Who'sWho in America®

Who's Who in America®

2010

64th Edition

Volume 2 ♦ M-Z

Geographic Index ♦ Professional Index

MARQUIS Who'sWho®
890 Mountain Avenue, Suite 300
New Providence, NJ 07974 U.S.A.
www.marquiswhoswho.com

Who's Who in America®

Marquis Who's Who

For information, contact: Marquis Who's Who, 890 Mountain Avenue, Suite 300
New Providence, New Jersey 07974
1-800-473-7020; www.marquiswhoswho.com

International Standard Book Number 978-0-8379-7023-3 (Classic Edition, Set)
978-0-8379-7020-2 (Classic Edition, Volume 2)
978-0-8379-7024-0 (Deluxe Edition, Set)
978-0-8379-7022-6 (Deluxe Edition, Volume 2)
International Standard Serial Number 0083-9396

Manufactured in the United States of America.

Table of Contents

Preface

"**WHO'S WHO IN AMERICA** *shall endeavor to list those individuals who are of current national reference interest and inquiry either because of meritorious achievement or because of the position they hold."*

Albert Nelson Marquis
Founder, 1899

Marquis Who's Who is proud to present the 2010 edition of *Who's Who in America*. This 64th edition features over 95,000 profiles of prominent individuals representing virtually every major field of endeavor.

In 1899, our first year of publication, Marquis biographees numbered 8,602. While the number of individuals profiled in *Who's Who in America* has grown substantially, our selection standards remain stringent. Fewer than one in 3,200 Americans are included in the 2010 edition of *Who's Who in America.*

On the pages that follow, you will find Nobel and Pulitzer Prize winners, legendary athletes, university presidents, accomplished artists, renowned entertainers, entrepreneurs, and leaders representing hundreds of industries. Our 2010 Edition includes some long-established biographees like Warren Buffett, Barbara Walters and Tiger Woods, as well as many intriguing first-time listees such as Captain Sully Sullenberger, the pilot who safely landed an airplane in the Hudson River, and Grammy award winning rapper, Lil Wayne.

Who's Who in America also includes the profiles of thousands of remarkable achievers who, despite extraordinary accomplishments in everything from breakthrough medical research to cutting-edge technological innovations, have not as yet become household names.

As in all Marquis Who's Who biographical volumes, the individuals profiled in *Who's Who in America* are selected on the basis of current reference value. Factors such as position, noteworthy accomplishments, visibility, and prominence in a field are all taken into account. While the vast majority of the individuals profiled on the following pages are American, *Who's Who in America* also includes the biographies of select individuals from around the world whose lives have had considerable impact and influence in America.

An individual's desire to be listed is not sufficient reason for inclusion. Similarly, wealth and social position are not relevant criteria. Of course, Marquis Who's Who has never charged a fee for publishing a biography, nor is purchase of the book ever a factor in the selection of biographees. Final decisions concerning inclusion or exclusion are made following extensive discussion, evaluation, and deliberation.

Biographical information is gathered in a variety of manners. In most cases, we invite our biographees to submit their biographical details. In many cases, though, the information is collected independently by our research and editorial staffs, which use a wide assortment of tools to gather the most complete, accurate, and up-to-date information available. Sketches researched by Marquis Who's Who are followed by an asterisk (*).

As a complement to the biographical profiles, the Geographic and Professional Indexes featured in Volume 2 make *Who's Who in America* an even more productive research tool. Through these indexes, users can identify and locate individuals in any of thirty-eight professional categories, as well as by country, state, or city. Each entry contains name and occupation description.

While the Marquis Who's Who editors exercise the utmost care in preparing each biographical sketch for publication, it is inevitable in a publication involving so many profiles that occasional errors will appear. Users of this publication are urged to notify the publisher of any issues so that adjustments can be made, which will not only be reflected in all subsequent editions of the book but which can now be immediately displayed via Marquis Who's Who on the Web.

All of the profiles featured in *Who's Who in America* are available on www.marquiswhoswho.com through a subscription. At the present time, subscribers to *Who's Who on the Web* have access to all of the names included in all of the Marquis Who's Who publications, as well as many new biographies that will appear in upcoming publications.

We sincerely hope that this volume will be an indispensable reference tool for you. We are always looking for ways to better serve you and welcome your ideas for improvements. In addition, we continue to welcome your Marquis Who's Who nominations. Feel free to submit these via our Web site (www.marquiswhoswho.com) or by e-mail and postal mail.

Without the cooperation and assistance of those profiled on the pages that follow, *Who's Who in America* would not be possible. We would like to specifically thank our biographees for reviewing and editing their profiles. As a consequence, *Who's Who in America* remains the unchallenged leader in the field of biographical reference works. For this we are truly grateful.

Key to Information

[1] GIBSON, OSCAR JULIUS, [2] physician, educator; **[3]** b. Syracuse, NY, Aug. 31, 1937; **[4]** s. Paul Oliver and Elizabeth H. (Thrun) G.; **[5]** m. Judith S. Gonzalez, Apr. 28, 1968; **[6]** children: Richard Gary, Matthew Lucas, Samuel Perry. **[7]** BA magna cum laude, U. Pa., 1960; MD, Harvard U., 1964. **[8]** Diplomate Am. Bd. Internal Medicine, Am. Bd. Preventive Medicine. **[9]** Intern Barnes Hosp., St. Louis, 1964-65, resident, 1965-66; clin. assoc. Nat. Heart Inst., NIH, Bethesda, Md., 1966-68; chief resident medicine U. Okla. Hosps., 1968-69; asst. prof. cmty. health Okla. Med. Ctr., 1969-70, assoc. prof., 1970-74, prof., chmn. dept., 1974-80; dean Coll. Medicine U. Okla., 1978-82; v.p. med. staff affairs Bapt. Med. Ctr., Oklahoma City, 1982-86, exec. v.p., 1986-88, chmn., 1988-95, chmn., CEO, 1995—; **[10]** mem. governing bd. Ambulatory Health Care Consortium, Inc., 1979-80; mem. Okla. Bd. Medicolegal Examiners, 1985—, Okla. Bd. Med. Ethics, 1994—. **[11]** Contbr. articles to profl. jours. **[12]** Bd. dirs., v.p. Okla. Arthritis Found., 1982—; trustee N. Ctrl. Mental Health Ctr., 1985—. **[13]** Served to lt. US Army, 1954-56. **[14]** Recipient R.T. Chadwick award Overlook Hosp., 1968; grantee Am. Heart Assn., 1985-86, 88, 1995-96. **[15]** Fellow Assn. Tchrs. Preventive Medicine; mem. AAAS, AMA, Am. Fedn. Clin. Rsch., Assn. Med. Colls., Masons, Shriners, Sigma Xi. **[16]** Republican. **[17]** Roman Catholic. **[18]** Achievements include research in the role of MMP inhibitors in the prevention of skin aging. **[19]** Avocations: swimming, weight lifting, traveling. **[20]** Home: 6060 N Ridge Ave Oklahoma City OK 73126 **[21]** Office: Bapt Med Ctr 1986 Cuba Hwy Oklahoma City OK 73120*

KEY

[1]	Name
[2]	Occupation
[3]	Vital statistics
[4]	Parents
[5]	Marriage
[6]	Children
[7]	Education
[8]	Professional certifications
[9]	Career
[10]	Career-related
[11]	Writings and creative works
[12]	Civic and political activities
[13]	Military
[14]	Awards and fellowships
[15]	Professional and association memberships, clubs and lodges
[16]	Political affiliation
[17]	Religion
[18]	Achievements
[19]	Avocations
[20]	Home address
[21]	Office address
[*]	Researched by Marquis Who's Who

Table of Abbreviations

The following abbreviations and symbols are frequently used in this book.

A

A Associate (used with academic degrees)
AA Associate in Arts
AAAL American Academy of Arts and Letters
AAAS American Association for the Advancement of Science
AACD American Association for Counseling and Development
AACN American Association of Critical Care Nurses
AAHA American Academy of Health Administrators
AAHP American Association of Hospital Planners
AAHPERD American Alliance for Health, Physical Education, Recreation, and Dance
AAS Associate of Applied Science
AASL American Association of School Librarians
AASPA American Association of School Personnel Administrators
AAU Amateur Athletic Union
AAUP American Association of University Professors
AAUW American Association of University Women
AB Arts, Bachelor of
AB Alberta
ABA American Bar Association
AC Air Corps
acad. academy
acct. accountant
acctg. accounting
ACDA Arms Control and Disarmament Agency
ACHA American College of Hospital Administrators
ACLS Advanced Cardiac Life Support
ACLU American Civil Liberties Union
ACOG American College of Ob-Gyn
ACP American College of Physicians
ACS American College of Surgeons
ADA American Dental Association
adj. adjunct, adjutant
adm. admiral
adminstr. administrator
adminstrn. administration
adminstrv. administrative
ADN Associate's Degree in Nursing
ADP Automatic Data Processing
adv. advocate, advisory
advt. advertising
AE Agricultural Engineer
AEC Atomic Energy Commission
aero. aeronautical, aeronautic
aerodyn. aerodynamic
AFB Air Force Base
AFTRA American Federation of Television and Radio Artists
agr. agriculture
agrl. agricultural
agt. agent
AGVA American Guild of Variety Artists
agy. agency
A&I Agricultural and Industrial
AIA American Institute of Architects
AIAA American Institute of Aeronautics and Astronautics
AIChE American Institute of Chemical Engineers
AICPA American Institute of Certified Public Accountants
AID Agency for International Development
AIDS Acquired Immune Deficiency Syndrome
AIEE American Institute of Electrical Engineers
AIME American Institute of Mining, Metallurgy, and Petroleum Engineers
AK Alaska
AL Alabama
ALA American Library Association
Ala. Alabama
alt. alternate
Alta. Alberta
A&M Agricultural and Mechanical
AM Arts, Master of
Am. American, America
AMA American Medical Association
amb. ambassador
AME African Methodist Episcopal
Amtrak National Railroad Passenger Corporation
AMVETS American Veterans
ANA American Nurses Association
anat. anatomical
ANCC American Nurses Credentialing Center
ann. annual
anthrop. anthropological
AP Associated Press
APA American Psychological Association
APHA American Public Health Association
APO Army Post Office
apptd. appointed
Apr. April
apt. apartment
AR Arkansas
ARC American Red Cross
arch. architect
archeol. archeological
archtl. architectural
Ariz. Arizona
Ark. Arkansas
ArtsD Arts, Doctor of
arty. artillery
AS Associate in Science, American Samoa
ASCAP American Society of Composers, Authors and Publishers
ASCD Association for Supervision and Curriculum Development
ASCE American Society of Civil Engineers
ASME American Society of Mechanical Engineers
ASPA American Society for Public Administration
ASPCA American Society for the Prevention of Cruelty to Animals
assn. association
assoc. associate
asst. assistant
ASTD American Society for Training and Development
ASTM American Society for Testing and Materials
astron. astronomical
astrophys. astrophysical
ATLA Association of Trial Lawyers of America
ATSC Air Technical Service Command
atty. attorney
Aug. August
aux. auxiliary
Ave. Avenue
AVMA American Veterinary Medical Association
AZ Arizona

B

B Bachelor
b. born
BA Bachelor of Arts
BAgr Bachelor of Agriculture
Balt. Baltimore
Bapt. Baptist
BArch Bachelor of Architecture
BAS Bachelor of Agricultural Science
BBA Bachelor of Business Administration
BBB Better Business Bureau
BC British Columbia
BCE Bachelor of Civil Engineering
BChir Bachelor of Surgery
BCL Bachelor of Civil Law
BCS Bachelor of Commercial Science
BD Bachelor of Divinity
bd. board
BE Bachelor of Education

BEE Bachelor of Electrical Engineering
BFA Bachelor of Fine Arts
bibl. biblical
bibliog. bibliographical
biog. biographical
biol. biological
BJ Bachelor of Journalism
Bklyn. Brooklyn
BL Bachelor of Letters
bldg. building
BLS Bachelor of Library Science
Blvd. Boulevard
BMI Broadcast Music, Inc.
bn. battalion
bot. botanical
BPE Bachelor of Physical Education
BPhil Bachelor of Philosophy
br. branch
BRE Bachelor of Religious Education
brig. gen. brigadier general
Brit. British
Bros. Brothers
BS Bachelor of Science
BSA Bachelor of Agricultural Science
BSBA Bachelor of Science in Business Administration
BSChemE Bachelor of Science in Chemical Engineering
BSD Bachelor of Didactic Science
BSEE Bachelor of Science in Electrical Engineering
BSN Bachelor of Science in Nursing
BST Bachelor of Sacred Theology
BTh Bachelor of Theology
bull. bulletin
bur. bureau
bus. business
BWI British West Indies

C

CA California
CAD-CAM Computer Aided Design–Computer Aided Model
Calif. California
Can. Canada, Canadian
CAP Civil Air Patrol
capt. captain
cardiol. cardiological
cardiovasc. cardiovascular
Cath. Catholic
cav. cavalry
CBI China, Burma, India Theatre of Operations
CC Community College
CCC Commodity Credit Corporation
CCNY City College of New York
CCRN Critical Care Registered Nurse
CCU Cardiac Care Unit
CD Civil Defense
CE Corps of Engineers, Civil Engineer
CEN Certified Emergency Nurse
CENTO Central Treaty Organization
CEO chief executive officer
CERN European Organization of Nuclear Research
cert. certificate, certification, certified
CETA Comprehensive Employment Training Act
CFA Chartered Financial Analyst
CFL Canadian Football League
CFO chief financial officer
CFP Certified Financial Planner
ch. church
ChD Doctor of Chemistry
chem. chemical
ChemE Chemical Engineer
ChFC Chartered Financial Consultant
Chgo. Chicago
chirurg., der surgeon
chmn. chairman
chpt. chapter
CIA Central Intelligence Agency
Cin. Cincinnati
cir. circle, circuit
CLE Continuing Legal Education
Cleve. Cleveland
climatol. climatological
clin. clinical
clk. clerk
CLU Chartered Life Underwriter
CM Master in Surgery
CM Northern Mariana Islands
cmty. community
CO Colorado
Co. Company
COF Catholic Order of Foresters
C. of C. Chamber of Commerce
col. colonel
coll. college
Colo. Colorado
com. committee
comd. commanded
comdg. commanding
comdr. commander
comdt. commandant
comm. communications
commd. commissioned
comml. commercial
commn. commission
commr. commissioner
compt. comptroller
condr. conductor
conf. Conference
Congl. Congregational, Congressional
Conglist. Congregationalist
Conn. Connecticut
cons. consultant, consulting
consol. consolidated
constl. constitutional
constn. constitution
constrn. construction
contbd. contributed
contbg. contributing
contbn. contribution
contbr. contributor
contr. controller
Conv. Convention
COO chief operating officer
coop. cooperative
coord. coordinator
corp. corporation, corporate
corr. correspondent, corresponding, correspondence
coun. council
CPA Certified Public Accountant
CPCU Chartered Property and Casualty Underwriter
CPH Certificate of Public Health
cpl. corporal
CPR Cardio-Pulmonary Resuscitation
CS Christian Science
CSB Bachelor of Christian Science
CT Connecticut
ct. court
ctr. center
ctrl. central

D

D Doctor
d. daughter of
DAgr Doctor of Agriculture
DAR Daughters of the American Revolution
dau. daughter
DAV Disabled American Veterans
DC District of Columbia
DCL Doctor of Civil Law
DCS Doctor of Commercial Science
DD Doctor of Divinity
DDS Doctor of Dental Surgery
DE Delaware
Dec. December
dec. deceased
def. defense
Del. Delaware
del. delegate, delegation
Dem. Democrat, Democratic
DEng Doctor of Engineering
denom. denomination, denominational
dep. deputy
dept. department
dermatol. dermatological
desc. descendant
devel. development, developmental
DFA Doctor of Fine Arts
DHL Doctor of Hebrew Literature
dir. director
dist. district
distbg. distributing
distbn. distribution
distbr. distributor
disting. distinguished

div. division, divinity, divorce
divsn. division
DLitt Doctor of Literature
DMD Doctor of Dental Medicine
DMS Doctor of Medical Science
DO Doctor of Osteopathy
docs. documents
DON Director of Nursing
DPH Diploma in Public Health
DPhil, Doctor of Philosophy
DR Daughters of the Revolution
Dr. Drive, Doctor
DRE Doctor of Religious Education
DrPH Doctor of Public Health
DSc Doctor of Science
DSChemE Doctor of Science in Chemical Engineering
DSM Distinguished Service Medal
DST Doctor of Sacred Theology
DTM Doctor of Tropical Medicine
DVM Doctor of Veterinary Medicine
DVS Doctor of Veterinary Surgery

E

E East
ea. eastern
Eccles. Ecclesiastical
ecol. ecological
econ. economic
ECOSOC UN Economic and Social Council
ED Doctor of Engineering
ed. educated
EdB Bachelor of Education
EdD Doctor of Education
edit. edition
editl. editorial
EdM Master of Education
edn. education
ednl. educational
EDP Electronic Data Processing
EdS Specialist in Education
EE Electrical Engineer
EEC European Economic Community
EEG Electroencephalogram
EEO Equal Employment Opportunity
EEOC Equal Employment Opportunity Commission
EKG electrocardiogram
elec. electrical
electrochem. electrochemical
electrophys. electrophysical
elem. elementary
EM Engineer of Mines
EMT Emergency Medical Technician
ency. encyclopedia
Eng. England
engr. engineer
engring. engineering
entomol. entomological
environ. environmental
EPA Environmental Protection Agency
epidemiol. epidemiological
Episc. Episcopalian
ERA Equal Rights Amendment
ERDA Energy Research and Development Administration
ESEA Elementary and Secondary Education Act
ESL English as Second Language
ESSA Environmental Science Services Administration
ethnol. ethnological
ETO European Theatre of Operations
EU European Union
Evang. Evangelical
exam. examination, examining
Exch. Exchange
exec. executive
exhbn. exhibition
expdn. expedition
expn. exposition
expt. experiment
exptl. experimental
Expy. Expressway
Ext. Extension

F

FAA Federal Aviation Administration
FAO UN Food and Agriculture Organization
FBA Federal Bar Association
FBI Federal Bureau of Investigation
FCA Farm Credit Administration
FCC Federal Communications Commission
FCDA Federal Civil Defense Administration
FDA Food and Drug Administration
FDIA Federal Deposit Insurance Administration
FDIC Federal Deposit Insurance Corporation
FEA Federal Energy Administration
Feb. February
fed. federal
fedn. federation
FERC Federal Energy Regulatory Commission
fgn. foreign
FHA Federal Housing Administration
fin. financial, finance
FL Florida
Fl. Floor
Fla. Florida
FMC Federal Maritime Commission
FNP Family Nurse Practitioner
FOA Foreign Operations Administration
found. foundation
FPC Federal Power Commission
FPO Fleet Post Office
frat. fraternity
FRS Federal Reserve System
FSA Federal Security Agency
Ft. Fort
FTC Federal Trade Commission
Fwy. Freeway

G

GA, Ga. Georgia
GAO General Accounting Office
gastroent. gastroenterological
GATT General Agreement on Tariffs and Trade
GE General Electric Company
gen. general
geneal. genealogical
geog. geographic, geographical
geol. geological
geophys. geophysical
geriat. geriatrics
gerontol. gerontological
GHQ General Headquarters
gov. governor
govt. government
govtl. governmental
GPO Government Printing Office
grad. graduate, graduated
GSA General Services Administration
Gt. Great
GU Guam
gynecol. gynecological

H

hdqs. headquarters
HEW Department of Health, Education and Welfare
HHD Doctor of Humanities
HHFA Housing and Home Finance Agency
HHS Department of Health and Human Services
HI Hawaii
hist. historical, historic
HM Master of Humanities
homeo. homeopathic
hon. honorary, honorable
House of Dels. House of Delegates
House of Reps. House of Representatives
hort. horticultural
hosp. hospital
HS High School
HUD Department of Housing and Urban Development
Hwy. Highway
hydrog. hydrographic

I

IA Iowa
IAEA International Atomic Energy Agency
IBRD International Bank for Reconstruction and Development
ICA International Cooperation Administration

ICC Interstate Commerce Commission
ICCE International Council for Computers in Education
ICU Intensive Care Unit
ID Idaho
IEEE Institute of Electrical and Electronics Engineers
IFC International Finance Corporation
IL, Ill. Illinois
illus. illustrated
ILO International Labor Organization
IMF International Monetary Fund
IN Indiana
Inc. Incorporated
Ind. Indiana
ind. independent
Indpls. Indianapolis
indsl. industrial
inf. infantry
info. information
ins. insurance
insp. inspector
inst. institute
instl. institutional
instn. institution
instr. instructor
instrn. instruction
instrnl. instructional
internat. international
intro. introduction
IRE Institute of Radio Engineers
IRS Internal Revenue Service

J

JAG Judge Advocate General
JAGC Judge Advocate General Corps
Jan. January
Jaycees Junior Chamber of Commerce
JB Jurum Baccalaureus
JCB Juris Canoni Baccalaureus
JCD Juris Canonici Doctor, Juris Civilis Doctor
JCL Juris Canonici Licentiatus
JD Juris Doctor
jg. junior grade
jour. journal
jr. junior
JSD Juris Scientiae Doctor
JUD Juris Utriusque Doctor
jud. judicial

K

Kans. Kansas
KC Knights of Columbus
KS Kansas
KY, Ky. Kentucky

L

LA, La. Louisiana
LA Los Angeles
lab. laboratory
L.Am. Latin America
lang. language
laryngol. laryngological
LB Labrador
LDS Latter Day Saints
lectr. lecturer
legis. legislation, legislative
LHD Doctor of Humane Letters
LI Long Island
libr. librarian, library
lic. licensed, license
lit. literature
litig. litigation
LittB Bachelor of Letters
LittD Doctor of Letters
LLB Bachelor of Laws
LLD Doctor of Laws
LLM Master of Laws
Ln. Lane
LPGA Ladies Professional Golf Association
LPN Licensed Practical Nurse
lt. lieutenant
Ltd. Limited
Luth. Lutheran
LWV League of Women Voters

M

M Master
m. married
MA Master of Arts
MA Massachusetts
MADD Mothers Against Drunk Driving
mag. magazine
MAgr Master of Agriculture
maj. major
Man. Manitoba
Mar. March
MArch Master in Architecture
Mass. Massachusetts
math. mathematics, mathematical
MB Bachelor of Medicine, Manitoba
MBA Master of Business Administration
MC Medical Corps
MCE Master of Civil Engineering
mcht. merchant
mcpl. municipal
MCS Master of Commercial Science
MD Doctor of Medicine
MD, Md. Maryland
MDiv Master of Divinity
MDip Master in Diplomacy
mdse. merchandise
MDV Doctor of Veterinary Medicine
ME Mechanical Engineer
ME Maine
M.E.Ch. Methodist Episcopal Church
mech. mechanical
MEd. Master of Education
med. medical
MEE Master of Electrical Engineering
mem. member
meml. memorial
merc. mercantile
met. metropolitan
metall. metallurgical
MetE Metallurgical Engineer
meteorol. meteorological
Meth. Methodist
Mex. Mexico
MF Master of Forestry
MFA Master of Fine Arts
mfg. manufacturing
mfr. manufacturer
mgmt. management
mgr. manager
MHA Master of Hospital Administration
MI Military Intelligence, Michigan
Mich. Michigan
micros. microscopic
mid. middle
mil. military
Milw. Milwaukee
Min. Minister
mineral. mineralogical
Minn. Minnesota
MIS Management Information Systems
Miss. Mississippi
MIT Massachusetts Institute of Technology
mktg. marketing
ML Master of Laws
MLA Modern Language Association
MLitt Master of Literature, Master of Letters
MLS Master of Library Science
MME Master of Mechanical Engineering
MN Minnesota
mng. managing
MO, Mo. Missouri
moblzn. mobilization
Mont. Montana
MP Member of Parliament
MPA Master of Public Administration
MPE Master of Physical Education
MPH Master of Public Health
MPhil Master of Philosophy
MPL Master of Patent Law
Mpls. Minneapolis
MRE Master of Religious Education
MRI Magnetic Resonance Imaging
MS Master of Science
MS, Ms. Mississippi
MSc Master of Science
MSChemE Master of Science in Chemical Engineering
MSEE Master of Science in Electrical Engineering
MSF Master of Science of Forestry

MSN Master of Science in Nursing
MST Master of Sacred Theology
MSW Master of Social Work
MT Montana
Mt. Mount
mus. museum, musical
MusB Bachelor of Music
MusD Doctor of Music
MusM Master of Music
mut. mutual
MVP Most Valuable Player
mycol. mycological

N

N. North
NAACOG Nurses Association of the American College of Obstetricians and Gynecologists
NAACP National Association for the Advancement of Colored People
NACA National Advisory Committee for Aeronautics
NACDL National Association of Criminal Defense Lawyers
NACU National Association of Colleges and Universities
NAD National Academy of Design
NAE National Academy of Engineering, National Association of Educators
NAESP National Association of Elementary School Principals
NAFE National Association of Female Executives
N.Am. North America
NAM National Association of Manufacturers
NAMH National Association for Mental Health
NAPA National Association of Performing Artists
NARAS National Academy of Recording Arts and Sciences
NAREB National Association of Real Estate Boards
NARS National Archives and Record Service
NAS National Academy of Sciences
NASA National Aeronautics and Space Administration
NASP National Association of School Psychologists
NASW National Association of Social Workers
nat. national
NATAS National Academy of Television Arts and Sciences
NATO North Atlantic Treaty Organization
NBA National Basketball Association
NC North Carolina
NCAA National College Athletic Association
NCCJ National Conference of Christians and Jews
ND North Dakota
NDEA National Defense Education Act
NE Nebraska
NE Northeast
NEA National Education Association
Nebr. Nebraska
NEH National Endowment for Humanities
neurol. neurological
Nev. Nevada
NF Newfoundland
NFL National Football League
Nfld. Newfoundland
NG National Guard
NH New Hampshire
NHL National Hockey League
NIH National Institutes of Health
NIMH National Institute of Mental Health
NJ New Jersey
NLRB National Labor Relations Board
NM, N.Mex. New Mexico
No. Northern
NOAA National Oceanographic and Atmospheric Administration
NORAD North America Air Defense
Nov. November
NOW National Organization for Women
nr. near
NRA National Rifle Association
NRC National Research Council
NS Nova Scotia
NSC National Security Council
NSF National Science Foundation
NSTA National Science Teachers Association
NSW New South Wales
nuc. nuclear
numis. numismatic
NV Nevada
NW Northwest
NWT Northwest Territories
NY New York
NYC New York City
NYU New York University
NZ New Zealand

O

ob-gyn obstetrics-gynecology
obs. observatory
obstet. obstetrical
occupl. occupational
oceanog. oceanographic
Oct. October
OD Doctor of Optometry
OECD Organization for Economic Cooperation and Development
OEEC Organization of European Economic Cooperation
OEO Office of Economic Opportunity
ofcl. official
OH Ohio
OK, Okla. Oklahoma
ON, Ont. Ontario
oper. operating
ophthal. ophthalmological
ops. operations
OR Oregon
orch. orchestra
Oreg. Oregon
orgn. organization
orgnl. organizational
ornithol. ornithological
orthop. orthopedic
OSHA Occupational Safety and Health Administration
OSRD Office of Scientific Research and Development
OSS Office of Strategic Services
osteo. osteopathic
otol. otological
otolaryn. otolaryngological

P

PA, Pa. Pennsylvania
paleontol. paleontological
path. pathological
pediat. pediatrics
PEI Prince Edward Island
PEN Poets, Playwrights, Editors, Essayists and Novelists
penol. penological
pers. personnel
PGA Professional Golfers' Association of America
PHA Public Housing Administration
pharm. pharmaceutical
PharmD Doctor of Pharmacy
PharmM Master of Pharmacy
PhB Bachelor of Philosophy
PhD Doctor of Philosophy
PhDChemE Doctor of Science in Chemical Engineering
PhM Master of Philosophy
Phila. Philadelphia
philharm. philharmonic
philol. philological
philos. philosophical
photog. photographic
phys. physical
physiol. physiological
Pitts. Pittsburgh
Pk. Park
Pky. Parkway
Pl. Place
Plz. Plaza
PO Post Office

polit. political
poly. polytechnic, polytechnical
PQ Province of Quebec
PR Puerto Rico
prep. preparatory
pres. president
Presbyn. Presbyterian
presdl. presidential
prin. principal
procs. proceedings
prod. produced
prodn. production
prodr. producer
prof. professor
profl. professional
prog. progressive
propr. proprietor
pros. prosecuting
pro tem. pro tempore
psychiat. psychiatric
psychol. psychological
PTA Parent-Teachers Association
ptnr. partner
PTO Pacific Theatre of Operations, Parent Teacher Organization
pub. publisher, publishing, published, public
publ. publication
pvt. private

Q

quar. quarterly
qm. quartermaster
Que. Quebec

R

radiol. radiological
RAF Royal Air Force
RCA Radio Corporation of America
RCAF Royal Canadian Air Force
Rd. Road
R&D Research & Development
REA Rural Electrification Administration
rec. recording
ref. reformed
regt. regiment
regtl. regimental
rehab. rehabilitation
rels. relations
Rep. Republican
rep. representative
Res. Reserve
ret. retired
Rev. Reverend
rev. review, revised
RFC Reconstruction Finance Corporation
RI Rhode Island
Rlwy. Railway
Rm. Room
RN Registered Nurse
roentgenol. roentgenological
ROTC Reserve Officers Training Corps
RR rural route, railroad
rsch. research
rschr. researcher
Rt. Route

S

S. South
s. son
SAC Strategic Air Command
SAG Screen Actors Guild
S.Am. South America
san. sanitary
SAR Sons of the American Revolution
Sask. Saskatchewan
savs. savings
SB Bachelor of Science
SBA Small Business Administration
SC South Carolina
ScB Bachelor of Science
SCD Doctor of Commercial Science
ScD Doctor of Science
sch. school
sci. science, scientific
SCV Sons of Confederate Veterans
SD South Dakota
SE Southeast
SEC Securities and Exchange Commission
sec. secretary
sect. section
seismol. seismological
sem. seminary
Sept. September
s.g. senior grade
sgt. sergeant
SI Staten Island
SJ Society of Jesus
SJD Scientiae Juridicae Doctor
SK Saskatchewan
SM Master of Science
SNP Society of Nursing Professionals
So. Southern
soc. society
sociol. sociological
spkr. speaker
spl. special
splty. specialty
Sq. Square
SR Sons of the Revolution
sr. senior
SS Steamship
St. Saint, Street
sta. station
stats. statistics
statis. statistical
STB Bachelor of Sacred Theology
stblzn. stabilization
STD Doctor of Sacred Theology
std. standard
Ste. Suite
subs. subsidiary
SUNY State University of New York
supr. supervisor
supt. superintendent
surg. surgical
svc. service
SW Southwest
sys. system

T

Tb. tuberculosis
tchg. teaching
tchr. teacher
tech. technical, technology
technol. technological
tel. telephone
telecom. telecommunications
temp. temporary
Tenn. Tennessee
TESOL Teachers of English to Speakers of Other Languages
Tex. Texas
ThD Doctor of Theology
theol. theological
ThM Master of Theology
TN Tennessee
tng. training
topog. topographical
trans. transaction, transferred
transl. translation, translated
transp. transportation
treas. treasurer
TV television
twp. township
TX Texas
typog. typographical

U

U. University
UAW United Auto Workers
UCLA University of California at Los Angeles
UK United Kingdom
UN United Nations
UNESCO United Nations Educational, Scientific and Cultural Organization
UNICEF United Nations International Children's Emergency Fund
univ. university
UNRRA United Nations Relief and Rehabilitation Administration
UPI United Press International
urol. urological
US, USA United States of America
USAAF United States Army Air Force
USAF United States Air Force
USAFR United States Air Force Reserve
USAR United States Army Reserve
USCG United States Coast Guard
USCGR United States Coast Guard Reserve
USES United States Employment Service

USIA United States Information Agency
USMC United States Marine Corps
USMCR United States Marine Corps Reserve
USN United States Navy
USNG United States National Guard
USNR United States Naval Reserve
USO United Service Organizations
USPHS United States Public Health Service
USS United States Ship
USSR Union of the Soviet Socialist Republics
USTA United States Tennis Association
UT Utah

V

VA Veterans Administration
VA, Va. Virginia
vet. veteran, veterinary
VFW Veterans of Foreign Wars
VI Virgin Islands
vis. visiting
VISTA Volunteers in Service to America
vocat. vocational
vol. volunteer, volume
v.p. vice president
vs. versus
VT, Vt. Vermont

W

W West
WA, Wash. Washington (state)
WAC Women's Army Corps
WAVES Women's Reserve, US Naval Reserve
WCTU Women's Christian Temper ance Union
we. western
WHO World Health Organization
WI Wisconsin, West Indies
Wis. Wisconsin
WV, W.Va. West Virginia
WY, Wyo. Wyoming

X, Y, Z

YK Yukon Territory
YMCA Young Men's Christian Association
YMHA Young Men's Hebrew Associa-tion
YM & YWHA Young Men's and Young Women's Hebrew Association
yr. year
YT Yukon Territory
YWCA Young Women's Christian Association
zool. zoological

Alphabetical Practices

Names are arranged alphabetically according to the surnames, and under identical surnames according to the first given name. If both surname and first given name are identical, names are arranged alphabetically according to the second given name.

Surnames beginning with De, Des, Du, however capitalized or spaced, are recorded with the prefix preceding the surname and arranged alphabetically under the letter D.

Surnames beginning with Mac and Mc are arranged alphabetically under M.

Surnames beginning with Saint or St. appear after names that begin Sains, and are arranged according to the second part of the name, e.g., St. Clair before Saint Dennis.

Surnames beginning with Van, Von, or von are arranged alphabetically under the letter V.

Compound surnames are arranged according to the first member of the compound.

Many hyphenated Arabic names begin Al-, El-, or al-. These names are alphabetized according to each biographee's designation of last name. Thus Al-Bahar, Neta may be listed either under Al- or under Bahar, depending on the preference of the listee.

Also, Arabic names have a variety of possible spellings when transposed to English. Spelling of these names is always based on the practice of the biographee. Some biographees use a Western form of word order, while others prefer the Arabic word sequence.

Similarly, Asian names may have no comma between family and given names, but some biographees have chosen to add the comma. In each case, punctuation follows the preference of the biographee.

Parentheses used in connection with a name indicate which part of the full name is usually omitted in common usage. Hence, Chambers, E(lizabeth) Anne indicates that the first name, Elizabeth, is generally recorded as an initial. In such a case, the parentheses are ignored in alphabetizing and the name would be arranged as Chambers, Elizabeth Anne.

However, if the entire first name appears in parentheses, for example, Chambers, (Elizabeth) Anne, the first name is not commonly used, and the alphabetizing is therefore arranged as though the name were Chambers, Anne.

If the entire middle name is in parentheses, it is still used in alphabetical sorting. Hence, Belamy, Katherine (Lucille) would sort as Belamy, Katherine Lucille. The same occurs if the entire last name is in parentheses, e.g., (Brandenberg), Howard Keith would sort as Brandenberg, Howard Keith.

For visual clarification:

Smith, H(enry) George: Sorts as Smith, Henry George
Smith, (Henry) George: Sorts as Smith, George
Smith, Henry (George): Sorts as Smith, Henry George
(Smith), Henry George: Sorts as Smith, Henry George

Who'sWho in America®

Biographees M-Z

MA, ADRIANNA, private equity firm executive; b. Beijing, 1973; arrived in US, 1982; BS in Elec. Engring. & Sciences, MS in Elec. Engring. & Sciences, MIT, 1996; MBA, Harvard Bus. Sch., 2000. Tech. project mgr. network server divsn. Hewlett-Packard Corp., 1996—98; v.p. Morgan Stanley, 2000—05; prin. energy/resources sector Gen. Atlantic, NYC, 2005—. Named one of 40 Under 40, Dealmaker mag., 2008. Office: Gen Atlantic Park Avenue Plz 55 E 52nd St 32nd Fl New York NY 10055 Office Phone: 212-715-4000. Office Fax: 212-759-5708.

MA, ALAN WAI-CHUEN, lawyer; b. Hong Kong, Apr. 20, 1951; s. Pak Ping and Qi Quon (Hung) Ma. BBA, U. Hawaii, 1975; MBA, Chaminade U., 1981; JD, Golden Gate U., 1983. Bar: Hawaii 1984, U.S. Dist. Ct. Hawaii 1984, U.S. Ct. Appeals (9th cir.) 1986, U.S. Supreme Ct. 1989. Ptnr. Oldenberg & Ma, Honolulu, 1984—90; prin. Law Offices Alan W.C. Ma, Honolulu, 1990—95, 1999—; counsel Goodsill Anderson Quinn & Stifel, Honolulu, 1995—99. Adj. prof. law U. Hawaii, Honolulu, 1988-95. Co-author: Real Estate Investment and Practices in the USA, 2007; co-editor: New Waves for Foreign Investors, 1990. Recipient Outstanding Vol. award Hawaii Cmty. Svc. Coun., 1990; named Best Lawyers in America, 1993-. Mem. ABA, Am. Immigration Lawyers Assn. (chpt. chair 1993-94), Internat. Bar Assn., Inter-Pacific Bar Assn., U.S. Japan Vols. Assn. (bd. dirs. 1989—), Overseas Chinese Am. Assn. (bd. dirs. 1993-94). Avocation: tennis. Office: PO Box 23014 Honolulu HI 96823 Office Phone: 808-944-1188. Business E-Mail: alanma@alanmalaw.com.

MA, BIANCA KIN-SAN, broadcast executive; b. Hong Kong; Sales & mktg. dir. Metro Broadcast Corp. Ltd., Kowloon, Hong Kong, 1994—98, 2001—05, dep. mng. dir., mng. dir., 2006—. Office: Metro Broadcast Corp Ltd Basement 2 Site 6 Whampoa Garden Kowloon Hong Kong Office Phone: 852-3698-8000. Office Fax: 852-3150-8625.

MA, FAI, mechanical engineering educator; b. Canton, People's Republic of China, Aug. 6, 1954; came to U.S., 1977, naturalized, 1988; s. Rui-Qi and Shao-Fen (Luo) M. BS, U. Hong Kong, 1977; MS, PhD, Calif. Inst. Tech., 1981. Sr. rsch. engr. Weidlinger Assocs., Menlo Park, Calif., 1981-82; rsch. fellow IBM, Yorktown Heights, N.Y., 1982-83; sr. engr. Standard Oil Co., Cleve., 1983-86; prof. mech. engring. U. Calif., Berkeley, 1986—. Vis. scholar Oxford U., Eng., 1992, U. Stuttgart, Germany, 1993. Co-author: Probabilistic Analysis, 1983, Computational Mechanics, 1989; co-editor Advances in Engring., 1995--; contbr. articles to profl. jours. Young Investigator award NSF, 1987; Humboldt fellow, 1992; Fulbright awardee, 2002. Fellow: ASME. Office: U Calif Dept Mech Engring Berkeley CA 94720-1740 Office Phone: 510-643-6527. Business E-Mail: fma@me.berkeley.edu.

MA, L. EVE ARMENTROUT, television producer, director, educator; b. Dec. 28, 1943; d. Edward Goodwin and Lucy McIver (Watson) Ballard; m. David Parker Armentrout, 1966 (div. 1969); 1 child, Lucy Ann; m. Jeong-Huei Ma, Jan. 1970 (div. 1986); children: William Marshall, Edward Benjamin. Student, Middlebury Coll., 1961-63; BA In English Lit., Creative Writing, San Francisco State Coll., 1968; postgrad. in Chinese, Stanford U., Calif., 1968; MA in US History, Calif. State U., Hayward, 1974; PhD in Modern Chinese History, U. Calif., Davis, 1976; JD, U. Calif. at Hastings, San Francisco, 1994. Bar: Calif., 1994. Tchg. asst. history dept. U. Calif., Davis, 1973-76; rsch. assoc. anthropology dept., 1977-79; asst. prof. history dept., 1980, 1982; rsch. assoc. applied behavioral scis. dept., 1982-83; asst. prof. Mills Coll., Calif., 1988-90; pvt. practice law, 1993—99; asst. prof. Calif. State U., Hayward, 1986—88; prodr.-dir. Palomino Prodns., 2004—. Cons. Golden Gate Nat. Rec. Area, San Francisco, 1979-80, Oakland Mus., 1981, 84, 2001, ARC Assocs., Inc., Oakland, 1981-82, James R. Moore Atty. at Law, San Francisco, 1982, Pacific Ocean divsn. U.S. Army Corps. Engrs. Hawaii, 1983-86, Japan Engr., dist. U.S. Army Corps Engrs. Camp Zama, Japan, 1986-89. Author: (with others) Chinese of Oakland, 1982, sole author: Revolutionaries, Monarchists and Chinatowns, 1990, Hometown Chinatown, 2000; editor, contbr.: Farms, Firms and Runways: U.S. Military Bases, 2001; editor, contbr.: One Day, One Dollar, 1984, Chung-Hsi Liao-way T'ai (newsletter), 1986; contbr. articles to scholary volumes and jours.; prodr., dir., host (TV series): Languages of Sound and Movement; prodr., dir. (TV series) Roots and Branches; prodr., dir., host (TV-DVD) Of Beauty & Deities, Arts that Cross Borders, Improvising Jerez-Style, Weaving with Spanish Threads, Pearls from the Sea; co-prodr. co-dir. (with Antonio de la Malena) Price of a Piece of Chocolate; profl. flamenco dancer. Hist. and interpretive rev. com. Calif. Dept. Pks. and Recreation Multicultural Ctr., 1982-84; design rev. com. Calif. State Railroad Mus., 1982-83; vol. tchr. pub. and pvt. schs., San Francisco Bay Area, 1973-86; leader Girl Scouts USA, 1976-79, Boy Scouts Am., 1985-98; officer neighborhood assn., Richmond, Calif., 1974-87; bd. dirs. Chinese/Chinese-Am. History Assn., El Cerrito, Calif., 1979-86, Chinese Hist. Soc. Am., 1983-90, Oakland Asian Culture Ctr., 1993-97, Celebrating Culture and Cmty., 1996-04; commr. Arts and Cultural Commn. Contra Costa County, 1998-2004, Arts and Cultural Commn. City of El Cerrito, 2004. Recipient States Calif. & Nev. TV Access Recognition award, Nat. Assn. Telecomm. Officers and Advisors, 2001, Western Access Video Excellence award, Alliance Cmty. Media, 2006, 2007; grantee, Kellogg Found., 1977—79, Calif. Coun. Humanities grantee, 1981, 1983—84, 1998, Calif. Arts Coun., 2000—04; Nat. Def. Fgn. Lang. fellow, Stanford U., 1971, Am.-East Asian Rels. fellow, U. Calif., Davis, 1972—73. Mem. Chinese Hist. Soc. Am. (bd. dirs. 1983-90), Calif. Bar Assn., Inst. Hist. Study, Ind. Scholars Asia, U. Calif.-Berkeley Inst., East Asian Studies, Film Arts Found., Oakland Asian Cultural Ctr. (bd. dirs. 1997-99), Bay Area Video Coalition. Democrat. Address: 1355 Arlington Blvd El Cerrito CA 94530-2514 also: Palomino Prodns Calle Benavente Bajo 3 11403 Jerez Spain Office: Palomino Prodns PO Box 8565 Berkeley CA 94707 Office Phone: 510-236-3257, 011 34 652 388586. Business E-Mail: palopro2004@yahoo.com.

MA (XUEZHENG), MARY, retired computer company executive; married; 1 child. BA, Capital Normal U., Beijing, 1976. Bureaucrat, Chinese Academy of Sciences' Internat. Corp. bureau China State Coun., 1978—90; with Lenovo Group, 1990—, sr. v.p. Beijing & Purchase NY, 1997—2007, CFO, 2000—07, non-exec. vice-chmn., 2007; ptnr., mng. dir. TPG Capital LP, Hong Kong & Beijing, 2007—. Bd. dirs. SOHU.com; bd. dir. Lenovo Group, 1997—2007. Named Best CFO, Finance Asia; named one of most powerful women, Forbes mag., 2005, 50 Most Powerful Women in Global Bus., Fortune mag., 2005, 50 Women to Watch, Wall St. Jour., 2006. Office: Lenovo Group Haidan District No 6 Chuang Ye Road Beijing 100085 China Office Phone: 86-10-58868888.

MA, SHENGQIAN, research scientist; s. Zhiping Cai; m. Rong Zhang, May 7, 2006. PhD, Miami U., Oxford, Ohio, 2008. Dirs. postdoc. fellow Argonne Nat. Lab., Ill., 2008—; grad. rsch. asst. Miami U., Oxford. Recipient award, Chinese govt., 2008, Young Investigator award, Am. Chem. Soc., Divsn. Inorganic Chemistry, 2008; Dirs. Postdoc. fellowship, Argonne Nat. Lab., 2008. Mem.: Sigma Xi (Rsch. award 2007—08). Achievements include patents for meshadjustable molecular sieve; research in metal organic framework from an anthracene derivative containing nanoscopic cages exhibiting high methane uptake. Office: Argonne Nat Lab 9700 S Cass Ave Bldg 205 Argonne IL 60439 Office Fax: 630-252-9917. Business E-Mail: sma@anl.gov.

MA, TIANWEI, engineering educator; b. Honolulu; s. YongXiang Ma and JingXia Zhang; m. David Ma; children: Andrew EnZe, Ariel EnYu. PhD, U. Calif., Santa Barbara, 2003. Cert. engr., Sichuan, China, 1996. Engr. ErZhong Machinery Co., Deyang, China, 1991—99; rschr. U. Calif., Santa Barbara, 2003—05; asst. prof. U. Hawaii, Honolulu, 2005—. Contbr. articles. Grant, NSF, 2008—. Mem.: ASCE. Achievements include research in decentralized approach for reduction of earthquake induced building vibrations; self-powered sensors; health monitoring of civil infrastructural systems. Office: Univ Hawaii Manoa Holmes 339 Honolulu HI 96822

MA, WENJING, application developer; d. Tongkuang and Linxia Ma. PhD, Pa. State U., Univ. Pk., 2007; studied with Frank Vavra, Wash. U.; studied with Wilbur Verhelst, Denver U.; studied with Edgar Britton, Angelo Di Benidetto. Cert. advanced programmer credential, SAS, 2006. Rsch. software developer Yahoo!, Santa Clara, Calif., 2007—. One-man shows include Beaux Arts Gallery, Denver, Internat. House, Denver, Contemporaries, Santa Fe, exhibited in group shows at Juried Arts Nat. Exhbn., Salt Lake City, Utah Mus., 53rd Ann. Arts Exhbn., Newport, numerous exhbns. and shows. Organizer Book Drive Troops in the Gulf; pres. Denver Coun. Arts & Humanities; v.p. Nat. Artists Equity; pres. Colo. Artists Equity; bd. trustee Denver Ctr. Performing Arts. Recipient Golden Mitten award, NY Cares Coat Dr., numerous awards; named Profl. & Bus. Women, 1994, Internat. Woman of Yr., Cambridge, Eng., 1994—95, 5000 Personalities of World, 1995, Foremost Women of 20th Century, Personality of America, Women of Yr., Am. Biog. Inst., 1998. Mem.: Women's Art Ctr. & Gallery (Denver), Asian Art Assn. (bd. mem.), Children's Diabetes Found. Denver (historian), Am. Med. Ctr., Nat. Coun. Jewish Woman (bd. mem.), Nat. Mus. Woman in Arts, Mus. Nat. History, Denver Art Mus., Rocky Mountain Liturgical Arts Assn., Friends Contemporary Art, Allied Sculptors (Colo.), Sigma Xi. Avocations: travel, singing, dance.

MA, WEN-XIU, mathematician, educator; b. Shanghai, June 20, 1962; s. Xiang-Fa Ma and Lan-Xian Zhao; m. Jian-Hong Hua, Mar. 12, 1992; 1 child, Tian-Xing. BSc in Math., U. Sci. and Tech. China, Hefei, 1982; MSc, Computer Ctr. Academia Sinica, Beijing, 1985, PhD, 1990. Asst. prof. dept. applied math. Shanghai Jiaotong U., 1985-87; postdoctoral fellow dept. math. Fudan U., Shanghai, 1990-92, assoc. prof. math., 1993-94; Humboldt Rsch. fellow dept. math. and computer scis. U. Paderborn, Germany, 1994-96; vis. scholar, dept. math. City U. Hong Kong, 1997—; vis. scholar dept. math. U. Manchester Inst. Sci. and Tech. Reviewer mathematical reviews; mem. work com. Shanghai Ctr. for Nonlinear Sci., 1993—. Editor Jour. Nonlinear Mathematical Physics; contbr. articles to profl. jours. Mem. Am. Math. Soc., Chinese Ctr. for Advanced Sci. and Tech. (assoc.), Chinese Soc. Indsl. and Applied Math., Chinese Mech Soc. (vice head youth work com. 1991—), Hong Kong Math. Soc. Avocations: ping pong/table tennis, badminton, swimming. Office: Univ of South Florida 4202 E Fowler Avbe Tampa FL 33620-5700

MA, WENXUE, medical scientist; s. Shumin Ma and Xiuqin Liu; m. Chunyang Hou, Dec. 12, 1992; children: Duli, Yiming. MS, Zhejiang Med. U., Hangzhou, China, 1997, MD, 1989; PhD, Zhejiang U., Hangzhou, 2002. Fellow U. Nebr. Med. Ctr., Omaha; rsch. assoc. U. Wis., Madison, 2004—05; with U. Calif., San Diego, 2005—. Mem.: AAAS (assoc.), Am. Assn. for Cancer Rsch. (assoc.), Sigma Xi (assoc.). Achievements include patents pending for transmembrane superantigen staphylococcal enterotoxin A. Office: Univ Calif San Diego 3855 Health Sciences Dr #0820 La Jolla CA Office Fax: 858-534-7061. Personal E-mail: mawenxue@hotmail.com. E-mail: wma@ucsd.edu.

MA, XINGMAO, environmental engineer, educator; m. Tzuting Kao. PhD, Mo. U. Sci. & Tech., Rolla, 2004. Cert. engr., Ohio, 2006. Asst. prof. Southern Ill. U., Carbondale, 2007—. Contbr. scientific papers to peer reviewed publs. Office: Southern IL Univ 1230 Lincoln Dr Carbondale IL 62901 Office Fax: 618-453-3044. Business E-Mail: ma@engr.siu.edu.

MA, XU, engineer, researcher; b. Beijing, Feb. 7, 1983; s. Genxi Ma and Huijuan Gao. PhD, U. Del., Newark, 2009. Rsch. asst. U. Del., 2005—09; post-doc. U. Calif., Berkeley, 2009—. Mem.: SPIE, JOSA. Home: 1704 Stone Gate Blvd Elkton MD 21921 Office: Univ Del 317 Evans Hall Newark DE 19716 Personal E-mail: maxu011156@hotmail.com. Business E-Mail: maxu@udel.edu.

MA, YO-YO, cellist; b. Paris, Oct. 7, 1955; m. Jill Hornor, 1977; children: Nicholas, Emily. Studied with Janos Scholz; studied with Leonard Rose, Juilliard Sch. Music, NYC, 1962; AB, Harvard U., 1976, MusD (hon.), 1991. Debut at age 9 Carnegie Hall, NYC; appeared with Pablo Casals, Isaac Stern, Leonard Bernstein, Emanuel Ax, Jaime Laredo, performs throughout world with maj. orchs.; rec. artist Sony Classical; founder & artistic dir. Silk Road Project Inc., Providence, 1998—. Messenger of peace UN, 2006—. (albums) Portrait of Yo-Yo Ma, Anything Goes (with Stephanie Grapelli), Yo-Yo Ma at Tanglewood, Cello Suites Inspired By Bach, Portrait of Cello Works, Premieres, Great Cello Concertos, 1989, Japanese Melodies, 1990, Hush, 1992, Made in America, 1993, The New York Album, 1994, Appalachia Waltz, 1996, Bach: Unaccompanied Cello Suites, 1997, The Protecting Veil/Wake Up...And Die, 1998, Plays Piazzolla, 1998, Soul of the Tango, 1998, Simply Baroque, 1999, Lulie the Iceberg, 1999, Solo, 1999, Appalachian Journey, 2000, Phantasmagoria, 2000, Yo-Yo Ma Plays the Music of John Williams, 2002, Silk Road Journeys: When Strangers Meet, 2002, Obrigado Brazil, 2003, Belle Epoque, 2003, Plays Ennio Morricone, 2004, Silke Road Journeys: Beyond the Horizon, 2004, The Dvorak Album, 2004, Vivaldi's Cello, 2004, Silk Road Journeys: Beyond the Horizon, 2005, Memoirs of a Geisha, 2005, The Essential Yo-Yo- Ma, 2005, Appassionato, 2006, New Impossibilities, 2007, Songs of Joy & Peace, 2008 Head Children's Orchestra Soc., Manhasset, NY. Named one of America's Best Leaders US News & World Report, 2007, Musician of the Yr., Musical America, 2008; recipient Avery Fisher prize, 1978, Glen Gould prize, 1999, Nat. Medal of the Arts, 2001, Dan David prize, 2006, Sonning Music prize, 2006; 15-time Grammy award winning artist. Mem.: AAAL (hon.). Office: Opus 3 Artists 470 Park Ave S 9th Fl New York NY 10016 also: Icm Artists 470 Park Ave S New York NY 10016-6819

MA, ZHENKUI, remote sensing applications scientist, consultant; b. Shenyang, Liaoning, China, Nov. 4, 1955; arrived in U.S., 1983; s. Deshan Ma and Shuxuan Zhang; m. Shufang Zhao; children: Bin, Jeanne. BS, Beijing Forestry Coll., 1982; MS, U. Mich., 1985, PhD, 1990. Sr. specialist Weyerhaeuser, Federal Way, Wash., 1996—2002, info. tech. cons., 2002—. Internat. cons. UN, Beijing, 1994—96. Mem.: Am. Soc. for Photogrammetry and Remote Sensing. Achievements include research in mapping large geographic areas using airborne data for forest inventory and biodiversity protection. Home: 21745 113th Place SE Kent WA 98031 Office: Weyerhaeuser 32275 32nd Ave S Fed Way Auburn WA 98001 Office Phone: 253-924-4772. Personal E-mail: zhenkui_ma@yahoo.com. Business E-Mail: zhenkui.ma@weyerhaeuser.com.

MA, ZHENQIANG, engineering educator; arrived in US, 1994, permanent resident, 2002; m. Shaoqin Gong, June 8, 1995; children: Alice Lily, David Liwei. BSEE in Elec. Engring., Tsinghua U., Beijing, China, 1991, BS in Applied Physics, 1991; MEE in Elec. Engring., U. Mich., Ann Arbor, 1997, MS in Nuc. Sci., 1997, PhD in Elec. Engring., 2001. Mem. faculty Tsinghua U., Beijing, 1991—94; engr. R&D Conexant Sys., Newport Beach, Calif., 2001—02, Jazz Semiconductor, Newport Beach, Calif., 2002; asst. prof. U. Wis., Madison, 2002—. Mem. rsch. panel tech. rev. MIT, Cambridge, Mass., 2004—; mem. sci. adv. bd. Lifeboat Found., 2007—; reviewer profl. jours. in field; panelist in field; presenter in field. Contbr. articles to profl. jours. Recipient award, Tsinghua U., 1992, Youth medal, 1992, Collaborative Disting. Pub. award, NASA, 2002, Best Student Paper award, Internat. Semiconductor Device Rsch. Symposium, 2005, Silicon Integrated Circuits in RF Sys. Topical Meeting, 2006; named Excellent Grad., Tsinghua U., 1991; grantee, NSF, 2003—07; fellow, Ohio State U., 1994. Mem.: IEEE (mem. exec. com. 2006—, co-chmn. tech. program 2005—06, chmn. pub. 2006—07, chmn. conf. 2007—), Electrochem. Soc., Lasers and Electro-Optics Soc., Comm. Soc., Microwave Theory and Techniques Soc., Electron Devices Soc. Achievements include the first flexible RF and the world's record-speed flexible transistors; discovery of analytical and graphical, full-frequency-range power gain relation between common-emitter and common-base configurations of bipolar junction transistors; recombination enhanced impurity diffusion process in SiGe heterojunction bipolar transistors; interplay relation between Kirk effect and early effect at high bias levels in bipolar transistors; unconditional stable design of common-base heterojunction bipolar transistors; correlation between doping profile and power gain of heterojunction bipolar transistors; analytical expression for parasitic effects on power gain degration of semiconductor power devices; power gain relation between common-source and common-gate configurations; novel radiation effects on SiGe power heterojunction bipolar transistors; new ballast resistor implementation rule in common-emitter and common-base bipolar transistors. Avocations: swimming, travel, running, ping pong/table tennis, multimedia entertainment. Home: 5520 Sandhill Dr Middleton WI 53562 Office: Univ Wis 1415 Engineering Dr Madison WI 53706 Business E-Mail: mazq@engr.wisc.edu.

MAA, JOHN, surgeon; b. Dallas; MD, Harvard Med. Sch., Boston, 1994. Cert. in gen. surgery Am. Bd. Surgery, 2003. Asst. prof. surgery U. Calif. San Francisco, 2002—, dir., surgery hospitalist program, 2005—08, dir., surgery hospitalist program med. ctr. Office: Univ Calif San Francisco 521 Parnassus Ave Rm C 341 San Francisco CA 94141-0790 Office Fax: 415-476-8694. Business E-Mail: maaj@surgery.ucsf.edu.

MAAS, COREY S., plastic surgeon; BS in Bio., Fla. St. Univ., Tallahassee, 1982; MD with hon., Univ. Fla. Coll. Med., Gainesville, Fla., 1986. Cert. Nat. Bd. Med. Examiners, 1987, Miss., 1987, Calif., 1991, Fla., 1996, Am. Bd. Otolaryngology, 1992, Am. Bd. Facial Plastic and Reconstructive Surgery, 1996. Gen. surg. intern St. Louis Univ. Med. Clinic, 1986—87, otolaryngology-head neck surgery resident, 1987—90, chief resident, 1990—91; fell. facial plastic and reconstructive surgery divsn. UC San Francisco Med. Clinic, 1991—92; private practice plastic surgeon San Francisco; founder, dir. Maas Clinic, 2001—. Clin. instr., divsn. plastic surgery UC, San Francisco, 1991, assoc. clin. prof., 1992—; dir., facial plastic surgery tng. fell. Am. Acad. Facial Plastic and Reconstructive Surgery, 2000. Recipient Gold Key Scholastic Leadership honor, FSU, 1982, Sir Harold Delf Gilles Rsch. award, Am. Acad. Facial and Plastic Surgery, 1992, Nat. Cmty. Svc. award, 1994. Fellow: Triologic Soc., Am. Coll. Surgeons, Am. Acad. Otolaryngology - Head and Neck Surgery, Am. Acad. Facial Plastic and Reconstructive Surgery; mem.: Calif. Soc. Facial Plastic Surgery, World Aesthetic Surgery Soc., San Francisco Med. Soc., Calif. Soc. Otolaryngology - Head and Neck Surgery, Calif. Med. Assn., Am. Rhinologic Soc., AMA. Office: The Maas Clinic 2400 Clay St San Francisco CA 94115 Office Phone: 415-567-7000. Office Fax: 415-567-7011.*

MAAS, JANE BROWN, advertising executive; b. Jersey City; d. Charles E and Margaret (Beck) Brown; m. Michael Maas, Aug. 30, 1957; children: Katherine, Jennifer. BA, Bucknell U., 1953; postgrad., U. Dijon, France, 1954; MA, Cornell U., Ithaca, N.Y., 1955; LittD, Ramapo Coll., 1986, St. John's U., 1988. Assoc. producer Name That Tune TV Program, NYC, 1957—64; v.p. Ogilvy and Mather Inc., NYC, 1964—76; sr. v.p. Wells, Rich, Greene, Inc., NYC, 1976—82; pres. Muller Jordan Weiss Inc., NYC, 1982—89, Earle Palmer Brown Cos., NYC, 1989—92, chmn., 1992—94, chmn. emeritus, 1994—. Co-author: (book) How to Advertise, 1975, Better Brochures, 1981, Adventures of a Advertising Woman, 1986, The New How to Advertise, 1992, Christmas in Wales: A Homecoming, 1994. Bd govs comt Scholastic Achievement, 1985—92; active Girl Scouts US, NY, 1970—76; mem adv bd William E Simon Grad Sch Bus, Univ Rochester, 1989—2005; pub dir AIA, 1993—95; trustee Bucknell Univ, Lewisburg, 1976—86, Fordham Univ, NY, 1983—91. Recipient Matrix Award, Women in Communications, 1980; named Woman of the Yr, NY Advert, 1986. Mem.: AIA (hon.), Am Assn. Advt. Agys. (bd govs), Am Archtl. Found (regent 1993—2000), Phi Beta Kappa. Avocations: creative writing, jogging. Home: 1775 York Ave New York NY 10128 Home Phone: 212-722-1221; Office Phone: 212-722-1221. Personal E-mail: janemaas@att.net.

MAAS, JOE (MELVIN JOSEPH MAAS), retired federal agency administrator; b. Washington, Feb. 29, 1940; s. Melvin Joseph and Katherine (Endress) M.; m. Constance Mary Haile, June 13, 1965; children: Christine, Michael, Kevin. BS, U. Md., 1965; postgrad., Stanford U., 1972—73. Dir. career edn. U.S. Dept. Labor, Washington, 1969-73; dep. dir. pers. SBA, Washington, 1973-76, dir. pers., 1976-82, asst. adminstr., 1982-95; founder, prin. Advancement Power, 2003—. Sr. v.p. Crave Entertainment Group, Inc., 2000 Bd. dirs., treas. Snowden Mill Assn., Silver Spring, Md., 1994-2002, pres. 2002-04; Wash. rep. Ind. Charities Am., 1995-96; bd. dirs. Amen Found., 1998—, Pres. Amen Found., 2003-05; chmn. Internat. Pers. Assn., 1982. With USMCR, 1957-64. Mem. Fed. Exec. Adminstrs. Assn., Sr. Exec. Assn., Pub. Employee Roundtable (bd. dirs. 1994—, chmn. Pub. Svc. Excellence awards 1996-98, treas. 1998-2002), Coun. Former Fed. Execs. (pres. 1997-99, bd. dirs. 1995-), Nat. Assn. Ret. Fed. Employees (chpt. pres. 1996-98, v.p. 1998-2000, state tng. officer 1997-01), Volkswagen Club (pres. Washington chpt. 1988-95, fiance chmn. Cath. Cmty. at Relay 2007-). Roman Catholic. Home: 2213 Aventurine Way Silver Spring MD 20904-5253 Personal E-mail: jm73bug@aol.com.

MAAS, KOREY DEVLIN, religious studies educator; s. Kenneth Leroy and Shirley Marie Maas; m. Cathryn Hope Werth, Aug. 3, 2002; 1 child, Atticus James Montgomery. BA, Concordia U., River Forest, Ill., 1993; STM, Concordia Sem., St. Louis, 1999; MST, U. Oxford, Eng., 2002, PhD, 2005; MDiv, Luth. Ch.-Mo. Synod, 2008. Prof. ch. history Concordia U., Irvine, Calif., 2005—. Editl. advisor Modern Reformation Mag., Escondido, Calif., 2007—. Contbr. articles to profl. jours. Vis. fellow, Cambridge U., Div. Faculty, 2009, Rsch. grant, Bibl. Charity Found., 2000. Mem.: Am. Soc. Ch. History, Soc. Reformation Rsch., Sixteenth Century Studies Soc. Lutheran. Office: Concordia Univ 1530 Concordia W Irvine CA 92612

MAAS, WERNER KARL, microbiology educator; b. Kaiserslautern, Germany, Apr. 27, 1921; came to U.S., 1936, naturalized, 1945; s. Albert and Esther (Meyer) M.; m. Renata Diringer, Oct. 15, 1960; children—Peter, Andrew, Helen. AB, Harvard U., 1943; PhD, Columbia U., 1948. Postdoctoral fellow Calif. Inst. Tech., Pasadena, 1946-48; commd. officer USPHS, Tb Research Lab., Cornell U. Sch., NYC, 1948-54; asst. prof. pharmacology NYU, 1954-57, assoc. prof. microbiology, 1957-63, prof., 1963-94, prof. emeritus, 1994—, chmn. dept. basic med. scis., 1974-81. Career grantee, USPHS, 1962—94. Mem.: Am. Soc. Microbiology, Genetics Soc. Am., Am. Soc. Biol. Chemists. Home: 86 Villard Ave Hastings On Hudson NY 10706-1821 Office: 550 1st Ave New York NY 10016-6402 Home Phone: 914-478-1839; Office Phone: 212-263-5322. E-mail: werner.maas@nyumc.org.

MAASCH, LLOYD PALMER, physician; b. Ashippun, Wis., June 16, 1928; s. Louis and Esther Maasch; m. Patricia Ruth Maasch, Dec. 23, 1950; children: Mary Pat, Thomas, Robert, Sue Ann, Patrick. BS, Marquette U., Milw., 1950; MD, Marquette Med. Sch., Milw., 1953; MD (hon.), Med. Coll. Wic., Milw., 2003. Health officer City of Weyauwega, Wis.; county coroner Waupaca County, Waupaca, Wis., 1952—95; mem. hosp. staff Riverside Med. Ctr., Waupaca, New London Family Med. Ctr., Wis.; family physician pvt. practice, Weyauwega. Adj. prof. U. Wis. Sch. Nursing, Oshkosh; med. dir. several nursing homes, Waupaca County, 1957—. Chmn. Weyauwega (20 acre) Pk., 1968—72. Lt. USN, 1955—57. Mem.: Wolf River Area Found., Lions (election chair, Melvin Jones fellow), Am. Legion. Republican. Lutheran. Avocations: painting, collecting Indian artifacts. Home: 208 W Clark St Weyauwega WI 54983-8920

MAATHAI, WANGARI, environmentalist, consultant; b. Nyeri, Kenya, Africa, Apr. 1, 1940; children: Waweru, Wanjira, Muta. BSc, Mt. St. Scholastica, Atchison, Kans., 1964; MS in Biol. Scis., U. Pitts., 1966; PhD in Anatomy, U. Nairobi, Kenya, 1971; LLD (hon.), Williams Coll., 1990; DSc (hon.), Hobart & William Smith Coll., 1994; DAgr (hon.), U. Norway, 1997; LLD (hon.), Yale U., 2004. Lectr. U. Nairobi, 1971-82, chair, dept. veterinary anatomy, 1976, assoc. prof., dept. veterinary anatomy, 1977; ran for presidency Kenya, 1997; founder Green Belt Movement, Nairobi, 1977, coord., 1984—2002; mem. Parliament, Tetu Constituency Republic of Kenya, 2002—, asst. min. of environ., natural resources & wildlife, 2003—. Bd. dir. UN Sec. Generals Adv. Bd. on Disarmament; mem. UN Commn. on Global Governance; founding mem. GROOTS Internat., 1985; endowed chair in gender and women's studies named "Fuller-Maathai", Conn. Coll., 2000; Montgomery Fellow, Dartmouth Coll., 2001; Dorothy McCluskey vis. fellow for conservation, Yale U., 2002. Author: The Green Belt Movement, 1985, The Green Belt Movement: Sharing the Approach and the Experience, 1988, The Green Belt Movement: Sharing the Approach, 2002, Unbowed, 2006; featured in many publs. Bd. dir. Kenya Red Cross Soc., 1973-80, Jane Goodall Inst., Women and Environment Develop. Orgn., World Learning for Internat. Develop., Green Cross Internat., Worldwide Network of Women in Environ. Work; bd. dir., chmn. Environ. Liaison Ctr. Internat., Kenya, 1974-84, Nat. Coun. Women, Kenya, 1976-87, chair 1981-87; active Friends of Kenyatta Nat. Hosp., Kenya, 1975; launched Kenya Jubilee 2000 coalition, 1998; mem. adv. bd. Democracy Coalition Project; mem. Earth Charter Commn.; mem. selection com., Sasakawa Environ. prize, UN Environ. Program., Kenya Recipient Women of Yr. award, 1983, Right Livelihood, 1984, Better World Soc. award, 1986, Windstar award for the Environment, 1988, Women of the World, 1989, Offeramus medal, 1990, Goldman Environ. prize, 1991, Africa prize for Leadership The Hunger Project, 1991, medal City of Edinburgh, Scotland, 1993, Jane Adams Leadership award, 1993, Golden Ark award, 1994, Juliet hollister award, 2001, Nobel Prize for Peace, 2004; co-recipient with Green Belt Movement Excellance award, Kenyen Cty. Abroad, 2001, Outstanding Vision and Commitment award, 2002, WANGO Environ. award, 2003, Sophie prize, 2004, Petra Kelly prize for Environment, 2004, J. Sterling Morton award, Conservation Scientist award, 2004, Arbor Day Found.; named to Global 500 Roll of Honor UN Environ. Program, 1990, 100 Heroines of the World, Internat. Women's Hall of Fame, 1995; elected by Earth Times as one of 100 persons in the World who have made a difference in the environ. arena, 1997; named one of 100 Most Influential People in World, Time Mag., 2005, one of most powerful women, Forbes mag., 2005. Mem. Club of Rome, Sasakawa Environ. Prize. Achievements include her work as a leader of the Green Belt Movement which has planted more than 30 million trees across Africa; awarded Nobel Peace Prize for her contribution to sustainable development, democracy, human rights, environmental conservation, peace and also for campaigning for broader women's rights; first East and Central African women to earn a PhD; first female chair and assoc. prof. of the Dept. of Veterinary Anatomy at the U. Nairobi; first female African to be awarded the Nobel Peace Prize. Office: care Green Belt Movement PO Box 67545 Nairobi Kenya

MAATMAN, GERALD LEONARD, insurance company executive; b. Chgo., Mar. 11, 1930; s. Leonard Raymond and Cora Mae (Van Der Laag) M.; children: Gerald L. Jr., Mary Ellen; m. Bernice Catherine Brummer, June 3, 1971. BS, Ill. Inst. Tech., 1951. Asst. chief engineer Ill. Inspection & Rating Bur., Chgo., 1951-58; prof., dept. chmn. Ill. Inst. Tech., Chgo., 1959-65; v.p. engring. Kemper Group, Chgo., 1966-68, pres. Nat. Loss Control Svc. Corp., 1969-74, v.p. corp. planning Long Grove, Ill., 1974-79, sr. v.p. info. svcs. group, 1979-85, exec. v.p. ins. ops., 1985-87; pres. Kemper Nat. Ins. Co., Long Grove, Ill., 1987-92, CEO, 1989-95, also bd. dirs., chmn. bd. dirs., 1991-95. Bd. dirs. Advs. for Auto and Hwy. Safety, 1992-98; chmn. bd. trustees Underwriters Labs., 1991-2002. Lt. (j.g.) USCGR, 1952-54. Mem. Knollwood Golf Club, Tau Beta Pi. Republican.

MAATMAN, MICAH JOEL, theater educator; b. Bowling Green, Ohio, Nov. 29, 1981; s. Vaughn and Janice Maatman; life ptnr. Jenn Zimmerman, Dec. 5, 1982. MFA in Theatre Design, Tech., and Mgmt., U. Ill., Urbana-Champaign, 2007. Grad. asst. U. Ill., 2004—07; asst. prof. theatre and dance Gustavus Adolphus Coll., Saint Peter, Minn., 2007—. Scenic designer (theatrical production) Topsy Turvy Mouse, Fefu, and Her Friends, A Funny Thing Happened on the Way to the Forum, columbinus, Intimate Apparel, As You Like It, The Other Shore, (opera) Madama Butterfly. Office: Gustavus Adolphus Coll 800 West College Ave Saint Peter MN 56082 Business E-Mail: mmaatman@gustavus.edu.

MAATSCH, DEBORAH JOAN, manufacturing executive; b. Lincoln, Nebr., Mar. 26, 1950; d. Leon F. Forst and Jarolyn J. Hoffman Forst Conrad; m. Gordon F. Maatsch, Mar. 14, 1969; children: Jason, Diana. BS, U. Nebr., Lincoln, 1976; MBA, U. Phoenix, 1997. Accredited tax advisor; IRS enrolled agt. Acct., supr. US Civil Svc., Heidelberg, Germany, 1971—73; paralegal Mattson Rickets Davies et al, Lincoln, Nebr., 1976—87; tax cons., 1981—; paralegal Wade Ash Woods & Hill, P.C., 1986—94; sr. trust adminstr. Investment Trust Co., 1994—96; compliance officer Nelson, Benson and Zellmer, Inc., 1995—96; pres. DGJD Inc., 1993—; contr. Arena Devel., Inc., 1996—2000; pres. Boyd Industries, Inc., 2001—. Contbr. articles to profl. jour. Event chmn., vol. Jefferson Cmty. Ctr., 1999—; bd. dirs. JCCA, 2001-03, pres., 2002-03; bd. dirs. Kids Roundup, 2002—; coord. Jefferson Hist. Preservation Fund; mem. South Park C. of C., Women's C. of C. Mem. Doane Coll. Alumni Assn. (dir. 1989-93), Nebr. Alumni Assn. Avocations: travel, outdoor activities, horses. Office: DGJD Inc PO Box 267 Jefferson CO 80456-0267 also: Boyd Industries Inc PO Box 315 Boyd TX 76023 Personal E-mail: dgjdinc@wildblue.net.

MAAZEL, LORIN VARENCOVE, conductor, composer, violinist; b. Neuilly-sur-Seine, France, Mar. 6, 1930; s. Lincoln and Marie (Barnet) Maazel; m. Miriam Sandbank (div.); m. Israela Margalit (div.); m. Dietlinde Turban, 1986; 3 children; 4 children from previous marriage. Studies with Vladimir Bakaleinikoff; student, U. Pitts., Mus. D. (hon.), 1968; HHD, Beaver Coll., 1973. Condr. Deutsche Oper Berlin, 1965—71, Berlin Radio Symphony Orch., 1965—75; music dir. Cleve. Orch., 1972—82; gen. mgr., chief condr. Vienna State Opera, 1982—84; music cons. Pitts. Symphony Orch., 1984—88, music dir., 1988—96; chief condr. Bavarian Radio Symphony Orch., Munich, 1993—2002; music dir. NY Philharm., 2002—09, Palau de les Arts Reina Sofia, Valencia, Spain, 2006—. Debut as condr., 1938; European debut, 1953; festivals include Bayreuth, Salzburg, Edinburgh; tours include S.Am., Australia, USSR, Japan, Korea, People's Republic China; albums include Holst: Planets, 2006. Decorated Comdr.'s Cross of Merit, Fed. Republic Germany, Legion of Honor, France, Knight Grand Cross, Italy, Comdr. of Lion, Finland; named a Goodwill Amb., UN. Achievements include 500 opera and concert performances with 150 orchestras; raising millions of dollars for benefit of UNESCO, World Wide Fund for Nature, Red Cross, and UN High Commisioner for Refugees. Avocations: tennis, swimming, collecting American paintings and Oriental art. Mailing: Palau de les Arts Reina Sofia Autopista del Saler 1 46013 Valencia Spain*

MABE, WALTER LEE, music educator; b. Reidsville, NC, Mar. 19, 1958; s. Morris and Ruth Mabe; m. DeLee Mabe; 1 child, Zach Micah. B in Music Edn., U. N.C., 1980, MusM, 1987. Lic. tchr. N.C. Tchr. Guildford County Sch., Greensboro, NC, 1980—81, Lexington City Sch., NC, 1981—. Dir. music 1st Meth. Ch., Lexington, 1994—. Named Tchr. of Yr., Lexington City Sch., 1997, 2005. Mem.: Am. Choral Dirs. Assn. (N.C. h.s. rep. 1998—2000), NC Music Educators Assn. (chmn. 2000—02, Music Tchr. of Yr. 2005). Home: 309 W 2nd Ave Lexington NC 27292 Office Phone: 336-242-1571. E-mail: lmabe@lexcs.org.

MABEE, CARLETON, historian, educator; b. Shanghai, Dec. 25, 1914; s. Fred Carleton and Miriam (Bentley) M.; m. Norma Dierking, Dec. 20, 1945; children: Timothy I., Susan (Mrs. Paul Newhouse). AB, Bates Coll., 1936; MA (Perkins scholar), Columbia U., 1938, PhD, 1942. With Civilian Pub. Svc., 1941-45; instr. history Swarthmore (Pa.) Coll., 1944; tutor Olivet (Mich.) Coll., 1947-49; asst. prof. liberal studies Clarkson Coll. Tech., Potsdam, NY, 1949-51, asso. prof., 1951-55; prof., 1955-61; dir. social studies divsn. Delta Coll., University Center, Mich., 1961-64; prof., chmn. dept. humanities and social scis. Rose Poly. Inst., Terre Haute, Ind., 1964-65; prof. history State U. Coll. at New Paltz, NY, 1965-80, prof. emeritus NY, 1980—. Participant in projects for Am. Friends Svc. Com., 1941-47, 53, 63; Fulbright prof. Keio U., Tokyo, 1953-54 Author: The American Leonardo, A Life of Samuel F.B. Morse, 1943, The Seaway Story, 1961, Black Freedom: The Nonviolent Abolitionists from 1830 through the Civil War, 1970, Black Education in New York State: From Colonial to Modern Times, 1979, (with Susan Mabee Newhouse) Sojourner Truth: Slave, Prophet, Legend, 1993, Listen to the Whistle: An Ancedotal History of the Wallkill Valley Railroad in Ulster and Orange Counties, N.Y., 1995; editor: (with James A. Fletcher) A Quaker Speaks from the Black Experience: The Life and Selected Writings of Barrington Dunbar, 1979, Bridging the Hudson: The Poughkeepsie Railroad Bridge and its Connecting Rail Lines, a Many-Faceted History, 2001, Gardiner and Lake Minnewaska, 2003, Promised Land: Father Divine's Interracial Cmtys. in Ulster County, NY, 2008, Gardiner Library: Its Beginning, Its Growing Energy, Its Struggle For Space, 2009; contbr. articles to profl. jours. Trustee Young-Morse Hist. Site, Poughkeepsie, N.Y., 1991-2002; ofcl. town historian, Gardiner, N.Y. Recipient Pulitzer prize in biography, 1944, Bergstein award for excellence in tchg. Delta Coll., 1963, Anisfield-Wolf award race rels., 1971, Gustavus Myers award for outstanding book on human rights, 1994; rsch. grantee Rsch. Found. SUNY, 1965, 67, 68, 80, Am. Philos. Soc., 1970, Nat. Inst. Edn., 1973-76, NSF, 1982-83. Mem. N.Y. State Hist. Assn., Phi Beta Kappa, Delta Sigma Rho. Methodist. Home: 2121 Route 44-55 Gardiner NY 12525-5808

MABEY, RALPH R., lawyer; b. Salt Lake City, May 20, 1944; s. Rendell Noel and Rachel (Wilson) M.; m. Sylvia States, June 5, 1968; children: Kathryn, Rachel, Elizabeth, Emily, Sara. BA, U. Utah, 1968; JD, Columbia U., 1972. Bar: Utah 1972, U.S. Dist. Ct. Utah 1972, U.S. Ct. Appeals (10th cir.) 1976, N.Y. 1985, U.S. Supreme Ct. 1988, U.S. Ct. Appeals (4th cir.) 1988, U.S. Ct. Appeals (3d cir.) 1993. Law clk. Atty. Gen., Salt Lake City, 1970, US Dist. Ct., Salt Lake City, 1972-73; ptnr. Irvine, Smith & Mabey, Salt Lake City, 1973-79; US bankruptcy judge US Ct., Salt Lake City, 1979-83; ptnr. LeBoeuf, Lamb, Greene & MacRae LLP, Salt Lake City and NYC, 1983—2005, Mabey & Murray LC, Salt Lake City, 2005—06; sr. of counsel Stutman Treister & Glatt, LA, 2006—. Sr. lectr. Brigham Young U. Sch. Law, Provo, Utah, 1983—2005; prof. law U. Utah Coll. Law, Salt Lake City, 2007—. Mng. editor Norton Bankruptcy Law Adviser, 1983-85. With USAR, 1968-74. Mem. ABA (bus. bankruptcy com.), Nat. Bankruptcy Conf., Am. Law Inst., Am. Bankruptcy Inst., Am. Coll. Bankruptcy, Internat. Insolvency Inst. (dir.). Republican. Mem. Lds Ch. Avocations: running, fly fishing. Home Phone: 801-295-0677. Business E-Mail: rmabey@stutman.com.

MABLI, PETER H., history educator; b. Englewood, NJ, May 21, 1984; s. Gerard M. Mabli and Linda Elfers-Mabli. BA in History, Fairleigh Dickinson U., Madison, NJ, 2006, MA in Tchg., 2007. Cert. creative instr. Apple Inc., 2008. Social studies tchr. Northern Highlands Regional HS, Allendale, NJ, 2006; creative instr. Apple Computer, Woodcliff Lake, NJ, 2007—; online prof. Fairleigh Dickinson U., Teaneck, NJ, 2007—. Mem.: Am. Hist. Assn., Phi Zeta Kappa, Phi Alpha Theta. Home: 684 Wyndemere Ave Ridgewood NJ 07450 Office: Fairleigh Dickinson Univ 1000 River Rd Teaneck NJ 07666 Personal E-mail: pmabli@me.com. Business E-Mail: pmabli@fdu.edu.

MABREY, RICK, science educator; b. St. Louis, Apr. 13, 1956; s. Harold Richard and Hazel Irene Mabrey; m. Misty Renee Barrera, Feb. 27, 1966. BSEd, U. Mo., Columbia, 1978; MFA in Writing, Lindenwood U., St. Charles, Mo., 2007. Tchr. Oakville Sr. HS, Mehlville, Mo., 1986—95, Epstein Hebrew Acad., St. Louis, 1997—99, Wright City HS, Mo., 1999—. Office: Wright City RII Sch Dist 520 Westwoods Rd Wright City MO 63390

MABRY, DONALD JOSEPH, retired academic administrator, history professor; b. Atlanta, Apr. 21, 1941; s. Jerry Leon and Eunice Leigh (Harris) M.; m. Susan Strong Johnston, July 28, 1962 (div. Oct. 1986); children: Scott, Mark; m. Paula Ann Crockett, Dec. 18, 1992. BA, Kenyon Coll., Gambier, Ohio, 1963; MEd, Bowling Green State U., 1964; PhD, Syracuse U., 1970. Instr. St. Johns River CC, Palatka, Fla., 1964—67; rsch. asst. fin. aid Syracuse U., NY, 1967—68, teaching fellow in history, 1968—69, Maxwell fellow, 1969—70, vis. lectr. dept. history, 1969—70; asst. to chancellor U. Kans., Lawrence, 1978—79; from. asst. prof. to prof. dept. history Miss. State U., Mississippi State, 1970—, asst. to pres., 1979—81, assoc. dean for budget and rsch., 1991—2001; now dir., assoc. dean Biol. Physical Sciences Rsch. Inst., Mississippi State, Miss.; ret. Sr. fellow, Ctr. for Internat. Security and Strategic Studies Miss. State U., 1981—91. Author: Mexico's Accion Nacional, 1973, The Mexican University and the State, 1982, (with others) Neighbors--Mexico and the United States, 1981; editor: The Latin American Narcotics Trade and U.S. National Security, 1989; contbr. articles to profl. jours. Mem. Am. Coun. on Edn. (exec. com. Coun. of Fellows 1980-83), South Ea. Coun. on Latin Am. Studies, Hist. Text Archive (founding editor) Avocation: computer telecommunications. Home: 206 Hiwassee Dr Starkville MS 39759-2105 Home Phone: 662-323-6852; Office Phone: 662-325-3604.

MABRY, JOSEPH M.(MIKE), JR., consumer products company executive; B math, Univ. No. Ala.; MBA, Okla. City Univ. Mgmt. positions through v.p. global services Wal-Mart, 1991—2003; sr. v.p. distbn. Lowe's Companies, Mooresville, NC, 2003—04, exec. v.p. logistics & distbn., 2004—. Office: Lowe's Companies 1000 Lowe's Blvd Mooresville NC 28117*

MABRY, PHILIP T., political scientist, consultant; b. Spartanburg, SC, Feb. 29, 1940; s. Roy T. and Eleanor Eva (Waddell) Mabry; m. Mary E. Byars, July 3, 1961 (div. Mar. 1980); children: Tammy Kay Waldrop, Phyllis Dianne Gibbons, Sonya Kowalski; m. Amy D. Mabry, June 18; stepchildren: Philip Singh, Tina Singh. Founder Ams. for Human Rights, Greenville, SC, 1975—79; pres. Western Rsch. Cons., Euless, Tex., 1982—; dir. Western Rsch., Euless, Tex., 2000—. Cons. U.S. Dept. State, Washington, 1982—87. Contbr. news articles, interviews on Iran/Contra and Iran hostage af. Polit. activist Rep. Party, Washington, 1962—. Recipient Cert. of Appreciation, Nat. Rep. Party, 2001, Cert. of Membership, Acad. Polit. Sci., 2001, Republican Commn. Accomplishment award, Nat. Rep. Senatorial Com., D.C., 2003, U.S. Congl. Order Merit award, Nat. Rep. Congl. Com., D.C., 2005. Mem.: Acad. Polit. Sci. Republican. Avocations: golf, coin collecting/numismatics, reading, history. Home: 125 Wanda Way Apt 119 Hurst TX 76053

MABRY, TOM J., retired biological chemistry professor; b. Commerce, Tex., June 6, 1932; s. Thomas Lee and Grace Mabry; m. Helga J. Mabry, Apr. 3, 1971; children: Michele, Patrick Thomas. MS in Chemistry, East Tex. State U., Commerce, 1953; PhD in Organic Chemistry, Rice U., Houston, 1960. Asst. prof. botany U. Tex., Austin, 1963—66, assoc. prof. botany, 1966—68, prof. botany, 1968—98, chmn. botany, 1980—86, prof. sect. molecular cell and devel. biology, 1998—2006, prof. emeritus, sect. molecular cell and devel. biology, 2006—; NIH postdoc. fellow Organic Chemistry Inst., Zurich U., Switzerland, 1960—62. Organizer and pres. Phytochem. Soc. N.Am., 1966—68; Guggenheim fellow Plant Biochemistry Inst., U. Freiburg, Germany, 1971—72. Author: (books) The Systematic Identification of Flavonoids, The Evolution of Centrospermous Families, Commercializing Biotechnology in the Global Economy, The Order Centrospermae; contbr. chapters to books. 1st lt. USAF, 1953—55, Wright Patterson Air Devel. Ctr., Dayton, Ohio. Recipient Plant Chemistry award, Am. Chem. Soc., 1986, Pergamon Phytochemistry prize, Phytochemical Soc. Europe, 1998, Rsch. Achievement award, Am. Soc. Pharmacognosy, 2001; named Distinguished Alumnus, Tex. A&M U. Commerce(Formerly East Tex. State U.), 1970, Outstanding Doctoral Tchg. award, U. Tex. Austin Grad. Sch., 1999, Ala. Lexander von Humboldt Sr. Scientist award. Office: Univ Tex 1 University Sta A6700 Austin TX 78712 Office Fax: 512-232-3402. Business E-Mail: mabry@mail.utexas.edu.

MABUS, RAYMOND EDWIN, JR., civilian military employee, former Governor of Mississippi; b. Starkville, Miss., Oct. 11, 1948; s. Raymond Edwin and Lucille M. (Curtis) M.; m. Julia Hines, Jan. 3, 1987 (div.); children: Elisabeth, Anne BA summa cum laude, U. Miss., 1969; MA, Johns Hopkins U., 1970; JD magna cum laude, Harvard U., 1976. Bar: Tex. 1976, DC 1978, Miss. 1982. Law clk. US Ct. Appeals (5th Cir.), Montgomery, Ala., 1976-77; legal counsel US House Agrl. Com., Wash., 1977-78; assoc. Fried, Frank et al., Wash., 1979-80; legis. aide to Gov. State of Miss., Jackson, 1980-83, state auditor, 1984-88, gov., 1988-92; US amb. to Saudi Arabia US Dept. State, Riyadh, 1994—96; of counsel Baker, Donelson, Bearman & Caldwell, 1996; pres. Frontline Global Resources, 1998—2002; non-exec. chmn. Foamex Internat. Inc., Linwood, Pa., 2004—07, interim pres., CEO, 2006—07; sec. Dept. of Navy US Dept. Def., Washington, 2009—. Chmn. So. Regional Edn. Bd., 1988-89 Lt. (j.g.) USN, 1970-72. Woodrow Wilson scholar Johns Hopkins U., 1969; named among Top 40 under 40 Esquire mag., 1987;

recipient Martin Luther King Jr. Social Responsibility award, 1990, King Ctr. in Atlanta, Miss. Assn. of Educators Friends of Edn. award, 1990, Disting. Pub. Svc. award, US Dept. Def., Disting. Civilian Svc. award, US Army, Nat. Wildlife Fedn. Conservation Achievement award, Friend of Edn. award, Miss. Assn. Educators' Mem. So. Govs. Assn. (chm. 1989-90). Democrat. Methodist. Avocations: spectator sports, walking, reading. Office: US Dept Def Dept Navy The Pentagon Rm 4E686 Washington DC 20350*

MACADAM, STEPHEN E., wholesale distribution executive; BS, Univ. Ky.; MS, Boston Coll.; MBA, Harvard Univ. Cons. positions through prin. McKinsey & Co., Charlotte, NC, 1988—98; sr. v.p. containerboard & packaging Georgia-Pacific Corp., 1998—2000; exec. v.p. pulp & paperboard Georgia-Pacific, 2000—01; pres., CEO Consolidated Container Co., 2001—05; CEO BlueLinx Holdings, Atlanta, 2005—08; pres., CEO EnPro Industries, Charlotte, NC, 2008—. Office: EnPro Industries 5605 Carnegie Blvd Charlotte NC 28209-4674

MÁCAL, ZDENÌK, conductor, music director; b. Brno, Czech Republic, Jan. 8, 1936; Student, Brno Conservatory; grad., Janácek Acad. Music, 1960. Prin. condr. Prague Symphony Orch.; condr. WDR Symphony Orch., Cologne, Germany, Sydney Symphony, 1986—87; music dir. Milw. Symphony Orch., 1986-96, NJ Symphony Orch., 1993—2002, music dir. emeritus, 2002—; chief condr. Czech Philharm., 2003—07. Winner Internat. Conducting Competition, Besancon, France, 1965, winner Dmitri Mitropoulos Competition, NYC, 1966. Office: NJ Symphony 2 Central Ave Newark NJ 07102-3119*

MACALALAG, EUFEMIO VERA, JR., urologist, researcher; b. Pagsanjan, Laguna, Philippines, Jan. 27, 1934; s. Eufemio Zaide Macalalag and Engracia Vera; m. Asuncion Tan Torres Lazaro, July 25, 1959; children: Mary Grace Macalalag Bustamante, Melissa Anne Macalalag Chan, Michael Eufemio Lazaro, Myra Michelle Macalalag Cruz, Mark Eufemio Lazaro IV. AA, U. Philippines, Quezon City, 1953, BA, 1954, BS in Medicine, 1955; MD, U. Philippines, Manila, 1958. Intern Philippine Gen. Hosp.; resident Columbia U. Presbyn. Med. Ctr.; chief urologist V. Luna Hosp. and Med. Ctr., Quezon City, 1967—, Capitol Med. Ctr., Quezon City, 1977—80. Med. dir. Medequal Systems and Supplies, Quezon City, 2000—. Physician Channel 4 Emergency unit EDSA Revolution, Quezon City. Col. Philippines Mil., 1997—2007. Fellow: Philippine Urol. Assn. (life), Am. Urol. Assn. (life); mem.: Soc. Male Reproduction and Urology (assoc.), Am. Assn. Gynecologic Laparoscopists. (assoc.), Internat. Coll. Surgeons (life). Achievements include research in urinary stone dissolution with irrigation of coconut water; human prostate cancer vaccine and for benign prostatic hyperplasia; artificial insemination with mixed donor; patents for catheter for outlet obstruction of urinary bladder; multiple ureteral stenting for drainage and dilatation of ureteral obstruction; design of bladder drainage of audio-visual M balder drainage; research in adjuvant immunotherapy for stage III prostate cancer. Home: 21 Laguna Street Barangay Bungad SFDM Quezon City 1105 Philippines Office: Medequal Systems and Supplies Inc 19A Laguna Street Barangay Bungad SFDM Quezon City 1105 Philippines Office Fax: (632) 3710651; Home Fax: (632) 3710651. Personal E-mail: bukomacmd@yahoo.com. Business E-mail: femy.macalalag@medequal.com.

MAC ALISTER, ROBERT JAMES, executive recruiter; b. NYC, Aug. 6, 1927; s. Ralph James and Ethel Burggraf Mac Alister; m. Nina Frances Koehler, Nov. 17, 1951; children: Hilary Lynn Stenger, James Kevin, Linda Ann Perez, Heather Ellen Smith. BA, Bard Coll., Annandale-on-Hudson, N.Y., 1950; MA, U. Chgo., 1958. Intern US Dept. State, Washington, 1950—51, info. specialist, 1951—52; cultural affairs assoc. US Info. Agy., Madras, India, 1952—54; steel salesperson Koehler Bros., Saginaw, Mich., 1954—55; county dir. Internat. Rescue Com., Saigon, Vietnam, 1955—57, exec. dir. NYC, 1955—59; campaign aide Pell for Senator Com., Providence, 1960; legis. asst. US Senator Claiborne Pell, Washington, 1961—62; county dir. Peace Corps, Abidjan, Ivory Ct., 1962—65; chief French spkg. Africa programs US Peace Corps, Washington, 1965—67, country dir. Fort Lamy, Chad, 1967—68, dir. staff tng. Washington, 1968—69; dean student svcs. Sangamon State U., Springfield, Ill., 1969—72; exec. dir. Group Health Plan N.E. Ohio, Cleve., 1973—75; cons. USAID, Washington, 1976—77; acting dir. US Peace Corps, Kinshasha, Zaire, 1977, spl. asst. to regional dir. Africa Washington, 1978—79; program analyst USAID, Washington, 1979—82, project mgr. Dakar, Senegal, 1982—86, desk officer, haili Washington, 1986—88, program officer, sahel regional divsn., 1988—89; internat. devel. cons. RJM Assocs., Frederick, Md., 1990—; pro bono rep. Vol. Assn. Bangldesh, Washington, 2006. Pro bono cons. US Peace Corps, 2003; pro-bono cons. Nat. Peace Corps Assn., Washington, 2003; pro bono cons. Africare, Washington. With USN, 1944—46. Recipient John Dewey award, Bard Coll., 2000. Mem.: Nat. Peace Corps Assn. Democrat. Unitarian-Universalist. Avocation: walking. Office Phone: 301-662-3497. Personal E-mail: bmaca@comcast.net.

MACALISTER, RODNEY J., former president African Development Foundation; Mgr. ops., bus. devel., cmty. devel. ConocoPhillips, Central Africa; founder, pres. Bus. & Conflict Ltd., London; pres. African Devel. Found. Mem. Corp. Coun. Africa, BCIU, Nat. Fgn. Trade Coun.; founding mem. Human Rights and Bus. Roundtable Fund of Peace.

MACALPIN, REX NERE, physician, educator; b. Glendale, Calif., Apr. 25, 1932; s. Frederic and Christine Capitola (Wright) MacA.; m. Carol Elizabeth White, June 22, 1957; children: David Ian, Anne Louise. Student, Harvard Coll., 1949-51; BA, Pomona Coll., Claremont, Calif., 1953; MD, U. Calif., San Francisco, 1957. Diplomate Am. Bd. Internal Medicine, Am. Bd. Cardiovasc. Disease. Med. intern, resident U. Calif. Sch. Medicine, San Francisco, 1957-60; cardiology fellow UCLA Sch. Medicine, 1960-61, prof. medicine, cardiology, 1963-88, prof. emeritus, 1988—. Contbr. over 100 articles to profl. publs. Lt. cmdr. USNR, 1961-63. Mem. Am. Heart Assn. (Svc. award 1981-84). Achievements include contribution to knowledge of the role of vasomotion in producing myocardial ischemia in coronary disease. Office: UCLA Divsn Cardiology 10833 Le Conte Ave Los Angeles CA 90095-1679 Office Phone: 310-206-5068. Business E-Mail: rmacalpi@ucla.edu.

MACALUSO, CHRISTIE A., bishop; b. June 12, 1945; B in Philosophy, St. Mary's Seminary, Balt., M in Sacred Theology; MA in Philosophy, Trinity U., Hartford; MA in Psychology, NYU; attended, New Sch. for Social Rsch., NYC. Ordained priest Archdiocese of Hartford, Conn., 1971, consecrated aux. bishop, 1997, aux. bishop, 1997—, ordained bishop, 1997; asst. pastor St. Thomas the Apostle Parish, West Hartford, St. Joseph Parish, New Britain; instr. philosophy St. Thomas Seminary Coll., academic dean, 1980—85, rector, pres., 1985; pastor Cathedral of St. Joseph, 1991—97; monsignor, Episcopal vicar Hartford, 1995. With Greater Hartford Consortium on Higher Edn., Asylum Hill Organizing Project, Christian Conf. of Conn. Roman Catholic. Office: 134 Farmington Ave Hartford CT 06105-3723

MACAN, WILLIAM ALEXANDER, IV, lawyer; b. Boston, Nov. 21, 1942; s. William A. and Carol (Whitten) M.; m. Jane Mitchell Ahern, Sept. 3, 1965; children: Sandi, Andrew. BA in Econs., Haverford Coll., 1964; LLB magna cum laude, U. Pa., Phila., 1967. Bar: Pa. 1968, US Tax Ct. 1970, NY 1999, Eng., 2000, Wales, 2000. Law clk. to judge U.S. Tax Ct., Washington, 1967-69; assoc. firm Morgan, Lewis & Bockius LLP, Phila., 1969-76, ptnr., 1976-2000, Allen & Overy LLP, NYC, 2000—04, of counsel, 2004—. Lectr. legal instns., seminars. Author publs. on tax-oriented equipment leasing, other tax subjects. Mem. ABA, NY State Bar Assn. Presbyterian. Office: Allen & Overy 1221 Ave of the Americas New York NY 10020 Home Phone: 618-687-3995; Office Phone: 212-610-6300. Business E-Mail: william.macan@newyork.allenovery.com.

MACARIN-MARA, LYNN, psychotherapist, consultant; b. Queens, NY, Feb. 27, 1948; d. David and Grace Macarin; m. Marvin Weingast, Sept. 2, 2000; 1 child, Leah Mara. MA, NYU, 1972; MSW, Hunter Sch. Social Work, 1980. Cert. psychoanalytic psychotherapy, hypnotherapy and hypnoanalysis. With Greenwich Inst. Psychotherapy and Psychoanalysis, 1984-87; pvt. practice, 1987—; pres. Face to Face Psychotherapy Svcs., Metuchen, N.J., 1987—; dir. family and children svcs. Ednl. Alliance, Inc., NYC, 1990-95. Adj. prof. SUNY, Staten Island, N.Y., 1972-73, New Sch. for Social Rsch., N.Y.C., 1980-81. Contbr. articles to profl. jours. Chairperson membership com. Temple Emanu-El, Edison, N.J., 1998-2001. Mem. N.J. Soc. for Clin. Social Work (newsletter editor 1997-99). Democrat. Jewish. Avocations: travel, dance, writing, painting. Office: Face to Face Psychotherapy Svcs 2 Blair Ave Metuchen NJ 08840

MACARTHUR, DIANA TAYLOR, advanced technology executive; b. Santa Fe, July 7, 1933; children: Elizabeth Tschursin, Alexander Tschursin. BA, Vassar Coll., Poughkeepsie, NY, 1955. Cons. economist Checchi & Co., 1957-61; v.p., dir. Thomas J. Deegan Co., 1961-62; dep. chief West Africa Peace Corps, 1963, reg. program officer for North Africa, Near East, South Asia, 1964, dir. divsn. pvt. and internat. orgns., 1965-66; pvt. cons., 1966-74; program mgr. Aerospace Divsn. Gen Elec. Co., 1974-76; pres. Consumer Dynamics, 1977-80; v.p., dir. Dynamac Internat. Inc., 1980-88, chmn., pres., CEO, 1988—; chmn., CEO Rsch. Analysis and Mgmt. Corp., 1988-92. Pres. Fgn. Traders, Inc., 1980—86. Trustee Menninger Found., Topeka, 1972-04, Santa Fe Inst., 2005-; bd. dirs. Sci. and Tech. Corp. U. N.Mex., 2004-; bd. visitors Menninger-Baylor Coll. Medicine, Meth. Hosp. Found., 2004-06; Lady Bird Johnson Wildflower Ctr., 1985-; mem. Pres.'s Com. of Adv. on Sci. and Tech., 1994-01; citizens adv. bd. to the Pres. Coun. on Youth Opportunity, 1966-70; served on CSIS Strengthening of Amer. Com., 1992, Nat. Benefits from Nat. Lab. Com., 1993, Sr. Policy on Nat. Challenges, 1996, Geopolitics of Energy Com., 2000; mem. The Chancellor's Adv. Coun. U. Sys. of Md.; bd. visitors U. Md. Biotech. Inst.; adv. com. Ctr. Strategic & Internat. Studies; bd. dirs. Atlantic Coun. USA; bus. adv. coun. Ctr. for China-US Coop., U. Denver. Mem. Coun. on Competitiveness, Business-Higher Edn. Forum (exec. com.), Tech. Coun. Md. (exec. com.), Los Alamos Nat. Lab. Found. (pres. bd. dirs.), Nat. Hispanic Cultural Ctr. Found., The Santa Fe Opera, Phi Beta Kappa. Office: Dynamac Internat Inc 1901 Research Blvd Rockville MD 20850-3268 Office Phone: 301-417-9800. Business E-Mail: dmacarthur@sfgrid.com.

MACARTHUR, JOHN RODERICK C. G. (RICK MACARTHUR), magazine publisher, journalist; b. NYC, June 4, 1956; s. J. Roderick and Christiane (L'Etendart) MacArthur. BA, Columbia Coll., 1978. Reporter Wall St. Jour., Chgo., 1977, Washington Star, 1978, Bergen Record, Hackensack, NJ, 1978—79, Chgo. Sun Times, 1979—82; asst. fgn. editor UPI, NYC, 1982; pres., pub. Harper's mag., 1983—. Bd. dirs. Com. to Protect Journalists, Overseas Press Club, Death Penalty Info. Ctr. Author: Second Front: Censorship and Propaganda in the Gulf War, 1992, The Selling of "Free Trade": NAFTA, Washington and the Subversion of Democracy, 1999. Fellow: NY Inst. Humanities; mem.: Econ. Club NY. Office: Harper's Mag 666 Broadway Fl 11 New York NY 10012-2394

MACASKILL, LLOYD EDWIN, systems analyst, consultant; b. Detroit, Jan. 24, 1944; s. Angus Duncan MacAskill and Catherine Mary MacLeod; m. Diane Elizabeth Axelson, Aug. 15, 1970; children: Meredith Lynn, Heather Elizabeth. BA, Alma Coll., 1966; BS, U. Wis., 1974; MS, U. Tenn., 1978. Programmer Berkeley Sci. Labs., Bethesda, Md., 1968—71; sys. programmer Johns Hopkins Sch. Medicine, Balt., 1978—80; project mgr. U. Md. Hosp., Balt., 1980—82; sys. analyst King Faisal Specialist Hosp., Riyadh, Saudi Arabia, 1982, Georgetown U. Med. Ctr., Washington, 1984, US Dept. of Navy, Washington, 1988—92, US Dept. Vets. Affairs, Silver Spring, Md., 1992—97, McKesson HBOC, Washington, 1997—99; sys. cons. Online Med. Networks, Springfield, Va., 1985—88; sr. sys. cons. Clin. Informatics Assocs., Carmel, Ind., 2005. Scout, lobbyist Am. Discovery Trail; author, publicist Gt. Ea. Trail. Recipient President's Call to Svc. award, President's Coun. Svc. and Civic Participation, 2004. Mem.: MacAskill Sept Soc. (pres.), Am. Med. Informatics Assn., W.Va. Scenic Trails Assn., Appalachian Trail Conservancy (registrar 1995), Am. Hiking Soc., Am. Discovery Trail Soc., Keystone Trails Assn., Potomac Appalachian Trail Club (trail mgr. 1993—2004, svc. awards 1991—2004). Episcopalian. Avocation: hiking trail development. Home: 1149 Veranda Ct Leland NC 28451-7790 Office: Del Labs 1830 Carver Rd Rocky Point NC 28457 Personal E-mail: lloydmaca@aol.com.

MACAULAY, JANICE MICHEL, music educator, composer; b. Providence, Aug. 19, 1949; d. Herbert John and Barbara Calland Michel; m. William Alfred Pastille, May 31, 1986; m. David Alexander Macaulay, June 13, 1970 (div. 1976); 1 child, Elizabeth Alexandra. MA in English, Brown U., Providence, 1972, MA in Music, 1977; MusD, Cornell U., Ithaca, NY, 1986. Organist Meml. Bapt. Ch., Seekonk, Mass., 1966; dir. music First Bapt. Ch., North Attleborough, Mass., 1968—72, Murray Universalist Ch., Attleborough, 1972—76, Ctrl. Congl. Ch., Fall River, Mass., 1977—79; tchg. asst., music theory Music Dept., Brown U., 1976—77; tchg. asst., piano, symphonic band, music appreciation Cornell U., Ithaca, 1980—83; lectr. music, coord. Wells Coll., Aurora, 1984—87; coord., assoc. prof. music dept. Anne Arundel C.C., Arnold, Md., 1987—93; lectr. Peabody Elderhostel, Balt, 1993—; music theory & appreciation U. Md., Balt. County, 1995—2001, instr., 2008—; vis. tutor,Grad. Inst., Liberal Edn. St. John's Coll., Annapolis, 1995—2005, continuing edn., cmty. programs tutor, 2003—. Composer songs. Recipient Residency award, Charles Ives Ctr. Am. Music, 1985, grant, Meet the Composer, 1984—86, Category prize, Internat Delius Composition Competition, 1989; Reading & travel grant, The Nat. Women Composers Resource Ctr., 1991, grant, Cornell U. Coun. Creative & Performing Arts, 1979, 1982, Grad. fellowship, Cornell U., 1984. Mem.: AAUW, RI Chpt.Am. Guild Organists (exec. bd. mem. 1978—80), Coun. Higher Edn. Music (v.p. 1991—93), Coll. Music Soc., Internat. Alliance Women Music, Soc. Music Theory, Soc. Composers, Inc., Broadcast Music Inc., Phi Beta Kappa. Home: 1061 Nova Cir Arnold MD 21012 Personal E-mail: jmacaulay@aol.com.

MACAULAY, LAWRENCE A., former Canadian government official, member of Parliament; b. St. Peters Bay, Sept. 9, 1946; s. Archibald and Bernadette MacAulay; m. Frances Elaine O'Connell, Aug. 16, 1972; children: Carolyn, Rita, Lynn. Mem. House of Commons, 1988—, apptd. assoc. critic for fisheries and oceans, 1989, apptd. critic for srs. and assoc. critic for fisheries, 1990; sec. of state for vets. Govt. of Can., 1993—96, min. labour, solicitor gen. of Can. Ottawa, 1998—2002. Mem. standing com. on forestry and fisheries, caucus com. on health and social devel.; acclaimed chair Atlantic Caucus, 1992. Roman Catholic.

MACAULAY, SUSAN JANE, lawyer, educator; b. Oceanport, NJ, Feb. 18, 1952; d. Gordon Livingston and Mary Forrest Macaulay; children: Lauren Mei, Anna Haiqiong. MusB, Oberlin Conservatory Music, 1974; JD, Loyola U., Chgo., 1984; LLM, Chgo.-Kent Coll. Law, 1990; M in Liberal Arts, U. Chgo., 1995. Bar: Ill. 1984, U.S. Dist. Ct. (no. dist.) Ill. 1984. Regional counsel Burroughs Corp., Lombard, Ill., 1984—86; atty. Borg-Warner Acceptance Corp., Chgo., 1986—86; assoc. gen. counsel Heller Fin., Inc., Chgo., 1986—94; gen. counsel ArcVentures, Inc., Chgo., 1994—95; v.p., corp. counsel Caremark Internat., Inc., Northbrook, Ill., 1995—96; sr. assoc. Skadden Arps Slate Meagher & Flom, Chgo., 1996—2001; ptnr. Gardner Carton & Douglas LLP, Chgo., 2001—06; gen. counsel Lamb Ptnrs., 2006—. Adj. prof. law Chgo.-Kent Coll. Law, 1992—. Contbr. chapters to books, articles to profl. jours. Named Ill. Leading Lawyer, The Law Bull. Ill. Superlawyers Chgo. Mag., 2004—06, Ill. Superlawyer, Chgo. Mag., 2004—06. Mem.: ABA, Chgo. Bar Assn., Families with Children from China. Avocations: classical music, local symphony orchestra member, writing. Office: Lamb Ptnrs 900 N Michigan Ste 1900 Chicago IL 60606 Office Fax: 312-915-3053. Business E-Mail: macaulay@lambllc.com.

MACAULAY, WILLIAM EDWARD, financial executive; b. NYC, Sept. 2, 1945; s. John H. and Ella M. (Cook) M.; m. Linda L. Rodger, June 17, 1967; children: Elizabeth R., Anne R. BBA cum laude, CCNY, 1966; MBA, U. Pa., 1968. Asst. v.p. Dominick & Dominick, NYC, 1968—71; v.p. Midlantic Bank, Newark, 1972—73, Oppenheimer Mgmt. Corp., NYC, 1973—75, exec. v.p., 1976—79; dir. corp. fin. Oppenheimer & Co., Inc., NYC, 1979—81, ptnr., 1976-81; gen. ptnr. Meridien Capital Co., Greenwich, Conn., 1981-92; pres., CEO, dir. First Res. Corp., Greenwich, 1982—. Chmn. Dresser Rand, Houston; bd. dirs. Weatherford Inc., So. Cross Holdings, Brisbane, Australia. Mem.: Indian Harbor Yacht Club. Presbyterian. Office: First Reserve Corp One Lafayette Pl Greenwich CT 06830-7165*

MACAULEY, KAREN ELIZABETH, nursing administrator, emergency nurse practitioner; b. Sayre, Pa., Mar. 12, 1965; d. Barry and Joie Rake; 1 child, Kelli Susan. BSN, Pa. State U., 1987, MEd, 1993. Cert. prehospital RN Pa. Emergency Med. Svcs. Coun.; RN pA., cert. critical care nurse, Am. Assn. Critical Care Nurses, emergency nurse, Emergency Nurses Assn. Staff nurse M.S. Hershey Med. Ctr., Pa., 1987—96; trauma program coord. Luther Hosp., Eau Claire, Wis., 1996—2001, Thomas Jefferson U. Hosp., Phila., 2001—04; trauma prevention and outreach dir. St. Christopher's Hosp. for Children, Phila., 2004—06; pediatric trauma program dir. All Children's Hosp., St. Petersburg, Fla., 2006—. Bd. dirs. Pa. State U. Coll. Health and Human Devel.; vol. Hosts for Hosps., Pa., 2001. Recipient Family Fun Vol. award, Family Fun Mag., 2005. Mem.: Am. Trauma Soc. (pres. to chair trauma nurse coun. 2000—07, bd. dirs. 2000—07), Soc. Trauma Nurses, Pa. State U. Alumni Assn. (life; pres. nursing All Alumni Group 2001—06, immediate past pres. 2006—08). Home: 3127 50th St N Saint Petersburg FL 33710 Office: All Children's Hosp 801 Sixth St N Saint Petersburg FL 33701 Office Phone: 727-767-4926. Personal E-mail: karenm@psualum.com. E-mail: macauleyk@allkids.org.

MACAVINTA-TENAZAS, GEMORSITA, physician; b. Numancia, Aklan, Phillippines, Dec. 18, 1938; arrived in U.S., 1967; d. Dominador Zalazar and Georgina Estrada (Tabanera) Macavinta; m. Salvador Torrefiel Tenazas Jr., Apr. 18, 1963; children: Alan, Alex, Albert, Alfred. BA, Far Ea. U., Manila, 1959, MD, 1964. Diplomate Am. Bd. Family Practice. Intern North Gen. Hosp., Manila, 1963-64; pvt. practice Manila, 1965-67; extern Chinese Gen. Hosp., Manila, 1965-67; with St. Joseph Med. Ctr., Burbank, Calif., 1967-69; chief cytotechnologist Cancer Screening Svcs., North Hollywood, Calif., 1969-73; resident in family practice medicine Health Scis. Ctr., Tex. Tech. U., Lubbock, 1974-75; staff physician VA Outpatient Clinic, LA, 1975—. Recipient physician recognition awards AMA, 1973-85, 92-94; named Mrs. Aklan, 1986, Disting. Alumna, Aklan Acad., Philippines, 1991, Most Outstanding Parent award Builders Lions Club, 1995, Citizen of Yr. Builders Lions Club, 1996, Outstanding Physician Club Filipino, 1996; named one of Ams. Top Family Drs. Consumers Rsch. Counc. Am., 2007; named to Asian Acad. Hall Distinction, Asian Leaders Assn., US Capital, 2007. Fellow Am. Acad. Family Physicians (bd. govs. 2003-05); mem. Philippine-Am. Assn. Family Physicians (bd. govs. 1996, 2003, 05-07, sec. 1998, sec. 1998-2002, Outstanding Leader award 2000, Mrs. Philippine Am. 2000), Am. Assn. Family Physicians (bd. govs., Phillipines 1996-), Calif. Acad. Family Physicians, Filipino Asian-Pacific VA Employees Soc. (pres. LA chpt. 1988—), Assn. Philippine Physicians in Am. (bd. govs. 2004, named Mrs. Mindanao 2002), Aklanons of Am. (pres. 1988—90, bd. govs. 1998-2000, 04-06, bd. dirs. 1990—, 1st Mrs. Aklan 1986-89), Far Ea. U. Med. Alumni Assn. (life mem., asst. sec. 1988—), Far Ea. U. Dr. Nicanor Reyes Alumni Found. (life). Roman Catholic. Avocations: dance, singing, sewing, piano playing, gardening. Office: VA Outpatient Clinic 351 E Temple Los Angeles CA 90012 Office Phone: 213-253-2677 ext. 4417. Business E-Mail: tenazas@va.gov.

MACAVOY, THOMAS COLEMAN, manufacturing executive, educator; b. Jamaica, NY, Apr. 24, 1928; s. Joseph V. and Edna M. Mac A.; m. Margaret M. Walsh, Dec. 27, 1952; children: Moira Mac Avoy, Ellen Mac Avoy Jennings, Christopher, Neil. BS in Chemistry, Queens Coll., 1950; MS in Chemistry, St. John's U., 1952, DSc (hon.), 1973; PhD in Chemistry, U. Cin., 1952. Chemist, Charles Pfizer & Co., Bklyn., 1957-60; mgr. electronics rsch. Corning Glass Works, NY, 1960-64, dir. phys. rsch., 1964-66, v.p. electronic products divsn., 1966-69, v.p. tech. products divsn., 1969-71, pres., 1971-83, vice-chmn., 1983-87; prof. mgmt. grad. sch. U. Va., 1988—. Patentee in field; contbr. articles to tech. jours. Trustee Corning Mus. Glass; past pres. Boy Scouts Am. With USN, 1946; with USAF, 1952-53. Recipient Silver Antelope award Boy Scouts Am., 1976, Silver Beaver award, 1975, Silver Buffalo award, 1982, Bronze Wolf award, 1988. Roman Catholic. Personal E-mail: tmacavoy@aol.com.

MACBAIN, WILLIAM HALLEY, minister, theology studies educator, academic administrator; b. Cambridge, Ont., Can., Aug. 12, 1916; s. George Alexander and Grace Ann (Wilkins) MacB.; m. Mary Ann Munday, Aug. 20, 1941; children: Grace Elizabeth MacBain Silvester, Constance Marilyn MacBain Parker. Licentiate in Theology, Toronto Baptist Sem., Ont., 1939; DD (hon.), Cen. Bapt. Sem., Toronto, 1962. Ordained to ministry Bapt. Ch., 1940. Pastor, founder Temple Bapt. Ch., Sarnia, Ont., 1937-64; pastor Forward Bapt. Ch., Toronto, 1964-73; dir., gen. sec. Fellowship Fgn. Missions, Toronto, 1973-81; chancellor Cen. Bapt. Sem., 1981-93, Heritage Bapt. Bible Coll. and Theol. Sem.,

Cambridge, Ont., Canada, 1993—. Pastor emeritus Forward Bapt. Ch., Toronto, 1994—; chmn. Can. Bd. Greater Europe Mission, 1963-73. Mem. Fellowship Evang. Bapt. Chs. in Can. (pres. 1953-54, 83-84) Conservative. Home: 1540 Kipling Ave Apt 903 Etobicoke ON Canada M9R 4C6 Office: Heritage Bapt Bible Coll and Theol Sem 175 Holiday Inn Dr Cambridge ON Canada N3C 3T2 Office Phone: 519-651-2869.

MACBENN, JOSEPH VERNON, director; b. Youngstown, Ohio, Aug. 31, 1979; s. Joseph Edison and Darlene MacBenn; m. Melissa Strouble, July 8, 2006. B in Music Edn., Mt. Union Coll., Alliance, Ohio, 2001; MEd, Ohio No. U., 2005. Tchg. lic. Ohio. Orch. dir. Lima (Ohio) City Schs., 2001—. Mem.: Am. String Tchrs. Assn., Internat. Trumpet Guild, Ohio Music Edn. Assn., Kappa Kappa Psi, Mu Phi Epsilon. Avocations: music, aquariums, travel. Home: 5097 Shields Rd Canfield OH 44406 Office: Lima Sr High Orch 1 Spartan Way Lima OH 45801 Personal E-mail: orchestrajoe@hotmail.com. Business E-Mail: jmacbenn@hotmail.com.

MACBETH, ANGUS, lawyer; b. LA, May 9, 1942; BA, Yale U., 1964, LLB, 1969. Bar: NY 1970, DC 1981. Law clk. to Hon. Harold R. Tyler, Jr. US Dist. Ct. (so. dist.) NY, 1969-70, asst. US atty. criminal divsn., 1975-77; chief pollution control sect. Land and Natural Resources Divsn., US Dept. Justice, 1977-79, dep. asst. atty. gen., 1979-81; ptnr. and sr. counsel environ. law Sidley Austin LLC, Washington, 1986—. Adj. prof. law NY Law Sch., 1985-2000; spl. counsel Wartime Relocation and Internment Civilians Commn., 1981-83. Mem. DC Bar (steering com. energy and natural resources divsn. 1982-84), NY State Bar Assn., Phi Beta Kappa. Office: Sidley Austin LLC 1501 K St NW Washington DC 20005 Office Phone: 202-736-8271.

MACCARTHY, TALBOT LELAND, civic volunteer; b. St. Louis, Jan. 28, 1936; d. Austin Porter Leland and Dorothy (Lund) Follansbee; m. John Peters MacCarthy, June 21, 1958; children: John Leland MacCarthy, Talbot MacCarthy Payne. BA, Vassar Coll., 1958. Sec., treas. Station List Pub. Co., St. Louis, 1975-85, pres., 1985-90. Hon. trustee Robert E. Lee Meml. Assn., Arts and Edn. Coun. Greater St. Louis, pres., 1978-80, emerita; past vestry mem. St. Michael and St. George Ch., 1997-00; past trustee St. Louis Art Mus., St. Louis Merc. Libr. Assn., Family & Children's Svc. Greater St. Louis, Health and Welfare Coun., Greater St. Louis, Jr. Kindergarten St. Louis Page Park YMCA, Scholarship Found. St. Louis, Friends St. Louis Art Mus. Bd., Ch. St. Michael and St. George Sch. Bd., Mid-Am. Arts Alliance; chmn. Mo. Arts Coun., 1980-85; past chmn. Vol. Action Ctr. Greater St. Louis; past vice chmn. bd. dirs. Mary Inst.; past pres. Jr. League St. Louis; mem. Nat. Coun. Arts, 1985-91; past mem. nat. coun. for Sch. of Art Washington U.; trustee, Seabury-Western Theol. Sem. Recipient Woman of Achievement citation St. Louis Globe Democrat, 1979, Mo. Citizens for Arts/Arts Advocacy award, 1987, Mo. Arts Award, 1993, Honor medal, Mary Inst. and Country Day Sch., 2005. Mem. Vassar Club St. Louis (past pres.), Mary Inst. Alumnae Assn. (past pres.), Colonial Dames Am., Garden Club St. Louis, Belvedere Club (Charlevoix, Mich.; former mem. bd. dirs.). Republican. Episcopalian. Avocations: tennis, visual arts, performing arts.

MACCARTHY, TERENCE FRANCIS, lawyer; b. Chgo., Feb. 5, 1934; s. Frank E. and Catherine (McIntyre) MacC.; m. Marian Fulton, Nov. 25, 1961; children— Daniel Fulton, Sean Patrick, Terence Fulton, Megan Catherine BA in Philosophy, St. Joseph's Coll., 1955; JD, DePaul U., 1960. Bar: Ill. 1960, U.S. Dist. Ct. (no. dist.) Ill. 1961, U.S. Ct. Appeals (7th cir.) 1961, U.S. Supreme Ct. 1966. Assoc. prof. law Chase Coll. Law, Cin., 1960-61; law clk. to chief judge U.S. Dist. Ct., 1961-66; spl. asst. atty. gen. Ill., 1965-67; exec. dir. Fed. Defender Program, U.S. Dist. Ct. (no. dist.) Ill., Chgo., 1966—. Mem. nat. adv. com. on criminal rules; 7th cir. criminal jury instrn. com.; chmn. Nat. Defender Com.; chmn. bd. regents Nat. Coll. Criminal Def.; faculty Fed. Jud. Ctr., Nat. Coll. Criminal Def., Nat. Inst. Trial Advocacy, U. Va. Trial Advocacy Inst., Harvard Law Sch. Trial Advocacy Program, Western Trial Advocacy Inst., Northwestern U., U. Ill. Defender Trial Advocacy course, Nat. Criminal Def. Coll., Loyola U. Trial Advocacy Program; lectr. in field Contbr. articles on criminal law to profl. jours. Bd. dirs. U.S.O. Served as 1st lt. USMC, 1955-57 Recipient Nat. Legal Aid and Defender Assn./ABA Reginald Heber Smith award, 1986, Alumni Merit award St. Joseph Coll., 1970, Cert. of Distinction USO, 1977, Harrison Tweed Spl. Merit award Am. Law Inst./ABA, 1987, Bill of Rights award Ga. chpt. ACLU, 1986, William J. Brennan award U. Va., 1989, Alumni Svc. award DePaul U. Coll. Law, 1994, Ann. Significant Contbns. award Calif. Attys. for Criminal Justice, Defender of the Century Fed. Defenders Assn., Inns of Ct. and Ct. of Appeals (7th cir.) Professionalism award; named to Outstanding Young Men of Am., 1970. Mem. ABA (past chmn. criminal justice sect., ho. of dels., bd. govs., Charles English award criminal justice sect.), Ill. Bar Assn., Chgo. Bar Assn., 7th Cir. Bar Assn., Nat. Assn. Criminal Def. Lawyers (Disting. Svc. award 1993), Nat. Legal Aid and Defender Assn., Nat. Coll. Criminal Def. (chair), Union League of Chgo. (pres.). Democrat. Roman Catholic. Office: US Dist Ct No Dist Ill 55 E Monroe St Ste 2800 Chicago IL 60603-5802

MACCHIAROLA, FRANK JOSEPH, academic administrator, educator; b. NYC, Apr. 7, 1941; s. Joseph John and Lucy (Bernardo) M.; m. Mary Teresa Collins, June 13, 1970; children: Joseph John, Michael Collins, Frank Joseph. BA, St. Francis Coll., 1962, L.H.D. (hon.), 1981; LL.B., Columbia U., 1965, PhD, 1970; L.H.D. (hon.), Coll. S.I., 1983; LL.D. (hon.), Dominican Coll., 1983, Manhattan Coll., 1983, St. Joseph's Coll., Molloy Coll., 1999; LL.D., Fordham U., 2009. From fellow to prof. polit. sci. CUNY, 1964-83, v.p., 1977-78; asst. v.p. Columbia U., NYC, 1973-74; dep. dir. N.Y. State Emergency Fin. Control Bd. for N.Y.C., 1976-77; chancellor of schs. N.Y.C. Public Sch. System, 1978-83; pres., chief exec. officer N.Y.C. Partnership, Inc., 1983-87; pres. Acad. of Polit. Sci., 1987-91; prof. bus. Columbia U., NYC, 1987-91; dean Benjamin N. Cardozo Sch. of Law, Yeshiva U., NYC, 1991-96; of counsel Tannenbaum, Helpern, Syracuse and Hirschtritt, NYC, 1991—; pres. St. Francis Coll., NY, 1996—2008, chancellor, 2008—. Trustee Manville Personal Injury Settlement Trust. Decorated cavalieri Order of Merit Italy; recipient cert. of merit Dirigible Soc. Am., 1976 Democrat. Roman Catholic. Office: 180 Remsen St Brooklyn NY 11201-4305 Office Phone: 718-489-5345. E-mail: fmacchia@stfranciscollege.edu.

MACCHIONE, NICK, city health department director; b. Catanzarro, Italy, Feb. 14, 1968; came to U.S., 1969; BA, Rutgers State U., 1990; MS, NYU, 1994; MPH, Columbia U., 1997. Program dir. Newark Dept. of Health and Human Services, 1993-97; chief, dir. Office AIDS Coord. County San Diego Dept. Health, 1997-98; gen. mgr. through dep. dir. & dir. County of San Diego Health and Human Services Agy., 1998—. Faculty mem. Grad. Sch. Pub. Health San Diego State Univ. John J. Hanlon Scholar, Pub. Health Leadership Scholar, Centers for Disease Control & Prevention. Fellow: Am. Coll. Healthcare Executives; mem.: Delta Omega of the Sigma (hon.). Avocations: domestic and international travel, chess, wine collecting. Office: San Diego HHSA Rm 207 MS-P501 1700 Pacific Hwy San Diego CA 92101 Office Phone: 619-515-6555.*

MACCINI, LOUIS JOHN, economist, educator; b. Cambirdge, Mass., Aug. 3, 1942; s. Joseph and Jennie (Leccacorvi) M.; m. Carol Monterisi, June 25, 1965; children: Michael S., Sharon L. BS in Economics, Boston Coll., 1965; PhD in Economics, Northwestern U., 1970. From asst. prof. to assoc. prof. economics The Johns Hopkins U., Balt., 1969-86, prof., 1986—, chair, 1992—2007. Ad hoc com. mem. graduate fin. aid, Johns Hopkins U., editorial bd., public interest investment adv. com., law sch. com., med. sch. com., and other coms.; mem. recruting chair dept. grad. student advisor dept., and other depts. Referee Am. Econ. Review, Jour. Econ. Dynamics and Control, Oxford Econ. Papers, and others; contbr. articles to profl. jours. Grantee NSF. Mem. Am. Econ. Assn., The Econometric Soc., Internat Soc. Inventory Rsch. Office: Johns Hopkins U 3400 N Charles St Baltimore MD 21218-2680 Home Phone: 410-433-7147; Office Phone: 410-516-7607. E-mail: maccini@jhu.edu.

MACCIONI, SIRIO, restaurant manager; b. Montecatini, Italy, 1932; s. Eugenio Maccioni; m. Egidiana Maccioni, 1964; children: Mario, Marco, Mauro. With Plaza Athénée, Maxim's, Paris, Hotel Atlantic, Hamberg; waiter cruise ship, 1956, Delmonico's, NYC; maître d' The Colony, NYC, 1961; founder, owner Le Cirque, Mayfair Hotel, NYC, 1974—97, Le Cirque 2000, Palace Hotel, NYC, 1997, Le Cirque, Bloomberg Tower, 2006—, Osteria del Circo, NYC, Las Vegas, Le Cirque, Las Vegas, Mexico City. Co-author: Sirio: The Story of My Life and Le Cirque, 2004; featured in (films) Le Cirque: A Table in Heaven, 2008. Office: Le Cirque 151 E 58th St New York NY 10022*

MACCLEAN, WALTER LEE, dentist; b. Sheridan, Wyo., July 10, 1935; s. Edward Satterlee and Eleanor Elizabeth (Weir) Mac.; m. Nancy Lee Strale, Sept. 4, 1965 (div. 1975); children: David Satterlee, Carrie Lynn. BS with honors, U. Wyo., 1957, postgrad., 1958; DMD, U. Oreg., Portland, 1962. Mil. dental adv. Korean Mil. Adv. Group, Wonju, 1962-63; chief dental svc. Dugway Chem. Testing Ctr., Utah, 1965-68; pvt. dental practice Cheyenne, Wyo., 1968-70; assoc. prof. Sheridan Coll., Wyo., 1970-76; staff dentist VA Hosp. Med. Ctr., Ft. Meade, S.D., 1976-93; ret., 1993. Cons., lectr. Health Edn. Program Svc., Ft. Meade, 1984-93. With U.S. Army, 1962-68. Mem. ADA. Jewish. also: Highbourne House 13 15 Marylebone High St London W1M 3PE England Home: 1898 Fort Rd Sheridan WY 82801

MACCORMACK, CHARLES FREDERICK, international relief organization executive; b. Oct. 27, 1941; married; two children. AB, Middlebury Coll., 1963, EdD (hon.), 1982; MIA, Columbia U., 1965, PhD, 1974. Staff assoc. internat. div. First Nat. City Bank, Caracas, Venezuela, 1964; instr. latin-Am. politics U. N.H., Durham, 1967; asst. to dean Internat. Fellows Program Columbia U., NYC, 1967-68; rsch. fellow fgn. policy studies Brookings Instn., Washington, 1969-70; dir. internat. career tng. program Experiment Internat. Living, Brattleboro, Vt., 1970-74; v.p. programs Save the Children Fedn./Community Devel. Found., Westport, Conn., 1974-77; pres. World Learning (formerly The Experiment Internat. Living/Sch. for Internat. Tng.), Brattleboro, 1977—92; pres., CEO Save the Children Fedn., Inc., Westport, Conn., 1993—. Bd. dirs. Arthur D. Little Mgmt. Edn. Inst., Ptnrs. Internat. Edn. and Tng., Am. Forum for Global Edn., Landmark Coll., Save the Children Fedn., Inc., 1993- Mng. editor Jour. Internat. Affairs. Mem. founding com. U., 1971-72, Vt. Commn. Edn. and the Econ. Future, 1982, coun. advisors Peace Corps Future Team, 1987, Coun. Fgn. Rels., N.Y.C., global awareness adv. bd. Wheaton Coll., Norton, Mass.; mem. exec. com., chair devel. assistance com., co-chair com. refugee svcs. Am. Coun. Voluntary Internat. Action. Universidad Cen. de Venezuela Fulbright fellow, Caracas, Venezuela, 1965-66, Universidad Nacional Autonoma de Mexico NSF fellow, Mexico City, 1968-69, Edward John Noble Leadership fellow, 1963-65; Gould scholar, Middlebury scholar, Travelli scholar, 1959-63. Office: Save the Children Fedn Inc 54 Wilton Rd Westport CT 06880

MACCORMACK, JEAN F., academic administrator; d. George and Helen MacCormack. BA, Emmanuel Coll., Boston, 1969; MEd, U. Mass., Amherst, 1978, EdD, 1979. Assoc. dean Coll. of Edn. U. Mass, Boston, 1984—87, acting dean Coll. of Edn., 1984—85, assoc. chancellor, 1987—88, vice chancellor arts and fin., 1988—95, interim chancellor, 1995—96, dep. chancellor and vice chancellor arts and fin., 1996—99, chancellor Dartmouth, 1999—. Mem. South Coast Econ. Devel. Partnership, 1999, Joint CEO Group, 2000, Racial and Ethnic Access and Fairness Adv. Bd., 2001; chair South Coast Edn. Compact, 2000; mem. vis. com. U. So. Maine New Eng. Assoc. of Sch. and Coll., 2000—01; ex-officio mem. U. Mass. Dartmouth Libr. Archive Campaign, 2001; bd. mem. South Coast Health Sys., Inc., 2002; mem. marine sci. com. Fall River CEO Group, 2003, mem. med. device com., 03, mem. south coast edn. com., 03; mem. Regional Competitiveness Coun., 2003. Vice chair bd. govs. New Bedford Oceanariun, 1999, chair edn and rsch. com., 1999, trustee, chair edn. com., 2000; trustee Artworks! at Dover St., 2000, mem. edn. com, 2000, mem. pers. com., 2000; trustee Global Learning Charter Sch., 2000; bd. mem. Greater New Bedford Workforce Investment Bd., 2000, mem. legis. affairs and pub. info. com., 2000, mem. youth coun., 2000; mem. New Bedford Econ. Devel. Coun., 2000; corporator Child and Family Svcs., Inc., 2002; incorporator Home Aged People in Fall river, 2003; corporator Narragansett Fin. Corp. Citizens - Union Savs. Bank, 2003; mem. pres.'s coun. New Bedford Symphony Orch., 2003; mem. leadership coun. New Bedford Whaling Mus. Mem.: YMCA of Southeastern Mass., WHALE, Am. Assn. of State Coll. and U., U. Mass. Dartmouth Libr. Assoc. E-mail: jmaccormack@umassd.edu.

MACCORMACK, SABINE GABRIELE, history educator; b. Frankfurt, Germany, Feb. 24, 1941; came to U.S., 1978; d. Alfred and Gabriele (Buhl) Oswalt; m. Geoffrey MacCormack, June 20, 1964; 1 child, Catherine. BA in History, Oxford U., Eng., 1964, PhD, 1974; diploma in archives, U. Liverpool, Eng., 1965. Asst. prof. history U. Tex., Austin, 1979-82; asst. prof. history and classics Stanford (Calif.) U., 1982-85, assoc. prof., 1985-89; Alice Freeman Palmer prof. history U. Mich., Ann Arbor, 1989-97, Mary Ann & Charles R. Walgreen Jr. prof. study human under., 1997—2008; Mellon vis. prof. Inst. for Advanced Study, Princeton, N.J., 1996-98; Theodore Hesborgh prof. Arts and Letters U. Notre, 2003—. Author: Art and Ceremony in Late Antiquity, 1981, Vision and Imagination in Early Colonial Peru, 1991, The Shadows of Poetry. Vergil in the Mind of Augustine, 1998; series editor Langs. and Cultures of the Spanish and Portuguese Worlds, 1997—; editl. cons. Viator, L.A., 1997—. Getty scholar Getty Ctr., L.A., 1991-92. Fellow Am. Acad. Arts & Scis., Medieval Acade Am.; mem. Am. Philos. Soc. Avocation: painting. Office: Kellog Institute Univ of Notre Notre Dame IN 46556

MACCRACKEN, MICHAEL CALVIN, atmospheric scientist; b. Schenectady, May 20, 1942; s. Calvin Dodd MacCracken and Martha (McCracken) MacCracken Howard; m. Sandra Ann Svets, Mar. 12, 1967; children: Christopher, Ronald. BS in Engring., Princeton U., 1964; MS in Applied Sci., U. Calif.-Davis/Livermore, 1966, PhD in Applied Sci., 1968. Atmospheric scientist Lawrence Livermore Nat. Lab., 1968—2002, prin. investigator, Bay Area air quality modeling study, 1973—76, dep. div. leader atmospheric and geophys. scis. div., 1974—87, div. leader atmospheric and geophys. scis. div., 1993—97; sr. scientist Office US Global Change Rsch. Program, 1993—2002, exec. dir., 1993—97, exec. dir. nat. assessment coord. office, 1997—2001, co-project leader study on global effects of nuclear exchange, 1983—88; prin. investigator Earth System Modeling Project, 1991—93; area mgr. CO2 research program Dept. Energy, 1979—90, project dir. multistate atmospheric power prodn. study, 1976—79; project leader bilateral environ. working group VIII Ukraine, 1984—90; mem. Internat. Com. Climate, 1987—2003, pres., 1995—2003; chief scientist climate change programs Climate Inst., Washington, 2002—. Mem. assesment investigation team Arctic Climate Impact Assessment, 2003—04. Co-author: Environmental Consequences of Nuclear War, Vol. 1: Physical and Atmospheric Effects, 1986; co-author: (co-editor) Projecting the Climatic Effects of Increasing Carbon Dioxide(US Dept. Energy State of the Arts reports), 1985; editor (assoc.): J. of Climate, 1987—95; co-editor: Sudden and Disruptive Climate Change: Exploring the Real Risks and How We Can Avoid Them, 2005; contbr. articles to profl. publs. Bd. dirs. Livermore Area Recreation and Park Dist., 1970—78, chmn., 1974, 1978. Grantee, Fannie and John Hertz Found., 1964—68. Mem.: AAAS (fellow, chair atmosperic and hydrosperic scis. 1996—97), Sci. Com. Oceanic Rsch., Internat. Assn. Meteorology and Atmospheric Scis. (pres. 2003—07), Am. Oceanography Soc., Am. Geophys. Union, Am. Meteorol. Soc. (chmn. com. on climate variations 1983—85).

MACCRATE, ROBERT, lawyer; b. Bklyn., July 18, 1921; s. John and Flora (MacNicholl) MacC.; m. Constance Trapp, May 4, 1946; children: Christopher Robert, Barbara Constance MacCrate Gatti, Thomas John. BA, Haverford Coll., 1943, LLD (hon.), 1987; LLB, Harvard U., 1948; LLD (hon.), Union U., 1986, Dickinson Sch. Law, 1987, William Mitchell Coll. Law, 1994, Quinnipiac Coll. Law, 1995, CUNY, 2002, U. S.C., 2003. Bar: N.Y. 1949, U.S. Supreme Ct. 1955, D.C. 1965. Assoc. Sullivan & Cromwell, NYC, 1948-51, 51-55, ptnr., 1956-59, 62-91, ret., 1991—96, sr. counsel, 1997—; law sec. N.Y. Appelate Divsn. Presiding Justice David W. Peck, 1951; counsel N.Y. Gov. Nelson A. Rockefeller, 1959-62; spl. counsel U.S. Army for Investigation Mylai incident, 1969-70; counsel N.Y. State Ct. on Judiciary, 1971; mem. jud. selection com. for fed. judgeships Senator Jacob K. Javits, 1972-80; mem. jud. nominating com. N.Y. 2d Jud. Dept., 1975-82. Trustee Lawyers Com. for Civil Rights Under Law, 1976—; chmn. emeritus Fund for Modern Cts., 1978—; cons. N.Y. Profl. Edn. Project, 1994-96. Co-author: Appellate Justice in New York, 1982, Legal Education and Professional Development--an Educational Continuum, 1992, Preserving the Core Values of the American Legal Profession, 2000; contbr. articles to profl. jours. Bd. mgrs. Haverford Coll., 1971-85, emeritus 1986—. Lt. USNR, 1943-46. Recipient Justice System Improvement award Coun. for Ct. Excellence, 1988, Gold medal Nat. Inst. Social Scis., 1989. Fellow Am. Bar Found. (chmn. N.Y. state 1973-80, bd. dirs. 1989—, sec. 1992-94, v.p. 1994-96, pres. 1996-98); mem. ABA (pres. 1987-88, del. 1972-78, 89—, N.Y. State del. 1979-81, bd. govs. 1981-84, 86-89, chair task force law schs. and the profession 1989-92, chair spl. adv. com. internat. activities 1988-89, 2d cir. mem. standing com. on fed. judiciary 1984-86, mem. commn. on opportunities in profession 1993-96, mem. coun. sect. individual rights and responsibilities 1997-2000, medal 2002), N.Y. State Bar Assn. (pres. 1972-73, del. 1972—, chair com. law governing firm structure and operation 1999-2002, medal 1999), Assn. Bar City of N.Y. (v.p. 1969-71, chmn. exec. com. 1968-69, chmn. libr. com. 1977-80, chmn. 2d century com. 1989-92), Bar Assn. Nassau County, D.C. Bar Assn., N.Y. County Lawyers Assn. (Disting. Svc. award 1991), Nat. Bar Assn., Am. Coll. Trial Lawyers, Am. Soc. Internat. Law (exec. coun. 1975-80), Union Internationale des Avocats, Acad. Polit. Sci. (bd. dirs. 1975-94), Am. Judicature Soc. (pres. 1979-81, bd. dirs. and mem. exec. com. 1974-83, Justice award 1989), Practising Law Inst. (trustee and mem. exec. com. 1972-95, emeritus trustee 1995—, Seligson award 1995), Am. Law Inst. (coun. 1975-2007, emeritus mem. coun. 2007-, ALI-ABA com. on continuing profl. edn. 1994-97, chair subcom. on future 1994-97), N.Y. Bar Found. (pres. 1976-91, Lifetime Achievement award, 2008), Phi Beta Kappa. Home: 40 The Terrace Plandome NY 11030-1349 Office: Sullivan & Cromwell Rm 2418 125 Broad St New York NY 10004-2498 Home Phone: 516-627-6255.

MACDEVITT, BRIAN, lighting designer; b. Oct. 6, 1956; s. William Gerard and Julie (Powers) MacDevitt. BFA, SUNY, Purchase; studies with Bill Mintzer. Guest instr. design dept. SUNY, 1986—87; faculty mem. NYU Tisch Sch. Lighting designer (Broadway plays) What's Wrong With This Picture?, 1994, Love! Valour! Compassion!, 1995, Master Class, 1995, Summer and Smoke, 1996, Sex and Longing, 1996, Present Laughter, 1996, Side Show, 1997, Proposals, 1997, The Diary of Anne Frank, 1997, Wait Until Dark, 1998, Night Must Fall, 1999, True West, 2000, The Ride Down Mt. Morgan, 2000, The Dinner Party, 2000, Judgment at Nuremberg, 2001, The Invention of Love, 2001, A Thousand Clowns, 2001, Major Barbara, 2001, Urinetown, 2001, The Women, 2001, Morning's at Seven, 2002, Into the Woods, 2002 (Tony award for Best Lighting Design of a Musical, 2002), Frankie and Johnny in the Clair de Lune, 2002, Short Talks on the Universe, 2002, Tartuffe, 2003, Nine, 2003, Long Day's Journey into Night, 2003, The Retreat From Moscow, 2003, Henry IV, 2003, Fiddler on the Roof, 2004, Match, 2004, A Raisin in the Sun, 2004, 'night Mother, 2004, Pacific Overtures, 2004, Good Vibrations, 2005, The Pillowman, 2005 (Tony award for Best Lighting Design of a Play, 2005), Sweet Charity, 2005, Dog Sees God: Confessions of a Teenage Blockhead, 2005, The Wedding Singer, 2006, The Vertical Hour, 2006, Inherit the Wind, 2007, Cymbeline, 2007, A Catered Affair, 2008, 13, 2008, Speed-the-Plow, 2008, American Buffalo, 2008, You're Welcome America, 2009, Blithe Spirit, 2009, Joe Turner's Come and Gone, 2009 (Tony award for Best Lighting Design of a Play, 2009), Accent on Youth, 2009, Race, 2009, (plays) Oh, Coward!, 1979, A Girl's Guide to Chaos, 1986, Seven Brides for Seven Brothers, 1984, Gigi, 1984, Oliver!, 1985, Brigadoon, 1986, Can-Can, 1988, The House in Town, 2006, The Coast of Utopia, 2006 (Outer Critics Cir. award outstanding lighting design, 2007, Drama Desk award outstanding lighting design, 2007, Tony award for Best Lighting Design of a Play, 2007). Mem.: United Scenic Artists.*

MACDONALD, ALAN HUGH, academic administrator; b. Ottawa, Ont., Can., Mar. 3, 1943; s. Vincent C. and Hilda C. MacDonald; children: Eric Paul Henry, Nigel Alan Christopher. BA, Dalhousie U., Halifax NS, 1963; BLS, U. Toronto, Ont., 1964. With Dalhousie U., 1964-78, law libr., 1965-67, 69-71, asst. univ. libr., 1970-72, health sci. libr., 1972-78, lectr. Sch. Libr. Svcs., 1969-78; with U. Calgary, Canada, 1979—2003, sr. advisor Info. Resources, 1999—2003, asst. to provost, 1999—2003, adj. prof. faculty comm. and culture, 2000—03, dir. Info Svcs., 1988—99, dir. librs., 1979-92, univ. orator, 1989—2003; dir. U. Calgary Press, 1984—90. Chair editl. bd. U. Calgary Press, 2001—03, libr. emeritus, 2003—; libr. N.S. Barristers Soc., 1969—74; mem. adv. bd. Nat. Libr. Can., 1972—76, Health Scis. Resource Ctr., Can. Inst. Sci. and Tech. Info., 1977—79; mem. Coun. of Prairie Univ. Librs., 1979—92, 1997—98, chair, 1984—85, 1989, 91; Bassam lectr. U. Toronto Faculty Info. Studies, 1994; Lorne MacRae lectr. Libr. Assn. Alta., 1996; mem. steering com. Alta. Libr. Knowledge Network, 1999—2002; steering com. Can. Digital Libr. Rsch. Initiative, 1999—2000. Mem. editl. bd. America: History and Life (ABC-CLIO), 1985-93. Pres. TELED Cmty. Media Access Orgn., Halifax, N.S.,

1972—74; mem. Minister's Com. on Univ. Affairs, Alta., 1979—83; bd. dirs. Alta. Found. for Can. Music Ctr., 1985—92, Can. Inst. for Hist. Microreprodn., 1990—98, pres., 1996—97; bd. dirs. Calgary Learning Ctr., 1997—2004, vice-chair, 2000—04. Coun. Libr. Resources fellow, 1975; exec. fellow Univ. Microfilms Internat., 1986; recipient Disting. Acad. Librarian award Can. Assn. of Coll. and Univ. Libraries, 1988, U. Toronto Faculty of Info. Studies Alumni Jubilee award, 1999. Mem.: Order of U. Calgary, Calgary Cmty. Network Assn. (bd. dirs. 1994—99, chair 1996—99), Can. Assn. Rsch. Librs. (bd. dirs. 1981—86, v.p. 1985—86, Disting. Svc. award to rsch. librarianship 2003), Can. Assn. Info. Sci. (pres. 1979—80), Foothills Libr. Assn., Atlantic Provinces Libr. Assn. (pres. 1977—78), Can. Libr. Assn. (treas. 1977—79, pres. 1980—81, Award for Outstanding Svc. to Librarianship 1997), Australian Libr. and Info. Assn. (assoc.), Can. Health Libr. Assn. (life; treas. 1977—79), Libr. Assn. Alta. (life; v.p. 1988—89, Pres.' award 1992), AeroSpace Mus. Assn. Calgary (bd. dirs. 2002—07, exec. dir. 2003—04, sec. 2004—07, libr. 2006—). Personal E-mail: ahmacdon@ucalgary.ca.

MACDONALD, ANNE, insurance company executive; b. NJ; BEd, Boston Coll.; MBA, Bath U., Eng. Account mgr. Grey Advt.; account mgr., exec. v.p., mng. dir. N.W. Ayer, Inc.; v.p. brand mgmt., Pizza Hut divsn. PepsiCo, 1993—97; mng. dir. global branding and comm., mng. dir. global mktg. consumer needs Citigroup Inc., 1997—2004, chief mktg. officer consumer divsn., 2004—06; pres., chief mktg. officer Macy's corp. mktg. Federated Dept. Stores, 2006—07; ptnr. The Rockefeller Consulting Group, 2007—09; exec. v.p., chief mktg. officer The Travelers Companies, Inc., 2009—. Bd. dirs. The Rentrak Corp., 2009—. Office: The Travelers Companies Inc One Tower Sq Hartford CT 06183*

MACDONALD, BRIAN, computer software company executive; Attended, U. Wash., 1980—82. Head Microsoft Project devel. team Microsoft Corp., Redmond, Wash., 1989, gen. mgr. Microsoft Outlook team, sr. v.p. subscription svcs., mgr. NetDos, 1999, corp. v.p. core search program mgmt., 2007—. Office: Microsoft Corp One Microsoft Way Redmond WA 98052-6399*

MACDONALD, BRIAN P., oil industry executive; BS, Mount Allison U.; MBA, McGill U. Treas. GM Canada GM Corp., 1998—2000, dep. CFO Izuzu Moters Ltd.; head mergers and acquisitions orgn. and global treasury group Dell, Inc., corp. v.p., treas., chmn. Dell Fin. Svcs., CFO comml. bus. unit, 2008—09; sr. v.p., CFO Sunoco, Inc., Phila., 2009—. Office: Sunoco, Inc 1735 Market St, Ste LL Philadelphia PA 19103*

MACDONALD, BRIAN SCOTT, management consultant; b. Sudbury, Ont., Can., June 6, 1939; s. David William and Katherine Lillian (McKinnon) MacD.; m. Margaret Louise Young, Aug. 11, 1962 (dec. Apr. 1985); children— Heather Anne, David Colin, Michael Alexander BA with honors, Royal Mil. Coll., Kingston, Ont., 1961; MBA cum laude, York U., Toronto, Ont., 1980; postgrad., U. Toronto, 1980—. Tchr., cons. Bd. Edn., Ont., Can., 1966-80; exec. dir. Can. Inst. Strategic Studies, Toronto, Ont., Can., 1982-89; pres. Strategic Insight Planning and Communications, 1989—; rsch. assoc. Queens U. Centre for Def. Mgmt. Studies, 2005—. Author: Military Spending in Developing Countries: How Much is Too Much, 1997; editor: Parliament and Defence Policy, 1982, War in the 80's: Men Against High Tech, 1983, Canada's Strategies for Space, 1984, The Grand Strategy of the Soviet Union, 1984, Defence and the Canadian Economy, 1984, Canada's Strategies for the Pacific Rim, 1985, High Tech and the High Seas, 1985, Canada, the Caribbean, and Central Am., 1986, Terror, 1986, Tactics and Technology, 1987, A Grand Strategy for the United States?, 1988, Airwar 2000, 1989, Canadian Strategic Forecast 1989, 1989, Space Strategy: Three Dimensions, 1989, The New World of Robust International Peacekeeping, 2005, Defence Requirements for Canada's Arctic, 2007, Canadians and Asia Pacific Security, 2008, The Strategic Impact of Energy Dependency, 2009; contbg. editor Def. Policy Rev., 1994-04. Pres. Royal Can. Arty. Assn., Toronto, 1976; vice chmn. Conf. Def. Assns., Ottawa, Ont., 1975, bd. dirs., 2005—, sr. def. analyst, 2006—; gov. Can. Corps of Commissionaires, Toronto, 1984-86; hon. aide de camp to Gov. Gen. Can., Ottawa, 1984-86; comdr. Toronto Militia Dist., 1984-86; bd. dirs. Atlantic Coun. Can., 1986—2005, sr. v.p., 1991, pres., 1999-2002; bd dirs. Royal Can. Mil. Inst., 1986-87, 2004—. Served to col. Can. Army, 1957-86. Marsh-McLennan scholar, 1977, Dept. Nat. Def. scholar, 1981-82 Mem. Toronto Bd. Trade. Office: 169 Newton Dr Toronto ON Canada M2M 2N6 Office Phone: 416-223-2192. Business E-Mail: strategicinsight@sympatico.ca.

MACDONALD, DON, psychology educator; b. Mar. 24, 1950; BA in Psychology, U. Tex., 1972; MS in Counseling, Ind. U., 1973; PhD in Psychology, Mich. State U., 1984. Tchr. 3rd grade Northshore Sch. Dist., Kenmore, Wash., 1975-76; staff psychologist Ho. of Commons, Lansing, Mich., 1976-80; grad. asst. Mich. State U., East Lansing, 1977-80; asst. prof. coun. and family therapy Seattle Pacific U., 1980-86, assoc. prof. coun. and family and cmty. therapy, 1986-96, prof. family therapy, 1996—. Office: Seattle Pacific Univ Watson Hall 112 Seattle WA 98119 Office Phone: 206-281-2107. Business E-Mail: eieio@spu.edu.

MACDONALD, DONALD ARTHUR, JR., physician, surgeon; b. Englewood, NJ, May 9, 1955; s. Donald Arthur and Ruth Moran M.; m. Florence Twombly Childs, June 14, 1980; children: Donald, Alexandra, Margaret, Ian. BA with highest honors, Williams Coll., 1977; MD, Dartmouth U., 1980. Diplomate Am. Bd. Ophthalmology. Intern Mary Imogene Bassett Hosp., Cooperstown, N.Y., 1980-81; resident Manhattan Eye Ear & Throat Hosp., NYC, 1981-84, attending physician, 1985—; fellow N.Y. Eye Ear & Throat Hosp., 1984-85; attending physician Riverview Med. Ctr., Red Bank, N.J., 1985—, chief dept. ophthalmology, 1995-97. Trustee Rumson (NJ) Country Day Sch., 1990-96, Monmouth County Vol. Ctr., 1996-98, Horizons Program, Rumson, 1996-98; trustee, bd. dirs. ALS Assn. Greater NY chpt.; bd. dirs. Burden Ctr. for the Aging, 2000-03. Mem. Lions, Rumson Country Club (commodore 1996-2003), Seabright Lawn Tennis and Cricket Club, St. Andrews Soc. N.Y., N.Y. Yacht Club, Monmouth Beach Club. Roman Catholic. Office: 21 Gilbert St N Tinton Falls NJ 07701-4913 Home Phone: 732-747-8217; Office Phone: 732-741-1902. E-mail: Drdonaldmadonald@mac.com.

MACDONALD, DONALD PAUL, lawyer; b. Newport, RI, Apr. 19, 1931; s. Bertram I. and Pauline E. (Toomey) MacD.; widowed; children: Theresa Carroll, Sheila Joan, D. Patrick. BA, Providence Coll., 1952; LLB, Georgetown U., 1956, LLM, 1963. Assoc. then ptnr. Smith & Pepper, Washington, 1957-61; asst. U.S. atty. Dept. Justice, Denver, 1962-67; ptnr. Carroll & MacDonald, Denver, 1967-72, Hornbein & MacDonald, Denver, 1972—. Dir. Legal Ctr., Denver, 1986—, pres., 1989—; dir. Qualife Wellness Com., Denver, 1994-2000; trustee, fellow Coll. Labor and Employment Lawyers, 1995—, pres. 1999, labor and employment law sect. mem. coun. 1985—, chair 1995-96, dir. Denver Children Advocacy Ctr., 2000-. With U.S. Army, 1952-54. Recipient Cath. Lawyers Guild St. Thomas More award, 1983. Fellow Am. Bar Found., Internat. Soc. Barristers; mem. ABA (mem. labor and employment sect., house dels. 1974-84), Denver Bar Assn. (pres. 1981-82), Univ. Club. Roman Catholic. Office Phone: 303-399-1617. Personal E-mail: dpmacdonald@netzero.com.

MACDONALD, DONALD STOVEL, public policy advisor; b. Ottawa, Ont., Can., Mar. 1, 1932; s. Donald Angus and Marjorie (Stovel) M.; m. Ruth Hutchison, Mar. 4, 1961 (dec.); children: Leigh, Nikki, Althea, Sonja; m. Adrian Merchant Lang, Sept. 10, 1988; stepchildren: Maria (dec.), Timothy, Gregory, Andrew, Elisabeth, Amanda, Adrian. Student, Ashbury Coll., Ottawa; BA, U. Toronto, Ont., 1951; LLB, Osgoode Hall Law Sch., 1955; LLM, Harvard, 1956; diploma internat. law, Cambridge U., 1957; LLD, St. Lawrence U., U N.B. Saint John, 1990, U. Toronto, 2000, Carleton U., 2003; DEng, Colo. Sch. Mines. Bar: Called to Ont. bar 1955. Assoc. McCarthy & McCarthy, Toronto, 1957-62; M.P. for Toronto-Rosedale, 1962; reelected, 1963, 65, 68, 72, 74; parliamentary sec. to Min. of Justice, 1963-65, to Min. of Finance, 1965, to Sec. of State for External Affairs, 1966-68, to Min. of Industry, 1968; pres. Privy Coun. and Govt. House Leader, 1968-70; min. of nat. def., 1970-72; min. energy, mines and resources, 1972-75; min. of fin., 1975-77; ptnr. firm McCarthy & McCarthy, Toronto, 1977-88; high commr. for Can. to U.K., 1988-91; counsel McCarthy Tetrault, Toronto, 1991-2000. Sr. advisor UBS Bunting Warburg, Toronto, 2000-02; sr. advisor pub. policy Lang Michener Barristers and Solicitors, 2002—; spl. lectr. U. Toronto Law Sch., 1978-82, 86-88; chmn. Royal Commn. on Econ. Union and Devel. Prospects for Can., 1982-85; chmn. adv. com. competition Ont. Electricity Sys., 1995-96; chmn. Inst. for Rsch. on Pub. Policy, Montreal, 1991-97, Siemens Can. Inc., 1991-04, Atlantic Coun. of Can., 1998-02; bd. dirs. Century Mining Corp. 2004-08, Boise Cascade Corp., 1995-04; chmn., trustee IPC US REIT, 2001-07; trustee Clean Power Operating Trust, 2001-07; chmn. Vector Wind Energy, 2005-06; trustee Energy Savs. Income Fund, 2005-06; co-chmn. Trudeau Ctr. Peace Conflict Studies, U. Toronto, 2006-; mem. adv. coun. Ctr. Am. Studies U. Western Ont., 2006-. Named Freeman of the City of London, 1990, hon. fellow Trinity Hall, Cambridge U., 1994, Companion of the Order of Can., 1994. Mem. Queen's Privy Coun. Can., Delta Kappa Epsilon. Liberal. Baptist. Office: Lang Michener Toronto Office Box 747 ste 2500 Brookfield 181 Bay St Toronto ON Canada m5j 2t7 Office Phone: 416-307-4241. Business E-Mail: dmacdonald@langmichener.ca.

MACDONALD, DOUGLAS ANDREW, psychologist, educator; b. Barrie, Can., June 2, 1967; s. David James and Rachel Marie MacDonald; m. Clementina Iampietro, Mar. 15, 1995; children: Moriah, Sarah. BA in Psychology (hon.), U. Windsor, Ont., Can., 1990, MA in Psychology, 1992, PhD in Psychology, 1998. Practicum student Guelph Assessment and Treatment Unit, Ont., Canada, 1991; intern U. Windsor Psychol. Svc. Clinic, 1992—93, Windsor Regional Hosp., 1994—95; behavioral cons. Essex County Dist. Sch. Bd., Ont., Canada, 1995—97; psychologist Greater Essex County Dist. Sch. Bd., Windsor, 1997—2004; prof. psychology U. Detroit, 2000—; dir. clin. MA program U. Detroit Mercy, 2003—. Rsch. asst. U. Windsor, 1987—88; faculty Saybrook Grad. Sch., San Francisco, 2001—; clin. cons. Glengarda Child Family Svc., 2004—. Co-editor: (novels) Approaches to Transpersonal Measurement and Assessment, 2002; editor (rsch. assoc.): Jour. Humanistic Psychology, 2002; co-editor: Humanistic Psychologist, 2003, Internat. Jour. Transpersonal Studies, 2003—06; assoc. editor: Jour. Transpersonal Psychology, 2001, consulting editor: Australian Gestalt Jour. Cons., bd. dirs. Glengarda Child & Family Svc., Windsor, Ontario, Canada, 2000—04. Grantee, Floraglades Found., 2000—04. Mem.: APA (Carmi Harari Early Career award 2006), Can. Psychol. Assoc. Achievements include research in expression, measurement, and devel. of spirituality and assessment tools. Avocations: gardening, music, martial arts. Home: 470 Frontenac Ave N9E1M1 Windsor ON Canada Office: U Detroit Mercy Dept Psychology 4001 W McNichols Rd Detroit MI 48221 Home Phone: 519-250-4723. Business E-Mail: macdonda@udmercy.edu.

MACDONALD, ELIZABETH HUTTON, artist, educator; b. Mpls., Dec. 3, 1926; d. Hugh McMillen and Dorothy (Wackerman) Hutton; m. Edward Holmes MacDonald, Sept. 15, 1951; children: Robert H., Dorothy E., Margaret M., Andrew H. BFA, U. Pa., Pa. Acad. Fine Arts, 1948; postgrad., U. Pa., 1948-49. Interior decorator Armstrong Cork Co., Lancaster, Pa., 1949-51; artist, designer Needlework Studio, Bryn Mawr, Pa., 1949, 51-78; tchr. painting Narberth, Pa., 1954-65; artist, designer, co-owner Bryn Mawr (Pa.) Needlework, 1978-80; artist, designer Narberth, 1980—. Vol. art in schs. program Phila. Art Mus., 1974-85. Leader, Girl Scouts Phila., Narberth, 1964-77. Mem. Orgn. Internat. Denteile au fuseauet à la Iguille, Embroiderers' Guild Am., Inc., (rec. sec. 1983-85, 1st place in profl. embroidery 1983, 2d v.p. 1985-86, editor newsletter 1987, 2d place area exhbn. 1987, Am. Color Print Soc. (sec. 1995-02, treas. 2002-, newsletter editor 2002-04), The Plastic Club (treas. 1990-92, pres. 1992-96, 2000-04, corr. sec. 1997-99, exhbn. co-chair 1998-2008, Monday morning painting tchr. 1982-86, print workshop tchr. 1988-91, also chmn. admissions 1984-85, chmn. exhbns. 1985-86, 1998-2006, newsletter editor 1994-2004, pres. 1999-2004, archivist, 2005—, membership chair, 2006-08, Silver medal 1952, 80, Gold medal 1981, Elizabeth MacDonald Print Studio award, 2009), Phila. Sketch Club (sec. 1994-95, pres. 1995-97, bd. dirs. 1997-01, house chmn. 2001-07, 2008-, bd. dirs., 2004-07, monitor print workshop, 2006-, Elizabeth H MacDonald award, First award, 2009), Pa. Acad. Fine Arts Fellowship (Hon. Mention award 2002, Glick award 2006), Chesapeake Regional Lace Group, Finger Lakes Lace Guild, Mortar Board, Internat. Old Lacers and Liberty Lacers (pres. 1994-98, 2006—, treas. 1998-2005, newsletter editor 1990-98, 02-04), Chi Omega. Republican. Office Phone: 610-664-1997. Personal E-mail: EHM205@verizon.net.

MACDONALD, HUGH IAN, economics professor, public policy professor, academic administrator; b. Toronto, Ont., June 27, 1929; s. Hugh and Winnifred (Mitchell) M.; m. Dorothy Marion Vernon, June 4, 1960; 5 children. B.Com., U. Toronto, 1952; MA, Oxford U., Eng., 1954, B.Phil., 1955; LLD (hon.), U. Toronto, 1974; D Univ. (hon.), Open U., UK, 1998; DLitt (hon.), Open U., Sri Lanka, 1999, Open U., Hyderabad, India, 2001, York U., Toronto, 2007. Lectr. U. Toronto, Ont., Canada, 1955—62, asst. prof., 1962—65; dean of men Univ. Coll. U. Toronto, 1956—65; chief economist Govt. Ont., Canada, 1965—67, dep. treas., 1967, dep. treas., dep. minister econ., 1968, dep. treas., dep. minister econs. and intergovtl. affairs, 1972; pres. York U., Toronto, Ont., Canada, 1974-84, prof. econ. and pub. policy, pres. emeritus, 1984—; dir. York Internat., 1984—94; dir. MPA program York U. Schulich Sch. Bus., 1994—. Past pres. World U. Svc. Can.; past chmn. Hockey Can., Commonwealth of Learning. Recipient Can. Centennial medal, 1967, Queen's Silver Jubilee medal, 1977, Commemorative medal, 125th Anniversary Can. Confedn., 1992, Vanier medal for distinction in pub. svc. and excellence in pub. adminstrn., 2000, Queen's Golden Jubilee medal, 2002, Senator Boorsma medal, Southeastern Conf. Pub. Adminstrn. in U.S., 2006; named Officer, Order of Can., 1977; Rhodes scholar, 1952. Fellow: The Commonwealth of Learning (past chmn.). Office: York U Schulich Sch Bus Rm N207 Seymour Schulich Bldg 4700 Keele St Toronto ON Canada M3J 1P3 Office Phone: 416-736-5632. Office Fax: 416-736-5643. Business E-Mail: yorkmpa@yorku.ca.

MACDONALD, J. RANDALL, information technology executive, human resources specialist; B in Polit. Sci., St. Francis Coll., M in Indsl. Rels. Human resources position Ingersoll-Rand Co., Sterling Drug Inc.; various human resources positions including exec. v.p. human resources and adminstrn. GTE (now Verizon Comm.), 1983—2000; sr. v.p. human resouces IBM, 2000—. Bd. dirs. Covance (formerly Corning Pharm. Svcs.); mem. Cornell U. Ctr. for Advanced Human Resources Study, chmn. exec. bd. Bd. trustees St. Francis Coll., Pa. Fellow: Nat. Acad. Human Resources (bd. dirs. 2000—); mem.: Labor Policy Assn. (vice chmn. bd. dirs.), Pers. Roundtable, Cowdrick Group.*

MACDONALD, JAMES ROSS, physicist, researcher; b. Savannah, Ga., Feb. 27, 1923; s. John Elwood and Antonina Jones (Hansell) Macdonald; m. Margaret Milward Taylor, Aug. 3, 1946; children: Antonina Hansell, James Ross IV, William Taylor. BA, Williams Coll., 1944; SB, MIT, 1944, SM, 1947; PhD, Oxford U., Eng., 1950, DSc, 1967. Staff Digital Computer Lab., MIT, 1946-47; physicist Armour Rsch. Found., Chgo., 1950-52; assoc. physicist Argonne Nat. Lab., 1952-53; with Tex. Instruments Inc., Dallas, 1953-74, v.p. corp. rsch. and engring., 1968-73, v.p. corp. R & D, 1973-74; cons., 1974—; dir. Simmonds Precision Products Inc., 1979-83; William Rand Kenan Jr. prof. physics U. N.C., Chapel Hill, 1974-91, prof. emeritus, 1991—. Adj. prof. biophysics U. Tex. Med. Sch., Dallas, 1954—74; mem. solid state scis. panel NRC, 1965—73; mem. adv. com. sci. edn. NSF, 1971—73; mem. vis. com. physics MIT, 1971—74; mem. external adv. com. Engring. Exptl. Sta. Ga. Inst. Tech., 1976—79. Editor, co-author: Impedance Spectroscopy-Theory, Experiment, and Applications, 2005, 2d edit., 2005; mem. editl. bd. Jour. Applied Physics, 1984—86; contbr. articles to profl. jours. Bd. dirs. League Ednl. Advancement Dallas, 1965—70; mem. Dallas Radio Commn., 1967—71; mem. sci. adv. coun. Callier Hearing and Speech Ctr., Dallas, 1974—78; mem. adv. com. Weber Rsch. Inst., 1985—90. Rhodes scholar, Oxford U., 1948—50. Fellow: AAAS, IEEE (editor Transactions Profl. Group Audio 1961—66, editor Transactions Audio and Electroacoustics 1966—73, award 1962, 1974, Edison Gold medal 1986), Am. Phys. Soc. (mem. com. edn. 1973—75, mem. com. applicaitons physics 1975—78, George E. Pake prize 1985); mem.: NAS (chmn. numerical data adv. bd. 1970—74, mem. com. motor vehicle emissions 1971—74, chmn. com. motor vehicle emissions 1973—74, mem. com. satellite power sys. 1979—81, mem. com. sci., engring., and pub. policy 1981—83, mem. commn. phys. scis., math. and applications 1985—88, mem. report rev. com. 1990—97), NAE (mem. coun. 1971—74, mem. exec. com. assembly engring. 1975—78), Audio Engring. Soc., Electrochemical Soc., Am. Inst. Physics (mem. governing bd. 1975—78), Sigma Xi, Phi Beta Kappa, Tau Beta Pi. Achievements include patents in field. Office: U NC Dept Physics and Astronomy Chapel Hill NC 27517-7549 Business E-Mail: macd@email.unc.edu.

MACDONALD, JOHN THOMAS, school system administrator; b. Utica, NY, Nov. 21, 1932; s. Gerald Clement and Mildred (Hayes) MacD.; m. Marcia Sprague Gallup; children: Terrence (dec.), Anthony, Elizabeth, Michele, Elise, Denise. BS, Northeastern U., 1958, EdM, 1960; PhD, U. Conn., 1970. Cert. elem. and secondary sch. tchr., prin., supt., Mass., Conn. Supervising prin. Noank, Ft. Hill. and Poquonnock Elem. Schs., Groton, Conn., 1962-66, Robert E. Fitch Jr. H.S., Groton, 1966-70; rsch. asst. Ednl. Resources and Devel. Ctr. U. Conn., Storrs, 1969-70; supt. schs. Wallingford (Conn.) Pub. Schs., 1970-73, Walpole (Mass.) Pub. Schs., 1973-78, Dartmouth (Mass.) Pub. Schs., 1978-86; commr. edn. State Dept. Edn., Concord, NH, 1986-90; asst. sec. for elem. and secondary edn. U.S. Dept. Edn., Washington, 1990-93; dir. state leadership ctr. Coun. of Chief State Sch. Officers, Washington, 1993-99, sr. advisor, 2000-01; prof. ednl. policy and leadership Neag Sch. Edn., U. Conn., 2001—06; dir. NE Ctr. for Ednl. Policy and Leadership. Mem. Postsecondary Edn. Commn., Concord, 1986-90, Coun. for Tchr. Edn., Concord, 1986-90, Profl. Stds. Bd., Concord, 1986-90; trustee Univ. System of N.H., Durham, 1986-90; mem. Surgeon Gen's Task Force, 1990-93; mem. White House Conf. on Indian Edn., 1990-93; mem. Interagy. Com. on Sch. Health, 1990-93, others; mem. dean's adv. coun. U. Conn., 1999—, Coll. Arts and Scis., Northeastern U., 1999—; mem. adv. coun. Va. Edn. Policy Inst., Va. Commonwealth U., 2000—; mem. adv. bd. ERIC, Washington, 1998—. Contbr. articles to profl. jours. Co-chmn. Emergency Sch.-Aide Proposals, U.S. Office Edn., 1973—75; mem. adv. com. external program rev. CDC, 1992—; mem. nat. adv. bd. ERIC Clearinghouse, 1999—; mem. Mass. Adv. Commn. for Ednl. TV, 1983—86, N.H. Task Force on Child Abuse, 1987—90; mem. Nat. Adv. Coun. Northeastern U., 1990—; mem. Galaxy Classroom Nat. Adv. Coun. Galaxy Inst. for Edn., 1992—; mem. sch. health policy initiative Ctr. for Population & Family Health Columbia U., 1992—; mem. Packard roundtable to children Ctr. for Health Policy George Washington U., 1992—; mem. adv. bd. Va. Commonwealth Policy Inst., 1999—; mem. Dean's adv. coun. Neag Sch. Edn. U. Conn., 1999—2005, Coll. Arts & Scis. Northeastern U., 1999—. Recipient Sears B. Condit award, 1958, Alumni award Northwestern U., 1973, Recognition award Coun. of Chief State Sch. Officers, 1990, Disting. Alumni award U. Conn., 2006. Fellow Phi Delta Kappa, Phi Alpha Theta; mem. N.H. Sch. Bldg. Authority, Mass. Assn. Sch. Supts. (pres. 1985-86). Office: U Conn Neag Sch Edn Dept Ednl Leadership 249 Glenbrook Rd Box U-2093 Storrs Mansfield CT 06269-2064 Personal E-mail: macmarjack@aol.com. Business E-Mail: john.macdonald@uconn.edu.

MACDONALD, KAREN CRANE, occupational therapist, geriatrics services professional; b. Denville, NJ, Feb. 24, 1955; d. Robert William and Jeanette Wilcox (Crane) M.; m. Geno Piacentini, Oct. 22, 1993. BS, Quinnipiac U., 1977; MS, U. Bridgeport, 1982; PhD, NYU, 1998. Cert. occupl. therapist. Occupational therapist, coord. of spl. care unit Jewish Home for the Elderly, Conn., 1987-92, N.Y. Inst., NYC, 1984-86; pvt. practice Fairfield County, Conn., 1977-88; occupl. therapist Rehab. Assocs., Fairfield, Conn., 1993-96. Instr. NYU, 1985—89, Quinnipiac Coll., 1986—92, Housatonic CC, Bridgeport, Conn., 2002—, Sacred Heart U., Fairfield, Conn., 2006—; lectr., cons. in field. Contbr. articles to profl. jours. Youth leader, deacon Union Meml. Ch., Stamford, Conn., 1980-88; deacon Southport Congl. Ch., 1992-94; chair consumer com. Alzheimer's Coalition of Conn., 1991-92. Teaching fellow NYU, 1983-86. Mem.: NOW, AAUW, PEO, AAAS, NY Acad. Scis., Am. Bd. Disability Analysts, Conn. Occupl. Therapy Assn. (gerontology liaison 1980—83), Am. Occupl. Therapy Assn. (coun. edn., scholar 1985), World Fedn. Occupl. Therapy, Grange, Toastmasters Internat., Pi Lambda Theta. Avocations: poetry writing, quilting. Home: 198 Glenbrook Rd Bridgeport CT 06610-1149 Personal E-mail: genokaren@aol.com.

MACDONALD, KEN CRAIG, geophysicist; b. San Francisco, Oct. 14, 1947; m. Rachel Haymon, 1984. BS in Engring. Geoscis., U. Calif., Berkeley, 1970; PhD in Marine Geophysics, MIT/Woods Hole, 1975. Cecil H. and Ida Green postdoctoral scholar Scripps Instn. of Oceanography, 1975-76, asst. rsch. geophysicist, lectr., 1976-80; assoc. prof. U. Calif., Santa Barbara, 1980-83, prof., 1983—. Chief scientist on over 30 deep sea expeditions; prin. ALVIN diver on over 40 dives to the mid-ocean ridge. Assoc. editor Jour. of Geophys. Rsch., 1979-82, Earth and Planetary Sci. Letters, 1978-88; mem. editorial bd. Marine Sci. Revs., 1986—; editor Marine Geophys. Rschs., 1986-90; contbr. over 100 articles to profl. jours. Mem. ALVIN Rev. Com., 1979-82; mem. Ocean Sci. Bd. of NAS, 1980-83, Lithosphere Panel Advanced Ocean Drilling Project, 1983-85, Ocean Scis. Panel, NSF, 1984-86, COSOD II planning com.; mem. various RIDGE coms., RIDGE steering com., 1987-90; mem. NSF Ocean Scis. Strategic Plan for Rsch. and Edn. Com., 1993-94, U.S. Geodynamics Comm., 1997—. Regents scholar U. Calif., Berkeley, 1966-70, Mineral Tech. scholar, 1967-70, Cecil H. and Ida Green scholar Inst. Geophysics and Planetary Physics/U. Calif., San Diego, 1975-76; NSF Grad. fellow, 1970-73, World Innovation Found. fellow, 2005; recipient AAAS Newcomb-Cleveland prize, 1980, Robert L. and Bettie P. Cody prize and medal Scripps Instn. Oceanography, 1994; ISI Highly Cited Rschr., 2004. Fellow Am. Geophys. Union, Geol. Soc. Am., Am. Assoc. Advancement Sci., 2007; mem. Phi Beta Kappa, Sigma Psi. Avocations: windsurfing, fly fishing. Office: U Calif Santa Barbara Dept Earth Sci Santa Barbara CA 93106 Business E-Mail: macdonald@geol.ucsb.edu.

MACDONALD, LAURIE, film company executive; m. Walter F. Parkes, 1983; 2 children. BA in English Lit., Sonoma State U., Calif. Documentary and news prodr. K-RON, NBC affiliate, San Francisco; creative exec. Columbia Pictures, 1984—85, v.p. prodn., 1985—88; head Aerial Pictures, 1988—94; exec. prodr. Amblin Entertainment, 1994; co-head motion pictures divsn. DreamWorks Pictures, 1994—. Prodr.: (films) Hayseed, 1997, Men in Black, 1997 (nominated Golden Globe best musical or comedy), Men in Black II, 2002, The Ring, 2002, The Terminal, 2004, Lemony Snicket's A Series of Unfortunate Events, 2004, The Ring Two, 2005, Just Like Heaven, 2005, The Legend of Zorro, 2005; (TV series) SFO; exec. prodr.: (films) How to Make an American Quilt, 1995, The Trigger Effect, 1996, Twister, 1996, The Mask of Zorro, 1998, Gladiator, 2000, The Time Machine, 2002, The Tuxedo, 2002, Catch Me If You Can, 2002; exec. prodr.: (films) The Island, 2005, The Lookout, 2007. Recipient Women in Hollywood Icon award, Premiere Mag., 1999; named one of 100 Most Powerful Women in Hollywood, Hollywood Reporter, 2003, 2005, 50 Most Powerful People in Hollywood, Premiere mag., 2004—05. Office: DreamWorks SKG 100 Flower St Glendale CA 91201 Office Phone: 818-733-7000. Office Fax: 818-695-7574.

MACDONALD, LELAND LLOYD, lawyer; b. Marfa, Tex., July 19, 1931; s. John Edward and Nannye Myrtle (Barnett) M.; m. Juanice L. Koen, Nov. 22, 1958; children: David Allen, Kathryn Ann. BBA, Baylor U., 1952, LLB, 1957. Bar: Tex. 1957, U.S. Dist. Ct. (we. dist.) Tex. 1960, U.S. Ct. Appeals (5th cir.). Title analyst Shell Oil Co., Midland, Tex., 1957—60; pvt. practice Midland, 1960—64; ptnr. Kerr, Fitz-Gerald & Kerr, Midland, 1964—73, Turpin, Smith, Dyer, Saxe & MacDonald, Midland, 1973—2003; pvt. practice, 2004—. Mem. admissions com. Tex. State Bar, 1978—80, grievance com., 1976—78. Author: Seven Sketches of Valor, 2006, Tejanos in the Texas Revolution, 1835-1836, 2008, Home Front, 2008. Past chmn. adv. bd. Salvation Army, 1962—82. Lt. USAF, 1952—54. Fellow: Tex. Bar Found. (life); mem.: Midland County Bar Assn. (pres. 1973—74), Baylor Law Alumni Assn. (bd. dirs. 1980—86), Tex. Assn. Def. Counsel, Tex. State Bar Assn., Midland County Jr. Bar Assn. (pres. 1964—65), The Alamo Soc., Midland Jaycees (v.p. 1960), Green Tree Country Club (bd. dirs. 1983—85), Rotary (pres. 1972—73), Freemasons (writer). Baptist. Home: 1515 Community Ln Midland TX 79701-4011 Office: Ste 1310 500 W Texas Midland TX 79701-4289 Office Phone: 432-684-9990.

MACDONALD, LENNA RUTH, executive lawyer, business advisor; b. Providence, July 16, 1962; d. Arthur Robert and Laina Ruth (Weake) M.; m. Robert Christopher Carew, Sept. 18, 1993. BA, Brown U., Providence, 1984; postgrad., London Sch. Econs. and Polit. Sci., 1984-85; JD, Emory U., Atlanta, 1988. Bar: Ohio 1988, RI, 1989, Mass. 1992, Ky. 1996. Assoc. Edwards & Angell, Providence, 1989-91, McDermott, Will & Emery, Boston, 1991-93; asst. gen. counsel, group mgr. BANC ONE N.H. Asset Mgmt. Corp., Manchester, NH, 1993-96, BANK ONE CORP., Louisville, 1996-98; real estate counsel Vencor, Inc., Louisville, 1998-99; v.p., gen. counsel, sec. Commonwealth Industries, Inc., Louisville, 1999—2004; pres. Balnakeil Ventures LLC, Charleston, SC, 2005—; chief strategy officer, gen. coun., sec. Force Protection Inc., Charleston, SC, 2007—. Mem. Charleston Angel Ptnrs. LLC, SC, 2005—. Mem. Mass. Bar Assn., RI Bar Assn., Ky. Bar Assn., Am. Friends London Sch. Econs., Phi Alpha Delta. Republican. Episcopalian. Personal E-mail: lenna.macdonald@forceprotection.net.

MACDONALD, LUNDEN ESCHELLE, language educator; b. Denver, Aug. 24, 1968; d. Kay Leedell and Ronald Fallis Rees (Stepfather); m. D. Patrick MacDonald, Apr. 22, 2000; children: Angus Dwyer, Murphy Carroll, Beatriz Maeve Ruth, Declan Hammond Rees. BA, U. Colo., Boulder, 1991, MA, PhD, Princeton U., NJ, 2006. Asst. prof. Spanish Met. State Coll., Denver, 2006—. Parent peer contact and events coord. Sudden Unexplained Death Childhood Program, CJ Found. SIDS, Hackensack, NJ, 2003—08. Mem.: AAUW, Colo. Congress Fgn. Lang. Tchrs., Am. Coun. Tchrs. Fgn. Lang., Modern Lang. Assn. Democrat. Avocations: family, travel, knitting, swimming, sports. Office: Met State Coll Campus Box 26 PO Box 173362 Denver CO 80217-3362 Office Fax: 303-556-8536. Business E-Mail: mannl@mscd.edu.

MAC DONALD, MICHAEL C., printing company executive; b. Phila., July 5, 1953; BA in Polit. Sci., Rutgers U., NJ, 1975. Dist. sales mgr. Xerox Corp., Stamford, Conn., 1977, pres. North Am. solutions group, 2000—04, sr. v.p., 2000—, pres. global accounts and mktg. ops., 2004—07, pres. mktg. ops., 2007—08, corp. sr. v.p. operational effectiveness, 2008—. Bd. dirs. Xerox Capital Svcs. Bd. trustees overseers Rutgers U.; mem. US C. of C. Named one of Best Marketers, BtoB Mag., 2008. Mem.: HealthRite (bd. dirs.), Jimmy V Found. (bd. dirs.). Office: Xerox Corp 800 Long Ridge Rd Stamford CT 06904 Office Phone: 203-968-3000.*

MACDONALD, PETER J., lawyer; b. 1957; BA, Northwestern U., 1980; JD cum laude, Boston U., 1984. Bar: Mass. 1985, NY 2001. Ptnr., vice chmn. Litigation dept, mem. exec. com. Wilmer Cutler Pickering Hale & Dorr, Boston. Former adj. prof. Northeastern Univ. Sch. Law. Editor: Boston Univ. Law Rev.; contbr. articles to profl. jours. Mem.: ABA, Boston Bar Assn. Office: Wilmer Cutler Pickering Hale & Dorr 60 State St Boston MA 02109 Office Phone: 617-526-6123. Office Fax: 617-526-5000. Business E-Mail: peter.macdonald@wilmerhale.com.

MACDONALD, R. FULTON SMITH, venture developer, business executive, educator, consultant; b. Monmouth County, NJ, Dec. 24, 1940; s. James Fleming Smith Macdonald and Jane Macfarlane Barnes Abbott; m. Carol Jean Archer (div.); 1 child, Paige Brubaker Smith; m. Laura Boswell; children: George Dewey Boswell, James Fleming Smith Macdonald II(dec.). AB, U. Pa., 1963, MBA, 1969; postgrad. in sr. mktg. mgmt., Stanford U., 1979; PhD (hon.), Ricker Coll., Maine. Systems mgr., mcht. John Wanamaker, Inc., Phila., 1969-74; prin. Booz, Allen & Hamilton, NYC, 1974-79; pres. Irwill Industries, NYC, 1979-82, Internat. Bus. Devel. Corp., NYC, 1982—; chmn. IBEX Mktg. Corp., NYC, 1988—. Adj. prof. Grad. Bus. Sch., Columbia U., NYC, 1984-85, Mgmt. Inst. NYU, 1992-98, chmn. globalization adv. bd., 1993-94; pres. Simfer Operational Internat., Inc., NYC, 1984; vice chmn. Neusteter Co., Denver, 1984-85; mng. dir. Stuyvesant Group Internat., Dutch Am. Bus. Advisors, NYC and Amsterdam, 1987-88; chmn. Am. Bus. Media, Inc., 1989-90, One Ams., Inc., Washington, 1990—; mng. dir. Synoptics Devel. Corp., NYC, 1992—; bd. dirs. C4SI, Inc., Ill., First Fin. M&A, Fla., Nisco Sys., Inc., Ga., Data Treasury Inc., NY, Vispron, Inc., Fla., 2002-05; vice chmn., dir. Close Out Now, NY, 1999-01; vice chmn. World Brand Mgmt., Jacksonville, Fla., 2000-01; CEO, Asia Am. Investments, Holdings Ltd., NY, 2000—; chmn., CEO Casa Caribe Devel. Corp., NY and Dominican Rep., 2002-05; chmn., CEO Global Fashion Close Outs, Inc., 2005—; chmn. Double Sport, Inc., 2005-06, Greater Caribbean Devel. Corp., 2005-06. Designer Manpower Mgmt. Concepts computer system, 1972—; author, pub. The IBD Quarterly Report, 1996—; author Dot.Comeback: Smarter, Tougher, Wiser, 2005; contbr. articles to bus. publs. Chmn. trustees Third Ch. of Christ Scientist, NYC, 2006-08. Capt. inf. U.S. Army, 1963-67, Vietnam. Decorated Bronze Star Mem. Inst. Mgmt. Consultants (cert. mgmt. cons. 1989), Global Econ. Action Inst., Soc. Mayflower Descendants, Soc. Coll. Alumni U. Pa. (pres. 1973-74, bd. mgrs. 1975—), NY Penn Club, NY Princeton Club. Republican. Avocation: squash. Home: 942 Portsmouth Dr Huntington Beach CA 92646 Home Phone: 212-755-0300. E-mail: fultonm@aol.com.

MACDONALD, ROBERT RIGG, JR., retired museum director; b. Pitts., May 11, 1942; s. Robert Rigg and Ruth (Johnson) M.; m. Catherine Ronan, Nov. 27, 1965; children: Matthew, Robert, Catherine. BA, U. Notre Dame, 1964, MA, 1965, U. Pa., 1970. Asst. curator Smithsonian Instn., Washington, 1965; curator Mercer Mus., Doylestown, Pa., 1966-70; dir. New Haven Colony Hist. Soc., 1970-74, La. State Mus., New Orleans, 1974-85; dir., CEO Mus. of City of N.Y., 1985—2002; ret., 2002. Adj. prof. mus. studies NYU, 1989—; adj. prof. pub. adminstrn. Coll. Charleston, 2006—; mem. Commn. Mus. for a New Century; vice-chmn. SC Aquarium, 2007-; bd. dirs. Internat. African Am. Mus.; mem. adv. bd. Riley Inst., Coll. Charleston, 2004-; vice chair Internat. Coms. Mus. of City, Internat. Coun. Mus., 2005-. Editor: Editor: New Haven Colony Furniture, 1973, Louisiana Images 1880-1920, 1975, Louisiana Black Heritage, 1977 Louisiana Portraitures, 1979, Louisiana Legal Heritage, 1981, The Sun King: Louis XIV and the New World, On Being Homeless, A Community of Many Worlds: Arab American New Society, 2002, City Museum & City Development, 2008; organizer (children's art, photographs) The Day Our World Changed: Children's Art of 9/11, The City Resilient: Photographs by Joel Meyerowitz. Decorated chevalier de l'Ordre des Arts et des Lettres (France), cruz de Caballero de la Orden de Isabel La Catolica (Spain); assoc. fellow Berkeley Coll., Yale U., 1978; Hagley fellow U. Del., 1970-71; Univ. scholar U. Notre Dame, 1964-65; named to Centennial Honor Roll Am. Assn. Museums, 2006. Mem.: Mus. City N.Y. (dir. emeritus 2002—), Am. Assn. Mus. (pres. 1985—88, chmn. ethics task force 1988—91, Disting. Svc. award 2003), Am. Assn. State and Local History (coun.), Century Assn. Roman Catholic. Home: 602 Island Walk East Mount Pleasant SC 29464 Home Phone: 843-388-1482; Office Phone: 843-670-7440. Personal E-mail: robertrm2@gmail.com.

MACDONALD, SALLY POLK BOWERS, retired addictions therapist; b. Memphis, Tenn., Feb. 23, 1930; d. Joel Polk and Sara Louise (Nee Zearing) Bowers; m. Lemuel Coover Shattuck, Jr. (div.); children: L. C. Shattuck III, Mark Bowers Shattuck, Melissa Polk Shattuck; m. Robert Donald Macdonald, Mar. 1, 1960; 1 child, Heather Stuart Macdonald LaMarre. BA, U. Ariz., Tucson, 1950. Lic. Alcohol and Drug Abuse Counselor State of Tenn. Adminstr. Clare Found., Santa Monica, Calif., 1978—88; counselor Wilder Youth Devel. Ctr., Somerville, Tenn., 1981—90; alcohol and drug abuse therapist Profl. Care Svcs., Inc., Somerville, 1983—2006; ret., 2006. Contbr. articles various profl. jours. Founding mem. Memphis Alcohol and Drug Coun., Memphis, 1984—86, Fayette County Animal Rescue, Somerville, Tenn., 1996—98; thriftshop chmn. Women's Symphony Assn., Ojai, Calif., 1967—69; precinct com. GOP, Tucson, 1952. Mem.: AOPA, Clare Found. (bd. mem. 1977—80), Assn. Preservation Tenn. Antiquities, Fayette County Hist. Soc. Republican. Episcopalian. Avocations: birdwatching, painting, interior decorating, dog rescue. Home: 113 W Marginal St Somerville TN 38068-1511

MACDONALD, SUSAN PRIEST, media specialist, writer; b. Lakeland, Fla., Sept. 24, 1958; d. Thomas Mitchell and Betty Jo Priest; m. Randall Malcolm MacDonald, Nov. 24, 1984; 1 child, Sarah Elizabeth. AA, South Fla. Jr. Coll., Avon Park, 1978; BA, Fla. State U., 1980, MS in Libr. Sci., 1984. Cert. profl. educator Fla. Media specialist Canal Point (Fla.) Elem. Sch., 1980—81; libr. assoc. I Del-Trail Br., Palm Beach County Libr. Sys., Delray Beach, Fla., 1981—82, libr. assoc. II West Atlantic Ave. Br., 1982—83; media specialist North Heights Elem. Sch., Rome, Ga., 1985—86, Jesse Keen Elem. Sch., Lakeland, 1986—98; sch. libr. media specialist Lawton Chiles Mid. Acad., Lakeland, 1998—. Author: Successful Keyword Searching: Initiating Research on Popular Topics Using Electronic Databases, 2001, Sebring: Images of America Series, 2008; prodr.: (TV documentary) Our Town: Lakeland, 2002. Adult vol. Campfire, Lakeland, 1986—88. Mem.: ALA, AASL, Sebring Hist. Soc., Polk County Hist. Assn., Polk Ednl. Media Assn. (legis. contact 1996—97, v.p. 2001—03, pres. 2003—05, 2d v.p. 2005—), Fla. Assn. for Media in Edn., Fla. So. Coll. Women's Club, Phi Theta Kappa. Avocations: bicycling, reading, geocaching. Home: PO Box 2501 Lakeland FL 33806-2501 Office: Lawton Chiles Mid Acad 400 N Florida Ave Lakeland FL 33801-4804

MACDONALD, WILLIAM BURKE, secondary school educator, consultant; b. Chgo., Dec. 19, 1942; s. William C. nad Jane (Burke) MacD.; m. Mary E. Kotre, Dec. 1968; children: Colleen, Kevin. AB, Regis U., Denver, 1964; MEd, Loyola U., Chgo., 1968. Nat. cert. counselor. Tchr. Lindop Sch., Broadview, Ill., 1964-68; guidance dir. Miner Jr. H.S., Arlington Heights, Ill., 1968-70; tchr. Addison Trail H.S., Addison, Ill., 1970—94, guidance dir., 1982-94; crises counselor Alexian Bros. Med. Ctr., 1996-99; field reporter Heartbeat Schaumburg Park Dist. Cable Access, 2000—. Mem. parish coun. Ch. of the Holy Spirit, Schaumburg, 1993-2004. Mem. AFT (pres. DuPage Coun. 1981-84), Suburban Dirs. Guidance (pres. 1993-94). Avocations: photography, computers. Office: 430 Greenhill Ln Schaumburg IL 60193-1764

MACDOUGAL, GARY EDWARD, corporate board member, foundation trustee; b. Chgo., July 3, 1936; s. Thomas William and Lorna Lee (McDougall) MacD.; children: Gary Edward, Michael Scott; m. Charlene Gehm, June 15, 1992. BS in Engring., UCLA, 1958; MBA with distinction, Harvard U., 1962. Cons. McKinsey & Co., LA, 1963-68, ptnr., 1968-69; chmn. bd., chief exec. officer Mark Controls Corp. (formerly Clayton Mark & Co.), Evanston, Ill., 1969-87; gen. dir. N.Y.C. Ballet, 1993-94; chmn. Gov. Task Force on Human Svcs. Reform State of Ill., 1993-97. Sr. advisor and asst. campaign mgr. George Bush for Pres., Washington, 1988; pub. del. alt. rep. U.S. Del. apptd. by Pres. Bush, UN 44th Gen. Assembly, 1989-90; chmn. Bulgarian-Am. Enterprise Fund, Chgo. and Sophia, Bulgaria, 1991-93, bd. dirs., 1991—; apptd. to U.S. Commn. on Effectiveness of UN, 1992-93; bd. dirs. United Parcel Svc. Am., Inc., Atlanta, 1973-07; adv. dir. Saratoga Ptnrs., N.Y.; instr. UCLA, 1969. Author: Make a Difference: How One Man Helped Solve America's Poverty Problem, 2000, 2nd edit. 2005; contbr. articles to Harvard Bus. Rev., Wall St. Jour., N.Y. Times, Chgo. Tribune, other publs., chpts. to books. Trustee Annie E. Casey Found., 1983-2006, UCLA Found., 1973-79, W.T. Grant Found., 1992-94, Russell Sage Found., 1981-91, chair, 1987-90; co-chmn. Americans for Bulgaria Found., 2008-; chmn. MacDougal Family Found.; commr. Sec. Labor's Commn. on Workforce Quality and Productivity, Washington, 1988-89; Lt. USN, 1958-61. Mem. Coun. Fgn. Rels., Author's Guild, Harvard Club, Kappa Sigma. Episcopalian. Home: 505 N Lake Shore Dr Apt 3611 Chicago IL 60611-3406 Personal E-mail: gemacd@aol.com.

MACDOUGALL, DIANA E., interpreter, educator, social sciences educator; children: Benjamin Alexander, Ian Scott. MA, U. Calif., Riverside, 2005. Cert. interpreter, translator Registry Interpreters Deaf, 1989. Assoc. prof. Riverside CC Dist., 1997—, ASL interpreter edn. program coord., 2000—, world langs. dept. chairperson, 2005—. ASL English pvt. practice, interpreting & transliterating, Calif., 1987. Exhbn., Photography, Colored Pencil; contbr. articles to profl. jours. Recipient Disting. Faculty Lectr. award. Mem.: Cmty. Scholars: Diversity, Phi Beta Kappa (Phi Betta Kappa 2003). Liberal. Avocations: art, scuba diving, boating, photography. Office: Riverside CC Dist 4800 Magnolia Ave Quad 22-B Riverside CA 92506 Office Phone: 951-222-8832. Office Fax: 951-222-8149. Personal E-mail: asllina@hotmail.com. Business E-Mail: diana.macdougall@rcc.edu.

MACDOUGALL, HARTLAND MOLSON, retired bank executive; b. Montreal, Que., Can., Jan. 28, 1931; s. Hartland Campbell and Dorothy (Molson) MacD.; m. Eve Gordon, Oct. 29, 1954; children: Cynthia, Wendy, Keith, Willa, Tania. Student, LeRosey, Switzerland, 1947-48, McGill U., 1949-53, Advanced Mgmt. Program, Harvard U., 1976. With Bank Montreal, various locations, 1953-84, dir., 1974, vice chmn., 1981; chmn., dir. Royal Trustco Ltd., Toronto, 1984-93. Dep. chmn. London Ins. Group, Inc., London Life Ins. Co., 1985-97; chmn., dir. Robert T. Jones Jr. Can. Scholarship Found. Founding chmn. Heritage Can., St. Michael's Hosp. Found., The Japan Soc.; past chmn. Can.-Japan Bus. Com.; gov., past pres. Coun. Can. Unity; past pres. Royal Agrl. Winter Fair; advisor Can. Sports Hall of Fame; bd. govs. Can. Olympic Found.; sen. Stratford Shakespearean Found.; former chmn. The Duke of Edinburgh Awards Internat. Coun.; v.p., dir. The Macdonald Stewart Found. Decorated Order of Can., comdr. Royal Victorian Order, Order of the Rising Sun, Gold and Silver Star (Japan); recipient Gabrielle Leger medal, 1978. Avocations: golf, gardening, tennis, farming. Office: BCE Place 181 Bay St Ste 300 PO Box 771 Toronto ON Canada M5J 2T3 Home: 16978 Shaws Creek Rd Belfountain ON Canada L7V OE8

MACDOUGALL, JOHN DUNCAN, thoracic surgeon; b. Indpls., Mar. 4, 1925; s. Duncan Campbell and Beulah Stewart (Ward) MacDougall; m. Inga Margaretha Tranberg, Oct. 6, 1951 (div. 1980); children: Duncan Campbell, Stewart Andrew, Eric Matthew, Victoria Suzanne MacDougall Oehmen; m. Barbara Lee Mayse, Nov. 1, 1980; children: Katherine Jane, James William. BS, Ind. U., Bloomington. Ind., 1948, MD, 1951. Diplomate Am. Bd. Surgery, Am. Bd. Thoracic Surgery. Pvt. practice, Indpls., 1957-93; pres. med. staff St. Francis Hosp., Beech Grove, Ind., 1975, pres. adv. bd., 1993-95, mem. governing bd. trustees, 2003—, chmn. governing bd. trustees, 1995—2003. Chmn. bd. dirs. Med. Assurance Ind., Indpls., 1987—2000, med. cons., 1993—. Mem. Ind. Gov.'s Task Force Organ Transplantation, Indpls., 1986—89; bd. dirs. Ind. Med. History Mus., 1989—2000, 2006—; active Ind. Hist. Soc., Indpls. Mus. Art; pres. Ind. Med. Polit. Action Com., Indpls., 1992—98; mem. exec. com. dean's coun. Ind. U. Sch. Medicine, Indpls., 1988—, mem. adv. com., 1989—96, pres. dean's coun., 1992—95; pres. English Speaking Union, 1987—2001. With US Army, 1943—46, ETO. Decorated Bronze Star. Fellow: ACS; mem.: AMA (del., chmn. Ind. delegation 1994—2003), Nat. Med. Vets. Assn. (bd. dirs. 1992—2004), Orgn. State Med. Assn. Pres. (pres. 1994—95), Indpls. Med. Soc. (pres. 1978—79), Ind. State Med. Assn. (pres. 1987—88), Purdue U. Pres.'s Coun., Ind. U. Sch. Medicine J. O. Ritchery Soc., Ind. U. Arbutus Soc., Univ. Club Indpls., Meridian Hills Country Club, Contemporary Club, Indpls. Lit. Club, Masons (33d degree), Am. Legion (comdr. Paul Coble Post #26 1999—2007), Soc. Ind. Pioneers. Republican. Episcopalian. Avocations: woodworking, golf, fishing. Home: 7202 Dean Rd Indianapolis IN 46240-3628

MACDOUGALL, PETER, retired lawyer; b. Boston, Sept. 22, 1937; s. Duncan Peck and Hildegard (Moebius) MacD. AB, Harvard U., 1958, LLB, 1963. Assoc. Ropes & Gray, Boston, 1964-73, ptnr., 1973-97, ret., 1997—. Sheldon fellow Harvard U., 1963-64. Mem.: Harvard (Boston). Avocations: concert and opera going, gardening, reading, travel. Home: 1720 Washington St Key West FL 33040-4916 also: 542 River Rd Westport MA 02790-5161 E-mail: pmacdougall@earthlink.net.

MACDOUGALL, PRISCILLA RUTH, lawyer; b. Evanston, Ill., Jan. 20, 1944; d. Curtis Daniel and Genevieve Maurine (Rockwood) MacDougall; m. Lester H. Brownlee, July 5, 1987. BA, Barnard Coll., 1965; grad. (hon.), U. Paris, 1967; JD, U. Mich., 1970. Bar: Wis. 1970, Ill. 1970. Asst. atty. gen. State of Wis., 1970—74; instr. Law Sch. and undergrad. campuses U. Wis., 1973—75; staff counsel Wis. Edn. Assn. Coun., Madison, 1975—; instr. Columbia Coll., Chgo., 1988—. Litigator, writer, speaker, educator women's and children's names and women's rights and employment issues. Author: Married Women's Common Law Right to Their Own Surnames, 1972; co-author: Booklet for Women Who Wish to Determine Their Own Names After Marriage, 1974, supplement, 1975, The Right of Women to Name Their Children, 1985; contbr. articles to profl. jours. Recipient Honor medal, Vet. Feminists Am., 2008. Mem.: ABA, Wis. State Bar (co-founder sect. on individual rights and responsibilities, chair 1973—75, 1978—79), Legal Assn. Women Wis. (co-founder). Home: 502 Engelhart Dr Madison WI 53713-4742 Office: 33 Nob Hill Dr Madison WI 53713-2198 Home Phone: 608-274-6729; Office Phone: 608-276-7711. Business E-Mail: macdougallp@weac.org.

MACDOUGALL, WILLIAM LOWELL, magazine editor; b. Des Moines, July 24, 1931; s. David Gregory and Elizabeth Jeanette (Dugan) MacD. AB, Willamette U., Salem, Oreg., 1952; M.J. in Journalism (Pulitzer scholar 1953-54), Columbia U., 1953. Reporter Washington Star, 1958-62; corr. Los Angeles Times, 1962-63; asso. editor, then London corr. U.S. News & World Report, 1964-68, asst. mng. editor Washington, 1978-86; mng. editor Artsreview mag. NEA, 1987; pres. Mid-Atlantic Media Co., Arlington, Va., 1989—. Author: American Revolutionary: A Biography of General Alexander McDougall, 1977. Served with USAF, 1954-57. Recipient George Washington medal Freedoms Found., 1978, citation U.S. Bicentennial Commn., 1976 Methodist. Office: Mid-Atlantic Media Co 5000 37th St N Arlington VA 22207-1823

MACDUFF, ILONE MARGARET, music educator; b. Berwyn, Ill., Jan. 30, 1938; d. Albert Kenneth Hinckle and Dorothy Lydia Ardina Lange; m. James Donald Macduff, Jr., Apr. 2, 1959; children: Gordon Scott, James Alexander, Charles Colin. MusB, U. Idaho, 1976. Internat. rep. Boy Scouts Am., 1983—93; mem. Thurston County (Wash.) Hist. Commrs., 1984—98; active Boy Scouts Am., Tumwater, Wash., 1968—93, dist. Cub Scout program chmn., 1973—75, mem. coun. Pow Wow staff, 1973—76; founder Cub Scout Day Camp, Tumwater Area Coun., 1973; chmn. Coun. Scout-O-Rama, 1979, 1980, 1981; mem. coun. Eagle bd. Boy Scouts Am., 1985—90; dir. monthly musicales State Captial Mus., 1970—74. Recipient Single and Double awards, Nat. Fedn. Music Clubs, 1969, 1977, Silver Beaver award, Boy Scouts Am., 1981, Disting. Commr. award, 1981, Lamb award, 1987. Mem.: Am. Coll. Musicians, Olympia Music Tchrs. Assn. (pres. 2003—04, student recitals chair 2005), Music Tchrs. Nat. Assn. (Olympia chpt. voice auditions chair 2001, 2004), Gordon Setter Club Am. (chmn. nat. dog show 2003), Puget Sound Gordon Setter Club (treas. 1998—2000, show chmn. 2003—04). Lutheran. Avocation: photography. Home: 8524 Delphi Rd SW Olympia WA 98512 Personal E-mail: delphimuse@msn.com.

MACE, MICHAEL JAY, architect; s. Delvin Lloyd and Jimalee Jay Mace; m. Donna Lee Lukow, Oct. 26, 1996; children: Seth Michael, Josiah Jay, Emily Kathleen, Erin Nalani Lukow. BArch, Wash. State U., Pullman, 1981. Lic. Mass., 1989, Okla., 2007, Mo., 2008. Archtl. intern Delvin L. Mace Architects, Vancouver, Wash., 1981—85, HRM Architects, Boston, 1985—86; project arch. DiNisco Kretsch & Assocs., Boston, 1988—89, Gazley, Plowman, Atkinson Arch., Portland, Oreg., 1989—93, Indsl. Design Corp., Portland, Oreg., 1993—96; assoc. prin. PageSoutherlandPage, Austin, Tex., 1996—. Contbr. articles to profl. jours. Mem.: AIA, NCARB.

MACE, STEVEN DOUGLAS, academic administrator, educator; s. Frank Mace and Betty Matluck; m. Belin da Maria Coello; 1 child, David E. BA, U. Wash., Seattle, 1971; MA, Tex. A&M U., Commerce, 1999; MEd, U. Tex., Austin, 1983. Cert. tchr. State Tex., 1982. Tchr. Am. Sch., Tegucigalpa, Honduras, 1976—82; adminstr. USHonduras Binational Ctr., Tegucigalpa, 1978—82. Translator FLAS USAId, Tegucigalpa, 1979—80. Active cmty. drives mem. HOA, Keller, Tex., 2000—03. Mem.: Phi Kappa Phi, Phi Alpha Theta. Evangelical. Office: Northlake Coll 5001 N MacArthur Irving TX 75062 Personal E-mail: sdmace@yahoo.com. Business E-Mail: sxm7420@dcccd.edu, sdmace@gmail.com.

MACEDO, PEDRO BUARQUE DE, physics professor, researcher; b. Copenhagen, July 16, 1938; s. Carlos Buarque and Maria Henriqueta Buarque de Macedo; m. Arlene Sheila Kromal, June 0, 1959; children: Pedro Steven, Michael Carlos, Charles Robert. BS in Physics, George Wash. U., Washington, 1959; PhD in Physics, Cath. U. America, Washington, 1963. GS12 postdoc. rschr. Nat. Bur. Standards, Washington, 1963—66, GS13 postdoc. rschr., 1967—72; assoc. prof., engring. Cath. U. America, 1967—70, prof., chem. engring., 1971—80, prof., engring., 1971—80, prof., physics, 1981—, co dir., vitreous state lab., 1972—2007, dir. emeritus, vitreous state lab., 2007—. Contbr. scientific papers to profl. jours., chapters to books. Recipient inventor of Yr., NY Intellectual Property Law Assn., 2008. Achievements include patents for fiber optics and strong Glass; immobolization vitrification nuclear waste, ion exchange, glass foam, vitrification of radioactive and hazardous waste. Home: 6100 Highboro Dr Bethesda MD 20817 Office: Cath Univ America VSL 620 MI Ave NE 405 Hannan Hall Washington DC 20064 Personal E-mail: pete@macedo.biz. Business E-Mail: macedo@cua.edu.

MACEDO DE LA CONCHA, RAFAEL, former Mexican government official; b. Mexico City, May 6, 1950; Grad., Heroic Mil. Coll.; law degree, U. Nacional Autónoma Mex., Mexico City; Dr Degree (hon.), Nat. Inst. Criminal Sci., Mex., 2003. With Mexican Army, advanced through grades to brig. gen.; legal, fiduciary and asst. dir. Nat. Bank of the Army, Air Force and Navy; judge, 1st magistrate Supreme Mil. Ct.; legal coun. fed. exec. br. Govt. of Mex., asst. chief legal counsel Presdl. staff, atty. gen. mil. justice, legal counsel Secretariat Nat. Def., atty. gen., 2000—05; prof. various subjects including Mexican positive law, polit., econ. and social problems of Mex., constl. law U. Nacional Autónoma Mex., Lat. Am. U., dir. law program. Rep. of Govt. of Mex. and Secretariat of Nat. Def. regarding arms and drug trafficking U.S. Dept. of State; rep. Secretariat of Nat. Def. before the Jt. Secretariat Com.; pres. drug abuse control commn. CICAD, 2002—03; chair, 5th mtg. mins. or justice mins. or atty. gen. Ams. REMJA, Washington, 2004. Decorated great cross Order of Isabella the Cath. Spain, Army 5th, 4th, 3d, 2d and 1st class medals, Army Spl. Class medal; recipient Mil. Tchg. award, Mexican Army, 1992, Melchor Ocampo, Nat. Acad., A.C., Blue Ribbon Gown and Eight-Cornered Academic Cap for univ. excellence, Benito Juarez knight's badge for profl. dignity, Jose Vasconcelos honor award for academic merits, Fed. Dist. Univ., award, Mex. Mil. Legion of Honor, 2000. Mem.: Mex. Nat. Legion of Honor.

MACEK, ROBERT JAMES, retired physicist; b. Rapid City, SD, July 14, 1936; s. Joseph Bernard and Esther Mary Macek; m. Anne R. Gullett, Dec. 29, 1962; children: Daniel Thomas, Karen Elizabeth Siegel. BS, SD State U., Brookings, 1958; PhD, Calif. Inst. Tech., Pasadena, 1964. Chemistry lab asst. SD State U., 1955—58; tech. staff mem. Los Alamos Nat. Lab., 1969—2003, alt. group leader, 1972—75, group leader, 1976—85, program mgr., 1985—86, assoc. divsn. leader, 1986—87, program mgr., 1987—93, facility ops. mgr., 1993—95, project leader, 1995—2003, guest scientist, 2003—; chemist Shell Devel. Corp, Emeryville, Calif., 1958; grad. rsch. asst. Calif. Inst. Tech., Pasadena, Calif., 1959—64; postdoc. rsch. assoc. U. Pa., Phila., 1966—69; sr. scientist TechSource, Inc., Santa Fe, 2003—, mem. dahrt red team, 2004—07. Mem. program rev. bnl high energy physics program US Dept. Energy, Brookhaven, NY, 1994, panel mem., accelerator physics and tech., Washington, 1995—96; expert cons. Atomic Energy Control Bd. Can., Ottawa, Ontario, Canada, 2000—01; mem. sci. adv. bd. HiEnergy Techs., Irvine, Calif., 2002—06; rev. panel mem. CERN, Geneva, 2002; accelerator adv. bd. Oak Ridge Nat. Lab., Tenn., 2007—. Contbr. scientific papers to profl. jours. Capt. Ordnance Corp US Army, 1964—66, Aberdeen Proving Ground and Yuma Proving Ground. SBIR Phase I grant, US Dept. Energy, 2004—05, SBIR Phase II grant, 2005—07. Mem.: IEEE, Am. Phys. Soc. Achievements include research in electron cloud instabilities in proton storage rings. Home: 163 Laguna St Los Alamos NM 87544 Office: Los Alamos Nat Lab PO Box 1663 Los Alamos NM 87545 Personal E-mail: rjmacek@comcast.net. Business E-Mail: macek@lanl.gov.

MACENCZAK, LEE ANDREW, air transportation executive; m. Kimberly Carol Macenczak, Dec. 11, 1982; children: Ansley Lauren, Austin Leigh. Grad. in Mgmt., Ga. State U., Atlanta. With Delta Air Lines, Inc., Atlanta, 1985—, v.p. reservation sales & distbn. planning, 1996—98, v.p. reservation sales, 1998—99, v.p. customer svc., 1999—2000, sr. v.p. sales & distbn., 2000—04, sr. v.p., chief human resources officer, 2004, sr. v.p., chief customer svc. officer, 2004—05, exec. v.p., chief customer svc. officer, 2005—06, exec. v.p. sales & customer svc., 2006—07, exec. v.p. sales & mktg., 2007—. Office: Delta Air Lines Inc PO Box 20706 Atlanta GA 30320-6001 Office Phone: 404-715-2600.

MACER, GEORGE ARMEN, JR., orthopedic hand surgeon; b. Pasadena, Calif., Oct. 17, 1948; s. George A. and Nevart Akullian M.; m. Celeste Angelle Lyons, Mar. 26, 1983; children: Christiana Marilu, Marina Lynn, Emily Sue. BA, U. So. Calif., 1971, MD, 1976. Diplomate Am. Bd. Med. Examiners; diplomate in orthop. surgery and hand surgery Am. Bd. Orthop. Surgery. Intern Meml. Hosp. Med. Ctr., Long Beach, Calif., 1976; Joseph Boyes Hand fellow, 1982; resident Orthop. Hosp./U. So. Calif., 1977-81; pvt. practice Long Beach, 1983—; vol. clin. faculty orthops. U. So. Calif., LA, 1983-89, 90—; cons. hand surgery svc. Rancho Los Amigos Hosp. Downey, 1990—. Cons. Harbor UCLA Med. Ctr., Torrance, 1983—; asst. clin. prof. U. Calif. Irvine, 2004-. Mem. AMA, Calif. Med. Assn., Los Angeles County Med. Assn., Calif. Orthop. Assn., Western Orthop. Assn., Am. Soc. for Surgery of Hand, Am. Acad. Orthop. Surgery, So. Calif. Soc. Surgery of Hand (pres. 2004-06). Republican. Avocations: boating, skiing, scuba diving, carpentry. Office: The Hand & Wrist Ctr 3918 Long Beach Blvd Ste 100 Long Beach CA 90807 Office Phone: 562-424-9000. Personal E-mail: macer4337@aol.com. Business E-Mail: george@handwristcenter.com.

MACER-STORY, EUGENIA ANN, writer; b. Mpls., Jan. 20, 1945; d. Dan Johnstone and Eugenia Loretta (Andrews) Macer; divorced; 1 child, Ezra Arthur Story. BS in Comms., Northwestern U., Evanston, Ill., 1965; MFA, Columbia U., NYC, 1968. Writing instr. Polyarts, Boston, 1970-72; theater instr. Joy of Movement, Boston, 1972-75; artistic dir. Magik Mirror, Salem, Mass., 1975-76, Magick Mirror Comm., 1977—. Author: Congratulations: The UFO Reality, 1978, Angels of Time, 1982, Project Midas, 1986, 2d edit., 2004, Dr. Fu Man Chu Meets the Lonesome Cowboy: Sorcery and the UFO Experience, 1991, 3d edit., 1994, Gypsy Fair, 1991, The Strawberry Man, 1991, Sea Condor/Dusty Sun, 1994, Awakening to the Light-After the Longest Night, 1995, Battles with Dragons: Certain Tales of Political Yoga, 1993, 2d edit., 1994, Legacy of Daedulus, 1995, The Dark Frontier, 1997, Troll and Other Interdimensional Invasions, 1999, Congratulations: The UFO Reality, 2000, Vanishing Questions, 2000, Carrying Thunder, 2002, Crossing Jungle River, 1998, Doing Business in the Adirondacks; True Tales of the Bizarre and Supernatural, 2003, The Merry Piper's Hollow Hills, 2003, Struck By Green Lightning aka Project Midas, 2004, reissued 2006; (poetry) Theatre Cosmos, 2005, Fast Luck Botanica & Other Such Poems, 2007, M7 Bus: The Circular Journey, 2008; (novels) The Sin of Love, 2006, OM/NADA, 2006, (non-fiction book) Pulse of the Dragon: The Secret Knowledge of the Pirates, 2009; (plays) Fetching the Tree, Archaeological Politics, 1986, Strange Inquiries, Divine Appliance, 1989, The Zig Zag Wall, 1990, The Only Qualified Huntress, 1990, Telephone Taps Written Up for Tabloids, 1991, Wars with Pigeons, 1992, Conquest of the Asteroids, 1993, Commander Galacticon, 1993, Meister Hemmelin, 1994, Six Way Time Play, 1994, Radish, 1996, Setting Up for the World Trade Centaur, 1996, Mister Shooting Star, 1998, Wild Dog Casino, 1999, Magic Mirror Space Installation at 515 Greenwich Street, 1999-2001, The Old Gaffer From Boise (at Gallery 113), 2000, The Redecoration According to Currier (at Gallery 113), 2001, Ars Chronicon Sylvestre, 2002, Swords of the Equinox, 2003, New Life Expo, New Yorker Hotel, NYC, 2003, Sayeed/Sayeeda, NYC, 2003, New Day, 2004, New Life Expo, 2005, Theatre For The New City, NYC, 2005, Honky Tonk Tornado Warnings, 2005, The Liberation of Little Lulu, Martin Luther King Detained in Limbo, 2006, Eternal Flowers of Ghost Mountain, Lower East Side Festival of Arts, 2006, Applied Ecological Authority, Staged Reading Theatre Cosmos, 2006, The Poison Man, 2007, "Tamuv Lenk" Theater for the New City, 2009, Ceremonies 17, 2008, others; editor Yankee Oracle Gazette, 1999; personal appearance as profl. clairvoyant (TV documentary) Haunted Houses, 1996, UFO Desk, Sta. WBAI radio shows, 1996-2001, Star People Confs., 1998—; exhbn. paintings Barcelona, Spain, 1999, 2000, 02, Magick Mirror Comm. Installation, 1999-2001, 515 Greenwich Gallery, So-Ho, NY, 1999, City Art Gallery, Stockholm, 2000, 04, Gam'Art Diffusion, Port Frejus, France, 2003, Kelikian Gallery, Beirut, 2002-03, Holland Art Fair, The Hague, 2003, BCN Art-Directe Gallery, Barcelona, Spain, 2003, Times Square Fashion Dist., Magick Mirror Space Fashion Ctr., 2003-06, Europ'art Expo, Geneva, 2006, The Other Side of Truth-Oak Island Nova Scotia, 2007, Varga Calley, 2008; author numerous poems; contbr. articles to profl. jours. and mags. Named Prof. and Corresponding Academician in Arts, Acad. Greci Marino, 2008; Shubert fellow, 1968. Mem. Am. Soc. Dowsers, Dramatists Guild (spkr., interviewer on radio shows and internet confs.), Theosophical Soc. Democrat. Avocations: swimming, outdoor activities, hiking. Office: Magick Mirror Comm PO Box 741 New York NY 10116-0741 Personal E-mail: e.macer-story@att.net. E-mail: magickmirr@aol.com.

MACEWAN, BONNIE, librarian, dean; b. Memphis, Sept. 10, 1950; m. Thomas Manig. BA, Whitter Coll., 1972; M, U. Denver, 1978. Humanities libr. Ctl. Mo. State Coll., Warrensburg, 1978—84; art, archaeology and music libr. U. Mo., Columbia, 1984—91; asst. dean scholarly comm. Pa. State U., University Park, 1991—98, dean collections and scholarly comm., co-dir. digital scholarly pub., 1998—2003; dean librs. Auburn U., Ala., 2006—. Mem.: ALA (vice chair, chair-elect collection mgmt. and develop. sect. 2001—02). Office: Auburn U Librs 231 Mell St Auburn University AL 36849 Office Phone: 334-844-1715. E-mail: macewbj@auburn.edu.

MACEWAN, NIGEL SAVAGE, retired merchant banker; b. Balt., Mar. 21, 1933; s. Nigel Savage and Ellen (Wharton) MacE.; children: Alison, Nigel, Pamela, Elizabeth; m. Judith Sperry, Sept. 2, 1995. BA, Yale U., 1955; MBA, Harvard U., 1959. Assoc. Morgan Stanley & Co., NYC, 1959-62, White, Weld & Co., NYC, 1962-63; v.p. R.S. Dickson & Co., Charlotte, NC, 1963-68; chmn. Fin. Cons. Internat. Ltd., Brussels, 1965-68; successively gen. ptnr., exec. v.p., pres., dir. White, Weld & Co., NYC, 1968-78; sr. v.p., dir. Merrill Lynch, Pierce, Fenner & Smith, NYC, 1978-87; chmn. Merrill Lynch Capital Ptnrs., NYC, 1985-87; pres., CEO Kleinwort Benson, N.Am. Inc., NYC, 1987-93, also bd. dirs.; ret., 1993. Chmn. Kleinwort Benson North Am., Inc., Kleinworth Benson Holdings, Inc., Alex Brown Kleinwort Benson Realty Advs.; bd. dirs. Kleinwort Benson Group plc, Kleinwort Benson Ltd., 1987-93, Kleinworth Benson Australian Income Fund, 1992-99; adj. prof. bus. adminstrn. NYU, 1973-75. Pres. Tokeneke Tax Dist., Darien, 1978-80, later treas.; bd. dirs. Islesboro (Maine) Health Ctr., 1994-2005, Sailors Mus. and Lighthouse, Islesboro, 1993-2000; trustee coun. Island Inst., 1997-02; adv. coun. Islesboro Island Trust, 1997-, Conservation Law Found., 1998-2006. Served with USN, 1955-57. Mem. Securities Industry Assn. (chmn. NY group 1975-76), NY Yacht Club, Yale Club NY, Harvard Club of Fairfield County, Conn., Wee Burn Country Club, Tokeneke Club, Tarrantine Club (Dark Harbor, Maine), Cruising Club Am., New Canaan Yacht Club. Republican. Episcopalian. Home: 153 Oenoke Ln New Canaan CT 06840-4518 Personal E-mail: nsmace@msn.com.

MACEWEN, SALLY, ancient language educator; d. John Eastburn and Isabelle Ewing McVaugh; life ptnr. Aaron Ruscetta; 1 child, Elaine Ruscetta. BA, Mt. Holyoke Coll., South Hadley, Mass., 1970; PhD, U. Pa., Phila. Prof. classics Agnes Scott Coll., Decatur, Ga., 1982—. Editor cloelia Women's Classical Caucus, co-chmn., 2006—08; mem., Faculty Exec. Com. Agnes Scott Coll., Decatur, Ga., 2005—, mem., Strategic Fin. Planning, 2008—. Bd. chmn. Friends Sch. Atlanta, Decatur, 1990—95. Recipient Human Rels. award, President's Com. on Cmty. Diversity, Agnes Scott Coll., 1999. Mem.: Am. Classical Assn., Classical Assn. Mid. West & South, Am. Philol Assn., Nat. Coalition Bldg. Inst. (coord. 1991—2008). Office: Agnes Scott Coll 141 E Coll Ave Decatur GA 30030 Business E-Mail: smacewen@agnesscott.edu.

MACEY, KITTY, costume designer, educator; MFA, Ohio U., Athens. Prof. costume design SUNY, Oswego, 1977—. Costume designer Sterling Rennisance Faire, NY. Office: SUNY Oswego 105 Tyler Hall Oswego NY 13126 Business E-Mail: macey@oswego.edu.

MACEY, WILLIAM BLACKMORE, oil industry executive; b. Buffalo, Aug. 1, 1920; s. Richard Charles and Doris (Bourne) M.; m. Jean Olive Mullins, Oct. 6, 1945; 1 dau., Barbara Jean. BS in Petroleum Engring, N.Mex. Sch. Mines, 1942; D.Engring. (hon.), N.Mex. Inst. Mining and Tech., 1984. Dist. engr. N.Mex. Oil Conservation Commn., 1946-48; dist. supt. Am. Republics Corp., 1948-52; chief engr. N.Mex. Oil Conservation Commn., 1952-54, state geologist, dir., 1954-56; v.p. Internat. Oil & Gas Corp. (and predecessor co., developers mineral properties), Denver, 1956-60, then pres., 1960-67; pres. Nielson Enterprises Inc., oil and gas prodn. and pipelines, livestock ranching, 1967-74; v.p., dir. Y-Tex Corp. (mfr. livestock identification tags), 1972-73; pres. GEN Oil Inc. (oil and gas prodn.), 1972-75, Col. Cody Inn (real estate and golf course devel.), 1970-73; pres., dir. Macey & Mershon Oil, Inc., 1974-93; dir. Juniper Oil and Gas Corp., Denver, 1981-83, Ruidoso (N.Mex.) State Bank Holding Co., 1987—; pres. The Macey Corp., Denver, 1985—99. Chmn. Pres.'s N.Mex. Inst. Mines and Tech., 1980-82; mem. adv. bd. U. Ariz. Heart Ctr., 1997-2002; mem. Pres.'s U. Ariz. Found. Served from 2d lt. to capt. USAAF, 1942-45. Mem.: N.Mex. Oil and Gas Assn. (exec. com. 1949—52, 1960—61), Popejoy & Pres.'s Club (U. N.Mex.), N.Mex. Jockey Club (bd. dirs. 1985—88, 1991—93, pres. 1993), Ruidoso, Tucson Country Club, Altolakes Golf and Country Club, Skyline Country Club (Tucson) (dir., treas. 1980—82, pres. 1982—83), Garden of the Gods. Episcopalian. Office: PO Box 2210 Denver CO 80201-2210 Home: 13605 Quaking Aspen Pl NE Albuquerque NM 87111-7166

MACFARLANE, DAVID GORDON, defense systems design and development executive; b. Portland, Oreg., June 2, 1947; s. Gordon August and Virginia Lorraine (Thompson) F.; m. Zella Mae Garber, Jan. 24, 1969 (div. Feb. 1987); children: Carol Anne, Nancy Jane; m. Kathryn June Kuhfahl, May 13, 1991(div. June, 2003); 1 stepson, Chad Patrick Hughes. BGS in Bus. Adminstrn., U. Nebr., Omaha, 1976; MBA, U. Nebr., 1980. Computer operator and programmer Data Systems, Inc., Portland, 1967-68; computer programmer Far West Fed. Savs. & Loan, Portland, 1968; programmer, system analyst PRC Data Svcs. Co., Virginia Beach, Va., 1970-71, San Diego, 1971-72; systems analyst PRC Info. Scis. Co., Bellevue, Nebr., 1972-81, project mgr., 1981-85; dept. mgr. PRC Govt. Info. Systems, Bellevue, 1985-90; ops. ctr. mgr. PRC Inc., 1991-93, v.p., gen. mgr., 1994-95; v.p. EER Systems, Inc., Seabrook, Md., 1995—2000; v.p. COO Kathal Tech. Mochen, Va., 2000—03; v.p. Data Computer Corp. America, Ellicott City, Md., 2003—04; pres. CEO Janovatine Info. Selection Inc., Neoburg, Va., 2004—; chmn. mem. Lonsdonne Home Gueness Assn. France Com., 2007—09; mem. london County Dallas Town Ctr. Cmty. Devel. Authority, 2008—, London County Rep. Cmty., 2009—. Bd. dirs., past pres. Bellevue Swim Club, 1979-84. With U.S. Army, 1968-70. Mem. Armed Forces Communications and Electronics Assn., Air Force Assn. Republican. Methodist. Office: Innovative Information Solutions Inc 525-K E Market St #282 Leesburg VA 20176

MACFARLANE, JOHN ALEXANDER, retired federal agency administrator; b. Winnipeg, Man., Can., Sept. 6, 1916; s. John MacKay and Annie Catherine (Smith) MacF.; m. Gladys Valda Church, Dec. 20, 1941; children: John Lane, Elizabeth Ann, Janet Christine. BA with honours, U. Man., Winnipeg, 1939. With stats. br. Wartime Prices and Trade Bd., Ottawa, Ont., Canada, 1940-46; supr. stats. dept. Cn. Mortgage and Housing Corp., Ottawa, 1946-65, asst. dir. econs. and stats. div., 1965-69, asst. dir. secretariat div., 1969-78; ret., 1978; treas. Caribbean and N.Am. area coun. World Alliance Ref. Chs., 1984—2002. Treas. Ottawa Valley Cricket Coun., 1946-70, 73-80, pres., 1970-73, 83-88; moderator Presbytery of Ottawa, Presbyn. Ch. Can., 1994-96, rep. elder, 1961-97. Recipient Long Svc. medal Boy Scouts Assn., 1945, Centennial medal Govt. of Can., 1967, spl. achievement award for amateur sport Govt. of Ont., 1991. Mem. Def. Cricket Club (sec.-treas. 1944-46, pres. 1951-76, 78-92). Address: New Edinburgh Square 420 Mackay St Apt 207 Ottawa ON Canada K1M 2C4 Personal E-mail: jamacf@sympatico.ca.

MACFARLANE, KEN, automotive executive; b. Glasgow, Scotland; BSChemE, U. Mich., 1971, MSChemE, 1972. With Ford Motor Co., 1973—, engring., quality & mfg. mgmt. positions in vehicle ops., Automotive Components Holding, Visteon, dir., truck mfg. ops., N.Am., v.p. mfg. Ford Europe, 2008—. Office: Ford Motor Co One American Rd Dearborn MI 48126 Office Phone: 313-322-3000. Office Fax: 313-845-7512.*

MACFARLANE, SETH WOODBURY, television producer, scriptwriter; b. Kent, Conn., Oct. 26, 1973; s. Ron and Perry MacFarlane. Grad., RI Sch. Design; degree (hon.), Harvard U., 2006, RI Sch. Design, 2007. Founder, owner Fuzzy Door prodn. co. Dir., writer, voice (films) The Life of Larry, 1995, Larry & Steve, 1996, writer Zoomates, 1998, exec. prodr., writer, voice Family Guy Presents Stewie Griffin: The Untold Story, 2005, exec. prodr., writer, dir., voice American Dad: The New CIA, 2005; actor: (films) Life Is Short, 2006, A Conversation with George, 2008, Hellboy II: The Golden Army, 2008; writer (TV series) Jungle Cubs, 1996, Ace Ventura: Pet Detective, 1996, Dexter's Laboratory, 1996—2003, Cow and Chicken, 1997, Johnny Bravo, 1997—2003, The Winner, 2006, exec. prodr., writer, voice Family Guy, 1999— (Emmy award for Outstanding Music and Lyrics, 2002, Emmy award for Outstanding Voice-Over Performance, Best Voice Acting in an Animated TV Prodn., Annie Awards, 2006), American Dad, 2005—, voice Crank Yankers, 2003—05, Robot Chicken, 2005—07, writer (TV films) Dexter's Laboratory Ego Trip, 1999, voice Robot Chicken: Star Wars, 2007, (video game) Family Guy, 2006. Avocations: piano, golf. Office: c/o Greater Talent Network 437 Fifth Ave New York NY 10016 also: c/o The Family Guy Twentieth TV PO Box 900 Beverly Hills CA 90213-0900

MACFERRAN, ERNEST LESLIE, mechanical engineer; b. Southbend, Ind., May 19, 1945; s. Ernest Leslie Macferran Sr. and Pearl Helen (Stook) Macferran; m. Janice Carol Carr. BS in Mech. Engring., U. South Fla., Tampa, 1967. Registered profl. engr., Fla., 1975. Mech. engr. Tenn. Valley Auth., Knoxville, 1968—71, Watson and Co., Tampa,

1972—79, Carastro Aguire and Assoc., Tampa, 1980—82, Lehr Assocs., Tampa, 1983—85, Prime Design A&E, Tampa, 1986—92, Carastro and Assocs., Tampa, 1993—2001, Sch. Dist. Hillsborough County, Tampa, 2002—. Spkr. in field. Recipient Engring. Excellence award, Fla. Inst. Consulting Engrs., 2000. Mem.: ASHRAE (Engr. of Yr. 2005), Assn. Energy Engrs. Republican. Presbyterian. Achievements include invention of smoke relief hatch; discovery of LogT method for correctly field measuring air flow in rectangular ducts; research in solar heating for dehumidification instead of standard electric heating. Avocations: bicycling, fishing. Office: Sch Dist Hillsborough County 901 E Kennedy Blvd Tampa FL 33602

MACGILLIVRAY, CATHERINE MARY, histologist; d. Angus Boyd and Anne Marie MacGillivray. Degree in Allied Health, North Shore Cmty. Coll., Beverly, 1990. Cert. Occupl. therapy Mass., 1990. Histologist Brigham & Womens Hosp., Cambridge, Mass., 2001—; occupl. therapy asst. Kindred Healthcare, Bridgewater, Mass., 2002—. Contbr. scientific papers. Office: Brigham & Womens Hosp 65 Landsdowne St Cambridge MA 02139 Office Fax: 617-768-8280. Business E-Mail: cmacgillivray@rics.bwh.harvard.edu.

MACGILLIVRAY, THOMAS E., cardiothoracic surgeon; b. Boston, May 14, 1961; s. Dougald C. and Dorothy M. MacGillivray; m. Leslie C. Lucchina, Sept. 4, 1994; 1 child, Caroline G. MD, Tufts U. Sch. Medicine, Boston, 1988. Cert. surgeon Am. Bd. Surgery, 1996, Am. Bd. Thoracic Surgery, 1999. Cardiac surgeon Mass. Gen. Hosp., 1998—. Co-dir. MGH Thoracic Aortic Ctr., Boston, 2009—. Fellow: ACS; mem.: Soc. Thoracic Surgeons, Am. Assn. Thoracic Surgery. Office: Mass Gen Hosp 55 Fruit St Cox 650 Boston MA 02114 Office Fax: 617-726-5804.

MACGINITIE, WALTER HAROLD, psychologist, educator; b. Carmel, Calif., Aug. 14, 1928; s. George Eber and Nettie Lorene (Murray) MacG.; m. Ruth Olive Kilpatrick, Sept. 2, 1950; children: Mary Catherine, Laura Anne. BA, UCLA, 1949; A.M., Stanford U., 1950; PhD, Columbia U., 1960. Tchr. Long Beach (Calif.) Unified Sch. Dist., 1950, 1955-56; mem. faculty Columbia U. Tchrs. Coll., 1959-80, prof. psychology and edn., 1970-80; Lansdowne scholar, prof. edn. U. Victoria, B.C., Canada, 1980-84. Research assoc. Lexington Sch. Deaf, N.Y.C., 1963-69; mem. sci. adv. bd. Ctr. for Study of Reading, 1977-80, chmn. 1979-80. Co-author: Gates-MacGinitie Reading Tests, 1965, 78, 89, 2000, Psychological Foundations of Education, 1968; Editor: Assessment Problems in Reading, 1972; co-editor: Verbal Behavior of the Deaf Child, 1969. Life mem. Calif. PTA. Served with USAF, 1950-54. Fellow APA, AAAS, Assn. Psychol. Sci., Nat. Conf. Rsch. on Lang. and Literacy, N.Y. Acad. Scis.; mem. Internat. Reading Assn. (pres. 1976-77, Spl. Svc. award 1981), Reading Hall of Fame (pres. 1989-90). Home and Office: PO Box 1789 Friday Harbor WA 98250-1789

MACGOWAN, BILL, information technology executive; BA in Polit. Sci., Claremont McKenna Coll., Calif. With Northrop Grumman, Allergan; v.p. human resources Corning Inc., Quest Diagnostics; head enterprise svcs. divsn. Sun Microsystems, Inc., Santa Clara, Calif., 1998, v.p. human resources Systems, Storage and Ops. bus. groups, v.p. human resources Global Ctrs. Expertise, sr. v.p. human resources, chief human resources officer, exec. v.p. people and places. Trustee Am. Found. for Blind. Office: Sun Microsystems Inc 4150 Network Cir Santa Clara CA 95054 Office Phone: 650-960-1300.

MACGOWAN, SANDRA FIRELLI, publishing executive, consultant; b. Phila., Nov. 9, 1951; d. William Firelli and Barbara (Gimbel) Kapalcik. BS in Biology, BA in English, Pa. State U., 1973, MA in English Lit., 1978. Cert. supervisory analyst N.Y. Stock Exch. Editor McGraw-Hill Pub. Co., NYC, 1979-81; sr. acquisitions editor Harcourt Brace Jovanovich, Inc., NYC, 1981-82; sr. editor The Coll. Bd., NYC, 1982-88; v.p., head editorial CS First Boston Corp., NYC, 1988-94; v.p., supervisory analyst internat. rsch. SBC Warburg, NYC, 1994-96; v.p., supervisory analyst internat. rsch. Arnhold and S. Bleichroeder, NYC, 1996—2003; mng. dir. Natixis Bleichroeder Inc. (formerly Arnhold and S. Bleichroeder), NYC, 2003—, mgr. Rsch. Dept., 2003—. Part time assoc. prof. pub. NYU Sch. Continuing Edn., N.Y.C., 1985-2006. Author: 50 College Admission Directors Speak to Parents, 1988. Democrat. Avocations: art, reading, travel. Office: Natexis Bleichroeder Fl 44 1345 Avenue Of The Americas New York NY 10105-4300 Home Phone: 212-534-5306; Office Phone: 212-698-3219. Business E-Mail: sandra.macgowan@blrnatixis.com.

MACGOWN, JOE A., entomologist, researcher; b. South Paris, Maine, June 21, 1964; s. Matthew W. MacGown and Mary E. Gregg; m. Julie D. Boyles, Mar. 16, 1989; 1 child, Joseph H. Rsch. technician to sci. illustrator Miss. State U., Starkvile, 1988—. Exhibition, Cotton District Arts Festival Juried Exhibition (hon. mention, 2006); Meridian Museum of Art-People's Choice Awards, Joe MacGown and Cetin Oguz Two Man show at the Meridian Museum of Art in Meridian. Vol. coach Starkville Acad., 2007—. Mem.: Miss. Entomol. Assn. Home: 2073 Sessums Rd Starkville MS 39759 Office: Miss Entomol Mus 100 Twelve Ln Mississippi State MS 39762 Office Phone: 662-325-9551. Personal E-mail: art@joemacgown.com. Business E-Mail: jmacgown@entomology.msstate.edu.

MACGREGOR, GEORGE LESCHER, JR., freelance/self-employed writer; b. Dallas, Sept. 15, 1936; s. George Lescher and Jean (Edge) MacG.; divorced; children: George Lescher III (dec.), Michael Fordtran. BBA, U. Tex., 1958. Asst. cashier First Nat. Bank in Dallas, 1960-64, asst. v.p., 1964-68; v.p. Nat. Bank of Commerce of Dallas, 1968-70, sr. v.p., 1970-73, exec. v.p., 1973-74; pres., chief exec. officer Mountain Banks Ltd., Colorado Springs, 1974-77; chief exec. officer Highfield Fin. (U.S.A.) Ltd., 1978-83; chmn. bd., chief exec. officer, dir. Dominion Nat. Bank, Denver, 1981-84; chmn. bd., chief exec. officer Royal Dominion Ltd., Denver; chmn. bd., chief exec. officer, dir. Market Bank of Denver, 1983-84; vice chmn., dir. Bank of Aurora, Denver, 1983-84; chmn., pres., chief exec. officer Alamosa Bancorp. of Colo., Denver, 1983-84; pres., chief exec. officer Am. Interstate Bancorp., 1984-88; pres. Banco, Inc., 1984-89; sr. mng. ptnr. Scotland Co., Denver, London, 1988-91; free-lance writer, 1992—. Served with M.C. AUS, 1958-60. Mem. Am. Inst. Banking (hon.), Young Pres.'s Orgn., Coon Creek Club, Broadmoore Golf Club, Oxford Club, Phi Gamma Delta. Anglican Catholic. Home and Office: 1736 Blake St Denver CO 80202-1226 Home Fax: 303-292-9794. Personal E-mail: twotatertotts@aol.com.

MACH, JAN ELLEN WALKENHORST, literature educator, editor; b. Madison, Nebr. d. Dale Edward and Mary Moyer Walkenhorst; m. Daniel Blount (div.); 1 child, Byron K. Rupp; m. Robert Mach, 2006. BS in English Edn., U. Nebr., 1974. Cert. tchr. Tex., 1982, Nebr., 2001, coll. bd. cert. 1995. Pres. Papillion (Nebr.) Edn. Assn., 1976—79; tchr. english Papillion (Nebr.) Pub. Schs., 1974—80, Richardson (Tex.) Ind. Sch. Dist., 1982—2000, Lincoln (Nebr.) Pub. Schs., 2001—04; instr. writing, asst. acad. counselor, tchr. theory of knowledge U. Nebr., Lincoln, 2004—. Mem. core team successful strategies, English Dept. chair, site-based facilitator, tchr. cadre; mem. project to convert curriculum to software Baylor U., 1994; rater statewide writing assessment Nebr., 2003. Editor: McGraw-Hill, 2000—, DC Health. Mem.: Nat. Assn. Acad. Advisors for Athletics. Avocations: reading, politics, travel. Office: Univ Nebr Athletic Dept 1 Memorial Stadium Lincoln NE 68588 Home: 1561 Rokeby Rd Pleasant Dale NE 68423 Home Phone: 402-826-5647; Office Phone: 402-472-9985. Personal E-mail: janwalk1952@aol.com. Business E-Mail: jwalkenhorst@huskers.com.

MACH, THOMAS S., history professor; b. Ohio; PhD, U. Akron, Ohio, 1996. Assoc. prof. history Mt. Vernon Nazarene Coll., Ohio, 1994—2000; prof. history Cedarville U., Ohio, 2000—; chair dept. history, govt. Mem.: Conf. Faith and History, Orgn. Am. Historians. Office: Cedarville Univ 251 N Main St Cedarville OH 45314 Business E-Mail: macht@cedarville.edu.

MACHA, KEN (KENNETH EDWARD MACHA), professional baseball manager; b. Monroeville, Pa., Sept. 29, 1950; m. Carolyn Virginia Macha; children: Eric, Kristin. BS in Civil Engring., U. Pitts. Infielder Pitts. Pirates, 1974—78, Montreal Expos, 1979—80, Toronto Blue Jays, 1981, Chunichi Dragons, Nippon Baseball League, 1983—85; minor league mgr. Boston Red Sox Org., 1995—98; bench coach Oakland Athletics, 1999—2002, mgr., 2002—06, Milw. Brewers, 2008—. Coach Am. League All-Star Team, 2005. Named Internat. League Mgr. Yr., 1998. Office: Milw Brewers Miller Pk One Brewers Way Milwaukee WI 53214*

MACHAN, POLLY JOSEPH, hotel manager; b. Cochin, Kerala, India, Jan. 29, 1952; s. Joseph Kurien and Alia Machan; m. Annamma Varughese, May 17, 1952; 1 child, John. B in Comms., Delhi U., India, 1980. Mgr. Claridges Hotel, New Delhi, Delhi, 2000—, Homran Ho., Salala, Muscat, Oman. Cons. updating sick hotel units, India, other countries. Mem.: Assocham. Home: 93 Esi Colony New Delhi 110015 India Office: Claridges Hotel 12 Aurangzeb Road Delhi New Delhi 110011 India Office Fax: 3010625. Personal E-mail: pollymachan@hotmail.com, aliason_2000@yahoo.com.

MACHAN, TIBOR RICHARD, college professor, newspaper columnist; b. Budapest, Hungary, Mar. 18, 1939; s. Tibor Gustav Machan and Ingeborg Doczy-Guendisch; children: Katherine Zupan, Thomas, Erin Elizabeth. Ph D, U. Calif., Santa Barbara, 1971. Prof. SUNY Coll., NY, 1972—81, Auburn U., Ala., 1986—96; harwood prof. Franklin Coll., Lugano, Ticino, Switzerland, 1984—86; vis. assoc. prof. U. San Diego, 1984—85, US Mil. Acad., West Point, NY, 1992—93; chair Chapman U., Orange, Calif., 1997—. Columnist Orange County Register, Santa Ana, Calif., 1966—. Contbr. articles to profl. jours. (Outstanding Scholarly Book, 1983). Editor, bd. mem. Reason Mag. Found., Santa Barbara, Calif., 1972—87. With USAF, 1958—62, Andrews AFB. Mem.: Mt. Pelerin Soc. Libertarian. Avocations: tennis, swimming. Office: Argyros Sch Business & Economics Chapman University One University Dr Orange CA 92866 Home Fax: 714-649-9225. Personal E-mail: tmachan@gmail.com. Business E-Mail: machan@chapman.edu.

MACHEN, JAMES BERNARD, academic administrator; m. Chris; children: Maggie, Michael, Lee. DDS, St. Louis U., 1968; MS, U. Iowa, 1972, PhD in Edn. Psychology, 1974. Prof., assoc. dean U. N.C., 1983-89; pres. Am. Assn. Dental Schs., 1987; dean U. Mich. Sch. Dentistry, 1989-95; provost, exec. v.p. acad. affairs U. Mich., 1995-97; pres. U. Utah, 1998—2003, U. Fla., Gainesville, 2004—. Mem. Inst. Medicine Com. in Future Dental Edn. Nat. Acad. Scis., 1993-95. Office: U Fla Office of the Pres 226 Tigert Hall PO Box 113150 Gainesville FL 32611-3150*

MACHEN, RONALD C., lawyer; b. May 6, 1969; AB, Stanford U., 1991; JD, Harvard U., 1994. Bar: Ill. 1994, DC 1995, US Supreme Ct. Clk. to Hon. Damon J. Keith US Ct. of Appeals, Sixth cir., 1995—97; asst. US Atty. US Dept. Justice, Washington, 1997—2001; ptnr. Wilmer Cutler Pickering Hale and Dorr LLP, Washington, 2001—. Lectr. on trial advocacy Howard U. Sch. Law, Washington, 1998. Recipient Spl. Achievement award, US Dept. Justice; named one of Top 40 Lawyers Under 40, Washingtonian Mag., Litigation's Rising Stars, The Am. Lawyer, 2007, 50 Most Influential Minority Lawyers in America, Nat. Law Jour., 2008; named to Washington DC Super Lawyers, 2007. Fellow: Am. Bar Found.; mem.: ABA (former co-chmn. Criminal Litig. com.), Nat. Bar Assn., Internat. Assn. Def. Counsel, Edward Bennett Williams Inn of Ct., Coun. Ct. Excellence. Office: Wilmer Cutler Pickering Hale and Dorr LLP 1875 Pennsylvania Ave NW Washington DC 20006 Office Phone: 202-663-6881. Office Fax: 202-663-6363. Business E-Mail: ronald.machen@wilberhale.com.*

MACHIDA, CURTIS A., research molecular neurobiologist, molecular virologist, oral biologist, educator; b. San Francisco, Apr. 1, 1954; AB, U. Calif., Berkeley, 1976; PhD, Oreg. Health Scis. U., 1982. Postdoctoral scientist Oreg. Health Scis. U., Portland, 1982-88; asst. sci. div. neurosci. Oreg. Nat. Primate Rsch. Ctr., Beaverton, 1988-95, assoc. scie. divsn. neurosci., 1995—2002; assoc. rsch. prof. integrative biosciences Sch. Dentistry Oreg. Health Scis. U., Portland, 2002—05, rsch. prof. integrative bioscis., 2005—07, tenured prof. integrative biosci., 2008—. Rsch. asst. prof. biochemistry and molecular biology Oreg. Health Sci. U., 1989-95, mem. faculty neurosci. and molecular and cell biology grad. programs, 1989—, adj. assoc. prof. biochemistry and molecular biology, 1995—; mem. grad. faculty biochemistry and biophysics Oreg. State U., Corvallis, 1997-01; mem. Institutional Ethics oversight com., Institutional Biosafety com., faculty bylaws com., preclin. curriculum com.; mem. Dental Sch. Rsch. Task Force; mem. biotech. program adv. com. Portland C.C. Editor Adrenergic Receptor Protocols, 1997-99, Viral Vectors for Gene Therapy: Methods and Protocols, 2000-03; mem. editl. bd. Molecular Biotechnology, Frontiers in Biosci., Internat. Jour. Biomed. Sci., World Medicine; ad-hoc reviewer Endocrinology, Molecular Pharmacology, Biochimica et Biophysica Acta, Am. Jour. Physiology, Lab. Animal Sci., NSF, BioTechs., Brain Rsch.; contbr. articles, revs., and abstracts to profl. jours. and internat. confs. Recipient Leukemia Assn. award, 1981, Tartar award Med. Rsch. Found. Oreg., 1980; NIH fellow, 1980-82, 85-87, grantee, 1989, 95, 98, 2002, 05; rsch. grantee, Am. Assn. Endodontists Found, Med. Rsch. Found. Oreg., Wills Found., Nat. Parkinson Found., Collins Med. Trust, Murdock Charitable Trust and Rsch. Corp., Nat. Am. Heart Assn. Mem. AAAS, Am. Soc. Biochemistry and Molecular Biology, Am. Soc. Microbiology, Soc. Neurosci., Am. Heart Assn. (basic scis. coun., established investigator 1994-99), Am. Soc. Gene Therapy, U.S.-Israel Binational Sci. Found. (reviewer). Achievements include patent on dopamine receptor and genes; cloning of several adrenergic receptor genes and simian retroviral infectious genomes; depositor, nucleotide sequence to EMBL and GenBank databases, and clones to American Type Culture Collection. Office: Oreg Health Sci U Sch Dentistry Dept Integrative Biosciences 611 SW Campus Dr Portland OR 97239-3097 E-mail: machidac@ohsu.edu.

MACHINA, MARK JOSEPH, economist; b. Detroit, Oct. 27, 1954; BA in Econs., Mich. State U., East Lansing, 1975, BA in Math., 1975; PhD in Econs., MIT, Boston, 1979. Asst. prof. econs. U. Calif., San Diego, 1979—84, assoc. prof. econs., 1984—88, prof. econs., 1988—. Vis. prof. econs. Duke U., Durham, NC, 1996; jr. rsch. officer Cambridge U., 1980—81; vis. asst. prof. econs. Princeton (N.J.) U., 1981—82; instr. People's U. China, Beijing, 1987, 90, 91, 93; Kaiser vis. prof. econs. Stanford (Calif.) U., 1999. Assoc. editor: Jour. Econ. Theory, 1983—91, Econometrica, 1984—91, Quarterly Jour. Econs., 1985—91, Jour. Econ. Perspectives, 1987—90, Jour. Econ. Surveys, 1987—91; co-editor: Theory and Decision, 1986—, Jour. Math. Econs., 1999—; founding co-editor: Jour. Risk and Uncertainty, 1988—90; contbr. articles to profl. jours. Trustee U. Calif. San Diego Found., 2001—04. Grantee, NSF, 1983—86, 1992—95, 1998—2001; fellow, Ctr. for Advanced Study in the Behavioral Scis., 1987—88; Grad. fellow, NSF, 1975—78, Vis. fellow, Australian Nat. U., Canberra, 1983, Rsch. fellow, Alfred P. Sloan Found., 1984—86, Erskine fellow, U. Canterbury, Christchurch, New Zealand, 1994. Fellow: Econometric Soc., Am. Acad. Arts and Scis.; mem.: Phi Beta Kappa. Business E-Mail: mmachina@ucsd.edu.

MACHLE, EDWARD JOHNSTONE, religious studies educator, philosopher; b. Canton, China, Sept. 29, 1918; s. Edward Charles and Jean (Mawson) M.; m. Neva Hull, Aug. 29, 1942; children— Stewart, Douglas, Kathi; m. Mary Lou Reynolds, Dec. 15, 1970; 1 adopted child, Michelle; stepchildren— Rebecca, Richard, Robin. Student, Pacific Lutheran Jr. Coll., 1937; BA, Whitworth Coll., 1939; B.D., San Francisco Theol. Sem., 1942, MA, 1944; PhD, Columbia U., 1952. Ordained to ministry Presbyn. Ch., 1942; minister Concrete, Wash., 1942-43; asst. minister San Francisco, 1943-44, Mineola, N.Y., 1944-46; instr. Columbia, 1946-47; asst. prof. U. Colo., 1947-53, asso. prof., 1953-63, prof., 1963-80, emeritus, 1981—, chmn. dept., 1951-52, 56-58, 66-69. Vis. lectr. U. Alta., summer 1960, Iliff Sch. Theology, 1962, Evergreen State, 1981, Peninsula Coll., 1985-86; in-parish research dir. San Francisco Theol. Sem.; dir. music St. Andrew Presbyn. Ch., Boulder, Colo., 1961-70; guest lectr. ch. music U. Colo. Sch. Music, 1950-65; disting. faculty fellow Sheldon Jackson Coll., 1986-88 Author: Nature and Heaven in the Xunzi, 1993; book, A Philosopher Looks at Jesus, 2008. Mem. Am. Phil. Assn., Soc. Asian and Comparative Philosophy, Acad. Religion. Presbyterian. Home: 11 Silver Canyon Place The Woodlands TX 77381 Personal E-mail: emachle@comcast.net. *Faith is largely willingness to learn of what can destroy us. Idolatry feeds on our fear of having faith. Research methods spring from the soil of our cultured idolatries. Thus, to learn, faith must at times be a traitor to "learning.".*

MACHON, MONIKA MARIA, insurance company executive, lawyer; b. Aschaffenburg, Fed. Republic of Germany, July 14, 1960; came to U.S., 1976; d. Lutz Guenter and B. Marie-Anne (Eriksson) M.; m. Kellett Jay Koch, May 23, 1987. BSBA, Rockhurst Coll., 1980; MBA, JD, Ind. U., Inpls., 1986. Bar: Wis. 1987. Credit analyst Ind. Nat. Bank, Indpls., 1980-82, loan rev. officer, 1982-84, internat. lending officer, 1984-85; atty. investments Northwestern Mut. Life Ins., Milw., 1986; investment mgmt. positions Providian, Barclays Capital; mgmt. positions Am. Internat. Group, NYC, 1998—; portfolio mgr., head emerging markets debt AIG Investments, CEO London based bus., gen. counsel, 2003, mng. dir., head global fixed income; sr. v.p., chief investment officer Am. Internat. Group, Inc. (AIG), NYC, 2009—. Instr. bus. law Marian Coll., Fond Du Lac, Wis., 1988. Campaign worker com. to re-elect justice Shirley Abrahamson, Milw., 1987. Mem. ABA, Wis. Bar Assn. (securities law com. 1988—), Milw. Young Lawyers Assn. (minority bus. certification appeals com. 1988—, chair corp. counsel com. 1988-89), Assn. Women Lawyers (chair membership com. 1988-89). Democrat. Episcopalian. Avocations: reading, theater, aerobic exercise. Office: AIG 70 Pine St New York NY 10270*

MACHOVEC, FRANK J., psychologist; b. Balt., May 16, 1930; s. James Joseph and Theresa Anna MacH.; m. Evelyn Mary Stultz, May 5, 1951; 1 child, Frank. BA, U. Md., 1964; MA, Loyola U., Balt., 1965; PhD, Fielding Inst., 1979. Diplomate Am. Bd. Psychol. Hypnosis, Am. Bd. Med. Psychotherapy; lic. clin. psychologist. Psychologist Victoria Hosp., Winnipeg, Man., Canada, 1975—76, Alta. Mental Health, Lethbridge, Canada, 1976—78, Alaska Psychol. Inst., Anchorage, 1978—80, State Hosp. South, Blackfoot, Idaho, 1979-81; dir. psychol. svcs. South Va. Mental Health Inst., Danville, 1981-86; dir. quality assurance Va. Dept. Mental Health, 1986-90; supr. psychology Va. Juvenile Corrections, 1991-95, ret., 1995. Prof. Piedmont Va. Com. Coll.; instr. Jefferson Inst. Author: Hypnosis Complications, 1986, Expert Witness Survival Manual, 1987, Humor Theories, History, 1988, Interview and Interrogation, 1989, Cults and Personality, 1989, Becoming Street Smart, 1994, Spiritual Intelligence, 2002, Light from the East, 2005, Private Investigative and Security Science, 2006, Divine Spark, 2007, Buddha, Tao, Zen, 2007, Lead and Manage, 2007, Whats Funny, Psychology of Humor, 2008, Cults and Terrorism, Zen Classics, 2009. With USMC, 1950—52. Avocations: writing, travel, teaching. Home Phone: 352-561-4525.

MACHOVER, CARL, computer graphics designer, engineer, consultant; b. Bklyn., Mar. 26, 1927; s. John Herman and Rose (Alter) M.; m. Wilma Doris Simon, June 18, 1950; children: Tod, Julie, Linda. BEE, Rensselaer Poly. Inst., 1951; postgrad., NYU, 1953-56. Mgr. applied engring. Norden div. United A/C Corp., 1951-59; mgr. sales Skiatron Electronics & TV, NYC, 1959-60; v.p. mktg., dir. Info. Displays, Inc., Mount Kisco, NY, 1960-73, v.p., gen. mgr., 1973-76; pres. Machover Assocs. Corp., White Plains, NY, 1976—. Adj. prof. Rensselaer Poly. Inst.; mem. RPI H&SS adv. bd. Bradford EIMC Indsl. Adv. Bd.; pres. bd. Art & Sci. Collaborations, Inc., 1994-2004. Author: Gyro Primer, 1957, Basics of Gyroscopes, 1958; mem. editl. bd., new products editor IEEE Computer Graphics and Applications; mem. editl. bd. Computers and Graphics; editor C4 Handbook, 1989, 2d edit., 1995, The CAD/CAM Handbook, 1996; co-editor Computer Graphics Rev.; co-exec. prodr. The Story of Computer Graphics, 1999; contbr. articles to profl. jours. Mem. adv. bd. Pratt Ctr. for Computer Graphics in Design. With USNR, 1945-46. Recipient Frank Oppenheimer award, Am. Soc. Engring. Edn., 1971, Orthagonal award, N.C. State U., 1988, Vanguard award, Nat. Computer Graphics Assn., 1993, Industry Lifetime Achievement award, CAD Soc., 2003; named to Computer Graphics Hall of Fame, Fine Arts Mus. of L.I., Hempstead, N.Y., 1988. Fellow Soc. for Info. Display (pres. 1968-70), Eurographics Assn.; mem. IEEE, Assn. for Computing Machinery, Am. Inst. Design and Drafting, Soc. Mfg. Engrs., Nat. Computer Graphics Assn. (bd. dir., pres. 1989-90), Computer Graphics Pioneer, Art and Sci. Collaborators Inc. (pres. 1995—), Sigma Xi, Tau Beta Pi, Eta Kappa Nu. Home: 152 Longview Ave White Plains NY 10605-2314 Office: Machover Associates 152A Longview Ave White Plains NY 10605-2314 Office Phone: 914-949-3777.

MACHOWSKI, LIISA ERVIN SHARPES, science educator; b. New Brunswick, NJ, Feb. 9, 1953; d. William and Gladys Ervin Sharpes; m. Daniel John Machowski, Oct. 6, 1979; children: Anne Marie, Michael Joseph. M in Curriculum & Instrn., The Citadel, Charleston, SC, 1992—96. Nat. Bd. cert. chemistry tchr. 2002. J.v. varsity girls basketball coach Titusville HS, Fla., 1975—76; jv girls basketball coach Palm Bay HS, 1977—78; head, sci. dept. Bishop Eng. HS, Charleston, SC, 1983—84; sponsor nat. honor soc. chpt. James Island Charter HS, Charleston, 1990—, sailing team sponsor, 2005—, sci. tchr. Contbr. for devel. of curriculum tchg. units for phys. sci. Charleston County Schs., 1999—2002; presenter of phys. sci. curriculum unit on chem. reactions S.C. Sci. Coun., Charleston, 2002—03. Mem.: Fla. Fedn. Tchrs., S.C. Sci. Coun., Charleston Ocean Racing Assn. (scorer 2005—). Roman Catholic. Avocations: sailing, bicycling, collector. Office: James Island Charter HS 1000 Fort Johnson Rd Charleston SC

MACIAS, EDWARD S., chemistry professor, dean, academic administrator; b. Milw., Feb. 21, 1944; s. Arturo C. Macias and Minette (Schwenger) Wiederhold; m. Paula Wiederhold, June 17, 1967; children: Matthew Edward, Julia Katherine. AB, Colgate U., 1966; PhD, MIT, 1970. From asst. prof. to Barbara and David Thomas Disting. prof. Arts and Scis. Washington U., St. Louis, 1970—2005, Barbara and David Thomas Disting. prof. Arts and Scis., 2005—, exec. vice chancellor and dean Faculty Arts and Scis., 1995—. Cons. Meteorology Rsch., Inc., Altadina, Calif., 1978-81, Salt River Project, Phoenix, 1980-83, Santa Fe Rsch., Bloomington, Minn., 1985-88, AeroVironment, Inc., Monrovia, Calif., 1986-88. Author: Nuclear and Radiochemistry, 1981; editor: Atmospheric Aerosol, 1981; contbr. numerous articles to profl. jours. Bd. dirs. Mark Twain Summer Inst., St. Louis, 1984-87, 88-90, The Coll. Sch., St. Louis, 1984-88, Colgate U., 1997—. Grantee NSF, EPA, Electric Power Rsch. Inst., So. Calif. Edison Co., Dept. Energy, AEC. Mem. Am. Chem. Soc., Am. Assn. Aerosol Rsch. (editorial bd.), Am. Phys. Soc., AAAS. Home: 6907 Waterman Ave Saint Louis MO 63130-4333 Office: Washington U Campus Box 1094 One Brookings Dr Saint Louis MO 63130 Office Phone: 314-935-6800.

MACIAS, LINDA C., legislative staff member; Chief of staff for Rep. Joe Bacca, US House of Reps., Washington, 2000—. Mem.: Congl. Hispanic Staffers Assn. (CHSA). Office: Office of Congressman Joe Baca 2245 Rayburn House Office Bldg Washington DC 20515-0542 Office Phone: 202-225-6161. Office Fax: 202-225-8671. E-mail: linda.macias@mail.house.gov.*

MACIAS, MICHAEL, research scientist; b. Atlanta, June 15, 1977; s. Salvador Macias III and Lucinda Macias. BS in Elec. Engring., Clemson U., SC, 2001; BS in Chemistry, U. SC., Columbia, 2004; PhD in Forensic Chemistry, Fla. Internat. U., Miami, 2004—. Grad. tchg. asst. Fla. Internat. U., Miami, 2004—06, rsch. assoc., 2004—. Rsch. assoc Internat. Forensic Rsch. Inst., Miami, 2004—. Contbr. scientific papers. Rsch. grant, Nat. Inst. Justice, 2006—08. Office: Florida International University 11200 SW 8th St Miami FL 33199 Business E-Mail: mmaci004@fiu.edu.

MACIEJOVSKY, BORIS, economist, researcher; s. Eduard Maciejovsky and Waltraut Elicker; m. Geeta Bhatia, Oct. 28, 1971. PhD, U. Vienna, 2000. Rsch. assoc. Max Planck Inst. Econ., Jena, Germany, 2001—04; rsch. fellow London Sch. Econ., London, 2007—. Contbr. articles to profl. jours. Mem.: Econ. Sci. Assn. Office: Imperial College Tanaka Building Rm 279 South Kensington Campus London SW72AV England

MACIEJUNES, NANNETTE V., museum director; b. Columbus, Ohio; m. George Maciejunes; 1 child. Grad. in Art History summa cum laude, Denison U., Granville, Ohio; grad., Ohio State U. Various positions including rsch. asst., collections and exhbns. dir., chief curator Columbus Mus. Art, 1984—89, 1990—2002, acting exec. dir., 2002—03, exec. dir., 2003—; collections and exhbns. curator Dixon Gallery and Gardens, Memphis, 1989. Grantee, Charles E. Burchfield Found., 1997. Office: Columbus Mus Art 480 E Broad St Columbus OH 43215 Office Phone: 614-221-6801.

MACIEL, GARY EMMET, chemistry professor, researcher; b. Fremont, Calif., Jan. 18, 1935; s. Manuel Morris and Beatrice Boyd Maciel; m. Maxine Ivy Nissen, Aug. 19, 1956; children: Eric Graham, Jennifer Ann Sanders. PhD, MIT, Cambridge, Mass., 1960. Asst., assoc. prof. to prof. U. Calif., Davis, 1961—71; prof. chemistry Colo. State U., Ft. Collins, 1971—. Contbr. scientific papers to profl. jours. Postdoc. fellowship, NSF, 1960—61, Rsch. grants, DOE, USGS, Phillip Morris, AFOSR, Cabot Corp., NIH, 1964—, Sabbatical fellowship, 1967—68. Fellow: Sigma Xi; mem.: Internat. Soc. Magnetic Resonance, Am. Chem. Soc. Achievements include development of nuclear magnetic resonance techniques, instrumentation and applications, especially in areas involving solid samples or surfaces, including systems based on silica or silica-like materials, coal, oil shale, plant samples, soils, synthetic polymers and resins, ceramics and sorbed pollutants. Avocations: swimming, scuba diving, skiing, gardening. Home: 1501 E Lake St Fort Collins CO 80524 Office: Colo State Univ Dept Chemistry Fort Collins CO 80523 Office Fax: 970-491-1801. Business E-Mail: gary.maciel@colostate.edu.

MACIEWSKI, BRYAN JON, finance educator, consultant; s. Margret Couture; m. Bonnie L. Pappen, June 11, 2003; children: Bobbie L., Marnie L. Johnson, Rebbeca L., Anthony V., LaReasha Johns, Natasha Francis, Naomi Francis, Nadia Torres. MBA, Embry-Riddle Aero. U., European Divsn., Germany, 1992. Faculty, bus. Fond du Lac Tribal and CC, Cloquet, Minn., 1998—2008; faculty Embry-Riddle Aero. U., European Divsn., Germany. Pastor Sawyer Chapel, Minn. With USAF, 1978—92, Germany. Master: Native Am. Ministerial Assn. (elder 2007—08). Office Fax: 218-879-0814. Business E-Mail: bryanjon@fdltcc.edu.

MAC INNES, DAVID HAROLD, artist, small business owner; s. Harold Boice and Julia (Storr) Mac Innes; m. Gloria Jean LePre; 1 child, Marisa Alley. Grad., Cleve. Inst. Art, 1946—49. Cert. fine art/applied art Cleve. Inst. Art, 1949. Art dir. Fuller, Smith & Ross, Pitts., 1958—62, Kenyon & Eckhardt, NYC, 1964—68; creative group supr. art dir., designer L.W. Frohlich, Inc. Pharms., NYC, 1968—72; sr. art dir. Wunderman, Ricotta & Kline, NYC, 1972—75, Conahay & Lyon, NYC, 1976—80, Barnum Comm., Inc., NYC, 1983—86, Chapman Advt., Inc. (Young & Rubicam), NYC, 1986—91; creative group & studio mgr. F. Scott Kimmich, Inc., Norwalk, Conn., 1980—83; owner, artist MacInnes Comm., Rancho Palos Verdes, Calif., 1992—. Contbg. artist (exhibitions) Three Rivers Centennial Exhibit, Pitts., 1955; exhibitions include Cleve. Mus. Art, 1958, 27th New Eng. Internat., Silvermine, Conn., 1959, In Retrospect, 1996, exhibitions include paintings, graphics, Larchmont Cmty. Ctr., 1997, exhibitions include paintings, plein-air oils, acrylics A Walk in the Park, Larchmont Art Gallery, one-man shows include, Ivy Sch. Art, Pitts., 1956, large scale acrylics, Art Directors Who Paint, artists guild, NY Big Apple Show (First Artist award, Mamaroneck Artists Guild, 1993); contbg. artist, editor, cinematographer (NY experimental film exposition); pvt. collections, NYC, Pitts., Ann Arbor, Mich., Cleve., Albuquerque. Pvt. 1st class USAF, 1943—45, US, Germany. Recipient First award, Pitts. Artists in Industry, 1960, LW Frohlich Competition, 1970, First prize award, Internat. Broadcasting Assn., 1970, First prize award for painting, Mamaroneck Artists Guild, 1992, Expect the Unexpected First award, Mamaroneck Artists Gallery, 1994, 2d Prize award for monoprint, Palos Verdes Art Ctr., 2003. Mem.: DuoDecimo Soc., Advt. Artists Pitts. (bd. mem. artist, editor, designer aap comm. 1955—59), Calif. Art Edn. Assn. (assoc.; contriuting mem. 2004—06), NY Art Dirs. Club Pa. (life; various com. positions 1972—2006, students scholarship com. mem. 1985—89), Palos Verdes Art Ctr., Paletteers (assoc.), Art Dirs. Club Pitts. (bd. mem. 1958—60). Avocations: travel, museums. Office: David Mac Innes PO Box 4711 Rancho Palos Verdes CA 90275 Office Fax: 310-541-1039. Business E-Mail: dmacinnes2@aol.com.

MACINNES, MARGARET E., retired art educator; b. Akron, Ohio, Mar. 28, 1931; d. William Paul and Florence E. Neal; m. Robert Lee Works (dec.); m. Margarate E. Macinnes. BFA, Carnegie Mellon U., Pitts., 1951; MS, U. So. Calif., LA, 1957. Cert. in art Calif., 1953, 1960; tchr. elem. and secondary art Pa., 1951. Tchr. LA Unified Sch. Dist., 1953—91; supr. art edn. fieldwork Calif. State U. Dominguez Hills, Calif., 1993—2004, instr. art, 1993—2004; ret., 2004. Mem. new tchr. com. LA Unified Sch. Dist., 1965—66, mem. review and revision art com., 1984—85, 1992—93; mem. com. Eveinings for Educators LA County Mus. Art, 1975—90; workshop leader in field; curatorial asst. Mingel Folk Art Mus., La Jolla, Calif., 1980, San Diego, 2002; judge advanced placement Ednl. Testing Svc., Princeton, NJ, 1989; tchr. mentor LA County Schs., 1993—2001. Exhibitions include Scaife House Gallery, 1952, LA County Mcpl. Art Gallery, 1983. Judge art shows So. Calif., 1965—2006; ofcl. election poll LA County Election Bd., 1991—2006. Mem.: Calif. Art Edn. Assn. (historian 2004—06, chmn. 2004—06, named Retired Educator of Yr. 2005), PVAC Paleteers. Avocations: printmaking, drawing, painting, travel, cooking. Studio: 27850 Longhill Dr Rancho Palos Verdes CA 90274 Office Phone: 310-541-1039.

MACINNIS, AL, professional sports team executive, retired professional hockey player; b. Inverness, NS, Can., July 11, 1963; Defenceman Calgary Flames, 1981-94, St. Louis Blues, 1994—2005, v.p. hockey ops., 2006—. Mem. Team Can., Olympic Games, Nagano, Japan, 1998, Salt Lake City, 2002; player NHL All-Star Game, 1985, 1987—92, 1994, 1996—2001, 2003. Recipient Max Kaminsky Trophy, 1983, Conn Smythe Trophy, 1989, James Norris Meml. Trophy, 1999; named to Sporting News All-Star First Team, 1990, 1991, First All-Star Team, NHL, 1990, 1991. Achievements include being a member of Stanely Cup Champion Calgary Flames, 1989; being a member of gold medal Canadian Hockey team, Salt Lake City Olympic Games, 2002; having his number, 2, retired by St. Louis Blues, 2006; being inducted into the Hockey Hall of Fame, 2007. Office: St Louis Blues Hockey Club Scottrade Ctr 1401 Clark Ave Saint Louis MO 63103

MACINNIS, FRANK T., construction and holding company executive, securities trader; b. Camrose, Alta., Can., Nov. 10, 1946; came to U.S., 1978; s. H. Frank and Adele M. (Irving) MacI.; m. Beverley J. McAndrews, Nov. 3, 1977; children: Christopher, Katrina, Lauren, Robbie. BA, Univ. Alta., Edmonton, 1968, LLB, 1971. Assoc. Liden, Ackroyd & Co., Edmonton, 1971-75; gen. counsel Banister-Price Internat., Tehran, Iran, 1975-77; dir. Banister-Price Overseas, London, 1977-78; exec. v.p. H.C. Price Co., Bartlesville, Okla., 1978-80; chmn., chief exec. officer H.C. Price Constrn. Co., Dallas, 1980-84; pres. Spie Group, Inc., Dallas, 1986—94; sr. v.p., CFO Comstock Group, Inc., Danbury, Conn., 1986—90, chmn., pres., CEO, 1990—94; pres. EMCOR Group Inc., Norwalk, Conn., 1994—97, chmn., CEO, 1997—. Mem. exec. com. Spie Batignolles, Paris, 1985-94; bd. dirs. The Williams Companies, ITT Industries, Inc. Served to lt. Royal Can. Navy, 1964-68; bd. dirs. Greater New York Chapter of the March of Dimes. Roman Catholic. Avocations: sports, coin collecting/numismatics, music. Office: EMCOR Croup Inc 301 Merritt Seven Corporate Park 6th Fl Norwalk CT 06851-1060 Office Phone: 203-849-7800. Office Fax: 203-849-7900.

MACINTYRE, NEIL ROSS, JR., medical educator; b. San Diego, Nov. 21, 1946; s. Neil Ross and Rebecca (Torrey) MacI.; m. Suzanne Artusio, June 20, 1970; children: Catherine, Neil III, Douglas, Charles, Elizabeth, Stephen. BS cum laude, U. San Francisco, 1968; MD, Cornell U., 1972. Diplomate Am. Bd. Internal Medicine, Pulmonary Disease, Critical Care Medicine; lic. physician, NC. Intern, jr. resident, sr. resident medicine Cornell U. Med. Ctr., N.Y. Hosp., NYC, 1972-75; fellow pulmonary diseases U. Calif., San Francisco, 1978-81; med. dir. respiratory care svcs., pulmonary function lab. Duke U. Med. Ctr., Durham, N.C., 1981—, asst. prof. medicine, 1981-89, assoc. prof., 1989-95, prof., 1995—. Editor: Complications of Mechanical Ventilation, 1992, Comprehensive Respiratory Care, 1994; editorial bd. Respiratory Care, 1986—, chmn., 1990-92; co-editor in chief Problems in Respiratory Care, 1988-91; med. editor Arkos, The Jour. of Mechanical Ventilation, 1989; editorial bd. Critical Care Medicine, 1992—; contbr. articles to profl. jours., chpts. to books. Trustee Am. Respiratory Care Found., 1988—, vice chmn., 1990—. With USN, 1975-78. Fellow Am. Coll. Chest Physicians; mem. Am. Thoracic Soc. (pres. NC chpt. 1989, lab. stds. com. 1992—), Am. Assn. Respiratory Care (chmn. bd. med. advisors 1990), Am. Lung Assn. (pres. Rsch. Triangle region 1988), Am. Heart Assn. (chmn. emergency cardiac care com. 1989-90, Silver Svc. medal 1978), Soc. Critical Care Medicine, Nat. Assn. Med. Dirs. Respiratory Care (pres. 1991-93), NC Soc. Respiratory Care (hon.), Alpha Omega Alpha. Office: Duke U Med Ctr PO Box 3911 Durham NC 27710-0001

MACIOCE, FRANK MICHAEL, lawyer, financial services company executive; b. NYC, Oct. 3, 1945; s. Frank Michael and Sylvia Maria (Morea) M.; children: Michael Peter, Lauren Decker, Theodore Kenneth; m. Helen Latourette Duffin, July 9, 1988. BS, Purdue U., 1967; JD, Vanderbilt U., Nashville, 1972. Bar: NY 1973, US Dist. Ct. (so. dist.) NY 1973, US Ct. Appeals (2d cir.) 1975, US Supreme Ct. 1976. Mem. law dept. Merrill Lynch, Pierce, Fenner & Smith Inc., NYC, 1972-80, v.p., 1978-88, 1st v.p., 1988-2000, Merrill Lynch Investment Mgrs., Plainsboro, NJ, 2000—03; councilman-at-large Summit, NJ, 2004—. Mgr. corp. law dept. Merrill Lynch & Co., Inc., NYC, 1980-93, asst. gen. counsel, 1982-2000; gen. counsel investment banking group, 1993-95, ops., svcs. and tech. counsel, 1995-2000, sec. of audit, compensation and nominating coms. bd. dirs., 1978-83, sec. exec. com., 1981-83; mng. dir. Merrill Lynch Overseas Capital, N.V., Netherlands Antilles, 1980-85; sec., dir. Merrill Lynch Employees Fed. Credit Union, NYC, 1978-82; dir. Merrill Lynch Pvt. Capital Inc., NYC, 1981-87, Teleport Comm. Group Inc., NYC, 1987-92, Enhance Fin. Services Inc, NYC, 1988-92; fin. planning adv. bd. Purdue U., 1996-2000. Pres. pro tem City of Summit Common Coun., 2004, pres., 2005—06. With US Army, 1969—70. Home and Office: 22 Essex Rd Summit NJ 07901-2802 Office Phone: 908-522-0903. Personal E-mail: fmacioce@comcast.net.

MACIUNAS, ROBERT JOSEPH, medical educator, researcher; b. Chgo., Mar. 15, 1955; s. Algirdas Kazimeras and Genevieve Strikas Maciunas; m. Ann Louise Failinger, Dec. 17, 1983; children: Nicholas Matas, Joseph Algirdas. BS, Northwestern U., Evanston, Ill., 1976; MD, U. Ill., Chgo., 1980; MPH, Vanderbilt U., Nashville, Tenn., 2004. Diplomate Ohio, 2001. Prof. neurosurgery and biomedical engring. Vanderbilt U., Nashville, 1986—98; Frank P. Smith prof. and chair neurosurgery U. Rochester, NY, 1998—2001; prof. and vice chmn. nuerosurgery U. Hospitals Case Med. Ctr. CWRU, Cleve. Dir. radiosurgery ctr. U. Hosps. Case Med. Ctr., CWRU, Cleve., 2001—, dir. brain tumor ctr., 2001—, dir. ctr. image guided neurosurgery, 2001—, dir. adult epilepsy surgery, 2001—, prof. neurology, radiology, radiation oncology, 2006—, dir. innovations, neurol. inst., 2008—. Contbr. chapters to books, articles to jours. Grant selection and funding mem. Oak Tree Philanthropic Found., Chgo., 2000—. Grantee, NIH, SDI, ONR, ACS, Codman, BrainLab, Medtronic, 1986—. Fellow: Am. Assn. Stereotactic and Functional Neurosurgeons, Am. Acad. Neurosurgery; mem.: ACS, Gamma Knife Soc., Cyberknife Soc., Soc. Neurol. Surgeons, Neurol. Soc. Am., Congress Neurol. Surgeons, Am. Assn. Neurol. Surgeons. Achievements include patents for image guided surgery. Avocations: soccer, reading, travel. Office: Univ Hosps Case Med Ctr 11100 Euclid Ave HH5 Cleveland OH 44106 Office Fax: 216-844-3014. Business E-Mail: robert.maciunas@uhhospitals.org.

MACK, ALAN WAYNE, interior designer; b. Cleve., Oct. 30, 1947; s. Edmund B. and Florence I. (Oleksa) M. BS in Interior Design, Case Western Res. U., 1969. Designer interior design dept. Halle's, Cleve., 1969, 71-73; designer Nahan Co., New Orleans, 1973-75, Hemenway's Contract Design, New Orleans, 1975-76; ptnr. Hewlett-Mack Design Assocs., New Orleans, 1976-85; prin., dir. interior design HLM Design, Inc., 1985—2001; prin., founding ptnr. Proteus Group, Chgo., 2001—. Mem. adv. com. interior design dept. Delgado Jr. Coll., New Orleans; mktg./merchandising adv. coun. St. Mary's Dominican Coll., New Orleans; mem. friends devel. coun. U. Iowa Mus. Art, 1986-91, chair, 1990-91; chmn. adv. com. interior design program Iowa State U., 1991-96; mem. design review com. City of Iowa City, 1992-93; mem. adv. bd. Healthcare Facilities Symposium & Expo, 2007—; mem. rev. com. Healthcare Design, 2004-07; mem. adv. bd. Healthcare Facilities Symposium, 2007—. Co-author: audiovisual presentation Nat. Home Improvement Coun. Conf., 1981; reviewer in field. Bd. dirs. Johnson County United Way, 1991-96. Served with U.S. Army, 1969-71. Mem. ASID (profl. mem., presdl. citation 1980, treas. La. dist. chpt. 1984), Vis. Nurses Assn. (bd. dirs. 1991-96), Found. for Interior Design Edn. Rsch. (standards com. 1972-76, bd. visitors 1977-80, accreditation com. 1981-95, trustee 1996-99, chmn. bd. dirs. 1998, pres. 1999). Home: 3800 N Lake Shore Dr Ste 2G Chicago IL 60613-3313 Office Phone: 312-573-4051. Business E-Mail: amack@proteusgroup.net.

MACK, CARL B., engineering executive; b. Jackson, Miss. m. Jamiyo Mack; children: Joshua, Jonathan. BS in Mech. Engring., Miss. State U., 1986. Engr. METRO-King County, Seattle; exec. dir. Nat. Soc. Black Engineers, 2005—. Named to Power 150, Ebony mag., 2008; Disting. Engring. Fellow, Miss. State U., 2006. Mem.: NAACP (pres. Seattle King County Br. 2003—04). Office: Nat Soc Black Engineers 205 Daingerfield Rd Alexandria VA 22314

MACK, CHRIS, men's college basketball coach; b. Cleve., Dec. 30, 1969; m. Christi Hester, Aug. 23; children: Lainee, Hailee. Attended, U. Evansville, Ind., 1988—90; B in Comm., Xavier U., Cin., 1992. Basketball player Athletes in Action, 1993, European Pro League, 1994; reserve coach McAuley HS, Cin., 1995; head coach Mount Notre Dame HS, Cin., 1995—99; dir. basketball ops. Xavier U. Musketeers, Cin., 1999—2001, asst. coach, 2004—09, head coach, 2009—; asst. coach Wake Forest U. Demon Deacons, Winston-Salem, NC, 2001—04. Participant Nike Villa 7 Consortium, Beaverton, Oreg., 2008. Named one of Top 25 Asst. Coaches, rivals.com, 2007. Office: Xavier Univ Mens Basketball 3800 Victory Pky Cincinnati OH 45207-7530 Office Phone: 513-745-3417. Business E-Mail: mackc@xavier.edu.*

MACK, CONNIE, IV, United States Representative from Florida; b. Ft. Myers, Fla., Aug. 12, 1967; s. Connie III and Priscilla Mack; m. Ann Mack (div.); children: Addison, Connie Mack V; m. Mary Bono, Dec. 15, 2007. BS, U. Fla., 1993. With LTP Mgmt. Inc., Ft. Myers, 1994—2000; ind. mktg. cons., 2000—; mem. Fla. Ho. of Reps., 2001—04, dep. majority leader, 2003—04; mem. US Congress from 14th Fla. dist., 2005—, mem. budget com., internat. rels. com., transp. & infrastructure com., fgn. affairs com. Founder Freedom Caucus; chair, founder Victims Compensation Coalition. Bd. dirs. Enterprise Fla., 2003, IT Fla., 2003—04. Republican. Roman Catholic. Office: US House Reps 317 Cannon House Office Bldg Washington DC 20515-0914 Office Phone: 202-225-2536. Office Fax: 202-225-0439.*

MACK, DAVID L., think-tank executive, former federal agency administrator; b. Portland, Oreg., June 10, 1940; s. Gilbert A. and Mildred V. (Canzler) M.; m. Rosamond E. Pratt, Aug. 20, 1966; children: Catherine, Sarah. BA, Harvard U., 1962, MA, 1964; postgrad., Am. U., Cairo, 1964-65. Internat. rels. officer Am. Embassy, Iraq, 1965-66, consular officer Jordan, 1966-67, US Consulate Gen., Jerusalem, 1967-68; attaché Am. Embassy, Lebanon, 1968-69, polit. officer Libya, 1969-72; internat. rels. officer US Dept. State, Washington, 1972-76; polit. officer US Interests Sect., Iraq, 1976-79; dep. chief mission Am. Embassy, Tunisia, 1979-82; office dir. US Dept. State, Washington, 1982-85, US amb. to United Arab Emirates Dubai, 1986-89, dep. asst. sec. for Near Ea. affairs Washington, 1990-93; internat. affairs adv. Nat. War Coll., 1993—95; sr. counselor C & O Resources, Inc., 1995—98; v.p. The Middle East Inst., Washington, 1998—. Diplomat-in-residence Howard U., 1989—90. Recipient Meritorious Honor award US Dept. State, Washington, 1977, Superior Honor award, 1978, 1983, Pres.'s Disting. Svc. award, 1992. Mem. Am. Fgn. Service Assn., Middle East Inst. Avocations: vegetable gardening. long distance running. Office: The Middle East Inst 1761 N St NW Washington DC 20036

MACK, EARLE IRVING, former ambassador, real estate company executive; b. NYC, July 11, 1939; s. H. Bert and Ruth (Kaufman) M.; m. Carol L. Dickey, July 26, 1990; children: Andrew, Beatrice. BS, Drexel U., 1959; attended, Fordham Law Sch., 1960-61; LHD (hon.), Yeshiva U., 1992; D in Bus. Adminstrn. (hon.), Drexel U., 2006. Sr. ptnr. The Mack Co., Fort Lee, 1964—2005; US amb. to Finland US Dept. State, Helsinki, 2004—05. Mem. adv. bd. N.Y. State Bus. Venture Partnership, 1988-98; mem. transition team for Gov. George Pataki, 1994-95; chmn., CEO, N.Y. State Coun. Arts, 1996-99, chmn. emeritus, 1999-. Prodr., co-dir. film The Children of Theater Street, 1977 (Acad. Award Feature Documentary nomination). Bd. dirs. Benjamin N. Cardozo Sch. of Law, N.Y.C., 1980-2004, chmn. exec. com., 1990, vice chmn. bd. dirs., 1991, chmn. bd. dirs., 1992-2004, chmn. emeritus, 2004; bd. dirs. N.Y.C. Ballet, 1988-2004; chmn. N.Y. State Racing Commn., 1983-89, The New 42d St., Inc., 1990-92; bd. dirs. Dance Theatre of Harlem, N.Y.C., 1987, co-chmn. bd., 1988-89; trustee N.Y. Racing Assn., Inc., 1990-2004; trustee, exec. com. Yeshiva U., 1992-2004. 1st lt. USAR, 1960—68. Recipient Can. Sovereign award Horse of Yr., 1993, Can. Sovereign award for best 3 yr. old horse, 1994, Ellis Island Medal of Honor, 1997; named One of Drexel 100, Drexel U., 1992, Commencement Spkr., 2006. Mem. Nat. Realty Com. (bd. dirs., exec. com. 1986-88), Urban Land Inst., Union League Club, Univ. Club, Reading Room Club. Achievements include international owner, breeder thoroughbred horses. Avocations: skiing, swimming, jogging, nutrition. Office: 2115 Linwood Ave Ste 110 Fort Lee NJ 07024

MACK, JEANNETTE ANA, medical technician; b. Jacksonville, Fla., July 14, 1951; d. Willie Lee and Dorothea Scott Mack; m. Luther Baker Jr. (div.); children: Luther Baker III, Calecia Baker Fowlers, Christopher

Baker. AS in Bus. Sci., Fla. Tech. Coll., Jacksonville, Fla., 1987, AS in Electronics Tech. with honors, 1986. Nurse's aide St. Lukes Hosp., 1974—79; monitor tech. and patient care Meml. Hosp., 1978—86, Riverside Hosp., 1987—89; neurodiagnostic tech. Meml. Hosp., 1986—88, U. Med. Ctr., 1989—96; supr. neurodiagnostic Meml. Hosp., 1996—. Baptist. Home: 98 Lake Run Blvd Jacksonville FL 32218-0806 Office: 3625 Univ Blvd S Jacksonville FL 32216

MACK, JOHN J., diversified financial services company executive; b. Mooresville, NC, Nov. 17, 1944; s. Charles and Alice (Azouri) Machoul; m. Christy King; children: John, Stephen, Jenna. BA, Duke U., 1968. Municipal bond trader and salesman Smith Barney; mem. bond dept. Morgan Stanley & Co., 1972, v.p., 1976—77, principal, 1977, mng. dir., 1979, head Worldwide Taxable Fixed Income Divsn., 1985—92; mem. bd. dirs. Morgan Stanley Group, NYC, 1987-97, chmn. operating com., 1992-97, pres., 1993-97; pres., COO Morgan Stanley Dean Witter & Co., NYC, 1997—2001; pres., CEO Credit Suisse First Boston, LLC, 2001—04; co-CEO Credit Suisse Group, NYC, 2003—04; chmn. Pequot Capital Mgmt. Inc., Westport, Conn., 2005; chmn., CEO Morgan Stanley, NYC, 2005—. Bd. dirs. Catalyst, Inc., Celiant Corp., Cousins Properties Inc.; bd. dir. NYSE, bd. exec., 2003—04; mem. internat. adv. panel Monetary Authority, Singapore; mem. chmn. adv. com. Nat. Assn. Securities Dealers (NASD); past mem. Beijing's Advisory Coun.; past dir. CICC (first investment bank in China), India Bus. Sch.; past bd. visitors Fuqua Sch. Bus., Duke U. Serves numerous positions of leadership for bus., civic and philanthropic org.; chmn. bd. trustees NY Presbyn. Hosp., U. Hosp. Columbia, Cornell; mem. bd. trustees Duke U.; trustee Doris Duke Charitable Found.; vice chmn. NYC2012; co-founder CJ Mack Found. Recipient Thomas F. Keller Disting. Leadership award, Fuqua Sch. Bus., Duke U., 1998. Republican. Office: Morgan Stanley 1585 Broadway New York NY 10036*

MACK, JULIA COOPER, retired judge; b. Fayetteville, NC, July 17, 1920; d. Dallas L. and Emily (McKay) Perry; m. Jerry S. Cooper, July 30, 1943; 1 dau., Cheryl; m. Clifford S. Mack, Nov. 21, 1957. BS, Hampton Inst., 1940; LLB, Howard U., 1951; JD (hon.), U. DC, 1999. Bar: DC 1952. Legal cons. OPS, Washington, 1952-53; atty.-advisor office gen. counsel Gen. Svcs. Adminstrn., Washington, 1953-54; trial appellate atty. criminal div. Dept. Justice, Washington, 1954-68; civil rights atty. Office Gen. Counsel, Equal Employment Opportunity Commn., Washington, 1968-75; assoc. judge Ct. Appeals, Washington, 1975-89; sr. judge DC Ct. of Appeals, Washington, 1989—2001. Mem. Am., Fed., Washington, Nat. Bar Assns., Nat. Assn. Women Judges. Home: 1610 Varnum St NW Washington DC 20011-4206

MACK, MARK PHILIP, chemical company executive; b. Buffalo, Jan. 14, 1950; s. Stanley Joseph and Florence M. Mack; m. Jean Ann Merrick, June 2, 1984; 1 child, Hannah Elizabeth. BS in Chemistry, Buffalo State Coll., 1971; PhD in Chemistry, SUNY, Buffalo, 1976. Rsch. assoc. Duke U., Durham, NC, 1975-77; rsch. chemist Conoco Inc., Ponca City, Okla., 1977-80, group supr., 1980-81; group leader Conoco/DuPont, Ponca City, 1982-85; sr. supr. DuPont Polymer Products, Wilmington, Del., 1985-89; rsch. mgr. OxyChem, Houston, 1989-90; dir. tech. Occidental Chem. Corp., Houston, 1990-95, Lyondell Petrochem. Co., Houston, 1995-97, v.p. licensing, 1996-97; dir. R&D Equistar Chems., LP, 1997-99, dir. catalyst R&D, analytical chemistry and polymer sci., 1999—2002; chief scientist Lyondell/Equistar, Cin., 2002—08; prin. Mark Mark LLC, 2009—. Patentee in field; contbr. articles to profl. jours. Recipient Linus Pauling award, SUNY-Buffalo, 1971, Outstanding Student in Chemistry award, Western N.Y. Sect. Am. Chem. Soc., 1971, Conoco Patent award, 1983, Equistar/Lyondell Inventor award, 2001, St. Labre Indian Sch. Ednl. Assn. award, 2002, Operational Excellence award, 2004; grantee Samuel B. Silbert fellowship, SUNY-Buffalo, 1974—75. Mem. AAAS, Am. Chem. Soc., Soc. Plastics Engrs., N.Y. Acad. Sci., Am. Mgmt. Assn., Product Devel. and Mgmt. Assn., World Future Soc., Sigma Xi. Home: 8483 Beckett Pointe Dr West Chester OH 45069-6440 Office Phone: 513-779-3926. Office Fax: 513-779-3926. Business E-Mail: markmack@cinci.rr.com.

MACK, MICHAEL EDWARD, physicist; b. Poughkeepsie, NY, May 28, 1939; s. Edward Joseph and Anita Eleanor (Barton) M.; m. Sarah Marie McManus, July 20, 1963; children: Patrick, Michael, Kathleen, Maura. BS, MIT, 1961, PhD, 1967. Prin. scientist United Technologies, East Hartford, Conn., 1967-73; dir. laser sys. Avco Everett (Mass.) Rsch. Lab., 1973-81; mgr. engring. Eaton S.E.B., Beverly, Mass., 1981-89; v.p. engring. Genus I.T.D., Newburyport, Mass., 1989-91; mgr. medium current engring. Varian Ion Implant Sys., Gloucester, Mass., 1991-96; R&D mgr. Eaton Ion Sys., Beverly, Mass., 1997—99; beamline mgr. Epion Corp., Billerica, Mass., 1999—2008; pres. Cape Ann Tech. LLC, 2008—. Lectr. Internat. Ion Implant Conf. Patentee in field; contbr. articles to profl. jours. Home: 7 Hidden Ledge Rd Manchester MA 01944-1228 Office: Cape Ann Tech LLC Manchester MA 01944 Personal E-mail: capeamtech@verizon.net.

MACK, MICHAEL J., JR., farm equipment manufacturing executive; B in Mech. Engring., M in Mech. Engring., Iowa State U., Ames; MBA in Fin., Ops. and Stats., U. Chgo. Registered profl. engr. Summer intern engr. John Deere Des Moines Works; various treasury positions Deere & Co., various positions in dealer systems, bus. devel., engring, purchasing, mfg. and mktg., sr. v.p. mktg. & adminstrn. Worldwide Comml. & Consumer Equipment Divsn., 2001—04, v.p., treas., 2004—06, sr. v.p., CFO, 2006—09, pres. worldwide construction & forestry divsn., John Deere Power Systems, 2009—. Mem. Engring. Coll. indsl. adv. bd. Iowa State U. Office: Deere & Co One John Deere Pl Moline IL 61265 Office Phone: 309-765-8000.*

MACK, RICHARD L., lawyer, software company executive; BS in Acctg., Moorhead State U.; JD, Hamline U. Bar: 1993. Counsel administrative div. Norwest Corp.; sr. atty. Cargill, Inc., 1994—2004; co-founder, Cargill's venture capital bus. unit Cargill; sr. v.p. The Mosaic Co., 2004—09, gen. counsel, corp. sec., 2004—, exec. v.p., 2009—. Mem.: Am. Corp. Counsel Assn., Hennepin County Bar Assn., Minnesota State Bar Assn. Office: Mosaic Co Atria Corp Ctr, Ste E490 3033 Campus Dr Plymouth MN 55441 Office Phone: 763-559-2860.

MACK, SARA ROHRBACH, librarian, educator; b. Topton, Pa., Nov. 20, 1921; d. Jonathan H. and Alda S. (Heffner) Rohrbach; m. George Mack, June 26, 1943 (wid. Jan. 1949); 1 child, Carol Mack Foy. BS, Kutztown State Tchrs. Coll., 1943; MS in Libr. Sci., Columbia U., 1955; postgrad., Temple U. and U. Pa. Elem. tchr. Chalfont (Pa.) Pub. Sch., 1943-45; libr. Mt. Penn Jr.-Sr. High Sch., Reading, Pa., 1949-58; prof. libr. sci. Kutztown (Pa.) State Coll., 1958-82, dept. chmn., 1977-82; retired, 1982. Adj. prof. Drexel U., Phila., 1968; bd. dirs. Friends of the Reading-Berks Pub. Librs., pres., 1983-84, exec. bd., 1985—. Compiler: Inspirational Readings for Elementary Grades, 1964; contbr. articles to profl. jours, book reviewer; contbg. author: American Reference Books Annual, Along the Saucony. Trustee Kutztown U. Coun., 1983-2001, chair, 1993-95; com. chmn. Kutztown Area Hist. Soc., 1983-93, 2002-05; ch. libr. Trinity Luth. Ch., Topton, 1966-05; del. to Pa. Govs. Conf. on Librs., 1990; mem. Berks Authors Bibliography Com., 1992-98. Recipient Superior Tchg. award Kutztown State Coll., 1962, Alumni Citation, 1980, 88, Award of Merit, Pa. Libr. Assn., 1969, Outstanding Libr. Contbn. award Loisa Gonser Cmty. Libr., 2002. Mem. ALA (com. mem. 1945), Pa. Libr. Assn., Pa. Sch. Librs. Assn. (pres. 1963-65, exec. bd. 1977-80 Named Outtanding Contbr. to Sch. Libr. Programs, 1981), Ch. and Synagogue Libr. Assn. (speaker and book reviewer), Pa. Citizens for Better Librs., Emeriti Faculty Kutztown U. (coord. 1989—), Phila. Children's Reading Roundtable, Am. Assn. Univ. Women, Delta Kappa Gamma. Home: 105 Dries Rd 34 Reading PA 19605

MACKALL, CRYSTAL L., medical researcher; BS/MD, Northeastern Ohio Universities Coll. Medicine, 1984. Medicine/pediatrics resident Northeastern Ohio U. Coll. Medicine, Akron, Ohio, 1984—88; clin. assoc. Pediatric Oncology Br., Ctr. Cancer Rsch., Nat. Cancer Inst., NIH, 1989—92, rschr., 1996—, acting chief, 2005—08, chief Pediatrics Oncology Br., head Immunology Sect., 2008—; postdoctoral sci. training Exptl. Immunology Br. Nat. Cancer Inst., 1990—96. Office: Nat Cancer Inst Bldg 10-CRC, Rm 1W-3750 10 Center Dr, MSC 1104 Bethesda MD 20892-1104 Office Phone: 301-402-5940. Office Fax: 301-451-7052. Business E-Mail: cm35c@nih.gov.*

MACKAY, ALFRED F., dean, philosophy educator; b. Ocala, Fla., Oct. 1, 1938; s. Kenneth Hood and Julia Horsey (Farnum) MacK.; m. Ann Nadine Wilson, Feb. 4, 1962; children: Douglas Kevin, Robert Wilson. AB, Davidson Coll., 1960; PhD, U. N.C., 1967. Prof. philosophy Oberlin Coll., Ohio, 1967-84, 96—, dean Coll. Arts and Scis. Ohio, 1984-95, acting pres. Ohio, 1991, provost Ohio, 2005—. Vis. asst. prof. philosophy dept. U. Ill., Urbana/Champaign, 1970-71; vis. prof. philosophy dept. Wayne State U., Detroit, 1983. Author: Arrow's Theorem: The Paradox of Social Choice, 1980; editor: Society: Revolution and Reform, 1971, Issues in the Philosophy of Language, 1976. Campaign cons. Buddy MacKay for U.S. Senate, Fla., 1988. 1st lt. U.S. Army, Airborne, 1961-63. Fellow Woodrow Wilson Found., 1963-66, Am. Coun. of Learned Socs., 1973, Humanities fellow Rockefeller Found., 1981. Democrat. Avocations: choral singing, automobiles. Office: Oberlin Coll Provost Cox Administration Building Oberlin OH 44074 Office Phone: 440-775-8410. Office Fax: 440-775-8944. E-mail: al.mackay@oberlin.edu.

MACKAY, CHARLES, opera company director; b. Albuquerque, N.Mex, May 1950; s. John and Margaret MacKay. Grad., U. Minn. Dir. fin. & adminstrn. Spoleto Festival USA, 1978—84; exec. dir. Opera Theatre St. Louis, 1984—85, gen. dir., 1985—2008, Santa Fe Opera, 2008—. Chmn. bd. dirs. OPERA America, 2004—08. Recipient Arts Mgmt. Career Svc. award, 1997. Office: Santa Fe Opera PO Box 2408 Santa Fe NM 87504-2408*

MACKAY, DAVID (A.D. DAVID MACKAY), food products executive; b. Hamilton, New Zealand, Aug. 16, 1955; m. Michelle Mackay; 2 children. B of Bus., Charles Stuart U., Australia, 1977. Group product mgr. Kellogg Australia, 1985—87; category dir. ready-to-eat cereals corp. hdqrs. Kellogg Co., Battle Creek, Mich., 1987—91; mng. dir. Sara Lee Bakery, Australia, 1992—98, Kellogg Australia, Battle Creek, 1998; mng. dir. U.K. and Republic of Ireland Kellogg Co., Battle Creek, 1998—2000; sr. v.p. Kellogg USA, Battle Creek, 2000, pres., 2000—03; exec. v.p. Kellogg Co., Battle Creek, Mich., 2000—03, pres., COO, 2003—06, pres., CEO, 2007—. Bd. dirs. Kellogg Co., 2005—, Fortune Brands Inc., 2006—. Office: Kellogg PO Box 3599 1 Kellogg Sq Battle Creek MI 49016-3599

MACKAY, EDWARD R., academic administrator; BA in Math., Bloomsburg U. of Pa.; PhD, Vanderbilt U. Joined U. Sys. of NH, Durham, 1979, vice chancellor, 1987—2009, treas., 2000—09, chancellor-elect, 2008—09, chancellor, 2009—. Chair NH Higher Edn. Loan Corp., 2006—08, Higher Edn. Savings Trust Commn.; mem. Havenwood-Heritage Heights Trust Fund Bd. Mem.: Nat. Assn. Coll. and Univ. Bus. Officers (NACUBO) (former chmn. bd.). Office: U Sys of NH Dunlap Ctr 25 Concord Rd Durham NH 03824-3545 E-mail: ed.mackay@usnh.edu.*

MACKAY, GREGORY JAMES, plastic surgeon; BA, Vanderbilt U., Nashville; MD, Med. U. SC, Charleston, 1987. Cert. Am. Bd. Plastic Surgery, 1998. Intern surgery Emory U., Atlanta, 1987, resident plastic surgery, 1988—93, resident craniofacial surgery, 1993—95, asst. prof., 1999—2002; fellow U. Pa., Phila., 1995—96; asst. prof. plastic surgery Mayo Clinic Grad. Sch. Medicine, 1999—2000; staff mem. Egleston Children's Hosp., Atlanta, 2000, staff mem. plastic surgery, 2003; staff mem. Scottish Rite Children's Hosp., Atlanta, 2000, 2003, Piedmont Hosp., Ga., 2003, Northside Hosp., Ga., 2003. Contbr. articles to med. jours., chapters to books; featured: magazines Atlanta Style & Design, Jezebel. Office: 5673 Peachtree Dunwoody Rd Ste 870 Atlanta GA 30342

MACKAY, HAROLD HUGH, lawyer; b. Regina, Sask., Can., Aug. 1, 1940; s. John Royden and Grace Madeliene (Irwin) MacK.; m. Jean Elizabeth Hutchison, Dec. 27, 1963; children: Carol, Donald. BA, U. Sask., 1960; LLB, Dalhousie U., Halifax, NS, 1963; LLD (hon.), U. Regina, 2002. Bar: Sask. 1964, Queen's Counsel 1981. Assoc. MacPherson Leslie & Tyerman LLP, Regina, 1963-69, ptnr., 1969—2004, mng. ptnr., 1989-96, chmn., 1997—2003, of counsel, 2005—. Bd. dirs. Mosaic Co., Toronto-Dominion Bank; chmn. task force Future of the Can. Fin. Svcs. Sector, 1997-98; Clifford Clark vis. economist Dept. of Fin., Govt. of Can., 2002-04; non-exec. chmn. bd. Domtar Corp. Recipient Officer Order of Can., 2002. Mem. Internat. Bar Assn., Can. Bar Assn., Law Soc. Sask. Mem. United Ch. Office: 1500 1874 Scarth St Regina SK Canada S4P 4E9 Home Phone: 306-586-4089; Office Phone: 306-347-8417.

MACKAY, HARVEY B., paper company executive, writer; b. St. Paul, 1932; s. Jack and Myrtle Mackay; m. Carol Ann Mackay. Grad. in History, U. Minn., 1954; grad., Stanford U. Grad. Sch. Bus. Founder, chmn., CEO MackayMitchell Envelope Co. (formerly Mackay Envelope Co.), 1959—. Spkr. in field. Author: (books) Sharkproof: Get the Job You Want, Keep the Job You Love..., 1994, Swim With The Sharks Without Being Eaten Alive, 1996, Beware the Naked Man Who Offers You His Shirt, 1996 (NY Times Bestseller), Dig Your Well Before You're Thirsty: The Only Networking Book You'll Ever Need, 1999, Pushing the Envelope: All the Way to the Top, 2000, We Got Fired! ...And It's The Best Thing That Ever Happened To Us, 2004; columnist: United Feature Syndicate. Former dir. Robert Redford's Sundance Inst.; past pres. Minn. C. of C.; bd. dirs. U. Minn. Carlson Sch. Mgmt., Minn. Orchestra. Recipient Horatio Alger award, Supreme Ct. Chambers, 2004; named to Minn. Bus. Hall of Fame, 2002. Mem.: Nat. Spkrs. Assn. (Hall of Fame), Envelope Mfrs. Assn. (pres. 1979—81), U. Minn. Nat. Alumni Assn. (past pres.), Toastmasters Internat. Achievements include being referred to as "Mr. Make Things Happen" by Fortune Magazine. Avocations: running, tennis, golf, travel. Office: MackayMitchell Envelope Co 2100 Elm St SE Minneapolis MN 55414 Office Phone: 612-331-9311.

MACKAY, JAMES COBHAM, museum director; BA in History, U. Va., 1983; MA in Am. History, George Mason U., 1995. Seasonal park ranger Nat. Park Svc./Bent's Old Fort NHS and Lowell NHP, LaJunta, Colo., Lowell, Mass., 1984-85; skilled craft interpreter Colonial Williamsburg Found., Va., 1985-87; rsch. intern Jamestown-Yorktown Found., Va., 1987-88; mus. aide The Lyceum, Alexandria History Mus., Va., 1988-89, dir. Va., 1995—; asst. dir. Gadsby's Tavern Mus., Alexandria, 1989-95. Bd. dirs. The Lee-Fendall House, Alexandria. Mem. Orgn. Am. Historians, Va. Assn. Mus., Am. Assn. Mus., Inst. Early Am. History and Culture. Office: The Lyceum Alexandria's History Mus 201 S Washington St Alexandria VA 22314-3625 Office Phone: 703-838-4994.

MACKAY, JAMES PETER HYMERS (LORD MACKAY OF CLASHFERN), retired university official; b. July 2, 1927; s. James Mackay and Janet Hymers; m. Elizabeth Gunn Hymers; 3 children. BA, Cambridge U., 1952; MA in Math. and Natural Philosophy with honors, Edinburgh U., 1948, LLB with distinction, 1955, LLD (hon.), 1983, Dundee U., 1983, Strathclyde U., 1985, Aberdeen U., 1987, St. Andrews U., 1989, Cambridge U., 1989; DCL (hon.), William and Mary Coll., 1989; LLD (hon.), Birmingham U., 1990, Newcastle U., 1990. Admitted to Faculty of Advocates, 1955; QC (Scot.), 1965. Sheriff prin. Renfrew and Argyll, 1972-74; vice-dean Faculty of Advocates, 1973-76, dean, 1976-79, Lord Advocate Scotland, 1979-84; Lord Appeal in Ordinary, 1985-87; senator Coll. of Justice Scotland, 1984-85; Lord Chancellor London, 1987-97; chancellor Heriot-Watt U., 1991—95. Standing jr. counsel to Queen's and Lord Treas.'s Remembrancer, Scottish Home and Health Dept., Commrs. Inland Revenue Scotland; mem. Scottish Law Commn., 1976-79 (part-time), Ins. Brokers' Registration Council, 1977-79. Named Hon. Master of the Bench, Inner Temple, 1979. Fellow Royal Soc. Edinburgh, Internat. Acad. Trial Lawyers, Inst. Taxation (hon.), trinity Coll. (hon.), Girton Coll. Cambridge U. (hon.), Am. Coll. Trial Lawyers (hon.); mem. Royal Coll. Physicians (hon.), Royal Coll. Surgeons (hon. fello w), Royal Coll. Ob-Gyns. (hon. fellow), Soc. Pub. Tchrs. Law (hon.), Law Soc. Scotland (hon.). Clubs: New (Edinburgh). Avocations: walking, travel. Address: Office of the Chancellor Heriot-Watt U Edinburgh EH14 4AS Scotland

MACKAY, JAMES ROBERT, psychiatric social worker, mayor, educator; b. Medford, Mass., May 8, 1930; s. James Alexander and Julia (MacNaught) MacK. BA, Tufts U., 1952, MA, 1954; MSW, Boston U., 1958; PhD, Union Inst., 1987. Social worker Peter Bent Brigham Hosp., Boston, 1958-60; dir. alcoholism N.H. Dept. Health and Welfare, Concord, 1960-63; dir. cmty. mental health State of N.H., Concord, 1963-64; pvt. practice psychotherapy Concord, 1964-97; exec. dir. Merrimack Valley Assistance Program, Concord, 2002; adj. faculty U. N.H., Durham, 1995—2001; mem. N.H. State Ho. of Reps., 1995—96, 2001—, chmn. com. on legis. adminstrn., vice chairperson com. on health and human svcs. Mem. bd. examiners mental health practice State of N.H., 1995-97; mayor City of Concord, N.H., 1986-88, 90-91; sr. lectr. psychotherapy Franklin Pierce Law Center, Concord, 1978; lectr. U. Conn. Grad. Sch. Social Work, 1981-88; adv. com. City of Concord Airport, 1992—. Contbr. articles on alcoholism, addiction, and juvenile delinquency to profl. jours. Chmn. N.H. Coun. Aging, 1969-83; chmn. Merrimack Valley AIDS Program, 2000-2002, treas., 2003—; pres. N.H. Social Welfare Coun.; chmn. N.H. del. to White House Conf. Aging, 1974, 80; chmn. N.H. Com. Older Am. Act, 1968-69; mem. Concord City Coun., 1980-91; chmn. Concord Pub. Transp. Adv. Bd., 1982-86; del. N.H. Rep. Conv., 1982; del. N.H. Constl. Conv., 1984; chmn. City of Concord Rep. Com.; mem. exec. com. State Rep. Com.; pres. Concord Outright Inc., 2000-02; commr. Christa McAuliffe Planetarium, 2001-; chmn. N.H. Mental Health Assn., 2006—. Recipient Am. award N.H. Social Welfare Coun., 1970, Vaughn award Activities in Aging, N.H., 1974; named Social Worker of Yr., State of N.H., 1997, Legislator of the Yr., NASW, 2003. Mem. NASW (pres. N.H. chpt. 1995-97), AAUP, Nat. League Cities (human devel. policy com. 1986). Office: 139 N State St Concord NH 03301-6414

MACKAY, KATHRYN LEILANI, social sciences educator; b. Honolulu, Mar. 23, 1947; d. Calvin Reynolds and Bertha Virginia MacKay. PhD, U. Utah, SLC, 1987. Coll. prof. Weber State U., Ogden, Utah, 1988—. Contbr. articles to hist. publs. Mem. Landmarks Commn., Ogden, 2000—08, Weber Reads, Ogden, Utah, 2007—08, Traditional Bldg. Skills Inst., Ephraim, Utah, 2004—08. Recipient Lindquist award, Weber State U., 2007; named Distinq. scholar, Utah Humanities Coun., 2006. Office: Weber State Univ 1205 University Cir Ogden UT 84408-1205 Business E-Mail: kmackay@weber.edu.

MACKAY, LEO SIDNEY, JR., healthcare company executive, former federal agency administrator; b. San Antonio, Tex., Aug. 15, 1961; s. Leo Sidney Sr. and Barbara Jean (Hodge) MacK.; m. Heather Lee Deebel, Jan. 9, 1993; children: Sarah Bley, Josiah Edward Earl. BS, U.S. Naval Acad., 1983; M Pub. Policy, J.F. Kennedy Sch. Govt., 1991; PhD, Harvard U., 1993. Commd. ensign USN, 1983, advanced through grades to lt. comdr., 1993; flight student Naval Aviation Tng. Comd., Pensacola, Fla., 1983-85; F-14 fighter pilot U.S. Navy, Virginia Beach, Va., 1985-89; grad./doctoral student Harvard U., Cambridge, Mass., 1989-92; instr. history dept. U.S. Naval Acad., Annapolis, Md., 1992-93; mil. asst. to sec. US Dept. Def., Washington, 1993-95; dir. market devel. Lockheed Martin Corp., Bethesda, Md., 1995-97; v.p. bus. devel. and strategic planning Bell Helicopter Textron, Inc., Ft. Worth, 1997—2001; dep. sec. U.S. Dept. Vets Affairs, Washington, 2001—03; COO, ACS State Healthcare Solutions Affiliated Computer Services, Inc., Atlanta, 2003—. Chair Advisory Com. on Minority Health US Dept. Health & Human Services, 2005—. Contbr. articles to profl. jours.; article reviewer Internat. Security Jour., Cambridge, Mass., 1991-94. Pres. congregation St. Martin's Luth. Ch., Annapolis, 1996-97. Kennedy fellow J.F. Kennedy Sch. Govt., Cambridge, 1989-90, guest fellow Brookings Inst., Washington, 1992-93, Internat. Affairs fellow Coun. Fgn. Rels., N.Y.C., 1995-96; MacArthur scholar MacArthur Found., Cambridge, 1991-92. Mem. Internat. Inst. Strategic Studies, U.S. Naval Inst., Coun. Fgn. Rels., Arlington C. of C. (bd. dirs.), U.S. Naval Acad. Alumni Assn. (nat. trustee 1995-98), Army and Navy Club. Republican. Lutheran. Avocations: reading, golf.

MACKAY, MALCOLM, executive search consultant; b. Bklyn., Nov. 6, 1940; s. John F. and Helen (Pflug) MacK.; children: Robert Livingston, Hope Winthrop. AB cum laude, Princeton U., 1963; JD, Harvard U., 1966. Bar: N.Y. 1967. Assoc. Milbank, Tweed, Hadley and McCloy, NYC, 1966-69; dep. supt. N.Y. State Ins. Dept., NYC, 1969-71, 1st dep. supt., 1971-73; vice chancellor L.I. U., Greenvale, N.Y., 1973-75; sr. v.p. Blue Cross & Blue Shield of Greater New York, 1975-77, N.Y. Life Ins. Co., NYC, 1977-89; mng. dir. Russell Reynolds Assocs., NYC, 1989—2009. Bd. dirs. Empire Fidelity Investments Life Ins. Co. Trustee Bklyn Conn. Found., Episcopal Social Svcs., NY. Mem. Century Assn., Piping Rock Club. Home: 184 Columbia Heights Brooklyn NY 11201 Home Phone: 718-855-0204. Business E-Mail: malcolm@brownmackog.com.

MACKAY, MARTIN, pharmaceutical executive; Microbiology First Class Honors Degree, Heriot-Watt U.; PhD in Molecular Genetics, U. Edinburgh, 1983. Mem., advanced drug delivery rsch. unit to head drug preformulation and delivery Ciba-Geigy, Sussex, England, head, molecular and cell biology, CNS Rsch. Basel, Switzerland, 1993—95; mem. antibacterial discovery Beecham Pharm., Surrey, England; dir., discovery biology Pfizer, Inc., England, 1995—97, sr. dir., head biology, 1997—98, v.p., UK discovery, 1998—99, sr. v.p., head worldwide discovery NY, 1999—2003, sr. v.p., head worldwide rsch. tech., 2003—07, v.p., global R&D, 2007, pres., global R&D, 2007—. Office: Pfizer Inc 235 E 42nd St New York NY 10017*

MACKAY, PATRICIA MCINTOSH, psychotherapist; b. San Francisco, Sept. 12, 1922; d. William Carroll and Louise Edgerton (Keen) McIntosh; m. Alden Thorndike Mackay, Dec. 15, 1945 (dec. June 2002); children: Patricia Louise, James McIntosh, Donald Sage; m. Richard John Rihn, July 26, 2003. AB in Psychology, U. Calif., Berkeley, 1944, elem. tchg. credential, 1951; MA in Psychology, John F. Kennedy U., Orinda, Calif., 1979; PhD in Nutrition, Donsbach U., Huntington Beach, Calif., 1981. Cert. marriage, family and child counselor. Elem. tchr. Mt. Diablo Unified Sch. Dist., Concord, Calif., 1950-60; exec. supr. No. Calif. Welcome Wagon Internat., 1960-67; wedding cons. Mackay Creative Svcs., Walnut Creek, Calif., 1969-70; co-owner Courtesy Calls, Greeters and Concord Welcoming Svcs., Walnut Creek, 1971-94; marriage, family and child counselor, nutrition cons., Walnut Creek, 1979—. Coord. Alameda and Contra Costa County chpts. Parents United Internat., 1985—, pres. region 2, bd. dirs., 1992; bd. dirs. New Directions Counseling Ctr., Inc., 1975-81, founder, pres. aux., 1977-79. Bd. dirs. Ministry in Marketplace, Inc., 1987—; founder, dir. Turning Point Counseling; active Walnut Creek Presbyn. Ch.; bd. dirs., counseling dir. Shepherd's Gate, shelter for homeless women and children, 1985-92, Contra Costa County Child Care Coun., 1993-95. Recipient award New Directions Counseling Ctr., 1978, yearly awards Neo-Life Co. Am. Prestige Club, 1977-856, Cmty. Svc. award Child Abuse Prevention Coun., 1990, 92, 94. Mem. AAUW, Am. Assn. Marriage and Family Therapists, U. Calif.-Berkeley Alunni Assn. (sec. 1979-94), Walnut Creek C. of C., Prytanean Alumnae, Soroptomists (bd. dirs. Walnut Creek 1976, 86), Delta Gamma. Republican. Home: 1101 Scots Ln Walnut Creek CA 94596-5432 Home Phone: 925-933-3126.

MACKAY, ROBERT BATTIN, museum director; b. Bklyn., Jan. 24, 1945; s. John French and Helen (Pflug) Mack; m. Anna V.; 1 child, Hale V. BS, Boston U., 1968, PhD in Am. Studies, 1980; MEd, Harvard U., 1972. With Archtl. Heritage, Inc., Boston, 1967-71; dir. Soc. Preservation of L.I. Antiquities, Cold Spring Harbor, NY, 1974—. Chmn. N.Y. State Bd. Hist. Preservation; mem. N.Y. State Coun. Parks, N.Y. State Heritage Areas. Editor: Long Island: An Illustrated History, 2000, AIA Architectural Guide of L.I., L.I. Country Houses and Their Architects, 1997, Author: America By the Yard, 2006 Treas. St. Giles Found.; v.p. Homeland Found.; adv. Gerry Charitable Trust; trustee Seatuck Enrivon. Assn. Mem. N.Y. Yacht Club (chmn. fine arts com.). Home: 59 Midland St Cold Spring Harbor NY 11724-1805 Office: Soc Preservation of LI Antiquities PO Box 148 Cold Spring Harbor NY 11724-0148

MACKELL, JAN, historian, writer; AA in English, Saddleback Cmty. Coll., 1984; degree in Comm., U. Colo., Colorado Springs, 1989. Owner, operator Homes With Histories, 1986—89, Gofer Tourism, 1996—98; owner, agent Cripple Creek Music Co., 1989—; docent, archivist Cripple Creek Dist. Mus., 1998—2006, dir., 2006—. Mktg. dir. Long Branch Casino, 1994—96; hist. rsch. cons. Teller County, Colo., 1994—; assoc. Colo. Preservation Inc., Denver, 1995—, vol. mem., 2003—; mem., co-chair Hist. Preservation Commn., City of Cripple Creek, 1999—2003. Columnist Colo. Gambler Mag., 1995—; contbg. writer: Ute Pass Courier/Gold Rush, 1996—, Kiva Mag., 1999—; author: Cripple Creek District: Last of Colorado's Gold Boons, 2003, Brothels, Bordellos, and Bad Girls: Prostitution in Colorado 1860-1930, 2004. Mem.: Old Colorado City Hist. Soc., Greenhorn Valley Hist. Soc. (sec. 1987—90), Colo. State Hist. Soc., Denver Posse of Westerners (hon.). Office: Cripple Creek Dist Mus 510 Bennett Dr Cripple Creek CO 80813 Office Phone: 719-689-2634. Business E-Mail: ccdmuseum@ccvnet.net.

MACKEN, JODI, real estate company executive; d. Lillian Macken; 1 child, Alexandra. Grad., Gold Coast Sch. Real Estate, Miami, 1988. Assoc. dir. Macken Realty, Inc., Macken Realty Comml., Macken Realty Signature Properties, Aventura, Fla., 1989—. Named a Power Woman in Real Estate, Miami SunPost, 2004, 2005. Office: Macken Realty Inc 18999 Biscayne Blvd Ste 105 Miami FL 33180 Office Phone: 305-933-3800. Office Fax: 305-933-3128. Business E-Mail: jmacken@mackenrealty.com.*

MACKENZIE, CHARLES ALFRED, lawyer; b. Houston, Sept. 20, 1965; s. Charles Lester and Glenda Faye M.; m. Gretchen Hartberg, Aug. 5, 1989; children: Katherine Ann, James Andrew. BA, Baylor U., 1987, MA, 1988, JD, 1991. Bar: Tex. 1991, 5th Cir. 1994, U.S. Supreme Ct. 1995; bd. cert. civil appellate law Tex. Bd. Legal Specialization Briefing & Rsch. Atty. 10th Ct. Appeals, Waco, Tex., 1991-94, Haley & Olson, Waco, Tex., 1994—. Grader Tex. Bd. Law Examiners, 1996-99; lectr. law Baylor U., Waco, 1991-92, 2000, 2004-09, civil appellate law adv. commn. Tex. Bd. Legal Specialization, 1999-2005. Mem.: Waco-McLennan County Young Lawyers Assn. (pres. 2000—01, named Outstanding Young Lawyer 1999), Abner V. McCall Am. Inn of Ct. (sec.-treas. 2000—02), State Bar Tex. (appellate sect. coun. 2001—04). Baptist. Avocation: photography. Office: Haley & Olson 510 N Valley Mills Dr, Ste 600 Waco TX 76710-6078 Office Fax: 254-776-6823. E-mail: AMackenzie@HaleyOlson.com.

MACKENZIE, CHARLES SHERRARD, academic administrator; b. Quincy, Mass., Aug. 21, 1924; s. Charles Sherrard and Dorothy MacKenzie; m. Florence Evelyn Phelps Meyer, Aug. 28, 1964 (dec. 1981); 1 child, Robert Walter Meyer; m. Lavonne Rudolph Gaiser, Mar. 30, 1985. Student, Boston U., 1942-43; BA, Gordon Coll., 1946; M.Div., Princeton Theol. Sem., 1949, ThD, 1955, PhD, 1957; LHD, Grove City Coll., 1997; postgrad., U. Paris, 1953. Ordained to ministry Congl. Christian Ch., 1949. Pastor Carversville (Pa.) Christian Ch., 1948-51; fellow faculty Princeton Theol. Sem., 1949-51, 53-54, Princeton U., 1954-64; pastor First Presbyn. Ch., Avenel, NJ, 1954-64, Broadway Presbyn. Ch., Columbia U., NYC, 1964-67, First Presbyn. Ch., Stanford U., San Mateo, Calif., 1967-71; pres. Grove City (Pa.) Coll., 1971-91, chancellor, 1991-92; advisor to pres., prof. philosphy Reformed Seminary, Orlando, Fla., 1992—; sr. min. Eastminster Presbyn. Ch., Wichita, Kans., 1993. Bd. dirs. Covenant Life Ins. Co., C.S. Lewis Inst.; cons. Oxford Project, 1992—, Provident Mutual Ins. Co.; lectr. Oxford U., 1965, U. Hamburg, 1968, Columbia U., 1964-67, Stanford U., 1967-71, U. Pitts., 1990-93; adv. Provident Mutual Ins. Co. Author: The Anguish and Joy of Pascal, 1973, Freedom, Equality, Justice, 1980, The Trinity and Culture, 1985. Bd. dirs. Knox Fellowship, Frontline, Orlando; mem. Human Relations Commn., San Mateo, 1968-70; mem. Indsl. Devel. Council, Grove City, 1972-75. Served with USAF, 1951-53. Mem. Presbyn. Coll. Union, Am. Assn. Pres.'s Ind. Colls. and Univs. (dir., pres.), Nat. Assn. Ind. Colls. and Univs. (mem. secretariat 1985-91), Freedoms Found. (nat. jury), Soc. Christian Philosphers, Duquesne Club (Pitts.), Univ. Club Boston, Citrus Club (Orlando), Evangelical initiative Notre Dame U., Rockford Inst. Main St. com. (De Toqueville award 1998). Republican. Address: 1231 Reformation Dr Oviedo FL 32765-7197

MACKENZIE, DONALD MURRAY, health facility administrator; b. Toronto, Ont., Can., June 5, 1947; s. Donald Alexander and June Cameron MacKenzie; m. Marilyn Adele McNaughton, Jan. 3, 1970; children: Jennifer, Katherine, Kenneth. BA in Econs., U. Toronto, 1968, MA in Polit. Sci., 1970, D Health Adminstr., 1974. Exec. asst. Mt. Sinai Hosp., Toronto, 1974-76, successively asst. exec. dir., assoc. exec. dir., v.p., 1974-89; pres. North York Gen. Hosp., Toronto, 1989—2002; asst. prof. U. Toronto, 1989—; internat. healthcare cons., 2002—. Chair Cardiac Care Network Ont., 2001-2002; founding dir. OH Africa, The Seeing Eye, North York Family Health Team. Editor: History of Canadian Hospitals, 1972; contbr. articles to profl. jours. Bd. dirs. Cancer Care Ont., 1989-99. Mem. Can. Coll. Health Svc. Execs. (cert., various coms.), Can. Cancer Soc. (hon. life, pres. Ont. div. 1989-91, award of merit 1988), Ont. Hosp. Assn. (chmn. 1999-2000), York Club. Anglican. Avocations: golf, tennis, canoe tripping. Personal E-mail: mmackenzie55@hotmail.com.

MACKENZIE, GEORGE ALLAN, company director; s. George Adam and Annette Louise MacKenzie; m. Valerie Ann Marchand, June 30, 1971; children from previous marriage: Richard Michael, Barbara Wynne. Student, Jamaica Coll., Kingston, 1944-48. Commd. flying officer Canadian Air Force, 1951, advanced through grades to lt. gen., 1978; comdr. Canadian Forces Air Command, Winnipeg, Man., 1978-80, resigned, 1980; exec. v.p., COO Gendis Inc., 1980-89, pres., COO, 1989-99, pres., CEO, 1999—2002; bd. dirs. Sony of Can. Ltd., Willowdale, Ont., Canada; pres., CEO CANUSA MedExpress Ltd., 2003—07. Mem. regional adv. bd. Carleton U. Decorated comdr. Order of Mil. Merit, Order St. Johns, Can. Decoration, Knight of St. Lazarus of Jerusalem. Mem. United Services Inst. Can. (hon. v.p.), Can. Corps Commissionaires (gov.), Police Chiefs Rsch. Found. (co-chmn.), Manitoba Club, Royal Mil. Inst. Manitoba. Home: 383 Christie Rd Winnipeg MB Canada R2N 4A5 Home Phone: 204-255-1337; Office Phone: 204-941-0675. Personal E-mail: gallanmac@hotmail.com.

MACKENZIE, KENDRA, art educator; d. Francis Waldo and Esther H. McKenzie. BA in Art History and Classics, Middlebury Coll., Vt., 1969; BFA, NS Coll. Art, Halifax, 1976; MA in Printmaking, U. N.Mex, Albuquerque, 1979; MFA in Printmaking, Rutgers U., New Brunswick, NJ, 1980; MA in Expressive Therapies, Lesley Coll., Cambridge, Mass., 1995. Cert. in K-12 tchg. art Mass., 1978. Grad. asst. Harvard Grad. Sch. Edn., Cambridge, Mass., 1969—70; chair, visual arts dept. Riverdale Country Sch., Bronx, NY, 2004—08, educator, visual arts dept., 1981—; intern, expressive therapies Children's Hosp., Boston, 1988—89. Steward, old growth forest Nature Conservancy Can., Cape Breton Island, NS, Canada, 1966—. Exhibitions include Drawings and A Cape Breton Daybook, exhibitions include U. N.Mex. Fractions and Wholecloth: A Series of Reconstructions, U. N.Mex. (Ford Found. grant, 1978). Independent. Avocations: painting, travel, drawing, environment.

MACKENZIE, LEWIS WHARTON, military officer; b. Truro, NS, Can., Apr. 30, 1940; s. Eugene Murdock and Shirley Helena (Wharton) MacK.; m. Dora Rosalie McKinnon; 1 child, Kimm Katheryn. Student, NATO Def. Coll., Rome, 1977; BA in Polit. Sci., U. Man., Winnipeg, Can., 1988; PhD (hon.), St. Francis Xavier U., 1993; LLB (hon.), St. Mary's U., 1993, Acadia U., 1993, U. Calgary, 2000. Commd. 2d lt. Can. Armed Forces, 1960, advanced through grades to major gen., 1992; teamsite comdr. Internat. Commn. Control and Supervision, Vietnam, 1972; co. comdr. UN Emergency Peace Keeping Force, Cairo, 1973; exec. asst. to comdr. Can. Forces Europe, Lahr, Fed. Republic Germany, 1974-77; comdr. Nicosia dist. UN Peacekeeping Force, Cyprus, 1978; commdg. officer 1st bn. Princess Patricia's Can. Light Infantry, Calgary, 1977-79; faculty mem. Can. Forces Staff Coll., Toronto, 1979-82; dep. chief staff for tng. Can. Army, Montreal, 1983-85; dir. pers. careers officers Can. Armed Forces, Ottawa, 1985-87; dir. Combat Related Employment of Women, Ottawa, 1987-88; comdr. combat tng. ctr. Can. Armed Forces, Gagetown Can. Forces Base, N.B., 1988-1990. Comdr. UN Peacekeeping Force, Ctrl. Am., 1990-91, chief of staff Unprotection force, Yugoslavia, 1992, comdr. UN forces to open Sarajevo airport for humanitarian relief, 1992; pres. MGen MacKenzie Enterprises Inc., MGen MacKenzie Comms. Inc., 1993—; host TV documentary A Soldier's Peace; bd. dirs. Crowflight Minerals Inc., Eurocontrol Technics, Inc., Allana Resources Inc., Norvista Resources Corp., Cymat Techs. Author: Peacekeeper, Road to Sarajevo, 1993, Soldiers Made Me Look Good, 2009. Bd. advisors Can. Fedn. for AIDS Rsch.; patron Saving Our Mil. Heritage, The Normandy Project, Internat. Comty. for Relief of Starvation and Suffering, Can., St. Anne's Vet.'s Hosp. Found., Tony Stacey Ctr.; bd. dirs. Last Post Fund, Vet.'s Rideln, Juno Beach Centre Assn. Decorated Meritorious Svc. Cross (2) (Can.); invested Order of Ont., 2002, Order of Can., 2007, Serving Brother Order of St. John, 1993; recipient Birks gold medal Xavier Jr. Coll., Sydney, N.S., Can., 1960, Vimy award, 1993, medal of honour UN Assn., 1994, World Peace award, 1993; named Canadian of Yr., Tourism Industry Assn. of Can., 1992; Internat. fellow U.S. Army War Coll., 1982-83; Nat. Sports Car champion, 1981; Nat. Formula Ford B Class champion, 1995-96, Formula Ford Diamond Class Champion, 2007, Formula Ford B Class Champion 2008; named to McLean's Honor Roll., 1993. Avocation: motor racing. Home and Office: RR2 Carp 2379 Upper Dwyer Hill Rd Ottawa ON K0A 1L0 Canada Office Phone: 613-256-1151. Business E-Mail: lewmack@xplornet.com.

MACKERODT, FRED, public relations specialist; b. Bklyn., Sept. 17, 1938; s. Leroy and Margaret (Murphy) M.; m. Christy Woods, June 7, 1987. Student, NYU, 1958-59. Freelance writer, photographer, NYC and Barcelona, Spain, 1968-73; editor Cars Mag., Popular Publs. Inc., NYC, 1973-76; pres. Fred Mackerodt, Inc. (pub. relations and publicity), NYC, 1976—, Stone House Farm, Inc., 2001—. Contbg. editor Popular Mechanics, 1987—; contbr. articles to popular mags. Spl. dep. sheriff Indian River County, Fla., 1994—2001; dir. Cornell U. Cooperative Ext. Orange County. Mem. Aviation and Space Writers Am., Internat. Motor Press Assn., Publicity Club N.Y., Wings Club, N.Y. Zool. Soc. (aquarium field assoc. 1971—) Home: 940 Craigville Rd Chester NY 10918 Address: Apt 612 205 W 86th St New York NY 10024-3362 E-mail: fmackerodt@fredmackerodt.com.

MACKERRAS, SIR CHARLES (ALAN MACLAURIN), conductor; b. Schenectady, NY, Nov. 17, 1925; s. Alan Patrick and Catherine Mackerras; m. Helena Judith Wilkins, 1947; 2 children. Student, Sydney Conservatorium Music, Australia, 1938-42; student with Vaclav Talich, Prague Acad. Music, 1947-48; DMus (hon.), U. Hull, 1990, U. Nottingham, 1991, U. Brno, Czech Republic, 1994, York U., Eng., 1994, Griffith U., Brisbane, Australia, 1994, Oxford U., Eng., 1997, Prague Acad. Music, 1999, Napier U., Scotland, 2000, U. Sydney, 2003, U. Melbourne, 2003, Janácek Acad. Music, Brno, 2004, U. London, 2005. Prin. oboist Sydney (Australia) Symphony Orch., 1943-46; staff condr. English Nat. Opera (formerly Sadler's Wells Opera), London, 1948-54, musical dir., 1970-77; prin. condr. BBC Concert Orch., 1954-56; first condr. Hamburg Opera, 1966-69; chief guest condr. BBC Symphony Orch., 1976-79; chief condr. Sydney Symphony Orch., Australian Broadcasting Commn., 1982-85; prin. guest condr. Royal Liverpool Philharm. Orch., 1986-88, Scottish Chamber Orch., 1992-95, condr. laureate, 1995—; music dir. Orch. of St. Luke's, 1998-2001, music dir. emeritus, 2001—; pres. Trinity Coll. Music, London, 2000. Freelance condr. with most Brit. and many continental orchs.,c oncert tours, Australia, 1957—66, U.S. coast-to-coast, 1983; prin. guest condr. San Francisco Opera, 1993—96, prin. guest condr. emeritus, 1996—; prin. guest condr. Royal Philharm. Orch., 1993—96, Czech Philharm. Orch., 1997—2003, Philharmonia Orch., 2002—; mus. dir. Welsh Nat. Opera, 1987—92, condr. emeritus, 1993—, Orch. of The Age of Enlightenment, 2007; condr. laureate Brno Philharm. Orch., 2007; hon. pres. Edinburgh Festival, 2008; condr. emeritus Royal Liverpool Philharmonic, 2009; appearances at internat. festivals and opera houses, frequent radio and TV broadcasts; condr. comml. recordings, notably Handel, Mozart operas and symphonies, Janáček, Brahms, Beethoven, Dvořák, Mahler and Schubert; hon. mem. Guildhall Sch. Music, 2007. Published ballet arrangements Pineapple Poll (Sullivan), Lady and the Fool (Verdi), reconstrn. Sullivan's Lost Cello Concerto, contbr. appendices to book Charles Mackerras: A Musicians' Musician, by Nancy Phelan, articles to Opera Mag., other jours. Decorated comdr. Order of Brit. Empire, Knight Bachelor, medal of merit Czech Republic, Companion Order of Australia, Companion of Honor; recipient Evening Std. award for opera, 1977, Janacek medal, 1978, Gramophone Record of Yr. award, 1977, 1980, 1999, Grammy award for best opera recording, 1981, 2007, Gramophone Best Opera Recording award, 1983, 1984, 1994, 1999, prix, Fondation Jacques Ibert, 1983, Record of Yr. award, Stereo Rev., 1983, Chocs de l'Année award, 1998, Edison award, Preis der Deutschen Schallplattenkritik, Prix Caecilia, 1999, Conducting award, Royal Philharm. Soc., 1999, Chopin prize and lifetime achievement award, Cannes Classical awards at Midem, 2000, award, Assn. Brit. Orchs., 2001, Disting. Musician award, Inc. Soc. Musicians, 2002, Gold medal, Royal Philharmonic Soc., 2005, Listeners' award, BBC Radio 3, 2005, 1st recipient Queen's medal for music, 2005, Classic FM Gramophone Lifetime Achievement award, 2006, MIDEM Music award, Orchestral Category, 2009, Classical BRIT award, 2009, Critics award, 2009, BBC Mag. award, 2009, Disc of Yr. award; named Australian of Yr. in the UK, 2007; hon. fellow, Royal Acad. Music, 1969, Royal Coll. Music, 1987, Trinity Coll. Music, London, 1999, Royal No. Coll. Music, 1999, St. Peter's Coll., Oxford, 1999, Cardiff U., 2003, Royal Welsh Coll. Music and Drama, 2005. Mem.: Orchestral Guildhall Sch. Music (hon.). Office: Lincoln House 300 High Holborn London WC1V 7JH England Office Phone: 44 0207 400 1710.

MACKESEY, DANIEL R., lawyer; b. Ithaca, NY, July 14, 1954; m. Jennifer Mackesey; 2 children. BA in Anthropology cum laude, Cornell U., 1977; JD, U. Va. Sch. Law, 1980. Bar: DC 1980, Va. 1980, admitted to practice: All Va. State Cts. Assoc. David & Hagner, 1982—85; v.p., sr. counsel Artery Organization, Inc., 1985—88, sr. v.p., gen. counsel, 1988—92; counsel Piper & Marbury, Washington, 1992—96; founding ptnr. Jefferson Law Firm, PLC, McLean, Va., 1996—2001; mng. mem. Womble Carlyle Sandridge & Rice PLLC, Tyson Corner, Va., 2001—, mem. firm mgmt. com. (ex-officio), chair firm. leadership com., mem. recruiting com., mem. professionalism com. Recipient NCAA Top Five award. Mem.: Va. State Bar (mem. real property sect., mem. corp. counsel sect.), ABA (mem. law practice mgmt. sect.). Office: Womble Carlyle Sandridge & Rice PLLC 8065 Leesburg Pike 4th Fl Vienna VA 22182-2738 Office Phone: 703-790-4682. Office Fax: 703-918-2242. Business E-Mail: dmackesey@wcsr.com.

MACKEY, BARBARA, museum association administrator, director; MA in Anthropology, U. Nev. Reno. Tchr. pub. sch.; owner retail bus.; hist. archeologist cultural resource mgmt. firms, Nat. Forest Svc., Nev., Calif.; exec. dir. Hist. Fourth Ward Sch., 2001—. Mem.: Nev. Museums Assn. (pres.). Office: Nev Museums Assn PO Box 97423 Las Vegas NV 89193-7423

MACKEY, ELIZABETH JOCELYN, music educator; b. Corbin, Ky., Oct. 30, 1927; d. Elbert Thomas and Flora (Bryant) M. BS in Music Edn., Peabody Coll., Nashville, 1948; MusB in Voice, Greensboro Coll., NC, 1953; MusM in Music History, U. Mich., Ann Arbor, 1956, PhD in Musicology, 1968. Instr. Indiana State Coll., Pa., 1956-58; assoc. prof. Minot State Coll., ND, 1964-67; asst. prof. Ball State U., Muncie, Ind., 1969-74, assoc. prof., 1974-80, prof., 1980-94, prof. emerita, 1994—. Contbr. articles to profl. publs. Fulbright scholar, 1961-62; AAUW fellow, 1963-64. Mem. Pi Kappa Lambda, Sigma Alpha Iota (Province pres. 1978-87, various awards). Lutheran. Avocations: travel, postcards, music stamps. Home: Westminster Village 142 5801 W Bethal Ave Muncie IN 47304

MACKEY, JEFFREY ALLEN, priest; b. Kingston, NY, July 12, 1952; s. Allen William and Vivian Mathilda (Hornbeck) M.; m. Martha LaVonne Webster, Dec. 18, 1971; children: Guy Linwood, Kenyon Paul, Geoffrey Joel. BS, Nyack Coll., 1974; D of Sacred Lit., Ridgedale Theol. Sem., 1975; MDiv, Macon Baptist Sem., Ga., 1976; D Ministry, Mansfield Div., 1985, Grad. Theol. Found., 1990; cert. of theol. studies, Gen. Theol. Sem., 1993; postgrad., Grad. Theol. Found., 1991—, U. of the South; DHL, St. Paul Theol. Sem., 2000; DLitt, Evangel U., 2003; DD, Grad. Theol. Found., 2005. Ordained to ministry Congl. Christian Ch., 1974; ordained priest Episcopal Ch., 1993. Min. music Neversink Valley Bapt. Ch., Huguenot, NY, 1969-70; pastor Ponckhockie Congl. Ch., Kingston, 1971-74, The Alliance Ch., Andover, 1974-76; acad. dean Macon (Ga.) Bible Inst., 1976-78; min. Oak Grove Gospel Tabernacle, Williamsport, Pa., 1977-80, 69th St. Alliance Ch., Phila., 1980-83; sr. min. Vestavia Alliance Ch., Birmingham, Ala., 1983-87, Hope Alliance Ch., New Hartford, NY, 1987-91; assoc. rector Grace Ch., Utica, NY, 1991-96, vicar Waterville, NY, 1995-96; rector Trinity Episcopal Ch., DeRidder, La., 1996-97, vicar Melrose, Fla., 2008—, Polk Meml. Episcopal Ch., Leesville, La., 1996-97; rector St. Mark the Evangelist Ch., North Bellmore, NY, 1997-99; registrar/Bible faculty Nyack Coll., Manhattan Campus, NYC, 1999-2000, assoc. dean for acad. affairs, 2000-2001, acad. dean, 2001—03, asst. v.p., dean Coll. Arts and Scis., 2003—05; v.p., acad. dean Trinity Sch. Ministry, 2005—07; interim rector St. Mark's Episcopal Ch., Orchard Park, NY, 2007—08. Adj. prof. Cranmer Theol. Ho., Shreveport, La., 1997, Nyack Coll., 1998—99; asst. priest St. John's Episcopal Ch., Kingston, NY, 2000—02; interim rector St. John's Ch., Kingston, 2002—03, St. Gregory's, Woodstock, NY, 2003—04; adj. Christ the King Seminary, East Aurora, NY, 2008. Author: A Worship Manifesto, 1986, Indicatives and Imperatives, 1987, Christ's Centripetal Cross, 1990; co-author: Where Love and People Are, 1990, Prophet of Justice, Prophet of Life: Essays on William Stringfellow, 1997, A Diary of Three Decades: Grace Church, Utica, N.Y., 1963-96, 1999, And Jesus Everything: Conversations with A.B. Simpson, 2000, A Heart for the Future, 2004, Hidden Mirth, 2005, A Mirrored Surprise, 2008; contbr. numerous articles to profl. jours. Mem. Alcohol and Drug Abuse Prevention Treatment Program, Birmingham, 1987—88; chaplain N. Bellmore Vol. Fire Dept., 1998—99; trustee Cathedral of St. John the Divine, NYC, 2002—05. Mem. Fellowship Christian Sch. Adminstrs., Evang. Theol. Soc., Am. Assn. Sch. Adminstrs., Am. Guild Organists, Anglican Assn. of Biblical Scholars, Order of Preachers (Anglican), Inst. for Advanced Theology, Soc. Biblical Lit. Avocations: piano, collecting art and statues, hymn writing, walking, auto restoration. Office Phone: 352-475-2177. Personal E-mail: parsonsmanor@comcast.net.

MACKEY, JOHN P., food products executive; s. Bill and Margaret Mackey; m. Deborah Morin. Student, Trinity Coll., San Antonio, Tex., U. of Texas, Austin. Owner Safer Way Natural Foods, Austin, 1978—80; co-founder, chmn., CEO Whole Foods Market Inc., Austin, 1980—, pres., 2001—04. Named Overall Nat. Entrepreneur of Yr., Ernst & Young, 2003. Achievements include hiking entire Applachian Trail (2168 miles), 2002. Avocations: yoga, meditation, scuba diving. Office: Whole Foods Market Inc 550 Bowie St Austin TX 78703-4677

MACKEY, PAMELA ROBILLARD, lawyer; b. Harlingen, Tex., July 16, 1956; d. Gregory Leo and Rosanne Elizabeth (Niland) Robillard; m. Craig W. Mackey, Dec. 30, 1983. BS in Journalism with honors, U. Colo., Boulder, 1981; JD with highest honors, George Washington U., 1985. Bar: Colo. 1985, US Dist. Ct. (dist. Colo.) 1985. Assoc. Davis, Graham & Stubbs, Denver, 1985-87, Haddon, Morgan & Foreman, P.C., Denver, 1987—89; dep. state pub. defender Office of State Pub. Defender, Colo., 1989—94; shareholder Haddon, Morgan, Mueller, Jordan, Mackey & Foreman, P.C., Denver, 1994—. Exec. editor George Wash. Law Rev., 1984-85. Fellow ABA; mem. Colo. Bar Assn., Denver Bar Assn. (mem. conciliation panel), Colo. Women's Bar Assn. (bd. dirs. 1986-90, 94-95; pres. 1995-96), Colo. Criminal Def. Bar (newsletter editor 1988), NACDL. Democrat. Roman Catholic. Avocations: skiing, golf. Office: Haddon Morgan Mueller Jordan Mackey & Foreman PC 150 E Tenth Ave Denver CO 80203 Office Phone: 303-831-7364. E-mail: pmackey@hmflaw.com.

MACKEY, SEAN CHARLES, anesthesiologist, electrical engineering consultan; b. Oceanside, Calif., Mar. 29, 1963; s. Ronald James and Susan (Fuller) M.; m. Lisa Ann Gordon, Nov. 26, 1990. BSE, MSE, U. Pa., 1986; MD, PhD, U. Ariz., 1994. Engring. tech. LaJolla (Calif.) Tech., 1985; rsch. assoc./biomed. engr. VA Med. Ctr., Phila., 1985-86; rsch. assoc. Univ. Med. Ctr./Anesthesiology, Tucson, 1986-88; owner Altech Cons., Sunnyale, 1987—; resident in anesthesiology Stanford U., 1995-98, fellow in pain mgmt., 1998. Cons. Univ. Med. Ctr. Anesthesiology, 1988—; rsch. assoc. sect. cardiology Am. Heart Assn., 1987—. GTE scholar, 1987, others; Am. Heart Assn. fellow, 1991. Mem. AMA, IEEE, Bioengring. Soc. Avocations: swimming, bicycling, computer programming, cooking, design of audio equipment. Home: 675 Belden Ct Los Altos CA 94022-1611

MACK-HARVIN, DIONNE L., library director; b. SC, June 18, 1972; BA in History and African-Am., SUNY, Brockport; MA in Africana Studies, SUNY, Albany, 1995, MLS in Info. Sci., 1996. Libr. Queens Coll., NY, 1996; libr. Crown Heights Libr. Bklyn. Pub. Libr., NY, 1996, asst. branch libr. NY, branch mgr. NY, regional libr. NY, dir. Ctrl. Libr. NY, chief of staff NY, 2005—06, interim dir. NY, 2006—07, exec. dir., 2007—. Office: Bklyn Pub Libr Ctrl Libr Grand Army Plaza Brooklyn NY 11238 E-mail: d.mack@brooklynpubliclibrary.org.

MACKIN, CHARLES PHILIP, JR., lawyer; b. Boston, Dec. 13, 1947; s. Charles Philip and Mary Patricia (Sparkes) M.; m. Deborah Ann Huey, Oct. 18, 1980; children: Emily K., Claire E.S. BA, St. Anselm Coll., 1969; JD, Loyola U., New Orleans, 1972; MGA, U. Pa., 1987; grad., U.S. Army War Coll., 1990. Bar: Pa. 1972, U.S. Ct. Mil. Appeals 1973, U.S. Ct. Appeals (D.C. cir.) 1977, U.S. Supreme Ct. 1977, U.S. Ct. Appeals (3rd cir.) 1985. Asst. dist. atty., Coudersport, Pa., 1978-81; sr. dep. atty. gen. Office of Atty. Gen. of Pa., Harrisburg, 1982-86, chief dep. atty. gen., 1986-89; dep. chief counsel for investigations Dept. Auditor Gen. of Pa., Harrisburg, 1989-91, dep. auditor gen., 1991-96. Capt. USMC, 1972-77. Mem. Pa. Bar Assn., Army Navy Club (Washington). Office: 3400 Trindle Rd Camp Hill PA 17011 Office Phone: 717-214-3700.

MACKIN, RANDAL THOMAS, literature and language professor; s. Mary Helen Ary; m. Lynda Ivanna Marie Garcia; children: Dylan Thomas, Hadley Carolyn Marie, Joseph William. ArtsD, Middle Tenn. State U., Murfreesboro, 2003. Newspaper editor Buffalo River Rev., Linden, Tenn., 1982—; asst. prof. Middle Tenn. State U., 1997—. Ch. elder First Christian Ch., Linden, Tenn., 2002—08. Recipient Meeman Foundation award. Mem.: Buffalo River Writers. Liberal. Avocations: writing, reading, gardening.

MACKINNON, ANN LAURIE, retired elementary school educator; 1 child, Brian John Stempel. BS, St. John's U., Jamaica, 1967, JD, 1996; MA in Edn., Hofstra U., NY, 1971. Elem. sch. tchr. Babylon Union Free Sch. Dist., NY, 1967—68, Connetquot Ctrl. Sch. Dist. of Islip, LI, NY, 1968—2000; ret., 2000. Mem. Connetquot Tchrs. Assn., Bohemia, NY, 1968—2000; v.p. S. Corp. Lauren-Curtis Assocs., d.b.a. Anne Lauren, Setauket, NJ, 1980. Avocations: fine arts, gardening. Home: 12 Harbor Hills Dr Port Jefferson NY 11777

MACKINNON, ARAN STUART, history professor; s. Victor and Ruth Ann MacKinnon; m. Elaine McClarnand, Aug. 6, 1999; 1 child, Kieran Stuart. BA with honors, Queen's U., Kingston, Ont., Can., 1988; MA, U. Natal, KawZulu-Natal, South Africa, 1991; PhD, U. London, 1996. Prof. history U. West Ga., Carrollton, 1997—, dir. global studies, 2001—07, dir. ctr. interdisciplinary studies, 2008. Contbr. chapters to books. Mem.: SERSAS (coord. 2001—08). Office: Univ West Ga 1601 Maple St Carrollton GA 30118 Business E-Mail: amackinn@westga.edu.

MACKINNON, CATHARINE ALICE, lawyer, educator, writer; d. George E. and Elizabeth V. (Davis) MacKinnon. BA in Govt. magna cum laude with distinction, Smith Coll., 1969; JD, Yale U., 1977, PhD in Polit. Sci., 1987; doctorate (hon.), Hebrew U., Jerusalem, 2008. Prof. law U. Mich., Ann Arbor, 1990—, Elizabeth A. Long Prof. Law. Long term vis. prof. U. Chgo., 1997-2005; co-dir. LAW Project Equality Now, 2001-05; fellow Ctr. for Advanced Study, 2005-06; Roscoe Pound Vis. Prof. Law, Harvard Law Sch., 2007; vis. prof. various univs. Author: Sexual Harassment of Working Women, 1979, Feminism Unmodified, 1987, Toward a Feminist Theory of the State, 1989, Only Words, 1993, Sex Equality, 2001, 2nd. edit., 2007, Women's Lives, Men's Laws, 2005, Are Women Human? and other international dialogues, 2006; co-author: In Harm's Way, 1997, Directions in Sexual Harassment Law, 2003. Mem.: AAAS (assoc.), Am. Bar Found. (Disting. Rsch. award 2007). Office: U Mich Law Sch 625 S State St Ann Arbor MI 48109-1215 Office Phone: 734-647-3595. Office Fax: 734-764-8309. E-mail: camtwo@umich.edu.

MACKINNON, DOLLY, historian, music educator; MusB, The U. Melbourne, Australia, 1987; PhD in History, The U. Melbourne, 1994; grad. cert., Queensland U. Tech., Australia, 2000. Sr. rsch. asst. U. Queensland, Brisbane, 1995—96, lectr., 1996—96, Queensland U. Tech., 1998—2002, U. Melbourne, 2002—08; faculty music U. Music, Melbourne, 2008—. Contbr. articles to profl. jours. Rsch. com. mem. UCCO, Melbourne, 2008—. Grantee, Queensland U. Tech., 2001—02; Marsden grant, Royal Soc. New Zealand Marsden Fund, 2003—05, Rsch. grant, Australian Rsch. Coun. Grant, 2007—09, Victorian Parliamentary Libr. fellowship, State Govt. Victoria, 2008. Mem.: Australian Soc. Muscology, Brit. Local History Assn., Australian and New Zealand Soc. History Medicine, Australian Soc. of Archivists Inc. Office: Univ Melbourne Sch Hist Studies & Faculty Music Victoria Melbourne 3010 Australia Business E-Mail: a.mackinnon@unimelb.edu.au.

MACKINNON, JAMES GORDON, economist, educator; b. Charlottetown, PEI, Can., Jan. 4, 1951; s. James William and Marion Elizabeth MacKinnon; m. Susan Gentleman, Nov. 23, 1985. BA with honors, York U., 1971; MA, Princeton U., 1974, PhD, 1975. Asst. prof. Queen's U., Kingston, Ont., Canada, 1975—78, assoc. prof., 1978—82, prof., 1982—, Sir Edward Peacock prof. econometrics, 1991—. Mem. editl. bd. Can. Jour. Econs., 1984—87, assoc. editor Jour. Applied Econometrics, 1989—91, Jour. Econometrics, 1991—2007, software rev. editor Jour. Applied Econometrics, 1991—. Fellow: Royal Soc. Can., Econometric Soc.; mem.: Can. Econs. Assn. (pres.-elect 2000—01, pres. 2001—02, past pres. 2002—03). Office: Queen's U Dept Econs Kingston ON Canada K7L 3N6 Home Phone: 613-531-9854; Office Phone: 613-533-2293. Business E-Mail: jgm@econ.queensu.ca.

MACKINNON, JOHN ALEXANDER, lawyer; b. Glen Ridge, NJ, Feb. 5, 1949; s. John and Carol McNeir (Cox) M.; m. Anne Rider Patterson, Aug. 19, 1972; children: Lindsay Rider, John William. BA, Williams Coll., 1971; JD, U. Va., Charlottesville, 1974. Assoc. Brown & Wood, NYC, 1974-82, ptnr., 1983-2001; ptnr. securities law Sidley Austin Brown & Wood LLP, NYC, 2001—06, Sidley Austin LLP, NYC, 2006—. Adv. bd. Mutual Fund Dir. Forum. Trustee, Tuxedo Park Libr., NY, 1982-89; mem. chmn., bd. zoning appeals, Tuxedo Park, 1987-89. Mem. ABA, Assn. of the Bar of NYC, The Tuxedo Club. Office Phone: 212-839-5300, 212-839-5534. Business E-Mail: jmackinnon@sidley.com.

MACKINNON, MALCOLM D(AVID), retired insurance company executive; b. Guelph, Ont., Can., Mar. 9, 1931; came to U.S., 1955; s. A.L. and Jean (Butchart) MacK.; m. Betty Campbell, June 18, 1955; children: Sandra, Katherine, Donald. BA, U. Toronto, 1953. Cert. CLU, chartered fin. analyst. With Prudential Ins. Co., 1954-94, v.p. Newark, 1979-81, sr. v.p., 1981—94; ret., 1994. Commentator pub. radio. Trustee Kean Coll., Union, N.J., 1990-93, Millburn Free Pub. Libr., 1996-2005, pres., 1997-2000; chmn. Milburn Short Hills chpt. ARC, 1992-94. Recipient Millburn Cmty. Svc. award, 2008. Fellow Soc. Actuaries; mem. Canoe Brook Country Club (Summit, N.J.). Home: 23 Grosvenor Rd Short Hills NJ 07078-1639

MACKINNON, RODERICK, neuroscientist, educator; b. Burlington, Mass., 1956; married. BA, Brandeis U., 1978; MD, Tufts U., 1982, PhD (hon.), 2002. Postdoctoral fellow Beth Israel Hosp., Harvard U., 1985—86, Brandeis U., 1986—89; from asst. to prof. dept. neurobiology Harvard Med. Sch., 1989—96; John D. Rockefeller Jr. prof. lab. molecular neurobiology and biophysics Rockefeller U., 1996—. Recipient W. Alden Spencer award, Young Investigator award, Biophysical Soc., 1995, Newcomb Cleveland prize, AAAS, 1998, Albert Lasker award for Basic Med. Rsch., Lasker Found., 1999, Lewis S. Rosentiel award, 2000, Gairdner Found. Internat. award, 2001, Nobel prize for chemistry, 2003; grantee, Howard Hughes Med. Inst. Chevy Chase, Md., 1997—. Mem.: NAS, Alpha Omega Med. Honor Soc. Avocation: trout fishing. Office: Rockefeller Univ 1230 York Ave New York NY 10021 also: Howard Hughes Med Inst 4000 Jones Bridge Rd Chevy Chase MD 20815-6789 Office Phone: 212-327-7288.*

MACKINNON, STEPHEN R., Asian studies administrator, educator; b. Columbus, Nebr., Dec. 2, 1940; s. Cyrus Leland and Helen (Wigglesworth) MacKinnon; children: Rebecca, Cyrus R.; m. Anne Feldhaus, Dec. 21, 2005. BA, Yale U., New Haven, Conn., 1963, MA, 1964; PhD, U. Calif., Davis, 1971. Acting instr. Chinese U., Hong Kong, 1968-69; dir. Asian Studies, prof. history Ariz. State U., Tempe, 1971—; vis. assoc. Chinese Acad. Social Sci., Beijing, 1979-81, 85. Mem. US State Dept. Selection Bd., Washington, 1991, Nat. Com. on US-China Rels., NYC, 1991—; cons. PBS film documentary "Dragon and Eagle." Author: Power/Politics China, 1980, Wuhan, 1938, 2008; co-author: Agnes Smedley, 1988, China Reporting, 1987; co-editor: Chinese Women Revolution, 1976 (ALA notable book 1976), Scars of War, 2001, China At War, 2007; lectr. on China to local orgns. and TV, 1981—. Commr. Phoenix Sister Cities, 1986-91; bd. dirs. Com. on Fgn. Rels., Phoenix, 1988—; bd. dirs. Marshall Fund Ariz., 1995—. Rsch. fellow Am. Coun. Learned Socs., Hong Kong, 1978, Fulbright Found., India, 1977-78; rsch. sr. Com. on Scholarly Com. People's Republic China, Washington-Beijing, 1992, Pacific Cultural Found., 1999, Am. Inst. Indian Studies, 2003, Fulbright-Hays ACLS, China, 2005-. Mem. Assn. Asian Studies (bd. dirs. 1990-91), Am. Hist. Assn. (program com. 1990-91). Avocations: tennis, hiking, jazz. Office: Ariz State U Dept History Tempe AZ 85287-4302 Office Phone: 480-965-5778. Business E-Mail: stephen.mackinnon@asu.edu.

MACKINNON, SUSAN, plastic surgeon; b. Can., Jan. 31, 1950; married; 4 children. MD, Queen's U., Kingston, Can., 1975. Cert. in plastic surgery. Surgery residency Queen's U., 1978; surgery residency divsn. plastic surgery U. Toronto, 1980, neurosurgery fellowship dept. surgery, 1981; hand surgery fellowship Union Meml. Hosp., Balt., 1982; Shoenberg prof., surgery chief divsn. plastic and reconstructive surgery Wash. U. Sch. Medicine. Surgeon Barnes-Jewish Hosp., St. Louis Children's Hosp.; with Barnes-Jewish West County Hosp. Contbr. chapters to books, articles to profl. jours. Recipient Medal award in surgery, Royal Coll. Physicians and Surgeons Can., 1988, Outstanding Clinician award, Wash. U. Sch. Medicine III Humanity Program; named a Top Dr., Wash. U.; named to, Best Doctors in America, 2002, 2005, 2006. Mem.: Inst. Medicine, Am. Assn. Plastic Surgeons (treas. 2003—05, v.p. 2005, pres. 2007—, awards com. chair), Am. Assn. Hand Surgery (v.p. 2003, pres.-elect 2004, pres. 2005). Achievements include completing the first donor nerve allotransplant, a procedure that can restore function to severely injured limbs that previously were considered irreparable; research in peripheral nerve surgery in hand/upper extremity and lower extremity; carpal tunnel syndrome; tarsal tunnel syndrome; thoracic outlet syndrome; nerve transplant; facial palsy. Office: Wash U Sch Medicine 600 S Euclid Ave Campus Box 8238 Saint Louis MO 63110 also: Plastic and Reconstructive Surgery Ctr Ctr for Advance Medicine 4921 Parkview Pl Ste G Fl 6 Saint Louis MO 63110 Office Phone: 314-362-4586. Office Fax: 314-362-4536.*

MACKINNON, VICTOR STUART, retired law educator; s. Norman and Edith MacKinnon; m. Ruth Ann MacKinnon, June 29, 1957; children: Gregor, Aran. MA, Glasgow U., Scotland, 1949, LLB, 1952; LLM, Harvard U., Cambridge, Mass., 1955, SJD, 1963. Solicitor: Scotland 1952. Lectr., then sr. lectr. faculty law U. Edinburgh, 1957—69; prof., dean faculty law Ahmadu Bello U., Zaria, Nigeria, 1966—69, Makerere U., Kampala, Uganda, 1971—72; prof. law Atkinson Coll., York U., Toronto, Canada, 1969—94. Vis. prof. law U. Zululand, South Africa, 1984, U. Cape Town, South Africa, 1985, U. Malaya, Kuala Lumpur, Malaysia, 1988—89; rsch. cons. U. South Pacific, Commonwealth Fund Tech. Cooperation, London, 1996. Author: Comparative Federalism, 1963; co-author: Materials in Public Administration, 1994; contbr. articles to profl. jours. Vol. mediator consumer law Office Atty. Gen., Augusta, Maine, 2000—. Recipient Spl. Commonwealth award, Ministry Overseas Devel., London, 1966—69, 1971—72; Sir Godfrey Collins scholar, U. Glasgow, 1954. Mem.: Law Soc. Scotland. Home: 268 Washington Rd Jefferson ME 04348 Office Phone: 207-549-5683. Personal E-mail: vmackinnon@roadrunner.com.

MACKINTOSH, FREDERICK ROY, oncologist; b. Miami, Fla., Oct. 4, 1943; s. John Harris and Mary Carlotta (King) MacK.; m. Judith Jane Parnell, Oct. 12, 1961 (div. Aug. 1977); children: Lisa Lynn, Wendy Sue; m. Claudia Lizanne Flournoy, Jan. 7, 1984; 1 child, Gregory Warren. BS, MIT, 1964, PhD, 1968; MD, U. Miami, 1976. Intern then resident in gen. medicine Stanford (Calif.) U., 1976-78, fellow in oncology, 1978-81; asst. prof. med. U. Nev., Reno, 1981-85, assoc. prof., 1985-92, prof. medicine, 1992—. Contbr. articles to profl. jours. Fellow ACP; mem. Am. Soc. Clin. Oncology, Am. Cancer Soc. (pres. Nev. chpt. 1987-89, Washoe chpt. 1988-90), No. Nev. Cancer Coun. (bd. dirs. 1981-92), No. Calif. Cancer Program (bd. dirs. alt. 1983-87, bd. dirs. 1987-91). Avocations: bicycling, sporting clays. Office: Med Sch Assocs North Ste 302 1500 E 2nd St Reno NV 89502 Home Phone: 775-853-2347; Office Phone: 775-784-7500. E-mail: roy.mackintosh@va.gov.

MACKLEM, MICHAEL KIRKPATRICK, publisher; b. Toronto, Ont., Can., July 12, 1928; s. Hedley Clark and Mary Eileen (Kirkpatrick) M.; m. Anne Woodburne Hardy, Dec. 30, 1950; children— Timothy Street, Nicholas Hardy. BA, U. Toronto, 1950; AM (Charles Scribner fellow), Princeton U., 1952, PhD (Porter Ogden Jacobus fellow, Royal Soc. Can. fellow), 1954. Instr., English Yale U., New Haven, 1954-55; staff editor Ency. Canadiana, 1955-58; asst. to dir. Humanities Research Council of Can., 1958-60; gen. mgr. Oberon Press, Ottawa, Ont., 1966-85. Pres. Michael, Hardy, Ltd., Ottawa, 1972—; elected mem., Order of Canada, 2007. Author: The Anatomy of the World: Relations Between Natural and Moral Law from Donne to Pope, 1958, God Have Mercy: The Life of John Fisher of Rochester, 1967, Cinderella, 1969, Voyages to New France 1615-1618, 1970, Voyages to New France 1599-1603, 1971, The Sleeping Beauty, 1973, Jacques the Woodcutter, 1977, Liberty and the Holy City, 1978, The Oberon Reader, 1991, The Oberon Poetry Collection, 1992. Can. Council fellow, 1964-65 Mem.: Order Can. (apptd. mem.). Home: 555 Maple Ln Ottawa ON Canada K1M 0N7 Office: Oberon Press 205-145 Spruce St Ottawa ON Canada K1R 6P1 E-mail: oberon@sympatico.ca.

MACKLIN, CROFFORD JOHNSON, JR., lawyer; b. Columbus, Ohio, Sept. 10, 1947; S. Crofford Johnson, Sr. and Dorothy Ann (Stevens) M.; m. Mary Carole Ward, July 5, 1969; children: Carrie E., David J. BA, Ohio State U., 1969; BA summa cum laude, U. West Fla., 1974; JD cum laude, Ohio State U., 1976. Bar: Ohio 1977, U.S. Tax Ct. 1978. Acct. Touche Ross, Columbus, 1976-77; assoc. Smith & Schnacke, Dayton, 1977-81, shareholder, 1988-89; sole practice Dayton, 1981-82; ptnr. Porter, Wright, Morris & Arthur, Dayton, 1983-88, Thompson, Hine LLP, 1989—, practice group leader pers. and succession planning, 2001—06. Adj. faculty Franklin U., 1977; adj. prof. U. Dayton Law Sch., 1981. Contbr. articles to profl. jours. Bd. dirs. Great Lakes Nat. Bank Ohio, 1997, Easter Seals, 1984-86. Served to capt. USMCR, 1969-74. Fellow Am. Coll. Trust and Estate Counsel; mem. ABA, Dayton Bar Assn. (chmn. probate com. 1981-83), Dayton Trust & Estate Planning (pres. 1983-84), Ohio Bar Assn. Presbyterian. Home: 7276 Wetherington Dr West Chester OH 45069 Office: Thompson Hine LLP 2000 Courthouse Pla NE PO Box 8801 Dayton OH 45402-1758 Home Phone: 513-759-0504; Office Phone: 937-443-6730.

MACKLIN, RUTH, bioethics educator; b. Newark, Mar. 27, 1938; d. Hyman and Frieda (Yaruss) Chimacoff; m. Martin Macklin, Sept. 1, 1957 (div. June 1969); children: Meryl, Shelley Macklin Taylor. BA with distinction, Cornell U., 1958; MA in Philosophy, Case Western Res. U., 1966, PhD in Philosophy, 1968. Instr. in philosophy Case Western Res. U., Cleve., 1967—68, asst. prof., 1968—71, assoc. prof., 1971—76; assoc. for behavioral studies The Hastings Ctr., Hastings-on-Hudson, NY, 1976—80; vis. assoc. prof. Albert Einstein Coll. Medicine, Bronx, NY, 1977—78, assoc. prof., 1978—84, prof. dept. epidemiology and social medicine, 1984—. Cons. NIH, 1986—; advisor WHO, Geneva, 1989—; mem. White House Adv. Com. on Human Radiation Experiments, Washington1994; chair ethical rev. com. UNAIDS, Geneva, 1996—2001. Author: Man, Mind and Morality, 1982, Mortal Choices, 1987, Enemies of Patients, 1993, Surrogates and Other Mothers, 1994, Against Relativism, 1999, Double Standards in Medical Research, 2004; contbr. articles to ethics, law and med. jours. Fellow: APHA, Am. Soc. Law, Medicine and Ethics, Inst. Medicine NAS, The Hastings Ctr., Am. Philosophs. Assn. (life); mem.: Am. Soc. Bioethics and Humanities (bd. dirs. 1997—99), Internat. Assn. Bioethics (bd. dirs., pres. 1999—2001). Democrat. Office: A Einstein Coll Medicine Dept Epidemiology Population Health 1300 Morris Park Ave Bronx NY 10461-1926 E-mail: macklin@aecom.yu.edu.

MACKLIS, ROGER MILTON, physician, educator, researcher; b. Stratford, Conn., Mar. 12, 1956; m. Carol Clark, July 25, 1987; children: Andrew Clark, Paul Clark. BS, MS, Yale U., 1978; MD, Harvard U., 1983. Diplomate Am Bd Radiation Oncology. Instr. Harvard Med. Sch., Boston, 1988-89, asst. prof. radiation oncology, 1989-93; dep. div. chief Children's Hosp., Boston, 1990-93; chmn. dept. radiation oncology Cleve. Clinic Found., 1993—. Biomedical consult, Boston, 1989—; assoc prof hist med Case Western Res Univ, 1995—; prof. medicine Cleve. Clin. Lerner Coll. of Medicine, 2004—. Author: (book) Manual of Introductory Clinical Medicine, 1984; contbr. articles to profl jours. Recipient Resident Research Award, ASTRO, 1988, Jr Faculty Research Award, Am Cancer Soc, 1990. Mem.: Soc Chairs of Acad Radiation Oncology Programs (treas, vpres, pres), Am Soc Therapeutic Radiology and Oncology, Am Soc Clin Oncology (Young Investigator Award 1987), Radiation Research Soc. Achievements include research in research on new approaches to cancer treatment involving radioactively labeled molecules and novel technologies for minimizing medical errors in oncology. Office: Cleve Clinic Found Dept Radiation Oncology 9500 Euclid Ave Cleveland OH 44195-0001 Home Phone: 440-442-4252; Office Phone: 216-444-5576. Business E-Mail: macklir@ccf.org.

MACKLOWE, HARRY B., real estate developer; b. Aug. 10, 1937; m. Linda Macklowe; children: Elizabeth Susan, William S. Student, U. Ala., NYU, Sch. Visual Arts, NYC. Founder, chmn. CEO Macklowe Properties, Inc., NYC, 1960—2008, chmn. emeritus, 2008—. Named one of Top 200 Collectors, ARTNews Mag., 2005—08. Avocations: yachting, art collection. Office: Macklowe Properties General Motors Bldg 767 Fifth Ave New York NY 10153 Office Phone: 212-554-5800.

MACKLOWE, WILLIAM S., real estate company executive; s. Harry B. and Linda Macklowe. Grad., NYU. Real estate fin. analyst Manufacturers Hanover; pres. Macklowe Properties, NYC, chmn., CEO, 2008—. Bd. governors Real Estate Bd. NY; exec. com. mem., real estate and constrn. divsn. State of Israel Bonds. Mem. Dia Art Found. Office: Macklowe Properties Gen Motors Bldg 767 Fifth Ave New York NY 10153 Office Phone: 212-265-5900. Office Fax: 212-554-5893.

MACKNIGHT, CAROL BERNIER, educational association administrator; b. Quincy, Mass., Apr. 12, 1938; d. Harold Nelson and Marguerite (Norris) Bernier; m. William J. MacKnight, Aug. 19, 1967. BS, Ithaca Coll., NYC, 1960; MM, Manhattan Sch. Mus., NYC, 1961; Dipl., Fontainebleau Sch. Music/Art, France, 1968; EdD, U. Mass., 1973. Asst. to supt. Falmouth (Mass.) pub. Schs., 1975—76; dir. bus., mgmt., engring. prog. Sch. Bus. Adminstrn. U. Mass., Amherst, 1976-79, assoc. dir. continuing edn., 1979-82, dir. Office Instructional Tech., 1982—93. Trustee New Eng. Regional Computer Program, Inc., 1986—92; bd. dirs. Info. Sys. and Bus. Exch., 1992—93; keynote spkr. Australian Soc. for Computers in Learning In Tertiary Edn. Conf., Adelaide, 1996; conf. chair various confs., 2002—. Editor: Jour. Computing in Higher Edn., 1988—2009, Jour. Info. Sys. for Mgrs., 1992—93; mem. editl. rev. bd.: Jour. of Computer-Based Instrn., 1988—2002, author/editor: computer progs.; contbr. articles to profl. jours. Grantee, CDC, 1986, Regents of Boston, 1988; Lilly Fellow Mentor, 1991—92. Mem. ACM, Assn. for Computing Machinery, Educom, Soc. Applied Learning Techs. (bd. dirs. 2003-05, bd. dirs. 2006- conf. chair e-learning 2004, conf. chair gaming and simulation 2006), New England Regional Computer Program. Avocations: music, photography, tennis, hiking, skiing. Office: Norris Consulting and Pub PO Box 2593 Amherst MA 01004 Business E-Mail: cmacknight@oit.umass.edu.

MACKNIGHT, WILLIAM JOHN, chemist, educator; b. NYC, May 5, 1936; s. William John and Margaret Ann (Stuart) M.; m. Carol Marie Bernier, Aug. 19, 1967 BS, Rochester U., 1958; MA, Princeton U., 1963, PhD, 1964. Rsch. assoc. Princeton U., 1964-65; asst. prof. chemistry U. Mass., Amherst, 1965-69, assoc. prof. chemistry, 1969-74, prof. chemistry, 1974-76, dept. head polymer sci., 1976-85, prof. polymer sci. and engring., 1985-88, 95-96, head dept. polymer sci. and engring., 1988-95, disting. univ. prof., 1996-98, Wilmer D. Barret disting. prof., 1998-99, Wilmer D. Barret Disting. prof. emeritus, 1999—. Mem. sci. and tech. adv. bd. Alcoa, Pitts., 1984-86, Diversitech Gen., Akron, Ohio, 1985-89; mem. panel for materials sci. Nat. Bur. Standards, Washington, 1983-89. Author: Polymeric Sulfur and Related Polymers, 1965; Introduction to Polymer Viscoelasticity, 3d edit., 2005. Served to lt. USN, 1958-61 Recipient Ford prize in high polymer physics Am. Phys. Soc., 1984, award for disting. svc. in the advancement of polymer sci. Japan Soc. for Polymer Sci., 1998; Guggenheim fellow, 1985, Internat. Rsch. award Soc. Plastics Engrs., 2007. Fellow: AAAS, Am. Phys. Soc. (exec. com. 1975—76); mem.: Am. Chem. Soc. (award in polymer chemistry 1997, Herman F. Mark award, polymers chemistry divsn. 2002, Flory award, polymer chemistry divsn. 2006), Nat. Acad. Engring., Cosmos Club. Avocations: music, sports. Home: 127 Sunset Ave Amherst MA 01002-2019 Office: U Mass Polymer Sci & Engring Dept Conte Bldg Amherst MA 01003 Home Phone: 413-549-5150; Office Phone: 413-577-1412. Business E-Mail: wmacknight@polysci.umass.edu.

MACKO, RICHARD FRANK, medical educator; married. Prof. neurology VA, Balt., 1994—. Office: Balt Vets Affairs 10 North Greene St Baltimore MD 21201 Business E-Mail: rmacko@grecc.umaryland.edu.

MACKWELL, STEPHEN JOSEPH, geophysicist, educator; b. Christchurch, New Zealand, June 5, 1956; arrived in U.S., 1984; s. Alan Gordon Mackwell and Mary Veronica (Carter) Francis; m. Kathleen Garland, March 27, 2004. BSc in Physics and Math., U. Canterbury, Christchurch, New Zealand, 1978, MSc in Physics, 1979; diploma of edn., Christchurch Tchrs. Coll., New Zealand, 1979; PhD in Geophysics, Australian Nat. U., Canberra, 1985. Postdoctoral assoc. Cornell U., Ithaca, NY, 1984—86, rsch. fellow, 1984—87; asst. prof. Pa. State U., University Park, 1987—92, assoc. prof., 1992—98; prof. exptl. geophysics Bayerisches Geoinst., Germany, 1998—2000, dir., 2000—02, Lunar and Planetary Inst., Houston, 2002—. Program dir. for geophysics, divsn. of earth sci., NSF, Washington, 1993-94, expert cons., 1995; panelist proposal rev. NASA, Houston, 1994-95; expert rev. Geoscis. Rsch. program, Dept. Energy, 1993; mem. rev. panel Planetary Geology and Geophysics program, NASA, 1994-96, 2002-, group chief, 1996-98, 2004, panel chief, 2005—. Assoc. editor Jour. Geophys. Rsch. - Solid Earth, 1992—97, mem. editl. bd. Physics of the Earth and Planetary Interiors, 1992—98, Tectonophysics, 2002; editor: (Solid Earth) Geophys. Rsch. Letters, 2000—01; editor-in-chief Geophys. Rsch. Letters, 2002—05; contbr. articles to profl. jours. Recipient Stipendiat der Alexander von Humboldt-Stiftung, Bayreuth, Germany, 1996; grantee, NSF, 1988—98, NASA, 1993—98. Fellow: Mineral. Soc. Am.; mem.: AAAS, Am. Geophys. Union (mem. meetings program com. 1988—91, mem. mineral acquisition and distbn. subcom. 1989—90, mem. phys. properties of Earth materials com., tectonophysics section 1989—91, mem. mineral physics com. 1990—92, mem. 75th anniversary com. 1992—94, mem. meetings com. 1992—96, mem. mineral and rock physics com. 2000—03, mineral physics editor for EOS trans. 1990—92, editor-in-chief, frontiers in mineral physics 1988). Office: Lunar & Planetary Inst USRA Ctr Advanced Space Studies 3600 Bay Area Blvd Houston TX 77058 Office Phone: 281-486-2128. Business E-Mail: mackwell@lpi.usra.edu.

MACLACHLAN, DOUGLAS LEE, marketing educator; b. Hollywood, Calif., Aug. 27, 1940; s. Alexander D. and Patricia E. (Culver) MacL.; m. Natalie Bowditch Knauth, July 23, 1966; children: Heather Bowditch, Trevor Douglas. AB in Physics, U. Calif., Berkeley, 1963, MBA, 1965, MA in Stats., 1970, PhD in Bus. Adminstrn., 1971; student, Hastings Sch. Law, 1965—66. Instr. bus. adminstrn. U. Calif., Berkeley, 1969-70; v.p. Hartec Corp., Newport Beach, Calif., 1965-70; from acting asst. prof. to Marion B. Ingersoll endowed prof. mktg. U. Wash., Seattle, 1970—2007, Marion B. Ingersoll endowed prof. mktg., 2007—, chair dept. mktg. and internat. bus., 2006—. Vis. prof. bus. adminstrn. U. Calif., Berkeley, 1974; vis. prof. Institut Europeen des Affaires, Fontainebleau, France, 1982—83, Cath. U. Leuven, Belgium, 1991—92, Koc U., Istanbul, 2001; dir. Univ. Book Store, 1985—2002, 2004—08. Contbr. articles to profl. jours.; mem. editl. bd.: Jour. Mktg. Rsch., 1975-81. Mem. Am. Mktg. Assn. (dir. Puget Sound chpt. 1975-77, 90-91, pres. 1978-79), Informs, Am. Statis. Assn., Assn. Consumer Rsch., Clan MacLachlan Soc. (pres. n.w. br. 1995—2009), Alpha Kappa Psi, Kappa Delta Rho, Beta Gamma Sigma. Home: 16305 Inglewood Rd NE Kenmore WA 98028-3908 Office: U Washington Box 353200 Seattle WA 98195-3200 Office Phone: 206-543-4369.

MACLACHLAN, KYLE, actor; b. Yakima, WA, Feb. 22, 1960; m. Desiree Gruber, Apr. 20, 2002; 1 child, Callum. BFA, U. Wash., 1982. Actor: (films) Dune, 1984, Blue Velvet, 1986, The Hidden, 1987, Don't Tell Her It's Me, 1990, The Doors, 1991, Twin Peaks: Fire Walk with Me, 1992, Where the Day Takes You, 1992, Rich in Love, 1993, The Trial, 1993, The Flintstones, 1994, Showgirls, 1995, The Trigger Effect, 1996, Mad Dog Time, 1996, One Night Stand, 1997, Hamlet, 1999, Perfume, 2001, Me Without You, 2001, Miranda, 2002, Northfork, 2003, Touch of Pink, 2004, (voice) Free Jimmy, 2006, (voice) Justice League: The New Frontier, 2008; TV series Twin Peaks, 1990-91 (Golden Globe award, 1991), Sex and the City, 2000-02, In Justice, 2006, Desperate Housewives, 2006-; TV movies: Against the Wall, 1994, Roswell, 1994, Moonshine Highway, 1996, Thunder Point, 1996, Route 9, 1998, The Spring, 2000, Jo, 2002, Mysterious Island, 2005; dir. (TV series) Tales from the Crypt, 1989; TV guest appearance Miami Vice, 1988. Address: Industry Entertainment Ste 300 955 S Carrillo Dr Los Angeles CA 90048 also: ICM 8942 Wilshire Blvd Beverly Hills CA 90211

MACLAINE, SHIRLEY, actress; b. Richmond, Va., Apr. 24, 1934; d. Ira O. and Kathlyn (MacLean) Beatty; m. Steve Parker, Sept. 17, 1954 (div. 1982); 1 child, Stephanie Sachiko. Broadway appearances include Me and Juliet, 1953, Pajama Game, 1954; actress (films) The Trouble With Harry, 1954, Artists and Models, 1954, Around the World in 80 Days, 1955-56, Hot Spell, 1957, The Matchmaker, 1957, The Sheepman, 1957, Some Came Running, 1958 (Fgn. Press award 1959), Ask Any Girl, 1959 (Silver Bear award as best actress Internat. Berlin Film Festival), Career, 1959, Can-Can, 1959, The Apartment, 1959 (Best Actress prize Venice Film Festival), Children's Hour, 1960, The Apartment, 1960, Two for the Seesaw, 1962, Irma La Douce, 1963, What A Way to Go, The Yellow Rolls Royce, 1964, John Goldfarb Please Come Home, 1965, Gambit and Woman Times Seven, 1967, The Bliss of Mrs. Blossom, Sweet Charity, 1969, Two Mules for Sister Sara, 1969, Desperate Characters, 1971, The Possession of Joel Delaney, 1972, The Other Half of the Sky: A China Memoir, 1975, The Turning Point, 1977, Being There, 1979, A Change of Seasons, 1980, Loving Couples, 1980, Terms of Endearment, 1983 (Acad. award for Best Actress, 1984, Golden Globe award for Best Actress), Cannonball Run II, 1984, Madame Sousatzka, 1988 (Best Actress Venice Film Festival, Golden Globe-Best Actress), Steel Magnolias, 1989, Waiting For the Light, 1990, Postcards From the Edge, 1990, Defending Your Life, 1991, Used People, 1992, Wrestling Ernest Hemingway, 1993, Guarding Tess, 1994, Evening Star, 1995, Mrs. Winterbourne, 1996, Carolina, 2003, Bewitched, 2005, In Her Shoes, 2005, Rumor Has It..., 2005, Closing the Ring, 2007; (TV appearances) Shirley's World, 1971-72, Shirley MacLaine: If They Could See Me Now, 1974-75, Gypsy in My Soul, 1975-76, Where Do We Go From Here?, 1976-77, Shirley MacLaine at the Lido, 1979, Shirley MacLaine...Every Little Movement, 1980 (Emmy award 1980), (TV movies) Out On A Limb, 1987, The West Side Waltz, 1995, Joan of Arc, 1999, These Old Broads, 2001, Hell on Heels: The Battle of Mary Kay, 2002, (TV mini-series) Salem Witch Trials, 2002; (directorial debut) Bruno, 2000; co-dir. documentary: China The Other Half of the Sky; star U.S. tour stage musical Out There Tonight, 1990; author: Don't Fall Off the Mountain, 1970, The New Celebrity Cookbook, 1973, You Can Get There From Here, 1975, Out on a Limb, 1983, Dancing in the Light, 1985, It's All in the Playing, 1987, Going Within: A Guide for Inner Transformation, 1989, Dance While You Can, 1991, My Lucky Stars: A Hollywood Memoir, 1995, The Camino: A Journey of the Spirit, 2000, Out On A Leash: Exploring The Nature of Reality and Love, 2003, Sage-ing While Age-ing, 2007; editor: McGovern: The Man and His Beliefs, 1972 Address: C/O ICM 8942 Wilshire Blvd Beverly Hills CA 90211-1934*

MACLAREN, ROY, retired Canadian government official; b. Vancouver, BC, Can., Oct. 26, 1934; s. Wilbur and Anne (Graham) MacLaren; m. Alethea Mitchell, June 25, 1959; children: Ian, Vanessa, Malcolm. BA, U. B.C., 1955; MA, U. Cambridge, Eng., 1957; postgrad., Harvard U., 1974; MDiv, U. Toronto, 1991, DCL (hon.), 1996; DHL (hon.), U. N. Ala.; LLD (hon.), U. N.B., U. P.E.I. Fgn. svc. officer Can. Diplomatic Svc., 1957-69; dir. corp. pub. affairs Massey-Ferguson Ltd., Toronto, Ont., 1969-74; chmn., CEO Ogilvy & Mather, Toronto, 1974-76; chmn. C.B. Media Ltd., 1976-93; mem. Parliament of Can., 1979-84, 88-96, parliamentary sec. to min. of energy, mines and resources, 1980-82, min. of state (fin.), 1983-84, min. of natl. revenue, 1984, min. of internat. trade, 1993-96; high commr. for Can. to U.K. of Gt. Britain and No. Ireland, 1996-2000; ret., 2000. Bd. dirs. Brookfield, Algoma Ctrl., Seaway Maritime Transport, Pacific Safety Products. Author: (book) Canadians in Russia: 1918-19, 1976, Canadians on the Nile, 1882-1898, 1978, Canadians Behind Enemy Lines, 1939-1945, 1981, Honourable Mentions, 1986, African Exploits: The Diaries of William Stairs, 1998, Commissions High, 2006; contbr. articles to profl. jours. Commr. Trilateral Commn.; chmn. Can. Inst. Internat. Affairs, Can.-India Bus. Coun., Atlantic Coun., Can. Europe Bus. Round Table; coun. mem. Internat. Inst. Strategic Studies, Ditchley Found. Former hon. col. 7th Toronto Rgt. Royal Can. Arty. Mem.: Pratt's (London), White's (London), Rideau Club (Ottawa), Toronto Club, Royal Can. Yacht Club. Address: 425 Russell Hill Rd Toronto ON Canada M5P 2S4

MACLAREN, WILLIAM GEORGE, JR., engineering executive; b. Chgo., May 6, 1928; s. William George, Sr. and Dorothy Pauline (Costello) MacLaren; m. Marie Lorraine Logan, Sept. 15, 1951 (div. Dec. 1977); children: Vanessa Ann MacLaren-Wray, Jon Mark, Scott William; m. Mary Patricia Loftus, Dec. 22, 1977 (div. Oct. 1995); m. Brigitte Hildegard Krakau, Apr. 19, 1997. BS in Indsl. Engring., U. Pitts., 1951; MS in Indsl. Engring., Syracuse U., NYC, 1958; PhD in Indsl. Mgmt., Columbia Pacific U., 1989. Commd. 2nd lt. USAF, 1951, advanced through grades to major gen., 1974; comdr. 5BW Minot AFB, ND, 1972-74; chief of staff 15 AF, 1975; comdr. Pacific Comm. Area, 1975-78; vice comdr. Air Force Comm. Command, 1978-79; dir. Command Control and Comm. Hdqs. USAF, 1979-81; dir. Comm. and Info. Sys. NATO, 1981-84; ret. USAF, 1984; v.p. Gia, Inc., Arlington, Va., 1984-90, 93-95; dir. gen. NATO/NATO Air Command and Control Mgmt. Agy., Brussels, 1990-93; v.p. BEI, Inc., Alexandria, Va., 1995—. Contbr. articles to profl. jours. Regional bd. dirs. Boy Scouts Am., Minot, ND, 1972—74. Named Disting. Engring. Alumnus, U. Pitts., 1986. Mem.: AIAA, Inst. Indsl. Engrs., Am. Def. Preparedness Assn., Armed Forces Comm. and Electronics Assn. (regional v.p. 1975—78, Gold medal 1983), Air Force Assn., Rotary, Order of Daedalians (chpt. pres. 1976—78, merit award 1979). Republican. Avocations: golf, bicycling, flying. Office: SAIC 1800 Diagonal Rd Ste 430 Alexandria VA 22314-2840 Home: 91 Clark Ct Dover DE 19901 Home Phone: 302-697-8975. Personal E-mail: wilmack@aol.com.

MACLAUGHLIN, DOUGLAS EARL, physicist, educator; b. Indiana, Pa., Nov. 18, 1938; s. William Donald and Mary Elizabeth (Prugh) MacL.; m. Catherine Elizabeth Graff, Mar. 2, 1967; 1 dau., Elizabeth Teresa. AB, Amherst Coll., 1960; PhD, U. Calif., Berkeley, 1966. NATO post-doctoral fellow Atomic Energy Research Establishment, Harwell, Eng., 1966-67; research asso. Faculte des Sciences, U. Paris, Orsay, 1967-69, U. Amsterdam, 1978, 80, 83; asst. prof. physics U. Calif., Riverside, 1969-73, assoc. prof., 1973-78, prof., 1978—2006, rsch. prof., 2006—, vice chmn. dept., 1976-81, 87-88. Vis. staff Los Alamos Nat. Lab., 1980—; vis. scholar Los Alamos Nat. Lab., 1997-98; vis. lectr. Kyoto U., 2005; vis. scientist MPICPS, Dresden, Germany, 2006; rschr. emeritus TRIUMF, Vancouver, Can., 2007-. Fellow: Am. Phys. Soc., AAAS; mem. Phi Beta Kappa, Sigma Xi. Office: Univ Calif Dept Physics and Astronomy Riverside CA 92521-0413

MACLAUGHLIN, FRANCIS JOSEPH, lawyer; b. Davenport, Iowa, Oct. 5, 1933; s. Francis Joseph and Sylvia (Boone) MacL.; m. Joan Elizabeth Pfeiffer, Oct. 17, 1959; children: Lisa Ann, Christine Ann, Francis Joseph BA, Yale U., 1955; JD, U. Mich., 1958. Bar: Ill. 1958, Calif. 1963. Assoc. Graham, Califf, Harper & Benson, Moline, Ill., 1958-59, Lillick, McHose & Charles, LA, 1963-70, ptnr., 1970-90, White and Case, 1990—97. Lt. USN, 1959—63. Mem. ABA, Calif. Bar Assn., Los Angeles County Bar Assn., Maritime Law Assn. U.S. Republican. Office: White & Case 633 W 5th St Ste 1900 Los Angeles CA 90071-2087 Home Phone: 310-459-2165; Office Phone: 213-553-7900. Personal E-mail: rusty1933@charter.net.

MACLAY, DONALD MERLE, retired lawyer; b. Belleville, Pa., Feb. 16, 1934; s. Robert Barr and Grace Virginia (Royer) M.; m. Nancy Margaret Hixenbaugh, Sept. 13, 1958; children: Susan Jo (dec.), Timothy Dean. AB magna cum laude, Grove City Coll., 1956; LLB, U. Pa., 1961. Bar: D.C. 1968, Pa. 1970. Commd. fgn. svc. officer U.S. Dept. State, 1961; assigned Am. embassy, Cotonou, Dahomey (Benin), 1962-64, Am. Consulate Gen., Frankfurt, Fed. Republic Germany, 1964-66, U.S. Dept. State, Washington, 1966-69; dir. courses of study Am. Law Inst.-ABA Com. on Continuing Profl. Edn., Phila., 1969-87, dep. exec. dir., 1987-99, ret., 1999. Served with U.S. Army, 1956-58. Mem.: Am. Law Inst. Democrat. Presbyterian. Home: 936 Church Rd Springfield PA 19064-3935

MACLAY, SARAH, poet, educator; d. H. Bruce and Mary Blair Maclay. B, Oberlin Coll., Ohio, 1978; MFA n Creative Writing, Vt. Coll., Montpelier, 2002. Lectr. U. So. Calif., LA, 2004; vis. asst. prof. Loyola Marymount U., 2006—. Book rev. editor Poetry Internat., San Diego, 2003—; artistic dir. Third Area: Poetry at Pharmaka, LA, 2008—. Author: (poetry book) Whore (Tampa review prize, 2003), The White Bride (prize, 2008).

MACLEAN, BRIAN W., insurance company executive; Dir. planning Corp. Fin. dept. The Travelers Companies, Inc., St. Paul, 1988, CFO claim services, 1993—96, CFO comml., 1996—99, pres. select accounts, 1999—2002, exec. v.p. claim services, 2002—05, co-COO, 2005, exec. v.p., COO, 2005—08, pres., COO, 2008—. Office: Travelers Cos Inc 385 Washington St Saint Paul MN 55102 Office Phone: 651-310-7911.

MACLEAN, DOUG, former professional hockey coach, former sports team executive; b. Summerside, PEI, Can., Apr. 12, 1954; m. Jill MacLean; children: Clark, Mackenzie. Student, P.E.I.; M in Ednl. Psychology, We. Ont. Asst. coach London Knights of OHL, 1984-85, St. Louis Blues, 1986-87, 87-88, Washington Capitals, 1988-89, 89-90, Detroit Red Wings, 1990-91, asst. gen. mgr., 1992-93, 93-94; gen. mgr. Adirondack, Red Wing orgn., 1992-93, 93-94; dir. player devel., scout Fla. Panthers, 1994-95, head coach, 1995—98; gen. mgr Columbus Blue Jackets, 1998—2007, pres., 1998—2007, head coach, 2003—04.

MACLEAN, JOHN, professional hockey coach, former professional hockey player; b. Oshawa, Ont., Can., Nov. 20, 1964; m. Adrienne MacLean; children: John Carter, Kyle Christopher. Right wing NJ Devils, 1983-97, San Jose Sharks, 1997-98, NY Rangers, 1998—2000, Dallas Stars, 2000—02; asst. coach NJ Devils, 2002—09; head coach Lowell Devils, 2009—. Named to Meml. Cup All-Star team, 1982-83; played in NHL All-Star game, 1989, 91. Achievements include being a member of Stanley Cup Champion New Jersey Devils, 1995; holding the New Jersey Devils franchise record for most points with 701, 1997-2009. Office: Lowell Devils 300 Martin Luther King Jr Way Lowell MA 01852*

MACLEAN, JOHN RONALD, lawyer; b. Pueblo, Colo., Jan. 19, 1938; s. John Ronald and Mary Victoria (Curlin) MacL.; m. Carol Jean Turner, Aug. 18, 1962; children— Leslie Carol, John Ronald. Student, U. Okla., 1956; BS, U.S. Mil. Acad., 1961; JD, Vanderbilt U., 1967. Bar: Tex. 1967; cert. in personal injury trial law Tex. Bd. Legal Splzn. Practicing atty. Turner & MacLean, Cleburne, Tex., 1967-68; county atty. Johnson County, Tex., 1968-76; dist. atty. 18th Jud. Dist. Tex., 1976-84; dist. judge 249th Jud. Dist. Tex., 1984-91; pvt. practice MacLean & Boulware, 1992—. Pres. Johnson County United Fund, 1976 With US Army, 1961—64. Fellow Tex. Bar Found.; mem. Tex. Bar Assn., Johnson County Bar Assn. (pres. 1969), Am. Bd. Trial Advocates (past nat. dir.), Vanderbilt U. Law Sch. Bar Assn. (past pres.), Elks. Democrat. Methodist. Home: 1216 W Westhill Dr Cleburne TX 76033-6021 Office: 11 N Main St Cleburne TX 76033-5543 Office Phone: 817-645-3700.

MAC LEAN, LLOYD DOUGLAS, surgeon; b. Calgary, Alta., Can., June 15, 1924; s. Fred Hugh and Azilda MacL.; m. Eleanor Colle, June 30, 1954; children: Hugh, Charles, Ian, James, Martha. B.Sc. (Viscount Bennett scholar), U. Alta., 1947, MD (Viscount Bennett scholar), 1949; PhD, U. Minn., 1957. Resident U. Minn. Hosp., Mpls., 1950-56; instr. dept. surgery U. Minn., Mpls., 1956-58, asst. prof. surgery, 1958-59, asso. prof., 1959-62; prof. McGill U., Montreal, Que., Canada, 1962—, chmn. dept. surgery, 1968-73, 77-82, 87-88. Surgeon-in-chief Ancker Hosp., St. Paul, 1957-62, Royal Victoria Hosp., Montreal, 1962-88; Edward Archibald prof. surgery McGill U., 1988-93, prof. surgery 1993—. Contbr. numerous articles on surgery, shock, host resistance and transplantation to profl. jours. Decorated officer Order Can. Fellow Royal Soc. Can.; mem. ACS (pres. 1993-94), Am. Surg. Assn. (pres. 1993), Ctrl. Surg. Assn. (pres. 1982-83), Am. Physiol. Soc., Am. Assn. Thoracic and Cardiovasc. Surgery, Soc. Surgery of Alimentary Tract. Home: # 1402-80 Berlioz Montreal PQ Canada H3E 1N9 Personal E-mail: lloydm@vdn.ca.

MACLEAY, THOMAS H., insurance company executive; married; 2 children. Various investment mgmt., corp. planning and fin. positions Nat. Life Group, 1976—91, CFO, 1991, bd. dirs., 1996—, pres., COO, 1996—2001, chmn., pres., CEO, 2001—08, chmn., 2009—. Chmn. Sentinel Group Funds, Inc.; bd. dirs. Chittenden Trust Co., Life Office Mgmt. Assn. Trustee, chmn. fin. com. Air Force Aid Soc.; bd. dirs. Ctrl. Vt. Econ. Devel. Corp. Office: Nat Life Group One National Life Dr Montpelier VT 05604 Office Phone: 800-732-8939.*

MACLEISH, RODERICK, JR., lawyer; b. Boston, Oct. 31, 1952; AB with honors, Vassar Coll., 1975; JD cum laude, Boston U., 1978. Bar: Mass. 1979, US Court Appeals, 1st Cir., US Court Appeals, 11th Cir., US Dist. Ct. for the Dist. Mass. Law clerk to Hon. Joseph L. Tauro US Dist. Ct. Mass., 1978-79; shareholder, atty. Greenberg Traurig, LLP, Boston. Lectr. and guest spkr. in the field. Editor Boston U. Law Rev., 1977-78; contbr.articles to profl. publs. Mem. civil justice adv. bd. US Dist. Ct., 1995; bd. dir. Cotting Sch., Lexington, Mass., 1990—, Internat. Assn. for the Right to Effective Treatment, 1988—92, Greater Boston Legal Svcs., 1988—90; founder, chmn. bd. dirs. The Mass. 9/11 Fund, Inc., 2002; mem. adv. com. Alliance for the Mental Ill of Mass. Inc., 1988—90. Recipient Award for Outstanding Advocacy in a successful 10-yr. pro bono litigation effort on behalf of Bridgewater State Hospital Clients, Alliance for the Mentally Ill of Mass., 1988, Civil Rights award, Mass. Coalition of Families and Advocates for the Retarded, 1997; named one of Top 10 Litigators, Nat. Law Jour., 2003. Fellow: Mass.

Bar Found. Office: Greenberg Traurig LLP One International Pl Boston MA 02110 Office Phone: 617-310-6000. Office Fax: 617-310-6001. Business E-Mail: macleishr@gtlaw.com.

MACLELLAN, STEVE, bank executive; Attended, Ariz. State U., 1978—80. CEO pvt. client svcs. J.P. Morgan Chase & Co., Bank One, J.P. Morgan Chase; nat. dir. wealth adv. svcs. Northern Trust, Chgo., CEO SW region Phoenix, 2009—.*

MACLENNAN, BERYCE WINIFRED, psychologist; b. Aberdeen, Scotland, Mar. 14, 1920; came to U.S., 1949, naturalized, 1965; d. William and Beatrice (MacRae) Mellis; m. John Duncan MacLennan, Nov. 29, 1944. BSc with honors, London Sch. Econs., 1947; PhD, London U., 1960. Diplomate Am. Bd. Clin. Psychology, cert. group therapist, trauma specialist. Group psychotherapist, youth specialist cons., NYC and Washington, 1949-63; dir. Ctr. for Prevention Juvenile Delinquency and New Careers, Washington, 1963-66; sect. chief NIMH, Mental Health Study Ctr., Adelphi, Md., 1967-70, chief, 1971-74; regional adminstr. Mass. Dept. Mental Health, Springfield, 1974-75; sr. mental health adv. GAO, Washington, 1976-90; pvt. practice, specialist psychotherapy Bethesda, Md., 1990—. Clin. prof. George Washington U., 1970-2002; group therapy cons. DC Mental Health Svcs., 1993-2002, Washington Assessement and Therapy Svcs., 1992-2006; lectr. Montgomery CC, 1988-91, Washington Sch. Psychiatry Geropsychiatric Program, 1997—; tech. adv. com. Prince George's County Mental Health Assn., 1968-84; cons. Washington Bus. Group on Health, 1990-91, KOBA, 1991; leader Trauma Psychotherapy Groups, 2002-03, Hebrew Home Rsch. Inst. Elder Housing Socialization and Memory Improvement Groups, 2000-02. Mem. NIMH Prevention Intervention Rsch. Task Force, 1990-91, Montgomery County Victims Assistance Programs, 1990-95; v.p. Compliance, Federally Employed Women, 1979-81; pres. Glenecho chpt. Older Women's League, 1993-94; mem. Montgomery County Disaster Outreach Team, 2004—. Fellow APA; disting. fellow Am. Group Psychotherapy Assn. Democrat.

MACLENNAN, DAVID HERMAN, research scientist, educator; b. Swan River, Man., Can., July 3, 1937; s. Douglas Henry and Sigridur (Sigurdson) MacL.; m. Linda Carol Vass, Aug. 18, 1965; children: Jessica Lynn (dec.), Jeremy Douglas, Jonathan David. BSA, U. Man., 1959; MS, Purdue U., 1961, PhD, 1963; DSc (hon.), U. Man., 2001. Postdoctoral fellow Inst. Enzyme Research, U. Wis., Madison, 1963-64; asst. prof. U. Wis., Madison, 1964-68; assoc. prof. U. Toronto, 1969-74, prof., 1974-93, J.W. Billes prof. med. rsch., 1987—2007, Univ. prof., 1993—, acting chmn., 1978-80, chmn., 1980-90; prin. investigator Can. Genetic Diseases Network Ctrs. Excellence, 1991—2006. Med. adv. bd. Muscular Dystrophy Assn. Can., 1976-87; scientists' rev. panel Med. Rsch. Coun. Can., 1988-90; chmn. molecular biology and pathology grants com. Heart and Stroke Found. Can., 1995-99; rsch. rev. panel U. Ottawa Heart Inst., 1991-95; med. rev. panel Gairdner Found., 1999-2001, med. adv. bd., 2001-2005; cons. Merck, Sharp and Dohme, West Point, Pa., 1992-98. Assoc. editor Can. Jour. Biochemistry, 1972-76; mem. editl. bd. Jour. Biol. Chemistry, 1975-80, 82-87; contbr. articles on muscle membrane biochemistry to profl. jours. Decorated Officer Order of Can., 2001, Order of Ont., 2008; recipient Gairdner Found. Internat. award, 1991; Can. Med. Rsch. Coun. scholar, 1969-71, I.W. Killam Meml. scholar, 1977-78; recipient I.W. Killam Meml. prize Health Scis., 1997, Jonas Salk award Ont. March of Dimes, 1998, Salute to the City award, City of Toronto, 2002, Rick Gallop award Heart and Stroke Found. Ont., 2002; fellow Internat. Soc. Heart Rsch., 2001. Fellow Royal Soc. Can., Royal Soc. London (Glaxo-Wellcome prize 2000), NAS (fgn. assoc.); mem. Can. Biochem. Soc. (Ayerst award 1974), Am. Soc. Biol. Chemists, Biophys. Soc. (Nat. Lectr. award 1990), Japanese Biochem. Soc. (hon.). Office: U Toronto-Banting & Best Med Rsch 112 College St Toronto ON Canada M5G 1L6 Home: 292 Airdrie Rd Toronto ON Canada M4G 1N3 E-mail: david.maclennan@utoronto.ca.

MACLEOD, GLEN GARY, language educator; b. Berea, Ohio, Oct. 10, 1948; s. William and Laura (Hall) MacL. BA, Wesleyan U., 1971; MA, Princeton U., 1978, PhD, 1981. From instr. to asst. prof. English Southampton Coll. L.I. Univ., Southampton, N.Y., 1980-83; from asst. prof. to prof. English U. Conn., Waterbury, 1983—. Mem. editl. bd. Paideuma, The Wallace Stevens Jour., William Carlos Williams Rev. Author: Wallace Stevens and Company, 1983, Wallace Stevens and Modern Art, 1993. NEH fellow, 1983; Huntington Libr. fellow, San Marino, Calif., 1984; Getty fellow, 1987-88.Boston Athenaeum fellow, 2002-03 Mem. MLA, AAUP, Am. Lit. Assn., Wallace Stevens Soc., William Carlos Williams Soc. Office: U Conn 99 E Main St Waterbury CT 06702-2311

MACLEOD, GORDON C., surgeon; b. Quincy, Mass., July 12, 1930; AB, Harvard U., Cambridge, Mass., 1952, MD, 1956. Diplomate Am. Bd. Surgery. Intern Madigan Army Hosp., Tacoma, 1956-57; resident Brigham-Childrens Hosps., Boston, 1957-59; surg. resident Boston Univ. Hosps., Boston, 1959-61; staff surgeon USAF Hosp., Tachi-Kawa AB, Japan, 1961-64, surgeon Westover AFB, Mass., 1964-68, David Grant USAF Med. Ctr., Calif., 1968-74; chmn. surgery USAF Med. Ctr., Scott AFB, Ill., 1974-76; active staff Washington Hosp., Fremont, Calif., 1976—2002, med. dir. oper. rm., 1998-2000. Instr. surgery Boston U., 1960-61; instr. U. Calif., Davis, 1969-71, asst. clin. prof. surgery, 1971-74; with US Air Force, 1956-76, colonel. Mem. ACS, AMA. Business E-Mail: gcmacleodmd56@post.harvard.edu.

MACLEOD, HUGH ANGUS MCINTOSH, optical science educator, physicist, consultant; b. Glasgow, Scotland, June 20, 1933; came to U.S., 1979; s. John and Agnes (Maclure) M.; m. Ann Turner, May 25, 1957; children: Hugh, Ivor, Charles, Eleanor, Alexander. BSc with honors, U. Glasgow, 1954; D of Tech., Coun. for Nat. Acad. Awards, 1979; D honoris causa, U. Aix-Marseille, 1997. Chartered physicist. Grad. apprentice Sperry Gyroscope Co. Ltd., Brentford, Eng., 1954-56, engr., 1956-60; chief engr. Williamson Mfg. Co. Ltd., London, 1961-62; sr. physicist Mervyn Instruments Ltd., Woking, Eng., 1963; tech. mgr. Sir Howard Grubb Parsons & Co. Ltd., Newcastle upon Tyne, Eng., 1964-70; reader in thin-film physics Newcastle upon Tyne Poly., 1971-79; assoc. prof. U. Aix-Marseille III, France, 1979; prof. optical scis. U. Ariz., Tucson, 1979-95, prof. emeritus, 1995—; pres. Thin Film Ctr., Inc., Tucson, 1992—; dir. Precision Optics Corp., Inc., 1997—2002. Author: Thin-Film Optical Filters, 2001; editor Jour. Modern Optics, London, 1988-93; contbr. over 200 articles to profl. jours., chpts. to books. Recipient John Matteucci award, Assn. Indsl. Metallizers, Coaters and Laminators, 2000, Life for Thin Film award, European Vacuum Coaters Workshop, 2004. Fellow Inst. Physics (London), Optical Soc. Am. (dir.-at-large 1987-89, Esther Hoffman Beller award 1997), SPIE-Internat. Soc. Optical Engring. (Gold medal 1987), Am. Vacuum Soc., Soc. Vacuum Coaters (Nathaniel H. Sugerman Meml. award 2002). Anglican. Avocation: piano. Home: 2745 E Via Rotunda Tucson AZ 85716-5227 Office: Thin Film Ctr Inc 2745 E Via Rotonda Tucson AZ 85716-5227 Business E-Mail: angus@thinfilmcenter.com.

MACLEOD, JOHN AMEND, lawyer; b. Manila, June 5, 1942; s. Anthony Macaulay and Dorothy Lillian (Amend); m. Ann Klee; children: Kerry, Jack. BBA, U. Notre Dame, 1963, JD, 1969. Bar: D.C. 1969, U.S. Supreme Ct. 1980. Assoc. Jones, Day, Reavis & Pogue, Washington, 1969-73, ptnr., 1974-79, Crowell & Moring LLP, Washington, 1979—. Mem. mgmt. com., 1979-82, 83-86, 91-94, 99-2000, 00-06, chmn.firm, 1984-85, 93-94., 2000-06, chmn. emeritus, 2006—. Editor-in-chief Notre Dame Law Rev., 1968-69; contbr. articles to profl. jours. Trustee Energy Mineral and Law Found., 1979—2002; bd. dirs. St. Francis Ctr., 1982—91, Notre Dame Law Assn., 1981—86. Served to lt. US Army, 1963—65. Recipient disting. mining lawyer award Nat. Mining Assn., 1995, forest industry victory of yr. award Am. Forest and Paper Assn., 1994. Mem. ABA, D.C. Bar Assn., Ptnrs. Leadership Forum, Metro. Club (Washington). Home: 4040 Swartz Rd Maurertown VA 22644-2320 Office: Crowell & Moring LLP 1001 Pennsylvania Ave NW Washington DC 20004-2595

MACLEOD, ROBERT ANGUS, retired microbiology educator, researcher; b. Athabasca, Alta., Can., July 13, 1921; s. Norman John and Eleonora Pauline Bertha (Westerhoff) MacL.; m. Patricia Rosemarie Robertson, Sept. 1, 1948; children: Douglas John, Alexander Robert, Kathleen Mary, David Gordon, Michael Norman, Susan Joan BA with honors in Chemistry, U. B.C., Vancouver, Can., 1943, MA in Chemistry and Biology, 1945; PhD in Biochemistry, U. Wis., Madison, 1949. Asst. prof. Queen's U., Kingston, Ont., Canada, 1949-52; sr. biochemist Fisheries Research Bd. Can., Vancouver, B.C., 1952-60; assoc. prof. to prof., chmn. dept. microbiology Macdonald Coll., McGill U., Ste. Anne de Bellevue, Que., Canada, 1960-86, prof. emeritus, 1986—. Cons. Def. Research Bd., Ottawa, Ont., 1965—75; assoc. editor Can. Jour. Microbiology, Ottawa, 1965—70. Author tech. papers. Recipient Harrison prize, Royal Soc. Can., 1960. Fellow: Royal Soc. Can.; mem.: Am. Soc. Microbiology (hon.), Can. Soc. Microbiologists (hon.; pres. 1976—77, award 1973). Avocations: swimming, fishing. Home: 10 Slate St Stittsville ON Canada K2S 1Y5

MACLEOD, WENDY, playwright, performing arts educator; d. Duncan Raasay and Marcella Teresa MacLeod; m. K. Read Baldwin, Aug. 11, 1990; children: Foss Kinloch Baldwin, Avery Duncan Baldwin. BA magna cum laude, Kenyon Coll., Gambier, Ohio, 1981; MFA, Yale Sch. Drama, New Haven, Conn., 1987. James E. Michael playwright-inresdience Kenyon Coll., Gambier, Ohio; vis. prof. film and theater Northwestern, Evanston, Ill., 2003. Author: (plays) Birnham Woods, Things Being What They Are, Juvenilia, The Water Children, Sin, Schoolgirl Figure, The House of Yes, Apocalyptic Butterflies, The Shallow End and The Lost Colony. Mem.: Writers Guild, East, New Dramatists, Dramatists Guild. Office: Kenyon Coll Dept Dance and Drama Gambier OH 43022 Office Fax: 740-427-5235.

MACLEOD, WILLIAM BENTLEY, economics, law professor; b. Iserlohn, Germany, 1954; came to U.S., 1995; m. Raisa Nones (div.); children: Raisa, Gabriela; m. Janet Marion Currie, May 18, 1997; children: Joana, Daniel. BA magna cum laude, Queen's U., Kingston, Ont., Can., 1975, MSc in Math., 1979; PhD in Econs., U. B.C., Vancouver, Can., 1984. From asst. prof. to assoc. prof. Queen's U., 1982-90; assoc. prof. U. Montreal, 1990-92, prof. econs., 1992-96, Boston Coll., 1996-97; prof. econs. and law U. So. Calif., LA, 1997—2006, dir. Ctr. for Law, Econs. and Orgn., 1997—2006, chair jr. recruiting, 2000—03; program dir., personnel and behavioral econs. IZA, Bonn, Germany, 2003—07; prof. dept. economics, SIPA & law sch. Columbia U., NY, 2005—; rsch. assoc. WBER, 2007—; co-dir., chair jr. recruiting Columbia U., 2005—06. Cons. Ind. Power Prodrs. Ont., Toronto, 1990-92, Human Resources Can., Ottawa, Ont., 1993-95; Harold Innis Meml. lectr., 1996; vis. prof. econs. and law Calif. Inst. Tech., 2002, Princeton U., 2003-04; bd. dirs. We. Econs. Assn. Assoc. editor: Jour. Econ. Behavior and Orgn., 2002—; editor: Jour. Labor Econs., 2003—; contbr. articles to profl. jours. NSF grantee, 1997-03, 06-. Fellow Econometric Soc.; mem. AAAS, Am. Econs. Assn., Soc. Labor Economists (H. Gregg Lewis prize 2002), Assn. Comparative Sys., Econ. Sci. Assn., Am. Law and Econs. Assn.(bd. dir. 2009-), Western Econs. Assn. (bd. dirs. 2003-06). Office: Columbia U Dept Econs MC3308 420 W 118th St New York NY 10027-7296

MACLIN, TODD (SAMUEL TODD MACLIN), diversified financial services company executive; b. Tex., 1956; BBA, U. Tex., 1978; MBA, U. Houston. Joined Chem. NY Corp., 1980; with Chem. Banking Corp., Chase Manhattan Corp.; exec. v.p. J.P. Morgan Chase & Co., chmn., CEO Tex. Region and head mid. market banking, then head comml. banking, 2004—. Advisory dir. Better Bus. Bur.; mem. advisory coun. McCombs Sch. Bus., U. Tex. Mem.: Young Presidents Orgn. Office: JP Morgan Chase & Co 270 Park Ave New York NY 10017-2070*

MAC LOW, MORDECAI-MARK, astrophysicist; b. NYC, Mar. 9, 1963; s. Jackson Mac Low and Iris Lezak. BA, Princeton U., 1983; PhD, U. Colo., 1989. Rsch. asst. U. Colo., Boulder, 1983—88; NRC fellow NASA Ames Rsch. Ctr., Moffett Field, Calif., 1989-90; rsch. assoc. U. Calif., Berkeley, 1991-92, U. Chgo., 1992-95; sci. Max-Planck-Inst. für Astronomie, Heidelberg, Germany, 1995-99, vis. sci., 2007, Zentrum für Astronomie der U., Heidelberg, 2007; asst. curator of astrophysics Am. Mus. Natural History, NYC, 1999—2002, assoc. curator astrophysics, 2002—07, curator-in-charge dept. astrophysics, 2005—, chair divsn. phys. scis., 2007—, curator astrophysics, 2007—. Adj. asst. prof. Columbia U., 1999—2002, adj. assoc. prof., 2003—07, adj. prof., 2007—; mem. grant rev. panels NSF and NASA, chair panels; mem. adv. com. tchr. renewal for urban sci. tchg. program Am. Mus. Natural History and CUNY, 2003—07; mem. several conf. sci. organizing coms.; spkr. in field; reviewer in field; lead curator Hayden Planetarium Space Show. Contbr. articles to popular mags. and profl. jours. Grantee, NSF, 1999—, NASA, 1999—. Mem.: Internat. Astron. Union, Am. Phys. Soc., Am. Astron. Soc. (mem. com. employment 2001—04). Office: Am Mus Natural History Dept Astrophysics CPW & 79th St New York NY 10024-5192 Home Phone: 212-932-2639. Business E-Mail: mordecai@amnh.org.

MACMEEKEN, JOHN PEEBLES, foundation executive, educator; b. Aug. 15, 1924; s. John West and Esther (Strong) M.; m. Mary Swanberg, Nov. 26, 1949; children: Carol B. Macmeeken Luther, John W., Susan G. Student, U. Calif., Berkeley, 1941-43, Ind. U., 1943-44; JD, Harvard U., 1948. Bar: Calif. 1948. Assoc. Chickering & Gregory, San Francisco, 1948-60, ptnr., 1960-82, Pettit & Martin, San Francisco, 1982-93; v.p. Zynk Indsl. Corp., 1995-98; pres. Found. for Books to China, 1993—, SOAR Bus. Inst., 1998—2008. Bd. dirs. Lanark West Corp.; pres. Clinton U., San Francisco, 1995-97; lectr. law Fudan U., Shanghai, China, East China Normal U., Shanghai, Nanking U., China, Zhongshan U., Guangzhou; sec. Twan Co. LLC, Sian Tien Dao Yuan. Sgt. U.S. Army, 1943-45. Mem. Nat. Com. on US-China Rels., Calif. Bar Assn., Outlook Club Calif. Republican. Congregationalist. Home: 5708 Glenbrook Dr Oakland CA 94618-1724 Office Phone: 510-428-2145. Personal E-mail: jmacmeeken@aol.com.

MACMILLAN, ROBERT SMITH, electronics engineer; b. LA, Aug. 28, 1924; s. Andrew James and Moneta (Smith) M.; m. Barbara Macmillan, Aug. 18, 1962; 1 child, Robert G. BS in Physics, Calif. Inst. Tech., 1948, MS in Elec. Engring., 1949, PhD in Elec. Engring./Physics cum laude, 1954. Rsch. engr. Jet Propulsion Lab., Calif. Inst. Tech., Pasadena, 1951-55, asst. prof. elec. engring., 1955-58; assoc. prof. elec. engring. U. So. Calif., LA, 1958-70; mem. sr. tech. staff Litton Sys., Inc., Van Nuys, Calif., 1969-79; dir. sys. engring. Litton Data Command Sys., Agoura Hills, Calif., 1979-89; pres. The Macmillan Group, La Canada Flintridge, Calif., 1989—. Treas., v.p. Video Color Corp., Inglewood, 1965-66; cons. fgn. tech. div. USAF, Wright-Patterson AFB, Ohio, 1957-74, Space Tech. Labs., Glendale, Calif., 1956-60, Space Gen. Corp., El Monte, Calif., 1960-63. With Air Corps US Army, 1943—46. Recipient Nat. Patriot's medal, Nat. Rifle Assn., 2002, Rep. Senatorial medal of freedom, 2004. Mem.: IEEE, Am. Phys. Soc., Am. Inst. Physics, Eta Kappa Nu, Tau Beta Pi, Sigma Xi. Republican. Presbyterian. Achievements include research in ionospheric, radio-wave, propagation; very low frequency radio-transmitting antennas; optical coherence and statistical optics. Home: 350 Starlight Crest Dr La Canada Flintridge CA 91011-2839 Office: The Macmillan Group 350 Starlight Crest Dr La Canada Flintridge CA 91011-2839 Home Phone: 818-790-4809; Office Phone: 818-790-4809. Office Fax: 818-952-1735. Personal E-mail: rsmacmillan08@aol.com.

MACMILLAN, STEPHEN P., health products executive; b. July 19, 1963; married; 2 children. BA in econ., Davidson Coll.; grad. advanced mgmt. program, Harvard Bus. Sch. Various mktg. positions Procter & Gamble; with over the counter div. McNeil Consumer and Specialty Pharm. Johnson & Johnson Corp., mktg. dir. J&J/Merck over-the-counter franchise worldwide England; mgr. dir. Johnson & Johnson MSD (Merck), England, 1995; v.p., mktg. and profl. sales McNeil Consumer and Splty. Pharm. Johnson & Johnson Corp., 1997; pres. Johnson & Johnson-Merck Consumer Pharmaceuticals; sector v.p. global splty. ops. Pharmacia & Upjohn, 1999—2003; COO Stryker Corp., 2004—05, pres., CEO, 2005—. Office: Stryker Corp 2725 Fairfield Rd Kalamazoo MI 49002*

MACMILLEN, RICHARD EDWARD, biological sciences educator, researcher; b. Upland, Calif., Apr. 19, 1932; s. Hesper Nichols and Ruth Henrietta (Golder) MacM.; m. Ann Gray, June 12, 1953 (div. 1975); children: Jennifer Kathleen, Douglas Michael; m. Barbara Jean Morgan, Oct. 23, 1980; 1 child, Ian Richard. BA, Pomona Coll., Claremont, Calif., 1954; MS, U. Mich., 1956; PhD, UCLA, 1961. From instr. to assoc. prof. Pomona Coll., Claremont, Calif., 1960-68, Wig Disting. prof., 1965; assoc. prof., then prof. U. Calif., Irvine, 1968—, chair dept. population and environ. biology, 1972-74, chair dept. ecology and evolutionary biology, 1984-90, prof. emeritus, 1993—. Award panel NSF, Washington, 1976-80; coord. U. Calif. Multi-Campus Supercourse in Environ. Biology, White Mountain Rsch. Sta., 1996-97, tchg. participant, 1998—; rev. panel, EPA Star grad. fellowship program, 2002, 04; budget com., Jackson County Fire Dist. 5, 2001—; Alumni Admissions vol., Pomona Coll., 2001—; SMART vol. Talent Elem. Sch., 2007-; vol. morphologist US Fish and Wildlife Svc. Forensics Lab., 2004—. Contbr. numerous articles to profl. jours; co-author: (with Barbara MacMillen) Meandering in the Bush: Natural History Explorations Outback Australia, 2007, 2nd edit., 2009. Chair sci. adv. bd. Endangered Habitats League, 1991-93. Recipient Rsch. award NSF, 1961-83; Fulbright-Hays Advanced Rsch. fellow Monash U., Australia, 1966-67. Fellow AAAS; mem. Am. Soc. Mammalogists (life), Ecol. Soc. Am. (cert. sr. ecologist), Am. Ornithologists Union (life), Cooper Ornithol. Soc. (life, bd. dirs. 1982-84). Democrat. Avocations: fly fishing, camping, hiking, nature photography. Home: 705 Foss Rd Talent OR 97540-9758 Home Phone: 541-512-9884. Business E-Mail: bidmac@jeffnet.org. *As world human populations continue to increase, our natural world continues to degrade. It is incumbent upon all of us to accept the responsibility of stewarding our land and its biota as precious and renewable resources.*

MACMINN, RICHARD DEAN, finance educator; b. Vancouver, Wash., Sept. 5, 1946; s. James Lewis and Lola Alice (Merritt) MacM.; m. Carole Ann Grimm, June 22, 1969; children: Sarah, Mark. BA, UCLA, 1967; MA, U. Ill., 1973, PhD, 1978. Asst. prof. econs. SUNY-Binghamton 1977-81; asst. prof. finance U. Tex.-Austin, 1981-85, assoc. prof. fin. 1986-87, Ambassador Edward A. Clark fellow; vis. prof. U. Mo., Columbia, 1987-88; assoc. prof. U. Tex., Austin, 1988—. Contbr. articles to profl. jours. Served to capt. USAF, 1967-71. Recipient research awards U. Tex., 1983, 84, 85. 86. Mem. Am. Econ. Assn., Am. Fin. Assn., Am. Risk and Ins. Assn. Presbyterian. Avocations: reading, running, racquetball, tennis. Office: Illinois State U Katie School Normal IL 61790 Personal E-mail: richard@macminn.org. Business E-Mail: richard.macminn@ilstu.edu.

MACMULLEN, NANCY JANE, critical care nurse, department chairman; d. Oliver H. and Susan A. Olson; m. Michael W. MacMullen; children: Michael H., Susan M. Williams, John P., Thomas C., Christopher P. BSN, Loyola U., Chgo., 1965, MSN, 1979, PhD, 1991. Cert. high risk obstetrics nurse, Nat. Certification Corp., 1993, nurse, Nat. League Nursing, 2009. Interim chairperson, nursing Govs. State U., U. Pk., Ill., 2007—. Contbr. articles to sci. jours. Interim v.p. CAAN Acad., Richton Pk., Ill., 2007—. Mem.: Sigma Theta Tau (pres. 2007—). Home: 5948 Liberty Sq Oak Forest IL 60452 Office: Govs State Univ 1 University Pky Oak Forest IL 60452 Office Fax: 708-235-2197. Business E-Mail: n-macmullen@govst.edu.

MACNAB, ALISTAIR MURDOCH, retired writer; s. Alexander Thom Macnab and Margaret Helen Murdoch; m. Mary Ann Maguire, July 31, 1976; children: Katriona Maura, James Alexander, Thomas Andrew. MS in Maritime Sci. (hon.), Royal Coll. Sci. & Tech., Glasgow, Scotland, 1963. Cert. Brit. Ministry Transport, 1963. Cadet to captain in command Bank Line Ltd, London, 1953—68; owner's USA rep. Andrew Weir Shipping, London, 1968—81; dir. logistics Maurice Pincoffs Co., Houston, 1993—98; pres. Greater Houston Port Bur., 1998—2007; self employed writer RVW Productions LLC, Houston, 2000—; adj. lectr. U. Houston Downtown, 2007—. Author: (text books, screenplays & novels) Breakbulk Fundamentals Running Away to Sea. Capt. Brit. Mcht. Navy, 1966—68. Master: Nautical Inst. (co pres. 2007—08). Independent. Avocations: travel, writing, winemaking. Business E-Mail: macnab6@aol.com.

MACNEIL, IAN, theatrical set & costume designer; Scenic & costume designer (Broadway plays) An Inspector Calls, 1994—95 (Drama Desk, Critic's Circle & Olivier awards for Best Set Design), scenic designer Via Dolorosa, 1999, Festen, 2006, Billy Elliot: The Musical, 2008 (Tony award for Best Scenic Design of a Musical, 2009), scenic & costume designer (Operas) Ariodante, English Nat. Opera (Olivier award), (plays) Machinal, English Nat. Theatre (Critic's Circle award), Afore Night Comes, Tin Tin, Vernon God Little, Young Vic, A Number, Plasticine, Far Away, Royal Ct. Theatre. Mailing: Imperial Theatre 249 W 45th St New York NY 10036*

MACNEIL, IAN RODERICK, lawyer, educator; b. NYC, June 20, 1929; s. Robert Lister and Kathleen Gertrude (Metcalf) Macneil; m. Nancy Carol Wilson, Mar. 29, 1952; children: Roderick, Jennifer, Duncan (dec.), Andrew. BA magna cum laude, U. Vt., 1950; LLB magna cum laude, Harvard U., 1955. Bar: N.H. 1956-02. Law clk. Hon. Peter Woodbury, 1955-56; asso. Sulloway Hollis Godfrey & Soden, Concord, NH, 1956-59; mem. faculty Cornell U. Law Sch., Ithaca, NY, 1959-72,

74-80, Ingersoll prof. law, 1976-80; Wigmore prof. law Northwestern U. Sch. Law, Chgo., 1980-99, prof. emeritus, 1999—. Vis. prof. U. East Africa, 1965-67, Duke U., 1971-72; prof. law, mem. Inst. Advanced Studies, U. Va., 1972-74; vis. fellow Centre for Socio-legal Studies and Wolfson Coll., Oxford U., 1979; hon. vis. fellow faculty law U. Edinburgh, 1979, 87; Rosenthal lectr. Northwestern U. Sch. Law, 1979; Braucher vis. prof. Harvard U., 1988-89. Author: Bankruptcy Law in East Africa, 1966, Contracts: Exchange Transactions and Relations, 3d edit., with Paul J. Gudel, 2001. The New Social Contract, 1980, American Arbitration Law: Reformation Nationalization Internationalization, 1992; co-author: Federal Arbitration Law, 1994. Served with U.S. Army, 1951-53. Guggenheim fellow, 1978-79. Fellow Soc. Antiquaries (Scotland), Am. Acad. Arts and Scis.; mem. Scottish Soc. No. Studies, The Scottish Medievalists, Standing Coun. Scottish Chiefs. Home: 95/6 Grange Loan Edinburgh EH9 2ED Scotland

MACNEIL, JUSTIN W., lawyer; b. Sacramento, Calif., Jan. 5, 1951; BA in English, Polit. Sci., U. Calif., Berkley, 1973; JD, U. Calif., Davis, 1976. Bar: State Bar Calif. (attorney at law). Attorney Law Office Justin W. Macneil, San Francisco, 1984—. Named Super Lawyer Bus. and Corporate Law, Jour. Law and Politics, 2005. Mem.: Bar Assn. San Francisco. Avocations: golf, hiking, Asian art. Office: Law Office Justin W Macneil PO Box 26024 San Francisco CA 94126-6024 Office Phone: 415-434-3490.

MACNEIL, ROBERT BRECKENRIDGE WARE, retired journalist, writer; b. Montreal, Que., Can., Jan. 19, 1931; came to U.S., 1963; s. Robert A.S. and Margaret Virginia (Oxner) MacN.; m. Rosemarie Anne Copland, 1956 (div. 1964); children: Catherine Anne, Ian B.; m. Jane J. Doherty, May 29, 1965 (div. 1983); children: Alison N., William H.; m. Donna P. Richards, Oct. 20, 1984. Student, Dalhousie U., 1949-51; BA, Carleton U., 1955; LHD (hon.), William Patterson Coll., 1977, Beaver Coll., Bates Coll., 1979, Lawrence U., 1980, Bucknell U., 1982, George Washington U., Kings Coll., Trinity Coll., U. Maine, 1983, Brown U., 1984, Colby Coll., Carleton Coll., U. S.C., 1985, Franklin and Marshall Coll., 1987, Nazareth Coll., Washington Coll., 1988, Kenyon Coll., 1990, U. Western Ont., 1992, U. Miami, Clark U., 1994, U. L.I., 1995, Columbia U., 1995, Princeton U., 1995, The Cooper Union, 1996, U. Toronto, 1997, Mt. Allison U., 1998; LHD (hon.), Dalhousie U., 2000. Radio actor CBC, Halifax, N.S., Canada, 1950-52, radio/TV announcer, 1954-55; announcer Sta.-CJCH, Halifax, 1951-52; announcer, news writer Sta. CFRA, Ottawa, Ont., Canada, 1952-54; sub-editor to filing editor Reuters News Agy., London, 1955-60; news corr. NBC, London, 1960-63, Washington, 1963-65, NYC, 1965-67; corr. Panorama program BBC, London, 1967-71, 73-75; sr. corr. Nat. Public Affairs Center for TV, Washington, 1971-73; exec. editor, co-anchor MacNeil/Lehrer Report, Sta. -WNET-TV, NYC, 1975—, MacNeil/Lehrer News Hour, PBS, 1983-95, ret., 1995; host America at a Crossroads, PBS, 2006—. Author: The People Machine, The Influence of Television on American Politics, 1968, The Right Place at the Right Time, 1982, Wordstruck, 1989, Burden of Desire, 1992, The Voyage, 1995, Breaking News, 1998, Looking For my Country, 2003; co-author: The Story of English, 1986, Do You Speak American?, 2005; editor The Way We Were 1963, 1988. Trustee Freedom Forum Newseum. Decorated Officer Order of Can., 1998; inductee TV Acad. Hall of Fame, 1999; recipient Lifetime Achievement award Overseas Press Club, 1995, Broadcaster of Yr. Internat. Radio and TV Soc., 1991, Paul White award Radio TV News Dirs. Assn., 1990, Medal of Honor U. Mo. Sch. Journalism, 1980; Catto fellow The Aspen Inst. Fellow AAAS, The MacDowell Colony (chmn. 1993); mem. AFTRA, Assn. Radio and TV News Analysts, Writers Guild Am., Century Club (NYC). Office: c/o MacNeil-Lehrer Prodns 2700 S Quincy St Ste 240 Arlington VA 22206-2226 E-mail: wordstruck2@cs.com.

MACNEILL, DANIEL SCOTT, library director; b. Abington, Pa., Oct. 8, 1945; s. William George and Ruth Scott MacNeill; m. Sylvia Toliver, Dec. 21, 1968; 1 child, Gwen Elizabeth. BA, LaSalle Coll., Phila., Pa., 1971; MS in Libr. Sci., U. Tenn., Knoxville, 1972. Cert. profl. libr. SC State Libr., 1996. Dean, learning resources Craven CC, New Bern, NC, 1972—74; libr. dir. Cannon Meml. Libr., Concord, NC, 1974—84; libr. Stony Brook Sch., NY, 1984—86; libr. dir. Meridian Pub. Libr., Miss., 1986—88; assoc. dir. Chattanooga Hamilton County Bicentennial Libr., 1988—91; libr. dir. Union County Pub. Libr., Monroe, NC, 1991—96; dir. librs. Lexington County Pub. Libr., SC, 1996—. Mem.: SC Libr. Assn., Mensa. Anglican. Avocation: reading. Home: 207 White Falls Dr Columbia SC 29212 Office: Lexington County Pub Libr 5440 Augusta Rd Lexington SC 29072 Business E-Mail: dmacneill@lex.lib.sc.us.

MACNEILL, FREDERICK DOUGLAS, artist; b. Boston, Sept. 28, 1929; s. Frederick Douglas and Agnes (Thompson) MacN.; m. Anita Concetta Venti, Sept. 1, 1961; children: John, Paul. Student, Vesper George Sch. of Art, 1952-54, Arthur Safford, Alphonse Shelton. One man shows include Guild Boston Artists, 1980, 82; exhibited in group shows at Springfield (Mass.) Mus. Fine Art, 1965, Hobe Sound Gallery, Miller Gallery, Cin., Guild Boston Artists, 1982, Hobe Sound N. Gallery (formerly Payson Waldron Gallery), Portland, Maine, 1982, Nat. Wildlife Art Mus, Jackson, Wyo., 1994, Mus. of SW, Midland, Tex., 1992, Gibbs Mus. Art, Charleston, SC, Mystic Maritime Gallery and Mus., Mystic, Conn., 1995; represented in permanent and pvt. collections; painting included in Crucifixion in American Art; also book cover. Recipient Marion Quimby award Ogunquit Art Assn., 1975, Elliot Liskin award Rockport Art Assn., 1984, John Chetcutti, 1985, Silver medal of honor, 1985, Guild of Boston Artists award, 1988, Arts for the Pk. Top 100 award, 1991-92, 94, 2004, Bernard Cory Meml. award Rockport Art Assn., 2007, Amee B. Davis Meml. award, 2007, others. Mem. Am. Artists Profl. League, Allied Artists Am., Acad. Artists of Am., Guild Boston Artists, Concord Art Assn., North Shore Art Assn. (Gloucester Coop. Bank award 2005, Gift Cert. award 2006, Alden Bryan Meml. award 2006), Rockport Art Assn. (Helen Van Wyk Gold medal, 2000, Marguerite Pearson Gold medal, 2002, Virginia Karl Meml. award 2004, Maurice E. Goldberg Meml. award 2005, Popular Vote award 2006, George O'Davies Silver medal 2008), Salmagundi Club (NYC, Martin Hannon Meml. award). Home: 23 Dana Rd Concord MA 01742-3408

MACNEILL, JAMES WILLIAM, environmental energy and management consultant; b. Sask., Can., Apr. 22, 1928; s. Leslie William and Helga Ingeborg (Nohlgren) MacN.; m. Phyllis Beryl Ferguson, Nov. 30, 1953; children: Catherine Anne, Robin Lynne. BA, U. Sask., 1949, BE Mech., 1958, LLD (hon.), 1988; Diplome, U. Stockholm, 1951; DSc (hon.), McGill U., 1992; D of Environ. Studies (hon.), U. Waterloo, 1993; LHD (hon.), Lakehead U., 1994. Spl. adv. on constl. rev. Privy Council Office, Govt. Can., Ottawa, Ont., 1969-70; asst. sec. Can. Ministry of State for Urban Affairs, Ottawa, 1970-73, permanent sec., 1973-76; Can. AEP, Can. commr.-gen. UN Human Settlements Conf., Vancouver, B.C., 1975-78; dir. environ. directorate OECD, Paris, 1978-84; sec. gen. World Commn. Environment and Devel., Geneva, 1984-87; sr. fellow Inst. Research Pub. Policy, Ottawa, 1987-93; pres. J.W. MacNeill and Assocs., 1987-98; chmn. Internat. Inst. for Sustainable Devel., 1994-99. Spl. advisor to adminstrn. UN Devel. Program, 1994-97; chmn. ind. insp. panel World Bank, 1997-2002; mem. adv. panel BP Caspian Devel., 2003--. Author: Environmental Management, 1971, Beyond Interdependence, 1991. Apptd. officer Order of Can., 1995. Recipient Saskatchewan Achievement award, 1984, Silver medal City of Paris, 1983, Climate Inst. award, 1991, Swedish WASA award, 1991, Lifetime Achievement award Govt. of Can., 1994, Candlelight award UN, 2002, Elizabeth Haub award for internat. environ. diplomacy, 2005. Mem. Assn. Profl. Engrs. Ont., Assn. Profl. Engrs. Sask. Office Phone: 847-491-8796. Personal E-mail: jwmacneill@hotmail.com, jwmdemill@hotmail.com.

MACO, PAUL STEPHEN, securities and exchange administrator; s. Paul and Rose Mary (McFadden) M.; m. Lisa M. Griglack, Aug. 23, 1997; 1 child, Claire Fiona. BA, Lehigh U., 1974; JD, NYU, 1977. Ptnr. Mintz, Levin, Cohn, Ferris, Glovesky & Popeo, Boston, 1988-94; faculty law Morin Ctr. for Internat. Banking Law Boston U., 1992-96, 99—; atty. fellow Office of Gen. Counsel SEC, Washington, 1994, dir. Office of Mcpl. Securities, 1995—. Adj. assoc. prof. Washington Coll. Law Am. U., 1999. Author: (with others) Bond Markets, Law and Regulation, 1999; bd. editors Jour. of Mcpl. Fin. Dir. Traditions for Tomorrow, Inc. Mem. ABA (co-reporter disclosure rules of counsel 1994), Nat. Assn. Bond Lawyers (dir. 1989-92, chair spl. com. on securities laws and disclosure 1987-89).

MACOMBER, DEBBIE, writer; b. Yakima, Wash., Oct. 22, 1948; m. Wayne Macomber; 4 children. Author: (novels) A Season of Angels, 1993, Morning Comes Softly, 1993 (Waldenbooks Bestselling Non-Series Debut Romance, Colo. Romance Writers Keeper award, 1996), Touched by Angels, 1994, The Trouble With Angels, 1994 (Waldenbooks Trend Book award), One Night, 1994, Someday Soon, 1995, Sooner or Later, 1996, Mrs. Miracle, 1996, This Matter of Marriage, 1997, Three Brides, No Groom, 1997, Nell's Cowboy, 1998, Lone Star Baby, 1998, Montana, 1998, Can This Be Christmas?, 1998, Caroline's Child, 1998, Texas Two-Step, 1998, Lonesome Cowboy, 1998, Dr. Texas, 1998, Shirley, Goodness & Mercy, 1999, Moon Over Water, 1999, Promise, Texas, 1999, A Season of Angels, 1999, The Touched by Angels, 1999, Dakota Born, 2000, Return to Promise, 2000, Dakota Home, 2000, Thursdays at Eight, 2001 (Named one Amazon.com's Top 10 Women's Fiction titles, 2001), Buffalo Valley, 2001, Always Dakota, 2001, 16 Lighthouse Road, 2001, 204 Rosewood Lane, 2002, Between Friends, 2002, The Christmas Basket, 2002 (Romance Writers of America RITA award), 311 Pelican Court, 2003, Those Christmas Angels, 2003, Changing Habits, 2003, The Snow Bride, 2003, 44 Cranberry Point, 2004 (Quill award for romance, 2005), The Shop on Blossom Street, 2004 (Publishers Weekly bestseller), When Christmas Comes, 2004, A Good Yarn, 2005, 50 Harbor Street, 2005 (Publishers Weekly bestseller), There's Something About Christmas, 2005, Navy Husband, 2005, Savannah's Garden, 2006, Christmas Letters, 2006, 74 Seaside Avenue, 2007 (No. 1 NY Times bestseller, 2007, No. 1 Publishers Weekly bestseller, 2007), Back on Bloom Street, 2007, Where Angels Go, 2007, Twenty Wishes, 2008, 8 Sandpiper Way, 2008 (No. 1 Publishers Weekly bestseller). Recipient Regional Svc. award, Romance Writers of Am., 1989, Career Achievement award for contemporary romance, Romantic Times, 1993, Woman of Distinction award, Soroptimist Internat., 1997; named Favorite Top 10 Author, Affaire de Coeur Mag., 1995; named a Tenn. Colonel for humanitarian svc., Gov. State of Tenn., 1994. Avocation: knitting. Mailing: c/o Author Mail Mira Books eHarlequin PO Box 5190 Buffalo NY 14240-5190

MACOMBER, JOHN D., investment company executive; b. Rochester, NY, Jan. 13, 1928; s. William Butts and Elizabeth Currie (Ranlet) M.; m. Caroline Morgan, Oct. 21, 1955; children: Janet Morgan, Elizabeth Currie, William Butts II. BA, Yale U., 1950; MBA, Harvard U., 1952. Mng. dir. McKinsey & Co., NYC, France and Switzerland, 1954-73; chmn., CEO Celanese Corp., NYC, 1973-87; chmn. J.D. Macomber & Co., NYC, 1987-89; pres., chmn. Export-Import Bank of U.S., Washington, 1989-92; prin. JDM Investment Group, Washington, 1992—. Bd. dirs. Lehman Brothers Holdings, Inc., 1994—. 1st lt. USAF, 1952-54. Mem. Links (N.Y.C.), River Club (N.Y.C.), Union Club (N.Y.C.), Metropolitan (Washington). Office: JDM Investment Group 2806 N St NW Washington DC 20007-3339

MACOMBER, JOHN D., former construction executive; b. Boston, Oct. 8, 1955; s. George and Ann L. Macomber; m. Kristin Hodgkins, June 11, 1983; children: Ian D., Eric C. BA, Dartmouth Coll., 1978; MBA, Harvard U., 1983. Project mgr. George B.H. Macomber Co., Boston, 1987-90, v.p., 1983-87, pres., chief exec. officer, 1990—. Lectr. MIT. Mem. exec. com. EBGH-TV Overseers, 1998—, Boys & Girls Clubs, Boston, 1989—, The Nature Conservancy, 1997—. Mem. U.S. Alpine Ski Team, 1974-76; NCAA All-America in skiing, 1974, 78. Mem. Harvard Bus. Sch. Assn., Young Pres. Orgn. Avocations: skiing, bicycling, tennis. Office: George BH Macomber Co 1 Design Center Pl Ste 600 Boston MA 02210-2327

MACOMBER, MARSHALL C., legislative staff member; b. Atlanta; ABJ cum laude, U. Ga., Athens, 1995. Dir. comm. & spl. legis. projects for Rep. Mike Rogers US House of Reps., Washington, chief of staff. Mem.: Theta Chi. Office: Office of Congressman Mike Rogers 324 Cannon House Office Bldg Washington DC 20515 Office Phone: 202-225-3261. Business E-Mail: marshall.macomber@mail.house.gov.*

MACOVSKI, ALBERT, electrical engineer, educator; b. NYC, May 2, 1929; s. Philip and Rose (Winogr) Macovski; m. Adelaide Paris, Aug. 5, 1950; children: Michael, Nancy. BEE, City Coll. N.Y., 1950; MEE, Poly. Inst. Bklyn., 1953; PhD, Stanford U., 1968. Mem. tech. staff RCA Labs., Princeton, NJ, 1950—57; asst. prof., then assoc. prof. Poly. Inst. Bklyn., 1957—60; staff scientist Stanford Rsch. Inst., Menlo Park, Calif., 1960—71; fellow U. Calif. Med. Center San Francisco, 1971—; prof. elec. engring. and radiology Stanford U., 1972—, endowed chair, Canon USA prof. engring., 1991—. Dir. Magnetic Resonance Sys. Rsch. Lab.; cons. to industry. Recipient award for color TV cirs., Inst. Radio Engrs., 1958; spl. fellow, NIH, 1971. Fellow: IEEE (Zworykin award 1973), Internat. Soc. Magnetic Resonance in Medicine (trustee 1991—94, gold medal 1997), Optical Soc. Am., Am. Inst. Med. Biol. Engring.; mem.: NAE, Am. Assn. Physicists in Medicine, Inst. Medicine, Eta Kappa Nu, Sigma Xi. Jewish. Achievements include patents in field. Office: Stanford Univ Dept Elec Engring Stanford CA 94305 Home: 620 Sand Hill Rd Apt 407B Palo Alto CA 94304 Office Phone: 650-723-2708. Business E-Mail: macovski@stanford.edu.

MACPHAIL, ANDREW B., professional sports team executive; b. Bronxville, NY, Apr. 5, 1953; m. Lark MacPhail; children: William Reed, Andrew Hamilton. Grad., Dickinson Coll., 1976. Bus. mgr. Gulf Coast League Bradenton Rookie affiliate Chgo. Cubs, 1976-77, asst. parks ops., 1977, with dept. player devel., 1978, asst. dir. dept. player devel., asst. dir. scouting, pres., CEO, 1994—2006; asst. gen. mgr. Houston Astros, 1982-85; v.p. player pers. Minn. Twins, 1985-86, exec. v.p., gen. mgr., 1986-94; pres. baseball ops. Balt. Orioles, 2007—. Named Maj. League Exec. of Yr., The Sporting News, 1991, Am. League Exec. of Yr., UPI, 1991; winner World Series Championship as general manager of the Twins, 1987, 91. Office: Balt Orioles Oriole Park at Camden Yards 333 W Camden St Baltimore MD 21201

MACPHERSON, GWENDOLYN LEE, geochemist, educator; d. Ronald H. and Ruth H. Cooper Macpherson; m. Mark R. Macpherson; children: Cooper Marie Farr, Elizabeth Jean Farr. PhD, U. Tex., Austin, 1989. Assoc. prof. U. Kans., Lawrence, 1989—. Office: Univ Kans 1475 Jayhawk Blvd Lawrence KS 66045

MACQUEEN, CHERIE K., interior designer, artist, retired newscaster, retired sportscaster; b. Kansas City, Mo., Mar. 20, 1952; d. Ira Raymond and Peggy Estelle (Turner) Milks. AA in Liberal Arts, L.A. Valley Coll., 1982; BS in Liberal Studies, Excelsior Coll., Albany, NY, 1993; postgrad., Calif. State U., San Bernardino, 1998—; cert. in Interior Design, U. Calif., Riverside, 2002. Pers. specialist US Army, Honolulu, 1973-75, adminstrv. specialist San Francisco, 1975-77, broadcast journalist Vicenza, Italy, 1977-80; radio traffic specialist Armed Forces Radio and TV, LA, 1980—84, radio prodn. specialist, 1984-86, supr. broadcast support specialist Sun Valley, 1986-90, broadcast support mgr, 1990-91, internal info. mgr., 1991-94, news and sports specialist, 1994-99; owner The Keilani Co., Highland, 2003—08, Ladysmythe Handcrafts, Highland, 2003—08. Mem.: DAV (life), Am. Soc. Interior Designers (student mem., Inland-Palm Springs chpt. 1999—2002, allied mem. 2002—04, bd. dirs., Inland-Palm Springs chpt. 2003—04, allied mem. Pasadena chpt. 2004—08), Pacific Pioneer Broadcasters (mem. 1999—), Women in Mil. Svc. for Am. (charter 1997—), Armed Forces Broadcasters Assn. (v.p. LA chpt. 1991—93). Avocations: crafts, crocheting. Home: 2887 Indian Canyon Ct Highland CA 92346-0276

MAC RAE, ALFRED URQUHART, physicist, electrical engineer; b. NYC, Apr. 14, 1932; s. Farquhar and Eliza J. (Urquhart) Mac R.; m. Peggy M. Hazard, May 13, 1967; children: Susan, Pamela. BS in Physics, Syracuse U., 1954, PhD in Physics, 1960. Dir. integrated circuit devel. Bell Labs., Murray Hill, NJ, 1979-83, dir. satellite communications systems Homdel, NJ, 1983-95; pres. Mac Tech., Berkeley Heights, NJ, 1995—. Sr. rsch. fellow Potomac Inst. New Zealand, 2000-07; chair NASA Internat. Technology Studies, 1997-98; mem. adv. com. to bd. trustees N.J. Inst. Tech., 1981-85. Bd. editor: Vacuum Sci. and Tech, 1965-67, Rev. Sci. Instruments, 1969-71; contbr. articles to jours.; patentee in field. Bd. dirs. Summit Area ARC, 1996-2004, chmn., 2001-02. Fellow IEEE (mem., chmn. numerous coms. 1969—, Third Millenium medal 2000), Am. Phys. Soc., Nat. Acad. Engring.; mem. Bohmische Phys. Soc., IEEE Electron Devices Soc. (pres. 1986-87, chmn. field awards coun. 1989-93, Ebers award 1994, Disting. Svcs. award 1996). Office: 72 Sherbrook Dr Berkeley Heights NJ 07922-2346 Personal E-mail: a.macrae@ieee.org.

MACRAE, CAMERON FARQUHAR, III, lawyer; b. NYC, Mar. 21, 1942; s. Cameron F. and Jane B. (Miller) MacR.; m. Ann Wooster Bedell, Nov. 30, 1974; children: Cathérine Fairfax, Ann Cameron. AB, Princeton U., 1963; LLB, Yale U., 1966. Bar: N.Y. 1966, D.C. 1967, U.S. Dist. Ct. (so. dist.) N.Y. 1975. Atty.-advisor Office of Gen. Counsel to Sec. Air Force, Washington, 1966-69; assoc. Davis, Polk & Wardell, NYC, 1970-72; dep. supt. and counsel N.Y. State Banking Dept., NYC, 1972-74, sr. ptnr., 1975—2004; vice-chmn. LeBoeuf, Lamb, Greene & MacRae, LLP, NYC, 1995—2000; sr. of counsel LeBoeuf, Lamb, Greene & MacRae, LLP, NYC, 2005—, Dewey & LeBoeuf LLP. Dir. Nat. Integrity Life Ins. Co., 2000—. Note and comment editor Yale Law Jour., 1965-66. Trustee, sec. St. Andrew's Dune Ch., 1982—; hon. chmn. Clear Pool Inc., 1990-94. Capt. USAF res., 1966-69. Mem.: DC Bar Assn., Jupiter Island Club, Cottage Club (Princeton, NJ), Shinnecock Hills Golf Club (Southampton), Bathing Corp. Southampton, Meadow Club (v.p., bd. govs.), Union Club (NYC). Democrat. Episcopalian. Office: Dewey LeBoeuf LLP 125 W 55th St New York NY 10019-5369 Office Phone: 212-424-8080. E-mail: cfmacrae@dl.com.

MACRAE, ELIZABETH (ELIZABETH MACRAE HALSEY), counselor, actor; b. Columbia, SC, Feb. 22, 1936; d. James and Dorothy (Hendon) MacRae; m. Charles Day Halsey, Jr., 1969; m. Nedrick Young, 1965 (dec. 1968); children: Benjamin Young(dec.), Beryl MacRae Young(dec.). Student, Herbert Berghof Studio, NYC, 1956—58, Arts Students League, 1958, U. So. Calif., LA, 1965, Marymount Manhattan Coll., NYC, 1989—91, Breakthrough at Gracie Sq. Hosp., 1990—91. Cert. Alcoholism and Alcohol Abuse, Credentialed Alcoholism Counselor 1992. Intern Arms Acres, Carmel, NY, 1990; counselor chem. dependency Breakthrough at Gracie Sq. Hosp., 1990; adult counselor Manhattan Bowery Corp., 1991—93; program dir., counselor alcoholism outpatient clinic Freedom Inst., 1993—98. Actor: (plays) off Broadway, 1956, New Eng. Stock, 1957, 1963, (as Elizabeth MacRae): (films) Everything's Ducky, 1961, Love in a Goldfish Bowl, 1961, The Incredible Mr. Limpet, 1964, The Wild Westerners, 1962, For Love or Money, 1963; (TV series) Route 66, 1969, 1972, 1974; (films) Francis Ford Coppola's The Conversation, 1974; (TV series) Naked City, 1960, 77 Sunset Strip, 1961, Harrigan and Son, 1961, Surfside 6, 1961, Maverick, 1961, Asphalt Jungle, 1961, Dr. Kildare, 1962, Hawaiian Eye, 1962, Stoney Burke, 1962, Death Valley Days, 1962, Sam Benedict, 1962, Gunsmoke, 1961—64, The Untouchables, 1962, Burke's Law, 1963, Rawhide, 1963, The Virginian, 1964, The Fugitive, 1964, I Dream of Jeannie, 1965, Gomer Pyle, USMC, 1966—68, Andy Griffith, 1967, Bonanza, 1968, Judd for the Defense, 1969, Rheingold Theatre - England, 1959, Kojak, 1974, Petrocelli, 1974, Mannix, 1974, Rhoda, 1976, Barnaby Jones, 1976, General Hospital, 1969, 1971; (TV films), 1974; (TV series) Days of Our Lives, 1976—77, All My Children, 1978, Guiding Light, 1980, Another World, 1980, 1989, Search for Tomorrow,: (live TV) The Verdict is Yours, 1958—60, Ellery Queen, 1960, Ninotshka, 1960. Vol. Help Line, NYC, 1982. Recipient Distinguished Counselor award, Freedom Inst., 2003. Mem.: AFTRA, SAG, Nat. Assn. Alcoholism and Drug Abuse Counselors, Actors Equity, Acad. Motion Picture Arts and Scis., Nat. Soc. Colonial Dames Am. (N.C. chpt.). Home: 1405 Raeford Rd Fayetteville NC 28305 Office: Manuscript Dept Univ NC CB 3926 Wilson Libr Chapel Hill NC 27514-8890 Office Phone: 910-485-5061. E-mail: chalsey@nc.rr.com.

MACRAE, IAN JOHN, medical educator, researcher; b. Santa Cruz, Calif., 1975; married. PhD, U. Calif., Davis. Asst. prof. Scripps Rsch. Inst., La Jolla, Calif., 2007—. Recipient Biomed. Scis. award, Pew Scholars Program, 2008—; Postdoc. fellowship, Life Scis. Rsch. Found., 2003—07. Achievements include research in crystal structure of dicer. Office: Scripps Rsch Inst 10550 N Torrey Pines Rd La Jolla CA 92037

MACRIS, ACHILLES O., bank executive; Student, U. Athens; MBA, Rice U. With Chase Manhattan, NYC, 1986—91, Bankers Trust, 1991—98; global head fgn. exchange, precious metals and commodities, internat. treasuries and local markets Dresdner Kleinwort Wasserstein Securities Ltd., London, 1998, global head credit products and fgn. exchange, 2002, global head capital markets, 2002—05, gen. mgr. London br., 1998—2002; ptnr. Cardinal Asset Mgmt. Ltd., London, 2005—06; internat. chief investment officer JP Morgan Chase & Co., NYC, 2006—. Office: JP Morgan Chase & Co 270 Park Ave New York NY 10017-2070*

MACRIS, JACK ACHILLES, surgeon; b. Highland Park, Mich., Nov. 3, 1924; MD, U. Mich., 1950. Diplomate Am. Bd. Surgery. Intern Grace Hosp., Detroit, 1950-51; resident in surgery U. Mich. Hosp., 1951-52,

1952-55, fellowship in surgery, 1955; hosp. staff mem. St. Anthonys Hosp., St. Petersburg, Fla. Fellow ACS (past pres. Fla. chpt.); mem. Fla. Med. Assn. (past pres.), Frederick A. Coller Surg. Soc. (past pres.), Fla. Surg. Soc. (past pres.). Home: # 822 555 5th Ave NE Saint Petersburg FL 33701

MACRIS, MICHAEL, lawyer; b. Jackson Heights, NY, July 12, 1949; Student, Cornell U.; BA with distinction, Stanford U., 1971; JD, Columbia U., 1974. Bar: N.Y. 1975, Conn. 1976. Mem. Cahill Gordon & Reindel LLP, NYC. Bd. editors Columbia Law Rev., 1973-74; co-editor ERISA & Benefits Law Jour., 1992-99. Harlan Fiske Stone scholar. Fellow: Am. Coll. Employee Benefits Counsel (charter); mem.: ABA (group chair), Phi Beta Kappa. Office: Cahill Gordon & Reindel LLP 80 Pine St Fl 19 New York NY 10005-1790 Office Phone: 212-701-3409. Business E-Mail: mmacris@cahill.com.

MACRITCHIE, FINLAY, chemistry professor, consultant; s. Finlay and Margaret MacRitchie; m. Sylvia Lina Bravo, Mar. 5, 1966; children: Sylvia Margaret MacRitchie-Hook, Jacqueline Aida. PhD, U. Sydney, 1962. Cert. in chemist Royal Australian Chem. Inst., 1986. Sr. prin. rsch. scientist CSIRO Australia, North Ryde, New South Wales, 1967—97; prof. Kans. State U., Manhattan, 1997—. Editor-in-chief jours. cereal Sci., 2007—. Author: (textbook) Chemistry at Interfaces, 1990; contbr. to numerous profl. jours. Recipient F.B. Guthrie medal, Royal Australian Chem. Inst., 1983, Thomas Burr Osborne medal. Fellow: AACC Internat. (George W. Scott Blair award 2008). Home: 1510 Williamsburg Dr Manhattan KS 66502 Office: Kans State Univ Shellenberger Hall 201 Manhattan KS 66506 Office Fax: 785-532-7010. Business E-Mail: finlay@ksu.edu.

MACSAI, JOHN, retired architect; b. Budapest, Hungary, May 20, 1926; came to U.S., 1947, naturalized, 1954; s. Ferenc and Margit (Rosenfeld) Lusztig; m. Geraldine Marcus, May 7, 1950; children: Pamela, Aaron, Marian, Gwen. Baccalaureate summa cum laude, Kolcsey Gimnasium, Budapest, 1944; student, Atelier Art Sch., Budapest, 1941-43, Poly. U., 1945-47; BArch magna cum laude, Miami U., Oxford, Ohio, 1949. Archtl. designer Skidmore, Owings & Merrill, Chgo., Pace Assos., Chgo., Raymond Loewy Assos., Chgo., 1949-55; ptnr. Hausner & Macsai, Chgo., 1955-71, Campbell & Macsai, Chgo., 1971-74; prin. John Macsai & Assocs. Architects, Inc., Chgo., 1975-90, O'Donnell Wicklund Pigozzi & Peterson, Chgo., 1991-2000, ret., 2000. Prof. architecture U. Ill., Chgo., 1970-76, prof. emeritus, 1997—. Author: High Rise Apartment Buildings: A Design Primer, 1972, Housing, 1976, Housing, 2d edit., 1982, Housing, Russian edit., 1980, Housing, Mexican edit., 1984; co-author: Designing Environments for the Aged, 1977, Housing for a Maturing Population, 1983, (ency.) Highrise Apartment Buildings, 1988, East European Modernism, 1996; contbr. articles to profl. jours.; prin. works include Nat. Opinion Rsch. Ctr., U.Chgo., 1967, High Energy Physics Bldg., 1968, Social Svcs. Ctr., 1970, Harbor House, 1965, Malibu East, 1972, Waterford apt. bldg., 1976, U. Chgo. faculty townhouses, 1986, Fairfield Ct. housing for the elderly, 1988, Evanston Pl. apt. bldg and city garage, 1991, 2960 N. Lake Shore Dr. Housing for the Elderly, 1991; staff arch. Tel Tanninim Archaeol. Project, Israel, 1996—2000, Elike Archaeol. Project, Greece, 2001; exhibitions include Gallery 1756, Chgo., 1991—2005, Chgo. Cultural Ctr., 2000, Cliffdwellers Club, 2002; author: (monthly article) Evanston Round Table. Fellow AIA (13 design award citations Chgo. chpt.). Jewish. Home: 1501 Hinman Ave Apt 3B Evanston IL 60201-4675 Personal E-mail: jgmacsai@uic.edu.

MACSKASSY, SOFUS ATTILA, computer scientist, educator; m. Laam Wong, Sept. 7, 1997. PhD, Rutgers U., New Brunswick, NJ, 2003. Dir., labs. Fetch Techs. Inc., El Segundo, Calif., 2005—; asst. adj. prof., dept. computer sci. U. Southern Calif., LA, 2006—. Office: Fetch Techs Inc 841 Apollo St Ste 400 El Segundo CA 90245 Personal E-mail: sofmac@gmail.com. Business E-Mail: sofmac@fetch.com.

MACTAGGART, TERRENCE JOSEPH, education educator, researcher, former academic administrator; b. Buffalo, Sept. 20, 1946; s. Joseph Carol and Genieve Mary (Quinn) MacT. BA in English and Philospohy, Canisius Coll., Buffalo, 1967; MA in Lit., St. Louis U., 1971, PhD in Lit., 1976; MBA, St. Cloud State U., Minn., 1986. Prof. Blackburn Coll., Carlinville, Ill., 1973-74; dir. Webster U., St. Louis, 1974-77; acting dean U. Alaska, Fairbanks, 1977-79; dean St. Cloud State U., Minn., 1979-83; v.p. Met. State U., St. Paul, 1983-86; vice chancellor Minn. State U. System, St. Paul, 1986-87, chancellor, 1991-95, U. Wis., Superior, 1987-91; prof. English Minn. State U., St. Paul, 1991-95; chancellor U. Maine Sys., Bangor, 1996—2001, interim chancellor, 2006—07; prof. U. Maine, 2002—. Fulbright Scholar in Thailand, 1996. Editor: Cost Effective Assessment of Prior Learning, 1983; contbr. articles on higher edn. to profl. jours. Sgt. U.S. Army, 1969-71, Viet Nam. NDEA fellow, 1968-72. Mem. Phi Beta Kappa. Avocations: cross country skiing, sailing. Office: U Maine Sys 16 Central St Bangor ME 04401-5106

MACTAVISH, CRAIG, former professional hockey coach, retired professional hockey player; b. London, Ont., Can., Aug. 15, 1958; m. Debbie MacTavish; children: Nathan, Sean, Brianna. Center Boston Bruins, 1980-85, Edmonton Oilers, 1985-94, NY Rangers, 1994, Phila. Flyers, 1994-96, St. Louis Blues, 1996-97; asst. coach NY Rangers, 1997—99, Edmonton Oilers, 1999—2000, head coach, 2000—09. Achievements include being a member of Stanely Cup Champion Edmonton Oilers, 1987, 1988, 1990, New York Rangers, 1994.

MACTAVISH, SUSANNE HANNA, retired library and information scientist; b. Atlanta, Jan. 6, 1947; d. Albert Kenneth and Mary Ann Hanna; m. Nelson Thomas Henderson, May 4, 1974 (div. Sept. 3, 1993); children: Russell Evan Henderson, Andrea Renee Henderson; m. Douglas Stewart MacTavish, Aug. 1, 1998; 1 child, Ian Stewart. BA, DePauw U., Greencastle, Ind., 1969; MS in Lib. Sci., Case Western Res. U., Cleve., 1970. Libr. Denver Pub. Libr., 1970—72; info. officer, libr. US CIA, 1972—81; mgr. libr. svcs. Gen. Electric Co., Gaithersburg, Md., 1981—93; project lead Lockheed Martin, Falls Church, Va., 1993—2001, ethics officer Gaithersburg, 2001—07; ret., 2007. Mem.: ALA (life), Internat. Orgn. Standardization/Internat. Electrotech. Commn. (joint tech. com., one sub com. twenty-four), Libr. Adminstrn. and Mgmt. Assn. (pres. 1990—91, councilor 2005—08), Ethics Officer Assn., Beta Phi Mu, Delta Zeta (v.p. 1968—69). Methodist. Home: 568 Rifes Ford Rd Verona VA 24482 Personal E-mail: sue.mactavish@northriver.coop.

MACTIER, ANN DICKINSON, state agency administrator; b. Ravenna, Nebr., June 29, 1922; d. Robert Smith and Carrie (Clark) Dickinson; m. James Allan Mactier, Feb. 26, 1944; children: James Allan II, Judith Ann, Robert Dickinson. BS, Northwestern U., 1944; BA, U. Nebr., Omaha, 1963, MA, 1969; EdD (hon.), U. Nebr., 2005. Owner, mgr. Ponca Hills Riding Acad., Omaha, 1966-73; cmty. coord. Coll. Fine Arts, U. Nebr., Omaha, 1974-75; mem. Nebr. State Bd. Edn., 1996—, v.p., 2001—. Mem. Omaha Jr. League, 1944—57; mem. exec. com. Riverfront Devel. Corp., Omaha, 1973—79; founder, pres. Florence Arts Coun., Omaha, 1975—79; mem. Omaha Pub. Schs. Bd. Edn., 1983—98; mem. steering com. Coun. Urban Bds. Edn., 1996—98; bd. dirs. Coun. Great City Schs., 1984—89. Home: 3811 N Post Rd Omaha NE 68112-1209 Office Phone: 402-453-4580. E-mail: ann@mactier.omhcoxmail.com.

MACURDY, JOHN EDWARD, bass; b. Detroit, Mar. 18, 1929; s. Blanchard Archibald and Dorathea Rosalie (Radtke) Macurdy; m. Justine May Votypka, Apr. 12, 1958; children: Allison Anne, John Blanchard. Student, Wayne State U., 1947; student of Avery Crew, Detroit, 1946. Mem. N.Y.C. Opera, 1959-62, Met. Opera, 1962—. Appeared in U.S., Europe, including San Francisco Opera, La Scala; performances include world premieres Mourning Becomes Electra, Met. Opera, 1967, opening night Anthony and Cleopatra, Met. Opera, 1966, Wuthering Heights, Santa Fe Opera, 1958, Six Characters in Search of an Author, N.Y.C. Opera, 1959, Griffalkin, Tanglewood Festival, 1957; Am. premieres Capriccio, Santa Fe Opera, 1958, Murder in the Cathedral, Empire State Music Festival, Bear Mountain Park, N.Y., 1959, Inspector General, N.Y.C. Opera, 1960; appeared with numerous orchs.; film Don Giovanni, 1979; participant 40th Anniversary Sud-Deutsche Rundfunk, 100th Anniversary Gala Met. Opera, 1983. Served with USAF, 1950-54. Recipient medal for artistic merit during Mich. Week City of Detroit, 1969, Arts Achievement award Wayne State U., 2003; inducted into Acad. Vocal Hall of Fame, 1985. Mem.: Bohemian Club of San Francisco. Presbyterian. Office: 73 Tall Oaks Ct Stamford CT 06903-1515

MACWHINNEY, BRIAN JAMES, psychology professor; b. NYC, Aug. 22, 1945; s. James Edwin and Julia Nanasy MacWhinney; m. Mary Kent Patteson, Dec. 22, 1968; children: Ross Alexander, Mark Ewan. PhD, U. Calif., Berkeley, 1965. Asst. prof. psychology U. Denver, 1975—81; prof. psychology Carnegie Mellon U., Pitts., 1981—. Dir. Child Lang. Data Exch. Sys., Pitts., 1984—. Organizer Voter Protection, Pitts., 2003—05; committeeman Allegheny County Dem. Party, Pitts., 2002—05. Grantee, NSF, NIH, 1976—2005. Fellow: Am. Psychol. Soc., Order of the Golden Bear; mem.: Soc. for Rsch. in Child Devel., Cognitive Sci. Soc., Psychonomic Soc. Democrat. Society Of Friends. Achievements include first to create the TalkBank data-exchange system; research in emergentist accounts of language learning; transformation of the logical problem of language acquisition. Avocations: travel, biking, languages. Office: Carnegie Mellon U Dept Psychology 5000 Forbes Ave Pittsburgh PA 15213 Personal E-mail: macw@mac.com.

MACWILLIAMS, KENNETH EDWARD, investment banker; b. Newburyport, Mass., Aug. 21, 1936; s. Harold Freeman and Helen (Melia) MacW.; children: Robert Hovey, James Stuart; m. Natalya V. Fedorova, Aug. 29, 2004. BA, Harvard U., 1958, MBA, 1962. V.p. Morgan Guaranty Trust Co., NYC, 1962-71; sr. assoc. Goldman Sachs & Co., NYC, 1971-74; mng. dir., domestic merchant banking group Manfacturers Hanover Trust Co., NYC, 1975-82; chmn., chief exec. officer Prudential Capital Corp. subs. Prudential Ins. Co. Am., Newark, 1982-90; pres. Prudential Equity Mgmt. Assn. subs. Prudential Ins. Co. Am., Newark, 1990-92; founder, pres. Woodrow Wilson Assocs., NYC, 1993—. Personal E-mail: macwilliams@earthlink.net.

MACY, WILLIAM H., actor; b. Miami, Mar. 13, 1950; m. Felicity Huffman, Sept. 6, 1997; children: Sofia Grace, Georgia Grace. Attended, Bethany Coll. Founding mem. St. Nicholas Theater, Chgo., Atlantic Theatre Co., NYC. Actor: (TV miniseries) The Awakening Land, 1978; (TV series) ER, 1994—98; actor, writer: Above Suspicion, 1995; actor: (TV films) The Cradle Will Fall, 1983, The Boy Who Loved Trolls, 1984, The Dining Room, 1984, The Murder of Mary Phagan, 1988, In the Line of Duty: Siege at Marion, 1992, A Private Matter, 1992, The Water Engine, 1992, The Heart of Justice, 1993, Texan, 1994, The Writing on the Wall, 1994, In the Shadow of Evil, 1995, Andersonville, 1996, The Night of the Headless Horseman, 1999, It's a Very Merry Muppet Christmas Movie, 2002, Reversible Errors, 2004, Family Man, 2008; actor, writer: The Con, 1998; A Slight Case of Murder, 1999; Door to Door, 2002 (Screen Actors Guild award best actor, 2003, Emmy award best actor in a TV movie, 2003, Emmy award best writing TV movie, 2003); The Wool Cap, 2004; actor, dir. Lip Service, 1988; actor: (TV appearances) Kate & Allie, 1984, Spenser: For Hire (3 episodes), 1985—88, The Equalizer, 1985, L.A. Law, 1986, Law & Order, 1990, Civil Wars, 1991, Bakersfield P.D., 1993, Frasier, 1993, Superman, 1996, King of the Hill, 1997, The Lionhearts, 1998, Hercules, 1998, Sports Night, 1998, Batman Beyond, 1999, Out of Order, 2003, The Unit, 2007, ER, 2009; (films) Foolin' Around, 1980, Somewhere in Time, 1980, Without a Trace, 1983, The Last Dragon, 1985, Radio Days, 1987, House of Games, 1987, Things Change, 1988, Homicide, 1991, Shadows and Fog, 1992, Benny & Joon, 1993, Searching for Bobby Fischer, 1993, Twenty Bucks, 1993, Being Human, 1993, The Client, 1994, Oleanna, 1994, Murder in the First, 1995, Roommates, 1995, Tall Tale, 1995, Evolver, 1995, Mr. Holland's Opus, 1995, Down Periscope, 1996, Fargo, 1996, Hit Me, 1996, Ghosts of Mississippi, 1996, Colin Fitz, 1996, Air Force One, 1997, Boogie Nights, 1997, Wag the Dog, 1997, Jerry and Tom, 1998, Pleasantville, 1998, Psycho, 1998, The Secret of NIMH 2: Timmy to the Rescue, 1998, A Civil Action, 1998, Happy, Texas, 1999, Mystery Men, 1999, Magnolia, 1999, Panic, 2000, State and Main, 2000, Jurassic Park III, 2001, Focus, 2001, Welcome to Collinwood, 2002, The Cooler, 2003, Seabiscuit, 2003, Cellular, 2004, Sahara, 2005, Edmond, 2005, Thank You for Smoking, 2006, (voice only) Doogal, 2006, Bobby, 2006, Inland Empire, 2006, (voice only) Everyone's Hero, 2006, He Was a Quiet Man, 2007, Wild Hogs, 2007, (voice only) The Tale of Despereaux, 2008, Shorts, 2009; (plays) American Buffalo, 1975, Speed-the-Plow, 2009; writer: (TV series) thirtysomething, 1987; writer: TV films Every Woman's Dream, 1996, Just a Walk in the Park, 2002; exec. prodr.: (films) Transamerica, 2005. Spokesperson United Cerebral Palsy. Office: Creative Artists Agy 2000 Ave of the Stars Los Angeles CA 90067*

MACZULSKI, MARGARET LOUISE, marketing professional; b. Detroit, Apr. 01; d. Bohdan Alexander and Olga Louise (Martinuick) Maczulski. BS, Mich. State U.; cert. E-Commerce Mgmt., DePaul U., 2000. Cert. meeting mgr. Mgr. meetings Nat. Assn. Realtors, Mktg. Inst., Chgo., 1977-82, mgr. mktg., 1982-83; regional sales mgr. Fairmont Hotels, Chgo., 1982; dir., mgr. trade shows and confs. Capital Cities Am. Broadcasting Co./Pub. Divsn., Wheaton, Ill., 1983-85; mgr. meeting and conf. planning Soc. Human Resource Mgmt., Alexandria, Va., 1985-90; mgr. meeting and conv. planning Kraft Foods, Glenview, Ill., 1990-95; cons. meetings and spl. events Chgo., 1996-98; sr. mgr. meeting and travel svcs. Coll. Am. Pathologists, Northfield, Ill., 1998-2000; conv. mgr. Common, A User Group, 2001—02, cons. spl. events, 2002—07; owner, dir., visiting angels Lake County, 2007—, Gurnee, Ill. Mem. Meeting Planners Internat., Greater Washington Soc. Assn. Execs. (past chmn. site inspection com.), Soc. Corporate Meeting Planners, Am. Soc. Assn. Execs., Mich. State U. Alumni Assn. (treas. DC chpt. 1987-90), Assn. Forum, Profl. Conf. Mgmt. Assn. Republican. Roman Catholic. Avocations: piano, swimming, skiing. Home: 16830 W Serranda Dr Libertyville IL 60048 Office Phone: 847-336-9666. Personal E-mail: maczulski@visitingangels.com, gwenraz@hotmail.com.

MADAN, DEEPAK S., engineering executive; s. S. M. and K. S. Madan; m. A. P. Madan; 1 child, N. S. B Technology/Metall. Engr., Indian Inst. Technology, Kanpur, India, 1982; MS Materials Engr., Rensselaer Poly. Inst., 1986, PhD Materials Engr., 1988. Rsch. fellow Rensselaer Poly. Inst., Troy, NY, 1982-87; sr. materials engr. Elkem Metals Co., Pitts., 1987-95; v.p. new product devel. F.W. Winter, Inc. & Co., Camden, NJ, 1995—2007; v.p. tech. and new bus. devel. Magnesium Elektron Powders, Manchester, NJ, 2007—. Spkr. at tech. meetings and seminars. Patentee in field; editor tech. books; contbr. articles to profl. jours. Mem.: Ctr. Innovative Sintered Products (ex-chmn. industry bd.), Metal Powder Prodrs. Assn. (dir., bd. dirs.), Am. Powder Metallurgy Inst. (past chmn. local chpt.), Am. Soc. Metals. Avocations: photography, travel, computers. Office: Magnesium Elektron Powders 100 Ridgeway Blvd Manchester NJ 08759 Office Phone: 908-330-8176.

MADAN, VISHAL, dermatologist; s. Suresh Madan; m. Savin Madan, Nov. 2003. MBBS in Medicine and Surgery with honors, NSCB Med. Coll., Jabalpur, 1997; MD in Dermatology, STD's and Leprosy, RDVV, Jabalpur, Madhya Pradesh, 2001. Sr. ho. officer Nscb Med. Coll., Jabalpur, Madhya Pradesh, India, 1998—2001, specialist registrar, 2001, U. Coll. Med. Scis., New Delhi, 2001—02; ho. officer Manchester Royal Infirmary, Lancashire, England, 2002—03; sr. ho. officer Addenbrookes Hosp. NHS Trust, Cambridge, Cambridgeshire, England, 2003—05; specialist registrar dermatology, fellow in cutaneous lasers Dermatology Ctr., Hope Hosp., Salford, Manchester, Lancashire, England, 2005—. Contbr. articles to peer reviewed jours. Recipient Bus Bhalla award, Indian Med. Assn., 1997, 7 Gold medals, Rdvv, Jabalpur, 1997; scholar, Rdvv Jabalpur, 1997. Master: Royal Coll. Physicians (life); mem.: British Cosmetic Dermatology Group, UK Dermatology Clin. Trials Network, North of Eng. Dermatology Soc., Med. Coun. India, Indian Assn. Dermatologists, Venereologists And Leprologists (life), Brit. Assn. Dermatologists (life). Hindu. Achievements include research in interstitial optical diffuser fibre in treatment of nodular basal cell carcinoma in Gorlin's syndrome; lasers in dermatology, skin cancer, general and medical dermatology; the significance of sodium metabisulfite in patch test reactions; contact allergy to Methylene-bis-methyloxazolidine; topical methotrexate in psoriasis and oral ivermectin in scabies. Avocations: running, golf, cooking. Office: Dermatology Ctr Hope Hospital Salford M6 8HD England Home Fax: 441612061018. Personal E-mail: vishalmadan@doctors.org.uk.

MADAPUSI, ARUN, educator, consultant; s. Chellu Madapusi; m. Viji ArunKumar, Nov. 1, 1992. PhD, U. North Tex., Denton, 2007. Faculty U. North Tex., 2000—. Recipient Ednl. awards, U. North Tex. Mem.: ISM. Office Fax: 940-565-4394. Business E-Mail: madapusi@unt.edu.

MADARA, JAMES LEE, dean, pathologist, educator, epitheliologist, CEO; b. Altoona, Pa., Sept. 16, 1950; s. Daniel Rodman and Margaret Jane (Hauser) M.; m. Victoria Mollenkopf, May 14, 1975; children: J. Maxwell, Alexis Lindsy. BA, Juniata Coll., 1971; MD, Hahnemann Med., 1975. Cert. anatomic and clin. pathology. Intern Deaconess Hosp., Boston, 1975—76, resident in pathology, 1976—78; fellow in internal medicine Harvard Med. Ctr., Boston, 1978—80; instr. pathology Harvard Med. Sch., Boston, 1980-81, asst. prof. pathology, 1981-85, assoc. prof. pathology, 1985-91, prof. pathology, 1993-97; assoc. prof. of health scis. and tech. Harvard-M.I.T., Boston, 1986-91; Timmie prof., chmn. dept. pathology & lab. medicine Emory U. Sch. Medicine, Atlanta, 1997—2002; dean, v.p. for medical affairs U. Chgo. Pritzker Sch. Medicine, 2002—, Sara and Harold Lincoln Thompson disting. svc. prof.; CEO U. Chgo. Med. Ctr., dean Biological Scis. Divsn. Assoc. editor Gastroenterology, 1986-91; mem. editl. bd. Jour. Clin. Investigation, 1987—; editor-in-chief Am. Jour. Pathology, 2000; contbr. over 160 articles to profl. jours. Grantee NIH, 1980—. Mem. Am. Soc. for Clin. Investigation (elected), Am. Soc. for Cell Biology, Am. Gastroenterological Assn. (rsch. coun. 1988-90, Ross Rsch. scholar award 1982), Am. Physiol. Soc., Am. Assn. Pathology (Parke/Davis award 1990), Assn. Am. Physicians. Achievements include description of functional sequellae of neutrophil-epithelial cell interactions; recognition that tight junctions between epithelial cells are regulated under physiological conditions. Office: Biological Sci U Chicago 5812 S Ellis St Chicago IL 60637 Office Fax: 773-702-1897. E-mail: jmadara@bsd.uchicago.edu.

MADDALONI, MARK A., toxicologist; b. NYC, Feb. 4, 1955; s. Daniel and Jean Maddaloni; m. Anne C. McConnell, Apr. 9, 1988; children: Amanda M., Caroline C. BS in Pharmacy, LI U. Coll. Pharmacy, NYC, 1980; MS in Toxicology, St. John's U., NYC, 1983; DPH, Columbia U. Sch. Pub. Health, NYC, 1998. Registered pharmacist NY State, 1981, diplomate Am. Bd. Toxicology, 1992. Poison info. specialist NYC Poison Control Ctr., NYC, 1983—91; toxicologist US EPA, NYC, 1991—. Instl. rev. bd. mem. NYC Dept. Health, 2000—; workshop chmn. AAAS, 2005. Contbr. scientific papers. Vice chmn. Planning Bd., Closter, NJ, 2002—08. Recipient Gold medal, US EPA, Environ. Scis. award, Columbia U.; Rsch. grant, US EPA, 2005, 2007. Mem.: Soc. Toxicology (Best Sci. Workshop award 2005). Avocations: tennis, golf, skiing. Office: US EPA 290 Broadway New York NY 10007 Business E-Mail: maddaloni.mark@epa.gov.

MADDALONI, MARTIN J., retired labor union administrator; BA, George Meany Ctr. Nat. Labor Coll., 2004. Bus. mgr. Steamfitters Local 420; v.p., Phila. internat. rep. United Assn. Journeyman and Apprentices Plumbing and Pipe Fitting Industry U.S. and Can., Wash., DC, 1988—97, gen. pres., 1997—2004. V.p. AFL-CIO, 1995. Office: United Assn 901 Massachusetts Ave NW Washington DC 20001-4307 also: 1717 K St NW Ste 207 Washington DC 20036 Office Phone: 202-628-5823.

MADDEN, CHERYL ANN, history professor; d. Robert George and Lydia Margaret Vredenburg; m. R. E. Madden, Apr. 6, 1974 (div. Sept. 11, 1997); children: Benjamin Arthur, John Edward. BA, U. RI, Kingston, 2002; MA, Providence Coll., Rhode Island, 2004. Cert. rschr. Nat. Archives & Records Adminstrn., 1999. Guest editor Can.-Am. Slavic Studies Holodomor Commemorative Editions, Idyllwild, Calif., 2003, 2008; adj. prof. history RI Coll., Providence, 2005—07, CC RI, Warwick, 2005—, keynote spkr., Holodomor Commemorative Event, 2008; annotated bibliographer Shevchenko Sci. Soc. Am., Inc., NYC, 2002—. Panelist Internat. Conf. Assn. Study Nationalities Harriman Inst., Columbia U., NYC, 2003; keynote spkr. Soyuz Ukrainok Holodomor Commemorative Event, Denver, 2003, Bus. & Profl. Assoc. Congress Holodomor Commemorative Event, Montreal, Quebec, Canada, 2007. Cochairperson Parents' Adv. Com., Charlestown, RI, 1980—86. Recipient Rumowicz Maritme Essay Contest award, English Dept. U.RI, 2003, Order Princess Olha medal, By Ukaze Pres. Ukraine Viktor Yushchenko, 2008; Michael P. Metcalf grant, RI Found., 1999, Yuri Kuziv grant, Shevchenko Sci. Soc. Am., Inc., 2002, 2003, 2008. Mem.: Am. Assn. Advancement Slavic Studies, Am. Assn. Ukrainian Studies, Shevchenko Sci. Soc. Am., Inc., Nat. Soc. Collegiate Scholars, Phi Alpha Theta, Golden Key Club. Liberal. Avocations: travel, writing, baking. Office: Community Coll Rhode Island 400 E Ave Warwick RI 02886-1807 Personal E-mail: ladyhistorian@yahoo.com.

MADDEN, DAVID, author; b. Knoxville, Tenn., July 25, 1933; s. James Helvy and Emile (Merritt) M.; m. Roberta Margaret Young, Sept. 6, 1956; 1 son, Blake Dana. BS, U. Tenn., 1957; MA, San Francisco State Coll., 1958; postgrad., Yale Drama Sch., 1959-60. Faculty Appalachian State Tchrs. Coll., Boone, NC, 1957-58, Centre Coll., Danville, Ky., 1960-62, U. Louisville, 1962-64, Kenyon Coll., Gambier, O., 1964-66, Ohio U., Athens, 1966-68; writer-in-residence La. State U., Baton Rouge, 1968-92, dir. creative writing program, 1992-94, dir. U.S. Civil War Ctr., 1992-99, Robert Penn Warren prof. creative writing, 2007—. Alumni prof. La. State U., 1994. Author: (novels) Cassandra Singing, 1969, Bijou, 1974, The Suicide's Wife, 1978, Pleasure Dome, 1979, On the Big Wind, 1980, Sharpshooter: A Novel of the Civil War, 1996, (stories) The Shadow Knows (Nat. Coun. on Arts selection), 1970, The New Orleans of Possibilities (lit. criticism) Wright Morris, 1964, Poetic Image in Six Genres, 1969, James M. Cain, 1970, A Primer of the Novel, 1980, Writers' Revisions, 1981, Cain's Craft, 1985, Revising Fiction, 1988, Rediscoveries II, 1988; asst. editor: The Kenyon Rev., 1964-66; editor: Remembering James Agee, 1974; co-editor: (with P. Bach) Classics of Civil War Fiction, 1991, Beyond the Battlefield, 2000, The Legacy of Robert Penn Warren, 2000, Thomas Wolfe's Civil War, 2004, Losses of the Sultana, 2004, Touching the Web of Southern Novelists, 2006, Primer of the Novel, 2006. Served with AUS, 1953-55. Recipient Rockefeller grant in fiction, 1969; John Golden fellow in playwriting, 1959; recipient Robert Penn Warren award for excellence in fiction. Mem. Authors League, Associated Writing Programs (bd. dirs.). Democrat. Office: La State U Dept English Baton Rouge LA 70803-0001 Home Phone: 225-344-3630. Business E-Mail: dmadden@lsu.edu.

MADDEN, DENIS JAMES, bishop; b. Carbondale, Pa., Mar. 8, 1940; BA, St. Benedict's Coll., Atchison, Kans.; MA in Psychology, Columbia U.; PhD in Clinical Psychology, U. Notre Dame. Lic. clin. psych. Md., DC. Ordained priest Order of St. Benedict, 1967; with Archdiocese of Balt., 1973—88; co-founder Accord Found., 1988; dir. Pontifical Mission for Palestine, Jerusalem, 1994—96; assoc. sec. gen. Cath. Near East Welfare Assn., Jerusalem, 1996—2005; ordained bishop, 2005; aux. bishop, urban vicar Archdiocese of Balt., 2005—. Prof. psychology U. Md. Sch. Med., Balt., 1973—88; marriage & family counselor Assoc. Cath. Charities, Balt. Roman Catholic. Office: Cath Ctr 320 Cathedral St Baltimore MD 21201 Office Phone: 410-547-5446. Office Fax: 410-727-8234.

MADDEN, JOHN, retired sportscaster, retired professional football coach; b. Austin, Minn., Apr. 10, 1936; s. Earl and Mary O'Flaherty M.; m. Virginia Madden; children: Mike, Joe. BS, Calif. Poly. U., 1959, MA, 1961. Profl. football player Phila. Eagles, 1959; asst. coach Hancock Jr. Coll., Santa Maria, Calif., 1960-62, head football coach, 1962-64; defensive coord. Calif. State U., San Diego, 1964-66; linebackers coach Oakland Raiders, Am. Football League (now Am. Football Conf., Nat. Football League), 1967-69, head football coach, 1969-79; sports commentator, football analyst CBS Sports, 1979-93, Fox Sports, 1994—2002, Monday Night Football (ABC), 2002—06, NBC Sunday Night Football, 2006—09. Author: Hey, Wait a Minute, I Wrote a Book!, 1984; One Knee Equals Two Feet (and Everything Else You Wanted To Know About Football), 1987, One Size Doesn't Fit All, 1993; co-author (with Dave Anderson) All Madden: Hey, I'm Talking Pro Football, 1996, (with Peter Kaminsky) John Madden's Ultimate Tailgating, 1998, (with Bill Gutman) John Madden's Heroes of Football, 2006; developer (software) John Madden Football, 1988, John Madden Football II, 1993. Recipient Emmy awards for sports broadcasting, 1982, 83, 85, 86, 87, 88, Pete Rozelle Radio-TV award, 2002; named NFL Coach of Yr. Am. Football League, Pro Football Weekly 1969, Sports Personality of Yr. Am. Sportscasters Assn., 1985, 1992; named one of The Most Influential People in the World of Sports, BusinessWeek, 2007, '08, Top 50 Sportscasters Am. Sportscasters Assn., 2009; named to The Pro Football Hall of Fame, 2006. Achievements include coaching the Oakland Raiders to seven AFC Western Division titles and one Super Bowl Championship, 1976, selected as head coach of the AFC Pro Bowl Team, 1971, 1972, 1973, 1974, 1975.*

MADDEN, JOHN, professional hockey player; b. Barrie, Ont., Can., May 4, 1973; m. Lauren Madden, July 1998; children: John Tyler, Reese. Grad., U. Mich., 1997. Center NJ Devils, 1999—2009, Chgo. Blackhawks, 2009—. Recipient Frank J. Selke Trophy, NHL, 2001. Achievements include being a member of NCAA National Championship Team, University of Michigan, 1996; being a member of Stanley Cup Champion New Jersey Devils, 2000, 2003. Office: Chicago Blackhawks United Ctr 1901 W Madison St Chicago IL 60612*

MADDEN, JOHN J., lawyer; b. NYC, May 27, 1946; s. John L. and Bertha M.; m. Mary A. O'Neill, June 19, 1976; children: Elisabeth, Samuel. BA, U. Pa., 1968; JD cum laude, Fordham U., 1975. Bar: NY 1976, US Dist. Ct. (So. Dist.) NY 1976; avocat a la cour de Paris 1994. From assoc. to ptnr. Shearman & Sterling LLP, NYC, 1975—83, ptnr., 1983—, co-head mergers and acquisitions group, 1987—91, head mergers and acquisitions group, 1995—2001, mng. ptnr. European Offices Paris, 1991-95, co-mng. ptnr., 2004—. Articles editor Law Review, Fordham Law Sch. Trustee St. David's Sch., N.Y.C., 1981-91 Served to 1st lt., Infantry platoon leader, 101st Airbourne Divsn. US Army, 1969—71, Vietnam. Mem. ABA, N.Y. Bar Assn., Assn. Bar City of N.Y., Internat. Bar Assn., Cercle de l'Union Interalliee (Paris), World Policy Inst. (bd. advisors 2004—) Office: Shearman & Sterling LLP 599 Lexington Ave New York NY 10022-6069 Office Fax: 646-848-7055. Business E-Mail: jmadden@shearman.com.

MADDEN, JOHN PATRICK, lawyer; b. NYC, Sept. 9, 1945; s. Eugene Patrick and Eileen Mary (Gaughan) M.; m. Sally Williams, Apr. 21, 1984; children: Samuel, Christopher. Student in Mechanical Engineering, U. Maine, 1966; student in Structural Engineering, U. Wash., 1967, Purdue Univ., 1968; student in Environmental Engineering, George Washington Univ., 1975; BCE, Manhattan Coll., 1967; MSCE, NYU, 1969; JD, St. John's U. Sch. Law, NYC, 1978; EC Trade Law, Trinity Coll., Cambridge Univ., England, 1976; Comecon Trade Law, Univ. Warsaw, Poland, 1976. Bar: US Patent and Trademark Office 1978, NY State Ct. 1979, NJ State Ct. 1982, US Dist. Ct. (so. and ea. dists.) NY 1982, US Dist. Ct. NJ 1982, US Supreme Ct. 1985; solicitor Law Soc. England and Wales, 2003; cert. Accredited Mediator Chartered Inst. Arbitrators, London, 2002; accredited mediator, CEDR, London, 2002; Large Complex Case Panel, Am. Arbitration Assn., 1996; constrn. arbitrator, 1983, Am. Arbitration Assn., comml. mediator, 1990, internat. arbitrator, 1993; US D.O.D. qualified instr., Nuclear Def. Design, 1967. Engr., 1966—75; law clk., assoc. Buckley, Treacy, Shaffel Mackey & Abbate, NYC, 1977-80; cons. Contractors Consulting Svcs. Inc., Greatneck, N.Y., 1980-81; ptnr. Madden, Sciarra & Muirhead, N.Y., N.J., 1981-82, Canfield, Venusti, Madden & Rossi, NYC, 1979—. Lectr. in field; arbitrator and mediator conciliator in field. Contbr. articles to profl. jours. V.p. N.Y.C. Jaycees, 1975-95. ROTC USAF, 1963-65. Mem. ABA (pub. contract law sect., forum com. on constrn. industry), Internat. Bar Assn. (mem. alternative dispute resolution com., internat. constrn. projects com.), London Ct. Internat. Arbitration, Swiss Arbitration Assn., Am. Trial Lawyers Assn., NY State Bar Assn., NY State Trial Lawyers Assn., Assn. of Bar of City of NY, Chartered Inst. Arbitrators, Union Internationale Des Avocats, Am. Arbitration Assn., NJ State Bar Assn., Nat. Arts Club, Fidelity & Surety Law com. Office: Canfield Venusti Madden & Rossi 230 Park Ave Rm 2525 New York NY 10169-2599 E-mail: johnpmadden@cs.com.

MADDEN, JOHN PHILIP, motion picture director, actor; b. Portsmouth, Hampshire, England, Apr. 8, 1949; Dir. (theatre prodns.) Grownups, Wings, Beyond Therapy, Caritas Christ, The Bundle, Measure For Measure, The Suicide, Beyond East And West, An American Comedy, Terry By Terry, Cinders, Salonka (Am. Premiere at Pub. Theatre), (TV films) The Pigman's Protege, Poppyland, A Wreath Of Roses, Sherlock Holmes, The Return Of Sherlock Holmes, Inspector Morse, The Storyteller, also directed episodes of After The War (PBS) and TV versions of Grownups and Wings; (films) Grown Ups, 1985, Ethan Frome, 1993, Meat, 1994, Golden Gate, 1994, Prime Suspect 4: The Lost Child, 1995, Truth or Dare, 1996, Mrs. Brown, 1997, Shakespeare in Love, 1998, Captain Corelli's Mandolin, 2001, Proof, 2005, Killshot, 2009; acted in films P.K. and the Kid, 1985, Little Giants, 1994, The Replacements, 2000.*

MADDEN, JOSEPH DANIEL, trade association executive; b. NYC, Dec. 25, 1921; s. Thomas A. and Margaret (McFadden) M.; m. Eileen M. MacDonnell, Sept. 8, 1951; children: Joseph Daniel, Jr., Maureen A. BS, Fordham U., 1951; MBA, N.Y. U., 1956. Credit investigator Dun & Bradstreet, NYC, 1947-48; credit mgr. Devoe & Raynolds Co., NYC, 1948-50, Admiral Corp., NYC, 1950-51; nat. credit mgr. Standard Toch Chems., Inc., SI, N.Y., 1951-52; with chems. and plastics div. Union Carbide Corp., Midland, Mich., 1952-62; mgr. Detroit sales office, 1958-60; sr. staff adminstr. Soc. Plastics Industry, Washington, 1962-69; exec. v.p. Drug, Chem. and Assoc. Techs. Assn., Robbinsville, NJ, 1969-88, cons. assn. mgmt., 1988—. With U.S. Army, 1942-43. Mem. AARP (past pres. local chpt.), Am. Soc. Assn. Execs. (cert.), N.Y. Soc. Assn. Execs. (past bd. dirs., Exec. of Yr. award 1988), Soc. Friendly Sons of St. Patrick, Kiwanis (past pres. Bayside, sec.), Am. Legion, Toastmasters Internat. (past pres. local club). Home: 211-37 18th Ave Bayside NY 11360-1529

MADDEN, MARIE FRANCES, marketing professional; b. Weatherby, Mo., Sept. 27, 1928; d. Truman E. and Hazel (Tiller) Wilford; m. Mertice A. Madden, July 20, 1974. Grad. high sch., Cameron, Mo. Cert. personnel cons. Office mgr. Bechtel Corp., San Francisco, Lawrence, Kans., 1948—52; adminstrv. asst. Milton P. Allen, Atty., Lawrence, 1952—56, Philip T. Sharples, Entrepreneur, Phila., 1956—74; corp. sec. Madden Aircraft Sales Corp., Dallas, 1974—81; pres., owner Madden Co., Inc. of Dallas, 1981—; exec. dir. TPC Madden Mktg. Group, Dallas, 1989—91; owner, pres. Madden Mktg. and Design Group, Dallas, 1991—. Pres. Innovative Sign Group, 1999-2002, CEO, 2002—; CEO Creative Foam Works, Richardson, Tex., 2004—. Bd. trustees Richardson Symphony Orch., 2003—; v.p. mktg. exec. commn. bd. Richardson Symphony Orch., 2003—06, 2008—; trustee 1st United Meth. Ch., Richardson, 2005—. Mem. Metroplex Assn. Pers. Cons. (bd. dirs. 1986-87), Tex. Assn. Pers. Cons. (bd. dirs. 1987-89), Apt. Assn. Greater Dallas, Nat. Apt. Assn., Nat. Assn. Home Builders, Tex. Apt. Assn. Avocations: reading, golf. Office: 1819 Firman Dr Ste 145 Richardson TX 75081-1868 Home: 1389 Shadow Creek Dr Fairview TX 75069 Office Phone: 972-671-6627. E-mail: mmadden@maddenmarketing.com.

MADDEN, MICHAEL DANIEL, finance company executive; b. Buffalo, Feb. 16, 1949; s. Daniel Francis and Miriam (Catron) M.; m. Mary Madden, May 1, 1976; children: Daniel, Kristina, Megan, Michael. BA in Econs. magna cum laude, Le Moyne Coll., 1971; MBA with distinction, U. Pa., 1973. Assoc. Kidder, Peabody & Co., NYC, 1973-77, v.p., 1977-80, mng. dir., 1980-85, global head investment banking, 1985-88; head investment banking Lehman Bros., NYC, 1989—93; exec. mng. dir. Global Capital Markets Kidder, Peabody Co., NYC, 1993-94; vice chmn., chief origination officer Paine Webber Inc., NYC, 1995-96; chmn., CEO Hanover Capital LLC, NYC, 1996—; ptnr. Beacon Group, NYC; sr. ptnr. Questor Mgmt., NYC, 1999—2005; mng. ptnr. Black Eagle Ptnrs., NYC, 2005—. Bd. dirs. Geologistics Corp., Transonic Sys. Inc., Chef Solutions Inc., Pinn Oak Mining, Freeport Properties, Inc. Bd. dirs. Cath. TV Ctr., NYC, 1981-85, Canisius Prep. Sch., Buffalo, 1992—; chmn. bd. trustees LeMoyne Coll., Syracuse, NY, 1987—. Mem. Am. Petroleum Inst., MBA Assn., Univ. Club, The Creek, Longboat Key Club. Republican. Roman Catholic. Avocations: boxing, hunting, tennis, coin collecting/numismatics, fishing. Office: Black Eagle Ptnrs 750 Lexington Ave 15 Fl New York NY 10022 Office Phone: 917-591-6060. Business E-Mail: mmadden@blackeaglepartners.com.

MADDEN, PALMER BROWN, lawyer; b. Milw., Sept. 19, 1945; m. Susan L. Paulus, Mar. 31, 1984. BA, Stanford U., 1968; JD, U. Calif., Berkeley, 1973. Bar: Calif. 1973, U.S. Dist. Ct. (no. dist.) Calif. 1973, U.S. Supreme Ct. 1982. Ptnr. McCutchen, Doyle Brown & Enersen, Walnut Creek, 1985-98; prin. ADR Svcs., Alamo, Calif., 1999—. Pres. State Bar Bd. Govs., 2000-01. Chair bd. govs. Continuing Edn. of the Bar, 1997; judge pro tem Contra Costa Superior Ct., 1991-98; pres. Contra Costa Coun., 1995, Kennedy-King Found., 1994; bd. dirs. Episcopal Homes Found., 2001-05, Bay Area Legal Aid, 2005-2007, Bar Fund, 2006-2007. Mem. Contra Costa County Bar Assn. (pres. 1996-97). Democrat. Episcopalian. Office: ADR Svcs 3000 Danville Blvd # 543 Alamo CA 94507 Office Phone: 925-838-8593. Business E-Mail: pbm@netvista.net.

MADDEN, RICHARD BLAINE, forest products executive; b. Short Hills, NJ, Apr. 27, 1929; s. James L. and Irma (Twining) M.; m. Joan Fairbairn, May 24, 1958; children: John Richard, Lynne Marie, Kathryn Ann, Andrew Twining. BS, Princeton U., 1951; JD, U. Mich., 1956; MBA, NYU, 1959; PhD (hon.), St. Scholastica Coll., 1994. Bar: Mich. 1956, N.Y. 1958. Gen. asst. treas.'s dept. Socony Mobil Oil Corp., NYC, 1956-57, spl. asst., 1958-59, fin. rep., 1960; asst. to pres. Mobil Chem. Co.; also dir. Mobil Chems. Ltd. of Eng., 1960-63; exec. v.p., gen. mgr. Kordite Corp.; also v.p. Mobil Plastics, 1963-66; v.p. Mobil Chem. Co., NYC, 1966-68, group v.p., 1968-70; asst. treas. Mobil Oil Corp., 1970-71; chmn. Mobil Oil Estates Ltd., 1970-71; pres., chief exec. Potlatch Corp., San Francisco, 1971-77, chmn. chief exec. officer, 1971-94; ret., 1994. From lectr. to adj. assoc. prof. fin. N.Y.U., 1960-63; bd. dir., Knight Grand Cross Magistral Grace in Obedience; dir. Order of Malta, Western Assn., former pres., chief exec. 2002-08; bd. govs., mem. audit com., mem. adminstrv. compensation and labor rels. com. San Francisco Symphony. Former bd. dir. Smith-Kettlewell Eye Rsch. Inst., trustee emeritus, former chmn. Am. Enterprise Inst.; former mem. bd. Nat. Park Found.; hon. trustee Con. Econ. Devel., PG&E Corp., URS Corp., DelMente Corp., Amfac Corp., Bank of Calif. Lt. (j.g.) USNR, 1951-54. Mem. N.Y. Bar Assn., Mich. Bar Assn. Clubs: Bohemian (San Francisco); Lagunitas (Ross, Calif.); Metropolitan (Washington). Roman Catholic. Office Phone: 415-453-9121.

MADDEN, STEVEN, footwear designer; b. NY, 1957; m. Wendy Madden. Attended, U. Miami. Founder Steven Madden Ltd., 1990, CEO, 1990—2002, creative & design chief, 2002—. Owner, Friedman accessories divsn. Steven Madden Ltd., 2006—, creative dir. Office: Steven Madden Ltd 52-16 Barnett Ave Long Island City NY 11104 Office Phone: 718-446-1800. Office Fax: 718-446-5655.

MADDEN, THOMAS JAMES, lawyer, educator; b. Trenton, NJ, Sept. 13, 1941; m. Irene Lyons. BEE, Villanova U., 1964; JD with honors, Cath. U., 1968. Bar: NJ 1968, DC 1968, US Patent Office 1968. Atty. adv. Naval Air Sys. Command, 1968—69; dep. gen. counsel Dept. Justice Law Enforcement Assistance Adminstrn., 1970—71, gen. counsel, 1972—79; dir. Nat. Adv. Commn. on Criminal Justice Stds. and Goals, 1971—73; adv. US Office Mgmt. and Budget on Fed. Assistance Programs, Washington, 1979—80; gen. counsel Dept. Justice Office Justice Assistance Rsch. and Stats., 1980; from assoc. to ptnr. Kay Scholer, Fierman, Hays and Handler, Washington, 1980—84; ptnr., gov. contract, intellectual property litig. Venable, LLP (formerly Venable, Baetjer, Howard & Civiletti), Washington, 1984—. Adj. prof. contract law Am. U., 1980-85; gen. counsel Nat. Coun. Juvenile and Family Ct. Judges; adv. panel on streamlining and codifying fed. acquisition laws Dept. Def., 1991-93; mem. Procurement Round Table, 1998—, vice chmn., 2002— Contbr. articles to profl. jours. Pres. US Ct. Fed. Claims Bar Assn., 1999-2000. Recipient Louis Brownlow award Am. Soc. for Pub. Adminstrn., 1982, Disting. Svc. award Dept. Justice Law Enforcement Assistance Adminstr., 1973, Wilson Cowen award US Ct. Fed. Claims, 1998. Fellow Am. Bar Found. (life); mem. ABA (chmn. pub. contract law sect. 1988-89, pres. fellows of pub. contract law sect. 1992-93), DC Bar Assn., Fed. Bar Assn. (pres. DC chpt. 1982-83). Office: Venable LLP 575 7th St N W Washington DC 20004 Office Phone: 202-344-4803. Business E-Mail: tmadden@venable.com.

MADDEN, WALES HENDRIX, JR., retired lawyer; b. Amarillo, Tex., Sept. 1, 1927; s. Wales Hendrix and Kathryn (Nash) Madden; m. Alma Faye Cowden, Nov. 8, 1952; children: Wales Hendrix III, Straughn. BA, U. Tex., 1950, LLB, 1952. Bar: Tex. 1952. Pvt. practice, Amarillo. Mem. Tex. Constl. Revision Commn., 1973. Mem. Tex. Coll. and Univ. Sys. Coord. Bd., 1964—69, Amarillo Area Found., Cal Farley's Boys Ranch, Pres.'s Export Coun., 1981, Select Com. Higher Edn., 1985, 1987; chmn. SWST regional panel Pres.'s Commn. White Ho. Fellowships, 1989—90; chmn. Tex. Water Devel. Bd., 2002; mem. Gov.'s Com. Ad Valorem Taxes, 1996; bd. regents Amarillo Coll., 1958—59, U. Tex., 1959—65; trustee Trinity U., San Antonio; chmn. bd. Internat. Food and Agrl. Devel., 1990—94. USNR, 1945—46, Pacific. Named Outstanding Man of Amarillo, 1972, Disting. Alumnus, U. Tex., 1979, U. Tex. Law Sch., 1986. Mem.: ABA, State Jr. Bar Tex. (pres. 1956), State Bar Tex. (Outstanding 50 Year Lawyer award 2003), Amarillo Bar Assn. (pres. 1956), Friar Soc., Amarillo C. of C. (pres. 1968), Tex. Philos. Soc., Sigma Alpha, Phi Eta Sigma, Phi Delta Theta, Phi Alpha Delta. Presbyterian. Avocations: mountain climbing, hiking. Home and Office: PO Box 15288 Amarillo TX 79105-5288 Office Phone: 806-374-2422.

MADDIN, ROBERT, metallurgist, educator; b. Hartford, Conn., Oct. 20, 1918; s. Isadore I. and Mae (Jacobs) Levine; married, July 8, 1945; children: Leslie, Jill. BS in Metall. Engring., Purdue U., 1942; DEng., Yale U., 1948. Registered profl. engr., Pa. Asst., assoc. prof. Johns Hopkins U., Balt., 1949-55; prof. U. Pa., phila., 1955-73, univ. prof., 1973-83; vis. prof. Harvard U., Cambridge, Mass., 1983-87, curator, 1987—; vis. prof. Oxford (Eng.) U., 1970, vis. fellow Wolfson Coll., 1987. Vis. prof. U. Birmingham, Eng., 1953-54; vis. scholar Hebrew U., Jerusalem, 1976; hon. prof. Beijing Sci. and Engring. U., 1986; hon. mem. Japan Metals, hon. prof. Dali U., 2006. Editor-in-chief Math., Sci., and Engring, 1965-82; contbr. more than 250 publs. to profl. jours. 1st Lt. USAF, 1942-45. Disting. Sr. Sci. fellow A. von Humboldt Found., Germany, 1989-90, Disting. Alumnus Purdue U., 1974; recipient Pomerance award Archaeol. Inst. Am., 1994, medal of merit U. Pa., medal, DBM, 2008. Fellow Am. Soc. Metallurgists, TMS. Avocation: history early metallurgy. Personal E-mail: maddin1511@yahoo.com.

MADDOCK, JEROME TORRENCE, library and information scientist; b. Darby, Pa., Feb. 7, 1940; s. Richard Cotton and Isobel Louise (Mezger) M.; m. Karen Rhueama Weygand, Oct. 2, 1965. BS in Biology, Muhlenberg Coll., 1961; MS in Info. Sci., Drexel U., 1968. Editl. assoc. Biol. Abstracts, Phila., 1962—63; mgr. rsch. info. Merck & Co., West Point, Pa., 1963—72; sr. cons. Auerbach Assocs., Inc., Phila., 1972—79; mgr. libr. and info. svcs. Solar Energy Rsch. Inst., Golden, Colo., 1979—88; mgr. info. svcs. Transp. Rsch. Bd., Washington, 1988—99; project mgr. IHS Enterprise Solutions, Boulder, Colo., 1999—2001; ind. cons., 2002—; faculty online U. Phoenix, 1999—. Del. Gov.'s Conf. on Libr. and Info. Svc., Pa., 1978; mem. blue ribbon panel to select archivist of U.S., Washington, 1979; U.S. del. to ops. com. on transp. rsch. info. Orgn. for Econ. Cooperation and Devel., 1988-99. Bd. dirs. Paoli (Pa.) Pub. Libr., 1976-77, Boulder Friends of Jazz, 2003—; bd. trustees Louisville County Pub. Libr., 2002-07, pres. 2004. With USAFR, 1962-68. Mem. AAAS, Am. Soc. Info. Sci. (chmn. 1974-75), Elks, Beta Phi Mu, Pi Delta Epsilon. Republican. Episcopalian. Achievements include projection of information science operations 10 years into the future. Home: 545 W Laurel Ct Louisville CO 80027-1116

MADDON, JOE (JOSEPH JOHN MADDON), professional baseball manager; b. Sept. 19, 1954; m. Jaye Sousoures, Nov. 8, 2008. BS in Economics, Lafayette Coll., Easton, Pa., 1976. Mgr. Idaho Falls Minor League Baseball, 1981, Salem Minor League Baseball, Peoria Minor League Baseball, Midland Minor League Baseball, 1985—86; coord. Calif. Angels Arizona Instrnl. League, 1984—93; roving hitting instructor Calif. Angels, 1987—93, dir. player develop., 1994, bullpen coach, 1994, first base coach, 1995, bench coach, 1996, interim mgr., 1996, 1999, bench coach, 2000—05; mgr. Tampa Bay Devil Rays, 2005—. Named Am. League Mgr. of Yr., Sporting News, 2008, Baseball Writers' Assn. America, 2008. Office: Tampa Bay Devil Rays One Tropicana Dr Saint Petersburg FL 33705*

MADDOW, RACHEL ANNE, radio and TV personality, political activist; b. Castro Valley, Calif., Apr. 1, 1973; d. Bob and Elaine Maddow. BA in Pub. Policy, Stanford U., Calif., 1994; DPhil in Polit. Sci., Lincoln Coll., Oxford U., Eng., 2001. Host Sta. WRNX-100.9 FM, Holyoke, Mass., co-host Dave in the Morning Show; host Big Breakfast, WRSI, Northhampton, Mass., 2002—04; co-host (with Chuck D. & Liz Winstead) Unfiltered, Air America Radio, NYC, host The Rachel Maddow Show, 2005—, MSNBC, 2008—. Regular panelist Tucker, 2005—, Race for the White House with David Gregory, 2008; regular contbr., former guest host Countdown with Keith Olbermann; polit. analyst MSNBC, 2008—. Named Lesbian/Bi Woman of Yr., AfterEllen.com's Visibility Awards, 2008; named one of Top 100 Gay Men & Women Who Moved Culture, Out mag., 2008, The 40 Under 40, Crain's NY Bus., 2009; grantee John Gardner Pub. Svc. Fellowship, 1994, Ludlam Health Policy Fellowship; fellow AIDS Legal Referral Panel, San Francisco; Rhodes Scholar, 1995. Office: Air America Radio 641 Ave Americas Fl 4 New York NY 10011-2038*

MADDOX, ALVA HUGH, retired state supreme court justice; b. Andalusia, Ala., Apr. 17, 1930; s. Christopher Columbus and Audie Lodella Maddox; m. Virginia Roberts, June 14, 1958; children: Robert Hugh, Jane Maddox, Hoesel. AB in Journalism, U. Ala., Tuscaloosa,

1952, JD, 1957. Bar: Ala. 1957. Law clk. to Judge Aubrey Cates, Ala. Ct. Appeals, Montgomery, 1957-58; field examiner Chief Atty.'s Office, VA, Montgomery, 1958-59; law clk. to Judge Frank M. Johnson, U.S. Dist. Ct., Montgomery, 1959-61; pvt. practice Montgomery, 1961-65; cir. judge, spl. cir. judge Montgomery Cir. Ct., 1963, asst. dist. atty., 1964; legal advisor to govs. including George C. Wallace, Lurleen B. Wallace, Albert P. Brewer, State of Ala., Montgomery, 1965-69; assoc. justice Supreme Ct. Ala., Montgomery, 1969-2001; ret., 2001. Author: Billy Boll Weevil: A Pest Becomes A Hero, 1976, Alabama Rules of Criminal Procedure, 1991, supplements, 1992—. Founder youth jud. program YMCA, Montgomery, 1978, also mem. metro. bd. dir. 2d lt. USAF, 1952-54, col. USAF Res. ret. Recipient Man of Yr. award YMCA, 1988, Disting. Program Svc. award, 1989, Srs. of Achievement award Montgomery Coun. on Aging, 1999, Sherman Christensen award Am. Arms Ct., 2009. Mem.: ABA, Am. Inns of Ct. (former trustee), Hugh Maddox Inn of Ct. Montgomery (charter, founding mem.), Christian Legal Soc., Inst. Jud. Adminstrn., Ala. Bar Assn. (Jud. award of merit 1997), Order of Samaritan/U. Ala. Law Sch., Kiwanis. Baptist. Office: 3137 Hathaway Pl Montgomery AL 36111-1707 Home Phone: 334-264-8732; Office Phone: 334-264-0505.

MADDOX, ODINGA LAWRENCE, II, head of religious order; b. Akron, Ohio, Aug. 23, 1964; s. Odinga Lawrence and Shirley Jean (Shavers) Maddox; m. Nancy Malone, Apr. 21, 1983; children: Terrell, Lawrence III, Shelly, Carissa, Joshua. AST in theology, Berean Bible Coll., 1995; BA in pastorial min., Bethany Divinity Coll., 2000; MA in pastoral min., Bethany Seminary, 2005. Ordained deacon 1996; cert. peace officer State of Ohio. Peace officer Comml. Protective Svcs., Akron, Ohio, 1984—96; pastor St. Paul AMEZ Ch., Coraopolis, Pa., 1996—98, Price Meml. AMEZ Ch., Atlantic City, 1998—. Auditor NJ Conf. AMEZ Ch., Atlantic City, 2002—; dean Camden Dist. Sch. of Min., Camden, NJ, 2002—. Mem. Salvation Army, Coraopolis, Pa., 1996—98. Recipient Black Hist. Acad. award, Asbury United Meth. Ch., 1999, Faithful Svc. award, Minister's Home Detention Program, 2003, Cmty. Involvement award, NAACP, 2005. Mem.: NAACP, Pan-Meth. Alliance (pres. 2001). Avocations: reading, fishing, power walking. Office: Price Meml AME Zion Ch 525 Atlantic Ave Atlantic City NJ 08401 E-mail: amezionite@aol.com.

MADDREY, WILLIS CROCKER, medical educator, internist, academic administrator, consultant, researcher; b. Roanoke Rapids, NC, Mar. 29, 1939; s. Milner Crocker and Sara Jean (Willis) M.; m. Ann Marie Matt; children: Jeffrey, Gregory, Thomas. BS, Wake Forest U., 1960; MD, Johns Hopkins U., 1964. Diplomate: Am. Bd. Internal Medicine. Intern Osler Med. Service Johns Hopkins Hosp., Balt., 1964-65, asst. resident, 1965-66, 68-69, chief resident, 1969-70; fellow in liver disease Yale U., 1970-71; asst. prof. medicine Johns Hopkins U., Balt., 1971-75, assoc. prof., 1975-79, prof., 1980—82, asst. dean Sch. Medicine, 1975-79, assoc. dir. dept. medicine, 1979-82; prof., chmn. dept. medicine Jefferson Med. Coll., Phila., 1982-90; v.p. clin. affairs U. Tex. Southwestern Med. Ctr., Dallas, 1990-93, exec. v.p. clin. affairs, 1993—. Assoc. editor: Medicine, 1972-82, Hepatology, 1988-95, mem. editl. bd., 1981-84, 86-87, Gastroenterology, 1982-87, Am. Jour. Medicine, 1978-88; contbr. articles to profl. jours. Bd. dirs. Am. Liver Found., 1978-81, Dallas County Med. Soc., 1996-98; trustee Magee Rehab. Hosp., Phila., 1982-87. With USPHS, 1966-68. Mem. ACP (bd. regents 1986-92, pres. 92-93), Am. Soc. Clin. Investigation, Am. Gastroenterol. Assn., Am. Assn. Study Liver Disease (pres. 1981). Republican. Office: U Tex Southwestern Med Ctr 5323 Harry Hines Blvd Dallas TX 75390-8570 Office Phone: 214-648-2024.

MADDUX, GREG (GREGORY ALAN MADDUX), retired professional baseball player; b. San Angelo, Tex., Apr. 14, 1966; m. Kathy Maddux; children: Amanda Paige, Chase Alan. Grad., H.S., Las Vegas. Pitcher Chgo. Cubs, 1986—92, 2004—06, Atlanta Braves, 1993—2003, LA Dodgers, 2006, 2008, San Diego Padres, 2007—08; ret., 2008. Co-founder Maddux Found., 1993—. Recipient Cy Young award, 1992—95, Gold Glove award, 1990—2002, 2004—08, William J. Slocum award, Baseball Writers' Assn. America, NY Chpt., 2009; named Nat. League Pitcher of Yr., The Sporting News, 1992—95; named to Nat. League All-Star team, Maj. League Baseball, 1988, 1992, 1994—98, 2000, All-Time Rawlings Gold Glove Team, 2007. Achievements include leading the National League in: starts, 1990-93, 2000, 03, 05; innings, 1991-95; wins, 1992, 94, 95; ERA, 1993-95, 98; complete games, 1993-95; shutouts, 1994, 95, 98, 2000, 01; being the first pitcher in Major League Baseball history to win the Cy Young award for four consecutive years, 1992-95; being a member of the World Series Championship winning Atlanta Braves, 1995; becoming 13th pitcher in MLB history to throw 3,000 strikeouts, 2005; holding the all-time record for Gold Glove awards with 18.*

MADDY, COLEEN, editor; b. Wilkinsburg, Pa., July 24, 1964; d. Jimmy Joe and Agnes (Prosser) M. BA in English Lit., U. N.Mex., Albuquerque, 1987; MA in English Lit., U. Iowa, Iowa City, 1989. Software tester Am. Coll. Testing, Iowa City, 1989-93; mgr. software quality assurance Breakthrough, Inc., Oakdale, Iowa, 1993-97; editor U. Iowa Hosps. and Clinics, Iowa City, 1997—99; mktg. comm. mgr., publs. editor Sun Healthcare Group, Inc., Albuquerque, 2000—. Adj. prof. Kirkwood C.C., 1992—99; instr. TVI C.C., 2000—06. Book rev. editor Iowa Woman, 1990-95; contbr. articles to ency. and mags. Mem. Phi Kappa Phi, Phi Beta Kappa. Roman Catholic. Avocations: writing, music. Office: Sun Healthcare Group Inc 101 Sun Ave NE Albuquerque NM 87109

MADDY, JIM, museum association administrator; MA in Economics, W. Va. U. Pres. League of Conservation Votes, Nat. Park Found., Wash., DC; with Resources Legacy Fund, Sacramento; pres., CEO Assn. Zoos and Aquariums, Silver Spring, Md. Office: Assn Zoos and Aquariums 8403 Colesville Rd Ste 710 Silver Spring MD 20910-3314

MADEIRA, FRANCIS KING CAREY, conductor, educator; b. Jenkintown, Pa., Feb. 21, 1917; s. Percy Childs and Margaret (Carey) M.; m. Jean E. Browning, June 17, 1947. Grad., Avon Old Farms, 1934; student, Julliard Grad. Sch., 1937-43; DFA (hon.), Providence Coll., 1966; DHL, R.I. Coll., 1969; MusD (hon.), Brown U., 1976. Instr. music Brown U., 1943-46, asst. prof. music, 1946-56, assoc. prof. music, 1956-66. Founder, condr. R.I. Philharm. Orch., 1945-78; concert pianist recitals and condr. concerts, U.S. and Europe; also guest condr. U.S. and fgn. orchs. World premiere Trilogy (JFK-MLK-RFK) (by Ron Nelson), R.I. Philharmonic Orch., 1969. Mem. music panel Maine State Arts Commn., 1987-90; bd. trustees Saco River Festival Assn., 1988-94; mem. adv. bd., trustee Portland (Maine) Symphony Orch., 1996—. Recipient Gov.'s award for excellence in arts, 1972; John F. Kennedy award for svc. to cmty., 1978, Maestro award R.I. Philharm. Orch., 1998, Millennium Reflections award R.I. Philharm. Orch., 1999, John Hazen White Sr. Leadership award R.I. Philharm. Orch., 2003, Citizen Citation award Mayor or Providence, R.I., 2003.

MADELIAN, VERGINE, biology professor; d. Garo Madenlian and Marie Medzikian. PhD, U. Mass., Amherst. Rsch. scientist Wadsworth Ctr. Labs and rsch., Albany, NY, 1978—2006; lectr. Calif. State U., Northridge, 2001—. Bd. dir. Armenian Bone Marrow Donor Registry, LA, 2001—. Grant, NIH, 1990, NSF, 1990. Avocations: gardening, music. Office: Calif State Univ Northridge 18111 Nordhoff Str Northridge CA 91330-83 Business E-Mail: vmadelian@csun.edu.

MADER, DOUGLAS PAUL, research administrator; b. Brookings, SD, May 16, 1963; s. Lawrence Harold Mader Jr. and Susan Margaret (Littleton) M.; m. Darla Sue Hower, Dec. 30, 1991; children: Alyssa, Megan, Matthew BS in Engring. Physics, S.D. State U., 1985; MS in Math., Colo. Sch. of Mines, 1990; PhD in Mech. Engring., Colo. State U., 1994. Quality control engr. Govt. Electronics Group, Motorola, Scottsdale, Ariz., 1985-87; integrated circuit test engr. Semiconductor Products sector, Motorola, Mesa, Ariz., 1987-88; sr. staff engr. Six Sigma Rsch. Inst., Motorola, Schaumburg, Ill., 1990-92, prin. staff scientist, 1992; cons. Rockwell Internat., Cedar Rapids, Iowa, 1992-93; quality engring. mgr. Advanced Energy Industries, Ft. Collins, Colo., 1993-95; instr. stats. and mech. engring. Colo. State U., 1993-94; statistician Hewlett-Packard Co., Greeley, Colo., 1995-96, sr. quality cons., 1996-97, quality engring. mgr., 1997; mfg. mgr. Hewlett-Packard Corporate Quality, Palo Alto, Calif., 1997-99, quality program mgr., 1999; dir. Seagate Technology, Longmont, Colo., 1999-2000; v.p. Six Sigma Acad., 2000—; pres., CEO SigmaPro Inc., Ft. Collins, 2000—. Author: Process Control Methods, 1993 (videotapes) Concurrent Engineering - The Foundation of Six Sigma Quality, 1992; mem. editl. bd. Internat. Jour. of Ops. and Quantitative Mgmt., 1994— Mem. Am. Statis. Assn., Inst. Indsl. Engrs., Am. Soc. Quality Control (cert. quality engr., standing rev. and mix media rev. bd. 1992—), Inst. Ops. Rsch. and Mgmt. Sci., Decision Scis. Inc Office: SigmaPro Inc 2038 Vermont Dr Ste 207 Fort Collins CO 80525 Business E-Mail: doug.mader@sigmapro.com.

MADERA URIBE, JOSE DE JESUS, bishop emeritus; b. San Francisco, Nov. 27, 1927; Student, Domus Studiorum of the Missionaries of the Holy Spirit, Coyoacan, D.F., Mexico. Ordained priest Missionaries of the Holy Spirit, 1957; ordained bishop, 1980; coadjutor to bishop Diocese of Fresno, 1980—91; aux. bishop Archdiocese for Mil. Svcs., Washington, 1991—2004, aux. bishop emeritus, 2004—. Roman Catholic. Office: 2330 John Still Dr Sacramento CA 95832 E-mail: maderajj@aol.com.

MADEWELL, JOHN EDWARD, radiologist; Student, Ctrl. State Coll., Oklahoma City, 1960-69; MD, U. Okla., 1969. Intern Madigen Gen. Hosp., Tacoma, 1969-70; resident in diagnostic radiology Walter Reed Med. Ctr., Washington, 1970-73; fellow in radiol. pathology Armed Forces Inst. Pathology, Washington, 1973-74; radiologist Pa. State Geisinger Health Sys.; prof., chmn. dept. radiology Milton S. Hershey Med. Ctr./Pa. State U., 1987—; exec. dir. Univ. Physicians/Pa. State U., Hershey, 1996-97. Mem. Am. Coll. Radiology, Am. Roentgen Ray Soc., Assn. Univ. Radiologists, Internat. Skeletal Soc., Radiologic Soc. N.Am. Office: Pa State U Coll Medicine Hershey MC Dept Radiol H066 PO Box 850 Hershey PA 17033-0850

MADGAR, ADAM JASON, engineering company executive; b. Warren, Ohio, Apr. 22, 1977; s. Gary and Jean Marie Gadzia; m. Allison DeVito, Aug. 18, 2007. BEE, Youngstown State U., Ohio, 2000, MBA, 2001; MA in Fin. Economics, Kent State U., Ohio, 2004. Six sigma black belt GE Consumer and Indsl. Products, Niles, Ohio, 1999—2004; corp. quality (six sigma black belt) MACtac - Divsn. Bemis, Stow, Ohio, 2004—06; corp. engring., process tech. Millwood Inc., Girard, Ohio, 2006—. Mem.: Biltmore Who's Who (VIP exec. mem. 2008—), Free & Accepted Masons, Ohio (master mason 2001—). Achievements include patents for the pallet repair and re-manufacturing industry. Home: 247 Portal Dr Cortland OH 44410 Office: Millwood Inc 986 Tibbetts-Wick Rd Girard OH 44420 Office Phone: 330-883-9626. Business E-Mail: amadgar@millwoodinc.com.

MADGETT, NAOMI LONG, poet, editor, publisher, educator; b. Norfolk, Va., July 5, 1923; d. Clarence Marcellus and Maude Selena (Hilton) Long; m. Julian F. Witherspoon, Mar. 31, 1946 (div. Apr. 1949); 1 child, Jill Witherspoon Boyer; m. William H. Madgett, July 29, 1954 (div. Dec. 1960); m. Leonard P. Andrews, Mar. 31, 1972 (dec. May 1996). BA, Va. State Coll., 1945; MEd, Wayne State U., 1955; PhD, Internat. Inst. for Advanced Studies, 1980; LHD (hon.), Siena Heights Coll., 1991, Loyola U., 1993; DFA (hon.), Mich. State U., 1994. Reporter, copyreader Mich. Chronicle, Detroit, 1946; svc. rep. Mich. Bell Telephone Co., Detroit, 1948-54; tchr. English pub. high schs. Detroit, 1955-65, 66-68; rsch. assoc. Oakland U., Rochester, Mich., 1965-66; lectr. English U. Mich., 1970-71; assoc. prof. English Eastern Mich. U., Ypsilanti, 1968-73, prof., 1973-84, prof. emeritus, 1984—; editor-pub. Lotus Press, 1974—. Editor Lotus Poetry Series, Mich. State U. Press, 1993-98. Author: (poetry) Songs to a Phantom Nightingale (under name Naomi Cornelia Long), 1941, One and the Many, 1956, Star by Star, 1965, 2d edit., 70, (with Ethel Tincher and Henry B. Maloney) Success in Language and Literature B, 1967, (textbook) Pink Ladies in the Afternoon, 1972, 2d edit., 90, Exits and Entrances, 1978, A Student's Guide to Creative Writing, 1980, (textbook) Phantom Nightingale: Juvenilia, 1981, Octavia and other Poems (Creative Achievement award Coll. Lang. Assn.), 1988, Remembrances of Spring: Collected Early Poems, 1993, Octavia: Guthrie and Beyond, 2002, Connected Islands, 2004, (autobiography) Pilgrim Journey, 2006; editor: (anthology) A Milestone Sampler: 15th Anniversary Anthology, 1988, Adam of Ife: Black Women in Praise of Black Men, 1992; In Her Lifetime tribute Afrikan Poets Theatre, 1989 Participant Creative Writers in Schs. program. Recipient Esther R. Beer Poetry award Nat. Writers Club, 1957, Disting. English Tchr. of Yr. award, 1967; Josephine Nevins Keal award, 1979; Mott fellow in English, 1965, Robert Hayden Runagate award, 1985, Creative Artist award Mich. Coun. for the Arts, 1987, award Nat. Coalition 100 Black Women, 1984, award Nat. Coun. Tchrs. English Black Caucus, 1984, award Chesapeake/Virginia Beach chpt. Links, Inc., 1981, Arts Found. Mich. award, 1990, Creative Achievement award Coll. Lang. Assn., 1988; Arts Achievement award Wayne State U., 1985, The Black Scholar Award of Excellence, 1992; Am. Book award, 1993, Mich. Artist award, 1993; Creative Contbrs. award Gwendolyn Brooks Ctr. Black Lit. and Creative Writing Chgo. State U., 1993, Lifetime Achievement award Furious Flower, 1994, George Kent award, 1995, Lifetime Achievement award Gwendolyn Brooks Ctr., 2003; Naomi Long Madgett Poetry award named for her, 1993—, Alain Locke award Detroit Inst. Arts, Friends of African and African Am. Art, 2003, Creative Scholarship award, Coll. Lang. Assn., 2007; inducted Sumner H.S. Hall of Fame, St. Louis, 1997, Nat. Lit. Hall Fame for Writers of African Descent, Chgo. State U., 1999, Mich. Women's Hall of Fame, 2002; named Poet Laureate, City of Detroit, 2001—, Mayor's award Literary Excellence, 2005; named one of 23 Enterprising Women, Detroit Hist. Soc., 2004; Bronze Bust created by Artis Lane unveiled at Charles H. Wright Mus. African Am. History, 2004. Mem. NAACP, Coll. Lang. Assn., So. Poetry Law Ctr., Langston Hughes Soc., Charles H. Wright Mus. of African Am. History, Detroit Working Writers, Detroit Inst. Arts, Fred Hart Williams Geneal. Soc., Alpha Kappa Alpha. Congregationalist. Home: 18080 Santa Barbara Dr Detroit MI 48221-2531 Office: PO Box 21607 Detroit MI 48221-0607 Office Phone: 313-861-1280. Personal E-mail: naomimadgett@comcast.net. *I have tried to set an example of excellence in the use of language, especially the language of poetry. If I can leave behind some enduring work—my own words and the words of others I have published—I will consider myself amply rewarded for my labors. The truly great people I have known have given a great deal of themselves in the service of others, have not been puffed up by their own importance, and have maintained integrity in their personal and professional lives. They have been my models.*

MADHAVAN, MURUGAPPA CHETTIAR, economics professor; b. Kandramanickam, Tamilnadu, India, Dec. 17, 1932; came to U.S., 1960; s. L. Murugappa Chettiar and Adaikkammai Achi (Meyyappan) M.; m. Nachammai Manickam, May 3, 1953; children: Nachiappa, Nataraj. BA with honors, Annamalai U., India, 1955, MA, 1958; MS, U. Wis., 1963, PhD, 1969. Lectr. in econs. Annamalai U., 1955-60; economist Europe and Mid. East World Bank, Washington, 1963-66, asst. sec. econ. com., 1966-68; dir. Ctr. for Rsch. in Econ. Devel. San Diego State U., 1969-85, prof. econs., 1974—2004, dir. Asian Studies, 1991-2000, chmn. dept. Asian Studies, 1999-2000. Prof. econs. Nat. Inst. Bank Mgmt., Bombay, 1971—72; vis. prof. econs. Indian Inst. Tech., Madras, 1979—80, Madras Sch. Econs., 1996, U. Putra, Malaysia, 2002; Father Carty Meml. lectr. U. Madras, 1980; vis. Fulbright prof. U. of the Philippines, 1987—88; cons. UN Devel. Program, NYC, 1987—88, Gen. Atomics, San Diego, 1993—99; advisor Gov. Sim Grinio, Philippines, 1988; vis. scholar IMF Inst., Washington, 2002; Fulbright sr. specialist Faculty of Law and Econs., Phnom Penh, Cambodia, summer, 2001. Co-author: The Transfer of Knowledge Through Expatriate Nationals, 1988. Chmn. World Affairs Coun. San Diego, 1991-93; pres. Tamil Nadu Found., Inc., Chgo., 1985-87, life mem.; advisor Mingei Internat. Mus., San Diego, 1985—; pres. San Diego Indian Am. Soc., 1984-99. Fulbright fellow, 1960; recipient Hon. Am. award Ams. by Choice, 1987, Leadership and Contbn. award Tamil Nadu Found., 1994; Fulbright sr. scholar Fulbright Program in Ho Chi Minh City, U. Econs., 2000, U. Putra Malaysia, 2000. Mem.: Am. Econ. Assn., Assn. Indian Econ. Studies (life), Indian Econ. Assn. (life), San Diego Indian Am. Soc. (life), Tamilnadu Found. (life), Fulbright Assn. (life). Democrat. Avocations: reading, walking, organizational activities. Home: 8727 Verlane Dr San Diego CA 92119-2033 Office: San Diego State U Coll Arts & Letters Ctr Asian Studies San Diego CA 92182 Home Phone: 619-698-5058; Office Phone: 619-594-1675. Business E-Mail: madhavan@mail.sdsu.edu.

MADHAVARAM, SREEDHAR, marketing educator; s. Jagapathi Rao and Sreedevi Madhavaram; m. Radha Appan, Dec. 14, 2003; 1 child, Ananya. PhD, Tex. Tech U., Lubbock, 2005. Asst. prof. mktg. Cleve. State U., 2005—. Contbr. articles to profl. jours. Mem.: Am. Mktg. Assn.

MADHRIRA, MACHAIAH M., nephrologist; s. Muthanna Mandanna and Janaki Muthanna Madrira; m. Nikhila Nanjappa Kullachanda, Nov. 12, 2006. MD, Mysore Med. Coll., India, 2001; MPH, U. SC., Columbia, 2004. Diplomate Am. Bd. Internal Medicine, 2007. Nephrology fellow Harlem Hosp. Ctr., Columbia U., NYC, 2007—09. Recipient prize, Columbia U. Coll. Physicians & Surgeons and Harlem Hosp. Ctr., 2009. Mem.: Renal Physicians Assn., Internat. Soc. Nephrology, Nat. Kidney found. (Resident Ednl. grant 2007, Fellows Ednl. grant 2008—09), Am. Soc. Nephrology, ACP. Office: Harlem Hosp Ctr Columbia Univ 506 Lenox Ave #12-101 New York NY 10037 E-mail: mmm2154@columbia.edu.

MADIGAN, JOHN WILLIAM, publishing executive; b. Chgo., June 7, 1937; s. Edward P. and Olive D. Madigan; m. Holly Williams, Nov. 24, 1962; children: Mark W., Griffith E., Melanie L. BBA, U. Mich., 1958, MBA, 1959. Fin. analyst Duff & Phelps, Chgo., 1960—62; audit mgr. Arthur Andersen & Co., Chgo., 1962—67; v.p. investment banking Paine, Webber, Jackson & Curtis, Chgo., 1967—69; v.p. corp. fin. Salomon Bros., Chgo., 1969—74; v.p., CFO, dir. Tribune Co., Chgo., 1975—81, exec. v.p., 1981—91; pub. Chgo. Tribune, 1990—94; pres., CEO Tribune Pub. Co., Chgo., 1991—94; pres., COO Tribune Co., Chgo., 1994—95, pres., 1994—2001, CEO, 1995—2002, chmn., 1996—2004; spl. ptnr. Madison Dearborn Ptnrs. LLC, 2005—. Bd. dir. AP, AT&T Wireless Svcs.; former dir. Morgan Stanley. Trustee Rush-Presbyn.-St. Luke's Med. Ctr., Mus. TV and Radio in N.Y., Northwestern U., Ill. Inst. Tech.; mem. bd. overseers Hoover Instn. Mem.: Chgo. Coun. on Fgn. Rels. (chmn.), Robert R. McCormick Tribune Found. Office: Madison Dearborn Partners 70 W Madison St Ste 4600 Chicago IL 60602-4215

MADIGAN, JOSEPH EDWARD, financial executive, director, consultant; b. Bklyn., June 26, 1932; s. James Peter and Mary (Goldman) M.; m. Catherine Cashman, July 26, 1980; children: Kerri Ann, Kimberly Ann Burquest, Elizabeth Ann Laginess. BBA cum laude, Baruch Coll., CUNY, 1958; MBA, NYU, 1963. Adminstrv. asst. Assoc. Metals & Minerals Corp., 1961-63; fin. analyst, fgn. exch. trader, corp. portfolio trader AMAX, Inc., 1963-65; mgr. corp. portfolio, dir. cash mgmt., asst. treas. TWA, Inc., 1965-68; treas. Borden, Inc., 1968-76, v.p., treas., 1976-80; exec. v.p., chief fin. officer, dir. Wendy's Internat., Inc., Dublin, Ohio, 1980-87. Bd. dirs Scioto Properties LLC; pres. Madigan Assocs., 1987—99. Chmn. bd. Lexford Residential Properties, 1997-99. With USN, 1951-55. Named Alumnus of Yr., Baruch Coll., CUNY. Mem. Fin. Execs. Internat., Nat. Investor Rels. Inst., Baruch Coll.-CUNY Alumni Assn. (Alumnus of the Yr. award), NYU Alumni Assn., Imperial Golf Club, Allendale Country Club, Beta Gamma Sigma. Republican. Roman Catholic. Home and Office: 5555 Heron Point Dr Unit 2102 Naples FL 34108

MADIGAN, KATHRYN GRANT, lawyer; b. Paterson, NJ, May 4, 1953; d. William Joseph and Patricia (McCaffrey) Grant; children: R. James III, Grant Daniel. BA, U. Colo., 1975; JD, Union U., Albany, NY, 1978. Bar: N.Y. 1979, U.S. Dist. Ct. (no. dist.) N.Y. 1979. Asst. gen. counsel Security Mut. Life Ins. Co. N.Y., Binghamton, 1978-85; law asst. trial part Broome County Surrogate's Ct., Binghamton, 1985-86; ptnr. Madigan & Madigan, Binghamton, 1986, Levene Gouldin and Thompson, Binghamton, ptnr. Elder Law Group. Mem. Harpur Forum, 1987—, chair 1997-98, Broome County Status of Women Coun., 1988. Recipient Bus. woman of the Yr. award Am. Bus. Women, 1988; named Woman Achievement Broome County Status of Women, Coun., 1988. Mem. N.Y. State Bar Assn. (chmn. subcom. on law student membership 1979-82, del. 1983-86, 89, exec. com. corp. counsel sect. 1982, pres., 2007-08, pres.-elect 2006-07, exec. com. 1990-98, 2002-, membership commn., 1979-89, 91, chair, 1997-02, ElderLaw Sec., chair, 1998-99, mem., 1991-, trust estates law sec., exec. com., 1999-2005; award of merit 1985, 86, named outstanding young lawyer award young lawyers sect. 1987), Broome County Bar Assn. (pres. 1988-89, bd. dirs. 1981-89, chmn. continuing edn. com. 1984-90, gender bias in cts. com. 1987), Ms. Demeanors Rugby Club (founder, pres. 1976-78), Binghamton Women's Rugby Club (founder, pres. 1978-82), Phi Beta Kappa, fellow NYS Bar Found.(life), Am. Bar Found., NH Acad. of Elder Law Attorneys, Am. Coll. Trust Estate Coun. Democrat. Roman Catholic. Avocations: hiking, music, literature. Mailing: Levene Gouldin and Thompson PO Box F 1706 Binghamton NY 13902 Office Phone: 607-763-9200. Office Fax: 607-763-9212. E-mail: kmadigan@binghamtonlaw.com.

MADIGAN, LISA, state attorney general; m. Pat Byrnes; 1 child, Rebecca. BA, Georgetown U., 1988; student, Loyola U. Asst. dean adult, continuing edn., dir. Sr. Acad. Lifelong Learning Wrights Family Coll. Wilbur Wright Coll., with positive alts. project; litigator Sachnoff & Weaver, Ltd., Chgo.; mem. Ill. Senate, Springfield, 1998—2002, mem. senate appropriations com., edn. com., joint com. adminstrv. rules; atty. gen. State of Ill., 2002—. Former vol. tchr., South Africa. Bd. dirs. AIDS Living Rememberance Com. Named one of Top 40 Lawyers Under 40, Nat. Law Jour., 2005. Mem. Ill. Bar Assn., Women's Bar Assn. Ill., Chgo. Bar Assn. Democrat. Office: Office of Atty General James R Thompson Ctr 100 W Randolph St Chicago IL 60601 Office Phone: 312-814-3000.*

MADIGAN, MICHAEL JOSEPH, state legislator, political organization administrator; b. Chgo., Apr. 19, 1942; m. Shirley Madigan; 4 children. Attended, U. Notre Dame; JD, Loyola U. Law Sch., Chgo. Pvt. practice atty.; mem. Dist. 22 Ill. House of Reps., 1971—, majority leader, 1977-80, minority leader, 1981-82, spkr. of the house, 1983-94, 1997—, Dem. leader, 1995-96. Sec. to Alderman David W. Healey; hearing officer Ill. Commerce Commn.; del. 6th Ill. Constnl. Conv.; trustee Holy Cross Hosp.; ex officio mem. adv. com. to pres. Richard J. Daley Coll.; adv. com. Fernley Harris Sch. for Handicapped; committeeman 13th Ward Democratic Orgn.; chmn. Dem. Party of Ill., 1998-. Mem. Coun. Fgn. Rels., City Club Chgo. Democrat. Office: Dist Office 6500 S Pulaski Rd Chicago IL 60629 also: Ill House Reps 300 State Capital Bldg Springfield IL 62706-0001 also: Dem Party Ill PO Box 518 Springfield IL 62705 Office Phone: 773-581-8000. Fax: 217-524-1794, 773-581-9414. E-mail: mmadigan@hds.ilga.gov.*

MADIGAN, WILLIAM CHARLES, literature and language professor, consultant; b. La Mesa, Calif., Oct. 20, 1957; s. William Charles and Annette Lucille Madigan; m. Apryl-kim Wold; children: Eric Lyle, Adriana Rose. BA, San Diego State U., 1986, MALA in Humanities, 1990. Cert. profl. clear tchg. credential Calif., 1986. Tchr. Grossmont Union HS, La Mesa, 1986—2007, Steele Canyon Charter, Spring Valley, Calif., 2007—. Ednl. cons. MADMAC, San Diego, 1995—2008; cons. AVID, San Diego, 1996—. Author: (book) Who is the Teacher, Anyway?. Named Golden Apple Tchr. of Yr., Grossmont Union HS, 1990, 2000. Mem.: Steele Canyon Big Picture Team. Liberal. Roman Catholic. Avocation: travel. Home: 3560 First Ave 14 San Diego CA 92103 Office: Steele Canyon HS 12440 Campo Rd Spring Valley CA 91978

MADIREDDI, MALLAREDDY, physiologist; b. Deveryamjal, India, Apr. 10, 1952; came to the U.S., 1984; s. Narsareddy and Laxmamma (Anthireddigari) M.; m. Sucharitha Ala, Dec. 15, 1983; children: Sunthosh P., Sundeep P. BS, Osmania U., Hyderabad, India, 1974, MSc, 1976, PhD, 1979; Longterm P.G. Electrophysiology, Czechoslovakia Acad. Scis., Prague, 1978-80. Asst. in physiology Inst. Physiology, Ludwig Maxmilions U. Munich, Germany, 1980-83; postgrad. rsch. electrophysiologist U. Calif., Divsn. Biomed. Scis., Riverside, 1984-85, asst. rsch. psysiologist Steps, 1985—, tchr., 1986—; prof. philosophy DEpt. Pediat., UCSD Sch. Medicine, U. Calif., San Diego. Tchr. Osmania U., Hyderabad, 1976-78, vis. scientist, 1983-84, spkr. in fields; presenter in field. Contbr. articles to profl. jours. & 66 rsch. articles, chpts. to books Recipient UNESCO and WHO postdoctoral award, 1978-80, UNESCO Travel grant, 1978, U.S. Cystic Fibrosis Found. travel grant, Verona, Italy, 1987, Dallas, 1981, Cystic Fibrosis Found. U.S. Postdoctoral Rsch. award, 1990, Cystic Fibrosis Found. grant, 1990-93, Cystic Fibrosis Inc. rsch. grant, Palo Alto, 1994, Rsch. awards, NIH Mem. AAAS, Am. Physiol. Soc., Biophys. Soc. Am. Office: U California San Diego 210 Dickinson St San Diego CA 92103 Home: 10569 Vorte Jardin Del Mar San Diego CA 92130 Office Phone: 619-543-5983. Business E-Mail: mmr@ucsd.edu.

MADIS, ERIC STEPHEN, musician; b. Derby, Conn., Dec. 5, 1953; s. Frederick Madis and Isabelle Bellis-Saran; m. Eileen Mercedes Damian, Sept. 2, 1989; 1 child, Alika Damian. BA in Physiol.-Psychology, U. Ill., Urbana, 1975. Luthier Rosewood Guitar Shop, Champagne, Ill., 1976—78; musician Dallas, 1978—81, Denver, 1981—84; pub. musician Seattle, 1984—; pres. Luna Records, Seattle, 1991—. Instr. Denver Free U., 1983—84, U. Wash., 1984—97, Nat. Guitar Workshop, 1998—; founder, sr. instr. Tang Soo Do MJH Seattle, Shoreline, Wash., 1992—. Contbr. articles to profl. jours.; composer, musician: albums Nine Shades of Blue, 1991, Traveling Light, 1997, Third Step, 2002, Wood, Wires & Bone, 2003, The Dues Will Never be Paid in Full, 2009. Steward Victory Creek Seattle Pub. Utilities, 2006—. Recipient New Folk award, Kerrville Nat. Folk Festival, Tex., 1981; scholar, Ill. Wesleyan U., 1971; Ill. Dept. Edn. scholar, 1971. Mem.: Victory Music (writer 1989—2007), Wash. Blues Soc., US Korean Martial Arts Fedn. (fourth degree black belt 2007). Avocations: martial arts, Hawaiian culture, running, languages, music. Home and Studio: 11756 12th Ave NE Seattle WA 98125

MADISETTI, VIJAY KRISHNA, electrical engineer, educator; PhD, U. Calif., Berkeley, 1989. Prof. Ga. Inst. Tech., Atlanta, 1989—. Author: (book) VLSI Digital Signal Processors. Fellow: IEEE. Office: Ga Inst Tech 777 Atlantic Dr NW ECE 0250 Atlanta GA 30332-0250 Business E-Mail: vkm@gatech.edu.

MADISON, ANNE CONWAY, marketing, public relations professional; b. Balt., Mar. 13, 1963; d. Earl Cranston Jr. and Nancy C.; 1 child, Ryan Douglas. BS in Comm., Wittenberg U., 1985. Pub. rels. specialist Springfield (Ohio) Met. Housing Authority, 1984-85; account rep. CT Corp. Sys., Washington, 1985-86; pub. rels. asst. Ryland, Columbia, Md., 1986-88, comm. coord., 1988-90, mgr. mktg. comm., 1990-92, dir. mktg. comm., 1992-94, v.p. comm., 1994—2003; v.p. mktg. & comm. ESIC, Inc., Columbia, 2003—05; v.p. corp. comm. Choice Hotels Internat., Inc., Silver Spring, Md., 2005—09, sr. v.p. corp. comm., 2009—. Bd. dirs., officer Domestic Violence Cr. of Howard County, Columbia, 1987-96; bd. dirs. Norbel Sch., Nat. Family Resiliency Ctr. Named Vol. of Yr. Domestic Violence Ctr., 1988, recipient Spirit award, 1992; named one of Top 100 Women in Md., The Daily Record, 1996. Mem. Pub. Rels. Soc. Am., Nat. Investor Rels. Inst. Republican. Roman Catholic. Office: Choice Hotels Internat Inc 10750 Columbia Pike Silver Spring MD 20901 Office Phone: 301-592-6723. Personal E-mail: acmadison@comcast.net. Business E-Mail: anne_madison@choicehotels.com.*

MADISON, EDDIE LAWRENCE, JR., public relations consultant, editor, writer; b. Tulsa, Sept. 8, 1930; s. Eddie Lawrence Sr. and Laverta (Pyle) M.; m. Davetta Jayn Cooksey, Nov. 17, 1956; children: Eddie Lawrence III, Karyn Devette, David Cooksey. B in Journalism, Lincoln U., Jefferson City, Mo., 1952; MA, U. Tulsa, 1959. Editor-in-chief, gen. mgr. Okla. Eagle, Tulsa, 1954-59; assoc. editor Chgo. Daily Defender, 1959-61; dep. editor Assoc. Negro Press, Chgo., 1961-63; sect. editor Chgo. Tribune, 1963-65; dir. domestic pub. affairs Paris Air Show Newsletter, U.S. Dept. Commerce; dep. dir. publs. divsn. Domestic and Internat. Bus., U.S. Dept. Commerce, Washington, 1965-69; mgr. cmty. svcs. Evening Star Broadcasting Co., Washington, 1969-78; asst. editor Bus. Am. Mag., Washington, 1978-81; press asst. Ho. of Reps., Washington, 1981-82; pub. affairs specialist U.S. Dept. HHS, Washington, 1982-92, mgr. HHS radio, 1991-92; asst. prof., chmn. dept. comm. Lincoln U., 1992-99; exec. editor, CEO, Okla. Eagle, Tulsa, 2001—; pres., CEO Three Elms & Assoc., Inc., Tulsa, 2001—. Founder Nat. Broadcast Assn. for Cmty. Affairs, Washington, 1974, 1st pres., 1974-77. Correspondent, Native Am. Times. Pres. Brightwood Civic Assn., Washington, 1969-72; mem. media adv. com. Mo. Arts Coun., 1996-99; mem. tobacco coalition and assist coms. Am. Cancer Soc., 1993-99; Hist. Preservation Commn., 1997-99; bd. dirs. Opportunities Industrialization Ctr., Washington, 1971-77, D.C. United Way, 1972-77, Boy Scouts Am., Washington, 1972-77. With U.S. Army, 1952-54; corr., Army Times, columnist, Recon Observer, Ellsworth AFB, S.D. Recipient Lifetime Achievement award, Tulsa Assn. Black Journalists, 2005. Mem. Alpha Phi Alpha (pres. Washington chpt. 1969-72, nat. dir. pub. rels. 1985-91, co-chair nat. pub. policy com. 1973, v.p. Montgomery County chpt. 1987-89, pres. Jefferson City Beta Zeta Lambda chpt. 1993, assoc. editor Sphinx mag., award of merit Ea. region 1992). Methodist. Avocations: photography, aerobics, jazz. Office: The Okla Eagle 624 E Archer St Tulsa OK 74120-1000 Home: 2335 Polk St Eugene OR 97405-1835 Office Phone: 918-582-7124 224. Fax: 918-852-8905. E-mail: emadsept@cox.net.

MADISON, GRACE LENORE, retired medical/surgical nurse, psychologist, educator; b. Albert Lea, Minn., July 29, 1924; d. Ernest and Gertrude Abbie (Gordy) Clubb; m. Eldon Harold Madison, June 15, 1946; children: Paul Ernest, Curtis John, Roger Dale, Carol Ann. BA in Psychology, So. Ill. U., Edwardsville, 1969, MA in Psychology, 1971. RN Minn., 1945; cert. clin. psychologist Ill., 1973. Pediat. staff nurse Sacramento City Hosp., 1945; spl. duty surg. nurse U. Minn. Hosp., 1945—46, nurse technician x-ray therapy, 1946—48, spl. duty heart surgery nurse, 1951—53; guest lectr. Coll. Home and Scis., Lahore, Pakistan, 1958; tchr. English Dacca, Bangladesh, 1959—60; staff nurse Mpls. Gen. Hosp., 1961—63, Alton Meml. Hosp., Ill., 1964; grad. rsch. asst. So. Ill. U., 1969—70, grad. tchr. asst., asst. project dir. Sch. Nursing, 1971—72. Psychology instr. Florissant Valley CC, Mo., 1973—77, Belleville Area Coll., Ill., 1974—75. Unitarian. Achievements include patent for Empathy Game. Avocations: travel, writing. Home: 1828 Stanford Pl Edwardsville IL 62025-2633

MADISON, JAMES RAYMOND, lawyer; b. White Plains, NY, Apr. 27, 1931; s. Raymond S. and Katherine (Sherwin) M.; m. Mary Massey, Sept. 19, 1953; children: Michael, Matthew, Molly. BS, Stanford U., 1953, LLB, 1959. Bar: Calif. 1960, U.S. Dist. Ct. (no. dist.) Calif. 1960, U.S. Ct. Appeals (9th cir.) 1960, U.S. Dist. Ct. (ctrl. dist.) Calif. 1970, U.S. Supreme Ct. 1973, U.S. Dist. Ct. (ea. dist.) Calif. 1981, U.S. Dist. Ct. (so. dist.) Calif. 1988. Assoc. Orrick, Herrington & Sutcliffe, San Francisco, 1959-67, ptnr., 1968-95; pvt. practice Menlo Park, Calif., 1996—. Trustee Antioch U., Yellow Springs, Ohio, 1980-87; bd. dirs. Planned Parenthood Alameda/San Francisco, 1984-89; pres. Calif. Dispute Resolution Coun., 2001; chair Calif State Bar ADR Com., 2009. Lt. (j.g.) USN, 1953-56. Mem. ABA, ASCE, State Bar Calif., Bar Assn. San Francisco, San Mateo County Bar Assn., Am. Arbitration Assn. (large complex case panel arbitrators and mediators, No. Calif. regional adv. coun.), Mediation Soc., Calif. Dispute Resolution Coun., Dispute Rev. Bd. Found., Coll. Comml. Arbitrators. Democrat. Episcopalian. Avocation: soccer. Office: 750 Menlo Ave Ste 250 Menlo Park CA 94025-4758 Office Phone: 650-614-0160. Personal E-mail: jrmcoach@aol.com.

MADISON, JOHN ROBERT, surgeon; b. Salineville, Ohio, 1935; MD, Ohio State U., 1960. Diplomate Am. Bd. Surgery. Rotating intern U. Tex. Med. Br., Galveston, 1960-61; resident Loma Linda Hosp., Riverside, Calif., 1963-68; staff Salem (Ohio) Cmty. Hosp. Fellow ACS. Office: 2094 E State St Salem OH 44460-2480 Office Phone: 330-337-7316.

MADISON, PAULA, broadcast executive; b. NYC, 1952; m. Roosevelt Madison; 1 child, Imani. Grad., Vassar Coll., 1974. Reporter Syracuse Herald Jour., 1974—80; investigative bur. reporter Ft. Worth Star - Telegram, 1980—82; asst. city editor Dallas Times Herald, 1982; cmty. affairs dir. WFAA-TV, Dallas, 1982—84, news mgr., 1984—86; news dir. KOTV-TV, Tulsa, 1986—87; exec. news dir. KHOU-TV, Houston, 1987—89; asst. news dir. WNBC, NYC, 1989—96, v.p., news dir., 1996—2000; v.p., sr. v.p. diversity NBC, NYC, 2000—02; pres., gen. mgr. KNBC, LA, 2000—07; regional gen. mgr. KVEA, KWHY, 2002—07; exec. v.p. diversity NBC Universal & Co., 2007—. Co. officer Gen. Electric. Bd. trustees Vassar Coll. Recipient Ida B. Wells award, Nat. Assn. Black Journalists', 1998, Ellis Island medal of honor, Nat. Ethnic Coalition of Orgns., 1999, President's award, NAACP, 2001, Frederick C. Patterson award, United Negro College Fund, 2001, Diversity award, Nat. Assoc. Minority Media Execs., 2002, Woman of the Year, Los Angeles County Commn. for Women, 2002, Excellence in Media Award, Calif. NOW Chap., 2003, TRISCCORT award, Tri-State Catholic Com. on Radio and TV, Asian-Pacific Am. Corp. Impact award, Org. Chinese Americans Greater Los Angeles Chap. Image award Corp. Achievement., Deborah award, Anti-Defamation League, 2003; named Disting. African-Am. New Yorker, N.Y.C. Comptroller Alan Hevesi, Citizen of Yr., City of LA Marathon, 2004; named to Power 150, Ebony mag., 2008. Mem.: N.Y. Assn. Black Journalists, Nat. Assn. Black Journalists. Office: NBC Universal 100 Universal City Plaza Universal City CA 91608

MADISON, ROBERT PRINCE, architect; b. Cleve., July 28, 1923; s. Robert J. and Nettie (Brown) M.; m. Leatrice L. Branch, Apr. 16, 1949; children: Jeanne Marie, Juliette Branch. Student, Howard U., 1940—43, HHD, 1987; BArch, Western Res. U., 1948; MArch, Harvard U., 1952; DFA (hon.), Cleve. State U., 2000; HHD (hon.), Kent State U., 2001; DSc (hon.), Case We. Res. U., 2004. Mem. various archtl. firms, 1948; instr. Howard U., Washington, 1952—54; chmn., CEO Robert P. Madison Internat., architects, engrs. and planners, Cleve., 1954—. Vis. prof. Howard U., 1961-62; lectr. Western Res. U., 1964-65; mem. U.S. architects del. Peoples Repub. China, 1974 Prin. works include U.S. Embassy Dakar, Senegal, West Africa, 1966, State of Ohio Computer Ctr., 1988, Cuyahoga County Jail, 1990, Continental Airlines Hub Concourse, Cleve. Internat. Airport, 1991. Mem. tech. adv. com. Cleve. Bd. Edn., 1960—; mem. adv. com. Cleve. Urban Renewal, 1963—; mem. fine arts adv. com. to mayor, Cleve.; mem. archtl. adv. coun. Cornell U.; trustee Case Western Res. U., Cleve. Opera, 1990, NCCJ, 1990, Commn. on Higher Edn., 1990, Cleve. (Ohio) Orch., 1998, Cleve. (Ohio) Arts Prize, 2001; bd. dirs. Jr. Achievement Greater Cleve.; trustee Cuyahoga County Hosp. Found., 1983—, Univ. Circle Inc., Midtown Corridor Inc.; mem. Ohio Bd. Bldg. Standards, 1986, Cleveland Heights City Planning Commn., 1987. 1st lt., inf. AUS, 1943-46. Decorated Purple Heart; Fulbright fellow, 1952-53; recipient Disting. Svc. award Case Western Res. U., 1989, Disting. Archtl. Firm award Howard U., 1989, Entrepreneur of Yt. award Ernst Young, Inc., Merrill Lynch, 1991, Arch. of Yr. Nat. Tech. Assn., 1996, Martin Luther King Jr. Corp. award African-Am. Archives Aux. Western Res. Hist. Soc., 1997, Disting. Alumni award Case We. Res. U., 1997; named to Corp. Hall of Fame, Ohio Assembly of Couns., 1991, Pres. award Kent State U., 1999; named to Cleve. Bus. Hall of Fame, 2002. Fellow AIA (chpt. pres., nat. task force for creative econs. 1976, mem. jury of fellows 1983-85, mem. nat. judicial coun. 1993, Gold Medal Firm award Ohio 1994, Gold Medal award Ohio 1997, Whitney M. Young Jr. award 2002); mem. Architects Soc. Ohio, Epsilon Delta Rho, Alpha Phi Alpha, Sigma Pi Phi. Office: Robert P Madison Internat Inc 2930 Euclid Ave Cleveland OH 44115-2416 Home: 18975 Van Aken Blvd Apt 410 Shaker Heights OH 44122-3539 Office Phone: 216-861-8195. Business E-Mail: rmadison@rpmadison.com.

MADISON, VICKI DIANNE, retired music educator; b. Paducah, Ky., July 17, 1947; d. Warren G. Dunkerson; m. David Norris Madison, June 6, 1969; 1 child, Philip Warren. MusB rank II, Murray State U., 1970. Yamaha Keyboard Lab Instr. Yamaha Corp., 2001, Orff/Schulwerk Level I Orff/Schulwerk, 2000. Music specialist k/12 Marshall County Schools, Benton, Ky., 1970—98, 1998—2005; adj. instr. Murray State U., Ky., 2001—; organist /pianist First Bapt. Ch. Calvert City, Ky., 1976—. Mem./sect. leader Paducah Symphony Chorus, Paducah, Ky., 1999—2002. Sec. Calvert City Lions Club, Ky., 1996—97, pres., 1998—99, dir., 2003—, pres., 1998—2000, dir., 2003—; councilwoman Calvert City City Coun., Ky., 1999—2004, coun. rep., 1999—; state historian for Ky. choral directors Am. Choral Directors Assn., Okla. City. Recipient Ky. Col., Commonwealth of Ky., 1996, Lion of the Yr., Calvert City Lions Club, 1998, Ky. Elem. Music Tchr. of the Yr., Ky. Music Educators Assn., 1996, Mid. Sch. Music Tchr. of the Yr., First Dist./Ky. Music Educators Assn., 1996—97. Mem.: Marshall County Arts Commn. (bd. dir. 2003—, pres. 2006—08), Music Educators Nat. Conf., Am. Choral Dirs. Assn. (historian 1996—2003, Ky. chpt.), Ky. Music Educators Assn. (elected/apptd. bd. rep. 1992—2005), Ky. Alliance Arts Edn. (treas. 2003, dir.), Ky. Cols. Democrat-Npl. Bapt. Avocation: travel. Home: 79 Camelot Dr Calvert City KY 42029

MADIX, ROBERT JAMES, chemical engineer, educator; b. Beach Grove, Ind., June 22, 1938; s. James L. and Marjorie A. (Strohl) M.; children: Bradley Alan, David Eric, Michaella Lynn, Evan Scott. BS, U. Ill., 1961; PhD, U. Calif., 1964. NSF postdoctoral fellow Max Planck Inst., Göttingen, Fed. Republic of Germany, 1964-65; asst. prof. chem. engr. Stanford (Calif.) U., 1965-72, assoc. prof., chem. engr., 1972-77; prof. chem. engring. Stanford U., 1977—, chmn., chem. engr., 1983-87, prof. chemistry, 1981—, Charles Lee Powell prof., 1990—2006, Charles Lee Powell prof. emeritus, 2006; sr. rsch. fellow divsn. engring. and applied sci. Harvard U., Cambridge, Mass., 2006. Cons. Monsanto Chem., St. Louis, 1975-84, Shell Oil Co., Houston, 1985-86; Peter Debye lectureship Cornell U., 1985; Eyring lectr. chemistry Ariz. State U., 1990; Barnett Dodge lectr. Yale U., 1996; disting. prof. lectr. U. Tex., Austin, 1980; Walter Robb Disting. lectr. Pa. State U., 1996; chmn. Gordon Rsch. Conf. on Reactions on Surfaces, 1995; sr. rsch. fellow divsn. engring. and applied scis. Harvard U., 2006; shah disting. leadership U. Fla., 2009. Assoc. editor Catalysis Rev., 1986—, Catalysis Letters, 1992—, Rsch. on Chem. Intermediates, 1994—; contbr. articles to profl. jours. Recipient Alpha Chi Sigma award AIChemE, 1990, Paul Emmett award Catalysis Soc. N.Am., 1984, Humboldt U.S. Sr. Scientist prize, 1978; Ford Found. fellow, 1969-72. Mem. AIChE, Internat. Precious Metal Inst. (Henry J. Alber award 1997), Am. Chem. Soc. (Irving Langmuir Disting. Lectr. award 1981, Arthur Adamson award 1997, Am. Phys. Soc., Am. Vacuum Soc., Calif. Catalysis Soc.

MADJD-SADJADI, ZAGROS, economics professor, consultant; 2 children. PhD, U. Southern Calif., LA, 1996. Sr. ptnr. Paragon Simulations Internat., 1984—; pres. Zagros Sadjadi Software, 1984—; adj. prof. polit. sci. and economics The Union Inst., LA, 1996—98; rsch. analyst, economics State Calif. Divsn. Labor Stats. and Rsch., San Francisco, 1998—99, rsch. program specialist, economics, 1999—2000, rsch. mgr. economics, 2000—03; adj. prof. economics and mgmt. Golden Gate U., San Francisco, 1999—2003; lectr. economics U. WI, Mona, St. Andrew, Jamaica, 2003—06, Kingston, Jamaica, 2003—06; assoc. prof. economics dir. Winston-Salem State U., NC, 2006—; chief economist San Francisco, 2006. Editor, chief and pub. Am. Rev. Polit. Economy, Winston-Salem, 2001—; dir. Internat. Confederation of Associations for Pluralism in Economics, Kansas City, Kans., 2004—, S.G. Atkins Cmty. Devel. Corp., Winston-Salem, 2007—; pres. Southern Assn. Can. Studies, Atlanta, 2006—08; chair, coun. affiliates Assn. Can. Studies, Washington, 2006—. Contbr. articles to profl. jours., chapters to books. State exec. com. rep. Libertarian Party of Calif., 1986—88. Pre-Doctoral Merit fellowship, U. Southern Calif., 1991—94, Haynes Dissertation fellowship, 1994—95, Occidental Petroleum Fulbright scholarship, Canada-US Fulbright Commn., 1994—95. Office: Winston-Salem State Univ 601 S Martin Luther King Jr Drive Winston Salem NC 27110 Office Phone: 336-750-2398. Business E-Mail: sadjadizm@wssu.edu.

MADJID, A. HAMID, retired science educator; b. Tashkent, Russia, Aug. 16, 1922; arrived in US, 1966; s. A. Madjid and Emilia (Madjid) Zabuli; m. Anni Neukomm-Madjid, Dec. 31, 1958; children: Torai, A. Hamid Jr. BA, Cornell U.; DSc, Swiss Fed. Inst. Tech. Sec., sci. adv. to pres., coord. Afghan scholarships, head indsl. planning Afghan Nat. Bank, Munich, 1948—55; sr. rsch. assoc. Swiss Fed. Inst. Tech., Zurich, 1955—66; asst. assoc. prof., dir. thermionic emission lab, co-head of sci. program Pa. State U., University Park, 1966—90; ret., 1990. Chair various com. Pa. State U., 1977—86. Contbr. articles various profl. jours. Mem. Am. European Swiss Phys. Soc., 1966—90; chair Harris Twp. Planning Commn., Pa., 1982—86; mem. State Coll. Area Sch. Dist. Curriculum Coun., 1987; dir. A.M. Zabuli Charitable Found., 1998, Renaissance Charitable Found., 1999. Mem.: AAAS, Am. Assn. of Naval Engrs., US Holocaust Meml. Mus., Heritage Found., Nat. Rifle Assn. Achievements include research in electron emission from metal, semi conductor and insulator surfaces and the transport and optical properties of such substances; patents for layer structured switching and negative resistance devices; development of methods of involving undergraduate students in basic scientific rsch. Avocation: growing bonsai trees. Home and Office: 326 Harris Dr State College PA 16801 Office Phone: 814-466-7127.

MADLE, ALLEN GEOFFREY, economics professor; b. NYC, Feb. 16, 1947; s. Geoffrey Albert and Ann Marie Madle; m. Agnes Dorothy Leslie, May 1, 1975; children: Patricia Ann Arevalos, Eileen Mary. PhD in Enviornamental Economics, Stratford, Conn., 1986. Pres. Ariz. Restaurant Assn., Flagstaff, 1995—2002; prof. economics SUNY IT, Marcy, 2004—; dir. A M Solutions Group Inc, Canastota, NY, 2005—. Dir. Flagstaff Chamber Commerce, Ariz., 1995—2005; bd. mem. Flagstaff Tourism Commn., Ariz., 1995—2005. Named Instr. of Yr., SUNY IT, 2007, Operator of Yr., Am. Restaurant Assn., 1991. Conservative. Methodist. Home: 251 S Peterboro St Canastota NY 13032 Office: A M Solutions Group Inc 251 S Peterboro ST Canastota NY 13032 Office Fax: 315-875-5073. Business E-Mail: amadle8143@aol.com.

MADLE, ROBERT ALBERT, writer; b. Phila., June 2, 1920; s. Vincent Robert and Mary Virginia (Kidwell) M.; m. Billie Franklin Lindsay, Nov. 7, 1943 (dec. Dec. 1997); children: Robert, Richard, Jane, Mary Anne; m. Ana Lisseth Martinez, Feb. 28, 2002; 1 stepchild, Sarah Nicole Martinez. BS, Drexel U., 1951, MBA, 1953. Asst. to sales mgr. Masland Duraleather, Phila., 1951—53; asst. to dir. indsl. rels. Chadbourne Hosiery, Charlotte, NC, 1953—54; mgr. pers. and credit Shaw Mfg. Co., Charlotte, 1954—56; pers. rsch. specialist U.S. Army, Washington, 1956—59; rsch. psychologist, program mgr. USN, Washington, 1959—80. Sci. fiction rsch. cons. Paramount Prodns., other film cos.; rsch. cons. projects Yesterday's Tomorrows and Study on Hugo Gernsback, Smithsonian Inst.; spkr. in field Co-author: Science Fiction Fandom, 1994; contbr. articles to sci. fiction and sports mags., (books) David A. Kyle:A Life of Scheme Fiction as & Drdrris, 2006, Tales of the Time Travellers, 2009; condr. search svcs. rare books in field of sci. fiction and fantasy lit.; cons. editor profl. fantasy mags., including Mag. of Horror, Bizarre Mystery, Startling Mystery, Famous Sci. Fiction. With U.S. Army, 1942-46. Named Guest of honor World Sci. Fiction Conv., Miami, 1977, U. Md. Sci. Fiction Conv., 1982, Boston Sci. Fiction Conv., 1996; rep. Am. sci. fiction Brit. Worldcon, 1957; recipient E.E. Evans Sci. Fiction Achievement award, 1974, Sam Moskowitz Achievement award, 2002 Mem.: Phila. Sci. Fiction Soc. (founder), First Fandom (pres. 1959—82, Hall of Fame 1990), Washington Sci. Fiction Assn., Sci. Fiction Writers Am. Achievements include development of survey on science fiction's predictions of atomic energy. Home: 4406 Bestor Dr Rockville MD 20853-2137 Office Phone: 301-460-4712.

MADOLE, RICHARD FRANK, geologist, consultant; b. Kirtland, Ohio, July 26, 1936; s. Frank Thomas and Frances Davis Madole; children: Mark Gregory, Thomas Richard, Christopher James. AB, Case-Western Reserve, Cleveland, 1958; MS, Ohio State U., Columbus, 1960, PhD, 1963. Geologist Chevron Standard Oil Tex. Divsn., 1963—65, Tex. Instruments, 1965—67; chairman dept. earth sci. Adrian Coll., 1967—71; rschr. Inst. Arctic and Alpine Rsch., 1972—74; vis. prof. dept. Geol. Sci. U. Colo.; geologist US Geol. Survey, Denver, 1974—97, scientist emeritus, 1997—. Mem. Geol. Soc. America, 1992; pres. Colo. Sci. Soc., 1996. Contbr. scientific papers to profl. jours. Recipient Omicron Delta Kappa, 1958, Cert. of Commendation, US Dept. Justice, 1991, US Dept. Interior Superior Svc. award, 1995, Meritorious Svc. award, 2004, Shoemaker award, USGS, 2006, Distinguished Career award, Geol. Soc. America, 2008; fellowship, Inst. Polar Studies Ohio State U., 1961—62, NSF, U. Colo, 1971—72. Fellow: Geol. Soc. America; mem.: Colo. Sci. Soc., Am. Quaternary Assn. Home: 3075 Fremont St Boulder CO 80304 Office: US Geol Survey MS 980 Box 25046 Denever Federal Ctr Denver CO 80225-0046 Office Fax: 303-236-5349. Business E-Mail: madole@usgs.gov, rmadole376@earthlink.net.

MADONNA, (MADONNA LOUISE VERONICA CICCONE), singer, actress, producer; b. Bay City, Mich., Aug. 16, 1958; d. Sylvio and Madonna Ciccone; m. Sean Penn, Aug. 16, 1985 (div. Sept. 14, 1989); m. Guy Ritchie, Dec. 22, 2000 (separated 2008); 1 child Rocco John; 1 child Lourdes Maria (with Carlos Leon); 2 adopted children, David, Mercy James. Student, U. Mich., 1976-78. Dancer Alvin Ailey Dance Co., NYC, 1979; CEO Maverick Records, LA, 1992—. Singer: (albums) Madonna, 1983, Like a Virgin, 1985, True Blue, 1986, You Can Dance, 1987, Like a Prayer, 1989, The Immaculate Collection, 1990, Erotica, 1992, Bedtime Stories, 1994, Something to Remember, 1995, Ray of Light, 1998 (Grammy award for Best Pop Album 1999), Music, 2000, GHV2: Greatest Hits Volume II, 2002, American Life, 2003, Remixed & Revisited, 2003, Confessions on a Dancefloor, 2005 (Grammy award for Best Electronic/Dance Album, 2007), I'm Going to Tell You a Secret, 2006, The Confessions Tour, 2007, Hard Candy, 2008; (soundtracks) Who's That Girl, 1987, I'm Breathless: Music From and Inspired by the Film Dick Tracy, 1990, Evita, 1996; actress: (films) A Certain Sacrifice, 1980, Vision Quest, 1985, Desperately Seeking Susan, 1985, Shanghai Surprise, 1986, Who's That Girl, 1987, Bloodhounds of Broadway, 1989, Dick Tracy, 1990, Shadows and Fog, 1992, Body of Evidence, 1992, A League of Their Own, 1992, Dangerous Game, 1993, Blue in the Face, 1995, Four Rooms, 1996, Girl 6, 1996, Evita, 1996 (Golden Globe award for Best Actress in Comedy/Musical, 1997), The Next Best Thing, 2000, Swept Away, 2002, (voice only) Arthur and the Invisibles, 2006; (TV appearances) Will & Grace, 2003; stage appearance: Speed-the-Plow, 1987, Up for Grabs, 2002; appeared in: (documentaries) Madonna: Truth or Dare, 1991, I'm Going to Tell You a Secret, 2005; writer, exec. prodr., I Am Because We Are, 2008; dir., exec. prodr.: (films) Filth and Wisdom, 2008; exec. prodr.: (films) Agent Cody Banks, 2003, Agent Cody Banks 2: Destination London, 2004; (TV films) 30 Days Until I'm Famous, 2004; author: Sex, 1992, (children's books) The English Roses, 2003, Mr. Peabody's Apples, 2003, Yakov and the Seven Thieves, 2004, Adventures of Abdi, 2004, Lotsa de Casha, 2005. Recipient Grammy award for Best Song Written for Motion Picture, 1999, World's Best Pop Artist award, World Music Awards, 2007, Best-Selling US Artist, 2007, 2008, Ivor Novello award for Internat. Hit of Yr., Brit. Acad. Composers & Songwriters, 2007, Style Icon award, Elle Mag., 2007; named one of The 100 Most Powerful Celebrities, Forbes.com, 2008; named to Rock & Roll Hall of Fame, 2008. Office: c/o Maverick Recirds LLC 9348 Civic Ctr Dr 3rd Fl Beverly Hills CA 90210*

MADORY, JAMES RICHARD, hospital administrator, retired military officer; b. Staten Island, NY, June 11, 1940; s. Eugene and Agnes (Gerner) M.; m. Karen James Clifford, Sept. 26, 1964; children: James E., Lynn Anne, Scott J., Elizabeth Anne, Joseph M. (dec.). BS, Syracuse U., 1964; MHA, Med. Coll. Va., 1971. Enlisted USAF, 1958; x-ray technician Keesler Area Med. Ctr., Biloxi, Miss., 1959-62; commd. 2d lt. USAF, 1964, advanced through grades to maj., 1979—; x-ray technician Keesler Area Med. Ctr., Biloxi, Miss., 1959-62; adminstr. Charleston (S.C.) Clinic, 1971-74, Beale Hosp., Calif., 1974-77; assoc. adminstr. Shaw Regional Hosp., S.C., 1977-79; ret. USAF, 1979; asst. adminstr. Raleigh Gen. Hosp., Beckley, W.Va., 1979-81; adminstr., dir., sec. bd. Chesterfield Gen. Hosp., Cheraw, S.C., 1981-87; pres., CEO Grand Strand Hosp., Myrtle Beach, S.C., 1987-95, trustee, 1987-95; elected vice chairman Horry County Planning Commn., 1996-98; cons. Healthcare Adminstrn., 1995—; med. dir., dept. pathology Lab. Informatics & LAb. Medicine, Med. U. SC. Adv. bd. Cheraw Nursing Home, 1984-85. Contbr. articles to profl. jours. Chmn. bd. W.Va. Kidney Found., Charleston, 1980-81; chmn. youth bd. S.C. TB and Respiratory Disease Assn., Charleston, 1972-73; county chmn. Easter Seal Soc., Chesterfield County, S.C., 1984-85; campaign crusade chmn. Am. Cancer Soc., Chesterfield County, 1985-86; chmn. dist. advancement com. Boy Scouts Am., 1987-90; bd. dirs. Horry County United Way, 1989-95, Horry County Access Care, 1989-91; trustee Cheraw Acad., 1982-85, Grand Strand Gen. Hosp., 1987-94, Coastal Acad., 1988-90; commr. Horry County Planning Commn., 1995-97, vice chmn., 1996-97; mem. Myrtle Beach AFB Redevel. Authority, 1997—; chmn. Horry County Boys & Girls Clubs Am., 1998-99, bd. dirs., 1998-2000; apptd. Myrtle Beach Air Base Redevel. Authority, 1998, Waccamaw Regional Workforce Investment Bd., 1998-01, vice-chmn., 1998—01; vice-chmn. Horry County Republican Party, 1998-99; S.C. fin. steering com.; campaign chmn. McCain 2000 for Pres., 1999-2000, Harry County. volunteer med. missionary Haiti Hosp. Lumieer, 2002, mem. Parish Coun., St. Mary Help Christians RC Ch., Auban, SC, 2007-. Decorated Bronze Star, Vietnamese Cross of Gallantry, Vietnamese Medal of Honor; named to S.C. Orders of Palmetto Gov. David Beasley, 1995. Fellow Am. Coll. Hosp. Adminstrs., Am. Coll. Health Care Execs; mem. S.C. Hosp. Assn. (com on legislation 1984-86, trustee 1989-94), Am. Acad. Healthcare Adminstrs., Cheraw C. of C. (bd. dirs. 1982-83), Rotary (pres. 1984-85). Republican. Roman Catholic. Home and Office: 341 Implement Dr Aiken SC 29803-6293 Office: Med Univ SC Dept Pathology & Lab Medicine 165 Ashley One Ste 309 Charleston SC 29425 E-mail: jmadory@yahoo.com.

MADORY, RICHARD EUGENE, lawyer; b. Kenton, Ohio, May 14, 1931; s. Harold Richard and Hilda (Strictland) Madory; m. Barbara Jean Madory, Sept. 25, 1955; children: Richard Eugene, Terry Dean, Michael Wesly. BS in Edn., Ohio State, Columbus, 1952; JD, Southwestern U., 1961. Bar: Calif. 1961, U.S. Ct. Mil. Appeals, U.S. Supreme Ct., U.S. Dist. Ct. (ctrl. dist.) Calif. With Madory, Booth, Zell & Pleiss, Santa Ana, Calif., 1962—, now pres., v.p., sec.-treas. Lectr. continuing edn. Bar of State of Calif. Col. USMC. Fellow: Am. Coll. Trial Lawyers; mem.: ABA, Nat. Bd. Trial Advocacy, Am. Bd. Trial Advs., So. Calif. Def. Counsel Assn., LA County Bar Assn., Orange County Bar Assn. Office: Ste 205 17822 17th St Tustin CA 92780-2152 Office Phone: 714-832-3772. Business E-Mail: madory@pacbell.net.

MADRA, SATBIR SINGH, materials researcher, mechanical engineer; arrived in U.S., 1995; s. Bhupinder Singh and Satwant Kaur Madra. BSME, Punjab U., 1993; MSME, San Jose State U., Calif., 1997. Lectr. San Jose State U., Calif., 1996—97; process devel. engr. R&D Watkins Johnson Co., Scotts Valley, Calif., 1997—99; sr. staff engr. Wj Comm., Inc., San Jose, 1999—2002, sr. rsch. scientist, 2002—05; sr. mgr. Semiconductor Package, 2005—06, RFID Engring., 2005—06; v.p. tech. Silitronics, Inc., San Jose, Calif., 2006—. sr. v.p., 2006—. Presenter in field. Contbr. articles to profl. jours. Mem.: ASME, IEEE, Materials Rsch. Soc., Internat. Microelectronics And Packaging Soc., Pi Tau Sigma. Avocations: tennis, travel, hockey. Office: Silitronics Inc 85 Great Oaks Blvd San Jose CA 95119 Business E-Mail: satbir.madra@silitronics.com.

MADRAS, BERTHA KALIFON, federal official, neuroscientist, researcher; b. Montreal, Que., Can., Dec. 9, 1942; m. Peter Madras, June 21, 1964; children: Cynthia Gumbert, Claudine D. BSc in Chemistry, with honors, McGill U., Montreal, 1963; PhD, McGill U., 1967. Chair divsn. neurochemistry New Eng. Primate Rsch. Ctr.; postdoctoral fellow Tufts U., Boston, 1966-67; postdoctoral fellow rsch. assoc. MIT, Cambridge, 1967-69, 72-74; asst. prof. U. Toronto, 1979—80, Harvard Med. Sch., Boston, 1986-90, assoc. prof., 1990-99, prof. psychobiology dept. psychiatry, 1999—2006, assoc. dir. pub. edn. divsn. addictions, 1998—2006; dep. dir. demand reduction Office Nat. Drug Control Policy, The White House, Washington, 2006—. Cons. Ont. Mental Health Found., 1984—90, chmn. fellowships/awards com., 1988—90; chmn. radiation safety com. Harvard U., 1995—99; acting dir. New Eng. Primate Rsch. Ctr., 1998—99; rev. com., cons. Nat. Inst. Drug Abuse, 1998—99; sci. adv. com. Brookhaven Nat. Lab., Upton, NY, 1998—; chmn. faculty affairs Harvard Med. Sch.; mem. Dana Alliance Brain Initiatives; mem. sci. adv. bd. Nat. Inst. Drug Abuse Medications Devel., Addiction Studies Inst. Journalists. Contbr. articles to profl. jours., chapters to books. Recipient Pub. Svc. award, Nat. Inst. Drug Abuse, Merit award, NIH; rsch. grantee, Parkinson's Disease Found., 1990—91, Nat. Inst. Drug Abuse, 1992—, Nat. Inst. Neurol. Disease & Stroke, 1994, 1999—. Mem.: Soc. Neurosci. Achievements include development of a marker for Parkinson's disease and attention deficit hyperactivity disorder; a probe for cocaine binding sites in brain; novel diagnostic and therapeutic agents for substance abuse and other brain disorders; research in how the brain responds and adapts to drugs; design of a CD-ROM on how drugs affect brain; 16 patents in field. Office: Office Nat Drug Control Policy 750 17th St NW Rm 609 Washington DC 20503*

MADRID, CIRILO L., health facility administrator; b. Clint, Tex., Mar. 18, 1945; s. Leandro L. and Felicitaz L. Madrid; m. Grace Avila Madrid, Jan. 23, 1971; children: Michelle, Melinda, Jesus. AA, Glendale CC, 1967; BA, Ariz. State U., 1969; MEd, U. Tex., El Paso, 1981; PhD, Hamilton U., 2002. Psychiat. tech. St. Mary's Hosp., Tucson, 1970—71; CEO Aliviane No-Ad, Inc., El Paso, 1971—, Family Reintegration Tex., El Paso, 1995—2000, New Beginnings of Tex., El Paso, 2000—. Mem. Lt. Gov. Drug Bd. State of Tex., Austin, 1978—81, Nat. Drug Coun. Ctr. Substance Abuse Tex., Wash., 2003—. Author: Mi India, 1981, Changing Heart of America, 2002; contbr. articles various profl. jours. Mem. Eastside Polit. Action Com., El Paso, 1995—; leg. chair. ASAP of Tex., Austin, 2002—; elected off. Ysleta Sch. Bd., El Paso, 1976—81. Combat medic US Army, 1969—70, South Vietnam. Recipient Carlos Finlay award, Pub. Health Svc., 1996, TCADA award, State of Tex., 1997, Tex. Chem. Found. award, 2000. Mem.: VFW, Tex. Assn. Drug Abuse Counselors, Assn. of Substance Svcs. Roman Catholic. Achievements include development of promising chem. dependence prevention approaches; evident based treatment approaches for hispanic addicts; chem. dependence training approaches for ethnic minorities. Avocations: running, weight training, poetry, comedy. E-mail: cmadrid@aliviane.org.

MADRID, PATRICIA A., former state attorney general; BA in English and Philosophy, U. N.Mex., 1969, JD, 1973; cert., Nat. Jud. Coll., U. Nev., 1978. Bar: N.Mex. Dist. judge State of N.Mex., 1978—84, atty. gen., 1999—2006. Chmn. Western Conf. of Attys. Gen.; exec. cons. Dickstein Shapiro, LLP, Washington, 2006—09; bd. chmn. Mexican Am. Legal Def. & Ednl. Fund, 2008—. Recipient Trailblazer award, N.Mex. Commn. on the Status of Women, Las Primeras award, MANA, 2004, Woman of the Yr. in Govt. award, Capital Bus. and Professional Women of Santa Fe, 2004, Exec. Dir. award, Animal Protection of N.Mex., 2004; named Latina Atty. of Yr., Nat. Hispanic Bar Assn., 2001, N.Mex. Power Broker, N.Mex. Bus. Weekly. Mem.: DNC Dem. Change Commn. Democrat. Mailing: 2219 Vista Larga Dr Albuquerque NM 87106 Office: 20 First Plaza Ctr NW Albuquerque NM 87102 Office Phone: 505-243-0503. E-mail: patriciamadrid100@yahoo.com.

MADRY-TAYLOR, JACQUELYN YVONNE, educational association administrator; d. Arthur Chester and Janie (Cowart) Madry; 1 child, Jana LeMadry. BA, Fisk U., 1966; MA, Ohio State U., 1969; EdD, U. Fla., 1975. Cert. Inst. for Ednl. Mgmt., Harvard U., 1981. Tchr. Spanish Terry Parker Sr. High Sch., Jacksonville, 1967-72; instr. U. Fla., Gainesville, 1972-75; asst. to v.p. for acad. affairs. Morris Brown Coll., Atlanta, 1975-76; dean for instructional svcs. No. Va. Community Coll., Annandale, Va., 1976-83; dean undergrad. studies Bridgewater (Mass.) State Coll., 1983-92, exec. asst. to acting pres., 1988, acting v.p. acad. affairs, 1988-90; dir. Acad. Leadership Acad. Am. Assn. State Coll. and Univs., Washington, 1992-94; dir. ednl. programs and svcs. United Negro Coll. Fund Hdqs., 1994-97; pres. JYM Assocs., 1999—; sr. advisor Nat. Assn. for Equal Opportunity in Higher Edn., 1997—2003. Cons. to colls., univs. and orgns., 1997-99; cons. W.K. Kellog Found., 1993-97; bd. dirs. Bridgewater State Coll. Early Learning Ctr., 1984-88; evaluator U.S. Dept. State/Fgn. Svc., Washington, 1982—, U.S. Dept. Edn., 1989—; pres. JYM Assocs., 1999—. Vice chmn. No. Va. Manpower Planning Coun., Fairfax County, Va., 1981. Recipient Cert. Achievement Bridgewater State Coll. Black Alumni, 1988, Women Helping Women award Soroptimist Internat., 1983, Outstanding Young Women Am. award, 1976, 78; named Personalities of South, 1977; recipient Outstanding Tchr./Student Rels. Humanitarian award B'nai B'rith, 1972. Mem. Pub. Mem. Assn. U.S. Fgn. Svc., Soroptimist Internat., Boston Club (v.p. 1986-88), Jack and Jill of Am., Inc., Am. Assn. of Univ. Women, Phi Delta Kappa, Alpha Kappa Alpha, Links Inc. (Reston, Va. chpt.). Methodist. Avocations: playing piano, bike riding. Home and Office: 12274 Angel Wing Ct Reston VA 20191-1119 Office Phone: 703-716-8746. Fax: 703-716-4364. Personal E-mail: jkemt@aol.com.

MADSEN, ANDREW H. (DREW MADSEN), food service executive; Grad., DePauw Univ., 1978. Various mktg. positions Gen. Mills, Inc., 1980—92; v.p., gen. mgr., Dixie consumer products James River Corp., 1993—97; pres. Internat. Master Publishers, 1997—98; exec. v.p. mktg., Olive Garden div. Darden Restaurants Inc., Orlando, Fla., 1998—2002, sr. v.p., pres. Olive Garden div., 2002—04, pres., COO, 2004—. Bd. dirs Darden Restaurants, Inc., 2004—. Mailing: Darden Restaurants Inc PO Box 593330 Orlando FL 32859-3330 Office: Darden Restaurants Inc 5900 Lake Ellenor Dr Orlando FL 32809 Office Phone: 407-245-4000. Office Fax: 407-245-4989.*

MADSEN, BARBARA A., state supreme court justice; b. Renton; BA, U. Wash., 1974; JD, Gonzaga U., 1977. Pub. defender King and Snohomish Counties, 1977—82; staff atty. Seattle City Atty.'s Office, 1982—84, spl. prosecutor, 1984—88; judge Seattle Mcpl. Ct., 1988—92; justice Wash. Supreme Ct., Olympia, 1993—. Chair Wash. State Gender and Justice Commn.; chair ct. pers. com., circulation com. Wash. State Supreme Ct., co-chair internal rules com., death penalty rules com., mem. ct. budget com., adminstrv. com., reporter of decisions com. Active Judges in the Classroom, Tacoma Pub. Sch. Recipient Vanguard award, Wash. Women Lawyers, 1998, Found. award, 2001, Jud. award, Equal Justice Coalition, 2004, Access to Justice award of distinction for pub. svc., 2006. Mem.: Judicature Soc., Nat. Assn. Women Judges (Presidents award 2002), Am. Judges Assn. Office: Wash Supreme Ct PO Box 40929 Olympia WA 98504-0929*

MADSEN, BRIGHAM DWAINE, history professor; b. Magna, Utah, Oct. 21, 1914; s. Brigham and Lydia (Cushing) M.; m. Betty McAllister, Aug. 11, 1939; children— Karen Madsen Loos, David B., Linda Madsen Dunning, Steven M.; m. Lola Kastler, Dec. 1, 2001; m. Mary Harriman, June 7, 2003. BA, U. Utah, 1938; MA, U. Calif., Berkeley, 1940, PhD, 1948. Prin. Grade Sch. and Jr. High Sch., Pingree, Idaho, 1938-39; assoc. prof. history Brigham Young U., Provo, Utah, 1948-54; pres., mgr. Madsen Bros. Constrn. Co., Salt Lake City, 1954-61; prof. history Utah State U., Logan, 1961-64; asst. dir. tng. Peace Corps, Washington, 1964-65; first dir. tng. Vols. in Service to Am., Washington, 1965; dean div. continuing edn. U. Utah, Salt Lake City, 1965-66, dep. acad. v.p., 1966-67, adminstrv. v.p., 1967-71, dir. libraries, 1971-73, prof. history, 1973-84, chmn. dept. history, 1974-75. Author: Bannock of Idaho, 1958, The Lemhi: Sacajawea's People, 1980, Corinne: Gentile Capital of Utah, 1980, The Northern Shoshoni, 1980, (with Betty M. Madsen) North to Montana: Jehus, Bullwhackers and Muleskinners on the Montana Trail, 1980; Gold Rush Sojourners in Great Salt Lake City, 1849 and 1850, 1983, The Shoshoni Frontier and the Bear River Massacre, 1985, Chief Pocatello: The "White Plume", 1986, Glory Hunter: A Biography of Patrick Edward Connor, 1990, Against the Grain: Memoirs of a Western Historian, 1998; editor: The Now Generation, 1971, Letters of Long Ago, 1973, A Forty-niner in Utah: Letters and Journal of John Hudson, 1982, B.H. Roberts: Studies of the Book of Mormon, 1985, Exploring the Great Salt Lake: The Stansbury Expedition of 1849-50, 1989, The Essential B.H. Roberts, 1999. 1st lt., inf. AUS, 1943-46. Mem. Phi Beta Kappa, Phi Kappa Phi, Phi Alpha Theta. Home: 451 Bishop Federal Ln Apt 4303 Salt Lake City UT 84115-2222 Home Phone: 801-480-0280. E-mail: mimih@01exmission.com.

MADSEN, CLIFFORD KIMBALL, music educator, therapist; b. Price, Utah, May 3, 1937; s. Charles Henry Sr. and Lenora (Kimball) M.; m. Mary Marakis, Aug. 17, 1956; children: Sitka, Cort, Katia. BA, Brigham Young U., 1959, MA, 1960; PhD, Fla. State U., 1963. Instrumental music Carbon County Schs., Helper, Utah, 1955-57; Robert O. Lawton disting. prof. music Fla. State U., Tallahassee, 1961—. Mem. editl. bds. Psychology of Music, 1989-96, Jour. of Rsch. in Music Edn., 1970-76, 2000-06, Jour. of Music Therapy, 1974—2000, Coun. for Rsch. in Music, 1991—; author: (books) Experimental Research in Music, 1970, Teaching/Discipline, 1970, Contemporary Music Education, 1978, Applications of Research in Music Behavior, 1987. Juv. Ct. Counselor, Leon County, Tallahassee, 1963-73, sr. citizens adv., 1984-91. Recipient Sr. Rschr. award Music Educators Nat. Conf., 1988; named to Nat. Assn. Music Edn. Hall of Fame, 2002. Mem. AAAS, Music Educators Rsch. Coun. (chmn. nat. conf. 1982-84), Nat. Assn. Music Therapy (chmn. rsch. com. 1980—, award of merit 1988, Lifetime Achievement award 2006), Am. Ednl. Rsch. Assn., Internat. Soc. Music Edn., Coll. Music Soc. Democrat. Office: Fla State U Ctr for Music Rsch Tallahassee FL 32306-1180 Office Phone: 850-644-3554. Business E-Mail: cmadsen@fsu.edu.

MADSEN, DOROTHY LOUISE (MEG), writer; b. Rochester, NY; d. Charles Robert and Louise Anna Agnes Meyer; m. Frederick George Madsen, Feb. 17, 1945 (dec.) BA, Mundelein Coll., Chgo., 1978; grad., U.S. Army Command and Gen. Staff Coll., 1960. Feature writer Gannett Newspapers, Rochester Democrat & Chronicle, NY, 1937—41; pub. rels. rep. Rochester Tel. Corp., 1941—42; exec. dir. LaPorte chpt. ARC, Ind., 1964; dir. adminstrv. svcs. Bank Mktg. Assn., Chgo., 1971—74; exec. dir. Eleanor Women's Found., Chgo., 1974—84; founder Meg Madsen Assocs., Chgo., 1984—88, women's career counselor; founder Eleanor Women's Forum, Clearinghouse Internat., Eleanor Intern Program Coll. Students and Returning Women. Chief global radiotelephone and radioteletype top secret encrypted conf. ctr. war dept. gen. staff Pentagon, Washington, 1944—46; conf. aide to Pres. Harry S Truman, Washington, 1945. Lt. col. WAC, 1942-47, 67-70 Decorated Legion of Merit, Meritorious Svc. award Mem.: Res. Officers Assn. (life), Mundelein Alumnae Assn., Ret. Officers Assn. (life), Phi Sigma Tau (charter mem. Ill. Kappa chpt.). Achievements include Aide to Pres. Truman during Sigsaly encoded phone conf. with Prime Min. Winston Churchill and U.S. Joint Chiefs Staff concerning terms of German surrender, WWII, Apr. 25, 1945. Home: 1030 N State St Apt 25H Chicago IL 60610-2831 E-mail: megmadsenchgo@aol.com.

MADSEN, GEORGE FRANK, lawyer; b. Sioux City, Iowa, Mar. 24, 1933; s. Frank O. and Agnes (Cuhel) M.; m. Magnhild Norstog; 1 child, Michelle Marie. BA, St. Olaf Coll., 1954; LLB, Harvard U., 1959. Bar: Ohio 1960, Iowa 1961, U.S. Dist. Ct. (no. and so. dists.) Iowa, U.S. Ct. Appeals (8th cir.), U.S. Supreme Ct. 1991. Trainee Cargill, Inc., Mpls., 1954; assoc. Durfey, Martin, Browne & Hull, Springfield, Ohio, 1959-61; assoc., then ptnr. Shull, Marshall & Marks, Sioux City, 1961-85; ptnr. Marks & Madsen, Sioux City, 1985-97, Marks, Madsen & Hirschbach, Sioux City, 1998-99, Mayne, Marks, Madsen & Hirschbach, LLP, Sioux City, 1999-2001. Author, editor: Iowa Title Opinions and Standards, 1978; contbg. author: The American Law of Real Property, 1991. Sec., bd.dirs. Sioux City Boys Club, 1969-76; mem. Sioux City Zoning Bd. Adjustment, 1963-65; active Iowa Mo. River Preservation and Land Use Authority, 1992-2001, pres., 1997-2001. Lt. USAF,

1954-56, capt. Iowa Air Nat. Guard, 1963-65. Fellow Iowa State Bar Found.; mem. ABA, Iowa Bar Assn., Woodbury County Bar Assn., Nat. Wildlife Assn., Mont. Wildlife Assn., Pheasants Forever, Phi Beta Kappa (past pres. Siouxland chpt.), Rotary Internat. Avocations: hunting, swimming, reading. Office: PO Box 3661 Sioux City IA 51102-3661

MADSEN, KAREN F., retired elementary school educator; b. Lincoln, Nebr., July 25, 1941; d. Carl William and Marjorie (Brandt) Friendt; m. James E. Madsen, June 25, 1961; children: Deborah L., Michael C. AA, Pasadena City Coll., Calif., 1961; BA, Calif. State U., LA, 1979. Cert. tchr. Calif. Elem. tchr. South Pasadena Unified Sch. Dist., Calif., 1980—2003, part-time tchr. gifted and talented, 1988—2003; ret., 2003. Producer News team, cable TV. Vol. Acad. Internat. Elem. Sch., Colorado Springs, 2003—. Recipient Hon. Svc. award, PTA, Disting Svc. award, 2003, Monterey Hills Sch. Tchr. of the Yr., (2). Mem. Internat. Reading Assn., Calif. Reading Assn., Santa Anita Reading Coun., So. Calif. Coun. Lit. Young People, East San Gabriel Valley Reading Coun., Tchrs. Assn. South Pasadena, Delta Kappa Gamma. Home: 2047 Wildwood Dr Colorado Springs CO 80918-1120

MADSEN, MATTHEW J., lawyer; b. Feb. 26, 1969; BBA in Fin., U. Iowa, 1991; JD, Stanford U., Calif., 1998. Bar: Mo. 1998. Atty. Lewis, Rice & Fingersh, LC, St. Louis, 2004—. Contbr. articles to profl. jours. Outside gen. counsel St. Louis Cmty. Found.; mem. planned giving adv. coun. Cardinal Glennon Childrens Hosp.; mem. gift planning coun. Variety Club of St. Louis. Recipient 40 under 40 award, St. Louis Bus. Jour., 2008; named one of Top 100 Attys., Worth mag., 2006, Best Lawyers, Am. Trust and Estate. Mem.: Estate Planning Coun. St. Louis, Bar Assn. Met. St. Louis, ABA (real property, probate and trust law sect.). Office: Lewis Rice & Fingersh LC 500 N Broadway Ste 2000 Saint Louis MO 63102 Office Phone: 314-444-7878. Office Fax: 314-612-7878. E-mail: mmadsen@lewisrice.com.

MADSEN, MICHAEL, actor; b. Chicago, Sept. 25, 1958; m. Georganne LaPierre (div.); m. Jeannine Bisignano (div.); 1 child, Christian; m. De Anna Morgan Apr. 15, 1996; 4 children. Films include: Wargames, 1983, The Natural, 1984, Racing with the Moon, 1984, The Killing Time, 1987, Shadows in the Storm, 1988, Iguana, 1988, Blood Red, 1989, Kill Me Again, 1990, The Doors, 1991, The End of Innocence, 1991, Thelma and Louise, 1991, Fatal Instinct, 1992, Inside Edge, 1992, Reservoir Dogs, 1992, Straight Talk, 1992, Almost Blue, 1992, Free Willy, 1993, A House in the Hills, 1993, Money for Nothing, 1993, Trouble Bound, 1993, Wyatt Earp, 1994, The Getaway, 1994, Dead Connection, 1994, Species, 1995, Free Willy II: The Adventure Home, 1995, The Winner, 1996, Red Line, 1996, Mullholland Falls, 1996, Man With a Gun, 1996, The Last Days of Frankie the Fly, 1996, Rough Draft, 1997, The Maker, 1997, Donnie Brasco, 1997, Catherine's Grove, 1997, Papertrail, 1997, The Girl Gets Moe, 1997, Executive Target, 1997, The Thief and the Stripper, 1998, Supreme Sanction, 1998, The Florentine, 1998, Species II, 1998, Fait Accompli, 1998, The Thief & the Stripper, 1998, Flat Out, 1998, Ballad of the Nightingale, 1998, The Florentine, 1999, Detour, 1999, The Stray, 1999, Luck of the Draw, 2002, The Alternate, 2000, The Price of Air, 2000, Love.com, 2000, Ides of March, 2000, The Ghost, 2000, Fall, 2000, Choke, 2000, Bad Guys, 2000, Extreme Honor, 2001, Pressure Point, 2001, Outlaw, 2001, L.A.P.D.: To Protect and to Serve, 2001, Die Another Day, 2002, Welcome to America, 2002, The Real Deal, 2002, Where's Angelo, 2003, My Boss's Daughter, 2003, Kill Bill: Vol. 1, 2003, Vampires Anonymous, 2003, Hunt for the Devil, 2003, Blueberry, 2004, Kill Bill: Vol. 2, 2004, Sin City, 2005, Chasing Ghosts, 2005, (voice) The Chronicles of Narnia: The Lion, the Witch and the Wardrobe, 2005, BloodRayne, 2005, All In, 2006, Scary Movie 4, 2006, Canes, 2006, UKM: The Ultimate Killing Machine, 2006, Cosmic Radio, 2007, Living & Dying, 2007, Machine, 2007, Boarding Gate, 2007, Strength and Honour, 2007, Afghan Knights, 2007, Tooth & Nail, 2007, Vice, 2008, House, 2008, Serbian Scars, 2008, Edgar Allan Poe's Ligeia, 2008, Hell Ride, 2008, Last Hour, 2008, Deep Winter, 2008, No Bad Days, 2008; TV movies include: Special Bulletin, 1983, War and Remembrance, 1988, Montana, 1990, Baby Snatcher, 1992, Beyond the Law, 1994, Supreme Sanction, 1999, The Inspectors 2: A Shred of Evidence, 2000, Sacrifice, 2000, High Noon, 2000, 44 Minutes: The North Hollywood Shoot-Out, 2003, Frankenstein, 2004, Croc, 2007, Crash and Burn, 2008; TV series include: Our Family Honor, 1985-86, Vengeance Unlimited, 1998, Big Apple, 2001, Tilt, 2005; author: The Complete Poetic Works of Michael Madsen, Vol 1: 1995-2005.

MADSEN, STEPHEN STEWART, lawyer; b. Spokane, Wash., Oct. 13, 1951; s. H. Stephen Madsen and Sarah Pope (Stewart) Ruth; m. Rebecca Wetherill Howard, July 28, 1984; children: Stephen Stewart Jr., Lawrence Washington, Christina Wetherill, Benton Howard. BA, Harvard U., 1973; JD, Columbia U., 1980. Bar: N.Y. 1981, U.S. Dist. Ct. (so. dist.) N.Y. 1981, U.S. Ct. Appeals (6th cir.) 1983, U.S. Ct. Appeals (8th cir.) 1985, U.S. Ct. Appeals (2d, 7th and D.C. cirs.) 1994, U.S. Supreme Ct. 1996. Law clk. to presiding judge U.S. Ct. Appeals 2d cir., NYC, 1980-81; assoc. Cravath, Swaine & Moore, NYC, 1981-88, ptnr., litig., 1988—. Bd. vis. Columbia U. Sch. Law, 1991—; bd. govs. Hill-Stead Mus., 1995-2002; mem. vestry St. Bartholomew's Ch., 1995-2004; bd. trustees La Scuola d'Italia, 2004—, chmn., 2005—, bd. dir. Episcopol Social Svcs., 2006-. Mem. ABA, N.Y. State Bar Assn. (exec. com. antitrust law sect. 1998—), New York City Bar Assn. (2007-), New York County Lawyers Assn., London Ct. Internat. Arbitration, Fedn. Bar Coun. Office: Cravath Swaine & Moore LLP Worldwide Pla 825 8th Ave Fl 38 New York NY 10019-7475 Office Phone: 212-474-1886. Office Fax: 212-474-3700. Business E-Mail: smadsen@cravath.com.

MADSEN, VIRGINIA, actress; b. Chgo., Sept. 11, 1963; d. Cal Madsen; m. Danny Huston, Sept. 2, 1989 (div. 1992); 1 child, Jack. Represented by Creative Artists Agy., Beverly Hills, Calif. Actor: (films) Class, 1983, Dune, 1984, Electric Dreams, 1984, Creator, 1985, Fire with Fire, 1986, Modern Girls, 1986, Slam Dance, 1987, Zombie High, 1987, Mr. North, 1988, Hot to Trot, 1988, Heart of Dixie, 1989, The Hot Spot, 1990, Highlander II—The Quickening, 1991, Becoming Colette, 1992, Candyman, 1992, Blue Tiger, 1994, Caroline at Midnight, 1994, The Prophecy, 1995, Ghosts of Mississippi, 1996, The Rainmaker, 1997, Ambushed, 1998, Ballad of the Nightingale, 1998, The Florentine, 1998, The Haunting, 1999, After Sex, 2000, Lying in Wait, 2000, Almost Salinas, 2001, American Gun, 2002, Artworks, 2003, Tempted, 2003, Nobody Knows Anything!, 2003, Sideways, 2004 (Screen Actors Guild Award, outstanding performance by cast in motion picture, 2005), Firewall, 2006, A Prairie Home Companion, 2006, The Number 23, 2007, The Astronaut Farmer, 2007, Diminished Capacity, 2008, The Haunting in Connecticut, 2009; (TV films) A Matter of Principle, 1984, The Hearst and Davies Affair, 1985, Long Gone, 1987, Gotham, 1988, Third Degree Burn, 1989, Ironclads, 1991, Victim of Love, 1991, Love Kills, 1991, A Murderous Affair: The Carolyn Warmus Story, 1992, Linda, 1993, Bitter Vengeance, 1994, The Apocalypse Watch, 1997, Children of Fortune, 2000, The Inspector General, 2000, Crossfire Trail, 2001, Just Ask My Children, 2001, Tempted, 2003, Brave New Girl, 2004; (TV miniseries) Mussolini: The Untold Story, 1985; (TV series) American Dreams, 2002-03, Smith, 2006-; TV appearances include The Hitchhiker, 1987, Moonlighting, 1989, Earth 2, 1994, Star Trek: Voyager, 1998, Frasier, 1999, The Practice, 2001, (voice) Justice League, 2002, Dawson's Creek, 2003, CSI: Miami, 2003, Boomtown, 2003. Democrat.

MADSON, PHILIP WARD, engineering executive, consultant; b. Atlantic, Iowa, Aug. 27, 1948; s. Philip Ward and Pearl Elaine (Thomson) M.; m. Maria Concepcion Casamitjana, Aug. 11, 1968; children: Peter Wesley, David Philip. BSChemE, Iowa State U., 1969, MSChemE, 1970. Registered profl. engr., Ohio. Process engr. Procter & Gamble, Cin., 1971-74, tech. brand mgr., 1974-76, sect. head, 1976-77, assoc. dir., 1977-79; cons. engr. Raphael Katzen Assocs., Cin., 1979-84, v.p., 1984-90, sr. v.p. tech. and mktg., 1990-92, pres., 1993-98; pres., CEO, COO KATZEN Internat., Inc., Cin., 1999—. Guest lectr. Alltech's Annual Internat. Short Course, 1983-2004, Lallemand's Ethanol Tech. Inst., 2005-, F. O. Licht's World Ethanol Prodn. Workshop, 1999-, founder, 1999-. Chmn. Police/Community Rels. Com. Kennedy Heights, 1978-84; chmn. media response team S.W. Ohio Sportsmen's Assn., 1990—; chmn. pub. rels. com. Firearms Facts Com., 1991—; founder, chmn. Kennedy Heights Concerned Citizens, Cin., 1979-85; mem. exec. bd. dirs. Kennedy Heights Community Coun., 1979-84. Recipient Spl. award Kennedy Heights Community Coun., 1984, Recognition Hamilton County Crime Prevention Assn., 1983, Ky. Col. Fellow Am. Inst. Chemists; mem. AIChE, Tech. Assn. Pulp and Paper Industry, New Uses Coun., Clean Fuels Devel. Coalition (exec. bds., chmn. mem. com. 1999—), Am. Chem. Soc., Internat. Inst. of Distillers (founding bd. dirs., v.p.), Ethanol Prodrs. and Consumers (mem. bd. dirs. 2008-), Internat. Exec. Svc. Corp. Avocations: music, hunting, target shooting. Home: 3749 Davenant Ave Cincinnati OH 45213-2218 Office: KATZEN Internat Inc 2300 Wall St Ste K Cincinnati OH 45212-2789 E-mail: madson@katzen.com.

MADTES, PAUL, biology professor; b. Allentown, Pa., May 24, 1955; s. Paul and Myrle Madtes; m. Judy Madtes, June 27, 1981; children: Sarah, Matthew. PhD, Tex. A&M U., Coll. Sta., 1980, Trinity Theol. Sem., Newburgh, Ind., 1990. Prof. and chair biology Mt. Vernon Nazarene U., Ohio, 1989—. Adj. faculty Ohio State U., Columbus, 1990—2005; pres.'s adv. bd. Master's Internat. Sch. Divsn., Evansville, Ind., 2002—, sr. sci. advisor, 2003—. Mem.: Soc. Neurosci. Office: Mt Vernon Nazarene Univ 800 Martinsburg Rd Mount Vernon OH 43050

MADU, LEONARD EKWUGHA, lawyer, human rights advocate, columnist; b. Ibadan, Nigeria, Mar. 17, 1953; came to U.S., 1977; s. Luke E. and Grace (Dureke) M.; m. Jaculine Stephanie Turner, June 4, 1980; children: Christine, Oscar. BA, Marshall U., 1980; JD, U. Tenn., 1988; MA, Am. U. Rsch. assoc. Lamberts Publs., Washington, 1980-82; data specialist Govt. Employees Ins. Co., Washington, 1982-85; law intern Knoxville (Tenn.) Urban League, 1986-88; cons. Morris Brown Coll., Atlanta, 1988; staff atty. East Carolina Legal Svc., Wilson, NC, 1989-90; cons. youth devel. Nat. Crime Prevention Coun., Washington, 1990; contract compliance officer Walters State C.C., Morristown, Tenn., 1990; examiner Dept. of Human Svc., Nashville, 1990-93; human rights officer Human Rights Commn., Nashville, 1993—; pres. Panafrica, Nashville, 1994—; CEO Madu and Assoc. Internat. Bus. Cons., 1996—; with Bus. Forum & Banquet, 1994—; 1st v.p. Nashville Multicultural Partnership, Inc., 2000—. Polit. cons. Embassy of Nigeria, Washington, 1995; cons. Embassy of Sierra Leone, Washington, 1995, Healthcare Internat. Mgmt. Co., 1996-2001, Embassy of Mozambique, 2000-01, Embassy of Togo, 2001—; bd. dirs. Peace and Justice Ctr., Nashville; pres. African Conglomerates Internat., Inc. Editor: African Nations Handbook, 1994, Directory of African Universities and Colleges, 1994; editor-in-chief Panafrican Digest, 1994, Panafrican Jour. of World Affairs, 1994; columnist Met. Times, Nashville, 1991—, The African Herald, Dallas, 1995—, U.S./African Voice, Balt., 1995—, African Sun Times, 1995—, The Nigerian and African, 1995—, The African Press, N.Y. Co-chmn. Clergy and Laity Concerned, Nashville, 1992-95; mem. curriculum and character com. Met. Sch. Bd., Nashville, 1994-97; co-coordinator The Haitian Project, 1991-94; vice-chmn. Nigerian Network Leadership awards N.Y., 1996; chmn. Internat. Women's Expo, Knoxville, 1996; co-chair Miss Nigeria Internat. Beauty Pageant, Washington, 1995, Miss Africa Internat. Beauty Pageant, Nashville, 1996, Igbo Union Chieftaincy Coronation Ceremony, Nashville, 1995; chmn. Nigerian Patriotic Front, 1997—; coord. United Nigeria Congress Party, 1997-98, Southeast U.S.; recruiter internat. students Tenn. State U., 1998-99; chmn. bd. dirs. Africa Found., Washington, 2001—2002. Recipient World Hunger Devel. Program award Marshall U., 1978-79, Hall of Nations scholar Am. U., 1980, 82, Mary Strohbel award United Way, 1994-95, Non-profit Vol. award Nat. Conf. of Christians and Jews, 1994. Mem. NAACP, U.S. Com. on Fgn. Rels., Soc. Profl. Journalists, UN Assn., Orgn. African Natonals (pres. 1994), African C. of C. (pres. 2000—). Avocations: reading, travel, soccer, ping-pong, tennis. Office: Panafrica 1016 18th Ave S Nashville TN 37212-2105

MADUREIRA, LUIS MANUEL, literature and language professor; b. Nampula, Mozambique, Mar. 20, 1960; s. Luiz Maria and Francelina Batista Madureira; m. Saylin Oquendo Alvarez, Nov. 21, 2006; 1 child, Leila Isabel. PhD, U. Calif., San Diego, 1991. Prof. U. Wis.-Madison, 1991—2008. Author: Imaginary Geographies in Portuguese and Lusophone-African Literature. Recipient Samuel Stone Disting. Alumnus award, U. Mass. Dartmouth, 2006; Rsch. grant, Luso-Am. Found. Devel., 2004, Inst. Arquivos Nacionais, Torre do Tombo, 2006. Avocations: running, travel, soccer, swimming, hiking. Office: Univ Wis-Madison 1220 Linden Dr 1018VH Madison WI 53705

MADURGA, GONZALO F., performing company executive, actor, singer, director; b. Havana, Cuba, Jan. 21, 1932; arrived in U.S., 1953; s. Bernabé Madurga and Matilde Barrena. MS, L.I. U., 1977; student, Tamara Daykarhanova Acting Sch., 1956. Cert. bilingual tchr., NY. Artistic dir. Counterpoint Theatre, NYC, 1972-75, Operatic, Concert & Theatre Artists, Inc., Miami, Fla., 1996—. Dir. Born Yesterday, Iceland, 1958, Miss Julie, NYC, 1975, The Stronger, NYC, 1975, The Odd Couple, RI, Street CAR Named Desire, RI, Fingernails Blue as Flowers, NYC, Uncle Vanya, NYC, 1975, Totalmente Shakespeare, 2000, La Verbena la Paloma, Zarzuela Pro Arte Grateli, Fla.; actor Debut off Broadway, Miami, King of the Dark Chamber, NYC, 1961, Romeo and Juliet, 1965, Macbeth, 1966, Original Company Fantasticks, NYC, 1971, Kismet, Lincoln Ctr., 1974, Sound of Music, 1975, Carmelina Bway, NYC, 1979, Ardientc Paciencia P.Rico, La Verbena de la Paloma, Queens, NY, 1985 (Best Actor, Moby Dick, NYC, 1973, Christmas Carol, donde esta el tenor, Miami, Fla., 2004, Esperando a mama, 2001, Alice Adventures in Wonderland, Miami, 2008, Assn. Cronistas de Espectaculos award 1985), The Death of Garcia Lorca, N.X. Shakespeare Festival, 1988, Romeo and Juliet, NYC, 1994, Coimbra, Miami, 1994 (Best Actor Assn. Críticos Cronistas de las Artes 1994), The Fantasticks, Miami, 1996, Macbeth, NY, Shakespeare Festival, 1997, The Merchant of Venice, 1997, NY, Drama, Death and the Maiden, Coconut Grove, Fla., 1999, Praying with the Enemy, Coconut Grove, 2000, Hamlet, Fla., New Theatre, 2000, 2002, Anna in the Tropics, Fla., 2002-03, Coconut Grove Playhouse, The Man of La Mancha, NJ, 1987 Anna in the Tropics- created the role santiago in the World Premier of Pulitzer Prize Play, The Most Happy Fella, 1987, NY, Broadway Opera Co., (TV Drama)One Life to Live, As the World Turns, 1982, The guiding Light, CBS, 1980-81, America's most Wanted, Fox TV NY, others. With U.S. Army, infantry, 1956-58. Mem. Actors' Equity, Screen Actors' Guild, Am. Fed. T.V. Radio Artists, Nat. Acad. T.V. & Sciences, Home and Office: Operatic Concert & Theatre Artists Inc 1315 SW 21st St Miami FL 33145 Fax: (305) 858-0365. E-mail: gonzalomadurga@msn.com.

MAEDA, AKIO, educator; b. Ichikawa, Chiba, Japan, Aug. 2, 1933; m. Mitsuko Nishiyama, Mar. 27, 1961; 1 child, Tomoko. PhD, Nagoya U., Japan, 1961. Asst. prof. U. Tokyo, 1961—68; assoc. prof. Kyoto U., 1968—93, prof., 1993—97. Office: Univ Ill 601 South Goodwin St Urbana IL 61801

MAEDA, JOHN, academic administrator, graphics designer, artist, computer scientist; b. Seattle, 1966; m. Kris Maeda. BS, MIT, 1988, MS; PhD in Design, Tsukuba U. Inst. of Art and Design, Japan, 1992; DFA (hon.), Md. Inst. Coll. Art, 2003; MBA, Ariz. State U., 2006. Assoc. prof., design and computation MIT, E. Rudge and Nancy Allen prof. media arts and sciences, coach, physical language workshop, dir., aesthetics & computation group; co-dir. SIMPLICITY; assoc. dir. MIT Media Libr.; pres. RI Sch. Design, 2008—. Lectr. on the topic of work and philosophy at numerous academic, cultural, and indsl. institutions. One-man shows include Design Machines, Axis Gallery, Tokyo, 1995, Deconstructing Cyberspace, Axis Gallery Annex, Tokyo, 1995, Paper and Computer, Ginza Graphic Gallery, Tokyo and Dai Nippon Dojima Gallery, Osaka, 1996, one-line.com, Ginza Graphic Gallery, Tokyo, 1999, maeda@media, Calif. Inst. Arts and Crafts, San Francisco and Inst. Contemporary Art, London, Post-Digital, Cristinerose Gallery, NY, 2000, Towards Post Digital, NTT Inter-communication Ctr., Tokyo, 2001, FooD, Cristinerose Gallery, NY, 2003, NATURE + Eye'm Hungry', Found. Cartier, Paris, 2005, exhibited in group shows at NHK Heart Exhibitions, Bukamura Gallery, Tokyo, 1996, Organic Computation, NY Art Director's Club, 1999, Design Triennale, Cooper-Hewitt Nat. Design Mus., 2000, 010101:Art in Technological Times, San Francisco Mus. Modern Art, 2001, Workspheres, Mus. Modern Art, NY, 2001; author: Reactive Square, 1995, Flying Letters, 1996, 12 o'clocks, 1997, Tap, Type, Write, 1998, Design By Numbers, 1999, maeda@media, 2000, Creative Code, 2004. Recipient Grand Prix, Interactive prize, Multimedia Assn. Japan, 1995, Gold prize, Tokyo Type Director's Club, 1996, Interactive prize, 1998, Japan Ministry of Culture, 1998, Gold prize, ID Magazine, 1998, NY Art Director's Club, 1998, DaimlerChrysler Design prize, 2000, Nat. Design award, Smithsonian Institution, 2001, Muriel Cooper prize, Design Mgmt. Inst., 2001, Mainichi Design prize, Japan, 2002, Raymond Loewy Found. prize, Germany, 2005; named Best Book in Computer Science, Am. Assn. Publishers, 2000, Köln Designer of Yr., 2001; named one of 21 Most Important People for the 21st Century, Esquire, 1999, 15 Master Graphic Designers, Yahoo, 1999, 10 To Watch, ResFest, 2001, 20 Masters of Design, Fast Company Design, 2004. Office: Office of the President RISD 20 Washington Pl 4th Fl Providence RI 02903 Office Phone: 617-253-3133, 401-454-6407. Fax: 617-258-5079; Office Fax: 617-258-6264. Business E-Mail: maeda@media.mit.edu. E-mail: jmaeda@risd.edu.

MAEDA, KAZUO, obstetrician, gynecologist, educator; b. Makizono-cho, Kirishima, Japan, Jan. 5, 1925; s. Sumi and Nao M.; m. Mariko Fuchiwaki; 1 son, Mahiro. M.D., Kyushu Imperial U., Fukuoka, Japan, 1947; PhD, 1955. Asst. prof. Kyushu U., 1957-68; chmn., prof. dept. obstetrics and gynecology Tottori U., Yonago, Japan, 1968—90, head Univ. Hosp., 1976-80; pres. 4th Asia-Oceania Congress Perinatology, 1986, 3d Internat. Congress The Fetus as a Patient, 1987, 2d Internat. Congress Computers in the Care of the Mother, Fetus and Newborn, 1989, 5th World Congress of Ultrasound in Obstetrics and Gynecology, 1995. Invention of Doppler fetal actocardiograph. Mem. Japan Soc. Obstetrics and Gynecology (mem. council 1971-75, 83-85, chmn. com. on med. engring. 1971-1990), Japan Soc. Perinatology (pres. 1984), Japan Soc. Med. Engring. (chmn. working group 1983-90), Japan Soc. Med. Ultrasound (chmn. working group 1983-90), Am. Inst. for Ultrasound in Medicine, Internat. Acad. Perinatal Medicine, World Assn. Perinatal Medicine, Ian Donald Interuniversity Sch. Med. Ultrasound (Japan dir., 1998-2008), Croatian Acad. Med. Sci., Croatian Soc. Ultrasound in Medicine and Biology (hon.). Home: 125 3-Chome Nadamachi Yonago Tottori Prefecture Japan Office Phone: 81826722500. Personal E-mail: maedak@mocha.ocn.ne.jp.

MAEDA, KENJI, medical researcher; b. Kumamoto, Japan, Apr. 17, 1970; MD, Kumamoto U., Japan, 1995, PhD, 2002. Diplomate Kumamoto U., 1995. Resident physician Kumamoto U., 1995—99, rsch. fellow, 2002—05; fellow NIH, Bethesda, Md., 2005—. Achievements include research in drug discovery for HIV and AIDS. Office Phone: 301-496-9238. Personal E-mail: maedak@verizon.net. Business E-Mail: maedak@mail.nih.gov.

MAEDA, KOICHI, pathologist; b. Tokyo, Aug. 30, 1942; s. Toyoji and Umeko (Goto) M.; m. Kimiko Sugiyama, Oct. 23, 1967; children: Yuko, Hayato, Chiaki. MD, Shinshu U., Matsumoto, Japan, 1967. Diplomate Am. Bd. Pathology, Clin., Anatomic and Hematology. Hematopathologist dept. pathology Henry Ford Hosp., Detroit, 1976—. Fellow Coll. Am. Pathologists, Am. Soc. Clin. Pathologists. Achievements include study of pathogenesis in familial crystalline dystrophy of retina with co-workers.

MAEHL, WILLIAM HARVEY, retired historian; b. Bklyn., May 28, 1915; s. William Henry and Antoinette Rose (Salamone) M.; m. Josephine Scholl McAllister, Dec. 29, 1941; children: Madeleine, Kathleen. BSc, Northwestern U., 1937, MA, 1939; PhD, U. Chgo., 1946. Asst. prof. history St. Louis U., 1941-42, Tex. A&M U., College Sta., 1943, De Paul U., Chgo., 1944-49; historian Dept. of Def., Karlsruhe, Stuttgart, Fed. Rep. Germany, 1950-52; chief briefing office U.S. hdqrs. U.S. Hdqs. European Command, Frankfurt, Germany, 1952-53; chief historian Arty. Sch., Okla., 1954; with War Plans Office, Hdqs. No. Air Materiel Area for Europe, Burtonwood, England, 1954-55; assoc. prof. European history Nebr. Wesleyan U., Lincoln, 1955-57, prof., 1958-62, 65-68; prof. German history Auburn (Ala.) U., 1968-81, prof. emeritus, 1981—. Vis. prof. U. Nebr., 1962, U. Auckland, New Zealand, 1963—64, Midwestern U., Wichita Falls, Tex., 1965. Author: German Militarism and Socialism, 1968, History of Germany in Western Civilization, 1979, A World History Syllabus, 3 vols., 1980, August Bebel, Shadow Emperor of the German Workers, 1980, The German Socialist Party: Champion of the First Republic, 1918-33, 1986; contbr. poetry to Question of Balance, Tears of Fire, Disting. Poets Am., Best Poems of 1995, Journey of Mind; contbr. articles to profl. jours.; chpts. to books. Grantee Nebr. Wesleyan U., 1959, Auburn U., 1969-73, 79-80, Am. Philosophical Soc., 1973-74, Deutscher Akademischer Austauschdienst, 1978. Mem.: Am. Hist. Assn., Phi Alpha Theta, Phi Kappa Phi.

MAEKAWA, KOJI OGURA, technology company administrator; b. Fukui, Japan, Sept. 11, 1954; s. Eiji and Toshiko M.; m. Yukiko Ogura, Nov. 30, 1995. BSChemE, Tokyo U. of Agr. & Tech., 1979; MBA, U. St. Thomas, St. Paul, 1992. Analytical engr., Analytical Lab. Sumitomo 3M,

Sagamihara, Japan, 1979-81, chem. engr., Corporate Lab., 1982-87; process engr., Optical Storage Divsn. 3M, St. Paul, 1988—92, sr. process devel. engr., 1993—96; technical team leader Imation Corp. Adv. Imaging Technology, St. Paul, 1997-98, bus. devel. mgr., 1998-99, program mgr., 1998—2000; program mgr., bus. devel. mgr. PDF Solutions, San Jose, Calif., 2000—05, acct. gen. mgr., 2006—08; v.p. Japan Bus. Devel., 2008—. Intellectual property translator (English/Japanese), language soc. Minn. Mining Mfg., 1993—; cons. Expert Magnetics Corp., Chiba, Japan, 1993—. Patentee in field. Mem. Am. Japanese Soc., Internat. Symposium Semicondr. Mfg. (Japan external com. mem. 2008-). Avocations: golf, gardening. Office: Ste 700 333 W San Carlos St San Jose CA 95110 Office Phone: 408-938-4409, 703-539-9382, 040-3573-0297. Business E-Mail: kojim@pdf.com, koji.maekawa@pdf.com.

MAES, PETRA JIMENEZ, state supreme court justice; widowed; 4 children. BA, U. N.Mex., 1970, JD, 1973. Bar: N.Mex. 1973. Pvt. pratice law, Albuquerque, 1973-75; rep., then office mgr. No. N.Mex. Legal Svcs., 1975-81; dist. judge 1st Jud. Dist. Ct., Santa Fe, Los Alamos, 1981-98; chief judge, 1984-87, 92-95; assoc. justice N.Mex. Supreme Ct., 1998—, chief justice, 2003—04. Mem. N.Mex. Commn. on Access to Justice. Mem.: Improved Task Force and Judical Info. Sys. Coun. (liason), Am. Law Instn., Am. Bar Assn., N. Mex Com. (co-chair), Nat. Hispanic Bar Assn., N. Mex. Hispanic Bar Assn., N. Mex. Women's Bar Assn., N. Mex. Bar Assn. Office: Supreme Court NMex PO Box 848 Santa Fe NM 87504-0848 Office Phone: 505-827-4883.*

MAESEN, WILLIAM AUGUST, development consultant; b. Albertson, NY, 1939; s. August and Wilhelmina (Gaska) M.; m. Carolee Patton, Nov. 21, 1989; m. Sherry Jaeger Maesen; children: Ryan, Betsy, Steven;children from previous marriage: Kimberly, Maureen. BA, Oklahoma City U., 1961; BS in Bus., 1961; MA, Ind. State U., 1968; PhD, U. Ill., Chgo., 1979; postgrad., 1982—83; PsyD, SC U., 2004; LLB, LaSalle Extension U., Chgo., 1965. LCSW, lic. clin. profl. counselor Ill. Instr. sociology Aquinas Coll., Grand Rapids, Mich., 1967—70; asso. prof. behavioral sci. Coll. St. Francis, Joliet, Ill., 1970—78; assoc. prof. M.S.W. program Grand Valley State U., Allendale, Mich., 1978—82; field instr. Jane Addams Coll. Social Work, 1982—83; city editor Denni Hlasatel, 1984—88; lectr. MSW program U. Ill., 1972; evening admissions coord. dept. mental health State of Ill., 1984—94, field liaison dept. mental health, 1994—97, contracts mgr. dept. mental health, 1997—2001; pvt. practise, 2001—. Dir. residential treatment Cathedral Shelter, Chgo., 1982—83; Cath. charities exec. bd. mem., chair, Joliet, 1987—95; exec. bd. mem., sec. lupus Found, 1995—2003; with Myasthenia Gravis Found, Blue Island, Ill., 1997—2001; mem. edtl. bd. GSC Pub., Calif., 2008—. Contbr. articles to profl. jours. Chairperson Joliet and Will County Homeless Task Force, 1988—90; pres. Cmty. Svc. Coun. Will County Inc., 2007—09; chmn. bd. RSVP program Catholic Charities, Diocese Joliet, 1974—2001, exec. bd., 1988—95. With USAFR, 1962—68. Recipient Disting. Svc. award, DEpt. Mental Health, Ill., 2002, Cmty. Svc. Coun. Will County Inc., 2008; named Outstanding Vol. Yr., RSVP, 2004. Mem.: The Sheperd's Table, Joliet (exec. bd. 1991—93), Alpha Kappa Delta, Beta Gamma. Avocations: dog breeding, gardening. Home: 1502 Waverly Pl Joliet IL 60435-4144 Office: Program Consultant PO Box 4380 Chicago IL 60680

MAESHIRO, MITZI (MIKILANI), literature and language educator; d. Roy Mitchell and Takako Hayes; m. Brian Morikazu Maeshiro, July 29, 1995. BA, U. of Hawaii at Hilo, 1982—83; Profl. diploma in Tchg., U. of Hawaii at Manoa, 1983—86, M in edn., 1995—2000. Hawaiian lang. specialist Kamehameha Schools, Honolulu, 1984—86, elem. sch. tchr., 1986—2003, literacy resource tchr., 2003—. Co-author: (book) Elevating Expectations: A New Take on Accountability, Achievement, and Evaluation, 2004. Mem.: ASCD (assoc.), Ka Hui Heluhelu (pres. 2001—02), Internat. Reading Assn. (assoc.), Nat. Coun. of Techers of English (assoc.). Home: 45-621 Puuluna Pl Kaneohe HI 96744-2841

MAFFEI, DANIEL B., United States Representative from New York, former investment company executive; b. Syracuse, NY, July 4, 1968; m. Abby Maffei. BA in History, Brown U., Providence; MS in Journalism, Columbia U., NYC; MPP in Govt., Harvard U., Cambridge, Mass. Reporter, prodr. Sta. WIXT-TV Channel 9 News, Syracuse, 1992—93; press. sec. Senator Bill Bradley, 1995—96, Senator Daniel Patrick Moynihan, 1997—98, US House of Representatives Ways and Means Com., 1998—2004, sr. policy advisor, 2004—05; campaign coord. Mayor Matt Driscoll, Syracuse, 2005; sr. v.p. corp. devel. Pinnacle Capital Mgmt., LLC, 2006—09; mem. US Congress from 25th NY Dist., 2009—. Former mem. NABET Local 211 the Comm. Workers America; mem. Tech Ctrl. Cmty. Adv. Bd. Active Spanish Action League, Donors Choose. Mem.: DeWitt Rotary Club. Democrat. Roman Catholic. Office: US Congress 1630 Longworth House Office Bldg Washington DC 20515-3225 also: Dist Office 1340 Federal Bldg PO Box 7306 100 S Clinton St Syracuse NY 13261 Office Phone: 202-225-3701, 315-423-5657. Office Fax: 202-225-4042, 315-423-5669.*

MAFFEI, GREGORY B., media company executive, former computer software company executive; b. NYC, May 24, 1960; s. Ralph J. and Sheila (Quinn) M. AB, Dartmouth Coll., 1982; MBA, Harvard U., 1986. Analyst Dillon, Read & Co., Inc., NYC, 1982-84, assoc.; pres. Beacon Hill Cons. Co., Boston, 1984; dir. bus. devel & investments Microsoft Corp., Redmond, Wash., 1993—94, treas., 1994—96, v.p. corp. devel., 1996—97, sr. v.p., fin. & adminstrn., CFO, 1997—2000; non-exec. chmn. Expedia, Inc., Bellevue, Wash., 1999—2002; pres., CEO 360 networks, Inc., Vancouver, BC, Canada, 2000—05, chmn., 2000—05; pres., CFO Oracle Corp., Redwood City, Calif., 2005; pres., CEO Liberty Media Corp., Englewood, Colo., 2006—. Bd. dir. Starbucks Corp., Seattle, 1999—, Electronic Arts Inc., Redwood City, Calif., 2003—, Liberty Media Corp., Englewood, Colo., 2005—. Bd. trustee Seattle Pub. Libr. George F. Baker scholar Harvard U., 1986. Roman Catholic. Office: Liberty Media Corp 12300 Liberty Blvd Englewood CO 80112

MAFFEO, ALPHONSE A., anesthesiologist; b. 1947; MD, SUNY Syracuse, 1972. Diplomate Am. Bd. Anesthesiology. Intern Harrisburg Hosp., 1972-73; res. anesthesiology Mass Gen. Hosp., Boston, 1973-75; physician Lehigh Valley Hosp., Allentown, Pa., 1977—, chmn. anesthesiology, 1990-2001. Clin. assoc. prof., assoc. chmn. anesthesiology Pa. St. U. Hershey Med. Ctr., 1994—2001. Fellow ABA, Am. Coll. Anesthesiologists, mem. Am. Soc. Anesthesiologists. Office: Allentown Anesthes Assn Inc 1245 S Cedar Crest Blvd Ste 301 Allentown PA 18103-6258

MAFFEO, PINO, chef; b. 1970; Grad., Newbury Culinary Coll., 1991. Task force chef Marriott Corp., 1991—92; chef Cafe Katie, San Francisco, 1992; chef de partie Molhern and Shackern, San Francisco; chef de cuisine Inn at the Opera, San Francisco; co-exec. chef Sage, Boston, 1996—99; chef de cuisine AZ, NYC, 1999—2002; co-exec. chef Pazo, NYC, 2002—03; exec. chef Boston Public Restaurant (formerly Restaurant L), Boston, 2004—. Guest appearances (TV series) The Early Show, Food Network, Simply Ming. Recipient Best New Chef award, Food and Wine Mag., 2006; named Best New Chef: Up and Coming, Boston Mag., 2005; named one of Boston's Rising Stars, StarChefs.com, 2006, Boston's Best New Faces, Boston Globe Mag., 2004, Boston's Top Tastemakers, Boston Mag., 2004. Office: Boston Public 234 Berkeley St Boston MA 02116 Office Phone: 617-266-4680.

MAFFEO, VINCENT ANTHONY, lawyer, director; b. NJ, Jan. 22, 1951; s. Michael Anthony and Marie Maffeo; m. Debra Maffeo, Dec. 16, 1972. BA summa cum laude, Bklyn. Coll., 1971; JD, Harvard U., 1974. Bar: NY 1975, Calif. 1982, Va. 1988, DC 1988, Mich. 1994. Assoc. Simpson Thacher & Bartlett, NYC, 1974—77; legal counsel Comms. Sys. divsn. ITT, Hartford, Conn., 1977—79; v.p., gen. counsel Bus. Comms. divsn. ITT, Des Plaines, Ill., 1979—80; asst. counsel western region ITT, 1980—83; group counsel ITT Europe, Inc., 1983—86; v.p. gen. coun. ITT Defense Inc., 1987—91; v.p., gen. coun. ITT Automotive, Inc., 1992—95; sr. v.p., gen. counsel ITT Corp., 1995—. Bd. dir. Fund for Modern Courts, 1997—. Trustee Sacred Heart Univ.; bd. dir. Pro Bono Partnership, Fundacion Chile. Lt. Judge Adv. Gen. Corps. USNR, 1975. Mem.: ABA, N.Y.State Bar Assn., Calif. State Bar, Phi Beta Kappa. Office: Itt 1133 Westchester Ave Ste N100 West Harrison NY 10604-3543 Business E-Mail: vince.maffeo@itt.com.

MAFFIA, JASON, health services administrator; b. NYC, June 23, 1977; s. Anthony and Gerri Maffia, Anthony and Gerri Maffia. MS in Psychology, Iona Coll., New Rochelle, NY, 2002. Diplomate cert. expert traumatic stress, cert. emergency crisis response, acute traumatic stress mgmt. Am. Acad. Experts Traumatic Stress, NY, cert. in health cons. Therapist Goodwill Industries, Queens, NY, 2002—03; applied behavior sci. specialist AHRC Nassau County, Brookville, NY, 2004—06; health svcs. adminstr., clin. supr. critical incident stress mgmt. team GEO Group Inc, Queens Pvt. Detention Facility, Jamaica, NY, 2006—. Team coord., mental health profl. Regional EMS Coun. NYC: Critical Incident Response Team; team leader, mental health profl. Nassau County Critical Incident Stress Mgmt. Team; team mem. Nassau County Cmty. Emergency Response Team: Office Emergency Mgmt.; presenter in field. Contbr. articles to profl. jours. Recipient Pioneering Sprit award, ICISF, 2009. Mem.: Nat. Scholars Honor Soc., Nat. Honor Soc. Psych., Nat. Ctr. Crisis Mgmt.: Premier Speakers Bur., Disaster Preparedness Emergency Response Assn., Internat. Critical Incident Stress Found., Am. Acad. Experts Traumatic Stress. Republican. Home: 722 Willow Rd Franklin Square NY 11010 Personal E-mail: jmaff72653@aol.com.

MAFFITT, JAMES STRAWBRIDGE, lawyer; b. Raleigh, NC, Oct. 29, 1942; s. James Strawbridge III and Lois (Handy) M.; children: Amy Maffitt Barkley, Margaret Maffitt Kramer; m. Frances Holton, Aug. 15, 1981. BA, Washington and Lee U., 1964, LLB, 1966. Bar: Va. 1966, Md. 1969. Assoc. Apostolou, Place & Thomas, Roanoke, Va., 1966-67; trust officer Mercantile-Safe Deposit & Trust Co., Balt., 1967-71; from assoc. to ptnr. Cable, McDaniel, Bowie & Bond, Balt., 1971-82; ptnr. Maffit & Rothschild, Balt., 1982-85, Anderson, Coe & King, Balt., 1986-90, Miles & Stockbridge, Easton, Balt., 1990—2008, James S. Maffitt, Esquire, LLC, Easton, Md., 2008—. Chmn. Acad. Art Mus., 1994—97, bd. dirs., 1993—99, Leadership Md., 1994—95; trustee Grayce B. Kerr Fund, Inc., 1998—; bd. dirs. Chesapeake Coll., 2002—, United Fund of Talbot County, 1994—98, pres., 1997—98. Fellow Md. Bar Found.; mem. ABA (ho. dels. 1986-88), Md. Bar Assn. (bd. govs. 1989-91), Va. Bar. Assn., Balt. City Bar Assn. (pres. 1985-86), Talbot Country Club. Republican. Episcopal. Avocation: golf. Home: 6272 Country Club Dr Easton MD 21601 Office: James S Maffitt Esquire LLC 114N West St Easton MD 21601 Business E-Mail: jim@maffittlaw.com.

MAGANA, MELANIE G, psychologist, consultant; b. New York, NY, Feb. 21, 1954; d. Anthony Dominic Thomas Guggenheimer; m. John R Magana, Oct. 4, 2003; children: Justin Anthony Moss, Timothy Andrew Moss. MS in Sch. Psychology, Nat. U., San Diego, Calif., 1995. Lic. Psychologist Calif., 2000. Sch. psychologist Oceanside Unified Sch. Dist., Oceanside, Calif., 1996, Chino Valley Unified Sch. Dist., Chino, Calif., 1996—2006; pvt. practice Resilience Through Edn., 2006—. Parenting instr. Chino Human Services, Chino, Calif., 2000—; cons. in trauma and loss in children. Mem.: APA (assoc.), Calif. Assn. Sch. Psychologists, Nat. Assn. Sch. Psychologists. Roman Catholic. Personal E-mail: ottermgm@sbcglobal.net.

MAGARGEE, W(ILLIAM) SCOTT, III, lawyer; b. Abington, Pa., Sept. 3, 1940; m. Annette Bruno, (dec.); children: Scott, Todd, Ashley. AB, Princeton U., 1962; LLB, Yale U., 1966. Bar: Pa. 1966, U.S. Dist. Ct. (ea. dist.) Pa. 1966, U.S. Tax Ct. 1973. Assoc. Dechert LLP, Phila., 1966-75, ptnr., 1975—2005, of counsel, 2006—. Bd. dirs. United Way Southeastern Pa., 2006—, CC Phila. Found., 1998—. Fellow Am. Coll. Employee Benefits Counsel; mem. ABA (sect. taxation), Phila. Bar Assn., Princeton Club Phila., Princeton Univ. Alumni Coun. (chmn. 1985-87), Phila. Club, Princeton club Phila. Office: Dechert LLP Cira Ctr 2929 Arch St Philadelphia PA 19104

MAGARIÑOS, CARLOS ALFREDO, international association administrator; MBA, Nat. U. Buenos Aires; postgrad., Internat. Devel. Law Inst. Rome, 1990; postgrad. mergers and acquisitions Wharton Sch., U. Pa., 1997; DHC (hon.), U. Econ. Sci. and Pub. Adminstrn., Budapest, 2000, U. Social and Bus. Scis. Buenos Aires, 2002. Assoc. prof. microeconomy, Buenos Aires, 1986; tech. coord. rsch. methodology in investigation, 1987; asst. prof. fgn. trade instns., 1989; assoc. prof. Argentine and Latin Am. Econ. Issues Salvador U., Buenos Aires, 1990; instr. U. Belgrano, Buenos Aires, 1990; dir.-gen. UN Indsl. Devel. Orgn., Vienna, 1997—; rep. Econ. and Trade Argentine Govt., Washington, 1990—96. Author: The Role of the State and Industrial Policy in the '90s, 1995, Reforming the UN System: UNIDO's Need-Driven Model, 2001, Gearing Up for a New Development Agenda-Marginalization vs Prosperity: How to Improve and Spread the Gains of Globalization, 2001, Updating and Fleshing Out the DevelopmentAgenda, 2002, China in the WTO-The Birth of a New Cathching-Up Stratgy, 2003; contbr. articles to profl. jours. Recipient Performance award, Inst. Superieur de Gestion, 2000. Office: UNIDO Vienna Internat Ctr PO Box 300 A-1400 Vienna Austria

MAGARY, ADAM J., legislative staff member; Grad., Wheaton Coll., Ill., 1997. Legis. asst. to congressman Donald Manzullo US House of Reps., Washington, 2000—01, legis. dir., 2001—02, chief of staff, 2003—, legis. liason, House Small Bus. Com., 2003—07. Republican. Mailing: US House Reps 2228 Rayburn House Office Bldg Washington DC 20515 Office Phone: 202-225-5676. Office Fax: 202-225-5284. Business E-Mail: adam.magary@mail.house.gov.*

MAGAZINE, CYNTHIA PENROSE, retired health care consultant; b. Manila, Philippines, Nov. 24, 1939; d. Douglas Lee Lipscomb Cordiner and Jane (Sturgeon) Edises; m. Douglas Francis Penrose, July 11, 1959 (div. 1981); children: Vicki, Lee Douglas; m. Alan Harrison Magazine, Aug. 30, 1984. BA, U. Calif., Berkeley, 1963; MBA, U. Santa Clara, 1977. LCSW. V.p., dir. employment Resource Ctr. for Women, Palo Alto, Calif., 1973-78; bus. planner Raychem Corp., Menlo Park, Calif., 1979; adminstrv. mgr. Electric Power Rsch. Inst., Palo Alto, 1979-83; sr. ptnr. MB Assocs., Washington, 1983—85; dir. ops. Utility Data Inst., Washington, 1985—86, Randmark, Inc., 1986-87; coord. market devel. for Mid-Atlantic states Kaiser Found. Health Plan, Washington, 1987-88, asst. to assoc. regional mgr., 1988-94; market planner MetraHealth, Vienna, Va., 1995; exec. staff asst. United HealthCare, Vienna, 1995, dir. strategic planning, splty. cos., 1996-97; dir. spl. projects MetraComp subs. United HealthCare, Vienna, 1997, v.p. regulatory affairs and compliance, 1997-99; ptnr. Penrose Mag. LLC, 2000—01; ret., 2001. Bd. dirs., treas. Unique Enterprises, Washington, 1985-87; sec. Wesley Property Mgmt. Co., 1987-89; bd. dirs. Wesley Housing Devel. Corp., 1988-89. Chair vol. com. Habitat for Humanity, No. Va., 2002—03, bd. dirs., 2003—06, chair Restore adv. com., 2003—05, v.p., exec. com., 2005—06; mem. Affirmative Action Adv. Com., Palo Alto, 1975—76; bd. dirs., sec. Am. Hospice Found., 1995—97, treas., 1998—2000; bd. dirs. Nat. Inst. for Med. Options, 1999—2001; bd. dirs., v.p. LWV, Berkeley, 1966—72, Palo Alto, 1972—73; chmn. program adv. com. Resource Ctr. for Women, Palo Alto, 1980—83. Mem. Peninsula Profl. Women's Network (v.p. 1981-82), U. Calif. Alumni Assn., AAUW (Bicentennial br. sec. 1986-88), Scottsdale, Ariz. (2008-), Fountain Hills, Ariz. (2007-), 4 Peaks Women's Club, Fountain Hills (2007-09), Fountain Hills Libr. Assn. (bd. dir. & mem. chair 2009-), Restore Com. Habitat Humanity Desert Foothills (chair 2009-), Capitol Area Soc. Healthcare Planning and Mktg., Nat. Capital Healthcare Execs., LWV. Democrat. Episcopalian. Avocations: nutrition and health, reading. Home: 16449 E Bainbridge Ave Fountain Hills AZ 85268 Home and Office: 16449 E Bainbridge Ave Fountain Hills AZ 85268 Home Phone: 480-219-6279. Personal E-mail: ccpenrose@cox.net.

MAGAZINER, ELLIOT ALBERT, musician, conductor, educator; b. Springfield, Mass., Dec. 25, 1921; m. Sari Fromkin; 2 children. Student, Nat. Orch. Assn., 1937-40, Princeton U., 1943, Juilliard School of Music, 1946-50. Music dir., prof. music Manhattanville Coll., Purchase, NY, 1970—. Faculty Westchester Conservatory Music, Summit Music Festival, 2001. Debut: Town Hall, NYC, 1952; staff artist, concertmaster CBS-TV and Radio; Networks: condrs. Reiner, Ansermet, Beecham, Stokowski; condr., sr. violin instr. Westchester Conservatory of Music; vis. condr. Dubuque Symphony; soloist N.Y. Philharm. Symphony, Symphony of the Air, Kol Visrael, symphonies in Chgo., Ft. Myers, Dubuque, York, St. Petersburg, Lincoln Ctr., NYC, 2002; recitals in N.Y.C., Washington, Detroit, Amsterdam, Paris, Jerusalem; star of CBS-TV, The Violin. Recs.: Charles Ives Sonata #2, Charles Ives Trio (with Frank Glazer and David Weber); Vivaldi Concerto in C and Concerto in B (with orchestre Symphonique de Paris); conductor Westchester All County Festival Orch. Mem. AAUP, N.Y. TV Musicians (pres.), CBS Musicians Fund (sec.) Achievements include Dec. 1 has been named the Elliot Magaziner Day by the Westchester County Legislature. Avocation: collecting unique and ancient instruments. Home: 250 Garth Rd Apt 2b3 Scarsdale NY 10583-3954 Office: Manhattanville Coll 2900 Purchase St Purchase NY 10577-2131 Office Phone: 914-694-2200 ext 6267, 914-323-3192.

MAGAZINER, HENRY JONAS, architect, writer; b. Phila., Sept. 13, 1911; s. Louis and Selma (Jonas) M.; m. Reba Henken, June 19, 1938; children: Ellen Louise (Mrs. Alan I. Widiss), Fred Thomas. BArch, U. Pa., 1936. Cert. Nat. Coun. Arch. Registration Bds. Draftsman Phila. City Planning Project, 1936-37; draftsman Louis Magaziner (Architect), Phila., 1937-39, architect, 1946-48; chief Architects' Squad, Day & Zimmermann, Inc., Burlington, Iowa, 1940-41; architect Albert Kahn (Architect), Detroit, 1942; designer Wright Aero. Corp., Wood Ridge, N.J., 1943-45; ptnr. Louis & Henry Magaziner, Phila., 1948-56; architect, planner pvt. practice, 1956-72; regional hist. architect, archtl. historian Mid-Atlantic region Nat. Pk. Svc., Phila., 1972-87; pvt. practice architecture, 1987—. Archtl. adviser Phila. Hist. Commn., 1970-75, mem. archtl. com., 1979-85, chmn. archtl. com., 1972-75. Author: The Golden Age of Ironwork, 2000, Our Liberty Bell, 2007. Mem. Carpenters' Co. of City and County of Phila., mem. mng. com. historic Carpenters' Hall, 2000-02; v.p. Phila. Health and Welfare Coun., 1957-61, Phila. chpt. Victorian Soc. Am., 1975; v.p. city planning Germantown Comty. Coun., 1957-62; bd. dirs. Downtown Children's (day care) Ctr., 1956-73, v.p., 1960-61; bd. dirs. Allens Ln. Art Ctr., 1945-67, Neighborhood Ctr. Phila., 1956-74, Hist. Soc. Pa., 1970-74, Chestnut Hill Hist. Soc., 1970-80, Phila. chpt. Assn. for Preservation Tech., 1991-98, Clean Air Coun., 1980-92, Center City Residents Assn., 1995-96; bd. dirs. Ebenezer Maxwell Mansion Mus., pres., 1964-67; trustee Stewardsom Meml. Fellowship in Arch., 1958-90. Recipient Presdl. award for Excellence in Design for the Govt., 1988, James Biddle award Preservation Alliance for Greater Phila., 1999; named to Germantown Hall of Fame, 1994. Fellow AIA (mem. com. on hist. resources, John Harbeson award 2000); mem. ASTM (mem. com. on hist. preservation stds. 1981-90), Am. Inst. Conservation, Assn. for Preservation Tech., Ea. Nat. Pk. and Monument Assn., Fellows in Am. Studies (pres. 1983-84), Nat. Trust for Hist. Preservation, Soc. Archtl. Historians (bd. dirs. 1977-80, mem. editl. bd. 58 vol. Buildings of the United States 1992-98), Bldg. Conservation Internat., Victorian Soc. Am., T-Square Atelier (pres. 1963-65), Pa. Soc. Architects, Pa. Acad. Fine Arts, Libr. Co. Phila., Sierra Club, Athenaeum of Phila., Preservation Action. Home: 2 Franklin Town Blvd Apt 2404 Philadelphia PA 19103-1237 *I do hope that we can pass on to future generations a prejudice-free America having a natural environment without pollution and a man-made environment with its best elements both preserved and appreciated. Achieving these objectives is an unending struggle but one certainly worth winning. God willing, I expect to continue to fight for these ends.*

MAGBOUL, MAGBOUL M., anesthesiologist, educator; MBBS, U. Khartoum, Sudan, 1974. Cons. anesthetist, asst. prof. King Saud U., Riyadh, Saudi Arabia, 1998—2001; asst. prof. U. Iowa, Iowa City, 2001—. Mem.: Royal Coll. Surgeons and Physcians Ireland. Achievements include invention of magboul laryngoscope. Office: Univ Iowa 200 Hawkins Dr Iowa City IA 62242 Business E-Mail: m-magboul@uiowa.edu. E-mail: mmagboul@gmail.com.

MAGDEN, RONALD EARNEST, education educator; b. Mountain Home, Idaho, Aug. 30, 1926; s. Roy Dennis Magden and Zoe (Bunnell) Cathrine; m. Joan Loraine Mulroney, Aug. 6, 1949. BA, U. Idaho, Moscow, 1949, MA, 1955; PhD, U. Wash., Seattle, 1964. Tchr. Am. history Orofino HS, Idaho, 1949—51, Renton HS, Wash., 1954—63; tchr. trainer Seattle U., 1962—64; chmn. social sci. divsn. Tacoma CC, 1964—83; tchr. trainer U. Zagreb, Croatia, 1972, SUNY, Buffalo, 1972; adj. instr. history, geography Tacomn CC, 1983—. Co-author: The Working Waterfront, 1983, Harts Lake School: Symbol of Pioneer Education, 1984, To Live in Dignity: Histories of Unions, 1985, More Voices, New Stories: Buddhism Comes to Seattle, 2002; author: A History of Seattle Waterfront Workers, 1991, The Working Longshoreman, 1991, Furusato: A History of the Tacoma and Pierce County Japanese, 1989; contbr. articles to profl. publs. Vol. tchr. McNeil Island Fed. Penitentiary, 1967—77, Women's Treatment Ctr., 1978—83. Scholar, Am. Coun. Learned Socs., 1960, Asian Soc., 1961, NEH, 1966—67, Civil Liberties Pub. Edn., 2001; fellow in history, Nat. Def. Act, 1962. Mem.: Tacoma Hist. Soc. (pres. 2000—05). Mailing: Tacoma Hist Soc 3703 N 22d St Tacoma WA 98406-5306

MAGDON-ISMAIL, MALIK, computer science professor; US, 1989; s. Hamim and Fathima Magdon-Ismail; m. Fathima Zainab Muhsin, July 17, 1999; children: Zain, Deen. BS summa cum laude, Yale U., New Haven, Conn., 1992; PhD, Calif. Inst. of Tech., Pasadena, 1998. Postdoctoral rsch. scholar Calif. Inst. of Tech., Pasadena, 1998—2000; prof. computer sci. Rensselaer Poly. Inst., Troy, NY, 2000—. CEO, chief tech. officer Swooge LLC, Albany, NY, 2006—; chief tech. officer Gold Finger Mgmt. LLC, Hong Kong, 2003—. Contbr. articles to profl. jours. Recipient Wilts prize for best PhD thesis in elec. engring., Calif. Inst. of Tech., 1998, Grant Funding awards to study social comm. networks, NSF, ONR, KDD, 2003, 2004, 2005, 2006. Mem.: IEEE, Assn. for Computing Machinary, Phi Beta Kappa. Achievements include patents pending for Remote Caller ID Projection Device. Avocations: bridge, squash, badminton, tennis, travel. Office: Rensselaer Poly Inst 110 8th St Troy NY 12180 Office Fax: 518-276-4033. E-mail: magdon@cs.rpi.edu.

MAGEE, ALAN, artist; b. Newtown, Pa., May 26, 1947; s. Richard Forrest and Rena (Cook) M.; m. Monika Gabriele Ruth Siekmann, Jan. 4, 1969. Student, Tyler Sch. of Art, 1965-66, Phila. Coll. Art, 1967-69. One-person shows include Allport Assocs. Gallery, Larkspur, Calif., 1978, 81, Clark Gallery, Lincoln, Mass., 1979, Staempfli Gallery, N.Y.C., 1980, 82, 90, FIAC Grand Palais, Paris, 1983, Norton Gallery and Sch. of Art, West Palm Beach, Fla., 1983, San Jose Mus. Art, 1983, Newport Art Mus., 1984, Farnsworth Art Mus., Rockland, Maine, 1984, Ark. Art Ctr., Columbus Mus. of Art, Ohio Chgo. Art Inst., U. Maine, 1985, Fresno Art Ctr., 1985, L.A., 1986, Schmidt-Bingham Gallery, N.Y.C., 1986, 88, 89, Allport Assocs. Gallery, San Francisco, 1986, Joan Whitney Payson Gallery at Westbrook Coll., Portland, Maine, 1990, Staempfli Gallery, NY, 1990, Farnsworth Art Mus., 1991, James A. Michener Art Mus., Bucks County, Pa., 1991, Ringling Sch. Art & Design, Sarasota, Fla., 1992, Fine Arts Ctr. at Cheekwood, Nashville, 1992, Edith Caldwell Gallery, San Francisco, 1992, 93, 95, 96, 97, Edith Lambert Gallery, Santa Fe, 1995, Hollis Taggart Gallery, N.Y.C., 2000, Berlin Philharm. Hall, 2000, Forum Gallery, L.A., 2001, 02, Forum Gallery, N.Y., 2003, James A. Michener Art Mus., 2003; 30-Yr. Retrospective traveling exhbn. James A. Michener Art Mus., 2003, Farnsworth Art Mus., 2004, Mus. of Tex. Tech U., 2004, Frye Art Mus., 2005, Luxemburg Embassy, Berlin, 2005, Forum Gallery, NY, 2006, Goethe Inst., NY, 2006, Sardoni Art Mus., Pa., 2006, Galerie Raab, Berlin, 2007, Ctr. for Maine Contemporary Art, Rockport, 2007, Forum Gallery, LA, 2007; group shows include Farnsworth Art Mus., Rockland, Maine, 1985, Akron (Ohio) Mus. of Art, 1985, Maine Coast Artists, Rockport, 1985, Ark. Art Ctr, Little Rock, 1985, Smithsonian Instn., Nat. Air and Space Mus., Washington, 1985, Wunderlich & Co., N.Y.C., 1986, Light Gallery, N.Y.C., 1986, Schmidt-Bingham Gallery, N.Y.C., 1986, 88, Mus. Fine Arts, Springfield, 1986, Butler Inst. Am. Art, Youngstown, Ohio, 1987, Am. Acad. and Inst. Arts and Letters, N.Y.C., 1987, Nat. Invitationnal Drawing Exhbn., 1989, Staempfli Gallery, N.Y.C., 1990, Albrecht Art Mus., St. Joseph, 1990, NAD, N.Y.C., 1990, Edith Caldwell Gallery, San Francisco, 1993, 94, 95, 96, Nora Eccles Harrison Mus. Art, Logan Utah, 1992, Portland Mus. of Art, 1993, Creiger Dane Gallery, Boston, 1995, Phila. Art Mus., 1995, Forum Gallery, N.Y.C, 1996, Nat. Mus. Am. Art, Washington, 1997, Hollis Taggart Gallery, N.Y., 1998, Hackett, Feedman Gallery, San Francisco, 1998, Portland Mus. Art, 1998, Farnsworth Art Mus., 1998, Art Inst. Chgo., 1999, Katonah Mus. Art, 1999, U. Rochester, 1999, O.P. FotoGalery, Hong Kong, 1999, others; prin. commd. works include portrait of Senate Majority Leader George Mitchell 2003 and Alan Magee, Maine, 2002, Tapestry for Riverview Psychiat. Ctr., Maine, and others; commns. include mural U. Maine, 1997, Maine State House, 1999; pub. collections include Farnsworth Art Mus., Rockland, Arco Collection, Lucasfilm, Bank of Japan, Mobil Oil, Janss Collection, L.A., Achenbach Collection, Palace of the Legion of Honour, San Francisco, Art Inst. Chgo., Portland (Maine) Mus. of Art, Rutgers U. Art Mus.; author: Stones and Other Works, 1987, Alan Magee 1981-91, Archive, Monotypes, Alan Magee, 2000, 03, Alan Magee - paintings, sculpture, graphics, 2003, Alan Magee: Maine Master, 2003, Time Pieces, 2006, Beyond Recognition: The Art of Alan Magee, 2006, Alan Magee: From the Underground River, 2007, (with Barry Lopez) Resistance, 2005; contbr. articles to profl. jours.; TV: Visions of Darkness and Light, 1988. Recipient Richard and Hinda Rosenthal Found. award N.Y.C., Am. Book award, Nevelson award, 1982; The Leo Meissner prize NAD, 1990. Personal E-mail: info@alanmagee.com.

MAGEE, CHARLES THOMAS, international consultant, retired diplomat; b. Clifton Forge, Va., Mar. 6, 1932; s. Charles Thomas and Dorothy Elizabeth (McPherson) M.; m. Maideh Mazda, May 30, 1959; 1 daughter, Maya. BA, Harvard U., 1953. Vice consul Am. Consulate, Windsor, Can., 1961-63; polit.-mil. affairs officer Am. Emb., Paris, 1964-66; polit. officer Soviet desk Dept. State, 1966-68; adv. Russian language and area studies Garmisch, Germany, 1968—69; polit. officer Am. Embassy, Moscow, 1969—71; dep. dir. for ops. Exec. Secretariat Dept. State, Washington, 1971-72, officer-in-charge French desk, 1972-74; chief internal polit. affairs, exec. asst. to amb. Am. Embassy, Paris, 1974—77, dep. chief mission Sofia, Bulgaria, 1977-80; chief jr. officer div. Bur. Pers. Dept. State, 1980-82, fgn. svc. insp., 1982-83; cons. gen. U.S. Consulate Gen., Leningrad, USSR, 1984-86; spl. asst. internat. affairs to mayor City of San Francisco, 1986-87; dir. Russian lang. ops. U.S. Del. to Negotiations on Nuclear and Space Arms with USSR, Geneva, 1988-91; sr. program officer for Russia Citizens Democracy Corps, Washington, 1992—93; amb. mission to Latvia Orgn. Security and Coop. Europe, 1994-97, amb. mission to Ukraine, 1998-99. Ofcl. election observer, Ukraine, 1998, 2002, 04, 06, Russia, 2000, 03, 04, Latvia, 2002, Azerbaijan, 2005, Ga., 2008; polling supr., Bosnia and Herzegovina, 2000; head Orgn. for Security and Coop. in Europe election observation mission to Macedonia, 2000, Azerbaijan, Moldova, Bulgaria, 2001, election expert Czech Republic, Malta, Ireland, 2009; field rep Census Bur., 2005; cons. Acad. Arrangements Abroad, N.Y.C., 1987—, Dept. of State, 1989—, Seabourn Cruise Line, San Francisco, 1989-92, Acad. Travel Abroad, Washington, 1995; asst. prof. Dept. Navy, 1959-61; election expert Czech Republic, Malta, Ireland, 2009. Active duty USN, 1953—59, lt. comdr. USNR. Mem. Am. Fgn. Svc. Assn., Harvard Club. Home and Office: 4518 Albemarle St NW Washington DC 20016-2016 Home Phone: 202-966-7038. Personal E-mail: ctmagee32@aol.com.

MAGEE, DONALD EDWARD, retired national park service administrator; b. Trenton, NJ, Sept. 24, 1937; s. Donald A. and Anna C. (Bocskowics) M.; m. Linda Kimball, June 27, 1964; children: Kevin, Bonnie Magee Burch, Gale. BS in Forestry Mgmt., U. Mass., 1964. Pk. ranger Bryce Canyon (Utah) Nat. Pk., 1966-68; area mgr. Sunset Crater Nat. Monument, Flagstaff, Ariz., 1968-73; mgmt. analyst Nat. Capital Region, Washington, 1973-80; supt. Stones River Nat. Battlefield, Murfreesboro, Tenn., 1980-89, USS Ariz. Meml., Pearl Harbor, Hawaii, 1989-95; ret., 1995. With USN, 1956-58. Recipient Excellence of Svc. award Dept. of Interior, 1991. Home: 95-457 Kaukoe St Mililani HI 96789-1865

MAGEE, ELAINE, dietician, consultant; BS in Nutrition, San Jose State U.; MPH in Nutrition, U. Calif., Berkeley. Registered Dietitian. Nutrition instr. Diablo Valley Coll.; nutrition mktg. specialist Calif. Dept. Health; host Light Cooking segment KSBW-TV NBC, Salinas, Calif.; nutrition expert & writer WebMD, SilverPlanet; nutrition expert & writer for nationally syndicated newspaper column The Recipe Doctor. Author: Eat Well for a Healthy Menopause, 1996, The Good News Eating Plan for Type II Diabetes, 1997, Someone's in the Kitchen with Mommy: 100 Easy Recipies and Fun Crafts for Parents and Kids, 1997, The Flax Cookbook: Recipes and Strategies for Getting the Most From the Most Powerful Plant on the Planet, 2003, Fry Light, Fry Right: Fried Food Flavor Without Deep Frying, 2004, The Change of Life Diet & Cookbook, 2004, Food Synergy: Unleash Hundreds of Powerful Healing Food Combinations to Fight Disease and Live Well, 2008, (med. nutrition series) Tell Me What to Eat If I Have...; regular contbr. to Women's Day and All You, written articles and recipes are featured in American Girl Mag. and Cooking Light, guest appearances on CBS Evening News, CNN, Caryl & Marilyn Real Friends, Good Morning NY and Debra Duncan Show.*

MAGEE, JOHN C., surgeon, educator; b. Jacksonville, NC, Jan. 15, 1962; s. John Thomas and Sarah Anne Magee; married. BA, U. Pa., Phila., 1984; MD, Jefferson Med. Coll., Phila., 1988. Diplomate Am. Bd. Surgery, 1997. Asst. prof. surgery U. Mich., Ann Arbor, 1998—2005, dir., adult kidney transplantation, 2000—08, dir., pediat. kidney transplantation, 2000—, dir., pediat. liver transplantation, 2001—, assoc. prof. surgery, 2005—. Sci. adv. bd. mem. Nat. Kidney Found. Mich., Ann Arbor, 2002—. Fellow: ACS, Soc. U. Surgeons, Am. Soc. Transplant Surgeons (chair, fellowship tng. com. 2007—); mem.: Internat. Pediat. Transplant Assn., Am. Soc. Transplantation, Transplantation Soc. Office: Univ Mich 1500 E Medical Center Dr Ann Arbor MI 48109 Business E-Mail: mageej@umich.edu.

MAGEE, JOHN FRANCIS, research and development company executive; b. Bangor, Maine, Dec. 3, 1926; s. John Henry and Marie (Frawley) M.; m. Dorothy Elma Hundley, Nov. 19, 1949 (dec. May 31, 2009); children: Catherine Anne, John Hundley, Andrew Stephen. AB, Bowdoin Coll., 1947; MS, U. Maine, 1952; MBA, Harvard U., 1948; LLD, Bowdoin Coll., 1996. With Arthur D. Little, Inc., Cambridge, Mass., 1950-98, v.p., 1961-72, pres., 1972-86, chief exec. officer, 1974-88, chmn., 1986-98, also dir., 1968-98. Author: Physical Distribution Systems, 1967, Industrial Logistics: Analysis and Management of Physical Supply and Distribution Systems, 1968, (with D. M. Boodman) Production Planning and Inventory Control, 1968; (with W. Capacino and W. Rosenfield) Modern Logistics Management, 1985. Former sec. to trustee Emerson Hosp.; emeritus trustee Thompson Island Outward Bound Edn. Ctr., chair, 1995—2000; emeritus trustee Bowdoin Coll.; hon. trustee Woods Hole Oceanographic Instn.; chmn. trustees Bowdoin Coll., 1990—94; overseer emeritus Mus. Sci., Boston. Officer USN, 1944—46. Recipient Disting. Leadership award, MIT, 1977. Fellow: Inst. for Ops. Rsch. and Mgmt. Sci., Phi Beta Kappa (life); mem.: Am. Soc. Metals (disting. life mem.), Inst. Mgmt. Scis. (pres. 1971—72), Ops. Rsch. Soc. Am. (pres. 1966—67, Kimball medal 1978), Comml. Club (pres. 1992—94), Somerset Club (Boston), The Country Club (Brookline, Mass.), Concord (Mass.) Country Club (gov. 1971—74), Phi Kappa Psi. Avocation: painting. Personal E-mail: magjfmagee@verizon.net.

MAGEE, THOMAS HENRY, radiologist, educator; b. Newport, RI, Nov. 26, 1958; s. Francis Robert and Anne Louise (Moriarty) M.; m. Christina Marie (Lapolla), June 7, 1987. BA, Wesleyan Univ., 1977-81; MD, NY. Med. Coll., 1982-86. Diplomate Am. Bd. Radiology. Staff radiologist Bethesda Naval Hosp., Md., 1991-94; asst. prof. medicine Uniformed Svc. Sch. of Med., Bethesda, Md., 1991-94, Kans. U. Sch. of Med., Kans. City, Kans., 1994—; staff radiologist Menorah Med. Pk., Overland Pk., Kans., 1994—; asst. prof. radiology U. Mo., Kans. City, Mo., 1997—2006; clin. prof. radiology U. Miami, 2006—. Pres. Rockhill Radiology, 1999; bd. examiner Am. Bd. Radiology; reviewer prof. jours., Am. Coll. Radiology. Contbr. articles to profl. jours. including Radiology, Jour. of Computer Assisted Tomography, Am. Jour. Roentgenology. Lt. comdr. USNR, 1991-94. Recipient: Jonas N. Muller Award, NY Med. Coll., 1986. Fellow Am. Coll. Radiology; mem. Am. Roentegen Ray Soc., Radiol. Soc. N.Am. (moderator, cert. of merit 1990); Kansas City Roentegen Ray Soc. (pres.), Internat. Skeletal Soc., Am. Bd. Radiology (bd. examiner, 2005). Avocations: stamp collecting/philately, tennis. Home: 185 Lanternback Island Dr Satellite Beach FL 32937-4704 Office: Neuroskeletal Imaging Melbourne FL Personal E-mail: tmageerad@cfl.rr.com.

MAGENTA, MURIEL, artist; b. NYC, Dec. 4, 1932; d. James E. and Sara (Wallman) Gellert; m. Gerald Zimmerman (dec.); children: Jean (dec.), Eric Vermilion. BA, Queens Coll., 1953; MA in Art History, Ariz. State U., 1962, MFA in Painting, 1965, PhD, 1970. Prof. art Ariz. State U., 1969—. One woman shows include Ariz. State U., 1976, Phoenix Art Mus., 1977, U. So. Calif., 1978, Marian Locks Gallery, Phila., 1979, Rutgers U., 1981, Yares Gallery, Scottsdale, Ariz., 1981, CitiBank, N.Y.C., 1984, U. Ark., 1984, L.A. Contemporary Exhbns., 1985, Scottsdale Ctr. for the Arts, 1990, 93, Kansas City (Mo.) Art Inst., 1991, Gallery 10, Washington, 1991, Ariz. State U. Art Mus., 1997, Computing Commons Gallery, Ariz. State U., 2002, Galvin Playhouse, Ariz. State U., 2005, 2009; group shows include L.A. Inst. Contemporary Art, 1978, Rutgers U., 1981, The Print Club Phila., 1983, Tweed Gallery, Plainfield, N.J., 1984, Tucson Art Mus., Ariz., 1988, Lawndale Art and Performance Ctr., Mus. of Fine Art, Santa Fe, N.Mex., 1990, Ctr. Simone De Beauvoir, Paris, 1992, Medien Operative Berlin, 1992, 8th Cadiz (Spain) Internat. Video Festival, 1992, South Bend (Ind.) Art Ctr., 1992, John Michael Kohler Art Ctr., Sheboygan, Wis., 1992, CAGE, Cin., 1993, Ctr. Simone DeBeauvoir, Paris, 1993, Drexel U., Phila., 1993, Artemisia Gallery, Chgo., 1996, U. Minn., Mpls., 1998, SIGGRAPH, Orlando, 1998, ZKM, Karlsruhe, Germany, 1998, Intermedia Art Gallery, Mpls., Minn., 1999, Tucson Mus. of Art, Ariz., 1999, United Nations, N.Y.C., 2000, Natl. Mus. of Photography, Film and TV, Bradford, U.K., 2002, Artemisia Gallery, Chgo., 2002, Savannah Coll. of Art and Design, Ga., 2002, Dallas Art Mus., Tex., 2003, Bklyn. Mus. Art, NYC, 2003, Anthology Film Archives, NYC, 2004, Victory Media Network, Am. Airlines Ctr., Dallas, 2006, Pioneer Theater, NY, 2006, Detroit Film Ctr., NY, 2006, Tempe Fine Ctr., Tempe, Ariz., 2007, Galvin Playhouse, Ariz., State U. Tempe, 2007, 09, Drexel U., Phila., 2007, 08, Scottsdale Innovation Ctr., Ariz, 2008; represented in permanent collections Ariz. State U., Valley Nat. Bank, Phoneix, Prudential Life, Scottsdale, SkySong Innovation Centre, Scottsdale, Ariz., 2008. Phoenix Art Mus. grantee, 1975-77; Ariz. State U. grantee, 1981-82, 92-93. Mem. NOW, Women's Caucus for Art (nat. pres. 1982-84, Mid-career achievement award 1991, Lifetime Achievement award 2002), Coll. Art Assn. Am., Mid-Am. Coll. Art Assn., Nat. Women's Polit. Caucus, Women in Animation, Inter-Soc. for the Electronic Arts, SIGGRAPH. Home: 8322 E Virginia Ave Scottsdale AZ 85257-1741 Studio: Ariz State U Tempe AZ 85287-1505 Office Phone: 480-965-4483. Business E-Mail: muriel.magenta@asu.edu.

MAGER, ARTUR, retired aerospace executive; b. Nieglowice, Poland, Sept. 21, 1919; arrived in U.S., 1939, naturalized, 1944; s. Herman and Ella (Kornbluh) M.; m. Phyllis R. Weisman, Aug. 19, 1942; 1 child, Ilana Gail. BS, U. Mich., 1943; MS, Case Inst. Tech., 1951; PhD in Aeros., Calif. Inst. Tech., 1953. Aero. rsch. scientist NASA Lewis Labs., Cleve., 1946-51; rsch. scientist Marquardt Corp., Van Nuys, Calif., 1954-60; dir. Nat. Engring. Sci. Co., Pasadena, Calif., 1960-61; dir. spacecraft scis. Aerospace Corp., El Segundo, Calif., 1961-64, gen. mgr. applied mechanics divsn., 1964-68, v.p., gen. mgr. engring. sci. ops., 1968-78, v.p. engring. group, 1978-82, cons., 1982—. Mem. BSD Re-entry Panel, 1961—63; mem. NASA com. missile and space vehicle aerodynamics, 1963—65; mem. adv. com. AFML, 1971—72; mem. NASA Adv. Coun., 1982—86; chmn. NASA Space Applications Adv. Com., 1982—86; mem. Aeros. and Space Engring. Bd. NRC, 1982—87; mem. Space Sta. Task Force NRC, 1983—87, mem. Shuttle Critically and Hazard Analysts Rev. Bd., 1986—88; mem. DSB NASP Task Force, 1987—88, AFSB Hypersonic Task Force, 1987—88. Contbr. articles to profl. jours. Mem. alumni fund coun. Calif. Inst. Tech., 1972—74; trustee West Coast U., 1980—92; mem. devel. disabilities bd. Area X, 1976—80, chmn., 1976—78; 1st v.p. Calif. Assn. Retarded, 1983—85; pres. Exceptional Children's Found., 1970—72; bd. councilors U. So. Calif. Sch. Engring., 1976—86. Recipient Disting. Alumni award, U. Mich., 1969, Golden Rule award, Calif. Assn. Retarded, 1977, 1989. Fellow: AAAS, AIAA (chmn. L.A. sect. 1967—68, bd. dirs. 1975—77, pres. 1980—81), Inst. Advanced Engring.; mem.: Nat. Acad. Engring., Technion Soc., Sigma Xi. Home and Office: 1353 Woodruff Ave Los Angeles CA 90024-5129 Personal E-mail: ap.mager1@verizon.net.

MAGER, EZRA PASCAL, investment company executive; b. NYC, Nov. 1, 1941; s. Harold and Naomi (Levinson) M.; m. Sarah Johnson, Mar. 25, 1964 9div.); 1 child, Emma Rachel; m. Reeva Starkman, May 14, 1972; children: Camilla Elizabeth, Michael Johanon. BA, Cornell U., 1963; MBA, Harvard, 1966. Successively v.p., sr. v.p., exec. v.p. and dir. Seiden & DeCuevas, Inc., NYC, 1966-73; exec. v.p., dir. Furman Selz Mager Dietz & Birney, Inc., NYC, 1973-90; vice chmn. United Auto Group, Inc., NYC, 1990-96, Cross Continent Auto Retailers, Inc., NYC, 1996-97, First Team Auto Corp., NYC, 1997-98; CEO EPM Advisory LLC, NYC, 1998—; pres. The Torrey Funds, 1998—2004. Trustee exec. com. The Textile Mus., Washington. Mem. N.Y. Soc. Security Analysts, Alpha Delta Phi. Clubs: Harvard (N.Y.C.), Hajji Baba Club (pres.). Democrat. Home: 141 E 72d St New York NY 10021-4315 Office: EPM Advisory LLC 509 Madison Ave Penthouse New York NY 10022 Office Phone: 212-223-2333. Business E-Mail: epmager@epmadvisory.com.

MAGERKO, MARGARET HARDY (MAGGIE), lumber company executive; b. Pitts., Dec. 7, 1965; d. Joseph Hardy; m. Peter Magerko. Student, W.Va. U. Pres. Nemacolin Woodlands Resort & Spa, 1987—, 84 Lumber Co., Eighty Four, Pa., 1994—. Named one of 400 Richest Ams., Forbes mag., 2006. Office: 84 Lumber Co 1019 Route 519 Eighty Four PA 15330 Business E-Mail: magerkom@84lumber.com.

MAGGETTE, COREY ANTOINE, professional basketball player; b. Melrose Pk., Ill., Nov. 12, 1979; s. Jimmie and Marguerite Maggette. Attended, Duke U., Durham, NC, 1998—99. Forward Orlando Magic, 1999—2000, LA Clippers, 2000—08, Golden State Warriors, 2008—. Achievements include leading the NBA in: freethrows (526), 2004. Office: Golden State Warriors 1011 Broadway Oakland CA 94607*

MAGGIO, THERESA GRIFFIN (TERRI MAGGIO), librarian; b. Shreveport, La., May 27, 1952; d. James Henry and Annie Laurie (Rosenblath) Griffin; m. Edward James Maggio, July 2, 1977; 1 child, Kelli Suzanne. BS in Social Studies Edn., La. State U., 1975, MLS, 1980; PhD in Libr. and Info. Studies, Fla. State U., 1988. Cert. Pub. Libr. Adminstr., 2008. Libr. La. State Libr., Baton Rouge, 1980—82; med. libr. Lallie Kemp Hosp., Independence, La., 1982—85; med. libr. cons. 7th Ward Hosp., Hammond, La., 1984—86; reference libr. Roddenbery Meml. Libr., 1988—89; dep. dir., pub. svc. libr. SW Ga. Regional Libr., Bainbridge, 1989—2005; collection devel. libr. State Libr. Fla., 2006, Jackson Correctional Inst., 2006—07; dir. Assumption Parish Libr., Napoleonville, La., 2007—. Recipient Baker and Taylor Grassroots award, 1980, Outstanding Reference Work award, 2000; named La. Libr. Assn. scholar, 1979; Title IIB fellow, 1985—86. Mem.: ALA. Democrat. Roman Catholic. Avocation: horse racing. Office: Assumption Parish Libr 293 Napoleon Ave Napoleonville LA 70390 Home Phone: 985-387-3156; Office Phone: 985-369-7070, Office Fax: 985-369-6019. Personal E-mail: terimaggio@hotmail.com. Business E-Mail: tmaggio@state.lib.la.us.

MAGGIPINTO, V. ANTHONY, lawyer; b. Tucson, Apr. 15, 1943; s. William Vito and Elizabeth Maria Maggipinto; m. Maria Teresa, Aug. 31, 1976; children: Marshall Albert Nicholas, Spencer William Jonathan. AB cum laude, Southampton Coll., 1970; JD, Fordham U., 1976. Bar: Fla. 1977, N.Y. 1978, U.S. Dist. Ct. (ea. and so. dists.) N.Y. 1979, U.S. Ct. Appeals (2d cir.) 1980; ordained deacon Cath. Ch., 2007. Asst. to pres. Interpub. Group of Cos., NYC, 1965-66; asst. dean of admission Southampton (N.Y.) Coll., 1971-73; investigative aide N.Y. State Com. on Jud. Conduct, NYC, 1974-76; asst. state atty. Dade County State Atty., Miami, Fla., 1977-78; asst. dist. atty. Suffolk Dist. Atty., Hauppage, N.Y., 1978-80; asst. county atty. Suffolk County Atty., Hauppauge, 1980-84; sole practice Riverhead and St. James, NY, 1982—2008, Southampton and St. James, NY, 2008—. Mem. spl. coms. on discovery, civil litigation U.S. Dist. Ct. (ea. dist.) N.Y., Bklyn., 1983-90, 95—, arbitrator, 1986—, Civil Justice Reform Act adv. group, 1990-95, chair jury task force, 1993—, commendation U.S. Dist. Ct., 1997. Mem. appeals bd. SSS, 1982—2001, vice chmn., 1986—97, chmn., 1997—2001. With submarine svc. USN, 1961—65. Recipient Disting. Alumni award L.I. U., 1990. Mem.: Southampton Coll. Alumni Assn. (exec. com. 1997—2004, pres. 2001—02), Navy League (judge adv. L.I. coun. 1992—), Fla. Bar Assn., Suffolk County Bar Assn., N.Y. State Bar Assn. (exec. com. real property sect. 1997—2002). Republican. Roman Catholic. Avocations: hiking, horseback riding. Office: Moricles Rd Box 471 Saint James NY 11780

MAGGS, PETER BLOUNT, lawyer, educator; b. Durham, NC, July 24, 1936; s. Douglas Blount and Dorothy (Mackay) M.; m. Barbara Ann Widenor, Feb. 27, 1960; children: Bruce MacDowell, Gregory Eaton, Stephanie Ann, Katherine Ellen. AB, Harvard U., 1957, JD, 1961; postgrad. (exchange student), Leningrad State U., USSR, 1961-62. Bar: D.C. 1962. Research assoc. Law Sch. Harvard U., 1963-64; asst. prof. law U. Ill., 1964-67, assoc. prof., 1967-69, prof., 1969-88, William and Marie Corman prof., 1988-98, Peer & Sarah Pedersen prof., 1998—2002, acting dean, 1990, Clifford M. and Bette A. Carney chair in law, 2002—; dir. Rule of Law Program Washington, 1994. Fulbright lectr. Moscow State U., 1977; reporter Uniform Simplification of Land Transfers Act, 1977; vis. prof. George Washington U., 1998. Author: (with others) The Mandelstam File, 1996; co-translator Civil Code of the Russian Federation, translation, 2003, Civil Code of the Republic of Armenia, translation, 1999, Intellectual Property (in Russian), 2000, Internet and Computer Law, 2001, Trademark and Unfair Competition, 2002; designer talking computers for the blind. Fulbright rsch. scholar, Yugoslavia, 1967; Fulbright disting. chair, Trento, 2002; East-West Ctr. fellow, 1972, Guggenheim fellow, 1979. Mem. ABA, D.C. Bar, Am. Assn. Advancement Slavic Studies, Assn. Am. Law Schs., Am. Law Inst.

(consultative group, UCC Article 2), Internat. Acad. Comparative Law. Office: U Ill Coll Law 504 E Pennsylvania Ave Champaign IL 61820-6909 Office Phone: 217-333-6711. Business E-Mail: p-maggs@illinois.edu.

MAGHELAL, PRAVEEN KUMAR, engineering educator; b. Chennai, Tamilnadu, India, Feb. 8, 1977; s. Maghelal Jain and Bhawari Bai Maghelal; m. Prathiba Natesan, Dec. 7, 2008. BArch, SRM Engring. Coll., Tamilnadu, 2001; MS in Infrastructure Planning, NJ. Inst. Tech., Newark, 2002; diploma in Civil Engring. (hon.), Valliammai Poly., Tamilnadu, 2006; PhD, Tex. A&M U., Coll. Sta., 2007. Grad. rsch. asst. Tex. A&M U., 2002—07; asst. prof. Fla. Atlantic U., Ft. Lauderdale, 2007—, grad. program coord., 2008—. Pres. Urban and Regional Sci. Student Orgn., Coll. Sta., 2005—06; grad. rep. Coll. Architecture Exec. Com., Coll. Sta., 2005—07. Contbr. articles to profl. jours. (Best Jour. Article of Yr., 2008). Bd. mem. Broward County Met. Planning Orgn., Ft. Lauderdale, 2008—. Recipient Gold medal, Valliammai Poly., 1996, Active Living Rsch. Dissertation award, 2005, Best Oral Presentation award, 2005, Outstanding Achievement award, Tex. A&M U., 2005, Honor Roll award, 2007; Grad. Student Recruitment grant, Fla. Atlantic U., 2008. Mem.: Assn. Collegiate Sch. Planning, Am. Planning Assn. Personal E-mail: pmaghelal@gmail.com. Business E-Mail: pmaghela@fau.edu.

MAGID, LAURIE, prosecutor; b. 1960; m. Jeffrey A. Miller; 3 children. BS in Economics, U. Pa. Wharton Sch. Bus., 1982; JD, Columbia Law Sch., 1985. Law clk. to Hon. James Hunter III US Ct. Appeals (3rd Cir.), 1985—86; asst. dist. atty. City of Phila., 1989—97, Delaware County, Pa., 1997—2001; dep. asst. US atty. (ea. dist.) US Dept. Justice, Phila., 2001—05, 1st asst. US atty., 2005—08, interim US atty., 2008—09. Commr. Pa. Commn. on Sentencing; notes & comments editor Columbia Law Review.

MAGIDIN, ARTURO, mathematics professor; BSc in Math., Nat. Autonom U. Mex., Mex. City, 1993; PhD, U. Calif., Berkeley, 1998. Assoc. investigator Nat. Autonomic U. Mexico, 1998—2002; vis. asst. prof. U. Mont., Missoula, 2002—03, adj. asst. prof., 2003—05; asst. prof. U. La. Lafayette, 2005—. Grantee R&D Rsch. Competitiveness Program, La. Bd. Regents, 2007—. Mem.: Math. Assn. Am., Am. Math. Soc. Achievements include research in dominions and amalgams of groups, capability of P-Groups. Office: Univ La Lafayette PO Box 41010 Lafayette LA 70504-1010

MAGIELNICKI, ROBERT L., lawyer; b. Perth Amboy, NJ, Mar. 28, 1947; s. Leon C. and Dorothy M. (Hudanish) M.; m. Kathleen J. Urban, June 14, 1969; children: Robert Jr., Kimberly, Peter, Matthew. AB with honors, Rutgers U., 1967; JD with distinction, Cornell U., 1970. Bar: N.Y. 1971, U.S. Supreme Ct. 1974, D.C. 1990. Commd. lt. USN, 1968; assoc. Donovan Leisure Newton & Irvine, NYC, 1970-71, 74-80; asst. staff judge advocate U.S. Naval Base Subic Bay, Republic of Philippines, 1971-73; asst. prof. law U.S. Naval Acad., Annapolis, Md., 1973-74; assoc. litigation and antitrust counsel Gen. Electric Co. Hdqrs., Fairfield, Conn., 1980-83, counsel, 1989-90; divsn. gen. counsel Gen. Electric Factory Automation Products, Charlottesville, Va., 1983-88; ptnr. Kutak Rock, Washington, 1990-2000, Schnader Harrison Segal & Lewis LLP, Washington, 2000—03, Sheppard Mullin Richter & Hampton LLP, Washington, 2003—. Avocations: tennis, golf, swimming, reading. Office: Sheppard Mullin Richter & Hampton LLP 11th Fl East 1300 I St NW Washington DC 20005-3314 Office Phone: 202-218-0002. E-mail: rmagielnicki@sheppardmullin.com.

MAGILL, ALAN JON, preventive medicine physician; b. Craig, Colo., Nov. 26, 1953; s. Reese Arnett and Rose (Zaccardo) M.; m. Janiine Grace Babcock, June 10, 1984; children: Lara, Sarah. BS in Biology, Chemistry, Environ. Sci., Lamar U., 1976; MS in Zoology, U. R.I., 1978; MD, Baylor U., 1984. Intern internal medicine Tripler Army Med. Ctr., Honolulu, 1984-85, resident, internal medicine, 1985-87; staff physician, internal medicine 5th Gen. Hosp., Bad Canstaat, Germany, 1987-89; fellow infectious diseases Walter Reed Army Med. Ctr., Washington, 1989-92, infectious disease officer dept. immunology, 1992-94, asst. chief, immunology, 1994—96, attending physician; chief dept. parasitology Naval Med. Rsch. Ctr. Detachment, Lima, Peru, 1996—99; head clin. rsch., malaria vaccine devel. unit NIH, 1999—2001; dir. divsn. exptl. therapeutics Walter Reed Army Inst. Rsch., Silver Springs, Md., rsch. coord., Leishmania rsch. program and anti-Malaria drug R&D program, Mil. Infectious Disease Rsch. Program. Assoc. prof. medicine and preventive medicine and biometrics Uniformed Services U. the Health Scis., Bethesda, Md. Asst. editor: Hunter's Tropical Medicine, 1995; contbr. articles to profl. jours., books. Maj. U.S. Army, 1984—. Fellow Am. Coll. Physicians; mem. Am. Soc. Tropical Medicine and Hygiene (pres. clin. group), Infectious Disease Soc. America, Royal Soc. Tropical Medicine and Hygiene, Internat. Soc. Travel Medicine (pres.). Avocations: mountain climbing, skiing. Office: Walter Reed Army Inst Rsch 503 Robert Grant Ave Silver Spring MD 20910-7500*

MAGILL, FRANK J., JR., prosecutor; b. 1959; m. Margaret Magill. BA magna cum laude, Georgetown U., JD magna cum laude, 1985. Accountant Arthur Andersen & Co., Denver; assoc. trial dept. Dorsey & Whitney; asst. US atty. Dist. Minn. US Dept. Justice, 1990—98, chief econ. crimes sect., 1998—2007, first asst. US atty., 2007—, acting US atty., 2008—09. Office: US Attys Office 300 S Fourth St Ste 600 Minneapolis MN 55415 Office Phone: 612-664-5600. Office Fax: 612-664-5787.*

MAGILL, KENT B., lawyer; b. Kansas City, Mo., Dec. 2, 1952; m. Teresa A. Magill. BS, Kent State U., 1975; JD, U. Iowa, 1977. Bar: Mo. 1977, Kans. 1987, US Dist. Ct. Dist. Kans. Assoc. Shughart, Thomson & Kilroy, Kansas City, Mo., 1977—80, atty., 1980—89; assoc. gen. counsel, v.p. The Marley Co., Mission Woods, Kans., 1989—92; v.p., gen. counsel, sec. Layne Christensen Co., Mission Woods, Kans., 1992—2000; assoc. gen. counsel Interstate Brands Corp., 2000—02, v.p., gen. counsel, sec., 2002—, Interstate Bakeries Corp., Kansas City, Mo., 2002—. Office: Interstate Bakeries Corp 12 E Armour Blvd Kansas City MO 64111

MAGILL, SAMUEL HAYS, academic administrator, consultant; b. Decatur, Ga., July 19, 1928; s. Orrin Rankin and Ellen Howe (Bell) M.; children: Samuel Hays Jr., Katherine Magill Walters, Suzanne Magill Weintraub; m. Eunice M. Brock. AB, U. N.C., 1950; BD, Yale U., 1953; PhD, Duke U., 1962; LHD (hon.), Stockton State Coll., 1990; EdD (hon.), Monmouth U., 2005. Ordained to ministry Congl. Christian Ch., 1953; gen. sec. Davidson Coll. YMCA, 1953-55; dir. student activities U. N.C., Chapel Hill, 1955-58, asst. dean student affairs, 1958-59; chaplain Dickinson Coll., 1962-63, asst. prof. religion, 1962-66, asso. prof. religion, 1966-68, dean coll., 1963-68; pres. Council Protestant Colls. and Univs., Washington, 1968-70; exec. asso., chief office acad. affairs Assn. Am. Colls., 1971-76; pres. Simon's Rock Early Coll., Great Barrington, Mass., 1976-79, Monmouth U., West Long Branch, NJ, 1980-93, pres. emeritus, 1993—; higher edn. cons., 1993-98; assoc. dir. gift planning U. N.C., 1999—2004, major gifts officer, 2004—06; vice chair Coker Hills Democratic Precinct, 2008—09; bd. dirs. Chapal Hill Carrboro YMCA, 2009—. Adj. prof. Duke U., 1996. Trustee Jersey Shore Med. Ctr., 1985-93; bd. overseers N.J. Gov.'s Schs., 1986-93; bd. dirs., pres. Falconbridge Homeowners Assn., 2003-06; bd. trustees, Chapel Hill Preservation Soc., 2007-; bd. dirs. Chapel Hill Carrboro YMCA, 2009-. Guerney Harris Kearns fellow in religion, 1960-61; Danforth Found. spl. grad. fellow, 1959-61. Fellow Soc. Values in Higher Edn. (dir. 1969-81); mem. Am. Assembly Collegiate Sch. Bus. (accreditation task force 1989-90), NCAA (pres.'s commn. 1990-93), Am. Coun. Edn. (commn. leadership devel. 1982-85, commn. on minority affairs 1986-89), Harvard Inst. Ednl. Mgmt., Assn. Ind. Colls. and Univs. N.J. (dir. 1980-93, exec. com. 1983-93, chair 1987-89), Order of Golden Fleece U. N.C., Fearrington Dem. Club (co-chair 1997-98), Delta Psi. Home: 319 Burlage Creek Chapel Hill NC 27514 Personal E-mail: sambomag@gmail.com.

MAGINNIS, ROBERT P., bishop; b. Phila., Dec. 22, 1933; Student, St. Charles Borromeo Sem., Overbrook, Pa. Ordained priest Archdiocese of Phila., 1961, auxiliary bishop, 1996—; ordained bishop, 1996; titular bishop Diocese of Siminina, 1996—. Roman Catholic. Office: 222 N 17th St Philadelphia PA 19103

MAGLACAS, A. MANGAY, nursing researcher, educator; BSN, Vanderbilt U.; MPH, U. Minn.; DPH, Johns Hopkins U.; DSc (hon.), U. Ill.; DSc (hon.), St. Paul U., Tuguegarao City, Philippines, 2008. Former chief sci. for nursing devel. health manpower divsn. WHO, Geneva, Switzerland, 1976-89, regional nurse adviser Southeast Asia Office Delhi, India, 1972-75. Internat. health/nursing cons., 1989—; adj. prof. Coll. Nursing, U. Ill., Chgo., 1990-2000; various vis. prof. positions in several countries, 1990—. Former mem., bd. dirs. Internat. Coun. Nurses, 1989-93; fgn. assoc. NAS Inst. Medicine, 1988—. Rockefeller fellow, 1964-67; Fulbright-Smith-Mundt scholar, 1952-54; recipient Outstanding alumni award Vanderbilt U., 1986, Internat. Pub. Health Leadership award Johns Hopkins U., 1992, Outstanding Profl. award for Nursing, Profl. Regulation Commn. of Philippines, 2000, Profl. Recognition award U. Philippines, 1989, Disting. Achievement award Philippine Nurses Assn., 1989, Outstanding Alumni award U. Philippines Sch. Nursing, 1987, Disting. Leadership award USA Commn. on Grads. of Fgn. Nursing Schs., 2002; named Woman of Yr. Am. Rsch. Inst. Bd. Internat. Rsch., 1988, named Most Outstanding Paulinian St. Paul's U., Philippines, 2002. Fellow Royal Coll. Nursing U.K. (hon.). Office: 147 Panay Ave Quezon City 1103 Philippines Personal E-mail: amelia_maglacas@yahoo.com.ph.

MAGLIOCCHETTI, PAUL, lobbyist; b. Pa., July 1946; Staff mem. Gen. Acctg. Office, Washington; sr. staff mem. US House of Reps. Appropriations Com., Washington, 1980—88; founder, pres. PMA Group, Arlington, Va., 1989—2009; lobbyist Gen. Atomics, 1998—99. Named one of 50 Top Lobbyists, Washingtonian mag., 2007. Office Phone: 703-415-0344. Office Fax: 703-415-0182.*

MAGLOIRE, ALIX J. (MAGLOIRE), internist; b. Port-au-Prince, Haiti, Feb. 26, 1953; arrived in U.S., 1969; s. Jean Gerard Magloire and Paulette Andrea Rigaud; m. Fanita Bryant Magloire, Dec. 31, 1986; children: Alix B., Joshua Yves. MD, U. Mex., Villa Hermosa, 1979. Diplomate Am. Bd. Internal Medicine, lic. physician Mass., Calif. Intern Elmhurst Hosp., Queens, NY, 1981—82; resident in internal medicine Bronx/Mt. Sinai Med. Ctr./NYU, Bronx, 1982—85; endocrinology fellow U. Calif., Davis, 1985—87; pvt. practice internal medicine; assoc. chief of medicine NCHCS VA, Oakland, Calif., 1995—. Contbr. articles to profl. jours. Vol. Drs. Without Borders; missionary Franciscan Orgn., 1996—. Recipient Jan Hart-Schuyers award, Richmond, Calif., 2002. Mem.: U. Calif.-Davis Alumni Assn., Endocrine Soc., Am. Diabetes Assn. Democrat. Avocations: painting, sculpting, poetry. Office: NCHCS Veterans Administration 2221 MLK St Oakland CA 94612

MAGNAN, MORRIS ALLEN, nursing researcher, educator; b. Port Huron, Mich., July 27, 1949; s. Mary Ann Fye and Morris R. Magnan. AS, St. Clair County CC, Port Huron, 1972; BSN, Madonna U., Livonia, Mich., 1984; MSN, Wayne State U., Detroit, 1993; PhD, 2001. Asst. prof. nursing Wayne State U., Detroit, 2002—04, assoc. rsch. prof., 2005—07; asst. prof. nursing Oakland U., Rochester, Mich., 2005—07. Contbr. rsch. articles to profl. jours. Cons. and sci. writer Agy. Health Care Policy & Rsch., 1992. Recipient E-Learning Instrn. award, Oakland U., 2007, Intramural Rsch. award, 2005, Sigma Theta Tau Rsch. award, 2006, Patient Safety Rsch. award, Blue Cross Blue Shield Found. Mich., 2005—07, Student Dissertation award, 2000—01, Student Rsch. award, Sigma Theta Tau - Lambda Chpt., 2000—01, Roberta S. Abruzzese Pub. award, 2008, Nurse Rschr. of Yr. award, Am. Assn. Clin. Nurse Specialists. Mem.: Emergency Nurses Assn., Nat. Assn. Clin. Nurse Specialists, Oncology Nursing Soc., Midwest Nursing Rsch. Soc., Sigma Xi, Sigma Theta Tau Internat. Achievements include co-authored and conducted initial psychometric testing of the sexuality attitudes and beliefs survey.

MAGNAN, SANNE, state agency administrator, public health service officer; b. NC; m. David Magnan; children: Grace, Hannah. BS in Pharmacy, U. NC, 1974; PhD in Medicinal Chemistry, U. Minn., 1978, MD, 1983. Cert. gen. internist. Staff physician various clinics; staff physician Lino Lakes Correctional Facility; lead physician Adult Care Clinic at Ramsey Clinic, Minn.; v.p. & med. dir., consumer health Blue Cross Blue Shield Minn.; clin. asst. prof. medicine U. Minn.; staff physician, TB clinic St. Paul-Ramsey County Dept. Pub. Health, Minn.; pres. Inst. Clin. Systems Improvement, Bloomington, Minn.; commr. Minn. Dept. Health, 2007—. Contbr. articles to profl. jours. Named one of 100 Influential Health Care Leaders, Minn. Physician, 2004, 2008; grantee Bush Fellowship, U. Minn., 1974—77. Office: Minn Dept Health PO Box 64975 Saint Paul MN 55164-0975 Office Phone: 651-201-5000.*

MAGNANO, SALVATORE PAUL, retired finance company executive, treasurer; b. Portland, Conn., Jan. 10, 1934; s. Salvatore and Lucy (Dimodica) M.; m. Lois Jewel Johnson, July 16, 1955; children: Paul C., Mark J., Peter E B.Metall. Engring., Rensselaer Poly. Inst., Troy, NY, 1955; MBA, Northwestern U., Chgo., 1959. Div. controller Sanders Assocs., Inc., Nashua, NH, 1962-73; v.p., controller Teledyne Mec, Palo Alto, Calif., 1973-75; div. controller Sanders Assocs., Inc., Nashua, 1975-79, grp. controller, 1979-81, grp. v.p., controller, 1981-86, v.p. fin. and treas., 1986-96; ind. fin. and adminstrv. cons., 1996—; ret. Pres. Boys and Girls Club of Greater Nashua, 1988-89, bd. dirs., 1981—, sec. bd. dirs., 2004-; trustee Boys and Girls Club Greater Nashua Charitable Found., 1991-, Daniel Webster Coll., Nashua, 1993-2008, Congl. Ch. of Hollis, 2002-08, bd. dirs., treas. N.H. Prostate Cancer Coalition, 2006—, trustee emeritus, Daniel Webster Coll., Nashua,2008-. Lt. USN, 1955-57 Mem. Fin. Execs. Inst. (life mem.), Beta Gamma Sigma (award for excellence 1959). E-mail: spm-ljm@charter.net.

MAGNANTI, THOMAS L., management and engineering educator; b. Omaha, Oct. 7, 1945; s. Leo A. and Florence L. Magnanti; m. Beverly A. McVinney, June 10, 1967; 1 child, R. Randall. BS in chem. engring., Syracuse U., 1967; MS in stats., Stanford U., 1969, MS in math., 1971, PhD in ops. rsch., 1972; Doktor honoris causa, Linköping U., 1995; PhD (hon.), U. Montreal, Universite Catholique de Louvain. Asst. prof. Alfred P. Sloan Sch. Mgmt. MIT, Cambridge, Mass., 1971-75, assoc. prof., 1975-79, prof., 1979-85, George Eastman prof. of mgmt. sci., 1985—, head mgmt. sci. area, 1982-88, co-dir. Ops. Rsch. Ctr., 1986—, founding co-dir. Leaders for Mfg. Program, 1988-94, prof. dept. elec. engring. and computer sci., 1995—, founding co-dir. Sys. Design and Mgmt. Program, 1995—, founding dir., Leaders for Mfg. Program, dean Sch. Engring., 1999—2007; rsch. fellow, vis. prof. Ctr. for Ops. Rsch. and Econometrics Univ. Catholique de Louvain, 1976-77, 89. Vis. scientist Bell Labs., 1977, GTE Labs., 1989; vis. scholar Grad. Sch. Bus. Adminstrn., Harvard U., 1980-81; mem. corp. mfg. staff Digital Equipment Corp., 1990; mem. editl. bd. Jour. Computational Optimization and Applications; mem. adv. bd. North Holland Handbooks in Ops. Rsch. and Mgmt. Sci.; bd. dirs. Ford Design Inst., Emptoris Inc; mem. internat. advisory bd., Linköping Univ. Author: Applied Mathematical Programming, 1977, Network Flows, 1993; editor: Jour. Ops. Rsch., 1983-87; co-editor: Math. Programming, 1981-83; assoc. editor SIAM Jour. Algebraic and Discrete Methods, 1981-83, Mgmt. Sci., 1978-81, Ops. Rsch., 1978-81, SIAM Jour. Applied Math., 1976-81, Math. Programming, 1988—; adv. editor Transp. Sci., 1985—, Mktg. Sci., Math. of Artificial Intelligence, 1987-91; contbr. numerous articles to profl. jours. Mem. NSF Sci. and Tech. Exchange Delegation to Soviet Union, 1977, NSF Rsch. Initiation Grant panels, 1985, 90; advisor NSF program on decision, risk and mgmt. sci., 1988, 89; mem. mfg. studies bd. Nat. Rsch. Coun., 1993—; mem. internat. adv. bd. Linkopeg U., Sweden; mem. pres. coun. Olin Coll.; mem. adv. bd. Harvard Bus. Sch., Stanford Sch. Engring. Recipient Gordon Billard award MIT, 1992, Irwin Sizer Award; Mgmt. Program Exch. grantee IREX, Curriculum Devel. grantee Sloan Found., 1990-94. Mem. IEEE (com. on large scale systems 1979-83), TIMS (mem. and chmn. various coms.), NAE, Am. Acad. Arts and Sciences, Ops. Rsch. Soc. Am. (pres. 1988-89, mem. and chmn. various coms., coun. mem. computer sci. tech. sect. 1983-87, co-organizer 1st doctoral consortium 1983, plenary speaker conf. on telecom. 1983, Lanchester prize 1993, Kimball medal 1994), Tau Beta Pi, Pi Mu Epsilon, Phi Kappa Phi. Achievements include research in network analysis and optimization, network design and combinatorial optimization, and applications in manufacturing, telecommunications, and transportation; development of new engineering/management programs. Home: 33 School St Hopkinton MA 01748-2003 Office: MIT Ops Rsch Ctr 77 Massachusetts Ave Cambridge MA 02139-4307

MAGNE, MICHEL JAQUES, dental educator, ceramist; b. La Chaux-de-Fonds, Neuchatel, Switzerland, July 3, 1958; s. Albin and Agnes Magne; m. Inge Munck; children: Julie, Charlotte, Marine. BS in Dental Tech., U. Ill., Chgo.; MS in Dental Ceramic, Switzerland, 1972. Dir., Ctr. Dental Tech. U. Southern Calif., LA, 2004—, assoc. prof. clin. dentistry, 2005—. Cons. in field dentistry Straumann ITI, Zhermack, Calif., 2004—. Contbr. articles to numerous profl. publs. Achievements include development of PMMA acrylic resin.

MAGNER, JEROME ALLEN, performing company executive; b. Bklyn., Mar. 14, 1929; s. Herman and Evelyn I. (Wolfe) M.; m. Frances Ogens, Mar. 22, 1953; children: Merrill, Steven. BBA cum laude, CCNY, 1951. Asst. to treas., chief acct. Grayson-Robinson Stores, Inc., S. Klein Dept. Stores, Inc., NYC, 1951-59; contr. Food Fair Properties, NYC, 1959-61; v.p., contr. Am. Leisure Products Corp., NYC and Providence, 1961-69; sr. v.p. fin., treas., CFO, Nat. Amusements Inc., NE Theatre Corp., Dedham, Mass., 1969—. Mem. Nat. Assn. Theatre Owners (bd. dirs.), CCNY Alumni Assn. Office: Nat Amusements Inc 200 Elm St Dedham MA 02026-4536 Business E-Mail: jmagner@nationalamusements.com.

MAGNER, MARJORIE J. (MARGE MAGNER), private equity firm executive; b. Bklyn., Apr. 29, 1949; BS in Psychology, Bklyn. Coll., 1968; MS in Indsl. Adminstrn., Purdue U., Ind., 1974. Various positions including mng. dir. Chem. Tech. Divsn. Chemical Bank, 1974—87; from comml. credit staff mem. to chmn., CEO Citigroup, Inc., NYC, 1987—2003; COO Citi Global Consumer Group, NYC, 2002—03, chmn., CEO, 2003—05; co-founder, mng. ptnr. Brysam Global Partners, LLC, NYC, 2007—. Bd. dirs. Gannett Co., 2006—, The Charles Schwab Corp., 2006—, Accenture, 2006—; chmn. bd. trustees Bklyn. Coll. Found.; mem. dean's adv. coun. Krannert Sch. Mgmt. Purdue U. Bd. dirs. Welfare to Work Partnership, Dress for Success Worldwide, Port Discovery Children's Mus., Balt., Md. Bus. Roundtable Edn. Recipient Am. Found. for the Blind Helen Keller Achievement award, 2001; named one of The 50 Most Powerful Women in Am. Bus., Fortune mag., 2001, 2002, 2003, 2004, The 25 Most Powerful Women in Banking, US Banker mag., 2003, 2004, 2005, The Top 20 Nonbank Women in Fin., 2007, 2008, The World's 100 Most Powerful Women, Forbes mag., 2005. Office: Brysam Global Partners LLC 277 Park Ave 35th Fl New York NY 10172 E-mail: marge.magner@brysam.com.*

MAGNER, TIMOTHY J., federal agency administrator, educator; married; 2 children. BA, Coll. William and Mary, 1988; MEd, Harvard U. Tchr. Walsingham Acad., Williamsburg, Va., Leysin, Switzerland, Paris, 1992—93; tech. training specialists Fairfax County Pub. Schs., Va.; Internet specialist, program mgr. K-12 ArtsEdge, Kennedy Ctr., 1995—97; dir. tech. Framingham Pub. Schs., Mass., 1997; with Nat. Retail Fedn., Washington, 1999; mgr. online learning PBS, Alexandria, Va.; dir. Schs. Interoperability Framework Assn., Washington, 2001—03; exec. dir. K-12 edn. Microsoft Corp., 2003—04; dep. dir. ednl. tech. US Dept. Edn., Washington, 2004—05, dir. Office of Ednl. Tech., 2006—; dep. exec. dir. Coun. of Chief State Sch. Officers, 2005—06. Prof. ednl. tech. Framingham State Coll.; adj. prof. George Mason U. Office: US Dept Edn 400 Maryland Ave, SW Washington DC 20202 Office Phone: 202-205-4280.*

MAGNES, HARRY ALAN, physician; b. Orange, NJ, Dec. 3, 1948; s. Sam and Shirley (Daniels) Magnes; m. Patricia Bruce, Mar. 25, 1989; 1 child, Carlos Fontiveros. AB in Biology magna cum laude, Brown U., Providence, 1970; MD, Yale U., New Haven, Conn., 1974; M in Med. Mgmt., Tulane U., New Orleans, 1998; cert. in med. mgmt., Am. Coll. Physician Execs., 1997. Diplomate Am. Bd. Internal Medicine. Intern, resident internal medicine U. Iowa Hosps. and Clinics, 1974—77; ptnr., med. dir., pres., CEO Gallatin Med. Clinic, Downey, Calif., 1997—2001; pres., CEO Gallatin Med. Corp., Downey, Calif., 1992—94; med. dir., bd. dirs. Gallatin Med. Found., Downey, Calif., 1993—2001; chief med. officer Gallatin Med. Group, 2000—01, Physician Assocs. of Greater San Gabriel Valley, Pasadena, Calif., 2001—05; CEO Lovelace Med. Group, Albuquerque, 2005—07; pres., CEO ABQ Health Ptnrs. Endoscopy Ctr., 2008—, ABQ Health Ptnrs. Med. Group, 2007—. Staff physician Downey Cmty. Hosp., 1977—96, Presbyn. Intercmty. Hosp., 1992—2001; clin. instr. Rancho Los Amigos Hosp., Downey, 1981—83; chairperson bd. dirs. Primehealth of So. Calif., 1997—99; sec.-treas. Calif. Health Network, 1998—99; project adv. bd. UCLA/UCLA/RAND Calif. Med. Group, IPA Governance Project, 1997—98; prin. investigator Reach Asthma Rsch. Project, 2002; bd. dirs. Calif. Health Network; bd. govs. Lovelace Clinic Found., 2006—, Lovelace Med. Ctr., 2006—07, ABQ Health Ptnrs., 2007—, Med. Group

Holding Co., 2007—; steering coms. N.Mex. Health Info. Collaborative, 2007—. Author: Rheumatic Fever in Connecticut, 1974. Bd. dirs. N.Mex. Symphony Orch., 2007—. James Manning scholar Brown U., 1968. Mem.: Greater Albuquerque Med. Assn., N.Mex. Med. Soc., Med. Group Mgmt. Assn., Am. Med. Group Assn. (policy com. 1994—98, legis. com. 1997—2000), Sigma Xi, Phi Beta Kappa, Delta Omega. Office Phone: 505-262-3085. Business E-Mail: harry.magnes@abqhp.com.

MAGNO, GIL D., music educator, personal development consultant; b. Funchal, Madeira Island, Portugal, June 14, 1934; s. Americo J. and Maria Franca DeJesus; life ptnr. Terezinha D. Dos Santos; children: Derek DeJesus, Lygeia DeJesus, Nydia DeJesus, Elyssia DeJesus. BA in Music Edn., Boston Conservatory of Music, 1959. Bassoonist Birmingham Symphony, Ala., 1959—62; band dir. Warrior H.S. Band, Warrior, Ala., 1959—61; classical guitar instr. U. Ala. Student Union, Tuscaloosa, 1961—62, New Eng. Conservatory of Music Prep Dept., Boston, 1964—65; vocal coach Magnoart Studio and Pubs., Coconut Grove, Fla., 1967—, author, 1985—. Author: (books) The Secret, 1999, Developing Confidence & Personal Magnetism, 2000, Autobiography: Transcending Their Lies, 2004, The Road to Victory: How to Start Your Own New World, 2007, (video) Magno Vocal Course #1, 2000; composer: (CD) A Tapestry of Love, 1998; author: (cassette book) Magno Vocal Technique Course #2, 2001. With USAR, 1954—62, Boston. Mem.: ASCAP, Music Tchr. Nat. Assn., Fla. Music Tchrs. Assn. Libertarian. Achievements include development of self transformation through personal magnetism. Avocation: gardening. Office Phone: 305-447-8660. Business E-Mail: gilmagno@magnoart.net.

MAGNUS, JEANETTE H., medical educator; m. Dagfinn Magnus, Feb. 1, 1980; children: Ragnhild E. Magnus Lindekleiv, Andreas J., Maria C. MD, Tromsø Med. Sch., Norway, 1983; PhD, U. Tromsø, 1992. Cert. in rheumatology Norway and EU, 1996. Clin. assoc. prof. Tromsø U., 1992—97, assoc. prof., 1997—99; clin. prof. pub. health Tulane U. Sch. Pub. Health and Tropical Medicine, New Orleans, 1999—2002, prof. pub. health, 2002—; clin. prof. medicine Tulane Med. Sch., 2000—. Dir. Tulane Xavier Nat. Ctr. Excellence Women's Health, 1999—, Mary Amelia Douglas-Whited Cmty. Women's Health Edn. Ctr., New Orleans, 2003—; prof. women's health Cecile USDIN, 2006. Contbr. articles to med. jours. Bd. mem. Kingsley House, New Orleans, 2007—, Trinity Counseling and Tng. Ctr., New Orleans, 2007—. Recipient Food and Drug Adminstrn.'s Leveraging, Collaboration award; named one of 10 Top Female Achievers in New Orleans, 2004; Women's Health Tng. Program grant, NIH, 2002, 2007, Maternal and Child Pub. Health Leadership Tng. grant, MCHB, HRSA, 2005. Mem.: APHA, Orgn. Study Sex Differences (coun. mem. 2006—07), Am. Soc. Bone Mineral Rsch., Am. Coll. Rheumatology, Internat. Soc. Gender Medicine, Delta Omega (mem., Nat. Pub. Health Hon. Soc.). Office: Tulane Univ 1440 Canal St New Orleans LA 70112

MAGNUS, P.D., philosopher, educator; married, July 22, 2001. BA, Tex. Christian U., Fort Worth, 1996; PhD, U. Calif. San Diego, La Jolla, 2003. Vis. asst. prof. Bowdoin Coll., Brunswick, Maine, 2003—04; asst. prof. U. Albany, SUNY, 2004—. Office: Dept Philosophy Univ Albany SUNY Albany NY 12222

MAGNUS, SANDRA H., astronaut; b. Belleville, Ill., Oct. 30, 1964; BS in Physics, U. Mo., Rolla, 1986, MS in Elec. Engring., 1990; PhD, Ga. Inst. Tech., 1996. Stealth engr. McDonnell Douglas Aircraft Co., 1986—91; fellow Inst. Tech. Ga., 1991—96; astronaut NASA Johnson Space Ctr., Houston, 1996—. Worked in Astronaut office payloads/habitability br. NASA, 1997—98; Russian Crusader for hardware testing and operational products develop., 1998; served as CAPCOM for Internat. Space Station, 2000; crew mem. STS-112 Atlantis Mission, 2002; flight engr., NASA sci. officer STS-126 Endeavour Mission, 2008. Recipient NASA Space Flight medal, 2002. Mem.: AAAS. Avocations: reading, soccer, travel, water-skiing. Office: Astronaut Office Johnson Space Ctr Houston TX 77058*

MAGNUSON, ERIC J., state supreme court chief justice; BA in History, U. Minn.; JD cum laude, William Mitchell Coll. Law. Law clerk, Judge Douglas K. Amdahl Hennepin County Dist. Ct.; law clerk, Chief Justice Robert Sheran Minn. Supreme Ct., St. Paul, 1976—77, chief justice, 2008—; atty, ptnr. Rider Bennett, Minn., 1977—2007, chair, appellate group practice Minn., mng. ptnr. Minn., 1999—2000; assoc. prof. law William Mitchell Coll. Law, U. St. Thomas Sch. Law. Chair Commn. on Jud. Selection; chair, screening committees Minn. Ct. Appeals, Minn. Supreme Ct.; co-reporter Minn. Supreme Ct. Appellate Rules Com. Co-author: Minnesota Practice: Appellate Rules Annotate, 2007; co-editor: Eighth Circuit Appellate Practice Manual, The Art of Advocacy: Appeals. Fellow: Am. Acad. Appellate Lawyers (past pres.); mem.: ABA (co-chair appellate practice com., sect. on litig., co-chair ppellate advocacy com., tort trial and ins. practice sect.), Minn. State Bar Assn. (chair ct. rules and jud. adminstrn. com., chair ct. appeals task force), 8th Cir. Bar Assn. (founding pres.). Office: Minn Jud Ctr 25 Rev Dr Martin Luther King Jr Blvd Saint Paul MN 55155 Office Phone: 651-297-7650.*

MAGNUSON, RACHEL, legislative staff member; Comm. dir. to Rep. Allyson Schwartz US House of Reps., Washington. Democrat. Office: 330 Cannon House Office Bldg Washington DC 20515 Office Phone: 202-225-6111. Office Fax: 202-226-0611. Business E-Mail: rachel.magnuson@mail.house.gov.*

MAGNUSON, ROGER JAMES, lawyer; b. St. Paul, Jan. 25, 1945; s. Roy Gustaf and Ruth Lily (Edlund) M.; m. Elizabeth Cunningham Shaw, Sept. 11, 1982; children: James Roger, Peter Cunningham, Mary Kerstin, Sarah Ruth, Elizabeth Camilla, Anna Clara, John Edlund, Britta Kristina. BA, Stanford U., 1967; JD, Harvard U., 1971; BCL, Oxford U., 1972. Bar: Minn. 1973, U.S. Dist. Ct. Minn. 1973, U.S Ct. Appeals (4th, 8th, 9th, 10th, 11th cirs.) 1974, U.S. Supreme Ct. 1978. Chief pub. defender Hennepin County Pub. Defender's Office, Mpls., 1973; ptnr., trial group Dorsey & Whitney, Mpls., 1972—, and head, nat. strategic litig. group. Dean Oak Brook Coll. of Law and Govt. Policy, 1995—; chancellor Magdalen Coll., 1999—. Author: Shareholder Litigation, 1981, Are Gay Rights Right, The White-Collar Crime Explosion, 1992, Informed Answers to Gay Rights Questions, 1994, Internat. Judicial Asst. in Civil Matters, 1999, Barracuda Bait, 2007; contbr. articles to profl. jours. Elder, Straitgate Ch., Mpls., 1980—. Fellow, Ctr. of Internat. Legal Studies, Mem. Christian Legal Soc., The Am. Soc. Writers of Legal Subjects, Mpls. Club, White Bear Yacht Club. Republican. Office: Dorsey & Whitney LLP 50 S 6th St Ste 1500 Minneapolis MN 55402-1498 Home Phone: 651-429-0579; Office Phone: 612-340-2738. Office Fax: 612-340-2807. Business E-Mail: magnuson.roger@dorsey.com.

MAGNUSON, TERRY R., geneticist, educator; Grad. in biology, U. Redlands. Postdoctoral work U. Calif., San Francisco; prof. genetics to dir. develop. biology ctr. Case Western Reserve U., 1984—2000; Sarah Graham Kenan prof., founding chair dept. genetics, Sch. Medicine U. NC, Chapel Hill, 2000—; dir. Carolina Ctr. for Genome Sciences, Chapel Hill; dir., cancer genetics Lineberger Comprehensive Cancer Ctr., Chapel Hill. Mem. adv. panels NIH Genetic Basis Disease Review Com., 1990—95, chair, 1993—95; program project site visits/RFA panels/Ad Hoc panel mem. (36), Ad Hoc counsel mem. NICHD, Mouse Chromosome 7 com., 1991—94, co-chair, 1992—93; mem. NRC panel on establishing guidelines for use of human embryonic stem cells; mem. adv. com., Human Embryonic Stem Cell Rsch. NRC and Inst. Medicine, 2006—; co-instructor, Molecular Embryology of the Mouse Cold Spring Harbor Lab., 1995—96, co-dir., Molecular Embryology of the Mouse, 1997—98; mem. organizing com. Cold Spring Harbor/Heidelberg Mouse Molecular Genetics Mtg., 2003—; bd. dir. Pharm. Products Developments Svc. Co., 2001—; bd. overseers Jackson Lab., 2004—. Contbr. articles to profl. jours.; co-editor-in-chief Genesis: The Journal of Genetics and Development, 1999—, mem. editl. adv. bd. Development, 1986—93, 1999—, Mammalian Genome, 1995—. Recipient Nat. Rsch. Svc. award, NICHD, 1979—82, New Investigator award, 1982—85, March Dimes Basil O'Conner award, 1984—86, NIH Merit award, 1999; Postdoctoral Fellow, NSF, 1978—79, Pew Scholar in Biomedical Sciences, 1985—89. Fellow: Am. Acad. Arts & Scis.; mem.: Genetics Soc. Am. (bd. dir. 2004), Soc. for Developmental Biology (bd. dir. 2000—06), Internat. Mammalian Genome Soc. (secretariat 1999—2001, founding mem.). Office: Dept Genetics U NC at Chapel Hill CB#7264 Lineberger Cancer Ctr 102 Mason Farm Rd Chapel Hill NC 27599-7264 Office Phone: 919-843-6475. Office Fax: 919-843-6365. Business E-Mail: trm4@med.unc.edu.

MAGNUSSON, INGVAR, periodontist, educator; s. Nils-Helge and Inga Magnusson; life ptnr. Jenny van Mill. DDS, U. Lund, Malmö, Sweden, 1970; PhD, U. Gothenburg, Sweden, 1976. Cert. periodontologist Sweden, 1982. Asst. prof. U. Gothenburg, 1972—76, assoc. prof., 1976—85, U. Fla., Gainesville, 1985—90, prof., 1990—, program dir., 2003—. Contbr. articles to profl. jours. Mem.: IADR. Office: Univ Fla Coll Dentist 1600 SW Archer Rd Gainesville FL 32610 Business E-Mail: imagnusson@dental.ufl.edu.

MAGONI, DESPO, artist; b. Feb. 17, 1943; MFA, Polytechnion of Athens, 1967. One-person shows include Henry-Hicks Gallery, Bklyn., 1976, Nonson Gallery, NYC., 1976, 78, Ora Gallery, Athens, 1978, 81, 83, Kouros Gallery, NYC., 1984, Alternative Mus., NYC., 1986, New Forms Gallery, Athens, 1988, 99, Bklyn. Coll. Art Gallery, 1994, Robeson Gallery, Rutgers U., Newark, 1994, André Zarre Gallery, NYC., 1997, Parsons Sch. of Design, NYC., 1999, John Jay Coll. Art Gallery, NYC., 1999, Shinsaegae Gallery, Kwangju, Republic of Korea, 2001; exhibited in group shows at Kouros Gallery, 1983, Mint Mus., Charlotte, NC, 1989, Mitchell Mus., Mt. Vernon, Ill., 1989, Haggerty Mus. Art, Marquette U., Milw., 1990, Pratt Inst. Gallery, NYC., 1990, André Zarre Gallery, 1997, Islip Mus., Oakdale, NY, 1997, Unit B Gallery, Chgo., 2004, Hellenic Mus., Chgo., 2006, Pelham Art Ctr., NY, 2006; pub. collections include Vorres Mus., Paiania, Greece, Mus. Modern Art, Guadalajara, Mexico, Mint Mus., Charlotte, NC, Alternative Mus., NYC., Pratt Inst. Libr., NYC, Vero Beach Art Ctr., Fla., Macedonian Mus. Contemporary Art, Thessaloniki, Greece, Pinakothec of the City of Athens, Greece, Kwangju Art Mus. Personal E-mail: magoni@earthlink.net.

MAGOON, PATRICK MICHAEL, hospital administrator; b. Chgo., Mar. 9, 1953; s. Albert George and Elizabeth Jane (Nolan) M.; m. Robin L. Gaeski, June 4, 1977. BA, Western Ill. U., 1976; MS in Urban Policy and Planning, U. Ill., Chgo., 1978. Asst. planner Children's Meml. Hosp., Chgo., 1977-78, adminstrv. svcs. mgr., 1978-80, dir. adminstrv. svcs., 1980-81, asst. v.p., 1981-83, v.p. adminstrn., 1983-90, v.p. adminstrn. ambulatory and satellite svcs., 1990, exec. v.p. corp. svcs., pres., CEO, 1998—. Bd. dirs. Nr. North Health Svcs. Corp., Chgo.; mem. profl. adv. com. Pediatric Excellence Program, Westchester, Ill., 1990—; chmn., Nat. Assn. Children's Hospitals and Related Instns., 2005-. Mem. Am. Hosp. Assn., Nat. Assn. Children's Hosp. and Related Instns., Ill. Hosp. Assn., Soc. for Ambulatory Care Profls, Met. Chgo. Healthcare Coun. (bd. dirs.), Comml. Club, Econ. Club, Exec. Club, City Club Chgo. Office: Children's Meml Hosp 2300 N Childrens Plz Chicago IL 60614-3394*

MAGOR, LOUIS ROLAND, conductor; b. Auburn, Nebr., May 16, 1945; s. John William and Eleanor Lucille (Niemann) M. B.Mus. Edn., Northwestern U., 1967, Mus.M., 1974. Choral dir. Avoca Jr. High Sch., Wilmette, Ill., 1968-70; choral dir. Niles North High Sch., Skokie, Ill., 1970-73; dir. San Francisco Symphony Chorus, 1974-82, Schola Cantorum, 1982-85, San Francisco Boys Chorus, 1985-88; artistic dir. Seattle Bach Choir, 1990—2001. Founder The Louis Magor Singers; mem. faculty San Francisco Conservatory of Music, 1976-78, San Francisco State U., 1979-80 Founder West Seattle Children's Chorus, 1990—; condr. Sing-It-Yourself Messiah, 1979-91, Calif. Symphony Chorus, 1990-92; exec. prodr. Sandy Bradley's Potluck, 1995-96; co-founder, mng. dir. Kenyon Hall, 1993—. Mem. Pi Kappa Lambda. Personal E-mail: louis@magor.com.

MAGORIAN, JAMES, poet, writer; b. Palisade, Nebr., Apr. 24, 1942; s. Jack and Dorothy (Gorthey) M. BS, U. Nebr., 1965; MS, Ill. State U., 1969; postgrad., Oxford U., 1972, Harvard U., 1973. Author children's books: School Daze, 1978, 17%, 1978, The Magic Pretzel, 1979, Ketchup Bottles, 1979, Imaginary Radishes, 1980, Plucked Chickens, 1980, Fimperings and Torples, 1981, The Witches' Olympics, 1983, At the City Limits, 1987, The Beautiful Music, 1988, Magic Spell #207, 1988; author numerous books of poetry, including: Ideas for a Bridal Shower, 1980, The Edge of the Forest, 1980, Spiritual Rodeo, 1980, Tap Dancing on a Tight Rope, 1981, Training at Home to Be A Locksmith, 1981, The Emily Dickinson Jogging Book, 1984, Keeper of Fire, 1984, Weighing the Sun's Light, 1985, Summer Snow, 1985, The Magician's Handbook, 1986, Squall Line, 1986, The Hideout of the Sigmund Freud Gang, 1987, Haymarket Square, 1998, Dragon Bones, 1999, Millennial Journal, 2000, Voices, 2006, (novels) America First, 1992, Hearts of Gold, 1996, (poetry) The Bookbinder's Daughter, 2007, Geographia, 2008.; contbr. poems and stories to numerous publs. Home and Office: 2626 North 49th St 402 Lincoln NE 68504

MAGOWAN, PETER ALDEN, professional sports team and retail executive; b. NYC, Apr. 5, 1942; s. Robert Anderson and Doris (Merrill) Magowan; m. Jill Tarlau (dec. July 1982); children: Kimberley, Margot, Hilary; m. Deborah Johnston, Aug. 14, 1982. BA, Stanford U., 1964; MA, Oxford U., Eng., 1966; postgrad., Johns Hopkins U., 1967—68. Store mgr. Safeway Stores Inc., Washington, 1968—70, dist. mgr. Houston, 1970—71, retail ops. mgr. Phoenix, 1971—72, divsn. mgr. Tulsa, 1973—76, mgr. internat. divsn. Toronto, Ont., Canada, 1976—78, mgr. western region San Francisco, 1978—79, CEO Oakland, Calif., 1980—93, chmn. bd. dirs., 1980—98; pres., mng. gen. ptnr. San Francisco Giants, 1993—; ret. Safeway Stores Inc., 2005. Bd. dirs. Daimler Chrysler Corp, Caterpillar. Office: San Francisco Giants 24 Willie Mays Plz San Francisco CA 94107-2199 Office Phone: 415-972-1950. Business E-Mail: scasabat@sfgiants.com.

MAGPILI, LUNA, systems engineer, consultant; b. Manila, Feb. 2, 1973; d. Marlo and Policarpia Magpili; m. Cesar A. Pinto, Jan. 6, 2001; children: Marlo Pinto, Luz Pinto. PhD, U. Va., Charlottesville, 2003. Cons. Brains Internat., Manila, 1998—2003; rsch. assoc. U. Va., 2004—; infrastructure officer Internat. Relief and Devel., Arlington, Va., 2005—06; grant writer, adminstrv. faculty Old Dominion U., Norfolk, Va., 2006—; dir. Devel. Action, Charlottesville, 2007—; cons. Ctrl. Pad, Norfolk, 2008—. Contbr. articles to profl. jours., chapters to books. Tchr. Filipino Am. Ctr., Norfolk, 2006—08, vol., 2006—08. Mem.: NSF (reviewer 2006—08), Am. Soc. Engring. Edn., Soc. Rsch. Adminstrs. Personal E-mail: luna_magpili@yahoo.com. Business E-Mail: magpili@virginia.edu.

MAGRAMM, IRENE, ophthalmologist; b. NYC, Jan. 24, 1955; BA, Columbia U. Barnard Coll., NYC, 1977; MD, Cornell U. Med. Coll., 1981. Diplomate Am. Bd. Ophthalmology, cert. Nat. Bd. Medical Examiners, lic. NY. Intern St. Luke's Hosp., NYC, 1981—82; resident ophthalmology North Shore U. Hosp., Manhasset, NY, 1982—85; fellowship pediat. ophthalmology, strabismus Manhattan Eye, Ear & Throat Hosp., NYC, 1985—86, asst. attending surgeon, 1986—89, assoc. attending surgeon, 1989—. Resident. instr. Manhattan Eye, Ear & Throat Hosp., 1986—90, resident selection com., 1987—93, asst. dir. Pediat. Ophthalmology Clinic, 1987—, quality assurance com., 1990—, continuing edn. com., 1996—; clin. instr. ophthalmology Weill Med. Coll. Cornell U., 1989—2000, clin. asst. prof., 2000—; asst. attending ophthalmologist NY Hosp. Cornell Med. Ctr., 1989—; assoc. adj. ophthalmologist NY Eye Ear Infirmary, 1999—. Contbr. articles to profl. jours. Fellow: Am. Acad. Medicine, Am. Acad. Ophthalmology; mem.: NY Soc. Clin. Ophthalmology, NY Soc. Pediat. Ophthalmology & Strabismus, Am. Assn. Pediat. Ophthalmology & Strabismus, NY State Ophthalmological Soc. Office: Irene Magramm MD 225 E 64th St New York NY 10065 Office Phone: 212-644-5100. Office Fax: 212-644-2520.

MAGRATH, C. PETER, academic administrator, educational association executive; b. NYC, Apr. 23, 1933; s. Laurence Wilfrid and Giulia Maria (Dentice) M.; m. Deborah C. Howell, 1988; children: Valerie Ruth, Monette Fay. BA summa cum laude, U. N.H., 1955; PhD, Cornell U., 1962. Faculty Brown U., Providence, 1961-68, prof. polit. sci., 1967-68, assoc. dean grad. sch., 1965-66; dean Coll. Arts and Scis. U. Nebr., Lincoln, 1968-69, dean faculties Coll. Arts and Scis., 1969-72, interim chancellor, 1971-72, prof. polit. sci., 1968-72, vice-chancellor for acad. affairs, 1972; pres. SUNY, Binghamton, 1972-74, prof. polit. sci., 1972-74; pres. U. Minn., Mpls., 1974-84, U. Mo. Sys., 1985-91, Nat. Assn. State Univs. and Land Grant Colls., Washington, 1991—2005, pres. emeritus, 2005—, sr. presdl. adv. to the Coll. Bd., 2006—; pres. W.Va. U., 2008—09. Author: The Triumph of Character, 1963, Yazoo: Law and Politics in the New Republic, The Case of Fletcher v. Peck, 1966, Constitutionalism and Politics: Conflict and Consensus, 1968, Issues and Perspectives in American Government, 1971; (with others) The American Democracy, 2d edit., 1973; (with Robert L. Egbert) Strengthening Teacher Education, 1987; contbr. articles to profl. jours. With AUS, 1955—57. Mem. Assn. Am. Univs. (chmn. 1985-86, bd. dirs. Salzburg Sem. 2000-05), Am. Assn. C.C.s (trustee), Phi Beta Kappa, Phi Kappa Phi, Pi Gamma Mu, Pi Sigma Alpha, Kappa Tau Alpha. Office: Coll Bd 1233 20th St NW Washington DC 20036-2375 Office Fax: 202-741-4743. Business E-Mail: pmagrath@collegeboard.org, pmargrath@collegeboard.org. *True personal success cannot be measured by public acclaim, recognition, or status. It grows out of an ability to recognize right from wrong, and to maintain principles of fairness and understanding in all human relationships - regardless of one's role in life. In my case I have tried to fulfill this ideal: I have been willing to exercise leadership by asserting my judgments and views openly and directly on the educational and human issues that came my way.*

MAGRATH, CHRISTI LEE, biology professor; b. Biloxi, Miss., Nov. 3, 1970; d. Lorraine Eleuterius Magrath. BS, U. Southern Miss., Hattiesburg, 1993; PhD in Molecular & Cell Biology, Tulane U., New Orleans, 1999. Asst. prof. Troy U., Ala., 1999—2004, assoc. prof., 2004—. Pres. Troy-Pike Habitat Humanity, 2003—09; bd. mem. Pike County Am. Cancer Soc., Troy, 2006—09; bd. mem., governance com. chair Ala. Assn. Habitat Affiliates, Auburn, 2006—09. Recipient Career award, Nat. Sci. Found., Troy U. Algernon Sydney Sullivan Humanitarian award, 2007. Mem.: Assn. Southeastern Biologists (chair, microbiology awards com. 2008—09), Beta Beta Beta (dist. dir. 2008—09, Faculty Advisor of Yr. 2005). Avocations: violin, computers, travel. Office: Troy Univ Biol Sci Univ Blvd Troy AL 36081 Office Fax: 334-670-3626. Business E-Mail: cmagrath@troy.edu.

MAGRATH, KATHLEEN BARRY, retired municipal official; b. Raymond, Neb., Aug. 10, 1930; d. Leo D. Barry and Eileen K. Larkin; m. Frank J. Magrath, June 6, 1953 (dec. Dec. 13, 1992); children: Maureen, Teresa, Patricia, Timothy, Cecilia, Mary Kathleen. BS in Chemistry, Mt. Marty Coll., Yankton, SD, 1952; MPA, Nova Southeastern U., Ft. Lauderdale, Fla., 1978, D in Pub. Adminstrn., 1979. Cert. med. technologist S.D., 1952. Med. technologist St. Catherine Hosp., McCook, Nebr., 1952—53, St. Joseph's Hosp., South Bend, Ind., 1953—54; adminstrv. asst. Dade County Sch. Bd., Miami, Fla., 1974—84; dir. child care ctr. Riviera Presbyn. Ch., Miami, 1980—82; mem. and vice chair Dade County Sch. Bd., Miami, 1984—86; coord. portfolio program Barry U., Miami, 1987—92, adj. prof. orgnl. comms., 1987—89. Founding mem. Greater Miami Urban League Fair Housing Group, 1966—70; mem. Dade County Cmty. Rels. Bd., Miami, 1983—90; dir. Fla. Sch. Bds. Assn., Tallahassee, 1985—86; mem. Dade County Property Adjustment Bd., Miami, 1986. Contbr. book reviews to Miami Herald, 1966—68; poet:. Mem. Archdiocese of Miami Synod, 1986—89; mem. local and state bds. PTA, 1970—74; vol. Fairchild Tropical Bot. Gardens, 1998—. Recipient Svc. award, Music Edn. Dade County Schs., 1985, Outstanding Svc. to Edn., Kappa Delta Pi, 1985, Recognition cert., Fla. Women's Hall of Fame, 1986, Women Helping Women cert. of Appreciation, Soroptimist Internat. of the Ams., 1991, Vol. of Yr., Homestead Mid. Sch., 2002—03. Democrat. Roman Catholic. Avocations: watercolor, drawing, volunteering, reading. Home: 7730 SW 134th St Miami FL 33156 E-mail: KBM810@aol.com.

MAGRATH, MICHAEL P., marketing executive, director; s. Paul E. and Carol A. Magrath (Stepmother); m. Danielle R. Gonzales, Oct. 11, 2003; 1 child, Erin E. BA, U. Mass., Amherst, 1988. Global product mgr. Pitney Bowes, Inc., Stamford, Conn., 2000—03; dir. product mgmt. SAMBA Holdings, Inc., Albuquerque, 2003—05; global product mktg. mgr. TallyGencom, Chantilly, Va., 2005; mktg. dir. Abraxas Corp., McLean, 2006—07; mktg. exec. govt. & healthcare mktg. Gemalto, Arlington, 2007—. Healthcare coun. sec. Smart Card Alliance, Princeton Junction, NJ, 2008—. Mem.: Am. Coun. Tech.: Info. Security Privacy Com., Am. Coun. Tech.: Health IT Com., Healthcare Info. & Mgmt. Systems Soc., Am. Mktg. Assn. Progressive. Office: Gemalto Inc 4401 Wilson Blvd Ste 210 Arlington VA 22203 Business E-Mail: michael.magrath@gemalto.com.

MAGRATH, SHARI MARIE, healthcare educator; b. Sept. 27, 1950; BS, Western Mich. U., Kalamazoo, 1991, M, 1996. HIV/AIDS/sexuality cert. instr. Mich. Dept. Edn., 1991, health edn. assessment cert. Mich. Dept. Edn., 2006, Project Alert cert. instr. Best Found., 1997. Mentor tchr. Mattawan Mid. Sch., Mich., Western Mich. U., assoc. instr.; trained peace jam instr., 2008. Presenter State Family Consumer Sci. Conf., 2005—06. Named Outstanding Tchr. of Yr., Life Mgmt. Educators of Mich., 1999—2000, Tchr. of Yr., Mattawan Sch. Dist., 1999—2000, 2005—06; Profl. Devel. grantee, 2006—07, Creative Instrn. grantee, Mattawan Found., 1998—99, 1999—2000, 2004—05, Career Prep grantee, Dept. Edn., State of Mich., 2001—02. Mem.: AAHPERD (Mich. Health Edn. Tchr. of Yr. 2006—07), Family Consumer Sci. (adv. coun.), Mich. Edn. Assn. (bargaining advisor 1991—). Office: Mattawan Mid Sch 56720 Murray St Mattawan MI 49071

MAGRILL, JOE RICHARD, JR., religious organization administrator, minister; b. Marshall, Tex., Aug. 7, 1946; s. Joe Richard and Mary Belle (Chadwick) M. BA summa cum laude, East Tex. State U., 1967; MDiv, Princeton Theol. Sem., 1970, MTh, 1972; MLS, Rutgers U., 1971. Ordained to ministry Cumberland Presbyn. Ch., 1970. Stated supply min. Newsome (Tex.) Cumberland Presbyn. Ch., 1966-67; Christian edn. asst. United Presbyn. Ch., Carlstadt, NJ, 1967-70; order libr. Princeton (N.J.) Theol. Sem., 1969-72; head libr., prof. Memphis Theol. Sem., 1972-79; pastor Brookhaven Cumberland Presbyn. Ch., Nashville, 1987-89; asst. to stated clk. Gen. Assembly Office, Cumberland Presbyn. Ch., Memphis, 1979-83, supr. ctrl. acctg. div., 1980-87, editor The Cumberland Presbyn., 1984-87, chief exec. bd. stewardship, 1989—2007, mem. Gen. Assembly Coun., 1993—2007, chief exec. Cumberland Presbyn. Investment Loan Program, Inc., 1999—2007, cons., 2007—. Mem. Trinity Presbytery of Cumberland Presbyn. Ch., 1970—; sec.-treas. Hist. Found. Cumberland Presbyn. Ch., Memphis, 1974—; bd. dirs. Hist. Found. Presbyn. Ch. U.S., Montreat, N.C., 1980-83, mem. Harrison County Historical Commn., 2009-. Editor: In the Valley of the Cauca, 1981, One Family Under God, 1982, Family of Faith, 1998. Recipient achievement award Hist. Found. Cumberland Presbyn. Ch., 1980; scholar Phi Alpha Theta, 1967, Am. Theol. Libr. Assn., 1970. Democrat. Avocations: computers, historical research. Home Phone: 903-928-0981. Business E-Mail: richardmargrill@att.net.

MAGRILL, ROSE MARY, library director; b. Marshall, Tex., June 8, 1939; d. Joe Richard and Mary Belle (Chadwick) M. BS, East Tex. State U., 1960, MA, 1961; MS, U. Ill., 1964, PhD, 1969. Asst. to dean women E. Tex. State U., Commerce, 1960-61, librarian II, 1961-63; teaching asst. U. Ill., Urbana, 1963-64; instr. to asst. prof. E. Tex. State U., Commerce, 1964-67; asst. prof. Ball State U., Muncie, 1969-70; asst. prof. to prof. U. Mich., Ann Arbor, 1970-81; prof. U. N. Tex., Denton, 1981-99; dir. libr. E. Tex. Bapt. U., Marshall, 1987-2001. Accreditation site visitor ALA, Chgo., 1975—; cons. in field. Co-author: Building Library Collections, 4th edit. 1974, Library Technical Services, 1977, Building Library Collections, 5th edit. 1979, Acquisition Management and Collection Development in Libraries, 2d edit. 1989; author: Family of Faith, 1998. Treas. Mission Synod of Cumberland Presbyn. Ch., 1989—2008; mem. bd. fin. Trinity Presbytery, 1989—98, presbyterial historian, 2008—; sec. Nat. Conv. Cumberland Presbyn. Women, 2000—02; co-moderator of gen. assembly Cumberland Presbyn. Ch., 2007; trustee Memphis Theol. Sem., 1988—98; sec.-treas. Harrison County Hist. Commn., 1995—; trustee Hist. Found., 1999—2008. Recipient award, Cumberland Presbyn. History, 1995, Spaulding History award, 2006. Mem.: ALA (RTSD Resources Sect. Pub. award 1978), Tex. Libr. Assn., Marshall (Tex.) Regional Med. Ctr. Aux. (treas. 2004—), Presbyn. Hist. Soc. of S.W. (bd. dirs. 2000—, chmn. bd. 2003—05, sec. 2005—). Home: 203 Pitts ave Marshall TX 75672-4719

MAGRO, CYNTHIA MARIA, pathologist; BS, U. Man., MD, 1985. Medical diplomate, diplomate Am. Bd. Cytopathology, Am. Bd. Dermatopathology, Am. Bd. Anatomic Pathology. Intern Harvard Med. Sch., Boston, 1985—87, resident, 1987—89, fellow, 1989—91; asst. prof. U. Winnipeg, 1991—93; asst. clin. prof. pathology Harvard Med. Sch., Boston, 1995—98; assoc. clin. prof. dermatology U. Hosps., Case Western Res. U., Cleve., 1998—99; assoc. prof. pathology Thomas Jefferson U., Phila., 1999—2000; prof. Ohio State U., Columbus, 2000—, dir. dermatopathology, 2000—. Author: (textbook) The Melanocytic Proliferations: A Comprehensive Textbook of Pigmented Lesions (Am. Assn. Pubs. award for Excellence, 2001); contbr. 133 publs. in field. Mem.: Am. Soc. Dermatopathology (chair edn. com. 2000—02). Achievements include research in neelanocyclic, lymphoproliferative and inflammatory disorders of the skin and malignant disorders of skin; inflammatory lung disease; interstitrol lung disease and lung transplantation.

MAGUIRE, BRIAN J., medical educator; DPH, George Washington U., Washington, 2004. Pres. dir. EMT BRAVO Ambulance, Bklyn., 1975—94; asst. prof. George Washington U., 1994—99; clin. assoc. prof. U. Md. Balt. County, 1999—; mgr. Global Secure Sys., Alexandria, Va., 2006—08. Dir. UMBC, Ctr. Emergency Edn. and Disaster Rsch., Balt., 2008—. Mem.: APHA. Achievements include research in occupational risks. Office: UMBC 1000 Hilltop Cr Baltimore MD 21250 Business E-Mail: maguire@umbc.edu.

MAGUIRE, CHARLOTTE EDWARDS, retired pediatrician; b. Richmond, Ind., Sept. 1, 1918; d. Joel Blaine and Lydia (Betscher) Edwards; m. Raymer Francis Maguire, Sept. 1, 1948 (dec.); children: Barbara, Thomas Clair II (dec.). Student, Stetson U., 1936—38, U. Wichita, 1938—39; BS, Memphis Tchrs. Coll., 1940; MD, U. Ark., 1944; LHD (hon.), Fla. State U., 2002. Intern, resident Orange Meml. Hosp., Orlando, Fla., 1944—46, med. staff., 1944—69, instr. nurses, 1947—57; resident Bellevue Hosp. and Med. Ctr., NYU, NYC, 1954—55; staff mem. Fla. Santarium and Hosp., Orlando, 1946—56, Holiday House and Hosp., Orlando, 1950—62; mem. courtesy and cons. staff West Orange Meml. Hosp., Winter Garden, Fla., 1952—67; active staff, chief dept. pediat. Mercy Hosp., Orlando, 1965—68; med. dir. childrens med. svcs., asst. sec. Fla. Dept. Health and Rehab. Svcs., 1969—71, med. dir. med. svcs. and basic care, 1975—84; med. exec. dir., med. svcs. divsn. worker's compensation Fla. Dept. Labor, Tallahassee, 1984—87; chief of staff physicians and dentists Ctrl. Fla. divsn. Children's Home Soc. Fla., 1947—56; dir. Orlando Child Health Clinic, 1949—58; pvt. practice Orlando, 1946—68; asst. regional dir. HEW, 1970—72; ret., 1987. Asst. dir. health and sci. affairs Dept. Health Edn. & Welfare, Atlanta, 1971-72, Washington, 1972-75; pediat. cons. Fla. Crippled Children's Commn., 1952-70, dir., 1968-70; med. dir. Office Med. Svcs. and Basic Care, sr. physician Office of Asst. Sec. Ops., Fla. Dept. Health and Rehab. Svcs.; clin. prof. dept. pediat. U. Fla. Coll. Medicine, Gainesville, 1980-87; mem. Fla. Drug Utilization Rev., 1983-87; real estate salesperson Investors Realty, 1982-2003; bd. dirs. Stavros Econ. Ctr. Fla. State U., Tallahassee; pres.'s coun. Fla. State U., U. Fla., Gainesville; Charlotte Edwards Maguire eminent scholar chair and scholarships for qualified students, 1999. Mem. profl. adv. com. Fla. Ctr. for Clin. Svcs. at U. Fla., 1952-60; del. to Mid-century White House Conf. on Children and Youth, 1950; U.S. del from Nat. Soc. for Crippled Children to World Congress for Welfare of Cripples, Inc., London, 1957; pres. of corp. Eccleston-Callahan Hosp. for Colored Crippled Children, 1956-58; sec. Fla. chpt. Nat. Doctor's Com. for Improved Med. Svcs., 1951-52; med. adv. com. Gateway Sch. for Mentally Retarded, 1959-62; bd. dirs. Forest Park Sch. for Spl. Edn. Crippled Children, 1949-54, mem. med. adv. com., 1955-68, chmn., 1957-68; mem. Fla. Adv. Coun. for Mentally Retarded, 1965-70; dir. ctrl. Fla. poison control Orange Meml. Hosp.; mem. orgn. com., chmn. com. for admissions and selection policies Camp Challenge; participant 12th session Fed. Exec. Inst., 1971; del. White House Conf. on Aging, 1980; dir. Stavros Econ. Ctr. Fla. State U.; trustee Fla. State U. Found., 1998—, mem. campaign com. Charlotte Edwards Maguire Eminent Scholarship named in her honor Fla. State U., Charlotte Edwards Maguire MLS Med. Libr., Fla. State U. Coll. Medicine named in her honor, 2005; named Outstanding Woman in Our Cmty. AAUW, Tallahassee, 2002; recipient David M. Solomon Disting. Pub. Svc. award Am. Geriatric Soc., 2005, Torch award Fla. State U., 2005. Mem. AMA (life), Nat. Rehab. Assn., Am. Congress Phys. Medicine and Rehab., Fla. Soc. Crippled Children and Adults, Ctrl. Fla. Soc. Crippled Children and Adults (dir. 1949-58, pres. 1956-57), Am. Assn. Cleft Palate, Fla. Soc. Crippled Children (trustee 1951-57, v.p. 1956-57, profl. adv. com. 1957-68), Mental Health Assn. Orange County (charter mem.; pres. 1949-50, dir. 1947-52, chmn. exec. com. 1950-52, dir. 1963-65), Fla. Orange County Heart Assn., Am. Med. Women's Assn., Am. Acad. Med. Dirs., Fla. Med. Assn. (life, chmn. com. on mental retardation), Orange County Med. Assn., Orange Med. Soc. (life), Fla. Pediat. Soc. (pres. 1952-53), Fla. Cleft Palate Assn. (counselor-at-large, sec.), Nat. Inst. Geneal. Rsch., Nat. Geneal. Soc., Assn. Profl. Genealogists, Tallahassee Geneal. Soc., Fla. State U. Found. Inc. (bd. dirs. Stavoris Ctr. for Econ. Edn.), Capital City Tiger Bay Club, Fla. Econs. Club, Francis Eppes Soc. Fla. State U., Econ. Club Fla., Governors Club. Home: 4158 Covenant Ln Tallahassee FL 32308-5765

MAGUIRE, GREGORY, writer; m. Andy Newman; children: Luke, Alex, Helen. PhD in English and Am. Lit., Tufts U., 1990. Fellow Bread Loaf Writers Conf., Middlebury, Vt., 1978; prof., assoc. dir. Ctr. for the Study of Children's Lit., Simmons Coll., 1979—86; co-dir., founding bd. mem. Children's Lit. New England, Inc., 1986—; artist-in-residence Isabella Stewart Gardner Mus., Boston, 1994; fellow Blue Mountain Ctr., NY, The Hambidge Ctr., Ga., 1998, The Va. Ctr. for the Creative Arts, 1999. Author: (novels) Wicked: The Life and Times of the Wicked Witch of the West, 1995, Confessions of an Ugly Stepsister, 1999, Lost, 2001, Mirror Mirror, 2003, Son of a Witch, 2005, (children's novels) The Dream Stealer, 1983 (named one of the Children's Books of the Yr., Child Study Children's Books Com., 1983, named a Nat. Coun. Tchrs. of English Tchr.'s Choice, 1984), Missing Sisters, 1994 (named a Parents Choice Hon. book, 1994), The Good Liar, 1996, The Hamlet Chronicles, Seven Spiders Spinning (named an ALA Notable book, 1994, Judy Lopez Meml. Award Hon. book, 1995), Six Haunted Hairdos, Five Alien Elves, Four Stupid Cupids, Three Rotten Eggs, A Couple of April Fools, Leaping Beauty: And Other Animal Fairy Tales, 2004; contbr. articles to profl. mags. including the Boston Rev., Christian Sci. Monitor, The Horn Book Mag., others. Office: William Reiss - Literary Agt John Hawkins and Assocs 71 W 23rd St Ste 1600 New York NY 10010 Address: Jennifer Suitor - Publicist HarperCollins 10 E 53rd St New York NY 10022

MAGUIRE, JANET, composer; b. Chgo. BA, Colo. Coll.; studied composition with René Leibowitz, Paris; student, Darmstadt Ferienkurse. Co-founder, pres. Venezia Nuova Musica, Venice, Italy, 1992—2003, Musica in Divenire, Venice, Italy, 2004—. Composer: Per Acqua, 1990, Shuffle, 1991, Ebb & Flow, 1992, Treize à Table, 1993, Cosi, 1993, Inno a Dio, 1994, Hark, 1995, La mia serra, 1995, Canzone d'Amore, 1996, Invenzione, 1996, Il fiume Tchirek, 1996, Glass, 1997, Discussion, 1997, Etude Osmotique, 1998, Fumées d'Ivresse, 1998, Lace Knots, 1998, Danza, 1999, L'altro Quartetto, 1999, Le Jardin de Versailles, 2000, L'intervista, 2000, Quest, 2000, Cummings Lieder, 2000, Five Chinese Poems, 2001, Hier bin Ich, Wo bist Du?, 2002, Un Momento, 2002, Moondust, 2002, A Trois, 2002, Southern Trees, 2002, Frills, 2002, Rain, 2003, Fingers, 2003, Vagheggiando, 2003, Gone, 2004, Sonata-Suonata, 2005, Variations, 2005, Tragedy, 2006, Please, 2007, Wisp, 2007, Lightly, 2002, (Operas) Envoys, 1996, HèRèSIE, 2008, (ballets) Taigà, 2001; orchestrator: Les Nuits Parisiennes, Die drei Pintos, arranger: Operas Turandot Finale by Giacomo Puccini. Fellow John Simon Guggenheim Meml. Found., 2008; Copland House resident, Aaron Copland Found., 2006. Mem.: European Soc. for Culture. Office: Musica in Divenire Via Fogazzaro 18 30172 Mestre Venezia Italy Personal E-mail: janetdmaguire@yahoo.com. E-mail: janetmaguire255@hotmail.com.

MAGUIRE, JOANNE M., aerospace transportation executive; BS, Mich. State Univ.; MS, UCLA. Positions with TRW Space & Electronics, 1975—2003, prog. mgr. Defense Support, dep. gen. mgr. Defense Systems div., v.p., gen. mgr. Space & Tech. div., v.p., gen. mgr. Space & Laser Programs div., v.p., dep. bus. develop.; with Lockheed Martin Corp., Bethesda, Md., 2003—, v.p. spl. programs, v.p., deputy Space Systems Co., exec. v.p. Space Systems Co., 2006—. Bd. dirs. Space Found., United Launch Alliance, INROADS Inc. Recipient Outstanding Leadership award, Women in Aerospace, 1999; named one of 50 Most Powerful Women in Bus., Fortune mag., 2006, 2007, 2008, Top 50 Women in Tech., Corp. Bd. Mem. mag., 2008. Mem.: AIAA, Soc. Women Engineers. Office: Lockheed Martin Corp 6801 Rockledge Dr Bethesda MD 20817*

MAGUIRE, JOSEPH F., bishop emeritus; b. Boston, Sept. 4, 1919; Student, Boston Coll., St. John's Sem., Boston. Ordained priest Archdiocese of Boston, 1945; ordained monsignor, 1964; asst. pastor St. Joseph Ch., Lynn, Mass., St. Anne Ch., Readville, Mass., Blessed Sacrament Ch., Jamaica Plain, Mass., St. Mary Ch., Milton, Mass.; sec. to Cardinal Cushing Boston, 1962-70; sec. to Archbishop Medeiros, 1970-71; ordained bishop, 1972; aux. bishop Diocese of Boston, 1972—76; coadjutor bishop Diocese of Springfield, Mass., 1976-77, bishop, 1977-91, bishop emeritus, 1991—. Cons., 1968—. Roman Catholic. Office: Chancery Office PO Box 1730 76 Elliot St Springfield MA 01105-1714

MAGUIRE, KIM D., retail executive; B, Indiana Univ. With Target, 1981—2001, sr. v.p. hardlines; exec. v.p., merchandising Circuit City, Richmond, Va., 2001—04; exec. v.p., chief merchandising officer QVC, 2004—07, Office Depot, Delray Beach, Fla., 2007—. Office: Office Depot 6600 N Military Trl Boca Raton FL 33496-2434

MAGUIRE, MARTIE (MARTHA ELENOR ERWIN MAGUIRE), musician; b. York, Pa., Oct. 12, 1969; d. Paul and Barbara Erwin; m. Ted Seidel, June 17, 1995 (div. 1999); 1 stepchild, Carter Seidel; m. Gareth MaGuire, Aug. 10, 2001; children: Eva Ruth, Kathleen Emilie, Harper Rose. Student, So. Meth. U. Performer Blue Night Express, 1984—89; fiddle player, violinist, vocalist Dixie Chicks, 1989—. Musician: (albums) Thank Heavens for Dale Evans, 1990, LIttle Ol' Cowgirl, 1992, Shouldn't a Told You That, 1993, Wide Open Spaces, 1998 (Album of Yr., Acad. Country Music, 1998, Best Country Album, Grammy Awards, 1998, Best Country Artist Clip of Yr., Billboard Awards, 1998, Maximum Vision Clif of Yr., Billboard Awards, 1998, Best Selling Album, Can. Country Music Award, 1999, Song of Yr. (Country), WB Radio Music Awards, 1999, Album of Yr., Acad. Country Music, 1999), Fly, 1999 (Best Country Album, Grammy Awards, 1999, Best Selling Album, Can. Country Music Awards, 2000, Internat. Album, British Country Music Awards, 2000, Country Album of Yr., Billboard Awards, 2000, Album of Yr., Acad. Country Music, 2000, Album of Yr., CMA, 2000), Home, 2002 (Favorite Country Album, Am. Music Awards, 2002, Best Recording Package, Grammy Awards, 2002, Best Country Album, Grammy Awards, 2002), Top of the World Tour: Live, 2003 (Best Country Group Vocal Performance, Grammy Awards, 2005), Taking the Long Way, 2006 (Album of Yr. and Best Country Album, Grammy Awards, 2007), (songs) Not Ready to Make Nice, 2006 (Record of Yr., Song of Yr., Best Performance by a Duo or Group with Vocal, Grammy Awards, 2007); performer: (documentary) Dixie Chicks: Shut Up and Sing, 2006. Recipient Horizon award, CMA, 1998, others; named Top New Country Artist, Billboard, 1998, Most Significant New Country Act, Country Monitor, 1998, Group of Yr., CMA, 1998, Top Vocal Group, Acad. Country Music, 1998, Internat. Rising Star, British Country Music Awards, 1999, Country Artist of Yr., Rolling Stone, 1999, Artist of Yr. (Country), WB Radio Music Awards, 1999, Favorite New Artist (Country), AMA, 1999, Vocal Group of Yr., CMA, 1999, Country Artist of Yr., Billboard, 1999, 2000, Vocal Group of Yr., CMA, 2000, Entertainer of Yr., 2000, ACM, 2000, 2001, Vocal Group of Yr., 2001, Favorite Musical Group or Band, People's Choice Awards, 2001, Favorite Country Band, Am. Music Award, 2002, Vocal Group of Yr., Country Music Assn. Award, 2002, Country Duo/Group of Yr., Billboard, 2002; named one of 100 Most Influential People, Time Mag., 2006.

MAGUIRE, MILDRED MAY, retired chemistry professor; b. Leetsdale, Pa., May 7, 1933; d. John and Mildred (Sklarsky) Magura. BS in Chemistry, Carnegie-Mellon U., 1955; MS in Phys. Chemistry, U. Wis., 1960; PhD in Phys. Chemistry, Pa. State U., 1967. Devel. chemist Koppers Co., Monaca, Pa., 1955-58; rsch. chemist Am. Cyanamid Co., Stamford, Conn., 1960-63; asst. prof. chemistry Waynesburg Coll., Pa., 1967-70, assoc. prof., 1970-74, prof., 1974—2006, prof. emerita, 2007; emeritus prof Waynesburg U., 2004; vis. prof. chemistry U. Wis. Cons. Pitts. Energy Tech. Ctr., summers 1978-86; faculty rsch. participant Oak Ridge Assoc. Univs., 1978-80, 82-85; Leverhulme vis. prof. U. Leicester, Eng., 1980-81, 1989; US del. Internat. Conf. Phys. Chemists, China, 1996, Sci. and Tech. Conf., India, 1997; vis. prof. chemistry U. Wis., Madison, 2004, 06, summer, 2005. Contbr. articles to sci. jours., chpt. to book. Sec. Waynesburg Women's Club, 1981-82; citizen amb. People to People Program, 1996, 97. Recipient Woman of the Yr. award AAUW, Waynesburg, 1983; Cottrell grantee Rsch. Corp. N.Y., 1970-71; Leverhulme vis. fellow U.K., 1980-81; Curie Internat. fellow AAUW, U.K., 1980-81; Robert West Superconductor Rsch. Grantee, Univ. Wis., 2001-05. Mem. AAUP, AAAS, Am. Chem. Soc.; Spectroscopy Soc. of Pitts.; Pitts. Soc. of Analytical Chemists. Avocations: gardening, painting, swimming, classical music, reading. Home: 1550 Crescent Hills 6th St Ext Waynesburg PA 15370-1654 Personal E-mail: mmaguire@alltel.net.

MAGURNO, RICHARD PETER, lawyer; b. Suffern, NY, June 29, 1943; s. Eugene and Rose (Foresta) M. BS, Georgetown U., 1964; MS, U. Wis., 1965; JD, Fordham U., 1968. Bar: N.Y. 1970, Fla. 1982, U.S. Supreme Ct. 1974, U.S. Ct. Appeals (2d, 5th, 11th cirs.) 1976, U.S. Dist. Ct. (so. and ea. dists.) N.Y. 1979. Atty. Eastern Air Lines, NYC, 1970-73, sr. atty., 1973-76, gen. atty., 1976-79, dir. legal Miami, Fla., 1980, v.p. legal, asst. sec., 1980-84, gen. counsel, sr. v.p. legal, sec., 1984-88; ptnr. Lord Day & Lord, Barrett Smith, 1989-94; gen. counsel, sr. v.p. legal Trans World Airlines, St. Louis, 1994-98; aviation cons., 1998-2000; gen. counsel, sr. v.p., sec. AirTran Airways, 2000—. Author: Romantic Suffern, 1773-1973, 1973. Served in Peace Corps, 1968-69. Mem. ABA, Fla. Bar Assn. Democrat. Roman Catholic.

MAH, SILVIA ARMITANO, director, educator; b. Caracas, Venezuela, Nov. 21, 1973; arrived in US, 1991; d. Ernesto Amadei and Shirley McDaniel Armitano; m. Edward Anthony Mah, June 27, 1998; children: Alexio Nicolas, Matteo Andreas, Sofia Alegria. BS in Biology with honors, Pepperdine U., Malibu, Calif., 1995; PhD, U. Calif. San Diego, La Jolla, 2004. Rsch. technician Abilene Christian U., Tex., field tchg. asst. marine biology, 1996; tchg. asst. invertebrate zoology and cell biology Pepperdine U., Malibu, Calif., 1993—95, lab coord., 1996; field technicain Smithsonian Instn., Washington, 1995; expdn. organizer Royal Ont. Mus., Ontario, Canada, 1997; grad. rsch. asst. U. Calif. San Diego, La Jolla, 1997—2004, head tchg. asst. structural biochemistry, 2003, teams in engring. svc. program dir., 2005—; terraclima outreach program coord. Scripps Instn. Oceanography, La Jolla, 2004—05; sci. cons. Encinitas Sch. Dist. - Mission Estancia Elem. Sch., Calif., 2004—05. Founding mem. Scripps Women in Sci. and Scripps Cmty. Outreach Program for Edn.ope) Scripps Instn. Oceanography, U. Calif. San Diego, La Jolla, 2000—02, career mentor, 2001—02; rsch. mentor U. Calif. San Diego, La Jolla, 2001—04, coord./instr. for sci. outreach, 2002—03; sci. fair judge Greater San Diego Sci. and Engring. Fair, 2004. Membersip chair Am. Women in Sci., San Diego, 2005. Recipient Tchg. Asst. Excellence in Tchg. award, Divsn. Biol. Scis., U. Calif. San Diego, 2003, Outstanding Sr. Rschr. award, Pepperdine U., 2005; fellow Travel award, Am. Soc. for Cell Biology Minorities Affairs Com., 2001—02; scholar, U. ND Alumni Found., 1996; Summer Undergraduate Rsch. in Biology Summer fellow, Pepperdine U., 1994, Advanced Tng. in Molecular Marine Biology fellow, Office Naval Rsch., 1995, Minority Grad. Rsch. fellow, NSF, 1997—2001, Shirley Boyd Meml. Fund fellow, Scripps Instn. Oceanography, U. Calif. San Diego, 2001. Mem.: Golden Key. Personal E-mail: samah@ucsd.edu. Business E-Mail: samah@uccsd.edu.

MAHABHASHYAM, SAI RAJESH, application developer; b. Hyderabad, Andhra Pradesh, India, Mar. 13, 1979; s. Madan Mohan and Shobha Mahabhashyam; m. Rohitha Kramadhati, Apr. 23, 2006. BTech, Indian Inst. Tech. Madras, 2000; M in Engring., Penn State U., Univ. Pk., 2001, MS, 2004, PhD, 2006. Cert. SCJP, 2006. Sr software engr. Oracle USA Inc., King Prussia, Pa., 2004—. Contbr. articles to profl. jours. (Best Paper award, 2003). Home: 1810 Wagon Wheel Dr Little Rock AR 72211 Personal E-mail: sairajesh@gmail.com.

MAHABIR, ERROL EDWARD, company executive; b. Feb. 25, 1931; m. Yvonne Lans; 3 children. BA in Adminstrn. and Mgmt., Columbia Pacific U. Formerly with Texaco Trinidad, Inc., asst. mgr. employee rels.; dep. mayor City of San Fernando, 1960-63, mayor, 1963-66; M.P. Parliament of Trinidad and Tobago, 1963—86, min. of labor and social security, 1969-71, min. of industry and commerce, 1973-76, min. Ministry of Fin., min. of petroleum and mines, 1976-79, min. Ministry of Fin., min. energy & energy-base industries, 1979-81, min. of labor, social security and co-operatives, 1981-85, min. of external affairs, 1985-86; chmn., mng. dir. Eminent Holdings, Eminent Svcs. Internat. Ltd., Gen. Pkg. Ltd., Damus Ltd. Chmn. Carib Containers Ltd.; bd. dirs. Brands Investments Ltd., Consol. Biscuits (Malta) Ltd. Office: PO Box 42 San Fernando Trinidad and Tobago Office Phone: 868-657-9142. Personal E-mail: ribahan@yahoo.com.

MAHABIR, RAMAN CHAOS, plastic surgeon, educator; b. Newcastle, NB, Canada, Aug. 14, 1975; s. Ray and Joan Ellen Mahabir. BSc, U. NB, Fredericton, 1996; MD, U. BC, Vancouver, Canada, 2000, MSc, 2001. Lic. Med. Coun. Can., 2002, cert. plastic surgeon Royal Coll. Physicians & Surgeons, Can., 2006. Clin. rsch. fellow Okanagan Plastic Surgery Ctr., Kelowna, British Columbia, Canada, 2000—01; plastic surgery resident U. Calgary, Alberta, Canada, 2001—05, chief plastic surgery resident, 2005—06; clin. asst. prof. U. Nev., Sch. Medicine, Las Vegas, 2006—07, aesthetic & breast surgery fellow, 2006—07, hand & microsurgery fellow, 2006—07; asst. prof. Tex. A&M and Scott & White, Temple, 2007—, chief microsurgery, 2007—, rsch. dir., 2007—, elective adminstr., 2008—. Contbr. articles to profl. jours. (Gaspar Anastasi award, 2004). Surgeon Las Vegas Med. Mission Philippines, Nev., 2007—09. Recipient Meml. Endowment award, U. BC, 2006; Can. Millennium scholarship, Govt. Can., 2000. Fellow: Royal Coll. Physicians & Surgeons, Can.; mem.: AMA, Can. Med. Assn., Am. Soc. Plastic Surgeons, Can. Soc. Plastic Surgeons, Alpha Omega Alpha. Office: Scott & White Dept Surgery 2401 S 31st St Temple TX 76504

MAHADEVA, MANORANJAN, financial executive, accountant; b. Colombo, Sri Lanka, Feb. 12, 1955; arrived in US, 1977; s. Kandiah and Rupavathy (Ponniah) M.; m. Donna Sue Martin, May 12, 1986; 1 child, Danielle. BBA, U. Tex., 1981; MBA, Tex. A&M U., 1985. Accrdited in bus. valuation, AICPA, cert. in fin. forensics, AICPA; mgmt. acct. and cert. fin. mgmt. Inst. Mgmt. Accts., fraud examiner, cash mgr., internal auditor 2002, lic. real estate broker Tex., cert. CPA. Asst. contr. Presbyn. Village North, Dallas, 1981-84; CFO Dallas Meml. Hosp., 1984-86; exec. dir. Associated Orthopedics & Sports Medicine, Plano, Tex., 1986-95; CFO Access Med. Supply Inc., Plano, 1988-95; mng. dir. YNM Corp., Plano, 1987-95; practice adminstr. Tex. Orthopaedic Assocs., Dallas, 1995-96; dir. project mgmt. Physician Reliance Network, Dallas, 1996-99; dir. valuations, bus. devel. US Oncology, Houston, 1999—2001, dirp. fin. planning, 2001—03, dir. regional fin., 2003—. CFO Access Med. Supply, Inc., 1988—96. Mem. editl. rev. bd. Jour. Accountancy and Strategic Fin., mem. editl. rev. bd., column editor Today's CPA; mem. editl. rev. bd.: Fin. Analyst Jour. Mem. Leadership Plano Class 8, 1990-91, bd. dirs., mem. exec. bd., 1991-97, chmn. exec. bd., 1992-93; mem. Mental Health Assn. Collin County, Tex. State Bd. of Physical Therapy Examiners; bd. dirs. Nat. Assn. Cmty. Leadership, vice chair, 1995-97, chair-elect, 1997-98, chair, 1998-99; bd. dirs. Am. Heart Assn., Inst. Mgmt. Accts., 2002—, Then, 2004; bd. dirs., treas. Crisis Ctr. of Collin County; chmn. emergency svcs. Coalition of Collin County; steering com. Leadership USA, 1996-97. Recipient Nat. Disting. Leadership award, 1994; Presdl. scholar Wayne (Nebr.) State U., 1977-78; Mano Mahadeva Day proclaimed in his honor Mayor of Plano, 1999. Mem. CFA Inst., Nat. Assn. Accts. (bd. dirs. North Dallas chpt. 1985-86), Am. Hosp. Assn., Internat. Students Assn., Am. Arbitration Assn. (mem. panel of neutrals), Houston Soc. Fin. Analysts, Plano C. of C. (chmn. cmty. edn. com.), Leadership Plano Alumni Assn. (bd. dirs.), Toastmasters, Lions (past pres. Plano, Lion of Yr. award 1993), Rotary (sec., program chmn., pres. Plano 1996-97, Rotarian of Yr. award 1995, Paul Harris fellow 1998), Delta Sigma Pi, Beta Gamma Sigma. Avocations: reading, tennis, playing drums, jogging, cooking. Home: 4113 Aldenham Dr Plano TX 75024 Office: US Oncology 4708 Alliance Blvd Ste 120 Plano TX 75093 Office Phone: 469-467-4372. Personal E-mail: mano.mahadeva@gmail.com.

MAHADEVAN, KUMAR, marine life administrator, researcher; b. Madras, Tamilnadu, India, Sept. 29, 1948; came to U.S., 1971; s. Sockalingam Ponnusamy and Pankajam (Nadar) M.; m. Linda Claire Goggin, Sept. 27, 1980; children: Andrew, Alexander, Chad, Vijayan. BS, Madras U., 1967; MS, Annamalai U., Chidambaram, India, 1971; PhD, Fla. State U., 1977. Instr. Chingleput (India) Med. Coll., 1967-68, Lakshman's Coll., Madras, 1968-69; rsch. asst. Fla. State U., Tallahassee, 1971-75; staff scientist Conservation Cons., Inc., Palmetto, Fla., 1975-78; sr. scientist Mote Marine Lab., Sarasota, Fla., 1978-79, dir. divsn., 1979—86, interim co-dir., 1984; pres. Mote Marine Found., Sarasota, Fla., 1986—; trustee Mote Sci. Found., Sarasota, Fla., 1999—. Mem. Coun. on Ocean Affairs, Washington, 1989-91, steering com. Gulf of Mex. Program, Atlanta, 1988-96; mem. South Atlantic and Gulf States Coastal Protection Commn., 1990-93; vice chmn. NOAA Marine Rsch. Bd., Gulf of Mex., 1992-96. Contbr. articles to profl. jours. Mem. sch. adv. bd., Sarasota, 1988-89; mem. tech. adv. bd. Myakka River, Sarasota, 1987-90; legis. liason Parents Assn. of Sarasota Schs., 1988-89; bd. dirs. Jason Found. for Edn., 1991-2004, Health Care Sarasota, 1997-98; vice chmn. Fla. Ocean Alliance, 2000—; mem. Fla. Gov.'s Ocean Com., 1997-98; mem. adv. bd. Harte Inst. for Gulf of Mex. Studies, 2001—; active Sarasota Cmty. Video Archives Hall of Fame, 2005. Nat. Merit scholar Univ. Grants Commn., India, 1969-71. Fellow Explorers Club (nat.); mem. N.Am. Benthological Soc., Oceanographic Soc., World Aquaculture Soc., Deep Sea Biol. Soc. (hon.), Fla. Acad. Scis. (councillor 1975), So. Assn. Marine Labs (pres. 1990, exec. bd. 1986-91, treas. 1995—), Assn. Marine Labs Caribbean (pres. 1987-88, exec. bd. 1984—), Nat. Assn. Marine Labs. (pres. 1994-95), Sci. and Environ. Coun. Sarasota (chmn. 2003-06, Fla. Coastal Ocean Observing Systems Rsch. Consortium (chmn. 2006-07), Greater Sarasota C. of C. (dir. 2005—), Sarasota Rotary Club, Nat. Marine Sanctuary Found. (dir., 2007—), Sarasota Convention & Visitor's Bur. (dir. 2008-), Sigma Xi. Republican. Avocations: racquetball, fishing, gardening. Office: Mote Marine Lab 1600 Ken Thompson Pky Sarasota FL 34236-1096 Home Phone: 941-346-9338. Business E-Mail: kumar@mote.org.

MAHADEVAN, UMA, physician; b. Colombo, Sri Lanka, Apr. 25, 1970; d. Ramasamy and Kanagam Mahadevan; m. Fernando S. Velayos, Apr. 14, 2007. BS, UCLA, 1991. Cert. physician NY, 1995. Asst. prof. medicine U. Calif., San Francisco, 2001—07, assoc. prof. medicine, 2007—. Chmn. patient edn. com. Crohn's Colitis Found. America, NYC, 2005—08. Recipient Sr. Investigator award, Crohn's Colitis Found. America, 2007—. Achievements include invention of pregnancy and inflammatory bowel disease. Office: Univ Calif San Francisco 2330 Post St #610 San Francisco CA 94115

MAHADY, JOSEPH MICHAEL, pharmaceutical executive; b. Apr. 27, 1953; BS in Pharmacy, St. John's U., 1977; MBA, Fairleigh Dickinson U., 1986. Pres. Am. Home Products Corp., Madison, NJ; pres. N. Am. & Global Bus. Wyeth Pharmaceuticals, Inc., 2002—05, pres. Americas & Global Bus., 2005—07, pres. Global Bus., 2007—08; sr. v.p. Wyeth, 2005—; pres. Wyeth Pharmaceuticals, Inc., 2008—. Office: Wyeth Pharmaceuticals Inc 500 Arcola Rd Collegeville PA 19426 also: Wyeth Five Giralda Farms Madison NJ 07940-0874 Office Phone: 484-865-5476, 973-660-5771.

MAHAFFEY, JOHN CHRISTOPHER, medical association executive; b. Jefferson City, Mo., July 20, 1953; s. Fred Turner and Betty Cord (Woodfill) Mahaffey; children: Michael, Katherine. BA, Western Ill. U., Macomb, 1975; MS, DePaul U., 1999. Cert. assn. exec. Legis. aide Congressman Harold R. Collier, Washington, 1972-73; legis. asst. Nat. Assn. Retail Druggists, Washington, 1975-76; dir. Commn. and Meetings Nat. Assn. Bds. of Pharmacy, Chgo., 1976-80; pres., CEO Assn. Forum, Chgo., 1980—2002; exec. dir. Am. Coll. Foot and Ankle Surgeons, Park Ridge, Ill., 2002—. Bd. dirs. Healthcare Assocs. Credit Union, 2003—. Commr. City of Park Ridge (Ill.) Econ. Devel. Commn., 1990—94, 1996—2000; mem. exec. com. Chgo. Convention and Tourism Bur., Chgo., 1993—2002. Recipient Disting. Alumni award, Western Ill. U., Macomb, 1993, Shapiro award, Assn. Forum, 2002. Fellow: Am. Soc. Assn. Execs. (Key award 1994); mem.: U. S. C. of C., Assn. Com. 100. Presbyn. Office: Am Coll Foot and Ankle Surgeons 8725 W Higgins Rd Chicago IL 60631 Office Phone: 773-693-9300. Business E-Mail: mahaffey@acfas.org.

MAHAFFEY, MARCIA HIXSON, retired educational administrator; b. Scobey, Mont. d. Edward Goodell and Olga Marie (Frederickson) Hixson; m. Donald Harry Mahaffey (div. Aug. 1976); 1 child, Marcia Anne (dec.); m. George Justin Fair, Mar. 26, 1997 (div. June 9, 2004). BA in English, U. Wash.; MA in Secondary Edn., U. Hawaii, 1967. Cert. secondary and elem. tchr., adminstr. Tchr. San Lorenzo (Calif.) Sch. Dist., 1958-59, Castro Valley (Calif.) Sch. Dist., 1959-63, vice prin., 1963-67, Sequoia Union HS Dist., Redwood City, 1967-77, asst. prin., prin., 1977-91, ret., 1991. Tchr. trainer Project Impact Sequoia Union HS Sch. Dist., Redwood City, 1986-91; supr.'s task force for dropout prevention, 1987-91, Sequoia Dist. Goals Commn. (chair subcom. staff devel. 1988) chair, Sequoia Union HS Dist. Grading Com., 1976-1984; mentor tchr. selection com., 1987-91; mem. Stanford Program Devel. Ctr. Com., 1987-91; chair gifted and talented Castro Valley Sch. Dist.; family svcs. bd., San Leandro, Calif. Vol. Am. Cancer Soc., San Mateo, Calif., 1967, Castro Valley, 1965; chair Carlmont H.S. Site Coun., Belmont, Calif., 1977—91; active Nat. Trust for Hist. Preservation; Neighborhood Beautification project dir. Bridle Trails Cmty. Club, 1999—2001; Golden Grads. scholarship com. Roosevelt HS, Seattle, 2000—, co-chair, 2004—07, chair, 2007—; founder Colonial Williamsburg, 2007—; Sunday sch. tchr. Hope Luth. Ch., San Mateo, 1970—76. Recipient Life Mem. award Parent, Tchr., Student Assn., Belmont, 1984, Svc. award, 1989, Exemplary Svc award Carlmont High Sch., 1989, 92; named Woman of the Week, Castro Valley, 1967, Outstanding Task Force Chair Adopt A Sch. Program San Mateo (Calif.) County, 1990. Mem.: DAR, AAUW, ASCD, Acad. Am. Poets, Sequoia Dist. Mgmt. Assn. (pres. 1975, treas. 1984—85), Assn. Calif. Sch. Adminstrs. (Project Leadership plaque 1985), The Heritage Found., Am. Heritage-The Soc. of Am. Historians, Smithsonian Instn., Met. Mus. Art, Libr. of Congress Assocs. (charter), Animal Welfare Advocacy, White Ho. Hist. Assn. (charter), Am. Mus. Natural History (charter), Woodrow Wilson Internat. Ctr. Scholars, Alpha Xi Delta (Order of Rose award 1997), Delta Kappa Gamma. Avocations: painting, travel, tap dancing, redecorating, poetry. *Personal philosophy: Life is short, so make haste to be kind to one another.*

MAHAFFEY, REDGE ALLAN, movie producer, director, writer, actor, scientist, business executive; b. Bethesda, Md., Dec. 15, 1949; s. George Newton and Lila Katherine (Drum) M.; m. Ellen Cecilia Cranston, May 30, 1973 (div. Dec. 1980); m. Patricia Jane Guy, Apr. 29, 1984 (div. Sept. 1994); children: Travis Guy, Morgan Nicole; m. Veronica Bird, Sept. 24, 1994; children: Ryan Alexander, Ramsey Blake. BS, U. Md., 1971, MS, 1973, PhD, 1976. Lic. series 7 2007, series 64 2007, Md. Real Estate, 2007. NRC postdoctoral fellow Nat. Acad. of Scis., Washington, 1976-77; research physicist Naval Research Lab., Washington, 1977-78; sr. research physicist Sachs/Freeman Assocs., Bladensburg, Md., 1978-79, dir. research Bowie, Md., 1979-81, exec. v.p., chief scientist Largo, Md., 1981-91, 1999—2007, also bd. dirs. Landover, Md., 1985—2007; mng. ptnr. Ramsway Pictures, 1991—; pres. WHOH, Davidsonville, Md., 1993—; investment cons. Inverness Real Estate Investments, Walnut Creek, Calif., 2007—. Instr. George Washington U., Washington, 1979-80, Prince George's Coll., 1987; pres. Capitol Contracts, Bowie, 1981-83. Author: A Higher Education, 1989, Me, Myself and I, 1992, Deadly Rivals, 1992; exec. prodr., writer Deadly Rivals, 1992, Quest of the Delta Knights, 1993; prodr., actor, writer, dir. Life 101, 1995 (hon. mention Atlantic City Film Festival 1997), First Encounter, 1997; prodr., actor, dir., writer She's Too Tall, 1998 (Best Comedy award Atlantic City Film Festival 1998); contbr. articles on lasers and particle beams to sci. jours., also short stories, essays and poems to mags.; patentee laser, x-rays and particle beams. Recipient Research Publ. award Naval Research Lab., 1978, 1st Place Novel Internat. Lit. Awards, 1988, award of merit Internat. Soc. for Advancement of Poetry, 1990. Mem. IEEE, Am. Phys. Soc., Mensa, Intertel, Nat. Writer's Club, Internat. Platform Assn., Internat. Soc. Phil. Enquiry, Writer's Assn. Anne Arundel County, Bethesda Writer's Ctr., Inst. Noetic Scis. Clubs: Sea Dragons Martial Arts(Washington) (treas. 1984-85, instr. 1987-91). Republican. Avocations: martial arts, softball, basketball. Office: SFA Inc 2200 Defense Hwy Crofton MD 21114 Office Phone: 301-858-1244. Business E-Mail: rmahaffey@invernessrei.com. E-mail: redge@sfa.com.

MAHAJAN, AJAY, engineering educator; PhD, Tulane U., New Orleans, 1994. Assoc. prof. Lake Superior State U., Sault Ste. Marie, Mich., 1994—98; prof. State Ill. U. Carbondale, 1998—. Office: State Ill Univ Carbondale 1230 Lincoln Dr Carbondale IL 62901 Business E-Mail: mahajan@engr.siu.edu.

MAHAJAN, ANITA, oncologist, educator; married. MD, McGill U., Montreal, 1988. Cert. Tex. Med. Bd. Assoc. prof. MD Anderson Cancer Ctr., Houston, 2002—. Mem.: ASTRO.

MAHAJAN, ARVIND, finance educator; b. Delhi, India, Nov. 24, 1951; arrived in U.S., 1974; s. Vedavrata and Shakuntala Mahajan; m. Vanita Mahajan, Jan. 16, 1983; children: Aseem K., Sia S. B of Commerce in Acctg. and Fin., U. Delhi, 1972; MBA in Fin., U. Scranton, 1975; PhD in Fin., Ga. State U., 1980. Fin. officer Raisina Press, Delhi, 1972—74; instr., rsch. asst. Ga. State U., Atlanta, 1976—79; sr. cons. Mfrs. Hanover Trust Co., NYC, 1987—88; asst. prof. fin. Tex. A&M U., College Station, 1980—86, assoc. prof., 1986—92, prof., 1992—94, Lamar Savings prof. fin., 1994—; dir. Aggies Wall St Program; assoc. dir. acad. programs Ctr. Internat. Bus. Studies and CIBER Tex. A&M U., College Station, 1990—99. Vis. prof. Group Ecole Superieure de Commerce, Rennes, France, 2000, Johannes Kepler U., Linz, Austria, 1992—99, Group Ecole Superieure de Commerce, Dijon, France, 1991, Indian Inst. Tech., New Delhi, 2003—; faculty mem. Acad. Future Internat. Leaders, 1998—2000. Contbr. articles to rsch. jours. and confs. Pres. Coalition Support Pub. Schs., College Station, 2003. Avocations: travel, reading, music. Office: Tex A&M U Mays Bus Sch College Station TX 77843

MAHAJAN, SUBHASH, electronic materials educator; b. Gurdaspur, India; m. Sushma Sondhi, Sept. 3, 1965; children: Sanjoy, Sunit, Ashish. BS with highest honors, Panjab U., India, 1959; BE in Metallyrgy with highest honors, Indian Inst. Sci., 1961; PhD in Materials Sci. and Engring., U. Calif., 1965. Rsch. asst. U. Calif., Berkeley, 1961-65; rsch. metallurgist U. Denver, 1965-68; Harwell fellow Atomic Energy Rsch. Establishment, Harwell, England, 1968-71; mem. tech. staff AT&T Bell Labs., Murray Hill, NJ, 1971-83, rsch. mgr., 1981-83; prof. electronic materials dept. material sci. and engring. Carnegie Mellon U., Pitts., 1983-97; prof. electronic materials Ariz. State U., Tempe, 1997—, assoc. chair, 1999, interim chair and chair dept. chem. and materials engring., 2000—06, dir. Sch. Materials, 2006—, Regents' prof., 2007. Mem. site panel Materials Rsch. Lab., 1993; vis. prof. U. Antwerp, Belgium, 1991, Ecole Ctrl. Lyon, Ecully, France, 1993; lectr., spkr., patentee, cons. in field. Editor: Handbook on Semiconductors, vol. 3, 1994, Acta Materialia, 2001; editor: (with V.G. Keramidas) Electrochemical Society Symposium Volume, 1983; editor: (with L.C. Kimerling) The Concise Encyclopedia of Semiconducting Materials and Related Technologies, 1992; editor: (with D. Bloor, R.J. Brook and M.C. Flemings) The Encyclopedia of Advanced Materials, 1994; editor: (with K.H. Jurgen Buschow, Robert W. Cahn et al) Encyclopedia of Materials: Science and Technology, 2001; coordinating editor: The Acta Materiala Jours., 2004—; contbr. more than 200 articles to profl. jours. Mem. materials rsch. adv. com. divsn. materials rsch. NSF, 1989-92. Fellow TMS, Am. Soc. Metals Internat. (trustee bd., Albert Sauveur Achievement award, Campbell Meml. Lectr.); mem. NAE, Materials Rsch. Soc. (editor symposium volume 1983, organizer symposium Am. Assn. Crystal Growers), Electrochem. Soc. (mem. electronics divsn. 1973-86, divisional editor 1976-86), Minerals, Metals and Materials Soc. (mem. phys. metallurgy com. 1976-83, vice chmn. mech. metallurgy com. 1978-79, mem. 1975-80, mem. electronic materials com. 1990-94, chmn. electronic, magnetic and photonic materials com. 1984-86, tech. dir. bd., John Bardeen award, The Educator award), Sigma Xi. Home: 8824 S Poplar St Tempe AZ 85284-4521 Office: Ariz State U Ira A Fulton Sch Engring Tempe AZ 85287 Home Phone: 480-345-9192; Office Phone: 480-727-9322. Business E-Mail: smahajan@asu.edu.

MAHALAWICH, ANNE MARY, retired mathematics educator; b. Norwich, Conn., Mar. 10, 1922; d. Dimitry and Emilia Pisarko; m. Nicholas Mahalawich, Nov. 24, 1945. BS, Willimantis State Tchrs. Coll., 1943, MS, 1967. Mem. RSVP, 1980—2006; mem. bd. Otis Libr.; pres. Taxpayer's Assn. Mem.: New London Retired Tchrs. (pres.), Norwich Tchrs. League (pres. 1972—73), AARP (pres.), Beta Sigma Phi (Profl. Woman of Yr. 1989), Phi Beta Kappa, Delta Kappa Gamma (pres.). Ea. Orthodox. Home: 7838 Naples Heritage Dr Naples FL 34112 Personal E-mail: amahalawich@aol.com.

MAHALEY-JOHNSON, HOSANNA, school system administrator; b. 1968; 3 children. BA, Marquette U., Milw., 1991; MEd, U. Ill., Chgo.; MBA, Northwestern U. Chief of staff Chgo. Pub. Schools, 2001—07, dir. New Schools Devel., dir. Renaissance 2010 initiative, 2006—07; pres. Atlanta Local Edn. Fund, 2007—. Bd. dirs. City Yr. Chgo.; bd. advisors Chgo. Comty. Trust; bd. dirs. Nat. Assn. Charter Sch. Authorizers. Named one of 40 Under 40, Crain's Chgo. Bus., 2006; fellow Entrepreneurial Leaders for Public Edn. Program, Aspen Inst., 2007. Office: 250 Williams St Ste 2115 Atlanta GA 30303 Office Phone: 773-553-1530. Office Fax: 773-553-2199.

MAHAN, CLARENCE, federal agency administrator, writer; b. Dayton, Ohio, Jan. 1, 1939; s. Clarence Mahan and Elsie (Crouch) Diltz; m. Suky Mahan, May 27, 1962; children: Sean M., Christiane Elizabeth. BA, U. Md., 1963; MA, Am. U., 1968; MBA, Syracuse U., 1969. Dep. comptroller U.S. Army, Japan, 1974-76; dep. chief program and budget Defense Commn. Agy., Arlington, Va., 1976; aide Asst. Sec. Army, Washington, 1976-77; chief operating appropriations Dept. AF, Washington, 1979-80; dir. fin. and acctg. Dept. Energy, Washington, 1980-81, dep. comptroller, 1981-82; dir. fiscal and contracts mgmt. EPA, Washington, 1982-83, dep. comptroller, 1983-85, dir. Rsch. Program Mgmt. Office, 1985-95. Instr., lectr. in field. Author: Classic Irises and the Men and Women Who Created Them, 2007; contbr. articles to profl. jours. and hort. mags. With U.S. Army, 1959-62, Korea. Mem. Am. Iris Soc. (bd. dirs., 2d v.p. 1991-95, 1st. v.p. 1995-98, pres. 1998-2001), Hist. Iris Preservation Soc. (pres. 1991-93), Soc. Japanese Irises (pres. 1989-92), Reblooming Iris Soc. (bd. dirs. 1986-94, pres. 2002-05). Democrat. Home and Office: 7311 Churchill Rd Mc Lean VA 22101-2001 Business E-Mail: cemahan@aol.com.

MAHAN, DAVID JAMES, retired academic administrator; b. St. Louis, May 29, 1934; s. John William and Eleanor (Johnson) M.; m. Jane E. Pyle, Nov. 28, 1957; children: Elizabeth Mahan-Shaw, Kathryn Goodman. BA, Okla. Baptist Coll., 1956; MA, Washington U., St. Louis, 1962, EdD, 1968. Cert. elem., secondary English tchr., Mo., cert. elem. prin., Mo., cert. supt., Mo. Adminstr., tchr. St. Louis Pub. Schs., 1958-90, supt., 1990-96; supt. in residence U. Mo., St. Louis, 1996-99. Co-author: The Faculty Team: School Organization for Results, 1971. Bd. dirs. Commerce and Growth Assn., St. Louis, 1990—, Asthma and Allergy Found. Am., St. Louis, 1990—, St. Louis Symphony Soc., 1992—, Boy Scouts Am., 1992—. Home: 5 Portland Ct Saint Louis MO 63108-1293

MAHAN, HUNTER, professional golfer; b. Orange, May 17, 1982; Student, Okla. State U., Stillwater. Mem. PGA Tour, 2003—. Mem. US Team Presidents Cup, 2007, Ryder Cup, 2008. Recipient Jack Nicklaus award, 2003, Fred Haskins award, 2003; co-recipient Ben Hogan award, 2003. Achievements include winning PGA Tour events: Travelers Championship, 2007; being a member of the Ryder Cup winning US team, 2008. Office: c/o PGA Tour 112 PGA TOUR Blvd Ponte Vedra Beach FL 32082*

MAHAN, JAMES E., archivist, educator; s. Lowell Edward Mahan and Ora Irene Lohmeyer; m. Janet Pike, Aug. 2, 1970; children: Adam, Abby E. Hammar. BA, Wichita State U., Kans., 1969; MS, Emporia State U., Kans., 1974. Prof. Mohave CC, Lake Havasu City, Ariz., 1975—. Bd. edn. Lake Havasu Charter Sch., 2004; sec treas. Lake Havasu Charter Sch., Inc, 2004; judge Brewers Competitions, Lake Havasu City, 2005—08. Home: 2864 Glengarry Dr Lake Havasu City AZ 86404 Office: Mohave CC 1977 W Acoma Blvd Lake Havasu City AZ Business E-Mail: jimmah@mohave.edu.

MAHAN, MARY HOYLE, retired physical educator; b. Boston, July 19, 1939; d. Frederick John and Mary Dwyer Hoyle; m. J. Roger Mahan Jr., Mar. 21, 1970 (dec. June 1999). BS in Phys. Edn., Bridgewater State Coll., 1960; MS in Phys. Edn., U. N.C., 1963; EdD, Nova Southeastern U., 1975. Tchr. phys. edn. Stoughton Jr. High Sch., Mass., 1960—62; tchr. phys. edn., coach Locust Valley Jr./Sr. High Sch., NY, 1963—65; prof. phys. edn., coach Ctrl. Conn. State U., New Britain, 1965—71, Miami-Dade C.C. North, 1971—2001, assoc. athletic dir., dept. chair, prof., ret., 2001; prof. emeritus Miami Dade Coll. CEO, pres. The Teaching Well, Ft. Lauderdale, Fla. Bd. trustees Bridgewater State Coll. Found., Lake Isle Woods Assn., Centerville; edn. found. Villanova U., Pa. Recipient 3 Outstanding Faculty awards, Miami-Dade C.C., Case Prof. of Yr., U. Tex., Endowed Tchg. Chair, Bowden award, Cheshire Acad., NATYCAA Bill Miller award, NAGWS Pathfinder award, Miami Sports Soc., Lifetime of Giving award, Fla. Assn. Health, Phys. Edn., Recreation, and Dance Hon. award, Delta Psi Kappa Alumna of Yr. award, Am. Red Cross Hon. award, Am. Assn. Health, Phys. Edn., Recreation, and Dance Aquatic Hon. award, Bridgewater State Coll. Nat. S. Elizabeth Pope Soc. Chair, Dr.Catherine Cornell Outstanding Alumni award; named Bridgewriter State Coll. Hall Fame, Fla. C.C. Activities Assn. Hall Fame; named to Weymouth High Sch. Hall Fame. Mem.: Nat. Assn. Two Yr. Coll. Athletics Admin., Delta Psi Kappa. Independent.

Roman Catholic. Avocations: golf, interior decorating, travel. Home (Winter): 3750 Galt Ocean Dr #2007 Fort Lauderdale FL 33308 Home (Summer): 30 Crestview Cir Centerville MA 02632

MAHAN, SUSAN THAYER, orthopedist; b. Eugene, Oreg., May 3, 1969; d. Gerald Dennis and Sally Spaugh Mahan; m. Steven John Kirincich; children: Sarah Thayer Kirincich, Abigail Spaugh Kirincich. AB, Harvard and Radcliffe Colls., Cambridge, Mass., 1991; MD, Albany Med. Coll., NY, 1999; MPH, Harvard Sch. Pub. Health, Boston, 2007. Diplomate orthop. surgeon Am. Bd. Orthop. Surgery, 2008. Orthop. surgeon Children's Hosp., Boston, 2005—. Referee USRowing, 1995—2008. Mem.: Alpha Omega Alpha. Achievements include patents for method and apparatus for ultrasound imaging using adaptive gray mapping and automatically adjust contrast in projected ultrasound. Office: Children's Hosp Boston 300 Longwood Ave Boston MA 02115 Business E-Mail: susan.mahan@childrens.harvard.edu.

MAHANEY, JACK, engineering educator; b. San Francisco, Sept. 24, 1949; s. Jack Morris and Jo Ann Mahaney; m. Colleen Hendrix, Mar. 26, 1977; children: Kathryn Leigh, Kristin Lara. BSME, Old Dominion U., Norfolk, Va., 1982, MSc in engring., 1985; PhD, U. Wales Swansea, 2002. Cert. profl. engr., Ga., 1993. Submarine missile technician US Navy, New London, Conn., 1967—78; prof. Mercer U., Macon, Ga., 1985—. Avocations: boating, bagpipes. Business E-Mail: jack.mahaney@mercer.edu.

MAHANEY, MICHAEL C., library director; m. Lee Mahaney; 1 child, Kate. BA with honors, SUNY, Buffalo, MLS with honors, 1976. With Buffalo & Erie County Pub. Libr., NY, 1973—, with Ctrl. Libr. NY, asst. dep. dir. cmty. rels. NY, 1990—2000, dep. dir., COO NY, 2000—02, dir. NY, 2003—. V.p. Explore and More, East Aurora, NY, pres.; bd. trustees NY Ctr. for Books and Reading. Mem. pres.'s adv. coun. Erie CC. Mem.: ALA, NY Libr. Assn. Office: Buffalo & Erie County Pub Libr 1 Lafayette Sq Buffalo NY 14203-1887 Office Phone: 716-858-7179. Office Fax: 716-858-6544. E-mail: mahaneym@buffalolib.org.

MAHANI, MOHAMMAD SHADBAKHT, engineering educator; b. Teheran, Iran; s. Mahmood Shadbakht and Shamsi Torkzad Sanian; children: Mehdi, Bita, Dariush. Degree in mgmt., Air Force Acad., Teheran, 1973; BS, U. Ill., Chgo., 1990; MS, U. Ill., 1991. Rsch. asst. U. Ill., Chgo., 1990—91; educator Wilbur Wright Coll., Chgo., 1991—93; dir., educator Acad. Lang. and Computer Sci., Chgo., 1993—; prof. DeVry U., Chgo., 1998—. Mem.: Alpha Chi Iota (advisor, award 2003), Eta Kappa Nu (award 1999). Achievements include design of unique method of teaching and learning English as a second language. Home: 6534 W Montrose Ave # 1-E Harwood Heights IL 60706 Office: DeVry Univ 3300 N Campbell Ave Chicago IL 60618 Office Phone: 773-777-7797. Business E-Mail: mmahani@devry.edu.

MAHANTHAPPA, KALYANA THIPPERUDRAIAH, physicist, researcher; b. Hirehalli, Mysore, India, Oct. 29, 1934; s. Kalyana and Thippamma (Maddanappa) T.; m. Prameela Talkerappa, Oct. 30, 1961; children: Nagesh, Rudresh, Mahesh. BSc, Central Coll. Bangalore, India, 1954; MSc, Delhi U., 1956; PhD (Faculty Arts and Scis. fellow), Harvard, 1961. Research assoc. U. Cal. at Los Angeles, 1961-63; asst. prof. U. Pa., Phila., 1963-66; mem. Inst. Advanced Study, Princeton, N.J., 1964-65; assoc. prof. physics U. Colo., Boulder, 1966-69, prof., 1969—, faculty research fellow, 1970-71, 76-77, 83-84, 93-94. Vis. prof./scientist U. Rome, 1970, Internat. Ctr. for Theoretical Physics, 1971, Cambridge U., 1976-77; cons. Aerojet-Gen., L.A., 1962-63; dir. Summer Inst. Theoretical Physics, Boulder, 1968-69, NATO Advanced Study Inst. in Elem. Particles, 1979, NATO Advanced Rsch. Workshop on Superstrings, 1987; gen. dir. Theoretical Advanced Study Inst. in Particle Physics, 1989—; sr. vis. rsch. fellow Imperial Coll., London, 1983-84. Contbr. articles to profl. jours. Recipient Rsch. Excellence award, Boulder Faculty Assembly, 2004. Fellow Am. Phys. Soc.; mem. AAAS, Sigma Xi. Achievements include research theoretical high energy and elementary particle physics. Home: 4760 Lee Cir Boulder CO 80303-1111 Office Phone: 303-492-8780. E-mail: ktm@pizero.colorado.edu.

MAHARAJ, DAVAN R., editor; b. 1962; BA in Polit. Sci. & Communications, U. Tenn., 1989; LLM, Yale U. Reporter LA Times, Orange County, Calif., LA, East Africa, asst. fgn. editor, dep. bus. editor, bus. editor, 2007—08, mng. editor, head fgn., nat., metro, sports and bus. depts., 2008—. Co-recipient Ernie Pyle Award for Human Interest Writing, 2005. Office: LA Times 202 W 1st St Los Angeles CA 90012 Office Phone: 213-237-5000. Office Fax: 213-237-7679.

MAHARIDGE, DALE DIMITRO, journalist, educator, writer; b. Cleve., Oct. 24, 1956; s. Steve and Joan (Kopfstein) Maharidge. Student, Cleve. State U., 1974—75. Freelance reporter various publs., Cleve., 1976, Cleve. Plain Dealer, 1978—80; reporter The Gazette, Medina, Ohio, 1977—78, Sacramento Bee, 1980—91; vis. prof. Stanford U., Palo Alto, Calif., 1992—2002; assoc. prof. Columbia U. Grad. Sch. Journalism, NYC, 2002—. Art colony resident Yaddo Residency, 2004, 07, MacDowell Colony, 2006. Author: Journey to Nowhere: The Saga of the New Underclass, 1985, Journey to Nowhere: The Saga of the New Underclass repub. with introduction by Bruce Springsteen, 1996, And Their Children After Them, 1989 (Pulitzer Prize for gen. nonfiction, 1990), The Last Great American Hobo, 1993, The Coming White Minority: California, Multiculturism and the Nation's Future, 1996, The Coming White Minority: California's Eruptions and the Nation's Future, Vintage Books edit., 1999, Homeland, 2004, Denison, Iowa: Searching for the Soul of America Through the Secrets of a Midwest Town, 2005; contbr. articles to profl. jours. Grantee, Open Soc. Inst., 2006; Freedom Forum grantee, 1995, Nieman fellow, Harvard U., 1988, Pope Found. grantee, 1994. Democrat. Office Phone: 212-854-3854. Personal E-mail: dmaharidge@yahoo.com.

MAHER, BILL (WILLIAM MAHER JR.), television personality and producer, comedian; b. NYC, Jan. 20, 1956; s. Bill and Julie (Berman) Maher. BA in English and Hist., Cornell U., NYC, 1978. Host Catch a Rising Star Comedy Club, NYC, 1979; creator, host Politically Incorrect Comedy Central, NYC, 1993-96, ABC, 1996—2002; host Real Time With Bill Maher, HBO, 2003—. Stand-up performances include The Bob Monkhouse Show, Late Night with David Letterman, The Tonight Show, (HBO spls.) One Night Stand, 1989, 1992, Stuff that Struck Me Funny, 1995, The Golden Goose Special, 1997, Be More Cynical, 2000, Victory Begins at Home, 2003, I'm Swiss, 2005, The Decider, 2007, film appearances: DC Cab, 1993, Rags to Riches, 1986, Club Med, 1986, Ratboy, 1986, House II: The Second Story, 1987, Out of Time, 1988, Cannibal Women in the Avocado Jungle of Death, 1989, Pizza Man, 1991, Say What?, 1992, Don't Quit Your Day Job, 1996, Bimbo Movie Bash, 1997, EDtv, 1998, Tomcats, 2001, The Aristocrats, 2005, Swing Vote, 2008, Religulous, 2008, TV appearances: Sara, 1985, Hard Knocks, 1987, Max Headroom, 1987, Murder She Wrote, 1989—90, The Midnight Hour, 1990, Charlie Hoover, 1991, Married With Children, 1992—93, MADtv, 2005, True Blood, 2008, The Man Show; author: True Story: A Novel, 1994, Does Anybody Have a Problem With That? Politically Incorrect's Greatest Hits, 1996, Does Anybody Have a Problem with That? The Best of Politically Incorrect, 1997, When You Ride Alone You Ride With Bin Laden: What the Government Should Be Telling Us to Help Fight the War on Terrorism, 2003, Keep the Statue of Liberty Closed: The New Rules, 2004, New Rules: Polite Musings from a Timid Observer, 2005. Adv. bd. mem. The Reason Project; bd. dirs. PETA. Recipient CableACE award, Nat. Acad. Cable Programming, 1990, CableACE award for best talk show series, 1995, CableACE award for best talk show host, 1995, Pres.'s award for Championing Free Speech, LA Times Press Club, 2002, Johnny Carson Prodr. of Yr. award, Prodrs. Guild of America, 2007; named one of Comedy Central's 100 Greatest Stand-Ups of All Time. Office: Brillstein Grey Entertainment Ste 350 9150 Wilshire Blvd Beverly Hills CA 90212*

MAHER, CORMAC OLIVER, neurosurgeon, pediatrician, researcher; s. Patrick Oliver and Mary Josephine Maher; m. Maya Lind Swenson, June 6, 1998; children: Caroline Loughrey, Oliver Lind, Evelyn Marie. MD, Georgetown U., Washington, DC, 1998. Lic. Minn., 1999, Mass., 2004, Mich., 2006. Neurosurgery resident physician Mayo Clinic, Rochester, Minn., 1998—2004; pediat. neurosurgery fellow Children's Hosp. Boston, Harvard Med. Sch., 2004—05; cerebrovascular neurosurgery fellow Brigham & Women's Hosp., Harvard Med. Sch., 2005—06; faculty pediat. neurosurgeon U. Mich., Ann Arbor. Contbr. scientific papers to profl. jours. Named one of Best Drs. America, 2007. Mem.: AMA, ACS, Alpha Omega Alpha, Congress Neurol. Surgeons, Am. Assn. Neurol. Surgeons (multiple com. memberships and liaison positions 1998). Roman Catholic.

MAHER, DAVID WILLARD, Internet company executive; b. Chgo., Aug. 14, 1934; s. Chauncey Carter and Martha (Peppers) M.; m. Jill Waid Armagnac, Dec. 20, 1954; children: Philip Armagnac, Julia Armagnac. BA, Harvard, 1955, LLB, 1959. Bar: NY 1960, Ill. 1961, Wis. 1996, US Patent Office 1961. Pvt. practice, Boston, NYC, 1958-60; assoc. Kirkland & Ellis, and predecessor firm, 1960-65, ptnr., 1966-78, Reuben & Proctor, 1978-86, Isham, Lincoln and Beale, 1986-88, Sonnenschein, Nath & Rosenthal, Chgo., 1988—2003; ret., 2003; chmn. bd. dirs. Publ. Interest Registry, 2003—04, sr. v.p law and policy, 2004—. Dir. BBB Chgo. and No. Ill., 2004—; lectr. DePaul U. Sch. Law, 1973—79, Loyola U. Law Sch., Chgo., 1980—84. Contbr. articles to profl. jours. Vis. com. U. Chgo. Div. Sch., 1986—. 2nd lt. USAF, 1955—56. Recipient Torch of Integrity award, Better Bus. Bureau, Chgo. and N. Ill., Inc. Fellow Am. Bar Found. (life); mem. ABA, Am. Law Inst., Wis. State Bar, Chgo. Bar Assn., Chgo. Lit. Club. Roman Catholic. Home: 501 N Clinton St Apt 1503 Chicago IL 60654-8886 Office: Pub Interest Registry 1775 Wiehle Ave Ste 102A Reston VA 20190 Office Phone: 312-876-8055. Business E-Mail: dmaher@pir.org.

MAHER, JAMES VINCENT, JR., physics professor, academic administrator; b. NYC, Aug. 25, 1942; s. James Vincent and Anne (Cunneen) M.; m. Angela Beth Braunstein, Aug. 13, 1966; children: Robin, James. BS in Physics, U. Notre Dame, 1964; MS in Physics, Yale U., 1965, PhD in Physics, 1969; PhD honoris causa (hon.), London Met. U., 2007. Postdoctoral fellow Argonne (Ill.) Nat. Lab., 1968-70; asst. prof. U. Pitts., 1970-74, assoc. prof., 1974-80, prof., 1980—, fellow Ctr. for Philosophy of Sci., dept. chair physics and astronomy, 1991-94, provost and sr. vice-chancellor, 1994—. Dir. Scaife nuclear physics lab., 1979-80. Contbr. over 100 articles to profl. jours. Intellectual property task force Assn. Am. Univs., 1998—99; task force on accreditation Nat. Assn. State Univs. and Land Grant Colls., 1997—2000; commr. Mid. States Commn. Higher Edn., 2004—. Grantee Dept. Energy, NSF. Fellow AAAS, Am. Phys. Soc.; mem. Am. Crystal Growth Assn. (pres. Pitts. chpt. 1989-92, exec. com. 1988-93), Sigma Xi. Democrat. Roman Catholic. Home: 1313 Denniston Ave Pittsburgh PA 15217-1330 Office: U Pitts Office of the Provost Pittsburgh PA 15260 Office Phone: 412-624-4223. Business E-Mail: jvmaher@pitt.edu.

MAHER, JOHN M., lawyer; b. Chgo., Sept. 10, 1970; BS magna cum laude, Bradley U., Peoria, Ill., 1992; JD magna cum laude, No. Ill. U. Coll. Law, 1996. Bar: Ill. 1996, DC 2004, US Dist. Ct. (no. and ctrl. dists.) Ill., US Ct. Fed. Claims, US Ct. Internat. Trade, US Army Ct. Criminal Appeals, US Ct. Appeals Armed Forces, US Ct. Appeals (7th and fed. cirs.), US Supreme Ct. Trial counsel, 1st inf. divsn. US Army Judge Advocate Gen.'s Corps, Germany, Macedonia, 1997—2000; trial atty., civil divsn. comml. litig. br. US Dept. Justice, Washington, 2001—04; litig. assoc. Mayer Brown Rowe & Maw LLP, 2004—06; ptnr. Epstein Becker & Green, P.C., 2006—08, Duane Morris LLP, Chgo., 2008, 2009—; gen. counsel US Office Pers. Mgmt., Washington, 2008—09. Former asst. prof. aviation law Embry-Riddle Aeronautical U.; adj. prof. law John Marshall Law Sch., Chgo. Contbr. articles to profl. jours. Serves as maj. US Army JAG Corps Res. Mem.: Ill. State Bar Assn. Office: Duane Morris LLP 190 S LaSalle St Ste 3700 Chicago IL 60603 Office Phone: 312-499-6735. Office Fax: 312-277-2343. Business E-Mail: jnmaher@duanemorris.com.*

MAHER, KATHY, museum director; BA in Art, SUNY, Coll. at Cortland, 1980—84; MA, NYU - Met. Mus. Art, 1989—93. Asst. to prodn. dir. Roman and Tannenholz, 1985—87; asst. dir., cur. Lockwood-Mathews Mansion Mus., 1987—98; cur. Barnum Mus., Bridgeport, Conn., 1999—, exec. dir., 2005—. Chmn. adv. com. Mus. State of Conn.; state del. Preservation Action, Wash., DC. V.p. Conn. Preservation Action, pres. Recipient Award of Excellence, Lower Hudson Conf., State of Conn. Gen. Assembly Official Citation, Conn. House of Representatives. Office: Barnum Mus 820 Main St Bridgeport CT 06604 Business E-Mail: KMaher@barnum-museum.org.

MAHER, L. JAMES, III, molecular biologist; b. Mpls., Nov. 28, 1960; s. Louis James and Elizabeth Jane (Crawford) M.; m. Laura Lee Moseng, July 2, 1983; children: Elizabeth Lillian, Christina Ailene. BS in Molecular Biology, U. Wis., 1983, PhD in Molecular Biology, 1988. Fellow U. Wis., Madison, 1983-84, rsch. asst., 1984-88; postdoctoral fellow Calif. Inst. Tech., Pasadena, 1988-91; asst. prof. molecular biology Eppley Inst., U. Nebr. Med. Ctr., Omaha, 1991-95; assoc. prof. biochem. molecular biology Mayo Clinic Coll. Medicine, Rochester, Minn., 1995-2000, prof., 2000—02, vice chmn., 2002—, assoc. dean for academic affairs, 2003—. Editorial bd. Antisense and Nuclear Acid Drug Design, 1991—, Nucleic Acids Rsch. Jour., 1988—; contbr. articles to profl. jours. Musician, Madison Symphony Orch., 1983-88, Calif. Inst. Tech. Symphony Orch., L.A., 1988-91. Gosney fellow, 1988; Am. Cancer Soc. postdoctoral fellow, 1988. Mem. AAAS, Phi Beta Kappa. Evangelical Christian Ch. Achievements include research in chemical and biochemical agents designed to artificially regulate the flow of genetic information in biological systems. Office: Mayo Clinic Coll Medicine Dept Biochem and Molec Biol 200 1st St SW Rochester MN 55905-0001 Home Phone: 507-287-0275; Office Phone: 507-284-9041. Business E-Mail: maher@mayo.edu.

MAHER, LOUIS JAMES, JR., geologist, educator; b. Iowa City, Iowa, Dec. 18, 1933; s. Louis James and Edith Marie (Ham) M.; m. Elizabeth Jane Crawford, June 7, 1956; children: Louis James, Robert Crawford, Barbara Ruth. BA, U. Iowa, 1955, MS, 1959; PhD, U. Minn., 1961. Mem. faculty dept. geology and geophysics U. Wis.-Madison, 1962—, prof., 1970—2003, chmn. dept., 1980-84, prof. emeritus, 2003—. Contbr. articles to profl. jours. With US Army, 1956—58, with counter intelligence corps US Army, 1957—58, Duty Sta., La Rochelle, France. Danforth fellow, 1955-61; NSF fellow, 1959-61; NATO fellow, 1961-62 Fellow AAAS, Geol. Soc. Am.; mem. Am. Quaternary Assn., Ecol. Soc. Am., Wis. Acad. Sci., Arts and Letters, Sigma Xi. Episcopalian. Office: U Wis Dept Geology and Geoph 1215 W Dayton St Madison WI 53706-1600 Office Phone: 608-262-9595. Business E-Mail: maher@geology.wisc.edu.

MAHER, THOMAS GEORGE, academic administrator, producer, media educator; b. St. Louis, Feb. 18, 1947; s. Dale Russell and Dorothy Leone M.; m. (div.). AB, St. Louis U., 1969, MA, 1971; PhD, U. So. Calif., 1985. Cert. C.C. tchr. and supr., Calif. Tchg. fellow St. Louis U., 1969-71; assoc. prof. Chaffey Coll., Rancho Cucamonga, Calif., 1974-79, media dir., 1980-84; assoc. producer Corp. for C.C. TV, Orange, Calif., 1979-80; assoc. dir. instrnl. tech. Calif. State Poly. U., Pomona, 1984-89; dir. office media svcs. U. Ill., Chgo., 1989-94; dir. office instrnl. svcs. Colo. State U., Ft. Collins, 1994—2006, interim v.p. divsn. ednl. outreach, 2000—02, dir. ebs and digital media, 2006—. Cons. Rsch. Comm., Ltd., Boston, 1984-94; book reviewer Focal Press, Inc., Boston, 1985-94. Writer: (TV series) Project: Universe, 1978 (Emmy award nomination 1979), The Business of Management, 1981; assoc. producer, dir., writer (TV series) Oceanus: The Marine Environment, 1979 (Emmy award 1980); exec. producer (TV program) For the People: Local Gov. Budget Making, 1992 (Cert. Merit, Chgo. Internat. Film/Video Festival 1992); producer, dir. (live nat. video teleconference, moderated by Sen. Bill Bradley) Campus Line-up with Carol Moseley Braun, 1992; instrnl. designer (interactive videodisc) Smog Check Multimedia Simulation Test, 1993 (INVISION Merit award, NewMedia Multimedia awards, 1993); prodr., dir. numerous additional refereed ednl. TV shows, 1974—. 1st lt. USAF, 1971-74. Grantee Air Force, 1967-69; Mary Clemmens scholarship St. Louis U., 1965-67, Educare scholar U. So. Calif., 1983-84; grantee numerous competitive contracts. Mem. Acad. TV Arts and Scis. (judge coll. Emmy awards, 1989), Am. Ednl. Research Assn., Assn. for Ednl. Comm. and Tech, Alpha Sigma Nu, Psi Chi. Democrat. Roman Catholic. Avocations: reading, computers, running, theater, piano. Office: Colorado State U Mail Stop 1018 Fort Collins CO 80523-1018 Home Phone: 970-568-3777; Office Phone: 970-491-3315. Business E-Mail: thomas.maher@colostate.edu.

MAHER, VIRGINIA JONES, art historian, educator; b. Milw., Oct. 11, 1941; d. Frederick Thomas Murphy and Virginia June Harmon; m. William H. Jones, Aug. 22, 1964 (dec. Nov. 23, 1982); children: William H. Jones Jr., Michael J. Jones, Megan Jones Townsend; m. J. Thomas Maher, III, May 14, 1994. BS, U. Wis., Milw., 1964, MA in Art History, 1994, cert. art mus. studies, 1994. Tchr. French and English Custer HS, Milw., 1964; curatorial asst. Kohler Art Ctr., Sheboygan, Wis., 1993; curator fine arts commn. Cathedral of St. John, Milw., 1995—2003; instr. art history Cardinal Stritch U., Milw., 1997—99, Peninsula Sch. Art, Fish Creek, Wis., 2001—; lectr. art history Milw. Art Mus., 2004—. Guest art curator Miller Art Mus., Sturgeon Bay, Wis., 2000—; bd. dirs. Peninsula Sch. Art, chmn. acquisitions com., 2002—, dir. Madeline Tourtelot Archives, 2007—; lectr. in field. Organizer Friends of Art History, Milw., 2000—03; hist. preservation Jr. League Evanston, Ill., 1980—81, lectr. art in the sch., 1978—80; mem. dean's adv. com. Inst. Visual Arts U. Wis. Milw., 2004; bd. dirs. Wis. Heritages Inc., Milw., 1996—99, Am. Heritage Soc. Milw. Art Mus., 1994—98. Recipient Grad. of Last Decade (G.O.L.D.) award, U. Wis., Milw., 2000; named Writer of Yr. award, Metalsmith Mag., 1998. Mem.: Nat. Mus. Women in Arts, Collectors' Corner Milw. Art Mus., Contemporary Art Soc. Milw. Art Mus., Womans Club Wis., Alpha Phi. Roman Catholic. Avocations: art collecting, painting, gardening. Home: 5611 Schauer Rd Sturgeon Bay WI 54235 Personal E-mail: vmaher@itol.com.

MAHERAS, THOMAS G., former diversified financial services company executive; b. Chgo., Nov. 25, 1962; BBA in Fin., U. Notre Dame, 1984. Various positions including head mortgage-backed securities, head high yield trading desk Salomon Smith Barney (Citigroup), 1984—96, vice chmn., head global fixed income, 1996—2004; CEO global capital markets, global corp. & investment banking group Citigroup Inc., NYC, 2004—06, co-pres. global corp. & investment banking group, 2007, co-chmn., co-CEO Citi Markets & Banking, 2007. Mem. borrowing adv. com. US Dept. Treasury. Mem.: Bond Market Assn. (bd. dirs., mem. exec. com.).

MAHERN, BRIAN, Councilman; Grad., Ind. U., Bloomington. Mem. Ind. Utility Regulatory Commn.; councillor, dist. 16 Indpls.-Marion County City-County Coun., 2007—. Democrat. Mailing: PO Box 2412 Indianapolis IN 46206 Office: 241 City-County Bldg 200 E Washington St Indianapolis IN 46204 Office Phone: 317-331-5011, 317-327-4242. Office Fax: 317-327-4230. Business E-Mail: brian@mahern.net.*

MAHERN, DANE, councilman; Grad., Ball State U., Muncie, Ind., 1994. Councillor, dist. 19 Indpls.-Marion County City-County Coun., 2003—. Chmn. met. devel. com. Indpls.-Marion County City-County Coun. Mem. grant bd. Indpls. Downtown, Inc. Democrat. Office: Indpls Marion County City County Coun 241 City Coun Bldg 200 E Washington St Indianapolis IN 46204 also: 2313 S Garfield DR Indianapolis IN 46203-4218 Office Phone: 317-506-2707, 317-327-4242. Business E-Mail: dmmahern@hotmail.com.*

MAHESH, VIRENDRA BHUSHAN, endocrinologist; b. India, Apr. 25, 1932; came to U.S., 1958, naturalized, 1968; s. Narinjan Prasad and Sobhagyawati; m. Sushila Kumari Aggarwal, June 29, 1955; children: Anita Rani, Vinit Kumar. BSc with honors, Patna U., India, 1951; MSc in Chemistry, Delhi U., India, 1953, PhD, 1955; DPhil in Biol. Sci, Oxford U., 1958. James Hudson Brown Meml. fellow Yale U., 1958-59; asst. rsch. prof. endocrinology Med. Coll. Ga., Augusta, 1959-63, assoc. rsch. prof., 1963-66, prof., 1966-70, Regents prof., 1970-86, Robert B. Greenblatt prof., 1979-99, chmn. endocrinology, 1972-86, chmn., Regents prof. physiology and endocrinology, 1986-99, chmn. physiology and endocrinology, 1986-99, regents prof., chmn. emeritus physiology and endocrinology, 1999—, Robert B. Greenblatt prof. emeritus endocrinology, 1999—. Dir. Ctr. for Population Studies, 1971-99; mem. reproductive biology study sect. NIH, 1977-81, mem. human embryology and devel. study sect. NIH, 1982-86, 90-93, chmn., 1991-93. Contbr. articles to profl. jours., chpts. to books; editor: The Pituitary, a Current Review, Functional Correlates of Hormone Receptors in Reproduction, Recent Advances in Fertility Research, Hirsuitism and Virilism, Regulation of Ovarian and Testicular Function, Excitatory Amino Acids: Their Role in Neuroendocrine Function; mem. editl. bd. Steroids, 1963—, Jour. of Clin. Endocrinology and Metabolism, 1976-81, Jour. Steroid Biochemistry and Molecular Biology, 1991—, Assisted Reproductive Tech./Andrology, 1993-98, Endocrinology, 1999-2003; mem. adv. bd. Maturitas, 1977-81; editor-in-chief Biology of Reprodn., 1999-2004, cons. editor, 2004-09. Recipient Rubin award Am. Soc. Study Sterility, 1962, Billings Silver medal, 1965, Best Tchr. award freshman class Sch. Medicine, Med. Coll. Ga., 1969, Outstanding Faculty award Sch. Medicine, 1992, Outstanding Faculty award Sch. Grad. Studies, 1981, 94, Disting. Tchg. award, 1988, Excellence in Rsch.

award Grad. Faculty Assembly, 1987-91, 93-95, Disting. Scientist award Assn. Scientist Indian Origin in Am., 1989, Lifetime Achievement award Sch. Medicine, 1997, Lifetime Achievement award Med.Coll. Ga. Rsch. Inst., 2006; rsch. grantee NIH, 1960-2000. Mem. Fedn. Am. Soc. Exptl. Biology (bd. dirs. 2004-07, 2008-), AAUP, Chem. Soc. (Eng.), Soc. Biochem. and Molecular Biol., Soc. Neurosci., Endocrine Soc., Soc. for Gynecologic Investigation, Internat. Soc. Neuroendocrinology, Soc. for Study Reproduction (Carl G. Hartman award 1996, Disting. Svc. award 2005), Am. Physiol. Soc. (chmn. endocrinology and metabolism sect. 2004-06), Internat. Soc. Reproductive Medicine (pres. 1980-82), Soc. Exptl. Biology and Medicine, Am. Fertility Soc., Am. Assn. Lab. Animal Sci., NY Acad. Scis., Sigma Xi. Business E-Mail: vmahesh@mail.mcg.edu.

MAHESHWARI, ADITYA V., orthopedist, educator; s. Vikram Bhan and Sushila Maheshwari; m. Nilima Maheshwari, Dec. 10, 2000; children: Eish, Krish. MS in Orthop., MAMC, New Delhi, MBBS, 1998, PGDPHA. Sr. resident Apollo Hosp., New Delhi, 2003—04, U. Delhi, 2004—05; fellow Dorr Arthritis Inst., Inglewood, Calif., U. Miami, Fla., 2006—07, Lenox Hill Hosp., NYC, 2007—08, U. Minn., Mpls., 2008—. Lectr. Jamia Hamdard U., New Delhi, 2003—04. Contbr. articles to presentation (SICOT/SIROT, 2005). Several Nat. Health Programs, New Delhi, 1992—2005. Recipient Best paper award, Delhi Orthop. Assn., 2003; rsch. fellowship, Dorr Arthritis Inst., 2006, U. Miami, 2007, Lenox Hill Hosp., 2008, U. Minn., 2008. Mem.: Indian Orthop. Assn. (life). Office: Orthops Univ Minn 2512 S 7th St Minneapolis MN 55454 Personal E-mail: adityavikramm@gmail.com.

MAHEY, JOHN ANDREW, retired museum director; b. DuBois, Pa., Mar. 30, 1932; s. Manasseh A. and Bernyce (Holdar) M. Student, Columbia U., 1950-52; BA, Pa. State U., 1959, MA, 1962. Asst. dir. Peale Mus., Balt., 1964-69; dir. E.B. Crocker Art Gallery, 1969-72, Cummer Gallery of Art, 1972-75, Meml. Art Gallery of U. Rochester, 1975-79; chief curator Philbrook Art Center, Tulsa, 1979-84; dir. San Antonio Mus. Art, 1984-89, Flint (Mich.) Inst. of Arts, 1989-96; ret., 1996. Contbr. articles on artists to art his. jours.; author exhbn. catalogs. Fulbright scholar, 1962 Mem. Phi Beta Kappa, Phi Alpha Theta. Home: 4645 N Progress Ave Harrisburg PA 17119 also: 3525 Canby St Apt 237 Harrisburg PA 17109 E-mail: mahey@aol.com.

MAHITAB, FRANK, librarian, director; m. Paula Bloodworth; 1 child, Immy Bloodworth. MLS, Clark Atlanta U., Ga. Coord. pub. svcs. Ft. Valley State U., Ga., 2002—04, interim libr. dir., 2004—. Office: Fort Valley State Univ Hunt Libr 1005 State Univ Dr Fort Valley GA 31030 Office Fax: 478-825-6663. Business E-Mail: mahitabf@fvsu.edu.

MAHLE, CHRISTOPH ERHARD, electrical engineer; b. Stuttgart, Germany, Mar. 7, 1938; came to U.S., 1968; s. Ernst Johannes and Else (Wurth) M.; m. Mary Heavenrich, Mar. 23, 1975; children: Lisa, Charles. Diploma engring., Swiss Fed. Inst. Polytech., Zurich, 1961, D of Sci. Tech., 1966. Rsch. asst. Swiss Fed. Inst. Tech., Zurich, Switzerland, 1961-67; with tech. staff Comsat Labs., Clarksburg, Md., 1968-71, sect. head, 1971-73, dept. mgr., 1973-81, dir., 1981-83, exec. dir., 1983-94, v.p., 1995-96; ret., 1996. Patentee in field; contbr. articles to profl. jours. Fellow IEEE. Avocations: music, mountain climbing. E-mail: chrismahle@usa.net.

MAHLE, WILLIAM T., pediatric cardiologist, educator; b. Nov. 19, 1966; Grad., Yale U., 1989; MD, U. Md. Sch. Medicine, 1993. Cert. Pediatrics, Pediatric Cardiology, Nat. bd. Med. Examiners. Resident, pediatrics Children's Hosp. Phila., 1993—96, fellow, pediatric cardiology, 1996—99; pediatric cardiologist, Sibley Heart Ctr. Cardiology Children's Healthcare Atlanta; assoc. prof. pediatrics Emory U. Sch. Medicine. Contbr. articles to profl. jours. Mem.: Am. Heart Assn., Am. Coll. Cardiology, Am. Acad. Pediatrics, Alpha Omega Alpha (v.p. 1992). Mailing: Childrens Healthcare Atlanta The McGill Bldg 2835 Brandywine Rd Ste 300 Atlanta GA 30341 Office: Childrens Healthcare Atlanta 790 Church St Ste 150 Marietta GA 30060 Office Phone: 404-256-2593. Office Fax: 678-547-9410.

MAHLENDORF, URSULA RENATE, literature educator; b. Strehlen, Silesia, Germany, Oct. 24, 1929; arrived in US, 1953; Student, Oberschule an der Hamburgerstraße, Bremen, Fed. Republic Germany, 1950, U. Tübingen, Fed. Republic Germany, 1950-52, Brown U., Providence, 1953-57, MA in English Lit., 1956, PhD in German Lit., 1958; student, Bonn U., Fed. Republic Germany, 1953, London U.; grad., New Directions in Psychoanalysis, Washington, 2002. Teaching asst. Brown U., Providence, 1953-57; from acting instr. to prof. German U. Calif., Santa Barbara, 1957—93, prof. women's studies, 1988—93, assoc. dir., campus coord. edn. abroad program, 1967—69, chmn. dept. Germanic and Slavic langs. and lits., 1980-83, assoc. dean Coll. Letters and Sci., 1986-89, emeritus, 1993—. Chmn. symposium in honor of Harry Slochower, 1977; campus coord. edn. abroad program U. Calif., 1967-69, assoc. dir., 1969-72; co-chair Nietzsche symposium Dept. Germanic and Slavic Langs. and Lits., U. Calif., Santa Barbara, 1981; Dickson Emeniti prof., 2009-. Author: The Wellsprings of Literary Creation, 1985; editor: (with John L. Carleton) Man for Man: A Multi-Disciplinary Workshop on Affecting Man's Social and Psychological Nature through Community Action (Charles C. Thomas), 1973, Dimensions of Social Psychiatry, 1979, (with Arthur Lerner) Life Guidance through Literature, 1992, The Shame of Survival: Working Nazi a Negi Childhood, 2009; assoc. editor Am. Imago, Am. Jour. Social Psychiatry, Jour. Evolutionary Psychology; contbr. more than 90 articles to profl. jours. Recipient Alumni Tchg. award, 1981; rsch. grantee, U. Calif., 1974—, Fulbright fellow, 1951—52, Festschrift named in her honor, Calif., 2004. Mem. MLA, Am. Assn. for Aesthetics and Art Criticism (past pres. Calif. div.), Assn. for applied Psychoanalysis (profl. mem.), Am. Assn. Social Psychiatry (councillor 1977-81), Internat. Assn. Social Psychiatry (treas. 1978-83) MLA, GSA, Women in German. Avocations: sculpting, woodcarving. Office: U Calif Dept Germanic Semitic Slavic Studies Santa Barbara CA 93106 Office Phone: 805-893-2131. Business E-Mail: mahlendo@gss.ucsb.edu.

MAHLER, HALFDAN THEODOR, physician, health organization executive; b. Vivild, Denmark, Apr. 21, 1923; s. Magnus and Benedicte (Suadicani) M.; m. Ebba Fischer-Simonsen, Aug. 31, 1957; children: Per Bo, Finn. MD, U. Copenhagen, 1948, degree in pub. health; LLD (hon.), U. Nottingham, Eng., 1975; MD (hon.), Karolinska Inst., Stockholm, 1977; Docteur, U. Scis. Sociales de Toulouse, France, 1977; DPH (hon.), Seoul Nat. U., 1979; ScD (hon.), U. Lagos, Nigeria, 1979, Emory U., 1989; MD (hon.), Warsaw Med. Acad., 1980; LHD (hon.), U. Nat. Federico Villareal, Lima, Peru, 1980, U. Gand, Belgium, 1983, CUNY, 1989; MD (hon.), Charles U., Prague, 1982, Mahidol U., Bangkok, Thailand, 1982, Aarhus U., Denmark, 1988, U. Copenhagen, 1988, Aga Khan U., Pakistan, 1989; LHD (hon.), U. Nat. Autonoma de Nicaragua, 1983; PhD (hon.), Semmelweis U., Budapest, Hungary, 1987; LLD (hon.), McMaster U., Can., 1989; DSc (hon.), SUNY, 1990; MD (hon.), U. Newcastle Upon Tyne, 1990; LLD (hon.), U. Exeter, 1990, U. Toronto, 1990; DPH (hon.), U. Goteborg, 2005. Specialized tng. in TB; active field of internat. pub. health work; planning officer mass Tb campaign Ecuador, 1950-51; sr. officer nat. Tb program WHO, India, 1951-61, chief Tb unit, Hdqrs., Geneva, 1962-69, sec. to expert adv. panel on Tb, 1962-69, dir. project systems analysis, 1969-70, asst. dir.-gen. div. health services and div. family health, 1970-73, dir.-gen., 1973-88, dir. gen. emeritus, 1988; sec. gen. Internat. Planned Parenthood Fedn., 1989-95. Contbr. articles to profl. jours. Decorated Grand Officier de l'Ordre Nat. du Benin, 1975, Grand Officier de l'Ordre Nat. du Voltaique, Upper Volta, 1978, comdr. de l'Ordre Nat. du Mali, 1982, Grand Officer de l'Ordre du Merite de la Rep. du Senegal, 1982, comdr. 1st class Order White Rose (Finland), Grand Officier de l'Ordre nat. malgache, Madagascar, 1987, Grand Cross Icelandic Order of the Falcon, 1988, Grand Cordon of Order Sacred Treasure, Japan, 1988, Bourgeoisie d'Honneur, Geneva, Switzererland, Grand Croix De L'Ordre De Merite, Luxenbourg, 1990, Grand Cross Ordem do Merito Medico, Brazil, 2003; recipient Jana Evangelisty Purkyne medal (Presdl. award) Prague, 1974, Comenius U. Gold medal Bratislava, 1974, Carlo Forlanini gold medal Federazione Italiana contro la Tubercolosi et le Malattie Polmonari Sociali Rome, 1975, Ernest Carlsens Found. Prize Copenhagen, 1980, Georg Barfred-Pedersen prize Copenhagen, 1982, Hagedorn medal and prize Denmark, 1986, Freedom From Want medal Roosevelt Inst., 1988, Storkors Af Dannebrogsordenen, Denmark, 1988; hon. prof. U. Nat. Mayor de San Marcos, Lima, Peru, U. Chile Faculty of Medicine, Beijing Med. Coll., Rep. of China, Shanghai Med. U.; Bartel World Affairs fellow Cornell U., 1988; U.N. Population award, 1995, Andrija Stampar award, 1995. Fellow Royal Coll. Physicians (London), Faculty Community Medicine of Royal Colls. Physicians U.K. (hon.), Indian Soc. for Malaria and other Communicable Diseases (hon.), Royal Soc. Medicine (London) (hon., U.K.-U.S. Hewitt award 1992), London Sch. Hygiene and Tropical Medicine (hon.); mem. Med. Assn. Argentina (hon.), Latin Am. Med. Assn. (hon.), Italian Soc. Tropical Medicine (hon.), Belgium Soc. Tropical Medicine (assoc.), Societe medicale de Geneve (hon.), Union Internat. contre la Tuberculose (hon.), Soc. Francaise d'Hygiene, de Medecine sociale et de Genie sanitaire (hon.), Uganda Med. Assn. (hon. life), Coll. Physicians and Surgeons, Bangladesh Royal Coll. Gen. Practitioners (ad eundem), List of Honour of the Internat. Dental Fedn., Am. Pub. Health Assn. (hon.), Nat. Acad. Medicine Mex. (hon.), Nat. Acad. Buenos Aires (hon.), Swedish Soc. Medicine (hon.), Brit. Medal Assn. (hon. fgn. corr. 1990), Inst. Medicine (NAS U.S.A.). Achievements include research in epidemiology and control of Tb, polit., social, econ, and technol. priorities in health sector, application of systems analysis to health care problems. Home and Office: Chemin de Pont-Céard 12 CH-1290 Versoix Switzerland Office Fax: 022 755 26 10. Business E-Mail: halfdan.mahler@bluewin.ch.

MAHLER, JASON M., legislative staff member; b. Hastings, Mich., July 8, 1965; m. Kimber Colton, June 30, 2001. AB, Duke U., Durham, NC, 1987; JD, U. NC, Chapel Hill, 1990. Bar: NC 1990, DC 1991. Assoc. Krivit & Krivit, 1992—93; legis. asst. and fellow for Senator Frank R. Lautenberg US Senate, Washington, 1994—95; legis. asst. and counsel for Rep. Zoe Lofgren US House of Reps., 1995—99, chief of staff for Rep. Anna G. Eshoo, 2003—; v.p. and gen. counsel Computer and Comm. Industry Assn., 1999—2003. Mem.: Sigma Alpha Epsilon. Presbyterian. Office: Office of Congresswoman Anna G Eshoo 205 Cannon House Office Bldg Washington DC 20515 Office Phone: 202-225-8104. Business E-Mail: jason.mahler@mail.house.gov.*

MAHLER, RONALD PAXTON SHEETS, engineer, mathematician; b. Great Falls, Mont., Aug. 15, 1948; s. Paxton Bowers and Edna Annabelle Sheets; m. Sue Ellen Cassel, Sept. 24, 1988 (div. Nov. 17, 2005); m. Deborah Jane Schreiber, Aug. 11, 1974 (div. Aug. 12, 1980). BA in Math., U. Chgo., 1970; PhD, Brandeis U., Waltham, Mass., 1974; BEE, U. Minn., Mpls., 1980. Sr. staff rsch. scientist Lockheed Martin Corp., Eagan, Minn., 1980—; asst. prof. math. U. Minn., Mpls., 1974—79. Author: (book) Statistical Multisource-Multitarget Information Fusion (Joseph Mignogna Data Fusion award, 2007); co-author: Mathematics of Data Fusion; co-editor: Random Sets: Theory and Practice; contbr. articles to profl. jours. (IEEE AESS Harry Rowe Mimno award, 2008). Recipient Author of Yr. award, Lockheed Martin Corp., 2004, 2008. Dfl. Achievements include patents for fuzzy logic classification system.

MAHLKE, AMY GERILYN, pre-school teacher; b. Winona, Minn., Jan. 21, 1959; d. Alan Eugene and Barbara Ann (Lelwica) Smith; m. David Allen Mahlke II; children: Katherine, David III. Student, Coll. St. Teresa, Winona, 1977-78; BS in Elem. Edn., Winona State U., 1982. Cert. tchr., Minn. Interim tchr. Jefferson Elem. Sch., Winona, 1985; tchr. learning disabled students Goodview Elem. Sch., Winona, 1985-86; tchr. of mildly handicapped Burlington Elem. Sch., Billings, Mont., 1986-88; tchr. Kid Kollege Preschool, Billings, 1988—. Mem. Mont. Edn. Assn. Republican. Roman Catholic. Avocations: cross country skiing, needlecrafts. Office: Kid Kollege Preschool PO Box 50232 Billings MT 59105-0232 Address: 2367 Maria Rd Winona MN 55987-9124

MAHMOOD, ARSHAD, former academic administrator; b. Pakistan, Aug. 10, 1940; married; 3 children. Student, Govt. Coll., Lahore, 1958—61; grad., Command and Staff Coll., Quetta, 1974; MSc in War studies, Quaid-e-Azam Univ., MSc in Def. and Strategies studies. Mng. dir., Overseas Employment Corp. and dir. gen., Emigration and Overseas Employment Bur., 1998—99; vice chancellor Punjab Univ., Pakistan, 1999—2008. Head Army Adv. Team to Qatar, 1985—87. Lt. gen. Pakistani Army (ret.). Decorated Sitara-i-Juraat for gallantry, Hilal-i-Imtiaz for meritorious svc. Avocation: cricket.

MAHMOOD, KHALID, civil engineer, researcher, consultant, educator; b. Lahore, Pakistan, July 13, 1943; s. Mahmood Ahmed Mahmood and Zahur Jehan Begum; m. Nasreen Khalid, Sept. 23, 1973; children: Bilal Khalid, Talal Khalid, Ammarah Khalid, Ammar Khalid. PhD, U. of NSW, Sydney, Australia, 1969—72; BSc (Civil Engring.), U. of Engring. & Tech., Lahore, Pakistan, 1961—65. Professional engineer, Pakistan Engring. Coun., Islamabad, 1982. Prof. of civil engring. King Abdulaziz U., Jeddah, Saudi Arabia, 1985—, U. of Engring. & Tech., Lahore, Pakistan, 1979—85. Cons. (structures and constrn.) Projects Directorate, King Abdulaziz U., Jeddah, Saudi Arabia, 1993—; project dir. (buildings & works) U. of Engring. & Tech., Lahore, Pakistan, 1981—85. Author: (journal paper) ACI Structural Journal, American Concrete Institute, Detroit, Michigan, Structural Engineering International, International Association for Bridge and Structural Engineering, Zurich, Structural Engineering and Mechanics - An International Journal, Taejon, Korea. Scholar Commonwealth scholarship, Australian Govt., 1969-1972. Fellow: Internat. Assn. for Bridge and Structural Engring., Zurich, Switzerland; mem.: Am. Concrete Inst., Detroit, Mich. Office: Univ of South Asia Tufail Road (Lahore Cantt) Lahore Pakistan

MAHMOOD, NAFEESA F., physician, consultant; MD, Punjab U., Lahore, Pakistan. Lic. Nat. Bd. Med. Examiners; cert. personal trainer Am. Coun. Exercise. Faculty, staff physician U. Minn., Mpls.; cons. internal medicine Mayo Clinic Outreach, Rochester, Minn.; med. dir., CEO, pres. New You Med. Aesthetics, LLC, St. Paul. Academic faculty, staff physician U. Ill., Urbana-Champaign, adviser, preceptor, clin. instructor, Chgo.; genomics liason Mayo Clinic, spkr. women's seminars in hypertention. Contbr. articles to profl. jours. Recipient Shield Healing Skills From God award, U. Ill. dept. medicine, Outstanding Clinician for Oustanding Diagnostic Skills & Clin. Achievement award, Certificate Commendation For Outstanding Clin. Performance award, U. Ill. dept. internal medicine. Mem.: Am. Soc. Laser Medicine and Surgery, Day Spa Assn., Am. Coll. Sports Medicine, ACP, Aerobics and Fitness Assn. of Am. (assoc.), Am. Acad. Aesthetic Medicine (assoc. Mem.), Am. Acad. Anti Aging Medicine (assoc. Membership), Am. Acad. Cosmetic Surgery (assoc.). Achievements include research in angiotensin II and amiodarone induced apoptosis of type 2 alveolar epithelail cells, duet to blockade of AT1 receptors by losartan and L compound. Avocations: jogging, exercise, reading, music, baking.

MAHMOODI, HAMID, engineer; s. Teimoor Mahmoodi and Fatemeh Dehghan. BSEE, Iran U. Sci. and Tech., 1998; MS in Elec. and Computer Engring., U. Tehran, 2000; PhD in elec. and computer engring., Perdue U., West Lafayette, Ind., 2005. Asst. prof. San Francisco State U., 2005—. Author: (tech. jour. paper) Estimation of Delay Variations Due to Random-Dopant Fluctuations in Nanoscale CMOS Circuits. Recipient Best Paper award, Internat. Conf. on Computer Design, 2004. Mem.: CICC, Tech. Program Com., ISQED Conf., IEEE. Achievements include patents for sense amplifier circuit; design of one delay fault testing technique using first level supply gating; research in low power, robust and high performance circuit design in nano-scaled technologies, low power and robust memory design, circuit design with nano-scaled devices. Avocations: swimming, travel. Office: 1600 Holloway Ave San Francisco CA 94132 Business E-Mail: mahmoodi@ecn.purdue.edu, mahmoodi@sfsu.edu.

MAHMOODI, SEYED NIMA, engineering educator; b. Tehran, Iran, June 30, 1975; s. Seyed Mohammad Naser and Mina Mahmoodi; m. Sahar Tabatabaei Sadeghi. PhD, Clemson U., SC, 2007. Rschr. Niroo Rsch. Inst., Tehran, 1998—2002; rsch. asst. Clemson U., 2004—07, postdoctrate, 2007—08; vis. asst. prof. Va. Tech, Blacksburg, 2008—. Contbr. articles to profl jours. Tchg. fellowship, Clemson U., 2006—07. Mem.: IEEE, ASME, SPIE. Achievements include research in nonlinear vibrations of nanomechanical cantilever beam sensors. Office: Ctr Vehicle Sys & Safety 3103 Commerce St Blacksburg VA 24061 Office Fax: 540-231-0730. Personal E-mail: mahmoodi@gmail.edu. Business E-Mail: mahmoodi@vt.edu.

MAHMOODIAN, ROZA, research scientist; BSc, U. Tehran, 2004; MSc, U. Va., Charlottesville, 2006; PhD student, Drexel U., Phila., 2006—. Contbr. articles to profl. sci. jours. Mem.: ASME, Internat. Soc. Biomechanics.

MAHMOODZADEGAN, NAVID A., investment banker; b. 1969; JD, Harvard U. Assoc., corp. securities dept. Irell & Manella Law; assoc. to ptnr., tech. group Donaldson, Lufkin & Jenrette, 1995; exec. dir., media and tech. Credit Suisse First Boston; head, media investment banking UBS Warburg, LA, 2000—06, global head, media investment banking, 2006—. Recipient Rainmaker Prize in media investment banking, Dealmaker mag., 2006. Office: UBS Media Investment Banking 1999 Ave of Stars Los Angeles CA 90067 Office Phone: 310-556-6700.

MAHMOUD, ADEL A., physician, molecular biologist, educator; b. Cairo, Aug. 24, 1941; arrived in US, 1972; s. Abdel Fattah and Fathia (Osman) Mahmoud; m. Sally L. Hodder, Jan. 31, 1993. Grad., Cairo U., 1958, MD, 1963; PhD, U. London, 1971. Asst. lectr. Ain Shams U., Cairo, 1965—68; WHO fellow U. London, 1969—72; rsch. assoc., prof. Case Western Res. U., Cleve., 1973—87, prof., chmn. dept. medicine, 1987—98; physician-in-chief Univ. Hosps., Cleve., 1987—98; pres. vaccines Merck & Co. Inc., Whitehouse Sta., NJ, 1998—2006; prof. dept. molecular biology and Woodrow Wilson Sch. Princeton U., 2007—. Editor: The Eosinophil in Health and Disease, 1979, Tropical and Geographical Medicine, 1990, Schistosomaisis, Tropical Medicine Sci. and Practice, Vol. 1, 2001, Biological Threats and Terrorism: Assessing the Science and Response Capabilities, 2002. Fellow: Infectious Diseases Soc. Am.; mem.: Inst. Medicine, Assn. Am. Physicians, Am. Soc. Clin. Investigations. Office: Princeton Univ 228 Lewis Thomas Lab Princeton NJ 08544 Office Phone: 609-258-8557. Business E-Mail: amahmoud@princeton.edu.

MAHMOUD, ALY AHMED, electrical engineering educator; b. Cairo, Jan. 25, 1935; came to U.S., 1960, naturalized, 1970; s. Ahmed Aly and Amina Mohammed (Rashwan) M.; m. Lucinda Lou Keller, Dec. 20, 1962; children: Ramy, Samy. B.Sc. with distinction and honors (Nat. Honor student), Ain Shams U., Cairo, 1958; MS, Purdue U., 1961, PhD, 1964. Diplomate: Registered profl. engr., Iowa, La. Instr. elec. engring. Ain Shams U., 1958-60; asst. prof. elec. engring. U. N.B., Fredericton, 1964; research engr. No. Electric Research and Devel. Lab., Ottawa, Ont., Can., summer 1964; asst. prof. elec. engring. U. Asyut, Egypt, 1964-66; sr. research elec. engr. Naval Civil Engring. Lab., Port Hueneme, Calif., 1968-69, summer 1970; asst. prof. elec. engring. U. Mo., Columbia, 1966-71, assoc. prof., 1971-73, prof., 1973-76; prof. elec. engring., dir. Iowa test and evaluation facility, program mgr. Power Affiliates Research Program; supr. Power System Computer Service, Iowa State U., Ames, 1976-85; dean Coll. Engring. U. New Orleans, 1985-88; dean Sch. Engring. and Tech. Ind. U.-Purdue U.-at Ft. Wayne, 1988—. With FPC, summer 1974; program mgr. NSF, 1975-76; cons. in field. Contbr. articles to profl. jours. Vice chmn. Water and Light Adv. Bd. City of Columbia, 1973-76. Am. Friends of Middle East fellow, 1960-68 Sr. mem. IEEE; Mem. Power Engring. Soc., Am. Phys. Soc., Egyptian Profl. Engring. Soc., Am. Soc. Engring. Edn., Sigma Xi, Tau Beta Pi, Eta Kappa Nu. Patentee in field. Office: Ind U-Purdue U-Ft Wayne Dean Sch Engring and Tech 2101 E Coliseum Blvd Fort Wayne IN 46805-1445 Home: 4981 Calle Arquero Oceanside CA 92057-2717 Home Phone: 760-754-9795. Business E-Mail: mahmoud@engr.ipfw.edu. *In this country there are outstanding opportunities for those who are willing to work hard to serve the society and their profession. I am thankful to be in the U.S. and to have found this type of opportunity.*

MAHMOUD, ENAD, civil engineer, researcher; b. Kuwait City, Kuwait, Apr. 5, 1981; arrived in US, 2004; s. Muhib Ahmad Mahmoud and Amal Nayef Abdulhadi. BS, U. Jordan, Amman, 2003; MS, Tex. A&M, Coll. Sta., 2005, PhD, 2009. Civil engr. Consol. Cons. Environ. and Engring., Amman, 2003—04; grad. rsch. asst. Tex. A&M U., 2004—05, Tex. Transp. Inst., Coll. Sta., 2005—09; rsch. assoc. U. Wis., Madison, 2009—. Contbr. articles to profl. jours. Recipient Academic Excellence award, Tex. A&M U., 2008; Rsch. Scholarship, Assn. Asphalt Paving Technologists, 2007, Internat. Edn. Fee scholarship, Tex. A&M U., 2007. Mem.: ASCE, Assn. Asphalt Paving Technologists, Assn. Former Students, Phi Kappa Phi (hon.). Achievements include development of experimental methods for the evaluation of aggregate resistance to polishing, abrasion and breakage. Personal E-mail: enad81@yahoo.com. Business E-Mail: emahmoud@wisc.edu.

MAHMOUD, HISHAM, research scientist; b. Fayoum, Egypt, Nov. 20, 1980; s. Abdelaziz Mesbah and A. Youssif; m. M. Kamal; 1 child, S. BS, Cairo U., Fayoumy Egypt, 1997—2002; MS, Cairo U., Egypt, 2005;

attending, U.South Fla., Tampa, 2009. Tchg. asst. Cairo U., 2002—05, Am. U. Cairo, 2004—05; rsch. asst. U. South Fla., 2005—, adj. faculty, 2008—. Contbr. articles to profl.jours. Achievements include patents pending for new algorithms to improve the performance of wireless communication systems. Office: Univ South Fla 4202 E Fowler Ave ENB118 Tampa FL 33620 Business E-Mail: hmahmoud@mail.usf.edu.

MAHMUD, JAMAL, psychiatrist; married. MD, King Edward Med. Coll., Lahore, Pakistan, 1987. DPM Coll. Physicians and Surgeons Ireland, 1999, DCP. Chief resident psychiatry Hahnemann U. Hosp., Phila., 2005—06; chief psychiatrist MHM, CFCF, Phila., 2006—. Clin. asst. prof. Drexel U. Coll. Medicine, Phila., 2008—. Contbr. articles to profl. jour. Recipient Martin Luther King freedom medal, Camden Freeholders NJ, 2006. Office: MHM 7901 State Rd Philadelphia PA 19136 Home Fax: 215-685-4796. Personal E-mail: jamalmfr@yahoo.com.

MAHMUD, SHIREEN DIANNE, photographer; b. Chittagong, Pakistan, Oct. 4, 1949; came to U.S., 1974; d. Mohammed Mazhurul Qudus and Mumtaz Mahal Begum; m. Abdul Wazed Mahmud, Apr. 10, 1966 (div. 1996); children: Sharmin, Anita. BA in Mass Comm., U. Hartford, 1982. Part-time med. sec., Middletown, Conn., 1979—82; freelance photographer, 1985—; typist Aetna Ins. Co., Middletown, 1991. Prodr. feature program Storer Cable Comm., Clinton, Conn., 1991-95; mem. Bridgeport Regional Bus. Coun., 1997; realtor Buyer's Capital. Literacy vol. Russell Libr., Middletown, Conn. Mem. AAUW, Nat. League Am. Pen Women, Internat. Soc. Poets (Hall of Fame award 1997), Conn. Soc. Poets, Conn. Songwriter's Assn., Internat. Platform Assn. Office Phone: 860-306-9090. E-mail: sdshireen@optonline.net.

MAHOLIC, NANCY L., nurse; b. Bradford, Pa., Jan. 25, 1937; d. George Edward and Leona Dolores Cuthbertson; m. James Andrew Maholic, Nov. 12, 1955; children: James Jr., Jeffrey, Julie. AA, Bucks County C.C., Newtown, Pa., 1980; degree, Upper Bucks Nursing Sch., Upper Black Eddy, Pa., 1981. Teller Bradford Nat. Bank, 1957—62, Springfield Bank, Ohio, 1964—66; office mgr. Woodrow Mfg. Co., Springfield, 1968—70; coord. adjustment svcs. for the blind, dept. head Bucks county Assn. for the Blind, 1970—78; staff nurse Doylestown Hosp., Pa., 1981—94; patient coord. Doylestown Women's Health, 1990—2003; pvt. duty nurse Bayada Nurses, Langhorne, Pa., 2003—. Preceptor Doylestown Hosp., 1983—2003. Youth choir dir. United Meth. Ch., Ivyland, Pa., 1970—74; parish nurse St. John's United Meth. Ch., 1999—, lay leader, 2005—. Recipient Nurse Excellence award, Doylestown Hosp., 1992; named Bayada Employee of Month, 2005. Republican. Avocations: music, reading. Home: 19 Meadow Ln Richboro PA 18954 Personal E-mail: nursecubby@aol.com.

MAHON, MALACHY THOMAS, SR., lawyer, educator; b. NYC, Jan. 4, 1934; s. James and Alice (Rooney) M.; m. Margaret Phyllis Kirwan, Jan. 25, 1958 (dec. 1993); children: Veronica Mahon Grover, Laura Mahon Chandonnet, Malachy. BA, Manhattan Coll., 1954; JD, Fordham U., 1960. Bar: N.Y. 1960. Law clk. to chief magistrate John M. Murtagh, NYC, 1959-60; law clk. to justice Tom C. Clark U.S. Supreme Ct., 1960-61; assoc. Hale Russell & Stentzel, NYC, 1961-62, Mudge Rose Guthrie & Alexander, NYC, 1979-80; of counsel Farrell, Fritz, Caemmerer, Cleary, Barnosky & Armentano, Mineola, NY, 1982-83, Havens & Lombard, Flushing, NY, 1994-95; prof. Fordham U. Law Sch., 1962-68; prof. law Hofstra U. Law Sch., 1968—, founding dean, 1968-73, S.B. Wilzig disting. prof. banking, 1985—. Vis. prof. U. Tex. Law Sch., 1973-74; exec. dir., spl. N.Y. State asst. atty. gen. Meyer Investigation of State Police Murder Coverup Charges Against the Spl. Attica Prison Riot Prosecutor's Office, 1975; chief counsel N.Y. Gov.'s Spl. Com. on Criminal Offenders, 1966; mem. Nassau County Bd. Ethics, 1983-96, chmn., 1989-96; chmn. merit selection com. EDNY Bankruptcy Judges, 1985-88. Staff author: Mental Illness, Due Process and the Criminal Defendant, 1968; monthly comml. law columnist: N.Y. Law Jour, 1976-78. Served with U.S. Army, 1954-56. Mem. ABA, N.Y. State Bar Assn., Assn. Bar City N.Y., Am. Law Inst. Home: 14 Duke Of Gloucester Manhasset NY 11030-3210 Office: Hofstra U Law Sch Hempstead NY 11550 Office Phone: 516-463-5864, 516-463-5868. Business E-Mail: lawmtm@hofstra.edu.

MAHON, ROBERT, photographer; b. Wilmington, Del., Dec. 28, 1949; s. Clifton and Mary Veronica (Figash) M.; m. Carol Joyce, Apr. 24, 1983. BA in Am. Studies, U. Del., 1971. One-man shows include Twining Gallery, N.Y.C., 1985, Mercer Coll., Trenton, N.J., 1993, Anne Reid Gallery, Princeton, 1996, N.J. State Mus., 1997, Dana Libr. Rutgers U., Newark, 1998, RVC Coll., N.J., 2001, PhilosophyBox, N.Y.C., 2004, Witherspoon Gallery, Princeton, NJ, 2005, 2008, Rittenhouse, Phila., 2006, 3000BC, 2007, Schotland Gallery, Flemington, NJ, 2007, Wither Spoon Gallery, Princeton, NJ, 2008, exhibited in group shows at Whitney Mus. Am. Art, 1982, Phila. Mus. Art, 1982, 1995, Am. Ctr., Paris, 1982, Mus. Modern Art, NYC, 1983—85, 1993, Kolnischer Kunstverein, 1983, Art Inst., Chgo., 1985, Twining Gallery, 1985—86, 1988—89, N.J. State Mus., 1990, 1997, 2002, 1999, Guggenheim Soho, 1994, Sandra Gering Gallery, N.Y.C., 1996, Newark Mus., 1997, 2002, Korn Gallery Drew U., Madison, N.J., 1999, N.Y. Pub. Libr., 1999, Guild Hall, East Hampton, N.Y., 1999, others, Represented in permanent collections Phila. Mus. Art, Mus. Modern Art, Met. Mus. Art, N.Y. Pub. Libr., Humanities Rsch. Ctr., U. Tex., Austin, Princeton U. Libr., Princeton U. Art Mus., Harvard U. Art Mus., N.J. State Mus., Newark Mus., Montclair Art Mus., Rutgers U., Dana Libr., Zimmerli Mus., Noyes Mus., also pvt. collections, exhibitions include 100 NJ Artists Nat. Tour, 2002—. Guggenheim grantee, 1985; RCIP Printmaking fellow, 1996. Home: PO Box Q Stockton NJ 08559-0390 E-mail: mailbox@robertmahon.net.

MAHONE, ANTONIO, elementary school educator; s. John Terry and Betty Jean Mahone; m. Stephanie Mahone, Nov. 24, 1994; children: Adanya Taylor Jenkins, Aysiah Chanell. Degree, Argosy U., Atlanta, 2008. Cert. in educational leadership Ga., 2008. Educator Fountain Elem. Sch., Forest Pk., Ga., 2000—03, Kendrick Mid. Sch., Jonesboro, Ga., 2003—. Sgt. US Army, 1991—2000, San Antonio. Office: Kendrick Mid Sch 7971 Kendrick Rd Jonesboro GA 30236 Home Fax: 770-477-6781. Business E-Mail: amahone@clayton.k12.ga.us.

MAHONE, GLENN R., lawyer; b. Apr. 22, 1945; m. Andrea Mahone; 2 children. BS, Pa. State U., 1968; JD, Duquesne U., 1973; LLM, Yale U., 1975. Bar: Pa. 1973. With Reed Smith LLP, 1973—80, 1991—; now ptnr., mem. exec. com.; broadcast industry exec., 1980—91. Dir. Matthews Internat. Corp.; chmn. Allegheny County Airport Authority. Trustee Duquesne U., Westminster Coll.; chmn. Manchester Bidwell Corp. Mem.: Homer S. Brown Law Assn., Allegheny County Bar Assn., Nat. Bar Assn., ABA. Office: Reed Smith LLP 435 Sixth Ave Pittsburgh PA 15219 Office Phone: 412-288-4240. Office Fax: 412-288-3063. Business E-Mail: gmahone@reedsmith.com.

MAHONEY, DAVID L., former pharmaceutical wholesale and healthcare management company executive; b. Brighton, Mass., June 24, 1954; s. Thomas H.D. and K. Phyllis (Norton); m. Winn Canning Ellis, Sept. 26, 1992. AB in English, Princeton U., 1975; MBA, Harvard U., 1981. Asst. gen. mgr. Ogden Food Svc. Corp., LA, 1975-76, concessions mgr. East Boston, Mass., 1976-77, gen. mgr., 1977-78, ops. analyst, 1978-79; assoc. McKinsey & Co., San Francisco, 1981-86, prin., 1986-90; v.p. strategic planning McKesson Corp., San Francisco, 1990-94, pres. HDS, Inc., 1994-95, pres. pharm. svcs., 1995-97, group pres. pharm svcs. & internat. group, 1997-99; exec. v.p., CEO pharm. svcs. bus. McKesson HBOC, 1999, co-CEO, 1999-2001; CEO iMcKesson, 2000-01. Bd. dirs. Symantec Corp., Corcept Therapeutics, KQED, Live Oak Sch., SFMOMA, Mercy Corps. Mem.: Young Pres. Orgn. Avocations: outdoor activities, photography. Office: Pier 5 The Embracadero Ste 102 San Francisco CA 94111

MAHONEY, GEORGE LEFEVRE, lawyer; b. Washington, Mar. 28, 1952; s. George Francis Xavier and Elaine (LeFevre) M.; m. Lucinda Stuart, July 11, 1986. BA, U. Va., 1974, JD, 1978. Bar: N.Y. 1979, U.S. Dist. Ct. (so. and ea. dists), N.Y. 1979, U.S. Ct. Appeals (5th cir.), 1980, U.S. Ct. Appeals (2d cir.) 1981, U.S. Ct. Appeals (D.C. cir.) 1991. Assoc. Satterlee & Stephens, NYC, 1978-82; asst. gen. counsel Dow Jones & Co., Inc., NYC and Princeton, N.J., 1982—93; corp. sec., gen. counsel Media General, Inc., Richmond, Va., 1993—, v.p., 2006—.

MAHONEY, JANE E., medical educator, director; m. Mark S. Brownfield; 1 child, Andrew Brownfield. BA, U. Va., Charlottesville, 1978; MD, U. Calif., San Francisco, 1986. Asst. prof., geriat. U. Wis., Sch. Medicine & Pub. Health, Madison, 1993—2004, assoc. prof., geriat., dept. medicine, 2004—, vice chair, women, medicine, 2005—; med. dir. Care Wis., Madison, 2003—. Academic award, Nat. Inst. Aging, 1993—98, grant, Ctrs. Disease Control & Prevention, 2002—. Mem.: Soc. Advancement Violence & Injury Rsch., Gerontol. Soc. America, Am. Geriat. Soc. Office: Geriat Sect Dept Medicine Univ Wis Sch Medicine & Pub Health 2870 University Ave Ste 106 Madison WI 53705 Office Fax: 608-263-7645. Business E-Mail: jm2@medicine.wisc.edu.

MAHONEY, JOHN, actor; b. Blackpool, Eng., June 20, 1940; MA in English, Western Ill. U.; student, Quincy Coll.; trained for the theater, St. Nicholas Theatre, Chgo. Stage performances include The Water Engine, 1977, The Hothouse, Taking Steps, Death of a Salesman, Orphans, 1985 (Theater World award), The House of Blue Leaves, 1986 (Tony award, Clarence Derwent award), The Subject Was Roses, 1991, The Drawer Boy, 2005, Prelude to a Kiss, 2007; films include Mission Hill, 1982, Voyeur, 1984, Code of Silence, 1985, The Manhattan Project, 1986, Streets of Gold, 1987, Tin Men, 1987, Suspect, 1987, Moonstruck, 1987, Frantic, 1988, Betrayed, 1988, Eight Men Out, 1988, Say Anything, 1989, Love Hurts, 1990, The Russia House, 1990, Barton Fink, 1991, Article 99, 1992, In the Line of Fire, 1993, Striking Distance, 1993, Reality Bites, 1994, The Hudsucker Proxy, 1994, The American President, 1995, Mariette in Ecstasy, 1996, Primal Fear, 1996, She's the One, 1996, Antz (voice), 1998, The Iron Giant (voice), 1999, The Broken Hearts Club, 2000, Almost Salinas, 2001, Atlantis: The Lost Empire (voice), 2001, Atlantis: Milo's Return (voice), 2003, Zodiac, 2007, Dan in Real Life, 2007; TV series: Lady Blue, 1985-86, H.E.L.P., The Human Factor, 1991, Frasier, 1993-2004; TV movies Chicago Story, 1981, Listen to your Heart, 1983, Dance of the Phoenix, 1984, The Killing Floor, 1984, First Steps, 1985, Trapped in Silence, 1986, Favorite Son, 1988, (TNT) Dinner at Eight, 1989, (HBO) The Image, 1990, The 10 Million Dollar Getaway, 1991, The Secret Passion of Robert Clayton, 1992; TV special The House of Blue Leaves, 1987. Served AUS Recipient award SAG, 2000.

MAHONEY, JOHN J., office supply company executive; BA, Coll. Holy Cross, Worcester, Mass.; MBA, Northeastern U., Boston. Ptnr. Ernst & Young; exec. v.p., CFO Staples Inc., Framingham, Mass., 1996—97, exec v.p., CFO, chief adminstrv. officer, 1997—2006, vice chmn., CFO, 2006—. Bd. dirs. ADVO, 2001—, non-exec. chmn. bd., 2004—; bd. dirs. Tweeter. Office: Staples Inc 500 Staples Dr Framingham MA 01701

MAHONEY, JOHN L., English literature educator; b. Somerville, Mass., Feb. 4, 1928; AB, Boston Coll., 1950, AM, 1952, DHL (hon.), 2003; PhD, Harvard U., 1957. From instr. English to prof. Boston Coll., 1955—94, Rattigan prof. English, 1994—2002, prof. emeritus, 2002—. Chmn. dept. English, Boston Coll., 1962-67, 69-70, dir. PhD program in English, 1970-75, 82-85, mem. ednl. policy com. Grad. Sch. Arts and Scis., 1985-87; vis. prof. English Harvard U. summer sch., 1963, 65, 67, 71, 80, 83, 86; cons. for self-study Weston Coll. Schs. of Philosophy and Theology, Boston Coll., 1965; sem. leader programs for women, Boston Coll., Newton Coll., 1976, 78, 79; mem. numerous acad. coms. and couns.; cons., mem. English adv. com. Commonwealth of Mass., 1968-70; mem. acad. coun. Woods Coll. of Advancing Studies, Boston Coll., 1969—, univ. core curriculum devel. com., 1991-97; trustee St. John's Sem., Brighton, Mass., com. on acad. affairs, 1980-86; sec. bd. trustees Katharine Gibbs Sch., Boston, 1982-90; mem. adv. bd. Jesuit Inst., Boston Coll., 1987—2005; mem. Boston Coll. Coun. the Arts, 1997-, mem. edn. com. Religion and the Arts. Author: The Whole Internal Universe: Imitation and the New Defense of Literature in British Criticism, 1660-1830, 1985, The Persistence of Tragedy: Episodes in the History of Drama, 1985, The Logic of Passion: The Literary Criticism of William Hazlitt, rev. edit., 1981, Wordsworth: A Poetic Life, 1997, Wordsworth and the Critics, 2001, Wordsworth of Rydal: Religious Experience and Religious Practice, 2003; editor, author intro. and notes: The Enlightenment and English Literature, 1980, The English Romantics: Major Poetry and Critical Theory, 1978, An Essay of Dramatic Poetry and Other Critical Writings by John Dryden, 1965, William Duff's Essay on Original Genius, 1964; contbr. Imagination and the Ways of Genius (in Approaches to Hazlitt), 1986, Teaching the Immortality Ode with Coleridge's Dejection: An Ode (in MLA Approaches to Teaching Wordsworth's Poetry), 1986, Teaching Shelley's Skylark and the Defence of Poetry (in MLA Approaches to Teaching Shelley's Poetry), 1990, and others; editor: (with J. Robert Barth, S.J.) Coleridge, Keats, and the Imagination: Romanticism and Adam's Dream, 1990, Seeing Into the Life of Things: Essays on Literature and Religion, 1998; CD recs. Boston College Poetry Reading Series: Poetry of Faith, 2003, Freedom: America's Literary Voices, 2005, Poetry of Ireland, 2007, Shakespeare's Sonnets, 2008; mem. editl. bd. Boston Coll. Mag., 1981-90; author articles, papers delivered at profl. confs.; reviewer for Studies in Romanticism, The Wordsworth Circle, European Romantic Rev., Nineteenth Century Contexts, So. Humanities Rev., Coll. Lit., Religion and the Arts 1650-1850; series editor Fordham U. Press Series on Religion and Lit., 1997-2005. Active Sacred Heart Parish, Lexington, Mass., del. to Lexington Coun. Chs., 1968, vice chmn. parish coun., 1969-72, mem. parish coun., 1995-98, 2005—, vice chmn., 1996-98, mem. religious edn. commn., 1974-79, 90-93, sem. leader Christian Youth Edn., 1969-73, lector, 1972—; mem. Archdiocese of Boston Commn. for Promotion of Parish Couns., 1969-74, Benjamin Mays Mentor Ahana program, 1993-2003. Boston Coll. Grad. Sch. fellow, 1950-52; Boston Coll. Faculty rsch. grantee, 1964, 68, 86, 92, 96, 97, 98, Mellon Found. grantee for rsch. and faculty devel., 1981-82; grantee rsch. Am. Philos. Soc., 1987; recipient Boston Coll. Campus Coun. Tchr. of Yr. award, 1966, Boston Coll. alumni award for excellence in edn., 1978, Andrè Favat award Mass. Coun. Tchrs. English, 1988, Prof. of Yr. award Coun. for Advancement and Support of Edn. Mass., 1989, Wordsworth Meml. Lectr., Rydal Ch., 2003. Mem. AAUP (pres. Boston Coll. chpt. 1962), MLA, N.E. Soc. Eighteenth Century Studies, Wordsworth-Coleridge Assn. Am., Keats-Shelley Assn. Am., The Johnsonians, Alpha Sigma Nu, Phi Beta Kappa (Tchg. award Boston Coll. 1994). Office Phone: 617-552-3720. Business E-Mail: mahoneyj@bc.edu.

MAHONEY, KATHLEEN MARY, lawyer; b. Methuen, Mass., Oct. 24, 1954; d. Joseph Patrick and Beatrice Evelyn (Blackington) M.; children: Alexis Anne Schmitt, Brynne Elizabeth Schmitt. BA, Keene State Coll., NH, 1976; JD, Syracuse U., NY, 1979. Bar: Minn. 1979, U.S. Dist. Ct. Minn. 1980, U.S. Ct. Appeals (8th cir.) 1985, U.S. Supreme Ct. 1988. Instr. Sch. of Law Hamline U., St. Paul, 1979-80; law clk. to hon. justice Douglas K. Amdahl Minn. Supreme Ct., St. Paul, 1980-81; law clk. to hon. judge Neal P. McCurn US Dist. Ct. (ND, NY), Syracuse, 1981-83; spl. asst. atty. gen. Atty. Gen.'s Office State of Minn., St. Paul, 1983-89; assoc. Oppenheimer, Wolff & Donnelly, St. Paul, 1989-91, sr. assoc., 1991-93, ptnr., 1994—2002, chair labor and employment practice group, 1995-97, mng. ptnr., 1997-2000, Larson-King, LLP, St. Paul, 2002—04; v.p., dep. gen. counsel Nash-Finch Co., Mpls., 2004—06, interim gen. counsel, sec., 2006, sr. v.p., gen. counsel, sec., 2006—. Cons. George Banzhaf Co., Milw., 1979-80; adj. prof. Hamline U. Sch. of Law, 1987-89. Mem. Dist. 621 Study Adv. Com., Shoreview, Minn., 1989-91, chair, 1991-93; mem. Turtle Lake Sch. Adv. Com., Shoreview, 1988-96; mem. exec. com., bd. dirs. Voyageurs Regional Nat. Park Assn., 1993-95; mem. Class of '93; bd. dirs. St. Paul Vol. Ctr., 1994-99; leader Girl Scouts Am., 1993-99; mem. Leadership St. Paul.; bd. dirs. Girl Scout Council St. Croix Valley, 2001-06, bd. chair 2004-06; bd. mem. Minn. Bd. Law Examiners, 2003-; dir. NFC Found., 2006-. Mem. ABA, Minn. Bar Assn., Ramsey County Bar Assn. Office: Nash-Finch Co 7600 France Ave S Minneapolis MN 55435

MAHONEY, KEVIN J., lawyer; b. Boston, Oct. 7, 1962; BA, U. Mass., 1986; JD, New Eng. Sch. Law, 1989. Bar: Mass. 1989, U.S. Dist. Ct. Mass. 1992; Black Belt 1981. Jud. law clk. Conn. Superior Ct., 1989—90; asst. dist. atty. Middlesex County, Mass., 1991—93; assoc. Lecomte, Emanuelson, Tick & Doyle, Boston, 1993; pvt. practice. Staff mem.: New Eng. Law Rev., 1987—88, symposium editor:, 1988—89; contbr. articles to profl. jours. Recipient Am. Jurisprudence Book award for Clin. Evidence, 1988. Mem.: Mass. Assn. Criminal Def. Lawyers, Nat. Assn. Criminal Def. Lawyers (mem. champion adv. com., mem. forensic evidence fraud task force, mem. law enforcement misconduct com.). Avocations: weightlifting, hunting, mountain climbing, literature, politics. Office: Law Offices of Kevin J Mahoney PC 545 Concord Ave Ste 22 Cambridge MA 02138 Office Phone: 617-492-0055. Fax: 617-492-6886.

MAHONEY, KEVIN J., social worker, educator; BA, St. Louis U.; MSW, U. Conn.; PhD, U. Wis., Madison. Chief rsch. and program devel. Conn. Dept. on Aging, 1978—87; prof. Boston Coll. Grad. Sch. Social Work, Chestnut Hill, Mass., 1999—, dir. nat. resource ctr. participant directed svcs.; nat. program dir. Cash & Counseling. Faculty mem. Yale U., U. Conn., U. Calif., San Francisco, U. Md.; spkr. in field. Contbr. articles to profl. jours. Recipient Flynn Prize for Social Work Rsch., 2007. Mem.: Gerontological Soc. Am. (sec., Maxwell Pollack award 2004). Office: Nat Resource Ctr Participant Directed Svcs Boston Coll Grad Sch Social Work 314 Hammond St Chestnut Hill MA 02467-3807 also: Boston Coll McGuinn Hall, Rm 527B 140 Commonwealth Ave Chestnut Hill MA 02467 Office Phone: 617-552-4039. Office Fax: 617-552-1975. E-mail: kevin.mahoney@bc.edu.

MAHONEY, KEVIN L., oceanographer; s. Richard L. Mahoney and Debbie M. Nettles, Jenny Mahoney (Stepmother); m. Maribel R. Ramos, Sept. 10, 2001; children: Aubrey Isabella, Keegan Patrick. BA, Miss. State U., Starkville, 1993; MS in Marine Biology, Nova Southeastern U., Davie, Fla., 1999; BA in Marine Sci., U. Hawaii, Hilo, 1995; D in Marine Sci., U. Southern Miss., Stennis Space Ctr., 2003. Postdoc. fellow, oceanographer Monterey Bay Aquarium Rsch. Inst., Moss Landing, Calif., 2003—05; oceanographer Naval Oceanog. Office, Stennis Space Ctr., 2003—. Achievements include research in marine optics. Avocations: guitar, gourmet cooking, travel, water sports. Office: Naval Oceanographic Office 1002 Balch Blvd Stennis Space Center MS 39529 Business E-Mail: kevin.l.mahoney@navy.mil.

MAHONEY, KIMBERLY LYNNE, event and facility executive; b. Johnson City, NY, Nov. 1969; d. Dewitt Duncan and Selina Faye Smith; m. Michael Mahoney, June 24, 2000. BA, U. Ky., 1992; MEd, U. Ga., 1994; PhD, Ohio State U., 2006. Facility mgmt. intern Charlotte Coliseum, NC, 1994; event coord. Charlotte Conv. Ctr., NC, 1994—95; account mgr. Show Pros Entertainment Svcs., Inc., Charlotte, NC, 1995—97, regional mgr. Greensboro, NC, 1997—98; guest services mgr. Schottenstein Ctr., Ohio State U., Columbus, 1998—2000, asst. dir. event svcs. and adminstrn., 2000—03; asst. commr. Ohio H.S. Athletic Assn., 2003—05; instr. Univ. S.C., 2005—06, asst. prof., 2006—07; vis. asst. prof. Ohio State U., 2007—08. Cons., trainer NFL Jacksonville Jaguars, 2002—03; cons. Mahoney, 2006—. Office: Ohio State Univ PAES Bldg A238 305 W 17th Ave Columbus OH 43210-1224 Personal E-mail: mahoney.kimberly@gmail.com.

MAHONEY, LINDA L., education educator, consultant; d. Frank Henry and Ruth Venus (Smith) M.; 1 child, Will Knight Hughes. BA in Elem. Edn., Goshen Coll., Ind., 1968; MEd in Edn., East Tex. State U., Commerce, 1992; EdD in Curriculum and Instrn., Tex. A&M U., Commerce, 1996. Tchr. Elkhart Cmty. Sch. Corp., Bristol and Elkhart, Ind., 1968—70, Quinlan Ind. Sch. Dist., Tex., 1985—93; tchg. asst. East Tex. State U., 1993—96; asst. prof. No. State U., Aberdeen, SD, 1996—98, U. West Ala., Livingston, 1998—2000, Stillman Coll., Tuscaloosa, Ala., 2000—05, Miss. U. for Women, Columbus, 2005—. Mem.: Coll. Reading Assn. Methodist. Avocations: crocheting, church choir. Office: Miss U for Women 1100 College St Columbus MS 39701 Personal E-mail: dreamonda@yahoo.com.

MAHONEY, MARGARET ELLERBE, foundation executive; d. Charles Hallam and Leslie Nelson (Savage) M. BS magna cum laude, Vanderbilt U., 1946; LHD (hon.), Meharry Med. Coll., 1977, U. Fla., 1980, Med. Coll. Pa., 1982, Williams Coll., 1983, Smith Coll., 1985, Beaver Coll., 1985, Brandeis U., 1989, Marymount Coll., 1990, Mt. Sinai Sch. Medicine, 1992, Rush U., 1993, SUNY, Bklyn., 1994, N.Y. Med. Coll., 1995. Fgn. affairs officer State Dept., Washington, 1946-53; exec. assoc., assoc. sec. Carnegie Corp., NYC, 1953-72; v.p. Robert Wood Johnson Found., Princeton, NJ, 1972-80; pres. Commonwealth Fund, NYC, 1980-94, MEM Assocs., Inc., NYC, 1995—. Spkr. in field. Contbr. articles to profl. jours. Trustee Carnegie Found. Advancement of Tchg., 1963—2001, John D. and Catherine T. MacArthur Found., 1985—2002, Smith Coll., 1988—93, Columbia U., 1991—96, Arthur Ashe Found., 1997—2005; vis. fellow Sch. Archtl. and Urban Planning, Princeton U., 1973—80; bd. dirs. Coun. on Found., 1982—88, Skillbuilders Fund, 1993—99, adv. dir., 1999—; bd. dirs. Alliance for Aging Rsch., 1986—99, Overseas Devel. Coun., 1988—2001, Nat. Found.

Ctrs. for Disease Control and Prevention, Inc., 1994—2004; mem. MIT Corp., 1984—89, N.Y.C. Commn. on the Yr. 2000, 1985—87; chmn. Nat. Found. Ctrs. for Disease Control and Prevention, Inc., 1996—98; bd. govs. Am. Stock Exch., 1987—92, Am. Skin Assn., 1994—, Classroom Inc., 1996—2005, Buckminster Fuller Inst., 2005, 2007—; mem. adv. bd. Office of Med. Examiner, NYC, 1987—; vice chmn. N.Y.C. Mayor's Com. for Pub./Pvt. Partnerships, 1990—93; mem. vestry Parish of Trinity Ch., 1982—89, 1991—95. Recipient Frank H. Lahey Meml. award, 1984, Women's Forum award, 1989, Walsh McDermott award, 1992, Disting. Grantmaker award Coun. Founds., 1993, Edward R. Loveland award ACP, 1994, Spl. Recognition award AAMC, 1994, Merit medal Lotos Club, 1994, Terrance Keenan Leadership award in health philanthropy Grantmakers in health, 1995, Distinction award Am. Skin Assn., 1998, Rsch. Am. award, 1999, Hon. Classmate Class of 1976 award Princeton U., 2001, Picker Inst. award, 2003. Mem. AAAS, Inst. Medicine of NAS, Am. Acad. Arts and Scis., Am. Philos. Soc., Coun. Fgn. Rels., Fin. Women's Assn. NY, NY Acad. Medicine, NY Acad. Scis., Alpha Omega Alpha. Office: MEM Assocs Inc 521 5th Ave 29th Fl New York NY 10175-0088 Office Phone: 212-297-0500.

MAHONEY, MARGARET ELLIS, advertising executive; b. Detroit, Mar. 17, 1929; d. Seth Wiley and Mildred Elizabeth (Hill) Ellis; m. Stephen Bedell Smith, Mar. 15, 1956 (div. Oct. 1962); 1 child, Laura Elizabeth; m. Patrick John Mahoney, Sept. 1, 1972 (dec.). BA, Butler U., 1953. Copywriter Hook Drugs Inc., Indpls., 1953; continuity dir. Sta. WXLW, Indpls., 1954-57; ptnr. Steve Smith and Assocs. Advt., Indpls., 1956-62; account mgr. Sive Advt., Cin., 1963-64, Associated Advt., Cin., 1964-65; copywriter SupeRX Drugs Inc., Cin., 1965-72; promotion writer U.S. News and World Report, Washington, 1974; asst. mgr. advt. Drug Fair, Alexandria, Va., 1975-82; dir. advt. Cosmetic and Fragrance Concepts Inc./DBA Cosmetic Ctrs., Beltsville, Md., 1982-89; advt., prodn. cons. Nat. Red Cross, Galladet U., Washington, 1989-94; real estate cons., 1964—65; asst. to real estate agt. Carmel, Ind., 1994-96; editl. cons., mem. svc. rep., acct. clk. Angie's List, Carmel, Ind., 1996—. Vestrywoman St. Matthews Episcopal Ch., Cin., 1969-71; vol. jr. achievement hosp. chmn. Sleepy Hollow Citizens Assn., Falls Church, Va., 1973; vol. resident assoc. program Smithsonian Instn., Washington, 1989-94; chmn. membership and pub. rels. Friends Chinn Park Regional Libr., Woodbridge, Va., 1991-94; vol. Indpls. Art Ctr. Gift Shop, 1997—, Prince William Symphony Orch., Prince William County Voter Registration Bd. Mem. Potomac Valley Aquarium Soc. (past treas., past sec., editor jour.), Am. Cichlid Assn. (nat. pub. rels. chair 1985-90), Delta Delta Delta. Avocations: swimming, reading, needlecrafts, travel, computers. Home: 9850 Greentree Dr Carmel IN 46032-9099 Office Phone: 317-803-3961.

MAHONEY, MARK, newspaper editor; children: Caitlin, Christa, Chelsea. BS in Comm. Mgmt., Ithaca Coll., NY. Radio reporter Sta. WEOK-WPDH, Poughkeepsie, NY; legis. corr. Albany, NY, 1987—88; reporter to city editor, then regional editor The Post-Star, Glens Falls, NY, 1988—99, editl. page editor, 1999—. Recipient Lee Enterprises Pres. award for editl. writing, 2003, Editl. Writing award, Am. Soc. Newspaper Editors, 2004, Pulitzer prize for editl. writing, 2009. Office: Post Star Lawrence & Cooper St Glens Falls NY 12801 Office Phone: 598-724-3131. Business E-Mail: mahoney@poststar.com.

MAHONEY, MAUREEN E., lawyer; b. Ind., Aug. 28, 1954; d. James Edward and Marian Ruth (Hanselman) M. m. William H. Crispin; children: Brad, Abigail. BA, Ind. U., 1974; JD, U. Chgo., 1978. Bar: Ill. 1978, Va. 1983, U.S. Dist. Ct. (no. dist.) Calif. 1980, U.S. Dist. Ct. D.C. 1981, U.S. Dist. Ct. (ea. dist.) Va., U.S. Ct. Appeals D.C. 1981, U.S. Ct. Appeals (8th cir.) 1982, U.S. Ct. Appeals (4th cir.) 1983, U.S. Ct. Appeals (5th cir.) 1986, U.S. Ct. Appeals (9th cir.) 1987, U.S. Supreme Ct. 1987. Law clk. to Hon. Robert Sprecher US Ct. Appeals (7th cir.), Chgo., 1978-79; law clk. to Justice William Rehnquist US Supreme Ct., Washington, 1979-80; ptnr. Latham & Watkins LLP, Washington, 1980—91, 1993—; dep. solicitor gen. US Dept. Justice, Washington, 1991—93. Recipient Rex Lee Advocacy award, J. Rueben Clark Law Soc.; named one of America's Top 50 Women Litigators, Nat. Law Jour., 100 Most Influential Lawyers in America, 2006, 50 Most Influential Women Lawyers in America, 2007. Mem. ABA, Washington Bar Assn., Ill. Bar Assn., Va. Bar Assn., Am. Acad. of Appellate Lawyers, Am. Coll. of Trial Lawyers. exec. comm. Supreme Court Historical Soc. Office: Latham & Watkins LLP 555 Eleventh St NW Suite 1000 Washington DC 20004-1305 Office Phone: 202-637-2250. Office Fax: 202-637-2201. Business E-Mail: maureen.mahoney@lw.com.*

MAHONEY, MAURICE JEREMIAH, medical educator; b. Washington, Aug. 4, 1935; s. Maurice Mahoney and Julia Johnson; m. Blanche Katz, May 23, 2004; children: Tatyana Renner, Karen, Cydney, Matthew, Allison, Linnea. AB, Cornell U., 1957; MD, U. Pitts., 1962; JD, U. Conn., 1994. Bar: Conn. 1994; diplomate Med.Genetics Am. Bd. of Med. Genetics, 1982, Pediats. Am. Bd. of Pediat., 1967. Prof. of genetics Yale U., New Haven, 1970—; dir. human investigation com. Yale U. Sch. of Medicine, 2000—. Editl. bd. Am. Jour. of Med. Genetics, NYC, 1977—94, Fetal Diagnosis and Therapy, Basel, Switzerland, 1984—, Jour. of BioLaw & Bus., Denville, NJ, 1997—; bd. dirs. Am. Soc. of Human Genetics, Bethesda, Md., 1981—84, Soc. for Inherited Metabolic Disorders, Washington, 1984—87; fellow Am. Pediat. Soc., The Woodlands, Tex., 1983—, Am. Coll. of Med. Genetics, Bethesda, Md., 1993—. Editor: (medical text book) Medicine of the Fetus & Mother. Capt. US Army, 1966—68, Ft. McClellan, AL USA. Fellow, AAAS, 1998—2005. Avocations: kayaking, triathlon, opera, bioethics. Home: 526 Riverdale Dr Stratford CT 06615 Office Fax: 203-785-7673. Personal E-mail: maurice.mahoney@yale.edu.

MAHONEY, MICHAEL JAMES, investment company executive; b. Spokane, Wash., July 18, 1960; s. James Lyle and Frances Edith (Castle) Mahoney; m. Ann Dickinson, May 29, 1993; children: James Junius Castle, Catherine Lane, Grace Dickinson, Christopher Michael Hayes. BA in History cum laude, Whitman Coll., 1982; MBA, Stanford U., 1991. Analyst corp. fin. dept. E.F. Hutton & Co., Inc., NYC, 1982—85; assoc. cons. Bain & Co., Inc., Boston, 1985—87, cons., 1987—89; summer assoc. Goldman, Sachs & Co., NYC, 1990; investment analyst G.T. Global (acquired by AIM Funds), San Francisco, 1991—93; portfolio mgr., lead mgr. G.T. Global Telecom. Fund, 1993—99; sr. portfolio mgr. AIM Funds, San Francisco, 1998—99; founding ptnr. J&M Investments, Menlo Park, Calif., 1996—; sr. analyst, portfolio mgr., dir. Dresdner RCM Global Investors, San Francisco, 1999—2000; chief strategy officer Neon Yoyo, Inc. (acquired by Interwoven, Inc.), San Francisco, 2000; dir. Interwoven, Inc., Sunnyvale, Calif., 2000—01; mng. dir., sr. portfolio mgr., bd. dirs. Falcon Point Capital LLC (formerly EGM), San Francisco, 2001—, sr. mng. dir., 2004—. Guest lectr. in investments Stanford Grad. Sch. of Bus., 1994—; frequent print and TV commentator on the telecomms. and tech.industries and investing, 1993—; profiled in Investment Visionaries by Peter Tanous, 2003. Pres. Spokane County Young Reps., 1976-78; campaign mgr. Malone for U.S. Senate, Boston, 1988; bd. overseers Whitman Coll., investment com. 1999—. Recipient Pete Reid award, Whitman Coll., 1997. Mem. O'Mahony Records Soc., Ea. Wash. Geneal. Soc., Pacific Rsch. Inst. for Pub. Policy (mem. tech. adv. bd.), Stanford Alumni Assn. (life), Guardsmen, Menlo Circus Club (Atherton, Calif.), Villa Taverna (San Francisco), Spokane Club (Washington), Lincoln Club of No. Calif., Hayden Lake Country Club (Idaho), Phi Beta Kappa, Sigma Chi (com. chmn. 1979-80). Office: Falcon Point Capital LLC Two Embarcadero Ctr Ste 1300 San Francisco CA 94111 Business E-Mail: mmahoney@fptcap.com.

MAHONEY, MICHAEL ROBERT TAYLOR, art historian, educator; b. Worcester, Mass., Jan. 24, 1935; s. Michael J. and Mary (Taylor) M. BA, Yale U., 1957; PhD, U. London, 1965. Finley fellow Nat. Gallery Art, 1962-64; fellow Harvard Center Italian Studies, Villa I Tatti, 1963; museum curator Nat. Gallery Art, 1964-69; prof. fine arts, chmn. dept. Trinity Coll., Hartford, Conn., 1969-86, Genevieve Harlow Goodwin prof. fine arts, 1974-99. Incorporator Hartford Pub. Library, 1970-99; elector Wadsworth Atheneum, Hartford, 1974-85 Author: The Drawings of Salvator Rosa, 1977, (with Jean Cadogan) Wadsworth Atheneum Paintings II: Italy and Spain; editor: National Gallery of Art Report and Studies in the History of Art, 1968-69. Trustee Cesare Barbieri Found., Trinity Coll., 1977-99, Watkinson Libr., Trinity Coll., 1985-99, Somerset House Art History Found., NYC, 1985-2004; bd. govs. Hill-Stead Mus., Farmington, Conn., 1992-95; mem. adv. coun. Am. Friends of Georgian Group, 1996—.

MAHONEY, PAUL G., dean, law educator; b. St. Louis, 1959; BS, MIT, 1981; JD, Yale Law Sch., 1984. Bar: NY 1987. Law clk. to Hon. Ralph K. Winter Jr. US Ct. Appeals 2nd Cir., New Haven, 1984—85; law clk to Hon. Thurgood Marshall US Supreme Ct., Washington, 1985—86; assoc. Sullivan & Cromwell, NYC, 1986—90; assoc. prof. U. Va. Sch. Law, Charlottesville, 1990—95, prof., 1995—, Albert C. BeVier rsch. prof., 1996, acad. assoc. dean, 1999—2004, Brokaw prof. corp. law, David and Mary Harrison disting. prof. law, Arnold H. Leon prof. law, dean, 2008—. Vis. prof. U. Chgo. Law Sch., U. So. Calif. Law Sch., U. Toronto Faculty of Law. Recipient All-Univ. Tchr. Award, U. Va., 1997. Office: U Va Sch Law 580 Massie Rd Charlottesville VA 22903-1789 Office Phone: 434-924-7343. E-mail: pmahoney@virginia.edu.*

MAHONEY, ROBERT WILLIAM, electronic and security systems manufacturing executive; b. NYC, Sept. 10, 1936; s. Francis Jospeh and Margaret (Colleton) Mahoney; m. Joan Marie Sheraton, Oct. 3, 1959; children: Linda Marie, Stephen Francis, Brian Michael. BS, Villanova U., 1958; MBA, Roosevelt U., Chgo., 1961. With sales dept. NCR, Inc., Phila., 1961—70, sales mgr. Allentown, Pa., 1971—76, v.p. Dayton, Ohio, 1977—80; pres. NCR Can. Ltd., Toronto, 1981—82; sr. v.p. Diebold, Inc., Canton, Ohio, 1983—84, pres., COO, 1984—85, pres., CEO, 1985—88, chmn. bd., 1988—2000, bd. dirs. Chmn. Fed. Res. Bank Cleve. Mem. adv. bd. C. of C. Leadership Canton, 1987, Firestone County, Arkon, Brookside County, Canton; bd. dirs. Timken Co., Sherwin-Williams Co., Cin. Bell., Akron U. Econ. Devel. Bd., Ohio, 1982, timken Mercy Med. Ctr., Canton, 1983—, Canton Symphony Orch., 1985, Northeast Ohio Coun., Cleve., 1986—, Stark County Devel. Bd., 1986—, Profl. Football Hall of Fame, Canton, 1987—, Jr. Achievement, 1984; trustee Canton City Sch.s, 1986, Mt. union Coll., 1988—, Ohio Found. Ind. Colls., 1988—. Served with USN, 1958—61. Republican. Roman Catholic.

MAHONEY, TIM (TIMOTHY EDWARD MAHONEY), former United States Representative from Florida; b. Aurora, Ill., Aug. 15, 1956; m. Terry Mahoney, 2008 (separated); 1 child. BA in Computer Sci & Bus., W. Va. U., 1978; MBA, George Washington U., 1983. Pres. Rodime Systems, Rodime Inc., 1986—89; co-founder Union Atlantic, 1995—98; co-founder, pres. Ctr. for Creative Entrepreneurship; pres. Highland Group, 1994—95; co-founder, COO, chmn. vFinance, Inc., Boca Raton, Fla., 1996—2006; mem. US Congress from 16th Fla. dist., 2006—09, mem. fin. svcs. com., agrl. com. Mem. New Dem. Coalition, Blue Dog Coalition. Mem. Venus United Meth. Ch. Recipient Friend of River award, Marin County Bd. Commrs., 2008. Mem.: Fla. Cattleman's Assn. Democrat. Methodist.*

MAHONEY, WILLIAM FRANCIS, editor, writer; b. Joliet, Ill., Jan. 24, 1935; s. Cletus George and Mildred Marie (Ochs) Mahoney; m. Carroll Frances Johnson, June 28, 1958 (dec. 1998); children: Erin Michele Alderfer, Kevin William, Megan Ann, Sheila Marie Startup, Nora Aileen Petchkofski; m. Indira Doobay, 2007 (dec. 2008). BS in Journalism, Marquette U., 1957. Reporter Ft. Wayne (Ind.) News Sentinel, 1958-59; pub. rels. mgr. Motorola, Inc., Franklin Park, Ill., 1959-66; sr. acct. exec. Young & Rubicam, Inc., Chgo., 1966-68; pub. info. dir. ABA, Chgo., 1969-71; investor rels. mgr. Chemetron Corp., Chgo., 1971-76; corp. comm. dir. Scott Paper Co., Phila., 1976-80; pub. rels. dir. Esmark Inc., Chgo., 1980-81; prin. Mahoney & Mitchell Incorp., Phila., 1981-89, Investor Rels. Ptnrs., Livingston, NJ, 1993—2001, prin., editl. dir. VI LLC, 2004—. Author: Investor Relations: The Professional's Guide to Financial and Marketing Communications, 1991, The Active Shareholder, 1993, The Strategy and Practice of Investor Relations, 1997, Theory and Practice of Investors Relations, 2007; author, editor: The Investor Relations Guide, 1999, The IR Book, Capital Markets and Valuation, 2003; exec. editor Shareholder Value Mag., 2000-2003; Investor Rels. Update, 1981-99, Valuation Issues. Mem.: Nat. Investor Rels. Inst. Republican. Roman Catholic. Home and Office: 716 S Brandywine St West Chester PA 19382 Office Phone: 610-247-6261. Personal E-mail: wfmahoney35@verizon.net. Business E-Mail: wfmahoney@vi-llc.com.

MAHONY, ROGER MICHAEL, cardinal, archbishop; b. Hollywood, Calif., Feb. 27, 1936; s. Victor James and Loretta Marie (Baron) Mahony. AA, Our Lady Queen of Angels Sem., 1956; BA, St. John's Sem. Coll., 1958, BST, 1962; MSW, Cath. U. Am., 1964. Ordained priest Diocese of Fresno, Calif., 1962; asst. pastor St. John's Cathedral, Fresno, Calif., 1962—64; diocesan dir. Cath. Charities and Social Svc., Fresno, 1964—70; exec. dir. Infant of Prague Adoption Svc., Cath. Welfare Bur., Fresno, 1964—70; adminstr. St. Genevieve's Parish, Fresno, Calif., 1964—67, pastor, 1967—68; asst. pastor St. John's Cathedral, Fresno, Calif., 1968—73, rector, 1973—80; chancellor Diocese of Fresno, 1970—77; ordained bishop, 1975; aux. bishop & vicar gen. Diocese of Fresno, Calif., 1975—80; bishop Diocese of Stockton, Calif., 1980—85; archbishop Archdiocese of LA, 1985—; elevated to cardinal, 1991; cardinal-priest Ss. Quattro Coronati, 1991—. Faculty extension divsn. Fresno State U., 1965—67; sec. U.S. Cath. bishops ad hoc com. on farm labor Nat. Conf. Bishops, 1970—75; chmn. com. on pub. welfare and income maintenance Nat. Conf. Cath. Charities, 1969—70; adminstrv. com. Nat. Conf. Cath. Bishops, 1976—79, 1982—85, 1987—90, 1992—95, 1998—2001, com. migration and refugees, 1976—95, chmn. com. farm labor, 1981—92, com. moral evaluation of deterrence, 1986—88, cons. com., chmn. for prolife activities, 1990—95; com. social devel. and world peace U.S. Cath. Conf., 1985—93, chmn. internat. policy sect., 1987—93; com. justice and peace Pontifical Couns., 1984—98, chmn. com. domestic policy, 1998—2001, pastoral care of migrants and itinerant people, 1986—91, social comms., 1989—. Active Mexican-Am. Coun. for Better Housing, 1968—72, Fed. Commn. Agrl. Workers, 1987—93, Urban Coalition of Fresno, Calif., 1968—72, Fresno County Econ. Opportunities Commn., Calif., 1964—65, Fresno County Alcoholic Rehab. Com., Calif., 1966—67, Fresno City Charter Rev. Com., 1968—70, Fresno Redevel. Agy., 1970—75, L.A. 2000 Com., 1985—88, Blue Ribbon Com. Affordable Housing City of L.A., LA, 1988; mem. commn. to draft an ethics code L.A. City Govt., 1989—90; trustee St. Agnes Hosp., Fresno, 1969—73, Cath. U. Am., 1984—88, 1998—; named chaplain to Pope Paul VI, 1967; chaplain St. Vincent de Paul Soc., 1964—70; bd. dirs. West Coast Regional Office Bishops Com. for Spanish-Speaking, 1967—70; chmn. Calif. Assn. Cath. Charities Dirs., 1965—69; trustee St. Patrick's Sem., Archdiocese of San Francisco, 1974—75; bd. dirs. Fresno Cmty. Workshop, 1965—67, Rebuild L.A., 1992—95. Named Young Man of Yr., Fresno Jr. C. of C., 1967. Mem.: Canon Law Soc. Roman Catholic. Office: Archdiocese LA 3424 Wilshire Blvd Los Angeles CA 90010-2241

MAHONY, SUSAN, pharmaceutical company executive; BS, Aston U., PhD in Pharmacy; MBA, London Bus. Sch. Sales and mktg. positions Amgen, Bristol-Myers Squibb, Schering-Plough; joined Eli Lilly and Co., global mktg. and new product devel. positions, gen. mgr. Lilly Canada, 2008—09, sr. v.p. human resources, 2009—. Office: Eli Lilly and Co Lilly Corp Ctr Indianapolis IN 46285*

MAHOOD, KEN, music educator; 2 children. BS Music, The King's Coll., 1969; MusM, Manhattan Sch. Music, 1971; PhD in Music Theory, Met. Coll., 1981; PhD in Music, Concordia Coll., 1999; EdD in Music Edn., Am. U., 2001. Assoc. dir. music Christian Fellowship Ch., Ashburn, Va., 1981—2005; founder, dir., prof. music svcs. KME Internat., Inc., Leesburg, Va., 1983—. Faculty mem. Northern Va. CC, 1995—; pianist Billy Graham Crusade, Washington, 1991. Recipient 20 yr. Achievement Award, Assn. Of Music Students, 2001. Mem.: Va. Music Tchrs. Assn., Music Educators Nat. Conf., Am. Coll. Musicians, Music Tchrs. Nat. Assn. Office: KME Internat Inc PO Box 1616 Leesburg VA 20177 Personal E-mail: drken@musikdok.com.

MAHOOD, MARIE L, counselor, educator; b. Hackensack, NJ, Aug. 25, 1961; d. James George and Marie Josephine (Karlovsky) Mahood. BA in English, Montclair State U., 1983, MA in Counseling and Sch. Social Work, 1991; LPC, BCPC, DAPA. Bd. cert. profl. counselor NJ; cert. secondary tchr. NJ. English tchr. Marylawn of the Oranges HS, South Orange, NJ, 1983—87; grad. asst., counselor Montclair State Coll., Upper Montclair, NJ, 1989—90, asst. to dir. Women's Ctr., 1990—91; counselor, tchr. Hudson County CC, Jersey City, 1992—. Mem.: APA, ACA, NEA, Am. Psychotherapy Assn., NJ Counseling Assn., NJ Edn. Assn., Nat. Acad. Adv. Assn., Psi Chi, Kappa Delta Pi, Phi Kappa Phi. Democrat. Roman Catholic. Avocations: reading, writing. Office: Hudson County CC 70 Sip Ave Jersey City NJ 07306 Office Phone: 201-360-4155. Business E-Mail: mmahood@hccc.edu.

MAHOOD, R. WAYNE, education educator; b. Maryville, Mo., July 16, 1934; s. Victor E. and Ruth D. (England) M.; m. Barbara Clark, Dec. 29, 1956; children: Bruce Lee, David Clark. AB, Hamilton Coll., 1956; MA, U. Ill., 1962; PhD, Syracuse U., 1969. Tchr. social studies York Community High Sch., Elmhurst, Ill., 1959-66; prof. edn. SUNY, Geneseo, 1969-94, chair dept. edn., 1980-83. Author: Government USA, 1985, The Plymouth Pilgrims, 1989, Teaching Social Studies in Secondary and Middle Schools, 1991, Charlie Mosher's Civil War, 1994, Written in Blood, 1997, Life and Times of Brevet Major General James S. Wadsworth, 2003, Alexander "Fighting Elleck" Hays, 2005; contbr. articles to profl. jours. Recipient Disting. Social Studies Educator award N.Y. State Coun. for the Social Studies, 1984. Mem. NY State Coun. for Social Studies (pres. 1977-78), Nat. Coun. Social Studies. Business E-Mail: mahood@geneseo.edu.

MAHORN, RICK (DERRICK ALLEN MAHORN), professional basketball coach, retired professional basketball player; b. Hartford, Conn., Sept. 21, 1958; BBA, Hampton U., Va., 1980. Ctr., forward Washington Bullets, 1980—85, Detroit Pistons, 1985—89, 1996—98, Phila. 76ers, 1989—91, 1998—99, Virtus Roma, Italy, 1991—92, NJ Nets, 1992—96; head coach Rockford Lightning, Continental Basketball Assn., 1999—2000; asst. coach Atlanta Hawks, 2001—02, Detroit Shock, 2005—09, head coach, 2009—. Color analyst, Detroit Pistons broadcasts Sta. WDFN; mktg. dept. Palace Sports and Entertainment. Achievements include member of the NBA Championship winning Detroit Pistons, 1989. Office: Detroit Shock Palace Sports & Entertainment 5 Championship Dr Auburn Hills MI 48326*

MAHORNER, JAMES G., lawyer; b. DeLand, Fla., Jan. 28, 1932; s. James Glennon and Sue Mahorner; m. Brenda Johnson (div. May 1992); children: John G., James G., Mary Christine Gore, Amy Caprice, Ted G. JD, Stetson U., DeLand, FL; BSEE, US Naval Acad., Annapolis, MD. Bar: Fla. Atty. Pvt. Practice, Fla., 1975—; gen. counsel Dept. of HRS, Fla., 1970—74; trial counsel Dept. of Agr., Fla., 1965; ptnr. Dickens, Linn, and Mahorner, Tallahassee, Fla., 1967—70, White, Phipps, Linn, Furnell and Mahorner, Tallahassee, Fla., 1965—67; atty. State Attorney's Gen. Office, Fla., 1960—65. Mem.: Mensa. Democrat-Npl. Avocations: chess, bridge, tennis. Office: 234 9th Avenue South Jacksonville Beach FL 32250 Home: PO Box 50774 Jacksonville Beach FL 32240-0774 E-mail: jgmahorner@netzero.net.

MAHOWALD, MARY BRIODY, humanities educator; b. NYC, Mar. 24, 1935; d. Thomas Michael and Mae Angela Briody; m. Anthony Peter Mahowald, Apr. 11, 1971; children: Maureen Elise, Lisa Marie, Michael Anthony. BA, St. Francis Coll., Bklyn., 1965; MA, Marquette U., Milw., 1967; PhD, Marquette U., 1969. Tchr. parochial schs., NYC, 1955—65; asst. prof. St. Joseph's Coll., Bklyn., 1969—70, Villanova U., Villanova, Pa., 1970—72; asst. prof./assoc. prof. Ind. U., Indpls., 1972—82; assoc. prof. to prof. Case Western Res. U., Cleve., 1982—90; prof. to prof. emeritus U. Chgo., 1990—. Cons. NIH, Washington, 1995, 2000—03, U.S. Dept. Def., Washington, 1993—97, Pres.'s Coun. on Bioethics, Washington, 2003. Author: Women and Children in Health Care, 1993, Genes, Women, Equality, 2000; contbr. articles to profl. jours. Adult lit. tutor Blue Gargoyle, Chgo., 2000—; hospice vol. Chgo., 1997—98. Grantee, NIH, 1992—97, U.S. Dept. Energy, 1995—98, Am. Coun. Learned Socs., 1997—98. Mem.: Am. Soc. Social Philosophy (pres. 1998), Am. Soc. for Bioethics and Humanities, Am. Philos. Assn. Avocations: reading, needlepoint. Office: University of Chicago 5841 S Maryland Ave Chicago IL 60637

MAHR, AARON LEE, government agency administrator; b. Canton, Ill., Jan. 4, 1947; s. Ivan Lee and Nina Berniece Mahr; m. Nicole Adrienne Bourque, June 30, 1987; children: Jennifer Ward, David Abba, Timothy. BA, Emory U., 1969; Sr. Ofcls. in Nat. Security, Harvard U., 1991. Cert. Army Acquisitions Corps. Inventory mgmt. specialist U.S. Army Weapons Command, Rock Island, Ill., 1969-70; supply sys. analyst Frankford Arsenal, Phila., 1970-71, U.S. Army Gen. Materiel & Petroleum Ctr., New Cumberland, Pa., 1971-74; Jordan/Kuwait country desk officer U.S. Army Internat. Logistics Command, Alexandria, Va., 1974-76; Mid-East program mgr. U.S. Army Security Assistance Command, Alexandria, 1976-82; Mid-East program mgr. Office Dep. Chief

Staff for Logistics Hdqs. Dept. of the Army, Pentagon, Washington, 1982-83; chief Israel and Turkey divsn. U.S. Army Security Assistance Command, Alexandria, 1983-85; dir. Internat. Coop. Programs Activity, Alexandria, 1986—2000. Diabetes hotline cons. Inst. for Peripheral Nerve Surgery, Balt., 2000—08. Mem. Order of DeMolay, Delta Tau Delta. Avocations: videography, photography, travel, fishing. Home: 1228 Vista Hills Dr Lakeland FL 33813-5641 Personal E-mail: aruba4us@earthlink.net.

MAHROOF, RIZANA M., biology professor; b. Kandy, Sri Lanka; d. Mohamed Mahroof Thamby Lebbe and Zulfa Mohamed Mahroof; m. Mohamed Hanas Abdul Cader. Diploma, IDM Computer Studies Ltd., 1996; BS (hon.), U. Peradeniya, Sri Lanka, 1996; MPhil, U. Edinburgh, UK, 1999; PhD, Kans. State U., Manhattan, 2004. Postdoc. fellow Okla. State U., Stillwater, 2005—07; asst. prof. SC. State U., Orangeburg, 2007—. Advisor Touchwood Investments Pvt Ltd, Colombo, Sri Lanka, 2000—01; cons. U. Peradeniya, Sri Lanka, 2000—01. Recipient C. C. Burkhardt award for best rsch., Rocky Mountain Conf. Entomologists, 2003, Fred Clute awrad for Rsch. in Integrated Pest Mgmt., Kans. State U., 2003, Honorory awrad for Rsch. in Molecular biology and biochemistry sect., Entomol. Soc. Am., 2003. Mem.: Gen. Coun. U. Edinburgh, Sri Lanka Advancement Sci., Entomol. Soc. Am., Gamma Sigma Delta, Honor Soc. Agr., Sigma Xi. The Hon. Reserach Soc. Office: South Carolina State Univ 300 College Street NE Campus PO Box 7365 Orangeburg SC 29117 Office Fax: 803-516-4685. Business E-Mail: rmahroof@scsu.edu.

MAHROUS, HISHAM, pharmacist, educator; PhD, NLU. Prof. Midwestern U., Glendale, Ariz., 1981—. Recipient award, Rep. House Majority US Congress. Office: Midwestern Univ 19555 N 59th Ave Glendale AZ 85308 Office Fax: 623-572-35550. Business E-Mail: smahro@midwestern.edu.

MAHSMAN, DAVID LAWRENCE, writer, church administrator; b. Quincy, Ill., Aug. 16, 1950; s. Alvin Henry and Dorothy Marie (Schnack) M.; m. Lois Jean Mohn, July 27, 1975. BS in Journalism, So. Ill. U., 1972; MDiv, Concordia Theol. Seminary, Fort Wayne, Ind., 1983; STM, Concordia Sem., St. Louis, 1995. Staff writer Paddock Publs., Arlington Heights, Ill., 1972-73, Decatur (Ill.) Herald & Rev., 1973-76; press asst. Hon. Tom Railsback U.S. Ho. Reps., Washington, 1976-79, campaign press sec. Hon. Dan Coats Ft. Wayne, Ind., 1979-80, 82; pastor Trinity Luth. Ch., Glen Cove, NY, 1983-85; dir. news and info. Luth. Ch.-Mo. Synod, St. Louis, 1985—2005; exec. editor, contbr. Luth. Witness, St. Louis, 1985—2005; exec. editor Reporter, St. Louis, 1985—2005; asst. to exec. dir. Bd. Mission Svcs. Mo. Synod, 2005—09; dir., spl. assignments Eurasia, Bd. Mission Svcs. Mo. Synod, 2009—. Mem. Inter-Luth. task force on pornography Luth. Coun. U.S.A., 1986; mem. Washington adv. coun. Mo. Synod, Office of Govt. Info., Washington, 1987-2000. Editor: Augsburg Today: This We Believe, Teach and Confess, 1997. Recipient Jacob Scher Investigative Reporting award Women in Comm., 1974, Commendation award Concordia Hist. Inst., 1988, 98, 1st Place Reporting award Evang. Press Assn., 2003. Mem. Concordia Hist. Inst. (life). Republican. Lutheran. Avocations: travel, photography. Office: Luth Ch-Mo Synod 1333 S Kirkwood Rd Saint Louis MO 63122-7226 E-mail: david.mahsman@lcms.org.

MAI, CHAO CHEN, engineer; b. Kwangchow, Canton, China, Feb. 26, 1936; came to U.S., 1962, naturalized, 1973; m. Shao Shen Yam; children: Glenn, Kenneth. MSEE, Oreg. State U., 1964; PhD in Elec. Engring., Utah State U., 1968. Project engr. Sylvania Electric Co., Woburn, Mass., 1967-70; mgr. R&D Mostek Corp., Carrollton, Tex., 1970-76, v.p. R&D, 1976-84; founder, sr. v.p. Dallas Semiconductor Corp., 1984-2000, pres. and COO, 2000—. Mem. IEEE, Electrochem. Soc. Achievements include patent for Silicon gate combined with depletion load process, method for making a semiconductor device, MOSFET Fabrication Process; research advanced processing technology in integrated circuits; subspecialty integrated circuits, microchip technology.

MAI, MARTIN, nephrologist, consultant; MD, U. Tex., Dallas, 1983. Diplomate Am. Bd. Internal Medicine, 1986, in nephrology 1988, in critical care medicine 1991. Cons. Mayo Clinic, Jacksonville, Fla., 2004—. Home: 241 Northwind Ct Ponte Vedra FL 32082 Office: Mayo Clinic 4500 San Pablo Rd Jacksonville FL 32224 Office Fax: 904-956-3220. Business E-Mail: mai.martin@mayo.edu.

MAIA, TIAGO VAZ, researcher; s. Paulo António Mendes Maia and Maria Helena Vasconcelos Vaz Maia; m. Sofia Carmen Faria Maia Cavaco, July 7, 2001; 1 child, Diogo Vaz Cavaco Maia. Licenciatura in Computer Sci. and Engring., U. Nova de Lisboa, Lisbon, 1994; MS in Computer Sci., SUNY, Buffalo, 2001; MS in Psychology, Carnegie Mellon U., Pitts., 2004, PhD in Psychology, 2007. Software engr. Edinfor, EDP Group, Lisbon, 1996—98; rsch. trainee European Space Agy., Noordwijk, Netherlands, 1998—99; vis. scientist Internat. Computer Sci. Inst. and U. Calif., Berkeley, 2000; postdoc. rsch. fellow Columbia U. and NY State Psychiat. Inst., NYC, 2007—. Bd. dirs. Internat. Forum Portuguese Rschrs., Lisbon, 2007—; mem. conf. program com. Brain, Life, and Culture Conf., Lisbon, 2008—. Contbr. articles to profl. jours. Recipient Herbert A. Simon Grad. Tchg. Award, Dept. Psychology, Carnegie Mellon U., 2005—06, Grad. Student Tchg. Award Hon. Mention, Carnegie Mellon U., 2006—07; Rsch. Fellowship, PRODEP (Portugal), 1994, Ministry Sci. and Tech., Portugal, 1998—99, Grad. Rsch. Fellowship, 2000—04, Calouste Gulbenkian Found. (Portugal), 2004—07, Postdoc. fellowship, Klingenstein 3rd Generation Found., 2008—. Mem.: Phi Kappa Phi. Office: Columbia Univ & NYSPI 1051 Riverside Dr Unit 74 New York NY 10032

MAIBACH, BEN C., JR., consumer products company executive; b. Bay City, Mich., 1920; With Barton-Malow Co., Detroit, 1938—, v.p., dir.-in-charge field ops., 1949-53, exec. v.p., 1953-60, pres., 1960-76, chmn. bd., 1976; chmn. and dir. Barton-Malow Ent.; chmn. bd. Cloverdale Equipment Co. Trustee Barton-Malow Found, Maibach Found., 1967—; chmn. Apostolic Christian Woodhaven, Detroit; bishop Apostolic Christian Ch., Mich., Ont., Fla.; bd. dirs. S.E. Mich. chpt. ARC, Rural Gospel and Med. Missions of India. Home: 29711 Wentworth St Apt 207 Livonia MI 48154-3887 also: 5525 Azure Way Sarasota FL 34242-1857

MAIDA, ADAM JOSEPH CARDINAL, cardinal, archbishop; b. East Vandergrift, Pa., Mar. 18, 1930; BA, St. Vincent Coll., Latrobe, Pa., 1952; STL, St. Mary's U., Balt., 1956; JCL, Lateran U., Rome, 1960; JD, Duquesne U., 1964. Bar: Pa., US Dist. Ct. (we. dist.) Pa., US Supreme Ct. Ordained priest Diocese of Pitts., 1956, assoc. pastor through vice-chancellor, gen. counsel, 1956—84; ordained bishop, 1984; bishop Diocese of Green Bay, Wis., 1984—89; archbishop Archdiocese of Detroit, 1990—2009, archbishop emeritus Mich., 2009—; elevated to cardinal, 1994; cardinal-priest Ss. Vitale, Valerian, Gervasio & Protasio, 1994—; superior Cayman Islands, Antilles, 2000—. Past asst. prof. theology, LaRoche Coll.; past adj. prof., Duquesne Univ. Sch. Law; Mem. Congregation for Catholic Edn., Congregation for the Clergy, Pontifical Council for Interpretation of Legis. Texts, Pontifical Council for Pastoral Care of Migrants & Itinerant Peoples, Cardinal Commn. for the Supervision of the Inst. for Works of Religion, Roman Curia. Author, Ownership Control & Sponsorship of Catholic Institutions, 1975, Church Property, Church Finances and Church-Related Corporations, A Canon Law Handbook, 1983; ed., The Tribunal Reporter, 1970, Issues in the Labor-Mgmt. Dialogue: Church Perspectives, 1983. Trustee, Basilica of the Nat. Shrine of the Immaculate Conception, Catholic Univ. Am., Mich. Catholic Conf., Papal Found. Phila.; chmn. bd. trustees, Sacred Heart Major Sem., S.S. Cyril & Methodius Sem.; mem. bd. gov. Ave Maria Sch. Law; bd. dir. Nat. Catholic Bioethics Ctr. Mem.: U.S. Conf. Bishops. Roman Catholic. Home and Office: Archdiocese of Detroit 1234 Washington Blvd Detroit MI 48226-1825*

MAIDEN, BARRY, chef; b. Saltville, Va., 1975; married; 1 child, Dylan. Grad., New England Culinary Inst., Montpelier, Vt., 2000. Chef l'Espalier, Boston; sous chef Sel de la Terre, Boston; chef de cuisine Lumiere, Newton; owner, exec. chef Hungry Mother, Cambridge. Served in USAR. Named one of America's Best New Chefs, Food & Wine Mag., 2009. Office: Hungry Mother 233 Carndinal Medeiros Ave Cambridge MA 02141 Office Phone: 617-499-0090.*

MAIDIQUE, MODESTO ALEX, engineering educator, former academic administrator; b. Havana, Cuba, Mar. 20, 1940; s. Modesto Maidique and Hilda Rodriguez; m. Nancy; children: Ana Teresa, Mark Alex. BS, MIT, 1962, MS, 1964, PhD, 1970. Instr. MIT, Boston, 1976-79; v.p., gen. mgr. Analog Devices Semiconductor, Boston, 1970-76; asst. prof. Harvard U., Boston, 1976-81; assoc. prof. Stanford U., Palo Alto, Calif., 1981-84; sr. ptnr. Hambrecht and Quist Venture Ptnrs., Palo Alto, Calif., 1981-86; co-founder, dir. U. Miami Innovation and Entepreneurship Inst., 1984-86; pres. Fla. Internat. U., Miami, 1986—2009, dir. Ctr. for Leadership, faculty mem. Coll. of Bus. Adminstrn., 2009—. Mem. Pres.'s Edn. Policy Adv. Com.; chmn. Beacon Coun., 1992-93. Recipient Citizenship award HEW, 1973, Teaching award Stanford U., 1983 Mem. IEEE, Assn. Cuban Engrs, Carnival Corp. (bd. dirs., 1994-), Nat. Semiconductor Corp. (bd. dirs., 1993-). Republican. Roman Catholic. Office: Fla Internat U Ctr for Leadership MARC 270 Miami FL 33199 Fax: 305-348-3660. E-mail: maidique@fiu.edu.*

MAIDMAN, RICHARD HARVEY MORTIMER, lawyer; b. NYC, Nov. 17, 1933; s. William and Ada (Seegle) M.; m. Lynne Rochelle Lateiner, Apr. 3, 1960 (div. Sept. 1987); m. Gail Lowe Haymes, Sept. 27, 1998; children: Patrick, Mitchel, Dagny. BA, Williams Coll., 1955; JD, Yale U., 1959; postgrad., NYU Grad. Sch. Bus., 1957, NYU Grad. Sch. Law, 1960-77. Bar: NY 1961, Fla. 1961, US Dist. Ct. 1962, 79, US Ct. Appeals 1966, US Supreme Ct. 1978. Assoc. Saxe, Bacon & O'Shea, NYC, 1962-64; ptnr. Weiner, Maidman & Goldman, NYC, 1964-67; pvt. practice NYC and Fla., 1968—96; mng. gen. ptnr. R & D Maidman Family Ltd. Partnership, NYC, 1972—; of counsel Maidman and Mittelman LLP, 1996—; chmn. Townhouse Mgmt. Co., 2002—, Fashion Wear Realty Co., Inc., 2004—. Of counsel Shwal, Thompson & Bloch, NYC and Geneva, 1976-87; pres. MBS Equities, Inc., 1970-88, Fashion Wear Realty Co., Inc., NYC, 1975-2004, chmn., 2004—; Barcelona Hotel Ltd., Miami Beach, Fla., 1975-84, New Haven Projects Co., 1987—97; dir., gen counsel The Farr Companies, Washington, 1990-92; legis. counsel Theodore R. Kupferman, 17th Congl. Dist. NY, 1966-68; receiver Halloran House Hotel, NYC, 1981; prin. Manhattan Parking Sys. Group, NYC, 1990-2007. Contbr. articles to profl. jours. Mem. ABA, NY State Bar Assn., Fla. Bar Assn., Assn. of the Bar of the City of NY, NYC Real Estate Bd. NY. Home: Steamboat Landing 27 Astor Ln Sands Point NY 11050-2602 also: 9 E 79th St New York NY 10021-0123 Office: 70 E 55th St New York NY 10022-3222 Office Phone: 212-755-0500. Personal E-mail: rhmm59@aya.yale.edu. Business E-Mail: richard@maidman.org.

MAIDMENT, KAREN E., bank executive; b. 1958; married; 2 children. Grad., Galt Collegiate Inst., 1977; B in Commerce, McMaster U. Chartered acct., 1983. With Clarkson Gordon, 1981; CFO Clarica Life Insurance Co., 1988; exec. v.p., CFO BMO Fin. Grp., 2000—03, sr. exec. v.p., 2003—. Mem., Mgmt. Bd. Exec. Com. BMO Fin. Grp. Pres. Canadian Fedn. U. Women; bd. mem. Cambridge Chamber of Commerce; hon. chair Easter Seals' Ball. Recipient Women of Distinction award, YWCA, 2001, Mgmt. Achievement award, McGill U., 2004, Wayne C. Fox Disting. Alumni award, McMaster U. Michael G. Degroote Sch. of Bus., 2004; named Canada's CFO of Yr., Fin. Executives Internat. Can. and PricewaterhouseCoopers LLP, 2006; named one of 25 Women to Watch, US Banker, 2006; named to Power 50 list, Fin. Post, 2004, 2005, 2006. Fellow: Inst. Chartered Accountants; mem.: Waterloo-Wellington Chartered Accountants Assn. (pres.). Office: BMO Financial Group Corporate Communications Media and Publi 302 Bay St 11th Fl Toronto ON Canada M5X 1A1 Office Phone: 416-867-3996.

MAIENSCHEIN, FRED, retired physicist; b. Belleville, Ill., Oct. 28, 1925; s. Fred and Ethel (Forsythe) M.; m. Joyce Kylander, Aug. 14, 1948; children: Jane, Jon. BS in Chem. Engring, Rose Hulman Inst. Tech., 1945; MS in Physics, Ind. U., 1948, PhD in Physics, 1949. Physicist Oak Ridge Nat. Lab., 1951-60, assoc. dir. engring. physics div., 1960-66; co-dir. Oak Ridge Electron Linear Accelerator, 1965-74, dir. engring. physics div., 1966-90, ret., 1990. Mem. com. reactor physics Nuclear Energy Agy., 1962-89; mem. adv. com. radiation aspects of SST, FAA, 1969-74; mem. subcoms. Nat. Com. Radiation Protection, 1959-71. Contbr. articles profl. jours., chpts. in books. Fellow Am. Nuclear Soc.; mem. Am. Phys. Soc., AAAS, Soc. Neurosci., Tau Beta Pi. Home: 2625 E Southern Ave C-247 Tempe AZ 85282

MAIER, CHARLES STEVEN, history professor; b. NYC, Feb. 23, 1939; s. Louis and Muriel (Krailsheimer) M.; m. Pauline Alice Rubbelke, June 17, 1961; children: Andrea Nicole, Nicholas Winterer, Jessica Elizabeth Heine. AB, Harvard U., 1960, PhD, 1967; postgrad., St. Anthony's Coll., Oxford, Eng., 1960—61. Instr. history Harvard U., Cambridge, Mass., 1967-69, asst. prof., 1969-73, lectr., 1973-75, prof. history, 1981-91, Krupp Found. prof. European studies, 1991—2002, Leverett Saltonstall prof. history, 2002—, dir. Ctr. for European Studies, 1994-2001, 2006; vis. prof. U. Bielefeld, Germany, 1976; assoc. prof. history Duke U., Durham, NC, 1976-79, prof., 1979-81. Rsch. fellow Lehrman Inst., NYC, 1975-76; mem. assoc. staff Brookings Instn., Washington, 1978-84; mem. coun. Fondation Jean Monnet pour l'Europe, Lausanne, Switzerland; mem. joint comm. on We. Europe Social Sci. Rsch. Coun. and Am. Coun. Learned Socs., 1978-84, chmn., 1979-81; mem. German Am. Acad. Coun., Bonn, Germany and Washington, 1998-2001; chair selection com., Am. Acad. Berlin, 2001-05; vis. prof. Sch. Advanced Studies in Social Scis., Paris, 2007. Author: Recasting Bourgeois Europe, 1975 (Am. Hist. Assn. George Louis Beer award 1976, Herbert Baxter Adams award 1977), In Search of Stability, 1987, The Unmasterable Past, 1988, Dissolution: The Crisis of Communism and the End of East Germany, 1997, Among Empires: American Ascendancy and its Predecesssons, 2006; editor: The Origins of the Cold War and Contemporary Europe, 1978, rev. edit., 1990, (with Dan S. White) The Thirteenth of May and the Advent of de Gaulle's Republic, 1967, (with Leon Lindberg) The Politics of Inflation and Economic Stagnation, 1985, Changing Boundaries of the Political, 1987, The Marshall Plan and Germany, 1991. contbr. numerous essays, chpts. to books, book reviews, 1970-2007. Decorated comdr.'s cross Order of Merit, Germany; fellow NEH, 1977-78, German Marshall Fund, 1980-81, Guggenheim Found., 1984-85; rsch. grantee MacArthur Found., 1988-89; recipient Alexander von Humboldt Found. Rsch. prize, 2003; fellow Woodrow Wilson Ctr. for Scholars, Washington, D.C., 1989. Mem. Coun. on Fgn. Rels., Am. Hist. Assn., Soc. Italian Hist. Studies, Soc. Historians of Am. Fgn. Rels., Am. Acad. Arts and Scis., Phi Beta Kappa. Office: Harvard U Ctr for European Studies Cambridge MA 02138 Office Phone: 617-495-4303. Business E-Mail: csmaier@fas.harvard.edu.

MAIER, GERALD JAMES, gas industry executive; b. Regina, Sask., Can., Sept. 22, 1928; s. John Joseph and Mary M. Student, Notre Dame Coll., Wilcox, U. Man., U. Alta., U. Western Ont.; LLD (hon.), U. Alta., 1999; LLD, U. Calgary, 2005. With petroleum and mining industries Can., U.S., Australia, U.K.; responsible for petroleum ops. Africa, United Arab Emirates, S.E. Asia; past chmn., pres., CEO TransCan. PipeLines, Calgary, Canada, 1985-99; vice-chmn. NOVA Chems. Corp., Calgary, 1998-2000. Chmn. Can. Nat. Com. for World Petroleum Congresses, 1991—94, Van Horne Inst. for Internat. Transp., 1992—2000; bd. dirs. Stream-Flo Industries, Ltd., 1998—, Master Flo Valve Inc., 1998—, Bow Valley Energy Ltd., 2006—09, GEM Inc., 2006—, Willbros Group, Inc., 2007—09, Gen. Magnetic Internat. Inc., 2008—. Chancellor Notre Dame Coll. Named Hon. Col. (ret.) King's Own Calgary Rgt., Resource Man of Yr. Alta. Chamber of Resources, 1990, Officer Order of Can., 2004; named to Can. Petroleum Hall of Fame, 1999; recipient Can. Engr.'s Gold medal Can. Coun. Profl. Engrs., 1990, Disting. Alumni award U. Alta., 1992, Mgmt. award McGill U., 1993, Centennial award Alta. Assn. Engrs., Geologists and Geophysicists, 1994, Hal Godwin award U. Calgary, 1999, Can. Bus. Leader award U. Alta., 1999, Can. Engring. Leader award U. Calgary, 2003, Alta. Centennial medal, 2005. Fellow Can. Acad. Engring.; mem. Assn. Profl. Engrs., Geologists and Geophysicists Alta. (past pres.), Can. Inst. Mining and Metallurgy (Past Pres.'s Meml. medal 1971), Legion of Honour, Soc. Petroleum Engr. (mem. CDN sect. 2006). Avocations: golf, downhill skiing, shooting, fishing. Office: Granmar Investments Ltd 88 Massey Pl SW Calgary AB Canada T2V 2G8

MAIER, PAUL LUTHER, history professor, minister, writer; b. St. Louis, May 31, 1930; s. Walter A. and Hulda (Eickhoff) M.; m. Joan M. Ludtke, 1967; children: Laura Ann, Julie Joan, Krista Lynn, Katherine Marie. MA, Harvard U., 1954; MDiv, Concordia Sem., St. Louis, 1955; postgrad., U. Heidelberg, Fed. Republic Germany; PhD summa cum laude, U. Basel, Switzerland, 1957; LittD (hon.), Concordia Sem., St. Louis, 1995, Concordia U., Irvine, 2007; LLD (hon.), Concordia U., Ann Arbor, 2000. Campus chaplain, 1958—99; prof. ancient history Western Mich. U., Kalamazoo, 1960—. Lectr. in field. Author: A Man Spoke, A World Listened, 1963, Pontius Pilate, 1968, First Christmas, 1971, First Easter, 1973, First Christians, 1976, The Flames of Rome, 1981, In the Fullness of Time, 1991, A Skeleton in God's Closet, 1994, More Than a Skeleton, 2003, The Da Vinci Code -Fact or Fiction?, 2004, (children's book) Martin Luther-A Man Who Changed The World, 2004; editor: The Best of Walter A. Maier, 1980; editor: Josephus—The Jewish War, 1982; editor, transl.: Josephus—The Essential Writings, 1988, Josephus—The Essential Works, 1995, Eusebius—The Church History, 1999; author, host: (video series)Jesus--Legend or Lord?, The Odyssey of St. Paul, Christianity, the First Three Centuries; contbr. 250 articles and revs. to profl. jours. Recipient Gold Medallion Book award ECPA, 1989, Disting. Faculty Scholar Western Mich. U., 1981, Alumni award tchg. excellence, 1974; named Outstanding Educator in Am., 1974-75, Prof. of Yr. Coun. for Advancement and Support of Edn., 1984, citation Mich. Acad. of Sci., Arts and Letters, 1985. Mem. Phi Beta Kappa. Office: Western Mich U Dept of History Kalamazoo MI 49008 Office Phone: 269-387-4816. Business E-Mail: maier@wmich.edu.

MAIER, PETER KLAUS, lawyer; b. Wurzburg, Germany, Nov. 20, 1929; came to U.S., 1939, naturalized, 1945; s. Bernard and Joan (Sonder) M.; m. Melanie L. Stoff, Dec. 15, 1963; children: Michele Margaret, Diana Lynn. BA cum laude, Claremont McKenna Coll., 1949; JD, U. Calif., Berkeley, 1952; LLM in Taxation, NYU, 1953. Bar: Calif. 1953, U.S. Supreme Ct. 1957; cert. specialist in taxation law, Calif. Atty. tax div. U.S. Dept Justice, Washington, 1956-59; pvt. practice tax law San Francisco, 1959-81. Prof. law Hastings Coll. Law, U. Calif., San Francisco, 1967-95; vis. prof. U. Calif. Boalt Sch. Law, Berkeley, 1988-89, Stanford U. Sch. Law, 1996-98; chmn. Maier, Siebel, Baber, Inc., San Francisco, 1981—2004; mng. dir. U.S. Trust Co. NA, San Francisco, 1998—2007; chmn. Fromm Inst. for Lifelong Learning, U. San Francisco, 1997—; pres. John B. Huntington Found., 1996—, Alfred and Hanna Fromm Found., 1974—. Author books on taxation; contbr. articles to profl. jours. Chmn. Property Resources Inc., Larkspur, Calif., 1968-77; pres. Calif. Property Devel. Corp., San Francisco, 1974-81. Capt. USAF, 1953-56, pres. Pvt. Wealth Ptnrs. Larkspur, 2003-. Mem. Calif. Bar Assn. (chmn. sect. taxation 1970-71), Order of Coif. Home: 2559 Clay St San Francisco CA 94115 Business E-Mail: pmaier@pwpart.com.

MAIER, ROBERT HENRY, retired real estate executive; b. Greenville, Tex., Nov. 19, 1932; s. William Lokey and Charlsie Lorraine (Nation) M.; m. Ruth Jean Chapman, Mar. 1, 1968; children: Alice, Joy Kupp. BA, So. Meth. U., 1964. Pers. dir. Atlantic Richfield Co., Dallas, 1954-69; v.p. adminstrn. ETMF Freight System, Dallas, 1969-78; chief pers. officer Varo, Inc., Garland, Tex., 1978-80; corp. v.p. adminstrn. Comml. Metals Co., Dallas, 1980-88; pres., COO The Staubach Co., Dallas, 1988-93; pres., CEO, bd. dirs. Cornerstone Mgmt. Co., 1993-96; pres., CEO ProblemSolvers, Inc., 1996—2004.

MAIER, RONALD VITT, surgeon, educator; b. Wheeling, W.Va., Oct. 23, 1947; BS, U. Notre Dame, 1969; MD, Duke U., 1973. Intern Parkland Meml. Hosp., Dallas, 1973-74; resident U. Wash. Hosps., Seattle, 1974-78; rsch. assoc. Scripps Rsch. Found., La Jolla, Calif., 1978-81; surgeon-in-chief HMC, Seattle, 1993—; vice chair U. Wash., Seattle, 1994—, Jane and Donald D. Trunkey prof., 2005—. Office: Dept Surgery 359796 Harborview Med Ctr 325 9th Ave Seattle WA 98104-2499 Office Phone: 206-744-3564. Business E-Mail: ronmaier@uw.edu.

MAIER, THEODORE JOSEPH, literature and language educator; life ptnr. Mary Magdalene, Dec. 25; 1 child, Jesus. PhD, Miami U. Ohio, Oxford, 2005. Cert. permanent secondary tchg. NY State, 1989. Assoc. prof. English Danville CC, Va., 2004—.

MAIER, WILLIAM BRYAN, II, physics professor; b. Okla. City, Jan. 30, 1937; s. William Bryan and Joan Maier; m. Ruth Maier, Sept. 21, 1958; children: William Christian, Alycia J. R. Turner, Terese S. Rainwater, Victoria E. PhD in Physics, U. Chgo., 1964. Staff mem. Los Alamos Nat. Lab., N.Mex., 1964—93; sr. lectr. dept. physics Naval Postgrad. Sch., Monterey, Calif., 1995—. Sci. rsch. coun. fellow U. Notttingham, Nottinghamshire, England, 1979—80. Contbr. scientific papers. Sr. fellow, Sci. Rsch. Coun., UK, 1979—80. Achievements include first to spectroscopy and chemistry in cold solutions, low-energy ion-neutral collisions, railgun technology. Office: Naval Postgrad Sch Dept Physics Monterey CA 93943 Business E-Mail: wmaier@nps.edu.

MAIESE, KENNETH, neurologist, neuroscientist; b. Audubon, NJ, Dec. 5, 1958; s. Charles and Margaret (Fioretti) M. BA summa cum laude, U. Pa., 1981; MD, Cornell U., 1985. Intern N.Y. Hosp., 1985—86, resident neurology, 1986—89, asst. attending physician, 1989—94; asst. prof. Cornell U. Med. Coll., NYC, 1989—94; assoc. prof. dept. neurology, anatomy and cell biology Ctr. Molecular Toxicology and Medicine Wayne State U., Detroit, 1994—99, dir. lab. molecular and cellular cerebral ischemia Ctr. Molecular Toxicology, 1994—, prof. dept. neurology, anatomy, cell biology Ctr. Molecular Toxicology, 1999—; prof. Barbara Ann Karmanos Cancer Inst., 2005—. Dir. neurol. diagnosis NY Hosp., 1991—94; chmn. nat. brain/stroke consortium Am. Heart Assn., 2000—01, exec. coun., 2001—, nat peer rev. steering com., 2002—, mem. rsch. com., 2003—; mem. study sect. cell death and injury NIH/CDIN, 2003—; mem. neurobiology study sect. Vet.'s Adminstrn., 2004—; spkr. in field. Author: Neurology and General Medicine, 1989, Neurological and Neurosurgical ICU Medicine, 1988; editor-in-chief Current Neurovascular Rsch., 2002—, Oxidative Stress and Cellular Longevity, 2007—; editor: Neuronal and Vascular Plasticity, 2003, Neurovascular Medicine, 2008-, Forkhead Transcripttion Factors, 2009, Aging & Oxidative Stress, 2009-; mem. editl. bd. Letters in Drug Design and Discovery, 2002—, Histology and Histopathology, 2002—, Jour. Histological Histopathology, 2002—, Drug Design Revs., 2003—, Medicinal Chemistry, 2004—, Current Drug Targets-Heme Agts., Jour. Heart Digest, 2005—, Internat. Jour. Molecular Medicine, 2005—, Ctrl. Nervous Sys. Agts., Medicinal Chemistry, 2006—, Open Neurosci. Letters, 2007—, Open Biochem. Jour., 2007—, Current Bioactive Components, 2007-, Open Neurology Jour., 2007-, Jour. Epithelial Biology and Pharmacology, 2008-, Jour. Interferon & Cytokine, 2008-, Jour. Coll Death, 2008-, Jour. Breast Cancer, 2009-, World Jour. Stem Cells, 2009-, World Jour. Diabetes, 2009-; editl. bd. contbr. The Merck Manual Profl. Home Edit., 2007; contbr. articles to profl. jours. Joseph Collins scholar, 1981-85, Grupe Found. scholar, 1985; grantee NIH, 1990—, Nat. Stroke Assn., 1992-94, Alzheimer's Assn., 1994—, Am. Heart Assn., 1995—, United Cerebral Palsy Found., 1995—, Janssen Found., 1995—; recipient Young Scientist award Jours. Cerebral Blood Flow, 1991, Hoechst Investigator award, 1993, Robert G. Siekert award in stroke, 1994, Johnson and Johnson Disting. Investigator award, 1996-98, Maiese Lab. Neurosci. Tng. award J & J/Janssen, 1998, Boehringer Investigator award, 1999, NIH/NIEHS award, Learn Found. award, 2002-03, MI Challenge award, Bugher Found. award, 2005, Am. Diabetes Assn. award, 2006, NIH/NIA award, 2007, NIH/NINDS/NIA award, 2009; named one of Am.'s Top Physicians, 2005-09, Best of US Physicians, 2006-08, Top Dr. 2009-. Mem. NIH (minority edn. tng. 2002—, spl. emphasis cellular pathophysiologyspl., emphasis panel cellular degeneration 2004—), Am. Acad. Neurology, NY Acad. Scis., Assn. for Rsch. in Nervous and Mental Diseases, Am. Neurol. Assn. (elected), Soc. Neurosci., Internat. Acad. Cardiology (sci. com. 2003-, Bugher Found. award 2005-), Am. Diabetes Assn. (Sr. Investigator award 2006), Alzheimer's Soc. UK, Diabetes Found. UK, Rsch. Coun. Hong Kong, Rsch. Coun. Spain, NIH Applied Metabolom Techs., Austrian Sci. Fund., Nat. Swiss Sci. Found., Wellcome Trust, UK, Alzheimers Rsch. Trust, UK, NMRC, Singapore, Natural Scis. & Engring. Rsch. Coun. Can, Am. Diabetes Assn. Rev. Roman Catholic. Achievements include rsch. in imidazole receptors, cerebral ischemia, nitric oxide toxicity, growth factor neuroprotection, signal cellular transduction mechanisms, metabotropic glutamate receptors, gene regulation, and gene therapy, patents in field. Office: Wayne State U Sch Medicine 8C-1 U Health Ctr Dept Neur 4201 Saint Antoine St Detroit MI 48201-2153 Business E-Mail: kmaiese@med.wayne.edu.

MAIKO, SANETA MORARA, educator and director; b. Nyamira, Nyanza, Kenya, Dec. 5, 1971; s. Zablon Maiko Aris and Britha Nyamisa Moraa Maiko; m. Beatrice M. Saneta, Feb. 24, 2001; 1 child, Rachael M. Morara. PhD in Missiology, Concordia Theol. Sem., Ft. Wayne, Ind., 2008. Cert. clin. pastoral educator Luth. Hosp. Ind., 2006, chaplain Ft. Wayne Police, 2006, victims asst. NVAA, 2006. Founder Crime Victim Care Allen County, Ft. Wayne, 2006—, exec. dir., 2006—; staff chaplain Select Splty. Hosp., Ft. Wayne, 2006—. Adj. prof. Ind. U.-Purdue U., Ft. Wayne, 2007—. Author: (book) Youth Faith and Culture. Mayor's commn. on domestic violence Mayor's Office, Fort Wayne, Ind., 2008. Mem.: Am. Acad. Religion. Avocation: reading. Office: Crime Victim Care Allen County 2117 E State Blvd Fort Wayne IN 46805 Business E-Mail: maikos@ipfw.edu.

MAIKON, MARC STEVEN, podiatrist; BA, Grinnell Coll., 1980; BS, U. Iowa, 1982; DPM, U. Osteo. Medicine, Des Moines, 1989. Cert. Am. Coun. Cert. Podiatric Physicians and Surgeons. Podiatrist, owner Family Foot Care Ctr. PLC, Cedar Rapids, Iowa, 1991—. Mem. Am. Coll. Foot Surgeons, Am. Podiatric Med. Assn., Iowa Podiatric Med. Soc., C. of C. Cedar Rapids, Rotary Internat. Office: Family Foot Ctr 3359 Center Point Rd NE Cedar Rapids IA 52402-5568 Home: 3359 Center Point Rd Ne Cedar Rapids IA 52402-5568

MAILLOUX, ROBERT JOSEPH, physicist; b. Lynn, Mass., June 20, 1938; s. Joseph H. and Nora S. M.; m. Marlene Schirf, Jan. 14, 1967; children: Patrice, Julie, Denise. BS, Northeastern U., 1961; SM, Harvard U., 1962, PhD, 1965. Physicist NASA Electronics Rsch. Ctr., Cambridge, Mass., 1965—70, Air Force Cambridge Rsch. Labs., Bedford, Mass., 1970—77, Rome Air Devel. Ctr., Bedford, 1977—80, chief antennas and components divsn., electromagnetic directorate, 1990—91; sr. scientist Air Force Rsch. Lab., 1992—2004. Lectr. Tufts U., Boston, 1985-, rsch. prof. U. Mass. Amherst, 2006-. Author: Phased Array Antenna Handbook and Elec. Scaning Arrays; editor History of Wireless; guest editor IEEE/AP-S Transactions Spl. Issue on Phased Array Antennas, 1999; contbr. chpts. to 8 textbooks, articles to sci. jours. Served with C.E. U.S. Army, 1966-68. Recipient Air Force Marcus O'Day paper award, 1971, Engineer of Yr. award Rome Air Devel. Ctr., 1988, fellow 1988 Fellow IEEE (chmn. tech. com. 1997 phased array symposium, spl. achievement award 1969, 76, nat. lectr., assoc. editor Trans. on Antennas and Propagation 1984-92, Harry Diamond award 1991, Fred Diamond award 1997, Third Millenium medal, 2000, Disting. Achievement award 2005); mem. Antenna and Propagation Soc. (chmn. Boston chpt. 1968, nat. meetings chmn. 1977-80, adcom mem. 1977-80, v.p. 1982, pres. 1983), Internat. Sci. Radio Union (Commn. B tech. activities chmn. 1980—), Sigma Xi (pres. Hanscom chpt. 1980-81), Eta Kappa Nu, Tau Beta Pi. Achievements include 12 patents in field. Office: AFRL/RYHA 80 Scot Dr Hanscom AFB MA 01731

MAILMAN, STANLEY, lawyer; b. NYC, Mar. 9, 1930; m. Mary Ann Banks, Aug. 9, 1963; children: Joshua, Alexander. BA, Cornell U., 1950, LLB, 1952; LLM in Internat. Law, NYU, 1956. Bar: N.Y. 1953, U.S. Dist. Ct. (so. dist.) N.Y. 1957, U.S. Ct. Appeals (2d cir.) 1960. Pvt. practice, NYC, 1955—89; mem. Satterlee Stephens Burke & Burke, NYC, 1989—, of counsel. Adj. prof. St. John's U. Law Sch., N.Y.C., 1986-88. Co-author: Immigration Law and Procedure, revised, 2009; columnist Immigration Law, NY, 1976-2006; editor The New Simpson-Rodino Law of 1986, 1986; contbr. articles to profl. jours. Bd. dirs. Internat. Rescue Com., N.Y.C., 1976-80, Lawyers Com. for Human Rights, N.Y.C., 1982-95. Served with U.S. Army, 1953-55. Mem. Am. Immigration Lawyers Assn. (pres. 1975-76), Consular Law Soc. (pres. 1985-86). Office: 230 Park Ave New York NY 10169-0005 Personal E-mail: stanley1mailman@aol.com.

MAIMON, ELAINE PLASKOW, academic administrator; b. Phila., July 28, 1944; d. Louis J. and Gertrude (Canter) Plaskow; m. Morton A. Maimon, Sept. 30, 1967; children: Gillian Blanche, Alan Marcus. AB, U. Pa., 1966, MA, 1967, PhD, 1970. Asst. prof. Haverford Coll., 1971-73; lectr. Arcadia U., Glenside, Pa., 1973-75, asst. prof., dir. writing, 1975-77, assoc. prof., 1977-83, assoc. dean, 1980-84, assoc. v.p., prof. English, 1984-86; adj. assoc. prof. U. Pa., Phila., 1982-83; assoc. dean of coll. Brown U., Providence, 1986-88; dean, prof. English Queens Coll. CUNY, Flushing, NY, 1988-96; campus CEO, provost Ariz. State U. West, Phoenix, 1996—2004; v.p. Ariz. State U., 1996—2004; chancellor U. Alaska, Anchorage, 2004—07; pres. Govs. State U., University Park, Ill., 2007—. Nat. bd. cons. NEH, 1977-81; mem. adv. bd. Cox Comm., 1997-2001; bd. dirs. Arrowhed Cmty. Bank. Co-author: Writing in the Arts and Sciences, 1981, A Writer's Resource, 2003; co-editor: Readings in the Arts and Sciences, 1984, Thinking, Reasoning and Writing, 1989, A Writer's Resource, 2003, 2d edit., 2007, The New McGraw Hill Handbook, 2007, Writing Intensive, 2007, The Brief McGraw Hill Handbook, 2008. Trustee Heard Mus., Phoenix, 1999—2005. Recipient Golden Heart award, Today's Ariz. Woman, 2000, Women of Distinction award, YMCA, Maricopa County, 2001, YWCA award in Edn., 2002, World award, Girl Scouts Am., Ariz. Cactus-Pine Coun., 2002, Woman of Vision award, Phoenix Bus. Jour.; Elaine Maimon award for Excellence in Writing named in her honor, Arcadia U., 1994. Mem.: MLA (exec. com., tchg. of writing divsn.), Am. Assn. Colls. and Univs. (exec. bd. 2002—06), Conf. on Coll. Composition Comm. (exec. com. 1985—87), ACE Nat. Commn. Women, Nat. Coun. Tchrs. English (nominating com. 1986—87, teaching of writing divsn. 1991), Phi Beta Kappa. Office: Govs State U Office of Pres 1 University Parkway University Park IL 60466-0975 Office Phone: 708-534-4130. Business E-Mail: emaimon@govst.edu.

MAIN, DAVID C., lawyer; b. Des Moines, Feb. 29, 1948; BA, DePauw Univ., 1970; MTS, Harvard Divinity Sch., 1973; JD, Georgetown Univ., 1976. Bar: DC 1977, Va., US Dist. Ct. (DC), US Ct. Appeals (DC cir.), US Supreme Ct. Staff mem. U.S. Senate Rep. Policy Com., 1974—76; health counsel to U.S. Senator Richard S. Schweiker, 1976—79; counsel U.S. Senate Subcom. on Health & Scientific Rsch., 1977—79; atty., chmn. managed care practice Gardner Carton & Douglas; atty., chmn. health care practice Crowell & Moring; ptnr., co-chmn. Healthcare practice Pillsbury Winthrop Shaw Pittman, McLean, Va. Founder & coord. Healthcare Tech. Network of Greater Washington; counsel Health Mgmt. Academy. Contbr. articles to profl. jours. Mem.: Am. Health Lawyers Assn., Md. BioScience Alliance, DC Hosp. Assn., Phi Beta Kappa. Office: Pillsbury Winthrop Shaw Pittman 1650 Tysons Blvd Mc Lean VA 22102-4859 Office Phone: 703-770-7518. Office Fax: 702-770-7901. Business E-Mail: david.main@pillsburylaw.com.

MAIN, EDNA DEWEY (JUNE MAIN), education educator; b. Hyannis, Mass., Sept. 1, 1940; d. Seth Bradford and Edna Wilhelmina (Wright) Dewey; m. Donald John Main, Sept. 9, 1961 (div. Dec. 1989); children: Alison Teresa Main Ronzon, Susan Christine Main Leddy, Steven Donald. Degree in merchandising, Tobe-Coburn Sch., NYC, 1960; BA in Edn., U. North Fla., Jacksonville, 1974, MA in Edn., 1979, M in Adminstrn. and Supervision, 1983; PhD in Curriculum and Instrn., U. Fla., Gainsville, 1990. Asst. buyer Abraham & Straus, Bklyn., 1960-61; asst. mdse. mgr. Interstate Dept. Stores, NYC, 1962-63; tchr. Holiday Hill Elem. Sch., Jacksonville, Fla., 1974-86; instr. summer sci. inst., 1984—92; prof. edn. Jacksonville U., 1992—, dir. masters program in integrated learning and ednl. tech. Instr. U. Fla., 1987—90, U. North Fla., 1990—92; cons. Assn. Internat. Schs. Africa, 1994—97. Co-author: (book) Developing Critical Thinking Through Science, Book I, 2001, Developing Critical Thinking Through Science, Book II, 2002. Rep. United Way, 1981—86; tchr. rep., chpt. leader White Ho. Young Astronaut Program, 1984—85; team leader NSF Shells Elem. Sci. Project. Recipient Innovative Excellence in Tchg., Learning and Tech. award, Internat. Coll. Conf., 1999, Outstanding Alumni award, U. North Fla., 1999, Eve award for Edn., 2001, Apple Disting. Educator award, 2003—; named Fla. Prof. of the Yr., Carnegie Found., 2002, Prof. of Yr., Jacksonville U., 2003. Mem.: Internat. Soc. Tech. Edn., Soc. Info. Tech. and Tchr. Edn., ASCD, NSTA (Sci. Tchrs. Achievement Recognition award 1983), Kappa Delta Pi, Phi Delta Kappa, Phi Kappa Phi. Office: Jacksonville U 2800 University Blvd N Jacksonville FL 32211-3394 Personal E-mail: main750@bellsouth.net.

MAIN, JAMES L., lawyer; b. Chgo., Sept. 24, 1947; BS in Engring. Sci., Fla. State U., 1969; JD with honors, U. Fla., 1974; LLM in Taxation, NYU, 1978. Ptnr. Holland & Knight LLP, Jacksonville, Fla., leader private equity funds practice group, pres. Mem. U. Fla. Law Review, 1973—74. Bd. dir., past pres. Rotary Club, Deerwood, 2006—07. Mem.: Jacksonville Bar Assn., ABA, Fla. Bar, Omicron Delta Kappa, Order of the Coif, Phi Kappa Phi. Office: Holland & Knight LLP 50 N Laura St Ste 3900 Jacksonville FL 32202 Office Phone: 904-798-7319. Business E-Mail: james.main@hklaw.com.

MAIN, ROBERT GAIL, communications educator, training services executive, television and film producer, retired military officer; b. Bucklin, Mo., Sept. 30, 1932; s. Raymond M. and Inez L. (Olinger) M.; m. Anita Sue Thoroughman, Jan. 31, 1955; children: Robert Bruce, David Keith, Leslie Lorraine. BS magna cum laude, U. Mo., 1954; grad. with honors, Army Commd. Gen. Staff Coll., 1967; MA magna cum laude in Comm., Stanford U., Calif., 1968; PhD, U. Md., 1978. Commd. 2d lt. US Army, 1954, advanced through grades to lt. col., 1968; mem. faculty Army Commd. Gen. Staff Coll., 1968-70; chief speechwriting and info. materials divsn. US Army Info. Office, 1971, chief broadcast and film divsn., 1972-73; dir. def. audiovisual activities Office of Info. for Armed Forces, 1973-76; ret., 1976; prof. instrnl. tech. Calif. State U., Chico, 1976—, dept. chair, 1993-98, prof. emeritus. Cons. in field. Author: Rogues, Saints and Ordinary People, 1988; prodr. (TV documentary) Walking Wounded, 1983, Army Info. Films, Army Radio Series, 1972-73; contbr. articles on computer based tng. and telecoms. to scientific and profl. jours. Decorated Legion of Merit, Meritorious Svc. medal, Commendation medal with oak leaf cluster, combat Inf. Badge; Vietnamese Cross of Gallantry; recipient Freedom Found. awards, 1972, 73, 74; Bronze medal Atlanta Film Festival, 1972; Best of Show award Balt. Film Festival, 1973; Creativity award Chgo. Indsl. Film Festival, 1973; Cine gold award Internat. Film Prodrs. Assn., 1974; named an Outstanding Prof. Calif. State U., 1987-88. Mem. Phi Eta Sigma, Alpha Zeta, Phi Delta Gamma, Omicron Delta Kappa, Alpha Gamma Rho. Personal E-mail: rmain75@aol.com.

MAIN, TERENA ANN, music educator, corporate financial executive; b. Torrington, Wyo., Feb. 23, 1977; d. Russell Alan and Nadine Fahye Kilmer; m. Gary Lee Main, Aug. 8, 2003. AA in Music Edn., Casper Coll., Wyo., 1998; MusB, U. Wyo., Laramie, 2001. Lic. in life ins. Primerica Fin. Svcs., Wyo., 2005. K-6 music tchr. Albany County Sch. Dist., Laramie, 2001—. Assoc. Primerica Fin. Svcs., Laramie, 2005—. Singer (vol. singer): Nat. Anthem; actor: (plays). Conservative. Roman Catholic. Avocations: travel, camping, snowmobiling.

MAIN, TIMOTHY L., electronics company executive; b. 1957; BS, Mich. State U.; M in Internat. Mgmt., Am. Grad. Sch. Internat. Mgmt. Comml. lending officer internat. divsn. Nat. Bank Detroit; mgr. prodn. control Jabil Circuit Inc., St. Petersburg, Fla., 1987, ops. mgr., 1987-89, project mgr., 1989-91, v.p. bus. devel., 1991, sr. v.p. bus. devel., pres., 1999—; CEO, 2000—. Bd. dirs. Jabil Circuit Inc., 1999—. Office: Jabil Cir 10560 9th St N Saint Petersburg FL 33716

MAINA, JOSHUA Y., electronics engineer, researcher; s. Yahi T. and Kwante F. Maina; m. Ladi Y. Jonathan, Jan. 2, 1999; children: Hyalladjira J., Galipu J., Katsalla J., Womi J. BS in Engring. Elec. and Electronics, U. Maiduguri, Nigeria, 1992; MS in Elec. Engring., U. Pitts., 1998; PhD, U. Pitts., Penn., 2004. Comm. engr. Kaborak Nigerian Ltd., Maiduguri, Borno State, 1992—95; broadcasting engr. Nigerian TV Authority, Kaduna, Kaduna State, Nigeria, 1995—96; sr. rsch. engr. Quintech Electronics and Comm., Inc., Ind., Pa., 2006—. Grad. rsch. asst. G U. Pitts., 1997—99, rsch. asst., 2002—05; prodn. engr. Sony Electronics, Inc., Mount Pleasant, Pa., 1999—2002; ind. cons. JYM Consulting, Pitts., 2005—06. Contbr. articles to profl. jours. (Innovators award, 2006). Gospel preacher. Mem.: IEEE, WiMAX Forum. Achievements include invention of conductive polymers; ultra wideband communications using virtual pulse; anti collision techniques. Home: 301 Long Rd Pittsburgh PA 15235 Office: Quintech Electronics and Comm 250 Airport Rd Indiana PA 15701-8944 Personal E-mail: joshysco@yahoo.com.

MAINELLA, FRAN (FRANCES P. MAINELLA), educator, former federal agency administrator; b. Groton, Conn., 1947; BS cum laude, U. Conn.; MS cum laude in Counseling, Ctrl. Conn. State Coll.; PhD in Pub. Svc. (hon.), Ctrl. Conn. State U., 2002. H.S. phys. edn. tchr. Vernon Pub. Sch., Rockville, Conn., 1969—77; asst. ctr. dir. Tallahassee Parks and Recreation Dept., 1977—78; dir. recreation Town of Lake Park, Fla., 1978—83; exec. dir. Fla. Recreation and Park Assn., Tallahassee, 1983—89; dir. divsn. Recreation and Parks Fla. Dept. Environ. Protection, Tallahassee, 1989—2001; dir. Nat. Park Svc. US Dept. Interior, Washington, 2001—06; vis. scholar Clemson U., SC, 2006—. Spkr. in field. Contbr. numerous articles to profl. publs. Co-chair Com. for Preservation of the White House, mem. adv. coun. on hist. preservation; bd. trustees John F. Kennedy Ctr. for Performing Arts; liaison White House Hist. Soc.; sec., treas. Nat. Park Found.; mem. Am. Folklife Bd.; past pres. Nat. Assn. State Park Dirs.; past bd. mem. Am. Acad. Park and Recreation Adminstr.; past mem. Fla. Commn. Ttourism; past officio bd. mem. Fla. Recreation and Park Assn.; past mem. Gov.'s Mansion adv. com.; past bd. mem. Fla. Gov.'s Coun. on Phys. Fitness and Sports; past sec., bd. dirs. Spl. Olympics; past pres. Tallahassee Soc. Assn. Execs.; past chair United Way Drive for Tallahassee Soc. Assn. Execs.; past bd. dirs. Tallahassee Leon County Convention and Visitors Bur.; bd. dirs. Ford's Theatre Soc., Wolf Trap Found. for Performing Arts. Recipient Disting. Svc. award, Nat. Assn. Recreation Resource Planners, 1996, Woman of Distinction award, Girl Scout Coun. of Apalachee Bend, 1998, Pugsley medal, Am. Acad. Park and Recreation Adminstrn., 1998, Disting. Svc. award, Nat. Assn. State Park Dirs., 1999, Senator Bob Williams award, State of Fla., 2001, Sheldon Coleman Outdoors award, 2002, Walter T. Cox Pub. Svc. Achievement award, Clemson U., 2002. Mem.: Nat. Recreation and Park Assn. (congress planning com. 1984, 1987, past chair coun. exec. dirs., pres. 1997—, Harold D. Meyer Profl. award 2000). E-mail: fmainella@clemson.edu.

MAINES, NATALIE LOUISE, musician; b. Lubbock, Tex., Oct. 14, 1974; d. Lloyd and Tina M.; m. Michael Tarabay, May 9, 1997 (div. Jan. 1999); m. Adrian Pasdar, June 24, 2000; children: Jack Slade, Beckett Finn. Student, Tex. Tech.; grad., Berklee Coll. Music, Boston, 1995. Performer Dixie Chicks, 1995—. Singer: (albums) Wide Open Spaces, 1998 (Maximum Vision Clip of Yr., Billboard, 1998, Best New Country Artist Clip of Yr., Billboard, 1998, Best Country Album, Grammy Awards, 1998, Album of Yr., Acad. Country Music, 1998, Best Selling Album, Can. Country Music Awards, 1999, Song of Yr. (Country), WB Radio Music Awards, 1999, Album of Yr., ACM, 1999), Fly, 1999 (Best Country Album, Grammy Awards, 1999, Best Selling Album, Can. Country Music Awards, 2000, Internat. Album, British Country Music Awards, 2000, Country Album of Yr., Billboard, 2000, Album of Yr., ACM, 2000, Album of Yr., CMA, 2000), Home, 2002 (Favorite Country Album, Am. Music Awards, 2002, Best Recording Package, Grammy Awards, 2002, Best Country Album, Grammy Awards, 2002), Top of the World Tour: Live, 2003 (Best Country Group Vocal Performance, Grammy awards, 2005), Taking the Long Way, 2006 (Album of Yr. and Best Country Album, Grammy Awards, 2007), (songs) Not Ready to Make Nice, 2006 (Record of Yr., Song of Yr., Best Performance by a Duo or Group with Vocal, Grammy Awards, 2007); performer: (documentary) Dixie Chicks: Shut Up and Sing, 2006. Recipient Horizon award, CMA, 1998; named Most Significant New Country Act, Country Monitor, 1998, Top New Country Artist, Billboard, 1998, Group of Yr., CMA, 1998, Top Vocal Group, Acad. Country Music, 1998, Country Artist of Yr., Rolling Stone, 1999, Top Country Artist, Billboard, 1999, Internat. Rising Star, British Country Music Awards, 1999, Artist of Yr., WB Radio Music Awards, 1999, Favorite New Artist (Country), AMA, 1999, Vocal Group of Yr., CMA, 1999, Country Artist of Yr., Billboard, 1999, Entertainer of Yr., CMA, 2000, ACM, 2000, 2001, Vocal Group of Yr., 2001, Favorite Musical Group or Band, People's Choice Award, 2002, Vocal Group of Yr., Country Music Assn. Awards, 2002; named one of 100 Most Influential People, Time Mag., 2006.

MAINI, SIR RAVINDER NATH, rheumatologist, educator; b. Ludhiana, Punjab, India, Nov. 17, 1937; arrived in U.K., 1955; s. Amar Nath and Saheli Ram (Mehra) M.; m. Marianne Pentz Gorm, 1963 (div. 1986); children: Mala, Ashwin, Nikul (dec.); m. Geraldine Rainier Walden Room, May 22, 1987; children: Alexander, Justin. BA, U. Cambridge, Eng., 1959; MB, BChir, U. Cambridge, 1962; Doctor (hon.), U. René Descartes, Paris, 1994; DSc (hon.), U. Glasgow, 2004. Jr. hosp. staff Guy's Hosp., Brompton Hosp., Charing Cross Hosp., London, 1962-70; cons. physician Charing Cross Hosp., West London Hosp., St. Stephen's Hosp., London, 1970-79; prof., head dept. immunology rheumatic diseases Charing Cross and Westminster Med. Sch., London, 1979—89, prof., head dept. rheumatology, 1989—2002; head divsn. clin. immunology Kennedy Inst. Rheumatology, London, 1979—2002, dir., 1990—2002, prof. rheumatology, 1989—2002, prof. emeritus, 2002—; mem. faculty of medicine Imperial Coll, U. London, 2000—02. Hon. cons. physician Charing Cross Hosp., London, 1970—2007, Hammersmith Hosps., London; European Union Med. Specialists Bd. in Rheumatology, 1994-98; past chmn. standing com. for investigative rheumatology European League Against Rheumatism (EULAR); mem. organizing com. European Workshop Rheumatology Rsch.-related European Workshops; trustee found. bd. Deutsches RheumaForschungsZentrum, Berlin; mem. sci. coun. Karolinska Hosp., Stockholm; mem. arthritis rsch. campaign Brit. Soc. for Rheumatology Clin. Trials Com., others; spkr. Nobel Asselbly symposium for inauguration of Ctr.

Molecular Medicine, Karolinska Hosp., Stockholm, 1997; inaugural Morris Ziff lectr. U. Tex. Health Scis., Dallas, 2001; Langdon Brown Lecture, Royal Coll. Physicians, 2005. Author (with D.N. Glass, J.T. Scott): Immunology of the Rheumatic Diseases, 1977; Modulation of Autoimmune Disease: The Penicillamine Experience, 1981; co-editor (with M. Feldmann, J.N. Woody): T-Cell Activation in Health and Disease: Disorders of Immune Regulation, Infection and Autoimmunity, 1989; co-editor: (with J.R. Kalden, J.S. Smolen) Rheumatoid Arthritis: Recent Research Advances, 1992; co-editor: (with W.V. van Venrooij) Manual of Biological Markers of Disease, 1996; co-editor in chief: Arthritis Rsch. & Therapy, 1999—; mem. editl. bd. Jour. Immunol. Methods, Annals Rheumatic Diseases, mem. adv. bd. Rheumatology Internat., Japanese Jour. Rheumatology, Scandinavian Jour. Rheumatology; contbr. articles to profl. jours. Recipient Disting. Investigators award, Am. Coll. Rheumatology, 1999, Crafoord Prize, Royal Swedish Acad. Scis., 2000, Outstanding Achievement in Clin. Rsch. award, Inst. Clin. Rsch., 2004, Fothergillian medal, Med. Soc. London, 2004, Cameron prize (with Prof. Feldmann), U. Edinburgh, 2004, Ambuj Nath Bose prize, Royal Coll. Physicians, 2005, Courtin-Clarins Prix award, 2000, Meritorious Svc. award in rheumatology, European League Against Rheumatism, 2005, Galen medal, The Worshipful Soc. Apothecaries London, 2006, RA award, Japan Rheumatism Found. Internat., 2007, Dr. Paul Janssen award, 2008; co-recipient Carol Nachman prize, Germany, 1999, Albert Lasker Clin. Med. Rsch. award, Lasker Found., 2003, EULAR Meritorious Svc. award in rheumatology, 2005; named Freyburg lectr. Hosp. for Spl. Surgery, NYC, 1993, Croonian Lectr. award, Royal Coll. Physicians, London, 1995, Lumleian Lectr. award, 1999; named to Knighthood, Queen Elizabeth II, 2003; Hon. fellow, Sidney Sussex Coll., U. Cambridge, 2004. Fellow Acad. Med. Scis., Royal Soc. Medicine, Royal Soc. UK, Brit. Soc. Rheumatology (Heberden Oration medal 1988), Slovakian Rheumatology Soc., Royal Coll. Physicians Edinburgh, Royal Coll. Physicians London; master Am. Coll. Rheumatology (hon.); mem. European League Against Rheumatism (hon.), Australian Rheumatism Assn. (hon.), Norwegian Soc. Rheumatology (hon.), Hellenic Rheumatology Soc. (hon.), Hungarian Rheumatology Soc. (hon.), Scandinavian Soc. Immunology (hon.), Mexican Soc. Rheumatology (hon.), Brit. Soc. Immunology, Assn. Physicians Gt. Britain and No. Ireland, Assn. Clin. Profs., Royal Soc. Medicine (Samuel Hyde lectr. 1999), Antibody Club, Reform Club, 1942 Club. Avocations: music appreciation, walking. Office: Kennedy Inst Rheumatology Imperial Coll ARC Bldg 65 Aspenlea Rd London W6 8LH England Office Phone: 44 (0) 20 8383 4403. Business E-Mail: r.maini@imperial.ac.uk.

MAINOUS, BRUCE HALE, foreign language educator; b. Appalachia, Va., Aug. 2, 1914; s. William Lazarus and Sibyl (Hale) M.; m. Ruth Marie Daugherty, June 7, 1941; children: Mary Michele (Mrs. Robert F. Chinn), Martha Hale (Mrs. Gary Dougherty). AB, Coll. William and Mary, 1935; MA, U. Ill., 1939, PhD, 1948; certificates, Sorbonne, Paris, 1958, U. Besançon, France, 1975. Asst. d'anglais Lycée de Nîmes, France, 1935-36; prin. Derby Grade Sch., Va., 1936-37; mem. faculty U. Ill., Urbana, 1937—, prof. French, 1964-84, prof. emeritus, 1984—, head dept., 1965-73, asst. dean, 1956-57; dir. Unit for Fgn. Lang. Study and Rsch., 1972-76, Lang. Learning Lab., 1976-84, acting dir. divsn. English as 2d lang., 1976-77. Author: (with H.C. Woodbridge) A Sainte-Beuve Bibliography, 1954, Basic French, 2d edit, 1968, (with Donald J. Nolan) Basic French, Workbook and laboratory Manual, 1968; co-author: Spanish for Agricultural Purposes, 1984, (with Maria T. Rund) A Glossary of Spanish-American Agricultural Terms, 1987. Served to lt. USNR, 1942-46; comdr. Res. ret. Decorated officier Ordre des Palmes Académiques; Camargo Found. fellow, 1975 Mem. MLA, Am. Assn. Tchrs. French, Ill. Fgn. Lang. Tchrs. Assn. (pres. 1966-68), Am. Council Teaching Fgn. Langs., Inst. d'Etudes Occitanes, N.Am. Catalan Soc., Corda Fratres Assn. Cosmopolitan Club, Phi Kappa Phi, Sigma Delta Pi, Pi Delta Phi. Clubs: Dial, Exchange. Methodist. Home: 502 W Washington St Urbana IL 61801-4052 Home Phone: 217-367-3160.

MAINSTER, MARTIN ARON, ophthalmologist, educator; b. Toronto, Ontario, Canada; s. Stanley and Mildred Mainster; m. Patricia Louise Turner; 1 child, Merrick Albert. PhD, NC State U., Raleigh, 1968; MD, U. Tex. Med. Br., Galveston, 1975. Diplomate Am. Bd. Ophthalmology, 1981, fellow Royal Coll. Ophthalmologists, 1990. Luther Fry prof. dept. ophthalmology U. of Kans. Sch. Medicine, Prairie Village, 1985—; dir., biomathematics divsn. Tech. Inc., San Antonio, 1968—72. Academic fellowship, Ford Found., 1964, NSF, 1965. Fellow: Royal Coll. Ophthalmologists, Royal Coll. Ophthalmologists, Am. Acad. Ophthalmology (Sr. Achievement award 1999); mem.: Macula Soc., European Soc. Cataract & Refractive Surgery, Am. Phys. Soc., Am. Soc. Cataract & Refractive Surgery, Assn. Rsch. Vision, Ophthalmology. Achievements include invention of UV,visible light blocking intraocular lenses & aspheric contact lens ophthalmoscopy and crossed dual-beam laser photodisruptor targeting; research in ocular light hazards and ophthalmic optics. Office: Ophthalmology U KS School Medicine 7400 State Line Rd Prairie Village KS 66208-3444

MAINWARING, THOMAS LLOYD, transportation executive, director; b. Cleve., Aug. 25, 1928; s. Hugh Trevor and Mary Beatrice (Ottman) M.; m. Gladys Fraser Mehr, June 10, 1983; children by previous marriage— Kevin, James, Eileen, Scott, Bruce BA, Albion Coll., 1950; MBA, Western Res. U., 1958. C.P.A., Ohio. Controller Cleve. Cartage Co., 1959-61, v.p., treas., 1961-64; controller Associated Truck Lines, Inc., Vandenberg Ctr., Grand Rapids, Mich., 1964-69; v.p. fin. Associated Transport, Inc., NYC, 1969-70, exec. v.p. fin. and adminstrn., 1970-72; pres. Ryder Truck Lines Inc., Jacksonville, Fla., 1972-78, exec. v.p., chief operating officer, 1978-81, chief exec. officer, 1981-84; pres. Freight System div. Ryder System Inc., Miami, Fla., 1984-86; cons. trucking industry affairs Arlington, Va., 1986-88; pres., chief oper. officer H & M Internat. Transp., Inc., 1989-91, vice chmn., 1991-92; transp. cons., 1992-93; pres., gen. mgr. E.I. Kane Intermodal Transport, Inc., Balt., 1993-95, vice chmn., 1995, transp. cons., 1996—99; COO, Am. C. of C. Execs., 2000—01; mgmt. cons., 2002—03; treas. & CFO AICHI-USA 2005 World Expn., Inc., 2003—06; exec. v.p. Shanghai-USA 2010 World Expo., Inc., 2006—07. Bd. dirs. Trucking Mgmt., Inc. Mem. exec. com. United Way Jacksonville, 1981-84; trustee Albion Coll., 1977; bd. dirs. Goodwill Industries North Fla. Served with AUS, 1950-53. Mem. Am. Trucking Assn. (nat. acctg. and fin. council 1964, pres. 1971, chmn. ATA Found. 1986-88, exec. com. 1985-88), Fla. Trucking Assn. (bd. dirs. 1973, pres. 1979), Am. Mgmt. Assn. (lectr. seminars), Jacksonville Area C. of C. (bd. govs., com. of 100, v.p. internat. 1984), Cen. and So. Motor Freight Tariff Assn. (bd. dirs. 1981-84, pres. 1983, exec. com. transp. rsch. bd. 1987-89), Sigma Nu. Home: 20 Beekman Place Queensbury NY 12804

MAINWARING, WILLIAM LEWIS, publishing company executive, author; b. Portland, Oreg., Jan. 17, 1935; s. Bernard and Jennie (Lewis) M.; m. Mary E. Bell, Aug. 18, 1962; children: Anne Marie, Julia Kathleen, Douglas Bernard. BS, U. Oreg., 1957; postgrad., Stanford U., 1957-58. With Salem (Oreg.) Capital Jour., 1958-76, editor, pub., 1962-76; pub. Oreg. Statesman, 1974-76; pres. Statesman-Jour. Co., Inc., Salem, 1974-76, Westridge Press, Ltd., 1977—, MediAmerica, Inc., Portland, 1981-96, CEO, 1988—91. Bd. dirs. MediAmerica, Inc. Author: Exploring the Oregon Coast, 1977, Exploring Oregon's Central and Southern Cascades, 1979, Exploring the Mount Hood Loop, 1992, Government, Oregon-Style, 1996, rev. edit., 1997, 99. Pres. Salem Beautification Coun., 1968, Marion-Polk County United Good Neighbors, 1970, Salem Social Svcs. Commn., 1978-79, Salem Hosp. Found., 1978-81, Marion Hist. Found., 2002-03. 2d lt. AUS, 1958; capt. Res. Ret. Mem. Salem Area C. of C. (pres. 1972-73), Oreg. Symphony Soc. Salem (pres. 1973-75), Salem City Club (pres. 1977-78), Sigma Chi. Republican. Presbyterian. Home and Office: 1090 Southridge Pl S Salem OR 97302-5947

MAIO, RONALD FRANK, emergency medicine physician; b. Chgo., Mar. 8, 1950; s. Joseph and Nora (Galli) M.; m. Jill Kristine Donovan, Dec. 6, 1975. BS, Regis Coll., 1972; DO, Mich. State U., 1976. Diplomate Am. Bd. Emergency Medicine. Intern Botsford-Zieger Hosps., Farmington Hills, Detroit, 1976-77; resident in emergency medicine Mich. State U., Univ. Affiliated Hosp., 1981-83; physician emergency medicine St. Lawrence Hosp., Lansing, Mich., 1983—. Clin. instr. human medicine Mich. Stte U., East Lansing, 1981—, Coll. Osteopathic Med., East Lansing, 1981—; med. advisor Delta Fire Service, Lansing, 1983—. Served to capt. U.S. Army M.C., 1977-80. Mem. Am. Osteo. Assn., Am. Coll. Emergency Physicians, Physicians for Social Responsibility. Avocations: running, reading, travel. Home: 1484 Sylvan Glen Rd Okemos MI 48864-3714 Office: St Lawrence Hosp Emergency Rm 1210 W Saginaw St Lansing MI 48915-1927

MAIOCCO, KENNETH JOSEPH, dermatologist; b. Bridgeport, Conn., Oct. 3, 1941; s. John Paul Maiocco and Jane Marie Pilgoste; m. Maxine Marie Gormley, Dec. 7, 1967; children: David, Mark, Dana, Adam. BS, Fairfield U., Conn., 1963; MD, U. Rochester, NY, 1967. Diplomate Am. Bd. Dermatology, 1976. Dir. pub. health Trumbull Health Dept., 1976—2006. Vol. skin cancer screening clinic Health Dept. Trumbull, Trumbull and Westport, Colo. Maj. US Army, 1971—73. Decorated Commendation medal; named Top Dr. for Women, Conn. Mag., 2002, Best Dr. in America, 2000—09, Top Dr. NY Metro Area, 2000—09. Mem.: Conn. Dermatology and Dermatol. Surgery Soc., Fairfield County Med. Assn., Conn. State Med. Soc., Am. Acad. Dermatology, Dermatology Found. Scholar's Cir., Gaelic Am. Club, Brooklawn Country Club. Avocations: golf, boating, skiing, model trains. Office: 4639 Main St Bridgeport CT 06606-1838 Office Phone: 203-374-5546.

MAIR, BRUCE LOGAN, interior designer, architectural firm executive; b. Chgo., June 5, 1951; s. William Logan and Josephine (Lee) M. BFA, Drake U., 1973; postgrad., Ind. Wesleyan U., 1990—. Mgr., head designer Reifers of Indpls., 1973-79; pres. Interiors Internat., Indpls., 1979-87; sr. designer Kasler Group, Indpls., 1987-89; dir. devel. Tillery Interiors and Imports, Greenwood, Ind., 1990, v.p. Indpls., 1990-92; owner Mair Interior Design Group, Indpls., 1992—. Pres. Tokens Inc., Indpls., 1982-88, Meg-A-Wat Enterprises Inc., Indpls., 1985-87, Luxury Ice Creams Inc., Indpls., 1986-87. Cover designer Indpls. Home and Garden mag., 1978, feature designer 1980; feature designer Builder mag., 1979; co-designer feature Indpls. At Home mag., 1979. Campaigner Anderson for Pres., 1980. Mem. Am. Soc. Interior Designers (profl., treas. Ind. chpt. 1982-83, Pres. awards 1981-82), U.S. Rowing Assn. (master 1987—), St. Joseph Hist. Neighborhood Assn., Columbia Club (rowing crew coxswain 1986—), Highland Model A Club, Tower Harbor Yacht Club (Douglas, Mich.), Royal Palm Yacht Club Ft. Myers, Alpha Epsilon Pi. Avocations: sculling, historic preservation, model a ford restoration, fishing, farming. Office Phone: 239-476-9404. Personal E-mail: brucemairid@aol.com.

MAIR, VICTOR HENRY, language and literature educator; b. East Canton, Ohio, Mar. 25, 1943; s. Joseph Charles and Esther Frieda Louise (Boyce) M.; m. Li-ching Chang, Dec. 15, 1969; 1 child, Thomas Krishna. BA, Dartmouth Coll., 1965; postgrad., U. Wash., 1967; BA in Chinese and Sanskrit with honors, U. London, 1972, MPhil in Chinese, 1984; MA in Chinese Lit., Harvard U., 1973, PhD in Chinese Lit., 1976; MA (hon.), U. Pa., 1985. Vol. Peace Corps, Nepal, 1965-67; lectr. English lang. and lit. Tunghai U., Taichung, Taiwan, 1970-72; tchg. fellow and lectr. Chinese religion and lit. Harvard U., Cambridge, Mass., 1973-77; asst. prof. Chinese religion and lit., 1977-79; asst. prof. Chinese U. Pa., Phila., 1977-79, assoc. prof. Chinese, 1984—88, prof. Chinese, 1989—, cons. scholar Mus. Archaeology and Anthropology; concurrent prof. dept. Chinese Sichuan U., Chengdu, China, 1997—, Peking U., China, 1998—. Vis. prof. dept. Asian and African studies Duke U., 1993-94, vis. rsch. prof., fellow Inst. Rsch. in Humanities Kyoto (Japan) U., 1995-96; mem. Sch. Hist. Studies Inst. Advanced Study, Princeton, N.J., 1998-99; humanities PhD nat. fellowship selection com. NEH, 1992-95, nat. fellowships for univ. tchrs. selection com.; Chinese studies fellowship selection com. Am. Soc. Learned Socs., 1993-97; mem. Inter-Univ. Bd. Chinese Lang. Studies, 1997—; disting. vis. prof. dept. U. Hong Kong, 2002-03; editor Encounters with Asia Series, Penn Press, 2003-; presenter, cons. in field. Co-author: The Tarim Mummies, 2000, The True History Of Tea, 2009; editor: The Columbia Anthology of Traditional Chinese Literature, 1994, The Bronze Age and Early Iron Age Peoples of Eastern Central Asia, 2 Vols., 1998, An Alphabetical Index to the Hanyu Da Cidian, 203, The Columbia History of Chinese Literature, 2001, Contact and Exchange in the Ancient World, 2006, The Prehistory of the Silk Road, 2008, others; co-editor: Hawai'i Reader in Traditional Chinese Culture, 2005; assoc. editor: Han-Ying cidian (ABC Chinese-English Dictionary), 1997, editor U. Hawaii Press, 1996-; editor, founder: Xin Tang Jour. Romanized Mandarin, 1982—, Sino-Platonic Papers, 1986—; contbr. articles to profl. jours., chpts. to books; translator and annotator: The Art of War: Sun Zi's Military Methods, 2007; co-translator numerous books; appeared in documentary on mummies of Ctrl. Asia NOVA, 1997, (film) Riddle of the Desert Mummies, 1998, Genetics of Central Asian Mummies, 2007; prin. investigator rsch. project on Bronze Age and Iron Age desiccated mummies of the Tarim Basin and surrounding areas, 1991—. Woodrow Wilson fellow, 1967-68, fellow Nat. Def. Fgn. Lang., 1968, 70, 72-75, Marshall fellow Sch. Oriental and African Studies U. London, 1968, Arthur Lehman fellow, 1974, Whiting fellow, 1975, Nat. Humanities Ctr., 1991-92, Swedish Collegium for Advanced Study, 2004, 08; grantee Alfred P. Sloan Found., 1992, U. Pa. Rsch. Found., 1994-95, Luce Found., 1994-97, Lang. Consortium, 1997-98, Freeman Found., 1997-2004, Dept. Edn., 2000-02. Mem. Am. Comparative Lit. Assn., Am. Oriental Soc., AAUP, Assn. Asian Studies, Am. Philos. Soc., Soc. Study Chinese Religion, T'ang Studies Soc. (dir. 1987—, pres. 2002-05), Chinese Lang. Soc. Hong Kong, Oriental Club Phila., Assn. Am. for Promotion Chinese Lang. Reform, Linguistic Soc. Am., World History Assn., Permanent Internat. Altaistic Conf., Inst. Ancient Equestrian Studies. Avocations: running, learning languages, playing french horn. Office: Dept East Asian Langs and Civilizations University of Pa Philadelphia PA 19104-6305 Home Phone: 610-543-6286; Office Phone: 215-898-8432. Office Fax: 215-573-9617. Business E-Mail: vmair@sas.upenn.edu.

MAISEL, DAVID, entertainment company executive; b. 1961; Mgr. entertainment and media practice The Boston Cons. Group; with Creative Artists Agy.; dir. corp. devel. and strategic planning The Walt Disney Co.; pres. Livent, Inc.; mng. dir. Chello Broadband, 1999—2001; head corp. strategy and bus. devel. Endeavor Talent Agy., 2001—03; pres., COO Marvel Studios, 2004—05, vice chmn., 2005—07, chmn., 2007—; exec. v.p. corp. devel., Office Chief Exec. Marvel Entertainment Inc., 2005—. Office: Marvel Studios 1600 Rosecrans Ave # 7A Manhattan Beach CA 90266-3708 also: Marvel Entertainment Inc 417 Fifth Ave New York NY 10016*

MAISEL, WILLIAM HOWARD, cardiologist, internist; b. Mar. 26, 1966; BS in Biology, MIT, Cambridge, Mass.; MPH, Harvard Sch Pub. Health, Boston, Mass.; MD, Cornell U., 1992. Cert. Am. Bd. Internal Medicine, 1995. Intern, internal medicine Brigham & Women Hosp., Boston, 1992—93, resident, internal medicine, 1993—95, fellow, cardiovascular, 1996—99, fellow, cardiac electrophysiology; clin. fellow, medicine Harvard Med. Sch., Boston, asst. prof. medicine; attending staff physician, cardiovascular divsn. Beth Israel Deaconess Med. Ctr., Boston. Chmn. circulatory system med. devices adv. panel FDA. Ad hoc reviewer Am. Jour. Cardiology, Annals Internal Medicine, Circulation, Jour. Am. Coll. Cardiology, Jour. Cardiovascular Electrophysiology, Jour. Interventional Cardiac Electrophysiology, New England Jour. Medicine, Pacing and Clin. Electrophysiology; contbr. articles tp profl. jours., chapters to books. Mem.: AMA, Heart Rhythm Soc., Am. Heart Assn., Am. Coll. Cardiology, Mass. Med. Soc. Office: Beth Israel Deaconess Med Ctr 185 Pilgrim Rd Baker 4 Boston MA 02215 Office Phone: 617-632-7457. Office Fax: 617-632-7620.*

MAISIN, JEAN RENÉ SIMON, medical researcher, educator; b. Leuven, Belgium, May 25, 1928; m. Claudine Derrider, Sept. 18, 1958; 3 children. MD, Cath. U. Louvain, 1954, dipl. Electro-Radiology, 1958, specialist in Pathology, 1959. Head radiobiology dept. CEN/SCK, Mol, Belgium, 1960-87; lectr., prof. Cath. U. Louvain, 1973-93, prof. emeritus, 1993—. Spkr. in field. Contbr. over 300 articles to sci. publs. Sec.-gen. European Late Effects Project Group, 1970-85, chmn. 1985-95, hon. mem., 1996—; mem. governing bd., v.p. Internat. Coun. Lab. Animal Sci., 1991, acting chmn., 1994-95, chmn. 1995-99, hon. mem., 1999—; rep. UN Sci. Com. on Effects Atomic Radiation, 1985—2008, pres. sessions, 1991-92; chmn. European Soc. Radiation Biology, 1986-88, hon. chmn., 1996-2003. Decorated gt. officer Order of Crown, comdr. Order of Leopold II, and officer Order of Leopold, Hanns-Langendorff Medaille, 1994; recipient Bacq and Alexander award, 1997. Mem. European Soc. Lab. Animal Sci. (former mem. governing bd.) European Assn. Late Effects (chmn. 1983-95), Internat. Assn. Late Effects. (former chmn.), Belgian Soc. Lab. Animal Sci. (hon.) Belgian Soc. Radiation Biology (former chmn.). Roman Catholic. Office: Unite Radiobiol Radioprotec 54 Ave Hippocrate B-1200 Brussels Belgium Home: Ave du Manoir 55 B-1410 Waterloo Belgium Personal E-mail: jrmaisin@skynet.be. Business E-Mail: maisin@rbnt.ucl.ac.be.

MAISTO, JOHN F., former ambassador; b. Braddock, Pa., Aug. 28, 1938; married; 3 children. BSFS, Georgetown U., 1961; MA, San Carlos Coll., Guatemala, 1962. With BiNational Ctr., Cordoba, Argentina, 1963-66; asst. cultural affairs officer USIA, Cochabamba, Bolivia, 1966-68; with Fgn. Svc., 1968—; adminstrv. asst. Fgn. Svc. Inst. Dept. State, 1968-69; econ. and comml. officer U.S. Embassy, La Paz, Bolivia, 1969-71; internat. rels. officer Ops. Ctr., 1971-72; spl. asst. Office of Counselor, 1972-73; internat. rels. officer office Andean affairs, bur. inter-Am. affairs Dept. State, 1973-75; polit. officer U.S. Embassy, San Jose, Costa Rica, 1975-78, Manila, 1978-82; dep. dir. office Philippine affairs, bur. East Asian and Pacific affairs Dept. State, 1982-84, dir., 1984-86; dep. chief of mission and charge d'affaires Am. Embassy, Panama, 1986-89; dep. permanent U.S. rep. to OAS, 1989-92; dep. asst. sec. state for Ctrl. Am. and Panama U.S. Dept. State, 1992-93; U.S. amb. to Nicaragua, 1993-96; U.S. amb. to Venezuela, 1997—2000; fgn. policy advisor U.S. so. commd., 2000—01; spl. asst. to Pres., sr. dir. for western hemisphere affairs Nat. Security Coun., 2001—03; U.S. permanent rep. to OAS US Dept. State, Washington, 2003—07. Office Phone: 202-742-6602. Personal E-mail: maistojn@aol.com.

MAITIN, IAN, physiatrist; BA in Biochemistry, Rutgers U., 1983; MD, Jefferson Medical Coll., 1989; MBA, Temple U., 2002. Intern, internal medicine Bryn Mawr Hosp., Bryn Mawr, Pa., 1989—90; resident, physical medicine and rehab. Robert Wood Johnson Rehab. Inst. UMDNJ, 1990—93, chief resident, 1993; assoc. prof. physical medicine and rehab. Temple U., 1993—, acting chair physical medicine and rehab., 2003—06, chair physical medicine and rehab., 2006—. Fellow: American Academy Physical Medicine and Rehab., American Assn. Electrodiagnostic Medicine; mem.: Assn. Academic Physiatrists. Office: Temple U 3420 N Broad St Philadelphia PA 19140 Office Phone: 215-707-2997. Business E-Mail: maitin@temple.edu.*

MAITLAND, GUY EDISON CLAY, lawyer; b. London, Dec. 28, 1942; (mother Am. citizen); s. Paul and Virginia Francesca (Carver) M. BA, Columbia U., 1964; JD, NY Law Sch., 1968; LLD (hon.), SUNY Maritime Coll., Ft. Schuyler, 2007. Bar: NY 1969, US Dist. Ct. (so. and ea. dists.) NY 1969, US Ct. Appeals (2d and DC cirs.) 1969. Assoc. Burlingham, Underwood & Lord, NYC, 1969-74; admiralty counsel Union Carbide Corp., NYC, 1974-76; exec. v.p., gen. counsel, officer Liberian Svcs., Inc., NYC and Reston, Va., 1976-99; pres. Trust Co. of the Marshall Islands, Inc., 1990—; mng. ptnr. Internat. Registries, Inc., 2000—. Del. UN Conf. on Trade and Devel., Manila, 1979, Belgrade, 1983; participant London Conf. on Limitation of Maritime Liability, 1976; mem. legal com. Internat. Maritime Orgn. (UN) London, 1980—; del. UN Conf. on Law of the Sea, 1976-82, London UN Maritime Law Conf., 1984; co-founder The Admiralty-Fin. Forum, NYC, 1986. Contbr. articles on maritime law, US shipping policy. Mem. NY Rep. State Exec. Com., 1974-76; del. Rep. Nat. Conv., Kansas City, 1976, UN Geneva Conf. on Arrest of Vessels, 1999; sec. NY Rep. County Com., 1976-87, vice chmn., 1988—, mem. exec. com., 1974-76; co-chmn. Citizens for Reagan, NY State, 1979-80; trustee Am. Mcht. Marine Mus. Found. at US Mcht. Marine Acad., King's Point, Nat. Maritime Hist. Soc., chmn., 2000-01; trustee NY Maritime Coll. at Ft. Schuyler Found., Inc.; bd. dirs. Seamen's Ch. Inst., NYC, Ctr. for Seafarers Rights, McLean Container Ctr. at King's Point, Inc., Coast Guard Found., Hellenic-Am. C. of C., NY Maritime Inc., SS US Conservancy; mem. adv. com. Am. Maritime History Project; mem. standing com. Soc. of City of NY; hon. dir. alumni assn. State of NY Maritime Coll.; founding chmn. N.Am. Marine Environ. Protection Assn.; chmn. industry adv. bd. N.Am. Marittime Ministry Assn.; chmn. internat. adv. com. Amistad Am., Inc.; mem. Pilgrims of the US; decorated Humane Order of African Redemption, Liberia, 1989. Mem. ABA, Assn. of Bar of City of NY (chmn. admiralty com. 1982-85), Maritime Law Assn. US (chmn. com. on intergovtl. orgns. 1987-95). Office: Internat Registries Inc 437 Madison Ave 32d Fl New York NY 10022-7001

MAIZE, JOHN CHRISTOPHER, dermatologist, educator; b. Elizabeth, NJ, July 23, 1943; s. Donald Adam and Caroline Marie (Costanzo) Maize; m. Janice Lee Bentley, May 21, 1966; children: Sandra Kristine Tolly, John C. Jr., Jennifer Lee. MD, U. Mich., 1968. Cert. Am. Bd.

Dermatology. Intern U. Mich., Ann Arbor, 1968—69, residency in dermatology, 1968—72; asst. prof. dermatology SUNY, Buffalo, 1972—77, assoc. prof., 1977—80, Med. U. SC, Charleston, 1980—83, prof., 1983—89, prof., chmn. dept. dermatology, 1989—2003, clin. prof., 2003—. Author: Pigmented Lesions of the Skin, 1987, Cutaneous Pathology, 1998; editor-in-chief Am. Jour. Dermatology, 1986—90. Fellow: Am. Soc. Dermapathology (pres. 1995), Am. Acad. Dermatology; mem.: Am. Bd. Dermatology (dir. 1990—99, pres. 1999), S.C. Dermatol. Assn. (pres. 2001), S.C. Med. Assn., Internat. Soc. Dermatopathology (sec. 1987—89, pres. 1989—91), Am. Dermatol. Assn. Roman Catholic. Avocations: fishing, golf, travel. Office: 266 W Coleman Blvd Unit 101 Mount Pleasant SC 29464 Home Phone: 843-881-1007; Office Phone: 843-388-6911. E-mail: jmaizesr@ameripath.com.

MAJEED, D. HADAYAI S., publishing executive, writer; b. Milwaukee, Wis., Jan. 14, 1955; d. Fred J. and Evelyn L. Spencer; m. Abdul H. Abdullah, Jan. 28, 1998. BA in Biology, U. Ark., 1976. Prin., owner Spencer-Majeed, Ltd., Conley, Ga., 1995—; adminstr. Baitul Salaam Network, Inc., Atlanta, 1997—. Author: Emerging Victorious: A Dialogue on Polygamy/Polygyny in America (nominated Writer of Yr., Ga. Writers, 2000). Mem. coun. Masjid Al Mu minun, Atlanta, 2002—04. Recipient Real Life is Drug Free award, State of Ga., 1997; nominee Noble Peace prize, 2005. Mem.: 1000 Peace Women 2005 (assoc.). Independent. Islam.

MAJERLE, DANIEL LEWIS, professional basketball coach, retired professional basketball player; b. Traverse City, Mich., Sept. 9, 1965; Attended, Ctrl. Mich. U., Mt. Pleasant. Forward Phoenix Suns, 1988-95, 2001—02, asst. coach, 2008—; forward Cleveland Cavaliers, 1995-96, Miami Heat, 1996—2001; ret., 2002; owner Majerle's Sports Grill, Phoenix, 1992—. Mem. US Basketball Team, 1988, 94. Named to NBA All-Defensive second team, 1991, 93, NBA All-Star team, 1992, 93, 95; recipient Bronze medal Olympic Games, Seoul, Republic of Korea, 1988, Gold medal World Championships, Toronto, 1994. Office: Phoenix Suns 201 E Jefferson St Phoenix AZ 85004 also: Majerle's Sports Grill 24 N 2nd St Phoenix AZ 85004*

MAJERUS, PHILIP WARREN, physician; b. Chgo., July 10, 1936; s. Clarence Nicholas and Helen Louise (Mathis) Majerus; m. Janet Sue Brakensiek, Dec. 28, 1957; children: Suzanne, David, Juliet, Karen; m. Elaine Michelle Flansburg, 1996. BS, Notre Dame U., 1958; MD, Washington U., 1961. Resident in Medicine Mass. Gen. Hosp., Boston, 1961—63; research assoc. NIH, Bethesda, Md., 1963—66; asst. prof. biochemistry Washington U., St. Louis, 1966—75, asst. prof. medicine, 1966—69, assoc. prof. medicine, 1969—71, prof. medicine, 1971—, dir. div. hematology, 1973—, prof. biochemistry, 1976—. Mem. editl. bd. numerous jours. and profl. mags.; contbr. articles to profl. jours. Recipient Faculty Rsch. Assoc. award, Am. Cancer Soc., 1966—75, Disting. Career award for contbns. to hemostasis, Internat. Soc. for Thrombosis and Hemostasis, 1985, Alumni Faculty award, Washington U. Sch. Medicine, 1986, The Robert J. and Claire Pasarow Found. award, 1994, Bristol-Myers Squibb prize for cardiovascular rsch., 1998, numerous others. Fellow: ACP; mem.: Inst. of Medicine of NAS, Am. Soc. Clin. Investigation (pres. 1981—82), Am. Soc. Biol. Chemists, Am. Fedn. Clin. Rsch., Am. Soc. Hematology (pres. 1991), Assn. Am. Physicians, Am. Acad. Arts and Scis., Alpha Omega Alpha, Sigma Xi. Home: 7220 Pershing Ave Saint Louis MO 63130-4248 Office: Wash Univ Sch of Med Dept Int Med Saint Louis MO 63110

MAJESTY, MELVIN SIDNEY, psychologist, consultant; b. New Orleans, June 6, 1928; s. Sidney Joseph and Marcella Cecilia (Kieffer) M.; m. Bettye Newanda Gordon, Dec. 18, 1955; 1 child, Diana Sue. BA, La. State U., 1949; MS, Western Res. U., 1951; PhD (USAF Inst. Tech. fellow), Case-Western Res. U., 1967. Commd. 2d lt. USAF, 1951, advanced through grades to lt. col., 1968; program mgr., ast. dir. tng. rsch. Air Force Human Resources Lab., 1967-69; dir. faculty and profl. ednl. rsch. USAF Acad., 1969-72; dir. plot tng. candidate selection program Officer Tng. Sch., Air Tng.Command, 1972-76; ret. USAF, 1976; personnel selection cons. to Calif. State Pers. Bd., Sacramento, 1976-92. Patentee listening center; founded pers. testing for ballistic missile and space systems; directed largest study of fighter pilot selection since World War II; pioneered use of phys. testing as replacement for the maximum age requirement in law enforcement jobs; developed phys. fitness tests and established psychol. screening standards for state highway patrol officer and police officers; contbr. numerous articles to profl. publs. With U.S. Army, WWII, 1944-46, Korea, Vietnam, USAF, 1951-76. Decorated Commendation medal (2), Meritorious Svc. medal (2), Am. Campaign medal, WWII Victory medal, WWII Overseas Occupation medal, Ballistic Missile badge, numerous others. Mem.: DAV, VFW, APA, Veterans for Peace, Reserve Officers Assn., Mil. Officers Assn. Am., Am. Family Assn., Am. Legion, Mil. Order Fgn. Wars, Vietnam Vets. Am., Amvets, Bible Soc., Nat. Assn. Uniformed Svc. Office: 801 Capitol Mall Sacramento CA 95814-4806

MAJOR, ALICE JEAN, lawyer; b. Denver; m. Kent H. Major, Feb. 16, 1997; children: David, Thomas, Kassie, Samantha, Cameron, Eve, Zoë, Emma. BS in Bus., U. Colo., 1984, MBA, 1986; JD, U. Kans., 1987. Bar: Mo. 1987, Kans. 1988, U.S. Dist. Ct. Kans. 1988, Colo. 1990, U.S. Dist. Ct. Colo. 1991, U.S. Ct. Appeals (3d cir.) 1993, U.S. Supreme Ct. 1994. Atty. Legal Aid of Western Mo., Kansas City, 1987-88, Spencer, Fane, Britt & Browne, Kansas City, 1988-91; mcpl. and county atty. City and County of Denver, 1991—. Spkr. Colorado Springs mtg. Colo. County Attys. Assn., 1992. Vol. Denver Dumb Friends League, Denver, 1996—. Recipient ribbons and awards for paintings. Mem. Alfred A. Arraj Inn of Ct. (barrister mem.). Avocations: art, skiing, fishing. Office: City Attys Office City and County of Denver 1437 Bannock St Rm 353 Denver CO 80202-5375

MAJOR, CLARENCE LEE, writer, painter, poet, educator; b. Atlanta, Dec. 31, 1936; s. Clarence and Inez (Huff) M.; m. Pamela Ritter, May 8, 1980. BS, SUNY, Albany; PhD, Union Inst. Prof. U. Colo., Boulder, 1977-89, U. Calif., Davis, 1989—. Author: All-Night Visitors, 1969, 2d version, 1998, Dictionary of Afro-American Slang, 1970, No, 1973, Reflex and Bone Structure, 1975, rev. edit., 1996, Emergency Exit, 1979, My Amputations, 1986, Such Was the Season, 1987, Painted Turtle: Woman with Guitar, 1988, Fun and Games, 1990, Calling the Wind, 1993, Juba to Jive: A Dictionary of African American Slang, 1994, Dirty Bird Blues, 1996; poetry: Swallow the Lake, 1970 (Nat. Coun. on the Arts award 1970), Symptoms & Madness, 1971, Private Line, 1971, The Cotton Club, 1972, Inside Diameter: The France Poems, 1985, Surfaces and Masks, 1988, Some Observations of a Stranger at Zuni in the Latter Part of the Century, 1989, Parking Lots, 1992, The Garden Thrives, 1996, Configurations: New and Selected Poems, 1958-1998, 1998 (Nat. Book Award Bronze medal 1999), Clarence Major and His Art: Portraits of an African American Postmodernist, 2001, Necessary Distance, 2001, Come By Here: My Mother's Life, 2002, Waiting for Sweet Betty, 2002, Conversations with Clarence Major, 2002, One Flesh, 2003, Myself Painting, 2008; one man shows include Kresge Mus., Mich., 2001, Hamilton Club Gallery, Paterson, NJ, 2006-07; group shows include Schacknow Mus. Fine Art, Plantation, Fla., 2003, Exploding Head Gallery, Calif., 2003-06; contbr. articles to Washington Post Book World, L.A. Times Book Rev., N.Y. Times Book Rev. Recipient Nat. Council on Arts award, Washington, 1970; Western States Book award, Western States Found., Santa Fe, 1986; Fulbright grantee, 1981-83. Office: Univ Calif Dept English 351 Voorhies Hall Davis CA 95616

MAJOR, HELEN E., physics professor, researcher; d. Romey B. and Annie Ephraim; children: Lawrence B., Hamilton R. BS, Clark Atlanta U., Ga., 1969; MS, U. Ill., Chapaign Urbana, 1971; PhD, Howard U., Washington, 2000. Assoc. staff GE Corporporate R & D, Schenectady, NY, 1976—79; assoc. prof. physics Lincoln U., Pa., 2004—. Faculty summer rsch. fellow NASA Goddard Space Flight Ctr., Greenbelt, Md., 2004—06. Contbr. chapters to books. Deacon St. Paul's Bapt. Ch., West Chester, Pa., 1993—2008. Mem.: Nat. Soc. Black Physicists, AAPT, Delta Sigma Theta. Baptist. Home: 1419 Hunter Ln West Chester PA 19380 Office: Lincoln Univ 1570 Baltimore Pike Lincoln University PA 19352

MAJOR, JOHN CHARLES, judge; s. William and Elsie M.; m. Hélène Provencher, 1959; children: Suzan, Peter, Paul, Steven. BComm, Loyola Coll., Montreal, 1953; LLB, U. Toronto, 1957, LLD (hon.), 2005, Concordia U., 2003, U. Calgary, 2005. Bar: Alta. 1958, Queen's Counsel, 1972. With Bennett, Jones & Verchere, Calgary, 1957-91, sr. ptnr., 1967; sr. counsel City of Calgary Police Svc., 1975-85; counsel McDonald Commn., 1978-82; sr. counsel Province of Alta., 1987, Alta. Ct. Appeal, 1991; justice Supreme Ct. of Can., Ottawa, Ont., Canada, 1992—95; with Companion of Order of Can., 2008. Fellow: Am. Coll. Trial Lawyers. Avocation: golf. Office: Bennett Jones LLP 4500 855-2 Str SW Calgary AB Canada T2P 4K7 Office Phone: 403-298-3166. Business E-Mail: majorj@bennettjones.ca.

MAJOR, PATRICK WEBB, III, principal; b. Wai, Maharastra, India, Mar. 12, 1947; s. Patrick W. Jr. and Alice (Seeland) M.; m. Daphnelynn Jantz, June 26, 1971; children: Mindy Joy, Matthew Patrick Webb. BA in BE, Columbia Internat. U., 1969; BA, Biola U., 1972; MA, Point Loma Nazarene U., 1979; postgrad., U. Calif., Irvine. Cert. secondary tchr., adminstr., Calif. Prin. Omega High Sch., Bakersfield, Calif., 1980-84; headmaster Bakersfield Christian Life Schs., 1984-86; prin. North Kern Christian Sch., Wasco, Calif., 1986-88; prin., adminstr. Yucaipa (Calif.) Christian Schs., 1988-2000; prin. Christian H.S., El Cajon, Calif., 2000—03; adminstr. First Bapt. Ch. of Lakewood (Calif.) Schs., 2003—. Chmn. ACSI So. Calif. Accreditation Comm., 1998-2003. Mem. ASCD, Assn. Christian Schs. Internat. (former dist. rep., exec. bd. 1992-2001), Ctrl. Redwood League (pres. 1985-86), CIF Ctrl Sect., Internat. Fellowship Christian Sch. Adminstrs. Business E-Mail: administrator@fbcoles.org.

MAJORAS, DEBORAH PLATT, consumer products company executive, former commissioner; b. 1963; m. John Majoras; 3 stepchildren. BA in Sociology, summa cum laude, Westminster Coll., 1985; JD, U. Va., 1989. Law clk. to Hon. Stanley S. Harris US Dist. Ct., DC, 1989—91; assoc. Jones Day, 1991—2001, ptnr. antitrust sec., mem. tech. issues practice Washington, DC, 2004; dep. asst. atty. gen. Antitrust Divsn., US Dept. Justice, Washington, 2001—02, prin. dep. asst. atty. gen., 2002—03; chmn. FTC, Washington, DC, 2004—08; v.p., gen. counsel Procter & Gamble Co., Cin., 2008—. Chair Internat. Competition Network's (ICN) Merger Working Group. Mem.: ABA (mem. Antitrust Law Sec.). Avocations: golf, shopping. Office: Procter & Gamble Co 1 Procter & Gamble Co Cincinnati OH 45202

MAJTENYI, STEVEN ISTVAN, retired civil engineer, consultant; b. Elek, Hungary, Jan. 20, 1936; came to U.S., 1962; s. Vilmos Gyorgy and Edit (Laczo) M.; m. Joan E. Zimmerman, Jan. 21, 1972; children: Vivian Claire, Juliet Eve. Student, U. Poitiers, France, 1962; MSc, Cornell U., 1965, PhD, 1969. Tchg. and rsch. asst. Cornell U., Ithaca, N.Y., 1964-68; soils engr. TAMS, NYC, 1968-71; hwy. rsch. engr. U.S. Dept. Transp./FHWA, Washington, 1971-76; hwy. engr. The World Bank, Washington, 1976-81; sr. cons. The World Bank, U.S. Dept. Transp./FHWA, Washington, 1981-95; procurement expert UN, NYC, 1995-98; civil engring. cons. Gahanna, Ohio, 1998—2006; ret., 2001. Speaker in field. Contbr. articles to profl. jours. Josephine de Karman scholar, 1962-64. Fellow: ASCE (life). Roman Catholic. Achievements include participation in the development of numerous technical ideas in the U.S. Government and private industry; improvement of procurement documents in numerous countries worldwide. Home: 167 Highmeadow Dr Gahanna OH 43230-1791

MAJUMDAR, ARUNAVA, mechanical engineer, educator; BTech, Indian Inst. Tech., Bombay, 1985; MS in Mech. Engring., U. Calif., Berkeley, 1987, PhD in Mech. Engring., 1989. Rsch. asst. U. Calif., Berkeley, 1985-89; asst. prof. Ariz. State U., 1989-92, U. Calif., Santa Barbara, 1992—96, prof. Berkeley, 1996—, vice chair Dept. Engring., 1999—2002, Almy and Agnes Maynard Chair Prof. mech. engring. Co-chmn. U.S.-Japan seminar on Molecular and Microscale Transport Phenomena, NSF, 1993; co-chmn. 22nd Internat. Thermal Conductivity Conf., Ariz. State U., Tempe, 1993. Reviewer Internat. Jour. Heat and Mass Transfer, Internat. Jour. Wear, NSF, Am. Chem. Soc. Petroleum Rsch. Fund, Solid State Electronics, Am. Inst. Physics, Soc. Photo-Instrumentation Engrs., Biotechnology Progress; contbr. over 20 articles to sci. jours. Scroeder-Scovill-Duncan scholar Indian Inst. Tech., 1982-84, D. K. Merchant scholar, 1984-85; Regents fellow U. Calif., Berkeley, 1985-86; recipient Young Investigator award NSF, 1992—; grantee NSF, 1990—, 91— (two grants), 92— (two grants). Mem. NAE, ASME (sec. K-8 com. fundamentals heat transfer heat transfer divsn., reviewer Jour. Heat Transfer, Jour. Tribology, Jour. Applied Mechanics, Melville medal 1992), AAAS, Am. Vacuum Soc., Materials Rsch. Soc. Achievements include research in heat generation and transport in nanometer scale devices and structures, nanomechanics of ductile grinding of brittle materials, contact mechanics of surfaces and application to microtribology, thermal and mechanical property measurement of very thin films. Office: U Callif Mailstop 1740 5131 Etcheverry Hall Berkeley CA 94720 Office Phone: 510-643-8199. E-mail: majumdar@me.berkeley.edu.

MAJUMDAR, SABITA, biology professor; d. Nara Narayan and Usha Rani Majumdar; 1 child, Shuman. PhD, Calcutta U., India, 1972; student, U. Paris, 1970—72. Assoc. prof. biology Barber-Scotia Coll., Concord, NC, 1998—2005, LeMoyne Owen Coll., Memphis, 2005—; rsch. assoc. U. Southern Calif., LA, 1978—79, Duke U. Med. Ctr., 1979—79. Scientist & head, electron microscope divsn. Indian Inst. Chem. Biology, Kolkata, West Bengal, 1982—98; vis. scientist French Acad. Sci., Lab. Microscope Electronic, U. Paris, 1998; adj. prof. physiology South West CC, Memphis. Educator YMCA, Memphis, 2009. Vis. scholar, French Acad. Sci., 1998; Scholarship, Govt. of India, 1978. Office: LeMoyne Owen Coll 807 Walker Ave Memphis TN 38126 Office Fax: 901-435-1424. Business E-Mail: sabita_majumdar@loc.edu.

MAK, I. TONG, biologist, educator; s. Sau L. Mak and Wai H. Siu; m. Titania Sea Mui, Aug. 6, 1982; 1 child, Tytus D.M. PhD, U. Wis., Madison, 1982. Nat. rsch. svc. award fellow Okla. Med. Rsch. Found., Okla. City, 1982—85; asst. rsch. prof. dept. medicine George Wash. U., Washington, 1986—97, assoc. rsch. prof. dept. physiology and medicine, 1998—2004, assoc. rsch. prof. dept. biochemistry and molecular biology, 2004—07, rsch. prof. depts. biochemistry & molecular biology and medicine, 2007—. Overseas external assessor U. Grants Com., Hong Kong Rsch. Grants Coun.; reviewer US Civilian Rsch. & Devel. Found., Arlington, Va., 2000—01. Contbr. articles to profl. publs. Fellow, NIH, 1982—85, grant, NIH-HLB, 1987—, NIH-NCCAM, 2006—. Mem.: Basic Cardiovasc. Rsch. Coun., Soc. Exptl. Biology & Medicine, Internat. Soc. Heart Rsch., Am. Heart Assn. (reviewer 2008—, grant 1986—88). Democrat. Office: George Washington Univ NW Ross Hall Rm 443 2300 Eye St Washington DC 20037 Office Fax: 202-994-2488. Business E-Mail: itmak@gwu.edu.

MAK, LINDA L., dermatologist; BSc with honors, U. Wis.; PhD, Johns Hopkins U. Contbr. articles to profl. jours. Mem.: Am. Acad. Pediats., Johns Hopkins Med. and Surg. Assn., Am. Acad. Cosmetic Surgery, Royal Coll. Surgeons Eng. Achievements include research in HIV vaccine development and gene therapy.

MAKADOK, STANLEY, management consultant; b. NYC, Mar. 30, 1941; s. Jack and Pauline (Speciner) Makadok; m. Neilia A. David, Nov. 12, 1989; 1 child from previous marriage, Richard. BME, CCNY, 1962; MS in Mgmt. Sci., Rutgers U., 1964. Bus. sys. analyst Westinghouse Electric Corp., Balt., 1964—65; project engr., corp. cons. Am. Cyanamid Corp., Pearl River, NY, Wayne, NJ, 1965—68; v.p., bus. devel. and planning Pepsico Inc. and affiliates, Purchase, NY, Miami, Fla., 1968—75; mgr. fin. and planning cons. Coopers & Lybrand, NYC, 1975—77; pres. Century Mgmt. Cons., Inc., Yardley, Pa., 1977—. Contbr. articles to profl. jours. Office: Century Mgmt Cons Inc 1449 Wheatsheaf Rd Yardley PA 19067-3939 Office Phone: 215-321-5699.

MAKASYUK, IGOR, physicist, consultant; b. Sochi, Russia, Mar. 17, 1964; s. Victor V. Makasyuk and Iraida N. Orlova; m. Guadalupe Montes, Mar. 24, 2002. MS, U. St.Petersburg, Russia, 1987, PhD, 1990. Cert. physicist Certifying Com. USSR, 1990. Assoc. prof. Mining Inst. Tech. U., St-Petersburg, 1990—2000, U. Civil Constrn. and Engring., St-Petersburg, 2000—03; rschr., lectr. San Francisco State U., 2003—07; dir., content devel. BOLT Sys., Inc., San Jose, 2007—08. Contbr. scientific papers. Active ASPCA, NYC, 2006. Grantee, Soros Found., 1993; Rsch. grant, Govt. Denmark, 1999. Mem.: Calif. Faculty Assn., Optical Soc. Am. Achievements include discovery of soliton beams in optical photrefractive lattices: vortex, dipole and vector solitons, confinement of light by defects in optically induced lattices; first to measure numerous rate constants for ion-atom-electron processes in noble gases with plasma and beam techniques. Avocations: music, reading, travel. Office: BOLT Sys Inc San Jose CA 95120 Home: 4274 Wilkie Way Apt Q Palo Alto CA 94306 Business E-Mail: imakasyu@stars.sfsu.edu.

MAKDISI, TONY, medical educator; b. May 1, 1968; s. Bahij and Badiah Makdisi; m. Fadia Rostom; children: Helen, Joyce. MD, Damascus U., Syria, 1992. Attending hospialist Berkshire Med. Ctr., Pittsfield, Mass., 2006—, assoc. prof. medicine, 2006—. Contbr. scientific papers. Recipient Best Tchg. Attending Of Yr. award, Berkshire Med. Ctr., 2008. Mem.: SHM, ACP, AMA.

MAKEEV, MAXIM A., physicist; b. Moscow, Mar. 11, 1970; s. Alexander N. and Vera M. Makeev. MS, Moscow Engring. Physics Inst., 1993; PhD, U. Notre Dame, 1999. Rsch., tchg. asst. U. Notre Dame, Ind., 1994—99; rsch. assoc. U. So. Calif., LA, 1999—2001, 2003—05; rsch. asssoc. La. State U., Baton Rouge, 2001—03; rsch. assoc. NASA Ames Rsch. Ctr., Moffett Field, Calif., 2005—. Mem.: Materials Rsch. Soc., Am. Phys. Soc. Achievements include contributions to development of methodologies for large-scale parallel simulations; research in statistical mechanics, surface science, nano-science. Office: NASA Ames Rsch Ctr MS 229-1 Moffett Field CA 94035-1000 Business E-Mail: makeev@usc.edu, mmakeev@mail.arc.nasa.gov.

MAKEL, LARRY A., lawyer; b. Vestaburg, Pa., Dec. 7, 1953; BA cum laude, Washington & Jefferson Coll., 1975; JD, W.Va. Univ., 1978; LLM, NYU, 1980. Bar: W.Va. 1978, Pa. 1978, Tex. 1981, DC. Asst. atty. gen. Commonwealth of Pa., 1978—79; ptnr., Banking, Bus. Law & Internat. Bus. Transactions practices, mem. exec. com. Patton Boggs LLP, Dallas. Former counsel & legis. liaison S.W. Chpt. Nat. Comml. Fin. Assn. Mem.: ABA (past chmn. Acquisition Fin. Subcommittee), State Bar Assn. Pa., State Bar Tex. (past vice chmn. Comml. Fin. Svc. Subcommittee), Dallas Bar Assn., Am. Coll. Comml. Fin. Attys. Office: Patton Boggs LLP Suite 3000 2001 Ross Ave Dallas TX 75201-8001 Office Phone: 214-758-1560. Office Fax: 214-758-1550. Business E-Mail: lmakel@pattonboggs.com.

MAKELA, JONATHAN JAMES, engineering educator; BS in Elec. Engring with honors, Cornell U., Sch. Elec. Engring., Ithaca, NY, 1999, PhD in Elec. & Computer Engring., 2003. Student researcher The Cleve. Clinic Found., 1995, 1996; co-op engr. 3M Co., 1997; undergraduate researcher Cornell U., Sch. Elec. & Computer Engring., Ithaca, NY, 1998—99, grad. rsch. asst., 1999—2002; Nat. Rsch. Coun. Rsch. Assoc., Thermospheric and Ionospheric Rsch. and Applications group Naval Rsch. Lab., Washington, 2002—04; with U. Ill, Urbana-Champaign, 2004—, asst. prof., dept. elec. & computer engring., 2004—, asst. rsch. prof., Coordinated Sci. Lab., 2004—. Mem. academic excellence workshop Cornell U., 1998, tchg. asst. fellow, 2000—01, head cooperative learning trainer, Learning Initiatives for Future Engineers, 2000—02; Discovery Station vol. Nat. Air and Space Mus., 2002—04; co-convener in the field, 2002—; sci. definition team member, Communication/Navigation Outage Forecasting System (C/NOFS) satellite, 2002—; team mem. calibration/validation effort for the Special Sensor Ultraviolet Spectrographic Imager (SSUSI), 2002—, Special Sensor Ultraviolet Limb Imager (SSULI) on the next generation Defense Meteorological Support Program (DMSP) satellites, 2002—; presenter in field; invited lectr. in field. Contbr. articles to profl. publications; referee for papers in several profl. publications, panel reviewer for proposals at NSF and NASA, reviewer for proposals Journal of Geophysical Research, Geophysical Research Letters, Radio Science, Annales Geophysicae, Planetary and Space Science, Journal of Atmospheric and Solar-Terrestrial Physics, and Advances in Space Research. Recipient Einwecther award for outstanding service to the Coll. Engring, 1999, Editors' Citation for Excellence in Refereeing for Geophysical Rsch. Letters, 2005; Cornell U. Grad. Rsch. Fellowship, 1999—2002, NSF Grad. Rsch. Fellowship, 1999—2002, NRC Post-Doctoral Rsch. Associateship, 2002—04. Mem.: Am. Geophysical Union, IEEE. Achievements include development of new instrumentation to forcast the weather in the ionosphere. Office: Dept Elec & Computer Engring U Ill 316 Coordinated Science Laboratory 1308 W Main St Urbana IL 61801-2307 Office Phone: 217-265-9470. Office Fax: 217-333-4303. Business E-Mail: jmakela@uiuc.edu.

MAKEN, SONNY, real estate company executive, developer; b. India, Sept. 27, 1975; arrived in U.S., 1989; s. Mani and Pam Maken; m. Debbie Maken, Mar. 2, 2002; children: Hannah, Abigail. BS in Internat. Econs., Georgetown U., 1997. Cert. commercial investment mgr. Chief legal assoc. No. Trust Inc., Chgo., 1997—99; lead subrogation specialist Grotefeld & Denenberg, LLC, Chgo., 1999—2001; pres., CEO The Maken Group, Inc., Palm Beach, Fla., 2001—; CEO Maken Hotel Group, Inc., Palm Beach, 2006—. Recipient Diamond Cir. award, Coldwell Banker Real Estate Inc., 2002, Pres. Cir. award, 2003, Coldwell Baker Real Estate Inc., 2004, 40 Under 40 award, South Fla. Bus. Jour., Real Estate Fla. Mag.; scholar, Gen. Mills Corp., 1995—97, United Meth. Ch., 1995—97. Mem.: CCIM (corr.), Realtor Assn. Greater Ft. Lauderdale (bd. dirs. 2009), Soc. Comml. Realtors (pres. 2009, bd. dirs.), Fla. Assn. Realtors (assoc.; bd. dirs.), C. of C. Palm Beaches, Georgetown Club Palm Beach (corr.), Georgetown Alumni Interviewer Program (corr.), Georgetown Club Miami (corr.). Avocations: golf, sailing, antique cars. Office: The Maken Group Inc Ste 215 6299 West Sunrise Blvd Sunrise FL 33313 also: Ste 203 2247 Palm Beach Lakes Blvd West Palm Beach FL 33409 Office Fax: 561-721-9854. Business E-Mail: sonnymaken@themakengroup.com.

MAKHIJA, MOHAN, nuclear medicine physician; b. Bombay, Oct. 1, 1941; came to US, 1969; m. Arlene Zambito, Nov. 11, 1978. MD, Bombay U., 1965. Diplomate Am. Bd. Nuc. Medicine, Am. Bd. Radiology; cert. spl. competence in nuc. radiology. Resident in radiology Morristown Meml. Hosp., NJ, 1972—75; resident in nuc. medicine Yale-New Haven Hosp., 1975; fellow Yale U. Sch. Medicine, New Haven, 1976—77; jr. attending physician Helene Fuld Med. Ctr., Trenton, NJ, 1977—78; acting dir. dept. nuc. medicine Monmouth Med. Ctr., Long Branch, NJ, 1978, dir. nuc. medicine sect., 1979—2000, asst. attending radiology, 1978—80, assoc. attending radiology, 1980—83, attending radiologist, 1983—2000, St. Peter's U. Hosp., New Brunswick, NJ, 2001—, Robert Wood Johnson U. Hosp., New Brunswick, 2001—. Sr. instr. Hahneman U., Phila., 1978-80, clin. asst. prof., 1980-83, clin. assoc. prof., 1983-91, clin. prof., 1991-94, clin. prof. radiologic scis. Med. Coll. Pa. and Hahnemann U., 1994-2000; clin. prof. radiology U. Medicine and Dentistry NJ-Robert Wood Johnson Med. Sch., 2002—; radiol. cons. to NJ State Bd. Med. Examiners., 1994. Contbr. articles to profl. jours. Mem. NJ Commn. on Radiation Protection, 2004—. Fellow: ACP (spkr. ho. of dels. 1992—93), Am. Coll. Radiology, Am. Coll. Nuc. Physicians; mem.: Med. Soc. NJ (trustee 2003—), Assn. Med. Specialties NJ (sec. 2001—02, pres. 2003—04), Soc. Nuc. Medicine (bd. govs. Gt. NY chpt. 1992—98), Indo-Am. Soc. Nuc. Medicine (pres. 1992—92), Radiol. Soc. NJ (chmn. nuc. medicine 1988—94, treas. 1994—95, sec. 1995—96, v.p. 1996—97, pres.-elect 1997—98, pres. 1998—99, chmn. nominting com. 2001—02, chmn. fellowship com. 2002—), Monmouth County Med. Soc. (pres. 1991—92). Home: 5 High Ridge Rd Ocean NJ 07712-3460 Office: St Peter's U Hosp 254 Easton Ave New Brunswick NJ 08901 Personal E-mail: mmakhija@aol.com.

MAKHLOUF, HALA R., pathologist, educator; d. M. Rashad Makhlouf and Aziza Sherif; m. Joseph A. Morris, June 26, 1996; children: Ryan Y. Morris, Malek J. Morris. MD, Ain Shams U. Sch. Medicine, Cairo, 1984, MS, 1987, PhD, 1990. Lectr. pathology Dept. Pathology, Ain Shams U. Sch. Medicine, 1991—96, assoc. prof., 1996—, prof., 2001; Callender-Binford fellow Hepatic and Gastrointestinal Pathology Dept., Armed Forces Inst. Pathology, Washington, 1996—98, pathologist, rschr., 2004—. Contbr. scientific papers. ICSU fellowship, 1991. Mem.: Am. Assn. Study of Liver Diseases. Achievements include research in cytotoxic effects of eosinophils on renal tubular epithelial cells: implication for renal allograft rejection; hepatic vascular neoplasms: K-RAS-2 mutations among sporadic angiosarcoma, thorotrust-induced angiosracoma, and epithelioid hemangioendotheliomas of the liver; morphological studies of human renal tubular epithelial cell injury following complement membrane attack: reversibility of lesions. Office: Armed Forces Inst Pathology 6825 16th St NW Bldg 54 Washington DC 20306 Office Fax: 202-782-4694. Personal E-mail: halaandjoe@yahoo.com. Business E-Mail: hala.makhlouf@afip.osd.mil.

MAKHLUF, HUDA A., research scientist; married. PhD, Med. U. SC., 1998. Postdoc. rschr. Harvard, Boston, 1998—2000; scientist Nat. U., Calif., 2007—. Nifty fifty participant San Diego Sci. Festival. Office: Nat Univ 11255 N Torrey Pines Rd La Jolla CA 92037

MAKI, ATSUSHI, economics professor; b. Kanagawa, Japan, Jan. 14, 1948; s. Sadao and Eiko (Yamaguchi) M.; m. Michie Yabu, Feb. 28, 1975; children: Chiori, Hisashi. BA, Keio U., Japan, 1971; MA, Keio U., 1973, PhD, 1993. Asst. prof. Keio U., Tokyo, 1973-79, assoc. prof., 1979-87, prof., 1987—2009, prof. emeritus, 2009—; prof. Tokyo Internat. U., 2009—. Guest rsch. officer Ministry Posts and Telecom., 1988-90; vis. scholar Harvard U., Cambridge, Mass., 1982-84, 2001, George Washington U., 2001, U. Sydney, Australia, 2002; vis. prof. Osaka U., Japan, 1989, Ecole Superieure des Scis. Econs. et Commls., France, 1994, 2005, Tokyo Internat. U., 2005-09, Kenya Sch. Monetary Studies, 2007; vis. fellow Australian Nat. U., Canberra, 1990, Massey U., New Zealand, 1991, U. Western Australia, Perth, 1993, Victoria U., Wellington, New Zealand, 1997, Bur. Labor Stats., Washington, 2001. Author: Consumer Preferences and Measurement of Demand, 1983, Japanese Consumer Behavior, 1998, Applied Econometrics, 2001, Empirical Analysis of Consumer Behavior, 2007. Recipient award Japan Found., 1996; Abe fellow SSRC, 2001; Ministry of Edn. grant-in-aid, 1997-99, 2003-. Mem. Am. Econ. Assn., Econometric Soc., Japanese Econ. Assn., Japan Assn. Stats., Japan Soc. Household Econs., Royal Econ. Soc. Home: 107-8 Terao Kawagoe-shi Saitama 350-1141 Japan Office: Tokyo Internat Univ 1-13-1 Matoba-Kita Kawagoe Saitama 350-1197 Japan Business E-Mail: makia@tiu.ac.jp, maki@fbc.keio.ac.jp.

MAKI, DENNIS G., epidemiology educator; b. River Falls, Wis., May 8, 1940; m. Gail Dawson, 1962; children: Kimberly, Sarah, Daniel. BS in Physics with honors, U. Wis., 1962, MS in Physics, 1964, MD, 1967. Diplomate Am. Bd. Internal Medicine, Am. Bd. Infectious Diseases, Am. Bd. Critical Care Medicine. Physicist, computer programmer Lawrence Radiation Lab., AEC, Livermore, Calif., 1962; intern, asst. resident Harvard Med. unit Boston City Hosp., 1967-69, chief resident, 1972-73; with Hosp. Infections sect. Ctrs. for Disease Control, USPHS, Atlanta, 1969-71; acting chief nat. nosocomial infections study Ctr. for Disease Control, USPHS, Atlanta, 1970-71; sr. resident dept. medicine Mass. Gen. Hosp., 1971-72, clin. and research fellow infectious disease unit, 1973-74; asst. prof. medicine U. Wis., Madison, 1974-78, assoc. prof., 1978-82, prof., 1982—; hosp. epidemiologist, U. Wis. Hosp. and Clinic, Madison, 1974—; Ovid O. Meyer prof. medicine U. Wis., Madison, 1975—, head sec. infectious diseases, 1979—2007, attending physician Ctr. for Trauma and Life Support, 1976—. Clinician, rschr., educator in field; mem. program com. Intersci. Conf. on Antimicrobial Agts. and Chemotherapy, 1987-94; mem. Am. Bd. Critical Care Medicine, 1989-95. Sr. assoc. editor Infection Control and Hosp. Epidemiology, 1979-93; mem. editl. bd. Jour. Lab. and Clin. Investigation, 1980-86, Jour. Critical Care, 1985-96, Jour. Infectious Diseases, 1988-90, Critical Care Medicine, 1989-94, 97—, Mayo Clinic Procs., 2002-07; contbr. articles to med. jours. Recipient 1st award for disting. rsch. in Antibiotic Rev., 1980, Internat. CIPI award, 1994, SHEA lectr., 1999, numerous tchg. awards and hon. lectrs. Master ACP; fellow Infectious Diseases Soc. Am. (coun. 1993-96, citation 2000), Am. Acad. Microbiology, Soc. for Critical Care Medicine, Surg. Infection Soc., Wis. Acad. Scis., Arts and Letters; mem. Soc. Hosp. Epidemiologists Am. (pres. 1990), Ctrl. Soc. for Clin. Rsch., Am. Soc. Microbiology, Am. Fedn. Clin. Rsch., Alpha Omega Alpha (nat. bd. dirs. 1983-89). Office: U Wis Hosp and Clinics H4/574 Madison WI 53792 Office Phone: 608-263-1545. Fax: 608-833-0327. Personal E-mail: dgmaki@yahoo.com. Business E-Mail: dgmaki@medicine.wisc.edu.

MAKI, HOPE MARIE (COUNTESS HOPE MARIE MAKI), artist, educator; b. St. Joseph, Mo., Jan. 14, 1938; d. Myrle Marie Howard; 3 children. Host TV art show Channel 6, Fort Walton Beach, Fla.; owner art sch., gallery; tchr. art, 1957—. Exhibited in shows at Arts-Inter-Salon Int des Sekneurs de L'Art, Chateauneuf du Pape, France, 1994, Salon Int des Seigneurs de L'Art, Palais des Congres Marseille, 1994, Mountserrat Gallery, N.Y.; represented in permanent pvt. and pub. collections; created art for the blind, 1963—; author, illustrator: Trader Jon His Life, 2001 Founder Art for the Blind, 1963. Named One of Best New Poets Am. Poetry Assn., 1987, 88, 89; recipient Award of Poetic Achievement, Amherst Soc., recognition of outstanding achievements in art edn. Cox Comm., 2000; poem placed in spl. collection Statue of Liberty Nat. Monument, 1992 Mem.: Nat. Mus. Women in Arts. Avocation: poetry. Home and Office: 3985 Langley Ave Pensacola FL 32504-8371 Office Phone: 850-478-4673.

MAKINEN, MARVIN WILLIAM, biophysicist, educator; b. Chassell, Mich., Aug. 19, 1939; s. William John and Milga Katarina (Myllyla) M.; m. Michele de Groot, July 30, 1966; children: Eric William, Stephen Matthew. AB, U. Pa., 1961; postgrad., Free U. Berlin, 1960-61; MD, U. Pa., 1968; DPhil, U. Oxford, Eng., 1976. Diplomate Am. Bd. Med. Examiners. Intern Columbia-Presbyn. Med. Ctr., NYC, 1968-69; rsch. assoc. NIH, Bethesda, Md., 1969-71; vis. fellow U. Oxford, Eng., 1971-74; asst. prof. biophysics U. Chgo., 1974-80, assoc. prof., 1980-86, prof. biochemistry and molecular biology, 1986—, chmn. dept., 1988-93. Established investigator Am. Heart Assn., 1975-80; lectr. in field. Contbr. numerous articles to profl. jours. Sr. surgeon USPHS, 1969-71. John Simon Guggenheim fellow 1997-98, John E. Fogarty Sr. Internat. fellow, 1984-85, European Molecular Biology Orgn. sr. fellow, 1984-85, NIH spl. fellow, 1971-74, Berquist fellow Am. Scandinavian Found., 1970. Fellow Am. Inst. Chemists; mem. Am. Chem. Soc., Biophys. Soc., Am. Soc. Biochemistry and Molecular Biology, The Protein Soc., AAAS. Office: U Chgo Center Integrative Science 929 E 57th St Chicago IL 60637-5415 Office Phone: 773-702-1080. Business E-Mail: makinen@uchicago.edu.

MAKKER, SUDESH PAUL, physician; b. Sargodha, Punjab, India, June 8, 1941; came to U.S., 1966; s. Manohar Lal and Daya Wati (Kharbanda) M.; m. Donna Mae Stohs, Feb. 15, 1969; children: Vishal, Kirin. Fellow of Sci., Panjab U., 1959; MD, All India Inst. med. Scis., New Dehli, 1964. Bd. cert. Am. Bd. Pediatrics, Am. Bd. Pediatric Nephrology. Intern in internal medicine All India Inst. of Med. Scis., New Dehli, 1965, resident in internal medicine, 1966; rotating intern Queens Gen. Hosp., NYC, 1966-67; resident in pediatrics U. Chgo. (Ill.) Hosps., 1967-69; rsch. fellowship in pediatric nephrology Case Western Res. U., 1969-71; fellowship in pediatric nephrology U. Calif., San Francisco, 1971; instr. to asst. prof. pediatrics Case Western Res. U., Sch. Medicine, Cleve., 1971-76, assoc. prof., div. head pediatric nephrology, 1976-83; prof., div. head pediatric nephrology U. Tex. Health Sci. Ctr., San Antonio, 1983-91; prof., sect. chief pediatric nephrology U. Calif., Davis Sch. Medicine, Davis, 1991—. Mem. ad hoc com. on nat. standards for dialysis and transplantation in children Am. Soc. Pediatric Nephrology; ad hoc com. on hypertension in the young Am. Heart Assn., N.E. Ohio Chpt.; mem. end stage renal disease program Crippled Children Svcs. State of Ohio; mem. rsch. grants com. and pub. edn. com. Kidney Found. of Ohio; vis. prof. U. Pa. Children's Hosp., Phila., 1981, U. So. Calif., L.A., 1981, U. Calif. Sch. Medicine, San Francisco, 1982, U. Mich., Ann Arbor, 1990, and many others. Editor: (textbook) Pediatric Nephrology, 1992, 2006; editorial bd.: Internat. Jour. Pediatric Nephrology, Indian Jour. Pediatrics; contbr. over 110 articles to profl. jours. Mem. AAAS, Am. Soc. Investigative Pathology, Am. Acad. Pediatrics, Am. Soc. Nephrology (elected fellow, 2004), The Soc. for Exptl. Biology and Medicine, Am. Assn. Immunologists, Soc. for Pediatric Rsch., Am. Pediatric Soc., Sigma Chi, Sigma Xi. Avocations: tennis, hiking, reading, photography. Office: Univ Calif Davis Med Ctr Pediatric Nephrology 2516 Stockton Blvd Sacramento CA 95817-2208 Office Phone: 916-734-8118. Business E-Mail: spmakker@ucdavis.edu.

MAKKI, S. KAMI, education educator; MS in Eng, U. NSW, 1991; PhD, U. Queensland, Australsia, 1997. Lectr. Royal Melbourne Inst. of Tech., Melbourne, Australia, 1997—2000, Queensland U. of Tech., Brisbane, Australia, 2000—03; asst. prof. U. Toledo, 2003—. Office Fax: 419-530-8146. Business E-Mail: kmakki@eng.utoledo.edu.

MAKKI, SHAMILA, project manager engineer, researcher; arrived in US, 2003; d. Seyed Rouholloh Mohammad Makki and Esmat Ghaem Maghami. M in Civil Engring., U. Queensland, Brisbane, 1999, grad. diploma in info. tech., 2002, M in Info. Tech. and Civil Engring., 2003; PhD in Elec. Engring., Fla. Internat. U., Miami. Civil engr., estimator Telecommunication Co., Tehran, 1990—95; civil engr. rsch. asst. Civil Engring. Dept., Brisbane, Australia, 1998—99; info. tech. rsch. scholar Sch. Info. Tech., Brisbane, 1999—2001, project mgmt. rsch., 2002—03; project mgmt. engr. Horizon Electronics, Inc., Miami Lakes, 2003—. Recipient several Tech. Contbn. and Leadership awards, NSF, 2003—07. Mem.: ACM, IEEE, Eta Kappa Nu, Phi Kappa Phi, Delta Epsilon Iota (life). Avocations: reading, sports, cooking. Office: Inst Electrical and Computer Engring Fla Internat U 10555 W Floyer St Miami FL 33174 Personal E-mail: shamilamakki@gmail.com.

MAKOGON, YURI F., engineering educator; BE in Oil Gas Prodn. Engring., Gubkin U., Moscow, 1956, MS, 1963; PhD, All Union Gas Rsch. Inst., Moscow, 1975. Sr. cons. natural gas hydrates Govt. India and Japan; assoc. prof. Gubkin U., Moscow, 1958—74; prof. petroleum dept. Indian Sch. Mines, Dhanbad, 1965—67; prof. Frayberg Mining Acad., Germany, 1973; head hydrate lab. All Union Gas Rsch. Inst., 1974—88; head gas hydrate lab. Oil and Gas Rsch. Inst. Russian Acad. Sci., Moscow, 1988—93; dir. Inst. Hydrocarbons and Environment, Moscow, 1991—98; vis. prof. Tex. A&M U., 1993—, rsch. assoc., 1993—. Operator Shebelinscoe Gas-Condensate Field, Ukraine, 1956—58, master, 1956—58, rsch. engr., 1956—58, chief engr., 1956—58; cons. gas hydrate problems in various orgns. Contbr. articles to profl. jours., chapters to books. Recipient Albert Einshtein medal, Russian Acad. Nat. Sc., 2002, V. Vernadsky Honor medal, 2003, Gold Crown & Eagle medal, 2005, Honor medal, 2007, Lifetime Achievement award, 6th Internat. Conf. Gas-Hydrates, 2008. Mem.: SPE (dep. chmn. student sci. 1953—56), Gubkin Petroleum Inst., Oil-Gas Sect. Russian Acad. (chmn. 1991—95), Geology Sect. Russian Acad., Nat. Geographic Soc., Internat. Soc. Petroleum Engr., Acad. Natural Sci. (Russia). Office: Gas Hydrate Lab Tex A&M Univ College Station TX 77843 Business E-Mail: makogon@tamu.edu.

MAKOUS, WALTER LEON, visual scientist, educator; s. Lawrence and Ruth Lorraine (Luehring) Makous; m. Marilyn Ann Carlson, Feb. 2, 1958 (div. 1973); children: Ann, James, Matthew; m. Joyce Brown Menconi, 1974 (div. 1981); m. Barbara Anne Duggins, Apr. 29, 1982. BS, U. Wis., 1958; MSc, Brown U., Providence, 1961, PhD, 1964. Mem. staff IBM, Yorktown Heights, NY, 1963-66; asst. prof. psychology U. Wash., 1966-69, lectr. in physiology and biophysics, 1966-69, assoc. prof. psychology, 1969-74, prof. psychology, 1974-79; prof. psychology, ophthalmology and visual sci. U. Rochester, 1979-95; prof. brain and cognitive sci., ophthalmology & visual sci., 1995—; dir. Ctr. for Visual Sci. U. Rochester, 1979-90. Northwest rep, charter mem steering comt West Coast Regional Consortium Univs in Neurosciences, 1976—79; mem coun on energy saving through more efficient lighting NAS-NRC, 1978—79, night vision coun, 1985—86; chmn ctr symp Univ Rochester, 1981—82; sensory processes panelist NSF, Washington, 1977—82, mem adv comt applied sci and research applicaitons policy, 1978—81; rev comt Presidential Young Investigator Award Program, 1984; vis scientist IBM Research, 1970—71. Editor (consult ed): Sensory Processes, 1977—79, Jour of the Optical Soc Am, 1982—86; contbr. articles to profl jours. With USNR, 1953—55. Grantee, Nat Eye Inst, 1969—2006, NSF, 1959—62, 1981—82. Fellow: AAAS, Optical Soc. Am. (ed vision and color 1982—86, mem coord vision and physiological optics comt 1983—89, coord vision and med optics comt 1983—89, publs comt 1985—89, chmn fellows and hon mems comt 1986, feature ed applied vision 1989—90); mem.: Am Nat Standards Inst/Human Factor & Ergonomics Soc-100 (rev comt 1992—2006, chmn. visual displays 2002—06), Assn. Rsch. in Vision and Ophthalmology (chmn sect psycho-physics 1977). Office: U Rochester Ctr for Visual Sci Rochester NY 14627 Office Phone: 585-275-8659. Business E-Mail: walt@cvs.rochester.edu.

MAKOVSKY, KENNETH DALE, public relations executive; s. Jack and Minnie (Freedman) Makovsky; m. Phyllis Ann Peck, Oct. 15, 1972; children: Evan, Matthew. BA, Washington U., St. Louis, 1962, JD, 1965. Asst. account exec. Curtis Hoxter Inc., NYC, 1965—66; account exec. Ruder & Finn Inc., NYC, 1966—69, Harshe-Rotman & Druck, NYC, 1970—72, v.p., 1973—75, sr. v.p., 1975—79, sr. v.p., dep. gen. mgr. N.Y. office, 1979; founder, pres. Makovsky and Co., Inc., NYC, 1979—; founder, past pres. Internat. Pub. Rels. Exch.; chmn. Makovsky & Co., Inc., NYC. Contbr. articles to profl. pubs. Nat. bd. govs. Am. Jewish Com. N.Y., 1999—, nat. pub. rels. com. chmn., 1981—; speechwriter 17th Dist. Congl. Campaign, NYC, 1972; v.p. Am. Jewish Com. N.Y., NYC, 1985—, N.Y. bd. dirs., 1978—; adv. com. S.I. Newhouse Sch. Pub. Commn., 1996—, Washington U. Nat. Arts and Sci. Coun., 1998—; bd. trustees Inst. PR, 2000—. Recipient Gold Quill IABC, 1990, Cipra award Inside Pub. Rels., 1994, PRSA's Silver Anvil, PRSA-NY's Big Apple award; named Pub. Rels. All Star, Inside Pub. Rels., 1992; co. named one of ten fastest growing pub. rels. firms in U.S., O'Dwyer Rankings, 1985, 86, 87, 89, 90, 91, one of four top pub. rels. firms in N.Y.C., Small Agy. Yr. Inside Pub. Rels., 1990, among 12 Best Managed Firms in U.S., 1993, 94, among the 12 top strategic counseling firms in U.S., 1995, one of the 8 hot bus.-to-bus. agys., 1996, one of the 8 best managed agys., 1997, one of the 12 top investor relations agys., 1997, among the 15 top tech. agys., 1997, best managed PR agy. in U.S., 1998, among 16 top investor relations agys., 1998, among 9 top bus.-to-bus., 1998, 16 nat. capabilities agys., 1998, among 12 best managed agys., 1999, one of 12 top bus.-to-bus. mktg., 1999, among 12 top investor relations agys., 1999, one of 15 top agys. in N.Y.C., 1999, among top 8 bus.-to-bus. mktg., 1999. Mem.: Inst. Pub. Rels. (bd. trustees), Arthur Page Soc., Nat. Investors Rels. Inst., Pub. Rels. Soc. Am. (Silver Anvil award for Chem. Spltys. Mfrs. Assn. 1978, award for Am. Superconductor 1994), Nat. Arts Sci. Coun., Washington U. Alumni Club N.Y.C. (pres. 1970). Avocations: theater, movies, travel. Office: Makovsky and Co Inc 575 Lexington Ave Fl 15 New York NY 10022-6104 Personal E-mail: kmakovsky@makovsky.com.

MAKOWSKI, CHRISTOPHER, marine biologist, educator; b. Paterson, Fla., Jan. 29, 1977; s. Arthur Makowski and Ann Marie Borowicz, Gary Borowicz (Stepfather). MS, Fla. Atlantic U., Boca Raton, 2004. Cert. underwater photographer instr. Profl. Assn. Diving Instrs., 2003, emergency 1st responder instr. 2003, master scuba diver trainer 2008, cert. marine mammal & protected species expert Nat. Marine Fisheries Svc. and Minerals Mgmt. Svc., 2007; registered diving safety officer Am. Acad. Underwater Scis., 2008. Rschr., tchg. asst. Fla. Atlantic U., Boca Raton, 2001—04; sr. marine biologist CPE Marine Sci. & Biol. Rsch., Boca Raton, 2003—, sci. cons. on sea turtles, 2003—, sci. seminar spkr., 2003—, diving coord., 2008—. Co-exhibitor The Glass Experience: A Glimpse Into the Paradigm Shifts Caused By Glass and the Innovators Who Use It; contbr. articles to numerous sci. jours., scientific papers to conf. presentation (1st Pl., Category of Conservation Rsch., 2002). Mem.: AAAS, Divers Alert Network, Am. Shore & Beach Preservation Assn., Coastal Edn. & Rsch. Found., Inc., Fla. Assn. Environ. Profls. (Boca Raton) (chpt. mem. 2008—), Profl. Assn. Diving Instrs. (Deerfield Beach) (underwater scuba diver instr. 2003—, emergency 1st responder instr. 2003—, underwater photography instr. 2003—, master scuba diver trainer 2008), Am. Acad. Underwater Scis. (diving safety officer 2008—), Internat. Soc. Reef Studies, Jour. Coastal Rsch. (Boca Raton) (editl. bd. mem. 2008—). Achievements include research in a new technique to estimate the abundance and distribution of juvenile sea turtles; using recycled glass to protect our shorelines and replenish our beaches; suitability of recycled glass cullet as an alternative sea turtle nesting substrate; design of creating the first interactive GIS sea turtle database for juvenile green turtles; research in the unknown marine resources of southwest Florida's nearshore reefs. Avocations: scuba diving, guitar, martial arts, photography. Office: CPE Marine Sci & Biol Rsch 2481 NW Boca Raton Blvd Boca Raton FL 33431 Business E-Mail: cmakowski@coastalplanning.net.

MAKRI, NANCY, chemistry professor; b. Athens, Greece, Sept. 5, 1962; came to the U.S., 1985; d. John and Vallie (Tsakona) M.; m. Martin Gruebele, July 9, 1992; children: Alexander Makris Gruebele, Valerie Gruebele Makri. BS, U. Athens, 1985; PhD, U. Calif., Berkeley, 1989. Jr. fellow Harvard U., Cambridge, Mass., 1989-91; from asst. prof. to assoc. prof. U. Ill., Urbana, 1992-99, prof., 1999—. Recipient Beckman Young Investigator award Arnold & Mabel Beckman Found., 1993, Ann. medal Internat. Acad. Quantum Molecular Sci., 1995, Camille Dreyfus Tchr.-Scholar award The Camille and Henry Dreyfus Found., 1997, Agnes Fay Morgan award Iota Sigma Pi, 1999, physics prize Bodossaki Found., 1999; named NSF Young Investigator, 1993; Packard fellow for sci. and engring. David and Lucile Packard Found., 1993, Sloan Rsch. fellow Alfred Sloan Found., 1994, Cottrell scholar Rsch. Corp., 1994; univ. scholar U. Ill., 1999. Fellow: AAAS, Am. Phys. Soc. Home: 2722 Valley Brook Dr Champaign IL 61822-7634 Office: U Ill Urbana Dept Chem 601 S Goodwin Ave Urbana IL 61801-3709 E-mail: nancy@makri.scs.uiuc.edu.

MAKRIS, MARGARET LUBBE, retired elementary school educator; b. Everett, Wash., July 17, 1930; d. Fred Roy and Edna (McFarland) Lubbe; m. Andreas Makris, June 12, 1959 (dec. Feb. 2005); children: Christos, Myron. BA, San Francisco State U., 1956; MEd, U. Md., College Park, 1970. Tchr. San Francisco Pub. Schs., 1954—56; recreation dir. U.S. Army Spl. Svcs. Staff, Germany, 1956—58; tchr. St. Louis Pub. Schs., 1959—61, Montgomery County Pub. Schs., Rockville, Md., 1961—86; ret., 1986. Achievements include co-sponsoring Makris Violin Competition, Salonika, Greece, 1996; founder Andreas Makris Music Endowment-Nat. Philharm., Strathmore Hall Music Ctr., 2005, Andreas and Margaret Makris Music Scholarship Fund, Md. Classic Youth Orchestras, Bethesda, 2006, Andreas & Margaret Makris Scholarship Fund, Colo. State U., Coll. Liberal Arts, Ft. Collins, Colo., 2006, Margaret and Andreas Makris Scholarship Fund, Am. Youth Phila. Orchestras, Annandale, Va., 2007; co-sponsor Makris Clarinet Competition, Colo. State U., Ft. Collins, 2003, Makris Wood Wind Competition, Colo. State U., 2004; pres., CEO Mediterranean Press, 2005; bd. dirs. Nat. Philharm., 2005; donation of Andreas Makris violin crafted by Nicolaus Gagliano in Italy 1732 to the Heritage Foundation Washington, 2006. Mem.: Am. Youth Philharmonic Orchs. (Annandale, Va.) (hon.; hon. bd. mem. 2008), Heritage Found. (Washington), Pres. Club. Republican. Home: 11204 Oak Leaf Dr Silver Spring MD 20901 Home Phone: 301-681-6817. Personal E-mail: mlmakris@yahoo.com.

MAKRIYANNIS, ALEXANDROS, medicinal chemist, educator; b. Cairo, Sept. 3, 1939; came to U.S., 1962; B Pharmacy and Pharm. Chemistry, U. Cairo, 1960; PhD, U. Kans., 1967. Postdoctoral fellow U. Calif., Berkeley, 1967-69; sr. chemist Smith, Kline and French Labs., Phila., 1967-70; rsch. assoc. dept. biochemistry and pharmacology Tufts Med. Sch., Boston, 1971-72, asst. prof. dept. biochemistry and pharmacology, 1972-74; from asst. prof. to prof. medicinal chemistry U. Conn., 1974-86, prof. medicinal chemistry and pharmacognosy, 1986—, prof. molecular and cell biology, 1994—, head medicinal chemistry and pharmacognosy Sch. of Pharmacy, 1981-87, dir. Ctr. for Drug Discovery, 1997—2004, Bd. Trustees Disting. prof. medicinal chemistry and molecular and cell biology, 2002—04; George D. Behrakis chair pharm. biotech., prof. chemistry, chem. biology and pharm. scis. dir. Ctr. for Drug Discover, Northeastern U., Boston, 2004—. Mem. Inst. Materials Sci., U. Conn., Storrs, 1976—, Polymer Sci. Program, 1980-87, Biomolecular Structure Ctr., Univ. Conn. Health Ctr., Farmington, 1987; vis. prof. R. Bitter Nat. Magnet Lab., MIT, Cambridge, 1983—; chmn. organizing com. 1st-6th Cyprus Conf. on New Methods in Drug Rsch., 1983, 85, 87, 89, 92, 94; sr. advisor NRC of Greece, 1985—; cons. NIAAA Intramural Rsch. Program, 1985-87; mem. spl. rev. com. NIDA, 1987—, ad hoc study sect., 1985-89; mem. ad hoc com. NIAID, 1990—; pres. Internat. Cannabis Rsch. Soc., 1993-94. Mem. editl. bd. El Farmaco, 2001—, Jour. Medicinal Chemistry, 2002—; sr. assoc. aditor for medicinal chemistry PharmSci, 1999—; contbr. numerous articles to profl. jours. Recipient Disting. Scientist award U. Conn. Alumni, 1996, Merit award NIH, 1997; McNeil Endowment fellow, 1964-67. Fellow AAAS, Am. Assn. Pharm. Scis. chair divsn. medicinal and natural products 1999-2000). Office Phone: 617-373-4200. E-mail: a.makriyannis@neu.edu.

MAKSEM, JOHN ADELBERT, pathologist; b. Garfield Heights, Ohio, Apr. 20, 1951; s. Celestyn and Jean Maksem; m. Mary Kay Satyshur, July 31, 1976. MD, Wash. U., St. Louis, 1977. Cert. in anatomic pathology Am. Bd. Pathology, in cytopathology Am. Bd. Pathology. Med. dir. gynecor divsn. Bostwick Labs., Inc., Orlando, Fla., 2005—07; dir. cytopathology Orlando Health, Fla., 2007—. Chief pathologist Mercy Med. Ctr., Des Moines, 1988—2005. Contbr. scientific papers to med. pubs. Fellow: Am. Soc. Clin. Pathology, Internat. Soc. Urologic Pathology; mem.: Papanicolaou Soc. Achievements include research in endometrial cytology and prostate cytology.

MAKSI, GREGORY EARL, engineering educator; b. Wilkes-Barre, Pa., May 9, 1939; s. Stephen Cedric and Laura Victoria (Pytell) M.; children: Sabrina, Jared, Joshua. BSME, Ga. Inst. Tech., 1961, MS in Indsl. Mgmt., 1964; PhD in Edn. Adminstrn., U. Miss., 1983. Registered profl. engr., Tenn. Mech. engr. Ellicott Machine Corp., Balt., 1961-62; project engr. Celanese Corp., Rock Hill, SC, 1964-67; assoc. prof. State Tech. Inst., Memphis, 1967-71, prof., 1971—2007, program chmn. of indsl. engring., 1973-90, chmn. dept. mech. engring./indsl. engring., 1990—2000; athletics coach S.W. Tenn. CC, 1972—85, chair dept. engring. technologies Memphis, 2001—07, prof. emeritus, 2007—. Cons. Tenn. Ednl. Alliance, Nashville, 1994, U. Ark., Millington, Tenn., 1988, instr., 1988—2005; curriclum coord. Memphis City H.S., 1993; quality-productivity adv., 1990; CAD/CAM cons., 1995. Hon. sheriff Shelby County Sheriff's Office, 1991; hon. state legis. Tenn. Ho. Reps., Nashville, 1992. Named Disting. Engr. Memphis Engrs. Coun., 1986, Outstanding Tech. Tchr. Am. Tech. Edn. Assn., 1998, Leadership Excellence award Nat. Inst. of Staff and Orgnl. Devel., 1997. Mem. Soc. Mfg. Engrs. (Outstanding Engr. 1998), Inst. of Indsl. Engrs., World Future Soc., Tenn. Profl. Engrs. Soc., Epsilon Pi Tau. Avocations: photography, tennis, racquetball, fishing. Office: SW Tenn CC 5983 Macon Cv Memphis TN 38134-7642

MALA, THEODORE ANTHONY, physician, consultant; b. Santa Monica, Calif., Feb. 3, 1946; s. Ray and Galina (Liss) M.; children: Theodore S., Galina T.; 1 adopted child, Christine A. Lindholm. BA in Philosophy, DePaul U., 1972; MD, Autonomous U., Guadalajara, Mex., 1976; MPH, Harvard U., 1980. Spl. asst. for health affairs Alaska Fedn. Natives, Anchorage, 1977-78; chief health svcs. Alaska State Divsn. Corrections, Anchorage, 1978-79; assoc. prof., founder, dir. Inst. for Circumpolar Health Studies, U. Alaska, Anchorage, 1982-90; founder Siberian med. rsch. program U. Alaska, Anchorage, 1982, founder Magadan (USSR) med. rsch. program, 1988; commr. Health and Social Svcs. State of Alaska, Juneau, 1990-93; pres., CEO Ted Mala, Inc., Anchorage, 1993-97; pres., ptnr. Mexican-Siberian Trading Co., Monterey, Mex., 1994-96; CEO, Confederated Tribes of Grand Ronde, Oreg., 1998-99; dir. tribal rels. Southcentral Found., Anchorage, 1999—, 2000—. Traditional healing dir. Southcentral Found., Anchorage, 2000—; Alaska rsch. and publs. com. Indian Health Svc., USPHS, 1987-90; advisor Nordic Coun. Meeting, WHO, Greenland, 1985; mem. Internat. Organizing Com., Circumpolar Health Congress, Iceland, 1992-93; chmn. bd. govs. Alaska Psychiat. Inst., Anchorage, 1990-93; cabinet mem. Gov. Walter J. Hickel, Juneau, 1990-93; advisor humanitarian aid to Russian Far East U.S. Dept. State, 1992-96; cons. USAID on U.S.-Russian Health Programs, 1994; apptd. adv. com. Sec. of Health and Human Svc. on Minority Health for the U.S., 2000—; mem. coun. pub. reps. NIH, 2002-05. Past columnist Tundra Times; contbr. articles to profl. jours. Trustee United Way Anchorage, 1978-79; chmn. bd. trustees Alaska Native Coll., 1993-96. Recipient Gov.'s award, 1988, Outstanding Svc. award Alaska Commr. Health, 1979, Ministry of Health citation USSR Govt., 1989, Citation award Alaska State Legislature, 1989-90, 94, Commendation award State of Alaska, 1990, Alaska State Legislature, 1994, Honor Kempton Svc. to Humanity award, 1989, citation Med. Comty. of Magadan region, USSR, 1989; named Physician of Yr. Nat. Assn. Am. Indian Physicians, 2008; Nat. Indian fellow U.S. Dept. Edn., 1979. Mem. Assn. Am. Indian Physicians (pres.), N.Y. Acad. Scis., Internat. Union for Circumpolar Health (permanent sec.-gen. 1987-90, organizing com. 8th Internat. Congress on Circumpolar Health 1987-90), Russian Acad. Polar Medicine (elected). Avocations: cross country skiing, hiking, photography, travel. Office Phone: 907-729-4955. E-mail: tmala@post.harvard.edu. *Personal philosophy: Progress in the North will come only when circumpolar countries put aside their geopolitical thinking and work together as one northern family.*

MALACH, MONTE, physician; b. Jersey City, Aug. 15, 1926; s. Charles and Yetta (Pascher) M.; m. Ann Elaine Glazer, June 15, 1952 (dec. June 1989); children: Barbara Sandra, Cathie Tara, Matthew David. BA, MD, U. Mich., 1949. Diplomate Am. Bd. Internal Medicine, Nat. Bd. Med. Examiners. Intern Beth Israel Hosp., Boston, 1949-50, resident, 1950-51, chief resident, 1951-52; chief med. resident Kings County Hosp., Bklyn., 1954-55; practice medicine specializing in internal medicine and cardiology Bklyn., 1955—2001; dir. CCU Bklyn. Hosp., 1965-91, dir. emeritus CCU, 1991—; med. dir., clin. coord. Medicare IPRO Downstate N.Y., 1990—2005; cardiology cons., 2005—. Pres. profl. staff Bklyn. Hosp., 1966-69, chmn. med. bd., 1971-72; attending staff Caledonian Hosp., pres. profl. staff, 1984-85; pres. profl. staff Bklyn. Hosp.-Caledonian Hosp., 1987-89, chmn. med. bd., 1988-89; cons. Kings County Hosp.; tchg. fellow Tufts U. Med. Sch., 1951-52; instr. medicine Downstate Med. Ctr., Bklyn., 1955-59, clin. asst. prof. medicine, 1959-68, clin. assoc. prof., 1969-76, clin. prof., 1976—; clin. prof. medicine NYU Med. Ctr., 1994—; bd. dirs. Bay St. Landing One Owners Corp., 1985-87; v.p. Ocean View Condos, 1989-90, pres., 1990-95; med. dir. IPRO Medicare Rev., N.Y. State, 1990—, IPRO N.Y. State Peer Rev., 1990-2006. Kings County committeeman Dem. Party, 1964, 65. Served with USNR, 1944-46, to 1st lt. M.C. U.S. Army, 1952-54. Recipient 1st Prize for Crisis Mgmt. Habitat Mag., 1987. Fellow Am. Coll. Chest Physicians, ACP (master, Laureate award 2000), Am. Coll. Cardiology (task force Health Care Quality Improvement Initiative 1996—); mem. AMA (chmn. sect. coun. internal medicine 1980), N.Y. Heart Assn., Am. Soc. Internal Medicine (master, trustee 1975-79, sec.-treas. 1979—, pres. elect 1981, pres. 1982-83, chmn. investment com. 1985-93), N.Y. State Soc. Internal Medicine (pres. 1973-74, dir. 1966-84, chmn. Bklyn. chpt., v.p. 1971, award of merit 1978), Bklyn. Soc. Internal Medicine (mem. council 1965, pres. 1969-72), Med. Soc. State of N.Y. (chmn. sect. internal medicine 1976, chmn. med. care ins. com. 1988-93), Federated Council for Internal Medicine (chmn. 1979-80), Med. Soc. County Kings (censor 1985-91). Office Phone: 917-522-1201. Office Fax: 917-522-1201. Personal E-mail: mmalach2@gmail.com. *There is a place for hard work, scrupulous ethics and pride of accomplishment. A great marriage and a fine close family are buffers against adversity.*

MALACHOWSKI, NICOLE, pilot; b. 1974; Grad., Air Force Acad., 1996. F-15E (Strike Eagle fighter jet) pilot Royal Air Force, Lakenheath, Eng., 494th Fighter Squadron; No. 3 right wing pilot Thunderbirds, US Air Force Air Demonstration Squadron, 2005—. Served in Operation Iraqi Freedom, 2005. Achievements include being the first female demonstration pilot in the 52 year history of the Thunderbirds, US military high performance jet team. Office: USAFADS 4445 Tyndall Ave Nellis AFB NV 89191

MALAFRONTE, DONALD, health planning consultant; b. Bklyn., Dec. 16, 1931; s. Pasquale and Amalia (Castaldo) M.; m. Diane Freedenberg, Jan. 7, 1960 (dec. Nov. 14, 1970); children: Philip, Victor.; m. Hillary Demby, Oct. 30, 1982. BS, NYU, 1954. Reporter L.I. Daily Press, 1956-58; reporter, editor Newark Star-Ledger, 1958-65, art columnist, 1963-70; adminstrv. asst. to mayor of Newark, 1965-70; dir. Newark Model Cities Program, 1967-70, Newark Community Devel. Adminstrn., 1968-70; chief urban field operations N.J. Regional Med. Program, 1970-73; pres. Urban Health Inst., Roseland, NJ, 1973—. Cons. to hosps., local govts., 1970— Author articles in field. Served with AUS, 1954-56. Recipient Joyce Kilmer fiction prize NYU, 1953 Office: Urban Health Inst 101 Eisenhower Pky Roseland NJ 07068-1028 Home: 1056 5th Ave New York NY 10028-0112 Office Phone: 973-228-9000. Business E-Mail: dmalafronte@uhi.org.

MALAFRONTE, JUDITH ADELIA, music educator; d. Albert Malafronte and Dorothy Hunter; children: Mario William Westenburg, Nadia Olivia Westenburg. BA, Vassar Coll., Poughkeepsie, NY, 1972; MA, Stanford U., Palo Alto, Calif., 1974. Lectr. music Yale U., New Haven, 2004—. Recipient First prize, Internat. Vocal Competition, 's-Hertogenbosch, Holland, 1981; Career grant, William M. Sullivan Found., 1980, Fullbright scholarship, 1982.

MALALAHALLI, JAYALAKSHMI S., history professor; d. Satyanarayana and Savithri Malalahalli; m. Mohan Tholakapalli; 1 child, Arjun Tholakapalli. MEd., Grand Valley State U., Allendale, 2003. Secondary tchg. cert. Dept. Edn., Mich., 1999. Tchr. Nat. English Sch., Bangalore, Karnataka, India, 1993—95; HS tchr. Jenison Pub. Sch., Mich., 1999—2001; adj. faculty Schoolcraft Coll., Livonia, Mich., 2005—. Vol. Gleaners Food Bank, Detroit, 2007—08. Mem.: Mich. Oral History Assn. Liberal. Hindu. Home: 1031 Wildwood Ln Canton MI 48188 Office: Schoolcraft Coll 18600 Haggerty Rd Livonia MI 48152 Business E-Mail: jmalalah@schoolcraft.edu.

MALAMUT, MYRA LEWINTER, music educator, director; d. Sidney William Lewinter and Ruth Cohn; children: Liza, Dennis. MM, Ithaca Coll., NY, 1977. Cert. NJ music tchr. State NJ, 1978. Instrumental music tchr. Chester Upland Sch. Dist., Pa., 1975—76, Berkeley Twp Sch. Dist., Bayville, NJ, 1978—81; flute and recorder instr. Settlement Music Sch., Phila., 1978—84; instr. music Georgian Ct. U., Lakewood, NJ, 1984—94, asst. prof. music, 1994—, chairperson music, 1996—97, chairperson, art, humanities and music, 1998—2000, chairperson, art and music, 2000—06, program dir. music, 2006—. Musician, flutist Strand Theater, Lakewood, 1979—2007, Ocean Wind Trio, Toms River, NJ, 1982—2005, Flutistically Yours Flute Quartet, Trenton, NJ, 1988—; musician, piccoloist Burlington Musical Soc. Concert Band, NJ, 2004—07. Author (power point creator): (textbook) America's Musical Landscape by Jean Ferris; composer: (musical arrangement) Danny Boy; musician (flutist): (recital) Benefit Performance for the Victims of 9/11. Chairperson, adult edn. com. Congregation Beth Tikvah, Marlton, NJ, 1992—94. Recipient Tech. and Tchg. award, Georgian Ct. U., 2005; Faculty Mini grant, 2005. Mem.: AAUP (local chpt. pres., Georgian Ct. Coll. 1995—97), Nat. Assn. Coll. Wind and Percussion Instructors, Music Educators Nat. Conf. and NJMEA. Achievements include being the first faculty member to create and implement narrated Power Points with sound and music for online teaching at Georgian Court University. Office: Georgian Court Univ 900 Lakewood Ave Lakewood NJ 08701 Office Phone: 732-987-2624.

MALANDRINO, CATHERINE, apparel designer; b. Grenable, France; m. Bernard Aiden. Grad., Esmond. With Dorothee Biss, Louis Feraud, Emanuel Ungaro, Et Vous; head designer Diane Von Furstenberg, NYC, 1998; founder, chief designer Catherine Malandrino brand, 1998—. Named to 500 People Who Most Impact the Hamptons list, Hamptons Mag., 2007. Achievements include designing famous Am. flag dress exhibited at Zandra Rhodes' Fashion and Textile Mus., London, 2003; opening boutiques all over the country and worldwide, including Paris and Tokyo. Office: Aidan Industries Inc 275 W 39th St Fl 3 New York NY 10018-3195

MALANEY, STEPHANIE J., reading specialist; b. Lafayette, Ind., Feb. 7, 1949; d. George Walter Joseph and Audrey (Fisher) Schneider; m. Michael J. Malaney; children: Amanda Lynn, Kyle Patrick, Ryan Elliot. BS Elem. Edn., U. Wis., Oshkosh, 1990, MS Elem. Edn., 1992; MSE Reading, U.Wis., Oshkosh, 1997; MS Ednl. Adminstrn., U.Wis., Madison, 2004. Tchr. grades 1-3 Appleton Area Sch. Dist., Wis., 1990—92, instrnl. lead tchr. and dist. leader social studies program, 1992—95, tchr. 6th grade, 1995—98, reading specialist, 1998—. Docent Ontagami Hist. Soc. Grigmon Mansion, Appleton, 2002—, Hearthstone (Hist. Site), Appleton, 2005—. Mem.: NEA, AAUW (pres. Appleton chpt. 2004—06, state nominating com.), Wis. Edn. Assn. (bd. dirs., mem. budget/fin. com.), Mid East Reading Coun. (pres. 2004—06). Avocations: reading, gardening, walking, travel, history research. Home: 307 E McArthur St Appleton WI 54911 Office: Appleton Area Sch Dist 2505 W Capitol Dr Appleton WI 54914 Office Phone: 920-832-4608. Office Fax: 920-993-7078. Business E-Mail: malaneystephan@aasd.k12.wi.us.

MALANGA, MICHAEL THOMAS, research scientist; b. Newark, Aug. 7, 1955; PhD, U. Mass., Amherst, Mass., 1982. Rsch. scientist Dow Chem. Co., Midland, Mich., 1982—. Achievements include patents for fields; research in syndiotactic polystryene and new business development; patents pending for the process and use of acicular mullite. Office: Dow Automotive 1250 Harmon Road Auburn Hills MI 48326

MALANGONI, MARK ALAN, surgeon, educator; b. East Chicago, Ind., Nov. 3, 1949; s. Roland G. and Cornelia (Marza) M.; m. Nancy Knapp, Aug. 12, 1972; children: Joseph, Michael, Jonathan. AB in Zoology cum laude, Ind. U., 1971, MD, 1975. MD; diplomate Am. Bd. Surgery. Asst. prof. surgery Med. Coll. Wis., Milw., 1980-84, assoc. program dir., gen. surgery, 1981-84; assoc. prof. Surgery U. Louisville, 1984-90, chief surgery Humana Hosp., 1985-90; prof. surgery Case Western Res. U., Cleve., 1990—. Chmn. dept. surgery MetroHealth Med. Ctr., Cleve., 1990—. Merit Rev. grantee VA, Louisville, 1985-88. Fellow Am. Coll. Surgeons; mem. Cen. Surg. Assn., So. Surg. Assn., Am. Surg. Assn., Phi Beta Kappa, Alpha Omega Alpha. Office: Metro-Health Med Ctr 2500 Metrohealth Dr # 914 Cleveland OH 44109-1998 Office Phone: 216-778-4558.

MALANI, ASHOK K., physician; b. Jadcharla, India, Dec. 17, 1969; s. Jugal K. and Kamala Malani; m. Hemalata Malani, Feb. 1, 1972; children: Khushi, Gyan. MBBS, Osmania Med. Coll., 1992; MS in Gen. Surgery, Postgraduate Inst. Med. Edn. and Rsch., 1996; MD in Internal Medicine, 2003. Jr. resident in gen. surgery Postgraduate Inst. Med. Edn. and Rsch., Chandigarh, India, 1993—96, sr. resident in surgery, 1996; sr. resident in surg. oncology Nizams Inst. Med. Scis., Hyderabad, India, 1996—97; resident in surgery and oncology Leighton Hosp., Crewe, England, 1998; resident in breast and surg. oncology Royal Free Hosp., London, 1998—2000; resident in internal medicine Coney Island Hosp., Bklyn., 2000—03, alt. del., com. interns and residents, 2001—03, mem. grad. med. edn. com., 2003, mem. quality control exec. com., 2003; attending physician, internal medicine St. Mary Hosp., Kankakee, Ill., 2003—05, mem. continuing med. edn., libr. and cancer com., 2004; attending physician, internal medicine Riverside Med. Ctr., Kankakee, 2003—05; pvt. practice Momence, Ill., 2003—05; hospitalist in hematology, oncology Heartlands Regional Med. Ctr., St. Joseph, Mo., 2005—. Hematology com. mem. US Oncology, Dallas, 2005—, US Oncology Rsch., Houston, 2005—. Contbr. scientific papers, abstracts, publs. in field. Com. mem. Coney Island Hosp., Bklyn., 2000—03, edn. com., quality control com., alt. del. com. of interns and residents New York, NY, 2001—03. Master: Post Grad. Inst. (life); fellow: Royal Coll. Surgeons, Royal Coll. Physicians and Surgeons of Glasgow (life); mem.: AMA (assoc.), ACP (assoc.). Office: St Joseph Oncology Inc 902 N Riverside Rd Saint Joseph MO 64507 Home: 2247 Legacy Trl Irving TX 75063-3846 Personal E-mail: drmalani@yahoo.com.

MALANSON, GEORGE PATRICK, geography educator; b. Clinton, Mass., July 12, 1950; s. Ernest Edward and Agnes Dorothy (Durkin) M.; m. Mary Margaret McCoy, Oct. 20, 1990; 1 child, Joseph Patrick. BA, Williams Coll., Williamstown, Mass., 1972; MS, U. Utah, 1978; PhD, UCLA, 1983. Vis. asst. prof. Okla. State U., Stillwater, 1982-84; researcher CNRS Centre Emberger, Montpellier, France, 1984-85; asst. prof. geography U. Iowa, Iowa City, 1985-89, assoc. prof. geography, 1989-96, prof. geography, 1996—2003, Coleman Miller prof., 2003—, IGBP-GCTE 2.2.3 task leader, 1997—99. Exec. coun. Ctr. for Global and Regional Environ. Rsch., Iowa City, 1990-99. Author: Riparian Landscapes, 1993; editor: Natural Areas Facing Climate Change, 1989; contbr. more than 100 articles to prof. jours. With U.S. Army, 1972-75. Faculty scholar U. Iowa, 1990. Fellow. AAAS, Assn. Am. Geographers, Ecol. Soc. Am., Internat. Assn. for Landscape Ecology, Arctic Antarctic & Alpine Rsch., Geography Compass, Phys. Geography (assoc. editor). Office: U Iowa Dept Geography 316 Jessup Hall Iowa City IA 52242-1316

MALARY, CLAUDE RHEAL, language educator; m. Amanda Lashaw. PhD, Brown U., Providence, 1997. Assoc. prof. St. Mary's Coll., Moraga, Calif., 1990—. Office: Saint Mary's Coll Calif Saint Mary's Rd Moraga CA 94575 Business E-Mail: cmalary@stmarys-ca.edu.

MALATACK, JAMES JEFFREY, pediatrician, liver transplant specialist; m. Catherine Malatack. BS in Physics, Villanova U., Pa., 1971; MD, Med. Coll. Pa., Phila., 1976. Diplomate Am. Bd. Pediat. Intern pediat. Children's Hosp., Pitts., 1976—77, resident, 1977—79, fellow, 1979—80, Phila., 1986—87; staff mem. St. Christopher's Hosp. for Children, Phila.; prof. Temple U. Sch. Medicine, Phila., dir. diagnostic referral svc., 1992—2000; chief pediat. diagnostic referral svc. Thomas Jefferson U. Sch. Medicine, Phila., 2000—. Dir. med. liver transplantation AI DuPont Hosp. Children, Wilmington, Del., 2006—. Dir. Malatack Meml. Scholarship, Muhlenberg Coll., Allentown, Pa., 2005. Recipient Thomas K. Oliver award, U. Pitt. Sch. Medicine, Victor C. Vaughn Tchg. award, Temple U. Sch. Medicine, Miracle Worker award, Children's Miracle Network, Residents Tchg. award, Thomas Jefferson Sch. Medicine, 2001; named Top Dr., Phila. Mag., 2001; named one of Best Drs. in Del., Del. Today Mag., 2005. Fellow: Am. Acad. Pediat.; mem.: Am. Bd. Pediat. Avocation: swimming. Office: AI duPont Hosp for Children 1600 Rockland Rd Wilmington DE 19803 Office Phone: 302-651-5638.

MALAVE, ANDRES, pharmacologist, educator; b. San Juan, Puerto Rico, Nov. 18, 1949; s. Andres Malave, Adela Nevarez; m. Lillian Arce, July 28, 1972; children: Jose A., Jaime E., Josue I., Jessica M. BS in Pharmacy, U. P.R., 1972; MS, Purdue U., 1981, PhD, 1983. Registered pharmacist P.R. Instr. U. P.R., San Juan, 1975—78, asst. prof., 1984—87, assoc. prof., 1988—91; prof., chmn. Nova Southeastern U.,

Ft. Lauderdale, Fla., 1992—2001, assoc. dean, 2001—04, dean Coll. Pharmacy, 2004—. CEO Malave Consulting Svcs., Inc., Ft. Lauderdale, 2001—04; dean coll. pharmacy U. P.R., 1987—91. Recipient Bristol Meyers/Squibb Faculty Devel. award, 1991—92; scholar, Fulbright, 2001. Mem.: Am. Assn. Pharm. Scientist, Peruvian Acad. of Pharmacy, N.Y. Acad. Sci., Soc. Neurosci., Am. Assn. Coll. Pharmacy. Achievements include development of simple non-radioactive assay for estimating protein kinase C and protein phosphatase-1. Avocations: sports, racquetball, basketball, music, guitar. Home: 224 La Costa Way Weston FL 33326 Office Phone: 954-262-1304. E-mail: amalave@nova.edu, copdean@nova.edu.

MALCHAU, HENRIK, orthopedist; b. Stockholm, Feb. 27, 1951; m. Britt Inger Malchau; children: Emma Louise Carlsen, Sara Sofia, Eric Christian. MD, U. Aarhus, Denmark, 1977; PhD, U. Goteborg, Sweden, 1995. Asst. prof. dept. orthop. Sahlgrenska U. Hosp., Goteborg U., 1983—95, asst. clin. head dept. orthop., 1991—2002, assoc. prof. dept. orthop., 1995—2002, clin. head dept. orthop., 1996—2004, prof. orthop. surgery, 2002—04; vis. prof. orthop. surgery Harvard Med. Sch., Boston, 2004—05, assoc. prof. orthop., 2006—. Co-dir. Swedish Nat. Total Hip Replacement Register, Goteborg, 1989—2004; external expert Nat. Bd. Health & Welfare, Stockholm, 1993—95; vis. rschr. orthop. biomechanics and biomaterials lab. Mass. Gen. Hosp., Boston, 2000—01, staff surgeon orthop. dept., 2004—; dir. Nat. Competence Ctr. Orthop., Stockholm, 2003—04; co-director Harris Biomaterials and Biomechanical Lab/Mass Gen. Hosp., Boston, 2004—; sec. Internat. Hip Soc., Stockholm, 2006—; pres. Internat. Soc. Registries, Stockholm, 2007—. Recipient Best Poster, European Orthop. Rsch. Soc., 1997, SICOT/SIROT World Congress, 2002. Mem.: Am. Hip Soc., Orthopaedic Rsch. Soc., Swedish Med. Assn., Nordic Orthop. Fedn., Danish Orthop. Soc., Swedish Orthop. Soc., Hip Soc. (adj. mem. 2006—08), Internat. Hip Soc. (nominating com. mem. 2003—08, sec. 2006—08), Am. Acad. Orthop. Surgeons (internat. affiliate mem. 2001—08, Otto Aufranc award 2004, Best Poster 2006), Goteborg Med. Assn. Achievements include patents for radial impaction grafting system; screw anchored joint prosthesis. Office: Mass Gen Hosp 55 Fruit St YAW 3922 Boston MA 02114-2696 Office Phone: 617-643-1322, 617-724-7548. Office Fax: 617-726-8770.

MALCOLM, ELLEN REIGHLEY, political advocacy association administrator; b. Hackensack, NJ, Feb. 2, 1947; d. William Ford Reighley and Barbara (Hamilton) Malcolm. BA, Hollins Coll., 1969; MBA, George Washington U., 1984. Regional mgr. Common Cause, Washington, 1971-74, nat. issues coord., 1974-75, so. states coord., 1975-76; pub. info. coord. Nat. Women's Polit. Caucus, Washington, 1978-79, project dir., 1979; media coord. Cambodia Crisis Ctr., Washington, 1980; press sec. to spl. asst. to pres. for consumer affairs White House, Washington, 1980-81; pres. Windom Fund, Washington, 1980—. EMILY's List, Washington, 1985—. Bd. dirs. Ctr. for Policy Alternatives, Washington, 1989—; chair Women's Legal Def. Fund, Washington, 1984—. Named a Woman of the Yr., Glamour, 1992; named Most Valuable Player, Am. Assn. Polit. Consultants; named one of America's Most Influential Women, Vanity Fair, 1998, 100 Most Important Women in America, Ladies' Home Jour., 1999. Mem. Washington Ednl. Telecomms. Assn. (bd. dirs. 1996—). Democrat. Office: Emilys List 1120 Connecticut Ave NW Ste 1100 Washington DC 20036-3949*

MALCOLM, GLORIA J., small business owner; b. Atlanta, Apr. 16, 1956; d. George and Norella Camp; m. Ericka Monique Malcolm-Davis. B in Bus. Mgmt., DeKalb Coll., Atlanta; PhD in Edn. Leadership, Nova Southeastern U. Cert. notary pub. Team leader MS Soc., Atlanta; cons., advisor Home Testing Inst., NYCq; rep., organizer Nielsen TV, Dunedin, Fla.; mem. Alliance Orgn., Memphis; assoc., advisor Joyner Hutcheson Rsch., Atlanta; owner, pres. GJM Profl. Cleaning Svc., Inc., Union City, Ga., College Park, Ga., 1988—2004; floor supr., U-scan coord. Kroger Co., Atlanta, 2005—. Bd. dirs. Atlanta FCU; asset mgmt. expert; strategic planning expert; investment planning expert; operational analysis expert. Mem. Peace Corps.; active United Food Comml. Unions, Home Inst., MS Walk Soc., Am. Stroke Assn.; mem. ARC, Nat. Geog. Soc.; mem. svcs. Mt. Carmel Bapt. Ch., Atlanta; bd. dirs. St. Matthew's Ch. With USMC, with US Army, corps engrs. US Army. Recipient Ga. Ministry Neophyle award, Ga. Ministry Business Tenacity award, Ga. Ministry Heritage award, Ga. Tech. award, Healthcare Industry award, Real Estate Industry award, Entertainment Industry award. Mem.: NAFE, The Leukemia and Lymphoma Soc., Contribute to Aides Walk of Atlanta, Internat. Rescue Com., Piedmaont Park Consevasy, Bldg. Trader Assn., United Negro Coll. Assns., Piedmont Conservancy Com., Rep. Senate Leadership, Am. Stroke Assn., Nat. Home Garden Club. Avocations: travel, reading, volleyball, tennis, bicycling. Office: GJM Profl Cleaning Svcs Inc 2171 Red Oak Cir Union City GA 30291

MALCOLM, MARK M., automotive executive; b. 1953; m. Patricia I. Malcolm; 2 children. Grad., Dartmouth Coll.; MBA, U. Chgo., 1977. Mgmt. positions through dir. worldwide acctg., Visteon CFO, & head vehicle ops. fin. Ford Motor Co., dir. fin. & strategy global purchasing, 2002—04; exec. v.p., contr. Ford Motor Credit, 2004—06; lead automotive analyst Cerberus Capital mgmt., 2006—07; pres., CEO Tower Automotive LLC, Novi, Mich., 2007—. Office: Tower Automotive Llc 17672 N Laurel Park Dr Livonia MI 48152-3984

MALCOLM, ROBERT JAMES, psychiatrist, educator, clinical investigator; m. Jane Young Young, July 11, 1969. MD, Med. U. SC, Charleston, 1970. Cert. Am. Bd. psychiatry and Neurology, 1976. Prof. psychiatry, family medicine and pediat. Med. U. SC, 1996—, assoc. dean, 2000—. Office: Med Univ SC 67 President St Charleston SC 29425 Office Fax: 843-792-7353. Business E-Mail: malcolmr@musc.edu.

MALCOLM, STEVEN J., petroleum pipeline company executive; b. St. Louis, Sept. 1948; m. Gwen Malcolm; 1 child. BCE, U. Mo.-Rolla, 1970; attended, Northwestern U. With Cities Gas Co.; dir., bus. develop. Williams Nat. Gas Co., 1984—86, dir. gas mgmt., 1986—89; v.p., gas mgmt. & supply Williams Field Svcs. Co., 1989—93, sr. v.p., gen. mgr., 1994—98; pres., CEO Williams Energy Svcs. LLC, 1998—2001; pres., COO Williams Companies, Tulsa, Okla., 2001—02, chmn., pres., CEO, 2002—. Bd. mem. Tulsa Area United Way, Tulsa Community Found., Tulsa Metro Chamber, St. John Medical Ctr.; bd. of trustees U. Tulsa. Mem.: Nat. Energy Svc. Assn., Gas Processors Assn. Office: Williams 1 Williams Ctr Tulsa OK 74172

MALDACENA, JUAN MARTIN, physicist, researcher; b. Buenos Aires, Sept. 10, 1968; married; 3 children. Student, U. Buenos Aires, 1985—88, Inst. Balseiro, U. Cuyo, Bariloche, Argentina, 1988—91; PhD program, Princeton U., 1992—96. Rsch. assoc. Rutgers U., 1996—97; vis. assoc. prof. Harvard U., 1997, Tomas D. Cabot assoc. prof., 1998—99, prof. physics, 1999—2001; prof. natural sci. Inst. for Advanced Study, Princeton, NJ, 2001—. Contbr. artilces to profl. jours. Recipient UNESCO Husein prize for Young Scientists, 1999, Sackler prize in Physics, 2000, Xanthopoulas prize in general relativity, 2001, Pius XI medal, 2002, Edward A. Bouchet award, Am. Phys. Soc., 2004, Dannie Heineman Prize for Math. Physics, 2007, ICTP Dirac medal, 2008; named a Disting. Lectr., Stanford U., 2004; Sloan Fellowship, 1998, Packard Fellowship in Sci. and Engring., 1998, MacArthur Fellowship, 1999. Fellow: Am. Acad. Arts & Scis., 2007. Office: Inst for Advanced Study Sch Natural Sciences Eliminate #1 1 Einstein Dr Princeton NJ 08540 Office Fax: 609-951-4489. E-mail: malda@ias.edu.

MALDE, MELISSA, singer, educator; d. Harold and Caroline Malde; life ptnr. Robert Lenk. BA in German Studies, Oberlin Coll., Ohio, 1984; MusB, Oberlin Conservatory, 1984; MusM, Northwestern U., Evanston, Ill., 1988; Meisterklasse diploma, Hochschule fur Musik, Munich, 1990; MusD, Cin. Coll. Conservatory of Music, 1998. Cert. in Body Mapping Andover Educators, 2001. Instr. U. Wis., Platteville, 1991—93; asst. prof. Luther Coll., Decorah, Iowa, 1995—2000; assoc. prof. U. Northern Colo., Greeley, 2000—. Gov. Colo., Wyo. NATS, 2001—05; auditions chair West Ctrl. Regional NATS, 2005—09. Musician (singer) opera, oratorio, mus. theatre; author (with Maryjean Allen, Kurt-Alexander Zeller): (textbook) What Every Singer Needs to Know About the Body. Vol. Continental Divide Trail Alliance, 2003—08. Office: Univ Northern Colo Campus Box 28 Greeley CO 80639

MALDONADO, ANTONIO, lawyer; Licenciatura en Derecho, Instituto Tecnologico Estudios Superiores, Monterrey, Mex., 2000; LLM, Am. U., Washington, 2002. Bar: Calif. 2005, NY 2004. Ptnr. Maldonado Leyva y Asociados S.C., Tijuana, Baja California, Mexico, 2003—05, Maldonado & Markham, LLP, San Diego, 2005—. Mem.: Colegio Abogados Constitucionalistas A.C., Am. Masters Laws Assn. (bd. dirs. 2004—06), Am. Immigration Lawyers Assn., Internat. Bar Assn., San Diego County Bar Assn. Independent. Avocations: golf, travel, deep sea fishing. Office Fax: 619-393-5515. E-mail: am@maldonadomarkham.com.

MALDONADO, CARLOS MANUEL, surgeon; b. Barcelona, Sept. 25, 1938; came to U.S., 1964. MD, U. Barcelona, 1964. Diplomate Am. Bd. Surgery. Intern Columbia Hosp., Milw., 1964—65; resident gen. surgery Marquette Affiliate Hosps., Milw., 1966—68; fellow thoracic cardiac surgery Newark Beth Israel Med. Ctr., 1969—70, resident gen. surgery, 1972—75. Mem. staff Martin Meml. Hosp., Stuart, Fla., Martin Meml. Hosp. South, Ft. Salerno, Fla., 1975—, chief surgery, 1983-85, chmn. quality coun., 1994— Fellow ACS; mem. AMA, Fla. Med. Assn., Internat. Soc. Cardiovasc. Surgery, Southeastern Surg. Congress, Martin County Med. Soc. (pres. 1999) Republican. Roman Catholic. Home: 2392 SE Ocean Blvd Stuart FL 34996-4230 Office Phone: 772-286-0050. Business E-Mail: carlosmmaldonado@bellsouth.net.

MALDONADO, FRANCISCO JAVIER, electrical research engineer; s. Sostenes Maldonado and Maria Díaz; m. Norma Angelica Portillo, Dec. 17, 1990; children: Mayra Lizeth, Frida Katherine, Samantha Melissa. B in Indsl. Engring. in Electronics, Inst. Tecnológico de Veracruz, Mexico, 1981—85; MSEE, Chihuahua Inst. Tech., Mexico, 1988; DEng, U. Tex. at Arlington, 2002. Rschr. Xomox S.A. de C.V., Chihuahua, 1987—88; tech. support engr. Zenith Data Systems, Chihuahua, 1988—90; rsch. prof. Chihuahua Inst. Tech., 1988—2001, 2003—05; rsch. asst. Automation and Robotics Rsch. Inst. at the UTA, Fort Worth, Tex., 1998—99, Image Processing and Neural Networks Lab., Arlington, 2000—01; elec. engr. Williams-Pyro, Inc., Fort Worth, 2001—02, elec. rsch. engr., 1995—. Reviewer neurocomputing jour. Elsevier, 2005; part-time prof. U. Autonoma de Chihuahua, 2005. Several grants for devel. of monitoring systems and control (Mex.), COSNET. Mem.: IEEE. Achievements include research in the development of pruning algorithm for designing MLP based upon a modified version of the Schmidt procedure. This pruning method was used for proposing two pseudogenetic algorithms; development of the principal investigator and collaborator in several SBIR projects (program of Small Business Research Innovations) developing hardware design in wireless applications and embedding neural networks; harware development and software simulation of industrial and mobile robots. Office: Williams-Pyro Inc 200 Greenleaf St Fort Worth TX 76107 Personal E-mail: frankmald@hotmail.com.

MALDONADO, GUSTAVO OMAR, engineering educator, researcher; s. Omar Ramon Maldonado and Vilma Norys Ferrero; m. Marcela Teresita Ruiz Funes, Dec. 17, 1985; children: Maria Virginia, Sofia Carolina. AA in Acctg., Colegio Corazon de Maria, Cordoba, Argentina, 1975; diploma in Profl. Civil Engring., U. Nat. Cordoba, 1981; MS in Engring. Mechanics, Va. Tech., Blacksburg, 1987, PhD in Engring. Mechanics, 1992. Cert. profl. engr., Calif., 1996, profl. civil engr., Cordoba, 1982; real estate broker NC, 1996. Postdoc. rsch. assoc. Va. Tech., 1992—93; earthquake engr. (assoc. seismologist) Calif. Strong Motion Instrumentation Program, Sacramento, 1993—95; assoc. prof. U. PR, Mayaguez, 1996—2000; lead faculty mem. engring. program Pima CC, Tucson, 2000—03; chairperson, engring. and faculty mem. Miami Dade Coll., Fla., 2003—04; lead faculty mem. engring. program Eastern Ariz. Coll., Thatcher, 2004—06; faculty mem. (interim coord. constrn. program) Ga. Southern U., Statesboro, 2006—. Cons. civil engr. Estudio Ing. Maldonado Torres, Cordoba, 1996—. Contbr. scientific papers (Paul E. Torgersen Rsch. Excellence award, Coll. Engring., Va. Tech., 1992, Hormix award, Cordoba, Robert J. McGrattan Lit. award, ASME, 1993). Lt. Argentinear Army, 1982—83, Buenos Aires. Ednl. Tech. grant, Pima County CC Dist., Tucson, 2001—02, Constrn. Tech. grant, Miami Dade Coll. Found., 2004, grants, Phelps Dodge Mining Co., 2006, Ga. Southern U., 2007—08. Mem.: Am. Inst. Steel Constrn., Constrn. Mgmt. Guild, Ga. Southern U. (academic advisor 2007—08), Sigma Xi, Sci. Rsch. Soc., Sigma Lambda Chi, Internat. Soc. Leaders in Constrn. (academic advisor 2007—08). Roman Catholic. Avocation: soccer.

MALDONADO-BEAR, RITA MARINITA, economist, educator; b. Vega Alta, PR, June 14, 1938; d. Victor and Marina (Davila) Maldonado; m. Larry Alan Bear, Mar. 29, 1975. BA, Auburn U., 1960; PhD, NYU, 1969. With Min. Wage Bd. & Econ. Devel. Adminstr., Govt. of P.R., 1969-70; asst. prof. econs. Manhattan Coll., 1970-72; assoc. prof. econs. Bklyn. Coll., 1972-75; assoc. prof. fin. & econs., undergrad./grad. divsn. Stern Sch. Bus. NYU, 1975-81, prof., 1981—2004, prof. emerita, 2004—. Vis. assoc. prof. fin. Stanford (Calif.) Grad. Bus. Sch., 1973-74; acting dir. markets, ethics & law, NYU, 1993-94; cons. Morgan Guaranty Trust Co., N.Y.C., 1972-77, Bank of Am., N.Y.C., 1982-84, Res. City Bankers, N.Y.C., 1978-87, Swedish Inst. Mgmt., Stockholm, 1982-91, Empresas Master of P.R., 1985-90. Author: Role of the Financial Sector in the Economic Development of Puerto Rico, 1970; co-author: Free Markets, Finance, Ethics and Law, 1994, Financing Economic Development in the Economy of Puerto Rico: Restoring Growth, 2006; contbr. articles to profl. jours. Bd. dirs. Medallion Funding Corp., 1985-87; mem. NYU Senate and Faculty Coun., 1995-2003, chair fin. com., 1996-2000; apptd. adv. bd. dirs. equity & diversity in edn. environs. Mid. States Commn. Higher Edn., 1991—; trustee Securities Industry Assn., N.Y. Dist. Econ. Edn. Found., 1994—; chair NSF, Nat. Vis. Com. Curriculum Devel. Project Networked Fin. Simulation, 1995—; econ. cons. Inst. Women of Color, Nat. Coun. Black Women Cmty. Svcs. Fund, 2000—; trustee Bd. Edn., Twp. Mahwah, N.J., 1991-92. P.R. Econ. Devel. Adminstrn. fellow, 1960-65, Marcus Nadler fellow, NYU, 1966-67, Phillips Lods Dissertation fellow, 1967-68. Mem. Am. Econs. Assn., Am. Fin. Assn., Metro. Econ. Assn. N.Y., Assn. Social Econs. (trustee exec. coun. 1994-96). Home: 95 Tam O Shanter Dr Mahwah NJ 07430-1526 Office: Mgmt Edn Ctr 44 W 4th St Ste 9-190 New York NY 10012-1106 Business E-Mail: rmaldona@stern.nyu.edu, rmaldona@stern-nyu.edu.

MALDONADO-CLASS, JOAQUIN, language educator; b. Manati, PR, Nov. 15, 1959; s. Juan Maldonado-Rodriguez and Albina Class-Santiago; m. Katherine Velez-Andujar, June 30, 1990; 1 child, Sebastian Gioachino Maldonado-Velez. BA, Universidad Central de Bayamon, PR, 1982, MA, 1993; PhD summa cum laude, U. PR, Rio Piedras, 2004. Cert. Spanish tchr. PR. Spanish tchr. Escuela Superior Catolica, Bayamon, 1986—89, Escuela Angel Sandin Martinez, Vega Baja, PR, 1989—93, Escuela Emilio R. Delgado, Corozal, PR, 1993—2000; assoc. prof. Spanish Truman State U., Kirksville, Mo., 2000—. Spanish instr. Universidad Interamericana, Bayamon, 1998—2000; texts author Editorial Norma, Catano, PR, 1998—2001. Author: (textbook) Sueños y Palabras 7, 2000, Sueños y Palabras 12, 2002. Tutor Casa Hogar Sagrados Corazones, Bayamon, 1985—86; missionary Fathers of Holy Spirit, French Guyana, 1984—85; co-dir. Servidores de Jesus, Vega Baja, PR, 1987—2000. Rsch. grantee, U. PR, 1999—2000. Mem.: L.Am. Studies Assn. Roman Catholic. Office: Truman State U 100 E Normal Kirksville MO 63501 Office Phone: 660-785-4500. Business E-Mail: jmaldona@truman.edu.

MALE, ALAN THOMAS, engineering educator, foundation administrator; b. Birmingham, Eng., Sept. 3, 1937; came to U.S., 1968; s. Albert Leslie and Olive (Caddel) M.; m. Beryl Glover, Sept. 20, 1958; children: Andrew James, Christopher John. BSc, U. Birmingham, 1958, PhD, 1962. Registered profl. engr. Pa., Ky.; chartered engr. U.K. Lectr. U. Birmingham, 1960-67; supr. Westinghouse Astronuclear Lab., Pitts., 1968-70; from mgr. metals processing to mgr. processing rsch. Westinghouse Rsch. Labs., Pitts., 1970-83; mgr. advanced processing Westinghouse Sci. & Tech. Ctr., Pitts., 1990-91; prin., tech. mgr. Concurrent Techs. Corp., Johnstown, Pa., 1992-96; dir. Ctr. for Robotics and Mfg. Systems U. Ky., assoc. dean rsch. and grad. studies College of Engring., 1996—2002, prof. mech. engring., 1996—. Pres. Anvil Techs. LLC, Lexington, Ky., 2003—. Holder 16 patents in field. Fellow Inst. Materials (award 1977), Soc. Mfg. Engrs. (life, internat. dir. 1991-99, pres. N.Am. mfg. rsch. inst. 1988-89, Frederick W. Taylor Rsch. medal 1989, internat. pres. 1997-98), ASM Internat. (life); mem. ASME, Am. Welding Soc. Republican. Methodist. Avocations: freemasonry, carpentry, fishing. Home: 3390 Mantilla Dr Lexington KY 40513-1039 Office Phone: 859-257-6262. Personal E-mail: blksmith@iglou.com. Business E-Mail: atmale@engr.uky.edu.

MALEC, WILLIAM FRANK, utilities company executive; b. Broadalbin, NY, June 22, 1940; s. Henry and Anna Frances M.; m. Sarah Powell, Sept. 11, 1965; children: Charles A., Mariah E. BS cum laude, Niagara U., 1962; MBA, Ind. U., 1967; AMP, Harvard U., 1987. Mgmt. trainee Marine Midland Bank, Buffalo, 1962-63; project budget analyst Cleve. Electric Illuminating Co., 1967-68; asst. treas. Mid-Continent Telephone Co., Hudson, Ohio, 1968-75; v.p., treas. Gulf States Utilities, Beaumont, Tex., 1975-78; treas. Cen. and S.W. Corp., C&W Leasing Inc., CSW Energy Inc., CSW Fin., Inc., Dallas; v.p., treas. Cen. and S.W. Services, Inc., Dallas, 1978-89; pres. C&W Credit, Inc., 1985-89; exec. v.p., CFO TVA, Knoxville, 1989-95. Pres. Paradise Ranch Homeowners Assn.; founder Fredericksburg New Comers Club. Served with U.S. Army, 1963-65. Mem. Nat. Mgmt. Assn., Leading Chief Fin. Officers. Republican. Roman Catholic. Office: 110 N Nilam St No PMB 123 Fredericksburg TX 78624

MALECH, HARRY LEWIS, immunologist, researcher; b. Carlstadt, NJ, Nov. 10, 1946; s. Morris and Freda M. (Lipowitz) M.; m. Emily Ann Root, June 4, 1972; children: Sarah Ruth, Dora Rachel, Daniel Lewis. BA, Brandeis U., 1968; MD, Yale U., 1972. Diplomate Am. Bd. Internal Medicine, 1974. Resident in internal medicine Hosp. of U. Pa., Phila., 1972-74; rsch. assoc. Nat. Cancer Inst., Bethesda, Md., 1974-76; fellow in infectious disease Yale U., New Haven, 1976-78, asst. prof. medicine, 1978-83, assoc. prof. medicine, 1983-86; sr. investigator, dep. chief Lab. Host Defenses Nat. Inst. Allergy and Infectious Diseases, Bethesda, 1986—. Mem. NIH patent policy bd. CRADA subcom.; meeting coord. yearly phagocyte workshop, Washington, 1989—; sci. adv. bd. Cadus Pharms., N.Y.C., 1992-95; cons. U.S. FDA, Bethesda, 1992, Idun Pharms., 1994—. Assoc. editor Jour. Immunology, 1986-91, Jour. Immunologic Methods, 1991-93; mem. editorial bd. Blood, 1996—; contbr. articles to sci. jours., chpts. to books. Fund raiser Yale U. Sch. Medicine Alumni Fund, 1973—, United Jewish Appeal Fedn., Rockville, Md., 1992; cons. Simon Wiesenthal Ctr., L.A., 1991. Surgeon USPHS, 1974-76. Recipient Dir.'s award NIH, 1990. Fellow Infectious Disease Soc. Am.; mem. AAAS, ACP, Am. Soc. Cell Biology, Am. Assn. Immunologists, Am. Soc. Clin. Investigation, Assn. Am. Physicians. Democrat. Jewish. Achievements include determination of genetic basis of two autosomal forms of chronic granulomatous disease, research on blood phagocytic cells, genetic therapy of immunodeficiency disorders. Office: Nat Insts Health 10/11N113 Bethesda MD 20892

MALECHA, MARVIN JOHN, architect, academic administrator; b. Lonsdale, Minn., June 26, 1949; s. George and Barbara Malecha; m. Cynthia Marie Miller, Aug. 8, 1970; children: Peter, Michelle. Student, St. Thomas Coll.; BArch, U. Minn.; MArch, Harvard U. Registered architect, Calif. Designer Wallace and Mundt Architects, Edina, Minn., 1969-73, Hugh Stubbins and Assocs., Cambridge, Mass., 1973-76; instr. Cambridge Urban Awareness Program, 1973-76, Boston Archtl. Ctr., 1974-76; asst. chmn., asst. prof. dept. arch. Coll. Environ. Design Calif. State Poly. U., Pomona, 1976-77, chmn., assoc. prof., 1979-82, prof., dean Coll. Environ. Design, 1982-94; dean Coll. Design N.C. State U., 1994—. Chmn. Univ. Fall Conf. com. Calif. State Poly. U., 1984; mem. steering com. Architects for Social Responsibility; mem. bd. advisors Tchrs. cert. program City Bldg. Edn. Program, planning com. So. Calif. Assn. Govts.; vis. critic UCLA, 1985, U., Minn., 1981-83, 87, U. So. Calif., 1980-87, Calif. Poly. State U., San Luis Obispo, 1979-87, Clemson U., 1988, Columbia U., 1993, U. Tenn., 1994, U. Md., 1995, Miss. State U., 1995, U. Wis., Milw., 1996, Roger Williams U., 1997; lectr. to schs. and archtl. assns.; cons. in architecture and research, Claremont, Calif., 1976—; master juror Nat. Council Archtl. Registration Bds.; mem. edn. equity com. Calif. State U. System, 1985-86; pres. Calif. Coun. Archtl. Edn., 1986-88; mem. accreditation vis. team for collegiate programs in landscape architecture, 1988—; bd. dirs. Nat. Archtl. Accreditation Bd.; campus architect cons. U. Calif., Riverside, 1990-94. Author: The Learning Organization and the Evolution of Practice Academy Concepts, Reconfiguration in the Study and Practice of Architecture, Form of Performance, The Fabric of Architecture, The Pomona Method; co-sgner, author internat. protocol for internat. exch. in arch. edn.; contbr. articles to profl. jours. Mem. Art and Liturgy com. Our Lady Assumption Ch., Claremont, Calif., 1982-94; mem. bldg. and real estate com. Archdiocese of Raleigh; bd. dirs. United Arts Raleigh, City Gallery Raleigh, 1995—; nat bd. dirs. Am. Inst. Architects; master juror workgroup, bd. dirs. Downtown Raleigh Alliance; pres. elect AIA, 2008-. Recipient Ellerbe Archtl. award, 1972, Hon. Mention Mass. Housing Dept., 1976, Topaz medallion for excellence in archtl. edn.,

2003, Prize for Creative Integration of Practice and Edn. in the Acad., Nat. Coun. Archtl. Registration, 2002, Jackson Rigney award, NCSU, 2006, Date prize, Cal-Pol, Pomona, 2007, Haecker Leadership award, 2008, William R June dale prize, 2008; Rotch scholar, 1980. Fellow AIA (bd. dirs. L.A. chpt. 1982-83, chmn. state and nat. awards coms. 1983-85, chmn. Monterey design conf. com., Henry Adams award 1973, mem. steering com. archs. in edn. com. 1991, chair archs. in edn. com. 1994-95, adv. bd. ArchVoices, presdl. citation L.A. chpt. 1987, mem. Calif. coun. 1994, nat. bd. dirs. 2005, Excellence in Arch. Edn. award), European Assn. for Arch. Educators (hon.), Soc. Am. Registered Archs., Assn. Collegiate Schs. Arch. (v.p. 1988-89, chair ann. meeting, pres. 1988-89, adminstrs. conf. Wash. 1985, Disting. Prof. 2002), Calif. Coun. Archtl. Edn. (pres. 1988-89), Golden Key (hon. mem. N.C. chpt.), Sigma X. Office: NC State U Coll Design PO Box 7701 Raleigh NC 27695-0001 Office Phone: 919-515-8300. E-mail: marvin_malecha@ncsu.edu.

MALECK, WOLFGANG HELMUT, anesthesiologist; b. Mannheim, Germany, Mar. 21, 1960; s. Helmut and Margot (Klein) Maleck; m. Katharina Patricia Koetter, June 29, 1998; children: David, Justus. MD/ARZT, U. Heidelberg, 1988. Diplomate Bd. Anesthesiology. Physician City Hosp., Frankenthal, Germany, 1989, Deaconess Hosp., Speyer, Germany, 1989-90, Med. Acad., Dresden, Germany, 1990, Ev. Stift, Koblenz, Germany, 1991-92, City Hosp., Ludwigshafen, Germany, 1992—2002, Spital Grenchen, Switzerland, 2003—05, Spital Menziken, Switzerland, 2005—08, Spital Aarberg, Aarberg, Switzerland, 2008, Spital Langenthal, Switzerland, 2008—. Mem. City Parliament, Mannheim, 1986-89. Mem. Reformed Ch. Office: Spital Langenthal St Urban Str CH-4900 Langenthal Switzerland Office Phone: 41-62-916-3111.

MALEK, FREDERIC VINCENT, finance company executive; b. Oak Park, Ill., Dec. 22, 1936; s. Fred W. and Martha (Smickilas) M.; m. Marlene A. McArthur, Aug. 5, 1961; children: Fred W., Michelle A. BS, U.S. Mil. Acad., 1959; MBA, Harvard U., 1964; D of Humanities (hon.), St. Leo Coll., St. Petersburg, Fla., 1970. Assoc. McKinsey & Co., Inc., LA, 1964-67; chmn. exec. com. Triangle Corp., Columbia, SC, 1967-69; dep. under sec. HEW, Washington, 1969-70; spl. asst. to Pres. U.S., Washington, 1970-73; dep. dir. U.S. Office of Mgmt. and Budget, Washington, 1973-75; with Marriott Corp., Washington, 1975-88, sr. v.p., 1975-77, exec. v.p., 1978-88; pres. Marriott Hotels and Resorts, 1981-88, Northwest Airlines, Mpls., 1989-90, vice chmn., 1990-91, also bd. dirs.; campaign mgr. Bush-Quayle '92, 1991-92; co-chmn. CB Richard Ellis, 1989-96; chmn. Lodging Opportunities Fund, 1991—, Thayer Capital Ptnrs., 1992—, Thayer Hotel Investors, 1994—. Chmn. 1996 Rep. Presdl. Trust, 1995-96; bd. dirs. Automated Data Processing Corp., CB Richard Ellis; dir. with rank of amb., 1990 Econ. Summit, 1989—; adj. prof. U. S.C., 1986-89; lectr. Kennedy Sch. Govt., Harvard U., 1976. bd. dirs. Automatic Data Processing, Inc., 1978-2009 Mem. Pres.'s Commn. on White House Fellows, 1971-75, White House Domestic Coun., 1974-75, Pres.'s Commn. on Pers. Interchange, 1974-76; dep. dir. com. for Re-election of Pres., 1972; Pres.'s Commn. on Pvt. Sector Initiatives, 1982-85, dir. conv. Bush for Pres., 1988; mem. Nat. Coun. on Surface Transp. Rsch., 1993-95; nat. adv. bd. Nat. Ctr. Econ. Edn. of Children, 1980-82; mem. Pres.'s Coun. on Phys. Fitness and Sports, 1986-91; bd. visitors US Mil. Acad., West Point; co-chmn., McCain Campaign, 2008; chmn. Rep. party, Va. Named Bus. Statesman of Yr. Harvard Bus. Sch. Club Washington, 2000, Citizen of Yr. Boy Scouts Am. Nat. Capitol Coun., 2000, Am. Friends of Czech Republic Civil Soc. Vision award, Woodrow Wilson award for corp. citizenship, 2004; named to Washington Bus. Hall of Fame, 2005; bd. trustees, Bush Libr. Found. Mem. Am.-Israel Friendship League (bd. trustees 1991—), Aspen Inst. (bd. trustees 1996—), Am. Friends Czech Republic (chmn. 2007-). Episcopalian. Avocations: bicycling, hiking. Office: 1455 Pennsylvania Ave NW Washington DC 20004-1008 Home Phone: 703-522-6848; Office Phone: 202-371-0150. Business E-Mail: fmalek@thayercapital.com.*

MALEK, MARLENE ANNE, foundation administrator; b. Oakland, Calif., June 22, 1939; d. William and Yolanda (Stella) McArthur; m. Frederic Malek; children: Frederic William, Michelle A. Olson. Degree in Nursing, Marymount U. Pres. Friends Cancer Rsch., Washington, 2000—. Vice chmn. bd. dirs. Marymount U., Arlington, Va.; presdl. appointee bd. dirs. Kennedy Ctr., 2002-08; bd. dirs. Nat. Mus. Women in Arts, Vital Voices Global Partnership, Best Friends Found., MD Anderson Cancer Ctr., Houston; bd. overseers Duke U. Cancer Ctr.; mem. C-Chang Nat. Dialogue Cancer. Episcopalian. Avocations: cross country skiing, bicycling.

MALENKA, BERTRAM JULIAN, physicist, researcher; b. NYC, June 13, 1923; s. Morris and Mollie (Wichtel) M.; m. Ruth D. Stolper, Mar. 28, 1948; children: David Jonathan, Robert Charles. AB, Columbia, 1947; MA, Harvard, 1949, PhD, 1951. Research fellow Harvard, 1951-54; asst. prof. physics Washington U., St. Louis, 1954-56; asso. prof. Tufts U., Medford, Mass., 1956-60; faculty Northeastern U., Boston, 1960—, prof. physics, 1962-93, prof. emeritus, 1993—. Mem. sci. adv. group Harvard-Mass. Inst. Tech. Cambridge Electron Accelerator, 1956— Mem. vis. com. dept. conservation Mus. Fine Arts, Boston, 1997—; mem. collections mgmt., 2004—; mem. vis. com. Art of the Ams. Dept. Mem. Am., Italian phys. socs., N.Y. Acad. Scis., Phi Beta Kappa, Sigma Xi. Achievements include research and publications on theory of nuclear forces and structure of nucleus, explanation polarization phenomena in high-energy scattering, gamma radiation, electric polarization deuteron, accelerator design. Home: 16 Rutledge Rd Belmont MA 02478-3323 Office: Northeastern Univ Dept Of Physics Boston MA 02115 E-mail: bjm11@verizon.net.

MALERNEE, JAMES KENT, JR., financial consultant; b. Durango, Colo., June 15, 1947; s. James Kent and Norma Virginia (Calhoon) M.; m. Charlean Ann Born, Aug. 21, 1971 (div. May 1, 1992). BS in Engring., U. Tex., Austin, 1970; PhD in Bus. Adminstrn., U. Tex., 1977; MBA, So. Meth. U., 1972. Petroleum engr. Tex. R.R. Commn., 1970-71; instr. fin. U. Tex., 1973-75; lectr. fin. U. Tulsa, 1975-76; assoc. Mgmt. Analysis Ctr., Northbrook, Ill., 1977-80, v.p., 1980—; sr. v.p. The MAC Group, 1987-89; also dir. MAC Rsch.; co-founder Cornerstone Rsch., NYC, mng. dir., 1989—2000, pres., CEO, 2000—07, chmn., 2007—. Lectr. mgmt. Stanford GSB, 1983; leader seminars on mergers and acquisitions and corp. strategy; guest speaker in field of strategy; speaker on damages in securities litigation P.L.I. and ABA; expert witness in securities and fin.; bd. dirs. RealPage, 2003-07; adv. bd. U. Tex. Bus. Sch., 2006-. Contbr. articles to profl. jours. Named one of Outstanding Young Men Am. U.S. Jaycees, 1977. Mem. Fin. Mgmt. Assn. (v.p. 1981-82, bd. dirs. 1983-85), Assn. Corp. Growth. Home: 208 E 51st St # 123 New York NY 10022-6557 Office: Cornerstone Rsch 599 Lexington Ave New York NY 10022-6030

MALET, DAVID SAMUEL, social sciences educator; m. Michelle Robin Ellis, Oct. 13, 2002; 1 child, Erica Dayana. BS, Boston U., Mass., 1998; MA, Georgetown U., Washington, DC, 1999; PhD student, George Wash. U., DC, 2003—. Cert. in tchg. with advanced standing Commonwealth Mass., 1998. Intern US Rep. Howard Berman, LA, 1993, US Senator John Kerry, Boston, 1995—96, Office Atty. Gen., Sydney, 1995; grad. tchg. asst. George Wash. U., 2003—08, lectr., 2008—; pub. rels. intern Rendon Group, Boston, 1997—98; student, tchr. Sharon HS, Mass., 1998; strategy and evaluation team intern Nat. Dem. Inst. Internat. Affairs, Washington, 1998—99; legislative corr. US Rep. Ruben Hinojosa, Washington, 2000; rsch. asst. US Senate Majority Leader Tom Daschle, Washington, 2000—03. Contbr. articles to profl. jours. Chpt. pres. Coll. Democrats, Boston, 1995—97. Recipient Disting. Sophomore award, Boston U., 1995; named Outstanding Svc., Jr. Statesmen America, 1994; Kraus Endowment fellowship in Polit. Sci., George Wash. U., 2007, Richards Endowment fellowship, 2007. Mem.: Internat. Studies Assn., Am. Polit. Sci. Assn., Sierra Club, Pi Sigma Alpha. Avocations: travel, cooking, tennis, photography. Office: George Washington Univ 714 21st St NW Washington DC 20052 Business E-Mail: dmalet@gwu.edu.

MALEWEZI, JUSTIN, Malawian government official; b. Ntchisi, Malawi, Dec. 23, 1944; married; 4 children. BA in Biology, Columbia U., 1967; cert. in edn., Econ. Devel. Inst., Washington, 1978. Tchr., headmaster, 1967-74; edn. adminstr., 1974-81; permanent sec. Ministry of Health, Malawi, 1981-83, Ministry of Edn., Malawi, 1984, Ministry of Treasury, Malawi, 1985-89; head civil svc. Govt. of Malawi, 1989-91; dir. planning and programs United Dem. Front, 1992-93, 2nd v.p., 1993; 1st v.p., min. of privatization Govt. of Malawi, Lilongwe, 1994—2004; M.P. (Ind.), chair parliamentary com. health, convener Malawi Nat. Assembly, 2004—. Home: PO Box B362 Capital City Lilongwe 3 Malawi Office: Office of 1st VP Private Bag 301, Capital City Lilongwe 3 Malawi Business E-Mail: jcmalewezi@sdnp.org.mw.

MALEWSKI, JENNIFER JEAN, clergy member; b. Deshler, Ohio, Dec. 31, 1946; d. David Edwards and Alberta Elsa (Ostrand) Parr; m. Charles William Malewski, Dec. 22, 1972; children; David Frank, John Charles, Jenelle Alberta. BA, U. Nebr., 1967; MDiv, St. Paul Sch. Theology, Kansas City, Mo., 1987. Ordained to ministry Christian Ch. (Disciples of Christ); chaplain. Tchr. correlated studies Omaha Pub. Schs., 1967-70; tchr. English Independence (Mo.) Pub. Schs., 1970-74; ministerial intern Overland Park (Kans.) Christian Ch., 1986-87; chaplain intern Bethany Med. Ctr., Kansas City, Kans., 1987-89; dir. interim pastoral care Spofford Home, 1988; staff chaplain U. Kans. Med. Ctr., 1989—. Facilitator critical incident response team, mem. donor adv. coun., tchr. U. Kans. Med. Ctr., mem. Palliative Care Teams; instr. and presenter in field, mem. Bridge Builders Quality Improvement Sub Com. Contbr. articles to profl. jours. Bd dirs. Grief Support Network Greater Kansas City, 1998—, pres., 1999—2002; facilitator summer workshops. Disciples Women's scholar, 1984-86. Mem. Funeral Consumers Alliance Kans. City (formerly Funeral and Meml. Soc. Am.) (bd. dir. Kansas City chpt., sec. 1997-98, bd. mem. 2007-), Kans. Assn. Chaplains (sec. 1991-92, 97-98, treas. 1994—, pres. 2003—04, historian 2007-), Kansas City Assn. Chaplains (treas. 1996—, facilitator 1997-98), Disciples Ministers Assn., Coll. of Chaplains, Assn. Profl. Chaplains (bd. cert.; chair state membership 2000-01, state rep. 2001-06), Assn. Death Educators and Counselors (cert. in thanatology; mem. cert. test com. 2002-04, cert. test comm., 2008), Scandinavian Assn. (pres. 2002-06), Pediatrics Ethics Com., Am. Psychotherapist Assn. Avocations: flower gardening, cultivating friendships, hiking, reading, writing, travel. Office Phone: 913-588-5033. Business E-Mail: jmalewsk@kumc.edu.

MALEY, SAMUEL WAYNE, electrical engineering educator; b. Sidney, Nebr., Mar. 1, 1928; s. Samuel Raymond and Inez (Moore) M.; m. Elizabeth Anne Green, June 11, 1963; children— Karen Margaret, Laura Elaine. BS, U. Colo., 1952, MS, 1957, PhD, 1959; student, U. N.Mex., 1957-58. Geophysicist Stanolind Oil Co., Lubbock, Tex., 1952; design engr. Beach Aircraft Corp., Wichita, Kans., 1952-53, Dynalectron Corp., Cheyenne, Wyo., 1953-56; research scientist U. Colo., Boulder, 1959-60, vis. lectr., 1960-61, asst. prof., 1961-62, assoc. prof. elec. engring., 1962-67, prof., 1967-91, prof. emeritus, 1991—, mem. Nat. Ctr. Computer Aided Design, Millimeter and Microwave Systems, 1988—. Cons. Nat. Center Atmospheric Research, 1964, Automation Industries Research Div., Boulder, Colo., 1960-71, Midwec Corp., Ogallala, Neb., 1969-70, IBM, Boulder, 1969— Author: Combinational Logic Circuits, 1969; contbg. author to 5 survey books on sci. and engring. Served with AUS, 1946-47; Served with USAF, 1947-48. Mem. IEEE, AAAS, Soc. Indsl. and Applied Math. Research electromagnetic theory; communication theory; computer design. Home: PO Box 1172 Boulder CO 80306-1172

MALGIERI, LEWIS JOSHUA, psychologist, consultant; b. Syracuse, NY, Nov. 10, 1943; s. Severino Vincenzino and Maria Francesca Malgieri; life ptnr. Kathleen Anne Stevens; children: Donald Wayne Stevens, Brian Michael Stevens, Scott Matthew Stevens. BA in Psychology, SUNY, Buffalo, 1968; MA in Psychology, Roosevelt U., 1974; PhD in Clin. Psychology (hon.), New Sch. For Social Rsch., 1991; postgrad. in Neuropsychology, Greystone Park Psychiat. Hosp., 1995. Neuropsychology cert. in biofeedback NJ Biofeedback Assn., 1981, cert. psychologist NJ State Bd. Psychol. Examiners, 1993, NY State Bd. Psychol. Examiners, 2001, hypnotherapist Wellness Inst. Seattle, 1995, lic. FCC amateur radio operator. Psychologist NY State Assn. for Retarded Citizens, Geneva, 1974—77, Rahway State Prison, NJ, 1985—93; prin. clin. psychologist Greystone Park Psychiat. Hosp., NJ, 1993—2001; chief psychologist Oswego Hosp., NY, 2001—. With US Army, 1969—71, Viet Nam. Named Grad. Asst., Roosevelt U., 1969—74; scholar, Syracuse U., 1962. Mem.: APA (Med. Corps. Psychologist Honor award 2002), Ctrl. NY Psychol. Assn. Roman Catholic. Home: 103 Pineledge Rd Camillus NY 13031 Office: Oswego Hospital 74 Bunner St Oswego NY 13126 Personal E-mail: fermi1001@aol.com.

MALGIERI, NICK, food service executive, educator, chef, writer; b. Newark, Sept. 30, 1947; s. Nufre and Antoinette (LoConte) M. BA in French, Seton Hall U., 1970; AOS in Culinary Arts, Culinary Inst., Hyde Park, NY, 1973. Pastrycook Seehotel Meierhof, Zurich, 1973-74, Hotel de Paris, Monte Carlo, 1974, Sporting Club, Monte Carlo, 1974-76, Hotel la Reserve, Beaulieu, France, 1974; pastry chef Windows on the World, NYC, 1976-79; asst. pastry chef Hotel Waldorf Astoria, NYC, 1979; chmn. baking dept. NY Restaurant Sch., NYC, 1979-83; dir. baking program Inst. Culinary Edn., NYC, 1984—; founder, owner Total Heaven Baking Co. Exec. chef Paine Webber; pastry chef Board Room; cons. Inhilco, Inc.; guest lectr. Smithsonian Instn.; Am. spokesperson for Switzerland tourism. Author: Nick Malgieri's Perfect Pastry, 1989, Great Italian Desserts, 1990, How to Bake, 1995 (James Beard Found. Cookbook award/Best Book on Baking/Desserts of 1995), Chocolate, 1998 (IACP/Julia Child cookbook award 1998, Salon Internat. du Livre award), Cookies Unlimited, 2000, Perfect Cakes, 2002 (100 Best Books of 2002 Pub. Weekly), A Baker's Tour: Nick Malgieri's Favorite Baking Recipes from Around the World, 2005, Perfect Light Desserts, 2006, The Modern Banker, 2008; contbr. articles and recipes to newspapers and profl. jours. Recipient Toque award City of Phila., 2006. Mem. Internat. Assn. Culinary Profls. Found. (former trustee), Internat. Assn. Culinary Profls. (cert. culinary profl., chmn. certification 1989-91), Amicale Culinaire de Monaco, Societe Culinaire Philanthropique N.Y., Federazione Italiana dei Cuochi, James Beard Found. (coord. competitions 1991-95), N.Y. Assn. Cooking Tchrs. (former bd. dirs., Ann. honor 2000), Bakers Dozen East (founding mem.). Home: 277 W 10th St New York NY 10014-2562 Office: Inst of Culinary Education 50 W 23d St New York NY 10010

MALHAS, FARIS AMIN, engineering educator; b. Jerusalem, Jan. 25, 1955; s. Amin F Malhas and Helweh A. Mahmoud; m. Fikrat H. Same, Nov. 22, 1995; children: Ameen F., Sami F., Tamara A., Layla J. PhD, U. Wis., Madison, 1987. Cert. in engring., FSPE, 2003. Founding prof. U. North Fla., Jacksonville, 2000—05; chair & prof. U. Dayton, Ohio, 2005—. Author: (textbook) Steel Structure Design and Theory. Recipient Martin P Korn award, Precast Prestressed Concrete Inst., 1990. Mem.: Am. Concrete Inst. (chair tech. com. 2008). Office: Univ Dayton 300 College Pk Dayton OH 45469 Home Fax: 937-229-3491. Business E-Mail: fmalhas@udayton.edu.

MALHOTRA, ANIL, psychiatrist, educator; AB, Cornell U., Ithaca, NY, 1985; MD, Bowman Gray Sch. Medicine, Winston-Salem, NC, 1989. Diplomate Nat. Bd. Med. Examiners, Am. Bd. Psychiatry and Neurology. Sr. staff fellow Exptl. Therapeutics Br. NIMH NIH, Bethesda, Md., 1993—98, chief, unit pharmacogenetics, 1996—98; guest rschr., lab. genetics NIAAA NIH, Bethesda, 1994—; chief, unit molecular psychiatry Zucker Hillside Hosp., Glen Oaks, NY, 1998—, dir., psychiatry rsch., 2003—; assoc. investigator Feinstein Inst. Med. Rsch., Manhasset, NY, 1999—2008, investigator, 2008—; assoc. prof., psychiatry Albert Einstein Coll. Medicine, Bronx, NY, 2001—; adj. assoc. prof., psychiatry Stony Brook U., NY, 2003—, Cold Spring Harbor Lab., NY, 2008—. Editl. bd. Molecular Psychiatry, 2008—, Schizophrenia Bull., 2008—, Clin. Neuropsychiatry, 2008—, Current Psychiatry Revs., 2008—, Open Psychiatry Jour., 2008—, Pharmacogenomics and Personalized Medicine, 2008—. Contbr. scientific papers to profl. jours. Recipient Sr. Scientist award, Tenth Biennial Winter Workshop Schizophrenia Rsch., 2000; K23 MH 01760-04 grant, NIMH NIH, 1999—2006, 1R01 MH 79800-01 grant, 2007—. Mem.: Am. Psychiat. Assn., Am. Coll. Neuropsychopharmacology. Office: Zucker Hillside Hosp 75-59 263rd St Glen Oaks NY 11004

MALHOTRA, ASHISH, medical researcher; b. Jalandhar, Punjab, India, Aug. 27, 1980; s. Prem Prakash and Kanta Malhotra; m. Ashu Sharma, Aug. 30, 2008. MBBS, Kasturba Med. Coll., Mangalore, Karnataka, India, 2003. Diplomate Am. Bd. Internal Medicine, 2007. Resident, house staff U. Conn. Sch. Medicine, Farmington, 2004—07, residency recruitment com. mem., 2005—07; advanced motility fellow Mayo Clinic Coll. Medicine, Rochester, Minn., 2007—08; fellow Banner Good Samaritan Med. Ctr., Phoenix, 2008—. Author: (story) Truth is Bitter. Vol. Internat. Advisor Coun., ECFMG, Phila., 2006—08, Colorectal Cancer Network, Balt., 2005—07; vol.-organizer Drug Deaddiction Coun. Students, Kasturba Med. Coll., 2000—03; vol. house officer Guru Nanak Mission Hosp., Jalandhar, Punjab, 2003; vol. Am. Liver found., New Haven, 2004—08. Recipient Gold medal, Outstanding Student award, Manipal Acad. Higher Edn., 2000, Young Investigator award, Letter of Commendation for Excellence Patient Care; named one of Best Orator, BSF Sch., Jalandhar, 1994—97, Best Spkr., All India 7th Nat. Sawan Pub. Sch. Elocution Contest, 1995, Best in Debates, Pub. Speaking, Kasturba Med. Coll., 2001—03, Best in Neurology Quiz, 2002. Mem.: ACP, Functional Brain Gut Rsch. Group, Am. Soc. Gastrointestinal Endoscopy, Am. Gastroent. Assn., Am. Coll. Gastroenterology, Nat. Scholars Honor Soc. (life). Hindu. Achievements include research in role of MII-pH for evaluating patients with extra esophageal reflux disease and role of inflammatory cytokines in irritable bowel syndrome; evaluating guideline adherence among primary care physicians for colorectal cancer screening; evaluating guideline adherence for osteoporosis prevention among women; meta analysis of evaluating celiac disease testing in IBS patients; validating BDQ7 for evaluating functional GI disorders. Home: 7810 N 14th Pl 2044 Phoenix AZ 85020 Office: Banner Good Samaritan Med Ctr 1111 E Mc Dowell Rd Phoenix AZ 85010 Personal E-mail: ashmalhotra@yahoo.com.

MALHOTRA, ASHOK KUMAR, philosophy educator; b. Ferozepur, India, 1940; came to the U.S., 1963, naturalized, 1977. s. Nihal Chand and Vidya (Wanti) M.; m. Nina Judith Finestone, Oct. 24, 1966 (dec.); children: Raj Kumar, Ravi Kumar. BA, U. Rajasthan, 1961, MA, 1963; PhD, U. Hawaii, 1969. Asst. prof. SUNY, Oneonta, 1967-70, assoc. prof., 1970-80, prof., 1980—, chmn. philosophy dept., 1975-80. Vis. prof. SUNY-Buffalo, summer 1970, Kurukshetra U. and Birla Inst., Pilani, India, spring 1980; grants reviewer NEH, 1978—; bd. dirs. SUNY Press editorial, 1989-93, dir. SUNY study abroad, program to India, 1980—; cons. TV series Kung Fu: The Legend Continues., 1992. Author: Sartre's Existentialism in Nausea and Being and Nothingness, 1978; Sartre's Existentialsim as Literature and Philosophy, 1995, Pathways to Philosophy: A Multidisciplinary Approach, 1996, Culture and Self, 1997, Transcreation of the Bhagavad Gita, 1998, Instant Nirvana, 1999, An Introduction to Yoga Philosophy, 2001, Wisdom of the Tao Te Ching, 2006, Instant Nirvana, 2nd edit, 2007, Yoga and Meditation, 2008; TV appearances include ABC World News Now, NBC News, JAIN TV, Doordarshan TV, ZEE TV (India), Natraj TV (Holland), All India Radio, NPR. Founder Ninash Found. Oneonta; established Indo-Internat. Sch., Dundlod, Rajasthan, Mahapura, Rajasthan and Kuran, Gujarat, India; founder, chmn. Yoga and Meditation Soc., SUNY, Oneonta. Recipient Excellence in Tchg. award and Disting. Tchg. Prof. award United Univ. Profession; Friend of Ednl. award City of Oneonta, 1998, Disting. Alumni award East-West Ctr., 2000, Jewel of India award 2002, Bharat Excellence award Friendship Forum of India, 2002, Spiritual Leadership award, 2006, Gullands NRI Exellence award, 2008; East-West Ctr. fellow, 1963-65, 66-67; N.Y. State Dept. Edn. grantee, 1967-69, NEH grantee, 1979. Mem. Am. Philos. Assn., Soc. Asian and Comparative Philosophy, Assn. Asian Studies, N.Y. State Asian Studies Soc., Internat. Phenomenol. Soc.,Soc. Comparative Study, Ctr. Yoga Relaxation (TV Show pub. access channel). Home: 17 Center St Oneonta NY 13820-1445 Office Phone: 607-436-3220. E-mail: malhotak@oneonta.edu.

MALHOTRA, MADHU BALA, psychiatrist; b. New Delhi, June 10, 1951; arrived in U.S., 1974; d. Faqir Chand and Krishna Khandpur; m. Amjed Hussain; 1 child, Saira H. Amjed. MBBS, India. Dir. Out Patient Dept. Psychiatry Brookdale U. Hosp. and Med. Ctr., NY. Mem.: Am. Assn. Psychiatrists from India, Am. Psychiat. Assn.

MALHOTRA, NARESH KUMAR, marketing educator; arrived in U.S., 1975; s. Har Narian and Satya (Kakkar) M.; m. Veena Bahl, Aug. 13, 1980; children: Ruth Veena, Paul Naresh. BTech with honors, Indian Inst. Tech., Bombay, 1971; MBA, I.I.M., Ahmedabad, India, 1973; MS, PhD, SUNY, Buffalo, 1979. Mgmt. cons. ASCI, Hyderabad, India, 1971-73; asst. prof. Ga. Tech. Inst., Atlanta, 1979—, assoc. prof. mgmt., coord. mktg., 1982-87, 89—, prof., 1988, Regents' prof., 1992—. Organizer several nat. and internat. mktg. mgmt. confs. Author: Marketing Research: An Applied Orientation (N.Am., European, Internat., Australia and New Zealand, Indian, Spanish, Portuguese, Chinese, Russian, French, Japanese, Bahasa Indonesia and Hungarian edits.), Basic Marketing Research: A Decision-Making Approach; contbr. articles to profl. jours. Recipient Outstanding Mktg. Educator, Acad. of

Mktg. Sci., 2005. Fellow Acad. Mktg. Sci. (disting., program chmn. 1984-85, 85-86, v.p. programs 1988-90, chmn. bd. 1990-92, pres. 1994-96, chmn. found. 1996-98, Top Rschr., Jour. Mktg. Rsch., Jour. Acad. Mktg. Sci., Jour. Healthcare Mktg., Internat. Mktg. Rev.), Decision Scis. Inst. (track chmn. 1984-86); mem. Am. Mktg. Assn. (track chmn. 1983-84), Am. Statis. Assn. Republican. Baptist. Achievements include globally top ranked A researcher based on six independent publication rankings. Avocations: reading, writing, outdoor activities. Home: 1956 Lenox Rd NE Atlanta GA 30306-3035 Office: Ga Tech Inst Coll Mgmt Atlanta GA 30332-0520 Office Phone: 404-894-4358. Business E-Mail: naresh.malhotra@mgt.gatech.edu.

MALHOTRA, NEIL, computer game company executive; B in Engring., U. Mich., Ann Arbor; MS in Applied Mechanics, Calif. Inst. Tech., Pasadena. With Orbital Sciences Corp.; dir. product develop. Axiom Champel Corp.; gen. mgr. video editing products Schafer Corp.; dir. tech. Icebox.com; chief tech. officer eMind, 1998—2005, Acclaim Games Inc., Beverly Hills, Calif., 2005—. Office: Acclaim Games 615 N Arden Dr Beverly Hills CA 90210

MALHOTRA, YOGESH, information scientist, management educator, information technology executive, management consultant, engineer; arrived in US, 1988, naturalized; BE in Mech. Engring. first class with distinction, U. Delhi, India, 1984; MBA in Econ. and Fin. first rank with nat. honors, U. Nev., Las Vegas, 1993; PhD in Info. Sys., Mgmt. Controls and Quantitative Methods with nat. honors, U. Pitts., 1998. Cert. CISA info. systems auditor Info. Systems Audit and Control Assn., Rolling Meadows, Ill., 2007, info. systems security profl. Internat. Info. Systems Security Cert. Consortium, Vienna, Va., 2005, computing profl.; C Eng chartered engr. Exec. engr., engring. and mgmt. systems Suzuki Maruti Udyog Ltd., Gurgaon, India, 1984—87; sys. analyst Tata Unisys Ltd., New Delhi, Bombay, 1987—89; software engr., mgmt. cons. Unisys Corp., Global Fin. Systmes Ctr., Norcross, Ga., 1988—89, Banque Indo Suez, Wan Chai, Hong Kong, 1989—90; mgmt. cons. info. systems Davenport Bank & Trust Co., Ill., 1988; sr. sys. analyst JK Technosoft, Neepz, India, 1990; sr. cons. info. sys. Bank Am., Nev., 1990—91; prin. founder, pres., chief knowledge architect BRINT, The Biztech Network, Pitts., 1994—98; founder, chmn., chief knowledge officer BRINT Inst., LLC, 1998—2001, founding chmn., chief knowledge architect, 2001—; asst. prof. mgmt. info. systems Syracuse U., 2001—08, assoc. prof. acctg. and info. sys., 2008—. Coun. ptnr., Inter-Agency Benchmarking & Best Practices Coun. US Fed. Govt., 1995—99; advisor, cons. Intel, Br. Telecom, Ziff Davis, Hewlett Packard, Arthur Andersen, South Korean, Vision Korea Nat. Campaign, Govt. of Netherlands, US Fed. Govt. and, Govt. of Mex., 1995—2001, NSF, 2002—05, UN, Philips, Netherlands, 2004—05; founder, editor-in-chief The Knowledge Mgmt. Think Tank, 1997—2001; advisor Govt. of Netherlands, 1998; mem. internat. advisory bd. Knowledge Mgmt. Jour., UK, 1998—2000; disting. faculty BrainTrust, San Francisco, 1998, advisory bd. mem., 98; invited rsch. faculty INSEAD, France, 1998; faculty exec. edn. program Carnegie Mellon U., 1998, Northwestern U., Kellogg Grad. Sch. Mgmt., 2000; founding mem. Ziff Davis Internet Commerce Standard, 1999—2000; assoc. editor Info. Resources Mgmt. Jour., Hershey, Pa., 2001—03; cons., advisor Intel Corp., 2001, NSF, 2002—05, Syracuse U., 2002—, UN, 2003; founder The Knowledge Mgmt. Network, 2002—; editl. adv. bd. The Learning Orgn., 2004—05; bd. dirs. Knowledge Mgmt. Consortium, Commonwealth Ctr. e-Governance, India; invited rsch. faculty lecture Queen's U. Sch. Bus., Canada, 2006; adv. bd. Emerald Pub. Group, UK, 2008—; spkr. in field. Author, editor: Knowledge Management and Virtual Organizations, 2000, Knowledge Management and Business Model Innovation, 2001; mem. editl. bds. ifo. tech. and mgmt. acad. and profl. jours.; contbr. articles to profl. jours. including Jour. Mgmt. Info. Systems, Jour. Knowledge Mgmt., Comm. of the ACM, IEEE, Jour. Global Info. Mgmt., others. Recipient First Best Reviewer award, Acad. Mgmt. OCIS Divsn., 1997, Networks Corp. Computing award, CNET, 2002; named exemplar of rsch. impact for bus. scholars, Assn. to Advance Collegiate Schs. of Bus.; grantee, Intel Corp., 2001, UN, 2003, Kaufman Found., 2003, SAP Univ. Alliance, 2003, Snyder Innovation Mgmt. Ctr., 2003, 2004, 2005, Ctr. for Creation and Mgmt. of Digital Ventures, 2003, 2004, Brethen Ops. Mgmt. Inst., 2005. Mem.: Info. Sys. Security Cert. Consortium, Info. Sys. Audit and Control Assn., Info. Sys. Security Assn., Assn. Info. Sys., Inst. Cert. Computing Profls., Inst. Engrs. (life), Phi Kappa Phi, Beta Gamma Sigma. Achievements include development of global research and practices for two new technology management disciplines, business technology and knowledge management; ranking of research impact among the top four, six, and three MIS scholars worldwide in studies on knowledge management published by the ASIS&T, U. of Minnesota, and Drexel U. Avocations: risk management, compliance, global finance, global financial markets, global financial systems. Office: Syracuse U Sch Mgmt Syracuse NY 13244 Home Phone: 315-798-4636; Office Phone: 315-443-3571, 315-382-7275. Business E-Mail: yogesh@syr.edu.

MALI, PAUL, publisher, retired management educator; b. Hartford, Conn., July 6, 1926; m. Mary S. Mali; children: Faith, Dawn. BS in Engring., U. Conn., 1953, MS, 1962, PhD in Mgmt. and Engring., 1967; postgrad., Cornell U., 1964. Cert. mgmt. cons. Inst. Mgmt. Cons. Elec. engr. Gen. Dynamics, Groton, Conn., 1953—67, dir., 1961—67; prof. mgmt. Entrepreneurial, New London, Conn., 1961—67, U. Hartford, Conn., 1967—94; minister/co-pastor Bible Student ch., New London, Conn., 1994—; prof. Swiss Inst. Tech., Hebrew U.; pub. Horizon Publs.; mgmt. cons. to IBM, Westinghouse, U.S. Steel, United Tech., Aetna, Hanes, Alcan Aluminum, Combustion Engring. Founding fellow Acad. Disting. Engrs. and Hall of Fame of U. Conn. Author: various profl. books, including Writing and Word Processing for Scientists and Engineers, 1981, MBO Updated, 1986, (ministerial books) Magnetic Amplifiers, 1960, The Bible as a Rising Civilization, 1998, Ten Bad Mistakes About God, 2000, Terrorism and the Permission of Evil, 2002, Biblical View on Human Cloning, others, 2002, Spirituality: The Roadmap to Heaven, Spiritual Leadership for Every Christian, 2007. Pres. Good Samaritan Fund, New London, Conn., 1994—; bd. dirs. 12 state cmty. colls., Conn., 1981—88. Named to, U. Conn. Acad. Disting. Engrs. and Hall of Fame, 2004. Mem.: Am. Mgmt. Assn., Tau Beta Pi, Beta Gamma Sigma, Phi Delta Kappa, Eta Kappa Nu. Achievements include having September 14th named Dr. Paul Mali day in Connecticut by Governer Rell and the state General Assembly. E-mail: malipnm@aol.com.

MALICAY, MANUEL ALABAN, physician; b. Zamboonga City, The Philippines, Aug. 13, 1947; arrived in US, 1973; s. Bernardino Malicay Agan and Juliana (Alaban) Malicay; m. Lourdes V. Manzano, Jan. 12, 1974; children: Mark, Marlo, Brian, Michael, Margaret. BS, Far Eastern U., Manila, 1967, MD, 1972. Rsch. and tchg. fellow Far Eastern U., Manila, 1972-73; intern St. Francis Hosp., Evanston, Ill., 1973-74; resident in internal medicine Vets. Hosp., Hines, Ill., 1974-76; pvt. practice Bolingbrook, Ill., 1976—; physician Hinsdale (Ill.) Hosp., 1976-97, 1976—, Good Samaritan Hosp., Downers Grove, Ill., 1977—, vice chmn. dept. medicine, 1998—2001, chmn. Clin. Quality Coun., 1999-2001; asst. prof. in medicine Rush Med. Coll., Chgo., 2004—. Chmn continuing med educ comt IPMS, 1998—; prin. clin. investigator Dynacirc Assessment Trial Analysis, 1990, The Safety and Efficacy of Cardizem SR as anti-anginal medication, 1991, Comparative Outcome Study of Metformin vs. conventional approach, 1996, Lantus GOAL AIC Clin. Trials, 2003, REACH Registry, 2004—; spkr., bureau mem. Novartis Pharm. Corp., 2003, Abbott Pharm. Editor: IPMS Today, 1989—91. Trustee Far Ea. U. Sch. Med. Alumni Found., 1993—2001, v.p., 2002—04; pres. Class of 1972 Far Ea. U. Dr. N. Reyes Med. Alumni Found.; chmn. continuing med. edn. Far Ea. U. DNR Sch. Med. Alumni Found., 2005—; co-chmn. physician adv. bd. Nat. Rep. Congl. Com., 2002—. Named Most Outstanding Silver Jubilarian, Far Eastern U. Dr N Reyes Med. Alumni Found., 1997, Physician of Yr., Nat. Rep. Congl. Com., 2003. Fellow: ACP; mem.: AMA, Far Eastern U. Med. Alumni Assn. Ill. (pres. 1991—93, co-chair conv. ann. reunion and sci. seminar 1993, Oustanding Alumnus 1995), Assn. Philippine Physicians Am. (co-chair 25th ann. conv. and sci. seminar 1996, gov. 1996—2001), Ill. Med. Soc. (del. 1990—, coun. on econs. com. 2002—), DuPage County Med. Soc. (bd. dirs. 1986—), Ill. Philippine Med. Soc. (seminar program dir. 1994, pres. 1994—96, chmn CME comt 1998—, program dir. Primary Care Update 1999, 2001, Disting Leadership Award 1996, Disting Physician Award Organized Med 1999, Disting Serv Award 2001). Avocations: tennis, dance. Home: 2 S 676th Ave Vendome Oak Brook IL 60521 Office: 402 W Boughton Rd Bolingbrook IL 60440-1872 also: 430 Sherwood Rd La Grange Park IL 60526-1968 Office Phone: 630-759-3782. Personal E-mail: mmalicaymd@hotmail.com.

MALICK, TERRENCE (DAVID WHITNEY II), film director; b. Waco, Tex., Nov. 30, 1943; m. Jill Jakes (div. 1978); m. Michele Malick, 1985 (div. 1998); m. Alexandra Wallace, 1998. Student, Harvard U., Oxford U.; MFA, Am. Film Inst. Dir., prodr., writer (films) Badlands, 1973 (Golden Seashell award 1974); dir., writer, Lanton Mills, 1969, Days of Heaven, 1978 (Best Dir. award Cannes Film Festival 1979, nominee Golden Globe award 1979, N.Y. Film Critics Circle award 1978), The Thin Red Line, 1998 (Acad. award nomination for Best Dir., Golden Berlin Bear award 1999, Chgo. Film Critics Assn. award 1999, Golden Satellite award, 1999), The New World, 2005; prodr. (films) Endurance, 1999, The Endurance, Shackleton's Legendary Antartic Expedition, 2000, Happy Times, 2001, The Beautiful Country, 2004, Undertow, 2004, Amazing Grace, 2006, The Unforseen, 2007; writer (films) Drive, He Said, 1971, Deadhead Miles, 1972, Pocket Money, 1972, The Gravy Train, 1974, Bear's Kiss, 2002

MALICKI, JAREMA, research scientist; s. Dariusz Malicki and Elzbieta Malicka. PHD, Yale U., New Haven, 1992. Asst. prof. Harvard Med. Sch., Boston, 1996—. Mem.: ARVO, Soc. Neuroscience. Office: Harvard Medical Sch/MEEI 243 Charles St Boston MA 02114 Office Fax: 617-573-4290. Personal E-mail: helix1@earthlink.net. E-mail: jarema_malicki@meei.harvard.edu.

MALIFRANDO, FRANK, healthcare executive, theater producer, consultant, film producer, international real estate investor, publisher; b. NYC, Feb. 16, 1954; s. Frank Malifrando and Michele Michelin Kuhn. BS, Southwest U., LA, 1986, MS in Health Scis., 2004. Cert. media comm. Boston U., 1991. CEO Spring Fed Corp., NYC, 1982—88, Kalanakila Prodns., Hawaii, 1985—91, Thunder Key Inc., 1982—89; mktg. dir. Mus. Edits. West, LA, 1988—91; dir. of devel. No. Calif. Svc. League, 1997—99; exec. dir. Keith Haring AIDS Interfaith Chapel, 1994—2000, Grace Cathedral, San Francisco; dir. devel. Life Lines Ministries, San Francisco, 1997—98; dir. of career svcs. Computer Learning Ctr., 1999—2001; project dir., designer Career Acceleration Mentor Program, 2000—01; exec. dir. fundraising arm Seton Med. Ctr., Seton Med. Ctr. Coastside, Dau. Charity Healthcare Sys., Seton Health Svcs. Found., Daly City, Calif., 2001—04, Sutter Marin-Marin Gen. Hosp., Novato Cmty. Hosp., Marin Cmty. Health Found., San Rafael, Calif., 2004—, regional exec. dir., 2007—08; owner Restaurant Spring Fed., NYC; personal mgr. of photographer Kenn Duncan; mem. Marin Gen. Hosp. found. bd.; mem. com. north and south Sutta Marin Found. Bd. Dir. of programs Alma DelFina Group, San Francisco, 1995—2000; CEO Artist Alliance Against AIDS, 1996; bd. dirs. Bethany Ctr., bd. vice chair, 2007; regional exec. dir. Sutter Marin Region, Marin Gen. Hosp., 2008—, Sutter Chartaible Found., Sutter Solano Med. Ctr., Sutter Regional Med. Found. Prodr.: Red Shoes, Kenn Duncan, 1984, (fine art reproductions) Hula Kahiko Series, 1986 (Pele Award of Excellence, 1986), Dance Cos., 1984 (Nat. Ann. Print award and Comm. Arts award, 1984); prodr., dir.: (documentaries) Poets and Painters, A Night at the Palace, 1994; Willie by Madaglia Cruz, starring Sean San Jose, 1996; In Conversation with David Henry Hwong, 1996; Awakening New Futures (behind bars), 1997; The making of an event: Charity Ball-150 Years for Daughters of Charity Seton Medical Center, 2001. Exec. dir., bd. mem. Marin Cmty. Health Found.; bd. dirs. Seton Health Svcs. Found., Bethany Ctr.; mem. adv. bd. Philanthropy Leadership Coun., Washington; chair CAPP; overseer Sutter Solano Charitable Found. Recipient Radiant Baby Gold Pin, Keith Haring Found., 1995, Canon Pastor award, Grace Cathedral, San Francisco, 1995, Pele award for excellence, Advertising Assn. of Hawaii, 1984, Cert. of Design Excellence, Print's Regional Design Annual, 1986, Black and White award, Assn. Honolulu Artist, 1987, Resolution recognition, State of Calif., 2003. Mem.: Dir.'s Coun. Devel.-Sutter Health, San Francisco C. of C., Seniors RSVP/San Francisco (adv. bd.), Brisbane C. of C., Half Moon Bay C. of C., Daly City C. of C. Achievements include creator and founder of the AIDS Interfaith Chapel in Grace Cathedral, San Francisco. Address: 4000 Civic Ctr Dr Ste 150 San Rafael CA 94903 Office: Sutter Marin-Marin Gen Hosp Found 4000 Civic Ctr Dr Ste 150 San Rafael CA 94903 Office Phone: 415-492-4735. E-mail: malifrf@sutterhealth.org.

MALIK, ABID, psychiatrist; s. Naimat K. Malik and Riaz Begum. MD, Dow Med. Coll., Karachi, 1995. Diplomate Am. Bd. Psychiatry & Neurology Inc., 2008. Psychiatry resident Albany Med. Ctr., NY, 2003—07, chief resident psychiatry, 2006—07; staff psychiatrist Area Mental Health Ctr., Garden City, Kans., 2007—. Contbr. rsch. papers to profl. publs. Recipient Scholarly paper award, Albany Med. Coll. Dept. Psychiatry Residency Program, 2007, Alan M. Kraft M.D. award, 2007. Mem.: AMA, Am. Bd. Med. Specialities, Am. Psychiat. Assn. Office: Area Mental Health Ctr 1111 E Spruce St Garden City KS 67846 Office Fax: 620-276-6117. E-mail: the_abid@hotmail.com.

MALIK, IMTIAZ, telecommunications industry executive, educator; BSc, U. Karachi, 1973, MS, 1974. Telecom specialist Ericsson, Stockholm, 1978—2002; telecom cons. Contracting, Dallas, 2003—08. Recipient Ericsson award. Achievements include patents in field. Home: 11300 Diablo Grande Dr Frisco TX 75035

MALIK, MALIK B., mathematics professor; m. Manal Salamabi, May 14, 1987. PhD, Essex U., Colchester, 1985. Dep. dean U. Khartoum, Sudan, 1993—94. Fulbright scholarship, CIES, 1994—95, Ga. State U., 1994—95. Office: UMES 1108 Kiah Hall Princess Anne MD 21853 Home Phone: 443-321-3661. Personal E-mail: mbmalik98@hotmail.com.

MALIK, MASROOR RASHEED, engineering executive; MS, U. Nebr., Lincoln, 1995. Project engr. Swagelok, Aurora, Ohio, 1998—, engring. supr. Solon, Ohio, 2003—. Prof., adj. Cleve. State U., 2003—. Mem.: Soc. Plastics Engr. (pres. 2004—05). Office: Swagelok Co 29500 Solon Rd Solon OH 44139 Business E-Mail: masroor.malik@swagelok.com.

MALIK, OM PARKASH, electrical engineering educator, researcher; b. Sargodha, Punjab, India, Apr. 20, 1932; arrived in Can., 1966; s. Arjan Dass and Kesar Bai (Ahuja) M.; m. Margareta Fagerstrom, Dec. 22, 1968; children: Ola Parkash, Mira, Maya. Nat. Diploma in Elec. Engring., Delhi Poly., India, 1952; M in Engring., Roorkee U., India, 1962; PhD, London U., 1965; D.I.C., Imperial Coll., London, 1966. Registered profl. engr., Ont., Alta. Asst. engr. Punjab State Elec. Bd., 1953-61, asst. to chief engr., 1957-59; rsch. engr. English Elec. Co., England, 1965-66; asst. prof. U. Windsor, Ont., Canada, 1966-68; assoc. prof. U. Calgary, Alta., Canada, 1968-74, prof. Alta., 1974-97, faculty prof. Alta., 1997—2000, assoc. dean student affairs, faculty engring. Alta., 1995-98, assoc. acad. dean faculty engring. Alta., 1979-90, acting dean Alta., 1981, prof. emeritus Alta., 1997—. Cons. prof. Huazhong U. Sci. and Tech., Wuhan, People's Republic China, 1986—; chief judge Can. Wide Sci. Fair, 2003; hon. prof. Tech. U. Cluj-Napoca, Romania, 2007—. Assoc. editor Can. Elec. and Computer Engring. Jour., 1988-97, mng. editor, 1998-2003; contbr. 700 articles to profl. jours. Indsl. tng. scholar Govt. India, 1952-53, sr. indsl. tng. scholar Confedn. Brit. Industries, 1959-60; recipient vol. svc. award APEGGA, 1990, Rsch. Excellence award Elec. and Computer Engring. Dept. U. Calgary, 1996, Can. Pacific Rwy. engring. medal Engring. Inst. Can., 1997, Disting. Lifetime Leadership award Faculty Engring. U. Calgary, 2001, Alberta Ingenuity Fund Rsch. Excellence award, 2002, L. C. Charlesworth Profl. Svc. award, APECGA, 2008; admitted Order of U. Calgary, 2006. Fellow IEEE (life, chmn. life mems. com. 2004-05, chmn. Western Can. coun. 1983-84, chmn. student activities Can. region 1979-82, chmn. life mems. com., mem. Found., Can. pres. elect 2008-, dir. Can. Found. 2005-, Centennial medal 1984, Western Can. Coun. Merit award 1986, Third Millennium medal 2000, A.G.L. McNaughton award 2001), Inst. Elec. Engrs., Can. Acad. Engring., World Innovation Found.; mem. IEEE Power Engring. Soc. (electric machinery com. 2002-, vice chmn. 2006-2007, chair 2008-, machine theory subcom. 1979-2004, excitation sys. subcom. 1988—, chmn. 2004-2007, sys. dynamic performance com. 1988-, energy devel. and power generation com. mem. 1990-, vice chmn. 2009-, sect. 2007-08), Assn. Profl. Engrs., Geologists and Geophysicists Alta. (Vol. Svc. award 1990, Alta. Ingenuity Rsch. Excellence award), Assn. Profl. Engrs. Ont., Am. Soc. Engring. Edn., Can. Elec. Assn. (assoc., controls com. 1977-92, chmn. digital control com. 1977-85, chmn. edn. com. 1983-85, mem. expert sys. com. 1989-94), Confederacion Panamericana de Ingenieria Mecanica, Electica y Ramas Afines (v.p. 1987-00, bd. dirs. region I, 1991-93), U. Calgary Emeritus Assn. (v.p. 2002-03, pres. 2003-04), Internat. Fed. Automatic Control (chmn. power plants and power sys. control commn. 2002-08). Hindu. Home: 4 6841 Coach Hill Rd SW Calgary AB Canada T3H 3T9 Office: U Calgary Dept Elec & Computer Engring 2500 University Dr NW Calgary AB Canada T2N 1N4 Home Phone: 403-217-6412; Office Phone: 403-220-6178. Personal E-mail: maliko@ucalgary.ca.

MALIK, PUNAM, medical educator; BSc in Zoology summa cum laude, Delhi U., India, 1979; MS in Nutritional Sci., U. Maryland, Balt., 1991; MBBS in Surgery, Delhi U. Lady Hardinge Med. Coll., 1985, MD, 1985. Lic. Med. Coun. India, Calif., Ohio, cert. Am. Bd. Pediat., 2005, Pediat. Hematology-Oncology, 2007. Intern, pediat. residency, Kalawati Saran Children's Hosp. Delhi U. Lady Hardinge Med. Coll., 1985—88; clin. instr. pediat. Children's Hosp. LA U. Southern Calif. Sch. Medicine, 1995—98, asst. prof. pediat. Keck Sch. Medicine, 1999—2005, assoc. prof. pathology, 2002—05, assoc. prof. pediat. and pathology, 2005—06; assoc. prof. pediat. U. Cin. Children's Hosp. Med. Ctr., 2006—, attending physician, divsn. hematology-oncology, 2008—; residency, pediat. Children's Hosp. LA, 1996—97, attending physician, divsn. hematology-oncology, 1998—2007. Chairperson Hematology-Oncology Jour. Club, CHLA, 1996—2006; assoc. dir. Cin. comprehensive sickle cell program CCHMC, 2006—, program leader, molecular and gene therapy program, exptl. hematology, 2007—, dir. hematology oncology fellowship program, 2007—08, dir. transnational cores, 2008—. Contbr. scientific papers. Recipient Rsch. Devel. award, CHLA, 2000—02, Pilot Project award, Specialized Ctrs. Rsch., 1997—99; Sickle Scholar, NIH-NHLBI, 1998—2003, Starter Scholar, John O' Conell Gene Therapy Program, 1997—99, Childrens Cancer Rsch. Fund fellowship, 2001—03, Wright Found. fellow, 2002—03. Fellow: Am. Acad. Pediat.; mem.: FDA (sci. adv. bd. 2008), NIH (sickle cell adv. com. 2007—), Internat. Soc. Exptl. Hematology (Travel awards 1998), NY Acad. Scis., Am. Assn. Advancement of Sci., Am. Soc. Hematology (Travel awards 1995, 1997), Cooley's Anemia Found. (sci. adv. bd. 2007—), Delhi Soc. Hematology, Blood, Am. Soc. Gene Therapy (ethics com. 2004—07, nominations com. 2005, Outstanding New Investigator award 2006). Office: Cin Children's Hosp Med Ctr TCHRF 6564 Divsn Exptl Hematology ML 7013 3333 Burnet Ave Cincinnati OH 45229 Business E-Mail: punam.malik@cchmc.org.

MALIK, SUDHIR, physics professor; s. Harish Chander and Janak Sundri Malik; m. Neeti Parashar; children: Priya, Prateek. PhD in Physics, Delhi U., New Delhi, 1997. Rsch. asst. prof. U. Nebr., Lincoln, 2005—. Home: 1701 Derby Dr Batavia IL 60510 Office: Fermilab PO Box 500 Batavia IL 60510

MALIK, WAHEED AHMAD, cardiologist; s. Gohar Sultana Malik; m. Samina Ahmed Malik, Oct. 24, 1996; children: Danial Ahmed, Harris Ahmed, Waleed Ahmed. MB & BChir, Army Med. Coll., Rawalpindi, Pakistan, 1986; MD, Ednl. Commn. Fgn. Med. Grads., 1993. Diplomate Am. Bd. Internal Medicine, 2001, Am. Bd. Nuc. Cardiology, 2002. Nuc. cardiologist and dir. Advanced Cardiology Ctr., Rockville, Md., 2002—. Mem.: Am. Soc. Nuc. Cardiology. Office: Advanced Cardiology Center 11119 Rockville Pike Ste 100 Rockville MD 20852 Office Fax: 301-816-8616; Home Fax: 301-816-8616. Personal E-mail: waheed5@verizon.net.

MALIN, HOWARD GERALD, podiatrist; b. Providence, Dec. 2, 1941; s. Leon Nathan and Rena Rose (Shapiro) M. AB, U. R.I., 1964; MA, Brigham Young U., 1969; BSc, Calif. Coll. Podiatric Medicine, 1969, DPM, 1972; MSc, Pepperdine U., 1978; MD (hon.), Internat. U. Sch. Medicine, Winnipeg, Man., Can., 2001. Diplomate Am. Bd. Podiatric Pub. Health, Am. Bd. Podiatric Orthopedics, Am. Acad. of Wound Care Mgmt. Extern in podiatry VA Med. Ctr., Wadsworth, Kans., 1971-72, Marine Corps Res. Dept., San Diego, 1972; resident in podiatric medicine and surgery N.Y. Coll. Podiatric-Medicine, NYC, 1972-73; resident in podiatric surgery, instr. in podiatric surgery N.Y. Coll. Podiatric Medicine, NYC, 1973-74; pvt. practitioner in podiatric medicine and surgery Bklyn., 1974-77; mem. staff Prospect Hosp., Bronx, NY, 1974-77; chief podiatry service, mem. staff, cons. sports medicine David Grant U.S. Air Force Med. Ctr., Travis AFB, Calif., 1977-80; chief podiatric sect. VA Med. Ctr., Martinsburg, W.Va., 1980—2009. Instr. ednl. devel. program VA Med. Ctr., Martinsburg,

W.Va., 1980—84; clin. prof. med. sci. Alderson-Broaddus Coll., U. Osteopathic Medicine and Health Scis.; adj. faculty Barry U. Sch. Podiatric Medicine; adj. clin. prof. Ohio Coll. Podiatric Medicine, dir. extern program; clin. asst. prof. surgery W.Va. U. Sch. Medicine. Mem. editl. rev. bd. Jour. Contemporary Podiatric Physician, 1991—. Lt. Col. USAFR, ret. Fellow Am. Soc. Podiatric Dermatology (past archivist)(life), Am. Coll. Foot Orthopedics (emeritus), Am. Coll. Podiatric Physicians, Am. Coll. Podiatric Radiology (archivist, past pres.)(life), Am. Soc. Podiatric Medicine (asst. exec. dir. emeritus, past pres., archivist, life), Am. Podiatric Med. Writers Assn. (pres., archivist), Am. Coll. Foot and Ankle Pediat. (past pres., archivist, historian, life), Am. Profl. Wound Care Assn., Royal Soc. for Promotion Health, Royal Soc. Medicine (life), Coll. Cert. Wound Specialists; mem. Am. Acad. Podiatric Sports Medicine (assoc.), Assn. Mil. Surgeons US (life), Am. Coll. Podiatric Surgery (life), Am. Hosp.& Healthcare POD,Am. Podiatric Med. Assn. (life), Phi Kappa Theta, Phi Kappa Psi. Home and Office: 2250 Bear Den Rd Ste 210 Frederick MD 21701-9408

MALIN, IRVING, language educator, critic; b. NYC, Mar. 18, 1934; s. Morris and Bertha (Silverman) M.; m. Ruth Lief, Dec. 18, 1955; 1 child, Mark. BA, Queens Coll., 1955; PhD, Stanford U., 1958. Acting instr. English Stanford U., 1955-58; instr. Ind. U., 1958-60; from instr. to prof. CCNY, 1960-72, prof., 1972—. Cons. Jewish Publ. Soc., 1964, Am. Quar., 1964, NEH, 1972, 79, 80, 81, 82, B'nai B'rith, 1974-75, Yaddo, 1975-77, Jewish Book Coun., 1976, 79, PEN, 1978-82, Princeton U. Press, 1979, Fairleigh Dickinson Press, 1980, Wayne State U. Press, 1980, Internat. Coun. Exch. of Scholars, 1980-81, Duke U. Press, 1981, Jewish Daily Forward, 1981, U. Pitts. Press, 1981, Papers on Lang. and Lit., 1981, U. Ga. Press, 1983, UMI Rsch., 1989, Gordian Press, 1990, Ctr. for Study of Higher Edn., 1990, Mosiac, 1991, MacArthur Found., 1996, U. of S.C. Press, 1998, Purdue U. Press, Lafayette, Ind., 1999; adv. bd. James Purdy Soc.; cons. U. Tex.2005 Author: William Faulkner: An Interpretation, 1957, New American Gothic, 1962, Jews and Americans, 1965, Saul Bellow's Fiction, 1969, Nathanael West's Novels, 1972, Isaac Bashevis Singer, 1972; co-editor: Breakthrough: A Treasury of Contemporary American Jewish Literature, 1964, William Styron's The Confessions of Nat Turner: A Critical Handbook, 1970, The Achievement of William Styron, 1975, William Goyen, 1997, Into the Tunnel, 1998, Garrett's Elizabethan Trilogy, 1998; editor: Psychoanalysis and American Fiction, 1965, Saul Bellow and the Critics, 1967, Truman Capote's in Cold Blood: A Critical Handbook, 1968, Critical Views of Isaac Bashevis Singer, 1969, Contemporary American-Jewish Literature: Critical Essays, 1973, Conrad Alken's Prose, 1982; co-editor: Underwords: Perspectives on Don DeLillo's Underworld, 2002; adv. editor: Studies in American Jewish Literature, Jour. Modern Literature, Review of Contemporary Fiction, Saul Bellow Jour., 20th Century Literature; reviewer: Hollins Critic, So. Quar.; co-editor Paul Bowles, 1986, Spl. Issue of 20th Century Lit., James Dickey Spl. Issue of S.C. Rev., 1994, Pynchon and Mason and Dixon, 2000, So. Novelists on Stage and Screen So. Quar., 1995, James Dickey's Fiction Spl. Tex. Rev., 1996, Leslie Fiedler and American Culture, 1999, Torpid Smoke: The Stories of Vladimir Nabokov, 2000. Fellow Yaddo, 1963, Nat. Found. for Jewish Culture, 1963-64, Huntington Libr., 1978. Mem. MLA, AAUP, Am. Studies Assn., Am. Jewish Hist. Soc., Melville Soc., Authors League Am., Soc. Study of So. Lit., Poe Studies Assn., English Inst., Nathaniel Hawthorne Soc., N.Y. Acad. Scis., Poetry Soc. Am., Popular Culture Assn., Nat. Book Critics Circle, Sherwood Anderson Soc., Internat. Assn. Univ. Prof. English, Kafka Soc., English-Speaking Union, Multi-Ethnic Lit. U.S. Soc., Hastings Ctr., Am. Jewish Congress, Assoc. Writing Programs, Nat. Coun. Tchrs. of English, Vladimir Nabokov Soc., Phi Beta Kappa. Jewish. Home: 96-13 68th Ave Forest Hills NY 11375-5039 Office: CCNY Dept English New York NY 10031

MALIN, ROBERT ABERNETHY, retired investment company executive; b. Mt. Vernon, NY, Dec. 13, 1931; s. Patrick Murphy and Caroline Cooper (Biddle) M.; m. Gail Lassiter, Nov. 5, 1960; children: Alison Campbell, Robert Lassiter. AB, Dartmouth Coll., 1953, MBA, 1954. Asst. to comptr. Biddle Purchasing Co., NYC, 1958-59; with Blyth & Co., Inc., NYC, 1960-71, v.p., 1965-71, dir., 1968-71, sr. v.p., mem. exec. com., 1971-72; sr. v.p. corp. fin. Reynolds Securities Inc., NYC, 1972-74, dir., 1973-74; mng. dir. First Boston Corp., NYC, 1974-90; gen. ptnr. Tiedemann Investment Group, NYC, 1991-96; mng. dir. SeaBridge Investment Advisors, Summit, NJ, 1997—2006; ret., 2006. Mem. adv. coun. Fin. Acctg. Stds. Bd., 1973-78. Served as lt. (j.g.) USNR, 1954-57. Mem.: Securities Industry Assn. (acctg. com.), Investment Bankers Assn. Am., The Moorings Club, Morris County Club, Beacon Hill Club. Republican. E-mail: malinrobta@aol.com.

MALING, GEORGE CROSWELL, JR., physicist; b. Boston, Feb. 24, 1931; s. George Croswell and Marjory Maling; m. Norah J. Horsfield, Dec. 29, 1960; children: Ellen P., Barbara J., Jeffrey C. AB, Bowdoin Coll., 1954; SB, MIT, 1954, SM, 1954, PhD in Physics, 1963. Rsch. asst., postdoctoral fellow MIT, 1957—65; adv. physicist IBM Corp., Poughkeepsie, NY, 1965—71, sr. physicist, 1971—92; pres. Empire State Software Sys., Ltd., 1992—93; dir. Noise Control Found., Inc., Poughkeepsie, 1975—2006; chmn. com. Sl-acoustics Am. Nat. Std. Com., 1976—79; dir. Internat. Noise Control Engring. Found., Inc., 1993—2006; mng. dir. Inst. of Noise Control Engring., 1994—2001; ret. Pres. Internat. Noise Control Engring. Found., 1999—. Editor: Noise/News, 1972—92; mng. editor: Noise/News Internat., 1993—, assoc. editor: Jour. Acoustical Soc. Am., 1976—83, editor tech. proc.; contbr. articles to profl. jours. Recipient Raleigh medal, Inst. Acoustics U.K., 1999, Dist. Noise Ctrl. Eng., INCE, 2001. Fellow: AAAS, IEEE, Audio Engring. Soc., Acoustical Soc. Am. (exec. coun. 1980—83, Silver medal in noise 1992); mem.: Nat. Acad. Engring., Internat. Inst. Noise Control Engring. (editor-in-chief 2002—, bd. dirs. 1980—86, v.p. comms. 1997—, bd. dirs.), Inst. Noise Control Engring. (bd. dirs. 1972—77, pres. 1975, award 2001). Personal E-mail: maling@alum.mit.edu.

MALINOWSKA-SEMPRUCH, KASIA, director; b. Bialystok, Poland, Mar. 5, 1966; d. Ryszard Malinowski and Irena Malinowska; m. Stas Sempruch, Apr. 28, 1996; children: Alan Sempruch, Kaya Sempruch. BA, Rutgers U., New Brunswick, NJ, 1990; MSW, U. Pa., Phila., 1992. Assoc. prof. Sch. Social Work, Crakow, 1992—93; program officer HIV Devel. Program, UN Devel. Program, NYC, 1993—95, program coord. Warsaw, 1995—98; program dir. Internat. Harm Reduction Devel. Program, Open Soc. Inst., NYC, 1999—. Vis. assoc. Albert Einstein Coll. Medicine, NYC, 2005—; task force mem. Millennium Project Task Force on HIV/AIDS, TB, Malaria and Access to Essential Medicines, 2002—05; reference group mem. UN Reference Group HIV/AIDS Prevention and Care Among Injecting Drug Users, 2002—; mem. subcom. Latin Am. grants program Tides Found., Fund Drug Policy Reform, NYC, 2002; mem. tech. rev. panel Global Fund to Fight AIDS, Tb and Malaria, 2002—05; vice chair bd. Internat. Coun. AIDS Svc. Orgns., Toronto, 2001—; mem. exec. bd. Social AIDS Com., Warsaw, 1996—; mem. steering com. AIDS and Mobility Project, Netherlands, 1987—88; regional organiser European Ctr. Social Welfare Policy, Vienna, 1993; internat. adv. com. mem. Awards Action on Human Rights and HIV/AIDS, 2004—; faculty mem. Salzburg Cornell Seminar, 2003—06; spkr. and present in field to numerous confs. on HIV/AIDS and related diseases. Editl. bd. mem. Internat. Jour. of Drug Policy; contbr. numerous articles to profl. jours. Recipient Gold Order medal, Polish Ministry Justice, 2000, Silve Badge award, Assn. Nurses for Malopolska Region, 2001. Mem.: Internat. AIDS Soc., Can. HIV/AIDS Legal Network. Office: Open Soc Inst 400 W 59th St New York NY 10019 Office Fax: 212-548-4617. Business E-Mail: kmalinowska@sorosny.org.

MALINOWSKI, ALEKSANDER, engineering educator; s. Szczepan Malinowski and Elzbieta Maria Malinowska; m. Dagmara Sniezek, Aug. 9, 1998; 1 child, Mateus Alexander. PhD, U. Louisville, Ky. Asst. prof. Bradley U., Peoria, Ill., 1998—2004, assoc. prof., 2004—. Recipient John Andrews award, Coll. Engring., Bradley U., 2004, 2008. Mem.: IEEE, Indsl. Electronic Soc. (adminstrv. com. mem. 2005—, Anthony J. Hornfeck Svc. award 2003). Office: Bradley Univ ECE Dept Peoria IL 61625

MALINOWSKI, ARTHUR ANTHONY, lawyer, arbitrator; b. Chgo., Apr. 4, 1929; s. Ignatius and Sophie (Data) M. BS in Econs., DePaul U., 1956, JD, 1960; MS in Indsl. Rels., Loyola U., 1958; PhD, Ill. Inst. Tech., 1972; LLM in Labor Law, Chgo. Kent Coll. Law, 1981. Bar: Ill. 1960. Instr. indsl. rels. Loyola U., Chgo., 1963-69, prof., 1969-94; prof. emeritus, 1994—; mem. Ill. Office Collective Bargaining, Chgo., 1973-83. Lectr. dept. econs. Ill. Inst. Tech., Chgo., 1965-68, with Gdansk U., Polish and Am.Ctr. Dispute Resolution Labor Mgmt. Disputes, 1992. Mem. Ill. Bar Assn., Indsl. Rels. Rsch. Assn., Nat. Acad. Arbitrators, Knights Malta, Phi Alpha Delta, Alpha Sigma Nu, Pi Gamma Mu, Iota Sigma Epsilon, Beta Gamma Epsilon. Home: 9240 Major Ave Morton Grove IL 60053-1552 Office: Loyola U of Chgo One E Pearson Ste 460 Chicago IL 60611-2147 Office Phone: 312-913-6613.

MALINOWSKI, DARIUSZ PIOTR, horticulturist, educator; s. Ryszard Wojciech Malinowski and Gabriela Maria Malinowska. Degree in Horticulture, Warsaw Agrl. U., Poland, 1989; PhD in Natural Scis., Swiss Fed. Inst. Tech., Zurich, Switzerland, 1995. Assoc. prof. Tex. A&M U., College Station, 2001—. Mem.: Am. Forage and Grasslands Coun. (assoc. Emerging Scientist award 1998, Merit award 2006), Am. Soc. Agronomy (assoc.). Achievements include research in discovery of chemical modifications in the rhizosphere of grasses infected with shoot-located Neotyphodium spp. fungal endophytes. Office: Texas Agrilife Research Stn 11708 Hwy 70W Vernon TX 76385 Business E-Mail: d-malinowski@tamu.edu.

MALINOWSKI, JEROME JOSEPH, design educator; b. Cleve., May 28, 1939; s. Joseph and Lottie Mary Malinowski. MFA, Syracuse U., NY, 1970. Cert. in indsl. design IDSA, 1970. Prof. U. La., Lafayette, 1967—98; prof. emeritus Syracuse U., 2009—. Indsl. design cons., Breaux Bridge, La. Designer, USA Olympic 4 Man Bobsled, 1988 (Worlds Most Aerodyn. Olympic Sled, 1992). Pres. Nat. Rural Electric Assn., Bouckville, NY, 1975—99. Recipient award, Ford Motors Corp., 1961, 1980. Mem.: Indsl. Designers Soc. America. Avocations: travel, weightlifting. Office: Univ La Lafayette PO Box 42811 Lafayette LA 70504-2811

MALINOWSKI, MARYELLEN, photographer, artist; b. Oak Park, Ill., Oct. 10, 1961; d. Richard A. and Mary Jo (Curran) Lamz; m. Preston Malinowski; children: Nicole, Brielle, Demi. Student, Internat. Acad. Merch./Design, Chgo., 1985, Maine Photog. Workshops, Rockport, 1996, Elgin CC, Ill., 1993—2004. Owner, dir. The Infrared Light Gallery, St. Charles, Ill., 1994—; prin., owner Enlighten Pub., St. Charles, 2004—. Spkr. in field. Author: The Sacred Light, 1999-2008; exhibited infrared photography in shows. Founder, bd. dirs. The Sacred Light Found. Recipient awards for photography; People's Choice award Women's Work Exhbn., Woodstock, 1995, 1st place Georgetown Internat. Fine Art Exhbn., Washington, 1997; recipient Ill. Women's Works Scholarship, 1996. Mem. Kodak Profl. Network, Nat. Assn. Profl. Woman, Profl. Photographers America, Theosophical Soc., Nat. Mus. Women in Arts. Home: 6N779 IL RT 31 Saint Charles IL 60175 Office: Infrared Light Gallery PO Box 1281 Saint Charles IL 60175 Home Phone: 630-584-8668; Office Phone: 800-571-2730, 630-584-8068. Business E-Mail: maryellen@infraredlight.com.

MALINS, DONALD CLIVE, biochemist, researcher; b. Lima, Peru, May 19, 1931; came to U.S., 1947; s. Richard Henry and Mabel (Madeline) M.; m. Mary Louise Leiren, 1962; children: Christopher W., Gregory S., Timothy J. BA, U. Wash., 1953; BS in Chemistry, Seattle U., 1954; PhD in Biochemistry, U. Aberdeen, 1967, DSc, 1976. Dir. environ. conservation div. Nat. Marine Fisheries Svc., Seattle, 1974-87; sr. scientific cons. U.S. Dept. Justice, Washington, 1989-91; sci. cons. NOAA, 1990-92; prin. scientist, dir. molecular epidemiology program Pacific N.W. Rsch. Inst., Seattle, 1992—2001, dir. biochem. oncology program, 2001—06, prin. scientist emeritus, 2006—; rsch. prof. dept. chemistry Seattle U., 1972-95. Affiliate prof. dept. environ. and occupl. health sci. U. Washington, 1984—, Coll. Ocean & Fishery Scis. U. Washington, 1974-91; editor-in-chief Aquatic Toxicology, 1980-95; lectr., speaker in field. Mem. editl. bd. Tech. in Cancer Rsch. and Treatment, 2001—; mem. editl. bd. Tech. in Cancer Rsch. and Treatment, 2001—; contbr. articles to profl. jours.; inventor in field. Bd. dirs. Am. Oceans Campaign, 1989-91; adv. bd. Internat. Jt. Commn., 1990-91. Recipient U.S. Dept. Commerce Gold medal, 1982. Mem. NAS, Am. Soc. Biochemistry and Molecular Biology, Am. Assn. for Cancer Rsch. Business E-Mail: fapyo@aol.com.

MALIPIERO, VICTORIA SCHNEIDER, opera singer; d. Donald Francis and Alice Eva (Billig) Snyder; m. Riccardo Malipiero, Dec. 21, 1988 (dec. Nov. 2003). MusB magna cum laude, Eastman Sch. Music, Rochester, NY, 1974, MusM, 1980; postgrad., U. Pisa, Italy, 1982; diploma in opera, Stuttgart Conservatory, Germany, 1984. Performer's cert. Eastman Sch. Music, 1978. Singer: (Operas) Stuttgart State Opera, 1980—85, La Scala, 1985, 1990, 1993, Genova Opera, 1986, 1988, Holland Festival Opera, 1987, 1990, Bologna Opera, 1987, 1988, 1995, Vienna Musikverein, 1992, Paris Chatelet Theater, 1993, Frankfurt Opera, 1999—2000, Rome Opera, 2001, others; singer: (soloist) Italian RAI Radio Broadcasts, 1984—2006, Schoenberg Festival, 2003, Musica in Alto Lario Festival, 2005, Master Classes on Lake Como, 2007—08, Flu Music Festival Miami, 2007, Villa Vigoni Internat. Twelve-Tone Music Convention, 2008; singer: (radio recs.) Schoenberg Lied der Waldtaube, Mahler Lieder eines fahrenden Gesellen, Dallapiccola An Mathilde, R. Malipiero Due Arie da L'Ultima Eva, Liederétudes. Flagstad Grant, Kirsten Flagstad Found., 1979—80. Mem.: Nat. Assn. Tchrs. Singing, Coll. Music Soc., Amici della Scala Milan (hon.), Pi Kappa Lambda, Sigma Alpha Iota. Home: 2848 Dove Pond Dr Grapevine TX 76051 Office: Via Pusgnano SNC 22010 Cremia Italy Office Phone: (011) 39-0344-82790.

MALIS, ANDREW GARY, telecommunications industry executive; ScB in Computer Sci., Brown U., Providence, 1975; ScM in Applied Math. and Computer Sci., Harvard U., Cambridge, Mass., 1979. Mem. tech. staff Mitre Corp., Bedford, Mass., 1975-78; divsn. engr. Bolt Beranek and Newman, Cambridge, Mass., 1979-93; cons. engr. Ascom Nexion, Acton, Mass., 1993-96; sr. cons. engr. Cascade Comm./Ascend Comm./Lucent Techs., Westford, Mass., 1996-2000; chief technologist Vivace Networks, Inc., San Jose, Calif., 2000—03, Tellabs, San Jose, 2003—06; dir. Verizon Commn., Waltham, Mass., 2006—. Chmn. working group Internet Engring. Task Force, Reston, Va., 1993—, ATM Forum, St. Louis, 1998-2000; mem. tech. adv. bd. Megisto Sys., Inc., Germantown, Md., 2000—; cons. Coun. Tech. Advisors, Gerson Lehrman Group, NYC, 2000—; pres., chmn. Multi-Protocol Label Switching Forum, Fremont, Calif., 2002-03; chmn., pres. IP/MPLS Forum, Fremont, Calif. 2003—, Internet Architecture Bd., Reston, Va., 2008-; spkr., chmn. numerous telecom.-related confs. Contbr. articles to sci. jours., including Procs. IEEE, IEEE Comm.; author telecom. stds. documents, 1981—. Bd. dirs., past pres. Temple Emanuel, Andover, Mass., 1986—. Recipient spl. tech. achievement award Frame Relay Forum, 1994, Disting. Svc. award, 1999; Spotlight award ATM Forum, 2000. Mem. IEEE, Internet Soc., Sigma Xi. Democrat. Jewish. Achievements include patent for method and apparatus for enabling flow control over multiple networks having disparate flow control capability. Office: Verizon Commn 117 West St Waltham MA 02451 Office Phone: 781-466-2362. Personal E-mail: amalis@gmail.com. Business E-Mail: andrew.g.malis@verizon.com.

MALISHENKO, TIMOTHY PETER, retired aerospace company executive; s. John and Myra Phillys (Morris) M.; m. Jane Baxter, Mar. 17, 1968; 1 child, Andrew. BSBA, Ohio State U., 1968; MBA in Supply Chain Mgmt., Mich. State U., 1969; MS in Sys. Mgmt., U. So. Calif., 1972; postgrad., Nat. War Coll., Washington, 1986. Commd. 2d lt. USAF, 1968, advanced through grades to maj. gen., 1998, chief contracts and acquisition NATO E-3A Early Warning Sy. Brunssum, Netherlands, 1979-82, dep. dir. R&D contracting Aero. Sys. Divsn. Wright-Patterson AFB, Ohio, 1982-84, dir. contracting, dep. aero. equipment, 1984-86, chief contract support divsn. Office Asst. Sec. Washington, 1987-88, chief, sys. and logistics contracting divsn., 1988-89, asst. dep. asst. sec. for contracting, 1989-90, dir. contracting Electronic Sys. Ctr. Hanscom AFB, Mass., 1990-93, dep. dir. contracting Hdqrs. Air Force Materiel Command Wright-Patterson AFB, Ohio, 1993-94, dir. contracting Hdqrs. Air Force Materiel Command, 1994-95; dep. asst. sec. for contracting USAF, Pentagon, Washington, 1995-97, dir. def. contract mgmt. agy., 1997—2001; v.p., contracts and pricing, integrated def. sys. Boeing Co., Seal Beach, Calif., 2001—03, corp. v.p., contracts and pricing Chgo., 2003—. Contbr. articles to profl. jours. Served to maj. gen. USAF. Decorated Def. Disting. Legion of Merit with oak leaf cluster, Def. Meritorious Svc. medal.

MALKAN, STACY, communications executive, director; b. Mass. d. Steven Anthony Grugnale and Diane Elizabeth Roche, James Nolan Roche (Stepfather); life ptnr. Henry Gerald Caldwell. BA, U. NH., Durham, 1990. Comm. dir. Health Care Without Harm, Arlington, Va., 2001—08; co-founder, comm. dir. Campaign Safe Cosmetics, San Francisco, 2002—. Pub., mng. editor Summit Free Press, Breckenridge, Colo., 1994—2000; mng. editor Breckenridge Pub., 1995—2000; editor, reporter Summit Newspapers, Frisco, Colo. Author: (book) Not Just a Pretty Face: The Ugly Side of the Beauty Industry (Silver medal IPPY, Ind. Book Pub. award, 2008). Personal E-mail: stacy@safecosmetics.org.

MALKASIAN, GEORGE DURAND, JR., obstetrician, educator; b. Springfield, Mass., Oct. 26, 1927; s. George Dur and Gladys Mildred (Trombley) M.; m. Mary Ellen Koch, Oct. 16, 1954; children: Linda Jeanne, Karen Diane, Martha Ellen. AB, Yale U., 1950; MD, Boston U., 1954; MS, U. Minn., 1963. Diplomate Am. Bd. Ob-Gyn. Intern Worcester (Mass.) City Hosp., 1954-55; resident in ob-gyn Mayo Grad. Sch. Hosp., Rochester, Minn., 1955-58, 60-61; mem. faculty Mayo Med. Sch., 1962—, prof. ob-gyn, 1976—, chmn. dept. ob-gyn, 1976-86. Author articles in field. Served to lt. comdr. M.C., USNR, 1958-60. Named Tchr. of Yr., Mayo Grad. Sch. Medicine, 1973, 77, Alumnus of Yr., Boston U. Sch. Med., 1990. Fellow Royal Coll. Obstetricians and Gynecologists (ad eundum); mem. ACS, Am. Coll. Ob-Gyn (pres. 1989-90), Am. Ob-Gyn Soc., Am. Radium Soc., Soc. Ob-Gyn, Assn. Profs. Ob-Gyn., N.Am. Ob-Gyn. Soc., Ctrl. Assn. Ob-Gyn, Minn. Soc. Ob-Gyn, Internat. Fedn. Ob-Gyn (v.p. 1997-2000), Zumbro Valley Med. Soc. (exec. dir. 1996-2002). Home: 211 NW 2nd St #503 Rochester MN 55901 Office: Mayo Clinic 200 1st St SW Rochester MN 55905-0001

MALKIEL, BURTON GORDON, economist, educator; b. Boston, Aug. 28, 1932; s. Sol and Celia (Gordon) Malkiel; m. Judith Ann Atherton, July 16, 1954 (dec. 1987); 1 child, Jonathan; m. Nancy Weiss, July 31, 1988. BA, Harvard, 1953, MBA, 1955; PhD, Princeton, 1964. Assoc. Smith Barney & Co., NYC, 1958—60; asst. prof. dept. econs. Princeton U., 1964—66, assoc. prof., 1966—68; prof., 1968—81, Rentschler prof. econs., 1969—81, chmn. dept. econs., 1974—75, 1977—81, Chem. Bank chmn.'s prof. econs., 1988—; dean Sch. Orgn. and Mgmt., Yale U., 1981—87. Mem. Pres.'s Coun. Econ. Advisors, 1975—77; bd. dirs. Vanguard Group Internat., Genmab, Theravance. Author: The Term Structure of Interest Rates, 1966, The Inflation-Beater's Investment Guide, 1980, Global Bargain Hunting, 1998, The Random Walk Guide to Investing, 2003, A Random Walk Down Wall Street, 9th edit., 2007, From Wall Street to the Great Wall, 2007; author: (with others) Strategies and Rational Decisions in the Securities Options Market, 1969, The Index Fund Solution, 1999. 1st lt. US Army, 1955—58. Mem.: Am. Fin. Assn. (dir., pres. 1978). Home: 76 North Rd Princeton NJ 08540-2430 Office: Princeton U Dept Econs Princeton NJ 08544-0001 Office Phone: 609-258-6445. Business E-Mail: bmalkiel@princeton.edu.

MALKIN, ALEXANDER J., biophysicist; b. Semipalatinsk, Kazakhstan, Jan. 20, 1958; PhD, Inst. Crystallography Russian Chemistry, Moscow, 1989. Rschr. U. Calif., Irvine, 1997—2003; sci. capability leader bionanosciences Lawrence Livermore Nat. Lab., Calif., 2003—. Assoc. rsch. biochemist U. Calif., Riverside, 1992—97. Mem.: Materials Rsch. Soc. Office: Lawrence Livermore Nat Lab 7000 E Ave Livermore CA 94551 Business E-Mail: malkin1@llnl.gov.

MALKIN, BARRY, film editor, consultant; b. NYC, Oct. 26, 1938; s. Richard and Helen (Kandix) M.; m. Stephanie Byer; 1 child, Sacha Janine. BA, Adelphi U., 1960. Freelance film editor Sacha Prodns., Inc., NYC, 1964—. Editor: (films) The Rain People, 1969, Cotton Comes to Harlem, 1970, They Might Be Giants, 1971, Who is Harry Kellerman?, 1971, Cops and Robbers, 1973, The Godfather Part 2, 1974, One Summer Love, 1976, Somebody Killed Her Husband, 1978, Last Embrace, 1979, One Trick Pony, 1980, Windows, 1980, Four Friends, 1981, Hammett, 1982, Rumble Fish, 1983, The Cotton Club, 1984 (Acad. award nominee for best film editing 1984), Peggy Sue Got Married, 1986, Gardens of Stone, 1987, Big, 1988, New York Stories ("Life Without Zoe"), 1989, The Freshman, 1990, The Godfather Part III, 1990 (Acad. award nominee for best film editing 1990), Honeymoon in Vegas, 1992, It Could Happen to You, 1994, Jack, 1996, The Rainmaker, 1997, Isn't She Great, 1999, Lucky Numbers, 2000, The Big Bounce, 2003, The Treatment, 2005, The Skeptic, 2006, The Disappeared, 2007. Mem. Acad. Motion Picture Arts and Scis., Motion Picture Editors Guild, Am. Cinema Editors. Home and Office: 275 Central Park W New York NY 10024-3015 E-mail: cpwblackie@aol.com.

MALKIN, CARY JAY, lawyer; b. Chgo., Oct. 6, 1949; s. Arthur D. and Perle (Slavin) Malkin; m. Lisa Kimley, Oct. 27, 1976; children: Dorothy R., Victoria S., Lydia R. BA, George Washington U., 1971; JD, Northwestern U., 1974. Bar: Ill. 1974, U.S. Dist. Ct. (no. dist.) Ill. 1974, N.Y. 2001. Assoc. Mayer, Brown & Platt, Chgo., 1974—80, ptnr., 1981—2002, Mayer, Brown, Rowe & Maw LLP, Chgo., 2002—, Mayer Brown LLP, Chgo., 2007—. Chmn. spl. events com. Mental Health Assn., 1984—85; mem. steering com. Endowment Campaign Latin Sch. Chgo., 1990—91, trustee, 1991—2000, nat. trustee, 2000—02, sr. trustee, 2002—; chmn. Campaign Latin Sch. Chgo., 1995—98; mem. exec. com. Friends Prentice Women's Hosp., 1991—92; bd. dirs. SOS Children's Village Ill., 1992—96; mem. M. S. Weiss fund bd. Children's Meml. Hosp., 1993—96, mem. Graziano fund bd., 1993—96; trustee Field Mus., 1999—, mem. fin. com., 2002—05, mem. investment com., 2003—05, mem. budget com., 2005—, mem. founder's coun., 1995—, chmn. founder's coun., 1999—2003. Mem.: Saddle and Cycle Club (bd. govs. 1998—2001, 2006—, sec. bd. govs. 2008—), Chgo. Club, Phi Beta Kappa, Order of Coif. Home: 233 E Walton St Chicago IL 60611-1526 Office: Mayer Brown LLP 71 S Wacker Dr Chicago IL 60606

MALKIN, EVGENI, professional hockey player; b. Magnitogorsk, Russia, July 31, 1986; s. Vladimir and Tatiana Malkin. Center Metallurg Magnitogorsk (Russian Super League), 2003—06, Pitts. Penguins, 2006—. Mem. Team Russia, Olympic Games, Torino, Italy, 2006; player NHL YoungStars Game, 2007. Recipient Calder Trophy, 2007, Art Ross Trophy, 2009, Conn Smythe Trophy, 2009; named NHL Rookie of Yr., Sporting News, 2007; named to All-Rookie Team, NHL, 2007, NHL All-Star Game, 2008, 2009, All-NHL team, Sporting News, 2009, First All-Star Team, NHL, 2009. Achievements include being drafted in the first round (2nd overall) in the NHL Entry Draft, 2004; being a member of silver medal Team Russia, World Junior Championships, 2006; being a member of Stanley Cup Champion Pittsburgh Penguins, 2009. Office: Pittsburgh Penguins 66 Mario Lemieux Pl Pittsburgh PA 15219*

MALKIN, MARJORIE J., recreational therapist, educator; b. New Haven, May 28, 1946; d. Jacob K. and Charlotte S. Malkin; m. Timothy J. Brossart, May 26, 1996; 1 child, Jace Andrew Brossart; 1 child from previous marriage, Daniel Jacob Klotz. BA cum laude, Mt. Holyoke Coll., South Hadley, Mass., 1967; MEd, U. Ga., Athens, 1983, EdD, 1986. Cert. therapeutic recreation specialist Nat. Coun. Therapeutic Recreation Cert., 1983. Recreation therapist Athens Gen. Hosp., 1983—87; dir. activity therapy CPC Palm Bay Hosp., Fla., 1987—88; dir. adjunctive therapy Charter Hosp., Paducah, NY, 1988—89; prof., grad. coord. Southern Ill. U., Carbondale, 1989—. Vis. asst. prof. Murray State U., Ky., 1988—89; cons. Ill. Dept. Human Svcs., Springfield, 1995—2002; cons. arts Peace Found., Ireland, 2007—09; cons., trainer U. Costa Rica, San Jose, 1996—97, Togliatti Social & Econ. Coll., Russia, 1998—2001, Samara Tech. Coll., Russia, 1998—2001; invited spkr., Barretstown, Ireland, 2007—. Contbr. chapters to books, articles to profl. jours. Recipient Profl. Knowledge award, Ill. Recreational Therapy Assn., 1997, 2001; named Outstanding Vol., Spl. olympics, 2002; scholar, Leisure Careers Found., 1985—86; Tom and Ruth Rivers grantee, World Leisure and Recreation Assn., 1985. Mem.: Am. Therapeutic Recreation Assn. (bd. dirs. 1992—94, internat. rels. team co-leader 2005—09, past chair rsch. com., Presdl. award for Outstanding Profl. Contbns. 1991—92, Best Rsch. presentation 1995), US Equestrian Fedn. (nat. lic. horse show judge and steward 1979—2009), Kappa Delta Pi. Achievements include research and publications concerning suicidal and depressed women; research in adolescent and family substance abuse and therapeutic recreation: concepts and methods in 1993; equine assisted therapy and cognitive behavioral therapy. Avocations: swimming, horseback riding, gardening, cooking, reading. Home: 335 Old US Hwy 51 Makanda IL 62958 Office: So Ill U 307 Pulliam Hall Carbondale IL 62901-4632 Office Fax: 618-453-1829. Business E-Mail: mmalkin@siu.edu.

MALKIN, MICHELLE, columnist, political commentator; b. Phila., Oct. 20, 1970; d. Apolo and Rafaela Maglalang; m. Jesse Dylan Malkin, July 23, 1993; 2 children. B, Oberlin Coll., Ohio, 1992. Editl. writer, columnist LA Daily News, 1992—94; columnist Seattle Times, 1996—99; nat. syndicated columnist Creators Syndicate, LA, 1999—. Regular contbr. FOX News Channel; former guest-host The O'Reilly Factor; founder, contbr. polit. web-blog MichelleMalkin.com, 2004—; founder, CEO Internet broadcast network Hot Air, 2006—. Author: Invasion: How America Still Welcomes Terrorists, Criminals and Other Foreign Menaces to Our Shores, 2002 (NY Times bestseller), In Defense of Internment: The Case for Racial Profiling in World War II and the War on Terror, 2004 (NY Times bestseller), Unhinged: Exposing Liberals Gone Wild, 2005, Culture of Corruption: Obama and His Team of Tax Cheats, Crooks, and Cronies, 2009 (#1 Publishers Weekly bestseller). Named a Warren Brookes Fellow, Competitive Enterprise Inst., 1995. Avocations: fishing, piano, crocheting. Mailing: Creators Syndicate Ste 700 5777 W Century Blvd Los Angeles CA 90045 E-mail: writemalkin@gmail.com.*

MALKIN, PETER LAURENCE, lawyer, investor; b. NYC, Jan. 14, 1934; s. Samuel and Gertrude (Greenberger) Malkin; m. Isabel L. Wien, July 10, 1955. Grad. cum laude, Poly. Prep. Country Day Sch., 1951; AB summa cum laude, Harvard Coll., Cambridge, Mass., 1955; LLB magna cum laude, Harvard U. Law Sch., Cambridge, 1958. Bar: NY 1958, Conn. 1976. Chmn. Wien & Malkin LLC, NYC, 1958—; mng. Empire State Bldg. Assocs. LLC, 1961—; chmn. W & M Properties, Inc., NYC, 1965—2009, Malkin Holdings, 2009—. Ptnr. NYC Partnership, NYC, 2001—; founding chmn. Grand Ctrl. Partnership Inc. & 34th Street Partnership, Inc.; founding dir. Fashion Ctr. Bus. Improvement Dist.; dir. Realty Found. NY, 1981—, v.p., 1995—; mem. adv. com. Greenwich Japanese Sch., Conn., 1992—2005; mem. NYC Mayor's Bus. Adv. Coun., 1997—2002; gov. Real Estate Bd., NYC, 1993—2005; co-founder, hon. co-chmn. Com. Encouraging Corp. Philanthropy, 1998—; emeritus dir. US Trust Corp. Mem. Bank America Global Wealth Investment Mgmt. Adv. Bd., Chmn. Met. Aircraft Noise Mitigation Commn., 1990—; vice-chmn. Harvard Law Sch. Fund, 1967-71, chmn. nat. scholarship com., 1975-76, chmn. NYC com., 1981-83; founder, bd. dir. Urban League Southwestern Fairfield County, 1969-73, treas., 1969-71; bd. dir., exec. com. Lincoln Ctr. Performing Arts, 1979—; bd. dir. Inst. Internat. Edn., 1983-89, hon. 1994—; bd. dir., vice-chmn. Greenwich Ctr. Arts, 2004-2009; mem. adv. bd. Conn. Trust Hist. Preservation, 2007—; trustee Nat. Trust Hist. Preservation, 1988-91, adv. coun., 1997—, trustee emeritus, 2005—; founding chmn. Greenwich Green & Clean, Inc., 1986—, Greenwich Adopt-A-Road, 1996-; founding pres. Greenwich Tree Conservancy, 2006—; chmn., co-founder Merritt Pkwy. Conservancy, 2002—; v.p., exec. com. Greenwich chpt. NAACP, 1967-69; trustee Citizens Budget Commn., NYC, 1971-91, Jewish Communal Fund, NY, 1976-81; dean's coun. Harvard U., 1987-95; chmn. capital campaign and chmn. dean's coun. Harvard Kennedy Sch. Govt., 1995—, overseers com. to visit Harvard Kennedy Sch. Govt., 1976-82, 83-89, 90—, to visit Harvard Law Sch. 1977-83; exec. com. Program Ctr. Jewish Studies, 1974-80; bd. overseers Harvard Coll., 1989-95, overseers com. univ resources, 1972—, exec. com., 1985—; dean's adv. com. Harvard Law Sch., 1988-90; elected dir. Harvard Alumni Assn., 1981-83; chmn. schs. and scholarship com. Harvard Coll., Greenwich, 1973-79; exec. com. Assn. Better NY, 1972—; founding chmn. NY leadership com. Harvard Coll. Fund. Brandeis U. fellow, 1970—; recipient Outstanding Young Man award, NYC Jaycees, 1969, Nat. Preservation Honor award Nat. Trust Hist. Preservation, 1987, Pres. award Grad. Sch. and Univ. Ctr. CUNY, 1989, Crain's All-Star award, 1994, Nacore Disting. Man of Yr. award, 1995; Murray Hill Archl. award, 1996, PENCIL award for outstanding commitment to NYC Pub. Schs., 2003, Lincoln Ctr. Outstanding Vol. Leader award, 2004, Olmstead award, Conn. Chpt. Am. Soc. Landscape Architects, 2008; Man of Yr., Greenwich Rotary, 2005, Outstanding Cmty. Leader Greenwich Conn. C. of C., 2008, Honor award Mcpl. Art Soc. NY, 2009. Mem. Harvard Law Sch. Assn. NYC (trustee 1968-70, v.p. 1973-74), Assn. Bar City NY, Century Assn., Links NY, The Hasty Pudding Inst. 1770, AD Hon., Harvard Varsity Club (Cambridge), Harvard Club NYC (bd. mgrs. 1979-81), Harvard Club (Fairfield County, Conn., v.p. 1974-75, bd. dirs. 1976-80), Bailwick Club (hon. life, founding pres.), Blind Brook Club, Conn. Golf Club, Indian Harbor Yacht Club, Phi Beta Kappa. Office: 60 E 42d St New York NY 10165-0015 Business E-Mail: plmalkin@wienmalkin.com.

MALKIN, STANLEY LEE, neurologist; b. Pitts., Nov. 11, 1942; s. Maurice and Bessie Beatrice (Serbin) M.; m. Candace N. Conard; children: Justin Ross, Keith Richard. BA with honors, U. Pa., 1964; MD, U. Pitts., 1968. Diplomate Am. Bd. Psychiatry and Neurology, Nat. Bd. Med. Examiners. Intern Montefiore Hosp., Pitts., 1968-69; resident in neurology Columbia-Presbyn. Med. Ctr., NYC, 1969-72; chief neurology svc., Wright-Patterson AFB, Dayton, 1972-74; practice medicine specializing in neurology NYC; attending staff Mt. Sinai Hosp.; former dir. Neuro-Diagnostic Lab., Englewood; assoc. clin. prof. neurology Mt. Sinai Sch. Medicine; founder Bergen-Passaic Tomography Ctr., Fairlawn, N.J. Neurology cons. Regent Hosp.; med. dir. Pain Suppression Labs., Inc.; med. dir. Efficient Health Systems, Inc.-N.Y.C. Healthline; founder, med. dir., exec. v.p. Hosp. Diagnostic Equipment Corp., 1987—; pres. Cancer Treatment Holdings, Inc, 1993-95, dir. 1993-94, sr. med. dir. 1995-97; founder Montvale Med. Imaging Assocs. (N.J.), N.Y. Med. Imaging, N.Y.C., Hosp. Diagnostic Equipment Corp. Co-mcpl. coord. Ft. Lee Citizens for McGovern, 1972; ptnr. Sall/Myers Med. Assocs., prin. 1995—; mem. Edgewater Rent Control Bd., 1978. Maj. M.C. USAF, 1972-74. Recipient Comdr.'s Recognition award for care of repatriated prisoners of war, 1973, award Am.'s Top Physicians Consumers' Rsch. Coun. Am., 2004-05, Conn. Vets. Wartime Svc. medal, 2008. Fellow Royal Soc. Medicine; mem. Am. Acad. Neurology, Am. Assn. Electrodiagnostic Medicine, Am. Soc. Neuro-Imaging (charter), EEG and Clin. Neurosci. Soc., Am. Headache Soc. (rev. bd.), Nat. Headache Found., Internat. Headache Soc., Nat. Neurotrauma Soc., N.Y. Acad. Scis., NYU Bellevue Psychiat. Soc., European Fedn. Neurol. Socs. Office: 60 E 42d St Ste 2214 New York NY 10165

MALKINE-FALVEY, FERN SYLVIE, writer, journalist, painter; b. Bklyn., Apr. 11, 1950; d. Georges Alexandre and Sonia May Malkine; m. Peter Anthony Falvey, June 20, 1992. AA in History/English, Ulster County CC, Stone Ridge, NY, 1972; BS in History/English Lit., NYU, NYC, 1974; MS in Spl. Edn., Fordham U., NYC, 1976. Rschr., writer Editions de la Difference, Paris, 1976—78; copy editor Look Mag., NYC, 1978—79; fgn. corr. Paris Match, NYC, 1979—81; copy editor Elle Mag., Paris, 1983—85; painter, freelance journalist Woodstock, NY, 1985—89; gallery dir. Isidore Ducasse Fine Arts, Manhattan, NY, 1989—92; art cons. Pavillon des Arts Mus., Paris, 1998—99; curator On-line Gallery, Woodstock, NY, 2001—, youth ctr. Dir., 2004—. Author: Georges Malkine: An Arbitrary Destiny; co-author: Georges Malkine: Le Vagabond du Surrealism; exhibitions include Tom Fletcher Gallery, Woodstock, 2001, The Art Gallery-Western New Eng. Coll., Springield, Mass., 2002—. Vol. Congressman Matt McHugh, Kingston, NY, 1981, Oglala Sioux Emergency Svcs., 1987, ARC, 2001—, Congressman Hinchey, Kingston, NY, 2004. Mem.: Hist. Soc. of Woodstock. Avocations: guitar, historical post cards, designing moccasins, designing tapestries. Home: PO Box 261 Shady NY 12409 Business E-Mail: fern@hvc.rr.com.

MALKINSON, FREDERICK DAVID, dermatologist, educator; b. Hartford, Conn., Feb. 26, 1924; s. John Walter and Rose Malkinson; m. Una Zwick, June 15, 1979; children by previous marriage: Philip, Carol, John. Student, Loomis Inst., 1937-41; 3 yr. cert. cum laude, Harvard U., 1943, DMD, 1947, MD, 1949. Intern Harvard-Beth Israel Hosp., Boston, 1949-50; resident in dermatology U. Chgo., 1950-54, from instr. to assoc. prof. dept. dermatology, 1954-68; prof. medicine and dermatology U. Ill., Chgo., 1968-71; chmn. dept. dermatology Rush Med. Coll. and Rush-Presbyn.-St. Luke's Med. Ctr. (now Rush U. Med. Ctr.), Chgo., 1968-92, Clark W. Finnerud, M.D. prof. dept. dermatology, 1981-95, 95—; trustee Sulzberger Inst. Dermatol. Comm. and Edn., 1976-96; pres. Sulzberger Inst. Dermatol. Communication and Edn., 1983-88, 93-96; prof. emeritus Rush U. Med. Ctr., Chgo., 2000—. Editor: Year Book of Dermatology, 1971-78; chief editor: AMA Archives of Dermatology, 1979-83; bd. editors, 1976-84, Jour. AMA, 1979-83; editorial cons. World Book Medical Encyclopedia, 1991-2000; contbr. articles to profl. jours., chpts. to books. Active Evanston (Ill.) Libr. Bd., 1988-94, pres., 1993-94. With M.C. USNR, 1950-52. Grantee, U.S. Army, 1955—61, USPHS, 1962—70. Fellow AAAS; mem. Am. Acad. Dermatology (v.p. 1987-89, dir. 1964-67), Am. Dermatol. Assn., Soc. Investigative Dermatology (v.p. 1978-79, dir. 1963-68), Am. Fedn. Med. Rsch., Cen. Soc. Clin. Rsch., Radiation Rsch. Soc., Assn. Profs. of Dermatology (dir. 1982-85), Dermatology Found. (exec. com., trustee 1980-93, pres. 1983-85, Lifetime Career Educator award 2006), Nat. Coun. on Radiation Protection and Measurements (mem. com. on cutaneous radiobiology 1986-92), Chgo. Dermatol. Soc. (pres. 1964-65, Gold Medal award 1992, established ann. lectureship, 2004), Chgo. Lit. Club (v.p. 1997-99, 2000-03, pres. 1999-2000). Office: Rush Univ Med Ctr Dept Dermatology 707 S Wood St 220 Annex Bldg Chicago IL 60612 Office Fax: 312-942-7778.

MALKOVICH, JOHN, actor; b. Christopher, Ill., Dec. 9, 1953; m. Glenne Headley, 1982 (div. 1988); m. Glenne Headly, Aug. 2, 1982 (div. 1988); m. Nicoletta Peyran, 1989; children: Amandine and Lorwy. Student, Eastern Ill. U., Ill. State U. Co-founder Steppenwolf Theatre, Chgo., 1976 Made N.Y.C. theatrical debut in True West, 1982 (Obie award, Clarence Derwent award); other theatrical appearances include: Death of a Salesman, 1984, Burn This, 1987, States of Shock; dir. Balm in Gilead, 1984-85, Arms and the Man, 1985, The Caretaker, 1986, Coyote Ugly, (Chgo., Kennedy Ctr. for Performing Arts, Washington) 1985, Libra, 1994, Steppenwolf, 1994; appeared in films Places in the Heart, 1984, The Killing Fields, 1984, Eleni, 1985, Making Mr. Right, 1987, Glass Menagerie, 1987, Empire of the Sun, 1987, Miles From Home, 1988, Dangerous Liaisons, 1988, The Sheltering Sky, 1990, Queen's Logic, 1991, The Object of Beauty, 1991, Shadows and Fog, 1992, Jennifer 8, 1992, Of Mice and Men, 1992, In The Line Of Fire, 1993 (Academy award nomination best supporting actor 1993), Alive, 1993, Touchstone, 1994, Para De La Nuages, 1994, Mary Reilly, 1994, Mulholland Falls, 1996, Der Unhold, 1996, The Portrait of a Lady, 1996, Primary Colors, 1997, Con Air, 1997, The Man in the Iron Mask, 1998, Rounders, 1998, Le Temps retrouvé, 1999, The Libertine, 1999, Ladies Room, 1999, Joan of Arc, 1999, Being John Malkovich, 1999 (American Comedy Award, 2000), Shadow of the Vampire, 2000, Les Ames Forte, 2001, Knockaround Guys, 2001, Je rentre a la Maison, 2001, Ripley's Game, 2002, Hotel, 2001, The Dancer Upstairs, 2002, Johnny English, 2003, The Hitchhiker's Guide to the Galaxy, 2005, Colour Me Kubrick, 2005, Klimt, 2006, The Call, 2006, Eragon, 2006, Drunkboat, 2007, Gardens of the Night, 2007, In Tranzit, 2007, Beowulf (voice), 2007, Burn After Reading, 2008, Changeling, 2008; exec. prodr. The Accidental Tourist, 1988, Somewhere Else, 2000; prodr. Ghost World, 2000, The Loner, 2001, Found in the Street, 2001, The Dancer Upstairs, 2002, Ripley's Game, 2002, Johnny English, 2003, A Talking Picture, 2003, The Libertine, 2004, Kill the Poor, 2006, Art School Confidential, 2006; co-exec. prodr. The Accidental Tourist, 1988; The Dancer Upstairs, 2002; appeared in TV films Word of Honor, 1981, American Dream, 1981, Death of a Salesman, 1985 (Emmy award 1986), Heart of Darkness, 1994, RKO 281, 1999, Les Miserables, 2000, Napoleon, 2002. Office: C/O MR MUDD 6333 W 3RD STE 902 Los Angeles CA 90003-3176

MALKOVICH, MARK PAUL, III, musician, performing company executive; b. Eveleth, Minn., July 10, 1930; s. Mark II and Mary Frances (Greben) M.; m. Joan Shewring, Feb. 7, 1959; children: Mark IV, Erik, Kent, Kara. BS in Chemistry, Columbia U., 1952, MS, 1953; studied piano with Dorothy Crost Bourgin, Chgo. Mus. Coll., 1947-50; William Beller ch. Piano Dept., Columbia U., 1951-54; Adele Marcus, Juilliard Sch., 1959-62; MusD (hon.), Salve Regina, 1993; DFA, U. RI, 1994; MusD, Cath. U. Am., 1999. Pres. Chem. Gum Industries, Ltd., NYC, 1964—69. Artistic and gen. dir. Newport Music Festival, 1975—; exec. dir. Palm Beach Festival, Fla., 1984-86; guest lectr. TV and radio appearances and adjudicator at music competitions; pres. Chopin Found. of U.S., Miami, Fla., 1985; presented N.Am. debuts of Bella Davidovich, Jean-Philippe Collard, Dmitry Sitkoveksky, Andrei Gavrilov, Mikhail Pletnev, others; founder Sports US*A*SR; negotiator/agt. for USSR leading hockey players Fetisov, Krutov, Larionov, Makarov, 1989. Recipient Individual Achievement award Bus. Vols. for the Arts, RI, 1998; named to RI Heritage Hall of Fame, 2000; named hon. citizen, Tbilisi, Republic of Ga., hon. prof. Tbilisi Conservatoire. Mem. Harvard Mus. Assn., Newport Reading Rm., Newport Hist. Soc., Spouting Rock Beach Assn., Royal Arts Found. (pres.), Clambake Club. Office: care Newport Music Festival PO Box 3300 Newport RI 02840-0992 Office Phone: 401-846-1133. Business E-Mail: staff@newportmusic.org.

MALKOWICZ, STANLEY BRUCE, urologist; b. Passaic, NJ; s. Stanley Jacob and Jeanne (iracki) M.; m. Denise Elaine Ewald, Sept. 22, 1985. BA, U. Vt., 1977; MD, U. Pa., Phila., 1981. Intern in surgery Hosp. U. Pa., Phila., 1981-82, resident in surgery, 1982-83, resident in urology, 1983-86, chief resident in urology, 1986-87; fellow in urologic oncology U. So. Calif., LA, 1987-88, Hosp. U. Pa., Phila., 1988-90, asst. prof. surgery, 1990-95, assoc. prof., 1995—2003, prof. urology, 2003—; chief urology Phila. VA Med. Ctr. Assoc. scientist Wistar Inst. Anatomy and Biology, Phila., 1988—; Nat. Kidney Found. rsch. fellow, 1983-84; Am. Found. Urologic Disease rsch. scholar, 1988-90. Contbr. articles to profl. jours. Mem. AAAS, Am. Urologic Assn., Am. Assn. GU Surgeons, Am. Soc. Clin. Oncology, Soc. Univ. Urologists, Urodynamics Soc., Assn. Academic Surgeons, Soc. Pelvic Surgeons (treas.-sec.), Soc. Urologic Oncology, Urol. Rsch. Soc., Phila. Urol. Soc. (pres.), S.E. Pa. Am. Cancer Soc. (pres.), Sigma Xi. Presbyterian. Avocations: camping, reading, cooking. Office: Hosp U Pa Philadelphia PA 19104-4206 Home Phone: 610-525-0117; Office Phone: 215-662-7330.

MALKS, BETTY F., social worker; d. Benjamin Fishman and Bertha Finkelstein; m. Joshua B. Malks, Aug. 28, 1988; children: Nicole Shana Rosen, Brannon Benjamin. BA, U. Md., College Park, 1967; MSW, Adelphi U., LI, NY, 1982. LCSW N.Y., 1982; cert. exec. mgmt. devel. U. Calif., Berkeley, 1994. Dir. enriched housing programs Associated Y's of Greater N.Y., NYC, 1983—88; social svcs. program mgr. County of Santa Clara, San Jose, Calif., 1993—97, dir. dept. aging and adult svcs., 1997—. Chair Elder and Dependent Adult Law Enforcement Protocol Task Force, San Jose, 1999—2002, Fin. Institutions Team to Combat Elder Fin. Abuse, San Jose, 2003—; founder Fin. Abuse Specialist Team, San Jose, 1999, Vets. Resource Faire, San Jose, 1999; panelist Second World Conf. on Family Violence, Prague, Czech Republic, 2003, Internat. Assn. Geriatrics and Gerontology Conf., Rio de Janeiro, 2005; N.Am. regional rep. Internat. Network for Prevention of Elder Abuse, 2003—; chair First Aging Summit Calif. Social Work Edn. Ctr., Long Beach, Calif., 2004; project dir. Archstone Found. Faith-based Initiative for Elder Abuse Awareness in Diverse Communities, San Jose, 2006—; presenter ASA/NCOA 0009 Conf., UCI Med. Conf.- Eldu Abuse 0008. Contbr. articles to profl. jours. Congl. del. White House Conf. on Aging, 2005; bd. dirs. Jewish Cmty. Rels. Coun., San Jose, 1990—93, Coun. on Aging, San Jose, 1992—93, Women's Fund of Silicon Valley, San Jose, 2002—04; chair Sr. Citizen's Commn., San Jose, 1992—94; charter mem. Nat. Holocaust, Washington, 1998—. Recipient commendation, Santa Clara County Bd. Dirs., 2000, award for outstanding svc. to the disabled cmty., Internat. Assn. Workforce Profls., Am.'s Crown Communities award for creation of the FAST team, Am. City and County mag., 2001, President's award, Nat. Assn. Adult Protective Svcs., 2004; named Woman of Achievement, Women's Fund of Silicon Valley, 2001. Mem.: Internat/Network for Prevention of Elder Abuse, Am. Soc. on Aging, Nat. Com. for Prevention of Elder Abuse. Avocations: exercise, travel. Business E-Mail: betty.malks@ssa.sccgov.org.

MALKUS, DAVID STARR, mathematician; b. Chgo., June 30, 1945; s. Willem V.R. Malkus and Joanne (Gerould) Simpson; m. Evelyn R. (div.); children: Christopher, Annelise, Byron, Renata. AB, Yale U., 1968; PhD, Boston U., 1976. Mathematician U.S. Nat. Bur. Standards, Gaithersburg, Md., 1975-77; asst. prof. math. Ill. Inst. Tech., Chgo., 1977-83, assoc. prof., 1983-84; assoc. prof. mechanics U. Wis., Madison, 1984-87, prof., 1987—2002, chmn. Rheology Rsch. Ctr., 1991-94, prof. emeritus, 2002—. Chair prof. Nanjing (People's Republic China) Aero. Inst., 1986. Co-author: Concepts and Applications of Finite Element Analysis, 1989; contbr. articles to Computer Methods Applied Mech. Engring., Jour. Computational Physics. Achievements include research on finite element methods--reduced and selective integration techniques, a unification of concepts. Home: 2710 Mason St Madison WI 53705-3716 Home Phone: 608-232-1455.

MALLAK, CRAIG T., pathologist; Chief, Armed Forces Med. Examiner Sys. Armed Forces Inst. Pathology. Capt. med. corps. USN. Mem.: Am. Acad. Forensic Sci. Office: Armed Forces Medical Examiners Systems 1413 Research Blvd Bldg 102 Rockville MD 20850 Office Phone: 301-319-0000. Office Fax: 301-319-0635. E-mail: mallak@afip.osd.mil.*

MALLAMO, J. LANCE, museum director; married. B in History, SUNY, Stony Brook; M in Urban Planning, Hunter Coll., CUNY. Dir. hist. svcs. Suffolk County Dept. Pks., 1980—98; historian Suffolk County, 1987—; exec. dir. Suffolk County Vanderbilt Mus., 1998—. Chmn. Suffolk County Hist. Trust Com.; co-chair North Shore Heritage Area Planning Commn.; mgr. hist. sites Town of Brookhaven, NY; grant reviewer Inst. Mus. and Libr. Svcs. Contbr. articles to books. Office: Suffolk County Vanderbilt Mus 180 Little Neck Rd Centerport NY 11721 Office Phone: 631-854-5555. Business E-Mail: director@vanderbiltmuseum.org.

MALLARD, CARRIE CHARLENE, science educator; b. Canton, Ill., Apr. 12, 1976; d. Robert Darwin and Barbara Charlene Mallard. BS, U. Ill., 1998, MS, 2001. Grad. tchg. asst. dept. agrl. and consumer econ. U. Ill., Champaign/Urbana, 1998—99, grad. rsch. asst. dept. animal scis., 1998—2001, vis. vet. rsch. asst. dept. clin. medicine, 2001—03; life sciences instr. Lincoln Trail Coll., Robinson, Ill., 2003—. Contbr. articles to profl. jours. Mem.: Nat. Mastitis Coun., Am. Dairy Assn. Avocations: travel, scrapbooking, reading. Office: Lincoln Trail Coll 11220 State Hwy 1 Robinson IL 62454

MALLCHOK, JEANNE, retired special education educator; b. Detroit, Dec. 3, 1936; d. Edward Lawrence and Marjorie (Kimball) Ruslander; m. Harry Mallchok, July 16, 1960; children: William, Marc, Mindy, Jeff. BA in Edn., Wayne State U., 1960; postgrad. studies, E. Carolina U., 1988-90, We. Oreg. State U., 1991-96. Cert. handicapped learner standard teaching lic.; basic endorsement k-12. Dancer Lemanis-Tillak Ballet Co., 1953-58; dancer-singer summer stock Botsford Inn., Detroit, 1957-58; dancer, vocal soloist Detroit Tambouitzans, 1957-61, 76-80; co-owner Haslett (Mich.) Pharmacy, 1963-83; artistic dir. Childrens Ballet Theatre, Lansing, Mich., 1975-84; choreographer Okemos H.S., Lansing Ballet, 1975-84; instr. dance Lansing C.C., 1975-84; owner, instr., mgr. The Ballet Corner, Mich., 1980-86; opera singer Eugene (Oreg.) Opera Co., 1991—97; instr. Children and Adult Dance Comty. Ctr., Eugene, 1991—2000; ednl. specialist Lane Edn. Svc. Dist., 1991—2001; ret., 2001; substitute tchr., K-12 Springfield Pub. Sch., 2001—, Eugene 4U Schs., 2001—. Instr. classical ballet Lansing (Mich.) CC, 1976-81, Lane CC, Eugene, 1998-2006, Shape Ctr., Eugene. Choreographer for classical ballets (adapted to HS or younger age groups) and musicals at Okemos (Mich.). HS, 1975-84. Vol. Morehead City, NC, 1975-84, Pet Ptnrs., R.E.A.D., Flying Doctors of Am., 2000-; bd. dirs. treas. Lansing (Mich.) Ballet Camp; bd. dirs. Children's Ballet Theatre, 1975-84. Mem. NEA, Oreg. Edn. Assn. Avocations: travel, dance, biking, hiking. Personal E-mail: jmallchok@hotmail.com.

MALLERY, CHARLES HENRY, college associate dean, biology educator; b. Southampton, NY, June 3, 1943; s. Harry F. and RosaLinda Mallery; m. Judy L. Kuehnell, Oct. 15, 1966; children: Jennifer M., Kimberly A. BS in Botany, U. Ga., 1965, PhD, 1970. Postdoctoral fellow Lab. Quantitative Biology, Coral Gables, Fla., 1970-72; vis. asst. prof. U. Miami, Coral Gables, 1972-73, asst. prof., 1973-79, assoc. prof. biology, 1979—, asst. dean Coll. Arts and Scis., 1986-89, assoc. dean, 1989—. Author lab. manual: General Studies in Biology, 1984; contbr. articles to profl. publs. Former rules chmn. US Swimming, Inc., Colorado Springs, Colo., 1988—, nat. events coord., 1990—. Mem. Am. Soc. Plant Physiologists, Fla. Acad. Scis., Japanese Soc. Plant Physiologists. Avocations: swimming refereeing, motorcycling. Office: U Miami PO Box 248004 Miami FL 33124-8004 Home Phone: 786-449-5442; Office Phone: 305-284-3188. Business E-Mail: cmallery@miami.edu.

MALLERY, DAVID, education leader, teacher seminars, consultant; b. Sugar Hill, NH, Aug. 3, 1923; s. Otto Tod and Louise Marshall Mallery; m. Judith Chappell Mallery, June 15, 1956; children: Roger, Diane Mallery Cusick. BA, Haverford Coll., Pa., 1945, PhD (hon.), 1995; MA, Middlebury Coll., Vt., 1950. Tchr. English Germantown Friends Sch., Phila., 1946-58; seminar leader Friends Coun. on Edn., Phila., 1959-94; dir. profl. devel. Nat. Assn. Ind. Schs., Washington, 1959—. Edn. cons., 1959—; tchr. Bell Tel./U. Pa. Inst. for Humanistic Studies for Execs., 1960's. Author: High School Students Speak Out, 1960's, Ferment on the Campus, 1960's. Edn. advisor Tracy S. Voorhees, Pres. Eisenhower's rep. on Cuban refugee crisis, 1959-60; founding trustee Am. Film Inst., 1967-79. Lt. (j.g.) USNR, 1943-46, WW II. Recipient Klingenstein award Columbia U. Tchrs. Coll., 1996. Avocations: films, theater, music, international networking. Home and Office: 9006 Crefeld St Philadelphia PA 19118-3607 Home Phone: 215-247-3113; Office Phone: 215-242-0731. Business E-Mail: mallery@davidseminars.com.

MALLETT, MARK EDMUND, theater educator; b. Kenton, Ohio, May 4, 1952; s. Edmund Irving and Winifred Mary Mallett; m. Patricia Kathleen Vandor, June 26, 1977. BA, U. Akron, Ohio, 1974; MA, U. Md., Coll. Pk., 1979; PhD, U. Ill., Urbana Champaign, 1994. Asst. prof. theater Morehead State U., Ky., 1996—2000; asst. prof. theater arts Richard Stockton Coll., Pomona, NJ, 2000—. Prodn. stage mgr. Cleve. Ballet, Ohio, 1980—86; co. mgr. Ft. Worth Ballet, 1986—87; prodn. mgr. instr. Emerson Coll., Boston, 1987—90. Home: 305 South Poplar Ave Galloway NJ 08205-4592 Office: Richard Stockton Coll NJ PO Box 195 Jimmie Leeds Rd Pomona NJ 08240 Office Fax: 609-652-4550. Business E-Mail: mark.mallett@stockton.edu.

MALLETT, VERONICA T., medical educator, director; b. Detroit, May 5, 1957; d. Conrad LeRoy and Claudia Gwendolyn Mallett; m. Kevin Isaac Briscoe, May 26, 2008; children: Leah Aldona Jackson, Simone Gwendolyn Jackson, Joseph Elliott Brisco, Paul Rollins Brisco; children: Kevin Isaac Jr. Brisco, Elise Isabell Brisco. BA, Barnard Coll., Columbia U., NY, 1979; MD, Coll. Human Medicine, Mich. State U., East Lansing, 1983. Lic. Medical Tenn., Ill. Clin. instr. dept. ob-gyn. Northwestern U. Med. Sch., Chicago, 1987—91, Wayne State U. Sch. Medicine, Detroit, 1991—93; asst. prof. dept. ob-gyn. Wayne State U., 1993—99; dir., women's continence & pelvic surgery ctr. Huntzel Hosp., Detroit, 1994—99; dir. Urogynecology & Reconstructive Pelvic Surgery, Huntzel Hosp., 1994—99, fellowship; dir., urogynecology Oakwood Health Sys., Dearborn, Mich., 1999—2005, program dir., ob-gyn. residency program, 2001—05; chair, dept. ob-gyn. med. group chair excellence, U. Tenn. Health Sci. Ctr., Memphis, 2005—; med. dir., healthcare excellence Regional Med. Ctr., Memphis, 2007—. Physician adv. bd. Lilly Pharm., Indianapolis, 1999—2001; physician advisor Kimberly-Clark, Atlanta, 2003—08. Contbr. chapters to books. Recipient Team Leader award, Patient Safety Improvement Corp., 2008; named one of America's Top 100 Leading Physicians, Black Enterprise Mag., 2008, Memphis' Top Doctors, Memphis Mag., 2006, 2008; Med. Leadership Program fellow, UHC, NAPH, 2007. Mem.: Tenn. Med. Assn., Bluff City Med. Soc. Home: 2421 Lennox Dr Germantown TN 38138 Office: Univ Tennessee College Medicine 853 Jefferson Av Rm E102 Memphis TN 38163 Office Fax: 901-448-4701. Business E-Mail: vmallett@utmem.edu.

MALLEY, CLAUDIA, publishing executive; B in Psych., U. Del. Mktg. dir. WNET, Newark; with Ziff-Davis Media Inc.; pub. Runner's World Rodale Mags. Inc., 1999—2003; assoc. pub. Nat. Geographic mag., 2003—05, v.p., US pub., 2005—; pub. Nat. Geographic Green Guide, 2008—. Mem.: NY Road Runners (bd. dirs.). Office: Nat Geographic Soc Hdqs 1145 17th Street NW Washington DC 20036

MALLEY, RAYMOND CHARLES, retired foreign service official, industrial executive; b. Cambridge, Mass., Dec. 22, 1930; s. William and Evangeline (Vautour) M.; m. Rita Ann Masse, May 26, 1951 (dec. June 1989); children: Keith, Bruce, Gregory; m. Josette Lucile Vidril Murphy, Aug. 11, 1995. AA, Boston U., 1950, BS, 1952; MA Equivalent, U. Geneva, 1955; MA, PhD ABD, Fletcher Sch. Law & Diplomacy, Tufts U. and Harvard U., Mass., 1956. Economist, fin. analyst Texaco, Inc., NYC, 1957—61; fgn. svc. officer US Dept. State, AID, Washington & fgn. posts, 1961—82, dir., US Trade and Devel. Program Washington, 1980; fed. exec. fellow Brookings Instn., 1973—74; v.p. Silopress, Inc., Sioux City, Iowa, 1982—87; pres. Silopress Can., 1985—87; cons., advisor Labat-Anderson Internat., Arlington, Va., 1988—93; sr. group advisor, N.Am. and S.Am. rep. Halla Bus. Group, Seoul, Republic of Korea, NYC, Washington, 1991—2004. Chmn. Halla Am. Inc., 1996—2004. Mem. exec. bd. Coll. Mgmt., L.I. U., Brookville, NY, 1994-2009. 2nd lt., 1st lt., capt. then maj. USAFR. Recipient Nat. Def. Svc. medal, USAFR, Korean War. Mem. Acadian Cultural Soc., Am. Fgn. Svc. Assn., Diplomatic and Consular Officers Ret., Harvard Club, Am. Legion, Res. Officers Assn. Roman Catholic. Avocation: tennis. Address: 6224 Loch Raven Dr Mc Lean VA 22101-3133 Office Phone: 703-893-8083. Personal E-mail: Rcmalley@aol.com.

MALLEY-MORRISON, KATHLEEN, psychology professor, researcher; d. Barbara and Edward Malley; m. Frank Morrison, Jan. 7, 1996. EdD, Boston U., Mass., 1970. Prof. psychology Boston U., 1970—. Author: (book) Family violence in a cultural perspective; editor: (scholarly book) International perspectives on family violence and abuse: A cognitive ecological approach; contbr. articles to profl. jours. Fellow: APA (assoc. Mentoring award 2006). Office: Boston Univ 64 Cummington St Boston MA 02215 Office Fax: 617-353-6933. Business E-Mail: kmalley@bu.edu.

MALLIA, MARIANNE, medical writer; b. Davenport, Iowa, Feb. 14, 1948; d. Norman Bramblett and Mary Jane (Hilkemeyer) Hagar; 1 child from previous marriage, Lindsay Sharyn. BA in English, U. Iowa, 1970. Cert. tchr., editor in life sci. Tchr. tech. writing Houston Ind. Sch. Dist., 1970—76; med. writer Tex. Heart Inst., Houston, 1976—; editl. cons. Tex. Heart Inst. Jour., Houston, 1977—87, head sci. publ., 1986—, sr. med. writer, 1994—. Instr. Sch. Allied Health Sci. and Sch. Pub. Health U. Tex., 1990—94. Editor: Techniques in Cardiac Surgery, 1984; editor: (with Denton A. Cooley) Surg. Treatment of Aortic Aneurysms, 1985; editor: (essays) Reflections and Observation, Denton A. Cooley, MD, 1985; author: (handbook) Heart Owner's Handbook, 1995; bd. editors: Life Sci., 2002. Fellow: Am. Med. Writers Assn. (core curriculum cert. 1984, instr. 1985—, advanced curriculum cert. 1989, honor roll workshop leader 1992—, bd. dir., exec. com. 1996—2005, pres. 2002—03, writer advanced core curriculum, Award Tchg. Excellence 1998); mem.: Women in Comm. (Matrix award 1996—2000), Coun. Biology Editors, Pi Beta Phi. Avocation: classic cars. Office: Tex Heart Inst PO Box 20345 Houston TX 77225-0345 Office Phone: 832-355-6776. Business E-Mail: mmallia@heart.thi.tmc.edu.

MALLIN, JOEL, lawyer; m. Sherry Vogel. BS, Cornell U.; LLB, Columbia U. Bar: NY 1961. Atty. Joel Mallin LLP, NYC. Chmn. Aldrich Mus., Conn. Named one of Top 200 Collectors, ARTnews Mag., 2004—08. Mem.: Manhattan Theatre Club. Avocation: collector of modern & contemporary art, particularly sculpture. Office: 110 East 59th St New York NY 10022-1304 Home: 60 Pound Ridge Rd Pound Ridge NY 10576 Office Phone: 212-715-0569, 212-486-0511. E-mail: jmallin@aol.com.

MALLIN, ROBERT, medical educator; b. New York, May 25, 1949; s. Henry Joseph and Clare Marie Mallin; m. Kimberly Norman Norman, July 20, 2002; children: Michael Patrick, Christopher Paul. Assoc. Applied Scis., State U. NY, Farmingdale, 1969; BA, U. S. C., Columbia, 1975, MD, 1981. Cert. family medicine Am. Bd. Family Medicine, 1984, addiction medicine Am. Bd. Addiction Medicine, 1998. Asst. prof. family medicine U. S. C. Sch. Medicine, 1984—86; med. dir. Harbison Med. Assocs., 1986—88; dir. emergency svcs. Providence Hosp., 1988—90; staff physician SC Dept. mental Health, 1991—98; prof. family medicine & psychiatry & behavioral medicine Med. U. SC., Charleston, 1998—. Contbr. articles to sci. jours. (Roe award: Outstanding Jour. Article, 1984), chapters to books. With USN, 1969—73, Charleston SC. Decorated Naval Achievment award USN. Mem.: Soc. Teachers Family Medicine, Am. Soc. Addiction Medicine, Am. Acad. Family Physicians. Avocations: bicycling, scuba diving, photography. Office: Medical Univ SC 295 Calhoun St Charleston SC 29425 Office Fax: 843-792-3598. Business E-Mail: mallinr@musc.edu.

MALLINSON, RICHARD GREGORY, chemical engineering educator; b. Indpls., Apr. 9, 1954; s. Harry and Susan Louise (Keckler) M. BSChemE, BS in Biomed. Engring., Tulane U., 1977; MSChemE, Purdue U., 1979, PhD, 1983. Rsch. asst. Purdue U., West Lafayette, Ind., 1977-83, Argonne Nat. Lab., Chgo., 1978; asst. prof. chem. engring. U. Okla., Norman, 1983-89, assoc. prof., 1989-99, dir. Inst. for Gas Utilization Techs., 1995—2002, prof., 1999—2006, C.M. Sliepcevich prof., 2006—. Faculty fellow NASA Kennedy Space Ctr., 2005-06, Lawrence Livermore Nat. Lab., Livermore, Calif., 1990; vis. prof. Tianjin (China) U., 1994—, Chulalongkorn U., Bangkok, 1994-2005; ptnr. OKKINETICS, Norman, 1996-2000; prin. investigator Univ. Technologists, Inc., Norman, 1988-91; Kerr McGee Disting. lectr. Kerr-McGee Found. U. Okla., 1989-94. Contbr. articles on energy and fuels. Bd. dirs. C.D. Mallory Found., Inc., Ala., 1994-99, Heartland Found., Inc., Okla., 1995-2001; mem. Okla. Found. for Excellence, 1993—. Officer USAR, 1977—84. Mem. AIChE (dir. local sect. 1989, symposia organizer 1986-, chair fueld and petrochems. divsn.,), Am. Chem. Soc. (symposia organizer). Achievements include patents in field for high density natural gas storage at high temperature, and chemical conversion of natural gas at low temperatures; other areas of expertise such as natural gas utilization, clean production of N204, biofuels, sustainability, alkane cracking modeling, coal conversion modeling. Home: 4631 Ridgeline Dr Norman OK 73072-1700 Office: U Okla 100 E Boyd St Rm T335 Norman OK 73019-1028 Office Phone: 405-325-4378. Business E-Mail: mallinson@ou.edu.

MALLIS, FERN J., fashion industry executive; b. Bklyn., Mar. 26, 1948; BFA, U. Buffalo. Merchandising editor Mademoiselle; prin. Fern Mallis Public Rels.; v.p. mktg. and comm. Design Ctr., NY; exec. dir. Coun. Fashion Designers of America, 1991—2001, 7th on Sixth, NYC; sr. v.p. IMG Fashion, NYC, 2001—. Head Mercedes Benz Fashion Week, NYC. Recipient Fashion Group Internat. award, 2003. Achievements include organizing the first NYC Fashion Week, 1993. Office: 7th on Sixth 304 Park Ave S Ste 1002 New York NY 10010-4306 Home: 40 E 68th St Apt 5B New York NY 10065-5946 also: 139 Big Fresh Pond Rd Southampton NY 11968-2211*

MALLISON, CRAIG T., research scientist; s. Tom Mallison and Judy Hendricks; m. Becky Mallison, June 26, 2000; children: Liberty, Douglas. BS in Natural Resources, Ohio State U., Columbus, 1989; MS in Fisheries and Aquatic Scis., U. Fla., Gainesville, 1999. Assoc. rsch. scientist Fla. Fish & Wildlife Conservation Commn., Lakeland, 1989—. Contbr. scientific papers to profl. jours. Mem.: Aquatic Plant Mgmt. Soc. Office: Fla Fish & Wildlife Conserv Comm 3900 Drane Field Rd Lakeland FL 33801 Business E-Mail: craig.mallison@myfwc.com.

MALLISON, HOWARD DANFORD, retired corporate communications specialist; b. Scotland Neck, NC, Sept. 13, 1932; s. Howard Winford and Myrtle Dean (Jernigan) Mallison; m. Norma Mae Gibbs, Apr. 30, 1955; children: Howard Danford II, N. Daniele Daniel. Lic. ins. agt. Va., 1958. Comm. specialist Dept. Army Civil Svc., 1953—58, 1962—79; life and casualty agt. Allstate Ins. Co., Portsmouth, Va., 1958—62; coord. support ctr. S.W.I.F.T., Belgian Internat. Co., Culpeper, Va., 1979—85; ret., 1985. Author of poems. Staff sgt. USAF, 1950—53. Decorated Korean Svc. medal USAF, Korean Svc. medal with 2 Bronze campaign stars; recipient Good Conduct medal. Mem.: NRA, Rivanna Rifle & Pistol Club. Avocations: walking, gun enthusiast, travel.

MALLON, THOMAS, writer; b. Glen Cove, NY, Nov. 2, 1951; s. Arthur Vincent and Caroline (Moruzzi) M. AB, Brown U., 1973; AM, Harvard U., 1974, PhD, 1978. Asst. prof. English Vassar Coll., Poughkeepsie, NY, 1979-85, assoc. prof., 1985-89, lectr. in English, 1989-91; lit. editor Gentlemen's Quar., NYC, 1991-95, writer-at-large, 1995-99; mem. Nat. Coun. on Humanities, 2002—05; dep. chmn. NEH, Washington, 2005—06; prof. English George Washington U., Washington, 2007—. Author: Edmund Blunden, 1983, A Book of One's Own, 1984, Arts and Sciences, 1988, Stolen Words, 1989, Aurora 7, 1991, Rockets and Rodeos, 1993, Henry and Clara, 1994, Dewey Defeats Truman, 1997, Two Moons, 2000, In Fact, 2001, Mrs. Paine's Garage, 2002, Bandbox, 2004, Fellow Travelers, 2007, Yours Ever, 2009. Recipient Ingram Merrill award, 1994, Nat. Book Critics Cir. citation for excellence in reviewing, 1998, Great Lakes Book award for fiction, 1998; Rockefeller Found. fellow, 1986-87, Guggenheim fellow, 2000-2001. Mem. PEN Am., Phi Beta Kappa. Home: 801 25th St NW Washington DC 20037 Personal E-mail: TVMallon@aol.com.

MALLORY, ARTHUR LEE, dean, retired state official; b. Springfield, Mo., Dec. 26, 1932; s. Dillard A. and Ferrell (Claxton) M.; m. Joann Peters, June 6, 1954; children: Dennis Arthur (dec.), Christopher Lee, Stephanie Ann, Jennifer Lyn. BS, S.W. Mo. State Coll., 1954; MEd, U. Mo., 1957, EdD, 1959; HHD, S.W. Bapt. Coll., Mo., 1972. History supr. U. Mo. Lab. Sch., Columbia, 1956-57; asst. to supt. schs. Columbia, 1957-59; asst. supt. schs. Parkway Sch. Dist., St. Louis County, Mo., 1959-64; dean evening div. U. Mo., St. Louis, 1964; pres. S.W. Mo. State U., Springfield, 1964-70, dean Coll. Edn., 1991-94; commr. edn. Mo. Dept. Edn., Jefferson City, 1971-87. Dir. Internat. House, U. Mo., Columbia, 1956-59; chmn. bd. Mo. Coun. on Econ. Edn., 2000—. V.p. Ozarks coun. Boy Scouts Am., 1967, pres. Gt. Rivers coun., 1972-73, Greene County Assn. for Retarded Citizens, 1989—; pres., 1991-96, mem. north ctrl. region exec. bd., 1984—; bd. dirs. Meml. Cmty. Hosp., Mid-Continent Regional Ednl. Lab., Ozark Pub. Telecoms. Inc., 1989—; chmn. bd. Mo. Coun. on Econ. Edn.; bd. regents Mo. State Univs.; trustee Pub. Sch. Retirement, William Jewell Coll., 1972-74; chmn. com. bds. So. Bapt. Conv., 1972-73, mem. com. or bds., 1981—; mem.exec. bd. Mo. Bapt. Conv., 1972-75, 77-80, 2d v.p., 1995-96, pres., 1996-97; trustee Southwestern Bapt. Theol. Sem., Fort Worth, 1995—; mem. adv. com. Young Audiences, Inc., 1986, ARC Bd., Greene County, 1986, Children's Svcs. Commn., chmn., 1986—, Edn. Commn. U.S.; bd. dirs. Ozark Pub. TV; chmn. bd. advisors Windemere Bapt. Assembly, 1992—, chmn. bd. trustees, 2000—; chmn. Mo. Coun. for Econ. Edn., 2000—. With U.S. Army, 1954-56. Recipient Disting. Service award Mo. Jr. C. of C., 1966; Disting. Service award U. Mo., 1976; Faculty/Alumni award U. Mo., 1976; Silver Beaver award Boy Scouts Am., 1983, Good Shepherd and Cross, 1986, Disting. Citizen award, 1986; hon. life mem. Mo. Congress Parents and Tchrs.; named Springfield's Outstanding Young Man of Yr., 1965; Champion of Excellence PUSH, 1978 Mem. Am. Assn. State Colls. and Univs., N. Central Assn. Colls. and Secondary Schs., Council Chief State Sch. Officers, Mo. Assn. Sch. Adminstrs., NEA, Mo. Tchrs. Assn. So. Baptist (deacon). Clubs: Masons (33 deg.), Rotary. Business E-Mail: arthurmallory@missouristate.edu.

MALLORY, FRANK LINUS, lawyer; b. Calgary, Alta., Can., May 5, 1920; s. Frank Louis and Anna Amy (Allstrum) M.; m. Jean Ellen (Lindsey), Jan. 29, 1944; children: Susan Mallory Remund, Ann M. Kenney, Bruce R. AB, Stanford U., 1941, LLB, 1947. Bar: Calif., 1948. Assoc. Gibson, Dunn, and Crutcher, LA, 1947-54; ptnr. L.A. and Orange County, 1955-88. Cert. specialist taxation law Calif. Bd. Legal Splty., 1973-89. Pres. town hall of L.A., 1970; Boys Republic, Chino, Calif., 1962-64; pres. Braille Inst. Am., L.A., 1988-92; Lt.(j.g.), USNR, 1942-46. Mem. ABA, Los Angeles County Bar Assn., Orange County Bar Assn., Newport Harbor Yacht Club, Big Canyon Country Club, Transpacific Yacht Club (staff commodore), Order of Coif, Phi Beta Kappa. Republican. Home: 25382 Sea Bluffs Dr 205 Dana Point CA 92629

MALLORY, GEORGE B., pulmonologist, educator; b. Greenwich, Conn., Mar. 11, 1948; s. George Barron Mallory and Eleanor Davis Spilman, Claude Spilman (Stepfather) and Margaret Mallory (Stepmother); m. Deborah Ann Mallory, Sept. 26, 2004; children: Elizabeth Bayliss Kenemore, Meredith Roedell. BA, Harvard Coll., Cambridge, Mass., 1970; MD, Albert Einstein Coll. Medicine, Bronx, NY, 1970. Cert. Am. Bd. Pediat., 1980, pulmonologist Am. Bd. Pediat., 1986. Pediat. resident Children's Hosp. Pitts., 1974—78, pulmonology fellow, 1981—83, asst. prof. pediat., 1983—84, Ark. Children's Hosp., Little Rock, 1984—90, St. Louis Children's Hosp., 1990—99, assoc. prof. pediat., 1990—99; dir., heart and lung transplantation Gt. Ormond St. Hosp. Children, London, 2000—01; assoc. prof. pediat. Tex. Children's Hosp., Houston, 2001—, prof. pediat., 2001—. Recipient Regional Champion award, Nat. Organd Donation and Transplantation Cmty., 2008; named Outstanding Clin. Tchr., St. Louis Children's Hosp., 1992. Mem.: Am. Soc. Transplantation, Internat. Soc. Heart and Lung Transplantation, Am. Coll. Chest Physicians (chair, sect. pediat. cardiopulmonary disease 1996—98), Am. Thoracic Soc., Christian Med. and Dental Assn., Alpha Omega Alpha. Avocations: bicycling, reading, politics. Home: 6506 Pickens St Houston TX 77007 Office: Tex Children's Hosp 6621 Fannin St CC 104000 Houston TX 77030 Business E-Mail: gbmallor@texaschildrens.org.

MALLORY, KATHLEEN NORRIS BROWN, literature and language professor; b. Carlisle, Ark., Apr. 4, 1934; m. Floyd Elves Mallory, Dec. 24, 1985; children: Robin Eugenia Jordan-Story, Thomasa Renee Jordan-Brunson. PhD, U. Nebr., Lincoln, 1983. Assoc. prof. English Southern Ark. U., Magnolia, 1974—2009, prof. English, 1974—. Named Kathleen Mallory Disting. Spkr., Southern Ark. U., English Dept., 2004—09. Mem.: Delta Sigma Theta Sorority, Inc. (pres. 1976—78, named Delta of Yr.). Home: 707 W University Magnolia AR

71753 Office: Southern Ark Univ 101 University Magnolia AR 71753 Home Phone: 870-234-6971; Office Phone: 870-235-4000. Personal E-mail: kathleen.mallory@sbcgloal.net. Business E-Mail: knmallory@saumag.edu.

MALLORY, KRISTIN L., community college administrator; BS, West Liberty State Coll., W.Va., 1985; Med, Salisbury U., Md., 1991; EdD, Marshall U., Charleston, W.Va., 2006. Registered dental hygienist W.Va., 1998. Chair, dept. dental hygiene CTC W.Va. U. Tech., Montgomery, 2003—06, v.p. academic affairs, 2006—. Cons. evaluator Higher Learning Commn., NCA, Chgo., 2006—. Recipient Outstanding Contbn. to CC Edn., W.Va. CC Assn., 2008. Mem.: Am. Dental Hygienists Assn.

MALLORY, MARK L., Mayor, Cincinnati, former state legislator; b. Cin., Apr. 2, 1962; s. William L. Mallory. Student, Xavier U.; BS in Adminstrv. Mgmt., U. Cin. Dept. mgr. Hamilton County Pub. Libr. Graphic Prodn., Cin., 1981—95; rep. dist. 31 Ohio Ho. Reps., Columbus, 1995—98; mem. Dist. 9 Ohio State Senate, Columbus, 1998—2005, asst. minority whip, 2000—03, asst. minority leader, 2003—05; mayor City of Cin., Ohio, 2005—. Bd. trustees Friar's Club; advisory coun. 4C for Children; advisory bd. Ronald McDonald House of Cin.; former chmn. Correctional Inst. Inspection Com. Bd. trustees Cin. Art Mus. Assn., 2007—08. Recipient Devel. Leadership award, Bowhay Inst. for Legis. Leadership, 1996, Myrl Shoemaker Legis. of the Year award, 1998, Excellence in Correctional Edn. award, Correctional Edn. Assn., 1999, Pub. Svc. award, Gothic Lodge 122, 2000, Legis. of the Year award, Nat. Assn. Social Workers, 2001, Wolfe award of Excellence, OH Assn. Elected Officials, 2002, Pub. Svc. award, Nat. Assn. Grad. & Profl. Students, 2003, Passport to Excellence award, Phi Delta Kappa, 2003, Andrew Carnegie award, OH Library Coun., 2003, Legis. of the Year award, OH Community Corrections Assn., 2004. Mem. NAACP, Libr. Staff Assn., Black Male Coalition, Friends of Pub. Libr., Urban League of Cin., Pub. Libr. Staff Assn., Internat. TV Assn., Mayors Against Illegal Guns Coalition Democrat. Achievements include being the first African American directly elected by the people of Cincinnati, 2005. Office: Office of Mayor 801 Plum St Rm 150 Cincinnati OH 45202-1979 Office Phone: 513-352-3250. Office Fax: 513-352-5201. Business E-Mail: mark.mallory@cincinnati-oh.gov.*

MALLORY, MICHAEL, art educator; b. Buffalo, Nov. 1, 1936; s. Thomas Deharte Mallory and Mary Downs; m. Rona Lynn Roisman; children: Juliet Catherine Rosenbaum, Alerxander Bradford. BA, Yale U., New Haven, 1959; MA, Columbia U., NYC, 1963, PhD, 1965. Prof. and chmn. art dept. Bklyn Coll. CUNY, NYC, 1965—. Office: Art Dept Bklyn Coll 2900 Bedford Ave Brooklyn NY 11210 Office Fax: 718-951-4728. Business E-Mail: mmallory@brooklyn.cuny.edu.

MALLORY, PATRICIA JODY, museum curator; b. De Ridder, La., Sept. 22, 1951; d. William Buford and Gwendolyn (singletary) M. BBA, La. State U., 1979. Mgr. Harpers Records, De Ridder, 1979-83; dir. pub. rels. Goldband Records, Lake Charles, La., 1983-89; mgr. Bargain Time, Baton Rouge, 1989-91, Hills Music, De Ridder, 1991-96; sales and mktg. exec. Krok Radio, De Ridder, 1996-97; mus. curator Beauregard Parish, De Ridder, 1997—. Leader blues band Blues Horizon. Drummer Goldband Studios, 1971-83, Lake Charles; drummer recs. include Blessed Rain (Blue Rain), 1987, Drenched (Blue Rain), 1989, Saturday Nights and Sunday Mornings (OFB), 1987. Active Beauregard Econ. Devel., De Ridder; mem. main street promotions com.; mem. bd. dirs. Downtown Mchts. Assn., Beauregard Assn. Retarded Citizens. Named one of Best Unsigned Drummers, Promark, 1995. Mem. Percussive Arts Soc., Daus. of Confederacy, Humane Soc., People for Ethical Treatment Animals, Nat. Geog. Soc., World Wildlife Fund, Beauregard Woman's Orgn. Avocations: music, travel. Home: 501 S Stewart St Deridder LA 70634-4955 E-mail: museum@beau.org.

MALLORY, ROBERT MARK, controller, retired finance company executive; b. Mattoon, Ill., Apr. 15, 1950; s. Robert Monroe and Betty Ann (Mudd) M.; m. Diana Marie Burde, Aug. 19, 1972; 1 child, Laura Elizabeth. BS in Accountancy, U. Ill., 1972; MBA, Northwestern U., 1985. CPA Ill. Staff acct. Price Waterhouse, Chgo., 1972-74, sr. acct., 1974-77, mgr., 1977-79; dir. internal audit Mark Controls Corp., Skokie, Ill., 1979-81, corp. contr., 1981-86, v.p., contr., 1986-88; contr., dir. planning Tribune Co., Chgo., 1988-91, v.p., contr., 1991—2008. Mem. AICPA (Elijah Watts Sells award 1972), Ill. CPA Soc., Fin. Execs. Internat., Beta Gamma Sigma. Methodist. Home: 3312 Lakewood Ct Glenview IL 60026-2505 Home Phone: 847-998-1467. Personal E-mail: mallory435@aol.com.

MALLORY, TIM, librarian; b. Berkeley, Calif., Apr. 4, 1949; s. James Irving and Margaret Peggy Mallory; m. Tita Lillegraven, Sept. 21, 1975; children: Megan Mallory Valentine, Sean Michael, Linsey Kindel. BA, Ft. Lewis Coll., Durango, Colo., 1978; MLIS, U. Calif., Berkeley, 1990. Cert. profl. life libr. Wash. State Libr. Commn., 1992. Materials testing technician Anamet Testing Labs, Port Costa Clay Products, Berkeley, 1968—70; film libr. technician Modern Talking Pictures, San Francisco, 1970—72; dir., project respond Youth Ednl. Svcs., Humboldt State U., Arcata, Calif., 1972—75; film libr. San Juan BOCS, Ft. Lewis Coll., Durango, Colo., 1976—78; non-profit coord., mgr., exec. dir. various agys., Redding, Calif., 1978—86; libr. literacy program dir. Shasta and Tehama County Librs., Redding, Calif., 1986—89, Red Bluff, 1986—89; libr. Shasta County Libr., Redding, 1990—92; libr., mgr., reference and adult svcs. coord. Timberland Regional Libr., Wash., 1992—. Dir. People of Progress, Redding, 1983—87; literacy program cons. Calif. State Libr., Peoples Computer Co., Berkeley, 1988—92. Trustee Buckeye Sch. Dist., Redding, 1986—91; pres. Self Help Home Improvement Project, Redding, 1980—89. Mem.: ALA, Wash. Libr. Assn. (interest group and strategic planning coord. 2003—07, v.p., pres. elect 2007—), Pacific NW Libr. Assn., Nature Conservancy. Avocation: philosophy. Office: Timberland Regional Libr 415 Tumwater Blvd Tumwater WA 98501 Office Fax: 360-586-6338. Personal E-mail: tim@tmallory.net. Business E-Mail: tmallory@trlib.org.

MALLORY, TROY L., accountant; b. Sesser, Ill., July 30, 1923; s. Theodore E. and Alice (Mitchell) M.; m. Magdalene Richter, Jan. 26, 1963. Student, So. Ill. U., 1941-43, Washington and Jefferson Coll., 1943-44; BS, U. Ill., 1947, MS, 1948. Staff sr. supr. Scovell, Wellington & Co., CPAs, Chgo., 1948-58; mgr. Gray Hunter Stenn CPAs, Quincy, Ill., 1959-62, ptnr., 1962-99. Mem. fin. com. United Fund, Adams County, 1961-64; bd. dirs. Woodland Home for Orphans and Friendless, 1970—2005, pres., 1981-84, 87-90. Served with 84th Inf. Divsn. AUS, 1942-45. Decorated Purple Heart, Bronze Star. Mem. AICPA, Ill. CPA Soc., Quincy C. of C. (bd. dirs. 1970-76), Rotary (bd. dirs. Quincy 1967-70, pres. 1978-79), Shriners (bd. dirs. Quincy 1982-85, pres. 1988), Royal Order Jesters (Ct. 20 dir. 1997), Railsplitters Soc. (pres. 1993). Home: 2229 Jersey St Quincy IL 62301-4341

MALLOW, MATTHEW J., lawyer; b. Bklyn., 1943; AB, Brown U., 1964; JD, NYU, 1967, LLM, 1968. Bar: NY 1967. Ptnr. corp. fin. Skadden, Arps, Slate, Meagher & Flom LLP, NYC. Guest lectr. Harvard Bus. Sch. Bd. trustee Brown U., 1990—96, 1997—, treas., 1999—; represented Bard Coll. in the creation of the Bard HS Early Coll., 2001; rep. of the city council pres. to the bd. trustees Metropolitan Mus. Art, 1978—85. Mem.: Assn. Bar City NY (exec. com. 1971—75, vice-chmn., grievance com. 1976—77, chmn. securities regulation com. 2003—06). Office: Skadden Arps Slate Meagher & Flom LLP 4 Times Sq New York NY 10036 Office Phone: 212-735-3930. Office Fax: 917-777-3930. Business E-Mail: mmallow@skadden.com.

MALLOY, DANNEL PATRICK, Mayor, Stamford, Connecticut; m. Cathy Malloy; children: Dan, Ben, Sam. LLB, Boston Coll. Bar: Conn., Mass., N.Y., U.S. Dist. Ct. Conn., U.S. Dist. Ct. (ea. and so. dists.) N.Y. Asst. dist. atty. Bklyn., N.Y. Dist. Atty.'s Office, 1980-84; ptnr. Abate & Fox, Stamford, Conn., 1984-95; mayor City of Stamford, 1995—. Mem. bd. fin. City of Stamford, 1983-94, Stamford Bd. Edn., 1994-95; spl. master Conn. Superior Ct.; lectr. Family Law Tng. Seminar. Past bd. dirs. Teen Life Ctr., Liberation Programs, Inc., CTE; treas. Conn. Conf. Municipalities, 1997-98, v.p.; vice chair mayors and pub. schs. task force U.S. Conf. Mayors; mem. fair policy steering com. Nat. League of Cities, 1997-98, mem. task force on youth and edn; chmn. Dem. Mcpl. Ofcls. Orgn.; mem. Dem. Nat. Com., mem. exec. com.; mem. adv. bd. U.S. Conf. Mayors. Mem. ABA, ATLA, Nat. Trial Lawyers Assn., Conn. Bar Assn., Conn. Trial Lawyers Assn. Democrat. Office: 10th Fl Govt Center 888 Washington Blvd Stamford CT 06902

MALLOY, EDWARD ALOYSIUS, academic administrator; b. Washington, May 3, 1941; s. Edward Aloysius and Elizabeth (Clark) Malloy. BA, U. Notre Dame, 1963, MA, 1967, ThM, 1969; PhD, Vanderbilt U., 1975. Ordained to ministry Cath. Ch., 1970. Instr. U. Notre Dame, South Bend, Ind., 1974—75, asst. prof., 1975—81, assoc. prof., 1981—88, prof. theology, 1988—, assoc. provost, 1982—86, pres. elect, 1986, pres., 1987—2005, pres. emeritus, 2005—. Established chair Cath. Studes in name of Edward A. Malloy Vanderbilt U., 1997; editl. adv. bd. The Presidency mag.; bd. dir. Nat. Com. on Higher Edn. and Health of Youth; co-chmn. Nat. Inst. on Alcohol Abuse and Alcoholism; chmn. Nat. Commn. on Substance Abuse and Sports; regent U. Portland, 1985—; bd. govs., trustee Notre Dame, Australia, 1990—. Author: Culture & Commitment: The Challenge of Today's University, 1992, Notre Dame: The Unfolding Vision, 1994, Monk's Reflection: A View from the Dome, 1999, Monk's Travels People, Places & Events, 2004, Monk's Notre Dame, 2005; co-author: Colleges and Universities as Citizens, 1999. Chmn. Am. Coun. Edn.; mem. Pres. Adv. Coun. on Drugs, 1989—; adv. bd. AmeriCorps and Nat. Civilian Cmty. Corps, 1994—97; interim chmn. Ind. Commn. Cmty. Svc., 1994—97; active Boys and Girls Clubs Am., 1997—; trustee U. St. Thomas, 1997—, Vanderbilt U., 1999; bd. advisors Bernadin Ctr., 1997—2005; founding dir., bd. dir. Points of Light Found.; past chmn. Campus Impact; bd. regents U. Portland, 1985; bd. govs. Notre Dame Australia, 1990; mem. Bishopps and pres. com. Assn. Cath. Colls. and Univs., 1988—2005; bd. dirs. Internat. Fedn. Cath. Univs., 1988—2005, NCAA Found., 1989—. Mem.: Nat. Assn. Ind. Colls. and Univs. (bd. dirs. 1997), The Conf. Bd., Assn. Governing Bds. of Univs. and Colls. (vice chair 1996—2004), Bus.-Higher Edn. Forum, Am. Soc. Christian Ethics, Cath. Theol. Soc. Roman Catholic. Office: Univ Notre Dame Pres Emeritus Notre Dame IN 46556 Office Phone: 574-631-6755.

MALLOY, ELLEN ANN, athletic trainer; d. William Francis Thomas and Janet Day Malloy. BS in Health and Phys. Edn., Bridgewater State Coll., Mass., 1977; MEd in Sports Medicine and Athletic Tng., U. Va., Charlottesville, 1979. Cert. EMT Mass., 1981; health and phys. edn. tchr. Mass., 1977, lic. athletic trainer Mass., 1984, cert. instr. ARC, 2003, Am. Heart Assn., 2000. Head women's athletic trainer, head baseball athletic trainer Duke U., Durham, NC, 1979—81; head athletic trainer Regis Coll., Weston, Mass., 1981—83, Sports Innovation and Diagostic Ctr., Charlottesville, 1984—86, Noble and Greenough Sch., Dedham, Mass., 1988—2003, Thayer Acad., Braintree, Mass., 2003—. Dir. sports medicine Europa Cup Hockey, Wellesley, Mass., 2001—. Vol. Spl. Olympics, Charlottesville, 1978—79; vol. athletic trainer Bay State Games, Boston, 1981—2000, Boston Marathon, Boston, 1981—2004, Jimmy Fund Walk, Boston, 2000—06; participant Doug Flutie Walk for Autism, Natick, Mass., 2004; vol. Meals on Wheels, Cohasset, Mass., 2000—06. Recipient Robert J. Agostini award, Noble & Greenough Sch., 1990, 1997. Mem.: Ind. Sch. Athletic Trainer's Assn. (pres. 1990—97), Ea. Athletic Trainer's Assn., Nat. Athletic Trainer's Assn. (cert.), State of Mass. - Allied Health (licentiate), Cohasset Golf Club (Mother-Daughter Champion 1975—79), Cohasset Golf Club (Father-Daughter Champion 1975—79), Cohasset Golf Club (Lincoln Bowl Champion 1975), Cohasset Golf Club (Women's Club Champion 1990—92), Cohasset Golf Club (Mixed Scotch Club Champion 1984), Cohasset Sailing Club (Lincoln Bowl Champion 1985, Father-Daughter Champion 1988—92, Mother-Daughter Champaion 1988—92, Mixed Scotch Club Champion 1989), Hatherly Country Club (Women's Tennis Club Champion 1969), South Shore Women's Golf League (Mother-Daughter Champion 1988), U. of Va. Alumni Assn. (life). Independent. Roman Catholic. Avocations: golf, tennis, hockey, sailing, sewing. Office: Thayer Acad 745 Washington St Braintree MA 02184 Office Fax: 781-848-1027. Business E-Mail: emalloy@thayer.org.

MALLOY, JOHN RICHARD, lawyer, chemicals executive; b. Boston, Nov. 26, 1932; s. Thomas Francis and Mary (Field) M.; m. Maraleta Ellerson, May 24, 1960; children: Maureen, John, Megan, Elizabeth. BA, St. John's Sem., Brighton, Mass., 1954; LLB, Boston Coll., 1957. Bar: Mass. 1957. With chief counsel's office IRS, 1961—64; atty. advisor Tax Ct. of U.S., 1964—65; legal dept. Du Pont, 1965—73, asst. comptroller taxes, 1973—75; v.p., dir. fin. Remington Arms Co., Inc., Bridgeport, Conn., 1975-78; chief counsel, energy and raw materials E. I. du Pont de Nemours and Co., Wilmington, Del., 1978-79, asst. gen. counsel legal, 1979-83, dir. pub. affairs, 1983-85, v.p. pub. affairs, 1983-85, sr. v.p. external affairs, 1985-92, sr. v.p., spl. counsel to chmn. bd., 1992-93; ret., 1993. Chmn. Jobs for Del. Grads, Wilmington, 1985-97, Del. Compensation Commn., 1988-96; trustee Med. Ctr. of Del., Christiana, 1985—, dir., 2004-2007, Del. Pension Fund, 1993-99; bd. dirs. Del. Cmty. Found., 1996-2000, Children's Beach House, 1993-2000; mem. Minner Commn., Del., 1993-96; chmn. Ursuline Acad., 1978-84, Del. Coun. on Transp., 1994-2001, Riverfront Devel. Corp., 2002—05; trustee Archmere Acad., 2001-05. With JAGC US Army, 1958—60. Mem. ABA, Fed. Bar Assn. Democrat. Roman Catholic. Avocations: tennis, golf, skiing.

MALLOY, KAOIME ELIN, costume designer, educator; b. Norfolk, Va. d. Barbara Ruth and Malcolm Adam Malloy; m. Patrick Alexander Turner. MFA, U. Iowa, Iowa City, 1990. Assoc. prof. costume design U. Wis., Green Bay, 2000—; adj. prof. design U. Iowa, 1997—2000. Mem.: IATSE, United Scenic Artists Local 829. Office: Univ of Wis Green Bay 2420 Nicolet Dr TH 331 Green Bay WI 54311-7001 Business E-Mail: malloyk@uwgb.edu.

MALLOY, MICHAEL HOWARD, pediatrician; b. Houston, Oct. 29, 1947; m. Carol Ann Schultz, Aug. 24, 1974; 1 child, Christopher Dillon. BS in Microbiology, Tex. A&M U., Coll. Sta., 1969; MD, U. Tex. Med. Br., Galveston, 1973; MS in Epidemiology, U. Tex. Sch. Pub. Health, Houston, 1986. Diplomate in neonatal-perinatal medicine Am. Bd. Pediat., 2005. Intern Norfolk Gen. Hosp., Va., 1973—74; pediatric resident U. Tex. Med. Br., 1974—76, asst. prof., 1980—85, prof., 1991—, neonatology fellow Houston, 1976—78; postdoc. fellow Columbia U., NYC, 1978—80; rsch. assoc. Nat. Ctr. Health Stats., Hyattsville, Md., 1985—87; rsch. med. officer Nat. Inst. Child Health and Human Devel., Rockville, Md., 1987—91. Office: Univ Tex Med Br 301 University Blvd Galveston TX 77555-0526 Business E-Mail: mmalloy@utmb.edu.

MALLOY, MICHAEL PATRICK, lawyer; b. Providence, July 18, 1959; s. Judge Edward Francis and Patricia Marie Malloy; m. Jamie Marie Azzara, Aug. 20, 1983. BA summa cum laude, Boston Coll., 1981, JD cum laude, 1984. Bar: Pa. 1984. Assoc. Drinker Biddle & Reath LLP, Phila., 1984-93, ptnr., 1993—, ptnr., head investment mgmt. group. Mem. ABA, Phila. Bar Assn. (past co-chair investment com.). Avocation: tennis and paddle tennis. Office: Drinker Biddle & Reath LLP One Logan Square 18th & Cherry Sts Philadelphia PA 19103-6996 Office Phone: 215-988-2978. Office Fax: 215-988-2757. Business E-Mail: michael.malloy@dbr.com.

MALLOY, MICHAEL TERRENCE, journalist, reporter; b. Chgo., Feb. 26, 1936; s. Medard Valentine and Lucille (Zehrol)M.; m. Ruth Gwendolyn Lor, June 5, 1965; children: Linda Jo, Terrence. Student, Reed Coll., 1953-54, Columbia U., 1966-67; BA, U. Toronto, 2001. Police reporter City News Bur. Chgo., 1956-58; reporter, then bur. chief and chief corr. S.E. Asia UPI, Japan, Laos, India, Vietnam and Thailand, 1960-66; reporter Nat. Observer, Washington, 1968-76, mng. editor, 1976-77; reporter Asian Wall St. Jour., Manila, 1977-80, mng. editor, Hong Kong, 1980-84; mng. editor Dow Jones Can., Toronto, Ont., 1984-94; chief corr. Dow Jones India Report, 1995-97. Author: Racing Today, 1967, The Art of Retirement, 1967. With U.S. Army, 1958-60. E-mail: mikemalloy@idirect.ca.

MALLOY, TOM, computer company executive; BS, Stanford U., Calif.; MS, Stanford U. Lead engr. Xerox Palo Alto Rsch. Ctr.; software developer Apple Computer; sr. engring. positions through head advanced tech. group Adobe Systems, 1986—, sr. v.p. & chief software architect, Advanced Tech. Labs. Bd. dir. Aklara. Mem.: Assn. Computing Machinery, IEEE. Office: Adobe Systems 345 Park Ave San Jose CA 95110

MALLUCHE, HARTMUT HORST, nephrologist, medical educator; b. Jan. 1, 1943; arrived in U.S., 1975, naturalized, 1985; s. Harald E. and Renate (Muenzberg) M.; children: Nadine, Danielle, Tiffany. Abitur, Albertus Magnus Coll., Koenigstein, Germany, 1963; postgrad., Phillips U., Marburg/Lahn, Fed. Republic Germany, 1963—65, U. Innsbruck, Austria, 1965—66, U. Vienna, 1966; MD, J.W. Goethe U., Frankfurt, Fed. Republic Germany, 1969. Diplomate German Bd. Internal Medicine. Intern County Hosp., Aichach, Germany, 1969—70; resident in internal medicine, fellow in nephrology Cen. Internal Medicine, Univ. Hosp., Frankfurt Am Main, Germany, 1970—75; asst. prof. medicine U. So. Calif., Calif., 1975—78, assoc. prof., 1978—81; prof., dir. divsn. nephrology, bone and mineral metabolism U. Ky. Med. Ctr., Lexington, 1981—. Cons. NIH, FDA; mem. Va. Merit Rev. Bd. Nephrology; program dir. Gen. Clin. Rsch. Ctr. Author: (monograph) Atlas of Mineralized Bone Histology, 1986; editor-in-chief Clinical Nephrology; contbr. articles to profl. jours. and books. Grantee, NIH, 1982—, Shriner's Hosp. for Crippled Children. Fellow: ACP; mem.: AAAS, Internat. Soc. Bone Morphometry (founder), Internat. Soc. Nephrology, Am. Fedn. Clin. Rsch., European Dialysis and Transplantation Assns., Am. Soc. Physiol. endocrinology, Am. Soc. Bone and Mineral Rsch., Am. Soc. Clin. Investigation, Am. Soc. Nephrology. Office Phone: 859-323-5049 221.

MALM, CARL ELMER, minister, educator; b. Omaha, Sept. 30, 1945; s. Clarence Franklin Malm and Opal Ferris; m. Becky Lu Ellis; children: Nathan Timothy, Cherise Noel Pilger. BA, U. Nebr., Omaha, 1967; MDiv, Lincoln Christian Sem., Ill., 1973. Cert. in ordination Christian Ch., 1973. Adj. lectr. U. Ala., Huntsville, 1985—; grief min. Ctr. Loss, Grief and Change, Huntsville, 1996—. With Huntsville Assn. Pastoral Care, Ariz., 1990. Home: 7725 Logan Dr Huntsville AL 35802 Office: Ctr Loss Grief and Change 8100 Whitesburg Dr Huntsville AL 35802 Personal E-mail: malmcarl@hotmail.com.

MALMGREN, HARALD BERNARD, economist; b. Boston, July 13, 1935; s. Berndt Birger and Magda Helena (Nilsson) M.; m. Patricia A. Malmgren, 1959 (div. 1975); children: Karen Philippa, Britt Patricia, Erika Nina; m. Linda V. Einberg, Oct. 3, 1987; children: Markus Harald, Liivia Linda, Viivianne Vaike. BA summa cum laude, Yale U., 1957; postgrad., Harvard U., 1959; PhD, Oxford U., 1961. Asst. prof. dept. engring. and econs. Cornell U., Ithaca, NY, 1961—62; head econ. group Inst. for Def. Analyses, Washington, 1962—64; asst. U.S. trade rep. Exec. Office Pres. The White House, Washington, 1964—69; sr. fellow Overseas Devel. Coun., 1969—71; amb., dep. U.S. trade rep., 1972—75; sr. fellow Woodrow Wilson Internat. Ctr. for Scholars, Washington, 1975—76; prof. George Washington U., Washington, 1976—77; pres. Malmgren, Inc., Washington, 1977—; mng. dir. Malmgren, Golt, Kingston, Ltd., London, 1979—99; chmn. Malmgren O'Donnell, London, 1998—2001, Cordell Hull Inst., Washington, 2001—. Adv. coun. Ctr. Strategic and Internat. Studies, Washington, 1987-97; adv. Senate Fin. Com., Washington, 1970-71, 75-76, Interaction Coun., 1985—. Author: International Economic Peace Keeping, 1972; co-author: Assisting Developing Countries, 1972; editor: Pacific Basin Development, 1972; bd. editors: The International Economy, 1987—, The Washington Quarterly, 1987-95, The World Economy, 1980-90; contbr. articles to profl. jours. Mem. Am. Econ. Assn., Met. Club, Reform Club. Home: Summerfield Farm 7620 Cannonball Gate Rd Warrenton VA 20186-7304 Office Phone: 202-466-8740. Business E-Mail: hm@malmgrenglobal.com.

MALMIN, CINDY LOU, music educator; b. Minocqua, Wis., Nov. 26, 1957; d. Elroy Vernon and Adeline I. Kriehn; children: Isaac V. Monson, Aaron A. Monson, Ruth L. Monson. Attended, U. Wis., River Falls, 1976—78. Cert. tchr. Am. Coll. Musicians, 2008. Mem. faculty The Studio Grand, Edina, Minn., 1987—93; music educator Monson Music Studio, Mpls., 1993—2002; mem. faculty MacPhail Ctr. for Music, Mpls., 2002—; dir. MacPhail Ctr. for Music, Suzuki Inst., 2006—. Mem.: Suzuki Assn. of Minn. (bd. mem. newsletter editor 2008—), Nat. Guild of Piano Tchrs. (Macphail ctr. auditions chairperson 2004—), Suzuki Assn. of Am. Avocations: reading, antiques. Office: 501 S 2nd St Minneapolis MN 55401 Business E-Mail: malmin.cindy@macphail.org.

MALMQUIST, CARL PHILLIP, psychiatrist; b. St. Paul, Mar. 10, 1934; s. Phillip C. and Lillian Viola (Kahler) M.; m. Arlyn Virginia Bodal (dec. 1984); children: Derek, Jay. BA summa cum laude, U. Minn., 1954, MD, 1958, MS in Philosophy of Sci., 1961. Diplomate Am. Bd. Psychiatry and Neurology, Am. Bd. Child Psychiatry, Am. Bd. Adult Psychiatry; cert. forensic psychiatry, added qualification in forensic psychiatry. Intern Columbia Med. Ctr., NYC, 1963—64, U. Minn.,

Mpls., 1962—63; assoc. prof. dept. psychiatry U. Mich., 1965—67; assoc. prof. Inst. Child Devel. U. Minn., 1967—70, prof., dir. child and adolescent psychiatry, 1971—72, prof. criminal justice, 1972—80, prof. social psychiatry, dept. sociology, 1980—. Cons. Hennepin County Dist. Ct., Mpls., 1967—; mem. commn. of mentally disabled ABA, 1985. Author: Handbook of Adolescence, 1980 (Guttmacher award 2007), Homicide: Psychiatric Perspectives, 1996, 2d edit., 2006; mem. editl. bd. Psychiat. Anns., 1981; contbr. articles to profl. jours. Fellow Am. Psychiat. Assn. (disting. sr.; commn. on jud. action 1994—), Am. Coll. Psychiatrists, Am. Orthopsychiat. Assn., Am. Acad. Child Psychiatry, Am. Acad. Psychiatry and Law (Segmour Pollock Disting. Achievement award 2004), Am. Coll. Forensic Psychiatry; mem. Group for Advancement Psychiatry, Am. Psychopathol. Assn. Episcopalian. Home: 5010 Bruce Ave Minneapolis MN 55424-1318 Home Phone: 952-926-6654; Office Phone: 612-624-4300. Business E-Mail: malmqu01@atlas.socsci.umn.edu, malmq001@umn.edu. E-mail: ma_mq001@umu.edu.

MALMSTAD, JOHN EARL, literature and language professor; b. Bismarck, ND, June 25, 1941; s. Manley Ellsworth and Joyce Evelyn (David) M. BA summa cum laude with distinction and departmental honors in Russian Lang. and Lit., Northwestern U., 1963; MA in Slavic Langs. and Lits., Princeton U., 1965, PhD in Slavic Langs. and Lits., 1969; AM (hon.), Harvard U., 1985. Instr. Columbia U., NYC, 1968-69, asst. prof. Russian Lit., 1969-73, assoc. prof., 1973-79, prof. dept. slavic langs. and lits., 1979-85; Samuel Hazzard Cross prof. Slavic langs. and lits. Harvard U., Cambridge, Mass., 1985—, assoc. dean, 1993-94. Vis. assoc. prof. Stanford U., 1971-72, U. Calif. Berkeley, 1977-78; vis. prof. Harvard U., fall 1982; cons., referee NEH translation awards; lectr. in field; attendee internat. symposia. Editor: (with others) The Poetry of Mikhail Kuzmin (3 vols.), 1977, The Poetry of Andrei Bely (3 vols.), 1982-85, Gibel Senatora, 1986, Vladislav Khodasevich Sobranie sochinenii, 1983, Andrei Bely, Spirit of Symbolism, 1987, Readings in Russian Modernism to Honor Vladimir Markov, 1993, Mikhail Kuzmin: Zhizn' Tvorchestvo, Epokha, 1996, Andrey Bely-Ivanov-Razumnik Perepiska, 1998, Mikhail Kuzmin: A Life in Art, 1999, K.N. Bugaeva Vospominaniia o Belom, 2001, Andrey Bely Stikhotvoeniia i poemy, 2 vol., 2006, Andrey Bely Perepiska s M.N. Moozovoi, 2006, Perepiska A.Belogo s A.Petrovskim, 2007, Mikhail Kuzmin, 2007; Russian book rev. editor Slavic Rev., 1975-86; assoc. editor Russian Rev., 1986-88; mem. editl. bd. Feniks, Opyty, Novoe Literaturnoe obozrenie, Experiment, Philologica, Diaspora; manuscript rev. profl. jours., univ. presses; contbr. articles to profl. jours. Woodrow Wilson fellow, 1963, NDFL fellow Columbia U., 1963-66, Princeton U., 1967-68, Fulbright-Hays fellow, 1966-67, spring 1981, spring 1987, Woodrow Wilson Dissertation fellow, 1966, ACLS rsch. fellow, 1972, Rsch. fellow Russian Inst. Columbia U., summer 1977, 79, 83, 84, IREX fellow, 1975, John Simon Guggenheim fellow, 1980-81; ACLS grant-in-aid, summer, 1980, IREX/ACLS grantee exch. Acad. Scis. USSR, fall 1981, spring 1987, 91, IREX travel grantee Moscow, 1992, Am. Coun. Internat. Edn. grantee, Moscow, 2003. Mem. MLA, Am. Assn. Advancement of Slavic Studies, Assn. Tchrs. of Slavic and East European Langs., Inst. d'Etudes Slaves (Paris), Phi Beta Kappa. Avocations: fine arts, ballet, reading. Home: 8A Cogswell Ave Cambridge MA 02140-2001 Office: Harvard U Dept Slavic Langs/Lit Barker Ctr, 12 Quincy St Cambridge MA 02138 E-mail: malmstad@fas.harvard.edu.

MALMSTADT, MARY JANE, music educator; b. Milw., Apr. 12, 1923; d. Daniel Monte and Angela Marie Monte-LaFata; m. Robert Guy, June 25, 1949 (dec. Mar. 1998); children: Keith Robert, Deborah Jean. BS in Music Edn., U. Wis., 1945; postgrad., U. Wis., Marinette and Madison, 1950—83. Music tchr. K-12 NeKoosa Pub. Schs., Wis., 1945—46; music tchr. 9-12 Marinette HS, Wis., 1946—51; pvt. piano tchr. Marinette, 1955—; music tchr. K-6 Elem. Schs., Marinette, 1965—2006; organist, pianist Pioneer Presbyn. Ch., Marinette, 1965—2008. Bd. dirs. Tri-City Cmty. Concerts, Wis. Mem.: Golden Soc. of Alumni/U. Wis. Milw., Gen. Fedn. of Women's Club (pres. 1988). Presbyterian. Avocation: oil painting, gardening, reading, travel, floral arrangements. Home: 1303 Elizabeth Ave Marinette WI 54143

MALONE, ALICIA JANE, minister, theologian; b. Akron, Ohio, July 7, 1953; d. Clifford David Malone, Sr. and Veralene Malone; 1 child, Aaron D. MA, Ashland Theol. Sem., Ohio, 1996, MDiv, 2001, D in Ministry, 2005; postgrad., Moody Bible Inst., Stow, Ohio, 1982—90, McCleary Theol. Ctr., Cleve., 1991—94. Cert. clin. pastoral edn. Stenographer Babcock & Wilcox Co., Barberton, Ohio, 1971—75, Navy nuc. corr., 1976—80; chaplain intern Akron Gen. Hosp., Ohio, 1995—, chaplain assoc. Acad. tchr. Mt. Olive Bapt. Ch., Akron, 1982—2006; execd. dir. Bondage Breakers, Inc., Akron, 1991—2006; mentor, counselor Cmty. Health Ctr., Akron, 2005—. Author: What God Can't Do Just Can't Be Done, 1996, Bondage Breakers, Inc. A Model, 2005. Recipient Harold K. Stubbs Justice award for social adv., Leona Ferris Caring award for social adv., Womens History award, Akron City Coun. Mem.: Am. Bapt. Akron Assn. (exec. com. 1991—2006). Avocations: chess, gardening, martial arts. Home: 1365 Peckham St Akron OH 44320 Office: Bondage Breakers Inc 680 E Market St Ste 305 Akron OH 44304

MALONE, BARBARA, councilwoman; BM, U. Cin.; JD, Ind. U. Sch. Law. Bar: Ind. Ptnr. Gonzalez, Saggio & Harlan LLP, Indpls.; councillor at-large Indpls.-Marion County City-County Coun., 2008—. Consumer rep. Ind. Med. Licensing Bd.; hearing officer Ind. Supreme Ct. Mem.: Marion County Bar Assn., Ind. Bar Assn., Nat. Bar Assn. Republican. Office: 6953 Bretton Wood Dr Indianapolis IN 46260 also: Indpls Marion County City County Coun 241 City County Bldg 200 E Washington St Indianapolis IN 46204 Office Phone: 317-291-4359, 317-327-4242. Business E-Mail: barbara_malone@sbcglobal.net.*

MALONE, CHRISTOPHER JOHN, statistician, educator; b. Spring Valley, Minn., July 19, 1971; s. Gregory John and Rita Maire Malone; m. Michelle Jean Heyer; children: Abbylyn Rose, Ellyson Louise, Emmalee Jean, Julianna Maire. BS in Math. & Stats., Winona State U., Minn., 1994; MS in Stats., Kans. State U., Manhattan, 1994, PhD in Stats., 2002. Asst. prof. Winona State U., 2002—09, assoc. prof., 2009—, dir., Statis. Consulting Ctr., 2009—. Mem.: Am. Statis. Assn. Home: 107 S Maple St Rushford MN 55971 Office: Winona State Univ PO Box 5838 Winona MN 55987 Business E-Mail: cmalone@winona.edu.

MALONE, CLAUDINE BERKELEY, financial and management consultant; b. Louisville, May 9, 1936; d. Claude McDowell and Mary Katharine (Smith) M.; BA, Wellesley Coll., 1963; MBA, Harvard U., 1972. CPA, Md. Systems engr. IBM Corp., Washington, 1964; sr. systems analyst Crane Co., Chgo., 1966; contr., mgr. data processing Raleigh Stores, Washington, 1967-70; asst. prof. Harvard U., 1972-76, assoc. prof., 1977-81; pres., CEO, Fin. & Mgmt. Consulting Inc., McLean, Va., 1981-; vis. prof., Georgetown U., 1982-84, U. Va., 1984-87; dir. Scott Paper Co., Houghton Mifflin Co., Campbell Soup Co., Boston Co., Dart Group Inc., Hasbro Inc., 1994-, Novell Inc., 2003-, Apollo Investment Corp., 2007-; trustee Penn Mut. Life Ins. Co. Chmn. Bus. for Reagan-Bush Com. Mass., 1980; trustee Wellesley Coll., 1982-. Recipient Candace award, 1982. Mem. Assn. Women CPA's, UN Assn., Wellesley Coll. Alumnae Assn., Washington Wellesley Club. Episcopalian.

MALONE, DAVID MICHAEL, diplomat, educator; b. Ottawa, Canada, Feb. 7, 1954; s. Paul Thomas Malone and Deirdre Lavalette Ingram. BA, U. Montreal, 1972; MPA, Harvard U., Cambridge, Mass., 1980; DPhil, Oxford U., Eng., 1997. Various positions in Can. fgn. ministry and at Can. diplomatic missions in Cairo, Amman and Kuwait Govt. of Can., 1975—90; Can. rep. UN/ECOSOC, NY and Geneva, 1990—92; amb., dep. permanent rep. Can. Permanent Mission to the UN, NYC, 1992—94; dir. gen., policy, internat. orgn. and global issues bureaus Can. Ministry of Fgn. Affairs and Internat. Trade, Ottawa, Canada, 1994—98; pres. Internat. Peace Acad., NYC, 1998—2004; asst. dep. min. global issues Fgn. Affairs Can., 2004—06; high commr. for Can. to India and amb. of Can. to Bhutan and Nepal, 2006—08; pres. Internat. Devel. Rsch. Ctr., Canada, 2008—. Adj. prof. law NYU Sch. Law, 1999—2004; adj. prof. internat. rels. Institut des Etudes Politiques (Sciences Po), Paris, 2001—04. Author: The UN Security Council from the Cold War to the Twenty First Century; contbr. articles to profl. jour. Address: C/O 1DRC 150 Kent St Ottawa ON KIG3H9 Canada Office Phone: 613-696-2599. Business E-Mail: dmalone@idrc.ca.

MALONE, DAVID ROY, public fund consultant retired educational association administrator, director; b. Beebe, Ark., Nov. 4, 1943; s. James Roy and Ila Mae (Griffin) M.; m. Judith Kaye Huff, June 20, 1965 (div. Feb. 1990); m. Deborah W. Thomas, Jan. 23, 2004; 1 child, Michael David. BSBA, U. Ark., 1965, JD, 1969, MBA, 1982. Bar: Ark. 1969, US Dist. Ct. (we. dist.) Ark. 1969, US Tax Ct. 1972, US Ct. Appeals (8th cir.) 1972, US Supreme Ct. 1972. Pvt. practice, Fayetteville, Ark., 1969-72; atty. City of Fayetteville, 1969-72; asst. prof. bus. U. Ark., Fayetteville, 1972-76, asst. dean law, 1976-91; mem. Ark. Ho. of Reps., 1980-84, Ark. Senate, 1984—2002; exec. dir. U. Ark. Found., 1991—2002, Ark. Tchr. Ret. Sys., 2003—06; ret., 2006; pub. fund cons. Beenstain Litounts Benyard Gross Ann LLP, NY. Chair Senate edn. com., 1997-2002, co-chair legis. coun., 1999-2000; bd. dirs. Bank of Elkins, 1976-98, S.W. Edn. Devel. Lab., Austin, Tex., 1988-94; legal adv. coun. So. Regional Edn. Bd., Atlanta, 1991-2002. Contbr. articles to profl. jours.; bd. dirs. Ark. Law Rev., 1978-92; contbg. author U. Ark. Press, 1989. Mayor City of Fayetteville, 1979-80; mem. Jud. Article Task Force, Little Rock, 1989-91; chair Motor Voter task force, 1994-95; bd. dirs. Music Festival Ark., 1989-91, Washington County Hist. Soc., 1993-96, 2008-09; bd. dirs. Walton Arts Ctr. Found., 1994-2000, chmn., 1994-98; chmn. bd. dirs. Washington County Law Libr., 1970-84; chmn. Ark. Tuition Trust Authority, 1997-99. Recipient Svc. award, Ark. Mcpl. League, 1980, Disting. Svc. award, U. Ark., 1988, Lucas Svc. award, Ark. Alumni Assn., 1998, award, Walton Coll. Bus., U. Ark., 2004. Mem. Ark. Bar Assn. (ho. of dels. 1977-81, award of merit 1980, exec. 1981-82, Outstanding Lawyer-Citizen award 1990), Washington County Bar Assn., Ark. Inst. Continuing Legal Edn. (bd. dirs. 1979-88), Fayetteville C. of C. (bd. dirs. 1984-89), Ark. Genealogy Soc. (bd. dirs. 1990-92). Democrat. Methodist. Avocations: genealogy, stamp collecting/philately. Home: 3411 Sassafras Hill Rd Fayetteville AR 72703 Mailing: PO Box 1366 Fayetteville AR 72702-1366 Personal E-mail: davidr_malone@yahoo.com.

MALONE, DOROTHY, actress; b. Chgo., Jan. 30, 1925; Actress: (feature films) Falcon and the Co-Eds, 1943, One Mysterious Night, 1944, Show Business, 1944, Hollywood Canteen, 1945, The Big Sleep, 1946, Night and Day, 1946, To the Victor, 1948, Two Guys from Texas, 1948, One Sunday Afternoon, 1949, Colorado Territory, 1949, South of St. Louis, 1949, The Nevadan, 1950, Mrs. O'Malley and Mr. Malone, 1950, Pushover, 1954, Private Hell 36, 1954, Young at Heart, 1955, Battle Cry, 1955, Five Guns West, 1955, Pillars of the Sky, 1956, Tension at Table Rock, 1956, Written on the Wind, 1956 (Acad. award 1956), Man of a Thousand Faces, 1957, Tip on a Dead Jockey, 1957, The Tarnished Angels, 1958, Too Much, Too Soon, 1958, Warlock, 1959, The Last Voyage, 1959, The Last Sunset, 1961, Beach Party, 1963, Gli Insaziabili, 1969, Abduction, 1975, The November Plan, 1976, Golden Rendezvous, 1977, Winter Kills, 1979, (TV movies) The Pigeon, 1969, Murder in Peyton Place, 1977, Little Ladies of the Night, 1977, Katie: Portrait of a Centerfold, 1978, Condominium, 1980, He's Not Your Son, 1984, Peyton Place: The Next Generation, 1985, (TV series) Fireside Theater, 1954-55, Peyton Place, 1964-68, (TV mini-series) Rich Man, Poor Man, 1976, (TV episodes) Lux Video Theatre, 1954, The Bob Hope Show, The Untouchables, others. Mem. Screen Actors Guild, AFTRA.*

MALONE, JEAN HAMBIDGE, educational consultant; b. South Bend, Ind., Nov. 23, 1954; d. Craig Ellis and Dorothy Jane (Piechorowski) Hambidge; m. James Kevill Malone, July 8, 1978; children: Julia Mae, James Kevill III, John Thomas. BS in Edn., Butler U., 1976, MS in Edn., 1977. Tchr. Indpls. Pub. Schs., 1977-78; dir. student center and activities Butler U., Indpls., 1978-87. Trustee Eisenhower Meml. scholarship, 1977-80; bd. dirs. Heritage Place of Indpls., 1983-88, Ind. Office Campus Ministries, 1985-87, 89—91, Campfire of Cen. Ind., 1980-84, 86-87, Intercollegiate YMCA, Indpls., 1985-87, 89-90, Indpls. Jr. League, 1989—, Indpls. Urban Parish Coop, 1987-90, v.p., pres., 1991, 92; bd. dirs. Gennesaret Free Clinic of Indy, 1992-94; mem. overseers coun. Camp Delafield Children with Dyslexia, 1993-95, bd. pres., 1997-2000; bd. dirs. Dyslexia Inst. Ind., 1996—, bd. pres., 1997-2000; mem. Commn. Youth Archdiocec, 2000-01; community adv. for the homeless of Indpls. Recipient Outstanding Faculty award, Butler U., 1980. Mem. Ind. Assn. Women Deans (v.p. bd. dirs. 1987-88), Adminstrs. and Counselors (bd. dirs. 1982-83), Internat. Dyslexia Assn. (mem. Ind. br. 1992—), Kappa Delta Pi, Phi Kappa Phi, Alpha Lambda Delta, Kappa Kappa Gamma. Roman Catholic. Office: 5256 N Illinois St Indianapolis IN 46208-2636 Personal E-mail: jhmalone2@aol.com.

MALONE, JOHN C., media company executive; b. Milford, Conn., Mar. 7, 1941; m. Leslie Malone; 2 children BS in Elec. Engring. and Econ., Yale U., 1963; MS in Indsl. Mgmt., John Hopkins U., 1964, PhD in Ops. Rsch., 1967; LHD (hon.), Denver U., 1992. With econ. planning rsch. and devel. Bell Telephone Labs/AT&T, 1963—68; joined McKinsey & Co., 1968; group v.p. Gen. Instrument Corp., 1970—73; formerly pres. Jerrold Electronics Corp. (subs. Gen. Instrument Corp.); pres., CEO Tele-Comms., Inc., Denver, 1973—96; chmn., CEO Tele-Comms., Inc. (merged with AT&T Corp.), Denver, 1996-99; chmn. Liberty Satellite, 1996—2000, Liberty Media Corp., Denver, 1990—, CEO, 2005—06. Bd. dirs. IAC/InterActiveCorp., 2001—04, Bank of New York, 1986—, UnitedGlobalCom, Inc., Discovery Communications, CATO Inst., Cablevision Systems Corp.; bd dirs. Liberty Media Corp.; bd. dirs. The Nature Conservancy; bd. dirs., chmn. emeritus Cable Television Laboratories, Inc. Bd. dirs. Nature Conservancy, CATO Inst. Recipient Wall Street Transcript's Gold award for cable industry's best CEO, 1982, 1985, 1986, 1987, Wall Street Transcript Silver award, 1984, 1989, NCTA Vanguard award, 1983, Women In Cable Betsy Magness Fellowship Honoree, U. Pa. Wharton Sch. Sol C. Snider Entrepreneurial Ctr. Award of Merit for Disting. Entrepreneurship, Am. Jewish Com. Sherrill C. Corwin Human Rels. award, Comm. Tech. Mag. Svc. and Tech. award, Bronze award, Fin. World CEO of Yr. Competition, 1993, Hopkins Disting. Alumnus award, 1994; named Man of Yr. award, TVC Mag., 1981; named one of Forbes' Richest Americans, 2006. Mem.: Nat. Cable. TV Assn. (dir. 1974—77, treas. 1977—78, dir. 1980—93, Vanguard award 1983). Office: Liberty Media Corp 12300 Liberty Blvd Englewood CO 80112

MALONE, JOSEPH JAMES, mathematics professor, researcher; b. St. Louis, Sept. 9, 1932; s. Joseph James and Aurelia Theresa (Schomaker) M.; m. Dorothy Sue Cleary, Nov. 24, 1960; children: Michael, Barbara, Philip, Patrick. BS, St. Louis U., 1954, MS, 1958, PhD, 1962. Instr. math. Rockhurst Coll., Kansas City, Mo., 1960-62; asst. prof. U. Houston, 1962-67; assoc. prof. Tex. A&M U., College Station, 1967-70, prof., 1970-71, Worcester (Mass.) Poly. Inst., 1971-2000, prof. emeritus, 2000—, chmn. dept. math., 1971-78. Contbr. articles to profl. jours. Mem. pub. schs. bd. Town of Westborough (Mass.), 1974-83, 84-87, fin. com., 1992-98, 2001-07, selectman, 1998-2001. With U.S. Army, 1954-56. Mem. Am. Math. Soc., Math. Assn. Am. Democrat. Achievements include research in near-ring theory and group theory. Home: 45 Adams St Westborough MA 01581-3610 Office: Worcester Poly Inst 100 Institute Rd Worcester MA 01609-2280 E-mail: jjmalone@wpi.edu.

MALONE, KELLY SCOTT, theology studies educator; s. Frank and Barbara Malone; m. Molly Elizabeth Fuller, Dec. 31, 1988; children: Maggie, Kevin. BA, Baylor U., Waco, TX, 1985; MDiv, Southwestern Bapt. Theol. Sem., Ft. Worth, 1988; PhD, 1995. Ordination ministry First Bapt. Ch., Royse City, TX, 1987. Asst. prof. intercultural studies SW Bapt. U., Bolivar, Mo., 2007—; missionary Internat. Mission Bd., So. Bapt. Conv., Japan, 1992—2007. Academic dean Christian Leadership Tng. Ctr., Tokyo, 2003—07. Author: (book) Hearing Christ's Voice. Mem.: Evang. Theol. Soc., Evang. Missiological Soc., Am. Soc. Missiology. Office: Southwest Bapt Univ 1600 Univ Ave Bolivar MO 65613 Business E-Mail: kmalone@sbuniv.edu.

MALONE, MIKE, dentist; m. Alma Malone; 3 children. DDS, La. State U., 1976. Pvt. practice, Lafayette, La. Official cosmetic dentist Miss Louisiana USA and Miss Louisiana Teen USA pageants. Contbr. articles to profl. jours. Fellow: Acad. Gen. Dentistry; mem.: ADA, Am. Acad. Cosmetic Dentistry (bd. dirs. 1997—2003, pres. 2003—04, mem. Bd. of Examiners for Accreditation), Am. Equilibration Soc., Pankey Alumni Assn. Office: Mike Malone, DDS & Assoc 300 Doucet Rd Lafayette LA 70503 Office Phone: 337-989-1268. E-mail: info@mikemalonedds.com.

MALONE, RICHARD JOSEPH, bishop; b. Salem, Mass., Mar. 19, 1946; BA, BD, MTh, St. John Sem., Boston; ThD, Boston U., 1981; STL, Weston Jesuit Sch. Theology, Cambridge, 1990. Ordained priest Archdiocese of Boston, 1972; assoc. pastor St. Patrick Parish, Stoneham, Mass., 1972—74; faculty St. Clement HS, Somerville, 1974—76; chaplain, mem. faculty Xaverian HS, Westwood, 1976—79; tchr. religious & theological studies, registrar, academic dean St. John Sem. Coll., Boston, 1979—90; chaplain Harvard-Radcliffe Cath. Student Ctr., 1990—93; dir. office religious edn. Archdiocese of Boston, 1993—95, sec. edn., 1995—2000, aux. bishop, South region, 2000—04; ordained bishop, 2000; bishop Diocese of Portland, Maine, 2004—. Chaplain Wellesley Coll., Regis Coll., Weston, Mass.; tchr. Emmanuel Coll., Boston. Roman Catholic. Office: 510 Ocean Ave Portland ME 04104-7559 Office Phone: 207-773-6471. Office Fax: 207-773-0182.

MALONE, ROBERT K., lawyer; b. Bklyn., 1959; BA, Cath. Univ. Am., 1981; JD, Seton Hall Univ., 1984. Bar: NJ 1985. Staff to Hon. Bill Bradley US Senate, Wash., 1979—81; law clk. to Hon. William H. Gindin US Bankruptcy Ct. Dist. NJ, 1985—86; ptnr., vice chmn. corp. restructuring practice group Drinker Biddle & Reath LLP, Florham Pk., NJ. Office: Drinker Biddle & Reath LLP 500 Campus Dr Florham Park NJ 07932-1047 Office Phone: 973-549-7080. Office Fax: 973-360-9831. Business E-Mail: robert.malone@dbr.com.

MALONE, ROBERT ROY, artist, educator; b. McColl, SC, Aug. 8, 1933; s. Robert Roy and Anne (Matthews) M.; m. Cynthia Enid Taylor, Feb. 26, 1956; 1 child, Brendan Trevor. BA, U. N.C., 1955; MFA, U. Chgo., 1958; postgrad., U. Iowa, 1959. Instr. art Union U., Jackson, Tenn., 1959-60, Lambuth Coll., 1959-61; asst. prof. art Wesleyan Coll., Macon, Ga., 1961-67, assoc. prof., 1967-68, W.Va. U., 1968-70, So. Ill. U., Edwardsville, 1970-75, prof., 1975—2000, prof. emeritus, 2000—. One-man shows at Gallery Illien, Atlanta, 1969, De Cinque Gallery, Miami, 1968, 71, Ill. State Mus., Springfield, 1974, U. Del., Newark, 1978, Elliot Smith Gallery, St. Louis, 1985, Merida Galleries, Louisville, 1985, Yvonne Rapp Gallery, Louisville, 1990, 92-93, 96, 98, 2000, 04, St. John's Coll., Santa Fe, 1991, Uzelac Gallery, Pontiac, Mich., 1997, others; group shows include Bklyn. Mus., 1966, Assoc. Am. Artists Gallery, NYC, 1968, Mus. d'Art Modern, Paris, 1970, DeCordova Mus., 1973-74, St. Louis Art Mus., 1985, Wake Forest U., 1985, New Orleans Mus. Art, 1990, Dakota Internat., Vermillion, 1994, Springfield Art Mus., Mo., 2004; represented in permanent collections including Smithsonian Instn., Washington, USIA, Washington, Libr. of Congress, Calif. Palace of Legion of Honor, San Francisco, NY Pub. Libr., NYC, Victoria and Albert Mus., London, Chgo. Art Inst., Indpls. Mus. Art, Humana Inc., Louisville, State of Ill. Ctr., Chgo., Speed Mus., Louisville, N. Ill. U., Capital Devel. Bd., Ill.; co-editor: Contemporary American Printmakers, 1999 (English and Chinese edits.). Recipient numerous regional, nat. awards in competitive exhbns.; Ford fellow, 1977, So. Ill. U. at Edwardsville sr. research scholar, 1976, 1984. Home: 600 Chapman St Edwardsville IL 62025-1260 Home Phone: 618-656-8987.

MALONE, THOMAS CHARLETON, oceanography educator; b. Banana River, Fla., Sept. 7, 1943; s. Thomas Earl and CArolyn (Underhill) M.; m. Mary Lou Malone, Jan. 13, 1964; children: Kelly Katharine, Michael Matthew. MS, U. Hawaii, 1967; PhD, Stanford U., 1971. Sr. rsch. assoc. Columbia U., Palisades, N.Y., 1976-80; oceanographer Brookhaven Nat. Lab., Upton, N.Y., 1980-82; assoc. prof. U. Md., Cambridge, 1982-83, prof. oceanography, 1983—, acting dir ctr. environ. and estuarine studies, 1988-90, dir. Horn Point Environ. Lab., 1990—. Adj. assoc. prof. CCNY, 1976-80; vice-chmn. system adv. coun. Univ.-Nat. Oceanographic Lab., Seattle, 1985-88; chmn., trustee Chesapeake Rsch. Consortium, Solomons, Md., 1988-90; mem. Gov.'s Chesapeake Bay Work Group, Annapolis, Md., 1988-90. Author: (with others) Algal Size and Phytoplankton Ecology, 1980, Size-Fractionated Primary Productivity of Marine Phytoplankton, 1980; contbr. articels to profl. jours. Grantee NSF, 1988-91, Md. Sea, 1989, Md. Dept. Natural Resources, 1990-91. Mem. Am. Soc. Limnology and Oceanography, Am. Geophys. Union, Phycological Soc. Am., Estuarine Rsch. Edn. Achievements include research in dynamics of coastal ecosystems, phytoplankton ecology, eutrophication. Home: 30448 Belmont Dr Trappe MD 21673-1521 Office: U Md Horn Point Environ Lab 2020 Horns Point Rd Cambridge MD 21613-3368

MALONE, THOMAS FRANCIS, academic administrator, meteorologist; b. Sioux City, Iowa, May 3, 1917; s. John and Mary (Hourigan) M.; m. Rosalie Doran, Dec. 30, 1942; children: John H., Thomas Francis, Mary E., James K., Richard K., Dennis P. BS, S.D. Sch. Mines, 1940,

D.Eng., 1962; Sc.D., MIT, 1946; L.H.D., St. Joseph Coll., West Hartford, Conn., 1965; Sc.D. (hon.), Bates Coll., 1988; Sc.D. (hon.), Wesleyan U., 2007. Instr. MIT, 1942-43, asst. prof., 1943-51, assoc. prof., 1951-56; dir. Travelers Rsch. Ctr., Travelers Ins. Co., Hartford, Conn., 1955-56, dir. rsch., 1956-69, sr. v.p., 1968-70, chmn. bd., 1961-70; dean Grad. Sch., U. Conn., Storrs, 1970-73; chmn. bd. Ctr. for Environment and Men, 1970-71; dir. emeritus Holcomb Rsch. Inst., Butler U., Indpls., 1983—; scholar in residence St. Joseph Coll., 1983-91; Nat. Scis. fellow Resources for Future, 1983-84; Univ. Disting. scholar N.C. State U., 1991—98. Chmn. bd. Univ. Corp. for Atmospheric Rsch., 1973—76; mem. Conn. Weather Control Bd., 1959—73; mem. panel on sci. and tech. com. on sci. and astronautics U.S. Ho. of Reps., 1960—70; nat. adv. com. cmty. air pollution HEW, 1962—66; mem. sci. info. coun. NSF, 1962—66; rep. Am. Geophys. Union to U.S. Nat. Commn. for UNESCO, 1963—73, chmn. U.S. Nat. Commn., 1965—67; mem. nat. adv. com. on oceans and atmosphere, 1972—75; mem. Conn. Rsch. Commn., 1965—71; mem. com. application sci. and tech. New Eng. Coun.; chmn. Nat. Motor Vehicle Safety Adv. Coun., 1967—70; mem. sci. adv. com. climate impact assessment and response program UN Environ. Program, 1992—; mem. adv. com. on accreditation Conn. Dept. Higher Edn., 2000—02; mem. acad. adv. bd. S.D. Sch. Mines and Tech., 1991—2002; bd. dirs. Conn. Acad. for Edn., 2001—02. Editor: Compendium of Meteorology, 1951; contbg. editor: Environment, 1992-99; bd. editors: Jour. of the Marine Tech. Soc., 1995-99. Bd. dirs. Engrs. Joint Coun., 1968-70; bd. govs. Ins. Inst. Hwy. Safety, 1968-70; mem. oversight rev. bd. Nat. Acid Precipitation Assessment Program, 1990-96; corporator Hartford Sem., 2003—. Recipient Spl. Citation for Patriotic Svc. US War Dept., 1946, Robert M. Losey award Inst. Aero. Sci., 1960, Charter Oak Leadership medal Greater Hartford C. of C., 1962, Charles Franklin Brooks award, 1964, Cleveland Abbe award Am. Meteorol. Soc., 1968, Conn. Conservationist of Yr. award, 1966, Guy E. March Silver medal S.D. Sch. Mines, 1976, Internat. Meteorol. Orgn. prize, 1984, Internat. St. Francis Assissi prize for environment, 1991, AAAS Internat. prize, 1994, Irving award Distance Edn. Consortium, 1997, Disting. Alumni award S.D. Sch. Mines, 1998, Living Legend award St. Joseph Coll., 2006; named to S.D. Hall of Fame, 2003; named KEN Practitioner of Yr., Entuovation Internat., 2003; N.C. State U. disting. scholar, 1990-99, emeritus, 1999-Fellow AAAS (internat. sci. coop., 1994), N.Y. Acad. Scis., Am. Meteorol. Soc. (pres. 1960-62), Am. Geophys. Union (past pres., sec. internat. participation 1964, Waldo E. Smith award 1986); mem. NAS (chmn. geophysics rsch. bd. 1969-76, chmn. bd. on internat. orgns. and programs, dep. fgn. sec. 1969-73, fgn. sec. 1978-82), NRC (space application bd. 1973-77), Am. Acad. Arts and Scis., Internat. Coun. Sci. Unions (v.p., sec.-gen. sci. com. problems environ. 1970-76, treas. 1978-82) Am. Geog. Soc. (coun. 1971-77), Royal Irish Acad. (hon.), Conn. Acad. Sci. and Engring. (exec. scientist 1987-91, 97-2000, Lifetime Disting. Svc. award, 2004, Traingle Fraternity inducted Men of Century, 2007), Acad. Polit. Scis., Sigma Xi (bd. dirs. 1983-96, pres. 1988-89, dir. Sigma Xi Ctr. 1992-95, chief scientist 1996-98). Home: 275 Steele Rd Apt 504B West Hartford CT 06117 Office Phone: 860-920-6357. Personal E-mail: tfmalone@aol.com.

MALONE, THOMAS W., business educator, researcher; b. Roswell, N.Mex., June 2, 1952; s. Ernest P. Jr. and Virginia Malone; m. Joan L. Goldberg, Aug. 28, 1988; children: Robert, Laura. BA in Math. Scis. magna cum laude, Rice U., 1974; MA in Psychology, Stanford U., 1977, MS in Engring.-Econ. Sys., 1979, PhD in Psychology, 1980. Cons. for computer-based instrn. Region IV Edn. Svc. Ctr., Houston, 1974-75; rsch. intern Xerox Corp., Palo Alto Rsch. Ctr., Calif., 1979-80, mem. rsch. staff, 1980-83; from asst. prof. to assoc. prof. MIT, Sloan Sch. Mgmt., Cambridge, Mass., 1983-89, Patrick J. McGovern prof. info. sys., 1989—2004, Patrick J. McGovern prof. mgmt., 2004—, dir. Ctr. Coord. Sci., 1989—2006, head info. tech. group, 2000—; dir. Ctr. Collective Intelligence, 2006—. Vis. prof. Harvard Bus. Sch., Boston, 1992, IESE Bus. Sch., Barcelona, 2001-02; co-dir. Initiative on Inventing the Orgns. of 21st Century, MIT, Sloan Sch. Mgmt., 1994-99, Douglas Drane Career Devel. assoc. prof. info. tech. and mgmt., 1985; co-founder, cons. Palladian Software, Cambridge, 1984-88, Agility Sys., Waltham, Mass., 1989-91; mem. adv. bd. Perot Sys. Corp., Dallas, 1992-98; co-founder, chmn. Phios Corp., Cambridge, 1996—, CEO, 1998-99; mem. adv. bd. ELance, Inc., Sunnyvale, Calif., 2000—2004, Oco Corp., Wayland, Mass., 2000—2006; bd. dir. Seriosity, Inc., 2006-; spkr. and presenter in field. Author: The Future of Work, 2004, others; contbr. articles to profl. jours.; patentee in field. Scholar U.S. Presdl. Scholars Commn., 1970; grad. fellow NSF, 1976. Mem. Assn. for Computing Machinery (program chair conf. on computer supported coop. work 1993-94), Phi Beta Kappa. Office: MIT Sloan Sch Mgmt E53-333 Cambridge MA 02142 Office Phone: 617-253-6843. Business E-Mail: malone@mit.edu.

MALONEY, CAROLYN BOSHER, United States Representative from New York; b. Greensboro, NC, Feb. 19, 1948; d. R.G. and Christine (Clegg) Bosher; m. Clifton H.W. Maloney, 1976; children: Christina, Virginia. BA, Greensboro Coll., 1968. Cmty. affairs coord. welfare edn. prog. Bd. Edn., NYC, 1972—75, spl. asst. ctr. career and occupl. edn., 1975—76; legis. aide housing com. NY State Assembly, 1977, sr. prog. analyst cities com., 1977—79; exec. dir. adv. coun. Office of NY State Senate Minority Leader Manfred Ohrenstein, 1979—82, dir. spl. projects, 1980—82; councilwoman Dist. 8 NYC, 1983-93; mem. US Congress from 14th NY Dist., 1993—; ranking mem. Joint Econ. Com., 2005—07, chair, 2007—, US House Dem. Caucus Task Force on Homeland Security, 2003—; mem. US House Financial Services Com., US House Oversight & Govt. Reform Com. Mem. US del. Fourth World Conf. on Women, Beijing, Internat. Conf. on Population and Devel., The Hague, Netherlands. Author: Rumors of Our Progress Have Been Greatly Exaggerated: Why Women's Lives Aren't Getting Any Easier -- and How We Can Make Real Progress for Ourselves and Our Daughters, 2008. Active Assn. for a Better NY, Manhattan Women's Polit. Caucus. Decorated Mil. Order of the Purple Heart; recipient Spl. Impact award, Healthy Mothers, Healthy Babies, 2000, Women's Leadership award, UN Family Planning, 2002, Disting. Pub. Svc. award, Nat. Family Planning and Reproductive Health Assn., Ellis Island Medal of Honor, Global Peace award, Peace Action, Queens Women of Distinction award, Queen's Women's Polit. Caucus. Mem.: Hadassah (Myrtle Wreath award), NOW, NAACP. Democrat. Presbyterian. Office: US House Reps 2332 Rayburn House Office Bldg Washington DC 20515-3214 also: Dist Office 1651 Third Ave Ste 311 New York NY 10128-3679 Office Phone: 202-225-7944, 212-860-0606. Office Fax: 202-225-4709, 212-860-0704.*

MALONEY, DON, professional sports team executive, retired professional hockey player; b. Lindsay, Ont., Can., Sept. 5, 1958; m. Toni Maloney; 1 child, Don. Left wing NY Rangers, 1979—89, Hartford Whalers, 1989, NY Islanders, 1989—91, asst. gen. mgr., 1991—92, gen. mgr., v.p. hockey ops., 1992—95; eastern profl. scout San Jose Sharks, 1996—97; asst. gen. mgr. NY Rangers, 1997—2007, v.p. player personnel, 2000—07; gen. mgr. Phoenix Coyotes, 2007—. Asst. gen. mgr. Team Can., World Hockey Championships, Helsinki, Finland, 2003, Czech Republic, 04. Office: Phoenix Coyotes Hockey Club 6751 N White Out Way, #200 Glendale AZ 85305

MALONEY, DOREEN M., performing arts educator; MFA, U. Wis., Madison, 1999. Assoc. prof. U. Ky., Lexington, 1999—. Office: Univ Ky 206 Fine Arts Lexington KY 40506

MALONEY, DREW, lobbyist; BA in Polit. Sci., Randolph-Macon Coll., Ashland, Va.; JD, Cath. U. Columbus Sch. Law, Washington. Campaign mgr. Va. State Senator Tommy Norment; field dir. Va. Atty Gen. Rep. Nominee Steve Agee; polit. dir. Carlyle Gregory Co.; Congl. liaison Robertson, Monagle and Eastaugh; legis. aide US Congressman Roger Wicker; legis. dir. US Congressman Ed Bryant; adminstrv. asst., legis. dir. Office the Rep. House Majority Whip; mng. dir., Ogilvy Govt. Rels. Ogilvy PR Worldwide Co., Washington, 2002—. Named one of Top Lobbyists in Washington, The Hill. Office: Ogilvy Govt Rels 1111 19th St NW Ste 1100 Washington DC 20036 Office Phone: 202-729-4200. Office Fax: 202-530-9777. Business E-Mail: info@drewmaloney.com.*

MALONEY, ELLEN CLAIRE, elementary school educator; b. Buffalo, Jan. 12, 1946; d. Eugene Michael and Norma Ann Gooley; m. John Charles Maloney, Aug. 9, 1986; children: Matthew Donovan Lennert, Elizabeth Anne Lennert, Patrick O'Neal Johnson. MEd, U. San Diego, Calif., 1978. Elem. tchr. San Diego Unified Sch. Dist., 1978—. Reader, sodality mem. St. Rita's Cath. Ch., San Diego, 1986—2006; mem. Whispering Winds Aux., San Diego, 2001—06. Named Tchr. of Yr., Encanto Elem., 1995, 1997, Zamorano Elem., 2002, 2004, 2005. Office: San Diego Unified Sch Dist 4100 Normal Ave San Diego CA 92105 Office Phone: 619-267-8007. Personal E-mail: malon63@aol.com.

MALONEY, JAMES HENRY, community development executive, former congressman; b. Quincy, Mass., Sept. 17, 1948; s. James Henry Jr. and Katherine Smith (Murphy) M.; m. Mary Angela Draper, Aug. 16, 1980; children: Adele, Anna, Ellen. BA cum laude, Harvard U., 1972; JD, Boston U., 1980. Vol. VISTA, Gary, Ind., 1969—70; exec. dir. Cmty. Action Com. Danbury, Conn., 1974—78; atty. Pinney, Payne, Van-Lenten, Burrell, Wolfe & Dillman, P.C., Danbury, 1980—86; ptnr. Dice, Maloney & Lenz, P.C., Danbury, 1986—93, Maloney, Leaphart & Assocs., PC, Danbury, 1995—97; mem. Conn. Senate, Hartford, 1987—95, 105-107th Congresses from 5th Conn. dist., 1997—2003, mem. armed svcs. com., mem. fin. svcs. com.; pres., gen. counsel Conn. Inst. Cmtys., Inc., 2003—; CEO Main St. Devel. Corp., 2003—. Democrat. Roman Catholic. Avocation: sailing. Office Phone: 203-743-9760 ext. 202. E-mail: JamesHMaloney@aol.com.

MALONEY, JOHN JOSEPH, writer; b. NYC, Jan. 15, 1929; s. John J. and Breda T. (O'Leary) M.; m. Helen Martin; children: Peter, Elizabeth, Mary Ellen. BA, Fordham Coll., 1951. City editor Patent Trader, Mt. Kisco, N.Y., 1953-59; news bureau mgr. N.Y. Stock Exchange, NYC, 1959-63; dir. pub. rels. Lehman Bros., NYC, 1963-71, Warnaco, Inc., Bridgeport, Conn., 1971-77; v.p. charge of media rels. Citigroup (formerly Citicorp/Citibank), NYC, 1977-91; writer Easton, Conn., 1991—. Cons. capital formation markets Kenyan govt., 1991, Bulgarian govt., 1999. With U.S. Army, 1951-53. Avocation: sailing. Home: 65 Sport Hill Pkwy Easton CT 06612-2239

MALONEY, MAUREEN MURPHY, social sciences educator; b. NYC, Nov. 16, 1941; d. Cyril Bernard Murphy and Monique Louissiane Jacques; m. Paul K. Maloney, Dec. 5, 1964; children: Jennifer, Paula, Edward. Diploma, Holy Name Sch. Nursing, 1962; BS in Psychology, Sacred Heart U., 1982; M in Applied Psychology, Fairfield U., 1986; D Ednl. Leadership summa cum laude, U. Bridgeport, 2003. RN N.J. Head nurse neurosurgery Columbia Presbyn. Med. Ctr., NYC, 1962—65; prof. Housatonic C.C., Bridgeport, Conn., 1993—, chmn. dept. behavioral and social scis., 2006—. Adj. prof. Norwalk C.C., 1987—93. Recipient award for Tchg. Excellence and Disting. Svc., Housatonic Coll., 2004. Mem.: APS, ASCD, APA, AAUP, Am. Psychological Soc. Roman Catholic. Avocations: reading, skiing, tennis, classical music, opera. Office: Housatonic CC 900 Lafayette Ave Bridgeport CT 06608

MALONEY, MILFORD CHARLES, retired internal medicine educator; b. Buffalo, Mar. 15, 1927; s. John Angelus Maloney and Winifred Hill; m. Dione Ethyl Sheppard. BS, Canisius Coll., 1947, postgrad., 1947-49; MD, U. Buffalo, 1953. Diplomate Am. Bd. Internal Medicine. Rsch. chemist Buffalo Electrochem. Co., 1947-49; intership Mercy Hosp./Georgetown U., 1953-54; med. residency Buffalo VA Hosp., 1954-56; cardiology fellow Buffalo Gen. Hosp., 1956-57; chmn. dept. medicine Mercy Hosp., 1969-94, program dir., internal medicine residency Buffalo, 1972-89; with steering com. Assn. Program Dirs. in Internal Medicine, 1976, coun. mem., 1977-80; clin. prof. medicine SUNY, Buffalo, 1981-94; trustee Am. Soc. Internal Medicine, 1984-90, edn. leader, European seminar, 1987, edn. leader, So. Am. seminar, 1988; faculty instr. Christopher Wren Assn. Coll. William and Mary, Williamsburg, Va., 1997—2008. Bd. dirs. Internal Medicine Ctr. for Advancement and Rsch. Edn., Ctr. Excellence in Aging and Geriatric Health, Williamsburg, Va., Heart Assn. Western NY, Buffalo, 1969; sr. cancer rsch. physician Roswell Park Meml. Cancer Inst., 1959-62; mem. internal medicine liaison com. NY State, 1980-90; faculty instr., mem. curriculum com. Christopher Wren Assn. Coll. William & Mary, Williamsburg, Va., 1997-99. Editor newsletter N.Y. State Soc. Internal Medicine, 1972-78. Bd. dirs. Health Sys. Agy. Western N.Y., Buffalo, 1981; mem. exec. com., bd. dirs. Blue Cross Western N.Y., Buffalo, 1987-1994; mem. bd. regents Canisius Coll., Buffalo, 1987—; mem. pres. assocs. SUNY, Buffalo; founding mem. Greater Williamsburg Va. Symphony Soc., 1998; bd. dirs. Va. Symphony, Norfolk, 2001; bd. dirs., dir. devel. Williamsburg Ctr. for Excellence in Aging and Geriatric Health, 2004. Capt. M.C., U.S. Army, 1957-59. Recipient award of merit N.Y. State Soc. Internal Medicine, 1980, Man of Yr. award Heart Assn. Western N.Y., 1982, ann. honoree award Trocaire Coll., 1986, Disting. Alumni award Canisius Coll., 1991, Berkson Excellence award in tchg. and art of medicine, SUNY at Buffalo, 1992, Outstanding Med. Tchg. Attending award Mercy Hosp./SUNY Med. Residents, 1994, Lifetime Career Achievement award Med. Alumni Assn. SUNY, Buffalo, 2005, Heritage award Mercy Hosp. Found., Buffalo, N.Y., 2005; named to Sports Hall of Fame, Canisius Coll., 1978. Master ACP (pres. emeritus, Upstate Physician Recognition award 1989); fellow Am. Coll. Cardiology; mem. AMA (SUNY rep. 1986-94, rep. to sect. med. schs. at ann. meetings 1984-94, chmn. sect. on internal medicine 1990-91), Am. Soc. Internal Medicine (bd. dirs. Internal Medicine Ctr. for Advancement of Rsch. Edn. 1988-91, trustee 1984-90, pres. 1990-91, chmn. long range planning com., rep. to Federated Coun. on Internal Medicine 1990-91, rep. nat. practice parameters and guidelines com. 1989-91, Scroll of Honor benefactor for Internal Medicine Ctr. for Advancement of Rsch. and Edn. 1991), Va. State Soc. Internal Medicine (ex officio mem. exec. com., bd. dirs.), N.Y. State Soc. Internal Medicine (pres. 1974-75), Alumni Assn. SUNY (pres. 1975), Med. Soc. County Erie (pres. 1991-82), Va. Soc. Internal Medicine (hon.), Greater Williamsburg Va. Symphony Soc. (founding mem. 1998, editor newsletter 1998-2003). Home: 116 Cove Point Ln Williamsburg VA 23185-8613 E-mail: mcmaloney@widomaker.com.

MALONEY, PAUL LEWIS, federal judge; b. Cleve., 1949; BA, Lehigh U., 1972; JD, U. Detroit, 1975. Bar: Mich. 1975. Asst. prosecutor Berrien County Prosecutor's Office, Mich., 1975—81, prosecuting atty. Mich., 1981—89; dep. asst. atty gen. criminal divsn. US Dept. Justice, 1989—93; spl. asst. to dir. State Mich. Dept. Corrections, 1993—95; dist. judge Berrien County Trial Ct., 1995—96, cir. judge, 1996—2007; judge US Dist. Ct. (we. dist.) Mich., 2007—. Office: 137 Federal Bldg 410 W Michigan Ave Kalamazoo MI 49007 Office Phone: 269-381-4741. Office Fax: 269-337-5700.

MALONEY, ROBERT E., JR., lawyer; b. San Francisco, Sept. 17, 1942; s. Robert E. and Mara A. (Murphy) M.; children: Michael, Sarah, Paul. BA magna cum laude, U. Portland, 1964; JD summa cum laude, Willamette U., Salem, Oreg., 1967. Bar: Oreg., Wash., U.S. Dist. Ct. Oreg., U.S. Dist. Ct. (we. dist.) Wash., U.S. Dist. Ct. (ea. dist.) Wash., U.S. Ct. Appeals (9th cir.). Shareholder Lane Powell PC, Portland, 1967—; chmn., profl. svcs. counsel Bounce Back Oreg., 2003. Mem. bd. visitors Willamette U. Law Sch., 1985-98, chair, 1993-95, mem. exec. com., 1992-97; past chair, mem. exec. com. Portland Trial Dept.; lawyers del. 9th Cir. Jud. Conf., 1995-98; chmn., pres. adv. coun. U. Portland, 2001—; mem. adv. com. Oreg. Ct. Appeals, 2004-. Bd. dirs. Oreg. chpt. Multiple Sclerosis Soc., 1995-02, Children's Cancer Assn., 2002—08, Oreg. Ind. Coll. Found., 2004—, chmn., Oreg. Lawyers Against Hunger, 1997-99; judge pro tem Multnomah County Cir. Ct., 1994-98. Mem. ABA (co-chair products liability com., trial practice com. 1988-93), Nat. Assn. R.R. Trial Counsel, Fedn. Ins. Corp. Counsel, Oreg. Assn. Def. Counsel (bd. dirs. 1988-95 sec. 1991-92, v.p. 1993-94, pres. 1994), Fed. Bar Assn. (exec. com. Oreg. divsn. 1988-96, pres. 1994-95), Multnomah Athletic Club. Republican. Roman Catholic. Office: Lane Powell PC 601 SW Second Ave Ste 2100 Portland OR 97204-3158 Office Phone: 503-778-2105. Office Fax: 503-778-2200. Business E-Mail: maloneyr@lanepowell.com.

MALONEY, ROBERT KELLER, ophthalmologist, medical educator; b. May 1, 1958; AB in Mathematics summa cum laude, Harvard U., 1979; MA in Philosophy, Politics and Econs., Oxford U., Eng., 1981; MD, U. Calif., San Francisco, 1985. Diplomate Am. Bd. Ophthalmology. Rsch fellow dept. physiology Cambridge (Eng.) U., 1985; intern U. Calif., LA, 1985-86; resident Wilmer Ophthal. Inst. Johns Hopkins Hosp., Balt., 1986-89; Heed fellow cornea and refractive surgery Emory U., Dept. Ophthalmology, Atlanta, 1989-91; clin. prof. ophthalmology Jules Stein Eye Inst. Sch. Medicine U. Calif., 2005—, assoc. prof. ophthalmology Jules Stein Eye Inst. Sch. Medicine, 1991—2004; dir. Maloney Vision Inst., LA, Calif., 1998—. Bd. dirs. Lasik Inst., Calhoun Vision; cons. in field. Contbr. numerous articles to profl. jours.; presenter and spkr. in field; assoc. editor (N.Am.) Jour. Refractive and Corneal Surgery, 1991-95; internat. editl. bd. European Jour. Implant and Refractive Surgery, 1995; reviewer Am. Jour. Ophthalmology, Ophthalmology, Archives of Ophthalmology, Jour. Cataract and Refractive Surgery, Ophthalmic Surgery and Lasers; editl. bd. Ophthalmology Times. Rhodes scholar, 1979, Heed Found. fellow, 1989-90, Heed/Knapp fellow, 1990-91, John Harvard scholar, 1978; recipient Detur and Edward Whitaker prizes, Harvard U., Rsch. to Prevent Blindness Career Devel. award, 1992, Mericos Whittier award, 1997, VISX Star Surgeon award, 1999, 2000. Mem. Am. Acad. Ophthalmology (long-range planning com. 1989-92, quality of care com. 1987-91, retina preferred practice pattern subcom., refractive errors preferred practice pattern subcom.; chmn. ann. meeting program com. for young ophthalmologists, 1990-92; adv. group to ad hoc com. on orgnl. design 1991, young ophthalmologists' com. 1992-94; Honor award 1993, 97, Sr. Achievement award 2002, Secretariat award 2003), Assn. Rsch. in Vision and Ophthalmology, Internat. Soc. Refractive Surgery (Disting. Lans Refractive Surgery award 2001), Calif. Assn. Ophthalmology, Max Fine Corneal Soc., Phi Beta Kappa. Office: Maloney Vision Inst Ste 900 10921 Wilshire Blvd Los Angeles CA 90024 Office Phone: 310-208-3937. Business E-Mail: info@maloneyvision.com.

MALONEY, SEAN M., electronics company executive; b. 1956; Mgr. applications engring. Intel U.K. Intel Corp., country mgr. Intel U.K., dir. mktg. Intel Europe, gen. mgr. Asia Pacific ops., tech. asst. to chmn. and chief exec., 1992—95, mgr. sales and mktg. activities Asia Pacific, 1995—98, sr. v.p., mgr. sales org., 1999—2001, exec. v.p., dir. sales org., 2001, exec. v.p., gen. mgr. Intel Comm. Group (ICG), 2001—04, exec. v.p., co-mgr. mobility group, 2004—06, exec. v.p., chief sales & mktg. officer, 2006—. Bd. dirs. Autodesk, Inc., 2007—, U.S./China Bus. Coun. Office: Intel Corp 2200 Mission College Blvd Santa Clara CA 95052*

MALONEY, WILLIAM JAMES, dentist, educator; b. White Plains, NY, Feb. 16, 1967; BS, Siena Coll., Loudonville, NY, 1989; DDS, NYU, 1992. Faculty NYU Coll. Dentistry, NY, 2000—. Contbr. articles to profl. jours. Mem.: ADA. Office: 12 Ellis Pl Ossining NY 10562 Business E-Mail: maloneydentistry@aol.com.

MALOOF, GAVIN PATRICK, professional sports team executive; b. Oct. 9, 1956; s. George and Colleen Maloof. Student, N.Mex. Mil. Inst., Roswell, N.Mex.; BA in Speech and Comm., Trinity U., San Antonio, 1979. Co-owner NBA Houston Rockets, 1979-82, Women's NBA Sacramento Monarchs, Sacramento Knights, ARCO Arena, NBA Sacramento Kings, 1999—; pres. World League of Am. Football Birmingham Fire, 1990—92; vice chmn. Maloof Cos. Co-recipient Most Involved Execs. award, World Sports Humanitarian Hall of Fame, 2001; named one of The Most Influential People in the World of Sports, Bus. Week, 2007. Avocation: golf. Office: Sacramento Kings Arco Arena One Sports Pky Sacramento CA 95834*

MALOOF, GILES WILSON, academic administrator, educator, author; b. San Bernardino, Calif., Jan. 4, 1932; s. Joseph Peters and Georgia (Wilson) M.; m. Mary Anne Ziniker, Sept. 5, 1958 (dec. Oct. 1976); children: Mary Jane, Margery Jo. BA, U. Calif., Berkeley, 1953; MA, U. Oreg., 1958; PhD, Oreg. State U., 1962. Petroleum reservoir engr. Creole Petroleum Corp., Venezuela, 1953—54; mathematician electronics divsn. rsch. dept. U.S. Naval Ordnance Rsch. Lab., Corona, Calif., 1958—59; asst. prof. math. Oreg. State U., Corvallis, 1962—68, rsch. assoc. dept. oceanography, 1963—68, vis. prof. math., 1977—78; prof. math. Boise State U., Idaho, 1968—, head dept., 1968—75, dean grad. sch., 1970—75. Author, reviewer of coll. textbooks; contbr. to profl. jours. Served with Ordnance Corps, AUS, 1950, 54-56. Recipient Carter award, 1963, Mosser prize, 1966, Oreg. State U., Alumni Found. scholar Tchg. award Boise State U., 2000. Mem. Math. Assn. Am., Am. Math. Soc., Soc. Indsl. and Applied Math., N.W. Coll. and Univ. Assn. for Sci. (dir., pres. 1990-92), N.W. Sci. Assn. (trustee 1977-80), Assn. We. Univs. (edn. and rsch. com. 1993-2001), Sigma Xi, Pi Mu Epsilon, Phi Kappa Phi. Home: 1400 Longmont Ave Boise ID 83706-3730 E-mail: giles@diamond.boisestate.edu.

MALOOF, JOSEPH, professional sports team owner; s. George and Colleen Maloof. Co-owner NBA Houston Rockets, 1979-82, NBA Sacramento Kings, 1999—, Women's NBA Sacramento Monarchs, Sacramento Knights, ARCO Arena; ptnr., pres. Maloof Cos. Bd. govs. NBA, 1999—; bd. mem. Coors Distbr. Coun. Co-recipient Most Involved Execs. award, World Sports Humanitarian Hall of Fame, 2001;

named one of The Most Influential People in the World of Sports, Bus. Week, 2007. Avocation: tennis. Office: Sacramento Kings Arco Arena One Sports Pky Sacramento CA 95834*

MALOOLEY, DAVID JOSEPH, electronics and computer technology educator; b. Terre Haute, Ind., Aug. 20, 1951; s. Edward Joseph and Vula (Starn) Malooley. BS, Ind. State U., 1975; MS, Ind. U., 1981. Supr. Zenith Radio Corp., Paris, Ill., 1978—79; assoc. prof., electronics and computer tech. Ind. State U., Terre Haute, 1979—; cons. in field. Served to 1st lt. US Army, 1975—78. Mem.: Nat. Fire Protection Assn., Assoc. Tech. Mgmt. and Applied Engring., Internat. Soc. Automation (sr.), Soc. Mfg. Engrs. (sr.), Phi Kappa Phi, Epsilon Pi Tau, Pi Lambda Theta, Phi Delta Kappa. Democrat. Home: 11420 Spring Creek Rd Terre Haute IN 47805-9679 Office: Ind State U Dept Electronics and Computer Tech Terre Haute IN 47809-0001 Office Phone: 812-237-3395. Business E-Mail: dmalooley@indstate.edu.

MALOOLY, WILLIAM FRANCIS, bishop; b. Balt., Jan. 18, 1944; BA, St. Mary's Coll., 1966; LHD (hon.), Mt. St. Mary's U., Emmitsburg, Md., 2006. Ordained priest Archdiocese of Balt., 1970; assoc. pastor St. Joseph, Tex., 1970—76, St. Anthony of Padua, Balt., 1976—81; assoc. adminstr., adminstr. CYO Retreat House, Sparks, Md., 1981—84; dir. clergy personnel Archdiocese of Balt., 1984—89, chancellor, vicar gen., 1989—2008; ordained bishop, 2001; aux. bishop, Western region vicar Archdiocese of Balt., 2001—08; bishop Diocese of Wilmington, Del., 2008—. Bd. trustees Good Samaritan Hosp., St. Mary's Sem. & U., Mt. St. Mary's U. Recipient Pres.'s medal, St. Mary's Sem. & U., 1999, Cardinal Shehan award, Balt. Archdiocesan Youth Office, 2006. Mem.: Knights of Malta. Roman Catholic. Office: Diocese of Wilmington 1925 Delaware Ave Wilmington DE 19899-2030 Office Phone: 302-573-3100. Office Fax: 302-573-3128.

MALOTT, JOHN RAYMOND, writer, consultant, not-for-profit executive; b. Kankakee, Ill., Nov. 5, 1946; s. Raymond Roderick and Ruth Pearl (Jacobs) M.; m. Hiroko Iwami, Nov. 23, 1971; children: David Iwami, Rumi Justine. BA, Northwestern U., 1967; grad., Nat. War Coll., 1983. Civilian advisor US Dept. State, Vietnam, 1969-70, China desk officer Washington, 1970-71, Am. consul Kobe, Japan, 1971-73, 1st sec. Am. Embassy Tokyo, 1974-77, Sri Lanka desk officer Washington, 1977-78, India desk officer, 1978-80; Am. consul Bombay, 1980-82; with Nat. War Coll. Washington, 1982-83; dep. dir. Japan Affairs, 1983-85; spl. asst. to Under Sec. State Econ. Affairs, 1985-86; Am. consul gen. Osaka, Japan, 1986-89; dir. Japan Affairs Washington, 1989-91; sr. seminar, 1991-92; dep. asst. sec. state South Asian Affairs, 1992-93; sr. advisor to Undersec. State for Econ. Affairs, Washington, 1993-95; U.S. amb. to Malaysia Dept. State, 1995-98; exec. chmn. Malott & Assocs., 1999—; pres. World Affairs/Coun. of Orange County, 2000—02; mng. dir. Manatt Jones Global Strategies, 2003—06; sr. advisor Manatt, Phelps & Phillips, LLP, 2003—06; pres., CEO Japan-Am. Soc. Wash., DC, 2006—. Author: Partners, 1992. Recipient Vietnam Svc. award, 1970, Meritorious Honor award Dept. State, 1982, Superior honor award, 1991. Presbyterian. Home: 5911 Reservoir Heights Ave Alexandria VA 22311-1017 Office Phone: 202-833-2210. Business E-Mail: jmalott@us-japan.org.

MALOUF, MARK E., structural engineer, consultant; s. John R. and Renée Malouf; m. Kimberley K. Skinner, May 10, 1984; children: Isabelle, John-Mark. BSCE, U. Okla., 1982, MSCE, 1984. Registered profl. engr. Project engr., mgr. Alpha Tower Design, Richardson, Tex., 1984—91, v.p. engring., 1991—92; pres. Malouf Engring. Internat., Dallas, 1992—. Exec. com. Electronics Industry Assn., Washington, 1988—, Telecom. Industry Assn., Washington, 1988; spkr. in field. Telecom com. City of Plano, Tex., 1997; treas. Tau Beta, Okla., 1982. Mem.: ASCE, Internat. Assn. Spatial Structures, Am. Coun. Cons. Engrs. Avocations: tennis, horseback riding, hiking. Office: Malouf Engring Internat Inc 17950 Preston Rd Ste 720 Dallas TX 75252

MALOVANY, HOWARD, lawyer, food products executive; b. Dayton, Ohio, July 6, 1950; m. Cynthia Jane Shilt, Sept. 18, 1976. BA, Ohio State U., 1972; JD, U. Toledo, 1977; MBA, U. Dayton, 1985. Bar: Ohio 1977, Ill. 1997. Staff atty., asst. sec. Nat. Cash Register Corp., Dayton, 1977-85; counsel Outboard Marine Corp., Waukegan, Ill., 1985-89, asst. sec., counsel, 1989—93, sec., sr. counsel, 1993—96; asst. sec., sr. counsel William Wrigley Jr. Co., Chgo., 1996-98, sec., gen. counsel, 1998-2001, v.p., sec., gen. counsel, 2001—07, sr. v.p., sec., gen. counsel, 2007—. Mem.: ABA, Am. Soc. Corp. Secretaries (mem. corp. practice & technology com. 1995—97), Toledo Internat. Law Soc. (founder), Ohio State Bar Assn., Ill. State Bar Assn. Office: William Wrigley Jr Co 410 N Michigan Ave Chicago IL 60611-4213 Office Phone: 312-645-4223. Business E-Mail: hmalovany@wrigley.com.

MALPHURS, ROGER EDWARD, biomedical marketing executive; b. Lake Worth, Fla., Dec. 15, 1933; s. Cecil Edward and Muriel Thelma (Ward) M.; m. Carolyn Sue Calapp, Feb. 2, 1963(div. 1993); children: Steven, Brian, Darren, Regina, Victoria. BS, U. Utah, 1961; D of Chiropractic, Palmer Coll. Chiropractic West, 1990. Cert. med. technologist; lic. chiropractor, Calif., Ariz. Supr. spl. chemistry Cen. Pathology Lab., Santa Rosa, Calif., 1968-73; mgr. lab. Cmty. Hosp., Santa Rosa, 1973-76; supr. chem., staff asst. Meml. Hosp., Santa Rosa, 1976-85; pres., CEO R.E. Malphurs Co., Sunnyvale, Calif., 1972—95; tech. writer Maximus, Inc., Rancho Cordova, Calif., 2004—07; clin. lab. scientist Marshall Med. Ctr., Placerville, Calif., 2007—. Owner, developer REMCO Mktg. Assocs., Santa Rosa, 1970—71; pvt. commodity trader, 1974—; owner Better Bus. Forms and Typeset, Santa Rosa, Calif., 1977—81; commodity pool operator, 1979—81; dept. mgr. immunochemistry Spectra Labs, Fremont, Calif., 1990—95; clin. trials cons. hematology, tech. writer Abbott Diagnostics, Santa Clara, Calif., 1995—2000; tech. writer Healtheon/WebMD, Santa Clara, Calif., 2000—01; tech. writer, project mgr. Hewlett-Packard, Roseville, Calif., 2000—04. Author: A New, Simple Way to Win at Blackjack, 1972. Served as squadron commdr. CAP USAF Aux., 1982-84. Mem. APHA, Am. Chiropractic Assn., Calif. Chiropractic Assn., Optimists Internat. (youth awards chmn. 1969-74), Toastmasters (sec./treas. 1988-89), Rep. Senatorial Inner Circle. Republican. Avocations: flying, computers, pistol shooting, painting, writing.

MALPHUS, EDWARD WILSON, pediatric gastroenterologist; b. Miami, Fla., Sept. 19, 1950; MD, U. South Fla. Coll. Medicine, Tampa, 1975. Diplomate Am. Bd. Pediat., cert. Pediat. Gastroenterology, lic. Calif. Intern pediat. Martin Luther King Jr. Gen. Hosp., LA, 1975—76, resident pediat. gastroenterology; fellowship Baylor U., Houston, 1980—82; pvt. practice in pediatric gastroenterology San Francisco. Contbr. articles to profl. jours. Avocations: boating, fishing, skiing. Office: Pvt Practice 2021 Santa Monica Blvd Ste 612 E Santa Monica CA 90404 Office Phone: 310-829-4403. Office Fax: 310-829-3279.

MALSHE, AJAY P., engineering educator; m. Savita A. Malshe; children: Harsha A., Ashvini A. PhD, U. Pune, India, 1992. Prof. U. Ark., Fayetteville, 2004—06, endowed chair prof., 2006—. Co-founder NanoMech LLC, Fayetteville, Ark., 2002—08, chief tech. officer, 2002—08. Contbr. articles to profl. jours. (Frost & Sullivan Tech. Excellence award, 2006). Recipient John A. Wagnon Tech. Achievement award, Internat. Microelectronics and Packaging Soc., 2007, Faculty Disting. Achievement award, Ark. Alumni Assn., 2007, John Imhoff Best Rschr. award, Coll. Engring. U. Ark., 2007. Mem.: ASME, Phi Tau Sigma. Achievements include invention of nanoparticles superabrasive cubic boron nitride coated cutting tool; patents for polishing of diamond substrates using chemical and lasers; patents pending for advanced nanolubricant and nanoengineered polymer; first to invent nano electromachining. Office: Univ Arkansas Dickson St MEEG 204 Fayetteville AR 72701 Business E-Mail: apm2@uark.edu.

MALT, RONALD BRADFORD, lawyer; b. Boston, Aug. 1, 1954; s. Ronald A. and Geraldine (Sutton) M.; m. Sharon Lynn Harford, Feb. 14, 1981; 2 children. AB, Harvard U., 1976, JD, 1979. Bar: Mass. 1979. Assoc. Ropes & Gray, Boston, 1979-86, ptnr., 1987—, policy com., 1993—, chmn., 2004—; dir. Fenway Ptnrs., Inc., NYC, 1999—. Asst. treas. Butler Capital Corp., N.Y.C., 1983—; sec. to adv. bd. Mezzanine Lending Assocs., N.Y.C., 1983—. Mem. corp. Mass. Gen. Hosp., Boston, 1989—; trustee Butler Found., 1989—, Butler Fund for the Environment, 2004-, Black River Environ. Improvement Assn., Inc., 1991—. Republican. Episcopalian. Office: Ropes & Gray One International Pl Boston MA 02110 Office Phone: 617-951-7318. Office Fax: 617-951-7050. Business E-Mail: bmalt@ropesgray.com.

MALTBY, KIRK, professional hockey player; b. Guelph, Ont., Can. married; 1 child, Ella. Left wing Edmonton Oilers, 1993—96, Detroit Red Wings, 1996—. Team rep. Detroit Police Athletic League (PAL). Achievements include being a member of Stanley Cup Champion Detroit Red Wings, 1997, 1998, 2002, 2008. Avocations: boating, golf, baseball, softball. Office: Detroit Red Wings Joe Louis Arena 600 Civic Ctr Detroit MI 48226

MALTESE, GEORGE JOHN, mathematics professor; b. Middletown, Conn., June 24, 1931; s. Giorgio and Sebastiana (Morello) M.; m. Marlene Erika Kunz, Apr. 14, 1956; children: Christopher, Michelle. BA, Wesleyan U., Middletown, Conn., 1953; postgrad., U. Frankfurt, Germany, 1953-54; PhD, Yale U., 1960. Instr. MIT, 1961-63; asst. prof. U. Md., College Park, 1963-66, assoc. prof., 1966-69, prof., 1969-73, U. Münster, Fed. Republic Germany, 1973—. Vis. prof. U. Frankfurt, 1966-67, 70-71, U. Palermo, Italy, 1967, 71, 76. U. Pisa, Italy, 1972, U. Kuwait, 1977, U. Bahrain, 1988, U. Oman, 1991. Contbr. articles to profl. jours. Served with AUS, 1954-56. Fulbright fellow, 1953-54; NATO postdoctoral fellow, 1960-61 Mem. Am. Math. Soc., Math. Assn. Am., Unione Matematica Italiana, Deutsche Mathematiker Verein. Home: 35 Orange Rd Middletown CT 06457-4913 Office: Dept Math Wesleyan U Middletown CT 06457 E-mail: gmaltese@wesleyan.edu.

MALTESE, SERPHIN RALPH, state legislator, lawyer; b. NYC, Dec. 7, 1932; s. Paul and Frances (Scafidi) Maltese; m. Constance Mary Del Vecchio, Aug. 27, 1955; children: Andrea Constance, Leslie Serphine, Serphin Ralph(dec.). BA, Manhattan Coll., 1958; LL.B., JD (War Service scholar 1958-62), Fordham U., 1962. Bar: N.Y. 1963. Trial atty. for ins. cos., 1963-66; asst. dist. atty., dep. chief homicide bur. Queens County, N.Y., 1966-69; asso. counsel N.Y. State Com. Campus Disorders, 1969-70; counsel N.Y. State Com. Deaf and Multiple Impaired, 1970; chmn. law com. Buckley for U.S. Senator, 1970; counsel N.Y. State Assembly, 1972-76, N.Y. State Senate, Albany, 1976-88, state senator, 1988—, chmn. senate standing com. on cities, mem. com. on civil svc. and pensions, codes, elections, fin., judiciary, higher edn., investigations and govt. ops. com. Past pres. N.Y. Conf. Italian Am. Legislators. Chmn. bd. trustees Christ the King Regional HS, 1976—; mem. exec. bd. Stuyvesant HS Alumni; exec. dir. N.Y. State Conservative Party, 1971—86, exec. vice chmn., 1978—86, state chmn., 1986—88; N.Y. state chmn. Conservatives for Ronald Reagan, 1980; chmn. Queens (N.Y.) Reps. With US Army, 1952—54, Korea. Recipient Charles Edison Meml. award, N.Y. State Conservative Party, 1977, Pres.'s medal, St. John's U., 1994, Pres.'s award, LaGuardia CC, 1998; named Man of the Yr., Commn. Social Justice, 1998. Mem.: VFW, Queens Asst. Dist. Attys. Assn., N.Y. State Bar Assn., Italian Am. Profl. Bus. Assn. (hon. chmn.), Queens C. of C., Young Ams. for Freedom (nat. sr. adv. bd.), Christopher Columbus Assn. (chmn. 1970—), Am. Conservative Union (nat. bd. dirs.), Harold Gray Collectors Soc. (pres.), Internat. Assn. Space Philatelists, Am. Legion, Cath. War Vets., Alpha Phi Delta. Republican. Roman Catholic. Office: 71-04 Myrtle Ave Glendale NY 11385-7254 also: 413 Capitol Albany NY 12247 Office Phone: 518-455-3281. Business E-Mail: maltese@senate.state.ny.us.*

MALTZ, ALLEN P., insurance company executive; B in Math, SUNY Albany. Actuary Travelers Ins. Co.; with Aetna US Healthcare; CFO Blue Cross Blue Shield Mass., 2001—. Fellow: Soc. Actuaries; mem.: Am. Acad. Actuaries. Office: Blue Cross Blue Shield Mass Landmark Ctr 401 Park Dr Boston MA 02215*

MALTZ, ROBERT, surgeon; b. Cin., July 21, 1935; s. William and Sarah (Goldberg) M.; m. Sylvia Moskowitz, Aug. 24, 1958; children: Mark Edward, Deborah Lynn, Steven Alan, David Stuart. BS in Zoology, U. Cin., 1958, MD, 1962. Diplomate Am. Bd. Otolaryngology. Intern Cin. Gen. Hosp., 1962-63; resident Barnes Hosp., St. Louis, 1965-69; asst. prof. surgery Stanford U. Med. Ctr., Palo Alto, Calif., 1969-71; asst. prof. otolaryngology U. Cin. Med. Ctr., 1971-75, assoc. prof. otolaryngology, 1975—; dir. dept. otolaryngology Jewish Hosp., Cin., 1992—. Chief divsn. head and neck surgery, dept. otolaryngology and maxillofacial surgery U. Cin. Med. Ctr., 1972-76; bd. dirs. Cancer Control Coun., U. Cin. Med. Cntr.; cons. Bur. Crippled Children's Svcs., State of Ohio; on staff Univ. Hosp., Cin., Jewish Hosp., Cin., Children's Hosp. Med. Ctr., Bethesda Hosp., Cin.; del. to numerous profl. confs.; mem. health affairs adv. com. Cmty. Mut. Ins. Co.; mem. mng. bd. PIE Mut. Ins. Co.; bd. dirs. UCATS, 1995-98; trustee Health Found. Greater Cin., 1997-2006, vice-chmn., 2000-01, chmn. 2001-03, chmn. program com., 2000-01; instr. short term courses in field; pres.-elect alumni exec. coun. U. Cin. Coll. Medicine, 1998-2000, pres., 2000-02. Contbr. articles to profl. jours. Bd. dirs. Jewish Cmty. Rels. Coun.; bd. trustees Cin. Art Acad., 1998-2007; faculty adv. com. U. Cin.; trustee Health Found. Fund, 2002-, vice-chmn., 2002-03, chmn., 2003—05. Capt. USAF, 1963-65. USPHS fellow, 1968-69; Eli Lilly Co. grantee, 1971-76, Burroughs Wellcome Co., 1972. Fellow ACS, Am. Acad. Facial and Reconstructive Surgery (edn. com. 1972, future plans com. 1973-75, sci. program com., budget and fin. com. 1975, chmn. credentials com., no. sect. 1980-85), Royal Soc. Health, Internat. Cosmetic Surgeons, Am. Acad. Cosmetic Surgeons, Am. Assn. Cosmetic Surgeons (sec.-treas. 1976-81); mem. Am. Acad. Otolaryngology and Head and Neck Surgery, Am. Coun. Otolaryngology, Soc. Univ. Otolaryngologists, Pan-Am. Assn. Oto-Rhino-Laryngology and Broncho-Esophagology, Ohio State Med. Assn., Cin. Acad. Medicine (trustee 1992-98, treas. 1993-95, pres. 1996-97, chmn. pub. rels. com. 1980, chmn. comm. com. 1994-96, chmn. sply. soc. com. 1995, legis. com. 1985, editl. bd. 1994-96, jud. com. 1995—2004, chmn. managed care med. dirs. com. 1997-2002), U. Cin. Alumni Assn. (bd. govs., sec. 1994, fin. v.p. 1995, 1st v.p. 1996, pres. 1997-98), Acad. Medicine Found. (bd. dirs., v.p., pres. 2002-2004), Cin. Ear, Nose and Throat Soc., Losantiville Country Club (bd. govs. 1996-2002, pres. 1999-2001), Omicron Delta Kappa, Sigma Sigma, Sigma Alpha Mu. Avocations: tennis, golf, travel. Home: 2601 Willowbrook Dr Cincinnati OH 45237-3725 Office: 11135 Montgomery Rd Cincinnati OH 45249 Office Phone: 513-793-9600.

MALTZMAN, IRVING MYRON, psychology professor; b. Bklyn., May 9, 1924; s. Israel and Lillian (Mass) M.; m. Diane Seiden, Aug. 21, 1949; children— Sara, Kenneth, Ilaine. BA, NYU, 1946; PhD, State U. Iowa, 1949. Mem. faculty UCLA, 1949—, assoc. prof., 1957—60, prof. psychology, 1961—94, chmn. dept., 1970—77, prof. emeritus, 1994—. Co-author: Handbook of Contemporary Soviet Psychology, 1969, Alcoholism: A Review of it Characteristics, Etiology, Treatments, and Controversies, 2000, author: Alcoholism: Its Treatments and Mistreatments, 2008. Fellow: APA, AAAS; mem.: Psychonomic Soc., APS, Phi Beta Kappa, Sigma Xi. Home: 11260-22B Overland Ave Culver City CA 90230-5559 Office Phone: 310-825-2909.

MALVEAUX, JULIANNE MARIE, academic administrator, economist, writer; b. San Francisco, Sept. 22, 1953; d. Paul and Proteone Marie (Alexandria) M. BA, Boston Coll., 1974, MA, 1975; PhD, MIT, 1980. Jr. staff economist Coun. Econ. Advisors, The White House, Washington, 1977-78; rsch. fellow Rockefeller Found., NYC, 1978-80; asst. prof. New Sch. Social Rsch., NYC, 1980-81, San Francisco State U., 1981-85; assoc. prof. U. Calif., Berkeley, 1989-91; syndicated columnist King Features Syndicate, 1990—2002; CEO Last Word Productions, Inc., 1996—2007; pres. Bennett Coll., Greensboro, NC, 2007—. Vis. scholar U. Calif., Berkeley, 1985-89, Stanford U., 1987-89; spkr. in field. Co-editor: Slipping Through the Cracks: The Status of Black Women, 1986, The Paradox of Loyalty: An African American Response to the War on Terrorism, 2002; author: Sex, Lies, and Stereotypes: Perspectives of a Mad Economist, 1994, Wall Street, Main Street, and the Side Street: A Mad Economist Takes a Stroll, 1999; editor: Voices of Vision: African American Women on the Issues, 1996; co-author: Unfinished Business: A Democrat and A Republican Take On the 10 Most Important Issues Women Face, 2002; contbr. articles to profl. jours. Founder, chmn. San Francisco Anti-Apartheid Com., 1985-86; bd. dirs. Coleman Advs. for Children and Youth, San Francisco, 1985-88, Dem. Women's Forum, San Francisco, 1986-88, San Francisco chpt. NAACP, 1984, Washington chpt. Nat. Rainbow Coalition, 1986-88; pres. San Francisco Bus. and Profl. Women's Club, 1987-89, San Francisco Leadership Forum, 1989-90; nat. v.p. Nat. Assn. Negro Bus. and Profl. Women's Clubs, Washington. Named one of Am.'s Top 100 Black Bus. and Profl. Women, Dollar and Sense Mag., 1985, one of 5 Black Women Who Make it Happen, Nat. Council Negro Women and Frito-Lay, 1987; postdoctoral fellow NRC, 1985-86. Roman Catholic. Office: Bennett Coll Office of Pres 900 E Washington St Greensboro NC 27401 also: Last Word Productions Inc 1318 Corcoran St NW Washington DC 20009 Office Phone: 202-462-1932, 336-517-2225.

MALVEAUX, SUZANNE, news correspondent; BA, Harvard U., Cambridge, Mass.; MA in Journalism, Columbia U., NYC. Prodr. documentaries, Egypt, Kenya; reporter FXT-TV, New Eng. Cable News, Boston, 1991—94; gen. assignment reporter WRC-TV, Washington; corr. NBC News, Chgo., Washington; White House corr. Cable News Network (CNN), Washington, 2002—. Recipient Emmy award, 1996; named Nat. Black MBA's Communicator of Yr., 2004; named one of America's Most Powerful Players Under 40, Black Enterprise mag., Outstanding Women in Marketing & Comm., Ebony mag.; named to Power 150, 2008. Achievements include breaking coverage of top news stories including the Sept. 11, 2001, terrorist attacks in Pennsylvania and the Pentagon, the Kosovo and Afghanistan wars from the Pentagon, Clinton's impeachment trial, retirement of Supreme Court Justice Sandra Day O'Connor and others. Office: 1 CNN Ctr Atlanta GA 30303 Office Phone: 404-827-1700. Office Fax: 404-827-1099.

MALY, KURT JOHN, computer science educator; b, Modling, Austria, Aug. 20, 1944; came to U.S., 1969; s. Anton and Editha (Gneist) M.; m. Christiana Peterlik, Mar. 18, 1972; 1 child, Angela Claudia. Diplom Ingenieur summa cum laude, U. Tech., Austria, 1968; MS, Courant Inst. NYU, 1970, PhD, 1973. Asst. prof. U. Minn., Mpls., 1972-78, assoc. prof., 1978-85, acting head, 1980-82, head, 1982-85; eminent prof., chmn. computer sci. Old Dominion U., Norfolk, Va., 1985—, Kaufman prof., 1991—. Hon. prof. Chengdu U. of Sci. and Tech., People's Republic of China, 1986—, Hefei U., People's Republic of China, 1991—, Guangxi Computer Inst., People's Republic of China, 1993—; bd. dirs. Inst. of Info. Tech., Ctr. for Innovative Tech., Blacksburg, Va., 1988-92; bd. dirs., exec. co-dir. Microelectronic and Info. Scis. Ctr., Mpls., 1980-85. Author: Fundamentals of the Computing Sciences, 1978; assoc. editor: Jour. for Microcomputer Application Tech., PRC; contbr. articles to profl. jours. Served with Austrian Air Force, 1963-64. Fellow Sorbonne U., Paris, 1966, Courant Inst., N.Y.C., 1968-72. Mem. Assn. Computing Machinery, IEEE, Sigma Xi. Roman Catholic. Office: Old Dominion U Norfolk VA 23529 Home Phone: 757-481-4986; Office Phone: 757-683-4817, 757-683-6001 68. E-mail: maly@cs.odu.edu.

MALY, MICHAEL KIP, lawyer; b. San Antonio, Tex., July 18, 1945; BA with honors, U. Tex., 1967; JD, U. Calif., 1975. Bar: Calif. 1975, U.S. Dist. Ct. Calif. (no., so., ea., ctrl. dist.). Mng. ptnr. Winston & Strawn LLP, San Francisco, 2003—. Spkr. in field; mem. arbitration panel San Francisco Superior Ct. Contbr. articles to profl. jours. Lt USN, 1967—72. Mem.: ABA. Office: Winston & Strawn LLP 101 California St San Francisco CA 94111-5802 Office Phone: 415-591-1424. Office Fax: 415-591-1400. Business E-Mail: mmaly@winston.com.

MALY, WOJCIECH P., engineering educator, researcher; b. Inowroclaw, Poland, Jan. 5, 1946; came to U.S., 1979; s. Feliks and Maria (Gordzialkowska) M.; m. Halina Zarembowska, Apr. 11, 1970; 1 child, Katarzyna. MSc, Tech. U. Warsaw, 1970; PhD, Polish Acad. Sci., Warsaw, 1975. Asst. prof. Tech. U. Warsaw, 1975-86; assoc. prof. dept. elec. and computer engring. Carnegie Mellon U., Pitts., 1986-90, prof., 1990-96, Whitaker prof., 1996—. Author: Atlas of IC Technologies, 1986; contbr. chpts. to books, numerous articles to profl. jours. Recipient Teare Tchg. award Carnegie Mellon U., 1989; SRC Tech. Excellence award Semicondr. Rsch. Corp., 1993. Fellow IEEE. Roman Catholic. Achievements include development of methodologies of design for manufacturability of integrated circuits; patents in field. Office: Carnegie Mellon U ECE Dept 5000 Forbes Ave Pittsburgh PA 15213-3890

MALYKHINA, ANNA P., medical educator; b. Novogrudok, Belarus, June 1, 1971; m. Alexander Malykhin, July 20, 1991; children: Katsiaryna, Pavel Alexander Malykhin. PhD, Inst. Radiobiology, NAS, Minsk, Belarus, 1998. Rsch. assoc. physiology U. Okla., Okla. City, 2004—06, asst. prof. rsch. physiology, 2006—08; asst. prof. urology in surgery U. Pa., Phila., 2008—. Grant, NIH, 2008—. Mem.: Functional Brain-Gut Rsch. Group, Am. Gastroent. Assn. Achievements include research in functional pelvic disorders and chronic pelvic pain. Office: Univ Pa 500 S Ridgeway #158 Glenolden PA 19036 Office Fax: 276-350-9609. Business E-Mail: anna.malykhina@uphs.upenn.edu.

MALZAHN, RAY ANDREW, chemistry professor, dean; b. Fort Madison, Iowa, July 8, 1929; s. Arnold Frederick and Inez (Russel) M.; m. Elizabeth Mae Barrett, Aug. 23, 1953; children— Karen Louise, Janet Elizabeth. BA, Gustavus Adolphus Coll., 1951; MS, U. N.D., 1953; PhD, U. Md., 1962. Research assoc. U. Ariz., Tucson, 1961-63; asst. prof. chemistry West Tex. State U., Canyon, 1963-65, assoc. prof., 1965-67, prof. chemistry, 1967-80, dean Coll. Arts and Scis., 1967-71, v.p. acad. affairs, 1971-77; prof., dean Sch. Arts and Scis. Mo. So. State Coll., Joplin, 1980-95, interim v.p. for acad. affairs, 1993-94. Served with AUS, 1954-56. Mem. Am. Chem. Soc. Home: 1215 Goetz Blvd Joplin MO 64801-1433

MAMANTOV, ANDREW, chemist; s. Galina and Igor Mamantov; m. Irina Kopaschikova, June 9, 1998. PhD, Rutgers U., 1971. Chemist U.S. EPA, Washington, 1980—. Editl. bd. Progress in Reaction Kinetics & Mechanism, St. Albans, 2004—09. Contbr. articles to profl. jours. Recipient Sci. & Technol. Achievement award, Office of R & D, 2007. Mem.: Am. Chem. Soc., Phi Lambda Upsilon. Achievements include development of equations for predicting hydrolysis. Office: US EVC 1200 Pennsylvania Ave Washington DC 20460

MAMAT, FRANK TRUSTICK, lawyer; b. Syracuse, NY, Sept. 4, 1949; s. Harvey Sanford and Annette (Trustick) M.; m. Kathy Lou Winters, June 23, 1975; children: Jonathan Adam, Steven Kenneth. BA, U. Rochester, 1971; JD, Syracuse U., 1974. Bar: D.C. 1976, U.S. Ct. Appeals (D.C. cir.) 1976, Fla. 1977, U.S. Supreme Ct. 1979, US. Dist. Ct. (ea. dist.) 1983, U.S. Ct. Appeals (6th cir.) 1983, Mich. 1984, U.S. Dist. Ct. (no. dist.) Ind. 1984. Atty. NLRB, Washington, 1975—79; assoc. Proskauer, Rose, Goetz & Mendelsohn, Washington, NYC and L.A., 1979—83, Fishman Group, Bloomfield Hills, Mich., 1983—85, ptnr., 1985—87; sr. ptnr. Honigman, Miller, Schwartz and Cohn, 1987—94; pres., CEO Morgan Daniels Co., Inc., West Bloomfield, Mich., 1994—; ptnr. Clark Klein & Beaumont, P.L.C., Detroit, 1995—96, Clark Hill, P.L.C., Detroit, 1996—2003, mem. exec. com., 1999—2001; ptnr. Dickinson Wright, PLLC, 2003—08, Foster, Swift, Collins & Smith, PC, 2008—. Bd. dirs. Mich. Food and Beverage Assn., Air Conditioning Contractors of Am., Air Conditioning Contractors of Mich., Am. Subcontractors Assn., Mich. Mfrs. Assn. Labor Counsel, Jewish Vocat. Svcs., Constrn. Fin. Mgmt. Assn., Mich. Assn. Home Builders. Gen. counsel Rep. Com. of Oakland County, 1986—; chmn. Constrn. Code Commn. Mich., 1993—; bd. dirs. 300 Club, Mich., 1984-90; pres. 400 Club, 1990-93, chmn., 1993—; mem. Associated Gen. Contractors Labor Lawyers Coun.; mem. Rep. Nat. Com. Nat. Rep. Senatorial Com., Presdl. Task Force, Rep. Labor Coun., Washington; city dir. West Bloomfield, 1985-87; pres. West Bloomfield Rep. Club, 1985-87; chmn. bd. trustees Am. Soc. Edn. Found., 2005—; fin. com. Rep. Com. of Oakland County, 1984-93; pres. Oakland County Lincoln Rep. Club, 1989-90; bd. dirs. camping svcs. and human resources com. YMCA, 1989-93, Anti-Defamation League, 1989—; vice chmn. Lawyers for Reagan-Bush, 1984; v.p. Fruehauf Farms, West Bloomfield, Mich., 1985-88; mem. staff Exec. Office of Pres. of US Inquiries/Comments, Washington, 1981-83. Fellow Coll. Labor and Employment Attys.; mem. ABA, FBA, Mich. Bar Assn., Fla. Bar Assn. (labor com. 1977—), Rep. Nat. Lawyers Assn., Mich. Bus. and Profl. Assn., Am. Acad. Constrn. and Labor Attys. (exec. dir. 1998—), Am. Subcontractors Assn. (Southeastern Mich., bd. dirs.), Founders Soc. Detroit Bar Assn., Assn. Corp. Growth (Detroit chpt.), Oakland County Bar Assn., Mich. Infrastructure and Transp. Assn., Constrn. Mgmt. Fin. Assn., B'nai B'rith (v.p. 1982-83, trustee 1987-88, bd. dirs. Detroit Barristers unit 1983-91, pres. 1985-87), Am. Soc. Employers (chmn. 2003-05, chmn. ednl. found. 2005—), Oakpointe Country Club, Detroit Soc. Clubs, Skyline Club, Fairlane Club, Detroit Athletic Club, Renaissance Club, Econ. Club Detroit. Office: Dickinson Wright PLLC 500 Woodward Ave Ste 4000 Detroit MI 48226 also: Morgan Daniels Co Inc 5484 Crispin Way Rd West Bloomfield MI 48323-3402 Office Phone: 248-539-9919. Personal E-mail: fmamat@aol.com. E-mail: fmatac@fosterswift.com.

MAMAUX, LALE M., legislative staff member; BA in Polit. Sci., Mary Baldwin Coll., Staunton, Va., 2000; MA in Polit. Sci., Am. U., Washington, 2002. Dep. dir. polit. affairs Kimball Stroud & Assoc., Inc., Washington; press. sec. to congressman Robert Wexler US House of Reps., Washington, 2003—04, comm. dir., 2004—07, comm. dir., Commn. Security & Cooperation in Europe, 2007—09, chief of staff to congressman Alcee Hastings, 2009—; dir. external rels. for digital TV transition Nat. Assn. Broadcasters, 2007. Press sec. Kerry-Edwards Presdl. campaign, Fla., 2004. Mailing: US House Reps 2353 Rayburn Office Bldg Washington DC 20515 Office Phone: 202-225-1313. Office Fax: 202-225-1171.*

MAMBULA, CHARLES J., finance educator, consultant; b. Gindiri, Plateau, Nigeria, Nov. 15, 1960; s. Jabani P. and Martha J. Mambula; m. Salamatu S. Machunga; children: Wadiamu J., Martha V., Charles J. BSc, Manchester Coll., Ind., 1983; MBA, U. Jos, Nigeria, 1989; PhD, U. Wales, Swansea, 1997. Cert. in new testament survey Ch. of Brethren, 1989. Asst. prof. Suffolk U., Boston, 2001—07; assoc. prof. Langston U., Okla., 2008—, chmn., 2008—. Cons. Jethro Mgmt. Consulting Co., Mashpee, Mass., 2007—; sr. ptnr. Global Venture Cons., Edmond, Okla., 2008—. Contbr. articles (Disting. Rsch. award, 2008). Nat. dep. chmn. Peoples Dem. Party Nigeria USA Chpt., Oklahoma City, 2006—. Summer Rsch. grant, Suffolk U., 2002. Democrat. Office: Langston Univ Sch Bus 33 Hwy E Langston OK 73050 Personal E-mail: mambula767@aol.com. Business E-Mail: cjmambula@lunet.edu.

MAMER, STUART MIES, lawyer; b. East Hardin, Ill., Feb. 23, 1921; s. Louis H. and Anna (Mies) M.; m. Donna E. Jordan, Sept. 10, 1944; children: Richard A., John S., Bruce J. AB, U. Ill., 1942, JD, 1947. Bar: Ill. bar 1947. Assoc. Thomas & Mulliken, Champaign, 1947-55; partner firm Thomas, Mamer & Haughey, Champaign, 1955—. Lectr. U. Ill. Coll. Law, Urbana, 1965-85; Mem. Atty. Registration and Disciplinary Commn. Ill., 1976-82 Chmn. fund drive Champaign County Community Chest, 1955; 1st pres. Champaign County United Fund, 1957; Pres., dir. U. Ill. McKinley Found., Champaign, 1957-69; trustee Children's Home and Aid Soc. of Ill., v.p., 1977-96. Served as pilot USAAC, 1943-45. Mem. Am. Coll. Trust and Estate Counsel (bd. regents 1984-90), Pillar of Champaign County Bar Assn., Phi Beta Kappa, Phi Gamma Delta. Republican. Presbyterian. Home: 101 W Windsor Rd # 3105 Urbana IL 61802-6663 Office: Thomas Mamer & Haughey LLP 30 E Main St Fl 5 Champaign IL 61820-3629 Office Phone: 217-351-1500. Business E-Mail: smamer@tmh-law.com.

MAMET, DAVID ALAN, playwright, scriptwriter; b. Chgo., Nov. 30, 1947; s. Bernard Morris and Lenore June (Silver) Mamet; m. Lindsay Crouse, Dec. 1977 (div.); m. Rebecca Pidgeon, Sept. 22, 1991. BA, Goddard Coll., Plainfield, Vt., 1969; DLitt (hon.), Dartmouth Coll., 1996. Artist-in-residence Goddard Coll., 1971-73; artistic dir. St. Nicholas Theatre Co., Chgo., 1973-75; guest lectr. U. Chgo., 1975, 79, NYU, 1981; assoc. artistic dir. Goodman Theater, Chgo., 1978; assoc. prof. film Columbia U., 1988. Chmn. bd. Atlantic Theater Co. Author: (plays) The Duck Variations, 1971, Sexual Perversity in Chicago, 1973 (Village Voice Obie award, N.Y. Drama Critics Cir. award), Reunion, 1973, Squirrels, 1974, American Buffalo, 1976, A Life in the Theatre, 1976, The Water Engine, 1976, The Woods, 1977, Lone Canoe, 1978, Prairie du Chien, 1978, Lakeboat, 1980, Donny March, 1981, Edmond, 1982 (Village Voice Obie award, 1983), The Disappearance of the Jews, 1983, The Shawl, 1985, Glengarry Glen Ross, 1984 (Pulitzer prize for drama, N.Y. Drama Critics Cir. award), Speed-the-Plow, 1987, Bobby Gould in Hell, 1989, The Old Neighborhood, 1991, Oleanna, 1992, The Cryptogram, 1994, Ricky Jay and His 52 Assistants, 1994, Death Defying Acts, 1995, Boston Marriage, 1999, Romance, 2005, November, 2007; dir.: (plays) Dangerous Corner, 1995; author: (screenplays) The Postman Always Rings Twice, 1979, The Verdict, 1980, The Untouchables, 1986, House of Games, 1986, We're No Angels, 1987, Homicide, 1991, Hoffa, 1991, Oleanna, 1994, The Edge, 1996, The Spanish Prisoner, 1996, Wag the Dog, 1997, Ronin, 1998, The Winslow Boy, 1999, State & Main, 2000, Lakeboat, 2001, Hannibal, 2001; co-author (with Shel Silverstein) Things Change, 1987; author: (novels) The Village, 1994, The Old Religion, 1996, Wilson: A Consideration of the Sources, 2001, (nonfiction) True and False: Heresy and Common Sense for the Actor, 1996, 3 Uses of the Knife: On the Nature and Purpose of Drama, 1996, The Wicked Son: Anti-Semitism, Self-Hatred and the Jews, 2006, Bambi vs. Godzilla: On the Nature, Purpose and Practice of the Movie Business, 2007, (children's books) Warm and Cold with drawings by Donald Sultan, 1985, Passover, The Duck and the Goat, 1996, The Duck and the Goat, Jafsie & John Henry, 1999, Bar Mitzvah, 1999, Henrietta, 1999, (essays) Writing In Restaurants, 1986, SomeFreaks, 1989, On Directing Film, 1990, The Cabin, 1992, Make-Believe-Town, 1996, (poetry) The China Man, 1999, The Hero Pony, 1990; dir.: (films) House of Games, 1986, The Winslow Boy, 1988, Things Change, 1988, Homicide, 1991, Oleanna, 1994, The Spanish Prisoner, 1996, State and Main, 2000, Catastrophe, 2000; dir., writer (films) Heist, 2001, Spartan, 2004, Redbelt, 2008, assoc. prodr. Hoffa, 1992; exec. prodr.: (TV films) Lansky, 1999, A Life in the Theater, 1993; prodr.: Lip Service, 1988; creator, writer (TV series) The Unit, 2006. Recipient Outer Critics Circle award for contbn. to Am. theater, 1978, Acad. award nominee for best screenplay adaptation, 1983, 1998, Common Wealth Award Distinguished Svc., 2004, Screen Laurel Award, Writers Guild Am., 2005; Rockefeller grantee, 1977, CBS Creative Writing fellow, Yale U. Drama Sch, 1976—77. Office: David Mamet 2 Northfield Plz Northfield IL 60093-1294

MAMIDWAR, SACHIN SURESHRAO, medical products executive; b. Nanded, Maharashtra, India, Aug. 12, 1975; s. Sureshrao Sambhappa and Nanda Sureshrao Mamidwar; m. Monika Belorkar; 1 child, Vedant. MS, Rutgers U., New Brunswick, NJ, 2002; MBBS, Byramjee Jeejeebhoy Med. Coll., Pune, Maharashtra, India, 1998. Lic. Maharashtra, 1998. Dir. product devel. Orthogen Corp., Springfield, NJ, 2004—07; gen. mgr. Orthogen LLC, 2007. Mem. editl. bd. Jour. Biomedical Materials Rsch., Springfield, NJ. Recipient Poster Presentation award, Rutgers U., 2001. Mem.: Am. Acad. Implant Dentistry, Acad. Osteointegration, Soc. Biomaterials. Achievements include patents for calcium sulfate based Bone grafts. Office: Orthogen LLC Suite 104 Springfield NJ 07081 Office Fax: 973 467-1218; Home Fax: 973 467-1218. Personal E-mail: sachin1275@hotmail.com. Business E-Mail: smamidwar@orthogencorp.com.

MAMLOK, WALTER JOSEPH, music educator, musician; b. Bronx, NY, Jan. 4, 1949; s. Julius Alvin and Ruth Mamlok; m. Carol Diane Rubin, Aug. 26, 1972; children: Charna Beth Westervelt, Elena Susanne. B in Music Edn., U. Hartford, 1971; MS, Ctrl. Conn. State U., 2000. Cert. profl. educator Conn. State Bd. Edn., 1994. Music tchr. Wethersfield (Conn.) Bd. Edn., 1971—75, 1976—80, Wolcott (Conn.) Bd. Edn., 1975—76; mgmt. Kemp Enterprises, South Windsor, Conn., 1980—88; music tchr. Newtown (Conn.) Bd. Edn., 1988—99, Meridan (Conn.) Bd. Edn., 1999—2001; music tchr. gr 6-12 Capitol Region Ednl. Coun., Hartford, Conn., 2001—04; mid. sch. music tchr. Bloomfield (Conn.) Bd. Edn., 2004—08, HS music tech. tchr., 2008—. Dir., condr. Strictly Swing Jazz Band, Bloomfield, 1977—; bass clarinetist Local 400 Pops Band, Rocky Hill, Conn., 1988—; musician Capital Winds Ensemble, Hartford, 1990—; clarinetist Klezical Tradition Klezmer Band, Fairfield, Conn., 1994—. Contbr. articles to profl. jours. Mem. Dem. Town Com., Bloomfield, 2004; v.p. bd. dirs. Temple Beth Sholom, Manchester, 1985—95, tchr., 1991—99; pres. Temple Beth Sholom Nursery Sch., Manchester, Conn., 1982—86. Mem.: Music Educators Technologists Assn. (treas., sec., charter), Conn Music Educators Assn., Conn. Edn. Assn. (assoc.), Music Educators Nat. Conf. (assoc.). Democrat. Jewish. Avocations: music, sports. Home: 1 South Ridge Dr Bloomfield CT 06002-5009 Office: Bloomfield Board of Education 390 Park Ave Bloomfield CT 06002 Home Phone: 860-243-1097. Personal E-mail: wmamlok@comcast.net. Business E-Mail: wmamlok@blmfld.org.

MAMMEL, MARK CRAWFORD, pediatrician, researcher; b. Hutchinson, Kans., Jan. 16, 1952; s. Russell Norman Mammel and Betty JoAnn Crawford; m. Nancy Ann Lauerman; children: Gordon Russell, Daniel Mark, Martin Dean. BA summa cum laude, U. Minn., Mpls., 1974, MD, 1978. Diplomate in pediat. Am. Bd. Pediat., 1982, in neonatology 1983. Ptnr. owner Assocs. Newborn Medicine, Pa., St. Paul, 1986—; prof. pediat. U. Minn., 1998—, co-dir. neonatal-perinatal fellowship program, 1990—. Dir., newborn rsch. & edn. Children's Hosps. & Clinics, St. Paul, 1994—, dir., Infant Diagnostic and Rsch. Ctr., 1994—. Contbr. scientific papers. Found. bd. mem. Children's Hosp. Found., St. Paul, 1996—2004; bd. mem. Children's Hosp., St. Paul, 1988—91. Fellow: Am. Acad. Pediat. (exec. com., perinatal sect. 2000—06, Young Investigator award 1985); mem.: Soc. Pediat. Rsch., Perinatal Rsch. Soc., Am. Pediat. Soc. Avocations: golf, travel, reading. Office: Assocs Newborn Medicine Pa 347 N Smith Ave 505 Saint Paul MN 55102 Office Fax: 651-220-7777. Business E-Mail: mamme001@umn.edu.

MAMMEL, RUSSELL NORMAN, retired food distribution company executive; b. Hutchinson, Kans., Apr. 28, 1926; s. Vyvian E. and Mabel Edwina (Hursh) M.; m. Betty Crawford, Oct. 29, 1949 (dec. Oct. 1994); children: Mark, Christopher, Elizabeth, Nancy. BS, U. Kans., 1949. With Mammel's Inc., Hutchinson, 1949-57, pres., 1957-59; retail gen. mgr. Kans. divsn. Nash Finch Co., Hutchinson, 1959-61, retail gen. mgr. Iowa divsn. Cedar Rapids, 1961-66, dir. store devel. Mpls., 1966-75, v.p., 1975-83, exec. v.p., 1983-85, pres., COO, 1985-91, also bd. dirs., 1991-97; pvt. investments, 1991—. With AUS, 1944-46. Office: Nash Finch Co 7600 France Ave S Ste 200 Minneapolis MN 55435-5920 Home: c/o B Howard 155 Gleason Lake Rd Apt 205 Wayzata MN 55391-1350

MAMUT, MARY CATHERINE, retired entrepreneur; b. Calabria, Italy, Oct. 17, 1923; came to U.S., 1928; d. Carmelo Charles and Caterina (Tripodi) Cogliandro; m. Michael Matthew Mamut, May 15, 1954; children: Anthony Carl, Charles Terrance. Student, Stenotype Comml. Coll., 1946-50. Sec. to pres. Thomas Goodfellow, Inc., Detroit, 1942-50; asst. to v.p. R.G. Moeller Co., Detroit, 1951-52; sec. to pres. United Steel Supply Co., Detroit, 1952-54; sec. to libr. Farmington (Mich.) Schs., 1962-68; real estate agt., 1969; owner, mgr. Crystal Fair, Birmingham, Mich., 1969-88, ret. Mich. Tchr. Stenotype Comml. Coll., Detroit, 1952-54. Vol. Henry Ford Mus., Dearborn, Mich., 1989-90, Greenfield Village, 1989-90, West Bloomfield Libr., 1993-95. Recipient World Lifetime Achievement award Am. Biog. Inst. U.S.A., 1993. Mem. Am. Bus. Women's Assn., Birmingham-Bloomfield C. of C., Profl. Secs. Internat, NAFE. Roman Catholic. Avocations: reading, music, art, theater. Home: 7423 Coach Ln West Bloomfield MI 48322-4022

MAN, DANIEL, plastic surgeon; married; 3 children. MD, Tel Aviv U., 1973. Lic. Maine, 1976, Del., 1976, Ky., 1978, Fla., 1981, diplomate in Plastic and Reconstructive Surgery Am. Bd. Plastic Surgery, 1981. Intern in gen. surgery Tel Hashomer Hosp., Ramat Gan, Israel, 1972—73; resident in gen. surgery Montefiore Hosp., Bronx, NY, 1974—76; resident in surgery Wilmington Gen. Hosp., Del., 1976—78; resident in plastic and reconstructive surgery U. Louisville, 1978—80; pvt. practice Boca Raton, Fla., 1981—. Presenter in field; profl. interviewed various mags., newspapers, and TV programs. Author: The Art of Man: Faces of Plastic Surgery, 1998, The New Art of Man: Faces of Plastic Surgery, 2002, Man at Work: A Photographic of Plastic Surgery and Art, 2006; contbr. books, anthologies, and profl. jours. in field. Recipient Humanitarian of Yr. award, Palm Beach County Victim Svcs., 2001, Letter of Recognition for Humanitarian Contbns., Fla. State Senator M. Mandy Dawson, 2001, Fla. State Senator Tom Rossin, 2001, US Congressman Robert Wexler, 2001, US Senator Bill Nelson, 2001, US Senator Bob Graham, 2001, Gov. Jeb Bush, Fla., 2001; named Dr. Man Day in his honor, Boca Raton, Fla., 2001; Hand fellowship, U. Louisville, 1978—80, Microvascular fellowship, 1980. Fellow: Am. Soc. Laser Surgery and Medicine; mem.: AMA, Y-ME Fla. (founding bd. mem. 1982—87, med. advisor 1982—87), Lipolysis Soc. N.Am., Broward County Soc. Plastic Surgeons, Palm Beach County Soc. Plastic Surgeons, Palm Beach County Med. Soc., Am. Soc. Aesthetic Plastic Surgery, Am. Soc. Plastic Surgeons. Office: 851 Meadows Rd Ste 222 Boca Raton FL 33486 Office Phone: 561-395-5508.

MAN, LAWRENCE KONG, architect, art dealer, entrepreneur; b. Kowloon, Hong Kong, July 4, 1953; s. Hon-Kwong Man and Sau-Ching Luk. Student, U. Redlands, 1971-72; BArch, U. Oreg., 1977; MArch, Harvard U., 1978. Registered architect, philanthropist, Dream Help Found., Calif. Designer, project architect Shepley Bulfinch Richardson & Abbott, Boston, 1978-86; project designer, project architect E. Verner Johnson & Assoc., Boston, 1987-91; owner Lawrence Man Architect, Cambridge, Mass., 1992-95, LA, 1994—. Prin. works include Kromka House, L.A., Calif., LMAN Studio, L.A., Chu House, Downey, Calif., Fong House, San Marino, Calif., Tighe Summer House, Sagamore Beach, Mass, Frozen Fusion Juice Bar, L.A. schs., Fed. Credit Union, L.A., Pub. Mus. Grand Rapids, Mich. (AIA Grand Valley Disting. Bldg. award 1997), LCP Studio, Somerville, Mass., New Asia Restaurants, Danvers and Arlington, Mass., Tai Pan Restaurant, Cambridge, Mass. (Honor award AIA 1993, New Eng. award Excellence in Architecture 1993, Design Excellence award Nat. Orgn. Minority Architects 1993), Ti-Sales Office, Sudbury, Mass. (Design Excellence award Nat. Orgn. Minority Architects 1993), Dental Clinic, Reading, Mass. (AIA Interior Architecture award 1992, Interior Design Project award Am. Soc. Interior Designers 1991, Boston Exports citation AIA 1990, Boston Soc. of Architects/New Eng. Healthcare Assembly honor award, 1994), Mus. Ctr. Union Terminal, Cin. (Reconstrn. award 1991), Ramesses Pavilion Boston Mus. Sci. (Double Vision award/Double Silver Soc. Environ. Graphics 1990), Smithsonian South Quadrangle Mus., Washington (Boston Exports award/citation AIA 1990, Honor award AIA 1989), U. Vt. Student Ctr., Burlington, Campus Ctr. Study and Libr. addition Franklin & Marshall Coll., Andover (Mass.) Co. Corp. Hdqs., Emerson Hosp., Concord, Mass., pvt. residences, others. Avocations: dance, travel, music. Office: 949 Chung King Rd Los Angeles CA 90012 Office Phone: 213-628-3883. Business E-Mail: info@lawrencemanarchitects.com. *There are ups and downs in life. It is more rewarding to experience them all, no matter how hard it may get sometimes. It allows you to become a more complete person. That is, in my view, a true achievement.*

MAN, PANG LING, retired psychiatrist; b. Hong Kong, China; arrived in U.S., 1963; s. Kwong Cheung and Loy-Ho Man; m. Hope Man, Mar. 8, 1958; children: Ching, Dick, Linda. Degree, Queen Coll., Hong Kong, 1953; MD, Sun Yat-Sen U., 1958. Intern, resident U. Hosp., Gongzhou, China, 1958—60; intern Grace Hosp., Winnipeg, Canada, 1963—64; resident Worcester State Hosp., Mass., 1964—67; instr. psychiatry U. Louisville, 1967—71; asst. prof. psychiatry Wayne State U., Detroit, 1971—78, assoc. prof. psychiatry, 1978—98, ret., 1998. Dir. rsch. Northville Regional Psychiatric Hosp., Mich., 1971—98, asst. dir. edn., 1971—90. Author: Handbook of Acupuncture Anesthesia, 1973; contbr. articles to profl. jours. Vol. physician Chinatown Free Clinic, Detroit, 1971—90. Fellow: Am. Psychiatric Assn., Am. Bd. Neurology and Psychiatry. Avocations: golf, travel, swimming, ping pong/table tennis, dance. Home: 6504 Horsemans Canyon Dr Walnut Creek CA 94595

MANABE, SYUKURO, meteorologist; b. Shingu, Shikoku-chuo-shi, Ehime-ken, Japan, Sept. 21, 1931; arrived in U.S., 1958; s. Seiichi and Sueko (Akashi) O.; m. Nobuko Nakamura, Jan. 21, 1962; children: Nagisa M., Yukari C. BS, Tokyo U., 1953, MS, 1955, PhD, 1958; DSc (hon.), McGill U., 2004. Rsch. meteorologist, gen. circulation rsch. sect. U.S. Weather Bur., Washington, 1958-63; sr. rsch. meteorologist Geophys. Fluid Dynamics Lab. Environ. Sci. Services Adminstrn., Washington, 1963-68; sr. rsch. meteorologist geophys. fluid dynamics lab. NOAA, Princeton, NJ, 1968-95, mem. sr. exec. svc. of U.S.A., geophys. fluid dynamics lab., 1979-95, sr. scientist, geophys. fluid dynamics lab., 1995-97; dir. global warming rsch. program Frontier Rsch. Sys. for Global Change, Yokohama, Japan, 1997—2001; sr. meteorologist Program in Atmospheric and Oceanic Sciences Princeton U., 2002—. Lectr. with rank of prof. Princeton U., 1968-98; vis. prof., faculty of sciences, Geophysical Inst., U. Tokyo, 1983, vis. prof. Sch. Environ. Sci., Nagoya (Japan) U., 2006. Contbr. articles to peer-reviewed publications. Recipient Gold medal U.S. Dept. Commerce, 1970, Presdl. Rank Meritorious Exec. award Pres. of U.S., 1989, Blue Planet prize Asahi Glass Found., 1992, Asahi prize Asahi Shimbun Cultural Found., 1995, Volvo Environ. prize Volvo Found., 1997, Milutin Milankovitch medal, European Geophys. Soc., 1998. Fellow AAAS, Am. Geophys. Union (Revelle medal 1993); mem. NAS, Acad. Europaea (fgn.), Royal Soc. Can. (fgn.), Japan Acad.(fgn.), Am. Meteorol. Soc. (hon., Meisinger award 1967, 2nd half century award 1977, C.G. Rossby Rsch. medal 1992), Royal Meteorol. Soc. (hon.), Japan Meteorol. Soc. (hon., Fujiwara award 1966). Achievements include first computers modeling study of global warming. Home: 6 Governors Ln Princeton NJ 08540-3666 Office: Princeton U Sayre Hall Forrestal Campus PO Box CN710 Princeton NJ 08544-0710

MANAF, MOHAMMED ZAINI, management consulting company executive; b. Muar, Johore, Malaysia, Feb. 24, 1941; s. Abdul Manaf Long and Azizah Thambi; m. Noor Aini Md. Zin, July 26, 1969; children: Sharifuddin, Aida Mastura, Shareen Adlina. Attended Maur HS & English Coll. at Johore Bahru, 1952-59, UK, 1960-67, attended Cornwall Tech. Coll., Redruth, Chiswick Poly.(now London Brunel U.), Isleworth Poly. (now Middlesex U.), City London Coll. (now London Met U.), London Sch. Econs. and Polit. Sci. U. London, DSc in Aero. Engring. (hon.), Pepperdine U., 1983; D.B.A., Pacific Western U., 1982,

LLD, 1983, D in Engring. Scis., 1987; DLitt. Clayton U., 1984, Colegio de Sto nino de jassan, 1999,PhD Kesington U., Calif., 1979; Dr. in Engring. Scis., Pacific Western U., 1987, D. Tech. Am. Coastline U., 1988, Litt.D. Summit U. La., 1993, D Faculty Commonwealth Open U., Brit. Virgin Islands, 1999. Cert. mfg. engr., mgmt. cons., professorship, 1992; profl. mgr. Can. Tech., adminstrv. asst. Borneo Co. (London) Ltd., Inchape Export Ltd., London, 1963-67; officer Chase Manhattan Bank, Kuala Lumpur, 1967-68; sales mgr. Wearne's Group of Cos., Kuala Lumpur, 1968-75; gen. mgr. Pernas Jardine Aviation Co., Kuala Lumpur, 1975-77; chmn. Manaf & Co., Kuala Lumpur, 1977—; gen. mgr. Seri Mechan Cons. Sdn. Bhd., Kuala Lumpur, 1983—; assoc. prof. Pacific Western U., Los Angeles, 1984-87, prof. and fellow, 1987—99; prof. engring. Clayton U., St. Louis, 1986, prof., 1986—87; mem. bd. advisors faculty engring. Nat. U. Malaysia, 1986—89; vis. lectr. Mara Inst. Tech., Shah Alam Selangor, Malaysia, 1970-73; hon. vis. fellow N.E. London Poly. (now called The U. East London), 1983—, vis. prof., 1986—; hon. cons. Imperial Coll. Sci. and Tech. U. London, 1986-96; prof., fellow Faculties of Engring. and Bus. Mgmt. Am. Coastline U., New Orleans, 1988—; assoc., Pepperdine U., 1984-. Author: Professional Organizations of Malaysia, 1979, chmn. bd. dirs. Manaf Sutter Inc. LA, 1983-89, The Malaysian Univs., 1981; contbr. articles to profl. jours. Com. mem. United Malay Nat. Orgn. Youth, Kuala Lumpur, 1971-77, Red Cross, 1975, UMNO Syed Putra Br., Kuala Lumpur, 1988. Recipient Disting. Svc. award U.S. Air Force, 1983, Pres. Disting. award, 1983, Hon. Citizen award Amb.-at-Large award eighteen govs., commrs. and mayors, Philippines, eight royal titles various Sultanates; named Hon. Admiral Gt. State Ala. Navy Gov. George C. Wallace, Gov. and Commdr.-in-Chief state Ala. Sec. State The Hon. Mr. D. Diegelman, 1983; created knight comdr. of merit Sovereign Order St. John of Jerusalem, 1986, knight grand comdr., 1987, appointed high commr. for Order St. John in Moslem countries with rank of brigadier in emergency med. corps, 1987, Baron of Hampstead and Petaling Jaya, 1993, named Hon. Mem. Louisiana Sheriff, 1996; diploma of honor Phi Kappa Phi, 1984; diploma Pi Epsilon Tau, 1981. Fellow AAIA, Brit. Inst. Mgmt., Inst. Chartered Shipbrokers U.K., Chartered Inst. Trasport UK, Chartered Inst. Arbitrators UK, Engring. Inst. Can., Can. Soc. Civil Engrs., Royal Soc. Arts London, Soc. Antiquaries Scotland, Royal Geog. Soc. London, World Lit. Acad.; hon. fellow Assn. Internat. Accts. U.K., Assn. Bus. Execs. U.K., Inst. Engrs. U.K. (Frank Haskell Silver medal 1982); mem. ASME, IEEE (founder, dep. pres. Malaysia chpt.), AAUP, Inst. Mgmt. Consultants Malaysia (founder, pres.) Nat. Soc. Prof. Engrs., 17 Am. acads. of sci. including N.Y. Acad. Scis., Phi Delta Kappa. Moslem. Clubs: Royal Overseas League (London); Royal Lake (Kuala Lumpur); Jaguar; Royal Commonwealth. Soc., Oxford U. Soc.(life)(hon. rep.), London Sch. Economics(life)(founder coun. mem. Malayasian Alumni) Home: Hampstead Lodge PO Box 1052 J Semangat Petaling Jaya 46860 Selangor Malaysia Personal E-mail: shareen.almanaf@gmail.com.

MANAFZADEH, SAEED, engineering educator, director; married. PhD, U. Ill., Chgo., 1983. Dir. undergrad. studies Dept. Mech. and Indsl. Engring., Chgo., 2005—. Office: Univ Ill Chgo 842 W Taylor St MC 251 Chicago IL 60607 Office Fax: 312-413-0447. Business E-Mail: saeedm@uic.edu.

MANANDHAR, GAURISHANKAR, cell biologist, educator; b. Kathmandu, Nepal, June 19, 1956; s. Shiva Shankar and Badri Kumari Manandhar; m. Minerva Manandhar, Dec. 12, 1984; children: Saurav, Nila. PhD, Moscow State U., 1991. Cert. cell biologist State Attestation Com., Russia, 1991. Asst lectr. Tribhuvan U., Kathmandu, 1982—92, lectr., 1992—99; vis. asst prof. Miyazaki Med. Coll., Japan, 1999—2002; rsch. asst prof. U. Mo., Columbia, 2005—. Contbr. scientific papers. Mem.: Soc. Study Reproduction (gen. mem. 1996—2008). Home: 911 Ashland Rd Apt E Columbia MO 65201 Office: Univ Mo 925 E Campus Dr Columbia MO 65211 Business E-Mail: manandharg@missouri.edu.

MANARA, JOCHEN WALTER, physicist, researcher; MS in Physics, Julius-Maximilians-U. Wuerzburg, Germany, 1997, PhD in Natural Scis., 2001. Rschr. ZAE Bayern, Wuerzburg, Germany, 2002—. Mem.: Assn. of German Engrs., German Phys. Soc. Office: ZAE Bayern Am Hubland Würzburg 97074 Germany Office Fax: 49(0)931/70564-60. Business E-Mail: manara@zae.uni-wuerzburg.de.

MANARY, MARK JOHN, pediatrician; b. Bay City, Mich., Apr. 5, 1956; BS in Chemistry and Chem. Engring.; MD, Wash. U. Sch. Medicine, 1982. Cert. Pediat., Pediat. Emergency Medicine. Resident, pediat. St. Louis Children's Hosp., 1983—85, attending physician, emergency unit; worked in Tanzania; med. officer, acting clin. dir. Cheyenne River Indian Reservation, SD; instr. pediat., divsn. pediat. emergency medicine Wash. U. Sch. Medicine, St. Louis, asst. prof. pediat., 1994, Helene B. Roberson Prof. Pediat. Contbr. several articles to prfl. jours. Mem.: Am. Soc. for Clin. Nutrition. Achievements include research interests that focus on different aspects of nutrition in populations of developing countries, especially in Malawi, Africa; founder of Peanut Butter Project. Office: Washington University Sch Medicine Campus Box 8116 660 S Euclid Ave Saint Louis MO 63110 Office Phone: 314-454-2341. Office Fax: 314-454-4345. Business E-Mail: manary@kids.wustl.edu.*

MANASSAH, JAMAL TEWFEK, electrical engineer, educator, management consultant; b. Haifa, Palestine, Feb. 23, 1945; s. Tewfek George and Alia Nasrallah (Kardoush) M.; m. Azza Tarek H.I. Mikdadi, Mar. 16, 1979; children: Tala, Nigh. BSc, Am. U., Beirut, Lebanon, 1966; MA, Columbia U., NYC, 1968, PhD, 1970. Mem. Inst. Advanced Study, Princeton, N.J., 1970-72, 74-79; asst. prof. Am. U. Beirut, 1972-75; chief sci. adviser Kuwait Inst. Sci. Rsch., 1976-81; COO Kuwait Found., 1979-81; prof. dept. elec. engring. CUNY, NYC, 1981—. Cons. Columbia Radiation Labs., N.Y.C., 1970-73, Ford Found., N.Y.C., 1973-79, NSF, Washington, 1978-83; chmn. Internat. Symposium Series, Kuwait, 1979-81; mng. dir. Khayatt and Co., Inc., N.Y.C., 1982; organizing com. Chem. Rsch. Applied to World Needs II, 1980-83; mem. Welfare Assn., Geneva, 1984-92; steering com. Internat. Workshop on Laser Physics, 1993-2000. Editor: Alternate Energy Sources (2 vols.) 1981; (with others) Advances in Food Producing Systems for Arid and Semiarid Lands (2 vols.), 1981, Innovations in Telecommunication (2 vols.), 1982, (with others) Transient Coherent Phenomena, 1995, Elementary Mathematical and Computational Tools for Electrical and Computer Engineering Using MATLAB®, 2001, 06, (with others) Coherent and Nonlinear Optics and Spectroscopy, 2002; mem. editl. bd. Internat. Jour. Laser Physics, 1994—, Laser Physics Letters, 2004—; contbr. articles to profl. jours. Commr. Lebanese Boy Scouts Assn., Beirut, 1972-75; adviser internat. program NSF, 1979-83; bd. dirs. CUNY Rsch. Found., 2001-03. Columbia U. faculty fellow, 1966-68, Pfister fellow, 1968-70; grantee NSF, 1982-87; recipient ABI Key award, 1987, Commemorative medal of honor, 1988; named Man of Yr., 1990. Mem. Assn. Mems. of Inst. for Advanced Study, Princeton Club. Christian Orthodox. Achievements include discovery of resonant absorption coefficient frequency shift; collective Lamb shift, pion minus condensation in nuclear matter, blackbody frequency shift; dynamical Lorenz shift, reflectivity frequency shift, induced coherent pulse compression, induced spectral broadening; induced frequency shift, three-photons frequency shift, twin peaks in second harmonics generation; induced waveguiding and focusing, time-space superspike, non-linear compression of noise correlation time, soliton phases; coherently inhibited amplification, induced channeling, delayed reflectivity, two-color photon echos; superradiance without inversion, pressure induced optical cavities, invisible gaps, periodicity enhanced precocious superradiant transition, acousto-induced reflectivity shift; metamorphosis of the emission angular profile; research in statistical field theory, nonlinear and quantum optics, photonics, ultrafast phenomena and new technologies assessment. Home: 55 E 87th St Apt 15G New York NY 10128-1051 Office: CUNY Dept Elec Engring Convent Ave New York NY 10031 Office Phone: 212-650-8133. Business E-Mail: manassah@ccny.cuny.edu.

MANASSE, HENRI RICHARD, JR., pharmaceutical executive; b. Amsterdam, The Netherlands, Nov. 27, 1945; came to U.S., 1954, naturalized, 1963; s. Henri David and Janny Lynn (Borst) M.; m. Arlynn Hem, Aug. 9, 1969; children: Bryan, Sheralynn. BS in Pharmacy, U. Ill., Chgo., 1968; MA, Loyola U., Chgo., 1972; PhD, U. Minn., 1974; DSc (hon.), Campbell U., 1997, Union U., 1997, Mercer U., 1998, LI U., NY, 2004. Lic. pharmacist, Ill. Rsch. pharmacist Xttrium Labs., Chgo., 1968-69; asst. to dean Coll. Pharmacy U. Ill., Chgo., 1969-72, asst. prof. pharmacy adminstrn., 1974-77, assoc. dean, 1977-80, acting dean, 1980-81, dean, prof., 1981-93, interim vice chancellor for health svcs., 1992-93; prof. coll. pharmacy and medicine U. Iowa, v.p. for health scis., 1993-96; exec. v.p.-designate Am. Soc. Health-Sys. Pharmacists, 1996—, CEO, exec. v.p., 1997—. Sr. policy fellow Ctr. on Drugs and Pub. Policy, U. Md., 1988—; mem. Ill. Bd. Pharmacy, Springfield, 1982-94; pub. mem. Am. Soc. Hosp. Pharmacists Commn. on Credentialling, Bethesda, Md., 1984-86; chair bd. dirs. Nat. Patient Safety Found., 1999-2001, chair bd. govs., 2006; mem. adv. bd. PEW Found. Health Professions Edn. Reform Commn.; bd. dirs. Am. Soc. Cons. Pharmacists Rsch. and Edn. Found.; pres. Coun. on Credentialing in Pharmacy, 1998—02; mem. quality quest prize selection com. Am. Hosp. Assn.; co-chair safe practices steering com. Nat. Quality Forum, 2001-04, adv. com. on exec. leadership; mem. sentinel events adv. com. JCAHO Sentinel, 2002—; cons. FDA Adv. Com. on Risk Mgmt. and Drug Safety, 2003-07; expert on patient safety Bd. Pharmacy Practice, profl. sec., 2005—, Internat. Pharm. Fedn., fellow, 2008; JCAHO mem. Internat. Adv. Com. on Patient Safety, with joint commn. resources, 2008-. Mem. editl. bd. Am. Jour. Hosp. Pharmacy, 1990-92; contbr. chpts. to books and articles to profl. jours. Pres. Downers Grove Sch. Bd. Caucus, Ill., 1984-85; bd. dirs. med. svc. Westside Holistic Ctr., Chgo., 1979-89. Recipient Lederle Faculty award Lederle Pharm. Co., 1975, Outstanding Achievement award U. Minn., 1998; named Alumnus of Yr., U. Ill. Alumni Assn., 1983. Jesse E Stewart Svc. award, U. of Illinois, 2004, Harvey A.K. Whitney Lecture award Am. Soc. Health Sys. Pharmacists, 2007. Fellow: Inst. Medicine Chgo.; mem.: NAS, AHRQ (ctrs. on edn. & rsch. therapeutics adv. com. mem. 2009—), Am. Soc. Assn. Execs., Am. Pharm. Assn., Inst. Medicine, Am. Soc. Health Sys. Pharmacists (H.A.K. Whitney award 2007), Am. Assn. Colls. Pharmacy (pres., adminstrv. bd. 1982—86, bd. dirs. 1984—86, pres. 1988—89). Baptist. Avocations: computers, international travel. Home: 10118 Vanderbilt Cir Rockville MD 20850-4674 Office: ASHP 7272 Wisconsin Ave Bethesda MD 20814 Office Phone: 301-657-3000, 301-664-8890. Business E-Mail: hrmjr@ashp.org.

MANATT, CHARLES TAYLOR, lawyer; b. Chgo., June 9, 1936; BS, Iowa State U., 1958; JD, George Washington U., 1962. Bar: Calif. 1962, U.S. Supreme Ct. 1967, D.C. 1985. Ptnr. Manatt, Phelps & Phillips, Washington, now chmn.; U.S. ambassador Dominican Republic, 1999—2001. Bd. editors George Washington Law Rev., 1960-62. Pres. Calif. Bankers Assn.; chmn. Nat. Democratic Inst., Calif. Dem. Com., Nat. Dem. Com., Internat. Found. for Election Sys.; chmn. bd. trustees George Washington U.; bd. dirs. Mayo Clinic, Wesley Found., Red Cloud Indian Sch.; gov. Iowa State Found.; trustee Mus. Am. History. Mem. ABA, Calif. State Bar, L.A. County Bar Assn., San Fernando Valley Bar Assn. (pres. 1971-72), Century City Bar Assn., Phi Delta Phi, Delta Sigma Rho. also: Manatt Phelps & Phillips Trident Ctr E Tower 11355 W Olympic Blvd Los Angeles CA 90064-1614 Office: Manatt Phelps Phillips 700 12th St NW Ste 1100 Washington DC 20005-4075

MANATT, RICHARD, retired education educator; b. Odebolt, Iowa, Dec. 13, 1931; s. William Price and Lucille (Taylor) M.; m. Sally Jo Johnson, Aug. 20, 1952; children— Tamra Jo, Ann Lea, Joel Price; m. Jacquelyn M. Nesset, Feb. 25, 1970; 1 child, Megan Sue. BSc, Iowa State U., 1953, MS, 1956; PhD, U. Iowa, 1964. Prin. Oskloosa (Iowa) Schs., 1959-62; rsch. assoc. U. Iowa, Iowa City, 1962-64; mem. faculty Iowa State U., Ames, 1964—, prof., 1972—, chmn. dept. ednl. adminstrn., 1970-80, 93-98, dir. Sch. Improvement Model Projects, 1980—, prof., 1998—2002, prof. emeritus, 2002—. Cons. performance evaluation for public and independent schs.; disting. vis. prof. Calif. State U., L.A. Author: Educator's Guide to the New Design, When Right is Wrong, Fundamentalists and the Public Schools, Clinical Manual for Teacher Performance Evaluation Compendias of Professional Growth Plans, (computer software program) Computer Assisted Teach Evaluation/Supervision. Served with AUS, 1953-55. Named Disting. Prof., Nat. Acad. Sch. Execs., 1979, Regents' Prof. Edn., 1994; recipient faculty citation Iowa State U. Alumni Assn., 1998, Margaret White Grad. Faculty award, 2001, Pres.'s award NAACP, 2002. Mem. NEA, NASSP, ASCD (Outstanding Cons. 1981), Am. Assn. Sch. Adminstrs., Phi Kappa Phi, Phi Delta Kappa, Delta Chi. Democrat. Methodist. Home: 2926 Monroe Dr Ames IA 50010-4362 Business E-Mail: rmanatt@iastate.edu.

MANCALL, ELLIOTT LEE, retired neurologist, educator; b. Hartford, Conn., July 31, 1927; s. Nicholas and Bess Tuch M.; m. Jacqueline Sue Cooper, Dec. 27, 1953; children: Andrew Cooper, Peter Cooper. BS, Trinity Coll., Hartford, 1948; MD, U. Pa., 1952. Diplomate Am. Bd. Psychiatry and Neurology. Intern Hartford Hosp., 1952-54; clk. in neurology Nat. Hosp. Nervous Disease, London, 1954-55; asst. resident neurology Neurol. Inst. NY, 1955-56; resident in neuropathology Mass. Gen. Hosp., 1956-57, clin. and rsch. fellow, 1957-58; tchg. fellow neuropathology Harvard Med. Sch., 1956-57; from asst. prof. neurology to assoc. prof. Jefferson Med. Coll., 1958-65; prof. medicine Hahnemann Med. Coll. and Hosp., 1965-76; prof. neurology Med. Coll. Pa.-Hahnemann U., 1993-95; prof. neurology, chmn. dept. Hahnemann Med. Coll. and Hosp., 1976-93; prof. neurology Jefferson Med. Coll., Phila., 1995—, interim chmn. dept. neurology, 1997—2003; prof. emeritus, 2006—. Dir. Hahnemann U. ALS Clinic, 1985-95; chmn. bd. dirs. Phila. Profl. Stds. Rev. Orgn., 1981-84. Author: (with others) The Human Cerebellum: A Topographical Atlas, 1961; (with B.J. Alpers) Clinical Neurology, 1971, Essentials of the Neurological Examination, 1971, 81; contbr. articles to profl. jours. With USN, 1945—47. Recipient Christian R. and Mary F. Lindback award, 1969, Oliver Meml. prize ophthalmology U. Pa., 1952. Fellow Am. Acad. Neurology (alt. del. to AMA 1982-86, gen. editor CONTINUUM 1991-2003, A.B. Baker award for excellence in neurol. edn. 1997, Presdl. award 2003); mem. Am. Neurol. Assn., Am. Assn. Neuropathology, Assn. Rsch. in Nervous and Mental Diseases, Soc. Neurosci., AAUP, Pa. Med. Peer Rev. Orgn. (dir. 1979-84), Phila. Neurol. Soc., Alpers Soc. Clin. Neurology, Coll. Physicians Phila., Sydenham Coterie, Phila. County Med. Soc., Pa. State Med. Soc., AMA (sec.-treas. sect. coun. neurology 1983-86), Am. Med. Soc. on Alcoholism, Neurology Intersoc. Liaison Group, Intersoc. Com. Neurol. Resources, Assn. Univ. Prof. Neurology (pres. 1988-90), Soc. for Exptl. Neuropathology, Am. Bd. Med. Specialities (exec. bd., chmn. com. study of evaluation procedures, 1992-99, rep. accreditation com. continuing med. edn. 1998-2004, chair accredidation coun., 2003-05), Am. Bd. Psychiatry and Neurology (v.p. 1990, del. to Am. Bd. Med. Spltys., dir. 1983-91, emeritus dir. 1991—, cons. 2004-), Pa. Blue Shield (profl. adv. coun. 1991-98). Democrat. Jewish. Home: PO Box 498 Lafayette Hill PA 19444-0498 Office: Ste 200 900 Walnut St Philadelphia PA 19107 Office Phone: 215-955-0707. Business E-Mail: elliott.mancall@jefferson.edu.

MANCALL, JACQUELINE COOPER, library and information scientist, educator; b. Phila., Mar. 31, 1932; d. Morris and Bertha Cooper; m. Elliott Lee Mancall, Dec. 27, 1953; children: Andrew Cooper, Peter Cooper. BA, U. Pa., 1954; MS, Drexel U. Sch. Libr. and Info. Sci., 1970, PhD, 1979. Adminstr. Miquon Sch., Pa., 1966—67, libr., 1967—76; tchg. asst. Drexel U., Phila., 1976—78, rsch. assoc., 1978, asst. prof., assoc. prof., 1979—89, prof., 1989—, prof. emeritus, 2007—. Chair Phila. Children's Reading Round Table, 1982—84, mem. steering com., 1979—89; mem. faculty coun. Drexel U., 1984—89, chair faculty coun., 1987—89, mem. senate, 2000—05, chair senate, 2001—02; mem. sch. libr. survey com. State Libr. Pa., 1993; cons. Author (with M.C. Drott): Measuring Student Information Use: A Guide for School Library Media Specialists, 1963; author: (with E.S. Aversa) Management of Online Search Services in Schools, 1989; author: (with Sandra Hughes-Hassell) Collection for Management Youth, 2005; rsch. editor: Sch. Libr. Media quar., 1982—88, mem. editl. bd.: Jour. Libr. and Info. Sci. Edn., 1981—86, mem. editl. adv. bd.: Multimedia Schs.; contbg. editor: Cath. Libr. World, 1981—85; contbr. chapters to books, articles to profl. jours. Bd. dirs. Friends of William Jeannes Meml. Libr., Plymouth Meeting, Pa., 1976—79; pres. bd. dirs. Miquon Sch., 1964—66. Recipient Harold M. Myers award for Outstanding Svc., Drexel U., 1990, Ann. award, Phila. Sch. Libr., 1994. Mem.: ALA (adv. com. office info. tech. 1995—97, continuing edn. task force 1995—98, co-chair ICONect evaluation com. 1996—2000, libr. congress nat. digital libr. adv. com. 1997, pub. awareness com. 1997—99, dir. KidsConnect 2000—02), Am. Assn. Sch. Libr. (chmn. continuing edn. com. 1985—87, rsch. stats. com. 1988—92, v.p./pres.-elect 1993, pres. 1994, Disting. Svc. award 1999), Pa. Sch. Librs. Assn. (chmn. profl. std. com. 1980—82, bd. dirs. 1984—87, chmn. profl. std. com. 1991—, Outstanding Contbr. award 1997), Phi Delta Kappa, Beta Phi Mu, Pi Gamma Mu. Democrat. Jewish. Office: Drexel U ISchool Philadelphia PA 19104 Business E-Mail: jackie.mancall@drexel.edu.

MANCERA AGUAYO, MIGUEL, retired banker; b. Mexico, Dec. 18, 1932; s. Rafael and Luisa (Aguayo) Mancera; m. Sonia Corcuera, July 18, 1959; children: Miguel, Carlos, Jaime, Alvaro, Gonzalo. Licenciado en Economla, Inst. Tecnilógico Autónomo, México, 1956; M in Econs., Yale U., New Haven, Conn., 1960; Dr. honoris causa, Instituo Tecnologico Autonomo de Mexico, 2006. With Banco De Comercio, S.A., 1953-56; economist Pub. Investment Commn., Presidency of the Rep., Mex., 1957-58, Banco De Mex., 1958-62, adminstr. export fin. and export credit guarantee fund, 1962-67, mgr. internat. affairs, 1967-71, dep. dir., 1971-73, gen. dep. dir., 1973-82, dir. gen., 1982-94, gov., 1994-97. Tchr. Free Sch. Law, 1957, L.Am. Ctr. Econ. Studies, 1962-64; bd. govs. Inst. Tecnológico Autónomo México, tchr. 1958-64. Bd. govs. Soc. Friends Nat. Mus. Art; mem. treasury com. Fundación para las letras Mexicanas; bd. dirs. Fundacion Mexicana para el Desarrollo Rural, Fundacion Mexicana para el Edn, la tech y la ciencia; bd. dirs. Fondo Mexicano para la Conservación de la Naturaleza, Fundación Gonzalo Río Arronte, Found. Merced, Centro Mexicano para la Filantropía; econ. adv. com. Inst. Mex. Ejecutivos Finanzas. Recipient Gran Oficial De La Orden De Rio Branco, Brasil, 1983; officer de la Legion de Honneur, France, 1990; recipient prize in econs., Rey Juan Carlos, Madrid, 1992, medal Ciudad de Mexico, 1993. Mem. Colegio Nacional de Economistas, Asociación Nacional de Ex-Alumnos del Inst. Tecnologico Autónomo de Méx, Yale U. Alumni Assn., Yale U. Club de Mex. Roman Catholic. Avocations: reading, classical music, riding.

MANCHESTER, KENNETH EDWARD, electronics executive, consultant; b. Winona, Minn., Mar. 22, 1925; s. Laurence Edwin and Daisy Idel (Finley) M.; m. Bonnie Lee Hardgrave, June 24, 1946; children: Cynthia Lee, David Scott. AB, San Jose State Coll., 1949; MS, Stanford U., 1950, PhD, 1955. Sr. chemist Shell Devel. Co., Emeryville, Calif., 1955-62; head chemistry sect. Sprague Electric Co., North Adams, Mass., 1962-63, head chemistry dept., 1963-69, dir. semiconductor rsch., devel. and engring., 1969-79, dir. quality assurance and reliability Worcester, Mass., 1979-85, v.p. corp. R & D North Adams, 1985-89, Sprague fellow, 1985; cons. semiconductor industry, 1989—. Lectr. Rensselaer Poly. Inst., Troy, N.Y., 1967. Contbr. articles to profl. jours.; patentee in field. Chmn. com. Troop 70 Boy Scouts Am. Sgt. U.S. Army Ground Forces, 1943-46, ETO. Named to Hall of Fame, Nat. Inventors, 2009. Mem. Am. Chem. Soc., AIME, Optimist Club, Sigma Xi. Democrat. Avocations: woodworking, golf.

MANCHESTER, LUCIEN CALEB, biology professor; married; children: Ella Bridgewater, Marissa Alexander. AA, BA, MA, U. Virgin Is. & U. Nebr. Med Ctr., St. Thomas, VI. & Omaha, PhD, 1983. Cert. math. & English London, 1965. Prof. anatomy, histology & physiology St. Mary's U., San Antonio, 1988—; adj. prof. U. Tex. Health Sci. Ctr., San Antonio, 1991—. Contbr. articles to profl. pubs. Sci. mentor to judson Upward Bound Program, San Antonio, 1988—2009. Rsch. grant, St. Mary's U., 1993—95. Mem.: Beta Beta Beta Biol. Soc. (advisor, mentor 1991—2009). Liberal. Methodist. Achievements include research in melatonin as an anti-oxidant & free radical scavenger; discovery of melatonin in procaryotes, seeds & bone marrow. Avocations: tennis, travel, volleyball, softball, golf. Office: St Mary's Univ 1 Camino Santa Maria San Antonio TX 78228

MANCHESTER, ROBERT W., psychologist; s. Diane M. Metz; m. Cynthia A. Smith, June 1, 1979; children: Jonathan A., Marcus R., Sara A. BS in Edn., Ohio State U., Columbus, 1981. Cert. ednl. therapist Nat. Inst. Learning Devel., 2006. Tchr. Living Vine Christian Sch., Newark, Ohio, 1981—84; mgmt. analyst Dept. Def., Washington, 1985—92; min. Newark, 1992—95; coord. religious edn. Ramstein AFB, 1996—99; tchr. third grade So. Md. Christian Acad., White Plains, 1999—2000, Grace Brethren Christian Sch., Clinton, Md., 2000—01, tchr. sixth grade, 2001—02, tchr. fourth grade, 2002—05, ednl. therapist, 2005—. Mem.: Nat. Forensic League, Assn. Christian Schs. Internat. (assoc.), Nat. Inst. Learning Devel. (assoc.). Conservative. Presbyterian. Avocation: reading. Office: Grace Brethren Christian Sch 6501 Surrats Rd Clinton MD 20735 Business E-Mail: robert.w.manchester@gbcseagles.org.

MANCIAS, PEEDRO, pediatrician; b. Sullivan City, Tex., Aug. 28, 1962; s. Raciel Armando and Martha Idalia Mancias; m. Beatriz Chavez, June 24, 1994; children: Pedro Jr., Mariana Isabelle, Paul Alexandro. BS, Pan Am. U., Edinburg, Tex., 1984. Cert. physician Tex. Med. Bd., 1988, in child neurology ABPN, 1998, in electrophysiology 1999. Clin. instr.

Dept. Pediat. UAMS, Little Rock, 1994—96; asst. prof. U. Tex. Med. Sch. Houston, 1996—2004, assoc. prof., 1996—. Recipient Humanism award, Leonard Tow Found., 2008; named Best Tchr., U. Tex. Med. Sch. Houston, 2006—08. Mem.: Peripheral Nerve Soc., Houston Neurol. Soc., AAEM, Tex. Med. Assn., Child Neurology Soc. Office: Univ Tex Med Sch-Houston 6431 Fannin Ste 7156a Houston TX 77030

MANCILLA, FAUSTINA RAMIREZ, retired psychologist; b. Tijuana, Mexico, Feb. 15, 1943; d. Domingo Gomez and Carmen Castillo Ramirez; m. Armando Hernandez Mancilla, Nov. 30, 1957; children: Irene M. Torres, Alice M. Kincaid, Edward, Sergio Armando, Jaime. BA in Liberal Studies, Loyola Marymount U., LA, 1980, MA in Counseling and Guidance, 1986, MA in Counseling Psychology, Marriage and Family, 1986, MA in Ednl. Psychology, 1987, MA in Sch. Adminstrn., 1993; MA in Profl. Adminstrv. Svcs., Azusa Pacific U., Azusa, Calif., 1999; PhD in Behavioral Studies, Azusa Pacific U., 2000. Guidance tech. Culver City Unified Sch. Dist., Calif., 1980—84; tchr. k-5, bilingual Lennox Sch. Dist., 1984—85, tchr. spl. edn., 1985—86; bilingual sch. psychologist Santa Monica/Malibu Unified Sch. Dist., 1986—90; asst. prin. Lennox Sch. Dist., 1990—91, sr. psychologist, 1991—93, dir. pupil pers. svcs., 1993—97; dist. psychologist Murrieta Valley Unified Sch. Dist., 1997—99; coord., prin., infant cir., presch. grasp Riverside County Office Edn., 1999—2003; interim dir. pupil svcs. Murrieta Valley Unified Sch. Dist., 1999—99; coord., site adminstr., interagency assessment and tng. ctr. Riverside County Office Edn., 2003—05. Early childhood devel. cons. Riverside County Office Edn., 2003—06. Cert. parent trainer instr. Ctr. Improvement Children, LA, 1986—90; trainer trainer Los Padres Richstone Family Ctr., Lawndale, 1987—90; cert. interpreter/translator trainer Loyola Marymount U., LA, 1990—2006; cert. trainer spl. projects bilingual edn. San Diego County Dept. Edn., 1995—96; trainer trainers tchg. strategies young children Dept. Edn. -Nat. Project, 1993—96. Recipient Outstanding Bilingual Psychologist award, Santa Monica/Malibu Unified Sch. Dist., 1989, Outstanding Svc. award, Supr. and Trainer, Loyola Marymount U., 1994, 1996, Outstanding Svc. award, Dist. Adv. Coun., Lennox Sch. Dist., 1997. Mem.: Calif. Assn. Sch. Psychologists, Assn. Calif. Sch. Adminstrs. (assoc.), Nat. Assn. Sch. Psychologists (assoc.), Kappa Delta Phi (hon.). Avocations: travel, dance, painting. Home: 31597 Vignes Court Winchester CA 92596 Office: Riverside County Office of Education 3939 Thirteenth Street Riverside CA 92502-0868

MANCINI, DERRICK CHARLES, physicist; b. Spokane, Wash., Sept. 11, 1956; s. Michael and Marjorie Lue (Delay) M.; m. Elizabeth Montgomery Gardner, july 23, 1994. AB in History, Cornell U., 1982, BS in Engring. Physics, 1982; MS in Materials Sci., U. Wis., 1983, MS in Physics, 1985; PhD, Uppsala U., 1994. Editor Plenum Pub., NYC, 1977-79; rsch. asst. CHESS Cornell U., Ithaca, N.Y., 1981-82, CXRL U. Wis., Madison, 1982-91; rsch. fellow Uppsala (Sweden) U., 1992-94, MAXLab, Lund, Sweden, 1994-95; staff scientist Argonne (Ill.) Nat. Lab., 1995—. Contbr. articles to profl. jours. Mem. Am. Phys. Soc., SPIE, Electrochem. Soc. Avocation: gourmet cooking. Office: Argonne Nat Lab APS/431 9700 Cass Ave # Aps/431 Argonne IL 60439-4803

MANCINI, ERNEST ANTHONY, geologist, educator, researcher; b. Reading, Pa., Feb. 27, 1947; s. Ernest and Marian K. (Filbert) M.; m. Marilyn E. Lee, Dec. 27, 1969; children: Lisa L., Lauren N. BS, Albright Coll., 1969; MS, So. Ill. U., 1972; PhD, Tex. A&M U., 1974. Petroleum exploration geologist Cities Svc. Oil Co., Denver, 1974-76; asst. prof. geology U. Ala., Tuscaloosa, 1976-79, assoc. prof., 1979-84, prof., 1984—, Disting. Rsch. prof., 2005—. State geologist, oil and gas supr. State Ala., Tuscaloosa, 1982-96; regional dir. Ea. Gulf Region of the Petroleum Tech. Transfer Coun., 1995-2007; founding dir. Ctr. Sedimentary Basin Studies, U. Ala., 1998—; interim chair, Dept. Geol. Scis. U. Ala. Contbr. articles to profl. jours. Geol. Soc. Am. fellow; recipient Nat. Coun. Citation Albright Coll., 1983, Pratt-Haas Disting. Lectr. Am. Assn. Petroleum Geologists, 1987-88, Blackman Moody Outstanding Prof. award, U. Ala., 2007. Mem. Geol. Soc. Am. (past chmn. S.E. sect.), Am. Assn. Petroleum Geologists (hon., A.I. Levorsen petroleum geology Meml. award Gulf Coast Assn., geol. socs. sect. 1980, chair rsch. com. 2001-04, assoc. editor, 2003-04, editor, 2004-07, Disting. Educator award 2000), Assn. Am. State Geologists (hon., past pres.), Am. Geol. Inst. (past pres., Ian Campbell medal 2004), Am. Geol. Inst. Found. (trustee), Nat. Assn. State Univs. and Land-Grant Colls. (past chair, mineral and energy resources sect. mem. bd. natural resources), Soc. Econ. Paleontologists and Mineralogists Gulf Coast sect. (hon., past pres.), Paleontol. Soc. (past pres. southeast sect.), Ala. Geol. Soc. (past pres.), Gulf Coast Assn. Geol. Scis. (hon., Outstanding Educator award 1998), Sigma Xi (past chpt. pres.), Phi Kappa Phi (past chpt. pres.), Phi Sigma. Presbyterian. Home: 15271 Four Winds Loop Northport AL 35475-3325 Office: U Ala Dept Geol Scis PO Box 870338 Tuscaloosa AL 35487-0338 Business E-Mail: emancini@geo.ua.edu.

MANCINI, JOHN, editor, publishing executive; b. NYC; m. Laura Litterello; 2 children. BA in Comm. Arts, LI Univ-C.W. Post. Reporter Greenwich Time, 1982—83; copy editor Stamford Advocate, Conn., 1983—85; presentation editor NY Times, 1995; dep. met. editor NY Post, 1995—96, met. editor, 1999—2001; founding editor-in-chief LI Voice, 1996—99; editorial asst. Newsday, 1980—82, copy editor, graphics editor, Sunday news editor, night city editor, day city editor, NY edition, 1985—95, met. editor, 2001—03, asst. mng. editor/NY, 2003—04, exec. v.p., editor, 2004—. Office: Newsday 235 Pinelawn Rd Melville NY 11747-4250 Office Phone: 631-843-4177. Office Fax: 631-843-4719. Business E-Mail: john.mancini@newsday.com.*

MANCINO, DOUGLAS MICHAEL, lawyer; b. May 8, 1949; s. Paul and Adele (Brazaitis) M.; m. Carol Keith, June 16, 1973. BA, Kent State U., 1971; JD, Ohio State U., 1974. Bar: Ohio 1974, U.S. Tax Ct. 1977, Calif. 1981, D.C. 1981. Assoc. Baker & Hostetler, Cleve., 1974-80; ptnr. Memel & Ellsworth, LA, 1980-87, McDermott, Will & Emery, LA, 1987—. Bd. dirs. Health Net of Calif. Inc. Author: Taxation of Hospitals and Health Care Organizations, 2000, (with others) Hospital Survival Guide, 1984, Navigating the Federal Physician Self-Referral Law, 1998; (with F. Hill) Taxation of Exempt Organizations, 2002; co-author quar. tax column Am. Hosp. Assn. publ. Health Law Vigil, (with L. Burns) Joint Ventures Between Hosps. and Physicians, 1987; contbr. articles to profl. jours. Chmn. bd. dirs. The Children's Burn Found.; bd. dirs. Kent State U. Found., Inc. Mem. ABA (tax, bus., real property, probate and trust sects., chair exempt orgns. com. 1995-97, coun. dir. 1999—), Calif. State Bar Assn. (tax, bus. law sects.), Ohio Bar Assn., Calif. State Bar, D.C. Bar Assn., Am. Health Lawyers Assn. (bd. dirs. 1986-95, pres. 1993-94), Calif. Soc. for Healthcare Attys., Bel Air Country Club, The Regency Club, Calif. Yacht Club. Office: McDermott Will & Emery 2049 Century Park E Fl 34 Los Angeles CA 90067-3101 E-mail: dmancino@mwe.com.

MANCOFF, NEAL ALAN, lawyer; b. Chgo., May 7, 1939; s. Isadore and Sarah (Leviton) M.; m. Alys Belofsky, June 26, 1966; children: Wesley, Frederick, Daniel. BBA, U. Wis., 1961; JD, Northwestern U., 1965. Bar: Ill. 1965, U.S. Dist. Ct. (no. dist.) Ill. 1965. Assoc. Aaron Aaron Schimberg & Hess, Chgo., 1965-72, ptnr., 1972-80, Schiff Hardin & Waite, Chgo., 1980—. Author: Qualified Deferred Compensation Plans, 1983, Nonqualified Deferred Compensation Agreements, 1987. Lst lt. U.S. Army, 1961-62. Mem. Chgo. Bar Assn. (chmn. employee benefits com. 1984). Office: Schiff Hardin LLC 7500 Sears Tower Chicago IL 60606

MANCUSO, FRANK G., entertainment and communications company executive; b. Buffalo, July 25, 1933; married Ed., SUNY. Film buyer, ops. supr. Basil Enterprises, 1959-63; joined Paramount Pictures Corp., 1963, booker Buffalo br., 1963-64, sales rep. Buffalo br., 1964-67, br. mgr., 1967-70; v.p., gen. sales mgr. Paramount Pictures Can. Ltd., 1970-72, pres., 1972-76; U.S. we. divsn. mgr. Paramount Pictures Corp., LA, 1976-77, gen. sales mgr. NYC, 1977, v.p. domestic distbn., 1977-79, exec. v.p. distbn. and mktg., 1979-83, pres. motion picture divsn., 1983-84, chmn., CEO NYC, 1984-91; chmn, CEO Metro-Goldwyn-Mayer, 1993-99. Bd. dirs. Metro-Goldwyn Mayer. Bd. dirs. Will Rogers Meml. Fund, N.Y.-Cornell Med. Ctr., Burke Rehab. Ctr., UCLA Med. Ctr., Mus. of Broadcasting, MGM Motion Picture TV Found. Mem. Acad. Motion Picture Arts and Scis. (bd. dirs.), Motion Picture Assn. (bd. dirs.), Am. Film Inst. (bd. dirs.), Motion Picture Pioneers (bd. dirs.), Variety Clubs Internat. (bd. dirs.). Office: Metro Goldwyn Mayer Inc 2500 Broadway Ste B-201 Santa Monica CA 90404-3065

MANCUSO, JOHN HENRY, retired lawyer, bank executive; b. Utica, NY, June 5, 1944; arrived in U.S., 1987; s. Sam A. and Frances H. (Nelson) M.; m. Etel Tumma, July 18, 1970; children: Christa E., John A. BA in English magna cum laude, Boston Coll., 1968; MA in English, Lehigh U., 1970; MS in Higher Edn. Adminstrn., Syracuse U., 1973, PhD in Higher Edn. Adminstrn., 1978, JD, 1975. Bar: (NY) 1999. Assoc. Hiscock & Barclay, Syracuse, 1976-80, ptnr., 1981-90; gen. counsel Key Bank of N.Y., Albany, 1992-94; sr. v.p., dep. gen. counsel KeyCorp, Cleve. and Albany, NY, 1990—2001, exec. v.p., gen. counsel, 2001—03; gen. counsel, sec. Key Bank Nat. Assn., Cleve., 1994—2003, vice chmn., 2001—03. Mem. U.S. Senate Banking Com. Task Force on Fin. Modernization Bill, 1998; adj. prof. law Syracuse U., 1976-87, tchr. higher edn. adminstrn. grad. sch.; English tchr. at various colls., secondary schs., 1968-73; spkr. in field; bd. dirs. Key Bank Nat. Assn., Key Corporate Capital Inc., KeyCorp Ins. Co. Ltd. Author: Home Equity Update: A Manual for Lenders and Lawyers, 1989; co-author: Compliance Examinations Update for Financial Institutions, 1985-2001, The Law of Truth in Lending: 1989, Supplement, Reporting to Bank Regulators: Requirements and Forms Manual, 1990, Bank Regulatory Update: Beyond Consumer Issues, 1995-97; contbr. numerous articles to profl. publs. Chmn. planning bd. Village of Manlius, N.Y., 1983-86; trustee Cleve. Hearing and Speech Ctr., 2000-03; bd. dirs. St. Mary's Sem., Cleve., 2003-05. Mem. Am. Bankers Assn. (bank counsel com. 1996-98), Am. Coll. Consumer Fin. Svcs. Lawyers (founding mem., 2001), N.Y. State Bar Assn. (chair bus. law sect. 1994-95, chmn. consumer fin. svcs. com. bus. law sect. 1988-91, chmn. subcom. on equal credit opportunity/truth-in-lending 1985-86, chmn. subcom. on credit cards/fair credit billing 1982-83), N.Y. State Bankers Assn. (mem. lawyers retail legis. com. 1992-94, ops. and payments sys. com. 1988-90, legal advisor to residential mortgage com. of consumer banking divsn. 1986-87, mem. lawyers adv. com. 1994-2003), Consumer Bankers Assn. (mem. ad hoc com. on bank investment products 1993-97, mem. lawyers com. 1987-97), Justinian Soc., Order of Coif. Republican. Avocations: skiing, golf, tennis, reading, chess.

MANCUSO, J(OHN) JAMES, librarian; b. Olean, NY, Apr. 19, 1958; s. Frank A. and Josephine (Romano) M. m. Kathleen M. Petrie, June 29, 1985; children: Nicholas, Victoria, Benjamin. BA, Syracuse U., 1979, MLS, 1983. Bibliographic asst. Ctrl. Libr. Coun., Syracuse, N.Y., 1980-83; quality control specialist BRS, Latham, N.Y., 1983-86; asst. dir. libr. Capital Dist. Libr. Coun., Albany, N.Y., 1986-2000; libr. Mid-Am. Bapt. Theol. Sem., Schenectady, N.Y., 2000—. Reference libr. Schenectady County Pub. Libr., Schenectady, N.Y., part-time 1993-2001; book reviewer Pub. Rsch. Quar., 1995-97. Editor, compiler: Directory of Repositories, 2000; contbr. articles to profl. jours.; inventor Orderly Arrangement of Knowledge (OAK)libr. classification sys. Ch. libr. 1st Presbyn. Ch., Schenectady, 1993— Mem. N.Y. Libr. Assn. (legis. com. 1992-97, sect. on mgmt. of resources and tech. smart Dewey fellow 1992), Hudson-Mohawk Libr. Assn. (pres. 1993-97), Capital Area Archivists N.Y. (v.p. 1992-94). Republican. Avocations: genealogy, seashells, calligraphy, writing. Office: Mid-Am Bapt Theol Sem 2810 Curry Rd Schenectady NY 12303 Office Phone: 518-355-4000. E-mail: jimancuso@mabtsne.edu.

MANCUSO, MARIO, lawyer, former federal agency administrator; b. 1969; BA, Harvard U., 1991; JD, NYU Sch. Law, 1995. Law clk. to Hon. Thomas C. Platt US Dist. Ct. (ea. dist.) NY; atty. Ropes & Gray Internat. Law Firm, 1995—2005; spl. counsel US Dept. Def., 2005, dep. asst. sec. for spl. ops. & combating terrorism, 2005—07; under sec. for industry & security US Dept. Commerce, 2007—09; vis. sr. fellow The Hudson Inst., Washington, 2009—; ptnr. Akin Gump Strauss Hauer & Feld LLP, Washington, 2009—. Mem. advisory bd. Boliven, 2009—. Served in US Army, Operation Iraqi Freedom. Office: Akin Gump Strauss Hauer & Feld LLP Robert S Strauss Bldg 1333 New Hampshire Ave Washington DC 20036 Office Phone: 202-482-4811, 202-887-4062. Office Fax: 202-887-4288. E-mail: mmancuso@akingump.com.*

MANCUSO, MICHAEL JOHN, corporate financial executive; BS, Villanova U.; MBA, Eastern Coll. Exec. in fin. mgmt. space systems divsn. GE; mgmt. positions through v.p. & CFO comml. engring., Pratt & Whitney group United Technologies Corp., 1986—93; CFO land systems divsn. Gen. Dynamics, Falls Church, Va., 1993-94, v.p., contr., 1994-97, sr. v.p., CFO, 1997—2006; v.p., CFO Computer Sciences Corp., Falls Church, Va., 2008—. Bd. dir. SPX Corp., 2005—, Shaw Group Inc., 2006—, LSI Corp. Office: Computer Sciences Corp 3170 Fairview Parl Dr Falls Church VA 22042*

MAND, MARTIN GARY, financial executive; b. Norfolk, Va., Sept. 26, 1936; s. Meyer J. and Lena (Sutton) M.; m. Shelly Cohen, Aug. 29, 1965; children: Gregory S., Michael E., Brian C. BS in Commerce, U. Va., 1958; MBA, U. Del., 1964. Various fin. staff and mgmt. positions E.I. du Pont de Nemours & Co., Wilmington, Del., 1961-81, v.p. taxes and fin. svcs., 1981-84, v.p., comptr., 1984-88, v.p., treas., 1989-90; sr. v.p., CFO, Nortel Networks, Mississauga, Ont., Canada, 1990—93, exec. v.p., CFO, 1993—94; chmn. pres., CEO Mand Assocs., Ltd., Wilmington, 1995—. Bd. dirs. Mizuho Corp Bank U.S.A., NYC, Townsends, Inc., Wilmington, Del.; pres. Fin. Execs. Rsch. Found., 1988—90. Co-author: (book) Partnering for Performance: Unleashing the Power of Finance in the 21st Century Organization, 2000. Lt. USN, 1958-61. Mem. Fin. Execs. Inst., Am. Mgmt. Assn. (chmn. fin. coun.). Office: 618 Berwick Rd Ste 100 Wilmington DE 19803-2204 Office Phone: 302-478-5644. Personal E-mail: mandassociates@comcast.net.

MANDAL, PRABIR KUMAR, biologist, educator; s. Paresh Chandra and Arati Mandal; m. Anita Choudhury, Jan. 29, 1988; 1 child, Sunny. BSc in zoology with honors, U. N.Bengal, India, 1978—81, MSc in Cytogenetics, 1981—84; PhD, Bhopal U., India, 1990—93. Rsch. scientist U. Hawaii, Honolulu, 1998—2006; vis. asst. prof. U. N.Fla., Jacksonville, Fla., 2003—; assoc. prof. Mountain State U., Beckley, W.Va., 2006—08; assoc. prof., chair, dept. biology Edward Waters Coll., Jacksonville, Fla., 2008—. Grantee Fla. Sea Grant Seminar grant award, U. Fla., 2005—06.

MANDAL, SUBHRANGSU S., chemistry professor, researcher; PhD, Indian Inst. Sci., Bangalore. Asst. prof. The U. of Tex. at Arlington, Arlington, Tex., 2005. Office: Dept Chemistry and Biochemistry 700 Plantarium Pl Arlington TX 76019 Business E-Mail: smandal@uta.edu.

MANDARICH, DAVID D., real estate corporation executive; b. 1948; With Majestic Savs. and Loan, 1966-67, MDC Holdings Inc., Denver, 1977—, bd. dir., 1980—89, 1994—, chmn. Richmond Am. Homes, 1990—93, exec. v.p. real estate, 1993—94, co-COO, 1994—96, COO, 1996—, pres., 1999—. Office: MDC Holdings 4350 S Monaco St Denver CO 80237

MANDEL, ANDREA SUE, packaging engineer; b. NYC, Mar. 25, 1951; d. Louis and Sylvia Polovsky; m. Richard Gordon Mandel, Aug. 30, 1970; 1 child, Lauren Rachel. BSME, CUNY, 1973; MS, Rutgers U., 1977. Cert. packaging profl. Scientist Johnson & Johnson, North Brunswick, N.J., 1973-78; chief packaging engr. Howmedica-Pfizer, Rutherford, N.J., 1978-80; mgr. packaging Drake Bakeries-Borden, Wayne, N.J., 1980-86; mgr. packaging engring. Lehn and Fink, Sterling Drug, Kodak, Montvale, N.J., 1986-88; sr. mgr. packaging devel. Church & Dwight, Inc., Princeton, N.J., 1988-93; pres. Andrea S. Mandel Assocs. Packaging Tech. Cons. Firm, Princeton Jct., N.J., 1993—. Chmn. Nat. Tamper Evidence Conf., 1983. Active Middlesex County Rep. Party, East Brunswick, N.J., 1977. Recipient Svc. award, Packaging Inst. N.J., 1985. Mem. ASME, Inst. Packaging Profls. (N.J. chpt. chmn. 1984-85, editorial adv. bd. Jour. Packaging Tech. 1988—, vice chairperson 1999—, chairperson cons. coun. 2001-03), Packaging Execs. Club, Soc. Plastics Engrs. Jewish. Achievements include pioneering use of personal computers in the packaging engineering field. Home and Office: 46 Ellsworth Dr Princeton Junction NJ 08550-3516 Personal E-mail: packagepro@comcast.net.

MANDEL, CAROL ANN, university librarian; b. Bklyn., Dec. 18, 1946; d. Irwin Daniel and Charlotte Mandel; m. Vincent T. Covello. BA magna cum laude, U. Mass., 1968; MSLS with honors, Columbia U., 1970, MA in Art History, 1975. Reference libr. Northeastern U. Libr., Boston, 1970; architecture and fine arts cataloger Columbia U. Librs., NYC, 1971-75, asst. to head original monographs cataloging dept., 1975-77, head original monographs cataloging dept., 1977-79, dir. tech. svcs., 1986-91, dir. tech. and networked info. svcs., 1991-93, dep. univ. libr., 1993—99; assoc. exec. dir. Assn. Rsch. Librs., Washington, 1979-83; asst., assoc. univ. libr. assess svcs. U. Calif., San Diego Librs., 1983-86; dean libr. NYU, 1999—. Cons. Libr. Congress, Coun. on Libr. and Info. Resources, Assn. Rsch. Librs.; mem. Rsch. Librs. Group, 2003-06; adv. bd. Portico; nat. digital strategy adv. bd. Libr. Congress; bd. dirs. Assn. for Rsch. Librs., 2005-, RLG Program Coun., Artstor, Portico, Libr. Congress Nat. Digital Info. Infrastructre Strategy Program, OCLC/RLG Bd. Com., Digital Libr. Fedn., pres. 2005-08; author and presenter in field. Contbr. articles to profl. publs. Recipient Margaret Mann Citation, ALA, 1999. Mem.: Am. Libr. Assn., Century Assn. Office: NYU Divsn Librs Bobst Libr 70 Washington Sq S New York NY 10012 Office Phone: 212-998-2444. Office Fax: 212-995-4070.

MANDEL, GAIL, immunologist; BS in Immunology, UCLA, PhD. Faculty Harvard Med. Sch., Tufts-New England Med. Ctr.; disting. prof. SUNY, StonyBrook, 1997—2006; investigator Howard Hughes Med. Inst., 2006—; sr. scientist Oreg. Health & Sci. Univ., Portland, 2006—. Recipient Jacob Javits award, NIH, McKnight Investigator award in Neurosciences. Fellow: AAAS, Am. Acad. Arts & Scis. Office: Oreg Health Sci Univ Vollum Inst L-474 3181 SW Sam Jackson Park Rd Portland OR 97239

MANDEL, HAROLD GEORGE, pharmacologist, educator; b. Berlin, June 6, 1924; came to U.S., 1937, naturalized, 1944; s. Ernest A. and Else (Crail) M.; m. Marianne Klein, July 25, 1953; children: Marcia Mandel Halgren, Audrey Lynn Todd. BS, Yale U., 1944, PhD, 1949. Lab. instr. in chemistry Yale U., 1942-44, 47-49; rsch. assoc. dept. pharmacology George Washington U. Sch. Medicine and Health Scis., 1949-50, asst. rsch. prof., 1950-52, assoc. prof. pharmacology, 1952-58, prof., 1958—, chmn. dept. pharmacology, 1960-96. Advanced Commonwealth Fund fellow Molteno Inst. Cambridge (Eng.) U., 1956; Commonwealth Fund fellow U. Auckland (N.Z.) and U. Med. Scis., Bangkok, Thailand, 1964; Am. Cancer Soc. Eleanor Roosevelt Internat. fellow Chester Beatty Research Inst. London, 1970-71; Am. Cancer Soc. scholar U. Calif., San Francisco, 1978-79; fellow Med. Research Council toxicology unit, Carshalton, Eng., 1986; Burroughs Wellcome Rsch. travel grant, Carshalton, 1988; hon. rsch. fellow dept. biochemistry and molecular biology U. Coll., London, 1993, 96, 97; mem. com. problems drug safety NRC-NAS, 1965-76, mem. com. on toxicology, 1978-82, mem. various panels, 1981-86; mem. cancer chemotherapy com. Internat. Union Against Cancer, 1966-73, fellow, Lyon, France, 1989; mem. external rev. com. Howard U. Cancer Research Center, 1972-74; cons. Bur. Drugs, FDA, 1975-79, EPA, 1978-82; mem. toxicology adv. com. FDA, 1975-78; mem. med. research service merit rev. bd. in alcoholism and drug dependence VA, 1975-78; mem. cancer spl. program adv. com. Nat. Cancer Inst., 1974-78, chmn., 1976-78; mem. Nat. Large Bowel Cancer Project Working Cadre, 1980-84; mem. Kettering award selection com. GM Cancer Rsch. Found., 1979-81; bd. advisors Roswell Park Cancer Inst., Buffalo, 1972-74. Editorial bd.: Jour. Pharmacology and Exptl. Therapeutics, 1960-65, field editor, 1978-94; editorial bd.: Molecular Pharmacology, 1965-69, Rsch. Comm. in Chem. Pathology, Pharmacology, 1972-98, Cancer Drug Delivery, Selective Cancer Therapeutics, 1983-92, Cancer Research, 1974-76, assoc. editor, 1977-81. Served with AUS, 1944-46. Recipient John J. Abel award in pharmacology Eli Lilly and Co., 1958, Disting. Achievement award Washington Acad. Scis., 1958, Golden Apple Teaching award AMA, 1969, 85, 97, Sci. Emeritus award Soc. Biology & Medicine, 1999. Fellow AAAS; mem. Am. Chem. Soc., Am. Soc. Biochemistry and Molecular Biology, Am. Soc. Pharmacology and Exptl. Therapeutics (pres. 1973-74), Am. Assn. Cancer Rsch., Assn. Med. Sch. Pharmacology Chairs (pres. 1976-78), Nat. Caucus of Basic Biomed. Sci. Chairs (chmn. 1991—), Citizens Pub. Rsch. and Edn. Funding (sec. 1996-99), Cosmos Club (Washington), Sigma Xi, Alpha Omega Alpha. Democrat. Achievements include research, numerous publs. on cancer chemotherapy, mechanism of growth inhibition, antimetabolites, drug disposition, chemical carcinogenesis. Home: Apt 302 4956 Sentinel Dr Bethesda MD 20816-3594 Office: George Washington U Sch Medicine and Health Scis Dept Pharmacology and Physiology 2300 I St NW Washington DC 20037-2336 Home Phone: 301-320-4450; Office Phone: 202-994-3542. Business E-Mail: phmhgm@gwumc.edu. E-mail: hgmandel@verizon.net.

MANDEL, HERBERT MAURICE, civil engineer; b. Port Chester, NY, May 11, 1924; s. Arthur William and Rose (Schmeiser) M.; m. Charlotte Feldman, Aug. 22, 1954; children: Rosanne Mandel Levine, Elliott D., Arthur M. BSCE, Va. Poly. Inst., 1948; M Engring., Yale U.,

1949. Registered profl. engr., N.Y., Conn., Fla., Md., Mich., Minn., Ohio, Pa., Va., W.Va. Structural engr. Madigan Hyland Co., LI, NY, 1949—50; mem. Parsons, Brinckerhoff, Quade & Douglas, Inc., 1950—86; v.p. GAI Cons., Inc., Monroeville, Pa., 1986—2004, prin. staff cons., 1993—2004, sr. staff cons., 2004—. Resident engr., Chgo., 1961, Atlanta, 1962, project. mgr., N.Y.C., 1963-70, Honolulu, 1970-74, v.p., 1974, sr. v.p., Pitts., 1977-86; mem. faculty Yale U., 1948-49; adj. faculty Bklyn. Poly. Inst., 1956-64, U. Pitts., 1986; gen. chmn. 6th Internat. Bridge Conf., Pitts., 1989. Prin. works include (prin.-in-charge) Williamstown-Marietta Bridge, W.Va.-Ohio, Dunbar Bridge, W.Va., I-64 Bridge over Big Sandy River, W.Va.-Ky., Davis Creek Bridge, Charleston, W.Va., Tygart R. Bridge, W.Va., Easley Bridge, Bluefield, W.Va., Fayette Sta. Bridge, Fayetteville, W.Va., Mon Valley Expwy., W.Va., King Coal Hwy, W.Va., Romney Bridge, W.Va., (project mgr.) Newport Bridge, Narragansett Bay, R.I., (designer/project engr.) Hackensack River Bridge, N.J., Housatanic River Bridge, Conn., Arthur Kill Vertical Lift R.R. Bridge, S.I., N.Y., 62d St. Bridge, Pitts., Savannah River Cantilever Bridge, Ga., I-84 Bridges, Danbury, Conn., (structural rehab. designer) Avondale Bridge, N.J, Lincoln Bridge, N.J., B&O R.R. Bridge, Vincennes, Ind., Hawk St. Viaduct, Albany, N.Y., Congress Ave. Bridge, Austin, Tex., Ohio St. Bridge, Buffalo, Panhandle Bridge, Pitts.; project dir. design and constrn. Pitts. Light Rail Transit Sys., 1977-84; designer Elizabeth R. Tunnel, Norfolk, Va., 1950. Served to 1st lt. U.S. Army, 1943-46, 50-52, ETO. Fellow ASCE, Soc. Am. Mil. Engrs.; mem. NSPE, Engrs. Soc. We. Pa. (exec. com. Internat. Bridge Conf. 1986—, gen. chmn. 1988-89), Am. Rlwy. Engring. and Maintenance of Way Assn. (steel structures specifications com. 1974—), Profl. Engrs. in Pvt. Practice (bd. govs. 1994-96, profl. devel. coun. 1995-97), Pa. Profl. Engrs. in Pvt. Practice (state vice-chmn. 1992-94, chmn. 1994-96), Pa. Soc. Profl. Engrs. (dir. Pitts. chpt. 1995-98), Internat. Assn. Bridge and Structural Engring., Assn. for Bridge Constrn. and Design, Engrs. Club Pitts., Tau Beta Pi, Chi Epsilon, Omicron Delta Kappa, Phi Kappa Phi, Pi Delta Epsilon, Scabbard and Blade. Jewish. Home: 920 Parkview Dr Pittsburgh PA 15243-1116 Office: GAI Cons Inc 385 Waterfront Dr E Homestead PA 15120-5005 Home: 1149 Hillsboro Mile Hillsboro Beach FL 33062 Home Phone: 412-561-4881. Personal E-mail: hmmcfm@aol.com.

MANDEL, IRWIN DANIEL, dentist; b. Bklyn., Apr. 9, 1922; s. Samuel A. and Shirley (Blankstein) M.; m. Charlotte Lifschutz, Apr. 1, 1944; children: Carol, Nora, Richard. BS, CCNY, 1942; DDS, Columbia U., 1945; DSc (hon.), U. Medicine and Dentistry N.J., 1981, U. Gothoburg, 1984, Columbia U., 1996. Rsch. asst. Dental Sch. Columbia U., 1946-48, mem. faculty Dental Sch., 1946—, prof. dentistry, dir. div. preventive dentistry Dental Sch., 1969-84, dir. Ctr. Clin. Rsch. in Dentistry Dental Sch., 1984-91, assoc. dean rsch., 1991-92; prof. emeritus Dental Sch., 1992—; pvt. practice dentistry, 1946-68; vis. prof. various dental schs.; chmn. oral biology and medicine study sect. Nat. Inst. Dental Rsch., 1974-76. Co-author: The Plaque Diseases, 1972; contbr. over 250 articles to profl. jours., chpts. to books. Active local chpt. Peace Action, Physicians for Social Responsibility. Lt. Dental Corps USNR, 1945-46, 52-54. Recipient Career Scientist award, N.Y.C. Health Rsch. Coun., 1969—72, Leadership award in periodontology, Tufts U. Dental Sch., 1971, Internat. award, U. Conn. Sch. Dental Medicine, 1979, Seymour J. Kreshover NIDR Lectr. award, 1986, Townsend Harris medal, CCNY, 2000. Fellow AAAS, Am. Coll. Dentists; mem. ADA (chmn. coun. dental rsch. 1978-80, Gold medal for excellence in rsch. 1985), Dental Soc. (Henry Spenadel award 1973, Jarvie-Burkhart Internat. award 1990), Am. Assn. Dental Rsch. (pres. 1980), Am. Assn. Pub. Health Dentists (Disting. Svc. award 1991), Fed. Dentair Internat. (W. D. Miller prize 1992), Internat. Assn. Dental Rsch. (Salivary Rsch. award 1994, Disting. Svc. award 2001), N.Y. Acad. Scis., Sigma Xi, Omicron Kappa Upsilon, Columbia U. Coll. Dental Medicine (Lifetime Achievement award, 2007). Home and Office: 1305 Holly Ln Cedar Grove NJ 07009 Office Phone: 973-239-0437. Personal E-mail: irwind.mandel@optonline.net.

MANDEL, JACK N., manufacturing executive; b. Austria, July 16, 1911; s. Sam and Rose M.; m. Lilyan, Aug. 14, 1938 (dec.) Student, Fenn Coll., 1930-33. Founder, former pres., chmn. Premier Indsl. Corp., Cleve.; chmn., pres. Manbro Corp.; exec. dir. Parkwood Corp.; gen. ptnr. Courtland Assocs. Former mem. exec. com. NCCJ; former life trustee Wood Hosp.; trustee Fla. Soc. for Blind; life trustee South Broward Jewish Fedn., Cleve. Jewish Welfare Fedn.; former pres., life trustee Montefiore Home for Aged; pres. adv. bd. Barry U.; hon. trustee Hebrew U.; trustee Tel Aviv U. Mus. of the Diaspora; life trustee The Temple, Woodruff Found.; trustee Cleve. Play House. Mem. Beachmont Country Club, Commede Club, Union Club. Office: Parkwood Corp 2829 Euclid Ave Cleveland OH 44115-2413

MANDEL, JEFFREY S., psychologist; MPH, UCLA, 1971; PhD, Wright Inst., LA, 1985. Cert. in clin. psychologist CA, 1991. Co-dir., internat. program UCSF Ctr. AIDS Prevention Studies, 1995—2009; dir. internat. tng. UCSF Inst. Global Health, 2008—. Contbr. articles to numerous profl. jours.

MANDEL, JOEL EMANUEL, orthopedist; b. BKlyn., Mar. 1, 1930; s. Morris and Minnie Mandel. BA, N.Y. U., 1951; MS, Ga. Inst. Tech., 1952; MD, Chgo. Med. Sch., 1956. Diplomate Am. Bd. Med. Examiners, Am. Bd. Orthop. Surgery, Am. Bd. Profl. Disabled Cons. Intern D.C. Gen. Hosp., 1956—57; resident in gen. surgery VA Hosp., 1957—58; resident in orthopedic surgery D.C. Gen. Hosp., 1958—60, N.Y. U., Bellevue, 1960—61; pres., founding ptnr. The New City (N.Y.) Orthopedic Group, P.C., 1961—85; med. dir. Post-Trauma Med. Svcs., New Windsor, NY, 1985—. Host weekly radio program Medicine Today, 1973—76. Mem. editl. bd. Jour. Disability, 1990—93, Disability, 1995—96. Bd. govs. Rockland County (N.Y.) Health Complex, 1977—88; mem. coord. coun. Rockland County Emergency Med. Svc., 1977—81. Recipient Rockland County Dist. Svc. award, 1973. Fellow: ACS, NY State Soc. Surgeons, Am. Acad. Orthop. Surgeons, Internat. Coll. Surgeons, Am. Acad. Disability Evaluating Physicians (bd. dirs. 1988—93, sec. 1990—93); mem.: Rockland County Med. Soc. (dir. pub. rels. 1967—73, exec. com. 1967—76, peer rev. com. 1973—85, pres. 1974—75, chmn. bd. censors 1975—76), Orange County Med. Soc. (peer rev. com. 1987—, exec. com. 1994—), Ea. Orthop. Assn., NY State Soc. Orthop. Surgeons (bd. dirs. 1976—82). Avocations: sailing, windsurfing, computer science, astronomy. Office: Post-Trauma Med Svc PC 833 Blooming Grove Tpk New Windsor NY 12553 Office Phone: 845-561-2000. Business E-Mail: jmandelmd@hvc.rr.com.

MANDEL, KARYL LYNN, accountant; b. Chgo., Dec. 14, 1935; d. Isador J. and Eve (Gellar) Karzen; m. Fredric H. Mandel, Sept. 29, 1956; children: David Scott, Douglas Jay, Jennifer Ann. Student, U. Mich., 1954-56, Roosevelt U., 1956-57; AA summa cum laude, Oakton Community Coll., 1979. CPA, Ill; registered investment advisor; lic. life ins. provider. Pres. Excel Transp. Service Co., Elk Grove, Ill., 1958-78; tax mgr. CTB, Ltd., CPAs, Northbrook, Ill., 1981-83; tax ptnr. Chunowitz, Teitelbaum & Mandel, CPAs, Riverwoods, Ill., 1984—. Sec-treas. Lednam, Inc., Coffee Break, Inc.; mem. acctg. curriculum adv. bd. Oakton C.C., Des Plaines, Ill., 1987—; pres. Lednam Enterprises, LLC, 2001—. Contbg. author: Ill. CPA's News Jour., Acctg. Today. Recipient State of Israel Solidarity award, 1976. Mem. AICPA, Am. Soc. Women CPA, Women's Am. ORT (pres. Chgo. region 1972-74, v.p. midwest dist. 1975-76, nat. endowment com., nat investment adv. com.), Ill. CPA Soc. (chmn. estate and gift tax com. 1987-89, legis. contact com. 1981-82, pres. North Shore chpt., bd. dirs. 1989-91, award for Excellence in Acctg. Edn.), Chgo. Soc. Women CPA, Chgo. Estate Planning Coun., Nat. Assn. Women Bus. Owners, Lake County Estate Planning Coun., Greater North Shore Estate Planning Coun. Office: 302 Saunders Rd Ste 300 Riverwoods IL 60015 Office Phone: 847-444-1040. Business E-Mail: klm@ctbltd.com.

MANDEL, LESLIE ANN, investment advisor, writer; b. Washington, July 29, 1945; d. Seymour and Marjorie (Syble) Mandel; m. Arthur Herzog III, Oct. 27, 1999. BA in Art History, U. Minn., 1967; cert., N.Y. Sch. Interior Design, 1969. Cert. Brailled Libr. Congress. Pres. Leslie Mandel Enterprises, Inc., NYC, 1968—; sr. v.p. Maximum Entertainment Network, L.A. and NYC, 1988-90; pres. Rich List Co., 1968—; pres., CEO Mandel Airplane Funding and Leasing Corp., NYC, Hong Kong, China and Mongolia, 1990—; CEO Mandel-Khan Inc., Ulaanbaatar, Mongolia, 1994—, Travel Safe: keep hers, keep his, 2002—. Fin. advisor Osmed, Inc., Mpls., 1986—, Devine Comm./Allen & Co., NY, Del., Utah, N.Mex., NY, N.Y. WUWV, Utah KBER, WKTC-AM-FM, 1984—89, Am. Kefir Corp., NYC, 1983—89, Shore Group (Internat., Guyana), Flight Internat., 1991—; owner The Rich List Co., 150 internat. catalogs, mags. and fundraising lists; joint venture Mongolian Ind. Broadcasting Channel, Ulaanbaatar, 1995; pres., owner Mandel Airplane Funding and Leasing Corp.; rep. Israeli Govt. IAI Satellite, China, Romania, Costa Rica, Mongolia, Amos Satellite Network, China, 1992—; advisor rep. Gt. Wall Corp., Long March Corp., China, 1992—, Chinese Silk, 1993—, Am. Oil Refinery, 1993—; bd. dirs. Coastal Equipment Co., Bristol Airlines; cons. Exclusive Miat Airlines, Mongolia; purchasing agt. People's Republic of China-Aircraft; advisor Aeropostalis, Mexico, 1994—95; photographer; lectr. UN Internat. Direct Mail; advisor Aruba Airlines, Mexicana Airlines; aircraft agt., bd. dirs. Lazorlines Landing Equipment, 1997—; lease Estafada Airlines 757-200-C, 2000—, Chile Airlines 757-200C, 2002; advisor Guyana 2000 Airlines; ptnr. Laserline/Vulcan Power Plant, China, 2005, Greece, 2005—, Nicaragua, 2005—, Trinidad and Tobago, 2005—, Pakistan, 2005—, Turkmenistan, 2005—, Hungary, 2005—. Photographer: Vogue, 1978, New Earth Times, 1995, Fortune mag.; Braille transcriber: The Prophet (Kalil Gibran), 1967, Getting Ready for Battle (R. Prawe Jhabuala), 1967; exec. prodr. film: Hospital Audiences, 1975 (Cannes award 1976); author: Hungry at the Watering Hole, Gardiners Island, 1636-1990, 1989, Expedition: In the Steps of Ghengis Kahn, 1994; advisor Port Liberté Ptnrs., 1988-94; contbr. articles to profl. jours. Fin. advisor Correctional Assn., Osborn Soc., 1977—; founder, treas. Prisoners Family Transportation and Assistance Fund, N.Y., 1972-77; judge Emmy awards of Acad. TV Arts and Scis., N.Y.C., 1970; bd. dirs. Prisoners Assn., 1990; chmn. U.S.A. com. Violeta B. de Chamarro for Pres. of Nicaragua Campaign. Recipient Inst. for the Creative and Performing Arts fellowship, N.Y.C., 1966, Appreciation cert. Presdl. Inaugural Com., Washington, 1981. Fellow N.Y. Women in Real Estate, Explorers Club (lectr. on Mongolia, fin. com., housing, student, hospitality and Lowell Thomas coms., reciprocity com., legacy com.); mem. Com. on Am. and Internat. Fgn. Affairs, Lawyers Com. on Internat. Human Rels., Bus. Exec. Nat. Security, Venture Capital Breakfast Club, The Coffee Club House, Sigma Delta Tau, Sigma Epsilon Sigma. Democrat. Avocations: painting, writing, fishing, canoeing, horseback riding, breeding cockatiels. Home: 4 E 81st St New York NY 10028-0235 Office: Mandel-Khan Inc PO Box 97 care Boldbaatar Mandel Kahn Ulaanbaatar 210648 Mongolia also: Leslie Mandel Enterprises PO Box 294 Wainscott NY 11975-0294 also: PO Box 294 Wainscott NY 11975-0029 Home Phone: 212-879-3089, 631-937-3068; Office Phone: 212-737-8917. Personal E-mail: mandelair@aol.com, richlistco@aol.com, leslie_mandel@yahoo.com.

MANDEL, MORTON, molecular biologist; b. Bklyn., July 6, 1924; s. Barnet and Rose (Kliner) M.; m. Florence H. Goodman, Apr. 1, 1952; children: Robert, Leslie. BCE, CUNY, 1944; MS, Columbia U., 1949, PhD in Physics, 1957. Scientist Bell Telephone Labs., Murray Hill, NJ, 1956-57; asst. prof. physics dept. Stanford (Calif.) U., 1957-61; scientist Gen. Telephone & Telegraph, Mountain View, Calif., 1961-63; rsch. assoc. dept. genetics Stanford U., 1963-64; rsch. fellow Karolinska Inst., Stockholm, 1964-66; assoc. prof. sch. of medicine U. Hawaii, Honolulu, 1966-68, prof., 1968—; founder, dir. Hawaii Biotechnology Group, Inc., 1982-95. Cons. Fairchild Semiconductor, Hewlett Packard, Lockheed, Rheem, Palo Alto, Calif., 1957-61. Contbr. articles to profl. jours. Lt. (j.g.) USN, 1944-46. Recipient Am. Cancer Soc. Scholar award Am. Cancer Soc., 1979-80, Eleanor Roosevelt Internat. Cancer fellowship, 1979; named NIH Spl. fellow Karolinska Inst., 1964-66. Fellow Am. Phys. Soc.; mem. Sigma Xi. Achievements include citation classics; optimal conditions for mutagenesis by N-methyl-N-nitro-N-nitrosoguanidine in E. coli K12; calcium dependent bacteriophage DNA infection. Office: Dept Biochemistry 1960 E West Rd Honolulu HI 96822-2319 Home: 250 Hammond Pond Pkwy Apt 303N Chestnut Hill MA 02467-1519 E-mail: mandel321@jacaro.com.

MANDEL, SHELDON LLOYD, dermatologist, educator; b. Mpls., Dec. 6, 1922; s. Maurice and Stelle R. M.; m. Patricia E., Oct. 15, 1978; 1 child, Melissa A. BA, U. Minn., Mpls., 1943, BS, 1944, BM, MD, U. Minn., Mpls., 1946; MA, St. Thomas U. Diplomate Am. Bd. Dermatology, 1953. Intern U. Okla., 1946-47; resident Valley Forge (Pa.) Gen. Hosp., 1947—49, VA Hosp., Mpls., 1949—51, VA Hosp. and U. Minn., Mpls., 1949—51; pvt. practice dermatology Mpls., 1951—; prof. clin. dermatology U. Minn., Mpls., 1970—. Contbr. articles to profl. jours. Capt. MC, U.S. Army, 1947-49. Fellow Royal Soc. Medicine (Britain), Am. Acad. Dermatology (life); mem. AMA, Minn. Med. Soc., Noah Worcester Dermatol. Soc. (bd. dirs. 1988-91), Internat. Dermatol. Soc. Office: Downtown Dermatology PA 7300 France Ave S Ste 400 Minneapolis MN 55435-4544 Office Phone: 952-374-5595. Personal E-mail: concha8@earthlink.net.

MANDEL, STEPHEN F., JR., hedge fund manager; b. Mar. 2, 1956; m. Susan Mandel; 3 children. AB, Dartmouth Coll., Hanover, NH, 1978; MBA, Harvard Bus. Sch., 1982. Sr. cons. Mars & Co., 1982—84; retail analyst Goldman, Sachs & Co., 1985—87, v.p., retail analyst NY, 1987—90; sr. mng. dir. Tiger Mgmt. Corp., 1990—97; founder, mng. dir. Lone Pine Capital, 1997—. Trustee Dartmouth Coll., 2007—, The Children's Sch., Stamford, Conn., Phillips Exeter Acad., NH, Teach for America; founder, chmn. Lone Pine Found. Named to 'The World's Billionaires' list, Forbes mag. Office: Lone Pine Capital LLC 2 Greenwich Plz Ste 2 Greenwich CT 06830-6353 Office Phone: 203-618-7878. Business E-Mail: smandel@lonepinecapital.com.*

MANDELBAUM, BERT ROLAND, orthopedist; m. Ruth Sorotzkin; children: Rachel, Jordan, Ava. MD, Wash. U. Med. Sch., St. Louis, Mich., 1980. Cert. AAOS Bds., 1998. Asst. prof., orthop. surgery UCLA, West Los Angeles, Calif., 1986—89; orthop. surgeon Santa Monica Orthop. Group, Santa Monica, Calif., 1989—. Asst. med. dir. Maj. League Soccer, 1995—. Contbr. chapters to books. Office: Santa Monica Orthop Group 2020 Santa Monica Blvd Santa Monica CA 90404 Office Fax: 310-315-0326.

MANDELBAUM, DAVID EZRA, pediatric neurologist; b. NYC, Oct. 24, 1952; s. Bernard Mandelbaum and Judith Louise Werber; m. Elana Katz, June 24, 1975 (div. Aug. 1992); 1 child, Danya Judith; m. Alison Speckman, Aug. 29, 2004. BA, Columbia U., 1974, MD, PhD, Columbia U., 1980. Diplomate Am. Bd. Pediatrics, Am. Bd. Psychiatry and Neurology; cert. child neurology, clin. neurophysiology, neurodevel. disabilities. Intern Yale-New Haven Hosp., 1980-81, resident in pediat., 1981-82; resident in neurology Neurol. Inst. Columbia-Presbyn. Med. Ctr., NYC, 1982-83, fellow pediat. neurology, 1983-85; dir. divsn. child neurology U. Med. & Dentistry N.J., New Brunswick, 1985—2003, asst. prof. pediat. and neurology, 1985-91, assoc. prof., 1991-2001, prof., 2001—03; prof. clin. neuroscis. and pediatrics Brown U., Providence, 2003—; dir., divsn. child neurology, dept. neurology R.I. and Hasbro Children's Hosps., 2003—; dir. Children's Neurodevel. Ctr., Hasbro Children's Hosp., 2005—. Chief child neurology svc. Robert Wood Johnson U. Hosp., New Brunswick, 1985-2003, St. Peters U. Hosp., New Brunswick, 1985-2003; chmn. profl. adv. bd. Epilepsy Found. N.J., 2002-03 cons., lectr. and presenter in field. Mem. editl. bd. Jour. Child Neurology, Pediatric Neurology; contbr. articles to profl. jours. Bd. dirs. YM/YWHA Raritan Valley, Highland Park, N.J., 1997-2001, Princeton (N.J.) Pro Musica, 1998. Grantee NIH, 1974-80, U. Medicine and Dentistry N.J. Found., 1986-88, Ortho-McNeil Pharm. Corp./Johnson & Johnson, 1997-98, Parke-Davis Corp., 1998, Nat. Alliance for Autism Rsch., 2002-04. Mem. Profs. Child Neurology, Child Neurology Soc., Am. Acad. Pediat., Am. Epilepsy Soc.; fellow: Am. Acad. Neurology. Jewish. Avocations: music, swimming. Office: Prof Office Bldg Ste 342 Providence RI 02906 Home Phone: 401-453-2570; Office Phone: 401-444-4345. Fax: 401-444-3236. E-mail: David_Mandelbaum@brown.edu, dmandelbaum@lifespan.org.

MANDELBAUM, JAY PHILIP, diversified financial services company executive; b. 1962; s. Joseph and Reva D. Mandelbaum; m. Lauren Beth Gordon, Feb. 5, 1994. BA, Princeton U., NJ, 1984; MBA, Harvard Bus. Sch. Cons. McKinsey & Co., 1984—92; v.p. corp. devel. Primerica Corp., 1992—94; sr. exec. v.p. Pvt. Client Sales and Mktg. Salomon Smith Barney, 1994—2000, vice chmn., CEO Pvt. Client Group, 2000—02; head strategy and bus. devel. Bank One Corp., 2002—04; head corp. strategy, mktg. and comm. J.P. Morgan Chase & Co., 2004—. Office: JP Morgan Chase & Co 270 Park Ave New York NY 10017-2070*

MANDELBROT, BENOIT B., mathematician, research scientist, educator; b. Warsaw, Nov. 20, 1924; arrived in US, 1958, naturalized, 2000; s. Charles and Belle (Lurie) M.; m. Aliette Kagan, Nov. 5, 1955; children: Laurent, Didier. Diploma, Ecole Polytechnique, Paris, 1947; MS in Aeronautics, Calif. Inst. Tech., 1948; PhD in Math., U. Paris, 1952; DSc (hon.), Syracuse U., 1985, Laurentian U., Ont., Can., 1986, Boston U., 1987, SUNY, 1988, U. Bremen, Germany, 1988, U. Guelph, Ont., Can., 1989, Pace U., 1989, U. Dallas, 1992, Union Coll., 1993, U. Buenos Aires, 1993, U. Tel Aviv, 1995, Open U., UK, 1998, Athens U. Bus. and Fin., 1998, U. St. Andrews, Scotland, 1999, Emory U., Atlanta, 2002, Politecnico di Torino, Italy, 2005; Dr. Medicine and Surgery (hon.), U. Bari, Italy, 2007; AM (hon.), Yale U., 2000. Postdoctoral mem. and Rockefeller scholar Inst. for Advanced Study, Princeton, NJ, 1953—54; jr. prof. math. U. Geneva, 1955-57, U. Lille and Ecole Polytechnique, Paris, 1957-58; rsch. staff mem. IBM Watson Rsch. Ctr., Yorktown Heights, NY, 1958-74, IBM fellow, 1974-93, IBM fellow emeritus, 1993—; vis. prof. engring. Yale U., New Haven, 1970, prof. math. scis., 1987—99, Sterling prof. math. sciences, 1999—2004, Sterling prof. math. sciences emeritus, 2005—; Battelle fellow Pacific Northwest Nat. Lab, 2005—07. Vis. prof. econs. Harvard U., 1962-63, applied math., 1963-64, math., 1979-80, 84-87, U. Paris, 1966, physiology Einstein Coll. Medicine, 1970, Coll. France, 1973, Inst. Hautes Etudes Sci. Bures, 1980, Mittag-Leffler Inst., Sweden, 1984, 2001, 02, 04, Max Planck Inst. Math, Bonn, Germany, 1988, Cambridge, 1990, 2005, Oxford U., 1990, Imperial Coll., London, 1991; Hitchcock prof. U. Calif., Berkeley, 1992; visitor MIT, 1953, Inst. lectr., 1964-; spkr. and organizer profl. confs. Author: Logique, langage et théorie de l'information, 1957, Les objets fractals: forme, hasard et dimension, 1975, 4th edit., 1995, Fractals: Form, Chance and Dimension, 1977, The Fractal Geometry of Nature, 1982, La Geometria della Natura, 1987, Fractals and Scaling in Finance: Discontinuity, Concentration, Risk, 1997, Fractales, hasard et finance, 1997, Multifractals and 1/f Noise: Wild Self-Affinity in Physics, 1999, Nel mondo dei frattali, 2001, Gaussian Self-Affinity and Fractals: Globality, The Earth, 1/f Noise and R/S, 2002, (with M.L. Frame) Fractals, Graphics and Mathematics Education, 2002, (with R.L. Hudson) The (Mis)Behavior of Markets: A Fractal View of Risk, Ruin, and Reward, 2004, Fractals and Chaos: The Mandelbrot Set and Beyond, 2004,; contbr. articles to profl. jours. Recipient Franklin medal Franklin Inst., 1986, Alexander von Humboldt Preis, 1987, Caltech disting. svc. award, 1988, Moet-Hennessy Sci. and Art prize, 1988, Harvey prize, 1989, Nev. prize U. Nev. Sys., 1991, Wolf prize for physics, 1993, Honda prize, 1994, Medal of City of Paris, 1996, John Scott award City of Phila., 1999, L.F. Richardson medal European Geophys. Soc., 2000, Sven Berggren prize, Lund, Sweden, 2002, Japan prize for Sci. and Tech., 2003, Fin. Times (Germany) award, 2004, Waclaw Sierpinski prize, 2005 Wladislaw Orlicz medal, 2005, Casimir Funk award Piasa, 2005; Guggenheim fellow, 1968. Fellow AAAS, IEEE (Charles Proteus Steinmetz medal 1988), Am. Acad. Arts and Scis., European Acad. Arts, Scis. and Humanities, Am. Phys. Soc., French Physics Soc. (hon.), Inst. Math. Stats., Econometric Soc., Am. Geophys. Union, Am. Statistic Assn.; mem. NAS U.S.A. (Barnard medal 1985), Am. Philos. Soc., Internat. Statis. Inst. (elected,), Am. Math. Soc., Norwegian Acad. Sci. and Letters (fgn. mem.), Sigma Xi (nat. lectr. 1980-82, Procter prize 2002). Achievements include origination of theory of fractals, a nascent interdisciplinary theory of roughness; many aspects this theory strongly attack young minds provides mathematical conjectures including very difficult ones, and also provides practical tools to handle financial data, mountains, clouds, fractures of metals, dynamic attractors, and all other shapes and phenomena in nature or man's works that are equally irregular or broken-up at all scales; the best known fractal is called Mandelbrot set. Office Phone: 617-620-6598. Personal E-mail: benoit.mandelbrot@yale.edu.

MANDELBROT, DIDIER A., physician, internist, educator; b. North Tarrytown, NY, Aug. 29, 1961; s. Benoit B. and Aliette (Kagan) M.; m. Catherine Mason Gordon, Aug. 20, 1994. AB, Harvard U., 1984; MD, U. Pa., 1989. Diplomate Am. Bd. Internal Medicine, Am. Bd. Nephrology. Resident in internal medicine U. Pa. Hosp., Phila., 1989-92; fellow in nephrology Brigham and Women's Hosp., Boston, 1992-96, instr. in medicine, 1996—. Recipient Nat. Rsch. Svcs. award NIH, 1993, Physician Scientist award, 1994. Mem. ACP, Am. Soc. Nephrology. Avocations: music, sports, movies. Office: Brigham and Women's Hosp 221 Longwood Ave Boston MA 02115-5804

MANDELKORN, ROBERT MARC, ophthalmologist; b. Detroit, Aug. 23, 1948; s. Ben and Rose Mandelkorn; m. Mary Beth Danneffel, Sept. 28, 2001; 1 child, Rachel Sophia. MD, U. Louisville, 1974. Ophthalmologist pvt. practice, Pitts., 1980—2000; dir. eye clinic VA Outpatient Clinic, Fort Myers, Fla., 2001—; med. internship Henry Ford Hosp., Detroit, 1974—76; opthalmology residency Sinai Hosp., Detroit, 1976—79; Glaucoma fellowship Ochsner Hosp., New Orleans, 1979—80. Fellow: ACS, Royal Coll. Ophthalmologists, Am. Glaucoma Soc., Am. Acad. Ophthalmology (Achievement award 2006). Achievements include patents for Mandelkorn Punctal Gauge/Dilator System; invention of Mandelkorn Suture Lysis Lens; Mandelkorn Iridotomy/Capsulotomy Lens. Office: Veterans Affairs Outpatient Clinic 3033 Winkler Ave Ext Fort Myers FL 33916

MANDELL, GERALD A., nuclear medicine physician; b. Phila., Dec. 20, 1943; s. Samuel Philip and Ida (Slutsky) M.; m. Susan Perilstein, June 13, 1964 (div. 1989); children: Nathan, Joshua, Geoffrey, Samantha; m. Joanna DiRenzo, Mar. 29, 1991; children: Christian Fermani, Brianne Dailey, Kyle Dailey. BA in Biology, U. Pa., 1965; MD, Jefferson Med. Coll., 1969. Diplomate Am. Bd. Radiology, Am. Bd. Nuclear Medicine, cert. added qualification Am. Bd. Pediatric Radiology. Intern in medicine Albert Einstein Med. Ctr., Phila., 1969-70; resident in diagnostic radiology Thomas Jefferson U. Hosp., Phila., 1970-73; fellow in pediatric radiology Thomas Jefferson U. Hosp./St. Christopher's Hosp. Children, Phila., 1973-74; fellow in nuclear medicine U. Pa. Hosp., 1981-83; assoc. dir. med. imaging A.I. duPont Inst., Wilmington, Del., 1983-93, chief nuclear medicine, 1993—2002; pediat. radiologist Phoenix Children's Hosp., 2002—. Instr. in radiology U. Pa., Phila., 1974-76, asst. prof., 1976-77, adj. assoc. prof. radiology, 1984-92, adj. prof. radiology, 1992-2007; assoc. prof. radiology, assoc. prof. pediatrics Hahneman Med. Coll. and Hosp., Phila., 1979; prof. radiology Jefferson Med. Coll., 1990-2002, prof. radiation therapy and nuclear medicine, 1991-2002; assoc. radiologist Children's Hosp. Phila., 1974-77, dir. radiology residency tng. program, 1974-77, assoc. staff dept. radiology, 1990-03; lectr., presenter in field. Co-author: Imaging Strategies in Pediatric Orthopaedics, 1990; editor Clin. Nuclear Medicine, 1996—; reviewer Jour. Nuclear Medicine, 1987, 94, 99-2001; contbr. numerous articles to profl. publs., chpts. to books. Trustee Samuel P. Mandell Found.; bd. dirs. Del. Guidance Svcs., Wilmington. Recipient Best Doctors in Am. award-N.E., 1997, Best Doctors in Del. award, 1997, Best Doctors in Am., 1998-2002, 2006-08, Top Doctors for Kids Phila. mag., 2001; grantee Soc. for Pediat. Medicine, 1991, Am. Heart Assn., 1991, Mallinckrodt Critical Care, 1992-93. Fellow ACP, Am. Acad. Pediatrics, Am. Coll. Radiology; mem. AMA, Pediatric Radiol. Soc., Soc. Nuclear Medicine (sec.-treas. pediat. coun. 1993, mem. healthcare com. 1993-2001, pres. pediat. coun. 1994-96, past-pres. pediat. coun. 1996-98, mem. ho. dels. 1996-98, Alavi-Mandell prize), Internat. Skeletal Soc., NY Acad. Scis., Phila. Roentgen Ray Soc., Del. Soc. Nuclear Medicine, New Castle County Med. Soc., Del. Radiol. Soc., Del. Med. Soc. (alt. del. 1993-2002). Jewish. Achievements include discovery of isotope method of scanning patients with neurofibromatosis. Home Phone: 602-237-6171; Office Phone: 602-546-1207. Personal E-mail: gmandell@phoenixchildrens.com.

MANDELL, GERALD LEE, internist, educator; b. NYC, Aug. 20, 1936; s. Herman and Sylvia (Keller) M.; m. Judith Rensin Mandell, Dec. 22, 1960; children: James, Pamela, Scott. BA, Cornell U., 1958; MD, Cornell U., NYC, 1962. Diplomate Am. Bd. Internal Medicine. Intern, resident NY Hosp. Cornell Med. Ctr., NYC, 1965-67; instr. Med. Coll., Cornell U., NYC, 1968-69; asst. prof. U. Va., Charlottesville, 1969-71, assoc. prof., 1972-75, prof., 1976—, Owen R. Cheatham prof. sci., 1981—, chief infectious diseases, 1970—2002. Editor: Principles and Practice of Infectious Diseases, 1979, 6th edit., 2005. Lt. comdr. USPHS, 1963-65. Recipient MERIT award NIH, 1986; named Outstanding Alumnus, Cornell Med. Coll, 2002. Master ACP; fellow AAAS, Infectious Diseases Soc. Am. (pres. 1994, Maxwell Finland award 2000), Nat. Inst. Allergy and Infectious Diseases (adv. coun.), Inst. Medicine; mem. Assn. Am. Physicians, Am. Soc. Clin. Investigation (emeritus prof. 2006—), Phi Beta Kappa, Alpha Omega Alpha, Coun. Am. Climatology Soc. (pres. elect 2009). Avocations: photography, tropical fish, sculling.

MANDELL, JAMES, health facility executive, urologist, educator; b. SI, NY, Feb. 20, 1945; s. Gustave and Rose (Zimmerman) M.; m. Valerie Steele, Jan. 20, 1967; children: Joshua Lindstrom, Jeremy Hill, Bethany Shalom. AA, U. Fla., 1965; MD, U. Fla. Coll. Medicine, 1970; MS, Union U., 1999. Am. Bd. Diplomate Urology 1979. Intern U. Fla. Sch. Medicine, Gainesville, 1970-71, resident in surgery, 1971-72; resident in urology U. NC Sch. Medicine, Chapel Hill, 1974-77, fellow in pediatric urology, 1977-78, asst. prof. surgery and pediatrics, 1979-84, assoc. prof., 1984-85; dir. pediatric urology NC Meml. Hosp., Chapel Hill, 1979-85; instr. surgery Harvard U. Med. Sch., Boston, 1978-79, asst. prof. surgery (urology), 1985-90, assoc. prof. surgery, urology, 1990-94, prof. surgery (urology); prof. surgery and pediat., chief divsn. urology, exec. med. dir. Albany Med. Coll., NY, 1994-97, dean NY, 1996-2000; fellow in surgery (urology) Children's Hosp., Boston, 1978-79, asst. in surgery (urology), 1985-90, sr. assoc. surgery, 1990-94, CEO, pres., 2000—. Contbr. numerous articles to med. jours., chpts. to books. Lt. comdr. M.C., USNR, 1972-74. Fellow ACS, Am. Acad. Pediatrics; mem. Am. Urol. Assn. (New England sec.), Soc. Pediatric Urology (exec. com. 1988-92), Soc. Univ. Urologists (pres. 2001-02). Avocations: fishing, skiing, tennis. Office: Children's Hosp Boston Dept Urology Hunnewell 3 300 Longwood Ave Boston MA 02115-5724 Office Phone: 518-355-2080, 617-355-6000. Office Fax: 617-730-0474. Business E-Mail: james.mandell@childrens.harvard.edu.*

MANDELL, MERCEDES SUSAN, anesthesiologist, educator; d. Carl and Sylvia Mandell; m. Paul-Michael David, June 9, 1988. BS, U. Toronto, 1975, PhD, 1982, MD, 1985; MS, Queen's U., Kingston, Can., 1978. Fellow U. Toronto, 1990—91; asst. prof. U. Colo., Denver, 1992—98, dir. anesthesia for liver transplantation, 1993—, assoc. prof., 1998—. Chair intraoperative com. on donation after cardiac death United Network of Organ Sharing, Richmond, Va., 2001—02. Scholar, Med. Rsch. Coun. Can., 1977—81, Med. Rsch. Coun. of Can., 1983; Scholarship for combined MD-PhD, 1981—82. Fellow: Royal Coll. Physicians and Surgeons Can.; mem.: Am. Hepato-pancreato Biliary Assn., Am. Soc. Anesthesiologists, Internat. Liver Transplant Soc. Avocations: marathon running, skiing, bicycling, travel. Office: University of Colorado 1945 Wheeling St Aurora CO 80045-2539 E-mail: susan.mandell@uchsc.

MANDELSTAM, STANLEY, physicist; b. Johannesburg, Dec. 12, 1928; came to U.S., 1963; s. Boris and Beatrice (Liknaitzky) M. BSc, U. Witwatersrand, Johannesburg, 1952; BA, Cambridge U., Eng., 1954; PhD, Birmingham U., Eng., 1956. Boese postdoctoral fellow Columbia U., NYC, 1957-58; prof. math. physics U. Birmingham, 1960-63; asst. rsch. physicist U. Calif., Berkeley, 1958-60, prof. physics, 1963-94, prof. emeritus, 1994—. Vis. prof. physics Harvard U., Cambridge, Mass., 1965-66, Univ. de Paris, Paris Sud, 1979-80, 84-85. Editorial bd. The Phys. Rev. jour., 1978-81, 85-88; contbr. articles to profl. jours. Recipient Dirac medal and prize Internat. Ctr. for Theoretical Physics, 1991. Fellow AAAS, Royal Soc. London, Am. Phys. Soc. (Dannie N. Heineman Math. Physics prize 1992). Jewish. Office: U Calif Dept Physics Berkeley CA 94720-7300

MANDELSTAMM, JEROME ROBERT, lawyer; b. St. Louis, Apr. 3, 1932; s. Henry and Estelle (London) M.; m. Carolyn A. White; stepchildren: John M. Gagliardi, Maria A. Amundson, Amy E. Gagliardi. AB, U. Pa., Phila., 1954; LLB, Harvard U., Cambridge, Mass., 1957. Bar: Mo. 1957. Since practiced in, St. Louis; ptnr. Greenfield, Davidson, Mandelstamm & Voorhees, 1969—81, Schmitz, Mandelstamm, Hawker & Fischer, 1981—82; pvt. practice St. Louis, 1982—. Bd. dirs. Legal Aid Soc. City and County St. Louis, 1967-75, pres. 1969-70; bd. dirs. Lawyers Reference Service Met. St. Louis, 1976-83, chmn., 1978-83; bd. dirs. Mo. Legal Aid Soc., 1977-82; mem. 22d Jud. Cir. Bar Com., 1983-85, gen. chmn., 1984-85. Mem. St. Louis County Bd. Election Commrs., 1973-77. Served with AUS, 1957. Mem. ABA, Mo. Bar Assn., Am. Arbitration Assn. (panel of arbitrators 1984-2003), Bar Assn. Met. St. Louis (v.p. 1974-75, treas. 1975-76, William L. Weiss award for Svcs. to the Bar and the Cmty. 2004), Legal Svcs. Ea. Mo. Inc. F. Wm. McCalpin Wall of Justice award, 2002. Home: 7217 Princeton Saint Louis MO 63130-3000 Office: 1010 Market St Ste 1600 Saint Louis MO 63101-2082

MANDERNACK, SCOTT BRYAN, librarian; b. Kenosha, Wis., Sept. 18, 1957; s. Ralph Gilbert and Shirley Ann Mandernack; m. Marilyn Louise Meyers, Sept. 12, 1997; m. Jeanna Kay LeSuer, Nov. 1, 1980 (div.); children: Morgan Leigh LeSuer-Mandernack, Leah Shaun LeSuer-Mandernack, Erin Rachel LeSuer-Mandernack, Jordan Bree LeSuer-Mandernack. BA in Sociology, Anthropology, U. Wis.-Parkside, Kenosha, 1979; MLIS, U. Wis., Milw., 1982. Reference libr., bibliographer Temple U., Phila., 1983—85; info. & instrn. libr. U. Wis., Whitewater, 1985—90; undergrad. reference and instrn. libr. Purdue U., West Lafayette, Ind., 1990—2002, head undergrad. libr., 2002—08; head rsch. & instrnl. svcs. Marquette U. Librs., Milw., 2008—. Recipient John H. Moriarty award, Purdue U. Librs., 2000, Spl. Boilermaker award, Purdue U. Alumni Assn., 2008. Mem.: ALA, Assn. Coll. and Rsch. Librs. Liberal. Avocations: bicycling, gardening. Office: Marquette Univ PO Box 3141 Milwaukee WI 53201 Business E-Mail: scott.mandernack@marquette.edu.

MANDERS, KARL LEE, neurosurgeon; b. Rochester, NY, Jan. 21, 1927; s. David Bert and Frances Edna (Cohan) Mendelson; m. Ann Laprell, July 28, 1969; children: Karlanna Butler, Maidena Fulford;children from previous marriage: Karl, Kristine Myers, Kerry. Student, Cornell U., 1946; MD, U. Buffalo, 1950. Diplomate Am. Bd. Neurol. Surgery, Am. Bd. Clin. Biofeedback, Am. Bd. Hyperbaric Medicine, Am. Bd. Pain Medicine, Nat. Bd. Med. Examiners. Intern U. Va. Hosp., Charlottesville, 1950-51, resident in neurol. surgery, 1951-52, Henry Ford Hosp., Detroit, 1954-56; pvt. practice Indpls., 1956—. Med. dir. Cmty. Hosp. Rehab. Ctr. Pain, 1973—92; chief hosp. med. and surg. neurology Cmty. Hosp., 1983, 93; coroner Marion County, Ind., 1977—85, 1992—96; with Ind. Med. Om Bund Sman, 2009. With USN, 1952—54, Korea. Recipient cert. Achievement, Dept. Army, 1969, Disting. Physician award, Cmty. Hosp., 1997, Cert. of Distinction, Ind. State Med. Assn., Am.'s Top Surgeon award, Cosumers Rsch. Coun. Am., 2002. Fellow: ACS, Harvey Cushing Soc., Am. Acad. Neurology, Internat. Coll. Surgeons; mem.: AMA, Med. Expert Soc. Sec. Adminstrn., Marion County Med. Soc., Ind. Med. Soc., James McClure Surg. Soc., Am. Bd. Med. Psychotherapists (mem. profl. adv. coun.), James A. Gibson Anat. Soc., Internat. Soc. Aquatic Medicine, Interurban Neurosurg. Soc., Ctrl. Neurol. Soc., Am. Acad. Pain Medicine, Midwest Pain Soc. (pres. 1988), Am. Pain Soc., Nat. Assn. Med. Examiners, Royal Soc. Medicine, Ind. Coroners Assn. (pres. 1979), Soc. Computerized Tomography and Neuroimaging, Am. Soc. Stereotaxic and Functional Neurosurgery, N.Am. Spine Soc., Internat. Back Pain Soc., Pan Am. Med. Assn., Acad. Psychosomatic Medicine, Biofeedback Soc. Am., Pan Pacific Surg. Assn., Soc. Cryosurgery, Am. Assn. Biofeedback Clinicians, Am. Acad. Forensic Sci., Undersea Med. Soc., Am. Holistic Med. Assn. (co-founder), Am. Soc. Contemporary Medicine and Surgery, Am. Coll. Angiology, NY Acad. Scis., Am. Assn. Study Headache, Internat. Assn. Study Pain, Congress Neurol. Surgery, Am. Legion, Highland Country Club, Brendonwood Country Club, Phi Chi Med. Fraternity (mem. vol. medicine). Home and Office: 5845 High Fall Rd Indianapolis IN 46226-1018 Home Phone: 317-547-2369; Office Phone: 317-546-6691. Personal E-mail: annlmanders@comcast.net.

MANDERSCHEID, LESTER VINCENT, agricultural economics educator; b. Andrew, Iowa, Oct. 9, 1930; s. Vincent John and Alma (Sprank) M.; m. Dorothy Helen Varnum, Aug. 29, 1953; children: David, Paul, Laura, Jane. BS, Iowa State U., 1951, MS, 1952; PhD, Stanford U., 1961. Grad. asst. Iowa State U., Ames, 1951-52, Stanford (Calif.) U., 1952-56; asst. prof. Mich. State U., East Lansing, 1956-65, assoc. prof., 1965-70, prof., 1970-73, prof., assoc. chmn., 1973-87, prof., chmn., 1987-92, prof., 1992-95, prof. emeritus, 1996—, coord. Grad. Sch., 1993—. Reviewer Tex. A&M Agrl. Econ. Program, College Station, 1989; cons. Consortium Internat. Earth Sci. Info. Network, Ann Arbor, 1990. Co-author: Improving Undergraduate Education, 1967; contbr. articles to jours. in field. Pres. parish coun. St. Thomas, East Lansing, 1984-87; coll. coord. United Way, East Lansing, 1983-84; pres. bd. dirs. Cristo Rey Cmty. Ctr., 1998-2001. Recipient Disting. Faculty award Mich. State U., 1977. Mem. Am. Agrl. Econ. Assn. (pres. 1988-89, bd. dirs. 1982-85, excellence in teaching award 1974), Am. Statis. Assn., Am. Econ. Assn., University Club, Sigma Xi (pres. 1986-87), Phi Kappa Phi (pres. 1979-80). Roman Catholic. Home: 2372 Burcham Dr East Lansing MI 48823-3885 Office: Mich State Univ Dept Agrl Food & Resource Economics Circle Dr East Lansing MI 48824-1039 Office Phone: 517-355-0301. Business E-Mail: mandersc@msu.edu.

MANDERSON, EASTON L., orthopedist, surgeon; arrived in U.S., 1963; s. Caleb Sterling and Beatrice Anita Manderson; m. Lois Constance Manderson; children: Tanya Michelle, Mario Sean, Keisha Anita Rochelle. BS cum laude, Howard U., 1967, MD, 1971. Diplomate Am. Bd. Orthopedic Surgery, Am. Bd. Ind. Med. Examiners. Rotating intern Freedmen's Hosp., Howard U., 1971—72; orthop. resident Howard U., 1972—75; pediat. orthop. fellow/resident Johns Hopkins U. Med. Sch.; med. officer DC Gen. Hosp., Washington, 1975—2001, chief orthopedic surgery, 1995—2001; pvt. practice Riggs Orthopedic Clinic, Washington, 1978—. Clin. instr. Howard U. Med. Sch., Washington, 1975—90, asst. prof., 1990—. Contbr. articles to profl. jours. Fellow: ACS, Am. Acad. Orthopedic Surgeons. Achievements include patents for extra medullary rod fixateur for long bone fracture; sub muscular and incision technique; jigless intra medullary nail with easy locking; intra medullary screw for fusion of ankles with complex deformities. Avocations: jogging, weightlifting, reading. Office: Riggs Orthopaedic Clinic 1140 Varnum St NE Washington DC 20017 Office Phone: 202-526-5300.

MANDL, ROBERT, application developer; b. Romania; s. Paul and Eva Mandl. BSc in Math., Physics, and Linguistics, Hebrew U., 1963, MSc in Math., 1965; student, MIT, Cambridge, Mass., MSEE, 1969, PhD in Engring., 1970. Sr. software engr. Softech, Waltham, Mass., 1980—83; mgr. software engring. Analogic Corp., Peabody, Mass., 1983—89; sr. software engr. Info. Engring., Bedford, Mass., 1990; cons. AT&T Bell Labs., North Andover, Mass., 1991—95; prin. engr. Digital Equipment Corp., Littleton, Mass., 1996—2001; ind. rschr. Cambridge, 2001—. Presenter in field. Author software; compiler, editor: MIT Folk Dance Club Song Book, 1975; contbr. articles to profl. jours. Mem.: IEEE (life), NY Acad. Sci., IEEE Computer Soc., Linguistic Soc. Am., Math. Assn. Am., Sigma Xi. Achievements include origination of TAXOR and complexity measure for Sudoku puzzles; development of Tonalized Pinyin and TASKMON. Avocations: languages, running, hambo, dance. Home: Box 397199 Cambridge MA 02139

MANDLE, ROGER, museum administrator, former academic administrator; BA in Studio Art/Art History, cum laude, Williams Coll., 1963; MA in Mus. Tng., NYU, 1967; PhD in Art History, Case Western Reserve U., 2002; DFA (hon.), U. Toledo, 1983, Kenyon Coll., 1986, Brown U., 2003. Assoc. dir. Minn. Inst. Arts, 1967—74; dir. Toledo Mus. Art, Ohio; dep. dir. Nat. Gallery Art, Washington, 1988—93; pres. RI Sch. Design, 1993—2008; exec. dir. Qatar Mus. Authority, 2008—. Mem. Nat. Coun. on the Arts; Robert Sterling Clark vis. prof. art history Williams Coll., 1993; US amb. Arts, 1996—2002. Recipient Am. Hellenic Ednl. Progressive award outstanding contr. to cultural world, 1983, Governor's award, Ohio, 1983, Marketer of Yr., Northwestern Ohio Chpt. Am. Mktg. Assn., 1983, Knight of the Order of Isabel the Catholic, His Majesty Juan Carlos, Spain, 1985; Andover Tchg. Fellowship, 1963—64.

MANDLER, GEORGE, psychologist, educator; b. Vienna, June 11, 1924; came to U.S., 1940, naturalized, 1943; s. Richard and Hede (Goldschmied) M.; m. Jean Matter, Jan. 19, 1957; children: Peter Clark, Michael Allen. BA, NYU, 1949; MS, Yale U., 1950, PhD, 1953; post grad., U. Basel, Switzerland, 1947-48; PhD (hon.), U. Vienna, 2009. Asst. prof. Harvard U., 1953-57, lectr., 1957-60; prof. U Toronto, 1960—65; prof. psychology U. Calif., San Diego, 1965-94, chmn. dept. psychology, 1965-70, disting. prof. emeritus, 1994—; dir. Ctr. Human Info. Processing, U. Calif., San Diego, 1965-90. Hon. rsch. fellow Univ. Coll. London., 1977-78, 82-90, vis. prof., 1990—. Author: Mind and Emotion, 1975, (German edit.), 1980, Mind and Body, 1984, (Japanese edit.), 1987, Cognitive Psychology, 1985, Japanese edit., 1991, Human Nature Explored, 1997, Interesting Times, 2001, Consciousness Recovered, 2002, A History of Modern Experiemental Psychology, 2007; co-author: (with W. Kessen) The Language of Psychology, (Italian edit.), 1959, (with J.M. Mandler) Thinking: From Association to Gestalt, 1964; contbr. articles and revs. to profl. jours.; editor: Psychol. Rev., 1970-76. Served with U.S. Army, 1943-46. Fellow Ctr. for Advanced Study in Behavioral Scis., 1959-60; vis. fellow Oxford U., Eng., 1971-72, 78; Guggenheim fellow, 1971-72. Fellow AAAS, Am. Acad. Arts and Scis.; mem. AAUP, Am. Assn. Advancement Psychology (1974-82); Psychonomic Soc. (governing bd., chmn. 1983), Am. Psychol. Soc., Am. Psychol. Assn. (pres. divs. exptl. psychology 1978-79, pres. div. gen psychology 1982-83, mem. coun. reps. 1978-82, William James prize 1986), Internat. Union Psychol. Scis. (U.S. com. 1985-90), Soc. Exptl. Psychologists, Fedn. Behavioral Psychol. and Cognitive Scis. (pres. 1981). Home: 1406 La Jolla Knoll La Jolla CA 92037-5236 Office: U Calif San Diego Dept Psychology La Jolla CA 92093-0109 also: 3 Perrins Lane London NW3 1QY England Business E-Mail: gmandler@ucsd.edu.

MANDLER, JEAN MATTER, psychologist, educator; b. Oak Park, Ill., Nov. 6, 1929; d. Joseph Allen and May Roberts (Finch) Matter; m. George Mandler, Jan. 19, 1957; children: Peter Clark, Michael Allen. Student, Carleton Coll., 1947-49; BA with highest honors, Swarthmore Coll., 1951; PhD, Harvard U., 1956. Rsch. assoc. lab. social rels. Harvard U., 1957-60; rsch. assoc. dept. psychology U. Toronto, Ont., Canada, 1961-65; assoc. rsch. psychologist, lectr. U. Calif. at San Diego, La Jolla, 1965-73, assoc. prof., 1973-77, prof. psychology, 1977-88, prof. cognitive sci., 1988—96, disting. prof., 1996—2000, disting. rsch. prof., 2000—; mem. adv. com. memory and cognitive processes NSF, 1978-81. Hon. rsch. fellow U. Coll., London, 1978-89, vis. prof., 1990—; hon. mem. Med. Rsch. Coun. Cognitive Devel. Unit, 1982-98. Author: (G. Mandler) Thinking: From Association to Gestalt, 1964, Stories, Scripts and Scenes, 1984, The Foundations of Mind: Origins of Conceptual Thought, 2004 (APA Divsn. 7 Eleanor Maccoby Book award 2005, Cognitive Devel. Soc. Best Authored Book award 2006); assoc. editor Psychol. rev., 1970-76; mem. editl. bd. Child Devel., 1976-89, Discourse Processes, 1977-94, Jour. Exptl. Psychology, 1977-85, Text, 1979-97, Jour. Verbal Learning and Verbal Behavior, 1980-88, Lang. and Cognitive Processes, 1985-2008, Cognitive Devel., 1990-99, Jour. Cognition and Devel., 1999-2008; contbr. articles to profl. jours Pres. San Diego Assn. Gifted Children, 1968-71; v.p. Calif. Parents for Gifted, 1970-71; mem. alumni council Swarthmore Coll., 1975-78. Recipient Disting. Scientific Contrbn. award, Am. Psychol. Assn., 2007; NIMH research grantee, 1968—81, NSF research grantee, 1981—99. Fellow: APA (mem. exec. com. divsn. 3 1983—85), Am. Acad. Arts and Scis.; mem.: Soc. Exptl. Psychologists, Cognitive Devel. Soc., Cognitive Sci. Soc., Psychonomic Soc. (mem. governing bd. 1982—87, chmn. 1985—86), Phi Beta Kappa. Office: U Calif San Diego Dept Cognitive Sci 9500 Gilman Dr La Jolla CA 92093-0515 Business E-Mail: jmandler@ucsd.edu.

MANDOCK, RANDAL LEE NICHOLAS, geophysicist, professor; PhD, Ga. Inst. Tech, Atlanta. Dir., Earth Sys. Sci. Program Clark Atlanta U., 1999—, assoc. prof., 2000—. Contbr. poster (Sci. Applications Internat. Corp. award, 2002). Dir. religious edn. St. Francis de Sales Ch., Mableton, Ga., 1995—2008. Sgt. USMC, 1972—76. Fellow Summer fellowship, Universal Energy Systems, 1987—89. Mem.: Am. Geophys. Union. Achievements include development of 3-D atmospheric turbulence imager. Office: Clark Atlanta Univ Rsch Ctr Sci & Tech Rm 2013 Atlanta GA 30314 Business E-Mail: edmac@cau.edu.

MANDOLINI-PESARESI, MASSIMO, classicist, educator; s. Bruna Mandolini-Pesaresi and Leandro Pesaresi. Laurea in Filosofia, U. Rome, 1980, Laurea in Letter Classiche, 1974; PhD in Italian Lit., Yale U., New Haven, 1990. Asst. prof. Emory U., Atlanta, 1988—90, Columbia U., NYC, 1991—2001, assoc. prof., 1991—2001; asst. prof. Georgetown U., DC, 1990—; assoc. faculty Saddleback Coll., Mission Viejo, Calif., 2004—. Author: Grecian Vistas: Giacomo Leopardi and Romantic Hellas, 1999, A Companion for Darkness: Classical Twilights in the II Millennium, 2006. Home: 55 Roswell Ave # 11 Long Beach CA 90803 Office: Saddleback Coll 28000 Marguerite Pky Long Beach CA 90803 Business E-Mail: mmp23@aya.yale.edu, mmandolinipesaresi@saddleback.edu.

MANDSAGER, RICHARD, hospital administrator; MD. Ret. asst. surgeon gen. USPHS Commissioned Corps; staff pediatrician Southcentral Found.; dir., Anchorage svc. unit Alaska Native Med. Ctr., dir., med. dir., pediatric svc. ctr. Anchorage, 2000—04; dir. Public Health Alaska Dept. Health & Social Svc., Juneau, 2004—06; exec. dir. Children's Hosp. at Providence, Anchorage, 2006—. Office: Children's Hosp 3200 Providence Dr Anchorage AK 99508 Office Phone: 907-561-2211.*

MANDY, STEPHEN HOWARD, dermatologist, educator; b. Balt., Jan. 6, 1943; s. Arthur Jennings and Sylvia Bliss Mandy; 1 child, Ashley Jacqueline. BA, George Washington U., 1962, MD, 1966. Cert. dermatology Am. Bd. Dermatology, 1972. Intern U. Fla., Gainesville, 1966—67; resident ob-gyn. Sinai Hosp., Balt., 1967—68; resident dermatology Johns Hopkins, Balt., 1968—69, U. Miami, Fla., 1969—71; pvt. practice South Miami, 1973—91, Aspen, Colo., 1991—2003, South Miami Beach, Fla., 2003—; chmn. bd. and founder DVM Pharm., 1976—92; clin. prof. dermatology U. Miami, Fla., 1982—; chmn. bd. Sirius Pharm., 2005—. Chmn. bd. Dermatologics For Vet. Medicine, Miami, 1976—92; pres. Am. Soc. for Dermatologic Surgery, Rolling Meadows, Ill., 2000—01. Contbr. articles to profl. jours. Maj. USAF, 1971—73. Jewish. Avocations: wine collector, skiing, equestrian, travel, photography. Office: South Beach Dermatology 555 Washington Ave Ste 210 Miami Beach FL 33139 Office Fax: 305-673-6422.

MANDYAM, GIRIDHAR DHATI, electronics engineer; b. Dallas, Tex., Oct. 15, 1967; s. Mandyam Dhati and Revathi Srinath; m. Chitra Mandyam, Feb. 1, 1973; 1 child, Atulya Dhati. BSEE, So. Meth. U., Dallas, 1985—89; MSEE, U. So. Calif., LA, 1991—93; PhD, U. N.Mex, Albuquerque, 1994—96. Engr. Rockwell Internat., Richardson, Tex., 1989—91, Qualcomm Inc., San Diego, Calif., 1993—94; mem. of group tech. staff Tex. Instruments, Dallas, Tex., 1996—98; sr. rsch. engr. Nokia Rsch. Ctr., Irving, Tex., 1998—2000, prin. scientist, 2000—02, dir., 2002—04, San Diego, 2004—06; chief technologist, N.Am. Nokia Mobile Phones, Irving, Tex., 2006; v.p. tech. Qualcomm Inc., San Diego, 2006; v.p. Qaulcomm Inc., San Diego, 2006—. Adj. prof. U. Tex. at Dallas, Richardson, 2001—. Mem.: IEEE. Achievements include patents for 14 issued US patents.

MANEKAS, JASON ARTHUR, lawyer; b. Lowell, Mass., June 30, 1970; BS summa cum laude, U. NH, 1992; JD cum laude, Suffolk U., 1995. Bar: NH 1995, US Dist. Ct. (Dist. NH) 1995, Mass. 1996, US Dist. Ct. (Dist. Mass.) 1996, US Ct. Appeals (1st Cir.) 1996. Law clk. Superior Ct. Mass., 1995—96; ptnr. Bernkopf Goodman LLP, Boston. Mem.: NH Bar Assn., Mass. Bar Assn. Office: Bernkopf Goodman LLP Ste 1300 125 Summer St Boston MA 02110 Office Phone: 617-790-3000. Office Fax: 617-790-3300. E-mail: jmanekas@bg-llp.com.

MANEKER, MORTON M., lawyer; b. NYC, Nov. 14, 1932; s. Arthur and Estelle (Hochberg) M.; m. Roberta S. Wexler, 1985; children: Meryl Colle, Amy Jill, Marion Kenneth. AB, Harvard U., 1954, LLB, 1957. Bar: NY 1957. Assoc. Shearman & Sterling, NYC, 1957—62; trial atty. antitrust divsn. Dept. Justice, 1962—63; ptnr. Proskauer Rose LLP, NYC, 1963—94; ret., 1994. Trustee Beth Israel Hosp., NYC, 1977—2001. Mem. Am. Law Inst., N.Y. State Bar Assn., Harmonie Club. Jewish. Home: 30 E 65th St New York NY 10021-7013 Office Phone: 212-439-9737. Personal E-mail: maneker@aol.com.

MANEKER, ROBERTA S(UE), public relations executive; b. NYC, July 9, 1937; d. Maxwell Roy and Esther (Gerson) Scheff; m. Hannan Wexler, June 4, 1961 (div. 1983); children: Daniel, Joanna Bayer; m. Morton M. Maneker, June 1, 1985. BA, Oberlin Coll., 1957. Ford Found. scholar, 1953-57; Mng. editor True Love mag., NYC., 1960-62; publicity dir. Capt. Kangaroo, CBS, NYC., 1962-66; syndicated columnist Oleg Cassini, NYC., 1967-69; freelance writer, NYC., 1967-70; dir. pub. rels. Direct Mktg. Assn., NYC, 1983-85, v.p. pub. rels., 1985-87; v.p. pub. rels. Christie's, NYC, 1987-91, sr. v.p. corp. comm./mktg., 1991-94; freelance cons. mktg. and pub. rels., 1995—; mktg. dir. Phillips Auctioneers, 2000-01; dir. 1991-2001, mktg. cons. Lechters, Inc., 2000; corr. Art & Antiques Mag., 1997—. Contbr. articles to publs. Trustee Jewish Home and Hosp., 1996-04, chmn. Manhattan Divsn., 2000-03; bd. trustee, Oberlin Coll., 1997-2006, mem. exec. com., 2004-2006, hon. trustee, 2006—; mem. vis. com. Allen Meml. Art Mus., 2002—, chmn. 2002-08; pres. Oberlin Coll. Alumni Assn., 1989-91, Phi Beta Kappa

MANELLA, NORA MARGARET, judge; BA with high honors, Wellesley Coll., Mass., 1972; JD, U. So. Calif., 1975. Bar: Calif. 1976, U.S. Ct. Appeals (5th cir.) 1976, D.C. Cit. Appeals 1978, U.S. Dist. Ct. (ctrl., so., no. and ea. dists.) 1980-81, U.S. Ct. Appeals (9th cir.) 1982. Law clk. to Hon. John Minor Wisdom U.S. Ct. Appeals (5th cir.), New Orleans, 1975-76; legal counsel Subcom. on Constn., Senate Com. on Judiciary, Washington, 1976-78; assoc. O'Melveny & Myers, Washington and L.A., 1978-82; asst. U.S. atty. U.S. Dept. Justice, LA, 1982—90, trial asst. major crimes, 1982-85, dep. chief, criminal complaints, 1986-87, chief criminal appeals, 1988-90; judge L.A. Mcpl. Ct., 1990—92, L.A. Superior Ct., 1992-93, U.S. Dist. Ct. (ctrl. dist.) Calif., LA, 1998—2006; justice pro tem Calif. Ct. of Appeal 2d appellate dist. LA, 1992, assoc. justice, 2006—; U.S. Atty. (ctrl. dist.) Calif. U.S. Dept. Justice, LA, 1994—98. Instr. U.S. Atty. Gen. Advocacy Inst., 1984-86, Calif. Jud. Coll., 1992-93; mem. Atty. Gen.'s Adv. Com., 1994-95. Mem. editl. bd. State Bar Criminal Law Newsletter, 1991-92. Mem. adv. bd. Monroe H.S. and Govt. Magnet, 1991-94; acad. specialist USAID Delegation, 1993; judge L.A. Times Cmty. Partnership Awards, 1993; bd. councilors Law Sch. U. So. Calif., 1996—. Mem. Am. Law Inst., Calif. Judges Assn., Nat. Assn. Women Judges, Calif. Women Lawyers, Women Lawyers LA, Order of Coif, Phi Beta Kappa. Office: Calif Ct of Appeal 2d Appellate Dist LA 300 South Spring St Los Angeles CA 90013 Office Phone: 213-830-7443. Business E-Mail: arlene.chavez@jud.ca.gov.

MANELLI, DONALD DEAN, scriptwriter, film and television producer; s. Daniel Anthony and Mignon Marie (Dean) M.; m. Susan Linda Allen, June 16, 1964 (div. Aug. 1973); children: Daniel, Lisa. BA, U. Notre Dame, 1959. Communications specialist Jewel Cos., Melrose Park, Ill., 1959; script writer Coronet Films, Chgo., 1960-62; freelance writer Chgo., 1962-63; creative dir. Fred A. Niles Communications Ctrs., Chgo., 1963-67; sr. writer Wild Kingdom NBC-TV, Chgo., 1967-70; freelance film writer, producer Chgo., 1970-76; pres. Donald Manelli & Assocs., Inc., Chgo. and Paris, 1976—. Screenwriter, prodr. more than 225 documentary films, 1970—, numerous episodes Wild Kingdom, 1967-82 (Emmy award 1969, 70). Recipient numerous awards various orgns. including N.Y. Internat. Film Festival, Houston Internat. Film Festival, Berlin, Paris, Venice Internat. Film Festivals, CINE, 1976—. Mem. Writers Guild Am. Roman Catholic. Avocations: photography, travel, tennis. also: 1 Rue Goethe 75116 Paris France Office: Donald Manelli and Assoc 8000 McConnell Ave Los Angeles CA 90045 Personal E-mail: dmanelli@earthlink.net. *A simple truth is played out in most lives: what we believe ourselves to be, we are. We may be tested with our own failed efforts and plain bad luck, but our personal vision gives us strength. Success brings satisfaction and the responsibility to help others form and follow their own visions.*

MANERA, ROSE ELLEN, music educator, elementary school educator; d. Gerald Stanley and Frances Ellen Wolcott; m. Michael A. Manera, Apr. 3, 1982; children: Matthew Gerald, Michelle Ellen. BA in Music, Calif. State U., Chico, 1976, BA in Liberal Studies, 1976. Single Subject Credential/Music-Life Calif. State U. Chico, 1977, Multiple Subject Credential-Liberal Studies-Life Calif. State U., Chico, 1977. Student tchr. 2nd grade (music emphasis) Chico Unified Sch. Dist., Calif., 1976—76; kindergarten, 1st grade tchr. Oroville Elem. Sch. Dist., Calif., 2004—05; student tchr. 5th grade (music emphasis) Chico Unified Sch. Dist., 1977—77; music specialist; k-8 gen. music, choir Manzanita Sch. Dist., Gridley, Calif., 1977—80; music specialist: k-8 gen. music, choir Bangor Sch. Dist., Calif., 1977—80, Pioneer Sch. Dist., Berry Creek, Calif., 1978—80; kindergarten tchr., music specialist: k-8 gen. music, choir, yearbook advisor-7th/8th grades Manzanita Sch. Dist., Gridley, Calif., 1980—84; part-time music tchr.: 4th-8th grades, choir Oroville Elem. Sch. Dist., 1987—94, full-time music tchr.: k-3rd gen. music; 4th-6th grade choirs, 7th-8th grade choir, 1987—94, full time music tchr.: k-3rd gen. music, 4th-6th choirs, 7th-8th grade choirs, 1994—2004. Dir. of the dist. music festival Oroville Elem. Sch. Dist., 1994—2004, mentor tchr., 1995—96. Accompanist for ch. choir Foothill Cmty. Ch., Oroville, 1994—2004. Recipient Tchr. Yr., Wal-Mart, 2004. Mem.: Calif. Kindergarten Tchrs. Assn. (assoc.), Calif. Music Educators Assn. (assoc.), Music Educators Nat. Conf. (assoc.). Avocations: reading, crafts, swimming. Office: Oroville Childhood Elem Sch Dist 2795 Yard St Oroville CA 95966 E-mail: emanera@ocesd.org.

MANESHNI, BAHMAN, economics professor; s. Farangis Pouladian; m. Farangis Zardoshty. MA in Economics, Vanderbilt U., Nashville, Tenn.; MA in Internat. Mgmt., Vanderbilt U., Glendale, Ariz., 1981. Adviser PVCC's Phi Beta Lambda Club, Phoenix, 1999—; mem. Am. Assn. Individual Investors, Chgo., 1996—; mem. econ instrnl. coun. Maricopa County Cmty. Colls. Dist., Tempe, Ariz., 2003—. Master: Phi Beta Lambda. Office: Paradise Valley CC 18401 N 32nd St Phoenix AZ 85032

MANESS, ELEANOR PALMER, researcher; b. Raleigh, NC, June 24, 1935; d. Oren Alston and Lillian Way Palmer; m. Charles B. Maness, Feb. 1, 1955 (dec. July 1989); children: Reid, Brian, Teresa. BA, Meredith Coll., 1958. Tchr. St. Timoth Sch., Raleigh, 1958—64; rsch. analyst N.C. State U., Raleigh, 1966—99; cons., 1999—. Contbr. articles to sci. jours. Recipient L.M. Ware Rsch. award, Am. Soc. for Hort. Sci., 1974, Excellence in Environment Rsch. award, Fed. Hwy. Adminstrn., 1997. Presbyterian. Avocations: hiking, swimming, gardening, rock hunting, fishing. Home: PO Box 655 Zebulon NC 27597

MANESS, THEODORE E. (TED MANESS), legislative staff member; m. Katie Winkeljohn; children: Elizabeth, Teddy. B in Polit. Sci., Francis Marion U., Florence, SC, 1980. Dir. legis. and polit. affairs US C. of C., 1987—93; chief of staff to John Kyl US House of Reps., US Senate, Washington, 1993—97; exec. dir. Nat. Republican Congl. Com., 1997—99; v.p. industry rels. Fannie Mae, 1999—2001; chief of staff to Rep. George Radanovich US House of Reps., Washington, 2004—. Recipient Outstanding Alumnus award, Francis Marion U., 2008. Republican. Office: 2410 Rayburn House Office Bldg Washington DC 20515 Office Phone: 202-225-4540. Office Fax: 202-225-3402.*

MANETTA, AMEDA AVRILL, social sciences educator; d. Malcolm James and Mabel Manetta; children: Lola P Sutherland, Morgan J. J. Sutherland. BA in Sociology, The U. of Western Ont., London, Ont., Can., 1988; BSW, The U. of Western Ont., 1989; MSW, U. of Windsor, Ont., 1990; PhD, Va. Commonwealth U., 1997. Faculty Stephen F. Austin State U., Nacogdoches, Tex., 1997—98; assoc. prof. Winthrop U., Rock Hill, SC, 1998—. Bd. dirs. Safe Passage, Inc, Rock Hill, SC, 2003—. Rev. editor Journal of Social Work in End-of-Life and Palliative Care, 2005—; contbr. articles to profl. jours., chapters to books. Mem. profl. adv. bd. Home Care Connections, Richmond. Grantee, Winthrop Faculty grantee, 1999, Stephen F. Austin Faculty grantee, 1998. Mem.: NASW (bd. dirs. 2001), Coun. on Social Work Edn., Am. Assn. of Suicidology. Office: Winthrop University 128 Bancroft Bldg Rock Hill SC 29733 Business E-Mail: manettaa@winthrop.edu.

MANEWITZ, MARK LEE, lawyer; b. St. Louis, Nov. 21, 1946; s. Robert and Irma Lee (Zarfas) M.; m. Sharon Faybelle Popovitz, June 22, 1969; children: Samantha Alexandra, Thomas Franklin. BA, U. Chgo., 1970; JD, Rutgers U., 1973. Bar: N.Y. 1974, U.S. Dist. Ct. (so. dist.) N.Y. 1974, U.S. Ct. Appeals (2nd cir.) 1975, N.J. 1982, U.S. Dist. Ct. (no. dist.) N.J. 1982, U.S. Ct. Appeals (3rd cir.) 1982, U.S. dist. Fed. (ea. dist.) N.Y., U.S. dist. N.J. Atty. Power Authority of State of N.Y., NYC, 1973-81; environ. counsel Exxon Co. USA, Linden, NJ, 1981-86; asst. gen. counsel Coltec Industries Inc., NYC, 1986-92; ptnr. Clapp & Eisenberg, Newark, 1992—, Reed Smith LLP, Newark, 2001; atty. Skadden, Arps, Slate, Meagher & Flom LLP, Newark; ptnr. Herrick Feinstein LLP, Newark. Adj. prof. law sch. Fordham U. 1987—, mem. faculty continuing legal edn. N.J. Inst. 1987-88, faculty mem. ALI-ABA Seminar on Environ. Litig. Contbr. Mem. NJ Bar Assn. (bd. dirs., chair environ. law com. 1989-90), NY State Bar Assn. (environ. com.), Assn. of Bar of City of NY (sci. and law com.). Republican. Avocations: theater, music. Office: Manewitz law Ste A1401 360 E 72nd St New York NY 10021 Office Phone: 212-592-5925, 917-733-5103. Personal E-mail: mmanewitz@gmail.com.

MANEY, MICHAEL MASON, lawyer; b. Taihoku, Japan, Aug. 13, 1936; s. Edward Strait and Helen M. M.; m. Suzanne Cochran, Oct. 22, 1960; 1 child, Michele. BA, Yale U., 1956; MA, Fletcher Sch. Law and Diplomacy, Tufts U., 1957; LL.B., U. Pa., 1964. Bar: N.Y. 1966, D.C. 1977. Case officer CIA, 1957-61; law clk. Justice John Harlan, Supreme Ct. U.S., Washington, 1964-65; asso. Sullivan & Cromwell, NYC, 1965-70, ptnr., 1971—77, 1981—2003, mng. ptnr. Washington, 1977-81, sr. counsel, 2004—. Law fellow Salzburg Seminar in Am. Studies, 1967; mem. bd. overseers Fletcher Sch. Law and Diplomacy. 1st lt. USAF, 1957-61. Mem. ABA, Am. Law Inst., Am. Coll. Trial Lawyers, N.Y. State Bar Assn., Union Club, Madison Beach Club, Madison Country Club, Met. Opera Club, Soc. of Cin. Address: 48 Neptune Ave Madison CT 06443-3210 Office: Sullivan & Cromwell LLP 125 Broad St New York NY 10004-2498

MANFREDA, JOHN J., federal agency administrator; b. DC; m. Rosemary Manfreda; 3 children. Grad., U. Md.; JD, Am. U., 1970; M in Tax Law, Georgetown U., 1974. Bar: DC, U.S. Ct. Appeals DC. With Bur. Alcohol and Tobacco Tax and Trade, US Dept. Treasury, 1970—2003, staff atty., 1970—78, assoc. chief counsel for alcohol and tobacco, 1978—96, chief counsel for alcohol and tobacco, 1996—2003, dep. adminstr., 2003—05, adminstr., 2005—. Office: Alcohol and Tobacco Tax and Trade Bur Pub Info Officer 1310 G St NW Ste 300 Washington DC 20220*

MANGA, MICHAEL, earth science educator, geophysicist; b. Hamilton, Ont., Can., July 22, 1968; s. Pran and Louise Manga; m. Susan Storch. BSc in Geophysics, McGill U., Montreal, Que., Can., 1990; SM in Engring. Scis., Harvard U., 1992, PhD in Earth and Planetary Scis., 1994. Miller rsch. fellow Miller Inst. Basic Rsch. in Scis., Berkeley, Calif., 1994—96; asst. prof. dept. geol. scis. U. Oreg., Eugene, 1996—2001; assoc. prof. dept. earth & planetary scis. U. Calif., Berkeley, 2001—. Contbr. articles to sci. jours.; assoc. editor: Jour. Geophys. Rsch., 2001—05, mem. editl. bd.: Geology, 2004—; editor: Revs. Geophysics, 2005—. Recipient CAREER award, NSF, 1997—2001, Ersted Award for Disting. Teaching, U. Oreg., 1999; named a MacArthur fellow, John D. and Catherine T. MacArthur Found., 2005; named one of Brilliant 10, Popular Sci. mag., 2003; fellow, Sloan Found., 2001. Fellow: Geol. Soc. Am. (Donath medal 2003), Am. Geophys. Union (James B. Macelwane medal 2002). Office: Dept Earth and Planetary Sci Univ Calif Berkeley 173 McCone Hall Berkeley CA 94720-4767 Office Phone: 510-643-8532. Office Fax: 510-643-9980. E-mail: manga@seismo.berkeley.edu.

MANGALPALLY, KIRAN KUMAR RAMCHANDER, medical researcher; s. Ramchander and Nimala Mangalpally; m. Kalpana Rama, Dec. 15, 2006. MD, Gandhi Med. Coll., Hyderabad, India, 2000; MB, BChir, Hyderabad, 2000. Cert. Am. Bd. Internal Medicine, 2007. Intern Mt. Vernon Hosp., NY, 2004—05, mem. rsch. com., 2006—07, resident physician, mem. pharmacotherapeutics com., 2005—07; rschr. Meth. Hosp., Houston, 2007—. Recipient Sidda Naik Best Resident award, 2007. Mem.: AMA, Cochrane Heart Group, Am. Coll. Physicians. Achievements include research in morphology of small and large platelets. Personal E-mail: kiranmrkumar@gmail.com.

MANGAN, JOHN LEO, retired electric power industry executive, international trade specialist; b. Lakewood, Ohio, May 24, 1920; s. Mark A. and Celia M. Mangan; m. Mildred J. Livingston, June 21, 1946; children: John, Scott. BSME, Carnegie Inst. Tech., 1942. Registered profl. engr., Mass., N.Y. Turbine design engr. Gen. Electric Co., Lynn, Mass., 1946-48, turbine application and sales engr. Fitchburg and Lynn, Mass., Schenectady, St. Louis, 1948-55, mgr. gas turbine indsl. sales Schenectady, 1955-60, mgr. gas turbine product planning, 1960-64, mgr. turbine bus. strategy devel., 1966-86; mgr. turbine indsl. customer requirements Boeing Co., Seattle, 1964-66. Contbr. articles profl. jours., chpts. in books; inventor in field. Mem. com. Boy Scouts Am., 1955-59, 64-66; bd. dirs. United Way Schenectady County, Inc., 1991-96, chmn., 1992-93. 1st lt. U.S. Army, 1942-46. Recipient Profl. and Social Activities award GE, 1977, cert. of merit N.Y. State Assembly, 1995. Fellow ASME (v.p. 1975-79, bd. govs. 1983-87, Gas Turbine citation, Centennial medal 1980, Dedicated Svc. award 1988); mem. Internat. Combustion Engine Coun. (permanent com. 1974-81, v.p. 1977-81). Home: 1345 Ruffner Rd Niskayuna NY 12309-2505 Home Phone: 518-372-9555.

MANGAN, MICHAEL D., corporate financial executive; BME, Gen. Motors Inst.; MBA, Amos Tuck Sch., Dartmouth Coll. Fin. mgmt. positions through group CFO GMAC Gen. Motors Corp., 1981—94; exec. v.p., CFO The Ryland Group Inc., 1994—99; v.p. investor rels. The Black & Decker Corp., Towson, Md., 1999—2000, sr. v.p., CFO, 2002—08, sr. v.p., pres. worldwide power tools, 2008—. Past. bd. dir. Gen. Motors Acceptance Corp. Office: The Black & Decker Corp 701 E Joppa Rd Towson MD 21286*

MANGANELLO, TIMOTHY M., auto parts company executive; B of Mech. Engring., U. Mich.; postgrad., Harvard U.; grad., Chrusler Inst. Program. Product engring. mgr. Chrysler Corp., 1973—81; sales mgr. PT Components, 1981—88; v.p. ops. BorgWarner TorqTransfer Systems, Inc., Muncie, Ind., 1995—99, pres., gen. mgr. Chgo., 1999—2001; v.p. BorgWarner, Inc., 1999—2001, exec. v.p., 2001—02, pres., COO, 2002—03, pres., CEO, 2003, chmn., CEO, 2003—. Mem. bd. dir. Bemis Co., Inc. Office: Borgwarner 3850 Hamlin Rd Auburn Hills MI 48326-2872

MANGANO, DENNIS THOMAS, science educator, director; b. NYC, Sept. 2, 1943; s. Thomas and Rose Mangano; m. Christina Mora, Aug. 15, 1993; children: Mark Thomas, Gabriella Elizabeth, Antonio Thomas, Luca Thomas. BSEE summa cum laude, Poly. Inst. NY, MS in Physics, PhD in Math. and Physics, 1971; MD, U. Miami, Fla., 1974. Cert. specialist Calif., 1977. Prof. tenured U. Calif., San Francisco, 1977—; dir. Ischemia Rsch. and Edn. Found., San Bruno, Calif., 1987—2008, founder, 2001—, prin. scientist, 2001—. Founder McSPI Rsch. Group, San Bruno, 1990—, dir., 1990—. Contbr. articles to profl. jours. Recipient Rsch. award, Julie Labs., 1965, MTS award, Bell Labs., 1965—72, Multiple Rsch. awards, 2008; Med. Rsch. grant, 1980—2001, Rsch. grant, NIH, 1985—90. Fellow: Am. Heart Assn. (hon.), NY Acad. Sci. (hon.). Independent. Roman Catholic. Avocations: running, basketball, competitive chess. Home: 30 Genevra Rd Hillsborough CA 94010 Office: Ischemia Rsch and Edn Found 1111 Bayhill Dr San Bruno CA 94066 Office Fax: 650-238-2181. Personal E-mail: dtmangano@gmail.com. Business E-Mail: dtm@ierf.org.

MANGANO, LOUIS, lawyer; b. Passaic, NJ, Sept. 19, 1939; s. Salvatore and Mary Mangano; m. Arlene M. Triolo, Sept. 20, 1964; children: Kenneth L., Eileen M., Louis M., Michael S. BS in Bus. Adminstrn., Seton Hall U., 1970; MA in Criminal Justice, John Jay Coll., 1973; JD, Seton Hall U., 1979. Bar: N.J. 1981, U.S. Dist. Ct. N.J. 1981, U.S. Supreme Ct. 1985. With Elmwood Park (N.J.) Police Dept., 1966-83; pvt. practice atty. Elmwood Park, 1981—. Adj. prof. Fairleigh Dickinson U., Rutherford, N.J., 1973-75, Jersey City (N.J.) State Coll., 1973-75; asst. prof. William Paterson Coll., Wayne, N.J., 1983-84. Trustee, pres. Elmwood Park (N.J.) Bd. Edn., 1980-83, 89-93; borough atty. for Elmwood Park, N.J., 2005-2007 With U.S. Army, 1959-61. Office: PO Box 305 395 River Dr Elmwood Park NJ 07407-1622 Office Phone: 201-796-2727.

MANGANO, MARK J., religious studies educator; b. Norwalk, Calif., Dec. 7, 1958; s. Alfio J. and Joann M. Mangano; m. Roberta H. McKinney, Aug. 6, 1983; children: Jonathan M., Joseph B., Jesse R., Joshua M. PhD, Hebrew Union Coll., Cin., 1990. Prof. Cin. Bible Coll. & Sem., 1988—90, Minn. Bible Coll., Rochester, 1990—2002, Lincoln Christian Coll. & Sem., Ill., 2002—. Author: (book) The Image of God, Esther & Daniel; editor: Old Testament Introduction. Office: Lincoln Christian Coll & Sem 100 Campus View Dr Lincoln IL 62656

MANGANO, PHILIP F., federal agency administrator; b. 1947; Dir. homeless services City of Cambridge, Mass.; with Soc. Action Ministries of Greater Boston; founding exec. dir. Mass. Housing and Shelter Alliance, 1990—2002; exec. dir. US Interagy. Coun. on Homelessness, 2002—. Breadline vol. St. Anthony's Shrine, Boston. Named a Pub. Official of Yr., Governing mag., 2006. Office: US Interagy Coun on Homelessness Fed Ctr SW 409 3rd St SW Ste 310 Washington DC 20024 Office Phone: 202-708-4663. Office Fax: 202-708-1216.

MANGANO, SALVATORE NICHOLAS, retired surgeon; b. Cambridge, Mass., 1922; s. Santo and Rose (Costa) M.; m. Anna Barney Stevenson, Apr. 28, 1956; children: Paul Stephen, John Joseph, Mary Ellen (dec.). AB, Harvard U., 1944; MD, Tufts U., 1947. Diplomate Am. Bd. Surgery. Intern Cambridge City Hosp., 1947-48, resident in surgery, 1949-51; resident Carney Hosp., Boston, 1948-49; pvt. practice gen. and colon-rectal surgery, 1953-90; cons. Mass. Dept. Correction, 1990—. Surgeon Lemuel Shattuck, Boston; asst. clin. prof. surgery Tufts U. Sch. Medicine, 1994—. Capt. USAF, 1951-53. Fellow ACS; mem. Am. Soc. Colorectal Surgery, Nat. Bd. Med. Examiners, Mass. Bd. Registration in

Medicine (sec. 1984-87), Fedn. State Med. Bds. (cert. of appreciation 1987), Middlesex Dist. Med. Soc. (exec. sec. 1970-2007). Roman Catholic. Personal E-mail: snmangano@gmail.com.

MANGER, WILLIAM, JR., federal agency administrator; BA in Polit. Sci., Trinity Coll., Hartford, Conn.; MBA, Columbia U., NYC, 1993—95. With mortgage-backed securities sale's desk Citicorp Securities; sr. policy advisor maritime adminstrn. US Dept. Transp.; regional adminstr., region II Small Bus. Adminstrn., 2005—07, assoc. adminstr. office field ops., 2007—. Mem. Bush-Cheney Presdl. Transition Team. Mem. village bd. Town of Southampton, NY, 1997; bd. mem. Riot Relief Fund, NYC. Office: US Small Bus Adminstrn 409 3rd St SW Washington DC 20416*

MANGER, WILLIAM MUIR, internist, educator, writer, research scientist; b. Greenwich, Conn., Aug. 13, 1920; s. Julius and Lilian (Weissinger) M.; m. Lynn Seymour Sheppard, May 30, 1964; children: William Muir, Jr., Lilian Wade (Mrs. Porter Fleming), Stewart Sheppard, Charles Seymour. BS, Yale U., 1944; MD, Columbia U., 1946; PhD, Mayo Found., U. Minn., 1958. Diplomate Nat. Bd. Med. Examiners, Am. Bd. Internal Medicine. Intern Presbyn. Hosp., NYC, 1946-47, resident, 1949-50, asst. physician, 1957—2001; fellow internal medicine Mayo Found., 1950-55; dir. Manger Rsch. Found., 1961-77; clin. asst. attending physician Columbia divsn. Bellevue Hosp., 1964-68; asst. attending physician NYU Bellevue Hosp., 1969-77, assoc. attending physician, 1977-83, attending physician, 1983—; instr. medicine Columbia U. Coll. Physicians and Surgeons, 1957-66, assoc. medicine, 1966-70, lectr. emeritus, 1991—. Asst. attending physician Presbyn. Hosp., 1966—68; asst. clin. prof. medicine NYU Med. Ctr., 1968—75, assoc. clin. prof. medicine, 1975—83, clin. prof. medicine, 1983—; mem. devel. com. Mayo Clinic, 1981; vice chmn. bd. Manger Hotels, Inc., 1957—73, 1990—2004; former mem. nat. high blood pressure edn. program NIH. Co-author: Chemical Quantitation of Epinephrine and Norepinephrine in Plasma, 1959, Pheochromocytoma, 1977, Clinical and Experimental Pheochromocytoma, 1996, 100 Questions and Answers About Hypertension, 2001, Our Greatest Threats, 2006; author: Catecholamines in Normal and Abnormal Cardiac Function, 1982; editor, co-author: Hormones and Hypertension, 1966; editor: Am. Lecture Series in Endocrinology, 1962-75; guest editor First Irvine H. Page Internat. Hypertension Rsch. Symposium, 1990; contbr. articles to profl. and lay jours. Mem. bd. govs. St. Albans Sch., Washington, 1958-64, 83-89, chmn., 1962-64, 67-69; trustee Found. Rsch. in Medicine and Biology, 1971-77, Buckley Sch., 1975-85, Lycee Francais, NY, 1996-98, Found. for Advancement Internat. Rsch. in Microbiology, 1977-82, Thyroid Found., 1980-85; mem. bd. visitors Boston U. Med. Sch., 1992—; trustee Found. for Depression and Manic Depression, 1978-89, pres., 1980-89; elder Presbyn. Ch., 1968-70, 92-93, trustee, 1962-67, 80-84, deacon, 1959-61; founder Values Initiative Tchg. About Lifestyle program to combat obesity, 2002. Lt. (j.g.) MC, USNR, 1947-49. Recipient Mayo Found. Alumni award for Meritorious Rsch., 1955, Disting. Alumnus award, 1992, Alumni Svc. award St. Albans Sch., 2007. Fellow ACP, Acad. Psychosomatic Medicine, Am. Geriatric Soc., Coun. on Geriatric Cardiology, NY Acad. Medicine (admission com. 1976-78, edn. com. 1979-92) Am. Coll. Cardiology, Am. Coll. Clin. Pharmacology, Royal Soc. Health, Am. Inst. Chemists; Nat. Hypertension Assn. (founder, trustee, chmn. 1977—), AMA, Am. Soc. Internal Medicine, NY State Med. Soc., NY County Med. Soc., Am. Heart Assn. (fellow coun. on circulation and coun. for high blood pressure rsch.), Inter-Am. Soc. Hypertension, Internat. Soc. Hypertension, Am. Soc. Hypertension (designated hypertension specialist), Am. Thoracic Soc., NY Acad. Sci., AAAS, Am. Physiol. Soc., Am. Chem. Soc., Am. Soc. Pharmacology and Exptl. Therapeutics, Am. Soc. for Clin. Pharmacology and Therapeutics, Clin. Autonomic Rsch. Soc., Am. Autonomic Soc., Med. Strollers, NYC, Endocrine Soc., Pan Am. Med. Assn., Harvey Soc., Soc. Exptl. Biology and Medicine, Rsch. Discussion Group (founding mem., sec.-treas. 1958-80), Am. Fedn. Clin. Rsch. Am. Soc. Nephrology, Royal Soc. Medicine (affiliate), Fellows Assn. Mayo Found. (v.p., pres. 1953), Mayo Alumni Assn. (v.p. 1981-82, exec. com. 1981-89, pres. elect 1982-85, pres. 1985-87), Chatecholamine Club (founder, sec.-treas. 1967-80, pres. 1981-82), Pheochromocytom Rsch. Support Orgn. (pres. and treas. 2005—), Drs. Mayo Soc., Plummer Soc., Albert Gallatin Assocs., The 1941 Soc., New Eng. Soc., SAR (chmn. admissions com. 1959-67, bd. mgrs. 1959-67, 69-70), Soc. Colonial Wars, Soc. of the Cin., Sigma Xi, Nu Sigma Nu, Phi Delta Theta, Explorers, Meadow (L.I., NY), Univ. Club, NY Athletic Club (NYC), Southampton Bathing Corp. Achievements include research on the mechanism of salt-induced hypertension, the mechanism whereby potassium lowers blood pressure and prevents stroke, and on pheochromocytoma. Home: 8 E 81st St New York NY 10028-0201 Home Phone: 212-772-3068; Office Phone: 212-689-0873. Fax: 212-447-7032. Personal E-mail: nathypertension@aol.com.

MANGES, JAMES HORACE, investment banker; b. NYC, Oct. 8, 1927; s. Horace S. and Natalie (Bloch) M.; m. Joan Brownell, Oct., 1969 (div.); m. Mary Seymour, 1974 (div. Oct. 2000); children: Alison, James H. Jr. Grad., Phillips Exeter Acad., 1945; BA, Yale U., 1950; MBA, Harvard U., 1953. With Kuhn, Loeb & Co., NYC, 1954-77, ptnr., 1967-77; mng. dir. Lehman Bros., Kuhn Loeb Inc., NYC, 1977-84, Shearson Lehman, Inc., NYC, 1984-90; adv. dir. Lehman Bros., NYC, 1990-96. Dir. Baker Industries, 1967—77, Proudfoot PLC (U.K.), 1996—98; dir., exec. com. Metromedia, Inc., 1970—86. Trustee The Episcopal Sch., 1978-92, St. Bernard's Sch., 1985-2000, Phillips Exeter Acad., 1985-89, mem. trustee coun., 1989-95; mem. Ctr. Strategic and Internat. Studies, Washington. Mem. Bond Club, Yale Club (N.Y.C.), Century Country Club (Purchase, N.Y.), Harvard Club (N.Y.C.). Home: 888 Park Ave New York NY 10075-0235 Office: #2016 45 Rockefeller Plz New York NY 10111-0100

MANGES, WAYNE WILLIAM, electrical engineer, researcher; b. Connellsville, Pa., Aug. 7, 1947; s. Wayne Browning and Hazel Thorpe Manges; m. JoAnn Therese Malinak, Oct. 3, 1962; children: Bryan Thomas, Lisa Michelle Hightower stepchildren: Rachel Leigh Glassell, Gregory Lee Glassell. BS in Edn., Calif. U., Pa., 1969; MEE, U. Tenn., Knoxville, 1984; MS in Natural Sci., Rensselaer Poly. Inst., Troy, NY, 1974; BEE, U. Pitts., 1977. Cert. profl. engr., Tenn., 1980. Chemistry, physics tchr. Avella HS, Avella, Pa., 1969—76; rschr., program mgr. Oak Ridge Nat. Lab., Tenn., 1977—. Bd. dirs. Wireless Indsl. Networking Alliance, Raleigh, NC, 2004—. Editor: Sensors Mag. Mem.: ISA (local pres. 2001—04, co-chair ISA standard automentation systems and automation soc.). Home: PO Box 4883 Oak Ridge TN 37831 Office: Oak Ridge Nat Lab PO Box 2008 MS6154 Oak Ridge TN 37831 Office Fax: 865-576-7523. Business E-Mail: mangesww@ornl.gov.

MANGIA, SILVIA, science educator; b. Rome, July 5, 1974; d. Anna Baldacci and Lanfranco Mangia. PhD in Biophysics, U. Rome, 2003. Cert. physics specialist U. Rome, 2005. Technologist Enrico Fermi Ctr., Rome, 2002—04; rsch. assoc. CMRR, U. Minn., Mpls., 2004—07, asst. prof., 2007—. Paintings and drawings, exhbhns., Hinckley Mus., Minn. Recipient Young Sci. Authors award, Inst. Nat. Fisica della Materia, Italy, 2001, Student Stipend award, ICBEM, 2006, ISMRM, 2006, Hot Topic Presentation award, GRC, 2006. Home: 1217 8th St SE Minneapolis MN 55414 Office: CMRR Univ Minn 2021 6th St SE Minneapolis MN 55455 Business E-Mail: mangia@cmrr.umn.edu.

MANGINI, ERIC, professional football coach; b. Hartford, Conn., Jan. 19, 1971; s. Carmine and Nancy Mangini; m. Julie Mangini; children: Jake, Luke. BA in Polit. Sci., Wesleyan Coll., 1994. Asst. coach Cleve. Browns, 1995—96, Balt. Ravens (formerly Cleve. Browns), 1996—97; defensive asst., quality control coach NY Jets, 1997—99, head coach, 2006—08; defensive backs coach New Eng. Patriots, 1999—2005, defensive coord., 2005—06; head coach Cleve. Browns, 2009—. Founder The Carmine & Frank Mangini Found., 2006—. Achievements include being a member of Super Bowl Championship winning New England Patriots, 2002, 2004, 2005. Office: Cleve Browns LLC 76 Lou Groza Blvd Berea OH 44017*

MANGINO, MARK THOMAS, college football coach; b. New Castle, Pa., Aug. 25, 1956; m. Mary Jane Mangino; children: Samantha, Tom. Grad., Youngstown State U., 1987. Coach Lincoln HS, Ellwood City, Pa.; offensive line coach, offensive coord. Geneva Coll., 1987—89; asst. coach Kans. State U., 1991—98; offensive line coach U. Okla., 1999, offensive coord., 2000—01; head coach U. Kans. Jayhawks, 2002—. Recipient Frank Broyles award, 2000, Eddie Robinson award, Football Writers Assn. Am., 2007, Walter Camp Coach of Yr. award, Walter Camp Football Found., 2007, Paul "Bear" Bryant award, Nat. Sportscasters & Sportswriters Assn., 2007, The Home Depot Coach of Yr. award, 2007; named Nat. Coach of Yr., AP, 2007, The Sporting News, 2007, Big 12 Coach of Yr., AP, 2007, Woody Hayes Nat. Coach of Yr., 2007, Am. Football Coaches Assn. Coach of Yr., 2007. Office: U Kans Football Allen Fieldhouse 1651 Naismith Dr Lawrence KS 66045

MANGLA, SUNDEEP, radiologist, research scientist; s. Kishan Chand and Sushila Mangla; m. Minh-Nhut Yvonne Dang, Oct. 4, 2003; children: Ronin Tai Satyam, Leila Mai Saraswati. BS, U. Akron, Ohio, 1988; MD, N.E. Ohio U., Rootstown, 1992. Resident in diagnostic radiology Coll. Medicine, N.E. OH U., Canton, 1992—97; fellow in diagnostic neuroradiology U. So. Calif., LA, 1997—98; fellow in interventional neuroradiology and neuroendovascular surgery Yale U., New Haven, 1998—99, U. Iowa, Iowa City, 1999—2000; asst. prof. interventional neuroradiology Columbia and Cornell Univs., NYC, 2000—03; dir. interventional neuroradiology, radiology rsch. SUNY Downstate Health Sci. Ctr., Bklyn., 2003—. Dir. radiology rsch. SUNY Downstate Health Sci. Ctr., 2006—. Contbr. articles to profl. jours. Local educator stroke awareness SUNY Health Sci. Ctr., Bklyn., 2003—06. Grantee, Columbia U., NY, 2002—03. Mem.: Neurocritical Care Soc., Am. Soc. Neuroradiology, Am. Soc. Interventional and Therapeutic Neuroradiology. Achievements include patents pending for endovascular and endoluminal robotics, nano-robotics. Avocations: tennis, basketball, travel, cooking, international and independent cinema. Office Fax: 718-270-7241. Business E-Mail: smangla@downstate.edu.

MANGLONA, JOHN A., commonwealth supreme court justice; b. Rota, Northern Marianas, June 12, 1959; m. Mona V. Monglona; 2 children. BA in Polit. Economy, U. Calif., Berkeley, 1981; JD, Creighton U. Sch. Law, Omaha, 1984; LLM in Taxation, U. Pacific McGeorge Sch. Law, 1988. Pvt. practice; assoc. judge Commonwealth Superior Ct., 1998—2000; assoc. justice Northern Mariana Islands Supreme Ct., 2000—. Designated justice Guam Supreme Ct., 1999—2003. Office: House Justice Guma Hustisia Imwaal Aweewe PO Box 502179 Saipan MP 96950-2179 Office Phone: 670-236-9820. Office Fax: 670-236-9897. Business E-Mail: supreme.court@saipan.com.*

MANGLONA, RAMONA V., judge, former attorney general; b. 1967; BA, U. Calif., 1990; JD, U. N.Mex., 1996. Bar: New Mex. Bar Assn. 1997, No. Mariana Islands Bar Assn. 1997. Asst. atty. gen., 1997—2002; atty. gen. No. Mariana Islands, Saipan, 2002—03; assoc. judge Commonwealth Superior Ct., 2003—. Home Phone: 670-235-5443; Office Phone: 670-236-9751.

MANGO, SUSAN E., biologist, educator; AB, Harvard U., 1983; PhD, Princeton U., 1990. Postdoctoral rsch. fellow Lab. of Molecular Biology U. Wis., Madison, 1990—95; asst. prof. to prof. oncological scis. U. Utah, Salt Lake City, 1996—2009, prof. molecular and cellular biology, 2009—. Contbr. articles to profl. jours. Named a MacArthur Fellow, The John D. and Catherine T. MacArthur Found., 2008. Office: U Utah Huntsman Cancer Inst Bldg 200 Circle of Hope, Rm LL376 Salt Lake City UT 84112 Office Phone: 801-581-7633. E-mail: susan.mango@hci.utah.edu.

MANGOGNA, RICHARD FREDERICK, federal agency administrator; b. Jamaica, NY, Jan. 29, 1940; s. Vincent and Violet (Sanders) Mangogna; m. Frances Ann Conroy, July 10, 1965; children: Donna, Ricky, Dawn, Kathleen, Suzanne. Sys. engr. IBM, Madison, Wis., 1961—64; supr. data processing Am. Airlines, Briarcliff Manor, NY, 1964—66; mgr. data processing NY Shipping Assn., NYC, 1966—67; v.p. AMF, Westbury, NY, 1967—69, Optimal Computer Svcs., NYC, 1969—71; sr. v.p. Chem. Bank, NYC, 1971, pres., COO electronic banking divsn.; pres., CEO COVIDEA; exec. v.p., CIO JP Morgan Chase; exec. cons. to under sect. Citizenship and Immigrations Svcs. US Dept. Homeland Security, exec. cons. office of CIO Immigration Customs Enforcement, CIO, 2008—. Mem. internat. policy com. US Coun. Internat. Bus., NYC, 1983; chair CIO coun. US Dept. Homeland Security, 2008—, chair enterprise architecture bd., 2008—. Mem.: Am. Bankers Assn. (exec. consumer fin. com. 1984), Data Processing Mgrs. Assn. Home: 3 Yellowbrick Rd Northport NY 11768-2644 Office: US Dept Homeland Security Seventh and D Streets SW Washington DC 20528*

MANGOLD, JOHN FREDERIC, manufacturing executive, retired military officer; b. La Grange, Ill., Jan. 24, 1927; s. John Frederic and Helvig Victoria (Anderson) M.; m. Margaret Ellen Gore, Oct. 25, 1947; children: John, Andrew, Jennifer. BS, U.S. Naval Acad., 1947; MSEE, U.S. Naval Postgrad. Sch., Monterey, Calif., 1958. Registered profl. engr., Conn. Commd. ensign USN, 1947, advanced through grades to comdr., 1962, comdg. officer nuclear submarine U.S.S. Halibut, 1962—63, comdg. officer nuclear tng. unit, 1963—67, ret., 1967; v.p. mfg. Combustion Engring., Inc., Windsor, Conn., 1972—78, group pres., 1982—86, v.p. utility boilers, 1990—91; pres. Vetco, Inc., Ventura, Calif., 1978—82; cons., 1992; pres. Detrex Corp., Southfield, Mich., 1992—93, ret., 1993. Bd. dirs. Detrex Corp. Mem. IEEE, U.S. C. of C. (energy com. 1984-87). Republican.

MANGONE, GERARD J., international maritime law educator; b. NYC, Oct. 10, 1918; s. Gerard Francis and Viola (Schumm) M.; m. Emma Haddad, Apr. 13, 1958; children— Cleopatra, Regina, Flaminia. AB, CCNY, 1938; MA, Harvard U., Cambridge, Mass., 1947, PhD (Charles Summer prize), 1949. Asst. prof. polit. sci. Wesleyan U., Middletown, Conn., 1948-51; assoc. prof. Swarthmore Coll., 1951-56; prof. polit. sci. and internat. relations Syracuse U., 1956-67; dir. grad. overseas tng. program, exec. officer Maxwell Center Study Overseas Operations, 1958-60; exec. asst. to dean Maxwell Grad. Sch., 1961-64, asso. dean dir. internat. relations program, 1961-67; dean Coll. Liberal Arts, v.p., provost Temple U., Phila., 1967-69; sr. fellow Woodrow Wilson Internat. Ctr., 1970-72; prof. internat. law U. Del., Newark, 1972-74, dir. Ctr. for Study of Marine Policy, 1973-89, H. Rodney Sharp prof. internat. law and orgn., 1975-89, univ. rsch. prof. internat. and maritime law, 1989—, prof. legal studies, 2001—, coord. grad. studies, 1976-79; adj. prof. Maine Maritime Acad., 1992—94. Vis. prof. Trinity Coll., Mt. Holyoke Coll., Yale, Princeton, Johns Hopkins; Tagore law prof. U. Calcutta, 1979; disting. lectr. U. Ind., 1980; vis. scholar U. Western Australia, 1983, 87, Peking U., 1984, Capetown U., 1986, 89, U. Natal, 1989, Hanyang U., 1994, Hong Kong U., 1997; mem. Presdl. Commn. Trust Territory Pacific, 1963; cons. AID, 1965-67, Nat. Commn. Marine Resources and Engring. and State Dept., 1967-73, UN, 1965, US Corps Engrs., 1975; vice chmn. exec. com. Commn. Study Orgn. Peace; exec. dir. Pres.' Commn. on UN, 1970-71; dir. diploma program, shipping and pt. mgmt. Pt. of Singapore, 1990-97; founder Gerard J. Mangone Marine Policy Ctr., 2003. Author: The Idea and Practice of World Government, 1951, A Short History of International Organization, 1954, The Elements of International Law, 2d edit, 1967, Marine Policy for America, 1977, 2d edit., 1989, Law for the World Ocean, 1981, Mangone's Concise Marine Almanac, 2d edit., 1991, United States Admiralty Law, 1997; co-author, editor: The Art of Overseasmanship, 1958, The Overseas Americans, 1960, European Political Systems, 1960, UN Administration of Economic and Social Programs, 1966, Energy Policies of the World, 3 vols, 1976-79, Internat. Straits of the World, 14 vols., 1978-2004; editor: Future of Gas and Oil from Sea, American Strategic Minerals, 1984; editor in chief: Marine Policy Reports, 1981-91, Internat. Jour. Marine and Coastal Law, 1991—. Capt. AUS, 1942-46, maj. res., 1946-54. Mem. Am. Soc. Internat. Law, Internat. Law Assn., Maritime Law Assn., Port of Wilmington Maritime Soc. (bd. dirs. 1980-, chmn. 1989, Francis Alison award 1983), Alison Soc. (founder, sec. 1990-), Del. Acad. Sci. (pres. 1993), Cosmos Club (Washington), Harvard Club (NYC). Home: 201 Unami Trl Newark DE 19711-7508 Office: Univ Del Coll of Marine and Earth Studies Newark DE 19716 Office Phone: 302-831-8087. Business E-Mail: gmangone@udel.edu.

MANGOPE, LUCAS MANYANE, tribal chief, politician; b. Motswedi, Zeerust, Dec. 27, 1923; s. Manyane and Semakaleng Mangope; m. Leah Tsholofelo, 1950; 4 sons, 3 daus. Student, St. Peter's Coll., Bethel Coll. Worked in Dept. Bantu Adminstrn. and Devel., taught at Motswedi; succeeded his father as chief of Bahurutshe-Boo-Manyane, Sept. 1959; vice-chmn. Tswana Territorial Authority, 1961-68, chief councillor, 1968-72; chief minister of Bophuthatswana, South Africa, 1972-77, pres. of Republic of Bophuthatswana, 1977-94; leader of the ofcl. opposition. Office: PO Box 3010 Mmabatho Northwest 2735 South Africa

MANGOUNI, NORMAN, publishing executive; b. Detroit, Oct. 19, 1932; s. Nazareth Lazarus and Isabelle (Garabedian) M.; m. Anahid Apelian, May 10, 1964; 1 child, Marie-Isabelle. AB, U. Mich., 1954; MS, Columbia U., 1955; postgrad., U. Mich., 1957-58. Reporter Ann Arbor (Mich.) News, 1957-59; editor Mich. Alumnus, U. Mich., Ann Arbor, 1959-62; sr. editor Coll. Entrance Exam. Bd., NYC, 1962-64; dir. fin. aid U. Miami, Coral Gables, Fla., 1965-66; dir. State U. N.Y. Press, Albany, 1966-78; pres., gen. editor Scholars' Facsimiles & Reprints, Ann Arbor, Mich., 1972—; pres. Caravan Books, Ann Arbor, Mich., 1972—, Acad. Resources Corp., Las Vegas, Nev., 1988—; corr. DuPont-Columbia Survey and Awards, 1976-78; rep. to com. on standards in field of library work, documentation and related pub. practices Am. Nat. Standards Inst., 1974-78. Exec. asst. to majority caucus Mich. State Senate, 1964; dir. summer session Am. Coll. Switzerland, 1979, 81, 82. Co-translator: The Gaucho Martin Fierro, 1974; contbr. articles to profl. jours.; mem. editorial bd. Ararat mag, 1962-66, 77-78. Served to lt. USAF, 1955-57. Mem. Mensa, Phi Sigma Kappa, Sigma Delta Chi, Phi Alpha Delta, Kiwanian. Home: PO Box 5934 Carefree AZ 85377 Office Phone: 480-575-9945. E-mail: maxinmin@umich.edu.

MANGRAVITE, RONALD, filmmaker, writer; MFA, UCLA; BA with high honors, U. Calif., Berkeley; prep., Lawrenceville Sch., NJ. Instr. Juilliard Sch., NYC, 1974—76; assoc. artistic dir. Attic Theater, Detroit, 1985—90; instr. Am. Film Inst., LA, 1991—2000, U. Miami, Coral Gables, 2001—09; theatre, film critic Miami New Times, New Times Broward/Palm Beach, Miami, 2001—05. Author: (plays) Back in the Saddle premiered NY, 1981, Behind the Chutes premiered NY, 1981, The Lewis & Clark Expedition, premiered Ashland, OR, 1983, The Rewrite premiered San Francisco, 1983, Jean Baptiste Pointe du Sable: Black Man in the Wilderness premiered Detroit, 1988, Madame Cadillac premiered Detroit, 1989, The Great Divide, 2005; co-author: The Screenwriter's Manual, 2005, The Complete Screenwriter's Manual, 2006; dir., writer: (short film) The Queen of the Sea, 2002; My Father's Hopes, 2004; writer, prodr. (feature film) All For Liberty, 2008. Recipient First prize, Fla. Press Assn., 2003, Silver Palmetto, Piccolo Spoleto Festival, 2004 for My Father's Hopes, Best Film, Miami Film Festival Collaboration Film Contest, 2002 for The Queen of the Sea, Best Screenplay, 2002 for The Queen of the Sea, Best of the Fest citation, Silver Images Film Festival, 2002 for My Father's Hopes, Accolade award of Excellence Feature Film, All For Liberty, 2008, Spl. Jury award, WorldFest Houston, All For Liberty, 2009, Audience award, Best Feature Film, Charleston Internat. Film Festival, All For Liberty, 2009. Personal E-mail: coralgatemedia@gmail.com.

MANGUM, GARTH LEROY, retired economist; b. Delta, Utah, July 23, 1926; s. James L. and Golda (Elder) M.; m. Marion Poll, Nov. 20, 1953; children: Stephen, David, Mary, Elizabeth. BS, Brigham Young U., 1956; MPA, Harvard U., 1958, PhD, 1960; JD, U. Utah, 1989. Instr. econs. Harvard U., 1960; asso. prof. econs. Brigham Young U., 1960-63; sr. staff analyst Presdl. R.R. Commn., 1961; research dir., subcom. employment and manpower U.S. Senate, 1963-64; exec. dir. President's Com. Manpower, 1964-65; exec. sec. Nat. Com. Tech., Automation and Econ. Progress, 1965-66; research prof. econs. George Washington U., 1967-71; co-dir. George Washington U. (Center Manpower Policy Studies), 1967-69; Max McGraw prof. econs. and mgmt. U. Utah, Salt Lake City, 1969-97, prof. emeritus, 1997—, dir. Inst. Human Resource Mgmt., 1969-90. Adj. prof. edn. leadership Brigham Young U., 2003—; lectr. U. Tel Aviv, Israel, 1969, 84, Am. Seminar at Salzburg, 1975, U. South Africa, 1977, Monash U., Australia, 1984; spl. mediator Fed. Mediation and Conciliation Svc., 1962-63; mem. Adv. Coun. Vocat. Edn., 1966-67; vice chmn. Nat. Manpower Policy Task Force, 1966-69, chmn., 1969-71; mem. Nat. Coun. on Employment Policy, 1976—, chmn., 1979-81, sec.- treas., 1990-2002; chmn. Nat. Inst. Career Edn., 1976-81; cons. internat. agencies, fed., state and local govts., bus. firms, govts. of, Saudi Arabia, Kuwait, Jordan, Oman, Yemen, Bahrain, United Arab Emirates, Indonesia, Yugoslavia, Romania, Uganda, Nigeria, Israel, South Africa, Russia, Brazil, Argentina, Chile, Uruguay, Mexico, Philipinnes, Taiwan, Republic of Korea, China, others; cons. AID, ILO, World Bank; also arbitrator; v.p. Retired Faculty Assn., U. SC, 2006-. Author: The Operating Engineers: Economic History of a Trade Union, 1964, MDTA, Foundation of Federal Manpower Policy, 1968, The Emergence of Manpower Policy, 1969, Federal Work and Training

Program in the 1960's, 1969, Economic Opportunity in the Ghetto, 1970, Human Resources and Labor Markets, 1971, Career Education: What It Is and How To Do It, 1972, A Decade of Manpower Development and Training, 1973, Career Education and the Elementary School Teacher, 1973, Career Education in the Middle/Junior High School, 1973, Manpower Planning for Local Labor Markets, 1974, Career Education for the Academic Classroom, 1975, Employability, Employment and Income, 1976, Career Education in the High School, 1976, Your Child's Career, 1977, The Lingering Crisis of Youth Unemployment, 1978, Coming of Age in the Ghetto, 1978, Job Market Futurity, 1979, The Coal Industry and its Industrial Relations, 1985, Capital and Labor in American Copper, 1992, Labor Struggle in The Post Office, 1992, The Mormons War on Poverty, 1993, Union Resilience in Troubled Times, 1994, Portable Pension Plans for Casual Labor Markets, 1995, Transnational Industrial Marriages, 1996, The Rise, Fall and Replacement of Industry-Wide Bargaining in the Basic Steel Industry, 1996, Programs in Aid of the Poor, 8th edit., 2003, On Being Poor in Utah, 1997, The Public Employment Svc. In a One Stop World, 1998, Poverty Ain't What It Used To Be, 1999, Confronting The Youth Demographic Challenge, 2000, The Persistance of Poverty in the United States, 2003, Struggling at the Golden Door: International Refugees in Utah, 2007; also articles, monographs.; editor: The Manpower Revolution: Its Policy Consequences, 1965, Automation and Economic Progress, 1966, Metropolitan Impact of Manpower Programs, 1973, The T in CETA, 1981, Of Heart and Mind: Social Policy Essays in Honor of Sar A. Levitan, 1996, Utah's Poor: Solutions for Today's Economy, 2005. With USAAF, 1944-45. Mem. Ch. of Jesus Christ of Latter-day Saints (missionary 1950-53, bishop 1971-78, other positions). Home: 2130 Ridgewood Way Bountiful UT 84010-1632 Home Phone: 801-296-9380. Personal E-mail: garthmangum@msn.com.

MANGUN, GEORGE R., psychology professor, director; PhD, U. Calif., San Diego. Prof. dept. psychology and neurology U. Calif., Davis, 2002—; founding dir. Ctr. Mind & Brain, Davis, 2002—. Office: Ctr Mind and Brain Univ Calif Davis 267 Cousteau Pl Davis CA 95618

MANHART, MARCIA Y(OCKEY), retired art museum director; b. Wichita, Kans., Jan. 14, 1943; d. Everett W. and Ruth C. (Correll) Yockey; children: Caroline Manhart Sanderson, Emily Manhart Morrison. BA in Art, U. Tulsa, 1965, MA in Ceramics, 1971. Dir. edn. Philbrook Art Ctr., Tulsa, 1972-77, exec. v.p., asst. dir., 1977-83, acting dir., 1983-84; exec. dir. Philbrook Mus. Art (formerly Philbrook Art Ctr.), Tulsa, 1984—2003; exec. dir., trustee The Judith and Jean Pape Charitable Foun., 2004—. Instr. Philbrook Art Ctr. Mus. Sch., Tulsa, 1963-72; gallery dir. Alexandre Hogue Gallery, Tulsa U., 1967-69; NEH Challenge Grant panelist, 1991, presenter to AAM Conv., 1991; MAAA Craft Fellowship panelist, 1988, 93, NEA Craft Fellowship panelist, 1990; NEA spl. exhbn. panelist, 1996; curator nat. touring exhibit Nature's Forms/Nature's Forces: The Art of Alexandre Hogue, 1984-85; co-curator internat. exhbn.: The Eloquent Object, 1987-90; curator Sanford and Diane Besser Collection exhbn., 1992. Author essays in field. Vis. com. Smithsonian Instn./Renwick Gallery, Washington, 1986; cultural negotiator Gov. George Nigh's World Trade Mission (Okla.), China., 1985; com. mem. State Art Coll. of Okla., 1985-99; mem. Assocs. of Hillcrest Med. Ctr., 1983-88, exec. com., 1985-88; com. mem. Neighborhood Housing Services, 1985-87; mem. City of Tulsa Arts Commn., 1996-2003; steering com. Harwelden Inst. for Aesthetic Edn., 1983; com. mem. River Parks Authority, 1976; mem. Jr. League of Tulsa Inc., 1974-78; adv. panel mem. Nat. Craft Planning Project, NEA, Washington, 1978-81; craft adv. panel mem. Okla. Arts and Humanities Council, 1974-76; juror numerous art festivals, competitions, programs; reviewer Inst. Mus. Services, Washington, 1985, 88, 92, 95, 98; auditor Symposium on Language & Scholarship of Modern Crafts, NEA and NEH, Washington, 1981; nominator MacArthur Fellows Program, 1988; panelist Lila Wallace Reader's Digest Internat. Artists Fellowship, 1992, panelist Pew Charitable Trust, 1996. Recipient Harwelden award for Individual Contbrn. in the Arts, 1989, Gov.'s award State of Okla., 1992. Mem. Gillespie County Hist. Soc. (bd. dirs. 2005-08), Phi Beta Kappa. Home: 105 S Cherry St Fredericksburg TX 78624 Office Phone: 830-997-7347. E-mail: mmanhart@austin.rr.com.

MANHEIM, CAMRYN, television and film actress; b. Caldwell, NJ, Mar. 8, 1961; d. Jerry and Sylvia Manheim; 1 child, Milo Jacob. BFA, UC Santa Cruz, 1984; MFA, NYU, 1987. Actor: (TV series) The Practice, 1997—2004 (Emmy award for Outstanding Supporting Actress in a Drama Series, 1998, Golden Globe award for Best Performance by an Actress in a Supporting Role, 1999); (TV films) Jackie's Back!, 1999, The Loretta Claiborne Story, 2000, Jenifer, 2001; (TV miniseries) The 10th Kingdom, 2000, A Girl Thing, 2001, Elvis, 2005; actor, prodr. (TV films) Kiss My Act, 2000; actor: (films) Bonfire of the Vanities, 1990, The Road to Wellville, 1994, Jeffrey, 1995, Eraser, 1996, Romy and Michele's High School Reunion, 1997, David Searching, 1998, Wide Awake, 1998, Mercury Rising, 1998, Happiness, 1998 (Nat. Bd. Rev. award, 1998), Fool's Gold, 1998, Joe the King, 1999, What Planet are You From?, 2000, East of A, 2000, The Laramie Project, 2002, Just Like Mona, 2003, Scary Movie 3, 2003, Twisted, 2004, Marilyn Hotchkiss' Ballroom Dancing and Charm School, 2005, Dark Water, 2005, An Unfinished Life, 2005; guest appearances Law and Order, Touched By an Angel, New York Undercover, Ally McBeal, Oh Baby, Chicago Hope, Will and Grace; writer: (off-Broadway play) Wake Up, I'm Fat, 1995; theater appearances include N.Y. Shakespeare Festival, Lincoln Ctr., Yale Repertory, N.Y. Theatre Workshop, Classic Stage Co., Home for Contemporary Theater. Office: Creative Artists Agency 2000 Avenue Of The Stars Los Angeles CA 90067-4700

MANHEIM, FRANK TIBOR, oceanographer; b. Leipzig, Germany, Oct. 14, 1930; came to U.S., 1937; s. Ernest and Anna Sophie (Vitters) M.; m. Ose Landergren, Sept. 12, 1960; children: Ose Jr., Leif, Francesca; m. Lucy McCartan, Nov. 21, 1998. AB, Harvard U., 1952; MSc, U. Minn., 1953; Dil.lic., U. Stockholm, 1962, DSc, 1974. Geologist Std. Vacuum Oil Co., Indonesia, India, 1956-58; analytical chemist Geol. Survey of Sweden, Stockholm, 1961-63; rsch. assoc. Dept. Geology, Yale U., New Haven, 1963-64; geologist U.S. Geol. Survey, Woods Hole, Mass., 1964-74; chmn. Dept. Marine Sci., U. South Fla., St. Petersburg, 1974-76; rsch. geochemist US Geol. Survey, 1977—2002. Mem. U.S.-Japan Natural Resources Commn., 1988—1993; adj. prof. Marine Sci. Rsch. Ctr., SUNY, Stony Brook, 1988-89, prof. sch. pub. policy George Mason U., Fairfax, Va., guest rschr. Marine Inst. Warnemunde U. Kiel Germany, guest rschr. Acad. Scis, USSR, 1982 Co-editor: The Dynamic Environment of the Ocean Floor, 1982, Chemical Composition of Ferromanganese Crusts in the World Ocean, 1989; compiler: (with others) Handbook of Geochemistry, 1978, Chemical Oceanography, 1976, Wastes in the Ocean, 1983, The Conflict Over Government Regulation, NY Springer, 2009 (CD Rom) Lake Pontchartrain Basin, 2002 Mem. planning coun. City of St. Petersburg, 1975-76; With U.S. Army, 1953-55. Exch. fellow Bulgaria U.S. Nat. Acad. Sci., 1972, Petterson Excellence medal Royal Swedish Acad. Sci., 1999; recipient rsch. grants. Mem. Am. Geophys. Union, Geochem. Soc. Achievements include rsch. on sediment and rock fluid extraction equipment and technique geochemistry, coastal contaminated sediments. Home: 13126 Pebble Ln Fairfax VA 22033-3419 Office Phone: 703-631-0166. Business E-Mail: fmanbei1@gmu.edu.

MANHEIM, MICHAEL, English literature educator; b. NYC, Mar. 4, 1928; s. Leonard F. and Eleanor (Blackman) M.; m. Martha Bradshaw, Mar. 6, 1955; children: James, Daniel. BA, Columbia U., 1949, MA, 1951, PhD, 1961. Instr. English U. Del., Newark, 1953-61; asst. prof. English U. Toledo, Ohio, 1961-63, assoc. prof., 1963-67, prof. English, 1967-91, prof. emeritus, 1991—, assoc. dean div. humanities, 1962-66, chmn. dept. English, 1966-72, 79-82, dir. Master's of Liberal Studies program, 1984-87. Vis. prof. Dartmouth, summer 1972; discussion leader Inst. Lifelong Learning, Dartmouth, 1994- Author: The Weak King Dilemma in the Shakespearean History Play, 1973, Eugene O'Neill's New Language of Kinship, 1982, Vital Contradictions: Characterization in Ibsen, Strindberg, Chekhov, and O'Neill, 2002; editor: The Cambridge Companion to Eugene O'Neill, 1998; contbr. articles and reviews in field. Mem. MLA, Shakespeare Assn., Eugene O'Neill Soc. (pres. 1990-92). Home: PO Box 63 Strafford VT 05072-0063

MANHEIMER, ERIC, medical researcher; Lab rsch. asst. dept. physiology U. Md. Sch. Medicine, 1993—95, database mgr & rsch. asst. dept. epidemiology, 1995—97, fellow Baltimore Cochrane Ctr., 1997—98, rsch. assoc. Ctr. for Integrative Medicine, 2003—; intern CDC Pub. Health Program Office, 1995; program analyst & intern NIH Office of Dietary Supplements, 1996—97; coord. & methodologist Brown U. New England Cochrane Ctr., 1998—2002; adminstr. Cochrane Collaboration Complementary Medicine Field, 2003—. Office: Kernan Hospital 2200 Kernan Dr Baltimore MD 21207-6997 Office Phone: 410-448-6871. Office Fax: 410-448-6875. E-mail: emanheimer@compmed.umm.edu.*

MANHOLD, JOHN HENRY, dental educator, consultant; b. Rochester, NY, Aug. 20, 1919; s. John Henry and Helen Martha (Shulz) Manhold; m. Beverly Schecter, 1953 (div. 1969); 1 child; m. Enriqueta Andino, Mar. 20, 1971. BA, U. Rochester, 1940; MD, Harvard U., 1944; MA, Washington U., 1956. Instr. Coll. Medicine Tufts U., Boston, 1948—50; asst. prof., chmn. gen. and oral pathology Coll. Dentistry U. Washington, St. Louis, 1954—56; from asst. prof. to prof., chmn. dept. gen. and oral pathology Seton Hall Coll. Medicine and Dentistry (now U. Medicine and Dentistry NJ), Newark, 1956—87; med. dir. Woog Internat., 1987—89; ret., 1989. Cons. Johnson & Johnson, New Brunswick, NJ, 1960—70, Richardson-Vicks, Shelton, Conn., 1981—87, Los Produits Associes, Geneva, 1965—87, Health Care Devel. Group NJ, 1990—2005, Health Care Devel. Group Pa., 1990—2005, Consumer Comm. Network NY, 1990—2005, Consumer Comm. Network Conn., 1990—2008; lectr. in field. Author: Introductory Psychosomatic Dentistry, 1956, Outline of Pathology, 1960; editor: Clinical Oral Diagnosis, 1965; author: Tissue Respiration and Oxigenating Agents, 1977, Practical Dental Management: Patients and Practice, 1984; author: (in 4 langs.) Illustrated Dental Terminology: A Lexicon for the Dental Profession, 1985; author: (with others) Handbook of Pathology, 1987; author: (novels) El Tigre, 2007, The Elymais Coin, 2008, Lobo, 2009; editor: Clinical Preventive Dentistry Jour., 1979—92; contbr. articles to profl. jours. Recipient Pres. award, Alumni Assn. U. Medicine and Dentistry NJ, 1980, Letter Appreciation, Asara Mihara former min. Japan, 1980, Cert. Achievement, U. Md., 1965, Hist. category book award, Nat. Indie Excellence, 2008, Western Category Book award, 2008, Best Book award, 2008, Suspense Category Book award, 2009, Lifetime Achievement award, 2009; named Disting. Alumni, Harvard U., 1989; named to Sr. Soc. Harvard Sch. Dental Medicine, 1984. Fellow: Acad. Psychosomatic Medicine (sec. 1975—76, treas. 1976—77, pres. 1977—78), Internat. Coll. Dentists, Am. Coll. Dentists; mem.: APA, AZ Book Pub. Assoc., Western Writers of Am., Soc. SW Authors, Internat. Assn. Dental Rsch., Am. Soc. Clin. Pathologists, St. Petersburg Yacht Club, Sigma Xi. Home and Office: 1590 N Dimaggio Path Hernando FL 34442 E-mail: kupferce@tampabay.rr.com.

MANI, INDERJEET, computer scientist, educator; married. PhD with distinction, Georgetown U., 1997; BSc, Delhi U., 1976; BSc hons., U. Sussex, 1979; MS, U. Pa., 1980. Mem. tech. staff Tex. Instruments, Dallas, 1984—88, MCC, Austin, Tex., 1988—92; sr. prin. scientist MITRE, McLean, Va., 1992—2003; assoc. prof. Georgetown U., Washington, 2003—. Author: Automatic Summarization, 2001, (magazine) WIND (Short Fiction award, 2003); contbr. articles to profl. jours., chapters to books; editor: Advances in Automatic Summarization, 1999; mem. editl. bd. Computational Linguistics, 2002—04. Achievements include patents for grammar tutoring computer system; research in natural language processing. Office: Linguistics Georgetown U 37th and O Sts Washington DC 20057

MANI, RAMESH G., physicist; s. Jagadisan GanapathiSubramaniam and Saroja Mani. PhD, U. Md., Coll. Pk., 1986. Rsch. assoc. U. Md., 1986—90; scientist Max-Planck-Inst. fuer Festkorperforschung, Stuttgart, Germany, 1990—97; rsch. engr. U. Calif., Santa Barbara, 1997—98; sr. rsch. assoc. Harvard U., Cambridge, Mass., 1998—2006; assoc. prof. physics Ga. State U., Atlanta, 2006—08. Contbr. articles to profl. jour. Achievements include invention of anti hall bar geometry to realize multiple hall effects in a single device; discovery of zero-resistance states induced by photo-excitation in semiconductors; multiple simultaneous quantum hall effects in a single device; patents for multiply connected Hall effect device for reducing resistive voltage offsets. Office: Ga State Univ 29 Peachtree Center Ave #400 Atlanta GA 30303 Business E-Mail: rmani@gsu.edu.

MANIKAS, KYLE G., prosecutor; b. Amsterdam, NY, Apr. 5, 1976; JD, Wash. Coll. Law, 2001. Pvt. practice, Washinton, DC, 2001—05; prosecutor Office Commonwealth's Atty., Fairfax, Va., 2005—08; atty. Manikas Law Offices,PLLC, McLean, Va., 2009—, mem., 2009—. Author: The Essential Guide to Understanding and Surviving the Criminal Process in Virginia. Mem.: ABA. Office: Manikas Law Offices PLLC 1660 Internat Dr Ste 400 Mc Lean VA 22102

MANION, BONNIE J., volunteer, poet, composer; b. South Bend, Ind., Apr. 13, 1942; d. Serge A. and Inez (Reed) Rivard; m. Paul T. Manion, Aug. 12, 1961; children: Christine, Sheila, Stephanie, Michael, Daniel, John Brian. BS in Elem. Edn., DePaul U., 1965; grad. lay ministry leadership program, Cath. Diocese, Peoria, Ill., 1988. Cert. elem. tchr. Ill. Author: Soul Search, 2002; contbr. of poetry to jours., 165 poems in 40 jours. Host family Rotary Internat., Hoopeston, Ill., 1985, 1995, 1996, 2002; vol. Hosp. Auxillary, Little League, United Way, Lions Club, local libr.; Hoopeston Music Boosters; vol. Dem. Party, Danville, Ill., 1972—2004; tchr. CCD programs St. Anthony's, Hoopeston, 1969—89, lay pastoral care min., 1985—; presenter diocesan programs Cath. Diocese, Peoria, Ill., 1980—2005. Recipient Pere Marquette Medal, Cath. Diocese, Peoria, 2001. Mem.: Ill. State Poetry Soc., St. Davids' Christian Writers' Assn., Mary Hartwell Catherwood Book Club. Avocations: painting, hiking.

MANION, DANIEL ANTHONY, federal judge; b. South Bend, Ind., Feb. 1, 1942; s. Clarence E. and Virginia (O'Brien) Manion; m. Ann Murphy Manion, June 29, 1984. AB, U. Notre Dame, 1964; JD, Ind. U., 1973. Bar: Ind., US Dist. Ct. (no. dist.) Ind., US Dist. Ct. (so. dist.) Ind. Dir., indsl. devel. Ind. Dept. Commerce, 1968—73; dep. atty. gen. State of Ind., 1973—74; from assoc. to ptnr. Doran, Manion, Boynton, Kamm & Esmont, South Bend, 1974—86; judge US Ct. Appeals (7th Cir.), South Bend, 1986—2007, sr. judge, 2007—. Mem. Ind. State Senate, Indpls., 1978—82; dir. St. Joseph Bank & Trust Co., 1979—86. With US Army, 1965—66. Office: US Ct Appeals US Courthouse & Federal Bldg 204 S Main St Rm 301 South Bend IN 46601-2122*

MANION, KAY DAUREEN, financial and office manager; b. St. Francis, Kans., Feb. 7, 1943; d. Edward William and Martha Dankenbring; children: Todd, Jon, Bandel. AS in Mktg. and Art, Western Nebr. C.C., 1990; postgrad., Colby CC, Kans., 1992-95, Fort Hayes State U., 1997—. Various banking positions, Kans. and Nebr., 1960-73; mgr. Alliance (Nebr.) Area C. of C., 1974-79; bridal cons., dept. mgr. Hatch Drug, Alliance, 1980-85; bridal cons. Herbergers, Scotts Bluff, 1986-88; salesperson, script writer Sta. KIMB, Kimball, 1989-90; med. records analyst Dunn Med. Equipment and Svcs., Inc., Colby, 1990-93; graphic designer Quad County Star, Oakley, Kans., 1993-95; news asst., advt. sales rep. Sherman County Star, Goodland, Kans., 1995-97; fin. and office mgr. Steinke Farm Svcs., Holdredge, Nebr., 2000—. Freelance creative designer, 1988—; dir. tng. H.S. Distributive Edn. Clubs Am., Alliance, 1980-85, CETA, Alliance, 1976-79; advt. mgr. Russell Daily News, Russell Record, 1997-99. Bd. dirs., sec. Alliance Cmty. Improvement Com., Alliance, 1974-79; mem. Oakley Tourism Com., 1994-96. Named Businesswoman of Yr. Alliance Area C. of C., 1978, One of the Oustanding Young Women in Am., 1976, 78; recipient Disting. Svc. award Jaycees, Alliance, 1979. Mem. Am. Legion Aux., Eagles Ladies' Aux., Phi Theta Kappa. Republican. Methodist. Avocations: art, drawing, photography, nature, music. Home: P O Box 193 Logan KS 67646-0193

MANION, MARK D., rail transportation executive; With Norfolk Southern Corp., Va., 1975—, v.p. transportation services and mechanical Va., sr. v.p. transportation ops. Va., 2003—04, exec. v.p. ops. Va., 2004—09, exec. v.p., COO Va., 2009—. Office: Norfolk Southern Corp Three Commercial Pl Norfolk VA 23510-2191 Office Phone: 757-629-2680. Office Fax: 757-629-2361.*

MANION, TOM, pharmaceutical executive; m. Janet Manion; children: Ryan, Travis (dec.). BA in Polit. Sci., Widener U., Chester, Pa.; M, Naval Postgraduate Sch. Fortune 500 cons.; bus. exec. including v.p. info. tech. Johnson & Johnson, 1990—. Served with USMC, ret. col. USMC Reserves, 2007. Republican. Mailing: PO Box 28 Doylestown PA 18901 Office Phone: 215-348-9080.

MANISCALCO-THEBERGE, MARY ELIZABETH, surgeon, medical educator; b. Portsmouth, Va., Sept. 1, 1956; d. Joseph Jack and Elizabeth Mary Maniscalco; m. Daniel Martin Theberge, June 23, 1984; children: Matthew John Theberge, Danielle Elizabeth Theberge. BS, Old Dominion U., 1978; MD, Ea. Va. Med. Sch., 1981. Diplomate Am. Bd. Surgery, Am. Bd. Critical Care. Intern gen. surgery Eisenhower Army Med. Ctr., 1981—82, resident gen. surgery, 1982—86; commd. 2d lt. US Army, 1981, advanced through grades to col., 1999; attending surgeon Frankfurt Army Regional Med. Ctr., 1986—89; trauma critical care fellow Washington Hosp. Ctr., 1989—90; surg. critical care fellow Walter Reed Army Med. Ctr., 1990—91, attending surg. intensivist, 1991—2003, attending surgeon, 1990—2006, spl. intensivist, 1991—2006, dir. surg. intensive care unit, 1993—95, chief gen. surgery svcs., 1994—2001, chair dept. surgery, 2001—06; sr. surg. investigator Office of Med. Insp., VA Health Adminstrn. Dept., Washington, 2007—08; dep. med. insp., profl. svcs., vet. health adminstr., 2008—. Cons. to surgeon gen. US Army, 1994—2002. Mem. forward in hope com. St. Thomas a Becket Cath. Ch., Reston, Va., 2003. Recipient William Clements award for excellence in edn., Uniformed Svcs. U., Bethesda, Md., 1994, Disting. Alumni award, Old Dominion U., 2003, Legion of Merit, 2006, commendation, Veterans Health Adminstrn., Gen. Claire L. Chennault award, 2006. Fellow: ACS (pres. Med. Washington chpt. 2003—04, mem. com.); mem.: AMA, Assn. Women Surgeons, Soc. Critical Care Medicine (chmn. coun. local chpt.), Am. Soc. Breast Surgeons. Office: Office of Med Insp VA Health Adminstrn VA Affairs 810 Vermont Ave NW Washington DC 20420 Business E-Mail: mary.maniscalco@va.gov.

MANISTA, RAYMOND J., lawyer, insurance company executive; b. Gary, Ind., June 23, 1965; m. Dawne Manista; 3 children. BA cum laude, Marquette Univ., 1987, JD magna cum laude, 1990. Bar: Wis. 1990, US Dist. Ct. Ea. & We. Wis. 1990, US Ct. Appeals Seventh Cir. 1992, US Supreme Ct. 1993. Atty. Godfrey & Kahn, 1990—98; asst. gen. counsel Northwestern Mutual, Milw., 1998—2001, dir. planning & projects, 2001—03, legal & mgmt. positions, 2003—06, v.p. corp. planning, 2006—08, sec., gen. counsel, 2008—. Mem.: ABA, State Bar Wis., Seventh Cir. Bar Assn., Milw. Bar Assn. Office: Northwestern Mutual 720 E Wisconsin Ave Milwaukee WI 53202 Office Phone: 414-271-1444. Office Fax: 414-665-7016.*

MANIVANNAN, DAKSHNAMOORTHY, computer scientist, educator; s. Munusamy and Radhammal Dakshnamoorthy; m. Bala Soulossana Manivannan; children: Suganya, Vasudevan. PhD, Ohio State U., Columbus, 1997. Vis. instr. Temple U., Phila., 1997—98; asst. prof. U. Ky., Lexington, 1998—2005, assoc. prof., 2005—. Referee NSF, Arlington, Va., 1998—. Grantee CAREER Award, NSF, 2000-2004. Mem.: IEEE, Assn. for Computing Machinery.

MANJI, HUSSEINI K., pharmaceutical company executive, neuropsychopharmacologist; BS, MD, U. BC. Fellow in psychopharmacology NIMH, Bethesda, Md.; fellow in cellular and molecular biology Nat. Inst. Diabetes and Digestive and Kidney Diseases; prof. psychiatry and behavioral neurosciences Wayne State U. Sch. Medicine; sr. investigator NIMH, 2000—08, chief Lab. Molecular Pathophysiology Bethesda, dir. Mood and Anxiety Disorders Prog., 2005—08; v.p. ctrl. nervous system and pain Johnson & Johnson Pharmaceutical Rsch. and Devel., Titusville, NJ, 2008—. Recipient A.E. Bennett award for Neuropsychiatric Rsch., Ziskind-Somerfeld award for Neuropsychiatric Rsch., Falcone prize, Nat. Alliance for Rsch. on Schizophrenia and Depression (NARSAD), 1999, Mougens Schou Disting. Rsch. award, Henry and page Laughlin Disting. Tchr. award, Disting. Rschr. award, Brown U. Sch. Medicine, Mentor of the Yr. award, NIHM, Supr. of Yr. award, Excellence in Clin. Care and Rsch. award. Fellow: Am. Coll. Neuropsychopharmacology (Joel Elkes award); mem.: Inst. Medicine, Soc. Biol. Psychiatry. Office: Johnson & Johnson Pharmaceutical Rsch and Devel 1125 Trenton Harbourton Rd Titusville NJ 08560*

MANJUNATH, PRASHANTH, anesthesiologist, researcher; b. Chitradurga, Karnataka, India, May 1976; MD, All India Inst. Med. Scis., New Delhi, 2005. Cert. Ednl. Comm. Fgn. Med. Grad., 2006. Sr. resident All India Inst. Med. Scis., New Delhi, 2004—05; sr. home officer Peterborough Dist. Hosp., Cambridgeshire, England, 2006—07; anesthesiology resident U. Miami and Jackson Meml. Hosp., Fla., 2007—. Contbr. articles to profl. jours. Recipient Best Rsch. Paper award, Indian Soc. Anesthesiologists, 2004, Prof Attiya Sakhi prize, Pakistan Soc. Anesthesiologists, 2004. Mem.: Am. Soc. Anesthesiologists. D-Liberal. Personal E-mail: pmanjunath@yahoo.com.

MANKE, DALE R., finance educator; MBA, Mo. State U., Springfield. Assoc. prof. Evangel U., Springfield, 1991—. Sgt. USAF, 1976—80. Office: Evangel Univ 1111 N Glenstone Springfield MO 65802 Business E-Mail: manked@evangel.edu.

MANKEL, FRANCIS XAVIER, retired principal, priest; b. Knoxville, Tenn., Nov. 8, 1935; s. George Whitehead Sr. and Willia Frances (Duncan) M. BA, St. Ambrose U., Davenport, Iowa, 1957; STB, St. Mary's Sem. and U., Balt., 1959, STL, 1961; MEd, Loyola Coll., Balt., 1965. Ordained priest, Roman Cath. Ch., 1961. Assoc. pastor Our Lady of Fatima Ch., Alcoa, Tenn., 1961—62, Holy Ghost Ch., Knoxville, 1962-67; tchr. Knoxville Cath. H.S., 1961—67, prin., 1967-79; pastor Sacred Heart Ch., Lawrenceburg, Tenn., 1979-84, St. John Neumann Ch., Knoxville, 1984-87, Sacred Heart Cathedral, Knoxville, 1987-97, Holy Ghost Ch., Knoxville, 1997—. Chancellor Cath. Diocese Knoxville, 1988-96, vicar gen., 1988-98, 1999-2007, 2009-; reverend monsignor, 2006; supt. Cath. Schs., Diocese of Knoxville, 1989-92. Bd. dirs. Knoxville area chpt. ARC, 1986—2005; sch. bd. Knoxville Cath. HS, 1967—79, 1984—85, 1987—; com. mem. Sacred Heart Cathedral Sch., Knoxville, 1987—97, St. Joseph Sch., Knoxville, 1997—. Mem. Knoxville Ministerial Assn. Home and Office: 111 Hinton Ave Knoxville TN 37917-6418 Office Phone: 865-522-2205. Personal E-mail: hgchurch@bellsouth.net.

MANKEY, GARY JAY, physics professor, director; b. Williamsport, Pa., Oct. 9, 1958; s. John L. and B. Jane Mankey; life ptnr. Janice Marie Fink. BA, Lycoming Coll., Williamsport, 1982; PhD, Pa. State U., University Pk., 1992. Postdoc. scholar Pa. State U., 1993—95; postdoc. rschr. La. State U., Baton Rouge, 1995—96; asst. prof. U. Ala., Tuscaloosa, 1996—2001, assoc. prof., 2001—05, prof., 2005—, grad. dir., 2008—. Contbr. articles to profl. jours. Mem.: Am. Phys. Soc., IEEE Magnetics Soc., AVS Sci. and Tech. Soc. Home: PO Box 866962 Tuscaloosa AL 35486 Office: Univ Ala Physics PO Box 870324 Tuscaloosa AL 35487 Office Fax: 205-348-2346. Business E-Mail: gmankey@mint.ua.edu.

MANKIN, ROBERT STEPHEN, diversified financial services company executive; b. NYC, Mar. 26, 1939; s. Samuel Harry Mankin and Dorothy (Rosenblum) Goldstein; m. Joyce Marie Cabel, June 13, 1971 (div.); children: Seth Howard, Laura Nicole, Gina Danielle; m. Ruth Irwin, July 20, 2002. BA cum laude, Bklyn. Coll., 1961; MBA, Bernard Baruch Coll., 1970; Dr. Profl. Studies with distinction, Pace U., 1982. Mgr. ABC, NYC, 1969-71, Babcock and Wilcox, NYC, 1971-74; mgr., v.p. Chase Manhattan Bank, NYC, 1974-84; sr. v.p. 1st Interstate Bank, NYC, 1984-87; mng. dir., co-head fixed income, mem. mgmt. com. Nomura Securities Internat., NYC, 1987-94; mng. dir. Paine Webber, NYC, 1994-95; pres., CEO Lakeside Fin. Svcs., Hoboken, NY, 1995—; COO Thomson Fin. Electronic Settlements Group, Boston, 1997-98; pres. Ocwen Tech. Exch., West Palm Beach, Fla., 1999; CEO Sutton Strategic, LLC, 2001—02; prin. advisor Tech Par Group, 2002—. Bd. dirs., sec. Nomura Mortgage Capital Corp., N.Y.C.; bd. dirs., pres., CEO Nomura Asset Capital Corp., N.Y.C., 1988-94, Paine Webber Real Estate, 1995-; trustee Hudson Inst., 2004, pres. Contbr. articles to profl. jours. Mem. Planning Forum, Assn. for Computing Machinery, Assn. Computer Programmers and Analysts (chmn. bd. 1971); Risk Mgmt. Assn. (NY)

MANKINEN, EDWARD A., geologist, researcher; b. Ft Bragg, Calif., May 20, 1939; m. Jeanne C. Weber, July 6, 1966; children: Julie M., Brian D. BS, San Jose State Coll., CA, 1963, MS, 1971. Rsch. geologist US Geol. Survey, Menlo Park, Calif., 1964—. Contbr. articles to profl. jours. Mem.: Geol. Soc. Am., Am. Geophys. Union. Office: US Geological Survey 345 Middlefield Rd Menlo Park CA 94025-3591 Office Fax: 650-329-4664. Business E-Mail: emank@usgs.gov.

MANKIW, NICHOLAS GREGORY (GREGORY MANKIW), economics professor, former federal official; b. Trenton, NJ, Feb. 3, 1958; s. Nicholas and Dorothy (Sawchak) Mankiw; m. Deborah Jean Roloff, June 16, 1984. AB, Princeton U., 1980; PhD, MIT, 1984. Staff economist Coun. Econ. Advisers, Washington, 1982-83; instr. MIT, Cambridge, 1984-85; asst. prof. economics Harvard U., Cambridge, 1985-87, prof., 1987—; mem., chmn. Coun. Econ. Advisers Exec. Office of the Pres., Washington, 2003—05. Research assoc. Nat. Bureau of Economic Research; adviser Fed. Reserve Bank of Boston, Congressional Budget Off.; mem. test devel. comm. ETS. Author: Macroeconomics, 1992, Principles of Economics, 1998; contbr. articles Am. Economic Review, Jour. of Polit. Economy, Quarterly Jour. of Economics, The NY Times, The Financial Times, The Wall Street Journal, Fortune. Recipient Presidential Young Investigator award NSF, 1986. Fellow Am. Acad. Arts & Scis. Office: Harvard U Dept Econs Littauer 223 Cambridge MA 02138

MANKO, JOSEPH MARTIN, SR., lawyer; b. Phila., Oct. 7, 1939; s. Horace David and Vivian (Greenberg) M.; m. Lynn Kimmelman, June 17, 1962; children: Joseph Jr., Glenn, Wendy. BA magna cum laude, Yale U., 1961; JD cum laude, Harvard U., 1964. Bar: Pa. 1964. Regional counsel EPA, Phila., 1973-75; assoc. Wolf, Block, Schorr & Solis-Cohen, Phila., 1964-72, ptnr., 1972-73, 75-89, chmn. environ. law dept., 1978-89; founding ptnr. Manko, Gold, Katcher, & Fox, LLP, Bala Cynwyd, Pa., 1989—. Adj. prof. U. Pa. Law Sch., 1988—2006, Grant Irey lectr., 1989—90, Thomas A. O'Boyle lectr., 2000—01; lectr. in law Vt. Law Sch., 1988—2005; dir. Pa. Environ. Coun., Phila., 1978—85, 1999—2001, chair, 1986—2001; dir. 10,000 Friends of Pa.; chair or co-chair numerous environ. bar assn. coms. Commr. Lower Merion Twp., Ardmore, Pa., 1980—91, 1994—2003, v.p., 2005—06, pres., 1993, 2004; mem. Com. of 70, Phila., 1978—88; chair Pa. Infrastructural Investment Authority, 2003—; commr. Fairmount Pk. Commn., 2007—09; dir. Fairmount Pk. Conservancy, 2007—; co-chair Phila. Sustainability Adv. Bd., 2008—; mem. Phila. Zoring Bd. Adjustments, 2008, Dem. State Com., 1985—90; pres. Beth David Reform Congregation, Gladwyne, Pa., 1983—86, trustee, 1978—83, 1986—, Fedn. Jewish Agys., Phila., 1982—86; bd. dirs. Golden Slipper Camp, 1981—84, 1988—, Jewish Cmty. Rels. Coun., 1983—88, Lower Merion Conservancy, 1976—2002, hon. dir., 2002—; bd. dirs. Abramson Ctr. for Jewish Life, 1990—98, Delaware River Basin Water Resources Assn., 1993—96, 21st Century Environ. Commn., 1997—98. Recipient Outstanding Conservation Profl. award Pa. Wildlife Fedn., 2000; named Disting. Environ. Neutral, CPR Inst. for Dispute Resolution, 1996—, Montgomery County (Pa.) Dem. of Yr., 2000. Mem.: ABA, Pa. Bar Inst. (bd. dirs. 1997—2000, 2001—), Phila. Bar Assn., Pa. Bar Assn. (Outstanding Environ. Atty. 2001), Vesper Club, Bala Golf Club (Phila.), Lambda Alpha, Phi Beta Kappa, Phi Gamma Delta. Avocations: tennis, golf, jogging, bridge, classical music. Office: Manko Gold Katcher & Fox LLP 401 E City Ave Ste 500 Bala Cynwyd PA 19004-1167 Home: 440 S Broad St Apt 2408 Philadelphia PA 19146 E-mail: Jmanko@mgkflaw.com.

MANKOFF, RONALD MORTON, retired lawyer; b. Gettysburg, SD, Oct. 13, 1931; s. Harry B. and Sarah (Frank) M.; m. Joy Faith Shechtman, Nov. 3, 1959; children: Jeffrey Walker, Douglas Frank. BSL, U. Minn., JD, 1954; LLM in Taxation, NYU, 1959. Bar: Minn. 1954, Tex. 1959. With Leonard, Street & Deinard, Mpls., 1957-58; research analyst Inst. Jud. Adminstrn., NYC, 1958-59; assoc. Lyne, Blanchette, Smith & Shelton, Dallas, 1959-60; ptnr. Durant and Mankoff, Dallas, 1960-85; pres. Brice & Mankoff P.C., Dallas, 1985-89, Mankoff, Hill, Held & Metzger, L.L.P., Dallas, 1989-95; chmn., gen. counsel RAC Fin. Group, Inc., 1994—96. Lectr. law So. Meth. U., 1974-77; speaker in field. Contbr. articles to profl. jours. Mem. Dallas Mcpl. Libr., 1973—75, Mayor's Task Force on Child Care, 1984; chmn. bd. Dallas chpt. Am. Cancer Soc., 1976—77, bd. dirs. Tex. divsn., 1981—94; chmn. Dallas Crusade, 1974—75, bd. dirs., mem. exec. com., 1963—88; mem. exec. com. Nat. Pooled Income Fund, Coun. Jewish Welfare Fedns. and Funds, 1975—77; adv. dir. Dallas Cmty. Chest Trust Fund, 1976—78; chmn. Found. Dallas Jewish Fedn., 1976—77; pres. Temple Emanu-el Dallas, 1977—79; bd. dirs. Jewish Fedn. Greater Dallas, 1977—79, 1999—2002, Dallas Civic Opera, 1981—83, World Union Progressive Judaism, 1981—90; mem. S.W. regional liaison com. IRS, 1980—83; mem. exec. com. Union Am. Hebrew Congregations, 1979—89, trustee, 1979—97, chmn. nat. coll. com., 1983—87, vice chmn. bd. dirs., 1984—88, vice chmn. devel. commn., 1997—99; sec. Dallas Assembly, 1979—84; mem. exec. com. Jewish Cmty Rels. Coun., 1982—83, Com. for Qualified Judiciary, 1982—; sec. Child Care Partnership, 1984—86, bd. dirs., 1986—88, Dallas Women's Found., 1985—89, mem. adv. coun., 1989—, chair adv. coun., 1997—99; bd. dirs. Am. Jewish Com., 1982—88, pres. Dallas chpt., 1986—90; bd. dirs. Tex. coun. Girl Scouts U.S., 1982—85; bd. dirs. Goodwill Industries of Greater Dallas, 1979—83, Title One Home Improvement Lender's Assn., 1994—96; bd. govs. Dallas Symphony Assn., 1988—92, 1998—; chmn. Temple Emanu El Found., 1988—95; bd. dirs. Dallas Inst. Humanities and Culture, 1998—2005, mem. adv. com., 2005—; bd. dirs. Ctr. for Interreligious Understanding, 2001—05, Cardio-Pulmonary Rsch. Inst., 2002—08, Jane's Due Process, Inc., 2002—07, Cmty. Home for Adults Found., 2001—, Am. Film Inst., Dallas, 2007—; adv. bd. Rockridge Inst., 2006—08. Lt. (j.g.) USN, 1954—57. Mem. ABA, State Bar Tex., Dallas Bar Assn., Honors Golf Club (bd. dirs. 1967-73), LaJolla Country Club, Crescent Club, Park Cities Club, Zeta Beta Tau, Delta Sigma Rho. Democrat. Jewish. Home: 22 Lakeside Pk Dallas TX 75225 also: 8510 El Paseo Grande La Jolla CA 92037 Home Phone: 214-368-6860. Personal E-mail: ron@mankoff.com.

MANLEY, AUDREY FORBES, retired academic administrator, pediatrician, military officer; b. Jackson, Miss., Mar. 25, 1934; d. Jesse Lee and Ora Lee (Buckhalter) Forbes; m. Albert Edward Manley, Apr. 3, 1970. AB with honors (tuition scholar), Spelman Coll., Atlanta, 1955; MD (Jesse Smith Noyes Found. scholar), Meharry Med. Coll., 1959; MPH, Johns Hopkins U.-USPHS traineeship, 1987; LHD (hon.), Tougaloo Coll., Miss., 1990, Meharry Med. Coll., Nashville, 1991; LLD (hon.), Spelman Coll., 1991, Tskegee U., 1998; DSc (hon.), Coll. New Rochelle, 1998, Morehouse Coll., 2002, U. Del., 2002. Diplomate: Am. Bd. Pediatrics. Intern St. Mary Mercy Hosp., Gary, Ind., 1960; from jr. to chief resident in pediatrics Cook County Children's Hosp., Chgo., 1960—62; NIH fellow neonatology U. Ill. Rsch. and Ednl. Hosp., Chgo., 1963—65; staff pediatrician Chgo. Bd. Health, 1963—66; practice medicine specializing in pediatrics Chgo., 1963—66; assoc. Lawndale Neighborhood Health Ctr. North, 1966—67; asst. med. dir., 1967—69; asst. prof. Chgo. Med. Coll., 1966—67; instr. Pritzker Sch. Medicine, U. Chgo., 1967—69; asst. dir. ambulatory pediatrics, asst. dir. pediatrics Mt. Zion Hosp. and Med. Center, San Francisco, 1969—70; med. cons. Spelman Coll., 1970—71, med. dir. family planning program, chmn. health careers adv. com., 1972—76; med. dir. Grady Meml. Hosp. Family Planning Clinic, 1972—76; commd. officer, advanced though grades to rear adm. USPHS, 1976—97; chief genetic diseases services br. Office Maternal and Child Health, Bur. Community Health Services, Rockville, Md., 1976—81; acting assoc. adminstr. clin. affairs Office of Adminstr. Health Resources and Services Adminstrn., 1981—83, chief med. officer, dep. assoc. adminstr. planning, evaluation and legis., 1983—85; sabbatical leave USPHS Johns Hopkins Sch. Hygiene and Pub. Health, 1986—87; dir. Nat. Health Service Corps.; asst. surgeon gen. US Dept. Health & Human Services, 1988, dep. asst. sec. for health, 1989—93, acting asst. sec. health, 1993, dep. asst. sec. health & intergovtl. affairs, 1993—94, dep. surgeon gen., acting dep. asst. sec. for minority health, 1994—95, acting surgeon gen., 1995—97; pres. Spelman Coll., 1997—2002, pres. emerita, 2003—. Mem. U.S. del. UNICEF, 1990-94, Am. Acad. Family Physicians (pub. adv. bd.), Am. Coun. Learned Socs., Am. Med. Assn. Minority Affairs Consortium (sr. advisor), Ctrs. for Disease Control Found. (bd. visitors), Morehouse Sch. Medicine (clin. Prof. Pediats., Pub. Health Lectr.), Rollins Sch. Pub. Health Emory U (Commrs., Adv. Coun., Ga. Leadership Commn. Organ, Tissue, Blood Marrow donation amont African Ams. Author numerous articles, reports in field; artist permanent collections Nat. Acads. Sci., Spelman Coll. Alumnae Hall of Fame, 2005. Trustee Spelman Coll., 1966-70; The Coll. Fund (UNCF com. Archives, Hist. Govtl. Affairs Com.), Coun. Fgn. Rels., bd. dirs. coun. Ind. Colls.; bd. dirs. March of Dimes, 1998, Nat. Merit Scholarship Corp., Nat. Minority Mil. Mus. Found. Edl. Adv. Coun., Am. Cancer Soc. Found., CDC Found., Compas Compact, Downtown Atlanta Chpt. Rotary, Atlanta 2000 Adv. Com., Quality Edn. for Minorities; adv. bd. Atlanta Regional Health Summit, Commerce Club, Ga. Found. Ind., Food and Drug Adv. Com., publ. advisory bd. Am. Acad. Family Physicians, sr. advisor AMA Minority Affairs Consortium, bd. visitors CDC Found., hon. advisor coun., charter mem. The Children's Inn at NIH, mem. Coun. on Fgn. Rels., Adv. Com., vaccine and biologics com. Food and Drug Adminstrn., mem. Health Careers Exploring Advisory Com., Tribal Colls.; chair, advisory group Univ. S.Carolina Rural Health Initiative. Rear adm. USPHS, ret. USPHS. Recipient Meritorious Svc. award USPHS, 1981, Mary McLeod Bethune award Nat Coun. Negro Women, 1979, Dr. John P. McGovern Ann. Lectureship award Am. Sch. Health Assn., Disting. Alumni award Meharry Med. Coll., 1989, Spelman Coll. 108 Founder's Day Convocation, 1989, Disting. Svc. medal USPHS, 1992, Hildrus A. Poindexter award OSG/PHS, 1993, numerous other svc. and achievement awards; named to African Americans in Sci., Engring., and Medicine Portrait Collection, Nat. Acads., 2005. Fellow Am. Acad. Pediatrics; mem. Nat. Inst. Medicine of Nat. Acad. Sci., Nat. Med. Assn., APHA, AAUW, AAAS, Coun. Fgn. Rels., Spelman Coll. Alumnae Assn. (Hall of Fame 2005), Meharry Alumni Assn., African Am. Collection Portraits of NAS, Operation Crossroads Africa Alumni Assn., Atlanta C. of C., Rotary, Delta Sigma Theta (hon.), Phi Beta Kappa. Mailing: 5820 Hannah Brook St Ardiente North Las Vegas NV 89081 Office Phone: 702-642-2088. Personal E-mail: amanley009@aol.com, amanley007@netaccess.com.

MANLEY, D. MARK, physics professor; b. Columbia, La., Sept. 1, 1954; s. Leslie Earl and Mable Ann (Lee) M.; m. Mari Takai, July 23, 1977. BS in Physics, U. La., Monroe, 1975; PhD in Physics, U. Wyo., Laramie, 1981. Lab. asst. U. La., 1972—75; grad. asst. U. Wyo., 1975—81; postdoc. rsch. assoc. Va. Tech, Blacksburg, 1981—84; postdoc. rsch. staff mem. Lawrence Livermore Nat. Lab., Livermore, 1984—86; asst. prof. Kent State U., Ohio, 1986—91, assoc. prof., 1991—97, undergrad. coord. dept. physics, 1995—2002, 2004—, prof., 1997—. Chair Baryon Resonance Analysis Group (BRAG) Steering Com., 2002—05. Contbr. articles to profl. jours. including Phys. Rev. C., Phys. Rev. D., Phys. Rev. Letters, Physics Letters B., Nuclear Instrumentation and Meth. A. NSF grantee 1989-2001, DOE grantee 2001-. Mem. Am. Phys. Soc., Sigma Xi (chpt. sec. 1989-93), Sigma Pi Sigma. Achievements include research in experimental nuclear physics concentrating on studies using electron scattering and charge-exchange reactions; experimental and phenomenological studies of baryon spectroscopy. Office: Kent State Univ Dept Physics Kent OH 44242-0001 Office Phone: 330-672-2407. Business E-Mail: manley@kent.edu.

MANLEY, EDWARD HARRY, JR., food safety and management trainer, professional association administrator, food products executive, retired military officer; b. SI, NY, Sept. 12, 1941; s. Edward H. and Dorothy I.; m. Judith Manley; children: Deborah Szymchack, Michael E. BS, Cornell U., 1975; MS, Rollins Coll., 1978. Cert. HACCP mgr., 2003. Joined USN, 1959, commd. ensign, 1970, advanced through grades to lt. comdr., 1979; food svc. dir. Naval Hosp., Annapolis, Md., 1972-73; asst. food svc. dir. Nat. Naval Med. Ctr., Bethesda, Md., 1971-72; food svc. dir. Naval Regional Med. Ctr., Orlando, Fla., 1975-80, ret., 1980; food svc. dir. North Broward Hosp., Pompano Beach, Fla., 1981-89; pres. Creative Food Concepts, Inc.; founder Workaholics Internat. Network, 1999—; pres. VIP Food Safety; founder Global Food Svc. Inst., 2009. Mem. adv. bd. Mid-Fla. Tech. Food Svc. Program, 1978-80, Atlantic Vo-Tech Dietetic Program, 1981-89; chmn. Skills Std. Bd., Hospitality and Tourism; presenter in field. Editor (publisher): HACCP Implementation Manual, 2006; author: Restaurant Manager's Handbook, 2007; editor: Food Safety 101, 2009. Mem. evaluation team Hennessey award US Air Force, 1982; mem. adv. bd. Broward C.C., 1985—. Ed Manley Scholarship Fund established, 1984; named Disting. Health Care Food Svc. Adminstr., 1985, Master Cert. Food Exec., 2002; recipient Peter Gust Economou award, 1987. Mem. Internat. Food Svc. Execs. Assn. (pres. Orlando br. 1979-80, pres. South Fla. br. 1983-84, internat. sec.-treas. 1986-87, chmn. bd. 1988-1989, pres. 1989-2008, Mem. of Yr. Orlando br. 1978, South Fla. br. 1984, Disting. Svc. award 1984, Dignified Order of Dinner Gong 2001, Chmn. award 2003, 05, 06, 08, Chmn., Mil. award 2008), Cornell Soc. Hotelmen (pres. Ctrl. Fla. chpt. 1976-80), Cornell Hotel Soc. (treas. Las Vegas 2001—03), Fla. Restaurant Assn. (bd. dir. 1980), Am. Soc. Hosp. Food Svc. Adminstrn. (sec. South Fla. chpt.), Cornell of Ctrl. Fla. Club, Naval Tng. Ctr. Officers Club (pres. 1978-80), Pompano Sq. Mall Walkers Club (founder). Home and Office: 2609 Surfwood Dr Las Vegas NV 89128-1282 Office Phone: 702-430-9217. Personal E-mail: hq@workaholic.org.

MANLEY, FRANK, language educator, writer; b. Scranton, Pa., Nov. 13, 1930; s. Aloysius F. and Kathryn L. (Needham) M.; m. Carolyn Mary Holliday, Mar. 14, 1952; children: Evelyn, Mary. BA, Emory U., 1952, MA, 1953; PhD, Johns Hopkins U., 1959. Instr., then asst. prof. Yale U., New Haven, 1959-64; assoc. prof., then prof. dept. English Emory U., Atlanta, 1964-2000, chmn. dept., 1968-70, Candler prof. English, 1982-2000, dir. creative writing program, 1990-2000, retired, 2000. Editor: The Anniversaries (John Donne), 1963, (with R. Sylvester) De Fructu qui ex Doctrina Percipitur Richard Pace, 1967, All Fools (George Chapman), 1968, A Dialogue of Comfort (St. Thomas More), vol. 12, 1977 (with Louis L. Martz) Epistola ad Pomeranum, vol. 7, 1990, Yale edit. More's complete works; author: Resultances, 1980 (Devins award for poetry 1980), Two Masters (co-winner Gt. Am. New Play Contest 9th Ann. Humana Festival New Am. Plays 1985), (with F. Watkins) Some Poems and Some Talk About Poetry, 1985, Within the Ribbons: 9 Stories, 1989, (play) The Trap, 1993, The Cockfighter: a Novel, 1998, Among Prisoners: Stories, 2000, (poems) The Emperors, 2001, True Hope: A Novel, 2002. With US Army, 1953—55. Guggenheim Found. fellow, 1966-67, 78-79; recipient NEH transl. program fellowship, 1981-83, Nat. Endowment Arts Creative Writing Fellowship in Fiction, 1995-97, Disting. Teaching award, 1984, Tchr.-scholar of Yr. award, 1989, Disting. Alumnus award The Marist Sch., 1993, Miller Playmaker award Theater Emory, 2007. Roman Catholic. Home: 401 Adams St Decatur GA 30030-5207 also: Doublehead Gap Rd Ellijay GA 30540 Business E-Mail: fmanley@emory.edu.

MANLEY, JOAN A(DELE) DANIELS, retired publishing executive; b. San Luis Obispo, Calif., Sept. 23, 1932; d. Carl and Della (Weinmann) Daniels; m. Jeremy C. Lanning, Mar. 17, 1956 (div. Sept. 1963); m. Donald H. Manley, Sept. 12, 1964 (div. 1985); m. William G. Houlton, May 31, 1991. BA, U. Calif., Berkeley, 1954; DBA (hon.), U. New Haven, 1974; LLD (hon.), Babson Coll., 1978. Sec. Doubleday & Co., Inc., NYC, 1954-60; sales exec. Time Inc., 1960-66, v.p., 1971-75, group v.p., 1975-84, also bd. dir.; circulation dir. Time-Life Books, 1966-68, dir. sales, 1968-70, pub., 1970-76; chmn. bd. Time-Life Books Inc., 1976-80. Vice chmn. bd. Book-of-the-Month Club, Inc., N.Y.C., until 1984; supervising dir. Time-Life Internat. (Nederland) B.V., Amsterdam, until 1984; mem. exec. bd. Coll. Letters and Sci. U. Calif., Berkeley, Calif., 2005— Past trustee Mayo Found., Rochester, Minn., Nat. Repertory Orch., William Benton Found.; former mem. adv. coun. Stanford U. Bus. Sch., Haas Sch. Bus. U. Calif. Named to Direct Mktg. Hall of Fame, 1993; U. Calif.-Berkeley fellow, 1989. Mem. Assn. Am. Pubs. (past chmn.).

MANLEY, JOHN FREDERICK, political scientist, educator; b. Utica, NY, Feb. 20, 1939; s. John A. and Gertrude Manley; children from previous marriage: John, Laura; m. Kathy Lynn Sharp, 1991; 1 child, Cole Sharp Manley. BS, Le Moyne Coll., 1961; PhD, Syracuse U., 1966. Asst. prof. polit. sci. U. Wis., 1966, assoc. prof., 1969-71; prof., chmn. dept. polit. sci. Stanford U., 1977-80. Fellow Center for Advanced Study in Behavioral Scis., 1976-77; vis. prof. Stanford in Oxford, 1996. Author: The Politics of Finance, 1970, American Government and Public Policy, 1976; author, co-editor: The Case Against the Constitution, 1987. Congressional fellow, 1963-64; Brookings Instn. fellow, 1965-66; Guggenheim fellow, 1974-75; Fulbright fellow U. Bologna, 1992. Office: 152 Greens Farms Rd Westport CT 06880-6215 Office Phone: 203-341-9410. E-mail: manley48@msn.com.

MANLEY, JUDITH L., director; b. Columbus; B in Bus., Ohio State U., 1970; MEd, Xavier U., 1986. Copy writer advt. agy., Columbus, 1970—74; program asst. Ohio State U., Columbus, 1974—. Advisor, counselor, tchr. dept. Spanish and Portuguese Ohio State U., Columbus, 1991—. Author poems. Commr. Greater Hilltop Area Commn., Columbus, 1989—; bd. dirs. Greater Hilltop Cmty. Devel. Corp., Columbus, 1989—2006; bd. mem. Greater Hilltop Comty. Theatre, Friends of Hilltop; alumnae Leadership Columbus, 1993; citizens' adv. coun. Columbus Devel. Ctr.; alumna Citizen's Police Acad., Columbus. Recipient Pres.'s Vol. Svc. award, Children's Hosp., Columbus, 2003,

2004, 2005, 2006, 2007—08, Va. Denman Vol. award, 2004; named Vol. of Month, 2002. Mem.: ACA, Am. Assn. Tchrs. Spanish and Portuguese. Avocations: writing, photography, music, theater.

MANLEY, LAWRENCE G., literature educator; BA, Dartmouth Coll.; MA, PhD, Harvard Univ. Faculty Yale Univ., 1976—, dir. grad. studies, Renaissance studies, 1985—86, dir. grad. studies, English dept., 1987—90, chair, Renaissance Studies program, 1991—98, dir., undergrad. studies in English, 2004—, William R. Kenan Jr. prof., English, 2005—. Grantee Andrew W. Mellon Found. Fellowship, Guggenheim Found. Fellowship. Fellow: Am. Acad. Arts & Scis. Avocation: instrument-rated pilot. Office: English Dept Yale Univ PO Box 208302 New Haven CT 06520-8302 Office Phone: 203-432-2249. Business E-Mail: lawrence.manley@yale.edu.

MANLEY, MICHAEL, automotive executive; b. Edenbridge, Eng., Mar. 6, 1964; BS in Engring., Southbank U., London, 1985; MBA, Ashridge Mgmt. Coll., Eng., 1998. Grad. mgmt. trainee Motor Industry Bus. Swan Nat. Motors, Aberdeen, Scotland, 1986—87, aftersales mgr., 1987—89; dir., gen. mgr. Olympian Renault, Bournemouth, England, 1989—92; sales and mktg. mgr. Lex Vauxhall, Portsmouth, England, 1992—97; gen. mgr. Wadham Kenning, Southampton, England, 1997—98; ops. dir. Lex Auto Sales RAC, London, 1998—2000; ops. dir. Mercedes Benz Direct DaimlerChrysler UK, 2000, dir. network devel., 2000—03; v.p. dealer ops. Chrysler Group LLC, Auburn Hills, Mich., 2003—06, v.p. sales strategy and dealer ops., 2006—07, exec. v.p. internat. sales, mktg., and bus. devel., 2007—08, exec. v.p. internat. sales and global product planning ops., 2008—09, pres., CEO Jeep Brand, 2009—. Office: Chrysler Group LLC PO Box 21-8004 Auburn Hills MI 48321-8004*

MANLOVE, BENSON, retired gas industry executive, secondary school educator; b. Detroit, Aug. 13, 1943; s. Steve and Eleanor Manlove; m. Sylvia Lynn Colding, Dec. 14, 1991; children: Kris Allison Manlove Simmons, Steven Benson, Nichole Levet. BBA, Wayne State U., 1969. Exec. asst. to pres. Wayne State U., 1968—70; co-owner L & M Office Products, Detroit, 1969—79; asst. to pres. Mich. Consol. Gas Co., Detroit, 1979—83, v.p. human resources, 1983—84, v.p. adminstrn., 1984—94, v.p. econ. devel., 1994—98; owner, operator Uniglobe Omni Travel, Tempe, 1998—2001; substitute tchr. Phoenix Union HS Dist., 2002—06; adj. faculty Gateway CC, Phoenix, 2006—. Dir. Detroit Econ. Growth Corp., 1976—96, acting pres., 1995—96. Dir. Greater Detroit C. of C., Detroit, 1975—80, St. Johns Hosp., Detroit, 1978—96, Am. Heart Assn., Detroit, 1994—95, Goodwill Industries Found., Detroit, 1994—96; chair Detroit Urban League, 1980—83, Blue Cross Blue Shield SE Mich., Southfield, 1993—96. Recipient Disting. Citizen award, Detroit City Coun., 1995; named Spirit of Detroit, Mayor's Office, 1996. Avocations: golf, fishing, photography, reading, travel. Personal E-mail: benson.manlove@yahoo.com.

MANLY, MARC EDWARD, lawyer, energy executive; b. Knoxville, Tenn., Mar. 11, 1952; s. William Donald and Jane (Wilden) M.; m. Colby A. Chapman, July 20, 1974; children: Justin C., Allison C. BA summa cum laude, Amherst Coll., 1974; MA in Econs., U. Mich., 1977, JD magna cum laude, 1977. Bar: Ill. 1978, DC 1988, US Dist. Ct. (no. dist. Ill.) 1978. Assoc. Sidley & Austin, Chgo., 1978—85, ptnr., 1986—94; v.p., solicitor gen. to v.p., chief counsel consumer svcs. group AT&T, 1995—2000; mng. dir. law & govtl. holdings, gen. counsel, sec. Newpower Holdings, Inc., 2000—02; exec. v.p., chief legal officer Cinergy Corp., 2002—06; group exec., chief legal officer Duke Energy, Charlotte, NC, 2006—. Mem. ABA, Order of Coif, Phi Beta Kappa. Office: Duke Energy 526 S Church St Charlotte NC 28202-1904 Office Phone: 704-594-6200.

MANLY, ROBERT W., IV, food products executive; Grad., Stanford U., Calif.; MBA, Harvard Bus. Sch. Asst. to pres. IBP, Inc., 1981—86; exec. v.p. Smithfield Foods, Inc., 1986—96; pres., COO Smithfield Packing, 1994—95; pres. Premium Std. Farms, 1996—2006; exec. v.p. Smithfield Foods, Inc., 2006—, interim CFO, 2007—08, exec. v.p., CFO, 2008—. Office: Smithfield Foods Inc 200 Commerce St Smithfield VA 23430 Office Phone: 757-365-3000.

MANN, BRUCE ALAN, lawyer, investment banking executive; b. Chgo., Nov. 28, 1934; s. David I. and Lillian (Segal) M.; m. Naomi Cooks, Aug. 31, 1980; children: Sally Mann Stull, Jonathan Hugh, Andrew Ross. BBA, U. Wis., 1955, SJD, 1957. Bar: Wis. 1957, N.Y. 1958, Calif. 1961. Assoc. Davis, Polk & Wardwell, NYC, 1957-60, Pillsbury, Madison & Sutro, San Francisco, 1960-66, ptnr., 1967-83; adminstrv. mng. dir. L.F. Rothschild Unterberg Towbin, 1983-87; ptnr. Morrison & Foerster, San Francisco, 1987—; sr. mng. dir. W.R. Hambrecht & Co., San Francisco, 1999—2003. Cons. SEC, 1978; vis. prof. law Georgetown U., 1978; lectr. in field. Author: (with Mattson) California Corporate Practice and Forms, 1999; contbr. articles to profl. jours. Served with USAR, 1957. Mem.: NASD (gov.-at-large 1981—83), ABA (chmn. fed. regulation of securities com. 1981—83, mem. bus. law sect. coun. 1996—99, standing com. on ethics and profl. responsibility 1997—2003, chmn. com. on venture capital 2000—03, chmn. com. investment strategies 2007—, coun. mem. sr. lawyers divsn. 2007—), Bar Assn. San Francisco (bd. dirs. 1974—75), State Bar Calif., Am. Law Inst., The Family Club. Office: Morrison & Foerster 425 Market St Ste 3100 San Francisco CA 94105-2482 E-mail: bmann@mofo.com.

MANN, C. GRIFFITH, curator; married; 3 children. BA in history and art history, Williams Coll., 1991; MA in art history, Johns Hopkins U., 1995, PhD in history of medieval art, 2002; grad., Mus. Leadership Inst., J. Paul Getty Mus., LA. From asst. to full curator medieval art Walters Art Mus., Balt., co-dir. curatorial divsn., asst. dir. curatorial affairs, dir. curatorial divsn., 2007—08; chief curator Cleve. Mus. Art, 2008—. Contbr. Picturing the Bible in the Thirteenth Century, The Lion Companion to Christian Art, Ethiopian Art: The Walters Art Mus., co-curator (exhibitions) Mything Persons: Historic Figures in Legends East and West, Walters Art Mus., Balt., 1998, The Book of Kings: Art, War and the Morgan Library's Medieval Picture Bible, 2002—03, curator Sacred Arts and City Life: The Glory of Medieval Novgorod, 2005—06. Office: Cleve Mus Art 11150 E Blvd Cleveland OH 44106*

MANN, CINDY, federal agency administrator, healthcare educator; Grad., Cornell U.; JD, NYU. Head fed. and state health policy work Ctr. on Budget and Policy Priorities; dir. Family and Children's Health Program Group Health Care Financing Adminstrn. (now Ctrs. for Medicare and Medicaid Svcs.), 1999—2001; rsch. prof., exec. dir. Ctr. for Children and Families Health Policy Inst., Georgetown U.; dir. Ctr. for Medicaid and State Ops. (CMSO) Centers for Medicare & Medicaid Services (CMS), US Dept. Health & Human Services, 2009—. Assoc. commr. Kaiser Commn. on Medicaid and the Uninsured. Contbr. articles to profl. jours. Office: Ctrs for Medicare and Medicaid Svcs 7500 Security Blvd Baltimore MD 21244*

MANN, DAVID SCOTT, lawyer, former congressman; b. Cin., Sept. 25, 1939; s. Henry M. and Helen Faye M.; m. Elizabeth Taliaferro, Oct. 5, 1963; children: Michael, Deborah, Marshall. AB cum laude, Harvard Coll., 1961, LLB magna cum laude, 1968. Bar: Ohio 1968. Assoc. Dinsmore & Shohl, Cin., 1968-74, ptnr., 1974-83, Taliaferro and Mann, Cin., 1983-92; councilman City of Cin., 1974-92, mayor, 1980-82, 91; mem. 103d Congress 1st Ohio dist., Washington, 1993-94; mem. armed svcs. com., mem. jud. com. Washington; of counsel Thompson, Hine and Flory, Cin., 1995-96; pvt. practice Mann & Mann, LLC, Cin., 1997—. Adj. prof. Coll. Law U. Cin., 1995—2002. Editor Harvard Law Rev., 1966-68, notes editor, 1967-68; contbr. articles to profl. jours. Mem., chmn. Cin. Bd. Health, 1972-74. With USN, 1961-65. Mem. Cin. Bar Assn. Democrat. Methodist. Home: 568 Evanswood Pl Cincinnati OH 45220-1527 Office Phone: 513-621-2888. Business E-Mail: david@mannandmannlaw.com.

MANN, DOUGLAS LOWELL, cardiologist; b. Oct. 31, 1951; MD, Temple U., 1979. Cert. Internal Medicine 1982, Cardiovascular Disease 1985. Resident in internal medicine Temple U. Hosp., Phila.; fellow in cardiology U. Calif., San Diego; rsch. fellow Mass. Gen. Hosp., Boston; chief cardiology divsn. Baylor Coll. Medicine, Houston, dir. Winters Ctr. Heart Failure Rsch. Office: Baylor Coll Medicine FC 9-83 1 Baylor Plz Houston TX 77030 Office Phone: 713-798-2545, 713-798-0285. Office Fax: 713-798-0270. E-mail: dmann@bcm.edu.

MANN, ERIC LOUIS, retired military officer, mathematics professor, researcher; b. July 22, 1952; BA in Math., Albion Coll., 1974; MSc in Sys. Mgmt. and Logistics Sys., U. So. Calif., 1980; MAT in Elem. Tchg. and Ednl. Tech., Colo. Coll., 1997; post grad. diploma in Ednl. Psychology, U. Conn., 2002, student, 2003—. Cert. Elem. Tchr. (kindergarten through eighth grade) NH, Elem. Tchr. (kindergarten through sixth grade) Conn., Mid. Sch. Math. Tchr. Conn., Mid. Sch. Earth Sci. Tchr. Conn. Advanced through grades to lt. col. USAF, 1975—96, ret. lt. col., 1996; intern tchr. Rockrimmon Elem., 1996—97; tchr. Atkinson Acad., NH, 1997—98, editor, pub. In Their Own Words; sci., math, Am. history tchr. Bow Meml. Mid. Sch., NH, 1998—2002, gifted and talented coord., 2001—02, mathcounts, math. team coach, Jason project coord., conv. coord., math. olympiads, continental math. league, Mandelbrot competition, space explorers mission to moon coord., bridge builders club supr., physics course coord., FIRST LEGO team organizer, gifted and talented resource website developer, editor lit. jour., chess club establisher; math. tchr. Hall Meml. Sch., Willington, Conn., 2002—03; vis. prof. Purdue U., 2005. Adj. prof. U. Conn., 2003—, webmaster project M3, 2003, editor project M3 newsletters, moderator on-line profl. discussion bd. project M3, rsch. assoc. project M3, 03, on-line course developer, mentor, 04; presenter in field, 2004—05. Contbr. articles to profl. jours. in field, manuals in field. Decorated Group Achievement award NASA, Commendation medals USAF, Achievement medals, Meritorious Svc. medals, Orgnl. Excellence awards, Outstanding Unit awards, Air Force Assn. award, Dept. Def. Joint Svc. Commendation medal, Master Space Ops. badge, Named one of Twelve Airmen of Air Force award, Named 1st Space Wing Jr. Officer of Quarter, Named Hdqs. North Am. Def. Command Jr. Officer of Quarter, Named Hdqs. Air Force Space Command Jr. Officer of Quarter, Named Strategic Air Command Communication Area Airman of Quarter; Quality of Life Improvement grant, USAF, New Boston Air Sta., 1990, Space Explorers On-line Simulation Project, Jefferson Pilot Fin. grant, Bow Meml. Mid. Sch., 1990, FIRST LEGO League grant, Bow PTO, 2001, Blue Chip Sch. Tech. grant, State of Conn., Hall Meml. Sch., 2003. Mem.: NSTA, Sch. Sci. and Math. Assn., Ind. Coun. Tchrs. Math., Nat. Coun. Tchrs. Math., Nat. Coun. Suprs. Math., Ind. Assn. for Gifted, Nat. Assn. Gifted Children, Assn. Supervision and Curriculum Devel., Kappa Delta Pi, Pi Lambda Theta.

MANN, FRANK, physics professor; s. Ernest and Reba Mann; m. Carolyn Amos, Nov. 22, 1969; children: Andrew Todd, Allison Marie. EdD, U. Ga., Athens, 1982. Assoc. prof. Emmanuel Coll., Franklin Springs, Ga., 1974—, elem. sci. cons., 1985—. Mem. Gideons Internat., Nashville, 1983. Mem.: Ga. Sci. Tchrs. Assn. Achievements include research in science materials for handicapped. Office: Emmanuel Coll 181 Spring St Franklin Springs GA 30639 Business E-Mail: fmann@ec.edu.

MANN, FRANK BERT, artist, educator; b. Washington, Apr. 22, 1950; s. Frank Bert and Wilda Vendetta Kaufman. BS, High Point Univ., 1972; BA, George Washington Univ., 1978; MFA, Pratt Inst., 1981. Guest lectr. Corcoran Sch. of Art, Washington, 1979, Pa. State U., Reading, 1986-87, Pratt Inst., Bklyn., 1987-88, Parsons Sch. Art & Design, NYC, 1996-97, Iona Coll., New Rochelle, NY, 2005. Exec. dir. Colaborative Projects, Inc., NY, 1987-88, Basicarts Network, NY, 1989-90; vis. artist Coalition for the Homeless Camp, 1997, Children's Friends for Life, NY, 1997, Project for St. Cyrils Ch., NY, 1992. Author: Eye of the Painter, 1997; illustrator (film) Nerves, 1993; exhibitions include Biennale Internat., Florence, Italy, 2001 (Lorenzo Il Magnifico medal in painting, 2001), US Rep. Internat. Festival of Contemporary Art, Chapel Salelles, St. Maurice D'lbie, France, 2007, Internat. Festival Contemporary Art, Chapel Salelles, 2007, Represented in permanent collections Guggenheim Mus., NYC, Mus. Contemp. Art, Nice, France, live interview series and DVD, A Special Program in Three Parts: The Art of Frank Mann, 2005, Ed McCormack, Frank Mann's Visual Music Spheres, 2006, Jeffrey C. Wright, Vision Mission: The Soft Edged Abstraction of Frank Mann, ASCA Bulletin, 2007. U.S. rep. Biennale Internazionale, Florence, 1999, 2001. Recipient Mable Sanger Webb award, Ford Found., 1980, Lorenzo le Magnifico medal, Internat. Dell'Arte Contemporanea, 2001; grantee, NY State Coun. Arts, 1988, NY City Dept. Cultural Affairs, 1989. Mem.: Assn. D'Art Internat., Contemporary Artists' Guild, Am. Soc. Contempoarary Artists (v.p. 2003—, art historian 2007), Drawing Soc., Artists Equity (bd. dirs. 2000—03, v.p. 2003—), Am. for the Arts. Lutheran. Home and Office: 212 E 34th St Apt 3E New York NY 10016-4846 Office Phone: 212-689-9003. Personal E-mail: fmann100@hotmail.com.

MANN, GEORGE STANLEY, diversified financial services company executive, real estate company officer; b. Toronto, Ont., Can., Dec. 23, 1932; s. David Philip and Elizabeth (Green) M.; children: Michael, Tracy. Attended, North Toronto Collegiate Sch.; LLD (hon.), U. Windsor. Ptnr. Mann & Martel Co. Ltd., 1959-68, CEO, 1968-70, United Trust Co., 1970-76; pres. Unicorp Canada Corp., Toronto, 1972-76, chmn. bd., 1976-90; dir. Nat. Bank Canada, 1978-91; chmn. bd. Union Gas Ltd., 1986-93; owner Townsview Properties Ltd., Toronto, 1984—. Bd. govs. Mt. Sinai Hosp., Toronto, Baycrest Hosp., Toronto. Mem. Oakdale Golf & Country Club (Toronto), High Ridge Country Club (Palm Beach, Fla.), Mar-a-Lago Club (Palm Beach, Fla.). Avocation: golf. Office: 1 St Thomas St Ste 3F Toronto ON M5S 3M5 Canada Home: 1 St Thomas Str Ste 22A Toronto ON M5S 3M5 Canada M5R 3T8 also: 505 South County Rd Palm Beach FL 33480 Office Phone: 416-922-1500.

MANN, JOAN ELLONA, artist, editor; b. Seattle, Aug. 21, 1931; d. Henry Hughes and Jeanetta Maurine (Baker)) Jacobsen; m. Hugh Mann, Sept. 2, 1955 (div. Aug. 1981); children: Susan, Kristi, Steven, Nancy, Roy. BA in Journalism, U. Wash., 1953, BFA in Sculpture, 1970, MFA in Sculpture, 1985. Reporter East Side Jour., Kirkland, Wash., 1953-55; med. editor Virginia Mason Med. Ctr., Seattle, 1965-69; info. specialist Continuing Edn. News Svc. U. Wash., Seattle, 1969-73; editor Seattle Arts Commn., 1973-77; pub. info. officer King County Arts Commn., Seattle, 1973-90; owner, mgr. Joan Mann, Editor, Seattle. Sculptures include multi-media floor sculpture Trident, Ship of Fools, 1988 (award); shows include U. Wash. Henry Gallery, 1971; group shows include Roscoe Louie Gallery, Seattle, 1975, Univ. Unitarian Gallery, 1978, U. Wash. Henry Gallery, 1987, U. Wash. Meany Hall, 1987, SJW Studios, Seattle, 1988, Seattle Ctr. Opera House, 1988, PNAC, Bellevue, 1988, Ctr. for Contemporary Art, Seattle, 1989. Precinct del. Wash. Dem. Com., Seattle, 1992. Recipient 2d and 3d place ann. awards Wash. Press Women, 1971, 1st prize Ctr. for Contemporary Art, 1989; travel grantee Goethe Inst., Berlin, 1988. Mem. Women in Comm. (Nat. Clarion award 1974), Allied Arts Seattle (adv. bd. 1990—), Seattle Art Mus. Roman Catholic. Avocations: photography, skiing, hiking on beaches, travel. Home Phone: 206-329-0813.

MANN, JOHN MARTIN, minister; b. McKeesport, Pa., Nov. 18, 1946; s. Glenn Grant and Mary Dorothy (Flaherty) M. BA, Clarion State Coll., 1967; MDiv, Duke U., 1970, ThM, 1972; D Ministry, Wittenberg U., 1976. Ordained to ministry Luth. Ch. in Am., 1972. Pastor 1st Luth. Ch., Edinboro, Pa., 1971-82; sr. pastor St. John's Luth. Ch., Erie, Pa., 1982-91; sem. pastor Luth. Theol. Sem., 2006—. Instr. Edinboro State Coll., 1971-82; adj. prof. religion Thiel Coll. Greenville, Pa., 1980-82, baccalaureate preacher, 1980-84, trustee, 1974-80, 82—; chmn. synod vocations examining com. NW Pa.-W.Va. Synod, 1984-88; chmn. intersynodical candidacy com. NW Pa.-Allegheny Synods, 1988-90; chmn. ch. vocations examining com. NW Pa. Synod, 1990—; chmn. Luth. Coalition of Erie, 1990-91; dean Cond. I, Northwestern Pa. Synod, 1991—, adj. faculty postgrad/ Family Systems Seminars, 2004; mem. faculty Clergy Seminars with Larry Foster. Contbr. articles to profl. jours. Bd. dirs. Luth. Home, Erie, 1976-79, 82—, Inter-Ch. Ministries NW Pa., 1979-84, South Erie Hillside Cmty. Orgn., 1982—, Holy Trinity Cmty. Ctr., Erie, 1984-88, Nesting Inn, 1988—, Hospice Met. Erie, 1988—, Westminster Counseling Ctr., Mpls.; chmn. Erie City Strategy for Luths., 1989—; pastor Trinity Luth. Ch., Canton, Ohio, 1992—2006; pres. UrbanArk Urban Ministry Coalition; active ELCA NE Ohio Synod, ecumenical com., chmn. synod outreach com., 1998—, dean conf., Canton, mission planner, Urban Strategy com.; founding chmn. Interfaith Roundtable of Canton and NW Neighborhood Assn.; covenant commr. Youngstown Roman Cath. Diocese, NE Ohio Synod; bd. dirs. Westminster Counseling Ctr. Recipient Outstanding Young Man of Am. award Jaycees, 1982. Mem. Luth. Assn. Larger Chs., Am. Assn. Pastoral Counselors, Luth. Campus Ministry Assn., Interdenominational Ministerial Assn. (sec.), Canton Downtown Pastors Assn., Synod Evangelism Com. Office: Trinity Luth Ch 415 Tuscarawas St W Canton OH 44702-2017 Office Phone: 651-641-3216. E-mail: jmann001@luthersem.edu. *In a global environment where fundamentalist religions create division and terrorism, we need a constructive, reappropriation of faith in God.*

MANN, KENNETH HENRY, marine ecologist; b. Dovercourt, Essex, Eng., Aug. 15, 1923; arrived in Can., 1967, naturalized, 1973; s. Harry and Mabel (Ashby) M.; m. Isabella Gilmour Ness, Apr. 18, 1946; children: Ian Malcolm, Sheila Helen, Colin Gilmour. BSc, U. London, 1949, DSc, 1964; PhD, U. Reading, 1953; LittD honoris causa, U. Cape Breton, 2008. Lectr. zoology, then reader U. Reading, Eng., 1949-64; 64-67; sr. biologist marine ecology lab. Bedford Inst. Oceanography, Dartmouth, Can., 1967-72, dir. marine ecology lab., 1980-87, sr. rsch. scientist, 1987-93, emeritus rsch. scientist, 1993—2008. Prof., chmn. biology Dalhousie U., Halifax, N.S., Canada, 1972—80, adj. prof. biology, 1980—2002. Author: Leeches: Their Structure, Physiology, Ecology and Embryology, 1961, Ecology of Coastal Waters: A Systems Approach, 1982, Ecology of Coastal Waters: Implications for Management, 2000; co-author (with J. Lazier): Dynamics of Marine Ecosystems: Biological-Physical Interactions in the Sea, 1991, 3d edit., 2005; co-author: (with R.S. Barnes) Fundamentals of Aquatic Ecology, 1991, Korean edit., 2002; editor, contbr.: (with T. Platt and R. Ulanowicz) Mathematical Models in Biological Oceanography, 1981, (with F. Wulff and J.G. Field) Network Analysis in Marine Ecology, 1989, (with A. Payne, K. Brink and R. Hilborn) Benguela Trophic Functioning, 1992; editor Jour. Animal Ecology, 1966—67. Served with Royal Air Force, 1942-46. Fellow Royal Soc. Can.; mem. Am. Soc. Limnology and Oceanography. Home: 23 Woodward Cres Halifax NS Canada B3M 1J6 Personal E-mail: ken.mann@ns.sympatico.ca.

MANN, KENNETH WALKER, retired minister, psychologist; b. Nyack, NY, Aug. 22, 1914; s. Arthur Hungerford and Ethel Livingston (Walker) M. AB, Princeton U., 1937; STB, Gen. Theol. Sem., NYC, 1942; MS, U. Mich., 1950, PhD, 1956. Ordained priest Episcopal Ch., 1942; diplomate Am. Assn. Pastoral Counselors; lic. clin. psychologist, Calif., Conn.; lic. marriage, family and child counselor, Calif. Vicar in Valley Cottage, Pearl River, NY, 1941-43; priest in charge Yonkers, NY, 1943-45; ret. minister, 1945—. Dir. youth work and Christian edn. Diocese L.A., 1945-47; curate in Beverly Hills, Calif., 1947-49; counselor Bur. Psychol. Svcs., U. Mich., 1951-52; chaplain, clin. psychologist dept. psychiatry St. Luke's Hosp., N.Y.C., also priest-psychotherapist Cathedral St. John Divine, N.Y.C., psychol. examiner ministerial candidates Diocese N.Y., 1952-58; assoc. chaplain Hosp. Good Samaritan, L.A., 1958-65; exec. pastoral svcs., exec. coun. Episc. Ch. N.Y.C., 1965-70; program officer Acad. Religion and Mental Health, N.Y.C., 1970-72; sr. adviser profl. affairs Inst. Religion and Health, 1972-74; sr. psychol. staff Silver Hill Found., New Canaan, Conn., 1974-84; pres. Rockland County (N.Y.) Mins. Assn., 1942-43; exec. sec. social svc. commn. Diocese N.Y., 1943-45; chmn. div. pastoral svcs. Diocese L.A., 1958-65; field dir. Western region Acad. Religion and Mental Health, 1958-61; assoc. nat. chaplain U.S. Power Squadrons, 1956-57. Author: On Pills and Needles, 1969, Deadline for Survival—A Survey of Moral Issues in Science and Medicine, 1970; contbr. articles to profl. jours. Pres. Adoption Inst. LA, 1964; edn. com. Calif. Heart Assn., 1962-64; trustee, treas. Acad. Religion and Mental Health, 1954-59, profl. bd., 1960-70; trustee Vis. Nurse Assn. LA, 1963-65, Children's Home Soc. Calif. in LA, 1964-65, North Conway Inst., 1966-80. USPHS grantee, 1950-51. Fellow AAAS; mem. APA (chmn. com. rels. between psychology and religion 1956-58), Western Psychol. Assn., Calif. Psychol. Assn., L.A. County Psychol. Assn., N.Y. Acad. Scis., Planetary Soc., Assembly Episc. Hosps. and Chaplains, Upper Nyack Tennis Club, Princeton Club N.Y., Exch. Club Beverly Hills (pres.). Republican. Home: 32 Tallman Ave Nyack NY 10960-1606 *I have strongly held to the principle that the total "health" of mankind cannot be considered apart from the values and aspirations by which people live, and by which they may even be prepared to die. Amidst the confusions that exist today over loyalties, traditions, and ideals, many are asking: What is the right way to behave? How should I think? What kind of person am I supposed to be? To help such people in quandary to live responsibly, and still be true to their individuality, is a large task, but it is one that is central to a religious ministry. It has always been my chief concern.*

MANN, LAURA ANN, soprano; MusB, Eastman Sch. Music, 1965, MusM, 1972; PhD in Mus. Arts., U. Md., 1995; studied with Herbert Brauer Kammeksaenger Dectsche Open, Berlin, Germany; studied with Edwin McArthur, NYC; studied with Edith Lang Kammeksaengerin, Lubeck, Germany; studied with David Garvey, studied with Julius Huehn, studied with Anna Kaskas, studied with John Maloy, studied with Kammeksanger Hans Hotter, studied with Louise Urban, studied with Canadian Nat. Opera Chgo. Lyric Open, studied with Rhoda Levine, studied with Ted van Griethaesen, studied with Sha 165 Pehro Theatre, performed vita with Stefan Scaggiari and Rayburn Wright, studied with Kammersanger Heinz Rehfuss, performed with Gerd Albrecht, performed with Christof Perick, performed with Richard Woitach. Prin., owner vocal studio Vocal Advancement, Fairfax, Va., 1979—. Prof. voice Tex. A&I U., Kingsville, Tex., 1984—85; asst. prof. voice Tex. Tech. U., Lubbock, Tex., 1984—86; vis. prof. voice We. Carolina U., Cullowhee, NC, 1986—88; prof. voice Anne Arundel Cmty. Coll., Annapolis, Md., 1989—94; adj. prof. voice and opera George Mason U., Fairfax, Va., 1995—2001, dir. opera, 1995—, mem. women's studies faculty, 1998—, tchr. stage movement, French, German diction; presenter in field; lectr. in field; clinician and adjudicator. Singer: (CDs) The Joy of Christmas, 1996, Laura Mann in Concert, 1999, (albums) Christ Is Born, Laura Mann In Recital, Songs of Light and Joy, 2002, (one-act, one-person opera/monodrama) The White Cliffs, Berlin Philharm., Swiss Chamber Orch., Prague Chamber Ensemble, Rochester Philharm., Buffalo Philharm., Richmond Symphony, Okla. City Symphony, Asheville Symphony, Dallas Baroque Ensemble, Kennedy Ctr. Concert Hall, German Embassy, French Embassy, Mexican Embassy. Broadcaster, Christian Sci. Media Svcs. Sta. WTNT-TV. Recipient Performer's Cert. in Voice and Opera, Eastman Sch. Music, Senatorial award, U. Md. Coll. Pl., 1995; named an Internat. Opera Singers Competition Semi-Finalist, Ctr. Contemporary Opera, NYC; grantee, Prince George's Arts Coun., 1993—96, Va. Commn. Arts, 2000—, Fulbright grant, Martha Rockefeller grant. Mem.: Music Tchrs. Nat. Assn., Internat. Alliance for Women in Music, Opera Am., Nat. Acad. Recording Arts and Scis., South Tex. Assn. Tchrs. Singing, Nat. Assn. Tchrs. Singing, Pi Kappa Lambda. Office: Music Dept George Mason Univ 4400 University Dr Fairfax VA 22030-4422 Office Phone: 703-217-8615, 703-995-1586. Personal E-mail: opera_tunity@peoplepc.com.

MANN, LESLIE, actress; b. San Francisco, Mar. 26, 1972; m. Judd Apatow, June 9, 1997; children: Maude, Iris. Actress (films) Virgin High, 1991, Bottle Rocket, 1996, The Cable Guy, 1996, She's the One, 1996, Last Man Standing, 1996, Things I Never Told You, 1996, George of the Jungle, 1997, Big Daddy, 1999, Timecode, 2000, Perfume, 2001, Orange County, 2002, Stealing Harvard, 2002, The 40 Year Old Virgin, 2005, Knocked Up, 2007 (nominated Best Supporting Actress, Chgo. Film Critics Assn., 2007), Drillbit Taylor, 2008, Seventeen Again, 2008, 17 Again, 2009, Funny People, 2009, Shorts, 2009, appearances on (TV series) Birdland, 1994, Freaks and Geeks, 2000. Office: c/o Endeavor Agy 9601 Wilshire Blvd 3rd Fl Beverly Hills CA 90212

MANN, MARY ANNEETA, author; b. Rockhampton, Queensland, Australia; came to US, 1965; d. Willie Augustus and Dorothy Louisa M.; 1 child, Attica Andrew. BA, Sydney U., Australia, 1964; MA, U. Calif., Berkeley, 1970; PhD, U. So. Calif., 1982. Author: Los Angeles Theatre Book, 1978, Los Angeles Theatre Book, 1984, The Construction of Tragedy, 1985, ThuGun and Natasha, 2003, Two Family Plays: Maria and the Comet The Round Table, 2004, Hubris, The Construction of Tragedy, rev., 2004, There Are No Enemies, 2007, Anzac to Understanding, 2008; author, editor: Science and Spirituality, 2004; playwrite: Tortoise Shell, Diana Devereaux, The Senator's Daughter, The Tongue-Cut Sparrow, Maria and the Comet, 1983, Anzac I and II, 1984, Thugun and Natasha, 1993 (Artistic Dir. achievement award Valley Theatre League 1994), The Round Table, 1995, The Right of the Womb-post 911, 2003. Mem. Australian Soc. Accts.

MANN, MICHAEL KENNETH, film director, producer; b. Chgo., Feb. 5, 1943; m. Summer Mann, 1974; 4 children. Student, U. Wis., London Film Sch. Dir.: (documentaries) 17 Days Down the Line, 1972; screenwriter, dir. (films) The Keep, 1983, Manhunter, 1986, screenwriter, exec. prodr., dir. Thief, 1981, screenwriter, prodr., dir. The Last of the Mohicans, 1992, Heat, 1995 (Dir., Screenwriter, Prodr. Acad. award nominee), The Insider, 1999, Ali, 2001, Miami Vice, 2006, Public Enemies, 2009, dir., prodr. Collateral, 2004, prodr. The Aviator, 2004, screenwriter (TV films) River of Promises, 1977, screenwriter, dir. The Jericho Mile, 1979 (Best Dir. award Dir. Guild Am., Emmy award, 1979), screenwriter Swan Song, 1980, screenwriter, exec. prodr., dir. L.A. Takedown, 1989, screenwriter, exec. prodr. (TV miniseries) Drug Wars: The Camarena Story, 1990 (Emmy award, 1990), screenwriter (TV series) Police Story, 1973, Starsky and Hutch, 1975, Bronk, 1975, screenwriter, dir. Vega$, 1978, screenwriter, exec. prodr. Miami Vice, 1984; exec. prodr.: (TV series) Robbery Homicide Division, 2002—03. Mem.: Dirs. Guild, Writers Guild. Office: c/o Creative Artists Agy 9830 Wilshire Blvd Beverly Hills CA 90212-1804*

MANN, NANCY JEAN, biology professor; b. Santa Monica, Calif., 1953; d. Mary and Farley Mann. BA, Calif. State U., Fullerton, MA in Biology, 1981. Cert.; life credential biologist Calif. Dept. Edn., 1981. Seasonal employee Morro Bay State Pk., 1984—85; naturalist Soc. Expeditions, SilverSea Cruises; prof. biology Cuesta Coll., San Luis Obispo, Calif., 1980—. Preparer & cons. Various Mus., Calif., 1980—86. Recipient M'May Diffley Tchg. Excellence award, Cuesta Coll. Democrat. Avocation: birdwatching. Office: Biology Dept Cuesta Coll PO Box 8106 San Luis Obispo CA 93403-8106

MANN, OSCAR, retired physician, internist, educator; b. Paris, Oct. 13, 1934; arrived in U.S., 1953; s. Aron and Helen (Biegun) Mann; m. Amy S. Mann, July 19, 1964; children: Adriana, Karen. AA with distinction, George Washington U., 1958; MD cum laude, Georgetown U., 1962. Diplomate Am. Bd. Med. Examiners, Am. Bd. Internal Medicine, Am. Bd. Cardiovasc. Disease, cert. advanced achievement in internal medicine. Intern Georgetown U. Med. Ctr., Washington, 1962-63, jr. asst. med. resident, 1963-64, clin. fellow in cardiology with Proctor Harvey program, 1965-66; sr. asst. resident in medicine Georgetown svc. D.C. Gen. Hosp., Washington, 1964-65; clin. prof. medicine Georgetown U. Sch. Medicine, 1985—; nat. chmn. med. alumni fund Georgetown U. Med. Sch., Washington, 1993-95; pvt. practice internal medicine and cardiology, Washington, 1966-99. Mem. med. nursing com. Georgetown U. Med. Ctr., mem. adv. com. CME, mem. tchg. adv. com., opthalmology dept. rev. com., surgery dept. rev. com., faculty com., search com. for a new dean for acad. affairs; appointed coun. to the dean Georgetown U. Sch. Medicine, 1977—; mem. Instnl. Self Study Task Force. Author: A Journey of Hope, 2005; contbr. articles to profl. jours. Nat. chmn. med. alumni fund Georgetown U., 1997—99. With US Army, 1953—55, with US Army, 1953—55. Recipient Mead Johnson Postgrad. Scholar ACP, 1964—65, Physicians Recognition award, AMA, 1987—96, Advanced Achievement in Internal Medicine, 1987, John Carroll award, Georgetown U., 1999. Fellow: ACP, Am. Coll. Chest Physicians, Am. Coll. Cardiology; mem.: AMA, Med. Soc. D.C., Am. Heart Assn. (coun. clin. cardiology), Am. Soc. Internal Medicine, Georgetown U. Alumni Assn. (bd. govs. 1993—, chair med. alumni bd. 1995—, nat. chmn. med. alumni fund 1997—99), Cosmos Club, Phi Delta Epsilon, Alpha Omega Alpha. Home: 5137 Yuma St NW Washington DC 20016 E-mail: oscarmann@comcast.net.

MANN, PAMELA A., lawyer; b. Chgo., Sept. 30, 1948; d. Fred and Sada Lea (Rudin) Mann; m. Walter M. Meginniss, Jr., July 25, 1982; 1 child, Emma E. Mann-Meginniss. BA in History, Oberlin Coll., 1970; JD, U. Pitts., 1973. Bar: Pa. 1974, N.Y. 1977, U.S. Supreme Ct. 1987. Jud. law clk. Judge Marion K. Finkelhor, Pitts., 1973-74; staff atty. Susquehanna Legal Svcs., Sunbury, Pa., 1974-76; sr. staff atty. Nat. Employment Law Project, NYC, 1976-82; clin. prof. Law Sch. Constnl. Litigation Clinic Rutgers U., Newark, 1982-84; dep. chief charities bur. N.Y. State Atty. Gen., NYC, 1984—85, chief charities bur., 1985—95; prin. Law Offices of Pamela A. Mann, NYC, 1995—. Lectr. in field. Co-author: Advising Non-Profits, 1988, 2d edit. 1995, Nonprofit Governance and Management, 2002; contbr. articles to profl. jours. Mem. govt. rels. com. Non-Profit Coording Com., 1996. Mem. Nat. Assn. State Charities Ofcls. (pres. 1994-95), Assn. Bar City NY (com. on non-profit orgns. 1984-94, chmn. 1998-2001). Office: 45 Broadway 31st Fl New York NY 10006-3007 Office Phone: 212-566-3200. Business E-Mail: pmann@pamelamann.com.

MANN, RAJINDER, entomologist, researcher; m. Kiran Mann. MS, Punjab Agrl. U., Ludhiana, 1997, PhD, 2001. Asst. prof. entomology Punjab Agrl. U., India, 1999—2005; postdoc. rsch. assoc. U. Fla., Gainesville. Pres. Punjab Agrl. U. Students Assn., 1995—99. Recipient Crop Rsch. award, 2004. Office: Univ Fla Entomology and Nematology Dept Gainesville FL 32611-0620 Office Phone: 863-956-1151.

MANN, RICHARD ALAN, physician, educator; b. Bklyn., Dec. 18, 1952; s. Daniel Isaac and Claire Ethel (Spiller) M.; m. Judith Fleischer, Aug. 6, 1977; 1 child, David Michael Mann. BS in Math., Union Coll., Schenectady, NY, 1973; MS in Biophysics, SUNY, Buffalo, 1975; MD, Albert Einstein Coll. Medicine, The Bronx, NY, 1979. Diplomate Am. Bd. Internal Medicine. Intern Grad. Hosp. U. Pa., Phila., 1979-80; resident Temple U. Hosp., Phila., 1980—82; clin. nephrology fellow Hosp. U. Pa., Phila., 1982—83, rsch. fellow, 1983—86; asst. prof. medicine Rutgers U. Med. Sch., New Brunswick, NJ, 1986—93; assoc. prof. medicine, microbiology and molecular genetics; physician Robert Wood Johnson Med. Sch., New Brunswick, 1993—, med. dir. Kidney/Pancreas Transplant Program, 1999—; mem. grad. program in microbiology and molecular genetics Rutgers U., Piscataway, NJ, 1989—. Antiviral drug adv. com. FDA, Rockville, Md., 1993—; spl. study sect. NIH, Bethesda, Md., 1994; NIH Reviewers Res.; State Dept. Task Force, Operation Desert Storm, 1991. Contbr. over 50 articles, chpts. and abstracts to profl. jours. Recipient Young Investigator award Nat. Kidney Found., 1987, Nat. Med. award Kidney and Urology Found. Am., 2004, named one of Best Drs. in Am., 1996-2008, Guide to Americas Top Physicians, Top Docs. in NJ, NJ Monthly Mag., njtopdocs.com, others; grantee NIH, 1988-93, William Lightfoot Schultz Found., 1987-88, UMDNJ Found., 1987-88. Mem. Am. Soc. Nephrology (co-chair basic immunology free comm. session 1989, 90), Am. Fedn. for Clin. Rsch., Am. Heart Assn. (Coun. on the Kidney in Cardiovascular Disease), Nat. Kidney Found., Nephrology Soc. N.J., Am. Assn. for Lab. Animal Sci., Am. Soc. Transplantation, Alpha Omega Alpha (Acad. Excellence and Outstanding Tchg. award 1995). Office: UMDNJ Robert Wood Johnson Med Sch Acad Health Sci Ctr CN-19 New Brunswick NJ 08903 Business E-Mail: mannri@umdnj.edu.

MANN, RICHARD O., public relations consulting company executive; b. NYC, July 1, 1933; s. Otto and Ruth (Buchwald) M.; m. Anne Marie Seidenschwang, Apr. 28, 1956; children: Melinda, Susan, Carolyn. BA in History and Polit. Sci., Hofstra U., Hempstead, NY, 1955. Reporter Newsday, Garden City, NY, 1951-56; pub. rels. v.p., cons. Carl Byoir & Assoc., NYC, 1957—76; v.p. corp. affairs Mack Trucks, Inc., Allentown, Pa., 1976-79; v.p. pub. rels. Transway Internat., NYC, 1979—85; pres. Mann Assoc., Danbury, Conn., 1985—. Track and field ofcl., U.S. Internat. meets, including 1984 Olympics, 1970—. 1st lt. US Army, 1956—57. Mem. Met. Golf Writers Assn. Republican. Presbyterian. Avocations: golf, sports. Home and Office: 63 Woodcrest Ln Danbury CT 06810 E-mail: romsport@sbcglobal.net.

MANN, ROANNE L., federal judge; b. 1951; BA, Yale U., 1972; JD, Stanford U., 1975. Bar: N.Y. 1975. Asst. dist. atty. Manhattan Dist. Atty.'s Office, NYC, 1975-76; law clk. U.S. Ct. Appeals for D.C. Circuit, Washington, 1976-77; spl. asst. to asst. atty. gen. civil divsn. U.S. Dept. Justice, Washington, 1977-78; asst. U.S. atty., chief appeals, sr. litigation counsel U.S. Atty.'s Office for So. Dist. N.Y., NYC, then dept. chief criminal divsn., 1978-86; ptnr. Stein, Zauderer, Ellenhorn, Frischer & Sharp, NYC, 1986-94; magistrate judge for ea. dist. N.Y., U.S. Magistrate Ct., Bklyn., 1994—. Mem.: Fed. Bar Coun. Office: US Magistrate Ct 225 Cadman Plz E Brooklyn NY 11201-1818 Office Phone: 718-613-2350.

MANN, SALLY M., photographer; b. Lexington, Va., May 1, 1951; married; children: Emmett, Jessie, Virginia. Student, Putney Sch., 1966-69, Bennington Coll., 1969-71, Praestegaard Film Sch., Denmark, 1971-72, Aegean Sch. Fine Arts, Greece, 1971-72; BA summa cum laude, Hollins Coll., 1974, MA, 1975; DFA (hon.), Corcoran Coll., 2006. Staff photog. Washington & Lee Univ., Lexington, Va. Guest lectr. Honolulu Acad. Arts, 1989, Women Photog. Conf., 1989, Md. Inst. Art, 1989, Bard Coll., 1989, San Francisco Cameraworks, 1990, Photog.-Retrospect/Prospect Conf., 1990, others; instr. Maine Photog. Workshops, 1985-89, Palm Beach Photog. Workshops, 1987-89, Ctr. Photog. Woodstock, 1988, 90, Internat. Ctr. Photog., N.Y., 1989, Image Found., Honolulu, 1989, Okla. Arts Found., 1989, Friends Photog. Workshops, 1990. One-woman shows include Cleve. Ctr. Contemporary Art, 1990, Edwynn Houk Gallery, Chgo., 1990, 92, Tartt Gallery, Washington, 1990, Md. Art Pl., Balt., 1991, Houk Friedman, NY, 1992-94, Mus. Contemporary Photog., Chgo., 1993-94, Mus. Modern Art, NY, 1991, Milw. Mus. Art, 1991, Whitney Mus. Am. Art, NY, 1991, Met. Mus. Art, NY, 1991, Frumpkin Adams Gallery, NY, 1994, Elizabeth Leach Gallery, Portland, Oreg., 1994, Bard Coll., Mass., 1994, Wellesley Coll., Mass., 1995, Edwynn Houk Gallery, NY, 1997, Gagosian Gallery, Calif., 1997; exhibited in group shows Corcoran Gallery Art, Washington, 1977, Va. Mus. Fine Arts, Richmond, 1988, New Orleans Mus. Art, 1990; represented in permanent collections Addison Gallery Am. Art, Andover, Mass., Balt. Mus. Art, Birmingham (Ala.) Mus. Art, Boston Mus. Fine Art, In Response to Place: Photographs from The Nature Conservancy's Last Great Places, Corcoran Gallery Art, 2001, Hirshhorn Mus. and Sculpture Garden, Nat. Mus. Am. Art, Smithsonian Inst., Washington, Met. Mus. Art, NY, Mus. Modern Art, NY, Whitney Mus. Am. Art, NY, San Francisco Mus. Art, Va. Mus. Fine Arts, Richmond, Gagosian Gallery, NYC, 2006, others; author/photographer: (with Ann Beattie) Second Sight: The Photographs of Sally Mann, 1984, (with Reynolds Price) At Twelve: Portraits of Young Women, 1988, Immediate Family, 1992, Still Time, 1994, What Remains, 2003, Deep South, 2005. Fellow Nat. Endowment Arts, 1982, 88, 92, Guggenheim Found., 1987, Southeastern Ctr. Contemporary Arts, 1989, Artists Visual Arts, 1989; named Best Photographer in Am., Time Mag., 2001. Mailing: c/o Mann Vita & Elrod 15 E Nelson St Lexington VA 24450

MANN, SAM HENRY, JR., retired lawyer; b. St. Petersburg, Fla., Aug. 2, 1925; s. Sam Henry and Vivian (Moore) M.; m. Mary Joan Bishop, Sept. 7, 1948; children: Vivian Louise, Sam Henry III, Wallace Bishop. BA, Yale U., New Haven, Conn., 1948; LLB, Fla. U., Gainesville, 1951, JD, 1967. Bar: Fla. 1951, U.S. Dist. Ct. (mid. and so. dists.) Fla. 1951, U.S. Ct. Appeals (5th cir.) 1955, U.S. Ct. Appeals (11th cir.) 1996, U.S. Supreme Ct. 1971. Ptnr. Greene, Mann, Rowe, Stanton, Mastry & Burton, St. Petersburg, 1951-84, Harris, Barrett, Mann & Dew, St. Petersburg, 1984—, ret., 2001. Trustee, v.p. Mus. Fine Arts, St. Petersburg, 1980-94, Eckerd Coll., St. Petersburg, 1976-79, Webb Sch., Bell Buckle, Tenn., 1966-75; bd. dirs. Regional Cmty. Blood Ctr., St. Petersburg, 1966-93, Fla. Blood Svcs., 1993-94, mem. emeritus 1996—; mem. Disting. Alumni Soc. Webb Sch.; mem., chmn. H. Milton Rogers Heart Found.; bd. dirs., pres. Family and Children's Svc., Inc., 1956-61. Lt. (j.g.) USNR, 1943-48. Fellow Am. Coll. Trial Lawyers, Am. Bar Found., Fla. Bar Found.; mem. ABA, Fla. Bar Assn., Fla. Supreme Ct. Hist. Soc., Am. Counsel Assn., Def. Rsch. Inst., Internat. Assn. Def. Counsel, Pinellas County Trial Lawyers Assn., Nat. Assn. Railroad Trial Counsel, Fla. Def. Lawyers Assn., Assn. Hostp. Attys., Bay Area Vanderbilt, St. Petersburg Bar Assn., Yale and U. Fla. Alumni Assns., Phi Alpha Delta, Delta Kappa Epsilon. Republican. Presbyterian. Avocations: travel, boating, gardening. Home: 531 Brightwaters Blvd NE Saint Petersburg FL 33704 Office: Harris Barrett Mann Dew Pa 8083 38th Ave N Saint Petersburg FL 33710-1029 Home Phone: 727-894-5713; Office Phone: 727-892-3100. Personal E-mail: mjbmann@aol.com.

MANN, THEODORE R., lawyer; b. Czechoslovakia, Jan. 31, 1928; came to U.S., 1929, naturalized, 1930; s. Aaron and Bertha (Schreiber) M.; m. Rowena Joan Weiss, 1954; children: Julie Ellen, Rachel Beth, Marcus Eliyahu. Pvt. practice, Phila., 1953—2005; counsel Pa. Securities Commn., 2005—07. Chmn., pres. Nat. Jewish Cmty. Rels. Adv. Coun., 1976-80; Conf. Pres. Major Am. Jewish Orgns., 1978-80; Nat. Conf. Soviet Jewry, 1981-83; Am. Jewish Congress, 1984-88; founding chmn. Mazon-A Jewish Response to Hunger, 1985-90, Project Nishma, 1988-97; exec. com. chair Israel Policy Forum, 1997-2001; dir.Jewish Social Policy Action Network, 2004-; trustee internat. coun. New Israel Fund, 2002-. Alumni fellow, Temple U. Home and Office: 2401 Pennsylvania Ave 17A4 Philadelphia PA 19130 E-mail: tedm@netreach.net.

MANN, THOMAS EDWARD, political scientist; b. Milw., Sept. 10, 1944; s. Edward Emil and Eleanor (Hoffman) M.; m. Sheilah Rosenhack, June 4, 1976; children: Edward Matthew, Stephanie Rachael. BA, U. Fla., 1966; MA, U. Mich., 1968, PhD, 1977. Staff assoc. Am. Polit. Sci. Assn., Washington, 1970-76, asst. dir., 1977-81, exec. dir., 1981-87; co-dir. congress project Am. Enterprise Inst., Washington, 1979-81; dir. govtl. studies Brookings Instn., 1987-99, W. Averell Harrimann sr. fellow in Am. governance, 1991—. Mem. bd. overseers Nat. Election Study, 1987-94, chmn., 1990-94. Author: Unsafe At Any Margin, 1978; co-author: Vital Statistics on Congress, 1980-2008; Renewing Congress, 1992, 93, The New Campaign Finance Sourcebook, 2005, The Broken Branch, 2006, 08; co-editor: The New Congress, 1981, The American Elections of 1982, 1983, Media Polls in American Politics, 1992, Values and Public Policy, 1994, Elections at Home and Abroad, 1994, Congress, the Press, and the Public, 1994, Intensive Care: How Congress Shapes Health Policy, 1995,Campaign Finance Reform, A Source Book, 1997, The Permanent Campaign and Its Future, 2000, Governance for a New Century: Japanese Challenges, American Experience, 2002, Inside the Campaign Finance Battle, 2003, Party Lines: Competition, Partisanship, and Congressional Redistricting, 2005; editor: A Question of Balance: The President, The Congress and Foreign Policy, 1990. Mem. Democratic Nat. Com.'s Commn. on Presdl. Nomination and Party Structure, 1975-78; mem. tech. com. Dem. Nat. Com. Commn. on Presdl. Nominations, 1981-82, The Fairness Commn., 1985. U. Mich. NDEA grad. fellow, 1966-69; Am. Polit. Sci. Assn. Congl. fellow, 1969-70 Fellow Am. Acad. Arts and Scis.; mem. Coun. on Fgn. Rels., Phi Beta Kappa (Frank J. Goodnow award, Charles E. Merriam award). Home: 6508 Goldleaf Dr Bethesda MD 20817-5837 Office: Brookings Instn 1775 Massachusetts Ave NW Washington DC 20036-2103 Home Phone: 301-229-8928. Business E-mail: tmann@brookings.edu.

MANN, TRUE SANDLIN, psychologist, consultant; b. Longview, Tex., Aug. 4, 1934; d. Bob Murphy and Stella True (Williams) Sandlin; m. Jack Matthewson Mann, Sept. 4, 1954 (div. Dec. 1989); children: Jack Matthewson Jr., Bob Sandlin, Daniel Williams, Nathaniel Currier. BS, Stephen F. Austin State U., Nacogdoches, Tex., 1973, MA, 1977; PhD, East Tex. State U., 1982. Lic. psychologist, Tex., Ark. Instr. Stephen F. Austin State U., 1975-76, vis. asst. prof. psychology, 1986-87; instr. East Tex. State U., Commerce, 1980-81; postdoctoral fellow Southwestern Med. Sch., Dallas, 1982-83; pvt. practice, Longview, Tex., 1983-92; psychologist dept. family practice U. Tex. Health Sci. Ctr., Tyler, 1990-92; dir. psychol. svcs. St. Michael's Hosp., Texarkana, Tex., 1992-93; cons. psychologist, Longview, 1993—. Weekly newspaper columnist HARBUS, Cambridge Mass., 1959-60; cons. Made-Rite Co., Longview, 1989—. Mem. candidate com. Assoc. Reps. Tex., Austin, 1990—; bd. dirs. Mental Health Assn. Tex., 1977-82, 84-92, Longview Symphony, 1995-99, Dallas Opera Guild, 1999—, Longview Mus. of. Art, 1995; mem. Leadership Tex., 1988—. Mem. APA, Tex. Psychol. Assn., N.E. Tex. Field Ornithologists. Episcopalian. Avocations: photography, travel, history. Home: 1906 N 4th St Longview TX 75601-3202 Office: 1203 Montclair St Longview TX 75601-3565

MANN, WENDY, librarian; BA in Polit. Sci., U. Pitts., 1989, MLS, 1990. Govt. docs. reference, electronic resources libr. U. Pitts., 1993—99, coord., govt. publications and maps, 1999—2007; edn. liaison libr. George Mason U., Fairfax, Va., 2007—. Co-editor: (book) Government Publications Unmasked: Teaching Government Information Resources in the 21st Century. Mem.: ALA. Office: George Mason Univ 4400 Univ Dr MS2FL Fairfax VA 22030

MANN, WILLIAM CRAIG, lawyer; b. Norwalk, Ohio, Nov. 17, 1953; s. Abraham and Shirley (Smith) M. BA, Case Western Res. U., Ohio, 1976; JD, U. Dayton, Ohio, 1979. Bar: Ohio 1979, U.S. Dist. Ct. (no. dist.) Ohio 1979, U.S. Supreme Ct. 1986, U.S. Dist. Ct. (so. dist.) Ohio 1988. Law clk. Ohio Supreme Ct., Ohio, 1985-86; pvt. practice Cleve., 1986-87; assoc. Wolske and Blue, Columbus, Ohio, 1987-97; ptnr. Sunbury, Mann & Young, Columbus, Ohio, 1997-99; of counsel Mitchell, Penchett, Fraley, Catalan & Boda Co. LPA, 1997—. Spkr. various orgns. in field, including Ohio Legal Ctr. Inst., Ohio Acad. of Trial Lawyers; mem. Ohio Supreme Ct. commn. on professionalism, 1997-2002 Contbr. articles to profl. jours. Bd. dirs. United Way, Huron County, Ohio, 1983; mem. exec. and cen. coms. Huron County Dem. Com., 1976-79. Mem. Ohio State Bar Assn. (ethics com. 1987—), Columbus Bar Assn., Ohio Acad. Trial Lawyers (pres. 2001—), Franklin County Trial Lawyers Assn. (pres. 2001-2002. Avocations: football, history, economics. Home: 2041 Ramblewood Ave Columbus OH

43235-7340 Office: Mitchell & Penchett Franley Catalano & Boda 580 S High St Ste 200 Columbus OH 43215 Office Phone: 614-224-4114. Personal E-mail: mannlaw99@aol.com.

MANNARD, JOSEPH GERARD, history professor; b. Chgo., Dec. 23, 1951; s. Thomas Wilbur Mannard and Isabella Fitzsimmons; m. Robin Leona Rohrer; children: Moira Elizabeth, Brigid Elizabeth, Ian Richard, Kathleen Margaret. AA, Manatee Jr. Coll., Bradenton, Fla., 1971; BA, U. South Fla., St. Petersburg, 1976; MA, U. South Fla., Tampa, 1979; PhD, U. Md., Coll. Pk., 1989. Asst. prof. history Indiana U. Pa., 1989—. Office: Indiana Univ Pa Keith Hall Rm 228 Indiana PA 15705-1014 Business E-Mail: jmannard@iup.edu.

MANNELLA, CARMEN A., research scientist; b. Buffalo, June 15, 1947; s. Patrick and Nicolina Mannella; m. Linda J. Thomann, Apr. 8, 1950; children: Marc P., Susan. BS in Physics, Canisius Coll., Buffalo, 1969; PhD in Biophysics, U. Pa., Phila., 1974. Rsch. scientist Wadsworth Ctr., Albany, NY, 1979—, dir. nat. resource visualization biol. complexity, 1989—, assoc. dir. rsch. and tech., 2007—. Prof. U. Albany, SUNY, 1986—; adj. prof. Rensselaer Poly. Inst., Troy, NY; mem., sr. health rsch. svc. Health Rsch., Inc., Rensselaer, NY, 2001—. Mem. editl. bd.: Jour. Bioenergetics and Biomembranes, 1992—. Co-chair grant rev. com. United Mitochondrial Disease Found., 2007—. Recipient Disting. Alumnus award, Canisius Coll., 2000, Nat. Rsch. Svc. award, Roswell Park Meml. Trust, 1974—76; grantee, NSF, 1981—99, 1991—99, NIH, 2001—06, 2008—; fellow, St. Louis U. Med. Sch., 1976—78; Peter Coleman fellow, Ben Gurion U., Beer Sheeva, Israel, 2006. Mem.: NY Acad. Sci., Ordway Rsch. Inst. (bd. dirs. 2008—), Albany Conf. Found. (bd. dirs. 1989—), Biophysical Soc. (chair bioenergetics subgroup 2001—04), DiGamma, Alpha Sigma Nu, Sigma Xi. Achievements include research in development of electron microscopy & application to mitochondrial membranes and ion channels. Office: Wadsworth Center Empire State Plaza Albany NY 12201-0509 Office Fax: 518-474-3439. Personal E-mail: carmmann@aol.com. E-mail: carmen@wadsworth.org.

MANNELLI, ITALO MARCELLO, physics professor; b. Florence, Italy, July 17, 1933; m. Mary Chapple, Aug. 6, 1959; 1 child, Marcello. Degree in physics, U. Pisa, Italy, 1957; diploma, Scuola Normale Superiore, Pisa, 1958. Asst. prof. U. Pisa, 1957-68; rsch. assoc. MIT, Cambridge, 1962-64; prof. U. Pisa, 1968-87; prof. physics Scuola Normale Superiore, Pisa, 1987—2009, dean classe of sci., 1999—2001; mem. Comitato Consulenza Scientifica Agenzia Spaziale Italiana, 1999—2001. V.p. INFN, 1974-76; sr. physicist CERN, Geneva, 1975-86, dir. rsch., 1978-80, chmn. sci. policy com., 1987-89. Contbr. rsch. articles to various jours. Recipient W.K.H. Panofsky prize in Exptl. Particle Physics, Am. Phys. Soc., 2007. Mem. Internat. Union Pure and Applied Physics (chmn. commn. on particles and fields 1982-87), Italian Phys. Soc., Soc. Corrispondents Accademia Lincei. Office: Scuola Normale Superiore Piazza Cavalieri 7 I 56126 Pisa Italy Home Phone: 39050 531125; Office Phone: 0039050509260. E-mail: mannelli@pi.infn.it.

MANNER, JENNIFER FOUSE, social worker; b. Balt., June 15, 1964; d. Richard Erb and Patricia Ann (Matthews) Fouse; m. David Bruce Manner, Aug. 16, 1986; 1 child, Jessica Lynn. BA in Psychology, Hope Coll., 1986; MS in Social Adminstrn., Case Western Reserve U., 1988. Lic. ind. social worker, Ohio, Vt; lic. alcohol and drug abuse counselor, Vt.; cert. chem. dependency counselor. Adolescent continuing care coord. Lakeland Inst., Lorain (Ohio) Cmty. Hosp., 1988-90; dir. Laurelwood Counseling Ctr., Mayfield Heights, Ohio, 1990-93; field instr. Mandel Sch. Applied Social Scis., Case Western Res. U., Cleve., 1991-95; ind. social worker, chem. dependency counselor Elyria, Ohio, 1993—2005; social worker Rutland Mental Health, Vt., 2005—06; asst. prof. Coll. St. Joseph, Rutland, 2006—. Adj. instr. Lorain County C.C., 1998-2005, Baldwin Wallace Coll., 2004-05, Coll. St. Joseph; lectr. in field. Mem. NASW, Psi Chi. Democrat. Avocations: canoing, skiing, singing.

MANNES, ELENA SABIN, film and television producer, television director; b. NYC, Dec. 3, 1943; d. Leopold Damrosch and Evelyn (Sabin) M. BA, Smith Coll., 1965; MA, Johns Hopkins U., 1967. Rschr. Pub. Broadcast Lab. Nat. Ednl. TV, NYC, 1968-70; writer Sta. WPIX-TV, NYC, 1970-73; assignment editor Sta. ABC-TV, NYC, 1973-76; prodr., writer Sta. WCBS-TV, NYC, 1976-80; prodr. CBS News, NYC, 1980-87, Pub. Affairs TV/Bill Moyers PBS Documentaries, NYC, 1987-90. Ind. documentary dir. and prodr., 1987—; exec. prodr. dir. writer TIME Music Inst. PBS. Recipient Emmy award NATAS, 1984, 85, 87, 90, 94, 96, 2002, Peabody award, 1985, Cine Golden Eagle award, 1988, 90, 93, 94, 95, 99, Robert F. Kennedy Journalism award, 1989, DGA awards, 1987, 90. Mem. Writers Guild Am., Dirs. Guild Am., Am. Film Inst. (dir. Workshop for Women). Avocations: tennis, still photography.

MANNICK, JOHN ANTHONY, surgeon; b. Deadwood, SD, Mar. 24, 1928; s. Alfred and Catherine Elizabeth (Schuster) M.; m. Alice Virginia Gossard, June 9, 1952; children— Catherine Virginia, Elizabeth Eleanor, Joan Barbara. BA, Harvard U., 1949, MD, 1953. Diplomate: Am. Bd. Surgery (dir. 1971-77). Intern Mass. Gen. Hosp., 1953-54, resident in surgery, 1956-60; instr. in surgery to asst. prof. Med. Coll. Va., 1960-64; asso. prof. to prof. surgery Boston U., 1964-76, chmn. div. surgery, 1973-76; Moseley prof. surgery Harvard U., 1976-94, Moseley Disting. prof. surgery, 1994—2008; dir. ednl. programs Harvard Med. Internat., 1994-96; chmn. dept. surgery Peter Bent Brigham Hosp. and Brigham and Women's Hosp., Boston, 1976-94. Mem. surgery, anesthesiology and trauma study sect. NIH, 1978-82, mem. medicine study sect., 1967-70; rsch. com. Med. Found., Inc., 1970-76. Author: (with others) Modern Surgery, 1970, Core Textbook of Surgery, 1972, Surgery of Ischemic Limbs, 1972, The Cause and Management of Aneurysms, 1990; mem. editorial bd. AMA Archives of Surgery, 1973-84, Clin. Immunology and Immunopathology, 1972-84, Surgery, 1982-97, Brit. Jour. Surgery, 1982-92, European Jour. Vascular Surgery, 1988-96, Shock, 1997—; mem. editl. bd. Advances in Surgery, 1979—, editor, 1984-86; mem. editl. bd. Jour. Vascular Surgery, 1984-97, assoc. editor, 1990-97; also articles. Served to capt. M.C. USAF, 1954-56. Markle scholar in acad. medicine, 1961-66, sci. leadership award, 2008 Fellow ACS (gov.), Royal Coll. Surgeons (hon., Eng.), Royal Coll. Surgeons (hon., Edinburgh), Royal Coll. Surgeons (hon. Ireland), Vascular Soc. Gt. Britain and Ireland (hon.); mem. Am. Fedn. Clin. Rsch., Am. Assn. Immunologists, Am. Soc. Exptl. Pathology, Soc. Clin. Investigation, Soc. Clin. Surgery, Soc. Univ. Surgeons (Lifetime Achievement award 2005), Soc. Surg. Chmn. (sec. 1985-87, pres. 1987-88), Am. Surg. Assn. (pres. 1989-90), Internat. Cardiovascular Soc. (recorder N.Am. chpt., 1973-76, pres. N.Am. chpt. 1991-92, internat. v.p. 1993, Disting. Svc. award 2002), Soc. Vascular Surgery (pres. 1981), N.E. Surg. Soc., (Nathan Smith Disting. award, 1999), New Eng. Soc. Vascular Surgery (pres. 1994-95), Royal Coll. Surgeons (hon., Australasia) So. Surg. Assn., So. Soc. Vascular Surgery (hon.), Surg. Infection Soc.(Sci. Leadership award, 2008), Halstead Soc., Lifeline Found. (pres. 1997-2002), Shock Soc. (Sci. Achievement award 2000), Uniformed Svcs. U. Health Scis. (dr. mil. medicine and surgery, Hon. 2003), Phi Beta Kappa. Home: 81 Bogle St Weston MA 02493-1056 Office Fax: 617-582-6169.

MANNING, AMY B., lawyer; b. Des Moines, July 19, 1967; d. Gerald and Beth Manning; m. Paul C. Ziebert; 3 children. BA in Biology, Monmouth Coll., Des Moines, 1989; JD, U. Chgo., 1992. Bar: Ill. 1992, US Dist. Ct. (no. dist.) Ill. 1992, US Ct. Appeals (7th cir.) 1993, US Ct. Appeals (6th cir.) 1996, US Ct. Appeals (8th cir.) 2000, US Ct. Appeals (2d cir.) 2006. Ptnr. McGuireWoods LLP (formerly Ross & Hardies), Chgo., 1992—. Recipient Thomas P. McAulrey award Outstanding Advocacy. Mem.: ABA (antitrust sect.), Chgo. Women in Tech., Nat. Assn. Women Bus. Owners (Chgo. chpt., Corp. Woman Acheivement award 2006), Chgo. Women Antitrust Atty. Network (founder), 7th Cir. Bar Assn., Ill. Bar Assn., Chgo. Bar Assn. (vice chmn. antitrust law com., call to action women com., Current Events newsletter). Office: McGuireWoods LLP 77 W Wacker Dr Ste 4100 Chicago IL 60601

MANNING, CHRISTOPHER ASHLEY, finance educator, consultant; b. LA, June 26, 1945; s. Ashley and Vivian LaVerne (Wagner) M.; m. Cathy Ann Nichols, July 30, 1977 (div. Sept. 1993). BS, San Diego State U., 1967; MBA, Northwestern U., 1971; PhD, UCLA, 1983. Corp. loan officer Security Pacific Nat. Bank, LA, 1971-75; v.p. fin. Solitude Ski Resort, Bravo Ski Corp., Salt Lake City, 1975-78; pres. Sequoia Spa Co., LA, 1976-79, Manning and Co., LA, 1971-86, Manning's Little Red Piano Shop, LA, 1971-86; instr. corp. fin. Pepperdine U., LA, 1979-83; instr. corp. fin. and real estate Long Beach State U., Calif., 1983-86; assoc. prof. fin. Loyola Marymount U., LA, 1986-92, prof. fin., 1992—. Mng. prin. Denver office Houlihan Valuation Advisors, 1993-94; founder, mng. prin. Manning Advisors. Mem. editl. bd. Jour. Real Estate Rsch., 1988-90, 91-93, 94-96, 97-99, 2003—; contbr. articles to profl. jours. 1st lt. US Army, 1967—70. Decorated Bronze Star. Mem.: Am. Real Estate Soc. (bd. dirs. 1994—96, 1997—99, v.p./program chair 2000—01, bd. dirs. 2000—, pres.-elect 2001—02, pres. 2002—03), Phi Eta Sigma, Beta Gamma Sigma. Republican. Episcopalian. Home and Office: Manning Advisors 29438 Quailwood Dr Palos Verdes Peninsula CA 90275-4929 Office Phone: 310-541-0353. Personal E-mail: chrismanning1@verizon.net. Business E-Mail: cmanning@lmu.edu.

MANNING, DANNY (DANIEL RICARDO MANNING), men's college basketball coach, retired professional basketball player; b. Hattiesburg, Miss., May 17, 1966; s. Ed and Darnelle; m. Julie Manning; children: Taylor, Evan. B in Comm., U. Kans., Lawrence, 1988. Forward LA Clippers, 1988-93, Atlanta Hawks, 1993-94, Phoenix Suns, 1994-99, Milw. Bucks, 1999—2000, Utah Jazz, 2000—01, Dallas Mavericks, 2001—02, Detroit Pistons, 2002—03; ret. NBA, 2003; dir. student/athlete devel., team mgr. U. Kansas Jayhawks, 2003—07, asst. coach, 2007—. Recipient Bronze medal US Olympic Basketball Team, 1988, Sixth Man of Yr. award NBA, 1998; named Player of Yr. Big Eight Conf., 1986-88, Most Outstanding Player NCAA Final Four, 1988, Naismith award, 1988, Wooden award, 1988; named to Sporting News NCAA All-Am. First Team, 1987, 88, Western Conf. All-Star Team NBA, 1993, 1994. Achievements include member of the NCAA Division I Final Four championship winning University of Kansas Jayhawks, 1988; being the first overall pick in the NBA Draft, 1988. Office: Univ Kansas Athletics Dept Allen Fieldhouse 1651 Naismith Dr Lawrence KS 66045 Office Phone: 785-864-3056.*

MANNING, DAVID GEOFFREY, former ambassador; b. Dec. 5, 1949; m. Catherine Manning. With Mex. and C.Am. Dept. British Fgn. and Commonwealth Office, 1972—74, third sec. to second sec. Warsaw, 1974—77, second sec. to first sec. New Delhi, 1977—80, with Soviet Dept., 1980—82, dep. head Policy Planning Dept., 1982—84, first sec. Paris, 1984—88, counselor-on-loan to Cabinet Office, 1988—90, counselor, head of chancery Moscow, 1990—93, head Ea. Dept., 1993—94, head Policy and Planning staff, 1994—95, dep. undersecretary, 1998—2000; fgn. policy adv. to Prime Min., London, 2001—03; amb., mem. UK Del. to NATO, Brussels, 2001; British amb. to Israel, Tel Aviv, 1995—98, to the US, Washington, 2003—07. UK mem. Internat. Conf. on Former Yugoslavia, 1994. Recipient Knight Comdr., Order of St. Michael and St. George.

MANNING, DENNIS J., insurance company executive; m. Kathy Manning; 3 children. BBA, Notre Dame U. Ins. agent Guardian Life Ins. Co. Am., Houston, 1983—91, v.p. life mktg., agy. distbn., 1991—2000, COO, 2000—02, pres., 2002—, CEO, 2003—. Bd. trustees Forman Sch., Litchfield, Conn. With US Army, in Vietnam. Office: 7 Hanover Sq New York NY 10004-2616

MANNING, ELI (ELISHA NELSON MANNING), professional football player; b. New Orleans, Jan. 3, 1981; s. Archie and Olivia Manning; m. Abby McGrew, Apr. 19, 2008. BA in Mktg., U. Miss., 2003. Quarterback NY Giants, East Rutherford, NJ, 2004—. Recipient Conerly trophy, 2001, 2003, Maxwell award, 2003, Johnny Unitas Golden Arm award, 2003; named Super Bowl XLII MVP, 2008; named to Nat. Football Conf. Pro Bowl Team, NFL, 2008. Mem.: Sigma Nu (Athlete the Yr. 2001). Achievements include being the first overall selection in the NFL Draft, 2004; leading the NFL in: passes intercepted, 2007; being a member of Super Bowl XLII winning New York Giants, 2008. Office: c/o New York Football Giants Giants Stadium East Rutherford NJ 07073*

MANNING, ERIC, computer scientist, educator, dean, researcher; b. Windsor, Ont., Can., Aug. 4, 1940; g. George Gorman and Eleanor Katherine (Koehler) M.; m. Betty Goldring, Sept. 16, 1961; children: David, Paula; m. Eileen Walker, Sept. 10, 2005. BSc, U. Waterloo, Ont., 1961, MSc, 1962; PhD, U. Ill., 1965. Registered profl. engr., B.C. With MIT and Bell Tel. Labs., 1965-68; prof. computer sci. U. Waterloo, 1968-86, founding dir. computer comms. networks group, 1973-82; founding dir. Inst. for Computer Rsch., 1982-86; prof., dean engring. U. Victoria, B.C., Canada, 1986-92, prof. computer sci., elec. engring., 1993-2000, New Media Ctr./Nortel Networks Prof. Network Performance, 2000—03; prin. scientist, strategic advisor Syscor R&D Inc., 2003—05. NewMIC Chief Scientist, Networks Cluster, 2000-03; dir. Natural Sci. and Engring. Rsch. Coun. Can., exec. com., chair strategic grants com., 1982-87; dir. Comm. Rsch. Ctr., Govt. of Can., 1995-97, Consortium for Software Engring. Rsch., Ottawa, 1997-99; trustee B.C. Advanced Sys. Found., 1986-93; dir. Sci. Coun. B.C., 1988-91; bd. dirs. Can. Microelectric Corp.; adv. com. on artificial intelligence NRC, 1987-91; internat. rsch. adv. com. Alta. Informatics Cir. Rsch. Excellence, 2002-, chair, 2007—; IBM chair computer sci. Keio U., Yokohama, 1992-93; hon. prof. South East U., Nanjing, China; guest prof. Tokyo U. Tech., 2005-07. Author: Fault Diagnosis of Digital Systems, 1970; contbr. articles to profl. jours V.p. Greater Victoria Concert Band, 1995-96; trumpet sect., Sooke Philharm. & 5th Field Arty. Band, Royal Can. Arty. Fellow IEEE, Engring. Inst. Can.; mem. Assn. Computing Machinery (mem. snowbird com. 1999-2001), Assn. Profl. Engrs. B.C., Soc. for Computer Simulation, Can. Inst. for Advanced Rsch. (adv. com. on artificial intelligence and robotics 1986-90), Can. Assn. for Computer Sci. (pres. 1994-2000), Can. Soc. for Fifth Generation Rsch. (trustee 1987-88), B.C. Microelectronics Soc. (bd. dirs. 1986-87). Avocations: amateur radio, scuba diving, sailing, flying, musical performance. Home: 440 Simcoe St #1431 Victoria BC Canada V8V 1L3 Office: U Victoria Faculty Engring PO Box 3055 Victoria BC Canada V8W 3P6 Home Phone: 250-386-8039. Business E-Mail: eric.manning@engr.uvic.ca.

MANNING, FREDERICK JAMES, insurance company executive; b. Chgo., Oct. 20, 1947; s. Herbert and June Betty (Cohen) M.; m. Gail Hilary Phillips, Feb. 9, 1980; children: Elizabeth Sarah, David Charles. BS, U. Pa., 1969; JD, Harvard U., 1972. CPA. Treas. The Marmon Group, Inc., Chgo., 1973-77; chmn. bd. dirs., chief exec. officer Celtic Life Ins. Co., Chgo., 1978—; also chmn. bd. dirs., pres., chief exec. officer Celtic Group, Inc., Chgo., chmn., pres., ceo. Bd. dirs. Engineered ControlsInternat.Inc., mem. of Adv. Com. Kellogg Grd. Sch. of Mgmt. (dispute resolution research ctr.). Trustee Michael Reese Health Trust; trustee, v.p., asst. sec. Pritzker Family Philanthropic Fund; mem., pres. coun. U. Pa.; mem. adv. com. Dispute Resolution Rsch. Ctr., Kellogg Grad. Sch. Mgmt., Northwestern U., Evanston, Ill.; bd. trustee, Michael Reese Health Trust, Newberry Library. Mem. World Pres.'s Orgn., Chief Exec. Orgn., Std. Club, East Bank Club, Met. Club, Northmoor Country Club (Highland Park, Ill.), member of bd. dir. Exec. Com., Governance Com., Policy Com., Membership Com. & Fin. Com.(co-chmn.) AHIP. Office: Celtic Insurance Co 233 S Wacker Dr Ste 700 Chicago IL 60606-6393 Office Phone: 312-332-5401.

MANNING, J. RICHARD, lawyer; b. Seattle, Nov. 2, 1932; BA, Seattle U., 1954; LLB, Gonzaga U., 1960. Bar: Wash. 1960. Pvt. practice, Seattle. Chmn. Seattle adv. coun. Am. Arbitration Assn., 1985—96, Bd. Govs., 1997—2000; Mem. Law Adv. Bd. Gonzaga U., 1988—; pres. Wash. State Bar Assn., 2002—03. Chair US Supreme Ct. Hist. Soc., Wash., 2005—. Recipient Nat. Outstanding Svc. award, Am. Arbitration Assn., 1988, Wash. Law and Politics Super Lawyer award, Top 100 Lawyers award, 2002—04. Mem.: ABA, Wash. State Bar Assn. (pres. 2003), Assn. Trial Lawyers Am., King County Bar Found. (pres. 1991—93), Am. Judicature Soc., King County Bar Assn. (pres. 1995—96). Office: 925 Logan Bldg 500 Union St Seattle WA 98101 Office Phone: 206-623-6302. Business E-Mail: jmb@seanet.com.

MANNING, JEROME ALAN, retired lawyer; b. Bklyn., Dec. 31, 1929; s. Emanuel J. and Dorothy (Levine) M.; m. Naomi Jacobs, Oct. 31, 1954; children: Joy, Stephen, Susan. BA, NYU, 1950, LLB, 1952; LLM, Yale U., 1953. Bar: N.Y. 1953, Fla. 1977. Assoc. Joseph Trachtman, NYC, 1956-61; ptnr. Stroock & Stroock & Lavan, NYC, 1961-96; prof. NYU Sch. Law, 1956-96. Editor: NYU Law Rev.; author: Estate Planning, 1980, rev. edit., 2005, Estate Planning for Laymen, 1992. Trustee N.Y.U. Sch. Law. Capt. USAF, 1953-56. Home: 1661 Pine St #911 San Francisco CA 94109-3457 Office Phone: 212-806-6030. Personal E-mail: jmanning@stroock.com.

MANNING, JOHN WARREN, III, retired surgeon, medical educator; b. Phila., Nov. 24, 1919; s. John Warren Jr. and Edith Margaret (Reagan) M.; m. Muriel Elizabeth Johnson, Oct. 11, 1944; children: John, Melissa, Susan. BS in Chemistry with honors, Ursinus Coll., 1940; MD, U. Pa., 1943; postgrad., 1978. Diplomate Am. Bd. Surgery. Naval intern Pa. Naval Hosp., 1946; resident Saginaw (Mich.) Gen. Hosp., 1947-50; preceptor Dr. H.M. Bishop, 1950-52; pvt. practice Saginaw, 1950—. Sr. staff mem. Saginaw Gen. Hosp., St. Luke's Hosp., Saginaw; past chief of surgery, chmn. tissue com. St. Mary's Hosp., Saginaw; cons. VA Hosp., Saginaw; assoc. clin. prof. surgery Mich. State U., assoc. prof. surgery, 1976-92, prof. emeritus, 1992—; mem. search com. Saginaw Coop. Hosp. Contbr. articles to profl. publs. Lt. USN, 1942-46, PTO. Fellow ACS; mem. AMA, Mich. State Med. Soc., Saginaw Surg. Soc., Soc. Abdominal Surgeons, Am. Coll. Angiology, Soc. Am. Gastrointestinal Endoscopic Surgeons.

MANNING, JUDITH HUBERT, state legislator, real estate company executive; b. Ga., Oct. 24, 1942; children: Hank, Elizabeth. Postgrad., Vienna U., Austria, 1963-64; BS in Edn., U. Ga., 1964. Tchr. soc. studies Coll. Pk. H.S., Fulton County, Ga., 1966-67, McEachern Middle Sch., Cobb County, Ga., 1967-69; real estate agent, broker Hubert Realty Co., 1982—91; past real estate agent, broker, co-owner Manning Properties, Marietta, Ga., 1991—; mem. Dist. 32 Ga. House of Reps., Atlanta, 1997—. Mem. Retirement Com., Natural Resources Com., Banks and Banking Com.; active Women Leaders Summit, 1995, 96; mem. edn. task force Am. Legis. Exch. Coun. Del. 7th dist. Rep. Party Convention; past adv. pres. ARC; mem. Atlanta Regional Commn., Cobb Emergency Aid, Cobb Youth Leadership; mem. Girls, Inc., past chair, bd.dirs.; bd. dirs. Jubilee Fine Arts Fesival, OpenGate, Gateway Vis. and Info. Ctr., Dept. Family and Children Svcs.; past bd. dirs. Cobb Symposium, Vol. Atlanta; publicity chair, past bd. dirs. YMCA; vol. Kennestone Hosp.; vol. task force, exec. mem. United Way; 1st pres. Vol. Cobb-Marietta; vice-chmn. Friends of the Park; historian, past bd. dirs. Ptnrs. Fund; participant Women Leaders Summit, 1995-96. W. Wyman Pilcher Jr. Meml. scholar; recipient Leadership Cobb Class of 1984-85, Leadership Ga. Class of 89-90, Disting. Leadership award Nat. Assn. Cmty. Leadership, 1989, Phoenix award Cobb County Bd. Realtors, 1996. Mem. Nat. Assn. Realtors, Cobb-Marietta Jr. League, Hon. Comdrs. Assn., The Walker Sch. Parents Assn., Assn. Metro Atlanta DFCS (co-vice chmn.). Republican. Office: Dist 32 480 Davis Carnes Ln NW Marietta GA 30064-4716 also: 401-E State Capitol Atlanta GA 30334 Office Phone: 404-656-7857. Business E-Mail: judy.manning@house.ga.gov.*

MANNING, KENNETH ALAN, lawyer; b. Buffalo, July 22, 1951; s. Jack Edwin and Dorothea Ann (Ruhland) Manning; children: Michael John, Kathyrn Ann. BS in Engring. Sci., SUNY, Buffalo, 1974, JD, 1977. Bar: N.Y. 1978, U.S. Dist. Ct. (we. dist.) N.Y. 1978, U.S. Dist. Ct. (no. dist.) N.Y. 1980, U.S. Ct. Appeals (2d cir.) 1983, U.S. Ct. Appeals (3d cir.) 1988. Confidential law asst. to assoc. justice Appellate Divsn. 4th Dept., Buffalo, 1977—79; assoc. Phillips, Lytle, Hitchcock, Blaine & Huber, Buffalo, 1979—84; ptnr. Phillips Lytle LLP, Buffalo, 1985—. Vol. Lawyers Project, Erie County, 1985-2002, Criminal Appeals Program, Erie County, 1988-89; mem. Western N.Y. region NCCJ. Woodburn fellow SUNY, Buffalo, 1973-76. Mem. ABA (TIP sect.), N.Y. State Bar Assn. (ins. negligence sect.), Erie County Bar Assn., Gyro Club (pres. 1988), Park Club. Avocations: sports, hunting. Home: 167 Leicester Rd Buffalo NY 14217-2113 Office: Phillips Lytle LLP 3400 HSBC Ctr Buffalo NY 14203-2887 Office Phone: 716-847-7041.

MANNING, KENNETH PAUL, specialty chemical company executive; b. NYC, Jan. 18, 1942; s. John Joseph and Edith Helen (Hoffmann) M.; m. Maureen Lambert, Sept. 12, 1964; children: Kenneth J., John J., Elise, Paul, Carolyn, Jacqueline. BME, Rensselaer Poly. Inst., 1963; postgrad., George Washington U., 1965-66; MBA in Ops. Rsch., Am. U., 1968. With W.R. Grace & Co., NYC, 1973-87, v.p. European consumer divsn., 1975-76, pres. ednl. products divsn., 1976-79, pres. real estate divsn., 1979-81, v.p. corp. tech. group, 1981-83, pres., CEO, Ambrosia Chocolate Co. divsn. Milw., 1983-87; group v.p. Sensient Technologies Corp., Milw., 1987-89, exec. v.p., dir., 1989-92, pres., COO, dir., 1992-96, pres., CEO, dir., 1996—, chmn., CEO, 1997—. Bd. dirs. Badger Meter, Inc., Milw., Sealed Air Corp., Saddle Brook, N.J. Served as lt. USN, 1963-67; rear adm. USNR, ret. Decorated Legion of Merit, Nat. Def. medal, others. Mem. ASME, Am. Chem. Soc., Navy League, US Naval Inst., Naval Res. Assn., Milw. Metro Assn. Commerce, Knights of Malta. Republican. Roman Catholic. Office: Sensient Technologies Corp 777 E Wisconsin Ave Milwaukee WI 53202-5304

MANNING, KEVIN JAMES, academic administrator; b. NYC, Nov. 8, 1944; s. James and Helen (Gurry) M.; m. Sara Garrity; children: Elizabeth Ann, Meagan Garrity, Kevin James. BA in Theatre, Webster U., St. Louis, 1967; MS in Pers., Shippensburg U., Pa., 1976; PhD in Ednl. Adminstrn., Ohio State U., 1982; attended, Inst. Ednl. Mgmt., Harvard U., 1989. Adminstr., intr. Webster U., St. Louis, 1967-68; mgmt recruiter L.S. Brady, Inc., St. Louis, 1969; adminstr. Washington U., St. Louis, 1969-71; admissions counselor Elizabethtown Coll., Pa., 1972-76, dir. admissions Pa., 1976-80, spl. asst. to pres. Pa., 1982-83; rsch. asst. Ohio State U., Columbus, 1980-82; chief staff Gov.'s Commn. Higher Edn., Harrisburg, Pa., 1983-84; v.p. devel. Immaculata Coll., Pa., 1984-2000; pres. Stevenson U. (formerly Villa Julie Coll.), Md., 2000—. Workforce adv. panel Commonwealth of Pa. Mem. attractions com. Phila. Econ. Devel. Coalition, 1988—; bd. trustees Peirce Coll., 1998—2001; mem. oversight com. Vision 2030; bd. dirs. Chester County Export Ctr., Exton, Pa., 1990. Mem. Sr. Devel. Officers Phila. (chmn. 1995-96), Great Valley C. of C. (bd. dirs. 2004-), Greater Balt. Com. (bd. dirs. 2007-), Maryland Bus. Roundtable (bd. dirs. 2007-). Avocations: reading, art, films, golf. Home: 1907 Billy Barton Cir Reisterstown MD 21136 Office: Stevenson U 1525 Greenspring Valley Rd Stevenson MD 21153-0641 Office Phone: 443-334-2203. E-mail: prs-mann@mail.vjc.edu.

MANNING, MICHAEL J., lawyer; b. Wichita, Kans., July 18, 1944; BA, U. Kans., 1966; JD, Washburn U., 1969. Bar: Kans. 1969, DC 1970. Mem. Fulbright & Jaworski LLP, Washington. Mem.: ABA, Fed. Energy Assn., D.C. Bar, Phi Alpha Delta. Office: Fulbright & Jaworski Market Sq 801 Pennsylvania Ave NW Fl 3-5 Washington DC 20004-2623

MANNING, PETER KIRBY, criminal justice educator; b. Salem, Oreg., Sept. 27, 1940; s. Kenneth Gilbert and Esther Amelia (Gibbard) M.; m. Victoria Francis Shaughnessy, Sept. 1, 1961 (div. 1981); children— Kerry Patricia, Sean Peter, Merry Kathleen; m. Betsy Cullum-Swan, Aug. 4, 1991 (div. 1997). BA, Willamette U., 1961; MA, Duke U., 1963, PhD, 1966; MA (hon.), Oxford U., Eng., 1983. Instr. sociology Duke U., 1964-65; asst. prof. sociology U. Mo., 1965-66, Mich. State U., East Lansing, 1966-70, assoc. prof. sociology and psychiatry, 1970-74, prof., 1974—; prof. criminal justice, 1993—. Beto chair lectr. Sam Houston State U., 1990; Ameritech lectr. E. Ky. U., 1993; vis. lectr. U. Las Andes, Meridá Venezuela, 2001—03, 2005; vis. prof. U. Victoria, 1968, MIT, 1982, SUNY, Albany, 1982, U. Mich., 1990—91, York U., Toronto, 1999; vis. sr. scholar Northeastern U. Coll. Criminal Justice, 2001, E.V. and E.M. Brooks chair, 2001—; cons. Nat. Inst. Law Enforcement and Criminal Justice, U.S. Dept. Justice, Rsch. Triangle Inst., NSF, Nat. Health and Med. Rsch. Coun., Australia, 1980—, Social Sci. Rsch. Coun. Eng., AID, Jamaica, 1991, Sheehy com. Police Pay and Performance, England, 1993. Author: Sociology of Mental Health and Illness, 1975, Police Work, 1977, 2d edit., 1997, The Narcs' Game, 1980, 2d edit., 2003, Semiotics and Fieldwork, 1987, Symbolic Communication, 1988, Organizational Communication, 1992, Private Policing, 1999, Policing Contingencies, 2003, The Technology of Policing, 2008; also book chpts., articles in profl. jours.; cons. editor series: Principal Themes in Sociology; co-editor Sage Series in Qualitative Methods, Crime, Law and Social Change, 2004—; mem. editl. bd. numerous jours. in social scis. Recipient Bruce Smith Sr. award Acad. Criminal Justice Scis., 1993, O.W. Wilson award, 1997, Charles H. Cooley award Mich. Sociol. Assn., 1994; NDEA fellow, 1962-64, NSF fellow, 1965, fellow Balliol Coll., Oxford U., 1982-83, vis. fellow Wolfson Coll., Oxford U., 1981, 82-83, fellow, 1984-86; Am. Bar Found. rsch. fellow, 1998; Rockefeller resident, Bellagio, Italy, 2000. Mem. Am. Soc. Criminology, Am. Sociol. Assn., Acad. Criminal Justice Scis., Brit. Soc. Criminology, Internat. Sociol. Assn., Midwest Sociol. Soc., Soc. Study Social Problems, Soc. Study Symbolic Interaction (spl. recognition award 1990, v.p. 1992-93, program chair 1993), Internat. Soc. Semiotics and Law. Office: Northeastern U Coll Criminal Justice Boston MA 02115 Office Phone: 617-373-7748. Personal E-mail: manningpk@hotmail.com.

MANNING, PEYTON WILLIAMS, professional football player; b. New Orleans, Mar. 24, 1976; s. Archie and Olivia Manning; m. Ashley Thompson, Mar. 17, 2001. BA in Speech Comm., U. Tenn., 1998. Quarterback Indpls. Colts, 1998—. Founder PeyBack Found., 1999. Recipient Am. Dream award, Hudson Inst., 2001, Henry P. Iba Citizen Athlete award, 2002, Bert Bell award, Maxwell Club, 2003—04, John Wooden trophy, Athletes for a Better World, 2004, ESPY award, Best NFL Player, ESPN, 2004, ESPY award, Best Championship Performance, 2007, Byron "Whizzer" White Humanitarian award, 2005, Walter Payton Man of Yr. award, 2005; named NFL MVP, AP, 2003, 2004, 2008, NFL Player of Yr., The Sporting News, 2003, 1st Team All-Pro, AP, 2003—05, 2008, NFL Offensive Player of Yr., 2004, NFL Pro Bowl MVP, 2005, Super Bowl XLI MVP, NFL, 2007; named one of The Most Influential People in the World of Sports, Bus. Week, 2007, 2008; named to Am. Football Conf. Pro-Bowl Team, NFL, 1999—2000, 2002—08. Achievements include leading the NFL in: interceptions, 1998, pass attempts, 1998, completions, 2000, 2003, passing yards, 2000, 2003, touchdown passes, 2000, 2004, 2006; setting the NFL single season record for most touchdown passes (49), 2004; member of Super Bowl XLI winning Indianapolis Colts, 2007. Office: Indianapolis Colts PO Box 535000 Indianapolis IN 46253-5000 also: Indianapolis Colts 7001 West 56th Strreet Indianapolis IN 46254*

MANNING, R. DAVIS, physiologist, educator; s. Roy D. and Beulah R. Manning; m. DeAnn L. Lewis. PhD, U. MS Med. Ctr, Jackson, 1973. Prof. U. MS Med. Ctr., 1973—. Mem.: The Am. Heart Assn. (Harry Goldblatt award 1995). Office: Univ MS Med Ctr 2500 N State St Jackson MS 39216 Business E-Mail: dmanning@physiology.umsmed.edu.

MANNING, ROBERT HENDRICK, retired audio-visual services director, retired communications educator; arrived in USA, 1947, naturalized, 1952; s. William and Gertrude (Unk) Manning. BS, No. Mich. U., 1974. Lic. capt. USCG. Instr. sailing USCG Acad., New London, Conn., 1959-63; dir. audio visual/media svcs. No. Mich. U., Marquette, 1965-93, capt. univ. rsch. vessel, 1977-79, dir. audio visual svcs. emeritus; dir. devel. Bresnan Comm. Co., Marquette, 1993-97; pub. rels. dir. Charter Comm., 2000—02; pvt. yacht capt., 2002—. Host (TV series) Ask the Doctors, Sta. WNMU-TV, 1977—98. With USCG, 1959—65. Mem.: Royal Nat. Lifeboat Inst., Navy League of the US, US Naval Inst., Marquette-Alger County Med. Soc. (hon.), USCG Acad. Alumni Assn. and Found., Northern Mich. U. Alumni Assn., Am. Radio Relay League. Avocations: astronomy, sailing, amateur radio. Home and Office: PO Box 309 Marquette MI 49855-0309

MANNING, ROBERT THOMAS, internist, educator; b. Wichita, Kans., Oct. 16, 1927; s. Thomas Earl and Mary Francis (Schlegel) M.; m. Jane Bell, July 29, 1949; children: Mary Kay Fausch, Phillip Trenton, Susan Ann Shiba. AB, Wichita U., 1950; MD, Kans. U., 1954; DHL, Med. Coll. Hampton Rds., 1991. Diplomate Am. Bd. Internal Medicine. Intern Kansas City (Mo.) Gen. Hosp., 1954-55; resident Kans. U., Kansas City, 1955-58; from asst. prof. to prof. Kans. U. Med. Ctr. Sch. of Medicine, Kansas City, 1958-71, assoc. dean students, 1969-71; dean Eastern Va. Med. Sch., Norfolk, Va., 1971-74, chmn., prof. internal medicine, 1974-77; prof. internal medicine U. Kans. Sch. of Medicine, Wichita, 1977-93; prof. emeritus U. Kans. Sch. Medicine, Wichita, 1993—; assoc. dean, clin. affairs U. Kans. Sch. of Medicine, Wichita, 1985-89; chmn. internal medicine U. Kans. Sch. Medicine, Wichita, 1987—89; pres. Wesley Med. Rsch. Inst., 1986-88. Nat. cons. surgeon gen. USAF, 1973-78. Author: Major's Physical Diagnosis, 9th edit., 1982; contbr. articles to profl. jours. Pres. Kans. Health Ethics, Inc., 1994-96. With US Army Air Corps, 1945—47. Recipient Advanced Achievement award Am. Bd. Internal Medicine, 1987. Fellow ACP (laureate Kans. chpt., bd. govs. Kans. 1984-88); mem. Am. Fedn. Clin. Rsch., Cen. Soc. Clin. Rsch., Am. Assn. Study Liver Disease, Sigma Xi, Alpha Omega Alpha. Presbyterian. Avocations: woodworking, golf. Home: 126 Trail Of The Flowers Georgetown TX 78633-4814 Personal E-mail: rmannsun@suddenlink.net.

MANNING, SYLVIA, academic administrator, language educator; b. Montreal, Que., Can., Dec. 2, 1943; came to U.S., 1967; d. Bruno and Lea Bank; m. Peter J. Manning, Aug. 20, 1967; children— Bruce David, Jason Maurice BA, McGill U., 1963; MA, Yale U., 1964, PhD in English, 1967. Asst. prof. English Calif. State U.-Hayward, 1967-71, assoc. prof., 1971-75, assoc. dean, 1972-75; assoc. prof. U. So. Calif., 1975-94, prof., assoc. dir. Ctr. for Humanities, 1975-77, assoc. dir. Ctr. for Humanities, 1975-77, chmn. freshman writing, 1977-80, chmn. dept. English, 1980-83, vice provost, exec. v.p., 1984-94; prof. English U. Ill., Champaign, 1994—, v.p. for acad. affairs, prof. English, 1994—, interim chancellor Chgo., 1999-2000, chancellor, 2000—08; pres. Higher Learning Commn., North Ctrl. Assn., 2008—. Author: Dickens as Satirist, 1971; Hard Times: An Annotated Bibliography, 1984. Contbr. essays to mags. Woodrow Wilson fellow, 1963-64, 66-67 Mem. MLA, Dickens Soc. Office Phone: 312-263-0456. Business E-Mail: smanning@hlcommission.org.

MANNING, TIMOTHY W., federal agency administrator; b. 1970; BS in Geology, Ea. Ill. U., 1993; grad., Naval Postgrad. Sch. Ctr. Homeland Def. & Security, Monterey, Calif. Dep. cabinet sec. N.Mex. Dept. Pub. Safety; homeland security adv. to Gov. Bill Richardson N.Mex.; various positions N.Mex. Dept. Homeland Security & Emergency Mgmt., chief Emergency Ops. Bur., state dir. emergency mgmt., 2003—05, dir., 2005—05, 2007—09; adminstr. for nat. preparedness, Fed. Emergency Mgmt. Agy. (FEMA) US Dept. Homeland Security, Washington, 2009—. Chair Gov.'s Homeland Security Adv. Com.; co-chair Nat. Homeland Security Consortium; commr. Emergency Mgmt. Accreditation Program. Mem.: Nat. Emergency Mgmt. Assn. (regional v.p., chair homeland security com.). Office: FEMA US Dept Homeland Security 500 C St SW Washington DC 20472 Office Phone: 202-646-2500.*

MANNING, W. ROBERT, JR., bank executive; B in Acctg. and Fin., U. Akron, Ohio, MBA, JD, U. Akron, Ohio; grad. with honors, Stonier Grad. Sch. Banking. With Nat. City Corp., 1977—, various mgmt. positions in fin. acctg., retail banking and trust and investments, mgr. retail delivery systems' planning and automation divsn., group mgr. customer focus initiative, sr. v.p., mgr. consumer loan svcs. and consumer lending divsns., exec. v.p., mgr. retail svcs. and direct banking, head Best in Class initiative, sr. v.p. lending svcs. Office: Nat City Corp Nat City Ctr 1900 E Ninth St Cleveland OH 44114-3484 Office Phone: 216-222-2000.

MANNING, WILLIAM DUDLEY, JR., retired specialty chemical company executive; b. Tampa, Fla., Mar. 7, 1934; s. William Dudley and Rebecca (Reid) M.; m. Carol Randolph Gillis, June 30, 1962; children: Carol Randolph, Rebecca Barrett, Anne Gillis. BA in Chemistry, Fla. State U., 1957. Sales rep. Amoco Chem. Co., St. Louis and Cleve., 1959-63; sales engr. The Lubrizol Corp., Tulsa, 1963-64, southwestern regional sales mgr., 1964-66, mgr. chem. product sales Wickliffe, Ohio, 1966-72, sales mgr., western U.S., 1972, gen. sales mgr., asst. div. head-sales, 1972-79, mktg. mgr., asst. div. head-sales, 1979-80, v.p. mktg., 1980-81, v.p., bus. devel. div., 1981-85, sr. v.p. sales and mktg., 1985-87; pres. Lubrizol Petroleum Chems. Co., Wickliffe, 1987-94; sr. v.p., asst. to pres. The Lubrizol Corp., 1994; cons., investor, 1994—. Bd. dirs. NYCO America LLC, CEO, Gates Mills, Ohio, Robbins and Myers, Dayton, Ohio. Trustee Vocat. Guidance Svcs., Cleve., 1991-2000, Borromeo Sem., 2000—2008. With USAR, 1957-63. Mem. Soc. Automotive Engrs. (assoc.), Kirtland Country Club (v.p. 1986-88, pres. 1988-89), Tavern Club (trustee 1986-91), Chagrin Valley Hunt Club. Republican. Roman Catholic. Office Phone: 440-423-0561. E-mail: wdmann4@cs.com.

MANNING-SMITH, KELLY ANN, dean of students; b. Dwight, Ill., Mar. 20, 1964; d. John Edwin Manning and Sue Ellen Jericho; m. Paul Vincent Smith, Sept. 4, 1982; children: Amanda Marie Smith, Jessica Lynn Smith, Joseph Paul Smith, Allyssa Nicole Smith. BEd, Ill. State U., Normal, 1994—98; MA in Ednl. Leadership, Aurora U., Ill., 2002—04. Cert. secondary edn. tchr. Ill., 1998, elem. edn. tchr. Ill., 1998. Learning behavior specialist Joliet Twp. HS, Ill., 1998—. Presenter in field, 2006. Coach Channahon Pk. Dist., Ill., 1995—2004; mem. Sch. PTO, Channhon, 1998—2006, Athletic Boosters, Channahon, 1998—2006, Music Boosters, Channhahon, 1998—2006; election judge Will County Ct. Ho., Channahon, 1999. Grantee Creative Classroom Proposal, JTHS Found., 2004; Creative Instrn. grant, Ill. Coun. Children Behavioral Disorders, 2000. Mem.: Assn. Curriculum & Instrn., Minooka Garden Soc., Ill. Coun. Exceptional Children (webmaster 1999—2000). D-Conservative. Meth. Avocations: reading, gardening, travel, hiking, bicycling. Office: Joliet Twp HS 201 E Jefferson St Joliet IL 60432 Office Phone: 815-727-6714. Business E-Mail: kmanning@jths.org.

MANNINO, EDWARD FRANCIS, lawyer, educator; b. Abington, Pa., Dec. 5, 1941; s. Sante Francis and Martha Anne (Hines) M.; m. Mary Ann Vigilante, July 17, 1965 (div. 1990); m. Antoinette K. O'Connell, June 25, 1993; children: Robert John, Jennifer Elaine. BA with distinction, U. Pa., 1963, LLB magna cum laude, 1966. Bar: Pa. 1967. Law clk. 3d cir. U.S. Ct. Appeals, 1966-67; assoc. Dilworth, Paxson, Kalish & Kauffman, Phila., 1967-71, ptnr., 1972-86, co-chmn. litigation dept., 1980-86, sr. ptnr., 1982-86; sr. prin. Elliott, Mannino & Flaherty, PC, Phila., 1986-90; chmn. Mannino Griffith PC, Phila., 1990-95; sr. ptnr. Wolf, Block, Schorr & Solis-Cohen, Phila., 1995-98; ptnr., chair litig. practice Akin, Gump, Strauss, Hauer & Feld LLP, Phila., 1998—2008; chair Mannino Law Firm, 2009—. Hearing examiner disciplinary bd. Supreme Ct. Pa., 1986—89, mem. adv. com. on appellate ct. rules, 1989—95; lectr. Temple U. Law Sch., 1968—69, 1971—72; mem. Phila. Mayor's Sci. and Tech. Adv. Com., 1976—79; project mgr. Pa. Environ. Master Plan, 1973; chmn. Pa. Land Use Policy Study Adv. Com., 1973—75; chmn. adv. com., hon. faculty history dept. U. Pa., 1980—85, lectr. Am. history, 2001—. Author: Lender Liability and Banking Litigation, 1989, Business and Commercial Litigation: A Trial Lawyer's Handbook, 1995, The Civil RICO Primer, 1996; mem. editl. bd. Litig. mag., 1985-87, Comm. Lending Litig. News, 1988-2001, Bank Bailout Litig. News, 1989-93, Bus. Torts Reporter, 1988-2005, Practical Litigator, 1989-2003, Civil RICO Report, 1991-2001; contbr. articles to profl. jours. Pres. parish coun. Our Mother of Consolation Ch., 1977-79; bd. overseers U. Pa. Sch. Arts and Scis., 1985-89, chmn. recruitment and retention of faculty com.; commonwealth trustee Temple U., 1987-90, audit, bus. and fin. coms. Named one of Nation's Top Litigators Nat. Law Jour., 1990, Pa.'s Top Ten Trial Lawyers, 1999, Best Lawyers in Am., Am.'s Leading Bus. Lawyers. Fellow Am. Bar Found., ABA (chmn. various coms.), Am. Law Inst., Hist. Soc. U.S. Dist. Ct. Ea. Dist. Pa. (bd. dirs.), Pa. Bar Assn., Phila. Bar Assn. (gov. 1975), Pa. Soc., Order of Coif, Phi Beta Kappa, Phi Beta Kappa Assocs. Democrat. Roman Catholic. Office: Mannino Law Firm Ste 400 600 W Germantown Pike Plymouth Meeting PA 19462 Office Phone: 610-940-1630. Office Fax: 610-825-7579. Business E-Mail: efmannino@comcast.net.

MANNINO, J. DAVIS, psychologist, educator, author; b. Patchoque, NY, Sept. 27, 1949; s. Joseph I. and Adrienne Adele (Davis) M. BA magna cum laude, SUNY, Stony Brook, 1971; MSW summa cum laude, San Francisco State U., 1974; EdD in Counseling and Ednl. Psychology, U. San Francisco, 1989. Lic. psychotherapist, Calif.; lic. clin. social worker, Calif., marriage, family and child counselor. Instr. U. Malaysia, 1974-76; dir. refugee programs City San Francisco, 1979-82; instr. U. San Francisco, 1979-85; pvt. practice specializing in psychology San Francisco, Sonoma Counties, 1979—. Cons. foster care Calif. State Legis., 1980, cmty. rels., San Francisco Police Dept., 1982-87, Hospice Sonoma County, 1990, Sonoma County Mental Health, 1990; forensic task force on AIDS, San Francisco Pub. Health Dept., 1984-85; child abuse investigation supr. City of San Francisco, 1985-88; supr. Reasonable Efforts to Families Unit; project coord. Edna McConnell Clark Found. Family Mediation Demonstration Grant, 1987-88; prof. human sexuality, death and dying, Intro. to Psychology Santa Rosa Jr. Coll., 1990—, chair dept. behavioral scis.; commr. Calif. Bd. Behavioral Sci. Examiners, 1990. Author: Grieving Days, Healing Days, 1997, Sexually Speaking, 1998, Sexual Themes and Variations, The New Millennium, 2000; contbr. articles to profl. jours.; local psychology columnist Art of Caregiving, 1986—. Mem. APA, NASW (diplomate clin. social work), Orthopsychiat. Assn., Am. Assn. Counseling and Devel., Am. Soc. Sex Educators, Counselors and Therapists, Soc. for Sci. Study Sexuality, Calif. Assn. Marriage Family and Child Therapists, Golden Gate Bus. Assn. (ethics com. 1986, Disting. Svc. award, 1985), Am. Assn. Marriage and Family Therapists, Nat. Register Clin. Social Workers, Lions (bd. dirs. San Francisco chpt. 1986). Avocations: running, gym and fitness, writing, gardening. Office: PO Box 2880 Guerneville CA 95446-2880 Office Phone: 707-524-1742. E-mail: psychdavis@aol.com. *Personal philosophy: A life is to be enjoyed not endured. How people get through life is a piece of art not a piece of cake. Everyday is a canvas and our actions brushstrokes, let our brushstrokes be bold each day.*

MANNINO, J(OSEPH) ROBERT, medical educator; b. Altoona, Pa., May 6, 1941; s. Joseph Robert and Helen La Rue (Menza) M.; m. Rosemary Kathleen McGrath, Apr. 8, 1978; 1 child, Angela Christine. BS, Juniata Coll., 1963; MA, East Carolina U., 1965; PhD, Colo. State U., 1974; DO, Kansas City Coll. Osteo. Med., 1971. Diplomate Am. Osteo. Bd. Family Practice. Intern Rocky Mountain Hosp., Denver, 1971-72; physician pvt. practice, Denver, 1972-77; dir. med. edn.nt Kansas City Coll. Osteo. Medicine, 1977-80; prof. family medicine Ohio U. Coll. Osteo. Medicine, Athens, 1981-94, Nova Southeastern U., Coll. Osteo. Medicine, North Miami Beach, Fla., 1994—2000. Teaching asst. physiology East Carolina U., 1965; coord. rsch. Phila. Coll. Osteo. Medicine, 1966-67; asst. dir. med. edn. Rocky Mountain Hosp., Denver, 1972-73, dir. med. edn., 1975-77, bd. trustees, 1975-77; dir. gen. practice residency Drs. Hosp., Columbus, 1980-94; dir. med. edn. & program dir. family practice residency North Broward Hosp. Dist., Ft. Lauderdale, Fla., 1994-96; clin. assoc. Cleveland Clinic, Ft. Lauderdale, 1996-2000; regional med. dir., Wexfold Health Sources, Ft. Lauderdale, Fla., 2002—2003; cons. in field. Contbr. articles to profl. jours. Rsch. fellow Colo. State U., 1968-69. Fellow Am. Coll. Osteo. Family Practice, Am. Soc. Colposcopy & Cervical Pathology, Am. Soc. Laser Medicine & Surgery; mem. Am. Osteo. Assn., Am. Coll. Cyrosurgery, N.Y. Acad. Scis., Fla. Soc. Osteo. Medicine, Fla. State Soc. Am. Coll. Osteo. Family Physicians, Broward County Acad. Fla. Soc. Osteo. Medicine, Endocrine Soc., Chi Beta Phi. Republican. Roman Catholic. Avocation: restoring antique cars.

MANNIX, CHARLES RAYMOND, law educator; b. Elizabeth, NJ, Aug. 2, 1950; s. Charles Raymond and Helen Joan (French) M. BA, Duquesne U., 1972, MA, JD, Duquesne U., 1976; MPA, Harvard U., 1998. Bar: Iowa 1976, NY 1996, Va. 1980, DC 1980, NH 2006, Vt. 2007, US Ct. Claims 1976, US Tax Ct. 1976, US Ct. Mil. Appeals 1976, US Ct. Internat. Trade 1976, US Ct. Appeals (4th and 5th cirs.) 1977, US Ct. Appeals (DC cir.) 1977, US Dist. Ct. Va. 1980, US Dist. Ct. NH 2006, US Supreme Ct. 1980, US Ct. Appeals (DC cir.) 1980, US Ct. Appeals (fed. cir.) 1982, NY 1996, Supreme Ct. Vt., 2007. Commd. 2d lt. USAF, 1973, advanced through grade to col., 2004; intern UN Office of Legal Affairs, NYC, 1975; res. legal advisor Air Force Surgeon Gen., 2001—06; assoc. dean, COO, Dartmouth Med. Sch., Hanover, NH, 2004—, asst. prof. medicine, 2004—. Adj. faculty Georgetown U., Washington, 1984-99; assoc. prof. and chmn. dept. med. jurisprudence, 1987-2004, asst. prof. mil. medicine, v.p. and gen. counsel Uniformed Svcs. U. Health Scis, 1987-2004. Decorated Commendation medal with 2 oak leaf clusters, USAF, 1978, Nat. Def. medal with 2 stars, Reserve medal with "m", 2002, Meritorious Svc. medal with 2 oak leaf clusters, 2003, Global War on Terror medal, 2004, Legion Merit, 2006, Army Commendation, 2004. medal of Outstanding Unit award, AF Organizational Excellence award, Uniformed Svcs. U. Helath Scis. Disting. Svc. medal. Mem. ABA, DC Bar Assn., Va. State Bar Assn., Vt. Bar Assn., NH Bar Assn., Am. Soc. Internat. Law, Am. Soc. Law and Medicine, Am. Arbitration Assn. (arbitrator), Am. Acad. Hosp. Attys., Nat. Assn. Coll. and Univ. Attys., NY State Bar Assn., Bar Assn. City of NY, Assn. Mil. Surgeons US, Harvard Club NY and Boston. Office: Office of the Dean Dartmouth Med Sch 1 Rope Ferry Rd Hanover NH 03755 Personal E-mail: charlesmannix@msn.com.

MANNIX, KEVIN LEESE, lawyer; b. Queens, NY, Nov. 26, 1949; s. John Warren Sr. and Editta Gorrell M.; m. Susanna Bernadette Chiocca, June 1, 1974; children: Nicholas Chiocca, Gabriel Leese, Emily Kemper. BA, U. Va., 1971, JD, 1974. Bar: Oreg. 1974, U.S. Ct. Appeals (9th cir.) 1976, U.S. Supreme Ct. 1978, Guam 1979. Law clk. to judge Oreg. Ct. Appeals, Salem, 1974—75; asst. atty. gen. Oreg. Dept. Justice, Salem, 1975—77, Govt. of Guam, Agana, 1977—79; judge adminstrv. law Oreg. Workers' Compensation Bd., Salem, 1980—83; assoc. Lindsay, Hart, Neil & Weigler, Portland, Oreg., 1983—86; pres. Kevin L. Mannix Profl. Corp., Salem, 1986—. Chmn. St. Joseph Sch. Bd., Salem, 1981-86; pres. Salem Cath. Schs. Corp., 1985; v.p. Salem Cath. Schs. Found., 1985-88, pres., 1988-90, 91-94, 2000—; chmn. bd. dirs. Blanchet Sch., 1995-; vice chair Oreg. Rep. Party, 1998-2000, chmn., 2003-05; state rep., 1989-97, 99-2001; state sen., 1998-99. Mem. Marion

Bar Assn., Rotary (bd. dirs. East Salem 1985-89, pres. 1987-88), KC. Republican. Avocations: photography, scuba diving, travel. Home: 375 18th St NE Salem OR 97301-4307 Office: 2009 State St Salem OR 97301-4349 Office Phone: 503-364-1913.

MANNWEILER, MARY-ELIZABETH, painter; b. Norwood, Ohio, June 23, 1916; d. Wilbur Lawrence Young Davis and Augusta Minnis (Newman) Davis; m. Robert Mays Lang, Sr., May 25, 1940 (dec. July 1981); children: Robert Mays Lang, Jr., Gary Davis Lang, Julianna Elizabeth Lang Crawford; m. Gordon Bannatyne Mannweiler, Apr. 17, 1982 (dec. Aug. 2001). Student, Miami U., Oxford, Ohio, 1935-37. Portrait painter; permanent collections; donated (with husband) stained glass window to Congl. Ch., Naugatuck, Conn. Past pres. Athena Club, Freeport, N.Y., Woodbury (Conn.) Woman's Club, 1977-78, Watertown (Conn.) Art League; past dir. Waterbury (Conn.) Symphony Orch.; pres. Mary Elizabeth and Gordon Mannweiler Found., Naugatuck, Conn.; trustee YMCA, Naugatuck; mem. scholarship com. Naugatuck H.S., 2003. Recipient blue ribbons for artwork; Paul Harris fellow Rotary, 2001; music room named in honor of Mr. and Mrs. Mannweiler Conn. Jr. Republic, Litchfield, 1997m Meml. Vol. award Naugatuck YMCA, 2005. Mem. DAR (regent Ruth Floyd Woodhull chpt. 1966-67, pres.). Home: 435 Hillside Ave Naugatuck CT 06770-2727

MANNY, CARTER HUGH, JR., architect, retired foundation administrator; b. Michigan City, Ind., Nov. 16, 1918; s. Carter Hugh and Ada Gage (Barnes) M.; m. Mary Alice Kellett, Dec. 6, 1942 (dec. Jan. 1994); children: Elizabeth, Carter Hugh III; m. Maya Moran, Dec. 27, 1995. AB magna cum laude, Harvard U., 1941, Indsl. Adminstr., 1942; Taliesin fellow, Scottsdale, Ariz., 1946; BS in Architecture, Ill. Inst. Tech., 1948. With Murphy/Jahn (name formerly Naess & Murphy and C.F. Murphy Assocs.), Chgo., 1948-83, partner, 1957-61; dir. 1st Citizens Bank, Michigan City, Ind., 1970-86; sr. v.p. Murphy/Jahn (name formerly Naess & Murphy and C.F. Murphy Assocs.), 1978-83. Mem. adv. com. on architecture Art Inst. of Chgo., 1982-2007, oversight com. Ill. Inst. Tech. Sch. of Architecture, Chgo., 1989-94; trustee Graham Found. Advanced Studies in Fine Arts 1956-74, exec. dir., 1972-93, hon. trustee, 1994—. Projects include O'Hare Internat. Airport, Chgo., FBI Hdqrs, Washington, First Nat. Bank Chgo, Chgo. Civic Center, Chgo. Bd. Trade. Fellow AIA (pres. Chgo. chpt. 1973, dir. Ill. coun. 1972-73), Soc. Archtl. Historians (dir. 1982-85), SAH, Chgo. Bldg. Congress (dir. 1978-83); mem. Phi Beta Kappa, Arts Club, Cliff Dwellers Club (Chgo., hon.). Home: 50 Parftridge Dr San Rafael CA 94901 Personal E-mail: cartermanny@hotmail.com.

MANOFF, RICHARD KALMAN, advertising executive, writer, public health service officer, consultant; b. Bklyn., June 24, 1916; s. Kalman and Sarah (Glatman) M.; m. Lucy B. Deutscher, Nov. 27, 1942; children: Robert K., Gregory P. BS, CCNY, 1937, postgrad., 1940. Asst. regional dir. War Manpower Commn., 1942-45; marketing dir. Welch Grape Juice Co., 1949-53; v.p. Kenyon & Eckhardt Advt., NYC, 1953-56; pres., chmn. bd. Richard K. Manoff Inc. Advt., NYC, from 1956; now pres. Manoff Internat. Inc.; spl. adv. mktg. and communications to exec. dir. UNICEF, 1980—. Dir. Thomas J. Lipton, Inc.; adj. prof. dept. health Scis. Sargent Coll. Allied Health Professions, Boston U., 1978—; lectr. pub. health Columbia U. Sch. Medicine, 1982-83; Mem. U.S. del. FAO World Conf., Rome, Italy, 1966; spl. advisor UNICEF and WHO, 1968-78; cons. spl. mission to Food and Agr. Ministry, Govt. India, AID, 1969; Ford Found. offices Pub. Edn. Pub. Broadcasting for children's TV; participant 1st World Conf. on Social Communication for Devel. Mass Communications, Mexico, 1970, 7th Asian Advt. Congress, Delhi, 1970, 3d Western Hemisphere Nutrition Congress, Fla., 1971, Internat. Conf. Nutrition, Nat. Devel. and Planning, Mass. Inst. Tech., 1971, Symposium Eating Patterns and Their Influence on Purchasing Behavior and Nutrition, Nev., 1971, Nutrition Workshop, AID, 1971, 9th Annual Summer Workshop Family Planning, 1971, 4th & 5th Seminar Workshop on Mgmt. and Planning of Population Family Planning Programs, 1971, New Products Symposium, 1971, Communication Seminar series Cornell U., 1971, Exploration The Frontiers of Nutritional Edn. Seminar, 1972, 9th Internat. Congress of Nutrition, Mexico, 1972, East-West Center Comml. Resources Conf. on Family Planning, Hawaii, 1972; Protein adv. group UN Systems Annual Mtg., 1973; mem. panel White House Conf. Food, Nutrition and Health, 1969; mem. Sec.'s Adv. Com. on Population Affairs, Dept. HEW, 1971-76; mem. adv. com. Population Reference Bur., Washington, 1977—, Population Inst., 1980—; mem. Nelson A. Rockefeller's Commn. on Critical Choices for Ams.; cons. HRSA Healthy Start Campaign to reduce infant mortality, 1991; bd. dirs. Population Comm. Internat.; Martin J. Forman Meml. lectr., Washington, 1993. Author: Social Marketing: New Imperative for Public Health, 1985. Bd. dirs. Planned Parenthood World Population, Pathfinder Fund, Boston, 1977-80, United Nutrition Edn. Found., Alexandria, Va., 1978—; mem. com. on internat. nutrition programs NAS-NRC, 1973; founder, mem. Com. for Shakespeare Festival, NYC; bd. visitors Grad. Sch. and Univ. Ctr., CUNY; mem. adv. bd., cons. to the pres. Henry J. Kaiser Family Found., 1987-91; dir. City Coll. Fund, 1990—. Recipient 5th Ann. Global award for media excellence Population Inst., China, 1985, Townsend Harris medal Alumni Assn. CCNY, 1986. Mem. Am. Assn. Advt. Agys. (gov. 1967—, sec.-treas. 1975—), Population Comms. Internat. (dir. 1992—), Friars Club, Harmonie Club (NYC), Century Assn. Home: 322 E 57th St New York NY 10022-2949

MANOLIO, TERI A., physician; d. Henry and Mary Jo Manolio. BS in Biochemistry, U. Md., Balt., 1976, MD, 1980; MHS in Epidemiology, Johns Hopkins Sch. of Hygiene and Pub. Health, Balt., 1987, PhD in Human Genetics and Genetic Epidemiology, 2001. Diplomate Nat. Bd. of Med. Examiners, 1981, Nat. Bd. of Internal Medicine, 1984, License to Practice Medicine Dept. of Health and Mental Hygiene/Md., 1987. Resident Boston City Hosp., 1980—84; chief resident DC General, 1983—84; fellow, divsn. internal medicine John Hopkins Hosp., 1984—87; med. officer, epidemiology and biometry program Nat. Heart, Lung, and Blood Inst., Bethesda, Md., 1987—94, dir., epidemiology and biometry program, divsn. epidemiology and clin. applications, 1994—2005; dir., office population genomics Nat. Human Genome Rsch. Inst., NIH, Bethesda, Md., 2005—, sr. advisor to the dir. for population genomics, 2005—. Prof. of preventive medicine and biometrics and clin. prof. of medicine Uniformed Services U. of the Health Sciences, Bethesda, Md., 1987—; active appointment, in-patient med. svcs. Nat. Naval Med. Ctr.; spkr. in field. Author several scientific research presentations, several book chapters; contbr. several sci. rsch. papers to profl. publs. Instr. NIH Tae Kwon Do Club, Bethesda, Md., 1996—2003. Recipient Presdl. Rank Award for Meritorious Svc., Pres., U.S., 2001, Phi Kappa Phi Honor Soc., U. Md., Coll. Pk., 1974, Phi Beta Kappa Honor Soc., 1976. Fellow: ACP, Am. Heart Assn. Office: Nat Human Genome Rsch Inst NIH Bldg 31 Rm 4B09 31 Center Dr MSC 2152 Bethesda MD 20892-2152 Office Phone: 301-402-2915. Office Fax: 301-402-4831. E-mail: manolio@nih.gov.*

MANOOGIAN, RICHARD ALEXANDER, consumer products company executive; b. Long Branch, NJ, July 30, 1936; s. Alex and Marie (Tatian) Manoogian; m. Jane Manoogian; children: James, Richard, Bridget. BA in Econs, Yale U., 1958. Asst. to pres. Masco Corp., Taylor, Mich., 1958-62, exec. v.p., 1962-68, pres., 1968-85, chmn. bd., CEO, 1985—2007, exec. chmn., 2007—. Chmn., dir. Mascotech, Inc., Trimas Corp.; dir. First Chgo. NBD Corp., Bank One Corp., Ford Motor Co., Metaldyne Corp., Detroit Renaissance, Am. Bus. Conf. Chmn. Alex & Marie Manoogian Found.; pres. & treas. Richard & Jane Manoogian Found.; co-founder Mackinac Island Cmty. Found., 2003; trustee U. Liggett Sch., State Dept. Fine Arts Comsn., Founder's Soc., Detroit Inst. Arts, Center for Creative Studies; trustee coun. Nat. Gallery Art. Named one of Top 200 Collectors, ARTnews, 2003—08. Mem. Yale Alumni Assn. Clubs: Grosse Pointe Yacht, Grosse Pointe Hunt, Country Club Detroit, Detroit Athletic. Office: Masco Corp 21001 Van Born Rd Taylor MI 48180-1300

MANOS, CHRISTOPHER LAWRENCE, lawyer, mediator; b. Ft. Bragg, NC, July 1, 1952; m. B.J. Osmon, June 14, 1974; children: Monica, Kelly. BS, U.S. Mil. Acad., 1974; JD, U. N.D., 1982. Bar: Mont. 1983, U.S. Dist. Ct. (Mont.) 1983, U.S. Ct. Appeals (9th cir.) 1983. Assoc. to ptrn. Moore, O'Connell, Refling & Manos, Bozeman, Mont., 1982-92; ptnr. Biglen & Manos, Big Timber, Mont., 1992—97, Manos law firm, 1997—2007; part-time dep. county atty. Sweet Grass county, 1992—98; county atty., 1998—2001. Trainer for mediators Ctr. for Collaborative Solutions and Alternative Dispute Resolution Assocs., Bozeman and Palo Alto, Calif., 1990—. Contbr. articles to profl. jours. Bd. dirs. Mont. Pub. TV, Bozeman, 1985-92, Mont. Coun. for Internat. Visitors, Bozeman, 1992; mem. Mont. Stat Bar Dispute Resolution Com., Helena, Mont., 1989-2001. Capt. U.S. Army, 1974-79. Col. USAR (ret.), 1979-2004. Mem. Mont. Mediation Assn., Am. Arbitration Assn., State Bar Mont. Office Phone: 406-442-7660.

MANOS, SARANTOS JOHN, physics educator; b. Bronx, NY, Dec. 7, 1941; s. Peter Sarantos and Carol Manos; m. Anna A. Manos; 1 child, Erika. AAS, Williamsville C.C., Buffalo, 1961; BS, U. So. Miss., 1968; MEd in Biology, Boston State Coll., 1972, MEd in Gen. Sci., 1982; MEd, Physics Inst., John D. O'Bryant Sch. Maths & Sci., 2006; postgrad., Pa. State U., U. Mass. Tchr. physics Boston Tech. H.S., 1969—; prof. physics Massasoit CC, Brock, Mass., 1983—. Coord. Simmons Math. Sci. Minority Enrichment Program, Boston Tech. H.S., 1998-2000; coord. after-sch. programs in elec. and mech. engring., biology and chemistry, Tufts U., 1978-84; instr. pre-engring. program North Shore C.C. Mem. Am. Assn. Physics Tchrs., Nat. Sci. Tchrs. Assn., Am. Inst. Physics Soc., New Eng. Sci. Tchrs. Assn., Mass. Assn. Sci. Tchrs., Greater Boston Physics Tchrs. Assn., N.Y. Acad. Scis. Home: 26 Kimberly Ln Randolph MA 02368-5524

MANOS, THOMAS G., investment company executive; b. Toronto, Ohio, Feb. 10, 1923; s. George A. and Louise G. (Clappas) Manos. BSBA, Kent State U., Ohio, 1950; MA, Hiram Coll., Ohio, 1950. Registered pub. acct., Ohio. Theater mgr. Manos Theatres Inc., Newton Falls, Ohio, 1940—41, 1946—49; open-hearth laborer Treadwell Constrn., Midland, Pa., 1941—42; with US mil. 11th Airborne Divsn., 1942—46; pub. acct. Data Processors Inc., Warren, Ohio, 1949—90; pres. Thedic Corp., Brookfield, Ohio, 2006—. 1st lt. US Army, 1942—46, PTO. Decorated Bronze star; recipient Nat. Leadership award, Bus. Adv. Coun., 2006. Home: 1076 S Park Dr Brookfield OH 44403

MANOSEVITZ, MARTIN, psychologist; b. Mpls., June 22, 1938; s. Julius and Ethel (Cohen) M.; m. Carolyn Heather Margulius, Sept. 17, 1959; children— Bradley, Jason. BA, U. Minn., Mpls., 1960, PhD, 1964. Diplomate in clin. psychology, psychoanalysis Am. Bd. Profl. Psychology. Asst. prof. psychology Rutgers U., 1964-67; asst. prof. psychology U. Tex., Austin, 1967-69, assoc. prof., 1969-75, prof., 1975-87; pvt. practice clin. psychology Austin, 1975-99, Aspen, Colo., 1999—. Adj. prof. psychology U. Tex., 1987-93; dir. psychol. svcs. CPC Capital Hosp., Austin, 1987-93, Shoal Creek Hosp., Austin, 1994-99; allied profl. staff Aspen Valley Hosp., 2000—; bd. dirs. Given Inst., Aspen. Trustee Austin-Travis County Mental Health-Mental Retardation Center, 1978-80. Fellow APA (bd. dirs. divsn. psychoanalysis, 1999-2000, membership chmn. 1997-2000, bd. mem. at large 1999-2000, treas. 2003-05), Acad. Psychoanalytic Psychology; mem. Colo. Psychol. Assn. (bd. dirs. 2005-06, pres.-elect 2006-07, pres 2007), Austin Soc. for Psychoanalytic Psychology (pres. 1994-95), Denver Psychoanalytic Soc. Office: 225 N Nill St Ste 203 Aspen CO 81611 Mailing: PO Box 7976 Aspen CO 81612 E-mail: mmanosev@earthlink.net.

MANOWITZ, PAUL, biochemist, researcher, educator; b. Monticello, NY, Dec. 13, 1940; s. Jacob M. and Rose (Levine) M.; m. Joyce L. Swartz, June 16, 1968; children: Neal J., Lauren H. BA in Chemistry with honors, Cornell U., 1962; PhD in Biochemistry, Brandeis U., 1967. Fellow NYU Sch. Medicine, 1967-70, instr., 1970-72; asst. prof. psychiatry U. Medicine and Dentistry N.J. Robert Wood Johnson Med. Sch., Piscataway, 1972-78, assoc. prof. psychiatry, 1978-96, prof. psychiaty, 1996—. Rsch. cons. VA Med. Ctr., Lyons, N.J., 1987—. Mem. editl. bd. Jour. of Studies on Alcohol, 1993—2003; contbr. articles to profl. jours. Mem. AAAS, Internat. Soc. for Biomed. Rsch. on Alcoholism, Am. Soc. Human Genetics, Am. Soc. Neurochemistry, Soc. Biol. Psychiatry, Rsch. Soc. on Alcoholism, Internat. Ombudsman Assn. Home: 7 Guernsey Ln East Brunswick NJ 08816-3506 Office: U Medicine and Dentistry NJ Robert Wood Johnson Med Sch 671 Hoes Ln Piscataway NJ 08854-5627 Office Phone: 732-235-4347. Personal E-mail: manowitz@comcast.net.

MANRIQUE, JAIME, writer, educator; b. Barranquilla, Atlantico, Colombia, June 16, 1949; came to U.S., 1966; became U.S. citizen, 1986. s. Gustavo Manrique and Soledad (Ardila) Reina; life partner William R. Sullivan. BA in English Lit., U. South Fla., Tampa, 1972; student, Columbia U., 1977. Instr. The Poetry Project, NYC, 1986, 90-92; vis. prof. writing The New Sch. U., Eugene Lang Coll., NYC, 1988-2000; assoc. prof. MFA program Columbia U., 2002—08. Writer-in-residence Yaddo, Saratoga Springs, N.Y., 1983-. 1991-98, The McDowell Colony, Peterborough, N.J., 1985-92, New Sch. for Social Rsch., 1989-91, Va. Ctr. for Creative Arts, 1990; bd. trustee PEN Am. Ctr., 2007-, chair membership com., 2008-, mem. exec. com., 2008-. Author: Los Adoradores de la Luna, 1976, Confesiones de un Critico Amateur, 1979, El Cadaver de Papa, 1980, Colombian Gold, 1983, Scarecrow, 1990, Latin Moon in Manhattan, 1992, Twilight at the Equator, 1997, My Night With Federico Garcia Lorca, 1999, Eminent Maricones: Arenas, Lorca, Puig, and Me, 1999, Mi Cuerpo Y Otros Poemas, 1999, Tarzan, My Body, Christopher Columbus, 2001, The Autobiography of Bill Sullivan, 2006, Our Lives Are the Rivers, 2006 (Internat. Latino Book award-Best Novel, Hist. Fiction, 2007). Recipient Nat. Poetry award Instituto de Cultura Y Bellas Artes, Cucuta, Colombia, 1975, EL awards, for El Diario, 2006, Commendation from the Office of Alan G. Heves, Controller of NYC for promoting and preserving Latino heritage and culture; grantee Found. for Contemporary Performance Arts, 1999; John Simon Guggenheim fellow 2000-01; named one of NY Most Disting. Latinos. Mem. PEN Am. Cen. (prison writing com., 1988-90, chmn. PEN Am. Ctr. fund for writers and editors with AIDS 1990-92). Democrat. Avocations: going to movies, hiking, travel, tennis, going to the beach. Personal E-mail: JMardila@aol.com.

MANRY, DAVID L., finance educator, consultant; 1 child, Jena Marie Ciers. PhD, U. Tex., Austin, 1992, MPA., 1990, BA. Asst. prof. U. Man., Winnipeg, Manitoba, Canada, 1992—94, Fla. Internat. U., Miami, Fla., 1994—2000, U. New Orleans, 2001—03, assoc. prof., 2003—07, prof., 2007—. Contbr. articles to rsch. jours. Fellowship, U. Tex., 1987—89. Office: Univ New Orleans Lakefront Campus KH-455 New Orleans LA 70148

MANSBACH, CHARLES, gastroenterologist, researcher; b. Norfolk, Va., Aug. 21, 1937; m. May Lynn Mansbach; children: Samuel Ross, Jonathan children: Harry. BA, Yale U., New Haven, 1963; MD, NYU, NYC, 1963. Lic. internal medicine Am. Bd. of Internal Medicine, gastroenterology Am. Bd. of Internal Medicine. Assoc. prof. of medicine Duke U. Med. Ctr., Durham, NC, 1970—86; prof. of medicine and physiology U. of Tenn., Memphis, 1986—. Lt. cdr. USNR, 1968—70. Recipient Merit Rev. grant, VA, 1971—2006; NIH rsch. grantee, 1975—. Achievements include research in Identified the pre-chylomicron transport vesicle. Office: Univ Tenn Ste 240 920 Madison Ave Memphis TN 38163 Business E-Mail: cmansbach@utmem.edu.

MANSBRIDGE, JANE JEBB, political scientist, educator; b. NYC, Nov. 19, 1939; d. Ronald and Georgia St. Claire (Mullen) Mansbridge; m. Christopher Jencks; 1 child, Nathaniel Mansbridge Jencks. BA, Wellesley Coll., 1961; MA, Harvard U., 1966, PhD, 1971. Asst. prof. polit. sci. U. Chgo., 1973-80; assoc. prof. Northwestern U., Evanston, Ill., 1980-86, prof. polit. sci., 1986-91, Jane W. Long prof. arts and scis., 1991-96; prof. J.F. Kennedy Sch. Govt. Harvard U., 1996-98, Adams prof. polit. leadership and democratic values, 1998—. Author: Beyond Adversary Democracy, 1980, Why We Lost the ERA, 1986; editor: Beyond Self-Interest, 1990; editor: (with Susan M. Okin) Feminism 2 vols., 1994; editor: (with Aldon Morris) Oppositional Consciousness, 2001; mem. editl. bd. Signs, Jour. Polit. Philosophy, Jour. Social Philosophy, Politics and Gender, Social Justice Rsch. Russell Sage Found. scholar, 1991-92; fellow Inst. for Advanced Study, 1985-86, Rockefeller Humanities, 1982-83, NSF, 1971-72, Ctr. Advanced Study in the Behavioral Scis., 1997-98, 2001-02, Radcliffe medal Radcliffe Grad. Soc., 2004; fellowship Radcliffe Inst. Advanced Study, 2004-05. Mem. Am. Acad. Arts and Scis., Am. Polit. Sci. Assn. (v.p. 1992-93, program chair 1990, exec. com. 1987-89, coun. 1987-89, pres. Women's Caucus 1996, Schuck award 1988, Kammerer award 1987), Soc. Advancement of Socio-Econs. (pres. 1992-93), Internat. Polit. Psychology Assn. (governing coun. 1993-94). Office: JF Kennedy Sch Govt 79 JFK St Cambridge MA 02138-5801 Office Phone: 617-495-9343.

MANSELL, DANNY EUGENE, construction executive; b. Flint, Mich., Mar. 18, 1957; m. Crystal Coleman. BA in History, Phys. Edn., U. Mich., Ann Arbor, 1979. Supr. Gen. Motors, 1978—87; sr. project mgr. Genesee Constrn. Services Co.; COO Domco Constrn. Services, 1991—. Mem. Johnston County Planning Bd., 2000—04; mem. exec. com. NC Rep. Party, 1995—2006; chmn. NC 2nd Congl. Dist., 2003—06; mem. Centenary United Meth. Ch., Selma, NC, coun. mem.; head Volunteers in Mission; bd. trustees Johnston Meml. Hosp., 2004—06; mem. adv. bd. Johnston County YMCA. Served with US Army, 1975—78, Ft. Bragg and Republic of Korea. Republican. Office: Domco Constrn Services 1139 Lehigh Ave Whitehall PA 18052 Office Phone: 610-266-5500.

MANSELL, DARREL LEE, JR., language educator; b. Canton, Ohio, Apr. 9, 1934; s. Darrel Lee and Virginia (Shepherd) M.; m. Elizabeth Meihack, Jan. 1957 (div. July 1970); 1 child, Benjamin Lloyd; m. Adriana Saviane, July 16, 1983. BA, Oberlin Coll., 1956; student, Oxford U., 1961—62; PhD, Yale U., 1963; MA (hon.), Dartmouth Coll., 1975. Instr. Dartmouth Coll., Hanover, NH, 1962-64, asst. prof., 1964-68, assoc. prof., 1968-74, prof., 1974-99, prof. emeritus, 1999—. Author: The Novels of Jane Austen, 1973; contbr. articles to scholarly jours. Mem.: Jane Austen Soc. N.Am. (founding patron), Phi Beta Kappa. Home: 2 Dana Rd Hanover NH 03755-2227 Office: Dartmouth Coll Dept English Hanover NH 03755

MANSELL, HENRY J., archbishop; b. NYC, Oct. 10, 1937; BA, St. Joseph Sem., Yonkers, 1959; attended, N.Am. Coll., Rome, Catholic U. America, 1965; Lic. in Sacred Theology, Gregorian U., Rome, 1963. Ordained priest Archdiocese of NY, NY, 1962, dir. Office of Parish Couns., 1972, vice-chancellor, 1985—88, chancellor, 1988—92, aux. bishop, 1993—95; ordained bishop, 1993; with various parishes NYC & Westchester County; bishop Diocese of Buffalo, NY, 1995—2003; archbishop Archdiocese of Hartford, Conn., 2003—. Roman Catholic. Office: Archdiocese of Hartford 134 Farmington Ave Hartford CT 06105-3784

MANSELL, KEVIN B., retail executive; b. St. Louis; Student, U. Mo. With Venture Store divsn. May Dept. Stores, 1975, positions in merchandising and buying; divisional mdse. mgr. Kohl's Corp., Menomonee Falls, Wis., 1982—87, gen. mdse. mgr., 1987, sr. exec. v.p. merchandising and mktg., 1998—99, pres., 1999—2008, pres., CEO, 2008—09, chmn., pres., CEO, 2009—. Bd. dirs. Kohl's Corp., 1999—. Office: Kohls Corp N56 W17000 Ridgewood Dr Menomonee Falls WI 53051-5660 Office Phone: 262-703-7000. E-mail: kevin.mansell@kohls.com.*

MANSERGH, GORDON DWIGHT, health maintenance and prevention researcher; b. St. Paul, Aug. 7, 1962; s. Gerald Gordon and Nancy Helen (Stuessy) M. BA, Gustavus Adolphus Coll., 1984; MA, Mich. State U., 1986; MEd, Boston U., 1991; postgrad., U. So. Calif., 1992—. Substance abuse counselor NORCAP Lodge, Foxboro, Mass., 1986-87; asst. dir. student affairs Chamberlayne Coll., Boston, 1987; asst. dir. orientation, off-campus svcs. Boston U., 1987-90, founding dir. Wellness Ctr., 1990-92; rsch. asst. U. So. Calif. Inst. for Prevention Rsch., 1992—; grant writer, program evaluator. Cons. EMT Calif. State Drug Prevention Tech. Assistance Project; rsch. asst. Kaiser Permanente So. Calif., 1992—, U.S. Ctrs. Disease Control and Prevention, 1995; co-founder, coord. Pasadena Area Colls. Together in Drug Prevention, 1993—; dir. PREVENT Consortium, 1991-92; drug prevention planning com. U.S. Dept. Edn., 1991-94; dir. Project DART, 1990-92; mem. N.W. Pasadena Health Coalition, L.A. Adolescent HIV Consortium, Mass. Coun. on Compulsive Gambling Prevention Coalition; chair Boston U. Substance Abuse Task Force, 1989-92; founding chair Boston AIDS Consortium Coll. Cmty. Edn. Com., 1988-90. Editor, co-author: The Wellness Resource Book, 1991, Adventures in Prevention, 1992, Wellnews, 1990-92. Vol. community svc. AIDS Action Com. Mass., Calif. AIDS Ride, AIDS Project L.A., Calif. AIDS Ride. Named Outstanding Young Man of Am., 1986-87; recipient Nat. Disting. Svc. Registry award, 1989-90; honoree Guild of St. Ansgar Gustavus Adolphus Coll., 1984; fellow Mich. State U., 1984-85. Mem. Am. Coll. Pers. Assn. (dir. wellness com. 1990-92), Am. Coll. Health Assn., Am. Psychol. Assn., Am. Pub. Health Assn., Soc. for Behavioral Medicine, Pi Lambda Theta.

MANSFIELD, ANGELA, councilwoman; b. Wolcott, Ind. 1 child, James. BS in Indsl. Mgmt., Purdue U.; JD, Ind. U., Indpls. Cert. pub. accountant in pub. acctg.; pvt. practice atty.; sect. chief, adminstrv., regulatory and tax litig. Office of the Atty. Gen., Ind.; gen. counsel Ind. State Budget Agency; councillor, dist. 2 Indpls.-Marion County City-County Coun.; mgr., tax adv. services DuCharme, McMillen & Associates. Vol. IndyFeral; bd. mem. Pk. Regency, Dance Kaleidoscope. Democrat. Office: 7836 Harcourt Springs Ct Indianapolis IN 46203 also: Indpls Marion County City County Coun 241 City County Bldg 200 E Washington St Indianapolis IN 46204 Office Phone: 317-872-3306, 317-327-4242. Business E-Mail: angelamansfield@aol.com.*

MANSFIELD, CHRISTOPHER CHARLES, lawyer; b. 1950; m. Laura Mansfield; children: Carolyn, Brendan. BA in Econs., Boston Coll., 1972, JD, 1975. Bar: Mass. 1975. With Liberty Mut. Ins. Co., Boston, 1975—, assoc. gen. counsel, 1981—83, v.p., gen. counsel, 1985—88, sr. v.p., gen. counsel, 1988—, bd. dirs. Bd. dirs. Employers Ins. Co., Wausau, New Eng. Legal Found.; bd. overseers RAND Corp. Inst. Civil Justice. Trustee Trust Fund Commn., Dedham, Mass.; bd. dirs. Pine St. Inn, Boston. Office: Liberty Mut Ins Co PO Box 140 175 Berkeley St Boston MA 02117-5066*

MANSFIELD, EDWARD PATRICK, JR., advertising executive; b. Warren, Pa., Oct. 29, 1947; s. Edward Patrick and Frieda (Dahler) M.; m. Norma L. Johnson, Apr. 17, 1971. AS in Acctg., Jamestown Bus. Coll., 1967; BS in Mktg. Advt., Myers U., 1970. Promotion mgr., ad dir. The News-Herald, Lake County, Ohio, 1973-77; dir. advt. The Eagle, Butler, Pa., 1977-78; dir. mktg. Baltimore Mag., 1978-79; dir. advt. The Washingtonian, Washington, 1979—. Founder, chmn. Warm-A-Heart Fund, 1988—; bd. dirs. Columbia Lighthouse for the Blind, 1988—, chmn., 1988-93; bd. dirs. The Lighthouse. Avocations: amateur radio, boating. Home: 347 Cottswold Pl Riva MD 21140-1528 Office: Washingtonian Mag 1828 L St NW Ste 200 Washington DC 20036-5169 Business E-Mail: emansfield@washingtonian.com.

MANSFIELD, GORDON HALL, former federal agency administrator; b. Pittsfield, Mass., Sept. 15, 1941; m. Linda Mansfield; 2 children. BA, Villanova U., 1964; JD, U. Miami, 1973. Staff atty. Marion County Legal Aid, 1975—78; pvt. law practice Ocala, Fla., 1979—81; assoc. legis. dir. Paralyzed Vets. America, Washington, 1981—83, nat. advocacy dir., 1983—86, assoc. exec. dir. govt. rels., 1986—89, exec. dir., 1993—2001; asst. sec. for fair housing & equal opportunity US Dept. Housing & Urban Devel. (HUD), Washington, 1989—93; asst. sec. for cong. & legis. affairs US Dept. Veterans Affairs, Washington, 2001—04, dep. sec., 2004—09, acting sec., 2007. Bd. dirs. Wounded Warrior Project, 2009—. Served in 101st Airborne Divsn. US Army, 1964—68, Vietnam. Decorated US Army Disting. Svc. Cross, Bronze Star, Purple Hearts (2), Combat Infantryman's Badge, Presdl. Unit Citation; recipient Presdl. Disting. Svc. award, The White House, Alumni Human Rels. medal, Villanova U., Disting. Pub. Svc. medal, US Dept. Def., Robert Dole Svc. to Our Nation award, Disabled Am. Veteran's Outstanding Disabled Veteran of the Yr. award; named to The US Army Officer Candidate Sch. Hall of Fame, 1997, The Nat. Spinal Cord Injury Hall of Fame, 2006, The Army Ranger Hall of Fame, 2007.*

MANSFIELD, HARVEY C., JR., political science professor; b. Mar. 21, 1932; s. Harvey Claflin Mansfield and Grace Winans Yarrow; m. Delba Winthrop; 2 children. AB, Harvard U., Cambridge, Mass., 1953, PhD, 1961. Asst. prof. U. Calif., Berkeley, 1960—62; lectr. Harvard U., 1962—64, asst. prof., 1964—66, assoc. prof., chmn., dept. govt., 1973—77, prof. govt., 1969—88, Frank G. Thomson prof. govt., 1988—93, William R. Kenan, Jr. prof. govt., 1993—. Mem. Coun. the Am. Polit. Sci. Assn., 1980—82, 2004; mem. bd. fgn. scholarships USIA, 1987—89; mem. adv. coun. NEH, 1991—94; pres. New Eng. Polit. Sci. Assn., 1993—94. Author: Statesmanship and Party Government, A Study of Burke and Bolingbroke, 1965, The Spirit of Liberalism, 1978, Machiavelli's New Modes and Orders: A Study of the Discourses on Livy, 1979, Taming the Prince; The Ambivalence of Modern Executive Power, 1989, Machiavel, L'art de la guerre, Introduction, 1991, America's Constitutional Soul, 1991, Machiavelli's Virtue, 1996, A Student's Guide to Political Philosophy, 2001, Manliness, 2006; editor: Selected Letters of Edmund Burke, 1984; translator: Machiavelli's The Prince, 1985; translator: (with L. Banfield) Machiavelli's Florentine Histories, 1988; translator: (with D. Winthrop) Alexis de Tocqueville, Democracy in America, 2000; co-author (with N. Tarcov): Niccoló Machiavelli, Discourses on Livy, 1996; contbr. articles to profl. jours. Recipient Joseph R. Levenson Tchg. award, 1993, Sidney Hook Meml. award, 2002, Nat. Humanities medal, 2004; named Jefferson Lectr. in the Humanities, 2007; Guggenheim Fellowship, 1970—71, NEH Fellowship, 1974—75, Nat. Humanities Ctr. fellow, 1982. Office: Harvard Univ Govt Dept 1737 Cambridge St CGIS N417 Cambridge MA 02138 Office Phone: 617-495-3333. Office Fax: 617-495-0438. Business E-Mail: hmansfield@gov.harvard.edu.*

MANSFIELD, JERRY W., literature and language professor; b. Oneida, Tenn. MFA, Vt. Coll., Montpelier, 1998. Cert. in creative writing pedagogy Antioch University, 2004. English prof. Moorpark Coll., Moorpark, Calif., 2004—08. Faculty sponsor Creative Writing Orgn., Moorpark. Recipient English award, U. Cumberland, 1996. Mem.: Sigma Tua Delta (life).

MANSFIELD, KAREN LEE, lawyer; b. Chgo., Mar. 17, 1942; d. Ralph and Hilda (Blum) Mansfield; children: Nicole Rafaela, Lori Michele. BA in Polit. Sci., Roosevelt U., 1963; JD, DePaul U., 1971; student, U. Chgo., 1959—60. Bar: Ill. 1972, US Dist. Ct. (no. dist.) Ill. 1972. Legis. intern Ill. State Senate, Springfield, 1966—67; tchr. Chgo. Pub. Schs., 1967—70; atty. CNA Ins., Chgo., 1971—73; law clk. Ill. Apellate Ct., 1973—75; sr. trial atty. US Dept. Labor, 1975—2008; rep. Danny K. Davis Mental Health Adv. Com., 2008—; mentor Adopt-a-Sch. Program, 1992—95; bd. dirs. Chgo. lawyer chpt. Am. Constn. Soc., 2006—. Contbr. articles to profl. jours. Vol. Big Sister, 1975—81; bd. dirs. Altgeld Nursery Sch., 1963—66; bd. dirs. Ill. div. UN Assn., 1966—72, Hull House Jane Addams Ctr., 1977—82, Broadway Children's Ctr., 1986—90, Acorn Family Entertainment, 1993—95; active Oak Park Farmers' Market Commn., 1996—2002; rsch. asst. Citizens for Gov. Otto Kerner, Chgo., 1964; com. mem. Ill. Commn. on Status of Women, 1964—70; del. Nat. Conf. on Status of Women, 1968; candidate for del. Ill. Constl. Conv., 1969. Mem.: 99's Internat. Orgn. Women Pilots (legis. chmn. Chgo. area chpt. 1983—86, legis. chmn. North Ctrl. sect. 1986—88, Legis. award 1983—85), Friends of Gamelan (performer), Am. Constn. Soc. (bd. dirs. Chgo. Lawyer chpt.), Women's Bar Assn. Ill., Chgo. Coun. Lawyers. Unitarian. Home: 204 S Taylor Ave Oak Park IL 60302-3307 Office: O KeefeLyons and Hynes LLC 30 Lasalle St Ste 4100 Chicago IL 60602

MANSFIELD, LORRAINE J., lawyer; JD, U. Wyo., Laramie, 1979. Bar: Wyo. 1979, Nev. 1981, US Ct. Appeals (10th cir.) 1980, US Ct. Appeals (9th cir.) 1983, US Ct. of Claims, 1990, US Supreme Ct. 1985. Law clk. Wyo. Supreme Ct., Laramie, 1980; sole practitioner law Las Vegas, 1981—. Arbitrator 8th Jud. Cir., Las Vegas, 1992—. Contbr. articles to profl. jours. Avocation: sailing. Office: Mansfield Law Office 6655 W Sahara Ave # B 200 Las Vegas NV 89146 Office Phone: 702-222-4009. Personal E-mail: lorrainemansfield1@yahoo.com.

MANSFIELD, STEPHEN LEE, writer, educator; b. Columbus, Ga., June 28, 1958; s. Eldon Leroy and Barbara Jane Mansfield; m. Beverly Darnall, Jan. 20, 2007; children: Jonathan Carter, Elizabeth Ann. BA, Oral Roberts U., Tulsa, Okla., 1981; MA, Abilene Christian U., Tex., 1988; PhD, Whitefield Theol. Sem., Lakeland, Fla., 1999. Pastor Fountain Gate Ch., Abilene, 1981—91, Belmont Ch., Nashville, 1991—2002; dir. Mansfield Group, Nashville, 2002—. Author: (books) The Faith of George W. Bush (NY Times Bestseller, 2004), The Faith of the American Soldier, Never Give In: The Extraordinary Character of Winston Churchill (Gold Medallion Finalist, 1996), Benedict XVI: His Life and Mission, The Faith of Barack Obama, 2008. Recipient Retailer Choice award, 2004; scholar Phi Alpha Theta, 1981. Conservative. Episcopalian. Avocations: hiking, travel, reading. Business E-Mail: stephen@mansfieldgroup.com.

MANSFIELD, WILLIAM L., manufacturing executive; BS, Drexel Univ.; MBA, Lehigh Univ. Mgmt. positions through v.p. Valspar Corp., Mpls., 1977—91, v.p. packaging & coatings, 1991—98, sr. v.p. packaging & indsl. coatings, 1998—2000, sr. v.p. arch., automotive, specialty & packaging coatings, 2000—02, exec. v.p., 2002—04, exec. v.p., COO, 2004—05, pres., CEO, 2005—. Office: Valspar Corp 1101 3d St S Minneapolis MN 55415

MANSI, JOSEPH ANNEILLO, public relations company executive; b. Oct. 8, 1935; s. Joseph C. and Vinnie (Chirico) M.; m. Mary P. Fusco, Aug. 1, 1959; children: Karen M. D'Attore, Jeanine V. Dimenna. BS, NYU, 1957. Newsman Internat. News Service, UPI, 1953-58; mem. pub. relations staff Lawrence Orgn., NYC, 1960-63; acct. supr. Philip Lesly Co., NYC, 1963-67; dir. corp. communications Ward Foods, Inc., NYC, 1967-72; dir. pub. relations Metromedia Inc., NYC, 1973-75; pres. Corp. Relations Network, Inc., NYC, 1975-80; mng. ptnr. KCSA Pub. Rels. Worldwide, NYC, 1980—2007. Trustee North Shore Hist. Mus., Five Towns Coll. With AUS, 1958—60. Mem. Pub. Rels. Soc. Am. (accredited). Home: 10 Beatrice Ln Glen Cove NY 11542-1202 Home Phone: 516-759-9007. Personal E-mail: jmansi@kcsa.com.

MANSO, LEIRA A., Latin American literature educator, poet, translator; BA cum laude, U. Puerto Rico, 1986; MA, NYU, 1989; PhD in Comparative Lit., Binghamton U., 1996. Prof. Broome C.C., SUNY, Binghamton, NY, 2000—, chairperson fgn. langs., ESL and speech dept., chair assessment and curriculum devel. for fgn. langs. and ESL com. Contbr. articles to profl. jours. Business E-Mail: manso_l@sunybroome.edu.

MANSON, BONITA YVONNE, nutritionist, educator; b. Decatur, Ala., Sept. 14, 1950; d. Will Henry and Joan Ann Jones; m. Tony James Manson, May 27, 1972; children: Tony James Jr., Gregory Keith. BSc, Wayne State U., 1975; MSc, Tex. So. U., 1984; PhD, Kans. State U., 1998. Nutrition splst. City of Riverside, Calif., 1986-95; program rep. U. Calif. Coop. Extension, Riverside, Calif., 1986-96; adj. instr. Chaffey Coll., Rancho Cucamonga, Calif., 1993-95; tchg. asst. Kans. State U., Manhattan, Kans., 1995-98; asst. prof. Austin Peay State U., Clarksville, Tenn., 1999, Middle Tenn. State U., Murfreesboro, 2000—01, SC State U., Orangeburg, 2002, 2007—, interim chair dept. family and consumer scis., 2006—07. Author: Downsizing Issues, 2000, Let's Take a Look at Gender Equity in the Classroom Teacher Education Preparation for Diversity.; author: (with T.J. Manson) The Teacher Education Program: Is There a Vision and Can They Accomplish It. Teacher Education Preparation for Diversity, 2002; contbr. chapters to books; author: Downsizing Issues: The Impact on Employee Morale and Productivity, 2004. Mem.: Assn. Fin. Counseling. Planning, Edn., Nat. Coun. Family Rels., Am. Edn. Rsch. Assn., Am. Assn. Family and Consumer Scis., Am. Dietetic Assn., Phi Delta Kappa, Kappa Omicron Nu. Democrat. Roman Cath. Office: SC State Univ 300 College St NE Orangeburg SC 29117 Office Phone: 803-536-7179. Business E-Mail: bmanson@scsu.edu.

MANSON, CONNIE JEANE, librarian; b. Seattle, Mar. 28, 1950; d. Richard A. and E. Elaine (Hereth) Manson. BA in English Lit., cum laude, U. Wash., 1972, M in Librarianship, with distinction, 1974. Reference libr. Mont. State Libr., Helena, 1974-75; libr. mgr. Wyo. Dept. Econ. Planning, Cheyenne, 1975-77; sr. geology/earth libr. Wash. Divsn. Natural Resources, Olympia, 1978—2004; now spl. projects libr. GeoRef Am. Geological Inst. Contbr. articles to profl. jours.; published more than one hundred bibliographies on the geology, mineral resources, urban planning, and natural hazards of the state, several volumes of Index to Geologic and Geophysical Mapping of Washington. Mem.: Western Assn. Map Librs., Assn. Engring. Geologists, Geosci. Info. Soc. (newsletter co-editor 1986—2007, v.p., pres. 1997—99, Meritorious Svc. award 1993, Mary B. Ansari Disting. Svc. award 2008). Office: Am Geological Inst 4220 King St Alexandria VA 22302*

MANSON, H. CRAIG (HAROLD CRAIG MANSON), law educator, former federal agency administrator, former judge; b. Mo., 1954; m. Penny Manson. Grad., USAF Acad., 1976; JD, U. Pacific McGeorge Sch. Law, 1981. Atty. Downey, Brand, Seymour & Rohwer, 1989—93; gen. counsel, Dept. Fish & Game State of Calif., Sacramento, 1993—98; judge Sacramento County Superior Ct., Calif., 1998—2002; asst. sec. for fish, wildlife & parks US Dept. Interior, Washington, 2002—05; Disting. visitor & lectr. in law U. Pacific McGeorge Sch. Law, Sacramento, 2006—. Editor -in-chief Pacific Law Review; adj. prof. employment law U. Pacific McGeorge Sch. Law, 1993—2001. Mem Calif. Rep. Party State Ctrl. Com., 1991—95. Served in USAF, 1976—89. Recipient Pacific McGeorge Alumnus of Yr. award, 2004; named Outstanding Graduating Sr., U. Pacific McGeorge Sch. Law, 1981. Office: U Pacific McGeorge Sch Law 3200 Fifth Ave Sacramento CA 95817 E-mail: cmanson@pacific.edu.

MANSON, JOANN ELISABETH, endocrinologist; b. Cleve., Apr. 14, 1953; d. S. Stanford and Therese (Palay) M.; m. Christopher N. Ames, June 12, 1979; children: Jennifer, Jeffrey, Joshua Simon. AB magna cum laude, Harvard U., 1975; MD, Case Western Res. U., 1979; MPH, Harvard Sch. Pub. Health, 1984, DPH, 1987. Bd. cert. internal medicine; bd. cert. in subspecialty of endocrinology and metabolism. Intern and resident internal medicine NEDH, Harvard Med. Sch., Boston, 1979-82; fellowship in endocrinology U. Hosp. Boston, Mass., 1982-84; rsch fellow in medicine Brigham and Women's Hosp., Boston, 1984-87, co-dir. women's health, divsn. preventive medicine, 1993—, chief divsn. preventive medicine, 1999—; staff physician, consulting endocrinologist Harvard Vanguard Med. Assocs., Peabody, Mass., 1986—2003; prof. medicine Harvard Med. Sch., Boston, 1999—, Elizabeth Brigham prof. women's health, 2003—. Mem. editl. bd.: Jour. Women's Health, 1996—, Menopause, 2004—; contbr. chapters to books, more than 700 articles to profl. jours.; author, editor: several books and textbooks. Vol. physician Lynn (Mass.) Shelter for the Homeless, 1989-93; med. adv. bd. Harvard Health Letter, Boston, 1992—, Greater Boston (Mass.) Diabetes Soc., 1993—, Harvard Women's Health Watch, Boston, 1993—; vol. Am. Heart Assn., 1992—. Recipient Connors award for oustanding leadership in women's health, 1999—, Woman in Sci. award, Am. Med. Women's Assn., 2003, Henry I. Bowditch award for excellence in pub. health, Mass. Med. Soc., 2002, Women's Profl. Achievement award, Harvard Coll., 2006; named Hero in Women's Health, Am. Health for Women Mag., 1997; named one of Top 10 Champions of Women's Health, Ladies Home Jour., 2000, Top Docs for Women, Boston mag., 2001. Fellow ACP, ACE; mem. AMA, Am. Med. Women's Assn., Am. Heart Assn., Am. Diabetes Assn., Women's Health Initiative (mem. steering com.), Assn. Am. Physicians, Alpha Omega Alpha. Avocations: reading, hiking, music, travel. Home: 14 Washington St Beverly MA 01915-5820 Office: Brigham and Women's Hosp 900 Commonwealth Ave E Fl 3 Boston MA 02215-1204 Home Phone: 978-927-6764; Office Phone: 617-278-0871. Business E-Mail: jmanson@rics.bwh.harvard.edu.

MANSON, NEIL ALAN, philosopher, educator; b. Annapolis, Md., Apr. 12, 1967; s. William Everett and Shirley Chance Manson. PhD, Syracuse U., NY, 1998. Gifford rsch. fellow, natural theology U. Aberdeen, Scotland, 1999—2001; postdoc. rsch. assoc. Ctr. Philosophy Religion U. Notre Dame, Ind., 2001—02; assoc. prof., philosophy U. Miss., University, 2003—. Office: Univ Miss Dept Philosophy and Religion University MS 38677-1848 Business E-Mail: namanson@olemiss.edu.

MANSON, PAUL NELLIS, plastic surgeon, educator; b. Kansas City, Mo., Dec. 28, 1943; s. Nellis Emanuel and Alice Winifred (Olson) Manson; m. Kathryn Garland, 1968; children: Ted, Jenner. BA in Chemistry, Northwestern U., 1965, MD, 1968. Cert. Gen. Surgery, 1978, Plastic Surgery, 1979. Intern gen. surgery Boston City Hosp., Mass., 1968—69; resident plastic surgery New England Deaconess Hosp., 1968—71, 1973—74; fellow Lahey Clinic, Boston, 1974—75; resident gen. surgery Johns Hopkins U., Balt., 1976—78; staff mem. Johns Hopkins Hosp. and Health Sys., 1987—, chief plastic surgery; prof., chmn. plastic surgery Johns Hopkins U. Sch. Medicine, 1990—. Maj. US Army, 1970—73. Republican. Presbyterian. Office: 8152 F McElderry Wing 601 N Caroline St Baltimore MD 21287-0981 Office Phone: 410-955-9477. Office Fax: 410-614-1296. Business E-Mail: pmanson@jhmi.edu.

MANSOUR, GREGORY JOHN, bishop; b. Flint, Mich., Nov. 11, 1955; AA, Mott CC, 1975; BA in Health Edn., Western Mich. U., 1977; STB, Cath. U. of Am., 1981; STL, Gregorian U., Rome, 1986. Ordained priest Eparchy of St. Maron, Bklyn., 1982; adminstr. St. Maron Parish, Phila., 1983; adminstr., pastor St. George Maronite Cath. Ch., Uniontown, Pa., 1983—84; incardinated Eparchy of Our Lady of Lebanon, LA, 1994; ordained bishop, 2004; bishop Eparchy of St. Maron, 2004—. Advocate, procurator Eparchial Marriage Tribunal. Roman Catholic. Office: 109 Remsen St Brooklyn NY 11201 Office Phone: 718-237-9913. Office Fax: 718-243-0444.

MANSOUR, MOHAMAD Y., structural engineer, researcher; s. Youssef J. and Rafia O. Mansour. PhD, U. Houston, 2001. Rsch. asst. prof. U. Houston, 2002—04, lectr. civil and environ. engring. dept., 2006—08; structural engr. Binkley and Barfiled, Houston, 2004—06; sr. structural engr. Bennett and Assocs., Houston, 2006—. Contbr. scientific papers (Best Tchr. award, 2002). Coach Shadow Creek Soccer Orgn., Pearland, Tex., 2007. Mem.: ASCE. Achievements include research in cyclic shear in the inelastic region.

MANSOUR, TAG ELDIN, pharmacologist, educator; b. Belkas, Egypt, Nov. 6, 1924; came to U.S., 1951, naturalized, 1956; s. Elsayed and Rokaya (Elzayat) M.; m. Joan Adela MacKinnon, Aug. 6, 1955; children— Suzanne, Jeanne, Dean. DVM, Cairo U., 1946; PhD, U. Birmingham, Eng., 1949, DSc, 1974. Lectr. U. Cairo, 1950-51; Fulbright instr. physiology Howard U., Washington, 1951-52; sr. instr. pharmacology Case Western Res. U., 1952-54; asst. prof., assoc. prof. pharmacology La. State U. Med. Sch., New Orleans, 1954-61; assoc. prof., prof. molecular pharmacology Stanford U. Sch. Medicine, 1961—, chmn. dept. pharmacology, 1977-91, Donald E. Baxter prof., 1977-98, prof. emeritus, 1999—. Cons. USPHS, WHO, Nat. Acad. Scis.; Mem. adv. bd. Med. Sch., Kuwait U.; Heath Clarke lectr. London Sch. Hygiene and Tropical Medicine, 1981 Author: Chemotherapeutic Targets in Parasites, 2002; contrbr. sci. articles to profl. jours. Commonwealth Fund fellow, 1965; Macy Found. scholar NIMR, London, 1982. Fellow AAAS; mem. Am. Soc. Pharmacology and Exptl. Therapeutics, Am. Soc. Biochemistry and Molecular Biology, Am. Heart Assn., Sierra Club, Stanford Faculty Club. Office: Stanford Sch Medicine Dept Chem and Sys Biology CCSR 269 Campus Dr Stanford CA 94305-5174

MANSOURI, LOTFOLLAH (LOTFI MANSOURI), retired performing company executive; b. Tehran, June 15, 1929; s. Hassan and Mehri (Jalili) M.; m. Marjorie Anne Thompson, Sept. 18, 1954; 1 child, Shireen Melinda. AB, UCLA, 1953. Asst. prof. UCLA, 1957-60; resident stage dir. Zurich Opera, 1960-65; chief stage dir. Geneva Opera, 1965-75; gen. dir. Can. Opera Co., Toronto, Ont., 1976-88, San Francisco (Calif.) Opera, 1988—2001, gen. dir. emeritus, 2001—; dramatic coach Music Acad. West, Santa Barbara, Calif., 1959; dir. dramatics Zurich Internat. Opera Studio, 1961-65, Centre Lyrique, Geneva, 1967-72; artistic adviser Tehran Opera, 1973-75; opera adviser Nat. Arts Centre, Ottawa, Ont., 1977; v.p. Opera America, 1979—. Operatic cons. dir. Yes, Giorgio, MGM, 1981; dir. opera sequence for film Moonstruck (Norman Jewison), 1987; stage dir. Fla. Grand Opera Mus. Acad. of West. Guest dir. opera cos. including Met. Opera, San Francisco Opera (70 prodns.), N.Y.C. Opera, Lyric Opera of Chgo., L.A. Opera, guest dir. opera cos. San Diego Opera, guest dir. opera cos. including Teatro Colon, Buenos Aires, Utah Opera, Canadian Opera Co. (30 new prodns.), Houston Grand Opera, La Scala, Covent Garden, Verona Opera, Kirov Opera, Australian Opera, Vienna Staatsoper, Vienna Volksoper, Salzburg Festival, Amsterdam Opera, Holland Festival, Nice (France) Opera, Festival D'Orange, France, Verona Arena Festival; co-author: An Operatic Life, 1982. Decorated chevalier Order Arts and Letters (France), 1992; recipient Nat. Endowment for the Arts Opera honor, 2009. Mem. Am. Guild Mus. Artists, Can. Actors Equity Assn. Achievements include initiating above-stage projection of subtitles as a simultaneous translation of opera, 1983. Office: Columbia Artists Management Llc 1790 Broadway # 6 New York NY 10019-1412 Home Phone: 415-386-3442; Office Phone: 415-387-9967. E-mail: lotfimansouri@hotmail.com.*

MANSOURI, NAZANIN, science educator; permanent resident, US, 2005; d. Javad Mansouri and Parvini Salek; m. Adrian Nunez, Sept. 6, 2002; 1 child, Maneli Nunez. PhD in Computer Engring., U. Cin., 2000. Asst. prof. Syracuse U., NY, 2000—. Mem.: IEEE. Office: Syracuse Univ Dept EECS 3-183 Ctr Sci and Tech Syracuse NY 13244-4100 Home: 2533 NW Biskendere S Portland OR 97229 Personal E-mail: nazanin.mansouri@gmail.com. Business E-Mail: namansou@ecs.syr.edu.

MANSUE, AMY, hospital administrator; s. Russell and Barbara Beaulieu. BS, MSW, U. Ala. Dep. commr. of state Dept. Human Svcs., 1989—92; v.p. Cablevision, NJ; sr. v.p. corp. devel. HIP, NY, pres., CEO NJ; dep. chief of staff to Gov. James McGreevey, NJ; pres., CEO Children's Specialized Hosp., Mountainside, 2003—. Bd. mem. Children's Specialized Hosp., 1995—99. Bd. mem. Planned Parenthood of Ctrl. NJ, Organ and Tissue Sharing Network, NJ Cmty. Devel. Corp. Recipient NJ Woman of Achievement award, NJ Fedn. Women's Clubs, 2007, Leadership award, Brain Injury Assn., 2007; named Garden State Women Leader in Non-Profits, Garden State Woman Mag., 2007. Office: Children's Specialized Hosp 150 New Providence Rd Mountainside NJ 07092*

MANSUETO, JOSEPH DANIEL, publishing executive; b. East Chicago, Ind., Sept. 3, 1956; s. Mario Daniel and Sara Wilda (Smart) M. BBA, U. Chgo., 1978, MBA, 1980. Securities analyst Harris Assocs., Chgo., 1983-84; founder, chmn., prin. Morningstar, Chgo., 1984—, CEO, 1984—96, 2000—. Recipient Rosenthal Award for Excellence in Investment Research, Univ. Chgo., 1992, KPMG Peat Marwick High Tech Entrepreneur of Yr. award, 1993, Disting. Entrepreneurial Alumnus award, Univ. Chgo., 2000; named one of Forbes' Richest Americans, 2006. Office: Morningstar Inc 225 W Wacker Dr Chicago IL 60606 Office Phone: 312-696-6000.*

MANSUR, LOUIS K., materials scientist, nuclear engineer; b. Lowell, Mass., Apr. 18, 1944; s. Louis Francis and Adele Mansur; m. Janice H. Spoone; children: Kendra Jane, Joanna Beth, Warren Keith. BS in Physics, U. Mass., Lowell, 1966; MS in Engring. Physics, Cornell U., Ithaca, NY, 1968; PhD in Materials Sci. and Nuclear Engring., Cornell U., 1974. Lab. instr. U. Mass., Lowell, 1964-66; reactor physicist (on loan from AEC) GE SEFOR Facility, Fayetteville, Ark., 1968-69; reactor engr. U.S. AEC, Washington, 1966-67, 70-71; staff mem. Oak Ridge (Tenn) Nat. Lab., 1974-82, group leader, 1982—99, team leader for materials R&D for spallation neutron source target, 1996—2003, rsch. program leader for shielding materials, 2002—. Mem. adv. bd. dept. nuclear engring. and radiol. scis. U. Mich.; sci. exchanges with European Countries, Japan and Russia; conf. organizer, proceedings editor, mem. coms. various internat. profl. orgns.; mem. steering com. Advanced Neutron Source; past chmn. ORNL Postdoctoral Program Com.; keynote speaker at internat. meetings; materials rsch. & devel. coord. Spallation Neutron Source. Author, co-author more than 260 sci. items, including book, chpts., and jour. articles; chmn. editors Jour. Nuclear Materials, Elsevier, 1990—. Co-recipient Materials Sci. Rsch. award Divsn. Materials Scis. U.S. Dept. Energy, 1985, 90, Publs., Tech. Achievement and R&D Accomplishment awards Oak Ridge Nat. Lab., 1985, 86, 87, 93, Outstanding Achievement award Am. Nuclear Soc. Fellow Am. Soc. Metals (past chmn. nuclear materials com., past. chmn. local chpt.), Am. Nuclear Soc.; mem. AAAS, Materials Rsch. Soc., Minerals, Metals and Materials Soc. (chmn. nuclear materials com.), Sigma Xi. Achievements include designing targets and materials for fission reactors and spallation accelerator facilities; patents on Hard Surface Polymers; work on development of theory of microstructural evolution relating structure and composition on atomic scale to materials properties; research in effects of neutron irradiation on dimensional, mechanical and physical properties, improved materials and properties by ion beam processing, shielding for neutrons and for galactic cosmic rays, integration of theoretical and experimental research on structural and compostitional basis of macroscopic properties.

MANSUROV, ZULKHAIR AIMUKHAMETOVICH, chemist; b. Sarkand, Kazakhstan, June 26, 1946; s. Aumukhamet Kopejanovich and Maken Tursynbekovna (Tursynbekova) M.; m. Raushan Magzumovna Tiesova, June 11, 1968; children: Kadyr (dec.), Batyr. PhD, Kazakh State Nat. U., 1973; DS, Inst. Structural Macrokinetics, Moscow, 1990. Jr. sr. scientist Kazakh U. Lab. Phys.-Chem., Almaty, Kazakhstan, 1973-79, head lab., 1979-88, sr. lectr., prof. dept. chem. kinetics and combustion, 1989-97; dept. head Kazakh State Nat. U., Almaty, Kazakhstan, 1997-2001, vice-rector on sci., 1992-98. Hon. rsch. asst. chem. and biochem. engring. dept. U. Coll. London, 1981; head lab. Hybridic Techs. Combustion Problems Inst., Almaty, 1988—, dir. 2000—, 1st vice rector, Al-Farabi Kazakh Nat. U., 2001— Co-author: Some Problems in Construction and Operation of the Chemical Processes, 1994, Physical Methods of Investigation, Kazsnu, 2000; contbr. articles to profl. jours. Recipient State Prize of Kazakhstan, 1992, Satpaev State prize, 2002, Higher Sch. Acad. Scis. medal, Russian Fedn., 2002, State prize, 2004; grantee Soros Internat. Sci. Found., 1993, DAAD, Germany, 1998, 2003, 06., Livermore Lab., U. Calif., 2001-02, INTAS, ISTC, UNESCO, 2005—. Mem. Internat. Higher Edn. Acad. Scis., Internat. Assn. for the Promotion of Cooperation with Scientists from former USSR, INTAS (coun. of scientists, grantee 2000), Ministry of Edn. and Sci. of Kazakhstan (grantee 2000). Avocations: swimming, chess. Home: Djandosov Str 34A Flat 174 480097 Almaty Kazakhstan Office: Kazakh Al-Faraby State Nat U Al-Faraby Prospect 71 480078 Almaty Kazakhstan Home Phone: 73272741817. E-mail: icp@nursat.kz.

MANSY, KHALED, engineering educator, architect; b. Zagazig, Sharkiah, Egypt, Mar. 10, 1962; arrived in U.S., 1996; s. Abdelmonem Mansy and Wagihah Massoud; m. Soha Elfeel, Mar. 15, 1995; children: Abdalrahman, Reem. BSc, Cairo U., 1984; MSc, Helwan U., Cairo, 1992; PhD with honors, Ill. Inst. Tech., Chgo., 2001. Lic. archtl. engr., Egyptian Syndicate Engrs., 1984. Lectr. Helwan U., Cairo, 1986—96; asst. prof. archtl. engring. Okla. State U., Stillwater, 2001—. Pvt. practice arch., Stillwater, Okla., 2003—. First Energy Star Home in Stillwater (Energy Star Label, 2004), ISS New Ctr.; contbr. scientific papers to profl. meetings, articles to profl. jours. Chair bldg. com. Islamic Soc. Stillwater, Okla., 2004—06. Recipient cert. of Merit Graphics, UNESCO, 1972, cert. Merit, Leading Edge Design Competition, 1999, Highest Std. Academic Achievement, Ill. Inst. Tech., 2001, Grand prize, NCARB, 2004, 6 certs. Merit, Egyptian Syndicate Engrs.; grantee, NSF, 2003—06. Mem.: Am. Soc. Engring. Edn., Illuminating Engring. Soc. N.Am., Soc. Bldg. Sci. Educators, Okla. Sustainability Network, US Green Bldg. Coun. Achievements include first to a new model design of the artificial sky dome. Office: Okla State Univ 124 Arch Bldg Stillwater OK 74078

MANTEGAZZA, SERGIO, finance company executive; b. Mendrisio, Switzerland, Oct. 31, 1927; s. Antonio and Angela (Ribolzi) M.; m. Sebastiana Hernandez, Feb. 25, 1955; children: Fabio, Dolores, Paolo. D of Bus. Adminstrn., Gademann Handelschule, 1945. With Globus Gateway Tours, Lugano, Switzerland, 1945-48, mgr., 1948-52, gen. mgr., 1952-56, dir., 1956-60; mng. dir. Globus and Cosmos Groups, Lugano, Switzerland, 1960—2008, pres.; main shareholder Monarch Airlines Ltd., 1967. Named Knight of the Order of St. Gregorio Magno Mem. Maxims Bus. Club, Mark's Club. Avocations: tennis, yachting, golf. Office: 7 Curzon Str Flat Nr 8 London WIJ 5HG England

MANTEI, LORRAINE E., school system administrator; b. Albuquerque, Feb. 27, 1961; d. Chester T. and Ella Strange Mantei; m. Richard E. Tuck, July 6, 2001; m. Donald G. Keene (div.); children: Cassandra D. Keene, Pamela Preston, Kendall Keene, Daniel Keene. BS, U. So. Ind., Evansville, 1986; MEd, Tex. A&M U., Commerce, 1999. Tchr. Duncanville Ind. Sch. Dist., Tex., 1994—2000, Arlington Ind. Sch. Dist., Grand Prairie, 2000—02; asst. prin. Dallas Ind. Sch. Dist., 2002—05; supr., prin. La Academia de Estrellas Charter Sch., 2006—. Mem. arts commn. bd. City of DeSoto, 2004—; precinct chair Dallas Dem. Party, 2004—; v.p. DeSoto Dining & Dialogue, Tex., 2005—. Mem.: ASCD, Hispanic Woman's Network, Tex. Elem. Prins. and Suprs. Assn. Democrat. Avocations: reading, walking, travel.

MANTEL, ALLAN DAVID, lawyer; b. NYC, June 27, 1951; s. Bernard and Ruth (Weichman) M.; m. Janet Mantel, June 17, 1985; children: Bernard, Elizabeth. BA, NYU, 1973; JD, SUNY, Buffalo, 1976. Bar: N.Y. 1977, U.S. Dist. Ct. (so. and ea. dists.) N.Y. 1977. Assoc. Rosenthal & Herman P.C., NYC, 1977-82; ptnr. Rosenthal, Herman & Mantel, NYC, 1983-94, Hofheimer, Gartlir & Gross, LLP, NYC, 1995-98, Stein Riso Mantel LLP, NYC, 1999—. Fellow Am. Acad. Matrimonial Lawyers (NY chpt. pres. 2007-08), AAML (nat. bd. govs. mem., 2007-), Internat. Acad. Matrimonial Lawyers; mem. ABA (Super Lawyers (NYC), Best Lawyers America), Ten Leaders (NYC), Buffalo Law Sch. SUNY (dean's adv. counsel 2007-). Jewish. Office: Stein Riso Mantel LLP 405 Lexington Ave New York NY 10174-0002 Office Phone: 212-599-1515. Business E-Mail: allan.mantel@steinrisomantel.com.

MANTEL, SAMUEL JOSEPH, JR., management educator, consultant; b. Indpls., Nov. 17, 1921; s. Samuel Joseph and Beatrice Smith (Talmas) M.; m. Dorothy Jean Friedland, June 28, 1950 (dec. July 27, 2005); children— Michael Lee, Samuel Joseph, III, Margaret Irene, Elizabeth Baer. AB, Harvard U., 1948, MPA, 1950, PhD, 1952. Asst. prof. social sci. Ga. Inst. Tech., 1953-56; asst. prof., then assoc. prof. econs., dir. Econs.-in-Action program, Case Western Res. U., 1956-69; prof. mgmt. and quantitative analysis U. Cin., 1969-89, prof. emeritus quantitative analysis and ops. mgmt., 1989—, Joseph S. Stern prof. mgmt., 1973—89, prof. emeritus, 1989, exec. dir. Grad. Ctr. for Mgmt. of Advanced Tech. and Innovation, 1987—89, emeritus, 1989. Mgmt. cons., condr. mgmt. seminars. Author: Cases in Managerial Decisions, 1964, Project Management: A Managerial Approach, 1985, 7th edit., 2009, Operations Management for Pharmacists: Strategy and Tactics, 1992, Project Management, 2008, Project Management in Practice 3d edit., 2008; contbr. chapters to books, articles to profl. jours. Vice pres. Jewish Fedn. Cin., 1978-80; past pres., life mem. Cin. Hillel Found., Cleve. Hillel Found.; historian Rockdale Temple, 1969-77; mem. mgmt. and adminstrn. com. Anti-Defamation League, B'nai B'rith, 1976; trustee Jewish Hosp., Cin., 1975-84, Sarah Marvin Found. for Performing Arts, 1990—; mem. mgmt. adv. com. Cin. Police Dept., 1991-92. Maj. USMCR, 1942-46, 51-53. Decorated D.F.C. with 2 oak leaf clusters, Air medal with 11 oak leaf clusters; Econs.-in-Action fellow, 1955; fellow Inst. Policy Rsch., 1980; named Prof. of Year, Delta Sigma Pi, 1974. Mem. IEEE, Project Mgmt. Inst., Iota Epsilon, Beta Gamma Sigma. Home: 608 Flagstaff Dr Cincinnati OH 45215-2525

MANTELL, MURRAY I., engineering educator; b. NYC, Sept. 6, 1917; s. John and Anna Mantell; m. Rose T. Plansky, Apr. 29, 1944; children: Melodie, Andrea, Tobi, John. B in Mech. Engring., U. Fla., 1940; MS in Civil Engring., So. Calif. U., 1945; PhD, U. Tex., 1952. Registered profl. engr., Fla. Pres. Mantell Constrn. Co., Miami, Fla., 1940—41, 1946; consulting engr. R. Belsham, Miami, Fla., 1941; naval arch. Charleston (S.C.) Navy Yard, 1941—43, Terminal Island Naval Shipyard, Long Beach, Calif., 1943—45; prof., dept. chmn. emeritus U. Miami, Coral Gables, Fla., 1946—. Chmn. Parks Planning Com., Miami Beach, Fla., 1950; vis. prof. U. Sheffield, England, 1965—66; mem. Fire Prevention and Safety Bd., Dade County, Fla., 1968; chmn. Adv. Panel on Planning and Zoning, Coral Gables, 1970; vice chmn. U.S. Dept. Agrl., County Farm Svc. Agy. Com., 2005—. Author: Ethics & Professionalism in Engineering, 1964, Strength of Materials, 1968, Handbook for Living, 1992; co-author: Orientation in Engineering, 1955, Structural Analysis, 1962, Engineering Properties and Construction Applications of Phosphogypsum, 1990. State sport chmn. Amateur Athletic Union, Fla., 1949; pres. Tigertail Civic Assn., Coconut Grove, Fla., 1960—62; v.p. Pine Ridge Civic Assn., Miami, 1966. Recipient Commendation for Engring. Achievement, Brit. Admiralty, 1942; named Engr. of Yr., Fla. Engring. Soc., 1961. Fellow: NSPE (life; chpt. v.p.), ASCE (life; chpt. pres.), Am. Soc. for Engring. Edn. (life; sect. pres., award for excellence in tchg. Western Electric Fund 1969). Avocations: stamp and coin collecting, sports, agriculture. Home: 5900 SW 84 Ave Miami FL 33143 Office: Dept Civil Engring Univ Miami Coral Gables FL 33124

MANTENA, RAVI, business educator; BS in Engring., Birla Inst. Tech. and Sci., Pilani, India, 1991; MBA, Indian Inst. Mgmt., Kolkata, 1993; PhD, NYU, NYC, 2004. Area sales mgr. Unilever India, Chennai, Tamil Nadu, India, 1993—94; mng. ptnr. Rajkamal Hatcheries, Visakhapatnam, Andhra Pradesh, India, 1994—98; asst. prof. computers and info. sys. U. Rochester, NY, 2004—. Contbr. articles to profl. jours. Recipient Harold McDowell award, NYU, 2005; Rsch. grant, Net Inst., 2006. Mem.: Assn. Info. Sys., Inst. Ops. Rsch. and Mgmt. Scis. Achievements include research in impact of digital convergence. Business E-Mail: mantena@simon.rochester.edu.

MANTEUFFEL, ROBERT LEE, lawyer; b. St. Francis, Kans., July 15, 1955; s. Walter Junior and Winnie Belle Manteuffel; m. Martha Ann Hatten, Mar. 8, 1980; children: Jessica Ann, Laura Alean. BA in Math. with distinction, Va. Mil. Inst., Lexington, 1977; MS in Ops. Rsch., USAF Inst. Tech., Wright-Patterson AFB, Ohio, 1985; JD, So. Meth. U., Dallas, 1991. Bar: Tex. 1991, US Dist. Ct. (no. dist.) Tex. 1992, US Dist. Ct. (so. dist.) Tex. 1994, US Dist. Ct. (ea. dist.) Tex. 1994, US Dist. Ct. (we. dist.) Tex. 1994. Commd. lt. US Army, 1977, advanced through grades to capt., interim comdr. and tng. officer fgn. liasion divsn. Armor Ctr. Ft. Knox, Ky., 1983, various positions in US & Germany, 1978—88; clk., atty. Bailey & Williams, Dallas, 1990—92; atty. Fowler, Wiles & Keith, LLP, Dallas, 1992—98, Kane Russell Coleman & Logan P.C., Dallas, 1998—. Mng. staff editor Southwestern Law Jour., 1990—91; author: Comment" The Quest for Efficiency: Public Sch. Funding in Texas" 43 Southwester Law Journal, 1990. Mem. adv. bd. West Dallas Youth and Family Ctr., 1995—2001; del. conf. world politics and economics Va. Mil. Inst., The Citadel, Charleston, SC, 1976. Recipient Mil. Parachute Badge, 1975, Silver medal for Army scholarship, Am. Legion, 1976, medal, Am. Vets. of WWII, 1977, John H. French medal, Va. Mil. Inst., 1977, Jackson-Hope medal (first honor), 1977, Army Svc. ribbon, 1977, Overseas Svc. ribbon, 1982, Army Commendation medal, 1982, Meritorious Svc. medal, 1988; named one of Outstanding Young Men of Am., 1985; Hatton W. Sumners scholar, So. Meth. U. and Hatton W. Sumners Found., 1988—91. Mem.: Dallas Bar Assn. (chair libr. com. 2002), State Bar Tex., Coll. State Bar Tex., Berkner Area Exch. Club (pres. club 2004—05), Rotary (bd. dirs. Dallas Market Ctr. club 2002—05), Kappa Alpha Order, Omega Rho, Va. Mil. Inst. Alumni Assn., Phi Delta Phi. Republican. Methodist. Avocations: music, reading, jogging, swimming, bicycling. Home: 4817 Copper Mountain Ln Richardson TX 75082 Office: Kane Russell Coleman & Logan PC 1601 Elm St Ste 3700 Dallas TX 75201 Office Phone: 214-777-4267. Office Fax: 214-777-4299. Business E-Mail: rmanteuffel@krcl.com.

MANTHEI, JOHN RICHARD, lawyer; s. Richard Dale and Karen Jane Manthei; m. Kimberly C. Manthei; children: Nathan, Nicholas, Sophia. BA in History & Polit. Sci. magna cum laude, Miami U., Oxford, Ohio, 1990; JD, U. Wis., Madison, 1994. Bar: Washington DC 1995. Senator John DanForth legis. aide US Senate, Washington, 1990—91; lawyer Spriggs & Hollingsworth, Washington, 1994—97, Morgan, Lewis & Bockius, Washington, 1997—98; majority counsel US House Reps. Com. Commerce, Washington, 1998—2000; ptnr. Latham & Watkins LLP, Washington, 2000—; global co-chair Healthcare and Life Sci. Practice Group, 2007—. Adv. bd. Food Drug Law Inst., Washington, 2005—. Contbr. articles to profl. legal jours. Bd. dirs. Stepping Stones, Rockville, Md., 2004—06. Named one of Top 40 Lawyers, Washington Magazine, 2006. Mem.: Phi Beta Kappa. Office: Latham & Watkins LLP 555 11th St NW Washington DC 20004

MANTHEI, RICHARD DALE, retired lawyer, health products executive; b. Olivia, Minn., Dec. 23, 1935; s. Alvin R. and Sidonia (Klatt) M.; m. Karen J. Peterson, Sept. 6, 1959 (dec. Mar. 1985); children: Steven, Jana, Kari, John, Rebecca; m. Lynn E. Graham, Aug. 9, 1986. BS in Pharmacy (Rexall award 1960), S.D. State U., 1960; JD, U. Minn., 1967. Bar: DC 1987, US Supreme Ct. 1987. Sales rep. Eli Lilly & Co., Indpls., 1962-64, atty., 1967-70; atty., then asst. corp. sec., dir. regulatory affairs Am. Hosp. Supply Corp., Evanston, Ill., 1970-79, corp. sec., dep. gen. counsel, 1979-85; assoc. gen. counsel Baxter Travenol Labs., Deerfield, Ill., 1986-87; ptnr. Burditt, Bowles & Radzius, Washington, 1987-90, McKenna & Cuneo, Washington, 1990-96; sr. v.p. regulatory scis. C.R. Bard, Inc., Murray Hill, NJ, 1996-2000. Author articles in field.; Editorial adv. staff: Med. Devices and Diagnostic Industry, 1979. Mem. bd. edn. Libertyville H.S., 1984-87; mem. governing bd. Spl. Edn. Dist. of Lake County, Ill., 1985-87; trustee N.J. Ctr. for Visual Arts. With AUS, 1954-56. Mem. Health Industry Mfrs. Assn. (chmn. law sect. 1976), Health Industry Assn. (chmn. legal com. 1973), Am. Soc. Corp. Secs. (corp. practices com. 1983-88, group pres. 1985-86, Chgo. regional group 1986-87), D.C. Bar Assn., Univ. Club (Evanston, Ill., bd. dirs. 1984-86). Home: 11608 Stonewall Jackson Dr Spotsylvania VA 22553

MANTHEY, FRANK ANTHONY, physician, director; b. NYC, Dec. 2, 1933; s. Frank A.J. and Josephine (Roth) M.; m. Douglas Susan Falvey, Sept. 14 1958 (div. 1979, dec. 1989); children: Michael P., Susan M., Peter J.; m. Doris Jean Pulley, Oct. 11, 1979. BS, Fordham U., 1955; MD, SUNY, Syracuse, 1958. Diplomate Am. Bd. Anesthesiology, Am. Bd. Med. Examiners. Intern Upstate Med. Ctr., Syracuse, 1958-59; resident in anesthesiology Yale-New Haven Med. Ctr., 1962-64; physician Yale-New Haven Hosp., 1964-75; pvt. practice medicine Illmo, Mo., 1975-79; dir. Manthey Med. Clinic, Elkton, Ky., 1979—. Clin. instr. anesthesiology Yale U. Med. Sch., New Haven, 1964-69, asst. clin. prof. anesthesiology, 1969-75; cons. Conn. Dept. Aeros., Hartford, 1969-70; sr. med. examiner Fed. Aviation Adminstrn., Illmo, 1975-79. Contbr. articles to profl. jours. Chmn. gen. works Little Folks Fair, Guilford, Conn., 1967-71; mem. Rep. Town Com., Guilford, 1969-75; chmn. Guilford Sch. Bldg. Com., 1973-75; mem. Todd County (Ky.) Bd. of Health, 1999—. Capt. USAF (M.C.), 1956-62. Mem.: Flying Physicians Assn. (v.p. NE chpt. 1973—75, v.p. nat. 1974—75, 1979—80, bd. dirs. 1970—73, 1975—78, bd. dirs. nat. 1975—78), Aerospace Med. Assn. (assoc. fellow 1973—75), Ky. Med. Assn., Aircraft Owners and Pilots Assn., Mercedes Benz ClubAm., Alpha Kappa Kappa. Avocations: stamp collecting/philately, coin collecting/numismatics, aviation, auto restoration, skiing. Home: 105 Sunset Dr Elkton KY 42220-9257 Office: Manthey Family Practice Clinic 203 Allensville St PO Box 368 Elkton KY 42220-0368

MANTHORNE, KATHERINE E., art historian, educator; d. Joseph Parker and Katherine Farrell Manthorne; m. James Lancel McElhinney. MA, Columbia U., NYC, 1979, PhD, 1985. Exec. editor Smithsonian Am. Art Mus., Washington, 1997—99, head rsch. office, 1997—99; prof. art history Grad. Ctr., CUNY, 2000—. Assoc. prof. Art History Program, U. Ill., Champaign, 1985—97, chair dept., 1985—97; prof. Am. art U. Venice, Italy, 1998. Contbr. to monographs. Adv. bd. mem. Archives Am. Art, Washington, 2000—; sec. Coll. Art Assn., NYC, 2006—08; adv. bd. mem. El Mus. Barrio, NYC, 2006—. Recipient Outstanding Faculty award, U. Ill., 1995; fellowship, US Capital Hist. Soc., 2006—07. Mem.: Fulbright Assn., Assn. Latin Am. Art, Assoc. Historians Am. Art (book rev. editor, newsletter 2007—08), Internat. Assn. Art Critics. Liberal. Roman Catholic. Office: Grad Ctr Art History Program 365 5th Ave New York NY 10016 Business E-Mail: kmanthorne@gc.cuny.edu.

MANTLE, RAYMOND ALLAN, lawyer; m. Judith Ann LaGrange, Nov. 26, 1967; children: Amanda Lee, Rachel Ann, Leah Amy. BSBA summa cum laude, BA summa cum laude, Kent State U., 1961; LLB cum laude, NYU, 1964. Bar: N.Y. 1964, Fla. 2005, U.S. Supreme Ct. Asst. counsel Gov. Nelson A. Rockefeller, NYC, 1964-65; assoc. Paul Weiss Rifkind Wharton & Garrison, 1967-69; mem. Varet & Fink P.C. (formerly Milgrim Thomajan & Lee, P.C.), NYC, 1969-95; ptnr. Piper & Marbury L.L.P., NYC, 1995-98; mem. Reitler Brown & Rosenblatt LLC (formerly Brock Silverstein, LLC), 1998—2003, counsel, 2004—06. Lectr. in computer law field. Contbr. author: Doing Business in China and Intellectual Property China, 1990—. Capt. US Army, 1965—67. Mem.: Fla. Bar, N.Y. State Bar Assn. (co-chmn. ann. meeting seminar on intellectual property 2000—05, co-chair intellectual property sect. internat. com. 2004—05, exec. com. intellectual property sect.). Republican. Methodist. Office: 808 Third St Suite C Neptune Beach FL 32266 Office Phone: 904-249-4370. Business E-Mail: rmantle@rmantlelaw.com.

MANTRAVADI, MURTY V., retired optics scientist; b. Perakalapudi, India, Oct. 4, 1929; came to U.S., 1956, 84; s. Gangadhara Sastry and Venkatalakshmi (Upadrasta) Mantravadi; m. Suryaprabhadevi Upadrasta, Mar. 12, 1952; children: Sandhyarani, Gangadhar, Lakshmi, Ravikumar, Suryanarayana, Padma. BSc, Andhra Christian Coll., India, 1949; diploma, Madras Inst. Tech., India, 1952; PhD, Inst. Optics, U. Rochester, NYC, 1959. Lectr. Madras Inst. Tech., 1952-55; asst. Inst. Optics, U. Rochester, 1956-59, asst. prof., 1959-64; prof. Madras Inst. Tech., 1964-66; scientist, engr. Bhabha Atomic Rsch. Ctr., Bombay, India, 1966-82; prof. Centro de inv en Optica, Leon, Guanajuato, Mex., 1982-84; chief scientist Halo Techs., Costa Mesa, Calif., 1984-86; prof. Ala. A&M U., Huntsville, 1986-87; rsch. engr./scientist Northrop Grumman Corp., Hawthorne, Calif., 1987-94; ret. Cons. in field. Contbr. articles to profl. jours.; patentee in field. Fellow Indian Acad. Scis., Optical Soc. India, Optical Soc. Am., Internat. Soc. Optical Engring. Home: 21610 Villa Pacifica Cir Carson CA 90745-1737 Personal E-mail: collimate@yahoo.com.

MANTSCH, HENRY HORST, chemistry professor; b. Mediasch, Transylvania, Romania, July 30, 1935; emigrated to Can., 1968; s. Heinrich Johann and Olga Augusta (Gondosch) M.; m. Amy Emilia Kory, Nov. 2, 1959; children: Monica, Marietta. BSc, U. Cluj, Transylvania, 1958, PhD, 1964. Rsch. scientist Romanian Acad. Sci., Cluj, 1958-65, Tech. U. Munich, Germany, 1966-68; with NRC, Ottawa, Can., 1968-72; prof. biochemistry U. Cluj, 1973-74, Liebig U., Giessen, Germany, 1975-76; head molecular spectroscopy NRC, Ottawa, 1977—; mem. Can. Rsch. Coun., Ottawa, 1977-91, Winnipeg, 1992—2002; sci. counsellor Can. Embassy, Berlin, 2002—07; sr. sci. advisor Foreign Affairs Can., Ottawa, 2008—. Adj. prof. Carleton U., Ottawa, 1978-90,

U. Ottawa, 1990-92, U. Manitoba, Winnipeg, 1992—. Contbr. articles to profl. jours.; patentee in field. Recipient medal Ministry of Edn., Bucharest, 1972, Humboldt Found. medal Bonn, 1980, Herzberg award, 1984, Marcus Marci medal, 1998; Chem. Inst. Can. fellow, 1979, Royal Soc. Can. fellow, 1982. Mem. Am. Biophys. Soc., Soc. Applied Spectroscopy, Chem. Inst. Can. (chmn. biol. chem. divsn. 1980-81), Can. Spectroscopy Soc. (nat. exec. com. 1981-90), Can. Biophys. Soc. (sec. 1999—). Office: Foreign Affairs Can 125 Sussex Dr K1A 0G2 Ottawa ON Canada Home Phone: 613-224-4936. Personal E-mail: henry.mantsch@international.gc.ca, henry.mantsch@rogers.com.

MANTYLA, KAREN, distance learning consultant; b. Bronx, NY, Dec. 31, 1944; d. Milton and Sylvia (Diamond) Fischer; 1 child, Michael Alan. Student, Rockland C.C., Suffern, NY, 1962, NYU, 1967, Mercer U., 1981. Coord. mktg. Credit Bur., Inc., Miami, Fla., 1973—79; dist. mgr. Rsch. Inst. Am., NYC, 1979—80, regional dir., 1980—85, mgr. field sales, 1985—86, mgr. nat. sales, 1986—87, mgr. nat. accounts, 1989; v.p. sales Bur. Bus. Practice/Paramount Comm., Inc., Waterford, Conn., 1989—93; pres. Quiet Power, Inc., Washington, 1993—. Author: Consultative Sales Power, 1995, Interactive Distance Learning Exercises That Really Work, 1999, The 2000/2001 ASTD Distance Learning Yearbook, 2000, Blending e-Learning: The Power is in the Mix, 2001; co-editor The 2001/2002 ASTD Distance Learning Yearbook; co-author: Distance Learning: A Step-By-Step Guide for Trainers, 1997, Blending E-Learning: The Power is in the Mix, 2001, The Learning Advantage, 2009. Bd. dirs. Federal Govt. Distance Learning Assn. Named to Distance Learning Hall of Fame, Fed. Govt. Distance Learning Assn., 2003. Mem. ASTD, Sales and Mktg. Execs. (past bd. dirs. NY chpt., v.p. Ft. Lauderdale chpt. 1979), US Distance Learning Assn. (editor Distance Learning News, mem. tech. and comm. com. Fla. chpt.), Nat. Assn. Women Bus. Owners, US C. of C., Women Entrepreneurs. Avocations: antiques, tennis, writing, swimming. Office: Quiet Power Inc South Bldg Ste 900 601 Pennsylvania Ave NW Washington DC 20004-2401 Office Phone: 202-661-4646. Business E-Mail: kmantyla@quietpower.com.

MANTZ, ARLAN W., physics professor; b. Slatington, Pa., July 25, 1940; s. Harold H. and Irene A. (Herber) M.; m. Barbara Dae Mantz, Dec. 28, 1963; 1 child, Yves Andre. BA, Catawba Coll., 1962; MSc, Ohio State U., 1966, PhD, 1969. Sr. scientist Air Force Avionics Lab., Ohio, 1966-73; postdoctoral fellow Labo Aime Cotton, Orsay, France, 1973-74; sr. scientist Digilab, Inc., Cambridge, Mass., 1974-76; engring. mgr. Laser Analytics Inc., Bedford, Mass., 1976-79, pres., gen. mgr., 1979-89; assoc. prof. Franklin and Marshall Coll., Lancaster, Pa., 1990-95; Oakes Ames prof. physics Conn. Coll., New London, 1995—. Editl. adv. bd. Spectrochemica Acta, 1990, revs. editor, 1995. Mem.: Am. Phys. Soc. Avocation: sailing. Office Phone: 860-439-5030. Business E-Mail: awman@conncoll.edu.

MANTZOROS, CHRISTOS SOCRATES, internist; b. Nafplion, Greece, May 28, 1963; MD, U. Athens, Greece, 1987, DSc, 1996; M Med. Sci., MSc in Clin. Epidemiology, Harvard U., 1997. Diplomate Am. Bd. Internal Medicine, Am. B. Endocrinology, Diabetes and Metabolism, Am. Bd. Nutrition. Intern Wayne State U., Detroit, 1990-91, resident in internal medicine, 1991-93; fellow Harvard U. Med. sch., Boston, 1993-96, instr. medicine, 1996-98, asst. prof., 1998—2003, assoc. prof., 2003—09. Recipient Wilhelm Friedrich Bessel award, Humboldt Found., Germany, 2005, award, Am. Assn. Clin. Endocrinology Frontiers Sci., 2005, Novartis, 2005, Lilly award, North Am. Assn. Study Obesity, 2006, HypoCCS award, 2006, Mead Johnson award, Am. Soc. Nutrition, 2007, Outstanding Investigator award, Am. Fedn. Med. Rsch., 2008. Office: Divsn Endocrinology Beth Israel Deaconess Med Ctr Boston MA 02215 Business E-Mail: cmantzor@bidmc.harvard.edu.

MANUEL, JERRY, professional baseball team manager; b. Hahira, Ga., Dec. 23, 1953; m. Renette Caldwell; children: Angela, Jerry, Anthony, Natalie. Switch-hitting infielder Class A Lakeland, Class AAA Toledo, 1973, Class AAA Evansville, 1974-75, Detroit Tigers, 1975-76, Montreal Expos, Canada, 1980-81, third base coach, 1991-96; switch-hitting infielder San Diego Padres, 1982, Class AAA Iowa, 1983, Class AAA Denver, 1984; scout Chgo. White Sox, 1985, mgr., 1997—2003; player, coach Indpls. orgn., 1986, infield instr., 1987; minor-league fielding coord. Expos orgn., 1988-89; mgr. Class AAA Indpls. Montreal Expos Sys., 1991; bench coach Fla. Marlins, 1996—97; first base and outfield coach NY Mets, 2005—06, bench coach, 2006—08, interim mgr., 2008, mgr., 2008—. Am. league coach MLB All-Star Game, Boston, 1999. Recipient C.I. Taylor award, Negro Leagues Legacy Awards, 2000; named Co-Mgr. of Yr., So. League, 1990, Am. League Mgr. of Yr., Baseball Writers Assn. America, The Sporting News, 2000, MLB Mgr. of Yr., AP, 2000; named to Calif. Black Sports Hall of Fame, 2000. Office: NY Mets Citi Field 126th St & Roosevelt Ave Flushing NY 11368*

MANUEL, KIMBERLY ANN, design educator; d. Charles and Mary-Ann Manuel. MFA, Calif. Inst. Arts, Valencia, 2004. Props master & scenic artist Burgess Meredith Theatre Bread Loaf Sch. English, Middlebury, Vt., 2003—; scenic artist U. Iowa, 2004—05; asst. prof. design Columbus State U., Ga., 2005—. Office: Columbus State Univ 4225 Univ Ave Columbus GA 31907 Office Fax: 706-571-4354. Personal E-mail: k_manuel78@hotmail.com. Business E-Mail: manuel_kimberly@colstate.edu.

MANUEL, PETER JAY, poet, singer/songwriter, dramatist, language professor, librettist; b. Framingham, Mass. s. John Lewis and Jane Dorothy (Bohlin) Manuel. BA in English, U. So. Maine, 1982, MFA in Creative Writing, 2005. Adj. prof. English So. Maine Cmty. Coll., South Portland, 2003—06. Organizer Geno's Live Poets' Soc., Portland, 2000—05, Word Cirkus, 2006—07. Mem. Trinity touring performance poetry act, 2002—05. Mem.: Acad. Am. Poets. Green Independent. Jewish. Avocation: art. Home: 312 Congress St # 4 Portland ME 04101 Business E-Mail: pmanuel@smccme.edu.

MANUEL, RALPH NIXON, retired private school executive; b. Frederick, Md., Apr. 21, 1936; s. Ralph Walter and Frances Rebecca (Nixon) M.; m. Sarah Jane Warner, July 22, 1960; children: Mark, David, Stephen, Bradley. AB, Dartmouth Coll., 1958, DHL (hon.), 2008; M.Ed., Boston U., 1967; PhD, U. Ill., 1971. Assoc. dean Dartmouth Coll., Hanover, NH, 1971-72, dean of freshmen, 1972-75, dean, 1975-82; pres. Culver (Ind.) Acad. and Culver Edn. Found., 1982-99. Bd. dirs. Ind. Sch. Cen. States, 1986-99, chair, 1993-95. Mem. Assn. Mil. Colls. and Schs. of U.S. (pres., bd. dirs.), Nat. Assn. Ind. Schs. (bd. dirs. 1995-99).

MANUELLA, FRANK, retired art and design educator; b. NYC; BFA, Cooper Union U., 1963; M in Comm. Design, Pratt Inst., 1982. Pres. Manuella & Assocs., NYC, 1963-82; prof. art & design U. Tex., Edinburg, 1982—2008, prof., 2006—08, prof. emeritus, 2008. Asst. prof. design Pratt Inst., N.Y.C., 1975-82; adv. bd. U. Tex. Press, 1982—, coun. mem., 1989-92, officer Phi Kappa Phi, 1990-92, faculty senator, 1986-93. Solo exhbns. include U. Tex. Gallery, 1991, 92, Reynosa, Mex., 1993, McAllen Internat. Mus., 1994; Artist, Other, Design New York City 9th Meml., 2003, One Man Show, Internat. Mus. Art Sci. McAllen, Tex., 2006. Recipient gov.'s award for acad. excellence, State of Tex., 1989; Fulbright grantee, 1993. Office: 1802 IVY Ln Edinburg TX 78539-5369

MANUTA, DAVID MARK, chemist, consultant; b. Bklyn., June 10, 1957; s. Gerald and Vivian Bernice (Chartoff) Manuta; m. Ruth Pauline Krog, Mar. 27, 1988 (dec. Dec. 1993). BS in Chemistry, SUNY, Oneonta, 1979; PhD in Chemistry, SUNY, Binghamton, 1985. Lab. tech. Sci. Process & Rsch., Somerset, NJ, 1980-81; from tchg. asst. to postdoctoral fellow SUNY, Binghamton, 1981-86; asst. prof. Upper Iowa U., Fayette, 1986-88; asst. prof. II Shawnee State U., Portsmouth, Ohio, 1989-90; mem. rsch. staff U.S. Enrichment Corp., Piketon, Ohio, 1990-2000; founder Manuta Chem. Consulting Inc., 1998; dir. Midwest Office Inter City Testing & Cons. Corp., 2004—; sr. cons. Boson Tech. Resources, LLC, 2005—. Tchr. Christ the King Regional HS, NYC, 1986; instr. Stanley Kaplan Exam. Prep. Svcs., Garden City, NY, 1986; mem. strategic planning com. Ohio Acad. Sci., 1996; expert witness, mediator, fire/explosion investigator; Hubzone reseller ThermoFisher Sci. LLC, 2006; cons. in field. Pres. Waverly Heights Crime Watch, 1995; sec. Big Bros./Big Sisters S. Ctrl. Ohio, 1996; pres. Pike County Humane Soc., Ohio, 1997; fin. chair Portsmouth employees chpt. Nat. Mgmt. Assn., 1997. With USN, 1978—79. IBM Corp. Grad. fellow, 1984—85. Fellow: Am. Inst. Chemistry (bd. dirs., pres., membership chmn., bd. chmn.); mem.: ASTM, AAAS, Ohio Acad. Sci., Internat. Assn. Arson Investigators, Nat. Fire Protection Assn., Nat. Forensic Ctr., Assn. Consulting Chemists Chem. Engrs. (bd. dirs.), Am. Chem. Soc. Avocations: chess, reading, running, bicycling, travel. Home: 431 Gordon Ave Waverly OH 45690-1208 Office: Am Inst Chemists 315 Chestnut St Philadelphia PA 19106-2702 Home Phone: 740-947-7998; Office Phone: 740-947-7998. Office Fax: 740-947-1565. Business E-Mail: mc2@dmanuta.com.

MANVILLE, GRETA CRAIG, writer; b. Clarinda, Iowa, June 12, 1932; d. William Donald Craig and Eunice Catherine Nolan; m. Wallace Carruthers Manville, Jr., Feb. 1, 1953. BA, San Jose State U., 1975, MA, 1978. Asst. treas. Argonaut Ins. Co., Menlo Park, Calif., 1962-75; exec. mgr. quality control Consol. Freightways, Menlo Park, 1977-91; freelance writer Sun City West, Ariz., 1991—. Bd. dirs., lit. contest coord. Ariz. Authors Assn., 2006—08; treas., 2009—. Author: Murder Online, 1998, Death Key, 2000 (1st place mystery/suspense category Authorlink website New Authors Awards Competition, 2000); co-author: The Purgatory Trail, 1995 (1st prize S.W. Writers Workshop 1993); author (poetry) Passage, 1999 (Grand prize Sparrowgrass Poetry Forum, 1999); bibliographer Steinbeck Review. Steinbeck fellowship, Martha H. Cox Ctr. Steinbeck Studies, San Jose State U., 2002—03. Avocation: duplicate bridge. Personal E-mail: gmanville@aol.com.

MANVILLE, STEWART ROEBLING, archivist; b. White Plains, NY, Jan. 15, 1927; s. Leo and Margaret (Roebling) Manville; m. Ella V. Grainger, Jan. 19, 1972 (dec.). Student, U. Wyo., 1944-46; BS, Columbia U., 1962. Various office positions, NYC, 1947-51, 56-58; asst. stage dir. several European opera houses, 1951-55; editor Jas. T. White & Co., 1959-63; archivist, curator Percy Grainger Library, White Plains, 1963—. Author: The Manville/Manvel Families in America; contbr. articles to mags. and newspapers. Mem.: SAR, Archivists Round Table Met. NY, St. Nicholas Soc. NY, Westchester Trails Assn. (pres. 2001—05), Brit. Music Soc., Société des Antiquaires de Picardie, Victorian Soc. Am. (past. dir. NY chpt.), Nat. Trust Hist. Preservation. Mem. Soc. Of Friends. Home: 46 Ogden Ave White Plains NY 10605-2323 Office Phone: 914-948-7436.

MANYAK, MICHAEL JOHN, urologist, educator, researcher; b. Flint, Mich., Mar. 25, 1951; m. Rebecca Bruning; children: Rachel, Susannah, Timothy. BA, U. Notre Dame, 1973; MD, U. of East, Manila, 1979. Intern, then resident in gen. surgery Booth Meml. Med. Ctr., Flushing, N.Y., 1980-82; resident in urology George Washington Univ. Med. Ctr., Washington, 1982-84, chief resident, 1984—85, instr. urology, 1988—89, asst. prof., 1989—91, assoc. prof., 1991—95, prof. urology engring. microbiology and tropical medicine, 1996—; v.p. med. affairs Cxtogen Corp., 2005—; v.p. US Med. Sci. EUSA Pharma(USA) Inc.; sr. med. advisor Global Rescue Inc. Mem. adv. bd. Nat. Kidney and Urological Disease, 1992—. Contbr. articles to profl. jours. Adv. bd. aerospace medicine NASA. Fellow Nat. Cancer Inst., 1985-88; scholar Am. Urol. Assn., 1986-88. Fellow Explorers Club (nat. bd. dirs. 1996-06, chmn. sci. adv. bd., Sweeney medal); mem. Am. Urol. Assn. (chmn. tech. coun. 1995). Office: Eusa Pharma 1717 Langhorne NE Newtown Rd Langhorne PA 19047 Office Phone: 215-867-4981. Business E-Mail: michael.manyak@eusapharma.com.

MANYAM, BALA VENKATESHA, medical researcher, neurology educator; arrived in US, 1972, naturalized, 1980; s. Kolar Venktesha and Swarnam (Venktesha) Iyer; m. Rani Manyam; 1 child, Shaila. MB, BS, Bangalore Med. Coll., 1967. Diplomate Am. Bd. of Psychiatry and Neurology. With Thomas Jefferson U., Phila., 1975-83, 83-84, asst. prof. pharmacology, 1981-83, assoc. prof. pharmacology, 1983-84; staff neurologist VA Med. Ctr., Wilmington, Del., 1975-80, asst. chief neurology, 1982-84; assoc. prof. neurology Sch. of Medicine So. Ill. U., Springfield, 1984-92, prof., 1992—99, dir. neurology residency program, 1993—99; prof., dir. Plummar Movement Disorder Ctr., Scott & White Clinic, Tex. A&M U. HSC Coll. Medicine, 1999—2005; disting. rsch. prof. Hindu U. of Am., 2006—. Founding dir. Parkinson's Disease & Movement Disorders Clinic, Springfield, 1984—99; mem. NIH/NCCAM Coun., 2004—07; adj. prof. neurology SI U. Sch. Medicine, 2006—. Contbr. numerous articles to profl. jours.; mem. editl. bd. Phytotherapy Rsch., patentee in field. Grantee NIH, VA, various founds. Fellow Am. Acad. Neurology; mem. Am. Neurologic Assn., Am. Assn. Physicians Indian Origin. Hindu. Achievements include research in drug development from herbs for neurological diseases; patents in field. Avocations: creative writing, history of medicine, collecting old coins and stamps, photography, Indian art. Personal E-mail: balavmanyam@yahoo.com.

MANYAME, COMFORT, systems administrator; b. Harare, Zimbabwe, Dec. 3, 1975; s. Naphtali Manyame and Julia Chigodoroa; m. Nyasha Razunguzwa, Feb. 27, 1999; children: Ngonidzaishe Comfort, Julia Mufaro. BS, U. Zimbabwe, Harare, 1999, MPhil, 2002; PhD, Tex. A&M U., Coll. Sta., 2006. Cert. GIS Certification Inst., 2008. GIS mgr. Mid-South Synergy, Navasota, Tex., 2007—09, mgr., system planning, 2009—. Conf. abstract reviewer Geospatial Info. & Tech. Assn., Aurora, Colo., 2008; asset mgmt. tech. workshop reviewer Urban and Regional Info. Sys. Assn., Pk. Ridge, Ill., 2008. Musician: (albums) Canaan, Pemberai, He Reigns; contbr. articles to jours. and mag. Recipient award, Environ. Sys. Rsch. Inst., 2006. Mem.: Urban and Regional Info. Sys. Assn., Geospatial Info. and Tech. Assn. E-mail: vamanyame@yahoo.com.

MANZ, JOHN R., bishop; BA in Philosophy, Niles Coll. Seminary, Loyola, Ill., 1967; MDiv, U. St. Mary of the Lake, Mundelein, Ill., 1971. Ordained priest Archdiocese of Chgo., 1971, aux. bishop, 1996—; assoc. pastor Providence of God, Chgo., 1971—78, St. Roman, Chgo., 1978—83; pastor St. Agnes of Bohemia, Chgo., 1983—96; dean Chgo.'s Lower West Side, 1987—96; ordained bishop, 1996; vicar for Vicariate III, 1996—. Mem.: US Conf. Catholic Bishops (chmn. Ch. Latin America, mem. adminstrv. com., mem. Migration and Refugee Svcs. Ch. Latin America). Roman Catholic. Home: 1850 S Throop St Chicago IL 60608-3149

MANZANARES, J. ROBERT, Permanent United States Representative to the Organization of American States; b. Colo. BA, Adams State Coll., Alamosa, Colo.; MPA in City Adminstrn., U. Colo., Boulder. Regional mgmt. officer US Dept. State, Abidjan, Cote d'Ivoire, mgmt. officer Mexico City, Reykjavik, Iceland, acting dep. chief of mission, mgmt. counselor Tel Aviv, advance officer for presdl. internat. visits Administrns. of Pres. Ronald Reagan and Pres. George H.W. Bush, sr. watch officer Ops. Ctr., dir. adminstrn. NSC, 1993—94, exec. dir. Bur. African Affairs, 1998—2000, exec. dir. to exec. secretariat Office of Sec. of State Colin Powell, dep. chief of mission, charge d'Affaires US Embassy Spain, 2003—06, acting nat. coord. for the Summits of the Ams., permanent US rep. to OAS, 2007—. Office: Bur Western Hemisphere Affairs US Dept State Rm 5914 2201 C St NW Washington DC 20520 Office Phone: 202-647-9422.*

MANZANO-RUIZ, JUAN JOSÉ, mechanical engineer, researcher; b. Caracas, Venezuela, Jan. 25, 1950; s. Juan Vicente and Carmen Teresa (Ruiz) Manzano; m. Lucila Sánchez; children: Juan Carlos, Anabella, Andres, Raul. Indsl. engr., U. Catolica, Caracas, Venezuela, 1974; MS of Mech. Engring., MIT, 1977, PhD in Mech. Engring., 1981. Registered profl. engr., Venezuela. Rsch. assoc. Inst. Venezuela Invest Sci., Los Teques, Venezuela, 1980-81; various engring. and mgmt. positions Intevep., Los Teques, Venezuela, 1981-83, cons., 1983-86, comml. mgr., 1986-88; engring. cons. PDVSA, Caracas, 1989-94; prof. mech. engring. U. Simon Bolivar, Caracas, 1981-96; various sr. engring. and exec. positions BP, Caracas, 1997—2001, sr. process engr. Houston, 2001—03; process engring. mgr. Jacobs Engring., Houston, 2006—. Contbr. about 40 articles and papers to tech. publs. Sci. fellow Inst. Venezuela Investigacion Cientifica, Los Teques, Venezuela, 1975-80, Mme Curie fellow European Econ. Com., U.K., 1991-92. Mem. Soc. Petroleum Engrs., Am. Biographical Inst.(rsch. bd. adv.). Achievements include patent for steam quality measurement using neutron-attenuation device. Office: Jacobs Engring 5850 Rodgerdale Rd Ste 150 Houston TX 77072 Home: 3903 Meagan Hills Ct Katy TX 77494-1612 Office Phone: 281-776-3961. Business E-Mail: juanmanzano@alum.mit.edu, juan.manzano@jacobs.com.

MANZARI, LAURA LYNN, law educator; b. NYC, Jan. 4, 1959; d. Charles John and Rose Marie (Lepik) Slepetis; m. Peter Michael Manzari, Aug., 19, 1988. BA, Queen's Coll., 1979, MLS, 1986; JD, St. John's U., 1982. Bar: N.Y. 1983. Claim atty. Allstate Ins. Co., Lake Success, N.Y., 1984-85; law libr. Parker Chapin Flattau & Klimpl, NYC, 1985; libr. Pace U., NYC, 1987-89; assoc. prof. L.I. U., Greenvale, 1989—, dept. head Libr. and Info. Sci. Libr., 2000—. Contbr. articles to profl. jours. Mem. ALA, AAUW, Greater N.Y. Assn. Coll. and Rsch. Librs., Nassau County Libr. Office: LI U B Davis Schwartz Meml Libr Greenvale NY 11548 Business E-Mail: manzari@liu.edu.

MANZI, JIM P., investment company executive; b. NYC, Dec. 22, 1951; s. Walter Edward and Ann (Smirka) M.; m. Glenda Baugh, May 20, 1978 BA, Colgate U., 1973; MAL.D., Fletcher Sch., Tufts U., 1979. Editl. asst. Nat. Rev. Mag., NYC, 1973-74; news reporter Gannet Newspapers, Port Chester, 1974-77; cons. McKinsey & Co., LA, Boston and NYC, 1979-83; v.p. mktg. and sales Lotus Devel. Corp., Cambridge, Mass., 1983-84, pres., 1984-86, 89-1996, CEO, 1986-1996; pres., CEO Industry Net, 1996; chmn. StoneGate Capital Group, LLC, Stanford, Conn., 1995—; bd. dirs. ThermoFisher Sci. Inc., Waltham, Mass., 2000—, chmn., 2004—06, 2007—. Recipient In-Depth Reporting award AP, N.Y., 1976, 77, Investigative Reporting award N.Y. State Pubs. Assn., 1976, 77 Office: ThermoFisher Sci Inc 81 Wyman St Waltham MA 02454-9046 also: StoneGate Capital Group LLC 20 Stanford Dr Farmington CT 06032*

MANZO, EDWARD DAVID, lawyer; b. NYC, 1950; BS in Physics, Poly. Inst. NYU, 1972; JD cum laude, SUNY, Buffalo, 1975. Bar: NY 1976, Ill. 1979, US Patent and Trademark Office 1976, US Ct. Appeals (fed. cir.) 1982, US Supreme Ct. 1982. Assoc. Darby & Darby, P.C., NYC, 1975-77; group patent counsel Schlumberger Ltd., NYC, 1977-79; ptnr. Cook, Wetzel & Egan, Chgo., 1979-85, 88-90, Jenner & Block, 1985-88; sr. ptnr. Cook McFarron & Manzo, Ltd., Chgo., 1990-99; sr. ptnr., exec. v.p., treas., CFO Cook Alex Ltd., Chgo., 1999—2005. Instr. DePaul U., Chgo., 1989-91, 2002-03; mem. adv. bd., CIPLIT Program DePaul U. Coll. Law, 2002-, adj. prof. law, 2009-. Author (with others): Intellectual Property Law in Illinois, 1988-90; editor-in-chief Claim Constrn. in Fed. Cir., Thomson Reuters (West) 2006-09, Patent Claim Interpretation-Global Edition, Thomson Reuters -West 2008-; contbr. articles to profl. jours. Bd. dirs. Concertante di Chgo., 1997-2004; Lake Forest Symphony, 2004-08; grantor Edward Manzo Patent Law scholarship DePaul Law Sch., 2001-03, Law Lectures, 2004-. Jaeckle Fleishman grantee, 1973. Mem. Am. Intellectual Property Law Assn., Intellectual Property Law Assn. Chgo. (v.p. 2008-09, pres.-elect 2009-), Stradivari Soc. Chgo., Sicilian Am. Cultural Assn. (treas. 1996-98, v.p. 1998-99, pres. 2000-02) Office: Cook Alex Ltd 200 W Adams St Ste 2850 Chicago IL 60606-5206 Office Phone: 312-236-8500. Business E-Mail: emanzo@cookalex.com.

MANZULLO, DONALD A., United States Representative from Illinois, lawyer; b. Rockford, Ill., Mar. 27, 1944; s. Frank A. Sr. and Catherine M.; m. Freda Teslik; children: Neil, Noel, Katie. BA in Polit. Sci./Internat. Rels., American U., 1967; JD, Marquette U. Law Sch., 1971. Atty., 1970—; mem. U.S. Congress from 16th Ill. Dist., 1993—. Mem. House Com. on Internat. Rels., subcom. internat. econ. policy and trade, subcom. on Asia and the Pacific, House Com. on small bus., chmn. on subcom. on tax, fin. and exports, Banking Com. and its capital markets, securities and govt.-sponsored enterprises subcom. Mem. No. Ill. Alliance for Arts, Friends of Severson Dells, Citizens Against Govt. Waste, Rep. Nat. Com. Recipient George Washington honor medal for excellence in pub. comm. Freedoms Found., Valley Forge, Pa., 1991. Mem. ABA, Ill. Bar Assn., Ogle County Bar Assn. (pres. 1971, 73), Nat. Legal Found., Acad. Polit. Sci., Ill. Press Assn., Ill. C. of C., Oregon City C. of C., Nat. Land Inst., Nat. Fedn. Ind. Bus., Ogle County Hist. Soc., Aircraft Owners and Pilots Assn., Ogle County Pilots Assn., Ill. Farm Bur., Ogle County Farm Bur. Republican. Office: US House Reps 2228 Rayburn House Office Bldg Washington DC 20515-1316*

MAO, LI, molecular biologist, educator; b. Nanjing, China, July 16, 1957; s. Xiqiu Mao and Yihe Huang; m. Jialing Xu, Dec. 25, 1982; children: Melissa Shanshan, Roger Tiger. MD, Nanjing Med. U., China, 1977—82. Diplomate China, 1982. Attending surgeon Nanjing Med. U. Hosp., China, 1989—95; rsch. fellow Johns Hopkins Med. Sch., Balt., 1992—95; asst. prof., medicine U. Tex., M.D. Anderson Cancer Ctr., Houston, 1995—99, assoc. prof., medicine, 1999—2004, prof., medicine, 2004—; exec. v.p., chief tech. officer Cangen Internat., Irvine, Calif., 2001—02. Advisor Panacea Pharmaceuticals, Washington,

2003—. Mem.: AACR (corr.). Office: Univ Texas MD Anderson Cancer Ctr Unit 432 PO Box 301402 Houston TX 77230-1402 Home: 6318 Kerne Ct Clarksville MD 21029-1557 Office Fax: 713-796-8655. E-mail: lmao@mdanderson.org.

MAO, RUIXUAN (RICK MAO), dean; arrived in US, 1986; s. Junye Mao and Wenhua Wu; m. Mi Hu, Oct. 6, 1980; m. Kangquan Zhou, Nov. 15, 1967 (div. May 9, 1980); children: Shufan, Guxia, Guyang Alex. BS, S.W. China Teachers U., Chongqing, 1964; MS, U. Tenn., Knoxville, 1986, PhD, 1993. Asst. prof. to assoc. prof. English S.W. China Teachers U., Chongqing, Sichuan, China, 1964—86; grad. asst. U. Tenn., Knoxville, 1986—89, instr. Chinese, 1989—90, grad. tchg. asst., 1990—92; asst. prof. English and coord. English edn. Philander Smith Coll., Little Rock, 1992—95, chair of divsn. of edn., assoc. prof. of edn., 1995—98; assoc. dir. instl. rsch. and planning The Ross Sch., East Hampton, NY, 1998—2002; dean liberal arts and social sci. Elgin C.C., Ill., 2002—05, dean comms. and behavioral sci., 2005—. Dir. instrn. and rsch. srs. S.W. China Teachers U., Chongqing, 1982—86, dir. internship program, 1982—86; English editor natural sci. series S.W. China Teachers U. Jour., 1979—86; translator Chinese edit. Sci. Am. Jour., 1980—85; editor Internat. Edn. Jour., Knoxville, Tenn., 1986—. Editor: (textbooks) English (Volumes I-VIII), 1973—75, Tunnel English (Volumes 1-3), 1974, Teacher's Manual for English (Volumes 1-6), 1976. Recipient Multicultural Presentation award, Little Rock Dist. U.S. Army Corps of Engrs., 1993, Extraordinary Contbn. award, The Ross Sch., 2002; grantee, Ark. State Dept. Higher Edn., 1995—98, Ill. C.C. Bd., 2003—, Historically Black Colls.and Univs., 1997; Hilton A. Smith fellow, U. Tenn., Knoxville, 1988—89. Mem.: Rotary (Elgin Breakfast chpt.). Avocations: bridge, ping pong/table tennis. Office: Elgin CC 1700 Spartan Dr Elgin IL 60123 Office Fax: 847-622-3048. Business E-Mail: rmao@elgin.edu.

MAO, SHIWEN, engineering educator; PhD, Poly. U., Bklyn. Rsch. scientist Va. Tech., Blacksburg, 2003—06; asst. prof. Auburn U., Ala., 2006—. Co-chair ICST Engring. Practice Sci. and Tech. Coun., 2007—, Wireless Comm. and Networking Symposium, Hangzhou, Zhejiang, China, 2007—08; tech. program com. co-chair 5th Internat. Conf. Testbeds and Rsch. Infrastructure Devel. Networks and Cmtys., Washington, 2008—, Ad Hoc Networks, Niagara Falls, Ont., Canada, 2008—. Author: (book) Broadband Mobile Multimedia: Techniques and Applications; co-author (with Shivendra S. Panwar): TCP/IP Essentials: A Lab-based Approach, 2004; contbr. articles. Recipient Leonard G. Abraham prize, IEEE Comm. Soc., 2004, Appreciation award, IEEE Computer Soc., 2007, Best Paper Runner-up award, QShine, Hong Kong, 2008. Mem.: IEEE, Eta Kappa Nu, Tau Beta Pi. Achievements include patents for method and apparatus for control and routing of wireless sensor networks. Office: Auburn Univ 200 Broun Hall Auburn AL 36849-5201 Personal E-mail: maoshiwen@hotmail.com.

MAO, WEIDONG, communications engineer, technology executive; arrived in U.S., 1986; BS, Beijing U., 1986; PhD in Elec. Engring., Princeton U., NJ, 1991. Sr. mem. rsch. staff Philips Electronics, Briarcliff Manor, NY, 1990—94; dir. telecom. unit Gen. Instrument, Horsham, Pa., 1994—97; co-founder, chief tech. officer MoreCom, Horsham, 1997—2000; v.p. tech. Liberate Tech., San Carlos, Calif., 2000—03; sr. fellow Comcast, Phila., 2003—. Key contbr. Moving Picture Expert Group, 1990—96; invited spkr. Nat. Cable TV Assn., 2004, 08; panelist Cable TV Labs., 2004. Wallace Meml. fellowship, Princeton U., 1989—90. Mem.: Soc. Motion Picture and TV Engrs., Soc. Cable Telecomm. Engrs., IEEE (sr.). Achievements include invention of digital TV system with synchronized www content; channel changer in a switched video system; apparatus and method for webcasting over digital TV; pioneer of digital cable, video on demand, and interactive television. Office: Comcast Cable 1 Comcast Ctr Philadelphia PA 19103 Office Phone: 215-286-7306, 215-286-7306. Business E-Mail: weidong_mao@cable.comast.com.

MAO, WEIDONG, science educator; b. Wuhan, Hubei, China, Apr. 27, 1970; s. Yilin Mao and Yu Sun; children: Ziwei, Mulan. BS, Wuhan U., 1992; MS, Wuhan U. Tech., 1999; PhD, Ga. State U., Atlanta, 2006. Asst. prof. Shippensburg U. Pa., Pa., 2006—07, Va. State U., Petersburg, 2007—. Author: (book) Genetic Epidemiology: Prediction of Susceptibility to Complex Diseases; contbr. articles to profl. jours. Grant, NIH, 2009.

MAO, YUAN, research scientist, educator; MS in Chemistry, Wuhan U., Hubei, China, 2005; Candidate, Fla. State U., Tallahassee, 2007—. Asst. lectr. Wuhan U. Sci. & Tech., Hubei, China, 2005—07; rsch. asst. Nat. High Magnetic Field Lab., Tallahassee, 2008—. Contbr. articles to profl. jours. Scholarship, Fla. state U., 2007. Mem.: Am. Soc. Mass Spectrometry. Business E-Mail: mao@magnet.fsu.edu.

MAO, ZHIQIANG, physics professor; b. Daiyang, Jiangsu, China, Dec. 5, 1965; s. Ligen Mao and Fengyin Tang; m. Yu Wang, Sept. 21, 1990; 1 child, Alice. PhD, U. Sci. & Tech. China, 1992. Asst. prof. Tulane U., New Orleans, 2002—07, assoc. prof., 2007—. Recipient Award, Rsch. Corp., 2005, Rsch. award, NSF, 2007. Mem.: Am. Phys. Soc. Office: Tulane Univ 6823 St Charles Ave New Orleans LA 70118 Office Fax: 504-862-8702. Business E-Mail: zmao@tulane.edu.

MAOCHENG, YAN, research scientist; married. PhD, China U. Petroleum, Beijing, 2005. Rsch. assoc. Inst. Metal Rsch., Chinese Acad. Scis., Shengyang, Liaoning, China, 2005—07; postdoc. rsch. assoc. ND State U., Fargo, 2007—. Contbr. scientific papers. Recipient Excellent Paper award, Chinese Soc. Corrosion and Protection, 2003. Mem.: Nat. Assn. Corrosion Engrs. Achievements include research in firstly demonstrate sacrificial (cathodic) protection of a metal by a fully organic coating — neutral and n-doped conjugated polymer and propose a cathodic protection mechanism; firstly characterize the stress corrosion cracking susceptibility of pipeline steel in a crevice by experimental E-pH diagrams and proved that the near-neutral pH SCC environment can be obtained. Office: Coatings and Polymeric Materials NDSU PO Box 6050 1735 Rsch Park Dr Fargo ND 58108-6050 Personal E-mail: maocheng.yan@yahoo.com. Business E-Mail: maocheng.yan@ndsu.edu.

MAPEL, DOUGLAS WAYNE, epidemiologist, educator, pulmonologist, critical care specialist; b. Torrejon U.S. AFB, Madrid, Spain, Apr. 14, 1961; m. Cynthia Caruso-Mapel (div.); children: Xena, Sierra. BS in Chemistry, U. Tex., Arlington, 1984; MD, U. Tex., Galveston, 1988; MPH, U. N.Mex., 1996. Diplomate Am. Bd. Internal Medicine, Am. Bd. Pulmonary Diseases, Am. Bd. Critical Care Medicine. Resident Tex. Tech. U., Lubbock, 1988—92; fellow U. N.Mex., Albuquerque, 1992—96, asst. prof., 1996—2000, clin. prof., 2001—; med. dir. Lovelace Respiratory Rsch. Inst., Albuquerque, 2001—03, Lovelace Clinic Found., Albuquerque, 2003—; sr. ptnr. Progressive Med. Intensivists, 2003—06; founding ptnr. Critical Care Cons. of Ariz., 2006—, Northern Ariz. Pulmonary Assn. Co-author: (book) Rom's Occupational Medicine, 1998, Occupational Disorders of the Lung, 2001; contbr. articles to profl. jours., scientific papers. Fellow: Am. Coll. Chest Physicians (Clin. Rsch. award 2004); mem.: ACP, Am. Thoracic Soc. Home: PO Box 67050 Albuquerque NM 87193 Office: Lovelace Clin Found 2309 Renard Pl SE Ste 103 Albuquerque NM 87106 Office Phone: 505-938-9900. Business E-Mail: doug.mapel@lcfresearch.org.

MAPEL, WILLIAM MARLEN RAINES, retired bank executive; b. Maryville, Mo., Sept. 17, 1931; s. William and Evelyn (Raines) M.; m. Gail Manchee, June 21, 1958; children: Daniel B., Susan L., Stephen W. BA, Yale U., 1953. Indsl. relations asst. Union Carbide Corp., NYC, 1953-57; with Citibank (N.A.), NYC, 1957-88, asst. cashier, 1959-62, asst. v.p., 1962-64, v.p., 1964-69, sr. v.p., 1969-88. Bd. dirs. Atlantic Salmon Fedn. Bd. Miramichi Salmon Assn. Mem. U.S. Srs. Golf Assn., Wentworth-By-The-Sea Country Club, Pine Valley Golf Club, Anglers Club, Wolf's Head, Delta Kappa Epsilon. Home: PO Box 2063 New Castle NH 03854

MAPES, GLYNN DEMPSEY, newspaper editor; b. NYC, July 15, 1939; s. John George and Dorothy (Glynn) M.; m. Elizabeth Adlum, Apr. 13, 1963; children— Timothy Glynn, Susannah Glynn. BA, Williams Coll., 1961. Reporter Wall St. Jour., San Francisco, 1965-67, bur. chief Phila., 1967-70, fgn. editor NYC, 1970-71, bur. chief, 1971-75, Page One editor, 1975-88, Reports editor, 1988-89, bur. chief London, 1989-93, money and investing editor NYC, 1993-99, asst. mgn. editor, 1999—. Bd. dirs., singer Bronx Opera Co. Lt. (j.g.) USN, 1961—65. Mem.: London Concert Choir, Collegiate Chorale. Democrat. Home: 37 W 12th St Apt 2H New York NY 10011-8503 Office: Wall St Jour 200 Liberty St New York NY 10281-1003 E-mail: gmapes@pipeline.com.

MAPLE, MARILYN JEAN, educational media coordinator; b. Turtle Creek, Pa., Jan. 16, 1931; d. Harry Chester and Agnes (Dobbie) Kelley; 1 child, Sandra Maple. BA, U. Fla., 1972, MA, 1975, PhD, 1985. Journalist various newspaper including Mountain Eagle, Jasper, Ala., Boise (Idaho) Statesman, Daytona Beach (Fla.) Jour., Lorain (Ohio) Jour.; account exec. Frederides & Co., NYC; prodr. hist. films Fla. State Mus., Gainesville, 1967-69; writer, dir., prodr. med. and sci. films and TV prodns. for 6 medically related colls. U. Fla., Gainesville, 1969—. Pres. Media Modes, Inc., Gainesville. Author: On the Wings of a Butterfly, The Refuge Two Bunny Tails; columnist Health Care Edn. mag.; contbr. Fla. Hist. Quar. Recipient Blakslee award, 1969, spl. award, 1979; Monsour lectr., 1979. Mem. Health Edn. Media Assn. (bd. dirs., awards 1977, 79), Phi Delta Kappa, Kappa Tau Alpha. Office: U Fla PO Box 16J Gainesville FL 32602-0016 Home: 125 Deep Lake Tr Melrose FL 32666 Personal E-mail: mmaple@atlantic.net.

MAPLES, KAREN ELIZABETH, obstetrician, gynecologist; b. June 24, 1954; MD (hon.), UCLA, 1980. Cert. Am. Bd. Ob-gyn. Intern, ob-gyn. U. So. Calif. Womens Hosp., LA, 1980—82; resident Harbor-UCLA Med. Ctr., Torrance, Calif., 1982—84; hosp. appointment Kaiser Permanente Med. Ctr., Bellflower, Calif.; asst. clin. prof. UCLA Sch. Medicine. Mem.: Assn. Black Women Physicians Office. Achievements include being the member of a California team of doctors that delivered the second set of octuplets ever born in the US. Responsible for delivering the 8th baby, when doctors only thought there were 7 babies. Office: Kaiser Permanente Med Ctr 9400 E Rosecrans Blvd Ste 4300 Bellflower CA 90706 Address: 9449 Imperial Hwy Downey CA 90242-2814 Office Phone: 562-461-4127.*

MAPLES, MICHAEL D., federal agency administrator, career military officer; b. Bonham, Tex., 1949; m. Lynn; children: Meredith, Katherine, Elizabeth. Graduate, US Mil. Acad., 1971; MA in Organizational Behavior, Pacific Lutheran U. Commd. 2d. lt. US Army, 1971, advanced through grades to lt. gen., 2005; stationed at Ft. Lewis, Wash., Republic of Korea; tng. mgmt. officer Ft. Sam Houston, Tex.; various assignments Desert Shield/Desert Storm; sr. military aide to sec. US Army; comdr. Babenhausen, Hungary; dep. chief staff ops. US Army Europe, Tazar, Hungary, asst. chief of staff G3, V Corps Heidelberg, Germany; asst. divsn. comdr. (support) 1st Armored Divsn. US Army Europe & Seventh Army, Germany; dir. mil. support, Office Dep. Chief of Staff for Ops. & Plans US Army, dir. ops., readiness & mobilization, Office Dep. Chief of Staff for Ops. & Plans Washington, 2000—01; commdg. gen. US Army Field Artillery Ctr., Ft. Sill, Okla., 2001—03; vice dir., dir. mgmt. The Joint Staff, The Pentagon, 2003—05; dir. Def. Intelligence Agy., Washington, 2005—. Decorated Legion of Merit with oak leaf cluster, Bronze Star medal, Def. Superior Svc. award with oak leaf cluster, Meritorious Svc. medal with three oak leaf clusters, Army Commendation medal with oak leaf cluster, Army Achievement medal, French Croix du Guerre with silver star. Office: Def Intelligence Agy 7400 Def Pentagon Washington DC 20301*

MAPLES, PHILIP G., retired museum director; s. Philip B Maples and Jessie Hazel Galligan; m. Karen E Ritz, Mar. 26, 1977; children: Philip C, Susan E. MA, SUNY, Brockport, NY, 1976. Curator of decorative arts Mattatuck Mus., Waterbury, Conn., 1971—72; asst. curator for registration Old Mus. Village of Smith's Clove, Monroe, NY, 1972; hist. rschr. and preparator Cayuga County Historian's Office, Auburn, NY, 1972—73; curator/dir. Arcade Hist. Soc., Arcade, NY, 1989—92, Baker-Cederberg Mus. and Archives, Rochester, NY, 1989—2009. Author: (institutional history) To Serve the Community: a Sesquicentennial History of Rochester General Hospital, 1847 to 1997, (monograph) Outline for an Emergency Medical Services History Program, Organizing a Healthcare History Program; contbr. articles in field to profl. jours. Fellow: Co. of Mil. Historians. Home Phone: 585-266-9034. Personal E-mail: p_maples@msn.com.

MAPLESDEN, CAROL HARPER, marriage and family therapist, music educator; b. Phila., Aug. 27, 1947; d. Emmitt Dewain and Helen Esther (Davison) Harper; m. James Paul Maplesden, May 27, 1967; children: Andrew James, Elizabeth Elvira. BA, Holy Family Coll., Phila., 1979; MA, La Salle U., Phila., 1984. Cert. counselor Nat. Bd. Cert. Counselors, lic. profl. counselor of mental health Del., Pa. Child, youth and family therapist People Acting To Help, Phila., 1983—86, Benjamin Rush Cmty. Mental Health, Phila., 1987-88; clin. dir. N.E. Treatment, Phila., 1988-89; outpatient supr. Interact Com. Mental Health, Phila., 1989; program supr. Cath. Charities Christopher House, Trenton, N.J., 1989-90; dir. Carden Family Inst., Phila., 1984—, CEO, 1984—, instr. keyboard, organist, vocal performer, vocal choir and handbell choir dir. Carden music div., 1993—. Seminar lectr. in Phila. area. Author: (piano course and audio tape) Young Beginnings Piano Course, Part I, 1993. Mem.: DAR, APA, DAC, NRC (hon. bus. chmn. 2004), Internat. Assn. Marriage and Family Counselors, Daus. Am. Colonists (chpt. regent 2006—), Daughters Union Vets. Civil War (Pa. state pres. 2001—02). Republican. Methodist. Avocations: history studies, genealogy, crafts. Office Phone: 215-741-4234.

MAPOSA, SITHOKOZILE, nursing researcher; b. Bulawayo, Zimbabwe, Nov. 15, 1959; d. Fayita Aaron Maphosa and Lainah Mpedzisi-Maphosa; 1 child, Linda Siphethokuhle. BA, U. South Africa, Pretoria, 1994; MSN, Case Western Res. U., Cleve., 1996; PhD, St. Louis U., 2009. RN Zimbabwe Nurses Coun., 1980. Asst. dir. svc. delivery Zimbabwe Nat. Family Planning Coun., Harare, 2001—02; program mgr. Advance Africa Zimbabwe, Harare, 2002—04; rsch. asst. St. Louis U. Sch. Nursing, 2004—. Sec. Ministry Health & Child Welfare-Reproductive Health Sect., Harare, 2000—04. Policy Communication Fellowship, Population Reference Bur., 2007—08, Margaret Ln. Fellowship, Margaret McNamara Meml. Fund., 2005. Mem.: Delta Lambda Chpt. Achievements include development of effective public health messages to prevent HIV/AIDS. Home: 4303 D Laclede Ave Saint Louis MO 63108 Office: St Louis Univ Sch Nursing 3525 Caroline Mall St Saint Louis MO 63104 Office Fax: 314-977-8949. Personal E-mail: teemaposa@yahoo.com. Business E-Mail: maposas@slu.edu.

MAPOTHER, THOMAS CRUISE See CRUISE, TOM

MAPP, ALF JOHNSON, JR., writer, historian, educator; b. Portsmouth, Va., Feb. 17; s. Alf Johnson and Lorraine (Carney) M.; m. Hartley Lockhart, Mar. 28, 1953; 1 son, Alf Johnson III; m. Ramona Hartley Hamby, Aug. 1, 1971. AA, Coll. William and Mary, 1945, AB summa cum laude, 1961; LLD (hon.), Old Dominion U., 2005. Editorial writer Portsmouth Star, 1945-46, assoc. editor, 1946-48, editorial chief, 1948-54; news editor, editorial writer Virginian-Pilot, Norfolk, 1954-58; free-lance writer, 1958—; lectr. Old Dominion U., 1961-62, instr., 1962-67, asst. prof. English and history, 1967-73, assoc. prof. English, journalism, creative writing, history, 1973-79, prof., 1979-82, eminent prof., 1982-89, eminent scholar, 1989-92, eminent scholar emeritus, 1992—, Louis I. Jaffe prof. English, 1990-92; Louis I. Jaffe prof. emeritus, 1992—. Radio commentator WSAP, Portsmouth, Va., 1947-48; profl. lectr., 1984—; frequent analyst or guest on radio and TV including individual stas. and Universal Studio and BBC radio networks, CBS-TV, 1985—, C-SPAN, 1998—, PBS, 2001, NPR, 2001, CNN, 2001—, World-Wide Ave Maria Network, 2005.; mem. Nat. Jefferson-Hemings Scholars commn., 2001-2002. Host (TV series) Jamestown to Yorktown, 1975—77; author: The Virginia Experiment, 1975, 4th edit., 2007, Frock Coats and Epaulets, 1963, 5th edit., 1996, America Creates Its Own Literature, 1965, Just One Man, 1968, The Golden Dragon: Alfred the Great and His Times, 1974, 4th edit., 1990, Thomas Jefferson: A Strange Case of Mistaken Identity, 1987, 3d edit., 1989 (Book-of-Month Club feature selection, 1987), Thomas Jefferson: Passionate Pilgrim, 1991, 3d edit., 1993 (Book-of-Month Club feature selection, 1991), (novel) Bed of Honor, 1995, 2d edit., 2000, Three Golden Ages: Discovering the Creative Secrets of Renaissance Florence, Elizabethan England, and America's Founding, 1998, Faiths of Our Fathers: What America's Founders Really Believed, 2003; co-author: Chesapeake Bay in the Revolution, 1981, Portsmouth: A Pictorial History, 1989, Constitutionalism: Founding and Future, 1989, Constitutionalism and Human Rights, 1991, Great American Presidents, 1995; mem. editl. bd. Jamestown Found., 1967—, author lyrics for symphonic composition, world debut with Va. Symphony, 1998; contbr. to NY Times, Wall St. Jour., other newspapers and mags. Mem. Portsmouth-Norfolk County Savs. Bond Com, 1948-51, Va. Com. on Libr. Devel., 1949-50; mem. publs. com. 350th Anniversary of Rep. Govt. in the Western World, 1966-69, War of Independence Commn., 1967-83; chmn. Portsmouth Revolutionary Bicentennial Com., 1968-81; chmn. awards jury Baruch award United Daus. Confederacy-Columbia U., 1976, mem., 1980; chmn. Portsmouth Mus. and Fine Arts Commn., 1983-85, Southeastern Va. Anglo-Am. Friendship Day, 1976, Bicentennial Commemoration of Cornwallis' Embarkation for Yorktown, 1981, World Premiere of Mary Rose Marine Archeol. Exhibit, 1985; mem. grant rev. com. Va. Commn. for the Arts, 1986-87; bd. dirs. Portsmouth Pub. Libr., 1948-58, v.p., 1954-56; bd. dirs. Va. Symphony, 1986-87, trustee, 1987—; mem. taxes and mandates com. City of Portsmouth, 1982-86; mem. adv. com. City Mgr. of Norfolk, 1988-94; bd. dirs. Portsmouth Area Cmty. Chest, 1948-52, Va. YMCA Youth and Govt. Found., 1950-52; mem. All-Am. cities com. for award-winning city Nat. League Municipalities, 1976; bd. advisors Ctr. Study Interactive Learning, Pasadena, Calif., 1993—; mem. steering com. Old Dominion U. Friends of the Libr., 1994-2002, dir., 1995-2002; trustee Coun. for Am.'s First Freedom, 1994-98; chair ad hoc com. Joint Portsmouth-Suffolk Libr., 1999-2004; dir. Va. R.R. Mus., 2000-. Named Portsmouth Young Man of Year, 1951; recipient honor medal Freedoms Found., 1951, Disting. Rsch. award Old Dominion U., 1987, Great Citizen award Hampton Roads 8 Cities, 2001, Notable Citizen award Portsmouth, Va., 1987; English award Old Dominion Coll., 1961; Troubadour, Great Tchrs. award, 1969; Outstanding Am. Educator award, 1972, 74; Nat. Bicentennial medal Am. Revolution Bicentennial Adminstrsn., 1976; medal Comité Francais du Bicentenaire de l'Independence des Etats-Unis, France, 1976; (with Ramona Mapp) Nat. Family Svc. award Family Found. Am., 1980; Laureate award Commonwealth of Va., 1981; Disting. Alumnus award Old Dominion U., 1982; Liberty Bell award Portsmouth Bar Assn., 1985; Old Dominion U. Triennial Phi Kappa Phi Scholar award, 1986, 91; History medal Great Bridge Chpt. DAR, Nat. Notary medal, 2007; Portsmouth Downtown Merchants award, 1984, 85, Nat. Founders and Patriots award, 1995; Old Dominion U. Outstanding Achievement award, 1995; Gladstone Hill Friend of the Arts award (with Ramona H. Mapp), 1995, Richard Hakluyt award for Am. history, 1996, First Freedom Tchg. Excellence awrd named in his honor Coun. for Am.'s 1st Freedom, 2005; named to Order of the Crown of Charlemagne, 1993. Mem. Am. Hist. Assn., Va. Hist. Soc., Portsmouth Hist. Soc. (historiographer 1975-82, v.p. 1982-84, pres. 1985), Norfolk Hist. Soc. (dir. 1965-72), No. Neck Hist. Soc., Hist. Socs. Eastern Va. (dir. 1971—), SAR, Am. Assn. U. Profs., Authors Guild, Va. Library Assn. (legislative com. 1950-51), Poetry Soc. Va. (pres. 1974-75, adv. com. 1976—), Va. Writers Club, Assn. Preservation of Va. Antiquities, Order of Cape Henry (dir. 1970—, nat. pres. 1975-76), Jamestowne Soc. (chief historian 1975-77, internat. sec. state 1978-79), English Speaking Union (dir. 1976-77), Modern Lang. Assn., Order of First Families Va. 1607-1624 (councillor 1996-99), Nat. Historians Circle, Phi Theta Kappa, Delta Phi Omega (chpt. pres. 1961), Phi Kappa Phi. Baptist. Home: Willow Oaks 2901 Tanbark Ln Portsmouth VA 23703-4828 Office Phone: 757-484-6273. Personal E-mail: amapp@cox.net.

MAPP, CATHERINE, performing arts educator, department chairman; d. Richard Custis Mapp and Martha Cory; m. Harvie S., Jan. 29, 1978. BA, Coll. William and Mary, Williamsburg, Va., 1975; MA, Tchrs. Coll., Columbia U., NYC, 1992. Asst. prof. Iona Coll., New Rochelle, NY, 1990—2004, chairperson, fine and performing arts dept., 1997—2004, 2007—, assoc. prof., 2004—. Curatorial dir. Art and Noon Dance Events Iona Coll., 1994—2007, Choreographer 's Symposium, Gender, Identity and Image Iona Coll., 2004; performers Peace, 2002—03. Soloist with Nancy Meehan Dance Company, 1986, 1989, 1990—93, Understudy, Erick Hawkins Dance Co., 1996; choreographer (solo) The Crossing, 1991, Emergence, 2002; group choreography, Selected Works-Joule, Dialogic Landscape, Hallelujah!, Short Stories, Calling Out, 1996—2008; author: (liner notes) Belief, Leon Parker Group, Sony Records, 1996. Recipient Hugh J. McCabe Meml. award, 2004, Merit Tchg. award, 1999—2003. Mem.: Internat. Baccalaureate Orgn. (intial document steering com. mem. 1998, examiner 2008), Nat. Dance Assn., Congress Rsch. Dance. Achievements include founder of dance program & curricula developmant Iona College.

MAPP, EDWARD CHARLES, speech educator; b. NYC, Aug. 17, 1929; s. Edward Cameron and Estelle Viola (Sampson) Mapp; children: Andrew, Elmer, Everett. BA, CCNY, 1953; MS, Columbia U., 1956; PhD, NYU, 1970. Tchr. Bd. Edn., NYC, 1957-64; dir. librs. N.Y.C. Tech. Coll. CUNY, 1964-77, dean of faculty Borough of Manhattan CC NYC, 1977-81, prof. speech and communication, 1983-92, prof. emeritus, 1994—; vice chancellor City Colls. Chgo., 1982-83. Treas. univ. faculty senate CUNY, 1974—77; commr. N.Y.C. Commn. Human Rights, 1987—94, vice chair, 1992—94; print model Funny Face Today, 1994—2002. Compiler Books for Occupational Education Programs, 1971, Directory of Blacks in Performing Arts, 1978, Directory of Blacks in Performing Arts, 2d edit., 1990; editor: (book) Puerto Rican Perspectives, 1974; author: African-Americans and the Oscar, 2008, Blacks in American Films: Today and Yesterday, 1972, Wednesday at Weeksville, 2005; co-author: (book) A Separate Cinema, 1992; columnist: Movie/TV Mktg., 1979—91. Mem. Bklyn. Borough Pres. Adv. Panel, 1981—84; mem. exec. com. Com. Pub. Higher Edn., NYC, 1978—81; bd. dirs. UN Assn. N.Y., 1975—78; trustee N.Y. Met. Ref. and Rsch. Agy., 1980—82. Recipient Founders Day award, NYU, 1970, award, Acad. Motion Picture Arts and Scis., 1996, Townsend Harris medal, City Coll. NY, 2009; named Comms. Educator of Yr., City Coll. N.Y., 2005; named to Black Collectors Hall of Fame, 1992. Mem.: Theatre Libr. Assn., Audelco, Friends Thirteen (bd. dirs. 2000—, 1st vice-chmn. 2003—05, chmn. 2005—07, co-chmn. Legacy Soc. 2007—), Archons Colophon (convenor 1985—86). Democrat.

MAQBOOL, ASIM, pediatrician, gastroenterologist; BS, MD, George Wash. U., Washington, 1997. Cert. in pediat. gastroent. Am. Bd. Pediat., 2005, nutrition specialist Am. Bd. Physician Nutrition Specialists, 2005. Resident physician Children's Hosp., Detroit, 1997—2000; fellow, pediat. gastroent. hepatology, and nutrition Johns Hopkins Hosp., JHU Sch. Medicine, JHU Bloomberg Sch. Pub. Health, Balt., 2003; attending physician and asst. prof. pediat. Children's Hosp. Phila. and U. Pa. Sch. Medicine, 2003—, clin. rschr., 2003—. Contbr. articles to profl. jours. Mem.: ASN, NASPGHAN. Office: Children's Hosp Phila 34th and Civic Ctr Blvd Philadelphia PA 19104

MAQSOOD, AHSAN, cardiologist, researcher; s. Maqsood Ul Hassan and Parveen Maqsood; m. Madiha Ahsan, Dec. 11, 1995; children: Mahnoor Ghumman, Aleena Ghumman. MD, Army Med Coll., Pakistan, 1994. Diplomate internal medicine Am. Bd. Internal Medicine, 2002, cardiology Am. Bd. Internal Medicine, 2005. Ho. staff CMH, Rawalpindi, Punjab, Pakistan, 1995, MH, 2005—06; med. officer KRL, 1996—97; medicine resident NBIMC, 1999—2002, cardiology fellow, 2002—05, interventional fellow, 2005—. Chief cardiology fellow NBIMC, Newark, 2004—05. Fellow: ACC (licentiate). Achievements include research in Qrs association with LV functin in paced rhythm; clinical significance of borderline elevated troponin. Office: Newark Beth Israel Med Ctr 201 Lyons Ave Newark NJ 07112 Office Fax: 973-926-7852. Personal E-mail: ahsanmaqsood@hotmail.com.

MAR, ERIC LEE, city supervisor, college professor; b. San Francisco, Aug. 15, 1962; m. Sandra Chin; 1 child, Jade. Assoc. prof. Asian Am./Ethnic Studies San Francisco State U., 1992—; supr., Dist. 1 San Francisco Bd. Supervisors, 2009—, vice-chair govt. audits & oversight com., land use & econ. devel. com. Acting asst. dean New Coll. Calif., San Francisco, 1993—97; elected mem. San Francisco County & Ctrl. Com. Dem. Party, 1998—; commr. San Francisco Bd. Edn., 2000—; past mem. human rights com. State Bar Calif.; past mem. civil rights com. Nat. Asian Pacific Am. Bar Assn.; past dir. Northern Calif. Coalition Immigrant Rights. Recipient Cmty. Svc. award, Asian Pacific Am. Labor Alliance, 1999. Mem.: Chinese Progressive Assn., Asians & Pacific Islanders for Cmty. Empowerment (founding mem.). Democrat. Office: City Hall 1 Dr Carlton B Goodlett Pl Rm 24 San Francisco CA 94102 Office Phone: 415-554-7410. Office Fax: 415-554-7415. Business E-Mail: Eric.L.Mar@sfgov.org.*

MARA, JOHN KEVIN, professional sports team executive; b. NYC, Dec. 1, 1954; s. Wellington Timothy and Ann (Mumm) Mara; m. Denise Walter; children: Lauren, Courtney, John Jr., Christine, Erin. BS in Mktg., Boston Coll., 1976; JD, Fordham U., 1979. Atty. Vedder, Price, Kaufman, Kammholz & Day, Shea & Gould; exec. v.p., gen. counsel NY Giants, East Rutherford, NJ, 1991—2005, pres., CEO, 2005—. Bd. dirs. St. Vincent's Hosp., The Sch. Holy Child, Catholic Community Services. Office: NY Giants Giants Stadium East Rutherford NJ 07073

MARADUDIN, ALEXEI A., physics professor; b. San Francisco, Dec. 14, 1931; BS, Stanford U., 1953, MS, 1954; PhD in Physics, Bristol U., 1957; D (hon.), U. Pierre et Marie Curie, Paris, 1986. Rsch. assoc. physics U. Md., College Park, 1956—57, rsch. asst. prof., 1957—58; asst. rsch. prof. Inst. Fluid Dynamics & Applied Math., 1958—60; physicist Westinghouse Rsch. Labs., Churchill Borough, Pa., 1960—65; cons. semiconductor br. U.S. Naval Rsch. Lab., Washington, 1958—60, Los Alamos Sci. Lab., N.Mex., 1965—67, 1983—89, Gen. Atomic Divsn. Gen. Dynamics Corp., 1965—71; prof. physics U. Calif., Irvine, 1965—, chmn. dept., 1968—71. Recipient Alexander von Humboldt U.S. Sr. Scientist award, 1980—81. Fellow: AAAS, Am. Phys. Soc., Optical Soc. Am., Inst. Physics (U.K.); mem.: Electromagnetics Acad., Phi Beta Kappa, Sigma Xi, Tau Beta Pi. Office: U Calif Irvine Dept Physics & Astronomy Rowland Hall 210 D Irvine CA 92697-4575 Office Phone: 949-824-5943. Business E-Mail: aamaradu@uci.edu.

MARALDO, USHANA, multimedia designer, artist, photographer, writer; b. Germany; BFA, Mich. State U.; MA in Psychology and Edn., U. Osnabruck; postgrad., U. Mexico; PhD in Metaphysical Sci., U. Sedona, 2005. Owner, dir. Sunstar Prodns., Santa Barbara, Calif., 1981—87; owner, pub. Luma Arts Pubs., Woodland Hills, Calif., 1982—92; owner, CEO Light World Pub. LLC, 2007—. Prodr. Arits in Edn. Program, San Francisco. Photographer, 2029 MAGAZIN, internat. edit., 1991—92, Art series: Humana, Cities of Light, Cosmic Calculus series: published in Printworld Directory of Contemporary Prints, 1988, Planet Earth, Kaiser Aluminum Corp., Represented in permanent collections Trump Tower, NYC, Warner Bros. Records, LA. Recipient Excellence award in Painting, Art Horizons, 1988, Excellence award, Photographer's Forum Mag., 1992. Mem.: Soc. Children's Book Writers and Illustrators.

MARAMAN, KATHERINE ANN, associate justice, Guam Supreme Court; b. Los Alamos, N.Mex., Aug. 13, 1951; d. William Joseph and Katherine Ann (Thorpe) Maraman. BA, Colo. Coll., Colo. Springs, 1973; JD, U. N.Mex., Albuquerque, 1976. Bar: N.Mex. 1976, Guam 1978, Trust Territory Pacific Islands, Commonwealth of No. Mariana Islands, US Ct. Appeals (9th cir.), US Supreme Ct. Draftsperson N.Mex. Legis. Coun. Svc., Santa Fe, 1976—77; atty. Brooks & Klitzkie, P.C., Agana, Guam, 1977—84; pvt. practice Agana, 1985—88; counsel Office of Gov., Agana, 1988—94; judge Superior Ct., Agana, 1994—2008; assoc. justice Guam Supreme Ct., 2008—. Mem. asst. legis. counsel Guam Legis., Agana, 1977—80, mem. minority counsel, 1981—87; bd. dirs. Pub. Defender Svc. Corp., Agana, 1988—94. Trustee Guam Ter. Law Libr., 1994—2006; counsel Rep. Party, Agana, 1981—94; deacon First Presbyn. Reformed Ch., Agana; bd. dirs. Guam Rehab. and Workshop, Inc., Tumon, Guam, 1983—95. Mem.: Guam Bar Assn. Office: Guam Supreme Ct Guam Judicial Ctr 120 W O'Brien Dr Ste 300 Hagatna GU 96910-5174 Office Phone: 671-475-3589. Business E-Mail: kamaraman@guamsupremcourt.com.*

MARAMOROSCH, KARL, virologist, educator; b. Vienna, Jan. 16, 1915; came to U.S., 1947, naturalized, 1952; s. Jacob and Stefanie Olga (Schlesinger) M.; m. Irene Ludwinowska, Nov. 15, 1938; 1 dau., Lydia Ann. MS magna cum laude in Entomology, Agrl. U., Warsaw, Poland, 1938; student, Poly. U. Bucharest, Rumania, 1944-46; fellow, Bklyn. Bot. Garden, 1947-48; PhD (predoctoral fellow Am. Cancer Soc. 1948-49), Columbia, 1949. Civilian internee, Romania, 1939—46; asst., then assoc. Rockefeller U., NYC, 1949-61; sr. entomologist Boyce Thompson Inst., Yonkers, NY, 1961-74, program dir. virology and insect physiology, 1962-74; disting. prof. microbiology Waksman Inst., Rutgers U., New Brunswick, NJ, 1974—85; prof. entomology Cook Coll., Rutgers U., New Brunswick, 1985—, Robert L. Starkey prof., 1983—; vis. prof. agr. U. Wageningen, Netherlands, 1953, Cornell U., 1957, Rutgers U., 1967-68, Fordham U., 1973, Hokkaido U., Sapporo, Japan, 1980, Justus Liebig U., Giessen, Ger., 1983. Mendel lectr. St. Peters Coll., Jersey City, 1963; virologist FAO to Philippines, 1960; Disting. Vis. prof. Fudan U., Shanghai, 1982; cons. FAO-UN, World-wide survey, 1963; chmn. U.S.-Japan Coop. Seminar, 1965, 74, 85; mem. panel food and fiber Nat. Acad. Scis., 1966; cons. rice virus diseases AID-IRRI, Hyderabad, India, 1971; cons. UNDP, Bangalore, India, 1978-79; virologist FAO/UNDP, Sri Lanka, 1981, 82, 83, Mauritius, 1985; AIBS lectr., 1970-72, Found. Microbiology Nat. lectr., 1972-73, Fulbright Disting. prof., Yugoslavia, 1972, 78; mem. tropical medicine and parasitology study sect. NIH, 1972-76; chmn. 1st-3d Internat. Confs. Comparative Virology, 1969, 73, 76. Author: Comparative Symptomatology of Coconut Diseases of Unknown Etiology, 1964; editor: Biological Transmission of Disease Agents, 1962, Insect Viruses, 1968, Viruses, Vectors and Vegetation, 1969, Comparative Virology, 1971, Mycoplasma Diseases, 1973, Viruses, Evolution and Cancer, 1974, Invertebrate Immunity, 1975, Legume Diseases in the Tropics, 1975, Invertebrate Tissue Culture: Research Applications, 1976, Invertebrate Tissue Culture: Applications in Medicine, Biology and Agriculture, 1976, Aphids as Virus Vectors, 1977, Insect and Plant Viruses: An Atlas, 1977, Viruses and Environment, 1978, Practical Tissue Culture Applications, 1979, Leafhopper Vectors and Plant Disease Agents, 1979, Vectors of Plant Pathogens, 1980, Invertebrate Systems in Vitro, 1980, Vectors of Disease Agents, 1981, Mycoplasma Diseases of Trees and Shrubs, 1981, Mycoplasma and Allied Pathogens of Plants, Animals and Human Beings, 1981, Plant Diseases and Vectors: Ecology and Epidemiology, 1981, Invertebrate Cell Culture Applications, 1982, Pathogens, Vectors and Plant Diseases: Approaches to Control, 1982, Subviral Pathogens of Plants and Animals, 1985, Viral Insecticides for Biological Control, 1985, Biotechnology Advances in Insect Pathology and Cell Culture, 1987, Mycoplasma Diseases of Crops, 1988, Invertebrate and Fish Tissue Culture, 1988, Biotechnology for Biological Control of Pests and Vectors, 1991, Viroids and Satellites: Molecular Parasites at the Frontier of Life, 1991, Plant Diseases of Uncertain Etiology, 1992, Insect Cell Biotechnology, 1994, Arthropod Cell Culture Systems, 1994, Forest Trees and Palms: Diseases and Control, 1996, Invertebrate Cell Culture: Novel Directions and Biotechnology Applications, 1997, Invertebrate Cell Culture: Looking Toward the XXI Century, 1997, Biotechnology and Plant Protection in Forestry Sci., 1998, Maintenance of Human, Animal, and Plant Pathogen Vectors, 1999; Methods in Virology, 1964-84, Advances in Virus Research, 1972—, Archives of Virology, 1973-78, Intervirology, 1973-77, Advances in Cell Culture, 1979-89, Jour. Virological Methods, 1980-; editor in chief Jour. NY Entomol. Soc. 1972-84; assoc. editor: Virology, 1964-68, 75-79. Recipient Sr. Rsch., Lalor Found., 1957, Nat. Ciba-Geigy award in agr., 1976, Wolf prize in agr., Wolf Found., Israel, 1980, Jurzykowski prize in biology, 1980, Disting. Svc. award, Am. Inst. Biol. Scis., 1983, Khailshanker Durlabhji award, Jaipur, 1993, Lifetime Achievement award, Soc. In Vitro Biology, 2001, Gold Shield award, Egyptian Soc. Biol. Control, 2007. Fellow AAAS (hon., Campbell award 1958), Entomol. Soc. Am. (hon., L.O. Howard Disting. Achievement award 2006), Am. Phytopath. Soc., NY Acad. Scis. (A. Cressy Morrison prize natural sci. 1951, chmn. divsn. microbiology 1956-60, rec. sec. 1960-61, v.p. 1962-63), Nat. Acad. Scis. India (hon.); mem. Harvey Soc., Growth Soc., Phytopath. Soc., Indian, Japan, Can. phytopath. socs., Leopoldina Acad., Internat. Com. Virus Nomenclature, Electron Microscopy Soc., Am. Soc. Microbiology (Waksman award 1978), Soc. In Vitro Biology (Tissue Culture Assn., pres. N.E. br. 1978-81, pres. history br. 1988-90, Disting. Lifetime Achievement award 2001), Soc. Invertebrate Pathology (hon., founder's lectr., Adelaide 1990, Founder's honoree Sapporo 1998, hon. mem. Warwick, 2008), Internat. Assn. Medicinal Forest Plants (pres. 1989—), Am. Soc. Virology, Sigma Xi (pres. Rugers chpt. 1978). Home: 17 Black Birch Ln Scarsdale NY 10583-7456 Office: Rutgers U Dept Entomology New Brunswick NJ 08901 Home Phone: 914-725-3336; Office Phone: 732-932-9329. Business E-Mail: maramors@rci.rutgers.edu, maramorosch@aesop.rutgers.edu.

MARAN, STEPHEN PAUL, astronomer; b. Bklyn., Dec. 25, 1938; s. Alexander P. and Clara F. (Schoenfeld) Maran; m. Sally Ann Scott, Feb. 14, 1971; children: Michael Scott, Enid Rebecca, Elissa Jean. BS, Bklyn. Coll., 1959; MA, U. Mich., Ann Arbor, 1961, PhD, 1964. Astronomer Kitt Peak Nat. Obs., Tucson, 1964-69; project scientist for orbiting solar observatories NASA-Goddard Space Flight Center, Greenbelt, Md., 1969-75; head advanced systems and ground observations br. NASA-Goddard Space Flight Ctr., 1970-77, mgr. Operation Kohoutek, 1973-74, sr. staff scientist Lab. for Astronomy and Solar Physics, 1977-95; asst. dir. Space Scis. for Info. and Outreach, 1995—2004. Cons. Westinghouse Rsch. Labs., 1966; vis. lectr. U. Md., College Park, 1969—70; sr. lectr. UCLA, 1976; A. Dixon Johnson lectr. sci. comm. Pa. State U., 1990; lectr. astronomy cruises and eclipse tours. Author (with John C. Brandt): New Horizons in Astronomy, 1972, 2d edit., 1979, Arabic edit., 1979; co-author (with Jacqueline Mitton): Gems of Hubble-Superb Images from the Hubble Telescope, 1996; co-author: (with Laurence A. Marschall) Galileo's New Universe, 2009, Pluto Confidential, 2009; author: Astronomy for Dummies, 1999, 2d edit., 2005, German edit., 2000, 2d German edit., 2004, French edit., 2001, Chinese edit., 2001, Russian edit., 2004, Dutch edit., 2005; editor: Physics of Nonthermal Radio Sources, 1964, The Gum Nebula and Related Problems, 1971, Possible Relations Between Solar Activity and Meteorological Phenomena, 1975, New Astronomy and Space Science Reader, 1977, A Meeting with the Universe, 1981, Astrophysics of Brown Dwarfs, 1986, The Astronomy and Astrophysics Encyclopedia, 1991, Astrophys. Letters, 1974—77; assoc. editor:, 1977—85, Earth, Extraterrestrial Scis., 1969—79, contbg. editor: Air & Space/Smithsonian, 1990—; mem. editl. adv. bd. Astronomy Mag., 1997—, Astronomy and Geophysics, 1997—2009; contbr. articles to pop. mags. Recipient Group Achievement award, NASA, 1969, 1974, Exceptional Achievement medal, 1991, Klumpke-Roberts award, Astron. Soc. Pacific, 1999; named Disting. Visitor, Boston U., 1970; vis. scholar, Univ. Ctr. Ga., 1997. Fellow: AAAS; mem.: Am. Geophys. Union, Am. Phys. Soc., Royal Astron. Soc., Internat. Astron. Union (editor daily newspaper 1988, Minor Planet 9768 named Stephenmaran in his honor 2000), Am. Astron. Soc. (Harlow Shapley vis. lectr. 1981—, press officer 1985—2009, George Van Biesbroeck prize 2007). Office: Am Astronomical Soc Ste 400 2000 Florida Ave NW Washington DC 20009 Office Phone: 202-328-2010 116.

MARANGELL, LAUREN BETH, psychiatrist, researcher; b. New Haven, Aug. 24, 1961; d. Frank and Susan (Melnick) M. BA, Trinity U., San Antonio, 1983; MD, Baylor Coll., 1987. Med. Lic., N.Y. Intern, resident, chief resident in neuropsychiatry Montefiore Med. Ctr., Albert Einstein Coll. Medicine, Bronx, NY, 1990; with Baylor Coll. Medicine, 1994—, Brown Found. chair in psychopharmacology of mood disorders, prof. psychiatry (with tenure), dir. mood disorders rsch. Contbr. articles to profl. jours.; scientific reviewer for most major journals in the field; author Concise Guide to Psychopharmacology. NIMH fellow, 1991-1994, Laughlin Fellowship, Am. Coll. Psychiatrists; named Disting. Lilly Scholar, Eli Lilly & Co., 2007-; recipient Young Investigators award, Nat. Alliance for Rsch. in Schizophrenia and Affective Disorders, Exemplary Psychiatrist award, Nat. Alliance for the Mentally Ill. Mem. AMA (in tng.), APA. Office: 6655 Travis St #560 Houston TX 77030

MARANO, ANTHONY JOSEPH, cardiologist; b. White Plains, NY, Apr. 14, 1934; s. Anthony Joseph and Mary Antoinette (Perrotta) M.; m. Mary Regina Marbach, Aug. 23, 1958; children— Thomas, Kathryn, Michele. BA, Williams Coll., 1956; MD, Cornell Med. Coll., 1960. Diplomate Am. Bd. Internal Medicine, Am. Bd. Cardiovasc. Disease. Intern Bellevue Hosp., NYC, 1960-61; resident St. Luke's Hosp., NYC, 1961-63; NIH fellow in cardiology Mt. Sinai Hosp., NYC, 1963-64, rsch. assoc., 1964-75; clin. assoc. in medicine Coll. Physicians and Surgeons, NYC, 1970-86; pres. med. staff White Plains Hosp., 1984-86, chief cardiology, 1985-91, chief cardiology emeritus, 1991—, bd. dirs., 1983-88; cons. in cardiology Burke Rehab. Ctr.; med. dir., founder Paramedic Ambulance, White Plains, 1976-82. Contbr. articles to profl. jours. Trustee Pace U., NYC, 1975—, Home Savs. Bank, White Plains, 1973-90; bd. dirs. YMCA, White Plains, 1978-82; team physician White Plains HS, 1967—; cons. physician Dept. Pub. Safety, White Plains, 1968—; cons. physician City of White Plains Sch. System, 1994-98; bd. dirs. Westchester County Sports Hall of Fame, 1993—; alumni trustee Tyng Found., Williams Coll., 1994—. Tyng scholar Williams Coll., 1952-59; recipient Outstanding Achievement award Emergency Med. Svcs. Coun., 1982, YMCA Ctrl. Westchester Cmty. Svc. award, 2006; named to White Plains HS Hall of Fame, 1998; Anthony J. Marano MD Cardiac Care Unit at White Plains Hosp. Ctr. named in his honor, 2005. Fellow ACP, Am. Coll. Cardiology; mem. AMA, Am. Coll. Sports Medicine, Am. Heart Assn., NY State Heart Assn. (bd. dirs. 1982-85), Westchester Heart Assn. (v.p. 1983-86, pres. 1987-90), Univ. Club (White Plains, pres. 1970-71) Westchester Country Club (Harrison, NY), Phi Beta Kappa. Avocations: gardening, swimming. Home: 46 Eagle Ct White Plains NY 10605-5116 Office: 15 North Broadway White Plains NY 10605 Office Phone: 914-948-8838.

MARANO, THOMAS, finance company executive; b. 1961; Grad., Columbia U., 1983. Joined Bear Stearns Companies Inc., 1983; temp. aide to CEO Bear Stearns Asset Mgmt.; global head of mortgages and asset-backed securities Bear Stearns Companies Inc., head high-grade structured credit strategies fund, 2007—08; mng. dir. Cerberus Capital Mgmt., L.P., 2008—; non-exec. chmn. Residential Capital LLC, 2008, chmn., CEO, 2008—. Office: Residential Capital LLC 1 Meridian Crossings Minneapolis MN 55423

MARANS, J. EUGENE, lawyer; b. Butte, Mont., May 26, 1940; s. Edward and Florence M.; m. Anne Marie Borger, Sept. 3, 1978; children: Julia C., John E. AB, Harvard U., 1962, LLB, 1965. Bar: N.Y. 1966, D.C. 1971. Law clk. to Judge Nim M. Wisdom U.S. Ct. Appeals (5th cir.), New Orleans, 1965-66; assoc. Cleary, Gottlieb, Steen & Hamilton, NYC, 1966-70, Paris, 1970-71, Washington, 1971-74, ptnr., 1975-90, 93-00, of counsel, 2001—, ptnr. Hong Kong, 1990-93. Mem. N.Y. State adv. com. U.S. Commn. Civil Rights, 1969-70; mem. nat. eval. com. on simplified method of determining eligibility in pub. assistance HEW, 1969-70; sec., counsel Bipartisan Com. on Absentee Voting, 1973— Contbr. articles to legal jours. Bd. dirs. New Leadership Fund, chmn. 1977-79; mem. Sabre Found., pres. 1990; trustee Internat. Inst. Rural Reconstrn., vice chair, 2001—. Mem. Assn. Ams. Resident Overseas, Ripon Soc. (nat. governing bd. 1962-2001, chmn. 1969-70), Coun. on Fgn. Rels., ABA, D.C. Bar (chmn. internat. sect. 1978-79), Assn. of Bar of City of N.Y., Am. Soc. Internat. Law, Union Internat. des Avocats, Washington Fgn. Law Soc. (pres. 1985-86), Am. Law Inst. E-mail: emarans@cgsh.com.

MARANTIS, DEMETRIOS J., federal official; b. May 28, 1968; AB in Pub. and Internat. Affairs, Princeton U., NJ, 1990; JD, Harvard Law Sch., 1993. Bar: 1993. Atty. Akin, Gump, Strauss, Hauer & Feld, Washington, Brussels; assoc. gen. counsel Office US Trade Rep., Exec. Office of the Pres., Washington, 1998—2002; chief legal adv. US-Vietnam Trade Coun., Hanoi, Vietnam, 2002—04; issues dir. Kerry-Edwards presdl. campaign, 2004; chief internat. trade counsel US Senate Fin. Com., 2005—09; dep. US Trade Rep. Office US Trade Rep., Exec. Office of the Pres., Washington, 2009—. Democrat. Office: US Trade Rep 600 17th St NW Washington DC 20508 Office Phone: 202-395-7360.*

MARASCO, WAYNE A., oncologist, educator; PhD, U. Conn. Sch. Medicine, 1980; MD, U. Mich. Med. Sch., 1986. Assoc. prof. Harvard Med. Sch.; assoc. prof. cancer immunology & AIDS Dana-Farber Cancer Inst. Founder Nat. Found. Cancer Rsch. Ctr. for Therapeutic Antibody Engring. Office: Dana-Farber Cancer Institute 44 Binney St Jimmy Fund 824 Boston MA 02115 Office Phone: 617-632-2153. Office Fax: 617-632-3889. E-mail: wayne_marasco@dfci.harvard.edu.*

MARASIGAN, RODEL CASTILLO, systems analyst; b. Cuenca, Batangas, Philippines, Feb. 2, 1963; s. Rodelio Jarlos and Marcelina Castillo Marasigan; m. Cieliza Roque Marasigan, Mar. 2, 1978; m. Ma. Corazon Marigmen De Laza, July 14, 1961 (div. Dec. 13, 2004); children: Hermione Kristine Roque, Lovelly de Laza, Hannah Kathrine Roque, Ar-em John de Laza, Robi James de Laza. BS in Arch., Far Ea. U., Philippines, 1984; Degree in Computer Programming, Sys. Technol. Inst., Philippines, 1989; Degree in Project Mgmt., FMEDGE Learning Zone, Australia, 2007. Archtl., structural draftsman F.F. Cruz & Co. Inc, Quezon, City, Manila, Philippines, 1981—85; it sys. engr., cost engr. McConnell Dowell South East Asia Pte, Ltd., Loyang Offshore Supply Base, Singapore, 1999—2000, it sys. engr., sr. cost engr. Ras Tanura, Al Khobar, Saudi Arabia, 2000—01, quantity surveyor, project control staff, 1996—97; sr. cost engr., database mgr., it sys. engr., subcontract mgr. McConnell Dowell Corp. Ltd., Ba Ria, Vung Tau, Vietnam, 2001—03, sr. cost engr., pcats adminstr., database mgr., it sys. engr. Melbourne, Victoria, Australia, 2003—04, sys. analyst, quantity surveyor, project control staff Mataput, Laem Chabang, Thailand, 1997—99; sr. cost engr., sys. engr. Simon Engring. Australia, Perth, Australia, 2004—05; sr. controls mgr. United Group Resources Pty Ltd, Gladstone, Queensland, Australia, 2005—06; project controls mgr. United Group Ltd., Infrastructure, Spring Hills, Queensland, 2006—; designer, contractor, developer LJMarasigan Constrn., Quezon City, Manila, 1985—91; cost estimator, quantity surveyor Tri-Realty Constrn. And Devel., Quezon City, 1988—89, constrn., project engr., 1989—91, constrn. project mgr., 1991—92; quantity surveyor, project control staff Mw Kellog Internat., Bintulu, Sarawak, Malaysia, 1993—95; project planning mgr. Metro Asia Resources Corp., Quezon City, 1995—96. Archtl. draftsman, estimator Topacio Realty, Manila, 1989—91. Author various software applications. Mem. Little Shepherds, Quezon City, 1984—2007. Mem.: Project Mgmt. Inst., Internat. Cost Engring. Coun. (assoc.), Australian Inst. Quantity Surveyor (assoc.). Home: 17 322 Sydenham Rd Victoria Sydenham 3037 Australia Personal E-mail: rcmarasig@bigpond.net.au. Business E-Mail: rodel.marasigan@unitedgroupltd.com.

MARATOS-FLIER, ELEFTHERIA, physician, educator; b. NYC, Dec. 15, 1951; d. Costas and Anna (Domenikos) Maratos; m. Jeffrey Scott Flier, Dec. 7, 1975; children: Sarah, Lydia. BS, NYU, 1972; MD, Mt. Sinai Sch. Medicine, NYC, 1976. Intern and resident George Washington U. Hosp., Washington, 1976-78; resident Beth Israel Hosp., Boston, 1978-79; rsch. fellow Harvard Sch. Pub. Health, Boston, 1980-81; fellow Joslin Diabetes Ctr., Boston, 1981-82; instr. Brigham & Women's Hosp., Harvard Med. Sch., Boston, 1982-87, asst. prof., 1987—. Contbr. articles to Sci., Jour. Cell Biology, Jour. Virology, Jour. Clin. Investigation. Mary K. Iacocca Rsch. fellow, 1981. Mem. Am. Soc. Virology, Am. Microbiol. Assn., Am. Diabetes Assn., Phi Beta Kappa. Office: Joslin Diabetes Ctr One Joslin Pl Boston MA 02215 also: Brigham & Womens Hosp 75 Francis St Boston MA 02115-6110

MARATSOS, MICHAEL PHILIP, psychology professor; b. San Francisco, June 26, 1945; s. Michael Demetrios and Helen Maratsos; m. Mary Anne Chalkley, Aug. 26, 1980; 1 child, Jessica Anne. BA in Psychology, Stanford U., Calif., 1967; MA in Social Psychology, Harvard U., Cambridge, Mass., 1968, PhD in Social Psychology, 1972. Asst. prof. U. Minn., Mpls., 1971—75, assoc. prof., 1976—79, prof., 1980—. Recipient McCandless Divsn. 7 award, APA, 1978, Early Disting. Scientific Contbn. award, 1979; fellow Sloan fellow, U. Calif. La Jolla, 1979, Ctr. Advanced Study Behavioral Studies, Stanford, Calif., 1980—81, Inst. Advanced Studies Hebrew U., Jerusalem, 1982—83. Fellow: Am. Psychol. Sci. Soc., Soc. Rsch. in Child Devel.; mem.: Linguistic Soc. Am. Achievements include theoretical work in distributional analysis in grammatical acquisition that formed the foundation for later work in statistical learning in the field of child development. Avocations: reading, travel, piano. Office: Inst Child Devel 51 E River Rd Minneapolis MN 55455

MARAVICH, MARY LOUISE, realtor; b. Ft. Knox, Ky., Jan. 4, 1951; d. John and Bonnie (Balandzic) M. AA in Office Adminstrn., U. Nev., Las Vegas, 1970; BA in Sociology and Psychology, U. So. Calif., 1972; grad., Realtors Inst. Cert. residential specialist. Adminstrv. asst. dept. history U. So. Calif., LA, 1972-73; asst. pers. supr. Corral Coin Co., Las Vegas, 1973-80; realtor Americana Group divsn. Better Homes and Gardens, Las Vegas, 1980-85, Jack Matthews and Co., Las Vegas, 1985-93, Realty Execs., Las Vegas, 1993—. Mem. NAFE, Nev. Assn. Realtors (cert. realtors inst.), Las Vegas Bd. Realtors, Nat. Assn. Realtors, Women's Coun. of Realtors, Am. Bus. Women's Assn., Million Dollar Club, Pres.'s Club. Office: Realty Execs 1903 S Jones Blvd Ste 100 Las Vegas NV 89146-1220 Home Phone: 702-732-3977; Office Phone: 702-873-4500.

MARAVIGLIA, BRUNO, physicist, researcher; b. Pescia/Pistoia, Tuscany, Italy, Apr. 29, 1938; s. Narciso and Nada (Guidi) M.; m. Maria Antonietta Macri, Jan. 31, 1992; 1 child, Beatrice. Master's degree, U. Florence, Italy, 1962; postgrad., La Sapienza U., Rome, 1964. Researcher Nat. Inst. Nuclear Physics, Rome, 1962-68; asst. prof. dept. physics Duke U., Durham, NC, 1969-70; assoc. prof. Inst. Physics La Sapienza U., Rome, 1970-79, prof. physics, 1980—, dir. Postgrad. Sch. Med. Physics, 1986—, dir. dept. physics, 1992-95. Vis. prof. dept. physics U. B.C., Vancouver, Can., 1977-78; dir. magnetic resonance and brain function E. Fermi Sch. Physics., 1998 Editor: Physics of NMR Spectroscopy, 1988, Nuclear Magnetic Double Resonance, 1992, (book procs.) XXIII Congress Ampere, 1986; contbr. over 180 articles to profl. jours.; mem. editorial bd. Jour. Magnetic Resonance, 1992-99, Magnetic Resonance in Medicine, 1986—, Applied Magnetic Resonance, 1990—, Solid State Nuclear Magnetic Resonance, 1995—. Mem. coun. Mus. of Physics and Sci. Ctr. E. Fermi, Rome, 2000—. Mem. Internat. Soc. Magnetic Resonance (com. mem. 1985—), Soc. Magnetic Resonance in Medicine, Italian Phys. Soc., Groupement Ampere (v.p. 1986-94, pres. 1994-2000). Avocations: skiing, hiking, archaeology. Home: Via Jacopo Sannazzaro 82 00141 Rome Italy Office: La Sapienza U Dept Physics P le Aldo Moro 2 00185 Rome Italy Office Phone: +39-06-4454859. E-mail: bruno.maraviglia@romal.infn.it.

MARAZITA, MARY LOUISE, genetics researcher; b. Cheboygan, Mich., June 13, 1954; m. Richard T. McCoy, 1984; 5 children. BS, Mich. State U., East Lansing, 1976; PhD in Genetics, U. NC, Chapel Hill, 1980. Fellow U. So. Calif., 1980-82; statistician, instr. UCLA, 1982-86; asst. prof. human genetics Med. Coll. Va., 1986-93; dir. Cleft Palate-craniofacial Ctr. U. Pitts., 1993-00, dept. chair oral biology, 1999—, asst. dean for rsch. Sch. Dental Medicine, 2000-2001, assoc. dean rsch., 2001—. Instr. biomath. U. Calif., 1984-86; asst. prof. dentistry Med. Coll. Va., 1992-93; assoc. prof. human genetics and oral biology U. Pitts., 1993-97, prof. human genetics and oral and maxillofacial surgery, 1997—, prof. psychiatry, 2003—. Fellow Am. Coll. Med. Genetics, Am. Cleft Palate Assn., Am. Soc. Human Genetics, Internat. Genetic Epidemiol. Soc., Internat. Assn. Dental Rsch. Achievements include research in genetics of cleft lip, cleft palate and other craniofacial anomalies, including statistical genetic analysis and gene mapping studies. Office: Univ Pitts Dept Oral Biology/Genetics Ste 500 Bridgeside Point 100 Technology Dr Pittsburgh PA 15219 Business E-Mail: marazita@pitt.edu.

MARBLE, DUANE FRANCIS, geography educator, researcher; b. Seattle, Dec. 10, 1931; s. Francis Augustus and Beulah Belle (Simmons) M.; m. Jacquelynne Hardester, Aug. 18, 1957; children: Kimberley Eileen Wood, Douglas Craig. BA, U. Wash., 1953, MA, 1956, PhD, 1959. Asst. prof. real estate U. Oreg., Eugene, 1959; asst. prof. regional sci. U. Pa., Phila., 1960-63; from assoc. prof. geography to prof. geography Northwestern U., Evanston, Ill., 1963-73, assoc. dir. Transp. Ctr., 1966-73; prof. geography and computer sci. SUNY at Buffalo, Amherst, NY, 1973-87; prof. geography and natural resources Ohio State U., Columbus, 1987-98, prof. emeritus, 1998—; Courtesy prof. U. Oreg., 2003—07, Geosciences Oreg. State U., 2007—. Chmn. com. on geog. data sensing and processing Internat. Geog. Union, 1980-88; founder Internat. Symposium Spatial Data Handling; founder Assn. Am. Geographers-Marble Fund Geographic Sci.; cons. on geog. info. systems to U.S. Bur. Census, UN, also pvt. orgns. Editor: Intro Readings in GIS, 1990, Taylor & Francis, 1990-95; author computer program (best software award Assn. Am. Geogs. 1990); mem. editl. bd. Annals of Assn. Am. Geography, 2000-05, Internat. Jour. of Geographic Info. Sys., 1987-97. Vice-chair Florence Urban Renewal Adv. Com., 2006—07; mem. Florence Transit Adv. Com., 2007—. Recipient Legend in Leadership award, Environ. Sys. Rsch. Inst., 1997, Making a Difference award, 2004; named GIS Educator of Yr., UCGIS, 2007. Mem.: Assn. Compititing Machinery, Assn. Am. Geographers (sr. assoc. 2005, honors 1993, Geog. and Info. Sci. and Sys. Disting. Career award 2007). Home: 2226 Primrose Ln Florence OR 97439-7627 Personal E-mail: dmarble@oregonfast.net.

MARBURGER, JOHN HARMEN, III, former federal official; b. SI, NY, Feb. 8, 1941; s. John H., Jr. and Virginia A. (Smith) M.; m. Carol Preston Godfrey, June 12, 1965; children: John Harmen, Alexander Godfrey. BA in Physics magna cum laude, Princeton U., 1962; PhD in Applied Physics (NASA trainee), Stanford U., 1967; LHD (hon.), Hofstra U., 2000; DS (hon.), Stony Brook U., 2002, Moscow State U., 2002. Physicist Goddard Space Flight Center, NASA, 1962—63; asst. prof. physics & elec. engring. U. So. Calif., Los Angeles, 1966—69, assoc. prof., 1969—75, prof., 1975—80, chmn. physics dept., 1972—75; interim dean Coll. Letters, Arts and Sciences, U. So. Calif., LA, 1976—77, dean, 1977—80; pres. SUNY, Stony Brook, 1980—94, prof. physics & elec. engring., 1994—98; pres. Brookhaven Sci. Assoc., 1998—2001; dir. Brookhaven Nat. Labs, 1998—2001; asst. to the Pres., dir. Office Sci. & Tech. Policy, Exec. Office of the Pres., Washington, 2001—09. Cons. laser fusion program Lawrence Livermore Labs., 1972-76; chmn. N.Y. State fact finding panel on Shoreham Nuclear Power Facility, 1983; chmn. bd. trustees Universities Rsch. Assn., 1988-94; co-chair NASULGC Bd. on Oceans and Atmosphere, 1992-93; bd. dirs. N.Y. State Edn. and Rsch. Network, Inc., 1986-98; bd. dirs., chair L.I. Rsch. Inst., 1989-95; bd. dirs. L.I. High Tech. Incubator Corp., 1992-98, chair 1994-98. Contbr. articles to tech. publs. Bd. dirs. Mus. at Stony Brook, 1980-92, 94-98, L.I. Assn., Inc., 1983-93, 98—, Action Com. for L.I., 1980-83, L.I. Forum for Tech., Inc., 1980—, Rsch. Found. SUNY, 1990—; bd. trustees Princeton U., 1985-89; chmn. N.Y. State Energy Office Rev. Commn., 1980-81, Suffolk County (N.Y.) Task Force on Priorities in Fin., 1980-81; campaign chmn. United Way of L.I., 1991-92. Recipient Shuichi Kusaka Meml. Prize Princeton U., 1962 Fellow AAAS, APS; mem. Assn. of Colls. and Univs. State of N.Y. (pres. 1988-90), Coleman Chamber Music Assn. (bd. dirs. 1969-80).*

MARBURY, RITCHEY MCGUIRE, III, engineering executive, surveyor; b. Albany, Ga., May 18, 1938; s. Ritchey McGuire and Shirley Kathryn (VanHouten) M.; m. Fonda Gayle Starnes, June 16, 1962; children: Mary Kathryn, Ritchey McGuire IV. BCE, Ga. Inst. Tech., 1960, M in City Planning, 1966. Registered profl. engr., Ga., Fla., Idaho, Ala.; land surveyor, Ga. V.p. Marbury Engring. Co., Albany, Ga., 1965-78, pres., chmn. bd., 1981—; pres. Marbury, Ritter, Scott & Turner, Inc., Albany, 1970-78, 81-92, Marbury Assocs., Inc., 1991—, Idaho Boise Mission of Latter-day Saints Ch., 1978-81, SRJ Engring., 2009—; sr. prin. EMC Engring. Svcs., 2004—08. Presenter seminars on total quality mgmt. to nat. convs. of Am. Cons. Engrs. Coun., Design Constrn. Quality Inst., Sml. Firm Coalition of Cons. Engrs., Assn. for Project Mgrs. Exec. bd. Boy Scouts Am., Southwest Ga., 1982—. Served to 1st lt. U.S. Army, 1963-65. Mem. NSPE (South Ga. chpt. pres. 1993-95), Am. Cons. Engrs. Coun., Surveying and Mapping Soc. of Ga. (bd. dirs. 1966-78), Ga. Planning Assn., Home Builders Assn. (bd. dirs. 1985-86), Rotary. Mem. Lds Ch. Avocations: fishing, writing, music, computer, golf. Home: 1824 Green Valley Dr Albany GA 31707-3116 Office: 1108 Maryland Dr Albany GA 31707 Office Phone: 229-436-9877. Business E-Mail: marbury@srjengineering.com. *Always be a role model of Christlike behavior and do those things that make a significant differenc for good. Do what's right simply because it's the right thing to do. The greatest results come through kindness.*

MARBUT, ROBERT GORDON, communications, electronic security and broadcast executive, investor; b. Athens, Ga., Apr. 11, 1935; s. Robert Smith and Laura Gordon (Powers) M.; m. Margo Susan Spitz, Sept. 24, 1989; children: Robert Gordon, Laura Dodd, Michael Powers, Marcy Lizbeth. B Indsl. Engring., Ga. Inst. Tech., 1957; MBA with distinction, Harvard U., 1963. Registered profl. engr., Calif. Engr. Esso Standard Oil Co., Baton Rouge, 1957; corp. dir. engring. and plans Copley Press, La Jolla, Calif., 1963-70; v.p. Harte-Hanks Newspapers, Inc., San Antonio, 1970-71; pres., CEO Harte-Hanks Comm., Inc., San Antonio, 1971-91, also dir., 1971-91, vice chmn. bd. dirs., 1991; founder, chmn., CEO Argyle Comm., Inc, San Antonio, 1992—; founder, CEO, dir. Argyle TV Holding, Inc., San Antonio, 1993-95; co-founder, chmn., CEO Argyle TV, Inc., San Antonio, 1994-97; chmn., co-CEO Hearst-Argyle TV, Inc., NYC, 1997-2000, chmn., 2001—02; co-mng. ptnr. Argyle Global, LP, 2001—; founder, chmn., CEO Sectec-GLOBAL, Inc., 2002—. Dir. AP, 1979—88, vice chmn., 1987—88; chmn. Newspaper Advt. Bur., 1988—90, exec. com. dir., 1974—89, 1982—90; bd. dirs. Valero Energy Corp., Tupperware, Inc., Hearst-Argyle TV, Inc., Bus. Execs. Nat. Security; mem. adv. bd. U. Ga. Henry W. Grady Sch. Journalism, 1975—83, Ga. Tech., 1978—81, 1998—; founding mem. Am. Bus. Conf., 1981—89; mem. U. Tex. Centennial commn., 1981—83; pres. adv. coun. U. Tex. Coll. Comm., 1982—83; bd. dirs. Up With People, 1983—2001, exec. com., 1984—2001; instr. Armstrong Coll., 1951, Calif. State U., LA, 1964, Woodbury Coll., 1964. Author: (with Healy, Henderson and others) Creative Collective Bargaining, 1965. Coordinating chmn. San Antonio Target 90 commn., 1983-84; campaign chmn. United Way, San Antonio, 1985, chmn. bd. trustees 1988-89; vice chmn. Tex. select com. on Tax Equity, 1987-89; mem select com. Tex. Revenues, 1991-92; mem. Tex. World Trade Coun., 1986-87. Capt. USAF, 1958-61. Salzburg Inst. Am. Studies sr. fellow, 1997—; recipient Isaiah Thomas award Rochester Inst. Tech., 1980, EXCEL award in comm., 1987, People of Vision award, 1991; selected to Acad. Disting. Engring. Alumni Ga. Tech., 1995. Mem. Am. Newspaper Publs. Assn. (chmn. task group on future, chmn. telecomm. com. 1974-81, bd. dirs. 1976-84, chmn. future task group), So. Newspaper Pubs. Assn. (pres. 1979-80, dir. 1975-81, treas. 1977), Am. Newspaper Pubs. Assn. Found. (trustee 1976-79), Tex. Daily Newspaper Assn. (pres. 1979, Tex. Newspaper Leader of Yr., 1981), N.Y. Met. Club, Doubles, San Antonio Country Club, Argyle Club, Greater San Antonio C. of C., Delta Tau Delta (Alumni Achievement award 2000), Omicron Delta Kappa, Phi Eta Sigma. Office: Hearst-Argyle Television Inc 200 Concord Plaza Dr Ste 700 San Antonio TX 78216-6941

MARC, DAVID TISCHLER, cardiologist, director; b. Phila., Nov. 21, 1960; m. Sarah Gentry; children: Jacob Scott Tischler, Ethan Stokes Tischler. BA, Swarthmore Coll., Pa., 1982; MD, Harvard Med. Sch., Boston, Mass., 1986. Cert. in cardiovasacular diseases ABIM, 1991. Dir., cardiac ultrasound lab. U. Vt. Coll. Medicine, Burlington, 1991—, assoc. prof., 1996—; co dir., cardiac MRI unit Fletcher Allen Health Care, Burlington, 2004—. Devel. com. mem. Lyric Theater, Burlington, 2007—. Named one of Best Doctors America, 2001—02. Fellow: ACC; mem.: ACP, ABIM, Am. Soc. Echocardiography, Am. Heart Assn. Independent. Achievements include research in stress echocardiography in the management of patients with mitral regurgitation. Avocations: bicycling, cross country skiing, acting, fly fishing. Office Fax: 802-847-0429. Business E-Mail: marc.tischler@vtmednet.org.

MARCALI, JEAN GREGORY, retired chemist; b. Jermyn, Pa., May 29, 1926; d. John Robert and Anna Marie Gregory; m. Kalman Marcali, Oct. 6, 1956; children: Coleman, Frederick. Student, U. Pa., 1948—52, U. Del., 1971—72. Microanalyst E.I. du Pont de Nemours & Co., Deepwater, NJ, 1943-60, tech. info. analyst, organic chems. dept., 1960-64, tech. info. analyst info. systems dept. Wilmington, Del., 1964-67, sr. adviser tech. info., 1967-70, supr. tech. info., 1970-82, 85-89, supr. adminstrv. svcs. Ctrl. Rsch. Dept., 1982-85, cons., 1989-92, ret., 1992. Sec. Alfred I. Dupont Elem. PTA, 1971, pres. 1972; pres. PTA Brandywine Sch. Dist., 1973; mem. Wilmington Dist. Rep. Com., 1976—, Winterthur Mus., 1996—. Mem. Am. Chem. Soc. (treas. divsn. chem. info. 1976-81, chmn.-elect 1981, chmn. 1982, 83, divsn. councilor 1983-90), Am. Chem. Soc. (com. on chem. abstracts svc. 1983-85, 87-93, mem. joint bd. coun. com. on chem. abstracts svc. 1994-96, 98, 99, 2000, Del. sec. chem. lit. topical group, chmn. 1979-80, chem. vets. chmn.-elect 1999), Order Ea. Star, Du Pont Country Club, Winterthur Mus. Guild. Lutheran. Home: 312 Waycross Rd Wilmington DE 19803-2950

MARCANTEL, BERNARD NORMAN, lawyer, judge; b. Oberlin, La., July 14, 1923; s. Emile Peter and Florence Ida (Reed) M.; m. Martha Tabb de Gravelles, June 23, 1946 (dec.); children: David Emile, Nancy Tabb, Gregory Norman, Peter Camille; m. Nancy Magoon, May 2, 1998 (dec.). BS, U. Southwestern La., 1946; JD, U. Chgo., 1949, Tulane U., 1950. Bar: La. 1950, U.S. Dist. Ct. (ea. and we. dists.) La. 1951, U.S. Ct. Appeals (5th cir.) 1978. Dist. atty. 31st Jud. Dist., Jennings, La., 1953-78; ptnr. Marcantel, Marcantel & Wall, Jennings, 1978—. Judge City of Jennings, 1985-93; judge pro tem 15th Jud. Dist., Crowley, Lafayette and Abbeville, La., 1990-91, 3d Cir. Ct. Appeals, Lake Charles, La., 1992, judge pro tem 1994—). Assoc. editor U. Chgo. Law Rev., 1947-48. With AUS, 1942-46, ETO. Mem. ABA, La. Bar Assn. Republican. Roman Catholic. Avocations: fishing, hunting. Home: 1331 N Cutting Ave Jennings LA 70546-4201 Office: 302 E Nezpique St Jennings LA 70546-5354

MARCANTEL, KEITH BERNARD, school psychologist, educator; m. Judith Ann Marcantel, June 22, 1985. BA in Psychology, SUNY, Stony Brook, 1978; MS in Ednl. Psychology and Stats., SUNY, Albany, 1979; MA in Counseling and Human Svcs., U. Colo., Colorado Springs, 1993. Cert. specialist sch. psychology SUNY, 1980, sch. psychologist Colo. Dept. Edn., 2005, elementary sch. counselor Colo. Dept. Edn., 2005, nat. cert. sch. psychologist NASP, 2009. Sch. psychologist Harrison Sch. Dist. Re-2, Colorado Springs, 1980—82, Centennial Mental Health Ctr., Fort Morgan, Colo., 1983—84, San Luis Valley BOCES, Alamosa, Colo., 1984—87, Woodland Park Sch. Dist. Re-2, Colo., 1987—. Program com. chairperson Pikes Peak Sch. Psychologists Orgn., Colorado Springs, 1988—90, pres., 1991—92; pikes peak liason Colo. Soc. Sch. Psychologists, Denver, 1997—98. Contbr. rsch. papers. Disaster action team vol. Red Cross, Colorado Springs, 2004—; bd. mem. North Teller Build a Generation, Woodland Park, 2001—. Mem.: NASP, Colo. Coun. Internat. Reading Assn., Colo. Soc. Sch. Psychologists, Colo. Mountain Club, Broadmoor Waltz Club (historian 2005—06). Avocations: skiing, hiking, jogging, travel, theater. Home: 925 N Baldwin St Woodland Park CO 80863-1374 Office: Woodland Park Sch Dist Re-2 PO Box 99 Woodland Park CO 80866-0099 Business E-Mail: kmarcantel@wpsdk12.org.

MARCDANTE, KAREN JEAN, medical educator; b. Milw., Sept. 15, 1955; d. Willard Karl and Beth Elaine (Maule) Kohn; m. Mark Wendelberger, Aug. 5, 1978 (div. Sept. 1985); m. Anthony Marcdante, Oct. 17, 1998. Student, Marquette U., Milw., 1973-76; MD, Med. Coll. Wis., Milw., 1980. Diplomate Am. Bd. Pediat. & Pediat. Crit. Care. Resident in pediat. Med. Coll. Wis. affiliated hosps., Milw., 1980-83; instr. pediat. Med. Coll. Wis., Milw., 1983-85, asst. prof. pediat., 1987-94, assoc. prof. pediat., 1994-2000, prof. pediat., 2000—, assoc. dean curriculum, 1997—2003, vice-chair edn. dept. pediat., 1994—; fellow in pediatric critical care U. Calif., San Francisco, 1985-87; vice chief staff Children's Hosp. Wis., Milw., 1995-97; chair rank and tenure com. Med. Coll. Wis., 2007—09. Dir. Respiratory Care Svcs., 1992-98, Transport Program, 1998-2008; chief dept. pediat. Children's Hosp. Wis., 1991-95, dept. critical care 1993-95, mem. numerous coms., including care mgmt. steering com., 1994-, critical care com., 1991—, pres.-elect, 2003-05; pres. med. dental staff, 2005-07. Contbr. numerous articles to profl. jours. Recipient New Investigator award Assn. Am. Med. Colls., 1992, Cert. Leadership award YWCA and Marquette Electronics Found., 1992, Laureate award Ctrl. Group Ednl. Affairs, 2004, Disting. Svc. award, 2009; grantee Dept. HHS, 1996—. Mem. Am. Acad. Pediat. (pub. rels. chair Wis. chpt. 1988-91, sec.-treas. 1990-95, v.p. 1995-96, chair careers and opportunities 1996-2001), Soc. Critical Care Medicine (chair task force on quality improvement pediat. 1994-96, quality indicator devel. work group 1997-98, Presdl. citation 1996, 97), Coun. on Med. Student Edn. in Pediat. (co-chair task force on tchg. methods 1991-96, nominating com. 1993-95, exec. com. 1996-99, sec.-treas. 1997-99). Business E-Mail: kwendel@mcw.edu.

MARCEAU, YVONNE, ballroom dancer, educator; b. Chgo., July 13, 1950; BFA, U. Utah, 1972; AA, Imperial Soc. Ballroom Dance. Ballet dancer Ballet West; ptnr. with Pierre Dulaine, 1976; founder, artistic dir. Am. Ballroom Theatre, NYC, 1984-93; educator dance divsn. Julliard Sch., NYC, 1993—. Guest tchr. Sch. Am. Ballet, NYC; tchr. ballroom dancing Juilliard Sch. Appearances include The Smithsonian Inst., JFK Ctr. for Performing Arts, N.Y. State Theater, N.Y.C., Sadlers Wells, London, (Broadway and London show) Grand Hotel, 1989-92, toured with Pierre Dulaine and Am. Ballroom Theatre worldwide, choreographer (films) Mona Lisa Smile, 2003. Recipient Recipient Brit. Theatrical Arts Championships 4 times, Spl. Astaire award, Dance Educator awards, Outstanding Achievement in Dance award Nat. Coun. Dance Am., 1992, Dance Mag. award, 1993, Edn. award, Americans for the Arts, 2005. Office: Am Ballroom Theater Co 4th Fl 25 W 31st St New York NY 10001 Office Phone: 212-244-9442. Office Fax: 212-244-9299. E-mail: info@dancingclassrooms.com.

MARCELIN, LOUIS HERNS, sociologist, educator; m. Louise Myrlande Placide. PhD, Fed. U. Rio de Janeiro, 1996; postdoc., U. Miami, Coral Gables, Fla., 1999. Cert. sociologist UFRJ, anthropologist 1996. Prof. U. Miami, 1999—; chancellor Interuniv. Inst. R & D, Miami, 2001—; rsch. dir. Family & Youth Cmty. Rsch. Ctr., Port-au-Prince, Haiti. Grant, Bur. Census, 2000—01, NIH, 2001—06, DHHS, 2002—03. Mem.: Am. Sociol. Assn., Am. Anthrop. Assn. Office: Univ Miami 5202 Univ Dr Coral Gables FL 33124-2005 Office Fax: 305-284-2110.

MARCELLA, JOSEPH, information scientist; BA in Biochemistry, Temple U., 1970. Computer operator/sys. programmer, asst. mgr. King Kullen Grocery Co./Gen. Fire & Casualty, LI, 1971-72; asst. v.p., electronic banking Bank of Am., Las Vegas, 1972-83; sr. v.p., dir. info. svcs. Norwest/Wells of Nev., Las Vegas, 1983-96; chief info. officer, dir. info. technologies City of Las Vegas, 1997—. Chair State Nev. Entities Tech. Alliance; adv. U. Nev. Las Vegas Grad. Sch. Bd. dirs., past pres. Bank Adminstrn. Inst.; past pres., v.p. Nev. Clearing House Assn.; bd. dirs. Western Payments Alliance; mem. Rules Com. Nat. Automated Clearning House, Task Force to Build Acad. Advanced Tech., Focus Sch. Partnership program. Named one of Top 25 CIO, Ctr. Digital Dept., 2008. Office: City Las Vegas Dept Info Techs City Hall 5th Fl 400 Stewart Ave Las Vegas NV 89101-2927

MARCELLO, PATRICK RYAN, dentist; b. Spartanburg, SC, Dec. 25, 1971; s. Theodore Joseph and Marjorie Marcello; m. Amy Madding Marcello, Sept. 2, 2001; children: Bella V, Marco II. BSc, Wofford Coll., Spartenburg, 1994; PhD in Dentistry, Med. U. SC, Charleston, 1999. Diplomate dental Med. U. SC. Assoc. dentist, Spartenburg, 2000—01; owner, operator Royal Crest Ctr. Advanced Dentistry, Greenville, 2001—. Mem.: ADA. Avocations: boating, fishing, hunting.

MARCH, BOYD LEE, dean, political science professor, researcher; b. Macon, Mo., Apr. 11, 1958; s. Virgil Boyd and Ruby Marceine March; m. Debra Lynn Branson, Apr. 21, 1984; children: William, Benjamin. BA, Truman State U., Kirksville, Mo., 1980, MA, 1983; PhD, U. Mo., Columbia, 1993. Asst. city mgr. City of Kirksville, 1983—84; city mgr. City of Marceline, Mo., 1984—85; asst. exec. dir. Mo. Local Govt. Retirement, Jefferson City, 1985—86; city adminstr. City of Willow Springs, Mo., 1986—87; adj. instr. Buena Vista Coll., Creston, Iowa, 1987—88; John H. Harland prof. polit. sci. Young Harris Coll., Ga., 1993—. Dir. Vietnam Vets. Oral History Project, Young Harris, 2001—; dean Divsn. Social & Behavioral Sci., 2007—. Author: If You Ain't Cav, 2005. Moderator candidate forum LWV, Hiawassee, Ga., 1993—; spkr. vets. support, 1995—. Recipient Vulcan Tchg. award, Vulcan Techs., 2005; named Faculty Mem. of Yr., Young Harris Coll., 1994, 1995, 1997, 2000, 2005, 2006, 2007, 2008. Methodist. Office: Young Harris Coll PO Box 456 Young Harris GA 30582 Office Phone: 706-379-5143. Office Fax: 706-379-4314. Business E-Mail: leem@yhc.edu.

MARCH, JAMES GARDNER, social sciences educator; b. Cleve., Jan. 15, 1928; s. James Herbert and Mildred (MacCorkle) M.; m. Jayne Mary Dohr, Sept. 23, 1947; children: Kathryn Sue, Gary Clifton, James Christopher, Roderic Gunn. BA, U. Wis., Madison, 1949; MA, Yale U., New Haven, Conn., 1950, PhD, 1953; PhD (hon.), Copenhagen Sch. Econs., Denmark, 1978, Swedish Sch. Econs., Helsinki, Finland, 1979, U. Wis., Milw., 1980, U. Bergen, Norway, 1980, Uppsala U., Sweden, 1987, Helsinki Sch. Econs., Finland, 1991, Dublin City U., Ireland, 1994, Göteborg U., Sweden, 1998, U. Poitiers, France, 2001, Budapest U. Econs., Hungary, 2003, York U., Toronto, 2007, Lappeenranta U., Finland, 2008, U. Alta., 2009, Stockholm Sch. Econs., 2009. From asst. prof. to prof. Carnegie Inst. Tech., 1953-64; prof. psychology, sociology, dean Sch. Social Scis. U. Calif., Irvine, 1964-70; prof. mgmt., higher edn., polit. sci. and sociology Stanford (Calif.) U., 1970-95, prof. emeritus, 1995—. Cons. in field; mem. Nat. Council Ednl. Research, 1975-78, Nat. Sci. Bd., 1968-74; mem. sociol.-social psychology panel NSF, 1964-66; social sci. tng. com. NIMH, 1967-68; mem. math. social sci. com. Social Sci. Research Council, 1958-60; mem. Assembly Behavioral and Social Sci., NRC, 1973-79, chmn. com. on aging, 1977-82, chmn. com. on math., sci., tech. edn., 1984-86 Author: (with H.A. Simon) Organizations, 1958, 2nd edit., 1993, (with R.M. Cyert) A Behavioral Theory of the Firm, 1963, 2nd edit., 1992, Handbook of Organizations, 1965; (with B.R. Gelbaum) Mathematics for the Social and Behavioral Sciences, 1969; (with M.D. Cohen) Leadership and Ambiguity, 1974, 2nd edit., 1986, Academic Notes, 1974; (with C.E. Lave) An Introduction to Models in the Social Sciences, 1975; (with J.P. Olsen) Ambiguity and Choice in Organizations, 1976, Aged Wisconsin, 1977, Autonomy as a Factor in Group Organization, 1980, Pleasures of the Process, 1980, Slow Learner, 1985; (with R. Weissinger-Baylon) Ambiguity and Command, 1986, Decisions and Organizations, 1988; (with J.P. Olsen) Rediscovering Institutions, 1989, Minor Memos, 1990, A Primer on Decision Making, 1994, Fornuft og Forandring, 1995; (with J.P. Olsen) Democratic Governance, 1995; The Pursuit of Organizational Intelligence, 1999, (with M. Schulz and X. Zhou) The Dynamics of Rules, 2000, Late Harvest, 2000; (with M. Augier) The Economics of Choice, Change and Organization, 2002, (with M. Augier), Models of a Man, 2004, Footprints, 2005, Valg, Vane ag Vision, 2005, (with T. Weil) On Leadership, 2005, Quiet Corners, 2008, Explorations in Orgn., 2008; contbr. articles to profl. jours. Fellow Ctr. Advanced Study in Behavioral Scis., 1955-56, 73-74; recipient Wilbur Lucius Cross medal Yale U., 1968, Viipuri prize, Finland, 2004, Herbert Simon award, Hungary, 2005; decorated knight 1st class Royal Norwegian Order of Merit, comdr. Order of Lion of Finland. Mem. NAS, APA, Nat. Acad. Edn., Accademia Italiana di Economia Aziendale, Royal Swedish Acad. Scis., Norwegian Acad. of Sci. and Letters, Am. Acad. Arts and Scis., Am. Econ. Assn., Am. Polit. Sci. Assn. (v.p. 1983-84, John Gaus award 1997, Wildavsky award 2004), Am. Sociol. Assn., Acad. Mgmt. (Disting. Scholar award 1999), Russell Sage Found. (trustee 1985-94, chmn. 1990-93), Finnish Soc. Scis. and Letters, Citigroup Behavioral Scis. Rsch. Coun. (chmn. 1994-2000), Am. Philos. Soc., Phi Beta Kappa, Sigma Xi. Home: 501 Portola Rd Box 8136 Portola Valley CA 94028 Office Phone: 650-424-4344. Business E-Mail: march@stanford.edu.

MARCH, KEVIN P., electronics executive; BS in Econs., U. Pitts., 1983, MBA, 1984. Various positions including dir. fin., contr. semiconductor units Tex. Instruments, Inc., Dallas, 1984—97, v.p. fin. planning, mgr. global ops., 1997—2002, contr., 2002—03, sr. v.p., CFO, 2003—. Mem. Fin. Exec. Internat., Conf. Bd.'s Coun. Fin. Exec. Office: Tex Instruments Inc PO Box 660199 Dallas TX 75266-0199 Office Phone: 972-995-2011. Office Fax: 972-995-4360.

MARCH, MICHAEL F., propulsion systems analyst, consultant; b. Detroit, Mar. 3, 1962; s. Stanley and Dorothy M. AAS in Archtl. Design, Macomb C.C., Warren, Mich., 1983; BS in Mech. Engring., Lawrence Technol. U., 1986; ME, U. Fla., 1994. Sr. analytical engr. United Techs. Corp.-Pratt & Whitney, West Palm Beach, Fla., 1986-93; pvt. practice propulsion analysis cons. Tullahoma, Tenn., 1994—. Mem. ASME.

MARCHAK, MAUREEN PATRICIA, retired anthropology and sociology educator, academic administrator; b. Lethbridge, Alta., Can., June 22, 1936; d. Adrian Ebenezer and Wilhelmina Rankin (Hamilton) Russell; m. William Marchak, Dec. 31, 1956; children: Geordon Eric, Lauren Craig. BA, U. B.C., Vancouver, Can., 1958, PhD, 1970. Asst. prof. U. B.C., Vancouver, 1972-75, assoc. prof., 1975-80, prof., 1980—, head dept. anthropology and sociology, 1987-90, dean faculty arts, 1990-96, disting. scholar in residence Peter Wall Inst., 2000—, prof., dean emerita of arts, 2001—; sr. rsch. fellow Ctr. Internat. Rels. Liu Inst. for Study of Global Issues, 2002—09, interim dir., 2005—06. Author: Ideological Perspectives on Canada, 1975, 2d edit., 1981, 3d edit., 1988, In Whose Interests, 1979, Green Gold, 1983 (John Porter award 1985), The Integrated Circus, The New Right and The Restructuring of Global Markets, 1991, Logging the Globe, 1995, Falldown, Forest Policy in British Columbia, 1999, Racism, Sexism and the University, the Political Science Affair at UBC, 1996, God's Assassins. State Terrorism in Argentina in the 1970's, 1999 (Wallace J. Ferguson prize, Hon. Mention), Reigns of Terror, 2003, No Easy Fix, Global Responses to Internal Wars and Crimes Against Humanity, 2008; author, co-editor: Uncommon Property, 1987; mem. editl. bd. Can. Rev. Sociology and Anthropology, Montreal, 1971-74, Studies in Polit. Economy, Ottawa, Ont., Can., 1980-87, Current Sociology, 1980-86, Can. Jour. Sociology, 1986-90, B.C. Studies, 1988-90, 2000-04. Bd. dir., chair ethics com. Univ. Hosp., 1992-93; trustee Cedar Lodge Trust Soc., 1989-92; mem. adv. coun. Ecotrust, 1991-93, bd. dir., 1993-97, Eco-trust Can., 1995-99; chmn. bd. dir. B.C. Bldgs. Corp., 1992-95; mem. B.C. Forest Appeals Commn., 1992-2002; bd. govs. U. B.C., 1999-2001; bd. dir. Pub. Svc. Employees for Environ. Ethics, 2002-04; mem. sector study steering com. Can. Coun. Profl. Fish Harvesters, 2002—05. Named Woman of Distinction, YWCA, 1999. Fellow Royal Soc. Can. (v.p. Acad. II 1994-98, pres. Acad. II 1998-2000); mem. Can. Sociology and Anthropology Assn. (pres. 1979-80, other offices), Internat. Sociol. Assn., Can. Polit. Sci. Assn., Assn. for Can. Studies, Forest History Soc. (mem. exec. com. 1991-92). Avocations: hiking, swimming, travel, listening to music. Home: 4455 W 1st Ave Vancouver BC Canada V6R 4H9

MARCHANT, BARBARA, performing arts educator, acting coach; d. Maurice and Maureen Marchant; m. Mel Howard, Feb. 7, 1977 (div. Feb. 10, 1997); children: Jessica Craig, Katie Orlinsky. BA in Theater Arts, SUNY, 1998. Cert. Meisner Tchr. William Esper Studio, 1997. Theater and TV acting coach Broadway, NBC, HBO, NYC, 1972—, West End, BBC, UK; theater, film and TV actor Broadway, CBS, ABC, PBS, NYC, 1979—2006; master tchr., meisner technique William Esper Studio, NYC, 1984—; film acting coach Miramax, Paramount, Columbia, Universal, NYC, 1992—; acting prof. Mason Gross Sch. Arts, Rutgers U., New Brunswick, NJ, 1997—, head acting program, 2002—; dir. Rutgers conservatory Shakespeare's Globe Theater, London, 2002—. Chair adv. com. London Acad. Theater Abroad, NYC, 1998—. Author: (book) Rowan and Littlefield A Young Actor's Scenebook: A Training Tool, 2000. Recipient Excellence in Undergrad. Tchg. award, Dialogues Grant, 2002; named Tchr. of Yr., Rutgers Parents Assn., 1997; nominee Obie award, Village Voice, 1972. Mem.: Am. Fedn. TV and Radio Artists, Actor's Equity Assn. Achievements include development of first year-long university program at Shakespeare's Globe Theater in London. Office Fax: 732-932-1409; Home Fax: 732-932-1409. Personal E-mail: bamarchant@aol.com. Business E-Mail: marchant@rci.rutgers.edu.rci.

MARCHANT, BYRON FRANK, lawyer, foundation administrator; b. Chgo., July 1, 1957; m. Ann Fairfax Walker, Dec. 10, 1994; 1 child, Rebecca. BS with merit, US Naval Acad., 1978; JD, U. Va., 1987. Bar: DC 1987, NY 1987, NJ 1988. Assoc. Sidney Austin Brown & Wood, Washington; with FCC, 1989—95; gen. counsel Telecommunications Systems, Inc., Annapolis, Md.; ptnr. Patton Boggs, Washington, 1996—97; sr. v.p., gen. counsel BET Holdings, Inc., Washington, 1997—98, exec. v.p., chief adminstrv. officer, gen. counsel, 1998—2008; pres., CEO US Naval Acad. Alumni Assn. and US Naval Acad. Found., 2009—. Chair, E-Commerce com. DC C. of C. Recipient Trailblazer award, Minority Corp. Counsel Assn., 1999. Mem.: PEN, Washington Lawyers Com. for Civil Rights and Law, Fed. Comm. Bar Assn., US Supreme Ct. Bar, ABA. Avocations: swimming, skiing, golf, bicycling. Office: US Naval Acad Alumni Assn 247 King George St Annapolis MD 21402 also: US Naval Acad Found Devel Divsn 291 Wood Rd Annapolis MD 21402-1254 Office Phone: 410-295-4090.*

MARCHANT, DONNA, cardiologist, director; b. NYC, Nov. 17, 1957; MD, NY Med. Coll., Valhalla, 1991. Dir. cardiology fellowship, interventional cardiologist North Shore U. Hosp., Manhasset, NY, 1999—, dir. CCU, 2006—. Fellow: Soc. Coronary Angiography and Intervention, Am. Coll. Cardiology; mem.: Hellenic Med. Soc., Am. Heart Assn. Office: North Shore Univ Hosp 300 Community Dr Manhasset NY 11030 Office Fax: 516-562-2087.

MARCHANT, KENNY, United States Representative from Texas; b. Bonham, Tex, Feb. 23, 1951; m. Donna Marchant; children: Luke, Matthew, Kenny, Dallas. BA, So. Nazarene U., Bethany, Okla., 1974; attended, Nazarene Theol. Sem., Kansas City, Mo., 1975—76; DHL (hon.), So. Nazarene U., Bethany, Okla., 1999. Mem. City Coun., Carrollton, Tex., 1980—84; mayor Carrollton, Tex., 1984—87; mem. Tex. State Ho. Reps., Austin, 1987—2004, US Congress from 24th Tex. dist., 2005—, mem. transp. and infrastructure com., mem. edn. and the workforce com., mem. govt. reform com. Mem. adv. bd. Children's Med. Ctr. Named Top Ten Legislator, Tex. Monthly mag., Citizen of Yr., Metrocrest C. of C., Legislator of Yr., Tex. Mcpl. League. Republican. Nazarene. Office: US Ho Reps 501 Cannon Ho Office Bldg Washington DC 20515-4324 Office Phone: 202-225-6605.*

MARCHASE, RICHARD BANFIELD, cell biologist, educator, research administrator; b. Sayre, Pa., Mar. 12, 1948; s. Nicholas and Vivian H. (Banfield) M.; m. Gail C. Andrews, Sept. 2, 2006; children: Nicholas Darrow, Allison Elizabeth. BS in Engring., Cornell U., 1970; PhD in Biophysics, Johns Hopkins U., 1976; postgrad., Duke U., 1978. Muscular Dystrophy Assn. postdoctoral fellow divsn. neurology Duke U. Med. Ctr., 1976-77, USPHS postdoctoral fellow dept. anatomy, 1977-78, asst. prof. anatomy, 1978-86; assoc. prof. cell biology U. Ala.-Birmingham, 1986—90, prof., 1990—, chmn., 1992—2000, sr. assoc. dean biomed. rsch., 2000—06, v.p. rsch. and econ. devel., 2004—. Contbr. chpts. to books, articles to profl. jours. Recipient Hamilton Watch award Cornell U., 1970, award Juvenile Diabetes Found., 1995-2002; Grad. fellow NSF, 1970-73, Danforth Found. grad. fellow, 1973-76; Nanaline H. Duke scholar, 1982-85; grantee USPHS 1979-, NSF, Presdl. Young Investigator grant, 1982-87. Mem. AAAS, Am. Soc. Cell Biology, Am. Soc. Zoology, Assn. of Anatomy, Cell Biology, and Neurobiology Chairpersons (pres. 1995-96), Am. Assn. Anatomists, Fed. Am. Soc. Exptl. Biology (bd. dirs. 2000— v.p. sci. policy, 2005, pres.-elect 2007), Sigma Xi. Office: U Ala Birmingham 720 AB Birmingham AL 35294-0001 Home: 4012 Lenox Rd Birmingham AL 35213 Office Phone: 205-934-1294. Business E-Mail: marchase@uab.edu.

MARCHENKO, TAMARA G., music educator; b. Nevelsk, Russia, Aug. 4, 1951; arrived in US, 1996; d. Georgy Davidovich and Galina Grigoryevna Khachikyan; 1 child, Leon;. BA in Piano, N.A. Rimskiy-Korsakov Coll. Music, Krasnodar, Russia, 1981; MusM, Kuban State U., Krasnodar, Russia, 1973. Care giver to elderly pvt. practice, LA, 1996—98; salesperson Jons Market, LA, 1998—99; tchr. music Sunflower Montessori Sch., LA, 2000—; pianist El Redentor Luth. Ch., LA, 2000—04; dir. choir, organist Ctrl. Luth. Ch., Van Nuys, Calif., 2002—05; tchr. aide LA Unified Sch. Dist., North Hollywood, Calif., 2005—; dir. music All Saints Luth. Ch., Sun Valley, Calif., 2005—; tchr. music Winds of Hope, Sun Valley, 2006—; tchr. missionary Okinawa Christian Sch. Internat., Japan, 2008—. Organist St. Barnabas the Apostle Anglican Ch., Sun Valley, 2006—. Mem.: Am. Guild Organists. Avocations: reading, exercise, music. Office Phone: 818-726-3310. Personal E-mail: marchenkomusic@netzero.com.

MARCHESE, LISA MARIE, lawyer, educator; b. Seattle, Sept. 13, 1962; d. John Sebastian and Joanne Spino Marchese. BA, Cath. U. Am., Washington, DC, 1984; JD, Georgetown U. Law Ctr., Washington, DC, 1987. Bar: Wash. 1988, Oreg. 2003, US Supreme Ct. 1998, US Dist. Ct. (ea. and we. dists.) Wash. 1998, US Ct. Appeals (9th cir.) 2003. Legis. counsel Hon. Daniel J. Evans, Washington, 1983—88; sr. dep. pros. atty. King County Prosecutor's Office, Seattle, 1989—98; ptnr. Stafford Frey Cooper, 1998—2006, Dorsey & Whitney LLP, Seattle, 2006—. Adj. law prof. U. Wash. Law Sch., 1999—, Seattle U. Sch. Law, 2000—; faculty mem. Nat. Inst. Trial Advocacy, 1999—; bd. mem. Wash. Women Lawyers, 2000—02; assoc. Am. Bd. Trial Advocates; fellow Litigation Coun. America; spkr. in field. Contbr. articles to various law jours. Mem.: Washington Women Lawyers, Phi Beta Kappa. Roman Cath. Avocations: sports, opera, reading, golf. Office: Dorsey & Whitney LLP US Bank Ctr 1420 Fifth Ave 3400 Seattle WA 98101 Office Phone: 206-903-8800, 206-903-2379. Business E-Mail: marchese.lisa@dorsey.com.

MARCHESE, MICHAEL JAMES, JR., radiation oncologist; b. NYC, Mar. 9, 1955; s. Michael James Sr. and Mabel Gladys (Rosero) M.; m. Kathryn Allen, Aug. 7, 1982 (div. May 1993); 1 child, Michael James III; m. Kathleen Spahr, Oct. 18, 1997; 2 children, Melissa June, Jessica Maria. BA magna cum laude, NYU, 1976; MD, Baylor Coll. Medicine, 1979. Diplomate Am. Bd. Radiology. Intern Monmouth Med. Ctr., Hahnemann Med. Coll., Long Branch, NJ, 1979—80; resident and chief resident radiation therapy Presbyn. Hosp., Columbia U. Coll. Physicians and Surgeons, NYC, 1980—83, asst. attending physician radiation oncology, 1983—87; resident brachytherapy svc. Meml. Sloan Kettering Cancer Ctr., Cornell U. Med. Coll., NYC, 1982; asst. clin. prof. radiation oncology Columbia U. Coll. Physicians & Surgeons, NYC, 1983—84, asst. prof. radiation oncology, 1984—87; attending staff radiology/radiation oncology Cmty. Med. Ctr., Toms River, NJ, 1987—96, Kimball Med. Ctr., Lakewood, NJ, 1994—, Med. Ctr. Ocean County, Brick, NJ, 1996—; dir. Ocean Radiation Therapy Ctr., Toms River, NJ, 1997—2005, Ctr. for Advanced Radiation Oncology, Toms River, NJ, 2005—08. Investigator Nat. Cancer Inst., 1983-87, investigator radiation therapy oncology group, 1983-87, 95—, physician surveyor, 1983-85, investigator cancer and leukemia group B, 1986-87, investigator Ea. Coop. Oncology Group, 1995—; physician surveyor practice accreditation program Am. Coll. Radiology, 1986-87; Cancer liason Am. Coll. Surgeons, Kimball Med. Ctr., 2001-04. Author: (with others) Radiation Therapy of Gynecological Cancers, 1987, Frontiers of Radiation Therapy and Oncology, vol. 22, 1988; contbr. articles to profl. jours. Bd. dirs. Am. Cancer Soc., Ocean County, N.J., 1993—2004, v.p., 1993-94, pres., 1994-98, chief med. officer, 2000-01. Recipient Resident/Fellow award Am. Radium Soc., Travel award European Soc. Therapeutic Radiology and Oncology, Clin. Oncology Career Devel. award Am. Cancer Soc., Physician of Yr., Am. Cancer Soc., 1998. Fellow Am. Coll. Radiation Oncology; mem. Am. Soc. Therapeutic Radiology and Oncology, Am. Soc. Clin. Oncology, Acad. Medicine N.J., Radiation Rsch. Soc., N.Y. Acad. Sci., Ocean County Med. Soc. (trustee 1997—, treas. 2005—), Med. Soc. N.J. (del. 2000—). Roman Catholic. Home: 44 Lake Shore Dr Red Bank NJ 07701-5840 Office: Shore Point Radiation Oncology 900 Route 70 E Lakewood NJ 08701 Office Phone: 732-901-7333. Personal E-mail: mjmmd44@yahoo.com.

MARCHESSOU, HELENE DAISY, English and American literature educator; b. Antwerp, Belgium, Mar. 20, 1939; arrived in France, 1940; d. Norbert and Anna (Schaechter) Bronner; m. François Jean Laurent Marchessou, Sept. 11, 1965; a child, Anne. Master's degree, U. Poitiers, France, 1961, PhD, 1964; doctorat d'etat, U. Paris VII, 1975. Asst. Faculty Arts, U. Poitiers, Poitiers, 1964-69, head dept. Am. studies, 1970-84, maître de confs., 1975, prof. Am. and English lit., 1977—. Instr. Hebrew to Jewish and non-Jewish adults; instr. Biblical Hebrew to Benedictines. Freelance journalist editor Sources, 1980-84, Mires, 1985-94; author poems under name Hélène Bronner, 1998; author: Le Jour dans la Nuit, Hélu Twin Sister's Painting, Le Renouveau du Lyrisme dans la Poésie americaine on William Carlos William, 1967; translator Louis Muhlstock's poems, bilingual edit., 2003; contbr. articles on Am. fiction writers from 1976-87 to profl. jours. Pres. Enquête sur la Tragique Histoire des Internements dans les Camps en France. Jewish. Avocation: sculpturing. Home: 199 rue de la Grève 86130 Dissay France

MARCHETTA, JEFFREY G., mechanical engineer, educator; s. Anthony S. and Linda C. Marchetta. BS in Mech. Engring., U. Memphis, 1997, MS in Mech. Engring., 1999, PhD, 2002. Rsch. assoc. Los Alamos (N.Mex.) Nat. Lab., 2002—02; asst. prof. U. Memphis, 2003—. Cons. Orbital Technologies Corp., Madison, Wis., 2000—05, Nat. Civil Rights Mus., Memphis, 2004—05. Contbr. articles to profl. jours. Grantee, Tenn. Space Grant Consortium, 2002—05. Mem.: ASME, AIAA (sec. microgravity and space processes tech. com. 2004—05), Am. Soc. Engring. Educators, PI Tau Sigma, Tau Beta PI. Office: University of Memphis 322D Engineering Sciences Bldg Memphis TN 38152 Business E-Mail: jmarchtt@memphis.edu.

MARCHETTA, MELINA, writer; b. Sydney, 1965; Former tchr. St Mary's Cathedral Coll., Sydney. Author: (novels) Looking For Alibrandi, 1992, Saving Francesca, 2003, On The Jellicoe Road, 2006 (Michael L. Printz award, ALA, 2009), Finnikin of the Rock, 2008 (Aurealis award for Best Young Adult Novel, 2008), (screenplays) Looking For Alibrandi, 2000 (Film Critics Circle of Australia award, Ind. Film award for Best Screenplay, Am. Film Inst. award, NSW Premier Lit. award); contbr. The Australian, Sydney Morning Herald, Australian Lit. Review. Mailing: c/o Sophie Hamley Cameron Creswell Agy Level 7 61 Marlborough St Surry Hills NSW 2010 Australia also: c/o Jill Grinberg & Assoc 244 Fifth Ave Fl 11 New York NY 10001 Personal E-mail: talk@melinamarchetta.com.au.*

MARCHI, JON, retired brokerage house executive, rancher, venture capitalist; b. Aug. 6, 1946; s. John Robert and Joan Trimble (Toole) M.; m. Mary Stewart Sale, Aug. 12, 1972 (div. 1999) Elizabeth Ann Harris, Aug. 06, 2006; children: Aphia Jessica, Jon Jacob. Student, Claremont Men's Coll., 1964-65; BS, U. Mont., 1968, MS, 1972. Sec., treas. Marchi, Marchi & Marchi, Inc., Morris, Ill., 1968-69; account exec. D. A. Davidson & Co., Billings, Mont., 1972-75, asst. v.p., office mgr., 1976-77, v.p. mktg. and adminstrn. Great Falls, Mont., 1977—. Sec., dir., v.p. fin. svcs. and exec. devel. D. A. Davidson Realty Corp., Great Falls, 1978-85, chmn. rsch. com., 1980; bd. dirs. Ligocyte Corp., Bozeman, Mont., Big Sky Airlines, Billings, chmn. bd. dirs., 1995; bd. dirs. Implemax Equipment Co., Inc., Bozeman, Energy Overthrust Found., Mansfield Found., Mont. Beverages, Mont. Venture Capital Network, Direct Advantage, Inc., Hamilton, Mont., Mont. Naturals Internat., Inc., Eclipse Techs., Inc., Mont. Small Bus. Investment Corp., Phillips Environ. Corp., Bozeman, Mont.; chmn., dir. Devel. Corp. Mont., Helena, 1995; cattle rancher, Polson, Mont., 1986—; dir. Mont. Econ. Devel. Action Group, 2001-; guest lectr. London Sch. Econs., London, 2004. Chmn. Mont. Gov.'s Subcom. for Venture Capital Devel., Mont. Cmty. Fin. Corp., Helena, Mont. Facility Fin. Corp.; chmn. investment com. State of Mont. Sci. and Tech. Alliance, 1985—; chmn. seed capital com. State of Mont., bd. dirs. job svc. com.; mem. Mont. Peoples Action; sec.-treas. Valley View Assn., 1987—; trustee sch. dist. # 35, Polson, Mont., 1990—, chmn., 1991—; bd. dirs. Mont. Entrepreneurship Ctr., Missoula, Mont., 1990—; pres., dir. sec.-treas. Mont. Pvt. Capital Network, Bozeman, Mont., 1990—, pres., 1992—, dir., 2007; chmn., dir. Mont. Naturals Internat., Inc., 1991; dir. Mont. State Rural Devel. Coun., 1992, Mont. SBA Adv. Coun., 1992; dir. Ctr. Econ. Renewal and Tech. Transfer Mont. State U., Bozeman, 1994—; del. to White House Conf. on Small Bus., Washington, 1994-95; chmn. Glacier Venture Fund, Helena, Mont., 1996—; treas., Mont. Ambassadors., 2007-; mem. investment adv. com. DCC Growth Fund, Washington, 1998—. With U.S. Army, 1969-71; dir. Mont. State U., Billings, Coll. of Bus. Bd., 1995-, Mont. Econ. Devel. Action Group, 2001-; mem. Gov.'s

Com. Tax Restructuring, 2002-, Gov.'s Task Force on Access to Capital, 2002-; mem. Frontier Fund, Kalispell, Mont., 2006; regional dir. Mus. of Rockies, Bozeman, Mont.; appointed chmn. Mont. Facility Fin. Auth., Founding Dir. & Share Holder, Bank of Montana, Missoula, 2007; dir. Greater Northern Drilling Corp., Billings, Mont., 2007, treas. Recipient Plenipotentiran of Yr., Mont. Ambassador; named Amb. of Yr., State of Mont., 2003, Alumni of Yr., U. Mont. Sch. Bus., 2004; named to Mont. Acad. Disting. Entrepreneurs, U. Mont., 2003. Mem. Nat. Cattlemen's Assn. (fgn. trade com.), Am. Wagyu Assn. (pres.), Can. Wagyu Assn., Polson C. of C. (bd. dirs.), Valley View Assn. (bd. dirs.), Mont. Cattle Feeders Assn., Mont. Angus Assn., Western Mont. Angus Assn., Am. Angus Assn., Western Mont. Stockgrowers Assn., Securities Industry Assn., Mont. Stock Growers Assn., Mont. Ambassadors (dir. 1995, pres. 2001—), Polson C. of C. (dir.), Acme Angels, Leadership Great Falls Club, Ski Club, Mont. Club, Helena Wilderness Riders Club, Rotary. Episcopalian. Office: Marchi Angus Ranches 7783 Valley View Rd Polson MT 59860-9302 Business E-Mail: jonmarchi@marchiangos.com.

MARCHIO, SAM, legislative staff member; Comm. dir., sr. legis. asst. to Rep. Sherwood Boehlert; dep. chief of staff, legis. dir. to chief of staff Rep. Michael Arcuri, US House of Reps., 2006—. Office: Office of Congressman Michael Arcuri 127 Cannon House Office Bldg Washington DC 20515 Office Phone: 202-225-3665. Office Fax: 202-225-1981. E-mail: Sam.Marchio@mail.house.gov.*

MARCHIOLI, NELSON JEROME, restaurant chain executive; b. 1949; BA in Comm., U. Ctrl. Fla. With General Mills Restaurant Group, 1972—86; mgr. trainee Red Lobster, v.p.; exec. v.p. internat. ops. Burger King Corp., sr. v.p. worldwide supply, 1995—96; exec. v.p., COO Bruegger's Corp., 1996—97; pres. El Pollo Loco, Inc., 1997—2001; pres., CEO Denny's Corp. (formerly Advantica Restaurant Group, Inc.), 2001—. Former dir. FRD Acquisition Co. (FDR). Office: Denny's Corp 203 E Main St Spartanburg SC 29319-9966*

MARCHIONINI, GARY JOSEPH, information science educator; b. Altoona, Pa., Sept. 12, 1949; s. Arthur and Claudia (Serventi) M.; m. Suzanne Bernhardt, July 10, 1970; children: Brian, Deanna. BA, Western Mich. U., 1971; MEd, Wayne State U., 1974, PhD, 1981. Tchr. math. East Detroit (Mich.) Pub. Schs., 1971-78; inservice specialist, rschr. Wayne State U., Detroit, 1978-82, asst. prof. inst. tech., 1982-83; asst. prof. info. sci. U. Md., College Park, 1983-90, assoc. prof. info. sci., 1990-95, prof. info. sci., 1995-98; Boshamer prof. info. sci. U. N.C., Chapel Hill, 1998—. Expert NSF, Washington, 1989-90; adj. prof. George Washington U., Washington, 1992. Author: Information Seeking in Electronic Environments, 1995; editor-in-chief: Transactions on Information Systems, 2002-2008; editor: Mongan Claypool Synthesis Series on Information Concepts, Retrieval & Services; contbr. articles to profl. jours. Grantee: NSF, 1987-90, Harvard U., Annenberg Corp. Pub. Broadcasting, 1988-93, Coun. on Libr. Resources, 1990-91, Nat. Libr. Medicine, 1992, NASA, 1993-94. Mem. Assn. for Computing Machinery, Am. Soc. for Info. Sci. (Rsch. award 1997), Am. Ednl. Rsch. Assn., Assn. for Advancement Computers in Edn., Am. Soc. Info. Sci. & Tech. (pres., 2009-). Office: U NC 203 Maning Hill Chapel Hill NC 27599-0001

MARCHUK, NEIL, automotive executive; First degree in Bus. Commerce, U. Windsor, Can.; MBA, U. Paisley, UK. Pers. and indsl. rels. mgr. ITT Can.; with DuPont, 1980—92, human resources dir. Greater China, 1995—99, dir. corp. human resources; v.p. human resources Can. bus. to dir. human resources and adminstrn. China ops. SC Johnson, 1992—95; exec. v.p. human resources TRW Automotive Holdings Corp. Mem. Overseas Schs. Adv. Bd. Office: TRW Automotive Holdings Corp 12001 Tech Center Dr Livonia MI 48150 Office Phone: 734-855-2600.

MARCIALIS, ANGELO VINCENT, musician, educator; b. Bronx, NY, Nov. 19, 1958; s. Vincent John and Mary Concetta Marcialis. BA in Music, Berklee Coll. Music, 1980; MA in Edn. and Music, Manhattanville Coll., 1991. Cert. state cert. adjudicator NY State Sch. Music Assn., tchr. mentor NY State Union Tchrs. Regional dir. Music on the Move, Staten Island, NY, 1982—84; dir. of bands Chester (N.Y.) Union Free Sch. Dist., 1985—87, Enlarged City Sch. Dist. Middletown, NY, 1987—2003; dir. ensembles Washingtonville (NY) Sch., 2003—. Historian, archivist, trumpeter, jazz clnician Orange County (N.Y.) Music Educators Assn., 1987—. Author: Supplementary Method for Beginning Trumpet Players, 1992. Recruiter Green Party, Orange County, 2000. Named Tchr. of Yr., Middletown, 1991. Mem.: N.Y. State Band Dirs. Assn., Internat. Trumpet Guild, N.Y. State Music Assn. Avocations: gardening, baseball, hiking, bicycling, herptology. Home: 3712 Whispering Hills Chester NY 10918-1530 Office: Washingtonville Sch 38 W Main St Washingtonville NY 10992 Office Phone: 845-497-2200 ext 21197, 845-497-4000 ext. 21197. Personal E-mail: trumpethead@hotmail.com.

MARCIALIS, ROBERT LOUIS, planetary astronomer; b. NYC, Sept. 14, 1956; s. Louis Angelo and Joan Regina (Dippolito) M. SB in Aero. and Astronautical Engring., MIT, 1978, SB in Earth and Planetary Scis., 1980; MS in Physics and Astronomy, Vanderbilt U., 1983; PhD in Planetary Scis., U. Ariz., 1990. Tchg. asst. dept. earth and planetary scis. MIT, Cambridge, 1976—80; lab. instr. dept. physics and astronomy Vanderbilt U., Nashville, 1981, 1982—83, rsch. asst. Arthur J. Dyer Obs., 1981—82; rsch. asst. Lunar and Planetary Lab. U. Ariz., Tucson, 1983—86, rsch. assoc., 1986—90; postdoctoral fellow Jet Propulsion Lab., Pasadena, Calif., 1990—92; adj. faculty Pima C.C., Tucson, 1992—; sr. rsch. specialist U. Ariz., 1996—. Founding mem. Pluto/Charon Mut. Eclipse Season Campaign. Contbr. articles to Nature, Bull. Am. Astron. Soc., Astron. Jour., Minor Planet Circular, Lunar and Planetary Sci., Sci., Jour. Brit. Astron. Assn., Astrophys. Jour., Icarus, also others. Instr. water safety ARC, 1981-82; ednl. counselor MIT, 1983—; fastpitch softball umpire, 1975—. Rsch. fellow NASA, 1986-89. Mem. AAAS, Am. Astron. Soc., Am. Geophys. Union, Astron. Soc. Pacific, Internat. Occultation Timing Assn., Sigma Pi Sigma. Roman Catholic. Achievements include discovery of water ice on surface of Pluto's moon Charon; construction of an albedo map for surface of Pluto; research on Pluto, Charon and Triton, icy satellites, outer solar system formation and evolution, solar system photometry, occultation astronomy, construction and calibration of Imager for Mars Pathfinder, cameras for the Mars Polar Lander and Mars Phoenix missions and Mars Odyssey gamma ray spectrometer. Office: U Ariz Lunar Planetary Lab Tucson AZ 85721-0001 E-mail: umpire@lpl.arizona.edu.

MARCIANO, GEORGES G., apparel executive; b. Jan. 1947; arrived in Calif., 1977; m. Megan Marciano. Co-founder Guess? Inc., 1981, chmn., CEO, designer, 1981—88, 1988—93. Office: Guess Inc 1444 S Alameda St Los Angeles CA 90021

MARCIANO, MAURICE, apparel executive; b. Morocco, 1948; arrived in Calif., 1977; Co-founder MGA, 1973; co-founder, dir. Guess? Inc., LA, 1981—, exec. v.p., 1981—90, pres., 1990—92, chmn. bd., CEO, 1993—99, co-CEO, co-chmn., 1999—2007, chmn. bd., 2007—; chmn. bd., CEO Pepe Clothing USA, Inc., 1993. Office: Guess Inc 1444 S Alameda St Los Angeles CA 90021-2433

MARCIANO, PAUL L., apparel executive; b. Marseilles, France; arrived in Calif., 1981; Co-founder MGA, 1973, Guess? Inc., LA, 1981—, creative dir., 1990—, sr. exec. v.p., 1990—92, pres., COO, 1992—2000, co-chmn., co-CEO, 1999—2006, CEO, vice chmn., 2007—. Office: Guess Inc 1444 S Alameda St Los Angeles CA 90021 Office Phone: 213-765-3100.

MARCIANO, SONIA, finance educator; d. Sital and Saroj Daryanani; m. Anthony Daryanani, Dec. 18, 1992; children: Samantha Ann, Alexa Noelle. PhD in Bus. Economics, U. Chgo. Clin. prof. Kellogg Sch. Mgmt., Evanston, Ill., 1996—2004, Stern Sch. Bus., NYC, 2007—; sr. lectr. Harvard Bus. Sch., Cambridge, Mass., 2004—07. Contbr. books and articles on strategy. Recipient Tchg. awards, Kellogg.

MARCINEK, CARA A., psychologist; d. Bernard F. and Margaret A. Marcinek. BS, Pa. State U., Univ. Pk., 2001; MS, Millersville U., Pa., 2004. Cert. sch. psychologist NASP, 2006, Pa. Dept. Edn., 2005. Intern sch. psychologist Chartiers Valley Sch. Dist., Bridgeville, Pa., 2004—05, sch. psychologist, 2005—. Vol. Dem. Party, Pitts., 2004; sec. Grad. Student Assn., Millersville U., Pa., 2003—04; vol. Animal Rescue League, Pitts., 2005—07; vol. tutor Study Buddies After-School Tutoring Program, Bridgeville, Pa., 2004—05. Mem.: NASP, Psi Chi, Golden Key. Liberal. Office: Chartiers Valley Sch District 50 Thoms Run Rd Bridgeville PA 15017 Business E-Mail: cmarcinek@cvsd.net.

MARCINKOSKI, ANNETTE MARIE, retired elementary school educator; b. Akron, Ohio, Aug. 2, 1933; d. Frank J. and Barbara (Popielarczyk) M. BS, U. Akron, 1955; MA, U. Mich., 1959. Tchr. Flint (Mich.) Pub. Schs., 1955-63; tng. tchr. Coop. Tchr. Edn. Program, 1963-69, elem. tchr., 1969—92. Active Big Sister program; sponsor Jr. Red Cross, 1959-63; tchr. Confraternity of Christian Doctrine; precinct del. Dem. Com. Mem. United Tchrs. of Flint (del. rep. assembly, instn./profl. devel. com.), Mich. Edn. Assn. (bd. dirs. 1978-90, pres. Region X, 1976-77, exec. com. 1986-90), NEA (regional dir. 1973-78), Elem., Kindergarten and Nursery Educators, Assn. Childhood Edn. Internat. (sec. Flint 1959-62, treas. Mich. 1970-72, pres. Mich. 1973-75), AAUW (v.p. 1967-69, area rep. in edn. 1969-72; Flint Br. Woman of Yr., 2008, DKG Woman of Discitation award, 2008, Flint Classroom Support Fund grant, 2009), Cath. Bus. Women (sec. 1970-72, del. Coun. State Orgns. 1974-76), Flint Area Reading Coun., Mich. Reading Assn., Mich. Edn. Spl. Svcs. Assn. (trustee 1983-92, v.p. 1990), Flint Cmty. Schs. Edn. Fund (bd. govs. 1984-88), Flint Classroom Support Fund (bd. trustees 1988-92, exec. dir. 1992—2008), Theta Phi Alpha (advisor GM Inst. chpt. 1973-85, chmn. bd. dirs. 1973-79, sec. Founders Found., 1978-80, nat. treas. 1980-82, chmn. nat. bd. dirs. 1986-88), Delta Kappa Gamma (pres. 1990-92), Phi Delta Kappa (del. 1981-84, 86-88). Office: 923 E Kearsley St Flint MI 48503-1900 Home: 26 Seaford Pl Okatie SC 29909-7110 Home Phone: 810-235-2989, 1-843-705-2181.

MARCOCCIA, LOUIS GARY, accountant, academic administrator; b. Syracuse, NY, Nov. 6, 1946; s. George A. and Rose J. (Misita) M.; m. Susan Evelyn Miller, June 21, 1974; 1 child: Rachel Kathryn. BS, Syracuse U., 1968, MS, 1969; EdD, U. Pa., 2003. CPA NY. Acct. Price Waterhouse & Co., Syracuse, NY, 1969-75; dir. internal audit Syracuse U., 1975-76, comptroller, 1976-82, v.p., comptroller, 1982-95, sr. v.p. bus., and fin., 1985—95, sr. v.p. bus., fin. and adminstrv. svcs., 1995—2006, exec. v.p., CFO, 2006—. Bd. dirs. Syracuse Bd. Chase Manhattan Bank, Syracuse Divsn., 1985-2001, Lincoln Life and Annuity Co. N.Y., Univ. Hill Corp., Upstate Med. Univ. Found.; pres. Syracuse U. Hotel and Conf. Ctr., LLC; spkr. Harvard U. Inst. Ednl. Mgmt., 1984-88, 90-91. Pres. parish coun. St. Michael's Ch., Syracuse, 1985-88; pres. Syracuse U. Theatre Corp., 1987—; bd. dirs. Friends of Burnet Park Zoo, 1987-93, Syracuse U. Press., 1982—, Syracuse Sports Corp., 1990-91. Mem. AICPA, N.Y. Soc. CPA, Nat. Assn. Accts., Fin. Execs. Inst., Inst. Internal Auditors. Clubs: Drumlins (pres. 1976—); Century. Republican. Roman Catholic. Avocations: swimming, tennis. Home: Hedge Ln Cazenovia NY 13035 Office: Syracuse U Off ExecVP and CFO 900 S Crouse AveSte 620 Syracuse NY 13244-2130 Business E-Mail: lmarcocc@syr.edu.

MARCOGLIESE, RICHARD J., energy executive; BSChemE, NYU. Various operational and tech. supervisory positions Benicia refinery, Baton Rouge refinery, refining and supply hdqs. and Bayway refinery Exxon; v.p., gen. mgr. Benicia refinery Valero Energy Corp., sr. v.p. strategic planning San Antonio, 2001—02, sr. v.p. refining ops., 2002, exec. v.p. refining ops., exec. v.p., COO, 2007—. Office: Valero Energy Corpn PO Box 696000 San Antonio TX 78269-6000*

MARCOM, PAUL KELLY, oncologist; MD, Baylor Coll. Medicine, Tex., 1989. Resident, medicine Duke U. Med. Ctr, 1989—92, resident, hematology and oncology, 1992—95, post-doctoral fellow, 1995—97, with med. oncology dept., 1997—. Contbr. several articles to profl. jours. Office: Duke U Med Ctr Box 3395 Med Ctr DUMC 3147 Durham NC 27710 Office Phone: 919-684-3877. Office Fax: 919-681-0874.*

MARCONI, DOMINIC ANTHONY, bishop emeritus; b. Newark, Mar. 13, 1927; s. Sabato Joseph and Antoinette (Ricciardi) Marconi BA, Seton Hall U., 1949; postgrad., Immaculate Conception Sem., Mahwah, NJ, 1952; STL, Cath. U., Washington, 1953. Ordained priest Archdiocese of Newark, NJ, 1953; assoc. pastor St. Anthony's Ch., Union City, NJ, 1953-66; assoc. dir. family life apostolate Archdiocese of Newark, 1966-70, dir., 1970-75, aux. and regional bishop, 1976—2002, aux. bishop emeritus, 2002—; co-dir. div. for services to elderly Associated Cath. Charities, 1975-76. Mem.: KC. Roman Catholic. Address: 71 Washington Ave Chatham NJ 07928-2014 Personal E-mail: damarcl@verizon.net.

MARCOSSON, THOMAS I., management consultant, advertising executive; b. NYC, Jan. 31, 1936; s. Mark and Mollie (Schreiber) M.; m. Carla F. Hunt, May 15, 1988; children: Mark, Susan, Samuel, Jill. Student, Union Coll., Schenectady, 1953-55; BS, NYU, 1959. CPA NY. Mgr. Touche Ross & Co., NYC, 1959-63; v.p. fin., dir. Superior Surg. Mfg. Co., Inc., Huntington, NY, 1964-66; div. pres., gen. mgr. OEI div., Vernitron Corp., Great Neck, NY, 1967-71; controller Allied Maintenance Corp., NYC, 1972-75, v.p. fin., 1975-82; chief fin. officer Remco Maintenance Corp., NYC, 1982-84, exec. v.p., chief operating officer, 1984-88; pres. MBW Advt. Network Inc., NYC, 1988-89; founder, pres. Dunmarc Assocs., Inc., NYC, 1989—; pres., dir. Square Arch Realty Corp., NYC, 1986—2004. Exec. v.p. Greater Talent Network, Inc., 1991—; co-founder, dir. Village Alliance Bus. Improvement Dist., 1993-2004. Office: 437 5th Ave 7th Fl New York NY 10016 Office Phone: 212-645-4200. Personal E-mail: tmarcosson@gmail.com.

MARCOTTE, MICHAEL STEVEN, municipal official; b. New Orleans, Jan. 17, 1951; s. Steven Stephen and Gloria Catherine (DeValcourt) Marcotte; m. Mary Jane Kilgore, May 28, 1972; children: Matthew David, Margaret Katherine. BA, M of Environ. Engring., Rice U., 1973. Cert. profl engr, Tex, Colo. Engr., sr. engr., mgr. Turner, Collie & Braden, Inc., Houston, 1973—82; chief maintenance engr. water divsn. City of Houston, 1982—83, mng. engr. water divsn., 1984—85, asst. to dir. Pub. Works dept., 1985—87, exec. asst. to dir. Pub. Works dept., 1987—88, acting dir. dept. planning and devel., 1988—89; dir. Dallas Water Utilities, 1989—95; dir. econ. devel. City of Dallas, 1995—97; chief engr. D.C. Water & Sewer Authority, 1997—2004; dir. pub. works City Houston, 2004—. Fellow: ASCE; mem.: Houston Galveston Area Coun., Am. Acad. Water Resource Engrs., Am Acad Environ Engrs (trustee), Tex Water Conservation Asn (bd dirs), Water Environ Fedn (life), Am Water Works Assn. (life; trustee Rsch. Found.). Presbyterian. Avocation: high school and college sports official. Home: 204 Travis St Apt 2D Houston TX 77002-1775 Office: City Houston 611 Walker 25th Fl Houston TX 77002 Home Phone: 713-226-8029; Office Phone: 713-837-0037. Personal E-mail: marcottem@prodigy.net.

MARCOTTE, PAUL JOHN, neurosurgeon, educator; b. Ottawa, Ont., Can., Oct. 15, 1958; (parents Can. and Am. citizens); s. Paul John and Elinor Ann (Simeone) M. BSc, U. Ottawa, 1980, MD, 1984. Intern Ottawa Civic Hosp., 1984-85; resident U. Ottawa, 1985-90, asst. prof., 1990-92; fellow in spinal surgery Barrow Neurol. Inst., Phoenix, 1991-92; assoc. prof. U. Pa., Phila., 1993—. Contbr. articles to profl. jours., chpts. to books. Fellow: ACS, Royal Coll. Physicians and Surgeons (Can.); mem.: Can. Congress Neurol. Surgeons, Am. Assn. Neurol. Surgeons, Congress Neurol. Surgeons. Roman Catholic. Avocations: hockey, model railroading, automobiles. Office: Hosp U Pa 3400 Spruce St Philadelphia PA 19104-4206

MARCOUX, CARL HENRY, former insurance company executive, writer, historian; b. San Francisco, Jan. 6, 1927; s. Henry Roderick and Margaret (Carlin) M.; m. Ana Virginia Penate-Melara, Nov. 11, 1967; children: Eric Henry, Grant Reynold. BA, Stanford U., 1950; MBA, Golden Gate U., San Francisco, 1958; MA in Latin Am. History, U. Calif., Irvine, 1988; PhD in Latin Am. History, U. Calif., Riverside, 1994. Gen. mgr. Nat. Union Ins. Co., Pitts., 1953-68; exec. v.p. Transam. Ins. Co., 1968-85. Author: (novels) Sailing West, 2001, A Few Years At Sea, 2009. Served with U.S. Mcht. Marine, 1944-46; USAF, 1951-53. Mem. Stanford Alumni Assn. Republican. Home: 1967 Port Cardigan Pl Newport Beach CA 92660-5347

MARCOUX, WILLIAM JOSEPH, lawyer; b. Detroit, Jan. 20, 1927; s. Lona J. and Anna (Ransom) C.; m. Kae Marie Sanborn, Aug. 23, 1952; children: Ann K., William C. BA, U. Mich., 1949, JD, 1952. Bar: Mich. 1953. Pvt. practice, Pontiac, Mich., 1953; assoc. McKone, Badgley, Domke and Kline, Jackson, Mich., 1953-65, ptnr., 1965-75; dir. Marcoux, Allen, Schomer, Bower, Nichols and Kendall PC, Jackson, Mich., 1975—. Mem. exec. bd. Great Sauk Trail council Boy Scouts Am., pres., 1965-66; bd. dirs. Jackson County United Way, pres., 1983-84; former fellow Am. Coll. Trial Lawyers. Served with USNR, 1945-46. Recipient Silver Beaver award Boy Scouts Am., 1969, Disting. Citizen award Land O'Lakes coun. Boy Scouts Am., 1991. Fellow Mich. State Bar Found.; mem. Mich. State Bar Assn., Jackson County Bar Assn. (pres. 1979-80), Jackson Rotary Club (pres. 1963-64), Country Club of Jackson, Clark Lake Yacht Club (commodore 1959). Methodist. Home: 1745 Malvern Dr Jackson MI 49203-5378 Office: Marcoux Allen et al PO Box 787 Jackson MI 49204-0787 Office Phone: 517-787-4100. Business E-Mail: wmarcoux@marcouxallen.com.

MARCOVITZ, LEONARD EDWARD, retail executive; b. Bismarck, ND, Sept. 6, 1934; s. Jacob and Frieda Marcovitz. Asst. mgr. Greengard's Clothing, Mandan, ND, 1955-58; mgr. K-G Men's Stores, Inc., Bismarck, 1958-61, Billings, Mont., 1961-69, v.p. store ops., 1969-73; pres. Leonard's Men's Stores, Yakima, Wash. and Billings, Mont., 1973-77; chief exec. officer K-G Retail div. Chromalloy Am. Corp., Englewood, Colo., 1977-81; pres. DeMarcos Men's Clothing, Casper, Wyo., 1982—, Idaho Falls, Idaho, 1984—, Billings, Mont., 1986-96, Twin Falls, Idaho, 1996—, Ft. Collins, Colo., 1999—, Boise, Idaho, 2000, DeMarcos, Men's Clothing, Boise Town Square, 2002, Bozeman, Mont., 2008. With N.D. Nat. Guard, 1954—61, with Mont. Nat. Guard, 1961—63. Mem. Menswear Retailers Am. (past dir.), Order of Demolay (Degree of Chevalier 1952, Internat. Master Councilor 1953, Demolay Dad 1959), Elks. Home: PO Box 777035 Henderson NV 89077

MARCU, AARON R., lawyer; b. Phila., Oct. 13, 1955; s. Howard Saul and Hinda Graubard Marcu; m. Mary Lu (Bilek), June 1, 1980; children: Adam, Benjamin. BS, Northwestern U., 1977; JD, Harvard Law Sch., 1980. Bar: NY 1981, US Dist. Ct. 1981, US Ct. Appeals 1984, US Supreme Ct. 1990. Law clk. for Hon. Richard Owen US Dist. Ct. (so. dist.) NY, 1980—82; assoc. Patterson, Belknap, Webb & Tyler, 1982—83; asst. US atty. US Atty.'s Office (so. dist.) NY, 1983—89, assoc. US atty., 1989; ptnr. Covington & Burling, 1989—2009, Freshfields Bruckhaus Deringer US LLP, 2009—; head US Litigation White Collar Def. Practice Group Covington & Burling. Court appt. receiver Milan Capital Corp., NY, NY, 2000—03, Eberhard Investment Assocs., 2003—. Mem. US Atty. Gen. Econ. Crimes Coun., 1988—89; commr. NYC Civilian Complaint Review Bd., NY, NY, 1995—98; trustee Fed. Bar Coun., 2000—06; dir. Lawyers Com. Violence, 1992—94, Fed. Bar Found., 1993—99, NY Coun. Defense Lawyers, 2000—03. Recipient Dirs. award Superior Performance, US Dept. Justice, 1987. Mem.: ABA, NYC Bar Assn. Home Phone: 646-509-8000; Office Phone: 212-841-1078, 212-284-4954. Office Fax: 212-841-1010. Business E-Mail: amarcu@cov.com, aaron.marcu@freshfields.com.

MARCUCCIO, PHYLLIS ROSE, retired educational association administrator, editor; b. Hackensack, NJ, Aug. 25, 1933; d. Filippo and Rose (Henry) Marcuccio. AB, Bucknell U., 1955; MA, George Washington U., 1976. Trainee Time, Inc., 1956—57; art prodn. for mags. of Med. Econs., Inc., 1958—60; mem. staff Nat. Sci. Tchrs. Assn., Washington, 1961—99; assoc. editor Sci. and Children, 1963, editor, 1964—93, dir. divsn. elem. edn., 1974—78, dir. divsn. program devel. and continuing edn., 1978—83, pub., 1993—99; dir. publs. Nat. Sci. Tchrs. Assn., 1983—99, assoc. exec. dir., 1990—99; pub. Dragonfly, 1996—99. Lectr., cons. in field. Author (photographer, illustrator numerous articles); co-author: Investigation in Ecology, 1972; editor: Science Fun, 1977, Science Fun, 2d edit., 1994; Selected Readings for Students of English as a Second Language, 1966; compiler: Opportunities for Summer Studies in Elementary Science, 1968, Opportunities for Summer Studies in Elementary Science, 2d edit., 1969, pub.: Sci. and Children, 1993—99, Dragonfly Mag., 1997—99. Apptd. commr. Rockville (Md.) Housing Authority, 1981—91, chairperson, 1984—86; bd. dirs. Nat. Sci. Resource Ctr., NAS, 1986—96, Hands on Sci. Outreach, Inc., 1991—2001; pres. East Rockville Civic Assn., 2000—; elected mem. City Coun. of Rockville, 2005—. Recipient Citizenship medal, DAR, 1951, Golden Lamp award, Edpress, 1998. Mem.: AAAS, NSTA (life), Pocono Environ. Edn. Ctr. (bd. dirs. 1989—98), Sci. Tchg. Assn. N.Y. (Outstanding Svc. to Sci. Edn. award 1987), Ednl. Press Assn. Am. (regional dir. 1969—71, sec. 1979—, Disting. Achievement award 1969, 1971—74, 1976, 1977, Eleanor Fishburn award 1978, Disting. Achievement award 1980, 1988, 1993, 1995), The Washington Forum, Washington edn. Press Assn. (treas. 1966—67, pres. 1975—76), Ohio Coun.

Elem. Sch. Sci. (life), Nat. Assn. Industry Edn. Coop. (bd. dirs. 1980—86), Nat. Press Club (Silver Owl), Am. Nature Study Soc., Coun. Elem. Sci. Internat. (Internat. award for outstanding contbns. sci. edn. 1971, 1972, 1986, 1994), Kiwanis Internat., Sigma Delta Chi, Phi Delta Kappa, Phi Delta gamma, Theta Alpha Phi. Home: 406 S Horners Ln Rockville MD 20850-1556 E-mail: marcu@erols.com.

MARCUM, JAMES ARTHUR, physiology and philosophy of science educator; b. Hamilton, Ohio, June 11, 1951; s. Richard C. and Madonna M. (Rohrkemper) M.; m. Sarah Hite Johnson, June 20, 1992. BSEd, Miami U., Oxford, Ohio, 1972, MS, 1974; PhD, U. Cin., 1978; MATS, Gordon-Conwell Sem., 1982; PhD, Boston Coll., 1995. Rsch. assoc. MIT, Cambridge, Mass., 1982-84; instr. Harvard U. Med. Sch., Boston, 1984-85, asst. prof., 1985-93; prof. Houghton (N.Y.) Coll., 1995—. Contbr. articles to profl. jours. including Jour. Clin. Investigation, Jour. Biol. Chemistry, Biol. Bull., Annals N.Y. Acad. Scis., Perspectives in Biology and Medicine, Perspectives in Sci., Jour. of Hist. of Medicine and Allied Scis., Am. Jour. Physiology. Predoctoral fellow U. Cin., 1974, postdoctoral fellow NIH, 1983, Frederik B. Bang fellow Marine Biol. Lab., Woods Hole, Mass., 1985; recipient Young Investigator award NIH, 1985; grantee-in-aid Am. Heart Assn., 1990. Achievements include demonstration that the non-thrombogenic property of the vascular endothelium is due in part to anticoagulantly active proteoheparan sulfate synthesized by endothelial cells. Office: Houghton Coll Dept Biology 1 Willard Ave Houghton NY 14744

MARCUM, JAMES WALTON, library director, educator; b. Crystal City, Tex., June 8, 1940; s. Clarence Edwin and Caroline (Koonce) M.; m. Judith Higginbotham, June 23, 1963 (div. 1986); children: Virginia Ann Marcum Lindhurst, Jessica Marcum; m. Rebecca Beavers, Feb. 14, 1987. BA, MA, Tex. A&I Coll., Kingsville, 1960-61; PhD, U. N.C., 1970; MPA, U. Okla., 1978; MLS, U. North Tex., 1991. History tchr. Donna (Tex.) High Sch., 1961-62; reporter-photographer Taylor (Tex.) Daily Press, 1962-63; instr. Pfeiffer Coll., Misenheimer, N.C., 1963-65; asst., assoc., prof. History Okla. Bapt. U., Shawnee, 1967-80; ptnr. Marcum Pontiac, Buick, GMC, Toyota, Pampa, Tex., 1980-81, owner, 1981-84; fin. cons. Shearson Lehman, Oklahoma City, 1984; owner, operator Fee Internat., Oklahoma City, 1985-86, Marcum Chrysler Dodge, Pampa, 1987-90; adj. prof. History U. North Tex., Denton, 1990-91; dir. libr. svcs., assoc. prof. history Centenary Coll., Shreveport, La., 1991-96; dir. libr.sr. lect. History, 1996—. Chair corp. faculty Okla. Bapt. U., 1979-80; instr. U. N.C., Chapel Hill, 1969-70; vis. prof. U. Okla., Norman, 1976-77; dir. continuing edn. Okla. Bapt. U., 1977-80, chair divsn. social scis., 1974-76, chair dept. History and Polit. Sci., dir. European study program, 1970-74. Contbr. articles, revs. to profl. jours. Mem. Shawnee Human Rels. Commn., 1970s; Dem. chair 4th Congl. Dist. Okla., 1975-77; chair resources com. Cmty. Partnerships, Shreveport, 1993—, West Tex. C. of C., Okla. Hist. Records Adv. Bd. Okla. Humanities grantee, 1975, 78. Mem. ALA, La. Libr. Assn., Am. Assn. for Advancement of Slavic Studies, World Future Soc. Democrat.

MARCUS, ABIR A., psychiatrist; arrived in US, 1995; d. Assaad Aziz Abdel-Sayed and Nadra Nassry Sourial; divorced; 1 child, Gina Marie. MD with honors, Ain Shams U., Cairo, 1991. Diplomate Am. Bd. Psychiatry and Neurology, Am. Bd. Med. Specialties, lic. psychiatrist NJ, NY. Intern Ain Shams Med. Sch., Cairo, 1992—93, instr. forensic medicine and toxicology, 1994—95; resident in psychiatry NJ Med. Sch., Newark, 1996—2000; fellow, asst. prof. Robert Wood Johnson, Piscataway, NJ, 2000—01; pvt. practice Little Silver and NYC, 1999—. Adj. asst. prof. Robert Wood Johnson Med. Sch., Piscataway, 2001—; task force com. for curriculum devel. in psychotherapy tng. for residents U. Medicine and Dentistry NJ Med. Sch., Newark, 1999—2000; cons. CPC Behavioral Health Care, Red Bank, NJ, 2001—; cons. in field. Contbr. articles to profl. jours. Recipient Physician's Recognition award, AMA, 1999, 2005; scholar, Nat. Inst. Drug Abuse. Mem.: Am. Psychoanalytic Assn. (assoc. mem.), Neurosci. Edn. Inst., Am. Soc. Clin. Psychopharmacology, NJ Psychiat. Assn. (pres. resident chpt. 1999, pres. 2000, early career psychiatry com., pub. edn. com., disaster preparedness com., resident and med. student com.), Am. Psychiat. Assn., Am. Acad. Addiction Psychiatry, Am. Soc. Addiction Medicine. Avocations: reading, travel, ballroom dancing, salsa dancing. Office: 34 Sycamore Ave # 2C Little Silver NJ 07739 Office Phone: 732-530-3122. Personal E-mail: doctor.marcus@hotmail.com. Business E-Mail: drmarcus@birovenusmedicalspa.com.

MARCUS, ALAN C., public relations consultant; b. NYC, Feb. 26, 1947; s. Percy and Rose (Fox) M.; m. Judith Lamel, June 21, 1979; 1 child, Allison. Student, Hun Sch. of Princeton, 1965. Dir. pub. rels. Bergen County Rep. Com., Hackensack, N.J., 1968; clk. N.J. Gen. Assembly, Trenton, 1969, sec. to majority party of assembly, 1970; pres. The Marcus Group, Inc., Secaucus, 1971—. Adj. prof. Rutger U. Grad. Sch., 1986-88. Trustee Nat. Leukemia Assn., 1978-82, Hun Sch. of Princeton, 1977-88, Passaic River Coalition, 1980-82. Recipient Youth Enterprise award Jim Waiter Corp., 1972. Mem. Pub. Rels. Soc. Am. (pres., bd. dirs. NJ chpt. 1976-77, NJ chpt. Pres. award 1975), NJ C. of C., NJ Bus. and Industry Assn., NJ Press Assn., Alpine Country Club. also: 50 W State St Trenton NJ 08608-1220

MARCUS, ALAN I., historian, educator; b. Red Bank, NJ, Aug. 15, 1949; s. Franklin Mitchell and Eunice Simels Marcus; m. Jean W. Marcus, Aug. 22, 1971; children: Gregory Vance, Jocelyn Claire. PhD, U. Cin., 1979. Prof. emeritus history Iowa State U., Ames, prof. history, 1980—2005, dir., history tech. and sci., 1991—2005, disting. humanities scholar, 1999—2000; prof. and head history Miss. State U., 2005—08. Author: (book) The Future is Now, Technology in America, 2nd ed. (Choice, Outstanding Academic Book, 1999), Building Western Civilization, Cancer From Beef, Plague Of Strangers, Technology in America, 1st.ed (Choice Outstanding Academic book, 1990), Agricultural Science and the Quest for Legitimacy; editor: Technical Knowledge in American Culture, The United States Department of Agriculture in Historical Perspective, Engineering in a Land-grant Context, Health Care Policy in Contemporary America; contbr. articles to profl. jours. Mem.: Am. Assn. History Medicine, Soc. History Tech., History Sci. Soc., Agrl. History Soc. (exec. com. mem. 1987—91, program com. mem. 1987—91), Am. Hist. Assn., Orgn. Am. Historians (program com. mem. 1999—2000, exec. com. mem. 1999—2000). Office: Dept History Miss State 242 Allen Hall PO Box H Mississippi State MS 39762 Office Fax: 662-325-1139. Business E-Mail: aimarcus@history.msstate.edu.

MARCUS, ANDREA CANDACE SILLS, lawyer; b. Brookline, Mass., Nov. 23, 1947; d. Benjamin and Mary Natalie (Rogers) Sills; m. Lawrence I. Marcus, Aug. 9, 1974; children: David, Anthony, Rebecca. Grad. with honors, Norwalk Hosp. Sch. Nursing, 1973; BSN, U. Miami, Coral Gables, Fla., 1985, MSN, 1987; JD, Sch. of Law, U. Miami, 1991. Bar: Fla., US Dist. Ct. (so. dist.) Fla., US Supreme Ct. 2004; cert. arbitrator, 2004, clin. nurse specialist oncology nurse/adult health, health care risk mgr., 2009; ARNP, Fla.; RN, Conn. Head nurse, mem. psychotherapeutic team Hall-Brooke Hosp., Westport, Conn., 1973-75; founder, bd. dir. Hospice of Boca Raton, Boca Raton, Fla., 1978—81; staff RN oncology Boca Raton Cmty. Hosp., 1983—84, psychiat. nurse liaison, 1984—89; patient care coord. Hospice by the Sea, Boca Raton, 1973-75; law clk. Legal Aid Soc. of Palm Beach County, 1989—91, atty., 1991—93; asst. counsel Interim Svcs. Inc., Ft. Lauderdale, Fla., 1993-95; assoc. atty. Krathen & Roselli, 1995-96; atty. Gary, Williams, Parenti, Lewis & McManus, Fort Pierce, Fla., 1996-97; assoc. Mitchell H. Katler & Assocs., P.A., Coconut Creek, Fla., 1997—98; trial atty. Figueroa, Gonzalez & Hoecker, West Palm Beach, 1998—2000; ptnr. McIntosh, Sawran, Peltz & Cartaya, Ft. Lauderdale, 2000—. Co-editor OnCare, 1987-88. Mem. Ambs. Program U. Miami; bd. dir. Estancia Homeowners Assn.; treas. Palm Beach County Med.Soc. Aux., Diabetes Assn. Palm Beach County; mem. svc. & rehab. com., steering com. Am. Cancer Soc.; mem. psychosocial support team Boca Raton Cmty. Hosp, Fla. Emergency Health vol. Fellow Fla. Bar Found.; mem. ABA, ATLA, ANA, Fla. Nurses Assn., Am. Assn. Corp. Counsel, Nat. Health Lawyers Assn., Am. Bd. Forensic Examiners, Am. Assn. Nurse Attys., Am. Soc. Law, Medicine and Ethics, Internat. Nurses Cancer Care, Am. Inn Ct. (Spellman chpt.), Oncol. Nurses Soc., Nurses Alliance Prevention Nuc. War, Health & Law Soc., Stephen Booher Inn of Ct., Def. Rsch. Inst., Fla. Def. Lawyers Assn., Broward County Bar Assn., Fla. Med. Malpractice Claims Coun., Am. Soc. Healthcare Risk Mgmt., U. Miami Alumni Club, Sigma Theta Tau, Phi Alpha Delta. Home: 6913 Corto Cir Boca Raton FL 33433-2730 Office Phone: 954-765-1001. Business E-Mail: cmarcus@mspcesq.com.

MARCUS, BERNARD, lawyer, arbitrator, mediator; b. Wilkes-Barre, Pa., Mar. 10, 1924; m. Frances Frank; children: Kate, Aaron, Charles, Mary. Student, U. Pa., 1941-43, Carnegie-Mellon U., 1943-44; LL.B., Harvard U., 1948; postgrad., Loyola U. of South, New Orleans, 1958. Bar: D.C. 1949, La. 1958. Atty. legis. reference service Library of Congress, 1949-50; acting counsel small bus. com. Ho. of Reps., 1950; atty. NLRB, Washington, Cin., Buffalo and New Orleans, 1950-57; assoc. Deutsch, Kerrigan & Stiles, New Orleans, 1957-58, ptnr., 1958-95, mng. ptnr., 1985-89, emeritus ptnr., 1995—2004; of counsel Lehmann, Norman & Marcus, New Orleans, 2004—. Cons. Dept. State, 1965-69; labor arbitrator Am. Arbitration Assn., 1960-; arbitrator Fed. Med. and Conciliation Svc., 1960-. Author: Congress and the Monopoly Problem, 1950; contbr. to casebooks. Pres. New Orleans Jewish Cmty. Ctr., 1973-75; active Nat. Jewish Welfare Bd., 1974-83; bd. dirs. New Orleans Jewish Welfare Fedn., Jewish Family and Children's Service, New Orleans, Communal Hebrew Sch.; v.p. New Orleans Home for Jewish Aged, 1978-80, Florence Heller Rsch. Found. With U.S Army, 1943-46. Mem. ABA, Fed. Bar Assn., La. Bar Assn., New Orleans Bar Assn. (exec. com. 1971-74), D.C. Bar Assn., Nat. Acad. Arbitrators. Home: 630 Burdette St New Orleans LA 70118-3937 Office: Texaco Bldg Ste 2050 400 Poydras St New Orleans LA 70130 Home Phone: 504-866-2929; Office Phone: 504-680-6045. Business E-Mail: bmarcus@lnmlaw.com.

MARCUS, BERNARD, foundation administrator, retired retail executive; b. Newark, 1929; married. BS, Rutgers U., 1954. V.p. Vornado Inc., 1952-68; pres. Odell Inc., 1968-70; v.p. Daylin Inc., 1970-73; with Handy Dan Home Improvement, LA, 1972-78; co-founder (ex. chmn. and CEO) Home Depot Inc., Atlanta, 1978—2002, ret., 2002. Exec. advisor Chief Exec. Leadership Inst., Yale U. Sch. Mgmt. Chmn., founder Marcus Found. Inc., Marcus Inst., 1991—; founder Ga. Aquarium, Marcus Devel. Resource Ctr., DC; bd. mem. City of Hope, Duarte, Calif., Shepherd Spinal Center, Atlanta, Am. Jewish Com., Atlanta Jewish Found. Recipient Golden Plate award, Acad. Achievement, 2006; named one of Forbes Richest Americans, 2006.

MARCUS, CLAUDE, advertising executive; b. Paris, Aug. 28, 1924; s. Jacques and Louise (Bleustein) M.; m. Claudine Pohl, May 27, 1948; children: Michele, Pierre, Anne-Marie, Isabelle. Diploma in Econs., U. Paris, 1947; Lic., Paris Law Sch., 1947. Sec. gen. Publicis, Paris, 1948-55, dir. comml. to dir. gen. adjoint, 1961, dir. gen., 1962-68; mng. dir. Publicis Conseil, Paris, 1968-83; pres. Publicis Internat., Paris, 1984-88; vice-chmn. Publicis Comm., Paris, 1988—96. Decorated chevalier de la Legion d'Honneur. Mem. Bur. Verification de la Publicite (vice-chmn.), Racing Club (France). Home: 12 Rue Felicien David 75016 Paris France Office: Publicis 133 Champs Elysees 75008 Paris France Personal E-mail: claudius6@wanadoo.fr.

MARCUS, ERIC ROBERT, psychiatrist; b. NYC, Feb. 16, 1944; s. Victor and Pearl (Maddow) M.; m. Eslee Samberg, Nov. 24, 1985; children: Max, Pia. AB, Columbia U., 1965; MD, U. Wis., 1969. Diplomate Am. Bd. Psychiatry and Neurology. Intern med. ctr. Bellevue hosp. NYU, 1969-70; resident NY state psychiat. inst. Columbia Presbyn. Med. Ctr.st., 1972-75; from co-dir. to dir. neuropsychiat//diagnostic treatment unit Columbia-Presbyn. Med. Ctr., NYC, 1975-84; dir. St. Marks Free Clinic, NYC, 1971-75; dir. med. student edn. in psychiatry coll. physicians and surgeons Columbia U., NYC, 1981—2007, bd. govs. student health, 1986—2003, supervising tng. analyst ctr. psychoanalytic training and rsch., 1994—, clin. prof. psychiatry and social medicine coll. physicians and surgeons, 1995—, dir. ctr. psychoanalytic tng. and rsch., 2007—, prof. clin. psychiatry, 2008—. Author: Psychosis and Near Psychosis, 1992, 2d edit., 2003; mem. editl. bd.: The Psychoanalytic Study of Society, 1989—94, Jour. Clin. Psychoanalysis, 1998—2002; co-editor: Psychiatry, 1998—2007; contbr. articles to profl. jours. Recipient Weber Rsch. award Columbia U. Psychoanalytic Ctr., 1991, O'Connor Tchg. award, 1995, Columbia U. Presdl. award for Outstanding Tchg., 1999. Fellow: NY Acad. Medicine, Am. Coll. Psychoanalysts, Am. Psychiat. Assn. (pres. NY County Dist. 2002—03, Roeske award 1991); mem.: Assn. Psychoanalytic Medicine (pres. 1999—2001), Am. Psychoanalytic Assn. (chmn. com. on univ. and med. edn. 1999—2005, mem. editl. bd. Jour. 2000—03, Sabshin award 2003). Avocations: classical music, photography, swimming, reading. Office: Columbia U Dept Psychiatry 1051 Riverside Dr New York NY 10032-1013 Office Phone: 212-427-0543.

MARCUS, FRANK ISADORE, cardiologist, educator; b. Haverstraw, NY, Mar. 23, 1928; s. Samuel and Edith (Sattler) M.; m. Janet Geller, June 30, 1957; children: Ann, Steve, Lynn. BA, Columbia U., 1948; MS, Tufts U., 1951; MD cum laude, Boston U., 1953. Diplomate Am. Bd. Internal Medicine (subspecialty cardiovasc. diseases). Intern Peter Bent Brigham Hosp., Boston, 1953-54, asst. resident, 1956-57, research fellow in cardiology, 1957-58; clin. fellow in cardiology Georgetown U. Hosp., 1958-59, chief med. resident, 1959-60; chief of cardiology Georgetown U. Med. Service, D.C. Gen. Hosp., Washington, 1960-68; instr. medicine Georgetown U. Sch. Medicine, 1960-63, asst. prof., 1963-68, assoc. prof., 1968; prof. medicine, chief cardiology sect. U. Ariz. Coll. Medicine, Tucson, 1969-82, disting. prof. internal medicine (cardiology), 1982-99, emeritus prof., 1999—, dir. electrophysiology, 1982—2001; prin. investigator multidisciplinary study of right ventricular dysplasia Nat. Heart, Lung and Blood Inst., 2001—08. Cons. cardiology VA Hosp., Tucson, 1969, USAF Regional Hosp., Davis-Monthan AFB, Tucson, 1969; mem. panel drug efficacy study, panel on cardiovascular drugs Nat. Acad. Scis.-NRC, 1967-68; chmn. undergrad. cardiovascular tng. grant com. HEW-NIH, 1970; dir. Arrhythmia Svcs., 1996-2001. Editor: Modern Concepts of Cardiovascular Disease, 1982—84; mem. editl. bd. Circulation, 1974—81, Current Problems in Cardiology, 1975—79, Cardiovascular Drugs and Therapy, 1986—2000, New Trends in Arrythmias, 1984—, Jour. Am. Coll. Cardiology, 1983—87, 1996—2000, Am. Jour. Cardiology, 1984—, Jour. Cardiovasc. Drugs and Therapy, 1991—2000, Pacing and Clin. Electrophysiology, 1995—, Annals of Noninvasive Electrocardiology, 1996—, Cardiology, 2000—, Jour. Electrocardiology, 2005—; contbr. articles to profl. jours. Chmn. Washington Heart Assn. High Sch. Heart Program, 1966-68. Capt. USAF, 1954-56. Recipient Career Devel. award NIH, 1965, Student AMA Golden Apple award Georgetown U. Sch. Medicine, 1968, Disting. Alumni award Boston U. Sch. Medicine, 2003, Master Clinician award Coun. Clin. Cardiology, 2005; Mass. Heart Assn. fellow, 1957-58; John and Mary Markle scholar, 1960-65; grantee Nat. Heart, Lung and Blood Inst., 2001—. Fellow Coun. on Clin. Cardiology Am. Heart Assn., ACP (Ariz. laureate award 1987), Am. Coll. Cardiology (bd. govs. Ariz. 1984-87, asst. sec. 1987-89, trustee); mem. Assn. Univ. Cardiologists, Inc. (v.p. 1989-90, pres. 1990-91), Ariz. Heart Assn. (dir. 1970, v.p. 1972-73, chmn. rsch. com. 1970-72), So. Ariz. Heart Assn. (dir. 1969), N.Am. Soc. Pacing and Electrophysiology, Alpha Omega Alpha. Home: 4949 E Glenn St Tucson AZ 85712-1212 Office: U Ariz Univ Med Ctr 1501 N Campbell Ave Tucson AZ 85724-0001 Home Phone: 520-327-1339; Office Phone: 520-626-1416. Business E-Mail: fmarcus@u.arizona.edu.

MARCUS, GREIL GERSTLEY, critic; b. San Francisco, June 19, 1945; s. Gerald Dodd and Eleanore (Hyman) M.; m. Jenelle Bernstein, June 26, 1966; children: Emily Rose, Cecily Helen. BA, U. Calif., Berkeley, 1967, MA, 1968. Record editor Rolling Stone mag., San Francisco and NYC, 1969-70, book columnist, 1975-80, Calif. Mag., LA, 1982-83, 88-90; pop music columnist Music Mag., Tokyo, 1978-94, New West mag., LA, 1978-82, Artforum mag., NYC, 1983—87, 1991—98, Village Voice newspaper, NYC, 1986—91, Interview Mag., NYC, 1992—; cultural columnist N.Y. Times, 1998, Esquire mag., 1998-99; interview Salon.com, 1992—2008, music columnist, 1999—2003, City Pages, 2003—04, The Believer, 2008—. Lectr. Princeton U., fall, 2000, 02, 06, U. Calif., Berkeley, spring, 2000, 06, 08, New Sch. U., fall, 2007, 09, U. Minn., 2008. Author: Mystery Train: Images of America in Rock 'n Roll Music, 1975, U.S. rev., 1982, 90, 97, 2008 (Brit., German, Greek, Dutch, Japanese, Italian, Chinese and French edits.), Real Life Rock (Japanese), 1984, Lipstick Traces: A Secret History of the 20th Century, 1989 US Rev. 2009(Brit., Italian, Spanish, German, French, Turkish, and Greek edits.), Dead Elvis: A Chronicle of a Cultural Obsession, 1991 (Brit., French, Japanese and German edits., rev. 1999), Ranters and Crowd Pleasers: Punk in Pop Music, 1977-92, 93, In The Fascist Bathroom: Writings on Punk, 1999 (Brit., German and US edits.), The Dustbin of History (Brit. and German edits.), 1995, Invisible Republic: Bob Dylan's Basement Tapes, 1997 (Brit., Italian, German, Dutch, French, and Chinese edits.), Double Trouble: Bill Clinton and Elvis Presley in a Land of No Alternatives, 2000, rev. edit., 2001 (Brit. edit.), The Old, Weird America: The World of Bob Dylan's Basement Tapes, 2001, The Manchurian Candidate (Brit. edit.), 2002, Like a Rolling Stone: Bob Dylan at the Crossroads (Brit., German, French, Japanese, Chinese, Italian edits.), 2005, The Shape of Things to Come: Prophecy and the American Voice (Brit., French edits.), 2006; editor: Stranded, 1979, rev. 1996, 2007, Psychotic Reactions and Carburetor Dung (Lester Bangs), 1987, (with Sean Wilentz) The Rose and the Briar: Death, Love and Liberty in The American Ballad, 2004, (with Werner Sallors) A New Literacy History of America; contbr. criticism to publs. including Creem, Express-Times, New Mus. Express, Another Room, RAW, Rock and Roll Confidential, Threepenny Rev., Representations, Common Knowledge, La Nouvelle Revue Francaise; curator Whitney Mus. Arm. Art, NY, 1998.

MARCUS, HARRIS LEON, materials science educator; b. Ellenville, NY, July 5, 1931; s. David and Bertha (Messite) M.; m. Leona Gorker, Aug. 29, 1962; children: Leland, M'Risa. BS, Purdue U., 1963; PhD, Northwestern U., 1966. Registered profl. engr., Tex. Tech. staff Tex. Instruments, Attleboro, Mass., 1966—68, Rockwell Sci. Ctr., 1968—70, group leader, 1971—75; prof. mech. engring. U. Tex., Austin, 1975—79, Harry L. Kent Jr. prof. mech. engring., 1979—90, Cullen Found. prof., 1980—95, dir. ctr. for Materials Sci. and Engring., dir. program, 1979—95; prof. materials sci. and engring., dir. Inst. for Material Sci., U. Conn., 1995—. Cons. numerous orgns. Contbr. more than 300 articles to profl. publs. Recipient U. Tex. faculty U. Tex. Engring. Found., 1983; Krengel lectr. Technion, Israel, 1983; Alumni Merit medal Northwestern U., 1988, Disting. Purdue Univ. Engring. Alumnus award, 1994. Fellow Am. Soc. Metals; mem. ACS, AIME (bd. dirs. Metall. Soc. 1976-78, 84-86), Materials Rsch. Soc., Conn. Acad. Sci. and Engring. Achievements include 24 patents. Home: 78 Ellise Rd Storrs Mansfield CT 06268-1424 Office: Inst Materials Scis 97 N Eagleville Rd Unit U-3136 Storrs Mansfield CT 06269-3136 Office Phone: 860-486-4623. Personal E-mail: harrismarcus@charter.net. Business E-Mail: hmarcus@mail.ims.uconn.edu.

MARCUS, JOHN RICHARD, lawyer; b. St. Helena, Calif., Apr. 28, 1930; s. Elias George Marcus and Dorothy Olive Jones; children: David, Debbie, Cathy, Nancy, Jonathan. BA, Walla Walla Coll., College Place, Wash., 1951; LLB, JD, UCLA, 1955. Bar: Calif. 1956, US Supreme Ct. 1963. Atty. Gen. Am. Ins., Panorama City, Calif., 1956—61; pvt. practice San Bernardino, Calif., 1961—. Pro-tem judge San Bernardino County, Riverside County. Past pres., bd. dirs. San Bernardion County Legal Aid Soc.; Rep. nominee Calif. State Senate, 1972. Recipient Achievement award, Calif. Supreme Ct., 2006, State Bar Calif., 2006. Mem.: Riverside County Bar Assn., Fed. Bar Assn., San Bernardino County Bar Assn., Lawyer Pilots Bar Assn., Law-Sci. Inst. Am., Am. Bd. Trial Adv. (pres. San Bernardino chpt. 1963—, bd. cert. 1963), Lake Arrowhead C. of C., Running Springs Area C. of C., Rotary. Avocations: hiking, cooking, travel, gardening, snow shoeing. Home: PO Box 1317 Running Springs CA 92382-1317 Office: 31564 Old City Creek Running Springs CA 92382-1317 Office Phone: 909-867-5445. Personal E-mail: jmarcus@verizon.net.

MARCUS, JOYCE (JOYCE MARCUS FLANNERY), anthropology educator; Student, U. Calif., Berkeley; MS, PhD, Harvard U. Prof. of anthropology, mus. anthropology U. Mich., Ann Arbor, curator, Latin American Archaeology. Serves on Smithsonian Coun. Contbr. articles to profl. jours. Mem.: Am. Acad. Arts and Sciences, NAS (councilor 2005—). Office: U Mich 101 West Hall 1092 Ann Arbor MI 48109 Office Phone: 734-763-5164. Business E-Mail: joymar@umich.edu.

MARCUS, KENNETH L., federal official; m. Stephanie Marcus. Grad., Willams Coll.; JD, U. Calif., 1991. Litigation ptnr.; gen. dep. asst. sec. fair housing and equal oppty. U.S. Dept. HUD; dep. asst. sec. edn. for enforcement U.S. Dept. Edn., delegated the authority of asst. sec. edn. for civil rights, 2003—05; staff dir. U.S. Commn. on Civil Rights, 2004—08. Office: America Bernard Baruch Coll 1 Bernard Baruch Way New York NY 10010 Home Phone: 703-669-0896. E-mail: ulmarcus@aol.com.

MARCUS, LARRY DAVID, broadcast executive; b. NYC, Jan. 27, 1949; s. Oscar Moses and Sylvia (Ackerman) Marcus; children from previous marriage: Julia Ilene, Barbara Maureen. BBA, CUNY, 1970, MBA, 1972. Computer systems analyst Johnson & Johnson, 1972—73; acctg. mgr. Sta. WPLG-TV, Miami, Fla., 1974-75; v.p., bus. mgr. Sta.

KPLR-TV-Koplar Comm., Inc., St. Louis, 1976-82; chief fin. officer Koplar Comm., Inc., St. Louis, 1982-88, River City Broadcasting Co., St. Louis, 1988-96; gen. ptnr. Marcus Investments, L.P., 1996—; CEO Peak Media Holdings LLC, San Diego, 1997—. Computer design cons. PriceWaterhouse Coopers, 1973—74; ptnr. San Diego Social Venture. Scholarship mktg. com. & chmn. Pro Kids, San Diego; vol. San Diego Hosp.; bd. dirs. St. Louis Nat. Pub. Radio, KPBS TV, FM, San Diego, Hero Broadcasting, MTV3; pres. Del Mar TV Found. Mem.: Comm. Strategic Equinox Ctr., Broadcast Cable Fin. Mgmt. Assn. (bd. dirs. 1976—89, treas. 1989—90, sec. 1990—91, v.p. 1991—92, pres. 1992—93). Avocations: skiing, golf, boxing, bicycling. Office: Peak Media LLC 13748 Pine Needles Dr Del Mar CA 92014 E-mail: ldmarcus@aol.com.

MARCUS, LINDA SUSAN, dermatologist; b. Bklyn. d. Nathaniel and Eugenia (Portnay) Marcus; m. Ronald Carlin, July 5, 1976; children: Robert Adam, Neal Marc. BS, Adelphi U., Garden City, NJ, 1970; MD, Downstate Med. Sch., Bklyn., 1975. Diplomate Am. Bd. Dermatology. Intern Long Island (N.Y.) Jewish Med. Ctr., 1975-76; resident in dermatology Columbia-St. Luke's, NYC, 1976-77, Boston U.-Tufts U., 1977-79; pvt. practice Wyckoff, NJ, 1980—. Dir. dermatology Valley Hosp., Ridgewood. Contbr. articles to profl. jours. Chair Nat. Psoriasis Found., NJ. Mem. Am. Acad. Dermatology (editor pamphlet editl. bd.), Am. Soc. Dermatol. Surgeons, Internat. Soc. Dermatol. Surgeons, NJ Dermatol. Soc. (program dir.), NJ North Dermatol. Soc. (co-chair, pres.), Dermatol. Soc. NJ (pres.). Avocations: swimming, ice skating. Office: 271 Godwin Ave Wyckoff NJ 07481-2057 Office Phone: 201-891-4373. Personal E-mail: sexyderm@verizon.net.

MARCUS, MARIA LENHOFF, lawyer, educator; b. Vienna, June 23, 1933; came to U.S., 1938, naturalized, 1944; d. Arthur and Clara (Gruber) Lenhoff; m. Norman Marcus, Dec. 23, 1956; children: Valerie, Nicole, Eric. BA, Oberlin Coll., 1954; JD, Yale Law Sch., 1957. Bar: N.Y. 1961, U.S. Dist. Ct. (so. and ea. dists.) N.Y. 1962, U.S. Ct. Appeals (2d cir.) 1962, U.S. Supreme Ct. 1964. Assoc. counsel NAACP, NYC, 1961-67; asst. atty. gen. N.Y. State, NYC, 1967-78; chief litigation bur. Atty. Gen. N.Y. State, 1976-78; adj. assoc. prof. NYU Law Sch., 1976-78; assoc. prof. Fordham U. Law Sch., NYC, 1978-86, prof., 1986—, Joseph M. McLaughlin prof., 1997—. Arbitrator Nat. Assn. Securities Dealers; chair subcom. interrogatories U.S. Dist. Ct. (so. dist.) N.Y., 1983-85. Contbr. articles to profl. jours. Named Tchr. of Yr., Fordham Law School Students, 2001. Fellow N.Y. Bar Found.; mem. Assn. Bar City of N.Y. (v.p. 1995-96, long range planning com. 1996-2000, exec. com. 1976-80, com. audit 1988-95, labor com. 1981-84, judiciary com. 1975-76, chmn. civil rights com. 1972-75), N.Y. State Bar Assn. (exec. com. 1979-81, ho. dels. 1978-81, com. constitution and by-laws 1984-93), N.Y. Women's Bar Assn. (Pres.'s award 1999). Office: Fordham U Law Sch 140 W 62nd St New York NY 10023-7485

MARCUS, MICHAEL B., mathematics professor; s. Harold Jacob and Jean Marcus; m. Jane Connor, Aug. 22, 1963; children: Lisa, Jason, Benjamin. PhD, MIT, Cambridge, Mass, 1965. Prof. Northwestern U., Evanston, Ill., 1967—81, Tex. A&M U., Coll. Station, Tex., 1981—86, CUNY, NYC, 1986—. Contbr. scientific papers. Grantee Rsch. Support, NSF, 1968—2008; fellow Guggenheim Found. Fellowship, 1993. Home: 253 W 73 rd St Apt 2E New York NY 10023 Business E-Mail: mbmarcus@optonline.net.

MARCUS, PAUL, law educator; b. NYC, Dec. 8, 1946; s. Edward and Lillian (Rubin) M.; m. Rebecca Nimmer, Dec. 22, 1968; children: Emily, Beth, Daniel. AB, UCLA, 1968, JD, 1971. Bar: Calif. 1971, U.S. Dist. Ct. (cen. dist.) Calif. 1972, U.S. Ct. Appeals (D.C. cir.) 1972, U.S. Ct. Appeals (7th cir.) 1976. Law clk. U.S. Ct. Appeals (D.C. cir.), 1971-72; assoc. Loeb & Loeb, LA, 1972-74; prof. law U. Ill., Urbana, 1974-83; dean Coll. Law U. Ariz., Tucson, 1983-88, prof., 1988-92; Haynes prof. law Coll. William and Mary, Williamsburg, Va., 1992—, Kelly prof. tchg. excellence, 1992—, interim dean, 1993-94, 97-98. Reporter, cons. Fed. Jud. Ctr. Commn., Nat. Com. on the Right to Counsel, 2004-07. Author: The Entrapment Defense, 1989, 4th edit., 2009, The Prosecution and Defense of Criminal Conspiracy, 1978, 6th edit., 2007, Gilbert Law Summary, 1982, 8th edit., 2004, Criminal Law: Cases and Materials, 1982, 6th edit., 2007, Criminal Procedure in Practice, 2001, 2d edit., 2003. Office: Coll William & Mary Law Sch PO Box 8795 Williamsburg VA 23187-8795 Home Phone: 757-253-0431; Office Phone: 757-221-3900. Business E-Mail: pxmarc@wm.edu.

MARCUS, PHILIP, associate dean; b. NYC, Nov. 26, 1946; s. Max and Rosaline Marcus; m. Rovena Shreck, Aug. 24, 1969; children: Mitchell Howard, Brian Seth, Alyssa Robyn. BS in Pharmacological Scis., Columbia U., NYC, 1969; MD, SUNY, Bklyn., 1973; MPH, Johns Hopkins U., Balt., 2001. Diplomate internal medicine Am. Bd. Internal Medicine, 1976, pulmonary diseases Am. Bd. Internal Medicine, 1978, critical care medicine Am. Bd. Internal Medicine, 1999. Assoc. dean, curriculum devel. NY Coll. Osteo. Medicine, Old Westbury, NY, 2001—; chief, divsn. pulmonary medicine St. Francis Hosp., Roslyn, NY, 2003—06. Contbr. articles various profl. jours. Fellow: ACP, Am. Coll. Chest Physicians (chair, practice mgmt. com. 2004—06). Avocation: travel. Office: NY Coll Osteo Medicine 233 E Shore Rd Great Neck NY 11023 Office Phone: 516-482-7810. Office Fax: 516-482-3760; Home Fax: 516-482-3760. Personal E-mail: pmarcus192@aol.com. E-mail: pmarcus@nyit.edu.

MARCUS, RANDALL EVAN, orthopaedic surgery educator; b. NYC, Feb. 10, 1950; s. Irwin and Dorthy (Mann) Marcus; m. Anne Mulligan, June 2, 1984; 1 child, Blair Mulligan. BS in Biochemistry, magna cum laude, Tulane U., 1972; MD, La. State U. Sch. Medicine, 1975. Diplomate Am. Bd. Orthopaedic Surgery, lic. Ohio. Fellow Nufield dept. orthopaedic surgery Oxford U., England, 1980-81; internat. fellow dept. surgery U. Basle, Switzerland, 1981; sr. fellow dept. orthopaedics U. Wash. Harborview Med. Ctr., Seattle, 1981; rotating surg. intern Case Western Res. U. Sch. Medicine, Cleve., 1975-76, asst. resident gen. surgery, 1976-77, resident orthopaedics, 1977-79, chief resident, 1979-80, postdoctoral fellow, 1977-80, instr. orthopaedic surgery, 1981-82, asst. prof., 1982-83, 86-91, assoc. prof., 1992-97, prof., 1998—. Dir. divsn. foot and ankle surgery Case Western Res. U. Sch. Medicine. Contbr. articles to med. jours. Recipient Tchg. Excellence award, Case Western Res. U. Sch. Medicine, 1996—97; named one of America's Top Surgeons, Consumers Rsch. Coun., 2001—07. Fellow: ACS, Am. Acad. Orthopaedic Surgeons; mem.: Pasteur Club Cleve., Cleve. Aesculapian Med. Soc., Innominatum Med. Soc. Cleve., Cleve. Orthopaedic Soc. (bd. dirs. 1986—89), Twentieth Century Orthopaedic Soc., Orthopaedic Trauma Assn., Am. Orthopaedic Foot & Ankle Soc., Assn. Bone & Joint Surgeons (pres. 2007—08), Am. Orthopaedic Assn., Am. Bd. Orthopaedic Surgery (pres. 2007—08, bd. dirs.). Achievements include patents for a multi-use femoral intramedullary nail. Avocations: golf, tennis, skiing. Office: Case Sch Med Dept Orthopaedic Surgery 11100 Euclid Ave Cleveland OH 44106 Office Phone: 216-844-3041.*

MARCUS, RICHARD SARGON, research scientist; AB, U. Pa., 1954, BSEE, 1955; MSEE, MIT, 1957, EE, 1958. Rsch. fellow MIT Rsch. Lab. for Electronics, 1955-58; prin. rsch. scientist MIT Lab. for Info. and Decision Systems, 1958-62, 67—; sr. systems engr. Itek Corp., 1962-67. Editl. bd. Info. Processing and Mgmt., Jour. of Intelligent Info. Systems; reviewer other jours. Mem. Am. Soc. for Info. Sci. (Best article of Yr. to Jour.), Assn. for Computing Machinery, Assn. for Computational Linguistics. Achievements include research on modeling of indexing and retrieval processes for bibliographic and textual databases and the application of those models in the development of expert search assistance systems. E-mail. Office: MIT LIDS 77 Mass Ave Rm 32D-558 Cambridge MA 02139-4307 Home Phone: 781-963-2792. Business E-Mail: rmarcus@mit.edu.

MARCUS, RUDOLPH ARTHUR, chemist, educator; b. Montreal, July 21, 1923; arrived in U.S., 1949, naturalized, 1958; s. Myer and Esther (Cohen) Marcus; m. Laura Hearne, Aug. 27, 1949 (dec. Jan. 2003); children: Alan Rudolph, Kenneth Hearne, Raymond Arthur. BS in Chemistry, McGill U., 1943, PhD in Chemistry, 1946, DSc (hon.), 1988, U. Chgo., 1983, Poly. U., 1986, U. Göteborg, Sweden, 1987, U. N.B., Can., 1993, Queens U., 1993, U. Oxford, Eng., 1995, Yokohama Nat. U., Japan, 1996, U. N.C., 1996, U. Ill., 1997, Technion-Israel Inst. Tech., 1998, Polytechnic U. Valencia, 1999, Northwestern U., 2000, U. Waterloo, Can., 2002. Rsch. staff RDX Project, Montreal, 1944—46; rsch. assoc. NRC of Can., Ottawa, Ont., 1946—49, U. N.C., 1949—51; asst. prof. Poly. Inst. Bklyn., 1951—54, assoc. prof., 1954—58, prof., 1958—64, acting head, div. phys. chem., 1961—62; prof. U. Ill., Urbana, 1964—78, head, div. phys. chem., 1967—68; Arthur Amos Noyes prof. chem. Calif. Inst. Tech., Pasadena, 1978—; vis. prof. theoretical chem. U. Oxford, 1975—76; Baker lectr. Cornell U., Ithaca, NY, 1991; Linnett vis. prof. chemistry Cambridge (Eng.) U., 1996; hon. prof. Fudan U., Shanghai, 1994—; hon prof. Inst. Chem. Chinese Acad. Scis., Beijing, 1995—; hon. fellow Univ. Coll., Oxford, 1995—; hon. prof. Tianjin U., China, 2002, China Ocean U., 2002, Dalian Inst. Chem. Physics, Dalian, China, 2005, Wenzhov Med. Coll., Wenzhov, China, 2005. Professorial fellow Univ. Coll., Oxford, 1975—76; mem. Courant Inst. Math. Scis., NYU, 1960—61; trustee Gordon Rsch. confs., 1966—69; assoc. mem. Ctr. Advanced Studies, U. Ill., Urbana, 1968—69; chmn. bd. dirs. Gordon Rsch. confs., 1968—69, mem. coun., 1965—68; mem. rev. panel Argonne Nat. Lab., 1966—72, chmn., 1967—68; mem. rev. panel Brookhaven Nat. Lab., 1971—74; mem. rev. com.Radiation Lab., U. Notre Dame Radiation Lab., U. Notre Dame, 1975—80; mem. panel on atmospheric chemistry climatic impact com. NAS-NRC, 1975—78, mem. com. kinetics of chem. reactions, 1973—77, chmn., 1975—77, mem. com. chem. scis., 1977—79; lectr. in field, 1982; mem. com. to survey opportunities in chem. scis., 1982—86; mem. math. panel Internat. Benchmarking of U.S. Rsch. Fields, 1996—97; mem. panel on accountability of federally funded rsch. Com. on Sci., Engring. and Pub. Policy, 2000—01; adv. com. for chemistry NSF, 1977—80; external adv. bd. NAS Ctr. Photoinduced Charge Transfer, 1990—; mem. presdl. chairs com., Chile, 1994—96; advisor, Ctr. for Molecular Scis. Chinese Acad. Scis. and State Key Lab. for Structural Chemistry of Unstable and Stable Species, Beijing, 1995—; co-hon. pres. 29th Internat. Chemistry Olympiad, 1997; hon. visitor Nat. Sci. Coun., China, 1999. Hon. editor Internat. Jour. Quantum Chemistry, 1996—, former mem. editl. bd. Jour. Chem. Physics, Ann. Rev. Phys. Chemistry, Jour. Phys. Chemistry, Accounts Chem. Rsch., Internat. Jour. Chem. Kinetics Molecular Physics, Theoretica Chimica Acta, Chem. Physics Letters, Faraday Trans., Jour. Chem. Soc., editl. bd. Laser Chemistry, 1982—, Advances in Chem. Physics, 1984—, World Sci. Pub., 1987—, Internat. Revs. in Phys. Chemistry, 1988—, Progress in Physics, Chemistry and Mechanics (China), 1989—, Perkins Transactions 2, Jour. Chem. Soc., 1992—, Chem. Physics Rsch. (India), 1992—, Trends in Chem. Physics Rsch. (India), 1992—, Internat. Jour. Molecular Chemistry, 2007—. Recipient Anne Molson prize in chem., McGill U., 1943, Sr. U.S. Scientist award, Alexander von Humboldt-Stiftung, 1976, Electrochem. Soc. Lecture award, 1979, 1996, Robinson medal, Faraday divsn. Royal Soc. Chemistry, 1982, Centenary medal, 1988, Chandler medal, Columbia U., 1983, Wolf prize in chemistry, Wolf Found., Israel, 1985, Nat. medal of Sci., 1989, Evans award, Ohio State U., 1990, Nobel prize in Chem., 1992, Hirshfelder prize in Theoretical Chemistry, U. Wis., 1993, Golden Plate award, Am. Acad. Achievement, 1993, Lavoisier medal, French Chem. Soc., 1994, Oesper award, U. Cin., 1997, Key to City of Taipei, Taiwan, 1999, William Jost lectr. and medal, Deutsche Bunsenges and Acad. Sci., Göttingen, 1999, Susquicentennial medal, Polytech U., Bklyn.; named Hon. Citizen, City of Winnipeg, 1994, Treasure of L.A., Ctrl. City Assn., 1995; fellow Alfred P. Sloan, 1960—61, NSF sr. postdoctoral, 1960—61; scholar Sr. Fulbright-Hays, 1972. Fellow: AAAS, Royal Soc. Can. (hon.), Internat. Acad. Quantum Molecular Sci. (hon.), Chinese Acad. Scis. (hon.), Internat. Soc. for Theoretical Chem. Physics (hon.), Internat. Soc. Electrochemistry (hon.), Royal Soc. Chemistry (hon.), Royal Soc. (London) (hon.), Am. Acad. Arts and Scis. (hon.; exec. com. western sect., co-chmn. 1981—84, rsch. and planning com. 1989—91); mem.: NAS (hon.), Am. Chem. Soc. (past divsn. chmn., mem. exec. com., mem. adv. bd. petroleum rsch. fund, Irving Langmuir award in chem. physics 1978, Peter Debye award in physic. chemistry 1988, Willard Gibbs medal Chgo. sect. 1988, S.C. Lind Lecture, East Tenn. sect. 1988, Theodore William Richards medal Northwestern sect. 1990, Edgar Fahs Smith award Phila. sect. 1991, Ira Remsen Meml. award Md. sect. 1991, Pauling medal Portland, Oreg., and Puget Sound sect. 1991, Auburn-Kosolapoff award 1996, Theoretical Chemistry award 1997, Top 75 Chem. & Engring. News award 1998), Am. Phys. Soc., Lit. and Hist. Soc., Univ. Coll. Dublin (hon.), European Acad. Scis. (hon.), Korean Chem. Soc. (hon.), Am. Philos. Soc. (hon.; coun. mem. 1990), Alpha Chi Sigma. Achievements include development of the Marcus Theory of electron transfer reactions in chemical systems and RRKM theory of unimolecular reactions. Home: 331 S Hill Ave Pasadena CA 91106-3405 Office Phone: 626-395-6566. Business E-Mail: ram@caltech.edu.*

MARCUS, RUTH BARCAN, philosopher, educator, writer, lecturer; b. NYC; d. Samuel and Rose (Post) Barcan; divorced; children: James Spencer, Peter Webb, Katherine Hollister, Elizabeth Post. BA, NYU, 1941; MA, Yale U., 1942, PhD, 1946; DLH (hon.), U. Ill., 1995. Rsch. assoc. in anthropology Inst. for Human Relations, Yale U., New Haven, Conn., 1945-47; AAUW fellow U. Chgo., 1947-48; vis. prof. (intermittently) Northwestern U., 1950-57, Guggenheim fellow, 1953-54; asst. prof., assoc. prof. Roosevelt U., Chgo., 1957-63; NSF fellow, 1963-64; prof. philosophy U. Ill. at Chgo., 1963-70, head philosophy dept., 1963-69; fellow U. Ill. Center for Advanced Study, 1968-69; prof. philosophy Northwestern U., 1970-73; Reuben Post Halleck prof. philosophy Yale U., 1973-93; sr. rsch. scholar, 1994—. Fellow Ctr. Advanced Study in Behavioral Sci., Stanford, Calif., 1979; vis. fellow Inst. Advanced Study, U. Edinburgh, 1983, Wolfson Coll., Oxford U., 1985, 86; vis. fellow Clare Hall, Cambridge U., 1988, lifetime mem. common rm., 1989—; past or present mem. adv. coms. Princeton U., MIT, Calif. Inst. Tech., Cornell U. Humanities Ctr., Columbia U., UCLA, Ohio State U., U. Calif. Santa Barbara, Carnegie Mellon U., Brown U., U. Va., U. Tex., others; disting. vis. prof. U. Calif., Irvine, 1995—. Author: Modalities, 1993; editor: The Logical Enterprise, 1975, Logic Methodology and Philosophy of Science VII, 1986; mem. editl. or adv. bds. Past or Present, Metaphilosophy, Monist, Philos. Studies, Signs, Jour. Symbolic Logic, Rev. Symbolic Logic, The Philosophers Annual; editor, contbr. to profl. jours. and books. Recipient Machette prize for contbn. to profession; Medal, College de France, 1986, Wilbur Cross medal Yale U., 2000, Launer prize, Switzerland 2007—, Quinn prize Am. Phi. Assn., 2007; Mellon sr. fellow Nat. Humanities Ctr., 1992-93; vis. disting. prof. U. Calif., Irvine, 1994, 96, 97, 98, 99, 2000 Fellow Am. Acad. Arts and Scis.; mem. Coun. on Philos. Studies (pres. 1988-90), Assn. for Symbolic Logic (past exec. coun., exec. com. 1973-83, v.p. 1980-82, coun. 1980-85, pres. 1982-84), Am. Philos. Assn. (past sec., treas., nat. bd. dirs. 1977-83, pres. ctrl. divsn. 1975-78, chmn. nat. bd. officers 1979-85), Philosophy of Sci. Assn., Inst. Internat. Philosophie (past exec. com., v.p. 1983-86, pres. 1990-93, hon. pres. 1994—), Fedn. Internat. Philosophy (exec. com., steering com. 1985-99), Elizabethan Club (v.p. 1989, pres. 1989-90), Phi Beta Kappa. Office: Yale U Dept Philosophy PO Box 208306 New Haven CT 06520-8306

MARCUS, STANLEY, federal judge; b. NYC, 1946; BA, CUNY, 1967; JD, Harvard U., 1971. Law clerk Hon. John Bartels, US Dist. Ct. (ea. dist.), NY; assoc. Botein, Hays, Sklar & Herzberg, NYC, 1974-75; asst. atty. US Dist. Ct. (ea. dist.)NY, 1975-78; spl. atty., dep. chief U.S. organized crime sect. Detroit Strike Force, 1978-79, chief U.S. organized crime sect., 1980-82; US atty. So. Dist. of Fla., Miami, 1982-85; judge US Dist. Ct. (so. dist.) Fla., Miami, 1985-97, US Ct. Appeals (11th cir.), 1997—. Mem. Fed. Bar Assn., Fla. Bar Assn, NY Bar Assn. Mem. US Army, 1968—74. Office: US Ct of Appeals 11th Cir 99 NE 4th St Rm 1262 Miami FL 33132-2185*

MARCUS, WILLIAM MICHAEL, rubber and vinyl products manufacturing company executive; b. Boston, Jan. 31, 1938; s. Richard and Diana (Litch) M.; m. Cynthia Steinman, Dec. 9, 1962; children: Melanie, Daniel, Richard. BS in Bus. Adminstrn., Babson Inst., 1959. With Am. Biltrite Inc., Wellesley Hills, Mass., 1960—, exec. v.p., treas., 1983—, also dir. Bd. dirs. Congoleum Corp., Aqua Bounty Tech. Served with US Army, 1960-61. Office: American Biltrite Inc 57 River St Wellesley Hills MA 02481-2013

MARCUSE, ADRIAN GREGORY, academic administrator; b. NYC, Mar. 25, 1922; s. Maxwell Frederick and Mildred Ann (Hitter) M.; m. Janet Constance Radlo, Oct. 28, 1945 (dec. Mar. 22, 1980); children: Nancy Ruth Marcuse Marshall, Sally Ann Marcuse Crawford, Elizabeth Susan Marcuse; m. Betty Jane Lieberman Rossman, Jan. 11, 1985; 1 stepchild, Amy Beth Rossman Schurtz. BS, MIT, 1942, MS, 1946; LLD (hon.), Lab Inst. Merchandising, 1992. Registered profl. engr. N.Y., Fla. Rsch. assoc. MIT, Cambridge, Mass., 1945-46; rsch. scientist United Aircraft Co., E. Hartford, Conn., 1946-47; application engr. Westinghouse Electric Corp., Boston, NYC, 1947-60; consulting engr. pvt. practice, NYC, 1955-62; v.p. mktg. and sales Corrosion Control Corp., NYC, 1960-62; sales and merchandising mgr. B. Altman & Co., NYC, 1962; v.p., COO Lab. Inst. of Merchandising, NYC, 1962-72, pres., CEO, 1972—2002, pres. emeritus, counsel to pres., 2002—, trustee, 1972—. Pres. LIM Fashion Edn. Found., N.Y.C., 1978—; chmn. Assn. Regionally Accredited Prvt. Colls. and Univs., Washington, 1990-93. Charter commr. City of Glen Cove, N.Y., 1964, chmn. bd. engrs., 1964-68, mem. planning bd., 1980-87; past treas. Community Concert Assn., Glen Cove; past trustee and budget chmn. North Country Reform Temple, Glen Cove; past mem. YMCA Fund-Raising Coun., Glen Cove; ranger, vol. JD McArthur Beach State Pk, Fla.; v.p., bd. dirs. Gov.'s Pointe Condominium, 2005-07. 1st lt. USAAF, 1942-45, PTO. Mem.: Assn. Proprietary Colls. (pres. 1975—76), Sigma Beta Delta, Sigma Xi. Republican. Avocations: sailing, bicycling, travel, theater. Office: Lab Inst of Merchandising 12 E 53rd St Fl 2 New York NY 10022-5268 Home: 356 Golfview Rd #306 North Palm Beach FL 33408 Home Phone: 561-776-7420. Business E-Mail: amarcuse@limcollege.edu.

MARCUSE, AIDA E., writer, translator, educator; b. Montevideo, Uruguay; arrived in U.S., 1985; d. Máximo Eimer and Sara Malek; m. Robert Marcuse, Mar. 16, 1957; children: Monique, Alain, Michel. Student, Maria S. de Munar Sch., Montevideo, 1950—54, Inst. Vázquez Acevedo, 1954—56, Inst. Artigas, 1954—56; degree in creative writing, SADE, Buenos Aires, 1975. Lectr., spkr. numerous workshops and confs. in field. Author: Caperucita y la luna de papel, 1996, 2000, The Jaguar and the Deer, 1991, Aventuras de Prudencio el prudente, 1997, Las aventuras de Alba, de la A a la Z, Un día en el mar, Qué es una mariposa blanca?, El ciempiés sin pies, El flamenco friolento, Mi gato se fue a la luna, Un modelo especial, Tio Jaguar no puede con Tio Mono, El mono y la banana, Antonio y su caballito de torno, Shhhh...es de noche, Smile, Mike!, Sopa!, 2001, What the Incas Say, 1999, 2d edit., 2001, An Old Indian Told Me..., 1994, The Travelling Kitchen, 1987, Yesteryear's Stories, 1987, A Kite for Grompón, 1985, A Dime for Judas, 1983, Steps in the Sand, 1982, A Mechanical Horse, 1982, Raggedy Doll, 3 edits., 1977—81, Watch Out, Mark!, 1976, Once Upon a Time...a Body, 4 edits., 1972—75, 1981, Había una vez un cuerpo..., 1996, Mi diccionario de juguete, 1996, Yo y los demás, Versos dispersos y cuentos diversos, Older than a Saying, 2000, Time to Be, 2001, El gato Ratonero, 2001, Ese día, en la selva..., 2003, Del Tío Jaguar y otros animales, 2004, Un Trozo de Pan, 2005 (Gold Honor Bilingual Category, Mom's Choice award, 2008); translator: numerous books, including Puss in Boots (Caldecott honor, 1991), The Little Red Hen, Dr. Seuss's Green Eggs and Ham, The Lorax, Oh, The Places You'll Go, The Tale of Peter Rabbit, The Very Hungry Caterpillar, 1993; contbr. poetry and short stories to anthologies, publs. in field. Recipient Order of Merit for Disting. Svcs., Govt. Peru, 2003, commendation, City of Miami, Fla., 1985. Mem.: PEN, Panama Linguistic Soc., Venezuelan Soc. Children's Lit. (founder), Argentine Soc. Children's Lit., Uruguayan Writers Soc., Argentine Writers Soc., Am. Translators Assn., Soc. Children's Book Writers and Illustrators (Fla. regional advisor 1989), Spanish Soc. of Del. (hon.). Personal E-mail: amarcuse@bellsouth.net.

MARCUSE, DIETRICH, retired physicist; b. Koenigsberg, East Prussia, Germany, Feb. 27, 1929; arrived in US, 1957; s. Richard and Gertrud (Solty) M.; m. Haide Schwarz, Jan. 13, 1959; children: Christina, Mikel. Diplom Physiker, Freie Universität, Berlin, 1954; Doktor Ingenieur, Karlsruhe Universität, 1962. Mem. tech. staff Siemens and Halske, Berlin, 1954-57, AT&T Bell Labs., Holmdel, NJ, 1957-94, dist. mem. tech. staff, 1982-94; ret., 1994. Vis. rsch. prof. U. Md., Balt. County, 1995-99. Author: Principles of Quantum-Electronics, 2d edit., 1980, Light Transmission Optics, 2d edit., 1982, Theory of Dielectric Optical Wave-guides, 1972, 2nd edit.,1991, Principles of Optical Fiber Measurements, 1981; also over 200 articles. Fellow IEEE (Quantum Electronics award 1981), Optical Soc. Am. (Max Born award 1989). Personal E-mail: dmarcuse@optonline.net.

MARCUSS, ROSEMARY DALY, economist; b. Stamford, Conn., Aug. 27, 1945; d. Eugene Lawrence and Margaret Mary (Murphy) Daly; B.A. in Econs. cum laude, Newton (Mass.) Coll., 1967; M.S., U. Md., 1973, Ph.D., 1979; m. Stanley J. Marcuss, July 6, 1968; children—Elena Daly, Aidan Stanley. Jr. staff economist President's Council of Econ. Advisers, 1968-70; economist, asst. to pres. Am. Fedn. State, County and Mcpl. Employees, Washington, 1973; economist, mgmt. cons. Data Resources, Inc., Washington, 1974-78; dep. asst. dir. tax analysis Congressional Budget Office, Washington, 1980-83, asst. dir. tax analysis, 1983-98; dep. dir. Bur. Econ. Analysis, Washington, 1998—; pres. Nat. Assn Bus. Econ., 2005-. NSF fellow, 1970-73. Mem. Am. Econ. Assn., Nat. Tax Assn., Tax Inst. Am., So. Econ. Assn., Soc. Govt. Economists, Nat. Economists Club, Nat. Assn. Business Economists (v.p. 2003-), Washington Women Economists. Home: 4616 29th Pl NW Washington DC 20008-2105 Office: Congressional Budget Office 2nd & D Sts SW Washington DC 20515-0001

MARCUSS, STANLEY JOSEPH, lawyer; b. Hartford, Conn., Jan. 24, 1942; s. Stanley Joseph and Anne Sutton (Leone) M.; m. Rosemary Daly, July 6, 1968; children: Elena Daly, Aidan Stanley. BA, Trinity Coll., 1963, Cambridge U., 1965, MA, 1968; JD, Harvard U., 1968. Bar: D.C., N.Y., Conn., U.S. Supreme Ct. Staff atty. office of gen. counsel HUD, Washington, 1968; atty. firm Hogan and Hartson, Washington, 1968-73; counsel to internat. fin. subcom. U.S. Senate Com. on Banking, Housing and Urban Affairs, 1973-77; dep. asst. sec. for trade regulation Dept. Commerce, Washington, 1977-78, sr. dep. asst. sec. for industry and trade, 1978-79, acting asst. sec. for industry and trade, 1979-80, acting asst. sec. for trade regulation, 1980; mem. firm Milbank, Tweed, Hadley & McCloy, Washington, 1980-93, Bryan Cave, 1993—. Former adj. prof. Am. U. Law Sch. Author: Effective Washington Representation, 1983; mem. bd. overseers U. Calif. Berkeley Law Jour.; contbr. articles to profl. jours. Former trustee Trinity Coll., Hartford. Marshall scholar. Mem. ABA, D.C. Bar (former chmn., steering com. internat. law div.), Phi Beta Kappa. Home: 4616 29th Pl NW Washington DC 20008-2105

MARCY, GEOFFREY W., astronomer, physicist, educator; BA in Physics & Astronomy summa cum laude, UCLA, 1976; PhD in Astronomy & Astrophysics, U. Calif., Santa Cruz, 1982. Fellow Carnegie Inst., Wash., 1982—84; full prof. physics & astronomy San Francisco State U., 1984—96, disting. prof., 1997—99, adjunct prof. physics & astronomy, 1999—; prof. astronomy U. Calif., Berkeley, 1999—. Mem. Com. on the Status of Women in Astronomy, 1994—97, NASA Working Group: Origins of Solar Systems, 1998—2000, NASA Working Group: Terrestrial Planet Finder, 1998—2001; dir. Ctr. for Integrative Planetary Sci., 2000—; Bunyan lectr., physics dept. Stanford U., 1997; G. Darwin Lecture Royal Astronomical Soc., 2000; NSF Disting. Lectr., 00; prin. investigator NASA Space Interferometry Mission, 2001; Sackler Lectr. U. Leiden, 2001; Niels Bohr Lecture N.B. Inst., 2005. Author numerous scientific articles in peer-reviewed jours., newspapers, and mag.; appearances include ABC Nightline, CBS Nightly News, NBC Today Show, BBC Horizons, CNN News, PBS, Late Show with David Letterman. Recipient Manne Siegbahn award, Swedish Acad., 1996, Internat. Assn. Universities Commn. 51 Bioastronomy Medal of Honor (First Ever Issued), 1997, Certificate of Recognition (First Ever Issued), Extrasolar Planetary Found., 1999, UCLA Alumni Profl. Achievement award, 1999, Carl Sagan award, Am. Astronautical & Planetary Soc., 2002, Exceptional Scientific Achievement medal, NASA, 2003, Shaw prize, 2005; named Person of Week, ABC News Hour, 1996, Alumnus Yr., U. Calif. Santa Cruz, 1997, Calif. Scientist of the Yr., 2000, Space Scientist Yr., Discover Mag., 2003. Fellow: Calif. Acad. of Sci.; mem.: NAS (Henry Draper medal 2001), Astronomical Soc. of Pacific (bd. dirs. 1997—99, pub. bd. 1997—2002), Am. Astronomical Soc. (bd. of councilors 1998—2000, Beatrice M. Tinsley prize 2002). Made First Zeeman Measurements of Magnetic Fields for Solor-Type Stars; found Pauncity of Brown Dwarfs Orbiting Stars; developed the method of Precise Doppler Measurements; discovered 70 of the first 100 Extrasolor Planets known; found evidence that the Solar System maybe peculiar; discoverd the first system of planets around a sun-like star; discovered first transiting planet around another star; discovered the first candidate Saturn-Mass planets; discovered the first extrasolar planet orbiting beyond 5AU; co-discovered the first Neptune-Sized Planets: Gliese 436b and 55 Cancri e. Office: U Calif 417 Campbell Hall Berkeley CA 94720 Office Phone: 510-642-1952. Office Fax: 510-642-3411.

MARCY, KEVIN MICHAEL, film producer, lawyer; BS, U. Nev., Reno, 1974—78; JD, U. So. Calif., LA, 1978—81. Bar: Calif. 1981, DC 2006. Atty. Kinsella, Boesch, Fujikawa & Towle, LA, 1981—83; assoc. prodr. Paramount Pictures, LA, 1983—87, 1995; asst. to Dan Aykroyd Applied Action Rsch., LA, 1987—95, prodr., 2003—, Snake River Productions, Malibu, Calif., 1996—2003; assoc. prodr. Miramax Films, LA, 2003. V.p., guest rels. Ho. of Blues, LA, 1994; cons. Hitplay Media, LA, 2000. Prodr.: (films) The Testimony Of Taliesin Jones, 2000, (short film) Mr. Bill Goes To Law School; assoc. prodr. (films) The Naked Gun, 1988, The Coneheads, 1993, Scary Movie 3, 2003. Mem.: Ho. of Blues Found. (life), Dan Aykroyd Biker Gang (life), Phi Kappa Phi (life), Beta Gamma Sigma (life), Phi Alpa Delta (life), Delta Sigma Pi (life).

MARDER, JOHN ADAM, lawyer; b. Fall River, Mass., Jan. 17, 1960; s. Everett Joseph and Brenda Joan (Leviss) M.; m. Bonnie Jane Webber, Nov. 11, 1989; 1 child, Max Phillip. BA, Bates Coll., 1982; JD, Calif. Western Sch. Law, 1985. Bar: Calif. 1986, U.S. Dist. Ct. (ctrl. dist.) Calif. 1989. Dep. dist. atty. San Bernardino D.A., 1985-87; atty. Home Ins. Co., LA, 1987; ptnr. Morris, Polich & Purdy LLP, LA, 1987-94; mng. ptnr. Manning & Marder Kass Ellrod Ramirez LLP (formerly Manning, Marder & Wolfe LLP), LA, 1994—. Gen. counsel Internat. Assn. Spl. Investigation Units, So. Calif. Chapter; bd. dirs. Athens Found. Named Calif. Atty. of the Yr., Calif. Lawyer mag., 2005; named a Super Lawyer, Law & Politics, 2005. Office: Manning & Marder Kass Ellrod Ramirez LLP 660 S Figueroa St 23rd Fl Los Angeles CA 90017

MARDER, MICHAEL V., philosopher, educator; m. Patricia Vieira. PhD in Philosophy, New Sch. Social Rsch., NY, 2007. Lectr., dept. Philosophy Georgetown U, Washington, 2008—. Author: (book) The Event of the Thing: Derrida's Post-Deconstructive Realism (University of Toronto Press, 2009), Groundless Existence: The Political Ontology of Carl Schmitt (Continuum Press, 2010). Office: Dept Philosophy Georgetown U 242 New N 37th And O St NW Washington DC 20057 Personal E-mail: michael.marder@gmail.com.

MARDER, MICHAEL ZACHARY, dental educator, researcher; b. NYC, Aug. 30, 1938; s. Jospeh Theodore and Rhea (Greenspun) M.; (widowed); children: Sherri Ellen, Robert Whitney. Student, Tufts U., 1959; DDS, Columbia U., 1963. Diplomate: Am. Bd. Oral Medicine. Practice dentistry, NYC, 1963-66, 68—; asst. Sch. Dental and Oral Surgery, Columbia U., NYC, 1963-66, instr., 1968, asst. clin. prof., 1968-72, assoc. clin. prof., 1972-76, NYC clin. prof. dentistry, 1976—, rschr., 1963—; dir. oral medicine, 1972-84; dir. clin. cancer tng., 1993—; attending dental surgeon Presbyn. Hosp., 1972-76; assoc. attending dentist, 1976-82; attending dentist, 1982—; cons. Good Samaritan Hosp., Suffern, NY. Lectr. field. Author 2 textbooks in dental medicine; contbr. chpts. to med. and dental textbooks, articles to profl. jours. Served to capt. US Army, 1966-68. Recipient Cert. Achievement US Army, 1968. Fellow NY Acad. Dentistry; mem. ADA, Internat. Assn. Dental Rsch., Am. Acad. Oral Medicine, Frist Dist. Dental Soc. NY, Omicron Kappa Upsilon, Sigma Xi. Office: 119 W 57th St New York NY 10019-2303 Office Phone: 212-265-8291. Business E-Mail: mzm2@columbia.edu.

MARDI, SHALVA JOSEF, research scientist; b. Lailashi, Ga., May 10, 1933; m. Rosa-Maria Mardi; 2 children. D of Med. Scis., Acad. Med. Scis., Ukraine, 1968, PhD, 1968. MD Nat. Russian Acad. Medicine, Moscow, 1959; prof. oncology Med. Sci. Acad., St. Petersburg, Russia, 1963; clin. prof. oncology Tbilisi, Georgia, 1970. Vis. lectr. in field. Contbr. over 250 sci. publs. to profl. jours. Mem.: WHO, UNO. Achievements include 12 international patents in medicine; invention of Mardi's Shark Caviar as an alternative for natural Beluga Caviar and as a food supplement for preventing cancer diseases as well as for the development of new lines in cosmeto-dermatology; new pharmaceutical product Mardil for the treatment of all types of skin neoplasmas to prevent and solve skin cancer epidemics globally. Business E-Mail: shalva33@tele2.ch.

MARDIKIAN, JACKIE, medical librarian; married. BA, York U., Toronto, Ont., Can., 1969; MLS, Western Mich. U., Kalamazoo, 1980. Cert. Acad. Health Info. Profls., Med. Libr. Assn., Chgo. Reference libr. Borgess Med. Ctr., Kalamazoo, 1981—83, dir., libr. svcs., 1983—85; collection devel., reference libr. SUNY Health Sci. Ctr., Syracuse, 1985—90; med. scis. libr. Rutgers State U. NJ, Piscataway, 1991—. Contbr. articles to libr. lit. jours. Mem.: Health Sci. Libr. Assn. NJ (pres. 1994—95). Office: Rutgers State Univ NJ 165 Bevier Rd Piscataway NJ 08854 Office Fax: 732-445-5703. Business E-Mail: mardikia@rci.rutgers.edu.

MARDILOVICH, IVAN P., education educator, researcher; b. Stolbtsy, Belarus, Sept. 21, 1952; s. Peter L and Elena I (Zvytsevich) Mardilovich; m. Galina A Semyonov, Apr. 23, 1977; children: Anastasia I, Katerina I. MSc, Belarus State U., 1975; PhD in phys. chemistry, Russian U. of Peoples' Friendship, 1982. Sr. rsch. scientist Nat. Acad. Sci. Belarus, Minsk, 1985—99; rsch. assoc. prof. Worcester Poly. Inst., Mass., 1999—. Sci. sec. of the divsn. of chem. and earth sciences NAS of Belarus, Minsk, Belarus, 1998—99. Sec.- gen. Internat. Fedn. of Chem. Societies, Minsk, Belarus, 1993—2000. Recipient Bronze medal, USSR Exhbn. of the Nat. Economy Achievements, 1985. Achievements include developed and characterized unique Pd and Pd-alloy membranes on porous supports for high temperature hydrogen separation and for a variety of hydrogen-related processes. Office: Worcester Poly Inst 100 Institute Rd Worcester MA 01609 Office Phone: 508-831-5474. Business E-Mail: ivanpm@wpi.edu.

MARDINLY, SUSAN J., musician, music educator; d. Ashe John Mardinly and Jane Elizabeth Fish; m. Fred Dale Shinkle, Feb. 21, 1998; children: Deborah Ruth Forish, Sarah Nancy McGaw. MusB, New Eng. Conservatory of Music, 1969; MusM, U. Hartford, 1991; D in Musical Arts, U. Conn., 2004. Voice tchr. Bungay Music Sch., Seymour, 1979—84, Ctr. Du Arts., Waterbury, Conn., 1985—91; dir. Woman Arts Program, 1992—96; voice tchr., dept. chair Hartford Conservatory, Hartford, Conn., 1992—99; voice tchr., arts adminstr. U. Conn., Storrs, 1992—96; voice tchr. The Hartt Sch. Cmty. Divsn., Hartford, Conn., 2005—. Lectr. recitals, 1978—; ch. soloist, choir dir., 1978—; dir. Chamber Musicians' Alliance, New Haven, 1979—83; operatic/oratorio soloist various cos., 1979—99; co-chair Ann. Concert of Music by Women Composers, Hartford, 2001—08. Author (editor, arranger): (book) Barbara Strozzi and The Pleasures of Euterpe, 30 other publ. vocal works by Barbara Strozzi; musician (soprano soloist, chorister): Conn. Opera, 1986—92; contbr. articles to profl. jours. Benefit concerts St. Vincent de Paul Shelter, Waterbury, Conn., 1978—; chair, var. com. Musical Club Hartford, 1981—. Recipient Nine Dir. Music awards, Naugatuck Teen Theater, Conn., 1991; Doctoral fellow, U. Conn., 1993—96, Wagenlis scholar, 1994, Rsch. grantee, 1995, WEL Found. grant, U. Hartford, 2009—. Mem.: Conn. Music Educators Assn. (cert. adjudicator 1995—), Conn. Nat. Assn. Tchrs. of Singing (judge 1981—, Conn. winner; NATSAA 1982), AGMA (profl. liason 1986—92), Mu Phi Epsilon (life; two term sec. 1966—68), Pi Kappa Lambda (life). Avocations: travel, poetry, cooking. Office: Hartt Sch Bloomfield Ave Hartford CT 06117 Home: 9 vILLAGE rD Southington CT 06489 Personal E-mail: susanmardinly@sbcglobal.net.

MARDON, AUSTIN, geographer, writer, researcher; arrived in U.S., 1985; s. Ernest George. BA in Geography, U. Lethbridge, Alta., 1985; MSc in Geography, S.D. State U., 1988; MEd in Edn. Curriculum and Instrn., Tex. A&M U., 1990; PhD in Geography, Greenwich U., Australia, 2000; postgrad., U. N.D., 1990, U. Alta., U. Calgary, U. Grenoble, Newman Theol. Coll., 2001, postgrad., 2003, Kharkov Nat. U., Ukraine, 2002—04, U. South Africa, 2009. Research scientist NASA/NSF, Antarctica, 1986-87; freelance writer, 1991—; dir., pres. Antarctic Inst. Canada, Edmonton, 1985—. Mem. meteorite recovery expedition, Antarctic, 1986-87; mem. Com. Space Rsch. Internat. Com. Sci. Unions; geoophys. con. Stargate Rsch. Lab., Calif., 1999-2002; self-help network coord. Alta. Mental Health Network, 1999-2003, self-help asst. program mgr. 2003—05; adj. faculty Greenwich (Australia) U., 2000-02, Greenwich (Calif.) U., 2002, Greenwich (Hawaii) U., 2003; sr. rsch. fellow Internat. Noble Acad., 2003—05; hon. prof. Penza State Pedagogical U., 2004; prof. geography Akamai U., Hawaii, 2005—. Author: A Conspectus of the Contribution of Herodotus to the Development of Geographical Thought, 1990, International Law and Space Rescue Systems, 1991, Kensington Stone and Other Essays, 1991, A Transient in Whirl, 1991, Political Networks in Alberta 1905-1992, 2002; co-author: Alberta Judicial Biographical Dictionary, 1990, Alberta Ethnic German Politicians, 1991, When Kitty Met the Ghost, 1991, Down & Out & On the Run in Moscow, 1991, Alberta Mormon Politicians, 1992, The Girl Who Could Walk Through Walls, 1991, Alberta General Election Returns & Subsequent Byelections 1882-1992, 1993, Edmonton Political Biography, 1994, Alberta Political Biographical Dictionary, 1994, Alberta Executive Council 1905-1990, 1994, Early Catholic Saints, 1997, Later Christian Saints, 1997, Childhood Memories & Legends of Christmas Past, 1998, Alone Against the Revolution, 1998, Community Names of Alberta, 1999, Men of Dawn, 1999, United Farmers of Alberta, 1999, Alberta Catholic Politicians, 2000, Alberta Anglican Politicians, 2001, Liberal Politicians in Alberta 1905-1921, 2002, What's in a Name?, 2002, Edmonton Federal Politicians, 2004, Edmonton Provincial Politicans, 2004, Edmonton Civic Politicans, 2004, Seven Days in Moscow, 2004, Alberta French Politicians, 2004; editor: Stygian Relics of the Lachrymose, 1998, The Spectral Carnival Show, 1998, A Wake of Evil, 1999, Lady Juanita, 2002, The Avengers Trilogy, 2004, Samson's Return, 2004; translator A Description of the Western Isles of Scotland (1549), 1990, contbr. more than 184 articles to profl. jours. Vol. Schizophrenia Soc. Alberta Edmonton Bd., 1999—2004, Schizophrenia Soc. Alberta Provincal Bd., 2000—04; bd. dirs. Regional Mental Health Adv. Com., 1999—2004, chair, 2000—01, mem. chairs com. for Alberta, 2000—01; trustee Edmonton Pub. Libr. Bd., Edmonton, 2001—; bd. dirs. Clubhouse Soc. Edmonton, 1993—99, chair bd. dirs., 1995—99; bd. dir. Nation Network for Mental Health, 1999—2000; bd. dirs. Clubhouse Demonstration Project Com., 1997—98. Recipient Antarctic Svc. medal, U.S. Navy, 1987, Duke of Edinburgh award, Can., 1987, Polar Continental Shelf Proj. Arctic Rsch. grantee, 1988, Tex. State Proclamation, 1989, personal audience with Pope in Rome, 1996; Gov. Generals Caring Canadian Award, 1998, Nadine Stirling award Can. Mental Health Assn., Alberta, 1999, hinks award, 2007, Flag of Hope award Schizophrenia Soc. Can., 2001, Jefferies award, 2007, Pres. award Can. Mental Health Assn., Alta., 2002, Disting. Alumni award U. Lethbridge, 2002, Queen Elizabeth II Golden Jubilee medal, 2002; named to U. Lethbridge Alumni Honor Soc., 2003. Fellow: Internat. Noble Acad. (sr.), Internat. Explorers Club; mem.: Order of Can., Russian Acad. Arts and Sci. (fgn. mem.), Antarctic Inst. Can., Schizophrenia Soc. Alta. (life) (hon.), Am. Polar Soc. (life), Internat. Acad. Astronauts, Sigma Pi Sigma, Gamma Theta Upsilon. Roman Catholic. Office: Post Office Sta Main PO Box 1223 Edmonton AB Canada T5J 2M4 Office Phone: 780-378-0063. Personal E-mail: aamardon@yahoo.ca.

MARECEK, JEANNE, psychologist, educator; b. Berwyn, Ill., May 28, 1946; d. Frank J. and Josephine (Serio) M. BS, Loyola U., Chgo., 1968; MS, Yale U., 1971, PhD, 1973. From asst. prof. to prof. psychology Swarthmore (Pa.) Coll., 1972—, chmn. dept., 1986—91, 1994—95, 1998—99, head women's studies program, 1996—99. Fulbright sr. lectr., Sri Lanka, 1988. Co-author: Making a Difference: Psychology and the Construction of Gender; contbr. numerous articles to profl. jours. and chpts. to books. Bd. dirs. Women in Transition, Phila., 1980-86; vice patron Nest, Hendala, Sri Lanka, 1995—; bd. dirs. Women's Therapy Ctr., Phila., 1996-2004, CHOICE, Phila., 2006—. Fellow Swedish Collegium for Advanced Study in Social Scis., 1997; various fed. research grants. Fellow: APA (internat. rels. psychology com., 2007-, chair 2009), Assn. Asian Studies, Am. Inst. Sri Lanka Studies (sec. 1995-2000, pres. 2001-07), Am. Overseas Rsch. Ctrs. (mem. exec. coun. 2002-09). Office: Swarthmore Coll Dept Psychology 500 College Ave Swarthmore PA 19081-1306 Business E-Mail: jmarecel@swarthmore.edu.

MARÉE, KATHLEEN NANCY, retired language educator; b. Belleville, NJ, Nov. 8, 1942; d. Jacobus and Marie Theresa (Lilore) Marée. BA, Rutgers U., Newark, NJ, 1965; MA in Tchg. magna cum laude, Fairleigh Dickinson U., Rutherford, NJ, 1970. Elem. French tchr. Freehold (N.J.) Elem. Schs., 1965—66, River Edge (N.J.) Elem. Schs., 1966—71, dept. head and fgn. langs. in elem. sch. rep.; elem. French tchr. Hanahouli Elem. Sch., Honolulu, 1971—73; pub. rels. coord. Oceanic Cablevision, Honolulu, 1974—75; pub. rels. rep., adminstrv. asst. Hawaii State Legis., Honolulu, 1975; ESL instr., head tchr., asst. coord. New Intensive Course in English program U. Hawaii at Manoa, Honolulu, 1976—79; founder, pres., dir. Lang. Inst. Hawaii, Honolulu, 1979—86; advisor, coord. study cultural tours Internat. Pacific Asian Consortium, Honolulu, 1979—86; ESL instr. Fairleigh Dickinson U., Seton Hall U., Rutgers U., NJ, 1987—89; ESL lectr. and adj. Bergen CC, Paramus, NJ, 1989—2000. Pub. rels. Fgn. Lang. Elem. Sch., 1966—71; chairperson N.J. Assn. Tchrs. Fgn. Langs. Elem. Sch., 1970—71. ESL tchr., coord. employment Vietnamese Immigrant Vol. Assistance, Honolulu, 1975; mem., ESL sponsor CIVITAN, Honolulu, 1980—86; com. mem. Save Our Schs., Nutley, NJ, 2006—07. Grantee, East-West Ctr.-Culture Learning Inst., 1975—76. Avocations: reading, oil painting. Home: 11 Newman Ave Nutley NJ 07110-2125 Home Phone: 973-661-4905.

MAREI, MAMDOUH MOHEY EDDINE, Egyptian government official; b. Alexandria, Egypt, Jan. 4, 1938; LLB, Ain Shams U., 1957. Prosecuting atty., 1957; counselor Emirates and Kuwait; asst. to Min. for Jud. Inspection Ministry of Justice; chief Alexandria Ct. of Appeal; pres. Cairo Ct. of Appeals, 2001—03; chief justice Egypt's Supreme Constl. Ct., 2003—06; min. justice Arab Republic of Egypt, 2006—. Chmn. Presdl. Election Commn. Office: Ministry of Justice Magles El Shaab St Justice Bldg Cairo Egypt

MAREINISS, DARREN PETER, lawyer, physician; b. Hoboken, NJ, Nov. 15, 1972; s. Martin Charles Mareiniss and Jeanette Schwarz Young; m. Alexandra Morgan, Aug. 16, 1997. AB cum laude, Dartmouth Coll., Hanover, NH, 1994; MD, NYU Sch. Medicine, NYC, 1999; JD, U. Pa., Phila., 2005; Master of Bioethics, U. Pa. Sch. Medicine, Phila., 2005. Lic. medicine/surgery N.Y., 2000, N.J., 2003, instr. advanced trauma and life support ACS, 2005, cert. MD 2008. Surg. intern NYU Med. Ctr./Bellevue Hosp., NYC, 1999—2000; surg. resident southwestern med. ctr. U. Tex., Dallas, 2001—02, instl. review bd. mem., 2008—; med. staff Gracie Sq. Hosp., NYC, 2002—03; assoc. atty. Bickel & Brewer, Dallas, 2004—07, Dechert LLP, Austin, 2007—09; sr. legal and med. policy cons. U. Md. Ctr. for Health and Homeland Security, 2006—; mem. IRB-U. Tex., 2008—09; adj. prof. U. Tex., 2009—. Lectr. Tex. Back Inst., Bioethics and Trauma. Contbr. articles to medical and legal jours. Recipient Letters Academic citation, Dartmouth Coll., 1991—93, N.Y. U. Sch. Medicine, 1996; Jaqua scholarship, Dartmouth Coll., 1993. Fellow: Am. Coll. Legal Medicine (mem. bioethics com 2004—, mem. grad. com. 2004—, chair, edn. com. 2008—); mem.: AMA, Alpha Omega Alpha. Achievements include research in disaster medicine, genetics and bioethics. Home: 100 Lancefield Rd Baltimore MD 21209 Office: Johns Hopkins Hosp Dept Emergency Medicine 5801 Smith Ave Davis Blvd Baltimore MD 21209 Personal E-mail: dpmmd@sbcglobal.net. Business E-Mail: d.marein1@jhmi.edu.

MAREN, STEPHEN, neuroscientist, psychologist, educator; PhD, U. Southern Calif. Prof. psychology U. Mich., dir. neuroscience grad. program. Assoc. editor various Neuroscience Jours. Fellow: Am. Psychological Assn. (Disting. Scientific award 2001). Office: Univ of Michigan Dept of Psychology 530 Church St 4046 East Hall Ann Arbor MI 48109-1043 Office Phone: 734-647-6980. E-mail: maren@umich.edu.*

MARENOFF, SUSAN, museum director, former professional athletics manager; B in Bus. Mgmt., SUNY, Binghamton. Various sales positions through v.p. Madison Square Garden; NY/NJ venue dir. FIFA Women's World Cup soccer tournament, 1998; dir. global mktg. Women's Tennis Assn. Tour, 1999; gen. mgr. New York Power, NYC, 2000—03; chief mktg. officer, exec. v.p. bus. devel. Intrepid Sea Air Space Mus., NYC, 2003—05, interim exec. dir., 2005, exec. dir., 2006—. Achievements include becoming the first woman executive at Madison Square Garden under 30. Office: Intrepid Sea Air Space Mus W 46th St and 12th Ave Pier 86 New York NY 10036 Office Phone: 212-957-3700. Business E-Mail: smarenoff@intrepidmuseum.org.

MARES, MICHAEL ALLEN, ecologist, educator, Museum Association Administrator; b. Albuquerque, Mar. 11, 1945; s. Ernesto Gustavo and Rebecca Gabriela (Devine) M.; m. Lynn Ann Brusin, Aug. 27, 1966; children: Gabriel Andres, Daniel Alejandro. BS in Biology, U. N.Mex., 1967; MD, Ft. Hays Kans. State U., 1969; PhD, U. Tex.-Austin, 1973. From asst. to assoc. prof. U. Pitts., 1973-81; assoc. prof., curator mammals U. Okla., Norman, 1981-83; dir. Okla. Mus. Nat. Hist., 1983—2003; assoc. prof. zoology U. Okla., 1983-85, prof., 1985—2003, presdl. prof., 2003—. Adj. prof. U. Nacional de Cordoba, Argentina, 1971-72, U. Nacional de Tucuman, Argentin, 1972, vis. prof., 1974; vis. scientist U. Ariz., Tucson, 1980-81; cons. Argentine Nat. Sci.

Found., Inst. Arid Zone Rsch., Mendoza, 1983, World Wildlife Fund, Brazil, 1986; mem. Coun. Internat. Exch. Scholars, Am. Republics Bd., Fulbright Commn., 1983-86, 88-91; bd. dirs. Coun. Internat. Exch. of Scholars, 1988-91; NUS cons., Venezuela, 1980-81; sci. cons. interim working group White House Biodiversity, Ecology, and Ecosystems, 1992-94; apptd. adv. bd. Ctr. Biol. Diversity, Dept. Interior; mem. Commn. on Future of Smithsonian Instns., 1993-96, Smithsonian Coun., 2000—. Contbr. articles to profl. jours. NSF grantee, 1974-79, 82-93, 99-2000; Nat. Fulbright Rsch. fellow, 1976; Nat. Geo. Soc. grantee, 1992-95, 99; rsch. fellow Chicano Coun. on Higher Edn., 1978, Ford Found. Minority Rsch., 1980-81; recipient Brazilian Nat. Acad. Sci. Rsch. award, 1975-78. Mem. AAAS (Western Hemispheric coop. com. 1989-93), Am. Soc. Mammalogists (1st. v.p. 1990-94, C. Hart Merriam award 2000), Am. Ecol. Soc., Interam. Assn. Advancement Sci., Am. Inst. Biol. Sci., Am. Soc. Naturalists, Soc. Study of Evolution, Southwestern Assn. Naturalists (Donald W. Tinkle rsch. excellence award), Paleontol. Soc., Natural Sci. Collections Alliance (pres), Sigma Xi, Phi Kappa Phi, Beta Beta Beta. Office: U Okla Hist and Dept Zoology 2401 Chautauqua Ave Norman OK 73072 Home: 505 Bethany Oaks Dr Norman OK 73071-2171 Office Phone: 405-325-9007. Office Fax: 405-325-7699.

MARETT, LOUIS J., lawyer; b. NYC, Mar. 17, 1947; AB magna cum laude, Harvard U., 1968, JD cum laude, 1972. Bar: Mass. 1972, US Dist. Ct. Mass., US Tax Ct., US Ct Fed. Claims. With Nutter, McClennen & Fish, Boston; ptnr. Choate, Hall & Stewart LLP. Chaired New England & Mass. Continuing Legal Edn. Trustee Mass. Taxpayers Found., Schepens Eye Rsch. Inst., St. Vincent de Paul Found. Named Best Lawyers Am. Mem.: ABA, Boston Bar Assn. Office: Choate Hall & Stewart 2 Internat Pl Boston MA 02110 Office Phone: 617-248-5091. Office Fax: 617-502-5091. Business E-Mail: lmarett@choate.com.

MARGALIT, EYAL, ophthalmologist, educator; b. Haifa, Israel, Feb. 3, 1960; s. Israel and Sara Margalit; m. Ruth Naomi Stashefsky; children: Noam, Tal Shlomit, Doron Sara. MD, Hebrew U., Israel, PhD, 1991. Cert. ophthalmologist Hebrew U., 1998, in retina specialist Johns Hopkins U., 2003. Retina svc. faculty U. Nebr. Med. Ctr., Omaha, 2003—. Capt. ARMY, 1978—82, Israel. Recipient Sinai award, Wilmer Eye Inst., 2001—02; Rsch. fellowship, Am. Friends Hebrew U., 1999, Clin. fellowship, Israel Med. Assn., 1999, Merit Rev. grant, Veterans Adminstrn., 2008. Mem.: Am. Soc. Retina Specialists, Am. Rsch. Vision and Ophthalmology, Am. Acad. Ophthalmology. Achievements include research in non-steroidal anti-inflammatory drugs for the eye; retinal electrophysiological mechanisms during electrical stimulation; federal funding for retina research. Office: Univ Nebr Med Ctr 3925 Dewey Ave Omaha NE 68198 Business E-Mail: emargalit@unmc.edu.

MARGALITH, HELEN MARGARET, retired librarian; b. NYC, Nov. 19, 1914; d. Louis and Caroline (Stern) Fleischer; m. Aaron Margalith, Jan. 26, 1947 (dec.); children: Carol Lenore, Joan Louise. BA, Hunter Coll., 1936, MA, 1944; MLS, Columbia U., 1958. Editl. corr. Book of the Month Club, 1936-47; rschr. libr. N.Y.C. Bd. Edn., 1955-80; prof. pibr. Touro Coll., NYC, 1980-90; mentor in libr. Empire State Coll., SUNY, 1991—. Cons. in field. Fellow Royal Soc. Medicine (libr. com., gerontology com., history of medicine com.); mem. Ch. and Synagogue Libr. Assn. (book reviewer), Internat. Honor Soc. Women in Edn., Am. Geolinguistic Assn. (bd. dirs. 2003—), Am. Soc. Geolinguistics, Delta Kappa Gamma Democrat. Avocations: reading, travel, research. Home: 205 W End Ave Apt 25S New York NY 10023-4804

MARGARITIS, JOHN PAUL, advertising and public relations executive; b. NYC, June 8, 1949; s. George H. and Mary (Liakos) Margaritis; m. Charlene Corenman, Feb. 21, 1982. BA in English, Washington & Jefferson Coll., Pa., 1971; MA in Media Studies, New Sch. Social Rsch., NYC, 1977. Account exec. Hank Boerner & Assocs., Uniondale, NY, 1974—76, Manning, Selvage & Lee, NYC, 1976—77; account supr. GE, NYC, 1977—79, Burson-Marsteller, Inc., Chgo., 1979—80, v.p., dir. client svcs. LA, 1980—82; exec. v.p., gen. mgr., sr. ptnr. Fleishman-Hillard, Inc., LA, 1982—88; chmn., CEO Ogilvy & Mather Pub. Rels., NYC, 1988—92; pres., COO Ogilvy Adams & Rinehart, NYC, 1992—94, pres., CEO, 1994—97, Hawthorn Grp. NY, 1998; owner, pres. Margaritis Assocs.; pres., CEO Rsch. Ptnrs. Internat., Inc., NYC, 2000; CEO Firebrand Fin. Grp., Inc., NYC; chief mktg. officer Asprey of London; exec. dir. to chmn. N.Am. Euro RSCG Worldwide Pub. Rels., 2005—07; sr. v.p. Marcus Grp. Inc., Little Falls, NJ, 2008—. Dir. emeritus Reasearch!America; bd. dirs. Arthur Ashe Found. Urban Health. 2nd lt. US Army, 1972—74. Mem.: Pub. Rels. Soc. America, Alpine Country Club. Republican. Greek Orthodox. Office: Marcus Grp Inc 150 Clove Rd Little Falls NJ 07424 Office Phone: 973-890-9590. Office Fax: 973-890-9130.*

MARGER, EDWIN, lawyer; b. NYC, Mar. 18, 1928; s. William and Fannie (Cohen) M.; m. Kaye Sanderson, Oct. 1, 1951; children: Shari Ann, Diane Elaine, Sandy Ben; m. L. Suzanne Smyth, July 5, 1968; 1 child, George Phinney; m. Mary Susan Hamel, May 6, 1987; 1 child, Charleston Faye. BA, U. Miami, 1951, JD, 1953. Bar: Fla. 1953, Ga. 1971, D.C. 1978. Pvt. practice, Miami Beach, Fla., 1953—67, Atlanta, 1971—90, Jasper, Ga., 1990—. Gen. counsel Physicians Nat. Risk Retention Group, 1988-91, Physicians Reliance Assn., 1988-91, Physicians Nat. Legal Def. Corp., 1988-91; spl. asst. atty. gen. Fla., 1960-61; atty., agt. Republic of Haiti, 1962-67, City of Port-au-Prince for Transp. and Housing, 1962, Dominican Republic for Trade and Industry, 1964-65; of counsel Richard Burns, Miami, 1967—. Contbr. articles to profl. jours. Tchr. Nat. Inst. Trial Advocacy; mem. Miami Beach Social Svc. Commn., 1957; chmn. Fulton County Aviation Adv. Com., 1980—; chmn. Pickens County Airport Adv. Com., 2004-06; trustee Forensic Scis. Found., 1984-88, v.p., 1986-88; lt. col., a.d.c. Gov. Ga., 1971-74, 80-84; col., a.d.c. Gov. La., 1977-87; Khan Bahador and mem. exiled King of Afghanistan Privy Coun., 1980—. With USAAF, 1946-47. Fellow Am. Acad. Forensic Scis. (chmn. jurisprudence sect. 1977-78, sec. 1976-77, bd. dirs. 1978-79, exec. com. 1983-86); mem. ATLA, ABA, Fla. Bar Assn. (aerospace com. 1971-83, bd. govs. 1983-87, 90-94, exec. com. 1993-94), State Bar Ga. (chmn. sect. environ. law 1974-75, aviation law sect. 1978, bd. govs. 1999-2005, stds. of the profession com.), Ga. Trial Lawyers Assn., Nat. Assn. Criminal Def. Lawyers, Ga. Assn. Criminal Def. Lawyers, Am. Judicature Soc., Am. Arbitration Assn. (commn. panel 1978), Inter-Am. Bar Assn. (sr.), World Assn. Lawyers (founding), Lawyer-Pilots Bar Assn. (founding, v.p. 1959-62), VFW, Am. Legion, Rotary, Lions, Navy League, U.S. Naval Inst., Advocates Club, Lawyers Club Atlanta, Martindale Hubbell Peer Rev. Rating AV. Office: 44 N Main St Jasper GA 30143-1501 Office Phone: 706-253-3060. Personal E-mail: admin@edmarger.com.

MARGESON, THEODORE EARL, judge; b. New Glasgow, NS, Can., Aug. 15, 1938; children: Theodore Jason, Mark Andrew Earl. BA, Mt. Allison U., Sackville, NB, Can., 1959, BEd, 1960; LLB, Dalhousie U., Halifax, NS, 1965. Barrister, solicitor, notary pub. Tchr. Shelburne HS, NS, 1960—61, New Glasgow HS, 1961-62; barrister, solicitor New Glasgow and Toronto, Ont., 1965-90; judge Tax Ct. of Can., Ottawa, 1990—. Bd. dirs. NS Legal Aid. Recipient Confedn. medal Govt. of Can., 1992; Jubilee medal, 2003. Mem. Can. Judges Conf., NS Barrister's Soc. (mem. of coun.), Continuing Legal Edn. Soc. (dir.). Avocations: golf, hockey, squash. Office: Tax Ct of Can 200 Kent St 2nd Fl Ottawa ON Canada K1A OM1 Office Phone: 613-943-2915, 613-947-4502, 613-947-0523.

MARGETON, STEPHEN GEORGE, law librarian; b. Elizabeth, NJ, Mar. 22, 1945; s. Louis George and Josephine A. (Bednarik) M.; m. Margaret Mary Salter, May 14, 1977; children: Catherine Ann, Elizabeth Ann. AB, Mt. St. Mary's Coll., 1967; JD, George Washington U., 1970; MSLS, Cath. U., 1973. Reference librarian Am.-Brit. law div. Library of Congress, Washington, 1968-72; law libr. Steptoe & Johnson, Washington, 1972-85; librarian Supreme Ct. of U.S., Washington, 1985-88; dir. Judge Kathryn J. DuFour Law Libr. The Cath. Univ. Am., 1988—. Instr. George Mason Law Sch., Arlington, Va., 1977-80. Mem. Am. Assn. Law Libraries, Internat. Assn. Law Libraries, Am. Soc. Internat. Law. Office: Cath U Am Judge Kathryn J DuFour Law Libr 3600 John Mccormack Rd NE Washington DC 20064-0001

MARGITIĆ, MILORAD R., language educator, researcher; b. Kragujevac, Serbia, June 6, 1934; arrived in USA, 1963; s. Radomir B. and Olga J. Margitić; m. Susan E. Kent, Oct. 5, 1969; children: Alexandra Margitic, Tatiana Margitic. MA Candidatus Degree, Univ. of Leiden, Leiden, the Netherlands, 1963; PhD French, Wayne State Univ., Detroit, Mich., 1971. Tchg. asst., instr., asst. prof. (French) Wayne State Univ., Detroit, 1963—72; asst. prof. (French) Univ. of Chgo., Chgo., 1972—78; asst. prof., assoc. prof., prof. (French) Wake Forest Univ., Winston-Salem, NC, 1978; ret., 2005. Author: (book) Essai sur la mythologie du Cid, 1976, La Suivante, comédie, de Pierre Corneille, édition critique, 1978, La Galerie du Palais, ou l'amie rivale, comédie, de Pierre Corneille, édition critique, 1981, Corneille comique: Nine Studies of Pierre Corneille's Comedy with an Intro. and a Bibliography., 1982, Actes de Wake Forest/ procs. of the NASSCFL 19th Ann. Conf., 1987, Le Cid, tragi-comédie, de Pierre Corneille, édition critique, 1989, Cornelian Power Games: Variations on a Theme in Pierre Corneille's Theater from "Mélite" to "Polyeucte", 2002. Recipient Scholarship (full stipend), Universitair Asyl Fonds/ Holland, 1960—63, Outside evaluator in tenure and promotion cases, UCLA, Vassar Coll., U. Ga., Loyola U.; grantee Publ. Subsidy Grant, Univ. of Chgo., 1975. Democrat. Serbian Orthodox. Avocation: play accordion as a hobby. Home: 5435 Stone Crossing Dr Winston Salem NC 27104-3744

MARGO, ADAIR, art association administrator, art gallery owner; BA in art history, Vanderbilt U.; studied Renaissance art and Italian, Syracuse U., Florence, Italy; MA in art history, N.Mex. State U. Founder, owner Adair Margo Gallery (now Adair Margo Fine Art), El Paso, Tex., 1985—; chmn. Pres.'s Com. on Arts and Humanities, Washington, 2001—. Mem. US Nat. Commn. UNESCO; hon. mem. US-Mex. Found. for Culture; instr. art history N.Mex. State U., U. Tex., El Paso; chmn. Tex. Commn. on the Arts; chmn. exhbns. USA Mid-America Arts Alliance; bd. dirs. Tex. Higher Edn. Coordinating Bd., Humanities Tex., Ctr. Medical Ethics and Humanities, U. San Antonio Med. Sch., Tex. Philosophical Soc., Tex. A&M U. Press; exec. com. Southern Assn. Colleges and Schools/Commn. on Colleges. Recipient Presdl. Citizens medal, 2008. Office: Pres's Com on Arts and Humanities Ste 526 1100 Pennsylvania Ave NW Washington DC 20506 also: Adair Margo Fine Art Ste 602 215 N Stanton El Paso TX 79901 Office Phone: 202-682-5409, 915-533-0048. Office Fax: 202-682-5608. E-mail: pcah@pcah.gov, amargo@adairmargo.com.*

MARGO, KATHERINE LANE, family physician, educator; d. Warren Wilson and Virginia (Penney) Lane; m. Geoffrey Myles Margo, Apr. 20, 1980; 1 child, Benjamin stepchildren: Jenny, Judy. BA, Swarthmore Coll., 1974; MD, SUNY Health Sci. Ctr., Syracuse, 1978. Cert. in family medicine. Resident physician St. Joseph's Hosp., Syracuse, 1979-82; attending physician Health Svcs. Assn., Syracuse, 1982-90, asst. med. dir. for quality assurance, 1985-90; asst. prof. family medicine SUNY-HSC at Syracuse, 1990-94; mem. residency faculty Harrisburg (Pa.) Hosp., 1994-2000; med. dir. Harrisburg Kline Family Practice Ctr., 1996-2000; assoc. residency dir. Harrisburg Family Practice Residency, 1997-2000; predoctoral dir., dept. family medicine & cmty. health U. Pa., 2000—, asst. prof., assoc. dir. family practice residency, 2000—, assoc. prof., 2009. Clin. assoc. prof. Allegheny Med. Sch., 1997—2000. Contbr. articles to profl. jours. Bd. trustees Pt. Choice, Syracuse, 1993—94; chair med. com. Planned Parenthood, Syracuse, 1984—94; bd. dirs. Planned Parenthood Susquehanna Valley, 1996—2000; active Friends of Chamber Music, Syracuse, 1985—94; keyboard player Old World folk Band. Recipient Exemplary Tchg. award, Pa. Acad. of Family Practice, 2003, Penn Pearls Tchg. award, U. Pa. Sch. Medicine, 2004. Mem.: Am. Acad. Family Practitioners (v.p. Syracuse chpt.), Soc. Tchrs. of Family Medicine (chair group on predoctoral edn. 2003—04). Democrat. Avocations: music, theater, gardening, birdwatching. Home: 426 Carpenter Ln Philadelphia PA 19119-3040 Office: Univ Pa Dept Family Practice Community Medicine 2 Gates 3400 Spruce St Philadelphia PA 19104 Office Phone: 215-662-8941. E-mail: margok@uphs.upenn.edu.

MARGO, ROD DAVID, lawyer; b. Johannesburg, Republic of South Africa, Feb. 14, 1950; came to US, 1978; s. Cecil Stanley and Marguerite Giselle (Polné) M. BCom, U. Witwatersrand, Johannesburg, South Africa, 1970, LLB cum laude, 1973; D Civil Laws, McGill U., Montreal, Que., Can., 1979. Bar: Ga. 1979, Calif. 1981, DC 1996, US Supreme Ct., 2005; solicitor, NSW, Australia, 2004. From assoc. to ptnr. Condon & Forsyth, LA, 1980—. Lectr. aviation law UCLA, 1981-98; adj. prof. law Inst. Air and Space Law, Montreal, Can. Author: Aviation Ins. 3d edit., 2000; co-author: Shawcross & Beaumont on Air Law, 4th rev. edit., 2009, co-author Montreal Convention, 1st edit., 2007. Fellow: Royal Aero. Soc.; mem.: LA County Bar Assn. Office: Condon & Forsyth 1901 Avenue Of The Stars Ste 850 Los Angeles CA 90067-6010 Office Phone: 310-557-2030. Business E-Mail: rmargo@condonlaw.com.

MARGOLIES-MEZVINSKY, MARJORIE, former congresswoman, political organization worker; b. Phila., June 21, 1942; d. Herbert and Mildred Margolies; m. Edward Mezvinsky, 1975; adopted children: Lee Heh, Holly; children: Marc, Andrew; 4 stepchildren; legal guardian of 3 other children. Grad., U. of Pa., 1963. Former TV reporter; corr. Sta. WRC-TV, Washington, Sta. WCAU-TV, Phila., Sta. WNBC-TV, NYC; contbg. corr. NBC Today Show, CNBC, A Closer Look, Real Life with Jane Pauley, Sunday Today, 1990-92; mem. US Congress from 13th Pa. Dist., Washington, 1993—95; dir., dep. chairwoman US Del. to UN 4th World Conf. on Women, 1995; chair Nat. Women's Bus. Coun.; pres. Women's Campaign Internat., Phila. Com. mem. Energy and Commerce, Small Bus., Govt. Ops. Author: They Came to Stay, 1976, A Woman's Place...the Freshmen Women Who Changed the Face of Congress, 1993. Active Penn Valley PTA, U. Pa. Women's Trustee Coun.; fund raiser Montgomery County Schs., Red Cross, Multiple Sclerosis Delaware Valley, Dystonia Med. Rsch. Found., Nat. Tay-Sachs Assn. Recipient five Emmy Awards, ABA award for disting. contbn. to public understanding Am. system of law and justice; CBS News Found. fellow Columbia U., NY, 1969-70. Mem. AFTRA, Women's Am. ORT, Am. Coun. Nationalities Svcs., Internat. Social Svcs. Democrat. Achievements include supporting refugee children and families. Office: Women's Campaign Internat 3701 Chestnut St Philadelphia PA 19104 Office Phone: 215-387-2603. Business E-Mail: marjorie@womenscampaigninternational.org.

MARGOLIN, ERIC MITCHELL, lawyer; b. NYC, Mar. 31, 1953; s. Benjamin and Muriel (Leibowitz) Margolin BA, SUNY, Buffalo, 1974; JD, Georgetown U., 1977. Bar: NY 1978. Staff atty. Met. Life Ins. Co., NYC, 1977-79; atty. Chesebrough-Pond's Inc., Greenwich, Conn., 1979—81, sr. atty., 1982—85; v.p., gen. counsel, sec., dir. Health-Tex Inc., NYC, 1985—92; sr. v.p., gen. counsel, sec. The He-Ro Group Ltd., NYC, 1992—93; v.p., gen. counsel, sec. Tire Kingdom Inc. (now TBC Corp.), West Palm Beach, Fla., 1993—2000; sr. v.p., gen. counsel, sec. Advance Auto Parts Inc., Roanoke, Va., 2001—07; sr. v.p., sec. gen. counsel CarMax Inc., Richmond, Va., 2007—. Mem.: ABA. Office: CarMax Inc 12800 Tuckahoe Creek Pkwy Richmond VA 23238

MARGOLIN, FRANCES MONGIN, clinical psychologist, educator; b. Montgomery County, Pa. d. Harry and Dorothy (Blanc) Mongin; m. Elias L. Margolin, Mar. 12, 1944; children: Janice, John, Carol, Paul. BA, Temple U., 1948; MA, Ohio U., 1955; PhD, US Internat. U., 1973. Lic. psychologist, marriage and family therapist Calif., diplomate Am. Bd. Clin. Psychology. Clin. psychologist Dayton State Hosp., Ohio, 1948—53; pvt. practice clin. psychology Dayton, 1953—55, La Jolla, Calif., 1974—; marriage counselor San Diego County Superior Ct., San Diego, 1955—74. V.p. AAUW, Dayton, 1954; asst. prof. psychology San Diego State U., 1975—76; prof. LaVerne Coll., San Diego, 1976—78, Chapman Coll., San Diego, 1978—88; chair psychology com. Harbor View Hosp., SD, 1985—88. Mem.: APA, San Diego Acad. Psychology, SD Nurses Coun. (Woman of Wisdom Leader 2004), Am. Women Psychology (San Diego rep. 1982—90), Assn. Psychologists Pvt. Practice, Calif. Psychol. Assn., Psi Chi. Home and Office: PO Box 3056 La Jolla CA 92038-3056

MARGOLIN, HAROLD, metallurgical educator; b. Hartford, Conn., July 12, 1922; s. Aaron David and Sonia (Krupnikoff) M.; m. Elaine Marjorie Rose, July 4, 1946; children: Shelley, Deborah, Amy. B in Engring., Yale U., 1943; M in Engring., Yale Univ., 1947, DEng, 1950. Rsch. assoc./scientist divsn. rsch. NYU, NYC, 1949-56, assoc. prof. metall. engring., 1956-62, prof., 1962-73; prof. phys. metallurgy Poly. U. N.Y., Bklyn., 1973-93, disting. rsch. prof., 1993—2003, 2004—05, emeritus prof., 2006. Theodore W. Krengel vis. prof. Technion, Haifa, Israel, 1983; cons. in field. Contbg. author books; contbr. articles to profl. publs.; patentee in field. With USNR, 1944-46. Fellow Am. Soc. Metals (edn. award N.Y. chpt. 1967); mem. Metall. Soc. (honoree symposium in his name San Francisco 1994), ASM Internat., TMS. Democrat. Jewish. Home: 81 Stony Run New Rochelle NY 10804-3415 Personal E-mail: hmemxox@aol.com. *Achievement, work, and refusal to accept defeat are intimately intertwined.*

MARGOLIN, ROBERT JEREMY, lawyer; b. Kansas City, Mo., Mar. 21, 1935; s. Abraham Eugene and Florence Margolin; m. Dorothy Ann Macy, Sept. 20, 1959; 1 child, Kathryn R. Margolin Richter. AB, Dartmouth Coll., 1957; JD, LLB, U. Mich., 1960. Bar: Mo., U.S. Ct. Appeals (8th cir.). Ptnr. Margolin and Kirwan, Kansas City, 1960—. Bd. dirs. Kansas City Kings, Feld Leasing. Asst. editor Mich. Law Rev. Bd. dirs. Menorah Med. Ctr., Kansas City, Kansas City Philharm. Assn.; exec. com. Jewish Vocat. Svc., Kansas City. Mem. ABA, Nat. Basketball Assn. (bd. govs.), Mo. Bar Assn., Kansas City Bar Assn. Avocations: golf, skiing. Home: 1628 River Ridge Williamsburg VA 23185-7546 E-mail: bobj757@aol.com.

MARGOLIS, BERNARD ALLEN, library administrator; b. Greenwich, Conn., Oct. 2, 1948; s. Sidney S. and Rose (Birkenfeld) M.; m. Amanda Batey, Nov. 2, 1973. BA in Polit. Sci., U. Denver, 1970, MA in Librarianship, 1973; D of Tech. (hon.), Wentworth Inst. Tech., 1999. Cert. libr., Mich. Asst. shelving supr. Denver Pub. Libr., 1968—70, libr. asst. I hist. divsn. lit. and hist. dept., 1970—72, br. head Va. Village Libr., 1972—73; dep. dir. Monroe County Libr. Sys., Mich., 1973—75, dir., 1976—88; dep. dir. SE Mich. Regional Film Libr., 1974—75, dir., 1976—88; asst. dir. Raisin Valley Libr. Sys., 1974—75, dir., 1976—78, Pikes Peak Libr. Dist., Colorado Springs, Colo., 1988—97; pres. Colo. Ctr. for the Book, 1989—92, 1993—97, Boston Pub. Libr., 1997—2008, State Librarian NY; asst. commr. State Edn. Dept. Lib., 2009—. Cons. in libr. pub. rels., 1976—; chmn. Colo. Gov.'s Conf. on Libr. and Info. Svcs., 1990; lectr. Western Mich. U., Kalamazoo, 1978-81; appraiser rare books, Monroe, Colorado Springs, 1970—. Contbr. articles to profl. jours.; mem. editl. bd. Bottom Line Mag. Fin. Mgmt. for Librs., 1986—, Jour. Libr. Adminstrn., 1997-. Bd. dirs. Mass. Ctr. for Book, 2008, Back Bay Assn.2008, Monroe Sr. Citizens Ctr., 1976-80, Monroe Fine Arts Coun., 1978-81, Am. the Beautiful Centennial Celebration, Inc., 1993, Boston Libr. Consortium, 1993-2008, Downtown Colorado Springs, Inc., 1994-97, Friends of Copley Sq., 2008, Care & Share, Inc., sec., 1994-95, vice chmn., 1995, chmn., 1995-97, Blue Cross-Blue Shield Consumer Coun., Detroit, 1984-88; adv. bd. Access Colo. Libr. and Info. Network, 1991-97, Mercy Meml. Hosp., Monroe, 1984-86, 5th Congl. Art Competition Com., 1992-97; Dem. candidate Mich. Senate, 1986; allocations com. Pikes Peak United Way, 1988-91, bd. dirs., 1990-91, 94-97, chmn., 1990-91, Great Pikes Peak Cowboy Poetry Gathering, 1990-92, 94-96; del. White House Conf. Libr. and Info. Scis.; mem. El Paso County Retirement Bd., Colo., 1995-97, sec., 1996-97; fellow Boston Found., 2006, 1998—; overseer Hancock Shaker Village, Pittsfield, Mass., 1999—; leadership mgmt. com. Assn. Rsch. Librs., 2003—06; bd. mem. Boston Pub. Libr. Found., Assocs. Boston Pub. Libr. Bd. Recipient Mayoral Cert. Commendation award Denver, 1972, 73, Commendation John F. Kennedy Ctr. Performing Arts, 1993, Frank Waters award Pikes Peak Writer's Conf., 1996; named Mich. Libr. of Yr., 1985, Colo. Libr. of Yr., 1990, Friend to Writers award Pen New England, 2007 Fellow: Mass. Hist. Soc.; mem.: ALA (cons. ann. swap and shop 1979—84, governing coun. 1985—, endowment trustee 1989—93, chmn. resolutions com. 1991—92, sr. endowment trustee 1993—2001, legislation com. 2008—, John Cotton Dana award 1977, 1991, Libr. Awareness Idea Search award Washington 1982), NY Lib. Assn., Assn. Ednl. Comm. and Tech., Pub. Libr. Assn., Libr. Adminstrv. Mgmt. Assn., Internat. Fedn. Libr. Assns. and Instns. (ofcl. US del. pub. libr. sect. 1997—2006), Mass. Libr. Assn. Democrat. Jewish. Office Phone: 518-474-5930. Personal E-mail: bernardmargolis@verizon.net.

MARGOLIS, DANIEL HERBERT, lawyer; b. 1926; s. Morris Abraham and Miriam M.; m. Anabel Tendler, Dec. 23, 1951 (dec.); children: Peter, Beth, Laura, James; m. Sidney Millman Moore, Feb. 5, 1983. BA, Johns Hopkins U., Balt., 1948; LLB, Harvard U., Cambridge, Mass., 1951. Bar: DC 1951, US Supreme Ct. 1959. Atty. adv. Office Price Stblzn., Washington, 1951-52; trial atty. Antitrust divsn. Dept. Justice, Washington, 1952-56; sr. ptnr. Bergson, Borkland, Margolis & Adler, Washington, 1962—86, McGuire, Woods, Battle & Boothe, Washington, 1986-89, Patton, Boggs LLP, Washington, 1989—2001; sr. counsel DC Office of Corp. Counsel, 2001—03; prin. Law Offices of Daniel H. Margolis, 2003—. With USN, 1945—46. Fellow: ABA, Coll. Comml. Arbitrators; mem.: Chartered Inst. Arbitrators. Avocations: sailing, skiing, cooking.

MARGOLIS, DAVID MICHAEL, medical educator; b. New Haven, Aug. 23, 1959; AB, Harvard Coll., Cambridge, Mass., 1981; MD, Tufts U. Sch. Medicine, Boston, 1985. Asst. prof. medicine, microbiology & immunology U. Md. Sch. Medicine and Inst. Human Virology, Balt., 1994—99; prof. medicine, microbiology & immunology U. Tex. Southwestern Med. Ctr., Dallas, 1999—2005; prof. medicine, microbiology & immunology, epidemiology U. NC, Chapel Hill, 2005—. Mem. AIDS Rsch. Adv. Com., DAIDS, NIH, Bethesda, 2004—08. Fellow: ACP, Infectious Diseases Soc. Am.; mem.: Am. Soc. Clin. Investigation. Achievements include research in demonstration of the role of HDACs in HIV latency. Office: Univ NC Sch Medicine 3302 Michael Hooker Rsch Ctr CB #7435 Chapel Hill NC 27599-7435

MARGOLIS, DORIS MAY ROSENBERG, editor, writer; b. Washington, May 10, 1936; d. Samuel Jacob and Eva (Mendelsohn) Rosenberg; m. Lawrence S. Margolis, Jan. 30, 1960; children: Mary Aleta, Paul Oliver. BA, George Wash. U., 1958. Founder, v.p., CEO Editorial Assocs., Washington, 1963-82, founder, pres., CEO, 1982—. Founder, pub., exec. editor Margolis Health Report, 1999—; bd. govs. Nat. Press Club, 1991-94; mem. adv. bd. Washington Journalism Conf., 1991-96; judge Biomedical Writing awards Am. Med. Writers Assn.-Mid-Atlantic, 1987-91, Blue Pencil Writing awards Nat. Assn. Govt. Contractors, 1992, 94, Rose Kushner Breast Cancer Writing award Am. Med. Writers Assn., 1992, Nat. Essay competition Pres.'s Com. on Employment of the Handicapped, Nat. Worker of Yr. competition Goodwill Industries of Am., Nat. Essay Competition Hospitalized Vets. Assn., others. Author: This Is Goodwill, 1968; editor-in-chief Jour. Rehab., 1960-67, (newsletters) Nat. Assn. Sheltered Workshops and Homebound Programs News, 1964-68, Jewish Occupational Coun. News, 1968-70, Aspen Update, 1976-80; contbg. editor (newspapers) Pediatric News, 1968-69, Ob-Gyn News, 1968-69, Internal Medicine News, 1968-69; columnist Jour. Rehab., 1960-67, Washington Jewish Week, 1968-73, Sports Medicine Monthly, 1984-85, Gazette Newspapers, 1999-2000; radio news corr. Physicians Radio News Network, 1969, 1976; contbr. articles to profl. jours.; editor: Concrete Facts Magazine, 1960, Rehabilitation of the Mentally Ill, 1961, Rehabilitation International, 1962, Rehabilitation of the Mentally Retarded, 1962, To Aid the Disabled, 1963, The Stroke Spectrum: Prevention, Treatment, and Rehabilitation, 1963, Workshops at the Crossroads, 1964, Sheltered Workshops: The Road Ahead, 1965, Sheltered Workshops, 1965, The Coronary Spectrum: Prevention, Treatment, and Rehabilitation, 1966, Medical Rehabilitation Model Delivery Systems, 1978; asst. editor NEA News, 1958-59. Singer, dancer Montgomery Light Opera Co., 1970's, Washington Civic Opera, 1978-84; singer, dancer, actress Hexagon Players, 1970-72; bd. dirs. Jewish Social Svcs. Agy., 1970-72; bd. govs. Am. Newspaper Women's Club, 1982-84, Woman's Nat. Dem. Club, 1983-88; exec. com. bd. dirs. People-to-People Com. on Disability, 1992-2000, vice-chmn., 1995-2000; pres. Inner Wheel Club of Washington, 1993-94. Recipient Ellen Woodhull scholastic scholarship George Washington U., 1957, Disting. Alumni Achievement award George Washington U., 1978, Nat. Press Club Vivian award, 1997, 99, 2007; personal commendations Pres. John F. Kennedy, 1963, Pres. Lyndon B. Johnson, 1966; Paul Harris fellow Rotary Internat. Fellow Am. Med. Writers Assn. (bd. dirs. 1989-94, chair pub. rels., advt. and mktg. sect. 1989-90, pres. Mid-Atlantic chpt. 1990-91, exec. com. bd. dirs. 1993-94); mem. Nat. Assn. Sci. Writers, Cosmos Club, Rotary Club of Washington, DC (Centennial pres. 2004-05, zone pub. rels. coord. Rotary Internat., 2006-07, rep. to OAS, 2006-07, rep. to World Bank, 2007-, pres. Rotary Found. of Washington, D.C., 2008-), Alpha Epsilon Phi Alumni Assn. (pres. 1959-60), Mortar Bd. (treas. 1957-58), Phi Delta Epsilon (v.p. 1957-58), Psi Chi, Alpha Theta Nu. Office: Editorial Assocs Nat Press Bldg Washington DC 20045

MARGOLIS, EMANUEL, lawyer, educator; b. Bklyn., Mar. 18, 1926; s. Abraham and Esther (Levin) Margolis; m. Edith Cushing (div.); m. Estelle Thompson, Mar. 1, 1959; children: Elizabeth Margolis-Pineo, Catherine Margolis, Abby Margolis Newman, Joshua, Sarah Margolis Marsh. BA, U. N.C., 1947; MA, Harvard U., 1948, PhD, 1951; JD, Yale U., 1956. Bar: Conn. 1957, U.S. Dist. Ct. Conn. 1958, U.S. Supreme Ct. 1969. Instr. dept. govt. U. Conn., 1951-53; assoc. Silberberg & Silverstein, Ansonia, Conn., 1956-60, Wofsey Rosen Kweskin & Kuriansky, Stamford, Conn., 1960-66, ptnr., 1966-96, of counsel, 1996—. Arbitrator State of Conn., 1984—85; adj. prof. Quinnipiac U. Sch. Law, 1986—. Sr. editor: Conn. Bar Jour., 1971—80, 1983—, editor-in-chief:, 1980—83, human rights columnist: Conn. Law Tribune, 2005—; contbr. articles to profl. jours. Nat. bd. dirs. ACLU, 1975—79; mem. Westport (Conn.) Planning and Zoning Commn., 1971—75; chmn. Conn. CLU, 1988—95, legal advisor, 1995—; mem. exec. com. Yale Law Sch., 2000—04. With US Army, 1944—46. Decorated Purple Heart; recipient 1st award for Disting. Svc. to Conn. Bar, Conn. Law Tribune, 1987, Champion of Liberty award, Conn. Def. Lawyers Assn, 2004. Fellow: Conn. Bar Found. (James W. Cooper fellow 1996); mem.: ABA, Am. Arbitration Assn. (arbitrator 1998—, trial referee 1985—), Nat. Assn. Criminal Def. Lawyers, Conn. Bar Assn. (chmn. human rigts sect. 1970—73). Home: 72 Myrtle Ave Westport CT 06880-3512 Office Phone: 203-327-2300. Personal E-mail: emesq@optonline.net.

MARGOLIS, GWEN, former state legislator; b. Phila., Oct. 4, 1934; d. Joseph and Rose Liedman; children: Edward, Ira, Karen, Robin. Grad., Temple U. Mem. Fla. House of Reps., 1975—80, Fla. State Senate, 1981—92, 2003—08, pres., 1990-92; mem. dist. 4 Metro-Dade County Commn., Fla., 1994—2002, chairperson Fla., commr. dist. 4 Fla.; realtor, appraiser. Bd. dirs. Holocaust Documentation Ctr. Fla., 1997—, bd. dirs. New Theater, 2009, Jewish Mus. LA, 2009. Recipient Econ. Devel. award Fla. C. of C., 1992, Legislator of Yr. award Fla. C. of C., 1992, Good Govt. award Dade League of Cities, 1992, Fla. Motion Picture and TV award, 1992, Glass Ceiling award Fla. Fedn. Bus. and Profl. Women, 1992. Named to Fla. Womens Hall of Fame, 2009, Women of Valor Greater Miami Jewish Fedn. Mem.: Miami Bd. Realtors. Democrat. Jewish. Home: 2 Grove ISLE Dr #209 Miami FL 33133 Home Phone: 305-285-7824; Office Phone: 305-790-1612. Personal E-mail: gwenmargois@comcast.net.

MARGOLIS, JAY M., former apparel company executive; b. NYC, Feb. 11, 1949; s. Mac and Sarah Margolis; m. Donna Brenda Polsky, June 12, 1972; children: Jared Michael, Stacey Allyse. BA, Queens Coll., NYC, 1971. Asst. mdse. mgr. Manhattan Shirt Co., NYC, 1972-74; mdse. mgr. Arrow Shirt Co., NYC, 1974-78; pres. Yves St. Laurent-Biderman Inc., NYC, 1978-81, Ron Chereskin div. Cluett Peabody, NYC, 1981-83, Claiborne Mens-Liz Claiborne Inc., NYC, 1983-86; group pres., exec. v.p. corp. Liz Claiborne Inc., NYC, 1986-88, vice chmn., 1988—92; pres., vice chmn. Tommy Hilfiger, 1992—95; chmn., CEO Esprit de Corp., 1995—99, E7th.com, 1999—2001; pres. splty. bus. group Reebok Internat. Ltd., 2001, pres., COO, 2001—04; group pres. apparel Limited Brands, Inc., 2005—07. Bd. dirs. Boston Beer Co., 2006—, Godiva Chocolatier, 2008—. Mem. bd. Fathers Day/Mothers Day Coun. Mem. City Athletic Club. Avocations: skiing, swimming, tennis, environmental studies.*

MARGOLIS, LAWRENCE STANLEY, federal judge; BSME, Drexel U., 1957; JD, George Washington U., 1961. Bar: DC 1963. Patent examiner US Patent Office, Washington, 1957-62; patent counsel Naval Ordnance Lab., White Oak, Md., 1962-63; asst. atty. gen. Washington, 1963—66; atty. criminal divsn., spl. asst. US atty. US Dept. Justice, Washington, 1966-68, asst. US atty. DC, 1968-71; US magistrate judge US Dist. Ct., Washington, 1971-82; judge US Ct. Fed. Claims, Washington, 1982—97, sr. judge, 1997—; chmn. task force on discovery reform US Claims Ct., Washington, chmn. alt. dispute resolution. Chmn. Space and Bldg. com., chmn. Ct. Security Com., mem. mgmt. com., mem. faculty Fed. Jud. Ctr. Editor-in-chief The Young Lawyer, 1965-66, DC Bar Jour., 1967-73; bd. editors The Dist. Lawyer, 1978-82. Trustee Drexel U., 1983-89; bd. govs. George Washington U. Alumni Assn., 1978-85, 93-96. Recipient Contbn. award DC Jaycees, 1966, Svc. award Boy Scouts America, 1970, Alumni Svc. award George Washington U., 1976, Disting. Alumni Achievement award George Washington U., 1985, Disting. Alumni Achievement award Drexel U., 1988, Drexel 100 award, 1992, Alternative Dispute Resolution award Ctr. for Public Resources, 1988, Alternative Dispute Resolution Svc. award Ct. of Fed. Claims, 1996, Alumni Recognition award George Washington U., 1996, Disting. Jud. Svc. award US Ct. Fed. Claims Bar Assn., 2007, Outstanding Svc. award Theodore Roosevelt HS, 2007-09. Fellow Inst. Jud. Adminstrn., American Bar Found.; mem. ABA (chmn. jud. adminstrn. divsn., Disting. Svc. award 1981), ABA Nat. Conf. Spl. Ct. Judges (chmn., Disting. Svc. award 1978), DC Jud. Conf., Bar Assn. DC (bd. dirs. 1970-72, jour. editor-in-chief, Chmn. of Yr. award, Contbn. award young lawyers sect. 1983), Fed. Bar Assn., George Washington U. Nat. Law Assn. (pres. DC chpt. 1974-76, nat. pres. 1983-84), U. Club., Rotary (bd. dirs. Washington 1984-90, pres. 1988-89, dist. gov. 1991-92, Rotarian of Yr. 1984, Rotary Internat. Rep. to the World Bank and Orgn. of American States, 1998-99, pres. Rotary Found. 1999-00, Rotarian of the Decade 2005), Charles Fahy American Inn of Ct. (Nat. Prog. award, 1997), Phila. Ctrl. HS Alumni (bd. mgrs. 2001-05, Hall of Fame Ctrl. HS, 2009), Rotary Club Washington (Excellence award, 2007-08) Office: US Ct Fed Claims 717 Madison Pl NW Ste 703 Washington DC 20005*

MARGOLIS, MARK NEAL, actor; b. Phila., Nov. 26, 1939; s. Isidore and Fanya (Fried) M.; m. Jacqueline Petcove, June 3, 1962; 1 child, Morgan. Studied with, Stella Adler, Lee Strasberg, Bill Hickey, Barbara Loden. Actor: (films) Short Eyes, 1977, Going in Style, 1979, Dressed to Kill, 1980, You Better Watch Out, 1980, The Avenging, 1982, Diner, 1982, Eddie Macon's Run, 1983, Scarface, 1983, Far From Poland, 1984, The Cotton Club, 1984, The Bedroom Window, 1987, The Secret of My Success, 1987, The Rosary Murders, 1987, White Hot, 1989, Glory, 1989, Tales from the Darkside: The Movie, 1990, Delta Force: The Colombian Connection, 1990, 1492: Conquest of Paradise, 1992, Where the Rivers Flow North, 1994, Ace Ventura: Pet Detective, 1994, Squanto: A Warrior's Tale, 1994, I Shot Andy Warhol, 1996, The Pallbearer, 1996, Absolute Power, 1997, Trouble on the Corner, 1997, Above Freezing, 1998, Pants on Fire, 1998, 18 Shades of Dust, 1999, The Thomas Crown Affair, 1999, Mickey Blue Eyes, 1999, End of Days, 1999, Flawless, 1999, Angela, 2000, Requiem for a Dream, 2000, Dinner Rush, 2000, Hannibal, 2001, The Tailor of Panama, 2001, Hard Ball, 2001, Bridget, 2002, Infested, 2002, Particles of Truth, 2003, Daredevil, 2003, 2BPerfectlyHonest, 2004, House of D, 2004, Stay, 2005, The Fountain, 2006, Gone Baby Gone, 2007, Defiance, 2007, The Wrestler, 2008; (TV series) NBC's Kings, Breaking Bad, The Guiding Light, 1994, Santa Barbara, 1990, Oz, 1998-99, Brotherhood, 2006, The Black Donnellys, 2007; (TV films) Muggable Mary, Street Cop, 1982, Rage of Angels, 1983, Doubletake, 1985, Almost Partners, 1987, Lady Mobster, 1988, Columbo: Columbo Cries Wolf, 1990, Descending Angel, 1990, Boss of Bosses, 2001; (broadway prodns.) The World of Sholom Aleichem, Infidel Caesar); (off-broadway prodns.) Three Americanisms, My Uncle Sam, Balm in Gilead, Hospitality, Child of the Clay Country, The Big Knife, others; (regional theatre) The Substance of Fire, Ghosts, Love Me or Leave Me, Once in a Lifetime, The Boys Next Door, A Shayna Maidel, Hunting Cockroaches, The Seagull, Split Decision, The Front Page, Broken Glass, Quills; TV guest appearances include Kojak, 1977, The Equalizer, 1986-88, Crime Story, 1987, Quantum Leap, 1989, Mancuso, FBI, 1990, Star Trek: The Next Generation, 1990, Jake and the Fatman, 1990, The Antagonists, 1991, Law & Order, 1992, 97, 2001, New York Undercover, 1994, Prince Street, 1997, 2000, Now and Again, 1999, 100 Centre Street, 2001, The Practice, 2002, Hack, 2002, Ed, 2003-04, Sex and the City, 2004, Law & Order: Criminal Intent, 2004, Crossing Jordan, 2005, Brotherhood, 2005, The Black Donellys, 2006, Californication, 2007. Mem.: Actors Studio (life). Office: Abrams Artists 275 7Ave New York NY 10001 E-mail: markmargolis1@mac.com.

MARGOLIS, PHILIP MARCUS, psychiatrist, educator; b. Lima, Ohio, July 7, 1925; s. Harry Sterling and Clara (Brunner) M.; m. Nancy Nupuf, July 26, 1959; children: Cynthia, Marc, David, Laurence. BA magna cum laude, U. Minn., 1945, MD, 1948. Diplomate Am. Bd. Psychiatry and Neurology, 1966 (examiner 1973—1999, 2003-), recert. com., 1998-2004. Intern Milw. County Hosp., 1948-49; resident VA Hosp. and U. Minn., 1949-52, Mass. Gen. Hosp. and Harvard U., Boston, 1952-54; instr. U. Minn., Milw., 1953-55; asst. prof. dept. psychiatry Med. Sch., U. Chgo., 1955-60, assoc. prof., 1960-66; prof. psychiatry Med. Sch. U. Mich., 1966—, prof. cmty. mental health, 1968—; prof. psychiatry emeritus L.S.A., 1997—, instr., 1977-97; chief psychiat. inpatient service U. Chgo. Hosps. and Clinics, 1956-66; dir. Civil Forensic Tng. Program, 1997—; cons. psychiatrist, co investigator Measuring Psychiatric Problems Mich. Correctional Facilities: Independent Study Mental Health & substance Abuse, 2009—; chair therapeutic U. Mich. Depression Ctr. Innovation Fund, 2009—; mem. Mich. Dept. State Med. Adv. Bd., 2009—. Cons. Forensic Psychiat. Ctr., State of Mich., 1972—, mem. dept. state med. adv. bd., 2009-, coord. med. student edn. program, 1975-78, dir., 1978-82; cons. Turner Geriatric Clin., 1978-86, cons. Breast Cancer Clinic, 1988, Powertrain subs. Gen. Motors, 1984—, Dept. Mental Health, U.S. Dept. Justice; assoc. chief clin. affairs U. Mich. Hosps., 1981-85, chair legis. govt. com., 1996—, chmn. ethics com.; profl. rev. com. PSRO Area VII, 1982-86, PROM, 2003—; mem. Mich. State Bd. Medicine, 1986-94, chmn. 1992-94, senate adv. com. Univ. Affairs., 1986-89; spl. com. on profl. conduct and ethics Fedn. of State Med. Bds., 1998—, Mich. del., 1988-96, FLEX Com. Nat. Bd. Med. Examiners, 1988-98; civil liberties bd. U. Mich., 1995-2004, chmn., 1996-2002, gen counsel adv. com., 2002-08; dir. Civil Forensic Tng. Program, 1997—. Author: Guide for Mental Health Workers, 1970, Patient Power: The Development of a Therapeutic Community in a General Hospital, 1974; also articles.; cons. editor: Community Mental Health jour, 1967—. Recipient Commonwealth Fund fellow award, 1964, Career Svc. award, 1992, Resident Appreciation award, 1991. Fellow: Am. Coll. Psychiatrists (chmn. bylaws com. 1997—, newsletter editor, Lifers 2003—), Am. Psychiat. Assn. (life; chmn. membership com. 1979—83, cons. ethics com. 1983—86, trustee 1985—88, sec. 1989—91, chmn. ethics appeals bd. 1989—, cons. steering com. on practical guidelines 1991—, budget com. 1991—, mem. assembly 1992, coun. med. edn. and career devel. 1993—, pres. Lifers 1994—, recertification com. 1998—, mem. pub. funding com. 2001—, assembly rep. 2003—, newsletter editor 2003—, cons. mem. com. 2004—, mem. audit com. 2004—, annual Lifers award 1999); mem.: Am. Acad. Psychiatry and Law (com. on psychoanalytic edn. 1995—, edn. com. 1998, treas. midwest chpt. 1998—2000, forensic tng. com. 2000—, pres. 2001—02), Am. Acad. Psychoanalysis, Mich. State Med. Soc. (bioethics com. 1989—, com. on med. licensure and discipline 1995—, mental health liaison com. 1995—, legis. and regulations com. 1995—, liaison com. Gen. Motors 1998—, chair 2000—, chair com. on med. licensure and discipline 2000—), Mich. Psychiat. Soc. (pres. 1980—81, chmn. ethics com. 1983—86, chmn. legislation and govt. com. 1996—2005, resolutions officer student rights responsibilities 1996—, v.p. 2000—, chmn. mem. com. 2004—, Career Achievement award 2000), Washtenaw County Med. Soc. (exec. coun. 1982—, chmn. ethics com. 1983—87, pres. 1987—88, editl. bd. 1995—, chair legis. commn. 1999—). Home: 228 Riverview Dr Ann Arbor MI 48104-1846 Office: 4250 Plymouth Rd Ann Arbor MI 48109 Office Phone: 734-647-8762. Business E-Mail: margolis@umich.edu.

MARGOLIS, SHERRY, newscaster; m. Jeffrey Zaslow, 1987; children: Jordan, Alexandra, Eden. BA in English, SUNY, Buffalo. Anchor and reporter WKBW-TV, Buffalo; reporter WJBK-TV, Detroit, 1984—, anchor "In the News", co-anchor 5am and noon news, anchor "Live at 11am", anchor "Fox-2 news at 5:30pm". Recipient Best News Anchor Emmys, NATAS, 1993, 1999, Cmty. Involvement award, U. Mich., 2002, Emmy Reporting, NATAS, 2002, 2006, Pub. Affairs Emmy, 2004, Award of Excellence, Mich. Assn. Broadcasters, 2004, Edward R. Murrow award, 2006; named Best Newscast in Mich., AP, 1990. Office: WJBK-TV Fox 2 PO Box 2000 Southfield MI 48037-2000

MARGOLIS, THOMAS IRA, vitreoretinal ophthalmologist; s. Herbert and Barbara M.; m. Robin Deborah Small, Mar. 12, 1989; children: Rebecca, Joshua, Jennifer. BA summa cum laude, U. Pa., 1984; MD magna cum laude, Harvard U., 1989. Cert. Am. Bd. Ophthalmology. Intern Cedars Sinai Med. Ctr., LA, 1989-90; resident Wills Eye Hosp., Phila., 1990-93; fellowship (vitreoretinal) Tufts U.-New Eng. Eye Ctr., Boston, 1993-95. Instr. ophthalmology Tufts U. Med. Sch., Boston, 1993-96; hosp. staff AtlantiCare Regional Med. Ctr., Shore Meml. Hosp., Somers Point, N.J.; prin. investigator Multi Ctr. Clin. Trials. Contbr. sci. articles to profl. jours. and chpt. to book. Pres. Atlantic County Med. Soc., 2007—08. Recipient Benjamin Franklin scholar U. Pa., 1980-84, Laurence B. Ellis scholar Harvard Med. Sch., 1987; named one of Top Docs, NJ Monthly, 2003, 05, Phila. Mag., 2004, 05, 06, 07, 08, 09, NJ Life, 2005. Mem. AMA, Am. Acad. Ophthalmology, N.J. Acad. Ophthalmology, N.J. Med. Soc., Wills Eye Hosp. Soc., N.J. Retina Soc., Am. Soc. Retina Specialists, Phi Beta Kappa. Jewish. Avocations: running, skiing, golf, tennis, travel. Office: Retinal and Ophthalmic Cons PC 1500 Tilton Rd Northfield NJ 08225-1827 also: 2466 E Chestnut Ave Vineland NJ 08360 also: Ste 102 211 S Main St Cape May Court House NJ 08210 Office Phone: 609-646-5200. Business E-Mail: vitrector@gmail.com.

MARGON, BRUCE HENRY, astrophysicist, educator; b. NYC, Jan. 7, 1948; 1 child Pamela. AB, Columbia U., 1968; MA, U. Calif.-Berkeley, 1971, PhD, 1973. Asst. rsch. astronomer U. Calif.-Berkeley, 1973—76; assoc. prof. astronomy UCLA, 1976—80; prof. astronomy U. Wash., Seattle, 1980—2001; chmn., 1981—87, 1990—95, sci. dir. Sloan Digital Sky Survey, 1998—99; assoc. dir. Space Telescope Sci. Inst., Balt., 2001—06; vice chancellor rsch., prof. astronomy and astrophysics U. Calif., Santa Cruz, 2006—. Bd. govs. Astrophys. Rsch. Consortium, Inc., Seattle; chmn. bd. dirs. AURA, Inc., Washington; co-investigator Hubble space telescope NASA, Washington, 1977—. NATO postdoctoral fellow, 1973-74; Sloan Found. rsch. fellow, 1979-83 Fellow AAAS, Am. Phys. Soc.; mem. Internat. Astron. Union, Am. Astron. Soc. (Pierce Prize 1981), Royal Astron. Soc. Office: Univ Calif Chancellors Office 1156 High St Santa Cruz CA 95064 Office Phone: 831-459-2425.

MARGOSHES, MIRIAM KAGAN, information specialist; b. Cambridge, Mass., Feb. 10, 1932; d. Baruch and Raizl (Rozinko) Kagan; m. Marvin Margoshes, Aug. 7, 1955; children: Bethia Anne, Sara Amy, Jessa Abi, Dan Raphael. BS, Simmons Coll., 1953; MS, CUNY, 1976. Cert. libr. media specialist NY. Libr. aide Harvard U. Librs., Cambridge, 1947-53; asst. libr. Wheelock Coll., Boston, 1954-57; libr., cons. Combined Book Exhibit, Briarcliff Manor, N.Y., 1971-73; instrnl. svcs. libr. Westchester C.C., Valhalla, N.Y., 1974-77; libr. dir., editor Pergamon Press, Inc., Elmsford, N.Y., 1978-83; libr. supr. Joseph E. Seagram & Sons, NYC, 1984-87; sr. rsch. assoc. House of Seagram, NYC, 1987-92; database specialist Towers Perrin, Valhalla, 1992—2004, ret., 2004; sr. database specialist IC/KM; part-time libr. Hastings Pub. Libr., 2005—. Cons. D.C. Welfare Dept., Washington, 1965-70; libr. cons. Pocantico Hills (N.Y.) Sch., 1973-74. Contbr. articles to profl. jours. Trustee Bethesda-Chevy Chase Libr. Bd., Md., 1968-71; dist. leader Tarrytown Dem. Com., 1972-74; trustee Temple Beth Abraham, Tarrytown, NY, 1980-89, 100th Anniversary publicity com., 1999-2000; chmn., sec. Warner Libr. Bd., Tarrytown, 1982, 84-94; trustee, sec. Westchester Libr. Sys. Bd., Elmsford, 1984-89, v.p. adv. com.; active Kerry/Edwards office, NYC, 2004; libr. vol. Anti-Defamation League, 2004-05; vol. Mus. Modern Art, 2005-. Recipient Luminary award Westchester Libr. Sys., 1999. Mem. Spl. Librs. Assn., Hadassah. Avocations: travel, cultural anthropology, aerobics. Personal E-mail: mirkamar@verizon.net.

MARGULES, CECELIA, composer, poet; b. Stockholm, Apr. 11, 1947; d. Morris Berkowitz; m. Rubin Margules, June 5, 1971; children: Julie, Rachyl, Adam. BA, Bklyn. Coll., 1970; Interior Design Degree, N.Y. Sch. Interior Design. Design cons. ARM Mgmt. Co., Bklyn., 1985—. Composer N.Y.C. Parks Dept., Emma Lazarus tribute, 2004, Celebration '350'. Contbr. articles and poetry to profl. jours.; contbg. editor: Harmony, 1987; composer: (songs) Guiliani, 1987, New Sinai Sound, 2005, Power of Good Concert, 2008 (Hon. Heroes of Holocaust), Emma Lazarus Tribute, 2008; Chords of Hope Concerts Robert Dielsky son of Defiance Movie, 2009. Chmn. Yossi Berger Holocaust Study Ctr., 1990—; cultural chmn. Jewish Heritage, NYC; bd. dirs. Jewish Cmty. Rels. Coun., NYC, 2000—. Recipient State of Israel Bonds award, 1996, Woman of Valor award, Coun. Jewish Orgns., 2003, 1st prize Zionist nat. song contest, Am. Zionist Movement, 1998. Mem.: Emunah of Am. (v.p., Kristallnacht Commemoration chmn. 2006, Woman of the Yr. 1991). Jewish. Personal E-mail: ceceliamar2@aol.com, ceceliaproductions@yahoo.com.

MARGULIES, BETH ZELDES, state attorney general; b. Hartford, Conn., Apr. 24, 1954; d. Benjamin and Edith Rose (Herrmann) Zeldes; m. Martin B. Margulies, July 26, 1981; children: Max, Adam. BA in Anthropology, McGill U., Montreal, 1976; JD summa cum laude, U. Bridgeport, 1983; LLM, Yale U., 1985. Bar: Conn. 1983, US Dist. Ct. Conn. 1983, US Ct. Appeals (DC cir.) 1988, US Supreme Ct., 1989, US Ct. Appeals (2d cir.) 1992. Asst. atty. gen. Atty. Gen.'s Office State of Conn., Hartford, 1985—. Contbr. articles to profl. jours. Office: Atty Gen Office State of Conn 55 Elm St Hartford CT 06106-1746 Office Phone: 860-808-5340. Business E-Mail: beth.margulies@po.state.ct.us.

MARGULIES, JAMES HOWARD, editorial cartoonist; b. Bklyn., Oct. 8, 1951; s. Henry Norman and Miriam Margulies; m. Martha Anne Golub, May 21, 1978; children: Elana, David. BFA, Carnegie-Mellon

U., 1973. Editorial cartoonist Jour. Newspapers, Springfield, Va., 1980-84, Houston Post, 1984-90, The Record, Hackensack, NJ, 1990—. Syndicated cartoonist various newspapers, 1985—. Author: My Husband Is Not a Wimp, 1988, Hitting Below the Beltway, 1998; contbr. columns to profl. jours.; cartoons featured on TV programs. Mem. leadership com. Jewish Community Ctr., Houston, 1987, 88. Recipient Best Cartoon award Population Inst., 1985, Global Media award, 1985, 2d Place Editl. award Pavillion of Humor, 1985, Judges award World Hunger Media awards, 1986, Katie award Press Club of Dallas, 1989, Best Black and White Illustration in Advt. and Graphic Arts Addy award Houston Advt. Fedn., 1990, John Peter Zenger award N.Y. State Bar Assn., 1992, Nat. Headliner award for editl. cartoons Press Club of Atlantic City, 1996, 1st prize Fischetti Editl. Cartoon Competition, Columbia Coll., Chgo., 1996, Deadline Club award for editl. cartoons N.Y. chpt. Soc. Profl. Journalists, 1998, 1st pl. for editl. cartoons Garden State Assn. of Black Journalists, 1999-2003, 3d Pl. Nat. Headliner awards for Editl. Cartoons. Press Club of Atlantic City, 2003, 04; named One of Texans Who Made the Eighties Winter, Ultra mag., 1990, Cartoonist of the Yr. Nat. Press Found., 2005, Berryman Cartoonist of Yr. Nat. Press Found., DC, 2005, Clarion award, for editl. cartoons, Assn. for Women in Comm., 2007, 08. Mem. Assn. Am. Editl. Cartoonists. Avocation: running. Office: The Record 7th Fl PO Box 471 1 Garret Mountain Plz Woodland Park NJ 07424-0471 E-mail: jimmarg@aol.com.

MARGULIES, JULIANNA, actress; b. Spring Valley, NY, June 8, 1966; m. Keith Lieberthal, Nov. 10, 2007; 1 child, Kieran Lindsay. BA, Sarah Lawrence Coll., 1989. Actress:(films) Out for Justice, 1991, Traveller, 1997, Paradise Road, 1997, A Price Above Rubies, 1997, The Newton Boys, 1998, The Big Day, 1999, What's Cooking, 2000, (voice only) Dinosaur, 2000, Ten Unknowns, 2001 (Lucille Lortel Award for outstanding featured actress, 2001), The Man From Elysian Fields, 2001, (voice only) Love Gets You Twisted, 2002, Ghost Ship, 2002, Evelyn, 2002, Slingshot, 2005, The Darwin Awrds, 2006, Snakes on a Plane, 2006; (TV series) Philly Heat, 1994, ER, 1994-2000 (Emmy award for supporting actress Drama, 1995, Golden Globe award winner, 1998, SAG award winner 1997, 98, 99), Canterbury's Law, 2008-; (TV mini-series) The Grid, 2004; (TV movies) The Mists of Avalon, 2001, Jenifer, 2001, Hitler: The Rise of Evil, 2003; (TV appearances) Law & Order, 1993, Murder, She Wrote, 1993, Homicide: Life on the Street, 1994, Scrubs, 2004, The Sopranos, 2006, '07; (theater appearances) The Substance of Fire, At Home, Fefu and Her Friends, The Substance of Fire, Living Expenses, Dan Drift, Book of Names, Balm in Gilead, In the Boom Boom Room, The Vagina Monologues, 2000, Festen, 2006.

MARGULIES, MARTIN B., lawyer, educator; b. NYC, Oct. 6, 1940; s. Max N. and Mae (Cohen) M.; m. Beth Ellen Zeldes, July 26, 1981; children: Max Zeldes, Adam Zeldes. AB, Columbia Coll., 1961; LLB, Harvard U., 1964; LLM, NYU, 1966. Bar: N.D. 1968, N.Y. 1974, Mass. 1977, Conn. 1988, U.S. Dist. Ct. Mass. 1977, U.S. Ct. Appeals (2d cir.) 1984, U.S. Supreme Ct. 1995. Asst. prof. law U. N.D., Grand Forks, 1966-69; editor-in-chief Columbia Coll. Today, Columbia U., NYC, 1969-71; assoc. editor Parade Mag., NYC, 1971-72; assoc. prof. law Western New Eng. Law Sch., Springfield, Mass., 1973-76; Bernard Hersher prof. law U. Bridgeport, Conn., 1977-92; Neil H. Cogan Pub. Svc. prof. law Quinnipiac U., 1997-99, prof. law, 1992—2005, prof. emeritus, 2005—. Author: The Early Life of Sean O'Casey, 1970, The Battle of Prestonpans 1745, 2007; contbr. articles to profl. jours. Cooperating atty. Conn. Civil Liberties Union, Hartford, 1979—, bd. dirs., 1982-94; bd. dirs. Conn. Attys. for Progressive Legislature, New Haven, 1982: bd. dirs. ACLU, 1987-94, mem. free speech-assn. and poverty constl. rights com., 1988-94; chmn. bd. dirs. Fairfield County Civil Liberties Union, 1982-87, Hampden County Civil Liberties Union, 1976-78; bd. dirs. Civil Liberties Union Mass., Boston, 1975-78, Greater Springfield Urban League, 1976-78, Conn. Civil Liberties Union, 1982-94, ACLU, 1987-94, Ctr. for First Amendment Rights, Inc., 1993—. Recipient Media award, NY State Bar Assn., 1972, Gavel award, ABA, 1973, Outstanding Tchr. award, U. Bridgeport Law Sch., 1986, 1987. Mem. Mass. Bar Assn., N.Y. State Bar Assn. Jewish. Home: 79 High Rock Rd Sandy Hook CT 06482-1623 Office: Quinnipiac Univ Sch Law 275 Mt Carmel Ave Hamden CT 06518-1947 Home Phone: 203-270-9255; Office Phone: 203-582-3252. Personal E-mail: mmargulies023@earthlink.net.

MARGULIS, ALEXANDER RAFAILO, physician, educator; b. Belgrade, Yugoslavia, Mar. 21, 1921; arrived in U.S., 1946; s. Rafailo and Olga (Weiss-Belic) Margulis; m. Hedvig Hricak, Feb. 26, 1983; 1 child, Peter Hricak. Student, U. Belgrade, 1939—41, student, 1945—46; MD, Harvard U., 1950; Doctorate (hon.), Aix-Marseille U., 1980, Med. Coll. Wis., 1986, Cath. U. Louvain, 1986, Karolinska Inst., Stockholm, 1986, U. Munich, 1987, U. Toulouse, 1987, U. Montpellier, 1993, U. Novi Sad, 2005. Diplomate Am. Bd. Radiology. Intern Henry Ford Hosp., Detroit, 1950—51; resident in radiology U. Mich. Hosps., 1951—53; jr. clin. instr. U. Mich., 1953—54; instr., then asst. prof. U. Minn., 1954—59; asst. prof. sch. medicine Washington U., St. Louis, 1959—60, assoc. prof. to prof., 1960—63; prof. radiology, chmn. dept. U. Calif., San Francisco, 1963—89, dir. magnetic resonance Sci. Ctr., assoc. chancellor spl. projects, 1989—93, spl. cons. to vice chancellor, 1993—2000; clin. prof. radiology Cornell U. Weill Med. Coll., NYC, 2000—; radiologist N.Y.-Presbyn. Med. Ctr., 2000—. Radiologist in chief U. Calif. Hosps., 1963—89; cons. VA Hosp., Letterman Gen. Hosp., San Francisco, U.S. Naval Hosp., Oakland, Calif.; cons. in radiology Office Surgeon Gen., 1967—71. Author (with others): Roentgen Diagnosis of Abdominal Tumors in Childhood, 1957; editor: Modern Alimentary Tract Radiology, Opinion in Radiology, 1988—91; co-editor: Alimentary Tract Roentgenology; editl. bd. Calif. Medicine, 1964—74, Radiology, 1975—93, assoc. editor Investigative Radiology, 1980—89; author: Be in Charge: A Leadership Manual, 2002, The Road to Success (How to get to the top of your profession), 2006. Capt. US Army, 1957—59. Recipient Cannon medal, Soc. Radiol., 1977, Gold medal, Am. Roentgen Ray Soc., 1988, J.P. Allyn medal, P. Roberts Rsch. Inst., 1989, Gold medal, Am. Coll. Radiology, 1999, UCSF medal, 2000; named to Hall of Honor, U. Mich. Med. Sch., 2006. Fellow: Internat. Soc. Mgmt. Res. Medicine, Hongkong Coll. Radiol., Royal Coll. Radiologists (hon.); mem.: AMA (cons. drugs 1961—), Radiol. Soc. Korea, Internat. Soc. Strategic Studies in Radiology (founding pres. 1995—), Royal Coll. Radiologists of Thailand, Polish Soc. Radiology, Thai Coll. Radiology, Chinese Radiol. Soc., Russian Radiol. Soc., Royal Coll. Surgeons Ireland, French Radiol. Soc., Swiss Radiol. Soc., Italian Radiol. Soc., Russian Acad. Scis. (fgn.), Serbian Acad. Scis. (fgn.), Soc. Magnetic Resonance in Medicine (pres. 1983—84), Calif. Acad. Medicine (pres. 1978), San Francisco Radiol. Soc. (pres. 1973—74), Radiol. Soc. N.Am. (Gold medal 1983), Rocky Mountain Radiol. Soc. (hon.), German Radiol. Soc. (hon.), Japan Radiol. Soc. (hon.), Soc. Chmn. Acad. Radiology Depts. (pres. 1968—69), Am. Gastroenterology Assn., Assn. Univ. Radiologists (pres. 1966—67, chmn. adv. com. acad. radiology 1971, pres. 1971), Roentgen Ray Soc., NAS-Inst. Medicine, U. Mich. Med. Sch. Hall Honor. Business E-Mail: arm2001@med.cornell.edu.

MARGULIS, GREGORY A., mathematics and science professor, researcher; b. Moscow, Feb. 24, 1946; came to U.S., 1991; s. Alexander Y. Margulis and Tsilya M. Osherenko; m. Raisa T. Kristal, Aug. 30, 1972; 1 child, Boris. Diploma, Moscow U., 1967, PhD, 1970; DSc, Belorrussian Acad. Scis., Minsk, 1983. Rschr. Inst. Problems in Info. Transmission, Soviet Acad. Scis., Moscow, 1970-91; prof. math. Yale U., New Haven, 1991—. Mem. sci. adv. coun. Math. Scis. Rsch. Inst., Berkeley, Calif., 1993-97; mem. sci. adv. bd. Clay Math. Inst., Cambridge, Mass., 2003. Author: Discrete Subgroups of Semisimple Lie Groups, 1991, Theory of Anosov Systems, 2004; mem. editl. bd. math. jours. Recipient prize for young mathematicians Moscow Math. Soc., 1968, Fields medal Internat. Math. Union, 1978, Humboldt Found. prize, 1995, Lobachevski prize Russian Acad. Scis., 1996, Wolf prize in math. Wolf Found., Israel, 2005. Mem. AAAS (fgn. hon.), NAS. Avocations: chess, jogging, swimming. Home: 20 Vista Ter New Haven CT 06515-2402 Office: Yale U Dept Math 10 Hillhouse Ave New Haven CT 06511-6814

MARGULIS, LYNN (LYNN ALEXANDER), evolutionist, educator; b. Chgo., Mar. 5, 1938; d. Morris and Leone Alexander; m. Carl Sagan, June 16, 1957; children: Dorion Sagan, Jeremy Sagan; m. Thomas N. Margulis, Jan. 18, 1967; children: Zachary Margulis-Ohnuma, Jennifer Margulis di Properzio. AB, U. Chgo., 1957; MS in Zoology and Genetics, U. Wis., 1960; PhD in Genetics, U. Calif., Berkeley, 1965; D (hon.), U. Montreal, Can., 1987, U. Valencia, Spain, 2001, U. Autonome Barcelona, 2007, U. Vigo, 2007; DSc (hon.), Southeastern Mass. U., North Dartmouth, 1989, Westfield State Coll., Mass., 1989, Plymouth State Coll., NH, 1991, Tulane U., New Orleans, 1996, U. Montreal, 1997, Autonomous U. Madrid, 1998, Union Coll., Schenectady, NY, 2001, San Francisco U., Quito, Ecuador, 2001, Rutgers U., New Brunswick, 2004, Bates Coll., Lewiston, Maine, 2005, Tufts U., Medford, Mass., 2006, NC State U., Raleigh, 2006; Dr.rer.nat (hon.), U. Oldenburg, Germany, 1999. Mem. faculty Boston U., 1966—68, asst. prof. biology, 1967—71, assoc. prof., 1971—77, prof., 1977—88, Univ. prof., 1986—88; Disting. Univ. prof. U. Mass., Amherst, 1988—. Sherman Fairchild Disting. scholar Calif. Inst. Tech., 1976—77; vis. prof. dept. microbiology U. Autónoma de Barcelona, Spain, 1986, Spain, 88; Disting. univ. prof. U. Mass.; mem. com. NASA, NYNEX Awards, Nat. Sci. Resource Ctr.; mem. OEB vis. com. Harvard Coll. Author: Origin of Eukaryotic Cells, 1970, Symbiosis in Cell Evolution, 1981, Early Life, 1982, 2d edit., 2002, Symbiosis in Cell Evolution, 2d edit., 1993, Microcosmos Videos, 1999, Luminous Fish: Tales of Science and Love, 2007; editor (with Mitchell Rambler and René Fester): Global Ecology, 1989; editor: (with others) Handbook of Protoctista, 1990; co-editor (with René Fester): Symbiosis as a Source of Evolutionary Innovation: Speciation and Morphogenesis, 1991; co-editor: Concepts of Symbiogenesis: A Historical and Critical Study of the Research of Russian Botanists, 1992, Environmental Evolution: Effects of the Origin and Evolution of Life on Planet Earth, 1992, Environmental Evolution: Effects of the Origin and Evolution of Life on Planet Earth, 2d edit., 2000, Glossary of Protoctista, 1993, What is Life?, 1995, Slanted Truths: Essays on Gaia, Evolution and Symbiosis, 1997; co-editor: (with Dorion Sagan) What Is Sex?, 1998; co-editor: Diversity of Life: The Illustrated Guide to the Five Kingdoms, 2d edit., 1999, Conversations with Ian McHarg: Dwelling in Nature, 2006; co-author: Five Kingdoms, 1982, 3d edit., 1998, Microcosmos, 1986; co-author: (with Dorion Sagan) Origins of Sex, 1986; co-author: Garden of Microbial Delights, 1988, 2d edit., 1998, Biospheres From Earth To Space, 1988, Mystery Dance: On the Evolution of Human Sexuality, 1991, What Happens to Trash and Garbage: An Introduction to the Carbon Cycle, 1993, Living Sands: Mapping Time and Space with Forams, 2000, Early Life, 2d edit., 2002, Acquiring Genomes: A Theory of the Origins of Species, 2002, Peces Luminosos: Historias de Ciencia y Amor, 2002, Una Revolucion en la Evolucion, 2002; co-author: (with Andrew Wier) Vol. I Cells and Reproduction, Vol. II Evolution and Diversity; co-author: (with Lorraine Olendzenski) (videos) Looking at Microbes, An Introduction to the Microbiology Laboratory for Students, Symbiotic Planet. A New Look at Evolution, 1997; co-author: (with D. Sagan) Dazzle Gradually: Reflections on Nature in Nature, 2007; contbr. chapters to books, articles to profl. jours. Recipient Nat. Medal Sci., 1999, Humboldt Prize, 2002, Commonwealth of Mass. award, Darwin-Wallace medal, Linnean Soc. London, 2008; Guggenheim fellow, 1979. Fellow: AAAS; mem.: NAS, Internat. Soc. Study of Life, Soc. Sci. Rsch., Soc. Evolutionary Protistology (co-founder), Sigma Xi (pres. 2005—06). Office: U Mass Dept Geosci 611 No Pleasant St Amherst MA 01003-9297 Mailing: PO Box 671 Amherst MA 01004-0671 Office Phone: 413-545-3244. *We must, as E. M. Forster admonished, "only connect" and lower our population's growth rate. The sciences, the quest for knowledge about the universe and life are intrinsically unified. Like all other species ever to have lived on Earth, ours too will become extinct our demise. The quality of our demise depends decrease number of people preservation of habitat of our planetmates directly on our own population growth rates by presentation of habitat of our planetmates.*

MARGULIS, VITALY, urologist; b. Kiev, Ukraine, Sept. 4, 1975; MD, UT Southwestern Med. Sch., Dallas, 2001. Cert. Am. Bd. Urology, 2006. Urologist UT Southwestern, 2001—06; urologic oncology M.D. Anderson Cancer Ctr., Houston, 2006—. Lead advisor Nano Biotech, Dallas, 2001—08. Achievements include research in molecular biology of renal cell cancer. Office: M D Anderson Cancer Ctr 1515 Holcombe Boulevard Houston TX 77030

MARHABA, TAHA FAROUK, engineering educator; PhD in Environ. Engring., Rutgers U., NJ, 1993. Cert. profl. engr., NJ, 1995. Prof. NJ. Inst. Tech., Newark, 1995—. Contbr. articles to profl. jour. Chair various coms., Dept. Civil & Environ. Engring. Named Prof. of Yr., NJ. Inst. Tech., Am. Water Works Assoc. Achievements include research in water quality and treatment; development of spectral fluorescent signatures technique for rapid determination of organic substances in water. Office: NJ Inst Tech 323 MLK Blvd Newark NJ 07102 Office Fax: 973-596-5790. Business E-Mail: marhaba@adm.njit.edu.

MARI, GIANCARLO, obstetrician, gynecologist, educator; b. Salerno, Italy, Apr. 17, 1957; s. Michele Mari and Cecilia Scola; m. Laura Detti, May 2006; children: Michael C, Camilla A. MD, U. Naples, Italy, 1982. Resident ob-gyn. U. Parma, Italy, 1982—84, U. Napoli, Italy, 1984—86; resident ob-gyn. Sch. Medicine Yale U., New Haven, 1990—94, fellow maternal-fetal medicine Sch. of Medicine, 1994—96, asst. prof. ob-gyn. Sch. of Medicine, 1995—2000, assoc. prof. ob-gyn. Sch. of Medicine, 1999—2000; assoc. prof. ob-gyn. U. Va., Charlottesville, Va., 2000—02; prof. ob-gyn. U. Cin., 2002—04, Wayne State U., Detroit, 2004—. Dir. diagnostic endoscopy and fetal therapy Wayne State U., mem.instl. rev. bd. Hutzel Hosp., 2006; dir. prenatal diagnosis and fetal therapy U. Cin., 2002—04, U. Va., 2000—02; rsch. fellow Baylor Coll. Medicine, Houston, 1997—2000. Author: Twin-Twin-Transfusion Syndrome International Registry (The best of SMFM 1998 award SGI, 1998); mem. editl bd.: European Jour. Ob-gyn. in Reproductive Biology, Prenatal Diagnosis and Fetal Therapy. Recipient Best Paper award, Soc. Perinatal Obstetricians, 1993, John J. Meehan-Clifford R. Miller award, Dept. Ob-gyn., Yale U., 1994; named Top reviewer, Am Jour. Ob-Gyn.; named one of Best Doctors in Am., 2004, 2006. Fellow: Am. Coll. Ob-gyn.; mem.: Internat. Soc. Ultrasound in Ob-gyn. (mem. editl. bd.), Soc. Gynecologic Investigation, Soc. Maternal Fetal Medicine. Roman Catholic. Achievements include discovery of non-invsive diagnosis of fetal anemia-Many children have and will have a happy life because of this discovery. Office: Wayne State University John R Detroit MI 48202 Personal E-mail: giancarlomari@hotmail.com. Business E-Mail: gmari@med.wayne.edu.

MARIA, BERNARD L., pediatric neurologist; b. Montreal, Que., Can., Jan. 23, 1958; s. Maurice A. and Margaret Maria; m. Barbara E. Maria, Nov. 28, 1983; 1 child, Alexander. DEC, Coll. Marguerite-Bourgeois, Montreal, 1976; MD, U. Sherbrooke, Can., 1981; MBA, U. Fla., 1995. Diplomate Am. Bd. Pediatrics, Am. Bd. Neurology and Psychiatry. Resident in pediatrics McGill U., Montreal, 1981-83; resident in neurology Johns Hopkins U., Balt., 1983-86; fellow in neuro-oncology M.D. Anderson, Houston, 1986-88; asst. prof. U. Toronto, Ont., Can., 1988-90; assoc. prof. U. Fla., Gainesville, 1990-98, prof., 1998—, divsn. chief, 1990—. Founding dir. neuro-oncology group Johns Hopkins Hosp., 1984-86; founding dir. neuro-oncology program U. Fla., 1990—; lectr. in field. Editor consensus in Child Neurology, 1997—, Current Mgmt. in Child Neurology, 1999, 2002, 05; guest-editor Seminar in Child Neurology, 1997; guest editor Jour. Child Neurology, 2002-; mem. editl. bd. Jour. Child Neurology, 1995—, Pediat. Neurology, 1997—; reviewer jours. in field; contbr. articles to med. jours., chpt. to book; author monographs in field. Grantee NSC Found., 1988-90, Brain Rsch. Found., 1988-90, U. Fla., 1990, ORDCR Found., 1990, 91-97, Sigma-Tau Pharms., 1992, Stop! Children's Cancer, Inc., 1991-92, 96-97, Abbot Pharms., 1992, Parke Davis Pharms., 1992, Nat. Cancer Inst., 1992, 93, Children's Miracle Network, 1995, Depotech, Inc., 1994, Glaxo, Inc., 1995, Genetic Therapy, Inc., 1995, 96, Sturge-Weber Found., 1995, LAVFW, 1997-98, Glaxo Wellcome, 1997, Parke Davis, 1997, State of Fla., 1997-99, NINDS, 1999—, Medeva, 1998-99. Mem. AMA, Child Neurology Soc. (bylaws com. 1990-95, fin. com. 1995—), Soc. for Pediat. Rsch., Soc. for Neurosci., Pediat. Oncology Group, Profs. of Child Neurology, Internat. Child Neurology Assn., Am. Acad. Pediat., Am. Acad. Neurology, Am. Soc. Clin. Oncology, Am. Pediat. Soc., Soc. Neuro-Oncology. Office: MUSC PO Box 250514 173 Ashly Ave Ste 409 Charleston SC 29425 Home Phone: 843-884-8329; Office Phone: 843-792-7715. Business E-Mail: mariabl@musc.edu.

MARIA ANTONELLA, PELIZZARI, art history educator; b. Genoa, Italy, Apr. 24, 1964; d. Pietro Pelizzari Antonella and Ida Mosca; m. Robert John Astle; 1 child, Leonardo Peter Pelizzari-Astle. MA, U. Genoa, 1986; PhD, U. NewMex., Albuquerque, 1998. Assoc. curator Canadian Ctr. Arch., Montreal, Quebec, 1998—2004; assoc. prof. Hunter Coll., NYC, 2006—. Editl. cons. History Photography, London, 2004—; peer reviewer Mac Arthur Found., 2007, J Paul Getty Found., LA, 2008. Author: (book) Traces of India: Photography, Architecture and the Politics of Representation (CAA book prize "Historians of British Art", 2004). Recipient Premio Friuli-Venezia Giulia Fotografia, CRAF, Spilimbergo, Italy, 2003, PSC Rsch. award, CUNY, 2008; Ansel Adams Rsch. fellowship, U. Ariz, 1995, Lisette Model, Joseph G. Blum fellowship, Nat. Gallery Canada, 1997. Mem.: Coll. Art. Assoc. Office: Hunter Coll 695 Pk Ave New York NY 10025

MARIAM, THOMAS FRED, public relations executive, radio producer; b. NYC, Feb. 26, 1957; s. Rudolph Karl and Lisa Gertrud (Silbermann) Mariam; m. Alyce Beth Appleman, Aug. 20, 2000; children: Michael Reese, Madison Leah. BA in Polit. Sci., Columbia U., 1978; MS in Broadcast Journalism, Boston U., 1980. News dir. Sta. WNBP, Newburyport, Mass., 1979-80; sports dir. Sta. WKCR-FM, NYC, 1976-78; editor, writer The Wall St. Jour. Report, NYC, 1980-84; nat. copy editor Dow Jones News Svc., NYC, 1984; dir. news svcs. Am. Stock Exch., NYC, 1984-95; sr. v.p. Rubenstein Assoc. Pub. Rels., NYC, 1995-96; sr. mgr. pub. rels. Booz-Allen & Hamilton, NYC, 1996-99; dir. mktg. and comm. Cadwalader, Wickersham & Taft, NYC, 1999-2000; dir. global comm. Clifford Chance Rogers & Wells LLP, 2000—02; pres. Mariam Comms. LLC, 2002—; prodr., co-host The Metro Golf Show, 2003—. Radio sports reporter Sports Final Radio Network, 1987—; NY corr. The Sports File, 1989-93. Producer, host (radio program) Amex Business Talk, 1985-94; freelance radio sports reporter, 1986—. Voting mem. Self-Help, Inc., N.Y.C., 1985-92; trustee Congregation Habonim. Mem. ABA, Legal Mktg. Assn., N.Y. Fin. Writers Assn. (bd. dirs. 1992-99), Radio-TV News Dirs. Assn., Pub. Rels. Soc. Am. (v.p. Westchester-Fairfield chpt. 2002—), Deadline Club N.Y., Nat. Assn. Broadcasters, Nat. Assn. Sportscasters and Sportswriters, Columbia Club N.Y. (dir.-at-large 1984-96, activities chmn. 1986-94, 1st v.p. 1988-96). Democrat. Jewish. Home and Office: 89 Country Ridge Dr Rye Brook NY 10573-1046 Office Phone: 914-939-4294. Business E-Mail: tom@mariam.biz.

MARIANI, MICHAEL MATTHEW, lawyer; b. West Pittston, Pa., Sept. 25, 1950; s. Stephen Francis and Tulia Felicia (DelCorso) M.; m. Patricia Mary Leptak, June 26, 1976; children: Kathryn Elizabeth, Michael Joseph. BS with honors, Wilkes Coll., 1972; JD, St. John's U., Jamaica, NY, 1975; LLM, NYU, 1980. Bar: NY 1976, US Dist. Ct. (so. and ea. dists.) NY 1976, US Tax Ct. 1980. Law sec. to presiding judge Surrogate's Ct., New City, NY, 1976-80; assoc. Law offices of Edward S. Schlesinger P.C., NYC, 1981-97; sr. v.p., dep. gen. trust counsel, dir. trust and estate svcs. Fiduciary Trust Co. Internat., NYC, 1997—. Adj. prof. law St. John's Univ. Sch. Law, Jamaica, NY, 2005—. Co-author: New York Probate, 1986, supplements 1987-2009; contbr. articles to profl. jours. Trustee Cath. Charities, Diocese of Bklyn., 1981—2005, treas., 1985—87, v.p., 1987—89, pres., 1989—91; bd. dirs. Mercy Home for Children, Bklyn., 1989—97, mem. adv. bd., 1997—; mem. profl. adv. bd. Calvary Hosp., 2002—; mem. Founders Affiliate bd. dirs. Am. Heart Assn., 2004—. Recipient Benemerenti medal Pope John Paul II, 1997. Mem. ABA (real property, probate and trust law sects.), NY State Bar Assn. (trusts and estates sects.), Assn. Bar City NY. Democrat. Home: 53-32 215th St Bayside NY 11364-1835 Office: 600 Fifth Ave New York NY 10020-2302 Office Phone: 212-632-3255. Business E-Mail: mmariani@ftci.com.

MARIANO, ANA VIRGINIA, retired pathologist; b. Baguio City, The Philippines, Nov. 20, 1938; came to US, 1963; d. Celestino Chuongco and Ana (Tanseco) Juan; m. Gregorio Torres Mariano, June 4, 1966; children: Joel, Eric, Greg, Anita. AA, U. St. Tomas, Manila, 1957, MD, 1962. Bd. cert. in anatomic pathology and clin. pathology Am. Bd. Pathology; lic. physician, NY, Pa. Med. intern Youngstown Hosp., Ohio, 1963; pathology resident I RI Hosp., Providence, 1964; pathology resident II-IV Wayne State U. Med. Sch., Detroit, 1965-68; assoc. pathologist Newark-Wayne Cmty. Hosp., Newark, NY, 1979-83; interim pathologist Clifton Springs Hosp., NY, 1983; lab. dir. and acting lab. dir. VA Med. Ctr., Altoona, Pa., 1995—97, staff pathologist, 1997-99. Locum tenens Altoona Hosp., Pa., 1999-2001; mem. courtesy med. staff Newark-Wayne Cmty. Hosp., 1983-92, Clifton Springs Hosp., NY, 1983-89; mem. adv. bd. Cath. Physicians Guild, Rochester, NY, 1991-92; cons. in pathology VA Med. Ctr., Altoona, 1993-96. Tchr. religious edn. St. Michael's Ch., Newark, 1978-80, 82-84. Fellow Am. Soc. Clin. Pathologists, Coll. Am. Pathologists. Roman Catholic. Avocations: swimming, aerobics, gardening.

MARI APARICI, CARINA, nuclear medicine physician; d. Gabriel Arcangel Mari and Dorita Aparici; m. William Monroe Whittle, July 15, 2000; 1 child, Brigitte Beatriz Whittle. MD, U. Valencia, 1992. Nuc. medicine specialist Stanford, Calif., 2005. Asst. prof. in residence U. Calif, San Francisco, 2005—08; chief nuc. medicine San Francisco VA, 2005—.

MARIASH, CARY NORMAN, medical educator, researcher; b. San Francisco, May 5, 1947; s. Irving Isadore and Estelle (Neiger) M.; m. Ami Nehira, June 20, 1970; children: Andrea, Evan. MD, U. Calif., San Diego, 1972. Diplomate Am. Bd. Internal Medicine. Diplomate Am. Bd. Endocrinology and Metabolism. Instr., medicine U. Minn., Mpls., 1979-80, asst. prof., 1980-85, assoc. prof., 1985-92, prof., 1992—, prof., cell biology and neuroanatomy, 1992—. Cons. Merit Rev. Bd., 1985-88; cons. physiologic chemistry, NIH, 1989-93; cons. London Diagnostics, Eden Prairie, Minn., 1988-89. Maj. U.S. Army, 1975-77. Recipient NIH rsch. grant, 1984—. Avocations: computer programming, commercial pilot. Office Phone: 317-962-0966. Business E-Mail: cmariash@clarian.org.

MARIENTHAL, GEORGE, telecommunications industry executive; b. Kansas City, Mo., Nov. 15, 1938; s. George and Sadie (James) M.; children: Shawn Ann Capon, Patrick James, Shannon Lee Van Winter. BS, U.S. Naval Acad., 1962; MS, Stanford U., 1963; MBA, Am. U., 1974. Sr. rsch. assoc. Logistics Mgmt. Inst., Washington, 1967-71; dir. regional ops. EPA, 1971-75, dir. water policy, 1984-85; dep. asst. sec. def. Dept. Def., Washington, 1975-81; v.p. Survival Tech., Inc., Bethesda, Md., 1981-84; dep. asst. sec. agr. Dept. Agr., Washington, 1985-86; dep. adv. programs Titan Systems, Inc., 1986-87; mgr. mktg. Computer Scis. Corp., Falls Church, Va., 1987-89; v.p. Verizon Business, Vienna, 1989—2007; pres. RTB Sys., Naples, Fla., 2007—. Bd. dirs. Home Security Title Ins. Co. Served with USAF, 1962-67. Mem.: Nat. Def. Indsl. Assn., Internat. Telephone Pioneers Assn., Armed Forces Comms. and Electronics Assn., Masons. Republican. Episcopalian. Home: 1280 10th Ave N Naples FL 34102-5428

MARIMOW, WILLIAM K. (BILL MARIMOW), editor; b. Phila., Aug. 4, 1947; s. Jay and Helen Alma (Gitnig) M.; m. Diane K. Macomb, Oct. 18, 1969; children: Ann Esther, Scott Macomb. BA, Trinity Coll., Conn., 1969. Asst. editor Comml. Car Jour., Chilton Co., Bala Cynwyd, Pa., 1969-70; asst. to econ. columnist Phila. Bull., 1970-72; staff writer Phila. Inquirer, 1972—, city hall bur. chief, 1979-81, editor Main Line Neighbors, 1986-87, NJ editor, 1987-89, city editor, 1989-91; city editor, asst. to pub. Phila. Inquirer & Daily News, 1991-93; met. editor Balt. Sun, 1993, assoc. mng. editor, 1993—95, mng. editor, 1995—2000, editor, sr. v.p., 2000—04; mng. editor Nat. Pub. Radio, Washington, 2004—05, v.p. news & info., 2006, ombudsman, 2006; editor Phila. Inquirer, 2006—. Instr. urban studies U. Pa., 1979; instr. English Rutgers U., Camden, NJ, 1981; nominating jury Pulitzer Prize, 1991—92, 1996—97, 2002—03, 2007; bd. fellows Trinity Coll., 1998—2000, bd. trustees, 2008—; mem. adv. bd. Knight Ctr. for Specialized Journalism at U. Md., 1999—2000; bd. visitors U. Md. Sch. Journalism, 2000—; mem. nat. adv. bd. Poynter Inst., 2004—. Recipient 1st place award for team reporting, Phila. Press. Assn., 1977, 1st place award for deadline reporting, AP Mng. Editors Pa., 1977, 1st place award for best news story, Sigma Delta Chi Phila., 1977, 2nd place award for deadline reporting, 1980, 2nd place award for investigative reporting, Keystone Press Assn., 1978, 1985, 1st place award for best news story, 1982, Pulitzer Prize for disting pub. svc., 1978, Nat. Pub. Svc. award, Sigma Delta Chi, 1978, Robert F. Kennedy Journalism award, 1978, Roy W. Howard Pub. Svc. award, Scripps-Howard Found., 1978, Silver Gavel award, ABA, 1978, 1982, Media Achievement award, Phila. Bar. Assn., 1982, William Schnader award, Pa. Bar Assn., 1982, Alumni Achievement award, Trinity Coll., 1984, Nat. Headliners award, 1985, Pulitzer Prize for investigative reporting, 1985; Nieman fellow, Harvard U., 1982—83. Mem. Am. Soc. Newspaper Editors, Pen & Pencil Club, Investigative Reporters & Editors, Inc. (1st place for radio reporting, 2004). Office: Phila Inquirer PO Box 8263 Philadelphia PA 19101 Office Phone: 215-854-4141.*

MARIN, CHEECH (RICHARD ANTHONY MARIN), actor, writer, director; b. LA, July 13, 1946; s. Oscar and Elsa Meza M.; m. Rikki Marin, Nov. 1, 1975 (div.); 1 child; m. Patti Heid, Apr. 1, 1986; 2 children. BS, Calif. State U., Northridge. Co-founder improvisational group, City Works, Vancouver; formed comedy duo with Tommy Chong called Cheech and Chong; appeared in clubs throughout U.S., Can., Europe and Australia including Carnegie Hall, JFK Ctr.; recs. include Sleeping Beauty, Cheech and Chong, Big Bamba, Los Cochinos (Grammy award best comedy), The Wedding Album, Get Out of My Room, Born in East L.A., (films) Up in Smoke, 1978, Cheech & Chong's Next Movie, 1980, Nice Dreams, 1981, It Came from Hollywood, 1982, Yellow Beard, 1983, Things Are Tough All Over, 1982, Still Smokin', 1983, The Corsican Brothers, 1984, After Hours, 1984 (Best Film award Havanna Film Festival 1987, Best Screenplay), Echo Park, 1985, Fatal Beauty, 1987, Rude Awakening, 1988, Oliver and Company (voice only), 1988, Troop Beverly Hills, 1989, Ghost Busters II, 1989, Shrimp on the Barbie, 1990, Fern Gully: The Last Rainforest (voice), 1993, The Lion King (voice), 1994, A Million to Juan, 1994, Ring of the Muscateers, 1994, Mr. Payback, 1995, Desperado, 1995, Dusk til Dawn, 1995, Tin Cup, 1995, Great White Hype, 1995, Santa Bugito (voice), 1995. Paulie, 1998, Luminarias, 2000, Spy Kids, 2001, Spy Kids 2: Island of Lost Dreams, 2002, Pinocchio (voice), 2002, Spy Kids 3-D: Game Over, 2003, Once Upon a Time in Mexico, 2003, Christmas with the Kranks, 2004, Underclassman, 2005, (voice) Cars, 2006, (voice) Tales from Earthsea, 2006, Grindhouse, 2007, Planet Terror, 2007, The Perfect Game, 2008, (voice) Beverly Hills Chihuahua, 2008; (video) Get Out of My Room, 1986 (Gold Cert. award); writer, dir., star (movie) Born in East L.A., 1987 (Grammy nomination 1986, Best Art Direction); co-writer title song Up in Smoke; producer, writer, actor, dir. (TV series) Culture Clash, 1991, Nash Bridges, 1996—2001, Lost, 2007-08; actor: Golden Palace, 1992; (TV movie) The Cisco Kid, 1994; concerts USA, Can., Europe and Australia; (TV) Latino Laugh Festival, 1997; dir. (Broadway) Latinologues, 2005. Recipient Grammy award for Los Cochinos, Best Comedy Rec., 1973

MARIN, DEBORAH B., psychiatrist, educator; b. Cleve., Oct. 9, 1957; d. Emanuel and Klara Blumenthal; m. Michael Marin; children: Lea, Max. BA, Wellesley Coll., 1979; MD, Mt. Sinai Med. Sch., 1984. Resident Mt. Sinai Med. Ctr., NYC, 1984—88; fellowship Cornell U., 1988—92; vice chair, prof. psychiatry Mt. Sinai Med. Ctr., NYC, 1992—, exec. v.p. for strategic devel., chief med. officer, 2004—; dean clin. rsch. Mt. Sinai Med. Sch., NYC, 2003—. Office: Mt Sinai Med Ctr 1425 Madison Ave New York NY 10029 E-mail: deborah.marin@mssm.edu.*

MARIN, ROSARIO, state agency administrator, former federal agency administrator; b. Mexico City, Mex., Aug. 4, 1958; m. Alex Marin; children: Eric, Carmen, Alvaro. BS bus. adminstrn., Calif. State U., LA, 1983, LLD (hon.), 2002; grad., Harvard U., 1998. With City Nat. Bank, Beverly Hills, 1981—86; chief legis. affairs Calif. Dept. Devel. Svcs., 1992—93; chair Calif. State Coun. Developmental Disabilities, 1994—96; asst. dep. dir. Calif. State Dept. Social Svcs., 1996—97; dep. dir. Gov.'s Office Cmty. Rels., LA, 1997—98; mayor City of Huntington Park, Calif., 1999—2000; 41st U.S. treas. U. S. Dept. Treasury, Washington, 2001—03. Mem. Calif. Integrated Waste Mgmt. Bd., Sacramento, 2004—, chmn., 2004—. Recipient Rose Fitzgerald Kennedy award, U.N., 1995, Excellence in Pub. Svc. award, Latino Perspective Conf., 2000, Alumna of the Year, Calif. State U., 2002. Address: State and Consumer Svcs Agy 915 Capitol Mall #200 Sacramento CA 95814

MARINA, NEYSSA, pediatrician, educator; MD, U. PR Med. Sci. Campus, 1983. Cert. Am. Bd. Pediat., 1990. Asst. mem. St. Jude Children's Rsch. Hosp., Memphis, 1989—95, assoc. mem., 1995—95; assoc. prof. Stanford U., Calif., 1996—2001, prof. pediat., 2001—. Mem.: Alfa Omega Alfa. Office: Stanford U Med Ctr 1000 Welch Rd Ste 300 Palo Alto CA 94304-1812 Office Fax: 650-723-5231. Business E-Mail: neyssa.marina@stanford.edu.

MARINACCIO, BRIDGET C., social sciences educator; d. Sandra A. Kennedy; m. Carmen Marinaccio, Aug. 14, 1993; children: Ashley A., Carmen, Andre F., Dominic, Julian A, Benjamin. PhD, SUNY, Buffalo, 2001. Rape crisis cousnelor NY, 1995. Chair social scis. Medaille Coll., Buffalo, 2003—, program dir., 2003—06. Clin. counselor Amherst Family Counseling, NY, 1995—. Author: (text book) Counseling Children and Adolescents. Scholar, Buffalo's Bus. First, 2006. Mem.: Am. Couseling Assn. (profl. standards com. 2004—06), NY Mental Health Counseling (assoc.; dir. buffalo/niagara region 2002—06). Office: Medaille Coll 18 Agassiz Cir Buffalo NY 14214 Personal E-mail: drbmarin@aol.com.

MARINATTO, JOHN, sports association executive; b. Providence; B in Bus. Mgmt., Providence Coll., 1979. Assoc. dir. alumni devel. Providence Coll., dir. sports info., athletic dir., 1988—2002; COO, sr. assoc. commr. Big East Conf., Providence, 2002—. Chmn. athletic dirs. fin. com. Big East Conf., 1992—93, chmn. athletic dirs. exec. com., 1996—2000, chmn. student-athlete adv. com., men's, women's basketball com., TV com., academic affairs com., championships and competition com.; mem. NCAA Mgmt. Coun., NCAA Bus. and Fin. Cabinet; Big East rep. NCAA Leadership Coun.; chief fin. and bus. officer Bowl Championship Series, 2002—04. Office: Big East Conf 222 Richmond St Ste 110 Providence RI 02903*

MARINCOLA, ELIZABETH MARK, nonprofit executive; b. New Haven, Conn., Aug. 31, 1959; d. James B.D. and Jean M. (Rambar) Mark; m. Francesco M. Marincola, Jan. 1, 1982; children: James Paul, Paula Rambar, Rachel Angela. AB, Stanford U., 1981, MBA, 1986. Dir. devel. Stanford (Calif.) U. Hosp., 1987-90; dep. dir. policy rsch. analysis NIMH, Rockville, Md., 1990-91; exec. dir. The Am. Soc. Cell Biology, Bethesda, Md., 1991—2005; pres. Soc. for Sci. & the Pub., 2005—; pub. Science News, Wash., DC. Mem. cell biology com. of visitors NSF, 2001; com. for divsn. on earth and life studies Nat. Acad. Sci., 2001—; mem. PubMed Ctrl. Nat. adv. com. Nat. Libr. of Medicine Nat. Inst. Health, 2000-03; 20th Annual Fae Golden Kass lectr. Harvard Med. Sch., 1999; mem. adv. bd. Krasnow Inst. for Advanced Study, George Mason U., 2002—; elected first citizen mem. Am. Soc. Cell Biology, 2003; mem. Coalition for Life Sci., 1991—, exec. dir., 1991-2005. Mem. stratetic adv. bd. Thomson Sci., 2005; bd. dirs., mem. fin. com. Pub. Libr. Sci., 2005—. Office: Soc for Sci & the Public 1719 N St NW Washington DC 20036 Office Phone: 202-785-2255. Business E-Mail: emarincola@societyforscience.org.

MARINE, CLYDE LOCKWOOD, agricultural products supplier, consultant; b. Knoxville, Tenn., Dec. 25, 1936; s. Harry H. and Idelle (Larue) M.; m. Eleanor Harb, Aug. 9, 1958; children: Cathleen, Sharon. BS in Agr., U. Tenn., 1958; MS in Agrl. Econs., U. Ill., 1959; PhD in Agrl. Econs., Mich. State U., 1963. Sr. market analyst Pet Milk Co., St. Louis, 1963-64; mgr. market planning agr. chems. div. Mobile Chem. Co., Richmond, Va., 1964-67; mgr. ingredient purchasing Central Soya Co., Ft. Wayne, Ind., 1970-73, corp. economist, 1967-70, v.p. ingredient purchasing, 1973-75, sr. v.p., 1975-90; pres. Marine Assocs., Ft. Wayne, 1991—; bd. dirs. SCAN, 1992—. Mem. agrl. policy adv. com. U.S.D.A. Bd. dirs. Ft. Wayne Fine Arts Found., 1976-79, Ft. Wayne Pub. Transp. Corp., 1975-83; chair, Libr. Found., Metro Human Rels. Commn., Kids First Found. Bd., v.p. Ft. Wayne Philharm., 1974-76. Served with U.S. Army, 1959-60. Mem. Nat. Soybean Processors Assn. (chmn.), U.S. C. of C., Am. Agrl. Econs. Assn., Am. Feed Mfrs. Assn. (chmn. purchasing coun.). Clubs: Ft. Wayne Country. Episcopalian. Office: Marine Assocs 4646 W Jefferson Blvd Fort Wayne IN 46804-6842 Office Phone: 260-436-4180. Business E-Mail: lmarine@proparkwest.com.

MARINE, MICHAEL W., former ambassador; b. NYC, 1947; m. Carmella Marine; adopted children: Jessica, Margaret. BA summa cum laude in Chinese Hist., U. Calif., Santa Barbara, 1974. With Fgn. Svc. US Dept. State, Washington, 1975—; polit. officer US Embassy, Hong Kong, 1982—85; various positions US Dept. State, Washington, 1985—91; dep. chief of mission US Embassy, Suva, Fiji, 1991—93, charge d' affaires, 1993—94, min. counselor for consular affairs Bonn, 1994—95, Moscow, 1995—97, dep. chief of mission Nairobi, Kenya, 1997—2000, charge d' affaires, 1999, dep. chief of mission Beijing, 2000—04; US amb. to Vietnam US Dept. State, Hanoi, 2004—07. Advanced through grades to capt. USMC, 1967—71. Recipient Superior Honor award, US Dept. State, 1981, 1990, 1993, 1999, 2001—02.

MARINE, SUSAN SONCHIK, analytical chemist, educator; b. Maple Heights, Ohio, Mar. 10, 1954; d. Stephen Robert and Gloria Ann (Hach) Sonchik; m. Michael David Marine; 1 child, Matthew Robert Marine. BS in Chemistry magna cum laude, John Carroll U., Cleve., 1975; MS in Analytical Chemistry, Case Western Res. U., Cleve., 1978; PhD in Phys. Chemistry, Case Western Res. U., 1980. Asst. chemist Horizons Research Inc., Beachwood, Ohio, 1974-75; chemist specialist Standard Oil of Ohio, Warrensville Heights, Ohio, 1975-79; organic chemistry br. mgr. Versar, Inc., Springfield, Va., 1980-83; mgr. gas chromatography program IBM Instruments Inc., Danbury, Conn., 1983-87, radiation safety officer, 1985-87; expert witness, cons. Martin, Craig, Chester & Sonnenschein, Chgo., 1981-83; adv. engr. in advanced lithography IBM Corp., Essex Junction, Vt., 1987-95; vis. assoc. prof. chemistry Centre Coll., Danville, Ky., 1995-98; asst. prof. chemistry and biochemistry, coord. tech. program Miami U., Middletown, Ohio, 1998—2004; spl. term appointment energy sys. divsn. Argonne Nat. Lab., Ill., 2003—05; assoc. prof. chemistry and biochemistry, coord. tech. program Miami U., Middletown, Ohio, 2004—. Vis. asst. prof. chemistry and math. Heritage Coll., 1991—92; vis. prof. Miami U. Dolibois European Ctr., 2008; spkr. in field. Author: African Walking Safari, 1985; editl. adv. bd. Jour. Chromatographic Sci., 1977-93, guest editor, 1987. Active Danbury Conservation Commn., 1986-87, tchr. and tutor chemistry, 1985-89, 91-92, 94; troop leader Lake Erie coun. Girl Scouts U.S.A., 1971-80, Southwestern Conn., 1983-87; leader explorer post Cleve. coun. Boy Scouts Am., 1977-78, venture crew co-leader Dan Beard coun., 2006—07; managerial advisor Jr. Achievement, Warrensville Heights, Ohio, 1977-78; judge State or Regional Sci. Fair, 1977, 80, 89-91, 99-2000, Odyssey of the Mind, 1994; asst. leader Internat. Folk Dancers, Newtown, Conn., 1985-87; tchr. religion, 1981-84, 87-90, 93-94; sch. bd. John XXIII Elem. Sch., 2004-07. Recipient Overall Best Paper award Eastern Analytical Symposium, 1984, First Gas Chromatograph award IBM Instruments Inc., 1985, contbn. award (tech. paper) 10th Internat. Congress of Essential Oils, Flavors, Fragrances, Washington, 1986, Centennial award for Excellence in Undergraduate Tchg, 2008. Mem. Am. Chem. Soc. (chmn. membership com. Green Mountain sect. 1988-89, chmn. 1990-91, local coord. Nat. Chemistry Week 1991, 93-98, 2002-04, nat. com. on technician affairs 2005—, nat. com. on cmty. activities 2005, subcom. chmn. 2007, chmn. edn. com. nat. tech. divsn. 2007-09, Phoenix award 1994, 97, Salute to Excellence award 2004), Iota Sigma Pi (pres. N.E. Ohio chpt. 1978-79, mem.-at-large fin. mgr. 1993-97, nat. v.p. 1996-99, nat. pres. 1999-2002, immediate past pres. 2002-05), Miami U. Middletown Chemistry Club (faculty advisor 2003-04), Miami U. Middletown Ski and Snowboard Club (faculty advisor 2004-06, 2009-), Phi Theta Kappa (faculty advisor Miami U. Middletown 2004—). Roman Catholic. Avocations: camping, dance, travel. Office: Miami U Middletown 4200 E University Blvd Middletown OH 45042-3458

MARINEAU, ERIC CHRISTIAN, research scientist; s. Lucien Marineau and Therese Deschesnes. BE in Mech. Engring., Ecole Poly. Montreal, Can., 2001, ME in Aerospace Engring., 2002; PhD in Aerospace Engring., Va. Poly. Inst. and State U., Blacksburg, 2007. Rsch. asst. Va. Poly. Inst. and State U., 2004—07, instr., 2007; postdoc. scholar Calif. Inst. Tech., Pasadena, 2007—. Reviewer Jour. Thermophysics and Heat Transfer, Reston, Va., 2008—. Contbr. scientific papers. Mem.: ASME, AIAA. Achievements include first to measurement of the temperature distribution over a laser heated target subjected to a supersonic turbulent flow using infrared thermography and fast response thermocouples; research in shock tunnel heat flux measurements on NASA's orion crew exploration vehicle at high enthalpy including the effect of turbulence and chemistry; computation and experiments of high enthalpy non-equilibrium nozzle flows to improve the characterization of free stream conditions and validation of modeling assumptions; new algorithm for the inverse heat transfer problem in a two-layer solid including the effect of temperature dependent material properties; shock tunnel measurements of bow shock oscillations on blunt bodies at hypervelocity. Business E-Mail: ermara@vt.edu.

MARINELLI, JANICE, broadcast executive; b. NY, 1958; m. Thomas Mazza; 3 children. BS in Comm., St. John's U., NY. Rsch. analyst TeleRep; sr. rschr. Lorimar TV, Katz TV Group; acct. exec. Disney-ABC Domestic TV (formerly Buena Vista TV), 1985, dir. sales western divsn., exec. v.p., 1996—99, pres. Burbank, Calif., 1999—. Named one of The 100 Most Powerful Women in Entertainment, Hollywood Reporter, 2006, 2007. Office: Disney-ABC Domestic TV 500 S Buena Vista St Burbank CA 91521

MARINELLI, ROD, professional football coach; b. Rosemead, Calif., July 13, 1949; m. Barbara Marinelli; children: Chris, Gina. Attended, U. Utah, 1968, Calif. Lutheran, 1970—72. Asst. coach Rosemead HS, Calif., 1973—75; defensive line coach Utah St. U. Aggies, 1976—81, offensive line/spl. teams coach, 1982; defensive line coach U. Calif. Golden Bears, 1983—91; asst. coach, defensive line coach Ariz. State U. Sundevils, 1993—95; defensive line coach U. So. Calif. Trojans, 1995—96, Tampa Bay Bucaneers, 1996—2006; head coach Detroit Lions, 2006—08; asst. head coach, defensive line coach Chgo. Bears, 2009—. Served in US Army, 1969, Vietnam. Recipient All-Am. honors, NAIA, 1972. Achievements include being a member of Super Bowl XXXVII winning Tampa Bay Buccaneers, 2003. Office: Chicago Bears 1000 Football Dr Lake Forest IL 60045*

MARINELLO, KATHRYN V., human resources company executive; b. 1956; married; 3 children. BS, SUNY, Albany; MBA, Hofstra U. Mgmt. positions with Barclay's, Citibank, Chemical Bank; pres. US Bank Card Services; pres. electronic payments group First Data Corp.; mgmt. positions with Gen. Electric, 1997—2006, exec. v.p. GE card services, pres. GE Capital cons. fin. services, pres., CEO GE Fin. Assurance Mktg. group, pres., CEO GE Fleet Services, 2002—06; chmn., CEO Ceridian Corp., Mpls., 2006—. Bd. dirs. Gen. Motors Corp., 2007—. Bd. dir. Greater Twin Cities United Way, Minn. Bus. Partnership. Named an Industry Leader, Mpls./St. Paul Bus. Journal, 2006. Mem.: The Bus. Roundtable. Office: Ceridian Corp 3311 E Old Shakopee Rd Minneapolis MN 55425*

MARINER, JONATHAN D., major league baseball executive; b. 1954; m. Mildred Mariner; children: Brian, Phillip, Matthew. BS in Acctg., U. Va.; MBA, Harvard U. CPA. Sr. fin. analyst to sr. mgr. MCI Comm., Washington; various positions including sr. mgr. mergers and acquisitions, strategic planning and budgets, and controller insurance ops. Ryder Truck Rental, Fla.; v.p. fin. and adminstrn. Greater Miami Convention and Visitors Bur.; v.p., CFO Fla. Panthers Hockey Club, 1993—94; CFO Pro Player Stadium; pres. Marlins Ballpark Devel. Corp.; exec. v.p., CFO Fla. Marlins Baseball Club, 1992—2000; COO, CFO Charter Schs. USA, 2000—02; exec. v.p. fin., CFO MLB, 2002—. Bd. dirs. Charter Schs. USA, BankAtlantic Bancorp, Ryan, Beck and Co., Steiner Leisure Ltd. Chmn. Broward Cmty. Coll. Found. Bd.; mem. advisory bd. U. Va. McIntire Sch. Commerce, Pine Crest Sch., Ft. Lauderdale, Fla. Named one of 101 Most Influential Minorities in Sports, Sports Illustrated mag. Avocation: martial arts. Office: Major League Baseball 245 Park Ave 31st Fl New York NY 10167

MARINETTI, GUIDO V., biochemistry professor; b. Rochester, NY, June 26, 1918; s. Michael and Nancy (Lippa) M.; m. Antoinette Francione, Sept. 19, 1942; children: Timothy D., Hope L. BS, U. Rochester, 1950, PhD, 1953. Research biochemist Western Regional Lab., Albany, Calif., 1953-54; instr. U. Rochester, NY, 1954-57, asst. prof., 1957-60, assoc. prof., 1960-66, prof. sch. medicine and dentistry, 1966—97; prof. emeritus dept biochemistry and biophysics, 1997—. Cons. Eastman Kodak, 1978, Rochester Gas & Electric, 1979 Author: Disorders of Lipid Metabolism, 1990, I Beat Heart Disease, So Can You, 2006; editor: Lipid Chromatographic Analysis, 3 vols., 1969, 2nd edit., 1976; contbr. over 165 pub. articles in sci. jours. Served with USAAF, 1942-46. Recipient Nat. Infantile Paralysis award, 1952; recipient Glycerine Research award, 1957; NSF grantee, 1953; recipient Lederle Med. Faculty award, 1955, 56 Mem. Am. Soc. Biol. Chemists, Am. Chem. Soc., AAAS, Sigma Xi, Phi Beta Kappa Achievements include research in membrane structure and function, biochemistry of phospholipids, phosphatidylinositiol metabolism in isolated synaptomsomes, membrane hormone receptors. Personal E-mail: gmarn19@frontiernet.net.

MARING, MARY MUEHLEN, state supreme court justice; b. Devils Lake, ND, July 27, 1951; d. Joseph Edward and Charlotte Rose (Schorr) Muehlen; m. David Scott Maring, Aug. 30, 1975; children: Christopher David, Andrew Joseph. BA in Polit. Sci., summa cum laude, Moorhead State U., Minn., 1972; JD, U. ND, 1975. Bar: Minn., ND. Law clk. to Hon. Bruce Stone, Mpls., 1975—76; assoc. Stefanson, Landberg & Alm, Ltd., Moorhead, Minn., 1976—82, Ohnstad, Twichell, Breitling, Rosenvold, Wanner, Nelson, Neugebauer & Maring, West Fargo, ND,

1982—88, Lee Hagan Law Office, Fargo, ND, 1988—91; pvt. practice Maring Law Office, Fargo, 1991—96; justice ND Supreme Ct., Bismarck, 1996—. Women's bd. mem. 1st Nat. Bank, Fargo, 1977-82; career day spkr. Moorhead Rotarians, 1980-83; mem. Court Svcs. Com., 1996-, Jud. Compensation, subcom. of Jud. Conf., 1998-, Five-State Jud. Conf. Planning Com., 1997-98, 99-2000; chmn. Gender Fairness Implementation Com., 1997-, Jud. Conf. Exec. Bd., 1998-, chair-elect, 2004-05, chair, 2005, Juvenile Drug Ct. Study, planning and Implementation Com., 1998-2000, Juvenile Drug Ct. Adv. Com., 2000-, Pers. Policy bd., 1999-2004, Govs. Drug and Alcohol Policy Adv. Bd., 1999-2001, ND Commn. Drug & Alcohol Abuse, 2002-, No. Plains Ethics Inst., 2000-, Juvenile Policy Bd., 2001-, Jud. Edn. Com., 2005-, Jud. Planning Com., 2001-, Harold Schafer Leadership Ctr. Com. Note editor ND Law Rev., 1975; contbr. articles to legal jours. Mem. ABA (del. ann. conv. young lawyers sect. 1981-82, bd. govs. 1982-83), Minn. Women Lawyers, ND State Bar Assn. (bd. govs. 1991-93), Clay County Bar Assn. (v.p. 1983-84), ND Trial Lawyers Assn. (pres. 1992-93), Internat. Soc. Barristers, Nat. Assn. Women Judges (dist. 10 dir. 2001-03). Roman Catholic. Office: ND Supreme Ct 600 E Boulevard Ave Dept 180 Bismarck ND 58505-0530 Office Phone: 701-328-4207. Business E-Mail: MMaring@ndcourts.gov.*

MARING-SIMS, MILA L., biology professor; d. Joel M. and Ester C. Maring; m. Kelley R. Sims, July 22, 2004. PhD in Physiology, Southern Ill. U., Carbondale, 1994. Biology instr. Southeastern Ill. Coll., Harrisburg, 1994—. Village trustee, Alto Pass, Ill., 2009—. Office: Southeastern Ill Coll 3575 Coll Rd Harrisburg IL 62946 Business E-Mail: mila.maring@sic.edu.

MARINI, KELLY JEAN, elementary school educator; d. Michael and Wendy Farrell; m. Kevin L. Marini, July 8, 2000; 1 child, Ava Farrell. BS, RI Coll., Providence, 1994—98. Cert. early childhood edn. RI Dept. Edn., 1998, spl. edn. K-8 RI Dept. Edn., 1998. Spl. educator, integrated kindergarten Fairlawn Early Learning Ctr., Lincoln, RI, 1999—2000, resource tchr., diagnostic prescriptive tchr., 2000—01, resource tchr., 2001—02, 1st grade tchr., 2001—. Mem.: Nat. Coun. Tchrs. Math. Office: Fairlawn Early Learning Ctr 3 Fairlawn Way Lincoln RI 02865 Business E-Mail: marinik@lincolnps.org.

MARINI, ROBERT CHARLES, environmental engineering executive; b. Quincy, Mass., Sept. 29, 1931; s. Larry and Millie (Cirillo) M.; m. Myrna Lydia Pellegrini, June 26, 1955 (dec. June 1994); children: Debra, Robert Charles, Larry; m. B. Anne Jones, May 27, 1995. BSCE (hon.), Northeastern U., 1954, doctorate (hon.), 1997; SMSE, Harvard U., 1955, postgrad. in advanced mgmt., 1985. Registered profl. engr., Mass. Jr. engr. Camp Dresser & McKee Inc., Boston, 1955-56, project engr., 1958-64, assoc., 1964-67, ptnr., sr. v.p., 1967-77, pres. environ. engring. div., 1977-82, exec. v.p., 1982-84, pres., 1984-90, CEO, 1989-98, chmn. bd. dirs., 1998—99, vice chmn. bd. dirs., 1999-2001, chmn. emeritus, 2001—09. Mem. civil engring. adv. com. Worcester (Mass.) Poly. Inst., 1985-90, U. Mass., 1986-90, U. Tex., Austin, 1989-91, chmn., 1991-92, mem. engring. found. adv. coun., 1991-98; trustee South Shore Savs. Bank, 1990—, audit com., 2001-. Contbr. articles to profl. jours. Dir. nat. coun. Northeastern U., Boston, 1983-2004, mem. corp. bd., 1983-2004, bd. overseers, 1985-89, trustee, 1989-2004; chmn. Leadership Phase Century II Fund, 1989-91, chmn. devel. com., 1991-98, vice chmn. bd. trustees, 1997-2004, vice chmn. emeritus, 2004-; bd. dirs. Mass. Bus. Round Table, 1991-99, vice chmn., 1995-97, chmn., 1997-99, Plimoth Plantation, 2005-09. Recipient Disting. Eagle Scout award Boy Scouts Am., 1986, Mass. Patriots award Old Colony Coun., 1998, W. Erwin Story award, 1991, Outstanding Civil Engring. Alumni award Northeastern U., 1992, Outstanding Alumni award, 1993; named Man of Yr., Don Orione, 1999. Mem ASCE (hon., disting. mem., Opal award 2003), fellow NAE, Boston Soc. Civil Engrs. (hon.); mem. Am. Pub. Works Assn. (Man of Yr. award New Eng. chpt. 1981), Am. Water Works Assn., Mass. Soc. Profl. Engrs. (Young Engr. of Yr. award 1966), Am. Acad. Environ. Engrs. (diplomate, trustee at large 1989-92, v.p. 1992-93, pres.-elect 1993-94, pres. 1994-95, Stanley E. Kappe award 1992, Gordon Maskew Fair award, 2005), Water Environment Fedn. (hon., N.E. chpt., Founders award 1999), Internat. Assn. Water Pollution Rsch. and Control, Engring. Soc. New Eng. (New Eng. award 1994), Greater Boston C. of C. (bd. dirs. 1997-99), Water Environ. Rsch. Found. (bd. dirs. 1998-2001), Tau Beta Pi, Phi Kappa Phi. Roman Catholic. Home: P O Box 1070 Boca Grande FL 33921 Home Phone: 941-964-2089; Office Phone: 617-452-6000. Business E-Mail: marinirc@comcast.net.

MARINIS, THOMAS PAUL, JR., lawyer; b. Jacksonville, Tex., May 31, 1943; s. Thomas Paul and Betty Sue (Garner) M.; m. Lucinda Cruse, June 25, 1969; children: Courtney, Kathryn, Megan. BA, Yale U., 1965; LLB, U. Tex., 1968. Bar: Tex. 1968. Assoc. Vinson & Elkins, Houston, 1969-76, ptnr., 1977—. Bd. dirs. Phoenix House of Tex., Inc. Fellow Tex. Bar Found.; mem. ABA (sec. taxation sect. 1986-87), Houston Country Club, Houston Ctr. Club, Coronado Club. E-mail: tmarinis@velaw.com.

MARINKOVIC, SERGE PETER, urologist, educator, surgeon; s. Sergio Fabian and Elsa Salvadora Marinkovic; m. Christina Mallusack Plymale, May 23, 2003. BA in Biology, NYU, 1985; MD, Wayne State U., Detroit, 1991. Diplomate Am. Bd. Urology, 2005. Gen. surgery internship Providence Hosp., Southfield, Mich., 1991—92; urology internship Brown Sch. Medicine, Providence, 1992—94, Geisinger Med. Ctr., Danville, Pa., 1995—98; female urology & prosthetics fellowship Smith Inst. Urology, LI Jewish Hosp., New Hyde Pk., NY, 1998—99; urogynecology fellowship Stuart L. Stanton Urogynecology Unit, St. George's Hosp., London, 1999—2001; assoc. prof. female urologist/female reconstructive surgery So. Ill. U. Sch. Medicine, Springfield, 2001—. Attending female reconstructive surgeon Women's & Children's Hosp., Lafayette, La., 2005—08; attending dept. female reconstructive surgery and women's medicine St. Francis Hosp., Indpls., 2008—. Contbr. articles to med. jours. Recipient Thirlby award, Am. Urol. Assn., 2004, 2005; Basic Sci. grantee, LI Jewish Hosp., 1999. Fellow: Am. Urogynecology Assn. (assoc.); mem.: Soc. Female Urology and Urodynamics. Republican. Roman Catholic. Avocations: piano, rare books. Office: St Francis Hosp Dept Urology Femal Reconstructive Surgeon and Women's Indianapolis IN 46259 Home Phone: 317-604-8600; Office Phone: 317-781-7391. Personal E-mail: urourogyn@yahoo.com.

MARINO, DAN (DANIEL CONSTANTINO MARINO JR.), sportscaster, retired professional football player; b. Pitts., Sept. 15, 1961; s. Daniel and Veronica Marino; m. Claire Veazey, Jan. 30, 1985; adopted children: Niki Lin, Lia children: Daniel Charles, Michael Joseph, Joseph Donald, Alexandra Claire. BA in Comm., U. Pitts., 1983. Quarterback Miami Dolphins, 1983—99; co-host Inside the NFL, HBO, 2000—, NFL Today, CBS, 2002—. Actor: (films) Ace Ventura: Pet Detective, 1994; co-author (with David Hyde): Dan Marino: My Life in Football, 2005. Founder Dan Marino Found., 1991—, Dan Marino Ctr., 1998—. Recipient Bert Bell Most Valuable Player award, Maxwell Club, 1984, NFL MVP award, AP, 1984, NFL Comeback Player of Yr., 1994, Walter Payton Man of Yr. award, 1998; named All-Am. Team Quarterback, The Sporting News, 1981, NFL Rookie of Yr., 1983, NFL All-Pro, 1984—86; named to Am. Football Conf. Pro Bowl Team, 1983—87, 1991—92, 1994—95. Achievements include holding the NFL record passing attempts (8,358) & single season passing yards, (5,084), 1984; NFL record for most games (12) with 400 or more yards passing; NFL records for most seasons (6) with 4,000 or more yards passing, most seasons (9) with 3,000 or more yards passing, 1984-92; most games (17) with four or more touchdown passes, 1984; most consecutive games (4) with four or more touchdown passes, 1984; lowest percentage (2.03) of passes interecepted by a rookie, 1983; inducted into the Coll. Football Hall of Fame, 2003, Pro Football Hall of Fame, 2005; design of. Office: Dan Marino Found PO Box 267640 Weston FL 33326

MARINO, DEIRDRE J., science educator; d. Corrado A. and Nancy Marino; 1 child, Daniella N. BA, Columbia U., NYC, 1988; MS, NYU, 1993, MPhil, 1991; MEd, Queens Coll., NYC, 2006. Sr. editor Plenum Sci. Pub., NYC, 1993—98; supervising editor Lippincott Williams & Wilkins, NYC, 1998—2003; educator sci. Steinway Ind. Sch. 141, Astoria, NY, 2003—. Patricia Harris Fellowship, NYU Grad. Sch. Arts & Scis., 1990—93. Mem.: NSTA, Kappa Delta Pi. Personal E-mail: deem345@aol.com.

MARINO, EUGENE LOUIS, publishing executive, director; b. NYC, Jan. 7, 1929; s. Salvatore A. and Florence M. (Casabona) M.; m. Patricia Ryan, Mar. 11, 1948; children: Jeanette, Anthony, John, Eugene III. Student, Columbia U., 1945-48. Credit mgr. Sears, Roebuck Inc., LI, NY, 1951-60; gen. credit mgr. Davison-Paxon div. R.H. Macy, Inc., Atlanta, 1960-63, Grand-Way div. Grand Union Co., NYC, 1963-66; v.p., gen. credit mgr. Consumer Products div. Singer Co., NYC, 1966-75, Grolier, Inc., Danbury, Conn., 1975-90; ret. Officer, v.p., gen. credit mgr., dir. numerous subsidiaries. Recipient Quarter Century cert. Internat. Consumer Credit Assn., 1981. Mem. Mchts. Rsch. Coun., Internat. Consumer Credit Assn., Nat. Assn. Credit Mgmt., Alpha Sigma Phi. Home: 4858 Tivoli Ct Sarasota FL 34235-3653 E-mail: elmarino1@verizon.net.

MARINO, JANE B., library director; m. Jim Marino; 3 children. BA, LeMoyne Coll.; MLS, Long Island U., 1989. Dir. Bronxville Pub. Libr., White Plains, NY. Author: Sing Us a Story: Using Music in Preschool and Family Storytime, 1992, Babies in the Library, 2003. Mem.: NY Libr. Assn., Assn. Libr. Svc. to Children (chair early childhood and parent edn. com. 2000—01, mem. bd. dirs., mem. preconference planning com., mem. Caldecott award com., mem. publications com., v.p./pres.-elect 2006—07, pres. 2007—), ALA. Office: Bronxville Public Library 60 Woodcrest Ave White Plains NY 10604 Office Phone: 914-337-7680. Office Fax: 914-337-0332. E-mail: jbmarino@optonline.net.

MARINO, JOSEPH, archbishop, diplomat; b. Birmingham, Ala., Jan. 23, 1953; s. Salvador and Josephine Marino. BA, Scranton Univ.; attended, Pius X Seminary; degree in Canon Law, Pontifical Gregorian Univ., Rome; attended, Pontifical Ecclesiastical Acad., Rome. Ordained priest Diocese of Birmingham, Ala., 1979, univ. chaplain; parochial vicar Cathedral of St. Paul, Birmingham; diplomatic positions Apostolic Nunciature to Philippines, 1988—91, Apostolic Nunciature to Uruguay, 1991—94, Apostolic Nunciature to Nigeria, 1994—97; diplomatic positions for rels. with Balkan nations Secretariat of State of Vatican City, Rome, 1997—2004; first counselor Apostolic Nunciature to England and Wales, London, 2004—08; ordained bishop, 2008; archbishop, apostolic nuncio to Bangladesh, 2008—. Roman Catholic. Mailing: Apostolic Nuncio PO Box 6003 Dhaka Bangladesh

MARINO, JOSEPH PAUL, SR., dean, chemist, researcher; s. Paul M. and Anella Marino; m. Yolanda Lucia Lizardi, Dec. 7, 1967; children: Joseph Paul Jr., Yolanda Maria Marino Swartz, Sylvia Maria Marino Chapman. BS, Pa. State U., State College, 1963; AM, Harvard U., Cambridge, Mass., 1965, PhD, 1967. Prof. chemistry U. Mich., Ann Arbor, 1969—2002, assoc. dean, 1994—97, chair dept. chemistry, 1997—2002; dean sci., prof. chemistry U. Notre Dame, Ind., 2002—. Fellow, NIH, 1967—69, US Govt., 1985. Mem.: Am. Chem. Soc. Home: 52219 Farmington Sq Rd Granger IN 46530 Office Fax: 574-631-8149; Home Fax: 574-631-8149. Business E-Mail: marino.12@nd.edu.

MARINO, MICHAEL FRANK, III, lawyer; b. Little Falls, NY, Feb. 19, 1948; s. Michael Frank and Betty (Roberts) M.; m. Catherine Viladesau, Aug. 31, 1970 (div. Nov. 1996); m. Ann Buttfield Feb. 15, 1997; children: Michael John, Lisa Kathryn, Matthew Christopher. BS, Cornell U., 1971; JD, Syracuse U., 1974; LLM, Georgetown U., 1982. Bar: D.C. 1975, U.S. Dist. Ct. D.C. 1975, U.S. Ct. Mil. Appeals 1975, N.Y. 1976, U.S. Dist. Ct. (ea. and we. dists.) Va. 1977, U.S. Dist. Ct. Md. 1980, U.S. Ct. Appeals (4th cir.) 1982, Va. 1982, U.S. Ct. Appeals (9th cir.) 1994. Civilian employee head rels. br. Office of the Judge Adv. of the Navy, Washington, 1975-76; spl. asst. to the gen. counsel Office of Sec. of Navy, Washington, 1977; asst. gen. counsel labor and employment Office of the Gen. Counsel of the Navy, Washington, 1978; assoc. Pierson, Ball & Dowd, Washington, 1978-81; ptnr. Boothe, Prichard & Dudley, Fairfax and Mc Lean, Va., 1981-87, McGuire, Woods, Battle & Boothe, Mc Lean, 1987-89, Reed, Smith, Shaw & McClay, NYC, 1989-2000, Hunton & Williams, McLean, Va., 2000—. Labor group head, Washington, Va.; mng. ptnr. McLean Office. Author: Virginia Employer's Guide to Labor Law, 1982; co-author: New York Employer's Guide, 1989, 1992—2001, Florida Labor and Emloyment Law, 2001, Labor Employment Law in Pennsylvania, 1994. Mem. planning com. SMU Multi State labor Law Conf., Dallas; chmn. Arlington (Va.) Chamber Employee Rels. Com.; bd. dirs. Arlington Chamber; mem. Va. Chamber Mgmt. Rels. Com. Richmond, 1980—; bd. dirs. Dan Marino Found. Capt. USMC, 1971-78. Mem.: ABA (labor law com. 1974—), Fairfax Bar Assn. (Pro Bono award 2000), N.Y. Bar Assn. (labor law com. 1974—), Va. Bar Assn. (labor law com. 1974—, sec.-treas. labor law sect. 1995, vice chair 1996—97), D.C. Bar Assn. (labor law com. 1974—). Roman Catholic. Avocations: exercise, boating. Office: Hunton & Williams 1751 Pinnacle Dr Ste 1700 Mc Lean VA 22102-3836 E-mail: mmarino@hunton.com.

MARINO, MICHELLE S., psychologist; b. Point Pleasant, NJ, Aug. 29, 1976; d. Walter Francis Michael and Ninon Bernadette Marino. MA in Counseling Psychology, Framingham State Coll., Mass., 2005; attending in Sch. Psychology, U. Mass., Boston, 2006—. Applied behavioral analyst New Eng. Ctr. Children, Southboro, Mass., 2002—04; behavior learning asst. Grafton Pub. Schs., Mass., 2004—06, sch. psychologist, 2006—. Achievements include development of ABA program at Grafton Middle School. Office: Grafton Pub Schs 30 Providence Rd Grafton MA 01519

MARINO, MIGUEL ANGEL, engineering educator; b. Cienfuegos, Cuba, Nov. 10, 1940; arrived in US, 1957; s. Ramon and Julia Marino; m. Irma Padovani, July 27, 1968; 1 child, Raquel Christina. AA, Andrew Coll., 1959; BS, N.Mex. Inst. Mining and Tech., 1962, MS, 1965; PhD, UCLA, 1972. Asst. geohydrologist N.Mex. State Engrs. Office, Santa Fe, 1964; asst. hydrologist Ill. State Water Survey, Champaign, 1965-69; from asst. prof. to assoc. prof. U. Calif., Davis, 1972—80, prof., 1980-99, dir. hydrology program, 1996-98, prof. above-scale, 1999—2003, disting. prof., 2003—. Author: Groundwater and Seepage, 1982, Regional Management of Water Resources, 2001, Integrated Water Resources Management, 2001, (monograph) Subsurface Flow and Contamination, 1987; contbr. articles to profl. jours. Pres./elect Am. Inst. of Hydrology, 2003—05; v.p. Internat. Commn. Water Resources Sys.; bd. dirs. Univs. Coun. Water Resources. Recipient Warren A. Hall medal, Univs. Coun. Water Resources. Fellow: Am. Geophys. Union, Am. Water Resources Assn. (hon.); mem.: ASCE (hon. Outstanding Jour. Paper awards 1986, 1990, Julian Hinds award 1996, Richard R. Torrens award 1986), Internat. Assn. Hydrol. Scis. (Best Paper award), Am. Inst. Hydrology (pres.-elect, cert.), Am. Water Resources Assn., N.Y. Acad. Scis., Sigma Xi, Tau Beta Pi. Home: 813 Harrier Pl Davis CA 95616-0173 Office: Univ Calif 139 Veihmeyer Hall Davis CA 95616 Office Phone: 530-752-0684. Business E-Mail: MAMarino@ucdavis.edu.

MARINO, PETER, architect; Grad. in Architecture, Cornell U., Ithaca, NY. With Skidmore Owings & Merrill, George Nelson, I.M. Pei/Cossutta & Ponte; founder, prin. Peter Marino Arch., PLLC, NYC, 1978—. Prin. works include Giorgio Armani NY (Excellence in Design award, AIA, 1997), Estée Lauder Plaza NY (Excellence in Design award, AIA, 1999), Chanel Osaka (Excellence in Design award, AIA, 2001), Private London Residence (Nat. Honor award, AIA, 2005), Chanel, rue Cambon (Merit in Design award, AIA, 2004, Nat. Honor award, AIA, 2005), Nassau County Mus. Art, NY (Merit in Design award, 2006). Chmn. bd. Young Concert Artists; bd. mem. NY Found. Architecture, Venetian Heritage Found. Fellow: AIA. Office: Peter Marino Arch PLLC 150 E 58th St New York NY 10022 Office Phone: 212-752-5444. Office Fax: 212-759-3727.*

MARINO, ROBIN L., multi-media company executive; b. July 26, 1954; BBA in Mgmt. and Mktg., Stetson U., DeLand, Fla., 1976. Mgmt. positions Federated Dept. Stores, Inc., 1977—89; pres. Polo Ralph Lauren Handbags & Luggage Polo Ralph Lauren Corp., 1989—96; pres. Donna Karan Collection Donna Karan Internat. Inc., 1996—97; sr. v.p. accessories worldwide Burberry Ltd., NYC, 1997—98; pres., COO Kate Spade LLC, NYC, 1999—2005; pres. merchandising Martha Stewart Living Omnimedia, Inc., NYC, 2005—08, co-CEO, 2008—. Recipient Disting. Alumni award, Stetson U., 2006. Office: Martha Stewart Living Omnimedia Inc 11 W 42nd St New York NY 10036 E-mail: rmarino@marthastewart.com.

MARINO, THOMAS A., lawyer, former prosecutor; b. 1952; AA, Williamsport Area C.C., 1983; BA, Lycoming Coll.; JD, Dickinson U. Assoc. McNemey, Page, Vanderlin & Hall, Williamsport, Pa., 1988—96; dist. atty. Lycoming County, Pa., 1996—2002; US atty. (mid. dist.) Pa. US Dept. Justice, 2002—07; in-house corp. counsel Keystone Sanitary Landfill, 2007—. Office: Keystone Sanitary Landfill 249 Dunham Dr Dunmore PA 18512

MARINO, WILLIAM FRANCIS, telecommunications industry executive, consultant; b. Phila., Dec. 28, 1948; s. William F. and Edith Ellen (Dougherty) M.; m. Mary Ellen Klems, Sept. 29, 1979; children: Kiersten Leigh, Meghan Lyn. Student, Ohio State U., 1967; BS in Fin. and Acctg., Widener U., 1970. Sr. acctg., fin. positions U.S. Steel Corp., Pitts., 1970-83; v.p. U.S. Steel Credit Corp., Pitts., 1983-85; dir. fin. programs CIS Corp., Syracuse, N.Y., 1985, v.p. instl. sales, 1986; pres. CIS Credit Corp., Syracuse, N.Y., 1987, v.p. fin., 1988; v.p., chmn. reorganization com. Continental Info. Systems Corp., Syracuse, N.Y., 1989; v.p. fin., CFO ITEC Corp., Lake Bluff, Ill., 1990-91, pres., CEO, 1991—, Global Telecom Svcs. Corp., 2000—. Advisor, cons. Chong & Assocs., N.Y.C., 1989. Advisor Hiawatha coun. Boy Scouts Am., Syracuse, 1987; dir. Cystic Fibrosis Found., Syracuse, 1987-88. Recipient Century award Boy Scouts Am., Syracuse, 1988. Mem. Am. Assn. Equipment Lessors, Am. Mgmt. Assn., Fin. Execs. Inst., Aircraft, Owners & Pilots Assn. Republican. Avocations: flying, cross country skiing. Home: 8763 Muirfield Dr Naples FL 34109-4352 Office: Global Telecom Svcs Corp 8763 Muirfield Dr Naples FL 34109-4352 Personal E-mail: billmarino@comcast.net.

MARINO, WILLIAM J., insurance executive; Various positions Prudential Ins. Co. Am., 1968-91, Horizon Blue Cross & Blue Shield of N.J., Inc., Newark, 1991-94; pres., CEO Horizon Blue Cross & Blue Shield of NJ Inc, Newark, 1994—. Mem. exec. com. Blue Cross/Blue Shield Assn. (BCBSA), chair Inter-Plan Operating Com. and Emerging Issues of BCBSA, bd. dirs. of Health Insurance Assn. of America, Nat. Inst. for Health Care Mgmt. Trustee, chmn. United Way of Essex and West Hudson, N.J., campaign chmn., 1993-94; chmn., bd. dirs., mem. exec. com. Regional Bus. Partnership; trustee N.J. Network Found., St. Peter's Coll., Newark Mus.; bd. pres. advisors Fairleigh Dickinson U.; mem. chief justice com. on efficiency N.J. Jud. Sys.; past trustee Kessler Inst. for Rehab., Inc. Mem. N.J. State C. of C., past chmn. bd. dirs., exec. com. Blue Cross/Blue Shield Assn. (BCBSA), Inter-Plan Operating Com., mem. Emerging Issues Com. of BCBSA, bd. dirs. Health Insurance Assn. of Amer., Nat. Inst. for Health Care Mgmt. Office: Horizon Blue Cross/Blue Shield NJ Inc 3 Penn Plz E Newark NJ 07105-2245*

MARINUCCI, RONALD E., history professor; b. Dearborn, Mich., Jan. 7, 1949; s. Fred and Doris Marinucci; m. Karen L. Lingenfelter, Dec. 13, 1974; children: Michael S., Matthew D. BA in History, Amherst Coll., Mass., 1971; MA in Counseling, East Mich. U., Ypsilanti, 1977, MA in History, 1983. Cert. MAT Wayne State U., Detroit, 1972. Tchr., HS history & govt. economics HVS, Highland, Mich., 1971—2005; varsity football & baseball coach Milford HS, Highland, 1974—81; adj. instr., history Oakland CC, Bloomfield Hills, Mich., 1995—; adj. prof., history C.S. Mott CC, Flint, Mich., 2005—. Contbr. articles to jours. (Motor City Striders Achievement award, 1999). Named Instr. of Yr., Oakland CC, 2006. Mem.: Phi Kappa Phi. Home: 4062 Cherry Garden Commerce Township MI 48382 Office: Mott CC 1401 E Ct St Flint MI 48503 Personal E-mail: ron_marinucci@comcast.net. Business E-Mail: ron.marinucci@mcc.edu.

MARION, ANNE WINDFOHR, rancher, museum administrator; b. Fort Worth, Tex., Nov. 10, 1938; d. James Goodwin Hall and Anne (Burnett) Hall Tandy; m. John Louis Marion, 1988; 1 child, Anne Phillips Grimes. Attended, Univ. Tex., Austin, Univ. Geneva, Switzerland. Chmn. Burnett Oil Co.; pres. Burnett Ranches Ltd., 6666 Ranch, Guthrie, Tex., Burnett Found., Forth Worth, Tex. Chmn. Georgia O'Keeffe Mus., Santa Fe; trustee Kimbell Art Mus., Forth Worth, Tex.; trustee, former chmn. & pres., chmn. acquisition com. Modern Art Mus., Forth Worth, Tex.; past trustee Mus. Modern Art, NYC; mem. bd. regents Texas Tech. Univ.; dir. emeritus Nat. Cowboy Hall of Fame; mem. exec. com. Forth Worth Stock Show; honorary bd. mem. Nat. Cowgirl Hall of Fame, West. Heritage Ctr. Recipient Charles Goodnight award, 1993, Golden Deed honoree, Fort Worth Exchange Club, 1993, Fern Sawyer award, Nat. Cowgirl Hall of Fame, 1994, Gov. award for excellence in the arts, New Mex., 1996, Boss of the Plains award, Ranching Heritage Ctr., 2003; named Great Woman of Texas, Fort Worth

Bus. Press, 1993; named one of Top 200 Collectors, ARTNews Mag., 2003—08, Forbes Richest Americans, 2006. Mem.: Tex. & S.W. Cattle Raisers Assn. (honorary v.p.), Am. Quarter Horse Assn. (honorary v.p., Merle Wood Humanitarian award 1999). Mailing: Burnett Ranches Ltd PO Box 130 Guthrie TX 79236

MARION, JOHN LOUIS, former fine arts auctioneer and appraiser; b. NYC, Nov. 27, 1933; s. Louis John and Florence Adelaide (Winters) Marion; m. Anne Burnett Windfohr, May 26, 1988; children from previous marriage: John L., Deborah Mary, Therese Marie, Michelle Marie. BS, Fordham U., 1956; postgrad., Columbia U., 1960—61. With Sotheby Parke Bernet Inc., NYC, 1960—, dir., 1965—, v.p., 1966—70, exec. v.p., 1970—72, pres., 1972—87; chmn. bd. Sotheby's Inc., NYC, 1975—, now hon. chmn. Bd. dirs. Sotheby Holdings Inc., London, Mus. N.Mex. Sys. Chmn. fine arts NYC divsn. Am. Cancer Soc., 1983—; vice chmn. bldg. steering com. Dobbs Ferry (NY) Hosp., 1975; bd. dirs. Internat. Found. Art Rsch.; Ctr. for Hope. Lt. (j.g.) USN, 1956—60. Named one of Top 200 Collectors, ARTnews Mag., 2003—08. Mem.: Appraisers Assn. Am., Vintage Club, Shady Oaks Club, Eldorado Club, Lotos Club. Avocation: Collector of 17th and 18th century European art; modern and contemporary art.

MARION, JOHN MARTIN, instructional technology educator; b. Fitchburg, Mass., Jan. 11, 1947; s. Don Louis and Violet Pearl Marion; m. Joann Elizabeth Marion, Aug. 8, 1970; children: Benjamin Andrew, Jessica Noelle. BS in Edn., Fitchburg State Coll., 1969, MEd, 1971; doctoral candidate in ednl. tech., Pepperdine U. Tchr. Groton Dunstable Regional Schs., Mass., 1969—84; computer tchr. Littleton Pub. Schs., Mass., 1985—86; computer coord. K-12th grades Newburyport Pub. Schs., Mass., 1986—90; assoc. dean Acad. Computing Endicott Coll., Beverly, Mass., 1990—98; dir. tech. Reading Pub. Schs., Mass., 1998—2000; media tech. specialist Dracut Pub. Schs., Mass., 2000—03; tech. edn. specialist Jefferson County Pub. Sch., Colo., 2003—. Instr. Merrimack Edn. Ctr., Chelmsford, Mass., 1980-90; trainer, cons. Logo Computer Sys., Inc., NYC, 1984-90; tchr. trainer Lego-Decta, Lego Sys., Inc., Enfield, Conn., 1987-90; mem. adv. bd. Claris Software Co.; bd. dirs. Mass. Computer Using Educator, 1989-90; master tchr. trainer Intel-Teach to the Future program Jefferson Pub. Schs., 2004—, info. literacy adv. com., 2004—. Bd. dirs. Reading Cmty. TV, Inc., 1998-99. Fulbright scholar tchr. exch., Southampton, Eng., 1973-74. Mem.: ASCD, Internat. Tech. Edn. Assn., Phi Delta Kappa. Office: Jeffco Schs 9201 W Columbine Dr Littleton CO 80128-4140 Home: 29191 Shadow Mountain Dr Conifer CO 80433-8612 Office Phone: 303-982-4130. Personal E-mail: jmarion@aol.com.

MARION, MARJORIE ANNE, literature and language professor, educational consultant; b. Winterset, Iowa, May 6, 1935; d. Virgil Arthur and Marilyn Ruth (Sandy) Hammon; m. Robert H. Marion, Dec. 20, 1964; 1 child, Kathryn Ruth BA, Colo. Coll., 1958; MA, Purdue U., 1969; postgrad., Inst. Mgmt. Lifelong Edn. Harvard U., 1981. Chairperson English dept. Lincoln-Way H.S., New Lenox, Ill., 1964—68; dir. pub. rels. U. St. Francis, Joliet, Ill., 1968—70, chairperson English dept., 1971—75, chairperson humanities and fine arts divsn., 1975—79, coord. instrnl. devel., 1979—80, dir. continuing edn., 1980—84, acting v.p. acad. affairs, 1984—85, dean faculty, 1985—89, assoc. prof. English, 1989—97, dir. Freshman Core Program, 1993—95, dir. Writing Ctr., 1996, prof. emeritus, 1997—. Cons. to presdl. search U. St. Francis, 2001—02; mem. vis. team North Ctrl. Assn., Joliet and Lockport, Ill., 1975—79; lectr. at ednl. workshops and instns.; condr. writing workshops for adults returning to coll., 1995—; TV and radio appearances regarding lifelong edn., Chgo., St. Louis, Albuquerque, Phoenix, 1982—85; lit. presenter in field, 2004—; lectr. writing workshops. Author: A Guide to Writing for the Faint at Heart, 1996; author monograph; drama critic Joliet Herald News, 1970-82 Chmn. Cath. Franciscan Charism Coun., 2005—06. Recipient Pres.'s award Coll. St. Francis, 1975 Mem. Am. Assn. Higher Edn., Nat. Coun. Tchrs. English, Nat. Acad. Advising Assn. Roman Catholic. Personal E-mail: mamarion1@msn.com.

MARION, SHAWN, professional basketball player; b. Waukegan, Ill., May 7, 1978; Student, Vincennes U., Ind., UNLV. Forward Phoenix Suns, 1999—2008, Miami Heat, Fla., 2008—09, Toronto Raptors, 2009, Dallas Mavericks, 2009—. Mem., Team USA Goodwill Games, Brisbane, Australia, 2001, World Championships, Indpls., 2002; mem. US Olympic Basketball Team, Athens, Greece, 2004. Recipient Gold medal, Goodwill Games, 2001, Bronze medal, men's basketball, Athens Olympic Games, 2004; named to All-Rookie Second Team, NBA, 2000, Western Conf. All-Star Team, 2003, 2005, 2007. Office: Dallas Mavericks 2909 Taylor St Dallas TX 75226*

MARIOTTO, MARCO JEROME, dean, psychology educator, researcher; b. Ill., Oct. 21, 1946; s. Marco Anibele and Sally (Hughes) M.; m. Danita Irene Czyzewski, May 4, 1985; children: Ana-Sofia Antonia, Marco Luca. BS, U. Ill., 1968, PhD, 1974. Diplomate Am. Bd. Sexology, Am. Bd. Forensic Examiners; lic. psychologist; cert. sex therapist, cert. health svcs. provider. Asst. rsch. dir. Adolf Meyer Ctr. Rsch. Units, Decatur, Ill., 1972-74; psychologist U.S. Army Acad. Health Scis., San Antonio, 1974; asst. prof. Purdue U., West Lafayette, Ind., 1975-79; assoc. prof. U. Houston, 1979-90, supervisory psychologist, 1979—, prof., 1990—, dept. chmn., 1994—99, founding dean grad. and profl. studies, 1999—; co-dir. Abramson Ctr. For Future of Health, 2007—. Cons. NIMH, Bethesda, Md., 1977—; NSF, Washington, 1980-84, Nat. Inst. Drug Abuse, Bethesda, 1986-89; adj. prof. U. Tex. Health Scis., Houston, 1980—. Contbr. chpts. to books and articles to profl. jours.; also rsch. monographs and tech. reports. Forensic cons. Harris County Dist. Atty.'s Office, Houston, 1988—, ABA, 1989—; founding mem. Gulf Coast Consortium on Mental Health, Houston and Galveston, Tex., 1989. Officer US Army, 1968—74. Named one of top 35 Young Scientist Profls. Jour. Cons. and Clin. Psychology, 1988; David Ross fellow Purdue U., 1977. Mem. APA, Am. Psychol. Soc.; mem. AAAS, Midwestern Psychol. Assn. (local rep. 1979—), Sigma Xi. Achievements include co-devel. of TSBC/SRIC planned access infosystem for rsch. and svc. for patients in residential treatment settings; rsch. in observational measurement in mental health, schizophrenia, chronic mental patients. Office: U Houston Office of the Dean Grad and Profl Studies Houston TX 77204-2012 Home Phone: 713-748-2783; Office Phone: 713-743-9088. Business E-Mail: mmariotto@uh.edu.

MARIS, MARGARET ATMA, psychotherapist, educator; d. Clarence Joseph and Catherine Nifa Bailey; life ptnr. Jeffery Raven; 1 child, Christian Joseph Kovac. MA in Psychology, Ctrl. Conn. State U., New Britain, 1991. Cert. psychodrama New Haven Ctr. Human Rels., 1990; gestalt therapist U. Bridgeport, 1987, thought feild therapy Hawaii, 2001, Psych-K Or., 2008. Exec. dir. Prudence Crandall Ctr. Women, New Britain, 1973—77, Susan B. Anthony Ctr. Women, Torrington, Conn., 1877—1981; dir. children svcs. U. Conn., Farmington, 1986—90; program dir. Child & Family Svc., Hilo, Hawaii, 1992—2000; coll. instr. Hawaii CC, Hilo, 1996—2005; sch. based behavioral health therapist Dept. of Edn., Hilo, Hawaii, 2000—; child & family therapist Hospice, Hilo, 2000—. Cons. Dept. Edn., Boston, 1990—91. Planning com. Nat. Coalition Aganist Domestic Violence, NYC, 1971—73; rev. com. United Way, Hartford, Conn., 1973—75. Mem.: APA, Nat. Assn. for Masters Psychology, Play Therapy Assn. Achievements include development of battered women's programs. Avocations: travel, yoga, reading, art, hiking. Home: PO Box 271 Pahoa HI 96778 Office: Dept Edn Waianuenue Ave Kaaawa HI 96730 Personal E-mail: atmamar@msn.com.

MARIS, ROBERT C., biologist, educator; b. Marlin, Tex., Feb. 9, 1954; s. Edward Luiell and Ava Copeland Maris; m. Leslie Yvonne Starkey, Aug. 21, 1976. BS, Tex. A&M U., Coll. Station, 1975; MS, U. Southern Miss., Hattiesburg, 1980; PhD, Old Dominion U., Norfolk, Va., 1986. Assoc. prof. biology Cheyney U. Pa., 1986—88, Mansfield U. Pa., 1988—96, biology prof., 1996—. Mem. & sec. Mansfield Lions Club, 1990—2009. Named one of Employee of the Yr., Mansfield U. Pa., 2006. Mem.: Commonwealth Pa. U. Biologists (pres. 1995—99), Crustacean Soc., Soc. Integrative & Comparative Biology. Home: 35 Sherwood St Mansfield PA 16933 Office: Mansfield Univ Pa Grant Sci Ctr Mansfield PA 16933 Office Fax: 570-662-4107. Business E-Mail: rmaris@mansfield.edu.

MARIS, STEPHEN S., lawyer, educator; b. Dallas, Dec. 19, 1949; children: Shane, Kara. BS, Stephen F. Austin State, Nacogdoches, Tex., 1971; JD, So. Meth. U., Dallas, 1975. Bar: US Dist. Ct. (no. dist.) Tex. 1975, US Dist. Ct. (ea. dist.) Tex. 1986, US Dist. Ct. (so. dist.) Tex. 1992, US Ct. Appeals (5th cir.) 1980, US Ct. Appeals (11th cir.) 1981, US Supreme Ct. Tex. 1975. Assoc. Passman & Jones, Dallas, 1975-80, ptnr., 1980-87, Fulbright & Jaworski, Dallas, 1987-97, Jenkens & Gilchrist, Dallas, 1997—2007, Hunton & Williams, 2007. Prof. So. Ill. U., 1979-80, So. Meth. U., Dallas, 1980—; mem. faculty Nat. Inst. Trial Advocacy, 1980—. Editor: Southwest Law Journal, 1973-75. Mem. ABA, State Bar Tex., Dallas Bar Assn., Barristers, Order Coif, Phi Delta Phi. Office: Hunton & Williams 1445 Ross Ave Ste 3700 Dallas TX 75202-2785 Office Phone: 214-468-3352. Business E-Mail: smaris@hunton.com.

MARISTUEN, KEITH A., lawyer; b. Malta, Mont., 1953; BA with high honors, U. Mont., 1975, JD with honors, 1978. Bar: Mont. 1978, US Tax Ct. 1980, US Ct. Appeals (9th Cir.). Mem. Bosch, Kuhr, Dugdale, Martin & Kaze PLLP, Havre, Mont. Mem.: ABA (mem. gen. practice sect. and small bus. sect.), Mont. State Bar Assn. (pres. 2004—05, chmn. bd. 2002—03, trustee 1992—, chmn. ethics com. 1995—2000, chmn. bankruptcy sect. legis. com. 1990—2002). Office: Bosch Kuhr Dugdale Martin & Kaze PLLP 335 Fourth Ave PO Box 7152 Havre MT 59501 Office Phone: 406-265-6706. Office Fax: 406-265-7578. Business E-Mail: kmaristuen@bkdlaw.org.

MARITZ, PAUL, computer software company executive; b. Rhodesia, Zimbabwe, 1955; married; 3 children. Grad. in Math. and Computer Sci., U. Cape Town. Programmer Burroughs; rschr. U. St. Andrews, Scotland; with Intel Corp., 1981—86; various positions through v.p. platform strategy and developer group Microsoft, 1986—2000, exec. mgmt. team; founder, CEO Pi Corp. (acquired by EMC), 2003—08; pres., gen. mgr. cloud computing divsn. EMC, 2008; pres., CEO VMware (subs. EMC), 2008—. Chmn. bd. Grameen Found. Office: VMware 3145 Porter Dr Palo Alto CA 94304 Office Phone: 650-475-5000. Office Fax: 650-475-5005.

MARK, HANS MICHAEL, physicist, former federal agency administrator; b. Mannheim, Germany, June 17, 1929; arrived in U.S., 1940, naturalized, 1945; s. Herman Francis and Maria (Schramek) M.; m. Marion G. Thorpe, Jan. 28, 1951; children: Jane H., Rufus J. AB in Physics, U. Calif., Berkeley, 1951; PhD, MIT, 1954; ScD (hon.), Fla. Inst. Tech., 1978; DEng (hon.), Poly. U. NY, 1982, Milw. Sch. Engring., 1991; LHD (hon.), St. Edward's U., 1993; ScD (hon.), Royal Mil. Coll. Sci., UK, 2004; DEng (hon.), Tri-State U., 2005. Rsch. assoc. MIT, Cambridge, 1954-55, asst. prof., 1958-60; rsch. physicist Lawrence Radiation Lab. U. Calif., Livermore, 1955-58, 60-69, exptl. physics divsn. leader, 1960-64, assoc. prof. nuc. engring. Berkeley, 1960-66, prof., 1966-69, chmn. dept. nuc. engring., 1964-69, lectr. dept. applied sci. Davis, 1969-73; cons. prof. engring. Stanford (Calif.) U., 1973-84; dir. NASA-Ames Rsch. Ctr., 1969-77; undersec. Air Force, dir. Nat. Reconnaissance Office USAF, Washington, 1977-79, sec. Air Force, 1979-81; dep. adminstr. NASA, Washington, 1981-84; chancellor U. Tex. Sys., Austin, 1984-92; prof. aerospace engring. and engring. mechanics U. Tex., Austin, 1988—; dir. defense rsch. and engring. Dept. Def., Washington, 1998-2001. Mem. Pres.'s Adv. Group Sci. and Tech., 1975-76; bd. dirs. Astronautics Corp. Am.; trustee Poly. U., 1984—. Author: (with N.T. Olson) Experiments in Modern Physics, 1966; (with E. Teller and J.S. Foster, Jr.) Power and Security, 1976; (with A. Levine) The Management of Research Institutions, 1983, The Space Station-A Personal Journey, 1987, (with Victor G. Szebehely) Adventures in Celestial Mechanics, 1998; also numerous articles; editor: (with S. Fernbach) Properties of Matter Under Unusual Conditions, 1969; (with Lowell Wood) Energy in Physics, War and Peace, 1988. Recipient Disting. Svc. medal NASA, 1972, 77, medal for exceptional engring. achievement, 1984, Exceptional Civilian Svc. award USAF, 1979, Disting. Pub. Svc. medal, Dept. Def., 1981, 2001, Sec.'s Gold medal Dept. Energy, 2001. Fellow AIAA (hon., Von Karman lectr. astronautics 1992), Am. Phys. Soc.; mem. NAE, Am. Nuc. Soc., Am. Geophys. Union, Coun. Fgn. Rels., Cosmos Club. Achievements include research on nuclear energy levels, nuclear reactions, applications, nuclear energy for practical purposes, atomic flourescence yields, measurement X-rays above atmosphere, spacecraft and experimental aircraft design. Office: U Tex Dept Aerospace Engring/Engr Austin TX 78712 Home Phone: 512-477-2753; Office Phone: 512-471-5077. Business E-Mail: hmark@mail.utexas.edu.

MARK, HON FONG LOUIE, cytogeneticist; m. Roger Mark; children: Yvonne, Roger Jr., Seamus. PhD, Brown U. Diplomate Am. Bd. Med. Genetics. Postdoctoral fellow in med. genetics R.I. Hosp., Providence, asst., assoc. dir. cytogenetics, fellow molecular biology, dir. cytogenetics, 1990-99, clin. cytogeneticist Cancer & Leukemia Group B, 1990—99; pres., CEO KRAM Corp., 1994—; dir. human genetics RIDOH, 1999—2001; exec. dir. RIACA, 2001—02; dir. cytogenetics dept. Presbyn. Lab. Svcs., Charlotte, NC, 2002—04; dir. cytogenetics Boston U. Sch. Medicine, 2004—07, clin. prof., 2004—07. Instr. pathology Brown U., Providence, asst. prof. pathology; clin. prof. Brown Med. Sch., 1998-2009; emeritus prof. Warren Alpert Med. Sch., Brown U., 2009-; assoc. mem. Maine Toxicology Inst., 1993-96; chair grants rev. com. mem., prenatal diagnosis com., chair cancer genetics com., steering com.; grant reviewer NIH, U.S. Army Breast Cancer Rsch. Program, U.S. Army Prostate Cancer Rsch. Program; reviewer numerous other panels. Author: Medical Cytogenetics, 2000; mem. editl. rev. bd. Applied Cytogenetics, Pathobiology, Exptl. and Molecular Pathology, Cancer Genetics and Cytogenetics; contbr. 200 articles to profl. jours. Recipient award Time Mag. Essay Writing Contest, Balfour award, Award R.I. Found.; NSF rsch. grantee Brown U., co-grantee Dept. Energy; Florence Seibert postdoctoral fellowship AAUW Ednl. Found.; North Providence Citizens scholar, Fruithill Jr. Women's Club scholar; others. Fellow Am. Coll. Med. Genetics; mem. AAAS, Am. Soc. Human Genetics, Assn. Genetic Technologists, Sigma Xi.

MARK, JAMES B. D., surgeon, educator; b. Nashville, Aug. 15, 1955; s. Julius and Margaret (Baer) M.; m. Jean Rambar, Aug. 18, 1955; children: Jonathan, Michael, Margaret, Elizabeth, Katherine. BA, Vanderbilt U., 1950, MD, 1953. Intern, resident in gen. and thoracic surgery Yale-New Haven Hosp., 1953-60; instr. to asst. prof. surgery Yale U., 1960-65; assoc. prof. surgery Stanford U., 1965-69, prof., 1969-97, prof. emeritus, 1997—, Johnson and Johnson prof. surgery, 1978—97, head div. thoracic surgery, 1972-97, assoc. dean clin. affairs, 1988-92; chief staff Stanford U. Hosp., 1988-92. Governing bd. Health Systems Agy., Santa Clara County, 1978-80; sr. Fulbright-Hays fellow, vis. prof. surgery U. Dar es Salaam, Tanzania, 1972-73 Mem. editl. bd.: Jour. Thoracic and Cardiovasc. Surgery, 1986-94, World Jour. Surgery, 1995-2003, The Pharos, 2002-; contbr. numerous articles to sci. jours. Bd. dirs. Stanford U. Hosp., 1992-94. With USPHS, 1955-57. Fellow ACS (pres. No. Calif. chpt. 1980-81), Am. Coll. Chest Physicians (pres. 1994-95); mem. Am. Assn. Thoracic Surgery, Am. Surg. Assn., Western Surg. Assn., Pacific Coast Surg. Assn., Halsted Soc. (pres. 1984), Western Thoracic Surg. Assn. (pres. 1992-93), Calif. Acad. Medicine (pres. 1978), Santa Clara County Med. Soc. (pres. 1976-77). Office: Stanford U Med Ctr CVRB Stanford CA 94305 Home: 81 Pearce Mitchell Pl Stanford CA 94305-8535 Office Phone: 650-723-6649. Business E-Mail: jbdm@stanford.edu.

MARK, KENNETH DEAN, museum director, educator; b. Harrisburg, Pa., Nov. 13, 1950; s. Clifford Kenneth and Catherine Elsie Mark; m. Beth L. Hostetler, July 15, 1972; children: Ryan, Sally Mark Young. BA, Messiah Coll., Grantham, Pa., 1972; MEd, Shippensburg U., Pa., 1975. Tchr. cert. Pa., 1972. 6th grade tchr. Mechanicsburg Area Sch. Dist., Pa., 1972—84, 5th grade tchr., 1984—2002, master tchr., 1990—2002; asst. dir. Oakes Mus., Messiah Coll., Grantham, Pa., 2001—05, dir., 2005—. Adj. lectr. in edn. Messiah Coll., Grantham, Pa., 1988—2001. Recipient Disting. Svc. to Pupils, Mechanicsburg Area Sch. Dist., 1974, 1976, 1982, 1989, Salute to Tchg. award, Pa. Acad. Profession of Tchg., 1990; named Elem. Tchr. of Yr., Mechanicsburg Area Sch. Dist., 1991. Mem.: NEA, Pa. State Edn. Assn., Pa. Sci. Tchrs. Assn., Mid-Atlantic Assn. Mus., Am. Assn. Museums. Independent. Protestant. Avocations: golf, reading, swimming, RVing. Office: Oakes Mus Natural History One College Ave Box 3029 Grantham PA 17027 Office Fax: 717-691-6046. Business E-Mail: kmark@messiah.edu.

MARK, LAURENCE MAURICE, film producer; b. NYC, Nov. 22; s. James Mark and Marion Lorraine (Huebner) Green. BA, Wesleyan U., 1971; MA, NYU, 1973. Exec. dir., publicity Paramount Pictures, NYC, 1978-80, v.p., West Coast mktg. LA, 1980-82, v.p., prodn., 1982-84; exec. v.p., prodn. Twentieth Century Fox, LA, 1984-86; pres. Laurence Mark Prodns., LA, 1986—. Exec. prodr.: (films) Black Widow, 1987, My Stepmother is an Alien, 1988, Working Girl, 1988, Mr. Destiny, 1990, Sister Act 2: Back in the Habit, 1993, As Good As It Gets, 1997, (TV) Sweet Bird of Youth, 1989, Oliver Twist, 1997, The Last Laugh, 2000, These Old Broads, 2001, (81st Acad. award, 2009); prodr.: (films) Cookie, 1989, True Colors, 1991, One Good Cop, 1991, The Adventures of Huck Finn, 1993, Cutthroat Island, 1995, Tom and Huck, 1995, Jerry Maguire, 1996, Romy and Michele's High School Reunion, 1997, Deep Rising, 1998, The Object of My Affection, 1998, Simon Birch, 1998, Anywhere But Here, 1999, Bicentennial Man, 1999, Hanging Up, 2000, Center Stage, 2000, Finding Forrester, 2000, Glitter, 2001, Riding In Cars With Boys, 2001, I, Robot, 2004, Last Holiday, 2006, Dreamgirls, 2006, The Lookout, 2007, Juliet Julia, 2009; prodr. (theatre) Brooklyn Laundry, 1991, (Broadway) Big, 1996. Mem. Acad. Motion Pictures Arts and Scis. Office: Columbia Pictures Sony Studios 10202 Washington Blvd Culver City CA 90232-3119 Home: 12437 Mulholland Dr Beverly Hills CA 90210-1336

MARK, MARSHA YVONNE ISMAILOFF, artistic director; b. Bridgeport, Conn., Mar. 15, 1938; d. Nicholas and Louba (Foullon) Ismailoff; m. Robert Louis Mark, June 25, 1960; children: Robert, William, Staci. Ballet tng. with, George Balanchine, 1946-50, George Volodine, 1945-60, 65-69; student, Skidmore Coll., 1978-80, Vaganova Method Sch., Minsk, USSR, 1983, U. of the Arts, 1990. Founder Marsha Imailoff Mark Sch. of Ballet, Newtown, Conn., 1969—; artistic dir. Com. for Ballet Miniatures, Newtown, Conn., 1974—, Malenkee Ballet Repertoire Co., Newtown, Conn., 1980—. V.p. Cmty. Arts Project Ext., Newtown, 1987-91; artistic dir. Danbury (Conn.) Music Ctr., 1989; instr. for neurologically impaired Ripton Sch., Shelton, Conn., 1992; choreographed section of Nutcracker Ballet for Special Children; toured Russia with Malenkee Ballet Repertoire Co. Choreographer including original works: Mademoiselle Angot, 1974, Circus, 1975, Haydn Concerto, 1976, Evening at the Zoo, 1977, Match Girl, 1978, The Four Seasons, 1979, Malenkee Waltz, 1980, Magic Key, 1981, Midsummer Night's Dream, 1982, Macbeth A Witches Haunt, 1983, Etudes, 1984, Toy Boutique, Etudes, 1985, Under the Sea, 1986, Nutcracker, 1987, 88, 89, 90, 91, 92, 93, 94, 95, 96, 97, Mere, Mere, Mere, 1988, Ellis Island Memoirs, 1991, Moonlight Etudes, 1992, Echoes of Soft Thunder, 1995, Coppelia, 1998; premiered in Baku USSR. Hostess for artists from Russia, translator UN Hostess Com., N.Y.C., 1988; Russian translator Friends of Music, Newtown, 1990, Sacred Heart U., Fairfield, Conn., 1994; founding pres. Seabranch Art League, Hobe Sound, Fla., 2006-; pres. Questors, Treasure Coast, Fla., 2006—. Achievements include first to perceived and instituted, a collaboration of art, dance for the Florida Art Dance Company. Home: 9221 SE Eldorado Way Hobe Sound FL 33455 Office Phone: 203-240-1967.

MARK, MARY ELLEN, photographer; b. Phila., Mar. 20, 1940; d. A. DeRoy and Beatrice (Silverman) M.; m. Frank Anthony Macaoge, 1963 (div. 1964); m. Martin Bell. BFA in Painting and Art History, U. Pa., 1962; MA in Photojournalism, Annenberg Sch. Communication, U. Pa., 1964; DFA (hon.), U. of Arts, Phila., 1992, U. Pa., 1994, Ctr. for Creative Studies, Detroit, 2001, Columbia Coll., Chgo., 2004, Kenyon Coll., Gambier, Ohio, 2004. Lectr., presenter workshops in field. One-woman shows include Photographers Gallery, London, 1976, Castelli Graphics, NYC, 1978, Olympus Gallery, London, 1981, Seson Art Gallery, U. Calif-Santa Cruz, Calif. Mus. Photography, Riverside, Drew U., NJ, 1982, Gallery of Fine Arts, Daytona Beach Community Coll., Fla., Friends of Photography, Carmel, Calif., 1983, Allen Street Gallery, Dallas, 1985, Birmingham (Ala.) Mus. of Art, 1989, numerous others; exhibited in group shows at Photokina, Cologne, 1973, Sidney Janis Gallery, NYC, 1976, Internat. Ctr. of Photography, NYC, 1979, Bibliotheque Nationale, Paris, 1979, Corcoran Gallery of Art and George Eastman House, NY, U. Colo., 1982, Eaton Shoen Gallery, San Francisco, 1983, Barbican Art Gallery, London, 1985, Munich Stadt Mus., 1985, Walker Art Ctr., Mpls., 1986, Portland (Maine) Mus. Art, 1986, Castle Gallery, New Rochelle, NY, Hillwood Art Gallery, Greenvale, NY, UN 40th Anniversary Photography Exhibit, 1985, Paris Opera, 1988, Zeitgenossischen Photography, Frankfurt, 1989, numerous others; author: Passport, 1974, Ward 81, 1979, Falkland Road: Prostitutes of Bombay, 1981, Mother Teresa's Missions of Charity in Calcutta, 1985, Streetwise, 1988, 25 Years, A Retrospective Book, 1992, Mary Ellen Mark: Indian Circus, 1993, A Cry for Help: Stories of Homelessness and Hope, 1996, Mary Ellen Mark: American Odyssey, 1999, Twins, 2003, Exposure, 2005, others; assoc. prodr. (films) American Heart, 1992; contbr. articles, photographs to profl. publs., mags. Fulbright scholar,

1965-66, Guggenheim fellow, 1994, Erna and Victor Hasselblad Found. grant, 1997; grantee USIA, 1975, NEA, 1977, 79-80, 1990, NY State Coun. for Arts, 1977; recipient Page One award The Newspaper Guild of NY, 1979, First Pl. Feature Picture Stroy U. Mo., 1980, Canon Photo Essayist award Life Mag., 1983, 1st prize Robert F. Kennedy Journalism, 1985, Philippe Halsman award ASMP, Photojournalism award George W. Polk, 1988, Internat. Ctr. Photog. Journalism award, 1997, Cornell Capa award, 2001.; Award of Excellence, Commun Arts Photog. Ann., 1998, 1999, Merit award, Art Dirs Club, 1998, Silver award, 1998.; Gold Medal award, Soc. Publ. Designers, 1998.; Leadership award, Internat. Photog. Coun., 1999.; Award for Excellence in Photojournalism, Photog. Adminstrs. Inc, 1999.; Merrill Panitt Citizenship award, Annenberg Sch. Comm., 2000.; Lucie award for Documentary Photog, 2003.; First Prize in the Arts, World Press Photo Awards, 2004; Photo Vision award, Photog. Ctr. Northwest, 2006; named Favorite Woman Photographer of All Time, Am. Photography mag. readers. Mem. Assn. Soc. Mag. Photographers. Office: Mary Ellen Mark Libr Fl 4 37 Greene St New York NY 10013-5915 Office Fax: 212-926-1532. Business E-Mail: library@falkland.com.

MARK, MELVIN, mechanical engineering educator, consultant; b. St. Paul, Nov. 15, 1922; s. Isadore William and Fannye (Abrahamson) M.; m. Elizabeth J. Wyner, Sept. 9, 1951; children: Jonathan S., David W., Peter B. B.M.E., U. Minn., 1943, MS, 1946; Sc.D. (Teaching, Research fellow), Harvard, 1950. Registered profl. engr., Mass., Minn. Instr. N.D. State U., 1943-44, U. Minn., 1945-47; project mgr. Gen. Electric Co., Lynn., Mass., 1950-52; mgr. Raytheon Co., Wayland, Mass., 1952-56; cons. engr., 1956—; prof. Lowell Technol. Inst., 1957-59, dean faculty, 1959-62; prof. mech. engring. Northeastern U., Boston, 1963-84, dean engring., 1968-79, provost, sr. v.p. for acad. affairs, 1979-84. Vis. lectr. Mass. Inst. Tech., 1955, Brandeis U., 1958; vis. prof. U. Mass., 1984-86; mem. Mass. Bd. Registration of Profl. Engrs. and Land Surveyors, 1990-2001. Author: Thermodynamics: An Auto-Instructional Text, 1967, Concepts of Thermodynamics, 1975, Thermodynamics: Principles and Applications, 1979, Engineering Thermodynamics, 1985; contbr. articles to profl. jours. Served with USAAF, 1944-45. Recipient prize Lincoln Arc Welding Found., 1947. Hon. fellow ASME (fellow 1948-50); mem. Am. Soc. Engring. Edn., Sigma Xi, Tau Beta Pi, Pi Tau Sigma, Phi Kappa Phi. Achievements include patents in field. Home: 70 Seminary Ave Apt 184 Auburndale MA 02466-2631

MARK, MELVIN M., psychology professor, department chairman; b. Grand Island, Nebr., 1953; BA in Psychology, U. Nebr., Lincoln; MA in Social Psychology, Northwestern U., Evanston, Ill., PhD in Social Psychology, 1979. Prof. psychology Pa. State U., sr. scientist, Inst. Policy Rsch. and Evaluation, head, dept. psychology. Co-author (with G. Henry and G. Julnes): Realist Evaluation, 1998, Evaluation: An Integrated Framework for Understanding, Guiding, and Improving Policies and Programs, 2000; editor emeritus: Am. Jour. Evaluation; contbr. articles to profl. jours. Named Outstanding Tchr., Pa. State U. Coll. Liberal Arts, 2000. Mem.: Am. Evaluation Assn. (pres. 2006). Office: Dept Psychology Pa State Univ 407 Monroe Bldg University Park PA 16802-3106 Office Phone: 814-863-1755. Office Fax: 814-863-7002. Business E-Mail: m5m@psu.edu.*

MARK, MICHAEL LAURENCE, retired music educator; b. Schenectady, NY, Dec. 1, 1936; s. David and Ruth (Garbowitz) M.; m. Lois Nitekman, Jan. 28, 1942; children: Michelle, Diana. BM, The Cath. U. of Am., 1958, DMA, 1969; MA, George Washington U., 1960; M in Music Edn., U. Mich., 1962. Tchr. Prince George's County, Md. Pub. Schs., 1958-60, 61-66; assoc. prof. music Morgan State U., Balt., 1966-70; supr. music Auburn (N.Y.) Enlarged Sch. Dist., 1970-72; dir. music Elmira (N.Y.) Enlarged Sch. Dist., 1972-73; assoc. prof., sch. music Cath. U. Am., Washington, 1973-81; dean grad. sch., prof. music Towson (Md.) U., 1981-95, prof. music, 1995-98, prof. emeritus, 1998; pres. Spectrum Assocs., Inc. Mem editl. com. five jours. in field. Author: Contemporary Music Education, 1978, 3rd rev. edit., 1996, Source Readings in Music Education History, 1982, 2nd edit., 2002, 3rd edit., 2007; co-author: A History of American Music Education, 1997, 3d edit., 2007. Pres. Balt. Neighborhood, Inc. Recipient Alumni Achievement award, Cath. U., 2009. Mem. Music Educators Nat. Conf. (numerous coms., Music Educators Hall of Fame), Coll. Music Soc., Md. Music Educators Assn. (pres. 1999-2003, Hall of Fame), U. Mich. Sch. Music Alumni Soc. (bd. govs., chair). Avocations: travel, woodworking. Personal E-mail: mimark@comcast.net.

MARK, PETER A., history professor; b. NYC, Dec. 30, 1948; s. Herbert and Avra Kessler Mark; life ptnr. Odile Goerg; children: Christopher Spencer, Joshua Tobias David. PhD, Yale U., New Haven, 1976. Alexander V. Humboldt fellow U. Frankfurt, Germany, 1983—86; prof. art history Wesleyan U., Middletown, Conn., 1986—. Program dir., culture peace, senegal Karuna Ctr. Peace-Bldg., Amherst, Mass. Author: (book) Portuguese Style and Luso-African Identity, The Wild Bull and the Sacred Forest.Senegambian Initiation Masks, A cultural, Economic and Religious History of the Casamance since 1500. Recipient Civil medal, Prefet de Paris, 2002. Avocations: mountain climbing, running, photography. Office: Wesleyan Univ Dept Art and Art History Middletown CT 06459 Business E-Mail: pmark@wesleyan.edu.

MARK, REUBEN, retired consumer products company executive; b. Jersey City, Jan. 21, 1939; s. Edward and Libbie (Berman) M.; m. Arlene Slobzian, Jan. 10, 1964; children: Lisa, Peter, Stephen. AB, Middlebury Coll., 1960; MBA, Harvard U., 1963. With Colgate-Palmolive Co., NYC, 1963—, pres., gen. mgr. Venezuela, 1972-73, Can., 1973-74, v.p., gen. mgr. Far East div., 1974-75, v.p., gen. mgr. household products div., 1975-79, group v.p. domestic ops., 1979-81, exec. v.p., 1981-83, COO, 1983-84, pres., 1983-86, CEO, 1984—2007, chmn., 1986—2008. Lectr. Sch. Bus. Adminstrn. U. Conn., 1977; bd. dirs. Time Warner, 1993—, Cabela's Inc., 2004—, Colgate-Palmolive Co., Pearson PLC. Served with U.S. Army, 1961. Mem. Soap and Detergent Assn. (bd. dirs.), Grocery Mfrs. Am. (dir.), Nat. Exec. Service Corp.*

MARK, SCOTT M., pharmacist, director, healthcare educator; s. Earl A. and Maureen M. Mark; m. Laura K. Mark, Feb. 14, 2000; children: Aaron, Olivia, Evan. BS in Pharmacy, Ferris State U., 1993; BA, U. Western Ont., 1994; PharmD, U. Ky., 1995; MS, Ohio State U., 1997; MEd, U. Ill., 2004. Cert. healthcare exec. Am. Coll. Healthcare Execs., 2003. Dir. pharmacy and respiratory care svcs. Children's Nat. Med. Ctr., Washington, 1997—2004; dir. pharmacy U. Pitts. Med. Ctr., 2004—; asst. prof. U. Pitts., 2005—, vice chair, 2005—. Chmn. bd. Nightingale Nursing Registry, Peterborough, Ont., 1999—. Fellow: Am. Coll. Healthcare Execs., Am. Soc. Health-System Pharmacists (chair sect. pharmacy practice mgrs. 2004—06). Office: U Pitts Med Ctr Ste G119 200 Lothrop St Pittsburgh PA 15213 Business E-Mail: marksm@upmc.edu.

MARK, WAYNE JOSEPH, lawyer; b. Humphrey, Nebr., Aug. 29, 1947; s. Gilbert Joseph and Evelyn Adelaide (Schroeder) M.; m. Mary Alice Kessler, June 7, 1969; children: Michaella, Christopher, Jeffrey, Marissa. BS in Bus., U. Nebr., 1969, JD with distinction, 1972. Bar: Nebr., 1972, US Dist. Ct. (Dist. Nebr.), US Ct. Appeals (8th Cir.). Mem. Fraser Stryker PC LLO, Omaha, 1972—, ptnr. Dir. Nebr. Continuing Legal Edn., Lincoln, 1991-94. Fellow Am. Coll. Trial Lawyers (state chmn. 2000-02, mem. Alternative dispute resolution com.), Nebr. State Bar Found.; mem. ABA, Nebr. State Bar Assn. (mem. ho. of dels. 1987-93, pres.-elect 2006-07, pres. 2007-08), Nebr. Def. Counsel Assn. (pres. 1990-92), Omaha Bar Assn., Def. Rsch. Inst. and Trial Lawyers Assn. (state chmn. 1992-95), Nebr. Assn. Trial Lawyers (dir. 86-88); US Supreme Ct. Historical Soc. (state chmn. 2002-04); Knights of Columbus; Delta Theta Phi. Office: Fraser Stryker PC LLO 500 Energy Pl 409 S 17th St Omaha NE 68102-2609 Office Phone: 402-978-5223. E-mail: wmark@fraserstryker.com, wmark@fslf.com.

MARKAKIS, NICK (NICHOLAS WILLIAM MARKAKIS), professional baseball player; b. Woodstock, Ga., Nov. 17, 1983; Attended, Young Harris Jr. Coll., Ga. Outfielder Balt. Orioles, 2006—. Named Jr. Coll. Player of Yr., Baseball America, 2002. Office: Balt Orioles Oriole Pk at Camden Yards 333 W Camden St Baltimore MD 21201*

MARKEE, KATHERINE MADIGAN, librarian, educator; b. Cleve., Feb. 24, 1931; d. Arthur Alexis and Margaret Elizabeth (Madigan) M. AB, Trinity Coll., Washington, 1953; MA, Columbia U., 1962; MLS, Case Western Res. U., 1968. Employment mgr., br. store tng. supr. The May Co., Cleve., 1965-67; assoc. prof. libr. sci., data bases libr. Purdue U. Libr., West Lafayette, Ind., 1968—96, libr. spl. collections, 1996—2006, oral history libr., 2006—. Contbr. articles to profl. jours. Mem. ALA, AAUP, Spl. Librs. Assn., Ind. Online Users Group, Sigma Xi (Rsch. Support award 1986), Oral History Assn., Soc. Am. Archivists. Avocations: photography, sailing, gardening. Office: Purdue U Libr 504 W State St West Lafayette IN 47907-2058 Office Phone: 765-496-1323. Business E-Mail: kmarkee@purdue.edu.

MARKEL, ANNA, pharmacist, educator; b. Russia, Apr. 18, 1982; d. Igor Shtrambrand and Kira Vinokur; m. Alex Vaysman. PharmD, Midwestern U. Chgo. Coll. Pharmcy, Downers Grove, 2007. Clin. pharmacist, clin. asst. prof. U. Ill. Med. Ctr., Chgo., 2008—. Business E-Mail: amarkel1@uic.edu.

MARKEL, GREGORY ARTHUR, lawyer; b. NYC, Aug. 6, 1945; s. Edward and Ann (Larkin) M.; m. Dorothy Flanagan (div. 1979); 1 child, Kimberly; m. Belinda Elizabeth Heym, May 3, 1981; children: Alexis, Amy, William. BA in Econs., Columbia U., 1967; MBA in Fin. and Acctg., U. Mich., 1968; JD, Yale U., 1972. Bar: N.Y. 1972, U.S. Dist. Ct. (so. and ea. dists.) N.Y. 1974, U.S. Ct. Appeals (2nd cir.) 1975, U.S. Ct. Appeals (3rd cir.) 1978, U.S Dist. Ct. (no. dist.) Calif. 1984, U.S. Ct. Appeals (9th cirs.) 1984, U.S. Ct. Appeals (11th cir) 1987. Assoc. Cravath, Swaine & Moore, NYC, 1972-80; ptnr. Davis, Markel & Edwards, 1980-93, Brobeck Phleger & Harrison LLP, NYC; ptnr., chmn. litig. dept., mem. mgmt. com. Cadwalader Wickersham & Taft LLP, NYC, 2002—. Tv, radio commentator on legal issues; mem. securities litig. panel Ann. Inst. Securities Regulation, 1999, 2000, 01, 02, 03, 04, 05, 06, 07, 08; bank commentator, instr., 2004—05. Contbr. articles to profl. jours. and chpts. to publs. in field. Named to Leading Securities Litig. Def. Attys., Chambers USA, Top Litigators for Comml. Litig., Best Lawyers in Am., Legal 500 Best Lawyers in NY, NY Super Lawyers, LawDragon 500 Top Lawyers in US. Fellow NY Bar Found.; Mem. ABA (mem. litig. and antitrust sects., litig. co-chair subcom. on fed. rules rev. of the pretrial practices and discovery com.), NY State Bar Assn. (mem. comml. litig. sect.), Fed. Bar Coun., Bar Assn. of City of NY, Bond Mkt. Assn. (due diligence com.), Securities Industry Assn. (compliance and legal divsn.). Office: Cadwalader Wickersham & Taft LLP 1 World Fin Ctr New York NY 10281 Home Phone: 212-759-4351; Office Phone: 212-504-6112. Office Fax: 212-504-6666. Business E-Mail: greg.markel@cwt.com.

MARKEL, HOWARD, physician, educator; b. Detroit, Apr. 23, 1960; s. Samuel and Bernice Markel; m. Marcia Deborah Gordin, Sept. 20, 1987 (dec. Oct. 1988); m. Kate Gelya Levin, Aug. 17, 1997; children: Bess Rachel, Samantha Louise. AB in English Lit. summa cum laude, U. Mich., 1982, MD cum laude, 1986; PhD in History of Sci., Medicine & Tech., Johns Hopkins U., 1994. Diplomate Am. Bd. Pediat., 1989. Intern, resident Johns Hopkins Hosp. & Sch. Medicine, Balt., 1986-89, fellow, gen. pediat. and adolescent medicine, 1989—91, fellow, history medicine, 1989—93; asst. prof. pediatrics, communicable diseases U. Mich., Ann Arbor, 1993-98, assoc. prof. pedicatrics, communicable diseases, 1998—2002, George E. Wantz disting. prof. history medicine, 2000—, prof. pediat. and communicable diseases, prof. history, 2002—, prof. pub. health, psychiatry, 2004—. Dir. Ctr. for History of Medicine, U. Mich., 1996—. Author: The H.L. Mencken Baby Book, 1990, The Portable Pediatrician, 1992, The Portable Pediatrician, 2nd edit., 2000, The Practical Pediatrician, 1996 (Child Mag. Book of Yr., 1997), Quarantine! East European Jewish Immigrants and the New York City, 1997 (Arthur Viseltear prize, APHA, 2003), When Germs Travel, 2004. Recipient Nat. Rsch. Svc. award, NIH, 1991, James A. Shannon Dirs. award, 1996, Burroughs Wellcome Fund 40th Ann. History Medicine award, 1996, History of Medicine award, Nat. Libr. Medicine, NIH, 2005—, Woodward award, Am. Clin. and Climatol. Assn., 2008; scholar Robert Wood Johnson Found., 1996—2000, 2008—. Fellow: Am. Acad. Pediat.; mem.: Inst. Medicine Nat. Academies Sci., Am. Pediat. Soc., Soc. Pediat. Rsch., Am. Assn. History Medicine (exec. coun. 1994—97). Democrat. Jewish. Office: U Mich Ctr for History of Medicine 100 Simpson Meml Inst 102 Observatory Ann Arbor MI 48109-0725 Office Phone: 734-647-6914. Business E-Mail: howard@umich.edu.

MARKEL, TANNA MICHELLE, design educator; b. Beaver, Pa., July 7, 1982; d. John Daniel and Beth Eleanor Mortimer; m. Todd Michael Markel, Oct. 26, 2002. AA, South Fla. CC, Avon Park, 2004. Cert. in autoCAD AutoDesk, 2008; in engring. and drafting, South Fla. CC, 2004. Drafter Germaine Surveying Inc., Sebring, Fla., 2000—03; instr., drafting & design South Fla. CC, 2003—. Vol. constrn. worker Fla. Regional Bldg. Com. 2, Ctrl. Fla., 1998—. Full time min. Jehovah's Witnesses, 1996—. Avocations: travel, sports, painting, music, reading. Home: 1804 N Highlands Blvd Avon Park FL 33825 Office: South Fla CC 600 W College Dr Avon Park FL 33825 Personal E-mail: tannamarkel@gmail.com. Business E-Mail: markelt@southflorida.edu.

MARKELL, JACK A., Governor of Delaware; b. Newark, Nov. 26, 1960; m. Carla Markell; children: Michael, Molly. BS in Economics, Brown U., 1982, MS in Devel. Studies, 1982; MBA, U. Chgo., 1985. Banker First Chgo. Corp., 1982—86; cons. McKinsey & Co., Inc., 1986—88; sr. v.p. corp. devel. Nextel Communications, 1989—95; sr. mgr. Comcast Corp., 1996—98; state treas. State of Del., Dover, 1999—2009, gov., 2009—. Chmn. Del. Coll. Investment Plan, 1999—, Info. Svcs. Task Force, 2001; founder Del. Money Sch. Named one of The Rising Stars of Democratic Party, Democratic Nat. Convention, 2000, The 10 Most Influential Tech. Leaders in Phila. Region, Philly Tech. Mag., 2001, The 10 Innovative Leaders from Around the Country under Age 40, New Democrat Mag. Democrat. Jewish. Office: Office of Governor Tatnall Bldg 3d Fl Dover DE 19901*

MARKER, MARC LINTHACUM, lawyer, investor, entrepreneur; b. LA, July 19, 1941; s. Clifford Harry and Voris (Linthacum) M.; m. Sandra Vocom. Aug. 29, 1965; children: Victor, Gwendolyn. BA in Econs. and Geography, U. Calif.-Riverside, 1964; JD, U. So. Calif., 1967. Asst. v.p., asst. sec. Security Pacific Nat. Bank, LA, 1970-73; sr. v.p., chief counsel, sec. Security Pacific Leasing Corp., San Francisco, 1973-92; pres. Security Pacific Leasing Svcs. Corp., San Francisco, 1977-85, dir., 1977-92. Bd. dirs., sec. Voris, Inc., 1973-86; bd. dirs. Refiners Petroleum Corp., 1977-81, Security Pacific Leasing Singapore Ltd., 1983-85, Security Pacific Leasing Can. Ltd., 1989-92; lectr. in field. Served to comdr., USCGR. Mem. D.C. Bar Assn; Club: Army and Navy. Republican. Lutheran.

MARKER, RHONDA JOYCE, librarian; b. Ft. Meade, Md., Sept. 25, 1956; d. James W. and Virginia Mae (Conaway) Marker; m. William F. Pittock, Oct. 1, 1983; children: Alexandra Mae Marker Pittock, Olivia Joy Marker Pittock. BA, Greenville Coll., Ill., 1978; MS in Libr. and Info. Sci., Pratt Inst., Bklyn., 1985. Catalog libr. Port Authority of NY and NJ, NYC, 1981—85, assoc. chief libr., cataloging svcs., 1985—89; head, original monographic cataloging Rutgers U. Librs., New Brunswick, NJ, 1989—96, head cataloging dept., 1996—2004, metadata libr., 2004—07, repository collection mgr., 2007—. Contbr. articles to profl. jours. Recipient Wilson R. King Sr. Religion award Greenville Coll., 1978. Mem.: NOW, ALA, NY Tech. Svcs. Libr. (pres. 2002—03), NJ Libr. Assn. (edn. com. 1991—93, sec. tech. svcs. sect. 1992, pres. tech. svcs. sect. 1993—94, 2008—09), Documents Assn. NJ (chmn. state documents task force 1990—91, pres. 1992, travel grantee 1991), Govt. Documents Round Table (cataloging com. 1991—95, chair 1992—93), Assn. Libr. Collections and Tech. Svcs. (support staff travel grant jury 2004—07, membership com. 2004—08, chair 2006—07, chair continuing edn. subcom. 2007—, RDA implementation task force mem. 2007—09), Beta Phi Mu, Alpha Kappa Sigma. Office: 169 Coll Ave New Brunswick NJ 08901 Office Phone: 732-932-8573 Ext. 195. Business E-Mail: rmarker@rci.rutgers.edu.

MARKERT, CYNTHIA ALLIN, artist; b. Oak Ridge, Tenn., Apr. 7, 1954; d. George Wilbur and Barbara Anderson Allin. BFA, U. Tenn., 1977. Exhibitions include So. Living Mag. Dream House, Atlanta, Bennett Gallery, Alexis Georges, New Orleans, Circa Gallery, Setting the Stage Artspace, Alexandria, Va., DC Space, Washington, Veni Vidi Vici, Zenith Gallery, Fla. Design Mag., Susan Key Gallery, Knoxville, Tenn., Vetrum Gallery, Asheville, NC, Michael B. Tusing Gallery, Staunton, Va., Impeccable Art, Winston Salem, NC, Kress Emporium, Asheville, Hanson Gallery, Knoxville, Studio E Gallery, Jupiter, Fla., Raiford Gallery, Roswell, Ga., C.J. Varnum Gallery, Palm Beach, Fla., Louis Aronow Gallery, San Francisco, Through the Lens Gallery, Knoxville, Tenn., World Grotto Marketplace, Vagabondia, Skirt Mag., Knoxville Mag., Studio 83, Nashville, archives, Nat. Mus. Women in the Arts, Washington, exhibitions include Three Flights Up Gallery, Knoxville, So. Lady Mag., Deka Bakari Gallery, Knoxville, Tenn., commns. include, Stanford U. Dept. Lively Arts, No. Ky. U. Dept. Dance, U. Tenn. Dept. Theatre, Pandora's Books, Knoxville, Tenn. Festival Ballet, Tressa'a Jazz Club, Asheville, New Millennium Writings, Image Conscious of San Francisco, Spiral Licensing of Cherre, France. Office: Markert Du Jour PO box 724 Knoxville TN 37901 Business E-Mail: cynthia@cynthiamarkert.com.

MARKESSINI, JOAN, research scientist, psychologist; b. NYC, Aug. 14, 1942; d. John Demetrios and Diana (Vlahos) M.; m. Kenneth W. Lucas, Aug. 14, 1999. BA in English and French, U. Del., 1964; MA in Linguistics, U. Wash., 1966; PhD in Cognitive Psychology, U. Del., 1979. Tng. analyst U.S. Dept. State, Washington, 1967-70; writer, editor-in-chief Edcom Systems, Inc., Princeton, N.J., 1970-72; ednl. psychologist U. Del., Newark, 1972-78; dir. corp. and found. rels. Cath. U. Am., Washington, 1978-84; asst. dir. resources devel. Nat. Trust for Hist. Preservation, Washington, 1984-85; sr. staff psychologist BDM Internat., Inc., McLean, Va., 1985-87; dir. publs. and communications Maxwell Communication Corp., McLean, 1987-90; psychologist Allen Corp., Alexandria, Va., 1990—95; dir. R&D, dep. dir. med. systems and distance learning L-3 Comm., Inc.: LINK Simulation and Tng., NYC, 1995—2002; founder, pres. WELLTrek Internat., LLC, 1995—. Author: The First Year of Life (13 vols.), 1971, The First Twelve Months of Life, 1973, Effects of Listener Familiarity and Topic Knowledge on Speech Communication, 1979, TeleMedicine Art and Practice: An Instructional Program Series, 1995, A Taxonomy of Cognitive Capabilities for Executives, 1991; (film) Meeting the Challenge, 2000; editor: Perspectives on Leadership, Vols. 1-5, 1993; contb. articles to profl. jours.; prodr. (film) Death of a Giant, 1967; Dream Work, 2009. numerous sci. and tech. reports. U. Wash. grad. fellow, 1965-66, U. Mich. fellow, 1965, U. Del. fellow, 1977-79. Mem. Am. Psychol. Assn., Assn. Psychol. Type (gen.), N.Y. Acad. Scis., Nat. Mus. Women in Arts (charter), Am. Film Inst. Club. Avocations: theater, opera, interior decorating, gardening. Home: PO Box 4218 Arlington VA 22204-0218 Office Phone: 703-684-4862.

MARKEY, BETSY (ELIZABETH HELEN MARKEY), United States Representative from Colorado; b. Cresskill, NJ, Apr. 27, 1956; d. Thomas Francis and Catherine A. (Dillon) Markey; m. James Francis Kelly, May 5, 1984; children: Katherine Angela, Erin Susan, Al. BA in Polit. Sci., U. Fla., 1978; MA in Pub. Adminstrn., Am. U., 1983; grad., Colo. Inst. Leadership Training, 2002. Staff asst. US Senator John Durkin, Washington, 1979, US Ho. of Reps., Washington, 1979-81; sr. asst. to v.p. Am. U., Washington, 1981-83; presdl. mgmt. intern US Dept. Treasury, Washington, 1983-84; chief policy and tng. divsn. office Info. Sys. Security US Dept. State, Washington, 1984-87; co-founder, CEO, CFO Syscom Svcs., Kensington, Mo., 1989—95; owner Huckleberry's, Fort Collins, Colo., 1995—2001; regional dir. 4th congl. dist. Senator Ken Salazar, 2005—07; mem. US Congress from 4th Colo. dist., 2009—. Founder No. Colo. Dem. Bus. Coalition, 2001; chair Larimer County Dem. Party, 2002—05; legis. aide Ho. Subcom. Post Office & Civil Svc. Vol. Christian Children's Fund, 1979—83, Poudre R-1 School Dist.; pres. bd. dirs. Food Bank Larimer County. Recipient Meritorious Honor award, US Dept. State, 1986; named a Presdl. Mgmt. Fellow, 1983. Mem.: NAFE, NOW, Nat. Assn. Women Bus. Owners, Internat. Network Women in Enterprise & Trade, Pi Alpha Alpha. Democrat. Avocation: outdoor sports. Office: US Congress 1229 Longworth House Office Bldg Washington DC 20515-0604 also: Dist Office 430 W Mountain Ave Fort Collins CO 80521-2605 Office Phone: 202-225-4676. Office Fax: 202-225-5870.*

MARKEY, EDWARD JOHN, United States Representative from Massachusetts; b. Malden, Mass., July 11, 1946; s. John E. and Christine M. Markey; m. Susan Blumenthal. BA, Boston Coll., 1968, JD, 1972. Bar: Mass. Mem. Mass. House of Reps., 1973-76, US Congress from 7th Mass. Dist., 1976—; chmn. US House Energy Independence & Global Warming Com., 2007—; mem. US House Nat. Resources Com., US House Energy & Commerce Com. Mem. editorial staff: Boston Coll. Law Rev. Served with USAR, 1968-73. Mem. Mass. Bar Assn. (Mass. Legislator of Year 1975) Clubs: K.C. Democrat. Roman Catholic. Office: US Congress 2108 Rayburn House Office Bldg Washington DC 20515-

2107 also: 188 Concord St Ste 102 Framingham MA 01702 Home: 7 Townsend St Malden MA 02148-6322 Office Phone: 202-225-2836, 508-875-2900. Office Fax: 202-226-0092.*

MARKEY, JAMES KEVIN, lawyer; b. Springfield, Ill., July 15, 1956; s. James Owen and Marjorie Jean (Diesness) M.; m. Allison Markey; children: Lauren, Katherine. BBA with highest honors, U. Notre Dame, 1977; JD cum laude, U. Mich., 1980; MBA, U. Chgo., 1987; LLM in Taxation, DePaul U., 1993. CPA Ill.; bar: Ill. 1980. Assoc. Chapman & Cutler, Chgo., 1980-81; atty. Quaker Oats Co., Chgo., 1981-84; corp. counsel Baxter Healthcare Corp., Deerfield, Ill., 1984-90; v.p. law and other positions Motorola, Inc., Schaumburg, Ill., 1990-2000; v.p., chief counsel-securities and internat. Kellogg Co., Battle Creek, Mich., 2000—06; v.p., sec., gen. counsel MAG Industrial Automation Sys., LLC, Sterling Heights, Mich., 2006—08; sr. v.p. & sr. corp. counsel Affiliate Computer Sci, Inc., 2008—. Mem. ABA, Beta Alpha Psi, Beta Gamma Sigma. Avocations: racquetball, running, bridge. Home: 8101 Greensboro Dr Plano TX 75025-2588 Office: 2828 N Haskell Plano TX 75024 Business E-Mail: jim.markey@att.net.

MARKEY, JOHN K., lawyer; b. Melrose, Mass., Aug. 1, 1947; BS cum laude, Boston Coll., 1969, JD, 1973. Bar: Mass. 1974. Asst. dist. atty. Middlesex County, 1974-77; asst. US atty. Dist. Mass., 1978; mem. Mintz, Levin, Cohn, Ferris, Glovsky and Popeo PC, ptnr., Litig., chmn., pro bono com. Mem.: Boston Bar Assn. (task force on drugs & the cts., com. on state cts.study, chmn. criminal law sect. 1990—92), Mass. Bar Assn., ABA. Address: Mintz Levin Cohn Ferris Glovsky & Popeo PC 1 Financial Ctr Fl 39 Boston MA 02111-2621 Office Phone: 617-348-1686. Office Fax: 617-542-2241. Business E-Mail: jmarkey@mintz.com.

MARKEY, WILLIAM ALAN, health facility administrator, consultant; b. Cleve., Dec. 29, 1927; s. Oscar Bennett and Claire (Feldman) M.; m. Irene Nelson, Oct. 31, 1954; children: Janet Ellen Markey-Hisakawa, Suzanne Katherine Markey-Johnson. Student, Case Inst. Tech., 1945—48; BA, U. Mich., 1950; MS, Yale U., 1954. Resident in hosp. adminstrn. Beth Israel Hosp., Boston, 1953-54; asst. dir. Montefiore Hosp., Pitts., 1954-56; asst. adminstr. City of Hope Med. Ctr., Duarte, Calif., 1956-57, adminstrv. dir., 1957-66; assoc. dir. cancer hosp. project, instr. pub. health U. So. Calif. Sch. Medicine, 1966-67, asst. clin. prof. pub. health and cmty. medicine, 1968-70, asst. prof., 1970-75, dep. dir. regional med. programs, 1967-71; adminstr. Health Care Agy., County of San Diego, 1971-74, health svcs. cons., 1974-75; dir. Maricopa County Dept. Health Svcs., Phoenix, 1975-79, cons., 1979-80; adminstr. Sonoma Valley Hosp., Calif., 1980—83. Lectr. pub. health Sch. Pub. Health, UCLA, 1969-74; lectr. cmty. medicine Sch. Medicine, U. Calif., San Diego, 1973-75; cons. LA County Dept. Hosps., 1966-71, cons. Hosp./Health Svcs., 1983—; CEO Chinese Hosp., San Francisco, 1985-86, 90-91; adj. instr. Golden Gate U., 1992-96. Mem. bd. edn. Duarte Unified Sch. Dist., 1967-72, pres., 1970-72; bd. dir. Hosp. Coun. So. Calif., 1963-67, sec., 1966-67, Duarte Pub. Libr. Assn., 1965-72, Duarte-Bradbury chpt. Am. Field Svc., 1965-72, Duarte-Bradbury Cmty. Chest, 1961-68, Ctrl. Ariz. Health Svcs. Agy., 1975-80, Vis. Nurse Assn. The Redwoods, Santa Rosa, Calif., 1985-86, Sonoma Greens Homeowners Assn., 1990-95, 2002-05, Sonoma City Opera, 1987, 93, United Way, Sonoma, 1996—; com. chmn. Sonoma County Bd. Realtors, 1990-92; active Sonoma County Multiple Listing Svc., 1987-97; mem. Sonoma County Human Svcs. Commn., 2003-. With AUS, 1950-52. Fellow Am. Coll. Health Care Execs. (life); mem. Am. Hosp. Assn. (life), APHA, Royal Soc. Health, Calif. Hosp. Assn. (trustee 1966-69, dir. 1966-69), Internat. Fedn. Hosps., Hosp. Coun. No. Calif. (dir. 1981-83), Kiwanis, Rotary (past pres. Duarte). Home: 866 Princeton Dr Sonoma CA 95476-4186

MARKEY, WINSTON ROSCOE, aeronautical engineering educator; b. Buffalo, Sept. 20, 1929; s. Roscoe Irvin and Catherine L. (Higgins) M.; m. Phoebe Anne Sproule, Sept. 10, 1955; children: Karl Richard, Katherine Ilse, Kristina Anne. BS, MIT, 1951, Sc.D., 1956. Engr. MIT, 1951-57, asst. prof., 1957-62, assoc. prof., 1962-66, prof., 1966—, undergrad. officer, 1988-2000, dir. Measurement Systems Lab., 1961-89. Chief scientist USAF, 1964-65, mem. sci. adv. bd., 1966-69 Author: (with J. Hovorka) The Mechanics of Inertial Position and Heading Indication, 1961; Assoc. editor: AIAA Jour, 1963-66. Recipient Exceptional Civilian Service award, USAF, 1965. Mem. Sigma Xi, Tau Beta Pi, Gamma Alpha Rho. Home: 11 Edgewood Rd Lexington MA 02420-3501 Office: MIT Bldg 33-208 Cambridge MA 02139 Office Phone: 617-253-2921. Personal E-mail: wrmarkey@earthlink.net. Business E-Mail: wrmarkey@mit.edu.

MARKEZICH, RON, computer software company executive; BA in Mgmt. Info. Sys., U. Notre Dame. With electronics and high tech. group Accenture (formerly Andersen Consulting); joined Microsoft, 1998; gen. mgr. fin. and adminstrn. info. tech. Microsoft Info. Tech., gen. mgr. info. tech. client svcs., gen. mgr. global tech. svcs.; CIO, v.p. managed solutions Microsoft Corp., Redmond, Wash., 2004, corp. v.p. Microsoft Online. Office: Microsoft Corp 1 Microsoft Way Redmond WA 98052-6399*

MARKHAM, CHARLES HENRY, neurologist; b. Pasadena, Calif., Dec. 24, 1923; s. Fred Smith and Maziebelle Valeta (Glover) M.; m. Kathleen Tiernan, Sept. 29, 1945 (div. 1971); children: Charles H., Arthur Tiernan, Daphne, James Daniel; m. Lisa Wells Overly, July 10, 1971; children: John Wells, Sara Brennan. Student, Colo. Sch. Mines, 1941-43; AB, Stanford U., 1947, MD, 1951. Intern, med. asst. resident Lane Hosp., San Francisco, 1950-52; fellow in neurology Children's Med. Ctr., Boston, 1952-53; asst. resident Boston City Hosp., 1953-54, chief resident, 1954-55; asst. prof. neurology UCLA Sch. Medicine, 1958-65, assoc. prof., 1965-70, assoc. prof. neurology, 1970-71, prof. neurology, 1971-94, prof. emeritus, 1994—; rsch. prof. dept. psychology U. Calif., Santa Barbara, 1995—. Sci. dir. Dystonia Med. Rsch. Found., Chgo., 1985-94, mem. bd. trustees, 1994—; sci. dir. Hereditary Disease Found., L.A., 1979-81; mem. adv. bd. Am. Parkinson Disease Assn., N.Y.C., 1976-83; attending physician UCLA Sch. Medicine, 1957—, cons. in neurology St. John's Hosp., Santa Monica, Calif., 1960-94. Contbr. articles to profl. jours.; author numerous books and abstracts. Trustee Westlake Sch. for Girls, L.A., 1965-74, St. Matthews Parish Sch., L.A., 1985-87; bd. dirs. Jubilee Christian Acad., 1996-99, Wildling Mus., 1997-2005, Las Positas Park Found., 1998-2000. With U.S. Army, 1943-45, ETO. Grantee NIH, NASA. Mem. Am. Acad. Neurology, AAAS, Am. Bd. Psychiatry and Neurology, Am. Epilepsy Soc., Am. Neurol. Assn., Am. Pain Soc., Am. Soc. for Gravitational and Space Biology, Bárány Soc. (Hallpike-Nylen prize 1990), Internat. Brain Rsch. Orgn., Internat. League Against Epilepsy, L.A. Soc. Neurology and Psychiatry, N.Y. Acad. Scis., Soc. for Neurosci., Western Inst. on Epilepsy, Rsch. Soc. for Parkinson Disease and Movement Disorders (pres. 1984-2000). Republican. Achievements include research in L-dopa and medical and surgical therapy for Parkinson's disease, dystonia, brain stem mechanisms for vestibular and quick and slow eye movements, long-term exposure to microgravity, space motion sickness, vestibular response to gravity, alcohol. Personal E-mail: cmarkham1@cox.net.

MARKHAM, CLAIRE AGNES (M. CLARE MARKHAM), retired chemistry educator, consultant; b. New Haven, Aug. 12, 1919; d. James J. and Agnes V. (Manning) M. BA, St. Joseph Coll., West Hartford, Conn., 1940, DHL (hon.), 1989; PhD, Cath. U. Am., 1952. Joined Sisters of Mercy, Roman Cath. Ch., 1940. Tchr. chemistry and math. Sacred Heart H.S., Waterbury, Conn., 1945-49; mem. faculty chemistry St. Joseph Coll., 1952-97, cons. instl. advancement, 1996—, prof. emeritus in chemistry, 1997—. Dept. chair St. Joseph Coll., 1959-70, dean Grad. Sch., 1979-87, asst. to pres. acad. affairs, 1987-95; dir. numerous tchr. insts., 1959-89; mem. vis. faculty Calvin's Lab., NSF, U. Calif., Berkeley, 1967-68. dir. CT Talent Prog., 2002-03. Contbr. articles to profl. jours.; editor sci. series McGraw Hill, 1956-60. Undersec. for Energy, Office of Policy and Mgmt., State of Conn., Hartford, 1977—79; mem. adv. com. Permanent Commn. Status of Women, Hartford, 1995—; mem. adv. coun. Dept. Higher Edn., State of Conn., Hartford, 1970—80; energy advisor Nat. Gov.'s Assn., 1977—79; bd. dirs. Conn. Energy Co-op, 2000—03. Recipient Equity award AAUW, 1992, Sci. Advocacy award, CSTA, 2002, award for outstanding sci. adv. Conn. Sci. Tchrs. Assn., 2002; Faculty fellow NSF, Trondheim, Norway, 1967, Travel grantee, cons., Madras, India, 1974-77. Fellow Conn. Acad. for Edn.; mem. AAAS, Am. Chem. Soc. (councilor 1968-88, chair Conn. Valley sect. 1955-67, 20 Yr. award 1988), Conn. Acad. Sci. and Engring. (founding mem., chair tech. bd. 1994-98), Sigma Xi (sect. chair 1993-95). Democrat. Avocations: photography, music, literature. Home: 1678 Asylum Ave West Hartford CT 06117-2791 Office: St Joseph Coll West Hartford CT 06117 Office Phone: 860-231-5501. Business E-Mail: cmarkham@sjc.edu.

MARKHAM, FRANK BELL, business educator; m. Marylin Vaz. BS in Mgmt., Embry-Riddle Aero. U., Daytona Beach, FL, 1978; MBA, Troy State U., Ala., 1980; D in Bus. Administrn., La. Tech U., Ruston, 1991. Maj., aviation US Army, 1968—88; asst. prof., mgmt. Radford U., Va., 1991—96; assoc. prof. bus. Lambuth U., Jackson, Tenn., 1996—98, NW Mo. State U., Maryville, 1998—2001, Mesa State Coll., Grand Junction, Colo., 2001—. Contbr. rsch. papers (Best Paper awrd, 1995). Cons. Jackson Area C of C, 1996—98. Decorated 3 DFC awards US Army, 101 Airborne Divsn., Master Aviator Badge award US Army; recipient Bronze Star award, US Army, 101 Airborne Divsn., 1969—70, Meritorious Svc. medal, US Army, 1984, 1988; named one of BSG Hall of Fame, McGraw-Hill & Glo-Bus Software, 2008. Mem.: SW Acad. Mgmt., Southern Mgmt. Assn. (dir. placement svcs. 1998—2008). Office: Mesa State Coll Dept Bus Admin 1100 North Ave Grand Junction CO 81501

MARKHAM, IAN STEPHEN, theology studies educator, dean; b. Crediton, England, Sept. 19, 1962; arrived in U.S., 2001; s. Stephen Keith Markham and Beryl Evelyn Walker; m. Lesley Patricia Dunn, July 4, 1987; 1 child, Luke Stephen Austin. BTh, Kings Coll., London, Eng., 1985; MLitt, Cambridge univ., Cambridge, Eng., 1990; PhD ethics, Exeter Devon, Exeter, Eng., 1994. Lectr. in theology Univ. Exeter, Devon, England, 1989—96; prof. of theology and pub. life Liverpool Hope Univ., Liverpool, England, 1996—2001; dean, pres. of the seminary, prof. of theology and ethics Hartford Seminary, Conn., 2001—07; dean, pres. Va. Theol. Seminary, 2007—. Coun. mem. and dir. Advt. Stds. Authority, London, 1993—99; Teape lectr., India, 2004; vis. prof. Leeds Metro. U., 2005. Author: Plurality and Christian Ethics, 1994, Truth and the Reality of God, 1999, Why Bother With Ethics, 2006; editor: September 11: Religious Perspectives on the causes and Consequences, 2002, Theology of Engagement, 2003, Globalization, Ethics and Islam: The Case of Bediuzzaman Said Nursi, 2005, Do Morals Matter?, 2007, Understanding Christian Doctrine, 2008, Liturgical Life Principles, 2009. Mem.: Am. Acad. of Religion. Home and Office: Va Theol Seminary 3737 Seminary Rd Alexandria VA 22304 Office Phone: 703-461-1701. Business E-Mail: imarkham@vts.edu.

MARKHAM, J. DAVID, secondary school educator, writer, historical consultant; b. Austin, Tex., Dec. 26, 1945; s. James Walter and Myrtle (Sturges) M.; m. Barbara Ann Munson, May 14, 1983. BS, U. Iowa, 1971; MA, U. No. Iowa, 1972; postgrad., So. Ill. U., 1972-74, U. Wis., 1981-82; MEd, Ariz. State U., 1991; postgrad., Fla. State U., 1996—97, Oxford U., Eng., 1996. Instr. sociology U. Wis., Fond du Lac/Stevens Point, 1974-76; dir. Vietnam edn. grants Wis. Dept. Vet. Affairs, Madison, 1979-83; coordinator internat. edn. AFSCME, Phoenix, 1983-84; vets. svc. officer Ariz. Vets. Service Commn., Phoenix, 1984-86; asst. to dir. Commn. on Ariz. Environ., Phoenix, 1986-88; div. supr. Ariz. Dept. Liquor Lics. and Control, Phoenix, 1988-89; world history and English tchr. Tolleson Union H.S. Dist., 1990-92; world history tchr. Lake Worth H.S., Palm Beach, Fla., 1992-2000; history tchr. Tumwater H.S., 2000—01, Centralia H.S., 2001—02, Orting H.S., 2002—07. Instr. sociology and polit. sci., Maricopa C.C. Dist., Phoenix, 1985-91; instr. Palm Beach C.C., 1993-95. Author: Napoleon's Road to Glory: Triumphs, Defeats and Immortality, 2003, Imperial Glory: The Bulletins of Napoleon's Grande Armée, 2003, Napoleon and Dr. Verling on St. Helena, 2005, Napoleon for Dummies, 2005; co-author: Napoleon: The Final Verdict, 1996; contbg. author: Ency. World History, 2005, Ency. Leadership, 2005, Ency. Am. Revolution, 2005, Ency. French Revolutionary and Napoleonic Wars, 2005; contbr. articles to profl. jours.; author: The Road to St Helena: Napoleon After Waterloo, 2008; editor: History Revisited: The Great Battles, 2008. Bd. dirs. World Affairs Coun. Ariz., 1987-90; v.p. Ariz. Com. for Bicentennial of the French Revolution, 1988-89; pres. Olympia World Affairs Coun., 2003—; bd. dirs. Friends of Ft. Lewis Mil. Mus., 2007-. With US Army, 1968-69, Vietnam. Decorated Bronze Star; recipient medal of Landtag of Badden-Württemberg, Germany, 1987, Spl. Svc. award Alliance Francaise of Phoenix, 1992, Marengo medal Province of Alessandria, Italy, 1997, medal City of Ajaccio, Corsica, France, 1997, 2008, Gen. Coun. Southern Corsica, 2008, Territorial Collection Corsica, 2008, Gold medal La Renaissance française. Fellow Internat. Napoleonic Soc. (exec. v.p. and editor-in-chief 1995—, pres. 2008-, Legion of Merit 1996); mem. Napoleonic Alliance (exec. v.p. 1992—2004, pres. 2004-07, editor conf. procs., editor bull., Pres. medal 1998), Inst. on Napoleon and the French Revolution, Western Soc. for French History, Sierra Club, Population Connection, Alpha Kappa Delta, Phi Kappa Phi, Phi Alpha Theta. Democrat. Avocations: collecting Napoleonic items, writing history, outdoor activities, travel, music. Home: 1841 52nd Way SE Olympia WA 98501-8000 E-mail: imperialglory@comcast.net.

MARKHAM, JOHN CHARLES, biologist; b. Hood River, Oreg., Apr. 2, 1943; s. Wilbur A. and Mamie L. (Graybill) M. AB in Biol. Scis., Stanford U., 1965; MA in Biol. Oceanography, Oreg. State U., 1967; PhD in Marine Biology, U. Miami, 1974. Cert. tchr., Oreg. Rsch. assoc. Bermuda Biol. Sta. for Rsch., St. Georges, 1974-79; researcher Centro de Investigaciones de Quintana Roo, Puerto Morelos, Mex., 1986-87; dir. Arch Cape (Oreg.) Marine Lab., 1979—. Courtesy rsch. prof. Oreg. State U., Corvallis, 1985—; rschr. systematics and distbn. of Isopoda Bopyridae. Contbr. articles to profl. jours. Advisor Haystack Rock Awareness Program, Cannon Beach, Oreg., 1985—. Recipient scholarship Stanford U., 1963-64, A.P. Giannini Found. scholarship, 1964-65; Fulbright scholar, 1967-68; rsch. grantee NSF, 1976-79, Christensen Rsch. Found., 1989, Govt. of France, 1991; Robert E. Maytag fellow U. Miami, 1968-71, Exxon Corp. fellow, 1975. Mem. Crustacean Soc., So. Calif. Acad. Scis. (life), Biol. Soc. Wash. Avocations: scuba diving, travel, photography. Office: Arch Cape Marine Lab 108 W Markham Ave Arch Cape OR 97102-0105

MARKHAM, REED B., speech communication professor; b. Alhambra, Calif., Feb. 14, 1957; s. John F. and Reeda (Bjarason) M. BA, MA, Brigham Young U., 1982; BS, Regents Coll., 1981, MA, 1982; MPA, U. So. Calif., 1983; MA, UCLA, 1989; PhD, Columbia Pacific U., 1991. Mem. faculty Brigham Young U., Provo, Utah, 1984, Calif. State U., Fullerton and Long Beach, 1984, Northridge, 1985, El Camino Coll., Torrance, Calif., 1986, Orange Coast Coll., Costa Mesa, Calif., 1986, Pasadena Coll., Calif., 1986, Fullerton CC, Calif., 1986; instr., mem. pub. rels. com. Chaffey Coll., Calif., 1986-87; prof., CARES dir. Calif. State Poly. U., Pomona, 1987-98; adj. prof. Calif. State U., LA, 1992-93, dir. Ctr. for Student Retention, 1995—; prof. East LA Coll., 1996—98, Salt Lake CC, 1998—99, Daytona Coll., 2005—06, Daytona State Coll., 2006—09, Daytona Beach CC, 2006—09; ret. Speechwriter US Supreme Ct., Washington, 1980; rsch. asst. to pres. Ctr. Study of Cmty. Coll., 1985; cons. gifted children program Johns Hopkins U./Scripps Coll., Claremont, Calif., 1987-88; mem. faculty Riverside (Calif.) Coll., 1989-90, Rio Hondo (Calif.) Coll., 1989-90, English Lang. Inst., 1994, Calif. Poly Summer Bridge, 1989-95; PACE Program East LA, 1995-96; adj. prof. Citrus Coll., 1998—, U. So. Calif., 1998—, Fla. CC, Jacksonville, 2004-05; mem. Pres.'s Coalition Am. Reads Challenge, 1999; mem. Olympic News Svc. 2002, 2001-; mem. governing bd. Coll. of Caribbean, 2005. Author: Power Speechwriting, 1983, Power Speaking, 1990, Public Opinion, 1990, Advances in Public Speaking, 1991, Leadership 2000: Success Skills for University Students, 1995, Excellence in Public Speaking, 1997; co-author: Student Retention: Success Models in Higher Education, 1996, Upward Bound Program Grant Proposal, 1996, Making Marriage Magnificent, 1998; editor Trojan in Govt., U. So. Calif., 1983; editl. bd. mem. Edn. Digest, Speaker and Gavel, Innovative Higher End., Pub. Rels. Rev., Nat. Forensic Jour., The Forensic Educator, Clearinghouse for the Contemporary Educator, Hispanic Am. Family Mag.; writer NY Times, Christian Sci. Monitor; ednl. columnist San Bernardino (Calif.) Sun., 1992-98. VOICE, 2000-01; contbg. editor Great Lives, 2002, American Lives, 2004; columnist, DeLand Forum, 2007; opinion editl. author, Orlando Sentinel, 2007; Co-Author: Money 911: Tested Strategies to Survive Financial Emergency, 2008. Pres. bd. trustees Regents Coll., 1986; appointed to Pres.'s Coalition for Am. Reads Challenge; mem. Coun. Study of Cmty. Colls., 2002—; torchbearer Olympic Winter Games, 2002; unit commr. Boy Scouts of Am., 2002—; bd. govs. Univ. Coll. of Caribbean, 2005. Mem. Am. Comm. Assn. (unit commr. Jour. editl. bd. 2007-08), Doctorate Assn. NY Scholars, Nat. Assn. Pvt. Nontraditional Colls. (accrediting com. 1989—), Pub. Rels. Soc. Am. (dir.-at-large inland empire 1992-93, faculty advisor), Ctr. Study Cmty. Colls., Middle States Commn. Higher Edn.(accrediter, 2008) Mem. Lds Ch. Mailing: 1155 CR 4139 Deland FL 32724 Office Phone: 386-785-2035. Personal E-mail: rljmarkham@comcast.net, reed_markham@hotmail.com, reed_markham@yahoo.com. Business E-Mail: markham@daytonastate.edu.

MARKHOTOK, ANNA, physics professor; b. St. Petersburg, Russia; married. PhD, Ioffe Physics Tech. Inst. Russian Acad. Scis., St. Petersburg. Cert. mountaineering & climbing instr. Moscow, 1993. Rsch. assoc. U. Wash., Seattle, 2003—06; asst. prof. MMA, Castine, Maine, 2006—. Contbr. articles & sci. papers to profl. jours. Mem.: AIAA, APS.

MARKISON, BRIAN A., pharmaceutical executive; BS, Iona Coll., 1982. Various mktg. and sales positions Bristol-Myers Squibb, 1982—98, sr. v.p., neuroscience/infectious disease, pres. neuroscience/infectious disease/dermatology, v.p., operational excellence and productivity, 1998—2001; pres. Bristol-Myers Squibb's Oncology, Virology and Oncology Therapeutics, 2001—04; COO King Pharm., Inc., Bristol, Tenn., 2004, pres. & CEO, 2004—07, chmn., pres., CEO, 2007—. Bd. dir. King Pharm., Inc., Bristol, Tenn., 2004—. Office: King Pharmaceuticals Inc 501 Fifth St Bristol TN 37620*

MARKLAND, ALAYNE DENISE, geriatrician, educator; m. Jason Kulvicki, May 29, 1999; children: Reid Eugene, Anna Marie. DO, U. North Tex. Health Sci. Ctr., Ft. Worth; MSc, U. Tex. Health Sci. Ctr., San Antonio. Diplomate Am. Bd. Internal Medicine. Asst. prof. U. Ala., Birmingham; staff physician Birmingham VA Med. Ctr. Recipient Career Devel. award, VA Rehabilitative Rsch. & Devel., 2008; Loan Repayment Program grant, NIH, 2005—08, Hartford Found. Geriat. Spl. Residents grant, John A. Hartford Found., 2008—. Mem.: ACP, Am. Geriat. Soc. Avocations: running, skiing, scuba diving. Office: Birmingham VA Med Ctr Univ Ala 1530 3rd Ave S Birmingham AL 35294 Office Phone: 205-934-3259.

MARKLAND, FRANCIS SWABY, JR., biochemist, educator; b. Phila., Jan. 15, 1936; s. Francis Swaby Sr. and Willie Lawrence (Averritt) M.; m. Barbara Blake, Jun. 27, 1959 (dec. April 5, 1996); children: Cathleen Blake, Francis Swaby IV; m. Wendy Jacquemin, Dec. 20, 2007. BS, Pa. State U., 1957; PhD, Johns Hopkins U., 1964. Postdoctoral fellow UCLA, 1964-66, asst. prof. biochemistry, 1966-73; vis. asst. prof. U. So. Calif., Los Angeles, 1973-74, assoc. prof., 1974-83, prof., 1983—, acting chmn. dept. biochemistry, 1986-88, vice-chmn., 1988-92, assoc. dean for sci. affairs, 2004—08. Cons. Clin. Lab. Med. Group, LA, 1977-88, Cortech, Inc., Denver, 1983-88, Maret Corp., Wayne, Pa., 1996-2000; co-founder Pivotal BioScis., Inc., 2003-; mem. biochem., endocrinology study sect. NIH, 1986-90, mem FLAIR prog., rev. NIH NCI, 2002-2003, 2008-09, ad hoc. mem. NIAD Spl. Jour. Review, 2008. Contbg. editor: Toxicon, Jour. Natural Toxins; contbr. articles to profl. jours.:. Mem. Angeles Choral, L.A. Capt. USNR, 1957-59, ret. Recipient NIH rsch. career devel. award USPHS, NIH, 1968-73, 2007-; rsch. grantee Nat. Cancer Inst., 1979-86, 91-93, Nat. Heart Lung and Blood Inst., 1984-88, 95-2002, State of Calif. Breast Cancer Rsch. Program, 1995-2002, State Calif. Cancer Rsch. Program, 2000-03, U.S. Army Prostate Cancer Rsch. Program, 2004—, Komen Found., 2004-, US Army Ovarian Cancer Program, 2007-; study sect. reviewer Western region Am. Heart Assn., 2003-06. Mem. AAAS, Am. Soc. Biochem. and Molecular Biology, Am. Chem. Soc., Internat. Soc. on Toxinology, Internat. Soc. on Thrombosis and Haemostasis (subcom. exogenous hemostatic factors, chair 1994-96, co-chair 1999—), Am. Assn. Cancer Rsch., Am. Soc. Hematology, Sigma Xi, Alpha Zeta. Avocations: singing, aerobics, bicycling. Office: U So Calif Keck Sch Medicine Cancer Rsch Lab Rm 106 1303 N Mission Rd Los Angeles CA 90033-1020 Business E-Mail: markland@usc.edu.

MARKLEY, JILL L., music educator; d. Robert E. and Susuan M. Graybill; m. Dennis L. Markley, Dec. 17, 1994; children: Alexander R., Lauren S. MusB, James Madison U., Harrisonburg, Va., 1992; MusM, West Chester U., Pa., 1998. Music tchr. Dallastown Area Sch. Dist., Pa., 1992—94; band dir. Palmyra Area HS, Pa., 1994—2000; instr. Harrisburg Area CC, Lancaster, Pa., 2005—. Home: 2491 Impala Dr Ronks PA 17572 Office: Harrisburg Area CC 1641 Old Philadelphia Pike Lancaster PA 17602

MARKLEY, WILLIAM C., lawyer; b. Salina, Kans., Dec. 21, 1945; m. Marcia A. Markley. BS, US Naval Acad., 1967; JD, Hastings Coll. Law, 1974. Sr. v.p., gen. counsel, sec. Jacobs Engring. Group Inc., Pasadena, Calif. Mem.: Am. Corp. Counsel Assn., State Bar Calif., ABA, LA County Bar Assn. Office: Jacobs Engring Group Inc 1111 S Arroyo Pky PO Box 7084 Pasadena CA 91109-7084 Office Phone: 626-578-6855. Office Fax: 626-578-6990. Business E-Mail: Bill.Markley@Jacobs.com.

MARKLIN, GEORGE, physicist; PhD, U. Md., Coll. Pk., 1983. Rsch. scientist U. Wash., Seattle, 2005—. Mem.: APS.

MARKMAN, RONALD, artist, educator; b. Bronx, NY, May 29, 1931; s. Julius and Mildred (Berkowitz) M.; m. Barbara Miller, Sept. 12, 1959; 1 dau., Ericka Elizabeth. B.F.A., Yale U., 1957, M.F.A., 1959. Instr. Art Inst. Chgo., 1960-64; prof. fine arts Ind. U., 1964—. Color cons. Hallmark Card Co., 1959-60 One-man shows Kanegis Gallery, 1959, Reed Coll., 1966, Terry Dintenfass Gallery, 1965, 66, 68, 70, 76, 79, 82, 85, The Gallery, Bloomington, Ind., 1972, 79, Indpls. Mus., 1974, Tyler Sch. Art, Phila., 1976, Franklin Coll., 1980, Dart Gallery, Chgo., 1981, Patrick King Gallery, Indpls., 1983, 86, John Heron Gallery, Indpls., 1985, New Harmony Gallery, 1985, Mitchell Gallery, St. John's Coll., Annapolis, Md., 2005; two-man show Dintenfass Gallery, 1984; group shows include Kanegis Gallery, Boston, 1958, 60, 61, Boston Arts Festival, 1959, 60, Mus. Modern Art, 1959, 66, Whitney Mus., N.Y.C., 1960, Art Inst. Chgo., 1964, Gallery 99, Miami, Fla., 1966, Ball State Coll., 1966, Butler Inst., 1967, Indpls. Mus., 1968, 69, 72, 74, Phoenix Gallery, N.Y.C., 1970, Harvard U., 1974, Skidmore Coll., 1975, Am. Acad. Arts and Letters, 1977, 89, Tuthill-Gimprich Gallery, N.Y.C., 1980, Patrick King Gallery, 1988, numerous others; represented in permanent collections Met. Mus. Art, Mus. Modern Art, Art Inst. Chgo., Library of Congress, Cin. Art Mus., Bklyn. Mus., Ark. Art Center, others; commns. include 5 murals Riley Children's Hosp., Indpls., 1986; installation Evanston (Ill.) Art Ctr., 1989, 2-part installation Ortho Child Care Ctr., Raritan, N.J., 1991; illustrator Acid and Basics-A Guide to Acid-Base Physiology, 1992. Served with U.S. Army, 1952-54. Recipient Ind. Arts Comm. award, 1990, 93; Fulbright grantee, Italy, 1962, grantee Ctr. for New TV, Chgo., 1992; Lilly Endowment fellow, 1989, honorable mention, Ohio Film Festival, 1995. Home and Office: 1623 Saint Margarets Rd Annapolis MD 21401-5540

MARKMAN, STEPHEN J., state supreme court justice; b. Detroit, June 4, 1949; s. Julius and Pauline Markman; m. Mary Kathleen Sites, Aug. 25, 1974; children: James, Charles. BA, Duke U., 1971; JD, U. Cin., 1974. Legis. asst. to Rep. Edward Hutchinson, Mich., 1975, Rep. Tom Hagedorn, Minn., 1976—78; chief counsel, staff dir. subcom. on constn. Senate Com. on Judiciary, 1978—85, dep. chief counsel, 1983; asst. atty. gen. Office Legal Policy, Dept. Justice, Washington, 1985-89; U.S. atty. U.S. Dept. Justice, Detroit, 1989-93; mem. Miller, Canfield, Paddock & Stone, Detroit, 1993—95; judge Mich. Ct. Appeals, 1995—99; justice Mich. Supreme Ct., Lansing, Mich., 1999—. Prof. constitutional law Hillsdale Coll. Author numerous articles appearing in Stanford Law Review, U. Chicago Law Review, U. Mich. Jour. of Law Reform, Am. Criminal Justice Law Review, Barrister's Law Jour., Harvard Jour. of Law & Public Policy, Detroit Coll. of Law Review. Fellow: Mich. Bar Found.; mem.: ABA, One Hundred Club, Am. Inns of Ct. Office: Mich Supreme Ct Hall of Justice 925 W Ottawa St Fl 6 Lansing MI 48915 Office Phone: 517-373-9449.*

MARKOE, FRANK, JR., lawyer, health facility administrator; b. Balt., Sept. 5, 1923; s. Frank and Margaret (Smith) M.; m. Margaret McCormack (div.); children: Andrée Markoe Caldwell, Ritchie Harrison Markoe Scribner. AB, Washington and Lee U., 1947; LLB, U. Md., 1950. Bar: Md. 1950. Pntr. Karl F. Steinmann, Balt., 1948-50, 50-53, Cable & McDaniel, Balt., 1954-55; gen. counsel, dir. Emerson Drug Co., Balt., 1955-56, adminstrv. v.p., 1957-58; v.p., sec., dir., gen. counsel Warner-Lambert Pharm. Co., 1958-67, exec. com., sr. v.p., dir., gen. counsel, sec., 1967-69, exec. asst. chmn. bd., 1970-71, sr. v.p., 1971-73; exec. v.p. Warner-Lambert Co., Morris Plains, NJ, 1973-77, vice chmn. bd., 1977-81; vice chmn. adv. bd. NY Hosp.-Cornell Med. Ctr., 1987—, also chmn. major gifts com. Capital Campaign; hon. holder Alfred E. Driscoll chair Fairleigh Dickinson U. Bd. dirs. NJ Coll. Medicine and Dentistry, Bd. Internat. Broadcasting, Radio Free Europe/Radio Liberty, Kips Bay Boys; bd. dirs., exec. com., pres. NJ Ballet. With USAAF, 1942-45, PTO. Mem. US C. of C., Proprietary Assn. (chmn., bd. dir., exec. com.), Pharm. Mfrs. Assn. (bd. dir., exec. com.), NJ State C. of C. (bd. dir.), Phi Beta Kappa. Home and Office: 201 Grenville Rd Hobe Sound FL 33455-2414

MARKOFF, BRAD STEVEN, lawyer; b. NYC, July 29, 1957; s. Daniel and Geri (Skitol) M.; m. Danna Kay Schmidt, May 17, 1980; children: Andrew David, Paul Steven, Samuel Joseph. AB, Duke U., 1979; JD, Washington U., St. Louis, 1982. Bar: Mo. 1982, U.S. Tax Ct. 1984, N.C. 1985. Assoc. Stolar Partnership, St. Louis, 1982-84; assoc., ptnr. Moore & Van Allen, Raleigh, NC, 1984-92; ptnr. Smith Helms Mulliss & Moore, Raleigh, NC, 1992-97, Alston & Bird LLP, Raleigh, NC, 1997—2005, ptnr. in charge Research Triangle Park, NC, 1997—2005, DLA Piper Rudnick Gray Cary US LLP, Raleigh, NC, 2005—; co-chair nat. REIT practice, mng. ptnr. Raleigh office. Bd. dirs. Coun. for Entrepreneurial Devel., Research Triangle Park, NC; spl. coun. apptd. by NC Gov. NC. R.R. Study Group, 1992-93; practice group head Alston & Bird's NC Bus. Practice, 1997—2005. Contbr. articles to profl. jours. Mem. ABA, Nat. Assn. Bond Lawyers, Nat. Assn. Real Estate Investment Trusts (mem. bd. advisors), Asian Pub. Real Estate Assn. (mem. bd. govs.), Mo. Bar Assn., N.C. Bar Assn. Avocations: golf, skiing. Office: DLA Piper US LLP 4141 Parklake Ave Ste 300 Raleigh NC 27612-2350 Home Phone: 919-787-5021; Office Phone: 919-786-2000. Office Fax: 919-786-2200. Business E-Mail: brad.markoff@dlapiper.com.

MARKOFF, JOHN, reporter; b. Oakland, Calif., Oct. 24, 1949; m. Leslie Terzian. Bachelors, Whitman Coll., Walla Walla, Washington, 1971; Masters, U. Oreg., 1976. Covered tech. and def. industry Pacific News Svc., San Francisco, 1977—81; reporter, editor Infoworld, 1981—83; wrote column on personal computers San Jose Mercury, 1983—85; west coast editor Byte Mag., 1984—85; reporter San Francisco Examiner, 1985—88; reporter, bus. sect., computer and tech. NY Times, 1988—. Adj. faculty Stanford U., 2002—; lectr. U. Calif. Berkeley Sch. Journalism. Co-author (with Lennie Siegel): The High Cost of High Tech, 1985; co-author: (with Katie Hafner) Cyberpunk: Outlaws and Hackers on the Computer Frontier, 1991; co-author: (with Tsutomu Shimomura) Takedown: The Pursuit and Capture of America's Most Wanted Computer Outlaw, 1996. Recipient award for best new reporting, Software Pub. Assn., 1988, Gerald Loeb award, UCLA Anderson Sch. Mgmt.; named one of most influential tech. reporters, Mktg. Computers mag., 2003; nominee Pulitzer prize. Office: NY Times 201 Spear St San Francisco CA 94105 Office Phone: 415-836-6700. Business E-Mail: markoff@nytimes.com.

MARKOPOLOS, HARRY M., financial investigator, former investment company executive; b. Erie, Pa., 1956; BABA, Loyola Coll., Balt., 1981; MS in Fin., Boston Coll., 1997. Chartered Fin. Analyst., Certified Fraud Examiner. Dist. mgr. ATFC Fin. Corp., Towson, Md., 1981—87; trader Makefield Securities Corp., Washington Crossing, Pa., 1987—88; asst. portfolio mgr. Darien Capital Mgmt., Greenwich, Conn., 1988—91; portfolio mgr. Rampart Investment Mgmt., Boston, 1991, chief investment officer, 2002—04; v.p. edn. Boston Security Analysts Soc., 2000—02, pres., 2002—03; fin. fraud investigator Boston, 2004—.

MARKOS, LOUIS A., language educator; b. East Orange, NJ, Jan. 22, 1964; s. Tom and Angie Markos; m. Donna M. Van Lare, Aug. 12, 1989; children: Alex, Stacey. BA, Colgate U., Hamilton, NY, 1986; MA, U. Mich., Ann Arbor, PhD, 1991; student, houston Bapt. U., 2009—. Prof. English Houston Bapt. U., 1991—. Author: (non-fiction book) Lewis Agonites: How C. S. Lewis can train us to wrestle with the modern and postmodern world, From Achilles to Christ: Why Christians should read the pagan classics, Pressing Forward: Alfred, Lord Tennyson and the Victorian Age. Pub. spkr., Houston, 2000—08. Recipient Outstanding Tchg. award, Houston Bapt. U., 1991. Conservative. Evangelical. Office: Houston Bapt Univ 7502 Fondren Rd Houston TX 77074 Office Fax: 281-649-3601. Business E-Mail: lmarkos@hbu.edu.

MARKOSKI, JOSEPH PETER, lawyer; b. Floral Pk., NY, Nov. 7, 1948; s. Stephen Nicholas and Josephine Veronica (Lapkofsky) Markoski; m. Julie Ann Angus, June 30, 1979; children: Katherine, Caroline, Peter. BSFS, Georgetown U., 1970, JD, 1973. Bar: DC 1973. Law clk. Hon. Thomas A. Flannery US Dist. Ct., Washington, 1973-74; assoc. Wilkinson, Cragun & Barker, Washington, 1975-80, ptnr., 1980-82, Squire, Sanders & Dempsey, Washington, 1982-96, mng. ptnr., 1991-96, mng. ptnr. Europe London, 1996—2000, mng. ptnr. DC & Tysons Corner, Va. Offices, 2003—09; mng. ptnr. Europe & Middle East, 2009—; chmn. Regulated Industries Practice Area, SS&D PAC, 2008—. Co-chmn. task force on open network initiatives Strategic Planning Group of U.S. CCITT Nat. Com., 1988-92. Co-author: Internat. Telecommunications Handbook, 1986; contbr. articles to profl. jours. Capt. USAR, 1970—78. Mem. ABA (vice-chmn. common carrier com. sci. and tech. sect. 1986-88, internat. common carrier project 1980-86), Fed. Commn. Bar Assn. (com. common carrier practice and procedure 1980—), Computer Law Assn. (bd. dirs., chmn. telecomm. bar liaison com. 1994-96), Internat. Bar Assn. (mem. comm. and internat. computer and tech. law coms.), Am. C. of C. (Eng.). Democrat. Roman Catholic. Office: Squire Sanders & Dempsey LLP Tower 42 25th Fl 25 Old Broad St London EC2N 1HQ England Office Phone: 44.20.71.898137. Office Fax: 44.20.7181.8111. Business E-Mail: jmarkoski@ssd.com.

MARKOV, ANDREI, professional hockey player; b. Voskresensk, Russia, Dec. 20, 1978; Defenseman Dynamo Moscow (Russian Premier League), 1998—2000, 2004—05, Montreal Canadiens, 2000—. Mem. Team Russia, World Championships, 2008. Named to NHL All-Star Game, 2008, 2009. Office: Montreal Canadiens 1275 St Antoine St W Montreal PQ H3C 5L2 Canada*

MARKOVICH, ALEXANDRIA, assistant principal; b. NYC, Jan. 18, 1954; d. Alexander and Mary Markovich; m. Robert Steven Young, Nov. 15, 1987; children: Anastasia Nicole Young, Christopher Robert Alexander Young. BA, SUNY, Stony Brook, NY, 1976; MPS in Creativity Devel.-Art Therapy, Pratt Inst., Bklyn., 1978; MEd, Coll. New Rochelle, NY, 2002. Cert. art tchr. NY State Bd. Edn., 1979, tchr. nursery, kindergarten, grades 1-6 NY State Bd. Edn., 1979, spl. edn. tchr. NY State Bd. Edn., 1982, specialization in staff devel. NY State Bd. Edn., 2001, asst. prin. spl. edn. day HS NYC Bd. Edn., 2003, health conservation tchr. NYC Bd. Edn., 1982, fine arts jr. HS tchr. NYC Bd. Edn., 1982, fine arts Day HS tchr. NYC Bd. Edn., 1982, spl. edn. tchr. NYC Bd. Edn., 1996, asst. prin. spl. edn. schs. NYC Bd. Edn., 2003, asst. prin. elem., intermediate, and jr. HS NYC Bd. Edn., 2003, asst. prin. in Fine Arts Day H.S. NYC Bd. Edn., 2003, supr. spl. edn. NYC Bd. Edn., 2003, sch. dist. adminstr. NY State Dept. Edn., 2002, cert. nat. official US Luge Assn., 2000. Spl. edn. tchr. Pub. Sch. 23 at Elmhurst Hosp., NY, 1980—82; spl. edn. tchr., art therapist Pub. Sch. 177 Queens, Fresh Meadows, 1982—2003; asst. prin. Pub. Sch. 4 at 179 Queens, Fresh Meadows, 2003—; asst. to prin., adminstrv. intern Saw Mill Elem. Sch., Bellmore, 2000—01. Contbr. articles to profl. jours.; actor: (plays) Little Shop of Horrors, Bye, Bye Birdie, Hello Out There, Plaza Suite;. Recipient Outstanding Spl. Educators award, Coun. Exceptional Children, 1982, Outstanding Performance as an Art Educator award, N.Y.C. Bd. Edn., 1984, Superior Art Instrn. award, A.A.A., Nat. Traffic Safety Program, 1986; named Tchr. of Yr., Coun. Exceptional Children, 1985, 1986; nominee N.Y. State Tchr. of Yr. award, N.Y. State Dept. Edn., 1985, 1986, 1987. Mem.: ASCD, Coun. Sch. Supervisors and Adminstrs., NYC Art Tchrs. Assn. (fin. sec. 1988—89, sec. 1987—88), NY State Alliance for Arts Edn., NY State Art Tchrs. Assn. (ad hoc com. mem. 1986—87), Girl Scouts Nassau County (del. 2001—05), Girl Scouts Merrick Assn. (treas. 2000—06, recruiter registrar 1995—2000). Russian Orthodox. Avocations: acting, art, camping, hiking. Personal E-mail: alexandria11566@yahoo.com.

MARKOVICH, PATRICIA H., economist; b. Oakland, Calif. MS in Econs., U. Calif., Berkeley; postgrad., Stanford U. Cert. emergency mgmt. planner. Pvt. practice polit. and econs. cons.; former aide to majority whip Oreg. Ho. of Reps.; lectr., instr. various Calif. instns., Chemeketa (Oreg.) Coll., Portland (Oreg.) State U.; commr. City of Oakland, Calif. Chairperson, bd. dirs. Cable Sta. KCOM; econ. and emergency mgmt. cons. Mem. Piedmont (Calif.) Gen. Plan Commn. NSF grant Oreg. Grad. Rsch. Ctr., Lilly Found. grant. Mem.: Armenian Rug Soc., Nat. Coordinating Coun. Emergency Mgmt., San Francisco Bay Area Rug Soc., Mensa.

MARKOVICH, VOYA R., information technology executive; arrived in US, 1969; s. Rista A. and Draga S. Markovic; m. Anita M. Sica, Jan. 9, 1951; children: Michael children: Steven. BS in Chemistry, U. Belgrade, Serbia, 1966; MS in Chemistry, Poly. Inst. N.Y., 1981. Analytical chemist Commodity Labs., Inc., NYC, 1969—81; devel. project mgr. IBM, Endicott, NY, 1981—2002; sr. v.p., chief tech. officer, gen. mgr. R&D and IP, Endicott Interconnect Techs., Inc., Endicott. Sr. tech. staff mem. IBM, Endicott, 1996—2002, mem. Acad. of Tech., 1997—2002. Contbr. chapters to books. Mem.: IEEE (assoc.), Electronic Components Tech. Conf. (assoc.), Internat. Printed Circuits (assoc.), Integrated Electronics Engring. Ctr. (assoc.), Internat. Microelectronics Packaging Soc. (assoc.). Achievements include 168 US patents in field; some of the patents include Direct Chip Attach on Laminate Packaging; Full Additive Process - Copper Bondable Surface (CBS); Z Interconnection for Organic Packaging; High Performance Core Board Technology; invention of High Speed Board design. Avocations: travel, technology, politics. Home: 3611 Joel Dr Endicott NY 13760 Office: Endicott Interconnect Technologies Inc 1701 North Street Endicott NY 13760 Personal E-mail: markovichv@yahoo.com, voyarm@aol.com. Business E-Mail: v.markovich@eitny.com. E-mail: voya.markovich@eitny.com.

MARKOVITS, ANDREI STEVEN, political science professor; b. Timisoara, Romania, Oct. 6, 1948; came to U.S., 1960, naturalized, 1971; s. Ludwig and Ida (Ritter) M. BA, Columbia U., NYC, 1969, MBA, 1971, MA, 1973, MPhil, 1974, PhD, 1976; PhD (hon.), Leuphana U., Lüneburg, Germany, 2007. Mem. faculty NYU, 1974, John Jay Coll. Criminal Justice, CUNY, 1974, Columbia U., 1975; rsch. assoc. Inst. Advanced Studies, Vienna, 1973—74, Wirtschafts und Sozialwissenschaftliches Inst., German Trade U. Fedn., Düsseldorf, Germany, 1979, Internat. Inst. Comparative Social Rsch., Sci. Ctr. Berlin, 1980; asst. prof. govt. Wesleyan U., Middletown, Conn., 1977—83; assoc. prof. polit. sci. Boston U., 1983—92; prof., chair dept. politics U. Calif., Santa Cruz, 1995—99; prof. dept. Germanic langs. and lit., dept. polit. sci., dept. sociology U. Mich., Ann Arbor, 1999—2003, Karl W. Deutsch Collegiate prof. comparative politics and German studies, 2003—, Arthur F. Thurnau prof., 2009—. Sr. rsch. assoc. Ctrl. European Studies Harvard U., 1975—99; vis. prof. Tel Aviv U., 1986, Osnabruck U., 1987, Bochum U., 1991; Fulbright prof. U. Innsbruck, Austria, 1996; vis. prof. Harvard U., 2002—03, St. Gallen (Switzerland) U., 2004, Hebrew U., 2005, Dortmund U., 2006, Webster U., Vienna Campus, 2008. Author, editor books and papers in field; TV and radio commentator. U. Pres.'s fellow Columbia U., 1969, B'nai B'rith Found. fellow, 1976-77, Kalmus Found. fellow, 1976-77, Ford Found. fellow, 1979, Hans Boeckler Found. fellow, 1982 Inst. Advanced Study Berlin fellow, 1998-99; Ctr. Advanced Study Behavioral Scis. Stanford U. Fellow, 2008-09, NY State scholar Columbia U., 1969; Winner Golden Apple award Best Tchr. U. Mich., 2007, Tronstein award Polit. Sci., 2007. Mem. N.Y. Acad. Scis., Am. Polit. Sci. Assn., Internat. Polit. Sci. Assn., AAUP. Home: 718 Onondaga St Ann Arbor MI 48104-2611 Office: Univ Mich 3110 Modern Lang Bldg 812 E Washington St Ann Arbor MI 48109-1275 Home Phone: 734-213-2226; Office Phone: 734-764-8018. Personal E-mail: andysmark@gmail.com. Business E-Mail: andymark@umich.edu.

MARKOWITZ, DEBORAH LYNN, Secretary of State, Vermont; b. Tarrytown, NY, Sept. 14, 1961; d. Gerald Harvey and Sandra Lee (Schulner) Markowitz; m. Paul William Markowitz, June 19, 1988; children: Aviva Lee, Sandra Rose, Ari David. BA with honors, U. Vt., 1982; JD magna cum laude, Georgetown U., 1987. Bar: Vt. 1988, US Dist. Ct. Vt. 1989. Assoc. Covington & Burling, Washington, summer 1986; jud. law clk. to Justice Peck Vt. Supreme Ct., Montpelier, 1987-88; assoc. Langrack, Sperry & Wool, Burlington, Vt., 1988-90; dir. Law Ctr. Vt. League Cities and Towns, Montpelier, Vt., 1990—97; devel. cons. Vt. Law Sch., South Royalton, 1997—; sec. state State of Vt., 1998—. Adj. faculty Vt. Law Sch., South Royalton, 1992; examiner Vt. Bd. Bar Examiners, Montpelier, 1994-98. Contbr. articles to profl. jours. Bd. dirs. Ctrl. Vt. Cmty. Action Agy., Vt. Hist. Soc.; trustee Woodbury Coll. Mem. ABA (state and local govt. sect.), Vt. Bar Assn. (mcpl. com.), Internat. Mcpl. Lawyers Assn. (chair pers. sect. 1993—), Nat. Assn. Secs. of State (pres.), Nat. Mus. Women in the Arts (bd. dirs. Vt. chpt.), Order of Coif. Democrat. Avocations: cross country skiing, singing, sketching, gardening. Office: Office Sec State Redstone Bldg 26 Terrace Street, PO Box 9 Montpelier VT 05609-0001 Office Phone: 802-828-2148. Office Fax: 802-828-2496. E-mail: dmarkowitz@sec.state.vt.us.

MARKOWITZ, HARRY MAX, finance and economics educator; b. Chgo., Aug. 24, 1927; s. Morris and Mildred (Gruber) M.; m. Barbara Gay. PhB, U. Chgo., 1947, MA, 1950, PhD, 1954. With research staff Rand Corp., Santa Monica, Calif., 1952-60, 61-63; chmn. bd., tech. dir. Consol. Analysis Ctrs., Inc., Santa Monica, 1963-68; prof. UCLA, Westwood, 1968-69; pres. Arbitrage Mgmt. Co., NYC, 1969-72; pvt. practice cons. NYC, 1972-74; prof. Wharton Sch Bus., U. Pa., 1972—74; with research staff T.J. Watson Research Ctr. IBM, Yorktown Hills, NY, 1974-83; prof. Rutgers U., 1980—82; Marvin Speiser Disting. Prof. of Fin. and Econs. Baruch Coll. CUNY, NYC, 1982-93; dir. rsch. Daiwa Securities Trust Co, Jersey City, 1990-2000; prin., owner Harry Markowitz Co., 1993—; rsch. prof. dept. econs. U. Calif. San Diego. V.p. Inst. Mgmt. Sci., 1960-62. adv. bd. Jour. Investment Mgmt. Author: Portfolio Selection: Efficient Diversification of Investments, 1959, Mean-Variance Analysis in Portfolio Choice, 1987; co-author: SIMSCRIPT Simulation Programming Language, 1963, (with Frank J. Fabozzi) The Theory and Practice of Investment Management, 2002; co-editor: Process Analysis of Economic Capabilities, 1963. Recipient John von Neumann Theory prize Ops. Rsch. Soc. Am. and Inst. Mgmt. Sci., 1989, Nobel Prize in Econs., 1990. Fellow Econometric Soc., Am. Acad. Arts and Scis., Am. Fin. Assn. Office: Ste 245 1010 Turquoise St San Diego CA 92109*

MARKOWITZ, LAWRENCE PETER, political science professor; b. New York, Ny, Jan. 14, 1970; s. Arnold and Janet Markowitz; m. Gulchiroy Zavkieva; 1 child, Timur. PhD in Polit. Sci., U. Wisconsin-Madison, 2005. Postdoc. fellow Georgetown U., Washington, 2005—06; vis. asst. prof. Oberlin Coll., Ohio, 2006—. Cons. World Bank, Washington, 1998—99. Fellow Fulbright-Hays, Dept Edn., 2002—03; Dissertation Completion fellowship, Social Sci. Rsch. Coun., 2003—04, Rsch. Grant, Nat. Coun. on Eurasian and East European Rsch., 2005—07. Avocations: travel, skiing. Office: Oberlin Coll Dept Politics 10 N Professor St Oberlin OH 44074 Business E-Mail: lawrence.markowitz@oberlin.edu.

MARKOWITZ, MARTY (MARTIN MARKOWITZ), city manager; b. Bklyn., Feb. 14, 1945; m. Jamie Markowitz, 1999. BA, Bklyn. Coll., 1970. Organizer Flatbush Tenants Coun., 1971; men. NY State Senate from Dist. 20, Albany, 1979—2002; borough pres. Brooklyn, 2002—. Chair Initiative for a Competitive Brooklyn; creator Seaside Summer Concert Series, Coney Island, Martin Luther King, Jr. Concert Series, Flatbush. Mem. NAACP (life), Midwood Jewish Ctr., City Urban League. Democrat. Jewish. Office: 209 Joralemon St Brooklyn NY 11201 Office Phone: 718-802-3700.*

MARKOWITZ, SAMUEL SOLOMON, chemistry professor; b. Bklyn., Oct. 31, 1931; s. Max and Florence Ethel (Goldman) M.; children: Michael, Daniel, Jonah; m. 2d Lydia de Antonis, Oct. 31, 1993. BS in Chemistry, Rensselaer Poly. Inst., 1953; MA, Princeton U., 1955, PhD, 1957; postgrad., Brookhaven Nat. Lab., 1955-57. Asst. prof. chemistry U. Calif., Berkeley, 1958-64, assoc. prof., 1964-72, prof., 1972—. Faculty sr. scientist Lawrence Berkeley Lab., 1958—; vis. prof. nuclear physics Weizmann Inst. Sci., Rehovot, Israel, 1973-74. Mem. Bd. Edn. of Berkeley Unified Sch. Dist., 1969-73, pres. bd., 1971-72. Recipient Elizabeth McFeely D'Urso Meml. Pub. Ofcl. award Alameda County Edn. Assn., 1973; LeRoy McKay fellow Princeton U., 1955, Charlotte Elizabeth Proctor fellow Princeton U., 1956, NSF postdoctoral fellow U. Birmingham, Eng., 1957-58, NSF sr. postdoctoral fellow Faculte des Scis. U. Paris a Orsay, Laboratoire Joliot-Curie de Physique Nucleaire, 1964-65. Fellow AAAS; mem. Am. Chem. Soc. (bd. dirs. Calif. sect., chmn. 1991, 93-94, Nat, Councilor, 1990-, Walter Petersen award 2003), Am. Phys. Soc., Am. Inst. chemists, N.Y. Acad. Scis., Calif. Inst. Chemists, Sigma Xi. Home: 555 Pierce St # 245 Albany CA 94706 Office: U Calif Dept Chemistry Berkeley CA 94720-1460 Office Phone: 510-642-2922. Business E-Mail: markowit@cchem.berkeley.edu.

MARKOWSKI, ELIZABETH M., lawyer; JD cum laude, NYU, 1978. Law clk. to Hon. Edward Weinfeld US Dist. Ct. (so. dist.) NY, 1978—79; sr. ptnr. Baker Botts LLP, NYC, 1992—2000; sr. v.p. legal Liberty Media Corp., Englewood, Colo., 2000—04; with Liberty Media Internat., Englewood, Colo., 2004—05; sr. v.p., gen. counsel, sec. Liberty Global Inc., Englewood, Colo., 2005—. Mem.: ABA, Assn. of Bar of City of NY. Office: Liberty Global, Inc 12300 Liberty Blvd Englewood CO 80112 Office Phone: 303-220-6600. Office Fax: 303-220-6601.

MARKS, BRUCE, performing company executive, choreographer; b. NYC, Jan. 23, 1937; s. Albert and Helen (Kosersky) M.; m. Toni Pihl Petersen, Jan. 27, 1966 (dec. May 1985); children: Erik Antony, Adam Christopher, Kenneth Rikard. Student, Brandeis U., 1954—55, Juilliard Sch., 1955—56; DFA, D, Northeastern U., 1997. Prof. U. Utah, 1981, 1984—86; artistic dir. Boston Ballet Co., 1985—97, artistic dir. emeritus, 1998—; artistic dir. Orlando Ballet, 2006—. Mem. dance adv. panel Nat. Endowment for Arts, 1979, chmn. internat. selection com., 1979, chmn. dance adv. panel, 1981, mem. nat. adv. bd. on arts and edn., 1989; bd. dirs., mem. exec. com., Dance/USA 1989, 92—, chmn., 1990-92, chmn. govt. affairs, 1992—; mem. U.S.-USSR Commn. on Dance and Theatre Studies, Am. Coun. Learned Socs./IREX; mem. jury Internat. Moscow Internat. Ballet Competition, 1989; mem. arts in edn. adv. coun. Harvard U., 1997; chmn. 3d Japan Internat. Ballet and Modern Dance competition, 1999; jury mem. Prague Internat. Ballet Competition, 2001; jury Shangh Internat. Ballet Competition, 2007; jury Seol Internat. Ballet Modern Dance Competition; artistic advisor Ft. Worth/Dallas Ballet, 2000-01; tchr. 1st Seoul (Korea) Internat. Dance Competition, 2004. Prin. dancer Met. Opera, 1956-6l, Am. Ballet Theatre, 196l-72, Royal Swedish Ballet, 1963, Festival Ballet, London, l965, Royal Danish Ballet, 197l-76; artistic dir. Ballet West, Salt Lake City, 1976-85; choreographer Eliot Feld Ballet Co., 1970, Royal Danish Ballet, 1971-76, Netherlands Dance Theatre, 1974, Ballet West, 1976-85; artistic fellow Aspen Inst. for Humanistic Studies, 1979—. Bd. dirs. Am. Arts Alliance, 1983-85, Am. Coun. for Arts, 1985—, Dance U.S.A., 1988-94, chmn., 1990-92; chmn. U.S.A. Internat. Ballet Competition, Jackson, Micc., 1990—, vice chair jury Helsinki, Finland, 1991, judge Helsinki Ballet Competition 1995; mem. nat. adv. bd. on arts and edn. NEA, 1989-91; mem. internat. jury 1st and 2d Japan Internat. Ballet Competition, Nagoya, Japan, 1993, 96, 2005, Am. jury for Prix de Lausanne, 1994, 98; mem. Brandeis Creative Arts Awards Commn., 1993, chmn. Brandeis Creative Arts Awards Dance, 1994; chair Grants to Dance Cos. panel NEA, 1993, overview panel, 1994; chmn. 3d Japan Internat. Ballet Competition, Nagoya, 1999; artistic advisor Ft. Worth/Dallas Ballet, 2000-2001; mem. Princess Grace Awards panel, 2005. Recipient Disting. Svc. award for artistic prodn. Nat. Govs. Assn., 1994, Capezio award Balletmakers, Inc., 1995, Dance Mag. award, 1997, Honors award Dance/USA, 1998, Proscenium award, Boston, 2001, Juilliard medal Svc. to Arts, 2005

MARKS, EMILIA ALONSO, language educator, researcher; PhD, U. Sevilla. Assoc. prof., instr. U. Sevilla, 1993—96; assoc. prof. Spanish Ohio U., Athens, 1996—; assoc. dir. Rsch. Inst. Empirical Study Lang., Ohio U. Dir. vocat. svc. Rotary Internat., Athens, 2006—. Office: Ohio Univ Dept Modern Lang 247 Gordy Hall Athens OH 45701 Office Fax: 740-593-0729. Business E-Mail: markse@ohio.edu.

MARKS, GERALD, surgeon, educator; b. Bklyn., Apr. 14, 1925; s. Maurice and Lee (Leib) M.; m. Barbara Ann Hendershot, Nov. 25, 1950; children: Richard M., James M., John H. Grad., Villanova U., 1945; MD, Jefferson Med. Coll., 1949. Diplomate: Am. Bd. Surgery, Am. Bd. Colon and Rectal Surgery (examiner). Intern Jefferson Med. Coll. Hosp., Phila., 1949-51, resident in surgery, 1952-57, resident in proctology, 1953-54, asst. dir. Tumor Clinic, 1959-68; practice medicine specializing in gen. and colorectal surgery Phila., 1957—; asst. chief surgery Phila. Gen. Hosp., 1957-70, chief Proctology Clinic, 1968-70, coordinator student surg. edn. Jefferson Surg. Service, 1960-70; attending physician in surgery Thomas Jefferson U. Hosp., 1957-95, sec. med. staff, 1974-77, dir. Comprehensive Rectal Cancer Ctr., Colorectal Surgery Residency Program, exec. dir. Colorectal Surgical Found., 1984-95, co-dir. Colorectal Cancer Genetics Ctr.; dir. div. internat. surg. edn. and practice Ctr. for Research in Med. Edn. and Health Care; instr. surgery Jefferson Med. Coll., 1958-67, assoc. in clin. surgery, 1967-68, clin. assoc. prof. surgery, 1974-78, prof., 1978-95; chief sect. colorectal surgery, cons. in colon-rectal surgery Pa. Hosp.; cons. in colon-rectal surgery VA Hosp., Coatesville, Pa., 1959—, San Juan, P.R., 1968—, Wilmington, Del., 1977—; cons in colon-rectal surgery USN Regional Med. Ctr., Phila., 1977—; Edgar Deissler prof. surgery Allegheny U. Health Scis., 1995—2001, dir. comprehensive rectal cancer ctr., 1995—98, dir. GI surg. endoscopy, 1995. Adj. prof. surgery U. Pa. Sch. Medicine; sr. investigator, Lankenan Inst. for Med. Rsch.; dir. Internat. Network Comprehensive Rectal Cancer Ctrs., 1997-; chmn. Marks Colorectal Surg. Found.; clin. prof. surgery Drexel U. Sch. Medicine, 2001; Deissler prof. surgery and founding dir. divsn. colorectal surgery Hahnemann Med. Coll. of Allegheny U., 1995-2000 Sr. editor Surg. Endoscopy, Ultrasound and Interventional Techniques Jour.; assoc. editor Diseases of the Colon and Rectum Jour., 1977—; cons. editor Pa. Medicine; editl. cons. bd. mem. Gen. Surgery News, 1991, Jour. Surg. Techn.; contbr. articles to profl. jours.; developed colonscopic colon teaching model; solo artist exhbn. in watercolor painting in Italy and U.S Chmn. Marks Colorectal Surg. Rsch. Found. Served with USN, 1943-46; served to capt. M.C. USAF, 1951-52. Recipient 7th Ann. Jonathan M. Wainwright award, Moses Taylor Hosp., Scranton, Pa., 1989; Ann. Alumni Achievement award, Jefferson Med. Coll.; named Man of the Yr., Jewish Nat. Fund, Lifetime Achievement award Northeast Soc. of Colon and Rectal Surgeons, 2004 Mem. ACS (rep. to bd. govs. 1983, council Met. Phila. chpt.), AMA, Pa. Soc. Colon and Rectal Surgery (pres. 1981-82), Am. Soc. Colon and Rectal Surgeons (v.p. 1989), Am. Soc. Clin. Oncology, Internat. Soc. Univ. Colon and Rectal Surgeons, Coll. Physicians Phila., Internat. Fedn. Socs. Endoscopic Surgeons (founding pres. 1991-2000), Royal Soc. Medicine (affiliate), Ea. Surg. Soc., Phila. Acad. Surgery (mem. council), Pa. Med. Soc., Phila. County Med. Soc. (bd. dirs., v.p., chmn. publs. com., pub. affairs com., v.p. 1986—), Soc. Surgery Alimentary Tract, Am. Soc. Gastrointestinal Endoscopy, Italian Soc. Gastrointestinal Endoscopy (hon.), Soc. Am. Gastrointestinal Endoscopic Surgeons (founder, pres. 1980, bd. govs., honoree Annual Gerald Marks Lectureship, former chmn. internat. rels. com., Dist. Svc. award, 1997, Lifetime Achievement award, 2004), Italian Soc. Surgery (hon.), Northeastern Soc. Colon and Rectal Surgeons (past pres.), Jefferson Vol. Faculty Assn. (pres. 1973-74, Brady Cancer Rsch. Inst. award, 1997), Am. Soc. Colon and Rectal Surgeons (v.p. 1989—), Abruzzi Surg. Soc. (hon.), European Assn. Endoscopic Surgeons, Endolaparoscopic Surgeons of Asia, Puerto Rico Chpt. Am. Coll. Surgeons, Alpha Omega Alpha Home: 45 Fairview Rd Narberth PA 19072-1328 Office: 100 Lancaster Ave # 3-west Wynnewood PA 19096-3411 Home Phone: 610-896-5900; Office Phone: 610-645-9093. E-mail: marksg@mlhs.org.

MARKS, HERBERT EDWARD, lawyer; b. Dayton, Ohio, Nov. 3, 1935; s. I.M. and Sarah S. M.; m. Marcia Frager; children: Jennifer L., Susan E. AB with high distinction, U. Mich., 1957; JD, Yale U., 1960; postgrad., George Washington U. Law Sch., 1965-67. Bar: Ohio 1960, D.C. 1964, U.S. Supreme Ct. 1965. Law clk. to chief judge U.S. Ct. Claims, 1964-65; assoc. Wilkinson, Cragun & Barker, Washington, 1965-69, ptnr., 1969-82, Squire, Sanders & Dempsey, Washington, 1982—2003, sr. counsel, 2004—. Assoc. gen. counsel Presdl. Inaugural Coms., 1969, 73, 81; chmn. U.S. State Dept. Adv. Panel on Internat. Telecom. Law, 1987—91; mem. adv. com. on internat. comm. and info. policy U.S. State Dept., 1988—91, 2002—; mem. U.S. del. ITU European Telecom. Devel. Conf., 1991, ITU Plenipotentiary Conf., 1998, ITU Coun., 2000, 04; mem. ITU Sec. Gen.'s Expert Group, 1999—2002; vice chmn. ITU Treaty Working Group, 2004—; bd. dirs. Vet. Legal Svc. Program, 2004—; polit. sci. adv. bd. U. Mich., 2002—. Contbr. articles to legal jours. Served to capt. JAG USAF, 1960-64. Mem. ABA (chair sci. and tech. sect. 1990-91), Internat. Tech. Law Assn. (pres. 1975-77, bd. dirs. 1972-85, adv. bd. 1985—), Fed. Comms. Bar Assn., Cosmos Club, Kenwood Golf and Country Club, Phi Beta Kappa. Office: Squire Sanders & Dempsey 1201 Pennsylvania Ave NW Washington DC 20044 also: 5317 Cardinal Ct Bethesda MD 20816-2908 Office Phone: 202-626-6624.

MARKS, HOWARD, computer game company executive, information technology executive; BS in Computer Engring., U. Mich., Ann Arbor. Co-founder Internet Consumer Techs., Activision 2.0; exec. v.p. Activision, 1991; founder, CEO eMind, 1998—2005; CEO Acclaim Games Inc., Beverly Hills, Calif., 2005—. Office: Acclaim Games 615 N Arden Dr Beverly Hills CA 90210

MARKS, JAMES GARFIELD, JR., dermatologist; b. Trenton, NJ, May 19, 1945; s. James Garfield and Lavinia May (Ellis) M.; m. Joyce Lynne Turner, Aug. 9, 1969; 1 child, Shannon. BA, Wilkes Coll., 1967; MD, Temple U., Phila., 1971. Intern Geisinger Med. Ctr., Danville, Pa., 1971-72; resident Wilford Hall USAF Med. Ctr., San Antonio, 1975-78; clin. instr. dermatology U. Tex. Health Sci. Ctr., San Antonio, 1978-80; staff dermatologist Pa. State U. Coll. Medicine, Hershey, 1980—, asst. prof., 1980-85, assoc. prof., 1985-91, prof. dermatology, 1991—; chair dept. dermatology Hershey Med. Ctr. Team leader Cosmic Ingredient Rev. Expert Panel; co-dir. Caribbean and Coastal Dermatology Symposia. Author: Atlas of Differential Diagnosis in Dermatology, 1998, Principles of Dermatology, 2006, Handbook of Contact Dermatitis, 2000, Contact and Occupational Dermatology, 2002, Principles and Practice of Dermatology, 1990, 2d edit., 1996, Occupational Skin Diseases, 1999, Conn's Current Therapy, 1988, 2d edit., 1989; author: (with others) Principles of Clinical Diagnosis, 1992, Dermatology, 2008; contbr. articles to profl. jours. Bd. dirs. Braun Sta. East Cmty., 1976. Maj. USAF, 1972-80. Decorated Meritorious Svc. Commendation meadl; Am. Acad. Dermatology Exch. fellow, 1984; recipient Roerig Pharms. Challenges in Dermatology Ednl. award, 1982. Mem. Am. Acad. Dermatology, Am. Contact Dermatitis Soc. (v.p. 1993, pres. 2001), N.Am. Contact Dermatitis Group, Pa. Acad. Dermatology, Phila. Dermatology Soc., European Soc. Contact Dermatitis, Soc. Investigative Dermatology, Assn. Mil. Dermatologists, Dermatology Found., Lions (v.p. 1982, pres. 1983). Office: Hershey Med Ctr 500 University Dr # 850 Hershey PA 17033-2360 Office Phone: 717-531-8307. Business E-Mail: jmarks@psu.edu.

MARKS, JAMES S., public health service administrator; b. Buffalo, May 13, 1948; AB cum laude, Williams Coll., 1969; MD, SUNY, Buffalo, 1973; MPH, Yale U., 1980. Diplomate Am. Bd. Pediatrics. Intern in pediat. U. Calif., San Francisco, 1973-74, resident in pediat., 1974-75, chief resident pediatric outpatient dept., 1975-76; fellow Robert Wood Johnson Clin. Scholars Program Yale U., New Haven, 1978-80; resident in preventive medicine Ctrs. for Disease Control, Atlanta, 1977-78, 1981-82, chief epidemiology and rsch. br., nutrition divsn., 1982-84, asst. dir. preventive medicine residency program, 1985-87, dir. divsn. reproductive health, 1987, coord. for chronic disease control activities, 1987-88, acting dir. divsn. diabetes transl., 1988-89, acting dir. divsn. chronic disease control, 1990-91, dir. divsn. reproductive health, 1992-95, dir. Nat. Ctr. Chronic Disease Prevention/Health Promotion, 1995—2004, acting dir., 2004; sr. v.p., dir. health group Robert Wood Johnson Found., 2004—. Clinic physician Planned Parenthood of San Francisco Teen Clinic, 1975-76; cons. physician Ohio Dept. Health Bur. Preventive Medicine, 1978-79; cons. PAHO Consultative Group on Perinatal Care, Washington, 1982, WHO Malaysia Ministry of Health, 1982, 83, WHO Maternal and Child Health Unit Geneva, 1983, World Bank China Program Third Health Project, 1988, 1991, World Bank Poland, Health Promotion/Chronic Disease Prevention, 1992, World Bank China, Seventh Health Project, 1993; adj. assoc. prof. Emory U. Sch. Pub. Health; asst. surgeon general, 1996—. Editor Chronic Disease Notes and Reports, 1989-92; contbr. articles to profl. jours, chpts. to books. Exec. sec. Diabetes Tech. Adv. com., 1989-92; liaison mem. Nat. Diabetes Adv. Bd., 1988-89; mem. Diabetes Mellitus Interagy. Coording. com., 1988-89; mem. subcom. adult edn., Am. Cancer Soc., 1987-92; staff White House Task Force on Infant Mortality, 1989; presenter in field. Epidemic Intelligence Svc. Officer USPHS Field Svcs. Divsn., 1976-78. Recipient Alexander D. Langmuir award, 1978, CDC Group award, 1984, Commendation Medal USPHS, 1984, and many other awards and citations. Fellow Am. Coll. Epidemiology; mem. APHA (active in com. work), Inst. Medicine, Am. Epidemiol. Soc., Soc. Epidemiol. Rsch., Am. Acad. Pediat. (com. pediatric rsch. 1994-95), Internat. Epidemiol. Assn., Physicians for Social Responsibility, Soc. on Med. Decision Making, Epidemic Intelligence Svc. Alumni Assn., Sigma Xi. Home: 15 Houghton Rd Princeton NJ 08540-3300 Office: Robert Wood Johnson Found PO Box 2316 College Rd East and Rte 1 Princeton NJ 08543*

MARKS, JOHN, engineer, consultant; adopted s. Cyril Bernard Marks and Laura Mary Kings. BS, U. Sussex, 1974. High Voltage Switching, C.e.g.b. Uk, 1990. Owners engr. Croatin Power Authority, Zagreb, Croatia, 2001—03; cons. engr. Tampa Electric Co, Tampa. Tech. dir. Cts (Uk) Ltd, Southampton, England, 1990—95. Sr. cons. (power) T.P.C., Taipei, Taiwan, 1979—84. Flt.lt. Brit. Mil., 1963—68. Mem.: ASME, IEEE. Conservative. Church Of England. Avocations: travel, swimming, rugby, music, reading. Home Fax: 34-96676165. Personal E-mail: johnmarks4@aol.com.

MARKS, JOHN R., retired science educator; s. Raymond W. and Ruth B. Marks; m. Diane K. Hulit, Aug. 26, 1972; children: Brian A., Jason A., David J. BS in Biology, Allegheny Coll., Meadville, Pa., 1968; MS in Biology, Bowling Green State U., Ohio, 1970; PhD in Biology, Bowling Green State U., 1974. Prof. Zane State Coll., Zanesville, Ohio, 1974—2009. Bell choir Grace United Meth. Ch., 1985—2009, trustee, 1985—2009, staff parish, 1985—2009, adminstrv. bd. mem., 1985—2009. Recipient W. D. Sheets award, Ohio Water Environment Assn., 1988, 2007; grant, NSF, 1991, 1998—2001, NFS ATEEC fellowship, Advanced Tech. Environ. Edn. Ctr., 1995, 1996, 1997, 2002, 2004. Mem.: Water Environment Fedn. (Lab. Excellence award 1994), Ohio Acad. Sci. Avocations: fishing, travel. Home: 3949 Skyline Dr Zanesville OH 43701 Home Phone: 740-454-7382. Personal E-mail: jrmarks@columbus.rr.com.

MARKS, JOHN R., III, mayor, Tallahassee, Florida, lawyer; m. Jane Marks; 1 child, John IV. BS, Fla. State U. Sch. Bus., 1969; JD, Fla. State U. College Law, 1972. Adminstrv. law judge Fla. Pub. Svc. Commn., served on, 1979, chmn.; regulatory atty. Katz, Kutter, et al., P.A., 1987, Knowles, Marks & Randolph, P.A., 1997; mng. ptnr. Adorno & Yoss, LLP; adj. prof. Fla. State U. Coll. Law; faculty mem. Nat. Assoc. Regulatory Utility Cmmrs. Utility Rate Sch.; mayor City of Tallahassee, 2003—. Bd. adv. U.S. Conf. Mayors; vice-chair Transp. & Comm. Com.; mem. Cmty. & Econ. Devel. Com., Nat. League Cities; pres. Fla. League Mayors, 2005—07; v.p. Fla. League Cities, pres. Judge adv. USAF. Named Super Lawyer, Fla. Super Lawyer Mag. Mem.: ABA, Am. Law Assn., Tallahassee Barristers Assn., Fla. Bar Assn., National Bar Assn., Omega Psi Phi Fraternity, Inc. Democrat. Office: City Hall Office of the Mayor 300 S Adams St Tallahassee FL 32301 Office Phone: 850-891-2000. Business E-Mail: john.marks@talgov.com.*

MARKS, JONATHAN H., law & bioethics educator; s. Ronald and Maxine D. Marks; m. Lisa R. Sternlieb, July 7, 2002; 1 child, Miranda J. MA, Oxford U., Eng., BCL, 1991. Bar: Bar Coun. Eng. & Wales 1992; cert. mediator CEDR, London, 2000. Barrister Verulam Bldg., London, 1993—2000; barrister founding mem. Matrix Chambers, London, 2000—; assoc. prof., bioethics, humanities and law Pa. State U., Univ. Pk., 2006—, dir. bioethics program, 2006—. Counsel Human Rights Watch Pinochet Case, London, 1998—99, Dr Nancy Olivieri European Ct. Justice, Luxembourg, 1999—2003. Greenwall fellowship, Johns Hopkins & Georgetown U., 2004—06, Edmond J. Safra Faculty fellowship, Safra Ctr., Kennedy Sch. Govt., Harvard U., 2009—. Mem.: Am. Soc. Bioethics & Humanities. Avocations: swimming, bicycling, cooking. Office: Pa State Univ 201E Old Botany University Park PA 16802

MARKS, KATHRYN ALLAN, dancer, educator; d. Morton and Helen W. Marks; m. George L. Merritt. A Applied Studies, U. Richmond, Va., 1992; Grad., SPARC, 2003. Dance specialist Henrico Recreation & Pks., Richmond, 1989—, Hanover Recreation & Pks.; arts tchr. Neighborhood Sch. Arts, 2000—03; guest artist Partner in The Arts, Blackwell Elem. Sch., Richmond, 2008—. Arts tchr. SPARC, Richmond, 2000—03. Personal E-mail: kathimarks13@gmail.com.

MARKS, LAWRENCE EDWARD, psychologist, educator; b. NYC, Dec. 28, 1941; s. Milton and Anne (Parnes) M.; m. Joya Ellen Cazes, Dec. 24, 1963; children: Liza, Laura. AB, Hunter Coll., NYC, 1962; PhD, Harvard U., Cambridge, Mass., 1965; PhD honoris causa, Stockholm U., 1994. Rsch.-assoc. prof. Yale U., New Haven, 1966-84; asst.-assoc. fellow John B. Pierce Lab., New Haven, 1966-84; prof. epidemiology and psychology Yale U., New Haven, 1984—; fellow John B. Pierce Lab., New Haven, 1984—, dir., 1999—2009. Author: Sensory Processes: The New Psychophysics, 1974, The Unity of the Senses, 1978. Named to Hall of Fame, Hunter Coll., N.Y.C., 1985; recipient Jacob Javits award NIH, Washington, 1987. Fellow AAAS, Am. Psychol. Assn., Am. Psychol. Soc., N.Y. Acad. Sci. Democrat. Jewish. Achievements include elucidation of common principles underlying sensory processes in various sense modalities; development of validational scheme for quantifying magnitudes of sensory experience; indication of role of cross-modal (synesthetic) perception in relation to language and literature. Home: 48 Maplevale Dr Woodbridge CT 06525-1118 Office: John B Pierce Lab 290 Congress Ave New Haven CT 06519-1403 Home Phone: 203-393-1565; Office Phone: 203-562-9901. Business E-Mail: marks@jbpierce.org.

MARKS, LOREN DEAN, psychology professor; b. Salt Lake City, July 4, 1972; s. James Lawrence and Renee Fluckiger Marks; m. Sandra Jody Martindale, Dec. 30, 1995; children: Mishonne M., Logan J., Haley R., Denton M. children: Aliyah J. PhD, U.Del., Newark, 2002. Cert. in CFLE Nat. Coun. Family Rels., 2004. Assoc. prof. LSU, Baton Rouge, 2002—. Contbr. articles to numerous profl. jours. (Jack Shand Rsch. award, 2005). Stake presidency counselor Ch. Jesus Christ Latter-day Saints, Baton Rouge, 2008—. Recipient Paper of Yr., NCFR Religion and Family Life Sect., 2005, Outstanding Undergrad. Tchg., Tiger Athletic Found., 2006, LSU Rainmakers - Top 100 Rsch. Faculty, 2008. Mem. Lds Ch. Office: LSU School Human Ecology Tower Dr Baton Rouge LA 70803 Business E-Mail: lorenm@lsu.edu.

MARKS, MALCULM WERNICK, plastic surgeon, educator; b. London, Oct. 6, 1950; s. Charles and Joyce Marks; m. Sharon Lynn Marks; children: Kevin, Lara, Eric, Nicole. BS, U. Wis., Madison; MD, louisiana State U. Asst. prof. surgery Tulane Med. Ctr., New Orleans, 1983—86, U. Mich. Med. Ctr., 1986—88, Wake Forest Baptist Med. Ctr., NC, 1988—98, prof. surgery, 1998—, chmn. dept surgery, 2006—. Author: (Text) Fundamentals of Plastic Surgery, 1997. Fellow: ACS; mem.: Am. Soc. Plastic Surgeons, Am. Assoc. Plastic Surgeons. Office: Dept Plastic Surgery Med Ctr Blvd Winston Salem NC 27157

MARKS, MELVIN I., physician, educator, hospital administrator, consultant; b. Montreal, July 30, 1940; came to U.S., 1979; s. Irving and Kate Marks; div. March 1999; children: Suzanne, Jennifer, Daniel. BSc, McGill U., 1961, MD CM, 1965; Cert. in Exec. Mgmt., UCLA, 1990. Diplomate Am. Bd. Pediat., Am. Bd. Pediat. Infectious Disease. Intern Montreal Gen. Hosp., 1965-66; resident in pediat. Montreal Children's Hosp., 1966-68; fellow in pediat. infectious diseases U. Colo. Med. Ctr., 1968-70; asst. prof. McGill U., Montreal, 1970-75, assoc. prof., 1975-79; prof. U. Okla., Oklahoma City, 1979-86; prof., vice-chmn. dept. U. Calif., Irvine, 1986—; clin. prof. U. So. Calif., 1997-99. Author: Pediatric Infectious Disease for the Practitioner, 1985; editor: Cystic Fibrosis, 1996. Bd. dirs. StarBright Found., L.A., 1995—. Office: Miller Childrens Hosp 2801 Atlantic Ave Long Beach CA 90806-1737 Home Phone: 714-402-3027; Office Phone: 562-933-8001. E-mail: mmarks@memorialcare.org.

MARKS, MERTON E., lawyer, international arbitrator, mediator, consultant; b. Chgo., Oct. 16, 1932; s. Alfred Tobias and Helene Fannie (Rosner) M.; m. Bernice H. Germaine, Aug. 21, 2007; children: Sheldon, Elise Marks Vazelakis, Alan, Elaine Marks Ianchiou (dec.). BS, Northwestern U., 1954, JD, 1956. Bar: Ill. 1956, U.S. Ct. Mil. Appeals 1957, Ariz. 1958, U.S. Dist. Ct. Ariz. 1960, U.S. Ct. Appeals (9th cir.) 1962, U.S. Supreme Ct. 1970; cert. arbitrator U.S. Dist. Ct. Ariz. Assoc. Moser, Compere & Emerson, Chgo., 1956-57; ptnr. Morgan, Marks & Rogers, Tucson, 1960-62; asst. atty. gen. State of Ariz., Phoenix, 1962-64, counsel indsl. commn., 1964-65; from assoc. to ptnr. Shimmel, Hill, Bishop & Gruender, Phoenix, 1965-74; ptnr. Lewis & Roca, Phoenix, 1974—2001; prin. Merton E. Marks PC Arbitration and Mediation Svcs., 2001—. Judge Pro Tempore Ariz. Ct. Appeals, 1994; CPR Inst. Dispute Resolution Inter-Insurer Arb. Panel; spl. master Ariz. Superior Ct., 2001—; US and internat. alternative dispute resolution; lectr. in field; arbitrator Internat panel Singapore Internat. Arbitration Ctr., 2003—09. Contbr. articles to profl. jours., columns. Past trustee Ariz. Opera Co., past chmn. endowment commn.; past mem. U.S. Olympic Com. for Ariz. Capt. JAGC, USAR, 1957-64. Fellow Chartered Inst. Arbitrators (London); mem. ABA (trial, tort and ins. practice sect., chmn. spl. com. on fed. asbestos legis. 1987-89, chmn. workers compensation and employers liability law com. 1983-84, dispute resolution sect.), Am. Bd. Trial Advs., Am. Coll. Legal Medicine, Am. Arbitration Assn., Financial Industry Regulatory Authority, Internat. Bar Assn. (arbitration com.), State Bar Ariz. (chmn. workers compensation sect. 1969-73), Fedn. Def. and Corp. Counsel (chmn. pharm. litig. sect. 1989-91, chmn. workers compensation sect. 1977-79, v.p. 1978-79, 81, bd. dirs. 1981-89, mem. products liability sect., mem. reinsurance sect., chmn. alternative dispute resolution sect. 2005-06), Internat. Assn. Def. Counsel, Ariz. Assn. Def. Counsel (pres. 1976-77), Maricopa County Bar Assn., Pima County Bar Assn., Def. Rsch. Inst. (drug and device com., chmn. workers compensation com. 1977-78), Reinsurance and Ins. Arbitration Soc., (cert. arbitrator). Office: 7868 E Via Marina Scottsdale AZ 85258-2852 also: 850 N Kolb Rd Tucson AZ 85710-1333 Office Phone: 480-991-3949. Business E-Mail: memarkspc@earthlink.net.

MARKS, MICHAEL E., electronics executive; BA, MA, Oberlin Coll.; MBA, Harvard U. Pres., CEO Metcal Inc., Menlo Park, Calif.; CEO Flextronics Internat. Ltd., Singapore, 1994—2005, chmn., 2006—; mem. Kohlberg Kravis Roberts & Co., Menlo Park, Calif., 2005—; interim CEO Tesla Motors. Bd. dir. SanDisk Corp.; mgr. Bigwood Capital. Office: KKR Ste 200 2800 Sand Hill Rd Menlo Park CA 94025

MARKS, PAUL ALAN, oncologist, cell biologist, educator; b. NYC, Aug. 16, 1926; s. Robert R. and Sarah (Bohorad) Marks; m. Joan Harriet Rosen, Nov. 28, 1953; children: Andrew Robert, Elizabeth Susan Marks Ostrer, Matthew Stuart. AB with gen. honors, Columbia U., 1945, MD, 1949, DSc (hon.), 2000; D in Biol. Sci. (hon.), U. Urbino, Italy, 1982; PhD (hon.), Hebrew U., Jerusalem, Israel, 1987, U. Tel Aviv, 1992; DSc (hon.), Ben Gurion U., Be'er Sheva, Israel, 2003. From fellow to prof. Coll. Physicians and Surgeons Columbia U., NYC, 1952—67, prof. medicine Coll. Physicians and Surgeons, 1967—82, dean faculty of medicine, v.p. med. affairs Coll. Physicians and Surgeons, 1970—73, dir. Comprehensive Cancer Ctr. Coll. Physicians and Surgeons, 1972—80, v.p. health scis. Coll. Physicians and Surgeons, 1973—80; prof. cell biology and genetics Coll. Medicine Cornell U., NYC, 1980—, prof. medicine Grad. Sch. Med. Scis., 1983—; pres., CEO Meml. Sloan-Kettering Cancer Ctr., NYC, 1980—99, pres. emeritus, 2000—. Instr. Sch. Medicine George Wash. U., 1954—55; cons. VA Hosp., NYC, 1962—66; attending physician Presbyn. Hosp., NYC, 1967—82; bd. dirs. Pfizer Inc., 1978—96, Shape Pharm., 2009—; attending physician Meml. Hosp. for Cancer and Allied Diseases, 1980—; prin. investigator, Devel. Cell Biology Sloan-Kettering Inst. for Cancer Rsch., 1980—; adj. prof. Rockefeller U., 1980—; vis. physician Rockefeller U. Hosp., 1980—; bd. sci. counselors divsn. cancer treatment Nat. Cancer Inst., 1980—83; hon. staff N.Y. Hosp., 1981—; steering com. Frederick Cancer Rsch. Facility Nat. Cancer Inst., 1982—86; chmn. prog. adv. com. Robert Wood Johnson Found., 1983—89; adv. com. on NIH to Sec. HHS, 1989—90, 1993—98; external adv. com. Intramural Rsch. Prog. Rev. NIH; gov. com. NYPRHA, 1996; tech. adv. grp. UN Assn. U.S.; coun. biol. scis. Pritzker Sch. Medicine U. Chgo., 1977—88; William Dameshek vis. prof. hematology Mt. Sinai Med. Ctr., 1985; nat. vis. com. CUNY Med. Sch., 1986—89; trustee Feinberg Grad. Sch. Weizmann Inst. Sci., Rehovot, Israel, 1986—; vis. prof. Coll. de France, 1988; Alpha Omega Alpha vis. prof. N.Y. Med. Coll., 1990; Mario A. Baldini vis. prof. Med. Sch. Harvard U., 1991; sci. adv. bd. City Hope Nat. Med. Ctr., Duarte, Calif., 1987—92, Raymond and Beverly Sackler Found., Inc., 1989, Jefferson Cancer Inst., Phila., 1989, PTC Biotech., Inc., 2002—, Ikonysis, 2004—08, Merck, Inc., 2004—05; mem. Found. Biomed. Rsch., 1989—; sci. adv. com. Imperial Cancer Rsch. Fund, 1994—2003; sr. adv. Lazard Freres, 2000—; co-founder, sec. and vice chmn. Aton Pharma, Tarrytown, NY, 2001—04, co-founder, chmn. bd.dir., 2006—; internat. adv. coun. Singapore Econ. Devel. Bd., 2000—03; dir. Dreyfus Mutual Funds, NC, 1998—2005; lectr. Nobel Forum, Karolinska Inst., Sweden, 2004. Author: 11 books; mem. editl. bd.: Blood, 1964—76, editor-in-chief:, 1978—82, mem. editl. bd.: Jour. Clin. Investigation, 1970—71, editor-in-chief: Jour. Clin Investigation, mem. editl. bd.: Cancer Treatment Revs., 1981—, Japanese Jour. Cancer Rsch., 1985—, Molecular Reprodn. and Devel., 1988—, Cancer Preventions, 1989, Sci., 1990, Current Opinion Oncologic Endocrine and Metabolic Drugs, 1998; mem. editl. bd. WTL Jour. Cell Biology; expert analyst: Chemistry and Molecular Biology edit. of Chemtracts, 1990—92, mem. adv. bd.: Internat. Jour. Hematology, 1992, Stem Cells, bd. contbg. editors: Blood Cells, Molecules and Diseases, 1994, Comité des Sages, 1994; contbr. over 400 articles to profl. jours. Trustee St. Luke's Hosp., 1970—80, Roosevelt Hosp., 1970—80, Presbyn. Hosp., 1972—80, Metpath Inst. Med. Edn., 1977—79, Hadassah Med. Ctr., Jerusalem, 1996; mem. jury Albert Lasker Awards, 1974—82; bd. dirs. Revson Found., 1976—91, Am. Found. for Basic Rsch. Israel, Israel Acad. Scis., 1991; mem. tech. bd. Milbank Meml. Fund, 1978—85; bd. govs. Friends of Sheba Med. Ctr., Tel Hashomer; mem. commn. sci. and tech. Mayor, NYC, 1984—87; mem. commn. Shoreham Nuc. Plant Gov., NYC, 1983; mem. task force biomed. rsch. and tech. Mayor, NYC, 1999. Recipient Stevens Triennial prize, 1960, Swiss-Am. Found. award, 1965, Centenary medal, Inst. Pasteur, 1987, Found. for Promotion of Cancer Rsch. medal, Japan, 1984, DSM, Robert Wood Johnson Found., 1989, Outstanding Achievement award, U. Innsbruck, 1991, Pres.'s Nat. Medal Sci., 1991, Japan Found. for Cancer Rsch. award, 1995, Lifetime Achievement award, Greater N.Y. Hosp. Assn., 1997, Am. Italian Cancer Found., 1999, Humanitarian award, Breast Cancer Rsch. Found., 2000, Disting. Lifetime Achievement award, Healthcare Chaplaincy, NY, 2001, John Stearns award, NY Acad. Medicine, 2002, Annie Blount Storrs Humanitarian award, Calvary Hosp., NY, 2002; fellow Commonwealth Fund fellow, Pasteur Inst., 1961—62; Ayrey fellow, 1985. Master: ACP, Coll. Physicians and Surgeons (Gold medal 1994); fellow: AAAS, Pasteur Inst. Paris (Commonwealth Fund fellow 1961—62), Am. Acad. Arts and Scis., Royal Soc. Medicine; mem.: NAS (chmn. Acad. Forum Adv. Com. 1980—81, chmn. sect. med. genetics, hematology and oncology 1980—83, coun. 1984—87, del. biol. warfare com. Internat. Security and Arms Control 1986—89, bd. dirs. 2002), Am. Philos. Soc., NY Acad. Sci. (bd. dirs. 2002), European Acad. Scis., UN Assn. (tech. adv. grp.), Weizmann Inst. Sci. (gov. emeritus, Israel), Third World Acad. Scis. (adv.), Soc. Study Devel. and Growth, Japan Soc. Hematology (Disting. lectr. 1989), Soc. Devel. Biology, Internat. Soc. Devel. Biologists, Harvey Soc. (pres. 1973—74), Assn. Am. Physicians, Am. Soc. Hematology (pres.-elect 1983, pres. 1984, chmn. adv. bd. 1985), Soc. Cell Biology, Assn. Am. Cancer Insts. (bd. dirs. 1983—88), Am. Assn. Cancer Rsch., Am. Soc. Human Genetics (past mem. prog. com.), Italian Assn. Cell Biology and Differentiation (hon.), Chinese Anti-Cancer Assn. (hon.), Japanese Cancer Assn. (hon.), Am. Soc. Biol. Chemists, Am. Soc. Clin. Investigation (pres. 1972—73), Am. Fedn. Clin. Rsch. (past councillor Ea. dist.), Red Cell Club (past chmn.), Inst. Medicine (coun. 1973—76, chmn. com. study resources clin. investigation with NAS 1988), Univ. Club, Soc. Interurban Clin. Club, Century Assn., Alpha Omega Alpha. Office: Meml Sloan-Kettering Cancer Ctr 1275 York Ave New York NY 10065-6094 Office Phone: 212-639-6568. Business E-Mail: marksp@mskcc.org.

MARKS, RAMON PAUL, lawyer; b. Washington, Dec. 9, 1948; s. Matthew J. and Simone V. (Van de Meulebroeke) Marks; m. Susan Eleanor MacCarthy; children: Robert Justin, Timothy Matthew, Fletcher. AB magna cum laude, Dartmouth Coll., 1971; MA in Internat. Rels. with high distinction, Johns Hopkins U., 1973; JD, U. Va., 1976. Bar: NY 1977, Tex. 1983, US Dist. Ct. (so. dist.) Tex. 1984, US Ct. Appeals (5ht cir.) 1984, US Ct. Internat. Trade 1988, US Dist. Ct. (so. dist.) NY 1989, US Ct. Appeals (fed. cir.) 1989. Assoc. Alexander & Green, NYC, 1976—77; corp. atty. Schlumberger Ltd., 1978, asst. gen. counsel Houston, 1986—87; asst. legal counsel svcs., techniques Schlumberger Paris, 1978—80; gen. counsel Schlumberger Well Svcs., Houston, 1980—84; sec., gen. counsel Dowell Schlumberger, Inc., 1984—85; ptnr. Marks & Murase, NYC, 1987, Dorsey & Whitney, 1997; ptnr., internat. litig. Arnold & Porter, 2005—. Mem.: Bus. Execs. Nat. Security (bd. dirs., chmn. governance com.), Assn. Bar City NY, Phi Beta Kappa. Office: Arnold & Porter 399 Park Ave New York NY 10022-4690 Office Phone: 212-715-1145. Office Fax: 212-715-1399. Business E-Mail: ramon.marks@aporter.com.

MARKS, ROBERTA BARBARA, artist, educator; b. Savannah, Ga.; d. Philip W. and Eleanore (Margolis) Dilner; children: Jeffery Allen, Steven Craig. BFA, U. Miami, Coral Gables, Fla., 1980; MFA, U. South Fla., Tampa, 1981. Instr., lectr. multi-media, lectr., vis. artist to numerous art schs., including U. South Fla., Tampa, 1998-05, Custom House Mus., Armory Art Ctr., Palm Beach, Fla., 2002, Key West, Fla., 2003, Galerie Jonas, Neuchatel, Switzerland, 2003, Chgo. Anderson Ranch Art Sch., Colo., 2004, U. South Fla., U. Miami Lowe Art Mus., Fla., Armory Art Ctr., Palm Beach, Fla., Valparaiso U., Ind., Rochester Inst. Tech. Am. Sch. of Crafts, NY, Galerie de Koull, Murten, Switzerland, Santa Fe Community Coll., Gainesville, Brookfield Craft Ctr., Conn., Fla. Keys Community Coll., U. Wis.-Milw., Parson Sch. Design, Key West C.C., Fla., 1991, Am. Embassy, Bern, Switzerland, 1993; juror Riverside Avondale Preservation Art Festival, Jacksonville, Fla., 1981, Ybor Square Art Festival, Tampa, 1980, Miami Lakes Art Festival, Fla., 1975. One woman shows include Brevard Community Coll., Melbourne, Fla., 1982, Cocoa, Fla., 1982, Coventry Galleries, Ltd., Tampa, 1983, Barbara Gillman Gallery, Miami, 1984, 87, Tennessee Williams Fine Arts Ctr., Key West, 1985, Garth Clark Gallery, NYC, 1985, Fred Gros Gallery, Key West, 1985, Key West Art and Historical Soc. East Martello Mus. and Gallery, 1985, U. Miami New Gallery, Fla., 1987, Katie Gingrass Gallery, Milw., 1987, Zimmerman Saturn Gallery, Nashville, 1987, Bern, Zurich Switzerland, 1988, Galerie Alte Krone, Altstadt, Biel, Switzerland, 1990, Helander Gallery, NYC, 1990, Gump's Gallery, San Francisco, 1990, Helander Gallery, NYC, 1991, LeMieux Gallery, New Orleans, 1991, Helander Gallery, Palm Beach, 1992, Galerie Etc., Bern, 1992, Galerie Bel Arte, Lengnau, Switzerland, 1992, Lucky Street Gallery, Key West, 1994-05, Barbara Gillman Gallery, Miami, 1994-05, Galerie Vinelz, Switzerland, 1994, Galerie Quattro, Zurich, 1994, many others; exhibited in group shows at Netsky Gallery, Miami, 1982, The Craftsman's Gallery, Scarsdale, NY, 1982, Garth Clark Gallery, Los Angeles, 1983, Nelson-Atkins Mus. Art, Kansas City, Mo., 1983, Am. Craft Mus., NYC, 1984, N. Miami Mus. and Art Ctr., 1985, Joanne Lyon Gallery, Aspen, Colo., 1984, Key West Art and Hist. Soc. East Martello Mus. and Gallery, 1985, Garth Clark Gallery, NYC and Los Angeles, 1985, 24X24, Ruth Siegel Ltd., NYC, 1987, Artforms Gallery, Louisville, 1986, The Pvt. Collection Women Artists, Ohio, 1987, East Martello Mus., Key West, Fla., 1990, East Martello Mus., Key West, Fla., 1990, Philharmonic Ctr. for Arts, Naples, Fla., 1993, Ctr. for Arts, Vero Beach, Fla., 1993, Helander Gallery, Palm Beach, 1993, Gingrass Gallery, Milw., 1993, many others; represented in permanent collections Mint Mus., Charlotte, NC, N.Mex Mus. Fine Arts, Sante Fe, Smithsonian Instn., Renwick Gallery, Rochester Inst. Tech. Fine Arts Dept., U. Utah Mus., U. South Fla. Fine Arts Dept., Galerie du Manoir, La Chaux-de-Fonds, Switzerland, Valencia Community Coll., Okum Gallery, Victoria and Albert Mus., London, IBM, Jacksonville, Fla., AT&T, NYC, Custom Ho. Mus., Key West, Fla., 2002, U. South Fla., Galerie Jonas, Neuchatel, Switzerland, 2003, Lucky St. Gallery, 2005, Mint Mus., Charlotte, NMex. Mus. Fine Arts, Sante Fe, others. Recipient Regional Visual Artist fellow, Miami, Fla., 1990, also numerous awards. Mem. World Craft Council, Artists Equity Assn., Internat. Sculpture Ctr.

MARKS, RONALD ANTHONY, communications industry executive; b. Portland, Oreg., Apr. 18, 1956; s. Nathaniel Frederick and Margaret Clara (Stuntebeck) Marks; m. Kathleen Suzanne Gray, Dec. 8, 1959. BS, Lewis and Clark Coll., 1978; MS in Econs., U. Oreg., 1982. Intelligence officer/liaison officer CIA, Langley, Va., 1983—99; intelligence advisor Senate Majority Leaders Dole and Lott, Wash., 1995—96; sr. intelligence advisor SAIC, Tyson Corner, Va., 1999—2001; dir. Intelligence Program Devel. SRA Internat., Fairfax, Va., 2001—02; dir. External Affairs British Telecom-Syntegra Federal, Rockville, Md., 2002—04; SVP govt. rels. Oxford Analytica, 2005—. Advisor Transitional Threats Initiative, Ctr. Strategic and Internat. Studies, Wash., 1998—, Homeland Security Advisory Com., Ctr. for Studies of the Presidency, Wash., 2002—; editl. advisory bd. Nat. Inst. Pub. Policy, Wash., 2002—; adj. prof. intelligence NH Defence U. Author: (essay) The Uses and Limits of U.S. Intelligence, Defining America's Brave New World. Mem.: Internat. Inst. Strategic Studies, Bus. Exec. for Nat. Security, Intelligence & NH Security Alliance, Assn. Former Intelligence Officers, Cosmos Club. Home: 7004 Dunningham Pl Mc Lean VA 22101 Office: Oxford Analytica 169 Thomas Jefferson St Washington DC 20007 Home Phone: 703-919-7419; Office Phone: 202-342-2860. Personal E-mail: rmarksster@gmail.com.

MARKS, SALLY JEAN, historian, educator; b. New Haven, Conn., Jan. 18, 1931; d. Percy and Margaret Ellen (Gates) Marks. AB, Wellesley Coll., Mass., 1952; AM, U. N.C., Chapel Hill, 1961; PhD, U. London, 1968. Policy planner U.S. Dept. Def., Washington, 1953—57; tchr. secondary schs., Conn., 1957—59; instr. U. N.C., Greensboro, 1960—62; from instr. to prof. history R.I. Coll., Providence, 1962—88; pvt. practice Providence. Author: The Illusion of Peace, 1976, 2d edit., 2003, Innocent Abroad, 1981 (George Louis Beer prize, 1981, Phi Alpha Theta book award, 1983), The Ebbing of European Ascendancy, 2002, Paul Hymans of Belgium Haus Press London, 2009; mem. editl. bd. H-Diplo; contbr. articles to profl. jours. Fellow Am. Coun. Learned Socs., Tauber Inst.; mem. Inst. Royal des Rels. Internat., Brussels, Am. Hist. Assn. (chmn. Beer prize com., program com.), Soc. French Hist. Studies, Soc. Historians of Am. Fgn. Rels. (chmn. Bernath prize com.), Conf. Group Ctrl. European History (chmn. prize com.); Providence Art Club, Royal Anglo-Belgian Club (London). Home and Office: 603 Hope St Providence RI 02906-2654

MARKS, STEPHEN J., neurologist, educator; b. Bklyn., Aug. 30, 1953; s. Ansel R. Marks and Frances L. Carpenter; m. Cindy G. Marks, Mar. 27, 1994; children: Jordan, Avery. BA, Colgate U., 1979. Diplomate Am. Bd. Neurology & Psychiatry. Intern Lenox Hill Hosp., NYC; resident Mt. Sinai Hosp., NYC; assoc. prof. N.Y. Med. Coll., Valhalla, 1987—. Team neurologist N.Y. Jets, Hempstead, 1986. Co-author: (chapter) Principle & Practice of Emergency Medicine, 1992, (book), 1997. Fellow: Am. Heart Assn. (mem. stroke coun.); mem.: Soc. Neuroscience, Nat. Stroke Assn., Am. Acad. Neurology. Avocations: skiing, windsurfing. Office: Dept Neurology Munger Pavilion, NYMC Valhalla NY 10595

MARKS, THEODORE LEE, lawyer; b. NYC, Oct. 18, 1935; s. Irving Edward and Isabel (Goodman) M.; m. Benita Cooper, July 13, 1958; children: Eric, Robert, Jennifer BS, NYU, 1956, LLB, 1958. Bar: N.Y. 1959, U.S. Dist. Ct. (so. dist.) N.Y. 1963, U.S. Supreme Ct. 1964, U.S. Ct. Appeals (2d cir.) 1975, U.S. Dist. Ct. (ea. dist.) N.Y. 1978. Assoc. Silver, Bernstein, Seawell & Kaplan, NYC, 1959-65; pvt. practice NYC, 1965-70; ptnr. Lee, Cash & Marks, NYC, 1970-76, Vogel, Marks & Rosenberg, NYC, 1976-79, Bromberg, Gloger, Lifschultz & Marks, NYC, 1979-85, Epstein Becker Borsody & Green, P.C., NYC, 1985-86, Gelberg & Abrams, 1986-87, Morrison Cohen Singer & Weinstein, 1987—2004; counsel Morrison Cohen LLP, NYC, 2004—. Speaker at meetings of profl. assns. Contbr. articles to profl. jours. Served with Army N.G., 1958-61. Mem. NY State Bar Assn. (mem. real property, banking, corp. and bus. law sects.), NY County Lawyers Assn., T&M. Office: Morrison Cohen LLP 909 Third Ave New York NY 10022 E-mail: tmarks@morrisoncohen.com.

MARKS, TOBIN JAY, chemistry educator; b. Washington, Nov. 25, 1944; s. Eli Sidney and Miriam (Heller) M.; m. Indrani Mukharji, May 19, 1985 BS in Chemistry, U. Md., 1966; PhD in Chemistry, MIT, 1970. Asst. prof., chemistry Northwestern U., Evanston, Ill., 1970-74, assoc. prof., chemistry, 1974-78, Charles E. and Emma H. Morrison prof. chemistry, 1985—99, prof. materials sci. and engring., 1987—, Vladimir N. Ipatieff prof. catalytic chemistry, 1999—. Invited lectr. in field; cons. or advisor for several major corporations and start-ups. Editor: Organometallics of the F-Elements, 1979; assoc. editor Organometallics, 1986—; editor: Fundamental and Technological Aspects of Organo-F-Element Chemistry, 1985; mem. several editl. boards; contbr. articles to profl. jours. Sloan Found. fellow, 1974, Guggenheim fellow, 1989-1990; Dreyfus Found. scholar, 1975; recipient Nat. Fesenius award Phi Lambda Upsilon, 1979, Mack award Ohio State U., 1987, Francis Clifford Phillips award, U. Pitts., 1998, Paolo Chini award, Italian Chem. Soc., 1999, Burwell award, N.Am. Catalysis Soc., 2001., Am. Inst. Chemists Gold medal, 2002, Evans medal, Ohio State U., 2003, Karl Ziegler medal, German Chem. Soc., 2003, 2005 Nat. Medal Sci., NSF, 2007; named to U. Md. Alumni Hall of Fame, 2005; named U. Pierre et Marie Curie Institut U. de France prof., 2005. Fellow Am. Acad. Arts and Scis., Royal Soc. Chemistry (Centenary medal, 1997, Sir Edward Frankland medal, Royal Soc. Chemistry (UK), 2003); mem. NAS, Am. Chem. Soc. (A.K. Doolittle award 1984, award in Polymeric Materials, 1983, award in Organometallic Chemistry 1989, award in Inorganic Chemistry 1994, Cotton medal Tex. A&M sect., 2000, Williard Gibbs medal, Chgo. sect., 2001, Linus Pauling medal, Oreg.-Washington sections, 2001, award in Chemistry of Materials, 2001, John C. Bailar medal, Urbana-Champaign sect., 2005, Disting. Svc. in the Advancement of Inorganic Chemistry, 2008), Soc. for Applied Spectroscopy, Materials Rsch. Soc., Leopoldina German Nat. Acad. Natural Scis., Phi Beta Kappa. Achievements include patents in field. Home: 2300 Central Park Ave Evanston IL 60201-1810 Office Phone: 708-491-5658. Office Fax: 847-491-2990. Business E-Mail: t-marks@northwestern.edu.

MARKULIS, HENRYK JOHN, career military officer; b. Columbia, SC, July 10, 1945; s. Henryk F. Markulis and Judith E. (Taylor) Kassman; m. Cathy F. Krawczyk; children: Mark C., Melinda L. BA, U. Buffalo, 1968; MA, Ctrl. Mich. U., 1977. Commd. USAF, 1969; advanced through ranks to col.; aircraft cmdr. 53d Weather Recon Squadron Ramey AFB, PR, 1970-74; gunship aircraft cmdr. 16th Spl. Ops. Squadron Korat RTAB, Thailand, 1974-75; cmdr. 437th Field Maintenance Squadron Sect. Charleston AFB, SC, 1975-78; exercise and contingency support 1701st Mobility Support Shaw AFB, SC, 1978-82; air staff action officer Joint Chiefs of Staff Pentagon, 1982-84; chief internat. programs Singapore, Malaysia & Brunei, 1984-93; dep. cmdr., chief staff Iceland Def. Force NATO, 1993-95, ret., 1995; pres., CEO Internat. Security and Mktg. Cons., 1996—. Cons. Nissan Motor Acceptance Corp., 1996—, Infiniti Fin. Svcs., 1996-, Project Boreas, 2006-08. Col. USAF, sr. pilot USAF. Mem. Am. Legion, VFW, Mil. Officers Assn. Am., Aircraft Owners and Pilots Assn., Army Navy Country Club, Order of Daedalians, Kiwanis, KC (4th degree). Avocation: golf. Office: 52 Union St Hamburg NY 14075 Home: 56 Union St Hamburg NY 14075-4910 Office Phone: 716-646-1589. Office Fax: 719-646-9589. Personal E-mail: colonelm@roadrunner.com.

MARKUS, LAWRENCE, retired mathematics professor; b. Hibbing, Minn., Oct. 13, 1922; s. Benjamin and Ruby (Friedman) M.; m. Lois Shoemaker, Dec. 9, 1950; children: Sylvia, Andrew. BS, U. Chgo., 1942, MS, 1946; PhD, Harvard U., Cambridge, Mass., 1951. Instr. meteorology U. Chgo., 1942-44; rsch. meteorologist Atomic Project, Hanford, 1944; instr. math. Harvard U., 1951-52; instr. Yale U., 1952-55; lectr. Princeton U., 1955-57; asst. prof. U. Minn., Mpls., 1957-58, assoc. prof., 1958-60, prof. math., 1960-93, assoc. chmn. dept. math., 1961-63, dir. control scis., 1964-73, Regents' prof. math., 1980-93, Regents' prof. emeritus, 1993—, dir. Control Sci. and Dynamical Sys. Ctr., 1980-89. Leverhulme prof. control theory, dir. control theory ctr. U. Warwick, Eng., 1970-73, Nuffield prof. math., 1970-85, hon. prof., 1985—; regional conf. lectr. NSF, 1969; vis. prof. Yale U., Columbia U., U. Calif., U. Warsaw, 1980, Tech. Inst. Zurich, 1983, Peking U. (China), 1983; dir. conf. Internat. Ctr. Math., Trieste, 1974; lectr. Internat. Math. Congress, 1974, Iranian Math. Soc., 1975, Brit. Math. Soc., 1976, Japan Soc. for Promotion Sci., 1976, Royal Instn., London, 1982, U. Beer Sheva, Israel, 1983; vis. prof. U. Tokyo, 1976, Tech. U., Denmark, 1979; mem. panel Internat. Congress Mathematicians, Helsinki, 1978; sr. vis. fellow Sci. Rsch. Coun., Imperial Coll., London, 1978; mem. UNESCO sci. adv. com. Control Symposium, U. Strasbourg, France, 1980; IEEE Plenary lectr., Orlando, Fla., 1982; Sci. and Engring. Rsch. Coun. vis. prof. U. Warwick, Eng., 1982-90; Neustadt Meml. lectr. U. So. Calif., 1985, prin. lectr. symposium U. Minn., 1988, dir. NSF workshop, 1989, prin. lectr. symposium in honor of his 75th birthday, 1997; Tate lectr. U. Cin., 1998; chmn. Conf. Markus-80, 2002; adv. bd. Office Naval Rsch., Air Force Office Sci. Rsch. Author: Flat Lorentz Manifolds, 1959, Flows on Homogeneous Spaces, 1963, Foundations of Optimal Control Theory, 1967, rev. edit., 1985, Lectures on Differentiable Dynamics, 1971, rev. edit., 1980, Generic Hamiltonian Dynamical Systems, 1974, Distributed Parameter Control Systems, 1991, Boundary Value Problems and Symplectic Algebra, 1998, Multi-Interval Linear Ordinary Boundary Value Problems and Complex Symplectic Algebra, 2001, Elliptic Partial Differential Operators and Symplectic Algebra, 2003, Infinite Dimensional Complex Symplectic Spaces, 2004; editor Internat. Jour. Nonlinear Mechanics, 1965-73, Jour. Control, 1963-67; mem. editl. bd. Proc. Georgian Acad. Sci. Math., 1993—; contbr. articles to profl. jours Lt. (j.g.) USNR, 1944-46. Recipient Rsch. prize Internat. Conf. Nonlinear Oscillations, Ukrainian Acad. Sci., Kiev, 1969, Festschrift volume, 1993; Fulbright fellow Paris, 1950; Guggenheim fellow Lausanne, Switzerland, 1963; Disting. Tchg. award, U. Minn., 1968. Fellow Royal Soc. Edinburgh (hon.); mem. Am. Math. Soc. (past mem. nat. coun.), Am. Geophys. Soc., Soc. Indsl. and Applied Math. (past nat. lectr.), Phi Beta Kappa, Sigma Xi. Office: 109 Vincent Hall 206 Church St S Minneapolis MN 55455 Business E-Mail: markus@math.umn.edu.

MARKUS, RICHARD M., judge, arbitrator; b. Evanston, Ill., Apr. 16, 1930; s. Benjamin and Ruby M.; m. Carol Joanne Slater, July 26, 1952; children: Linda, Scott, Kent. BS magna cum laude, Northwestern U., 1951; JD cum laude, Harvard U., 1954. Bar: D.C. 1954, Ohio 1956, Fla. 1994. Appellate atty., civil div. Dept. Justice, Washington, 1954-56; ptnr. civil litigation law firms Cleve., 1956-76, 89-98; judge Cuyahoga County (Ohio) Common Pleas Ct., 1976-80, Ohio Ct. Appeals, 1981-88. Instr. M.I.T., 1952-54; adj. prof. Case Western Res. U. Law Sch., 1972-78, 84-87, Cleve. State U. Law Sch., 1960-80, prof. 1999-2000; prof. Harvard Law Sch., 1980-81; mem. Nat. Commn. on Med. Malpractice, 1971-73; chmn. Nat. Inst. Trial Advocacy, 1978-81, trustee 1971—. Author: Trial Handbook for Ohio Lawyers, all edits., 1971—, Ohio Evidence Rules with Commentary, 1999; contbr. articles to profl. jours.; editor Harvard U. Law Rev, 1952-54. Republican nominee Justice of Ohio Supreme Ct., 1978; bd. dirs. Luth. Metro Ministry, 1988—, Fairview Luth. Hosp., 1985—. Mem. Ohio State Bar Assn. (pres. 1991-92), Cuyahoga County Bar Assn., Greater Cleve. Bar Assn. (trustee 1967-70, 85-90), Assn. Trial Lawyers Am. (nat. pres. 1970-71), Ohio Acad. Trial Lawyers (pres. 1965-66), Phi Beta Kappa, Pi Mu Epsilon, Delta Sigma Rho, Phi Alpha Delta. Home and Office: Pvt Judicial Svcs Inc 3903 N Valley Dr Cleveland OH 44126-1716 E-mail: judgemarkus1@cs.com.

MARKUS, ROBERT MICHAEL, retired journalist; b. Chgo., Jan. 30, 1934; s. David White and Anna (Tonkonogy) M.; m. Leslie Winnifred Ator, Aug. 25, 1962; children— Catherine Mary, Patricia Anne, Michael Hughes. B.J., U. Mo., 1955. Gen. assignment reporter Moline (Ill.) Dispatch, 1955-59; successively copy editor, sports columnist, feature writer, baseball writer, coll. sports writer, hockey writer Chgo. Tribune, 1959-96, ret., 1996. Mem. Northbrook (Ill.) Caucus, 1967. Served with U.S. Army, 1956-58. Recipient Nat. Headliner award as best columnist, 1973; named Ill. Sports Writer of Year, 1970, 71, 72 Mem. Football Writers Assn. Am., Baseball Writers Assn. Am., Am. Auto Racing Writers and Broadcasters Assn. Home: 3000 Holiday Dr 1501 Fort Lauderdale FL 33316 Personal E-mail: bobmarkus34@gmail.com.

MARK-VIVERITO, MELLISA, Councilwoman; b. San Juan, PR; BA in Polit. Sci., Columbia U., 1991; MA in Pub. Adminstrn., Baruch Coll., 1995. Strategic organizer 1199SEIU, NY; dir. Hispanic Edn. & Legal Fund; dep. dir. ASPIRA Assn., 1996—99; local mgr. US Census Bur. (Manhattan), 2000; vol. Howard Dean presdl. campaign, Davenport, Iowa, 2004; field ops. coord. John Kerry presdl. campaign, St. Petersburg, 2004; councilwoman, Dist. 8 NY City Coun., 2006—. Former mem. Cmty Bd. 11, Cmty. Bd. 2; former treas. El Barrio Revolving Loan Fund; prodr & co-host WBAI Pacifica Radio; cmty. adv. bd. mem. El Diario/La Prensa; mem. civil svc. & labor, contracts, environ. protection, immigration, waterfronts, women's issues, youth svcs. coms. Founding mem. Women of El Barrio; chmn. Violence Intervention Program; bd. mem. Boricua Initiative; del. Internat. Women's Conf., China, 1995, World Conf. Against Racism, South Africa, 2001. Democrat. Office: 105 E 116th St New York NY 10029 also: 250 Broadway New York NY 10007 Office Phone: 212-828-9800, 212-788-6960. Office Fax: 212-722-6378, 212-442-1564. Business E-Mail: viverito@council.nyc.ny.us.*

MARKWAY, BARBARA GERTH, psychologist, writer; d. Vernon William and Erika Schulze Gerth; m. Gregory Patrick Markway, Apr. 22, 1989; 1 child, Jesse William. BA, Valparaiso U., 1982; MA, U. Mo., St. Louis, 1986, PhD, 1990. Lic. psychologist State Com. Psychologist, Mo., 1991. Fellow St. Louis U. Med. Ctr., 1990—91; psychologist, owner Markway Psychol. Assoc., St. Louis, 1991—95; psychologist St. Mary's Health Ctr., Jefferson City, 1996—2000, Capital Region Med. Ctr., Jefferson City, 2000—04; psychologist, owner Anxiety & Stress Mgmt. Ctr., Jefferson City, 2004—. Author: (non-fiction books) Dying of Embarrassment: Help for Social Anxiety and Phobia, 1992, Illuminating the Heart: Steps Toward a More Spiritual Marriage, 1996, Painfully Shy: How to Overcome Social Anxiety and Reclaim Your Life, 2000, Nurturing the Shy Child, 2005; appeared on (TV shows) Good Morning America, The Today Show. Mem.: APA. Achievements include being featured in numerous newspapers and magazines. Office: Markway Psychol Assoc 428 E Capitol Ave # 313 Jefferson City MO 65101-3164 Business E-Mail: barbmarkway@gmail.com. E-mail: markways1@mchsi.com.

MARKWOOD, STEPHEN ERNEST, educator, college president; b. Glasgow, Ky., Nov. 26, 1942; s. Chester Ray and Mary (Tandy) M.; m. Susan Hendee, Dec. 26, 1965; children: Christopher M., Kathryn M. BS in Edn., Bowling Green U., 1964, MA, 1968; EdD, Pa. State U., 1983. Asst. dean student life Waynesburg Coll., Pa., 1968-70; assoc. dean students Dickinson Coll., Carlisle, Pa., 1970-77; dean student devel. Rio Grande Coll., Ohio, 1977-80; v.p. Marietta Coll., Ohio, 1980—92; provost Ottawa U., 1992-95; pres. Alderson-Broaddus Coll., 1995—2008, cons., Academic vice chair W.Va. Ind. Colls., 2000-03; chair Appalachian Coll. Assn. 2003-05. Contbr. articles to prof. jours. Served to capt. U.S. Army, 1964-66. Recipient Disting. Leadership award Pa. State U., 2005; Edn. Leadership award, 2007. Mem. Nat. Assn. Student Personnel Adminstrs., Am. Coll. Personnel Assn. (commn. 1983-84), Ohio Coll. Personnel Assn. (pres. 1983-84, outstanding leadership 1984, 87), Am. Coll. Personnel Assn. (mem. com. 1983-87), Ohio C. of C. (v.p.), Marietta C. of C. (pres.), Ohio Assn. Student Personnel Adminstrs, Ottawa C. of C. (treas.), W.Va. Intercoll. Assn. (chair 2002-04), Philip/Barboul C. of C. (dir.), Kiwanis (bd. dirs.). Avocations: golf, running. Office: 12 Raindrop Ln Bluffton SC 29909 Home Phone: 843-705-0960; Office Phone: 843-304-6502. Business E-Mail: markwoodse@ab.edu.

MARKWORTH, NORMAN, astronomer, educator; b. Palatine, Ill. married. PhD, U. Fla., Gainesville, 1977. Asst. prof., astronomy SW Mo. State U., Springfield, 1977—78, Stephen F. Austin State U., Nacogdoches, Tex., 1978—84, thesis dir., 14 MS students, 1978—2008, dir., observatories, 1982—, assoc. prof., astronomy, 1984—89, prof., astronomy, 1989—2000, regents prof., astronomy, 2000—. Dir., co-dir. Tchg. Excellence Ctr. Actor: (cmty. theater) More than 25 prodns.; singer (dir., performer): After 5; contbr. articles to profl. jours. Recipient Tchg. Excellence award, Coll. Scis. and Math., 1995, 2000; named Prof. of Yr., Student Govt. Assn., 1990—91. Mem.: Internat. Astron. Union. Achievements include development of design and construction of 41-inch telescope at SFASU observatory. Office: Stephen F Austin State Univ 1901 Raguet St N Nacogdoches TX 75962 Business E-Mail: nmarkworth@sfasu.edu.

MARLAND, ALKIS JOSEPH, leasing company executive, computer scientist, educator, financial planner; b. Athens, Greece, Mar. 8, 1943; arrived in U.S., 1961, naturalized, 1974; s. Basil and Maria (Pervanides) Mouradoglou; m. Anita Louise Malone, Dec. 19, 1970 (dec. Mar. 27, 2003); children: Andrea Weber, Alyssa. BS, Southwestern U., 1963; MA, U. Tex., Austin, 1967; MS in Engring. Adminstrn., So. Meth. U., 1971. CLU; cert. data processing, enrolled agt., fund specialist, ChFC, CFP, accredited tax advisor, accredited tax preparer. With Sun Co., Richardson, Tex., 1968-71, Phila., 1971-76; mgr. planning and acquisitions Sun Info. Svcs. subs. Sun Co., Dallas, 1976-78; v.p. Helios Capital Corp. subs. Sun Co., Radnor, Pa., 1978-83; pres. ALKAN Leasing Corp., Wayne, Pa., 1983—, also bd. dirs. Prof. dept. computer scis. and bus. adminstrn. Ea. Coll., St. Davids, Pa., 1985—87; prof. math. Villanova (Pa.) U., 1987—89. Contr. Christian Counseling and Ednl. Found., 2003—05; bd. dirs. Radnor Twp. Sch. Dist., 1987—91, Delaware County Intermediate Unit, 1988—91. Mem.: IEEE, Assn. Investment Mgmt. and Rsch., Phila. Union League, World Affairs Coun. Phila., Fgn. Policy Rsch. Inst., Phila. Fin. Assn. (mem. award 1988, sec. 1989—92, bd. dirs. 1989—92), Fin. Planning Assn. (treas. 2000—01, bd. dirs. Phila. Tri-State Area 2000—04, pres.-elect 2002, pres. 2003, chmn. 2004), Fin. Analysts Phila., Nat. Assn. Pub. Accts., Nat. Assn. Tax Practitioners, Nat. Assn. Enrolled Agts., Inst. Cert. Fin. Planners (bd. dirs. Phila. Tri-State Area 1993—99, v.p. membership 1994—95, treas. 1995—99), Am. Assn. Equipment Lessors, Fin. Svc. Profls., Data Processing Mgmt. Assn., Assn. Computing Machinery, Main Line C. of C., Wayne Club, Rotary Club (pres. 1989—90, asst. gov. 1990—92, 1993—94, treas. dist. 7450 2002—07, dist. 7450 gov. elect 2008—09, gov. 2009—), Masons. Republican. Home and Office: 4 Starling Ct Phoenixville PA 19460 Office: PO Box 1063 Oaks PA 19456-1063 Personal E-mail: almarland@aol.com.

MARLAR, DONALD FLOYD, lawyer; b. Little Rock, Jan. 15, 1944; s. Floyd Howard and Ruth May (Lawson) M.; m. Janet Jeanne Clark, Mar. 29, 1963; children: Jennifer Clark, Christopher Decker. BA, Ark. State U., 1966; JD, U. Tulsa, 1969; Masters in Taxation, George Washington U., 1972. Bar: Okla. 1969. Ptnr. Pray, Walker, Jackman, Williamson & Marlar, Tulsa, Okla., 1973-96, pres., 1996—. Chmn. Okla. Bar Tax Section, 1979-80. Dir. Tulsa Ballet Theatre, 1987—, pres., 1991-92; gen. coun., v.p. Gilcrease Mus., Tulsa, 1989—, pres., 2000-01, chmn. bd. dirs., 2001—; trustee Grace and Franklin Bernsen Found., Tulsa, 1992—, Tulsa C.C. Found.; dir. Tulsa Hist. Soc., 2006-. Capt. U.S. Army, 1969-73. Mem. Am. Bar Assn., Tulsa Bar Assn., The Summit Club (bd. govs. 1986-92, pres. 1992). Home: 3517 E 70th Pl Tulsa OK 74136-2647 Office: Moyers Martin Imel Santee 401 Southern Boston Ave Ste 1100 Tulsa OK 74103 Home Phone: 918-492-6608; Office Phone: 918-582-5281. Personal E-mail: marlar@moyersmartin.com. Business E-Mail: marlar@moyersmartinimelsantee.com.

MARLAS, JAMES CONSTANTINE, diversified financial services company executive; b. Chgo., Aug. 22, 1937; s. Constantine J. and Helen (Cotsirilos) M.; m. Kendra S. Graham, 1968 (div. 1971); m. Glenn Close, 1984 (div. 1987); m. Marie Nugent-Head, 1993. AB cum laude, Harvard U., 1959; MA in Jurisprudence, Oxford U., Eng., 1961; JD, U. Chgo., 1963. Bar: Ill. 1963, NY 1966. Assoc. firm Baker & McKenzie, London and NYC, 1963-66; exec. v.p. South East Commodity Corp., NYC, 1967-68; chmn. bd. Union Capital Corp., NYC, 1968—; vice chmn. bd. Mickelberry's Food Products Co., NYC, 1970-71; pres., dir. Mickelberry Comm. Corp., NYC, 1972—, chief exec. officer, 1973—, chmn. bd., 1984—; chmn. bd., CEO Newcourt Industries, Inc., 1976—. Chmn. bd. dirs. Bowmar Instrument Corp., chmn. exec. com., 1983-92. Co-editor: Univ. Chgo. Law Rev, 1962-63; Contbr. articles to profl. jours. Bd. dirs. NYC Opera, Commanderie de Bordeaux, Brasenose Coll. Charitable Found. Mem. Am. Fgn. Law Assn., Young Pres.'s Orgn. Clubs: Boodle's (London); Knickerbocker (NYC), Racquet and Tennis (NYC). Office: Union Capital Corp 445 Park Ave 14th Fl New York NY 10022-4405 Office Phone: 212-832-0944.

MARLEAU, PATRICK, professional hockey player; b. Aneroid, Sask., Can., Sept. 15, 1979; m. Christina Marleau. Center San Jose Sharks, 1997—, capt., 2003—09. Mem. Team Can., World Cup of Hockey, 2004. Recipient NHL All-Star Game, 2007; named San Jose Mercury News South Bay Sportsperson of Yr., 2006; named to NHL All-Star Game, 2004, 2009. Achievements include being a member of World Cup Champion Team Canada, 2004. Office: San Jose Sharks 525 W Santa Clara St San Jose CA 95113*

MARLEN, JAMES S., chemical, plastics and building materials manufacturing company executive; b. Santiago, Chile, Mar. 14, 1941; came to U.S., 1961; m. Carolyn S. Shields, Jan. 23, 1965; children: James, Andrew, John. BSChemE, U. Ala., 1965; MBA, U. Akron, 1971. With GenCorp., Akron, Ohio, 1965-93, engring., mktg. and gen. mgmt. positions domestic and internat. ops., 1977—80; group pres. fabricated plastics GTR Coated Fabrics Co., 1980-87; pres. consumer and indsl. sects. GenCorp Polymer Products, Akron, Ohio, 1988—; v.p. and officer GenCorp, Akron, 1988-93; pres., CEO Ameron Internat. Corp., Pasadena, Calif., 1993—. Bd. dirs., Ameron, Inc., chmn. bd. dirs., pres. and CEO, 1995—; dir. A. Schulman, Inc., Tamco Steel, Parsons Corp.; gen. and hon. chmn. Nat. Inventors Hall of Fame Induction, 1993. Bd. dirs. YMCA Met. L.A., The Employers Group of Calif., Town Hall of L.A., gov.; mem. the Beavers; dir. L.A. Sports Coun.; mem. bd. visitors Anderson Sch. Bus., UCLA, 1999-2001. Mem. Chem. Mfrs. Assn. (past pres.), Assocs. Caltech, Calif. C. of C., L.A. C. of C. (dir.), Portage Country Club (Akron, Ohio), Calif. Club (L.A.), Annandale Golf Club (Pasadena), L.A. Country Club, Valley Hunt Club (Pasadena), Soc. Fellows of Huntington Libr. (L.A.), Birnam Wood Golf Club (Santa Barbara, Calif.). Office: Ameron Internat Corp 245 S Los Robles Ave Pasadena CA 91101-2820

MARLER, JEFFREY ALLEN, neuroscientist; s. Kay Doreen Jeffries, Robert Hugh Jeffries (Stepfather); m. Edith Sutherland Marler, Aug. 29, 1981; children: Daniel Rinn, Joseph Edmund, Alexandra Beatrice, Marielle Natasha. PhD, U. Tex., Austin, 1999. Asst. prof. Mich. State U., East Lansing, 1999—2004; assoc. prof. James Madison U., Harrisonburg, Va., 2004—. Contbr. articles to profl. jours. Williams Syndrome grant, NIH, Child Health and Devel., 2003—06. Mem.: Nat. Williams Syndrome Assn. (grant 2006), Internat. Evoked Response Audiometry Study Group, Acoustical Soc. America, Am. Speech-Lan. Hearing Assn. (Editors' award 1998). Office: James Madison Univ 701 Carrier Dr MSC 4304 Harrisonburg VA 22807 Business E-Mail: marlerja@jmu.edu.

MARLETT, JUDITH ANN, nutritional sciences educator, researcher; b. Toledo; BS, Miami U., Oxford, Ohio, 1965; PhD, U. Minn., 1972; postgrad., Harvard U., 1973-74. Registered dietitian. Therapeutic and metabolic unit dietitian VA Hosp., Mpls., 1966-67; spl. instr. in nutrition Simmons Coll., Boston, 1973-74; asst. prof. U. Wis., Madison, 1975-80, assoc. prof. dept. nutritional scis., 1981-84, prof. dept. nutritional scis., 1984—. Cons. U.S. AID, Leyte, Philippines, 1983, Makerere U., Kampala, Uganda, 2005; acting dir. dietetic program dept. Nutritional Scis. U. Wis., 1977-78, dir., 1985-89; cons. grain, drug and food cos., 1985—, adv. bd. U. Ariz. Clin. Cancer Ctr., 1987-95; sci. bd. advisors Am. Health Found., 1988—; reviewer NIH, 1982-2004; vis. prof. Makerere U., Kampala, Uganada, 2005; spkr. in field. Mem. editl. bd. Jour. Sci. of Food and Agrl., 1989—, Jour. Food Composition and Analysis, 1994-2000, Jour. of Nutrition, 2002-08; contbr. articles to profl. jours. Mem. NIH (Diabetes amd Digestive and Kidney Disease spl. grant rev. com. 1992-96), Am. Soc. Nutrition, Am. Dietetic Assn. Achievements include research on human nutrition and disease, dietary fiber and gastrointestinal function. Office: U Wis Dept Nutritional Sci 1415 Linden Dr Madison WI 53706-1527 Home Phone: 623-972-5221; Office Phone: 623-972-5221. Business E-Mail: jmarlett@nutrisci.wisc.edu.

MARLETTA, MICHAEL A., biochemistry educator, researcher; b. Rochester, NY, Feb. 12, 1951; m. Margaret Gutowski, 1991. BA, SUNY, Fredonia, 1973; PhD in Pharm. Chemistry, U. Calif., San Francisco, 1978. NIH postdoctoral fellow, dept. chem. MIT, Cambridge, 1978-80, from asst. prof. to assoc. prof. toxicology, 1980-87; assoc. prof. med. chemistry U. Mich., Ann Arbor, 1987-91, assoc. prof. biol. chemistry, 1989-91, John G. Searle prof. med. chemistry, prof. biol. chemistry, 1991—2001; prof., chemistry, biochemistry and molecular biology U. Calif., Berkeley, 2001—, Aldo DeBenedictis disting. prof., chmn. dept. chemistry, 2005—, Joel Hildebrand disting. prof. chem., 2005—. Investigator Howard Hughes Med. Inst., 1997—2001; Miller vis. rsch. prof. U. Calif., Berkeley, 2000. Recipient George H. Hitchings award for innovative methods in drug discovery & design, 1991, Faculty Recognition award, U. Mich., 1992, Outstanding Achievement award, SUNY, Fredonia, 1993, Disting. Faculty Leadership award in biomed. rsch., U. Mich. Med. Sch., 2000, Disting. Faculty Achievement award, U. Mich., 2000, Emil Thomas Kaiser award, Protein Soc., 2007; named State of Mich. Scientist of Yr., 2000; named to Alumni Honor Roll, SUNY, 1996; MacArthur fellow, John D. and Catherine T. MacArthur Found., 1995. Fellow: Am. Acad. Arts and Scis., Mich. Soc. Fellows (sr.); mem.: NAS, Inst. Medicine, Am. Chem. Soc. (Repligen award in chemistry of biol. processes 2007, Esselen award for chemistry in pub. interest 2007), Am. Soc. Biochem. and Molecular Biology. Achievements include research in protein/structure function with a particular interest in enzyme reaction mechanisms and molecular mechanisms of signal transduction, study of nitric oxide synthase, guanylate cyclase and related enzymes in this signaling system. Office: Univ Calif Chemistry Dept 570 Stanley Hall Berkeley CA 94720-1460 Office Phone: 510-666-2763. Office Fax: 510-666-2765. Business E-Mail: marletta@berkeley.edu.

MARLOW, JAMES ALLEN, lawyer; b. Crossville, Tenn., May 23, 1955; s. Dewey Harold and Anna Marie (Hinch) M.; m. Sabine Klein, June 9, 1987; children: Lucas Allen, Eric Justin. BA, U. Tenn., 1976, JD, 1979; postgrad., Air War Coll., Maxwell AFB, Ala., 1990-91, Internat. Studienzentrum, Heidelberg, Germany, 1985-86. Bar: Ga. 1979, D.C. 1980, Tenn. 1980, U.S. Dist. Ct. (mid. dist.) Tenn. 1984, U.S. Ct. Fed. Claims 1987, U.S. Ct. Internat. Trade 1988, U.S. Tax Ct. 1987, U.S. Ct. Mil. Appeals 1980, U.S. Ct. Appeals (fed. cir.) 1987, U.S. Supreme Ct. 1987. Assoc. Carter & Assocs., Frankfurt, Fed. Republic Germany, 1984-85; chief internat. law USAF, Sembach AFB, Germany, 1986-96; pvt. practice Crossville, 1997—. Instr. Ctrl. Tex. Coll., 1997-2005; asst. prof. Embry-Riddle Aero. U., Kaiserslauten, Fed. Republic Germany, 1985-1999 Capt. USAF, 1980-84, Col. USAFR. Mem. Phi Beta Kappa. Avocations: genealogy, german and spanish languages. Home and Office: 5746 Highway 127 S Crossville TN 38572 Personal E-mail: james.marlow@jamesamarlow.com.

MARLOW, PATRICIA BAIR BOND, realtor; b. Altoona, Pa., Dec. 3, 1932; d. John Lesley and Gladys Marie Bair; m. Neal Nelson Jensen Bond, Aug. 7, 1953 (dec. July 1963); children: John Scott Bond, Lisa Suzanne Moody, Lesley Ann Stephen; m. Laurin Purcell Marlow, Apr. 4, 1967. Student, Mary Washington Coll., 1950-52. Realtor Everitt/Luby, Dallas, 1971-80; with Merrill Lynch, Dallas, 1980-89; realtor Adleta Fine Properties, 1989—. Contbr. poetry to anthologies. Recipient Diamond Summit. Mem. Dallas Mus. Art, Dallas Arboretum, Les Femmes du Monde, Dallas Mus. Art League, Tex. Kidney Found., Salvation Army (women's aux.). Avocation: watercolor painting. Home: 5336 Mission Cir Granbury TX 76049 Office: Adleta Fine Properties 5950 Berkshire Ln Dallas TX 75225 Home Phone: 817-326-3263. Personal E-mail: patti@pattimarlow.com.

MARLOWE, WILLIE, artist, fine arts educator; b. Whiteville, NC, Jan. 17, 1943; d. John David and Tessie Ernestine (McLawhorn) M.; m. Thomas Blakeslee Speight, July 11, 1980. Student, Pa. Acad. Fine Arts, Phila., 1964; BS, East Carolina U., 1965; MFA, U. Idaho, 1969; postgrad., Peace Coll., 1993. Instr. dept. art Skidmore Coll., Saratoga Springs, NY, 1970-74, mentor univ. without walls, 1972-74; instr. dept. art Columbia-Greene C.C., Hudson, NY, 1973-74; instr. Empire State Coll. SUNY, Albany, 1974; prof. emerita Dept. Visual Arts Sage Coll., Albany, 1977—2008; chmn. The Sage Colls., Albany, 1979-81, artist in residence, 2007—08. Co-founder, tchr. Saratoga Arts Workshop, Saratoga Springs, N.Y., 1970-74; watercolor tchr. abroad Sage Colls., Scotland, Ireland, 2001; tchr. Somerville Coll., Oxford U., Eng., 1992; vis. artist U. Ga. studies abroad program, Cortona, Italy, 1989; vis. artist, Wexford Arts Ctr., Ireland, 1998, Tula State Lev Tolstoy Pedagogica L U., Tula, Russia, artist-in-residence for Ptnrs. of the Americas, Barbados, W.I., 1986, The Millay Colony for the Arts, Austerlitz, N.Y., 1999; artist selection com. Albany Ctr. Gallery, 1998; internat. artists' residency Cill Rialaig Project, Ballinskelligs, Ireland, 2005, Emily Harvey Found., Venice, 2006, 2008; del. to Russia with Albany Tula Alliance; lectr. in field. One-woman shows include The Mint Mus. Art, Charlotte, NC, 1971, Schenectady Mus., NY, 1975, Marist Coll., Poughkeepsie, NY, 1976, Stockton State Coll., Pomono, NJ, 1977, Greenville Mus. Art, NC, 1982, 97, Ann Grey Gallery The Casino, Saratoga Springs, NY, 1985, The Barrett Art Gallery Utica Coll. Syracuse U., NY, 1986, The Atrium Gen. Electric Corp. R&D Ctr., Schenectady, 1988, Forum Gallery, Gütersloh, Germany, 1992, Albany Ctr. Gallery, 1992, 97, McHenry County Coll., Crystal Lake, Ill., Main St. Gallery, Dobbs Ferry, 1995, The Wexford Arts Ctr., Ireland, 1998, The Saratoga Arts Ctr., Saratoga Springs, NY, 2000, Fondo del Sol Gallery and Visual Arts Ctr., Washington, 2002, Barrett Arts Ctr., Poughkeepsie, NY, 2002, Gallery C, Raleigh, 2003, Color and Space traveling solo show, NC, 2006, Ai Genovesi, Venice, Italy, 2008; exhibited in group shows, 20th St. Art Gallery, Sacramento, Ca., 2008, Albany Ctr. Gallery, NY, 2008, Martinez Gallery, Troy, NY, 2008, Art Upstairs, Wexford, Ireland, 2007, Adirondack CC, Queensbury, NY, 2006, Gallery Neptune, Bethesda, Md., 2008, Wexford (Ireland) Arts Ctr., 2004, Art Ctr. for the Capital Region, Troy, NY, 2002, Reprize Internat. Invitational Show, Wexford Arts Ctr., Ireland, 2002, Martinez Gallery, Troy, NY, 2002, Artemisia Gallery, Chgo., 2000, 03, Nexus Gallery, NYC, 1997-99, Gang Gallery, NYC, Eng. & Co., London, 1993, Steinbaum-Krauss Gallery, NYC, 1990, Stux Gallery, Boston, 1987, Nat. Mus. Women Arts, Washington, 1987, Westbeth Gallery, NYC, 1994, Clocktower, NYC, 1986, Rice Gallery The Albany Inst. History & Art, 1986, Deborah Davis Fine Arts, Hudson, 2003-04, 06, Firlefanz Gallery, Albany, 2004, Gallery 100, Saratoga Springs, 2004, U. West Eng., Bristol, 2004, Nat. Coll. Art and Design, Dublin, Ireland, 2004, Art ten 20, Sacramento, Calif., 2009, Riverfront Studios, Schuylerville, NY, 2009, Gallery C, Releigh, NC, 2009; represented in pvt. collections; represented in permanent collections Legis, Nat. Orgn. Women in th Arts, Zimmerili Art Museum, Rutgers U., NJ. Offices Empire State Plz., Albany, First Albany Corp., Md. Dept. Econ. & Cmty. Devel., Balt., Quad Graphics, Boston, SUNY Albany, NC Nat. Bank, Charlotte, Greenville Mus. Art, East Carolina U., Greenville, NC, Boston Pub. Libr., Budapest Gallery, Russell Sage Coll., Troy, Mint Mus. Art, Charlotte, NC, Four Winds Ctr., Saratoga Springs, U. Mus. SUNY Albany, Bullard and McLeod & Assocs., Inc., Albany, NY, Rocky Mount Art Ctr., NC, Adirondack CC, NY, represented by Art Upstairs, Wexford, Ireland, Gallery C, Raleigh, NC, Martinez Gallery, Troy, NY, Denorah Davis Fine Art, Hudson, NY, Gallery Neptune, Bethesda, Md., Art Forms, Guiderland, NY, Art Gallery Ltd., New Bern, NJ; co-curator and curator for mail art shows. Recipient Purchase award in painting Hudson Mohawk Regional Ann., SUNY Albany, 1977, 95, 97, medal Internat. Art Competition Metro Arts, Inc., Scarsdale, N.Y., 1986, honorable mention in painting Third Ann. Nat. C.C. Miniature Painting Show, Lexington, 1987, Sywer award, 1995, and numerous others; N.Y. State Coun. on the Arts grantee Barrett Art Gallery Syracuse U., 1986, grantee Artists' Space, 1988, Spl. Opportunity grant N.Y. Found. Arts. Mem.: Nat. Assn. Women Artists, Albany Inst. History and Art, Fulton St. Gallery, Albany Ctr. Gallery, Woman's Caucus For Art. Avocations: painting, visual poetry, mail art. Personal E-mail: info@williemarlowe.com.

MARMER, ELLEN LUCILLE, pediatrician, cardiologist; b. Bronx, NY, June 29, 1939; d. Benjamin and Diane (Goldstein) M.; m. Harold O. Shapiro, June 5, 1960; children: Cheri, Brenda. BS in Chemistry, U. Ala., 1960; MD, U. Ala., Birmingham, 1964. Cert. Nat. Bd. Med. Examiners; diplomate Am. Bd. Sports Medicine, Bd. Pediat., Bd. Qualified and Eligible Pediatric Cardiology, Bd. cert. sports medicine. Intern Upstate Med. Ctr., Syracuse, NY, 1964-65, resident, 1965-66; fellow in pediatric cardiology Columbia Presbyn. Med. Ctr.-Babies Hosp., NYC, 1967-69; pvt. practice Hartford, Vernon, Conn., 1969—. Examining pediatrician child devel. program Columbia Presbyn. Med. Ctr.-Babies Hosp., N.Y.C., 1967, instr. pediat., 1967-69; dir. pediatric cardiology clinic St. Francis Hosp., Hartford, 1970-80; asst. state med. examiner, Tolland County, Conn., 1974-79; sports physician Rockville (Conn.) High Sch., 1976—; advisor Cardiac Rehab. com., Rockville, 1984-90; mem. bd. examiners Am. Bd. Sports Medicine, 1991—, chmn. credentials com., 1991-93. Mem. Vernon Town Coun., 1985-89; bd. dirs. Child Guidance Clinic, Manchester, Conn., 1970—; life mem. Tolland County chpt. Hadassah, v.p., 1969-70, pres., 1970-72, bd. dirs., 1973-74; mem. B'nai Israel Congregation and Sisterhood, Vernon, 1969—, chmn. youth commn., 1970-72; mayor Town of Vernon, 2003-05, 05-. Recipient Outstanding Svc. award Indian Valley YMCA, 1985. Fellow Am. Acad. Pediat., Am. Coll. Cardiology, Am. Coll. Sports Medicine; mem. Conn. Med. Soc., Am. Heart Assn. (mem. coun. cardiovasc. disease in young 1969—, chmn. elect New Eng. regional heart com. 1990-91, mem. Heritage affiliate 1998—), Conn. Heart Assn. (bd. dirs. 1974-75, 83-84, pres. 1986-88), Heart Assn. Greater Hartford (bd. dirs. 1970-89, mem. exec. com. 1972-73, 79-84, pres. 1982-84), Tolland County Med. Assn. (sec. 1971-72), Vis. Nurse and Cmty. Care Tolland County, LWV (state program chairperson Vernon chpt. 1971-73). Democrat. Jewish. Avocation: sports. Office: 520 Hartford Tpke Vernon Rockville CT 06066 Office Phone: 860-870-9366.

MARMER, NANCY, editor; b. NYC, Nov. 19, 1932; d. Carl and Frances Marmer; m. Gerald Jay Goldberg, Jan. 23, 1954; 1 child, Robert. BA magna cum laude, Queens Coll., 1954; postgrad., U. Minn., 1954-57, UCLA, 1968-71. L.A. corr. Art Internat., 1965-67; West Coast editor Artforum, 1976-77; sr. editor Art in America, NYC, 1979-81, exec. editor, 1981-83, book rev. editor, 1983-97, mng. editor, 1983-97, editor-at-large, 1997-98, contbg. editor, 1998—. Lectr. Mellon seminar R.I. Sch. Design, 1983; lectr. art criticism Visual Arts dept. U. Calif., San Diego, 1978; faculty expository writing Dept. English, U. Minn., 1954-57. Author: The Modern Critical Spectrum, 1962; contbr. numerous articles to profl. jours.; art critic/reviewer for Art in America, Art Internat., Artforum, L.A. Times. Recipient Samuel Kress Found. Award in Art History; Nat. endowment for the Arts fellow in art criticism. Mem. Phi Beta Kappa. Personal E-mail: nmarmer@verizon.net.

MARMET, GOTTLIEB JOHN, lawyer; b. Chgo., Mar. 24, 1946; s. Gottlieb John and Margaret Ann (Saylor) M.; m. Jane Marie Borkowski, Sept. 12, 1970; children: Gottlieb John, Philip Stanley, Thomas Jacob. BS with distinction in Acctg., San Diego State U., 1967; JD, Northwestern U., 1970. Bar: Ill. 1970, U.S. Dist. Ct. (no. dist.) Ill. 1970, U.S. Tax Ct. 1981; CPA, Calif., Ill., Minn. Tax acct. Touche Ross & Co., Chgo., 1970-75; assoc. atty. Howington, Elworth, Osswald & Hough, Chgo., 1975-79; tax mgr. Peat, Marwick, Mitchell & Co., Mpls., 1979-81; assoc. Shefsky, Saitlin & Froelich, Ltd., Chgo., 1981-83; prin. G. John Marmet, Glenview, Ill., 1983—. Lectr. corp. law William Rainey Harper Coll., Arlington Heights, Ill., 1984; instr. Ill. Soc. CPAs, 1976, 77, Minn. Soc. CPAs, 1980. Author: Farm Corporations and Their Income Tax Treatment, 1970, 74; contbr. articles to jours., pubs. Active Northeast Ill. Coun. Boy Scouts Am., 1984—, dist. chmn. Skokie Valley, 1988, mem. exec. bd., 1989-91, 99-2006; bd. dirs. North Shore Sr. Ctr., 1995-99. Recipient Hon. Mention Chgo. Bar Assn. Art Show, 1972, Boy Scouts Am. Dist. award of merit, 1990, Silver Beaver award, 1997. Mem. AICPA, ABA, Ill. Bar Assn., Chgo. Bar Assn., Rotary (Service Above Self award 1986, 96, bd. dirs. 1988-90, v.p. 1990-91, pres. 1991-92, 2004—05, 2008-), Internat. Fellowship Scouting Rotarians (life, chmn. Inter-Am. region 2005—7, Silver Wheel award 2005, Cliff Dochterman award 2006), Beta Gamma Sigma, Beta Alpha Psi, Phi Alpha Delta. Office: 950 Milwaukee Ave Ste 318 Glenview IL 60025-3779 Home Phone: 847-724-5196; Office Phone: 847-298-9428. Personal E-mail: gmarmet@aol.com.

MARMOLEJOS, POLI A., federal agency administrator; m. Laura Cordero; children: Sofia, Cecilia, Amalia. Joined US Dept. Justice, Washington, 1981, spl. asst. and spl. counsel, Civil Rights Divsn., dep. spl. counsel, Office Spl. Counsel Immigration Related Unfair Employment Practices, prosecutor, Office of the US Attorney, DC, sr. trial lawyer, voting sect., Civil Rights Divsn.; dir., Office Civil Rights and Diversity US Dept. Energy, Washington, dir., Office Hearings and Appeals. Mediator, fed. dist. ct. DC Mediation Program; past pres. Dept. Justice Assn. Hispanic Employees, DC Hispanic Bar Assn. Mailing: US Dept Energy 1000 Independence Ave SW Washington DC 20585 Business E-Mail: poli.marmolejos@hq.doe.gov.*

MARMOR, MICHAEL FRANKLIN, ophthalmologist, educator; b. NYC, Aug. 10, 1941; s. Judd and Katherine (Stern) M.; m. C. Jane Breeden, Dec. 20, 1968; children: Andrea K., David J. AB, Harvard U., Cambridge, Mass., 1962, MD, 1966. Diplomate Am. Bd. Ophthalmology. Med. intern UCLA Med. Ctr., 1967; fellow neurophysiology NIMH, 1967-70; resident in ophthalmology Mass. Eye and Ear Infirmary, Boston, 1970-73; asst. prof. ophthalmology U. Calif. Sch. Medicine, San Francisco, 1973-74; asst. prof. surgery (ophthalmology) Stanford U. Sch. Medicine, Calif., 1974-80, assoc. prof. Calif., 1980-86, prof. Calif., 1986—, head. div. ophthalmology Calif., 1984-88, chmn. dept. Calif., 1988-92, dir. Basic Sci. Course Ophthalmology Calif., 1993—2005. Faculty mem. program in human biology Stanford U., 1982—; chief ophthalmology sect. VA Med. Ctr., Palo Alto, Calif., 1974-84; mem. sci. adv. bd. No. Calif. Soc. to Prevent Blindness, 1984-92, Calif. Med. Assn., 1984-92, Nat. Retinitis Pigmentosa Found., 1985-95; affiliate Stanford Ctr. for Biomedical Ethics, 2008-. Author: The Eye of the Artist, 1997, Degas Through his own Eyes, 2002; editor: The Retinal Pigment Epithelium, 1975, The Effects of Aging and Environment on Vision, 1991, The Retinal Pigment Epithelium: Function and Disease, 1998; editor-in-chief Doc. Ophthalmologica, 1995-99; history editor: Survey of Ophthalmology, TimeOph; contbr. more than 250 articles to peer-rewiewed jours., 50 chpts. to books. Mem. affirmative action com. Stanford U. Sch. Medicine, 1984-92. Sr. asst. surgeon USPHS, 1967-70. Recipient Svc. award Nat. Retinitis Pigmentosa Found., Balt., 1981, Rsch. award Alcon Rsch. Found., Houston, 1989; rsch. grantee Nat. Eye. Inst., Bethesda, Md., 1974-94. Fellow Am. Acad. Ophthalmology (bd. councillors 1982-85, pub. health com. 1990-93, rep. to NAS com. on vision 1991-93, mus. com. 2004—, Honor award 1984, Sr. Honor award 1996), Cogan Ophthalmology Hist. Soc. (pres. 2003—), Assn. Rsch. Vision & Ophthalmology; mem. Internat. Soc. Clin. Electrophysiology of Vision (v.p. 1990-98, dir. stds.), Internat. Soc. for Eye Rsch., Retina Soc., Macula Soc. (Green lectr. 2007). Democrat. Avocations: tennis, bicycling, chamber music (clarinet), art, history. Office: Stanford U Sch Medcine Dept Ophthalmology Stanford CA 94305-5308

MARMOR, THEODORE RICHARD, political science professor, writer; b. Bklyn., Feb. 24, 1939; s. James and Mira Bernice (Karpf) M.; m. Jan Schmidt, Oct. 20, 1961 (dec. 2003); children: Laura Carleton, Sarah Rogers; m. Kieke G.H. Okma, May 11, 2007. BA, Harvard U., 1960, PhD, 1966; postgrad., Wadham Coll., Oxford U., Eng., 1961-62. Asst. and assoc. prof. polit. sci. U. Wis.-Madison, 1967-69; assoc. prof. pub. affairs U. Minn.-Mpls., 1970-73; prof. U. Chgo., 1973-79; prof. polit. sci. Yale U., New Haven, 1979—, chmn. Ctr. Health Studies, 1979-85, prof. pub. mgmt. Sch. Orgn. and Mgmt., 1983—2007; adjunct prof. JF Kennedey Sch. Gov., Harvard U., 2007—. Vis. fellow Russell Sage Found., 1987-88; cons., lectr. in field. Author: The Politics of Medicare, 1973, 2d edit., 2000, Political Analysis and American Medical Care, 1983, Understanding Health Care Reform, 1994, Fads, Fallacies and Foolishness: Medical Care Management and Policy, 2007; co-author: Health Care Policy, 1982, America's Misunderstood Welfare State, 1992; editor: Poverty Policy, 1971, National Health Insurance, 1980, Social Security: Beyond the Rhetoric of Crisis, 1988, Why Some People Are Healthy and Others Not, 1994, Jour. Health Politics Policy and Law, 1980-84, Jour. Health Politics and Law Policy; contbr. articles to profl. jours. Mem. Coun. Fgn. Rels., NYC, 1979-85, Pres.' Commn. on 1980s, 1980; social policy adviser Walter Mondale Presdl. Campaign, 1984. Can. Inst. Advanced Rsch. fellow, 1987-1994; fellow Adlai Stevenson Inst., J.F.K. Inst. Politics. Fellow Inst. Medicine, Nat. Acad. Social Ins.; mem. U.S. Squash Racquets Assn. (bd. dirs. 1983-93), Century Assn., United Oxford and Cambridge Club, Lawn Club, Univ. Club. NY. Democrat. Jewish. Office: Yale U Sch Mgmt 135 Prospect St New Haven CT 06520-8200 Home: 434 E 52 St 6G New York NY 10022

MARMORSTEIN, VICTORIA E., lawyer; BA with distinction, U. Okla., 1973; JD, Am. U., 1977; LLM, U. Va., 1978. Bar: DC 1977, NY 1980, Calif. 1989. Ptnr., global chair, fin. and real estate dept. Latham & Watkins, LA. Adj. prof., UCLA Sch. of Law. Editor: Va. Jour. of Internat. Law; author: numerous articles in profl. publications. Named in Chambers & Partners Guide to America's Leading Lawyers for Bus., 2004, in Euromoney's Legal Group Guide to the World's Leading Securitization Lawyers; named one of Top Women Lawyers in LA, LA mag., 2004. Mem.: Phi Beta Kappa. Fluent in Spanish. Office: Latham Watkins 355 S Grand Ave Los Angeles CA 90071-1560

MARNEY, BRENDA JOYCE, reverend, computer programmer; b. Welch, W. Va., Sept. 15, 1952; d. Franklin Garfield Brown and Anna Sarah Toler; m. Barry Lynn Marney, Oct. 3, 1970; children: Joecina Lynn Dasher, Brian Paul. B in Computer Programming, Topeka Tech., 1982; B in Theology, Destiny Coll., Scotland, M in Theology, 2008; diploma in Art, Topeka Tech. Ordained Licensed Minister. Pres., spkr. Women's Aglow, Topeka, 1983—95; pastor/founder Good Shepherd Family Ch., Topeka, 1995—; partnership The Diamond House, Topeka, 1999—; radio show Good Shepherd Min., Topeka, 1994; sister Topeka. Area dir. World Harvest Fellowship, Columbus, Ohio, 2003—. Avocation: water-skiing. Office: Good Shepherd Family Ch 7630 SW 21st Topeka KS 66615 also: 2054 SE California Ave Topeka KS 66607 Office Phone: 785-273-6830. Business E-Mail: good@shepherd.kscoxmail.com.

MARNEY, SAMUEL ROWE, JR., retired allergist, immunologist, educator; b. Bristol, Va., Feb. 15, 1934; m. Elizabeth Ann Bingham, Oct. 1, 1966; children: Samuel Rowe III, Annis Morison. BA in Chemistry, U. Va., 1955, MD, 1960. Diplomate Am. Bd. Internal Medicine, Am. Bd. Allergy and Immunology; cert. in Diagnostic Lab. Immunology, 1988. Staff physician VA Hosp., Nashville, 1968—69, clin. assoc., 1969—71, clin. investigator, 1971—74, staff physician, infectious disease and allergy cons., 1974—; asst. prof. medicine Med. Ctr. Vanderbilt U., Nashville, 1971—76, assoc. prof., 1976—2008, dir. allergy and immunology, 1974—2008. Vis. investigator Scripps Clinic and Rsch. Found., La Jolla, Calif., 1973-74. Capt. USAF, 1962—64, Korea. Fellow ACP, Am. Acad. Allergy and Immunology, Am. Coll. Allergy and Immunology; mem. Southeastern Allergy Assn. (pres. 1986-87, Hal M. Davison Meml. award, 1981, 99), Tenn. Soc. Allergy and Immunology. Home: 4340 Sneed Rd Nashville TN 37215-3242

MAROHN, WILLIAM D., consumer products company executive; BSME, Univ. Toledo, 1964. With Whirlpool Corp., 1964—98, division v.p., 1979—84, v.p., 1984—87, pres. Kenmore appliance group, 1987—89, exec. v.p. No. Am. ops., 1989—91, pres. Whirlpool Europe, 1992, pres., COO, 1992—97, vice chmn., 1997—98; dir. Newell Rubbermaid, Atlanta, 1999—, chmn., 2004—. Bd. dir. Cooper Tire & Rubber, Hanson Cold Storage. Dir. Mich. Jobs Commn.; chmn. Whirlpool Found., Lake Mich. Coll. Found.; mem. vis. com. Univ. Mich. Sch. Bus. Served USAF, Ohio & Mich. Air Nat. Guard. Recipient Gold T award, Univ. Toledo, 1997. Office: Newell Rubbermaid Ste 600 10 B Glendale Pkwy Atlanta GA 30328

MAROLDA, ANTHONY JOSEPH, management consulting company executive; b. Winthrop, Mass., Sept. 7, 1939; s. Daniel Arthur and Rose Marie (Pagliarulo) M.; m. Maria Theresa Rizzo, Oct. 10, 1970; children: Matthew, Ria. BS in Physics, Northeastern U., 1962; MS in Physics, Northeaster U., 1968; MBA, Harvard U., 1970. Lic. coast guard master 2008. Rsch. physicist High Voltage Engring. Corp., Burlington, Mass., 1962-65; sr. scientist E.G. & G. Inc., Wellsley, Mass., 1965-68; v.p. Arthur D. Little, Inc., Cambridge, Mass., 1970-85; pres. The Winbridge Group, Inc., Harvard, Mass., 1985—; officer US Merchant, Marine, 2008. Bd. advs. Daetwyler N.Am., Burlington, N.J., Altdorf, Switzerland, 1995-96; bd. dirs. Stratbridge, Inc., Cambridge, Mass. Inventor Apparatus High Density Plasma, 1965; co-author: Business Problem Solving, 1980, Modern Marketing, 1986, Regional Resiliance and Defense Conversion, 1997; author: Inventor and Inventor's Son, 2007, The Rdidon H.M.S. Vindicator, 2009. Adv. Waterbury-Leningrad. Intersport, Waterbury, Conn., 1988-92; mem. comty. action program Harvard Bus. Sch. Alumni Orgn., 1997-. Recipient Hayden Meml. Scholarship, Northeastern U., 1957. Mem. Harvard Club, Harvard Bus. Sch. Alumni Assn. Republican. Roman Catholic. Avocations: hiking, sailing, tennis.

MARON, DAVID JOEL, cardiologist, educator; b. Nov. 1, 1920; Undergraduate degree, Stanford Univ.; MD, Keck Sch. Medicine, Univ. Southern Calif. Sch. Medicine, 1981. Cert. Internal Medicine, Cardiovascular Disease. Intern, internal medicine UCLA Med. Ctr., 1981—82, resident, medicine, 1982—94; fellow, cardiology Stanford Univ., fellow; staff mem. St. John's Hosp., Santa Monica, 1991—93, Santa Monica Hosp., 1991—93, Vanderbilt Univ. Hosp., Nashville, 1993, Nashville VA Hosp.; clin. instr. Stanford U., 1984—89, UCLA, LA, 1992—93; asst. prof. medicine Vanderbilt Univ. Med. Ctr., Nashville, 1993—2002, assoc. prof. medicine, 2002—; med. dir. Kim Dayani Ctr. for Health Promotion. Mem. scientific adv. bd. Physician Nutrceutical Co., 2002; co-founder Cardiovascular Services of Am. Contbr. articles to profl. jours. Office: Vanderbilt Univ Med Ctr 2311 Pierce Ave Nashville TN 37232

MARON, MARC, comedian, actor, writer; b. NJ, Sept. 27, 1963; m. Mishna Wolff. Stand-up comic, 1986—; host Short Attention Span Theater, Comedy Central; co-host (with Mark Riley) Morning Sedition, Air Am. Radio, 2004—05. Performer: (one-man show) Jerusalem Syndrome, 2000; author: (book) Jerusalem Syndrome: My Life as a Reluctant Messiah, 2001; actor: (films) Los Enchiladas!, 1999, Almost Famous, 2000; guest appearances (comedian) Late Show with David Letterman, Late Night with Conan O'Brian, (documentaries) Left of the Dial, 2005. Jewish.

MARONE, ANTHONY F., JR., quality assurance professional; b. Framingham, Mass., Aug. 9, 1982; s. Anthony and Denise Marone. BS, Rutgers U., New Brunswick, NJ, 2000—04; MS in Bus. Adminstrn., Rutgers U., Newark, NJ, 2004—05. CPA NJ Bd. Accountancy, 2007. Assurance assoc. PricewaterhouseCoopers, LLP, NYC, 2005—. Editor: (internet newsletter) Tomorrow's CPA Newsletter; actor: (promotional video) Take The Next Step; contbr. articles to mags. Mem.: Am. Inst. CPAs, NJ Soc. CPA's (Merit scholarship 2000), Mensa, Nat. Soc. Collegiate Scholars, Tau Kappa Epsilon (pres. 1998—99).

MARONI, DONNA FAROLINO, biologist, researcher; b. Buffalo, Feb. 27, 1938; d. Enrico Victor and Eleanor (Redlinska) Farolino; m. Gustavo Primo Maroni, Dec. 16, 1974. BS, U. Wis., 1960, PhD, 1969. Project assoc. U. Wis., Madison, 1960-63, 68-74; Alexander von Humboldt fellow Inst. Genetics U. Cologne, Fed. Republic Germany, 1974-75; Hargitt fellow Duke U., Durham, NC, 1975-76, rsch. assoc., 1976-83, rsch. assoc. prof., 1983-87; sr. program specialist N.C. Biotech. Ctr., Research Triangle Park, 1987-88, dir. sci. programs div., 1988-92, v.p. for sci. programs, 1992-94, ret., 1995. Mem. adv. com. MI-CROMED at Bowman Gray Sch. Medicine, Winston-Salem, NC, 1988—94; mem. sci. adv. bd. NC Biosci. Fund, LLC, 1998—99, Minority Sci. Improvement Alliance for Instrn. and Rsch. in Biotech, Ala. A&M U., Normal, 1990—91. Contbr. articles to profl. jours. Grantee NSF, 1977-79, NIH, 1979-82, 79-83, 82-87. Mem. Genetics Soc. Am., N.C. Acad. Sci., Inc. (bd. dirs. 1983-86), Sigma Xi (mem. exec. com. Duke U. chpt. 1989-90). Achievements include research in electron microscopy, evolution of chromosomes, chromosome structure, evolution of mitosis, and mitosis and fungal phylogeny. Home: 355 Carolina Meadows Villa Chapel Hill NC 27517 Business E-Mail: dmaroni@email.unc.du.

MAROON, MICHELE SENGA, dermatologist; b. Wheeling, W.Va., Feb. 26, 1960; d. Michael Charles and Agnes Immaculate (Acierno) M.; m. Marc Leon Baranouski, Apr. 21, 1990; children: Elise, Calli. BA in Chemistry, W.Va. U., 1982, MD, 1986. Bd. cert. dermatologist. Assoc. Geisinger Med. Ctr., Danville, Pa., 1990—. Dir. residency dept. dermatology Geisinger Med. Ctr., 1990—. Contbr. articles to profl. jours. Mem. Am. Acad. Dermatology, Women's Dermatologic Soc., Alpha Omega Alpha, Phi Beta Kappa. Office: Dept Dermatology Geisinger Med Ctr Danville PA 17822-0001 Office Phone: 570-271-8050. Business E-Mail: mmaroon@geisinger.edu.

MAROONE, MICHAEL E., automotive executive; b. 1962; CEO Maroone Car & Truck Sales, Pembroke Pines, Fla.; COO, pres. AutoNation Inc., Ft. Lauderdale, Fla., 1999—. Bd. dir. Intercontinental Bank; chmn. South Fla. Internat. Auto Show, 1995. Bd. dir. Dan Marino Found., Boys and Girls Club of Broward County, Children Cancer Caring Ctr., Police Athletic League. Recipient Chmn.'s award, Ford Motor Co., Quality Dealer award, Time mag.; named Humanitarian of Yr., Transflorida Bank. Mem.: Fla. Automotive Dealers Assn. (bd. dir.), South Fla. Chevrolet Dealers Mktg. Assn. (pres. 1994), South Fla. Auto Truck Dealers Assn. (pres. 1994). Office: AutoNation Inc 110 S E 6th St Fort Lauderdale FL 33301

MAROTTA, JOSEPH THOMAS, medical educator; b. Niagara Falls, NY, May 28, 1926; emigrated to Can., 1930; s. Alfred and Mary (Montemuro) M.; m. Margaret Hughes, Aug. 31, 1953; children: Maureen, Patricia, Margaret, Fred, Thomas, Jo Anne, Michael, Martha, John, Virginia. MD, U. Toronto, 1949. Trainee in internal medicine U. Toronto, 1949-52; trainee in neurology Presbyn. Hosp., NYC, 1952-55, U. London, Eng., 1955-56; mem. faculty U. Toronto, 1956—, prof. medicine, 1969—; former assoc. dean clin. affairs U. Toronto Faculty of Medicine, 1981-89; hon. prof. of neurology U. Western Ont., 1990—. Fellow Royal Coll. Physicians (Can.); mem. Alpha Omega Alpha, Phi Chi. Home and Office: 46 Carnforth Rd London ON Canada N6G 4P6 Office Phone: 519-642-4698.

MAROUGI, SALAM D., engineering educator; MS, U. Birmingham, England; PhD in engring., U. Birmingham, Eng., 1978. Expert devel. engr. Agilent Technologies, Santa Rosa, Calif., 2004—. Adj. prof. Sonoma State U., Rohnert Pk., Calif., 2004—. Achievements include development of high technology test and measurment instruments; research in synchronization, phase-locked loops, pulse modulation and microwave antennas and published numerous papers on these topics. Office: Agilent Technologies 1400 Fountain Grove Pky Santa Rosa CA 95403

MAROVITZ, SANFORD EARL, English language and literature educator; b. Chgo., May 10, 1933; s. Harold and Gertrude (Luster) M.; m. Eleonora Dimitsa, Sept. 1, 1964. BA with honors, Lake Forest Coll., 1960; MA, Duke U., 1961, PhD, 1968. Instr. English Temple U., 1963-65; Fulbright instr. U. Athens, Greece, 1965-67; from asst. prof. English to prof. Kent State U., Ohio, 1967-96, prof. emeritus, 1996—. Vis. prof. English, Shimane U., Matsue, Japan, 1976-77, chair, 1987-92; co-dir. Melville Among the Nations, Greece, 1997. Co-editor: Artful Thunder: Versions of Romanticism in American Literature in Honor of Howard P. Vincent, 1975, Melville Among the Nations: Proceedings, 2001; co-author: Bibliographical Guide to the Study of the Literature of the U.S.A., 5th edit., 1984; author: Abraham Cahan, 1996; contbr. articles to profl. jours. Nat. trustee Lake Forest Coll., 1990-98. With USAF, 1953-57. Woodrow Wilson fellow, 1960-61; recipient Disting. Svc. Citation Lake Forest Coll., 1985, Disting. Tchg. award Kent State U., 1985, Presdl. Citation Shimane U., 1998. Mem.: MLA, Jack London Soc., Coll. English Assn. (Robert Miller award for best article in CEA Critic 2000), R.W. Emerson Soc., Saul Bellow Soc., W.D. Howells Soc. (v.p. 2000—01, pres. 2002—03, editor The Howellsian 2004—07), Aldous Huxley Soc. (curator 1998—), Nathaniel Hawthorne Soc., Melville Soc. (sec. 1994—96, pres. 1998), Phi Beta Kappa, Phi Beta Delta, Omicron Delta Kappa. Democrat. Jewish. Home: 1155 Norwood St Kent OH 44240-3342 Office: Kent State U Dept English Kent OH 44242-0001 E-mail: smarovit@kent.edu.

MARPLE, DOROTHY JANE, retired church executive; b. Abington, Pa., Nov. 24, 1926; d. John Stanley and Jennie (Stetler) M. AB, Ursinus Coll., 1948; MA, Syracuse U., 1950; Ed.D., Columbia U. Tchrs. Coll., 1969; L.H.D., Thiel Coll., 1965, Gettysburg Coll., 1979, Ursinus Coll., 1981; D. Humanitarian Services, Newberry Coll., 1977; DD, Trinity Luth. Sem., 1987. Counselor, asst., office dean undergrad. women Women's Coll., Duke, 1950-53; dean women, fgn. student adv. Thiel Coll., 1953-61; asst. social dir. Whittier Hall, Columbia Tchrs. Coll., 1961-62; exec. dir. Luth. Ch. Women, Luth. Ch. Am., Phila., 1962-75; asst. to bishop Luth. Ch. Am., 1975-85; coord. Transition Office Evang. Luth. Ch. Am., 1986-87; asst. gen. sec. ops. Nat. Coun. Chs. of Christ in U.S., NYC, 1987-89. Coord. Luth. Ch. in Am. commn. on function and structure, 1970-72; chairperson Luth. World Fedn. Commn. Ch. Cooperation, 1983-90; mem. bd. dirs. Luth. Theol. Sem., Gettysburg, 1989-98; bd. trustees United Bd. Christian Higher Edn. in Asia, 1989-98. Home: 8018 Anderson St Philadelphia PA 19118-2936

MARQUAND, JEAN MACMURTRY, educational association administrator; b. Schenectady, NY, Feb. 1, 1947; d. Louis Frederick, Jr. and Eleanore Jean (Noyes) McMurtry. BA in Edn. with honors, Simmons Coll., Boston, 1969; MEd, U. Vt., Burlington, 1975; cert. advanced studies in mgmt., Harvard U., Cambridge, Mass., 1993. Elem. tchr., Pittsford, 1969-70; reading specialist Lincoln, Vt., 1971-73, Pembroke, Mass., 1976; grad. teaching asst U. Vt., 1975; elem tchr. Chatham, Mass., 1977-80; with Arthur D. Little, Cambridge, Mass., 1981-82; exec. sec. Meredith & Grew, Inc., Boston, 1982—2003; prin. On Holiday, LLC, 2003—. Bd. mgrs. Jr. League, Boston, 1990—92, v.p., 1993—94, sustaining com., 1997—, dir. sustainer mem., 2006—07; active Philanthropic Ednl. Orgn., Orleans, Mass., 1983—, treas., 2005—08, chair Mass. state bylaws com., 1998. Recipient Vol. Recognition award, Jr. League Boston, 1989, 2006. Mem.: Internat. Alliance, PEO, Chowder Soc., Boston Jr. League Garden Club, Coll. Club (pres. 1994—98, chair bylaws com. 1998—2003, parliamentarian 2001—03). Personal E-mail: jean@onholidaydresswear.com.

MARQUARDT, CHRISTEL ELISABETH, judge; b. Chgo., Aug. 26, 1935; d. Herman Albert and Christine Marie (Geringer) Trolenberg; children: Eric, Philip, Andrew, Joel. BS in Edn., Mo. Western Coll., 1970; JD with honors, Washburn U., 1974. Bar: Kans. 1974, Mo. 1992, U.S. Dist. Ct. Kans. 1974, U.S. Dist. Ct. (we. dist.) Mo. 1992. Tchr. St. John's Ch., Tigerton, Wis., 1955-56; pers. asst. Columbia Records, LA, 1958-59; ptnr. Cosgrove, Webb & Oman, Topeka, 1974-86, Palmer & Marquardt, Topeka, 1986-91, Levy and Craig P.C., Overland Park, Kans., 1991-94; sr. ptnr. Marquardt and Assocs., L.L.C., Fairway, Kans., 1994-95; judge Kans. Ct. Appeals, 1995—; bd. regents Washburn U. Topeka, 2007—. Mem. atty. bd. discipline Kans. Supreme Ct., 1984—86; mem. Kans. Sentencing Commn., 2004—, Kans. Criminal Justice Recodification, Rehab. and Restoration Com., 2004—; bd. regents Washburn U. Tokeka, 2007—. Mem. editorial adv. bd. Kans. Lawyers Weekly, 1992-96; contbr. articles to legal jours. Bd. dirs. Topeka Symphony, 1983-92, 96-, Arts and Humanities Assn. Johnson County, 1992-95, Brown Found., 1988-90; hearing examiner Human Rels. Com., Topeka, 1974-76; local advisor Boy Scouts Am., 1973-74; bd. dirs., mem. nominating com. YWCA, Topeka, 1979-81; bd. govs. Washburn U. Law Sch., 1987-2002, v.p., 1996-98, pres., 1998-2000, disting. alumni, 2004; mem. dist. bd. adjudication Mo. Synod Luth. Ch., Kans., 1982-88. Named Woman of Yr., Mayor, City of Topeka, 1982; Obee scholar Washburn U., 1972-74; recipient Jennie Mitchell Kellogg Atty. of Achievement award, 1999, Phil Lewis medal of Distinction, 2000, Atty. of Achievement award Kans. Women Attys. Assn., Disting. Svc. award Washburn U. Law Sch., 2002, 04; named Disting. Alumni, Washburn U. Fellow: Kans. Bar Found. (trustee 1987—89), Am. Bar Found.; mem.: ABA (mem. ho. dels. 1988—, chmn. specialization com. 1991—93, lawyer referral com. 1993—95, state del. 1995—99, bar svcs. and activities 1995—99, bd. govs., program and planning com. 1999—2002, bd. govs. 1999—2002, ctrl. and ea. European law initiative 2001—02, SCOPE com. 2001—08, African law coun. 2002—04, del-at-large ho. of dels. 2002—, standing com. on jud. independence 2004—, SCOPE com. chair 2006—07), Scape and Correlation of Work, Law and Organizational Econ. Ctr. (bd. dirs. 2000—02), Am. Bus. Women's Assn. (lectr., corr. sec. 1983—84, pres. career chpt. 1986—87, named one of Top 10 Bus. Women of Yr. 1985), Topeka Bar Assn., Kans. Trial Lawyers Assn. (bd. govs. 1982—86, lectr.), Kans. Bar Assn. (sec., treas. 1981—85, bd. dirs. 1983—, v.p. 1985—86, pres. 1987—88, mem., lawyer referral com. 1999—). Home: 3408 SW Alameda Dr Topeka KS 66614-5108 Office: 301 SW 10th Ave Topeka KS 66612-1502 Business E-Mail: marquardtc@kscourts.org.

MARQUARDT, DAVID F., venture capitalist; BSME, Columbia U., 1973; MBA, Stanford U., 1979. Design engr., devel. mgr. Diablo Systems; assoc. Instl. Venture Associates, 1979—80; founding ptnr. Tech. Venture Investors, 1980—95; founding gen. ptnr. August Capital, Menlo Park, Calif., 1995—. Founding mem. bd. dirs. Microsoft Corp., 1981—; bd. dirs. Alibre Inc., AutoTradeCenter Inc., NetCell Corp., Seagate Tech. Inc., Westbridge Tech. Inc., Netopia Inc., 1990—, Tumbleweed Comm. Corp. Inc., 1997—, Six Apart Ltd., 2004—. Mem.: Nat. Venture Capital Assn. (past dir.), We. Assn. Venture Capitalists (past pres.). Office: August Capital 2480 Sand Hill Rd Ste 101 Menlo Park CA 94025 Office Phone: 650-234-9900. Office Fax: 650-234-9910.

MARQUARDT, R. NIELS, United States Ambassador to the Comoros and Madagascar; Grad., Lewis & Clark Coll., Portland, Oreg., 1975, Am. Grad. Sch. Internat. Mgmt., 1980, Nat. War Coll., 1994; attended sr. seminar, econ. and comml. studies program, US State Dept. Fgn. Svc. Inst. Vol. Peace Corps., Rwanda, 1977—79; joined fgn. svc. US State Dept., Washington, 1980, country risk analyst, US Export-Import Bank, with bur. East Asian & Pacific affairs, econ. officer Thailand, 1981—83, 1987—90, Brazzaville, Republic of the Congo, 1983—85, France, 1990—94, Germany, 1995—98, dir. counseling & assignments divsn., bur. human resources, 1998—2001, spl. coord. diplomatic readiness, 2001—04, US amb. to Equatorial Guinea, 2004—06, US amb. to Cameroon, 2004—07, US amb. to the Comoros and Madagascar, 2007—. Recipient Meritorious and Superior Honor awards, US State Dept., Presdl. Performance Pay award. Office: c/o Am Embassy Port Louis Dept State Washington DC 20521-2450*

MARQUARDT, SHIRLEY MARIE, retired management consultant; b. Orlando, Okla., Aug. 20, 1941; d. Arthur Theodore Jack and Eleanor Lou Hurst; m. Donald Lee Marquardt, June 7, 1960; 1 child, Shirley Marie. Diploma, Army Mgmt. Staff Coll., 1994; A in Gen. Studies, Ctrl. Tex. Coll., 1983; BS in Gen. Studies, Am. Technol. U., 1987; MS in Human Resource Develop., U. Ctrl. Tex., 1988; diploma in Orgnl. Effectiveness, US Army Orgnl. Effectiveness Ctr. and Sch., 1985. Cert. Journeyman Mgmt. Analyst Civilian Career Intern Program, Dept. Army, Info. Mapping Course Instr. Info. Mapping, Inc., Prevention Sexual Harassment Course Instr. III Corps, Ft. Hood, Number Skills Course Instr. Mc-Graw Hill Book Co., Investment in Excellence Course Facilitator Pacific Inst. Sec. First Meth. Ch., Perry, Okla., 1959—60; exec. sec. YMCA, El Paso, Tex., 1960—62; clk. typist Hdqs., US Army Ryukyu Islands, Okinawa, Japan, 1963—66; mil. personnel clerk III Corps., Ft. Hood, Tex., 1968—70, sec. computer sys. command, 1970—72, adminstrv. specialist, sec. stenographer, 1978, pers. clk., Civilian Pers. Dir., 1980—81, mgmt. analyst, Directorate of Resource Mgmt., 1981—84, asst. dir., Dir. Program Integration, Leadership, 1984—94, divsn. chief, Adminstrn. Svc. Divsn. Dir. Info. Mgmt., 1994—98; mil. pers. clk., adj. gen. office, hdqrs. Berlin Brigade, 1966—68; sec. US Army Corps Engrs., Frankfurt, Germany, 1976—78; clk. stenographer VII Corps Arty., Aschaffenburg, Germany, 1975; pers. clk. Test, Evaluation Command Civilian Pers. Office, Aberdeen Proving Ground, Md., 1978—79; supr. mgmt. asst. U.S. Army Toxic, Hazardous Materials Agy., Aberdeen Proving Ground, 1979—80; office svcs. supr. Facilities Engring. Divsn., Aberdeen Proving Ground, 1979; ret., 1998. Prodr.: (30 minute TV film) Waverley Historic District; editor: Enid Oklahoma Waverley Wind. Mem. City Spl. Tax Oversight Com., Enid, 1999—2005, City Enid Comprehensive Planning Com., 2000—05, City Enid Cmty. Rels. Bd., 2003—08, Enid A.M. Too Am. Bus. Club, 2004—06, City Enid Hist. Preservation Commn., 2004—08, Garfield County Rep. Women's Club, Enid, 2004—06; bd. mem. Horn of Plenty, Enid, 2004—07; mem. Am. Bus. Club. Decorated Achievement medal for Civilian Svc. US Army, III Corps, Ft. Hood, Army Individual Superior Civilian Svc. award, Army Comdr. award with two oak leaf clusters United States Army, III Corps, Ft. Hood; recipient Employee of Yr., III Corps, Ft. Hood, 1987. Mem.: AARP, Pub. Edn. Govt. Access Sys. TV, Waverley Hist. Dist. Neighborhood Assn. (pres. 1999—2005), The Ret. Enlisted Assn. Aux., Sons & Daughters the Cherokee Strip Assn. (bd. mem., edn. com. chair 2005—06), Nat. Trust Hist. Preservation, Okla. Hist. Soc., Garfield County Rep. Women's Club. Republican. Methodist. Avocations: historic preservation, cmty. volunteerism. Home: 1323 W Broadway Ave Enid OK 73703-5720

MARQUARDT, STEVE ROBERT, advocate; b. St. Paul, Sept. 7, 1943; s. Robert Thomas and Dorothy Jean (Kane) M.; m. Judy G. Brown, Aug. 4, 1968; 1 child, Sarah. BA in History, Macalester Coll., 1966; MA in History, U. Minn., 1970, MLS, 1973, PhD in History, 1978. History instr. Macalester Coll., St. Paul, 1968—69; cataloger N.Mex. State U. Libr., Las Cruces, 1973—75; acting univ. archivist, acting dir. Rio Grande Hist. Collections N. Mex. State U. Libr., Las Cruces, 1973—74; acquisitions librarian Western Ill. U. Libr., Macomb, 1976—77, head cataloger, Online Computer Libr. Ctr. coord., 1977—79; asst. dir. resources & tech. svcs. Ohio U. Libr., Athens, 1979—81; dir. librs. U. Wis., Eau Claire, 1981—89; dir. univ. librs. No. Ill. U., DeKalb, 1989—90; dir. librs. U. Wis., Eau Claire, 1990—96; dean of librs. S.D. State U., Brookings, 1996—2006. Editor Jour. Rio Grande History, 1974; contbg. editor: Library Issues, 1994-2003; contbr. articles to profl. jours. Coord., adoption group 275 Amnesty Internat., Eau Claire, 1985—88, legis. coord. Minn., 2007—, freadom co-chair, 2006—; pres. Chippewa Valley Free-net, 1994—96. Mem.: ALA. Lutheran. Avocation: bicycling. Home and Office: Rancho Mosquito 9383 123rd Ave SE Lake Lillian MN 56253-4700 Home Phone: 605-690-6113; Office Phone: 320-664-4231. E-mail: marquardt.steve@gmail.com.

MARQUES, CHRISTINE SCHON, political organization administrator; b. Oct. 26, 1958; Internat. vice chair Democrats Abroad, 2005—07, internat. chairwoman, 2007—. Democrat. Office: Democrats Abroad 430 S Capitol St SE Washington DC 20003 Office Phone: 202-488-5073. Office Fax: 202-863-8174. E-mail: chair@democratsabroad.org.*

MARQUES, NADEJDA, language educator, interpreter; d. Jarbas and Tercia Marques; m. James Cavallaro, Dec. 30, 1998; 1 child, Mara Cavallaro. BA in Economics, Faculdade Ciencias Gerenciais UNA, Belo Horizonte, Brazil; MBA in Fin., Fundacao Getulio Vargas, Rio de Janeiro; degree in Human Rights and Devel., U. Pablo Olavide, Seville, Spain; Internat. Baccalaureate, United World Coll., N.Mex. Angola rschr. Human Rights Watch, NYC; spl. corr. & interpreter Wash. Post, Rio de Janeiro; lang. and culture instr. U. Mass., Boston; Portuguese instr. Harvard U., Cambridge, Mass., Bentley U., Waltham, Mass., 2008—; Portuguese interpreter Office Ct. Interpreter Svcs., Boston, 2008—. Cons. AJPD, Luanda, Angola. Contbr. articles; translator: (book) Race in Another America. Vol., human rights documentation Justica Global, Rio de Janeiro. Achievements include research in documenting transit and resettlement of refugees; initiating and developing Portuguese program. Avocations: dance, travel, movies. Office: Bentley Univ Modern Langs 175 Forest St Morison 109 Waltham MA 02452 Business E-Mail: nmarques@bentley.edu.

MARQUESS, LAWRENCE WADE, lawyer; b. Bloomington, Ind., Mar. 2, 1950; s. Earl Lawrence and Mary Louise (Coberly) M.; m. Barbara Ann Bailey, June 17, 1978; children: Alexander Lawrence, Michael Wade. BSEE, Purdue U., 1973; JD, W.Va. U., 1977. Bar: W.Va. 1977, Tex. 1977, U.S. Dist. Ct. (so. dist.) W.Va. 1977, U.S. Dist. Ct. (no. dist.) Tex. 1977, Colo. 1980, U.S. Dist. Ct. Colo. 1980, U.S. Ct. Appeals (10th cir.) 1980, U.S. Supreme Ct. 1984, U.S. Dist. Ct. (no. dist.) Ohio 1988, U.S. Ct. Appeals (DC cir.) 1997, U.S. Dist. Ct. Nebr. 1999. Assoc. Johnson, Bromberg, Leeds & Riggs, Dallas, 1977-79, Bradley, Campbell & Carney, Golden, Colo., 1979-82, ptnr., 1983-84, Stettner, Miller & Cohn P.C., 1984-87, Nelson & Harding, Denver, 1987-88, Heron, Burchette, Ruckert & Rothwell, 1989-90, Harding & Ogborn, 1990-94, Otten, Johnson, Robinson, Neff & Ragonetti, Denver, 1994-2001, Littler Mendelson, P.C., Denver, 2001—, mng. shareholder, 2001—08. Mem. faculty Am. Law Inst. - ABA Advanced Labor and Employment Law Course, 1986, 87. Mem.: ACLU, ABA (labor, antitrust and litig. sects.), Hist. Soc. 10th Jud. Circuit (founding mem.), Colo. Bar Found., Coll. Labor and Employment Lawyers, 1st Jud. Dist. Bar Assn., Denver Bar Assn., Colo. Bar Assn. (co-chmn. labor law com. 1989—92), Nat. Rlwy. Hist. Soc., Sierra Club. Democrat. Methodist. Home: 11883 W 27th Dr Lakewood CO 80215-7000 Office: Littler Mendelson PC 1200 17th St Ste 1000 Denver CO 80202 Office Phone: 303-362-2840. Business E-Mail: lmarquess@littler.com.

MARQUEZ, ALBERTO, industrial engineering educator, researcher; b. Mexico, Distrito Federal, Mexico, June 8, 1965; s. Jose Luis Marquez and Venus de la Paz Uribe; m. Ana Cristina Pereda, Feb. 26, 2000; children: Ana Isabel, Cristina. BSc in Indsl. Engring., Tecnologico de Monterrey, 1986, MSc in Mgmt. Sciences, 1992; PhD, Ariz. State U., 1999. Traffic and distbn. dept. mgr. Procter & Gamble, Distrito Federal, Mexico, 1987—90; ops. planning mgr. Grupo Vitro, Mexico, Distrito Federal, 1990—94; rsch. asst. Ariz. State U., Tempe, 1995—99; indsl. engr. Tefen USA, Tempe, 1997—98; sr. cons. IBM Can. Ltd., Toronto, Ontario, 1999—2000; prof. Tecnologico de Monterrey, Mexico, Distrito Federal, 2000—03, indsl. engring. dept. chair, 2003—. Founder, CEO Tecnologia Para la Productividad, Mexico, 1994—. Scholar, Procter and Gamble, 1988-89; Fulbright Conacyt scholar, 1994—99. Mem.: Inst. Indsl. Engrs., Informs. Office: Lamar Univ Indsl Engring Dept 2203 Cherry Engring Bldg Beaumont TX 77710-0032 Personal E-mail: alberto_marquez@hotmail.com. Business E-Mail: alberto.marquez@lamar.edu.

MARQUEZ, ALFREDO C., federal judge; b. 1922; m. Linda Nowobilsky. BS, U. Ariz., 1948, JD, 1950. Bar: Ariz. Practice law Mesch Marquez & Rothschild, 1957-80; asst. atty. gen. State of Ariz., 1951-52; asst. county atty. Pima County, Ariz., 1953-54; adminstrv. asst. to Congressman Stewart Udall, 1955; judge U.S. Dist. Ct. Ariz., Tucson, 1980-91, sr. judge, 1991—. Served with USN, 1942-45 Office: 23416 Everett Pl Ramona CA 92065-4211

MARQUEZ, MERCEDES M., federal agency administrator; b. San Francisco, 1959; m. Mirta Ocana. BA, U. So. Calif., 1982; JD, Georgetown U. Law Ctr., 1985, LLM, 1987. Ptnr. Litt & Márquez, 1992—97; sr. counsel to sec., dep. gen. counsel for civil rights & fair housing US Dept. Housing & Urban Devel. (HUD), 1997—2001; v.p. McCormack Baron Salazar, Inc., 2001—04; gen. mgr. L.A. Housing Dept., 2004—09; asst. sec. for cmty. planning & devel. US Dept. Housing & Urban Devel. (HUD), Washington, 2009—. Advisory bd. mem. The Eleanor Roosevelt Papers & Human Rights Project. Office: US Dept Housing & Urban Devel 451 7th St Washington DC 20410*

MARQUEZ, VICTOR E., medical researcher; naturalized, US, 1987; BS in pharmacy, Ctrl. U. of Venezuela, Caracas, 1966; MS in medicinal chemistry, U. Mich., Ann Arbor, 1968, PhD, 1970. Postdoctoral training Nat. Cancer Inst., NIH, 1970—71; positions in pvt. industry Venezuela, 1971—76; vis. scientist Nat. Cancer Inst., NIH, 1977—87, granted tenure, 1987, now chief Lab. Medicinal Chemistry, Ctr. Cancer Rsch., head Organic Chemistry Sect. Achievements include holding over 20 US patents. Office: Nat Cancer Inst 376 Boyles St, Rm 104 Frederick MD 21702-1201 Office Phone: 301-846-5954. Office Fax: 301-846-6033. E-mail: marquezv@dc37a.nci.nih.gov.*

MÁRQUEZ-MAGAÑA, LETICIA MARIA, biology professor; b. Sacramento, Aug. 15, 1963; d. Jesús José and Guadalupe María Márquez; married; children: Joaquín, Elías. BS,MS in Biol. Scis., Stanford U., 1986; PhD in Biochemistry, U. Calif., Berkeley, 1991. Postdoctoral fellow Stanford (Calif.) U., 1991—94; asst. prof. biology San Francisco State U., 1994—99, assoc. prof. biology, 1999—2004, prof. biology, 2004—, microbial geneticist, 1994—. Contbr. articles to profl. jours., including Jour. Bacteriology, Jour. Biol. Chemistry, Cell Biology Edn. Motivational spkr. to minority students, No. Calif., 1994—; mem. task force Hispanic-Serving Inst. Hispanic Assn. Colls. and Univs.; mentor to UC San Fransico Tchg. postdoctoral fellows, 2002—. Named Hispanic Powerhitter, Hispanic Engr. mag., 2003; named one of 100 Most Influential Hispanics, Hispanic Bus. mag., 1998; NSF grant. Mem.: AAAS (Mentor award 2001), Soc. Advancement of Chicanos and Native Americans in Sci. (sci. ptnr. K-12 educators 2001—, bd. dirs. 1989—91), Am. Soc. Microbiology. Office: San Francisco State U Dept Biology 1600 Holloway Ave San Francisco CA 94132 E-mail: marquez@sfsu.edu.

MARQUIS, WILLIAM OSCAR, lawyer; b. Fort Wayne, Ind., Feb. 26, 1944; s. William Oscar and Lenor Mae (Gaffney) M.; m. Mary Frances Funderburk, May 11, 1976; children: Lenor, Kathryn, Timothy Patrick, Daniel, Ann. BS, U. Wis., Madison, 1973; JD, South Tex. Coll. Law, 1977. Bar: Wis. 1979, U.S. Dist. Ct. (we. dist.) Wis. 1979, U.S. Dist. Ct. (ea. dist.) Wis. 1982, U.S. Tax. Ct. 1983, U.S. Ct. Appeals (7th cir. 1985). With Wis. Dept. Vet. Affairs, Madison, 1977-79; corp. counsel Barron County, Wis., 1979-80; assoc. Riley, Bruns & Riley, Madison, 1980-81, Jastroch & LaBarge, S.C., Waukesha, Wis., 1981-84; ptnr. Groh, Hackbart & Marquis, 1984-93. Named Hubbell's Am. Lawyers; named one of Best Lawyers, Milw. Mag. Mem. ATLA, Wis. Trial Lawyers Assn. Office: 230 W Wells St Ste 327 Milwaukee WI 53203-1866 Home Phone: 414-962-3210; Office Phone: 414-276-4766. Personal E-mail: william.marquis@sbcglobal.net.

MARR, JAMES JOSEPH, venture capitalist; b. Hamilton, Ohio, Oct. 21, 1938; s. J. Joseph and Mildred Adele Marr; m. Martha Eleanor Marr, June 29, 1963; children: Kathleen, Joseph, John, Kerry, James. BS, Xavier U., 1959; MD, Johns Hopkins U., 1964; MS, St. Louis U., 1968. Diplomate Am. Bd. Internal Medicine, Am. Bd. Infectious Diseases. Intern Johns Hopkins Hosp., Balt., 1964-65; resident Barnes Hosp., Washington U., St. Louis, 1969-70; postdoctoral fellow in microbiology St. Louis U., 1967-69; asst. prof. medicine and microbiology Washington U., St. Louis, 1970-75, assoc. prof., 1975-76; prof. medicine and microbiology St. Louis U., 1976-82; prof. medicine and biochemistry U. Colo., Denver, 1982-89; sr. v.p. drug discovery Monsanto/Searle, Skokie, Ill., 1989-93; v.p. R&D Ribozyme Pharms., Boulder, Colo., 1993-96; CEO Immunologic Pharm. Corp., Waltham, Mass., 1996-99; gen. ptnr. Pacific Rim Ventures, Inc., 2000—. Bd. dirs. Sequitur, Inc., Immunologic Pharms., Primal, Inc. Contbr. articles to profl. jours.; patentee in field. Bd. trustees Estes Park (Colo.) Med. Ctr., 1994-96; bd. dirs. Estes Park Med. Ctr. Found., Larimer County Dept. Health, Am. Red Cross (Northern Colo.); advisor Cub Scouts/Boy Scouts Am., St. Louis, 1975-82. Capt. U.S. Army Spl. Forces, 1966-68. Fellow ACP, Am. Acad. Microbiology, Infectious Diseases Soc. of Am., Am. Assn. of Physicians; mem. Am. Soc. Clin. Investigation, Am. Coll. Physician Execs., Phi Beta Kappa, Alpha Omega Alpha, Sigma Xi. Avocations: scuba diving, climbing, skiing, martial arts (2 black belts), poetry, writing. Home and Office: 14885 Irving St Broomfield CO 80020 Personal E-mail: marrj@imho.com.

MARR, PHEBE ANN, retired historian, educator; b. Mt. Vernon, NY, Sept. 21, 1931; d. John Joseph and Lillian Victoria (Henningsen) Marr. BA, Barnard Coll., NYC, 1953; PhD, Harvard U., Cambridge, Mass., 1967. Rsch. assoc. ARAMCO, Dhahran, Saudi Arabia, 1960-62; dir. mid. east program Fgn. Svc. Inst., 1963-66; asst. prof. Stanislaus State Coll., Turlock, Calif., 1970-71, assoc. prof., 1971-74; assoc. prof. history U. Tenn., Knoxville, 1974—85, chmn. Asian studies program, 1977—79. Cons. ARAMCO, 1979-83. Author: The Modern History of Iraq, 1985, 2d edit., 2003; co-editor: Riding the Tiger: Middle East Challenge After the Cold War, 1993; contbr. articles to profl. jours. Bd. dirs. Mid. East Policy Coun., 2004, Hollings Inst., 2008. Rsch. fellow Mid. East Ctr., Harvard U., Cambridge, Mass., 1968-70, sr. fellow Nat. Def. U., Washington, 1985-97, Woodrow Wilson Ctr. fellow, 1998-99, Coun. on Fgn. Rels., U.S. Inst. Peace fellow, 2004-06. Mem. Mid. East Inst., Mid. East Studies Assn. Home and Office: 3637 Upton St NW Washington DC 20008-3126 Office Phone: 202-462-3580. Personal E-mail: marrphebe@aol.com.

MARR, ROBERT BRUCE, physicist, researcher; b. Quincy, Mass., Mar. 25, 1932; s. Ralph George and Ethel (Beals) M.; m. Nancy Rosa Parkes, June 12, 1954; children: Richard, Jonathan, Rebecca. BS, MIT, 1953; MA, Harvard U., 1955, PhD, 1959. Research asso. Brookhaven Nat. Lab., Upton, NY, 1959-61, asso. physicist, 1961-64, physicist, 1964-68, sr. physicist, 1968-95, assoc. chmn. applied math. dept., 1974-75, 83-88, chmn., 1975-78; ret., 1995. Adj. assoc. prof. Columbia U., 1969; lectr. SUNY at Stony Brook, 1969-70, vis. prof. dept. computer sci., 1979; guest mathematician U. Colo., 1970; vis. mathematician Lawrence Berkeley Lab., 1978; cons. NSF, NIH, 1969— Contbr. articles to profl. jours. Served with U.S. Army, 1958-59. NSF grantee, 1974 Mem. Soc. for Magnetic Resonance in Medicine (trustee 1982-87, sec.-treas. 1984-86, treas. 1986-87). Home: 368 Private Rd Patchogue NY 11772-5827

MARRA, VINCENT J., JR., economics professor; b. Wilmington, Del., Jan. 24, 1958; Lectr. U. Del., Newark, 2001—; rate analyst Delmarva Power, Wilmington, 1986—2000. Mem.: Delcastle Men's Golf Assn. (pres. 2006—).

MARRACK, PHILIPPA CHARLOTTE, immunologist, researcher; b. Ewell, Eng., June 28, 1945; m. John Kappler, 1974; children: Kate, Jim. BA, U. Cambridge, 1967, PhD in Biology, 1970. Post-doctoral fellow, lab. rschr. U. Calif., San Diego, 1971-73; post-doctoral rschr. fellow U. Rochester, NY, 1973-79, assoc. rschr. NY, 1974-75, asst. prof. immunology NY, 1975-79, assoc. prof. NY, 1980-85; prof. dept. microbiology and immunology U. Colo. Health Scis. Ctr., Denver, 1988—94, prof. integrated dept. of Immunology, 1994—, prof., dept. biochemistry and molecular biology, prof. medicine; head, div. of basic immunology Nat. Jewish Ctr. for Immunology and Respiratory Medicine, Denver, 1988—90; prof. dept. biophysics, biochemistry and genetics U. Colo. Health Scis. Ctr., Denver, 1985-88; head, div. of Basic Immunology Nat. Jewish Medical and Rsch. Ctr., Denver, 1998—99, sr. faculty mem., Integrated Dept. of Immunology; investigator Kappler and Marrack Rsch. Lab. Howard Hughes Med. Inst., Chevy Chase, Md., 1986—. Mem. dept. medicine Nat. Jewish Hosp. and Rsch. Ctr., Denver, 1979—. Contbr. articles to profl. jours.; mem. editl. bds. Cell, Science, and Journal of Immunology. Served on panels for Am. Cancer Soc., US NIH, Burroughs Wellcome Fund. Recipient Feodor Lynen medal, 1990, William B. Coley award Cancer Rsch. Inst., 1991, Wellcome Found. lecturer Royal Soc., 1990, Paul Ehrlich and Ludwig Darmstädter prize, 1993, Louisa Gross Horwitz prize, 1994, Women's Excellence Scis. award Fedn. Am. Socs. Exptl. Biology, 1995, Women in Sci. award, L'Oreal-UNESCO, 2004. Mem. NAS, Inst. Medicine, Royal Soc., Am. Assn. Immunologists (pres. 2000-2001, Lifetime Achievement award, 2003), Brit. Soc. Immunology, Internat. Union of Immunological Societies (past pres.). Office: Howard Hughes Med Inst Natl Jewish Med and Rsch Ctr 1400 Jackson St 5th fl Goodman Bldg Denver CO 80206*

MARRA ORAM, DIANA MARIE, microbiologist, educator; d. Lawrence and Carol Marra; m. Mark Oram; children: Peter Albert Oram, Tbd Oram. BS, GA Tech, Atlanta, 1992; PhD, Emory U., Atlanta, 1999. Asst. prof. U. Md., Balt., 2005—; postdoc. fellow U. Colo. Health Scis. Ctr., Denver, 2000—05. Office: Univ Md Balt 650 W Baltimore St Rm 9211 Ellicott City MD 21042

MARRERO, BENJAMIN, electrical engineer, educator; b. Humacao, PR, June 4, 1953; s. Epifanio and Theodosia Marrero; married; children: Teneen Sharise, Deandreus Lamar, Tamishia Latoya, Benjamin Timothy, Wilfredo Velez. BSEE, Purdue U. Calumet, Hammond, Ind., 1999, MEd, 2007. Cert. in A+ Comptia, 2000, in network+ 2008. Instr. Purdue U. Calumet, 1999—, elec. engring. lab supr., 2003—. Elec. supr. Mittal Steel Co., East Chgo., Ind. Bd. mem. Assembly God, East Chgo., 1995. Mem.: IEEE, Soc. Hispanic Profl. Engrs. Home: 6161 Brie Ave Portage IN 46368 Office: Purdue Univ Calumet 2200 169th St Hammond IN 46323 Business E-Mail: marrero@calumet.purdue.edu.

MARRERO, VICTOR, federal judge, lawyer; b. Santurce, PR, Sept. 1, 1941; s. Ezequiel Marrero and Josefina (Sanabria) Santos M.; m. Veronica M. White, Dec. 1987. BA, NYU, 1964; LLB, Yale U., 1968; postgrad. (Fulbright scholar), U. Sheffield, Eng., 1966-67. Bar: N.Y. 1982. Exec. dir. NYC Dept. City Planning, 1973-74; spl. counsel to comptroller City of N.Y., 1974-75; 1st asst. counsel to gov. State of N.Y., Albany, 1975-76; chmn. NYC City Planning Commn., 1976-77; commr. N.Y. State Divsn. Housing and Cmty. Renewal, NYC, 1977-79; undersec. HUD, Washington, 1979-81; ptnr. Tufo & Zuccotti, NYC, 1982-85, Brown & Wood, NYC, 1986-93; amb., U.S. rep. UN Econ. and Social Coun., NYC, 1993-97; amb., permanent U.S. rep. OAS, Dept. State, Washington, 1998-99; judge U.S. Dist. Ct. (So. Dist.), NYC, 1999—. Vis. lectr. Yale U. Law Sch., New Haven, 1986, Columbia U. Law Sch., 1991-93. Trustee N.Y. Pub. Libr., 1989—, SUNY, Albany, 1985-93, Cooper Union, 1989-93, Consolidated Edison Co., 1988-93; bd. dirs. P.R. Legal Def. and Edn. Fund., N.Y.C., 1972-86, N.Y. Telephone Co., 1987-93; chmn. N.Y. State Chief Judge's Com. to Improve Availability of Legal Svcs., 1988-90. Mem. ABA (Pro Bono Publico award 1993), N.Y. State Bar Assn. (Root/Stimson Pub. Svc. award 1992), Assn. Bar City N.Y. (mem. com. modern cts. 1980-93, exec. com. 1986-89, judiciary com. 1991-92, v.p. 1992-93). Office: US Courthouse 500 Pearl St Rm 660 New York NY 10007-1502 Office Phone: 212-805-6374.

MARRETT, MICHAEL MCFARLENE, chaplain; b. Greenwich Town, Surrey, Jamaica, Oct. 7, 1935; s. Kenneth Louis and Ivy Lynmae (McFarlane) M.; m. Margery Eva Mugford, Jan. 29, 1984. Cert. gen. ordination, Oxford U., Eng., 1961; cert. edn. in English lang., London U., 1967; MDiv, Gen. Theol. Sem., 1969, STM, 1970, N.Y. Theol. Sem., 1972; postgrad., Princeton Theol. Sem., 1972-73, Columbia U., 1973-75; BA, Fordham U., 1974; postgrad., The Coll. of Preachers, 1979, Yale U., 1979-81; PhD, NYU, 1980; MS, So. Conn. State U., 1982. Lic. pastoral counselor, Md.; cert. profl. mental health clergy, chaplain and fellow of Coll. Chaplains; nat. cert. bereavement facilitator Am. Acad. Bereavement; diplomate Am. Psychotherapy Assn. Staff chaplain St. Elizabeths Hosp., Washington, 1986-99; ret., 1999. Author: The Lambeth Conferences and Women Priests, 1981. Appointed commissary Diocese of Akoko, West Africa, 1984, appointed hon. canon St. Stephens Cathedral, 1987. Mem. Assn. Clin. Pastoral Edn. (clin.), Am. Assn. Christian Counselors, Am. Assn. Family Counselors. Home: PO Box 48232 1902 C St NE Washington DC 20002-6714

MARRI, PRADEEP REDDY, research scientist; b. Hyderabad, Andhra Pradesh, India, Aug. 6, 1976; s. Pratap Reddy and Nalini Marri; m. Sujatha Panyala, Apr. 24, 2004; 1 child, Anshi. PhD, U. Hyderabad, India, 2004. Rsch. assoc. U. Ariz., Tucson, 2006—07, asst. rsch. scientist, 2007—. Rsch. Associateship, Indian Coun. Agrl. Rsch., 2001—04, Sr. Rsch. fellowship, 1998—. Office: BIO5 Inst Univ Ariz 1617 E Helen St Tucson AZ 85719 Personal E-mail: pradeepm@email.arizona.edu.

MARRIN, CHARLES AINSWORTH STAVELEY, cardiovascular and thoracic surgeon, educator; b. Santa Monica, Calif., Dec. 19, 1947; s. Charles Ainsworth and Cecilia Margaret (Staveley) M.; m. Marian Anthon Bruen, Apr. 19, 1976; 1 child, Minet A. B. MB, BS, U. London, Royal Free Hosp. Sch. Medicine, London, 1971. Ho. physician Willesden Gen. Hosp., London, 1971, Royal Free Hosp., London, 1972; resident in gen. surgery St. Luke's Hosp. Ctr., NYC, 1973-76, chief resident, 1976-77, fellow in cardiovasc. surgery, asst. physician, 1977; fellow in cardiovasc. surg. rsch. Coll. Physicians and Surgeons, Columbia U., NYC, 1978; resident in cardiovasc. and thoracic surgery Columbia-Presbyn. Med. Ctr., NYC, 1979-80, chief resident, 1980; staff surgeon Hitchcock Clinic and Dartmouth-Hitchcock Med. Ctr., Lebanon, N.H., 1981—; prof. surgery Dartmouth (N.H.) U. Med. Sch., 2000—. Author chpts. to books; contbr. articles to profl. jours. Co-prin. investigator Am. Heart Assn., 1993—; co-investigator U.S. Agy. for Health Care Policy and Rsch., 1993—. Fellow ACS, Am. Coll. Cardiology, Am. Coll. Chest Physicians; mem. AMA, Am. Assn. Thoracic Surgery, Soc. Thoracic Surgeons.

MARRIOTT, JOHN W., III, hotel executive; BS, Univ. Utah, 1985. With Marriott Internat. Inc., Washington, 1976—, sr. v.p. mid-Atlantic region, exec. v.p. global sales & mktg., bd. dir., 2002—, exec. v.p. lodging, 2003—05, vice chmn., 2005—. CEO J.W.M. Family Enterprises, 2006. Named one of Forbes Richest Americans, 2006. Office: Marriott internat Inc Marriott Dr Washington DC 20058

MARRIOTT, JOHN WILLARD, JR., lodging and senior living executive; b. Washington, Mar. 25, 1932; s. John Willard and Alice (Sheets) M.; m. Donna Garff, June 29, 1955; children: Deborah, Stephen Garff, John Willard, David Sheets. BS in Banking and Fin., U. Utah, 1954. V.p. Marriott Hot Shoppes Inc., 1959-64, exec. v.p., bd. dirs., 1964; pres. Marriott Corp., 1964—, CEO, 1972—; chmn. bd. Marriott Internat., Inc. (formerly Marriott Corp.), 1985—. Bd. dirs. GM, U.S.-Russia Bus. Coun., Host Marriott Svcs. Corp., Naval Acad. Endowment Trust. Trustee Nat. Geog. Soc.; mem. nat. adv. bd. Boy Scouts Am.; mem. Bus. Coun., Bus. Roundtable.; exec. com. World Travel and Tourism Coun. Lt. USNR, 1954-56. Recipient Bus. Leader of Yr. award, Georgetown U. Sch. Bus. Adminstrn., 1984, Svc. Above Self award, Rotary Club at JFK Internat. Airport, 1985, Am. Mgr. of Yr. award, Nat. Mgmt. Assn., 1985, Golden Chain award, Nations's Restaurant News, 1985, Hall of Fame award, Consumer Digest Mag., 1985, Citizen of Yr. award, Boy Scouts of Am., 1986, Restaurant Bus. Leadership award, Restaurant Bus. Mag., 1986, Gold Plate award, Am. Acad. Achievement, 1986, Hall of Fame, Am. Hotel and Motel Assn., 1986, Hall of Fame award, Culinary Inst. of Am., 1987, Hospitality Exec. of Yr. award, Pa. State U., 1987, Bronze winner in Fin. World's Chief Exec. Officers award, 1988, Silver Plate award Lodging Hospitality Mag., 1988, Chief Exec. Officer of Yr. Chief Exec. Officer Mag., 1988, Signature award CA chpt. Nat. Multiple Scelerosis, 1988, Excellence Cmty. award Suburban Hosp., 1993, Silver Plate award Internat. Foodsvc. Mfrs. Assn., 1993, Good Scout award Boy Scouts Am. Greater N.Y. Coun., 1990, Trendsetter award Foodsvc. Cons. Soc., 1989 Mem. Conf. Bd., U.S. C. of C., Bald Peak C.C. (N.J.), Avenel Golf Club, Sigma Chi. Mem. LDS Ch. Clubs: Burning Tree (Washington), Met. (Washington). Office: Marriott Intl Inc 1 Marriott Dr Washington DC 20058-0001

MARRIOTT, MICHEL, reporter; married; 3 children. BA in Philosophy and Journalism, Morehead State U., 1976; MA in Journalism, Northwestern U., 1977. Reporter Marion Chronicle-Tribune, Ind., 1977, Courier-Jour., Louisville, Washington Post, Phila. Daily News; gen. editor Newsweek mag., NY, 1994—95; reporter NY Times, 1987—94, reporter, Style Dept., 1995—98, tech. reporter Circuits Sect., 1998—. Adj. prof. Grad. Sch. Journalism Columbia U.; prof., Dept. Communication, Film & Video City Coll. NY; frequent contbr. Ann. Men's Issue Essence mag.; contbr. Esquire mag.; prof. Antioch Writer's Workshop. Author: Hedz; co-author: (screenplays) (based on his NY Times series) New Jersey Drive, 1995 (Pulitzer prize nominee). Recipient Outstanding Achievement award, Nat. Assn. Black Journalists, 1981; Nieman fellow, Harvard U., 2002. Office: Circuits Sect NY Times 229 West 43rd St New York NY 10036 Office Phone: 212-556-7803. Office Fax: 212-556-1448.

MARRIOTT, RICHARD EDWIN, hotel and contract services executive; b. Washington, Jan. 9, 1939; s. John Willard and Alice Taylor (Sheets) M.; m. Nancy Peery, Mar. 20, 1962; children: Julie Ann, Sandra, Karen, Mary Alice. BS, U. Utah, 1963; MBA, Harvard U., 1965. With Marriott Corp., Washington, 1965—, group v.p. restaurant ops., 1976-78, corp. group v.p. restaurant and theme park ops., 1979-84, exec. v.p., 1984, vice chmn., 1986—92; chmn. Host Hotels & Resorts, Bethesda, Md., 1992—. Chmn. bd. dirs. Media Corp., 1973—; bd. dirs. Riggs Nat. Bank of Washington. Mem. Nat. Commn. Against Drunk Driving; trustee Boys Clubs Am., Dole Found. for Employemnt of Persons with Disabilities; chmn. Marriott Found. People with Disabilities. Named one of Forbes Richest Americans, 2006. Mem. Nat. Restaurant Assn., Sigma Chi. Mem. Lds Ch. Office: Host Hotels & Resorts Suite 1500 6903 Rockledge Dr Bethesda MD 20817

MARRIOTT, SUSAN, research scientist; b. Ft. Madison, Iowa, Mar. 31, 1959; d. Richard S. and H. Irene (Garner) M. BS in Microbiology, Iowa State U., 1981; PhD, Kans. State U., 1986, postgrad., 1986-87. Assoc. prof. dept. molecular virology and microbiology Baylor Coll. Medicine, Houston, 1991—2006, prof. dept. molecular virology and microbiology, 2007—. Pres., CEO BioScience Writers. Contbr. chpts. to books, articles to profl. jours.; spkr. at numerous confs. NIH fellow, 1985-86. Mem. AAAS, Am. Soc. Virology, Am. Soc. Microbiology (Cora M. Downs award for excellence in sci. rsch. Missouri Valley br. 1982), Sigma Xi (rsch. grantee 1986, bd. dirs. 1992-96). Office: Baylor Coll Medicine Dept Molecular Virology and Microbiology One Baylor Plaza Houston TX 77030 Home Phone: 713-516-7228; Office Phone: 713-798-4440. E-mail: susanm@bcm.edu.

MARRISON, BENJAMIN J., editor-in-chief; b. Ashtabula, Ohio; BA, Bowling Green State U. With Toledo Blade, Cleve. Plain Dealer, 1990—99, Columbus bur. chief, 1996—99; mng. editor news Columbus Dispatch, Ohio, 1999, editor, 1999—. Named to Bowling Green State U. Hall of Fame. Mem.: AP Soc. Ohio, Columbus Met. Club. Office: Columbus Dispatch 34 S 3rd St Columbus OH 43215 Office Phone: 614-461-5200. E-mail: bmarrison@dispatch.com.*

MARRO, ANTHONY JAMES, retired newspaper editor; b. Middlebury, Vt., Feb. 10, 1942; s. Francis James and Esther Martha (Butterfield) M.; m. Jacqueline Helen Cleary, June 5, 1965; 1 child, Alexandria. BA in History, U. Vt., 1965; MS in Journalism, Columbia U., 1968. Reporter Rutland (Vt.) Herald, 1964-67, Newsday, LI, NY, 1968-74, chief Washington bur., 1979-81, mng. editor, 1981-86, exec. editor, 1986-87, editor, 1987—2003; reporter Newsweek, Washington, 1974-76, N.Y. Times, Washington, 1976-79. Co-recipient Pulitzer prizes for Pub. Service Reporting, 1970, 74.

MARRON, DONALD BAIRD, SR., venture capitalist; b. Goshen, NY, July 21, 1934; m. Gloria Swope Marron, 2 children; m. Catherine D. Calligar, 2 children. Student, Baruch Sch. Bus., 1949-51, 55-57. Investment analyst NY Trust Co., NYC, 1951-56, Lionel D. Edie Co., NYC, 1956-58; mgr. research dept. George O'Neill & Co., 1958-59; pres. D.B. Marron & Co. Inc., NYC, 1959-65, Mitchell Hutchins & Co. Inc. (merger with D.B. Marron & Co. Inc. 1965), NYC, 1965-69, pres., chief exec. officer, 1969-77; pres. PaineWebber Inc. (merger with Mitchell Hutchins & Co. Inc. 1977), NYC, 1977—80, CEO, 1980—2000, chmn. bd., 1981—2000; co-founder, former chmn. Data Resources, Inc., 1969—79; chmn. UBS Am., 2000—03; founder, chmn., CEO, mem. investment com. Lightyear Capital, LLC, NYC, 2000—. Dir. NYSE 1974-81; bd. mem. Fannie Mae 2001-06, Shinsei Bank 1999-2005; chmn. Collegiate Funding Svcs. 2004-06; gov., vice chmn. Securities Industry Assn. 1974-77; gov. NASD 1997-2001. Chmn. Emeritus Ctr. for Study of the Presidency; vice chmn. & former pres. bd. trustees Mus. of Modern Art, N.Y.C; mem. adv. bd. UBS Art Collection; mem. bd. overseers and mgrs. Meml. Sloan-Kettering Cancer Ctr.; trustee Charles A. Dana Found., Ctr. for Strategic & Internat. Studies (private sector co-chmn. Nat. Commn. on Retirement Policy); bd. dirs. NYC Partnership; mem. Govs.'s Sch. and Bus. Alliance Task Force, NY; former mem. Pres. Commn. on The Arts and The Humanities; former vice chmn. Calif. Inst. for the Arts. Named one of Top 200 Collectors, ARTnews Mag., 2004—08. Mem.: Council on Fgn. Rels. Avocation: collector of 19th century European, modern & contemporary art. Office: Lightyear Capital LLC 11th Fl 375 Park Ave New York NY 10152 Office Fax: 212-328-0516. Business E-Mail: dbmarron@lycap.com.*

MARRON, DONALD BAIRD, JR., economist; b. 1965; s. Donald Baird and Gloria Marron. BA in Mathematics, Harvard U., 1987; PhD in Economics, MIT, 1994. Asst. prof. economics U. Chgo. Grad. Sch. Bus., 1994—98; prin. Charles River Associates, Washington, 1998—2000; exec. dir., chief economist Joint Econ. Com. US Congress, 2002—04; chief economist Coun. Econ. Advisors, Exec. Office of the Pres., 2004—05, cons., sr. econ. adviser, 2007—08, mem., 2008; dep. dir. Congl. Budget Office, 2005—07, acting dir., 2005—07. Vis. prof. Georgetown U., 2009—. Contbr. articles to profl. jours. Personal E-mail: donald_marron@yahoo.com.

MARRON, PAMELA ANNE, artist; b. Hackensack, NJ, Nov. 16, 1945; d. Chester Charles and Edith Anne Marron. AA, Parsons Sch. Design, NYC, 1968; postgrad., Stanford U., Calif., 1970. Mem. art com. Stratton Art Festival, Stratton Mountain, Vt.; founder, art com. Elm St. Arts, Manchester, Vt. Archtl. Digest, 1998, Women Artists Calendar, 1999, one-woman shows include Stratton Arts Festival, 1974—94, Park McCullough House, Bennington, Vt., 1976, The Hoosac Sch., N.Y., 1978, Garden Gallery, Londonderry, Vt., 1980, AVA Gallery, Hanover, N.H., 1984, Castleton State Coll., Vt., 1986, Pindar Gallery, N.Y.C., 1987, Northstar Gallery Show, Stratton Mountain, 1989—2002, Avanti Gallery, Lambertville, N.J., 1990, Nicholas Roeruch Mus., N.Y.C., 1990, Lotus Gallery, Cambridge, Mass., 1990, Vt. State House, Montpelier, 1992, Chaffee Art Ctr., Rutland, Vt., 1994, Elm St. Arts, Manchester Center, Vt., 1994, 95, 1994, 1995, Gallery Two, Woodstock, Vt., 1995, Olde Moon Gallery, Breckenridge, Colo., 1998, Grayson Gallery, Woodstock, 1999, Gardner Colby Gallery, Naples, Fla., 2001, Schenectady Mus., 2004, Haddad Lascano Gallery, Greater Barrington, Mass., 2005, Redux Gallery, Dorset, Vt., 2005, Nancy Price Gallery, Jamaica, Vt., 2005, Dorset Theater Festival, 2005, So. Vt. Art Ctr., 2006, Vt. Art Gallery, Brattleboro, 2006, So. Vt. Coll., Manchester Center, 1975, 79, 2006, Beside Myself Gallery, Arlington, Vt., 1982, 86, 90, Cove Gallery, Wellfleet, Mass., 1991, 97, The Artisans Gallery, Brattleboro, Vt., 2007, Brattleboro Mus., 2007, Represented in permanent collections Lotus Corp., Omni Corp., N.Y.C., Yoder Bros. Internat., Barberton, Ohio, Brandon Artist's Guild, Vt., Lake Shore Gallery, Bolton Landing, NY, numerous group exhbns., one-woman shows include Southern Arts Ctr., 1976—2008. Recipient Max Beckman scholarship, 1967, 1968, Jurors award, Berkshire Mus., 1978, Stratton Art Festival, 1983, 1988, Jay Conaway award, 1987, 1990. Mem.: Vt. Coun. on Arts, So. Vt. Art Ctr. (art com., numerous art exhbns., Jurors award 1998). Avocations: singing, swimming, walking. Home: Box 563 Dorset VT 05251 Office Phone: 802-867-2246.

MARROW, DEBORAH, foundation administrator; d. Seymour Arthur and Adele M.; m. Michael J. McGuire; children: David Marrow McGuire, Anna Marrow McGuire. BA cum laude, U. Pa., PhD; MA, Johns Hopkins U. With Phila. Mus. of Art, 1974-75, Chrysalis Mag., LA, 1978-80, The J. Paul Getty Trust, LA, 1983—. Various positions including program officer Getty Grant Program; interim dir., The Getty Rsch. Inst.; dean for extern relations, The J. Paul Getty Trust, interim pres., CEO; dir. The Getty Found. Mem. Save Am.'s Treas. com., Nat. Trust for Historic Preservation (in partnership with White House Millenium Coun.), 1998-2001; bd. govs. U. Calif Humanities Rsch. Inst., 2000-05; mem. internat. com. for History of Art; mem. bd. trustees U. Pa., 2003-. Office: The Getty Found 1200 Getty Center Dr Ste 800 Los Angeles CA 90049 Office Phone: 310-440-7320.

MARROW, TRACY **See ICE-T**

MARRS, CAROL FAYE, performing arts educator, writer; b. Fairbanks, Alaska, Sept. 22, 1955; d. Morris Elton Robinson and Mary Emogene Hall; m. Gregory Evan Marrs; children: Matthew, Haley. BSc, West Tex. State U., Canyon, 1977. Tchr. English/Speech Hereford Ind. Sch. Dist., Tex., 1979—81; tchr. speech/drama/English River Rd. Ind. Sch. Dist., Amarillo, Tex., 1981—82, Canyon Ind. Sch. Dist., Tex., 1982—90; tchr. grade 1 Lewisville Ind. Sch. Dist., Carrollton, Tex., 1996—98, tchr. creative dramatics, 1998—2005, Flower Mound, 2005—. Workshop presenter Tex. Educators Theatre Assn., Austin, 2005; author, pub. spkr. Tex. Panhandle Penwomen, Amarillo, 1988—; dir. summer music theatre camp for children; tchr. music class for toddlers. Author: (children's poetry) Pet Cobwebs, 1988, (speech textbook) The Complete Book of Speech Communication, 1991. Mem. Grace Cmty. Assembly of God, Flower Mound, 2005—. Named Elem. Tchr. of Yr., Indian Creek Ind. Elem. Sch., Lewisville Ind. Sch. Dist., 2003—04; finalist Tchr. of Yr., LISD, 2003, 2004; grantee, Lewisville Edn. Found., 2003—04; 3 nominations Tchr. of Yr., Disney. Mem.: PTA, Tex. Educators Theatre Assn., Mothers In Touch (campus coord. 2005—06). Home: 420 Moran Dr Highland Village TX 79070 Office: Wellington Elem Flower Mound TX Office Phone: 469-713-5989.

MARS, FORREST E., JR., candy company executive; s. Forrest Mars Sr.; m. Virginia Cretella, Oct. 20, 1955 (div. Jan. 1990); children: Victoria B., Valerie A., Pamela D., Marijke E. BA, Yale U., 1953, BS. Chmn. bd. dirs., former CEO Mars Inc., Mc Lean, Va. Named one of World's Richest People, Forbes Mag., 1999—, Forbes Richest Americans, 1999—. Office: Mars Inc 6885 Elm St Mc Lean VA 22101-3810

MARS, JOHN FRANKLYN, candy company executive; b. 1935; m. Adrienne Mars; 2 children. BA, Yale U., 1957, BS. Chmn. Kal Kan Foods Inc.; co-pres. Mars Inc., 1973—, CEO, 2000—, chmn. Named one of World's Richest People, Forbes Mag, 1999—, Forbes Richest Americans, 1999—. Office: Mars Inc 6885 Elm St Mc Lean VA 22101

MARSAL, BRYAN PAUL, restructuring company executive; b. New Orleans, Mar. 26, 1951; m. Kathleen Marsal; 2 children. BA in Bus., U. Mich., 1973, MBA, 1975. V.p. loan recovery divsn. Citibank, NA; dir. ops. control Norton Simon Inc., 1982; co-founder, co-CEO Alvarez & Marsal LLC, NYC, 1983—; pres., CEO Republic Health Corp., Dallas; chief exec. Bidermann Industries USA Inc., Anthony Mfg., Gitano; COO Alexander's Dept. Store; chmn, CEO Cluett Am. Corp.; chief restructuring mgr. Arthur Andersen LLP; chief restructuring officer HealthSouth Corp, 2003, Lehman Brothers Holdings Inc., 2008—, CEO, 2008—09, chmn., CEO, 2009—. Bd. dirs. Timex Corp., Cluett Am. Corp., Essent Healthcare, Inc. Office: Alvarez & Marsal LLC 6th Fl 600 Lexington Ave New York NY 10022 Office Phone: 212-759-4433. Office Fax: 212-759-5532.*

MARSALIS, WYNTON, musician; b. New Orleans, Oct. 18, 1961; s. Ellis and Dolores Marsalis. Studied with John Longo; student, New Orleans Ctr. for Performing Arts, Berkshire Music Ctr., Juilliard Sch. Music, 1979-81. Music dir. Lincoln Ctr. Jazz Orch. Trumpet soloist with New Orleans Philharm. Orch., 1975, recitalist with New Orleans Ctr. for Creative Arts, 1979, played with various New Orleans and NYC orchs., with Art Blakey's Jazz Messengers, 1980—81, Herbie Hancock's V.S.O.P. quartet, formed own group, 1981, albums Fathers and Sons, 1982, Hummel/Haydn/L. Mozart Trumpet Concertos, 1983 (Grammy award, 1983), Wynton Marsalis (Best Jazz Record, Downbeat readers' poll, 1982), Think of One, 1983 (Grammy award), Handel, purcell, Torelli, Fasch, Moler, Trumpet Concertos, 1983, Hot House Flowers, 1984, Black Codes from the Underground, 1985 (2 Grammy awards), J Mood, 1986, Carnaval, Marsalis Standard Time, Vol. 1, 1987 (Grammy award), Majesty of the Blues, 1989, Standard Time, Vol. 3, 1990, Intimacy Calling Standard Time, Soul Gestures in Southern Blue, Vols. 1, 2, 3, 1991, Blue Interlude, 1992, Citi Movement, 1993, In This House, On This Morning, 1994, Wynton Marsalis, 1995, Popular Songs: The Best Of Wynton Marsalis, 2001, All Rise, 2002, Unforgivable Blackness, 2004, The Magic Hour, 2004, Baroque Music For Trumpets, 2005, Trumpet Concertos, 2005, Live At The House Of Tribes, 2005, (with others) The All-American Hero, Live at Bubba's, In Gabriel's Garden, Sound of Jazz, All American Hero, 1996, Blood on the Fields, Jump Start and Jazz, Crescent City Xmas Card, 1997, Standard Time, Vol. 5: The Midnight Blues, One by One, Gold Collection, 1998. Recipient Grammy award for best solo jazz instrumental, 1983—85, Grammy award for best solo classical performance with orch., 1984—85, Grammy award for best jazz instrumental performance with group, 1985, 1987, musician of the Year, Down Beat Readers, 1992, Pulitzer prize for music, 1997, Algur H. Meadows award, Southern Meth. Univ., 1997, Nat. Medal of Arts, Nat. Endowment for the Arts, 2005, Most Influential Black Americans, Ebony mag., 2006; named Jazz Musician of Yr., Downbeat readers' poll, 1982, 1984—86, 1989, Best Trumpet Player, Downbeat critics' poll, 1984, Acoustic Jazz Group of Yr., 1984, Best Trumpet Player, Downbeat readers' poll, 1985; named one of America's 25 Most Influential People, Time mag., 1996, 100 Most Influential People, Time Mag., 2006; named to Power 150, Ebony mag., 2008. Office: Jazz at Lincoln Ctr 33 West 60 St Fl 11 New York NY 10023

MARSANO, JOSEPH D., physicist; s. Daniel T. and Linda J. Marsano; m. Denise K. Malkowski, Oct. 8, 2005. BS in Math., U. Mich., Ann Arbor, BS in Physics, 2001; MA, Harvard U., Cambridge, Mass., PhD, 2006. John A. Mccone postdoc. fellow Calif. Inst. Tech., Pasadena, 2006—. Recipient Wiley Book Physics award, U. Mich., 2001, Outstanding Achievement Math. award, 2001, Harold T. White Tchg. prize, Harvard U., 2002, Distinction Tchg. award, Derek Bok Ctr. Tchg. and Learning, Harvard U., 2002. Mem.: Phi Beta Kappa. Office: Calif Inst Tech 1200 E California Blvd Mail Code 452-48 Pasadena CA 91125

MARSCHKE, SEAN M., chief of police, emergency management director; s. Gregory G. and Catherine A. Marschke; m. Laurel L. Lischka, Oct. 22, 1994 (dec.); 1 child, Caylyn C. AS in Police sci., Waukesha County Tech. Coll., Pewaukee, Wis., 1991; BS in Criminal Justice Adminstrn., Mt. Senario Coll., Ladysmith, Wis., 2000; grad., Northwesten U. Sch. Police Staff and Command, 2001, FBI Law Enforcement Exec. Devel. Seminar, Wis., 2003, Nat. Fire Acad., Md., 2005. Cert. Unified Tactical Instr. Wis. Dept. Justice. Law enforcement ranger Wis. Dept. Natural Resources, Eagle, 1991—92; police officer Village of Merton, Wis., 1991—97; police chief Village of Sturtevant (Wis.) Police Dept., 1992—; emergency mgmt. dir. Village of Sturtevant, 1998—. Tng. and mgmt. cons. Fall River (Wis.) Police Dept., 1996—; tng. cons. Randolph (Wis.) Police Dept., 1996—2006, Fox Lake (Wis.) Police Dept., 1996—2006, Rio (Wis.) Police Dept., 1996—2006; spl. dep. US Marshal, FBI Safe Sts. Task Force GRGTF, 2006—08; interim Fire Chief, Sturtevant, Wis., 2007—08. Appointee Racine County Local Emergency Planning Com., 2002—. Recipient Traffic Safety Enforcement award, Wis. Dept. Transp., 1996, Commendation, Office of Dir. of Pub. Safety, Village of Sturtevant, 1999, John Edgar Hoover Meml. award, Am. Police Hall of Fame, 2001, Commendation, Office of Dir. of Pub. Safety, Village of Sturtevant, 2001, 2002, Office of Dir. Pub. Safety, Village of Sturtevant, 2003; named Law Enforcement Officer of Yr., VFW Post # 9929, 1994. Mem.: NRA (life; police firearms instr. 1992—), Internat. Assn. Chiefs of Police, FBI Law Enforcement Exec. Devel. Assn. (assoc.), Internat. Law Enforcement Educators Trainers Assn. (assoc.), Nat. Fire Acad. Alumni Assn., Harbor Lite Yacht Club (assoc.), Loyal Order of Moose (assoc.). Roman Catholic. Avocations: camping, hunting, boating, hiking. Office: Village of Sturtevant 2801 89th St Sturtevant WI 53177 Personal E-mail: sgtsmm@yahoo.com.

MARSCIARELLI, GARRY KENT See MARSHALL, GARRY

MARSDEN, BRIAN GEOFFREY, astronomer; b. Cambridge, Eng., Aug. 5, 1937; arrived in US, 1959; s. Thomas and Eileen (West) M.; m. Nancy Lou Zissell, Dec. 26, 1964; children: Cynthia Louise, Jonathan Brian. BA, Oxford U., UK, 1959, MA, 1963; PhD, Yale U., 1965. Rsch. asst. Yale U., New Haven, 1959-65; lectr. astronomy Harvard U., Cambridge, Mass., 1966-83; astronomer Smithsonian Astrophys. Obs., Cambridge, 1965—; assoc. dir. planetary scis. Harvard-Smithsonian Ctr. for Astrophysics, Cambridge, 1987—2002. Dir. Ctrl. Bur. Astron. Telegrams, 1968-2000, Minor Planet Ctr. Internat. Astron. Union, 1978-2006. Editor: The Earth-Moon System, 1966, The Motion, Evolution of Orbits and Origin of Comets, 1972, Catalogue of Orbits of Unnumbered Minor Planets, 1996, Catalogue of Cometary Orbits, 2008. Recipient Merlin medal Brit. Astron. Assn., 1965, Goodacre medal, 1979, Alcock lectureship, 2003; Van Biesbroeck award U. Ariz., 1989, Camus-Waitz prize Societé astronomique de France, 1993, Dirk Brouwer award Am. Astron. Soc., 1995, Lacchini prize Unione Astrofili Italiani, 2001. Fellow Royal Astron. Soc. (Svc. award astronomy and geophysics 2006, space pioneer award, Nat. Space Soc.); mem. Am. Astron. Soc. (chmn. div. on dynamical astronomy 1976-78), Internat. Astron. Union (pres. commn. 1976-79, 2000-03), Astron. Soc. Pacific, Sigma Xi. Office: Harvard-Smithsonian Ctr Astrophysics 60 Garden St Cambridge MA 02138-1516 Home Phone: 781-862-6549; Office Phone: 617-495-7244. Business E-Mail: bmarsden@cfa.harvard.edu.

MARSDEN, HERCI IVANA, classical ballet artistic director; b. Omis-Split, Croatia, Dec. 2, 1937; d. Ante and Magda (Smith) Munitic; m. Myles Marsden, Aug. 10, 1957 (div. 1976); children: Ana, Richard, Mark.; m. Dujko Radovnikovic, Aug. 27, 1977; 1 child, Dujko. Student, Internat. Ballet Sch., 1955. Mem. corps de ballet Nat. Theatre, Split, 1954-58; founder Braecrest Sch. Ballet, Lincoln, RI, 1958—, State Ballet of R.I., Lincoln, 1960—, artistic dir., 1976—. Artistic dir. U. R.I. Classical Ballet, Kingston, 1966—, lectr., 1966—. Office: Brae Crest School of Ballet 52 Sherman Ave Lincoln RI 02865-3809 Office Phone: 401-334-2560. Business E-Mail: hmarsden@stateballet.com.

MARSDEN, JAMES PAUL, actor; b. Stillwater, Okla., Sept. 18, 1973; m. Lisa Linde Marsden, July 22, 2000; children: Jack, Mary James. Student, Okla. State U. Actor: (films) No Dessert Dad, Til You Mow the Lawn, 1994, Public Enemies, 1996, Campfire Tales, 1997, Disturbing Behavior, 1998, Gossip, 2000, X-Men, 2000, Sugar & Spice, 2001, Zoolander, 2001, Interstate 60, 2002, X2, 2003, The 24th Day, 2004, The Notebook, 2004, Heights, 2004, The Alibi, 2006, 10th & Wolf, 2006, X-Men: The Last Stand, 2006, Superman Returns, 2006, Hairspray, 2007, Enchanted, 2007, 27 Dresses, 2008, Sex Drive, 2008; (TV films) In the Line of Duty: Ambush in Waco, 1993, Search and Resume, 1994, 919 Fifth Avenue, 1995, Gone in a Heartbeat, 1996, One the Edge of Innocence, 1997, Bella Mafia, 1997; (TV series) Boogies Diner, 1994, Second Noah, 1996—97, Ally McBeal, 2001—02. Office: Bwr Public Relations 5700 Wilshire Blvd Los Angeles CA 90036-3659

MARSH, BENJAMIN FRANKLIN, lawyer; b. Toledo, Apr. 30, 1927; s. Lester Randall and Alice (Smith) M.; m. Martha Kirkpatrick, July 12, 1952; children: Samuel, Elizabeth. BA, Ohio Wesleyan U., 1950; JD, George Washington U., 1954. Bar: Ohio 1955. Pvt. practice law, Toledo, 1955—88; assoc., ptnr. Doyle, Lewis & Warner, Toledo, 1955—71; ptnr. Ritter, Boesel, Robinson & Marsh, Toledo, 1971—88; mem. Marsh & McAdams, Maumee, 1988—98; pers. officer AEC, 1950—54; asst. atty. gen. State of Ohio, 1969—71; asst. solicitor City of Maumee, 1959—63, solicitor, 1963—92; mem. Marsh McAdams, Ltd., Maumee, 1999—. Mem. U.S. Fgn. Claims Settlement Commn., Washington, 1990-94; counsel N.W. Ohio Mayors and Mgrs. Assn., 1990-2000; regional bd. rev. Indsl. Commn. Ohio, Toledo, 1993-94; mem. Ohio Dental Bd., 1995-2000; trustee Corp. for Effective Govt., 1998-2003; mem. Ohio Elections Commn., 2001-07, chmn. 2003-04 U.S. rep. with rank spl. amb. to 10th Anniversary Independence of Botswana, 1976; past pres. Toledo and Lucas County Tb Soc.; past co-chmn. citizens for metro pks.; past mem. Judges Com. Notaries Pub.; former mem. Lucas County Bd. Elections; former chmn. bldg. commn. Riverside Hosp., Toledo; past trustee Com. on Rels. with Toledo, Spain; past chmn. bd. trustee Med. Coll., Ohio; past treas. Coglin Meml. Inst.; chmn. Lucas County Rep. Exec. Com., 1973-74; precinct commiteeman, Maumee, 1959-73; legal counsel, bd. dirs. Nat. Coun. Rep. Workshops, 1960-65; pres. Rep. Workshops, Ohio, 1960-64; alt. del. Rep. Nat. Conv., 1964; candidate 9th dist. U.S. Ho. of Reps., 1968; adminstrv. asst. to Rep. state chmn. Ray C. Bliss, 1954; chmn. Lucas County Bush for Pres., 1980; co-chmn. Reagan-Bush Com. for Northwestern Ohio, 1980, vice chmn. fin. com. Bush-Quayle, 1992; co-chmn. Ohio steering com. Bush for Pres., mem. nat. steering com., 1988; del. Rep. Nat. Conv., 1988; past bd. dirs. Ohio Tb and Respiratory Disease Assn.; apptd. Ohio chmn. UN Day, 1980, 81, 82; adminstrv. asst. Legis. Svc. Commn., Columbus, 1954-55; mem. Lucas County Charter Commn., Toledo, 1959-60; vice-chmn. U.S. Nat. Commn. for UNESCO, mem. legal com., del. 17th gen. conf., Paris, 1972, U.S. observer meeting of nat. commns., Africa, 1974, Addis Ababa, Ethiopia; past mem. industry functional adv. com. on stds. trade policy matters; mem. nat. def. exec. res. Dept. Commerce; active Am. Bicentennial Presdl. Inauguration, Diplomatic Adv. Com. With USNR, 1945-46. Named Outstanding Young Man of Toledo, 1962. Mem. ABA, Maumee C. of C. (past pres.), UN Assn., Ohio State Bar Assn., Toledo Bar Assn., Ohio Mpcl. League (past pres.), Am. Legion (past comdr. Toledo Post), Lucas County Maumee Valley Hist. Soc. (past pres.), Internat. Inst. Toledo, Ohio Mcpl. Attys. Assn. (past pres.), Orgn. Security and Cooperation in Europe (registration supr., adjudicator, elections supr. in Bosnia), Western Lake Erie Hist. Soc., Ohio Hist. Soc., Canal Soc. Ohio, Toledo Mus. Art, Ohio Wesleyan U. Alumni Assn. (past pres.), Ohio State Bar Found., Toledo Bar Found., Rotary, Toledo Country Club, Torch Club Toledo, Navy League, Omicron Delta Kappa, Delta Sigma Rho, Theta Alpha Phi, Phi Delta Phi, English Speaking Union(Toledo), US6 Grand Canyon Sailors Assn. Presbyterian. Home: 1624 Swan Creek Ln Toledo OH 43614 Office: 204 W Wayne St Maumee OH 43537-2125 Office Phone: 419-893-4880. Personal E-mail: bmarsh124@aol.com.

MARSH, BRUCE DAVID, geologist, educator; b. Munising, Mich., Jan. 4, 1947; s. William Roland and Audrey Jane (Steinhoff) M.; m. Judith Anne Congdon, Jan. 24, 1970; children: Hannah Eyre, William Noah. BS, Mich. State U., East Lansing, 1969; MS, U. Ariz., Tucson, 1971; PhD, U. Calif., Berkeley, 1974. Geologist, geophysicist Anaconda Co., Tucson, 1969-71; asst. prof. dept. earth/planet sci. Johns Hopkins U., Balt., 1974-78, assoc. prof., 1978-81, prof., 1981—. Chmn., 1989-93; vis. prof. Calif. Inst. Tech., Pasadena, 1985, U. Maine, 1992-93; co-chmn. Gordon Rsch. Conf. on Inorganic Geochemistry, Holderness, N.H., 1983-84; advisor NASA, Washington, 1975-84, NSF, Washington, 1978-90, NRC, 1985-91; Hallimond lectr. Mineral. Soc. Great Britain and Ireland, 1995. Assoc. editor Geology, 1981-83, Jour. Volcanology and Geothermal Rsch., 1978—, Jour. Petrology, 1986—; editor Jour. Volcanology and Geothermal Rsch., 1985—. Fellow Geol. Soc. Am. (assoc. editor Bulletin 1986-92), Royal Astron. Soc., Mineral. Soc. Am., Am. Geophys. Union (sec. sect. on volcanology, geochemistry and petrology 1984-86, pres. elect 1988-90, pres. 1990-92, Bowen award 1993, Daly lecture 2000); mem. Model A Ford Club Am. Achievements include being named in honor of research in Antarctica, Marsh Cirque, a glacial valley in the Olympus Mountains. Office: Johns Hopkins U Dept Earth-Planetary Scis 322 Olin Hall Baltimore MD 21218 Office Phone: 410-516-4652. Business E-Mail: bmarsh@jhu.edu.

MARSH, CARYL AMSTERDAM, retired curator, psychologist; b. NYC, Mar. 9, 1923; d. Louis and Kitty (Weitz) Amsterdam; m. Michael Marsh, Sept. 3, 1942 (dec. 1993); children: Susan E., Anna L. BA, Bklyn. Coll., 1942; MA, Columbia U., NYC, 1946; PhD, George Washington U., 1978. Lic. psychologist DC. Asst. cultural attache Am. Embassy, Paris, 1946-48; psychologist D.C. Recreation Dept., 1957-69; spl. asst. Smithsonian Instn., Washington, 1966-73; curator exhbns. Nat. Archives, Washington, 1978-85, sr. exhbns. specialist, 1985-86; dir. traveling psychology exhbn. Am. Psychol. Assn., 1986-93, sr. advisor, 1993-95; chair humanities seminars in sci. mus. Assn. Sci. Tech. Ctrs., 1994—2001; ret., 2003. Rsch. fellow exptl. gallery Smithsonian Instn., 1992; rsch. cons. Nat. Zoo, 1981-92, Smithsonian Folk Life Festival, Nat. Mus. Am. History, 1977-78; organizer Discovery Room Nat. Mus. Natural History, 1969-73; cons. Meyer Found., 1964-66; advisor Lemelson Ctr. for Study of Invention and Innovation, Nat. Mus. Am. History, 1999-2000. Editor: Exhibition: The American Image, 1979. Organizer Anacostia Neighborhood Mus., Washington, 1967, bd. dirs., 1974—, v.p. 1993—; sec. D.C. Commn. on Arts and Humanities, 1969-72; pres. Pre-Sch. Parents Coun., Washington, 1956-57; adv. bd. Youth Alive, 1997-99. Fellow Nat. Mus. Am. Art, 1975-77; vis. scholar Nat. Mus. Am. Art, 1978—; grad. fellow CUNY, 1945-46; scholar George Washington U.; noted for Disting. Contbn. to Pub. Understanding of Psychology, APA, 1993. Mem. AAAS, APA (Outstanding Svc. award 1992, Disting. Contbn. to Pub. Understanding of Psychology award 1993), D.C. Psychol. Assn., Am. Assn. Mus., Mus. Edn. Roundtable (bd. dirs. 1983-87), Prince George's Plulharmonic (bd. mem. 2007-). Home and Office: 10450 Lottsford Rd # 3011 Mitchellville MD 20721-2734

MARSH, CLARE TEITGEN, retired school psychologist; b. Manitowoc, Wis., July 7, 1934; d. Clarence Emil and Dorothy (Napiezinski) Teitgen; m. Robert Irving Marsh, Jan. 30, 1955; children: David, Wendy Marsh Tootle, Julie Marsh Domino, Laura Marsh Beltrame. MS in Sch. Psychology, U. Wis., Milw., 1968. Cert. nationally cert. sch. psychologist. Sch. psychologist Milw. Pub. Schs., 1976; lead psychologist West Allis (Wis.)-West Milw. Pub. Schs., 1968-95; sch. psychologist Wauwatosa (Wis.) Pub. Schs., 1987; instr. Milw. Sch. Engring., 1989-90, Alverno Coll., 1990-91, ret., 1995. NDEA fellow, 1966-68. Mem. Suburban Assn. Sch. Psychologists (pres. 1976-77, 86-87), Wis. Assn. Sch. Psychologists (pres. 1990-91, chmn. membership com. 1980-84, sec. 1985-89, chmn. conv. 1987), Wis. Fedn. Pupil Svcs., Menomee Falls Symphony Orch., Our Lord's United Meth. Ch., United Meth. Women (pres. 2003-06, spl. mission recognition mem. 2008), Phi Kappa Phi, Pi Lambda Theta (past pres. 1992), Kappa Delta Pi, Phi Delta Kappa, Sigma Tau Delta, Alpha Chi Omega. Home: 14140 W Honey Ln New Berlin WI 53151-2442 Personal E-mail: claremarsh@wi.rr.com.

MARSH, CLAY BRADEN, pulmonologist, researcher; b. Charleston, W.Va., Nov. 15, 1958; s. Don and Geraldine Marsh; m. Gail Marsh; children: Cameron, Matthew, Rachel. BS, W.Va. U., 1981, MD, 1985. Diplomate Am. Bd. Internal Medicine, 1988, Am. Bd. Pulmonary Medicine, 1993, Am. Bd. Critical Care Medicine, 1994. Clin. instr. rsch. divsn. pulmonary and critical care medicine Ohio State U., Columbus, 1993—95, asst. prof. medicine, 1995, assoc. prof. medicine, 1998—2004, prof. medicine, 2004—, vice chmn. rsch. dept. internal medicine, 2000—, interim dir. divsn. pulmonary, allergy and critical care medicine, 2002—03, dir. divsn. pulmonary, allergy, critical care and sleep medicine, 2003—; investigator Davis Heart and Lung Rsch. Inst., Columbus, 1998—; dir. Ctr. Critical Care and Respiratory Medicine, 2005—; assoc. dir. Davis Heart and Lung Rsch. Inst., Columbus, 2000—; resident in internal medicine Ohio State U., Columbus, 1985—88, chief resident in internal medicine, 1989—90, fellow in pulmonary and critical care medicine, 1990—92. Mem. sect. study lung, biology and pathology NIH, Washington, 2003—04. Recipient Presdl. award, Am. Lung Assn. Ohio, 2003. Mem.: Am. Soc. Biochemistry and Molecular Biology, Stanley Sarnoff Found. (sci. bd.), Fedn. Am. Soc. Exptl. Biology, Ohio Thoracic Soc., Am. Thoracic Soc. Home: 2266 Club Rd Columbus OH 43221 Office: Pulmonary Critical Care OSU 473 W 12th Ave Columbus OH 43210 Business E-Mail: clay.marsh@osumc.edu.

MARSH, DON ERMAL, supermarket executive; b. Muncie, Ind., Feb. 2, 1938; s. Ermal W. and Garnet (Gibson) M.; m. Marilyn Faust, Mar. 28, 1959; children: Don Ermal, Jr., Arthur Andrew, David Alan, Anne Elizabeth, Alexander Elliott. BA, Mich. State U., 1961. With Marsh Supermarkets, Inc., Indpls., 1961—2006, pres., 1968—2006, chmn. CEO; ret. Chmn. FoodPAC, Washington, 1991; bd. dirs. Nat. City Bank, Indpls., Ind. Energy, Inc., Indpls.; gov. World Econ. Forum—Food & Agro, Geneva. Bd. dirs. Corp. Community Coun., Culver Fathers Assn., Food Industry Crusade Against Hunger, Charlene S. Lugar Birth Defects Grant Fund, Am. Arbitration Assn, Ctrl. Ind. Corp., Econ. Club Indpls., Hanover Coll., other; bd. mem. Ind. Assn. Cities and Towns; mem. adv. com. on food distbn. Western Mich. U.; mem. Conner Prairie Pioneer Settlement Adv. Coun.; mem. Indpls. Mus. Art.; mgmt. coun. Am. Mgmt. Assn. Mem. Am. Mgmt. Assn., Mgmt. Execs. Soc., Gen. Mgmt. Coun., Internat. Food Congress, Assn. of Publicly Traded Cos. (bd. dirs., past chmn.), Food Mktg. Inst. (bd. dirs.), Indpls. C. of C., Ind. State C. of C. (bd. dirs.), Ind. Retail Coun. (bd. dirs.), Ind. Soc. Chgo., Chief Execs. Orgn., World Bus. Coun., Newcomen Soc. N.Am., Internat. Ctr. for Cos. of Food Trade and Industry (past chmn., bd. dirs.), Food Merchandisers Edn. Coun., Nat. Assn. Convenience Stores, Nat. Assn. Food Rsch., World Pres. Orgn., Young Pres. Orgn. Alumni, Nat. Soc. Fund Raising Execs., Well House Soc., Am. Bus. Club, Ind. Fiscal Policy Inst., Ind. Soc. Chgo., Ind. U. Varsity Club, Crooked Stick Golf Club, Columbia Club, Delaware Country Club, The Hundred Club Indpls., Indpls. Athletic Club, Marco Polo Club, Meridian Hills Country Club, Skyline Club, Masons, Elks, Pi Sigma Epsilon, Lambda Chi Alpha Found., Sigma Phi Omega. Republican. Presbyterian.

MARSH, FREDRIK, photographer; b. Quantico, Va., 1957; BFA in Photography, Ohio State U., 1980, MFA in Printmaking, 1984. One-man shows include U. Notre Dame, Ind., 2000, Gallery Sink, Denver, 2003, Tex. Tech. U., Lubbock, 2004, U. Arts, Phila., 2006, 9th Internat. Photo Gathering, Aleppo, Syria, 2007, exhibited in group shows at Latest Development, Huntington Mus., W.Va., 2000, Trading Places, Ohio State U., 2003, Photographers, ART-Galerie, Siegen, Germany, 2005, Image as Evidence, Dayton Visual Arts Ctr., Ohio, 2006, Nat. Prize Show, Kathryn Schultz Gallery, Cambridge, Mass., 2007, Heroes of Horticulture, George Eastman House, Rochester, NY, 2007, FotoFest, Fine Print Auction, Houston, 2008. Recipient Ford Found. award, Ohio State U., 1983; grantee Sächsichen Ministeriums für Wissenschaft und Kunst, Dresden, Germany, 2003; fellow Arts Midwest/Nat. Endowment Arts, 1985, John Simon Guggenheim Meml. Found., 2008. Mem.: Greater Columbus Arts Coun. (bd. trustees, Individual Artist fellowship in photography 2004, Individual Excellence award in photography 2007, Spl. Projects grant 2007), Ohio Arts Coun. (Profl. Devel. Assistance award 1988, Individual Artist fellowship in photography 1991, Artists Projects grant 2002, Individual Artist fellowship in photography 2004, Individual Excellence award in photography 2007). Office: Greater Columbus Arts Coun Ste 2250 100 E Broad St Columbus OH 43215 E-mail: fredrik.marsh@fredrikmarsh.com.*

MARSH, HAROLD MICHAEL, anesthesiologist; b. Sydney, Mar. 7, 1939; came to U.S., 1974; m. Elizabeth Eleanor. BSc in Medicine, U. Sydney, 1956, MBBS, 1963. Intern Royal Prince Alfred Hosp., Sydney, 1964, resident, 1965—68, Mayo Grad. Sch. Medicine, Rochester, Minn., 1969—71; clin. assoc. dept. anesthesiology Toronto We. Hosp., 1971; dir. dept. intensive care Royal Prince Alfred Hosp., 1972—74; instr. anesthesiology Mayo Med. Sch., Rochester, 1975—76, asst. prof. anesthesiology, 1976—83; assoc. prof. anesthesiology Mayo Grad. Sch., Rochester, 1981—89, prof. anesthesiology, 1989; chmn. dept. anesthesiology Henry Ford Hosp., Detroit, 1989—98; prof. chmn. dept. anesthesiology Wayne State U., 1998—; spec.-in-chief anesthesiology Detroit Med. Ctr., 1998—2007; chief, anesthesia svc. Karmanos Cancer Inst., 2006—; anesthesiologist John D. Dingell VAMC, 2007—. Part-time lectr., tutor faculty medicine U. Sydney, 1972-74; cons. anesthesiology Mayo Clinic, 1974-89, med. dir. surg. and respiratory intensive care units, 1977-81, dir. critical care svcs., 1981-83, 87-89, assoc. dir. critical care svcs., 1984-87, chmn. divsn. intensive care & respiratory therapy, 1985-89; vis. prof. dept. anesthesia U. Pa., 1976, Nat. Naval Med. Sch., 1981, Northwestern U., 1982, 89, Royal Prince Alfred Hosp., 1983, Sir Charles Gairdner Hosp., 1984, U. Md., 1987, Sloan-Kettering Inst., 1990, Rush-Presbyn.-St. Luke's Med. Ctr., Chgo., 1991, U. Hosp., London, Ont., 1993; invited lectr. dept. anesthetics IV Pan Am. Congress of Diseases of Chest, Caracas, Venezuela, 1987, Uniformed Svcs. U. Health Scis. Med. Sch., Bethesda, Md., 1987, Walter Reed Amry Med. Ctr., 1987, Naval Hosp., 1987, Bethesda, World Congress Intensive Care, Kyoto, Japan, 1989, Uddevalla (Sweden) Hosp., 1993, Karolinska Hosp., Stockholm, Sweden, 1993, Nat. Inst. Cardiology, Mexico City, Mexico, 1993; presenter in field. Contbr. chpts. to books and articles to profl. jours. With Australian Mil., 1958-61. Faculty of Anaesthetists, Royal Australasian Coll. Surgeons fellow, 1968. Fellow Am. Coll. Chest Physicians; mem. AAAS, Am. Bd. Anesthesiology, Am. Coll. Anesthesiologists, Wayne County Med. Soc. (pres. 2002). Achievements include research on general anesthesia and the lung, acute lung injury, metabolism, epidemiology in critical care, anesthesia education, anesthetic drugs and neurochemistry. Office: Detroit Med Ctr DRH/UHC Dept Anesthesiolog 4201 Saint Antoine St Detroit MI 48201-2153 Office Phone: 313-745-4300.

MARSH, JACK, JR., (JOHN OTHO MARSH), lawyer, former United States Representative from Virginia; b. Winchester, Va., Aug. 7, 1926; s. John Otho and Nell Virginia (Wayl) M.; m. Glenn Ann Patterson, July 22, 1950; children: John O., Rebecca Patterson, Scot Wayland. LLB, Washington and Lee U., 1951; degree (hon.), The Citadel, James Madison U., Shenandoah U., Hampden-Sydney Coll. Bar: Va. 1952, D.C. 1970. Pvt. practice, Strasburg, 1952; town judge, 1954-62; town atty. New Market, Va., 1954-62; mem. US Congress from 7th Va. dist., 1963—71; asst. sec. for legis. affairs US Dept. Def., Washington, 1972-73; asst. to the v.p. for nat. security affairs The White House, Washington, 1973-74, counselor to Pres. with Cabinet Rank, 1974—77; ptnr. Mays, Valentine, Davenport & Moore LLP, Washington, 1977-81; sec. Dept. Army, Washington, 1981-89; asst. sec. for spl. ops./low intensity conflict US Dept. Def., Washington, 1987-88, legis. counsel to sec., 1989-90; mem. Hazel & Thomas, P.C., Winchester and Falls Ch., Va., 1990-94, of counsel Winchester, Va., 1995—96; chmn., interim CEO Novavax, Inc., Rockville, Md., 1996—97. Mem. Shenandoah County (Va.) Sch. Bd., 1958-60; chmn. Res. Forces Policy Bd., 1989-94; chmn. Sec. Def.'s Panel on Quality of Life, 1995-; co-chmn., ind. rev. goup Walter Reed Hosp., Bethesda Naval Hosp.; vis. prof. ethics, Va. Mil. Inst., 1998-99, adj. prof. law, Coll. William & Mary, 1999-2000, disting. adj. prof. law, George Mason U., 2005- Mem. Am. Revolution Bicentennial Commn., 1966-70. Served with AUS, 1944-47; lt. col. Va. N.G., ret. Recipient Disting. Pub. Svc. medal US Dept. Def. (5), Presdl. Citizen's medal, 1989, Outstanding Virginian award Va. Press Assn., 1990; named to Outstanding Young Man of Yr., 1959. Mem. Va. State Bar, Va. Jaycees (life), Am. Legion, VFW, N.G. Assn. U.S., Va. N.G. Assn., Masons, Phi Kappa Psi, Phi Delta Phi, Omicron Delta Kappa. Presbyterian (past elder).

MARSH, JOAN KNIGHT, educational film company executive, video company executive, publishing executive; b. Apr. 8, 1934; d. E. Lyle and Ruth (Hopkins) Knight; m. Alan Reid Marsh, Sept. 27, 1958; children: Alan Reid, Clayton Knight. BA, Tex. Tech U., 1956. Owner, pres. MarshMedia, Kansas City, Mo., 1969—. Mem. ctrl. governing bd. Children's Mercy Hosp., 1996-05; mem. coun. Family Study Ctr., U. Mo., Kansas City, 1983-89, Children's Relief Assn. Mercy Hosp., Kansas City, 1984—, pres., 1989-91; chmn., hon. co-chmn. Rose Brooks Ctr. Cabaret, 1995, 2000; pres. Friends of Children's Mercy Hosp., 1996-98; chmn. The Jewel Ball, 1997, Nelson-Atkins Mus. Art: Great Ball of China II, 1999, An Asymmetrical Evening GAla Opening of Bloch Bldg., 2007; Genevieve Byrne spkr. Series ARC Kansas City chpt., 2004. Mem. Jr. League (sustaining chmn. 1982-84, Cmty. Svc. award 1999), Gamma Phi Beta. Republican. Presbyterian. Avocations: egyptology, filmology. Office Phone: 816-523-1059.

MARSH, JOSEPH FRANKLIN, JR., retired academic administrator; b. Charleston, W.Va., Feb. 24, 1925; s. Joseph Franklin and Florence (Keller) M. Student, Concord Coll., 1941-42, W.Va. U., 1942-43; AB, Dartmouth Coll., 1947; student, Nat. Inst. Pub. Affairs, Washington, 1947-48; M.P.A., Harvard U., 1949; LL.D., Davis and Elkins Coll., 1968; L.H.D., Alderson-Broaddus Coll., 1982. Cons. Hoover Commn., Washington, 1948; instr. in gt. issues Dartmouth, 1952—54, instr. econs., 1953—55, asst. prof., 1955—59; pres. Concord U., Athens, W.Va., 1959—73, pres. emeritus, 1985—; ednl. cons., 1973—74; pres. Waynesburg (Pa.) U., 1974—83, pres. emeritus, 1983—; v.p. The Armand Hammer United World Coll. of the Am. West, Montezuma, N.Mex., 1984—85; pres. Marsh Edn Cons., Athens, W.Va., 1985—. Dir. One Valley Bank of Mercer County, 1987-98, hon. dir., 1998-2000. Contbr. articles to profl. jours. Mem. State Dept. Ednl. Mission to U.A.R., 1964, Mercer County (W.Va.) Planning Commn., 1964-74, 83-94, hon., 1994—; vice chmn. W.Va. Com. for Constl. Amendments, 1966; mem. regional coun. Internat. Edn. Study Mission to Europe, 1970; bd. dirs. Am. Assn. State Colls. and Univs., 1972-73, Regional Coun. for Internat. Edn., 1973, Hospice Care Mercer County, W.Va., 1987-91, Faculty Merit Found. W.Va., 1990—, Greater Mercer County Charitable Found., Inc., W.Va., 1998-02, exec. com. 2001-02, chmn., pres., 1998-2001; bd. dirs. Charitable Found. of the Virginians, Inc., 2002-05, Pa. Assn. Colls. and Univs., 1974-83, exec. com., 1980-82; bd. dirs. Pa. Commn. for Ind. Colls. and Univs., 1974-83, sec.-treas., 1976-77, vice chmn., 1977-80, chmn., 1980-82; trustee Found. Ind. Colls. Pa., 1974-83, mem. exec. com., 1979-82; bd. visitors Midway Coll., Ky., 1979-93; adv. com. Pa. State Coun. Higher Edn., 1980-82; trustee Concord U. Found., 1986, bd. dirs., 1987—; active Town of Athens Planning Commn., 1986-94, pres. commn. 1987-94; bd. trustees, Princeton (W.Va.) Cmty. Hosp. Found., 1989-98, vice chmn., 1989-97; Gov's. appointee to bd. dirs. State Coll. System W.Va., 1989-96, chmn. adminstrv. com., 1990-91, vice chmn. of bd., 1991-95, chmn., 1995-96; gov.'s appointee to the W.Va. Parkways, Econ. Devel. and Tourism Authority, 1998—2006, asst. sec., 2001-02, sec., 2002-03, vice chmn., 2003-04; gov.'s appointee Edn. Commn. of the States, 1998-2002. Served as gunnery officer USNR, 1943-46. Named Outstanding Young Man, W.Va. Jr. C. of C., 1960; recipient Alumnus of Yr. award Concord U., 1973, Golden Alumnus award, 1992, Outstanding Alumnus award for Career Achievement, 1996; Outstanding Citizen award Athens Woman's Club, 1992, Total Community Involvement Award, Town of Athens, WV, 2001; Rotary fellow Oxford (Eng.) U., 1950-52. Mem. AAUP, Am. Assn. Univ. Adminstrs., Am. Econ. Assn., Royal Inst. Pub. Adminstrn., Oxford Union Debating Soc. (life), Oxford Soc. (life), Pa. Soc., Duquesne Club (Pitts.), Univ. Club (Bluefield), Masons, Rotary (dist. gov. 1992-93), The Guild of Carillonneurs N.Am. (hon.), Phi Beta Kappa, Phi Tau, Phi Delta Pi, Phi Sigma Kappa, Alpha Kappa Psi (hon.). Methodist. Home: 106 First Ave Athens WV 24712 Office: PO Box 734 Athens WV 24712-0734 Home Phone: 304-384-9816; Office Phone: 304-384-9816.

MARSH, JOSEPH VIRGIL, investment advisor, analyst, broker, consultant, research scientist; b. Winston-Salem, NC, Apr. 28, 1952; s. Gilliam Hughes and Dovie Elizabeth (Watson) Marsh. Student, Surry CC, 1970-72, US Govt. Schs., Md., SC, Washington, 1972-74; BSEE, U. Md., 1976; diploma, NY Inst. Fin., 1978, NYU, 1978, MBA, 1980. Cert. comml. real estate broker NC. With Joint Armed Svcs. Tech. Liaison, Washington, 1974-75; cons. US Govt., 1975-76; corr., cons. individuals, bus. on tech. matters Ararat, NC, 1977—. Registered advisor SEC, 1981—2000. Active U.S. Presdl. Task Force, 1981—2000; founder Marsh Found., 1989; tech. liaison NASA, 1992. Recipient Presdl. medal of merit, Pres. of US, 1988, 1990. Mem.: VFW (hon.), Coun. Civilian Tech. Advisers, Internat. Assn. Sci. Devel., Ind. Cons. Assn., Internat. Entrepreneurs Assn., Armed Forces Assn. Republican. Office: Hwy 2019/2026 Ararat NC 27007-0178 Office Phone: 336-374-4405.

MARSH, KARYN B., lawyer; b. St. Louis, Sept. 13, 1964; d. Robert Lewis and Dorothy Eleanor Bergmann; m. Barry Douglas Marsh, Oct. 22, 2006. BS, Pa. State U., University Park, 1986; MBA, Villanova U., Pa., 1994; JD, U. Md., Balt., 2003. Bar: Md. 2003, U.S. Dist. Ct. Md. 2004, DC 2008. Geologist Woodward-Clyde Cons., Plymouth Meeting, Pa., 1988—91, SMC Environ. Svcs., King of Prussia, 1991—92, ICF Kaiser Engrs., Fairfax, Va., 1994—97; paralegal Gibson Dunn & Crutcher, Washington, 1998—2000; law clk. Md. Dept. Environment, Balt., 2001; honors law clk. US EPA, Washington, 2002; atty. Law Offices of Peter G. Angelos, Balt., 2004—07, Gibson Dunn & Crutcher, 2007—. Contbr. articles to profl. jours. Recipient Ellen Steidle Achievement award, Coll. Earth & Mineral Scis., Pa. State U., 1986, Pub. Svc. award, U. Md. Sch. Law, 2003; fellow, Villanova U., 1992—94, U. Md. Ctr. Health and Homeland Security, Balt., 2003—04; Peter Aiello Meml. scholar, Italian Am. Associated Charities, 2002. Mem.: ABA, Environ. law Inst. Avocations: kayaking, camping, birdwatching. Business E-Mail: kmarsh@gibsondunn.com.

MARSH, MILTON R.W., composer; b. Hamilton, Bermuda, Sept. 29, 1945; arrived in U.S., 1964; s. Milton Murray and Gwendolyn Isadora Marsh; children: Tanya, Jonathan Milton, Milton Andre. Cert. in Edn., London U., 1964; MB, Berklee Coll. Music, Boston, 1969; MusM, New Eng. Conservatory, Boston, 1971. Cert. tchr., adminstr. Calif. Music cons. Nat. Ctr. for Afro-Am. Artists, Boston, 1970—71; vis. prof. SUNY, Oneonta, 1972—73, prof., dir. Afro-Am. music studies Buffalo, 1973—77. Cons. Nat. Ctr. for Afro-Am. Artists, Boston, 1970—71. Author: (music) Monism, 1975, Continuum, 1985, We Are Not Separate, 2003. Recipient grant, Artist Found. Office: Alankara Records PO Box 230635 Boston MA 02123-0635 Office Phone: 781-979-2417. Office Fax: 781-324-4922. Personal E-mail: mmarsh8113@aol.com. E-mail: alankara@msn.com.

MARSH, PATRICIA A., business educator; b. Phoenix, June 5, 1947; d. Emma R. and L. Thomas Peart (Stepfather), Wallace M. Anderson; m. James L. Marsh, June 28, 1980; children: Melissa L., Tyler J. BS in Edn., Northern Ariz. U., Flagstaff, 1969; MA in Edn., Ariz. State U., Tempe, 1973. Cert. Ariz. CC Bd., 1973. Bus. tchr. Moon Valley HS, Phoenix, 1970—85; adj. bus. faculty Maricopa Tech. Coll., Phoenix, 1973—76, Phoenix Coll., 1985—88, bus. faculty, 1988—90; computer info. sys., bus. faculty Paradise Valley CC, Phoenix, 1990—. Named PVCC Woman Distinction, Women's Leadership Group, 2005; named to Innovator of Yr., PVCC Innovation Com., 1995, 2000. Mem.: Internat. Soc. Bus. Educators, Nat. Bus. Edn. Assn. Meth. Avocations: gardening, reading, hiking. Office: Paradise Valley CC 18401 North 32 St Phoenix AZ 85032 Office Fax: 602-787-6725. Business E-Mail: patti.marsh@pvmail.maricopa.edu.

MARSH, RICHARD H., energy executive; BA, Kent State U.; MA in Clinical Psychology, U. Akron, MBA. CFA. Joined Ohio Edison, 1980, various financial positions, 1980—91; treasurer Ohio Edison (merged with Centerior Energy to form FirstEnergy), 1991—97; v.p. finance FirstEnergy Corp., Akron, Ohio, 1997, v.p., CFO, 1998—2001, sr. v.p., CFO, 2001—. Chmn. Utility Pension Fund Study Group; mem. fin. adv. com. Edison Elec. Inst. Mem. advancement coun. Coll. Bus. Admin. U. Akron, v.p. alumni coun.; chair We. Reserve Girl Scout Coun.; trustee FirstEnergy Found., H.M. Life Opportunity Services; mem. advisory com. for Master of Sci. in Fin. Engring. prog. Kent State U. Mem.: Cleve. Soc. Security Analysts. Office: First Energy Corp 76 S Main St Akron OH 44308-1890

MARSH, ROBERT HARRY, chemicals executive; b. Camden, NJ, Sept. 6, 1946; s. Harry Louis and Margaret Charlotte (Starke) M. BA, BSME, Rutgers U., 1969; MBA in Mgmt. and Fin., Temple U., 1980. Lic. profl. engr., NJ, Pa., Del. From mech. engr. to mech. specialist and project engr. Rohm & Haas Engring., Bristol, Pa., 1967—76; from staff engr. to sr. engring. specialist Hercules, Inc., Wilmington, Del., 1976—80, sr. fin. analyst for corp. strategic planning, 1980—81, sr. bus. analyst bus. group, 1982—83; mgr. bus. analysis Himont, Inc., 1983—86, dir. strategy and planning, 1986—88, dir. bus. mgmt., 1988—91, mng. dir. China, 1991—95, dir. strategy, 1991—95; founder R.H. Marsh & Assoc. Internat. Mgmt., Bethlehem, Pa., 1995—; pres., prin., CEO, chmn. bd. dirs. Internat. Bus. and Mktg. Mgmt., 1996—. Founder, bd. dirs. various cos., 1995—. Contbr. articles to profl. jours. Active Haddonfield (N.J.) Civic Affairs, Bethlehem (Pa.) Civic Affairs, Wesley Meth. Ch., Bethlehem, Pa., 2001—. Mem.: NSPE, ASME (vice chmn. awards com. 1980, membership chmn. 1982, nat. power com. 1977—84), Engrs. Club Phila., Pyramid Club Phila., Beta Gamma Sigma. Home and Office: 225 Flagstone Dr Bethlehem PA 18017 Personal E-mail: rbtmarsh@verizon.net, rbtmarsh@aol.com.

MARSH, ROBERT MORTIMER, sociologist, educator; b. Everett, Mass., Jan. 22, 1931; s. Henry Warren and Ruth (Dunbar) M.; children: Eleanor L., Christopher S.H., Diana E. Student, Boston U., 1948-50; AB, U. Chgo., 1952; MA, Columbia, 1953, PhD, 1959. Fellow Ford Found., Japan, Taiwan, Hong Kong, 1956-58; instr. sociology U. Mich., 1958-61; asst. prof. sociology Cornell U., 1961-65; asso. prof. Duke, 1965-67; mem. faculty Brown U., 1967—, prof. sociology, 1968—, chmn. dept., 1971-75. Manpower personnel and tng. rsch. prof. U.S. Naval Acad., Annapolis, 1987-88; vis. prof. Nat. Tsing Hua U., Taiwan, 1991. Author: The Mandarins: The Circulation of Elites in China, 1961, Comparative Sociology: A Codification of Cross-Societal Analysis, 1967; (with H. Mannari) Modernization and the Japanese Factory, 1976, Organizational Change in Japanese Factories, 1988, The Great Transformation: Social Change in Taipei, Taiwan Since the 1960s, 1996; also articles; assoc. editor Adminstrv. Sci. Quar., 1963-67, Jour. Comparative Family Studies, 1970-74; co-editor: (with J. Michael Armer) Comparative Sociological Research in the 1960s and 1970s. East Asian Inst. summer fellow Chinese Columbia, 1955; Ford Found. and Guggenheim Found. fellow Japan, 1969-70; Japan Soc. Promotion Sci. fellow, 1976, 83; Chiang Ching Kuo Found. and Nat. Sci. Coun. fellow (Taiwan, Republic of China). 1991-93. Mem. Am. Sociol. Assn., Ea. Sociol. Assn., Assn. Asian Studies, Internat. Studies Assn. (exec. com. comparative interdisciplinary studies sect. 1971-76), Japan Human Rels. Assn. (councilor 1970—). Office: Dept Sociology Brown Univ Providence RI 02912-0001

MARSHAK, ALAN HOWARD, electrical engineer, educator; b. Miami Beach, Fla., Mar. 21, 1938; s. Jerome and Yetta (Feiner) M.; children: Jerry Brian; m. Joan Grode Milner, May 25, 1997. BScEE, U. Miami, 1960; MS, La. State U., 1962; PhD, U. Ariz., 1969. Asst. prof. elec. engring. La. State U., Baton Rouge, 1969-73, assoc. prof., 1973-78, prof., 1978—2002, chmn. dept. elec. and computer engring., 1983—2002, prof. emeritus, 2002—. Vis. prof. Electron Device Rsch. Ctr., U. Fla., Gainesville, 1979-80; tech. reviewer NSF, 1976—, panelist, 1993-96; panelist NRC, 1993, 2001, 04; mem. Southeastern Ctr. Elec. Engring. Edn., 1984-2002, life mem., 2002—, chmn., CEO, 1992-2001, trustee, 1994—; spkr. profl. confs. Tech. referee various jours. including Solid-State Electronics, Jour. Applied Physics; editor: Device and Process Modeling, IEEE Trans. Electron Devices, 1991-2001; author: (with D. J. Hamilton and F. A. Lindholm) Principles and Applications of Semiconductor Device Modeling, 1971, Basic Experiments in Electronics: A Laboratory Manual, 1978, also 56 jour. articles and conf. proceedings. NSF grad. trainee, 1967-69; grantee, 1970, 73, 75, 78; named F.H. Coughlin/CLECO prof. of elec. engring., 1993. Fellow IEEE (life); mem. Electron Devices Soc., Sigma Xi, Eta Kappa Nu. Home: 113 Clipper Cove Lafayette LA 70508-7023

MARSHAK, HARRY, plastic surgeon; b. LA, Oct. 1, 1961; s. Herbert and Pearl (Engelson) M. BS, U. Calif., Riverside, 1981; MD, UCLA, 1984. Diplomate Am. Bd. Surgery, Am. Bd. Plastic Surgery. Pvt. practice, Beverly Hills, Calif., 1991—. Fellow ACS (hon.), Internat. Coll. Surgeons; mem. Am. Soc. Plastic and Reconstructive Surgeons, Calif. Soc. Plastic Surgery, Am. Soc. for Aesthetic Plastic Surgery. Republican. Avocation: sports. Office: 120 S Spalding Dr Ste 300 Beverly Hills CA 90212-1841 Office Phone: 310-657-7600.

MARSHAK, MARVIN LLOYD, physicist, researcher; b. Mar. 11, 1946; s. Kalman and Goldie (Hait) M.; m. Anita Sue Kolman, Sept. 24, 1972; children: Rachel Kolman, Adam Kolman. AB in Physics, Cornell U., 1967; MS in Physics, U. Mich., PhD in Physics, 1970. Rsch. assoc. U. Minn., Mpls., 1970-74, from asst. prof. to assoc. prof., 1974-83, prof. physics, 1983-96, dir. grad. studies in physics, 1983-86, prin. investigator high energy physics, 1982-86, head Sch. Physics and Astronomy, 1986-96, sr. v.p. for acad. affairs, 1996-97, Morse-Alumni disting. tchg. prof. physics, 1996—, Inst. of Tech. prof., 2004—, dir. residential coll., 1997—2005, faculty legis. liason, 1997—2001, chair univ. senate consultative exec. com., 2004—05, dir. undergrad. rsch., 2007—. Contbr. articles to profl. jours. Trustee Children's Theater Co., 1989-94. Fellow: Am. Phys. Soc. Home: 2855 Ottawa Ave S Minneapolis MN 55416-1946 Office Phone: 612-624-1312. Business E-Mail: marshak@umn.edu.

MARSHAK, ROBERT REUBEN, retired dean, medical educator, veterinarian; b. NYC, Feb. 23, 1923; s. David and Edith (Youselovsky) Marshak; m. Ruth Emilie Lyons, Dec. 4, 1948 (div. 1983); children: William Lyons, John Ball, Richard Best; m. Margo Post Marshall, June 25, 1983. Student, U. Wis., 1940—41; DVM, Cornell U., 1945; DVM (hon.), U. Bern, 1968; MA (hon.), U. Pa., 1971. Diplomate Am. Coll. Vet. Internal Medicine (charter). Practice vet. medicine, Springfield, Vt., 1945—56; prof., chmn. dept. medicine Sch. Vet. Medicine, U. Pa., Phila., 1956—58; prof. medicine Grad. Sch. Medicine, 1957—64; chmn. dept. clin. studies Sch. Vet. Medicine, 1958—73; dir. Bovine Leukemia Research Center, 1965—73; dean Sch. Vet. Medicine, 1973—87; co-dir. Center on Interactions Animals and Soc., 1975—79, also mem. grad. group com. in comparative med. scis.; prof. medicine, chief sect. epidemiology and pub. health Sch. Vet. Medicine U. Pa., 1990—93, prof. medicine emeritus, 1993—, dean emeritus, 1987—. Adv. bd. Pa. Dept. Agr., 1973—87; chmn. Gov.'s STudy Group on Horse Racing Industry in Pa., 1979; del. to evaluate vet. med. and rsch. Chinese Ministry Agr.; adv. com. Stroud Water Rsch. Ctr., 1992; adv. coun. Coll. Vet. Medicine, Cornell U., 1993—; animal use and care com. Calif. Inst. Tech., 2003—. Contbr. articles to profl. jours. Sci. adv. bd. Sch. Vet. Medicine The Hebrew U., Jerusalem, 1984—, rev. com., 1997—; trustee Upland Country Day Sch., 1988—91; animal adv. com. City of Phila., 1989—93; pres. rev. com. Koret Sch. Vet. Medicine Hebrew U. Jerusalem, 1997—98; bd. dirs. Humane Soc. U.S., 1978—82, Bide-a-wee Home Assn., 1980—85. With US Army, 1943—44. Recipient Disting. Vet. award, Pa. Vet. Med. Assn., 1984, Barnraiser award, Pa. Farmers Assn., 1987. Fellow: Phila. Coll. Physicians; mem.: Pa. Vet. Med. Assn., Am. Vet. Med. Assn., Nat. Acad. Inst. Medicine (sr.), John Morgan Soc. (pres. 1967—68), Phila. Zool. Soc. (bd. dirs. 1986—87), James A. Baker Inst. for Animal Health (mem. adv. coun. 1977—), Westminster Kennel Club, Phi Zeta, Sigma Xi. Personal E-mail: rmarshak@caltech.edu.

MARSHALL, ALAN GEORGE, chemistry and biochemistry educator; b. Bluffton, Ohio, May 26, 1944; s. Herbert Boyer Marshall and Cecil (Mogil) Rosen; m. Marilyn Gard, June 13, 1965; children: Gwendolyn Scott, Brian George. BA in Chemistry with honors, Northwestern U., 1965; PhD in Phys. Chemistry, Stanford U., 1970. Instr. II U. B.C., Vancouver, Can., 1969-71, asst. prof., 1971-76, assoc. prof., 1976-80; prof. chemistry and biochemistry, dir. Chem. Instrument Ctr. Ohio State U., Columbus, 1980—93; prof. chemistry and biochemistry Fla. State U., Tallahassee, 1993—, disting. rsch. prof., 1999, Kasha prof., 2000—06, Robert O. Lawton prof., 2006—. Dir. Ion Cyclotron Resonance Program Nat. High Magnetic Field Lab., 1993. Author: Biophysical Chemistry, 1978, Fourier Transforms in NMR, Optical and Mass Spectroscopy, 1990; editor: Nat. High Magnetic Field Lab. ICR/ION Trap newsletter, 1986—97, Rapid Comm. in Mass Spectrometry, 1998—2005; mem. editl. bd. Rapid Comm. in Mass Spectrometry, 2005—; mem. editl. adv. bd.: Analytical Chemistry, 1990—92, mem. editl. bd.: Internat. Jour. Mass Ion Procs., 1987—, Mass Spectrometry Rev., 1994—, Jour. Magnetic Resonance, 1996—2000, Chemometrics and Intelligent Lab. Systems, 1986—89, Ency. of Mass Spectrometry, 2000—, mem. internat. editl adv. bd.: ACS Ency. of Chem. Instrumentation, 1992—95; mem. internat. editl adv. bd. Ann. Review Analytical Chemistry, 2009—; contbr. 485 articles to profl. jours. Recipient Disting. Scholar award, Ohio State U., 1988, award in analytical chemistry, Ea. Analytical Symposium, 1991, Maurice F. Hasler award, Spectroscopy Soc. Pitts., 1997, Two-Yr. Creativity award, NSF, 1997, gold medal, N.Y. Soc. Applied Spectroscopy, 1998, Pitts. Spectroscopy award, Spectroscopy Soc. Pitts., 2002; grad. fellow, NSF, 1965—69, Alfred P. Sloan rsch. fellow, 1976. Fellow: AAAS, Am. Inst. Chemists (Chem. Pioneer award 2007), Soc. Applied Spectroscopy, Am. Phys. Soc., Am. Chem. Soc. (Akron Sect. award 1988, award in chem. instrumentation 1990, Frank H. Field and Joe L. Franklin award in mass spectrometry 1995, award in analytical chemistry 2002, Herty medal (Ga. sect.) 2003, Fla. sect. award 2003, So. Chemist award (Memphis sect.) 2004, Ralph Helen Oesper award 2008); mem.: Eni (New Frontiers in Hydrocarbons award 2009), Soc. Applied Spectroscopy (hon.; chmn. local sect. 1990—93), Eastern Analytical Symphony (award Mass Spectrometry 2009), Am. Soc. Mass Spectroscopy (bd. dirs. 1991—93, 2003—, pres. 2004—06, mem. jour. editl. bd. 1987—89, 1999—2004, Disting. Contbn. award 1999), Internat. Mass Spectrum Soc. (Thomson medal 2000). Office: Fla State U Nat High Magnetic Field Lab 1800 E Paul Dirac Dr Tallahassee FL 32310-4005 Office Phone: 850-644-0529. Business E-Mail: marshall@magnet.fsu.edu.

MARSHALL, ALISON BUELL, lawyer; b. Poughkeepsie, NY, Aug. 6, 1959; d. Howard Drake and Natalie (Junemann) Marshall; m. Allen Lee Schirm, July 27, 1985; 2 children: Karen Anne, Janet Lynn. AB, Princeton U., NJ, 1981; JD, U. Pa., 1984. Bar: Pa. 1984, U.S. Dist. Ct. (ea. dist.) Pa. 1986, Mich. 1986, U.S. Ct. Appeals (2d cir.) 1988, (6th cir.) 1989, D.C. 1990. Law clk. to judge U.S. Dist. Ct. (ea. dist.) Pa., Phila., 1984-86; assoc. Miller, Canfield, Paddock & Stone, Detroit, 1986-91, ptnr. Washington, 1991—98, Jones Day, 1998—. Chair diversity task force Jones Day, Washington, 2003—08. mem., 2008—. Editl. adv. bd. mem.: Employee Rels. Law Jour., 2000—. Mem. ABA (labor and employment law sect., EEO com.), Mich. Bar Assn., Pa. Bar Assn., D.C. Bar Assn., Nat. Assn. for Perinatal Addiction Rsch. and Edn. (chair bd. dirs. 1990-95). Democrat. Home: 6500 Monique Ct Mc Lean VA 22101-1648 Office: Jones Day 51 Louisiana Ave NW Washington DC 20001-2105 Office Phone: 202-879-7611. Fax: 202-626-1700. Business E-Mail: abmarshall@jonesday.com.

MARSHALL, ALLEN WRIGHT, III, communications executive, financial consultant; b. Griffin, Ga., Dec. 4, 1941; s. Allen Wright and Evelyn Louise (Halliburton) Marshall; m. Monica Hodgins McKellar; 1 child, Allen Wright IV. BA in Journalism, U. Ga., 1964; diploma, Elkins Inst. Radio, Atlanta, 1964; postgrad., Ga. State U., 1968, MBA, 1988; cert., Coll. Fin. Planning, Denver, 1991. 1st class radio telephone lic. FCC; cert. fin. planner. Pres. Sta. WKEU-AM-FM, Griffin, 1954-86;

co-founder, v.p. Griffin Cable TV, 1971-74; co-founder, pres. Custom Svcs. Inc. (now Marshall Plans Inc.), Griffin, 1974—; co-founder, v.p. Cobbwells Marshall Inc., Griffin, 1982-87, Page One, Griffin, 1983-87; co-founder, pres. Toolware Inc., Griffin, 1993-97; co-founder, sec./treas. Magnolia Broadcasting Inc., laGrange, Ga., 1993-95; founder, mng. mem. Spalding Speculators LLC, Griffin, 1995—, Carpediem Ventures, LLC, Griffin, 2005—, Renaissance Griffin LLC, 2006. Bd. dirs. Madame's Fine Dining LLC, Griffin, 2008, Face Internat. Corp., Norfolk, Va.; spkr. in field. Author radio progrms, editorials (Ga. AP award 1969-84); also articles. Bd. dirs. Goals for Griffin and Spalding Counties INc., 1981-92, pres. 1991; mem. adv. com. Griffin Vocat.-Tech. Sch., 1982-87; bd. dirs. Jr. Achievement, Griffin, 1977-87; chmn. Griffin-Spalding Indsl. Authority, 1984; mem. Gov.'s Adv. Com. on Area Planning and Devel. Commns., 1971-72, Downtown Devel. Authority, 2009-; bd. dirs. McIntosh Trail Area Planning and Devel. Commn., Ga., 1971-73; founding trustee, vice chair, treas. St. George's Episc. Sch., 1995-2001; chair, Main St. Adv. Bd., 2000-; treas., trustee Nat. Episc. Radio/TV Found., 1986-93. Sgt. U.S. Army, 1966-68. Named Man of Yr., Exch. Club of Griffin, 1984. Mem. Ga. Assn. Broadcasters 9bd. dirs. 1970-74, Radio Sta. of Yr. 1977), Griffin Area C. of C. (bd. dirs. 1980, chmn. indsl. com. 1980, 81), C.C. (charter mem. 1966), Rotary (pres. 1976-77). Avocations: photography, architecture. Home and Office: 1800 Maple Dr Griffin GA 30224-7405

MARSHALL, ANNE BRADLEY, lawyer; b. Hartford, Conn., May 29, 1952; d. George A. and Anne Elizabeth (Bradley) M.; m. Bruce Rea Elworthy, Aug. 25, 1979. BA, Wellesley Coll., 1974; JD, Yale U., 1977. Bar: Calif. 1980, Tex. 1977, Wyo 1994, Mt. 1994; Calif. Bd. Legal Specialization; cert. tax specialist; cert. estate planning, trust and probate law specialist, legal socialist, 2005. Assoc. Bracewell and Patterson, Houston, 1977-79; assoc. Pettit and Martin, San Francisco, 1981-82, Bronson, Bronson & McKinnon, San Francisco, 1982-83; ptnr. Elworthy and Marshall Profl. Corp., Carmel, Calif., 1983-86, Tahoe City, Calif., 1987—97, Elworthy & marshall Proth Corp., Sheridon, 1998-; lectr. World Trade Inst., N.Y.C., 1978-80, Am. Mgmt. Assn., 1979, Calif. Continuing Edn. of Bar, Berkeley, 1982, Trust and Tax Forum, 1992, Trust and Probate Forum, 1994. Durant scholar, Wellesley Coll., 1974, Trustee scholar, 1974, Named one of Best Lawyers Bay Area, San Francisco, 2005. Mem. State Bar Tex., State Bar Mt., Wyo. State Bar, State Bar Calif., Soc. Trust & Estate Practioners London, CPE Forum Ctrl. Coast(bd. dirs.),Greater Carmel Valley C. of C. (past bd. dirs.), Elizabethan (New Haven) Club, Yale Club (past bd. dirs. Monterey), Monterey Bay Wellesley Club(past pres.), Phi Beta Kappa. Home: 1001 Pioneer Rd Sheridan WY 82801-3435 Office Phone: 307-674-0101. Business E-Mail: emlaw@empclaw.com.

MARSHALL, BRIAN LAURENCE, federal official; b. Kingston-on-Thames, Eng., Apr. 6, 1941; arrived in US, 1949, naturalized, 1955; s. John and Marguerite Elizabeth (Sandele) Marshall. BA in European History, U. N.C., 1963; MS in Internat. Mgmt., Thunderbird Grad. Sch. Internat. Mgmt., Glendale, Ariz., 1973. Commd. 2d lt. USAF, 1964, advanced through grades to capt., 1972; instr. Armed Forces Air Intelligence Tng. Ctr., Denver, 1965-68; intelligence analyst Task Force Alpha, Nakhon Phanom, Thailand, 1968-69; intelligence systems analyst Hdqs. Tactical Air Command, Langley AFB, Va., 1969-72, resigned, 1972; sr. analyst Computer Scis. Corp., Falls Church, Va., 1974-87; dir. U.S. membership and pubs. U.S.-Mexico C. of C., Washington, 1987-91; v.p. pub. affairs, bd. dirs. N.Am. Free Trade Assn., Washington, 1991-96; v.p., bd. dirs. N.Am. Trade and Investment Group, Washington, 1991-97; with U.S. Dept. State, 2005—; dept. state adviser Govt. of Iraq, US Embassy, Baghdad, 2005—, dept. state sr. advisor, elections in Kirkuk, Iraq, 2008—. Contract team leader strategic planning studies and analyses U.S. Dept. Def., Joint Chiefs Staff, Washington, 1976—82; regional oper. supr. elections in Bosnia Orgn. Security and Coop. in Europe (OSCE), 1997, election supr., Bosnia and Kosovo, 1997—98, Bosnia and Kosovo, 2000; internat. trade cons., 1998—2005; long and short term observer, Belarus, 2001, Belarus, 04, Azerbaijan, 03, Ukraine, 04. Contbr. articles to booklets and newsletters. Bd. dirs. Columbia Plz. Tenants Assn., Washington, 1981—84; vol. Republican Nat. Com., 1994, Pres. Ford Com., Washington, 1976. Mem.: VFW (chaplain Post 5633 2001—05), Washington Mgmt. and Bus. Assn. (vice chmn. 1981—83, treas. 1987—91), Thunderbird Alumni Assn. (pres. Washington chpt. 1980—87, Achievement award 1987), Fgn. Policy Assn. (team leader Great Decisions discussion series 1986—97), World Affairs Coun., Assn. Former Intelligence Officers, Has House Harriers. Republican. Roman Catholic. Avocations: jogging, travel, discussion groups, reading. Home: 5304 Albemarle St Bethesda MD 20816-1827 Mailing: Provincial Reconstruction Team FOB Hammer APO AE 09308 Personal E-mail: brnmarsh@hotmail.com. Business E-Mail: marshallbl@state.gov.

MARSHALL, BRIDGET, literature and language professor; PhD, U. Mass., Amherst, 2004. Asst. prof. U. of Mass., Lowell, Lowell, Mass., 2005—. Office: Univ Mass Lowell English Dept 61 Wilder St Lowell MA 01854

MARSHALL, BRYAN WILLIAM, educator; PhD, Mich. State U., East Lansing. Prof. Miami U., Oxford, Ohio, 1994—. Office: Miami Univ 214 Harrison Hall Oxford OH 45056-2807 Office Fax: 513-529-1709. Business E-Mail: marshabw@muohio.edu.

MARSHALL, CAPRICIA PENAVIC, federal official; b. Cleve., 1964; d. Frank and Mary Penavic; m. Robert Marshall; 1 child, Cole. BA in Polit. Sci. & Internat. Studies, Purdue U., West Lafayette, Ind., 1986; student, U. Madrid; JD, Case Western Res. U. Sch. Law, Cleve., 1990. Spl. asst. to Hillary Clinton Bill Clinton Presdl. campaign, 1992; spl. asst. to First Lady Hillary Clinton The White House, 1993—97, dep. asst. to Pres., social sec., 1997—2001; cons., 2001—06; sr. advisor Hillary Clinton Presdl. Campaign, 2006—08; exec. dir. HillPAC, 2008—09; chief of protocol US Dept. State, 2009—. Office: Office of Chief of Protocol 2201 C St NW Rm 1238 Washington DC 20520*

MARSHALL, CHARLES NOBLE, rail transportation executive; b. Phila., Feb. 18, 1942; s. Donnell and Cornelia Lansdale (Brooke) M.; m. Ann Shaw Donovan, Jan. 12, 1971; children— Elizabeth, Caroline, Cornelia, Edward BS in Engring., Princeton U., 1963; JD, U. Mich., 1967. Bar: Md. 1967, D.C. 1975, Pa. 1978. Atty. Balt. & Ohio R.R., Balt. and Cleve., 1967-73; gen. atty. So. Ry., Washington, 1973-78; gen. counsel commerce Conrail, Phila., 1978-83, v.p. mktg., 1983-85, sr. v.p. mktg. and sales, 1985-89, sr. v.p. devel., 1989-95; pres., COO Genesee & Wyoming Inc., 1997—2005, vice chmn., 2005—06; sr. v.p. industry affairs Farmrail Sys., Inc., 2006—. Bd. dirs. Rails to Trails Conservancy.

MARSHALL, CINDY LOU, science and social studies educator; b. Elkhart, Ind., Sept. 7, 1956; d. James Allen (Stepfather) and Georgiane Pearl Mitchell; m. Thomas James Marshall, July 16, 1977; children: Jennifer Lillian Emerson, Christy Leigh, Lori Anne. A in Animal Health, Abraham Baldwin Agrl. Coll., Tifton, Ga., 1976; B in Mid. Sch. Edn., Ga. Southwestern, Americus, 1991, M in Edn., 1992. Gifted cert. Ga. Southwestern U., 1999. Animal health technician Cutler Ridge Vet. Clinic, Miami, 1972—79; tchr. remedial math grade 9-12 Terrell HS, Dawson, Ga., 1991—92; tchr. sci. grade 7 Lee County Mid. Sch., Leesburg, Ga., 1992—2003; tchr. sci./social studies grade 8 Merry Acres Mid. Sch., Albany, Ga., 2003—04; tchr. sci./social studies grade 6 Robert Cross Mid. Magnet Sch., Albany, 2004—. Sci. dept. chairperson Lee County Mid. Sch., 1991—2003, sci. fair organizer, 1992—98, club advisor, 1992—94, sci. fair advisor (regional/state/internat.), 1992—98, sci. olympiad coach, 1995—2000, sci. club advisor, 1995—2000; sci. olympiad coach Robert Cross Mid. Magnet Sch., 2004—, beta club advisor, 2004—, chairperson Honors Day, 2005—; organizer sci. curriculum grade 6 Dougherty County Sch. Sys., Albany, 2005—07. Vol. Dawson Manor Nursing Home, Ga., 1987—91; Secret Santa for foster children First Bapt. Ch., Dawson, 1987—92, tchr. Bible sch., 1988—2001, tchr. Sunday sch., 1995—99, tchr. Girls in Action, 1992—98, dir. summer youth camp, 1997—2000. Named Tchr. of Yr., Lee County Mid. Sch., 2001—02; named to Wall of Fame, 2003. Mem.: Delta Kappa Gamma (life; 2d v.p. 2002—03, corr. sec. 2006). Baptist. Office: Robert Cross Middle Magnet Sch 324 Lockett Station Rd Albany GA 31721-4005 Business E-Mail: cindy.marshall@dougherty.k12.ga.us.

MARSHALL, DEBRA LYNN, secondary school educator; b. Charleston, W.Va., July 7, 1956; d. James L. Marshall and Lena B. Bailey. BA in English cum laude, Ohio State U., Columbus, 1998; MEd in English, Ohio State U., 1999. Tchr. H.S. English Piqua (Ohio) City Sch., 1999—2003, Moreno Valley (Calif.) Unified Schs., 2003—. Adj. faculty Edison C.C., Piqua, 2001—03; coord. Ohio Writing Project, Piqua, 2000—02. Author: (short stories) Super Boy, 2003 (Hon. Mention award Sinclair C.C., 2003). Mem. pub. rels. team Spring Arts Show The Piqua (Ohio) Arts Coun., 2003. Mem.: NEA, Nat. Coun. Tchrs. English, Calif. Assn. Tchrs. English, Calif. Tchrs. Assn. Avocations: dog training, painting, cello. Office: CanyonSprings High School 23100 Cougar Canyon Dr Moreno Valley CA 92557 Office Phone: 951-571-4760. Personal E-mail: marshalld4@adelphia.net, marshalld4@roadrrunner.com.

MARSHALL, DONALD GLENN, English language and literature educator; b. Long Beach, Calif., Sept. 9, 1943; s. Albert Louis and Margaret Corinne (Morrison) M.; m. Kathleen Bonann, June 21, 1975; children: Stephanie Deborah, Zachary Louis AB summa cum laude, Harvard U., 1965; MPhil, Yale U., 1969, PhD, 1971. Asst. prof. English UCLA, 1969-75; from assoc. prof. to prof. English U. Iowa, Iowa City, 1975-90; honors dir. U. Iowa Coll Liberal Arts, 1981-85; prof. English dept. U. Ill., Chgo., 1990—2003, head dept., 1990—2000; prof. Great Books Pepperdine U., Malibu, Calif., 2003—. Editor: Philosophy as Literature/Literature as Philosophy, 1986, The Force of Tradition: Response and Resistance in Literature, Religion, and Cultural Studies, 2005; compiler: Contemporary Critical Theory: A Selective Bibliography, 1993; translator: (with Joel Weinsheimer) Truth and Method by Hans-Georg Gadamer, 1989; contbr. articles and revs. to profl. jours. Recipient Bell prize Harvard U., 1965, Webster prize Yale U., 1967; NEH Younger Humanist fellow, 1973-74; grantee UCLA, U. Iowa, Howard A. White award, Pepperdine U., 2008. Mem.: MLA, Ill. Humanities Coun. (bd. dirs. 1994—2000, Chgo. Humanities Festival bd. dir. 1997—2003), The Poetry Found. (trustee 1996—, pres. 1998—2000), Conf. Christianity and Lit. (bd. dirs. 2000—03). Democrat. Roman Catholic. Office: Pepperdine U Divsn Humanities and Tchr Edn 24255 Pacific Coast Hwy Malibu CA 90263 Office Phone: 310-506-7654. Business E-Mail: Donald.Marshall@pepperdine.edu.

MARSHALL, DOUGLAS WILLIAM, health research administrator, educator; b. Indpls., July 1, 1943; s. William Pryor and Virginia (Guthrie) M.; m. Heidi Christina Amenda, May 30, 1985; 1 child, W. Parker. BA, Denison U., Granville, Ohio, 1965; AM, U. Mich., 1967, PhD, 1976. Western field mgr. U. Mich. Alumni Assn., San Francisco, 1967-69; assoc. curator W.L. Clements Libr. Am. History U. Mich., Ann Arbor, 1970-82; project dir. Campbell-Ewald Co., Warren, Mich., 1982-83; sr. account exec. N.W. Ayer, Inc., Detroit, 1984; mgr. strategic planning GM, Detroit, 1985-91; program mgr. GM Internat., Detroit, 1991-96; CEO Onkoservices, Detroit, 1996-97; v.p. new bus. devel. Innovative Solutions in Healthcare, Detroit, 1997-99; prin. Blitz and Assoc. LLC, 2000—; v.p. bus. devel. Idetix Inc., 2005—06; dir. automotive divsn. Al-Ahel Co., 2006—08; ptnr. HealthCURE Inc., 2008—, DeBruicker & Assoc., 2008—. Adj. assoc. prof. radiation oncology Sch. Medicine, Wayne State U., Detroit, 1996-2000; coord. program in history of discovery U. Mich., Ann Arbor, 1973-81. Co-author: (with H.H. Peckham) Campaigns of the American Revolution: An Atlas Manuscript Maps, 1976; exec. editor Terrae Incognitae: Annals of the Soc. for the History of Discoveries, 1975-82; editor: Research Catalog of Maps of America to 1860, 4 vols., 1972; writer, narrator: (ednl. TV series) Maps: Horizons to Knowledge, 1981. Dir. Gt. Lakes region Am. Cancer Soc. Found., 1996-05; mem. dean's adv. bd. Rackham Grad. Sch., U. Mich., 1999-06; mem. S.E. Mich. strategic planning bd. United Found., Detroit, 1982-83; trustee City of Grosse Pointe Found., 2004-08; mem. recruiting adv. bd. USN, Great Lakes, 2007- Rsch. fellow Nat. Geog. Soc., 1977; recipient Bicentennial award Bicentennial Commn., State of Mich., 1974; Fulbright lectr. U.S. Fulbright Commn., Helsinki U., 1980-81; William Andrews Clark postdoctoral fellow UCLA, 1979. Mem. Mich. Map Soc. (pres. 1984-85), Soc. for the History of Discoveries (coun. 1979-81), Bohemian Club Calif. Episcopalian. Achievements include development of circular array ultrasound scanner for early breast cancer detection; commercialization trials for a process to inhibit the spread of nosocomial infection. Home: 545 University Pl Grosse Pointe MI 48230-1639 Home (Summer): PO Box 152 7090 Windemere Harbor Springs MI 49740 Personal E-mail: dwmarshall652003@yahoo.com.

MARSHALL, ELAINE FOLK, Secretary of State, NC; b. Lineboro, Md., Nov. 18, 1945; d. Donald and Pauline Folk; m. Bill Holdford; 5 stepchildren. BS in Textiles and Clothing, U. Md., 1968; JD, Campbell U., 1981, LLD (hon.), 2008; D (hon.), Meredith Coll., 2004, Lees McRae Coll., 2004. Bar: N.C., U.S. Dist. Ct. (ea. and mid. dists.), U.S. Ct. Appeals (4th cir.), U.S. Supreme Ct. Tchr., 1968—75; owner retail bus., 1968-79; assoc. Bain Law Firm, Lillington, NC, 1981-84; ptnr. Bain & Marshall, Lillington, 1985-92, Marshall & Marshall, Lillington, 1993-96; mem. N.C. State Senate from 15th dist., 1993—94; sec. state State of N.C., Raleigh, 1997—. Legal advisor Bus. and Profl. Women, N.C., 1982-90; mem., N.C. Capital Planning Commn., 1993-94, 1997-, N.C. Cts. Commn., 1993-94, bd. mem. Nat. Electronic Commerce Coord. Coun., 2001-03, 2005—, v.p., 2005-06, pres., 2007, bd. mem. Nat. Assn. Secretaries of State, 2001-04. Bd. dirs. Harnett County United Way, 1987-97, N.C. 4-H Devel. Fund, Inc., 1990—, N.C. Rural Econ. Devel. Fund, 1993-95, N.C. Bd. Econ. Devel., 1993-94, 97—, N.C. Ctr. Pub. Policy Rsch., 1994-99, N.C. Justice Acad. Found., 1994-98; mem. Divine St. United Meth. Ch.; founding chmn., hon. chmn. Harnett HelpNet Children, 1992—; trustee Meredith Coll., 1997-2002. Recipient N.C. Friends Ext. award, 1992, Spl. Achievement award, N.C. Acad. Trial Lawyers, 2000, Alumni of Yr. award, N.C. 4-H Found., Lifetime Achievement award, 2003, Best of Breed, In the Arena awards, Ctr. Digital Govt., 2002, Top 25 award, Govt. Tech. Mag., 2003, Atty. of Yr. award, N.C. Assn. Women Attorneys, 2004, Women in Bus. award RBC Centura Bank and Triangle Bus. Jour., 2005, Hon. Gold Record award Recording Industry Am., 2005, U.L. Lab. award, 2005, Get Real award Internat. Anti Counterfeit Coalition, 2005, US C. of C. Anti-Counterfeiting award, 2007. ETA State Founders award, 2007, Professionalism award Campbell U. Sch. Law, 2008. Fellow N.C. Inst. Polit. Leadership (bd. dirs. 1996-2006); mem. Women's Forum N.C., Gamma Sigma Delta, Delta Kappa Gamma. Democrat. Office: 2 S Salisbury St Raleigh NC 27601 Office Phone: 919-807-2005. Business E-Mail: emarshall@sosnc.com.

MARSHALL, ELLEN RUTH, lawyer; b. NYC, Apr. 23, 1949; d. Louis and Faith (Gladstone) M. AB, Yale U., 1971; JD, Harvard U., 1974. Bar: Calif. 1975, D.C. 1981, N.Y. 1989. Assoc. McKenna & Fitting, LA, 1975-80; ptnr. McKenna, Conner & Cuneo, LA and Orange County, Calif., 1980-88, Morrison & Foerster, LLP, Orange County, 1988—2003, Manatt, Phelps & Phillips LLP, Orange County, 2003—. Mem. ABA (bus. law sect., mem. savs. inst. com., mem. asset securitization com., tax sect., mem. employee benefits com.), Orange County Bar Assn., Center Club (Costa Mesa, Calif.), Yale Club (N.Y.C.). Office: Manatt Phelps & Phillips LLP 695 Town Ctr Dr Costa Mesa CA 92626

MARSHALL, FRANCIS JOSEPH, aerospace engineer; b. NYC, Sept. 5, 1923; s. Francis Joseph and Mary Gertrude (Leary) M.; m. Joan Eager, June 14, 1952; children— Peter, Colin, Stephen, Dana. BS in Mech. Engring, CCNY, 1948; MS, Rensselaer Poly. Inst., 1950; Dr. Eng. Sci., N.Y. U., 1955. Engr. Western Union Co., NYC, 1948, Gen. Electric Co., Schenectady, 1948-50; engr. Wright-Aero Corp., Woodridge, NJ, 1950-52; group leader Lab. for Applied Scis., U. Chgo., 1955-60; instr. Ill. Inst. Tech., 1957-59; prof. Sch. Aeros. and Astronautics, Purdue U., West Lafayette, Ind., 1960—. Engr. U.S. Naval Underseas Warfare Center, Pasadena, Calif., 1966-68; faculty fellow NASA-Langley, 1969-70; vis. prof. Inst. Tech. Mara-Midwest Univs. Consortium for Internat. Activities, Malayasia, 1989. Contbr. articles to profl. jours. Served with U.S. Army, 1943-46. Decorated Combat Inf. badge.; Rsch. grantee NASA, 1970-76; Fulbright scholar, Turkey, 1988-89. Asso. fellow AIAA; mem. Am. Soc. Engring. Edn., AAUP. Office: Sch Aeros and Astronautics Purdue U West Lafayette IN 47907 Home: Marshall 4405 Bellvue Ave Austin TX 78756-3418 Home Phone: 512-366-5695.

MARSHALL, FRANK W., film producer, director; b. LA, Sept. 13, 1946; m. Kathleen Kennedy. Student, UCLA. Location mgr.: The Last Picture Show, 1971, What's Up Doc?, 1972; assoc. prodr.: Paper Moon, 1973, Daisy Miller, 1974, At Long Last Love, 1975. Nickelodeon, 1976, The Driver, 1978; line prodr.: Orson Welles' The Other Side of the Wind (unreleased), Marin Scorsese's The Last Waltz, 1977; prodr.: (films) Raiders of the Lost Ark, 1981 (Academy award nomination for best picture 1981), Noises Off, 1992; (with Steven Spielberg) Poltergeist, 1982; (with Spielberg, Quincy Jones, and Kathleen Kennedy) The Color Purple, 1985 (Academy award nomination for best picture 1985), (with Kathleen Kennedy and Kane Startz) Indian in a Cupboard, 1995; (with Spielberg and Kennedy) Empire of the Sun, 1987, Always, 1989; (with Robert Watts) Who Framed Roger Rabbit, 1988; (with Kennedy and Gerald R. Molen) Hook, 1991; (with Kennedy) Milk Money, 1994, The Sixth Sense, 1999, Snow Falling on Cedars, 1999, A Map of the World, 1999, Signs, 2002, The Young Black Stallion, 2003, The Bourne Supremacy, 2004, Roving Mars, 2006; exec. prodr.: (films) The Warriors, 1979, Twilight Zone-The Movie, 1983; (with George Lucas) Indiana Jones and the Temple of Doom, 1984; (with Kennedy and Spielberg) Gremlins, 1984, The Goonies, 1985, Back to the Future, 1985, Young Sherlock Holmes, 1985, *batteries not included, 1987, Dad, 1989, Back to the Future Part II, 1989, Gremlins 2: The New Batch, 1990, Back to the Future Part III, 1990, Joe Versus the Volcano, 1990, Cape Fear, 1991, We're Back! A Dinosaur's Story, 1993; (with Kennedy) Fandango, 1985; (with Kennedy, Spielberg, and David Kirschner) An American Tail, 1986; (with Kennedy and Art Levinson) The Money Pit, 1986; (with Kennedy, Spielberg, Peter Guber, and Jon Peters) Innerspace, 1987; (with Kennedy, Lucas, and Spielberg) The Land Before Time, 1988; (with Kennedy and Lucas) Indiana Jones and the Last Crusade, 1989; (with Kennedy and Kirschner) An American Tail: Fievel Goes West, 1991; (with Chris Meledandri) Swing Kids, 1993; (with Kennedy and Molen) A Far Off Place, 1993, Swing Kids, 1993, Congo, 1995, The Sports Pages, 2001, The Bourne Identity, 2002, Mr. 3000, 2004; exec. prodr. (with Spielberg, Robert W. Cort, and Ted Field), dir.: Arachnophobia, 1990; dir.: Alive, 1993, Congo, 1995, Eight Below, 2006; exec. producer: TV Roger Rabbit and the Secret of Toontown; prodr., dir. TV Johnny Bago. Recipient David O. Selznick Achievement award in Theatrical Motion Pictures, Producers Guild Am., 2008.

MARSHALL, FREDDIE RAY, former United States Secretary of Labor; b. Oak Grove, La., Aug. 22, 1928; Grad., La. State U.; PhD in Econs., U. Calif., Berkeley. Prof. La. State U., U. Ky., U. Tex., Austin, now prof. emeritus, Audre and Bernard Rapoport centennial chair economics & pub. affairs; sec. US Dept. Labor, 1977—81; co-founder Econ. Policy Inst., 1986. Author: Thinking for a Living: Education and the Wealth of Nations, 1992; editor: Back to Shared Prosperity: The Growing Inequality of Wealth and Income in America, 1999. Fulbright Scholar.

MARSHALL, FREDERICK J., neurologist, educator; BA in Psychology, Swarthmore Coll., 1983; MD, Harvard Med. Sch., 1989. Fellow Brigham & Women's Hosp. Harvard Med. Sch., 1986; resident Harvard-Longwood Neurological Training Program; assoc. prof. dept. neurology U. Rochester Med. Ctr., 1997—. Mem.: Nat. Alzheimer's Assn., Huntington Disease Soc. America (Leadership award 2000), Alpha Omega Alpha, Sigma Xi, Phi Beta Kappa. Office: 919 Westfall Rd Bldg C Ste 220 Rochester NY 14618 Office Fax: 585-760-6236.*

MARSHALL, GAILEN DAUGHERTY, JR., allergist, educator; b. Houston, Sept. 9, 1950; s. Gailen D. and Evelyn C. (Gresham) M.; m. Elizabeth M. Marek, Nov. 5, 1978; children: Sarah Elizabeth, Jonathan David, Rebecca Marie. BS, U. Houston, 1972; MS, Tex. A&M U., 1975; PhD, U. Tex., 1979, MD, 1984. Rsch. sci. U. Tex., Galveston, 1981-84; rsch. fellow U. Iowa, Iowa City, 1985-86; lab. dir. Biotherapeutics Inc., Memphis, 1986-88; chief med. resident Bapt. Meml. Hosp., Memphis, 1988-89; assoc. dir. Rsch. for Health Inc., Houston, 1989-90; dir. divsn. allergy and immunology U. Tex., Houston, 1990—2004, clin. asst. prof. medicine, 1990-91, asst. prof. medicine, 1991—98, assoc. prof. medicine and pathology, 1998—2003, prof., 2003—04; vice chair medicine, dir. divsn. clin. immunology and allergy U. Miss. Med. Ctr., Jackson, Miss., 2004—, prof. medicine and pediatrics. Mem. sci. adv. com. Carrington Labs., Dallas, 1992-94; mem. Merck Rhinitis Adv. Bd., 2002-05, Genentech/Novartis Adv. Bd., 2003—. Mem. editl. bd. Molecular Biotherapy, 1992-93, Cancer Biotherapy, 1994-96, Allergy Procs., 1994-2003, Annals Allergy, Asthma and Immunology, 1995-99, Jour. Interferon Cytokin Rsch., 1999-2005, Clin. Immunology, 2001-05, Jour. Clin. Immunology, 2002-05, Cellular Molecular Allergy, 2003-05; editor-in-chief Annals of Allergy, Asthma and Immunology, 2006—; contbr. articles to profl. jours. Judge Greater Houston Sci. Fair, 1992—; adv. bd. Merck Rhinitis, 2002-04, Grenentech Worch's, 2003-05. Fellow ACP, Am. Coll. Allergy and Immunology, Am. Acad. Allergy-Immunology (chair com.); mem. Tex. Allergy-Immunology Soc. (chair com., bd. dirs. 1999-2002), Greater Houston Allergy Soc. Republican.

Baptists. Avocations: classical music, fishing. Office: U Miss Med Ctr 2500 N State St Jackson MS 39216 Home Phone: 601-899-1793; Office Phone: 601-815-5527. Business E-Mail: gmarshall@medicine.umsmed.edu.

MARSHALL, GARRY K. (GARRY KENT MARSCIARELLI), film producer, director, writer; b. NYC, Nov. 13, 1934; m. Barbara Marshall, Mar. 1963; children: Lori, Kathleen, Scott. BS, Northwestern U. Writer Jack Paar Show, Joey Bishop Show, Danny Thomas Show; writer (TV series) Make Room For Daddy, 1953, The Dick Van Dyke Show, 1961, The Lucy Show, 1962, Gomer Pyle, USMC, 1964, I Spy, 1965, Barefoot in the Park, 1970, Love, American Style, 1969; writer (TV films) Sheriff Who, 1967 (also prodr.), The Murdocks and the McClays, 1970; writer, creator, prodr. (TV series) Hey Landlord, 1966; writer, creator (TV film) Wednesday Night Out, 1972; dir., exec. prodr. (TV series) The Odd Couple, 1970; creator, dir., prodr. Evil Roy Slade, 1972; creator, writer, exec. prodr., dir. Happy Days, 1974, Laverne and Shirley, 1976 (co-creator), Mork and Mindy, 1978; writer, prodr.(films) How Sweet It Is, 1968, The Grasshopper, 1970; screenwriter, dir. (films) Flamingo Kid, 1984, The Other Sister, 1999; dir. (films) Young Doctors in Love, 1982 (also exec. prodr.), Nothing in Common, 1987 (also prodr.), The Lottery, 1987, Overboard, 1987, Beaches, 1988, Pretty Woman, 1990, Frankie & Johnny, 1991 (also prodr.), Exit to Eden, 1994 (also prodr.), Dear God, 1996, Runaway Bride, 1999, The Princess Diaries, 2001, Raising Helen, 2004, The Princess Diaries 2:Royal Engagement, 2004, Georgia Rule, 2007; dir. (TV series) Me and the Chimp, 1972 (also creator, exec. prodr.), Blansky's Beauties, 1977 (also prodr.), Herndon, 1983 (also exec. prodr.), Murphy Brown, 1988; creator, dir., exec. prodr. (TV films) Dominic's Dream, 1974; actor (film) The Phony American, 1961, Maryjane, 1968, Psych-Out, 1968, Grand Theft Auto, 1977, Lost In America, 1985, Jumpin' Jack Flash, 1986, Secret Agent OO Soul, 1990, Soapdish, 1991, A League of Their Own, 1992, Statistically Speaking, 1995, With Friends Like These, 1998, Never Been Kissed, 1999, This Space Between Us, 2000, It's a Shame About Ray, 2000, Can't Be Heaven, 2000, Tomcats, 2001, The Hollywood Sign, 2001, (voice) The Majestic, 2001, Orange County, 2002, Mother Ghost, 2002, Devil's Knight, 2003, The Long Ride Home, 2003, They Call Him Sasquatch, 2003, Lucky 13, 2005, (voice) Chicken Little, 2005; actor (TV films) But Seriously, Folks, 1986, The Last Shot, 1993, The Twilight of the Golds, 1997 (also exec. prodr.), Frank Capra's American Dream, 1997, CHiPs '99, 1998; exec. prodr. (TV series) Who's Watching the Kids, 1978, Angie, 1979, Joanie Loves Chachi, 1982; (TV films) Beanes of Boston, 1979; guest appearances include Dick Van Dyke Show, 1965, 1966, Hey Landlord, 1967, The Odd Couple, 1974, Happy Days, 1975, Laverne & Shirley, 1976, Vega$, 1980, Murphy Brown, 1994-1997 (several episodes), The Naked Truth, 1997, The Simpsons (voice) 1999, Mad TV, 2000, Three Sisters, 2001, 2002, Monk, 2002, Sabrina, The Teenage Witch, 2002, Father of the Pride (voice), 2004, Unscripted, 2005; actor (TV series) On the Lot, 2007, Brothers and Sisters, 2007, and several others. Office: Pkwy Prodns 10202 Washington Blvd Culver City CA 90232-3119

MARSHALL, GERALD FRANCIS, optical engineer, consultant, physicist; b. Seven Kings, Eng., Feb. 26, 1929; BSc in Physics, London U., 1952. Physicist Morganite Internat., London, 1954—59; sr. rsch. devel. engr. Ferranti Ltd., Edinburgh, 1959—67; project mgr. Diffraction Ltd. Inc., Bedford, Mass., 1967—69; dir. engring. Medical Lasers, Inc., Burlington, Mass., 1969—71; staff cons. Speedring Sys., Troy, Mich., 1971—76; dir. optical engring. Energy Conversion Devices, Inc., Troy, Mich., 1976—87; trained cancer counselor, 1976—; sr. tech. staff specialist Kaiser Electronics, San Jose, Calif., 1987—89; cons. in optics design and engring., 1989—. Editor, contbg. author: Laser Beam Scanning, 1985, Optical Scanning, 1991, Handbook of Optical and Laser Scanning, 2004. Fellow: Inst. Physics, SPIE - Internat. Soc. Optical Engring. (bd. dirs. 1991—93), Optical Soc. Am. Achievements include patents in field. Home and Office: 410 Dusenbury St Niles MI 49120-1468 Office Phone: 269-687-1692.

MARSHALL, GERALD LEE, mathematician, educator; b. Franklin County, NC, June 27, 1947; s. George Eugene Marshall and Roberta Odell Perry; m. Judy Faye Beck, Nov. 24, 1991; 1 child, Kera Beck; m. Karen Louise Gebhart, June 19, 1971 (div.); children: Katharine Elizabeth, Katrina Marie. BSChE, N.C. State U., 1969; ThM in Christian Theology, Luther Rice Sem., 1975; MLS, Fla. State U., 1977; MDiv in New Testament Greek, Luther Rice Sem., 1976, DMin Theol. Libr., 1979; AA, C.C. Chgo., Wiesbaden, Germany, 1985; MA in Math., U. Ala., 1997; PhD in Math. Edn., Ill. State U., 2000. Ordained Christian min. So. Bapt. Conv., 1985. Pastor Aschaffenburg Bapt. Ch., Germany, 1985—87; adj. lectr. C.C. Chgo., Wiesbaden, Germany, 1984—87; min. edn. Hillsboro Heights Bapt. Ch., Huntsville, Ala., 1987—89; supr. environ. svcs. Huntsville Hosp. Sys., 1989—98; adj. instr. Calhoun C.C., Decatur, Ala., 1989—98, Heartland C.C., Bloomington, Ill., 1998—2000; head dept. math. Tri-County Tech. Coll., Pendleton, SC, 2001, v.p., 2002—03, pres., 2007—08. Master presenter Nat. Inst. for Staff and Orgnl. Devel., Austin, Tex., 2002; presenter S.C. Tech. Edn. Assn., Myrtle Beach, SC, 2002—08. Contbr. articles to profl. jours. Capt. USAF, 1969—72, U.S. and Thailand. Grantee NSF, 2000—02, Sustainable Univs. Initiatives, 2002. Mem.: S.C. Math. Assn. Two-Yr. Colls. (pres. 2004—07), S.C. Coun. Tchrs. Math., Assn. Math. Tchr. Educators, Am. Math. Assn. Two-Year Colls., Nat. Coun. Tchrs. Math., Math. Assn. Am. Baptist. Avocations: travel, mathematics history. Home: 2701 Bellview Rd Anderson SC 29621 Office: Tri-County Tech Coll P O Box 587 Pendleton SC 29670 Office Phone: 864-646-1368. Business E-Mail: gmarshal@tctc.edu.

MARSHALL, GRAYSON WILLIAM, JR., materials scientist, biomedical engineer, health sciences educator, dentist; b. Balt., Feb. 12, 1943; s. Grayson William and Muriel Marie Marshall; m. Sally Jean Rimkus, July 4, 1970; children: Grayson W. III, Jonathan Charles. BS in Metall. Engring., Va. Poly. Inst., 1965; PhD in Materials Sci., Northwestern U., 1972, DDS, 1986; MPH, U. Calif., Berkeley, 1992. Cert. dentist. Rsch. assoc., design and devel. ctr. Northwestern U., Evanston, Ill., 1972-73, NIH fellow, 1973, instr. Dental and Med. Schs. Chgo., 1973-74, asst. prof. Dental Sch., 1974-78, assoc. prof. Dental Sch. and Grad. Sch., 1978-87; prof. preventive and restorative dental scis. U. Calif., San Francisco, 1987—, chief biomaterials sect., 1988-92, chmn. biomaterials and bioengring. divsn., 1992—, vice chmn. rsch. preventive and restorative dental scis., 2005—. Chmn. oral and craniaofacial scis. program U. Calif., San Francisco, 2002-07, UCSF Grad. Coun., 2003-05, UCSF Inst. Regenerative Medicine, 2007-; guest scientist Lawrence Livermore Nat. Lab., 1989-2000, Lawrence Berkeley Nat. Lab., 1989—; cons. oral biology and medicine study sect. NIH, 1988-92; dir. Clin. Rsch. Unit, 1992-96, Dentist-Sci. Award Program, 1996-2004, Integrated DDS-PhD Program, 1996—2009, Comprehensive Oral Health Rsch. Tng. Program, 2001-08. Contbr. articles to profl. jours. and books. Mem. City of Larkspur Heritage Preservation Bd., 1998—, chmn., 2006—08, mem. centennial com., 2007—08. Recipient Spl. Dental Rsch. award Nat. Inst. Dental Rsch., 1975, Rsch. Lectr. award U. Calif., San Francisco, 1994, IADR Wilmer Souder Disting. Scientist award, 2007; vis. fellow U. Melbourne, Australia, 1981. Fellow: AAAS, Acad. Dental Materials (exec. sec. 1983—85, chmn. credentials 1984—91, bd. dirs. 1985—93, mem. editl. bd. Scanning Microscopy 1987—93, pres. 1991—93, Cells and Materials 1992—2000, sect. editor 1993—2000, Jour. Oral Rehab. 1994—, Dent Mater 1998—, Am. Jour. Dentistry 2004—), Am. Coll. Dentists, Internat. Coll. Dentists; mem.: APHA, ADA (assoc. editor Jour. ADA 2002—05), U.S. Power Squadrons, U.S. Naval Inst., Calif. Pub. Health Assn.-North, Calif. Acad. Scis., N.Y. Acad. Scis., Am. Assn. Dental Rsch. (bd. dirs. 1996—98, San Francisco coun. 1997—2007, v.p. 2007—08, pres. elect 2008—09, pres. 2009—), Microscopy Soc. Am., Am. Coll. Sports Medicine, Internat. Assn. Dental Rsch. (Chgo. sect. officer 1978—80, dental materials coun. 1990—96, pres. 1998—99), Soc. Biomaterials, Am. Dental Edn. Assn. (sect. officer 1981—83), Omicron Kappa Upsilon, Sigma Gamma Epsilon, Sigma Xi, Alpha Sigma Mu. Avocations: swimming, sailing, hiking, travel. Office: U Calif Dept Preven & Restor Dental Scis San Francisco CA 94143-0758 Business E-Mail: gw.marshall@ucsf.edu, gwmarshall@lbl.gov.

MARSHALL, HELEN M., city official; b. NYC, Sept. 30, 1929; m. Donald E. Marshall; children: Donald Jr., Agnes Marie. BA, Queens Coll., 1979; attended, L.I. U. Dir. Langston Hughes Libr., 1969, Elmcor Testing Assessment and Placement Program; mem. NY State Assembly, Dist. 35, 1983—91; city councilwoman Dist. 21, NYC, 1992—2001; borough pres. Queens, 2001—. Chmn. stds. and ethics com., mem. edn., housing and bldg. and environ. protection coms. Dem. nat. committeewoman, N.Y., 1975; del. Dem. Nat. Conv., 1980; mem. Nat. Dem. Exec. Com., N.Y. State assemblywoman, Dist. 35, 1983-91 past mem. cities, election law, higher edn., labor and transp. coms., chairwoman airport devel. subcom., 1985; vice chairwoman Women's Legis. Caucus, 1985, past chairwoman standing com. on state-fed. rels. Democrat. Office: 120-55 Queens Blvd Kew Gardens NY 11424 Office Phone: 718-286-2870. E-mail: Marshall4Queens@aol.com, info@queensbp.org.

MARSHALL, HEMAN ALEXANDER, III, lawyer; b. Roanoke, Va., Feb. 15, 1950; s. Heman Alexander Jr. and Jeanne (Martin) M.; children: Alexander Tevis, Claiborne Henebry, Courtney Littlepaige; m. Judith Skaff, July 6, 1996. BA, U. Va., 1972, JD, 1975. Bar: Va. Assoc. Woods, Rogers, Muse, Walker & Thornton, Roanoke, Va., 1975-80, ptnr., 1981-85, Woods, Rogers & Hazlegrove, P.L.C., Roanoke, Va., 1985-93, prin., 1994—, pres., 1995—2001, chmn., 1997—2002. Contbr. articles to profl. jours. Bd. dirs. Binaba Found., 2003—06, Nat. Conf. Cmty. and Justice, Roanoke, 2000—04, Art Mus. Western Va., 2000—04. Fellow Va. Law Found., Am. Bar Found.; mem. ABA, Va. State Bar (chmn. health law sect. 1988-89, antitrust law sect. 1989-90), Va. Bar Assn. (chmn. health law sect. 1991-92, bd. govs. 2000-04, chmn. law practice mgmt. divsn. 2002-04), Health Law Sect. Governing Coun. 2007-, Roanoke Bar Assn., Am. Health Lawyers Assn. Home: 6629 Cotton Hill Rd Roanoke VA 24018-6915 Office: Woods Rogers PLC 10 S Jefferson St Ste 1400 Roanoke VA 24011-1331 Office Phone: 540-983-7654. Business E-Mail: marshall@woodsrogers.com.

MARSHALL, JEFFREY SCOTT, mechanical engineer, educator; b. Cin., Feb. 10, 1961; s. James C. and Norma E. (Everett) M.; m. Marilyn Jane Patterson, July 16, 1983; children: Judith K., Eric G., Emily J., Paul E. BS summa cum laude, UCLA, 1983, MS, 1984; PhD, U. Calif., Berkeley, 1987. Asst. rsch. engr. U. Calif., Berkeley, 1988; engr. Creare, Inc., Hanover, NH, 1988-89; from asst. to assoc. prof. dept. ocean engring. Fla. Atlantic U., 1989-93; from assoc. prof. to prof. dept. mech. engring. U. Iowa, Iowa City, 1993—2001, prof., 2001—06, chair dept. mech. and indsl. engring., 2001—06; prof. U. Vt., Burlington, Vt., 2006—, dir. Sch. Engring., 2006—07. Assoc. editor Jour. Fluids Engring.; contbr. articles to profl. jours.; textbook author. Recipient ARO Young Investigator award, 1992-95. Fellow ASME (assoc. editor jour. Fluids Engring. 2001-04, Henry Hess award 1992); mem. Am. Phys. Soc., Tau Beta Pi. Achievements include research in fluid mechanics, three-dimensional vortex dynamics and vortex-structure interaction, particulate flows, and thin film flows. Office: Vt Sch Engring Burlington VT 05405 Office Phone: 802-656-3826. Business E-Mail: jeffm@cems.uvm.edu.

MARSHALL, JIM (JAMES CREEL MARSHALL), United States Representative from Georgia; b. Ithaca, NY, Mar. 31, 1948; s. Robert Creel and Mary Elizabeth (Pie) M.; m. Camille Hope, Mar. 17, 1976; children: Elizabeth, Robert Creel III. AB, Princeton Univ., 1972; JD, Boston Univ., 1977. Bar: Ga. 1977. Mayor City of Macon, 1995—99; mem. US Congress from 3rd Ga. dist., 2003—06, US Congress from 8th Ga. dist., 2006—, mem. Agrl. and Armed Svcs. Coms. Contbr. articles to profl. jours. Pres. Macon Heritage Assn., 1989-90, Leadership Macon, 1988-90; commn. Macon Housing Authority, 1989-95; mem. bd. govs. State Bar Ga., 1995—, mem. adv. bd. US Conf. of Mayors, 1997—; co-chair econ. devel. Nat. Conf. of Dem. Mayors, 1996—, chair criminal justice com. Ga. Mcpl. Assn., 1997—. With US Army, 1968-70, Vietnam. Mem. Macon Bar Assn. (pres. 1992-93), Palaver Club of Macon, League of Women Voters. Democrat. Roman Catholic. Avocations: reading, sports, hunting, piddling. Office: US Ho Reps 502 Cannon Ho Office Bldg Washington DC 20515-1003 also: 682 Cherry St, Ste 300 Macon GA 31201*

MARSHALL, JO TAYLOR, social worker; b. NYC; BA, Sarah Lawrence Coll., Bronxville, NY, 1957; MSW, Columbia U., NYC, 1959. Cert. clin. social worker, NY, NJ; bd. cert. diplomate. Caseworker Youth Cons. Svcs., 1960-62; program cons. Social Work Recruiting Ctr., 1962-63; casework supr. Louise Wise Svcs., 1963-68; faculty field instr. sch. social work Columbia U., NYC, 1968-70; coord. social work vol. and student tng. programs St. Lukes/Roosevelt Hosp. Ctr., 1970-75; asst. dir. fieldwork, faculty lectr. in health care Columbia U., NYC, 1975-78; dir. social work and psychiat. emergency svcs. Morristown Meml. Hosp., 1978—95; social worker pvt. practice, 1995—2002; ret., 2002. Adj. prof. Columbia U.; adv. bd., faculty Nat. Discharge Planning Inst. SUNY, Buffalo; prin. speaker, cons. Hosp. Assn. Pa., 1983, Mid-Atlantic Health Congress, 1985, VA, East Orange, N.J., 1986, Hosp. Assn. Tenn., 1987; adv. com. Rutgers GGrad. Sch. Social Work; mem. multidisciplinary state rev. com. for discharge planning standards in NJ. Contbr. articles to profl. jours.; produced and cons. on numerous film and TV prodns. Named Dir. of Yr., NJ Hosp. Social Work, 1989-90. Mem.: NASW, Acad. Cert. Social Workers, Soc. Hosp. Social Work Dirs. (pres. NJ chpt. 1988—89, exec. bd., chmn. nat. media task force). Achievements include The Weleome Terrace at Columbia Grad. Sch. of Social Work named in her honor in 2004. Home (Winter): 1230 Hillsboro Mile Hillsboro Beach FL 33062-1344 Home (Summer): PO Box 40 Far Hills NJ 07931-0040 Office Phone: 908-553-5444. Personal E-mail: jomase@msn.com.

MARSHALL, JOHN CROOK, internal medicine educator, researcher; b. Blackburn, Lancashire, Eng., Feb. 28, 1941; came to US, 1976; s. Albert Acey and Marion Miller (Crook) M.; m. Marilyn Dallas Parry, Sept. 20, 1969; children: Samantha Jane, Susannah Crook. BS, Victoria U., Manchester, Eng., 1962, MB, ChB, 1965, MD, 1973. Diplomate Am. Bd. Internal Medicine, Am. Bd. Endocrinology and Metabolism. Intern Manchester Royal Infirmary, 1965-66; resident Brompton Hosp., Nat. Heart Hosp., Nat Hosp. Queen Sq., London, 1966-69, Hammersmith Hosp., London, 1966-69, rsch. fellow, 1969-72; lectr. U. Birmingham, Eng., 1972-76; assoc. prof. internal medicine U. Mich., Ann Arbor, 1976-79, prof., 1979-91, chief endocrinology and metabolism, 1987-91; prof. U. Va., Charlottesville, 1991—, dir. Ctr. for Rsch. in Reprod., 1996—. Sci. counselor NIH, Bethesda, Md., 1983-84. Editor: Endocrinology Jour., 1979-84, Endocrinology Text, 1990—; contbr. articles to profl. jour. Grantee NIH, 1977-. Fellow ACP, Royal Coll. Physicians, Royal Soc. Medicine; mem. Ctrl. Soc. for Clin. Rsch. (coun. 1983—), Assn. Am. Physicians, Am. Soc. for Clin. Investigation, Am. Clin. and Climatological Soc. Anglican. Avocations: vintage racing cars, golf. Office: U Va Sch Medicine Dept Internal Medicine Charlottesville VA 22908-0001 Business E-Mail: jcm9h@virginia.edu.

MARSHALL, JOHN DAVID, lawyer; b. Chgo., May 19, 1940; s. John Howard and Sophie (Brezenk) M.; m. Marcia A. Podlasinski, Aug. 26, 1961; children: Jacquelyn, David, Jason, Patricia, Brian, Denise, Michael, Catherine. BS in Acctg., U. Ill., 1961; JD, Ill. Inst. Tech., 1965. CPA Ill.; bar: Ill. 1965, U.S. Tax Ct. 1968, U.S. Dist. Ct. (no. dist.) Ill. 1971. Ptnr. Mayer, Brown & Platt, Chgo., 1961—2006. Bd. dirs. Levinson Ctr. for Handicapped Children, Chgo., 1970—75. Mem. Ill. Bar Assn., Chgo. Bar Assn. (agribus. com. 1978—, trust law com. 1969-95, probate practice com. 1969—2007, com. on coms. 1983-00, vice chmn. 1988-89, chmn. 1989-90, legis. com. of probate practice com. 1983—, chmn. and vice chmn. legis. com. of probate practice com. 1983-84, rules and forms com., 1996-, chmn. exec. com. probate practice com. 1982-83, vice chmn. exec. com. 1981-82, sec. exec. com. 1980-81, div. chmn. 78-79, div. vice chmn. 1977-78, div. sec. 1976-77, Appreciation award 1982-83), Union League Club (Chgo.); ret. fellow ACTEC. Roman Catholic. Home: 429 N Willow Wood Dr Palatine IL 60074-3831 Office: Attorney at Law 1300 E Woodfield Rd Schaumburg IL 60173 also: 520 N Hicks Rd Palatine IL 60069 Office Phone: 847-991-3150. Business E-Mail: jmarshall@bsd-cpa.com.

MARSHALL, JOHN ELBERT, III, foundation executive; b. Providence, July 2, 1942; s. John Elbert Jr. and Millicent Edna (Paige) M.; m. Diana M. Healy, Aug. 16, 1968; children: Nelson John, Priscilla Anne. BA, Brown U., 1964. Advt. mgr. U.N. Alloy Steel Corp., Boston, 1968-70; devel. officer Brown U., Providence, 1970—72, assoc. dir. devel., 1972—75; exec. dir. R.I. Found., Providence, 1975—79; v.p. Kresge Found., Troy, Mich., 1979-82, exec. v.p., 1982-87, pres., 1987—, trustee, 1991—, CEO, 1993—2006. Former chmn. Mich. Cmty. Found. Youth Project. Bd. dirs. United Way Cmty. Svcs., Detroit Downtown Partnership, New Detroit, City Year Detroit, Detroit 300 Conservancy Endowment, Detroit Riverfront Conservatory, Health Found. for the Ams., Assn. Hole in the Wall Camps Found.; former bd. dirs. Mich. Campus Compact, Mich. Nonprofit Forum, Coun. Mich. Founds., Detroit Cmty. Devel. Funders Collaborative; former bd. dirs., vice chmn. Family Svc. Detroit and Wayne County; past pres. Bloomfield Village Assn.; former trustee Coun. on Founds., Washington; mem. com. CFSEM Greenways Initiative; mem. capital improvement program Detroit Pub. Schs.; mem. pres.'s leadership coun. Brown U. Office: The Kresge Foundation 3215 W Big Beaver Rd Troy MI 48084-2818

MARSHALL, JOHN HARRIS, JR., geologist, oil industry executive; b. Dallas, Mar. 12, 1924; s. John Harris and Jessie Elizabeth (Mosley) Marshall; m. Betty Eugenia Zarecor, Aug. 9, 1947 (dec. 2003); children: John Harris III, George Z., Jacqueline Anne. BA in Geology, U. Mo., Columbia, 1949, MA in Geology, 1950; LHD, Garrett Evang. Theolgical, Evanson, Ill., 1996. Registered geologist Calif., Wyo., Ky., Tex. Geologist Magnolia Oil Co., Jackson, Miss., 1950-59; assoc. geologist Magnolia/Mobil Oil, Okla. City, Okla., 1959-63; from dist. and divsn. geologist to chief geologist worldwide Mobil Oil Corp., various, 1963-81, gen. mgr. exploration for Western Hemisphere NYC, 1981-82; chief geologist Ambrex, 1982—84; prin., owner Marshall Energetics, Inc., Dallas, 1982—. Dir. exploration Anschutz, 1985-91; pres. Summit Oil and Gas Worldwide, 1993-99, Madera Prodn. Co., 1992—; adv. bd. Salvation Army, Manhattan, 1980-82; trustee Sci. Place, Dallas, 1995-2002, pres. adv. coun. U. Mo., plan giving com., 2004— Geology devel. bd. U. Mo., past pres., 1982-, pres. Coll. Arts and Sci. devel. program, 1996—, devel. coun., 1996-2000, arts and scis. strategic devel. bd., 2000—; councilman, City of Warr Acres Okla., 1962-63; active United Meth. Ch., 1951—, Boy Scouts Am., 1960-68; trustee Found. of Evangelism, United Meth. Ch., 1984-, chair, 1988-96, AAPG Found., 2004—. With US Army, 1943—46. Decorated 3 Battle Stars US Army; recipient Curator's medal, U. Mo., 1949, Disting. Alumni Svc. award, 1996, Arts and Sci. award, The Mosaic Soc., U. Mo., 2000, Faculty-Alumni award, U. Mo., 2001, Hon. Life Mem., Geology Devel. Bd., U. Mo., 2004. Mem. Am. Assn. Petroleum Geologists (trustee AAPG Found. 2004—, Pub. Svc. award 2000), Am. Geol. Inst., Am. Geol. Soc. (Dallas, Alaska, Oklahoma City; LA Basin pres. 1969-70), Rocky Mountain Assn. Geologists, NY Acad. Sci., Pacific Petroleum Geologists, Am. Sci. Affiliation, Assn. Christian Geologists, United Meth. Gen. Bd. of Discipleship (nat. hispanic evangelization com., 2003-), Meth. Men Club, Denver Petroleum Club, Sigma Xi. Democrat. Office: 4831 W Lawther Dr Apt 221 Dallas TX 75214

MARSHALL, JOHN HENRY, lawyer; b. Paterson, NJ, July 31, 1949; s. Henry Leland and Elizabeth Marion (Bates) M.; m. Jan (Eastman), May 4, 1979. BA, Dartmouth Coll., 1971, Cambridge U., Eng., 1973; JD, Yale U., 1977. Bar: Vt. 1977, U.S. Dist. Ct. Vt., 1978. Assoc. Downs Rachlin Martin, St. Johnsbury, Vt., 1977—82, ptnr., 1982—, mng. ptnr., 2003—09. Mem. Vt. Health Care Authority Adv. Com. Universal Access Plan, 1992. Chmn. Dist. Environ. Commn., St. Johnsbury, 1981-90; mem. Governor's Blue Ribbon Commn. on Health Care, 1991; chmn. Vt. Cmty. Found., 2000-02; chmn. Vt. Pub. TV, 2002-04. Capt. U.S. Army, 1973-74. Mem. Vt. Bar Assn. (chmn. environ. law com. 1987-92, chmn. health law com. 1994-96). Office: Downs Rachlin Martin PLLC 90 Prospect St Saint Johnsbury VT 05819-0099 Home: PO Box 19 Peacham VT 05862-0019 Business E-Mail: jmarshall@drm.com.

MARSHALL, JOHN LINDSAY, medical educator; b. Frankfort, Ky., June 23, 1961; s. Ernest David and Jane Snyder Marshall, Virginia Dyson Marshall (Stepmother); m. Elizabeth Alexander Alexander, June 16, 1984; children: Charles Alexander, Emma Elizabeth. BS, Duke U., Durham, NC, 1982; MD, U. Louisville, 1988. Prof. Georgetown U., Washington, 2008—, assoc. prof., 2003—08. Dir., devel. therapeutics gi cancer Lombardi Cancer Ctr., Washington, 2000—; chief, hematology oncology Georgetown U., 2005—; dir., clin. rsch. Lombardi Cancer ctr., 2000—; pres., internat. soc. gi oncology ISGIO, 2008—. Contbr. scientific papers to profl. jours. Elder Georgetown Presbyn. Ch., 2008—; sci. advisor The Wellness Cmty., Washington, 2003—. Recipient award, AOA, 1988, Gallo, The Cancer Inst. NJ., 2001, Living Wellness award, Wellness Cmty., 2004; named one of Top doctors award, Washingtonian Mag., 2005, America's Top doctors, 2008; grants, Georgetown U., 2006. Mem.: ASCO. Office: Georgetown Univ 3800 Reservoir Rd Washington DC 20007 Office Fax: 202-444-1229. Business E-Mail: marshalj@georgetown.edu.

MARSHALL, JOHN PAUL, broadcast engineer; came to U.S., 1967. Degree, U. Grenoble, 1963; student, U. Munich, 1964—65, San Francisco State U., 1969—71, John O'Connell Tech. Inst., 1973—74. Cert. Novell adminstr., cert. broadcast technologist, A+ computer svc. technician Microsoft Cert. Profl.; cert. Networkplus Tech., Microsoft Cert.

Profl., Microsoft Cert. Sys. Engr. Mem. faculty law and econ. scis. U. Grenoble, France, 1963—64; mem. Expo '67 staff City of Montreal, Que., Canada, 1967; filmmaker Cinemalab, San Francisco, 1970; engr. film and TV Able Studios, San Francisco, 1971—73; engr. radio and TV Sta. KALW-FM (Nat. Pub. Radio), San Francisco, 1973—74; broadcast engr. Sta. KRON-TV (NBC), San Francisco, 1974—91; intern Centre d'Informatique et de Maintenance Automatisme, 1993; founder Marshall U.S.A., San Francisco, 1994; freelance broadcast engr. KPIX-TV (CBS), KGO-Radio (ABC), KSFO-Radio (ABC), KPST-TV, San Francisco, 1995—2001; adminstr. Thomson Prometric, San Francisco, 2003—. Freelance audio visual tech. advisor, San Francisco area, 1975—, lectr. radio, TV, motion pictures, 1975—, cons. customized electronic effects; tech. advisor, assoc. Broadkast Skills Bank. Translator tech. pubs. and manuals, 1975—. Mus. dir., participant in theater prodns., 1950-59; active Boy Scouts Am. Govt. of France scholar, 1960-63. Mem. Rolls Royce Owners Club Found. (life), Internet Soc., Soc. Broadcast Engrs. (cert. broadcast networking technologist), Elec. Tech. Assn. Avocations: classical pianist, polyglot, world traveler. Personal E-mail: jpm1221@sbcglobal.net. *Personal philosophy: (French proverb) Aide toi, le ciel t'aidera--Use your own resources and you will always receive a helping hand from heaven.*

MARSHALL, JOHN STEVEN, artist, educator, museum administrator; b. Oct. 20, 1957; Spl. studies, U. of the South, 1979-80; AA, Motlow State Community Coll., Tullahoma, Tenn., 1981; BFA, Middle Tenn. State U., 1983; MFA, U. N.C., Greensboro, 1985. Art instr. Meridian Cmty. Coll.; curator Meridian Cmty. Coll. Art Gallery; registrar, curatorial asst. Weatherspoon Art Gallery, U. N.C., Greensboro, 1983-85, asst. curator, lectr., 1985, acting curator, 1986; instr./curator Meridian C.C., 1986—; dir. Meridian Mus. Art, 1986-89; represented by Artworks Gallery, Laurel, Miss., Sylvia Schmidt Gallery, New Orleans, Miss.; co-owner Horne-Marshall Gallery, Meridian. Lectr. art various Tenn. and Miss. orgns.; curator, jury mem. various exhbns. One-man shows include Meridian Mus. Art, 1989, 2008, Miss. State U., 1990, 92, Miss. U. for Women, 1990, Tusculum Coll., 1992, Gen. Art Gallery, Miss., 1993, Coleman Art Ctr., Ala., 1995, Meridian C.C., 1995, Lauderdale Cmty. Gallery, 1995, Meridian Underground Gallery, 1996, Arts in the Park, 1996, Eula Bass Lewis Gallery, Miss., 1996, Dauphin Way Gallery, Mobile, Ala., 1997, Horne-Marshall Gallery, Meridian, 1997, Sylvia Schmidt Gallery, New Orleans, 1997, Casteel Gallery, Meridian, Miss., 1997, Bi-State Comp. Meridian Museum of Art, 1998, East Central Cmty. Coll., Meridian Mus. Art, 2008; 2-person show Winfield Gallery, 1991; exhibited in group shows Elliot U. Ctr. Gallery, Brentwood and Nashville, 1984, Weatherspoon Art Gallery, Greensboro, 1985, 86, Waterworks Gallery, Winston-Salem, N.C., 1985, Meridian Mus. Art, 1987, 89, Casteel Art Gallery, Meridian, 1987, U. So. Miss., 1988, Greenville Art Gallery, 1988, Space-One-Eleven Gallery, 1990, Birmingham-So. Coll., 1990, Winfield Gallery, 1991, Marie Hall Gallery, Jackson, Miss., 1998, East Ctrl. CC, 2008, Miller Art Gallery, 2008; represented in pvt. collections. Mem. Meridian Mus. Art, Meridian Coun. for the Arts. Named Arts Educator of the Yr., Meridian, Miss., 1996; recipient Lamplighter Ednl. Excellence award, 1996. Mem.: Miss. Teachers Assn. Avocations: sailing, guitar, scuba diving. Office: Meridian Community Coll 910 Highway 19 N Meridian MS 39307-5890 Business E-Mail: jmarshal@mcc.cc.ms.us.*

MARSHALL, JOHN TREUTLEN, lawyer, educator; b. Macon, Ga., Nov. 1, 1934; s. Hubert and Gladys (Lucas) Marshall; m. Katrine White, May 1, 1959; children: Allison, Rebecca, Paul, Mary Anne. BA, Vanderbilt U., 1956; LLB, Yale U., 1962. Bar: Ga. 1962, US Dist. Ct. (no., mid. and so. dists.) Ga. 1962, US Ct. Appeals (5th cir.) 1962, US Supreme Ct. 1978, US Ct. Appeals (11th cir.) 1982. Of counsel Bryan Cave LLP, Atlanta, 1962—. Chmn. bd. visitors Ga. State U. Law Sch., 2005—; chmn. No. Dist. Ga. Bar Coun., 1989, Ga. State Bar Commn. Continuing Lawyer Competency, 1991—93, Ga. State Commn. Stds. Profession, 1996—; bd. dirs. Ga. Eye Bank, Inc., Atlanta Bar Found. Bd. editor Yale Law Jour. Trustee Ga. Inst. Continuing Legal Edn., 1983—90; bd. dirs. Atlanta Legal Aid, 1972—73. Capt. USMC, 1959—62. Recipient S. Phillip Heiner award, Atlanta Vol. Lawyers Assn., 1992, A. Gus Cleveland award, Ga. Commn. Continuing Legal Edn., Tradition of Excellence award, State Bar Ga., 1995, Disting. Svc. award, Ga. State Bar, 2006, Professionalism award, Am. Inns of Ct. (11th Jud. Cir.), 2005, Ben F. Johnson, Jr. award for Pub. Svc., 2007. Fellow: Ga. Bar Found., Atlanta Bar Found. (bd. dirs.), Am. Acad. Appellate Lawyers, Am. Coll. Trial Lawyers (state chmn. 1985—86); mem.: ABA (ho. of dels. 1976—86, Harrison Tweed award 1986), Ga. Inst. Trial Advocacy (chmn. 1982—83), Atlanta Bar Assn. (pres. 1974—75, Charles E. Watkins Jr. award 1988, Leadership award 1996), Atlanta Bar Found. (bd. dirs.), State Bar Ga. (chmn. stds. profession com., Disting. Svc. award 2005, Lifetime Achievement award Anti Defamation League 2009), Am. Arbitration Assn. Office: Powell Goldstein One Atlantic Ctr Fl 14 1201 W Peachtree St NW Atlanta GA 30309-3488 Office Phone: 404-572-6615. Business E-Mail: jmarshall@pogolaw.com.

MARSHALL, JOSHUA MICAH, publisher, blog writer, columnist, editor, political journalist; b. St. Louis, Mo., Feb. 15, 1969; m. Millet Israeli, 2005. Grad., Princeton U., 1991; PhD in American History, Brown U. Assoc. editor to Washington editor The American Prospect, 1998—2001; founder, editor, publisher Talking Points Memo (talkingpointsmemo.com); editor, publisher TPMCafe.com, 2005—; contbg. editor The Washington Monthly, Washington; contbg. writer, columnist The Hill, Washington; columnist Time.com. Blog writer TPMmuckraker.com. Contbg. writer Salon.com; contbr. articles to the Atlantic Monthly, Boston Globe, Financial Times, Foreign Affairs, LA Times, NY Republic, New Yorker, NY Post, NY Times and Slate; guest appearances CNN, CNBC, C-Span, Fox and MSNBC. Recipient George Polk award for Legal Reporting, 2007. Office: The Hill 1625 K St NW Ste 900 Washington DC 20006 also: TPM Media LLC 805 Ave of the Americas New York NY 10001 also: Washington Monthly 5471 Wisconsin Ave Ste 300 Chevy Chase MD 20815-3563

MARSHALL, KATE, state treasurer; b. San Francisco, July 22, 1959; m. John Marshall; 2 children. Student, Univ. Calif. Boalt Hall, Berkeley, 1982; BA, Univ. Calif., Berkeley, 1982, JD. Law intern Laxalt, Washington, Perito & Debuc, Washington; tchr. English &, Commerce Peace Corps, Kenya; with field offices Dept. Justice, Washington, San Francisco; in-house counsel ATG Inc., 2000; pvt. practice atty.; sr. dep. atty. gen. State of Nev., 1997—2000, state treas., 2007—. Named Woman of Achievement, Nev. Women's Fund, 2001. Democrat. Office: State Treas Capitol Bldg 101 N Carson St Ste 4 Carson City NV 89701 Office Phone: 775-684-5600. Office Fax: 775-684-5781. Business E-Mail: statetreasurer@nevadatreasurer.gov.*

MARSHALL, KATHLEEN, choreographer, theater director; Mem. exec. bd. Soc. Stage Dirs. and Choreographers. Asst. choreographer (Broadway plays) Kiss of the Spider Woman, 1993—95, She Loves Me, 1993—94, Damn Yankees, 1994—95, choreographer Swinging on a Star, 1996 (Drama Desk nomination), 1776, 1997—98, Ring Round the Moon, 1999, Kiss Me, Kate, 1999—2001 (Tony nom. best choreography, 2001, Laurence Olivier nom. best choreography, 2002, Drama Desk nomination, Outer Critics Circle nomination, Astaire Award nomination), Seussical, 2000—01, Follies, 2001 (Outer Critics Circle award nomination), Little Shop of Horrors, 2003; dir.: (Broadway plays) Wonderful Town, 2003 (Tony nom. best dir. musical, 2004, Drama Desk award best choreography, 2004); choreographer (Broadway plays) Wonderful Town, 2003 (Tony award best choreography, 2004), The Pajama Game, 2005 (Outer Critics' Cir. award, outstanding choreography, 2006, Drama Desk award outstanding choreography, 2006, Tony award, best choreography, 2006), (TV films) The Music Man, 2003. Recipient Mr. Abbott Award, Stage Directors & Choreographers Found., 2005.

MARSHALL, KATHRYN SUE, lawyer; b. Decatur, Ill., Sept. 12, 1942; d. Edward Elda and Frances M. (Minor) Lahniers; m. Robert S. Marshall, Sept. 5, 1964 (div. Apr. 1984); children: Stephen Edward, Christine Elizabeth; m. Robert J. Arndt, June 25, 1988 (dec. 1999). BA, Lake Forest Coll., 1964; JD, John Marshall Law Sch., Chgo., 1976. Intern U.S. Atty.'s Office, Chgo., 1974—76; mng. ptnr. Marshall and Marshall Ltd., Waukegan, Ill., 1976—84; pvt. practice Waukegan, 1984—93, Preemptive Solutions Leadership Consulting, Wash., 2007—. Contbr. articles to profl. jours. Bd. dirs., v.p. Lake Forest (Ill.) Fine Arts Ensemble; bd. dirs. Island Hosp. Health Found.; mem. steering com. Equal Justice Coalition; cert. jud. Dem. candidate Lake County, Ill.; bd. dirs. Camerata Soc., Lake Forest. Fellow: ABA (gov. 1993—96), Coll. Law Practice Mgmt., Ill. Bar Assn.; mem.: RSVP (dir.), Navy League (life). Avocations: boating, reading, travel. Office: 7610 Mid Town Rd # 302 Madison WI 53719

MARSHALL, KENNETH ROBERT, music educator; b. Aurora, Ill., May 18, 1939; s. John Redman and Gladys Marie Marshall. MusB, U. Ill., 1961, BS in Music Edn., 1962, MusM, 1963; BS in Hospitality Mgmt., Fla. Internat. U., 1980. Cert. evaluator Fla. Dept. Revenue. Choral dir. various high schs., Ill., Fla., 1963—68; dir. choral activities Brevard C.C., Cocoa, Fla., 1968—75; dir. choral activities, tchr. English Internat. Sch. Bangkok/Thai U., 1975—79; U.S. customs product clearance/tangible personal property Sunbelt Internat. Shoppers/Osceola Co. Property Dep. Appraiser, Orlando and Kissimmee, Fla., 1979—90; full time ch. musician, organist, dir. 1st United Meth. Ch., Sanford, Fla., 1990—92; med. records transcriptionist Leesburg (Fla.) Regional Med. Ctr., 1992—95; assoc. prof. humanities Valencia C.C., Orlando, Fla., 1995—2003; organist, dir. music Faith Viera (Fla.) Luth. Ch., 2004—. Tchr., counselor various high schs. and coll.s, Fla., 1963—2003; part-time ch. musician, 1975—95. Named Prof. of the Semester, Phi Theta Kappa, 1999—2000. Mem.: Am. Guild Organists (assoc.; regional officer 1968—75), Am. Choral Dirs. Assn. (life; state and conv. planning positions 1965—75), Phi Mu Alpha. Republican. Methodist/Lutheran. Avocations: animals, stamp collecting/philately. Home: 1470 Malibu Cir NE Apt 107 Palm Bay FL 32905-6312 Personal E-mail: jsbach2@gmail.com.

MARSHALL, KEVIN A., director; b. Bronx, NY, June 9, 1950; s. Aldon Eddie and Winifred Ann Marshall; m. Marlene Ann Cassella, Dec. 30, 1972; children: Jeffrey Aldon, Bryan Matthew. BA, William Paterson U., Wayne, NJ, 1972; MFA, Ohio U., Athens, 1974. Head grad. program in theatre mgmt. and arts adminstrn. U. Ala./Ala. Shakespeare Festival, Tuscaloosa, 1982—98; dir. Sch. Theatre and Dance U. Fla., Gainesville, 1998—. Bus. mgr. Festival Players, Chattanooga, 1979—82; house mgr. Manhattan Theatre Club, NYC, 1979; exec. dir. Johnson City Area Arts Coun., Tenn., 1982; ho. mgr. Ala. Shakespeare Festival, Anniston, Ala., 1983—84. Co-author: Theatre Management: A Successful Guide to Producing Plays on Commercial and Non-Profit Stages; editor: Theatre Mgmt. Jour. V.p. Chattanooga Wine Tasters, 1981—82; active Assn. Arts Adminstrn. Educators, Pitts., 1991—92, Tenn. Theatre Assn., Nashville, 1981—82, Appalachian Coun. for the Arts, Bristol, Tenn., 1982. Recipient Druid Arts award, Arts Coun. Tuscaloosa County, 1992. Mem.: Southeastern Theatre Conf., Assn. for Theatre in Higher Edn. (treas. 1990—95). Roman Catholic. Avocation: travel. Home: 4064 SW 98th Ter Gainesville FL 32608 Office: Univ Fla PO Box 115900 Gainesville FL 32611 Office Fax: 352-392-5114. Business E-Mail: kmarshall@arts.ufl.edu.

MARSHALL, LUCILLE RUTH, retired mathematics professor; b. Waukegan, Ill., Mar. 20, 1941; d. James Arthur and Emily Ruth Cunnington; AA, Santa Rosa Jr. Coll., 1990; BA, Sonoma State U., 1994; MS, Mo. State U., 2000; post grad. in math., U. Mo., 2003. Tchg. asst. Mo. State U., Springfield, Mo., 1998—2000; grad. tchg. asst. U. Mo., Rolla, 2000—03; ret., 2004. Adj. faculty Ozarks Tech. Coll., Springfield. Vol. income tax cons. Southcentral Mo. Cmty. Action Agy., Mo. Mem.: Order Eastern Star (sec. Current River chpt. # 239). Home: PO Box 8 Winona MO 65588

MARSHALL, MARGARET BLAIR, thoracic surgeon; MD, Georgetown U. Sch. Medicine, Washington, 1991. Chief thoracic surgery Georgetown U. Hosp., 2004—. Chairperson workforce patient safety practice edn. Soc. Thoracic Surgeons, 2008. Named Best Drs. Am., 2007—08. Mem.: Soc. Thoracic Surgeons. Office: Georgetown Univ Hosp 3800 Reservoir Rd NW 4 PHC Washington DC 20007 Office Fax: 202-444-5227.

MARSHALL, MARGARET HILARY, state supreme court chief justice; b. Newcastle, Natal, South Africa, Sept. 1, 1944; came to U.S., 1968; d. Bernard Charles and Hilary A.D. (Anderton) M; m. Samuel Shapiro, Dec. 14, 1968 (div. Apr. 1982); m. Anthony Lewis, Sept. 23, 1984. BA, Witwatersrand U., Johannesburg, 1966; MEd, Harvard U., 1969; JD, Yale U., 1976; LHD (hon.), Regis Coll., 1993. Bar: Mass. 1977, U.S. Dist. Ct. Mass., U.S. Dist. Ct. N.H., U.S. Dist. Ct. D.C., U.S. Dist. Ct. (ea. dist.) Mich., U.S. Tax Ct., U.S. Ct. Appeals (1st, 11th and D.C. cirs.), U.S. Supreme Ct. Assoc. Csaplar & Bok, Boston, 1976-83, ptnr., 1983-89, Choate, Hall & Stewart, Boston, 1989-92; v.p., gen. counsel Harvard U., Cambridge, Mass., 1992-96; justice Mass. Supreme Jud. Ct., 1996-99, chief justice, 1999—. Mem. jud. nominating coun., 1987-90, 92; chairperson ct. rules subcom. Alternative Dispute Resolution Working Group, 1985-87; mem. fed. appts. commn., 1993; mem. adv. com. Supreme Judicial Ct., 1989-92, mem. gender equality com., 1989-94; mem. civil justice adv. group U.S. Dist. Ct. Mass., 1991-93; spl. counsel Jud. Conduct Commn., 1988-92; trustee Mass. Continuing Legal Edn., Inc., 1990-92. Trustee Regis Coll., 1993-95; bd. dirs. Internat. Design Conf., Aspen, 1986-92, Boston Mcpl. Res. Bur., 1990-94, Supreme Judicial Ct. Hist. Soc., 1990-94, sec., 1990-94. Fellow Am. Bar Found. (Mass. state chair); mem. Boston Bar Assn. (treas. 1988-89, v.p. 1989-90, pres.-elect 1990-91, pres. 1991-92), Internat. Women's Forum, Mass. Women's Forum, Boston Club, Phi Beta Kappa (hon.). Office: Supreme Judicial Court 1 Pemberton Sq Ste 2-500 Boston MA 02108-1717*

MARSHALL, MARK F., lawyer; b. 1954; BS, U. SD, 1977, JD, 1981. Bar: SD 1981, US Dist. Ct. SD 1981, US Ct. Appeals (8th cir.) 1981, US Supreme Ct. 1984. Law clk. hon. Fred J. Nichol, 1981-83; ptnr. Bangs, McCullen, Butler, Foye & Simmons, Rapid City, SD, 1983-96; of counsel Johnson, Heidepriem, Miner, Marlow & Janklow, Sioux Falls, SD, 1996—2000; magistrate judge U.S. Dist. Ct. S.D., Sioux Falls, 1996-2000; ptnr. Davenport Law Firm, Sioux Falls, 2000—. Office: 206 W 14th St Sioux Falls SD 57105 Office Phone: 605-336-2880. Business E-Mail: mmarshall@dehs.com.

MARSHALL, MARY JONES, civic worker; b. Billings, Mont.; d. Leroy Nathaniel and Janet (Currie) Dailey; m. Harvey Bradley Jones, Nov. 15, 1952 (dec. 1989); children: Dailey, Janet Currie, Ellis Bradley; m. Boyd T. Marshall, June 27, 1990. Student, Carleton Coll., 1943-44, U. Mont., 1944-46, UCLA, 1959. Owner Mary Jones Interiors. Founder, treas. Jr. Art Coun., LA County Mus., 1953-55, v.p., 1955-56; mem. costume coun. Pasadena (Calif.) Philharm.; co-founder Art Rental Gallery, 1953, chmn. art and architecture tour, 1955; founding mem., sec. Art Alliance, Pasadena Art Mus., 1955-56; benefit chmn. Pasadena Girls Club, 1959, bd. dirs., 1958-60; chmn. LA Tennis Patron's Assn. Benefit, 1965; sustaining Jr. League Pasadena; mem. docent coun. LA County Mus.; mem. costume coun. LA County Mus. Art, program chmn. 20th Century Greatest Designers; mem. blue ribbon com. LA Music Ctr.; benefit chmn. Venice com. Internat. Fund for Monuments, 1971; bd. dirs. Art Ctr. 100, Pasadena, 1988—; pres. The Pres.'s LA Children's Bur., 1989; co-chmn. benefit Harvard Coll. Scholarship Fund, 1974, steering com. benefit, 1987, Otis Art Inst., 1975, 90th Anniversary of Children's Bur. of LA, 1994; mem. Harvard-Radcliffe scholarship dinner com., 1985; mem. adv. bd. Estelle Doheny Eye Found., 1976, chmn. benefit, 1980; adv. bd. Loyola U. Sch. Fine Arts, LA, Art Ctr. Sch. Design, Pasadena, 1987—; patron chmn. Benefit Achievement Rewards for Coll. Scientists, 1988; chmn. com. Sch. Am. Ballet Benefit, 1988, NYC; bd. dirs. Founders Music Ctr., LA, 1977-81; mem. nat. adv. coun. Sch. Am. Ballet, NYC, nat. co-chmn. gala, 1980; adv. coun. on fine arts Loyola-Marymount U.; mem. LA Olympic Com., 1984, The Colleagues; founding mem. Mus. Contemporary Art, 1986; chmn. The Pres.'s Benefit LA Children's Bur., 1990; exec. com. LA Alive for LA Music Ctr., 1992; mem. exec. com. Children's Bur. of LA Found., 1992; chmn. award dinner Phoenix House, 1994, 96; bd. dirs. Andrews Sch. Gerontology, U. So. Calif., 1996—, Leakey Found., 1996—; bd. regents Children's Hosp. LA, 1996—. Mem. Am. Parkinson Disease Assn. (steering com. 1991), Valley Hunt Club (Pasadena), Calif. Club (LA), Kappa Alpha Theta. Home: 10375 Wilshire Blvd Ste 8B Los Angeles CA 90024-4712

MARSHALL, NATALIE JUNEMANN, economics professor; b. Milw., June 13, 1929; d. Harold E. and Myrtle (Findlay) Junemann; m. Howard D. Marshall, Aug. 7, 1954 (dec. 1972); children: Frederick S., Alison B.; m. Phillip Shatz, May 27, 1988. AB, Vassar Coll., 1951; MA, Columbia U., 1952, PhD, 1963, JD, 1994. Instr. Vassar Coll., Poughkeepsie, NY, 1952-54, 59, 59-60, 63, dean studies, prof. econs., 1973-75, v.p. for student affairs, 1975-80, v.p. for adminstrn. and student services and prof. econs., 1980-91, prof. econs., 1991-94; teaching fellow Wesleyan U., Middletown, Conn., 1955-56; from asst. prof. to prof. SUNY, New Paltz, 1964-73; prof. econs. Vassar Coll., Poughkeepsie, NY, 1973-94; of counsel Donoghue, Thomas, Auslander & Drohan, Hopewell Junction, NY, 1997—. Editor (with Howard Marshall): The History of Economic Thought, 1968; editor: Keynes, Updated or Outdated, 1970; author (with Howard Marshall): Collective Bargaining, 1971. Trustee St. Francis Hosp., 1979-88, Area Fund Dutchess County, 1981-87, Coll. New Rochelle, 1994-2000, Hudson Valley Philharm., 1985-92, pres., 1989-91. Mem. AAUP, Am. Assn. Higher Edn., Am. Econ. Assn., AAUW (v.p. N.Y. State div. 1964-66), Poughkeepsie Vassar Club (pres. 1965-67). Home: 157 Skidmore Rd Pleasant Valley NY 12569-5001

MARSHALL, PATRICK C., lawyer; b. San Francisco, Aug. 8, 1954; BA, Whitman Coll., 1976; JD with honors, U. Wash., 1979. Bar: Wash. 1979, Calif. 1984. Ptnr. Pillsbury Winthrop Shaw Pittman, San Francisco, 1984—, office mng. ptnr., 2004, co-leader Litigation sect., leader San Francisco Litigation sect. Mem.: San Francisco Bar Assn. Office: Pillsbury Winthrop Shaw Pittman 50 Fremont St San Francisco CA 94105 Office Phone: 415-983-7233. Office Fax: 415-983-1200. Business E-Mail: patrick.marshall@pillsburylaw.com.

MARSHALL, PENNY (C. MARSHALL, CAROLE PENNY MARSHALL), director, actress; b. NYC, Oct. 15, 1943; d. Anthony W. and Marjorie Irene (Ward) M.; m. Michael Henry (div.); 1 child, Tracy Lee; m. Robert Reiner, Apr. 10, 1971 (div. 1979). Student, U. N.Mex., 1961-64. Appeared on numerous television shows, including The Odd Couple, 1972-74, Friends and Lovers (co-star), 1974, Let's Switch, 1974, Wives (pilot), 1975, Chico and the Man, 1975, Mary Tyler Moore, 1975, Heaven Help Us, 1975, Saturday Night Live, 1975-77, Happy Days, 1975, Battle of Network Stars (ABC special), 1976, Barry Manilow special, 1976, The Tonight Show, 1976-77, Dinah, 1976-77, Mike Douglas Show, 1975-77, Merv Griffin Show, 1976-77, Blansky's Beauties, 1977, Network Battle of the Sexes, 1977, Laverne and Shirley (co-star), 1976-83, Entertainment Tonight's Presents: Laverne and Shirley Together Again, 2002; TV films More Than Friends, 1978, Love Thy Neighbor, 1984, Challenge of a Lifetime, 1985, The Odd Couple: Together Again, 1993; guest appearances include Mary Tyler Moore, 1975, Happy Days, 1975, Chico and the Man, 1975, Mork & Mindy, 1978, Bosom Buddies, 1982, Taxi, 1983, The Simpsons (voice), 1990, Frasier, 2004, I'm With Her, 2004; appeared in motion pictures How Sweet It Is, 1967, The Savage Seven, 1968, The Grasshopper, 1970, 1941, 1979, Movers and Shakers, 1985, She's Having a Baby, 1988, The Hard Way, 1991, Hocus Pocus, 1993, Get Shorty, 1995, Special Delivery, 1999, Stateside, 2004, Looking for Comedy in the Muslim World, 2005, Everybody Wants to Be Italian, 2007, Alice Upside Down, 2007, Blonde Ambition, 2007; dir. films: Jumpin' Jack Flash, 1986, Big, 1988, Awakenings, 1990 (exec. prodr.), A League of Their Own, 1992 (exec. prodr.), Renaissance Man, 1994 (exec. prodr.), The Preacher's Wife, 1996, The Time Tunnel: The Movie, 1999, Special Delivery, 1999, Riding in Cars with Boys, 2001; appeared in TV movie Jackie's Back, 1999; prodr. TV series A League of Their Own, 1993 (also dir. pilot), Dynasties, 2003, Crossover, 2004; dir. (TV Series) Working Stiffs, 1979; prodr. films Getting Away With Murder, 1996, With Friends Like These, 1998, Risk, 2003, Cinderella Man, 2005, Bewitched, 2005; exec. prodr. Calender Girl, 1993. Avocations: needlepoint, jigsaw puzzles, antique shopping. Office: c/o William Morris Agy 151 El Camino Dr Beverly Hills CA 90212

MARSHALL, PHILIP JAMES, astrophysicist; b. Melton Mowbray, Leicestershire, Eng., Feb. 28, 1978; s. Clifford James Marshall and Pauline Tavener. MSc in Natural Sci., U. Cambridge, 2000, PhD in Astrophysics, 2004. Postdoc. rsch. assoc. KIPAC, Stanford U., 2003—06; tabasgo prize fellow astrophysics U. Calif., Santa Barbara, 2006—. Contbr. scientific papers. Mem.: Am. Astron. Soc. Office: Univ Calif Dept Physics Santa Barbara CA 93101 Business E-Mail: pjm@physics.ucsb.edu.

MARSHALL, RICHARD TREEGER, lawyer; b. NYC, May 17, 1925; s. Edward and Sydney (Treeger) M.; m. Dorothy M. Goodman, June 4, 1950; children: Abigail Ruth Marshall, Stanley Marshall; m. 2d Sylvia J. Kelley, June 10, 1979. BS, Cornell U., 1948; JD, Yale U., 1951. Bar: Tex. 1952, U.S. Ct. Appeals (5th cir.) 1966, U.S. Ct. Appeals (10th cir.) 1980, U.S. Supreme Ct. 1959; lic. Tex. Dept. Ins. Pvt. practice, El Paso, Tex., 1952-59, 61-79; assoc. Fryer & Milstead, El Paso, 1952; sr. ptnr. Marshall & Wendorf, El Paso, 1959-61, Marshall & Volk, El Paso, 1979-81; sr. atty. Richard T. Marshall & Assocs., PC, El Paso, 1981-85; sr. ptnr. Marshall, Thomas & Winters, El Paso, 1985-87; sr. atty. Marshall & Winters, 1987-88, Marshall, Sherrod & Winters, 1988-90; pvt. practice El Paso, 1990—. Instr. polit. sci. U. Tex., El Paso, 1961-62; instr. ins. law C.L.U. tng. course Am. Coll.; officer, dir. Advance Funding, Inc., El Paso Editor El Paso Trial Lawyers Rev., 1973-80; contbr. articles to profl. jours. Mem. ABA, ATLA (sec. personal injury law sect. 1967-68, nat. sec. 1969-70, sec.-treas. environ. law sect. 1970-71, vice chmn. family law litigation sec. 1971-72), El Paso Bar Assn., El Paso Trial Lawyers Assn. (pres. 1965-66), Roscoe Pound-Am. Trial Lawyers Found. (commn. on profl. responsibility 1979-82). Office: 4110 Rio Bravo St Ste 100 El Paso TX 79902-1026 Office Phone: 915-779-6627. Business E-Mail: rtmlaw@gmail.com.

MARSHALL, ROBERT CHARLES, computer company executive; b. Berwyn, Ill., June 19, 1931; s. Joseph H. and Rose M.; m. Sarane Virruso, Aug. 1, 1954; children— Joseph, Lisa, Jim. BSE.E., Heald Engring. Coll., 1956; MBA, Pepperdine U., 1976. Engr. Lawrence Radiation Lab., Livermore, Calif., 1956-64; systems engr. Electronics Assos., Palo Alto, Calif., 1964-69; v.p. mfg. Diablo Systems, Hayward, Calif., 1969-75; with Tandem Computers, Inc., Cupertino, Calif., 1975—, sr. v.p., chief operating officer, dir., 1979-96; pres., CEO Info Gear, 1996-97; gen. ptnr. Selby Venture Ptnrs., 1998—. Served with U.S. Army, 1952-54. E-mail: Bob@selbyventures.com.

MARSHALL, ROBERT HERMAN, retired economics professor; b. Harrisburg, Pa., Dec. 6, 1929; s. Mathias and Mary (Bubich) M.; m. Billie Marie Sullivan, May 31, 1958; children: Mellisa Frances Hansen, Howard Hylton Irion, Robert Charles. AB magna cum laude, Franklin and Marshall Coll., 1951; MA, Ohio State U., 1952, PhD, 1957. Teaching asst. Ohio State U., 1952-57; mem. faculty, then prof. econs. U. Ariz., Tucson, 1957-95, prof. emeritus, 1995; dir. Internat. Bus. Studies Project, 1969-71. Research observer Sci.-Industry Program, Hughes Aircraft Co., Tucson, summer 1959 Author: Commercial Banking in Arizona: Structure and Performance Since World War II, 1966, (with others) The Monetary Process, 2d edit, 1980. Bd. dirs. Com. for Econ. Opportunity, Tucson, 1968-69. Faculty fellow Pacific Coast Banking Sch., summer 1974 Mem. Am. Econ. Assn., Phi Beta Kappa, Beta Gamma Sigma, Pi Gamma Mu, Phi Kappa Phi, Delta Sigma Pi. Democrat. Roman Catholic. Home: 6700 N Abington Rd Tucson AZ 85743-9795 Office Phone: 520-621-6224.

MARSHALL, ROBERT LEWIS, musicologist, educator; b. NYC, Oct. 12, 1939; s. Saul and Pearl (Shapiro) M.; m. Traute Maass, Sept. 9, 1966; children— Eric, Brenda. AB, Columbia U., 1960; M.F.A., Princeton U., 1962, PhD, 1968; postgrad., U. Hamburg, W. Ger., 1965. Instr. dept. music U. Chgo., 1966-68, asst. prof., 1968-71, assoc. prof., chmn. dept., 1972-78, prof., 1978-83, Brandeis U., 1983-2000, chmn. dept., 1985-93, incumbent endowed chair Louis, Frances and Jeffrey Sachar prof. music, 1986-2000; emeritus, 2000—. Vis. assoc. prof. Princeton U., 1971-72; endowed prof. Univ. Ala., 1994; mem. rev. bd. rsch. materials program NEH, 1982, rev. bd. edits., 1991. Author: The Compositional Process of J.S. Bach, 2 vols., 1972, The Music of Johann Sebastian Bach: The Sources; The Style; The Significance, 1989, Mozart Speaks: Views on Music, Musicians and the World, 1991, Dennis Brain on Record: A Comprehensive Discography of His Solo, Chamber, and Orchestral Recordings, 1996; editor New Bach Edit., Eighteenth Century Keyboard Music, 1994, 2d edit., 2003; co-editor: Variations on Canon: Essays on Music from Bach to Boulez in Honor of Charles Rosen, 2008; contbr. articles to musical jours. in U.S., Gt. Brit., Germany. Mem. music adv. bd. Ill. Arts Council, 1977-79. Recipient Deems Taylor award ASCAP, 1990; NEH fellow, 1978-79; Hon. Harold Spivacke consultantship Library of Congress. Mem. Am. Musicol. Soc. (bd. dirs. 1974-75, v.p. 1985-86, editl. bd. jour. 1975-80, rev. editor 1986-89, chmn. publs. com. 1991-94, Otto Kinkeldey prize 1974, hon. 2003), New Bach Soc. (chmn. Am. chpt. 1977-80), Phi Beta Kappa. Home: 100 Chestnut St Newton MA 02465-2538 E-mail: rmarshal@brandeis.edu.

MARSHALL, ROBERT NORMAN, hotel executive; b. Atlantic City, Dec. 13, 1943; s. Al and Frances Moskowitz; m. Gayle Robertson, June 14, 1970; 1 child, Rudi Lee. BS, NYU, 1965; MBA, LI U., Bklyn., 1968. Cert. hotel exec. Calif., 1973, cmty. coll. instructor Ca., Ariz. Exec. dir. Miami Conv. Bur., Fla., 1977—79; gen. mgr. Quadna Mountain Resort, Hill City, Minn., 1980—81; dir. sales Sheraton Hotels Hawaii, Honolulu, 1982—86; pres. Pacific Resorts Internat., Scottsdale, Ariz., 1986—. Nat. dir. Easter Seals, Miami, 1977—78. Business E-Mail: marshallsoffice@hotmail.com.

MARSHALL, RON, retail executive; b. 1954; BS with honors, Wright State U., 1976. V.p., CFO Barnes & Noble Bookstores; sr. v.p., CFO Dart Group Corp., Md., 1991-94; exec. v.p., CFO, Pathmark Stores, Inc., NJ, 1994-98; pres. Nash Finch Co., Mpls., 1998—2002, CEO, 1998—2006; prin. Wildridge Capital Mgmt., 2006—08; pres., CEO Borders Group, Inc., Ann Arbor, Mich., 2009—. Bd. dirs. Claire's Stores, Inc., 2007—, Borders Group, Inc., 2009—. Recipient Outstanding Alumni award, Wright State U., 2003. Mem. Food Mktg. Inst. (bd. dirs.). Office: Borders Group Inc 100 Phoenix Dr Ann Arbor MI 48108*

MARSHALL, SIMONE VERNIERE, psychologist, psychoanalyst; b. Paris; came to U.S., 1951; d. Urbain and Gabrielle (Cadiergues) Verniere; m. Robert J. Marshall, Sept. 13, 1953; childrren: Gabrielle, Annette. Lic. psychology, Sorbonne U., 1948; MA in Devel. Psychology, Columbia U., 1951, PhD in Clin. Psychology, 1959. Cert. in psychoanalysis, White Inst., N.Y.C., 1970. Rsch. sch. psychologist Nat. Bd. of Edn., Paris, 1948-51; child clin. psychologist Children's Hosp., Buffalo, N.Y., 1953-54; clin. psychologist N.J. Dept. of Instns., Trenton, N.J., 1956-58; clin. instr. Rutgers Univ. Psychology Clinic, New Brunswick, N.J., 1958-59; part-time cons. Bd. of Edn., Ossining, N.Y., 1960-64; child therapist Rockland Mental Health Ctr., Monsey, N.Y., 1961-65; pvt. practice psychologist, psychoanalyst Westchester, N.Y., 1960-90, NYC, 1966—. Tng. analyst Blanton Peale Inst. Religion & Health, N.Y.C., 1984-90; supr. Inst. for Contemporary Psychotherapy, N.Y.C., 1974-97; faculty Nassau County Med. Ctr., L.I. Inst. for Psychoanalysis, 1980-94; lectr. Union Theol. Sem., N.Y.C., 1983-8 6. Co-aauthor: (with R.J. Marshall) The Transference-Countertransference Matrix, 1988. Coord., founder Croton-Cortlandt Women's Ctr., Croton-on-Hudson, N.Y., 1976-81. Recipient Fullbright scholarship Columbia Univ., 1951-52. Mem. Am. Psychol. Assn., Am. Group Psychotherapy Assn., White Psychoanalytic Soc. Avocations: photography, painting. Home and Office: 300 E 74th St Apt 33D New York NY 10021-3746 Office Phone: 212-988-0634.

MARSHALL, SOPHIA S.L., director; b. Jackson, Miss., Apr. 30, 1970; d. Floyd Marshall, Sr. and Mamie A. Marshall. BS in Edn., Jackson State U., Miss., 1992; MS in Edn., U. Kans., Lawrence, 1996; EdS, Jackson State U., Miss., 1998; PhD, U. So. Miss., Hattiesburg, 2003. Lic. tchr. Miss. Dept. Edn. Tchr. elem. Jackson Pub. Schs., Miss., 1993—95; sr. specialist edn. Miss. Dept. Edn., Jackson; asst. prin. Vicksburg- Warren Sch. Dist., Miss.; tchr., coord. quality enhancement project Jackson State U.; asst. prof. Tougaloo Coll., Miss.; dir. tchr. edn. preparation program Hinds C.C., Utica, Miss. Dir. project Children Def. Fund Freedom Scholl, Tougaloo; cons. in field. Author: (poem) Child Protege, 1996 (named to Nat. Libr. Poetry, 1996). Recipient Dr. Edgar E. and Inez W. Smith Tchg. and Rsch. Faculty award; fellow, U. Kans., 1990; Kettering scholar. Mem.: ASCD (assoc.), Tri State Evaluative Rsch. and Capacity Bldg. (assoc.), Consortium Rsch. Ednl. Accountability and Tchr. Evaluation Nat. Evaluation Inst. (assoc.), Phi Kappa Phi (life), Delta Sigma Theta (life; chair 1994—95). Missionary Baptist. Office: Teacher Edn Preparation Program 34175 Hwy 18 PO Box 1109 Utica MS 39175-9638 Office Fax: 601-885-7183. Personal E-mail: ssl_marshall@yahoo.edu. Business E-Mail: ssmarshall@hindscc.edu.

MARSHALL, TERRYLYNNE, art educator, painter, sculptor; b. Murphy, NC, June 27, 1951; d. Robert A. and Dora Jo (Moreland) Marshall. EdS, U. Ga., Athens, 1996. Art instr. Truett-McConnell Coll., Cleveland, Ga., 1996—2001, 2005—. Pres. Towns County Hist. Soc., Hiawassee, Ga., 2004—, Yonah Art Guild, 2007—. Mem.: Ga. Art Edn. Assn. (Bus. Rep. 1994—2003, Gov. Exhibit chmn. 1997—2003, charter mem., Grassroots grantee, Disting. Svc. award 2000, 2004). Baptist. Avocation: art. Personal E-mail: terrylynnemarshall@yahoo.com.

MARSHALL, THOMAS CARLISLE, retired applied physics professor; b. Cleve., Jan. 29, 1935; s. Stephen Irby and Bertha Marie (Bieger) M.; children: Julian, John B.Sc., Case Inst. Tech., 1957; M.Sc., U. Ill., 1958, PhD, 1960. Asst. prof. elec. engring. U. Ill., 1961-62; mem. faculty Columbia U., 1962—2006, asst. prof. elec. engring., 1962-65, assoc. prof., 1965-70, prof. engring. sci., 1970-78, prof. applied physics, 1978—2006, prof. emeritus, 2007—. Author: Free Electron Lasers, 1985, Book of the Toade, 1992; contbr. more than 170 articles to profl. jours. Research grantee Dept. Energy, Office Naval Research, NSF. Fellow: Am. Phys. Soc. (study group on directed energy weapons 1985—87); mem.: Free Election Lasers and Advanced Concepts in Accelerator Physics. Office Phone: 212-854-3116, 914-953-2544. E-mail: tcm2@columbia.edu.

MARSHALL, TOM, publishing executive; b. Shreveport, La., 1954; With Lousiana Life; pub. Alaska mag., 1987—89; gen. mgr. Cooking Light, 1991—98; v.p. mktg. So. Living, 1998—2003; v.p., pub. Sunset, NYC, 2003—. Recipient Gen. Excellence Nat. Mag. award, 1983. Office: Sunset Time and Life Bldg 20th Fl 1271 Avenue of the Americas New York NY 10020 Office Phone: 212-522-9058. Business E-Mail: marshallt@sunset.com.

MARSHALL, VINCENT DE PAUL, industrial microbiologist, researcher; b. Washington, Apr. 5, 1943; s. Vincent de Paul Sr. and Mary Frances (Bach) M.; m. Sylvia Ann Kieffer, Nov. 15, 1986; children from previous marriage: Vincent de Paul III, Amy. BS, Northeastern State Coll., Tahlequah, Okla., 1965; MS, U. Okla. Health Sci. Ctr., Oklahoma City, 1967, PhD, 1970. Rsch. assoc. U. Ill., Urbana, 1970, postdoctoral fellow, 1971-73; rsch. scientist The Upjohn Co., Kalamazoo, Mich., 1973-74, rsch. head, 1975, sr. rsch. scientist, 1976-91, sr. scientist, 1991-2000; cons., 2000—. Mem. editl. bd. Jour. of Antibiotics, 1990-2001, Jour. Indsl. Microbiology, 1989-2001, Devels. in Indsl. Microbiology, 1990; contbr. numerous articles to profl. jours., chpts. to books; patentee in field. Served with U.S. Army Nat. Guard, 1960-65. NIH predoctoral fellow, 1967-70; NIH postdoctoral fellow, 1971-73. Fellow Am. Acad. Microbiology; mem. Soc. for Indsl. Microbiology (membership com. 1988-90, co-chair edn. com. 1989-93, local sects. com. 1991-96, chair nominating com. 1993-94, mem. nominating com. 1999-2000, co-chair program com. 1993-94, dir. 1994-96, pres. So. Great Lakes sect. 1992-95), Am. Soc. Microbiology, Am. Soc. Biochemistry and Molecular Biology, Internat. Soc. for Antimicrobial Activity of Non-Antibiotics (sci. adv. bd.), Sigma Xi. Republican. Lutheran. Home and Office: 203 Paisley Ct Kalamazoo MI 49006-4359 Home Phone: 269-349-3795; Office Phone: 269-349-3795. E-mail: vince3795@aol.com.

MARSHALL, WAYNE KEITH, anesthesiology educator; b. Richmond, Va., Feb. 9, 1948; s. Chester Truman and Lois Ann (Tiller) M.; m. Dale Claire Reynolds, June 18, 1977; children: Meredith Reynolds, Catherine Truman, Whitney Wood. BS in Biology, Va. Poly. Inst. and State U., 1970; MD, Va. Commonwealth U., 1974. Diplomate Am. Bd. Anesthesiology, Nat. Bd. Med. Examiners; bd. cert. in pain mgmt. Surg. intern U. Cin., 1974-75, resident in surgery, 1975-77; resident in anesthesiology U. Va. Coll. Medicine, Charlottesville, 1977-79, rsch. fellow, 1979-80; asst. prof. anesthesia Pa. State U. Coll. Medicine, Hershey, 1980-86, assoc. prof., 1986-95, assoc. clin. dir. oper. rm., 1982-95, dir. pain mgmt. svc., 1984-95, chief divsn. pain mgmt., 1992-95; prof., chmn. dept. anesthesiology Med. Coll. Va., Richmond, 1995-99; med. dir. operating rms. MCV Hosp., 1995-99; prof. anesthesiology Coll. Medicine Pa. State U., Hershey, 1999—2004; pvt. practice, 2004—. Moderator nat. meetings. Mem. editorial bd. Am. Jour. Anesthesiology, 1987-99, Jour. Neurosurg. Anesthesiology, 1988—2004; contbr. articles and abstracts to med. jours. Recipient Antarctic Svc. medal NSF, 1980. Mem. AMA, Soc. Neurosurg. Anesthesia and Critical Care (sec.-treas. 1985-87, v.p. 1987-88, pres. 1989-90, bd. dirs. 1985-91), Assn. Univ. Anesthetists, Am. Soc. Anesthesiologists (del. ASA ho. of dels. 1990-92), Internat. Anesthesia Rsch. Soc., Pa. Soc. Anesthesiology. Republican. Baptist. Office Phone: 717-766-1127. Personal E-mail: wmarsh2723@aol.com.

MARSHALL, WILLIAM, III, think-tank executive; b. Norfolk, Va., 1952; m. Katryn S. Nicolai; children: Olivia, William. BA in English and History, U. Va., 1975. Reporter Richmond Times-Dispatch; various positions on Capitol Hill and electoral politics; policy dir. Dem. Leadership Coun., 1985-89; pres. Progressive Found., 1989—; pres., founder Progressive Policy Inst., Washington, 1989—. Sr. editor 1984 House Dem. Caucus policy, Renewing America's Promise; participant in drafting nat. legis., including a demonstration project for vol. nat. svc. Nat. Cmty. Svc. Act of 1990; press sec., spokesman, speechwriter for 1984 U.S. Senate campaign of current N.C. Gov. Jim Hunt; speechwriter, policy analyst for late U.S. Rep. Gillis Long of La., chmn. of House Dem. Caucus; spokesman, speechwriter 1982 U.S. Senate campaign of former Va. Lt. Gov. Dick Davis. Co-editor: Mandate for Change, 1992; editor: Building the Bridge: 10 Big Ideas to Transform America, 1997, With All Our Might: A Progressive Strategy for Defeating Jihadism and Defending Liberty, 2006; contbr. articles to profl. jours. Office: Progressive Policy Inst 600 Pennsylvania Ave SE Ste 400 Washington DC 20003-4350 Office Phone: 202-547-0001.*

MARSHALL, WILLIS HENRY, psychiatrist; b. Covington, Ky., Nov. 28, 1936; s. Willis Henry Sr. and Pauline Elizabeth (Murphy) M.; m. Carolyn Mae Kowalski; children: Louann Lorinda Marshall Johnson, John Willis. AB cum laude, U. Evansville, Ind., 1958; MD, Ind. U., Bloomington, 1961. Cert. psychiatry Am. Assn. Psychiat. Medicine, 2005. Intern Detroit Meml. Hosp., 1961-62; resident psychiatry Mental Health Inst., Cherokee, Iowa, 1965-67, 69-70, staff psychiatrist, 1967-69, Mental Health Ctr., Muskegon, Mich., 1970-71; pvt. practice psychiatry Madison, Tenn., 1974-85, Bowling Green, Ky., 1987-98; staff psychiatrist chief admission svc., staff psychiatrist treatment unit Mid. Tenn. Mental Health Inst., Nashville, 1981—85, staff psychiatrist evaluation unit forensic svcs. div., 1985—87, chief of staff, 1986-87; forensic psychiatrist State of Tenn., 1981—87; staff psychiatrist Moccasin Bend Mental Health Inst., Chattanooga, 1998—2003; staff psychiatrist, med. dir. Crisis Stabilization Unit Vol. Behavioral Health Svcs. Ctr., Chattanooga, 2003—05, outpatient psychiatrist, 2005—. Part-time staff psychiatrist Ottawa County Mental Health Ctr., Grand Haven, Mich., 1971-73, Tenn. Dept. Mental Health and Mental Retardation Mid. Tenn. Mental Health Inst., Nashville, 1981-87, Lifeskills, Inc., Glasgow, Ky., Franklin, Ky., 1987-89; psychiat. cons. Allegan County Mental Health Ctr., Allegen, Mich., 1973; med. svcs. cons. dept. of forensic svcs. Mid. Tenn. Mental Health Inst., Nashville, 1983-84; clin. asst. prof. psychiatry dept. allied health Trevecca Nazaraene Coll., Nashville, 1985-87; part-time pvt. practice psychiatry, Muskegon, Mich., 1970-74, Madison, Tenn., 1974-87; assoc. clin. dir. mental health unit Med. Ctr., Bowling Green, Ky., 1987-91; preceptor, asst. clin. prof. resident physician asst. program U. Ky., 1988-91; acting med. dir. Rivendell Children's Psychiat. Hosp., Bowling Green, 1989; med. dir. adult mental health unit Rivendell of Ky., 1992-94. Prin. works include several sculptures and paintings. Commd. officer, surgeon USPHS, 1962-65. Recipient AMA Physicians Recognition award, 1969, 79, 83, 86, 89, 92, Exemplary Psychiatrist award Nat. Alliance for Mentally Ill, 1993; named to Am. Top Psychiatrists, 2007, 08. Mem. Am. Psychiat. Assn. (life, art assn. 1976—), Ky. Med. Assn., Warren County Med. Soc., Am. Profl. Practice Assn., Am. Acad. Clin. Psychiatrists, Am. Assn. of Psychiat. Medicine, Am. Physicians Art Assn., NRA, Nat. Geog. Soc., AAA Automobile Club, Gallatin Gun Club, Alpha Omega Alpha. Republican. Adventist. Avocations: sculpture, photography, painting, hunting, fixing old guns. Home: 5115 Silver Ln Apison TN 37302-9594 Office: 420 Bell Ave Chattanooga TN 37405 also: Pub Consumers Rsch Coun Am 2020 Pennsylvania Ave NW Ste 300-A Washington DC 20006 Office Phone: 423-634-8884 ext. 1193.

MARSHALL-BEASLEY, ELIZABETH, landscape architect; d. Hamilton West Marshall, Jr. and Mary Barno Marshall; m. James W. Beasley, Jr., Nov. 28, 1986. BA, Princeton U., 1981; M in Landscape Arch., Fla. Internat. U., 1998. Policy analyst N.J. Legislature, 1981; field devel. dir. The Rouse Co., 1984; devel. mgr. Disney Devel. Co., Orlando, Fla., 1988; devel. dir. Norton Mus. Art, West Palm Beach, Fla., 1995; state orgn. dir. Jeb Bush for Gov., Tallahassee, 1996; project mgr., apprentice Morgan Wheelock Inc., West Palm Beach, 1999—2001; cons. Elizabeth Marshall-Beasley, West Palm Beach, 2001—02; pres. Elizabeth Marshall-Beasley, MLA, West Palm Beach, 2003—. Pres. coun. Nat. Pub. Radio, Washington, 2001—; gov. apptd. Bd. Landscape Arch., Tallahassee, 2002—; bd. dirs. Habitat for Humanity, West Palm Beach, New Horizon Svc. Dogs, Orlando. Sponsor Nantucket Conservation Found.; mem. curriculum com. Fla. A&M U. Grad. Sch. Arch.; active US VA Task Force Health and Rehab. Gardens; apptd. mem. City West Palm Beach Art in Pub. Places Commn.; mayor Art in Pub. Places Commn., 2006—. Recipient, ADDY, 1987, Comml. Project of 1989, Architecture Record, 1989; Fairchild Tropical Gardens: Off Site Collection Grad. scholar, 1997. Mem.: Am. Soc. Landscape Arch. (cert.), Sigma Alpha Lambda, Phi Kappa Phi. Episcopalian. Avocations: travel, theater. Office: Ste 1500 505 S Flagler Dr West Palm Beach FL 33401 E-mail: em-b@landplandesign.com.

MARSHALL TRAINO, HEATHER M., researcher; d. Warren D. Marshall and Lewellyne C. Blanchard; m. Anthony J. Traino, June 2, 2007. PhD, SUNY, Buffalo, 2006. Asst. prof. Rochester Inst. Tech., NY, 2006—07; postdoc. fellow Va. Commonwealth U., Richmond, 2007—09, instr., 2009—. Mem.: Nat. Communication Assn. Office: Va Commonwealth Univ PO Box 980149 Richmond VA 23298 Office Fax: 804-828-5440.

MARSHBURN, THOMAS H., astronaut, emergency physician; b. Statesville, NC, Aug. 29, 1960; m. Ann. M. Sanders; 1 child. BS in Physics, Davidson Coll., NC, 1982; M in Engring. Physics, U. Va., 1984; MD, Wake Forest U., 1989; M in Med. Sci., U. Tex. Med. Br., 1997. Lic. private, instrument, aerobatic and commercial pilot. Tng. in emergency medicine St. Vincent's, Toledo, 1989—92, life flight physician; worked as emergency physician Seattle; accepted into first class of the NASA/UTMB Space Medicine Fellowship Galveston, Tex.; emergency physician in area hospitals Houston; emergency physician Mass. Gen. Hosp., Boston; attending in emergency medicine U. Tex.-Houston; flight surgeon, Space Shuttle Med. Ops. and Joint US/Russian Space Program NASA, 1994; flight surgeon Cosmonaut Tng. Ctr., Star City, Russia, 1996—97, Flight Control, Carole, Russia; co-chair, med. ops. Shuttle/Mir Space Program, 1997—98; dep. flight surgeon STS-98 Mission (Neuronal), 1998—2000; lead flight surgeon STS-101 Mission to Internat. Space Station, Expedition 7 to Internat. Space Station, 2003; med. ops. lead for Internat. Space Station; completed astronaut candidate tng. NASA, 2006; crew mem. STS-127 Mission (Endeavour), 2009. NASA rep. to Harvard/MIT Smart Med. Systems Team of Nat. Space Biomedical Rsch. Inst., Boston. Recipient NASA Superior Achievement award, 1998, Space and Life Sciences Divsn. Spl. Space Flight Achievement award, 2003, 2004, Lyndon B. Johnson Space Ctr. Superior Achievement award, 2004. Mem.: Aircraft Owners and Pilot's Assn., Am. Acad. Emergency Medicine, Aerospace Med. Assn. Avocations: backpacking, mountain climbing, scuba diving, swimming, snowboarding, guitar, reading. Office: NASA-Astronauts Office Johnson Space Ctr 2101 NASA Parkway Houston TX 77058*

MARSTON, CHRISTOPHER M., federal agency administrator; b. Grosse Pointe, Mich., 1974; m. Michelle Marston; 1 child, Abby. AB in Govt., cum laude, Dartmouth Coll., Hanover, NH, 1996; JD cum laude, Georgetown U. Law Ctr., DC, 2003. Congl. intern to staff mem. com. govt. reform and oversight US Ho. of Reps., 1996—97, asst. to Rep. Rob Portman, 1998, sys. analyst office of parliamentarian, 1998—2001; chief of staff Office Nat. Drug Policy, 2001—04; dir. Ohio state/fed. rels. Office Gov. Bob Taft, DC, 2004—06; White House liaison US Dept. Interior, 2006—07; dep. asst. sec. for mgmt. US Dept. Edn., 2007—08, asst. sec. Office of Mgmt., 2008—. Past pres. Alexandria Vol. Bur.; chmn. Alexandria Rep. City Com. Recipient Gov.'s award, Va. Rep. Party, 2007. Office: US Dept Edn 400 Maryland Ave SW Washington DC 20202

MARSTON, DOUGLAS ROBERT, engineering educator; b. Pitts., May 24, 1948; s. Douglas Robert and Margaret Haas Marston. Lic. radiotelephone Fed. Comm. Commn., 1965. Elect. tech, instr. Northrop Aircraft, Hawthorne, Calif., 1972—84; prof. electronics El Camino Coll., Torrance, Calif., 1982—. Mem.: Spectrum Mgt. Assoc. (pres. 2004—05). Avocation: skeet shooting. Office: El Camino Coll 16007 Crenshaw Blvd Torrance CA 90506-0003 Business E-Mail: dmarston@elcamino.edu.

MARSTON, EDGAR JEAN, III, lawyer; b. Houston, July 5, 1939; s. Edgar Jr. and Jean (White) M.; m. Graeme Meyers, June 21, 1961; children: Christopher Graham, Jonathan Andrew. BA, Brown U., 1961; JD, U. Tex., 1964. Bar: Tex. 1964. Law clk. to presiding justice Supreme

Ct. Tex., Austin, 1964-65; assoc. Baker & Botts, Houston, 1965-71; ptnr. Bracewell & Patterson, L.L.P., Houston, 1971-89, 96—. of counsel, 1990-96; exec. v.p., gen. counsel Southdown, Inc., Houston, 1987-95, also bd. dirs. Mem. ABA, Tex. Bar Assn., Tex. Bar Found., Houston Bar Assn., Houston Country Club, Coronado Club. Episcopalian. Avocations: hunting, fishing, stamp collecting/philately, reading. Office: Bracewell & Giuliani LLP 711 Louisiana St Ste 2300 Houston TX 77002-2770 Office Phone: 713-221-1315. E-mail: edgar.marston@bgllp.com.

MARSTON, MICHAEL, economist, consultant; b. Oakland, Calif., Dec. 4, 1936; s. Lester Woodbury and Josephine (Janovic) Marston; m. Alexandra Lynn Geyer, Apr. 30, 1966; children: John, Elizabeh. BA, U. Calif., Berkeley, 1959; postgrad., London Sch. Econs., 1961—63. Cert. rev. appraiser Nat. Assn. Rev. Appraisers and Mortgage Underwriters, 1984. V.p. Larry Smith & Co., San Francisco, 1969—72, exec. v.p. urban econ. divsn., 1969—72; chmn. bd. Keyser Marston Assocs., Inc., San Francisco, 1973—87; gen. ptnr. The Sequoia Partnership, 1979—91; pres. Marston Vineyard and Winery, 1982—, Marston Assocs., Inc., 1982—. Pres. The Ctr. Individual and Instnl. Renewal, 1996—. Contbr. articles to profl. jours. Mem. spkr. bus. Am. Embassy, London, 1961—63; mem. Gov.'s Issue Anlysis Com. and Spkr. Bur., 1966; v.p., bd. dirs. Dem. Forum, 1968—72; chmn. San Francisco Waterfront Com., 1969—86; v.p. People for Open Space, 1972—87, mem. exec. com., 1972—87; chmn. fin. com. San Francisco Planning and Urban Rsch. Assn., 1976—87, bd. dirs., 1976—87, mem. exec. com., 1976—87, treas., 1976—87; bd. trustees Cathedral Sch. Boys, 1981—82, Marin Country Day Sch., 1984—90; pres. Presidio Heights Assn. Neighbors, 1983—84; mem. Napa Valley Vintners, 1986—, mem. gov. affairs com.; v.p. St. Luke's Sch., 1986—91; chmn. Presidio Com., 1991—; v.p., trustee Youth for Svc. Served to lt. USNR. Mem.: Napa Valley Vintners, Calif. Vintage Wine Soc., World Congress Land Policy, Urban Land Inst., Pacific Union Club, Bohemian Club, Order of Golden Bear, Chevalier du Tastevin, Lambda Alpha. Home: 3375 Jackson St San Francisco CA 94118-2018 *Personal philosophy: Success is what you do with what you have not what others think or what is in vogue.*

MARSTON, MICHELLE PRESSON, legislative staff member; b. New Brunswick, NJ, Feb. 18, 1970; m. Christopher Michael Marston, June 2008. BA, Mt. Holyoke Coll., 1991; JD, Coll. of William and Mary, 1998. Bar: Va. 1998, US Ct. Appeals for Armed Forces 1998. Legis. asst. for Rep. Chris Smith US House of Reps., Washington, 1992—95, legis. counsel for Rep. Tillie Fowler, 1999—2000, legis dir. for Rep. Ander Crenshaw, legis dir. for Rep. Randy Forbes, 2001—02, chief of staff for Rep. Scott Garrett, 2006—08, chief of staff for Rep. Michele Bachmann, 2008—; field dir. Rep. Nat. Com., 2005. Clk. US Ct. Appeals for the Armed Forces, 1998—99. Roman Catholic. Office: Office of Congresswoman Michele Bachmann 107 Cannon House Office Bldg Washington DC 20515 E-mail: michelle.presson@mail.house.gov.*

MARSZALEK, ELIZABETH A., computer graphics designer, educator; b. Davenport, Iowa; BS, Marycrest Coll., Davenport, Iowa, 1985; MS, No. Ill. U., DeKalb, Ill., 1987. Dir. mail computer programmer Gen. Bus. Forms, Skokie, Ill., 1987—89; sys. operator ProData, Des Plaines, Ill., 1989—90; sr. sys. operator Techtron Studio, Chgo., 1990—91; sr. trainer Linotype-Hell Co., Chgo., 1991—93; prof. Coll. DuPage, Glen Ellyn, Ill., 1993—. Mem.: Graphic Arts Tchrs. Ill., Soc. Am. Artists, Graphic Arts Tech. Found. Office: College of DuPage 425 Fawell Blvd Glen Ellyn IL 60137 Home Fax: 630-942-4472. Personal E-mail: marszale@cod.edu.

MARSZALEK, WIESLAW, electrical engineering educator; b. Nowa Deba, Poland, Dec. 10, 1957; s. Stanislaw and Kazimiera (Trzaska) M.; m. Alina Marianna Jemielita, Oct. 24, 1981; children: Joanna, Adam. MS, Tech. U., Warsaw, Poland, 1981, PhD, 1984, Habilitation, 1990. Asst. prof. elec. engring. Tech. U., Opole, Poland, 1984-90, prof., 1991—; postdoctoral fellow Alexander von Humboldt Found., Bonn, Fed. Republic of Germany, 1990-92. Vis. asst. prof. U. Thrace, Xanthi, Greece, 1988; organizer sci. confs.; parenter in field; reviewer various sci. jours. Author: Analysis and Synthesis of Dynamical Systems, 1986, Structure Analysis of Singular Systems with Orthogonal Functions, 1990, (with Z. Trzaska) Theory of Electrical Signals and Circuits, 1987; also articles. Recipient 3d class award Min. Edn., Warsaw, Poland, 1986, 89. Mem. Am. Math. Soc. (jour. reviewer 1988—). Roman Catholic. Avocation: travel. Office: DeVry Univ 630 US Highway 1 North Brunswick NJ 08902

MARTA, DAWN RENEÉ, psychologist; b. Ottawa, Ill., Sept. 10, 1963; d. Bruce Roger Rooks and Marsha Ann (Meade) Monroe; m. David Lee LeBeau (div. Oct. 1987); 1 child, Nicholas Scott LeBeau; m. Scott Kennedy Echols (dec. Feb. 1996); m. Anthony John Marta, Dec. 21, 2001. Student, Fla. C.C., Jacksonville, 1990—93; AA in Medicine, Ctrl. Fla. C.C., Ocala, Fla., 1994; student, Santa Fe C.C., Gainesville, 1994; BA in Philosophy with high honors, U. Fla., 1997; MDiv in Theology, Duke U., 2000; postgrad., George Fox U., 2000; D in Psychology, Argosy U., 2004. Cert. personal trainer Am. Coun. Exercise. Membership dir. Duval County Med. Soc., Jacksonville, Fla., 1987—93; emergency rm. admissions rep. Munroe Regional Med. Ctr., Ocala, Fla., 1993—94; admissions rep. Shands Hosp. U. Fla., Gainesville, 1994; adminstr. Covenant Presbyn. Ch., Gainesville, 1994—95; chaplain Duke U. Med. Ctr., Durham, NC, 1998—2000; personal trainer Ottawa, Elgin, 2000—04; resident Meridian Behavioral Health Svcs., 2004—05; clin. psychologist, owner, operator Ctr. Human Flourishing, Andrews, 2005—. Usher First United Meth. Ch., Chgo., 2002, Elgin, 2003—04, trustee edn. com., 2003—04; mem. Andrews Methodist Ch, Andrews, NC. Mem.: APA, NC Psychology Assn. Avocations: bodybuilding, bicycling, hiking, kayaking, travel. Office: Ctr Human Flourshing 34 First St Box 2462 Andrews NC 28901 Office Phone: 828-321-9900. E-mail: drmarta11@verizon.net.

MARTE-BAUTISTA, HELEN I., retired performing arts educator; d. Diosdado and Modesta Inocencio Marte; 1 child, Andreliz Marte Bautista. MA, San Francisco State U., 1970. Cert. Calif. State credential. Educator, staff devel. San Francisco Unified Sch. Dist., 1968—98. Commr. San Francisco Pub. Libr., 2000—; trustee Am. Libr. Trustee Assn., Chgo., 2002—. Choreographer (prodn.) dance drama, Santa Cruzan (Dance-in-Residence award, 1968). Pres. City Celebration, Inc. Ethnic Dance Festival, San Francisco, 1984—88; sec., bd. mem. Kearny St. Housing Corp., Inc., San Francisco, 1986; pres. Friends of the San Francisco Commn. and Status of Women, 1986—88; treas. YWCA - San Francisco, Marin and San Mateo County, 1990—96; treas. Mayor's Protocol Office San Francisco/Manila Sister City Com., 1996; citizen adv. mem. Presidio Redevel. U.S. Dept. of Interior, San Francisco, 1997—99; sec., mem. bd. Internat. Hotel Sr. Housing Corp., Inc., San Francisco, 1998. Recipient Summer/Residence Citizenship award, Ethical Union Soc., Philippine Scouts Assn., U. Calif., Berkeley, 1961, Merit award outstanding pub. svc., San Francisco Mayor's Office Diane Feinstein, 1984, Human Rights award, San Francisco, Human Rights Commn., 1985; grantee Spl. Edn. program bilingual tchrs., U. San Francisco, 1979; Melvin Jones fellow, Lion's Found., 2005. Mem.: Delta Kappa Gamma (assoc.; pres. 1982—84, Beta Chi chpt.), Am. Fedn. of Teachers (assoc.; mem. of the bd. 1971—76), Fil-Am. Lions Club San Francisco (pres.), Am. Lions Club San Francisco (assoc.; mem. of the bd. 1988, Presdl. award 1996). Avocations: travel, art, music, literature, dance.

MARTEL, JOHN SHELDON, lawyer, writer, musician; b. Stockton, Calif., Jan. 1, 1931; s. Henry T. and Alice L. M.; m. Bonnie Martel; children: John Sheldon, Melissa Ann. BS, U. Calif.-Berkeley, 1956, JD, 1959. Bar: Calif. 1959. Dep. dist. atty., Alameda County, 1960-61; assoc. trial atty. firm Bronson, Bronson & McKinnon, San Francisco, 1961-64; ptnr. firm Farella, Braun & Martel, San Francisco, 1964—. Lectr., mem. adv. bd. Hastings Ctr. for Trial and Appellate Adv., 1983—. Author: (novels) Partners, 1988, Conflicts of Interest, 1994, The Alternate, 1999, Billy Strobe, 2001, screenplay, 2009; author, editor legal publs.; composer-writer popular songs and CDs; profl. musician. Pilot USAF, 1951-54. Winner Am. Song Festival awards, 1978-80, 82, 85, 87. Fellow Am. Coll. Trial Lawyers (state chmn. 1985-87, bd. regents 1993-98); mem. ABA (litigation, antitrust, tort and ins. sects.), Calif. Bar Assn., San Francisco Bar Assn. (former chair litigation sect.), Am. Bd. Trial Lawyers (bd. dirs. 1991-93), Am. Fedn. Musicians, Phi Delta Phi, Kappa Sigma. Office: Farella Braun & Martel 235 Montgomery St Ste 3100 San Francisco CA 94104-2902 Office Phone: 415-954-4422. Personal E-mail: johnwriter@aol.com. E-mail: jmartel@fbm.com.

MARTEL, MARCI, mental health services professional; b. Corvallis, Oreg., Nov. 15, 1971; d. Burlie Allen and Lois Louise Brunson; m. Allan Joseph Martel; children: Katherine Elizabeth, Alexander Joseph, Christopher Michael. BS in Human Svcs., Springfield Coll., Mass., 1996, MS in Cmty. Psychology, 1998; PhD, Capella U., Mpls., 2008. Lic. clin. mental health counselor State NH Bd. Mental Health Practice, 2001. Social worker Abenaki Indian Ctr., Inc., Manchester, NH, 1994—96; clin. treatment coord. Easter Seal Soc. NH, Manchester, 1998—2000; regional dir. Familystrength, Nashua, NH, 2000—02; asst. prof. Hesser Coll., Manchester, 2001—05; adj. faculty Southern NH U., Manchester, 2005—, Rivier Coll., 2009—; owner NE Counseling Assocs., LLC, Nashua, 2001—. Cons. Nashua Pastoral Care Ctr., NH, 2001—. Vol. Salvation Army, Manchester, 1996—2009. Office: Northeast Counseling Assocs LLC 6 Concord St Nashua NH 03064 Personal E-mail: marcimartelphd@aol.com.

MARTEL, ROLAND M., engineering executive; BA in Math., Colby Coll., Waterville, Maine, 1976; MBA in Ops. Mgmt., Cornell U., Ithaca, NY, 1982. Gen. mgr. Anchor Stampings Ill. Tool Works Inc. (ITW), Glenview, Ill., 1994, various v.p. and pres. positions Metal Components divsn., pres. Global Automotive Divsn., 2005—06, exec. v.p. global automotive components businesses, 2006—. Office: Ill Tool Works 3600 W Lake Ave Glenview IL 60026-1215 Office Phone: 847-724-7500. Office Fax: 847-657-4572.*

MARTELET, FRANCOIS R., pharmaceutical executive; b. Dijon, France, Feb. 17, 1960; m. Marie Santiard, July 9, 1991; children: Marie-Alix, Alexandre, Astrid-Marie. M in Bus., Dijon U., MD. Degree in med. law: France; cert. Advanced Gen. Mgmt. Program. Internat. mktg. trainee F. Hoffmann-La Roche, 1991—92, product mgr. Stockholm, 1992—94, group product mgr., 1994—95, internat. product mgr. Basel, Switzerland, 1996—96; head regional oncology, Europe, Middle East, Africa Eli Lilly Corp., London, 1996—99; bus. unit head Benelux Schering-Plough, Brussels, 1999—2000; v.p. pharma oncology intercontinental region, Latam, Asia-Pacific, CEE, Middle East, Africa) Novartis Pharma, East Hanover, NJ, 2001—03; regional head, Cen. and Ea. Europe, Mid. East, Africa Novartis, Munich, 2003—, Basel, Switzerland, 2003—05; v.p. oncology worldwide, human health divsn. Merck & Co., Inc., Whitehouse Station, NJ, 2005—06; French instr. US Mil. Acad., West Point, NY, 2006—; CEO AVAC Tech., 2007—. Lt. col. French Army Res., 2005—. Decorated Military Svcs. medal France. Mem.: Chem. Pharm. Assn., Internat. Execs. Resource Group, INSEAD Alumni, Greater Phila. Execs. Club, NJ Execs. Club. Roman Catholic. Avocations: skiing, horseback riding, jumping. Home: 9 Washington ST FL 2 Morristown NJ 07960-9490 Office Phone: 908-500-5549. Personal E-mail: francoismartelet@yahoo.com.

MARTELL, TERRENCE F., stock exchange executive; Sr. v.p. Commodity Exchange, Inc.; staff Zicklin Sch. of Bus., Baruch Coll., 1992—; dep. dept. chair Baruch Coll. Faculty Senate, 1992—2004; pub. dir. New York Bd of Trade, 2001—; mem. Exec. Com. and Audit Com., New York Bd of Trade; mem. bd. dir. IntercontinentalExchange (ICE), 2007—, vice-chmn., 2007—. Bd. mem. Manhattan Chamber of Commerce, Reuters/Jefferies CRB Index Oversight Com. Office: ICE Futures US World Fin Ctr One North End Ave 13 th Fl New York NY 10282 Office Phone: 212-748-4000.*

MARTELLA, ROGER ROMULUS, JR., lawyer, former federal agency administrator; b. 1970; m. Ann Martella; 3 children. BA, Cornell U., 1992; JD, Vanderbilt U., 1995. Law clk. to Hon. David Ebel US Ct. Appeals (10 Cir.), 1995—96; assoc. Sidley Austin LLP, Washington, 1996—98; prin. counsel Complex Litig. Natural Resources Sect. US Dept. Justice, Washington; prin. dep. gen. counsel EPA, Washington, 2005—06, acting gen. counsel, 2006—07, asst. adminstr., gen. counsel, 2007—08; ptnr. Sidley Austin LLP, Washington, 2008—. Mem. Warrenton Town Coun. Named Ctr. Dist. Citizen of Yr. Mem.: Knights of Columbus. Office: Sidley Austin LLP 1501 K St Washington DC 20005 Office Phone: 202-736-8097. Office Fax: 202-736-8711. E-mail: rmartella@sidney.com.*

MARTELLI, PHIL, men's college basketball coach; m. Judy Martelli; children: Phil Jr., Jimmy, Elizabeth. Grad., Widener U., Chester, Pa., 1976, D (hon.) in Pub. Svc., 2004; LHD (hon.), Cabrini Coll., Radnor, Pa., 2006. Head basketball coach Bishop Kenrick HS; asst. coach Widener U. Pioneers, St. Joseph's U. Hawks, Phila., 1985—95, head coach, 1995—. Asst. coach Goodwill Games, 1998, FIBA World Championship for Young Men, 2001; head coach USA Under-21 World Championship Team, 2005. Active Coaches vs. Cancer, Phila. Chpt. Recipient Harry Litwack award, 2004; named Big 5 Coach of Yr., 1996, 1997, Coach of Yr., Atlantic 10 Conf., 1997, 2001, 2004, 2005, USBWA Dist. I, 2003, 2004, NABC Dist. 2, 2004, Consensus Nat. Coach of Yr., 2004, Citizen of Yr., March of Dimes, 2004; named to CYO Hall of Fame, Archdiocese Phila., Pa. Sports Hall of Fame, 2000. Office: Saint Joseph's U Athletic Dept 5600 City Ave Philadelphia PA 19131 Office Phone: 610-660-1706.*

MARTEN, GORDON CORNELIUS, agronomist, educator, federal agency administrator; b. Wittenberg, Wis., Sept. 14, 1935; s. Clarence George and Cora Levina (Verpoorten) M.; m. Lynette Joy Hanson, Sept. 9, 1961; 1 dau., Kimberly Joy. BS, U. Wis., 1957; MS, U. Minn., 1959, PhD, 1961; postgrad., Purdue U., 1962; DSc (hon.), U. Minn., 2006. Rsch. agronomist U.S. Dept. Agr., U. Minn., St. Paul, 1961-72, supervisory rsch. agronomist, rsch. leader, 1972-89; adj. prof. agronomy U. Minn., St. Paul, 1971-96; assoc. dir. USDA-Agr. Rsch. Svc., Beltsville, Md., 1989-96; prof. emeritus U. Minn., St. Paul, 1996—. Mem. governing body and U.S. rep. to OECD Biol. Resource Mgmt. Program, Paris, 1990-96; adminstrv. coun. USDA Sustainable Agrl. Rsch. and Edn. Program, 1993-95. Assoc. editor: Crop Sci., 1972-74; sr. editor USDA Handbook Near Infrared Reflectance Spectroscopy: Analysis of Forage Quality, 1985, rev. edit., 1989; mem. edit. bd. Sci. of Food and Agriculture, 1985-90; contbr. numerous articles to profl. jours. NSF grad. fellow, 1959-61; recipient Merit award Am. Forage and Grassland Coun., 1976, Outstanding Svc. award, 1981, Civil Servant of Yr. award Twin Cities, Minn., 1976, Cert. of Merits, USDA Agrl. Rsch. Svc., Northrup King Faculty Outstanding Performance award U. Minn., 1986, Superior Svc. award USDA, 1987; named to Hall of Fame, Wausau Wis. Sch. Dist., 1998. Fellow: Crop Sci. Soc. Am. (bd. dirs. 1975—77), Am. Soc. Agronomy; mem.: Agronomic Sci. Found. (trustee 1984—89), Coun. Agr. Sci. and Tech. (bd. dirs. 1985—90), Am. Forage and Grassland Coun. (bd. dirs. 1977—80), North Suburban St. Paul Golden K Kiwanis (bd. dirs. 1998—2001), Biol. Club, Sigma Xi, Phi Kappa Phi, Delta Theta Sigma, Alpha Zeta, Gamma Sigma Delta (Adminstrn. award of merit Nat. Capital Area 1994). Lutheran. Home: 1312 Willow Cir Roseville MN 55113-3235

MARTEN, TIMOTHY JAMES, plastic surgeon; b. Kingstown, RI, Jan. 7, 1956; MD, U. Calif., Davis, 1982. Cert. Plastic Surgery, 1993. Intern surgery Kaiser Found. Hosp., Oakland, Calif., 1982—83, resident plastic surgery, 1983—87; resident U. Ill., Chgo., 1987—89; staff mem. Calif. Pacific Med. Ctr., San Francisco, 1990—, St. Mary's Hosp. Med. Ctr., San Francisco, 1990—, St. Francis Hosp. Med. Ctr., San Francisco, 1990—; pvt. practice Marten Clinic of Plastic Surgery, San Francisco. Office: Marten Clinic Of Plastic Surgery 450 Sutter St Rm 2222 San Francisco CA 94108-4201 Office Phone: 415-677-9937. Office Fax: 415-677-9473. E-mail: info@martenclinic.com.

MARTENS, LESLIE VERNON, retired dentistry educator, consultant; b. Peoria, Ill., Oct. 15, 1938; s. Vernon Christ and Lydia Rachel (Weisenburger) M.; m. Judith A., June 15, 1961 (div. Nov. 1988); children: Michael J., Philip S., Eric W., Pamela A. Student, Bradley U., Peoria, Ill., 1956—59; DDS, Loyola U. Chgo., 1963; MPH, U. Minn., Mpls., 1969. Dental officer, maj. U.S. Army Dental Corps., Tex., 1963-68; asst. prof., assoc. dir. Grad. Program in Dental Pub. Health U. Minn., Mpls., 1969—72, from assoc. prof. to prof. emeritus Schs. Dentistry and Pub. Health, 1972—2005, prof. Schs. Dentistry and Pub. Health, 1982—2005, prof. emeritus, 2006—, chmn. dept. preventive scis. Sch. Dentistry, 1982—2001. Cons. to 21 dental schs. and 40 other health related agys. and orgns., 1972—. Contbr. over 95 articles to profl. jours.; patentee in field. Chmn. Red Cross Vol. Program, U.S. Army, 1963-67; merit badge counselor Boy Scouts Am., Anoka, Minn., 1972-89. Maj. U.S. Army, 1963-68, Germany. Grantee, U. Minn., 1970—; recipient commanding gen. citation U.S. Army, Fort Campbell, Ky., 1968, 84. Mem. ADA, Am. Assn. for Dental Rsch., Internat. Assn. for Dental Rsch., Am. Assn. Dental Schs., Omicron Kappa Upsilon, Delta Omega. Achievements include patents in field. Avocation: thoroughbred racing. Business E-Mail: marte001@umn.com.

MARTENSEN, ROBERT LAWRENCE, emergency physician, educator, historian, ethicist, writer; b. Lake County, Ohio, Jan. 1, 1947; s. Lorenz Thomas and Bernice Helen (Sommer) M.; m. Phoebe Cutler (div.); m. Anne Carver (div.); children: Bayard Cutler, Charles Carver, Robert Maxwell. BA, Harvard U., 1969; MD, Dartmouth Coll., 1974; PhD, U. Calif., San Francisco, 1993. House officer U. Calif., San Francisco, 1974-77; staff physician Calif. Pacific Med. Ctr., San Francisco, 1977-93; asst. prof. Harvard Med. Sch., Cambridge, Mass., 1993, faculty mem., dept. social medicine; prof., chair, history and philosophy of medicine dept. U. Kansas Med. Ctr., dir., Clendening Libr. and Mus. of History of Medicine; James A. Knight Chair in Humanities and Ethics in Medicine, prof. surgery Tulane U. Sch. Medicine; dir. Office NIH History, Office of Intramural Rsch., 2007—. Invited presenter in field. Author The Brain Takes Shape: An Early History, 2004, A Life Worth Living: A Doctor's Reflections on Illness in a High-Tech Era, 2008; Contbr. articles to profl. jours., chpts. to books. Med. advisor on disaster planning, San Francisco, 1977-79. Guggenheim Fellowship, 2002. Mem. Soc. for Acad. Emergency Medicine, History of Sci. Soc., Am. Assn. for the History of Medicine, Am. Soc. of 18th Century Studies, Bohemian Club, Knickerbocker Club, Olympic Club. Office: Office NIH History National Institute Health Bldg 45 3AN38 MSC 6330 Bethesda MD 20892-6330 Office Phone: 301-496-6610. Business E-Mail: martensenr@mail.nih.gov.

MARTENSON, EDWARD ALLEN, theater manager; b. Paris, Ky., May 4, 1949; s. Milton A. and Bettye (Hudnall) M.; m. Gina Franz, Mar. 18, 1979; children: Benn, Hallie. AB, Princeton U., 1971. Mgr. McCarter Theater, Princeton, N.J., 1973-79; mng. dir. Yale Repertory Theater, New Haven, 1979-82; dir. theater program NEA, Washington, 1982-86; exec. dir. Guthrie Theater, Mpls., 1986—. Adj. assoc. prof. Sch. Drama Yale U., New Haven, 1979-82, co-chmn. adminstrn., 1979-82. Home: PO Box 946 Taos NM 87571-0946 Office: Guthrie Theater 725 Vineland Pl Ste 2 Minneapolis MN 55403-1187

MARTH, WILLIAM S., pharmaceutical executive; BSc in Pharmacy, U. Ill., 1977; MBA, Keller Grad. Sch. of Mgmt., Chgo. Ill., 1989. Various positions with Apothecon Divsn. of Bristol-Myers Squibb; v.p., sales and mktg. Teva Pharm. USA, North Wales, Pa., 1999—2002, exec. v.p., 2002—05, pres., CEO, 2005—. Office: Teva Pharm USA 1090 Horsham RD POB 1090 North Wales PA 19454*

MARTI, KURT, chemistry professor; b. Berne, Switzerland, Aug. 18, 1936; came to U.S., 1965; s. Werner Marti and Emma H. (Habegger) M.; children: Andres Niklaus, Stefan Kurt, Lorenz Roman. MS, U. Berne, 1963, PhD, 1965. Postgrad. research chemist U. Calif.-San Diego, La Jolla, 1965-68, asst. prof., 1969-74, assoc. prof., 1974-80, prof., 1980—; vis. prof. phys. rsch. lab. Ahmedabad, India, 1977, U. Berne, Switzerland, 1977, 95. Vis. prof. U. Bordeaux, France, 1983, 94; mem. rev. panel Lunar Sci. Inst., Houston, 1971-74, 91-93; lunar sample analysis planning team mem. Johnson Space Ctr., Houston, 1975-78; lectr. in field. Assoc. editor Geochim. Cosmochim. Acta, 1985-95. Grantee NASA, 1971—; Guggenheim fellow, 1976. Fellow Meteoritical Soc.; mem. AAAS, Am. Geophys. Union, Am. Chem Soc. Home: 13424 Calais Dr Del Mar CA 92014-3524 Office: U Calif San Diego Dept Chemistry La Jolla CA 92093-0317 E-mail: kmarti@ucsd.edu.

MARTI, PAUL EDGAR, JR., architect, educator; b. Wichita, Sept. 7, 1929; s. Paul Edgar and Edna Clareen (Conley) M.; m. Audrey Lee Marti, Mar. 15, 1933; children: Dane Eric, Kara Lynn. BArch, Kans. State U., 1953; MA, U. Calif., Berkeley, 1958. Architect Murphy-Mackey, St. Louis, 1955—57, Hellmuth-Obata-K, St. Louis, 1958—62; v.p. Smith-Entzeroth, Clayton, Mo., 1962—88, Paul Marti Assocs. Architects, St. Louis, 1988—. Juror Am. Plywood Assn. awards, Seattle, 1973; instr. archtl. tech. Washington U., St. Louis, 1979—85. Contbr. articles in field to profl. jours. Alderman, 1986—; chmn. bd. St. Louis U. Cupples Hist. Mansion, 1995-2000; mayor, City of Oakland, Mo., 2001-; pres. Mayors Small Cities of St. Louis, 2004. Served with USAF, 1953-55. Citation of merit Am. Plywood Assn., 1978; Honor award, landmarks Assocs., 1996. Mem. AIA (award of merit St. Louis 1970, bd. dirs.), Alpha Tau Omega, Clayton Mo. Optimists (pres. 1968). Home:

105 Minturn Ave Saint Louis MO 63122-4842 Office: Paul Marti Architects 34 N Brentwood Blvd Ste 1 Saint Louis MO 63105-3746 Office Phone: 314-725-9006. Business E-Mail: martiarchitect@mailstation.com.

MARTIKAINEN, A(UNE) HELEN, retired health specialist educator; b. Harrison, Maine, May 11, 1916; d. Sylvester and Emma (Heikkinen) M. AB, Bates Coll., 1939, DSc (hon.), 1957; MPH, Yale U., 1941; DSc, Harvard U., 1964; DSc (hon.), Smith Coll., 1969. Health edn. sec. Hartford TB and Pub. Health Assn., 1941; cons. USPHS, 1942—49; chief health edn. WHO, Geneva, 1949—74; ret., 1974; chair internat. affairs AAUW-NC, 1986—94, rep. to NC Coalition on Aging, 2001—, bd. dirs., 2001—08; mem. NC Health Adv. Bd. Aging, 2001—08. Hon. trustee Bridgton Acad., North Bridgton, Maine; mem. NC Women's Forum, 1984—; bd. dirs. NC Ctr. of Laws Affecting Women, Inc.; bd. dirs. West Triangle chpt. UNA-USA; chair residents health and social svcs. com., residents coun., residents com. for cmty. rels. Carol Woods. Recipient Delta Omega award Yale U., Nat. Adminstrv. award Am. Acad. Phys. Edn., Key award Bates Coll., Internat. Svc. award, France, 1953, Prentiss medal, 1956, Spl. medal, cert. for internat. health edn. svc. Nat. Acad. Medicine for France, 1959, Profl. award Soc. Pub. Health Educators, 1963, Benjamin Elijah Mays award Bates Coll. Alumni Assn., 1989, Legacy of Leadership honoree Pines of Carolina coun. Girl Scouts U.S., 2002; named to Bridgeton Acad. Hall of Fame, Maine, 2003. Fellow APHA (chmn. health edn. sect., Excellence award 1969); mem. AAUW, LWV, Women's Internat. League for Peace and Freedom, U.S. Soc. Pub. Health Educators, Internat. Union Health Edn. (Parisot medal, tech. adviser), Acad. Phys. Edn. (assoc.), NC Coun. Women's Orgns. (mem. coun. assembly 1988-92, Women of Distinction award 1989), Phi Beta Kappa. Home: 3113 Carol Woods 750 Weaver Dairy Rd Chapel Hill NC 27514-1443

MARTIN, ALBERT CHARLES, manufacturing executive, lawyer; b. San Lucido, Italy, Sept. 20, 1928; s. Joseph and Carmela M.; m. Jean Perrin, Aug. 22, 1953 (dec.); children: Lynne, Ken; m. Frances Doughty, June, 1996. BS, Mich. State U., 1952; MS, U. Mich., 1953; JD, Detroit Coll. Law, 1962. Bar: Mich. 1962. Corp. counsel, sec. Udylite Corp., Detroit, 1963-68; corp. counsel Hooker Chem. Corp., NYC, 1968-70, Grow Chem. Co., NYC, 1970-71; group v.p. Leeds & Northrup Internat., North Wales, Pa., 1971-79, pres., 1979—. Served with U.S. Army, 1946-48. Mem. Mich. Bar Assn. Personal E-mail: amartin001@verizon.net. E-mail: franal8@aol.com.

MARTIN, ALICE HOWZE, former prosecutor; b. Memphis, Apr. 25, 1956; married; 3 children. BSN, Vanderbilt U., 1978; JD, U. Miss., 1981. Bar: Tenn. 1981, Miss. 1981, Ala. 1989. Asst. US atty. US Attys. Office, Memphis, 1983-89; ptnr. Harris Harris & Martin, Florence, Ala., 1992—94; dist. mcpl. judge City of Florence, Ala., 1993—97; judge Cir. Ct. State of Ala., 1997—99; US atty. (no. dist.) Ala. US Dept. Justice, 2001—09. Avocations: travel, skeet shooting.

MARTIN, ALLEN, retired lawyer; b. Manchester, Conn., Aug. 12, 1937; s. Richard and Ruth Palmer (Smith) M.; m. Bonnie Reid, Sept. 8, 1979; children: Elizabeth Palmer, Samuel Bates. BA, Williams Coll., 1960, Oxford U., 1962; LLB, Harvard U., 1965. Ptnr. Downs, Rachlin and Martin, Burlington, Vt., 1971—2002. Chmn. bd. dirs. Wicor Ams., 1991-2007; bd. dirs., chmn. compensation com. IDX Systems Corp., 1999-2006; bd. dirs., chmn. fin. com. Union Mut. Ins. Co., New Eng. Guaranty Ins. Co.; mem. Vt. Jud. Responsibility Bd., vice-chmn., 1978-80; trustee Vt. Law Sch., 2000-04. Chmn. Vt. Bd. Edn., 1978-83; chmn. Vt. Rep. Party, 1991-95; mem. Rep. Nat. Com., 1991-95, 97-99. Mem.: ABA, Am. Law Inst. (life). Republican. Home: PO Box B Six Chimneys Orford NH 03777 Office Phone: 603-640-6100. E-mail: amartin@valley.net.

MARTIN, ANDREA LOUISE, actress, comedienne, writer; b. Portland, Maine, Jan. 15, 1947; m. Bob Dolman, 1980 (div.); children: Joe, Jack. Grad., Emerson Coll. Appearances include (plays) Hard Shell, 1980 (off-Broadway debut), Sorrows of Stephen, 1980, What's a Nice Country Like You Doing in a State Like This?, 1974, She Loves Me, (Broadway shows) My Favorite Year, 1992 (Tony award, Featured Actress in a Musical, 1993), Candide, 1997, Oklahoma!, 2002, Funny Girl, 2002, Fiddler on the Roof, 2005, Young Frankenstein, 2007, Exit the King, 2009, (films) Cannibal Girls, 1973, Black Christmas, 1974, Wholly Moses!, 1980, Soup for One, 1982, Club Paradise, 1986, Innerspace, 1987, Martha Ruth and Eddie, 1988, Worth Winning, 1989, Boris and Natasha, 1989, Rude Awakening, 1989, Too Much Sun, 1991, Stepping Out, 1991, All I Want for Christmas, 1991, (voice) The Itsy Bitsy Spider, 1992, Striking Distance, 1993, Bogus, 1996, (voice) Anastasia, 1997, Wag the Dog, 1997, The Rugrats Movie (voice), 1998, Bartok the Magnificent, 1999, Believe, 2000, Loser, 2000, Recess: Schools Out (voice), 2001, All Over the Guy, 2000, Jimmy Neutron: Boy Genius, 2001, My Big Fat Greek Wedding, 2002, New York Minute, 2004, The Producers, 2005, The TV Set, 2006, How to Eat Fried Worms, 2006, Young Triffie's Been Made Away With, 2006, Black Christmas, 2006, (TV series) Second City TV, 1977-81, Kate and Allie, 1982, The Martin Short Show, 1994, (voice) Earthworm Jim, 1995-96, Life...and Stuff, 1997, Recess, 1997, Damon, 1998, George and Martha, 1999, The New Woody Woodpecker Show, 1999, (voice) Superman, 1998-2000, Committed, 2001, (voice) The Adventures of Jimmy Neutron: Boy Genius, 2002-06, My Big Fat Greek Life, 2003, (voice) Kim Possible, 2002-07, (TV films) That Thing on ABC, 1978, Torn Between Two Lovers, 1979, The Robert Klein Show, 1981, Charles Dickens' David Copperfield, 1993, Gypsy, 1993, In Search of Dr. Seuss, 1994, Harrison Bergeron, 1995, My Funny Valentine, 2000, The Kid, 2001, Sick in the Head, 2003, Kim Possible: A Sitch in Time, 2003, (voice) Jimmy Neutron: Attack of the Twonkies, 2005; TV host Women of the Night II, 1988, Second City Fifteen Anniversary Special, 1988, Andrea Martin: Together Again, 1989; actress/writer: TV series SCTV Network 90, 1981-83 (2 Emmy awards 1982, 83), SCTV Channel, 1983-84, TV pilot From Cleveland, 1980; also The Completely Mental Misadventures of Ed Grimley, 1988-90 (voice of Mrs. Freebus).

MARTIN, ARIC DOYLE, lawyer; m. Ellen Dympna Lang, Oct. 14, 2006. BA in Econs., Miami U., Oxford, Ohio, 1992; JD, Ohio State U., Columbus, 1995. Bar: Ohio 1995, US Dist. Ct. (no. dist.) Ohio 1996, US Ct. Appeals (6th cir.) 1996. Assoc. Rolf & Goffman Co., LPA, Cleve., 1995—2001, ptnr., 2001—05, mng. ptnr., 2005—. Spkr. in field. Author: The Survey Book for Nursing Facilities, 2000, The Nursing Home Risk Management Checklist, 2000, The HIPAA Privacy Rule: A Nursing Facility Manual, 2001, The HIPAA Privacy Rule: An Assisted Living Manual, 2001, The HIPAA Privacy Rule: An ICF/MR Manual, 2001, The HIPAA Security Rule: A Long-Term Care Manual, 2003; editor: (DVD) A Time of Transition: Moving Your Loved One Into a Nursing Home, 2005. Atty. adviser Health Policy Inst. Ohio, Columbus, 2006—07. Named Ohio Super Lawyer, Law & Politics Mag., 2004—07. Mem.: Cleve. Bar Assn., Ohio State Bar Assn., Am. Assn. Home and Svcs. for the Aging, Am. Health Care Assn., Am. Health Lawyers Assn., Assn. Ohio Philanthropic Homes and Housing for the Aging, Ohio Health Care Assn. Office: Rolf & Goffman Co LPA 30100 Chagrin Blvd Ste 350 Pepper Pike OH 44124-5705 Office Fax: 216-514-0030. Business E-Mail: martin@rolfgoffman.com.

MARTIN, ARTHUR MEAD, lawyer; b. Cleve. Heights, Mar. 29, 1942; s. Bernard P. and Winifred (Mead) M. AB, Princeton U., 1963; LLB, Harvard U., 1966. Bar: Ill. 1966, U.S. Dist. Ct. (no. dist. Ill.) 1969, U.S. Ct. Appeals (7th cir.) 1970, U.S. Supreme Ct. 1980, U.S. Ct. Appeals (fed. cir.) 2000. Instr. law U. Wis., Madison, 1966-68; assoc. Jenner & Block, Chgo., 1968-74, ptnr., 1975—2003. Co-trustee Dille Family Trust, 1982—. Author: Historical and Practice Notes to the Illinois Civil Practice Act and Illinois Supreme Court Rules, 1968-88. Trustee 4th Presbyn. Ch., Chgo., 1996-99, sec. 1997-99, exec. com. 1997-99, mem. nominating com., 2006-07; bd. dirs. Stop Colon/Rectal Cancer Found., 1998—; founding bd. mem. Alliance for the Great Lakes, 2005—, chair nominating com., 2005-09, transition com. mem., 2009-. Mem. ABA, Am. Law Inst. (mem. consultative group principles of law nonprofit orgns. 2004-), Ill. Bar Assn., Chgo. Bar Assn. (bd. editors 1972-86), Ill. State Hist. Soc. (adv. bd. 1998-99, bd. dirs. 1999—, exec. com. 1999—, fin. com. 1999—, treas. 2002—), Ill. Centennial Bus. Com., Lake Mich. Fedn. (bd. dirs. 1993-02, 03-, exec. com. 1994-02, treas. 1994-99, 01-02, sec. 1999-01), Law Club Chgo., Legal Club Chgo. Office: Jenner & Block 330 N Wabash Ave FL 4400 Chicago IL 60611 Business E-Mail: amartin@jenner.com.

MARTIN, BENJAMIN GAUFMAN, ophthalmologist; b. Louisville, Aug. 18, 1937; s. Benjamin and Catherine L. Martin; m. Caroline Sue Martin, May 25, 1975; children: Benjamin, Lori, Tamara, Farrell, Steven, David. BME, U. Louisville, 1954, M. Engring., 1973; MD, U. So. Calif., 1964. Design engr. Philco/Ford, Palo Alto, Calif., 1957-60; rsch. engr. N.Am./Rockwell, Inglewood, Calif., 1961-63; intern Wright-Patterson Med. Ctr., Dayton, Ohio, 1964-65; ophthalmology resident Wilford Hall Med. Ctr., San Antonio, 1968-71; commd. USAF, 1963, advanced through grades to col., ret., 1980; CEO Cape Coral (Fla.) Eye Ctr., 1980—. With USN, 1954-57. Decorated Legion of Merit, DFC, Bronze Star, Air medal. Mem.: DFC Soc., Daedalions, Elks, Shriners, Masons. Republican. Lutheran. Office: Cape Coral Eye Ctr 4120 Del Prado Blvd S Cape Coral FL 33904-7165 Office Phone: 239-542-2020.

MARTIN, BIDDY (CAROLYN ARTHUR MARTIN), academic administrator; BA in English, Coll. of William and Mary, 1973; MA in German Lit, Middlebury Coll., 1974; PhD in German Lit. summa cum laude, U. Wis., Madison, 1985. Instr. German studies & women's studies Cornell U., Ithaca, NY, 1983—85, asst. prof., 1985—91, assoc. prof., 1991—97, chair Dept. German Studies, 1994—97, co-dir. Inst. German Studies, 1995—96, sr. assoc. dean Coll. Arts and Scis., 1996—2000, prof., 1997—, provost, 2000—08; chancellor U. Wis., Madison, 2008—. Grad. field rep. for German studies Cornell U., 1991—96, grad. field rep., co-founder lesbian and gay studies, 1992—96, assoc. dir. program women's studies, 1993—94; mem. steering com. for strategic plan III Weill Cornell Med. Coll., NYC, 2004—, mem. sci. adv. bd. for Cornell Ithaca. Author: Women and Modernity: The (Life)Styles of Lou Andreas-Salomé, 1991, Femininity Played Straight: The Significance of Being Lesbian, 1996; mem. edtl. bd.: Studies in Gender and Sexuality, New German Critique, Gay and Lesbian Quar., Diacritics, Signs, Women in German; contbr. articles to profl. jours. Fellow: Soc. for Humanities; mem.: Phi Beta Kappa. Office: U Wis / Office of Chancellor 161 Bascom Hall 500 Lincoln Dr Madison WI 53706 Office Phone: 608-262-9946. E-mail: chancellor@news.wisc.edu.*

MARTIN, BOBBY C., graphics designer, educator; b. Tahlequah, Okla., May 10, 1957; s. Billye and Bonnie Martin; m. Stephanie Van Riper, June 6, 1990; children: Melissa Wallis, Alex, Samantha Hope. BA, Northeastern State U., Tahlequah, 1992; MFA, U. Ark., Fayetteville, 1995. Graphic design coord. Gilcrease Mus., Tulsa, Okla., 1995—2000; assoc. prof. art Northeastern State U., 2000—08; assoc. prof. visual arts John Brown U., Siloam Springs, Ark., 2008—. Owner Berean Intermedia, Tahlequah, 1997—. Exhibitions include Through Our Ancestors' Eyes. Profl. Devel. fellowship, Coll. Art Assn., 1995—96. Mem.: Christians in Visual Arts, Gideons Internat. Office: John Brown Univ 2000 W University St Siloam Springs AR 72761 Personal E-mail: bcmartin@bobbycmartin.com. Business E-Mail: bmartin@jbu.edu.

MARTIN, BOE WILLIS, lawyer; b. Texarkana, Ark., Oct. 6, 1940; s. E.H. and Dorothy Annette (Willis) M.; m. Carol J. Edwards, June 12, 1965; children: Stephanie Diane, Scott Andrew. BA, Tex. A&M U., 1962; LLB, U. Tex., 1964; LLM, George Washington U., 1970. Bar: (Tex.) 1964. Law clk. Tex. Supreme Ct., 1966-67; assoc. Snakard, Brown & Gambill, Ft. Worth, 1967-69, assoc., ptnr., 1971-72; asst. counsel US Senate Labor and Pub. Welfare Com., 1969; legal asst. U.S. Senator Ralph W. Yarborough, 1969-71; assoc., ptnr. Stalcup & Johnson, Dallas, 1972-77; assoc. ptnr. Coke & Coke, Dallas, 1977-80; ptnr., shareholder Johnson & Gibbs, Dallas, 1981—95, Bell, Nunnally & Martin, Dallas, 1996—. Vis. prof. law So. Meth. U. Sch. Law, 1972-73, 75, 88-89, 95, 99-2000, 02-09, U. Tex. Sch. Law, 1977, 79, U. Houston Law Ctr., 2005. Contbr. articles to profl. jours. Staff Carter-Mondale Campaign, 1976, 80; cons. to v.p. of US, 1977-80; cons. Mondale for Pres. Campaign, 1983-84, Dukakis for Pres. Campaign, 1988; dep. coord. of visit of Pres. Mikhail Gorbachev to State of Minn., 1990. Capt. US Army, 1964-69. Mem. ABA, Tex. Bar Assn., Dallas Bar Assn. Democrat. Episcopalian. Home: 4055 Sweetwater Dr College Station TX 77845-964 Office: Bell & Nunnally & Martin 3232 Mckinney Ave Ste 1400 Dallas TX 75204-2426 Business E-Mail: boem@bellnunnally.com.

MARTIN, BOSTON FAUST, neurosurgeon; b. Tampa, fla., June 1, 1927; s. Boston Francis and Cantherina Heidi Martin; m. Roselle Bayot, May 26, 1988; children: Sandrine, Nathalie, Samantha, Arielle. BS, Howard U., 1949; BMS, U. Fribourg, Switzerland, 1954; MD, U. Geneva, 1958. Diplomate Am. Bd. Neurological and Orthopedic Surgeons, Am. Bd. Minimally Invasive Spinal Surgery. Intern in gen. surgery Danbury (Conn.) Hosp., 1959-60; resident in gen. surgery Stamford (Conn.) Hosp.-Yale U. Affiliate, 1960-61; resident in neurology Met. Hosp., NYC, 1961-62; resident in neurosurgery NYU Bellevue Med. Ctr., NYC, 1962-65; chief resident in neurosurgery NYU Med. Ctr., NYC, 1965-66, fellow in neurosurgery, 1966-67; interim chief neurol. surgery sect. Sch. Medicine and Univ. Hosp., U. P.R., San Juan, 1969-70, asst. prof. neurosurgery, 1969-75; clin. instr. in neurol. surgery NYU, 1966-67; clin. instr. in rehab. medicine U. Medicine and Dentistry N.J./N.J. Med. Sch., Newark, 1978-86, clin. instr. surgery, 1996—; attending neurosurgeon Hosp. Ctr. at Orange, NJ, 1976—, Meadowlands Hosp. Med. Ctr., Secaucus, NJ, 1981—, chief neurol. surgery, 1998—; attending neurosurgeon Christ Hosp., Jersey City, 1987—. Pvt. practice, West Orange, 1976—; attending neurosurgeon Doctors Hosp., Santuce, 1970-75, Matilde Brenes Hosp., Bayamon, P.R., 1970-75, San Jorge Hosp., Santice, P.R., 1970-75, Tchrs. Hosp., Haty Rey, P.R., 1971-75, Auxilio Muto Hosp., Hato Rey, 1971-75, Presbyn. Hosp., Santuce, 1972-75; asst. attending neurosurgeon Knud-Hansen Meml. Hosp., St. Thomas, V.I., 1967-69, U. P.R. Univ. Hosp., 1969-75; attending neurosurgeon East Orange Gen. Hosp., 1976-86, chief neurol. surgery, 1990-2000; chief spinal cord injury svc. VA Med. Ctr., East Orange, 1975-84; active attending neurosurgeon Newark Beth Israel Med. Ctr., 1998—; presenter in field. Co-author: the Conus Medullaris: Physiological Anatomy and Clinical Considerations. 1987; contbr. articles to profl. jours. Lt. col., flight surgeon USAF, 1984-90. Recipient Cert. of Merit Lions Club Internat., 1969, Disting. citation DAV, 1977, spl. trophy for disting. svc. DAV, 1979. Mem. ACS, AAUP, Internat. Coll. Surgeons, Acad. Medicine N.J., Congress Neurol. Surgeons (mem. internat. com. 1974, socio-econ. com. 1974-76, med. legal subcom. 1978-84), Societe de Neuro-Cirurgie De Langue Francaise, N.J. Neurosurg. Soc., Assn. Mil. Surgeons U.S., Am. Acad. Neurol. and Orthopedic Surgeons, Air Force Assn., Orange Mountain Med. Soc., Alpha Phi Alpha. Office: 81 Northfield Ave West Orange NJ 07052-5338

MARTIN, BOYCE FICKLEN, JR., federal judge; b. Boston, Oct. 23, 1935; s. Boyce Ficklen and Helen Artt Martin; children: Mary V.H., Julia H.C., Boyce Ficklen III, Robert C.G. II; m. Anne B. Ogden, Jan. 6, 2000. AB, Davidson Coll., 1957; JD, U. Va., 1963; D of Laws, Hanover Coll., Ind., 2006. Bar: Ky. 1963. Law clk. to Hon. Shackelford Miller, Jr. US Ct. Appeals (6th cir.), Cin., 1963—64, judge Cin. and Louisville, 1979—; asst. to US atty (we. dist.) Ky US Dept. Justice, Louisville, 1964, U.S. atty. (we dist.) Ky., 1965; instr. Louisville Law Sch., 1965—67; pvt. practice Louisville, 1966—74; 1st asst. Office the County Atty., Jefferson County, 1970—74; judge Jefferson Circuit Ct., Louisville, 1974—76; chief judge Ky. Ct. Appeals, Louisville, 1976—79. Jud. coun. US Ct. Appeals (6th cir.), 1979—96, chmn., 1996—; mem. Jud. Conf. of US, 1996—, exec. com., 1998—2003. Chmn. Isaac W. Bernheim Found., Louisville, 1982—95; trustee Blackacre Found., Inc., Louiville, 1983—94, chmn., 1986—94; trustee Hanover Coll., Ind., 1982—, vice-chmn. Ind., 1992—97, chmn. Ind., 1998—2006; exec. bd. Old Ky. Home coun. Boy Scouts of Am., 1968—72; pres. Louisville Zool. Commn., 1971—74; trustee Isaac W. Bernheim Found., Louisville, 1981—97, 2006—; vestry mem. St. Francis in the Fields Episcopal Ch., Harrods Creek, Ky., 1979—83; bd. vis. Davidson Coll., NC, 1980—86, trustee NC, 1994—98. Capt. JAGC US Army, 1958—66. Fellow: Am. Bar Found.; mem.: ABA (com. effective appellate advocacy Conf. Appellate Judges), Nat. Assn. Criminal Def. (Lawyers award 2007), Metro. Louisville Ky. Bar Assn. (Judge Yr. 2001), Louisville Bar Assn., Ky. Bar Assn. (Judge Yr. 2007), Fed Bar Assn., Am. Judicature Soc., Inst. Jud. Adminstrn. Office: US Ct Appeals 209 US Courthouse 601 W Broadway Louisville KY 40202-2227*

MARTIN, C. ALAN, utilities executive; b. Birmingham, Ala., 1949; m. Cheryl Martin; children: Ryan, Lindsey. BA in English, U. Ala.; MA in Psychology, U. Ala., Birmingham. Right-of-way agent, Ala. Power Southern Co., asst. to the pres., v.p. mktg., v.p., Birmingham divisn., v.p. human resources, exec. v.p., CMO, exec. v.p. corp. services, Ala. Power, exec. v.p., pres., CEO Southern Co. Services, 2008—. Mem. mgmt. coun. Southern Co. Active Boy Scouts America; chmn. Ctrl. Ala. United Way Campaign, 1995; bd. dirs. Ala. Sports Found., Jr. Achievement, Met. Devel. Bd., Operation New Birmingham; bd. dirs., exec. com. Birmingham Area C. of C.; exec. adv. coun. U. Ala., Birmingham, Birmingham Southern Coll.; bd. governors 191 Club, Atlanta. Office: Southern Co 30 Ivan Allen Jr Blvd NW Atlanta GA 30308 Office Phone: 404-506-5000.*

MARTIN, CARMEL M., federal agency administrator; b. 1967; BA in Economics & Internat. Studies, Manhattan Coll., Riverdale, NY, 1989; MPA, U. Tex. LBJ Sch. Pub. Affairs; JD, U. Tex. Sch. Law. Law clk. to Hon. Thomas Reavley US Ct. Appeals (5th cir.); assoc. Hogan & Hartson LLP; trial atty, civil rights divsn., ednl. opportunities sect. US Dept. Justice; spl. counsel to Senator Tom Daschle US Senate, chief counsel & sr. policy advisor to Senator Jeff Bingaman, chief edn. advisor to Senator Ted Kennedy, 2005—08; assoc. dir. domestic policy Ctr. for Am. Progress, 2004—05; asst. sec. for planning, evaluation & policy devel. US Dept. Edn., Washington, 2009—. Democrat. Office: US Dept Edn 400 Maryland Ave SW Washington DC 20202*

MARTIN, CAROL JACQUELYN, artist, educator; b. Ft. Worth, Tex., Oct. 6, 1943; d. John Warren and Dorothy Lorene (Coffman) Edwards; m. Boe Willis Martin, Oct. 6, 1940; children: Stephanie Diane, Scott Andrew. BA summa cum laude, U. North Tex., 1965; MA, U. Tex., El Paso, 1967; studied at, Art Students League NY, 2007. Tchr. English Edgemere Elem. Sch., El Paso, 1965—66; tchr. Fulmore Jr. H.S., Austin, Tex., 1966—67, Monnig Jr. H.S., Ft. Worth, 1967—68, Paschal H.S., Ft. Worth, 1968—69; instr. English Tarrant County Jr. Coll., Ft. Worth, 1968—69, 1971—72, Eastfield C.C., Dallas, 1981, Richland C.C. Dist., 1982; instr. art Meml. Student Ctr. UPlus Tex. A&M U., 2002—03; instr. art Brenham Fine Arts League, 2006, 2009, Galerie Pavilion, Wichita Falls, Tex., 2008. Artist Vt. Studio Ctr., 1998; press sec. Senator Gaylord Nelson, Washington, 1969—71. Editor The Avesta Mag., 1964-65; various group art exhbns., Solo Artist Exhbn. Galerie Pavilion, 2008. Mem. Nat. Mus. Women in Arts; mem. Friends of Meml. Student Ctr.-OPAS (Opera and Performing Arts Soc.), The Woman's Club. Mem. Lone Star Art Guild (sec. 2006-07, bd. mem. 2007-08), Brazos Valley Art League, Brazos Valley Symphony Soc., Mortar Board, Opera and Performing Arts Soc. Guild, Alpha Chi, Sigma Tau Delta, Kappa Delta Pi, Delta Gamma. Democrat. Episcopalian. Avocations: travel, photography, skiing, painting. Address: 4055 Sweetwater Dr College Station TX 77845-9650

MARTIN, CHARLES JOHN, professor; b. Sloatsburg, NY, Apr. 3, 1935; s. Kenneth Irving and Jean (Law) M.; m. Carole Jean Rising, June 13, 1959; children: Scott David, Keith Bradley. BS, Union Coll., 1956; MS, Mich. State U., 1957; PhD, Rensselaer Polytechnic Inst., 1961. Grad. teaching asst. dept. math. Mich. State U., East Lansing, 1956-57; instr. dept. math Union Coll., Schenectady, N.Y., 1957-58; grad. rsch. asst. dept. math. Rensselaer Polytechnic Inst., Troy, N.Y., 1958-61; sr. staff scientist R&D div. AVCO, Lowell, Mass., 1961-66; from assoc. prof. to prof. dept. math. Mich. State U., East Lansing, 1966-75; prof., head dept. math. Western Carolina U., Cullowhee, N.C., 1975-88; dean coll. engring. and aviation sci. Embry-Riddle Aero. U., Daytona Beach, Fla., 1989-90, provost, 1990—92; dean of faculty U. Daytona Beach, 1992—94; prof. emeritus, 2005—. Contbr. articles to profl. jours. NSF grantee, 1972, 78-79, 80-82, 81-82, 83-86, 88-90—, NASA grantee, 1966-70. Mem. Am. Math. Soc., Math. Assn. Am., Computer Soc. IEEE, ASME, Sigma Xi, Pi Mu Epsilon. Avocations: photography, golf. Home: 127 Oak Ln Ormond Beach FL 32174-2633 Personal E-mail: cjrml@earthlink.net.

MARTIN, CHARLES NEIL, JR., health care management company executive; b. Florence, Ala., Dec. 11, 1942; s. Charles Neil Sr. and Hazel Lucy (Hawkins) M. BS, So. Coll., Chattanooga, 1964. Adminstr. El Reposo Nursing Home, Florence, 1964-66, Parkwood Convalescent Ctr., Chattanooga, 1966-67; project dir. Tenn. Hosp. Assn., Nashville, 1967-68, asst. dir., 1968-69; v.p. Gen. Care Corp., Nashville, 1969-76, exec. v.p., 1976-79, pres., COO, 1979-80; sr. v.p. HCA, Nashville, 1980-85, exec. v.p., 1985-87, also bd. dirs.; pres., chief operating officer Health-Trust, Inc., Nashville, 1987—92; chmn., pres., CEO OrNda Health-

Corp., 1992—97; chmn., CEO Vanguard Health Sys., Nashville, 1997—. Bd. dirs. Equicor, Nashville, 1986—. Bd. dirs. Cystic Fibrosis Found., Nashville, 1987. Office: Vanguard Healthcare 20 Burton Hills Blvd Nashville TN 37215*

MARTIN, CHESTER Y., sculptor, painter; b. Chattanooga, Nov. 2, 1934; s. Woodfin Ballenger and Mabel Willett (Young) M.; m. Patricia Ann Parnell, Aug. 15, 1963; 1 child, Sharon Elizabeth (Mrs. Christopher Pruitt). Student, U. Chattanooga, 1952-55, 60-61, Internat. Medallic Workshop-Pa. State U., 1984. Freelance artist, Chattanooga, 1967-86; sculptor, engraver U.S. Mint, Phila., 1986-92. One-man shows include Hunter Mus. Art, Chattanooga, 1979; group shows: Kottler Galleries, N.Y.C., 1966; Internat. Exposition Contemporary Medals, Italy, 1983, Sweden, 1985, Finland, 1990; U.S. Dept. State, 1984, Nat. Sculpture Soc., N.Y.C., 1984, 85, 99, Cast Iron Gallery, N.Y.C., 1992, Internat. Exhbn. of Contemporary Medals, Brit. Mus., London, 1992, Hungarian Nat. Gallery, Budapest, 1994, Neuchatel, 1996, Nat. Sculpture Soc., N.Y.C., 1999, Weimar, 2000, Paris Mint, 2002, Lisbon, 2004, numerous others; permanent collections: British Mus., London; Smithsonian Instn.; Food and Agrl. Orgn., Rome; Am. Numismatic Soc., N.Y.C.; Julius Wile Sons and Co., N.Y.C.; Brookgreen Gardens, S.C., U.S. Mint, Phila., Belmont U., Nashville; major comms.: World Food Day Medal, UN, 1984, others; other major works: History of Chattanooga Mural, 1974; theme painting of Br. Colonial Ft. Loudon, 1975; Centennial Mural for Chattem Inc., Chattanooga, 1980; sculptured Congl. Bicentennial Silver Dollar, 1989, Eisenhower Centennial Dollar reverse, Mt. Rushmore Dollar obverse, 1991; designer Andrew Wyeth Congl. medal, 1989, George H.W. Bush Presdl. medal reverse; designer Yosemite Nat. Park Centennial Congressional Medal, 1991, Gen. Colin L. Powell Congressional Medal, 1992, White House Bicentennial Dollar reverse, 1992; designer mural Chattanooga Met. Airport, 1999. Served with USAF, 1956-60. Recipient numerous art awards, most recent being Purchase award Benedictine Art Competition, 1975, Medallic Sculpture award Am. Numismatic Assn., 1993. Mem. Fedn. Internationale de la Medaille (Am. del.), Am. Medallic Sculpture Assn. (v.p. 1987). Methodist. Avocation: modern languages. Mailing: 4110 Sunbury Ave Chattanooga TN 37411-5232 Office Phone: 423-698-3561. E-mail: cymppm@comcast.net.

MARTIN, CHRIS, singer; b. Devon, England, Mar. 2, 1977; m. Gwenyth Paltrow, 2003; children: Apple Blythe Alison, Moses. Student in Ancient World Studies, U. Coll. London. Sign painter; vocalist, pianist, rhythm guitarist Coldplay, 1998—. Singer: (albums) Parachutes, 2000 (Grammy award for Best Alternative Music Album, 2001), A Rush of Blood to the Head, 2002 (Grammy award for Best Alternative Music Album, 2002), Live 2003, 2003, X&Y, 2005 (Juno award for Best Internat. Album, 2006), Love, Actually, 2006; musician Viva La Vida, 2008 (Grammy award for Rock Album of Yr., 2009), (songs) In My Place, 2002 (Grammy award for Best Rock Performance By A Duo Or Group With Vocal, 2002), Clocks, 2002 (Grammy award for Record of Yr., 2003), Speed of Sound, 2005 (MTV Europe award for Best Song, 2005), Viva La Vida, 2009 (Grammy awards for Song of Yr. and Best Group Pop Vocal Performance, 2009). Recipient Favorite Alternative Artist (Coldplay), Am. Music Awards, 2005; named World's Best Rock Act, World's Best-Selling Rock Act, and Best-Selling Brit. Artist, World Music Awards, 2008. Office: Capital Records 1750 North Vine St 10th Fl Hollywood CA 90028*

MARTIN, CLAUDE RAYMOND, JR., marketing consultant, educator; b. Harrisburg, May 11, 1932; s. Claude R. and Marie Teresa (Stapf) M.; m. Marie Frances Culkin, Nov. 16, 1957; children: Elizabeth Ann, David Jude, Nancy Marie, William Jude, Patrick Jude, Cecelia Marie. BS, U. Scranton, Pa., 1954, MBA, 1963; PhD, Columbia U., NYC, 1969. Newsman Sta. WILK-TV, Wilkes-Barre, Pa., 1953-55; news dir. Sta. WNEP-TV, Scranton, Pa., 1955-60; dir. systems Blue Cross & Blue Shield Ins., Wilkes-Barre, 1960-63; lectr. mktg, St. Francis Coll., Bklyn., 1964, U. Mich., Ann Arbor, 1965-68, asst. prof., 1968-73, asso. prof., 1973-77, prof., 1977-80, Isadore and Leon Winkelman prof. retail mktg., 1980—92, chmn. mktg. dept., 1986-90, prof. retail mktg. Isadore and Loen Winkerman, 1992—. Bd. dirs. Perry Drug Stores, cons. mktg., 1983-89; spl. cons. on rsch. changes in U.S. currency Fed. Res. Sys., 1978—; pub. mem. Nat. Advt. Rev. Bd., 1989-94. Contbr. articles to profl. jours. Trustee U. Scranton, 1996—. Served with USNR, 1955-57. Mem. Acad. Mktg. Sci., Am. Mktg. Assn., SW Mktg. Assn., Bank Mktg. Assn., Assn. Consumer Rsch., Am. Collegiate Retailing Assn., Am. Acad. Advt. (Disting. Fellow). Roman Catholic. Home: 1116 Aberdeen Dr Ann Arbor MI 48104-2812 Office Phone: 734-971-1897. Personal E-mail: claudemartinjr@hotmail.com.

MARTIN, CLYDE F., engineering educator; b. Wichita, Kans., Nov. 6, 1943; BSE, Kans. State Tchr. Coll., 1965; PhD, U. Wyo., Laramie, 1971; D (hon.), Royal Inst. Tech. Sweden, 1998. With NASA, 1971—73, 1976—77; asst. prof. Utah State U., 1973—76; assoc. prof. Case Western Reserve U., 1978—83; P.W. Horn prof. Tex. Tech U., Lubbock, 1983—. Office: Texas Tech U 1400 Boston Ave Lubbock TX 79409

MARTIN, CRAIG LEE, engineering company executive; b. Dodge City, Kans., Nov. 23, 1949; s. Ray N. and Nadia C. Martin; m. Diane E. Hensley, Mar. 19, 1977. BSCE, U. Kans., 1971; MBA, U. Denver, 1982. Project mgr. Martin K. Eby Constrn. Co., Wichita, Kans., 1972-83; exec. v.p., COO CRSS Constructors, Inc., Denver, 1983-89; exec. v.p. CRSS Comml. Group, Houston, 1989-90; sr. v.p. CRSS Capital, Houston, 1990-92, CRSS Inc., Houston, 1992-94; pres. CRSS Architects, Inc., Houston, 1992-94; sr. v.p. ops. Jacobs Engring. Group Inc., 1994-95; pres. Jacobs Constructors, Inc., 1994-95; sr. v.p. gen. sales and mktg. to pres. Jacobs Engring. Group, Inc., Pasadena, Calif., 1995—2000, exec. v.p. global sales, 2000—02, pres., 2002—06, CEO, pres., 2006—. Adv. bd. Constrn. Bus. Rev., 1993—. Bd. govs. Woodbury U. Sch. Bus. Mem. ASCE. Avocations: golf, clay shooting. Home: 930 S El Molino Ave Pasadena CA 91106-4414 Office: Jacobs Engring Group Inc 1111 S Arroyo Pkwy Pasadena CA 91105-3254 Office Phone: 626-578-6813. Business E-Mail: craig.martin@jacobs.com.

MARTIN, DANIEL C., surgeon, gynecologist, educator; b. St. Louis, Apr. 7, 1946; s. Dan Allen and Ruth Keel (Fields) M.; m. Glenn Ann Blakemore, July 7, 1970; children: Josh, Adam. BS in Physics, Emory U., Atlanta, 1968, MD, 1972. Diplomate Am. Bd. Ob-Gyn. Rsch. asst. physics and radiology Emory U., Atlanta, 1968-69; intern, resident, fellow, instr. The Johns Hopkins Med. Instns., Balt., 1972-77; from asst. prof. to clin. asst. prof. U. Tenn., Memphis, 1977-90, clin. assoc. prof., 1990—2005, clin. prof., 2005—06, prof., 2006—; surgeon Reproductive Surgery, P.C., Memphis, 1977—2006, UT Med. Group, Memphis, 2006—. Gynecologist, reproductive surgeon Bapt. Meml. Hosp., 1977—; Axel Munthe presenter, Naples, Italy, 1992; guest spkr.Annual Japanese Endometrosis Symposium, Osaka, 1994, 2004; dir. gynecologic laser and endoscopy workshops, 1982-93. Editor: (textbooks) Lasers in Endoscopy, 1990, Laparoscopic Appearance of Endometriosis, 1990, Manual of Endoscopy, 1990, Atlas of Endometriosis, 1993, Endoscopic Management of Gynecologic Disease, 1996. Picker Found. fellow Emory U., 1969; Tex. Assn. Ob-Gyn. hon. fellow, 1989; recipient Bridges trophy for athletics Emory U., 1968, Codman surg. award, 1982, 83, Video award Am. Fertility Soc., 1992, Physician Recognition awrd Endometriosis Assn., 1995; named one of Best Drs. Am. Woodward and White Inc., 1992, 94, 96, 98, 00, 02, 04, 06, 08; Hon. mem. Australian Gynecol. Endoscopy Soc., 1993, named to Sports Hall of Fame, Emory Coll., 2002. Mem. ACOG (sect. chair jr. fellows Md.), Tenn. Med. Assn., Memphis and Shelby County Med. Soc. (comm. com.), Am. Nat. Std. Inst. (subcom. on laser safety in med. facility), Am. Assn. Gynecol. Laparoscopists (pres. 1990-91, Videoendoscopy award 1993), Gynecologic Surgery Soc. (pres. 1994-96, chmn. bd. 1996-98), Australian Gynecol. Endoscopy Soc. (hon.), Argentinian Ob-Gyn. Soc. (hon.). Office Phone: 901-347-8331.

MARTIN, DANIEL RICHARD, pharmaceutical executive; b. Lima, Peru, June 9, 1937; s. James Marion and Clementine Caroline (Valencia) M.; m. Barbara Artemis Cyrus, June 23, 1962; children: Daniel Richard Jr., John Alexander, Christopher Andrew. BA, Cornell U., 1958; MS, Columbia U., NYC, 1959. Area sales supr. Schering Corp., Bloomfield, NJ, 1960-64; assoc. McKinsey & Co., NYC, 1964-69; treas. Harper & Row, Pubs., NYC, 1969-72; mng. dir. Merck & Co., Rahway, NJ, 1972-77; group v.p. Bell & Howell Co., Chgo., 1977-80; pres. Howland Martin Corp., NYC, 1980-85; pres. Sterling Europe, Middle East, Africa Sterling Drug, Inc., NYC, 1986-89; pres., CEO, also bd. dirs. E-Z-EM, Inc., Westbury, NY, 1990-97; pres., also bd. dirs. Milestone Scientific, Inc., Livingston, NJ, 1998-99. Adj. prof. mgmt. Pace U., NYC, 1996—; bd. mgrs. Country Life LLC, 2005; bd. dir. DelMonte Ltd., Asia. Co-chmn. Accion Internat., Cambridge, Mass., 1988-98; trustee Bangor (Maine) Theol. Sem., 1991-2000, Key and Candle Found., 2006-; dir. Americas Found., 1995-; bd. dirs., fin. com. White Plains Hosp., NY, 1997-, sec. treas. NGO Alliance, 2008-. Decorated Order of Merit (Ecuador). Mem. Coun. on Fgn. Rels., Americas Found., Cornell Club NYC Independent. Congregationalist. Home: 31 Rochambeau Dr Hartsdale NY 10530-3017 E-mail: drm1937@aol.com.

MARTIN, DAVID ALAN, lawyer, law educator; b. Indpls., July 23, 1948; s. C. Wendell and Elizabeth Bowman (Meeker) M.; m. Cynthia Jo Lorman, June 13, 1970; children: Amy Lynn, Jeffrey David. BA, DePauw U., 1970; JD, Yale U., 1975. Bar: D.C. Law clk. to Hon. J. Skelly Wright U.S. Ct. Appeals (D.C. cir.), 1975—76; law clk. to Hon. Lewis F. Powell U.S. Supreme Ct., Washington, 1976—77; assoc. Rogovin, Stern & Huge, Washington, 1977—78; spl. asst. bur. human rights & humanitarian affairs US Dept. State, Washington, 1978—80; from asst. prof. to assoc. prof. U. Va. Sch. Law, Charlottesville, 1980—86, prof., 1986—91, Henry L. & Grace Doherty prof. law, 1991—2003, F. Palmer Weber Rsch. prof. civil liberties and human rights, 1992—95, F. Palmer Weber Rsch. prof. civil liberties & human rights, 2000—03, Warner-Booker disting. prof. internat. law, 2003—09, Class of 1963 rsch. prof., 2004—07; gen. counsel US Immigration & Naturalization Svc. (INS), US Dept. Justice, Washington, 1995—98; dep. gen. counsel US Dept. Homeland Security, Washington, 2009—, acting gen. counsel, 2009. Cons. Adminstrv. Conf. U.S., Washington, 1988-89, 91-92, US Dept. Justice, 1993-95, US Dept. State, 2003-04 Author: Forced Migration: Law and Policy, 2007, Immigration: Process and Policy, 1985, 6th edit., 2008, Asylum Case Law Sourcebook, 1994, 7th edit., 2007, The Endless Quest: Helping America's Farm Workers, 1994, The United States Refugee Admissions Program: Reforms for a New Era of Refugee Resettlement, 2005; editor: The New Asylum Seekers, 1988, Immigration Admissions, 1998, Immigration Controls, 1998, Rights and Duties of Dual Nationals: Evolution and Prospects, 2002, Immigration Stories, 2005; bd. editors Am. Jour. Internat. Law, 2004-; contbr. articles to profl. jours. Nat. governing bd. Common Cause, Washington, 1972-75; elder Westminster Presbyn. Ch., Charlottesville, 1982-84, 89-92; bd. dirs. Internat. Rescue Com., 2000-03. German Marshall Fund Rsch. fellow, Geneva, 1984-85. Mem. Am. Soc. Internat. Law (v.p. 2003-05, Book award 1986), Internat. Law Assn. Democrat. Office: US Dept Homeland Security 3801 Nebraska Ave Washington DC 20528

MARTIN, DAVID ALLEN, application developer, computer scientist; b. Louisville, Oct. 27, 1953; s. Philip Allen and Finas Ellen Martin; m. Rhonda Faye Martin, Apr. 12, 1998; children: Benjamin Lloyd, Sarah Beth Richert, Patricia Ellen, Bradley Alan Richert. BS in Computer Sci., U. Louisville, 1975, MS in Computer Sci., 1977. Field rep. Compugraphic Corp., Wilmington, Mass., 1977—80; chief tech. officer A. L. Sewell Co., Inc., Louisville, 1980—92, Computer Contractors Internat., Dana Point, Calif., 1992—97, e-PULSETrak.com, Louisville, 1997—. Cons. software bus. solutions Computer Contractors Internat., Dana Point, Calif., 1992—97. Author: (software) Traker; co-author: e-PULSETrak.com. Deacon Midlane Pk. Bapt. Ch., Louisville, 2004—06. Bapt. Avocations: travel, computers, reading, investments. Office: e-PULSETrakcom 4220 Bardstown Road Louisville KY 40218 Office Fax: 502-459-2955; Home Fax: 502-459-2955. Business E-Mail: davidm@e-pulsetrak.com.

MARTIN, DAVID BRITON HADDEN, JR., lawyer; b. Beverly, Mass., Dec. 9, 1946; s. David Briton Hadden and Mary Louise (Ward) Martin; m. Martha Bacon, June 21, 1969; children: Charlotte, Jessica, Benjamin Ward. BA, Yale U., 1969; JD, U. Va., 1976. Bar: Va. 1976, DC 1977. Spl. counsel SEC, Washington, 1980—84, spl. counsel to chmn., 1984—85, dir., divsn. corp. fin., 2000—02; assoc. Hogan & Hartson, Washington, 1985—87, ptnr., 1987—99, Covington & Burling, Washington, 2002—, co-head, securities practice group, co-head corp. practice area. Mng. editor: U. Va. Law Rev., 1975—76. Bd. dirs. Jubilee Jobs, 1998—2008; trustee Westover Sch., 1998—; mem. bd. dirs. SEC Hist. Soc., 2004—, chmn., bd. dirs., 2009—. Mem.: Metro. Club. Office: Covington & Burling LLP 1201 Pennsylvania Ave Washington DC 20004-2401 Home Phone: 703-836-4915; Office Phone: 202-662-5128. Office Fax: 202-778-5128. Business E-Mail: dmartin@cov.com.

MARTIN, DAVID CHARLES, materials science engineering educator; b. Kalamazoo, Sept. 24, 1961; s. Ernest Charles and Shirley Jean (Calkins) M.; m. Kim Louise, May 12, 1990; children: Nathaniel Ernest, Timothy Walker. MS, U. Mich., 1985; PhD, U. Mass., 1989. Process devel. staff IBM, Burlington, Vt., 1983; rsch. engr. GM Corp., Warren, Mich., 1983-85; vis. scientist E.I. duPont De Nemours & Co., Inc., Wilmington, Del., 1989-90; asst. prof. materials sci. U. Mich., Ann Arbor, 1990—. Named Nat. Young Investigator NSF, 1992. Mem. Am. Soc. Metals Internat. (chpt. ops. com. 1992), Mineral, Metals, and Materials Soc. (exec. com. 1992, pres. Detroit chpt.), Am. Phys. Soc., Am. Chem. Soc., Materials Rsch. Soc., Microscopy Soc. Am. Home: 3111 Tiger Lily Ct Ann Arbor MI 48103-8703 Office: Univ of Mich 2022 H H Dow Bldg Ann Arbor MI 48109

MARTIN, DAVID EDWARD, health sciences educator; b. Green Bay, Wis., Oct. 1, 1939; s. Edward Henry and Lillie (Luckman) M. BS, U. Wis., 1961, MS, 1963, PhD, 1970. Ford Found. research trainee Wis. Regional Primate Ctr., Madison, 1967-70; asst. prof. health scis. Ga. State U., Atlanta, 1970-74, assoc. prof., 1974-80, prof., 1980-91, regents prof., 1992—2000, regents prof. emeritus, 2000—. Affiliate scientist Yerkes Primate Rsch. Ctr., Emory U., Atlanta, 1970—98; US rep to Internat. Olympic Acad., 1978; sport medicine rsch. assoc. US Olympic Com., 1981—84; chmn. sports scis. USA Track and Field; mem. coaching staff US teams to world championships in distance running, Rome, 1982, Gateshead, England, 83, Budapest, Hungary, 94, Vilamoura, Portugal, 2000, Fukuoka, Japan, 06, head coach, Paris, 1980, Madrid, 84, Hiroshima, Japan, 85, Warsaw, 87, Antwerp, Belgium, 91; mem. Olympic med. support group Atlanta Olympic Games. Author: Laboratory Experiments in Human Physiology, 4th edit., 1980, The Marathon Footrace, 1979, La Corsa Di Maratona, 1982, The High Jump Book, 1982, The High Jump Book, 2d edit., 1987, Respiratory Anatomy and Physiology, 1987, Training Distance Runners, 1991, Training Distance Runners, 2d edit., 1997, Training Distance Runners, German edit., 1992, Training Distance Runners, Spanish edit., 1995, Training Distance Runners, Japanese edit., 2001, The Olympic Marathon, 2000. Trustee Ga. Found. for Athletic Excellence. Named Disting. prof. Ga. State U., 1975, 81, 85 Fellow Am. Coll. Sports Medicine; mem. Internat. Soc. Olympic Historians, Am. Physiol. Soc., Atlanta Track Club. Home: 510 Coventry Rd Apt 13A Decatur GA 30030-5038 Office: Ga State U Dept Cardiopul Care Atlanta GA 30303 Office Phone: 404-413-1272. Business E-Mail: drdave@gsu.edu.

MARTIN, DAVID HUBERT, internist, epidemiologist, educator; b. Detroit, Mar. 24, 1943; s. Hubert Cillis and Mable Anita (Stewart) M.; m. Jane Ellen Schlichtemeier, Nov. 22, 1970; children: Jennifer, Jason. BA with distinction, U. Kans., 1965; MD cum laude, Harvard Coll., 1969. Diplomate Nat. Bd. Med. Examiners, Am. Bd. Internal Medicine, Infectious Disease Subspecialty Bd. Am. Bd. Internal Medicine. Intern Bronx (N.Y.) Mcpl. Hosp. Ctr., 1969-70; staff assoc. Nat. Inst. Allergy and Infectious Diseases, Mid. Am. Rsch. Unit, NIH, Panama Canal Zone, 1970-73; med. resident U. Wash. Affiliated Hosps., 1973-75; sr. fellow in infectious diseases U. Wash., 1976-78; chief resident in medicine USPHS Hosp., Seattle, 1975-76, staff internal medicine clinic, 1975, attending physician internal medicine, 1976-78, staff dept. internal medicine New Orleans, 1979-81; staff Hotel Dieu Hosp., New Orleans, 1982-94; clin. asst. prof. medicine La. State U. Med. Sch., New Orleans, 1979-81, asst. prof. medicine divsn. infectious diseases, 1981-82, assoc. prof. medicine divsn. infectious diseases, 1982-88, assoc. prof. microbiology, 1986-88, prof. internal medicine and microbiology, 1988, asst. chief sect. infectious diseases, 1988-89, chief sect. infectious diseases, 1990—, Harry E. Dascomb M.D. prof. of medicine, 1990—. Instr. dept. medicine U. Wash. Sch. Medicine, Seattle, 1975-78, acting asst. prof. medicine, 1978-79; chmn. infection control com., chmn. instnl. rev. bd. human rsch. com., chmn. antibiotic utilization com., sec. rsch. and editl. com., sec. animal welfare com. USPHS Hosp., New Orleans, 1979-81, dep. chief clin. rsch. dept., 1979-81, chmn. credentials com., 1980-81; mem. infection control com. Hotel Dieu Hosp., New Orleans, 1983-84, chmn. pharmacy and therapeutics com., 1988-94, mem. infection control com., 1990-94; vis. physician Charity Hosp. (now Med. Ctr. of La. at New Orleans), New Orleans, 1982—, chmn. antiobiotics com., 1982—, dir. infection control program, 1993—, chmn. infection control com., 1993—, vice chmn. pharmacy and therapeutics com., 1995—; chmn. comprehensive medicine head search com. La. State U. Med. Sch., 1989-90, dept. medicine faculty promotion com., 1988—, AIDS policy com., 1992; adv. bd. La. State Labs., 1993—, State La. Pub. Health Lab. Adv. Com., 1994—, U.S. Pub. Health Region 6 Infertility Prevention Adv. Com., 1995—; mem. nat. STD treatment guidelines com. Ctrs. Disease Control, 1993, 98, nat. Chlamydia and gonorrheadiagnosis guidelines com., 1997—; dir. La. STD/HIV rsch. ctr., 2001-04, Gulf South STI/TM Collaborative Rsch. Ctr., 2004—. Peer reviewer various jours. including Sexually Transmitted Diseases, The Jour. of Infectious Diseases, The Am. Jour. of the Med. Scis., Archives of Internal Medicine, Clin. Infectious Diseases, New Eng. Jour. Medicine, Annals Internal Medicine, Jour. AMA; contbr. chpts. to books and articles to profl. jours. Dir. La. STD/HIV Rsch. Ctr., 2002—. With USPHS, 1970-82. Fellow ACP (La. chpt. program chmn. 1994-95), Infectious Diseases Soc. Am.; mem. Internat. Soc. for Sexually Transmitted Disease Rsch. (bd. dirs. 1991-99, chmn. 1995 meeting organizing com., pres. 1993-95, sec.-treas. 1999—), Am. Fedn. for Clin. Rsch., Am. Sexually Transmitted Diseases Assn. (v.p. 1992-94, pres. 1994-96), Am. Soc. for Microbiology, European Soc. for Clin. Microbiology and Infectious Diseases, So. Soc. for Clin. Investigation, La./Miss. Infectious Diseases Soc. (bd. dirs., sci. program chmn. 1993, pres. 1997-99), Phi Beta Kappa. Achievements include research in the effect of sexually transmitted microorganisms on pregnancy outcome, antibiotic treatment of sexually transmitted diseases and in particular C. trachomatis, epidemiology of C. trachomatis in normal populations, chancroid and other genital ulcer diseases; establishment of first chlamydia laboratory in the Gulf South. Office: La State U Med Sch 1542 Tulane Ave New Orleans LA 70112-2825 Office Phone: 504-568-5031.

MARTIN, DAVID JULIAN, medical association administrator; Cert. Assn. Exec. Positions related to acctg. and bus. mgmt.; with Bands of America; asst. exec. dir. Am. Assn. Neurol. Surgeons; exec. dir. Urban and Regional Info Systems Assn., Park Ridge, Ill.; CEO, exec. v.p. Soc. Critical Care Medicine. Mem.: Assn. Forum Chicagoland, Am. Assn. Med. Soc. Execs., Coun. Engring. and Sci. Soc. Execs., Am. Soc. Assn. Execs. Office: Soc Critical Care Medicine 500 Midway Dr Mount Prospect IL 60056 Office Phone: 847-827-6869. Office Fax: 847-827-6886. Business E-Mail: dmartin@sccm.org.*

MARTIN, DAVID STANDISH, education educator; b. New Bedford, Mass., Aug. 24, 1937; s. Theodore Tripp and Elinor Louise (Raymond) M.; m. Susan Katherine Orowan, June 30, 1962. BA, Yale U., 1959; MEd, Harvard U., 1961, CAS, 1968; PhD, Boston Coll., 1971. Cert. tchr., prin. Tchr. Newton (Mass.) Pub. Schs., 1961-68, asst. prin., 1969-70; teaching asst. Boston Coll., Chestnut Hill, Mass., 1968-69; curriculum dir. Beverly (Mass.) Pub. Schs., 1970-73; prin. Mill Valley (Calif.) Pub. Schs., 1973-75, curriculum dir., 1975-80; chmn. dept. edn. Dominican Coll., San Rafael, Calif., 1978-80; coordinator undergrad. tchr. edn. Gallaudet U., Washington, 1980-85, dean sch. edn. and human svcs., 1985-95, prof. edn., 1995—2001, prof., dean emeritus, 2002—. Cons. Curriculum Devel. Assocs., Washington, 1975-2001; mem. bd. examiners Nat. Coun. Accreditation Tchr. Education; bd. dirs. USA-SINO Tchr. Education Consortium, Western Pa. Sch. for the Deaf; Fulbright fellow U. Witwatersrand, South Africa, 2003, 04, Open U., 2005, vis. rsch. prof. Author: Case Studies in Curriculum, 1989; editor: Cognition, Education and Deafness, 1985, Advances in Cognition Education and Deafness, 1991; co-editor, author: Assessing Deaf Adults, Curriculum for Deaf Learners; contbr. articles to profl. jours. Grantee Dept. Edn., 1970, 85, Knight Found., 1995-2001, Ford Found., 1998-2001. Mem. D.C. Assn. Colls. Tchr. Edn. (pres. 1989-92), Assn. for Supervision and Curricum Devel., Nat. Coun. for Social Studies, Am. Ednl. Rsch. Assn., Am. Assn. Colls. for Tchr. Edn. (bd. dirs.), Coun. for Exceptional Children, Phi Delta Kappa, Kappa Delta Pi (chair publ.), Ednl. Consulting Schs. and Univs. (prof., dean emeritus 2002-), Cape Cod Geneal. Soc. (co-pres. 2006-). Democrat. Unitarian Universalist. Avocations: genealogy, sailing, classical organ, astronomy. Home and Office: 10 Colonial Farm Cir Marstons Mills MA 02648 Home Phone: 508-420-0224; Office Phone: 508-527-0460. Personal E-mail: davidchina_2000@yahoo.com, davidmartindr@aol.com.

MARTIN, DEAN, state treasurer; m. Kerry Martin. Degree in Small Bus. Mgmt. & Entrepreneurship, Ariz. State U. Founder Digital Media Develop. Co.; ptnr. Mktg. Consulting Firm; mem. Dist. 24 Ariz. State Senate, 2001—02, mem. Dist. 6, 2002—07; state treas. State Ariz., 2007—. Mem.: Young Republicans, Phoenix Rotary 100, 100 Club. Office: 1700 W Washington St 1st Fl Phoenix AZ 85007 Office Phone: 602-604-7800. Office Fax: 602-542-7176.*

MARTIN, DEAN FREDERICK, retired chemistry professor; b. Woodburn, Iowa, Apr. 6, 1933; s. Herman A. and Frances M. (Rausis) M.; m. Barbara Bursa, Dec. 22, 1956; children: Diane, Bruce, John, Paul, Brian, Eric. BA, Grinnell Coll., 1955; PhD, Pa. State U., 1958. NSF postdoctoral fellow Univ. Coll., London, 1958—59; instr. inorganic chemistry U. Ill., Champaign-Urbana, 1959—61, asst. prof., 1961—64; assoc. prof. chemistry U. South Fla., Tampa, 1964—69, prof., 1969—, Disting. Svc. prof. chemistry, 1992—2006, prof. emeritus, 2006—. Vis. prof. physiology and pharmacology Duke, 1970-71 Author: (with Barbara B. Martin) Coordination Compounds, 1964, (with Therald Moeller) Laboratory Chemistry, 1965, Marine Chemistry, 2 vols, 1968, 70; editor (with George M. Padilla) Marine Pharmacognosy, 1973; editor Fla. Scientist, 1984—. Recipient Alumni award Grinnell Coll., 1971; USPHS rsch. career award, 1969-74; amed Disting. Svc. prof., 1992—, Disting. U. Prof. Emeritus, 2006-. Fellow AAAS; mem. Am. Chem. Soc., Royal Soc. Chemistry (London), Aquatic Plant Mgmt. Soc., Alpha Chi Sigma, Phi Beta Kappa, Sigma Xi. Roman Catholic. Avocation: woodworking. Home: 3402 Valencia Rd Tampa FL 33618-3950 Office: U South Fla Dept Chemistry CHE 205 4202 E Fowler Ave Tampa FL 33620-5205 Office Phone: 813-974-2374. Business E-Mail: dmartin@cas.usf.edu.

MARTIN, DEMETRI (DEMITRI MARTIN), comedian, scriptwriter; b. NYC, May 23, 1973; Ed., Yale U.; attended, NYU Law Sch. Stand-up comedian Boston Comedy Club, NYC, writer (TV series) Late Night with Conan O'Brien, 2003—04, The Wrong Coast, 2004, youth correspondent The Daily Show, Comedy Central, 2005—, writer, actor (TV episode) Comedy Central Presents Demetri Martin, 2004, Invite Them Up, 2005; actor: (TV episode) 12:21, 2004; writer, actor If I..., 2004 (Perrier Comedy award, Edinburge Internat. Fringe Festival, 2003), These Are Jokes, 2005, Dr. Earnest Parrot Presents Demetri Martin, 2006, Melbourne Internat. Comedy Festival, 2006 (Barry award, 2006), host Across the Narrows Music Festival, Coney Island, 2005; actor: (films) Paper Heart, 2009, Taking Woodstock, 2009. Recipient Nightlife award for male comic stand-up, 2007; named one of 25 Funniest People in America, Entertainment Weekly, 40 Under 40, Crain's NY Bus., 2006. Avocation: skateboarding. Mailing: c/o The Daily Show Comedy Central 1775 Broadway New York NY 10019-1903 E-mail: demetrimartin@hotmail.com.*

MARTIN, DIANNA LUISE, retired school administrator; b. Ft. Sill, Okla., Oct. 17, 1950; d. Dutch and Anneliese Martin. MEd, Coll. NJ, Trenton, 1980. Cert. elem. tchr. Murray State U., 1972, reading specialist Coll. NJ, 1980, chief sch. adminstrn. Georgian Ct. Coll., 1993, learning disabilities specialist Rowan Coll., 1983. Tchr. Pemberton Twp. Schs., Browns Mills, NJ, 1972—80; child study team mem. Lacey Twp. Schs., Forked River, NJ, 1980—88; dir. spl. svcs. Plumsted Twp. Schs., New Egypt, NJ, 1988—93, Manchester Twp. Sch. Dist., Whiting, NJ, 1993—98; adj. prof. Fla. Atlantic U., Boca Raton, 1998—, Lynn U., Boca Raton, Fla., 2005—07. Author: (book) Getting Extra Help For Your Child. Mentor Big Bros. and Big Sisters Broward County, Ft. Lauderdale, Fla., 1999—2009; juvenile ct. vol. NJ. Supreme Ct., Manchester Township, NJ, 1995—98; foster parent dogs Grateful Paws, Ft. Lauderdale, 2005—09; broward spl. olympic bd. mem. Spl. Olympics, Ft. Lauderdale, 1999—2000; trustee exec. bd. NJ. Assn. Sch. Administr., Trenton, 1995—97. Recipient Quarterback Club award, Miami Dolphins, 2004, Big Sister of Yr., Big Brother and Big Sisters Broward County, 2006. Home: 842SE 19th Ave Apt 1 Deerfield Beach FL 33441 Home Phone: 954-571-8494. Home Fax: 854-571-8494. Personal E-mail: diannamartin7@hotmail.com.

MARTIN, DONNA LEE, retired publishing company executive; b. Detroit, Aug. 7, 1935; d. David M. Paul and Lillian (Paul); m. Rex Martin, June 5, 1956; children: Justin, Andrew. BA, Rice U., 1957. Mng. editor trade dept. Appleton-Century-Crofts Co., NYC, 1961-62; dir. publs. Lycoming Coll., Williamsport, Pa., 1966-68; editor Univ. Press of Kans., Lawrence, 1971-74; mng. editor Andrews McMeel Publ., Kansas City, Mo., 1974-80, v.p., editorial dir., 1980-95, v.p., editor-at-large, 1995-98; v.p. Universal Press Syndicate, Kansas City, 1980-98. Lectr. U. Mo., Kansas City, Johnson County Cmty. Coll., Kans.; free-lance writer, editor; cons. editor Kans. City Star Books. Author: (adaptation) Charles Dickens' A Christmas Carol: Adapted for Theatre; co-author (with Melissa Hayden) The Nutcracker Ballet; contbr. articles to profl. jours. Named Disting. Alumna Rice U., 1990. Mem. Ctrl. Exchange (Kansas City), The Groucho Club (London), Phi Beta Kappa. Home: 6810 W 66th Ter Shawnee Mission KS 66202-4147 Business E-Mail: donnamartin@kc.rr.com.

MARTIN, EARL F., dean, law educator; married; 2 children. BA, U. Ky., 1984, JD, 1987; LLM, Yale U., 1996. Atty. JAG Corps US Air Force; prof. law Tex. Wesleyan U. Sch. Law, Fort Worth, 1997—2005, assoc. dean, 2003—05; dean Gonzaga U. Sch. Law, 2005—. Office: Gonzaga U Sch Law PO Box 3528 721 N Cincinnati St Spokane WA 99220-3528 Office Fax: 509-313-3700. E-mail: emartin@lawschool.gonzaga.edu.*

MARTIN, EDWARD CURTIS, JR., landscape architect, educator; b. Albany, Ga., Aug. 21, 1928; s. Edward Curtis and Mildred Lee (Tyler) M.; m. Roberta Inman Parker, Mar. 18, 1967; children: Edward Curtis III, Andrew Parker. BFA, U. Ga., 1950, M of Landscape Architecture, 1969. Landscape arch. Norman C. Butts Landscape Contractor, Atlanta, 1950, M.T. Brooks Office of Landscape Architecture, Birmingham, Ala., 1950—55; Univ. landscape arch., horticulturist Miss. State U., 1956-70, prof. landscape architecture, 1970-92, Disting. prof., 1988, prof. emeritus, 1993—. Originator, chmn., lectr. Edward C. Martin Jr. Landscape Design Symposium, 1957-2005; guest lectr. U. San Luis Potosi, Mex., 1990, U. Mex. Sch. Architecture, Mexico City, 1991, La. State U., 1990-92, 94, 96, Biendenharn Found., Monroe, La., 1991, Longue Vue Found., New Orleans, 1991; prof. Miss. State U., 1992-93; guest instr. in field; originator, lectr. Garden Design Workshops, Miss. State U., 1988-2001; host numerous flower and garden shows and tours abroad; So. hist. gardens lectr. Miss. U. for Women, 1997-2000; photog. landscape archtl. rsch. study: Europe, 1958, 66, 74, 85, S.Am., 1960, Israel, 1993, 95, Greece, Turkey, 1998; vis. prof. La. State U., 1990-94, 97; instr. landscape design Bot. Gardens, Huntsville, Ala., 1996; instr. ecology tour Copper Canyon, Mex., 1994; spkr. and lectr. in field. Author: Landscape Plants in Design, A Photographic Guide, 1983; co-author: Home Landscapes, Planting Design and Management, 1994; invited to participate in Attingham Summer Program in Hist. Preservation (English country houses and gardens) Eng., 1985; author/photographer of 80-captioned slide series, one on Home Landscapes, another on Urban Landscape Design for use by Nat. Coun. State Garden Clubs, Inc., 1994; guest spkr. 53rd Ann. Landscape Design Symposium, Miss. State U., 2008. Mem. Miss. State Bd. Landscape Archs. for Profl. Registration, 1973-74; mem. Starkville Park and Recreation Bd., Miss., 1973-79; civic beautification com. Black Mountain, NC, 2002—; bd. visitors Warren Wilson Coll., Asheville, NC, 2002—; elder Trinity Presbyn. Ch., Starkville, Miss., Warren Wilson Presbyn. Ch. and Coll. Chapel, Asheville; garden tour guide Biltmore Estate, Asheville, 2003— Recipient Silver Seal award Nat. Coun. State Garden Clubs 1969, honoree 1995, Landscape Heritage award Fraser Found. Calif. 1986, Helent S. Hull Lit. award, 1996; Paul Harris fellow Rotary Internat., 1998; reception area (lobby) of Miss. State U. Dept. Landscape Architecture donated in his honor by Garden Clubs Miss. Inc., 2003. Fellow Am. Soc. Landscape Archs. (chmn. edn. com. 1960-61, pres. Miss. sect. S.W. chpt. 1975, chmn. S.W. chpt. ann. awards com. 1976, trustee Miss. chpt. 1977-81, nominated Jot Carpenter Tchg. medal Miss. chpt. 2006); mem. So. Garden History Soc., Nat. Coun. State Garden Clubs (chmn. landscape design 1993-97, Appreciation cert. 2005), Garden Clubs Miss. (bd. dirs. 1958-2005, Silver Trophy 1961, Spl. Silver award 1980, Gold trophy 1993, Appreciation citation 2005), Am. Soc. Landscape Archs. (spkr., spring conf. NC chpt., Asheville, 2009). Presbyterian. Home: 464 Chapel Rd Black Mountain NC 28711-2640 Office: Dept Landscape Architecture Box 9725 Mississippi State MS 39762-9725 Home Phone: 828-669-0321. Personal E-mail: edonthemountain@bellsouth.net.

MARTIN, EDWIN WILSON, mayor; b. Oceanside, NY, Sept. 3, 1931; s. Edwin Wilson and Jean (Carbone) Martin; m. Peggy Smith, Sept. 5, 1953; children: Scott Andrew, Bruce Leslie. AB, Muhlenberg Coll., Pa., 1953; MA, U. Ala., 1955; PhD, U. Pitts., 1961; D of Sci. Edn. (hon.), Muhlenberg Coll., Pa., 1981; DHL (hon.), Emerson Coll., Boston, 1984, LI U., 1995. From asst. to assoc. prof. speech pathology U. Ala., 1960—66; dir. sub-com. on handicapped US Ho. Reps., 1966—67; dep. assoc. commr. edn. US Office of Edn., 1967—69; assoc. commr., dir. Bur. Edn. Handicapped, 1969—79; dep. commr. edn. US Dept. HEW, 1979—80; asst. sec. edn. US Dept. Edn., 1980—81; lectr. in edn. Harvard U., 1979—81; adj. prof. edn. Columbia U., 1982—91; pres., CEO Nat. Disability Svcs., NY, 1981—94, pres. emeritus NY, 1994—; ret., 1994; mayor Venice, Fla., 2007—. Bd. dirs. Pall Corp., NY, Roslyn Savs. Bank, 1993—2003; adv. bd. Roslyn Bank divsn. NY Cmty. Bank, 2004—07. Columnist: Venice Gondolier Sun, 2003—; contbr. articles to profl. jours., chapters to books. Chmn. Internat. Study Group on Spl. Needs Children, Southampton, England, 1982—92; active Mayor's Adv. Com. on Spl. Edn., NYC, 1987—89, Govs. Adv. Com. on Rehab., NY, 1990—94, Bd. Zoning Appeals, Venice, 2004—05; bd. mem. Golden Beach Assn., Inc., Venice, 1995—98, 2007—. Recipient Alexander Graham Bell award, Alexander Graham Bell Assn. for the Deaf, 1978, Disting. Leadership award, US Dept. Edn., 1986. Fellow: Am. Speech, Lang. and Hearing Assn.; mem.: Coun. for Exceptional Children (v.p., pres.-elect, pres., past pres. divsn. learning disabilities 1996—2000, Wallin award 1979), Jacaranda West Country Club (mem. nominating com. 2005, mem. green com. 2006, mem. bylaws and planning com. 2007). Office Phone: 941-486-2626. Business E-Mail: emartin@ci.venice.fl.us.

MARTIN, ELLIOT EDWARDS, theatrical producer; b. Denver, Feb. 25, 1924; m. Marjorie Cuesta, Oct. 7, 1949; children: Richard, Linda Lisa. Student, U. Denver, 1943-46. Actor, singer London Co. Okla.; actor, singer, stage mgr., assoc. producer Theatre Guild, NYC and London, 1947-53; prodn. stage mgr. 20 Broadway plays and musicals, 1953-61; theatrical producer Never Too Late, Nobody Loves an Albatross, NYC, 1962-66; theatre producer London, 1963; mng. dir. Center Theatre Group, Music Ctr., Los Angeles, 1966-71; producer Elliot Martin Prodns., NYC, 1972—. Mem. exec. bd. Nat. Theatre of the Deaf, Chester, Conn., 1981-, Westport-Weston Arts Council, 1976- Prodns. on Broadway include: Dinner at Eight, 1966, More Stately Mansions, 1967, Abelard and Heloise, 1971, Emperor Henry IV, 1973, A Moon for the Misbegotten, 1973 (spl. Tony award), When You Comin' Back, Red Rider, 1974 (Outer Critics award), Of Mice and Men, 1975, Touch of the Poet, 1976, Dirty Linen and New Found Land, 1977, Caesar and Cleopatra, 1977, Kingfisher, 1979, Clothes for a Summer Hotel, 1980, Kingdoms, 1981, American Buffalo, 1981, Angels Fall, 1983, Glengarry Glen Ross, 1984 (Pulitzer prize), Woza Albert, 1984, American Buffalo, 1984, Harrigan 'n' Hart, 1985, Arsenic and Old Lace (Broadway and nat. tour), 1986-87, Joe Turner's Come and Gone (7 Tony nominations, NY Drama Critic's award best play), 1988, Steel Magnolias (nat. tour), 1989, The Circle, 1989-90, Shadowlands, 1990-91, Breaking Legs, 1991-92, She Loves Me (9 Tony noms.), 1993-94, Death of a Salesman, 1995-96, A Moon For the Misbegotten, 2000, Down the Gaden Paths, 2001, I'm Not Rappaport, 2002, The Oldest Living Confederate Widow Tells All, 2003, (London) Moon for the Misbegotten at the Old Vic, 2006, A Moon For The Misbegotten NYC Broadway, 2007. Mem. bd. assocs. U. Bridgeport, 1978-83. Recipient Tony award for most innovative revival, 1977-78, Larry Tajiri award for outstanding contbn. to arts Denver Post, 1970, Congl. commendation, 1970, Profl. Achievement award U. Denver, 1987. Mem. Platform Speakers Am., League NY Theatres and Prodrs. (gov.), Am. Friends of Theatre (pres.), Players Club, NY Athletic Club (NYC). Republican. Home Phone: 212-245-4177; Office Phone: 212-245-4176. Personal E-mail: eemmar@vorizon.net.

MARTIN, FRANK C., II, art educator; s. Frank C. Martin and Leola Glisson-Martin; m. Shirley Ann Fields, June 18, 1988. BA in History Art, Yale U., New Haven, 1976; MA in History Art, CUNY, Hunter Coll., 1986. Assoc. mgr., edn. svcs. The Met. Mus. Art, NYC, 1984—91; instr. history art SC. State U., Orangeburg, 1991—; curator I. P. Stanback Mus., Orangeburg, 1991—2004; exec. cons. curatorial affairs McCrory Galleri, Columbia, SC, 2004—. Mem. Assn. Internat. des Critiques d'Art, NYC, 2003—. Author (curator): (exhibition and catalogue) Art in an Age of Authenticity. Recipient, SC. Humanities Coun., 1992—94; grantee, 1999—2000. Mem.: Southeastern Coll. Art Conf., Coll. Art Assn., Assn. Internationale des Critiques d'Art. Christian Ch. Achievements include research in critical assessment of aesthetic response and ethnocentrist experience. Avocations: horseback riding, travel, swimming. Home: 145 Lovell St Orangeburg SC 29115 Office: SC State Univ 300 Coll St NE Orangeburg SC 29117

MARTIN, FRED, artist, academic administrator; b. San Francisco, June 13, 1927; s. Ernest Thomas and Leona (Richey) M.; m. Genevieve Catherine Fisette, Jan. 29, 1950 (dec.); children: T. Demian, Fredericka C., Anthony J.; m. Stephanie Zuperko Dudek, 1992. BA, U. Calif., Berkeley, 1949, MA, 1954; postgrad., Calif. Sch. Fine Arts, 1949—50. Registrar Oakland (Calif.) Art Mus., 1955-58; dir. exhbn. San Francisco Art Inst., 1958-65, 1965-75, dir. coll., 1983-92, dean acad. affairs. Exhibited one man shows, Zoe Dusanne Gallery, Seattle, 1952, M.H. deYoung Meml. Mus., San Francisco, 1954, 64, Oakland Mus. Calif., 1958, 2003, San Francisco Mus. Modern Art, 1958, 73, Dilexi Gallery, San Francisco, 1961, Minami Gallery, Tokyo, 1963, Royal Marks Gallery, NYC, 1965-70, Hansen Fuller Gallery, San Francisco, 1974, 75, 76, Quay Gallery, San Francisco, 1979, 81, 84, Natsoulas Gallery, Davis, Calif., 1991, Belcher Studios Gallery, San Francisco, 1994, Frederick Spratt Gallery, San Jose, 1996, Ebert Gallery, San Francisco, 1997, 98, 99, 2001, 2003, Art and Consciousness Gallery/John F. Kennedy U., Berkeley, 1997, Shasta Coll., 1998, Han Art Contemporaine, Montreal, 1999, Sanchez Art Ctr., 2003, Collector's Gallery of Oakland Mus., 2004, Paul Sunderholm Gallery, 2004, Gallery Denovo, Sun Valley, Idaho; represented in permanent collections, Mus. Modern Art, NYC, San Francisco Mus. Modern Art, Oakland Art Mus., Whitney Mus., Fogg Mus.; author: Beulah Land, 1966, Log of the Sun Ship, 1969, Liber Studiorum, 1973, A Travel Book, 1976, From an Antique Land, 1979; Bay area corr.: Art Internat., 1967-69, 75-76; contbg. editor Art Week, 1976-93. Recipient prizes Oakland Art Mus., 1951, 58, prizes San Francisco Mus. Art, 1957, 58, prizes Richmond (Calif.) Art Ctr., 1962, prizes Nat. Found. for Arts, 1970. Home: 232 Monte Vista Ave Oakland CA 94611-4922 Office: San Francisco Art Inst 800 Chestnut St San Francisco CA 94133-2206

MARTIN, FUSI FONKIJOM, film director, educator; s. Andrew Tita and Grace Mandofi Fusi; m. Lucie Gwannulla Fusi; children: Phoebe Akumbom Fusi, Lema Nyingmah Fusi, Tita Ntune Fusi, Nahnine Vibain Fusi. BA, Yaounde U., Cameroon, 1987, MA, 1988, Hull U., Eng., 1989, PhD, 1994. Adj. asst. prof. George Wash. U., Washington, 1995—96; asst. prof. Ky. State U., Frankfort, 1996—2000, U. So. Calif., LA, 2000—05, Coll. William & Mary, Williamsburg, Va., 2006—. Dir.: (screenplay) The Outsider. Office: Coll William & Mary 601 Jamestown Rd Williamsburg VA 23187 Business E-Mail: mffusi@wm.edu.

MARTIN, GALE D., adult education educator; b. Detroit, Sept. 18, 1957; d. Shirley J. Martin. MS, U. Mich., Ann Arbor, 1985. Prof. C.C. So. Nev., Las Vegas. Adj. instr. Schoolcraft Coll., Livonia, Mich., 1980—89. Vol. Red Rock Conservation Area, Las Vegas, 2004—06. Mem.: Nat. Sci. Tchrs. Assn. (assoc.), S.E.P.M. (assoc.), G.S.A. (assoc.). Office: Community College So Nev 700 College Dr H3C Henderson NV 89002 Office Fax: 702-651-3161. E-mail: gale_martin@ccsn.edu.

MARTIN, GARY WAYNE, lawyer; b. Cin., Feb. 14, 1946; s. Elmer DeForrest and Nellie May (Hughes) M.; m. Debra Lynn Goldsmith, June 25, 1982; children: Christopher, Jeremy, Joie, Casey. BA, Wilmington Coll., 1967; JD, U. Cin., 1974. Bar: Fla. 1974. With Fowler White Boggs, Tampa, Fla., 1974—. Lt. USNR, 1967-73. Mem. Harbour Island Athletic Club. Republican. Presbyterian. Avocation: tennis. Office: Fowler White Boggs 501 E Kennedy Blvd Ste 1700 Tampa FL 33602-5240 Home Phone: 813-287-0079; Office Phone: 813-228-7411. Business E-Mail: gmartin@fowlerwhite.com.

MARTIN, GEORGE (WHITNEY), writer; b. NYC, Jan. 25, 1926; s. George Whitney and Agnes Wharton (Hutchinson) M. BA, Harvard U., 1948; student, Trinity Coll., Cambridge U., Eng., 1950; LL.B., U. Va., 1953. Bar: N.Y. 1955. With firm Emmet, Marvin & Martin, NYC, 1955-59; engaged in writing, 1959—. Author: The Opera Companion, A Guide for the Casual Operagoer, 1961, 6th edit., 2008, The Battle of the Frogs and Mice, An Homeric Fable, 1962, 2d edit., 1987, Verdi, His Music, Life and Times, 1963, 4th edit., 2001, The Red Shirt and The Cross of Savoy, The Story of Italy's Risorgimento, 1748-1871, 1969, Causes and Conflicts, The Centennial History of the Association of the Bar of the City of New York, 1870-1970, 1970, 2d edit., 1997, Madam Secretary: Frances Perkins, 1976, The Damrosch Dynasty, America's First Family of Music, 1983, Aspects of Verdi, 1988, 2nd edit., 1993, Verdi at the Golden Gate, San Francisco in the Golden Years, 1993, Twentieth Century Opera, A Guide, 1999, CCB: The Life and Century of Charles C. Burlingham, New York's First Citizen, 1858-1959 (Erwin N. Griswold award US Supreme Ct. Hist. Soc., 2006), 2005; contbr. articles to profl. jours., mags. Home: 53 Crosslands Dr Kennett Square PA 19348-2010 Office Phone: 610-388-0529.

MARTIN, SIR GEORGE HENRY, recording industry executive; b. London, Jan. 3, 1926; s. Henry and Bertha Beatrice Martin; m. Sheena Rose Chisolm, 1948; 2 children; m. Judy Lockhart Smith, 1966; 2 children. DMus (hon.), Berklee Coll. Music, Boston, 1989; MA (hon.), Salford U., Manchester, 1992. With BBC, 1950, EMI Records Ltd., London, 1950—65, head of Parlophone label; founder Associated Ind. Recording (AIR), London, 1965; founder, chmn. AIR Studios, London, 1969, Montserrat, France, 1979, George Martin Music; prodr. The Beatles, 1962—70; ret., 2002. Prodr. all Beatles records, records produced include Off the Beatle Track, 1964, Ferry Cross the Mersey, 1965, George Martin Plays "Help", 1965, Sgt. Pepper's Lonely Hearts Club Band, 1967 (Best Contemporary Album, Album of Yr., Grammy Awards, 1968), London by George, 1967, Live and Let Die, 1973 (Best Arrangement Accompanying Vocalist, Grammy Awards, 1974), The Who's Tommy, 1993 (Best Musical Show Album, Grammy Awards, 1994), George Martin Instrumentally Salutes the Beatle Girls, 1994, In My Life, 1998, Love, 2007 (Best Compilation Soundtrack Album, Best Surround Sound Album, Grammy Awards, 2008); author: All You Need is Ears, 1979, Making Music, 1983, Summer of Love: The Making of Sgt. Pepper, 1993. Sub-lt. Royal Naval Vol. Res., 1944—47. Recipient Comdr., Order Brit. Empire, 1988, Knight Bachelor, 1996; named Man of the Yr., Brit. Phonographic Industry, 1998; named to Rock & Roll Hall of Fame, 1999; fellow (hon.), Guildhall Sch. Music. Mem.: Royal Acad. Music (hon.). Office: AIR Studios Lyndhurst Hall London NW3 5NG England Office Phone: (20) 7794-0660. Office Fax: (20) 7794-8518.

MARTIN, GILES, recording industry executive; b. London, Oct. 9, 1969; s. George Henry Martin. Bassist, songwriter, prodr. Velvet Jones; A&R prodr. Instant Karma record label, 1999—2002; co-exec. George Martin Music, London. Prodn. asst. The Beatles Anthology, 1996, prodr. albums including The K's, 1994, My Life Story, 1994, The Glory of Gershwin, 1995, The Choir, 1995, The Great Music Experience, 1995, Monorail, 1996, INXS, 1996, George Martin: In My Life, 1996—97, The Alice Band, 2000—01, Imagine the Concert, 2001, Party at the Palace, 2001, Hayley Westenra: Pure, 2003, Willard White: My Way, 2004, Hayley Westenra: Odyssey, 2004—05, The Beatles: Love, 2004—06 (Best Compilation Soundtrack Album, Best Surround Sound Album, Grammy Awards, 2008), Kim Richey: Chinese Boxes, 2007, Paco Peña, 2007. Office: C A Mgmt PO Box 379 Lymington SO41 1AU England

MARTIN, GINA LYNN, lawyer; BS cum laude, St. Michael's Coll., 1992; JD, Fordham U., 1995. Bar: NY 1996, Mass. 1999. Assoc. Fried, Frank, Harris, Shriver & Jacobson, NYC; ptnr. Bus. Law Dept. Goodwin Procter LLP, Boston. Mem.: Am. Bankruptcy Inst., ABA, Boston Bar Assn. Office: Goodwin Procter LLP Exchange Place 53 State St Boston MA 02109 Office Phone: 617-570-1330. E-mail: gmartin@goodwinprocter.com.

MARTIN, GRACE BURKETT, psychologist; b. Sumter, S.C., Aug. 27, 1939; d. John Hazel and Grace Thomasine (Briggs) Burkett; BA magna cum laude, Armstrong State Coll., 1976; MS, Fla. State U., 1979, PhD, 1980; m. H. Russell Martin, Jr., Oct. 9, 1957; children— H. Russell, Carolyne, Melinda. Lic. psychologist. Hist. preservationist, 1962—; dir. Christian edn. St. Thomas Parish, Savannah, Ga., 1970-74; prof. psychology Armstrong State Coll., Savannah, 1980-2001, prof. emeritus, 2002-, dept. head psychology, dir. gen. studies degree program; head. divsn. social and behavioral scis., interim dean arts and scis.; pres. Orgn. Cons.; lectr.; radio and TV appearances. Author, collaborator nat. and cross-nat. studies of women and work; co-author UNESCO manual for nat. leaders and policy makers; cons. editor Jour. Supplementary Abstract Svc., 1980, 81. Bd. dirs. Coastal Empire YMCA, 1972-75; mem. Savannah Symphony Soc.; mem. commn. on mission Episcopal Diocese of Ga., 1972-74, mem. liturg. commn., 1972-74, also lic. lay reader; pres. Operation Return, 1972-76. Named Mrs. Ga., 1962. Mem. Am. Psychol. Assn., Am. Psychol. Soc. (charter), Southeastern Psychol. Assn., Soc. Indsl. Organizational Psychology, Am. Mgmt. Assn., Nat. Assn. Women Deans and Administrators, Ga. Assn. Women Deans and Adminstrators, Commerce Club Savannah (charter), Ga. Ednl. Research Assn. Home: 50 Shipwatch Rd Savannah GA 31410-2950 Personal E-mail: martingrace@comcast.net.

MARTIN, GUY, lawyer; b. LA, Jan. 22, 1911; s. I.G. and Mary Pearl (Howe) M.; m. Edith Kingdon Gould, Oct. 12, 1946; children— Guy III, Jason Gould, Christopher Kingdon, Edith Maria Theodosia Burr. AB, Occidental Coll., 1931; BA (1st class hons.), Oxford U., 1934, MA, 1944; LL.B., Yale, 1937. Bar: N.Y. 1938, D.C. 1947. Practiced with Donovan, Leisure, Newton & Lumbard, NYC, 1938-41; gen. counsel All Am. Aviation, Inc., 1942, Am. Mexican Claims Commn., U.S. Dept. State, 1945-47; ptnr. Martin, Whitfield, Smith & Bebchick (and predecessors), Washington, 1952-80; counsel Martin and Smith (and predecessors), 1981-86; pres., vice chmn. bd., dep. chief exec. officer Internat. Bank, 1981-86; with Law Office of Saltzstein & Martin, 1988-99. Served with USN; sea duty 1942-45. Mem. ABA, Assn. of Bar of City of N.Y., Bar Assn. D.C, Phi Beta Kappa, Sigma Alpha Epsilon. Clubs: Yale, Brook, Knickerbocker (N.Y.C.); Metropolitan, City Tavern (Washington). Episcopalian. Home: 3300 O St NW Washington DC 20007-2813

MARTIN, HARRY C., lawyer; Grad., U. Va.; JD with honors, George Washington U. Ptnr. Fletcher, Heald, Hildreth PLC, Arlington, Va. Columnist Broadcast Engring. mag., 1981—, Radio mag., 1997—, frequent spkr. NAB, state broadcast industry conventions, regular panelist Kagan Radio Summit seminars. Bd. dir. Univ. Va. Club of Washington. Mem.: Fed. Comm. Bar Assn. (asst. secy-secy. 1997—99, asst. treas.-treas. 2000—02, pres.-elect 2003—04, pres. 2004—05, exec. com. 1994—2002). Office: Fletcher Heald & Hildreth 11th Fl 1300 N 17th St Arlington VA 22209 Office Phone: 703-812-0415. Office Fax: 703-812-0486. Business E-Mail: martin@fhhlaw.com.

MARTIN, HARRY CORPENING, lawyer, retired state supreme court justice; b. Lenoir, NC, Jan. 13, 1920; s. Hal C. and Johnsie Harshaw (Nelson) M.; m. Nancy Robiou Dallam, Apr. 16, 1955; children: John, Matthew, Mary. AB, U. N.C., 1942; LLB, Harvard U., 1948; LLM, U. Va., 1982. Bar: N.C. 1948. Pvt. practice, Asheville, NC, 1948-62; judge NC Superior Ct., Asheville, 1962-78, NC Ct. Appeals, Raleigh, 1978-82; justice NC Supreme Ct., 1982-92; ptnr. Martin & Martin, Attys., Hilllsborough, 1992—99. Adj. prof. U. N.C. Law Sch., 1983-92, Duke U., 1990-91, Dan K. Moore disting. vis. prof., U. N.C. Law Sch., 1992-94; sr. conf. atty. U.S. Ct. Appeals for 4th Cir., 1994-99; chief justice Supreme Ct. ea. bd. of Cherokee Indians, 2000-2007, ret. With U.S. Army, 1942-45, South Pacific. Mem. U.S. Supreme Ct. Hist. Soc., N.C. Supreme Ct. Hist. Soc. (pres.). Democrat. Episcopalian. Home: 1 Hilltop Rd Asheville NC 28803-3017 Office: Martin Law Firm Asheville NC 28803 Office Phone: 828-274-4633. Personal E-mail: judgemartin@bellsouth.net.

MARTIN, HOWARD W., JR., lawyer; b. Norfolk, Va., Mar. 10, 1942; BS in Bus. Adminstrn., Washington & Lee U., 1964; LLB, U. Va., 1967. Sr. ptnr. Crenshaw Ware & Martin PLC, Norfolk, Va., mng. ptnr. Mem. Norfolk Divsn. Bd. Hampton Roads C. of C., 2001—05; adminstrv. bd. mem. Ghent United Methodist Church, Norfolk, Va., 1978—, chmn., 1984—86; bd. dirs. Tidewater YMCA, 1978—84. Line officer USN, navy lawyer Judge Advocate General's Corp. USN. Mem.: Va. Law Found. (bd. mem. 1990—97, sec. 1993—94, pres. 1995—96, fellow 1997—), Norfolk & Portsmouth Bar Assn. (treas. 1994—96, pres. 1997), Va. Bar Assn. (exec. com. mem. 1987—90, sec. 1989—90), Va. State Bar (coun. mem. 2000—, exec. com. mem. 2003—, pres. 2007—08), ABA. Office: Crenshaw Ware & Martin PLC One Commercial Pl 1200 Bank of America Ctr Norfolk VA 23510-2111 Office Phone: 757-623-3000. Office Fax: 757-623-5735. E-mail: hmartin@cwm-law.com.

MARTIN, IONIS BRACY, artist, educator; b. Chgo., 1936; d. Francis Wright and Hattie Robinson Bracy; m. Allyn Aubrey Martin; 1 child, Allyn Bracy-Fletcher. BS, Fisk U., 1957; MEd, U. Hartford, 1968; MFA, Pratt Inst., Bklyn., 1987. Y-teen assoc. dir. YWCA of Greater Hartford, 1957—59; homefinder Conn. Child Welfare Assn, New Haven, 1959—61; art tchr. Arsenal elem sch. Hartford Bd. Edn., Conn., 1961, art tchr. Weaver H.S., 1961—67; h.s. art tchr. Bloomfield Bd. Edn., Conn., 1971—2001; lectr., adj. prof. Ctrl. Conn. State U., New Britain, 1985—2003. With Gall Rschr. African Am. Almanac, 1994; co-founder, sec. treas., v.p. bd. dirs., hon. mem. Artist Collective, Hartford, 1972—; trustee Wadsworth Athenaeum Mus. Art, Hartford, 1978—97; corporator Hartford Art Sch., U. Hartford, West Hartford, 2001—06; with Links Inc. & Sch. Art Inst. Chgo., 2008—. Author: A Curriculum Sampler. Docent DuSable Mus.; co-trustee, chmn. Ella Burr McManus Trust, Hartford, 1985—2006; bd. dirs. Ancient Burial Ground, Hartford, 1998—2005, Huntington House Mus., Windsor, Conn., 2001—05., DuBois Inst. fellow Harvard U., 1994, Through Young Black Eyes grantee, Conn. Commn. on the Arts, Artist fellow, Skidmore Coll. Mem.: Art Inst. Chgo., Canton Gallery on the Green, The Links, Art Works Gallery, Delta Sigma Theta. Home: 3120 S Indiana Ave Unit 404 Chicago IL 60616-3762 Personal E-mail: ionismartin@mac.com.

MARTIN, J. CLARK, lawyer; b. Washington, May 10, 1940; BSEE, La. State U., 1963, JD, 1966. Bar: La. 1966, Tex. 1970. Ptnr., co-head Intellectual Property / Technical Litig. Sect. Vinson & Elkins LLP, Houston. Fellow: Tex. Bar Found. Office: Vinson & Elkins LLP First City Tower 1001 Fannin St, Ste 2300 Houston TX 77002 Office Phone: 713-758-2400. E-mail: cmartin@velaw.com.

MARTIN, JACK, educational services company executive, former federal agency administrator; b. Frendale, Mich. m. Bettye Martin; children: Randy, Ingrid. BS, MBA, Wayne State U.; postgrad., U. Minn. CPA. With GM Corp., Detroit; various mgmt. positions Control Data; cons. acct. Touche Ross & Co. (now Deloitte and Touche); mng. dir., CEO, founder Jack Martin and Co. P.C., CPAs, 1975—2002; chmn., acting CEO Home Fed. Savings Bank, Detroit, 1995—2002; chmn. Provider Reimbursement Rev. Bd. US Dept. Health & Human Services, 1991—94; CFO US Dept. Edn., Washington, 2002—05; acting dir. Selective Svc. System, Arlington, Va., 2004; exec. v.p. White Hat Mgmt., Akron, Ohio, 2005—. Chmn. of bd. Health Alliance Plan; mem. investment com. Mercy Health Sys. (now Trinity Health); chair Mich. adv. com. U.S. Civil Rights Commn.; v.p. Merrill Palmer Inst. Wayne State U. Trustee, Alzheimer's Assn. Recipient Pres. Quality award for Improved Fin. Performance, US Dept. Edn., Certificate of Excellence in Accountability Reporting, Assn. Govt. Accountants, Alexander Hamilton award for Tech., Treasury & Risk Mgmt. mag. Mem.: AICPA (mem. practice stds. subcom.), Det. Athletic Club (bd. dirs.). Office: White Hat Mgmt 159 S Main St Ste 600 Akron OH 44308

MARTIN, JACQUELINE BRIGGS, writer; b. Maine; m. Rich Martin; children: Sarah, Justin. Author: Bizzy Bones and Moosemouse, 1986, Bizzy Bones and the Lost Quilt, 1988, Bizzy Bones and Uncle Ezra, 1984, Button, Bucket, Sky, 1998, The Finest Horse in Town, 1992, Grandmother Bryant's Pocket, 1996 (Lupine award 1996), The Green Truck Garden Giveaway: A Neighborhood Story and Almanac, 1997, Good Times on Grandfather Mountain, 1992, Higgins Bend Song and Dance, 1997, Snowflake Bentley, 1998 (Caldecott Award 1999, Lupine Award 1998), Washing the Willow Tree Loon, 1995, The Lamp, The Ice and The Boat Called Fish, 2001, The Water Gift and the Pig of the Pig (Lupine award 2003), 2003, On Sand Island, 2003, (with Sarah Martin Bosse) Banjo Granny, 2006, Chicken Joy on Redbean Road, 2007.

MARTIN, JACQUES, professional hockey coach, former professional sports team executive; b. St. Pascal, Ont., Can., Oct. 1, 1952; children: Angela, Nathalee. Head coach St. Louis Blues, 1986—88; asst. coach Chgo. Blackhawks, 1988—90; assoc. coach Quebec Nordiques, 1990—93, asst. coach, 1994—95, Colo. Avalanche, 1995—96; head coach Ottawa Senators, 1996—2004, Fla. Panthers, 2004—08, gen. mgr., 2006—09; head coach Montreal Canadiens, 2009—. Assoc. coach Team Can., Olympic Games, Salt Lake City, 2002, Torino, Italy, 06. Founder Jacques Martin Hockey Sch.; host Jacques Martin Omnium Golf Tournament. Recipient Jack Adams Award, 1999. Office: c/o Montreal Canadiens 1275 St Antoine St West Montreal PQ Canada H3C 5L2*

MARTIN, JAMES GRUBBS, healthcare consultant, Former United States Representative, NC; b. Savannah, Ga., Dec. 11, 1935; s. Arthur Morrison and Mary Julia (Grubbs) M.; m. Dorothy Ann McAulay, June 1, 1957; children: James Grubbs, Emily Richey, Arthur Benson. BS, Davidson Coll., 1957; PhD, Princeton U., 1960. Assoc. prof. chemistry Davidson (N.C.) Coll., 1960-72; mem. US Congress from 9th N.C. Dist., 1973-85; gov. State of N.C., 1985-92; v.p. Carolinas HealthCare System, Charlotte, NC, 1993—2008. Mem. Mecklenburg (NC) Bd. County Commrs., 1966-72, chmn., 1967-68, 70-71; pres. NC Assn. County Commrs., 1970-71; tuba player Charlotte Symphony, 1961-66; bd. dirs. Family Dollar Stores, Inc., Palomar Med. Techns., Inc. Chmn. Global TransPark Found., 1993—; trustee Davidson Coll., 1998-2005; trustee Union Theol. Sem., Va., 2002-07. Danforth fellow, 1957—60. Mem. Beta Theta Pi (v.p., trustee 1966-69, pres. 1975-78), Masons (33 deg., Grand Cross), Shriners. Presbyterian. Office: Carolinas Med Ctr PO Box 32861 Charlotte NC 28232-2861 Office Phone: 704-355-5310. E-mail: jgmartin@carolinas.org.

MARTIN, JAMES JOHN, JR., systems analyst, retired research and development company executive; b. Paterson, NJ, Feb. 3, 1936; s. James John and Lillian M.; m. Lydia Elizabeth Bent, June 11, 1954; children: David, Peter, Laura, Daniel, Lucas. BA, U. Wis.-Madison, 1955; postgrad., Div. Sch., Harvard U., 1955-57; MS, Navy Postgrad. Sch., 1963; PhD, MIT, 1965. Commd. ensign USN, 1957, advanced through grades to comdr., 1971, ret., 1977; sector v.p. Sci. Applications Internat. Corp., La Jolla, Calif., 1977-95. Author: Bayesian Decision Problems and Markov Chains, 1967; editor: On Not Confusing Ourselves, 1991; contbr. articles to profl. jours. Bd. dirs. Mil. Conflict Inst., 1986-92. Decorated Legion of Merit. Mem. Internat. Inst. Strategic Studies, Ops. Research Soc. Am., Mil. Ops. Research Soc. (bd. dirs. 1974-77) Democrat. Avocation: cooking. Home: 6603 Aranda Ave La Jolla CA 92037-6216

MARTIN, JAMES KAY, policy and management consultant; b. Montreal, Sept. 20, 1948; s. Douglas and Margaret Martin; m. Emma Lim Abrenica, Sept. 12, 1986. B of Math., U. Waterloo, Ont., 1970; PhD, U. Toronto, 1974. Sr. analyst Health & Welfare, Ottawa, 1974-79; asst. dir. transfer payments Social Devel. Ministry, Ottawa, 1980-84; exec. dir. planning Dept. Agr., Ottawa, 1984-90; exec dir. regulatory affairs Treasury bd. Can., Ottawa, 1990-96; dir. gen. Internal Audit and Risk Mgmt. Human Resources Can., Ottawa, 1997—2004; dir. gen. audit and evaluation Human Resources and Skills Devel., Ottawa, 2004—05; pres. JK & E Martin Cons., Inc., Ottawa, 2005—. Chmn. regulatory mgmt. group OECD, Paris, 1993-96. Contbr. articles to profl. jours. Chmn. grad. students union U. Toronto, 1973, mem. bd. govs., 1974. Fellow Nat. Rsch. Coun., 1970, Ont. Inst. for Edn., 1971, Can. Coun., 1972, 73. Mem. Ottawa Humane Soc. Roman Catholic. Avocations: running, canoeing, skiing, swimming. Office Phone: 613-614-3012. Personal E-mail: jmartin@betterpolicyonline.com.

MARTIN, JAMES KIRBY, historian, educator; b. Akron, Ohio, May 26, 1943; s. Paul Elmo and Dorothy Marie (Garrett) M.; m. Karen Wierwille, Aug. 7, 1965; children: Darcy Elizabeth, Sarah Marie, Joelle Kathryn Garrett. BA summa cum laude, Hiram Coll., 1965; MA, U. Wis., 1967, PhD, 1969. Asst. prof. history Rutgers U., New Brunswick, NJ, 1969-73, assoc. prof., 1973-79, prof., 1979-80, asst. provost, 1972-74, v.p. acad. affairs, 1977-79; vis. prof. Rutgers Ctr. of Alcohol Studies, 1978-88; prof. history U. Houston, 1980-97, disting. univ. prof., 1997—, chmn. dept., 1980-83; vis. prof. history Rice U., Houston, 1992. Chmn. bd. sponsors Papers of Thomas Edison Project, 1977-80; founding ptnr. PastQuest Rsch. Svcs., 1999. Author: Men in Rebellion, 1973, In the Course of Human Events, 1979, (with M.E. Lender) A Respectable Army: The Military Origins of the Republic, 1982, 2d edit., 2006, (contemporary mil. reading list), Drinking in America: A History, 1982, rev. edit. 1987, (with others) America and Its Peoples, 1989, 5th edit. 2004, concise edit. 1995, Benedict Arnold: Revolutionary Hero, 1997 (Homer D. Babbidge, Jr. award), audio edit., 2001,(with J.T. Glatthaar) Forgotten Allies: Oneida Indians and the American Revolution, 2006; editor: Interpreting Colonial America, 1973, 2d edit. 1978, The Human Dimensions of Nation Making, 1976, (with K. Stubaus) The American Revolution, Whose Revolution?, 1977, 81, (with M.E. Lender) Citizen-Soldier: The Revolutionary War Journal of Joseph Bloomfield, 1982 (R.P. McCormick prize), Ordinary Courage: The Revolutionary War Adventures of Joseph Plumb Martin, 1993, 2d edit., 1999, 3rd edit., 2008; mem. editl. bd. Papers of William Livingston Project, 1973-80, Houston Rev., 1981-2003, N.J. History, 1986—, Conversations with the Past Series, 1993-95; gen. editor Am. Social Experience Series, 1983-2002; advisory editor, Critical Historical Encounters Series, Oxford U., 2007-. Recipient N.J. Soc. of the Cin. prize for Disting. Achievement in Am. History, 1995, Hiram Coll. Alumni Achievement award, 1996. Mem. Tex. Assn. for Advancement History (bd. dirs. 1981-93, v.p. 1986-90), Inst. for Internat. Bus. Analysis (adv. coun. 1982-86), Am. Hist. Assn. (Beveridge-Dunning prize com. 1990-93), Orgn. Am. Historians, So. Hist. Assn., Soc. Historians Early Am. Republic (adv. coun. 1985-88), Soc. for Mil. History, Phi Beta Kappa, Phi Kappa Phi, Pi Gamma Mu, Omicron Delta Kappa, Phi Alpha Theta. Office: U Houston Dept History 524 Arnold Hall Houston TX 77204-3003

MARTIN, JAMES LARENCE, dentist, educator; b. Dubuque, Iowa, Sept. 3, 1940; s. James Larence and Ada Virginia (Boone) M.; m. Willie Mae Walker, Jan. 23, 1941; children: Linda Gail, James Larence III, John Lance. BS, Loras Coll., Dubuque, 1959, LittD, 1982; MS, Tenn. State U., 1960; DDS, Meharry Med. Coll., 1966; MPH, U. Mich., 1975. Dental dir. children and youth Meharry Med. Coll., Nashville, 1967-72, acting dir. children and youth program, 1972-73, dir. primary dental svcs., 1973-75, coord. dental component Ctr. for Health Care Rsch., 1975-77, prof., 1981—; owner Martin Dental, Nashville, 1980—. Dental cons. Medically Dedicated, Washington, 1992—; pres. faculty senate Meharry Med. Coll., 1989-93, mem. pres.'s exec. mgmt. team, 1989-93, dir. divsn. dental public health 1999—, chmn. dept. dental pub. health, 1999—. Contbr. articles to profl. jours., chpts. to books. Bd. regents Loras Coll., 1997—. Recipient Meritorious Svc. award Acad. Oral Medicine, 1977. Mem. ADA, Am. Pub. Health Assn. (med. com.), Am. Assn. Pub. Health Dentistry, Nat. Assn. Cmty. Health Ctrs., Am. Acad. Goil Foil Operators, Soc. of the Upper 10th, Nashville Area C. of C., Beta Kappa Chi, Phi Sigma. Achievements include discovery of leukoedema in childrem. Avocations: reading, swimming, photography. Home: 3515 Geneva Cir Nashville TN 37209-2524 Office: 908 34th Ave N Nashville TN 37209-2502 Office Phone: 615-327-4499. Personal E-mail: jmarti3817@aol.com.

MARTIN, JAMES RUSSELL, lawyer; b. Columbus, Ohio, June 24, 1947; s. Robert Wells and Gwendolyn (Collins) M.; m. Susan Virginia Jarman, Aug. 4, 1973; children: James Russell Jr., Elizabeth Collins. BA in History, Denison U., Granville, Ohio, 1969; JD, U. Denver, 1972. Bar: Colo. 1972, U.S. Dist. Ct. Colo. 1972. Assoc. Brundage & Yates, Denver, 1973; asst. atty. gen. State of Colo., Denver, 1974-76; assoc. Thomas & Esperti PC, 1976—78; v.p. Butterwick Enterprises Ltd., Denver, 1978-81, pres., 1981-83; ptnr. Baker & Hostetler LLP, Denver, 1985—2004; sr. v.p., gen. counsel, clerk Bluegreen Corp., Boca Raton, Fla., 2004—. Mem.: ABA, Authorized House Coun., Fla., Assn. Corp. Counsel, Denver Bar Assn., Colo. Bar Assn., Am. Resort Devel. Assn. Avocations: skiing, tennis, bicycling. Office: Bluegreen Corp 4960 Conference Way N Ste 100 Boca Raton FL 33431 Business E-Mail: jim.martin@bluegreencorp.com.

MARTIN, JAY (ROBERT JOSEPH MARTIN), legislative staff member; b. Cin., June 4, 1979; BA, U. Dayton, Ohio, 2001. Staff asst. and legis. corr. for Rep. Steve Largent, US House of Reps., Washington, 2001; legis. asst. for Rep. John Sullivan, 2002, Rep. Dennis Rehberg, 2002—04, dep. chief of staff, 2004—08, chief of staff, 2008—. Recipient Rower award, Crew Team, 2001. Roman Catholic. Avocations: sports, reading. Office: Office of Congressman Dennis Rehberg 2448 Rayburn House Office Bldg Washington DC 20515 Office Phone: 202-225-3211. Business E-Mail: jay.martin@mail.house.gov.*

MARTIN, JAY HERBERT, psychoanalyst, literature professor, political science professor; s. Sylvester K. and Ada M. (Smith) M.; m. Helen Bernadette Saldini, June 9, 1956; children: Helen E., Laura A., Jay Herbert. AB with honors, Columbia U., 1956; MA, Ohio State U., 1957, PhD, 1960; PhD in Psychoanalysis, So. Calif. Psychoanalytic Inst., 1983. Instr. English Pa. State U., 1957-58; instr., then asst. to assoc. prof. English and Am. Studies Yale U., New Haven, 1960-68; prof. English and comparative culture U. Calif., Irvine, 1968-79; asst. prof. psychiatry and human behavior, clin. supr. residency program Calif. Coll. Medicine Calif. Coll. Medicine U. Calif.-Irvine, 1978—96; Leo S. Bing prof. English and Am. lit. U. So. Calif., LA, 1979-96, dir. undergrad. program in Am. studies, 1968-69, dir. program in comparative culture, 1969-71, dir. edn. abroad program, 1971-75; prof. govt., Edward S. Gould prof. humanities Claremont McKenna Coll., 1996—; dir. civilization program Claremont (Calif.) McKenna Coll., 1996—2000, acting dir. Gould Ctr. for Humanistic Studies, 1998-2000, prof., English, grad. sch., 2004—. Instr. psychoanalysis So. Calif. Psychoanalytic Inst., 1984-96; Bicentennial prof. Am. lit. and culture Moscow State U., USSR, 1976, Dai Ho Chun (Wisdom) chair Prof. U. Hawaii, 2000-01; dir. NEH summer sems., 1976, 77; mem. evaluation com. dept. pvt. post-secondary edn. State of Calif., 1986; lectr. in field; cons. in field Author: (criticism and biography) Conrad Aiken: A Life of His Art, 1962, Harvests of Change: American Literature 1865-1914, 1967, Nathanael West: The Art of His Life, 1970 (U. Calif. Friends Libr. award), Robert Lowell, 1970, Always Merry and Bright. The Life of Henry Miller, 1978, (U. Calif. Friends of Libr. award, Phi Kappa Phi Best Faculty Publ. prize U. So. Calif., transl. in French, Japanese and German), (fiction) Winter Dreams: An American in Moscow, 1979, Who Am I This Time, Uncovering the Fictive Personality, 1988 (trans. Portuguese), Burlington No. Found. award 1989); Swallowing Tigers Whole, 1996, A Corresponding Leap of Love: Henry Miller, 1996, Henry Miller's Dream Song, 1996, Journey to Heavenly Mountain, 2002 (ForeWord mag. Book of Yr. prize), The Education of John Dewey, 2003; author Baseball Magic (short stories) 2008, Live All You Can: Alexander Joy Cartwright And the Invention of Modern Baseball, 2009, one hour radio drama, William Faulkner. Sound Portraits of Twentieth-Century Humanists, starring Tennessee Williams, Glenn Close, Colleen Dewhurst, Nat. Pub. Radio, 1980; author one-act docudrama Trial Days in Coyocoan, Antioch Rev., 2001; author sects. 24 books including most recently American Writing Today, vol. I, 1982, The Haunted Dusk: American Supernatural Fiction, 1820-1902, 1983, Frontiers of Infant Psychiatry, vol.II, 1986, Centenary Essays on Huckleberry Finn, 1985, Robert Lowell: Essays on the Poetry, 1987, William Faulkner: The Best from American Literature, 1989, The Homosexualities: Reality, Fantasy and the Arts, 1991, Life Guidance Through Literature, 1992, Biography and Source Studies, 1995, William Faulkner and Psychology, 1995, Psychotherapy East and West, 1996, Readings on Huckleberry Finn, 1999, John Fante: A Critical Gathering, 2000, Uncollected Works By...Paul Laurence Dunbar, 2000, American Literature of the Civil War, 2004, Blackwell Companion to Modernist Literature and Culture, 2004,Cases as Catalysts, 2005, Only God: A Biography of Ramsuratkumar, 2005, International Research on Global Affairs, 2005, Psychoanalytic Rev., Contemporary Psychoanalysis Jour., Am. Imago; editor: Winfield Townley Scott (Yale series recorded poets), 1962, Twentieth Century Interpretations of the Waste Land: A Collection of Critical Essays, 1968, Twentieth Century Views of Nathanael West, 1972, A Singer in the Dawn: Reinterpretations of Paul Laurence Dunbar (with intro.), 1975, Economic Depression and American Humor (with intro.), 1986; mem. editl. bd. Am. Lit., 1978-81, Humanities in Society, 1979-1983; editor-in-chief Psychoanalytic Edn., 1984-89; editor Humanitas/Communitas, 1998-2000; appearances on TV and radio including Connie Martinson Talks Books, Barbara Brunner Nightline, Sonya Live in LA, Oprah Winfrey Show, C-SPAN, 1988-89; contbr. numerous articles and revs. to profl. jours., bulls. Pres. Friends of Irvine Pub. Libr., 1974-75; mem. Com. for Freud Mus. Recipient Fritz Schmidl Meml. prize for rsch. applied psychoanalysis Seattle Assn. Psychoanalysis, 1982, Marie H. Briehl prize for child psychoanalysis, 1982, Franz Alexander prize in psychoanalysis, 1984, Disting. Writers award Antioch Rev., 2004; Morse rsch. fellow, 1963-64, Am. Philos. Soc. fellow, 1966, J.S. Guggenheim fellow, 1966-67, Rockefeller Found.humanities sr. fellow, 1975-76, Rsch. Clin. fellow So. Calif. Psychoanalytic Soc. 1977-81, Rockefeller fellow, Bellagio, Italy, 1983, NEH sr. fellow, 1983-84; Durfee Found. fellow to China, 2004; fellow Bogliasco Found. Liguria Ctr. for Arts and Humanities, 2004. Mem. So. Calif. Am. Studies Assn. (pres. 1969-71), Am. Studies Assn. (exec. bd. 1969-71, del. to MLA Assembly 1974, chmn. Ralph Gabriel prize com. 1975-77), MLA (chmn. prize com. Jay B. Hubbell Silver medal in Am. lit. 1978-84), Nat.

Assn. Arts and Letters (prize com. 1987-88), Nat. Humanities Faculty (advisor to Valhalla High Sch., El Cajon, Calif. 1979-81), Nat. Am. Studies Faculty, Internat. Psychoanalytic Assn., Internat. Assn. Empirical Aesthetics, Internat. Assn. U. Profs. English, Internat. Karen Horney Soc., Newport Psychoanalytical Inst., Phi Beta Kappa. Home: 748 Via Santo Tomas Claremont CA 91711-1569 Home Phone: 909-624-8155; Office Phone: 909-398-0193. Personal E-mail: helenjay@ca.rr.com.

MARTIN, JEANINE KAY, retired elementary school educator; d. John Albert and Virginia Grace (Smith) Hawthorne; m. Earl John Martin, June 20, 1962; children: Gregory, Christine. BA, Marycrest Coll., Davenport, Iowa, 1965. Cert. early childhood educator Iowa, reading endorsement Iowa. Kindergarten tchr. Bettendorf Schs., Iowa, 1958—60; 1st grade tchr. DeWitt Cmty. Schs., 1960—68; presch. tchr. Sugar Plum Presch., 1st Congl. Ch., DeWitt, 1971—78; Title I reading tchr., reading recovery tchr. West Liberty Cmty. Sch., Iowa, 1984—2003; ret., 2003. Pres. West Liberty Edn. Assn., 1990; coord. bus./sch. book giveaway West Liberty Schs., 1998—2005; activities coord. West Liberty Children's Festival, 2004—06; pres. ladies bd. West Liberty Country Club, 1981; pres. West Liberty Choral Aux., 1987; chmn. West Liberty After Prom, 1987; organizer, coord. Treats for Troops, West Liberty, 2003; Sunday sch. tchr. West Liberty, De Witt, 1976—81; bd. dirs. Iowa Assn. Edn. of Young Children, Des Moines, 1973—75, Louis and Ida Rich Day Care Ctr., West Liberty, 1990—95, West Liberty Cmty. Ctr., West Liberty, 1995—. Recipient award, Carver Trust, 1998, Comdr.'s award for pub. svc., Dept. of Army, Camp Dodge, Johnston, Iowa, 2005, Cmty. Svc. award, West Liberty C. of C., 2005; named Reading Tchr. of Yr., Old Capitol Reading Assn., 2003, Rotary Citizen of Month, West Liberty Rotary Club, 2004; grantee, West Liberty Schs. Found., 1997—2002. Mem.: Nat. Reading Recovery Assn., Nat. TTT Soc. (pres. 1977, 1995, 2000). Avocations: golf, reading, travel.

MARTIN, JOANNE, social sciences educator; b. Salem, Mass., Sept. 25, 1946; d. Richard Drake and Nathalie (Ashton) M.; m. Beaumont A. Sheil, July 9, 1977; 1 child, Beaumont Martin Sheil. BA, Smith Coll., 1968; PhD in Social Psychology, Harvard U., 1977; PhD in Econs. and Bus. Adminstrn. (hon.), Copenhagen Bus. Sch., 2001; PhD (hon.), Vrije U., Amsterdam, 2005. Assoc. cons. McBer & Co. (formerly Behavior Sci. Ctr. of Sterling Inst.), 1968-70, dir. govt. mktg., 1970-72; asst. prof. orgnl. behavior Grad. Sch. Bus., Stanford (Calif.) U., 1977-80; assoc. prof. grad. sch. bus. Stanford U., 1980-91, prof. grad. sch. bus., 1991—, dir. doctoral programs, grad. sch. bus., 1991-95, Fred H. Merrill prof. orgn. behavior and, by courtesy, sociology, 1996—, prof. emeritus, 2008—. Sec. univ. adv. bd. Stanford U., 1995—96, vice chair adv. bd., 1996—97; vis. scholar Australian Grad. Sch. Mgmt. U. N.S.W., 1989—90, Copenhagen Bus. Sch., 1998, 2004; vis. scholar dept. psychology Sydney (Australia) U., 1989—90; Ruffin fellow bus. ethics Darden Grad. Sch. Bus. Adminstrn. U. Va., 1990; mem. bd. advisors iMahal, 1990—2000; bd. dirs. C.P.P., Inc., 1993—2003; mem. internat. adv. bd. Internat. Ctr. for Rsch. in Orgnl. Discourse, Strategy and Change; Bus. Sch. rep. Stanford U., 1995—; vis. scholar U. Tech. Sydney, 2004—05. Mem. editl. bd. Adminstrv. Sci. Qtrly., 1984—88, Jour. Social Issues, 1981—83, Acad. Mgmt. Jour., 1984—85, Social Justice Rsch., 1985—90, Jour. Mgmt. Inquiry, 1991—2004, Orgn., 1994—2005, Jour. Mgmt. Studies, 1996—2004, Gender, Work and Organization, 1998—, Orgn. Studies, 2003—07, Scandinavian Jour. Mgmt., 2003—, consulting editor Internat. Jour. Mgmt. Reviews, 1998—2007; co-author: five books; contbr. over 60 articles to profl. jours. and edited books. Recipient Centennial medal for contbns. to soc. Harvard U. Grad. Sch. Arts and Scis., 2002; Lena Lake Forrest Rsch. fellowship Bus. and Profl. Women's Found., 1978, James and Doris McNamara Faculty fellowship Grad. Sch. of Bus., Stanford U., 1990-91, Grad. Sch. Bus. Trust Faculty fellow, 2005-06. Fellow: APA, Am. Psychol. Soc., Acad. Mgmt. (nat. rep.-at-large 1983—85, divsn. program chair 1985—87, divsn. chair 1987—89, nat. bd. govs. 1992—95, we. divsn. Promising Young Scholar award 1982, Nat. Disting. Educator award 2000, We. Divsn. Disting. Scholar award 2003, Nat. Orgn. and Mgmt. Divsn. Disting. Scholar career achievement award 2005, Joanne Martin Trailblazer award, Orgn. and Mgmt. Theory Divsn. 2007); mem.: Nat. Assn. Corp. Dirs. (adv. bd. 2000—04). Office: Stanford U Grad Sch Bus Littlefield Ctr 353 Stanford CA 94305 Business E-Mail: martin_joanne@gsb.stanford.edu.

MARTIN, JOHN BRUCE, chemical engineer; b. Auburn, Ala., Feb. 2, 1922; s. Herbert Marshall and Lannie (Steadham) M.; m. Mildred Jane Foster, Aug. 7, 1943 (dec. Nov. 1960); children— Shirlie Martin Briggs, John Bruce; m. 2d, Phyllis Barbara Rodgers, June 25, 1963; 1 child, Richard Kipp BS, Ala. Poly. Inst., 1943; M.Sc., Ohio State U., 1947, PhD, 1949. With Procter & Gamble Co., Cin., 1949-82, coordinator orgn. devel., research and devel., 1967-77, mgr. indsl. chem. market research, 1977-82; sr. assoc. Indumar Inc., Cin., 1982-86, sr. v.p., 1986-87. Lectr. U. Cin., 1982-88; adj. assoc. prof. Auburn U., 1983-88. Author: Martin's Mini Mysteries, 1998, Killing is Murder, Pseudonym Pleiades, 2003, Defending Donald Harvey, 2005; contbr. articles to profl. jours.; patentee in field Served with AUS, 1943-46 Decorated Air Medal, Bronze Star with oak leaf cluster; recipient Disting. Alumnus award Coll. Engring., Ohio State U., 1970, Disting. Engr. award Tech. Socs. Council Cin., 1982 Fellow AIChE (bd. dirs. 1968-70, chmn. mktg. divsn. 1985, Mktg. Hall of Fame 1988, Chem. Engr. of Yr. award Ohio Valley 1971); mem. Am. Chem. Soc., Am. Soc. Engring. Edn., Engring. Soc. Cin. (pres. 1972-73), Tech. and Sci. Socs. Cin. (pres. 1972-73), Comml. Devel. and Mktg. Assn., Barbershop Harmony Soc.(named barbershopper of the year, 2003), Mystery Writers Am., Sisters in Crime, Sigma Xi, Tau Beta Pi, Phi Kappa Phi, Phi Lambda Upsilon Republican. Presbyterian. Home: 5513 Evergreen Ridge Dr Cincinnati OH 45215 E-mail: jmartin660@cinci.rr.com.

MARTIN, JOHN C., pharmaceutical company executive; b. 1952; MBA in Mktg., Golden Gate U., 1974; PhD in Organic Chemistry, U. Chgo., 1977. With Syntex Corp., 1978-84; dir. antiviral chemistry Bristol-Myers Squibb Co., 1984-90; v.p. R&D Gilead Sciences, Inc., Foster City, Calif., 1990-95, COO, 1995-96, pres., CEO, 1996—2008, chmn., CEO, 2008—. Bd. dirs. Gilead Sciences, Inc., 1996—, Gen-Probe Inc., 2007—; chmn. Bay Area Bioscience Ctr., 1999—2001; mem. Nat. Inst. Allergy & Infectious Diseases Coun., 2000—03, Presdl. Advisory Coun. on HIV/AIDS, 2005—; bd. dirs. Calif. Healthcare Inst., 2003—, chmn. bd., 2005—06, 2008—. Bd. trustee U. Chgo., Golden Gate U. Recipient Isbell award, Am. Chemical Soc., Gertrude B. Elion award for Scientific Excellence, Internat. Soc. for Antiviral Rsch.; named to Nat. Acad. Engring. Nat. Academies, 2008. Mem.: Internat. Soc. for Antiviral Rsch. (pres. 1998—2000). Office: Gilead Scis Inc 333 Lakeside Dr Foster City CA 94404*

MARTIN, JOHN CARL, astronomer, educator; married. PhD in Astronomy, Case Western Res. U., Cleve., 2003. Postdoc. rsch. assoc. U. Minn., Mpls., 2003—06; asst. prof. astronomy-physics U. Ill., Springfield, 2006—, dir. Henry Barber astron. obs., 2009—. Mem.: Am. Assoc. Physics Tchrs., Astron. Soc. Pacific, Am. Astron. Soc.

MARTIN, JOHN CHARLES, judge; b. Durham, NC, Nov. 9, 1943; s. Chester Barton and Mary Blackwell (Pridgen) Martin; m. Margaret Rand; children: Lauren M. Smith, Sarah, Susan M. Prince stepchildren: Louise Short, Carl (Trip) Short. BA, Wake Forest U., 1965, JD, 1967; postgrad., Nat. Judicial Coll., Reno, 1979; cert. justice execs. program, U. NC, 1982. Bar: NC 1967, US Dist. Ct. (mid. dist.) NC 1967, US Dist. Ct. (ea. dist.) NC 1972, US Dist. Ct. (we. dist.) NC 1975, US Ct. Appeals (4th cir.) 1976, US Supreme Ct. 2002. Assoc. Haywood, Denny & Miller, Durham, N.C., 1969-72, ptnr., 1973-77; resident judge Superior Ct. 14th Jud. Dist. N.C., Durham, 1977-84; judge N.C. Ct. Appeals, Raleigh, 1985—88, 1993—2004, chief judge, 2004—; ptnr. Maxwell & Hutson, P.A., Durham, 1988-92; arbitrator U.S. Dist. Ct. (mid. dist.) N.C., 1988-92. Study com. rules of evidence and comparative negligence N.C. Legis. Research Commn., 1980; mem. N.C. Pattern Jury Instrn. drafting com., 1978-84, N.C. Trial Judge's Bench Book Drafting Com., 1984-87, N.C. News Media-Adminstrn. of Justice Coun., 1987, state/fed. Jud. Coun. N.C., 1985-87, chmn., 1987; bd. visitors Wake Forest U. Sch. Law, 1986—; mem. alumni coun. Wake Forest U., 1993-96, 2001—04; mem. N.C. Jud. Coun., 2004-; mem. N.C. State Jud. Edn. Study Com., 2000-2003, NC Jud. Coll.(Adv. Com.); chmn. N.C. Jud. Stds. Commn., 2001—; exec. com. mem. Chief Justice's Commn. Professionalism. Mem. Durham City Coun., 1975—77, chair pub. works com.; panel of arbitrators Duke U. Pvt. Adjudication Ctr., 1988—92; mem. parent adv. bd. Chatham Hall Sch., 2003—05; mem. parent coun. Wake Forest U., 2006—09. With Mil. Police Corps USAR, 1967—69. Recipient Disting. Svc. award Durham Jaycees, 1976. Mem. ABA, Appellate Judges Conf., Coun. of Chief Judges State Ct. Appeals, N.C. Bar Assn. (chmn. adminstrn. of justice study com. 1990-92, bench, bar and law sch. com. 1987-91, jud. campaign oversight com. 1990, Lit. Sect. Coun. 1991-94, conv. planning com. 1995-98, adminstrn. justice task force 1996-98, appellate rules study com. 1999-2001, strategic planning/emerging trends com. 2002-04, endowment com. 2004—, v.p. 1997-98), Durham County Bar Assn. (bd. dirs. 1991-92), Wake County Bar Assn., 10th Jud. Dist. Bar Assn., NC Jud. Conf. (v.p. 1999-00), Appalachian State U. Parents Assn. (bd. dirs. 1997-01), Phi Delta Phi. Democrat. Methodist. Office: PO Box 888 Raleigh NC 27602-0888 Office Phone: 919-831-3700. Business E-Mail: mnj@coa.state.nc.us.

MARTIN, JOHN F., academic administrator; b. Chico, Calif., June 20, 1959; s. E. Milo and Esther (Foster) M.; m. Karen L. Beeman, June 11, 1982; 1 child, Kristen Joy. BA in Bus., So. Nazarene U., Bethany, Okla., 1982; MA, Fuller Theol. Sem., Pasadena, Calif., 1999. Sales rep. Met. Life Ins. Co., Oklahoma City, 1982—85; mgr. Enterprise Rent A Car, Shreveport, La., 1985—90; dir. devel. Le Tourneau U., Longview, Tex., 1990—99; assoc. vice pres. U. Advancement, 1999—; chartered advisor philanthropy, 2009. Instr. philanthropy Southwestern Christian U., Bethany, 2007—; presenter in field. Sec. bd. dirs. Servant Heart Ministries, Tulsa, Okla., 1992—; mem. Leadership Longview, 1997, Leadership Bethany, 2001 Mem. Christian Leadership Alliance, Kiwanis (pres.), Downtown OKC Club(pres. 2007-08), OK Chapter of Assoc. Fund Raising Profls., (Outstanding Profl. Fundraiser, 2007).Downtown Longview Club Avocations: music, gardening, genealogy.

MARTIN, JOHN K., communications executive; b. 1968; married; 1 child. BS in Econ., Wharton Sch. Bus., U. Pa., 1989; MBA in Fin. & Orgnl. Behavior, Columbia U., 1994. CPA Ernst and Young LLP, NY; mgr., SEC fin. reporting Time Warner Inc., 1993, dir., Fin. Special Projects, dir., Office of Pres., v.p. investor rels., 1999—2000; dir., Equity Rsch. Grp. ABN AMRO Securities LLC, 2000—02; sr. v.p. investor rels. Time Warner Inc., 2002—05; exec. v.p., CFO Time Warner Cable, 2005—07, Time Warner Inc., 2007—. Client adv. bd. Thomson Fin. Services; mem. Conf. Bd. Global Coun. of Investor Rels. Executives. Named Next Generation analyst for cable TV industy, Institutional Investor, 2001; named one of 40 Executives Under 40, Multichannel News, 2006. Mem.: Mus. TV & Radio, Nat. Investor Rels. Inst. Office: Time Warner Cable Inc 290 Harbor Dr Stamford CT 06902-6732 Office Phone: 203-328-0600. Office Fax: 203-328-0690.*

MARTIN, JOHN LEWIS, state legislator; b. Eagle Lake, Maine, June 5, 1941; s. Frank and Edwidge (Raymond) M. BA in History and Govt., U. Maine, 1963, postgrad., 1963-64. Tchr. Am. govt. and history Ft. Kent (Maine) Community High Sch., 1966-72; instr. U. Maine, Ft. Kent, 1972-89, asst. prof., 1989—; mem. from Eagle Lake and St. Francis dist. Maine Ho. of Reps., 1964-94, minority fl. leader, 1970-74, speaker of ho., 1975-94, chmn. com. on energy & natural resources, 1994-95, mem. from dist. 151, 1998-2000. Mem. Maine Senate, Dist. 1, 2000—, chmn. com. natural resources, 1999-2004, human svcs., chmn. rules com.; adj. lectr.; mem. intergovtl. rels. com. Nat. Legis. Conf., 1970-74; chmn. Maine Land Use Regulation Commn., 1972-73, Maine Bur. Human Rels., 1972, State Legis. Leaders Found., 1979-83; mem. exec. bd. Nat. Conf. State Legislatures, chmn. state-fed. assembly, 1985-86, chair task force on reapportionment, 1987-88, vice chmn. budget, fiscal and rules com., 1986-87, v.p., 1988-89, pres.-elect, 1989-90, pres., 1990-91, immediate past pres., 1991-92; mem. exec. com. New Eng. Caucus of State Legislatures, 1978-95, chmn., 1982; mem. regional exec. com. Nat. Dem. State Legis. Leaders Assn., 1991-95, chmn., 1987-89; bd. dirs. Found. for State Legislatures, 1988-94; mem. exec. com. Dem. Nat. Com., 1991-94; pres. Ambulance Svc. Inc., 1975—. Trustee Eagle Lake Water and Sewer Dist., 1966—, No. Maine Gen. Hosp., Eagle Lake, Ea. Maine Health Care, 1991-92, No. Maine Med. Ctr., 1966—; mem. rural health steering com. Nat. Acad. for State Health Policy; advisor White House Task Force on Health Care Reform; dir. intergovtl. affairs Nat. Health Care Campaign, 1994; trustee Maine Med. Ctr., Ft. Kent. Mem. New Eng. Polit. Sci. Assn. Democrat. Home: PO Box 250 Eagle Lake ME 04739-0250 Office: Maine Senate State House Augusta ME 04333-0003 Office Phone: 207-287-9406.

MARTIN, JOHN WILLIAM, JR., retired lawyer, automotive executive; b. Evergreen Park, Ill., Sept. 1, 1936; s. John William and Frances (Hayes) M.; m. Joanne Cross, July 2, 1966; children: Amanda Hayes, Bartholomew McGuire. AB in History, DePaul U., 1958, JD, 1961. Bar: Ill. 1961, D.C. 1962, N.Y. 1964, Mich. 1970. Antitrust trial atty. Dept. Justice, Washington, 1961-62; assoc. Donovan, Leisure, Newton & Irvine, NYC, 1962-70; sr. atty. Ford Motor Co., Dearborn, Mich., 1970-72, assoc. counsel, 1972-74, counsel, 1974-76, asst. gen. counsel, 1976-77, assoc. gen. counsel, 1977-89, v.p., gen. counsel, 1989-99; ret., 1999. Contbr. articles to profl. jours. Trustee DePaul U., 1998—2007, life trustee, 2007—; bd. dirs. Ctr. Social Gerontology, Inc., Nat. Women's Law Ctr., Friends of Legal Svcs. Corp. Mem.: Am. Law Inst., Assn. Gen. Counsel, Little Traverse Yacht Club (commodore 2006—08). Republican. Roman Catholic. Personal E-mail: jwmartinjr@gmail.com.

MARTIN, JOSEPH BOYD, neurologist, educator, retired dean; b. Bassano, Alta., Can., Oct. 20, 1938; s. Joseph Bruce and Ruth Elizabeth (Ramer) Martin; m. Rachel Ann Wenger, June 18, 1960; children: Bradley, Melanie, Douglas, Neil. BSc, Eastern Mennonite Coll., Harrisonburg, Va., 1959; MD, U. Alta., 1962; PhD in Anatomy, U. Rochester, NY, 1971; MA (hon.), Harvard U., 1978; ScD (hon.), McGill U., 1994, U. Rochester, 1996, U. Wis., 1997, U. Alta., 1998. Mem. faculty McGill U. Faculty Medicine, Montreal, Canada, 1970—78, chair, dept. neurology and neurosurgery, 1977—78; prof. medicine and neurology, neurologist-in-chief Montreal Neurol. Inst., 1976—78; Bullard prof. neurology, chief dept. neurology svc. Mass. Gen. Hosp., Boston, 1978—89; Julieanne Dorn prof. neurology Harvard U. Med. Sch., 1984; dean Sch. Medicine U. Calif., San Francisco, 1989—93; chancellor U. Calif., San Francisco, 1993—97; dean faculty medicine Harvard U. Med. Sch., Boston, 1997—2007, Lefler prof. neurobiology, 2007—09. Chmn., bd. dirs. New Eng. Healthcare Inst., 2002—. Editor: Harrison's Principles of Internal Medicine, 1980—99. Recipient Moshier Meml. gold medal, U. Alta. Faculty Medicine, 1962, John W. Scott gold med. award, 1962, Abraham Flexner award, AAMC, 1999, Henry Friesen Internat. prize, 2006. Fellow: Am. Acad. Arts and Scis.; mem.: NAS, Inst. of Medicine, Assn. Am. Physicians, Soc. Neurosci., Royal Coll. Phys. and Surg. Can., Am. Neurol. Assn. (pres. 1990). Office: Department of Neurobiology Goldenson Bldg Long Wood Ave Boston MA 02115 Office Phone: 617-432-7197. E-mail: joseph_martin@hms.harvard.edu.

MARTIN, JOSEPH ROBERT, retired corporate executive; b. Phila., Dec. 9, 1947; s. Robert and Elva Ruth (Griffin) M.; m. Catherine Marie Kelly, Sept. 5, 1970; children: Joseph Robert Jr., Jennifer H., Patrick F., Kathleen K., Mariah E. BS, Embry Riddle U., 1974; MBA, U. Maine, 1976. Sr. corp. fin. analyst Keyes Fibre Co., Waterville, Maine, 1976—80; mgr. fin. analysis and planning Schlumberger, Fairchild, South Portland, Maine, 1980—83; divsn. contr. Schlumberger, Factron, Clifton Park, NY, 1983—84; corp. contr. VTC, Inc., Bloomington, Minn., 1984—87, v.p. fin., CFO, 1987—88, sr. v.p., CFO, 1989—90; dir. fin. Nat. Semiconductor, South Portland, Maine, 1990—91; v.p. fin. std. products group Nat. Semicondr., Santa Clara, Calif., 1991—95; v.p. fin. worldwide ops. Nat. Semiconductor, Santa Clara, Calif., 1995—96; exec. v.p., CFO, vice chmn. bd. dirs. Fairchild Semiconductor, South Portland, Maine, 1996—2006; ret., 2006. Bd. visitors U. So. Maine, 1998—2001; pres.'s bd. advisors Embry-Riddle Aero. U., 2000—04, trustee, 2004—; chmn. bd. dirs. Brooks Automation LLC, Chelmsford, Mass.; bd. dirs. Synqor, Inc., Hudston, Mass., Soitec, Inc., Bernin, France. Served to capt. U.S. Army, 1967-72, Vietnam. Decorated D.F.C., Purple Heart, Bronze Star medal, Air medal, Vietnamese Cross of Gallantry, Army Commendation medal. Home: 17 Stornoway Rd Cumberland Foreside ME 04110 Office: JR Martin Co 14 Lantern Ln Cumberland Foreside ME 04110 Office Phone: 207-781-2825. E-mail: joe@jrmandco.com.

MARTIN, JOSEPH VINSON, neuroscientist, educator; b. Boston, Sept. 17, 1952; s. James Cullen and Mary Louise (Echols) M.; m. Jean Ann Rusteberg, Apr. 27, 1989; 1 child, Lara Jean. BA, Northwestern U., Evanston, Ill., 1973; PhD, U. So. Calif., 1987. Rsch. asst. LA Harbor Commn., 1978—79; chemist NIMH, Bethesda, Md., 1982—87; post-doctoral rsch. assoc. SUNY, Stony Brook, 1987—88, rsch. instr.; asst. prof. Biology Dept., Rutgers U., Camden, NJ, 1989—95, assoc. prof., 1995—2004, prof., 2004—, chair, 2006—, acting dir. ctr. computational and integrative biology, 2007—. Manuscript reviewer European Jour. Pharmacology, Hormones and Behavior, Pharmacology Biochemistry and Behavior, Sleep; lectr. in field. Contbr. articles to profl. jours. Recipient NSF Undergrad. Summer Rsch. fellowship, 1972, NIMH Predoctoral Rsch. fellowship, 1977-78, NSF grantee, 1994-97, 98-2001, 2002-04, 2004—, Dean's Citation, UMDNJ. Mem. AAAS, Assn. Profl. Sleep Socs., Internat. Brain Rsch. Orgn., NJ Acad. Sci., NY Acad. Scis., Sleep Rsch. Soc., Soc. for Neuroscience. Business E-Mail: jomartin@camden.rutgers.edu.

MARTIN, JUDITH SYLVIA, journalist; b. Washington, Sept. 13, 1938; d. Jacob and Helen (Aronson) Perlman; m. Robert Martin, Jan. 30, 1960; children: Nicholas Ivor, Jacobina Helen. BA, Wellesley Coll., 1959; DHL (hon.), York Coll., 1985, Adelphi U., 1991. Reporter-critic, columnist Washington Post, 1960—83; syndicated columnist United Feature Syndicate, NYC, 1978—; columnist Microsoft, 1996—. Critic-at-large Vanity Fair, 1983—84. Author: The Name on the White House Floor, 1972, Miss Manners' Guide to Excruciatingly Correct Behavior, 1982, Gilbert, 1982, Miss Manners' Guide to Rearing Perfect Children, 1984, Common Courtesy, 1985, Style and Substance, 1986, Miss Manners' Guide for the Turn-of-the-Millennium, 1989, Miss Manners on (Painfully Proper) Weddings, 1996, Miss Manners Rescues Civilization, 1996, Miss Manners' Basic Training: Communications, 1997, Miss Manners' Basic Training: Eating, 1997, Miss Manners' Basic Training: The Right Thing to Say, 1998, Miss Manners' Guide to Domestic Tranquility, 1999, Star-Spangled Manners, 2002, Miss Manners Guide to Excruciatingly Correct Behavior (Freshly Updated), 2005, No Vulgar Hotel, The Desire and Pursuit of Venice, 2007, Miss Manners Guide to a Surprisingly Dignified Wedding, 2009. Bd. dirs. Friends of Scuola San Rocco. Recipient Nat. Humanities medal, 2005, Alumni Achievement award, Wellesley Coll., 2007. Mem. Cosmos Club, Literary Soc. Office: United Feature Syndicate 200 Madison Ave Fl 4 New York NY 10016-3911 Business E-Mail: MissManners@unitedmedia.com.

MARTIN, JUDSON PHILLIPS, retired education educator; b. Butler, Wis., Feb. 4, 1921; s. Charles H. and Emma (Phillips) M.; m. June Ruth Elletson, June 19, 1948 (dec. June 1993); children: Christopher Alan, Karen Marie; m. Mary Belle Jepson, Sept. 23, 1971 (dec. Apr. 1995); stepchildren: Stephen, Susan (dec. 1998), Sandra, Christopher; m. Kathryn L. Tompkins, Feb. 17, 1996; stepchildren: David (dec. 2004), Dale. BS, U. Wis., Madison, 1942, MA, 1946, PhD, 1955. Registrar, acad. dean Bemidji State U., Minn., 1946—67; dean grad. study, prof. edn. N.E. Mo. State U., 1968-71, prof. edn., 1971-80, 82-85, head div. edn. and head tchr. edn., 1980-82. Substitute tchr. Seminole County, Fla., 1990-96. Dist. officer Minn. Boy Scouts Am.; mem. Bemidji City Coun., 1951; pres. Red Barn Cmty. Arts Coun.; sch. vol. Seminole County, Fla., 1994-96; newspaper reader for the blind Sta. WMFE, Orlando, Fla. With AUS, 1943-45. Decorated Bronze Star; Croix de Guerre (France) avec etoille. Mem. NEA, Am. Legion, Minn. Edn. Assn. (past pres. higher edn. sect.), Mo. Edn. Assn., Am. Assn. Higher Edn., Mo. Fiber Artists Assn., Fla. Storytellers Assn., Weavers of Orlando, Handweavers of Am., Fla. Tropical Weavers, Spacecoast Weavers, Masons, Moose, K.T., Elks, Kiwanis (dist. lt. gov. 1974-75), Phi Delta Kappa, Voices of Brevard. Presbyterian.

MARTIN, JUNE JOHNSON CALDWELL, journalist; b. Toledo, Oct. 06; d. John Franklin and Eunice Imogene (Fish) Johnson; m. Erskine Caldwell, Dec. 21, 1942 (div. Dec. 1955); 1 child, Jay Erskine; m. Keith Martin, May 5, 1966. AA, Phoenix Jr. Coll., 1941; BA, U. Ariz., 1943-59; postgrad., Ariz. State U., 1939-40. Freelance writer, 1944—; columnist Ariz. Daily Star, Tucson, 1956-59, 70-94, book reviewer, 1970-94, co-founder Ann. Book and Author Event; editor Ariz. Alumnus mag., Tucson, 1959-70; ind. book reviewer, audio tape columnist Tucson, 1994—; coord. S.W. Books of Yr. sponsored by Pima Pub. Libr., Ariz., 2000—06; columnist So. Ariz. Authors, Ariz., 2005—. Panelist, co-producer TV news show Tucson Press Club, 1954-55, pres., 1958. Contbg. author: Rocky Mountain Cities, 1949; contbr. articles to World Book Ency., and various mags. Mem. Tucson CD Com., 1961; vol. campaigns of Samuel Goddard, U.S. Rep. Morris Udall, U.S. amb. and Ariz. gov. Raul. Castro. Recipient award Nat. Headliners Club, 1959, Ariz. Press Club award, 1957-59, 96, Am. Alumni Coun., 1966, 70, 2007, Lawrence Clark Powell Outstanding Contbn. Southwest Lit.

Mem. Nat. Book Critics Circle, Ariz. Press Women, Jr. League of Tucson, Tucson Urban League, PEN U.S.A. West, Planned Parenthood So. Ariz., Tucson Press, Pi Beta Phi. Democrat. Methodist. Home: Desert Foothills Sta PO Box 65388 Tucson AZ 85728-5388

MARTIN, KAREN LYNN MATTHEWS, biology professor; m. Robert Douglas Martin; children: Gregory D., Alexander D. BS, MS, U. Okla., Norman; PhD, UCLA, 1990. Prof. Pepperdine U., Malibu, Calif., Frank R. Seaver chair in biology, 1991—. Exec. dir. Grunion Greeters, Grunion. org, Malibu, 2002—. Editor (with M. Horn and M. Chotkowski): (sci. book) Intertidal Fishes: Life in Two Worlds; editor: (with S. Sumida) Amniote Origins: Completing the Transition to Land. Bd. mem. Westside Food Bank, Santa Monica, Calif., 1994—97; mem., bd. govs. South Calif. Acad. Scies., LA, 1996—2006. Recipient Environ. Partnership award, Am. Shore and Beach Preservation Assn., 2006; named Outstanding Grad. student, UCLA Alumni Assn., 1989; scholar John D. Isaacs Undergraduate Rsch., Calif. Sea Grant Coll., 2006; Friday Harbor Postdoc. fellowship, U. Wash., 1990—91. Fellow: Am. Inst. Fishery Rsch. Biologists; mem.: AAAS, Am. Fisheries Soc., Soc. Integrative and Comparative Biology (life; sec., dcpb 1996—98), Am. Soc. Ichthyologists and Herpetologists (life). Achievements include research in studies on physiological ecology of coastal marine animals, particularly fishes. Office: Pepperdine Univ 24255 Pacific Coast Hwy Malibu CA 90263 Business E-Mail: karen.martin@pepperdine.edu.

MARTIN, KATE M., history professor; b. Lowell, Mass., Dec. 30, 1959; d. Edward F. and Louise S. Martin; m. John A. Simpson, Apr. 21, 1990. BA, Northeastern U., Boston, 1982; MA, Boston U., 1997. Asst. dir. Boston U. ISCIP, 1989—2003; vis. lectr. Bridgewater State Coll., Mass., 2007—08; instr. Cape Cod CC, West Barnstable, Mass., 2008—. Co-editor (with Uri Ra'anan): (book) Russia: A Return to Imperialism?, Russian Pluralism: Now Irreversible?. Mem.: Am. Conf. Irish Studies, Berkshire Conf. Women Historians, New Eng. Hist. Assn., Cumann Na Gaeilge I mBoston. Office: Cape Cod CC 2240 Iyannough Rd West Barnstable MA 02668 Business E-Mail: kmartin@capecod.edu.

MARTIN, KATHRYN A., endocrinologist; b. Adams, Mass., Mar. 15, 1955; d. John J. and Agnes Martin; m. David M. Systrom, June 15, 1985; children: Hannah Systrom, Conor Systrom. BA, Dartmouth Coll., Hanover, 1977; MD, Dartmouth Med. Sch., 1980. Lic. Physician Bd. registration, MA, 1983. Endocrinologist, faculty Mass. Gen. Hosp., Boston, 1988—; sr. dep. editor UpToDate, Waltham, Mass., 2000—. Mem.: Endocrine Soc. (com. chair 2005—08).

MARTIN, KENNETH E., electrical engineer, cônsultant; b. Colo. Springs; BSEE, Colo. State U., Ft. Collins, 1970; MA, U. Wash., Seattle, 1974. Cert. profl. engr., Wash. & Oreg., 1979. Field engring. Bonneville Power Adminstrn., Olympia, Wash., 1977—82, rsch. engr. Vancouver, Wash., 1982—2008; consulting engr. Electric Power Group, Pasadena, Calif., 2008—. Cons. instr. U. Wis., Madison, 2003—. With US Army, 1970—72, Yuma, Ariz. Recipient Adminstrs's award, Bonneville Power Adminstrn., 2003. Fellow: IEEE (fellow 2008). Unitarian Universalist. Achievements include development of phasor data concentrator. Avocations: windsurfing, soccer, skiing, music. Office: KenM Consulting 2306 NE 46th Ave Portland OR 97213 Business E-Mail: martin@electricpowergroup.com.

MARTIN, KENYON, professional basketball player; b. Saginaw, Mich., Dec. 30, 1977; BA in Criminal Justice, U. Cin., 2000. Player NJ Nets, 2000—04, Denver Nuggets, 2004—. Mem. sr. nat. team USA Basketball, 2003. Recipient John R. Wooden award, 2000; named Nat. Player of Yr., AP, 2000; named to All-Rookie First Team, NBA, 2001, Western Conf. All-Star Team, 2004. Office: c/o Denver Nuggets 1000 Chopper Cir Denver CO 80204*

MARTIN, KEVIN JEFFREY, former federal official; b. Charlotte, NC, Dec. 14, 1966; m. Catherine Jurgensmeyer Martin. BA in Polit. Sci., U. N.C., Chapel Hill, 1989; MA in Pub. Policy, Duke U., 1990; JD, Harvard U., 1993. Bar: Fla., D.C. Law clk. to Hon. William M. Hoeveler US Dist. Ct. (so. dist.) Fla., Miami, 1993—94; assoc. Wileu, Rein & Fielding, Washington, 1994—97; legal advisor to commr. Harold Furchtgott-Roth FCC, 1997—99; deputy gen. counsel Bush Campaign, 1999—2000; mem. Bush-Cheney Transition Team; spl. asst. to the Pres. for econ. policy The White House, Washington, 2000—01; commr. FCC, 2001—09, chmn., 2005—09. Named one of Top 40 Lawyers Under 40, Nat. Law Jour., 2005, 50 Who Matter Now, CNNMoney.com Bus. 2.0, 2006, 50 Most Important People on the Web, PC World, 2007, 50 Most Powerful People in DC, GQ mag., 2007. Mem.: D.C. Bar Assn., Fla. Bar Assn., Fed. Comm. Bar Assn. Republican.*

MARTIN, KRISTIN EMILY, librarian; b. Springfield, Ill., Sept. 13, 1975; d. James E. and Karen B. Martin; m. Joshua Martin Drucker, Sept. 24, 2000. BA, MusB, U. Mich., Ann Arbor, 1998; MS in Libr. Sci., U. NC, Chapel Hill, 2000. Asst. archivist Cleve. Mus. Art, 2000—02; metadata mgr., docs. cataloger State Libr. NC, Raleigh, 2002—06; electronic resources cataloger U. NC, 2006—08; metadata libr. U. Ill., Chgo., 2008—. Office: Daley Libr Univ Ill Chgo Catalog Dept MC 234 Chicago IL 60607 Office Fax: 312-413-0424. Business E-Mail: kmarti@uic.edu.

MARTIN, LAURA, secondary school educator; b. Syracuse, NY, Mar. 8, 1983; d. James and Kathy Keller; m. Ryan Martin, Sept. 6, 2003; 1 child, Jed. AS, Bemidji State U., Minn., 2003; BS in Math. Edn., ND State U., Fargo, 2005. Mid. sch. tchr. St. John's Prep. Sch., Collegeville, Minn., 2005—. Mem.: NCTM. Avocations: soccer, camping, backpacking.

MARTIN, LAURA KEIDAN, lawyer; b. Detroit, Oct. 8, 1964; BA, U. Mich., 1986; JD, Harvard U., 1989. Bar: Ill. 1989. Ptnr. Katten Muchin Rosenman LLP, Chgo. Mem.: ABA, Nat. Health Lawyers Assn., Ill. Assn. Healthcare Attys. (bd. dirs. 2001—07, pres. 2006), Chgo. Bar Assn. (chair antitrust law com. 2004—05). Office: Katten Muchin Rosenman LLP 525 W Monroe St Chicago IL 60661 Office Fax: 312-902-5487, 312-577-8951. E-mail: laura.martin@kattenlaw.com.

MARTIN, LAURABELLE, property manager; b. Jackson County, Minn., Nov. 3, 1915; d. Eugene Wellington and Mary Christina (Hansen) M. BS, Mankato State U., 1968. Tchr. rural schs., Renville County, Minn., 1936-41, 45-50, Wabasso (Minn.) Pub. Sch., 1963-81; pres. Renville Farms and Feed Lots, 1982-86. Author: Hist. Biography of Joseph Renville, 1996; poet: Nat. Libr. Poetry (Silver Cup award, 2003). Pres. Wabasso (Minn.) Edn. Assn., 1974-75, publicity chmn., 1968-74; sec. and publicity agt. Hist. Renville Preservation Com., 1978-86; publicity chmn., sec. Town and Country Boosters, Renville, 1982-83. Recipient Outstanding Achievement in Poetry Award, Internat. Soc. Poets. Mem. Genealogy Soc. Renville County, Am. Legion Aux. Democrat. Lutheran. Avocations: antique furniture, travel, sewing, poetry. Home and Office: 334 NW 1201st Rd Holden MO 64040-9378

MARTIN, LELAND MORRIS (PAPPY), historian, educator; b. Patrick Springs, Va., Aug. 8, 1930; s. Rufus Wesley and Mary Hilda (Biggs) M.; m. Mildred Greer, May 12, 1956 (dec. June 2007); children: Lee Ann Geneve, Mitzi Jo. AB, Berea Coll., 1953; MS, U. Tenn., 1954; grad., Air War Coll., Maxwelll AFB, Ala., 1978; MA in History, U Tex. Pan-Am., 1993; cert. machinist, Tex. State Tech. Coll., 1997, AAS in Machining Technology-Tool and Die Making, 1999. Enlisted USAF, 1954, advanced through grades to col., 1977; comdr. RAF, Greenham Common, Welford, 1974-76; comdt., comdr. Noncommd. Officers Acad., McGuire AFB, NJ, 1976—79; vice comdr., comdr. RAF Mildenhall and RAF Chicksands, England, 1979-83; chief of staff 21st Air Force, McGuire AFB, 1983-84; pres. Air Force Phys. Evaluation Bd., Randolph AFB, NJ, 1984-86; ret., 1986; dep. exec. dir. Confederate Air Force, Harlingen, Tex., 1986-88; exec. dir. Am. Airpower Heritage Found., Harlingen, 1986-88; tchg. asst., lectr. in history U. Tex. Pan Am., Edinburg, 1989-93; adj. prof. history Tex. State Tech. Coll., Harlingen, 1994—2001. Co-chair (with Sir Douglas Bader) 1976 Internat. Air Tatoo at RAF Greenham Common; chair Air Fete 80 and 81, RAF Mildenhall, Eng. Co-editor: History of Military Assistance Command, Vietnam, 1970. Decorated Legion of Merit with two oak leaf clusters, Bronze Star; Cross of Gallantry (Vietnam); recipient Amb.'s award Ct. St. James, London, 1974, 83. Mem. Air Force Assn., Am. Watchmakers and Clockmakers Inst., Nat. Assn. Watch and Clock Collectors, Brit. Officers Club Phila. (hon.), Rotary (gov. internat. dist. 5930 1995-96), Phi Alpha Theta, Phi Kappa Phi. Republican. Presbyterian. Avocations: clock repairs, photography, golf, fishing. Home: 90 Elizabeth Dr Ridgeway VA 24148

MARTIN, LENORE MARIE, bioorganic researcher, educator; b. Ann Arbor, Mich., June 26, 1963; d. Donald Leigh and Alice Fay (Opaskar) M. BA, Northwestern Univ., 1983; PhD, UCLA, 1988. Rsch. assoc. The Rockefeller Univ., NYC, 1988-94; asst. prof. U. R.I., 1994—. Safety com. UCLA Chem. dept., 1985-87; orgn. symposium Am. Chem. Soc., L.A., 1987. Contbr. articles to profl. jours. Recipient Best Paper in Organic Chem. award Am. Chem. Soc., 1983. Mem. Am. Chem. Soc., Am. Peptide Soc., Am. Assn. Advancement of Sci., Sigma Xi., Phi Lambda Upsilon, Sigma Delta Epsilon. Achievements include first synthesis of an oligonucleotide on solid polystyreme support; pioneer in the use of capillary electrophoresis on antibodies. Office: U RI Coll Pharmacy Dept Pharmacognosy Kingston RI 02881-0809

MARTIN, LINDA GAYE, demographer, economist; b. Paris, Ark., Dec. 17, 1947; d. Leslie Paul and Margie La Verne (Thomas) Martin. BA in Math., Harvard U., 1970; MPA, Princeton U., 1972, PhD in Econs., 1978; DHL (hon.), Marlboro Coll., 2002; D in Pub. Policy (hon.), Rand Grad. Sch., 2006. Dir. mgmt. info. sr. ctrs. bur. purchased social svcs. for adults City of N.Y., 1972—74; rsch. assoc., rsch. dir. U.S. Ho. of Reps. Select Com. on Population, Washington, 1977—79; rsch. assoc. East-West Population Inst., Honolulu, 1979—89, asst. dir., 1982—84; asst. prof. econs. U. Hawaii, Honolulu, 1979—81, assoc. prof., 1981—89, prof., 1989; dir. com. on population Nat. Acad. Scis., Washington, 1989—93; dir. domestic rsch. divsn., v.p. RAND, Santa Monica, Calif., 1993—95, v.p. for rsch. devel., 1995—99, sr. fellow, 2007—; pres. Population Coun., NYC, 1999—2004; scholar in residence Inst. Medicine, 2004—07; adj. prof., Bloomberg Sch. Pub. Health Johns Hopkins U., 2007—. Neurosci. behavior and sociology of aging rev. com. Nat. Inst. on Aging, Bethesda, 1991—95; chair panel on aging in developing countries NAS, Washington, 1987, com. on population, 1993—99, panel on internat. aging data, 1999—2001; peer rev. oversight group NIH, 1998—2004. Editor: The ASEAN Success Story, 1987; co-editor: Demographic Change in Sub-Saharan Africa, 1993, The Demography of Aging, 1994, Racial and Ethnic Differences in the Health of Older Americans, 1997; contbr. articles to profl. jours. Mem. adv. coun. Woodrow Wilson Sch. Pub. and Internat. Affairs, Princeton U., NJ, 2000—08. Recipient Fulbright Faculty Rsch. award, Coun. for Internat. Exch. of Scholars, 1988. Mem.: AAAS (adv. coun. 2003—06, chair social, econ. and polit. scis. sect. 2007—08), Population Assn. Am. (bd. dir. 1991—93), Internat. Union for Sci. Study Population, Gerontol. Soc. Am. Democrat. Home: 3419 Mansfield Rd Falls Church VA 22041 Office: RAND Corp 1200 S Hayes St Arlington VA 22202

MARTIN, LYNN MORLEY, former United States Secretary of Labor; b. Evanston, Ill., Dec. 26, 1939; d. Lawrence William and Helen Catherine (Hall) Morley; children from a previous marriage: Julia Catherine, Caroline; m. Harry D. Leinenweber, Jan. 1987; stepchildren: Jane, John, Stephen, Justin, Thomas Leinenweber. BA, U. Ill., 1960. Tchr. pub. schs. Winnebago County, Ill., 1972—76; mem. Ill. House of Reps., 1977-79, Ill. State Senate, 1979-81, US Congress from 16th Ill. Dist., 1981-91; sec. US Dept. Labor, Washington, 1991-93; prof. J.J. Kellogg Grad. Sch. Mgmt. Northwestern U., 1993—2000. Bd. dirs. Dreyfus Funds, Procter & Gamble Co., Constellation Energy Group; mem. Coun. Fgn. Relations, Chgo. Network. Co-chmn. Bush-Quayle Presdl. campaign, 1988. Named one of Outstanding Young Women in Am., U.S. Jaycees; named Rep. Woman of the Yr., 1989; named a Mother of the Yr., Nat. Mother's Day Com., 1992; 1st woman elected to leadership post in House of Reps., 1982. Mem. AAUW, Jr. League, Phi Beta Kappa (hon. doctorate). Republican.

MARTIN, MALCOLM ELLIOT, lawyer; b. Buffalo, Dec. 11, 1935; s. Carl Edward and Pearl Maude (Elliot) M.; m. Judith Hill Harley, June 27, 1964; children: Jennifer, Elizabeth, Christina, Katherine. BA, U. Mich., Ann Arbor, 1958, JD, 1962. Bar: N.Y. 1963, U.S. Ct. Appeals (2nd Cir.) 1966, U.S. Supreme Ct. 1967. Assoc. Chadbourne & Parke LLP (formerly Chadbourne Parke Whiteside & Wolff), NYC, 1962-73, ptnr., trusts, estates, pvt. clients practice groups, 1974—2006, of counsel, 2007—. Dir., sec. Carl and Dorothy Bennett Found., Inc.; sec., counsel Copper Devel. Assn., Inc. With US Army, 1958—60. Mem. ABA, NY State Bar Assn., Assn. Bar City NY, St. Andrew's Soc. NY, Rockefeller Ctr. Club, Copper Club (NYC). Office: Chadbourne & Parke LLP 30 Rockefeller Plz Fl 31 New York NY 10112-0129 Office Phone: 212-408-1040. Office Fax: 212-541-5369. Business E-Mail: mmartin@chadbourne.com.

MARTIN, MARCELLA EDRIC, retired community health nurse; b. Rosedale, Miss., Jan. 25, 1930; d. Amos and Alma Allen; m. Reuben Clifton Martin, Jan. 25, 1969; children: Brunetta, Jacqueline, Cornell, Constance. Student, Marygrove Coll., Detroit, 1971; ADN, Highland Park Sch. Nursing, Mich., 1979; ThB, Cmty. Bible Coll., Detroit, 1968. Lic. LPN. Nurse VA Hosp., Ann Arbor, Mich., Crittendon Hosp., Detroit, Vis. Nurses Assn., Detroit. Instr. Charles H. Mason Bible Sch., Detroit, 1991—95; mem. C.O.G.I.C. Bus. owners Assn., 1982—. Author: Women Who Struggle, 2001; prodr.: (plays) And Didn't Those Knees Bow, 2004. Founder Prime of Life Adult Foster Care Home, 1979, Somebody's Got To Care Min., 2003; mem. Nat. Campaign Tolerance-The Wall of Tolerance, 2003; missionary over women Chs. of God in Christ, 1986—2002; vol. Redford Geriatric Home, Mich., 1999—. Recipient Spirit of Detroit award, City of Detroit, 1978, 2000, 2002, Disting. Citizen of Detroit award, 1980, Testimonial Resolution award, 1985; named to Wall of Tolerance, New Civil Rights Meml. Ctr., Montgomery, Ala., 2003. Mem.: Detroit Writers Guild. Democrat. Pentecostal Ch. Avocations: reading, writing. Home: 25332 Shiawassee Cir Apt 106 Southfield MI 48034 Personal E-mail: reumarone@comcast.net.

MARTIN, MARCIA D., science educator; d. James David Davis and Mary Louise Merriman; m. Francis P. Martin (div.); children: Marc Jon, Scott Anthony. Grad., U. So. Miss., Hattiesburg, 1986. Cert. tchr. Miss., Ark. Tchr. asst. remedial reading Pascagoula Sch. Dist., Miss., 1983—85; tchr. remedial reading Moss Point H.S., Miss., 1986—88; tchr. TLC program Pulaski County Sch. Dist., Little Rock, 1989—92, tchr. math., sci., 1992—95, 1995—97, tchr. 6th grade sci., 1997—. Sci. fair sponsor Daisy Bates Elem., Little Rock, 1989—93; tchr., curriculum writer MAST Program, Daisy Bates Elem., Little Rock, 1992—94; mem. West Nile Virus study County Sch. Dist., 2003. Recipient Disting. Leadership award, Ark. Leadership Acad., 1986; grantee, Pulaski County Sch. Dist., 2003. Mem.: Pulaski Assn. Classroom Tchrs. Avocations: classical piano, needlecrafts. E-mail: marcia_martin2002@yahoo.com.

MARTIN, MARCIA GRAY, retired architecture educator, artist, designer; b. Chgo., May 18, 1932; d. Harry Gray and Emma Bernstein; children: Elizabeth Anne, Charles Brandon. BArch, Ill. Inst. Tech., 1956; attended, De Paul Law Sch., 1957—58, U. Chgo., 1948—50; MA in Liberal Studies, North Ctrl. Coll., 1997. Freelance architect designer, Chgo., 1956—79; instr. architecture Coll. Dupage, Glen Ellyn, Ill., 1980—88, prof. architecture, 1989—2004, coord. architectural programs, 2000—04, prof. emeritis, 2004—; asst. art gallery Inspire Fine Art, Chgo., 2004—07. Head traveling exhibition Coll. Dupage, 2001—; illustrator, artist Wheaton History Ctr., Ill., 1985—. Author: (books) Wheaton, USA, 1991, Architectural Drafting, 1997; exhibitions include drawings water color paintings Wheaton: A Visual Experience, 2008. Sec. Wheaton Historic Preservation Coun.; mem. City Wheaton Historic Com., Ill., 1992—93, Landmark Preservation Coun., Wheaton, 1990—2004; pres. Waterford Condominium Assn., Wheaton, 2005—; mem., bd. dirs. Dupage Art League, Wheaton, 1980—85; mem. bd. dirs. Wheaton Historic Preservation Coun.; pres. bd. dirs. Waterford Condominium Assn., Wheaton. Recipient Wisdom and Counsel award, Wheaton Youth Outreach, 1990, Julia Beverage award, Ill. Inst. Tech., 2007. Achievements include the creation of one of the few undergraduate historic preservation education programs. Home: 455 W Front St #302 Wheaton IL 60187 Personal E-mail: marciagraymartin@yahoo.com.

MARTIN, MARGARET M., artist, educator, Author; b. Buffalo, Aug. 15, 1940; d. Earl and Margaret L. (Milley) M. BFA, Boston U., 1962; student, John Pike, Rex Brandt, Robert E. Wood, John Pellew, Milford Zornes; DFA (hon.), D'Youville Coll., Buffalo, NY, 2004. Graphic designer Wagner Folding Box, Buffalo, 1962-64; art director Manhardt Alexander Inc., Buffalo, 1964-77; freelance designer MMMartin Design, Buffalo, 1977-79; artist, tchr. Buffalo, 1979—. Cons. Niagara Frontier Watercolor Soc., Buffalo, 1986—. One-woman shows include Performing Arts Ctr., Buffalo, 1996, Kenan Gallery, Lockport, NY, 1997, D'Youville Coll., Buffalo, 2001, Garret Club, Buffalo, 2003, Buffalo Club, 2005; exhibiited in group shows at Taiwan Art Inst., Taipei, 1994, Catharine Lorillard Wolfe Art Club, 1996-97, 03, 05, 07, Balt. Watercolor Soc., 1996, Burchfield Penney Art Ctr. Buffalo, 2004, Am. Watercolor Soc., NYC, 2002, F.G Burroughs-S.B. Chapin Art Mus., Myrtle Beach SC, 2007; author: No More Wishy-Washy Watercolor, 1999, Watercolor Secrets, 2009; featured painting in the Movie "Bruce Almighty", Universal Studios, 2003. Recipient Morrison award Adirondacks Nat. Exhbn. Am. Watercolor, 1991, Adriana R. Zahn award Catharine Lorillard Wolfe Art Club, 1992, Cynthia Shipp Goodgal Meml. Watercolor award Catharine Lorillard Wolfe Art Club, 2003, Best of Show award Internat. Plein Air Painters Worldwide Paintout, Niagara Falls, Ont., Can., 2004, Frank and Mary Anderson Cassidy Meml. award Catharine Lorillard Wolfe Art Assn., 2005, Mary LaGreca Meml. award Hudson Valley Art Assn. 75th Ann. Exhbn., 2006; featured painting in the Movie "Bruce Almighty", Universal Studios, 2003. Mem. Met. Mus. Art, Albright-Knox Art Gallery, Met. Opera Guild, Nat. Trust, Niagara Buffalo Partnership, Midwest Watercolor Soc. (bd. dirs. 1985-87, Grumbacher Gold Medal 1988), Nat. League Am. Pen Women, (exhbn. chmn. 1980-82, Biennial Award Excellence 1988), Salmagundi Club (Ogden Pleissner Meml. award), Nat. Arts Club (exhbn. com. award solo exhbn. 1985), Catharine Lorillard Wolfe Art Club (Anna Hyatt Huntington award painting 1985). Presbyterian. Avocations: horticulture, music. Studio: 69 Elmwood Ave Buffalo NY 14201-2018

MARTIN, MARK D., state supreme court justice; b. Apr. 29, 1963; s. M. Dean and Ann Martin. Student, U. Dayton; BS summa cum laude, We. Carolina U., 1985; JD (hon.), U. NC, 1988; grad., Nat. Jud. Coll., 1993; LLM, U. Va., 1998. Bar: NC, US Dist. Ct. (ea. and mid. dists.) NC, US Ct. Appeals (4th cir.), US Supreme Ct. Law clk. to Hon. Clyde H. Hamilton US Dist. Ct., Columbia, SC, 1988-90; pvt. practice McNair Law Firm, Raleigh, NC, 1990-91; legal counsel to gov. Office of Gov., Raleigh, NC, 1991-92; superior ct. judge Jud. Dist. 3A, Greenville, NC, 1992-94; judge NC Ct. Appeals, 1994-99; assoc. justice Supreme Ct. NC, Raleigh, 1999—2006, sr. assoc. justice, 2006—. Mem. legis. and law reform com. Conf. Superior Ct. Judges; sec. NC Jud. Conf., co-chair legis. liaison com.; adj. prof. law U. NC, Chapel Hill; adj. faculty NC Ctrl. U. Sch. Law; sr. lecturing fellow Duke U. Law Sch.; chair Chief Justice's Commn. Future NC Bus. Ct. Editor-in-chief: Jour Internat. Law and Comml. Regulation. Office coord. United Way Ann. Combined Campaign, 1991, 1992; mem. master plan adv. com. N.C. Dept. Correction, 1992; mem. N.C. Coun. Women, 1992. Recipient Order Long Leaf Pine, Disting. Alumnus award, Western Carolina U., Svc. award, City of Raleigh Cmty. Svc. Dept., Book award, Sci. Methods for Lawyers; Lloyd C. Balfour fellow, N.C. Inst. Polit. Leadership fellow, Coun. State Govt. Toll fellow. Mem.: ABA (editl. bd. Judges' Jour., coalition justice com., commn. state ct. funding, John Marshall award rev. com., nominating com., com. to develop nat. issues forum programs on Am. jury, coalition for justice rep., com. to develop nat. issues forum programs on separation of powers, adv. commn. World Justice Project, program chair jud. divsn., edn. chair appellate judges conf., exec. com., Appellate Judges Conf., sec. Appellate Judges Conf., co-chair presidential commn. on fair and impartial ct., vice chair Appellate Judges Conf.), Am. Law Inst., Am. Judicature Soc. (nat. adv. coun. mem.), Appellate Judges Ednl. Inst. (chair, program planning com., bd. dirs.), Mortar Bd., Wake County Bar Assn. (bd. dirs., continuing legal edn. presenter), Assn. NC Women Attys., NC Assn. Black Lawyers, NC Bar Assn. (strategic planning emerging trends com., litig. sect. coun., v.p., multidisciplinary practice task force, minorities profession com., program com. 2004 Brown v. Bd. Edn. 50th anniversary), Carolina Law Alumni Assn. (bd. dirs.), U. NC Law Davis Soc., Rotary, Internat. Hon. Soc., Beta Gamma Sigma, Delta Sigma Phi (scholar), Phi Alpha Delta, Omicron Delta Epsilon, Pi Gamma Mu, Phi Kappa Phi, Alpha Lambda Delta. Office: NC Supreme Ct PO Box 1841 Raleigh NC 27602-2170 Office Phone: 919-831-5712. Business E-Mail: maj@sc.state.nc.us, mmartin@sc.state.nc.us.*

MARTIN, MARK OWEN, biology professor; b. Compton, Calif., June 16, 1958; s. Jack Sevard and Wanda Jean Martin; m. Jennifer Jean Quinn, Dec. 19, 1998; children: Anson Robert Quinn, Zachary Vincent Quinn. PhD, Stanford U., Calif., 1986. Assoc. prof. Biology Dept. U. Puget Sound, Wash., 2005—. Office: Univ Puget Sound Biology Dept 1500 N Warner St 1088 Tacoma WA 98416 Business E-Mail: momartin@ups.edu.

MARTIN, MARSHALL WAYNE, finance educator; b. Halifax, Va., July 24, 1946; s. Marshall Webb Martin; m. Elsie Linda Long. A in Arts and Scis., Danville CC, Va., 1970; BS in Mktg. and Economics, Va. Poly. Inst. & State U., Blacksburg, 1973, MBA, 1973. Assoc. prof. bus. adminstrn. Danville CC, 1973—. Cons. Danville Regional Med. Ctr., 2001—04. E-5 US Army, 1966—67, Vietnam. Decorated Vietnam Svc. medal US Army. Mem.: Va. Assn. Economist. Office: Danville CC 1008 South Main St Danville VA 24541

MARTIN, MELISSA CAROL, radiological physicist; b. Muskogee, Okla., Feb. 7, 1951; d. Carl Leroy and Helen Shirley (Hicks) Paden; m. Donald Ray Martin, Feb. 14, 1970; 1 child, Christina Gail. BS, Okla. State U., Stillwater, 1971; MS, UCLA, 1975. Cert. radiol. physicist Am. Bd. Radiology, radiation oncology Am. Bd. Med. Physics. Asst. radiation physicist Hosp. of the Good Samaritan, LA, 1975-80; radiol. physicist Meml. Med. Ctr., Long Beach, Calif., 1980-83, St. Joseph Hosp., Orange, Calif., 1983-92, Therapy Physics, Inc., Gardena, Calif., 1993—. Cons. in field. Editor: (book) Current Regulatory Issues in Medical Physics, 1992. Fund raising campaign divsn. mgr. YMCA, Torrance, Calif., 1988-92; dir. AWANA Youth Club-Guards Group, Manhattan Beach, Calif., 1984—. Named Dir. of Symposium, Am. Coll. Med. Physics, 1992. Fellow Am. Coll. Med. Physics (chancellor western region 1992-95, treas. 2004-05, vice-chair, 2009, Marvin Williams award, 2009), Am. Assn. Physicists in Medicine (profl. coun. 1990-95, 2006—, treas. 1998-2003, bd. dirs. 1994-2003, co-dir. summer sch. 2007, vice-chair ednl. coun. 2009-), Am. Coll. Radiology (econs. com. 1992-95, councilor at large 2001-06, commn. on med. physics 2002-07, mem. mammogrtaphy accreditation com., 2006—), Govt. Relative Comm. (vice chair 1998-07); mem. Calif. Med. Physics Soc. (treas. 1991-98), Am. Soc. for Therapeutic Radiology and Oncology, Health Physics Soc. (pres. So. Calif. chpt. 1992-93), Am. Brachytherapy Soc. Baptist. Avocation: christian youth group dir. Home: 507 Susana Ave Redondo Beach CA 90277-3953 Office: Therapy Physics Inc 879 W 190th St Ste 419 Gardena CA 90248 Office Phone: 310-217-4114. Personal E-mail: melissamartin@compuserve.com. Business E-Mail: melissa@therapyphysics.com.

MARTIN, MICHAEL THOMAS, humanities educator, writer; b. Detroit, May 3, 1962; m. Bonnie Shanburn, Aug. 16, 1967; children: Brendan, Dylan, Thomas, Mae, Aidan, Zelie, Isabel, Gabriel. BA Summa Cum Laude, Marygrove Coll., Detroit; MA, U. Detroit Mercy. Catechesis cert. Byzantine Cath. Eparchy Parma, 2007. Tchr. Detroit Waldorf Sch., 1991—2007; instr. Marygrove Coll., 2007—. Dir. curriculum devel. Inst. Art-Infused Edn., Detroit, 2006—08. Contbr. to scholarly articles (Publ. in LOGOS, 2008); author: (creative nonfiction) Music of the Spheres, (poetry) It All Comes down to Laundry (Publ. in RELIEF, 2008). Catechist St Stephen's Byzantine Cath. Ch., Allen Park, Mich., 2006—. Fellow: Fellowship Cath. Scholars; mem.: Intercollegiate Rsch. Inst. Independent. Roman Catholic. Office: Marygrove Coll 2485 W McNichols Rd Detroit MI 48221 Office Phone: 313-927-1432. Business E-Mail: mmartin@marygrove.edu.

MARTIN, MICHAEL TOWNSEND, sports association executive, marketing professional, consultant; b. NYC, Nov. 21, 1941; s. Townsend Bradley and Irene (Redmond) M.; m. Jennifer Johnston, Nov. 7, 1964 (div. Jan. 1977); children: Ryan Bradley, Christopher Townsend; m. Jean Kathleen Meyer, Mar. 1, 1980 Grad., The Choate Sch., 1960; student, Rutgers U., 1961-62. Asst. gen. mgr. N.Y. Jets Football Club, NYC, 1968-74; v.p. NAMANCO Prodns., NYC, 1975-76; v.p., gen. mgr. Cosmos Soccer Club, NYC, 1976-77; exec. asst. Warner Communications, NYC, 1978-84; owner, operator Martin Racing Stable, NYC, 1983—; pres. Sports Mark, Inc., NYC, 1990—2003. Bd. dirs. Mote Marine Lab., Sarasota, Fla., Animal Rescue Coalition, Coun. of Visitors, Woods Hole Marine Biol. Lab., Nat. Lighthouse Ctr. and Mus., Lemur Conservation Found., Sta. WEDU PBS, Tampa Fla.; bd. mem. Ringling Coll. Bd. Art and Design; program com. Sta. WNET Channel 13; bd. advisors The Pennington Sch., Dir.'s Cir., Scripps Instn. Oceanography Mem. Athletics Congress (life, cert. official 1984—), U.S. Tennis Assn. (life), Internat. Oceanographic Found. (Miami life mem.), Fla. Thoroughbred Breeders Assn., Quogue Field Club, The Union Club. Republican. Episcopalian. Avocation: collecting inuit (eskimo) art. Home: 131 E 69th St Apt 11A New York NY 10021-5158 Office: 400 Pk Ave 6th Fl New York NY 10022-2511 Office Phone: 212-980-9525. Personal E-mail: mmarti1237@aol.com.

MARTIN, MICHAEL V., academic administrator, economics professor; b. Crosby, Minn., Jan. 29, 1947; s. Ben F. and Dorothy A. Martin; m. Janis R. Roeglin, Aug. 15, 1970; children: Amanda C., Samuel J. BS in Econs., Mankato State Coll., 1969, MA in Econs., 1971; PhD in Applied Econs., U. Minn., 1977. Instr. in econs. U. Wis., Eau Claire, 1972-74; from asst. prof. to prof. Oreg. State U., Corvallis, 1977-92; assoc. dean U. Minn., St. Paul, 1992-95, v.p., dean Coll. Agrl., Food and Environ. Scis., 1995—98, acting dir. Agrl. Experiment Station, 1997—98, v.p. agrl. policy, 1997—98; v.p. agrl. and natural resources U. Fla., Gainesville, 1998—2004, sr. v.p., 2004; pres. N.Mex. State U., Las Cruces, 2004—08; chancellor La. State U. and A&M Coll., Baton Rouge, 2008—. Recipient Diversity Recognition award USDA-NRCS, 1997, Agrl. Achievement award Oreg. Dept. Agr., 1992, Minn. Forest Preserve, 1998, Social Justice award, N.MEx. State U., 2005; named Weekly Power Broker, N.Mex. Bus., 2006. Mem. Am. Econs. Assn., Am. Agrl. Econ. Assn., Internat. Assn. Agrl. Economists, Internat. Agrl. Trade Rsch. Consortium, Econ. Hist. Assn., Sigma Xi. Democrat. Avocations: reading, golf. Office: La State U Office of Chancellor 156 Thomas Boyd Hall Baton Rouge LA 70803 Office Phone: 225-578-6977. Office Fax: 225-578-5982. E-mail: chancellor@lsu.edu.*

MARTIN, MURRAY D., manufacturing executive; b. Hawkesville, Ontario; s. John and Melissa Martin. Studied computer sci. and mathematics, U. Waterloo. Joined Litton Industries; various positions to v.p., gen. mgr. Monroe Office Systems; pres. Dictaphone Canada subs. of Pitney Bowes, 1987—90; pres. Pitney Bowes copier systems, 1990—98, Pitney Bowes Internat., 1998—2001; group pres. global mailstream solutions Pitney Bowes Inc., Stamford, Conn., 2001—04, exec. v.p., 2003—04, pres., COO, 2004—07, pres., CEO, 2007—08, chmn., pres., CEO, 2009—. Bd. dir. Brink's Co., 2005—. Bd. dir. United Way Internat., Forum of World Affairs. Named first disting. fellow, Waterloo U. Centre for Applied Cryptographic, 2001. Office: Pitney Bowes Inc 1 Elmcroft Rd Stamford CT 06926-0700*

MARTIN, MYRON GREGORY, foundation administrator; b. Houston, Jan. 14, 1958; s. Monty Gene and Vera Mae (Saurage) M. MusB, U. North Tex., 1980; MBA, Golden Gate U., 1989. Various sales and mktg. positions Baldwin Piano Co., NYC, 1980-1990, dir. concert and artists, 1990-95; exec. dir. Liberace Found., Las Vegas, Nev., 1995-98; dir. U. Las Vegas, 1998—. Mem. adv. bd. Thelonious Monk Inst., Washington, D.C., 1994-95; bd. dirs. Cystic Fibrosis Found., Chgo., 1990, Liberace Found., 1993-95, Museums and Attractions, Las Vegas, 1996—. Recipient Special award Cystic Fibrosis Found., 1990. Mem. Nev. Mus. Assn. (bd. dirs. 1997—). Avocations: tennis, judging scholarship pageants for miss america organization. Home: 3996 Placita Del Rico Las Vegas NV 89120-2629 Office: U Las Vegas Performing Art Ctr 4505 S Maryland Pkwy Las Vegas NV 89154-9900

MARTIN, NORMAN MARSHALL, computer science educator; b. Chgo., Jan. 16, 1924; s. Harry Eugene and Fay Cohen; m. Emilia Regina van Deene, Aug. 16, 1950; children: Gabrielle Block, Gwenwyn Janett. Student, Central YMCA Coll., 1941-42; MA, U. Chgo., 1946; postgrad., U. Amsterdam, Netherlands, 1949-50; PhD, U. Calif. at Los Angeles, 1952. Instr. philosophy U. Ill. at Urbana, 1950-51, UCLA, 1952-53; research asso. Willow Run Research Center, U. Mich., 1953-55; mem. tech. staff Space Tech. Labs., El Segundo, Calif., 1955-61, head logic techniques group, 1957-61; staff logician, dir. Logicon, Inc., LA, 1961-65, treas., 1962-65; assoc. prof. philosophy U. Tex. at Austin, 1965-68, assoc. prof. computer sci., 1966-68, prof. philosophy and computer sci., 1968-74, prof. philosophy, computer sci. and elec. and computer engring., 1974-90, prof. emeritus, 1990—, assoc. chmn. computer sci., 1975-78. Lectr. engring. U. Calif. at Los Angeles, 1956-65; cons. Logicon, Inc., 1965-71. Author: Systems of Logic, 1989, Closure Spaces and Logic, 1996. Served with F.A. AUS, 1943-45. Decorated Purple Heart.; Fulbright grantee Netherlands, 1949 Mem. Am. Math Soc., Am. Philos. Assn., Assn. Symbolic Logic, Assn. Computing Machinery, Sigma Xi. Democrat. Unitarian Universalist. Home: 6804 Mesa Dr Austin TX 78731-2820 E-mail: martin@cs.utexas.edu.

MARTIN, OLIVIA JEAN, social studies educator; b. LA, Nov. 08; d. Henry and Stella Martin. BA in Clin./Physiol. Psychology, U. So. Calif., 1990; MA in Edn. Adminstrn., Azusa Pacific U., 2005. Mgr. Eastman West, Montebello/Buena Park, Calif.; asst. mgr. Hortman Jewelers; peer coll. tutor East LA Coll., Monterey Park, Calif., 1985—86; facilitator U. So. Calif.-Biomed. Rsch. Program, LA, 1987—91; behavioral counselor, nutritional specialist Nutri Sys., West Covina, Calif.; tchr. asst. Franklin Adult H.S., LA; elem. tchr. L.A. Unified Sch. Dist., 1994—2001; asst. dir. curriculum L.A. Archdiocese/San Gabriel Mission H.S., 2001—02, sci. tchr., 2000—01; mid. sch. social studies and sci. tchr. Azusa (Calif.) Unified Sch. Dist., 2002—06, dist. mgmt. trainee, 2004—06. Participant Olive Crest Cruise for Kids, LA, 2004; hon. mem. exec. bd. Azusa PTA Coun., 2004—06; fundraiser Corvettes United Spl. Wish Found., LA, 1999—2005. Recipient Merit award, Gov. of Calif., 1998—2000, Congl. award, Rep. Edward Roybal, L.A., 1986, Best Facilitator AP Biology award, U. So. Calif., 1989. Mem.: ASCD, NEA, Calif. Assn. Bilingual Edn. (pres. Azusa Canyon chpt. 2006—07), Nat. Coun. Social Studies, Assn. Calif. Supts. and Adminstrs., Corvettes Ltd. Club, Pi Lambda Theta. Republican. Roman Catholic. Avocations: racquetball, auto shows, auto racing. Home: PO Box 80892 San Marino CA 91118-9982

MARTIN, PAUL, former Prime Minister of Canada; b. Windsor, Ont., Can., Aug. 28, 1938; s. Paul Joseph and Eleanor (Adams) M.; m. Sheila Ann Cowan, Sept. 11, 1965; children: Paul William, Robert James, David Patrick. BA in Philosophy and History, U. Toronto, Can., 1962, LLB, 1965. Bar: Ont. 1966. Exec. asst. to pres. Power Corp. Can. Ltd., 1966-69, v.p., 1969-71; v.p. spl. projects Consol.-Bathurst Ltd., 1971-73; v.p. planning and devel. Power Corp., Can., 1973-74; pres. Can. S.S. Lines Ltd., Montreal, 1974-80, CEO, 1976-80; pres., CEO CSL Group Inc., 1980-88; M.P. Ho. of Commons, 1988—; min. for fed. office of regional devel. Govt. of Can., Ottawa, 1993-95, min. fin., 1993—2002, prime min., 2003—06; leader Liberal Party Can., 2003—06. Co-chair Nat. Platform Com. of Liberal Party of Can. Author: Making History: The Politics of Achievement; co-author (with Chaviva Hosek): Creating Opportunity: The Liberal Plan for Canada. Former mem. C.D. Howe Inst. Policy Analysis Com., Birt, N.Am. Com., Ctr. Rsch. Action on Race Rels.; former bd. dirs. Can. Coun. Christians and Jews; founding dir. emeritus North-South Inst., Can., Coun. Native Bus.; bd. govs. Concordia U., coun., v.p., past mem. bd. advisors; inaugural chair G-20, 1999. Liberal. Avocations: sports, reading.

MARTIN, PAUL EDWARD, lawyer; b. Atchison, Kans., Feb. 5, 1928; s. Harres C. and Thelma F. (Wilson) M.; m. Betty Lou Crawford, Aug. 28, 1954; children: Cherry G., Paul A., Marylou. BBA, Baylor U., 1955, LLB, 1956; LLM, Harvard U., 1957. Bar: Tex. 1956, Pa. 1958. Assoc. Ballard, Spahr, Andrews & Ingersoll, Phila., 1957-58; ptnr. Fulbright & Jaworski, Houston, 1959-77; shareholder Chamberlain, Hrdlicka, White, Williams & Martin, 1977—; instr. in estate planning U. Houston. Exec. com. Met. Houston March of Dimes, 1980-82; chmn. deacons West Meml. Bapt. Ch., 1979-80; trustee Baylor U., 1970-89, Meml. Hosp. Sys., 1975—, Fgn. Mission Bd., So. Bapt. Conv.; pres. Baylor U. Devel. Coun., 1973-74. Lt. comdr. USN, 1947-53. Fellow Am. Coll. Trust and Estate Coun.; mem. ABA (sect. real property, probate and trust law and sect. taxation), State Bar Tex., Houston Bar Assn., Houston Estate and Fin. Forum (pres. 1965-66), Houston Bus. and Estate Planning Coun., Houston Club, Phi Delta Phi. Republican. Co-author: How to Live and Die with Texas Probate. Home: 126 Lakeside Dr Montgomery TX 77356 Office: 3200 SW Freeway Ste 1400 Houston TX 77027 Office Phone: 713-622-9455. Office Fax: 713-655-1527. Personal E-mail: paul.martin07@yahoo.com.

MARTIN, PETER GERARD, computer technician, consultant, secondary school educator; b. Weymouth, Mass., May 2, 1952; s. John Augustine and Jean Anita (Murphy) M.; m. Elizabeth Anne Collins, Aug. 24, 1974; children: Derek Grant, Erin Jean. BA, Nasson Coll., 1974; MS, U. R.I., 1979; postgrad., Boston Coll., U. So. Maine, 1977-79; MA, Columbia Pacific U., 1991; PhD, U. Heriseau, 2000. Computer programmer Baybank Data Services, Waltham, Mass., 1975-76; mathematician Factory Mut. Engring., Norwood, Mass., 1976-78; tchr. Kennebunk (Maine) High Sch., 1978-79; v.p. strategic planning The Foxboro (Mass.) Co., 1979-84, systems cons., 1984-85, mgr. system product planning, 1986-88, v.p. market strategies and comm., 1996-99, v.p. corp. mktg., 1999—; v.p. mktg. Intec Controls Corp., 1993-94; v.p. Automation Rsch. Corp., 1996. Instr. Dean Jr. Coll., Franklin, Mass. 1980-96; tech. cons. Balance Inc., Wiscassett, Maine, 1985-89. Author: Dynamic Performance Management: A Path to World Class Manufacturing, 1992, Bottom-Line Automation, 2001; contbr. articles to profl. jours. Pres. East Woonsocket Sch. Parent Council, R.I., 1983-85; mem. Parents Involvement Com., Woonsocket, 1985; Cub Scout den leader, Woonsocket, 1985-86; instr. religious edn. Our Lady of Lourdes Ch. Mem. Soc. Mfg. Engrs., Mfrs. Automation Protocol Users Group, Inst. Soc. of Am. Roman Catholic. Avocations: camping, tennis, boating. Office: The Foxboro Co Bristol Park 351-2C Bristol Park Foxboro MA 02035 Business E-Mail: peter.g.martin@ips.invensys.com. E-mail: pmartin@foxboro.com.

MARTIN, PETER ROBERT, psychiatrist, pharmacologist; b. Budapest, Hungary, Sept. 6, 1949; came to U.S., 1980; s. Nicholas M. and Eva (Horvat) M.; m. Barbara Bradford, Dec. 23, 1985; 1 child, Alexander Bradford. BSc with honors, McGill U., Montreal, Que., Can., 1971, MD, CM, 1975; MSc, U. Toronto, Ont., Can., 1978. Diplomate Am. Bd. Psychiatry and Neurology, Psychiatry, Addiction Psychiatry. Resident in internal medicine U. Toronto, 1975-76, resident in psychiatry, 1978-80; fellow clin. pharmacology Addiction Rsch. Found., Toronto, 1976-78; chief sect. clin. sci. Nat. Inst. on Alcohol Abuse & Alcoholism, Bethesda, 1983-86; assoc. prof. Vanderbilt U. Sch. Medicine, Nashville, 1986-92, prof., 1992—, dir. divsn. addiction psychiatry, 1986—, dir. addiction ctr., 1994—; dir. Vanderbilt Inst. for Coffee Studies, 1999—. Vis. scientist Lab. of Clin. Sci., NIMH, Bethesda, Md., 1980-83; investigator John F. Kennedy Ctr. for Rsch. on Human Devel., Nashville, 1993—. Fellow Royal Coll. Physicians (Can.), Am. Psychiat. Assn. (disting.); mem. AAAS, Am. Soc. Clin. Pharmacology and Therapeutics, Am. Acad. Addiction Psychiatry, Rsch. Soc. on Alcoholism, Internat. Soc. Biomed. Rsch. in Alcoholism. Office: Vanderbilt Psychiat Hosp Ste 3068 1601 23rd Ave South Nashville TN 37212 Office Phone: 615-322-3527. E-mail: peter.martin@vanderbilt.edu.

MARTIN, PHILLIP DWIGHT, bank consulting company executive, mayor; b. Nevada, Mo., Jan. 4, 1943; s. E. Dwight and Berniece E. (Leedy) M. BS, U. Mo., 1964, MBA, 1965, cert. math. and bus. edn., 1966. Tchr. Warsaw (Mo.) Pub. Schs., 1966—68; investment analyst Bus. Men's Assurance Co. Am., Kansas City, Mo., 1968—70; exec. v.p. Farmer's Bank Walker, Mo., 1970—71; banking cons. Howard J. Blender Co., Dallas, 1971—84; chmn. Profit Motivators Internat., Inc., Boulder, Colo., 1984—2002; mayor City of Walker, 1986—2008, 2002—09; math. tchr. El Dorado Springs, Mo., 2002—; pres. CTAS of El Dorado Springs RII. Chair technology com. NRMC. Bd. dirs. Nev. Regional Med. Ctr., 2004—. Mem. Walker R-4 Alumni Assn. (cofounder, life mem. scholarship com., pres. 1994-96), Cmty. Tchr. Assn.(pres., 2009-) Home: 214 E Marvin Ave Walker MO 64790-9106 E-mail: pdm19@neighborlink.us.

MARTIN, PHILLIP HAMMOND, lawyer; b. Tucson, Jan. 4, 1940; s. William P. and Harriet (Hammond) M.; m. Sandra S. Chandler, June 17, 1961 (div. Mar. 1989); children: Lisa, Craig, Wade, Ryan; m. Erika Zetty, May 9, 1990. BA, U. Minn., 1961, JD, 1964. Bar: Minn. 1964, U.S. Tax Ct. 1967, U.S. Dist. Ct. Minn. 1968, U.S. Ct. Appeals (8th cir.) 1973, U.S. Supreme Ct. 1981, U.S. Claims Ct. 1983, U.S. Ct. Appeals (fed. cir.) 1988, U.S. Ct. Appeals (7th cir.) 1989. Assoc. Dorsey & Whitney, Mpls., 1964-69, ptnr., 1970—. Home: 487 Portland Ave Saint Paul MN 55102-2216 Office: Dorsey & Whitney LLP Ste 1500 50 S 6th St Minneapolis MN 55402-1498 Office Phone: 612-340-2845. Business E-Mail: martin.phil@dorsey.com.

MARTIN, R. KEITH, business and information systems educator, consultant; b. Seattle, Sept. 5, 1933; s. Jerome Milton and Winifred (Gifford) Martin; m. Carolyn Joanne Carosella, June 15, 1957; children: Jefferson, Sean, Jennifer, Katherine. AB, Whitman Coll., 1955; MBA with high honors, CCNY, 1965; PhD, U. Wash., 1973. Registered, lic. profl. engr.; cert. data processing, cert. systems profl., cert. computer profl. Div. mgr. Campus Merchandising Bur., Inc., NYC, 1955-56; sales rep. IBM, Seattle, 1956, Svc. Bur. Corp. subs. IBM, NYC, 1957-58; specialist mgmt. adv. svcs. Price Waterhouse & Co., NYC, 1959-65, Seattle, 1965-66, mgr., 1966-67; dir. mgmt. systems dept. U. Wash., 1967-71, lectr. dept. acctg. Sch. Bus. Adminstrn., 1971-73; asst. prof. dept. accountancy Baruch Coll., CUNY, 1973-76, assoc. prof., 1977-79; prof. acctg. Fairfield U., 1979-84, prof. acctg. and info. systems, 1984-94, assoc. dean Sch. Bus., 1980-82, dean, 1982-93, acting dean grad. Sch. of Communications, 1988-90, prof. info. systems, 1994-2001, prof. info. systems and ops. mgmt., 2001—05, prof. emeritus, 2005—, dept. chmn., 1999—2002, holder Stephen and Camille Schramm chair in bus., 2000—04. V.p. Eastalco Systems, 1971-72; faculty fin. div. Am. Mgmt. Assn., 1963-64; part-time lectr. Bellevue C.C., 1967-69, Shoreline Community Coll., 1968-72, Seattle U., 1971-72; program dir., summer program at Heslier (Rotterdam) 2000, 2001, Nat. Univ. Galway, 2003. Author: Management Information Systems in Higher Education: Case Studies at Three Universities, 1973, Effective Business Communications, 1976, 79, 91, Systems Development and Computer Concepts, 1977; Co-author: Management Control of Electronic Data Processing, 1965; assoc. editor: Industry Guides for Accountants and Auditors, 2 vols., 1980; mem. editorial rev. bd. Dickenson Pub. Co., 1974-75, Prentice-Hall, Inc., 1977-78, 87-88, 90-91, Reston Pub. Co., 1977-78, Jour. Acctg. Edn., 1981-83; featured roles (Amateur Comedy Club prodns.) Guys and Dolls, 1997, Our Town, 1997, The Fantastics, 1998, The Night of the Iguana, 2002, The Rainmaker, 2002, My Fair Lady, 2004; stage mgr. Some Assembly Required, 1999, Arcadia, 2000, Murder by the Book, 2002, Night Watch, 2005; house mgr.(plays) The Real Thing, 1997, The Tempest, 1997, play com., 2004-07, chmn., 2005-06; lead and featured roles (Warner Stage Co.) Footloose: The Musical, 2007, On Golden Pond, 2007. Death of a Salesman, 2008,(Goshen Players) Li'l Abner, 2008, The Rainmaker, 2008, Lysistrata, 2009, (Riverton Players) A Christmas Carol, 2008, (Thomaston Opera House Arts) 45 Seconds from Broadway; author numerous monographs; contbr. numerous articles to profl. jours. Mem. Mendelssohn Choir of Conn., Conn. Choral Soc.; Westchester Chordsmen, Litchfield Norwestones; bd. dirs. Goshen Players, 2009-. Recipient cert. of appreciation Am. Mgmt. Assn., 1966, cert. of merit for disting. service to Mgmt. Scis., 1969, for disting. service to info. systems profession, 1973; Merit award Assn. Systems Mgmt., 1971, Achievement award, 1972, Internat. award World Assn. for Case Method Rsch. and Application, 1996, 2002; cert. for service City of Seattle, 1973; named Outstanding Young Man Am., 1970, One of 300 Outstanding Alumni, Whitman Coll., 1979; Kellogg fellow, 1971-72, Price Waterhouse faculty fellow, 1976. Mem.: NSPE, AAUP, Am. Acctg. Assn., Soc. Mgmt. Info. Systems, NY Soc. Profl. Engrs., Soc. Cert. Data Processors, Assn. Computing Machinery, Data Processing Mgmt. Assn., Assn. Systems Mgmt. (sec. 1968—69, v.p. 1969—70, pres. Pacific NW chpt. 1970—71), Inst. Mgmt. Accts. (assoc. dir. NY chpt. 1963—64, Seattle chpt. 1967—70, assoc. dir. NY chpt. 1975—85), Acad. Creative Tchg. (exec. bd. 1998—), World Assn. Case Method Rsch. and Application (adv. bd. 1996—99, exec. bd. dirs. 1999—, vice-chair internat. case stds. setting com. 2001—), Am. Inst. Indsl. Engrs. (dir. Seattle chpt. 1967—70, chmn. regional conf. 1969), Oliver Wolcott Libr., Westchester County Hist. Soc. (trustee 2005—, treas. 2009—), Litchfield Hist. Soc. (mus. vol.), Amateur Comedy Club (play com. mem. 2004—07, exec. com. mem. 2005—06, chmn. 2005—06), Bronxville Field Club, Beta Alpha Psi, Phi Delta Kappa, Mu Gamma Tau, Beta Gamma Sigma, Phi Delta Theta (province pres. 1986—87). Avocations: theater, singing. Home: 39 Sheldon Ln Litchfield CT 06759 Personal E-mail: rkmartin6221@msn.com.

MARTIN, RICHARD H., principal; b. Washington, Pa., Feb. 25, 1956; s. Henderson E. and Margaret Roxena Martin; m. Lori Confer Martin, Nov. 6, 1982. BS in Edn., Calif. State Coll., 1978, MA in Comms., 1980; EdD in Edn. Adminstrn., W.Va. U., 1991. Cert. tchr., supr., prin., supt. schs. Asst. to dean Calif. State Coll., 1978-80; tchr. Turkeyfoot Sch. Dist., Confluence, Pa., 1980-81, Somerset (Pa.) Sch. Dist., 1981-82, Frazier Sch. Dist., Perryopols, Pa., 1982-85, dept. chair, 1985-90, prin., 1990-96, Mt. Lebanon Sch. Dist., Pitts., 1996-99, Bethlehem Ctr. High Sch., 1999—. Cons. W.Va. Dept. of Edn., Charleston, 1990—, Intermediate Unit #1, Calif., 1982-90; mem. safety coun. Mt. Lebanon Sch.

Dist., Pitts., 1997—; trainer in IDEA Allegheny Intermediate Unit, Pitts., 1998—; adj. asst. prof. W.Va. U., 1991—. Contbr. articles to profl. jours. Recipient Cmty. Svc. award Perrypolis Heritage Soc., 1991. Mem. NASSP/PASSP, AASA, ASCD, CEFPI, Mt. Lebanon Found., Masons (floor officer 1985—), Monessen Commandary Knights Templar (floor officer 1985—), Shriners, Uniontown Masons, Phi Delta Kappa. Avocations: fly fishing, hunting, good cigars. Home: 225 Nobles Rd Brownsville PA 15417-9283 Personal E-mail: martinlm@peoplepc.com.

MARTIN, RICHARD JAY, medical educator; b. Detroit, May 16, 1946; s. Peter Aaron and Tillie Jean (Munch) M.; m. Helene Iris Horowitz, Dec. 23, 1967; children: Elizabeth Hope, David Evan. BS, U. Mich., 1967, MD, 1971. Diplomate Am. Bd. Internal Medicine and Pulmonary Disease. Intern, Ariz., 1971-72; resident Tulane U., New Orleans, 1974-76; pulmonary fellow, 1976-78; asst. prof. medicine U. Okla., Okla. City, 1978-80, U. Colo., Denver, 1980-85, assoc. prof., 1985-92, prof., 1992—. Dir. Cardiorespiratory Sleep Rsch., Nat. Jewish Health, Denver, 1980-89, staff physician, 1980-, head divsn. pulmonary medicine, 1993-2005, vice-chair dept. medicine, 1997-2004, acting chair dept. medicine, 2004-2005, chair dept. medicine, 2006—. Author: Cardiorespiratory Disorders During Sleep, 1984, 2d edit., 1990, (with others) Current Therapy in Internal Medicine, 1984, Clinical Pharmacology and Therapeutics in Nursing, 1985, Interdisciplinary Rehabilitation of Multiple Sclerosis and Neuromuscular Disorders, 1984, Drugs for the Respiratory System, 1985, Current Therapy in Pulmonary Medicine, 1985, Abnormalities of Respiration During Sleep, 1986, Mitchell's Synopis of Pulmonary Medicine, 1987, Pulmonary Grand Rounds, 1990, Asthma and Rhinitis, 1994, The High Risk Patient: Management of the Critically Ill, 1995, Manual of Asthma Management, 1995, 2000, Severe Asthma: Pathogenesis and Clinical Management, 1995, Curret Pulmonology, 1995, Pulmonary and Respiratory Therapy Secrets, 1996, (book chpts.) Lung Biology in Health and Disease, 1995, 3d edit., 2000, Allergy, 1997, Asthma, 1997, Emergency Asthma, 1999, Difficult Asthma, 1999, Asthma and Rhinitis, 1999, Imaging of Diffuse Lung Disease, 2000, Manual of Asthma Management, 2000, Severe Asthma, 2001, Asthma Critical Debates, 2002, Inhaled Steroids in Asthma, 2002, The Merck Manual, 2002, Current Review of Asthma, 2003; editor: Nocturnal Asthma: Mechanisms and Interventions, 1993, Cardiothoracic Interrelationships in Clinical Practice, 1997; author, editor: Nocturnal Asthma: Mechanisms and Treatment, 1993, Combination Therapy for Asthma and Chronic Obstructive Pulmonary Disease, 2000; mem. editl. bd. Chronobiology Internat., 1997—, Am. Jour. Respiratory and Critical Care Medicine, 1994-98, Bronchial Asthma: Index and Review, 1996-97; assoc. editor: Clinical Care for Asthma, 1995-97; contbr. articles to profl. jours. Pres. Congregation Rodef Shalom, Denver, 1984-85; regional v.p. United Synagogues of Am., Denver, 1988-89. Recipient Best Paper in Internal Medicine award, Okla. Soc. Interna. Medicine, 1977—78, U. Okla. Gastroenterology sect, 1977, Amb. award, Nat. Jewish Med. and Rsch. Ctr., 2002; named Disting. Lectr., Royal Coll. Physicians and Surgeons Can., 1998, Cardio-Pulmonary Congress, Argentina, 1998, Assn. Argentina Allergy and Immunology, 2001; grantee Am. Lung Assn., Va., U. Okla. Lung Assn., NIH, Parker B. Francis Found.; Pulmonary fellow, Am. Lung Assn., 1977—79, James F. Hammarsten Outstanding fellow, U. Okla. Health Scis. Ctr., 1978. Mem. ACP, Am. Thoracic Soc., Am. Fedn. for Clin. Rsch., Am. Coll. Chest Physicians (Disting. scholar in respiratory health 2003-07, Colorado Pulmonary Hall of Fame, 2007), Colo. Trudeau Soc., Western Soc. Clin. Investigation. Avocations: biking, golf, Karate. Office: Nat Jewish Health 1400 Jackson St Denver CO 80206-2761 Office Phone: 303-398-1847, 303-398-1095. Business E-Mail: martinr@njhealth.org.

MARTIN, RICHARD KELLEY, lawyer; b. Tulsa, June 30, 1952; s. Richard Loye and Maxine (Kelley) M.; m. Reba Lawson, June 12, 1993; children from previous marriage: R. Kyle, Andrew J. BA, Westminster Coll., 1974; JD, So. Meth. U., 1977. Bar: Tex. 1977, U.S. Tax Ct. 1979. Ptnr. Akin, Gump, Strauss, Hauer & Feld, LLP, Dallas, 1977-95, Haynes and Boone LLP, Dallas, 1995—. Bd. dirs. Goodwill Industries, Dallas, 1986-2000, v.p., 1986-91; bd. dirs. Greater Dallas Youth Orchs., 1987-90; bd. dirs., v.p., pres. Big Bros. and Sisters Met. Dallas, 1988-91; bd. dirs. Tejas coun. Girl Scouts U.S., 1997-2001, Salvation Army, Dallas, 2003--. Mem. Tex. Bar Assn., Salesmanship Club Dallas. Republican. Methodist. Office: Haynes and Boone LLP 2505 N Plano Rd Ste 4000 Richardson TX 75082-4101 Office Phone: 972-739-8634. Business E-Mail: rick.martin@haynesboone.com.

MARTIN, RICHARD L., retired insurance executive; b. Franklin, NJ, Feb. 2, 1932; s. Richard Lewis and Elizabeth (Roe) M.; m. Susan Mazuy, June 20, 1970; children: David Cory, Scott Mazuy; m. Victoria Lee Morton, May 30, 1998; 1 stepchild, Robert M. Ferguson. BEd, U. Miami, 1958; MA, Columbia U., 1963. Chartered Property Casualty Underwriter. Educator Franklin (N.J.) Sch. Dist., 1958-60; mng. dir. Sparta (N.J.) Sch. Dist., 1960-66; adminstr. Orange (N.J.) Sch. System, 1966-71; chief exec. officer Montague (N.J.) Sch. Dist., 1971-72, Stanhope (N.J.) Sch. System, 1972-73; v.p. Selective Ins. Group, Branchville, N.J., 1973-87; pres., chief exec. officer Med. Malpractice Ins. Assn., NYC, 1987-98; ret., 1998. Chmn. N.J. Anti-Car Theft Com., Trenton, 1980-87; treas. N.J. Ins. News Svc., Newark, 1982-87; chmn. AIA-N.J. State Conf., Trenton, 1983-87. Contbr. several articles to mags. With USMC, 1952-54. Mem. CPCU, Am. Mgmt. Assn., Soc. Ins. Research, Soc. for Corp. Planning, City Midday, Newton Country, Branchville Rotary, Sons of Am. Revolution, Mayflower Soc. Presbyterian. Avocations: golf, hunting. Home: Two Plains Rd Augusta NJ 07822

MARTIN, RICHARD PETER, classics educator, consultant; b. Boston, May 19, 1954; s. Nicholas Richard and Marie Eileen (Daly) M.; children: Catherine, Thomas. AB, Harvard U., 1976, AM, 1978, PhD, 1981. Teaching fellow Harvard U., Cambridge, Mass., 1978-81; from asst. to assoc. prof. Princeton (N.J.) U., 1981-94, prof., 1994—99; Antony and Isabelle Raubitschek Prof. of Classics Stanford U., 2000—. Author: Healing, Sacrifice and Battle, 1983, The Language of Heroes, 1989, Myths of the Ancient Greeks, 2003; editor: Bulfinch, Mythology, 1991. Class of 1936 preceptor Princeton U., 1984-87. Devel. grantee Apple Computer Co., 1989. Fellow Onassis Found.; mem. Am. Philol. Assn., Celtic Studies Assn. of N.Am., Irish Texts Soc. Democrat. Roman Catholic. Office: Stanford Univ Bldg 110 Main Quad Stanford CA 94305-2145 Home Phone: 650-823-4771; Office Phone: 650-723-0479. Business E-Mail: rpmartin@stanford.edu.

MARTIN, RICKY (ENRIQUE MARTIN MORALES IV), vocalist, actor, producer, composer; b. San Juan, Dec. 24, 1971; children: Valentino, Matteo. Mem. Menudo, 1984—89; solo artist, 1991—. Singer: (albums) Ricky Martin (Spanish), 1991, Me Amaras, 1993, A Medio Vivir, 1995, Vuelve, 1998 (Grammy award for Best Latin Pop Album, two Billboard Latin Music awards), Ricky Martin, 1999 (two MTV Video Music awards, Teen Choice award Favorite Male Artist, two Billboard Music awards, Am. Latino Media Arts award for Male Entertainer of Yr., two World Music awards, two Latin MTV Video Music awards, two Latin Billboard awards, People's Choice award, five Grammy nominations), Sound Loaded, 2000 (Latin Grammy Award, three World Music awards, Blockbuster award, Radio Music award, MTV Europe award, two ACE awards, Alma award), La Historia, 2001, The Best of Ricky Martin, 2001, Almas del Silencio, 2003 (Am. Music award, Premio Lo Nuestro award), Life, 2005, Live: Black & White Tour, 2007, Ricky Martin MTV Unplugged, 2006 (Best Male Pop Vocal Album, Best Long Form Music Video, Latin Grammy awards, 2007); actor: (TV series) General Hospital, 1994—95; (Broadway plays) Les Miserables, 1996; (films) Les Diables, 2002. Founded Ricky Martin Found., San Juan, 2000, launched People for Children Initiative, 2004; Goodwill Ambassador UNICEF, 2004—. Recipient Hispanic Heritage award, Hispanic Heritage Found., 2002, Lifetime Achievement award, Univision Premios Lo Nuestro, 2004, Latin Billboard Spirit of Hope award, 2002, Alma Awards Lifetime Achievement award, 2003, Internat. Humanitarian award, Internat. Ctr. Missing & Exploited Children, 2005, State Dept. Internat. Hero, 2005, The Others prize for social svc., Salvation Army, 2006, Person of Yr., Latin Recording Acad., 2006, star, Hollywood Walk of Fame, 2007. Mem.: Latin Acad. Recording Arts and Scis., Nat. Acad. Recording Arts and Scis. Office: RM Entertainment Group 228 E 45th St Fl 11 New York NY 10017-3338 Business E-Mail: management@rmentgroup.com.

MARTIN, ROBERT BRUCE, chemistry professor; b. Chgo., Apr. 29, 1929; s. Robert Frank and Helen (Woelffer) M.; m. Frances May Young, June 7, 1953. BS, Northwestern U., 1950; PhD, U. Rochester, 1953. Asst. prof. chemistry Am. U., Beirut, Lebanon, 1953-56; research fellow Calif. Inst. Tech., 1956-57, Harvard U., 1957-59; asst. prof. chemistry U. Va., Charlottesville, 1959-61, assoc. prof., 1961-65, prof., 1965—, chmn. dept., 1968-71. Spl. fellow Oxford U., 1961-62; Program dir. Molecular Biology Sect., NSF, 1965-66 Author: Introduction to Biophysical Chemistry, 1964. Fellow AAAS; mem. Am. Chem. Soc. Home: 620 Sand Hill Rd #314D Palo Alto CA 94304

MARTIN, ROBERT DAVID, judge, educator; b. Iowa City, Oct. 7, 1944; s. Murray and G'Ann (Holmgren) Martin; m. Ruth A. Haberman, Aug. 21, 1966; children: Jacob, Matthew, David. AB, Cornell Coll., Mt. Vernon, Iowa, 1966; JD, U. Chgo., 1969. Bar: Wis. 1969, US Dist. Ct. (we. dist.) Wis. 1969, US Supreme Ct. 1973, US Dist. Ct. (ea. dist.) Wis. 1974. Assoc. Ross & Stevens, S.C., Madison, Wis., 1969-72, ptnr., 1973-78; chief judge U.S. Bankruptcy Ct. We. Dist. Wis., 1978—. Instr. gen. practice course U. Wis. Law Sch., 1974, 76, 77, 80, lectr. debtor/creditor course, 1981-82, 83, 85, 87, 2001, 07, 08, 09, farm credit seminar, 1985, advanced bankruptcy problems, 1989, 91, 96; co-chmn. faculty Am. Law Inst.-ABA Fin. and Bus. Planning for Agr., Stanford U., 1979; faculty mem. Fed. Jud. Ctr. Schs. for New Bankruptcy Judges, 1985-96; chmn. Ann. Continuing Legal Edn. Wis. Debtor Creditor Conf., 1981—. Author: (book) Bankruptcy: Annotated Forms, 1989; co-author: Secured Transactions Handbook for Wisconsin Lawyers and Lenders, Bankruptcy-Text Statutes Rules and Forms, 1992, Ginsberg and Martin on Bankruptcy, 4th edit, 1996. Chmn., bd. dirs., mem. exec. com. Luth. Social Svc. Wis. and Upper Mich.; bd. dirs., mem. exec. com. Turnaround Mgmt. Assn., 1997—2007. Mem.: Wis. State Bar, Nat. Bankruptcy Conf., Nat. Conf. Bankruptcy Judges (bd. govs. 1989—91, sec. 1993—94, v.p. 1994—95, pres. 1995—96), Am. Coll. Bankruptcy. Office: 120 N Henry Rm 340 PO Box 548 Madison WI 53701-0548 Office Phone: 608-264-5188.

MARTIN, ROBERT EDWARD, architect; b. Dodge City, Kans., Mar. 17, 1928; s. Emry and Alice Jane (Boyce) M.; m. Billie Jo Lange, Aug. 16, 1952 (div. Feb. 1970); m. Kathryn M. Arvanitis, June 26, 1971; children: Lynn, Amy, Blaine. Student, McPherson Coll., 1946-48; BArch, U. Cin., 1954. Registered architect, Ohio. Architect Samborn, Steketee, Otis & Evans, Inc., Toledo, 1956-58; prin. Schauder & Martin, Toledo, 1958-72, The Collaborative, Inc., Toledo, 1972-93. Mem. Bd. Examiners Archs., Ohio, 1985-95, pres., 1989-94; bd. examiners Nat. Coun. Archtl. Registration Bds., 1986-95, edn. com., 1992; chmn. site design divsn. Archtl. Registration Exam., 1989, 90, 91; mem. Nat. Coun. Archtl. Registration Bds. Grading, 1987-94; chmn. study of Toledo Fire & Rescue Dept., Corp. for Effective Govt., 1994. Artist numerous paintings. Mem. Toledo Planning Commn., 1971-74, Toledo Zoning Appeals Bd., 1973, Toledo Bd. Bldg. Stds., 1967-84, Citizens Fire Adv. Commn., 1974-80, Citizens Urban Area Adv. Commn., 1962, Toledo Area Coun. Govts., 1977-80, Com. of 100, Toledo, 1987-89, Spectrum Friends Fine Arts, Inc., Toledo; chmn. bd. Toledo Area Govtl. Rsch. Assn., 1981-90; chmn. Corp. for Effective Govt., Study of Toledo Fire and Rescue Dept., 1994; chmn. Cystic Fibrosis, Toledo. 1985. Served to capt. USAF, 1954-56. Recipient numerous watercolor awards. Fellow AIA (pres. Toledo chpt. 1966, Arch. of Yr. 1993), Archs. Soc. Ohio (pres. 1975), Ohio Watercolor Soc. (trustee 1999—), N.W. Ohio Watercolor Soc., Toledo Fedn. Art Socs. (pres. 1989, 90), Spectrum, Tile Club (pres. 2006—), Toledo Artists Club, NOONERS (pres. 2008) Sylvania Country Club, Toledo Club, Rotary, Masons, Shriners, Jesters. Mem. Ch. of Brethren. Avocation: painting. Home: 5119 Regency Dr Toledo OH 43615-2946 Office: 1700 N Reynolds Rd Toledo OH 43615-3628 Office Phone: 419-531-5753.

MARTIN, ROBERT WILLIAM, retired utilities executive; b. Toronto, Ont., Can., June 7, 1936; s. William George and Evelyn Irene (Phillips) M.; m. Patricia Lorraine Norris, June 27, 1959; children: Stephen Gregory, Robert Scott, Adrienne Christine Teron. BASc., U. Toronto, 1958. Pres., CEO, Consumers Gas, Toronto, 1980—92. Bd. dirs. Enbridge Inc., HSBC Bank Can., Allied Properties Income Trust. Hon. gov. York U.; bd. dir. York U. Found.; past chmn. Toronto Symphony Orch. Recipient Meritorious Svc. award, U. Toronto, 1983, Arbor award, U. Ontario, Queen's Jubilee medal, 125 Yrs. Confederators medal, Govt. of Can., 1992. Mem.: Assn. Profl. Engrs. Ont., Toronto Club, Mad River Golf Club. Home: 118 Farnham Ave Toronto ON Canada M4V 1H4 Office Phone: 416-972-0970.

MARTIN, ROBERT WILLIAM, econometrician; b. Elizabeth, NJ, Nov. 14, 1961; s. Edward Robert Martin and Vivienne Angela Schaul; m. Nancy Lee Lannan, Sept. 16, 2006. BA in English, U. N.C., 1984, BA in Econs., 1985; MA in Econs., Clemson U., 1989. Rsch. asst. dept. econs. Clemson (S.C.) U., 1988-89, lectr., policy analyst Ctr. Policy Studies, 1989-90; econometrician, exec. mgr. Bd. Econ. Advisors, Columbia, S.C., 1990—. Cons. Clemson U., 1990; adj. instr. Midlands Tech. Coll., Columbia, 1994—97; adj. faculty mem. of the yr. Sch. of Social & Behavioral Sciences, 1997; mem. S.C. budget and control bd. Grad. Leadership Acad., 2003. Contbr. articles to profl. jours. Mem. Am. Econ. Assn., Nat. Assn. Bus. Economists (Carolinas chpt. regional v.p. and sec., Omicron Delta Epsilon, Sigma Tau Delta. Avocations: golf, woodworking, music. Home: 6503 Christie Rd Columbia SC 29209-2049 Office: Bd Econ Advisors Rembert Dennis Bldg 1000 Assembly St Ste 442 Columbia SC 29201 Office Phone: 803-734-4637. Business E-Mail: robert.martin@bea.sc.gov.

MARTIN, ROBLEE BOETTCHER, retired cement manufacturing executive; b. St. Louis, Apr. 21, 1922; s. Henry W. and Esther (Boettcher); m. M. Lillian Seegraves, July 15, 1940; children: Mary Katherine (dec.), Bruce Daniel, Amy Lee. BS in Chem. Engring., Columbia U., 1943, MS in Chem. Engring., 1947; D.Sc. in Bus. Adminstrn. (hon.), Cleary Coll., 1962. Prodn. supr. Monsanto Chem. Co., St. Louis, 1946-49; dir. research and devel. Miss. Lime Co., Ste. Genevieve, Mo., 1949-59; pres. Dundee Cement Co., Mich., 1959-69; v.p. Fruehauf Corp.; gen. mgr. (Fruehauf Bldgs. div.), Detroit, 1969-72; pres. Presidents Assn. div. Am. Mgmt. Assn., NYC, 1972-74; pres. insulation div. Keene Corp., Princeton, NJ, 1974-76; chmn., chief exec. officer Keystone Cement Co., Bath, Pa., 1976-89, Giant Cement Co., Harleyville, SC, 1985-89; sr. v.p., dir. Giant Group Ltd., Beverly Hills, Calif., 1985-89. Served to lt. (j.g.) USNR, 1944-46, PTO. Mem.: Phi Lambda Upsilon, Tau Beta Pi, Sigma Xi. Baptist. Home: 2590 Elms Plantation Blvd Charleston SC 29406

MARTIN, RODNEY O., JR., insurance company executive; b. Portland; BSBA, Alfred U., 1974. Various mgmt. positions including pres. Conn. Mut. Ins. Svcs., 1975—95; pres., CEO Am. Gen. Life Ins. Co., NY, 1995—97, chmn., CEO, 1997—2000; sr. vice chmn. AIG Am. Gen. Co., 2000—01; pres., CEO AIG Am. Gen. Corp., 2001—06; exec. v.p. life ins. Am. Internat. Group, Inc. (AIG), NYC, 2002—; COO AIG Worldwide LIfe Ins., 2006—09; chmn. AIG Internat. Life & Retirement Services, 2009—. Office: American Internat Group Inc (AIG) 70 Pine St New York NY 10270*

MARTIN, ROGER BOND, landscape architect; b. Virginia, Minn., Nov. 23, 1936; s. Thomas George and Audrey (Bond) M.; m. Janis Ann Kloss, Aug. 11, 1962; children: Thomas, Stephen, Jonathan. BS with high distinction, U. Minn., 1958; M. Landscape Arch., Harvard U., 1961. Asst. prof. U. Calif.-Berkeley, 1964-66; from assoc. prof. to prof. emeritus U. Minn., Mpls., 1966—99, prof. emeritus, 1999—; owner Roger Martin & Assoc., Mpls., 1966—68, 1999—; prin. InterDesign, Inc., Mpls., 1968-84, Martin & Pitz Assocs., Inc., Mpls., 1984-98. Vis. prof. U. Melbourne, Australia, 1979—80; vis. prof. coll. design U. Minn., Mpls., 2000—; sr. rsch. fellow Ctr. for Changing Landscapes, Mpls., 2003—. Prin. works include Minn. Zool. Gardens, 1978 (merit award Am. Soc. Landscape Archs., 1978, Classic 25 Yrs. award, 2008), Mpls. Pkwy. Restorations, 1972—87 (merit award, 1978, Minn. Classic award Am. Soc. Landscape Archs., 1994), South St. Paul Ctrl. Sq., 1978 (merit award, 1978), Festival Park, Chisholm, Minn., 1986 (merit award, 1986), Miss. Wildlife Refuge Visual Image assessment (merit award, 1989), Nicollet Island Park, Hennepin Avenue Master Plan, 1995 (merit award, 1995), North Shore Scenic Byway Plan, 2005 (Honor award, 2005), Gitchi Gammi Trail Master Plan, 2005 (Honor award, 2006), Red Lake River Access Master Plan, 2007 (Honor award, 2007). Recipient Fredrick Mann award for svc. to edn. U. Minn., 1990, Disting. Educator award Sigma Lambda Alpha, 1990, Bradford Williams medals for outstanding articles in landscape Architecture mag., 1968, 69, Minn. chpt. Lob Pine award for outstanding svc. to Landscape architecture, 1988, Mpls. Com. on Urban Environ. award for design of Whittier Park, 1997, exe. award Minn. River Trails Master Plan, 2008; fellow Am. Acad. in Rome, 1962-64, Vawed Pl. award Minn. Zool. Gardens, 2008. Mem. Am. Soc. Landscape Archs. (pres. Minn. chpt. 1970-72, trustee 1980-84, nat. pres. 1987, chmn.-elect coun. fellows 1991, chmn. 1992-94, past chmn. 1994-96, Pub. Svc. award 1985, Minn. chpt. Classic award 1994, 1st Valued Places award 2005, Mpls. Pky. Reconstrn. Sys. Design, Minn. Chpt. ASLA Valued Places award, 2008 Nat. Coun. Instrs. Landscape Architecture (pres. 1973-74), Can. Soc. Landscape Archs. (hon.). Home and Office: 2912 45th Ave S Minneapolis MN 55406-1829 Business E-Mail: marti009@umn.edu.

MARTIN, ROGER HARRY, retired college president; b. NYC, June 26, 1943; s. Edwin Diller and Emma (Neuenburg) M.; m. Susan Bradford, Aug. 29, 1970; children: Katherine R., Emily G. BA, Drew U., 1965; BD, Yale U., 1968, STM, 1969; DPhil, Oxford U., Eng., 1974. Program officer Edn. Incentive Program, NYC, 1969-70; devel. officer NYU, 1970-71, 75-76; asst. dir. devel. Rensselaer Polytech Inst., Troy, NY, 1974-75; asst. prof. history, exec. asst. to pres. Middlebury (Vt.) Coll., 1976-80; assoc. dean Harvard Div. Sch., Cambridge, Mass., 1980-86; prof. history, pres. Moravian Coll., Bethlehem, Pa., 1986-97; pres. Randolph-Macon Coll., 1997—2006, ret., 2006. Pres. Academic Collaborations, Inc. Author: Evangelicals United: Ecumenical Stirrings in Pre-Victorian Britain, 1795-1830, 1983. Bd. dirs. Brit. Schs. and Univs. Found., NYC. Mem. Harvard Club (N.Y.C.). Mem. Soc. Of Friends. Avocations: skiing, running. Home: 1321 Crown Ct Mamaroneck NY 10543

MARTIN, ROGER HEMENWAY, artist, educator; b. Sept. 3, 1925; s. Roger Hemenway and Ellie Emelia (Oker) M.; m. Joan Catherine Fertig, June 19, 1954; children: Christopher, Rachel, Mari; m. Ann O'Grady, Sept. 23, 1990. Diploma with honors, Boston Mus. Sch., 1950; DFA (hon.), Montserrat Coll., 1998. Tchr. New Eng. Sch. Art, Boston, 1966-70; founding mem., assoc. prof. Montserrat Coll. Art, Beverly, Mass., 1970—91, prof. ameritus, 1991—; mem. faculty Gordon Coll., Wenham, Mass., 1976-84. One-man shows include Carl Siembab Gallery, Boston, 1969, Eugenics Gallery, Magnolia, Mass., 1969, Manchester (Mass.) Art Assn., 1970, 83, Marion (Mass.) Art Ctr., 1975, Galleria Roseanna, Boston, 1976, Stagecoach Ho. Gallery, Gloucester, Mass., 1977, Montserrat Sch. Visual Art Gallery, Beverly, 1979, Retrospective, 1990, Pingree Sch. Gallery, South Hamilton, Mass., 1980, Orphanos Gallery, Boston, 1987-88; exhibited in group shows at Rockport Art Assn., 1954-75, 80—, De Cordova and Dana Mus., 1965, Inst. Contemporary Art, Boston, 1964, Carl Siembab Gallery, Boston, 1968, 69, Eugenics Gallery, Magnolia, 1969, Phoenix Gallery, 1969, Montserrat Sch. Visual Art, 1970-83, Doll and Richards Gallery, Boston, 1973-75, Sch. St. Gallery, Rockport, 1983, 85, Orphanos Gallery, Boston, 1987-88, Judi Rotenberg Gallery, Boston, 1988-89; commns. include Prose and Poetry, Child Life Mag.; contbr. articles to profl. jours.; illustrator Beacon Press, New Yorker Mag., N.Y. Times, Atlantic Monthly; woodcuts and paintings United Ch. Christ; case designer and carvings Fisk pipe organs Harvard U., Cambridge, Mass., Ho. Hope Presbyn. Ch., St. Paul, Pohick Ch., Lorton, Va., Stanford (Calif.) U., New Bern, N.C.; author: Rockport Remembered, 1997, A Rockport Album, 1998, Rockport Recollected, 2001. Mem. Rockport Fire Dept., 1960-83, capt. 1970-83; mem. Planning Bd. and Appeals Bd., Rockport. With USCG, 1942-46. Democrat. Home: 29 Penryn Way Rockport MA 01966 Personal E-mail: boppi2@comcast.net.

MARTIN, ROGER JOHN, computer scientist; b. Ft. Atkinson, Iowa, Sept. 11, 1947; s. Raymond Charles and Linda R. (Kuennen) M.; m. Jane Degnan, Nov. 21, 1970; children: John, Kathryn, Susan, Jacquelyn. BS in Computer Sci., Iowa State U., 1969, MS in Computer Sci., 1971. Computer specialist Naval Ship R & D Ctr., Bethesda, Md., 1971-76; supervisory sys. analyst Exec. Office of Pres., Washington, 1976-82; computer scientist, mgr. software engring. group Inst. Computer Scis. and Tech., Nat. Inst. Stds. and Tech., Washington, 1982-92, chief sys. and software tech. divsn., 1993-95, mgr. software methods, 1995-96; mgr. stds. strategy. Sun Microsys., Palo Alto, Calif., 1996—2002; dir. stds. AOL, LLC, Dulles, Va., 2002—. Program co-chmn. Conf. on Software Maintenance, 1985, gen. mgr., 1987; gen. chmn. Computer Stds. Comf., 1988. Soccer coach Montgomery Country Recreation Dept., Rockville, Md., 1979-83; treas., del. Mill Creek Towne Elem. Sch. PTA, Rockville, 1981-84, pres., 1986-87; Magruder clustr PTA coord., 1984-856; leader Cub Scouts Am., Rockville, 1983-84, asst. troop scoutmaster, 1984-92. Recipient award for tech. excellence Interagy. Com. on Info. Resources Mgmt., 1989, Fed. Computer Week 100 award, 1992, cert. of recognition Nat. Bur. Stds., 1983, bronze medal Dept. Commerce, 1984, silver medal, 1989, Hans Karlsson award IEEE, 1995, Standards Medallion, 1992. Mem. Assn. for Computing Machinery, IEEE Computer Soc. (chmn. working group on test methods for POSIX 1986-93, tech. com. on conformance testing 1989-94, mem. tech. com. on operating sys. project mgmt. com. 1991-93, cert. of recognition 1987, Meritorious Svc. award 1991, Stds. medal 1992). Home: 1102 Round Pebble Ln Reston VA 20194-1002 Office: AOL 44900 Prentice Dr Sterling VA 20166 Office Phone: 703-265-6203. E-mail: roger.martin@corp.aol.com.

MARTIN, ROLAND S., journalist, former editor; b. Houston, Nov. 14, 1968; m. Jacquie Hood. BS in Journalism, Tex. A&M, 1991; student, La. Bapt. U. Owner, pub. Dallas-Fort Worth Heritage; mng. editor Houston Defender, Dallas Weekly; county govt. & neighbors reporter Austin Am.-Statesman, 1991—93; city hall reporter Fort Worth Star-Telegram, 1993—95; morning drive reporter KRLD-AM, 1995; news dir., morning anchor KKDA-AM, Dallas, 1995—98; founding editor BlackAmericaWeb.com, 2001, Savoy mag., 2002—04; exec. editor, gen. mgr. Chgo. Defender, 2004—07; host The Roland S. Martin Show, WVON-AM, Chgo.; commentator TV One Cable Network, 2005—; contbr. CNN, 2007—. Author: (books) Speak, Brother! A Black Man's View of America, 2002, Listening to the Spirit Within: 50 Perspectives on Faith, 2007; appeared on MSNBC, FOX News, Court TV, BET Nightly News, NPR, and numerous others. Recipient Edward R. Murrow award, Radio TV News Dirs., Image award, NAACP, 2008; named to Power 150, Ebony mag., 2008. Mem.: Am. Soc. Newspaper Editors, Nat. Assn. Black Journalists, Alpha Phi Alpha. Office: TV One Cable Network Creators Syndicate 5777 W Century Blvd Ste 700 Los Angeles CA 90045 also: WVON-AM 1000 E 87th St Chicago IL 60619 Office Phone: 310-337-7003. Office Fax: 310-337-7625.

MARTIN, RUSSELL (NATHAN COLTRANE JEANSON), JR., professional baseball player; b. East York, Ont., Feb. 15, 1983; s. Russell Martin, Sr. and Suzanne (Jeanson) Martin. Attended, Chipola Jr. Coll., Marianna, Fla. Catcher LA Dodgers, 2006—. Recipient Gold Glove award, 2007, Silver Slugger award, 2007; named to Nat. League All-Star Team, 2007. Achievements include breaking the Dodgers' franchise record for stolen bases by a catcher. Mailing: LA Dodgers 1000 Elysian Park Ave Los Angeles CA 90012

MARTIN, RUTH L., pharmacologist; b. Cuba, Mo. d. Alfred J. and Violette J. Heyer; m. Ron Martin; 1 child, Nathaniel. PhD, Nothwestern U., Evanston, Ill., 1993. Sr. rsch. pharmacologist Abbott, Abbott Pk, Ill., 2002—03, assoc. rsch. investigator, 2003—. Rsch. pharmacologist Abbott, 2000—02. Office: Abbott 100 Abbott Pk Rd Abbott Park IL 60064-6119 Office Fax: 847-938-5286.

MARTIN, SANDRA HANCOCK, language educator; b. Washington, Aug. 7, 1940; d. Hugh Trenwith Hancock and Rose Alice Todd; m. John David Martin, Nov. 8, 1939; children: Todd David, Andrew Thomas. BA in Spanish, Coll. William and Mary, Williamsburg, Va., 1962; MAT in Spanish, U. Fla., Gainesville, 1966. Cert. tchr. NJ, 1973. Spanish tchr. Ramsey Sch. Dist., NJ, 1973—2003; adj. prof. Spanish Ramapo Coll. NJ., Mahwah, 2004—. Contbr. articles to profl. jours. Taught art history, vol. Bergen County Jail, Hackensack, NJ, 1995—2006. Mem.: Am. Assn. Tchrs. Spanish and Portuguese. Office: Ramapo Coll NJ AIS 505 Ramapo Valley Rd Mahwah NJ 07430 Business E-Mail: smartin@ramapo.edu.

MARTIN, SIVA, lawyer; b. Chgo., Oct. 26, 1925; s. Leon and Goldie (Baronian) M.; m. Mary Kaprelian, Aug. 12, 1952; children: Robert, Jack. BS, Loyola U., 1950; MA, Northwestern U., 1951; JD, DePaul U., 1953. Bar: Ill. 1953. Loan officer Nat. Blvd. Bank, Chgo., 1955-62; v.p. Ill. State Bank, Chgo., 1962-73; sole practice Chgo., 1973—. Dist. chmn. Boy Scouts Am., Chgo., 1957; pres. Chgo. Chpt. Armenian Gen. Benevolent Union, 1978-80. Mem. ABA, Ill. State Bar Assn., Chgo. Bar Assn., Chgo. Mortgage Attys., Northwest Real Estate Bd. Democrat. Mem. Apostolic Ch. Club: Lions. Home: 6550 N Kenton Ave Lincolnwood IL 60712-3433 Office Phone: 773-283-5688.

MARTIN, STANLEY ALLEN, lawyer; b. Logansport, Ind., Apr. 9, 1955; s. Richard James and Helen Elizabeth M.; m. Kellie Lea McCabe, Aug. 14, 1988. BS, MIT, 1977; JD, Boston Coll., 1984. Bar: Mass. 1985, U.S. Dist. Ct. Mass. 1985, U.S. Ct. Appeals (1st cir.) 1985, N.H. 1986, U.S. Dist. Ct. N.H. 1987. Prin. Stan Martin, Designer/Builder, Andover, Mass., 1977-84; assoc. Gadsby & Hannah LLP, Boston, 1984-91, ptnr., 1992—2001, Holland & Knight LLP, Boston, 2001—. Lectr. Northeastern U., Boston, 1989—95, MIT, 2000—01. Author: Mechanic's Liens, Performance and Payment Bonds under Massachusetts Law, 1989, 7th rev. edit., 1996; co-author: Architect-Engineer Liability Under Massachusetts Law, 1985, 5th rev. edit., 1990; editor: Construction Law handbook, 2nd edit.(Wolters Kluwer), 2008; contbg. author ann. Aspen Construction Law Update, 1995—; contbr. articles to profl. jours. Bd. dirs. Andover Com./A Better Chance-ABC, 1981—84, Associated Gen. Contractors of Mass., 1999—2001, Boston Archtl. Ctr., 2000—04, Edgewood Retirement Cmty., 2001—. Mem. ABA (pub. contract sect., chair region I 1990-96), Am. Arbitration Assn. Constrn. Industry Panel, Mass. Bar Assn. (chair pub. law sect. 1993-94), Internat. Bar Assn., N.H. Bar Assn. Home: 7 Pendant Ct Andover MA 01810-6305 Office: Holland & Knight LLP 10 St James Ave Boston MA 02116 E-mail: stan.martin@hklaw.com.

MARTIN, STEVE, actor, comedian; b. Waco, Tex., Aug. 14, 1945; s. Glenn and Mary Lee Martin; m. Victoria Tennant, Nov. 20, 1986 (div. 1994); m. Anne Stringfield, July 28, 2007 Student, Long Beach State Coll., UCLA. Exec. prodr. TV show Domestic Life, 1984. TV writer for Smothers Bros. (co-winner Emmy award 1969), Sonny and Cher, Pat Paulsen, Ray Stevens, Dick Van Dyke, John Denver, Glen Campbell; nightclub comedian; guest and host appearances NBC's Saturday Night Live, Tonight Show; appeared on Carol Burnett Show; starred in TV spls. Steve Martin: A Wild and Crazy Guy, 1978, Comedy is Not Pretty, 1980, Steve Martin's Best Show Ever, 1981; rec. comedy albums Let's Get Small, 1977 (Grammy award 1977), A Wild and Crazy Guy, 1978 (Grammy award 1978), Comedy is Not Pretty, 1979, The Steve Martin Brothers, 1982; actor: (films) The Absent Minded Waiter, 1977, The Jerk, 1979, Pennies From Heaven, 1981, Dead Men Don't Wear Plaid, 1982, The Man With Two Brains, 1983, All of Me, 1984 (Nat. Soc. Film Critics award best actor 1984, New York Film Critics' Circle award best actor 1984), Three Amigos, 1986 (also exec. prodr.), Roxanne, 1987 (also exec. prodr.), (Nat. Soc. Film Critics award best actor 1988, Los Angeles Film Critics' award best actor 1988), L.A. Story, 1991; actor (films) Sergeant Pepper's Lonely Hearts Club Band, 1978, The Muppet Movie, 1979, The Kids Are Alright, 1979, The Lonely Guy, 1984, Little Shop of Horrors, 1986, Planes, Trains and Automobiles, 1987, Dirty Rotten Scoundrels, 1988, Parenthood, 1989, My Blue Heaven, 1990, Father of the Bride, 1991, Grand Canyon, 1991, Housesitter, 1992, Leap of Faith, 1993, Mixed Nuts, 1994, A Simple Twist of Fate, 1994, Sgt. Bilko, 1995, The Spanish Prisoner, 1998, Bowfinger, 1999, Joe Gould's Secret, 2000, Novocaine, 2001, Bringing Down the House, 2003, Looney Tunes: Back in Action, 2003, Cheaper by the Dozen, 2003, Jiminy Glick in La La Wood, 2004, Shopgirl, 2005 (also writer, prodr.), Cheaper by the Dozen 2, 2005, The Pink Panther, 2006 (also writer), Baby Mama, 2008, The Pink Panther 2, 2009 (also writer); (theatre) Waiting For Godot, 1988; (TV movies) And the Band Played On, 1993, Rutles 2: Can't Buy Me Lunch, 2002; (TV appearances) 30 Rock, 2008; screenwriter (films) Easy Money, 1983, Bowfinger, 1999, Traitor, 2008; author: Cruel Shoes, 1977, Pure Drivel, 1998, Shopgirl, 2001; playwright Picasso at the Lapin Agile, 1993; author: (children's books) The Alphabet From A To Y With Bonus Letter Z!, 2007, (autobiography) Born Standing Up, 2007; musician (albums) The Crow: New Songs for the Five-Sting Banjo, 2009. Trustee L.A. Mus. Art. Recipient Georgie award, Am. Guild Variety Artists, 1977, 1978, Grammy award, 1978, Mark Twain prize for Am. Humor, 2005, Kennedy Ctr. Honors, John F. Kennedy Ctr. for Performing Arts, 2007; named one of 50 Most Powerful People in Hollywood, Premiere mag., 2006. Office: PO Box 929 Beverly Hills CA 90213

MARTIN, SUE ANN, theater educator; BA, Wayne State U., 1963, MA, 1965, PhD, 1969. Prof. speech & theatre U. Windsor, Ont., Canada, 1971—81, dir. sch. drama, 1981—91, dean arts, 1991—97; dean comm. & fine arts Ctrl. Mich. U., Mt. Pleasant, 1997—; prodr., host Arts Almanac Ctrl. Mich. U. Pub. Radio, 1997—2008, co-host, Children's Bookshelf, 2006—. Exec. prodr. Mich. Story Festival, Mt. Pleasant, 2003—08. Co-author: Sprouts: Projects for Creative Growth in Children, 1981, Treasure Hunts: Classica. Literature for Children, 1983, Research Workout: Creative Training in Research Skills, 1984; contbr. articles in area of creativity and the creative process in artists profl. jours. Mem. Bd. Exec. Mich.Humaiti Coun., Mich. Assn. Broadcasters (award for radio feature 1999). Avocations: children's literature, storytelling. Office: Ctrl Mich U Dept of Comm & Dramatic Art 364 Moore Hall Mount Pleasant MI 48859 Business E-Mail: marti1sa@cmich.edu.

MARTIN, SUSAN KATHERINE, librarian; b. Cambridge, Eng., Nov. 14, 1942; came to U.S., 1950, naturalized, 1961; d. Egon and Jolan (Schonfeld) Orowan; m. David S. Martin, June 30, 1962. BA with honors, Tufts U., 1963; MS, Simmons Coll., 1965; PhD, U. Calif., Berkeley, 1983. Intern libr. Harvard U., Cambridge, Mass., 1963-65, systems libr., 1965-73; head systems office gen. libr. U. Calif., Berkeley, 1973-79; dir. Milton S. Eisenhower Libr. Johns Hopkins U., Balt., 1979-88, exec. dir. Nat. Commn. on Libraries and Info. Sci., 1988-90; univ. libr. Georgetown U., Washington, 1990-2001, tchr., cons., 2001—; pres. SKM Assocs., 2001—; cons. dir. Marstons Mills Pub. Libr., 2003—05, dir., 2005—08. Mem. libr. com. Princeton (N.J.) U., 1987—95; mem. vis. com. Harvard U. Libr., 1987—93, 1994—2000; bd. overseers for univ. libr. Tufts U., 1986—2001, Tufts U. Sch. Arts and Scis., 2001—06; cons. various librs. and info. cos., 1975—; mem. libr. adv. com. Hong Kong U. Sci. Tech., 1988—95; mem. acad. libr. adv. group U. Md. Sch. Librs. and Info. Scis., 1994—96; mem. adv. bd. ERIC, 1990—92; mem. Chadwyck-Healey N.Am. Adv. Com. on Lit. Online, 1997—99; vice chair, chair Chesapeake Info. and Rsch. Libr. Alliance, 1996—98; cons. libr. devel. & fundraising, 1998—; spkr. in field; mem. adv. bd. Georgetown U. Libr., 2001—. Author: Library Networks: Libraries in Partnership, 1986—87; editor: Jour. Libr. Automation, 1972—77; co-editor: Portal: Libraries and the Academy, 2000—04; mem. editl. bd. Portal: Libraries and the Academy, 2005—; mem. editl. bd.: Advanced Tech./Librs., 1973—93, Jour. Libr. Adminstrn., 1986—2000, Libr. Hi-Tech., 1989—93, Jour. Acad. Librarianship, 1994—99; contbr. articles to profl. jours. Trustee Phila. Area Libr. Network, 1980—81; bd. dirs. Universal Serials and Book Exch., 1981—82, v.p., 1983, pres., 1984; trustee Capital Consortium, 1992—95; mem. bd. Potomac Internet, 1995—96; pres., trustee Marstons Mills Pub. Libr., 2002—03, 2008—. Recipient Simmons Coll. Disting. Alumni award, 1977; named Samuel Lazerow disting. lectr., Drexel U., 1984, L.I. U., 2002; Coun. on Libr. Resources fellow, 1973. Mem.: ALA (coun. 1988—92, structure revision TF 1995—97, chair task force on external accrediting body 1999—2002), Assn. Coll. and Rsch. Librs. (pres. 1994—95, vis. program officer for scholarly com. 2002—03), Coalition for Networked Info. (leader working group 1990—92), Assn. Jesuit Colls. and Univ. Librs. (chair 1997—98), Libr. of Congress (optical disk pilot project adv. com. 1985—89), Assn. Rsch. Librs. (info. policy com. 1995—97, stats. com. 1998—2000), Libr. and Info. Tech. Assn. (pres. 1978—79, chair Frederick Kilgour award com. 2006—07), Rsch. Librs. Group (bd. govs. 1981—88, exec. com. 1985—87), Internat. Fedn. Libr. Assns. Commn. on Access to Info. and Freedom of Expression, Cranberry Shores Chorus (publicity coord. 2002—05, webmaster 2004—, pres. 2005—07), Sweet Adelines Internat. (region 1 mgmt. team 2005—), Cosmos Club (libr. com. 1988—2005), Phi Beta Kappa (chair Georgetown U. chpt. 2000—01). Home: 10 Colonial Farm Cir Marstons Mills MA 02648 Business E-Mail: martin@skmassociates.net.

MARTIN, TERRY MALONE, assistant principal; s. Perry Malone and Ruby Joan Martin; m. Malia Crystal Cowen, Nov. 1, 1997; 1 child, Jeremiah T. stepchildren: Stephen A. Sargent, Sean A. Sargent. EdB, Taccoa Falls Coll., Ga., 1982; MEd, Ga. State U., Atlanta, 1987, EdD in Adminstrn. and Supervision, 1996. Tchr. Clayton County Bd. Edn., Jonesboro, Ga., 1982—95; asst. prin. Fayetta County Schs., Fayetteville, Ga., 1995—96, Fulton County Schs., Fairboro, Ga., 2000—, Bethlehem Area Sch. Dist., Pa., 1997—98, prin., 1998—2000. Part-time prof. Clayton State U., Morrow, Ga., 2001—, adv. bd., 2004—. Coord. PRISE Video Series, 2000 (Telly award). Pres. Whitewater HS Tip Off Club, Fayetteville, 2005—06. Named Outstanding Young Man Am., 1982; named to Hall of Fame, Toccoa Falls Coll., 1993. Mem.: ASCD. Conservative. Baptist. Avocations: helicopter flight, auto restoration. Office: Bear Creek Mid Sch 7415 Herdon Rd Fairburn GA 30213

MARTIN, THOMAS CHARLES, pediatrician; b. Detroit, Jan. 3, 1951; s. Robert Clark and Therese Martin Martin; m. Judith Avery Josian Martin, Sept. 20, 1987; children: Nicole Marie, Lavren Therese. BA, Cornell U., Ithaca, 1973; MD, U. Mich., Ann Arbor, 1977. Cert. pediatrics, in addiction medicine. Pediat. resident Wash. U., St. Louis, 1977—79, pediat. cardiac fellow, 1979—83, asst. prof., 1984—91; cons. pediat. Holbertion Hosp., St. Johns, 1991—2007; coord. rsch. Crossroad Ctr., St. Johns, 1998—; pediat. hospitalist Eastern Main Med. Ctr., Bangor, Maine, 2007—. Asst. prof. U. Rochester, 1994—2004; clin. prof. Am. U., Coll. Medicine, Antigua, 2005—07. Contbr. articles to numerous profl. jours. Physician- Devel. Assesment Clin. Amazing Grace Home, Antigua, 1994—2007. Fellow: Am. Soc. Addiction Medicine, Am. Acad. Pediat., Am. Coll. Cardiology. Avocations: reading, writing. Office: Eastern Main Med Ctr 489 State St, P O Box 404 Bangor ME 04402

MARTIN, THOMAS JOHN, pediatrician, sports medicine physician; b. Greensburg, Pa., July 4, 1934; s. John William and Mary DeTar Martin; m. Lois Darlene Miller, June 20, 1992; children: Jack T., Susan L. O'Malley, James S., David S. BS, Franklin and Marshall Coll., Lancaster, Pa., 1956; MD, U. Pitts., 1960. Diplomate Am. Bd. Pediats. Gen. practice medicine, Slippery Rock, Pa., 1961—62, 1964—65; pediat. resident Children's Hosp. of Pitts., 1965—67; assoc. in pediats. Geisinger Med. Ctr., Danville, Pa., 1967—75, chmn. pediats., 1975—95; dir. inpatient pediats. Aultman Hosp., Canton, Ohio, 1995—97; team physician, prof. Pa. State U., University Park, 1997—2004, clin. prof. pediats., Milton S. Hershey Med. Ctr., 2005—; assoc. program dir. family practice residency The Williamsport (Pa.) Hosp., 2004—; prof. emeritus dept. orthop. and rehab. Hershey Med. Ctr., 2005—; dir. pediat. hosp. level II nursery svc., 2004—; vice chmn. pediat., 2008—. Adj. clin. assoc. prof. Jefferson Med. Coll., Phila.; team physician football, wrestling Pa. State U., University Park, 1997—2004; courtesy staff Lewistown (Pa.) Hosp., 1999—2004; active staff Nittery Med. Ctr., State College, Pa., 1997—2004, Children's Hosp. Med. Ctr. of Akron, Ohio, 1995—97; lectr. in field. Contbr. articles to profl. jours. Pres. Riverside Home and Sch., Pa., 1968—69; coach, organizer Danville H.S. Swim Team, 1974; pres. Riverside Home and Sch. Assn., 1968—69; mem. global mission com. Upper Susquehanna Synod Coun., 1999—; fin. com. Pine St. Luth. Ch., Danville, 1994—96, coun. mem., 1993—95, chmn. religious com., 1993—95; bd. dirs. Sunbury Area YMCA, Pa., 1976—84. Capt. US Army, 1962—64. Recipient Honors for Exceptional Svc. to Children and Youth, Nat. Child Labor Com., N.Y.C., 1995; named Citizen of the Yr., Elks, 1995; named to Geisinger's Pediat. Wall of Fame, 2005. Mem.: AMA, Nat. Wrestling Coaches Assn., Pa. Med. Soc. (continuing med. edn. accreditation surveyor 1988—93), Am. Coll. Sports Medicine, Am. Acad. Pediats. (com. on sports medicine and fitness 1998—2004, exec. com. sect. on sports medicine 1997—2003, chpt. chmn. 1980—82), Lycoming County Med. Soc., Am. Bd. Pediats. Lutheran. Avocations: running, skiing, swimming, concerts. Home: 23 E Hayes Crossing Belleville PA 17004 Office: Susquehanna Health System 777 Rural Ave Williamsport PA 17701 Home Phone: 717-667-2580; Office Phone: 570-321-2810. Business E-Mail: tmartin@susquehannahealth.org.

MARTIN, THOMAS LYLE, JR., academic administrator; b. Memphis, Sept. 26, 1921; s. Thomas Lyle and Malvina (Rucks) M.; m. Helene Hartley, June 12, 1943 (dec. Sept. 1983); children: Michele Marie, Thomas Lyle; m. Mildred L. Moore, June 5, 1984. B.E.E., Rensselaer Poly. Inst., 1942, M.E.E., 1948, D.Eng., 1967; PhD, Stanford U., 1951; DSc (hon.), So. Meth. U., 2004. Prof. elec. engring. U. N.Mex., 1948-53; prof. engring. U. Ariz., 1953-63, dean engring., 1958-63, U. Fla., Gainesville, 1963-66, So. Meth. U., Dallas, 1966-74; pres. Ill. Inst. Tech., Chgo., 1974-87, pres. emeritus. Capt. Signal Corps AUS, 1943-46. Mem. ASEE Hall of Fame. Fellow IEEE; mem. Nat. Acad. Engring. Achievements include being one of the founders of Dallas-Ft. Worth Internat. Airport. Home and Office: PO Box 167845 Irving TX 75016-7845

MARTIN, THOMAS MACDONALD, lawyer; b. Huntington, NY, Dec. 17, 1947; s. Raleigh Lloyd and Elizabeth Battle (Gutwein) M.; m. Sheila Lynn Wilkens, July 13, 1968. AAS in Bus. Adminstrn., SUNY, Selden, 1967; BS in Criminal Justice, SUNY, Westbury, 1976; JD, Touro Coll., 1986. Bar: Va. 1988, U.S. Ct. Appeals (4th cir.) 1988, U.S. Supreme Ct. 1993, U.S. Ct. Fed. Claims 1993, U.S. Ct. Appeals (fed. cir.) 1993, U.S. Ct. Mil. Appeals 1993; U.S. Dist Ct. (ea. dist.) Va. 2002; cert. fraud examiner. Customs officer, sky marshall U.S. Customs Agy. Svc., NYC, 1971-75; spl. agt. U.S. Dept. Agr., NYC, 1975-78; supervisory spl. agt. Office of Insp. Gen., NYC, 1978-81, asst. regional insp. gen. then regional insp. gen., 1981-86, dep. div. dir. Washington, 1986-88, chief internal affairs, 1988-91, sr. spl. agt. gen. investigations divsn., 1991-93, sr. spl. agt. program investigation divsn., 1993-98; ret. Fairfax, Va., 1998; pvt. practice law, 1998—; magistrate 19th Jud. Dist., Fairfax County, Va., 1999—2001. With USN, 1967-71. Mem. ATLA, ABA (litigation sect. 1989—), Fed. Bar Assn., Fairfax Bar Assn., Nat. Geog. Soc., Fed. Law Enforcement Officers Assn., Nat. Assn. Fraud Examiners. Methodist. Avocations: Karate, marksmanship, golf, fishing, reading. Personal E-mail: MARTINLAW1@excite.com.

MARTIN, THOMAS REED, medical educator, medical association administrator; b. Cin., Oct. 27, 1947; BA in Chemistry, Macalester Coll., St. Paul, 1969; MD, U. Pa., 1973. Cert. Pediat. Critical Care Medicine, Pediat. Pulmonology. Intern, pulmonary medicine U. Wash., Seattle, 1973—74, resident, 1974—77, fellow, pulmonary and critical care medicine, 1978—80, asst. prof. medicine, 1982-85, assoc. prof. medicine to prof. medicine, 1985—, vice chair dept. medicine, dir., Pulmonary Rsch. Training Prog., 1990—; chief medicine svc., prof. medicine VA Pugent Sound Health Care Sys., Seattle, 2000—. Vis. scientist, dept. immunology Scripps Rsch. Inst., La Jolla, Calif., 1989—90; vis. scientist, dept. biochemsitry Geneva Biomedical Rsch. Inst. & Hosp. U. Geneva (Switzerland), 1997—98. Contbr. several articles to profl. jours. Mem.: Am. Thoracic Soc. (former pres.). Office: Pulmonary Rsch Lab VA Med Puget Sound Heath Care Sys U Wash Box 358280-151L 1660 S Columbian Way Seattle WA 98108 Office Phone: 206-764-2504, 206-764-2219. Office Fax: 206-768-5289. E-mail: trmartin@u.washington.edu.

MARTIN, THOMAS RHODES, communications executive, writer, educator; b. Memphis, July 10, 1953; s. Otis Knox and Joe Anne Coggin Martin; m. Wanda C. Benderman, Dec. 1, 1984; children: Seth Knox, Cyrus Rhodes. BA, Vanderbilt U., Tenn., 1975. Sales communication writer Schering and Plough Corp., Memphis, 1976-78; media devel. specialist, Fed. Express Corp., Memphis, 1978-81, sr. media devel. specialist, 1981-82, mgr. of mgmt. comm., 1982-84, mng. dir. employee comm., 1984-92, mng. dir. pub. rels., 1992-95, v.p. corp. comm., 1995-96; v.p. corp. rels., ITT Industries, White Plains, NY, 1996-99, sr. v.p., dir. corp. rels., 1999—2007; sr. counselor Pulse Point Group, LA, 2007—; chair Adv. Coun. Dept. Comm., Coll. of Charleston, SC. Exec.-in-residence Dept. Comm. Coll. Charleston, 2007—. Contbg. editor Memphis mag., 1984—94, contbr. PR Week mag.; contbr. articles to profl. jours. Bd. dirs. Big Bros. and Big Sisters, Memphis, 1983—87, Memphis Oral Sch. for the Deaf, 1985—91, Leadership Memphis, 1986—87, 1992—96, Pub. Rels. Soc. Am. Found, 1999—2001; trustee Inst. for Pub. Rels., 1999—; bd. govs. Josephson Inst. Ethics. Recipient Journalism award, Sigma Delta Phi, 1983, Mobius Advt. award, 1998, NY ADDY Award, 2001; named to PR News Hall of Fame, 2006. Mem.: Arthur W. Page Soc. (bd. dirs. 2001—, pres. 2004—05), Pub. Rels. Soc. Am. (Silver Anvil award 1995, Bronze Anvil award 1996), Internat. Assn. Bus. Communicators, The Wisemen. Avocations: writing, backpacking, sailing, skiing, bicycling. Office: Coll Charleston Dept Comm 66 George St Charleston SC 29424 also: Pulse Point Group Ste 2000 8491 Sunset Blvd Los Angeles CA 90069 Office Phone: 843-953-6383. E-mail: tom@pulsepointgroup.com, martintr@cofc.edu.

MARTIN, THOMAS STEPHEN, lawyer; b. NYC, Aug. 31, 1946; s. Stephen Paul and Kathleen Mary (Redmond) M.; m. Lynne Kathryn Mallory, Oct. 2, 1968; children: Laura Kathryn, Mallory Anne. BA maxima cum laude, King's Coll., 1968; JD, U. Chgo., 1972. Bar: DC 1973. Assoc. Steptoe & Johnson, Washington, 1972-75; spl. asst. to asst. atty. gen., civil div. Dept. Justice, Washington, 1975-76, asst. to solicitor gen., 1976-78, dep. asst. atty. gen. civil div., 1978-80, acting asst. atty. gen. civil div., 1981-82; ptnr. Venable, Baetjer, Howard & Civiletti, Washington, 1982-83, Jenner & Block, Washington, 1983-90; ptnr. litigation group Shearman & Sterling LLP, Washington, 1990—, mng. ptnr., dir. Appellate and Supreme Ct. Practice Group; mem. adv. com. fed. rules of civil procedure, 1980-84. Chmn. com. admissions and grievances US Ct. Appeals (DC cir.), 1991—. Comment editor: U. Chgo. Law Rev, 1971-72. Mem. ABA, DC Bar Assn., Am. Law Inst. Office: Shearman & Sterling LLP 801 Pennsylvania Ave NW Ste 900 Washington DC 20004-2604 Office Phone: 202-508-8040. Office Fax: 202-508-8100. Business E-Mail: tmartin@shearman.com.

MARTIN, TOM, mayor, Lubbock, Texas; m. Karen Martin, 1969. Public information officer City of Lubbock, 1970—74, police officer, 1974—90, councilman from Dist. 5, 2002—06, mayor Tex., 2008—; chief of police San Marcos, Tex., 1990—92, Grapevine, Tex., 1992—98. Bd. mem. Lubbock Met. Transp. Planning Orgn., Ports-to-Plains Trade Corridor Coalition, Lubbock Scottish Rite Dyslexia Learning Ctr. Deacon Cumberland Presbyterian Church, fin. com.; mem. and past pres. Lubbock Internet Bus. Assn. Named Volunteer of Yr., Lubbock C. of C., 2000. Presbyterian. Office: Office of Mayor PO Box 2000 Lubbock TX 79457 Office Phone: 806-775-2010. Business E-Mail: TMartin@mail.ci.lubbock.tx.us.*

MARTIN, TONY, retired humanities educator; b. Port of Spain, Trinidad and Tobago, Feb. 21, 1942; arrived in U.S., 1969, naturalized; s. Claude G. and Vida Beryl M. Barrister in Law, Hon. Soc. Gray's Inn, London, 1965; BSc in econ. with honors, U. Hull, 1968; MA, Mich. State U., 1970, PhD, 1973. Bar: England 1966, Trinidad 1968. Asst. prof. history, African-Afro Am. studies U. Mich., Flint, 1971—73; assoc. prof. history and Africana studies Wellesley Coll., 1973—75, assoc. prof. Africana studies, 1975—79, prof. Africana studies, 1979—2007, prof. emeritus, 2007. Vis. prof. history U. Minn., 1975, The Colo. Coll., Colo. Springs, 1985-86; vis. prof. African-Am. Studies, Brown U., Providence, R.I., 1991, Brandeis U., Waltham, Mass., 1974, 81; hon. rsch. fellow U. of West Indies, Trinidad, 1986-87; lectr. DuBois-Padmore-Nkrumah, Ghana, 1990; cons. founds.; expert witness Congl. Hearings, 1987; guest lectr. numerous univs., U.S., Can., Caribbean, Australia, Africa, Eng.; featured spkr. Conf. of Intellectuals of Africa and its Diaspora, Dakar, Senegal, 2004; mem. editl. bd. Jour. African American History, Jour. Black Studies, Afro-Americans in NY Life and History. Author: Race First, 1976, Literary Garveyism, 1983, The Pan-African Connection, 1983, Amy Ashwood Garvey, 2007, Marcus Garvey, Hero, 1983, Rare Afro-Americana (with Wendy Ball), 1981, The Jewish Onslaught, 1993; editor or compiler: Poetical Works of Marcus Garvey, 1983, African Fundamentalism, 1991, Message to the People, 1986, In Nobody's Backyard:The Grenada Revolution in its Own Words 1985;reviewer articles for profl. jours.; contbr. articles to profl. jours., encys., and other ref. books, intro. to E. Franklin Frazier and Eric Williams, eds, The Economic Future of the Caribbean, 2004; contbg. editor profl. jours.; reviewer of manuscripts for various publishers. Pres. Union of West Indian Students in Gt. Britain and No. Ireland, 1966—68. Recipient Rsch. award Am. Philos. Soc., Phila., 1990, Cmty. award Henry Sylvester Williams award from the Emancipation Support Com., Trinidad; disting. historian award, African American Inst., Northeastern U. Mem. Assn. of Caribbean Historians (exec. bd. mem. 1985-87), African Heritage Studies Assn., Assn. for the Study of Classical African Civilizations (John Henrik Clarke Living Legacy award), Organ. Am. Historians, Nat. Coun. Black Studies (v.p. New Eng. region, 1984-86), Caribbean Cultural Ctr., NY (bd. dir. 1988-90), Assn. for Study of African Am. Life and History. Personal E-mail: amartin@wellesley.edu.

MARTIN, VICKI JOAN, biology professor; BS, U. N.C., Charlotte, 1970—74; MS, Wake Forest U., NC, 1974—76, PhD, 1977—80. Postdoctoral fellow U. Alta., Edmonton, Canada, 1980—81; asst. prof. U. Louisville, Ky., 1981—83; asst. to assoc. prof. U. Notre Dame, Ind., 1983—99; prof. biology Appalachian State U., Boone, NC, 1999—, chair, dept. biology, 1999—2004. Dir., optical lab. U. Notre Dame, Notre Dame, 1983—99, dir. grad. studies, dept. biology, 1990—92; cons. Earth and Sky NPR, 1999—. Contbr. chapters to books, articles to profl. jours. and pubs. Recipient Career Advancement award, NSF, 1987—90, Frank O'Malley Undergraduate Tchg. award, U. Notre Dame, 1995—96, 100 Scholar's Rsch. award, Appalachian State U., 2004. Mem.: Am. Micros. Soc. (pres. 2009—), Nat. Coun. on Undergraduate Rsch. (elected councilor 2005—). Achievements include research in demonstration of visual pigments in primitive eyes of invertebrates. Office: Appalachian State Univ 572 Rivers St Boone NC 28608

MARTIN, W. TERRY, librarian; b. Tuscaloosa, Ala., Sept. 5, 1948; s. W. Harry and Eleanor (Ambrose) M.; m. Carol Prewitt, May 25, 1973; 1 child, W. Brian. AB, Samford U., 1970; MA, SAmford U., 1977; MLS, U. Ala., 1973. Libr. tech. svcs. Samford U., Birmingham, Ala., 1973-79; circulation and tech. svcs. libr. Southeastern Bapt. Theol. Sem., Wake Forest, N.C., 1979-85; dir. libr. svcs. Georgetown (Ky.) Coll., 1985-93; dir. libr. La. Coll., Pineville, 1993—. Contbr. articles to profl. jours. Mem. So. Bapt. Libr. Assn. (pres. 1990-91), Am. Libr. Assn., Assn. Christian Libr., Assn. Baptist Libr. & Archivists, La. Libr. Assn. Baptist. Avocations: camping, travel, genealogy, local history. Office: LA Coll Lib 1140 Coll Dr Pineville LA 71359-0001

MARTIN, WILFRED WESLEY FINNY, psychologist, property owner and manager; b. Rock Lake, ND, Dec. 3, 1917; s. William Isaac and Anna Liisa (Hendrickson-Juntunen) M.; m. Stella Helland, Sept. 25, 1943; children: Sydney Wayne, William Allan. BA, Jamestown Coll., 1940; army specialized tng. program, Hamilton Coll., 1944; MS, EdD, U. So. Calif., 1956. Highsch. prin., coach pub. sch., Nekoma, ND, 1940—42; contact rep., psychologist VA, LA, 1946—49, psychologist, chief rehab., 1972—77; guidance dir. Moorhead (Minn.) Pub. Schs., 1951—53; instr. Concordia Coll., Moorhead, 1952—53; from intern to resident Fargo VA Hosp., ND, 1953—58; psychologist VA, Fargo, 1953—58; assoc. Sci. Rsch. Assoc./IBM, Boulder, Colo., 1958—65, regional dir. LA, 1966—72; owner, mgr. Martin Investments, Huntington Beach, Calif., 1977—. Adjutant U. Miss., Oxford, 1942; trustee Wilfred W. and Stella Martin Trust, Huntington Beach, 1991. Author: Veterans Administration Work Simplification, 1948, 57. Charter mem. Rep. Presdl. Task Force, 1980; adv. sr. ptnrs. bd. dirs. U. Calif. Med. Sch., Irvine, 1990; donor Dr. and Mrs. W.W. Martin Endowment, Jamestown Coll., N.D., 1985; mem. Assocs. of James Ford Bell Libr., U. Minn., Pres.'s Cir. Finlandia U. With U.S. Army, 1942-45. Mem. Am. Psychol. Assn., Cardinal & Gold U. So. Calif., Jamestown Coll. Heritage Circle (charter, Pres.'s Cir.), Finlandia U. Suomi Coll. Second Century Soc., Elks. Republican. Lutheran. Avocations: reading, Finnish heritage, swimming, sports, card playing. Home: PO Box 5445 Huntington Beach CA 92615-5445 *The dominant force in my life is described by the Finnish word SISU, which means perseverence, determination, competitiveness, and tenacity toward goal-oriented achievements. Due to SISU, faith, and hard work I enjoy an active happy successful life.*

MARTIN, WILLIAM A., environmental engineer, researcher; BSChemE, Purdue U., West Lafayette, Ind., 1995; MS in Environ. Engring., U. Ill., Urbana-Champaign, 2003. EIT Ind., 1995. Engr. officer US Army, 1995—2003; staff scientist, environ. engr. Applied Rsch. Assocs. Inc., Vicksburg, Miss., 2004—06; rsch. environ. engr. US Army ERDC-EL, Vicksburg, 2006—07, supr. environ. engr., 2007—. Author. Recipient Army Commendation medal, US Army, 1995—2003, Army Achievement medal; named ESTCP Project of Yr., 2007. Mem.: ASCE, AIChE, AEA, Internat. Humic Substances Soc. Achievements include patents pending for passive reactive berm; biopolymer production. Avocations: running, travel, golf. Office: US Army ERDC-EL 3909 Halls Ferry Rd Vicksburg MS 39180 Business E-Mail: andy.martin@usace.army.mil.

MARTIN, WILLIAM COLLIER, hospital administrator; b. Atlanta, Aug. 16, 1926; s. William Henry and Lillian (Collier) M.; m. Alice Elizabeth Nickle, Jan. 12, 1952 (dec.); children: Mary Anne, Patricia Jean, William Collier, Nancy Lee; m. Carol J. Sullivan, July 25, 1998. BS, U. Ga., 1950; diploma, Charlotte Meml. Hosp., 1952; postgrad., U. Okla., 1969. Operating room technician Athens Gen. Hosp., Ga., 1949-50; hosp. adminstrn. intern/resident Charlotte Meml. Hosp., NC, 1950-52; hosp. adminstr. Rockmart-Aragon Hosp., Rockmart, Ga., 1952-54; asst. hosp. adminstr. St. Agnes Hosp., Raleigh, NC, 1954-56; hosp. adminstr. Florence-Darlington Tb. Sanitorium, Florence, SC, 1956-58; commd. 1st lt., MSC US Army, 1959; advanced through grades to lt. col.; adj. US Army Hosp. Ft. Campbell, Ky., 1959; comdg. officer med. co. US Army Hosp., 1959-61; comdg. officer US Army Med. Svc. Detachment Ft. Gulick, Canal Zone, Panama, 1961-64; exec. officer 5th Evacuation Hosp. Ft. Bragg, NC, 1964; comdg. officer, 1964-65; adj. personnel officer 55th Med. Group Ft. Bragg, NC, 1965-66, Qui Nhon, Vietnam, 1966-67; comdg. officer 47th Gen. Hosp., Fitzsimons Gen. Hosp. Denver, 1967-68; exec. officer Evans Health Care Facility Ft. Buckner, Okinawa, Japan, 1968-69; dir. security plans and ops. U.S. Army Med. Ctr., Camp Kue, Okinawa, Japan, 1969-71; med. ops. officer VII Corps Moehringen, Germany, 1971-73; chief tng., exercise and readiness US Army Med. Command Heidelberg, Germany, 1973-74; dir. security plans and tng. Fitzsimons Army Med. Ctr., 1974-77; ret., 1977—. Guest lectr. healthcare adminstr. US Army Med. Command in Europe, 1973-74; exec. dir. Thoms Rehab. Hosp., Asheville, NC, 1977-78; pres./chair Escambia County Pub. Health Trust, 1978-86; founder Hospice of Northwest Fla. and Exec. Dir., 1979-86. Mem. Pres.'s Com. on Employment of the Handicapped, 1978; sec. United Meth. Bd. Pastoral Care and Counseling, 1988-90; mem., v.p., bd. ministries Pensacola Dist. United Meth. Ch., Inc., 1988-98; dir. lay speaking, bd. laity, coun. on ministries Pensacola Dist. United Meth. Ch., Inc., 1988-98; dir. lay speaking, bd. laity Ala.-West Fla. Conf. United Meth. Ch., 1988-97; mem. Health and Human Svcs. task force citizens goals for Pensacoloa, 1981-86; vice chmn. adminstrv. bd. Pine Forest United Meth. Ch., Pensacola, 1979-86; mem. fin. com., 1979-86; dir. lay speaking Pensacola Dist. United Meth. Ch., 1985-88; bd. dirs. Hispanic Ministries, Inc., 1986-93, Meth. Homes for the Aging, Inc., 1990—2006. Served with USN, 1944-46. Decorated Legion of Merit, Bronze Star, Meritorious Svc. medal (3); Vietnam Royal Cross of Gallantry with bronze palm; cert. lay speaker United Meth. Ch. Fellow Am. Acad. Med. Adminstrs.; mem. Am. soc. Tng. and Devel. (dir. 1977-78), Ret. Officers Assn., Assn. US Army (dir. Denver-Centennial chpt. 1974-77, Greater Gulf Coast chpt. 1979-86), US Power Squadrons, Ret. Officers Assn. (bd. dirs. Bob Sikes chpt. 1996-2000, bd. dirs. Escarosa chpt. 1985-99, pres. ESCAROSA chpt. 1989-90), VFW, Masons, Phi Delta Theta. Republican.

MARTIN, WILLIAM FRANCIS, JR., lawyer; b. Lowell, Mass., 1961; s. William F. and Patricia A. Martin; m. Martha Doherty, 1988; children: William F. III, Daniel J., Jacqueline E. BA in English, Coll. of Holy Cross, Worcester, Mass., 1983; JD, Boston Coll., 1986. Bar: Mass. 1986, N.H. 1991. Law clk. to Hon. Joseph R. Nolan Mass. Supreme Jud. Ct., Boston, 1986-87; assoc. Hale and Dorr, Boston and Manchester, 1987-93; ptnr. Eno, Boulay, Martin Donahue, LLP (and predecessor firm), Lowell, 1994—. Bd. dirs. Lowell Parks and Conservation Trust, Lowell, 1991—; mem. Lowell Conservation Commn., 1993-94, chmn., 1994-99. Articles editor Boston Coll. Law Review, 1985-86. Mem. Lowell City Coun., 2000-2005, 2008-; mayor City of Lowell, 2006—07; bd. dirs. D'Youville Sr. Care, 1997—. Mem. Omicron Delta Epsilon, Order of the Coif. Home: 173 Clark Rd Lowell MA 01852 Office: Eno Boulay Martin & Donahue LLP 21 George St Lowell MA 01852 Home Phone: 978-441-2203; Office Phone: 978-452-8902. Business E-Mail: b.martin@ebmdattorneys.com.

MARTIN, WILLIAM H., medical educator, director; b. Charleston, SC, Feb. 12, 1949; s. William H. and Beverly Baker Martin; m. Cynthia R. Richardson; children: Lauren Emily, David William. BS, Coll. William & Mary, Williamsburg, Va., 1971; MD, Med. U. SC., Charleston, 1975. Diplomate Am. Bd. Internal Medicine, 1978, endocrinology & metabolism 1981, Am. Bd. Nuc. Medicine, 1995, Bd. Nuc. Cardiology, 1999. Endocrinologist Fronk Clinic, Honolulu, 1980—83, Endocrine Assocs., Oak Ridge, Tenn., 1983—90, Sole Propr., Oak Ridge, 1990—93; resident, dept. radiology Vanderbilt U. Med. Ctr., Nashville, 1993—95, asst. prof., dept. radiology, 1995—2002, dir., clin. nuc. medicine tng. program, 1998—, co-dir., clin. nuc. cardiology, 1998—, med. dir., nuc. medicine, 2000—, assoc. prof., 2002—, chmn., quality improvement com. dept. radiology, 2006—. Coord., continuing med. edn. SE Chpt. Soc. Nuc. Medicine, 1998—2008, fin. chmn., 2001—, pres., 2003—04; cons. to editor Jour. Nuc. Medicine, 1999—2005; editl. bd. Clin. Nuc. Medicine, 2002—05; fellow Am. Soc. Nuc. Medicine, 2006—. Editor: (book) Practical FDG Imaging; contbr. chapters to books and numerous articles (Tchg. award, 2008). Mem.: Soc. Nuc. Medicine (house dels. 2003—04). Office: Vanderbilt Univ Med Ctr 1161 21 Ave S Nashville TN 37232-2675

MARTIN, WILLIAM R. (BILLY MARTIN), lawyer; b. Pitts., 1949; m. Michel McQueen Martin; children from previous marriage: Nikki, Erica. BA, Howard U., 1973; JD, U. Cin., 1976. Bar: Ohio 1976, DC 2000, admitted to practice: US Supreme Ct., US Ct. Appeals, DC Cir., US Ct. Appeals, 4th Cir., US Ct. Appeals, 6th Cir., US Ct. Appeals, 9th Cir., US Dist. Ct. DC, US Dist. Ct. Md., US Dist. Ct., So. Dist. Ohio. Asst. city prosecutor City Cin., Ohio, 1976—78; asst. US Atty. (so. dist.) Ohio US Dept. Justice, Ohio, 1978—80, spl. atty., organized crime strike force San Francisco, 1980—84, asst. US Atty. Washington, 1984—88, exec. asst. US atty., 1988—90; ptnr., litig. dept. Eckert Seamans Cherin & Mellott, LLC, Washington, 1990—94; ptnr., prin. William R. Martin & Assocs., Washington, 1994—97; ptnr., litig. dept. Manatt Phelps & Phillips, LLP, Washington, 1997—2000, Dyer Ellis & Joseph (merged with Blank Rome LLP, 2003), Washington, 2000—03; ptnr., comml. litig. group Blank Rome LLP, Washington, 2003—07; ptnr., litig. dept. Sutherland Asbill & Brennan LLP, Washington, 2007—09; ptnr. Howrey LLP, Washington, 2009—. Lead atty. for critical witness Office Independent Counsel (Starr) investigation of Pres. William Jefferson Clinton; instr. Trial Advocacy Inst., Justice Dept.; advisor NBA and NFL Players Assn. Offers commentary and legal analysis on major TV networks such as: CNN, NBC, CNBC, Court TV and BET. Recipient Disting. Alumni award, Howard U., U. Cin. Coll. Law; named one of The 75 Best Lawyers in Washington, Washingtonian Mag., 2002, 50 Most Influential Minority Lawyers in America, Nat. Law Jour., 2008; named to The Power 150, Ebony mag., 2008, The Morehouse Coll. Internat. Bd. Renaissance Leaders. Mem.: Washington Bar Assn., Nat. Bar Assn., DC Bar Assn., ABA. Achievements include defending celebrity clients such as Jayson Williams, Allen Iverson, Juwan Howard, Rod Strickland, Riddick Bowe, and Michael Vick; represented the parents of murdered government intern Chandra Levy and former White House intern Monica Lewinsky and her mother Marcia. Office: Howrey LLP 1299 Pennsylvania Ave NW Washington DC 20004 Office Phone: 202-383-6618. Office Fax: 202-383-6610. E-mail: MartinBilly@howrey.com.*

MARTIN, WILLIAM RAYMOND, retired financial manager; b. Phila., Oct. 16, 1939; s. Clyde Davis and Mary Anna (Coates) M.; m. Michaela Roberta Smink, Sept. 8, 1962 (div. 1969, dec. 2002); 1 child, James; m. Margaret Scouten, Oct. 16, 1970 (div. 1983); children: Mary Frances, Susanna; m. Joan Friedman Kennedy, Jan. 29, 1988 (div. 1999). BSME, Lehigh U., 1960; MBA, U. Pa., 1973. Mem. engring. staff Pa. R.R., 1960-65; asst. gen. mgr. Excelsior Truck Leasing, Phila., 1965-71; sr. policy analyst Assn. Am. R.R.s, Washington, 1973-76, mgr. engring. econ., 1976-78; mgr. fin. analysis So. Ry., Washington, 1978-83; dir. fin. planning Norfolk (Va.) So. Corp., 1984-92, asst. v.p. fin., 1992-95. Contbr. articles to profl. jours. Bd. dirs. Williams Sch., Norfolk, 1988—96, pres., 1992—96; bd. dirs. Va. Stage Co., Norfolk, 1995—2001, Feldman Chamber Music Soc., 2001—05, Norfolk Chamber Consort, 1998—2004, treas., 2001—04. Mem. ASME, Soc. Automotive Engrs., Mid Atlantic Roadracing Club. Home: 118 Woody's Ln Weems VA 22576

MARTIN, WILLIAM ROYALL, JR., retired professional society administrator; b. Raleigh, NC, Sept. 3, 1926; s. William Royall and Edith Ruth (Crocker) M.; m. Betty Anne Rader, June 14, 1952; children: Sallie Rader Martin Busby, Amy Kemp Martin Lewis. AB, U. N.C., 1948, MBA, 1964; BS, N.C. State U., 1952. Chemist Stamford (Conn.) rsch. labs. Am. Cyanamid Co., 1952—54; chemist Dan River Mills, Danville, Va., 1954—56, Union Carbide Corp., South Charleston, W.Va., 1956—59; rsch. assoc. Sch. Textiles N.C. State U., 1959—63; tech. dir. Am. Assn. Textile Chemists and Colorists, Research Triangle Park, NC, 1963—73, exec. dir., 1974—96. Adj. asst. prof. Coll. Textiles, N.C. State U., 1966-88, adj. assoc. prof., 1989-97; del. Internat. Orgn. Standardization, Pan Am. Standards Commn. With USNR, 1944—46. Fellow Am. Inst. Chemists, Soc. Dyers and Colourists, Textile Inst.; mem. Am. Chem. Soc., Coun. Engring. and Sci. Soc. Execs. (past pres. 1992-93), Fiber Soc., Am. Assn. Textile Chemists and Colorists, Masons, Rotary, Phi Kappa Phi, Phi Gamma Delta. Methodist. Home and Office: 224 Briarcliff Ln Cary NC 27511-3901 Office Phone: 919-467-9946. Personal E-mail: wrbrm195z@gmail.com.

MARTIN, WILLIAM RUSSELL, nuclear engineering educator; b. Flint, Mich., June 2, 1945; s. Carl Marcus and Audrey Winifred (Rosene) M.; m. Patricia Ann Williams, Aug. 13, 1967; children: Amy Leigh, Jonathan William. BSE in Engring. Physics, U. Mich., 1967; MS in Physics, U. Wis., 1968; MSE in Nuclear Engring., U. Mich., 1975, PhD in Nuclear Engring., 1976. Prin. physicist Combustion Engring., Inc., Windsor, Conn., 1976-77; asst. prof. nuclear engring. U. Mich., Ann Arbor, 1977-81, assoc. prof. nuclear engring., 1981-88, prof. nuclear engring., 1988—, dir. lab. for sci. computation, 1986—2001, chmn. nuclear engring., 1990-94, assoc. dean for acad. affairs Coll. Engring., 1994-99, dir. Ctr. for Advanced Computing, 2002—04; acting dir. Mich. Grid Ctr., 2002—04, chmn. nuclear engring., 2004—. Cons. Lawrence Livermore Nat. Lab., Livermore, Calif., 1982—, Los Alamos (N.Mex.) Nat. Lab., 1980-89, 2001—, IBM, Inc., Kingston, N.Y., 1984, Rockwell Internat., Pitts., 1985. Author: Transport Theory, 1979; author tech. and conf. papers. Recipient Glenn Murphy award Am. Soc. for Engring. Edn., 1993; Disting. scholar U. Mich. Coll. Engring., 1967; vis. fellow Royal Soc., London, 1989. Fellow Am. Nuclear Soc.; mem. Am. Phys. Soc., Soc. for Indsl. and Applied Math., IEEE. Avocations: running, reading, skiing, sailing. Home: 420 Huntington Dr Ann Arbor MI 48104 Office: U Mich Dept Nuclear Engring Ann Arbor MI 48109 Home Phone: 734-665-3776; Office Phone: 734-764-5534. Business E-Mail: wrm@umich.edu.

MARTINA, CARLO JACK, lawyer; b. Wyandotte, Mich., Jan. 1, 1954; s. Carlo and Matilda M.; m. Marie A. Pulte; children: Raphael, Ariel. BS with high distinction, U. Mich., 1976; JD, Wayne State U., 1979. Bar: Mich. 1979, U.S. Dist. Ct. (ea. dist.) Mich. 1980. Assoc. Provisor, Eisenberg et al, Southfield, Mich., 1979-81, Auslander, Babcock & Weiss, Southfield, Mich., 1981-83; atty. pvt. practice, Southfield, Mich., 1983—. Mem. adv. bd. Legal Alternatives for Women, Southfield, 1985-87; co-founder Mich. br. Justice for Children, 1995-97; co-founder, co-publisher, co-owner MetroParent Mag., Southfield, 1987-95; mem. task force Oakland County Family Ct., 2001-03; lectr. in field. Legal expert (video) Latchkey Kids: Home Alone & Safe, 1994; author: Effective Discovery in Domestic Violence Litigation, 2002; contbr. chpts. to books, articles pub. to profl. jour. Mem. adv. bd. Gov.'s Internat. Yr. of Family Coun., Lansing, Mich., 1994-95, Roundtable of Christians, Muslims & Jews, Detroit, 1989-91, Anti-Defamation League, Southfield, 1988-90, Coalition Against Domestic Violence; scoutmaster Cub Scout Pack 1016, Birmingham, Mich., 1993-97. James P. Angel scholar U. Mich., 1977-79. Mem. Mich. Trial Lawyers Assn., Mich. Bar Assn. (bd. dirs., family law coun. 2001—, chmn. child support, alimony and friend of ct. com. 2002—, exec. bd. mem. state bar family law coun. 2003--, lectr.), Oakland County Bar Assn. (co-chair family support com., friend of ct. subcom. 2000-03), Wayne County Bar Assn. (family law divsn., liaison to Mich. Bar Assn., family law coun. 2001—, pres. 2004-05). Avocations: reading, fishing, furniture refinishing and home remodeling, model building. Office: 1158 S Main St Plymouth MI 48170-2214 Business E-Mail: MartinaLawOffice@aol.com.

MARTIN-BERG, LAUREY, literature and language professor; b. Chgo., Mar. 23, 1950; d. Frederick Richard Kramer and Marilyn Jean Kramer Benson; m. John Wesley Martin (div.); children: Stirling Brooke Martin, Hunter Kirk Martin; m. William James Berg, Feb. 1, 1986; stepchildren: Jennifer Anne Berg Duffy, Jessica Lyn Berg Prosser. BA, Stanford U., Palo Alto, Calif., 1972; MA, U. Wis., Madison, 1975, PhD, 1982. Vis. asst. prof. U. Wis., Madison, 1983—86, lectr., 1986—92, sr. lectr., 1992—2000, disting. lectr., 2000—. Co-author: Images, 1990, Emile Zola Revisited, 1992, Gustave Flaubert, 1997, Paroles, 1999, 3d edit., 2006. Recipient Hilldale award for Excellence in Tchg., U. Wis., Madison, 1998, UW-Madison Student Ser. award, 2002, Disting. Svc. award, Madison Coll. Letters & Scis, 2009; grantee, U. Wis., Madison, 1997. Mem.: Phi Kappa Phi, UW-Madison Humanities & Social Sci. Area Review Com. (chair), UW-Madison Disting. Prefix Review Com., Com. Inst. Cooperation Roman Lang. (prog. dir.), Am. Assn. U. Coord. & Supervisors, Wis. Assn. Fng. Lang. Tchrs., Am. Assn. Tchrs. French, Am. Coun. Tchrs. Fgn. Langs., Phi Beta Kappa. Office: U Wis Dept French and Italian 618 Van Hise Hall 1220 Linden Dr Madison WI 53706

MARTINDALE, KENNETH ALLEN, retail executive; b. 1960; Joined as courtesy clk. Smith's Food & Drug Centers, Inc., 1975, various positions including dist. mgr. store ops. & sr. v.p. mktg., then sr. v.p. sales & procurement, 1996—98; exec. v.p. sales & procurement Fred Meyer, Inc., 1998—99; pres., CEO, chmn. bd. dirs. Intesource, Inc., 2004—06; co-pres., chief merchandising & mktg. officer Pathmark Stores, Inc., 2006—07; sr. exec. v.p. merchandising, mktg. & logistics Rite Aid Corp., 2008—. Founder, mng. dir., CEO Orchard Street, Inc.,

Salt Lake City, 1999—2003; prin. Martindale Devel. Group, LLC, 1999—2004; bd. dirs. Intesource, Inc., 2000—04. Office: Rite Aid Corp 30 Hunter Ln Camp Hill PA 17011 Business E-Mail: kmartindale@riteaid.com.*

MARTIN DE CAMILO, JODY ELIZABETH, biology professor; m. Gerardo R. Camilo. PhD, St. Louis U., 2001. Asst. prof. St. Louis CC Meramec, 2001—07, assoc. prof., 2007—. Sci. spkr. St. Louis Acad. Scis., 2001—09. Recipient Excellence award, CC Nat. Ctr. Cmty. Engagement Svc. Learning & Civic Engement, 2004, Faculty Innovation award, Mo. Cmty. Colls. Assn., 2006, NISOD Excellence award, 2009; named Outstanding Instr. of Yr., Phi Theta Kappa CC Honor Soc., 2003, Outstanding Biology Instr., 2003. Mem.: NSTA, Nat. Assn. Biology Tchrs., Sigma Xi Sci. Honor Soc. Office: St Louis CC Meramec 11333 Big Bend Blvd Saint Louis MO 63122-2810 Business E-Mail: jmdecamilo@stlcc.edu.

MARTINEAU, ROBERT JOHN, retired law educator; b. Oconto, Wis., May 18, 1934; s. Francis Joseph and Gertrude (Schauer) Martineau; m. Constance Ann Zimmerman, Dec. 21, 1957; children: Robert John, Renee, Anne, Jeanne. BS, Coll. Holy Cross, 1956; JD, U. Chgo., 1959. Bar: Md. 1960, U.S. Supreme Ct. 1964, Iowa 1969, Wis. 1974. Law clk. to chief judge Md. Ct. Appeals, 1959-60; pvt. practice Md., 1960-68; asst. atty. gen. Md., 1964-65; assoc. prof. U. Iowa, 1968-71; prof., 1971-72; cir. exec. U.S. Ct. Appeals (8th cir.), Mo., 1972-74; exec. officer Wis. Supreme Ct., 1974-78; prof. U. Dayton, Ohio, 1978-80; prof. law U. Cin., 1980-88, disting. rsch. prof., 1988-93, emeritus, 1994—, assoc. dean, 1980—83, acting dean, 1985—86. Cons. Inst. Jud. Adminstrn., 1970—72, Fed. Jud. Ctr., 1978, Nat. Ctr. State Cts., 1978—79, 1987, Inst. Jud. Adminstrn., 1987—88, UN Devel. Program, Bhutan, 1999; spl. prof. U. Birmingham, England, 1987. Author: Wisconsin Appellate Practice, 1978, Judicial Reform in Wisconsin, in Court Reform in Seven States, 1980, Modern Appellate Practice-Federal and State Civil Appeals, 1983, Fundamentals of Modern Appellate Advocacy, 1985, Cases and Materials on Appellate Practice and Procedure, 1987; author: (with others) 2d edit., 2005; author: Appellate Justice in England and the United States: A Comparative Analysis, 1990, Drafting Legislation and Rules in Plain English, 1991; author: (with M. Salerno) Legal, Legislative, and Rule Drafting in Plain English, 2005. Reporter Wis. Supreme Ct. Com. Discipline Attys., 1975—77, Wis. Jud. Coun. Com. Appellate Practice and Procedure, 1976—78, Com. Contempt and Extraordinary Remedies, 1979—80; sec. Md. Constl. Conv. Commn., 1965—67, Md. Constl. Conv., 1967—68, Wis. Supreme Ct. Com. Study State Bar, 1975—77; mem. Iowa Mcpl. Laws Study Com., 1970—71, Wis. Legis. Coun. Com. Ct. Reorganization, 1977, Ohio Supreme Ct. Adv. Com. Rules, 1988—91; mem., reporter ABA Appellate Judges Conf. Com. Appellate Skills Tng., 1984—85, Com. Appellate Skills Tng., 1984—85; co-chair Com. Appellate Practice, 1986—88. Mem.: Am. Jud. Soc. (bd. dirs. 1966—68), Md. Bar Assn. (reporter com. jud. selection 1962—64, v.p. 1967), Assn. Am. Law Schs. (ho. reps. 1982—87). Democrat. Roman Catholic. Home Phone: 941-488-0455; Office Phone: 941-488-0455. Personal E-mail: r.j.martineau@gmail.com.

MARTINEN, JOHN A., travel company executive; b. Sault Ste Marie, Mich., June 26, 1938; s. John Albert and Ina Helia (Jarvi) M. BS with highest honors, Mich. State U., 1960; JD, NYU, 1963. Asst. purser Grace Line Inc., NYC, 1963—65, chief purser, 1965—69; cons. Empresa Turistica Internat., Galapagos Cruises, Quito, Galapagos Islands, Ecuador, 1969—70; regional mgr. Globus & Cosmos (Group Voyagers Inc.), NYC, 1970—73, v.p., 1974—76, exec. v.p., 1977—78, pres., CEO, 1979—92, Littleton, Colo., 1993—98, chmn., 1998; pres., CEO Vista Travel Ventures, Inc., Denver, 1999—2001; pres. Trafalgar Tours, Long Island City, NY, 2002; prin. Safe Passage Internat., Lakewood, Colo., 2003—. Bd. dirs. 366 Broadway Homeowners Assn., NYC, 1983—92, sec., 1987—92; bd. dirs. Edbrooke Homeowners Assn., Denver, 1992—2002, sec., 1994—97, pres., 1997—2002. Root-Tilden Scholar, N.Y.U. Law Sch., 1960—63. Mem. Am. Soc. Travel Agts. (chmn. tour operating program 1995-99), U.S. Tour Operators Assn. (bd. dirs. 1993-99, treas. 1996-97, sec. 1998-99, chmn. travel automation com., 1990-1998), Acad. Travel and Tourism (bd. advisors 1987-92, NY, 1992-01, Denver), Lotos Club NY, Wings Club (NY), Columbine Country Club (Colo.), Denver Athletic Club, Skal Club, NY, Am. Tourism Soc. Democrat. Home: 915 W End Ave Apt 7 A New York NY 10025 Office: Safe Passage Internat 3609 S Wadsworth Blvd Ste 565 Lakewood CO 80235 Home Phone: 212-678-7998; Office Phone: 800-777-7665. E-mail: JohnMartinen@TravelStrategies.net.

MARTINETTI, RONALD ANTHONY, lawyer; b. NYC, Aug. 13, 1945; s. Alfred Nathan and Frances Ann (Battipaglia) M.; m. Ky Le Du, June, 2002. Student, Columbia U., NYC, 1966—68, U. Chgo., 1981-82; JD, U. So. Calif., LA, 1982. Bar: Calif. 1982; U.S. Dist. Ct. (cen. southern and no. dists.) Calif. 1982, U.S. Dist. Ct. Ariz., 1992; U.S. Ct. Appeals (9th cir.) 1982. Ptnr. Kazanjian & Martinetti, Glendale, Calif., 1986—. Co-founder Am. Legends Website, 1995, Am. Legends Pub., 1996. Author: Nine Easy Ways to Strengthen Your Bad Faith Case in Discovery, 1991; co-author: (with M. Slattery) Rights of Owners of Lost, Stolen or Destroyed Instruments Under UCC Section 3-804: Can They Be Holders in Due Course?, 1993, James Dean Story, 1995; contbr. articles to profl. jours. and popular mags. Mem. Calif. Bar Assn. Office: 520 E Wilson Ave Glendale CA 91206-4374 Office Phone: 818-241-1011. Office Fax: 818-241-2193. Personal E-mail: amlegends@aol.com.

MARTINETTO, JOSEPH R., investment company executive; BA, Claremont McKenna Coll.; MBA, Univ. Calif., Berkeley. Fin. mgmt. positions through sr. v.p. asset & liability mgmt. First Interstate Bank, 1984—96; sr. asst. treas. Transamerica Corp., 1996—97; sr. v.p. Transamerica Fin. Corp., 1996—97; sr. v.p., treas. Charles Schwab Corp., San Francisco, 1997—2001, sr. v.p. retail fin., 2001—07, exec. v.p., CFO, 2007—. Office: Charles Schwab Corp 101 Montgomery St San Francisco CA 94104

MARTINEZ, ADRIANA, photographer; Student, U. Nev., Las Vegas; BA, Brooks Inst. Photography. Photography instr. C.C. So. Nev.; wedding photographer So. Nev. News Bur.; chair Nev. State Dem. Party, Las Vegas, 2003—06. Mem.: PTA. Mailing: 1499 Sunair Cir Las Vegas NV 89110

MARTINEZ, ALEX J., state supreme court justice; b. Denver, Apr. 1, 1951; m. Kathy Carter; children: Julia, Maggie. Diploma, Phillips Exeter Acad., NH, 1969; student, Reed Coll., 1969-72; BA, U. Colo., 1973, JD, 1976. Bar: Colo. 1976. Dep. state pub. defender, Pueblo and Denver, 1976-83; county ct. judge Pueblo, 1983-88; dist. ct. judge, 1988-97; justice Colo. Supreme Ct., Denver, 1997—. Supreme Ct. liaison Colo. Criminal Rules Com., Colo. Criminal Jury Instns.; chmn. Pub. Access Com., Jud. Edn. Com.; bd. dirs. Servicios de la Raza. Chmn. Pueblo adv. bd. Packard Found., 1993-96; chmn. site-based governing coun. Pueblo Sch. Arts and Scis., 1994-95; mem. site-based governing coun. Roncalli Mid. Sch., 1993-94; bd. dirs. Colo. U. Law Alumni. Mem. Colo. Bar Assn. (regional v.p. 1995-96), Colo. Hispanic Bar Assn., Pueblo Bar Assn. (mem. exec. coun. 1994-96), Pueblo Hispanic Bar Assn. Office: Colo Supreme Ct 2 E 14th Ave Denver CO 80203-2115*

MARTINEZ, ALVARO IGNACIO, science educator; s. Ignacio and Emma Martinez; m. Susana Gonzalez, Oct. 3, 1970; children: Juan Manuel, Maria Paula Barnard. PhD, U. Ctrl. Fla., Orlando, 1993. Sr. rschr. Ecopetrol ICP, Bucaramanga, Santander, Colombia, 1993—2000; assoc. prof. Tex. A&M U. Kingsville, 2001—. Office: Tex A&M Univ Kingsville MSC 213 University Blvd Kingsville TX 78363

MARTINEZ, ANDRES MANUEL, JR., mathematics educator; s. Andres and Agustina (Garcia) M.; m. Jennifer Dolores Fuller, Oct. 2, 1977 (div. Aug. 1986); children: Andres M. III, Antonio D.; m. Barbara E. Raleigh, Oct. 22, 1988. MEd, Pace U., White Plains, NY, 1997. Cert. tchr. math, grades 7-12, N.Y. Sgt. US Army, 1972—83; prin. upper sch. Dorado Acad., PR, 2004—07; math. tchr. Port Jervis City Sch. Dist., NY, 2007—. Lacrosse ofcl. NCAA, New Windsor, NY, 1983—2003. Mem. Nat. Coun. Tchrs. Math., Nat. Collegiate Athletic Assn., Phi Delta Kappa, Pi Lambda Theta. Roman Catholic. Avocations: sports official for football and lacrosse, coaching football, basketball, lacrosse. Office: Port Jervis City Sch Dist 118 East Main St Port Jervis NY 12771

MARTINEZ, ARTHUR C., bank executive, retired retail executive; b. NYC, Sept. 25, 1939; s. Arthur F. and Agnes (Caulfield) M.; m. Elizabeth Rusch, July 30, 1966; children: Lauren, Gregory. BSME, Polytech. U., 1960; MBA, Harvard U., 1965; LLD (hon.), U. Notre Dame, 1997. Dir. planning Internat. Paper Co., NYC, 1967-69; asst. to pres. Talley Industries, Mesa, Ariz., 1969-70; dir. fin. RCA Corp., NYC, 1970-73, v.p., 1973-80; sr. v.p., CFO Saks Fifth Ave. Inc., NYC, 1980-84, exec. v.p., 1984-87, vice chmn., 1990-92; sr. v.p. & group chief exec. Batus Inc., Louisville, 1987-90; chmn., CEO Sears Merchandise Group, Chgo., 1992-95, Sears, Roebuck and Co., 1995—2000, chmn., CEO emeritus, 2000—; interim chmn., CEO Internat. Flavors & Fragrances Inc., NYC, 2006; mem. supervisory bd. ABN AMRO Holdings N.V., 2002—, chmn., 2006—. Bd. dirs. Saks Fifth Avenue, Inc., 1990-92, PepsiCo, Inc., 1999-, Internat. Flavors & Fragrances, 2000-, Liz Claiborne, Inc., 2001-, IAC/InterActiveCorp., 2005-, Martha Stewart Living Omimedia, Inc., 2001-04, Am. Internat. Group, Inc. (AIG), 2009-; bd. dirs. Fed. Res. Bank Chgo., 1996-2002, chmn., 2000-01 Bd. dirs. Defenders of Wildlife, 1992—, Nat. Urban League; chmn. bd. trustees Polytech. U., 1990—; trustee Art Inst., Orch. Assn. Chgo. Symphony Orch.; bd. dirs. Northestern Meml. Hosp., Chgo. 1st lt. U.S. Army, 1961-63. Named CEO of Yr., Fin. World Mag., 1996; recipient T.C. and Elizabeth Clarke medallion Sch. of Bus., Coll. William and Mary, 1997, Olin Sch. of Bus. Excellence in Bus. award, Washington U., St. Louis, 1997. Mem. Nat. Retail Fedn. (chmn. bd. dirs.). Avocations: tennis, golf, gardening. Office: ABN AMRO Holdings NV Gustav Mahlerlaan 10 1082 PP Amsterdam Netherlands*

MARTINEZ, BELINDA, health insurance company executive; MBA, U. So. Calif.; MPH, Loma Linda U. With Delta Ins.Co., 1988—, dir. acct. svcs. Delta Dental; v.p. profl. svcs. PMI Dental Health Plan Delta Ins.Co., v.p. underwriting and fin., 1999—2001, sr. v.p., COO, 2001—; COO Delta Ins.Co., 2003—. Named one of Top 10 Latinos in Healthcare, LatinoLeaders mag., 2004. Office: Delta Dental Calif 100 1st St San Francisco CA 94105

MARTINEZ, BENJAMIN RAY, security firm executive, public relations executive, retired military non-commissioned officer; b. Bakersfield, Calif., Apr. 13, 1955; s. Raymond Dominguez and Reba Lori Martinez; m. Carmencita Bugtong Adriatico, Dec. 6, 1986. Tech. cert., CC of Air Force, Gunther AFB, Ala., 1986, US Army Ordnance, Camp Roberts, Calf., 1999; tech. instr. cert., U. Calif., Long Beach, 2004. Lic. security officer Calif. Security policeman USAF, San Antonio, 1973—86; wheel and track vehicle repairer Calif. Army N.G., Gardena, Calif., 1994—2002. Mentor North HS Army JROTC, Torrance, Calif.; mem. Easter Seals, USO; founder, CEO We Stand For Am.; supporting mem. The Carter Ctr., The Ronald Reagan Presdl. Found., Reagan Presdl. Libr.; life mem. Rep. Nat. Party, San Bernardino, Calif., 1986—2004; mem. Rep. Presdl. Task Force. Staff sgt. USAF, 1973—86, staff sgt. Calif. Army Nat. Guard, 1994—2002. Decorated Jts. Svcs. Commendation medal Supreme Hdqs. NATO, US Army 94th Engrs. Divsn. Coin; recipient letter of commendation and coin, US Dep. Sec. of Def. Hon. Rudy De Leon, 2000; named Honor recipient, Eisenhower Commn., Rep. Nat. Party, 2006, Nat. Rep. Senatorial Com. Commn. Mem.: AARP, VFW, World Wildlife Fund, Nat. Law Enforement Meml./Mus. (founding mem.), Retired Res., Carter Ctr. (sustaining mem.), The Heritage Found., The Cousteau Soc., Nat. Geog. Soc., Air Force Assn. (life), Air Force Sgts. Assn. (life), Inventors Workshop Internat. (assoc.), US Army 9th/10th Cavalry (assoc.; sustaining mem. 1998—2004), Nat. Inventors Hall of Fame, Disabled Am. Vets., Planetary Soc., Nat. Space Soc., Paralyzed Vets. of Am., World Heritage Ctr., George H.W. Bush Presdl. Libr. (sustaining mem.), World Fedn. of UN, UN Assn. of the USA, Am. Legion. Republican. Christian. Achievements include invention and patent for object retrieving device; contributor to the US Forces Coalition during Operation Iraqi Freedom. Avocations: world travel, ancient military histories, archaeology, paleontology-geology, arts and humanities. Home: 1250 Kendall Dr D-305 San Bernardino CA 92407-5832 Personal E-mail: rangerthree@hotmail.com.

MARTINEZ, BOB, former federal official, former governor; b. Tampa, Fla., Dec. 25, 1934; s. Serafin and Ida (Carreno) Martinez; m. Mary Jane Marino, 1954; children: Sharon, Alan. BS, U. Tampa, 1957; MA in Labor and Industrial Rels., U. Ill., 1964. Tchr. Hillsborough County, 1957-62, 63-66; exec. dir. Hillsborough County Tchrs. Assn., 1966-75; pres. Cafe Sevilla Spanish Restaurant, 1975-83; mayor City of Tampa, 1979-86; gov. State of Fla., 1987-91; dir. Office Nat. Drug Control Policy, Washington, 1991—93; mng. dir. govt. cons. Carlton Fields, PA; pres. Bob Martinez & Co.; sr. policy adv. Holland & Knight LLP, Tampa, 2007—. Lead gov. on drug trafficking and substance abuse, chmn. so. states energy bd. Nat. Govs. Assn., 1989; dir. Hillsborough Edn. Found.; hon. dir. Fla. Coun. on Econ. Edn. Pres. Fla. League of Cities, 1985—86; dir. Harmony Inst., Greater Tampa C. of C.; dir. emeritus The Collins Ctr.; bd. advisors Moffitt Cancer Ctr. & Rsch. Inst.; dir., chmn. devel. com. Tampa Bay History Ctr.; trustee emeritus U. Tampa. Recipient Tree of Life award, Nat. Jewish Fund, Svc. Dedication & Loyalty award, Boys & Girls Club of Greater Tampa, Effective Govt. award, Greater Tampa C. of C., State award, Fla. Architects, Tampa Bay Internat. Businessman's award, Top Mgmt. award, Sales & Mktg. Execs. Fla., cert. commendation, Nat. Trust Hist. Preservation US. Mem.: Rotary Club of Tampa, Tampa's Lowry Park Zoological Soc. (dir., exec. com. mem.), Fla. Coun. of 100 (hon.). Republican. Roman Catholic. Office: Holland & Knight LLP 100 N Tampa St, Ste 4100 Tampa FL 33602-3644 Office Phone: 813-227-6308. Office Fax: 813-229-0134. E-mail: bob.martinez@hklaw.com.

MARTINEZ, CARLOS, museum director; b. 1963; Grad., Calif. State U.-Dominguez Hills, 1981—86. Exec. dir. Fresno Art Mus., Calif., 2007—. Mem. Calif. Arts Coun., 2006—. Office: Fresno Art Mus 2233 N 1st St Fresno CA 93703 Office Phone: 559-441-4221 103. Business E-Mail: carlos@fresnoartmuseum.org.

MARTINEZ, DAVID ROGER, chemist, researcher; b. Toledo, Jan. 22, 1954; s. Daniel and Herlinda (Ramirez) M. BS, U. Toledo, Ohio, 1978. Rsch. chemist S.W. Rsch. Inst., Houston, 1978-80; lab. tech. Shilstone Engrng. Testing Lab., Houston, 1981-82; quality control technician Pepsi-Cola Bottling Group, Houston, 1982-83, Chardonol divsn. Freeman Chem. Co., Houston, 1985-86; rsch. asst. U. Tex. Health Sci. Ctr., Houston, 1987—91, 1996—2004, Baylor Coll. Medicine, Houston, 1991-93; rsch. technician Howard Hughes Med. Inst., Houston, 1993—96, 1997—98; rsch. assoc. II, U. Tex. Med. Br., Galveston, Tex., 2005—07; assoc. scientist II Cogenics, a Beckman Coulter Co., Houston, 2007—. Active Harris County Tejano Dems. Mem. Am. Chem. Soc. Democrat. Roman Catholic. Avocations: radio-electronics, computers, science fiction. Office: Cogenics Beckman Coulter Co Ste 103 9441 W Sam Houston Pky S Houston TX 77099 Personal E-mail: genescreen@aol.com. Business E-Mail: dmartinez@cogenics.com, david.martinez@beckman.com.

MARTINEZ, EDUARDO VIDAL, lawyer; b. Travis AFB, Calif., Sept. 27, 1955; s. Vidal and Isidora (Lee) M.; m. Mary Kim Sullivan, Apr. 7, 1984; children: Anthony Michael, Linda Michelle. BA, U. Tex., 1978; MA, Antioch Ctr. for Legal Studies, Washington, 1983; JD, Miss. Coll., 1990; MA in Strategic Studies, U.S. Army War Coll., 2003. Bar: Miss. 1991, U.S. Dist. Ct. (no. and so. dist.) Miss. 1991, U.S. Ct. Mil. Appeals 1991, U.S. Ct. Appeals (5th cir.) 1991, U.S. Supreme Ct. 1994, cert. Mediator, Miss. Supreme Ct., 2005. Gen. counsel Home-Land Title & Abstract Co. Inc., Jackson, Miss., 1991; pvt. practice Jackson, 1991-92; spl. asst. atty. gen. Office of the Atty. Gen., Jackson, 1992-97; legal counsel, site adminstr. SkyTel Corp., 1997—2005, corp. counsel, 1999—2005; dir. site leasing and acquisition WorldCom Broadband Solutions, Inc., 2001. Editor: Legal Eye, 1989—90. Capt. USN, 2007—. Scholar Miss. Bar Found., 1988, scholar in environ. law Am. Law Inst., 1990; recipient Stanford Young Outstanding Atty. award, 2007 Mem. ABA, Miss. Bar Assn., Naval Res. Assn. (chpt. pres.), Navy League, Res. Officer Assn. (chpt. pres., nat. naval sect. committeeman 2000-02), Sea Svs. (nat. v.p. 2002-03), Nat. Jr. Officer (co-chmn., 1996-97.), Miss. Coll. Sch. Law Alumni Assn (pres.-elect 2004-05, pres. 2005-06). Roman Catholic. Office: PO Box 2469 Jackson MS 39225-2469 Home Phone: 601-853-4571. Personal E-mail: evmart@juno.com.

MARTINEZ, GUSTAVE See SOLOMONS, GUS JR.

MARTINEZ, HERIBERTO, human resources and management professional; m. Migdalia Centeno. BA in Mgmt., Inter Am. U., PR, 1983. Labor law cons. Dept. Labor, Arecibo, PR, 1979—83; human resources mgr. Casera Foods Inc., Barceloneta, PR, 1983—93, Cardinal Health, Manati, PR, 1996—2006. Dir. Coop. Ahorro y Credito de Manati, 1996—2003. Recipient Recognition award for work performance, Adminstrn. Accion Juvenil, 1976, Recognition award, Ideas Program, 1981, Chmn. award, Cardinal Health, 1997; named Dir. of Yr., Coop. Ahorro y. Credito, Manati, PR, 1998; nominee Manuel A. Perez award, Dept. of Labor, 1983. Mem.: Puevias de Esperanza Manati (exec. dir. 2007—), Mustang Club America, PR Mustang Club (former sec. 2002—04). Democrat. Roman Catholic. Avocations: guitar, electrical bass, writing, cars. Home: 222 Montecarlo St Monaco 3 Manati PR 00674 Business E-Mail: esperanza3@prtc.net.

MARTINEZ, HERMINIA S., economist, banker; b. Havana, Cuba; came to U.S., 1960, naturalized, 1972; d. Carlos and Amelia (Santana) Martinez Sanchez; m. Mario Aguilar, 1982; children: Mario Aguilar, Carlos Aguilar. BA in Econs. cum laude, Am. U., 1965; MS in Fgn. Svc. (Univ. fellow); MS in Econs., Georgetown U., 1967, PhD in Econs., 1969; postgrad., Nat. U. Mex. Instr. econs. George Mason Coll., U. Va., Fairfax; economist, devel. econs. dept. World Bank, 1969-71; economist World Bank Latin Am. (Ctrl. Am., Mex., Venezuala, Equador, Panama and Dominican Republic, Washington, 1971-79; sr. loan officer for Middle East and North Africa World Bank, 1977—84, sr. loan officer, economist Africa Region, 1988-91, prin. ops. officer pvt. sector fin. group Africa region, 1992-96, lead specialist, regional mgr., 1996—2001; pvt. practice fin., econ. devel. Africa and Latin Am., 2001—. Contbg. author: The Economic Growth of Colombia: Problems and Prospects, 1973, Central American Financial Integration, 1975. Mid-Career fellow Princeton U., 1988-89. Mem. Am. Econ. Assn., Soc. Internat. Devel., Brookings Inst. Latin Am. Study Group. Roman Catholic. Home: 5145 Yuma St NW Washington DC 20016-4336 Office: World Bank 1818 H St NW Washington DC 20433-0001

MARTINEZ, IRIS, state legislator; b. Chgo., Ill. 1 child. Grad., Northeastern U., U. Ill., Chgo. Former asst. majority leader Ill. State Senate, Ill.; state ctrl. com. woman 4th Congressional Dist. State Dem. Party; human svcs. asst.; mem. Dist. 20 Ill. State Senate, Springfield, 2003—. Liaison to Hispanic Ministry. Committeewoman Ill. Dem. State Com.; mem. Dem. Nat. Com. Democrat. Catholic. Office: Capitol Senator 20th Dist 413A Capitol Bldg Springfield IL 62706 also: District 2845 N Kedzie Ave Chicago IL 60618 Home: 3154 W Grace St # 1 Chicago IL 60618-4529 Office Phone: 217-782-8191, 773-489-2020. Office Fax: 773-489-2024. E-mail: martinez@senatedem.state.il.us.*

MARTINEZ, KATHLEEN M. (KATHY MARTINEZ), federal agency administrator; Supr. tech. assistance, internat., employment, poverty reduction, and tng. programs World Inst. Disability, Oakland, Calif., 2000—05, exec. dir., 2005—09; asst. sec. for disability employment policy US Dept. Labor, Washington, 2009—. Head Internat. Leadership Forum for Women with Disabilities, Washington, 1997; mem. Nat. Coun. Disability, 2002—; mem. steering com. Nat. Inst. Disability and Rehab. Rsch., 2003; mem. adv. com. disability and fgn. policy US Dept. State, 2005; mem. bd. dirs. US Inst. Peace, 2007—; charter mem. AT&T Adv. Panel on Access and Aging; bd. mem. Connected Nation. Co-author: (articles) Change from Within, Rd. to Ind. Living in the USA: An Hist. Perspective and Contemporary Challenges, Latinos with Disabilities in the United States: Understanding and Addressing Barriers to Work. Office: US Dept Labor 200 Constitution Ave NW Washington DC 20210*

MARTINEZ, LEO, dean, law educator; b. Santa Fe; m. Sharon Martinez; children: Jennifer, Elizabeth. BS in Math., Physics, U. Kans.; MS in Systems Analysis, U. Southern Calif., LA; JD, U. Calif. Hastings Coll. of the Law. Asst. US atty.; pvt. practice atty., tax law Howard Rice, et. al.; faculty mem. U. Calif. Hastings Coll. of the Law, 1985—, academic dean, 1994—2006, prof. contract, tax and ins. law, 2006—, acting chancellor and dean, 2009—. Contbr. articles to profl. jours. Trustee Hastings 1066 Found.; past bd. mem. St. Paul's Sch., Oakland, Calif., Berkeley Law Found., World Affairs Coun.; bd. mem. Access Group, St. Francis Hosp. Found., Pub. Radio Capital, Pub. Advocates, bd. chmn.; bd. mem., past bd. chmn. Northern Calif. Pub. Broadcasting.

Served with US Army Judge Advocate General's Corps. Mem.: Am. Law Inst., Thurston Soc., Order of the Coif. Office: Univ Calif Hastings Coll of the Law 200 McAllister St San Francisco CA 94102 Office Phone: 415-565-4700. Business E-Mail: martinez@uchastings.edu.*

MARTINEZ, LUCY, lawyer; b. Townsville, Queensland, Australia, Aug. 18, 1977; arrived in US, 2001; BA, LLB, U. Queensland, Brisbane, Australia, 1998; LLM, Columbia U., 2003. Bar: Supreme Ct. Queensland, Australia (Solicitor) 2001, N.Y. 2004. Assoc., judge's clk. Queensland Ct. of Appeal, Brisbane, 1999—2000, High Ct. of Australia, Sydney, NSW, 2000—01; lectr. U. NSW, Sydney, 2001—01; assoc. Columbia Law Sch., NYC, 2001—03; atty. White & Case LLP, NYC, 2003—07, Freshfields Bruckhaus Deringer LLP, 2007—. Contbr. articles to profl. jours. Mem.: ABA, Bar Assn. NY, Am. Soc. Internat. Law. Office: Freshfields Bruckhaus Deringer LLP 520 Madison Ave 34th Fl New York NY 10022 Business E-Mail: lucy.martinez@freshfields.com.

MARTÍNEZ, MARTHA C., language educator; d. Donaldo and Elvia Martínez; m. Juan A. Herrera, Sept. 3, 2004; children: Gabriel Herrera, Isabela Herrera. BA, Eastern Wash. U., Cheney, 1998; MA in Spanish Lit., Ariz. State U., Tempe, 2003. Adminstrv. asst. Eastern Wash. U., 1998—99; tchg. asst. Ariz. State U., Tempe, 1999—2002, rsch. asst., 2001—02, faculty assoc., 2002—03; faculty adj. Spanish Mesa CC, Ariz., 2002—03; prof. Spanish Ariz. Western Coll., Yuma, 2003—. Active mem. Ariz. Assn. Chicanos Higher Edn., Yuma, 2004—08. Recipient Chicano award, Eastern Wash. U., 1998; named to Dean's List, 1998; finalist Dean's Tchr. of Yr., Ariz. State U., 1999. Mem.: Am. Assn. Tchrs. Spanish and Portuguese (Ariz. chpt.) (sec. 2006—08), Am. Coun. Tchg. Fgn. Langs., Ariz. Lang. Assn. (Western Ariz. rep. 2003—08). Avocations: reading, travel, sports. Office: Ariz Western Coll 2020 S Ave 8E Yuma AZ 85365 Office Fax: 928-344-7678. Personal E-mail: martham75@yahoo.com. Business E-Mail: martha.martinez@azwestern.edu.

MARTINEZ, MEL (MELQUIADES RAFAEL MARTINEZ), former United States Senator from Florida, former United States Secretary of Housing and Urban Development; b. Sagua La Grande, Cuba, Oct. 23, 1946; arrived in US, 1962, naturalized, 1971; s. Melquiades C. and Gladys V. (Ruiz) M.; m. Kathryn Tindal, June 13, 1970; children: Lauren Elizabeth, John Melquiades, Andrew Tindal. AA, Orlando Jr. Coll., 1967; BA in Internat. Affairs, Fla. State U., 1969, JD, 1973. Bar: Fla. 1973, US Dist. Ct. (mid. dist.) Fla. 1973, US Supreme Ct. 1979, US Dist. Ct. (so. dist.) Fla. 1986; cert. Nat. Bd. Trial Advocacy. Civil trial atty., ptnr. Martinez, Dalton, Dellecker and Wilson, Orlando, Fla., 1973-85; ptnr. Martinez, Dalton, Dellecker, Wilson and King, 1985-98; chmn. Orange County, Fla., 1998-2001; sec. US Dept. Housing & Urban Devel., Washington, 2001—03; US Senator from Fla., 2005—09; mem. US Senate Armed Services Com., 2005—09, US Senate Banking Housing & Urban Affairs Com., 2005—09, US Senate Commerce, Sci. & Transp. Com., 2005—09, US Senate Spl. Com. on Aging, 2005—09; gen. chmn. Rep Nat Com., 2007. Mem. Fla. Utilities Commn., 1994—97, pres., 1995—97; chmn. Fla. Growth Mgmt. Study Commn.; mem. com. banking, housing and urban affairs US Senate, com. energy and natural resources, com. fgn. relations, congressional-exec. commn. China, spl. com. aging. Bd. dirs. Cath. Social Svcs. Orlando, 1978-86; founder, chmn. Mayor's Hispanic Adv. Com., Orlando, 1981-82; chmn. bd. commrs. Orlando Housing Authority, 1983-86. Named one of 25 Most Influential Hispanics, Time Mag., 2005 Mem. Fla. Bar (bd. govs. young lawyers sect. 1980-81), Acad. Fla. Trial Lawyers (dir. 1981-85, treas. 1986-87, pres. 1988-89), 9th Jud. Cir. (jud. nomination commn. 1986), Congressional Hispanic Leadership Inst. Republican. Roman Catholic.*

MARTINEZ, MIGUEL ACEVEDO, urologist, consultant, lecturer; b. Chihuahua, Mex., Aug. 18, 1953; came to US, 1956; s. Miguel Nuñez and Velia (Acevedo) M. AB, Stanford U., 1976; MD, Yale U., 1983. Diplomate Am. Bd. Urology. Intern U. SC Med. Ctr., 1983—84; resident in urology White Meml. Med. Ctr., LA, 1984-89, urologist, 1989—. Cons., lectr. physician asst. program U. So. Calif., LA, 1990—, clin. instr.; patient edn. cons. ICI Pharm., Del., 1991—, Zeneca's Speaker Forum; patient edn. and med. cons., lectr. Abbott Labs., 1991—; mem. edn.cons. several radio/TV stas., 1991—; mem. subcom. for diseases on kidney and transplantation NIH, Washington, 1991; mem. nat. Hispanic adv. bd. Pfizer Pharms., Inc., 1998—; mem. adv. bd. Glaxo Smith Kline, 2002—; cons. spkrs. bur. Pfizer, Bayer/ESK. Author: Intercellular Pathways, 1981, editor: Contributing Winter optimizing the Treatment of Design Prostatic Hyperplasia in African American And Latin American Men the American Journal Medicine, supplement, 2008. Polit. cons. Xavier Becerra, US Congress, 1992, Martin Gallegos, Gil Cedillo, Calif. State Assembly, 1993, others; bd. dirs. Latino Ctr. for Prevention and Action in Health, Orange County, calif.; bd. govs., sec., rep. Zeneca Urology Econ. Summit, Washington, 1993; mem. Pfizer Nat. Hispanic Adv. Bd. Named Nat. Male Outstanding Teenage of Am., 1971, One of Outstanding Young Men of Am., 1981; named one of America's Top Physicians, 2005, 06; recipient Philanthropic Leadership award Philanthropic Svc. Instns., 2006; Nat. Hispanic Med. Assn. Pub. Policy fellow, 2000-01. Mem. AMA, Nat. Hispanic Med. Assn. (public policy fellow), Am. Urological Assn., Calif. Med. Assn. (polit. action com. bd. dirs. 1997—, del.), LA Med. Assn. (polit. action com. 1992—), LA County Med. Assn., Yale Alumni Assn., Stanford Alumni Assn., LA Athletic Club. Office: White Meml Med Ctr Rm 500 1701 Cesar Chavez Ave Los Angeles CA 90033-2438 Office Phone: 323-224-6202. Personal E-mail: uromd@earthlink.net.

MARTINEZ, PEDRO JAIME, professional baseball player; b. Manoquayabo, Dominican Republic, July 25, 1971; Pitcher LA Dodgers, 1992—93, Montreal Expos, 1994—97, Boston Red Sox, 1998—2004, NY Mets, 2005—08, Phila. Phillies, 2009—. Recipient Nat. League Cy Young award, 1997, Am. League Cy Young award, 1999, 2000; named Minor League Player of Yr., The Sporting News, 1991, Pitcher of Yr., 1997, 1999, 2000, All-Star Game MVP, Maj. League Baseball, 1999; named to Nat. League All-Star Team, 1996, 1997, 2005, 2006, Am. League All-Star Team, 1998—2000, 2002. Achievements include leading the National League in: earned run average, complete games, 1997; leading the American League in: wins, 1999; earned run average, 1999-2003; strikeouts, 1999, 2000, 2002; shutouts, 2000; capturing Major League Baseball's Triple Crown for a pitcher (leading a league in wins, earned run average and strikeouts), 1999; member of World Series Championship winning Boston Red Sox, 2004. Office: Phila Phillies Citizens Pk One Citizens Bank Way Philadelphia PA 19148*

MARTINEZ, RAUL L., public relations executive; b. Santiago, Oriente, Cuba, Mar. 6, 1949; arrived in US, 1960; s. Chin and Aida Martinez; m. Angela Callava, Jan. 10, 1970; children: Aida, Raul Jr. AA, Miami Dade Coll.; BS in Criminal Justice, Fla. Internat. U., Miami, 1977. Pub., founder Spanish lang. newspaper El Sol de Hialeah, Fla., 1969—; pres. Martex Realty, Inc., 1975—91; council mem. City of Hialeah, 1977-81, mayor, 1981—90, 1993—2005; pres. Martinez & Fernandez Pub. Rels., Miami Lakes, 2005—. Chmn. Fla. Hispanic Commn., 1976—83; mem. Fla. State Commn. Hispanic Affairs, 1979—82, Gov.'s Commn. Statewide Prosecution Function, 1984—85, Fla. State Comprehensive Plan Com., 1985—87; mem. Roundtable on Defense & Fgn. Policy Dem. Policy Commn., 1985—86; chmn. Dade County Council Mayors, So. Fla. Employment & Tng. Consortium, Hialeah Dade Devel. Inc. Hon. adv. Miami Dade Cmty. Coll., Hialeah Ctr. Fedn. Hispanic Students; bd. advs. Barry U., Miami Shores; mem. cmty. devel. com. United Way Dade County. Recipient Legion of Honor award, 1977, Citizen Involvement award, Crime Commn. Greater Miami, 1977, Over the Top award, Hialeah-Miami Springs YMCA, 1979, Orden del Merito de Duarte Sanchez y Mella award, President of Dominican Republic, 2003; named Pub. Adminstr. of Yr., South Fla. chpt. Am. Soc. Pub. Adminstrn., 1984. Mem.: Dade County Assn. Chiefs of Police, Fla. League Cities (past pres., Lifetime Achievement award 2006), Nat. League Cities (bd. dirs.), Dade County C. of C., Hialeah Latin C. of C., Kiwanis. Democrat. Catholic. Office: Martinez & Fernandez Public Relation 11900 Biscayne Blvd Ste 630 North Miami FL 33181-2734 Office Phone: 305-558-6555. Office Fax: 305-820-9906.*

MARTINEZ, RONALD L., literature and language professor; b. Washington, May 19, 1948; s. Rafael Humberto and Esther Lorenson Martinez; m. Mary Therese Royal, July 23, 1988; children: Liliana, Marina, Cecilia. PhD, U. Calif., Santa Cruz, 1977. Asst. prof. italian and comparative lit. U. Calif., San Diego, 1977—80; prof. italian U. Minn., Mpls., 1980—2002; prof. italian studies Brown U., Providence, 2002—. Fellowship for U. Tchrs., Nat. Endowment Humanities, 1993—94. Mem.: Dante Soc. (exec. coun. 2000—03). Democrat.

MARTINEZ, RUEBEN, entrepreneur; b. Miami, Ariz., 1940; Profl. barber; owner, founder Libreria Martinez Books and Art Gallery, 1993—. Co-founder Latino Book Festival; founding mem. Santa Ana's Reading com.; spkr. in field. Named MacArthur Fellow, John D. and Catherine T. MacArthur Found., 2004; named one of 26 Fascinating Entrepreneurs, Inc. Mag., 2005. Office: Libreria Martinez 1110 N Main St Santa Ana CA 92701 Office Phone: 714-973-7900.

MARTINEZ, TODD J., chemistry professor; b. Mar. 22, 1968; BS, Calvin Coll., 1989; PhD, U. Calif., 1994. Fulbright fellow Fritz Haber Inst. Molecular Dynamics, Jerusalem; presdl. postdoctoral fellow U. Calif., LA, 1994—96; asst. prof. U. Ill., Urbana-Champaign, 1996—2002, assoc. prof., 2002—04, prof., 2004—, Gutsgell Chair of Chemistry, 2006—. Faculty affiliate theoretical and computational biophysics group Beckman Inst. Advanced Sci. and Tech.; ad hoc reviewer for numerous sci. journals; vice-chair ACS Theoretical Chemistry Subdivision, 2005—. Recipient CAREER Award, NSF, 1998, Rsch. Innovation award, Rsch. Corp., 1998, Beckman Young Investigator award, Beckman Found., 1999, Camille Dreyfus Teacher-Scholar award, Camille & Henry Dreyfus Found., 2000—05; named a MacArthur fellow, John D. and Catherine T. MacArthur Found., 2005. Mem.: Biophysical Soc., Am. Assn. for the Advancement of Sci., Am. Physical Soc., Am. Chem. Soc. Office: U Ill Dept Chemistry MC 712 600 S Mathews Urbana IL 61801 E-mail: tmartine@uiuc.edu.

MARTINEZ, VICTOR JESUS, professional baseball player; b. Ciudad Bolivar, Venezuela, Dec. 23, 1978; s. Margot Martinez; m. Margret Martinez; 1 child, Victor Jesus Jr. Catcher, first baseman Cleve. Indians, 2004—09, Boston Red Sox, 2009—. Co-chmn. Esperanza Fiesta of Hope Program, 2004; active Tribe Loving & Care Hosp. Visits. Recipient Silver Slugger award, 2004, 2005; named Man of Yr., Cleve. Chpt., Baseball Writer's Assn. Am., 2004; named to Am. League All-Star Team, Maj. League Baseball, 2004, 2007, 2009. Achievements include setting a new Indian's franchise record for a catcher with 101 RBIs in 2004; being the first catcher in Indian's franchise history to win a Silver Slugger award, 2004. Office: Boston Red Sox 4 Yawkey Way Boston MA 02215 Office Phone: 216-420-4200.*

MARTINEZ, VILMA SOCORRO, lawyer; b. San Antonio, Oct. 17, 1943; d. Salvador and Marina (Pina) Martinez; m. Stuart R. Singer, Nov. 1968; children: Carlos, Ricardo. BA, U. Tex., 1964; LLB, Columbia U., 1967. Bar: NY 1968, Calif. 1975. Staff atty. gen. civil rights litig. NAACP Legal Def. and Edn. Fund, 1967—70; EEO counsel NY State Divsn. Human Rights, 1970—71; litig. assoc. Cahill, Gordon & Reindel, 1971—73; pres., gen. counsel Mex.-am. Legal Def. & Ednl. Fund, Inc., 1973—82; ptnr. Munger, Tolles & Olsen LLP, LA, 1982—. Dir. Anheuser-Busch Cos., Inc; cons. US Commn. on Civil Rights, 1969—74, US Census Bur., 1975—81, US Treasury Dept., 1976, Calif. Fed. Jud. Selection Com., 1977—80, Presdl. Adv. Bd. on Ambassadorial Appointments, 1977—81, US Hispanic-Mex. Govt. Internat. Commn., 1980—82; bd. dirs. Fluor Corp., 1993—2009. Regent U. Calif., 1976—90, chmn., 1984—86; mem. corp. bd. Shell Oil co., 1997—2005, Sanwa Bank Calif., 1990—2005; trustee Edward W. Hazen Found. Recipient Jefferson award, Am. Idst. Pub. Svc., 1976, John D. Rockefeller III Youth award, Rockefeller Found., 1977, U. medal of Excellence, Columbia U., 1978, Valerie Kantor award, Mex. Am. Legal Def. Edn. Fund, Inc., 1982, Lex award, Mex.-Am. Bar Assn., 1983, Excellence medal, Columbia U. Law Sch., 1992, Maynard Toll award, Legal Aid Found.; named one of Boardroom Elite, Hispanic Bus. Mag., 2007; John Hay Whitney fellow, 1964, Samuel Rubin fellow, Columbia U. Sch. Law, 1983. Office: Munger Tolles & Olson LLP 355 S Grand Ave Fl 35 Los Angeles CA 90071-1560*

MARTINEZ, WALFRIDO (WALLY MARTINEZ), lawyer; BS magna cum laude, Seton Hall U., South Orange, NJ, 1988; JD, U. Pa. Law Sch., Phila., 1991. Bar: NJ, Fla., US Ct. Appeals (11th cir.), US Dist. Ct. (no., mid., so. Fla. dists.), US Dist. Ct. (NJ dist.). Ptnr. Holland & Knight, Miami, 1991—99; founding ptnr. Hunton & Williams LLP, Miami, 1999—2004, mng. ptnr., 2006—; sr. v.p., gen. counsel Diageo North America, Inc., 2004—06. Mem. adv. com. rule and procedures, atty. examination com. US Dist. Ct. (so. Fla.), 2000—04, chmn. ad hoc com. on atty. grievance, admissions and discipline, 2002—04; mem. Fla. Bar Atty. Grievance Com., 2003—04. Bd. mem. U. Pa. Alumni Soc., 2008—; bd. trustees Nat. Assn. Law Placement Found., 2008—. Named one of 50 Most Influential Minority Lawyers in America, Nat. Law Jour., 2008; named to Fla. Super Lawyers, bus. lawyers, 2007, 2008. Office: Hunton & Williams 111 Brickell Ave Ste 2500 Miami FL 33131 Office Phone: 305-810-2507. Office Fax: 305-810-2460. Business E-Mail: wmartinez@hunton.com.*

MARTINEZ BLAND, VERONICA KAY, elementary school educator; b. Chillecothe, Ohio, Apr. 7, 1953; d. Robert Charles and Martha Josephine Fannin; m. Ralph Edward Bland, Oct. 4, 2003; 1 stepchild, Sarah Rachel Bland;children from previous marriage: Amadeo Enrico Martinez, Miguel Domingo Martinez. Student, Urbana U., Ohio, 1971—72; BS in Elem. Edn. summa cum laude, Cumberland U., Lebanon, Tenn., 1991. Tchr. 6th grade reading/lang. Rosebank Elem. Sch., Nashville, 1991—98, 1999—2000, 2d grade tchr., 1998—99, 4th grade tchr., 2000—02, reading specialist, 2002—. Sponsor Student Writers' Club, Nashville, 1991—2001; mentor intern program Belmont U., 1995—2000, mem, faculty adv. com., 1999—2000, chmn. faculty adv. com., 2001—02; curriculum developer Metro Nashville Pub. Schs., 1997, Time to Rise YMCA program, 2003. Author: (reading material for ednl. software) Bredex Corp., 2002. Rosebank chair United Way Giving Campaign, Nashville, 1993—2004; faculty rep. PTA, 1999—2000, 2004—; mem. Tying Nashville Together, 2005. Recipient Disting. Classroom Tchr. award, Metro Nashville Edn. Assn., 1994—95, Elem. Edn. award, Mayor's Coun. for Disabilities, Nashville, 1996—97; named Rosebank Tchr. of Yr., Metro Nashville Pub. Schs., 1996—97, 2005—06; grantee, Met. Nashville Pub. Edn. Found., 1996—97, 1997—98. Mem.: Nat. Staff Devel. Coun., NCTE, Mid. Tenn. Reading Assn., Internat. Reading Assn., Tenn. State PTA (hon. life), Kappa Delta Pi, Delta Kappa Gamma. Disciples Of Christ. Avocations: reading, gardening, pottery. Office: I Litton Middle Sch 4601 Hedgewood Dr Nashville TN 37216 Office Phone: 615-262-6700 ext 207. Office Fax: 615-262-6717. E-mail: veronica50@msn.com.

MARTINEZ-CONDE, SUSANA, neurologist, researcher; married. PhD in Neuroscience, U. Santiago de Compostela, Spain, 1996. Fellow Harvard Med. Sch.; dir. & prin. investigator Visual Neuroscience Lab. Barrow Neurological Inst. Founding mem. & executive chmn. Neural Correlate Soc. Mem.: Assn. for Scientific Study of Consciousness. Office: Barrow Neurological Institute St Josephs Hospital 350 W Thomas Rd Phoenix AZ 85013*

MARTINEZ DIEZ, FERNANDO, engineer; b. Tuxtla Gutierrez, Chiapas, Mexico, May 7, 1978; s. Fernando Martinez Gordillo and Maria Diez Camacho; m. Bianca Pucci Wessel, May 26, 2006. BS, ITESM, Monterrey, Mexico., 2000; Diploma in Ethics and Socio-Cultural Values, U. Pontificia Comillas, Madrid, 2000; PhD, ME, Colo. Sch. Mines, Golden, 2004. Cert. PE, SEP Mex., 2000, CWI, AWS, 2000. Quality control mgr. Estructuras y Perfiles Especiales SA, Tuxtla Gutierrez, 1997—2000; postdoctoral fellow Colo. Sch. Mines, 2004; sr. engr. rsch. and devel. Caterpillar Inc., 2004—07, engr. project team leader, 2008—. Cons. CSIM, Monterrey, 1998—2000, Estructuras y Pertiles Especiala SA, Tuxtla Gutierrez, 1999—2004, Avios Metalicos Mexicanos SA de CV, 1999—2004. Contbr. to numerous profl. jours. publ. Vol. Red Cross, Tuxtla Gutierrez, 1995—96, CEFAC, Tuxtla Gutierrez, 1999. Recipient Granjon (B), Internat. Inst. of Welding, 2007. Mem.: Sci. Rsch. Soc., ASNT, ASM, AWS. Achievements include patents for manufacturing processes and apparatuses. Personal E-mail: a_gadget@hotmail.com.

MARTINEZ-FONTS, ALFONSO, federal agency administrator; Degree in Polit. Sci., Villanova U., 1971; MBA in Fin., LI U., 1974. Mgr. Chem. Bank, Manila, Philippines, 1976—79, Mex. City, 1982—88, regional mgr. Argentina, Chile, Uruguay, Paraguay, and Bolivia NYC, 1980—82, lending officer met. divsn., lending officer internat. divsn.; pres. JP Morgan Chase, San Antonio, chmn., CEO El Paso, Tex.; spl. asst. to sec. pvt. sector office US Dept. Homeland Security, asst. sec. pvt. sector office, 2005—. Mem. comm. coun. Am. Bankers Assn.; bd. mem. Greater El Paso Chamber Found., Project ARRIBA, ACCION Internat., ACCION USA; mem. Hispanic/Latino adv. bd. Frito-Lay; mem. adv. bd. Fannie Mae. Pres. Am. C. of C., Mex. City, 1988; chmn. Greater San Antonio C. of C., 1993; bd. mem. United Way of El Paso; mem. devel. bd. U. Tex. El Paso. Recipient Humanitarian award, Nat. Conf. Christians and Jews, 1995. Office: US Dept Homeland Security 12th & C St SW Washington DC 20024*

MARTINEZ-FRAGA, PEDRO J., lawyer; b. Havana, Cuba, Sept. 9, 1960; BA with high honors, St. John's Coll., 1984; JD, Columbia U., 1987. Bar: Fla. 1988, DC 1988, US Dist. Ct. (so., mid. districts) Fla. 1988, US Ct. Appeals (11th cir.) 1989, US Dist. Ct. (Colo. dist.) 1991, US Supreme Ct. 1999. Adj. prof. law U. Miami, 2002—04; mem. com. Fla. Bar Rules of Civil Procedure, 1990—97, Fla. Bar Rules of Judicial Adminstrn., 1996—97; chair com. Fla. Bar Code & Rules of Evidence, 1996; mem. ad hoc com. on rules and procedures US Dist. Ct., So. Dist. Fla. Author, editor Florida Civil Procedure, 2000, 2001, (chapters to books); contbr. articles to profl. journals. Dir. Cuban-Am. Endowment for Arts; bd. dirs. Miami Lighthouse for Blind, New World Sch. Arts; bd. mem. bd. visitors and governors St. John's Coll. Recipient Harlan Fiske Stone scholarship, 1987; named 2001 Lawyer of the Americas, U. Miami Inter-Am. Law Review; named one of Top Lawyers in So. Fla., So. Fla. Legal Guide, 2001—05, Fla. Legal Elite, Fla. Trend Mag., 2004—05, Top Lawyers in Fla., Fla. Monthly Mag., 2004, Best Lawyers in Am., 2005—07; named to, Am. Law Inst., 1999, Best of the Bar, So. Fla. Bus. Jour., 2003—05. Fellow: Am. Bar Found.; mem.: Hispanic Bar Assn., Am. Trial Lawyers Assn., Cuban-Am. Bar Assn., Dade County Bar Assn. (chair internat. law com. 2001—02, chair fed. ct. com. 1996), Internat. Bar Assn. Office: Greenberg Traurig LLP 1221 Brickell Ave Miami FL 33131 Office Phone: 305-579-0595. Office Fax: 305-579-0717. Business E-Mail: martinezp@gtlaw.com.

MARTÍNEZ-LÓPEZ, CARMEN LEONOR, management consultant, educator; b. Aracataca, Magdalena, Colombia, Oct. 13, 1956; d. Domingo Ramón Martínez and Alicia Esther Acosta de Martínez; m. Iván R. López, May 26, 2000. Licenciate in Ednl. Adminstrn., U. San Buenaventura, Medellín, Colombia, 1980; M in Ednl. Adminstrn., U. Antioquia, Medellín, 1989; specialist in Pub. Adminstrn., U. Escuela de Adminstrn. Publica, Medellín, 1995; specialist in Indsl. Rels., U. Escuela de Adminstrn. and Fin., Medellín, 1983, MBA, 2003; PhD in Internat. Bus., U. Tex.-Pan Am., Edinburg, 2003. Bd. dirs. Inst. Polictectico Jaime Isaza Cadavid, Medellín, 1980—82; dep. and bd. dirs. budget commn. Dept. de Antioquia, Medellín, 1982—84; regional mgr. Nat. Agy. Social Security, Medellín, 1983—86; pres. External Orgnl. Cons., Medellín, 1987—93; prof., rsch. and cons. U. Escuela de Adminstrn. and Fin., Medellín, 1989—92; adminstrv. mgr. Am. Med. Holding, Medellín, 1992—93; dept. chair Inst. Colombiano de Edn. Superior de Incolda, Cali, Colombia, 1993—96; rschr. and tchr. asst. U. Tex.-Pan Am., Edinburg, 1998—2003; asst. prof. CUNY, 2004—. Strategic planning cons. Am. Med. Holding, Medellín, 1989—92; strategic mgmt. cons. U. ICESI, Cali, 1995—96; strategic planning cons. Ednl. Cooperative Uraba, Apartadó, Antioquia, Colombia, 1999—2001; vis. prof. U. Monterrey, Mexico, 1999—2000. Dep. Dept. of Antioquia, Medellín, 1982—84; v.p. Colombian Conservative Party, Medellín, 1981—83; active Poly. Inst. Jaime Isaza, Medellín, 1980—82. Fellow: Ptnrs. of the Ams. (assoc.); mem.: Acad. Internat. Bus., Bus. Assn. L.Am. Studies, Acad. Mgmt. Conservative. Roman Catholic. Avocations: golf, soccer, travel. Office: CUNY S661 199 Chambers St New York NY 10007-1097 Home: Apt 3A 450 Pelham Rd New Rochelle NY 10805 Home Fax: 914-637-9305. Personal E-mail: carleo13@aol.com.

MARTINEZ-LOPEZ, JORGE IGNACIO, internist, educator, cardiologist, consultant; b. Santurce, PR, Oct. 5, 1926; s. Jorge Martinez-Rivera and Dolores (Lopez) Martinez; m. Mona Hagan, June 12, 1950 (div. 1982); children: Jorge Alan, Anthony James, Ricardo, Matthew Joseph; m. Glenda Gayle Tomlinson, Mar. 4, 1983. MD, La. State U., 1950. Diplomate Am. Bd. Internal Medicine, Am. Bd. Cardiovascular Diseases. Intern Arecibo Dist. Hosp., PR, 1950-51; resident in internal medicine La. State U. Medicine Svc., Charity Hosp. La., New Orleans, 1954-57; trainee in cardiology, instr. dept. medicine La. State U. Med. Ctr., 1957-59, asst. prof., 1960-63, assoc. prof., 1963-70, prof., 1970-86, prof. emeritus, 1986—; clin. prof. dept. internal medicine Tex. Tech. U. Health Scis. Ctr., Lubbock, 1988; prof. dept. internal medicine Tex. Tech. U. Health Sci. Ctr., El Paso, 1988—; mem. staff R. E. Thomason

Gen. Hosp., El Paso. Cardiologist Heart Sta., Charity Hosp. La., 1960-75, dir. dept. cardiology, 1975-86, vis. physician, 1957-64, sr. vis. physician, 1964-86; cardiologist Hotel Dieu, New Orleans, 1961-86, dir. cardiology dept., 1970-75; dir. cardiac work evaluation unit Delgado Rehab. Ctr., New Orleans, 1967-86; cons. cardiology Edward F. Hebert Meml. Hosp., USN, Gretna, La., 1977-78; bd. govs. Orleans Parish Med. Soc., 1974-76; v.p. New Orleans Acad. Internal Medicine, 1969-70, pres., 1970-71. Contbr. more than 300 articles to profl. jour. Col. U.S. Army, 1951-53, 86-88, res. 1953-88, ret. Scholar Govt. P.R., 1947-50. Fellow Am. Coll. Cardiology, Am. Coll. Chest Physicians, Am. Coll. Physicians, Am. Heart Assn., Coun. Clin. Cardiology; mem. Am. Heart Assn. (fellow Coun. Clin. Cardiology, La. bd. dir. 1965-86, v.p. 1972-73, pres.-elect 1973-74, pres. 1974-75, El Paso div. pres.-elect 1989-90, pres. 1990-91, bd. dir. 1989—), Assn. Army Cardiology, La. State Med. Soc., Res. Officers Assn. (La. dept. surgeon 1963-69, 74-75, pres. Chpt. 19, 1963-69), Mil. Officers Assn. Am. Avocations: photography, music, painting. Office: Tex Tech U Health Science Ctr 4800 Alberta Ave El Paso TX 79905-2709 Home Phone: 915-751-3020; Office Phone: 915-545-6626 ext 258.

MARTINEZ-MALDONADO, MANUEL, academic administrator, dean, medical and science educator; b. Yauco, PR, Aug. 25, 1937; s. Manuel and Josefa Maldonado (Josefa Maldonado) Martinez; m. Nivia Elena Rivera, Dec. 18, 1959; children: Manuel, David, Ricardo, Pablo. BS, U. PR, 1957; MD, Temple U., 1961. Diplomate Am. Bd. Internal Medicine, Am. Bd. Nephrology. Intern St. Charles Hosp., Toledo, 1961—62; resident VA Hosp., San Juan, 1962—65, chief resident, 1964—65, chief med. svcs., 1973—90, co-dir. renal metabolic lab., 1973—90; instr. U. Tex. Southwestern Med. Sch., Dallas, 1967—68; from asst. prof. to prof. medicine, co-dir. renal sect. Baylor Coll. Medicine, Houston, 1968—73; prof. medicine U. PR Sch. Medicine, 1973—90, prof. physiology, 1974—90; prof. medicine U. Caribbean, Bayamon, PR, 1980—90; prof., vice chmn. dept. medicine Emory U. Sch. Medicine, 1990—98; chief med. svcs. and clin. affairs Atlanta VA Med. Ctr., 1990—98; v.p. for rsch., prof. medicine Oreg. Health Scis. U., Portland, 1998—99, v.p. rsch., 1999—2000; pres., dean, prof. medicine and physiology Ponce Sch. Medicine, 2000—06; prof. medicine, pharmacology, toxicology U. Louisville, 2007, exec. v.p. rsch., 2007—. Assoc. mem. nephrology com. Am. Bd. Internal Medicine, 1982—86; nat. adv. bd. gen. medicine B study sect. Nat. Inst. Arthritis, Metabolism and Digestive Diseases NIH; bd. sci. counselors, sci. advisors com. Nat. Heart, Lung and Blood Inst., NIH. Author: La Voz Sostenida, 1984, Palm Beach Blues, 1986, Por Amor al Arte, 1989, Hotel Maria, 1989, Isla Verde, 1999, Novela de Medicdia, 2003; film critic: El Reportero, 1983—86, El Mundo, 1987—90, editor/co-editor: in field, mem. editl. bd.: U. P.R. Press; editor: Am. Jour. of Med. Scis., 1994—98, Am. Jour. Kidney Disease, 1997—2002; contbr. over 200 articles to profl. jours. Com. mem. 500th Anniversary of Discovery Am., PR, 1987—92; pres. bd. trustees Inst. Puerto Rican Culture and Performing Arts Ctr., 2001—05; trustee Corp. Musical Arts, 2001—05, Inst. Puerto Rican Lit., 2001—05; chair culture and recreation panel PR 2025; health com. Popular Dem. Com., PR, 1982—84; bd. dirs. Alliance for PR, Inc., bd. sec., 2004—06. Recipient Lederle Internat. award, Lederle Corp., 1966—67, Macy Faculty Scholar award, The Josiah Macy Jr. Found., 1979—80, Grand Mobil prize medicine, Mobil Oil Corp., 1981, Disting. Alumnus award, Temple Med. Sch., 1988, Presdl. award, Nat. Kidney Found., 1988, Donald W. Seldin award, 1994, Disting. Physician award, PR Hosps. Assn., 1988, Orden del Cafetal award, Municipality of Yauco, 1989, Abelardo Díaz Alfaro award, Medicine & Humanites Acad. of Family Medicine, 2002, Svc. Exec. award, PR Mfrs. Assn., 2005, Svc. Exec. of Yr. award, PR Mfrs. Assn. (So. region), 2006; named one of Outstanding Young Men, PR C. of C., 1976. Master: ACP; fellow: AAAS, Am. Heart Assn. (hypertension rsch. coun.), Coun. for High Blood Pressure Rsch.; mem.: Am. Acad. Arts and Scis. (hon. fgn.), Nat. Kidney Found. (chmn. pub. policy com. 1992—94, chmn. sci. adv. com. 1987—91, Pub. Svc. medal, Donald W. Seldin award), Consortium Southeastern Hypertension Ctrs. (bd. dirs.), Assn. Am. Physicians, Inter-Am. Soc. Hypertension Assn. (bd. govs., chmn. 8th Sci. Congress 1989, U.S. Pharmacopeial Conv. Cardio Renal Drugs com. 1990—96), L.Am. Soc. Nephrology (v.p. 1987—91, pres.-elect 1991—94, pres. 1994—96, Miatello award 1999), Am. Soc. for Clin. Investigation, So. Soc. Clin. Investigation (sec.-treas. 1983—85, pres. 1985—86, Founders medal 1990), Am. Soc. Nephrology (legis. liaison com., chmn. audit com. 1988), Inst. Medicine of NAS (com. on human rights 1987—92), Alpha Omega Alpha. Roman Catholic. Achievements include research in kidney physiology and pathophysiology, treatment of clinical disturbances of blood composition, clinical use of diuretics, mechanisms of the devel. of hypertension. Avocations: theater, art, music, poetry, films. Office: U Louisville Rm 200 Jouett Hall 2310 S Third St Louisville KY 40292 Home Phone: 502-749-0339; Office Phone: 502-852-8373. Personal E-mail: martinem_pms@hotmail.com. Business E-Mail: m0mart10@louisville.edu.

MARTINEZ-MUNOZ, GLORIA ANGELICA, biochemist, researcher; b. Mexico City, May 28, 1968; d. Armando Martinez-Ramos and Amalia Munoz-Escobar; m. Juan Manuel Morgan, Dec. 16, 1992 (div.); 1 child, Carolina Morgan-Martinez. B in Chemistry, U. Nacional Autónoma de Méx., Mexico City, 1990, MD in Chemistry, 1999, PhD in Chemistry, 2005. Asst. prof. dept. chemistry U. Nacional Autónoma de Méx., Mexico City, 1995—96; assoc. rschr. Procter and Gamble, Mexico City, 1995—96; assoc. technician Cellular Physiology Inst., Mexico City, 1997—99; postdoctoral assoc. SUNY Upstate Med. U., Syracuse, 2005—. Contbr. articles to profl. jours. Achievements include research in K+/H+ antiporter in the vacuole of yeast; model of permeabilized spheroplasts for bioenergetics studies in yeast; application of fluorescent dyes to the study of internal pH and membrane potential in yeast; study of link between plasma membrane Ht-ATPase and V-ATPase on yeast. Avocations: literature, piano, painting. Office Fax: 315-464-8750. Personal E-mail: gloria_martinez2006@yahoo.com.mx. Business E-Mail: martineg@upstate.edu.

MARTINEZ-PONS, MANUEL, educational psychologist; b. Dominican Republic, Apr. 19, 1940; arrived in US, 1954; s. Manuel and Alsacia (Gorsd) Martinez. AA, U. State of N.Y., 1973, BS, 1975; BGS, U. Nebr., Omaha, 1973, MS, 1975; PhD, U. Nebr., Lincoln, 1977; MPh, CUNY, 1985, PhD, 1988; postgrad., Bklyn. Coll., 2006—. Rsch. assoc. CUNY, 1982-85, instr. computer programing, 1985-86, assoc. prof. Sch. Edn., Bklyn. Coll., 1986—2004, prof. Sch. Edn., Bklyn. Coll., 2004—, grad. dep. Sch. Edn. Bklyn. Coll., 2006—. Adj. instr. U. Nebr., Lincoln, 1975—77, Omaha, 1978; adj. instr. City Coll. CUNY, 1980—81, adj. asst. prof. Medgar Evers Coll., 1985, adj. asst. prof. Queens Coll., 86. Author (with others): (book) Student Perceptions in the Classroom: Causes and Consequences, 1992; author: Research in the Social Sciences and Education: Principles and Process, 1997, Statistics in Modern Research: Applications in the Social Sciences and Education, 1999, The Psychology of Teaching and Learning: A Three-Step Guide, 2001, Le tranfert effectiv comme un processus d'auto-regulation, 2002, Continuum Guide to Successful Teaching in Higher Education, 2003; cons. editor: Jour. Exptl. Edn., 1997—; contbr. articles to profl. jours. Transport mission pilot USAF, civil air patrol USAF. Recipient numerous grants. Mem.: Am. Psychol. Soc., Am. Ednl. Rsch. Assn., Am. Mensa. Avocation: aviation. Home: 453 Beach 138th St Rockaway Park NY 11694-1341 Office: Brooklyn Coll Sch of Edn Brooklyn NY 11210 Office Phone: 718-951-5447. Personal E-mail: mpons@msn.com.

MARTINEZ SOMALO, EDUARDO CARDINAL, cardinal, archbishop; b. Banos de Rios Tobia, Spain, Mar. 31, 1927; Licentiate in Theology & Canon Law, Pontifical Gregorian Univ., Rome; attended, Pontifical Ecclesiastical Acad., Rome; D in Canon Law, Pontifical Lateran Univ., Rome, 1956. Ordained priest Diocese of Calahorra y La Calzada, Spain, 1950; diplomatic positions Secretariat of State, Vatican City, 1956—70, assessor, 1970—75, substitute, 1979—88; prof. Pontifical Ecclesiastical Acad., Rome; counselor Apostolic Delegation to Great Britain, 1970; ordained bishop, 1975; archbishop, apostolic nuncio to Colombia, 1975—79; prefect Congregation for Divine Worship & Discipline of the Sacraments, Rome, 1988—92; elevated to cardinal, 1988; cardinal-deacon Ss. Nome di Gesu, 1988—99; prefect Congregation for Institutes of Consecrated Life and Societies of Apostolic Life, Rome, 1992—2004; chamberlain of the Apostolic Chamber Rome, 1993—2007; cardinal-priest Ss. Nome di Gesu, 1996—; chamberlain emeritus of the Apostolic Chamber, 2007—. Roman Catholic. Office: Vatican City 00120 Vatican City Italy

MARTINEZ TORRES, RAFAEL L., territorial supreme court justice; b. Humacao, PR, Feb. 14, 1959; s. Luis Martinez and Aurea Torres; m. Sandra S. Cruz Rodriguez. BA magna cum laude, Univ. PR, JD cum laude, 1983. Legal adv. PR Supreme Ct.; atty. Cestero Marchand & Quintero Rivera; atty. litigation div. Fiddler, Gonzalez & Rodriquez; exec. dir. Govt. Commn. PR House Reps., 1993—95; judge PR Cir. Ct. Appeals, 1995—2009; assoc. justice PR Supreme Ct., 2009—. Mailing: Rama Judicial de Puerto Rico PO Box 9022392 San Juan PR 00902-2392*

MARTINI, JASON, academic administrator; b. Lubbock, Tex., Mar. 8, 1973; s. John William Martini, Jr and Sue Ann Martini; children: Loryn N'cole Terry, Alyssa Brooke, Kellee Elise. BS in Emergency Med. Svc., AAS in Allied Health, AA in Pre Nursing Studies, MS in Computer Info. Sys. Cert. network+ CompTIA, A+ CompTIA. Network adminstr. Patterson-UTI Energy, Inc.; staff sgt. paramedic USAF; computer maintenance instr. Western Tex. Coll., interim dean, tech. & telecom. Snyder, dir. tech. & telecom., 2006—. Trampoline coach Cheer Star Athletics, Snyder, Tex. With Air Force, 1996—2001, Lackland AFB. Office: Western Tex Coll 6200 College Ave Snyder TX 79549

MARTINI, JOHN, engineering educator, department chairman; b. Orange, NJ, Dec. 6, 1951; s. Vincent James and Rose Ida Martini; m. Janet Lee Chitwood, Aug. 31, 1974; children: Cara Lee Whedbee, Gabriel Vincent Martine. AAS in Electronics Tech., U. Ark., Ft. Smith, 1977; BA in Liberal Studies, U. Okla., Norman, 1990; MA, Webster U., Ft. Smith, 1994. Lt. col. USAF, Ark. Air N.G., Ft. Smith, 1979—2005; dir. facility svcs. St. Edward Mercy Med. Ctr., Ft. Smith, 1992—96; advance program instr. John Brown U., Ft. Smith, 1995—98; dir. facility svcs. Holt Krock Clinic, Ft. Smith, 1996—98; lead asst. prof. mfg. tech. mgmt. U. Ark., 1998—2004, asst. prof. electronics tech., dept. chair, 2004—. Dir. river valley best and frontier trails best robotics championships, U. Ark. BEST Robotics Inc., Ft. Smith, 2004—, bd. mem. dist. 1 rep., Dallas, 2005—; stem adv. com. mem. Ark. Sci. and Tech. Authority, Little Rock, 2005—. Recipient Master Tchr. award, U. Ark., 2006—07, Rose award, Hospitality Ptnr. of Yr., City of Ft. Smith, 2006; named Advisor of Yr., U. Ark., 2003—04. Mem.: Nat. Assn. Indsl. Tech. (Ann Arbor, Mich.) (pres. exec. bd. 2008—, pres., C.C. and Tech. Inst. Divsn. 2007—, Outstanding Indsl. Tech. Faculty award, Region 4 2007). Conservative. Baptist. Avocations: guitar, golf.

MARTINKOSKY, JESSICA, art educator; b. Va. d. Beverly and John Martinkosky. BFA, James Madison U., Harrisonburg, Va., 2001; MFA, Va. Commonwealth U., Richmond, 2003. Educator Peninsula Fine Arts Ctr., Newport News, Va., 2004—07; asst. prof. fine art ceramics Blue Ridge CC, Weyers Cave, Va., 2007—. Exhibition, The Winter Solstice: Borrowed (Ceramics Biennial Exhbn. award, Manchester, NH, 2008), A Pox on Both Your Houses (Clay3 (Cubed): 2008 Nat. Juried Ceramics Exhbn. award, Warrenville, Ill.), My Pie! (Carbondale Clay Nat. award, 2008). Mem.: Nat. Coun. Edn. Ceramic Arts. Avocations: horseback riding, hiking, gardening, reading. Office: Blue Ridge CC Box 80 Weyers Cave VA 24486 Business E-Mail: martinkoskyj@brcc.edu.

MARTIN-LOWRY, BEVERLY ANNE, writer, columnist; b. Washington, Oct. 25, 1948; d. James Aubrey and Gertha Mae Martin; m. Courtland Alan Milner, Apr. 20, 1968 (div. Oct. 17, 1989); children: Jennifer Anne Litton, Martin Alan Milner; m. Peter Hans Lowry, Dec. 29, 1999. CEO Pen 2 Paper, Ink, Live Oak, Tex., 2003—. Author: In October, I Turn Fifty! A Satirical Look Back on Life, 2000, Memoirs and Confessions: From Europe to the USA, 2001, (novels) Strong Appetites, 2004, Can't Cook Anonymous, 2004, The Most Unlikely Angel: A Trilogy of Love, Life, and Laughter, 2005, The Reel Thing; editorial columnist: Sounding Off; contbr. articles to local newspapers. Mem.: Am. Legion (life). Republican. Presbyterian. Avocations: swimming, reading, travel. Personal E-mail: n2books@satx.rr.com.

MARTINO, JOSEPH F., bishop; b. Phila., May 1, 1946; s. Joseph F. and Eleanor Rose Martino. Grad., St. Charles Borromeo Sem., Overbrook, Pa.; Licentiate in Sacred Theology, Gregorian U., Rome, D in Ecclesiastical History. Ordained priest Archdiocese of Phila., 1970, dir. office for ecumenical and interreligious affairs, 1990—93, 1997—2003, dir. office for renewal of pastoral life, 1992—97, aux. bishop, 1996—2003; asst. pastor Epiphany of Our Lord Parish, Phila., 1971—75, Our Lady of Grace Parish, Penndel, Pa., 1975—77, Immaculate Conception Parish, Jenkintown, Pa., 1977—81, St. Barbara Parish, Phila., 1987; faculty mem. Bishop Shanahan High Sch., 1982—84; dean of formation, Theology Divsn. St. Charles Borromeo Sem., Overbrook, Pa., 1986—92, asst. prof. ch. history, 1986—92; rev. monsignor, 1991; ordained bishop, 1996; titular bishop Diocese of Cellae, Maurotania, 1996—; bishop Diocese of Scranton, Pa., 2003—. Co-chair Pa. Conf. on Interchurch Cooperation; Cath. co-chair Internat. Cath. Mennonite Dialogue; mem. Eccles. Adv. Com., Cardinal Newman Soc. for Preservation of Cath. Higher Edn., Adv. Coun. Catholics United for the Faith; bd. trustees Basilica Nat. Shrine of Immaculate Conception, Washington, 2004; rep. diocesan priests, Region III, Nat. Adv. Coun. Adminstrv. Com. Nat. Conf. Cath. Bishops, mem. Evangelization com., mem. Ecumenical and Interreligious Affairs com. Roman Catholic. Office: 300 Wyoming Ave Scranton PA 18503 Office Phone: 610-667-3394.

MARTINO, JOSEPH PAUL, research scientist, researcher; b. Warren, Ohio, July 16, 1931; s. Joseph and Anna Elizabeth (Kubina) M.; m. Mary Lou Bouquot, May 18, 1957 (dec. Jan. 1988); children: Theresa, Anthony, Michael; m. Nancy McCoy, Dec. 28, 2000. AB in Physics, Miami U., Ohio, 1953; MSEE, Purdue U., 1955; PhD in Stats., Ohio State U., 1961; grad., Air War Coll., 1972. Commd. 2d lt. USAF, 1953, advanced through grades to col., 1973, project engr. armament lab. Wright-Patterson AFB, Ohio, 1955-58, mathematician Office Sci. Rsch. Washington, 1961-62, staff scientist Avionics Lab. Wright-Patterson AFB, 1972-73, dir. engring. standardization Def. Electronics Supply Ctr. Dayton, Ohio, 1973-75, ret., 1975; sr. scientist, rsch. inst. U. Dayton, 1975-93. Author: Technological Forecasting for Decisionmaking, 1972, rev. edit., 1983, 3d edit., 1992, A Fighting Chance-The Moral Use of Nuclear Weapons, 1988, Science Funding: Politics and Porkbarrel, 1992, Research and Development Project Selection, 1995, (novel) The Justice Cooperative, 2004; assoc. editor: Tech. Forecasting and Social Change Jour., 1968—. With USAF, 1953—75, col., 1973—75. Fellow IEEE (Centennial medal 1984), AAAS, AIAA (assoc.); mem. Inst. for Ops. Rsch. and Mgmt. Sci., Am. Soc. Engring. Mgmt., Engrs. Club of Dayton. Roman Catholic. Office Phone: 937-492-4729. Business E-Mail: j.p.martino@ieee.org.

MARTINO, MICHAEL CHARLES, entertainer, musician, actor; b. Phila., Sept. 10, 1950; s. Salvatore Joseph and Marie Angela (Langone) M. Grad. high sch., Upper Darby, Pa. Spokesperson/rep. Petosa Accordion Co., Seattle, 1979—; featured TV entertainer Mike Martino Show, Delaware County, Pa., 1987-89; accordion tchr. Drexel Hill, Pa., 1989—; featured artist Am. Accordion Soc. Conv., King of Prussia, Pa., 2003; actor TV series Hack, Channel 3, 2003. Entertainer, host, prodr. St. Jude's Children's Hosp. Marathon, King of Prussia, Pa., 1973; opening act comedian Morty Gunty, 1973, Pat Cooper, Phila., 1981; guest artist, entertainer Internat. Platform Assn. Conv., Washington, 1979, Am. Accordion Musicological Soc. Festival and symposium, King of Prussia, 2003; nite club performer Glen Mills, Pa., 1989; actor TV commls., Elkton, Md., 1979, Halloween Spl. KYW-TV, Phila., 1986, TV show Hack, 2003; performed radio contest jingle Sta. KISS 100 radio, Media, Pa., 1992; featured soloist Am. Accordian Festival, King of Prussia, Pa., 2003; opening act for Donna Theodore Fundraiser for Joe Theodore, Glassboro, NJ, 2005, Charlie Graci Rock and Roll Pioneer, Del. County, Pa., 2004. Author: (movie) Forever Fiftys, 1990; composer, dir., prodr., actor: (video) Forever Fiftys; composer: (movie) That First September; creator, performer Suspended Triple Bellows Shake Technique for the Accordion, 1994; composer (ballad) Through the Music, Through the Words I Sing, 1995, (sung by Donna Theodore) Through the Music Through the Words I Sing, 1998; actor: (movie) Jesus' Son, 1999, (TV show) Hack, 2003; guest performer Accordion Conv., King of Prussia, 2003; featured in various articles. Recipient citation U.S. Ho. Reps., 1989, Proclamation Mike Martino Day Mayor Ward, Del. County, 1988, Danny Thomas Hon. award St. Jude's Hosp., Del. County, 1973, Mayor's Svc. award Upper Darby, Pa., 1994. Roman Catholic. Avocations: antique cars, dogs. Home: 2530 Stoneybrook Ln Drexel Hill PA 19026-1610

MARTINO, PAULA L., government agency administrator, art historian, educator; BS in Bus., U. Md., Coll. Pk., 2001, MA in Art History, 2005. Pres. Md. County & Mcpl. Svc., La Plata, Md., 1993—; govt. affairs cons. Southern Md. Assn. Realtor, Hughesville, 2002—; adj. prof. art history Coll. Southern Md., La Plata, 2004—. Charter mem. Southern Md. Women's League, Inc., Waldorf; pres. Charles County Archaeological Soc., La Plata, Md., 2008—; sec. Southern Md. Women's League Found., Waldorf, 2008—; mem., maj. gifts com. Coll. Southern Md. Found., La Plata, 2008—. Office: Maryland County & Mcpl Svc 101 Burning Bush Pl La Plata MD 20646

MARTINO, RENATO RAFFAELE CARDINAL, cardinal, archbishop, diplomat; b. Salerno, Italy, Nov. 23, 1932; Attended in Philosophy and Theology, Pontifical Gregorian U.; attended in Civil and Canon Law, Pontifical Lateran U.; attended Pontifical Pastoral Inst., Lateran U.; postgrad., Sacra Romana Rota, Pontifical Eccles. Acad.; PhD in Canon Law, Pontifical Lateran U., 1962; PhD, Saint John's U., New York, USA, Malloy Coll., Rockeville Ctr, New York, USA, St. Thomas U., Miami Gardens, Florida, USA, Seton Hall U., South Orange, USA, Marywood U., Scranton, USA, Christendom Coll., Front Royal, USA, Sacred Heart U., Connecticut, USA, Catholic U., Sao Salvador, Brazil, Catholic U., Salta, Argentina, Gonzaga U., Spokane, USA, Assumption U., Bangkok, Thailand, State U., Salerno, Italy. Ordained priest Archdiocese of Salerno-Campagna-Acerno, Italy, 1957; attaché, 2d sec. Apostolic Nunciature, Nicaragua, 1962-64, from 2d to 1st sec. Philippines, 1964-66, 1st sec., 2d auditor Lebanon, 1966-70, counselor Canada, 1975-78, Brazil, 1978-80, pro-nuncio Thailand, 1980-86, apostolic del., 1980, 1st apostolic pro-nuncio Singapore, 1981; head dept. internat. orgns. Secretariat of State, Vatican City, 1970-75; ordained bishop, 1980; permanent observer Holy See to UN NYC, 1986—2002; pres. Pontifical Council for Justice and Peace, Rome, 2002—, Pontifical Council for Pastoral Care of Migrants & Itinerant Peoples, Rome, 2006—09; elevated to cardinal, 2003; cardinal-deacon S. Francesco di Paola ai Monti, 2003—. Mem., head Holy See; del. to numerous confs. Decorated Chaplain Grand Cross Conventual ad honorem Sovereign and Mil. Order Malta, Knight Grand Cross Most Exalted Order White Elephant, Grand Officer in the Order of Merit of the Italian Republic, Knight Comdr. with Star of Equestrian Order Sepulchre Jerusalem, Knight Comdr. Order of Cedar, Lebanon, Cross Pro Piis Meritis Sovereign and Mil. Order Malta, Bailiff Grand Cross of Honor and Devotion, Knights Of Malta, Knight Grand Cross Order of Christ, Portugal, Francisco de Miranda, Venezuela, Order of Libertado Gen. San Martin, Argentina, Grand Officer, Order of Sts. Maurice and Lazarus. Roman Catholic. Office: Piazza S Calisto 16 Vatican City Italy 00120*

MARTINO, ROBERT SALVATORE, orthopedic surgeon; b. Clarksburg, W.Va., May 31, 1931; s. Leonard L. and Sarafina (Foglia) M.; m. Lenora Cappellanti, May 22, 1954; children: Robert S. Jr., Leslie L. Reckziegel. AB, W.Va. U., 1953, postgrad., 1955-56, BS in Medicine, 1958; MD, Northwestern U., 1960. Diplomate Am. Bd. Orthop. Surgery; lic. Ill., Calif., Ind. Intern Chgo. Wesley, 1960-61; resident dept. orthopaedic surgery Northwestern U., 1961-65, Chgo. Wesley Meml., 1961-62, Am. Legion Hosp. for Crippled Children, 1962-63, Cook County Hosp., Chgo., 1964, 64-65; orthopaedic surgeon Gary, Ind., 1965-67; orthopaedic surgeon Merrillville, Ind., 1967—. Fellow Nat. Found. Infantile Paralysis, 1956, Office of Vocat. Rehab., Hand Surgery, 1965; chief of staff St. Mary Med. Ctr., 1976, chief of surgery, 1974-85; chief of staff Gary Treatment Ctr./Ind. Crippled Children's Svcs., 1974-84; adj. asst. prof. anatomy Ind. U., 1978, clin. asst. prof. orthop. surgery, 1980, emeritus asst. prof. anatomy and cell biology Ind. U., 2003, emeritus clin. asst. prof. orthop. surgery, 2003; mem. Zoning Bd., 1989-90. Chmn. Planning Bd. Town of Dune Acres, 1992-96; bd. dirs. United Steel Workers Union Health Care Plan, 1994—, St. Mary's Med. Ctr., Hobart, Ind.; com. on Health Care Reform. Capt. infantry US Army, 1953—55, active duty USAR, 1955—58. Fellow ACS (emeritus), Am. Acad. Orthop. Surgery (emeritus); mem. AMA, NRA, Ind. Med. Soc., Ill. Med. Soc., Chgo. Med. Soc., Ill. Orthop. Soc., Ind. Orthop. Soc., Mid-Am. Orthop. Assn., Tri-State Orthop. Soc., Clin. Orthop. Soc. Republican. Roman Catholic. Home: 22 Oak Dr Chesterton IN 46304-1016 Personal E-mail: indorth@aol.com, brutabobm@aol.com.

MARTINO, SAL, medical association administrator; 3 children. BA in Polit. Sci., CUNY: Queens Coll., Flushing; grad., NY Hosp. Sch. Radiography, 1976; M in Hosp. Adminstrn., 1979; M in Health Edn., CUNY: Lehman Coll., Bronx, 1986; M in Higher Edn., Columbia U., NYC, 1989, EdD, 1991. Cert. Am. Soc. Assn. Execs., 2005. Darkroom tech. Queens Gen. Hosp.; asst. prof. to prof. radiologic tech. CUNY:

Hostos CC, NYC, 1979—99, dir. radiologic tech. program, chmn. allied health dept., assoc. dean academic affairs; dir. edn. Am. Soc. Radiologic Technologists, Albuquerque, 1999—2000, v.p. edn. rsch., 2000—01, COO, Edn. Rsch. Found., 2001—, exec. v.p., chief academic officer, 2001—08, CEO, 2008—. Bd. dirs. NYC Soc. Radiologic Technologists, 1982—86; bd. trustees Am. Registry Radiologic Technologists, 1987—95; vice chmn. exam com. Am. Soc. Assn. Execs., mem. health care cmty. com. Fellow: Am. Soc. Radiologic Technologists; mem.: Commn. Accreditation Allied Health Edn. Programs, Acad. Radiology Rsch. Office: Am Soc Radiologic Technologists 15000 Ctrl Ave SE Albuquerque NM 87123-3909*

MARTINO, SILVANA, osteopath, medical oncologist; b. Guardia Piemontese, Italy, Sept. 7, 1948; came to U.S., 1958; d. Antonio and Elena (Iannuzzi) M. BS in Psychology, Wayne State U., 1970; DO, Mich. State U., 1973. Bd. cert. internal medicine and med. oncology. Intern Detroit Osteo. Hosp., 1973-74; resident in internal medicine Botsford Hosp., Farmington, Mich., 1974-77; fellow in oncology Wayne State U. Sch. Medicine, Detroit, 1977-79, asst. prof. med., 1979-88, assoc. prof., 1988-93; med. dir. Westlake Comprehensive Breast Ctr., Westlake Village, Calif., 1993-97, Breast Ctr., Van Nuys, Calif., 1997-99; med. oncologist John Wayne Cancer Inst., Santa Monica, Calif., 1999—. Full-time staff Harper-Grace Hosps., Detroit, 1979-93, coord. oncology housestaff 1979-83; univ. affiliate, sect. of oncology, dept. medicine, Hutzel Hosp., Detroit, 1979-93; clin. advisor breast cancer prognostic study Mich. Cancer Found., Detroit, 1981-86; univ. affiliate dept. medicine Detroit Receiving Hosp., 1983-93; adj. faculty dept. medicine Wayne State U. 1989-92; mem. oncology drug adv. com. FDA, 2002—, chair, 2005—; spkr. in field. Co-author: Diet & Cancer: Markers, Prevention and Treatment, 1994; contbr. articles to profl. jours., chpt. to book. Bd. dir. Wellness Cmty., Conjeo Valley/Ventura, Calif., 1995-99; bd. dir. ACS Greater Conjeo Valley Unit, Thousand Oaks, Calif., 1994-99. Fellow Am. Coll. Osteo. Internists; mem. AAAS, Am. Osteo. Assn., Am. Soc. Clin. Oncology, Internat. Assn. Breast Cancer Rsch., Am. Soc. Preventive Oncology, Am. Assn. for Cancer Rsch., Inc., Southwest Oncology Group (chair breast com. 1992-2000, co-chair cancer control rsch. com. 87-92, oncology drug adv. com. 2002-2006, chmn. com. 2005-06). Office Phone: 310-582-7900. Business E-Mail: smartino@theangelesclinic.org.

MARTINOVSKI, BILYANA, language educator, researcher; d. Milorad Simeonovich Martinovsky and Ekaterina Terzieva Malmborg; 1 child, Josef Benjamin. Dr (hon.), Goteborg U., 2000. Asst. prof. U. Coll. Boras, Sweden, 2006—; lectr. Goteborg U., Sweden, 2000. Sr. rschr. Inst. Creative Techs., USC, Marina del Rey, Calif., 2000—07; bd. editors Jour. Intercultural Comm., Group Decision and Negotiation Jour., NYC, 2007. Translator: (poetry) Saga of Emgyon, History of the idea of the Underworld. Mem. Marston Hill: Internat. Found. for the Quality of Life, Mullsjo, Sweden. Fellow Book project: Uncertainty in Wittgenstein and Buddhism, Swedish Treasury Bank, 2000; Cognitive processes discourseing fellowship, STINT, 2000. Office: Goteborg Univ Dept Of Linguistics Box 200 Goteborg 41282 Sweden

MARTIN-RUIZ, BEATRIZ, music company executive; b. Bilbao, Vizcaya, Spain, Dec. 7, 1972; d. Luis Martin Felipe and Maria Ines Ruiz Iparraguirre; m. Michael J. Hughes, May 21, 1999; 1 child, Gabriel Martin Hughes. Profl. diploma, Real Conservatorio Superior Musica, Madrid, 1992, diploma in Art, 1995; MusB, U. Ill., Urbana, U. Ill., Champaign, 1996. Admissions counselor U. Ill., Champaign, 2001—05, Iona Coll., New Rochelle, NY, 2005—07; conservatory music coord. Purchase Coll., SUNY, Purchase, 2007—. Office: Conservatory Music Purchase Coll 735 Anderson Hill Rd Purchase NY 10577 Office Fax: 914-251-6739. Business E-Mail: beatriz.martin-ruiz@purchase.edu.

MARTINS, ALEX, professional sports team executive; b. Kearny, NJ; m. Julia Martins; children: Sophia, Gabrielle. BSBA, Villanova U., 1986; MBA, U. Ctrl. Fla. Asst. pub. rels. dept. NBA Phila. 76ers, 1986—88; asst. sports info. dir. Georgetown U., 1988—89; dir. publicity/media rels. NBA Orlando Magic, 1989—96, sr. dir. comm., 1996—98, exec. v.p. mktg. and franchise rels., 2005—06, COO, 2006—; sr. v.p. mktg. and branding NBA New Orleans Hornets; v.p. comm. and pub. affairs NFL Cleve. Browns; v.p. sports ventures Tavistock Grp., 2003—05. Former chmn. bd. Magic Action Team Cmty. Fund (now Orlando Magic Youth Fund). Office: Orlando Magic 8701 Maitland Summit Blvd Orlando FL 32810*

MARTINS, DAVID, medical researcher; s. Richard Ayodele and Felicia Asabi Martins. MBBS, U. Ibadan, Nigeria, 1989; MS, UCLA, 2005. Cert. in internal medicine Calif. Med. Bd., 1989. Med. dir. To Help Everyone Clinic, LA, 2000—08; dir., Clin. Rsch. Ctr. Charles Drew U., LA, 2000—. Founding dir. Knight Inst., LA, 2008—. Contbr. articles to med. jours. Elder-in-charge Fountain Blessing, LA. Recipient Best Tchg. Resident award, Charles Drew U., 1998, Best Clinician award, 2000, Excellence award, 2002. Mem.: AMA. Achievements include research in clinical hypertension. Home: 326 North Western Ave #125 Los Angeles CA 90004 Office: Charles Drew Univ 1731 W 120th St Los Angeles CA 90059 Home Fax: 213-480-3364. Personal E-mail: dsomartins@yahoo.com. Business E-Mail: davidmartins@cdrewu.edu.

MARTINS, JACK M., mayor; m. Paula Martins; children: Kaitlin, Vanessa, Emma, Caroline. Grad., Am. U.; JD, St. John's U. Sch. Law. Mayor Inc. Village of Mineola, LI, NY, 2003—. Mem. fin. policy com. NY State Conf. Mayors' Legis. Com., 2006—, mem. exec. com., 2007—, Nassau County Village Ofcls. Assn. Former pres. NYS Portuguese Civic Assn.; mem. Corpus Christi Sch. Bd., Mineola Libr. Bd.; zone chair Lions Dist. 20 K-2; bd. mem. Am. Found. Charities of Portugal, Mineola Portuguese Ctr., Escola Julio Dinis, Mineola, Heart Coun. LI. Recipient Ambassador's award, Heart Coun. LI, Smart Growth award, Vision LI, 2005. Mem.: LI Portuguese Lions Club, County Seat Kiwanis Club. Republican. Office: Village of Mineola Mayor Gen Offices 155 Washington Ave Mineola NY 11501

MARTINS, NELSON, physics professor; b. Santos, Brazil, Oct. 18, 1930; s. Aniceto and Angelica Martins; m. Maria Lucia, Jan. 8, 1959 (div. Sept. 1983); children: Flavia, Paulo. BS in Physics, Mackenzie U., São Paulo, Brazil, 1958; D in Physics, Pontifica U., Campinas, Brazil, 1977. Cert. physicist. Dir. engring. Mackenzie U., 1971-73, dir. Exact Sci., 1983-90; gen. dir. Ednl. Found., Barretos, Brazil, 1973-76; chief physics dep. Engring. Sch., Araraquara, Brazil, 1991; chief physics dept. U. Santo Amaro, São Paulo, 1990-92; dir. CCET Ctr. Exact Scis. and Tech., São Paulo, 1992-95. Author: (with others) Electriciy and Magnetism, 1973, Dimensional Analysis, 1980, Dynamics, 1982. Mem. Am. Assn. Physics Tcrhs., Brazil Soc. Physics. Office: Sorocaba Engring Sch Rod Sen Jose Ermirio Moraes Sorocaba 18001970 Brazil Personal E-mail: nelson_martins30@yahoo.com.br. Business E-Mail: nmartins@uniabc.br.

MARTINS, PETER, performing company executive, choreographer; b. Copenhagen, Oct. 27, 1946; arrived in U.S., 1967, naturalized, 1970; m. Lisa LaCour (div.); 1 child, Nilas; m. Darci Kistler. Pupil of Vera Volkova and Stanley Williams with Royal Danish Ballet. With NYC Ballet, 1967—, tchr., 1975, ballet master, 1981-83, co-ballet master-in-chief, 1983-89, ballet master-in-chief, 1990—. Tchr. Sch. Am. Ballet, NYC, 1975, chmn., 1983—; artistic advisor Pa. Ballet, 1982—; co-founder & artistic dir. NY Choreographic Inst., 2000—; participant, Voices of the Arts Kennedy Ctr. for Performing Arts, Washington, 2006. Mem. Royal Danish Ballet, 1965—67, prin. dancer including Bournonville repertory, 1967, guest artist NYC Ballet, 1967—70, prin. dancer, 1970—83, guest artist regional ballet cos. U.S., guest artist Nat. Ballet Can., Royal Ballet London, Grand Theatre Geneva, Paris Opera, Vienna State Opera, Munich State Opera, London Festival Ballet, Ballet Internat., Royal Danish Ballet, TV appearances in series of Balanchine works, 1974, appeared on PBS Dance in Am. series A Choreographer's Notebook: Stravinsky Piano Ballets by Peter Martins, 1984; choreographer Broadway musicals Dream of the Twins, 1982, On Your Toes, 1982, Song and Dance, 1985, Calcium Light Night, 1977, Tricolore-Pas de Basque sect., 1978, Rossini Pas de Deaux, 1978, ice ballet Tango-Tango, 1978, Dido and Aeneas, 1979, Sonate di Scarlatti, 1979, Eight Easy Pieces, 1980, Lille Suite, 1980, Suite from Histoire du Soldat, 1981, Capricio Italien, 1981, The Magic Flute, 1981, Symphony No. 1, 1981, Delibes Divertissement, 1982, Piano-Rag-Music, 1982, Concerto for Two Solo Pianos, 1982, Waltzes, 1983, Rossini Quartets, 1983, Tango, 1983, A Schubertiad, 1984, Mozart Violin Concerto, 1984, Poulenc Sonata, 1985, La Sylphide, 1985, Valse Triste, 1985, Eight More, 1985, We Are the World, 1985, Eight Miniatures, 1985, Ecstatic Orange, Tanzspiel, 1988, Jazz, 1993, Symphonic Dances, 1994, Barber Violin Concerto, 1994, Mozart Piano Concerto No. 17, 1994, X-Ray, 1995; author (autobiography): Far From Denmark, 1982. Recipient Dance Mag. award, 1977, Golden Apple award, Cue, 1977, Merit award, Phila. Art Alliance, 1985, Liberty award, NYC, 1986, H.C. Andersen Ballet prize, Royal Danish Theatre, 1988; named Knight of Order of Danneborg, Denmark, 1983. Office: NY State Theater NYC Ballet 20 Lincoln Center Plz New York NY 10023-6913*

MARTINSON, BRADLEY JAMES, lawyer; b. Ortonville, Minn., Oct. 16, 1945; s. Edwin James and Helen Eleanor (Christenson) M.; m. Beth Louise Nelson, June 24, 1967; children: Sara, Timothy. BA, Concordia Coll., Moorhead, Minn., 1967; JD, U. Minn., 1973. Assoc. Robert Hillstrom & Assocs., Mpls., 1973-80; shareholder Hillstrom, Bale & Martinson, Mpls., 1980-85, Martinson, Schwartz & Corey, Mpls., 1985-87, Salmen, Brinkman & Martinson, St. Paul, 1987-90; shareholder, mng. ptnr. Tews, Squires, Martin & Martinson, Mpls., 1990-97; shareholder Law Offices of Bradley J. Martinson, Mpls., 1998—. 1st lt. U.S. Army, 1968-71. Mem. Midland Hills Country Club (pres. 1997-98). Home: 1928 29th Ave NW New Brighton MN 55112-1737 Office: 333 S 7th St Ste 1170 Minneapolis MN 55402 Office Phone: 612-335-9300. Business E-Mail: bmartinson@martinsonlaw.com.

MARTINSON, IDA MARIE, retired medical/surgical nurse, physiologist; b. Mentor, Minn., Nov. 8, 1936; d. Oscar and Marvel (Nelson) Sather; m. Paul Varo Martinson, Mar. 31, 1962; children: Anna Marie, Peter. Diploma, St. Luke's Hosp. Sch. Nursing, 1957; BS, U. Minn., 1960, M.N.A., 1962; PhD, U. Ill., Chgo., 1972. Instr. Coll. St. Scholastica and St. Luke's Sch. Nursing, 1957—58, Thornton Jr. Coll., 1967—69; lab. asst. U. Ill. at Med. Ctr., 1970—72; lectr. dept. physiology U. Minn., St. Paul, 1972—82, asst. prof. Sch. Nursing, 1972—74, assoc. prof. rsch., 1974—77, prof., dir. rsch., 1977—82; prof. dept. family health care U. Calif., San Francisco, 1982—2003, chmn. dept., 1982—90. Vis. rsch. prof. Nat. Taiwan U., Def. Med. Ctr., 1981; vis. prof. nursing Sun Yat-Sen U. Med. Scis., Guang Zhou, China, Ewha Women's U., Seoul, Republic of Korea, Frances Payne Bolton Sch. Nursing, Case Western Res. U., Cleve., 1994—96; chair, prof. dept. health scis. Hong Kong Poly. U., 1996—2000. Author: Mathematics for the Health Science Student, 1977; editor: Home Care for the Dying Child, 1976, Women in Stress, 1979, Women in Health and Illness, 1986, The Child and Family Facing Life Threatening Illness, 1987, Family Nursing, 1989, Home Health Care Nursing, 1989, Home Health Care Nursing, 2d edit., 2002; contbr. chapters to books, articles to profl. jours. Active Am. Cancer Soc. Recipient Book of Yr. award, Am. Jour. Nursing, 1977, 1980, 1987, 1990, Humanitarian award for pediat. nursing, 1993; fellow, Fulbright Found., 1991. Mem.: ANA, Inst. Medicine, Am. Acad. Nursing, Coun. Nurse Rschrs., Sigma Theta Tau, Sigma Xi. Lutheran. Address: 12149 E Movil Lake Rd NE Bemidji MN 56601 *The challenge of quality health care to all of society and the critical role nursing has to play in order to achieve this goal has motivated me throughout my professional life. The richness of talent in this country spurs me on.*

MARTINSON, JACOB CHRISTIAN, JR., academic administrator; b. Menomonie, Wis., Apr. 15, 1933; s. Jacob Christian and Matilda Kate (Wisner) M.; m. Elizabeth Smathers, Apr. 29, 1962; children— Elizabeth Anne, Kirsten Kate. BA, Huntingdon Coll., Ala., 1954, LLD (hon.), 1993; MDiv, Duke U., 1957; DDiv, Vanderbilt U., 1972; grad., Inst. Ednl. Mgmt., Harvard U., 1981. Ordained elder United Methodist Ch. Minister Trinity United Meth. Ch., Lighthouse Point, Fla., 1960-67; sr. minister First United Meth. Ch., Winter Park, Fla., 1967-71; supervising instr. Vanderbilt U. Div. Sch., Nashville, 1971-72; pres. Andrew Coll., Cuthbert, Ga., 1972-76, Brevard Coll., NC, 1976-85, High Point (N.C.) U., 1985—2005, hon. chancellor, 2005—; interim pres. Garrett-Evang. Theol. Sem., Evanston, Ill., 2006. Chmn. bd. dirs. 1st Union Nat. Bank, High Point, 1989; lectr. St. Mary's Theol. Soc., U. St. Andrews, Scotland. Chmn. N.C. Friends of Higher Edn., 1986; mem. W.I.H. and Lula E. Pitts Found., Atlanta, 1972-76. Recipient Hickman Preaching award Duke U. Div. Sch.; Glen Slough scholar Vanderbilt U., 1971; hon. fellow Westminster Coll., Oxford, Eng., 1994; Rotary Paul Harris fellow. Mem. Brevard C. of C. (pres. 1979), High Point C. of C. (chmn. 1992), Piedmont Ind. Coll. Assn. (chmn. 1991-93), Carolinas Intercollegiate Athletic Conf. (pres. 1991-93), Phi Theta Kappa. Methodist. Avocation: mountain hiking. Home: 556 Crum Dr Lake Junaluska NC 28745 Office Phone: 828-456-5457. Personal E-mail: jmartinson@bellsouth.net.

MARTINUZZI, LEO SERGIO, JR., banker; b. Newton, Mass., Aug. 1, 1928; s. Leo Sergio and Jessica (Stewart) Martinuzzi; m. Helen Renfrew Gibson, Oct. 26, 1957 (dec. Oct. 1996); children: John James, Georgiana Gibson, Samuel Stewart; m. Sandra Stetson, Nov. 18, 2004. BA, Harvard U., 1950; B.Litt., Oxford U., 1952. With Chase Manhattan Bank, NYC, 1956-81, asst. treas., 1960, asst. v.p. Japanese brs., 1961-64, v.p. Japanese brs., 1964-68, marketing exec. internat. staff, 1968-72, sr. v.p., 1971-81; corporate devel. officer Chase Manhattan Corp., 1972-75, group exec. info. services, 1975-81; chmn. Chase Econometric Assocs. Inc., 1975-80; sr. v.p. strategic planning Squibb Corp., NY, 1981-87, cons., 1988-91. Chmn. Strategic Dimensions, Inc., 1990—; adj. prof. econs. Edison CC, 1993—97. Lt. (j.g.) USNR, 1952—56. Home: 336 Galleon Dr Naples FL 34102-7638 Home Phone: 239-430-1475. Personal E-mail: jmartinuzzi@yahoo.com.

MARTIN-VEGA, LOUIS A., dean, engineering educator; b. NY; B in Indsl. Engring., U. PR, Mayaguez, 1968; M in Ops. Rsch., NYU, 1971; M in Systems Engring., U. Fla., Gainesville, 1973, PhD in Indsl. and Systems Engring., 1975. Registered profl. engr., Fla., PR. Faculty mem. U. PR, Mayaguez; prof. dept. indsl. and systems engring. U. Fla., dir. Ctr. Electronics Mfg.; Lockheed prof. Coll. Engring. Fla. Inst. Tech., Melbourne; chair dept. indsl. and mfg. systems engring. Lehigh U., Bethlehem, Pa.; dir. divsn. design, manufacture and indsl. innovation NSF, 1998—2000, acting head engring. directorate, 2000—01; prof., dean engring. U. South Fla., Tampa, 2001—06; dean Coll. Engring. NC State U., Raleigh, 2006—. Recipient Hispanic Engr. Nat. Achievement award, 2000. Mem.: Nat. Engring. Deans Coun., Pan Am. Acad. Engring., Soc. Mfg. Engrs., Inst. Indsl. Engrs. (pres. 2007—08, Albert Holtzman Disting. Educator award 1999). Office: NC State U Coll Engring 113 Page Hall Box 7901 Raleigh NC 27695-7901 Office Phone: 919-515-2311.

MARTON, TUTZI, artist; b. Bucharest, Romania, Oct. 13, 1936; s. Samuil and Terezia (Roth) Marton Chereji; m. Meszesi Ervin, July 10, 1957 (div. 1972). Grad. Cluj Coll., Romania, 1956, Acad. Journalism, Budapest, 1971. Came to U.S. 1972. Art dir. Foaia Noastra mag., Budapest, 1959-71; textile designer Loweinstein Inc., N.Y.C., 1972-75. One-man shows Romania Library, N.Y.C., 1978, Kar Gallery Fine Art, Toronto, Ont., Can., 1978, Galeria Laurina, The Hague, Netherlands, 1981, Galeria Star, Gallarate, Italy, 1982, Galeria Dania, Haifa, Israel, 1983; exhibited in group shows Gallerie Rosenau, Bern, Switzerland, 1977, York Gallery, Ottawa, Ont., 1978, Mus. Art, Long Beach, N.Y., 1979, Profile Gallery, N.Y.C., 1980, Gallery Alfa, Sunshine Coast, Australia, 1981, Romana Kramoris Gallery, Sag Harbor, N.Y., 1981; represented in permanent collection Nat. Archives Washington, Statue of Liberty, Mus. Art Fla., Palm Beach, Tomaquag Indian Memorabilia Mus., R.I., Vatican, Rome, Haifa Mus. Music and Ethnology, Israel, Musee Petit Format, Couvin, Belgium, 1987—. Bd. dirs. Nat. Council on Art in Jewish Life, N.Y.C., 1983. Recipient 1st prize Mus. Art Long Beach, 1981, Passatore award Rome, Italy 1982, Bronze medal Internat. Symposium Cantacuzziono, Vienna, 1983; Ioan and Maria Constantinescu grantee, Hague, Nederlands, 1981. Fellow Anglo Am. Acad. (hon.); mem. Internat. Assn. Art, Artists Equity Assn., Fgn. Press Assn. (assoc.). Home: 110 Riverside Dr Apt 7B New York NY 10024

MARTONE, BARBARA, school psychologist; b. Mt. Kisco, NY, Oct. 27, 1977; d. Joseph and Lauri Martone; m. Kevin Hynes. BA, Pace U., Pleasantville, NY, 2000; MS, Coll. New Rochelle, NY, 2002. Cert. sch. psychologist NY, 2004. Sch. psychologist Del. Autism Program, Newark, Del., 2003, Mahopac Ctrl. Sch. Dist., NY, 2004—. Office: Mahopac Ctrl Sch Dist 421 Baldwin Pl Rd Mahopac NY 10541

MARTONE, ERIC ANTHONY DOMENIC, history educator; b. Nuremberg, Bavaria, Germany, Sept. 29, 1978; s. Maria and Robert Cordery (Stepfather), Anthony Martone; m. Nicole Martone; 1 child, Domenic John Agateno. BA in History cum laude, Pace U., Pleasantville, NY, 2000; MA in Global History, Iona Coll., New Rochelle, NY, 2003; tchr. cert., Western Conn. State U., Danbury, 2003, MA in European History, 2007; French cert., U. Toronto, Canada, 2006. Cert. provisional educator history/social studies grades 7-12 Conn., 2006. Rsch. analyst Pitney Bowes, Stamford, Conn., 1999—2002; tchr. Enlightenment Sch., Waterbury, 2004; history tchr. John F. Kennedy HS, Waterbury, 2004—; instr. Sch. Prof. Devel., SUNY, Stony Brook, 2008—. Creative cons. Teacher's Discovery, Auburn Hills, Mich., 2005—; vis. scholar Dickinson Coll., Carlisle, Pa., 2005, U. Mass. Dartmouth, North Dartmouth, 2006; grad. asst. Stony Brook U., 2007—. Author: (books) With a Little Help From My German Friend: Leopold II of Belgium and the Berlin Conference, 1884-85, 2003, Encyclopedia of Blacks in European History and Culture, 2009; translator: (drama) The Vampire/Catilina: Two Plays by Alexandre Dumas, 2003; contbr. encys. in field. Named Outstanding History Maj., History Dept., Pace U., 2000; grantee, Freeman Found., Wesleyan U., 2005, NEH, 2005—09; Presdl. scholar, Pace U., 1996—2000, All-American scholar, US Achievement Acad., 1999, All-Academic Team scholar, Tau Kappa Epsilon, 1999. Mem.: Am. Hist. Assn., Western Soc. for French History, Conn. Educators' Assn., Waterbury Tchrs.' Assn., Nat. Educators' Assn., French Hist. Soc., Societe des Amis d'Alexandre Dumas, Alpha Chi, Pi Gamma Mu, Phi Alpha Theta, Tau Kappa Epsilon. Office: John F Kennedy HS 422 Highland Ave Waterbury CT 06708 Business E-Mail: emartone@waterbury.k12.ct.us.

MARTONE, PATRICIA ANN, lawyer; b. Bklyn., Apr. 28, 1947; d. David Andrew and Rita Mary (Dullmeyer) Martone; m. Barbara Ann Rosen, Sept. 2, 2006. BA in Chemistry, NYU, 1968, JD, 1973; MA in Phys. Chemistry, Johns Hopkins U., Balt., 1969. Bar: NY 1974, US Dist. Ct. (so. and ea. dists.) NY 1975, US Ct. Appeals (2d cir.) 1975, US Ct. Appeals (1st cir.) 1981, US Patent and Trademark Office 1983, US Ct. Appeals (fed. cir.) 1984, US Supreme Ct. 1984, US Dist. Ct. (ea. dist.) Mich. 1985, US Dist. Ct. (no. dist.) Calif. 1995, US Dist. Ct. Colo. 2004. Tech. rep. computer timesharing On-Line Sys., Inc., NYC, 1969-70; assoc. Kelley Drye & Warren, NYC, 1973-77, Fish & Neave, NYC, 1977-82, ptnr., 1983—2004, Ropes & Gray LLP, NYC, 2005—. Adj. prof. NYU Sch. Law, 1990—; mem. adv. coun. Engelberg Ctr. Innovation Law & Policy, 1996—; participating atty. Cmty. Law Offices, NYC, 1974—78; atty. Pro Bono Panel US Dist. Ct. (so. dist.) NY, 1982—84; lectr. Practising Law Inst., NYC, 1995—, Aspen Law & Bus., 1990—95, Franklin Pierce Law Sch., 1992—97, Lic. Exec. Soc.; chair, bd. dirs. NY Lawyers for the Pub. Interest, 1996—98, vice chair, 1998—2000, 2002—06, emeritus bd., 2006—. Mng. editor NYU Law Sch. Rev. Law and Social Change, 1972-73; contbr. articles to profl. jours. Past bd. mem. Nat. Orgn. Italian Am. Women. Recipient Founder's Day award NYU Sch. Law, 1973, award NY Lawyers for Pub. Interest, 2006, Women Power Influence award, 2009; NSF grad. trainee Johns Hopkins U., 1968-69; NYU scholar, 1964-68; fellow Litig. Counsel Am., 2007. Mem. ABA, Am. Intellectual Property Law Assn., Assn. Bar City NY (mem. environ. law com. 1978-83, trademarks, unfair competition com. 1983-86), Fed. Bar Coun., Fed. Cir. Bar Assn., Am. Chem. Soc., Licensing Execs. Soc., NY Intellectual Property Law Assn., Litig. Counsel America, Univ. Club. Office: Ropes & Gray LLP 1211 Ave of the Americas Fl 35 New York NY 10036-8704 Office Phone: 212-596-9021. Business E-Mail: patricia.martone@ropesgray.com.

MARTONE, S. MICHAEL, computer company executive; B, U. Miami; grad. advanced mgmt. prog., Northwestern U. Kellogg Sch. Mgmt., Evanston, Ill. Various ops. mktg. and sales positions Xerox Corp., 1970—87; with Automatic Data Processing, Inc., Roseland, NJ, 1987—, group pres. claims svcs., 1995—98, group pres. dealer svcs., 1998—2004, group pres. employer svcs., 2004—06, COO, 2006—. Office: Automatic Data Processing Inc 1 ADP Blvd Roseland NJ 07068*

MARTONOSI, SUSAN E., mathematics professor; PhD, MIT, Cambridg, 2005. Asst. prof. Harvey Mudd Coll., Claremont, Calif., 2005—. Office: Harvey Mudd Coll 301 Platt Blvd Claremont CA 91711

MARTORANA, BARBARA JOAN, retired secondary school educator; b. NYC, Oct. 18, 1942; d. Samuel and Joan Renee (Costello) M. BA, St. John's U., Jamaica, NY, 1970, MS in English Edn., 1972; advanced cert. computers in edn., LI U., 1988, profl. diploma in edn. adminstrn., 1990. Cert. sch. dist. adminstr., sch. adminstr. and supr., tchr. English grades 7-12, NY, Ed.D, Lit. Studies, Hofstra U., Hempstead, NY, 2003.

Exec. sec. Am. Petroleum Inst., NYC, 1960-65; exec. asst. to v.p. Goldring, Inc., 1965-67; exec. asst. Rsch. Inst. for Cath. Edn., 1967-69; English tchr. St. Martin of Tours Sch., Amityville, 1970-77, Oceanside Jr. HS, 1977-78, Freeport HS, 1979—2008. Rec. sec. Freeport Tehr. Ctr. Policy Bd., NY, 1986-89; co-chair Middle States Steering Com., Freeport, 1988-90; chair Freeport H.S. Shared Decision Team, 1992-93, site-based mgmt. team, 2005-08; adv. bd. LI Writing Project, Garden City, N.Y., 1993—, co-leader Summer Insts.; adj. prof. literacy studies dept. Hofstra U., NY, 1999—. Co-author: (textbooks) Writing Competency Practice, 1980, rev., expanded edit., 1989, 3d edit., 2007. With Seaford Rep. Club, NY, 1975—. Mem. Nat. Coun. Tchrs. English (conf. on English edn.), NY State English Coun., LI Writing Project. Avocations: reading, writing, travel. Personal E-mail: engteech@aol.com.

MARTORE, GRACIA C., publishing company executive; b. 1951; m. Joseph Martore; 2 children. BA, Wellesley Coll. Asst. treas. Gannett Co., Inc., Mc Lean, Va., 1985—93, v.p. Treasury Svcs., 1993, head Investor Rels., 1996—98, treas., v.p. Investor Rels., 1998—2001, sr. v.p., 2001—06, CFO, 2003—06, exec. v.p., CFO, 2006—. Office: Gannett Co Inc 7950 Jones Branch Dr Mc Lean VA 22107-0910*

MARTORI, JOSEPH PETER, lawyer; b. NYC, Aug. 19, 1941; s. Joseph and Teresa Susan (Fezza) M. BS summa cum laude, NYU, 1964, MBA, 1968; JD cum laude, U. Notre Dame, 1967. Bar: DC 1968, U.S. Dist. Ct. DC 1968, U.S. Dist. Ct. Ariz. 1968, U.S. Ct. Appeals (9th cir.) 1969, U.S. Supreme Ct. 1977. Assoc. Sullivan & Cromwell, NYC, 1967-68, Snell & Wilmer, Phoenix, 1968-69; pres. Goldmar Inc., Phoenix, 1969-71; ptnr. Martori, Meyer, Hendricks & Victor, P.A., Phoenix, 1971-85, Brown & Bain, P.A., Phoenix, 1985-94, chmn. corp. banking & real estate dept., 1994—; chmn. bd. ILX Resorts, Inc., Phoenix. Chmn. ILX Inc., Varsity Clubs Am. Inc. Author: Street Fights, 1987; also articles. Trustee Boys' Clubs Met. Phoenix, 1974-99; consul for Govt. of Italy, State of Ariz., 1987-97. Mem. ABA, State Bar Ariz., Maricopa County Bar Assn., Lawyers Com.for Civil Rights Under Law (trustee 1976—), Phoenix Country Club, Plaza Club (founding bd. govs. 1979-90). Republican. Roman Catholic. Office: ILX Resorts Inc 2111 E Highland Ave Ste 200 Phoenix AZ 85016-4786 Business E-Mail: jmartorisr@ilxresorts.com.

MARTUCCI, WILLIAM CHRISTOPHER, lawyer; b. Asbury Park, NJ, Mar. 10, 1952; s. Frank and Evelyn (Gerrity) M.; children: Daniel Robert, William Sessions, John Andrew, James Christopher, Andrew Michael, Matthew Peter, Caroline Kenney. AB magna cum laude, Rutgers U., 1974; JD with honors, U. Ark., 1977; LLM with honors, Georgetown U., 1981; LLM in Exec. Edn., Harvard Bus. Sch., 1997. Bar: Mo. 1977. Law clk. to presiding justice Mo. Ct. Appeals, Kansas City, 1977-78; assoc. Spencer, Fane, Britt & Browne, Kansas City, 1981-86, ptnr., 1987-99, Shook, Hardy & Bacon LLP, Kansas City, 2000—, leader Nat. Employment Litig. & Policy Group. Charter mem. Am. Employment Coun., 1993—; adj. prof. employment law U. Mo. Law Sch., Kansas City, 1988-95, chair minority affairs com. 1992-2002. Editor-in-chief Ark. Law Rev., 1976-77; contbr. articles to profl. jours. Chmn. adv. coun. Urban League Greater Kansas City Tng. Ctr., chmn. mentor program, 1988-2005; mem. Kansas City Civic Coun.; mem. Kansas City Tomorrow Leadership Program, 1992-93; adv. bd. Boys and Girls Club Kansas City, Reviving Baseball in the Inner City. Served to lt. JAGC, USN, 1978-81. Recipient Navy Commendation medal, Navy Achievement medal. Mem. ABA (employment and labor rels. com., EEO litigation com.), Mo. Bar Assn. (exec. com. continuing legal edn. 1987—, chair 1993-2000), Kansas City Bar Assn. (chmn. continuing legal edn. 1984-86, mem. exec. com. 1985-98, leadership award 1985, chmn. labor and employment law com. 1988-90, Pres. award 1992, 97), Lawyers Assn. Kansas City (mem. exec. com. young lawyers sect. 1981-82), Kansas City Club, Homestead Country Club, Rotary, Williams Club NY. Clubs: Kans. City. Republican. Roman Catholic. Office: Shook Hardy and Bacon 2555 Grand Blvd Kansas City MO 64105-2613 Home: 6429 Overbrook Rd Mission Hills KS 66208-1939 Office Phone: 816-474-6550. Business E-Mail: wmartucci@shb.com.

MARTY, ALVIN LEONARD, retired economist, educator; b. NYC, Jan. 29, 1927; s. Harry and Pearl (Ballin) Marty. AB, UCLA, 1947; postgrad., Cambridge U., 1947—50; PhD, U. Calif., Berkeley, 1955. Mem. faculty Northwestern U., Evanston, Ill., 1955—60; prof. econs. and fin. Ctr. Study Bus. and Govt. Baruch Coll. CUNY, NYC, 1960—2008; emeritus prof. Grad. Sch. U. Ctr., 2008. Vis. prof. U. Chgo., 1962, U. Hawaii, 1973, Columbia U., 1974, City U. London, 1987-88, U. N.S.W., Australia, 2002; vis. scholar Fed. Res. Bank of St. Louis, 1993; Simon rsch. prof. Manchester U., 1975-76 Mem. editl. bd. Am. Econ. Assn.; contbr. articles to profl. jours. Ehrman student Cambridge U., 1947-50; Ford Found. fellow, 1956-57. Home: 545 W End Ave New York NY 10024-2713 Personal E-mail: amarty@nyc.rr.com.

MARTY, MARTIN EMIL, theology studies educator; b. West Point, Nebr., Feb. 5, 1928; s. Emil A. and Anne Louise (Wuerdemann) Marty; m. Elsa Schumacher Marty, 1952 (dec. 1981); children: Frances, Joel, John, Peter, James, Micah, Ursula; m. Harriet Lindemann Marty, 1982. MDiv, Concordia Sem., 1952; STM, Luth. Sch. Theology, Chgo., 1954; PhD in Am. Religious and Intellectual History, U. Chgo., 1956; LittD (hon.), Thiel Coll., 1964; LHD (hon.), W.Va. Wesleyan Coll., 1967, Marian Coll., 1967, Providence Coll., 1967; DD (hon.), Muhlenberg Coll., 1967; LittD (hon.), Thomas More Coll., 1968; DD (hon.), Bethany Sem., 1969; LLD (hon.), Keuka Coll., 1972; LHD (hon.), Willamette U., 1974; DD (hon.), Wabash Coll., 1977; LLD (hon.), U. So. Calif., 1977, Valparaiso U., 1978; LHD (hon.), St. Olaf Coll., 1978, De Paul U., 1979; DD (hon.), Christ Sem.-Seminex, 1979, Capital U., 1980; LHD (hon.), Colo. Coll., 1980; DD (hon.), Maryville Coll., 1980, North Park Coll. Sem., 1982; LittD (hon.), Wittenberg U., 1983; LHD, Rosary Coll., 1984; LHD (hon.), Rockford Coll., 1984; DD (hon.), Va. Theol. Sem., 1984; LHD (hon.), Hamilton Coll., 1985, Loyola U., 1986; LLD (hon.), U. Notre Dame, 1987; LHD (hon.), Roanoke Coll., 1987, Mercer U., 1987, Ill. Wesleyan Coll., 1987, Roosevelt U., 1988, Aquinas Coll., 1988; LittD (hon.), Franklin Coll., 1988, U. Nebr., 1993; LHD (hon.), No. Mich. U., 1989, Muskingum Coll., Coe Coll., Lehigh U., 1989, Hebrew Union Coll. and Governors State U., 1990, Whittier Coll., 1991, Calif. Luth. U., 1993; DD (hon.), St. Xavier Coll. and Colgate U., 1990, Mt. Union Coll., 1991, Tex. Luth. Coll., 1991, Aurora U., 1991, Baker U., 1992; LHD (hon.), Luth. U., 1993; LHD, Calif. Luth. U., 1993, Midland Luth. Coll., 1995; DD, Hope Coll., 1993, Northwestern Coll., 1993; LHD (hon.), George Fox Coll., 1994, Drake U., 1994, Centre Coll., 1994, Fontbonne Coll., 1996; DD, Yale U., 1995; LHD (hon.), Otterbein Coll., 1996; ThD (hon.), Lycoming Coll., 1997; LHD, Dana Coll., 1998; LittD (hon.), Alma Coll., 1998, Concordia U. Portland, 1998, Niagara U., 1998; LHD (hon.), Kalamazoo Coll., 1999, William Jewell Coll., 1999; LittD, Lynchburg Coll., 2003; DD (hon.), Trinity Coll., 2001, Wake Forest U., 2003; DHum (hon.), Westminster Choir Coll., 2001; LHD (hon.), U. Scranton, 2001; DD (hon.), Wake Forest U., 2003; LHD (hon.), Ea. Mennonite U., 2003, Iona Coll.; LLD (hon.), Fordham U., 2005; LHD (hon.), Ill. Coll., 2007, Augsburg Coll., 2007. Ordained to ministry Luth. Ch., 1952. Pastor, Washington, 1950—51; asst. pastor River Forest, Ill., 1952—56; pastor Elk Grove Village, Ill., 1956—63; prof. history of modern Christianity Div. Sch. U. Chgo., 1963—, Fairfax M. Cone Disting. Svc. prof., 1978—98, prof. emeritus, 1998—; assoc. editor Christian Century mag., Chgo., 1956—85, sr. editor, 1985—98; co-editor Ch. History mag., 1963—97. Pres. Park Ridge Ctr. for Study of Health Faith and Ethics, Ill., 1985—89, sr. scholar-in-residence, 1989—98; pres. Am. Inst. for Study of Health, Faith and Ethics, 1985—89; dir. The Pub. Religion Project, 1996—99; interim pres. St. Olaf Coll., 2000—01. Author: A Short History of Christianity, 1959, The New Shape of American Religion, 1959, The Improper Opinion, 1961, The Infidel, 1961, Baptism, 1962, The Hidden Discipline, 1963, Second Chance for American Protestants, 1963, Church Unity and Church Mission, 1964, Varieties of Unbelief, 1964, The Search for a Usable Future, 1969, The Modern Schism, 1969, Righteous Empire, 1970, Protestantism, 1972, You Are Promise, 1973, The Fire We Can Light, 1973, The Pro and Con Book of Religious America, 1975, A Nation of Behavers, 1976, Religion, Awakening and Revolution, 1978, Friendship, 1980, By Way of Response, 1981, The Public Church, 1981, A Cry of Absence, 1983, Health and Medicine in the Lutheran Tradition, 1983, Pilgrims in Their Own Land, 1984, Protestantism in the United States, 1985, Modern American Religion, The Irony of it All, Vol. 1, 1986, An Invitation to American Catholic History, 1986, Religion and Republic, 1987, Modern American Religion: The Noise of Conflict, Vol. 2, 1991, Lutheran Questions, Lutheran Answers, 2007, The Mystery of the Child, 2004; author: (with R. Scott Appleby) The Glory and the Power, 1992; editor (with Jerald C. Brauer): The Unrelieved Paradox: Studies in the Theology of Franz Bibfeldt, 1994; editor: (with Micah Marty) Places Along the Way, 1994; editor: Our Hope for Years to Come, 1995, Modern American Religion, Under God, Indivisible, Vol. 3, 1996, The One and the Many, 1997, The Promise of Winter, 1997, When True Simplicity is Gained, 1998, Politics, Religion, and the Common Good, 2000, Education, Religion, and the Common Good, 2001, Speaking of Trust, 2003, Vision of Utopia, 2003;: When Faiths Collide, 2004, Protestant Voice in American Pluralism, 2004, Martin Luther, 2004; editor: (jours.) Context, 1969—; editor: Second Opinion, The Mystery of Child, 2007, The Christian World: A Global History, 2008; sr. editor: The Christian Century, 1956—98; contbr. articles to religious publs. Chmn. bd. regents St. Olaf Coll., 1996—2001, sr. regent, 2002—; dir. The Pub. Religion Project, 1996—2000. Recipient Nat. Medal Humanities, 1997, Alumni medal, U. Chgo., 1998. Fellow: Am. Acad. Political and Social Scis. (Mohandas K. Gandhi Fellow, Mohandas K. Gandhi fellow), Soc. Am. Historians, Am. Acad. Arts and Scis. (dir. fundamentalism project 1988—94); mem.: Am. Antiquarian Soc., Am. Acad. Religion (pres. 1987—88), Am. Cath. Hist. Assn. (pres. 1981), Am. Soc. Ch. History (pres. 1971), Am. Philos. Soc. Lutheran. Personal E-mail: memarty@aol.com.

MARTY, RAYMOND, nuclear physician; b. Oct. 26, 1929; s. Harry Kenneth and Pearl (Bailin) M.; m. Carole M. Perry, Jan. 25, 1960. BA, UCLA, 1952; MD, U. Lausanne, Switzerland, 1959. Intern Hosp. Good Samaritan, LA, 1960-61; resident in diagnostic radiology Albert Einstein Sch. Medicine, Bronx, N.Y., 1962; fellow radiation therapy Stanford Med. Sch., 1962-63; dir. out patient clinic St. Joseph's Hosp., San Francisco, 1963-65; fellow Tumor Inst., Seattle, 1965-66, mem. staff, 1966—, dir. nuclear medicine/ultrasound, 1967—. Assoc. clin. prof. nuclear medicine tech. Seattle U. Med. Sch., 1972—; asst. clin. prof. nuclear medicine U. Wash. Med. Sch., Seattle, 1974—. Contbr. articles to profl. jours. Fellow Am. Coll. Radiology, Am. Coll. Nuclear Physicians; mem. AMA, Radiol. Soc., N. Am. Soc. Nuclear Medicine, Seattle Yacht Club, Columbia Tower (Seattle) Club, La Chaine des Rotisseurs. Home: 4607 103rd Ln NE Kirkland WA 98033-7638 Office: 1229 Madison St Ste 1150 Seattle WA 98104-3587

MARTYL, (MRS. ALEXANDER LANGSDORF JR.), artist; b. St. Louis, Mar. 16, 1917; d. Martin and Aimee (Goldstone) Schweig; m. Alexander Langsdorf, Jr., Dec. 31, 1941; children: Suzanne, Alexandra. AB, Washington U., St. Louis, 1938. Instr. art dept. U. Chgo.; artist in residence Tamarind Inst., U. N.Mex., Albuquerque, 1974, artist in residence Ucross Found. Wyoming, 2008 Solo shows include, Calif. Palace of Legion of Honor, 1956, Chgo. Art Inst., 1949, 76, Feingarten Galleries, NYC, Beverly Hills and Chgo., 1961, 62, 63, St. Louis, 1962, Feingarten Gallery, NYC, 1963, LA, 1964, Kovler Gallery, Chgo., 1967, Washington U., St. Louis, 1967, U. Chgo. Oriental Inst. Mus., 1970, Deson&Zaks Gallery, 1973, Fairweather-Hardin Gallery, 1977, 81, 83, Ill. State Mus., 1978, Fermilab, 1985, 91, Bklyn. Mus., 1986, Oriental Inst. Mus., 1987, Gibbes Art Mus., Charleston, SC, 1988, Fairweather-Hardin Gallery, 1988, Tokyo Internat. Art Expo, 1990, State of Ill. Art Gallery, Chgo., 1990, Expo Navy Pier, Chgo., 1993, Printworks Gallery Ltd., Chgo., 1995, 97, 99, 2002, 04, 07, Navy Pier, Chgo., 2003, 04, Oriental Inst. Mus., Chgo., Martyl: Nature/Artifice Ft. Wayne Mus. Art, 2000; represented in permanent collections Chgo. Art Inst., Pa. Acad. Fine Arts, Ill. State Mus., Bklyn. Mus., DuSable Mus., Chgo., LA County Mus., Whitney Mus. Am. Art, Davenport Mcpl. Mus., Iowa, St. Louis Art Mus., Washington U., U. Ariz., Arnot Gallery, Elmira, NY, Greenville Mus., SC, Nat. Coll. Fine Arts, Hirshhorn Mus. and Sculpture Gallery, Rockford Mus., Ill; artist in resident Ucross Found. Clearmont Wyomins, 2008. Recipient prize, Kasas City Art Inst., 1940, prizes, St. Louis Art Mus., 1942—43, 1st Disney prize, Drawing LA Mus., 1946, Armstrong prize, Chi Art Inst., 1949, Wm. Bartels award, Art Inst. Chi, 1961, Logan medal, Art Inst. Chgo., 1950, award, Am. Inst. & Archtl. Unitarian Ch., Evanston, Ill., Artist Residence, Oxbow, Mich., U. N.Mex., Ucross Found. Mem. Arts Club (Chgo.). Unitarian Universalist. *To be an artist means devoting a lifetime to an intensely difficult activity— one that requires concentration and skill. I've spent my time learning the power of color, line, shape and meaning. I like to think that I have opened out experiences people cannot reveal by themselves.*

MARTYN, EVI, musician, educator; b. Athens, Greece, Nov. 12, 1941; arrived in U.S., 1965; d. Anastasios and Sophia (Alivizatos) Giannatos; BA, Royal Conservatory Athens, 1959; MA, Royal Conservatory Athens, Greece, 1959; PhD Music, Hochschule fur Musik, Munich, Germany, 1963. Owner, founder Martyn Sch. Music, Los Alamitos, Calif., 1973—, chair keyboard dept., 1973—. Lectr., adjudicator, demonstrator numerous competitions, seminars, workshops etc. Author: Art of Piano Playing, 1988, The Root of Evil, 2005; contbg. author: Hellenic Voice; contbr. articles to profl. mags.; internat. performances include Wigmore Hall, London, Playel Hall, Paris, Merkin Hall, NYC, soloist SW Symphony of Utah, St. George, 2006; author: Captain Philip Markopoulos a Patton's Hero: An Incredible True Story When Fate and Destiny Outpower Weapons, 2009. Performer at numerous benefit concerts including: D.C. Performing Arts Ctr., 1983, KLON Pub. Radio, Long Beach, Calif., Rotary Club Benefit for Needy, Huntington Beach, Calif., 1985, Hellenic U. Club, Loyola Marymount U., Calif., 1996. Recipient Excellent Artistic Evaluation, Internat. Comm. Agy., Washington, 1980, Award of Merit, Rotary Club of So. Calif., 1986, Knights of Pythias, 1993, The Andreas Sygros Gold medal, Greece Minister of Culture, First prize with gold medal, Royal Conservatory, Athens, 1959. Mem.: Internat. Assn. Music Competitions, Nat. Assn. Music Tchrs., Nat. Guild Piano Tchrs. (Named to Hall of Fame 1989). Avocation: swimming. Personal E-mail: evimartyn@aol.com.

MARTZ, CLYDE OLLEN, retired lawyer; b. Lincoln, Nebr., Aug. 14, 1920; s. Clyde O. and Elizabeth Mary (Anderson) M.; m. Ann Spieker, May 29, 1947; children: Robert Graham, Nancy. AB, U. Nebr., 1941; LLB, Harvard U., 1947. Bar: Colo. 1948, U.S. Ct. Appeals (D.C. cir.) 1968, U.S. Supreme Ct. 1969. Prof. U. Colo., Boulder, 1947-58, 60-62; jud. adminstr. State of Colo., Denver, 1959-60; ptnr. Davis, Graham & Stubbs, Denver, 1962-67, 69-80, 81-87, of counsel, 1988—2008; asst. atty. gen. U.S. Dept. Justice, Washington, 1967-69; solicitor U.S Dept. Interior, Washington, 1980-81; exec. dir. dept. natural resources State of Colo., 1987. Adj. prof. U. Denver, 1961-79, U. Colo., Boulder, 1988-96; cons. Pres. Materials Policy Commn., 1951; mem. Colo. Adv. Bd. Bur. Land Mgmt., 1967-69; bd. dirs., adv. bd. Natural Resources Law Ctr., 1982-2003. Author: Cases and Materials on Natural Resources Law, 1951, Water for Mushrooming Populations, 1954; co-author: American Law of Property, 1953, Water and Water Rights, 1963; editor, co-author: American Law of Mining, 1960. Co-chmn. Jud. Reorganization Commn., 1961-63; elder Presbyn. Ch., Boulder; pres. Rocky Mountain Mineral Law Found., 1961-62, others. Comdr. USN, 1942-58, PTO, with Res. Decorated Silver Star, Bronze Star, Letter of Commendation, Disting. Svc. award; honored by creation of Clyde O. Martz Natural Resources Scholarship Fund, 2002. Mem. ABA (chmn. natural resources sect. 1985-86), Fed. Bar Assn., Am. Health Lawyers Assn., Colo. Bar Assn. (chmn. water sect. 1957, chmn. mineral sect. 1961, award of merit 1962), Nat. Mining Assn. (Disting. Svc. award 1997), Order of Coif, Phi Beta Kappa. Democrat. Avocations: horticulture, woodworking, mountain climbing, skiing. Home: 1620 Indian School Apt 255 Albuquerque NM 87107 also: 1620 Indian School Rd NE Apt 255 Albuquerque NM 87102-1755

MARTZ, MIKE J., former professional football coach; b. Sioux Falls, SD, May 13, 1951; s. Betty; m. Julie Martz; children: Chris, David, Tim, Emily. Attended, San Diego Mesa Coll., U. Calif., Santa Barbara; BS summa cum laude, Fresno State, 1972. Head coach Bullard High, Fresno, Calif., 1973, San Diego Mesa Coll. Olympians, 1974, 1976—77, San Jose State U. Spartans, 1975, Santa Ana Coll. Dons, Calif., 1978, Fresno State U. Bulldogs, 1979, U. of the Pacific Power Cats, 1980—81, U. Minn. Golden Gophers, 1982; quarterbacks and receivers coach Ariz. State U. Sun Devils, 1983—87, offensive coord., 1988—91; offensive asst. LA Rams, 1992—93, quarterbacks coach, 1994; wide receivers coach St. Louis Rams, 1995—96, offensive coord., 1999—2000, head coach, 2000—05; quarterbacks coach Washington Redskins, 1997-98; offensive coord. Detroit Lions, 2006—07, San Francisco 49ers, 2008. Mem. competition com. NFL, 2004—. Featured spkr. Blanchette Rockefeller Neurosciences Institute Black-Tie Gala, 2004; active Make-a-Wish Found.; hon. co-chair Nat. Coun. Jewish Women's Back to School Store; co-chair St. Louis Rams Super Blood Drive. Named Most Pro-Active Coach, World Sports Humanitarian Hall of Fame, 2003. Achievements include member of Super Bowl XXXIV Championship winning St. Louis Rams, 2000.*

MARUPUDI, SAMBASIVA RAO, surgeon, educator; b. Chintalapudi, India, July 1, 1952; arrived in US, 1976; s. Venkateswarlu and Nagendramma (Gaddipati) M.; m. Usha Nandipati, Mar. 25, 1976; children: Neena, Neelima. MB, BS, Guntur Med. Coll., India, 1974. Diplomate Am. Bd. Surgery, Am. Bd. Colon and Rectal Surgery. Rotating internship St. Clare's Hosp., Schenectady, NY, 1976-77; resident in gen. surgery St. Agnes Hosp., Balt., 1977-78, Franklin Sq. Hosp., Balt., 1978-82; fellow in colon and rectal surgery U. Tex. Health Scis. Ctr., Houston, 1982-83; pvt. practice Amarillo, Tex., 1983—. Clin. asst. prof. dept. surgery Tex. Tech. U. Health Scis. Ctr., Amarillo, 1984—. Fellow ACS, Am. Soc. Colon and Rectal Surgeons, Internat. Coll. Surgeons; mem. AMA, Tex. Med. Assn., Potter-Randall County Med. Soc. (past pres.), Tex. Soc. Colon and Rectal Surgeons (past pres.). Republican. Hindu. Office: 800 Quail Creek Dr # 103 Amarillo TX 79124-1634 Office Phone: 806-358-7911. Personal E-mail: smarupudi@aol.com, drmarupudi@hotmail.com.

MARUS, ROBERT, dentist; m. Patricia Marus; children: Drew, Caroline. DDS, NYU, 1985. Resident Jamaica Hosp., NYC; pvt. practice Yardley, Pa. Featured cosmetic dentist It's Your Call, CN8; cons. 3M; spkr. in field. Mem.: ADA, Pa. Dental Assn., Am. Acad. Cosmetic Dentistry, Montgomery-Bucks Dental Soc. Office: 1003 Floral Vale Blvd Yardley PA 19067 Office Phone: 212-504-9119. E-mail: info@drmarus.com.

MARUSTER, ROBERT ALAN, air transportation executive; b. 1971; BA in Polit. Sci., Auburn U., Ala., 1993; MBA, Emory U., Ga. Airport customer svc. agent Delta Air Lines Inc., 1993, various positions to dir. airport strategy, planning & devel., 2002—04, v.p. airport customer svc., Hartsfield-Jackson Atlanta Internat. Airport, 2004—05; v.p. operational planning JetBlue Airways Corp., 2005—06, sr. v.p. airports & operational planning, 2006—07, sr. v.p. customer svcs., 2007—09, COO, 2009—. Office: JetBlue Airways Corp 29 Queens Blvd Ste 118 Forest Hills NY 11375*

MARUYAMA, MAGOROH, business educator, researcher, consultant; b. Tokyo, Apr. 2, 1929; came to U.S., 1950; s. Shinsaku and Toyoko (Takashima) M.; m. Pierrette Duriez, Apr. 1966 (div. 1974); 1 child, Yukon; m. Kuniko Sakakibara, July 23, 1976; 1 child, Yuki. BA in Math., U. Calif., Berkeley, 1951; postgrad., U. Munich, U. Heidelberg, Fed. Republic of Germany, 1954-55, U. Copenhagen, 1955-57; PhD, U. Lund, Sweden, 1959. Asst. prof. human devel. U. Calif., Berkeley, 1960-62; rsch. assoc. psychology Stanford U., Calif., 1962-64; assoc. prof. psychology San Francisco State U., 1965-70; prof. computer sci. Antioch Coll., 1971-72; prof. systems sci. Portland (Oreg.) State U., 1973-76; vis. prof. anthropology and architecture U. Ill., Urbana, 1976-77; vis. prof. anthropology U. Uppsala, Sweden, 1982; vis. prof. mgmt. UCLA, 1983, Nat. U., Singapore, 1983-84; vis. prof. bus. adminstrn. U. Hawaii, Honolulu, 1984-86; prof. internat. bus. Aoyama Gakuin U., Tokyo, 1987-96, Aomori (Japan) Koritsu Daigaku, 1996—. Vis. prof. U. Oreg., U. Montpellier, France, 1986; cons. U.S. Dept. Commerce 1971, Can. Fed. Ministry Urban Affairs, 1974, NASA, 1975, Monsanto Chems., 1980, Volvo, Sweden, 1982, Fed. Motors of Indonesia, 1984, Technopolises Japan, 1984, MITI of Japan, 1985, Fujitsu, Japan, 1985, Hakuhodo, Japan, 1985, Gadelius, Sweden, 1988, Michelin, France, 1989, NEC, Japan, 1989-90, C. Itoh, Japan, 1990, OECD, France, 1990, Ministry of Rsch. and Tech., France, 1992. Author: The Second Cybernetics, 1963, Mindscapes and Science Theories, 1980, Mindscapes in Management, 1994, Heterogram Analysis, 1999, Interactive Heterogeneity, 2003. Sgt. USMC, 1952-54. Grantee NSF, NIMH, 1965-76. Fellow AAAS, APA; mem. Acad. Mgmt., Internat. Sociol. Assn., Sigma Xi, Pi Mu Epsilon Avocations: architecture, art design, music composition theory. Office Phone: 858-452-3826. Office Fax: 858-452-3826. Personal E-mail: kuniko_maruyama@sbcglobal.net.

MARUYAMA, WARREN H., federal official, lawyer; m. Karen Chittenden; children: Hana, Noah. BA, Carleton Coll., Northfield, Minn., 1976; JD, Cornell Law Sch., NYC, 1980. Bar: DC, US Ct. Appeals (4th cir.), US Ct. Appeals (fed. cir.), US Ct. Internat. Trade. Atty.'s adv. US Internat. Trade Commn., Washington; assoc. gen. counsel Office US Trade Rep., The White House, Washington,

1983—86, lead US negotiator for Uruguay Round Subsidies & Countervailing Measures Negotiating Grp., 1986—89; dep. assoc. dir. internat. econ. policy Office Policy Devel., The White House, 1989—91, assoc. dir., 1992; ptnr. Hogan & Hartson LLP, Washington, 1993—2007; gen. counsel Office US Trade Rep., Exec. Office of the Pres., 2007—. Recipient Excellence in Legal Profession award, Mex. Am. Legal Def. Fund, 2003; co-recipient Disting. Svc. award, Asian Am. Justice Ctr., 2004; named to Best Lawyers in America, 2005, 2006. Republican. Office: Office US Trade Rep 600 17th St NW Washington DC 20508*

MARVEL, KEVIN BOYD, professional society administrator, astronomer; b. Colorado Springs, Colo., Sept. 29, 1967; s. Kenneth Barry and June Anne (Neaves) M. BS in Astronomy and Physics, U. Ariz., Tucson, 1990; MS in Astronomy, N.Mex. State U., Las Cruces, 1994; PhD in Astronomy, N.Mex. State U., 1996. Summer rsch. asst. Nat. Radio Astronomy Obs., Socorro, N.Mex., 1988, predoctoral rschr., 1994—96; summer rsch. asst. Commonwealth Sci. and Industry Orgn. - Divsn. Radio Physics, Sydney, 1989; postdoctoral scholar Owens Valley Radio Obs. Calif. Inst. Tech., 1996—98; assoc. exec. officer policy programs Am. Astron. Soc., Washington, 1998—2001, dep. exec. officer, 2002—06, exec. officer, 2006—. Contbr. articles to sci. jours. Recipient Undergraduate Rsch. grant U. Ariz., Tucson, 1988, 89. Mem. AAAS, Am. Assn. Variable Star Observers, Am. Astron. Soc., Am. Geophys. Union, Astron. Soc. of Pacific, Sigma Xi, Internat. Dark Sky Assn., Nat. Radio Astronomy Obs., Commonwealth Sci. and Indsl. Rsch. Orgn. Office: Am Astron Soc 2000 Florida Ave NW Ste 400 Washington DC 20009 Office Phone: 202-328-2010. Office Fax: 202-234-2560. E-mail: marvel@aas.org.

MARVEL, L. PAIGE, federal judge; b. Dec. 6, 1949; BA magna cum laude, Notre Dame Coll., 1971; JD with honors, U. Md., 1974. Bar: Md. 1974, US Dist. Ct. Md. 1974, US Tax Ct. 1975, US Ct. Appeals (4th circuit) 1977, US Supreme Ct. 1980, US Ct. Claims 1981, DC 1985. Assoc. Garbis & Schwait, P.A., Balt., 1974-76, shareholder, 1976-85, Garbis, Marvel & Junghans, P.A., Balt., 1985-86; mem. Melnicove, Kaufman, Weiner, Smouse & Garbis, P.A., Balt., 1986-88; ptnr. Venable, Baetjer and Howard LLP, Balt., 1988-98; judge US Tax Ct., Washington, 1998—. Mem. U. Md. Law Sch. Bd. Vis., 1995—2001; mem. advisory com. US Dist. Ct. Md., 1991—93; mem. Commr.'s Review Panel on IRS Integrity, 1989—91. Co-editor procedure dept. Jour. Taxation, 1989-98; contbr. chpts. to books, articles to profl. jours. Active Women's Law Ctr., 1974-85, Md. Dept. Econ. and Cmty. Development Advisory Com., 1978-80; trustee Loyola-Notre Dame Library, Inc., 1996-2003. Recipient Recognition award Balt. Is Best Prog., 1981, MSBA Taxation section's Tax Excellence award, 2002, Pres. medal Coll. Notre Dame, 2006; named One of Maryland's Top 100 Women, The Daily Record, 1998. Fellow American Bar Found., Md. Bar Found., American Coll. Tax Counsel (regent 1995-98); mem. ABA (sect. taxation coun. dir. 1989-92, vice-chair com. ops. 1993-95, Disting. Svc. award, Jules Ritholz award 2004), American Law Inst. (advisor restatement of law third, law governing lawyers), Md. Bar Assn. (chmn. taxation sect. 1982-83, bd. dirs. 1988-90, 96-98, Disting. Svc. award), Balt. Bar Assn. (at-large exec. coun.), American Tax Policy Inst. (trustee 1997-98), Serjeant's Inn. Avocations: golf, music, travel. Office: US Tax Ct 400 2nd St NW Washington DC 20217-0001 Office Phone: 202-521-0740.*

MARVENTANO, DAVID, engineering and construction management company executive; B, SUNY, Oswego; law degree, Union U., Albany, NY. With Staff of Assemblyman Michael F. Nozzolio, Albany; with legis. counsel's office Staff of Assembly Minority Leader Clarence Rappleyea; v.p., sr. dir. govt. affairs Securities Industry Assn.; leadership position Staff of US Rep. Bill Paxon, Staff of US Rep. Billy Tauzin; staff dir. Energy & Commerce Com. US House Reps.; sr. v.p. govt. rels. Fluor Corp., 2003—. Office: Fluor Corp 403 E Capitol St SE Washington DC 20003 Office Phone: 202-548-5800. Office Fax: 202-548-5810.

MARVIN, CHARLES ARTHUR, law educator; b. July 14, 1942; s. Burton Wright and Margaret Fiske (Medlar) Marvin; m. Elizabeth Maureen Woodrow, July 4, 1970 (div. July 1987); children: Colin, Kristin; m. Elizabeth Dale Wilson, Mar. 20, 1999. BA, U. Kans., Lawrence, 1964; postgrad., U. Toulouse, France, 1964-65; JD, U. Chgo., 1968, M of Comparative Law, 1970. Bar: Ill. 1969. Legal intern EEC, Brussels, 1970; lectr. law U. Kent, Canterbury, England, 1970-71; asst. prof. law Laval U., Quebec City, Que., Canada, 1971-73; legal adv. Constnl., internat. and adminstrv. law sect. Can. Dept. Justice, Ottawa, Ont., 1973-76, dir. Adminstrv. Law Reform Project, 1983-85; assoc. prof. law U. Man., Winnipeg, Canada, 1976-77; dir. adminstrv. law project Law Reform Commn., Ottawa, 1977-80; prof. law Villanova U., Pa., 1980-83, Ga. State U., 1985—, assoc. dean, 1987-89. Legal advisor on adminstrv. code revision Govt. of Kazakhstan, 1993; law faculty devel. adviser, Bulgaria, 93; dir. internat. human rights law summer program Regent U. Sch. Law., 1998; USIS lectr., Ivory Coast, 98; Fulbright prof. Riga Grad. Sch. Law, Latvia, 2000—03; vis. prof. law Vytautas Magnus U., Lithuania, 2004—06. Fulbright scholar, U. Toulouse, 1964—65, Summerfield scholar, U. Kans., 1961—64, Ford Found. Comparative Law fellow, 1968—70. Fellow: Am. Bar Found.; mem.: ABA, Can. Coun. Internat. Law, Internat. Law Assn., Internat. Bar Assn., Am. Fgn. Law Assn., Am. Soc. Internat. Law, Chgo. Bar Assn., Ill. Bar Assn., Phi Beta Kappa, Phi Delta Phi, Phi Beta Delta, Omicron Delta Kappa. Office: Ga State U Coll Law PO Box 4037 Atlanta GA 30302-4037 Office Phone: 404-413-9186. Business E-Mail: cmarvin@gsu.edu.

MARVIN, DAVID EDWARD SHREVE, lawyer; b. Jan. 6, 1950; s. George Charles Marvin and Shirley Mae (Marvin) Schaible; m. Mary Anne Kennedy, Sept. 16, 1972; 1 child, John. BS cum laude, Mich. State U., East Lansing, 1972; JD cum laude, Wayne State U., Detroit, 1976. Bar: Mich. 1976, U.S. Dist. Ct. (ea. dist.) Mich. 1976, U.S. Dist. Ct. (we. dist.) Mich. 1978, U.S. Ct. Appeals (7th cir.) 1977, U.S. Ct. Appeals (6th cir.) 1979, U.S. Supreme Ct. 1979, U.S. Ct. Appeals (D.C. cir.) 1982, D.C. 1982. Asst. mgr. Alta Supply Co., Lansing, 1972-73; rsch. asst. Wayne State U., Detroit, fall 1975; jud. intern U.S. Dist. Ct., Detroit, summer 1975; shareholder Fraser Trebilcock Davis & Dunlap, P.C., Lansing, 1976—, v.p., 1997—2005, also bd. dirs. Pres. Red Rock Prodns., Inc., 1990-94; lectr. Inst. CLE, 1989; mem. qualifications rev. com. U.S. Dist. Ct. (we. dist.) Mich., 2001—. Exec. editor Wayne Law Rev., 1975-76; contbr. articles to law jours. Commr. Mich. Solar Resource Adv. Panel, Lansing, 1978-81, Mich. Commn. Profl. and Occupl. Licensure, 1981-83; chmn. Ingham County Energy Commn., Mason, Mich., 1978-80 (state bar rep. assembly 1985-88); dir., corp. sec. Friends Mich. Hist. Ctr., Inc., 1988-92; treas. Lansing Lawyer Referral Svc., 1981; state del. Nat. Solar Congress, Washington, 1978; hearing officer City of East Lansing, 1985; Tri-County Coun. of Bar Leaders (chmn. 1986); bd. dirs. East Lansing Edn. Found., 1990-92, Impression Five Sci. Mus., 1991-97; regional fin. chmn. Abraham for U.S. Senate, 1993-94, Abraham Senate 2000, 1995-2000; mem. transition team, Gov. Engler, 2000—03, Atty. Gen. Cox, 2002-03; exec. bd. chief Okemos coun. Boy Scouts Am., 1996—, pres., 2001-03. Recipient Disting. Vol. award Tri-County Voluntary Action Ctr., 1990, Gov.'s Minuteman award, 1990, John W. Cummiskey award State Bar Mich., 1990, George Washington Honor medal Freedoms Found., 1990; named Outstanding Young Man Am., 1984, The Outstanding Young Lawyer in Mich., 1985-86, Small Bus. Adv. Yr., C. of C., 1991, Silver Beaver award Boy Scouts Am., 2003, Disting. Citizen, Cmty. Svc. award, 2007, Boy Scouts Am., 2005, Cmty. Svc. award, C. of C., 2007; Wm. D. Traitel scholar, 1975. Fellow ABA, Am. Bar Found., Mich. State Bar Found. (life); mem. ABA, State Bar Mich. (com. chmn., sect. coun. 1982—, state chmn. 1988-89), Energy Bar Assn., Mich. Soc. Assoc. Execs., Energy Bar Assn., Ingham County Bar Assn. (pres. 1985-86), Pro Bono Lawyers Svc. (pres. 1982-83), Lansing Regional C. of C. (v.p. 1987), Mich. Audubon Soc. (bd. dirs. 1991-93), Mich. State Univ. Alumni Assn. (nat. bd. dirs. 1992—), State Capital Law Firm Group (nat. bd. dirs. 1989—, chmn. com. Can. 1990-93, chair pub. utility, energy and comm. sect. 1994-2007, nat. sec. 1996-97, vice-chmn. 1997-98, chmn. 1998-99), Downtown Coaches Club (bd. dirs., pres. 1987), Nat. Resource Ctr. on State Laws and Regulations (nat. bd. dirs. 1993-99, chmn. 1998-99), Mich. Wind Working Group, Mich. State U. Pres.'s Club, Rotary (bd. dirs. 1995-97, pres. 2004-05, Paul Harris fellow), Phi Alpha Delta, Phi Eta Sigma, Theta Delta Chi (pres. 1972), Mich. Wind Working Group. Republican. Home: 1959 Groton Way East Lansing MI 48823-1347 Office: Fraser Trebilcock Davis & Dunlap PC Boji Tower Fl 10 124 West Allegan Street Lansing MI 48933 Office Phone: 517-377-0830, 517-377-0825. Business E-Mail: dmarvin@fraserlawfirm.com.

MARVIN-BASTA, LAURA LYNN, art educator; b. Balt., Jan. 30, 1975; d. Donald Elbert and Esther Mae Head; m. Brian Marvin, July 6, 2002 (div. Mar. 4, 2006); children: Kyle Everett Marvin, Colin Christopher Basta; m. Dustin Basta, July 19, 2008. Assoc., Balt. County C.C., 1996; Bachelors, Towson U., 2002; Masters, Goucher Coll., Balt., 2002. Cert. elem., reading tchr. Md. Art/tech. tchr. Colgate Elem. Sch., tech integration tchr. Balt. County Pub. Schs., 2002—; with TABCO Rep., 2008—. Mentor tchr. Balt. County Pub. Schs., 2005—06. Nominee Dundalk Tchr. of Yr., 2008; Meml. scholarship, Vietnam Vets. of Am. Chpt. 451, 1997. Mem.: NEA (life), Tchrs. Assn. of Balt. County (life), Md. State Tchrs. Assn. (life). Avocations: painting, drawing, decorating, sculpting.

MARX, ANTHONY W., academic administrator; b. NYC, Feb. 28, 1959; s. Peter and Marion E. (Mankin) M.; m. Karen Barkey, Sept. 7, 1992; children: Joshua, Anna-Claire. Student, Wesleyan U., Middletown, Conn., 1977-79; BA, Yale U., 1981; MPA, Princeton U., 1986, MA, 1987, PhD, 1990. Adminstrv. aide to the pres. U. Pa., Phila., 1981-84; cons. SACHED Trust, Johannesburg, 1984, 86; vis. scholar Community Agy. for Social Enquiry, Johannesburg, 1988, 90; prof. polit. sci. Columbia U., NYC, 1990—2003; pres. Amherst Coll., 2003—. Rsch. asst. Ctr. for Ednl. Rsch. and Devel., Santiago, Chile, 1985; cons. UNDP, N.Y.C., 1991; vis. scholar Ctr. for Afro-Asian Studies, Rio de Janeiro, Brazil, 1993. Author: Lessons of Struggle, 1992, Making Race and Nation: A Comparison of the United States, South Africa and Brazil, 1998 (Ralph J. Bunche award Am. Polit. Sci. Assn., 1999, Barrington Moore prize Am. Sociol. Assn., 2000), Faith in Nation: Exclusionary Origins of Nationalism, 2003; contbr. articles to profl. jours. Trustee, treas. Fund for Edn. in South Africa, N.Y.C., 1991—94. Grantee J. D. and C.T. MacArthur Found., Chgo., 1989-90, Social Sci. Rsch. Coun., N.Y.C., 1992-93, U.S. Inst. Peace, Washington, 1992-93; named fellow H.F. Guggenheim Found., N.Y.C., 1994.; John Simon Guggenheim fellow, 1997. Office: Office of Pres 103 Converse Hall PO Box 5000 Amherst MA 01002-5000 Office Phone: 413-542-2234. E-mail: marx@amherst.edu.

MARX, GARY DEAN, educational consultant, futurist, think-tank executive; b. Manchester, SD, Nov. 28, 1938; s. Harvey Frederick and Lucille (Stemple) Marx; m. Judy Rae Marx, June 18, 1961; children: John Fredrick, Daniel Winston. BA, U. S.D., 1960. Cert. Pub. Rels. Soc. Am., Nat. Sch. Pub. Rels. Assn., Am. Soc. Assn. Execs. Newscaster, announcer, dir. KSOO radio and TV sta., Sioux Falls, SD, 1958-61; newscaster, announcer WOW radio and TV sta., Omaha, 1961-71; dir. comms. Westside Cmty. Schs., Omaha, 1971-77; exec. dir. comms. Jefferson County Pub. Schs., Denver, 1977-79; sr. assoc. exec. Am. Assn. Sch. Adminstrs., Arlington, Va., 1979-96, exec. dir. Leadership for Learning Found., 1996-98; pres. Ctr. for Pub. Outreach, Inc., Vienna, Va., 1998—. Sr. rsch. fellow Health, Energy and Productivity in Sch. project, Bethesda, Md., 2000-02; pub. rels. cons. Nat. Sch. Pub. Rels. Assn., Rockville, Md., 1972—; v.p., owner Sta. KOAK Radio, Red Oak, Iowa, 1977-82; v.p. Comms. Devel. Inc., Denver, 1974-76; evaluator CIVITAS Internat. Exch. Program, Calabasas, Calif., 2000—; cons., internat. spkr. in field. Author: Radio...Your Publics are Listening, 1976; Radio...Get the Message, 1977; Excellence in Our Schools...Making it Happen, 1984; Public Relations for Administrators, 1984, 88; Working with the News Media, 1993; Preparing Students for the 21st Century, 1996, 99; The Future of Cmty., 1999; Preparing Schools and School Systems for the 21st Century, 1999; Ten Trends...Educating Children for a Profoundly Different Future, 2000, Future Focused Leadership...Preparing Schools, Students and Communities for Tomorrow's Realities, 2006, Sixteen Trends...Their Profound Impact on Our Future, 2006; contbr. articles to profl. jours. Founder, chmn. Keystone Cmty. Task Force, Omaha, 1970-77; mem. Omaha Parks and Recreation Bd., City of Omaha, 1975-77; mem. urban growth policy bd., 1976; mem. nat. edn. adv. com. for restoration Statue of Liberty-Ellis Island Found,. NYC, 1984-86; founder Nat. Supr. of Yr. program, 1987; mem. Horace Mann League, 1985-, bd. dirs. 2005—; mem. exec. com. edn. Commn. of Bicentennial of the US Constitution, Washington, 1986-92,; bd. dir. Campaign New Priorities, Washington, 1992-93, US Coalition Edn. for All, 1993-1997, Manchester Monument Adv. Coun., SD, 2006-07, bd. dirs., Laura Ingalls Wilder Meml. Soc., 2007—, Harvey Dunn Soc. SD, 2009-, founder Coalition for America's Children, Washington, 1992-98; mem. steering com. Libr. of Congress, Ctr. for the Book, Washington, 1992-99, Goals 2000 Arts Edn. Partnership NEA, Washington, 1993-98, Civitas Internat., Brussels, Belgium, 1996—, Fulbright Scholars, selection com., 1998-; mem. design arts program steering com. NEA, Washington, 1993-94; mem. grants selection com. Alliance for Arts Edn., John F. Kennedy Ctr. for the Performing Arts, Washington, 1993-96, selection com. advisor Nat. Tchr. of Yr. Program, Washington, 1979-99; mem. steering com., mem. selection com., judge Disney Salute to the Am. Tchr., Burbank, Calif., 1993-97; Emmy awards judge NATAS, NYC, 1995-97; mem. nat. adv. bd. NBC The More You Know campaign, NYC, 1992-98; mem. nat. adv. bd. PBS, 1990-98; judge USA Today All USA Acad. Team, Arlington, Va., 1995-2000, judge Nat. History Day, 2002-; internat. cons., spkr., Ctr. Civic Edn., Calabasas, Calif., 1996—, USIA, US Dept. State, Washington, 1996—; mem. steering com., facilitator Nat. Ctr. Energy Mgmt. and Bldg. Techs., 2004—, twelve-mem. alternative futures panel Washington Metro Area in 2025, Washington Post, 2007-2008. Recipient Radio Advertising Bureau Commercial award, 1967, Pres. award, Nat. Sch. Pub. Relations Assn., 1999, Disting. Svc. award, Am. Assn. Sch. Administrs., 2000. Mem. Nat. Sch. Pub. Rels. Assn. (numerous coms. 1971—, accredited, Pres.'s award 1999), Pub. Rels. Soc. Am. (accredited), Am. Soc. Assn. Exec. (cert.), Edn. Writers Assn. (bd. dir. 1983-86), Am. Assn. Sch. Adminstrs. (Disting. Svc. award 2000), World Future Soc. (profl. mem.), Assn. Supervision and Curriculum Devel., Horace Mann League (bd. dirs. 2005-, Ambs. award 2009). Avocations: folk art, travel, reading, writing, photography. Office: Ctr for Pub Outreach 1831 Toyon Way Vienna VA 22182-3355 Office Phone: 703-938-8725. Personal E-mail: gmarxcpo@aol.com.

MARX, GARY T., sociologist, writer; b. Hanford, Calif., Oct. 1, 1938; BA, UCLA, 1960; MA, U. Calif., Berkeley, 1962, PhD, 1966. Rsch. assoc. U. Calif., Berkeley, 1965-67, lectr. dept. sociology, 1966-67; rsch. assoc. Harvard-MIT Joint Ctr. for Urban Studies, 1967-73; asst. prof., lectr. dept. social rels. Harvard U., 1967-73; sr. rsch. assoc. Ctr. for Criminal Justice Harvard Law Sch., 1973-75; assoc. prof. MIT, 1973-79, prof., 1979-94, emeritus prof. dept. urban studies and planning, 1994; prof. U. Colo., Boulder, 1992-98, chair dept. sociology, 1992-96; vis. scholar U. Wash., 1999—. Vis. prof. U. Calif., San Diego, 1977-78, SUNY, Albany, 1980, Cath. U., Louvain, and Louvain La Neuve, Belgium, 1991, Tech. U., Vienna, Austria, 1993, Nankai U., China, 1995, U. Calif. Irvine, 2000, Berkeley, 2001, Northwestern U., 2001; A.D. Carlson disting. vis. prof. in social scis. W.Va. U., 2003; Hixon Riggs prof. sci., tech. & soc. Harvey Mudd Coll., 2007-08; mem. exec. com. Am. Sociol. Assn., 1973-76; mem. adv. bds. Office of Tech. Assessment, 1985-87, NAS, 1989-91, Electronic Privacy Info. Ctr., 1992—; presenter testimony U.S. Congress, 1981, 91, 97; mem. Nat. Rsch. Coun. Panel, 1989-91, 2002-04. Author: Protest and Prejudice, 1967, rev. edit., 1969, Japanese edit., 1971, Undercover: Police Surveillance in America, 1988, Chinese edit., 1995; co-author: (with others) Inquiries in Sociology, 1972, (with N. Goodman) Society Today, rev. edit., 3d. edit., 1978, 4th edit., 1982, (with Doug McAdam) Collective Behavior and Collective Behavior Process, 1993; contbr. numerous articles to profl. jours.; editor: (book) Racial Conflict: Tension and Change Am. Soc., 71, Muckracking Sociology: Research as Social Criticism, 1972, (jours.) Social Problems, 1969-75, Am. Sociol. Rev., 1972-75, Ann. Rev. Sociology, 1978-84, 97-98, Jour. Conflict Resolution, 1984-91, Crime Law and Social Change, 1987-97, Qualitative Sociology, 1988-96, Justice Quar., 1990-93, Sociol. Forum, 1991-96, Criminology, 1991-93; co-editor: (books) (with others) Confrontation: Psychology and Problems of Today, 1970, (with N. Goodman) Sociology: Classic and Popular Approaches, 1980, (with C. Fijnaut) Undercover: Police Surveillance in Comparative Perspective, 1995, (with J. Alexander and C. Williams) Self, Social Structure, and Beliefs, 2004; mem. editl. bd. The Info. Soc., 1995—, The Am. Sociologist, 1997—, Policing and Society, 1997—, Ethics and Info. Tech., 1998—, Contingencies and Crisis Mgmt., 1991-, Surveillance and Soc., 2002-, Internat. Polit. Sociology, 2006-, Identity Info. Soc., 2008-, Intelligence Ethics, 2008-. Recipient Disting. Scholarship award Am. Sociol. Assn., 1990, named Jensen lectr., 1989; Outstanding Book award Acad. Criminal Justice Scis., 1990, Bruce Smith Lifetime Achievement award, 1999; Silver Gavel award ABA, 1991; Guggenheim fellow, 1970-71, rsch. fellow Ctr. for Advanced Study in the Behavioral Scis., 1987-88, 96-97, fellow Woodrow Wilson Internat. Ctr. for Scholars, Washington, 1997-98; rsch. grantee NSF, 1973-75, 85-86, 91-95, 2006-09, 20th Century Fund, 1982-87, Austauschdienst, Whiting Found., Deutscher Akademischer, 1991; resident scholar Rockefeller Study and Conf. Ctr., Belagio, Italy, 1990, Stice Meml. lectr. in social scis. U. Wash., 1992, Appel Disting. lectr. in law and tech., Denver U., 1994; Chancellor's Disting. fellow U. Calif., 2000.

MARX, KENNETH R., music educator; b. Evergreen Park, Ill., May 10, 1957; s. Robert P. and Katherine B. Marx; m. Darrelyn M. Brawders, Apr. 2, 1991. MusB, DePaul U., Chgo., 1979; MusM Edn., Vandercook Coll. Music, Chgo., 1982. Cert. tchr. Type 10 Music and Type 03 Classroom Ill. State Bd. Edn., 1979. Dir. instrumental music edn. Lemont (Ill.)-Bromberek Sch. Dist. 113A, 1979—. Mem. alumni bd. DePaul U. Sch. Music, Chgo., 1997—99; instrumental music adjudicator, clinician Ill. Grade Sch. Music Assn., Ill. Music Assn.; condr. Ill. State Champion Mid. Sch. Band, 2005. Author: Rehearsal Techniques for Young Bands. Dir. Lemont Band Boosters, 1979—2006; pres. Beau Ridge Homeowner's Assn., Park Ridge, Ill., 1995—99; cons. S.E. DuPage Ednl. Conf., Lemont. Recipient Excellence in Edn. award, Ill. State Bd. Edn., 1991, Chicagoland Outstanding Educator award, Quinlan & Fabish Music, 1996, PTA Tchr. of Yr. award, 1995. Mem.: ASBDA, Nat. Band Assn., Music Educators Nat. Conf. (assoc.), Ill. Music Educators Assn. (assoc.), Phi Beta Mu. Home: 1219 Beau Dr Park Ridge IL 60068 Office: Old Quarry Middle School 16100 W 127th St Lemont IL 60439 Personal E-mail: kdmarx@comcast.net. E-mail: kenmarx@lemontschools.com.

MARX, MICHAEL WILLIAM, language educator, writer; b. Phila., Nov. 1, 1951; s. Elmer Edward and Katharine Scott Marx. Student, Loyola U.; BA in Polit. Sci., Hobart Coll., 1973; MFA in Film Making, NYU, 1976; MA in English, Ind. State U., Terre Haute, 2001. Freelance writer, Calif., 1976-90; owner, head chef Freelandville Novelist Cafe, Ind., 1990—95; pub. Marx & Marx Writers & Pubs., 1998—99; instr. English lang. and lit. Ind. State U., Terre Haute, 1999—2001; instr. Lakeland Coll., Danville, Ill., 2000—01, Ivy Tech State Coll., Terra Haute & Greenfield, Ind., 2000—01, Mira Costa Coll., Oceanside, Calif., 2001—03, Southwestern Coll., Chula Vista, Calif., 2001—02, San Diego City Coll., 2001—, Palomar Coll., San Marcos, Calif., 2001—03, Miramar Coll., San Diego, 2001—03, Cuyumaca Coll., El Cajon, Calif., 2001—03, Inter-Am. Coll., National City, Calif., 2001—03, San Diego State U., 2002—04, Nat. U., 2002—04; instr. lit., film Webster U., 2004—; instr. Chapman U., 2004—05; instr. humanities, English composition, English lit., effective speaking Art Inst. Calif., San Diego, 2004—08, chair libr. com., 2006—08; English instr. ITT Tech., 2009—. Tchr. Vincennes U., Ind., 1991—93, Ind. Bus. Coll., 1995. Author: (book) A War Ends, 1977, A War Ends, 2d edit., 1985 (Artisan award Acad. Fine Arts and Friends), Eric Greenfield: Middle American, 1987, Justus: A Utopia, 1999; columnist: North Knox Leader, 1997—98, Knox County Daily News, Wabash Weekly News, 1991—92; movie reviewer Cine-Marx. Personal E-mail: michael@michaelmarx.com.

MARX, NICKI DIANE, sculptor, painter, jeweler; b. LA, Oct. 3, 1943; d. Donald F. and Ruth H. (Ungar) M. Student, U. Calif., Riverside, 1965, U. Calif., Santa Cruz, 1973. Represented by Nicki Marx Studio, Taos, N.Mex., Fred Kline Gallery, Santa Fe, N.Mex. One-woman shows include Palm Springs Desert Mus., 1977, Julie Artisans Gallery, NYC, 1975, Phoenix Art Mus., 1975, Weston Gallery, Carmel, Calif, 1981, Kirk de Gooyer Gallery, LA, 1982, Rocklands Gallery, Monterey, Calif., 1983, Fetish Gallery, Taos, 1988, Fenix Gallery, Taos, 1991, Earthworks, 1993, Lamberts, 1994, Stables Gallery, Taos, 1995, Fred Kline, 1995, Sun Cities Mus. Art, Ariz., 1996, Harwood Mus. Art, Taos, 1999, others; group exhbns. include E.P. Smith Gallery, Santa Cruz, 1994, Lumina Gallery, Taos, 1994, Cafe Gallery, Albuquerque, 1991, Bareiss Gallery, Taos, 1990, Ctr. for Contemporary Art, Santa Fe, 1989, Jordan Gallery, Taos, 1988-89, Stables Art Gallery, Taos, 1988, 94, Albuquerque State Fair Grounds, 1986, San Francisco Mus. Modern Art, 1977-78, Elements Gallery, Greenwich, Conn., 1977, Pacific Design Ctr., LA, 1976, Lester Gallery, Inverness, Calif., 1976, others; represented in pub. collections IBM, Milford, Conn., NYC, San Jose, Calif., Bank of Am., San Francisco, The Continental Group, Inc., Stamford, Conn., Cedars-Sinai Hosp., LA, Farm Bur. Fedn., Sacramento, Calif., Sherman Fairchild Sci.

Ctr., Stanford, Calif., Palm Springs Desert Mus., Calif., U. Mus., Ariz. State U. at Tempe, Mills Coll. Art Gallery, Berkeley, Calif.; exhibited in pvt. collections of Estate of Eugene Klein, Estate of Louise Nevelson, Estate of Georgia O'Keeffe, Fritz Scholder, Ray Graham, Bunny Horowitz, Sue and Otto Meyer, Burt Sugarman, Craig Moody, Paul Pletka, others; subject of numerous articles in jours. and mags. MacDowell Colony fellow, 1975; recipient Adolph and Esther Gottleib Found. grant, 1985. Studio: PO Box 128 Penasco NM 87553 Office Phone: 505-587-2383. Business E-Mail: marx@laplaza.org.

MARX, OWEN COX, lawyer; b. Grosse Pointe, Mich., Oct. 17, 1947; s. Leo A. and Anne (Cox) M.; m. Patricia Windschill, Aug. 14, 1971; children: Patrick Cox, Molly Simser, Anne Windschill. BA, Coll. of St. Thomas, St. Paul, 1969; JD, Cath. U., Washington, 1972. Bar: Minn. 1972, N.Y. 1973. Law clk. to presiding justice Minn. Supreme Ct., St. Paul, 1972-73; assoc. Mudge, Rose, Guthrie & Alexander, NYC, 1973-75, Dorsey & Whitney, Mpls., 1975-78, ptnr., 1979-86, ptnr., head London office, 1986-90, ptnr., corp. fin., internat. practice groups NYC, 1990—, and co-chmn., project devel. and fin. Bd. dirs. Bush Mfg. Co., Detroit, Off Site Tech. Inc., Detroit, OFLA Receivables Corp., San Diego, Hercules (Cayman) Ltd., Cayman Islands. Mem. Internat. Bar Assn., Minn. Bar Assn., N.Y. Athletic Club. Republican. Roman Catholic. Office: Dorsey & Whitney 250 Park Ave New York NY 10177-1500 Office Phone: 212-415-9285. Office Fax: 212-953-7201. Business E-Mail: marx.owen@dorsey.com.

MARX, ROBERT G., orthopedic surgeon, educator; b. May 1, 1965; BSc in Biology, U. Montréal, 1987; MD, McGill U., 1991; MSc in Clin. Epidemiology, U. Toronto, 1996. Cert. Am. Bd. Orthop. Surgery, Royal Coll. Surgeons Can. Resident U. Toronto; fellow, sports medicine/shoulder and knee surgery Hosp. Spl. Surgery, assoc. attending orthop. surgeon; dir., Foster Ctr. for Clin. Outcome Rsch. Hosp. for Spl. Surgery, Weill Med. Coll., Cornell U.; assoc. prof. orthop. surgery Weill Med. Coll., Cornell U., assoc. prof. pub. health. Orthop. dir. Sports Medicine Inst. for Young Atheletes; invited lectr. or vis. prof. in the field. Contbr. several articles to profl. jours., chapters to books; mem. editl. adv. bd. Muscle and Fitness Mag. Recipient O'Donoghue Sport Injury Rsch. award, Am. Orthop. Soc. for Sports Medicine, 2003; Royal Coll. Physicians and Surgeons Can. Detweiler Traveling Fellowship, Am. Acad. Orthop. Surgeons Health Services Rsch. Fellowship. Mem.: Knee Surgery and Orthop. Sports Medicine (mem. scientific adv. com.), Canadian Orthop. Assn., Am. Orthop. Soc. for Sports Medicine, Am. Acad. Orthop. Surgeons, Internat. Soc. Arthroscopy (mem. scientific adv. com.). Office: 519 E 72nd St New York NY 10021 Address: Hosp Spl Surgery 535 E 70th St New York NY 10021 Office Phone: 212-606-1645. Office Fax: 212-774-7822. Business E-Mail: MarxR@HSS.EDU.

MARX, THOMAS GEORGE, economist; b. Trenton, NJ, Oct. 25, 1943; s. George Thomas and Ann (Szymanski) Marx; m. Arlene May Varga, Aug. 23, 1969; children: Melissa Ann, Thomas Jeffrey, Jeffrey Alan. BS summa cum laude, Rider Coll., 1969; PhD, U. Pa., Phila., 1973. Fin. analyst Am. Cyanamid Co., Trenton, 1968; economist FTC, Washington, 1973; econ. cons. Foster Assocs. Inc., Washington, 1974-77; sr. economist GM, Detroit, 1977-79, mgr. indsl. econs., 1980-81, dir. econs. policy studies, 1981-83, dir. corp. strategic planning group, 1984-86, gen. dir. market analysis and forecasting, 1986-88, gen. dir. econ. analysis, 1988-90, gen. dir. issues mgmt. on industry govt. rels. staff, 1990-96, dir. econ. issues and analysis corp. affairs staff, 1996-97, dir. global climate issue, 1997—2005; coll. prof., dir. bus. adminstrn. doctorate program Coll. Mgmt. Lawrence Technol. U., 2005—. Mem. faculty Temple U., Phila., 1972—73, U. Pa., Phila., 1972—73; adj. prof. Wayne State U., 1981—89, U. Detroit, 1988—2005; prof., dir. bus. adminstrn. doctorate program Lawrence Technol. U., 2005—; dir. Ctr. Study Global Leadership & Understanding, 2005—. Assoc. editor: Bus. Econs., 1980—98, mem. editl. bd.: Akron Jour. Bus. and Econs., 1981—90; contbr. articles to profl. jours. With USAF, 1961—65. Mem.: Assn. Pub. Policy Analysts, Planning Forum, Western Econ. Assn., So. Econ. Assn., Econ. Soc. Mich., Detroit Area Bus. Economists (v.p.), Nat. Assn. Bus. Economists, Am. Econ. Assn., Nat. Econs. Club, Beta Gamma Sigma, Pi Gamma Mu. Roman Catholic. Home: 3312 Bloomfield Park Dr West Bloomfield MI 48323-3514 Office Phone: 248-204-3081. Business E-Mail: tmarx@ltu.edu.

MARY, DIANE BRADLEY, elementary school educator, secondary school educator; d. William Joseph and Mary Ann Bradley; children: William Bradley, James Corbett, Megan Shannon Mary. Degree, Stanford U., Calif.; MA in Edn., U. Calif., Berkeley, 1965. Cert. counselor U. Calif. Berkley; tchr. San Francisco State U. Tchr. 7th grade sci., biology Sullivan Mid. Sch., Fairfield, 1989—2007, counselor, 2007—. Mentor tchr. U. Calif., Davis. Recipient Tchr. Yr., Sullivan Middle Sch., Disting. Alumni award, Stanford U. Home: 2889 St Andrews Rd Fairfield CA 94534 Office: Sullivan Middle Sch 2195 Union Ave Fairfield CA 94533 Office Fax: 707-421-3964. Personal E-mail: dmscience@aol.com.

MARYA, MANUEL PAUL CLAUDE, metallurgical and materials engineer, researcher; b. Nantes, France, July 1, 1972; s. Surendar Kumar and Annie Jeanne Suzanne (Crouau) Marya; m. Noriko Yao, Nov. 3, 2003. DUT in Mech. & Mfg. Engring., Inst. U. Nantes, France, 1990—92; BEng in Mech. Engring., U. Quebec, Can., 1992—95; MS in Metall. & Materials Engring., Colo. Sch. Mines, Golden, 1996—99, PhD in Metall. & Materials Engring., 2001. Rsch. asst. Colo. Sch. Mines, Golden, Colo., 1996—2001, postdoctoral fellow, 2002, rsch. asst. prof., 2002—04; vis. scientist Gen. Motors Rsch. & Devel., Warren, Mich., 2002—04; sr. mem., tech. staff Nanocoolers Inc., Austin, Tex., 2004—09; mgr., materials and process engring. dept. Schlumberger, Rosharon, Tex., 2008—. Engring. trainee ECN Centre LASER, Nantes, France, 1990—92; rsch. asst. U. Nottingham, England, 1995; material & welding rsch. cons. Ecole Centrale Nantes, France, 1996—. Contbr. over 50 articles to profl. jours. and internat. conf. proceedings, chapters to books. Recipient Henry Granjon award, Internat. Inst. Welding, 2002, AWS William Spraragen award, 2006; grantee, Ford, Visteon, Gen. Motors, 1999—2004. Fellow: Am. Welding Soc.; mem.: Am. Soc. for Materials. Achievements include research in Magnesium Joining, Laser Processing Research, Alloy and Liquid Metal Development, Materials Processing, Coatings and Corrosion, etc; patents in field. Avocations: travel, art, reading. Office: Materials Engring Dept Bldg 45 Office 1227 14910 Airline Rd Rosharon TX 77583 Office Fax: 281-285-5177. Personal E-mail: mpmarya@hotmail.com.

MARYNIUK, MELINDA DOWNIE, medical educator, director; d. George Laurence and Joan Voorman Downie; m. George Alexander Maryniuk; children: Andrew Laurence, Adam Downie. MEd, Tufts U., Medford, Mass., 1979. Registered dietitian Commn. Dietetic Registration, 1979. Dir., clin. & edn. programs Joslin Diabetes Ctr., Boston, 1993—. Elected mem. Am. Diabetes Assn., Alexandria, Va., 1995—99. Recipient Excellence Clin. Nutrition award, Am. Dietetic Assn., 2004, Outstanding Educator Diabetes award, 2005. Home: 308 Pond St Jamaica Plain MA 02130 Office: Joslin Diabetes Ctr One Joslin Pl Boston MA 02215 Personal E-mail: mmaryniuk@hotmail.com.

MARZIO, PETER CORT, museum director; b. Governor's Island, NY, May 8, 1943; s. Francis and Katherine (Mastroberte) M.; m. Frances Ann Parker, July 2, 1979; children: Sara Lon, Steven Arnold. BA, Juniata Coll., 1965; MA, U. Chgo., 1966, PhD, 1969. Rsch. asst. to dir., then historian Nat. Mus. History and Tech., Smithsonian Instn., 1969-73, assoc. curator prints, 1977-78, chmn. dept. cultural history, 1978; dir., CEO Corcoran Gallery Art, Washington, 1978-82; dir. Mus. Fine Arts, Houston, 1982—. Instr. Roosevelt U., Chgo., 1966-68; assoc. prof. U. Md., 1967-77; chmn. Fed. Coun. on Arts and Humanities, 1997-2000. Author: Rube Goldberg: His Life and Works, 1973, The Art Crusade, 1976, The Democratic Art: An Introduction to the History of Chromolithography in America, 1979; editor: A Nation of Nations, 1976. Bd. dirs. Wallace Found. Sr. Fulbright fellow, Italy, 1973-74. Mem. Cosmos Club (Washington), Coronado Club (Houston), Assn. of Art Museum Directors (pres. 1988-89). Office: Mus Fine Arts 1001 Bissonet St PO Box 6826 Houston TX 77265-6826 Office Phone: 713-639-7300. E-mail: pmarzio@mfah.org.

MARZORATI, GERALD, editor; b. Patterson, NJ, Feb. 8, 1953; BA in Humanities, with honors, Villanova U., Pa., 1975. Sr. editor SoHo News, NYC; dep. editor Harper's mag., NY; non-fiction editor The New Yorker mag. Condé Nast Publs.; articles editor NY Times Mag., NYC, 1994—98, editl. dir., 1998—2003, editor, 2003—; asst. mng. editor NY Times, NYC, 2006—. Author: A Painter of Darkness: Leon Golub and Our Times, 1990 (PEN/Martha Albrand award). Recipient Nat. Mag. award for Reporting, Am. Soc. Mag. Editors, 2009. Office: New York Times 620 8th Ave New York NY 10018-1405 Office Phone: 212-556-1234.*

MÁS, BEVERLEY BERLIN, counseling advisor, career planning advisor; d. Hobart Irl Willis and Irene Ethel Holeman; m. Oscar Más, Apr. 30, 1977. BA in Psychology summa cum laude, Fla. Atlantic U. Harriett L. Wilkes Honors Coll., 2002. Secretarial supr. Irell & Manella Law Firm, Century City, Calif., 1981—91; freelance manuscript editor Palm Beach Gardens, Fla., 1991—99; academic advisor and counselor Palm Beach C.C., Palm Beach Gardens, 2002—, tutor English, biology, anatomy/physiology, 1996—99; freelance life coach Palm Beach Gardens, 2002—. Trainer-recruiter Literacy Coalition Palm Beach County, Jupiter, Fla., 2000—02; presenter in field. Author short stories and poems; contbr. articles to profl. jours.; author: Aging and Memory for Self-performed Task: Effects of Task Difficulty and Time Pressure, Songs of Honour, 2006. Group facilitator Murder and Suicide Survivors, LA, 1994—95, Suicide Survivors, LA, 1994—95; organizer, ofcl. Psychology Club Palm Beach C.C., Palm Beach Gardens, 1998—99, contbg mem. of president's strategic planning team, 1998—99, coll. amb. and student liaison; organizer of svc. of food and fin. svc. to needy families in cmty., v.p. of svc. Phi Theta Kappa Internat. Honors Soc., Palm Beach Gardens, 1998—99, organizer svc. food & fin. svc. to needy families in cmty., v.p. svc., 2008—09; ann. neighborhood vol. Am. Heart Assn., Palm Beach Gardens, 1999—, Am. Cancer Soc., Palm Beach Gardens, 1999—2006; leader Spl. Olympics, North Palm Beach, Fla., 1999—; organizer Halloween and Christmas parties for abused and underprivileged children Palm Beach County, Palm Beach Gardens, 1999—99; leader, vol. program for after-school tutorage Am. Reads Program, Jupiter, Fla., 2000—02; honoree, spkr., program presenter Nat. Collegiate Honors Coun. Nat. Convention, Chgo.; presenter Cognitive Aging Conf., Atlanta, 2000; v.p. Glenwood Homeowners' Assn., Palm Beach Gardens, 1998—99. Recipient Spl. commendation as outstanding scholar in Ho. Resolution No. 9053, State Fla. Ho. Reps., 1999, State Poetry award, Fla. Collegiate Honors Coun., 2002, winning short story, Twentieth Century Lit. Conf., U. Louisville, Ky., 2002, Editors Choice award, Internat. Poetry Assn., 2005; named Disting. Alumna, Harriet L. Wilkes Honors Coll., Fla. Atlantic U., 2004, 2005, Fla. Atlantic U., 2005; named to All USA Academic First Team, USA Today, 1999, All Fla. Academic First Team, Fla. State Legislature, 1999; finalist Exemplary Practice award, Fla. Assn. C.C.s, 2006; scholar, Harriet L. Wilkes Honors Coll., Fla. Atlantic U., 2001; Guistewhite Scholar of the Yr., Phi Theta Kappa Internat. Honor Soc., 1999, Frederick DeHon scholar. Mem.: APA (life), SAG (life), Women in Edn. (assoc.), Fed. Assn. Cmty. Colls. (assoc.), Greater Found. Women's Coun. (life), People for the Ethical Treatment of Animals (life), Physicians' Com. for Responsible Medicine (life), Soc. for the Study of Peace, Conflict, and Violence (life), Nat. Alliance for the Mentally Ill (life), Am. Fed. Variety Artists (life), Amnesty Internat. (life; women's action coun.), Psi Beta (v.p. and chair edn. activities), Golden Key, Phi Kappa Phi, Phi Theta Kappa (Guistewhite scholar of the Yr. 1999), Nat. Soc. Collegiate Scholars (life). Achievements include research in age difference in effects of gaze avers; effects of age and encoding context on recognition of nouns and verbs; Organizer, motivational lecturer and consultant for the first Dream It Do It Club in nation (support group for non traditonal students). Home: 1502 15th Ter Palm Beach Gardens FL 33418-3613 Office: Palm Beach CC 3160 PGA Blvd Palm Beach Gardens FL 33410-2893 Business E-Mail: masb@pbcc.edu.

MASAND, PRAKASH S., psychiatrist, researcher; b. Bombay; US, 1984; s. Sham Masand; m. Sonia Masand; 1 child, Natasha. MD, Topiwala Nat. Med. Coll., Bombay, 1982. Cert. Am. Bd. Psychiatry and Neurology, 1990. Resident in psychiatry SUNY Upstate Med. U., Syracuse, 1985—88, prof. psychiatry, 1989—2001; fellowship in consultation liaison psychiatry Mass. Gen. Hosp., Harvard Med. Sch., 1988—89; consulting prof. psychiatry Duke U. Med. Ctr., Durham, NC, 2001—. Sect. editor Current Psychiatry Reports, Phila., 2002—. Contbr. chapters to books, articles to profl. jours. Local candidate fund raiser, Chapel Hill, NC. Named Tchr. of Yr., Dept. Psychiatry SUNY Upstate Med. U., 1990, 1996; named one of Americas Top Psychiatrists, 2004—05, Best Doctors in Am., 2005—06. Fellow: Am. Psychiat. Assn. Office: DUMC Dept Psychiatry 2218 Elder St 2B STe 202 Durham NC 27705

MASANEK, MICHELE, secondary school educator, soccer coach; s. Ronald Julian and Stephanie Ann Masanek; BE, Bowling Green State U., Ohio, 1992; ME, Wright State U., Dayton, 2004. Tchr. Winston Woods Sch., Forest Pk., Ohio, 1994—95, Fairfield City Schs., 1995—2005. Girl's soccer coach Fairfield HS, 1994—2004, boy's asst. soccer coach, 2004—; coach Odyssey of the Mind, Ohio, 1995—98; asst. weight rm. supr., 2008—. Supporter Young Life, Fairfield, 1995—, Athletes in Action, Fairfield, 1999—, Fellowship of Christian Athletes, Fairfield, Ohio, 1999—. Recipient Fairfield Sch. Bell award, Fairfield City Schs., 1999, 2000, 2001, 2002, 2003, 2004, 2005, 2006, 2007—08, Fairfield Amb. award, 2004; named Asst. Coach of Yr., Ohio HS, 2006, Cin. HS, 2006, Tchr. of Yr., Fairfield Rotary Club, 2007; nominee Ashland Tchr. of Yr., 1994, Tchr. of Yr., Walt Disney, 2000, 2004, 2006, Fairfield City Schs., 2004, Tchr. of Week, WMOH, 2004. Mem.: Pi Lambda Theta, Phi Kappa Phi. Democrat. Avocations: soccer, running. Office: Fairfield City Schs 255 Donald Dr Fairfield OH 45014 Personal E-mail: mro717@msn.com.

MASCARENAS, PAUL A., automotive executive; Degree in Mech. Engring., King's Coll., U. London. Joined Ford Motor Co., 1982, various positions in product planning, prog. mgmt., body engring. and powertrain to chief prog. engr. Mondeo model sedan, then exec. dir. product devel. N.Am. Dearborn, Mich., v.p. N.Am. engring./global product devel., 2005—. Office: Ford Motor Co N Am Hdqs 1 American Rd Dearborn MI 48126 Business E-Mail: pmascarenas@ford.com.*

MASCETTA, JOSEPH ANTHONY, principal; b. Canonsburg, Pa., Sept. 2, 1931; s. Joseph Alphonso and Amalia (Ciavarra) M.; m. Jean Verrone, June 18, 1960; children: Lisa Marie, Linda Jo, Lori Jean. BS, U. Pitts., 1954; MS, U. Pa., 1963; cert. advanced study, Harvard U., 1970. Cert. tchr. math., phys. scis., adminstr. secondary sch., Pa. Tchr. chemistry Canonsburg High Sch., 1956-59, Mt. Lebanon High Sch., Pitts., 1959-75, chair sci. dept., 1967-75; coord. secondary curriculum Mt. Lebanon Sch. Dist., Pitts., 1975-81; prin. Mt. Lebanon Sr. High Sch., Pitts., 1981-91; ret., 1991; ednl. cons., 1991—. Vis. team Mid. States Assn. Colls. and Schs., Phila., 1967-78, chair vis. teams, 1981-96, Pa. state adv. com., 1988-91; sch. bd. and edn. commn. St. Patrick Sch., Canonsburg, 1972-85, 95-2002; tchr. undergrad. and grad. courses Duquesne U., Pitts., 1975-81; regional dir. Pa. Jr. Acad. Sci., Pitts., 1976-82; ednl. cons. Pitts. area schs., 1992—; quality edn. com. Pitts. Diocese, 1995-97. Author: Modern Chemistry Review, 1968, Chemistry the Easy Way, 1989, 5th rev. edit., 2003-, Barrews E-Z Chemistry, 2009, Barrows Sat Subject Test Chemistry, 2009, Barron's SAT II, Chemistry, 1994, 9th rev. edit., 2008; contbg. author: (ency.) Barron's Student Concise Ency., 1988, rev. 1994, Barron's New Student's Concise Ency., 1993, Perry Como Commemorative Booklet, 1998. Recipient Outstanding Tchr. award Spectroscopy Soc., 1973; grantee NSF, 1961, 62-63, 63, 67, 69-70, 73; sci. fellow GE, 1959. Mem. ASCD, Nat. Assn. Secondary Sch. Prins. (cert. recognition 1991), Pa. Assn. Curriculum & Supervision (exec. bd. dirs. 1985-87, regional pres. 1987), Western Pa. Assn. Curriculum and Supervision (v.p. 1983-85, pres. 1985-87, exec. bd. dirs. 1989-2001), Greater Canonsburg Heritage Soc., Italian-Am. Heritage and Cultural Soc. Washington County (chair scholarship com. 1992—, Man of Yr. award 2006), Phi Delta Kappa. Roman Catholic. Avocations: painting, writing. Home: 451 McClelland Rd Canonsburg PA 15317-2258 E-mail: jmascett@verizon.net.

MASCHERIN, TERRI LYNN, lawyer; b. Trenton, NJ, July 9, 1959; d. Anthony Americus and Kathryn Eleanor Mascherin; m. Thomas Warren Abendroth, Aug. 31, 1985. AB, Duke U., 1981; JD, Northwestern U., 1984. Bar: Ill. 1984, U.S. Dist. Ct. (Ariz.) 1999, U.S. Dist. Ct. (no. dist. Calif.) 1991, U.S. Dist. Ct. (Colo.) 1999, U.S. Dist. Ct. (no. dist. Ill.) 1984, U.S. Dist. Ct. (ea. dist. Mich.) 1998, U.S. Dist. Ct. (we. dist. Mich.) 1998, U.S. Dist. Ct. (ea. dist. Wis.) 1998, U.S. Ct. Appeals (6th cir.) 1999, U.S. Ct. Appeals (7th cir.) 1987, U.S. Ct. Appeals (9th cir.) 1999, U.S. Ct. Appeals (10th cir.) 2000, U.S. Supreme Ct. 1995. Assoc. Jenner & Block LLP, Chgo., 1984—92, ptnr., mem. litig. dept., 1992—, chair Assoc. Retention Subcommittee of Diversity Com., mem. Mgmt., Diversity and Women's Forum Steering Com. Chair law bd. Nothwestern U., 2006—08. Contbr. articles to law jours. Vice chair Law Bd. Northwestern U., 2004—06. Recipient Charles A. Duke award, Duke U., 1996, Outstanding Legal Svc. award, Nat. Coalition to Abolish Death Penalty, 2002, Cunningham-Carey award, Ill. Coalition to Abolish Death Penalty, 2004; named one of The 50 Most Influential Women Lawyers in Am., Nat. Law Jour., 2007. Fellow: Am. Bar Found.; mem.: ABA (chair Death Penalty Representation Project 2003—06), Women's Bar Assn. Ill., Ill. Bar Assn., Chgo. Bar Assn. (bd. mgrs. 2002—04, chair strategic planning com. 2005—06, treas. 2006—, 2nd v.p. 2008—09, first v.p. 2009—). Office: Jenner & Block 330 N Wabash Chicago IL 60611 Office Phone: 312-923-2799. Office Fax: 312-840-7799. Business E-Mail: tmascherin@jenner.com.

MASCI, JOSEPH RICHARD, physician; b. New Brunswick, NJ, Nov. 27, 1950; s. Joseph Nicholas and Delfina (Musa) M.; m. Elizabeth Bass, May 21, 1993; 1 child, Jonathan Samuel. BA, Cornell U., 1972; MD, NYU, 1976. Diplomate Am. Bd. Internal Medicine, Am. Bd. Infectious Diseases. Instr. medicine Boston U. Sch. Medicine, 1979—80, Mt. Sinai Sch. Medicine, NYC, 1982—84, asst. prof. clin. medicine, 1984—88, asst. prof. medicine, 1988—90, assoc. prof. medicine, 1990—2003, prof. medicine, 2003—, prof. cmty. and preventive medicine, 2006—; assoc. dir. medicine Elmhurst Hosp. Ctr., NY, 1987—2002, chief, infectiious disease, dir. medicine, 2002—. Peer reviewer NIH, 1994—. Author: Primary and Ambulatory Care of the HIV-Infected Adult, 1992, Outpatient Management of HIV-Infection, 2d edit., 1996, 3d edit., 2001, Bioterrorism: A Guide for Hospital Preparedness, 2005. Recipient Dr Linda Laubenstien award for Excellence in AIDS Care, 2002, Presdl. Voluntary Svc. Gold award. Fellow Am. Coll. Chest Physicians, US Agy. Internat. Devel. (Faculty Coun. award), NY Acad. of Medicine, ACP; mem. Am. Soc. Microbiology, Assn. Program Dirs. Internal Medicine, Assn. Profs. of Medicine. Office: Elmhurst Hosp Ctr 79-01 Broadway Elmhurst NY 11373-1329

MASCOLO-DAVID, ALEXANDRA, music educator; d. Vittorio Ferreira David and Anna Maria Mascolo; m. Patrick M. Donnelly, Sept. 29, 2000. MusD, U. Kans., Lawrence, 1997. Instr. piano Iowa State U., Ames, 1993—95; asst. prof. piano Ctrl. Mich. U., Mt. Pleasant, 1995—2002, assoc. prof. piano, 2002—07, prof. piano, 2007—. Musician: (piano performance) Carnegie Hall, (cd recording and release) 24 Brazilian Waltzes of Francisco Mignone, Piano Concertos of David Maslanka; contbr. articles to profl. jours. Recipient Provost's award, Ctrl. Mich. U., 2001, President's award, 2007. Office: Ctrl Mich Univ Sch Music Campus Dr Mount Pleasant MI 48859 Business E-Mail: david1am@cmich.edu.

MASE, RAYMOND JAMES, musician, educator; b. Meriden, Conn., May 12, 1951; s. James G. and Angelina (Evilia) M. BMus, New Eng. Conservatory, Boston, 1973. Trumpter Am. Brass Quintet, NYC, 1973—, Am. Composers Orch., NYC, 1976—, N.Y.C. Ballet Orch., 1987—, Summit Brass, 1986—, Orpheus Chamber Orch. Trumpet instr. Aspen Music Festival, 1973-; instr. The Juilliard Sch., N.Y.C., 1987—, chmn. of brass, 1991—. Editor: Editions of Early Brass Music.

MASEAR, CLAUDE, music educator, musician; b. Bklyn., Mar. 16, 1964; s. Clyde Benjamin and Elizabeth Demetriades Masear. MusB cum laude, Bklyn. Coll., 1988, MusM, 1991—91; cert. in Sch. Adminstrn. and Supr., Bklyn. Coll., 1993; EdD, Columbia U., 1999; diploma in Ednl. Adminstrn., Coll. New Rochelle, 2001. Cert. music tchr. N.Y., 1992, sch. adminstr./Supervisor N.Y., 1998. Music educator Intermediate Sch. N.Y. City Schs., Hollis, NY, 1988—90, music educator Intermediate Sch Bklyn., 1990—91; music educator Lawrence (N.Y.) Pub. Schs., 1992, Hicksville (N.Y.) Pub. Schs., 1992—93, 1994—95, Huntington (N.Y.) Pub. Schs., 1993—94, 1995—. Asst. dir. Salute To Music Program NY. State Schs., Bklyn., 1990—93; concert master Spirit Improvisation Ensemble Columbia U., NYC, 1995—; lectr. music edn. Bklyn. (N.Y.) Coll., Bklyn., 1996; presenter, balanced Mind Conf. L.I. U. C.W. Post Coll., 2001. Author: The Development And Field Test Of A Model For Evaluating Elementary String Programs, 1999; composer: (songs) Funky Town (Gold award N.Y. State Maj. Orgn. Festival, 1997), Rock Around The Clock (Silver award N.Y. State Maj. Orgn. Festival, 2000); musician Bouree For Solo Violin; conducted: Queens Borowide Concert, 1999. Coach 68 Precint Police Athletic League Youth Coun., Bklyn., 1981—93. Scholar, Teachers Coll., Columbia U., 1994. Mem.: N.Y. State Sch. Music Assn. (assoc.), Kappa Delta Pi (assoc.). Greek

Orthodox. Achievements include development of standards for string instruction grades3-12; design of program evaluation models for public school music programs. Avocations: exercise, music, travel, cooking, languages. Office: Huntington Public Schools Woodhul Road Huntington NY 11743 Home: 12 College Dr Stony Brook NY 11790-2724 Personal E-mail: clmaedd@aol.com.

MASEFIELD, OLIVER LESLIE PETER, aerospace transportation executive, aerospace engineer; b. London, June 10, 1948; BSc in Aero. Engring., Loughborough U. of Tech., Loughborough, Leics, Eng., 1972; PhD in Aerodynamics, Loughborough U. of Tech., 1991. Chartered engr., Royal Aero. Soc., UK, 1978. Future projects engr. Hawker Siddeley Aviation, Kingston, Surrey, England, 1972—73; v.p. R & D Pilatus Aircraft Ltd, 6370 Stans, Switzerland, 1973—99; v.p. eclipse engring. Williams Internat., Walled Lake, Mich., 2000—01; v.p. engring. Eclipse Aviation Corp., Albuquerque, 2000—04, sr. v.p., 2004—09, sr. fellow, 2004—09; bus. devel. mgr. PhostrEx, 2008; owner Masefield Consulting LLC, 2009. Study group mem. Joint Aviation Authority, 1991—99; bd. mem., dir. Dynamic Test Centre, Biel, Bern, Switzerland, 1997—99; adv. bd. Mech. Engring., U. N.Mex., Albuquerque, 2002—09; designated engring. rep., mech. sys., flight analyst FAA, 2006. Internat. editor (periodical) Jour. of Aircraft. Fellow: Royal Aero. Soc.; mem.: AIAA, Internat. Coun. of Aero. Scis. (program com. mem. 1990—2007), Internat. Coun. of Aero. Scis. (coun. mem. 1986—99), Swiss Soc. of Aero. Scis. (coun. mem. 1986—99). Achievements include led team which developed Pilatus PC-7, PC-9, PC-12 and PC-7 Mk II aircraft; program manager and led Pilatus team in partnership with Beech Aircraft, which obtained contract for JPATS trainer aircraft for USAF & USN, TGA; led team which first introduced Friction Stir Welding production in aviation; led team which developed revolutionary Eclipse 500 personal jet aircraft program manager and chief engineer for eclipse concept jet development. Avocations: reading, snowboarding, squash, windsurfing, walking. Office: Eclipse Aviation Corp 2503 Clark Carr Loop SE Albuquerque NM 87106 Home: 8716 Warm Springs Rd Nw Albuquerque NM 87120-3238 E-mail: oliver.masefield@eclipseaviation.com.

MASEKELA, BARBARA JOYCE MOSIMA, former ambassador; 2 children. B, U. Ohio. Chief of staff to Nelson Mandela, 1990—94; exec. dir. for pub. and corp. affairs De Beers Consol. Mines (ret. 2003); South African amb. to France and UNESCO, 1995—99; South African amb. to the US Washington, 2003—07. Asst. prof. English lit. Staten Island CC, NY, Rutgers U., NJ; trustee Nelson Mandela Children's Fund, Nelson Mandela Found.; various exec. and non-exec. directorships including Standard Bank of South Africa, South African Broadcasting Corp., and Internat. Mktg. Coun., 1999—2003. Achievements include founding African Nat. Congress Office of Arts and Culture.

MASELLI, JOHN ANTHONY, food products executive; b. NYC, Feb. 18, 1928; s. Anthony and Livia M.; m. Brigitta Degenkolb, Dec. 26, 1948; children: Elisa, John A. Jr. BS in Chemistry, CCNY, 1947; MS in Chemistry, Fordham U., 1949, PhD in Chemistry, 1952. Dir. research and devel. Standard Brands, Stamford, Conn., 1952-64; mgr. product devel. M&M/Mars, Hackettstown, NJ, 1964-67; pres. OZ Food Corp., Chgo., 1967-79; v.p. tech. Nabisco Brands, East Hanover, NJ, 1979-85; v.p. corp. research and devel. RJR Nabisco, Winston-Salem, NC, 1985-87; sr. v.p. tech. Planters LifeSavers Co., Winston-Salem, 1987-91, cons., 1991—. Bd. dirs. Cultor Food Scis. (Finland), NC Biotech. Ctr., Sci-Works, Winston Salem, Winston Salem Symphony. Patentee in field. Bd. dirs. Chgo. Boy's Club, 1975-79, YMCA, Wilton, Conn, 1980-84. Mem. AAAS, ACS, Inst. Food Tech., Am. Soc. Bakery Engrs., Indsl. Biotechnology Assn., Indsl. Research Inst. Republican. Avocations: sailing, photography, music. Home: 529 Knob View Pl Winston Salem NC 27104-5107

MASER, DOUGLAS JAMES, legal and governmental operations lawyer; b. Canton, Ohio, Nov. 21, 1951; s. David James and Mardell Margaret (Getz) M.; 1 child, Courtney Leigh. BA, Ohio State U.; JD, Capital U., Columbus, Ohio. Bar: Ohio 1976, U.S. Dist. Ct. (so. dist.) Ohio 1977. Asst. pros. atty. Franklin County Pros. Attys. Office, Columbus, 1975-80; assoc. Janes and Jack Law Offices, Columbus, 1980-85; pvt. practice, Columbus, 1985-88; ptnr. Day, Ketterer, Raley, Wright & Rybolt, Columbus, 1988-95; dep. adminstr. med. mgmt. and cost containment Ohio Bur. Worker's Compensation, Columbus, 1995-98, gen. counsel, dir. govtl. rels., occupl. health rsch., 1998-99; v.p. bus. devel. Ohio Employee Health Partnership, 1999—2001; assoc. Blaugrund, Herbert & Martin, Inc., Dublin, Ohio, 2001—02, Workers' Compensation Mgmt. Solutions, Independence, Ohio, 2002—. Legis. cons. Ohio Assn. Chiefs Police, Columbus, 1983-86, Franklin County Bd. Mental Health, Columbus, 1988-90, Ohio Fire Chiefs Assn., Columbus, 1985-90. Ret. col. USAR, 2004. Mem. DMEC, Ohio State Bar Assn., Cleve. Bar Assn, Cleve. Diocese Lawyers Guild. Republican. Avocations: computer simulations, war gaming, bicycling, hiking, swimming. Home: 6731 Hidden Lake Trl Brecksville OH 44141-3189 Office: Workers Compensation Mgmt Solutions Ste 530 5005 Rockside Rd Independence OH 44131-6808 Office Phone: 216-643-6954. Office Fax: 216-520-6376. Business E-Mail: djmaser@wcmsinc.com.

MASEY, JACK, exhibition designer; b. NYC, June 10, 1924; s. Max and Anna Masey; m. Beverly Payeff-Masey, March 20, 2003. Student, Cooper Union, 1941-43; BFA, Yale U., 1950. Pres. MetaForm LLC, NYC, 1979—; project mgr. design La. Pavilion World Expo., New Orleans, 1984, Statue Liberty Exhibit, NYC, 1986; project mgr. for design Johnstown (Pa.) Flood Mus., 1988, Ellis Island Immigration Mus., NYC, 1990; project mgr. design Nat. D-Day Mus., New Orleans, 1994, designer D-Day Invasion, Pacific Exhbn., 2000; project mgr. design Harry S. Truman Mus., Independence, Mo., 2001. Lectr. Sch. Art and Arch., Yale U., 1968—69; design cons. State Hermitage Mus., St. Petersburg, Russia, 1998; project mgr. design Fly-Girls of WWII exhibn. The Mighty Eighth Air Force Mus., Savannah, Ga., 2005. Cartoonist Esquire mag, 1946; exhibits officer, USIS, New Delhi, 1951-56; designer U.S. Pavilion, Kabul Internat. Fair, 1956; dir. design Am. Nat. Exhbn., Moscow, 1959, chief, East-West exhibits br. USIA, Washington, 1960-65; chief design U.S. Pavilion, Montreal (Que., Can.) World Expo, 1967, dep. commr. gen. for planning and design Osaka (Japan) World Expn., 1970; dir. design Am. Revolution Bicentennial Commn., Washington, 1971-73; dir. design and exhbns. Am. Revolution Bicentennial Adminstrn., 1974-77, design dir. Internat. Communication Agy., Washington, 1977—79; designer: Medicine-U.S.A. exhbn. for, USSR exchange program, 1962, Tech.-Books exhbns., 1963; co-designer Visitor Center, UN, 2001; co-writer: Cold War Confrontations: US Exhibitions and Their Role in the Cultural Cold War, Lars Muller, 2008. Served with AUS, 1943-45, ETO. Recipient Meritorious Service award USIA, 1959, Superior Service award, 1964, Superior Honor award, 1967, 75; award of excellence Fed. Design Council, 1975; Outstanding Achievement award, 1979; award of excellence Soc. Fed. Artists and Designers, 1971; Gold medal Art Dirs. Club, 1965; cert. of excellence Am. Inst. Graphic Arts, 1964; two Fed. Design Achievement awards for Contributions to Excellence in Design, U.S. Govt., 1984, Presdl. awards for Statue of Liberty Mus., 1986, for Ellis Island Immigration Mus., 1990. Home: 131 E 66th St Apt 3A New York NY 10065-6129 also: 137 E 25th St New York NY 10010-2314 Office Phone: 212-532-8580. E-mail: jackmasey@cs.com.

MASH, DONALD J., college president; b. Oct. 12, 1942; children: Maria, Christina, Donnie (dec.). BS in Edn., Ind. U. Pa., 1960; MA in Geography, U. Pitts., 1966; PhD, Ohio State U., 1974. Teaching fellow U. Pitts., 1964-65; instr. geography U. Pitts.-Bradford, 1965-68; dean for student svcs. Ohio Dominican Coll., 1968-75; v.p. for student affairs George Mason U., Fairfax, Va., 1975-85, exec. v.p. adminstrn., 1985-88; pres. Wayne (Nebr.) State Coll., 1988-98; chancellor U. Wis.-Eau Claire, 1998—2005; exec. sr. v.p. U. Wis. Sys. Office: U Wis 1730 Van Hise Hall 1220 Linden Dr Madison WI 53706-4004 Office Phone: 608-262-4049. Business E-Mail: dmash@uwsa.edu.

MASHBERG, ARTHUR, medical educator; b. Nov. 1925; m. Edna Mashberg; children: Marc, Debra. AB cum laude in Biology and Chemistry, Bklyn. Coll., 1945; DDS, NYU, 1949; postgrad., U. Pitts., 1958—59. Diplomate Am. Bd. Oral and Maxillofacial Surgery. Resident in oral & maxillofacial (OMF) surgery VA Hosp., Pitts., 1958-61; chief OMF surgery sect. VA Med. Ctr., East Orange, NJ, 1961-90; clin. prof. to prof. emeritus of surgery U. Medicine and Dentistry, N.J. Med. Sch., 1977—; clin. assoc. prof. to clin. prof. to vis. prof. OMF surgery U. Medicine and Dentistry, N.J. Dental Sch., 1961—90; clin. assoc. prof. to clin. prof. OMF surgery Fairleigh Dickinson U., NJ, 1976—89. Attending, dept. oral surgery and anesthesiology Martland Hosp., 1969—75; cons. staff St. Joseph's Hosp. and Med. Ctr., Paterson, NJ, 1978—; dep. dir. Cancer Ctr., Va. Med. Ctr., E. Orange, NJ, 1988—90; cons. Vets. Affairs Med. Ctr., 1990—99, Rsch. Epidemiol. Diagnosis and Treatment Head & Neck Cancer; scientist US-Italy Cancer exch.; lectr. in head and neck oncology numerous univs. and orgns. Contbr. articles to profl. jours., chpts. to books, monographs, abstracts. Capt. US Army, 1951—52, Korea. Grantee VA, 1967-72, 71-73, 72-77, NIH, NIDR, 1973-80, NIH, 1980-82, Nat. Cancer Inst., 1981-84, Smokeless Tobacco Rsch. Inst., 1995. Fellow Am. Coll. Dentists; mem. ADA, Acad. Medicine of NJ, Am. Cancer Soc. (profl. edn. com. 1983, med. com. 1993-94, Cancer Achievement award), Am. Soc. OMF Surgery, Am. Coll. OMF Surgeons, Nat. Assn. V.A. Dentists (pres.), Cancer Inst. NJ (edn. com. 1976-77), NJ Soc. Oral Surgeons, Oncology Soc. NJ, Soc. of Head and Neck Surgeons, NY Head and Neck Soc., Soc. of Educators in OMF Surgery. Achievements include patents for cancer detection; consultant pharmaceutical identificationate of erythroplasia as the earlies visual sign of squamous cancer; establishment of alcohol as a primary risk factor in oral and pharyngeal cancer. Personal E-mail: aartmash@comcast.net.

MASHBERN, WILLIAM ALLEN, minister, retired religious organization administrator; b. Sept. 15, 1947; MusB, Carson-Newman Coll., Jefferson City, Tenn., 1969; MCM in Ch. Music, So. Bapt. Theol. Sem., Louisville, 1972, D of Musical Arts, 1988; MusM, Memphis State U., 1980. Min. of music and youth East Hill Bapt. Ch., Pensacola, Fla., 1972—74; min. of music Audubon Pk. Bapt. Ch., Memphis, 1974—81; min. of music and youth Evergreen Bapt. Ch., Frankfort, Ky., 1981—86; dir. worship and ch. music Ill. Bapt. State Assn., Springfield, Ill., 1986—2007; ret., 2007. Mem. (men's choir) The CenturyMen, 1987— (Grammy nominees, 2000). Mem.: Nat. Assn. Tchrs. of Singing, State Music Leaders Fellowship (treas. 2003—07). Home: 601 Gladney Ct Mahomet IL 61853-2775 Home Phone: 217-590-4200. Personal E-mail: amashbern@gmail.com.

MASHBURN, JAMAL, sportscaster, retired professional basketball player; b. NYC, Nov. 29, 1972; Grad., Ky. Coll. Forward Dallas Mavericks, 1993-97, Miami Heat, 1997-99, Charlotte Hornets, 1999—2004, Phila. 76ers, 2005—06; ret., 2006; studio analyst ESPN, 2006—. Named to NBA All-Rookie First Team, 1994; Eastern Conf. All-Star Team, 2003. Office: ESPN Plz Bristol CT 06010

MASHECK, JOSEPH DANIEL, art critic, educator; b. NYC, Jan. 19, 1942; s. Joseph Anthony and Dorothy Anna (Cahill) M. AB, Columbia U., 1963, MA, 1965, PhD, 1973; MLitt, U. Dublin, 2001. Editorial researcher Bollingen Found.-Princeton U. Press, 1967-69; lectr. liberal studies Maidstone Coll. Art, Kent, England, 1968-69; preceptor in art history Columbia U., 1970-71; instr. art history Barnard Coll., 1971-73, asst. prof., 1973-82; lectr. visual and environ. studies Harvard U., Cambridge, Mass., 1983-86; assoc. prof. art history Hofstra U., Hempstead, NY, 1987-94, prof., 1994—. Coord. grad. program in humanities Hofstra Mus., Hempstead, 1991—99, curatorial cons., 1991—; vis. prof. art history Colombia U., 2002; adj. prof. art history Fordham U., 2003; centenary fellow, visiting prof. art history Edinburgh Coll. Art, Scotland, 2006—. Author: Historical Present: Essays of the 1970s, 1984, Smart Art (Point 1), 1984, Modernites: Art-Matters in the Present, 1993, Building-Art: Modern Architecture Under Cultural Construction, 1993, C's Aesthetics: Philosophy in the Painting, 2004; editor: Marcel Duchamp in Perspective 1975, reprint, 2002, Van Gogh 100, 1996, A.W. Dow's Composition, 1997; editor-in-chief Artforum mag., 1977-80; columnist Boston Rev, 1985-87; contbr. Art in America, 1987-. Bd. dirs. Crosby St. Project, N.Y., 1995-96; mem. adv. bd. Annals of Scholarship, 1998—; cons. ed. Bklyn. Rail, 2004-. Samuel H. Kress Found. fellow, 1968-69, Nat. Endowment Arts fellow, 1972-73, 75-76, Guggenheim fellow, 1977-78, Centenary fellow Edinburgh Coll. Art, 2006-; grantee Malevich Soc., 2003; Hon. Armiger, Coll. Arms, London Fellow Royal Soc. Arts, Soc. Antiquaries of Scotland; mem. AAUP, Internat. Assn. Art Critics. Roman Catholic. Democrat. Office: Hofstra U Dept Fine Arts and Art History Calkins Hall Hempstead NY 11549

MASHHOON, BAHRAM, physicist, researcher; b. Tehran, Iran, Sept. 9, 1947; s. Hassan Mashhoon and Nosrat Dargahi; 1 child, Yasmin. BA, U. Calif., 1969; PhD, Princeton U., 1972. Assoc. prof. U. Mo., physics dept., Columbia, 1985—95; prof. U. Mo., 1995—. Author: (nonlocal theory of accelerated observers) Physical Review A, 1993. Home: 404 Victoria Dr Columbia MO 65201 Office: Dept Physics and Astronomy Univ Mo Columbia MO 65211 E-mail: mashhoonb@missouri.edu.

MASHIN, JACQUELINE ANN COOK, health facility consultant; b. Chgo., May 11, 1941; d. William Hermann and Ann (Smidt) Cook; m. Fredric John Mashin, June 7, 1970; children: Joseph Glenn, Alison Robin. BS, U. Md., 1984; BSN, Cath. U., Washington, 1993. Cert. realtor. Adminstrv. asst. CIA, Washington, 1963-66; asst. to mng. dir. Aerospace Edn. Found., Washington, 1966-74; exec. asst. to asst exec. dir. Air Force Assn., Washington, 1974-79; v.p., ptnrship. owner Discount Linen Store, Silver Spring, Md., 1979-81; asst. regional polit. dir. Office of Pres.-elect, Washington, 1980-81; confidential asst. to dir. Office of Personnel Mgmt. (US), Washington, 1981-83; spl. asst. to dep. dir. Office of Mgmt. and Budget, Washington, 1983-86; dir. internat. communications and spl. asst. to commr. Dept. of the Interior, Washington, 1986-89, cons., 1989-93; with Washington Hosp. Ctr., 1993—2009. Chmn., vol. coord. Mo. County Rep. Party, 1999; chmn. Bayclub, Mo. County Fedn. Rep. Women, 1999, 2000. Pres. Layhill Civic Assn., Silver Spring, Md., 1980; state chmn. Md.'s Reagan Youth Delegation, Annapolis, Md., 1980; state treas., office mgr. Reagan-Bush State Hdqrs. of Md., Silver Spring, 1980; mem. Women's Com. Nat. Symphony Orch.; pres. Rock Creek Women's Rep. Club, 1998, Montgomery County Rep. Party, 1999, Montgomery County Fedn. Rep. Women, 1999—; steering com. Wheaton Redevel. Program, 2001—07; gov.'s adv. bd. Md. Bd. Health and Mental Hygiene Balt., 2003- Mem.: White House Vols., Air Force Assn. (life), U.S. Capital Hist. Soc., Aux. Salvation Army (life), Indian Spring Country Club. Republican. Avocations: golf, horseback riding, collecting wine glasses, hibel plates, lithos and lalique crystal. Home and Office: 2429 White Horse Ln Silver Spring MD 20906-2243 Home Phone: 301-871-6063. Personal E-mail: Jaguar041@aol.com.

MASHNIK, STEPAN G., physicist; b. Brinzeni, Moldova, June 1, 1952; arrived in U.S., 1996, naturalized, 2004; s. George I. and Natalia G. Mashnik; m. Nadejda I. Sukhlova; children: Polina, Daria. BS, Kishinev State U., 1972; MS, Moscow State U., 1974; PhD, Joint Inst. Nuc. Rsch., Dubna, Russia, 1981; sr. rsch. diploma, Presidium Acad. Sci. USSR, Moscow, 1989. Jr. rsch. scientist Joint Inst. Nuc. Rsch., Dubna, 1975—82, sr. rsch. scientist, 1991—97; sr./jr. rschr. Acad. Sci. Moldova, Kishinev, 1982—91, leading rsch. scientist, 1991—2004; long term vis. staff mem. Los Alamos Nat. Lab., N.Mex., 1997—2001, staff mem., 2001—. Country coord. XXVIII Internat. Conf. High Energy Physics, Hamburg, 1996—97; mem. internat. sci. coun. Joint Inst. Nuc. Rsch., Dubna, 1992—95; mem. intermediate energy data group NEA/OECD, Paris, 1994—, liaison officer between Paris, and JINR, Dubna, 1996—97; vis. rschr. Oak Ridge Nat. Lab., Tenn., 1995—96, Centre d'Etudes de Bruyers-le-Chatel, France, 1996. Contbr. articles to profl. jours. Recipient Several Excellent Work and Dubna County awards, Joint Inst. Nuc. Rsch., 1975—82, Investigations in Theoretical Physics award, Inst. Applied Physics, Acad. Sci. Moldova, 1983, Moldova Award for Young Scientists, 1984, Am. Medal of Honor, 2003, Svc. award, Los Alamos Nat. Lab., 2007; CRDF Grant, Devel. of a Universal Intranuclear Cascade Type Model for Heavy Ion and Nucleon Induced Reactions at Intermediate Energies, 2001—04, NASA Grant, Propagation Model for Cosmic Ray Species in the Galaxy, 2002—. Mem.: Internat. Nuc. Soc., Am. Nuc. Soc., Am. Phys. Soc. Avocations: swimming, travel, skiing, jogging. Office Phone: 505-667-9946. Office Fax: 505-667-3726. Personal E-mail: sgmnim@gmail.com. Business E-Mail: mashnik@lanl.gov.

MASI, ALFONSE THOMAS, medical educator; b. NYC, Oct. 29, 1930; s. Antonio and Mary (Genese) M.; m. Nancy Ann Bouton, Aug. 27, 1960; children: Anthony Mark, Christopher Maurice, Maria Lisa, Amy Elizabeth. BS, CUNY, 1951; MD, Columbia U., 1955; Dr.P.H., Johns Hopkins U., 1963. Intern Johns Hopkins Hosp., 1955-56; resident Johns Hopkins Hosp. and UCLA Med. Ctr., 1958-60; practice medicine specializing in rheumatology; asst. prof. epidemiology Johns Hopkins Sch. Hygiene, 1963-65, asso. prof., 1965-67; prof. medicine, dir. div. connective tissue diseases Coll. Medicine, U. Tenn., Memphis, 1967-78, prof. dept. health care scis., 1967-78; prof. dept. medicine U. Ill. Coll. Medicine-Peoria, 1978—, head dept. medicine, 1978-85; prof. epidemiology U. Ill. Sch. Pub. Health, Chgo., 1978—. Cons. various divs. NIH, 1971—; com. mem. various projects NRC, 1972— Served with USPHS, 1956-58. Sr. investigator Arthritis Found., 1966-71; also Russell L. Cecil fellow. Fellow ACP, APHA, Am. Coll. Epidemiology, Am. Coll. Rheumatology (master), Am. Rheumatism Assn. Home: 6710 N Skyline Dr Peoria IL 61614-3127 Office: U Ill Coll Medicine-Peoria Dept Medicine One Illini Dr Box 1649 Peoria IL 61656-1649 Office Phone: 309-671-8428. Business E-Mail: amasi@uic.edu. *"To thine own self be true" is a principle which helps one have a confident, enthusiastic and satisfied attitude in life. Faith in our Creator, sense of individual purpose and sensitivity to the needs of others nurture the important commitments and compassion which help one achieve difficult and worthy goals. Love is one of life's highest attainments and is facilitated by giving and serving. Life's rewards are generous to those who are blessed with health, love and opportunities for serving to one's best abilities.*

MASI, DALE A., social sciences educator, research and development company executive; b. NYC; d. Alphonse E. and Vera Avella; children: Eric, Renee, Robin. BS, Coll. Mt. St. Vincent; MSW, U. Ill.; PhD Social Work, Cath. U. Lectr. Sch. Social Svcs., Ipswitch, Eng., 1970-72; project dir. occupational substance abuse program, asso. prof. Boston Coll. Grad. Sch. Social Work, 1972-79; dir. Office Employee Counseling Svc., Dept. Health/Human Svcs., Washington, 1979-84; pres. Masi Research Cons., Inc., 1984—2005; prof. emeritus U. Md. Grad. Sch. Social Work, 1980—2004; adj. prof. U. Md. Coll. Bus. and Mgmt., 1980—2004, prof. emeritus, 2004—; lectr. Boccon U., Milan, 2004—; project dir. NIH Rsch. grantee coll. bingo drinking Northeastern U., 2005—08. Mem. IBM Mental Health Adv. Bd., 1990-95; cons. IBM, Toyota, Mobil Chm., The Washington Post, U.S. Ho. Reps., U.S. Postal Svc., White House, WHO, Bechtel Corp., other orgns. in pub. and pvt. sector; bd. advisors Nat. Security Inst., Wayside Youth and Family Support Network; USIA Ampart lectr. on alcohol, drugs and AIDS in the workplace; chair CMHS Joint Industry Alliance, 2002—; acad. advisor Northwestern U. Author: Human Services in Industry, Organizing for Women, Designing Employee Assistance Programs, Drug Free Workplace, AIDS Issues in the Workplace: A Response Model for Human Resource Management, The AMA Handbook for Developing Employee Assistance and Counseling Programs, Evaluating Your Employee Assistance and Managed Behavioral Care Program, Internat. Employee Assistance Anthology, I, II and III edits., Productivity Lost: Alcohol and Drugs in the Workplace; co-author: Shrink to Fit: Answers to Your Questions About Therapy; also over 40 articles. Recipient award, Employee Assistance Program Digest; named Disting. Scholar, Nat. Acad. Practice, 2001—; named to Employee Assistance Program Hall of Fame; fellow Fulbright scholar, 1969—70, Fulbright fellow, 1994, AAUW postdoctoral fellow, NIMH, 1962—64; Fulbright Sr. Specialist, Japan, 2002, Italy, 2005, Eng., 2008. Mem. AAUW, NASW (Internat. Rhoda G. Sarnat award 1993), Acad. Cert. Social Workers, Employee Assistance Profls. Assn. (nat. individual achievement award 1983), Fulbright Assn. (nat. bd.). Democrat. Roman Catholic. Office: PO Box 990268 Boston MA 02199

MASI, JANE VIRGINIA, marketing and sales consultant; b. June 6, 1947; d. Vincent Joseph and Virginia Marie (Beddow) Masi; m. Charles Walter Friedman, Feb. 14, 1976 (div. Sept. 1998); m. Charles W. Friedman, July 29, 2006 (dec. Sept. 2006). BA in Comms. and Psychology, Mercy Coll., NYC, 1969; MA, New Sch. Social Rsch., 1979, postgrad., 1994. Asst. sales mgr. Chevron Chem., NYC, 1969-71; writer, 1973-75; ptnr. Masi-D'Angelo Constrn. and Devel. Assocs., NYC, 1979-83; pres., founder Beddow Mills Inc., NYC, 1982-85, Beddow Mfg. Inc., NYC, 1983-85; co-pres. TRS Mktg. Inc., NYC, 1985—. Founder Energy Works, 1985, Did You Know, 1989, Range Burgers, 1989, Terramor, 1989, In the Pink!, 1991, The Profl. Salon, 1991, Terramor Foods, 1991, Terramor Catering, 2003; founder, dir. TRS Inc. Profl. Suite, 1986—; pub. The Planetary Gazette, 2002-Happy Healing Hours cmty. svc. events concert, 2001-; WTRS Met Radio, 2008, TRS Media, 2008, Terramn Commn., 2008 N.Y. Regents scholar, 1965-69. Mem. Soc. Ethical Treatment of Animals. Avocations: woodworking, carpentry, advocating animal rights, design psychology. Office: TRS Mktg Inc 44 E 32nd St Fl 11 New York NY 10016-5508 Office Phone: 212-685-2848. E-mail: terramor@earthlink.net.

MASI, JULIA A., elementary school educator; d. Ralph and Frances Marie Masi. MS, Adelphi U., 1987; MA, Adelphi U., 1991; cert. in Chinese, NYU, 1994; cert. in non-profit mgmt., U. Ill., Chgo., 2005. Cert. diamond appraiser Gemological Inst. Am. Tchr. Pub. Sch. 169, NYC Dept. Edn., Bklyn., 1988—97; sci. tchr. Pub. Sch. 24, NYC Dept. Edn., Bklyn., 1997—. Mng. editor: Fanzeen Mag., contbr.: Dance Pages; exhibitions include Brooklyn Hist. Soc., 2002. Vol. editor newsletter, website Magic Mgmt. Hosp.; vol. GourmetSoupKitchens Website; mem. Jane Godall Inst.; bd. dirs. Children of the City, Bklyn., 2005—; jr. assoc. Mus. of Modern Art, NYC, 1996—; mem. young collectors coun., aquisitons com. Guggenheim Mus., NYC, 1993—; vol., team leader NY Cares, NYC, 2005—. Mem.: APA (assoc.). Democrat. Roman Catholic. Avocations: writing, ballet, mentoring, drawing, languages.

MASICH, ANDREW EDWARD, museum director, historian; b. Yonkers, NY, Feb. 7, 1955; s. Edward John and Mary Gibson (Friedlander) M.; m. Deborah Jean Niermeyer, Dec. 27, 1978; children: Matthew, Molly, Max. BA in History/Anthropology, U. Ariz., 1977, MA in History, 1984. Dir. Rio Colo. divsn. Ariz. Hist. Soc., Yuma, 1978, dir. ctrl. divsn. Phoenix, 1985; v.p. Colo. Hist. Soc., 1990-98, acting pres., 1997; pres., CEO Hist. Soc. Western Pa., Pitts., 1998—. Founder, pres. Ft. Yuma Press, Denver, 1980—, Gorton Toy Soldiers, 1988-91; cons. Am. Assn. Museums-Mus. Assessment Program, Washington, 1981—; pres. Friends Ariz. Hwys., Phoenix, 1987-90; lectr. and cons. in field. Author: Halfbreed, The Remarkable True Story of George Bent, 2004, The Civil War in Arizona, 2006; co-author: (with David Halaas) Cheyenne Dog Soldiers, 1997 (Choice award for best acad. book in history 1997), The Real West, 1996 (Am. Assn. Museums award 1997); co-author: (CD-ROM) Cheyenne Dog Soldiers, 1997. Mem. Santa Fe Trail Adv. Coun., 1993—98; chmn. Ft. Pitt dist. Boy Scouts Am., 2001—; bd. dirs. Greater Pitts. Conv. and Visitors Bur., 2001—; mem. faculty Williamsburg Seminar for Hist. Adminstrn., 2001—. Mem. Am. Assn. State and Local History (mem. coun. 1995—), Am. Assn. Mus. (accreditation commn. 2004—), Phi Beta Kappa. Avocations: living history, historical research and writing. Office: Heinz History Ctr 1212 Smallman St Pittsburgh PA 15222-4208 Office Phone: 412-454-6371. E-mail: aemsich@hswp.org.

MASIELLO, ROCCO JOSEPH, air transportation executive, consultant; b. NYC, Jan. 9, 1922; s. Joseph and Armanda (Mansueti) M.; m. Rita Elizabeth Amoruso, Feb. 11, 1945; children: Richard, Robin, Janet. Student, CCNY, 1946-48, Hofstra U., 1951-54. Registered profl. engr., Maine. With Pan. Am. World Airways, NYC, 1950-59; v.p. maintenance and engring. U.S. Air Group, Pitts., 1959—73, Am. Airlines, Tulsa, 1973-82, sr. v.p. ops. Dallas, 1982-86; co-founder, exec. v.p. USAfrica Airways, 1990—94, also bd. dirs; founder The Reston Group; aerospace cons., prin. R.J. Masiello and Assoc. Mem. Soc. Aerospace Engr., Royal Aero. Soc. Roman Catholic. Personal E-mail: rjmasiello@aol.com.

MASIH, TARA LYNN, book editor, writer; b. Syracuse, NY, Aug. 22, 1963; d. Lalit Kumar and Sandra Kolyer Masih; m. Robert Edward Padykula, Aug. 29, 1993 (div. May 2000); 1 child, Arun Padykula; m. Michael Gilligan, Oct. 25, 2008. BA, C.W. Post Coll., 1985; MA, Emerson Coll., 1986. Editl. asst. Little, Brown & Co., Boston, 1987-88; asst. editor STORIES Mag., Boston, 1987-88; sr. book editor Bedford Books, Boston, 1988-93; freelance book editor Boston, 1993—. Author: essays, poems and short stories; author: (editor) (book) The Rose Metal Press Field Guide to Writing Flash Fiction. Recipient 1st pl. for fiction, The Ledge mag., 1995; scholar, Bookbuilders of Boston, 1985. Avocations: gardening, tennis, canoeing, travel, reading. Personal E-mail: masiht@aol.com.

MASKAEV, OLEG, professional boxer; b. Zhambul, Kazakhstan, Mar. 2, 1969; arrived in US, 1999, naturalized, 2004; m. Svetlana Maskaev; 4 children. Profl. boxer, 1993—. Winner vacant title vs. Nikolai Kulpin by unanimous decision, heavyweight divsn. Pan Asian Boxing Assn., 1995, winner vacant title vs. Toakipa Tasefa by knockout, heavyweight divsn., 98, winner title def. vs. Jeff Wooden by tech. knockout, heavyweight divsn., 99, winner title def. vs. Shane Sutcliffe by tech. knockout, heavyweight divsn., 99; winner title eliminator vs. Sinan Samil Sam by unanimous decision, heavyweight divsn World Boxing Coun., 2005, winner title def. vs. Hasim Rahman by tech. knockout, heavyweight divsn., 06, winner title def. vs. Peter Okhello by unanimous decision, heavyweight divsn., 06. Named Comeback Fighter of Yr., The Ring Mag., 2006.

MASKET, EDWARD SEYMOUR, television executive; b. NYC, Mar. 3, 1923; s. Isadore and Jennie (Bernstein) M.; m. Frances Ellen Rees, June 11, 1958 (div.); children: Joel Daniel, Johanna Rees Bettaeib, Kate Isobel Smiley. BS, CCNY, 1942; LLB, JD, Harvard U., 1949. Bar: N.Y. 1949. Atty., dir. bus. affairs, v.p. bus. affairs ABC, 1951-68; v.p. to exec. v.p. Columbia Pictures TV, Burbank, Calif., 1968-81; sr. v.p. adminstrn. Universal TV, 1982-86, exec. v.p. adminstrn., 1986-90, MCA TV Group, 1990-93; TV cons., 1994—98; ret., 1998. Served as 2d lt. AUS, 1942-46, PTO. Mem. Motion Picture Pioneers, Phi Beta Kappa. Personal E-mail: telemogul@aol.com.

MASKIN, ERIC STARK, economics professor; b. NYC, Dec. 12, 1950; m. Gayle Sawtelle; children: Joseph, Charlotte. AB in Math., Harvard U., 1972, AM in Applied Math., 1974, PhD in Applied Math., 1976; MA (hon.), Cambridge U., 1977. Rsch. fellow Jesus Coll. Cambridge U., England, 1976-77; prof. econs. MIT, Cambridge, Mass., 1981, 1981-84, Harvard U., Cambridge, 1985—2000; Albert O. Hirschman prof. social sci. Inst. for Advanced Study, Princeton, NJ, 2000—. Louis Berkman prof. econs. Harvard U., 1997—2000. Editor Quar. Jour. Econs., 1984—90, Econs. Letters, 1992—; contbr. articles to profl. jours., chapters to books. Recipient Galbraith Tchg. prize, Harvard U., 1990, 1992, Kempe award, 2007, Nobel Meml. prize in Econ. Scis., 2007; Guggenheim fellowship, 1980—81, Sloan Rsch. fellowship, 1983—85. Fellow: European Econ. Assn., Am. Acad. Arts and Sci., Brit. Acad. (corr.), Econometric Soc. (mem. coun. 1999—2004, v.p. 2001—02, pres. 2003); mem.: Nat. Acad. Sci., Soc. Social Choice and Welfare (mem. coun. 1995—2001), Am. Econ. Assn. (mem. nominating com. 1995—96), Game Theory Soc. (mem. coun. 2001—03, exec. v.p. 2008—). Office: Inst for Advanced Study Einstein Drive Princeton NJ 08540 Office Phone: 609-734-8309.

MASLACH, CHRISTINA, psychology professor; b. San Francisco, Jan. 21, 1946; d. George James and Doris Ann (Cuneo) M.; m. Philip George Zimbardo, Aug. 10, 1972; children: Zara, Tanya. BA, Harvard-Radcliffe Coll., 1967; PhD, Stanford U., 1971. Prof. psychology U. Calif.-Berkeley, 1971—, vice provost for tchg. & learning, 2001—08, 2008—. Author: Burnout: The Cost of Caring, 1982; co-author: Influencing Attitudes and Changing Behavior, 1977, Maslach Burnout Inventory (rsch. scale), 1981, 2d edit., 1986, 3d edit., 1996, Experiencing Social Psychology, 1979, 4th edit., 2001, Professional Burnout, 1993, The Truth About Burnout, 1997, Preventing Burnout and Building Engagement, 2000, Banishing Burnout, 2005. Recipient Disting. Teaching award, 1987, Best Paper award Jour. Orgnl. Behavior, 1994, Prof. of Yr. award Carnegie/CASE, 1997. Fellow AAAS, APA, Assn. Psychol. Sch., Soc. Clin. and Exptl. Hypnosis (Henry Guze rsch. award 1980), We. Psychol. Assn. (pres. 1989); mem. Soc. Exptl. Social Psychology. Democrat. Office: U Calif Office of Chancellor 200 California Hall # 1500 Berkeley CA 94720-1500 Business E-Mail: maslach@berkeley.edu.

MASLAK, PETER GEORGE, hematologist; MD, Mt Sinai Sch. Medicine, NYC, 1984. Diplomate hematology Am. Bd. Internal Medicine, 1990. Attending physician Meml. Sloan-Kettering Cancer Ctr., NYC, 1991—; chief, hematology lab. svc. Meml. Sloan-Kettering, New York, NY, 2002—. Fellow: ACP. Achievements include research in Leukemia therapy. Office: Memorial Sloan-Kettering Cancer Ctr 1275 York Ave New York NY 10065 Office Phone: 212-639-5518.

MASLEN, ERIC HARVEY, engineering educator, researcher; b. Lakewood, Ohio, Oct. 10, 1957; s. Stephen Harold and Lee Howeth Maslen; m. Sandra Faye McKamey, July 7, 1990; children: Benjamin Eric Smith, Travis Lee. BS in Mech. Engring., Cornell U., Ithaca, NY, 1980; PhD in Mech. and Aerospace Engring., U. Va., Charlottesville, 1990. R & D engr. Koppers Co., Glen Arm, Md., 1980—85; prof. U. Va., 1990—. Office: Univ Va 122 Engr's Way Charlottesville VA 22904-4746 Business E-Mail: ehm7s@virginia.edu.

MASNYK, IHOR JAREMA, chemist, director; s. Gregory Nmi and Olga Nmi Masnyk; m. Olga Nmi Shevchenko, Feb. 11, 1956; children: Taras Wolodymyr, Katya Areta Duvalko. BA, U. Chgo., 1953, MS, 1958, PhD, 1962. Sect. head Endocr. Eval. Br.CCNSC, NCI, NIH, Bethesda, Md., 1962—66, chemist, 1967—73. Chief planning analysis br. Div. Can. Bio. Anal. Br. NCI. NIH, Bethesda, 1973—77. With US Army, 1955—57, Ft. Know, KY Germany. Mem.: Sci. Soc. Taras Shevchenko. Avocations: music, painting, soccer, volleyball, tennis. Home: 8614 Hidden Hill Ln Potomac MD 20854 Office: Crurebddegncinih 6120 Exec Blvd Bethesda MD 20892 Business E-Mail: masnyki@mail.nih.gov.

MASOCHA, WALTER, finance educator; b. Harare, Zimbabwe, Feb. 9, 1964; s. Adolf Mangwiro and Julliana Masocha; m. Judith Lewis, July 23, 1965; children: Tinashe Munyaradzi Blessing, Tafadzwa Tichaona. B in Acctg. with honors, U. Zimbabwe, 1987; MSc in Fin., U. Strathclyde, Scotland, 1993, PhD in Acctg. & Fin., 2000. CPA, registered public accountant. Mgmt. auditor UN Devel. Program, Harare, Zimbabwe, 1994—96; lectr. acctg. & fin. U. Stirling, Scotland, 2000—. Audit dir. Office Comptr. & Auditor Gen., Harare, 1990—94. Ordained min. Forward in Faith Ministries, Stirling, 2000—. Recipient Best Student award, U. Strathclyde, 1993. Mem.: Zimbabwe Inst. Mgmt., Zimbabwe Inst. of Pers. Mgmt. (assoc.), Inst. Chartered Secs & Adminstrs. (assoc.). Avocations: golf, travel, soccer, ping pong/table tennis, tennis. Home: 9 Forth Park Bridge of Allan Stirlingshire Stirling FK9 5NT Scotland Office: U Stirling Dep of Accounting & Finance Stirling FK9 4LA Scotland UK Office Fax: 44 (0) 1786 467308; Home Fax: 44 (0) 1786 831181. Personal E-mail: vamasocha@yahoo.com. E-mail: walter.masocha@stir.ac.uk.

MASON, ALEXANDER TAYLOR, finance company executive; b. 1951; BA, Princeton U., 1973. Mng. dir., co-head corp. fin. Bankers Trust; COO global corp. fin. Deutsche Bank, vice chmn. Americas; joined Mercantile Bankshares Corp., 2003, vice chmn., COO, 2005—07; pres., COO, mem. exec. com. CIT Group, Inc., 2008—. Bd. dirs. Mercantile Bankshares Corp., 2005—07. Bd. mem. Mercy Health Svc., Balt.; chmn. bd. trustees Md. Sci. Ctr., 2006—; chmn. bd. Bus. Volunteers Unlimited. Office: CIT Group, Inc 505 Fifth Ave New York NY 10017 also: One CIT Drive Livingston NJ 07039

MASON, BOBBIE ANN, writer; b. Mayfield, Ky., May 1, 1940; d. Wilburn A. and Christianna (Lee) M.; m. Roger B. Rawlings, Apr. 12, 1969. BA, U. Ky., 1962; MA, SUNY, Binghamton, 1966; PhD, U. Conn., 1972. Asst. prof. English Mansfield (Pa.) State Coll., 1972-79. Writer-in-residence, U. Ky., Lexington, 2001—. Author: Nabokov's Garden, 1974, The Girl Sleuth: A Feminist Guide to the Bobbsey Twins, Nancy Drew and Their Sisters, 1975, 2d edit., 1995, Shiloh and Other Stories, 1982 (PEN Hemingway award, Nat. Book Critics Circle award nominee, Am. Book award nominee, PEN Faulkner award nominee), 2d edit., 2001, In Country, 1985, 2d edit., 2005, Spence + Lila, 1988, 2d edit., 1998, Love Life, 1989, Feather Crowns, 1993 (Nat. Book Critics Cir. award nominee, So. Book Critics Cir. award), Midnight Magic, 1998, Clear Springs, 1999 (Pulitzer prize finalist), Zigzagging Down a Wild Trail, 2001 (So. Book Critics Cir. award), Elvis Presley, 2003 (Ky. Literary award), An Atomic Romance, 2005; editor: Missing Mountains, 2005, Nancy Culpepper, 2006; contbr. New Yorker, 1980—, The Atlantic, Redbook, Paris Rev., Mother Jones, Harpers, N.Am. Rev., Va. Quar. Rev., Story, Ploughshares, So. Rev., Crazyhorse, DoubleTake; contbr. works Best American Short Stories, 1981, 83, The Pushcart Prize, Best of the Small Presses, 1983, 86, 97. Recipient O. Henry Anthology awards, 1986, 88, Hillsdale prize, 1999; grantee Pa. Arts Coun., 1983, 89, Nat. Endowment Arts, 1983, Am. Acad. and Inst. Arts and Letters, 1984; Guggenheim fellow, 1984. Mem.: PEN, Author's Guild, Fellowship of So. Writers. Office: Internat Creative Mgmt care Amanda Urban Agt 825 8th Ave New York NY 10128 Business E-Mail: aurban@icmtalent.com.

MASON, CHARLES ELLIS, III, magazine editor; b. Boston, Oct. 31, 1938; s. Charles Ellis, Jr. and Ada Brooks (Trafford) M. BA, Yale U., 1960. Loan officer State St. Bank, Boston, 1963-68; asso. editor Sail mag., Boston, 1968-74, exec. editor, 1974—. Author: (with Buddy Melges) Sailing Smart, 1983; editor: Best of Sail Trim, 1976, Best of SAIL Navigation, 1981. Mem. exec. com. Sierra Club Greater Boston Group, 1992-. Served with USNR, 1960-62. Office: 16 Joy St Boston MA 02114 Business E-Mail: cmason@sailmagazine.com.

MASON, CHARLES EUGENE, entomologist, educator; b. Brighton, Colo., Aug. 28, 1943; s. Carl Hastings Mason and Mildred Mae Brouhard Mason; children: Thomas C. M., Christina L. G. Johnston, Rosemary K. T. Archangelo. PhD, Kans. State U., Manhattan, 1973. Col. Arm Res., Phila., 1969—2003; prof. U. Del., Newark, 1975—. Decorated Legion of Merit US Army; recipient Faculty Senate Commendation, U. Del., 2007. Mem.: Am. Entomol. Soc. (pres. 1981—84), Entomol. Soc. America. Home: 38 The Horseshoe Newark DE 19711-2067 Office: Univ Del Entomology 531 S College Ave Room 250 Newark DE 19716-2160 Office Fax: 302-831-8889. Business E-Mail: mason@udel.edu.

MASON, CHIP See MASON, RAYMOND

MASON, CHRISTOPHER MAY, lawyer; b. Orange County, NC, Nov. 4, 1957; s. Julian Dewey and Elsie (May) M. BA summa cum laude, U. N.C., 1979; JD magna cum laude, Duke U., 1983. Bar: N.Y. 1985, D.C. 1985, U.S. Dist. Ct. (so. and ea. dists.) N.Y. 1985, U.S. Dist. Ct. (no. and we. dists.) N.Y., 1989, U.S. Dist. Ct. D.C., 1995, U.S. Ct. Internat. Trade 1985, U.S. Temporary Emergency Ct. of Appeals 1985, U.S. Ct. Appeals (4th, 6th, 8th cirs.) 1985, U.S. Ct. Appeals (2d, 3d, 5th, 7th and 9th cirs.) 1988, U.S. Ct. Appeals (D.C. cir.) 1991, U. S. Supreme Ct. 1988. Law clk. to judge J. Clifford Wallace U.S. Ct. Appeals (9th cir.), San Diego, 1983-84; assoc. Cravath, Swaine & Moore, NYC, 1984-89, Hunton & Williams, NYC, 1989-91, ptnr., 1992-2000, Nixon Peabody LLP, NYC, 2000—. Contbr. articles to profl. jours. Bd. mem., bd. persons Presbyn. Ch. (US). Mem. ABA, Assn. of Bar of City of N.Y., N.Y. State Bar Assn., Fed. Bar Coun., Phi Beta Kappa, Order of Coif, Lawyers' Com. Civil Rights Under Law (bd. mem.). Presbyterian. Office: Nixon Peabody LLP 437 Madison Ave New York NY 10022-7001 Office Phone: 212-940-3000. E-mail: cmason@nixonpeabody.com.

MASON, CONNIE JEANNE, writer; b. Niles, Mich., Apr. 22, 1930; d. Frank G. and Frances (Coda) Roti; m. Lewis Gerald Mason, July 1, 1950; children: Jeri A. Vlasicak, Michelle A. Osborn, Mark. Author: Promise Me Forever, 1990, Brave Land, Brave Love, 1990, Surrender to The Fury, 1990, Ice @ Rapture, 1991, A Promise of Thunder, 1991, Lord Of The Night, 1991, Treasures Of The Heart, 1992, Tears Like Rain, 1993, Wind Rider, 1993, Sierra, 1994, The Lion's Bride, 1994, Taken By You, 1995, pure Temptation, 1995, Flame, 1996, A Love To Cherish, 1996, Shadow Walker, 1997, To Love A Stranger, 1997, Sheik, 1997, Viking!, 1998, The Black Knight, 1999 (NY Times Extended Bestseller List), Pirate, 1998, Gunslinger, 1999, To Tempt a Rogue, 1999, The Black Knight, 1999 (NY Times Extended List 1999), The Outlaws: Rafe, 2000, A Taste of Sin, 2000, The Outlaws: Jess, 2000, A Breath of Scandal, 2001, The Outlaws: Sam, 2001, The Dragon Lord, 2001, The Rogue and the Bastion, 2002, Lionheart, 2002, Seduced by a Rogue, 2003, The Laird of Stonehaven, 2003, The Last Rogue, 2004, The Pirate Prince, 2004, Gypsy Lover, 2005, A Knight's Honor, 2005, A Taste of Paradise, 2006, Highland Warrior, 2007, The Price of Pleasure, 2007, Viking Warrior, 2008, also novellas. Recipient Career Achievement award, Romantic Times, 1994; named Story Teller of Yr., 1990. Mem. Romance Writers Am., Novelists, Inc. Avocations: reading, travel.

MASON, DAVID MARION, commissioner; b. Aiken, SC, June 9, 1958; s. John Eber Jr. and Frances Marie (Hooper) Mason; m. Margaret Donna Boersig, Dec. 29, 1984; 10 children. Student, Lynchburg Coll., Va., 1976-77; BA in Polit. Sci. cum laude, Claremont McKenna Coll., Calif., 1979. Asst. dir. research Obenshain/Warner for Senate, Richmond, Va., 1978; legis. asst. to Senator John Warner US Senate, Washington, DC, 1979-80; legis. dir. to Rep. Thomas J. Bliley Jr. US Congress, DC, 1981-84, staff dir. to Rep. Trent Lott, 1984-86; freelance polit. writer Lynchburg, Va., 1986; pres. Commonwealth Found. Va., Richmond, 1986-87; exec. asst. to asst. sec. US Dept. Def., 1987-88, dep. asst. sec. Washington, 1988-89; dir. exec. branch liaison, dir. US Congress assessment project, v.p. govt. rels., sr. fellow in congressional studies The Heritage Found., Washington, 1990—98; chmn. Fed. Election Commn., Washington, 1998—. Mem. faculty Leadership Inst. seminars, Washington, 1984; lectr. USOPM seminars, Washington, 1984-88. First vice chmn. Young Rep. Fedn. Va., Richmond, 1983; chmn. Arlington Area Young Reps., Va., 1984; active Arlington County Rep. com., 1980-86, 10th dist. Rep. com., Falls Church, Va., 1985. Named one of Outstanding Young Men of Am., 1980, 85. Republican. Roman Catholic. Office: Fed Election Commn 999 E St NW Washington DC 20463

MASON, DEAN TOWLE, cardiologist; b. Berkeley, Calif., Sept. 20, 1932; s. Ira Jenckes and Florence Mabel (Towle) M.; m. Maureen O'Brien, June 22, 1957; children: Kathleen, Alison. BA in Chemistry, Duke U., Durham, NC, 1954; MD, Duke U., 1958. Diplomate Am. Bd. Internal Medicine, Am. Bd. Cardiovasc. Diseases, Nat. Bd. Med. Examiners. Intern, then resident in medicine Johns Hopkins Hosp., 1958-61; clin. assoc. cardiology br., sr. asst. surgeon USPHS, Nat. Heart Inst., NIH, 1961-63, asst. sect. dir. cardiovascular diagnosis, attending physician, sr. investigator cardiology br., 1963-68; prof. medicine, prof. physiology, chief cardiovascular medicine U. Calif. Med. Sch., Davis-Sacramento Med. Center, 1968-82; dir. cardiac ctr. Cedars Med. Ctr., Miami, Fla., 1982-83; physician-in chief Western Heart Inst., San Francisco, 1983—2000; chmn. dept. cardiovascular medicine St. Mary's Med. Ctr., San Francisco, 1986-99, hon. med. staff, 2000—. Co-chmn. cardiovascular-renal drugs U.S. Pharmacopeia Com. Revision, 1970—75; mem. life scis. com. NASA; med. rsch. rev. bd. VA, NIH; prof. medicine (hon.) Peking Med. U., China, 1987; vis. prof. numerous univs.; cons. in field. Editor-in-chief Am. Heart Jour., 1980—96; contbr. chapters to books, articles. Recipient rsch. award, Am. Therapeutic Soc., 1965, Theodore and Susan B. Cummings Humanitarian award, Dept. State-Am. Coll. Cardiology, 1972, 1973, 1975, 1978, Skylab Achievement award, NASA, 1974, U. Calif. Faculty Rsch. award, 1978, Symbol of Excellence, Tex. Heart Inst., 1979, Disting. Alumnus award, Duke U. Sch. Medicine, 1979, award of Honor, Wisdom Soc., 1997, Medal of Honor, Winston Churchill Soc., 1998, Armand Hammer Creative Genius award, 1998, Dwight D. Eisenhower Admirable Am. of Achievement award, 1998, Eternal Jesus Christ award, 1998, Blessed Lord's Prayer award, 1998, Dean Towle Mason Eminent Physician of Wisdom award, 1998, Dean Towle Mason, M.D. Medal of Wisdom award, 2001, Cardiologist of the Century Wisdom award, 2001, Albert Schweitzer world Humanitarian of Wisdom award, 2002, Jonas Salk award for med. rsch., 2003, Albert Einstein Sci. Rsch. award, 2003, John Wayne Pioneer of Am. award, 2003, Ernest Hemingway award for maj. contbns. to med. lit., 2003, Will Durant Philosopher-Physician award, 2004, Paul Dudley White award for disting. svc. in cardiovasc. medicine, 2004, Newton Kugelmass Children's Cardiology Crusader award, 2004, Norman Vincent Peale Healing Power of Prayer award, 2005, Lifetime Achievement award, U. Calif., Davis, 2008. Master Am. Coll. Cardiology (pres. 1977-78); fellow ACP, Am. Heart Assn., Am. Coll. Chest Physicians, Royal Soc. Medicine; mem. Am. Soc. Clin. Investigation, Am. Physiol. Soc., Am. Soc. Pharmacology and Exptl. Therapeutics (Exptl. Therapeutics award 1973), Am. Fedn. Clin. Research, NY Acad. Scis., Am. Assn. U. Cardiologists, Am. Soc. Clin. Pharmacology and Therapeutics, We. Assn. Physicians, AAUP, We. Soc. Clin. Rsch. (past pres.), El Macero Country Club, Phi Beta Kappa, Alpha Omega Alpha. Republican. Methodist. Home: 44725 Country Club Dr El Macero CA 95618-1047 Office: Western Heart Inst St Marys Med Ctr 450 Stanyan St San Francisco CA 94117-1079

MASON, DWAYNE L., lawyer; s. Leroy and Tillie Mason. BSChemE, Purdue U., 1984; JD, U. Houston, 1993. Bar: Tex. Supreme Ct. 1993, U.S. Patent & Trademark Office 1995. Ptnr. Matthew Joseph Shaddox & Mason, Houston, 1995—99, Winstead Secrest & Minick, Houston, 1999—2001, Akin Gump Strauss Hauer & Feld, Houston, 2001—. Dir. Harris Coutny MUD 222, Houston, 1995—2006. Editl. bd.: Nanotechnology Law and Bus. Mem. Greater Houston Ptnrship., 2001—; bd. mem. Houston Strategic Forum, 2005—, Kiwanis Club. Named Top Minority IP Ptnr., AIPLA/MCCA, 2003, Top Lawyer, Tex. mag., 2004. Mem.: Kiwanis (chair legal com. 2001—, bd.). Office: Akin Gump Strauss Hauer & Feld LLP 1111 Louisiana St 44th Fl Houston TX 77002 Office Phone: 713-220-8186. Office Fax: 713-236-0822. Business E-Mail: dmason@akingump.com.

MASON, EDWARD EATON, surgeon; b. Boise, Idaho, Oct. 16, 1920; s. Edward Files and Dora Bell (Eaton) M.; m. Dordana Fairman, June 18, 1944; children— Daniel Edward, Rose Mary, Richard Eaton, Charles Henry. BA, U. Iowa, 1943, MD, 1945; PhD in Surgery, U. Minn., 1953.

Intern, resident in surgery Univ. Hosps., Mpls., 1945-52; asst. prof. surgery U. Iowa, 1953-55, asso. prof., 1956-60, prof., 1961-91, prof. emeritus, 1991—, chmn. gen. surgery, 1978-91. Cons. VA Hosp.; trainee Nat. Cancer Inst., 1949-52 Author: Computer Applications in Medicine, 1964, Fluid, Electrolyte and Nutrient Therapy in Surgery, 1974, Surgical Treatment of Obesity, 1981; developer gastric bypass and gastroplasty for treatment of obesity; contbr. articles profl. jours. Served to lt. (j.g.) USNR, 1945-47. Fellow ACS; mem. AMA, Am. Surg. Assn., Western Surg. Assn., Soc. Univ. Surgeons, Internat. Soc. Surgery, Ctrl. Surg. Assn., Soc. Surgery Alimentary Tract, Am. Thyroid Assn., Am. Soc. Bariatric Surgery, Sigma Xi, Alpha Omega Alpha. Republican. Presbyterian. Home: 5 Melrose Cir Iowa City IA 52246-2013 Office: Univ Hosp Dept Surgery Iowa City IA 52242 Business E-Mail: edward-mason@uiowa.edu. *Continuity of interest and planning weaves the daily decisions into a whole cloth that does more than cover one's imperfections.*

MASON, ELLSWORTH GOODWIN, retired librarian; b. Waterbury, Conn., Aug. 25, 1917; s. Frederick William and Kathryn Loretta (Watkins) Mason; m. Rose Ellen Maloy, May 13, 1951 (div. Oct. 1961); children: Kay Iris Morice, Joyce Iris Lande; m. Joan Lou Shinew, Aug. 16, 1964; 1 child, Sean David. BA, Yale U., 1938, MA, 1942, PhD, 1948; LHD, Hofstra U., 1973; diploma, Inst. Children's Lit., 1996. Cert. Christian Writer's Guild. Reference asst. Yale Library, 1938-42; export license officer Bd. Econ. Warfare, 1942-43; instr. English Williams Coll., 1948-50; instr. humanities Marlboro (Vt.) Coll., 1951-52; serials libr. U. Wyo. Libr., 1952-54; reference libr. Colo. Coll. Libr., Colorado Springs, 1954-58; lectr., libr. Colo. Coll., 1958-63; prof., dir. libr. svcs. Hofstra U., Hempstead, NY, 1963-72; prof., dir. U. Colo. Librs., Boulder, 1972-76; freelance writer children's lit., 1995—. Libr. cons., 1958—; vis. lectr. Northwestern U., 1961, Colo. Coll., 1965, Syracuse U., 1965—68, Elmira Coll., 1966, Columbia U., 1966—68, Lincoln U., 1969, U. BC, Canada, 1969, U. Toronto, 1970, U. Tulsa, 1971, 76, U. Rutgers, 1971, U. Ill., 1972, Colgate U., 1972, Simmons Coll., 1972, U. Oreg., 1973, Hofstra U., 1974, U. N.C., 1976, U. Ala., 1976, Ball State U., 1977, U. Lethbridge, Canada, 1977, U. Ariz., 1981, Ariz. State U., 1981, Victoria U., New Zealand, 1983, U. Canterbury, New Zealand, 1983, U. Nev., Las Vegas, 1992, Remember Pearl Harbor Assn., 1993, 94; rsch. assoc. U. Calif., Berkeley, 1965; adj. prof. U. Ill., Urbana, 1968; pres. Mason Assocs., Ltd., 1977—; libr. value engr., 1992—. Author (with Walter and Jean Shine): A MacDonald Potpourri, 1988, The University of Colorado Library and Its Makers, 1876-1972, 1994; editor (with Stanislaus Joyce): The Early Joyce, 1955; editor Xerox U.M. edit., 1964, Norwood: Norwood Editions, 1977, Philadelphia (R. West), 1978, editor with Richard Ellmann The Critical Writings of James Joyce, 1959, 2d edit., 1989, editor Colorado College Studies, 1959—62, Critical Commentary on a Portrait of the Artist as a Young Man, 1966, The Bookover's Bounty, 1977—82; translator: Recollections of James Joyce (S. Joyce), 1950, Essais de J. Joyce, 1966, Escritos Criticos de James Joyce, Portuguese edit., 1967, Spanish edit., 1973, 1975, James Joyce's Ulysses and Vico's Cycle, 1973, Krittische Schriften v. James Joyce, 1975, Mason on Library Buildings, 1980; editor, compiler: Focus on Robert Graves, 1972—88, adv. editor: Focus on Robert Graves and His Contemporaries, 1988—; mem. editl. bd. Serial Slants, 1957—59, Choice, 1962—65, Coll. and Rsch. Librs., 1969—72, Serials Libr., 1977—98; contbr. articles to profl. jours. Mem. chancellor's coun. U. Tex., Austin, 1982—; exec. bd. U. Ky. Libr. Assocs., 1991—94, Concerned Christians in Ky., 1993—98, Littlefield Soc. U. Tex., Austin, 2004—. With USN, 1943—46. Recipient Harry Bailly Spkr.'s award, Assn. Colls. Midwest, 1975; named Ky. Col., 1993; grantee, Am. Coun. Learned Socs., Edn. Facilities Labs., Hofstra U., U. Colo.; fellow, Coun. Libr. Resources, 1969—70. Mem.: ALA (councilor-at-large 1961—65), Am. Christian Writers, Nat. Assn. Scholars, James Joyce Found. (chmn. sect. translation from Joyce 2d Internat. James Joyce Symposium 1969), Inst. Vico Studies, New Zealand Royal Forest and Bird Protection Soc., Conf. Editors Learned Jours., Alcuin Soc. Vancouver, Pvt. Librs. Assn., New Zealand Libr. Assn., Libr. Assn. (London), Bibliog. Soc. Am., Colo. Libr. Assn. (pres. so. dist. 1960—61), Black Am.'s PAC, Colo. Book Collectors (founder, pres. 1975—86), Ghost Town Club, Caxton Club, Archons of Colophon, Sigma Kappa Alpha (pres. 1969—70), Alpha Sigma Lambda. Home: 736 Providence Rd Lexington KY 40502-2267 also: 39 Discovery Dr Whitby New Zealand

MASON, FRANK HENRY, III, automotive and rental company executive; b. Paris, Tenn., Nov. 16, 1936; s. Frank H. and Dorothy (Carter) M.; children: Robert C., William C. B of Elec. Engring., Vanderbilt U., 1958; MS in Indsl. Mgmt., MIT, 1965. With Ford Motor Co., 1965-71; asst. controller Ford Brazil, Sao Paulo, 1971-74; mgr. overseas fin. dept. Ford Motor Co., Dearborn, Mich., 1974-76, asst. controller engine divsn., 1976-78, mgr. facilities and mgmt. svcs., 1978-81; controller Ford Motor Credit Co., Dearborn, Mich., 1981-87; dir. fin. Ford Fin. Svcs. Group, Dearborn, Mich., 1987-89; exec. v.p., chief fin. officer U.S. Leasing, Internat., San Francisco, 1989-92; retired, 1992. Lt. USN, 1958-63.

MASON, GEORGE ROBERT, retired surgeon, educator; b. Rochester, NY, June 10, 1932; s. George Mitchell and Marjorie Louise (Hooper) M.; m. Grace Louise Bransfield, Feb. 4, 1956 (dec.); children: Douglas Richard, Marcia Jean, David William; m. Rosemary Harrison, Feb. 16, 2002. BA, Oberlin Coll., 1955; MD with honors, U. Chgo., 1957; PhD in Physiology, Stanford U., 1968. Diplomate: Am. Bd. Surgery (examiner 1977-80, dir. 1980-86), Bd. Thoracic Surgery. Teaching asst. pathology U. Chgo., 1954-56; rotating intern U. Chgo. Clinics, 1957-58; tchg. asst. surgery, NIH postdoctoral fellow, USPHS fellow surgery Stanford U., 1960-62; from asst. resident in surgery to sr. and chief resident in surgery Stanford U. Hosps., 1962-66; mem. faculty Stanford Med. Sch., 1965-71, assoc. prof., 1970-71; prof., chmn. dept. surgery U. Md. Med. Sch., Balt., 1971-80; also prof. physiology; prof., chmn. dept. surgery U. Calif., Irvine, 1980-89; chief surgical svc. Hines VA Hosp., Ill., 1990—95; prof. surgery and thoracic cardiovascular surgery Loyola U. Med. Ctr., Maywood, 1990—2001, chmn. dept. thoracic and cardiovasc. surgery, 1995—97; ret., 2001. Mem. residency review com. for surgery, 1981-87. Contbr. to profl. jours., med. textbooks. Served to capt. M.C., USAF, 1958-60. Giannini fellow Stanford U., 1966-67; recipient Markle scholarship in acad. medicine, 1968-74 Mem. ACS, Am. Assn. Thoracic Surgeons, Am. Coll. Chest Physicians, Am. Physiol. Soc., Am. Gastroent. Assn., Pacific Coast Surg. Assn., Assn. Acad. Surgery, Ctrl. Surg. Soc., So. Surg. Soc., Chgo. Surg. Soc., Am. Surg. Assn., Western Surg. Assn., Soc. Thoracic Surgeons, Ill. Thoracic Surg. Soc. (pres. 1994-95), Halsted Soc., Chesapeake Vascular Soc., Soc. Internat. Chirurgie, Soc. Clin. Surgery, Soc. for Surgery Alimentary Tract, Soc. Univ. Surgeons. Home: 846 Bonnie Brae PL River Forest IL 60305-1510 Personal E-mail: grmason@earthlink.net.

MASON, GREGG CLAUDE, orthopedic surgeon, researcher; b. Schenectady, NY, July 28, 1958; s. George and Maureen (Murphy) M.; m. Dina Marie Sokolowski, June 16, 1990. BS in Chemistry magna cum laude, Allegheny Coll., 1980; MD, U. Pitts., 1984. Diplomate Am. Bd. Orthop. Surgery, Nat. Bd. Med. Examiners. Gen. surgery intern U. Colo./U. Colo. Med. Ctrs., Denver, 1984-85; orthopaedic rsch. fellow U. Pitts., 1985-86, resident in orthopaedic surgery, 1986-89; orthopedic surgeon U.S. Naval Hosp., Okinawa, Japan, 1989-92; pvt. practice, Erie, 1992—. Active staff St. Vincent Med. Ctr., St. Vincent Surgery Ctr., Hamot Med. Ctr., Union City Meml. Hosp.; lectr. in field. Contbr. articles to profl. jours. Comdr. M.C. USNR, 1980—. Recipient Outstanding Student Rsch. award U. Pitt. Sch. Medicine, 1984, Harold Henderson Sankey Orthop. award, 1984; rsch. grantee Competitive Med. Rsch. Fund., Presbyn.-Univ. Hosp. of Pitts., 1986-87, U. Pitts. Rsch. Devel. Fund, 1986-87. Disting. Alden scholar 1977, 78, 79, 80, Sandra Doane Turk scholar, 1979, Armed Svcs. Health Professions scholar, 1981-84. Fellow ACS, Internat. Coll. Surgeons, Mil. Soc. Orthop. Surgeons, Am. Acad. Orthop. Surgeons (tchg. seal 1993); mem. AMA, Pa. Orthop. Soc. (Best Rsch. Paper 1987, 88), Erie Orthop. Soc., U. Pitts. Med. Ctr. Orthop. Alumni., Am. Orthop. Soc. of Sports Medicine (Cabaud award 1988), Ea. Orthop. Assn. (Founders award 1988), Phi Beta Kappa. Office: Orthopaedic Surgeons Inc 204 W 26th St Erie PA 16508-1898 Office Phone: 814-454-2401.

MASON, GREGORY WESLEY, JR., secondary school educator; b. Chgo., Jan. 21, 1963; s. Gregory Wesley and Diana (Burton) M.; m. LaTanya Yvonne Brown, June 8, 1991; children: Gregory Arthur, Timothy Michael. BS, Ill. State U., 1986; MEd, U. Ill., Chgo., 1996. Cert. secondary tchr., gen. adminstr., Ill. Instr. City Coll. Chgo., 1986-89; instr. project alert Roosevelt U., Chgo., 1989-91, counselor project upward bound, 1991-93; tchr. math. Bowen High Sch., Chgo., 1993-95, chmn. profl. planning adv. com., 1994-95; tchr. math. Whitney M. Young Magnet H.S., Chgo., 1995-2000, chmn. dept. math., 1997-2000; adminstr. Chgo. Pub. Schs., 2000—05; asst. prin. Sir Miles Davis Acad., 2005—08; prin. Philip Murray Lang. Acad., 2008—. Instr. Ill. Math. and Sci. Acad., Aurora, summers 1993-96; lectr. Coll. Edn., Loyola U., Chgo., 1999-2001; tchr. coord. Golden Apple Found., 2000-01; mem. nat. adv. bd. Schs. and Scholars Program, Woodrow Wilson Nat. Fellowship Found. Mem. pres.'s coun. edn. com. Mus. Sci. and Industry; mem. Ill. Robotic Competition Adv. Bd. Named to Outstanding Young Men of Am., 1985. Mem. ASCD, Nat. Coun. Tchrs. Math., Ill. Coun. Tchrs. Math., Ill. Coun. for Coll. Attendance (bd. dirs. 1993-97), Nat. Assn. Secondary Sch. Prins., Benjamin Banneker Assn., Masons, Phi Delta Kappa. Avocations: swimming, chess, reading, stock trading, computers. Home: 10500 S Oakley Chicago IL 60643 Office: Philip Murray Lang Acad 5335 S Kenwood Chicago IL 60615 Business E-Mail: gmason@crs.k12.il.us.

MASON, HERBERT WARREN, JR., religion and history educator, author; b. Wilmington, Del., Apr. 20, 1932; s. Herbert Warren and Mildred Jane (Noyes) M.; m. Jeanine Young, June 25, 1982; children from previous marriage: Cathleen, Paul, Sarah. AB, Harvard U., Cambridge, Mass., 1955, AM, 1965, PhD, 1969. English tchr. Am. Sch. Paris, 1959-60; asst. prof. St. Joseph's Coll., Gorham, Maine, 1960-62; vis. lectr. Simmons Coll., Boston, 1962-63; vis. lectr. in Islamic Hist. Tufts U., Medford, Mass., 1965-66; teaching fellow in English Harvard U., Cambridge, Mass., 1962-66, teaching fellow in Islamic Hist., 1966-67; translator Bollingen Found., NYC, 1968-72; prof. History and Religion Boston U., 1972-2000, William Goodwin Aurelio prof. history and religious thought, 2000—; emeritus prof., history. U.K. cons. editor Banipal; dir. inst. study muslim socs. and civilians Boston U., 2006—. Author: Reflections on the Middle East Crisis, 1970, Two Statesmen of Medieval Islam, 1971, Gilgamesh, 1971, 2d edit., 2003, The Death of al-Hallaj, 1979, Moments in Passage, 1979, (novel) Summer Light, 1980; translator: La Passion d'al-Hallaj, 4 vols., Bollingen Series (Louis Massignon), 1983, abridged 1 vol., 1994, A Legend of Alexander, 1986, Memoir of a Friend: Louis Massignon, 1988, Testimonies and Reflections, 1989, al-Hallaj, 1995, Haythu Taltaqi al-Anhar (novel in Arabic "Where the Rivers Meet"), 1999, English edit., 2003, (poems) Disappearances, 1999; co-editor: Humaniora Islamica; cons. editor Banipal, London; contbr. articles, essays, revs., fiction and poetry to popular fiction mags. Sec. Inter-racial Riverside Assn., Cambridge, Mass., 1965-67; trustee Bd. Charity of Edward Hopkins, Boston Athenaeum. Fellow Soc. for Values in Higher Edn.; mem. PEN (bd. dirs. Delos chpt.), Medieval Acad. Am., Am. Oriental Soc., Am. Acad. Religion, Mark Twain Soc., Inst. Internat. des Recherches Louis Massignon in Paris (dir. edn., v.p.), Am. Acad. Poetry, Japan Poetry Mus. (Iwate-Ken). Home: 9 Seaview Lane Newbury MA 01951 Office: Boston U 745 Commonwealth Ave Boston MA 02215-1401 Personal E-mail: herbertwmason@comcast.net, herbertmason@mac.com.

MASON, JAMES ELIOT, energy executive, director; b. El Dorado, Ark., Sept. 29, 1951; s. George Washington and Mary Arden Mason; m. Janice Gail White, Mar. 21, 1975; 1 child, Calin Elaine. PhD, Cornell U., Ithaca, NY, 1996. Asst. prof. U. Ctrl. Ark., Conway, 1996—97; dir. Am. Solar Action Plan (formerly Solar Energy Campaign), Farmingdale, NY, 1998—. Organizer Assn. Cmty. Orgns. Reform Now, New Orleans, 1978—90. Contbr. articles to profl. jours. Home and Office: Am Solar Action Plan 52 Columbia St Farmingdale NY 11735 Personal E-mail: je_mason@verizon.net. Business E-Mail: asap@solarplan.org.

MASON, JAMES HAMILTON, surgeon; b. Kokomo, Ind., June 5, 1930; d. Lorne Wilfred and Alice Hamilton Mason; m. Anabel Russell, Dec. 22, 1951; children: James Russell, Daniel Hamilton, John Lorne, Seth Gordon, Amy Alice. BA, DePauw U., Greencastle, Inc., 1952; MD, Cornell U., Med. Coll., NYC, 1956. Diplomate Am. Bd. Surgery. Intern U. Ill, Chgo., 1956, resident, 1959—63; attending surgeon St. Francis Hosp., Evanston, Ill., 1963—, chief surgery, 1967—, dir. edn., 1967—; pres. Am. Cancer Soc., Ill. Divsn., 1977. Assoc. prof. surgery U. Ill., Coll. Medicine, Chgo., 1967—; clin. assoc. prof. surgery Loyola U., Stritch Sch. Medicine, Ill., clin. prof. surgery, Ill., 1970—. Lt. USN, 1957—59. Mem.: AMA, Ill. State Med. Inter-Ins. Exch. (bd. govs.), Chgo. Inst. Medicine, Pan Pacific Surg. Assn., Ill. Surg. Soc. (2d v.p. 1978, counselor), We. Surg. Soc., Soc. Surgery of Alimentary Tract, Chgo. Surg. Soc. (recorder 1971—74, v.p. 1981—82), Chgo. Med. Soc., Ill. State Med. Soc. (pres. 1981—82), Am. Cancer Soc. (pres. N. Shore br. 1970—71, 1971—72, pres 1973), Warren H. Cole Soc. (sec. 1967—69, pres. 1972), Midwest Surg. Assn., Am. Coll. Surgeons (v.p. Chgo. met. chpt. 1973—74, pres. Chgo. met. chpt. 1976—77). Protestant. Home: 4620 N Catamount Tr NE Ada MI 49301

MASON, JANICE M., principal, director; d. George W. and Delores M. (Phillips) Mason. B, Ill. State U., Normal, 1978; M in Curriculum and Instrn., Concordia U., River Forest, Ill., 1996; cert. of advanced studies, Lewis U., Romeoville, Ill., 1999. Tchr. 6th-8th grade phys. edn., computer Antioch Upper Grade Sch., Ill., 1978—86; tchr. 5th grade self contained classroom W. C. Petty Elem. Sch., Antioch, 1986—92, 1998—2001, tchr. 5th grade sci., computer, 1992—98; asst. prin., dir. tech. Fox Lake Grade Sch. Dist. 114, Spring Grove, 2001—06, prin., dir. tech., 2007—. Scholar, P. E. O., 1998. Mem.: ASCD, NAESP, Ill. Prins. Assn. Home: 7002 247th Ave Salem WI 53168 Office: Fox Lake Grade School District 114 29067 West Grass Lake Rd Spring Grove IL 60081 Office Fax: 847-973-4110. Personal E-mail: jmmason56@aol.com. Business E-Mail: masonj@flgs.lake.k12.il.us, jmason@foxlake114.org.

MASON, JERRY, finance educator, consultant; b. Bell, Calif., May 31, 1941; s. Wilton Ira and Esther Evelyn (Brown) M.; m. Joyce Hurst, Sept. 5, 1968; children: Matthew, Amy, Belinda, Andrew, Laurie, Julie. BS, Brigham Young U., Provo, Utah, 1965; MBA, Stanford U., Palo Alto, Calif., 1967; PhD, U. Mo., Columbia, 1980. CFP, CLU, ChFC. Vis. prof. Shippesburg U., Pa., 2005—06; assoc. prof., fin. planning Coll. St. Rose, Albany, NY, 2007—. Bd. dirs. Nat. Found. for Consumer Credit, Balat.; founder, dir. Accredited Fin. Counselor Cert. Program, 1992-94; monthly workshop leader for individuals filing chpt. 13 bankruptcy, Lubbock, 1991—. Editor: Personal Finance: Study Guide, 1992; author: The Easy Family Budget Book, 1990; contbr. articles to profl. jours. Bd. mem. Nat. Found. for Consumer Credit, Balt., 1985—95. Named Tchr. of Yr., Tex. Tech U., 1994. Mem. Internat. Assn. for Fin. Planning (chpt. pres. 1991-94, Paper of Yr. 1985), Assn. for Fin. Counseling and Planning Edn. (charter, founder, past pres. 1983-86, Fin. Counseling and Educator of Yr. 1993). Lds Ch. Avocations: gardening, hiking, travel, backpacking, walking. Office: Coll St Rose 432 Western Ave Albany NY 12203 Personal E-mail: jmason41@yahoo.com. Business E-Mail: masonj@strose.edu.

MASON, JOAN ELLEN, nurse; b. Reading, Pa., June 29, 1947; d. Richard Lenhart and Mary Jane (Miller) Fritz; m. W. Davis Mason, Feb. 12, 1977 (dec. Jan. 2002). RN, Temple U. Hosp. Sch. Nursing, 1968; BS in Nursing Edn., Temple U., 1971, EdM in Health Edn., 1981; postgrad., U. Pa. Staff nurse Temple U. Hosp., Phila., 1968-71; nursing instr. Phila. Gen. Hosp. Sch. Nursing, 1971-76; coord. staff devel. Meml. Hosp., Roxborough, Pa., 1976-84; clin. editor Springhouse Corp., Pa., 1984-94; nurse cons. Kelly Sci. Resources, 1995-98; adminstrn., profl. nurse Bed and Breakfast Inn, Cape May, NJ, 1982—2003; nurse cons. Reading, 1999—2003, Orwigsburg, 2003—05. Mem. exhibit com. Mus. Nursing History, Inc., 1988-2001. Editor Congl. Free Ch. of Chirst newsletter; devel.: Bible Fellowship Group; contbr. articles to profl. jours. Vol. Reading Mus., Berks Arts Coun. Mem. Mid-Atlantic Ctr. for Arts, Orwigsburg Women's Libr. Soc. Republican. Home: 225 Eisenhower Dr Orwigsburg PA 17961-1605

MASON, JOEL BERNARD, internist, gastroenterologist; b. Syracuse, NY, June 17, 1955; B in General Biology, U. Ill.-Urbana, 1977; MD, U. Chgo.-Pritzker Sch. Medicine, 1981. Cert. internal medicine, gastroenterology, nutrition. Intern, gastroenterology U. Iowa Hosps., Iowa City, 1981—82, resident, 1982—84; fellow U. Chgo. Hosp., 1984—86; gastroenterologist Tufts-New England Med. Ctr., Boston; assoc. prof. medicine and nutrition Tufts Sch. Medicine; dir., vitamins and carcinogenesis lab., USDA Human Nutrition Rsch. Ctr. Tufts U. Cons. Mead-Johnson Nutritional; editorial bd. Jour. Parenteral & Enteral Nutrition. Mem.: Am. Soc. for Nutritional Sciences. Office: Tufts-New England Med Ctr Medicine Clin Nutrition 711 Washington St Boston MA 02111-1524 also: Tufts New England Med Ctr Medicine Gastroene 750 Washington St #218 Boston MA 02111 Office Phone: 617-556-3194. Office Fax: 617-556-3234. E-mail: joel.mason@tufts.edu.

MASON, JOHN LATIMER, engineering executive; b. LA, Nov. 8, 1923; s. Zene Upham and Edna Ella (Watkins) Mason; m. Frances Howe Draeger, Sept. 1, 1950 (dec. June 1951); m. Mary Josephine Schulte, Nov. 26, 1954; children: Andrew, Peter, Mary Anne, John Edward. BS in Meteorology, U. Chgo., 1944; BS in Applied Chemistry, Calif. Inst. Tech., 1947, MS in Chem. Engring., 1948, PhD, 1950. Registered profl. engr., Calif. Engr. AiResearch Mfg. Co., Los Angeles, 1950-60; dir. engring. AiResearch Mfg. Co. div. Garrett Corp., Los Angeles, 1960-72; v.p. engring. Garrett Corp., Los Angeles, 1972-87; v.p. engring. and tech. Allied-Signal Aerospace Co., Los Angeles, 1987-88, cons., 1989-96; chmn. tech. adv. com. Indsl. Turbines Internat., Inc., Los Angeles, 1972-81, bd. dirs., 1980-88; adj. prof. engring. Calif. State U., Long Beach, 1992-96. Tech. adv. bd. Tex. Ctr. for Superconductivity, U. Houston, 1989-02, Ceryx Inc., 1998-2001; chair Calif. Coun. Sci. and Tech. Panel on Transp. R&D Ctr., 1993-94; bd. dirs. Planetary Sci. Inst., sec., 1998—; cons. Capstone Turbine Corp., 1994-98; workshop com. Transp. Rsch. Bd., 1998.; cons. Cleaire, Inc., 2001-03, Applied Rsch. and Tech., 2001-; ptnr. Applied Rsch. and Tech., 2001-06. Patentee in field. Chmn. energy and environment com. FISITA Coun., 1990-94. 1st lt. USAAF, 1943-46, PTO. With USAF, 1946—57. Fellow AIAA, assoc. Soc. Automotive Engrs., bd. dirs. 1984-87, 90-93, pres.-elect 1989-90, pres. 1990-91, Performance Rev. Inst. chmn. 1990-91, bd. dirs. 1992-93; mem. AAAS, NRC of NAS, com. on alternative energy R&D strategies 1989-90, Office Sci. and Tech. Policy, Nat. Critical Techs. panel 1992-93, Inst. Medicine of NAS, com. on health effects of indoor allergens 1992-93, Nat. Acad. Engring., US Advanced Ceramics Assn. chmn. tech. com., bd. dirs. 1985-88, Am. Chem. Soc., Am. Ceramic Soc., Caltech Assocs., Sigma Xi assoc., Am. Soc. Mech. Engrs., Eco Power, Inc. (mem. engrg. adv. bd. 2008-), Univ. of So. Calif. Office Phone: 310-375-5161. Personal E-mail: JL-Mason@cox.net.

MASON, JOHN MURWYN, JR., bank executive; b. St. Louis, Mar. 1, 1940; s. John Murwyn and Clara Frances (Shaffer) M.; m. Mary Jean Martell; children: Anne Elizabeth, John Martell. BA, Mich. State U., 1962, MBA, 1964, PhD, 1971. Sr. economist Fed. Res. Bank, Cleve., 1968-71; spl. asst. to Sec. HUD, Washington, 1971-72; asst. prof. fin. Wharton Sch., U. Pa., Phila., 1971-83; exec. v.p., chief fin. officer Wilmington Savs. Fund Soc., Del., 1983-87; exec. v.p., chief oper. officer 1st Am. Savs. F.A., Jenkintown, Pa., 1987-89; pres., chief exec. officer Flagship Fin. Corp. and 1st Am. Savs. F.A., 1989—. Author: Financial Management of Commercial Banks, 1979. Vestryman St. David's Episcopal Ch., Radnor, Pa., 1986—; bd. dirs. Nat. Conf. Christians and Jews, Phila., 1989—; bd. advisors Annenberg Ctr. U. Pa., 1989—, Hagley Mus. and Library, 1984-87. Mem. Am. Econs. Assn., Am. Statis. Soc., Econometric Soc. Republican. Episcopalian. Avocations: golf, running. Office: First Am Savs FA 500 Old York Rd Jenkintown PA 19046-2852

MASON, JOHN WAYNE, psychoneuroendocrinologist, retired medical educator; b. Chgo., Feb. 9, 1924; s. John Ralph and Frances Elsie (Swedman) Mason; m. Joyce Ann Towne; children: John Mark, Victoria Joyce, Peter Brooke. AB, Ind. U., Bloomington, 1944; MD, Ind. U., Indpls., 1947; MA (hon.), Yale U., New Haven, 1977. Diplomate in pathol. anatomy Am. Bd. Pathology. Surg. intern NY Hosp.-Cornell Med. Ctr., NYC, 1947—48, resident in pathology, 1948—50; chief dept. neuroendocrinology Walter Reed Army Inst. Rsch., Washington, 1953—74; prof. emeritus psychiatry Yale U. Sch. Medicine, New Haven, 1977—. Cons. and dir. psychoendocrine lab. Adult Psychiatry br. NIMH, Bethesda, Md., 1960—65; sci. advisor, neurosychiatry br. Walter Reed Army Inst. of Rsch., Washington, 1974—77; dir. psychoendocrine lab. Nat. Ctr. for PTSD, VA Med. Ctr., West Haven, Conn., 1977—2000; lectr. and invited lectr. in field. Contbr. more than 170 sci. rsch. publs. to profl. jours., 24 chpts. to books, also revs. in field; author: (monograph) Organization of Psychoendocrine Mechanisms, 1968 (Med. Lit. Citation Classic award). Faculty sponsor, Campus Crusade for Christ ministry Yale U., 1983; Bible tchr. Trinity Evang. Free Ch., Woodbridge, Conn., 1978—. Served to maj. M.C. US Army, 1948—53. Recipient Rsch. Scientist Career award, NIMH, 1981-1991, medal, Pavlovian Soc., 1985, Meritorius Civilian Svc. award, Dept. of Army, 1960, Sustained Superior Performance Civil Svc. awards, 1960, 1966, 1969, Lifetime Achievement award, 21st Century Traumatology Conf., Georgetown U. Med. Ctr. Founds., 1996; grantee, NIMH, 1989-2000. Mem.: Assn. Psychosomatic Medicine (editl. bd. mem. 1963—91),

Internat. Soc. Psychoneuroendocrinology (Lifetime Achievement award 2005), Endocrine Soc., Am. Psychosomatic Soc. (pres. 1969—70, Pres.'s award 2000), Alpha Omega Alpha, Phi Beta Kappa. Achievements include long term systematic basic and clinical research on the importance of psychosocial influences upon a wide range of endocrine systems in relation to stress and stress-related clinical disorders; major pioneering contributions to the development of the field of psychoneuroendocrinology and to exploring its far-reaching clinical implications for psychiatry and medicine; development of psychoendocrine strategies using concurrent hormonal and psychological measurements providing new leverage for the interdisciplinary study of; intrapsychic processes including emotional states, psychological defenses and coping styles; established that psychosocial and physical stress stimuli produce broadly organized multihormonal patterns of change involving many interdependent endocrine systems; received national and international recognition as a leader providing landmark experimental and conceptual contributions in the fields of psychoendocrinology and stress research; development of an unusual profile of thyroid hormonal alterations in PTSD patients, which provides compelling leads concerning the pathogenesis and possible treatment of this disorder. Home: 32 Maple Vale Dr Woodbridge CT 06525 Personal E-mail: jwmason@pol.net.

MASON, JOSEPH See BUSHINSKY, JAY

MASON, KEIRA, anesthesiologist; BS, MD, Yale U., Conn. Dir. radiology anesthesia and sedation, assoc. prof. anesthesia Harvard U. Boston Children's Hosp., 1996—. Chmn. pediat. com. World Soc. Intravenous Anesthesia. Office: Childrens Hosp Boston 300 Longwood Ave Boston MA 02115

MASON, LINDA, physical education educator, coach; b. Indpls., Jan. 29, 1946; d. Harrison Linn and Hazel Marie (Bledsoe) Crouch; divorced; children: Cassandra, Andrew. BS, Ind. U., 1968, MS, 1977. Cert. phys. edn. tchr., K-12, Ind. Tchr. phys. edn. Woodview Jr. H.S., Indpls., 1968—71; tchr. phys. edn., coach Ind. U.-Purdue U. Indpls., 1972—76; basketball coach Butler U., Indpls., 1976—84; head softball coach, asst. basketball coach Westfield Washington High Sch., Westfield, Ind., 1985; tchr. phys. edn., basketball coach Orchard Park Elem. Sch., Carmel, Ind., 1985—; tchr. elem. physical edn. Carmel-Clay Schs., Carmel, 1985—; asst. varsity coach softball Carmel H.S., 1993—95, head varsity softball coach, 1996—99. Head coach Ind. Girls' H.S. All-Stars Basketball Team, Indpls., 1980. Named Coach of Yr. Dist. 4, Nat. Collegiate Athletic Assn., 1983, Coach of Yr. for softball ICGSA, 1997, coach ICGSA Girls All Stars, 1998. Mem. Delta Psi Kappa. Personal E-mail: peteacherl@msn.com, peteacherl@indy.rr.com. Business E-Mail: lmason@ccs.k12.in.us.

MASON, LOIS E. (J. DAY MASON), painter, poet, actress, educator; b. Boston, May 4, 1919; d. Harold Monroe and Orpah Cecil (Smith) Scheibe; m. Lucien Bunce Day, June 21, 1941 (div. 1954); children: Felicity, Christopher, Sarah; m. Frederick Dike Mason, Apr. 27, 1964 (dec.); children: Frederick Dike III, Victoria, Johanna. Student, U. Leiden, Netherlands, 1939; BA, Oberlin, Ohio, 1940; postgrad., Cranbrook Acad. Art, Bloomfield Hills, Mich., 1941. Set-up and tchr. art dept. Pingree Sch., Hamilton Mass.; TV, lectr. creative arts and writing, Mass. and Conn., 1949-58. Actress appearing in Alien Corn, Twelfth Night, Crucible, George Washington Slept Here, Philadelphia Story, Auntie Mame, Skin of our Teeth, Spoon River, Anything Goes, Call Me Madame, Seven Keys to Baldpate, Other People's Money, Quilters, Golden Pond, Cat on a Hot Tin Roof, Little Foxes, Lettice and Lovage, Close Ties, Grace and Glorie, others; set designer, decorator Auntie Mame, See How They Run, Tea House of the August Moon, Spoon River, Archie and Mehitable; author: Speaking to Strangers, 1987-88; one-woman shows include New Britain (Conn.) Mus., Am. Ballet, N.Y., Green Mountain Gallery, N.Y.C., Essex (Mass.) Inst., Marblehead Arts, Quadrom, Mast Cove, 6 Deering, Miles Hosp., Afty. Gen.'s Office, Kennebec Valley Art Assn., Chocolate Ch. Art Ctr., Maine Gallery, Kristina's, Oliver's, Islesboro Historic Soc., West Island Gallery, Bath, Maine. Ch. ladies com. Hamilton Hall, Salem, Mass., 1975—78; set designer Cmty. Theater, Swampscott, Mass., 1973—78. Recipient C. Law/Watkins fellowship Phillips Gallery, Mus., Washington, 1944-46. Mem. Nat. Assn. Women Painters, Conn. Acad., Silvermine, Maine Gallery, Kennebec Valley Arts, Chocolate Ch. Art Ctr., Marblehead Arts, Conn. Acad., Maine Writers and Publs. Avocations: cooking, sailing, gardening.

MASON, MARILYN GELL, retired library administrator, writer, consultant; b. Chickasha, Okla., Aug. 23, 1944; d. Emmett D. and Dorothy (O'Bar) Killebrew; m. Carl L. Gell, Dec. 29, 1965 (div. Oct. 1978); 1 child, Charles E.; m. Robert M. Mason, July 17, 1981. BA, U. Dallas, 1966; MLS, N. Tex. State U., Denton, 1968; MPA, Harvard U., 1978. Libr. N.J. State Libr., Trenton, 1968-69; head dept. Arlington County Pub. Libr., Va., 1969-73; chief libr. program Metro Washington Coun. Govts., 1973-77; dir. White House Conf. on Librs. and Info. Svcs., Washington, 1979-80; exec. v.p. Metrics Rsch. Corp., Atlanta, 1981-82; dir. Atlanta-Fulton Pub. Libr., Atlanta, 1982-86, Cleve. Pub. Libr., 1986-99; founder, exec. dir. WebJunction Online Computer Library Ctr., 2002—08; ret., 2008. Evalene Parsons Jackson lectr. divsn. librarianship Emory U., 1981; trustee Online Computer Library Ctr., 1984—97; commr. Nat. Commn. Libr. Info. Scis., 1999—2002. Editor: Survey of Library Automation in the Washington Area, 1977; author: The Federal Role in Library and Information Services, 1983, Strategic Management for Today's Libraries, 1999. Bd. visitors Syracuse U. Sch. Info. Studies, 1981—85, U. Tenn. Sch. Libr. and Info. Sci., Knoxville, 1983—85; trustee Coun. Libr. Resources, Washington, 1992—2000. Recipient Disting. Alumna award, N. Tex. State U., 1979; named to Ohio Libr. Coun. Hall of Fame, 1999. Mem.: ALA (council mem. 1986—90, Herbert and Virginia White award 1999), DC Library Assn. (pres. 1976—77), Ohio Library Assn., Am. Assn. Info. Sci. Home and Office: 2929 First Ave 1122 Seattle WA 98121 Office Phone: 206-714-3009. Business E-Mail: m.g.mason@earthlink.net.

MASON, MARSHALL W., theater director, educator, author; b. Amarillo, Tex., Feb. 24, 1940; s. Marvin Marshall and Lorine (Chrisman) M. BS in Speech, Northwestern U., 1961. Prof. Ariz. State U., 1994-2005, prof. emeritus, 2005; chief drama critic New Times, Phoenix, 1994-96. Founder, artistic dir. Circle Repertory Co., 1969-87, guest artistic dir., Ctr. Theater Group, 1988; dir. Broadway prodns. Redwood Curtain, 1993, The Seagull, 1992, Solitary Confinement, 1992, Burn This, 1987, As Is, 1985 (Drama Desk award, Tony nomination), Passion, 1983, Angels Fall, 1983 (Tony nomination), Fifth of July, 1981 (Tony nomination), Talley's Folly, 1980, 2008 (Pulitzer Prize, N.Y. Drama Critics Circle award, Tony nomination), Murder at the Howard Johnsons, 1979, Gemini, 1977, Knock Knock, 1976 (Tony nomination); Off-Broadway prodns. Book of Days, 2002, Sympathetic Magic, 1997, Robbers, 1997, Cakewalk, 1996, A Poster of the Cosmos/The Moonshot Tape, 1994, The Destiny of Me, 1992, Sunshine, 1989, Talley and Son, 1985, Childe Byron, 1980, Hamlet, 1979, Serenading Louie, 1976 (Obie award), Knock Knock, 1976 (Obie award), The Mound Builders, 1975 (Obie award), Battle of Angeles, 1974 (Obie award), The Sea Horse, 1974, The Hot L Baltimore, 1973 (Obie award); dir. numerous prodns. including Who's Afraid of Virginia Woolf?, Tokyo, 1985, Talley's Folly, 1982, London, Home Free! and The Madness of Lady Bright, 1968, Nat. Tour Sleuth, 1988, Regional Summer and Smoke, 1988, Whisper in the Mind, 1990(Arizoni award), King Lear, 1998 (Arizoni award), The Elephant Man, London, 1998, Long Day's Journey into Night, 1998 (Arizoni award), Riga, 1999, Ginger, 2000; transl. Pirandello's Enrico IV, 2001; dir. Ghosts, 2001, Private Lives, 2002, The Drawer Boy, 2003, The Cherry Orchard, 2004, The Cripple of Inishman, 2004, The Member of the Wedding, 2005, Cat on a Hot Tin Roof, 2005, The Goat, 2006 (Arizoni award); dir. TV prodns. including Picnic, 1986, Kennedy's Children, 1982, Fifth of July, 1983, The Mound Builders, 1975; author: Creating Life on Stage, 2006. Recipient Vernon Rice award, 1975, Drama Desk award, 1977, Margo Jones award, 1977, Outer Critics Circle award, 1978, Theatre World award, 1979, Shubert's Vaughan award, 1980, Obie award for Sustained Achievement, 1983, Inge Festival award for lifetime achievement, 1990, Last Frontier award, 1994, award Ariz. Press Club, 1995, Erwin Piscator award, 1996, Millennium Mr. Abbott award, 1999, Creative Achievement award Ariz. State U., 2001. Mem. Soc. Stage Dirs. and Choreographers (pres. 1983-85), Dirs. Guild Am., Actors Equity Assn., Coll. Fellow of Am. Theater. Address: 165 Christopher St 5U New York NY 10014 Office Phone: 213-446-4144. E-mail: mwm@asu.edu.

MASON, MICHAEL A., telecommunications industry executive, former FBI agent; b. Chgo. married; 2 children. BS in Accounting, Ill. Wesleyan U., 1980. Supr. pers. resources unit FBI, New Haven, 1985, asst. insp., supr. Syracuse Resident Agy. NY, 1994—98, asst. spl. agent-in-charge Buffalo divsn., 1998—2000, chief applicant processing sect., 2000—01, spl. asst. to dir., 2001—02, spl. agent-in-charge Sacramento divsn., 2002—03, asst. dir.-in-charge DC field divsn., 2003—06, acting exec. asst. dir., adminstrn., 2006, exec. asst. dir. for criminal investigations, cyber, response & svcs. br, 2006—08; chief security officer Verizon Comms. Inc., Basking Ridge, NJ, 2008—. Capt. USMC, 1980—84. Recipient Presdl. Rank award, FBI, 2004, Disting. Alumnus award, Ill. Wesleyan U., 2007. Office: Verizon Ctr 1 Verizon Way Basking Ridge NJ 07920-1097 Office Phone: 908-559-2000.

MASON, PHILIP JOHN, geneticist; b. Rochdale, Lancashire, England, Feb. 3, 1954; s. Frank Mason and Winifred Ashworth. BSc, Edinburgh U., Scotland, 1976, PhD, 1980. Embo fellow U. Geneva, 1980—82; rsch. fellow Imperial Cancer Rsch. Fund, London, 1982—85; sr. lectr. Royal Postgrad. Med. Sch., London, 1985—2000; reader in molecular genetics Imperial Coll., London, 2000—03; prof. Washington U. Sch. Medicine, St. Louis, 2004—. Contbr. articles to profl. jours. Achievements include research in the molecular genetics of G6PD deficiency; the molecular genetics of PNH; the molecular genetics of Dyskeratosis Congenita; the molecular genetics of Goodpasture's disease. Office: Washington U Med Sch Dept Internal Medicine Box 8125 660 S Euclid Ave Saint Louis MO 63110 Business E-Mail: pmason@dom.wustl.edu.

MASON, PHILLIP HOWARD, aircraft company executive, retired military officer; b. Cash, Va., Mar. 13, 1932; s. Phillip Howard and Mary Armisted (Hogg) M.; m. Frances Murray Gallogly, Mar. 3, 1962 (dec. 1995); children: Mary Catherine, Patrick Howard, Susan Frances, Sheryl Ann; m. Barbara Martin, Sept. 23, 2006. BS in BA, magna cum laude, St. Benedicts, 1966; MBA, Shippensburg State Coll., 1976; postgrad., U.S. Army Command and Gen. Staff Coll., 1965-66, U.S. Army War Coll., 1975-76. Enlisted in U.S. Army, 1948, advanced through grades to brig. gen., 1980, bn. comdr. 1st Bn., 1st ADA Ger., 1971-73, sec. gen. staff 32d Army Air Def. Command, 1974, systems coordinator ODCS-RDA, Dept Army Washington, 1975; project mgr. AD Command and Control Redstone Arsenal, Ala., 1976-78; comdr. 11th ADA Bde Fort Bliss, Tex., 1978-79; project mgr. STINGER Redstone Arsenal, 1979-83; dir. combat support system ODCSRDA, Dept. Army Washington; ret. U.S. Army, 1983; v.p. bus. devel. Sanders Assocs., Nashua, N.H., 1984-90; project mgr. Hughes Aircraft Co., 1990—; ret., 1998. Decorated Disting. Svc. medal, Legion of Merit with oak leaf cluster, Bronze star, Meritorious Svc. medal with two oak leaf clusters, Joint Svcs. Commendation medal, Army Commendation medal. Home: 3514 Gulf Blvd Saint Petersburg Beach FL 33706 Office Phone: 978-725-8044. Personal E-mail: phmason@verizon.net.

MASON, RAYMOND ADAMS (CHIP MASON), diversified financial services company executive; b. Lynchburg, Va., Sept. 28, 1936; s. Raymond Watsi and Marion (Adams) M.; married; children: Paige Adams, Pamela Ann, Carter Meade, Morgan Rand. BA in Econs., Coll. William and Mary, 1959. Rep. Mason & Lee Inc., Richmond, Va., 1960-62; founder, pres. Mason & Co. Inc., Newport News, Va., 1962-70; pres. Legg, Mason & Co., Inc., Washington, 1970-73, Legg, Mason Wood Walker, Inc., Balt., 1978—81, chmn.; chmn., pres., CEO Legg Mason, Inc., Balt., 1981—2008, non-exec. chmn., 2008—. Chmn. regional firms com. N.Y. Stock Exchange, 1978-81. Trustee emeritus Endowment Assn., Coll. William and Mary; bd. dirs. emeritus William and Mary Sch. Bus. Adminstrn. Sponsors, Inc.; former trustee Balt. Mus. Art; former bd. dirs. Nat. Aquarium, Balt.; bd. dirs., exec. com., chair fin. com. Johns Hopkins Hosp.; chmn. bd., exec. com. Johns Hopkins U.; former chmn. bd. sponsors Sch. Bus. & Mgmt. Loyola Coll., Balt., 1980-88; bd. dirs. Greater Balt. Com., 1982-84, chmn., 1987-89; chmn. United Way Ctrl. Md. Mem. Nat. Assn. Securities Dealers (bd. govs. 1971-75, chmn. bd. govs. 1974-75), Securities Industry Assn. (bd. dirs. 1982—, chmn. 1985-86, bd. govs. 1984-88, chmn. bd. govs. 1987). Clubs: Ctr., Md., Balt. Country, L'Hirondelle, Elkridge Club, Balt. Country Club, New Orleans Country Club. Office: Legg Mason Inc Bldg 100 Light St Baltimore MD 21202-6189

MASON, RAYMOND E., JR., distributing company executive; b. Columbus, Ohio, Mar. 20, 1920; s. Raymond E. and Lula Estella (Potter) Mason; m. Margaret E. Edwards, Feb. 6, 1942; children: Raymond E. III, Michael D., Bruce R. BS, Ohio State U., 1941; grad., U.S. Command and Gen. Staff, 1962, U.S. Army War Coll., 1965; D of Bus. Sci. (hon.), Ohio State U., 2001; D (hon.), Franklin U., 2004; D of laws (hon.), Cumberland Coll., 2003. Ops. mgr. Suburban Motor Freight, Columbus, 1946-47; pres., gen. mgr. CFL Lines, Columbus, 1947-48; pres., chmn. Columbus Truck & Equipment Co., 1949—. Pres., chmn. REM Realty, Columbus, 1962—, Bode-Finn Co., Cin., 1966—99; chmn. Ford Bros. Inc., Ironton, Ohio, 1975—79; mem. distbr. adv. coun. Mack Trucks; mng. dir. J. D. Ranch, Myakka City, Fla. Active Boy Scouts Am.; former trustee Freedoms Found. Valley Forge, Ohio Hist. Found.; vice-chmn. New Coll. Found.; dir. Mote Marine Lab. Ohio State U. Found.; chmn. bd. trustees emeritus Franklin U. With US Army, 1941—45, maj. gen. USAR. Decorated Bronze Star medal with V for Valor, Legion of Merit, Silver Star; recipient Pres. Unit citation, Truck Dealer of the Yr. award, Time mag., 1972, Good Scout award, Ctrl. Ohio Coun. Boy Scouts Am., Silver Beaver award, Boy Scouts Am., Silver Antelope award, Disting. Citizen of Yr. award, Centennial medal, Ohio State U., Pacesetters award, Coll. Bus. ISU, 1996, Virginia Steckler Internat. Svc. award, ARC, 1998, Lifetime Achievement award, Ohio State U., 1999, Harrison Sayre award, 2001, Philanthropist of the Yr., Columbus Found., 2001; named State of Ohio Vet. Hall of Fame, 1997, Buckeye Boys State Hall of Fame, 1999, Ohio State U. ROTC Hall of Fame, Jr. Achievement Ctrl. Ohio Bus. Hall of Fame, 2000; Baden-Powell fellow, World Scout Found. Mem.: Ohio Truck Assn., Am. Truck Dealers, Ohio State U. Alumni Assn., Army War Coll. Alumni Assn., Armor Assn., U.S. Army Arty. Assn., Columbus Club, Rotary (past dist. gov., Man of Yr., Paul Harris fellow), Masons. Office: Columbus Truck Equipment Co PO Box 83250 Columbus OH 43203-0250 Home: 85 Sugar Mill Dr Osprey FL 34229-9067

MASON, ROBERT MCSPADDEN, information scientist, educator, dean; b. Sweetwater, Tenn., Jan. 16, 1941; s. Paul Rankin and Ruby May (McSpadden) M.; m. Betty Ann Durrence (div. 1980); children: Michael Dean, Donald Robert; m. Marilyn Killebrew Gell, July 17, 1981. SB, MIT, Cambridge, 1963, SM, 1965; PhD, Ga. Inst. Tech., Atlanta, 1973. Tech. staff mem. Sandia Labs., Livermore, Calif., 1965-68; rsch. scientist Ga. Inst. Tech., Atlanta, 1971-75, sr. rsch. scientist, 1975; prin. Metrics, Inc., Atlanta, 1975-80; pres. Metrics Rsch. Corp., Atlanta, 1980-86, Cleve., 1986-98, Tallahassee, 1998—2005, Seattle, 2005—; adj. prof. Weatherhead Sch. Mgmt. Case Western U., 1987-88, vis. prof., 1988-91, prof. for practice of tech. mgmt., 1991-98; dir. Ctr. Mgmt. Sci. and Tech., 1988-96; Sprint prof. mgmt. and prof. mgmt. info. sys. Coll. Bus. Fla. State U., Tallahassee, 1998—2005, chair mgmt. info. sys., 1998—2002; prof. info. sch. U. Wash., Seattle, 2006—, assoc. dean rsch., 2006—. Co-author: The Impact of Office Automation on Clerical Employment, 1985-00, 1985, Library Micro Consumer, 1986; co-editor: Information Services: Economics, Management, and Technology, 1981, Management of Technology V: Technology Management in a Changing World, 1996, Management of Technology, Sustainable Development, and Eco-Efficiency, 1998, Management of Technology: The Key to Prosperity in the Third Millenium, 2001; Am. editor Technovation, 1994-2005, sr. editl. bd., 2005—; contbr. articles to profl. jours. Mem. Internat. Assn. for Tech. Mgmt. (newsletter editor 1992-93, program chair internat. conf., 1996, pres. 1996-98, mem. exec. com. 1998—, Disting. Achievement award 2007). Republican. Presbyterian. Avocations: flying, skiing, sailing, scuba diving, photography. Home: 2929 1st Ave Unit 1122 Seattle WA 98121 Office: Info Sch U Wash Seattle WA 98195-2840

MASON, SALLY KAY FROST, academic administrator, biology professor; b. NYC, May 29, 1950; d. Michael and Alberta Viparina; m. John S. Frost, Aug. 1975 (div. Feb. 1982); m. Kenneth Andrew Mason, Mar. 17, 1990. BA in Zoology, U. Ky., 1972; MS in Cell/Devel. Biology, Purdue U., 1974; PhD in Cell/Devel. Biology, U. Ariz., 1978. Rsch. assoc. Ind. U., Bloomington, 1978-80; asst. prof. biology U. Kans., Lawrence, 1980—86, assoc. prof. biology, 1986-91, prof. biology, 1991-2001, chair dept. physiology and cell biology, 1986-89, assoc. dean scis., 1990-95, dean arts and scis., 1995-2001; provost, prof. biology Purdue U., West Lafayette, Ind., 2001—07; pres. U. Iowa, 2007—. Chmn. bd. Inproteo, 2003—07; chmn. EHR adv. bd. NSF, 2005—06; mem. exec. com. Nat. Assn. State U. and Land Grant Colls., 2002—; mem. Pres.'s Nat. Medal of Sci. Selection Com., 2006—. Mem. editl. bd. Pigment Cell Rsch., 1988-99; contbr. chpts. to books and articles to profl. jours. Dissertation fellow AAUW, 1977-78, Kemper Tchg. fellow U. Kans., Lawrence, 1997; grantee NSF, NIH, Washington, 1981—; Wesley Found. grantee Welsey Health Found., Wichita, Kans., 1991-93. Mem. Internat. Fedn. Pigment Cell Scis. (coun. mem. 1997-2000), Pan Am. Soc. for Pigment Cell Rsch. (coun. mem. 1988-98, pres. 1996-98), Coun. Colls. Arts and Scis. (bd. mem. 1997-99, pres. elect 1999-2000, pres. 2000-2001), Chgo. Coun. Global Affairs Energy & Midwest Competitiveness Task Force (co chair 2008), Am. Coun. Edn. (bd. dirs. 2008-), Herbret Hoover Presdl. Libr. Assn. (bd. trustee, 2009-). Avocations: travel, reading, writing. Office: U Iowa Office of Pres 101 Jessup Hall Iowa City IA 52242-1316

MASON, SCOTT MACGREGOR, entrepreneur, inventor, consultant; b. NYC, Feb. 11, 1923; s. Gregory Mason and Mary Louise Turner; m. Mildred Davidson, Mar. 13, 1949 (div. 1970); children: Alan Gregory, Phoebe Louise, Caleb; m. Virginia Frances Perkins, May 5, 1970 (dec. 1990). AB, Princeton U., 1943; MS, NYU, 1947. Control chemist Firestone Tire & Rubber Co., Akron, Ohio, 1943-44; R & D chemist Am. Cyanamid Co. Rsch. Labs., Stamford, Conn., 1948-52; mgr. stearate dept. Warwick Chem. div. Sun Chem. Corp., Wood River Junction, R.I., 1952-58; cons., Stonington, Conn., 1958-59; instr. Williams Meml. Inst., New London, Conn., 1959-63; NSF fellow Brown U., Providence, 1963-64; tchr. Moses Brown Sch., Providence, 1964-70; owner, mgr. Innoventures, Wakefield, R.I., 1970—. Cons. Greene Plastics Corp., Canonchet, R.I., 1972-80, Dorette Inc., Pawtucket, R.I., 1982-83. Trustee Pine Point Sch., Stonington, 1956-62, pres. bd., 1959-61. With AUS, 1944-46, ETO. Named Tchr. of Week, Sta. WICE, Providence, 1967; summer rsch. fellow NSF, U. R.I., 1960. Mem. AAAS, N.Y. Acad. Scis. Achievements include patents in field. Avocations: tennis, fishing, snorkeling, photography, music. Office: Innoventures PO Box 369 Wakefield RI 02880-0369 Office Phone: 401-789-8073. Personal E-mail: smason19@cox.net.

MASON, STEVE, professional hockey player; b. Oakville, Ont., Can., May 29, 1988; Goaltender London Knights (OHL), 2005—08, Kitchener Rangers (OHL), 2008, Columbus Blue Jackets, 2008—. Goaltender Team Can., World Jr. Championships, Pardubice, Czech Republic, 2008. Recipient Calder Meml. Trophy, 2009; named NHL Rookie of Yr., Sporting News, 2009; named to NHL YoungStars Game, 2009, All-Rookie Team, NHL, 2009, Second All-Star Team, 2009. Achievements include being a member of Gold Medal Team Canada, World Junior Championships, 2008. Office: Columbus Blue Jackets Nationwide Arena 200 W Nationwide Blvd, Ste Level Columbus OH 43215*

MASON, TERRY, city health department administrator, urologist; BS, Loyola U., 1974; MD, U. of Ill. Abraham Lincoln Sch. Medicine, 1978. Pres., ptnr. Prairie Med. Associates; chief Urology Mercy Hosp., Chgo.; assistant prof. surgery Abraham Lincoln Sch. Medicine U. of Ill.; commr. dept. public health City of Chgo., 2006—. Host radio prog. Doctor in the House WVON, Chgo. Author: Making Love Again, Renewing Intimacy & Helping Your Man Overcome Impotence, 1988. Recipient Physician of the Year, Nat. Med. Assn., 1999, Black Enterprise Best in Medicine award, 2001. Fellow: Am. Coll. Surgeons; mem.: World Impotence Assn. (regional dir.), Am. Urological Assn., Nat. Med. Assn. (nat. chmn.), AMA, Saltpond Redevelopment Inst., Ghana West Africa, NAACP. Office: City of Chgo Dept Health 333 S State St Ste 200 Chicago IL 60604 also: Prairie Med Assocs Ltd 2600 S Michigan Ste 303 Chicago IL 60616*

MASON, THOMAS ALBERT, retired lawyer; b. Cleve., May 4, 1936; m. Elisabeth Gun Sward, Sept. 25, 1965; children: Thomas Lewis, Robert Albert. AB, Kenyon Coll., 1958; LLB, Case-Western Res. U., 1961. Bar: Ohio 1962. Assoc. Thompson Hine LLP, 1965-73, ptnr., 1973—2001, ret., 2002—. Trustee Cleve. YMCA, 1975-94. Capt. USMCR, 1962-65. Mem. Am. Coll. Real Estate Lawyers, Ohio Bar Assn., Cleve. Bar Assn.

MASON, THOMAS ALEXANDER, historian, educator, author; b. Port Huron, Mich., Oct. 29, 1944; s. Frank Hallgren and Charlotte (Hamilton) M.; m. Christine Huguette Guyonneau, Aug. 11, 1984; 1

child, Charlotte Guyonneau. BA in History with highest honors, Kenyon Coll., 1966; MA, U. Va., 1970, PhD, 1975. Asst. prof. history Pembroke (N.C.) State U., 1976-79; assoc. editor Papers of James Madison, U. Va., 1979-86, acting editor, 1986-87; dir. publs. Ind. Hist. Soc., 1987—2001, v.p. publs., 2001—02; v.p. Ind. Hist. Soc. Press, 2002—06; adj. faculty mem. Ind. U., Indpls., 2007—. Author: Serving God and Mammon: William Juxon, 1582-1663, 1985; exec. editor: Traces of Indiana and Midwestern History, 1989-2006; editor: Documentary Editing, 1989-93, Mag. of Albermarle County History, 1984-86; co-editor: Papers of James Madison, congl. series, vols. 14-16, 1983-89, presdl. series, vol. 1, 1984; project dir.: Papers of Lew and Susan Wallace, 4 DVDs, 2009; mem. editl. bd. Jour. of the Early Republic, 1991-95, Ency. of Indpls., 1990-94, Documentary Editing, 2002-06, AASLH Book Series, 2006-; contbr. articles to encys. and scholarly jours. Served with USMC, 1966-68. Mem. Am. Assn. for State and Local History (publs. com. chair 2006-08), Am. Hist. Assn., N.Am. Conf. on Brit. Studies, So. Hist. Assn., Ind. Assn. Historians (pres. 2008-09), Assn. Documentary Editing (councillor-at-large 1999-2002, dir. publs. 1995-98, Disting. Svc. award 1993), Hist. Soc. of the Episcopal Ch. (sec. 1995-2005, bd. dirs. 1993-2005), English-Speaking Union U.S. (chmn. region VI 1996-2002, bd. dirs. 1995-2002, pres. Indpls. br. 1989-96, Lily Dabney scholar 1972, Merit award 2002), Raven Soc., Rotary (Indpls., bd. dirs. 1998-2000), Colonnade Club (Charlottesville), Royal Commonwealth Soc. (London), Omicron Delta Kappa (faculty sec. Va. Cir. 1984-86), Alpha Delta Phi. Episcopalian. Home: PO Box 20331 Indianapolis IN 46220-0331

MASON, THOMAS P., lawyer; BA with high distinction, U. Nebr., 1978; JD with honors, U. Tex., 1981. Bar: Tex. 1981. Ptnr. Andrews & Kurth, Houston; sr. energy and securities ptnr. Vinson & Elkins, Houston, 2001—07; gen. counsel Energy Transfer Partners, LP, Dallas, 2007—. Office: Energy Transfer Group Ptnrs LLP 3738 Oak Lawn Ave Dallas TX 75219 Office Phone: 214-981-0700. Business E-Mail: tom.mason@energytransfer.com.

MASON, THOMASINE GRAYSON, judge; b. Summerton, SC, Nov. 7, 1918; d. James Fulton Grayson and Martha Anne Gentry; m. Edgar Fleming Mason, June 30, 1939 (dec.). BA, U. S.C., Columbia, 1938, LLB, 1942, JD, 1970. Certificate in cotton classing N.C. State Coll., 1956. Tchr., West Columbia, SC, 1938—39; civil svc. rep. during World War II Atlanta, Athens and Charleston Navy Yard; gen. practice of law Manning, SC; trial atty. Dept. Justice, Washington, 1969—71; fed. adminstrv. law judge Office of Disability Adjudication and Review, 1971—2009; hearing office chief adminstrv. law judge, 1985—2002. Bd. trustees Clarendon Meml. Hosp., Manning, SC; state senator SC; del. Nat. Dem. Conv., 1960. Mem.: Richland County Bar Assn., S.C. Bar Assn., ABA, DAR, Am. Legion Aux., Alpha Delta Pi. Republican. Baptist. Avocation: jet-skiing. Business E-Mail: thomasine.g.mason@ssa.gov.

MASON, WILLIAM, opera company director; b. Chgo. m. Diana Davis; 2 children. MusB, Roosevelt U. Chgo. Musical Coll. Asst. to co-artistic dir. Lyric Opera Chgo., 1962—66, asst. stage mgr., 1968—70, prodn. dir., 1974—78, dir. ops., artistic & prodn., 1981—97, gen. dir., 1997—; asst. to music adminstr. NYC Opera, 1971; prodn. stage mgr. Cin. Opera, 1972; musical preparation asst., stage mgr. Light Opera Manhattan, 1972; prod. mgr., asst. dir. Corbett Found., Ohio, 1973; artistic adminstr. San Francisco Opera, 1979—80. Mem. Lyric Children's Chorus, 1954—56. Decorated Comdr. dell'Ordine Della Stella Della Solidarieta' Italiana, Italy, 2003; recipient Dushkin award, Music Inst. Chgo., 2005. Office: Lyric Opera Chgo 20 N Wacker Dr Chicago IL 60606-2806 Office Phone: 312-332-2244.*

MASON, WILLIAM A(LVIN), psychologist, educator, researcher; b. Mountain View, Calif., Mar. 28, 1926; s. Alvin Frank and Ruth Sabina (Erwin) M.; m. Virginia Joan Carmichael, June 27, 1948; children: Todd, Paula, Nicole, Hunter. BA, Stanford U., 1950, MS, 1952, PhD, 1954. Asst. prof. U. Wis.-Madison, 1954-59; research assoc. Yerkes Labs. Primate Biology, Orange Park, Fla., 1959-63; head dept. behavioral sci. Delta Primate Research Ctr., Tulane U., Covington, La., 1963-71; prof. psychology, research psychologist U. Calif., Davis, 1971-91, leader behavioral biology unit Calif. Primate Rsch. Ctr., 1972-96, prof. emeritus, 1991. Bd. dirs. Jane Goodall Inst., 1978-92, Karisoke Rsch. Ctr., 1980-86. Mem. Editorial bd. Animal Learning and Behavior, 1973-76, Internat. Jour. Devel. Psychobiology, 1980-92, Internat. Jour. Primatology, 1980-90; contbr. numerous articles to profl. jours., chpts. to books. With USMC, 1944-46. USPHS spl. fellow, 1963-64. Fellow AAAS, APA (pres. divsn. 6 1982, disting. sci. contbn. award 1995), Am. Psychol. Soc., Animal Behavior Soc.; mem. Internat. Primatological Soc. (pres. 1976-80, 81-84), Am. Soc. Primatologists (pres. 1988-90, disting. primatologist award), Internat. Soc. Devel. Psychobiology (pres. 1971-72, Best Paper of Yr. award 1976), Sigma Xi. Home: 2809 Anza Ave Davis CA 95616-0257 Office: U Calif Regl Primate Rsch Ctr 1 Shields Ave Davis CA 95616 Home Phone: 530-756-2479. Business E-Mail: wamason@ucdavis.edu.

MASONER, JASON R., hydrologist; s. Sue Winters; m. Tammy K. Biggs, Feb. 14, 1993; children: Hanna, Jasey, Masoner Rylee. BS, East Ctrl. U., Ada, Okla., 1997. Hydrologist US Geol. Survey, Oklahoma City, 1997—. Achievements include patents for floating evaporation pan.

MASONIS, TODD, Internet company executive; BS, Stanford Univ. Systems developer e-steam Inc.; co-founder netElement, 1999, Natient Technologies; co-founder, v.p. products Plaxo Inc., Mountain View, Calif., 2001—. Office: Plaxo Inc 203 Ravendale Dr Mountain View CA 94043 Office Phone: 650-254-5402. Office Fax: 650-254-1435. Business E-Mail: todd@plaxo.com.

MASON-LIPTON, HOLLI MARIE, pathologist, educator; b. Grangeville, Idaho, Nov. 21, 1963; d. Lynn David and Joan Karen Bircher Mason; m. Dennis Arthur Lipton, June 27, 2004; children: Samantha Ashley Lipton, Kimberly Hope Lipton; m. Scott Michael Mathews, May 28, 1988 (div. Sept. 11, 2003); children: Paige Erin Mathews, Mason James Mathews, Grant Michael Mathews. MD, Med. Coll. Va., Richmond, 1995; BA in Linguistics, U. Oreg., Eugene, 1986, BA in Speech Pathology and Audiology, 1986. Lic. physician and surgeon Calif., 1996. Assoc. clin. prof. pathology David Geffen Sch. Medicine, UCLA, 2001—. Dir., transfusion medicine and serology Harbor UCLA Med. Ctr., Torrance, 2001—, chair, blood utilisation com., 2001—, chair pathology quality improvement com., 2003—, dir., pathology residency tng. program, 2006—. Contbr. articles to profl. jours. Mem. ARC, Southern Calif. Divsn., Pomona, 2001—08, bd. dirs., 2001—08, med. adv. com. mem., 2003—, exec. bd. dirs., 2007—08; mem. Hemorrhage Task Force, Calif. Maternal Quality Care Collaborative, San Francisco, 2007. Mem.: Calif. Blood Bank Soc. (Sacramento, Calif.) (bd. dir. 2006—), Am. Assn. Blood Bankers, Woodland Hills Rock Chippers. Independent. Office: Harbor UCLA Med Ctr 1000 W Carson St Torrance CA 90509 Personal E-mail: hmm_md@yahoo.com.

MASOTTI, LOUIS HENRY, real estate educator, consultant; b. NYC, May 16, 1934; s. Henry and Angela Catherine (Turi) Masotti; m. Iris Patricia Leonard, Aug. 28, 1958 (div. 1981); children: Laura Lynn, Andrea Anne; m. Ann Randel Humm, Mar. 5, 1988. AB, Princeton U., 1956; MA, Northwestern U., 1961, PhD, 1964. Fellow Nat. Ctr. Edn. in Politics, 1962; asst. prof. polit. sci. Case Western Res. U., Cleve., 1963-67, assoc. prof., 1967-69, dir. Civil Violence Rsch. Ctr., 1968-69; sr. Fulbright lectr. Johns Hopkins U. Ctr. Advanced Internat. Studies, Bologna, Italy, 1969-70; assoc. prof. Northwestern U., Evanston, Ill., 1970-72, prof. polit. sci. and urban affairs, 1972-83, dir. Ctr. Urban Affairs, 1971-80, dir. Program in Pub. and Not-for-Profit Mgmt., Kellogg Sch. Mgmt., 1979-80, prof. mgmt. and urban devel. Kellogg Sch. Mgmt., 1983-94, dir. Real Estate Research Ctr. Kellogg Sch. Mgmt., 1986-88. Cons. in field; vis. assoc. prof. U. Wash., 1969; exec. dir. Mayor Jane Byrne Transition Com., Chgo., 1979; vis. prof. Stanford Sch. Bus., 1989—92, UCLA Sch. Mgmt., 1989—92; prof., dir. real estate mgmt. program U. Calif. Grad. Sch. Mgmt., Irvine, 1992—98; bd. dirs. Mfd. Home Cmtys., Inc., Facilities Mgmt. Internat., S. Calif. Physicans Ins. Co. Author: (book) Educaiton and Politics in Suburbia, 1967, Shootout in Cleveland, 1969, A Time to Burn?, 1969, Suburbia in Transition, 1973, The New Urban Politics, 1976, The City in Comparative Perspective, 1976; co-editor: Metropolis in Crisis, 1968, Metropolis in Crisis, 2d edit., 1971, Riots and Rebellion, 1968, The Urbanization of the Suburbs, 1973, After Daley: Chicago Politics in Transition, 1981, Downtown Development, 1985, Downtown Development, 2d edit., 1987; editor: Edn. and Urban Soc., 1968—71, Urban Affairs Quar., 1973—80; sr. editor: Econ. Devel. Quar., 1986—92, vice chmn. bd.: Ill. Issues Jour., 1986—92, BOMA Office Mag., 1990—95. Mem. Cleveland Heights Bd. Edn., 1967—69; devel. coord. high tech. State of Ill. - City of Chgo., 1982—83; Rsch. dir. Carl Stokes for Mayor Cleve., 1967; advisor to various congl., gubernatorial and mayoral campaigns Ohio, Ill., NJ, Calif. Lt. USNR, 1956—59. Recipient Disting. Svc. award, Cleve. Jaycees, 1967; fellow, Homer Hoyt Inst. Advanced Real Estate Studies; numerous rsch. grants, 1963—2000. Mem.: Internat. Econ. Devel. Coun., Nat. Assn. Indsl. Office Properties, Internat. Devel. Rsch. Coun., Internat. Assn. Corp. Real Estate Execs., Nat. Trust Hist. Preservation, Habitat, Urban Land Inst., Lambda Alpha Internat. Address: 2010 W Twinoaks Dr Prescott AZ 86305 Office Phone: 619-750-1703. Personal E-mail: louismasotti@mac.com.

MASRANI, BHARAT B., bank executive; Grad., York U., Canada, 1978; MBA, 1979. Vice chair, pres., CEO TD Waterhouse Europe; sr. v.p. Toronto-Dominion Bank; pres., CEO TD Waterhouse Internat., 2002, e.Bank, 2002; exec. v.p., Toronto-Dominion Bank, 2002—03; vice chair Credit Asset Mgmt. TD Securities LLC, 2002—03; exec. v.p. risk mgmt. Toronto-Dominion Bank, 2003—05, vice chmn., chief risk officer, 2005—06; dir. TD Banknorth Inc., 2005—06, pres., 2006—07, pres., CEO, 2007—. Office: TD Banknorth Inc Two Portland Square 7th Fl Portland ME 04101 Office Phone: 207-761-8541. Office Fax: 207-761-6673.

MASRI, MERLE SID, biochemist, consultant; b. Jerusalem, Palestine, Sept. 12, 1927; came to U.S., 1947; s. Said Rajab and Fatima M.; m. Maryjean Loretta Anderson, June 28, 1952 (div. 1974); children: Kristin Corinne, Allan Eric, Wendy Joan, Heather Anderson. BA in Physiology, U. Calif., Berkeley, 1950; PhD in Mammalian Physiology and Biochemistry, U. Calif. Berkeley, 1953. Rsch. asst. Dept. Physiology, Univ. Calif., Berkeley, 1950-53; predoctoral fellow Baxter Labs., Berkeley, 1952-53; rsch. assoc. hematology Med. Rsch. Inst., Michael Reese Hosp., Chgo., 1954-56; sr. rsch. biochemist Agrl. Rsch. Svc., USDA, Berkeley, 1956-87; supervisory rsch. scientist Agrl. Rsch. Svc., USDA, N.D. State U. Sta., Fargo, ND, 1987-89; pvt. practice as cons. Emeryville, Calif., 1989—. Lectr. in field. Contbr. articles to profl. jours.; chpts. to books. Recipient Spl. Svc. and Merit awards USDA, 1966, 76, 77, Superior Svc. award USDA, 1977. Mem. AAAS, Am. Chem. Soc., Am. Oil Chemists Soc., Am. Assn. Cereal Chemists, N.Y. Acad. Scis., Inst. Food Technologists, Commonwealth Club Calif., Internat. Platform Assn., World Affairs Coun. of No. Calif., Sigma Xi. Achievements include patents for detoxification of aflatoxins in agricultural crops and aflatoxin contaminated milk, improved dyeability of cotton fabrics and reduced dye and electrolyte discharge in plant effluent, new closed-circuit raw wool scouring technology to conserve water and energy and control pollution, synthesis and use of polymers and modification of biopolymers for wastewater treatment, and for encapsulation, enzyme immobilization, toxic heavy metals removal and textile finishing treatment, non-polluting new technology for scouring raw wool in a closed circuit with water recycling and re-use and waste effluent control; studied chlorination of water in food processing operations and water re-use and recycle and the generation of mutagens and means of improving disinfection efficiency and reducing mutagen formation, pharmacology, metabolism, and toxicology of natural and synthetic compounds, cereal and baking technology and wheat and durum quality, carbohydrate chemistry, fermentation and enology, confectionery, ceramic chemistry and digital graphic art image production; discovery of new methods and reagents for protein and amino acid residue modification and analysis, new mammalian metabolic pathways; development of other non-polluting textile finishing treatments (shrink, wrinkle, insect and fire resistance). Home: 9 Commodore Dr Emeryville CA 94608-1652

MASRI, TAHER NASHAT, Jordanian government official; b. Nablus, Jordan, Mar. 5, 1942; s. Nashat and Hadiyyah (Solh) M.; m. Samar Bitar Masri, Dec. 31, 1967; children: Nashat, Nadine. BBA, North Tex. State U., Denton, 1965. Dep. chief dept. fin. Cen. Bank of Jordan, 1965-73; mem. Lower House of Parliament, Jordan, 1973-74, 84-88, 89-93, 93-97; min. of state for occupied ter. affairs, 1973-74; amb. to Spain, 1975-78; amb. to France, 1978-83; rep. UNESCO, 1978-83, EEC, 1978-80; amb. to U.K., 1983-84; min. fgn. affairs, 1984-88, 91; dep. prime min., min. econ. affairs, 1989; chmn. fgn. rels. com., 1989-91; prime min., min. def., 1991; speaker Lower House of Parliament, 1993-94, 2005—; mem. Upper House of Parliament (senate), 1998—2001, 2005—. Mem., reporter Royal Com. for Drafting Nat. Chpt. Chmn., bd. trustees Jordan U. Sci. and Tech., 1998—. Named Grand Cordon of the Jewelled Al-Nahda, Jordan, Al-Nahda 1st degree, Jordan, Al-Kawkab 1st degree, Jordan, Grande Officier de Legion d'Honeur, France, Commandre Legion d'Honeur, France, Grand Brit. Empire, Grande Officier de l'Order Nat. Merite, Knight of Grand Cross of The Order of the Republic if Italy, Grande Cordon de l'Ordre Nat. de Cedre, Lebanon; recipient Isabela Catolica award Spain, Merito Civil award Spain, Grand Decoration of Honour in Gold with Sash for Svcs. to Republic of Austria, Merit Gwanghawa medal Order of Diplomatic Svc., Korea; named to Grand Brit. Empire. Office: PO Box 5550 Amman 11183 Jordan Office Phone: 962-6-4642227.

MASS, MYRON FRANK, allergist, immunologist; b. Phila., Feb. 24, 1945; m. Marilyn Halpern, June 12, 1966; children: Ellis, David. Student, U. Fla., 1963; BA, Brandeis U., 1966; MD, U. Fla., 1970; postgrad., U. Colo., Albany, NY, 1972, U. Colo., Denver, 1975. Intern Albany Med. Ctr., NY, 1970-71, residency, 1971-72; sr. residency U. Colo. Med. Ctr., Denver, 1972-73, postgrad. fellow/allergy-immunology, 1973-75; assoc. clin. prof. medicine U. Fla., Jacksonville, 1977—. Past chmn. dept. medicine Meml. Med. Ctr., Jacksonville; prin. investigator Jacksonville Ctr. for Clin. Rsch. Inventor skin chamber. Chmn. Duval County Environ. Protection Bd.; trustee Fla. CC at Jacksonville, 1999-2007, also bd. trustees. Maj. USAF, 1975-77. Health Professions scholar U. Fla. Fellow ACP, Am. Acad. Allergy and Immunology, Am. Coll. Allergy; mem. Duval County Med. Soc. (v.p., pres.-elect, pres.). Office: 3636 University Blvd S Ste B2 Jacksonville FL 32216-4223 Office Phone: 904-733-8200. E-mail: massjax@comcast.net.

MASSA, CONRAD HARRY, retired religious studies educator; b. Bklyn., Oct. 27, 1927; s. Harry Frederick and Josephine W. (Lepold) M.; m. Anna W. Rossi, Aug. 19, 1951; children: Stephen Mark, Barbara Ann. AB with honors, Columbia U., 1951; M.Div., Princeton Theol. Sem., 1954, PhD, 1960; HHD, Lafayette Coll., 1987. Ordained to ministry Presbyn. Ch., 1954. Pastor Elmwood Presbyn. Ch., East Orange, NJ, 1954-57; asst. prof. homiletics Princeton Theol. Sem., 1957-61; sr. pastor Old First Ch., Newark, 1961-66, Third Presbyn. Ch., Rochester, NY, 1966-78; dean acad. affairs Princeton Theol. Sem., 1978-94, dean emeritus, 1994—, Charlotte W. Newcombe prof., 1978-95, Charlotte W. Newcombe prof. emeritus, 1995—. 1st moderator Synod of the Northeast, United Presbyn. Ch.; vis. prof. St. Bernard's Roman Cath. Sem., Rochester, 1968-70; keynote speaker 11th ann. conf. Inst. Theology, Yonsei U., Seoul, Republic of Korea, 1991, pres. Marion County Audubon Soc. Author articles and book revs. Trustee Lafayette Coll., Easton, Pa., 1982-93. Served with U.S. Army, 1946-47. Mem. Acad. Homiletics, Am. Acad. Religion, Internat. John Bunyan Soc. Home: 9583 SW 90th St Ocala FL 34481-7495 E-mail: chm1@sprynet.com. *I have learned to try to understand all events and persons in terms of their relationships to other things, persons and events. While it is sometimes fruitful to isolate a particular and study it in its solitude, nothing and no one really exists in such isolation. This has become a guiding principle in my continued research and growth in those areas of greatest interest - religion, education and society.*

MASSA, ERIC J.J., United States Representative from New York, retired military officer, former congressional aide; b. Charleston, SC, Sept. 16, 1959; m. Beverly Massa; children: Alexandra, Justin, RiChard. Grad., US Naval Acad., Annapolis, Md., 1981. Commd. officer US Navy, spl. asst. to Gen. Wesley Clark; with photonics divsn. Corning Inc., with automotive environ. divsn.; profl. staff mem. US House Armed Services Com.; mem. US Congress from 29th NY Dist., 2009—. Served in USN, 1981—2001. Decorated Gold Star, Def. Meritorious Svc. Medal, Navy Commendation Medal, Navy Achievement Medal, Legion of Merit, Meritorious Service Medal. Democrat. Roman Catholic. Office: US Congress 1208 Longworth House Office Bldg Washington DC 20515-3229 also: Dist Office 101 Grove St Ste 101 Pittsford NY 14534 Office Phone: 202-225-3161, 585-218-0040, 607-654-7566. Office Fax: 202-226-6599. Business E-Mail: eric.massa@mail.house.gov.*

MASSAD, STEPHEN ALBERT, lawyer; b. Wewoka, Okla., Dec. 20, 1950; s. Alexander Hamilton and Delores Jean (Razook) Massad; children: Caroline, Sarah, Margaret. AB, Princeton U., 1972; JD, Harvard U., 1975. Bar: Tex. 1975. Assoc. Baker Botts LLP, Houston, 1975-82, ptnr., 1983—, corporate dept. chair, 1994—2002, mem. exec. com., 1995—2001. Office: Baker Botts LLP 3000 One Shell Plz 910 Louisiana St Houston TX 77002 Office Phone: 713-229-1475. Business E-Mail: stephen.massad@bakerbotts.com.

MASSAD, TIMOTHY G., lawyer; b. New Orleans, July 30, 1956; s. Alexander H. and Delores Massad. AB magna cum laude, Harvard U., 1978, JD magna cum laude, 1984. Bar: NY 1985. Assoc. Cravath Swaine & Moore LLP, NYC, 1984—92, ptnr., corp., 1992—, resident ptnr. Hong Kong, 1998—2002. Corp. counsel Covenant House; vice chmn. Norwalk Redevel. Agy.; pres. Norwalk CC Found.; bd. dirs. and exec. com. US-India Bus. Coun. Mem.: ABA, Internat. Bar Assn., NYC Bar Assn., NY State Bar Assn., Phi Beta Kappa. Office: Cravath Swaine & Moore LLP Worldwide Plz 825 Eighth Ave New York NY 10019-7475 Office Phone: 212-474-1154. Office Fax: 212-474-3700. Business E-Mail: tmassad@cravath.com.

MASSARO, TONI MARIE, retired dean, law educator; BS highest distinction, Northwestern U., 1977; JD, Coll. William and Mary, 1980. Assoc. Vedder, Price, Kaufman and Kammholz, Chgo., 1980—82; asst. prof. Washington and Lee U., U. Fla., 1982—84; prof. law U. Ariz., Tucson, 1989—, regents prof., Milton O. Riepe chair constl. law James E. Rogers Coll. Law, 1997—, dean James E. Rogers Coll. Law, 1999—2009. Vis. asst. prof. law U. Fla., 1984—85; vis. prof. Johann Goethe U., Frankfurt, Germany, 1988, U. NC, 1989, Stanford U., 1989. Author: Constitutional Literacy: A Core Curriculum for a Multi-Cultural Nation; co-author: Civil Procedure: Cases and Problems, 4thedit., 2009; contbr. articles to law revs. Recipient Women on the Move award, YWCA, 2002, Leslie F. and Patricia Bell Faculty Award, 1998, Judge Leonard hand Pub. Svc. award, 2009. Fellow: Am. Bar Found.; mem.: Ariz. State Bar (Access to Justice com. 2003—04, Professionalism com. 2002—), Am. Law Inst., Am. Assn. Law Schs. (Academic Freedom and Tenure com. 2000—04), Order of the Coif. Office: U Ariz Coll Law 1201 E Speedway PO Box 210176 Tucson AZ 85721-0176 Office Phone: 520-626-2687. Office Fax: 520-621-9140. Business E-Mail: massaro@law.arizona.edu.

MASSE, WILLIAM BRUCE, archaeologist; b. San Diego, July 10, 1948; s. Gerald John Masse and Viola Hope Bumgarner; m. Judith Lee Peters, Sept. 12, 1971; 1 child, Jeffrey Alan. BA in Anthropology, Stanford U., 1971; MA in Anthropology, U. Ariz., 1977; PhD in Anthropology, So. Ill. U., 1990. Archeologist Nat. Park Svc., Tucson, 1977-79, Ariz. State Mus., Tucson, 1985-86; field archaeologist State Historic Preservation Office, Honolulu, 1988-89; pacific area archaeologist Dept. of Navy, Pearl Harbor, Hawaii, 1990-94; archaeologist Dept. Air Force, Luke Air Force Base, Ariz., 1995-98, Los Alamos (N.Mex.) Nat. Lab., 1999—. Editor: The Protohistoric Period in the North American Southwest, 1981; contbr.: Chaco and Hohokam: Prehistoric Regional Systems in the North American Southwest, 1991, Natural Catastrophes During Bronze Age Civilizations: Archaeological, Geological, Astronomical, and Cultural Perspectives, 1998; editor (spl. issue) Jour. S.W., 1996; contbr. articles to profl. jours. Mem.: AAAS, Soc. Am. Archaeology (repatriation com. 1998—2001), Am. Anthrop. Assn., Sigma Xi. Office: Los Alamos Nat Lab RRES-ECO Ecology Group Mail Stop M887 Los Alamos NM 87545 Fax: (505)667-0731. E-mail: wbmasse@lanl.gov.

MASSENET, NATALIE, internet entrepreneur; b. LA; m. Arnaud Massenet; children: Isabella, Ava. Grad., UCLA, 1987. Prodn. asst. film co.; stylist Moda mag.; with Women's Wear Daily, 1993; sr. fashion editor Tatler mag., London; freelance stylist Isabella Blow; founder, chmn. Net-a-Porter, London, 2000—. Recipient award, MBE Svcs. Fashion Industry, 2009; named Entrepreneur of Yr., Harpers & Queen/Chanel, 2005, European Bus. Leaders, 2008. Office: Net-a-Porter The Dome Whiteleys Cen 15 Queensway London W2 4YN England

MASSENGALE, MARTIN ANDREW, agronomist, educator, university president; b. Monticello, Ky., Oct. 25, 1933; s. Elbert G. and Orpha (Conn) M.; m. Ruth Audrey Klingelhofer, July 11, 1959; children: Alan Ross, Jennifer Lynn. BS, Western Ky. U., 1952; MS, U. Wis., 1954, PhD, 1956; LHD (hon.), Nebr. Wesleyan U., 1987; DS (hon.), Senshu U., Tokyo, 1995. Cert. profl. agronomist, profl. crop scientist. Research asst. agronomy U. Wis., 1952-56; asst. prof., asst. agronomist U. Ariz., 1958-62, assoc. prof., assoc. agronomist, 1962-65, prof., agronomist, 1965-76, head dept., 1966-74, assoc. dean Coll. Agr. assoc. dir. Ariz. Agr. Expt. Sta., 1974-76; vice chancellor for agr. and natural resources U. Nebr., 1976-81; chancellor U. Nebr.-Lincoln, 1981-91, interim pres., 1989-91; pres. U. Nebr., 1991-94, pres. emeritus, 1994, found. disting. prof. and dir., 1994—. Chmn. pure seed adv. com. Ariz. Agrl. Expt. Sta.; past chmn. bd., pres. Mid-Am. Internat. Agrl. Consortium; coord. com. environ. quality EPA-Dept. Agrl. Land Grand U.; past chmn. bd. dir. Am. Registry Cert. Profls. in Agronomy, Crops and Soils; bd. dir. Ctr. for Human Nutrition, Lincoln Ins. Group., Woodmen Accident & Life Co., LIG, Inc., Am. First, LLC, All Am. Enterprises, LLC; chair bd. dir. Agronomic Sci. Found., chmn. selection com; dir. devel. Secretariat, Filippo Maseri Florio World Prize Disting. Rsch. in Agr.; exec. com. U. Nebr. Tech. Park, LLC; mem. adv. bd. Nat. Agrl. Rsch., Ext., Edn. and Econs., 1998—, chair secs. nat. adv. bd., exec. com.; nat. adv. bd. Trees Am., 1998—. Chmn. NCAA Pres.'s Commn., 1988-91; distbn. revenue com., standing com. on appointments North Ctrl. Assn. Commn. on Insts. Higher Edn., 1991; trustee Nebr. Hist. Soc. Found.; bd. dir. Nebr. Hist. Soc.; bd. govs. Nebr. Sci. and Math. Initiative; mem. Knight Found. Commn. on Intercollegiate Athletics; bd. dir. Great Plains Funds, IBP; hon. life trustee Nebr. Coun. on Econ. Edn.; hon. lifetime trustee Nebr. Coun. on Econ. Edn.; bd. dir., trustee U. Nebr. Found. With U.S. Army, 1956-58. Named Midlands Man of Yr., 1982, to We. Ky. U. Hall of Disting. Alumni, 1992, DeKalb Crop Sci. Disting. Career award, 1996, Outstanding Educator Am., 1970, Wayne County H.S., Monticello, Ky., Charter Hall of Fame, 2002; recipient faculty recognition award Tucson Trade Bur., 1971, Ak-Sar-Ben Agrl. Achievement award, 1986, Agrl. Builders Nebr. award, 1986, Walter K. Beggs award, 1986, Vol. of Yr. award for disting. svc. Nebr. Coun. on Econ. Edn., IANR Team Initiation award, Agri award Triumph of Agr. Expn., 1999, Exemplary Svc. to Agr. award Nebr. AgRels. Coun., 2000, Friend of LEAD award Nat. LEAD Alumni Assn., 2001, Outstanding Pres. award All-Am. Football Found., 2001, Wagonmaster award Nebraskaland Found., 2006; named to Charter Hall of Fame, USDA, 2004; hon. state farmer degrees Ky., Ariz., Nebr. Future Farmers Am. Assn. Fellow AAAS (sect. chmn.), Crop Sci. Soc. Am. (past dir., pres. 1972-73, past assoc. editor, pres. western soc., Disting. Career award 1996), Am. Soc. Agronomy (past dir., vis. scientist program, past assoc. editor Agronomy Jour., Disting. Svc. award 1984); mem. Am. Grassland Coun., Ariz. Crop Improvement Assn. (bd. dir.), Am. Soc. Plant Physiology, Nat. Assn. Colls. and Tchrs. Agr., Soil and Water Conservation Soc. Am., Ariz. Acad. Sci., Nebr. Acad. Sci., Agrl. Coun. Am. (bd. dirs., issues com.), Coun. Agrl. Sci. and Tech. (bd. dir. budget and fin. 1979-82, 94-2005, treas., exec. com. 1997-2005), Nat. Assn. State Colls. and Land Grant Univs. (chmn. com. on info. tech. 1987-94, exec. com. 1990-92, bd. dir. 1992-94), Edn. Engring. Professions (mem. commn.), Coll. Football Assn. (chmn., bd. dir. 1986-88), Am. Assn. State Coll. and Univs. (task force instl. resource allocation), AAFL Enterprises LLC (bd. dir., 2004—), Assn. Am. Univs. Rsch. Librs. (steering com. 1992-94), Nebr. Crop Improvement Assn. (Disting. Svc. award), Grazing Lands Forum (pres.), Nebr. C. of C. and Industry, Nebr. Diplomats Inc. (hon. diplomate), Nebr. Vet. Med. Assn. (hon.), Sigma Xi, Phi Kappa Phi, Gamma Sigma Delta (Merit award, 1997, Agriculture award, 2008), UNL Coll. Agrl. Scis. & Natural Resources(Alumni Assoc. Svc. award, 2009), Alpha Zeta, Phi Sigma, Gamma Alpha, Alpha Gamma Rho (bd. dir. ednl. found. 2004—, Bros. of the Century award), Phi Beta Delta, Golden Key, Innocents Soc. Office: U Nebr 306 Biochemistry Hall Lincoln NE 68583-0736 Office Phone: 402-472-4101. Business E-Mail: mmassengale1@unl.edu.

MASSETTI, TONY J., computer services company executive; With IBM, CFO tech. group; CEO Aurum Solutions, Ltd., Hong Kong, 2000—01; sr. dir., v.p. fin. Sandisk Corp., 2001—02; v.p. fin. QLogic Corp., 2002—04, sr. v.p., CFO, 2004—08; CFO NCR Corp., Dayton, Ohio, 2008—. Office: NCR Corp 1700 S Patterson Blvd Dayton OH 45479 Office Phone: 937-445-1936.

MASSEY, CHARLES KNOX, JR., advertising agency executive; b. Durham, NC, Jan. 16, 1936; s. Charles Knox and Louise (Southerl) M.; m. Mary Ann Keith, Aug. 27, 1960; children: Elizabeth, Knox, Louise. BS in Bus. Adminstrn, U. N.C., Chapel Hill, 1959. Account exec. Tucker Wayne & Co., advt. agy., Atlanta, 1964-78, pres., 1978-88, Tucker Wayne/Luckie & Co., Atlanta, 1988-95; chmn., CEO West Wayne, Inc., Atlanta, 1996—2000; mng. gen. ptnr. Keith Massey Family Investments LLLP, 2000—. Trustee The Lovett Sch., Atlanta. Mem. Piedmont Driving Club (pres. 1990-92), Highlands (N.C.) Country Club, Univ. Club (N.Y.C.). Episcopalian. Home: 67 Brighton Rd NE Atlanta GA 30309-1518 Office: PO Box 77388 Atlanta GA 30357

MASSEY, DENISE MCLAIN, theology studies educator; d. Dennis Ray and Eltimae Laird McLain; m. Charles Patrick Massey, Jan. 8, 1983; children: Patrick Thomas, Christopher Aaron. BA, La. Coll., Pineville, 1980; MDiv, Southern Bapt. Theol. Sem., Louisville, Ky., 1984, ThM, 1987, PhD, 1991. Cert. ordination to pastoral ministry Highland Bapt. Ch., 1988, supr. Assn. Clin. Pastoral Edn., 1998. Tchg. fellow, group supr. Southern Bapt. Theol. Sem., 1984—89, asst. prof. psychology religion, pastoral care, 1991—96, clin. assoc., vis. assoc., vis. prof. psychology religion, pastoral care, 1996—2001; chaplain Twinbrook Nursing Home, Louisville, 1986—88, Veterans Affairs Med. Ctr., Louisville, 1988—91; clin. pastoral edn. supr. Louisville Cluster Clin. Pastoral Edn., 1987—93, 1996—98; supr. pastoral care Kindred Hosp. Louisville, 1998—2003; pastoral counselor Pastoral Counseling & Consultation Ctr., Louisville, 2000—03; assoc. prof. pastoral care, counseling McAfee Sch. Theology; Mercer U., Atlanta, 2003—; coach life, spiritual, dreams-guided Internat. Coaching Fedn., Atlanta, 2007—. Editl. bd. Jour. Pastoral Care & Counseling. Contbr. articles to profl. jours., sermon to be sermons voices Womens Spirituality. Task force Ky. Hosp. Assn., Louisville, 2002—03; parent tchr. assn. mem. Mountain Pk. Elem., Trickum Mid., Parkview High, Lilburn, Ga., 2003—09; respondent Nat. Summit Torture, Atlanta, 2008; workshop leader Inst. Healthy Congregations, Atlanta, 2008; deacon, worship leader, tchr. Oakhurst Bapt. Ch., Decatur, Ga.; profl. adv. com. Care & Counseling Ctr. Ga., Decatur, 2004—09, Children's Healthcare, Atlanta, 2008—09; mem. bd. dirs. Jefferson Alcohol & Drug Abuse Ctr., Louisville, 1992—96. Recipient Outstanding Svc. award, Dept. Veterans Affairs, 1991. Mem.: Bapt. Women Ministry Ga., Soc. Pastoral Theology, Internat. Coaching Fedn., Assn. Clin. Pastoral Edn. (spkr. 1991—2008, certification commn., SE region 2006, certification commn., east ctrl. region, sem. adv. coun.). Avocations: reading, cooking. Office: McAfee Sch Theology 3001 Mercer University Dr Atlanta GA 30341 Home: 5255 Country Lake Ct Lilburn GA 30047 Office Fax: 678-547-6478. Business E-Mail: denise.massey@gmail.com.

MASSEY, JAMES EARL, retired clergyman, educator; b. Ferndale, Mich., Jan. 4, 1930; s. George Wilson and Elizabeth (Shelton) M.; m. Gwendolyn Inez Kilpatrick, Aug. 4, 1951. Student, U. Detroit, 1949-50, 55-57; BTh, BRE, Detroit Bible Coll., 1961; AM, Oberlin Grad Sch. Theology, 1964; postgrad., U. Mich., 1967-69; DD, Asbury Theol. Sem., 1972, Ashland Theol. Sem., 1991, Huntington Coll., 1994; HumD, Tuskegee U., 1995; DD, Warner Pacific Coll., 1995; LittD, Anderson U., 1995; DD, Wash. and Jefferson Coll., 1997, North Park Theol. Sem., 1999. Ordained to ministry Ch. of God, 1951. Assoc. min. Ch. of God, Detroit, 1951-53; sr. pastor Met. Ch. of God, Detroit, 1954-76, pastor-at-large, 1976; spkr. Christian Brotherhood Hour, 1977-82; prin. Jamaica Sch. Theology, Kingston, 1963-66; campus min. Anderson Coll., Ind., 1969-77, asst. prof. religious studies Ind., 1969-75, assoc. prof. Ind., 1975-80, prof. N.T. and homiletics Ind., 1981-84; dean of chapel and univ., prof. religion and society Tuskegee U., Ala., 1984-89; dean, prof. preaching and bibl. studies Anderson Sch. Theology, 1989-95, dean emeritus, prof. at large, 1995—; dean emeritus Tuskegee U. Chapel, 1998—; ret., 1998. Chmn. Comm. on Higher Edn. in the Ch. of God, 1968-71; vice chmn. bd. publs. Ch. of God, 1968-78; dir. Warner Press, Inc.; rsch. scholar Christianity Today Inst. Author: When Thou Prayest, 1960, The Worshipping Church, 1961, Raymond S. Jackson, A Portrait, 1967, The Soul Under Seige, 1970, The Church of God and the Negro, 1971, The Hidden Disciplines, 1972, The Responsible Pulpit, 1973, Temples of the Spirit, 1974, The Sermon in Perspective, 1976, Concerning Christian Unity, 1979; gen. editor: Christian Brotherhood Hour Study Bible, 1979, Designing the Sermon, 1980; co-editor: Interpreting God's Word for Today, 1982; editor: Educating for Service, 1984, The Spiritual Disciplines, 1985, The Bridge Between, 1988, Preaching From Hebrews, 1992, The Burdensome Joy of Preaching, 1996, Sundays at The Tuskegee Chapel, 1999, Aspects of My Pilgrimage: An Autobiography, 2002, Remembering William L. Dawson, 2004, African Americans and the Church of God, 2005, Stewards of the Story, 2005; mem. editl. bd. The Christian Scholar's Rev. Leadership mag.; mem. editl. bd., contbg. editor Vol I New Interpreter's Bible, 1990—; contbg. editor Preaching mag.; sr. editor Christianity Today mag. Mem. Corp. Inter-Vrsity Christian Fellowship; bd. dirs. World Vision. Served with AUS, 1951-53. Mem. Nat. Assn. Coll. and Univ. Chaplains, Nat. Com. Black Churchmen, Nat. Negro Evang. Assn. (bd. dirs. 1969-86). Office: 367 Beverly Rd Greensboro AL 36744-6034 Home Phone: 334-624-4297.

MASSEY, KEITH ANDREW, language educator; s. William Frederick Massey and Nancy Lou Dodge; m. Adriana Toma, Dec. 18, 2004. BA, U. Wis., Madison, 1987, MA, 1992, PhD, 1998; MA, Luther Sem., St. Paul, 1990. Arabic linguist Nat. Security Agy., Ft. Meade, Md., 2002—06; tchr. Leonia HS, NJ, 2006—. Author: (book) Intermediate Arabic for Dummies. Greek Orthodox. Avocation: travel.

MASSEY, PATRICK BABER, internist, health facility administrator; BS, U. Ill., 1975; MS in Microbiology, Roosevelt U., 1977; PhD in Immunology/Microbiology, Northwestern U., 1982; MD, Rush U., 1986. Cert. Internal Medicine, Alternative Medicine. Intern Rush-Presbyterian St. Luke's Med. Ctr., Chicago, resident, asst. prof., med. attending, 1989—92; med. dir. Skin Rsch. Inst., La Grange Park, Ill., 1990—92; fellowship in integrative medicine U. Ariz., 2000—02; med. dir., alternative and complimentary medicine Alexian Brothers Med. Ctr., Elk Grove Village, Ill., 2002—, dir. physician acupuncture training program. Clinical instructor Loyola U. Med. Sch.; columnist Daily Herald, Arlington Heights, Ill.; mem. Diabetes Initiative Task Force Alexian Brothers Hospital Network, mem. Health Care Advisory Bd., mem. Health Initiative Commt. Fellow: Coll. of Physicians; mem.: Am. Bd. of Internal Medicine, Am. Assn. of Integrative Medicine, Am. Pain Soc., Midwest Pain Soc. Office: 9301 N 76th St Milwaukee WI 53223 Office Phone: 847-923-0046. Office Fax: 847-923-0047.*

MASSEY, RAYMOND DAVID, lawyer; b. Goldsboro, NC, Oct. 13, 1946; s. Raymond L. and Dorris L. (Grant) Massey; m. Barbara A. Warner, Aug. 16, 1967; children: Suzanne, Christine. BA, Wofford Coll., Spartanburg, SC, 1968; JD, U. S.C., Columbia, 1971; LLM in Taxation, Emory U., Atlanta, 1985. Bar: S.C. 1971, U.S. Dist. Ct. S.C. 1971, cert.: S.C. Supreme Ct. (specialist estate planning and probate law). Assoc. Perrin, Perrin & Mann, Spartanburg, Spartanburg, 1971—74; trust officer Bankers Trust of S.C., Columbia, SC, 1974—78; shareholder Brown, Massey, Evans, McLeod & Haynsworth, PA, Greenville, SC, 1978—. Pres. Greenville Estate Planning Coun., 1982; chair Cmty. Found. of Greater Greenville, 2001—02; dir. Greenville Hosp. Sys. Found., 2002—. Named to trusts and estates section, Best Lawyers in Am. Fellow: Am. Coll. Trust and Estate Counsel; mem.: S.C. Bar Assn. (chmn. probate, estate planning and trust sect. 1983), Greenville Bar Assn. (pres. tax sect. 1980—81), Poinsett Club, Greenville Country Club. Presbyterian. Office: PO Box 2464 Greenville SC 29602-2464 Office Phone: 864-271-7424.

MASSEY, RICHARD, astrophysicist; b. Sutton Coldfield, West Midlands, England, Oct. 14, 1977; s. Ian and Stephenie Massey. MS in Math. & Physics, U. Durham, England, 2000; PhD, U. Cambridge, England, 2004. Sr. postdoctoral scholar Calif. Inst. Tech., Pasadena, 2004—. Achievements include research in mapping the large-scale distribution of dark matter. Office: Calif Inst Tech 105-24 1200 E Calif Blvd Pasadena CA 91125 Business E-Mail: rjm@astro.caltech.edu.

MASSEY, RICHARD N., lawyer, telecommunications industry executive; JD with honors, Univ. Ark. Ptnr. Kutak Rock, 1998—2000; mng. dir. Stephens Inc., Little Rock, 2000—05; exec. v.p., gen. counsel, corp. sec. Alltel Corp., Little Rock, 2005—07, chief strategy officer, gen. counsel, 2007—. Office: Alltel Corp One Allied Dr Little Rock AR 72202

MASSEY, ROBERT UNRUH, internist, educator, dean; b. Detroit, Feb. 23, 1922; s. Emil Laverne and Esther Elisabeth (Unruh) M.; m. June Charlene Collins, May 28, 1943 (dec. July 2005); children: Robert Scott (dec.), Janet Charlene. Student, Oberlin Coll., 1939-42, U. Mich. Med. Sch., 1942-43; MD, Wayne State U., 1946. Intern, resident in internal medicine Henry Ford Hosp., Detroit, 1946-50; assoc. Lovelace Clinic, Albuquerque, 1950-68, chmn. dept. medicine, 1958-68, bd. govs., 1957-68; dir. med. edn. Lovelace Found. for Med. Edn. and Research, 1960-68; clin. assoc. U. N.Mex. Sch. Medicine, 1961-68; prof. medicine U. Conn. Sch. Medicine, Farmington, 1968-92, prof. emeritus, 1992—, assoc. dean for grad edn., 1968-71, dean Sch. Medicine, 1971-84, currently prof. emeritus dept. community medicine and health care, acting univ. v.p. for health affairs, 1975-76. Chief staff Newington VA Hosp., Conn., 1968-71; trustee Am. Assn. Med. Clinics, 1966-68; exec. com., regional adv. group Conn. Regional Med. Program, 1971-76; trustee, v.p. Capitol Area Health Consortium, 1974-78, pres., 1980-81. Editor-in-chief Conn. Medicine, 1986-99; editor Jour. of the History of Medicine and Allied Scis., 1987-91. Bd. dirs. Health Planning Coun., Inc., 1974-76; bd. dirs. Hartford Inst. for Criminal and Social Justice, 1976-80, Conn. Easter Seal Soc., 1977-85, Hospice Inst. Edn., Tng. and Rsch., 1979-81. With AUS, 1955-57; maj. Res. Fellow ACP; mem. Am. Group Practice Assn. (accreditation commn. 1968-78), Assn. Am. Med. Colls., Am. Assn. History of Medicine, Hartford County Med. Assn., AMA, Conn., Hartford med. socs., Am. Osler Soc., Beaumont Med. Club, Soc. Med. Adminstrs., Twilight Club (Hartford), Acorn Club, Sigma Xi, Alpha Omega Alpha. Roman Catholic.

MASSEY, STEPHEN CHARLES, rare book dealer, consultant; b. London, May 9, 1946; s. Charles Dudley and Sheila Florence (Browne) M.; divorced; 1 child, Sarah Louise. Grad. high sch., UK. Cataloguer books and manuscripts Christie's, London, 1964-75, sr. dir. rare books and manuscripts dept. NYC, 1975-96, sr. internat. cons., 1997-99. Mem. The Grolier Club, The Old Book Table. Avocations: cinema, reading, running, music, forestry. Office Phone: 212-628-6850. Personal E-mail: scmassey@aol.com.

MASSEY, THOMAS BENJAMIN, retired university president; b. Charlotte, NC, Sept. 5, 1926; s. William Everard and Sarah (Corley) M.; m. Bylee Hunnicutt Massey, July 10, 1968; children: Pamela Ann, Caroline Forest. AB, Duke U., 1948; MS, N.C. State U., 1953; PhD, Cambridge U., 1968. Assoc. dean students Ga. Inst. Tech., Atlanta, 1950-58; lectr. U. Md. Univ. Coll., 1960-66, dir. London, 1966—69, dir. Toyko, 1969-71, dir. Heidelberg (Fed. Republic of Germany), 1971-76, vice chancellor, 1976-78, chancellor, 1978-88, pres., 1988-98, pres. emeritus, 1998—. Served with USN, 1943-46. Mem. APA, Univ. Continuing Edn. Assn., Am. Assn. Higher Edn., Internat. Confs. on Improving Learning and Tchg. at the Univ. (chair 1975—). Personal E-mail: benmassey@mac.com.

MASSEY, WALTER EUGENE, bank executive, retired academic administrator; b. Hattiesburg, Miss., Apr. 5, 1938; s. Almor and Essie (Nelson) M.; m. Shirley Ann Streeter, Oct. 25, 1969; children: Keith Anthony, Eric Eugene. BS in Math & Physics, Morehouse Coll., 1958; MA, PhD, Washington U., St. Louis, 1966. Physicist Argonne Nat. Lab., Ill., 1966-68; asst. prof. physics U. Ill., Urbana, 1968-70; assoc. prof. Brown U., Providence, 1970-75, prof., dean, 1975-79; prof. physics U. Chgo., 1979-93; dir. Argonne Nat. Lab., 1979-84; v.p. for rsch. Argonne Nat. Lab. U. Chgo., 1984-91; dir. NSF, Washington, 1991-93; sr. v.p. acad. affairs U. Calif. System, 1993-95; pres. Morehouse Coll., Atlanta, 1995—2007, pres. emeritus, 2007; chmn. Bank of America Corp., Charlotte, NC, 2009—. Bd. dirs. Bank of America Corp. 1998-, McDonald's Corp., 1998-, BP p.l.c., 1998-2008, Delta Air Lines, Inc., 2007-08; cons. NAS, 1973-76; mem. NSB, 1978-84; chair Sec. Energy Adv. Bd., 1997-99; mem. Gates Millennium Scholars Adv. Coun.; mem. coun. visitors Marine Biol. Lab.; mem. Pres.'s Coun. Advisors on Sci. and Tech., 1990-92, 01-. Contbr. articles on sci. edn. in secondary schs. and in theory of quantum fluids to profl. jours. Bd. fellows Brown U., 1980-90, Mus. Sci. and Industry, Chgo., 1980-89, Ill. Math. and Sci. Acad., 1985-88; bd. dirs. Urban League RI, 1973-75; mem. Salzburg seminar, 1997—, Atlanta Symphony Orch., 1996—; Woodruf Art Ctr., 1995—, Atlanta Com. Pub. Edn., 1996-2004, Bd. Project GRAD, Gt. Schs. Atlanta Bd., 2004-; trustee U. Chgo; active Atalnta Com. for Progress, 2003—. Recipient over 25 hon. degrees; NAS fellow, 1961, NDEA fellow, 1959-60, AAAS fellow, 1962; recipient Disting. Svc. Citation Am. Assn. Physics Teachers, 1975, Archie Lacey Meml award NY Acad. Sci., 1992, Bennie Trailblazer award Morehouse Coll., 1992, Disting. Achievement award MOrgan State U., 1992, Golden Plate award, 1992 Mem. AAAS (bd. dirs. 1981-85, pres.-elect 1987-88, pres. 1988-89, chmn. 1989-90), Am. Phys. Soc. (councillor-at-large 1980-83, v.p. 1990), Smithsonian Inst. (bd. regents), Sigma Xi. Office: Bank of America Corp 100 N Tryon St, 18th Fl Charlotte NC 28255*

MASSIE, CLIFFORD MICHAEL, music company executive; b. Bklyn., May 11, 1957; s. Michael and Jennifer Massie. BA cum laude with honors, Brandeis U., 1979. Pres. The Hit House, Levittown, NY, 1987—, Shoot No Blanks Music Publishing, Bethpage, NY, 1987—. Producer/remixer Teena Marie, Gloria Gaynor, David Hasselhoff, Evelyn Champagne King, Promoter Jay-Z, Ja Rule, DMX, Ludacris, Ashanti, Janet Jackson, Mariah Carey, Aaliyah, Snoop Dogg, Brian McKnight. Recipient Songwriter 1st Place Billboard Mag. contest, 1988. Mem.: NMPA, NARAS, ASCAP. Achievements include numerous Gold and Platinum singles/albums. Home: 3700 Mallard Rd Levittown NY 11756 Office: The Hit House 3700 Mallard Rd Levittown NY 11756 also: Shoot No Blanks Music Pub PO Box 102 Bethpage NY 11714 Office Phone: 516-735-3452. Office Fax: 516-735-3329. Personal E-mail: cliffmassie@optonline.net.

MASSIE, MARIBETH LEIGH, nursing educator; b. Cleve., Aug. 27, 1962; d. Raymond Jospeh and Marianne Jeanette Hrach; m. Steven Joseph Massie, May 23, 1992. BSN, Ohio State U., Columbus, 1986; MS, Columbia U., NYC, 1998; PhD, Va. Commonwealth U., Richmond, 2008. CRNA, COA, 1998. Asst. program dir. asst. prof. clin. nursing Columbia U., NYC, 1999—2006; dir. clin. edn. staff nurse anesthetist Johns Hopkins U., Balt., 2001—. Dir. Md. Assn. Nurse Anesthetists, Balt., 2000—08. Mem.: Columbia U. Sch. Nursing Alumni Assn., Ohio State U. Alumni Assn. (Outstanding Sr. award 1986), Md. Assn. Nurse Anesthetists (pres. sec. 2004—08), Am. Assn. Nurse Anesthetists, SigmaTheta Tau, Mortar Bd. (sec. 1985—86). Home: 219 E Churchill St Baltimore MD 21230 Personal E-mail: mbsmassie@yahoo.com.

MASSIER, PAUL FERDINAND, mechanical engineer; b. Pocatello, Idaho, July 22, 1923; s. John and Kathryn (Arki) M.; m. Miriam Parks, May 1, 1948 (dec. Aug. 1975); children: Marilyn Massier Schwegler, Paulette Massier Holden; m. Dorothy Hedlund Wright, Sept. 12, 1978. BSME, U. Colo., 1948; MSME, MIT, 1949. Cert. U. Idaho, So. Branch, 1943. Engr. Pan-Am. Refining Corp., Texas City, Tex., 1948; design engr. Maytag Co., Newton, Iowa, 1949-50; research engr. Boeing Co., Seattle, 1951-55; sr. research engr., supr. and dep. sect. mgr. Jet Propulsion Lab. Calif. Inst. Tech., Pasadena, 1955-84, task mgr., 1984-88, mem. tech. staff, 1989-94. Contbr. articles to profl. jours. Moderator Arcadia Congl. Ch., 1996-98; mem. Arcadia High Sch. Music Club, 1966-71. With U.S. Army, 1943-46. Recipient Apollo Achievement award NASA, 1969, Basic Noise Rsch. award NASA, 1980, Life Mem. Svc. award Calif. PTA, 1970, Layman of Yr. award Arcadia Congl. Ch., 1971, Mil. Unit Citation award, 1946. Fellow AIAA (assoc., Sustained Svc. award 1980-81); mem. AAAS, NY Acad. Scis., Planetary Soc., Nat. Space Soc., Order of Engr., Bukovina Soc. of the Ams., Sigma Xi, Tau Beta Pi, Pi Tau Sigma, Sigma Tau. Congregationalist. Achievements include 50% reduction of cooling requirements for rocket engines, experimental evaluation of heat transfer from thermally ionized gases at temperatures up to 13,000 degrees; experimental determination of starting characteristics, shock-wave structures, heat transfer and pressure distributions in supersonic diffusers led to the development of criteria for their design and their use as a means of simulating altitude conditions at ground level for static testing of rocket engines; experimental/analytical determination of the relationships of large-scale turbulent structures, density and temperature fluctuations, inverted velocity profiles, internally generated pure tones, twin jet shielding, and aircraft flight on noise emitted from aircraft supersonic jets; understanding of the formation of cenospheres during the combustion of heavy oils by analysis of electron microscope photo images of droplets, and stages of formed globules and cenospheres gathered on slides during combustion experiments. Home: 764 Lava Falls Dr Las Vegas NV 89110

MASSIMINO, JULIA A., legislative staff member, lawyer; b. Dallas; BA, Trinity U.; JD, U. Tex., Austin, 1998, MPA, 1999. Staff asst. for Rep. Howard Berman, US House of Reps., Washington, 2000—01, legis. counsel, 2003—07, chief counsel, 2007—09, chief of staff, 2009—; legis. counsel for Rep. William Delahunt, Washington, 2003—08; counsel Subcommittee on Courts, the Internet, and Intellectual Property US House Com. on the Judiciary, Washington, 2007—. Office: Office of Congressman Howard Berman 2221 Rayburn House Office Bldg Washington DC 20515 Office Phone: 202-225-4695. Office Fax: 202-225-3196. E-mail: julia.massimino@mail.house.gov.*

MASSIMO, ANNA GEORGIEVA, medical educator; d. Georgi Kotsev Chobanov and Ivanka Pateva Chobanova; m. Nicholas Anthony Massino III; 1 child, Andrea Nicole. MD, Varna U. Medicine, Bulgaria, 1991; postgrad, SHEBA Med. Ctr., Tel-Aviv, 1994. In devel. & function endocrine & immune sys. teratology Ednl. Com. Teratology Soc., San Diego, CA, 1998; cert. in exptl. approaches for studying mechanisms for abnormal devel. Palm Beach, 1997. Physician nephrology & hemodialysis dept. Russe Regional Hosp., Bulgaria, 1991—95; scientist, reproductive toxicology dept. Huntington Life Scis., East Milstone, NJ, 1996—97, sr. scientist, supr. -fetal pathology dept., 1997—2000; med. cons. Net Alliance, Inc., Washington, NJ, 2001—02; adj. prof., sci. dept. anatomy & physiology Warren County CC, Washington, 2003—08, sr. adj. prof., sci. dept. anatomy & physiology, 2008—. Contbr. scientific papers including collection of amniotic fluid & maternal, fetal blood in the pregnant rat for toxicokinetic studies, jours. includes abnormal devel., teratology, vol. 57. Mem.: Soc. Toxicology (mid. Atlantic chpt., Outstanding Poster Presentation award 1998), Mid Atlantic Soc. Toxicology, Israel Med. Assn. (physicians exch. program), Teratology Soc. US (Outstanding Poster Presentation award 1998). Independent. Home: 38 W Johnston St Washington NJ 07882 Business E-Mail: amassimo@warren.edu.

MASSIN, EDWARD KRAUSS, physician; b. Houston, 1939; MD, Washington U., St. Louis, 1965; BA, Rice U., 1961. Intern Barnes Hosp., St. Louis, 1965-66, resident, 1966-67; with St. Lukes Episcopal Hosp., Houston. Clin. prof. Baylor Coll. Medicine. Cardiology fellow U. Colo. Med. Ctr., 1969-71. Fellow Am. Coll. Cardiology Office: Cardiology Cons Houston 6624 Fannin St Ste 2310 Houston TX 77030-2335 Office Phone: 713-796-2668.

MASSMAN, RICHARD ALLAN, lawyer; b. Beaumont, Tex., Aug. 19, 1943; s. Irwin Massman and Sylvia (Schmidt) Schwartz; m. Barbara Elaine Kessler; children: Jason Todd, Karen Faye. BS cum laude, U. Pa., 1965; JD cum laude, Harvard U., 1968. Bar: Tex. 1968; cert. in taxation, Tex. Bd. Legal Specialization. Assoc. Coke & Coke, Dallas, 1968-70, Johnson & Wortley, P.C. (formerly Johnson & Gibbs, P.C.), Dallas, 1970-71, ptnr., 1971-88, shareholder, 1988-94; of counsel Johnson & Wortley P.C., Dallas, 1994-95; sr. v.p., gen. counsel Hunt Consolidated, Inc., Dallas, 1994—2009, gen. counsel emeritus, 2009—. Lectr. So. Meth. U., Dallas, 1973; trustee Am. Beacon Funds, 2004—, chmn., 2008—; bd. dirs. Retina Found. Southwest, 2004—; chmn., 2008—. Chmn. Dallas Civil Svc. Bd., 1983; trustee Greenhill Sch., Dallas, 1985-92, vice chmn., 1990-92; trustee Dallas Opera, 1999—; chmn. Dallas Opera Found., 2007—; bd. dirs. Presbyn. Hosp. Found., 2007—; chmn. Temple Emanu-El Found., 2006—. Recipient Jurisprudence award Anti-Defamation League, 2000, Best Gen. Counsel award Dallas Bus. Jour., 2006. Mem. Am. Coll. Tax Coun., Tex. State Bar (chmn., sec. taxation 1983-84), Dallas Bar Assn. (chmn., sec. taxation 1978), Trophy Club, Bent Tree Country Club. Office: Hunt Consolidated Inc 1900 N Akard St Dallas TX 75201-2300

MASSOUD, YEHIA, science educator; PhD, MIT, Cambridge, Mass., 1999. Prof. Rice U., Houston, 2003—. Contbr. articles to profl. jours. Recipient Career award, NSF, 2005. Office: Rice University 6100 Main St MS 380 Houston TX 77005

MASSOUDI, BAHRAM BARRY, management consultant; b. Tehran, Iran, 1960; arrived in U.S., 1977; BS, Syracuse U., NYC, 1981; MEng, McGill U., Montreal, 1983; MBA, U. Wash., Seattle, 1992. Internat. compensation mgr. Schlumberger Ltd., Paris, 1984—90; principal Gemini Consulting, Morristown, NJ, 1992—99; founder, mng. ptnr. Cubicon LLC, Seattle, 1999—2007; sr. mgr., strategic trans. Bearing Point Mgmt. and Tech. Cons., 2007—. Author: Do the Right Deal, Do the Deal Right: 35 Success Factors for Mergers and Acquisitions, 2006; contbr. articles to profl. jours. Chmn. Arts Commn., Mercer Island, Wash., 2004—06; commr. City of Mercer Island, 2006—. Avocations: jogging, photography, restoring old houses, gardening.

MASSY, WILLIAM FRANCIS, education educator, consultant; b. Milw., Mar. 26, 1934; s. Willard Francis and Ardys Dorothy (Digman) M.; m. Sally Vaughn Miller, July 21, 1984; children by previous marriage: Willard Francis, Elizabeth BS, Yale U., 1956; SM, MIT, 1958, PhD in Indsl. Econs., 1960. Asst. prof. indsl. mgmt. MIT, Cambridge, 1960-62; from asst. prof. to prof. edn. and bus. adminstrn. Stanford U., Calif., 1962-96, assoc. dean Grad. Sch. Bus. Calif., 1971, vice provost for rsch. Calif., 1971-77, v.p. for bus. and fin. Calif., 1977-88, v.p. fin. Calif., 1988-91, prof. emeritus, 1996—; prof. edn., dir. Stanford Inst. Higher Edn. Rsch., Calif., 1988-96; sr. v.p. P.R. Taylor Assocs., 1995-99; sr. rschr. Nat. Ctr. for Postsecondary Imrprovement, 1996—2002; pres. The Jackson Hole Higher Edn. Group, Inc., 1996—. Bd. dirs. MAC, Inc., 1969-84, Stanford Mgmt. Co., 1991-93; mem. u. grants com. Hong Kong, 1990-2003; mem. coun. Yale U., 1980-95; mgmt. cons. Stanford Mgmt. Co., 1991-93.bd. dirs. Diebold, Inc., chmn. audit com., 2003-07. Author: Stochastic Models of Buying Behavior, 1970, Marketing Management, 1972, Market Segmentation, 1972, Planning Models for Colleges and Universities, 1981, Endowment, 1991, Resource Allocation in Higher Education, 1996, Honoring The Trust, 2003, Remaking the American University, 2005, Academic Quality Work, 2007; mem. editl. bd. Jour. Mktg. Rsch., 1964-70, Harcourt, Brace Jovanovich, 1965-71; contbr. articles to profl. jours. Bd. dirs. Palo Alto-Stanford chpt. United Way, 1978-80, Stanford U. Hosp., 1980-91, EDUCOM, 1983-86. Ford Found. faculty rsch. fellow, 1966-67; recipient Frederick W. Lanchester prize, Operations Rsch. Soc., 1981; Outstanding Contributions to Coll. and Univ. Planning award, Soc. Coll. Univ. Planning., 1995. Mem. Am. Mktg. Assn. (bd. dirs. 1971-73, v.p. edn. 1976-77), Inst. Mgmt. Scis., Tau Beta Pi, Sigma Xi. Avocations: hiking, scuba diving, travel. Office: The Jackson Hole Higher Edn Group Inc PO Box 9849 Jackson WY 83002-9849 Personal E-mail: bill@jhheg.com.

MAST, GREGORY LEWIS, lawyer; b. Waterloo, Iowa, July 29, 1954; s. Kenneth Edgar and Shirley Louise (Crandall) M.; m. Jennifer Lynn East, Dec. 30, 1978; children: Millicent Ashley, William Robert. BA, De Pauw U., 1976; JD, Harvard U., 1979. Bar: Ariz. 1979, U.S. Dist. Ct. Ariz. 1979. Ptnr. Evans, Kitchel & Jenckes, P.C., Phoenix, 1979-85, Jones, Jury, Short & Mast, P.C., Phoenix, 1986-88, Gallagher & Kennedy, P.A., Phoenix, 1988—2008; shareholder Mast Law Firm PC, Phoenix, 2008. Mem. Ariz. Town Hall, Phoenix C. of C. (spl. events com.), Ariz. Baseball Commn., Valley Partnership, White Mountain Country Club, Thunderbirds, Phoenix Country Club, Real Estate Investment Adv. Coun. Named Am's. Leading Bus. Lawyers, by Chambers USA, Best Lawyers Valley, by Phoenix mag., Best Lawyers Am., by Woodward/White, Inc., 2007. Mem.: DePauw U. Alumni Assn., Phi Beta Kappa, Maricopa County Bar Assn., State Bar Ariz. Office: Mast Law Firm PC 2415 E Camelback Rd Ste 1050 Phoenix AZ 85016 Office Phone: 602-852-5950. Office Fax: 602-530-8500. Business E-Mail: gmast@mastlawfirm.com.

MAST, JOY NYSTROM, biogeographer educator; b. Mpls., July 19, 1967; d. Paul C. and Carol J. (Lewis) Nystrom; m. Jerald C. Mast, Aug. 5, 1989; children: Erik Nystrom Mast, Colin Nystrom Mast. BS, Univ. Wis., 1989; M, Univ. Colo., 1991, PhD, 1993. Lab. rschr. Univ. Wis., Madison, 1986-89; grad. asst. Univ. Colo., Boulder, 1989-91, instr., 1991-93; asst. prof. Northern Ariz. Univ., Flagstaff, 1993—99, assoc. prof., 1999—2002, prof., 2006—; assoc. prof. Carthage Coll., Kenosha, Wis., 2002—06. Educator Continuing Edn. for Ecosystem Mgrs., 1995—2002; jour. reviewer Annals of the Assn. of Am. Geographers, 1996. Contbr. articles to profl. jours. Bd. dirs. Nat. Biogeography Speciality Group, Washington, 1996—98, pres., 2005—07; judge Assn. of Am. Geographers, Washington. Recipient Outstanding Tchr. award Univ. Colo., Univ. Colo., 1993, numerous rsch. grants., NSF. Mem.: Ecological Soc. Am., Assn. of Am. Geographers. Office: Carthage Coll 2001 Alford Park Dr Kenosha WI 53140

MAST, KANDE WHITE, artist; b. St. Louis, Mar. 10, 1950; d. Elliott Maxwell and Mary (Barritt) W. Student, U. Mo., Kansas City, 1968-70, Longview C.C., Kansas City, Mo., 1970-71. Portrait painter, free-lance artist, Albany, NY, 1973-74, Kansas City, 1974—; dir., tchr. Studio Kande, Sch. Fine Arts, Kansas City, 1983-86; founder, exec. dir. Art Ctr. Kansas City, 1986-90; behavioral foster parent, 1989—2005; master foster parent, 1992—2005. Mem. psychiat. diversion team, mental health rev. team Jackson County Divsn. Family Svcs., 1992-95. Portrait painter and free-lance artist. Pres., bd. dirs. Advocates for Children, Inc., 1996—; vol. Ozanam Home for Boys, Kansas City, 1987—, mem. adv. bd., 1991—; mem. Cmty. Response Team, Jackson County, Divsn. Family Svcs.; founding mem. Nat. Campaign for Tolerance. Named Therapeutic Foster Parent of Yr., 1992. Mem.: Code Pink: Women for Peace, Nat. Campaign for Tolerance, Nat. Mus. of Women in Arts (charter). Home and Studio: 12406 Baltimore Ct Kansas City MO 64145 Personal E-mail: kande@kc.rr.com.

MASTASCUSA, EDWARD JOHN, electrical engineering educator; b. Pitts., June 27, 1938; s. Nick S. Mastascusa and Thelma W. Lutz; m. Mary Noreen Mastascusa, Sept. 3, 1960; children: Noreen, Edward, Martin, Diana, Maria, Joan. BSEE, Carnegie Mellon U., Pitts., 1960, MSEE, 1961, PhD in Elec. Engring., 1964. Elec. engr. Harry Diamond Labs., Washington, 1964-66; asst. prof. elec. engring. U. Wyo., Laramie, 1966-68; prof. elec. engring. Bucknell U., Lewisburg, Pa., 1968—. Author: Computer Assisted Network & System Analysis, 1989. With U.S. Army, 1964-66. Avocations: barbershop singing, running, photography. Home: 141 Spencer Pl Lewisburg PA 17837 Office: Bucknell U Elec Engring Dept Lewisburg PA 17837

MASTEN, BARBARA JEAN, education educator, department chairman; b. Toledo, Jan. 14, 1948; d. Joseph Anthony Czyzewski and Angela Rose Piorkowski; m. William Leonard Masten, Sept. 18, 1971; 1 child, Todd Michael. B in Edn., U. Toledo, 1970, M in Edn. Adminstrn., 1979. Sr. accountant and edn. and tchg. specialist Gen. Motors, Toledo, 1970—82; English instr. St. Ursula Acad., Toledo, 1983—89; instr. U. Toledo Cmty. Coll., 1989; assoc. prof./dept. chair Lourdes Coll., 1989—. Mem. adv. bd. Sch. Edn. Lourdes Coll., Sylvania, Ohio, 2003—, pres. faculty senate, 2005—06. Recipient Faculty Excellence award, Lourdes Coll., 1995, 1999, 2004. Mem.: Nat. Coun.Tchrs. English, Ohio Assn. Develop. Edn. Avocations: flower arranging, golf, reading. Office: Lourdes Coll 6832 Convent Blvd Sylvania OH 43560 Office Phone: 419-824-3758. Business E-Mail: bmasten@lourdes.edu.

MASTEN, JACQUELINE GWENDOLYN, small business owner; b. Brunswick, Maine, Oct. 24, 1941; d. Ralph Henry Bennet and Phyllis Estelle Crooker; children from previous marriage: Geraldine Frances Bullwinkel, Jennifer Lynn. Diploma in Bus., Pluss Sch. of Business, Portland, Maine, 1966. Shop owner Hudson Chair Caning Svcs., Hudson, NH, 1982; data entry operator Digital Corp., Nashua, NH, 1980; real estate landlady Hudson, NH, 1996—. Author: A Shaker Poetry Poetic History Book: A Tribute to My Aunt Eldress Gertrude Soule Shaker, 2003; contbr. poems to books. Recipient Shakespear medallion of Excellence, Internat. Soc. of Poets, 2002; named 1999 Poet of the Year, Famous Poets Soc., Nev., 1999, World Champion Amature, Internat. Soc. of Poets, 2001. Mem.: New Eng. Saddlebred and Pony Assn., Quartzsite Roadrunner Gem and Mineral Club. Avocation: Shaker poetry writing, shaker tape chair seating, silversmith, gem faceting, lapidary.

MASTER, ROBERT JEFFERY, consumer products company executive, marketing professional; s. Joseph and Carol Master; m. Lori Heather Blackman, Dec. 13, 2003; 2 children. B Polit. Sci., U. Wis., Madison; MBA, Washington U. Olin Sch. Bus., St. Louis. Various brand mktg. positions Young & Rubicam, Inc., PepsiCo, Inc.; dir. mktg. eHobbies.com; various mktg. dir./mgmt. positions Unilever US, Inc. (subs. Unilever NV), 2003—07, dir. N. Am. media, 2007—. Office: Unilever US Inc Hdqs 700 Sylvan Ave Englewood Cliffs NJ 07632*

MASTERN, DEAN SCOTT, personal growth and development consultant; b. Warren, Ohio, Aug. 26, 1961; s. Kenneth Richard and Joyce Eileen Mastern; m. Sheree Diane Grier, Aug. 21, 1987; children: Aaron Keith, Rachel Colleen. PhD in Psychology, SW Acad. of Mental Health, 1987, PhD (hon.) in Quantum Biophysics, 1987; DD (hon.), World Christianship Ministries, 1987. Cons. Dean S. Mastern, PhD, Tyler, Tex., 1987—. Author: Theory of Quantum Biophysics, 1987. Mem.: Am. Assn. of Religious Counselors (life). Republican. Avocations: flying, sailing, sports cars, motorcycles. Office: DSM Cons PO Box 133012 Tyler TX 75713 Personal E-mail: dsmphd@yahoo.com.

MASTERS, ANN BROWNING, educator, poet; d. Shirley A. and William T. Browning; m. Jeremy A. Masters; 1 child, Forrest J. BA, U. Fla., 1973, MEd, 1976, PhD, 1992, EdS, 1976. Exec. dir. Jan House Drug Abuse Prevention and Edn. Ctr., St. Augustine, Fla., 1976—77; consultation edn. coord. Tri-County Mental Health Svcs., St. Augustine, 1979—80; sr. case mgr., staff coord. St. Johns County Coun. Aging, 1981—85; academic advisor St. Johns River C.C., St. Augustine, 1985—96, prof. edn. program coord., 1996—. Author of poems; contbr. articles to profl. jours. Founding bd. dirs. Los Floridanos Soc., St. Augustine, Fla., 2000—03. Recipient Tchg. Excellence award, Nat. Inst. for Staff and Orgnl. Devel., 1998. Mem.: AAUW, Edn. Law Assn., Fla. Assn. of C.Cs. (chpt. pres. 1993), Los Floridanos Soc., Menorcan Cultural Soc., St. Augustine Hist. Soc. (bd. dirs. 2004—).

MASTERS, ANNE, library director; With Pioneer Libr. System, Okla. Recipient Outstanding Alumni award, U. Okla. Sch. Libr. and Info. Studies, 2007. Mem.: Continuing Libr. Edn. and Networking Exchange Round Table (pres. 2006—07), Pub. Libr. Assn. (mem. trainer cadre), Urban Libraries Coun. (exec. leadership inst. sponsor, Joey Rodger Leadership award 2005), Okla. Libr. Assn. (Disting. Svc. award, Meritorious Svc. award, named Okla. Libr. Legend 2007), Norman Sooner Rotary. Office: Pioneer Libr System 225 N Webster Norman OK 73069 Office Phone: 405-701-2642. Office Fax: 405-701-2649. Business E-Mail: amsters@pls.lib.ok.us.

MASTERS, BLYTHE, bank executive; b. England, 1970; BA in economics, Trinity Coll., Cambridge U. With JP Morgan Chase & Co., NYC, 1991—, co-head of N.Am. credit portfolio, 1998—99; head of global credit derivatives mktg. JP Morgan Securities, Inc.; co-head of asset backed securitization JP Morgan Chase & Co., NYC, head of N.Am. structured credit products, head of global credit portfolio and credit policy and strategy, CFO investment bank, 2004—06, head of global commodities, 2006—. Exec. com. JP Morgan Chase & Co. NYC. Chmn. bd., NY affiliate Susan G. Komen for the Cure. Named one of 40 Under 40, Crain's NY Bus., 2004. Mem.: Securities Industry and Fin. Markets Assn. (former chair credit derivatives market practices com., chmn.). Office: JP Morgan Chase & Co 270 Park Ave New York NY 10017-2070

MASTERS, CLAUDE BIVIN, lawyer; b. Cleburne, Tex., July 25, 1930; s. Claude Pinkney and Ola Mae (Rollins) M.; m. Jenita Whites, June 1, 1949 (div.); children: C. Thomas, Cl Danette Masters McClanahan, Teresa Masters Lebeck; m. Cynthia McCormack, Nov. 4, 1983 (div.). BS, U. Houston, 1953, JD, 1969, LLM, 1985. Bar: Tex. 1969, U.S. Dist. Ct. (so. dist.) Tex. 1972, U.S. Dist. Ct. (we. dist.) Tex. 1972, U.S. Ct. Appeals (5th cir.) 1971, U.S. Ct. Appeals (11th cir.) 1983, U.S. Supreme Ct. 1978. Ptnr. Martin & Masters, Houston, 1971-73; v.p., gen. counsel Summit Ins. Co. N.Y., NYC, 1973-75; sr. atty. Ashland Oil Co., Ky., 1975-78; v.p. Houston Oil and Minerals Co., 1978-84; assoc. Dunnam & Strong, Houston, 1984-85; risk mgmt. cons. Masters & Assocs., Houston, 1975—. Bd. dirs. Alford & Assocs., Houston; adj. prof. law U. Houston, 1984—. Dir.-gen. Tex. Safety Assn., Austin, 1959. Served with U.S. Army, 1946-47. Named Outstanding Speaker, Southwest Ins. Info. Svc., Dallas, 1961-62. Fellow Tex. Bar Found. (life), Houston Bar Found (life); mem. Jaycees (bd. dirs. Tulsa 1962; named Outstanding Mem. Tex. 1960), Phi Delta Phi. Republican. Mem. Ch. of Christ. Home: 314 College Ave Cleburne TX 76033 Office: 5444 Westheimer Rd Ste 1775 Houston TX 77056-5325 E-mail: claudemasters@charter.net.

MASTERS, EDWARD EUGENE, association executive, former foreign service officer; b. Columbus, Ohio, June 21, 1924; s. George Henry and Ethel Verena (Shaw) M.; m. Allene Mary Roche, Apr. 2, 1956; children: Julie Allene, Edward Ralston. Student, Denison U., 1942—43; BA with distinction, George Washington U., 1948; MA, Fletcher Sch. Law and Diplomacy, 1949; grad., Nat. War Coll., 1964. Joined U.S. Fgn. Svc., 1950; intelligence rsch. analyst Near East Dept. State, 1949-50; resident officer Heidelberg, Germany, 1950-52; polit. officer embassy Karachi, Pakistan, 1952-54; Hindustani lang. and area tng. U. Pa., 1954-55; consul, polit. officer Madras, India, 1955-58; intelligence rsch. specialist South Asia Dept. State, 1958-60, chief Indonesia-Malaya br. Office Rsch. Asia, 1960-61, officer-in-charge Thailand affairs Bur. Far Eastern Affairs, 1961-63; counselor for polit. affairs Am. embassy, Djakarta, 1964-68; country dir. for Indonesia Dept. State, 1968-70; dir. Office East Asian Regional Affairs, 1970-71; minister Am. embassy, Bangkok, 1971-75; amb. to Bangladesh, 1976—77; amb. to Indonesia, 1977—81; adj. prof. diplomacy Fletcher Sch. Law and Diplomacy, 1981-82; sr. v.p. Natomas Co., 1982-84; pres. Nat. Planning Assn., 1985—92, Edward Masters & Assocs., Washington, 1992—2009; founder US Indonesia Soc., 1994, pres., 1994—2000, chmn., 2000—09, chmn. emeritus, 2009—. Adj. prof. Sch. Advanced Internat. Studies, 2000—02. With US Army, 1943—46. Mem. Am. Fgn. Svc. Assn., Cosmos Club, Phi Beta Kappa, Omicron Delta Kappa, Pi Gamma Mu, Delta Phi Epsilon. Home: 4101 Cathedral Ave NW Apt 1001 Washington DC 20016-7500 Personal E-mail: mastersdc@att.net.

MASTERS, GARY, dancer, choreographer; Grad., Juilliard Sch. Cofounder, co-artistic dir. Mathews-Masters Dance Co., NYC, 1977; artistic assoc. Limón Dance Co., NYC, 1987—94; dir. Limón West Dance Project, San José, Calif., 1994—98. Artist lectr. San Jose State U., Calif., 1990—. Performed with Ethel Winter Dance Co., Juilliard Dance Ensemble; former mem. Pa. Ballet; with Limón Dance Co. roles include Emperor Maximillian in Carlota, Black Hawk in The Unsung, title role in Orfeo; choreographer various works for Nashville Ballet, Newcomb Dance Co., Dancer's Repertory Co., (with Fred Mathews) Mathews-Masters Dance Co., choreographed: Echoes 1968, Mask, 1969, Places (I), 1971, Celebration, 1972, Untitled Solo, 1975, Triptych, 1975, Places (II), 1975, Quest, 1976, Tribute to Limón, 1977, Summer Spill, 1978, Tabuh Tabuhan, 1979, Scapegoat, 1979, Bolero, 1980, Concerto for Paris, 1980, many others. Recipient Sustained Achievement honors, Isadora Duncan Dance Awards, 2009. Mailing: 1578 Santa Maria Ave San Jose CA 95125*

MASTERS, GEORGE WINDSOR, JR., electrical engineer, educator; b. Annapolis, Md., Mar. 11, 1930; s. George and Ruby Lena (Jess) Masters; m. Barbara Lyons Wilson; children: Barbara Anne, George W. III. BS, MIT, 1952, MS, 1954; PhD, U. Fla., 1966. Mem. tech. staff Instrument Lab., MIT, Cambridge, 1952-55; chief engr. Dynamic Instrument Co., Cambridge, 1955-58; sect. head Electromech. Rsch. Inc., Princeton, NJ, 1958-62; mem. sr. staff, sect. head flight control sect. The Aerospace Corp., El Segundo, Calif., 1962-75; chief engr. airborne sys. dept. USN Test Pilot Sch., Patuxent River, Md., 1975—2004; assoc. prof. elec. engring. Fla. Inst. Tech., Melbourne, 1984—2004; adj. assoc. prof. aviation sys. U. Tenn. Space Inst., Tullahoma, Tenn., 2004—. Recipient Meritorious Civilian Svc. award, Dept. of Navy, 2004. Mem. AIAA, IEEE, US Naval Inst., Elks, Kappa Sigma. Republican. Episcopalian. Home Phone: 770-537-8700. Business E-Mail: mastersgw@att.net.

MASTERS, GUY, science educator; s. Joyce and Thomas Masters; m. Vrginia Flemming; children: James Wiseman, Katie Wiseman. PhD, Cambridge U., England, 1979. Prof. UCSD, 1979—. Mem.: FRS, London. Office: SIO UCSD 9500 Gilman Dr La Jolla CA 92093-0225 Business E-Mail: gmasters@ucsd.edu.

MASTERS, JOHN CHRISTOPHER, psychologist, educator; b. Terre Haute, Ind., Oct. 25, 1941; s. Robert William and Lillian Virginia (Decker) M.; m. Mary Jayne Capps, June 6, 1970; children— Blair Christopher, Kyle Alexander. AB, Harvard Coll., 1963; PhD, Stanford U., 1967. Asst. prof. Ariz. State U., Tempe, 1968-69; from asst. prof. to prof. U. Minn., Mpls., 1969-79; assoc. dir. Inst. Child Devel., 1974-79; Luce prof. pub. policy and the family, prof. psychology Vanderbilt U., Nashville, 1979-87, interim chair dept. psychology, 1986-88; pres. Profl. Mgmt. Group, Inc., 1991—; dir. Master Ventures, 1989—, Master Travel, 1989—. Assoc. editor: Child Development, 1973-76, Behavior Therapy: Techniques and Empirical Findings, 1974, 79, 88; editor: Psychol. Bull., 1987-89. Home: 4923 Old Oakleaf Dr Sarasota FL 34233-3947 Office Phone: 800-767-6162.

MASTERS, JON JOSEPH, corporate governance specialist, management consultant; b. NYC, June 20, 1937; s. Arthur Edward and Esther (Shady) M.; m. Rosemary Dunaway Cox, June 16, 1962; children: Brooke Alison, Blake Edward. BA, Princeton U., 1958; JD, Harvard U., 1964. Bar: N.Y. 1965, U.S. Dist. Ct. (so. dist.) N.Y. 1965, U.S. Ct. Appeals (2d cir.) 1965. Cons. asst. to under sec. Dept. Army, 1961; mem. policy planning staff asst. sec. for internat. security affairs Dept. Def. Washington, 1962; mem. Pres. Johnson's Spl. Polit. Research Staff, Washington, 1964; assoc. Shearman & Sterling, NYC, 1965-68, 69; mem. staff Bedford-Stuyvesant D & S Corp., Bklyn., 1968-69; v.p., sec., gen. counsel, dir. Baker, Weeks & Co., Inc., NYC, 1969-76; co-founder, ptnr. Christy & Viener, NYC, 1976-96; Vice-chmn. Robb, Peck, McCooey Specialist Corp., NYC, 1996—98; prin. Lear, Yavitz & Assocs., NYC, 1996-2001, mng. prin., 1998—2001; prin. Mercer Delta Cons., NYC, 2001—02; chmn. Masters Governance Cons., LLC, NYC, 2002—05; co-founder, prin. Masters-Rudnick & Assocs., LLC, NYC, 2005—. SEC adv. com. broker-dealer compliance, 1972-74; legal advisor NACD Blue Ribbon Commn. on CEO and Dir. Performance Evaluation, 1994; chmn. bd. Clear and Present Prodns., 1992-93; dir. Harris & Harris Group, Inc., 1992-98; mem. pvt. sec. adv. group IFC Global Corp. Governance Forum 2007-. Mem. implementation com. Econ. Devel. Task Force of N.Y. Urban Coalition, 1968; mem. bd. Internat. Social Service, Am. Br., Inc., 1978-83, pres., 1979-83; bd. dirs. The Arts Connection, 1979-85; mem. steering com. N.Y. Lawyers Alliance for Nuclear Arms Control, 1983-96. Served with USN, 1958-61. Mem. ABA, Assn. Bar City N.Y. (com. mcpl. affairs 1977-80). Office: 350 E 82 St New York NY 10028 Office Phone: 212-879-0872. Business E-Mail: jjmasters@mastersrudnick.com.

MASTERS, JONATHAN EDWARD, clinical psychologist; b. Northport, NY, Sept. 27, 1962; s. Edward Joseph and Janet (Pendleton) Masters. BA, Marist Coll., Poughkeepsie, NY, 1985; grad., Gutter Inst. of Tech., 1986; MA, Pepperdine U., LA, 1991, PsyD, 1998; PhD candidate, Inst. Contemporary Psychoanalysis, LA, 2003—. Cert. psychologist Ariz. Bd. Psychologist Examiners, 1999. Part-time lectr. in astronomy Vanderbilt Planetarium, Centerport, NY, 1979—84; psychology trainee NY State Office Mental Health, Poughkeepsie, 1985; behavioral specialist Psychol. Support Svcs., Mission Hills, 1990—94, Prairie Group Home, Hawthorne, 1991—94, Only a Place to Start, Inglewood, 1991—94, John B. Kelley Residential Treatment Ctr. for Men, LA, 1992—94, John B. Kelley Residential Treatment Ctr. for Women, LA, 1992—94; psychology trainee Cath. Psychol. Svcs., LA, 1993, U. So. Calif. Med. Ctr., LA, 1994; predoctoral intern Pederson-Kraig Ctr., Huntington, NY, 1994—95; staff psychotherapist Advanced Ctr. Psychotherapy, Jamaica Estates, 1996—98; staff psychotherapist/psychologist New Hope Guild Ctr. for Children, Howard Beach, NY, 1996—99; clin. psychologist Paradise Valley Psychiat. Assocs., Phoenix, 2000—. Vol. Hurricane Katrina ARC, Phoenix, 2005. Mem.: APA (assoc.), SW Psychoanalytic Soc. (assoc.; practice com. mem. 2000, jour. group mem. 2000—01, chair program com. 2001—03, treas. 2004—05, bd. dirs. 2004—05). Office: Paradise Valley Psychiatric Assocs 4232 E Cactus Rd Ste 207 Phoenix AZ 85032 Personal E-mail: jmast99@cox.net.

MASTERS, JOSEPH, lawyer, engineering company executive; b. 1956; BSCE, Cleveland State U., 1979; JD, Case Western Reserve U., 1982. Bar: Ohio 1982. Pvt. practice; with URS Corp.; San Francisco, 1992—, v.p., gen. counsel, 1997—2006, v.p., gen. counsel, corp. sec., 2006—. Mem.: ABA. Office: URS Corp 26th Fl 600 Montgomery St San Francisco CA 94111 Office Phone: 415-774-2700.

MASTERS, ROGER DAVIS, political scientist, toxicologist, educator; b. Boston, June 8, 1933; s. Maurice and S. Grace (Davis) M.; m. Judith Ann Rubin, June 6, 1956 (div. 1984); children— Seth J., William A., Katherine R.; m. Susanne R. Putnam, Aug. 25, 1984 (dec. 2006). BA, Harvard U., Cambridge, Mass., 1955; MA, U. Chgo., 1958, PhD, 1961; MA (hon.), Dartmouth Coll., Hanover, NH, 1974. Instr. dept. polit. sci. Yale U., 1961-62, asst. prof., 1962-67; assoc. prof. dept. govt. Dartmouth Coll., Hanover, NH, 1967-73, prof., 1973-98, John Sloan Dickey Third Century prof., 1980-85, chmn. dept., 1986-89, Nelson A. Rockefeller prof., 1991-98, prof. emeritus, 1998—, rsch. prof., 1999—. Cultural attache Am. Embassy, Paris, 1969—71; chmn. France-Am. Commn. Ednl. and Cultural Exch., 1969—71; vis. lectr. Yale U. Law Sch., 1988—89, Vt. Law Sch., 1993—94; sect. editor Social Sci., Info., 1971—; chmn. exec. com. Gruter Inst. Law and Behavioral Rsch., 1995—98; pres. Found. for Neurosci. and Soc., 1998—; mem. Get the Lead Out of Vt. Task Force, 2006. Author: The Nation Is Burdened, 1967, The Political Philosophy of Rousseau, 1968, The Nature of Politics, 1989, Beyond Relativism, 1993, Machiavelli, Leonardo, and the Science of Power, 1996, Fortune is a River, 1998; editor: Rousseau's Discourses, 1964, Rousseau's Social Contract, 1978; co-editor: Ostracism: A Social and Biological Phenomenon, 1986, Collected Writings of J.J. Rousseau, 1990—, Primate Politics, 1991, The Sense of Justice, 1992, The Neurotransmitter Revolution, 1994; editor Gruter Inst. Reader in Biology, Law, and Human Social Behavior, 1992. Served with AUS, 1955-57. Fulbright fellow Inst. d'Etudes Politiques, Paris, 1958-59, joint Yale U.-Social Sci. Rsch. Coun. fellow, 1964-65, Guggenheim fellow, 1967-68, Hastings Ctr. for Ethics and Life Scis. fellow, 1973-78. Mem. AAAS, Am. Polit. Sci. Assn., Assn. Polit. and Life Sci., Am. Soc. for Legal and Polit. Philosophy, Internat. Soc. Human Ethology, Human Behavior Evolution Soc., Am. Acad. Environ. Medicine. Office: Dartmouth Coll Dept Govt Silsby Hall HB6108 Hanover NH 03755 Home: The Greens 53 Lyme Rd Unit #21 Hanover NH 03755 Office Phone: 603-646-1029. Business E-Mail: roger.d.masters@dartmouth.edu.

MASTERS, STANLEY H., economics professor; b. Boston, Feb. 11, 1940; s. Malcolm H. and Claire M. Masters; m. Julie J. Jones, July 2, 1966; children: Sarah K., Joseph D. BA, Amherst Coll., Mass., 1961; PhD, Princeton U., NJ, 1965. Rsch. assoc. U. Wis., Madison, 1974—81; prof. economics Binghamton U., NY, 1981—. Contbr. articles to profl. jour. Unitarian Universalist. Home: 2641 Lynnhurst Dr Vestal NY 13850 Office: Binghamton Univ Binghamton NY 13902 Personal E-mail: masterssj@aol.com.

MASTERSON, CARLIN See GLYNN, CARLIN

MASTERSON, JAMES FRANCIS, psychiatrist; b. Phila., Mar. 25, 1926; s. James Francis and Evangeline (O'Boyle) M.; m. Patricia Cooke, Jan. 28, 1950; children: James F., Richard K., Nancy. BS, U. Notre Dame, 1947; MD, Jefferson Med. Sch., Phila., 1951. Diplomate Am. Bd. Psychiatry, Am. Bd. Neurology. Intern Phila. Gen. Hosp., 1951-52; resident in psychiatry Payne Whitney Clinic, N.Y. Hosp., N.Y.C., 1952-55, chief resident, 1955-56, dir. adolescent OPD, 1956-66, head adolescent program, 1968-75, asst. attending psychiatrist, 1956-60, assoc. attending psychiatrist, 1960-70, attending psychiatrist, 1970—, dir. The Symptomatic Adolescent Research Project, 1957-67; dir. Masterson Group, P.C. for Study and Treatment Personality Disorders, N.Y.C., 1977—. Author: Psychotherapy of the Borderline Adolescent, Psychotherapy of the Borderline Adult, Countertransference, Narcissistic Personality Disorder, The Real Self, The Psychiatric Dilemma of Adolescence, The Test of Time: From Borderline Adolescent to Functioning Adult, The Personality Disorders: As Seen Through the Lens of Attachment Theory and Neurobiology Development of the Self, 2005; contbr. articles to profl. jours. Fellow Am. Psychiat. Assn., Am. Coll. Psychoanalysts; mem. AMA, Am. Coll. Psychoanalysis, N.Y. Soc. Adolescent Psychiatry (founder, past pres.), N.Y. County Med. Soc. Office: 60 Sutton Pl S New York NY 10022-4168 Office Phone: 212-751-4992. Business E-Mail: mastersnin@aol.com.

MASTERSON, JOHN PATRICK, retired language educator; b. Chgo., Mar. 15, 1925; s. Michael Joseph and Delia Frances (Dolan) M.; m. Jean Frances Wegrzyn, Aug. 18, 1956; children: Mary Beth, Michael, Maureen, Laura. BA, St. Mary of the Lake, 1947; MA, De Paul U., 1952; PhD, U. Ill., 1961. Chmn. English dept. De Paul U., Chgo., 1964-67, head humanities div., 1967-70, prof. English, 1970, dean Coll. Liberal Arts and Scis., 1970-76, prof. mgmt., 1976-80, 82-87, dean Grad. Sch., 1980-82; emeritus, 1988—. Cons. in field. Recipient award Shell Oil Co., 1968, Via Sapientiae award De Paul U., 1987; fellow adminstrn. program Am. Coun. Edn. Roman Catholic. Home: 1922 Belleview Ave Westchester IL 60154-4345

MASTERSON, JOSEPH DANIEL, lawyer; b. Amirillo, Tex., Feb. 11, 1953; s. Thomas Murray and Elizabeth Francis (Leu) M.; m. Doris I. Owen, Aug. 8, 1981; children: Jeffrey S. Owen, Michele O. Ramirez. BS Bus. Adminstrn. summa cum laude, Culver-Stockton Coll., 1975; JD magna cum laude, Harvard U., 1978. Bar: Wis. 1978. Assoc. Quarles & Brady, Milw., 1978—, ptnr. Contbr. Mem.: ABA, State Bar Wis. United Methodist. mem. Harvard Law Rev. 1977-1978. Office: Quarles & Brady 411 E Wisconsin Ave Milwaukee WI 53202-4497 Office Phone: 414-277-5169. Office Fax: 414-978-8969. Business E-Mail: jdm@quarles.com.

MASTERSON, KENNETH RHODES, lawyer; b. Kennett, Mo., Feb. 22, 1944; s. H. Byron and Mary (Rhodes) M.; children— Michael K., Elizabeth Megel, Grace Megel BA, Westminster Coll., 1966; JD, Vanderbilt U., 1970. Bar: Mo. 1970, Tenn. 1976. Ptnr. Thomason, Crawford & Hendrix, Memphis, 1976-79; v.p. legal Federal Express, Memphis, 1980-81, sr. v.p., gen. counsel, 1981-93, sr. v.p., gen. counsel and sec., 1993-96, exec. v.p., gen. counsel and sec., 1996-98, FedEx Corp., Memphis, 1998—2005, cons., 2005—. Mem. ABA, Mo. Bar Assn., Am. Corp. Counsel Assn. Home: 8679 Classic Dr Memphis TN 38125-8824 Office: FedEx Corp 942 S Shady Grove Rd Memphis TN 38120-4117 Fax: 901-818-7590.

MASTERSON, KLEBER SANLIN, JR., physicist; b. San Diego, Sept. 26, 1932; s. Kleber Sandlin and Charlotte Elizabeth (Parker) M.; m. Sara Ann Cooper, Dec. 21, 1957; children: Thomas Marshall, John Cooper. BS in Engring., US Naval Acad., Annapolis, 1954; MS in Physics, US Naval Postgrad. Sch., Monterey, Calif., 1961; PhD in Physics, U. Calif., San Diego, 1963; grad. in advanced mgmt. program, Harvard Bus. Sch., 1982. Commd. ensign USN, 1954, advanced through grades to rear adm., 1979, comdg. officer USS Preble Pearl Harbor, Hawaii, 1969-71, mgr. antiship missile def. project Washington, 1974-77, exec. asst. to sec. of Navy, 1977-79, asst. dep. comdr. Naval Sea Systems Command, 1979-81, chief Studies, Analyses and Gaming Agy., 1981-82, ret., 1982; prin. Booz, Allen and Hamilton, Inc., Arlington, Va., 1982-87, v.p. and ptnr., 1987-92; sr. v.p. Sci. Applications Internat. Corp., 1992—96; pres. The Riverside Group, Ltd., 1994—2005; ret. Bd. control, editl. bd. US Naval Inst., Annapolis, Md., 1971-82, chmn. editl. bd. 1974-82; bd. dirs. Mil. Ops. Rsch. Soc., 1984-90, pres., 1988-89; mem. divsn. rev. com. TSA divsn. Los Alamos Nat. Lab., 1996-2001, chmn. 1998-2001. Editor: Book of Navy Songs, 1954; contbr. articles on plasma and theoretical nuclear physics, computer science, radars, ops. rsch. to profl. publs. Active Historic Alexandria Resources Commn., 1998—2008, vice-chmn. 2001-02, chmn., 2002-04. Decorated Defense Superior Svc. medal, Legion of Merit with 2 gold stars, Navy Commendation medal with combat V and 2 gold stars. Mem. Am. Phys. Soc., US Naval Acad. Alumni Assn. (pres. Washington chpt. 1989-90), US Naval Acad. Found. (trustee 1991—), Soc. of Cin. (chmn. edn. com. 1997-2001, asst. sec. gen. 2001-04, editor Cin. Fourteen 2001-04, treas. gen. 2004-07, v.p. gen. 2007-), Mass. Soc. of Cin. (mem. standing com., v.p. 1999-2001, pres. 2001-04), Sigma Xi. Achievements include development of NELIAC computer program and strategic simulation methodology. Home and Office: 101 Pommander Walk Alexandria VA 22314-3844 Home Phone: 703-548-4464; Office Phone: 703-548-6183. Personal E-mail: skidmasterson@cs.com.

MASTERSON, LISA M., gynecologist, obstetrician; married; 1 child. Grad., Mt. Holyoke Coll.; MD, U. So. Calif. Pvt. practice, Santa Monica, Calif.; founder, med. dir. Ocean Oasis Med. Spa, Santa Monica, Calif.; staff mem. Cedars-Sinai Med. Ctr., LA. Med. expert The Doctors, 2008—. Founder Maternal Fetal Care Internat. (MFCI). Office: Ocean Oasis Med Spa 1333 Ocean Ave Santa Monica CA 90401 Office Phone: 310-451-9900.*

MASTERSON, MARY STUART, actress; b. NYC, June 28, 1966; d. Peter and Carlin Glynn Masterson; m. George Carl Francisco, May 25, 1990 (div. 1992); m. Damon Santostefano, May 20, 2000 (div. 2004); m. Jeremy Davidson, 2006. Attended, NYU. Theatre appearances include Alice in Wonderland, 1982, Been Taken, 1985, The Lucky Spot, 1987, Lily Dale, 1987, Three Sisters, 1991, Nine, 2003; actress: (TV movies) City in Fear, 1980, Love Lives On, 1985, Lily Dale, 1996, On the 2nd Day of Christmas, 1997, Black and Blue, 1999, Three Blind Mice, 2001, R.U.S./H., 2002, Something the Lord Made, 2004; (films) The Stepford Wives, 1975, Heaven Help Us, 1984, At Close Range, 1985, My Little Girl, 1986, Gardens of Stone, 1987, Some Kind of Wonderful, 1987, Mr. North, 1988, Chances Are, 1989, Immediate Family, 1989, Funny About Love, 1990, Married To It, 1990, Fried Green Tomatoes, 1991, Mad at the Moon, 1992, Benny and Joon, 1993, Bad Girls, 1994, Radioland Murders, 1994, Heaven's Prisoners, 1996, Bed of Roses, 1996, Digging to China, 1997, Dogtown, 1997, The Postman, 1997, The Florentine, 1998, The Book of Stars, 1999, The Book of Stars, 2000, Leo, 2002, West of Here, 2002, The Sisters, 2005, Whiskey School, 2005, The Insurgents, 2006; (TV appearances) Amazing Stories, 1986, Hallmark Hall of Fame, 1996, Kate Brasher (6 episodes), 2001, Gary the Rat, 2003, Blue's Clues, 2004, Law & Order: Special Victims Unit (5 episodes), 2004-07, Waterfront (5 episodes), 2006; dir, prodr.: (films) The Cake Eaters, 2009; prodr. (films) Last Man Running, 2003 Office: PO Box 240002 Los Angeles CA 90024*

MASTERSON, PETER, actor, film producer; b. Houston, June 1, 1934; s. Carlos Bee and Josephine Yeager (Smith) M.; m. Carlin Glynn, Dec. 29, 1960; children: Carlin Alexandra, Mary Stuart, Peter Carlos. BA in History, Rice U., 1957. Appeared in Broadway plays Marathon '33, 1963, Blues for Mr. Charlies, 1964; title role in Trial of Lee Harvey Oswald, 1967; appeared in The Great White Hope, 1968, That Championship Season, 1974, The Poison Tree, 1975, (films) The Exorcist, 1972, Man on a Swing, 1973, The Stepford Wives, 1974; playwright The Best Little Whorehouse in Texas, 1978; dir. Broadway prodns. The Best Little Whorehouse in Texas, 1978 (Drama Desk award for Best Dir. of Musical 1978); co-dir., co-writer The Best Little Whorehouse Goes Public, 1994; dir. off-Broadway prodns. The Cover of Life, 1994, The Young Man from Atlanta (Pulitzer prize 1995); screenwriter The Best Little Whorehouse in Texas, 1980; prodr. (TV film) City in Fear, 1980; dir. films The Trip to Bountiful, 1985, Blood Red, 1986, Full Moon in Blue Water, 1987, Night Game, 1988, Convicts, 1989, Arctic Blue, 1993, Lily Dale, 1996, The Only Thrill, 1997, Mermaid, 1999, Lost Junction, 2001, Whiskey Sch., 2005. Mem. AFTRA, SAG, Actors Equity Assn., Soc. Stage Dirs. and Choreographers, Writers Guild Am., Actors Studio, Dirs. Guild Am., Seawanhaka Club, Corinthian Yacht Club, Tex. Corinthian Yacht Club.

MASTERSON, WILLIAM A., retired judge; b. NYC, June 25, 1931; s. John Patrick and Helen Audrey (O'Hara) M.; m. Julie Dohrmann Cosgrove; children: Mark, Mary, Timothy, Barbara. BA, UCLA, 1953, JD, 1958. Bar: Calif. 1959, U.S. Supreme Ct. 1965. Assoc. Sheppard, Mullin, Richter & Hampton, LA, 1952-62, pntr., 1962-79; ptnr. Rogers & Wells, 1979-83, Skadden, Arps, Slate, Meagher & Flom, 1983-87; judge L.A. Superior Ct., 1987-92; justice Ct. Appeal, 1993-2000; ret., 2000. Author, editor: Civil Trial Practice: Strategies and Techniques, 1986. With inf. U.S. Army, 1953-55. Fellow Am. Coll. Trial Lawyers; mem. Order of Coif. Office: PO Box 190 Mendocino CA 95460

MASTO, CATHERINE MARIE CORTEZ, state attorney general, former county official; b. Nev., Mar. 29, 1964; d. Manny and Joanna Cortez; m. Paul E. Masto. BS in Fin., U. Nev., Reno, 1986; JD cum laude, Gonzaga U. Sch. Law, Spokane, Wash., 1990. Bar: Nev. 1990, US Dist. Ct. (dist. Nev.) 1991, US Ct. Appeals (9th cir.) 1994. Law clk. to Judge Michael J. Wendell 8th Jud. Dist. Ct., 1990—91; assoc. Raleigh, Hunt & McGarry, P.C., Las Vegas, 1991—95; staff mem. to Gov. Bob Miller State of Nev., Carson City, 1995—98, chief of staff, 1998—2000; asst. US atty. Dist. Nev. US Dept. Justice, Las Vegas, 2000—02; asst. county mgr. Clark County, Nev., 2002—05; atty. gen. State of Nev., Carson City, 2007—. Mem. So. Nev. Domestic Violence Ct. Task Force, Supreme Ct. Nev. Ct. Funding Commn. Democrat. Office: Office of Atty Gen Nev Dept Justice 100 N Carson St Carson City NV 89701-4717 Office Phone: 775-684-1100.*

MASTOVSKA, KATERINA, chemist, researcher; m. Jan Mastovsky, June 10, 2000; 1 child, Richard Mastovsky. MS in Chemistry, Inst. Chem. Tech., Prague, Czech Republic, 1998, PhD, 2001. Rschr. Inst. Chem. Tech., 1995—2001, Drexel U., Phila., 2003—04; vis. scientist USDA, Agrl. Rsch. Svc., Wyndmoor, Pa., 2002—03, rsch. chemist, 2004—. JMPR expert UN, FAO, Rome, 2006—; cons. Gen. Mills, Mpls., 2006—. Contbr. chapters to books, articles to profl. rsch. jours. Recipient Rector award, Inst. Chem. Tech., 1998, award, Josef Hlavka Found., 1998, Extra Effort award, USDA, 2005, Excellence Govt. award, Fed. Exec. Bd., 2008. Mem.: AOAC Internat., Am. Soc. Mass Spectrometry, Am. Chem. Soc., Sigma Xi, Sci. Rsch. Soc. Office: USDA Agrl Rsch Svc 600 E Mermaid Ln Wyndmoor PA 19038 Business E-Mail: katerina.mastovska@ars.usda.gov.

MASTRANGELO, MATT, publishing executive; Ad dir. Rolling Stone mag.; assoc. pub. Men's Jour., 2005—07, pub., 2009—; exec. dir. corp. sales and mktg. Wenner Media, 2007—09. Office: Wenner Media Men's Jour 1290 Ave Americas New York NY 10104 Office Phone: 212-484-1616. E-mail: matt.mastrangelo@mensjournal.com.*

MASTRIAN, JAMES P., retail executive; BS in Pharmacy, U. Pitts., 1965. Lic. pharmacist Pa., Md., Ohio, Va. Pharmacist People's Drug Stores, Inc., 1965; pres., gen. mgr. Gray Drug Fair Stores Sherwin-Williams Co., 1983—89, sr. v.p. merchandising and mktg. Paint Stores Group, 1983—89; positions up to exec. v.p. mktg. Revco Drugstores, 1990—97; sr. exec. v.p. merchandising and mktg. OfficeMax; exec. v.p. category mgmt. Rite Aid Corp., Camp Hill, Pa., 1998-99, exec. v.p. mktg., 1999—2000, sr. exec. v.p. mktg., logistics and pharmacy svcs., 2000—05, COO, 2005—07, spl. advisor corp. strategy, 2007—. Office: Rite Aid Corp 30 Hunter Ln Camp Hill PA 17011-2410 Office Phone: 717-761-2633.

MASTRO, CHRISTOPHER P., secondary school educator; b. Schenectady, NY, Oct. 17, 1946; s. George and Evelyn Mastro; m. Linda Mary Condon, June 27, 1981. BA in English, St. Michaels Coll., Winooski, Vt., 1968, MAT in English, 1969. English tchr. Mohonason H.S., Rotterdam, NY, 1969—71, Clayton Bouton H.S., Voorheesville, NY, 1971—98; edn. supr. St. Rose Coll., Albany, NY, 2001—02, SUNY, Albany, 2002—. H.S. basketball coach, 1971—86; spkr. in field; vol. writing/English instr. Hope House Residential Adolescent Facility, Colonie, NY, 2002—. Recipient Outstanding Tchr. award, Golub, 1990, Vol. Tchg. award, Albany County Exec., 2008. Mem.: NY State United Tchrs.

MASTROMARCO, DAN RALPH, lawyer, consultant; b. Saginaw, Mich., Jan. 18, 1958; s. Victor and Helen (Finkbeiner) M. Student, London Sch. of Econs., Eng., 1982; JD, U. Toledo, 1983; LLM, Georgetown U., 1985. Bar: Mich. 1983, DC 1984, Md., 2009. Counsel US Senate, Permanent Subcom. on Investigations, Washington, 1983-85; trial atty. Tax div. US Dept. of Justice, Washington, 1985-86; asst. chief counsel for tax policy US SBA, Washington, 1986-92; dir. tax and fiscal policy Jefferson Group, Washington, 1992-94; pres., CEO The Argus Group, Washington, 1994—. Coord. Nat. Adv. Coun. for Small Bus., Tax Com., 1986-88; hon. mem. tax com. Small Bus. Legis. Coun., 1986-90; adj. prof. internat. mgmt. program U. Md.; exec. dir. Travel Coun. Fair Competition; pres. Prosperity Inst. Author: The Art of Lobbying in Poland, 1995, Out by Its Roots, 1999, The Secret Chamber on the Public Square?, 2006; contbr. author, editor profl. jours., reports. Mem. Nat. Italian Am. Bar Assn. (trustee scholarship fund, counsel, v.p.), US C. of C. (tax policy com.). Roman Catholic. Office: 7764 Armistead Rd Lorton VA 22079 Office Phone: 703-521-3900. Personal E-mail: argusgroupdrm@aol.com.

MASTROMONACO, ALYSSA, federal official; b. 1976; BA in Polit. Sci., U. Wis., Madison, 1998. Press sec. for Representative Rick Boucher US Congress; dir. scheduling presdl. campaign for Senator John Kerry US Senate, 2004, dir. scheduling for Senator Barack Obama, 2005—06; polit dir. Hopefund com., 2006; dir. scheduling & advance Barack Obama Presdl. Campaign, Chgo., 2007—08, The White House, Washington, 2009—. Office: The White House 1600 Pennsylvania Ave NW Washington DC 20500 Office Phone: 202-456-1414.*

MASTROPIETRO, GAIL, psychologist, consultant; d. Francis and Evelyn O'Connor; children: Stepahnie York, Joseph. CAGS in psychology, RI Coll., 1991. Consulting psychologist AVATAR Residential Svc., Warwick, RI, 1990—; sch. psychologist Providence Sch. Dept., 1993—. Dir. RI Teen Inst., Cranston, 1988—92. Legislative chairperson RI Sch. Psychologist Assn., Warwick, 2007—. Recipient Profl. Svc. award, RI Sch. Psychologist Assn., 1996, Profl. Recognition award, OSARR, 1999. Office: Providnece Sch Dept 234 Daboll St Providence RI 02909 Personal E-mail: gail.mastropietro@ppsd.org.

MASUCCI, CARMINE, retired electrical engineer; b. Jan. 29, 1923; s. Anthony and Luigia (Capozzi) M.; m. Carmela Marie Greco, July 14, 1951; children: Mary Lou Masucci Rothfuss, Melinda Masucci Di-Napoli. BSEE, CCNY, 1944; postgrad., Poly. Inst. N.Y., 1948-56. Assoc. gen. mgr. intelligence sys. dept. CBS Labs., Stamford, Conn., 1960-69, gen. mgr. govt. and indsl. sys., 1973-75; v.p. tech. ops. Sequential Info. Sys., Elmford, N.Y., 1969-70; mgr. advanced electro-optical sys. Astro Electronics divsn. RCA, Hightstown, N.J., 1970-73; v.p. gen. mgr. EPSCO Labs., Wilton, Conn., 1975-76; v.p. engring. IZON Corp., Stamford, 1976-79, New Brunswidk Sci. Co, Inc., Edison, N.J., 1979-84; engring. mgr. Hartman Sys. divn. Figgie Internat. Inc., Huntington Station, NY, 1984—89; group mgr. Cardion Electroinics Inc. divsn. Siemens Inc., Woodbury, N.Y., 1989-94; ret., 1994. Cons. in field, historian Polytechnic Alumni Assn. Contbr. articles to profl. jours. Pres. parents coun. Manhattanville Coll., Purchase, N.Y., 1979-80, voice, Eastchester Town Bd. Meetings, Eastchester Union Free Sch. Dist. Bd. of Edn., Annual Interfaith Holocaust Commemoration in Bronxville, Eastchester and Tuckahoe; writer local papers. With USNR, 1944-46. Mem. IEEE (life), Soc. Photog. Instrumentation Engrs., Soc. Photog. Sci. Engrs., Soc. Info. Display, Poly. Inst. Alumni Assn. (dir., historian). Roman Catholic. Home: 64 Hickory Hill Rd Eastchester NY 10709-1439 Personal E-mail: cmasucci@aol.com.

MASUCCI, MICHAEL JAMES, artist; b. NYC, Nov. 24, 1952; s. Allen A. and Frances Masucci; life ptnr. Kate Johnson, Sept. 30, 1969. Student, Arts Students League of N.Y., Parsons Sch. of Design, CUNY, 1972—74, Columbia U., 1974—76. Studio mgr. Alan Kaplan Studios, NYC, 1978—79; master printer Modernage Photographics, NYC, 1979—2002; CEO/dir. EZTV, Santa Monica, Calif., 1983—; video artist Bethune Theaterdanse, LA, 1986—2002, Loretta Livingston and Dancers, LA, 2001—05. Co-creator, v.p. Rock Against Racism-USA, NYC, 1978—80; faculty Otis Coll. of Art and Design, LA, 2002—05; adv. bd. DV Expo, LA, 2003—05; curator Hacking the Timeline, Santa Monica, Calif., 2006—. Prodr.: (feature film) Exile in Paradise, 1989 (AFI Retrospective, 1999); dir.: Quantum Entanglement, 2003; contbr. book,; cinematographer (documentary film) The Sharpest Girl in Town, 1989 (commd. Mus. of Modern Art, NY, 1999); dir.: (documentary film) Zina Bethune in China, 1989 (AFI retrospective, 1999), Outside Looking In, 1996 (ICA-London Screening, 1996); contbr. articles to mags. and profl. jours. Judge for grants Roy Dean Film Awards, LA, 2002—06; adv. bd. LA Theater Ctr., 1990—92, West Hollywood Mktg. Corp., Calif., 1990—92; bd. mem. Avaz Internat. Dance Theater, LA, 2005—06; adv. bd. LA Free Clinic. Recipient Artistic and Cmty. Svc. award, Dance Outreach/Bethune Theaterdanse, 1987, award, Changchun Film Studios, China, 1987, Artistic and Cmty. Svc. award, City of West Hollywood, 2001, Directing Award for Quantum Entanglement, Telly Awards, 2004, Curating award, James Irvine Found., 2005-6; named one of Top 100 Prodrs., Prodr. Mag., 2000; Prodn. grant, Milken Found., 1989, Inst. of Contemporary Art, London, 1997, Exhbn. grant, West Hollywood Mktg. Com., 2000, Calif. Arts Coun., 2000, Online Exhbn. grant, Adobe Software, 2004-5, Artist grant, French Ministry of Culture, 2005-6, Prodn. grant, Santa Monica Cultural Affairs Dept., 2006, LA County Arts Commn., 2006. Mem.: L.A. Assn. of Ind. Video and Filmmakers (pres. 2006), Assn. of Ind. Video and Filmmakers, Assn. of Ind. Feature Film Prodrs., Assn. Computing Machinery Spl. Interest Group in Computer Graphics (chmn. digital video commitee 2002—03), Digital Video Expo (adv. bd. 2003—05). Achievements include invention of LiteCrane projection technology. Office: Eztv 1629 18th St #6 Santa Monica CA 90404 E-mail: mmasucci@eztvmedia.com.

MASUI, YOSHIO, zoology educator; b. Kyoto, Oct. 6, 1931; arrived in Can., 1969; s. Fusa and Toyo Masui; m. Yuriko Masui, May 9, 1959; children: Sayuri, Hitoshi. BSc, Kyoto U., 1953, MSc, 1955, PhD, 1961; DSc (hon.), U. Toronto, 1999. Asst. prof. Konan U., Kobe, Japan, 1965; rsch. staff biologist Yale U., New Haven, 1966-69, lectr., 1969; assoc. prof. U. Toronto, Ont., 1969-78, prof. Ont., 1978-97, prof. emeritus, 1997—, Konan U., 1999—. Recipient Manning award Manning Found., Calgary, Alta., 1991, Gairdner Internat. award Gairdner Found., Toronto, 1992, Albert Lasker award for Basic Med. Rsch., Lasker Found., 1998; named Officer, Order of Canada, 2003. Fellow Royal Soc. London., Royal Soc. Can. Achievements include discovery of Maturation Promoting Factor (MPF) and Cytostatic Factor (CSF) and their roles in cell divison control. Office: Univ Toronto Dept Cell and Sys Biology 25 Harbord St Toronto ON Canada M5S 3G5 Home Phone: 647-343-0497; Office Phone: 416-978-3493. Business E-Mail: masui@rogers.com.

MASUNAGA, DAVID K., mathematics professor; s. Frances Masunaga. BA, Northwestern U., Evanston IL, 1979; EdM, Harvard U., Cambridge MA, 1986. Sr. master math. Iolani Sch., Honolulu, 1979—. Pres. Hawaii Coun. Tchrs. Math., Honolulu, 1981—82. Contbr. articles to jours. Bd. dirs. Oahu Civic Orch., Honolulu, 2002—. Recipient Presdl. award, NSF, 1985, Edyth May Sliffe award, Math. Assn. Am., 2000; fellowship, Woodrow Wilson Nat. Found., 1986, Nat. Tech. Grantee, Hewlett-Packard Corp., 1992, Fallingwater Tchr. fellowship, Western Pennsylvaia Conservancy, 1992. Mem.: Hawaii Coun. Tchrs. Math., Oreg. Coun. Tchrs. Math., Internat. Double Reed Soc., Math. Assn. Am., Am. Math. Soc., Nat. Coun. Tchrs. Math. Achievements include design of correlation between modular origami techniques and isonemal fabric polytopes. Avocation: professional musician. Office: Iolani School 563 Kamoku Street Honolulu HI 96826

MASUR, HENRY, internist; b. NYC, Mar. 8, 1946; s. Jack and Barbara (Forsch) Masur; m. Grace Steinacker, Jan. 14, 1979; children: Carrie, Jack, Julia. AB, Dartmouth Coll., 1968; MD, Cornell U., 1972. Diplomate Am. Bd. Internal Medicine, Am. Bd. Infectious Diseases. Intern, resident N.Y. Hosp., 1972—74; resident Johns Hopkins Hosp., Balt., 1974—75; asst. prof. Cornell Med. Coll., NYC, 1978—82; asst. chief critical care medicine NIH, Bethesda, Md., 1982—83, dep. chief critical care medicine, 1983—89, chief critical care medicine, 1989—. Clin. prof. George Washington U. Med. Sch., Washington. Mem.: Infectious Diseases Soc. Am. (pres. 2006—07), Assn. Am. Physicians, Am. Soc. Clin. Investigation. Office: NIH Rm 2C145 9000 Rockville Pike Bethesda MD 20892-1662 Home Phone: 301-229-1111. Business E-Mail: hmasur@nih.gov.

MASUR, KURT, conductor, music director; b. Brieg, Silesia, Germany, July 18, 1927; Grad., Nat. Music Schule, Breslau, Germany, 1944, Leipzig Conservatory, 1946-48; degree (hon.), U. Mich., Cleve. Inst. Music, Leipzig U., Westminster Choir Coll., Hamilton Coll. Repetiteur and conductor Halle Nat. Theatre, 1948-51; conductor Erfurt City Theatre, 1951-53, Leipzig City Theatre, 1953-55, Dresden Philharm., 1955-58; gen. music dir. Mecklenburg Staatstheater, 1958-60; mus. dir. Komische Oper Berlin, 1960-64; chief conductor Dresden Philharm., 1967-72; conductor Leipzig Gewandhaus Orch., 1970-96; mus. dir. NY Philharmonic, NYC, 1991—2002; conductor London Philharm. Orch., 1989-92, 2000—; music dir. Orchestre National de France, Paris, 2002—; music dir. emeritus Philharmonic Soc. of NY, 2002—. Prof. Leipzig Acad. Music, 1975—; hon. guest condr. Israel Philharm. Orch., 1992. Musician (tours include): Europe, S.Am., Japan, U.S., Can., Mid. East; musician: (rec. artist) Symphonies by Mendelssohn, Symphonies by Brahms, Symphonies by Bruckner, Symphonies by Beethoven, Symphonies by Schumann, Symphonies by Tchaikovsky, Prokofiev's Piano Concertos, Beethoven's Missa Solemnis. Mailing: The London Philharmonic Orchestra 89 Albert Embankment London SE1 7TP England

MASUYAMA, KAZUE, literature and language professor; b. Yokohama, Kanagawa, Japan; PhD, SUNY, Buffalo, 2001. Coord. Japanese lang. program SUNY, 1993—; Japanese lang. specialist Mary Tsukamoto Calif. Japanese Lang. Acad., Elk Grove, 1999—2000; asst. to assoc. prof. Calif. State U., Sacramento, 2002—. AP Japanese lang. and culture exam devel. com. Coll. Bd., NYC, 2007—. Recipient Tchr. award, Nat. Coun. Japanese Lang. Tchrs., 2006; named Outstanding Tchr., Fgn. Lang. Assn. Greater Sacramento, 2005. Fellow: Northern Calif. Japanese Tchrs. Assn. (v.p. 2006—). Office: Calif Univ Sacramento 6000 J St Sacramento CA 95819-6087

MASYS, DANIEL RICHARD, medical educator, department chairman; b. Columbus, Ohio, Mar. 6, 1949; s. Paul John and Jane Marie (Mollenauer) M.; m. Linda Suzanne Bross, June 2, 1974; 1 child, Christopher. AB in Biochemistry, Princeton U., 1971; MD, Ohio State U., 1974. Diplomate Am. Bd. Internal Medicine. Staff hematologist, oncologist U.S. Naval Hosp., San Diego, 1980-84; chief ICRDB br. NIH, Bethesda, Md., 1984-86; dir. Lister Hill Nat. Ctr. Nat. Libr. Medicine, Bethesda, Md., 1986-94; dir. biomed. informatics, prof. Sch. Medicine U. Calif., San Diego, 1994—2004; prof., chair dept. biomedical informatics Vanderbilt U., 2005—. Assoc. editor Acad. Medicine jour., 1988-91, Jour. Am. Med. Informatics, Assn., 1994-2004. Mem. high performance computing White House Office of Sci., Washington, 1991-94; rep. Fed. Networking Coun., Washington, 1991-94. Capt. USPHS, 1984-94; NASA Adv. Aerospace Medicine, 2004-. Fellow: ACP, Am. Coll. Med. Informatics (exec. com. 1989—92, pres. 2006—); mem.: Nat. Acad. Scis., Inst. Medicine, Am. Med. Informatics Assn. (bd. dirs. 1992—95, assoc. editor jour. 1993—2004, Pres.'s award 1992), Alpha Omega Alpha. Office: Vanderbilt Univ 416 EBL 2209 Garland Ave Nashville TN 37232-8340

MATA, DAVID JOSEPH, physician; b. Houston, Feb. 3, 1956; s. José and Josephine M.; m. Patricia M. Mata; children: Daniel José, Timothy John. BA in Biology, Point Loma Coll., 1978; postgrad., Calif. State U., LA, 1978-80; MD, U. Minn., 1987. Diplomate Am. Bd. Family Practice, Nat. Bd. Med. Examiners. Resident in family medicine San Bernardino County Med. Ctr., Calif., 1987-90; med. dir. Salud Med. Ctr., Woodburn, Oreg., 1990-96; pvt. practice Hemet, Calif., 1996—. Adj. asst. prof. Oreg. Health Scis. U. Sch. Medicine, Portland, 1991—96; active staff mem. Salem Hosp., Oreg., 1992—96, Silverton Hosp., Oreg., 1992—96, Hemet Valley Med. Ctr., 1997—; vice-chair Family Medicine, 2000—02; cons., steering com. mem. Am. Lung Assn., Salem, 1992—94; med. dir. Birth Choice, Hemet, 2001—07, Ramona Manor Convalescent Hosp., 2002—, Heartland Hospice, Hemet, 2005—06. Expert witness to U.S. Congress, Oreg. Supreme Ct., 1992; counselor East L.A. Task Force, 1979-80; chaplain Boy Scouts Am., Hemet, 1998—; adv. com. San Jacinto Head Start, 1998—; vol. physician 20th World Jamboree Boy Scouts Am., Thailand, 2002-03. Geriatric Medicine fellow U. Minn., 1985, Med. Student Rsch. tng. grantee NIH, 1985, scholar Nat. Hispanic Scholarship Found, 1987; named one of 10 Outstanding Young Ams., U.S. Jr. C. of C., 1993, Outstanding Young Person of World, 1993; recipient Golden Aztec award Oreg. Human Devel. Corp., 1993, Citation of Merit award Oreg./Pacific Dist. Ch. of Nazarene, 1993, Mentorship award Dept. Family Medicine Oreg. Health Scis. U., 1993, Disting. svc. award Ch. of the Nazarene, Woodburn, Oreg., 1996; named Family Doctor of the Yr., Oreg., 1995; recipient Congl. Tribute, U.S. Ho. of Reps., 1994. Fellow Am. Acad. Family Physicians; mem. Nazarene Health Care Fellowship, Am. Acad. Family Physicians, Northwest Regional Primary Care Assn. (clinicians com. 1990-93), Riverside County Med. Assn., Calif. Med. Assn. Democrat. Mem. Ch. Of The Nazarene. Avocations: drawing, camping, church activities, public speaking. Office: Bldg B, Ste A 255 N Gilbert St Hemet CA 92543-4066

MATA, LINDA SUE PROCTOR, writer, consultant; b. Topeka, Oct. 22, 1950; d. Frank Robert and Anabelle Simpson Proctor; m. Robert William Mata, Aug. 29, 1980; children: Adrian Robert-Proctor, Christiana Nicole. BA in Sociology, U. Ctrl. Okla., 1973; BA in Edn., Pacific Luth. U., 1983; MBA, City U., Renton, Wash., 1999; postgrad., Capella U. Tchr. North Thurston Sch. Dist., Olympia, Wash., 1986—88; cons. Wash. Dept. Social and Health Services, Olympia, 1988—. Tchr. Kid's Outreach, Olympia, 2001—. Author: Roads and Reminiscences, 2002; co-author (with Christiana Mata): Upon the Stars, 2004, Flowers in Bloom, 2006, Evening Shadows, 2006. Mem. NAACP, Thurston County Diversity Coun. With US Army, 1977—81. Recipient Diversity award for State Employees, Washington State, 2004, Cert., South Sound Poets, 2004, Toastmaster Speakers award, 2005. Mem.: U. Okla. Alumni Assn. (assoc.), Toastmasters Internat. (sec.). Avocations: travel, doll collecting, reading, camping, poetry. Personal E-mail: mata222@comcast.net. Business E-Mail: matals@dshs.wa.gov.

MATALIN, MARY JOE, political consultant, editor; b. Chgo., Aug. 19, 1953; d. Steven and Eileen Matalin; m. Artie Arnold (div.); m. James Carville, Nov. 25, 1993; 2 children. BA in Polit. Sci., Western Ill. U.; student, Hofstra Law Sch., Hempstead, NY. Voter contact dir. Reagan-Bush re-election campaign, 1984; chief staff to co-chmn. RNC, 1985; Midwest regional political dir. primary elections Bush-Quayle election campaign, 1988, dir. nat. victory '88 gen. election, 1988; polit. dir. George Bush's 1992 re-election campaign; co-host Equal Time, CNBC, 1993—96; host The Mary Matalin Show, CBS Talk Radio Network, 1996—98; co-host Crossfire, 1999—2001; asst. to Pres. & counselor to v.p. The White House, 2001—02; chief editor Threshold Editions (Simon & Schuster), 2005—. Author: All's Fair: Love, War and Running for President, 1992, Letters to My Daughters, 2004; appearances include (TV series) K-Street, (documentaries) Boogie Man: The Lee Atwater Story. Named one of 25 Most Influential Republicans, Newsmax Mag., 2008. Republican. Office: The Office of Mary Matalin 424 S Wash St Lower Level Alexandria VA 22314 Office Phone: 703-739-6006. E-mail: mary@matalin.info.*

MATALLANA, LYNNE, patient advocacy association administrator; m. Richard Matallana. BA in Polit. Sci., UCLA, 1977; MA in Internat. Politics, London Sch. Economics & Polit. Scis., 1985. Former ptnr. advt. agy., Calif.; co-founder, pres. Nat. Fibromyalgia Assn., Calif., 1997—; cmty. devel. coord, adminstrative asst. City Ont., 1980—83; v.p. mktg. devel Cmty. Sys. Assocs. Inc., 1983—84; mktg. dir. Main Place Mall, JMB Inc.; gen. mgr. Mission Viejo Mall, Edward J. DeBartolo Corp., 1986—89; dir. promotions & pub. relations Raging Waters Amusement Inc., 1989—90; ptnr, v.p. Diversified Mktg. Concepts Inc.; pres. Cause Mktg. LLC, 2005—. Mem. FDA Ctr. for Drug Evaluation Rsch., Arthritis Adv. Com., Nat. Inst. Arthritis & Musculoskeletal & Skin Diseases Coalition. Pub., editor-in-chief Fibromyalgia AWARE mag, 2002—; co-author: The Complete Idiot's Guide: Fibromyalgia, 2005. Office: National Fibromyalgia Association 2121 S Towne Centre Pl Ste 300 Anaheim CA 92806-6124 Office Phone: 714-321-0150. Office Fax: 714-921-6920.*

MATALLY, MOSES, minister; b. Dyede-dein, Grand Bassa, Liberia, Feb. 28, 1964; arrived in US, 1991; s. Garswa Zawodo-gbo and Martha Nyonon-Chean Garswa; m. Harriet Mamie Cooper, Aug. 25, 1992; children: Daneto Abba, Tojyea Garswa, Favor Jahnjay. BTh summa cum laude, Liberia Bapt. Theol. Sem., Paynesville, 1989; MDiv, So. Bapt. Theol. Sem., Louisville, 1993. Cert. Profl. Career Devel. Inst., 1999, A+ profl. CompTIA, 2001, computer tech. Ky. Cmty. and Tech. Coll. Sys., 2001, web page design I and II Ky. Cmty. and Tech. Coll. Sys., 2001; ordained Bapt. Ch., 1989. Pastor Grace Bapt. Ch., Monrovia, Liberia, 1987—90, Cedar St. Bapt. Ch., Owensboro, Ky., 1994—97, Wing Ave. Bapt. Ch., Owensboro, 1999—2004, Ch. for All, Inc., Owensboro, 2004—; assoc. min. Beargrass Bapt. Ch., Louisville, 1991—93. Summer missionary, ch. planter Christian County Bapt. Assn., Hopkinsville, Ky., 1992; co-founder, ch. planter Liberia Inter-Denominational Assembly, Buduburam, Ghana, 1990—91. Author: (book) Color Marriage: Mixed Couples of the Bible Uncovered, 2006; musician: (concerts, recordings on radio & tv) Glorious Harmony singing group. Organizer, cons. Helping Hand Owensboro, 2003—04, Fresh Start for Life, Inc., Owensboro, 2004—07; coord. relief supplies Liberian refugee camp, Buduburam, Ghana, 1990—91. Scholar, Am. Women Liberia, 1986—89, So. Bapt. Conv., 1991—93. Mem.: Am. Assn. Pastoral Counselors, Am. Assn. Christian Counselors. Achievements include founded churches in Liberia, Ghana and United States. Home: 3635 Legacy Run Owensboro KY 42301 Personal E-mail: mogama@gmail.com. Business E-Mail: attend@church4all.com.

MATANO, SALVATORE RONALD, bishop; b. Providence, Sept. 15, 1946; BA in Philosophy, Our Lady of Providence Sem. Coll.; STL, Pontifical Gregorian U., Rome, 1972, D in Canon Law, 1983. Ordained priest Diocese of Providence, 1971, vicar gen., moderator of Curia, 1992—97; asst. pastor Johnston, RI, 1972—73; ordained bishop, 2005; coadjutor bishop Diocese of Burlington, Vt., 2005, bishop Vt., 2005—. Prof. Our Lady of Providence Sem. Coll., 1972—77, diocesan dir. priests' personnel, 1977, diocesan asst. chancellor, 80, vicar adminstrn., co-chancellor; spl. lectr. dept. theology Providence Coll., 1995—2000. Roman Catholic. Office: Diocese of Burlington 351 North Ave PO Box 526 Burlington VT 05402-0526 Office Phone: 802-658-6110. Office Fax: 802-658-0436.

MATARANGLO, ROBERT PATRICK, artist, educator; b. South Amboy, NJ, Mar. 17, 1947; s. Christopher Joseph and Kathleen Rita Mataranglo; m. Sabina Dougherty (div.); 1 child, Sabina. BS in Engring., Newark Coll. Engring., 1968; BS in Engring. Mgmt., NJ Inst. Tech., Newark, 1995; MA in Painting, Montclair Coll., NJ, 1999; MFA in Visual Arts, Vt. Coll., Montpelier, 2002. Sr. engr. John's Manville Corp., NJ, 1968—73, Interpace Corp., Parsippany, NJ, 1973—79; project engr. Ford Motor Co., Edison, NJ, 1979—81, Chanel Perfumes, Piscataway, NJ, 1981—85; sr. project engr. Sandoz Pharm., East Hanover, NJ, 1988—95. Adj. prof. Ocean County Coll., Toms River, NJ, 2000—, Brookdale CC, Lincroft, NJ, 2000—07, Monmouth U., Long Branch, NJ, 2003—05, Kean U., Union, NJ, 2008; artist-in-residence Health Farm, Middletown, NJ, 2004—. Mem. Monmouth County Arts Coun., Art Alliance, 2006; co-founder, past v.p. Shore Inst. Contemporary Art; co-founder Black Box Asbury Pk.; founder, past pres. Chanel Employees Fed. Credit Union. Mem.: Mensa. Avocations: sculpting, movies. Home and Office: 335 Norwood Ln Avon By The Sea NJ 07717

MATARASSO, ALAN, plastic and reconstructive surgeon; b. NYC, Oct. 19, 1953; s. Daniel and Ethel M. BA magna cum laude, Boston U., 1975; MD, U. Miami Sch. Medicine, Miami, Fla., 1979. Diplomate Nat. Bd. Med. Examiners, 1980, Am. Bd. Plastic Surgery, 1986. Intern, dept. gen. surgery Albert Einstein Coll. Med., Montefiore Med. Ctr., Bronx, NY, 1979-80, resident, dept. gen. surgery, 1980—83, chief resident, dept. gen. surgery, 1982—83, resident and chief resident dept. of plastic surgery, 1983—85; fellow aesthetic surgery Manhattan Eye, Ear and Throat Hosp., 1985, asst. attending surgeon, 1985—, attending surgeon, 1986—, NY Eye and Ear Infirmary, 1986—, Beth Israel North Hosp., 1988—; surgeon St. Luke's/Roosevelt Hosp. Ctr., 1986—; asst. attending surgeon Lenox Hill Hosp., 2000—; clin. prof. plastic surgery Albert Einstein Coll. Medicine, 1996—. Expert cons., State NY, Dept. Health, Office of Profl. Med. Conduct. Contbr. chpt. Encyclopedia of Flpas, Mastery in Plastic Surgery; instrnl. course vol. Plastic Surgery Ednl. Found.; editor Clinics in Plastic Surgery on Non Operative Techniques for Facial Rejuvenation and Liposuction and Body Contouring for Operative Techniques in Plastic Surgery; sr. sci. editor Aesthetic Surgery Jour.; numerous profl. presentations; contbr. several articles to profl. jours.; quoted in numerous mags. and newspapers including NY Times, Wall Street Jour., Vogue, Elle, Marie Claire, Hapers Bazaar, Ladies Home Jour., Self, InStyle, GQ, Newsweek, Time and Economist; featured on TV broadcasts including 20/20, Lifetime LIVE, Fox 5 TV, CNN and others. Bd. dirs. Sephardic Home For The Aged, Bklyn.; NE reg. coord., Ultrasonic Assisted Lipoplasty Reg. Workshops, 1996-98. Recipient Physicians Recognition award AMA, 1994, 2004; named one of Best Drs. in Am. Am. Health Mag., 1996, Best Doctors in N.Y., N.Y. Mag., 1996, 98-2005, Castle-Connolly Guide to the Best Drs., NY Metro Area. Fellow ACS, NY Acad. Medicine, Internat. Coll. Surgeons (USA) in Plastic Surgery; mem. Am. Assn. Plastic Surgeons (chair videotape com., 1996-99, symposium com., 1997-99, mem. teaching course subcom., 1996-, vice chair, 1998-99, program com., 1996-, Strategic Planning com., 1999-, travelling prof., 1999-2001, edu. commn., 1999-2000, time and place com., 2000-, chair, corp. sponsorship com., 2000-, rep. to products/svcs. workshop, 2000, parliamentarian, 2001-2002); mem. Am. Soc. Aesthetic Plastic Surgery (bd. dirs.), Fla. Soc. Plastic and Reconstructive Surgeons (corr. mem.), Internat. Soc. Aesthetic Plastic Surgeons (pub. edu. com., 2000), Nat. Endowment for Plastic Surgery, Lipoplasty Soc. N.Am., Assn. for Academic Surgeons, Northeastern Soc. Plastic Surgeons (chmn., aesthetic symposium, 1998-99, bd. dirs.), NY Reg. Soc. of Plastic and Reconstructive Surgery (treas., sec., program chair, pres.), Soc. for Acad. Surgeons, Royal Soc. Medicine, England Oversee Fellow, Am. Cleft Palate Assn., Pan Am. Med. Soc. (mem., sect. on Plastic and Reconstructive Surgery), Pan Pacific Surgical Assn., NY County Med. Soc. (Young Physician's Com., 1992-94, peer review com. I & II, 1993-, grievance com., 1993-, media com., 1993-), Med. Soc. State NY (social discipline com., 1994-, state legis. com., 1994-96), NY Reg. Soc. Plastic Surgeons, (exec. com. 1988-, sci. com. med. program chair, 1988-), NY State Soc. Surgeons, Rhinoplasty Soc. (bd. dirs., historian, pres. elect, 2008), Soc. of Laparoendoscopic Surgeons, So. Med. Assn., AMA, Am. Soc. Plastic Surgeons (Young Plastic Surgeons, 1987-89, Plastic Surgery Product Assessment Commn., 1991-92, CPT/ICD 9 Coding Workshop, 1991-96, Ad Hoc Com. 1992, mktg. com, 2000), Plastic Surgery Edu. Found. (Computerized Exam, 1989, EF Teleplast, 1992-95, vis. scholar, 1993-94, Edu. Assessment, 1992, Internat. Symposia, 1993, chair, Resource Book Subcom. of Resident Information Com., 1995-98, rep. on Domsestic Clin. Symposia, 1997-, In-service Examination Com., Aesthetic and Breast Subcom., 2000, Device and Technique Assessment Com., 2000, Domestic Clin. Symposia Com., 2000), Aesthetic Surgery Edu. and Rsch. Found. (charter mem.), Skin Cancer Found. (med. adv. com., 1986-), Cancers and Careers.org (adv. bd. 2000), Northeastern Soc. Plastic Surgeons. Developed a new technique of muscle tightening and liposuction for flattening the stomach. Office: Manhattan Eye Ear and

Throat Hosp 1009 Park Ave New York NY 10028-0936 Home Phone: 212-628-0900; Office Phone: 212-249-7500. Office Fax: 212-628-5000. Personal E-mail: matarasso@aol.com.

MATARASSO, SETH L., dermatologic surgeon; b. Oct. 12, 1957; MD, U. Buffalo, 1984. Intern Beth Israel Med. Ctr., NYC, 1984-85; resident Baylor Coll. Medicine, Houston, 1985-88; fellowship U. Calif. Sch. Medicine, San Francisco, 1989-90; clin. prof. dermatology Sch. Medicine U. Calif., San Francisco, 1990—. Lectr. in field. Contbr. articles to profl. jours. Fax: 415-362-7745.

MATARAZZO, JOSEPH DOMINIC, psychologist, educator; b. Caiazzo, Italy, Nov. 12, 1925; (parents Am. citizens); s. Nicholas and Adeline (Mastroianni) M.; m. Ruth Wood Gadbois, Mar. 26, 1949; children: Harris, Elizabeth, Sara. Student, Columbia U., 1944; BA, Brown U., 1946; MS, Northwestern U., 1950, PhD, 1952. Fellow in med. psychology Washington U. Sch. Medicine, 1950-51; instr. Washington U., 1951-53, asst. prof., 1953-55; rsch. assoc. Harvard Med. Sch., assoc. psychologist Mass. Gen. Hosp., 1955-57; prof., head med. psychol. dept. Oreg. Health Scis. U., Portland, 1957-96, prof. behavioral neurosci., 1996—2007, prof. emeritus behavioral neurosci., 2007—. Mem. behavioral medicine study sect. NIH; nat. mental health adv. coun. NIMH; bd. regents Uniformed Svcs. U. Health Scis., 1974-80. Author: Wechsler's Measurement and Appraisal of Adult Intelligence, 5th edit., 1972, (with A.N. Wiens) The Interview: Research on its Anatomy and Structure, 1972, (with Harper and Wiens) Nonverbal Communication, 1978; editor: Behavioral Health: A Handbook of Health Enhancement and Disease Prevention, 1984; mem. editl. bd.: Jour. Clin. Psychology, 1962-96; cons. editor: Contemporary Psychology, 1962-70, 80-93, Intelligence: An Interdisciplinary Jour, 1976-90, Jour. Behavioral Medicine, 1977—, Profl. Psychology, 1978-94, Jour. Cons. and Clin. Psychology, 1978-85; editor: Psychology series Aldine Pub. Co, 1964-74; editor Williams & Wilkins Co, 1974-77; contbr. articles to profl. jours. With USNR, 1943-47; capt. Res. Recipient Hofheimer prize Am. Psychiat. Assn., 1962 Fellow AAAS, APA (pres. 1989-90, divsn. health psychology 1978-79, mem. coun. reps. 1982-91, bd. dirs. 1986-90, Ann. Disting. Profl. Contbn. award 1991, Ann. Gold Medal for Life Achievement in the Application of Psychology 2001); mem. Western Psychol. Assn. (pres. 1986-97), Am. Assn. State Psychology Bds. (pres. 1963-64), Nat. Assn. Mental Health (bd. dirs.), Oreg. Mental Health Assn. (bd. dirs., pres. 1962-63), Internat. Coun. Psychologists (bd. dirs. 1972-74, pres. 1976-77), Am. Psychol. Found. (pres. 1994-2000). Home: 1934 SW Vista Ave Portland OR 97201-2455 Office: Oreg Health Scis U Sch Medicine 3181 SW Sam Jackson Park Rd Portland OR 97239 Home Phone: 503-228-3215; Office Phone: 503-494-8644. Office Fax: 503-494-5972. Business E-Mail: matarazz@ohsu.edu.

MATARAZZO, MARIA C., management educator, department chairman; b. Somerville, Mass., Nov. 9, 1945; d. Anthony Samuel and Rose Matarazzo. BS in Bus. Edn. cum laude, So. NH U., Manchester, 1974, MBA, 1983; postgrad., Nova Southeastern U., 1993—94. Instr. So. NH U., Manchester, 1980—84; prof. NH Cmty. Tech. Coll., Manchester, 1984—88; divsn. chair, assoc. prof. Rivier Coll., Nashua, NH, 1988—. Presenter in field. Named Bus. Tchr. of Yr., Dept. Edn., 2005. Mem.: Acad. Mgmt., Bus. and Profl. Women (bd. dirs. 2001—, legis. chair 2002—), Ea. Bus. Edn. Assn., Nat. Bus. Edn. Assn., NH Bus. Edn. Assn. (pres., v.p., bd. dirs., Achievement award 2004), Alpha Delta Kappa, Alpha Sigma Lambda, Pi Omega Pi. Office: Rivier Coll 420 Main St Nashua NH 03060

MATARAZZO, RUTH GADBOIS, behavioral neuroscience and psychiatry professor emerita; b. New London, Conn., Nov. 9, 1926; d. John Stuart and Elizabeth (Wood) Gadbois; m. Joseph D. Matarazzo, Mar. 26, 1949; children: Harris, Elizabeth, Sara. AB, Brown U., 1948; MA, Washington U., St. Louis, 1952, PhD, 1955. Diplomate in clin. psychology and clin. neuropsychology Am. Bd. Examiners Profl. Psychology. Rsch. fellow pediat. Washington U. Med. Sch., 1954-55; rsch. fellow psychology Harvard U. Med. Sch., 1955-57; asst. prof. med. psychology Oreg. Health Scis. U., Portland, 1957-63, assoc. prof., 1963-68, prof. dept. med. psychology, 1968—, prof. emerita, 1997. Woman liaison officer to Assn. Am. Med. Coll.s, 1979—90; cons. Tillamook Job Corps, Oreg. Bd. Med. Examiners, Social Security Adminstrn., Portland Ctr. Hearing and Speech. Author (E. Greif): (book) Behavioral Approaches to Rehabilitation: Coping with Change, 1982; contbr. chapters to books, articles to profl. jours., book reviews to jours. Bd. dirs. Portland Opera Assn., Portland Mental Health Assn., Morrison Child Guidance Clinic, Portland Chamber Orch., Neskowin Valley Sch., Hoover-Minthorn Mus.; gov. Soc. of Mayflower Desc. Oreg. Fellow: APA (mem. policy and planning bd., mem. edn. and tng. bd., vice-chair accreditation bd., chair accreditation task force, mem. accreditation bd., site visitor APA accreditation of grad. programs, mem. coun. of reps., Oreg. rep. to coun. rep., Annual Presdl. award 2007), Oreg. Psychol. Assn. (past pres.), We. Psychol. Assn. (bd. dirs.); mem.: AAAS, Nat. Soc. Colonial Dames Oreg. (treas., fin. chair, bd. dirs.), Portland Psychol. Assn. (past pres.), Sigma Xi. Home: 1934 SW Vista Ave Portland OR 97201-2455 Business E-Mail: matarazr@ohsu.edu.

MATASAR, ANN B., retired dean, finance educator; b. NYC, June 27, 1940; d. Harry and Tillie (Simon) Bergman; m. Robert Matasar, June 9, 1962; children— Seth Gideon, Toby Rachel AB, Vassar Coll., 1962; MA, Columbia U., 1964, PhD, 1968; M of Mgmt. in Fin., Northwestern U., 1977. Assoc. prof. Mundelein Coll., Chgo., 1965-78; prof., dir. Ctr. for Bus. and Econ. Elmhurst Coll., Elmhurst, Ill., 1978-84; dean Roosevelt U., Chgo., 1984-92; prof. Internat. Bus. and Fin. Walter E. Heller Coll. Bus. Adminstrn. Roosevelt U., 1992—2005, prof. bus. emerita, 2005—. Dir. Corp. Responsibility Group, Chgo., 1978-84; chmn. long range planning Ill. Bar Assn., 1982-83; mem. edn. com. Ill. Commn. on the Status of Women, 1978-81 Author: Corporate PACS and Federal Campaign Financing Laws: Use or Abuse of Power?, 1986; (with others) Research Guide to Women's Studies, 1974, (with others) The Impact of Geographic Deregulation on the American Banking Industry, 2002, Women of Wine: The Rise of Women in the Global Wine Industry, 2006; contbr. articles to profl. jours. Dem. candidate 1st legis. dist. Ill. State Senate, no. suburbs Chgo., 1972; mem. Dem. exec. com. New Trier Twp., Ill., 1972-76; rsch. dir., acad. advisor Congressman Abner Mikva, Ill., 1974-76; bd. dirs. Ctr. Ethics and Corp. Policy, 1985-90. Named Chgo. Woman of Achievement, Mayor of Chgo., 1978. Fellow AAUW (trustee ednl. found. 1992-97, v.p. fin. 1993-97); mem. Am. Polit. Sci. Assn., Midwest Bus. Adminstrn. Assn., Acad. Mgmt., Women's Caucus for Polit. Sci. (pres. 1980-81), John Howard Assn. (bd. dirs. 1986-90), Am. Assembly of Coll. Schs. of Bus. (bd. dirs. 1989-92, chair com. on diversity in mgmt. edn. 1991-92), North Ctrl. Assn. (commr. 1994-97), Beta Gamma Sigma. Democrat. Jewish. Avocations: walking, biking, opera, crosswords. Home Phone: 847-498-5959. E-mail: amatasar@roosevelt.edu.

MATCHAR, DAVID B., physician, researcher; b. Balt., Sept. 29, 1955; s. Joseph Charles and Evelyn M.; m. Barbara Fran Goldfinger, May 4, 1980; children: Emily Ruth, Benjamin Jacob, Daniel William. MD, U. Md., 1980. Diplomate Am. Bd. Internal Medicine. Prof. medicine Duke U. Med. Ctr., Durham, NC, 1985—, dir. Duke Ctr. Clin. Health Policy Rsch., 1985—; dir., program health svcs. rsch. Duke Nat. U. Singapore Grad. Med. Sch., 2008—. Fellow ACP, Soc. Gen. Internal Medicine (pres. so. sect. 1988), Am. Heart Assn., Soc. for Med. Decision Making (editl. bd., chair 1993 ann. meeting, trustee), Am. Acad. Neurology. Office: Duke Ctr Clin Health Policy Rsch 2200 W Main St Ste 220 Tower Durham NC 27705 Office Phone: 919-286-3399. Business E-Mail: match001@mc.duke.edu.

MATCHETT, WILLIAM H(ENRY), English literature educator; b. Chgo., Mar. 5, 1923; s. James Chapman and Lucy H. (Jipson) M.; m. Judith Wright, June 11, 1949; children: David H., Katherine C., Stephen C. BA with highest honors, Swarthmore Coll., 1949; MA, Harvard U., 1950, PhD, 1957. Teaching fellow Harvard U., Cambridge, Mass., 1953-54; instr. English lit. U. Wash., Seattle, 1954-56, asst. prof., 1956-61, assoc. prof., 1961-66, prof., 1966-82, prof. emeritus, 1982—. Author: Water Ouzel, 1955, The Phoenix and the Turtle, 1965, Fireweed, 1980, Shakespeare and Forgiveness, 2002, Elementary, 2004; numerous poems and articles; co-author: Poetry: From Statement to Meaning, 1965; editor: Modern Lang. Quar., Seattle, 1964-82. Mem. Soc. Friends. Home: 1017 Minor Ave Apt 702 Seattle WA 98104-1303

MATECKI, PAUL L., lawyer; b. 1955; BA, Grinnell Coll., 1978; JD, St. Louis U., 1981. Bar: Mo. 1981, Fla. 1987. Corp. counsel Raymond James Fin., Inc., St. Petersburg, Fla., 1989—97, sr. v.p., 1989—, gen. counsel, dir. compliance, 2004—, corp. sec., 2006—. Mem.: ABA, Assn. Corp. Counsel West Fla. Chpt. Office: Raymond James Fin Inc 880 Carillon Pky Saint Petersburg FL 33716 Office Phone: 727-567-1000. Office Fax: 727-567-8053.

MATECZUN, JOHN MATTHEW, career military officer; b. Albuquerque, Aug. 29, 1946; s. Alfred Jospeh and Margaret Ellen Mateczun; m. Elizabeth Kathleen Holmes; children: Erin Johnson, Adam Johnson, Laura. MD, U. N.Mex., 1978; MPH, U. Calif., Berkeley, 1982; JD, Georgetown U. Law Ctr., 1988. Diplomate Am. Bd. Psychiatry & Neurology, cert. in forensic psychiatry. Asst. divsn. surgeon, divsn. psychiatrist 3rd Marine Divsn., USN, Okinawa, Japan, 1982—83, med. staff, Nat. Naval Med. Ctr. Bethesda, Md., 1983—85, intern adv, dir. transitional internship, 1985—87, chmn. dept. psychiatry, 1989—90, dir. med. svcs., 1990—91, force surgeon, USMC Forces Pacific Camp Smith, Hawaii, 1991—94, chmn. dept. psychiatry, Naval Regional Med. Ctr. Portsmouth, Va., 1987—89, dir. TRICARE Region 1 Washington, 1994—95, prin. dir. clin. svcs., office asst. sec. of def. (health affairs), 1995—97, chief med. officer Tricare Mgmt. Activity, 1997—98, comdg. officer Naval Hosp. Charleston, SC, 1998—2000, asst. chief ops., Bur. Medicine & Surgery Washington, 2000—01, chief staff, Bur. Medicine & Surgery, 2003, comdr. Naval Med. Ctr. San Diego, 2003—05, dep. surgeon gen., 2005—07, vice chief, Bur. Medicine & Surgery, 2005—07, comdr. Joint Task Force Nat. Capital Region Med., 2007—. Assoc. prof. clin. psychiatry Uniformed Svcs. U. Health Scis. Contbr. chapters to books. Decorated Navy Disting. Svc. medal, Def. Superior Svc. Medal with Oak Leaf Cluster, Legion Merit with three gold stars, Bronze Star, Def. Meritorious Svc. medal, Meritorious Svc. medal with gold star, Navy/Marine Corps Commendation medal, Army Commendation medal, Navy/Marine Corps Achievement medal. Fellow: APA (disting.); mem.: Am. Coll. Physician Execs., Am. Acad. Psychiatry & Law, Assn. Mil. Surgeons of US (life). Office: Joint Task Force CAPMED Bldg 27 8901 Wisconsin Ave Bethesda MD 20889*

MATELES, RICHARD ISAAC, biotechnologist; b. NYC, Sept. 11, 1935; s. Simon and Jean (Phillips) M.; m. Roslyn C. Fish, Sept. 2, 1956; children: Naomi, Susan, Sarah. BS, MIT, 1956, MS, 1957, DSc, 1959. USPHS fellow Laboratorium voor Microbiologie, Technische Hogeschool, Delft, The Netherlands, 1959-60; mem. faculty MIT, 1960-70, assoc. prof. biochem. engring., 1965-68; dir. fermentation unit Jerusalem, 1968-77; prof. applied microbiology Hebrew U., Hadassah Med. Sch., Jerusalem, 1968-80; vis. prof. dept. chem. engring. U. Pa., Phila., 1978-79; asst. dir. rsch. Stauffer Chem. Co., Westport, Conn., 1980, dir. rsch., 1980-81, v.p. rsch., 1981-88; sr. v.p. applied scis. IIT Rsch. Inst., Chgo., 1988-90; proprietor Candida Corp., Chgo., 1990—. Editor: Jour. Chem. Tech. and Biotech., 1972—2008; editor: (N.Am. edit.) Biotech., 2001—08; editor: Penicillin: A Paradigm for Biotechnology, 1998, Directory of Toll Fermentation and Cell Culture Facilities, 2005; contbr. articles to profl. jours. Mem. Conn. Acad. Sci. Engring., 1981—; mem. vis. com., dept. applied biol. sci. MIT, 1980-88; mem. exec. com. Coun. on Chem. Rsch., 1981-85. Fellow Am. Inst. Med. and Biol. Engring.; mem. AICE, AAAS, SAR, Am. Chem. Soc., Am. Soc. Microbiology, Inst. Food Technologists, Union League. Home: 222 E Chestnut St Apt 10B Chicago IL 60611 Office: Candida Corp Ste 1616 77 W Washington St Chicago IL 60602 Office Phone: 312-346-3335. Business E-Mail: rmateles@candida.com.

MATELIC, CANDACE TANGORRA, museum director, educator, organizational consultant; b. Detroit, Aug. 21, 1952; d. Paul Eugene and Madeline Marie (Tangora) M.; m. Steven Joseph Mrozek, Sept. 17, 1983 (div. Sept. 1987); 1 child, Madeline Rose. BA, U. Mich., 1974; MA, SUNY, Oneonta, 1977; PhD in Orgnl. Studies, SUNY, Albany, 2007. Interpretive specialist Living History Farms, Des Moines, 1978-80; mgr. adult edn. Henry Ford Mus./Greenfield Village, Dearborn, Mich., 1981-82, mgr. interpretive tng., 1982-84; dir., prof. mus. studies Cooperstown grad. prog. SUNY, Oneonta, 1985-94; exec. dir. Mission Houses Mus., Honolulu, 1994-96, Historic St. Mary's City, Md., 1997-98; pres./CEO CTM Profl. Svcs., Inc., 1998—; founder, prin. The Cherry Valley Grp., 2002—04. Cons. history mus., 1979—; lectr., tchr. nat. and regional confs., workshops, seminars, 1979—; frequent keynote spkr.; grant reviewer NEH and Inst. for Mus. Svc., Washington DC, 1982—, PEW Charitable Trusts, 2003; mem. guest faculty U. Victoria, BC, 1993, 2000, 02, 03, 04, 06; faculty Distance Course, 2004, 05, 08, 09. Author: (with others) Exhibition Reader, 1992, Distance Learning Course, 2002-, Strategic Interpretation and Program Plan for the Mill and Anselma, 2005; co-author: A Pictorical History of Food in Iowa, 1980, Survey of 1200-Plus Museum Studies Graduates, 1988, Naper Settlement Strategic Interpretation and Program Plan, 2006; contbr. articles and videos on mus. interpretation, tng., orgnl. change and mentoring in mus., 1979—; author conf. procs. Trustee Motown Hist. Mus., 1985—2004; bd. dirs. Hawaii Youth Opera Chorus, 1996; project mgr. prog. plan for the Richard and Sarah Allen Ctr. for Faith, Freedom and Cmty., Mother Bethel Found., 2004-05. Mem. Am. Assn. State and Local Hist. (sec., bd. dirs. 1988-93, prog. chmn. ann meeting 1988, mem. edn. com. 1996-99, co-chair task force on edn. and tng. 1994-96, faculty nat. workshop series 2001-04, Historic House Initiative), designed profl. tng. workshop series, 1999-00, Assn. Living Hist. Farms and Agrl. Mus. (bd. dirs. 1980-88, pres. 1985, John T. Schlebecker award Lifetime Disting. Svc. 1996), Midwest Open Air Mus. Coordinating Coun. (founder, bd. dirs., pres. 1978-80, Candace Tangorra Matelic essay award competition established by MOMCC 2002), Am. Assn. Museums (mus. studies com. 1986-94), Internat. Coun. Museums, Nat. Trust for Hist. Preservation, Hawaii Museums Assn. (bd. dirs. 1994-96), So. Md. Mus. Assn. (bd. dirs. 1997-98). Democrat. Roman Catholic. Home and Office: 338 Navigators Dr Pawleys Island SC 29585-7068 Office Phone: 843-655-0216. E-mail: candace@transformorg.com.

MATENAER, TEGWIN A., artist, retired educator, consultant; BA in Art, Calif. State U., Fresno, 1978. Cert. tchg. Calif. Dept. Edn., Art, 1979, LH Fresno St. U., 1980, RSP Fresno St. U., 1982. Art tchr., grant participant Fresno City Elem. Dist., 1980; tchr. Fresno County Office Edn., 1980—82, Redding, Calif., 1982—89; art tchr. Sequoia Mid. Sch., Redding Elem. Sch. Dist., 1989—95; art and photography tchr. Shasta Coll. Cmty. Edn., 1996—98; art. coord., artist in residence Redding Sch. of Visual and Performing Arts, 1999—2006. Mentor tchr. Shasta County Office Edn., 1986—88; art grant coord. Calif. arts project Sequoia Mid. Sch., Redding Elem Sch. Dist., 1994—95; pvt. art tchr., juror local and regional art and photography shows, exhibits, and competitions. Exhibited in one-woman and group juried shows, 1982—. Recipient awards, Acad. Scis., Moscow, 1990, Redding City Hall Civic Ctr., 1998, 2001—05, Redding Airport, 2001, 2003—04, Category award pastel for Summer Rains, 2002, Best of Show for River Run, 2005, Whiskeytown Visitors Ctr., 2005—06, Category award pastel for Funnel Follies, 2006, Best of Photography Ann. award, Calif. Art Rev., awards, Internat. Ctr. Design, NYC, SCAC, 2009. Mem.: AAUW (artist participant annual home tour scholarship fundraiser 1998—2009, past cultural coord.), Austin Pastel Soc., Sierra Pastel Soc., Pastel Soc. West Coast, Pastel Soc. SW, Pastel Soc. N.Mex, Pastel Soc. Colo. (signature mem.), NW Pastel Soc. Office: Tegwin Matenaer Fine Arts PO Box 992538 Redding CA 96099-2538 Business E-Mail: tegsmail@tegwinart.com.

MATENOPOULOS, DEBBIE, television personality; m. Jay Faires, July 2003 (separated 2008). Student, Va. Commonwealth U., 1992-94; BA in Journalism, N.Y. Univ., 1997. From intern to prodn. asst. MTV News, NYC, 1994-97; co-host The View, NYC, 1997—99.*

MATERA, CRISTINA M, gynecologist, educator; b. Englewood, NJ, Sept. 29, 1960; MD, NYU, 1986. Cert. in ob-gyn. and reproductive endocrinology and infertility. Resident ob-gyn. Columbia Presbyn. Med. Ctr./Presbyn. Hosp., NYC, 1986—90, fellow, 1990—92; asst. prof. Columbia P&S, 1990—. Office: 50 E 77th St New York NY 10075 Office Phone: 212-639-9122. E-mail: cmateramd@mac.com.

MATERA, FRANCES LORINE, retired elementary school educator; b. Eustis, Nebr., June 28, 1926; d. Frank Daniel and Marie Mathilda (Hess) Daiss; m. Daniel Matera, Dec. 27, 1973. Luth. tchrs. diploma, Concordia U., Seward, Nebr., 1947, BS in Edn., 1956; MEd, U. Oreg., Eugene, 1963. Elem. tchr. Our Savior's Luth. Ch., Colorado Springs, Colo., 1954—57; tchr. 5th grade Monterey Pub. Schs., Calif., 1957—59; tchr. 1st grade Roseburg Schs., Oreg., 1959—60; tchr. several schs. Palm Springs Unified Sch. Dist., Calif., 1960—93; tchr. 3rd grade Vista del Monte Sch., Palm Springs, Calif., 1973—93; ret., 1993. Named Tchr. of the Yr., Palm Springs Unified Schs. Mem. Kappa Kappa Iota (chpt. and state pres.). Personal E-mail: franmatera7@aol.com.

MATERIA, KATHLEEN PATRICIA AYLING, nurse; b. Jersey City, Nov. 7, 1954; d. Donald Anthony and Muriel Cecilia (Joyce) Ayling; m. Francis Peter Materia, June 5, 1983; children: Christopher Michael, Donna Nicole. BSN, Fairleigh Dickinson U., 1976. RN, N.J. Critical care nurse Palisades Gen. Hosp., North Bergen, N.J., 1976-87; grad. nurse, 1976-77; nurse critical care unit North Hudson Hosp., Weehawken, NJ, 1977-78. Mem. Alpha Sigma Tau. Democrat. Avocations: bowling, dance.

MATERNA, JOSEPH ANTHONY, lawyer; b. Passaic, NJ, June 13, 1947; s. Anthony E. and Peggy Ann (Popowich) Materna; m. Dolores Corio, Dec. 14, 1975; children: Jodi, Jennifer, Janine. BA, Columbia U., 1969, JD, 1973. Bar: NY 1975, Fla. 1977, US Dist. Ct. (ea. and so. dists.) NY 1977, US Supreme Ct. 1977, US Tax Ct. 1978, US Ct. of Claims 1978. Trusts and estates atty. Chadbourne Parke Whiteside & Wolff, NYC, 1973-76, Dreyer & Traub, NYC, 1976-80, Finley Kumble Wagner Heine Underberg & Casey, NYC, 1980-85; ptnr., head trusts and estates dept. Newman Tannenbaum Helpern Syracuse & Hirschtritt, NYC, 1985-90, Shapiro Beilly Rosenberg Aronowitz Levy & Fox LLP, NYC, 1990—2004, Solomon, Blum, Heymann & Stich, LLP, NYC, 2004—. Lectr. in field; expert witness in trusts and estate field ct. litigations, N.Y., 1999—. Contbr. articles to profl. jours. Chmn. planned giving com., mem. bd. govs. Arthritis Found. NY Chpt., NYC, 1980—; mem. bd. trustees, corp. treas. Cath. Interracial Coun., NYC, 1992—; mem. bequests and planned gifts com. Cath. Archdiocese of NY, NYC, 1988—; corp. sec. Arthritis Found. NY chpt., NYC, 1997—, mem. budget and fin. com., 2001—; mem. Meml. Sloan-Kettering Nat. Trusts and Estates Assocs. Recipient Planned Giving award Arthritis Found.-NY Chpt., NYC, 1994, Discovery Alliance award Arthritis Found.-NY Chpt., NYC, 1995; named Accredited Estate Planner, Nat. Assn. Estate Planners, Marietta, Ga., 1995. Mem. ABA, Fla. Bar (trusts and estate com.), NY State Bar Assn. (com. on estates and trusts, com. on surrogate's ct.), Bar Assn. of NYC (mem. com. on surrogate's ct., mem. con. on estate taxation), NYC Estate Planning Coun. (lectr., author), NY County Lawyers Assn. (mem. com. on trusts and estates 1979—, com. on profl. ethics, com. on taxation 2000—, com. on surrogate's ct. 2007, con. on estates and trusts 2007), Queens County Bar Assn. (mem. com. trusts and estates 1990—, mem. com. on taxation, mem. com. on profl. ethics, com. on surrogate's ct.), Am. Judges Assn. (civil ct. arbitrator NYC), Am. Arbitration Assn. (panel of arbitrators), NY State Trial Lawyers Assn., Richmond County Bar Assn. (com. on surrogates ct., com. on estate taxation, com. on estates and trusts), Columbia Coll. Alumni Assn. of Columbia U. (class pres. 1969—), Columbia Law Sch. Assn., SI Richmondtown Hist. Soc., Archdiocese NY, Regina Coeli Legacy Soc., Phi Delta Phi. Republican. Roman Catholic. Avocations: music, history, theater, lecturing, politics, antique cars. Home: 155 Johanna Ln Staten Island NY 10309-3604 Office: Solomon Blum Heymann & Stich LLP 40 Wall Street 35th Fl New York NY 10005 Office Phone: 212-267-7600. Business E-Mail: jmaterna@solblum.com.

MATES, LAWRENCE A., II, medical company executive, consultant; b. Toledo, Oct. 10, 1954; s. Lawrence A. and Phyllis A. (Thomas) M.; m. Ulrike D. Heermann, Dec. 23, 1977; children: Lawrence A. III, Jessica M. BS in Mktg. cum laude, Princeton U., 1976, MBA, 1977. Sales mgr. Technicare Corp., Cleve., 1977-80; dist. sales mgr. Siemens Med. Systems, Iselin, N.J., 1981-85; regional sales mgr. Digital Equipment Corp., Detroit, 1985-88; v.p. sales Cemax, Inc., Fremont, Calif., 1988—92; exec. v.p. Philips Electronics, Cin., 1992-2000; sr. v.p. Siemens, 2000—. Bd. dirs. Provident Nat. Bank. Bd. dirs. Cin. City Planners, 1994—, United Way, 1985-86, 92-96, Am. Cancer Soc., 1997-99; mem. Ea. Pa. Planning Commn., 2006—; v.p. West Chester Citizen's Bd., 2006—; mem. banker's bd., Malvern, Pa., 2006—. Mem. Med. Researchers Assn., Am. Hosp. Assn., Toledo Bus. Assn. (v.p. 1984-85), Ohio Young Men's Bus. Assn. (pres. 1985, chmn. 1992-93), Cin. Profl. Bus. Assn. (v.p. 1993—), Cin. Health Profls. (dir. 1994-95), Cin. Investors Ltd. (dir. 1994-98), Toledo Investors Ltd. (pres. 1986, 92), Cin. Bankers Club, Cin. Club, Univ. Club (v.p. 1993-96, pres. 1998-02), Sycamore Athletic Boosters (pres. 1996-98, bd. dirs. 1996—). Republican. Roman Catholic. Avocations: swimming, travel, wine collecting, automobiles, golf. Office Phone: 610-448-1517. E-mail: LMATES@aol.com.

MATES, ROBERT EDWARD, mechanical engineering educator; b. Buffalo, May 19, 1935; s. Cyril S. and Ruth Elizabeth Mates; m. Gail Paxson, June 4, 1960; children: Robert E., Elisabeth, Steven. BS, U. Rochester, 1957; MS, Cornell U., 1959, PhD, 1963. Lic. profl. engr., NY, 1962. Instr. Cornell U., Ithaca, NY, 1958-61; asst. prof. SUNY, Buffalo, 1962-65, assoc. prof., 1965-69, chmn. mech. and aero. engring., 1967-70, 79-82, prof. mech. engring., 1969-97, dir. Ctr. Biomed. Engring., 1989-96, prof. emeritus, 1997—. Editor various symposium proceedings; contbr. articles to profl. jours. Mem. supt. adv. com. vocat. edn. Buffalo Pub. Schs., 1990—98. NIH spl. rsch. fellow, 1970-71, 78-79, H.R. Lissner award Am. Soc of Mechanical Engineers, 1995. Fellow ASME (chmn. winter ann. meeting com. 1989-93, mem.-at-large bd. comm. 1988-93, v.p. bd. comm. 1994-98), Am. Inst. for Med. and Biol. Engring. (founding, chmn. acad. coun. 1996-97); mem. AAUP, Biomed. Engring. Soc. (bd. dirs. 1991-94, chmn. awards com. 1991-92, mem. pub. bd. 1992-94), Am. Soc. Engring. Edn. Democrat. Episcopalian. Avocations: woodworking, tennis, sailing, bridge. E-mail: matesr@asme.org.

MATES, SUSAN ONTHANK, physician, educator, musician, writer; b. Oakland, Calif., Aug. 8, 1950; d. Benson and Lois (Onthank) M.; m. Joseph Harold Friedman, Dec. 10, 1978; children: Rebecca, Deborah, William. Student, Juilliard Sch. Music, 1967-69; BA magna cum laude with distinction, Yale Coll., 1972; MD, Albert Einstein Coll. Medicine, 1976. Cert. Am. Bd. Internal Medicine, Nat. Bd. Med. Examiners. Intern Boston City Hosp., 1976-77; fellow in gen. medicine Coll. of Physicians and Surgeons-Columbia U., NYC, 1977-78; resident/fellow in infectious diseases Montefiore Hosp., Bronx, 1978-82; asst. prof. medicine Brown U., Providence, 1982-85, asst. prof. biochemistry, 1985-86, clin. assoc. prof. medicine, 1993-98, vis. lectr., 2006; staff mem., former dir. R.I. State Tb Clinic, R.I. Dept. Health, Providence, 1986-96, cons. Tb program, 1987-96. Judge short story contest Providence Jour., 1994, 98; mem. jury R.I. Coun. Arts Fellowship; contbg. editor Pushcart Prize, Pushcart Press, 1995, 96, 97, 98, 99. Author: (fiction) The Good Doctor, 1994 (John Simmons Short Fiction Award, U. Iowa Press, 1994); contbr. sci. articles to profl. jours., stories to revs. and jours. and anthologies. Recipient Recognition award for young scholars AAUW, 1985, Clin. Investigator award NIH, 1984, R.I. Found. award, 1983; McDowell Colony fellow, 1995, Yaddo fellow, 1996; Symposium scholar in lit. and medicine for 21st Century, Brown U., 1997. Mem. Am. Med. Women's Assn., Poets and Writers, Alpha Omega Alpha.

MATESKY, ELISABETH ANNE, international solo violinist, educator, composer, arranger; b. LA, Oct. 1, 1946; d. Ralph and Betty (Blumberg) M.; m. Allen Leslie Odens, Feb. 18, 1973 (div. Nov. 1979). BMus and spl. degree in violin performance, U. So. Calif., 1964; pvt. study, with Jascha Heifetz, LA, 1962—63, with Nathan Milstein, London, 1969-71, study, 1969—71. Artist in residence in violin Syracuse (N.Y.) U., 1971-72; concertmaster Syracuse Symphony Orch., 1971-72; violinist Chgo. Symphony Orch., 1972-73; concertmaster Rockford Symphony Ill., 1981—87; artist tchr. violin, chmn. dept. string Am. Conservatory Music, Chgo., 1986-91; spl. lectr. in violin Chgo. Musical Coll., 1991-93; in residency artist Trinity Coll. Music, London, 1996—. Mistress of ceremonies Stradivari Soc. Concert Series, Chgo., 1993—; entrepreneur young artists concerts, London, 1994—; mem. bd. patrons Sascha Lasserson Meml. Trust, London, 1996—; guest tchr., performer Sibelius Acad. Music, Helsinki, 1999; concertmaster City Symphony Chgo., 2001—. Writer The Strad Mag., Asta Jour., Sun-Scandinavia Newspaper; interviewer Internat. Young Artists; guest artist Ravinia Music Festival; guest soloist Grant Park Music Festival; violinist (PBS TV) Heifetz Master Class Film: Elisabeth Matesky in Khachaturian Violin Concerto (JH-7), N.Y., 1963; rec. artist BBC of various concertos and recitals, 1967—; solo violinist, artist (TV London film) Grace Under Pressure, 1970-71; dedicatee (PBS TV concert) Bradshaw Violin Concerto, 1981, Hawk! by Doug Lofstrom, 1991; recorded for WFMT Radio, 1991; London '71 (winner popular composition contest, Chgo., 1993); violinist (TV comml.) Sta. WFMT Radio, 1985 (1st prize N.Y. TV Comml. 1986); guest violinist (WFMT Radio) Salute to My Teachers: Heifetz & Milstein, 1995; artist tchr. (film) Elisabeth Matesky Violin & Chamber Music Master Classes at Trinity College of Music, London, 1996; soloist, composer, arranger (films) Ageless for Life, Chgo., CAN TV Films: 1999-London'71, 2000-Fantasia for Solo Violin on Themes from Rimsky Korsakov's Capriccio Espagñol, 2000-Schindler's List for Solo Violin, 2001-Chicagoiananna/Le Cygne for Solo Violin from Saint Saens Carnival of the Animals in "Homage a Sadelle", 2002 (soloist, arranger/music consult to prodr.), "Chicago Baseball Post 9/11--It's More Than a Ballgame", Performance of "To The Chicago White Sox with Love--Elisabeth Matesky's Memorial Transcription for Solo Violin of the Star Spangled Banner", Performance at U.S. Cellular Field (formerly Comiskey Park), Chgo., Chgo. White Sox vs. Chgo. Cubs Classic Baseball Game, 2002. Guest violinist at State Dinner with Pres. Jimmy Carter, White House, Washington, 1977. Named Woman of the Yr. Syracuse Jour. Newspaper, 1971; Fulbright scholar Royal Coll. Music, London, 1964-65, 65-66; NEA grantee Sacramento Symphony Orch., 1979-80; Performing Arts Award for "Chicagoiananna" in "Homage a Sadelle", Hometown Nat. Video Festival, U.S.A., 2002, Special Performance award, Sibelius Internat. Violin competition, Findland, 1965. Mem. Fulbright Alumni Assn. (honoree 1996), Am. String Tchrs. Assn., Chgo. Symphony Alumni Assn. Home: 227 E Walton Place Unit 11 W Chicago IL 60611 Personal E-mail: violinplus@yahoo.com.

MATHAS, THEODORE A. (TED MATHAS), insurance company executive, lawyer; b. Apr. 4, 1967; m. Keryn Mathas; 3 children. AB, Stanford U., 1989; JD, U. Va., 1992. Atty. Debevoise & Plimpton; corp. v.p. NY Life Ins. Co., NYC, 1995—98, pres. Eagle Strategies Corp. subs., 1996—99, pres. NYLIFE Securities, 1997—99, sr. v.p., 1998—2004, COO agy. dept., 1999—2001, COO life & annuity, 2001—04, exec. v.p., co-head life & annuity, 2004—06, vice-chmn., COO, mem. exec. mgmt. com., 2006—07, pres., COO, 2007—08, pres., CEO, 2008—09, chmn., pres., CEO, 2009—. Bd. dirs. Haier NY Life Ins. Ltd., NY Life Ins. Co., 2006—, Am. Coun. Life Insurers, 2007—. Mem. Univ. Va. Law Review. Mem.: Order of the Coif. Office: NY Life Ins Co 51 Madison Ave New York NY 10010 E-mail: theodore_mathas@newyorklife.com.*

MATHENY, ADAM PENCE, JR., child psychologist, educator, consultant, researcher; b. Stanford, Ky., Sept. 6, 1932; s. Adam Pence and Dorotha (Steele) Matheny; m. Ute I. Debus, July 10, 1962 (div.); m. Mary P. Tolbert, June 24, 1967 (div.); children: Laura Steele, Jason Gaverick. BS, Columbia U., 1958; PhD, Vanderbilt U., 1962. Sr. human factors engr. Martin Aerospace divsn., Balt., 1962—63; instr. Johns Hopkins U. Med. Sch., Balt., 1963—65; staff fellow Nat. Inst. Child Health and Human Devel., 1965—67; from asst. prof. to prof. pediat. U. Louisville Med. Sch., 1967—75; assoc. dir. to dir. Louisville Twin Study, 1986—. Mem. rev. panel NIH, 1991—95. Co-author: Genetics and Counseling in Medical Practice, 1969; contbr. articles to profl. jours. With USN, 1951—55. Recipient Outstanding Rsch. medal, U. Louisville. Fellow: APA, Am. Psychol. Soc., Am. Assn. Applied and Preventive Psychology, Internat. Soc. Twin Studies; mem.: AAAS, Internat. Soc. Infant Study, Internat. Soc. Behavior Devel., Behavior Genetics Assn., Soc. Rsch. Child Devel., Sigma Xi, Phi Beta Kappa. Office Phone: 502-634-0050. Business E-Mail: apmathol@louisville.edu. E-mail: adammatheny@aol.com.

MATHENY, EDWARD TAYLOR, JR., lawyer; b. Chgo., July 15, 1923; s. Edward Taylor and Lina (Pinnell) Matheny; m. Marion Elizabeth Shields, Sept. 10, 1947; children: Nancy Elizabeth, Edward Taylor III; m. Ann Spears, Jan. 14, 1984. BA, U. Mo., 1944; JD, Harvard, 1949. Bar: Mo. 1949. Pvt. practice, Kansas City, 1949-91; ptnr. firm Blackwell, Sanders, Matheny, Weary & Lombardi, 1954-91. Pres. St. Luke's Hosp., Kansas City, 1980-95; bd. dirs. Dunn Industries, Inc. Author: The Presence of Care (History of St. Luke's Hospital, Kansas City), 1997, A Long and Constant Courtship (The History of a Law Firm), 1998, The Rise and Fall of Excellence, 2000, The Pursuit of a Ruptured Duck (When Kansas Citians Went to War), 2001. Pres. Cmty. Svc. Broadcasting of Mid-Am., Inc., 1971—72; chmn. Citizens Assn. Kansas City, 1958; chmn. bd. dir. St. Luke's Found., 1989—95; trustee U. Kansas City, 1980—96, Kansas City Cmty. Found., 1983—94, Eye Found., 1990—2000, H&R Block Found., 1996—, Jacob L. and Ella C. Loose Found., 1996—2005. Mem. Kansas City Bar Assn., Mo. Bar, River Club, Mo. Acad. Squires, Mission Hills Country Club, Phi Beta Kappa, Sigma Chi (Balfour Nat. award 1944) Episcopalian (chancellor emeritus Diocese West Mo.). Home: 4900 Central St Kansas City MO 64112

MATHENY, RUTH ANN, editor; b. Fargo, ND, Jan. 17, 1918; d. Jasper Gordon and Mary Elizabeth (Carey) Wheelock; m. Charles Edward Matheny, Oct. 24, 1960. BE, Mankato State Coll., 1938; MA, U. Minn., 1955; postgrad., Universidad Autonoma de Guadalajara, Mex., 1956, Georgetown U., 1960. Tchr., U.S. and S.Am., 1938-61; assoc. editor Charles E. Merrill Pub. Co., Columbus, Ohio, 1963-66; tchr. Confraternity Christian Doctrine, Washington Court House, Ohio, 1969-70; assoc. editor Jr. Cath. Messenger, Dayton, Ohio, 1966-68; editor Witness Intermediate, Dayton, 1968-70; editor in chief, assoc. pub. Today's Cath. Tchr., Dayton, 1970—2002, editor-in-chief emeritus, 2002—; editor in chief Catechist, Dayton, 1976—89, Ednl. Dealer, Dayton, 1976-80; v.p. Peter Li, Inc., Dayton, 1980—. Editl. collaborator: Dimensions of Personality series, 1969—; co-author: At Ease in the Classroom; author: Why a Catholic School?, Scripture Stories for Today: Why Religious Education?; freelance writer, 1943— Bd. dirs. Friends Ormond Beach Libr. Mem.: 3d Order St. Francis (eucharistic min. 1990—2006), Nat. Coun. Cath. Women. Home: 26 Reynolds Ave Ormond Beach FL 32174-7043 Office: Peter Li Ednl Group 2621 Dryden Rd Ste 300 Dayton OH 45439 Personal E-mail: chilermat@aol.com. *In a world that is constantly changing, a strong religious faith is a dependable compass through which we are able to stay on a positive, forward course.*

MATHER, ELIZABETH VIVIAN, healthcare executive; b. Richmond, Ind., Sept. 19, 1941; d. Willie Samuel and Lillie Mae (Harper) Fuqua; m. Roland Donald Mather, Dec. 26, 1966. BS, Maryville Coll., Tenn., 1963; postgrad., Columbia U., 1965-66. Tchr. Richmond Cmty. Schs., 1963-67, Indpls. Pub. Schs., 1967-68; systems analyst Ind. Blue Cross Blue Shield, Indpls., 1968-71, Ind. Nat. Bank, Indpls., 1971; med. cons. Ind. State Dept. Pub. Welfare, Indpls., 1971-78, cons. supr., 1978-86; systems analyst Ky. Blue Cross Blue Shield, Louisville, 1988-89; contracts specialist Humana Corp., Louisville, 1989—. Active Rep. Cen. Com. Montgomery County, Crawfordsville, 1976-86, Centenary Meth. Ch., adminstrv. bd., 1990. Mem. DAR (treas. 1963-66, sec. 1978-86). Avocation: designing and sewing clothes. Home: 6106 Partridge Pl Floyds Knobs IN 47119-9427 Office: 500 W Main St Fl 6 Louisville KY 40202-2946 Office Phone: 502-580-2519. Business E-Mail: emather@humana.com.

MATHER, JOHN CROMWELL, astrophysicist; b. Roanoke, Va., Aug. 7, 1946; s. Robert Eugene and Martha Belle (Cromwell) Mather; m. Jane Anne Hauser, Nov. 22, 1980. BA in Physics, Swarthmore Coll., Pa., 1968; PhD in Physics, U. Calif., Berkeley, 1974; DSc (hon.), Swarthmore Coll., 1994. NAS/NRC rsch. assoc. NASA/Goddard Inst. Space Studies, NYC, 1974—76; lectr. astronomy Columbia U., NYC, 1975—76; astrophysicist NASA/Goddard Space Flight Ctr., Greenbelt, Md., 1976—, prin. investigator FIRAS on COBE, 1976—, study scientist Cosmic Background Explorer Satellite, 1976—82, project scientist COBE, 1982—, head infrared astrophysics br., 1988—89, 1990—93, sr. scientist Greenbelt, Md., 1989—90, 1993—; head Office of Chief Scientist NASA, Washington, 2007—. Chmn. external adv. bd. U. Chgo. Ctr. Astrophys. Rsch. in the Antarctic, 1992—95; mem. lunar astrophysics mgmt. ops. working group NASA, Washington, 1992; study scientist Next Generation Space Telescope, 1995—2002; mem. NRC Bd. Physics and Astronomy, 1998—2001; sr. project scientist James Webb Space Telescope, 2002—; mem. astrophysics subcommittee NASA Adv. Coun., 2006—. Co-author (with John Boslough): The Very First Light: The True Inside Story of the Scientific Journey Back to the Dawn of the Universe, 1996; contbr. articles to profl. jours. Recipient NSF Fellowship, hon. Woodrow Wilson Fellowship, 1968—70, Hertz Found. fellowship, 1970—74, Nat. Space Achievement award, Rotary Club, 1991, Nat. Air & Space Mus. Trophy, 1991, Aviation Week & Space Tech. Laurels award for space/missles, 1992, John Scott award, City of Phila., 1995, Marc Aaronson Meml. prize, 1998, Benjamin Franklin medal in physics, Franklin Inst., 1999, Presdl. Rank award, NASA, 2003, Cosmology prize, Peter Gruber Found., 2006; co-recipient Nobel Prize in Physics, Nobel Found., 2006; named a Goddard Fellow, 1994; named one of The World's Most Influential People, TIME mag., 2007; named to Aviation Week & Space Tech. Hall of Fame, 1997, Newton HS Hall of Fame, NJ, 2003; finalist Discover Mag. Tech. award, 1993. Fellow: Am. Phys. Soc.; mem.: AIAA (Astronautics Space Sci. award 1993), NAS, Am. Acad. Arts & Scis. (Rumford prize 1996), Soc. Photo-Optical Instrumentation Engrs. (George W. Goddard award 2005), Internat. Astron. Union, Am. Astron. Soc. (councilor 1998—2001, Dannie Heineman prize astrophysics 1994), Phi Beta Kappa, Sigma Xi. Democrat. Unitarian Universalist. Achievements include proposing Cosmic Background Explorer Satellite, led team to successful launch in 1989; measured spectrum of cosmic microwave background radiation to unprecedented accuracy. Office: NASA/Goddard Space Flight Code 443 Observational Cosmology Greenbelt MD 20771 also: Office of Chief Scientist NASA 300 E St NW Washington DC 20546-0001 Office Phone: 301-286-8720, 301-286-6885. E-mail: john.c.mather@nasa.gov.*

MATHER, MILDRED EUNICE, retired archivist; b. Washington, Iowa, July 25, 1922; d. Hollis John and Delpha Irene (Cummings) Whiting; m. Stewart Elbert Mather, Aug. 7, 1955 (dec. Jan. 3, 2006); children: Julie Marie, Thomas Stewart(dec.). Cert., Burlington and Des Moines, 1941, 1947, Stenotype Inst., 1948. Typist Burlington Willow-Weave, 1941-42, Burlington Basket Co., 1942; clk. typist U.S. Dept. War, Washington, 1942-43; supr. internat. conf. U.S. Dept. State, Washington, 1949-52; bookkeeper Iowa Wesleyan Coll., Mt. Pleasant, 1952-55; clk. typist Herbert Hoover Presdl. Libr., West Branch, Iowa, 1964-69, archives technician, 1964-72, archivist, libr., 1972-92, ret., 1992. With WAC US Army, 1943—46. Mem.: Am. Legion, Order Ea. Star. Republican. Home: 1794 Garfield Ave West Branch IA 52358-9403 Home Phone: 319-643-5471.

MATHER, RICHARD BURROUGHS, retired Chinese language and literature educator; b. Baoding, Hebei, China, Nov. 11, 1913; s. William Arnot and Grace (Burroughs) M.; m. Virginia Marjorie Temple, June 3, 1939; 1 dau., Elizabeth Temple. BA, Princeton U., 1935; B.Th., Princeton Theol. Sem., 1939; PhD in Oriental Langs, U. Calif., Berkeley, 1949. Ordained to ministry United Presbyterian Ch. U.S., 1939; pastor Belle Haven (Va.) Presbyterian Ch., 1939-41; asst. prof. Chinese U. Minn., Mpls., 1949-57, assoc. prof., 1957-64, prof., 1964-84. Mem. Am. Council Learned Socs. Com. on Study of Chinese Civilization, 1979-81 Author: Shih-shuo hsin-yu, A New Account of Tales of the World, 1976, rev. edit., 2002, The Poet Shen Yueh (441-513), the Reticent Marquis, 1988, The Age of Eternal Brilliance: Three Poets of the Yung-ming Era, 2003; contbr. articles to profl. jours. Guggenheim fellow, 1956-57; Fulbright Hays grantee, 1956-57, 63-64; Am. Council Learned Socs. grantee, 1963-64 Mem. Am. Oriental Soc. (pres. 1980-81), Assn. Asian Studies. Democrat. Achievements include research in medieval Chinese lit. and religion. Home: 1666 Coffman St Apt 108 Saint Paul MN 55108

MATHER, ROGER FREDERICK, retired music educator, writer; b. London, May 27, 1917; came to U.S., 1938; s. Richard and Marie Louise (Schultze) M.; m. Dorothea Meinen, Sept. 11, 1943 (div. Sept. 1971); children: Arielle Diane, Christopher Richard; m. Betty Louise Bang, Aug. 3, 1973. BA with honors, Cambridge U., 1938; MSc, MIT, Cambridge, 1940; MA in Metallurgy, U. Cambridge, 1941. Registered profl. engr., Ohio, Mich., Pa. Rsch. metallurgist Inland Steel Co., East Chicago, Ind., 1940-42; chief metallurgist Willys-Overland Motors, Toledo, 1942-46, Kaiser-Frazer Corp., Willow Run, Mich., 1946-50; project mgr. U.S. Steel Corp., Pitts., 1950-61; dir. rsch. engring. Mine Safety Appliances Co., Pitts., 1961-62; rsch. staff Du Pont Co., Wilmington, Del., 1962-63; chief nuclear power tech. br. NASA, Cleve., 1963-73; adj. prof. music U. Iowa, Iowa City, 1973-96; ret., 1996. Instr. pub. speaking and stage fright U. Iowa, 1983-85, Kirkwood C.C., Iowa City, 1983-85; cons. Miyazawa Flutes, U.S.A., Coralville, Iowa, 1985-90; lectr. U. Toledo; Mich. state examiner Registration of Profl. Engrs.; condr. numerous workshops, clinics, classes, and flute recitals regionally, nationally, Europe and Asia. Author: The Art of Playing the Flute, 1980, Vol. 2, 1981, Vol. 3, 1988; contbr. chpts. to several woodwind anthologies; pub., exec. editor The Romney Press, 1980—; contbr. poems to numerous poetry anthologies in US, Eng., numerous articles to sci. and music jours. Mem. Internat. Soc. Poets (Hall of Fame 1998, Poet of Merit 2002, Featured Artist 2005), Nat. Flute Assn. (life, coms.), The Pa. Assn., Mensa Episcopalian. Avocations: semi-professional photography, high fidelity sound reproduction contributions, alternative medicine. Home: 715 George St Iowa City IA 52246 Personal E-mail: bangmather@mchsi.com.

MATHERN, TIM, state legislator; b. Edgeley, ND, Apr. 19, 1950; m. Lorene Randall, Feb. 12, 1971; children: Reba, Tonya, Josh, Zach. BA in Sociology, ND State U., 1971; MSW, U. Nebr., Lincoln, 1980; MPA, Harvard U., 2000. Social worker Cath. Family Svc., Fargo, ND, 1973—78, supr. child welfare, 1980—85, family life dir., 1985—95, exec. dir., 1996—99; mem. Dist. 11 ND State Senate, Bismarck, 1986—, asst. majority leader, 1993, minority leader, 1995-99. Mem. Kennedy Sch. Student Govt., Cambridge, Mass., 1999—2000; adminstr. & devel. dir. Church of the Nativity, 2000—06; mem. health care task force Coun. State Govts., 2003—; v.p. pub. policy Prairie St. Johns, 2006—. Mem. Fargo-Cass County Econ. Devel. Corp., 1993—99; bd. dirs. Prairieland Home Care, 1993—99, Charism Cmty. Ctr., 1997—2007; pres., bd. dirs. Kaleidoscope, 2001—02; sch. coun. Martin Luther King Jr., Cambridge, 1999—2000; bd. dirs. Villa Nazareth, 2005—06; treas. Clara Barton Neighborhood Assn., 2004—; dir. Bush Found., 2006—; adv. coun. UND Sch. Medicine & Health Scis., 2003—, New Items State Commn. Nat. Cmty. Svc., 2007—, Metro Youth Partnership, 2008—; mem. exec. com. ND Dem. Nonpartisan League Party, 1995—99; bd. dirs. Am. Diabetes Assn., 2004—07. Recipient N.D. Prairie Peacemaker award, 2000, Pub. Svc. award, U. Nebr. Alumni Assn., 2002, Advocate award, Nat. Assn. Psychiat. Health Care Sys. Grassroots, 2009; named Social Worker of Yr., Nat. Assn. Social Workers, N.D. Chapter, 1987, Legislator of the Yr., Red River Valley Mental Health Assn., 1989, 1991, N.D. Children's Caucus, 1993, 1998; Bush fellow, 1999, Littauer fellow, 2000. Mem.: NASW (Social Worker of the Yr. award 1987, Lifetime Achievement award 1998), Coun. Faith Based & Cmty. Initiatives, Mental Health Assn. Democrat. Roman Catholic. Office: 429 16th Ave S Fargo ND 58103 also: State Capitol 600 E Blvd Bismarck ND 58505 Office Phone: 701-328-3373, 701-476-7825. Office Fax: 701-280-5795. Business E-Mail: tmathern@nd.gov.

MATHERNE, G. PAUL, medical educator; b. Lafayette, La., Oct. 30, 1958; s. Gaynell Paul and Marie Annette Matherne; m. Linda Ann Binko, June 21, 1980; children: Gregory James, Benjamin Thomas, Stephanie Leigh, Nicholas Scott. MD, Tex. A&M U., College Sta., 1982. Pediatric resident U. Okla., 1982—85. Pediatric cardiology fellow U. Iowa, 1985—88; prof. pediat. U. Va., Charlottesville, 1988—, dept. chair, 1988—, divsn. head, 2003—. Fellow: Am. Coll. Cardiology, Am. Heart Assn. (chair congenital cardiac defects sect.); mem.: Cardiovasc. Disease of Young Coun. (vice chair), Soc. Pediat. Radiology, Am. Pediat. Soc., Am. Acad. Pediat. Home: 1533 Surry Hill Ct Charlottesville VA 22901 Office: Univ Va Dept Pediat Charlottesville VA 22908 Business E-Mail: gpm2y@virginia.edu.

MATHERS, MARGARET, senior copy editor; b. Ada, Okla., Feb. 16, 1929; d. Robert Lee and Josiephine Margaret (Reed) Erwin; m. Coleman F. Moss, Sept. 1956 (div. 1966); children: Carol Lee Gibson-Taylor, Marilyn Frances; m. Boyd Leroy Mathers, Apr. 10, 1967 (div. 1987). BS in Music, Tex. U., 1950. Svc. rep. Gen. Tel. Co., Santa Monica, Calif., 1955-58; tchr. pvt. sch. Santa Monica, 1958-60; computer program and data analyst System Devel. Corp., Santa Monica, 1961-66; computer programmer Inst. Def. Analyses, Arlington, Va., 1966-70; typist, transcriber Edgewater, Md., 1971-80; sec. People Assisting the Homeless, 1992-94; proofreader, copy editor Farmington Daily Times, 2004—06, sr. copy editor, 2006—, mem. editl. bd., libr., office mgr., 1999—. Pres. San Juan Coun. Cmty. Agys., 1986-87, treas., 1987-89, sec., 1989-90; cons. in field. Dir. San Juan Cath. Charities, Farmington, N.Mex., 1984-93, asst. dir., 1993-96, sec. bd. dirs., 1997-2000; chmn. county Libertarian Party N.Mex., San Juan County, 1985-99, sec., 2005-, sec. ctrl. com., 1988-92, 2005—, mem. ctrl. com., 1988—; mem. jud. coun. Libertarian Party, N.Mex.; mem. selection com. Habitat for Humanity, 1990; mem. San Juan County Task Force on Housing, 1991, Task Force on Transp., 1991; mem. social justice com. Sacred Heart, Farmington, 1992; mem. adv. bd. San Juan County DNA Legal Aid, 1992, sec., 1993; sec. Cmty. Network Coun., 1992-94, treas., 1994—; treas. Neighborhood Watch, 1998-2005; minister Secular Franciscan Order, 1997-2001; formation trainer Secular Franciscans, 2005—08. Roman Catholic. Avocations: puzzles, politics, philosophy. Office: The Daily Times PO Box 450 Farmington NM 87499-0450

MATHERS, MARSHALL See EMINEM

MATHES, RACHEL CLARKE, voice educator, singer; b. Atlanta, Mar. 14, 1941; d. Frank Alfred and Jacqueline Woolfolk Mathes. MM, U. S.C., 1988, DMA, 1991. Leading soprano Stadttheater, Basel, Switzerland, 1966—66, Deutsche Oper am Rhein, Duesseldorf, Germany, 1967—73, Met. Opera, NYC, 1974—77; prof. voice U. Ala., Birmingham, 1983—. Elder, tchr. bible South Highland Presbyn. Ch., Birmingham, 1999—. Recipient Birmingham News Obelisk award, 1979, 1981, Ala. Music Hall Fame Contemporary award, 1987; scholar, Fulbright Found., 1962—63. Mem.: Nat. Fedn. Music Clubs, Nat. Assn Tchrs. Singing, Pi Kappa Alpha.

MATHES, STEPHEN JON, lawyer; b. NYC, Mar. 18, 1945; s. Joseph and Beatrice M.; m. Michele Marshall, Oct. 22, 1972 (div. 1992); children: Aaron, Benjamin; m. Maria McGarry, Dec. 19, 1992; 1 child, Sara. BA, U. Pa., 1967, JD, 1970. Bar: NY 1971, Pa. 1972, US Dist. Ct. (ea. dist.) Pa. 1971, US Ct. Appeals (3d cir.) 1972, US Supreme Ct. 1978, US Ct. Appeals (5th cir.) 1985, US Ct. Appeals (4th cir.) 1985, US Ct. Appeals (9th cir.) 2000. Law clk. US Ct. Appeals (3d cir.), Phila., 1970-71; asst. dist. atty. major felony unit, spl. investigation unit Office of Phila. Dist. Atty., 1975; assoc. Dilworth, Paxson, Kalish & Kauffman, Phila., 1971-74, 76-77, sr. ptnr., 1977-91, mem. exec. com., 1987-90, co-chmn. litig. dept., 1987-91; ptnr. Hoyle, Fickler, Herschel & Mathes (formerly Hoyle, Morris & Kerr), Phila., 1992—; bd. dirs. The Levitt Found., 1990—, sec., 1991—2006, pres., 2006—. Mgmt. com. Hoyle, Morris & Kerr, Phila., 1992-97, 2001—. Bd. dirs., exec. com. Acad. Vocal Arts, 1993-2000, mem. exec. com., chmn. student aid com.; mem. legal and compliance divsn. Securities Industry Assn., 1998—, Am. Law Inst. 1995; trustee Harvard Review of Philosophy, 2004-; pres. Levitt Found., 2006-. Mem. ABA, Am. Law Inst., Securities Industries Assn., Pa. Bar Assn., Phila. Bar Assn. (mem. litig. divsn.), Thanatopsis Soc., Racquet Club, Germantown Cricket Club. Home: 199 Lynnebrook Ln Philadelphia PA 19118-2706 Office: Holye Fickler Herschel & Mathes Ste 1500 One S Broad St Philadelphia PA 19107 Office Phone: 215-981-5880. Business E-Mail: smathes@hoylelawfirm.com.

MATHESON, ALAN ADAMS, law educator; b. Cedar City, Utah, Feb. 2, 1932; s. Scott Milne and Adele (Adams) M.; m. Milicent Holbrook, Aug. 15, 1960; children: Alan, David Scott, John Robert. BA, U. Utah, 1953, MS, 1957, JD, 1959; postgrad., Columbia U. Bar: Utah 1960, Ariz. 1975. Asst. to pres. Utah State U., 1961-67; mem. faculty Ariz. State U., Tempe, 1967—, prof. law, 1970—, dean, 1972, 1978-84, 89, 97-98. Bd. dirs. Ariz. Found. for Legal Svcs. and Edn. Pres. Tri-City Mental Health Citizens Bd., 1973-74. With AUS, 1953-55. Mem. ABA, Utah Bar Assn., Ariz. Bar Assn., Maricopa County Bar Assn., Phi Beta Kappa, Order of Coif. Democrat. Mem. Lds Ch. Home: 720 E Geneva Dr Tempe AZ 85282-3737 Office: Ariz State U Coll Law Tempe AZ 85287 Office Phone: 480-965-6503.

MATHESON, JAMES DAVID (JIM), United States Representative from Utah; b. Salt Lake City, 1960; m. Amy Matheson; 2 children. BA in Govt., Harvard U., Cambridge, Mass., 1982; MBA, UCLA, 1987. Worked in energy industry, 12 yrs.; founder Matheson Grp., 1998; mem. US Congress from 2nd Utah dist., 2001—, mem. fin. svcs. com., mem. transp. and infrastructure com., mem. sci. com. Mem. Salt Lake Pub. Utilities bd., Scott M. Matheson Leadership Forum. Democrat. Mem. Lds Ch. Office: US Ho Reps 1222 Longworth Ho Office Bldg Washington DC 20515 Office Phone: 202-225-3011.*

MATHESON, JEAN KING, neurologist, educator; b. Boston, Oct. 28, 1949; d. Daniel Nicholson and Isabella (Mills) M.; m. Mark David Aronson, Aug. 17, 1981; children: Alexander, Benjamin. BS, Antioch Coll., Yellow Springs, Ohio, 1972; MD, Harvard U., 1976. Intern in medicine Beth Israel Hosp., Boston, 1976-77; resident in neurology Lonwood Tng. Program in Neurology Harvard Med. Sch., Boston, 1977-80, chief resident in neurology, 1979-80; fellow in clin. neurophysiology Brigham and Women's Hosp., Boston, 1980-82; neurologist Beth Israel Hosp., Boston, 1982—, co-dir. Sleep Disorders Ctr., 1982-98; med. dir. Sleep Disorders Ctr. Beth Israel Deaconess Med. Ctr., Boston, 1998—. Asst. prof. neurology Harvard Med. Sch., Boston, 1997—. Contbr. chpts. to books and articles to profl. jours. Fellow: Am. Acad. Sleep Medicine; mem.: Am. Acad. Neurology, Alpha Omega Alpha. Office: Beth Israel Deaconess Med Ctr Sleep Disorders Center, CCE 866 330 Brookline Ave Boston MA 02215-5400 Business E-Mail: jmatheso@bidmc.harvard.edu.

MATHESON, JOHN H., lawyer, educator; b. Chgo., Mar. 9, 1952; s. George F. and Dorothy S. Matheson; m. Judith M. Surleta, Aug. 30, 1970; children: Dean T., Jack H., Adam C. BS in Econs., Ill. State U., Normal, 1974; JD, Northwestern U., Chgo., 1977. Bar: Ill. 1978, Minn. 1987. Jud. law clk. US Ct. Appeals, Chgo., 1977—78; atty. Hedlund, Hunter & Lynch (now Latham and Watkins), Chgo., 1978—82; prof. law U. Minn. Law Sch., Mpls., 1982—; of counsel Kaplan, Strangis & Kaplan, P.A., Mpls., 1987—. Founder Bus. Law Inst. U. Minn. Author: (books) Publicly Traded Corporations: Governance, Operation and Regulation, 1993, Business Law Deskbook, 2d edit., 2003, Corporation Law and Practice, 2d edit., 2004; contbr. articles to profl. jours. Recipient Winner for Legal Excellence in Writing award, Burton Found., 2007, Disting. Law Alumni award, U. Minn. Law Sch., 2008; named to Acad. Disting. Tchrs., U. Minn., 2008. Mem.: Am. Law Inst. (life). Office: Univ Minn Law Sch 229 19th Ave S Minneapolis MN 55455 Business E-Mail: mathe001@umn.edu.

MATHESON, LINDA, retired social worker; b. Martna, Estonia, Mar. 29, 1918; came to U.S., 1962, naturalized, 1969; d. Endrek and Leena Endrekson; m. Charles McLaren Matheson, Feb. 5, 1955. Diploma, Inst. Social Scis., Tallinn, Estonia, 1944; MS, Columbia U., 1966, D in Social Work, 1974. Diplomate clin. social work. Social work officer UN Rehab. and Resettlement Assn., Germany, 1946-48; social worker Victorian Mental Hygiene, Australia, 1955-62; rsch. assoc., social work project dir. Arthritis Midway House, NYC, 1966-68; rsch. Columbia Presbyn. Med. Ctr., NYC, 1971-75; field instr. Columbia U. Sch. Social Work, 1977-79, Columbia Presbyn. Med. Ctr., NYU Sch. Social Work, 1989-90; ret., 1992. Family Found. fellow, 1966, 89-90; grantee NIMH, 1969-72. Mem. Nat. Assn. Social Workers, Nat. Wildlife Fedn., BATUN, Baltic-Am. Freedom League, Smithsonian Assn., English Spkg. Union, Alliance Francaise, Columbia U. Alumni Assn., Met. Mus. N.Y. Lutheran. Home: 60 Broad St FL 39 New York NY 10004-2394

MATHEU, FEDERICO MANUEL, university chancellor; b. Humacao, PR, Mar. 17, 1941; s. Federico Matheu-Baez and Matilde Delgado-Vazquez; m. Myrna Delgado-Miranda, May 30, 1963; children: Federico Antonio, Rosa Myrna, Alfredo Javier, David Reinaldo. BS in Chem. Engring, U. P.R., 1962; PhD in Phys. Chemistry, U. Pitts., 1971. Chem. engr. Commonwealth Oil Refining Co., 1962-63; mem. adminstrv. staff and faculty U. P.R., 1963-78, dir. Humacao Coll., 1976-78; chancellor San German campus Inter Am. U. P.R., 1978-91; exec. dir., gen. coun. on edn. Commonwealth of P.R., Hato Rey, 1991-96; chancellor U. Metropolitana-Ana G. Méndez U. System, 1996—. Cons. in field. Author papers, reports in field. Named Disting. Educator P.R. Jaycees, 1974 Mem. Colegio de Quimicos P.R., Am. Chem. Soc., Sci. Tchrs. Assn. P.R. (pres. 1975-76), P.R. Acad. Arts and Scis., Phi Delta Kappa, Phi Tau Sigma. Home: Parque de Villa Caperra No 17 Zuania St Guaynabo PR 00966 Office: UMET PO Box 21150 San Juan PR 00928-1150 Office Phone: 787-766-1743. Business E-Mail: um_fmatheu@suagm.edu.

MATHEUS, CHRISTOPHER JOHN, computer scientist, researcher; b. Milw., Dec. 21, 1960; s. Jerald Theodore and Rosemarie Matheus; m. Genoveva Torres, May 1988; 1 child, Kayla Marie. BA in Physics, Lawrence U., Appleton, Wis., 1983; MS in Computer Sci., U. Ill., Urbana-Champaign, 1987, PhD in Computer Sci., 1989. Devel. & tech. assoc. Oak Ridge Nat. Labs., Tenn., 1983—87; prin. mem. tech. staff GTE Labs., Waltham, Mass., 1989—98, sr. mgr., 1998—2000; v.p. advanced techs. Redwood, Inc., Boston, 2000; arch., mgr. Verilytics, Inc., Burlington, Mass., 2000—02; chief tech. officer VIStology, Inc., Framingham, Mass., 2002—. Contbr. articles to profl. jours. Recipient Leslie H. Warner Tech. Achievement award, GTE Corp., 1995, Excellence award, GTE Labs., 1997; fellowship, Thomas J. Watson Found., 1983—84, Tchg. Incentive grant, Gen. Electric, 1989. Mem.: IEEE. Office: 5 Mountainview Dr Framingham MA 01701 Business E-Mail: cmatheus@vistology.com.

MATHEW, JAMES M., immunologist, educator; s. Mathew C. Muthuplackal and Thresia Mauthuplackal; m. Rosamma J. Mathew; children: M. Sunil, George J. PhD, Madurai Kamaraj U., Tamil Nadu, India, 1988. Postdoc. fellow Wash. U., St. Loius, 1989—94; rsch. asst. & assoc. prof. U. Miami, Fla., 1994—2007; assoc. prof. surgery & microbiology-immunology Northwestern U., Chgo., 2007—, dir., immune monitoring lab., 2007—. Grant, NIH, Pharmas, 1995—2009. Mem.: Intestinal Transplant Assn., Transplantation Soc., Am. Soc. Histocompatibility & Immunogenetics (com. mem. 1997—2009), Am. Soc. Transplant Surgeons. Conservative. Roman Cath. Office: Northwestern Univ 300 E Superior St Tarry 11-727 Chicago IL 60611 Office Fax: 312-503-3366.

MATHEW, REVI PUTHENPURACKAL, pediatrician, educator; s. Mathen P. and Thankamma Mathew; m. Saramma John; children: Kavitha Mariamma, Anitha Elizabeth, Arun Mathen. MBBS, Kasturba Med. Coll., Mangalore, India, 1968, MD, 1972. Diplomate Am. Bd. Pediat., 1997, pediatric endocrinology 1999, 2006. Asst. prof., pediat. Vanderbilt U. Med. Sch., Nashville, 1999—2004, assoc. prof., pediat., 2005—. Attending pediatric endocrinologist ARAMCO, Dhahran, Saudi Arabia, 1982—95. Contbr. scientific papers to profl. jours. Recipient award, Best Drs. Inc., 2006—07. Fellow: Royal Coll. Physicians; mem.: Royal Coll. Physicians (DCH 1977), Lawson Wilkins Pediatric Endocrine Soc., Endocrine Soc., Soc. Pediatric Rsch. Achievements include research in genetics of persistent hypoglycemia of infancy. Office: Vanderbilt Univ Med Sch 11136 C-DOT 2200 Children's Hosp Nashville TN 37232 Office Fax: 615-343-5845. Business E-Mail: revi.mathew@vanderbilt.edu.

MATHEW, SARA, corporate financial executive; BS, Univ. Madras, India; grad degree in acctg., Inst. Cost & Works Accountants, India; MBA, Xavier U. Brand mgmt., investor rels. Procter & Gamble, comptroller., paper products divsn., CFO, global baby care bus. unit, 1998—2000, v.p., fin. ASEAN region, Australia, Asia & India, 2000—01; CFO The Dun & Bradstreet Corp., 2001—07, pres., US, 2006—07, pres., internat., 2006—06, pres., COO, 2007—. Bd. dirs. The Dun & Bradstreet corp., 2008—. Mem.: The Inst. of Cost & Works Accountants in India (assoc.). Office: The Dun & Bradstreet Corp 103 JFK Parkway Short Hills NJ 07078 Office Phone: 973-921-5500. Office Fax: 866-560-7035.*

MATHEWS, BARBARA EDITH, gynecologist; b. Oct. 5, 1946; d. Joseph Chesley and Pearl (Cieri) Mathews. AB, U. Calif., 1969; MD, Tufts U., 1972. Diplomate Am. Bd. Ob-Gyn. Intern Cottage Hosp., Santa Barbara, Calif., 1972-73, Santa Barbara Gen. Hosp., 1972-73; resident in ob-gyn Beth Israel Hosp., Boston, 1973-77; clin. fellow in ob-gyn Harvard U., Boston, 1973-76, instr., 1976-77; gynecologist Sansum Med. Clin., Santa Barbara, 1977-98; sr. scientist Sansum Med. Rsch. Inst., 1998—; med. dir., gynecologist Women's Health Svcs., Santa Barbara, 1998—. Faculty mem. ann. postgrad. course Harvard Med. Sch.; bd. dirs. Sansum Med. Clinic, 1989-96, vice chmn. bd. dirs., 1994-96; dir. ann. postgrad course UCLA Med. Sch. Bd. dirs. Meml. Rehab. Found., Santa Barbara, Channel City Club, Santa Barbara, Music Acad. of the West, Santa Barbara, St. Francis Med. Ctr., Santa Barbara; mem. citizen's contg. edn. adv. coun. Santa Barbara C.C.; moderator Santa Barbara Cottage Hosp. Cmty. Health Forum. Author: (with L. Burke) Colposcopy in Clinical Practice, 1977; contbg. author Manual of Ambulatory Surgery, 1982. Bd trustees Furman U., Greenville, SC, 2005—, bd. dirs., 2005—. Fellow ACOG, ACS; mem. AMA, Am. Soc. Colposcopy and Cervical Pathology (dir. 1982-84), Harvard U. Alumni Assn., Tri-counties Obstet. and Gynecol. Soc. (pres. 1981-82), Birnam Wood Golf Club (Santa Barbara), Phi Beta Kappa. Home: 2105 Anacapa St Santa Barbara CA 93105-3503 Office: 2235 De La Vina St Santa Barbara CA 93105-3815 Office Phone: 805-687-7778. Office Fax: 805-687-0012.

MATHEWS, DAVID (FORREST DAVID MATHEWS), foundation executive, former United States Secretary of Health Education and Welfare; b. Grove Hill, Ala., Dec. 6, 1935; s. Forrest Lee and Doris (Pearson) M.; m. Mary Chapman, Jan. 24, 1960; children: Lee Ann Mathews Hester, Lucy Mathews Heegaard. AB, U. Ala., 1958; PhD, Columbia U., 1965; LL.D., U. Ala., 1969, Mercer U., 1976; L.H.D., William and Mary Coll., 1976, Med. U. S.C., 1976, Samford U., 1978, Transylvania U., 1978, Stillman Coll., 1980, Miami U., 1982; H.H.D., Birmingham-So. Coll., 1976, Wash. U., St. Louis, 1984; L.H.D., Ctr. Coll., 1985; L.L.D., Ohio Wesleyan U., 1987, Lynchburg Coll., 1987; L.H.D., U. New Eng., 1988, Hofstra U., 1999; LL.D., Aquinas Coll. Exec. v.p. U. Ala., 1968-69, pres., 1969-80, prof. history, 1977-81; sec. US Dept. Heath, Edn. & Welfare, Washington, 1975—77; pres., CEO Charles F. Kettering Found., Dayton, Ohio, 1981—. Dir. Birmingham br. Fed. Res. Bank of Atlanta, 1970-72, chmn., 1973-75; mem. council SRI Internat., 1978-85; chmn. Council Public Policy Edn., 1980— Contbr. articles to profl. jours.; author: Politics for People: Finding a Responsible Public Voice, 1994 Trustee Judson Coll., 1968-75, Am. Univs. Field Staff, 1969-80; bd. dirs. Birmingham Festival of Arts Assn., Inc., 1969-75; mem. Nat. Programming Council for Public TV, 1970-73, So. Regional Edn. Bd., 1969-75, Ala. Council on Humanities, 1973-75; vice chmn. Commn. on Future of South, 1974; mem. So. Growth Policies Bd., 1974-75; mem. nat. adv. council Am. Revolution Bicentennial Adminstrn., 1975; mem. Ala. State Oil and Gas Bd., 1975, 77-79; bd. dirs. Acad. Ednl. Devel., 1975—, Ind. Sector, 1982-88,; chmn. Pres.'s Com. on Mental Retardation, 1975-77; chmn. income security com. aging com. Health Ins. Com. of Domestic Council, 1975-77; bd. govs. nat. ARC, 1975-77; bd. govs., bd. visitors Washington Coll., 1982-86; trustee John F. Kennedy Center for Performing Arts, 1975-77, Woodrow Wilson Internat. Center for Scholars, 1975-77; fed. trustee Fed. City Council, 1975-77; bd. dirs. A Presdl. Classroom for Young Americans, Inc., 1975-76; trustee Tchrs. Coll., Columbia U., 1977—85, Nat. Found. March of Dimes, 1977-83, Coun. om Learning, 1977-84, Miles Coll., 1978—; mem. nat. adv. bd. Nat. Inst. on Mgmt. Lifelong Edn., 1979-84; mem. Ala. 2000, 1980—; spl. adviser Aspen Inst., 1980-84; mem. bd. trustees Gerald R. Ford Found., 1988—, bd. visitors Mershon Ctr. Ohio State U., 1988-91; bd. dirs. Nat. Civic League, 1996—. Served with U.S. Army, 1959-60. Recipient Nicholas Murray Butler medal Columbia U., 1976, Ala. Adminstr. of Year award Am. Assn. Univ. Adminstrs., 1976, Educator of Year award Ala. Conf. Black Mayors, 1977, Brotherhood award NCCJ, 1979 Mem. Newcomen Soc. Am., Phi Beta Kappa, Phi Alpha Theta, Omicron Delta Kappa, Delta Theta Phi. Home: 6050 Mad River Rd Dayton OH 45459-1508 Office: Charles F Kettering Found 200 Commons Rd Dayton OH 45459-2788 Office Phone: 937-434-7300. E-mail: jenkyn@kettering.org.

MATHEWS, E. ANNE JONES, retired library educator, academic administrator; b. Phila. d. Edmond Fulton and Anne Ruth (Reichner) Jones; m. Frank Samuel Mathews, June 16, 1951; children: Lisa Anne Mathews-Bingham, David Morgan, Lynne Elizabeth Bietenhader-Mathews, Alison Fulton Sawyer. AB, Wheaton Coll., 1949; MA, U. Denver, 1965, PhD, 1977. Field staff Intervarsity Christian Fellowship, Chgo., 1949-51; interviewer supr. Colo. Market Rsch. Svcs., Denver, 1952-64; reference libr. Oreg. State U., Corvallis, 1965-67; program dir. Ctrl. Colo. Libr. Sys., Denver, 1969-70; inst. dir. U.S. Office of Edn., Inst. Grant, 1979; dir. pub. rels., prof. Grad. Sch. Librarianship and Info. Mgmt. U. Denver, 1970-76, prof., dir. continuing edn., 1977-80; dir. office libr. programs, office ednl. rsch., improvement US Dept. Edn., Washington, 1986-91; dir. Nat. Libr. Edn., Washington, 1992-94; cons. Acad. Ednl. Devel., Washington, 1994—; cons. mil. installation vol. edn. rev. Am. Coun. on Edn., 1990—; from asst. prof. to prof., 1977—85; ret., 2004. Mem. adv. com. Golden H.S., 1973—77; faculty assoc. Danforth Found., 1974—84; mem. secondary sch. curriculum com. Jefferson County Pub. Schs., Colo., 1976—78; vis. lectr. Simmons Coll. Sch. L.S., Boston, 1977; mem. book and libr. adv. com. USIA, 1981—91; spkr. in field; cons. USIA, 1984—85; del. Internat. Fedn. Libr. Assns., 1984—93; mem. adv. coun. White House Conf. on Librs. and Info. Svcs., 1991; cons. Walden U., Mpls., 2001. Author, editor 6 books; contbr. articles to profl. jours., numerous chpts. to books. Mem. rural librs. and humanities program Colo. planning and resource bd. NEH, 1982—83; bd. mgrs. Friends Found. of Denver Pub. Libr., 1976—82; pres. Faculty Women's Club, Colo. Sch. Mines, 1963—64; bd. dirs. Jefferson County Libr. Found., 1996—, v.p., 1997—2000. Mem.: ALA (visionary leaders com. 1987—89, mem. coun. 1979—83, com. on accreditation 1984—85, orientation com. 1974—77, 1983—84, pub. rels. com.), English Speaking Union, Assn. Libr. and Info. Sci. Edn. (comm. com. 1978—80, program com. 1977—78), Colo. Libr. Assn. (pres. 1974, bd. dirs. 1973—75, continuing edn. com. 1976—80), Mountain Plains Libr. Assn. (profl. devel. com. 1979—80, pub. rels. and publs. com. 1973—75, continuing edn. com. 1973—76), Am. Soc. Info. Sci. (chmn. pub. rels. 1971), Naples Philharm. League, Pelican Bay Women's League Fla., Mountain Rep. Women's Club (v.p. 1997—2000), Mt. Vernon (Colo.) Country Club, Cosmos Club (Washington). Avocations: travel, reading, museum and gallery activities, volunteer work. E-mail: afmathews2@earthlink.net.

MATHEWS, HARRY BURCHELL, poet, writer, educator; b. NYC, Feb. 14, 1930; s. Edward James and Mary (Burchell) M.; m. Niki de Saint Phalle, June 6, 1949 (div. 1964); 2 children; m. Marie Chaix, July 29, 1992. BA cum laude, Harvard Coll., 1952. Faculty Bennington Coll., Vt., 1978-80; vis. lectr. Hamilton Coll., Clinton, NY, 1979, Columbia Coll., NYC, 1982-83; Musée du Louvre, Paris, 1992; French Inst., London, 1996; vis. writer Brown U., Providence, 1988, Temple U., Phila., 1990, Magdalene Coll., Cambridge, England, 1992, Berliner Literarisches Colloquium, Berlin, 1994, Duke U., 1996, New Coll. of Calif., Brown U., San Francisco Art Inst., 1997, Key West Literary Seminar, 1999, Key West Writers Workshops, 2000, New Sch. U., 2002—05; Regents lectr. U. Calif., San Diego, 2001. Founding dir. Shakespeare & Co., Lenox, Mass.; bd. dirs. Dalkey Archive Press; lectr. in field at nat., internat. colls, art ctrs. and instns. Author: The Conversions, 1962, Tlooth, 1964, The Sinking of the Odradek Stadium, 1975, Country Cooking and Other Stories, 1980, Cigarettes, 1987, 20 Lines A Day, 1988, The Orchard, 1988, The Way Home, 1988, The American Experience, 1991, Singular Pleasures, 1993, The Journalist, 1994, The Human Country, 2002, My Life in CIA, 2005, (with A. Brotchie) Oulipo Compendium, 1998, (in French) Sainte Catherine, 2000; (poetry) The Ring, Poems 1956-69, 1970, The Planisphere, 1974, Trial Impressions, 1977, Selected Declarations of Dependence, 1977, Armenian Papers: Poems 1954-84, 1987, Out of Bounds, 1989, A Mid-Season Sky: Poems 1954-89, 1991, (in French) Le savoir des rois: poèmes à perverbes, 1976, Ecrits français, 1990; (essays) Immeasurable Distances: The Collected Essays, 1981, The Case of the Persevering Maltese: Collected Essays, 2003; trans.: A Man in a Dream (Georges Perec) 1975, The Laurels of Lake Constance (Marie Chaix) 1977, The Life: Memoirs of a French Hooker (Jeanne Cordelier), 1978, Blue of Noon (Georges Bataille), 1978, Ellis Island (Georges Perec) 1996, The Dust of Suns (Raymond Roussel) 1991, various jour. articles; pub., co-editor Locus Solus, 1960-62; Paris editor The Paris Review, 1989-2003; contbr. poems, stories to anthologies, articles, criticisms, reviews to profl. jours. Decorated officer Ordre Arts et Lettres (France); recipient award Fiction Writing Am. Acad. Inst. Arts and Letters, NY, 1991, Am. award for lit., 1994; grantee Deutsche Akademische Austausch Dienst, Berlin, 1991; fiction writing grantee NEA, 1982. Mem. Ouvroir de Littérature Potentielle (Paris), Bielefelder Colloquium Neuer Poesie. Avocations: music making, back-country skiing, hiking, cooking. Home (Winter): Key West FL Home (Summer): Paris France Home and Office: 619 Grinnell St Key West Key West FL 33040 Home: 67 Rue De Grenelle 75007 Paris France E-mail: hmathews2@cs.com.

MATHEWS, IRIMPAN ITTOOP, macromolecular crystallographer; b. Ernakulam, Kerala, India, July 30, 1962; S. Irimpan Mathew Ittoop and Marium Ittoop Irimpan; m. Sheji Mathews Sheji, May 23, 1994; 1 child, Ervin. BS, Calicut U., Kerala, India, 1982, MSc, 1984; PhD, Indian Inst. Sci., Bangalore, 1993. Postdoctoral rsch. assoc. Mich. State U., Lansing, 1991-96; postdoctoral assoc. Cornell U., Ithaca, N.Y., 1996—. Contbr. articles to profl. jours. Sr. rsch. fellow U. Grants Commn., India, 1988-91, jrs. rsch. fellow, 1985-87. Mem. AAAS, Nat. Geog. Soc., Am. Crystallographic Assn. Office: Stanford Univ 2475 Sand Hill Rd Menlo Park CA 94025

MATHEWS, JACK SHERMAN, foundation administrator, retired insurance company executive; b. Jacksonville, Ill., Aug. 28, 1924; s. Franklin Roosevelt and Helen Adeline Mathews; m. Elizabeth Caldwell Mathews, Jan. 17, 1943; children: Constance Lee Paige, John Harlan. BA, Ill. Coll., 1948; grad. Sch. Ins., Purdue U., 1988. Ins. agt. Equitable Life of NY, Jacksonville, 1948—55; agy. v.p. Ctrl. Nat. Life, Jacksonville, 1955—68; gen. agt. Franklin Life, Springfield, Ill., 1969—84; dir. tng. John Deere Ins. Co., 1984—90, ins. broker, 1990—95; exec. dir. Jacksonville Pub. Schs. Found., 1995—. Pres. Jacksonville C. of C., 1951—52; consistery Valley of Springfield; alderman City of Jacksonville, 1953—61, bd. police and fire com., 1981—88. With Air Corps US

Army, 1943—44. Mem.: Elks, Shriners, Masons. Republican. Presbyterian. Avocations: reading, golf, travel. Home: 404 Westwinds Dr Jacksonville IL 62650 Office: Jacksonville Pub Schs Found 516 Jordan Jacksonville IL 62650

MATHEWS, JACK WAYNE, journalist, film critic; b. LA, Dec. 2, 1939; s. Walter Edwin and Dorothy Helen (Friley) M.; m. Lucinda Lucille Herbert, Nov. 5, 1971; children: Darren Brady, Shelby Kay. BA, San Jose Coll., Calif., 1965; MS, UCLA, 1966. Reporter Riverside (Calif.) Press, 1967-69; mktg. exec. Riverside Raceway, 1969-75; columnist, editor Rochester (N.Y.) Democrat & Chronicle, 1975-78; columnist, film critic Detroit Free Press, 1978-82, USA Today, LA, 1982-85; columnist L.A. Times, 1985-89, film editor, 1989-91; film critic Newsday, LI, 1991-99, N.Y. Daily News, 1999—2008, movie editor, 1999—2006. Co-host Cinema, PBS, 1995-98; juror Montreal World Film Festival, 1993. Author: The Battle of Brazil, 1987. Democrat. Office Phone: 845-621-1837. Business E-Mail: jmath30031@aol.com.

MATHEWS, JESSICA TUCHMAN, think-tank executive, former federal official, columnist; b. NYC, July 4, 1946; d. Lester Reginald and Barbara (Wertheim) Tuchman; m. Colin D. Mathews, Feb. 25, 1978 (div.); children: Oliver Max Tuchman, Jordan Henry Morgenthau; m. Charles G. Boyd, Dec. 31, 2005. AB magna cum laude, Radcliffe Coll., 1967; PhD, Calif. Inst. Tech., 1973. Congrl. sci. fellow AAAS, 1973—74; profl. staff mem. Energy and Environ. subcom., House Com. on Interior and Insular Affairs US Ho. of Reps., Washington, 1974—75; dir. issues and rsch. Udall Presdl. campaign, 1975—76; dir. Office of Global Issues NSC, Washington, 1977—79; mem. editorial bd. Washington Post, Washington, 1980—82, columnist, 1991—97; v.p., dir. rsch. The World Resources Inst., Washington, 1982—92; dep. to undersec. for global affairs US Dept. State, Washington, 1993; sr. fellow Coun. on Fgn. Rels., Washington, 1993—97; pres. Carnegie Endowment Internat. Peace, Washington, 1997—. Mem. numerous adv. panels Office Tech. Assessment, NAS, AAAS, EPA; adv. com. Air Products Corp., 1995—99; bd. dirs. Somalogic Inc., HanesBrands Inc. Trustee Rockefeller Found., Century Found., Nuc. Threat Initiative; mem. Coun. Fgn. Rels.; bd. dirs. Joyce Found., Chgo., 1984—91, Inter-Am. Dialogue, 1991—2000, Surface Transp. Policy Project, 1991—2003, Radcliffe Coll., 1992—96, Carnegie Endowment for Internat. Peace, Washington, 1992—, Rockefeller Bros. Fund, NYC, 1992—96, Brookings Instn., Washington, 1995—2001. Mem.: Inst. Internat. Econs. (adv. com.), Fedn. Am. Scientists (bd. dirs. 1985—87, 1988—92), Trilateral Commn. Democrat. Jewish. Office: Carnegie Endowment Internat Peace 1779 Massachusetts Ave NW Washington DC 20036-2109 Office Phone: 202-939-2210. Office Fax: 202-332-0925. E-mail: jmathews@CarnegieEndowment.org.*

MATHEWS, JOAN HELENE, pediatrician; b. Manchester, NH, Feb. 3, 1940; d. John Barnaby and Helen A. Wlodkoski; m. Ernest Stephen Mathews, June 1, 1965; 3 children. BS, U. N.H., 1961; MD, Columbia U., 1965. Diplomate Am. Bd. Pediatrics. Med. intern Roosevelt Hosp., NYC, 1965-66; pediatric resident Babies Hosp. Columbia Presbyn. Med. Ctr., NYC, 1966-68, pediatric endocrine fellow Babies Hosp., 1968-70; instr. clin. pediat. Columbia U. Coll. Physicians and Surgeons, NYC, 1973-77; asst. prof. pediat. Cornell U. Med. Coll., NYC, 1977-81; clin. instr. pediat. Harvard Med. Sch., Boston, 1985—2003, clin. asst. prof. pediat., 2003—; clin. assoc. children's svc. Mass. Gen. Hosp., Boston, 1985—. Fellow: Am. Acad. Pediat.; mem.: Phi Beta Kappa. Office: 777 Concord Ave Cambridge MA 02138-1053 Office Phone: 617-876-6800. Office Fax: 617-876-5713. E-mail: joan.mathews@childrens.harvard.edu.

MATHEWS, LINDA MCVEIGH, newspaper editor; b. Redlands, Calif., Mar. 14, 1946; d. Glenard Ralph and Edith Lorene (Humphrey) McVeigh; m. Thomas Jay Mathews, June 15, 1967; children: Joseph, Peter, Katherine. BA, Radcliffe Coll., 1967; JD, Harvard U., 1972. Gen. assignment reporter L.A. Times, 1967-69, Supreme Ct. corr., 1972-76, corr. Hong Kong, 1977-79, China corr. Beijing, 1979-80, editor op-ed page, 1980-81, dep. nat. editor, 1981-84, dep. fgn. editor, 1985-88, editl. writer, 1988-89, editor L.A. Times Mag., 1989-92; corr. Wall Street Jour., Hong Kong, 1976-77; sr. prodr. ABC News, NYC, 1992-93; nat. editor N.Y. Times, NYC, 1993-96; editor USA Today, McLean, Va., 1997—. Lectr.; freelance writer. Author (with others): Journey into China, 1982, One Billion: A China Chronicle, 1983. Mem. Women's Legal Def. Fund, 1972-76; co-founder, pres. Hong Kong Montessori Sch., 1977-79; bd. dirs. Ctr. for Childhood. Mem.: Fgn. Corrs. Club Hong Kong. Office: USA Today 7950 Jones Branch Dr Mc Lean VA 22108 Office Phone: 703-854-5581. Personal E-mail: LiMathews@aol.com. Business E-Mail: lmathews@usatoday.com.

MATHEWS, LINNEA KOONS, science educator, librarian; b. Waterville, Maine, Jan. 27, 1957; d. Edwin Donaldson and Elizabeth (Ortquist) Koons; m. Thomas Joseph Mathews, Oct. 11, 1986. BA, Colby Coll., 1979. Cert. phys. sci. and life sci. Dept. of Edn., Maine, 1988. Science tchr. SAD 39, Buckfield, Maine, 1987—2002, Mt Blue HS, Farmington, Maine, 2002—. Digital libr. Math. and Sci. Tchg. Excellence Collaborative, Portland, Maine, 2001—. Educator (devel. assessment tasks) Maine Assessment Portfolio, Local Assessment Development (Maine Math. and Sci. Alliance Tchr. Leader, 2004). Grantee MMSTEC Digital Libr., Nat. Science Found. Mem.: NSTA, Nat. Coun. Tchrs. Math., US Eventing Assn., Am. Connemara Pony Soc. Democrat. Achievements include development of MMSTEC Digital Library. Avocations: horseback riding, cooking, gardening. Home: 230 Lovejoy Pond Rd Fayette ME 04349 Office: Mt Blue HS 129 Seamon Rd Farmington ME 04938 Home Fax: 207-685-4465. Personal E-mail: tayfarm@aol.com. Business E-Mail: lkoons@msad9.org.

MATHEWS, MARY KATHRYN, retired government official; b. Washington, Apr. 20, 1948; d. T. Odon and Kathryn (Augustine) M. Student, Pa. State U., 1966-68; BBA, Am. U., 1970, MBA, 1975. Personnel mgmt. specialist, coordinator coll. recruitment program, GSA, Washington, 1971-75, adminstrv. officer, 1975-78; personnel mgmt. specialist Office of Personnel Mgmt., Washington, 1978; employee devel. specialist Office Sec. Transp., Washington, 1978-80, dep. chief departmental services and spl. programs div., 1980-81; asst. dir. adminstrv. div. Farm Credit Adminstrn., Washington, 1981-84, dir. adminstrv. div. McLean, Va., 1984-86, chief adminstrv. services div., 1987-88; dep. staff dir. for mgmt. U.S. Commn. Civil Rights, Washington, 1988-90, asst. staff dir. for mgmt., 1990-91, asst. staff dir. for congl. affairs, 1991-94, staff dir., 1994-97; ret., 1997. Chief spl. programs staff and homebound handicapped employment program GSA, Washington, 1973-74; mem. task force Presdl. mgmt. intern program U.S. Office Pers. Mgmt., Washington, 1977-78; coord. mgmt. devel. program for women Office Sec. Transp., Washington, 1979-81. Vol. mentor, speaker Alexandria Commn. on Women, 1991-93. Mem. Exec. Women in Govt. (treas. 1993-94, v.p. 1994-95, pres. 1995-96, bd. dirs.), Small Agy. Coun. (exec. com. 1990-91, 94-96, chmn. micro agy. group 1990-91), Internat. Alliance (bd. dirs. 1996-97), Nat. Trust Hist. Preservation, Nat. Assn. Mus. Women in Arts (charter), Delta Gamma (rush advisor 1971-73, pres. bd. dirs. local chpt. house corp. 1972-73).

MATHEWS, MICH, computer company executive; married; 2 children. Grad., U. Brighton, England. With GM, 1987—89; pub. rels. cons., UK divsn. Microsoft Corp., 1989, gen. mgr. corp. pub. rels. grp. Redmond, Wash., 1993—99, v.p. corp. pub. rels. group, 1999, mem. bus. leadership team, 1999—, v.p. corp. comm., v.p. ctrl. mktg. orgn., sr. v.p. ctrl. mktg. group, 2002—. Named Marketer of Yr., BtoBonline mag., 2006, Power Player, Advt. Age, 2008; named one of Best Marketers, BtoB Mag., 2008. Office: Microsoft Corp One Microsoft Way Redmond WA 98052-6399 Office Phone: 425-882-8080. Business E-Mail: michm@microsoft.com.*

MATHEWS, MICHAEL STONE, investment banker; b. Ohio, Oct. 23, 1940; s. Robert Green and Dallas Victoria (Stone) M.; m. Cecilia Aall, May 13, 1967; children: Brandon, Mark, Alexander. AB, Princeton U., 1962; JD, U. Mich., 1965. Bar: N.Y. 1966. Assoc. White & Case, NYC, 1965—69; v.p. Smith Barney Harris Upham & Co., NYC, 1969—77; sr. v.p. Scandinavian Securities Corp., NYC, 1977—79, DNC Am. Banking Corp., NYC, 1979—89; pres. DNC Capital Corp., 1986—89; ptnr. Bradford Assocs., 1989—92; mng. dir. Westgate Capital Co., 1993—. Bd. dirs. Particle Drilling Tech., Inc., Antioch Co. Home: 149 Bedens Brook Rd Skillman NJ 08558 Office: 115 E 69th St New York NY 10021 Office Phone: 212-991-9015. Personal E-mail: michaelsmath@cs.com.

MATHEWS, PEGGY ANNE, nurse, consultant; b. Oakdale, La., Sept. 10, 1941; d. Howard Douglas and Huldah Mary (Hicks) Tyler; children: Joseph, Mark, Debra. A.Nursing, La. State U., Alexandria, 1975; BSN Northwestern State U., La. Cert. legal nurse cons., Legal Nurse Cons. Inst., Houston. R.N., La. Nurse intensive care unit St. Frances Cabrini Hosp., Alexandria, 1975-78, 78-80, staff educator nurse edn. dept, 1978-80, dir. noninvasive cardiology dept, 1980-85, nurse edn. dept., 1979-80, dir. cardiology, 1980—, established cardiac rehab. program, 1982, dir. Cardiac Catheterization Lab.; med. dir. TRACE Detection Svcs. Mem. Am. Assn. Critical Care Nurses, Am. Heart Assn. Democrat. Roman Catholic. Avocations: dancing, fishing, horse back riding, gardening, hunting. Home: 122 Cedar Point Ln Boyce LA 71409-8798 Office: St Frances Cabrini Hosp 3330 Masonic Dr Alexandria LA 71301-3899 Personal E-mail: pmrn41@yahoo.com.

MATHEWS, SHARON WALKER, performing company executive, secondary school educator; b. Shreveport, La., Feb. 1, 1947; d. Arthur Delmar and Nona (Frye) Walker; m. John William (Bill) Mathews, Aug. 14, 1971; children: Rebecca, Elizabeth, Anna. BS, La. State U., 1969, MS, 1971. Dance grad. asst. La. State U., Baton Rouge, 1969-71, choreographer, 1975-76; 6th grade tchr. East Baton Rouge Parish, 1971-72, health phys. edn. tchr., 1972-74; dance instr. Magnet High Sch., Baton Rouge, 1975—; artistic dir. Baton Rouge Ballet Theatre, 1975—; dance dir. Dancers' Workshop, Baton Rouge, 1971—; choreographer Baton Rouge Opera, 1989-94, Univ. H.S. Musical Theatre, 1998—; choreographer Baton Rouge Gilbert and Sullivan Soc. summer musical La. State U., 2000, 2001; choreographer Baton Rouge Little Theater, 2000, 2002. Tchr. Am. Ballet Teheatre, NY, 2008. Author: East Baton Rouge Parish Dance Curriculum. Mem. La. Supts. Task Force Arts in Edn., 1999—2001, La. Content Stds. Com. Dance, 2001, East Baton Rouge Parish Curriculum Com. Dance, 1997, La. Arts Consortium, 2000—, La. Arts Content Stds. Com., 2002—, La. Arts Content Revision Com., 2002—03. Recipient Stream award for Artistic Excellence, S.W. Regional Ballet Assn., 1991, Mayor's Pres.'s award for Excellence in the Arts, 1999, Creative Ticket award for excellence in the arts, Kennedy Ctr., 2005, John W. Barton Sr. Excellence in Nonprofit Mgmt. award, Baton Rouge Area Found., Standford Financial award, 2007; named Dance Educator of the Yr., La. Alliance Health, Phys. Edn., Recreation and Dance; named to Univ. HS Hall of Distinction, 2003, Baton Rouge Magnet HS Hall of Fame, 2003. Mem.: SW Regional Dance Am. (parlimentian 2007—), La. Assn. Health, Phys. Edn., Recreation and Dance (dance chairperson 1995), Southwestern Regional Ballet Assn. (bd. dirs. 1981—, treas., exec. bd. dirs. 1989—92). Republican. Baptist. Office: Baton Rouge Ballet Theater 10745 Linkwood Ct Baton Rouge LA 70810 Office Phone: 225-767-5814.

MATHEWSON, CHRISTOPHER COLVILLE, engineer, geologist, educator; b. Plainfield, NJ, Aug. 12, 1941; s. George Anderson and Elsa Rae (Shrimpton) M.; m. Janet Marie Olmsted, Nov. 2, 1968; children: Heather Alexis, Glenn George Anderson. BSCE, Case Inst. Tech., 1963; MS in Geol. Engring., U. Ariz., 1965, PhD in Geol. Engring., 1971. Registered profl. engr., Tex., Ariz.; profl. geologist Tex., Oreg., Alaska. Officer, lt. Nat. Ocean Survey, 1965-71; prof. Tex. A&M U., College Station, 1981—, Regents prof., 2005—. Mem. coun. of examiners Assn. State Bds. Geology, 1994—; cons., speaker in field. Author: Engineering Geology, 1981 (C.P. Holdredge award); contbr. articles to profl. publs. Chmn. College Station Planning and Zoning Commn., 1973—81; trustee Geol. Soc. Am. Found., 2001—03. Fellow Geol. Soc. Am. (chmn. engring. geology divsn. 1986-87, Meritorious Svc. award 1991), Soc. Am. Mil. Engrs.; mem. Assn. Engring. Geologists (editor bull. 1981-88, pres. 1988-89, C.P. Holdredge award 1981, F.T. Johnston Svc. award 1995, Karl & Ruth Terzachie Outstanding Mentor award 2008, exec. dir. 1998-2002), Am. Geol. Inst. (pres. 1991-92), Nat. Coal Coun., Internat. Assn. Engring. Geologists (chmn. U.S. nat. com. 1995-98). Office: Tex A&M U Dept Geology And Geophysics College Station TX 77843-3115 Office Phone: 979-845-2488. E-mail: mathewson@geo.tamu.edu. *Commitment and dedication to the mission will lead to its successful completion regardless of the odds.*

MATHEWSON, DAVID, religious studies educator; b. Wellsboro, Pa., Nov. 6, 1963; s. Ruth Mathwson; m. Joyce Harkins, June 13, 1987; children: Caleb, Jordan, Ally. PhD, U. Aberdeen, Scotland, 1998. Instr. Oak HIlls Christian Coll., Bemidji, Minn., 1998—2003; assoc. prof. Bibl. studies Gordon Coll., Wenham, Mass., 2003—; adj. prof. Gordon-Conwell Theol. Sem., South Hamilton, Mass., 2004—. Author: (book) A New Heaven and a New Earth. Sch. coun. Pentucket Regional HS, West Newbury, Mass., 2008—. Mem.: Soc. Bibl. Lit. Independent. Home: 14 Thorndike Ave Merrimac MA 01860 Office: Gordon Coll 255 Grapevine Rd Wenham MA 01984

MATHEWSON, GEORGE ATTERBURY, retired lawyer; b. Paterson, NJ, Mar. 31, 1935; s. Joseph B. and Christina A. (Atterbury) M.; m. Ann Elizabeth, July 31, 1975' 1 child, James Lemuel. AB cum laude, Amherst Coll., Mass., 1957; LLB, Cornell U., Ithaca, NY, 1960; LLM, U. Mich., 1961. Bar: NY 1963. Atty office spl. legal assts., trial atty. FTC, Washington, 1963-65; regional atty. NY State Dept. Environ. Conservation, Liverpool, 1972-73; pvt. practice Syracuse, 1967—72, 1973—2002; of counsel Banac and Mathewson, Manlius, NY, 2002—04; ret., 2004. Adj. instr. bus. law Onondaga C.C., Syracuse, 1979-84. Author: 1984 Arrives in America, 2005. Bd. dirs. South Side Businessmen, 1971-72, 88-91, v.p., 1992, pres. 1993; elder Onondaga Hill Presbyn. Ch., 1979, 82-85; dir. Manilus C. of C., 1995, v.p., 1997; trustee Steuben County Hist. Soc., 2002—05, v.p. 2005; bd. dirs. Yates County Arts Coun., Inc., 2003-06, sec., 2004; dir. Finger Lakes Chamber Music Festival, 2007, 2008; dir. Milly's Pantry, Inc., 2009. Mem. ACLU, Fed. Bar Assn., NY State Bar Assn. (former mem. state and county bar assn. coms.), Onondaga County Bar Assn., Kiwanis (bd. dirs. Onondaga club 1988-89, v.p. 1989, pres. 1989-91). Patentee safety device for disabled airplanes. Home: Po Box 435 Penn Yan NY 14527-0435 Home Phone: 315-536-4052.

MATHEWSON, MARK STUART, lawyer, editor; b. Pana, Ill., Mar. 6, 1955; s. Raymond Glenn and Frances (King) M.; m. Barbara Jean Siegert, Oct. 30, 1980; children: Margie, Molly. BA, U. Wis., Madison, 1978; JD, U. Ill., 1984; MA, U. Iowa, 1985. Bar: Ill. 1985. Reporter Ill. Times, Springfield, 1985; asst. prof. Culver Stockton Coll., Canton, Mo., 1985—86; pvt. practice Pana, Ill., 1987—88; mng. editor Ill. Bar Jour., Ill. State Bar Assn., Springfield, 1998—2000, dir. pub., 2000—. Office: Ill State Bar Assn Ill Bar Journal Ill Bar Ctr Springfield IL 62701 Home: 401 E Hargrave St Athens IL 62613-9787

MATHIA, MARY LOYOLA, parochial school educator, nun; b. Hempstead, N.Y., Sept. 14, 1921; d. Paul John and Laura Marie (Linck) Mathia. BA, Coll. Mt. St. Joseph, 1953; M in Pastoral Studies, Loyola U.-Chgo., 1980. Joined Sisters of Charity of Cin., Roman Cath. Ch., 1941. Tchr. various schs. Ohio and Mich., 1943-62, St. John Bapt. Sch., Chillum, Md., 1962-63; social studies tchr. and dept. chmn. Holy Name H.S., Cleve., 1963-69; ednl. cons. Diocese of Cleve., 1970-78; dir. edn. St. Benedict Ch., Crystal River, Fla., 1979-86; founding prin. Cen. Cath. Sch. of Citrus County, Lecanto, Fla., 1985-90, v.p. devel. and pub. rels., 1990-91; parish cons. and dir. adult edn., St. Scholastica, 1986-2007, RCIA dir. St. Frances Xavier Cabrini Ch., 2007-. Recipient Mother Seton award, 1998, St. Jude medal Award for Svc. to St. Scholastic Ch., presented by Rev. Robert Lynch, Bishop of the Diocese of St. Petersburg, 2002, St. Jude award, Dick Ribble/Bert Miller award, Interfaith Coun. of Citrus County, 2004; dir., cons. St. Frances Cabrini Ch., Spring Hill, Fla., 2007. Republican. Office: St Frances Cabrini Ch Spring Hill FL 34609 Office Phone: 352-683-9666. *Society today is crying out for stability and a purpose for life. Only a God-centered education can fill the void created by the noise of external forces and the deadening of creative ideas stemming from a computer, media-saturated environment. As ministers of the Gospel our "quiet whispers" must penetrate the minds of a weary people, inspire them and bring them safely to the harbor of salvation in Christ Jesus Our Lord.*

MATHIAS, ALICE IRENE, business management consultant; b. NYC, Mar. 2, 1949; d. Murray and Charlotte (Kottle) Mathias. BS in Math., Western New Eng. Coll., 1972. Programmer Carnation Co., LA, 1973-78; programmer/analyst Cedars-Sinai Med. Ctr., LA, 1978-79, Union Bank, LA, 1979-81; group leader Kaiser Found. Health Plan, Pasadena, Calif., 1981-98; sr. cons. KPMG LLP, LA, 1998—99; prin. Info. Tech. Mgmt., LA, 1999—. Mem. LA Ctr. Theatre Group Patron (Inner cir.), Nat. Women's History Museum (charter mem.), LA County Mus. Art (sponsor), Smithsonian Inst., KCET Pub. TV, Compassion & Choices, U.S. Holocaust Meml. Mus. (charter mem.), Caithness Collectors Soc., Statue of Liberty Ellis Island Found. Home: 2031 Dracena Drive Apt 320 Los Angeles CA 90027 Office: Info Tech Mgmt 2031 Dracena Dr Ste 320 Los Angeles CA 90027

MATHIAS, LYNDA ROWELL, retired secondary school educator; b. Orangeburg, SC, Aug. 31, 1943; d. Harold Deland and Edna (Hancock) Rowell; m. Ervin McDonald Mathias Jr., June 26, 1965; children: Ervin M. III, Michael K. BA, Newberry Coll., 1964; MEd, U. SC, 1985. Cert. tchr., SC. Tchr. bus. edn. Orangeburg HS, 1964—65; tchr. English Saluda Mid. Sch., SC, 1965—67; tchr. econs. St. Andrews HS, Charleston, SC, 1968; tchr. bus. edn. Allendale Vocat. Edn. Ctr., SC, 1970—73; tchr. English, guidance counselor Allendale Acad., 1976—88; instr. continuing edn., adj. prof. Trident Tech. Coll., Charleston, 1989, 1990; tchr. gifted and talented Charleston County Schs., 1989—92; guidance counselor Moultrie Mid. Sch., Mt. Pleasant, SC, 1992—93; counselor Sullivan's Island Elem. Sch., SC, 1993—95; guidance counselor Myrtle Beach Mid. Sch., 1995—98. Solo vocalist, various local church, sch. and civic functions. Inactive Am. Cancer Soc., Am. Heart Assn. Former mem. NEA, SC Edn. Assn., Charleston County Edn. Assn., SC Ind. Sch. Assn. (workshop presenter, tchr. improvement com., advanced accreditation evaluator, judge 1989 tchr. of yr. award, named SC Indep. Schs. Tchr. of Yr. 1988). Republican. Avocations: tennis, aerobics, needlecrafts, reading. Home: 1633 Wells Branch Rd Ulmer SC 29849 Personal E-mail: emmathias@bellsouth.net.

MATHIAS, MARGARET GROSSMAN, manufacturing company executive, leasing company executive; b. Detroit; d. D. Ray and Lila May (Skinner) Grossman; children: Deborah, Robert, Lesley, Jennifer, Mary. BA, Mt. Holyoke Coll.; cert., Am. Acad. Art. Artist and co-mgr. Mary Chase Marionettes, NYC; exec. v.p. Star Five Corp., Elkhart, Ind., 1975-88, pres., treas., chmn. bd., 1985-90; sec., chmn. bd. L & J Press Corp., Elkhart, 1985-91, also chmn. bd. dirs.; chmn., pres., CEO Magland Co., Elkhart, 1986—2002, Magco Inc., Elkhart, 1986—; pres., chmn., CEO Tech Products, Inc., Elkhart, 1992—. Mem. fin. com. United Fund, Elkhart; mem. parents adv. bd. Furman U., Greenville, SC, 1978-83, mem. art adv. bd. Mt. Holyoke Coll., South Hadley, Mass., 1982—; pres. Tri Kappa Svc. Orgn., Elkhart, 1965-66; trustee Stanley Clark Sch., South Bend, Ind., 1977-87; bd. dirs. Bridgework Theatre, Goshen, Ind., also Balt., 1996—2009; mem. adv. bd. Ruthmere 1910 House Mus. designated one of Am.'s castles, 1998—2008; instr., spkr. etiquette Montessori Schs., Elkhart, 1998—; vol. Dept. Edn., 2003, Art Inst. Chgo., 2003; weekly vol. dept. edn. Art Inst. Chgo. Recipient Lawson Top Sculpture Purchase award Midwest Mus. Am. Art, 1990. Mem. Elkhart C. of C., Elcona Country Club (Elkhart), Woman's Athletic Club (Chgo.), Thursday Club (Elkhart, pres. 1976). Republican. Avocations: sculpting, travel, skiing. Home: 1077 Greenleaf Blvd Apt 101 Elkhart IN 46514-3562 Office: 429 S Main St Elkhart IN 46516-3210

MATHIAS, MICHAEL G., insurance company executive; Various managerial, tech. and application devel. positions Prudential Ins., Macmillan Pub., Ednl. Testing Svc., Verizon, UBS/PaineWebber Inc.; systems engring. mgr. Aetna Information Systems, head tech. architecture and strategy, 2006—07, head enterprise architecture, 2007—08; v.p., chief tech. officer Aetna, Inc., 2008—. Office: Aetna Inc 151 Farmington Ave Hartford CT 06156 Office Phone: 860-273-0123.*

MATHIAS, REUBEN VICTOR (VIC MATHIAS), organization executive, real estate investor; b. Copperas Cove, Tex., Mar. 5, 1926; s. Alvin E. and Ella L. (Teinert) M.; m. Helen I. Thoresen, Jan. 28, 1950; children: Mona, Mark, Matt. BBA, U. Tex., 1950. Cert. Chamber Exec. Dist. mgr. W.A. Shaeffer Pen Co., Youngstown, Ohio, 1950-51; mgr. Cen-Tex Fair, Temple, Tex., 1951-52; dir. info. Tex. Assn. Soil Conservation Suprs., Temple, 1952-53; mgr. membership dept. Austin (Tex.) C. of C., 1953-56, chief exec. officer, 1956-82; dir. corp. devel. Hardin Corp., Austin, 1983-86; real estate and investments, 1987-92; pres. Tex. Travel Industry Assn., Austin, 1992-96. V.p. Austin Tours, Inc.; sec. Longhorn Caverns, Inc.; chmn. bd., instr. Inst. for Orgn. Mgmt., U. Houston; mgmt. cons. not-for-profit orgns., 1997-2003, retired and serving as vol. cons. to non-profit orgns., 2004-. Contbr. monthly editorial Thoughts While Thinking to Austin Mag., 1961-82. Pres. Austin USO Council, 1958-59; v.p. Beautify Tex. Council, 1975-77; founding pres. Discover Tex. Assn., 1969-71; chmn. Central Tex. Blood

Donor Fund, 1979. Served with U.S. Army, 1944-46. Mem. Am. C. of C. Execs., Tex. C. of C. Execs. (pres. 1965), Rotary (pres. Austin 1985-86). Lutheran. Home: 3100 Mistywood Cir Austin TX 78746-7861 Home Phone: 512-327-6077. *You can find happiness only by giving it to others. Much of my life has been devoted to community building through voluntary action. The fact that my career has allowed me to stay in one community has made it possible for me to make and carry out long-term plans, both for the community and personally.*

MATHIAS, ROBERT S., pediatric nephrologist; b. Bklyn., Mar. 22, 1955; MD, Rush U. Med. Coll., Chgo., 1983. Diplomate Am. Bd. Pediat., cert. Am. Bd. Pediat. Nephrology. Intern pediat. U. Calif. Med. Ctr., San Diego, 1983—84, resident pediat., 1984—85, resident pediat. nephrology, 1986—87; fellowship Children's Hosp., Boston, 1987; clin. prof. Children's Renal Ctr. U. Calif. Med. Ctr. Contbr. articles to profl. jours. Mem.: Am. Acad. Pediat. Office: UCSF Med Ctr 533 Parnassus Ave Rm U585 S San Francisco CA 94143 Office Phone: 415-476-2423. Business E-Mail: rmathias@peds.ucsf.edu.

MATHIASON, JOHN ROLAND, political science professor, consultant; b. Willmar, Minn., Aug. 5, 1942; m. Jan Elizabeth Clausen, Aug. 5, 2004; m. Maria Cristina Sara-Serrano, Nov. 15, 1966 (dec. July 15, 2004); children: John Michael, Pablo Andres. BA summa cum laude, St. Olaf Coll., Northfield, Minn., 1963; PhD, MIT, Cambridge, Mass., 1968. Expert social aspects agrarian reform UN Bur. Tech. Cooperation, Caracas, Venezuela, 1966—67; asst. prof. comm. U. Wash., Seattle, 1968—71; assoc. social affairs officer UN Secretariat, NYC, 1971—74, social affairs officer, 1976—80, sr. program officer, 1980—87, dep. dir. divsn. advancement of women, 1987—97; asst. resident rep. UN Devel. Program, Islamabad, Pakistan, 1974—76; adj. prof. pub. adminstrn. NY U., NYC, 1994—2001; prof. internat. rels. Syracuse U., NY, 1999—. Mng. dir. Assocs. Internat. Mgmt. Svcs., NY, 1997—. Author: Eliminating Weapons of Mass Destruction: Prospects of Effective International Verification, 2004, Invisible Governance: International Secretariats in Global Politics, 2007, Internet Governance: The New Frontier of Global Institutions, 2008. Bd. chair, comprehensive planning com. Shandaken, NY, 2001—03. Mem.: Assn. Former Internat. Civil Servants (life). Democrat. Lutheran. Avocation: hiking. Home: 538 Fayette Blvd Syracuse NY 13224 Office: Maxwell Sch Syracuse Univ 225 Eggers Hall Syracuse NY 13244-1090 Business E-Mail: jrmathia@maxwell.syr.edu.

MATHIESON, GARRETT ALFRED, insurance brokerage executive; b. Bronxville, NY, June 12, 1952; s. William Frederick and Susan (Prager) M.; m. Doris King, June 21, 1980; children: Christine, William. BA, Hobart Coll., 1974; MBA, N.Y. U., 1980. Account rep. Marsh & McLennan, NYC, 1974-77; sr. broker Frank B. Hall & Co., NYC, 1977-78; risk mgmt. cons. Marsh & McLennan, NYC, 1978-80, cons. mgr.-asst. v.p., 1980-82, v.p., mgr. world consulting svcs., 1982-85; mng. cons. Towers Perrin Forster & Crosby, NYC, 1985-86; sr. v.p. Jardine Ins. Brokers, NYC, 1986-90; exec. v.p. Rollins Burdick Hunter, NYC, 1990-92; chmn., CEO, Rollins Hudig Hall Pa., Phila., 1992-94; vice chmn. Aon Risk Svcs., 1994—99; pres., CEO Willis Risk Solutions, NYC, 1999—2005; pres. Lockton Co. LLC, NYC, 2006—. Seminar mgr. World Trade Inst., 1982-84. Contbr. articles to profl. jour. Mem.: Univ. Glee Club, Kiawah Island Club, Shenorock Shore Club, Siwanoy Country Club. Presbyterian. Avocations: vocal music, theater, golf, tennis. Office: Lockton Co LLC 7 Times Sq New York NY 10036

MATHIEU, GAIL DENNISE, United States Ambassador to Namibia; b. NJ; m. Erick Mathieu; 1 child, Yuri. BA in Spanish and Latin Am. Studies, Antioch Coll., Yellow Springs, Ohio, 1973; JD, Rutgers U. Sch. Law, Newark, 1976; attended, Johns Hopkins Sch. Advanced Internat. Studies. Bar: NJ 1976, DC 1977. Asst. prosecutor City of Newark, NJ; US observer UNESCO, 1991—95; dep. office dir. Pacific Island affairs US Dept. State, 1995—97, dep. office dir. West African affairs, 1997—99, dep. chief of mission Accra, Ghana, 1999—2002, US amb. to Niger Niamey, 2002—05, dir. office tech. specialized agencies, bur. internat. orgn. affairs, 2005—07, US amb. to Namibia Windhoek, 2007—. Recipient Performance Pay award, US Dept. State, Meritorious Honor award, Superior Honor award. Office: DOS Amb 2540 Windhoek Pl Washington DC 20521*

MATHIEU, MICHELE SUZANNE, grant writer, computer scientist, consultant; b. Chgo., Mar. 24, 1950; d. Joseph Edward Mathieu and Mary Ellen Fisher; m. Robert Steven Harris, May 1, 1988 (dec. Sept. 2000); m. Kathryn Ruth Huff, June 28, 2008. BS in Mktg., Regents Coll., Albany, NY, 1998; cert. web site design, Columbia Coll., Chgo., 2000; cert. in Perl and CGI Scripting, San Diego C.C., 2003, Microsoft cert. profl.; cert. in regulatory essentials UCSD, 2008. Broadcast coord. Grey-North Advt., Chgo., 1967-71; head drama dept. Patricia Stevens Coll., Chgo., 1972; instr. beginning acting Ted Liss Sch. Performing Arts, Chgo., 1973-75; project coord. grants and contracts Am. Dietetic Assn., Chgo., 1974-81, adminstr. govt. affairs, 1981-86, mgr. licensure comm., 1986-90, adminstr. nutrition svcs. payment systems, 1990-94, team leader, health care fin. team, 1994-97, dir. health care fin. team, 1998—2000, dir. mem. web, 2000—01, dir. applications devel., 2001—02; technician Networks Plus Tech. Group, San Diego, 2003—04; pc imaging technician Knowledge Info. Solutions, San Diego, 2004; dir. grants and contracts Virtual Reality Med. Ctr., San Diego, 2004—08; coord., grants & cmty. Rady Children's Hosp., San Diego, 2008—. Grant proposal cons. Chgo., 1978, San Diego, 2008-; med. reporter, writer various internat. clients, 1994-; PC cons., Chgo., 1994-2002, San Diego, 2002—. Editor Legis. Newsletter, 1981-86; contbg. editor Nutrition Forum, 1986, Courier, 1987—2002; contbr. articles to profl. jours., mags., newspapers. Website project mgr. DigitalEve, Chgo., 2001. Ill. Arts Coun. grantee, 1981. Mem. Am. Med. Writers Assn., Am. Soc. Assn. Execs. (Excellence in Govt. award 1989), WebSanDiego. Avocations: reading, fitness walking, sailing.

MATHIEU, SUSAN LEIFER, recreational therapist, educator; b. Long Beach, Calif., Nov. 13, 1952; d. Sally and Oscar Solomon Leifer; m. Jeff Mathieu, Mar. 20, 1976; children: Joseph Gabriel Mathieu 18, Daniel Jacob Mathieu 16. BA, Calif. State U., Long Beach, 1975, MS, 1992; EdD, U. La Verne, 1999. Cert. therapeutic recreation specialist Nat. Coun. Therapeutic Recreation, 1984. Lectr. Calif. State U., Dominquez Hills, 1990—2002, asst. prof. Long Beach, 2002—. Therapeutic recreation tng., cons. ChildNet, Long Beach, 1989—. Contbr. articles to profl. jours. Recreation commr. City of Long Beach, Parks, Recreation and Harbor Recreation Commn., 1981—85; bd. dirs. Jr. League, Long Beach, 1983—2005, PTA, Rancho Palos Verdes, Calif., 1994—99; sisterhood bd. dirs. Congregation Ner Tamid, Rancho Palos Verdes, Calif., 2000—04. Recipient Spl. Recognition award, Cath. Charities Family Shelter for Homeless, 1996, Golden Rule award, JC Penny, 1998. Mem.: Nat. Recreation and Pk. Assn. (assoc.; spkr. 1996—2005, Profl. award Pacific S.W. region 1984, 1994), Long Beach Area Child and Domestic Violence Coun. (assoc.; spkr.), Calif. Pk. and Recreation Soc. (assoc.; com. chair 1998—99, Outstanding Therapeutic Recreation Educator award 1996), Calif. State U. Long Beach Alumni Assn. (bd. dirs. 2004—05), Guild for Infant Survival (assoc.; parent support 1990—95), Chi Kappa Rho Gamma (assoc.; scholarship com. 2002—04, mem. women in leisure svcs.). Jewish. Achievements include first to introduced reading to former gang members in a residential treatment facility. Avocations: kayaking, drums, international folk dancing, developing comedy routines as a teaching tool, guitar. Office: Calif State Univ Long Beach 1250 Bellflower Blvd Long Beach CA 90840 Office Fax: 562-985-8154. Business E-Mail: smathieu@csulb.edu.

MATHIS, ALICIA, biologist, department chairman; b. Meridian, Miss., May 7, 1960; d. Shirley Broadhead. BS, U. So. Miss., 1982, MS, 1985; PhD, U. La., Lafayette, 1989. Tchg. asst. U. So. Miss., Hattiesburg, 1983—85; biologist U.S. Army Corps of Engrs., Vicksburg, Miss., 1985; tchg. asst. U. La., Lafayette, 1985—89; post-doctoral fellow U. Sask., Saskatoon, Canada, 1990—93; prof. Mo. State U., Springfield, 1993—, head dept. biology, 2005—. Rev. panel NSF, 2001—01; mem. adv. bd. Ozark Ctr. for Wildlife Rsch., Reeds Spring, Mo., 1994—97. Editor: Herpetologica, 2004—; assoc. editor: Jour. Herpetology, 1997—2000, Behavioral Ecology and Sociobiology, 2000—03; contbr. articles to profl. jours., chapters to books. Grantee, Sigma Xi, 1987, 1988, NSF, 1996, Mo. Dept. Conservation, 1997—99, US Fish and Wildlife Svc., 2001—03, 2005—; fellow, Mountain Lake Biol. Sta., 1988. Mem.: Herpetologists League (councilor 2001—03), Am. Soc. of Ichthyologists and Herpetologists (symposium organizer 1997), Internat. Soc. for Behavioral Ecology, Animal Behavior Soc. (travel grantee 1993). Avocation: singing. Office: Mo State U Dept Biology 901 S National Ave Springfield MO 65897 Personal E-mail: aliciamathis@missourstate.edu.

MATHIS, CATHERINE J., publishing executive; b. Aug. 2, 1953; BS in Bus. Adminstrn., U. Minn., 1975, MBA in Mktg., Mgmt. Info. Sys., 1979. Mkt. rsch. analyst Internat. Paper Co., Purchase, NY, 1980—81, mgr. bus. sys., 1981—84, mgr. sales analysis, 1984—87, mgr. shareholder comm., 1987—92; v.p. corp. rels. Overseas Shipholding Group Inc., 1992—97; dir. investor rels NY Times Co., NYC, 1997—2000, v.p. corp. comm., 2000—07, sr. v.p. corp. comm., 2007—; spokesperson NY Times and The Times Co., 2000—. Bd. dirs. Nat. Investor Rels. Inst., 2005—; pres. Investor Relations Assn. Named Communicator of Yr., Internat. Assn. Bus. Communicators (NY chapter), 2006. Office: Corp Comm The NY Times Co 620 8th Ave New York NY 10018 Office Phone: 212-556-1981. Business E-Mail: mathis@nytimes.com.

MATHIS, DOLORES, special education educator; PhD, U. Mich., Ann Arbor, 1975. Prof. edn. Tenn. State U., Nashville, 1976—, program coord. of spl. edn., 1977—82. Mem. Links, Inc., Hendersonville Area, Tenn., 1979—. Mem.: Coun. Exceptional Children. Episcopalian. Office: Tenn State Univ Coll Educ 3500 John Merrit Blvd Nashville TN 37208

MATHIS, JOHN PRENTISS, lawyer; b. New Orleans, Feb. 10, 1944; s. Robert Prentess and Lena (Horton) M.; m. Karen Elizabeth McHugh, May 31, 1966; children: Lisa Lynne Mathis Kirkpatrick, Andrew P. BA magna cum laude, So. Meth. U., 1966; JD cum laude, Harvard U., 1969. Bar: Calif. 1970, DC 1975, US Ct. Appeals (DC cir.) 1972, US Ct. Appeals (5th cir.) 1975, US Ct. Appeals (3d cir.) 1980, US Supreme Ct. 1982. Assoc. Latham & Watkins, LA, 1969-71; spl. asst. to gen. counsel FPC, Washington, 1971-72; gen. counsel Calif. Pub. Utilities Commn., San Francisco, 1972-74; assoc. Baker & Botts, Washington, 1974-76, ptnr., 1976-92, Hogan & Hartson, Washington, 1992—2000; v.p., assoc. gen. counsel regulatory affairs Edison Mission Energy, Washington, 2000—06. Bd. dirs. Chesapeake Wildlife Heritage, Easton, Md., Talbot Preservation Alliance, Easton, Mid-Atlantic Symphony Orch., Ocean City, Md., 2004—08. Mem. ABA (litig. sect., chmn. energy litig. com. 1985-89, divsn. dir. 1989-90, chmn. legis. com. 1990-94, rep. to coord. group energy law 1992-97, v.p.), Fed. Energy Bar Assn., Harvard U. Law Sch. Assn. DC (past pres.), Congl. Country Club, Talbot Country Club (Easton, Md.). Republican. Episcopalian. Home Phone: 410-822-4209. Personal E-mail: john.p.mathis@gmail.com.

MATHIS, KAREN J., lawyer, legal association administrator; b. Providence, Nov. 7, 1950; d. Charles H. Young and Elizabeth L. (Kriegal) Ballard; m. Stan A. Mathis, Sept. 7, 1970 (div. 1978). BA cum laude, U. Denver, 1972; JD, U. Colo., 1975; LLD (hon.), Sienna Coll., 2003, Sturm Law Sch., U. Denver, 2005, Mich. State U., 2006, Southwestern Sch. Law, 2006. Bar: Colo. Supreme Ct. 1975, U.S. Dist. Ct. 1975, U.S. Ct. Appeals (10th cir.) 1978, U.S. Tax Ct. 1980. Tax acct. Peat Marwick Mitchell, Denver, 1975-76; ptnr. Rothenberg & Mathis, Denver, 1976-79; sole practitioner Denver, 1979-80; assoc. Sterling & Simon PC, Denver, 1980-83; ptnr. Hughes & Dorsey, Denver, 1983-84; shareholder, dir. Sterling & Miller, Denver, 1984-86; pres. The Mathis Law Firm, Denver, 1986—2004; pres., CEO Mathis Asset Mgmt., Inc., Denver, 1989—2004; ptnr. McElroy, Deutsch, Mulvaney & Carpenter, LLP, Denver, 2004—. Contbr. articles to profl. jours. Bd. dirs. CORRA, Denver, Planned Parenthood Rocky Mountains, Denver; bd. dirs., v.p. Rocky Mountain Meml. Soc., Denver; mem. adv. com. Colo. Dept. Social Svcs., Denver. Named Disting. Alumni U. Colo., 1992; recipient Order of the Coif (hon.) U. Colo., 2002; named one of The 50 Most Influential Women Lawyers in America, Nat. Law Jour., 2007. Mem. ABA (ho. of dels. 1982-, interim Colo. state del. 1992-2000, chair standing com. on mem., 1994-97, chair commn. on women in the profession, 1997-2000, chair ho. dels., 2000-02, chair gen. practice, solo & small firm section, 2002-03, pres-elect, 2005-06, pres., 2006-2007), Colo. Bar Assn. (1st v.p. 1992-93, bd. govs. 1983-, outstanding young lawyer in Colo.), Denver Bar Assn. Office: McElroy Deutsch Mulvaney & Carpenter LLP Mile High Ctr 1700 Broadway Ste 1900 Denver CO 80290 Office Phone: 303-293-8800 Ext. 242. Office Fax: 303-839-0036. E-mail: kmathis@mdmlawco.com.*

MATHIS, LISA, federal agency administrator; Assoc. dir. & pediatric & maternal staff FDA Office of New Drugs. Office: 10903 New Hampshire Ave Rm 6414 Silver Spring MD 20903 E-mail: lisa.mathis@fda.hhs.gov.*

MATHIS, LUSTER DOYLE, academic administrator, political scientist, educator; b. Gainesville, Ga., May 5, 1936; s. Luster and Fay Selena (Wingo) M.; m. Rheba Burch, June 5, 1958; children— Douglas James, Deborah Jane. AB, Berry Coll., 1958; MA, U. Ga., 1958, PhD (Univ. Alumni Found. fellow), 1966. Asst. prof. polit. sci. Brenau Coll., Gainesville, 1960-61; asso. prof. Calif. Baptist Coll., 1961-62, Belmont Coll., Nashville, 1962-64; asso. prof., head dept. polit. sci. W.Ga. Coll., Carrollton, 1965-68, prof., 1969-75, head dept., 1969-71, chmn. div. grad. studies, 1970-73; assoc. dean, 1972-75; research asso., asst. editor Papers of Thomas Jefferson Princeton U., 1968-69; v.p., dean of coll. Berry Coll., Mt. Berry, Ga., 1975-93, v.p. acad. affairs, 1993-99, provost, 1999-2000, coll. historian, prof. govt., 2000—03. Cons. Citizens Com. on Ga. Gen. Assembly. Co-author: Courts as Political Instruments, 1970. Mem. Ga. Democratic Charter Commn., 1974-75; mem. consumer adv. com. Floyd Med. Center, 1978-80. Fellow, Nat. Hist. Publs. Commn., 1968—69. Mem. Am. Assn. Higher Edn., Am. Conf. Acad. Deans, Ga. Polit. Sci. Assn. (pres. 1968-69). Democrat. Baptist.

MATHISEN, DOUGLAS J., thoracic surgeon; b. Spring Valley, Ill., 1948; MD, U. Ill. Diplomate Am. Bd. Thoracic Surgery, Am. Bd. Surgery. Thoracic surgeon Mass. Gen. Hosp., Boston, 1995—; prof. thoracic surgery Harvard U. Med. Sch., 1989—99, Hermes C. Grillo prof. thoracic surgery, 1999—; chief cardiac thoracic surgery Mass. Gen. Hosp. Fellow Am. Coll. Surgeons; mem. AMA, ACCPA, Am. Assn. Thoracic Surgery, Soc. Thoracic Surgery (bd. mem., 2nd v.p.), Cardiothoracic Surgery Network, Thoracic Surgery Directors Assn., Thoracic Surgery Found. for Rsch. & Edn., Soc. Thoracic Surgeons (treas.). Office: Mass Gen Hosp Thoracic Surgery Blake 1570 55 Fruit St Boston MA 02114 Office Phone: 617-726-6826. Business E-Mail: dmathisen@partners.org.

MATHISEN, HAROLD CLIFFORD, foundation administrator; b. East Orange, NJ, Apr. 1, 1924; s. Harold and Ottilie Christine (Nordland) Mathisen; m. Dora Elizabeth Bachtel, Sept. 14, 1946; children: Margaret Bennett, Harold, Elizabeth Mathisen Andersen, Barbara Ramsland. AB, Princeton U., 1943; MBA, Harvard U., 1948. Asst. to contr. Kaiser Frazer Corp., Willow Run, Mich., 1948—52; investment analyst Smith Barney & Co., NYC, 1952—61; pres. Alliance Found., NYC, 1961—. Treas. AGF Mgmt. Co., NYC, 1969—85; portfolio mgr. Legg Mason Wood Walker, Inc., NYC, 1967—78, NYC, 1982—2005, Citigroup, NYC, 2005—07. Pres. Alliance Growth Fund, NYC, 1968—78; trustee, pres. McAuley Water St. Mission, NYC, 1967—99; asst. treas., investment mgr. Christian and Missionary Alliance, Nyack, 1978—80; asst. treas. NY Internat. Bible Soc., NYC, 1980—82. Lt. USNR, 1944—46. Mem.: Inst. Chartered Fin. Analysts, NY Soc. Securities Analysts, Sigma Xi, Phi Beta Kappa. Home: 36 Runnymede Rd Chatham NJ 07928-1374 Office: One New York Plaza New York NY 10004

MATHISEN, HOWARD, psychologist, educator, minister; b. Bklyn., June 3, 1938; s. Olaf and Hjordis K. (Skjaerum) Mathisen; m. Sue Jane Andrews, June 13, 1960 (div. 1975); m. Kathleen Ann Poce, Sept. 20, 1980 (dec. 1987); m. Carolynn Anne Burroughs, Aug. 22, 1992. BA in Psychology, Taylor U., Upland, IN, 1956—60; MDiv, Phila. Theol. Sem., 1960—63; postgrad. in Theology, Luth. Theol. Sem., 1964—65; MA in Religion, Concordia Sem., St. Louis, 1966—67; postgrad. Alcoholism studies, Rutgers U., 1975; postgrad. in Psycholody, Assumption Coll., Worcester, MA, 1971—76; DMin in Psychology, Andover Newton Theol. Sch., 1972—76. Lic. psychologist, Mass., marriage and family therapist, Mass.; cert. diplomate of sex therapy Am. Assn. Sexuality Educators, Counselors and Therapists; diplomate in marital and sex therapy Am. Bd. Family Psychology; diplomate Am. Bd. Sexology. Pastor Christ Meml. Ch., Phila., 1962-66, Zion Luth. Ch., Webster, Mass., 1967-73; dir. Human Svcs. Ctr. Hubbard Regional Hosp., Webster, 1973-81; pvt. practice psychology Boylston, Mass., 1976-81; co-dir. Counseling Affiliates, Worcester, Mass., 1981-97; dir. pastoral counseling Boston Road Clinic, Worcester, 1997—2001; dir. credentialing svcs. Capstan, Worcester, 1998-99; asst. pastor Concordia Luth. Ch., Worcester, 1976-98; dir. min. asst. program New Eng. Synod, Evangelical Luth. Ch., 1991—; psychologist Prescott Health Care, 2002—. Adj. instr. psychology Nichols Coll., Dudley, Mass., 1981, Assumption Coll., Worcester, 1983-86. Dean ctrl. Mass. conf. New Eng. Synod, Luth. Ch., 1988-90; bd. dirs. Luth. Svc. Assn. New Eng., 1973-87, vice chmn., 1983-85, chmn., 1985-87; bd. dirs. Luth. Home of Worcester, 1987-92, chmn., 1987-89; chmn. bldg. com. Luth. Nursing Home, Worcester, 1977-79; chmn. Family Svcs. Com., 1981-83; mem. Mass. Adv. Com. Continuing Edn. for Nursing, 1979-81; bd. dirs. Family Planning Svcs. Ctrl. Mass., 1975-81; mem. tech. adv. subcom. substance abuse Ctrl. Mass. Health Sys. Agy., 1979-80. Fellow Acad. Family Psychology, Am. Acad. Clin. Sexologists; mem. APA, Am. Assn. Marriage and Family Therapy, Mass. Psychol. Assn., Mass. Assn. Marriage and Family Therapy, Acad. Managed Care Providers. Lutheran. Avocations: travel, photography. Office: Prescott Health Care 95 Lincoln St Worcester MA 01605 Home: 18 Emily Dr West Boylston MA 01583-2122 Office Phone: 508-754-1803. E-mail: mathisen@charter.net.

MATHISEN, LAUREN J., psychologist; d. Eric and Diane Briscoe; m. Jason L. Mathisen, July 29, 1995; children: Tristan, Peyton, Aidan. BA, U. Md., Coll. Pk, 1999; MS, Northeastern U., Boston, Mass., 2001, CAGS (hon.), 2002. Cert. in sch. psychology Mass. Dept. Edn., 2002, NASP, 2007. Sch. psychologist Hull Pub. Schs., Mass., 2002—. Contbr. chapter to book. Com. mem. First Bapt. Christian Sch., Weymouth, Mass., 2005—08. Mem.: NASP, Nat. Honors Soc., Phi Kappa Phi. Conservative. Office: Hull HS 180 Main St Hull MA 02045 Office Fax: 781-925-3071. Business E-Mail: lmathisen@town.hull.ma.us.

MATHOG, ROBERT HENRY, otolaryngologist, educator; b. New Haven, Apr. 13, 1939; s. William and Tiby (Gans) M.; m. Deena Jane Rabinowitz, June 14, 1964; children: Tiby, Heather, Lauren, Jason. AB, Dartmouth Coll., 1960; MD, NYU, 1964. Diplomate Am. Bd. Facial Plastic and Reconstructive Surgery. Intern Duke Hosp., Durham, NC, 1964-65, resident surgery, 1965-66, resident otolaryngology, 1966-69; practice medicine, specializing in otolaryngology Mpls., 1971-77, Detroit, 1977—; chief of otolaryngology Hennepin County Med. Center, Mpls., 1972-77; asst. prof. U. Minn., 1971-74, asso. prof., 1974-77; prof., chmn. dept. otolaryngology Wayne State U. Sch. Medicine, 1977—. Chief otolaryngology Hennepin County Hosp., Mpls., 1972-77, Harper-Grace Hosps., Detroit, 1977—, Detroit Receiving Hosp., 1977-92; cons. staff VA Hosp., Allen Park, Minn., 1977—, Children's Hosp., Detroit, 1977—, Hutzel Hosp., Detroit, 1966, St. Joseph Mercy Hosp., Oakland, Mich., 2001; mem. adv. coun. Nat. Inst. Deaf and Other Communicable Disorders NIH, 1992-96; chief otolaryngology, head and neck surgery June Hosp., 1994-95. Author: Otolaryngology Clinics of North America, 1976, Textbook of Maxillofacial Trauma, 1983; editor in chief Videomed. Edn. Systems, 1972-75; editor: Atlas of Craniofacial Trauma, 1992; contbr. articles to med. jours. Bd. dirs. Bexer County Hearing Soc., 1969-71; adv. coun. WIDCB, 1993; pres. and chmn. Lions Hearing Ctr., 1999-, Mich. Maj. USAF, 1969-71. Recipient Valentine Mott medal for proficiency in anatomy, 1961, Recognition award Wayne State Bd. Govs. Faculty, 1993; Deafness Rsch. Found. grantee, 1979-81, NIH grantee, 1986, 92, 96, Lawrence M. Weiner Alumni award Wayne State U. Sch. Med., 1999. Fellow ACS, Am. Acad. Otolaryngology, Head and Neck Surgery (Cert. award 1976, Cert. of Appreciation 1978), Am. Soc. Head and Neck Surgery, Triological Soc. (v.p. 1995-96, mtg. guest of honor 2002, Vice Presdl. Citation award 2004), Am. Otol. Soc., Am. Acad. Facial Plastic and Reconstructive Surgery (v.p. 1980), Am. Neurotology Soc.; mem. AMA, Am. Laryngol. Soc. (coun. 1994—), Am. Laryngol. Assn., Mich. Med. Soc., Am. Head and Neck Soc., Soc. Univ. Otolaryngologists (pres. 1995), Assn. Acad. Depts. Otolaryngology, Assn. Rsch. Otolaryngology (pres. 1981). Home: 27115 Wellington Rd Franklin MI 48025-1329 Office: 43494 Woodward Ste 210 Bloomfield Hills MI 48312 Also: Wayne State U Sch Med 540 E Canfield St Detroit MI 48201-1928

MATHRE, LAWRENCE GERHARD, minister, federal agency administrator; b. Vancouver, BC, Can., Mar. 24, 1925; s. Lawrence Alfred and Nellie Josephine (Thompson) M.; m. Blanche Kathleen Brudevold, Sept. 2, 1951; children: James Lawrence, Jerome Keigh, John Mark, Joel David. BA, St. Olaf Coll., 1948; MDiv., Luther Sem., 1952; MA,

Phillips U., 1962. Ordained to ministry Evang. Luth. Ch. in Am., 1952. Pastor First Luth. Ch., Fargo, N.D., 1952-54, Bethlehem Luth. Ch., Buffalo Center, Iowa, 1952-57; founder, pastor Prince of Peace Luth. Ch., Oklahoma City, 1957-63; chaplain fed. prison system U.S. Dept. Justice, Okla., Wash., Ill. and Calif., 1963-73, chaplain dir. Western and N.C. regions, 1973-83; pastor Hope Luth Ch., San Mateo, Calif., 1984-87, Zion Luth. Ch., Stockton, Calif., 1987-91; ret., 1991. Assoc. prof. Pacific Luth. U., Parkland, Wash., 1970-72; chaplain St. Joseph's Regional Med. Ctr. Nat. chaplain Fed. Prison Retirees Assn., 1999—. With AUS, 1943—45, ETO. Decorated Bronze Star. Mem. Am. Protestant Correctional Chaplains Assn. (nat. pres. 1974), Am. Correctional Chaplains Assn. (nat. pres. 1977), Assn. Clin. Pastoral Edn. (regional chmn. 1979-83, v.p. 1977-79, treas. 1984-89), Winnebago Itasc Travelers (chaplain), Lions (chaplain San Mateo club 1985-87). Republican. Home: 43850 Venice Dr La Quinta CA 92253 *It is not nearly as important what happens to you as it is what you do about what happens to you. A life lived for oneself is empty; a life lived with and for others is full. You truly find yourself when you are well related—to God and to others.*

MATHUR, NARESH CHANDRA, retired engineering educator; b. Gurgaon, India, Oct. 12, 1935; s. Avinash Chandra and Vidyavati Mathur; m. Madhur Mathur; children: Suchitra, Sharad Chandra. BA with honors, Delhi U., India, 1955; diploma, Indian Inst. Sci., Bangalore, 1958; MS, U. Ill., Urbana, 1961, PhD, 1963. Vice chancellor U. Roorkee, UP, India, 1987—90; vice chmn. U. Grants Commn., New Delhi, 1994—98. Mng. dir. Ednl. Cons. India Ltd., New Delhi, 1984—86. Fellow: Astron. Soc. India, Instn. Electronics and Telecom. Engrs. (India); mem.: IEEE. Office: Univ Mo Kans City 5100 Rockhill Rd Rm 560A FH Kansas City MO 64110 Business E-Mail: mathurn@umkc.edu.

MATHUR, RYAN, social sciences educator; b. Lancaster, Pa., Feb. 6, 1976; s. Dilip and Carolyn Mathur; m. Amy Heptner; 1 child, Nathan. PhD, U. Ariz., Tucson, 2000. Prof. Juniata Coll., Huntingdon, Pa., 2001—. Contbr. articles to profl. jours. Mem.: GSA, SGE, SEG. Office: Juniata Coll 1700 Moore St Huntingdon PA 16652

MATHYS, GORDON D., accountant, educator; b. Hawkeye, Iowa, Jan. 15, 1947; s. Clarion and Darlene M Mathys; m. Janice R. Beltz, Aug. 30, 1969; children: Dalen M. Mathys-Cook, David M. BA, Upper Iowa U., Fayette, 1969; MEd, Iowa State U., Ames, 1992. Instr. Gates Bus. Coll., Waterloo, Iowa, 1969—71, Cedar Rapids Bus. Coll., Cedar Rapids, 1971—74; prof. Hawkeye C.C., Waterloo, 1974—. Author: (book) Computerized Accounting using Peachtree, Computerized Accounting using QuickBooks. Mem.: Iowa State Alumni Assn., Phi Kappa Phi. Avocation: gardening. Office: Hawkeye Comm College PO Box 8015 Waterloo IA 50704-8015

MATIA, PAUL RAMON, lawyer; s. Leo Clemens and Irene Elizabeth (Linkert) M.; m. Nancy Arch Van Meter, Jan. 2, 1993. BA, Case Western Res. U., 1959; JD, Harvard U., 1962. Bar: Ohio 1962, US Dist. Ct. (no. dist.) Ohio 1969, US Ct. Appeals (6th cir.), 2007. Law clk. Common Pleas Ct. of Cuyahoga County, Cleve., 1963-66, judge, 1985-91; asst. atty. gen. State of Ohio, Cleve., 1966-69, adminstrv. ast. to atty. gen. Columbus, 1969-70; senator Ohio State Senate, Columbus, 1971-75, 79-83; ptnr. Hadley, Matia, Mills & MacLean Co., L.P.A., Cleve., 1975-84, Porter Wright Morris & Arthur LLP, Cleve., 2005—; judge U.S. Dist. Ct. (no. dist.) Ohio, 1991-99, chief dist. judge, 1999—2004, sr. judge, 2005; mem. 6th Cir. Jud. Coun., 1999—2004. Candidate Lt. Gov. Rep. Primary, 1982, Ohio Supreme Ct., 1988. Named Outstanding Legislator, Ohio Assn. for Retarded Citizens, 1974, Watchdog of Ohio Treasury, United Conservatives of Ohio, 1979; recipient Heritage award Polonia Found., 1988. Mem. Fed. Bar Assn., Ohio State Bar Assn., Cleve. Met. Bar Assn., Sixth Cir. (life), Judge John M. Manos Inn of Ct., Club at Key Ctr., Vineyards Country Club, Naples, Fla. Republican. Avocations: skiing, gardening, travel. Office: Porter Wright Morris & Arthur LLP 925 Euclid Ave Ste 1700 Cleveland OH 44115-1483 Office Phone: 216-443-2548. Business E-Mail: pmatia@porterwright.com.

MATIENZO, LUIS J., chemical engineer; b. Lima, Peru, Jan. 30, 1944; came to U.S., 1967; s. Luis J. Matienzo and Elsa (Bustamante) M.; m. Paula M. Roth, Mar. 20, 1970; children: Gregg, Timothy, Mark. BSChemE, San Marcos U., 1967; MS in Chemistry, Mich. State U., 1969; PhD in Chemistry, U. Md., 1973. Postdoctoral fellow Case Western Res. U., Cleve., 1974; rsch. chemist E.I. duPont de Nemours & Co., Exptl. Sta., Wilmington, Del., 1974-79; sr. scientist Martin Marietta Labs., Balt., 1979-85; adv. engr. IBM Corp., Endicott, N.Y., 1985-95; sr. engr., 1995—. Asst. prof. La Molina U., Lima, 1969-70; vis. prof. Nat. U. Engring., Lima, 1977-78; lectr. material sci. and engring. Cornell U., Ithaca, N.Y., 1987—; vis. prof. materials sci. & engring. Cath. U., Lima, 1996. Author 6 book chpts., 120 tech. articles; reviewer tech. contbns. to profl. jours. W.R. Grace Chem. Engring. scholar, 1965-66, Ford Found. scholar, 1967-69. Fellow Böhmische Physikalische Gesellschaft; mem. Am. Vacuum Soc., Am. Inst. Physics, Sigma Xi (grad. studies award 1973), Materials Rsch. Soc. Achievements include 23 filed patents in field; research in applied surface analysis. Office: IBM Corp 1701 North St Bldg 257-3 Endicott NY 13760-5598

MATIJEVIC, EGON, chemistry professor; b. Otocac, Croatia, Apr. 27, 1922; came to U.S., 1957; s. Grgur and Stefica (Spiegel) M.; m. Bozica Biscan, Feb. 27, 1947. Diploma in Chem. Engring., U. Zagreb, 1944, PhD in Chemistry, 1948, D Habilitation in Phys. Chemistry, 1952; DSc (hon.), Lehigh U., 1977, M. Curie-Sklodowska U., Lublin, Poland, 1990, Clarkson U., 1992, Zagreb U., Croatia, 1998, Nat. U. San Martin, Buenos Aires, 2003, U. Ljubljana, Slovenia, 2003. Instr. chemistry U. Zagreb, 1944-47, sr. instr. phys. chemistry, 1949-52, privat dozent in colloid chemistry, 1952-54, dozent in phys. and colloid chemistry, 1955-56, on leave, 1956-59; rsch. assoc. Inst. Cinematography, Zagreb, 1948; rsch. fellow dept. colloid sci. U. Cambridge, England, 1956-57; vis. prof. Clarkson Coll. Tech., Potsdam, NY, 1957-59, assoc. prof. chemistry Postdam, NY, 1960-62; prof. Clarkson U., Postdam, NY, 1962-86, disting. univ. prof., 1986-99, LaMer prof. colloid and surface sci., 2000—; assoc. dir. Inst. Colloid and Surface Sci. Clarkson Coll. Tech., 1966-68, dir. inst., 1968-81, chmn. dept. chemistry, 1981-87. Vis. prof. Japan Soc. for Promotion Sci., 1973, U. Melbourne, Australia, 1976, Sci. U. Tokyo, 1979, 84, fgn. guest Inst. Colloid and Interface Sci., 82; vis. scientist U. Leningrad, Russia, 1977; advisor IAEA, Buenos Aires, 1978, Buenos Aires, 80; lectr. in field. Author: (with M. Kesler) General and Inorganic Chemistry for Senior High Schools, 11 edits., including Croatian, Macedonian, Hungarian, Italian, 1943-63; translator: Einfuhrung in die Stochiometrie (Nylen and Wigern), 1948; editor: (with Alter J. Weber) Adsorption from Aqueous Solution, 1968, Surface and Colloid Science, vols. 1-17, 1969-2002; contbr. numerous articles to profl. publs. Recipient Gold medal, Am. Electroplaters Soc., 1976, guest of honor 56th and 63d Colloid and Surface Sci. Symposia, Blacksburg, Va., 1982, Seattle, 1989, Boston, 2002, Egon Matijevic chair endowed in his name, Clarkson U., 1992. Mem. Am. Chem. Soc. (councilor divsn. colloid and surface chemistry 1982-87, chmn. 1969-70, Kendall award 1972, Langmuir Disting. Lectureship award 1985, Ralph K. Iler award 1993), Kolloid Gesellschaft (hon. life, Thomas Graham award 1985), Internat. Assn. Colloid Interface Sci. (pres. 1985-87), Chem. Soc. Japan, Inst. Colloid and Interface Sci. of Sci. U. of Tokyo (hon.), Phalanx Soc., Croatian Acad. Scis. and Arts (fgn.), Am. Ceramic Soc. (hon.), Materials Rsch. Soc. Japan (hon.), Acad. Ceramics (Italy), Croatian Chem. Soc. (hon., Bozo Tezak medal 1991), Sigma Xi (Clarkson Coll. Tech. chpt. award 1972, nat. lectr. 1987-89). Roman Catholic. Office: Ctr Advanced Materials Proc Clarkson U Dept Chem Potsdam NY 13699-5814 Home Phone: 315-265-2263. Business E-Mail: matiegon@clarkson.edu.

MATILSKY, TERRY ALLEN, astrophysicist, educator; b. Bklyn., Mar. 29, 1947; s. Ben and Dorothy Matilsky; m. Ruth Friedner, May 25, 1973; children: Sarabeth, Jacob, Athena, Matthew, Loren. BS, U. Mich., Ann Arbor, 1967; PhD, Princeton U., NJ, 1971. Sr. scientist Am. Sci. & Engring., Cambridge, 1971—74; astrophysicist MIT, Cambridge, 1974—76; prof. physics Rutgers U., Piscataway, NJ, 1976—. Cons. NASA, Washington, 1976—2008. Bd. mem. Rutgers Fed. Credit Union, NB, NJ, 1990—2008. Rsch. grant, NASA, 1976—90. Mem.: AAS. Achievements include discovery of 100 sec. variability in quasars; time variability in various galactic X-ray sources. Office: Rutgers Univ Dept Physics Piscataway NJ 08854

MATIS, NINA B., lawyer; b. NYC, June 23, 1947; AB cum laude, Smith Coll., 1969; JD, NYU, 1972. Bar: Ill. 1973. Ptnr., nat. co-chair real estate practice Katten Muchin Zavis Rosenman LLP, Chgo.; chief investment officer, gen. counsel, exec. v.p. iStar Financial Inc. Adj. prof. law Northwestern U., 1984-87. Named one of 500 Leading Lawyer in America, Lawdragon, 100 Most Influential Lawyers in America, Nat. Law Jour., 2006, 50 Most Influential Women Lawyers in America, 2007. Mem. Am. Bar Assn., Am. Coll. Real Estate Lawyers, Chicago Fin. Exchange, Chicago Real Estate Exec. Women, Chicago Real Estate Women, Econ. Club of Chicago, Lambda Alpha Internat. (Ely Chpt.), Internat. Coun. of Shopping Centers, Lakefront SRO, Pension Real Estate Assn., Real Estate Fin. Forum, The Chicago Network, Urban Land Inst. Office: Katten Muchin Zavis Rosenman 525 W Monroe St Ste 1600 Chicago IL 60661-3693 Office Fax: 312-577-8686. E-mail: nina.matis@kmzr.com.*

MATISE, JOHN J., investment company executive; s. Salvatore A. and Patricia M. Matise; m. Ann Hayden, 1994; 1 child, Anthony Joseph. BA with high honors, U. Calif., Davis, 1992; MBA, Anderson Sch. UCLA, 2000. Sr. consulant Andersen Cons., San Francisco, 1992—94; mgr. Deloitte Consulting, San Francisco, 1994—97, Accenture, San Francisco, 1997—99; v.p. Encore Venture Partners, LA, 1999—2001; v.p. pvt. equity Wedbush, Inc., LA, 2001—04; prin. Matise Capital, Playa Del Rey, Calif., 2004—; v.p. internat. and s7 Saleen, Inc., Irvine, Calif., 2004—05; COO Small World Kids, Inc., Culver City, 2006; mng. dir. Stone Canyon Venture Partners, L.P., Beverly Hills, 2007—. Mem. The Karma Found., Beverly Hills, Calif., 2005; chmn. UCLA Venture Capital and Pvt. Equity Alumni Assn., Los Angeles, Calif., 2001; mem. UCLA Anderson Sch. Alumni Rels. Bd., Los Angeles, Calif., 2001—05; bd. dir. Small World Kids, Inc., Culver City, Calif., 2004—06. Avocations: travel, outdoor activities. Office: Stone Canyon 1316 S Centinela Ave Apt 5 Los Angeles CA 90025-1961 Office Fax: 720-228-1848. Business E-Mail: jmatise@scvp.com.

MATIYA, JIM, psychology professor; b. Chgo., Mar. 2, 1947; s. Roy and Lorraine Matiya; m. Susan M. Green, July 29, 1978; children: Mike, Alissa. BS, Ill. State U., Normal, 1972; M in Family Therapy, Calif. State U., Los Angeles, 1979. Instr. Fla. Gulf Coast U., Ft. Myers, 2008—. With Psychology Connection Video Series, John Wiley & Sons. Recipient Moffett award, Soc. Tchg. Psychology, 2003; nominee, Golden Apple Found. Chgo., 2001. Business E-Mail: jmatiya@fgcu.edu.

MATKIN, JUDITH CONWAY, product designer; b. Ontario, Oreg., Jan. 26, 1943; d. Edward Owen and Lois Lorraine Conway; m. Eltjo Emile Witkop, Feb. 23, 1963 (div. Jan. 1970); children: Gregory Lyn, Joella Monique, Bradley Michael; m. Reuel P. Matkin, Mar. 20, 1995; stepchildren: Chris, Marcie, Ryan. Designer, sales rep. Jerome I. Silverman, Inc., NYC, 1970-86, Gem East Corp., Seattle, 1986-87; designer Nova Stylings, Van Nuys, Calif., 1987-91, Bagley & Hotchkiss, Santa Rosa, Calif., 1991-94; designer, owner Judith Conway, Windsor, Calif., 1994—. Design cons. Jade and Gem Corp., Hong Kong, 1986; career fair advisor Gemol. Inst. Am., L.A., N.Y.C., 1990-99. Designer Diamond Internat. Awards, 1990, Jewelers of Am. Awards, 1991, Platinum Guild Internat., 1998. Lobbiest Parents of Blind Children, Oreg., 1978-79; pres. Lambda Chi Alpha Parents Orgn., Oreg. State U., Corvallis, 1983-84, Lakeridge Parents Music Orgn., Lake Oswego, Oreg., 1984-85; adv. coun. Couture Internat. Jewelry Collections and Conference. Finalist Design awards, Couture Town & Country, 2000, Couture Internat. Design Coll. Conf., 2008. Mem. Calif. Jewelers Assn., Womans Jewelers Assn. (chairperson annual dinner 1990, Designer of the Yr. 1998), Jewelry Info. Ctr., Contemporary Design Group, Chaine Des Rotisseurs (dame de la chaine). Avocations: art collecting, wine and food, musical instruments and listening, boating. Office: Judith Conway Inc PO Box 956 Windsor CA 95492-0956 Office Phone: 707-838-8760.

MATKOWSKY, BERNARD JUDAH, mathematician, educator; b. NYC, Aug. 19, 1939; s. Morris N. and Ethel H. M.; m. Florence Knobel, Apr. 11, 1965; children: David, Daniel, Devorah. BS, CCNY, 1960; M.E.E., NYU, 1961, MS, 1963, PhD, 1966. Fellow Courant Inst. Math. Scis., NYU, 1961-66; mem. faculty dept. math. Rensselaer Poly. Inst., 1966-77; John Evans prof. applied math., mech. engring. & math. Northwestern U., Evanston, Ill., 1977—, chmn. engring. sci. and applied math. dept., 1993-99; Lady Davis vis. prof. Technion, 2007. Vis. prof. Tel Aviv U., 1972-73; vis. scientist Weizmann Inst. Sci., Israel, summer 1976, summer 1980, Tel Aviv U., summer 1980; cons. Argonne Nat. Lab., Sandia Labs., Lawrence Livermore Nat. Lab., Exxon Research and Engring. Co. Editor Wave Motion—An Internat. Jour., 1979-99, Applied Math. Letters, 1987—, SIAM Jour. Applied Math., 1976-95, European Jour. Applied Math., 1990-96, Random and Computational Dynamics, 1991-97, Internat. Jour. SHS, 1992—, Jour. Materials Synthesis and Processing, 1992-2002, SIAM Mongraphs Math. Modeling and Computation, 2005—, Mathematical Modeling of Natural Phenomena, 2007—; mem. editl. adv. bd. Springer Verlag Applied Math. Scis. Series; contbr. chpts. to books, articles to profl. jours. Fulbright grantee, 1972-73; Guggenheim fellow, 1982-83 Fellow: AAAS, Am. Phys. Soc., Am. Acad. Mechs.; mem.: Soc. Natural Philosophy, Com. Concerned Scientists, Conf. Bd. Math. Scis. (coun., com. human rights math. scientists), Am. Assn. Combustion Synthesis, Combustion Inst., Am. Math. Soc., Soc. Indsl. and Applied Math., Eta Kappa Nu, Sigma Xi. Home: 3704 Davis St Skokie IL 60076-1745 Office: Northwestern U Technological Institute Evanston IL 60208-0001 Office Phone: 847-491-5396. Business E-Mail: b-matkowsky@northwestern.edu.

MATLAK, MICHAEL EDWARD, pediatric general surgeon; b. Chgo., Jan. 30, 1944; MD, Loyola U., 1968. Cert. Am. Bd. Surgery, Am. Bd. Pediatric Surgery. Intern, gen. surgery Cook County Hosp., Chgo., 1968—69; resident, gen. surgery Mayo Clinic, Minn., 1971—75; resident, pediatric surgery Children's Nat. Med. Ctr., Washington, 1975—77; staff mem., divsn. pediatric gen. surgery U. Utah Health Sciences Ctr., Salt Lake City, prof. surgery (clin.), pediatrics. Mem.: Pacific Assn. Pediatric Surgeons, Am. Pediatric Surgical Assn., Am. Coll. Surgeons, Am. Acad. Pediatrics. Address: List 2nd Womens and Childrens Clinic 1034 N 500 W Provo UT 84604 also: U Utah Health Sciences Ctr 50 N Medical Dr Salt Lake City UT 84132 Office: Primary Childrens Med Ctr Ste 2600 100 N Mario Capecchi Dr Salt Lake City UT 84113-1103 Office Phone: 801-662-2950.

MATLIN, MARLEE BETH, actress; b. Morton Grove, Ill., Aug. 24, 1965; d. Don and Libby M.; m. Kevin Grandalski, Aug. 29, 1993; children Brandon Joseph, Tyler Daniel, Sara Rose, Isabelle Jane. Attended William Rainey Harper Coll. Spokeswomen Nat. Captioning Inst. Appeared in films Children of a Lesser God, 1986 (Acad. award for best actress, Golden Globe award), Walker, 1987, Linguini Incident, 1991, The Player, 1992, Hear No Evil, 1993, Snitch, 1996, It's My Party, 1996, In Her Defense, 1998, When Justice Fails, 1998, Freak City, 1999, Two Shades of Blue, 2000, Askari, 2001; TV films: Bridge to Silence, 1989, Against Her Will: The Carrie Buck Story, 1994, When Justice Fails, 1997, Dead Silence, 1997, Where the Truth Lies, 1999 (also exec. prodr.), Kiss My Act, 2001, Sweet Nothing in My Ear, 2008; TV series: Reasonable Doubts, 1991-93; guest star: Picket Fences, 1993, 94-96 (Emmy nomination, Guest Actress-Drama Series, 1994), Seinfeld, 1993 (Emmy nomination Guest Actress-Comedy Series, 1994), The Larry Sanders Show, 1992, Spin City, 1996, ER, 1999, Judging Amy, 1999, The West Wing, 2000—2006, The Practice, 2000, Gideon's Crossing, 2001, Extreme Makeover: Home Edition, 2003, The Division, 2003, Law & Order: Spl. Victims Unit, 2004-05, Desperate Housewives, 2005, My Name is Earl, 2006-07, CSI: NY, 2006, The L Word, 2007-08; performer Dancing with the Stars, 2008; author: Deaf Child Crossing, 2002; (voice) Baby Einstein: Baby Wordsworth, 2005, Baby Einstein: My First Signs, 2007 (also prodr.). Bd. dirs. Very Spl. Arts, Starlight Found. Office: c/o Spanky Taylor 3727 W Magnolia Ste 300 Burbank CA 91505 also: Fifteen Minutes Public Relations 8436 W Third St Ste 650 Los Angeles CA 90048*

MATLINS, STUART M., management consultant, publisher; b. NYC, July 25, 1940; s. Louis Karl and Lillian M. m. Andrea Cines, June 20, 1960 (div.); children: Seth, Andrew; m. Antoinette Leonard, Oct. 9, 1977. Attended, London Sch. Econs., 1958—59; BS, U. Wis., Madison, 1960; AM, Princeton U., NJ, 1962; postgrad., Princeton U., 1962—63. Internat. economist Bur. Internat. Commerce, U.S. Dept. Commerce, Washington, 1963-66; cons. Booz Allen & Hamilton, Inc., NYC, 1966-67, asst. to pres. internat./adminstrv. dir., 1967-70, v.p. internat. ops., 1970-71, v.p./mng. officer, instl. and pub. mgmt. div., 1971-74; pres., mgmt. cons. Stuart Matlins Assocs., Inc., Woodstock, Vt., 1974—. Chmn. bd. dirs. LongHill Ptnrs., Inc.; publisher Gemstone Press, Jewish Lights Pub., SkyLight Paths Pub. Bd. dirs. Health Edn. Found., Woodstock Area Jewish Cmty., Vt.; former chmn. overseers NY Sch., Hebrew Union Coll.-Jewish Inst. Religion; bd. govs. Hebrew Union Coll.; capital budget com. Town of Woodstock; adv. bd. Abraham Geiger Coll., Germany; dir. Jewish Book Coun. Woodrow Wilson fellow, 1960-61, Herbert O. Peet fellow, 1961-62, Phillip A. Rollins fellow, 1962-63; recipient Am. Jewish Disting. Svc. award Hebrew Union Coll., 2006. Mem. Princeton Club. Office: LongHill Ptnrs Inc PO Box 237 Woodstock VT 05091-0237 also: Sunset Farm Offices Rt 4 Woodstock VT 05091

MATLOCK, B. JANE, science educator; b. Kankakee, Ill., Jan. 31, 1953; d. Richard Lea Mann and Edith Lucille Joy-Mann; m. Michael Dean Matlock, July 15, 1972; 1 child, Leslie Joy Matlock-Starling. BS in Psychology and Elem. Ed., Olivet Nazarene U., 1989. Cert. K-9 tchr. Ill. State Bd. Edn., 1989, in mid. sch. endorsements Ill. State Bd. Edn., 1991. Tchr. 3rd grade Bruning Elem. Sch., Wilmington, Ill., 1989—90; edn. coord. Ideal Computer Systems, Kankakee, Ill., 1990—91; social studies methods tchr. Olivet Nazarene U., Kankakee, 1991; sci. tchr. 7th grade L.J. Mid. Sch., Wilmington, 1991—92, Oster-Oakview Jr. High, New Lenox, Ill., 1992—94, L.J. Stevens Mid. Sch., Wilmington, 1994—2005; tchr. 5th grade Plainfield Sch. Dist. 202, Ill., 2006—08, tchr. 5th grade sci. curriculum com., 2006—08. Sch. improvement team Oster-Oakview Jr. High, New Lenox, Ill., 1992—94; sch. leadership team Wilmington SD# 209-U, 1995—2002; Jr. Beta Club sponsor L.J. Stevens Mid. Sch., 1997—2000, head volleyball coach, 1998—99, sci. club sponsor, 1999—2005; Challenger team trainer Will County Aerospace Team, 2000—; tchr. Jason Expdn., 2004—07; MAD sci. tchr. River View Elem. Sch., 2006—07; mem. Astronomy Resources Connecting Schs., 2005—, mem. sci. curriculum com., 2006—. Night coord. Family Fun Sci., 2007—; chancel choir First United Meth. Ch., Wilmington, 1986—, worship com., 2001—06. Recipient Bright Idea award, Oster-Oakview PTO, 1993, Extra Mile award, L.J. Stevens Mid. Sch., 2005, CAPE award, 2007. Mem.: AAUW, NSTA, Wilmington Comm. Band, Space Exploration Educators Conf., Ill. Sci. Tchrs. Am., Kappa Delta Pi, Mensa (assoc.). Methodist. Home: 817 Mae St Wilmington IL 60481 Office: River View Elem Sch 2097 Bronk Rd Plainfield IL 60586 Personal E-mail: matlock817@msn.com. Business E-Mail: jmatlock@learningcommunity202.org.

MATLOCK, DAVID LOUIS, obstetrician, gynecologist, reconstructive surgeon; b. St. Louis, Mo. BA in Chemistry, Coll. St. Louis Univ., Mo., 1974; MD, St. Louis Univ. Sch. Medicine, Mo., 1978; MBA, U. Calif. Irvine Grad. Sch. Mgmt., 2000. Lic. Bd. Med. Quality Assurance, 1979, cert. Am. Bd. Obstetrics and Gynecology, 1987, re-cert. Am. Bd. Obstetrics and Gynecology, 1997. Intern, internal medicine U. So. Calif. Med. Ctr., LA, 1978—79, King/Drew Med. Ctr., LA, 1980, resident, obstetrics & gynecology, 1980—83; private practice Ross Loos, Torrance, Calif., 1979—80, Calif., 1985—; dept. chmn., obstetrics and gynecology Mission Hosp., Huntington Park, Calif., 1984—85; med. dir. Women's Ctr., LA, 1986—88; dir., laser surgery program Marina Hills Hosp., LA, 1988—89; med. dir. Beverly-Wilshire Surgery Ctr., 1990—90, dir., laser surgery program, 1991; med. dir. Beverly Hills Ambulatory Surgery Ctr., Inc., 1995—, So. Calif. Surgery Ctr., LA, Beverly Hills Sunset Surgery Ctr.; CEO, founder Laser Vaginal Rejuvenation Inst. Med. Associates, Inc. Resident coun. on admissions So. Calif. Med. Ctr., 1978; resident program evaluation, obstetrics & gynecology King/Drew Med. Ctr., 1982; presenter in field. Contbr. articles to profl. jours.; author: (book) Sex By Design; featured on Dr. 90210. Fellow: Am. Acad. Cosmetic Surgery, Am. Coll. Obstetricians and Gynecologists; mem.: Am. Soc. Gynecological Laparoscopists, LA County Med. Assn., Calif. Med. Assn., AMA, Am. Soc. Liposuction Surgery. Avocations: tennis, jogging, publishing, travel, entrepreneurial healthcare. Office: Lasar Vaginal Rejuvenation Inst LA 9201 Sunset Blvd Ste 406 Los Angeles CA 90069 Office Phone: 310-859-9052. Office Fax: 310-859-7792. Business E-Mail: drmatlock@drmatlock.com.*

MATLOCK, JACK FOUST, JR., diplomat; b. Greensboro, NC, Oct. 1, 1929; s. Jack Foust and Nellie (McSwain) M.; m. Rebecca Burrum, Sept. 2, 1949; children: James, Hugh, Nell, David, Joseph. AB summa cum laude, Duke U., 1950; MA, Columbia U., 1952; cert., Russian Inst., 1952; LLD (hon.), Greensboro Coll., 1989, Albright Coll., 1992, Conn. Coll., 1993; LLD (hon.), Latvian Acad. Scis., 2002. Instr. Dartmouth, 1953-56; fgn. service officer Dept. State, 1956-91; assigned Washington, 1956-58, Am. Embassy, Vienna, 1958-60; Am. consul. gen. Munich,

1960-61; assigned Am. Embassy, Moscow, 1961-63, Accra, Ghana, 1963-66, Am. Consulate, Zanzibar, 1967-69, Am. Embassy, Dar es Salaam, Tanzania, 1969-70, Sr. Seminar in Fgn. Policy, Dept. State, 1970-71; country dir. for USSR State Dept., 1971-74; minister-counselor, dep. chief mission Am. Embassy, Moscow, 1974-78; diplomat-in-residence Vanderbilt U., Nashville, 1978-79; dep. dir. Fgn. Service Inst., Washington, 1979-80; chargé d'affaires ad interim Am. Embassy, Moscow, 1981; ambassador to Czechoslovakia, 1981-83; spl. asst. to pres., sr. dir. European and Soviet Affairs Nat. Security Council, 1983-87; U.S. ambassador to the Soviet Union, Moscow, 1987-91; sr. rsch. fellow Columbia U., NYC, 1991-93, Kathryn and Shelby Collum Davis prof. Practice Internat. Diplomacy, 1993-96; George F. Kennan prof. Inst. for Advanced Study, Princeton, NJ, 1996-2001; John L. Weinberg/Goldman Sachs and Co. vis. prof. pub. and internat. affairs Princeton U., 2001—02; Sol Linowitz prof. internat. rels. Hamilton Coll., 2006, 2009; Cyrus Vance prof. internat. rels. Mt. Holyoke Coll., 2007—. Adj. prof. Columbia U., 2007—. Author: Autopsy on an Empire: The American Ambassador's Account of the Collapse of the Soviet Union, 1995, Reagan and Gorbachev: How the Cold War Ended, 2004; compiler, editor: Index to J.V. Stalin's Works, 2d edit., 1971. Mem. Am. Acad. Diplomacy, Coun. on Fgn. Rels., Century Assn. N.Y., Am. Philos. Soc. Home: 32 Wagoner Hill Rd Fayetteville TN 37334 Office Phone: 609-252-1953. Business E-Mail: matlock@ias.edu.

MATLOCK, JOHN HUDSON, retired science administrator, materials engineer; b. San Angelo, Tex., Nov. 23, 1944; s. Lee Hudson Jr. and Harriett (Kidder) M.; m. Kathe Lynne Reep, Sept. 3, 1966; children: Michelle, Joseph. B in Engring. Sci., U. Tex., 1967, MSME, 1969, PhD in Material Sci. and Engring., 1970; MBA, So. Ill. U., Edwardsville, 1976. Registered profl. engr., Mo., Wash., Oreg. Sr. rsch. engr. Monsanto Co., St. Peters, Mo., 1970-72, rsch. specialist, 1972-74, supt. tech. svcs., 1974-79; sr. staff engr. Mostek Corp., Carrollton, Tex., 1979-80, mgr. material tech. group, 1980-83; v.p. tech. SEH Am., Inc., Vancouver, Wash., 1983-90, exec. v.p., 1990-96, Komatsu Silicon Am., Hillsboro, Oreg., 1996, pres., CEO, 1997—2005; global officer Komatsu, Ltd., 1999—2003, sr. adv., 2006—07; dir. Komatsu Electronic Metals, Ltd., 1999—2006; ret., 2007. Adj. asst. prof. physics So. Ill. U., Edwardsville, 1973-76; mem. engring. adv. bd. Wash. State U., Pullman, 1984-96, adj. lectr., 1985; adj. prof. mech. engring., mem. grad. faculty Oreg. State U., Corvallis, 1985-90; mem. vis. com. Engring. Coll., U. Wash., Seattle, 1985-94, mem. indsl. adv. bd. Material Sci. and Engring., 1988-2000; bd. dirs. Wash. Tech. Ctr., 1990-96. Contbr. approximately 40 articles on silicon crystal growing and the effect of silicon properties on electronic device performance to profl. and trade jours. Bd. trustees 1st Ch. of God, Vancouver, 1988-91, tchr. adult ch. sch., 1986-91, 2001-02, spl. assignment missionary to Tanzania, 2006-; sch. bd. Kingsway Christian Sch., Vancouver, 1990-91; bd. dir., Wash. Tech. Ctr., 1990-96; elder Sonrise Ch., Hillsboro, 2004-06. Mem. Electrochem. Soc., Metall. Soc., AIME, Am. Soc. for Materials, Soc., Tau Beta Pi, Pi Tau Sigma, Phi Kappa Phi, Beta Gamma Sigma. Personal E-mail: johnmatlock97124@gmail.com.

MATLOCK, PAMELA DURBIN, special education educator; d. Bennie and Doris Dunaway Durbin; m. William Matlock; 1 child, Billie June Matlock-Farrell. M, Murray State U., KY, 1980. Cert. in tchg. Ky., 1975. Spl. edn. tchr. Paducah Ind. Schs., 1976—2002; spl. edn. lectr. & edn. coord. Murray State U. Coll. Edn., 2002—. Presenter Profl. Devel. Seminars Edn. Author: (support book) Bully Free Lesson Plans for High School. Ofcl. referee US Swimming. Recipient Tchg. Excellence award, Murray State U. Bd. Regents, 2007; named Outstanding Advisor, Ky. Edn. Assn., 2008. Mem.: Coun. Exceptional Children, Phi Delta Kappa (sec. MSU chpt. 2007—). Avocation: travel. Office: Murray State Univ 3240 Alexander Hall Murray KY 42071 Business E-Mail: pam.matlock@coe.murraystate.edu.

MATOAX, LOUISE, mathematics educator curriculum development, consultant; b. Gainesville, Aug. 13, 1961; d. Mary Leigh and George St.Clair Beers; 1 child, Canpaza. BS in Computer Sci., Mid. Tenn. State U., 1984, MS in Math., 1990. Cert. profl. math. educator State Fla. Dept. Edn.; Software Quality Engr. # 324, Am. Soc. for Quality, 1997. Grad. tchg. asst. devel. studies dept. Mid. Tenn. State U., Murfreesboro, 1988—90; adj. prof. math. Santa Fe CC, Gainesville, 1990—91; adj. prof. math. and phys. edn. Pellissippi State Tech. CC, Knoxville, Tenn., 1992—93; hardware dept. Lowe's, Durham, NC, 1993; butcher, produce, grocery, front end, bakery delivery Whole Foods Market, Durham, NC, 1993; sr. product quality assurance test engr. WallData, Inc., Bellingham, Wash., 1994; math. instr. Bellingham (Wash.) Tech. Coll., 1994—95; sr. software quality engr. Component Internat., Inc., Mason, Ohio, 1996—98; prof. math. and physics in English ITESM, Colima, Mexico, 2000; sr. quality assurance engr. Raytheon Missile Sys., Tucson, 2001—02; math. instr. Hazard CC, Jackson, Ky., 2002—03, Miami Dade Coll., Kendall Campus, Fla., 2003—07; math. tchr., curriculum cons. Gibbs HS, South St. Petersburg, Fla., 2007—; math. educator St. Petersberg Coll., Gibbs HS. Rev. panel mem. The Ky. Jour. of Excellence in Coll. Tchg. and Learning, Jackson, Ky., 2002—03; math. curriculum cons. Educo, Inc., Miami, 2005; math. textbook reviewer Thompson, Brooks-Cole, Miami, 2005, McGraw-Hill Higher Edn., Miami, 2005—; math. curriculum cons. Edusun, Inc., Miami, 2006—. Author: (algorithmic automated computer test book) Test Bank, 2004. Mem. ACLU, Miami, 2004—06. Avocations: sewing, rug hooking, woodworking, writing, music. Personal E-mail: louise.matoax@gmail.com.

MATROS, RICHARD K., insurance company executive; b. Queens, NY; m. Adrienne Matros; children: Carly, Chelsea, Alex. BA in Psychology, Alfred U.; MA in Gerontology, U. S.C. Facility adminstr. Extended Care Inc., Catered Living Inc.; regional adminstr., v.p. We. Ops. Beverly Enterprises Inc.; exec. v.p. ops. Care Enterprises, 1988—91, pres., COO, 1988—91, 1991—94, pres., CEO, 1994; pres., COO Regency Health Svcs. Inc., 1994—95, pres., CEO, 1995—97, Bright Now! Dental, 1998—2000; chmn., CEO Sun Healthcare Group, 2001—. Office: Sun Healthcare Group Ste 400 18831 Von Karman Ave Irvine CA 92612*

MATROSOV, SERGEY, senior research scientist; b. Vladikavkaz, Ossetia, U.S.S.R., Oct. 21, 1956; arrived in U.S., 1989; s. Yuri Matrosov and Eugenia Matrosova; m. Natalia Potashnik, Oct. 4, 2001; 1 child, Eugeni. BA in Physics, Leningrad State U., Russia, 1977, MS in Atmospheric Physics, 1979; PhD in Geophysics, Main Geophys. Observatory, Russia, 1985. Rsch. scientist Main Geophys. Observatory, Leningrad, 1979—89, U. Colo., Boulder, 1990—. Sci. team mem. NASA, Dept. Energy, 1996—. Author: Microwave Radiowaves in Meteorology; contbr. articles to profl. jours. Mem.: Am. Geophys. Union, Am. Meteorol. Soc. Achievements include patents in field. Avocation: skiing. Office: Univ Colo 216 UCB Boulder CO 80309 Office Phone: 303-497-6393. Business E-Mail: sergey.matrosov@noaa.gov.

MATSCHULLAT, DALE LEWIS, lawyer; b. Ft. Sill, Okla., May 1, 1945; s. Wayne Emil and Harriet Jane (Bowman) M.; m. Eileen Joanne Davidson, Aug. 26, 1967; children— Robert Charles, Stephen Francis. AB, Stanford U., 1967, JD, 1970. Bar: NY, Wis. Law clk. US Dist. Ct. (ea. dist. NY), Bklyn., 1970-71; assoc. firm Davis, Polk & Wardwell, NYC, 1972-77; sector counsel Allis Chalmers Corp., Milw., 1977, v.p., gen. counsel, Newell Rubbermaid Inc., Rockford, Ill., 1989—2007, corp. sec., 2003—07, sr. v.p., sec., gen. counsel, 2007—. Roman Catholic. Office: Newell Rubbermaid 3 Glenlake Pkwy Atlanta GA 30328*

MATSCHULLAT, ROBERT W., former consumer products company executive; b. Nov. 21, 1947; married. BA, Stanford U., 1969, MBA, 1972. CFO The Seagram Co. Ltd., 1995—99, vice chmn., 1995—2000; head worldwide investment banking Morgan Stanley & Co. Inc., 2000—04; non-exec. chmn. The Clorox Co., Oakland, Calif., 2004—05, interim chmn., CEO, 2006. Bd. dirs. The Clorox Co., 1999—, The Walt Disney Co., 2002—, McKesson Inc.

MATSEN, FREDERICK ALBERT, III, orthopedic educator; b. Austin, Tex., Feb. 5, 1944; s. Frederick Albert II and Cecilia (Kirkegaard) M.; m. Anne Lovell, Dec. 24, 1966; children: Susanna Lovell, Frederick A. IV, Laura Jane Megan. BA, U. Tex., Austin, 1964; MD, Baylor U., 1968. Intern Johns Hopkins U., Balt., 1971; resident in orthopaedics U. Wash., Seattle, 1971-74, acting instr. orthopaedics, 1974, asst. prof. orthopaedics, 1975-79, assoc. prof. orthopaedics, 1979-82, prof., 1982-85, 86—, adjunct prof. Ctr. Bioengring., 1985—, dir. residency program orthopaedics, 1978-81, vice chmn. dept. orthopaedics, 1982-85, acting chmn. dept. orthopaedics, 1983-84, prof., chmn. dept. orthopaedics, 1981—. Mem. Orthopaedic Residency Rev. Com., Chgo., 1981-86. Author: Compartmental Syndromes, 1980; editor: The Shoulder, 1990; contbr. articles to profl. jours., chpts. to textbooks; assoc. editor Clin. Orthopaedics, Jour. Orthopaedic Rsch., 1981—. Lt. comdr. USPHS, 1969-71. Recipient Traveling fellowship Am. Orthopaedic Assn., 1983, Nicholas Andry award Assn. Bone and Joint Surgery, 1979, Henry Meyerding Essay award Am. Fracture Assn., 1974. Mem. Am. Shoulder and Elbow Surgeons (founding, pres. 1991—), Am. Acad. Orthopaedic Surgeons (bd. dirs. 1984-85), Orthopaedic Rsch. Soc., Western Orthopaedic Assn., Phi Beta Kappa. Office: U Wash Dept Orthopaedics RK 10 1959 NE Pacific St Seattle WA 98195-0001 Office Phone: 206-543-3690. Business E-Mail: matsen@u.washington.edu.

MATSUDA, FUJIO, retired academic administrator; b. Honolulu, Oct. 18, 1924; s. Yoshio and Shimo (Iwasaki) M.; m. Amy M. Saiki, June 11, 1949; children: Bailey Koki, Thomas Junji, Sherry Noriko, Joan Yuuko, Ann Mitsuyo, Richard Hideo. BSCE, Rose Poly. Inst., 1949; DSc, MIT, 1952; DEng (hon.), Rose Hulman Inst. Tech., 1975. Rsch. engr. MIT, 1952—54; rsch. asst. prof. engring. U. Ill., Urbana, 1954—55; asst. prof. to prof. engring. U. Hawaii, Honolulu, 1955—62, chmn. dept. civil engring., 1959—62, v.p. bus. affairs, 1973-74, pres., 1974-84, exec. dir. Rsch. Corp., 1984-94; pres. Japan-Am. Inst. Mgmt. Sci., Honolulu, 1994-96. Bd. dirs. First Hawaiian Bank, Jaims Uresenke Found. Hawaii; past dir., trustee Aloha Airlines, HEI & Hawaiian Elec. Co., Buyco & Brewer Ltd., UAL & United Airlines, First Hawaiian, Inc., Bankwest, PICHTR, Pacific Buddhist Acad., Hawaiian Cmty. Found., Honolulu Symphony, Kuakini Hosp., Rehab Hosp. Pacific. Sgt. US Army, 1943—45. Recipient Honor Alumnus award Rose Poly. Inst., 1971, Disting. Svc. award Airport Ops. Coun. Internat., 1973; Disting. Alumnus U. Hawaii, 1974, 91, Hawaii Engr. of Yr., 1972, Order of Sacred Treas. 2nd Class Govt. Japan, 1984. Mem. NAE, NSPE, ASCE (Parcel-Sverdrup Engring. Mgmt. award 1986), Social Sci. Assn., Japan-Am. Soc. Hawaii (trustee 1976-84, adv. coun. 1984—), UH Coll. Engring (Living Treas. Hawaii 2003, Outstanding Svc. award 2007), Sigma Xi, Tau Beta Pi. Personal E-mail: fmatsuda@hawaii.rr.com.

MATSUDA, MASAFUMI, research scientist, educator; b. Yanai-shi, Japan, Jan. 15, 1956; s. Akimasa and Hiroko Matsuda; m. Yoshiko Kawamura, June 3, 1984; 1 child, Momoyo. MD, U. Tokyo, 1982; PhD, Yamaguchi U., Japan, 1989. Cert. Nat. Bd. Japan, 1982, Ecfmg, 1991, Bd. Cert. in Internal Medicine Japanese Soc. of Internal Medicine, Japan, 1991, Bd. Cert. in Diabetology Japan Diabetes Soc., Japan, 1993, Bd. Cert. in Endocrinology and Metabolism Japan Endocrine Soc., 1994. Resident U. Tokyo Hosp., 1982—83, Yamaguchi U. Hosp., Ube-shi, Japan, 1983, staff physician, 1984—87, 1989—90; resident Shuto Gen. Hosp., Yanai-shi, Japan, 1983—84; asst. Internal Medicine, Yamaguchi U., Ube-shi, Japan, 1987—88; staff physician Saiki Hosp., Nagato-shi, Japan, 1988—89; vis. scientist Diabetes Divsn., U. Tex. Health Sci. Ctr. at San Antonio, 1990—93, clin. instr., 1993—96, asst. prof., 1996—98; lectr. Diabetes Divsn., Internal Medicine, Kawasaki Med. Sch., Kurashiki-shi, Japan, 1999—2000, Endocrine and Diabetes Divsn., Internal Medicine, Kawasaki Med. Sch., Kurashiki-shi, Japan, 2000—05; dir. diabetes and endocrine dept. Kameda Med. Ctr., Kamogawa-shi, Japan, 2006—. Diabetes rsch. dir. Clin. Rsch. Ctr., Tex. Diabetes Inst., San Antonio, 1997—98. Grantee Rsch. Fellowship, Juvenile Diabetes Found. Internat., 1991—93, Grant-in-Aid for Sci. Rsch., Japan Soc. for the Promotion of Sci., Ministry of Edn., Culture, Sports, Sci., and Tech., Japan, 2001—02. Fellow: Japan Soc. Internal Medicine. Office: Kameda Med Ctr Diabetes and Endocrine Dept 929 Higashi-cho Kamogawa-shi Chiba 296-8602 Japan Office Fax: 81-4-7099-1198. Personal E-mail: matsudam-ind@umin.ac.jp. Business E-Mail: mmatsuda@kameda.jp.

MATSUDA, MASATAKE, former rail transportation executive; b. Hokkaido, Japan, 1936; Student, Hokkaido U. Chmn. E. Japan Rlwy. Co., Tokyo; joined Japan Nat. Rlwy., 1961, formerly Planning Mgr. of Office of Planning Mgmt., Planning Mgr. Hokkaido Hdqs., Dir.-Gen. Reconstruction Promotion Hdqs.; Mgmt. Dir. Corpn. Planning Hdqs. E Japan Rlwy Co. (Japan Rlwy. East-co. created after privatization of JNR 1987), Gen.-Mgr., V.P, Pres., 1993; former Chmn. Japan Rlwy. East. Dir. Mizuho Holdings Inc.; Pres. World Exec. Coun., Internat. Union of Railways (UIC); V.P. UIC, 2003—04; mem. Prime Min. Adv. Panel to oversee Privatization of Semi Governmental Expressway Corporations, 2003, resigned in protest of privatization scheme.

MATSUDA, TAKAYOSHI, surgeon, educator, biomedical researcher; b. Tonan, Japan, 1937; came to U.S., 1965; MD, Keio Gijuku U., Tokyo, 1963. Diplomate Am. Bd. Surgery. Rotating intern Cook County Hosp., Chgo., 1965-66, resident in surgery, 1966-71, dir. burn ctr., 1975-93; asst. prof. surgery Kyorin U., Tokyo, 1971-75; asst. prof. U. Ill., Chgo., 1977—; pres. TM & Assocs., Oak Park, Ill., 1994—. Cons. alternative medicine, cons. leadership devel., fin. freedom; investigator renewable energy; spkr. in field. Editl. bd. Jour. Burn Care Rehab., 1987-93; contbr. articles to profl. publ., chpt. to books. Recipient Jerry and Thelma Stergios award for Excellence in Basic Rsch., U. Ill. at Chgo., 1979, The Superior Pub. Serv. award, County of Cook, State of Ill., 1993. Fellow ACS; mem. Internat. Soc. Surgery, Internat. Soc. Burn Injuries, Am. Burn Assn., Am. Assn. Surgery Trauma, Soc. Critical Care Medicine, Chgo. Surg. Soc. Achievements include research in and devel. of a novel approach for the production of electricity without pollution; established the first human skin bank in the State of Illinois at the Burn Unit of Cook County Hospital, 1977. Office: TM & Assocs Alternative Medicine Cons 103 Bishop Quarter Ln Oak Park IL 60302-2672 Office Phone: 708-386-2522. Personal E-mail: takimatsuda@hotmail.com.

MATSUDA, WAKOTO, neurosurgeon, researcher; b. Onomichi, Hiroshima, Japan, Apr. 6, 1968; s. Tadao and Fujiko (Makihata) Matsuda; m. Kiyoe Nakazawa, Mar. 22, 1991; children: Shin, Nako, Tei. MD, U. Tsukuba, Japan, 1996; PhD, Kyoto U., Japan, 2009. Diplomate in neurosurgery Japan Neurosurg. Soc., 2002. Resident dept. neurosurgery U. Tsukuba Hosp., 1996—2002; clin. fellow dept. neurosurgery Tsukuba Med. Ctr. Hosp., 2002—03; postgrad. dept. morphological brain sci. Grad. Sch. Medicine, Kyoto U., 2003—06; asst. prof. divsn. anatomy and cell biology, dept. anatomy Shiga U. Med. Sci., 2006—. Recipient Best Resident award, Inst. Clin. Medicine, U. Tsukuba, Dept. Neurosurg., 2002; scholar, Iwadare Scholarship Found., 2003. Mem.: Soc. Neuroscis., Japanese Assn. Anatomists, Japan Neuroscience Soc., Japanese Congress Neurological Surgeons, Japan Neurosurg. Soc. Office: Shiga Univ Med Sci Divsn Anatomy Cell Biology Dept Anatomy Tsukinowa-cho Seta Otsu Shiga 520-2192 Japan Office Fax: 81-77-548-2139. Personal E-mail: wako@mua.biglobe.ne.jp. Business E-Mail: matsuda2@belle.shiga-med.ac.jp.

MATSUHISA, NOBUYUKI, chef, restaurant owner; b. Saitama, Japan; Chef, owner Matsuhisa, Beverly Hills, 1987—, Aspen, Colo., 1997—, Nobu, NYC, 1994—, London, 1997—, Tokyo, 1998—, Malibu, Calif., 1999—, Las Vegas, 1999—, Nobu Next Door, NYC, 1998—, Ubon, LA, 1999—. Author: Nobu: The Cookbook, Nobu Now, 2005. Recipient 2008 Am.'s Top Restaurant award for Nobu, Zagat Survey; named one of America's Best New Chefs, Food & Wine mag., 1989, So. Calif.'s Rising Stars, LA Times Mag., 1998. Office: Nobu 105 Hudson St New York NY 10013-2331

MATSUI, CONNIE L., pharmaceutical executive; b. Piedmont, Calif. m. William Beckman; 2 children. BA, Stanford U., MBA, 1977. Various positions Wells Fargo Bank, 1977—91; sr. dir., planning and resource devel. IDEC Pharm., 1992—94, v.p., planning and resource devel., 1994—2000, sr. v.p., planning and resource devel., 2000—03; exec. v.p. corp. strategy and communication Biogen Idec Inc., 2003—. Bd. dirs. Halozyme Therapeutics, Inc., 2006—. Nat. pres. Girl Scouts Am., 1999—2002. Office: Biogen Inc 14 Cambridge Ctr Cambridge MA 02142

MATSUI, DORIS OKADA, United States Representative from California; b. Dinuba, Calif., Sept. 25, 1944; m. Robert Takeo Matsui, Sept. 17, 1966 (dec. Jan. 1, 2005); 1 child, Brian. BA in Psychology, U. Calif., Berkeley, 1966. Sr. adv. to Pres. White House, Washington, 1993—99; govt. rels. adv. Collier, Shannon & Scott PLLC, Washington, 1999—2005; mem. US Congress from 5th Calif. dist., 2005—; mem. energy and commerce com., rules com. Mem. Clinton-Gore Transition Team, 1992—93; past pres., bd. chair KVIE Pub. TV, Sacramento. Bd. trustees Woodrow Wilson Ctr., Meridian Internat. Ctr.; past bd. trustees Crocker Art Mus., Arena Stage, Sacramento Children's Home; bd. regents Smithsonian Inst. Recipient Action for Breast Cancer Awareness award, Advocates award, Nat. Assn. Mental Health, Mentor award, U. So. Calif. Sacramento Sch. Pub. Adminstrn., Newmyer award, Sidwell Friends Sch., Rosalie Stern award, U. Calif. Alumni Assn. Mem.: Junior League Sacramento, Women's Club Sacramento. Democrat. Methodist. Office: US House Reps 222 Cannon House Office Bldg Washington DC 20515-0505 also: Robert T Matsui Fed Courthouse 501 I St Ste 12 600 Sacramento CA 95814*

MATSUI, HIDEKI, professional baseball player; b. Kanazawa, Japan, June 12, 1974; married, Mar. 26, 2008. Outfielder Yomiuri Giants, Tokyo, 1992—2002, NY Yankees, 2003—. Donor Japanese Red Cross Soc. for Tsunami Relief, 2004; amb. NYC Tourism. Recipient Golden Spirit award, 1999, 2000, Matsutaro Shoriki award, 2000; named MVP, Japanese Ctrl. League, 1996, 2000, 2002; named to Am. League All-Star Team, Maj. League Baseball, 2003; finalist Am. League Rookie of Yr. award, 2003. Achievements include member of Japanese League championship winning Yomiuri Giants, 1994, 2000, 2002; nine-time Japanese League All-Star. Office: NY Yankees Yankee Stadium One E 161st St Bronx NY 10451

MATSUMOTO, ALAN H., radiologist, educator; m. Julie A. Matsumoto; children: Mallory, Monica. MD, Wake Forest Bowman Gray Sch. Medicine, Winston-Salem, NC, 1980. Diplomate Am. Bd. Internal Medicine, Va., 1983, Am. Bd. Radiology, 1987, in added qualification 1995, cert. in vascular & interventional Va., 2005. Dir., interventional radiology H.C.A. Blake Hosp., Bradenton, Fla., 1989—91; asst. prof. Georgetown U. Hosp., Washington, 1988—89, UVA Health Scis. Ctr., Charlottesville, 1991—93, dir., fellowship program, 1993—98, assoc. prof., 1993—98, prof., radiology, 1998—2006, exec. vice chair, 2001—08, prof., 2001—08, UVA Health Sys., 2008—, interim chair, 2008—. Editor: (book) Endovascular Today, Radiologic Clinics of North America; contbr. articles to profl. jours. Recipient Disting. Faculty award, SCVIR, 2001; named Best Dr. in America, 2005—07, Best Dr. in Va.; Rsch. grant, Gen. Electric Inc., 2002—04, Commonwealth Health Rsch. Bd., 2003—04, NIH NHLBI, 2004—. Mem.: AMA, CIRSE, Med. Soc. Va., Am. Heart Assn., Southeastern Angiographic Soc., Am. Coll. Radiology, Radiol. Soc. N.Am., Soc. Interventional Radiology (Disting. Faculty award 2002). Office: UVA Dept Radiology 1215 Lee St Rm 1076 Charlottesville VA 22908 Office Phone: 434-982-0211.

MATSUMOTO, CAROLEE SETSUKO, researcher, education developer and administrator; b. Denver, Feb. 13, 1943; d. Harry Katsumi and Pearl Shizuho (Nakamura) M.; m. David Luther Gilbertson, Oct. 20, 1990. BA, Ea. Mich. U., 1965; MEd, Wayne State U., 1968; EdD, Harvard Univ., 1991. Cert. biology, sci. tchr., adminstr., Mass. Sci. tchr. Greenburgh Sch. Dist. #8, Hartsdale, NY, 1965-67; sci. dept., head tchr. Nagoya Internat. Sch., Japan, 1968-70; tchr. sci. grades 7-8 Brookline HS, Mass., 1970—73, tchr. biology, 1976—79, sci. supr., 1979-81; sci. dept. head Graded Am. Sch., Sao Paulo, Brazil, 1973-76; asst. supt. curriculum, instrn. Concord and Concord/Carlisle Pub. Schs., Mass., 1981-87; teaching fellow Harvard U., Cambridge, Mass., 1984-85; curriculum dir., prin. investigator Edn. Devel. Ctr., Newton, Mass., 1987-93, sr. project dir., sr. scientist, 1993—. Bd. dir. New Eng. & Islands Reg. Lab., Andover, Mass., 1985-96, Lloyd Environ. Ctr., S. Dartmouth, Mass., 1990-97; mem. adv. coun. Collaboration Equity, Am. Assn. for Advancement Sci., Washington, 1994-96; mem. Mass Dept. Edn. Cultural Proficiency Steering Com., 2006-; vis. scholar Stanford U., Palo Alto, Calif., 1993; rep. Carpe Vitam Found., Sweden; co-dir. U. Mass., Dartmouth, K-12 Rsch. Devel. Dissemination Ctr. Bd. dir. Tchrs. 21, Wellesley, Mass., 1993-2006; bd. govs. New Bedford Ocean Explorium, adv. bd. mem., Women Fund South Coast, Mass. Mem.: ASCD, Nat. Staff Devel. Coun., Am. Ednl. Rsch. Assn., Nat. Sci. Tchrs. Assn. Avocations: travel, photography. Home: 17 Arnold Pl New Bedford MA 02740-3634

MATSUMOTO, KIYO ANN, federal judge; b. Raleigh, NC, 1955; BA, U. Calif., Berkeley, 1976; JD, Georgetown U. Law Sch., 1981. Litig. assoc. MacDonald, Hoague and Bayless, Seattle, 1981—83; asst. US atty. (ea. dist.) NY US Dept. Justice, 1983—2004, dep. chief, first dep. chief, chief civil divsn., chief financial litig. unit, civil health care fraud coord., sr. trial counsel; magistrate judge US Dist. Ct. (ea. dist.) NY, 2004—08, judge, 2008—. Instr. civil litigation, financial litigation and trial advocacy Atty. General's Advocacy Inst., Nat. Advocacy Ctr., Office Legal Education US Dept. Justice; adj. prof. legal rsch. and writing Brooklyn Law Sch., 1998—2004; adj. prof. govt. civil litigation clinic and seminar NYU Law Sch. Mem.: Nat. Asian Pacific American Bar Assn., Asian American Bar Assn. NY, Eastern Dist. New York's Com. Civil Litigation, Assn. Bar of the City NY, Fed. Bar Coun. Office: US Dist Ct 225 Cadman Plaza E Brooklyn NY 11201 Business E-Mail: kiyo_matsumoto@nyed.uscourts.gov.

MATSUMOTO, SHINICHI, surgeon, researcher; b. Sakai, Osaka, Japan, Mar. 17, 1963; s. Takeshi and Hiroko (Fukai) M.; m. Eriko Amano, Oct. 10, 1991; children: Kyohei, Hana. Bachelor's degree, Kobe U., Japan, 1988, PhD, 1996. Med. lic., Japan. Physician Kobe U. Hosp., 1988-89, Osaka Red Cross Hosp., 1989-90, Kanzaki (Japan) Hosp., 1991, Kasai (Japan) Citizen Hosp., 1992; with dept. surgery U. Minn. Med. Sch., Mpls., 1997-99, U. Wash. Med. Ctr., Seattle, 1999—; sr. rsch. scientist Puget Sound Blood Ctr., 1999—, 2000—; rsch. assoc. U. Wash. Med. Ctr., Seattle, 2000—, clin. cons., 2001—, rsch. assoc., clin. assoc., 2001—. Vis. scientist U. Wash. Med. Ctr.; rsch. assoc. Puget Sound Blood Ctr.; cons. Islet Isolaiton Facility. Contbr. articles to med. jours. Mem. Internat. Soc. Surgery, Internat. Pancreas and Istet Transplant Soc., Japanese Surg. Soc., Japanese Gastroenterol. Surgery, Am. Soc. Transplantation. Avocations: golf, skiing. Office: Baylor All Saints Medical Ctr 1400 8th Ave Fort Worth TX 76104 Personal E-mail: shinichim@mac.com. E-mail: shinichim@psbc.org, shinichimatsumo@hotmail.com.

MATSUMURA, VERA YOSHI, pianist; b. Oakland, Calif. d. Naojiro and Aguri Tanaka; m. Jiro Matsumura, Aug. 8, 1942; 1 son, Kenneth N. BA in Piano Pedagogy, Coll. Holy Names, Oakland, 1938; pvt. studies with F. Moss, M. Shapiro, L. Kreutzer, P. Jarrett. Mem. staff, pianist Radio Sta. KROW, Oakland, 1938-39. Numerous concert performances in Far East (Japan, Thailand), 1940—; numerous tchg. appointments, 1940—; dir. Internat. Music Coun., Berkeley, Calif., 1969—. Named to Hall of Fame, Piano Guild, 1968. Mem. Nat. Music Tchrs. Nat. Assn., Music Tchrs. Assn. Calif., Internat. Platform Assn., Alpha Phi Mu. Methodist. Home: 2 Claremont Cres Berkeley CA 94705-2324

MATSUOKA, YOKY, medical educator; d. Mizuko and Takashi Matsuoka; m. Simon Baker; 3 children. BS in Elec. Engring. and Computer Sci., U. Calif., Berkeley, 1993; MS in Elec. Engring. and Computer Sci., MIT, Artificial Intelligence Lab, 1995, PhD in Elec. Engring. and Computer Sci. in the field of Artificial Intelligence and Computational Neuroscience, 1998. Sr. product engr. Barrett Tech., Inc., Cambridge, Md., 1995—97; postdoctoral fellow in mech. engring. Harvard U., Cambridge, 1998—2000; asst. prof., Robotics Inst., Dept. Mechanical Engring., Ctr. for the Neural Basis of Cognition & biomedical engring. (by courtesy) Carnegie Mellon U., Pitts., 2001—06, dir., neurobotics lab., 2001—06, Anna Loomis McCandless Faculty Chair, 2004; clin. asst. prof., dept. phys. medicine and rehabilitation U. Pitts., Pa., 2002; assoc. prof., dept. computer sci. and engring. U. Wash., Seattle, 2006—. Cons. Barrett Tech., Inc., Bodymedia, Psychology Software Tools, Inc.; mem. scientific adv. bd. Z-KAT; temporary mem. NIH-Musculoskeletal Rehabilitation Scis.; co-private investigator and investigator for several rsch. studies. Contbr. several articles to profl. jours. Recipient NSF Career award, 2003, Presdl. Early Career award for Scientists and Engineers (PERCASE), NSF, 2004, IEEE Early Career award in Robotics and Automation, 2005; named a MacArthur Fellow, John D. and Catherine T. MacArthur Found., 2007. Mem.: Soc. Neural Conrol Movement, Soc. Neuroscience, IEEE, Sigma Xi. Achievements include being the leader in the emerging field of neurorobotics; hoping to understand, assist, rehabilitate, and enhance the human neuromuscular systems of both healthy and motor-impaired people. Office: CSE650 Computer Science and Engineering Box 352350 University of Washington Seattle WA 98195 Office Fax: 206-543-2969. Business E-Mail: yoky@cs.washington.edu.

MATSUSHIRO, NOBUHITO, engineering executive, researcher; b. Ashiya, Hyogo, Japan, Feb. 27, 1957; s. Kotaro and Emi Matsushiro; life ptnr. Junko Matsushiro, Oct. 8, 1965. BE, U. Electro-Comm., Tokyo, 1980, ME, 1982, PhD in Info. Engring., 1996; PhD in Color Sci., Chiba U., Japan, 2006; part-time PhD student, Chiba U. Sch. Medicine, Japan, 2007—. Mgr. Oki Data Corp., Takasaki, Gunma, Japan, 1995—99, gen. mgr. position rschr., 2000—04, exec. sr. rschr., 2004—. Guest scientist Rochester Inst. Tech., NY, 2005—. Co-author: Encyclopedia of Imaging Science and Technology vol. 1, 2002, Color Desktop Printer Technology, 2006; contbr. articles to prof. jours. Mem.: Soc. Imaging Sci. and Tech. Achievements include patents in field. Office: Oki Data Cor 3-1 Futaba-cho Gunma Takasaki 370-8585 Japan Home: 3-24-4 Mirokuji Fujisawa-shi Kanagawa 251-0016 Japan Office Fax: 81-27-328-6168. Business E-Mail: no-matusiro@oki.com.

MATSUURA, KENNETH RAY, counseling administrator; b. Urbana, Ill., July 17, 1954; s. George Shigeo and Sally Sueko (Kawasaki) M.; m. Peggy Ai Iwata, May 27, 1995; 1 child, Claire Miya Sara. BA, U. Calif., Santa Barbara, 1976; MA, UCLA, 1978, PhD, 1996. Career counselor Calif. State U. Dominguez Hills, Carson, 1984-85; grad. recruitment coord. U. Calif., Irvine, 1985-90; counselor/articulation officer Cerritos Coll., Norwalk, Calif., 1990—. Mem. accreditation teams Western Assn. Schs. and Colls., L.A., 1994, Alameda, 1999, mem. accreditation task force Project Renewal; chair South Coast Higher Edn. Coun.; co-chair region 8 articulation officers and transfer ctre. dirs.; program reviewer Am. Coll. Pers. Assn. Ann. conf., Washington, 1988; presenter to confs. UCLA grad. advancement program fellow, 1977—78. Avocations: singing, music. Home: 101 Santa Ynez Dr Arcadia CA 91007 Office Phone: 562-860-2451 2141. Business E-Mail: matsuura@cerritos.edu.

MATSUZAKA, DAISUKE, professional baseball player; b. Tokyo, Sept. 13, 1980; m. Tomoyo Shibata; 1 child, Niko. Pitcher Seibu Lions, Japan, 1999—2006, Boston Red Sox, 2007—. Mem. Japanese nat. team Athens Olympic Games, Greece, 2004, World Baseball Classic, 2006, 09. Recipient Sawamura award, 2001, Bronze medal, baseball, Athens Olympic Games, 2004; named Pacific League Rookie of Yr., Nippon Profl. Baseball League, 1999, All-Star Game MVP, 2004, MVP, World Baseball Classic, 2006, 2009; named to All-Star Game, Nippon Profl. Baseball League, 1999, 2000, 2001, 2004, 2005, 2006. Achievements include member of World Baseball Classic winning Japanese national team, 2006; breaking the Red Sox rookie record for the most strikeouts in a season with 156, 2007; member of World Series championship winning Boston Red Sox, 2007. Office: Boston Red Sox 4 Yawkey Way Boston MA 02215-3496 Fax: 617-375-0944.*

MATTA, CHÉRIF FARID, chemistry professor; b. Alexandria, Egypt, Sept. 8, 1963; arrived in Can., 1995, naturalized; s. Farid Alphonse Matta and Nabila Nassif Abdel Nour. BSc in Pharm. Sci., Alexandria U., 1987; PhD in Theoretical, Computational Chemistry, McMaster U., Hamilton, Ont., Can., 2002. Registered pharmacist 1987, cert. in health and hosp. adminstrn. Sadat Acad., Nat. Inst. Higher Mgmt., Alexandria, 1994. Pharmacist Matta Pharmacy, Alexandria, 1987—91; asst. to chief pharmacist Naval Forces HQ, Egypt, 1988—90; med. supplies specialist World Health Orgn., 1991—94; post-doctoral fellow U. Toronto, 2002—04; I.W. Killam post-doctoral fellow Dalhousie U., Halifax, 2004—06; asst. prof. Mt. St. Vincent U., Halifax, 2006—. Adj. prof. Dalhousie U., Halifax, 2006—, McMaster U., Hamilton, Ont., 2004—05; invited asst. and assoc. prof. U. Henri Poincare, Nancy, France, 2007, Nat. Ctr. Scientific Rsch., 2007. Author: The Quantum Theory of Atoms in Molecules: From Solid State to DNA and Drug Design, 2007; mem. editl. bd.: Internat. Jour. Applied Chemistry, 2005—, reviewer for profl. jours.:; contbr. scientific papers, chapters to books. Mem. academic rev. bd. Internat. Jour. Computational Sci., 2007—; mem. adv. bd. Scientific Jours. Internat., 2007—; mem. bd. gov. McMaster U., 2000—01; mem. bd. trustees Dalhousie Legal Aids, 2007—. 1st lt. Naval Med. Corps., 1988—90. Recipient John C. Polanyi Prize, Can., 2004, Chemistry Tchg. award, U. Toronto, 2003—04; fellow, World Biol. Forum, 2003—05. Mem.: Scientific Rsch. Soc., European Soc. Computational Methods in Sci. and Engring., Am. Chem. Soc., Can. Chem. Soc., Ont. Pub. Health Assn., Chem. Inst. Can., Sigma Xi. Avocations: astronomy, philosophy, painting, politics, exercise. Office: Mt St Vincent U Dept Chemistry and Physics Halifax NS B3M 2J6 Canada Home Fax: 902-457-6134. Personal E-mail: quantumjazz@hotmail.com.

MATTA, FABIO, structural engineer, educator; s. Giovanni Matta and Nadia Campesato. Laurea in Civil Engring., U. Padova, Italy, 2003; PhD in Civil Engring., Mo. U. Sci. and Tech., Rolla, 2007. Cert. profl. engr., Italy, 2004. Grad. rsch. asst. Mo. U. Sci. and Tech., Ctr. Infrastructure Engring. Studies, 2004—07; rsch. asst. prof. dept. civil, archtl., and environ. engring. U. Miami, Coral Gables, Fla., 2007—. Assoc. dir. NSF Industry/U. Coop. Rsch. Ctr. Repair Bldgs. and Bridges with Composites, Coral Gables, 2007—. Contbr. articles to profl. jour. (ASCE-CERF Charles J. Pankow award, 2nd pl., 2006). Recipient Author Travel award, Am. Composites Mfrs. Assn., 2007; finalist NOVA award, Constrn. Innovation Forum, 2006. Mem.: ASME, ASCE (assoc.), Soc. Exptl. Mechanics, Internat. Inst. FRP in Constrn., Engrs. Without Borders, Am. Concrete Inst., ACI Com. 440 Fiber Reinforced Polymer Reinforcement (assoc.). Office: Univ Miami 1251 Memorial Dr MEB-317 Coral Gables FL 33146-0630 Business E-Mail: fmatta@miami.edu.

MATTA, THAD MICHAEL, men's college basketball coach; b. Hoopeston, Ill., July 11, 1967; s. Jim Matta; m. Barbara Matta; children: Ali, Emily. Student, So. Ill. U.; BS, Butler U., 1990. Grad. asst. coach Ind. State U., 1990—91; academic coord., adminstrv. asst. Butler U., Indpls., 1991—94, asst. coach, 1997—2000, head coach, 2000—01; asst. coach Miami U., Ohio, 1994—95, 1996—97, Western Carolina U., 1995—96; head coach Xavier U., Cin., 2001—04, Ohio State U., Columbus, 2004—. Named Nat. Rookie Coach of Yr., CBS SportsLine.com and Coll. Insider.com, 2001, Coach of Yr., Midwestern Collegiate Conf., 2001, Atlantic 10 Conf., 2002, Columbus Dispatch, 2004, Big Ten Conf. and US Basketball Writers Assn. Dist. V, 2006. Office: Ohio State U Jerome Schottenstein Ctr 555 Borror Dr Columbus OH 43210 Office Phone: 614-292-0505. E-mail: matta.5@osu.edu.

MATTANO, REBECCA L., environmentalist, educator; b. Milw., July 16, 1977; d. Joe M. and Nancy J. Mattano; m. Brian P. Thomas, Aug. 5, 2006; children: Sierra Rose Thomas, Madeline Sage Thomas. MS in Natural Resources, UW Stevens Point, 2005. Environ. sci. instr. Carroll U., Waukesha, Wis., 2005—; author pres. Little Environmentalists, Hartland, Wis., 2008—. Water action vol. Waukesha Co. Govt., 2008—. Author: (books) Nature Discovery Go Green With Me. Vol. Retzer Nature Ctr., Waukesha, 2006—. Grant, Environ. Protection Agy. GEM WEEB, 2003—04. Mem.: Hartland C. of C. Democrat. Personal E-mail: rmattano@cc.edu.

MATTAR, MARY ANNE Y., biology professor; b. NB, NJ, Aug. 22, 1978; d. Hafez and Laila Youssef; m. Raafat Mattar, Aug. 31, 2002; children: Daniel, Christopher. MS in Biomed. Engring., Rutgers & UMDNJ, NB, 2003. Adj. prof. Coastline CC, Westminister, Calif., 2006—. Office: Coastline CC 14120 All Am Way Westminster CA 92683 Business E-Mail: mmattar@coastline.edu.

MATTAUCH, ROBERT JOSEPH, retired electrical engineering educator, retired dean; b. Rochester, Pa., May 30, 1940; s. Henry Paul and Anna Marie (Mlinarcik) M.; m. Frances Sabo, Dec. 29, 1962; children: Lori Ann, Thomas J. BS, Carnegie Inst. Tech., Pitts., 1962; MEE, N.C. State U., Raleigh, 1963, PhD, 1967. Asst. prof. elec. engring. U. Va., Charlottesville, 1966-70, assoc. prof. elec. engring., 1970-76, prof. elec. engring., 1976-83, Wilson prof. elec. engring., 1983-86, Standard Oil Co. prof. sci. and tech., 1986-89, chmn. dept. elect. engring., 1987-95, BP Am. prof. sci. and tech., 1989-95; Commonwealth prof., founding chair dept. elec. engring. Va. Commonwealth U., Richmond, 1995-99, dean engring., Commonwealth prof., 1999—2006, dean emeritus, Commonwealth prof., 2006—. Cons. The Rochester Corp., Culpepper, Va., 1983—88, Milltech Corp., Deerfield, Mass., 1985. Patentee: infrared detector; solid state switching capacitor; thin wire pointing method, whiskerless Schottky diode, controlled in-situ etch back growth technique. Bd. dirs. U. Va. Patent Found., 1989-95, Greater Richmond Tech. Coun., 2001—, Va. Bioscis. Devel. Ctr., 2000—06, Richmond Symphony Orch., 2003-. Recipient Excellence in Instruction of Engring. Students award Western Electric, 1980, Greater Richmond Tech. Coun. Leadership award, 2006; named one of Top Ten Talents of 1990 Wash. Tech. Fellow IEEE (Centennial medal 1984); mem. Eta Kappa Nu (recipient Oustanding Prof. in Elec. Engring. 1975), Sigma Xi, Tau Beta Pi, Sigma Pi Sigma, Phi Kappa Phi. Office: Va Commonwealth U PO Box 843072 Richmond VA 23284-3072 Home Phone: 804-741-0142; Office Phone: 804-334-8245. Business E-Mail: rjmattau@vcu.edu.

MATTERN, DOUGLAS JAMES, think-tank executive; b. Creede, Colo., May 19, 1933; s. John A. and Ethel (Franklin) Mattern; m. Noemi E. Del Cioppo, May 4, 1963. Student, San Jose State U., 1956-58. Reliability engr. Intersil, Sunnyvale, Calif., 1973-80; sr. engr. Data Gen. Corp., Sunnyvale, 1981-87; staff engr. Apple Computer, Cupertino, Calif., 1987-97; sr. engr. Trimble Navigation, Sunnyvale, 1998-2000. Sec. Gen. World Citizens Assembly, San Francisco, 1975—86; dir. World Citizens Diplomats, Palo Alto, Calif., 1988—90; pres. Assn. World Citizens, San Francisco, 1989—; CEO World Citizens Found., San Francisco, 1979—; chmn. World Citizens Assembly, San Francisco, 1995, Taipei, Taiwan, 2001, Internat. Peace Conf., San Francisco, 2005. Author: Resolution to End the Arms Race, 1982, Looking for Square Two-Moving from War and Violence to Global Community, 2006, Looking for Square Twin a Path to the Future, 2008; contbg. author: Building a More Democratic United Nations, 1991; editor: World Citizen Newsmag., 1973—; contbr. Bd. dirs. War/Peace Found. With USN, 1951—55. Recipient Albert Einstein Peace award, Internat. World Educators for World Peace, 2001, Lifetime Achievement award for Love and Peace, Fowpal, 2005. Home: 2671 South Ct Palo Alto CA 94306-2462 Office: 55 New Montgomery St Ste 224 San Francisco CA 94105-3421 Office Phone: 415-541-9610. Business E-Mail: info@worldcitizens.org. E-mail: worldcit@best.com.

MATTERS, CRAIG, editor; m. Sara Matters; 2 children. Grad., Vassar Coll. Sr. editor Intercorp Associated Media Corp, Stamford, Conn., 1985—88; mng. editor Manhattan Lawyer mag., 1988; ran newsrooms in San Francisco and Miami, editor online community American Lawyer Media; sr. editor Money mag. Time Inc., 1998, asst. mng. editor Money mag., 1999, editor CNNMoney.com, 2001, exec. editor Money mag., 2004, exec. editor Fortune mag., mng. editor Money mag., 2008—. Office: Money Time and Life Bldg Rockefeller Ctr New York NY 10020*

MATTERSON, JOAN MCDEVITT, physical therapist; b. Bryn Mawr, Pa., Feb. 24, 1949; d. William J. and Wanda Jean (Edwards) McD.; children: Brian, Jennie, Kira. BS in Biology, St. Joseph's U., Phila., 1973; cert. in Phys. Therapy, U. Pa., 1974. Assoc. pharmacologist, rschr. immunology and arthritis Prog. Phys. Therapy, P.A., Wilmington, Del., 1976-93, pediatric phys. therapist, 1974-81, pres., 1976-95; rehab. dir. Achievement Rehab.; phys. therapist Liberty Home Health, 1995—; rehab. dir. Office of Joan Matterson, 1995—, Integrated Health Svcs.-Kent, Smyrna, Del., 1996—; dir. rehab. Keystone Care Therapies, Media, Pa., 1997—, with Pain Mgmt. Ctr. Chester, Pa., 1999; with Hands on Health, Wilmington, 1999—2000; phys. therapist Hickory House Nursing and Rehab. Ctr., Honeybrook, Pa., 2000—; pvt. practice Wilmington, 2000—. Lectr. in field of low level laser therapy. Dep. gov. Am. Biog. Rsch. Inst.; mem. adv. bd. Internat. Biog. Rsch. Inst., Cambridge, Eng. Mem. NAFE, Am. Soc. Laser Medicine and Surgery, Internat. Platform Assn., Am. Acad. Pain (assoc.), Inst. Noetic Sci., Am. Bd. Forensic Examiners, N.Am. Assn. Laser Therapy, Internat. Exec. Service Corp. Avocations: dance, skiing, cooking. Office Phone: 610-457-9158. Personal E-mail: jnmttrsn711@aol.com.

MATTESON, CAROL J., academic administrator; BS in Health Edn., Slippery Rock U. of Pa.; MS in Psychomotor Learning, U. Oreg.; PhD in Bus. Adminstrn., U. Pitts. Faculty Sturt Coll. of Edn., South Australia, Slippery Rock U., U. Maine, Augusta, Rowan U., NJ; asst. to pres. Slippery Rock U. of Pa.; dean coll. of bus. Bloomsburg U., Pa., provost and v.p. academic affairs Pa., 1992—95; exec. v.p. and provost Rowan U., NJ, 1995—2000; pres. Mt. Ida Coll., Newton, Mass., 2000—. Office: Mt Ida Coll 777 Dedham St Newton MA 02459 Office Phone: 617-928-4502. E-mail: cmatteson@mountida.edu.

MATTESON, JOHN THOMAS, English educator, lawyer; b. San Mateo, Calif., Mar. 3, 1961; s. Thomas Dickens and Rosemary Ann (Hamilton) M.; m. Michelle Marie Rollo, Apr. 6, 1991; 1 child, Rebecca Ann. AB in Hist., Princeton U., 1983; JD, Harvard U., 1986; MPhil, Columbia U., 1995, Ph.D. in English, 1999. Bar: NC, Calif. Law clk. to Hon. Terrence Boyle U.S. Dist. Ct. (ea. dist.) N.C., Elizabeth City, 1986-87; atty., assoc. Titchell, Maltzman et al, San Francisco, 1987-88, Maupin, Taylor, Ellis & Adams, Raleigh, N.C., 1988-91; rschr., instr. composition Columbia U., NYC, 1991—2001; prof. John Jay Coll. of Criminal Justice, NYC. Author: (book) Eden's Outcasts: The Story of Louisa May Alcott and Her Father, 2007 (Pulitzer prize for biography, 2008). Mem. Calif. Bar Assn., NC Bar Assn., Princeton Club of NY, Phi Beta Kappa. Democrat. Home: 3438 Corlear Ave Bronx NY 10463-3702 Office: John Jay Coll Criminal Justice 619 54th St Apt 734 New York NY 10019 Office Phone: 212-237-8586. Business E-Mail: matteson151@earthlink.net.

MATTESON, WILLIAM BLEECKER, lawyer; b. NYC, Oct. 20, 1928; s. Leonard Jerome and Mary Jo (Harwell) M.; m. Marilee Brill, Aug. 26, 1950; children: Lynn, Sandra, Holly. BA, Yale U., 1950; JD, Harvard U., 1953. Bar: N.Y. 1954. Clk. to judge Augustus N. Hand U.S. Ct. Appeals, 1953-54; clk. to U.S. Supreme Ct. Justice Harold H. Burton, 1954-55; assoc. firm Debevoise & Plimpton (and predecessors), NYC, 1955-61, ptnr., 1961—98, Debevoise & Plimpton (European office), Paris, 1973-78; presiding ptnr. Debevoise & Plimpton, 1988-93. Lectr. Columbia U. Law Sch., 1972-73, 78-80. Trustee Peddie Sch., Hightstown, N.J., 1968-73, Kalamazoo Coll., 1972-77, Miss Porter's Sch., Farmington, Conn., 1977-83, N.Y. Inst. Spl. Edn., 1981-2004, Salk Inst., La Jolla, Calif., 1993-96, vice-chair, 1994-96, Statue of Liberty Ellis Island Found., 1996—2008, Hartford Found., 1996-2004; active USA Bus. and Industry Adv. Com. to the Orgn. for Econ. Coop. and Devel., Paris, 1986-2000; chmn. Worldwide Bus. and Industry Adv. Com., 1994-96; vice chmn. U.S. Coun. for Internat. Bus., 1990-2000, hon. trustee. Mem. ABA, FBA, Internat. Bar Assn., N.Y. State Bar Assn., Assn. Bar City of N.Y. (chmn. securities regulation com. 1968-71), Harvard U. Law Sch. Assn. N.Y.C. (trustee 1968-73), Coun. Fgn. Rels., Union Club, Sankaty Head Club, John's Island and Windsor Clubs. Office: Debevoise & Plimpton 919 3d Ave 47th Fl New York NY 10022 E-mail: wbmatteson@debevoise.com.

MATTESSICH, RICHARD VICTOR (ALVARUS), business administration researcher; b. Trieste, Venezia-Julia, Italy, Aug. 9, 1922; s. Victor and Gertrude M.; m. Hermine Auguste Mattessich, Apr. 12, 1952. Mech. engr., Engring. Coll., Vienna, Austria, 1940; Diplomkaufmann, Hochschule für Welthandel, Vienna, 1944; Dr.rer.pol., Hochschule für Welthandel, 1945; Accademico Ordinario, Accademia Italiana di Economia Aziendale, Bologna, 1980—; D honoris causa, U. Complutense, Madrid, 1998, U. Montesquieu, Bordeaux, 2006, U. Malaga, 2006, U. Graz, 2008. Rsch. fellow Austrian Inst. Econ. Rsch., Vienna, 1945-47; instr. Rosenberg Coll., St. Gallen, 1947-52; dep. head Mt. Allison U., Sackville, Canada, 1953-59; assoc. prof. U. Calif., Berkeley, 1958-67; prof. econs. Ruhr U., Bochum, Germany, 1966-67; prof. indsl. adminstrn. U. Tech., Vienna, 1976-78; prof. bus. adminstrn. U. B.C., Vancouver, Canada, 1967-87, prof. emeritus, 1988—, Arthur Andersen & Co. Disting. chair, 1980-87. Vis. prof. Free U., Berlin, 1965, U. Social Scis., St. Gallen, Switzerland, 1965-66, U. Canterbury, 1970, Austrian Acad. Mgmt., 1971, 73, City Univ. Hong Kong, 1992, Chuo U., Tokyo, 1992; hon. prof. Centro Univ. Francesco de Vitoria, Madrid; mem. bd. nominations Acctg. Hall of Fame, Columbus, Ohio, 1978-87, 2004—; bd. govs. Sch. Chartered Accountancy, Vancouver, 1981-82; bd. dirs. Can. Cert. Gen. Accts. Rsch. Found., 1984-90, internat. adv. bd., 1993—. Author: Accounting and Analytical Methods, 1964, in German, 1970, in Japanese, 1972, in Spanish, 2002, Simulation of the Firm Through a Budget Computer Program, 1964, Instrumental Reasoning and Systems Methodology, 1978, Critique of Accounting: Foundational Research in Accounting, 1995, Professional Memoirs and Beyond, 1995, The Beginnings of Accounting and Accounting Thought, 2000, Two Hundred Years of Accounting Research, 2008; editor: Modern Accounting Research History, Survey and Guide, 1984, 89, 92, Accounting Research in the 1980s and Its Future Influence, 1991, French transl., 1993, others; mem. editl. bd. Theory and Decision Libr., Jour. Bus. Adminstrn., Economia Azlendale, Praxiology, Acctg., Bus. and Fin. History. Sec.-treas. Internat. House, U. B.C., 1969-70. Served to lt. Orgn. Todt., 1944-45. Recipient Lit. award AICPA, 1972, Haim Falk award Can. Acad. Acctg. Assn., 1991, highest rsch. award Acad. Accounting Historians, 2003, Hourglass award; Ford Found. fellow, 1961-62; Disting. Erskine fellow U. Canterbury, 1970; Killam sr. fellow U. B.C., 1971-72; nominated Nobel Meml. prize in Econs., 2002. Fellow Accademia Italiana di Economia Aziendale (accademico ordinario 1980—); mem. Am. Acctg. Assn. (lit. award 1972), Schmalenbach Gesellschaft, Verb. d. Hochschullehrer für Betriebswirtschaft (exec. adv. coun. 1976-78), Inst. Chartered Accts. of B.C. (bd. of govs. 1981-82), Austrian Acad. Scis. (corr.), Acad. Acctg. Historians (life). Achievements include pioneering analytical methods in accounting and the computerized spreadsheet. Office: U BC Sauder Sch Bus Vancouver BC Canada V6T 1Z2 Business E-Mail: richard.mattessich@sauder.ubc.ca. *Cautious optimism is the best long-run strategy.*

MATTEUCCI, DOMINICK VINCENT, real estate developer; b. Oct. 19, 1924; s. Vincent Joseph and Anna Marie (Zoda) M.; m. Emma Irene DeGuia, Mar. 2, 1968; children: Felisa Anna, Vincent Eriberto. BS, Coll. of William and Mary, 1948, MIT, 1950. Registered profl. engr., Calif.; lic. gen. bldg. contractor, real estate broker. Owner Matteucci Constrn. Co., Newport Beach, Calif.; pres. Nat. Investment Brokerage Co., Newport Beach. Home: 2104 Felipe Newport Beach CA 92660-4040 Office: PO Box 10474 Newport Beach CA 92658-0474

MATTHAEI, GAY HUMPHREY, interior designer; b. NYC, Mar. 13, 1931; d. Robert Louis and Ethel Gladys Humphrey; m. Konrad Henry Matthaei, Nov. 16, 1956; children: Marcella, Leslie, Konrad. BA, Mt. Holyoke Coll., 1952; MIA, Columbia U., 1954, MA, cert. Russian Inst., 1954; grad., Parsons Sch. Design, 1970. Lectr., cons. NBC, 1956; dir. Radrick Prodns., Where Time Is a River, 1966—67; cons. N.Y.C. Parks Recreation and Cultural Adminstrn., 1970—72; assoc. Pearl R. Mitchell A.S.I.D., 1972—74, owner, 1974—97; owner, mgr. Gay Matthaei Interiors, NYC, 1975—2003. Ptnr. Two Fold Graphics, 1992—96. Restorations include Town Farms Inn, 1978, State Capital of Conn., 1977-78, Pres.'s House, Mt. Holyoke Coll., 1982, Samuel Russell House, Wesleyan Coll., 1984, Courtly Manor, Greenwich, Conn., 1987 Buhl Family Found., 1993; author: The Ledgerbook of Thomas Blue Eagle, 1994, 1995, (CD-Rom) The Journey of Thomas Blue Eagle, 1995, Sketchbook of Thomas Blue Eagle (Best Books for Teenagers NY Pub. Libr. 2002). Trustee Mt. Holyoke Coll.; mem. Commn. on State Capital Preservation and Restoration, Conn., 1997-82, Greenwich Bd. Realtors, Nat. Bd. Realtors; literacy vol., Greenich, Conn., 2005. Recipient Christopher award, 1994, Internat. Readers Assn. award, 1995, EMMA award, best CD-Rom award Multimedia Asia, others. Mem.: Nat. Mus. Am. Indian (charter), Mt. Holyoke Club, Phi Beta Kappa. Home: 710 Riverbank Rd Stamford CT 06903-3514 Office: Capital Properties and Estates Weichert Realtors 25 Field Point Rd Greenwich CT 06830-5335 Office Phone: 203-249-1459. Personal E-mail: tphq@optonline.net.

MATTHEI, EDWARD HODGE, architect; b. Chgo., Dec. 21, 1927; s. Henry Reinhard and Myra Beth (Hodge) M.; m. Mary Nina Hoffmann, June 30, 1951; children: Edward Hodge, Suzanne Marie, Christie Ann, Laura Jean, John William. BS in Archtl. Engring, U. Ill., 1951. Registered arch. 17 states, including Ariz., Fla., Ill., Mich., N.Y., Wis., Calif.; cert. NCARB. Dir. health facilities planning and constrn. Child & Smith (architects and engrs.), Chgo., 1951-60; sr. v.p. health facilities planning Perkins & Will, Chgo., 1960-74; ptnr. firm Matthei & Colin Assoc., Chgo., 1974-96; planning and archtl. design cons. Chgo., 1996—. Com. chmn. Am. Nat. Standards Inst., 1983-89; lectr. 1st Internat. Conf. on Rehab. of Handicapped, Beijing, 1986, Design USA, Novosbirsk and Moscow, USSR, 1990. Editor: Inland Architect, 1956-58; prin. works health facilities projects, med. ctr. master plans including Akron (Ohio) Gen. Hosp., Heritage Hosp., Taylor, Mich., Rose Meml., Denver, Silver Cross Hosp., Joliet, Ill., Shands Tchg. Hosp. & Med. Sch., U. Fla., Gainesville, Mercy Hosp., Davenport, Iowa, Westlake Cmty. Hosp., Chgo., Highland Park (Ill.) Hosp., Ctrl. DuPage Hosp., Winfield, Ill., Nebr. Meth. Hosp., Omaha, Rockford (Ill.) Meml. Hosp., U. Ala. Med. Ctr., Birmingham, U. Calif. Sch. Medicine, Irvine, Kent Hall, U. Chgo., Holy Cross Hosp., Md., West Mich. Cancer Ctr. Mem. profl. adv. com. Nat. Easter Seal Soc., 1965-1970, chair, 1988-89, 1st v.p., bd. dirs., 1978; mem. bd. dirs. St. Scholastica H.S., Chgo., 1973-83, 86-96; mem. Welfare Coun. Greater Met. Chgo., 1965-72. With AUS, 1946-47. Recipient Leon Chatelain award for barrier-free environ. Nat. Easter Seals Soc., 1979, Disting. Svc. award, 1990, 99, Meritorious Svc. award Am. Nat. Standards Inst., 1987, Speedy award Paralyzed Vets. Am., 1993. Fellow: AIA (chmn. bldg. affairs com. Chgo. chpt. 1959—66, chmn. com. on arch. for health 1963—74, co-chmn., AMA joint com. on environ. health 1967—70, Disting. Svc. award Chgo. chpt. 1988); mem.: Builders Assn. Chgo., Nat. Center Barrier Free Environment (dir.), Internat. Hosp. Fedn., Am. Assn. Hosp. Planning, Am. Hosp. Assn., Chgo. Assn. Commerce and Industry. Office: Matthei & Colin Assocs 332 S Michigan Ave Chicago IL 60604-4434 Home: 890 Audubon Way Apt 502 Lincolnshire IL 60069 Home Phone: 847-793-0939. Personal E-mail: ematthei@sbcglobal.net.

MATTHEW, LYN, sales executive, consultant, marketing professional; b. Long Beach, Calif., Dec. 15, 1936; d. Harold G. and Beatrice (Hunt) Matthew; m. Wayne Thomas Castleberry, Aug. 12, 1961 (div. Jan. 1976); children: Melanie Castleberry, Cheryl Castleberry, Nicole Castleberry, Matthew Castleberry. BS, U. Calif., Davis, 1958; MA, Ariz. State U., 1979. Cert. hotel sales exec., meeting profl., hospitality mktg. exec., hospitality mgmt. exec. Pres. Davlyn Cons. Found., Scottsdale, Ariz., 1979-82; cons., vis. prof. Art Bus., Scottsdale, 1982—; pres., dir. sales and mktg. Embassy Stes., Scottsdale, 1987-98; pres. Matthew Enterprises, Inc., Scottsdale, 1998—. Vis. prof. Maricopa CC, Phoenix, 1979—, Ariz. State U., Tempe, 1980—83; cons. Women's Caucus Art, Phoenix, 1983—88; coun. adminstr. Lynn Andrews Prodns., 2001—07. Author: The Business Aspects of Art, Book I, 1979, Book II, 1989, Marketing Strategies for the Creative Artist, 1985, Moxibustion Manual, 1999. Bd. dirs. Rossom Ho. and Heritage Sq. Found., Phoenix, 1987—88; trustee Hotel Sales and Mktg. Assn. Internat. Found., 1988—90, chmn., 1991—93, mem. exec. com., 1993—95. Recipient Cmty. Bldg. award, 2000. Mem.: Flagstaff Artist's Coalition (gallery mgr. 2008—), Am. Orgn. Bodywork Therapies Asia (pres., state dir. 1999—2003, nat. bd. dirs. 2009—, nat. bd., regional dir. 2009—), Ariz. Acad. Performing Arts (v.p. bd. dir. 1987—88, pres. 1988—89), Soc. Govt. Meeting Planners (charter bd. dir. 1987, nat. conf. co-chair 1993—94, Sam Gilmer award 1992), Meeting Planners Internat. (v.p. Ariz. Sunbelt chpt. 1989—91, pres. 1991—92, CMP cert. trainer 1995—2000, Supplier of the Yr. award 1988), Cert. Hospitality Mktg. Execs. (profl. designation tng. chair 1995), Hotels Sales and Mktg. Assn. Internat. (bd. dir. 1985—90, pres. Great Phoenix chpt. 1988—89, regional dir. 1989—90, mktg. exec. 1998—), Ariz. Vocat. Edn. Assn. (sec. 1978—80), Ariz. Women's Caucus Art (pres. 1980—82, hon. advisor 1986—87), Nat. Women's Caucus Art (v.p. 1981—83), Women in Higher Edn., Ariz. Visionary Artists (treas. 1987—88), Women Image Now (Achievement and Contbn. in Visual Arts award 1983), Coun. Whistling Elk (worldwide coun. adminstr. 2001—06). Personal E-mail: lynmatthew@mo.com.

MATTHEWS, ALEXANDER, health facility administrator; b. NYC, Sept. 8, 1924; s. Matthew and Helen (Tertis) Fotopoulos; m. Ann Koutsatsa Matthews (dec.); m. Linda Kay Warren, Dec. 30, 1999; children: Andrew Philip, Lydia Ann. BA, Boston U., 1948; MD, SUNY, 1952. Diplomate Am. Bd. Surgery, Bd. Thoracic Surgery. Pvt. practice, 1960—90; med. dir. Des Moines Med. Exchange Program, Stavropal, Russia, 1990—95; chief med. officer Mil. Entrance Processing Sta., Des Moines, 1995—. Chief surgery, med. staff, bd. dirs. Iowa Luth. Hosp., Des Moines, 1962—90. Comdr. USPHS, 1952—59. Fellow: ACS, Am. Coll. Chest Physicians; mem.: Soc. Thoracic Surgeons. Home: 505 Glenview Dr Des Moines IA 50312 Office: Mil Entrance Processing Sta Dept Defense 2500 U Ave West Des Moines IA 50266-1480

MATTHEWS, ALLAN FREEMAN, geologist; b. Wakefield, Mass., May 27, 1916; s. Ralph Freeman Matthews and Mary (Morrill) Hill; m. Shirley Jean Spencer, Dec. 23, 1937 (div. Oct. 1955, dec. 1989); children: David Allan, Kim; m. Mary Cerantonio Thomas, Feb. 24, 1956, (div. Jan. 5, 1962); m. Doris Olive Haignere, June 26, 1962 (Dec. 2003). BA, Carleton Coll., Northfield, Minn., 1937; MS, Antioch Coll., Yellow Springs, Ohio, 1939; postgrad., Johns Hopkins U., Balt., 1939-40. Tech. editor Ceramic Industry Jour., Chgo., 1940-41; editor, sect. chief US Bur. Mines, Washington, 1941-51; asst. dir., staff Pres.'s Materials Policy Commn., Washington, 1951-52; materials cons. Nat. Security Resources Bd., Washington, 1952-53; ops. analyst Johns Hopkins Ops. Rsch. Office, Chevy Chase, Md., 1953-54; program officer US Agy. Internat. Devel., Washington, 1954—75, Germany, Liberia, Yemen; editor, pub. Developing Country Courier, McLean, Va., 1978-85. Del. UN Global Modeling Conf., Paris, 1982; initiated citizens transnat. constl. conv., The Hague, Netherlands, 1998; chmn. constn. action group Alliance for Democracy, Waltham, Mass., 1997-99; minerals cons. Global 2000 Project, 1978-80; participated in Global Exch. Reality Tour supporting grassroots social justice, Venezuela, 2007; cons. and presenter in field. Author: Sovereigns Peacefully Take Charge, 1997, 2nd edit., 2005, Compiled History of Atlantic Federation Movement, 2008; editor: Minerals Yearbook, 1947-50; contbr. article Physical Natural Resources, Encyclopaedia Britannica, 1959. Dir. Streit Coun. for a Union of Democracies, Washington, 1957-2009; core planner 20/20 Vision, Washington, 1991-97; a founder The Reston Forum, 1990-92; pres. Waterford Sq. Condominium Assn., Reston, 1992; apptd. adv. bd. Phila. Two Orgn. Direct Democracy, 2001, Signatory of Natl. Initiative for Democracy, 2002. Lt. (j.g.) USN, 1944-46. Recipient Meritorious award US Agy. for Internat. Devel., 1955, Commendation for Devel. Analysis, 1957; named Fellow in Geology, 1937-39. Mem. AAAS, ACLU, Democratic Socialists Am., Natural Resources Def. Coun., U N Assn., World Federalist Movement, Unitarian Universalist Assn., Fed. Am. Scientists, Phila. Two Direct Democracy, Soc. for Internat. Devel. (proposer continental fed. unions at N.Am. regional conf. 2000), Initiative and Referendum Inst. Green Party. Achievements include evaluation of mineral resources adequacy and advancement of transnational constitutions. Home: Apt 624 900 N Taylor St Arlington VA 22203-1863 Personal E-mail: allan_matthews@comcast.net.

MATTHEWS, BARBARA CARIDAD, lawyer; d. Frederick Lawrence and Caridad Ofelia Matthews; m. Andrew Michael Danas, Nov. 6, 1999; 1 child, Lydia Marguerite Danas. B.Sc.F.S., Georgetown U., 1986; JD with honors, Duke U., 1991, LLM, 1991. Bar: N.Y. 1992. Assoc. banking advisor Inst. Internat. Fin., Washington, 1992—94, banking advisor, regulatory counsel, 1996—2003; assoc. Morrison & Foerster, Washington, 1994—96; sr. coun., Fin. Svc. Com. House of Rep., 2003—05; sr. advisor to the asst. sec. internat. U.S. Dept. Treasury, Washington, 2006, attaché U.S. treasury Mission to European Union & MInister Counseior Fin. Affairs Brussels, 2006—08; founder, mng. dir. BCM Internat. Regulatory Analytics LLC, 2008—. Mem. editl. bd. Jour. Derivatives Use, Trading and Regulation, 1997—2003; contbr. articles to profl. jours., chapters to books. Pres. Friends Assisting the Nat. Symphony, Washington, 1998—99; bd. dirs. Young Audiences, Washington, 2000—04; mem. exec. com. women's leadership group Boys & Girls Clubs Greater Washington, 2000—. Fellow internat. law, Ford Found., 1991—92. Mem.: ABA, Coun. Fgn. Rels., Internat. Assn. Fin. Engrs., Women in Housing & Fin., Women's Fgn. Policy Group, NY State Bar Assn., NY Bar, Pi Sigma Alpha, Alpha Sigma Nu. Avocations: photography, tennis, travel. Office Phone: 202-379-2920. E-mail: matthewsb@bcmstrategy.com.

MATTHEWS, BRIAN W., molecular biology educator; b. Mount Barker, Australia, May 25, 1938; came to U.S., 1967; s. Lionel A. and Ethlinda L. (Harris) M.; m. Helen F. Denley, Sept. 7, 1963; children: Susan, Kristine. BS, U. Adelaide, Australia, 1959, BS with honors, 1960, PhD, 1964, DSc, 1986. Mem. staff Med. Rsch. Coun., Cambridge, Eng., 1963-66; vis. assoc. NIH, Bethesda, Md., 1967-69; prof. molecular biology U. Oreg., Eugene, 1969—, chmn. dept. physics, 1985-86, dir. Inst. Molecular Biology, 1980-83, 90-92; Drummond lectr. U. Calgary (Can.), 1995. Advisor NSF, Washington, 1975-77; investigator Howard Hughes Med. Inst., 1989—2008; mem. U.S. Nat. Commn. for Crystallography, Washington, 1980-86, 88-90. Editor: Protein Science, 2007—. Rsch. fellow Alfred P. Sloan Found., 1971, Guggenheim fellow, 1977; recipient Career Devel. award NIH, 1973, Faculty Excellence award Oreg. Bd. Edn., 1984, Discovery award Med. Rsch. Found. Oreg., 1987, Reed Coll. Vollum award, 1994, Stein and Moore award Protein Soc., 2000. Mem. NAS (coun. mem. 2009-), AAAS, Crystallographic Assn., Am. Chem. Soc., Protein Soc. (pres. 1995-97), Biophysical Soc. (nat. lectr. 2001). Office: U Oreg Inst Molecular Biology Eugene OR 97403 Office Phone: 541-346-2572. E-mail: brian@uoxray.uoregon.edu.

MATTHEWS, CHARLES, school disciplinarian; b. Hoboken, NJ, Nov. 19, 1954; s. David Joseph and Eileen Matthews; m. Janice Stolte, Nov. 3, 1984; 1 child, Trace Poggioli. BA, St. Peter's Coll., Jersey City, 1977, MEd, 2003. Prin.'s cert. NJ, 2003. Grammar sch. tchr. T.G. Connors Sch., Hoboken, 1977—87; varsity head baseball coach Hoboken HS, 1986—2008, tchr., 1988—2000, disciplinarian, 2001—. Named Baseball Coach of Yr. Mem.: Hoboken B.P.O.E. Home: 15 Church Towers Hoboken NJ 07030 Office: Hoboken HS 8th And Clinton St Hoboken NJ 07030 Office Fax: 201-356-3704. Business E-Mail: cmatthews@hoboken.k12.nj.us.

MATTHEWS, CHARLES W., JR., oil industry executive, lawyer; b. Houston, Feb. 27, 1945; BA, U. Tex., 1967; JD, U. Houston, 1970. Bar: Tex. 1970, Tenn. 1980, admitted to: U.S. Dist. Ct., So. Dist. Tex. 1975, U.S. Supreme Ct., U.S. Ct. Appeals, Dist. Columbia Circuit, U.S. Ct. Appeals, Fifth and Eleventh Circuits 1981. Trial atty. law dept. Exxon Corp., 1971-78, region atty. southeastern and southern region mktg. offices, 1978-81, assoc. gen. atty. litigation sect., gen. counsel & dir. Petroleum Casualty Co. and Exxon Risk Mgmt. Svcs., 1981-92; from assoc. gen. counsel law dept. to gen. counsel law dept. Exxon U.S.A., 1992; v.p., gen. counsel Exxon Mobil Corp., 1995—. Instr. State Bar Tex. Profl. Develop. Program, Litigating the Oil and Gas Case, 1988, U. Houston Law Found., mem. bd. trustees. Author: Recent Developments in Liability for Oil and Gas Operations, 1987. Nat. trustee Southwest Region Boys and Girls Club Am.; chair U. Tex. Chancellor's Coun., 2002; mem. bd. overseers Rand Inst. Civil Justice; mem. develop. bd. U. Tex. Recipient Alumnus of the Yr., Univ. of Houston, 2000. Fellow: Tex. Bar Found.; mem.: ABA (fellow, mem. com. corp. gen. counsel), Tex. Access Justice Commn. (commr. 2004—), Chief Legal Officers Roundtable, Am. Inns Ct. Found. (trustee, mem. leadership coun.), Nat. Ctr. State Courts (co-chair gen. counsel com. 2002—), Defense Rsch. Inst., State Bar Tex. (vice chmn. adminstrn. justice com. 1988, corp. counsel liaison to litigation section 1988—89), Ctr. Am. and Internat. Law (chmn. exec. com. 2002—, trustee), Internat. Assn. Def. Counsel Found. (chmn. corp. counsel com. 1991, v.p. 1993—95, bd. dirs.), Assn. Gen. Counsel, Dallas Bar Assn., Dallas Bar Found. (fellow, v.p., gen. counsel), Houston Bar Assn. (bd. dirs. 1994—95, fellow), Order Barons. Office: Exxon Mobil Corp Law Dept 5959 Las Colinas Blvd Irving TX 75039-2298*

MATTHEWS, CHRISTIAN WILLIAM, JR., minister; b. Jersey City, Oct. 12, 1934; s. Christian William and Lydia Louise (Weller) M.; m. Elaine Louise Ochs, June 18, 1955; children: Christian William III, Patricia Louise, Judith Ann, Barbara Jean. BA, King's Coll., 1956; MRE, Palmer Theol. Sem., 1960, MDiv, 1962, MEd, U. Del., 1961; ThM, Princeton Theol. Sem., 1965; DD, Grove City Coll., 1988. Ordained to ministry Presbyn. Ch. (U.S.A.), 1962. Dir. Christian edn. United Presbyn. Ch. of Manoa, Havertown, Pa., 1959-62; asst. min. 1st Presbyn. Ch., Norristown, Pa., 1962-65; assoc. min. Marble Collegiate Ch., NYC, 1965-68; sr. min. Fox Chapel Presbyn. Ch., Pitts., 1968-79, Christ Presbyn. Ch., Toledo, 1979-2000, 2d Presbyn. Ch., Balt., 2000—04, 1st Presbyn. Ch., Grand Haven, Mich., 2004—. Mem. The Fellowship, Washington, Synod Gen. Coun. Presbyn. Ch. U.S.A.; chmn. Synod Evangelism; leader marriage and family seminars; mem. alumni fund bd. Princeton Theol. Sem.; mem. Kirk coun., Alma Coll.; cons. Presbyn. Ch. in U.S.A., Nat. Com. for Prison Reform, County Human Svc. Commn. Author: Lingering with Luke—A Study of the Life of Christ, 1976, Marriage and Family Study Course, 1983; developer (nat. program for Presbyn. chs.) Risk Evangelism; signer Lausanne Covenant of Internat. Congress on World Evangelization. Chmn. Com. for Ecol. Instrn.; founding pres. Samaritan Counseling Ctr.; sec. The Ability Ctr.; bd. dirs. area coun. Boy Scouts Am., Toledo Rotary Club, James C. Caldwell Cmty. Ctr., Toledo Area Min., AASK-Mid Am., Toledo Leadership Found.; mem. Coun. for Religion and Psychiatry. Mem.: Rotary Club of Toledo. Home and Office: 337 Sawgrass Ct Holland OH 43528-9210 Office Phone: 443-418-5593. Business E-Mail: drcwmatthews@aol.com. *As I reflect upon life, I believe that God is at work in our world bringing together people of faith to meet the complex challenges confronting us at this time of history. Working together, we are able to encourage, strengthen, and support one another in meeting the needs of our world.*

MATTHEWS, CHRISTOPHER JOHN, political commentator, writer; b. Phila., Dec. 17, 1945; s. Herbert Charles and Mary Teresa (Shields) Matthews; m. Kathleen Ann Cunningham, 1980; children: Michael, Thomas, Caroline. BA in Econs., Coll. Holy Cross, Worcester, Mass., 1967, LLD (hon.), 2003; grad. studies, U. NC; doctorate (hon.), St. Leo U., Loyola Coll., Md., Niagara U., Fontbonne Coll., Beaver Coll., New England Sch. Law, Anna Maria Coll., Chesnut Hill Coll. Legis. asst. to Utah Senator Frank Moss, 1971—73; staff mem. Maine Senator Edward Muskie; staff asst. US Senate Budget Com., 1974—77; speechwriter for Pres. Jimmy Carter, 1977—79; aide to Spkr. Tip O'Neill US House Reps., 1981—87; polit. analyst CBS This Morning, 1987; bur. chief, columnist San Francisco Examiner, Washington, 1987—2000; former nat. syndicated columnist San Francisco Chronicle; host Hardball with Chris Matthews CNBC, 1997—2002, MSNBC, 1999—; host syndicated program, The Chris Matthews Show, 2002—. Author: Kennedy & Nixon: The Rivalry That Shaped PostWar America, 1996, Hardball: How Politics is Really Played- Told By One Who Knows the Game, 1999, Now, Let Me Tell You What I Really Think, 2001, American: Beyond Our Grandest Notions, 2002, Life's a Campaign: What Politics Has Taught me About Friendship, Rivalry, Reputation and Success, 2007; contbr. articles to The New Republic, US News & World Report, NY Times, Christian Sci. Monitor, Am. Politics; actor: (films) Man of the Year, 2006. Trade devel. advisor US Peace Corps, Swaziland, 1968—70. Recipient Lincoln Award, Union League of Phila. Democrat. Office: Hardball With Chris Matthews 30 Rockefeller Plz New York NY 10112*

MATTHEWS, CRAIG GERARD, retired energy executive; b. Bklyn., Mar. 8, 1943; m. Carol O. Olsen, Sept. 10, 1971; children: Kenneth C., Bradford P., Melinda M. BCE, Rutgers U., NB, 1965; MS in Indsl. Mgmt., Polytech. Inst. Bklyn., 1971; PhD (hon.), NYU, Poly. U.; PhD in Engring., NYU Poly., 2009. Vice chmn., COO, KeySpan Corp. (formerly Bklyn. Union Gas Co.), 1965—2002, ret., 2002; pres., CEO NUI Corp., 2004; ret., 2004—. Bd. dirs. Hess Corp., Nat. Fuel Gas, Republic Fin. Bd. dirs. Salvation Army, Bklyn. Philharm., Greater NY, NJ, nat. bd. dirs. NJ, Poly. U., Bklyn. Republican. Presbyterian. Home: 132 Canterbury Way Basking Ridge NJ 07920 Office Phone: 908-719-4290. E-mail: craiggmatthews@aol.com.

MATTHEWS, DAN, dentist; Grad., U. Tex.; DDS, U. Tex. Health Sci. Ctr. Gen. practice resident Audie Murphy Vets. Hosp., San Antonio; pvt. practice Austin, Tex. Vol. Christina's Smiles, The Theo Project, Round Rock Health Clinic. Fellow: Am. Acad. Gen. Dentistry; mem.: ADA, Capital Area Dental Soc., Am. Equilibration Soc., Am. Acad. Cosmetic Dentistry, Tex. Dental Assn. (delegate), Rio Grande Valley Dental Soc. (former pres. and v.p.), L.D. Pankey Inst. Alumni Assn. Avocations: poetry, fishing. Office: The Park at Eanes Creek Bldg 2, Ste 221 4407 Bee Cave Rd Austin TX 78746-6410 Office Phone: 512-452-2273. E-mail: texasmiles@austin.rr.com.

MATTHEWS, DANIEL B., air transportation executive; BA in Bus. Adminstrn. and Econs., Lewis U., Romeoville, Ill., 1976; MBA, Loyola U., Chgo., 1977. Various comml. lending and tax-oriented lease financing positions Borg-Warner Leasing, Chgo., Sears Bank & Trust Co.; various corp. fin. and treasury-related positions Ea. Air Lines, Inc., 1982—90, staff v.p., treas.; asst. treas. Ryder Sys., Inc., 1990—93; with NW Airlines Corp., Minn., 1993—, v.p. aircraft transactions, v.p., asst. treas., 1999—2000, sr. v.p., treas. Bd. mem. DARTS, Mpls. Mem. spl. adv. coun. Lewis U. Office: NW Airlines Corp 2700 Lone Oak Pky Eagan MN 55121 Office Phone: 612-726-2111.

MATTHEWS, DARRYL R., SR., not-for-profit fundraiser; m. Allison Paige Stinson; children: Julian, Blake, Darryl Jr. BSc in Polit. Sci. and Sociology, Ctrl. Mo. State Univ., 1977. Claims adjuster USF&G, Kansas City, Mo., 1977—78; asst. exec. sec. Alpha Phi Alpha Fraternity, Inc., Chgo., 1978—81, dir. mktg., membership Balt., 1983—93, dep. exec. dir., 1993—94, interim exec. dir., 1994—95, exec. dir., COO, 1995—96, sr. gen. pres. Baltimore, Md., 2005—; account exec. AT&T, Southwestern Bell, Am. Bell, Kansas City, 1981—83; exec. dir. mktg. Bingwa Software Co., Norcross, Ga., 1996—97; ind. cons. White House Presdl. Advance Office, 1997—98; exec. dir., COO Nat. Assn. of Black Accts., Inc., Greenbelt, Md., 1998—. Vice-chmn. bd. dirs. Martin Luther King Jr. Nat. Meml., Washington. Named one of Most Influential Black Americans, Ebony mag., 2006; named to Power 150, 2008. Office: Nat Assn Black Accountants Inc 7474 Greenway Center Dr Greenbelt MD 20770-3504 Office Phone: 410-554-0040, 301-474-6222. Office Fax: 410-554-0054, 301-474-3114.

MATTHEWS, DAVE, singer, musician; b. Johannesburg, Jan. 9, 1967; s. John and Val Matthews; m. Jennifer Ashley Harper, Aug. 10, 2000; children: Grace Anne, Stella Busina, August Oliver. Vocalist, guitarist The Dave Matthews Band, 1991—; founder ATO Records, 2000—. Bd. dirs. Farm Aid, 2001—. Musician: (albums) Remember Two Things, 1993, Under the Table and Dreaming, 1994, Crash, 1996, Live at Red Rocks, 9-15-95, 1997, Before These Crowded Streets, 1998, Live at Luther College, 1999, Listener Supported, 1999, Live in Chicago 12-19-98, 2001, Everyday, 2001, Live at Folsom Field, Boulder Colorado, 2002, Busted Stuff, 2002, The Central Park Concert, 2003, (solo) Some Devil, 2003, The Gorge, 2004, Stand Up, 2005, Live at Radio City

Music Hall, 2007, (songs) So Much to Say, 1996 (Grammy award Best Rock Performance by A Duo Or Group, 1996), The Space Between, 2001, Gravedigger, 2003 (Grammy award Best Male Rock Vocal Performance, 2003); actor: (films) Where the Red Fern Grows, 2003, Because of Winn-Dixie, 2005, I Now Pronounce You Chuck and Larry, 2007, You Don't Mess with the Zohan, 2008. Recipient Best Live Act award, My VH1 Awards, 2000, Favorite Group award & Must-Have Album award, 2001; named one of 100 Sexiest Artists, VH1, 2002. Office: IFA Talent Agy Ste 490 8730 Sunset Blvd Los Angeles CA 90069 also: Ato Records 44 Wall St Fl 23 New York NY 10005-2426

MATTHEWS, DAVID, clergyman; b. Indianola, Miss., Jan. 29, 1920; s. Albert and Bertha (Henderson) M.; m. Lillian Pearl Banks, Aug. 28, 1951; 1 dau., Denise. AB, Morehouse Coll., Atlanta, 1950; student, Atlanta U., 1950, Memphis Theol. Sem., 1965, Delta State U., Cleveland, Miss., 1969, 71, 72; D.D. (hon.), Natchez Jr. Coll., Miss., 1973, Morris Booker Meml. Coll., 1988. Ordained minister Nat. Baptist Conv. U.S.A., 1946; pastor chs. in Miss., 1951—, Bell Grove Baptist Ch., Indianola, 1951—, Strangers Home, Greenwood, 1958—. Tchr., chmn. dept. social sci. Gentry H.S., Indianola, 1958-83; moderator Sunflower Bapt. Assn., 1957—; v.p. Gen. Bapt. Conv. Miss., 1958—, former lectr., conv. congress religious edn.; v.p. Nat. Bapt. Conv. U.S.A., 1971-94; del. to Nat. Coun. Chs., 1960, supr. oratorial contest, 1976; pres. Gen. Missionary Bapt. State Conv. Miss., 1974-98. Mem. Sunflower County Anti-Poverty Bd., 1965-71, Indianola Bi-Racial Com., 1965—; mem. Gov.'s Advisory Com.; col. on staff Gov. Finch, 1976-80; mem. budget com. Indianola United Fund, 1971—; chmn. bd. Indianola FHA, 1971—; trustee Natchez Jr. Coll.; mem. Miss. Gov.'s Research and Devel. Council, 1984—; apptd. mem. So. Govs. Ecumenical Coun. Infant Mortality, 1987. Served with U.S. Army, 1942-45, PTO. Recipient citation Morehouse Coll., 1950, citation Miss. Valley State Coll., 1956, J.H. Jackson Preaching award Midwestern Baptist Laymen Fellowship, 1974, Gov.'s Merit award, 1975, Human Svc. award Miss. Valley State U., 2004. Mem. NEA, Miss., Indianola Tchrs. Assns., Am. Bible Soc. (adv. coun. 1991-2000, student reform theol. sem. centennial edn. 1990—). Democrat. Baptist. Home: PO Box 627 Indianola MS 38751-0627 Fax: 662-887-9078. Personal E-mail: matthews3463@bills.net. *I have learned not to seek honors and success but to become so involved in worthwhile works that I lose myself and by such actions success and honors have come.*

MATTHEWS, DAVID FORT, career officer; b. Lancaster, NH, Sept. 25, 1944; s. Clinton Fort and Mabel Sawin (Oaks) M.; m. Eva Mae Horton, Nov. 10, 1990. BA, Vanderbilt U., 1966; MA, Mid. Tenn. U., 1973. Cert. acquisition mgr. Rsch. and devel. officer U.S. Army Rsch. Inst., Washington, 1974-77; exec. officer 194th Maintenence Battalion-Camp Humphreys, Korea, 1978-79; career program mgr. U.S. Army Mil. Pers. Ctr., Washington, 1979-82; logistics staff officer Dep. Chief of Staff Logistics, Washington, 1982-83; team chief Chief of Staff Army Study Group, Washington, 1983-85; logistics div. chief Multiple Launch Rocket System Project Office, Huntsville, Ala., 1985-88; comdr. Ordnance Program Div., Riyadh, Saudi Arabia, 1988-90; project mgr. Army Tactical Missile System, Huntsville, 1990-94; sr. lectr. weapon systems acquisition Naval Postgrad. Sch., Monterey, Calif., 1994—. Decorated Legion of Merit, Bronze Star; recipient award as project mgr. of yr. Sec. of Army, 1991. Mem. Nat. Def. Indsl. Assn., Assn. U.S. Army. Avocations: sports, water-skiing, reading, scuba diving. Home: 83 High Meadow Ln Carmel CA 93923 Office: Naval Postgrad Sch Monterey CA 93943 Office Phone: 831-656-2360. Business E-Mail: dmatthews@nps.edu.

MATTHEWS, ELIZABETH WOODFIN, law librarian; b. Ashland, Va., July 30, 1927; d. Edwin Clifton and Elizabeth Frances (Luck) Woodfin; m. Sidney E. Matthews, Dec. 20, 1947; 1 child, Sarah Elizabeth Matthews. BA, Randolph-Macon Coll., 1948, LLD (hon.), 1989; MS in Libr. Sci., U. Ill., 1952; PhD, So. Ill. U., 1972; LLD, Randolph-Macon Coll., 1989. Cert. law libr., med. libr., med. libr. III. Libr. Ohio State U., Columbus, 1952-59; libr., instr. U. Ill., Urbana, 1962-63; lectr. U. Ill. Grad. Sch. Libr. Sci., Urbana, 1964; libr., instr. Morris Libr. So. Ill. U., Carbondale, 1964-67; classroom instr. So. Ill. U. Coll Edn., Carbondale, 1967-70; med. libr., asst. prof. Morris Libr. So. Ill. U., Carbondale, 1972-74, law libr., asst. prof., 1974-79, law libr., assoc. prof., 1979-85, law libr., prof., 1985-92, prof. emerita, 1993—. Author: Access Points to the Law Library, 1984, 17th Century English Law Reports, 1986, Law Library Reference Shelf, 1988, 5th edit., 2003, Lincoln as a Lawyer: An Annotated Bibliography, 1991. Mem. AAUW (pres. 1976-78, corp. rep. 1978-88), Am. Assn. Law Librs., Postdoctoral Acad. Higher Edn., Beta Phi Mu, Phi Kappa Phi. Methodist.

MATTHEWS, GILBERT ELLIOTT, investment banker; b. Brookline, Mass., Apr. 24, 1930; s. Martin W. and Charlotte (Cohen) M.; m. Anne Lisbeth Barnett, Apr. 20, 1958 (div. 1975); children: Lisa Joan, Diana Kory (dec. 1995); m. Elaine Rita Siegal Pulitzer, Jan. 2, 1978 (div. 1999); 1 child, Jennifer Rachel. AB, Harvard U., 1951; MBA, Columbia U., 1953. Chartered fin. analyst. Dept. mgr. Bloomingdale's, NYC, 1953, 56-60; security analyst Merrill Lynch, NYC, 1960; investment banker Bear, Stearns & Co., NYC, 1960-95, gen. ptnr., 1979-85; mng. dir. Bear, Stearns & Co. Inc., 1985-86, sr. mng. dir., 1986-95, Sutter Securities Inc., San Francisco, 1995—, chmn. bd. dirs., 1997—. Served as lt. (j.g.) USN, 1953-56. Mem. N.Y. Soc. Security Analysts. Democrat. Jewish. Office: Sutter Securities Inc 220 Montgomery St Ste 1700 San Francisco CA 94104 Office Phone: 415-352-6336. Business E-Mail: gil@suttersf.com.

MATTHEWS, JACK (JOHN HAROLD MATTHEWS), language educator, writer; b. Columbus, Ohio, July 22, 1925; s. John Harold and Lulu Emma (Grover) M.; m. Barbara Jane Reese, Sept. 16, 1947; children: Cynthia Ann Matthews Warnock, Barbara Ellen Matthews Saunders, John Harold. BA, Ohio State U., 1949, MA, 1954. Clk. U.S. Post Office, Columbus, 1950-59; prof. English Urbana Coll., Ohio, 1959-64, Ohio U., Athens, 1964-77, disting. prof., 1977—2003, disting. prof. emeritus, 2003—. Author: Bitter Knowledge, 1964 (Ohioana fiction award 1964), Hanger Stout, Awake!, 1967, The Charisma Campaigns, 1972, Collecting Rare Bodies For Pleasure and Profit, 1977, Sassafras, 1983, Crazy Women, 1985, Booking in the Heartland, 1986 (Ohioana Non-fiction award 1986), Ghostly Populations, 1986, Memoirs of a Bookman, 1989, Dirty Tricks, 1990, On The Shore of That Beautiful Shore (play), 1991, An Interview with the Sphinx (play), 1992, Storyhood As We Know It and Other Tales (stories), 1993, Booking Pleasures, 1996, (essays) Reading Matter, 2000, Schopenhauerova Vule, 2002, others. Served with USCG, 1943-45. Recipient numerous ind. artist awards Ohio Art Council, Major Artist award, 1989-90, Ohioana Career award, 2005; Guggenheim fellow, 1974-75 Mem. Phi Beta Kappa Home: 4314 Fisher Rd Athens OH 45701-9333 Office: Ohio U Dept English Athens OH 45701 Home Phone: 740-593-8915. Business E-Mail: matthej1@ohio.edu.

MATTHEWS, JOHN, human resources specialist, wholesale distribution executive; M in Finance. Various positions in human resources Costo Wholesale Corp., Issaquah, Wash., 1990—, sr. v.p., human resources and risk mgmt. Former comdr., logistics expert USN. Office: Costco Wholesale Corp 999 Lake Dr Issaquah WA 98027 Office Phone: 425-313-8100. Office Fax: 425-313-8103.*

MATTHEWS, KATHLEEN SHIVE, biochemistry educator; b. Austin, Tex., Aug. 30, 1945; d. William and Gwyn Shive; m. Randall Matthews. BS in Chemistry, U. Tex., 1966; PhD in Biochemistry, U. Calif., Berkeley, 1970. Post doctoral fellow Stanford (Calif.) U., 1970-72; mem. faculty Rice U., Houston, 1972—, chair dept., 1987-95, Wiess prof., 1989-96, Stewart Meml. chair, 1996—, dean natural scis., 1998—2008. Mem. BBCB study sect. NIH, Bethesda, Md., 1980-84, 86-88, BRSG adv. com., 1992-94; mem. adv. com. on rsch. programs Tex. Higher Edn. Coord. Bd., Austin, 1987-92; mem. undergrad. edn. initiative rev. panel Howard Hughes Rsch. Inst., Bethesda, 1991, mem. rsch. resources rev. panel, 1995, mem. predoctoral fellowships rev. panel, 2001, trustee S.W. Rsch. Inst., 2003—, steering com. adv. bd. Vinson & Elkins Women's Initiative, 2001-06. Mem. editl. bd. Jour. Biol. Chemistry, 1988-93, assoc. editor, 1994-99; contbr. 150 reviewed papers. Fellow AAAS; mem. Am. Soc. Biochemistry and Molecular Biology (nominating com. 1993-94, 96-97, fin. com. 2001-2002), Protein Soc., Biophys. Soc. (pub. affairs com. 2002-05), Am. Chem. Soc., Phi Beta Kappa. Office: Rice Univ Dept Biochem Cell Biology PO Box 1892 6100 Main St MS140 Houston TX 77005-1892 Office Phone: 713-348-4871. Business E-Mail: ksm@rice.edu.

MATTHEWS, KELLY E., chemistry professor; b. Pa. BS in Chemistry, Lehigh U., Bethlehem, Pa., 1988; PhD in Chemistry, Va. Tech., Blacksburg, 1992. Asst prof. chemistry Newberry Coll., SC, 1995—97; chemistry and physics tchr. Warwick HS, Lititz, Pa., 1997—2002; prof. sci. HACC, Lancaster, Pa., 2002—, chair, sci. dept, 2007—. Office: HACC Ctrl Pa CC 1641 Old Philadelphia Pike Lancaster PA 17602 Business E-Mail: kematthe@hacc.edu.

MATTHEWS, MILDRED SHAPLEY, retired editor; b. Pasadena, Calif., Feb. 15, 1915; d. Harlow and Martha (Betz) Shapley; m. Ralph Vernon Matthews, Sept. 25, 1937; children: June Lorrain, Bruce Shapley, Melvin Lloyd, Martha Alys. AB, U. Mich., 1936. Rsch. asst. Calif. Inst. Tech., Pasadena, 1950—61; bilingual editor, rsch. asst. Astron. Obs. Merate-Milan and Trieste, Italy, 1960—70; rsch. asst. Lunar-Planetary Lab., editor space sci. series U. Ariz., Tucson, 1970—96; ret., 1996. Contbr. articles to Sky and Telescope, Astronomia. Recipient Masursky Meritorious Svc. award div. planetary sci. Am. Astron. Soc., 1993. Avocations: classical music concerts, especially opera, travel. Home: 3154 Del Vina St Pasadena CA 91107

MATTHEWS, NORMAN STUART, retail executive; b. Boston, Jan. 13, 1933; s. Martin W. and Charlotte (Cohen) M.; m. Joanne Banks, June 11, 1956; children: Gary S., Jeffrey B., Patricia A. BA, Princeton U.; MBA, Harvard U. Ptnr. Beacon Mktg. and Advt. Assocs., NYC, 1956-71; sr. v.p. Broyhill Furniture Co., Lenoir, NC, 1971-73, E.J. Korvettes, NYC, 1973-78; chmn., chief exec. officer Gold Circle Stores, Columbus, Ohio, 1978-82; vice chmn. Federated Dept. Stores, Cin., from 1982, pres., chief oper. officer, 1987-88, retail cons., 1988—. Dir. Progressive Corp., Finlay Fine Jewelry, NYC, Henry Schein, Inc., Melville, NY. Office Phone: 212-308-5605. Personal E-mail: normanmatthews@yahoo.com.

MATTHEWS, PAMELA R., literature and language professor, dean; b. Bryan, Tex., Oct. 4, 1953; d. Blanche L. and Jack R. Matthews; m. Dennis A. Berthold, June 23, 1984; 1 child, Matthew Erich Berthold. BA in English, U. Houston, 1977; MA in English, Tex. A&M U., Coll. Sta., 1981; PhD in English, Duke U., Durham, NC, 1988. Prof. English Tex. A&M U., Coll. Sta., 2006—, assoc. dean liberal arts, 2006—. Contbr. articles to profl. jours.; editor: (documentary) Perfect Companionship: Ellen Glasgow's Selected Correspondence with Women. Liberal. Avocations: travel, piano, reading. Home: 1204 Marsteller Ave College Station TX 77840-2519 Office: Tex A&M Univ Coll Liberal Arts 4223 TAMU College Station TX 77843-4223 Business E-Mail: p-matthews@tamu.edu.

MATTHEWS, PHILIP RICHARD, lawyer; b. San Francisco, Aug. 27, 1952; s. Richard Thomas and Marjorie Hilda (Dean) M.; m. Dana Lynn Meier, Aug. 8, 1981; children: Lauren Alison, Lyndsey Ann. BA in Polit. Sci., George Washington U., 1974; JD, U. Calif.-San Francisco, 1977. Bar: Calif. 1978, US Ct. Appeals (9th cir.) 1978, US Dist. Ct. (no. and so. dists.) Calif. 1978, US Dist. Ct. (ea. dist.) Calif. 1980. Assoc. Dinkelspiel, Plevin, Steefel & Levit, San Francisco, 1978—80, Hancock, Rothert & Bunshoft LLP, San Francisco, 1980—85, ptnr., 1985—2005, mng. ptnr., 1992—94, 1997—99, chairperson, 2004—05; ptnr. Duane Morris, LLP, 2006—, mem. ptnr.'s bd., 2006—. Spkr. in field. Bd. govs. U. Calif., Hastings Coll. of Law. Mem.: ABA, State Bar Assn. of Calif., Bar Assn. of San Francisco, Commonwealth Club. Democrat. Episcopalian. Avocations: sports, outdoors, genealogy, travel, hiking. Office: Duane Morris LLP Ste 2000 One Market, Spear Tower San Francisco CA 94105-1104 Home Phone: 925-930-6043; Office Phone: 415-957-3174. Office Fax: 415-520-5640. Business E-Mail: prmatthews@duanemorris.com.*

MATTHEWS, ROBIN ADELE, environmental scientist, educator; b. Missoula, Ga., Mar. 3, 1952; d. Ervin W. and Lura A. Maetche; m. Geoffrey B. Matthews, June 15, 1973; children: Guinevere A., Elizabeth A. BS, U. Calif., Riverside, 1973; MS, Ind. U., Bloomington, 1978; PhD, Va. Poly. Inst., Blacksburg, 1981. Environ. scientist DuPont-Savannah River Lab., Aiken, SC, 1981—84, Kennedy, Jenks Engrs., Irvine, Calif., 1985; lectr. Western Wash. U., Bellingham, 1986—90, prof., 1990—, dir., Inst. Watershed Studies, 2008—. Office: Inst Watershed Studies 516 High St Bellingham WA 98225 Office Fax: 360-650-6470. Business E-Mail: robin.matthews@wwu.edu.

MATTHEWS, RONDRA J., publishing executive; b. Inglewood, Calif., July 13, 1955; d. Nedra Plummer; m. Keith Matthews. BS in Behavioral Sci., High Point U.; MBA, Rollins Coll. Former pres. Better Bus. Bur. Ctrl. Fla.; various mgmt. positions Orlando (Fla.) Sentinel Comms., 1980—99, v.p., gen. mgr., 1999—2000; pres., pub., CEO Daily Press, Newport News, Va., 2000—06; publisher, CEO Baltimore Sun Co., 2006—07. Bd. dirs. Peninsula Alliance for Econ. Devel., Hampton Roads Partnership, Greater Peninsula NOW; bd. advisors Christopher Newport U. Sch. Bus.; chair-elect bd. dirs. United Way of the Va. Peninsula.

MATTHEWS, STEVE ALLEN, lawyer; b. Columbia, SC, Oct. 11, 1955; s. Philip Garland and Vernecia Neely (Wilson) M.; m. Caroline Elizabeth FitzSimons, Sept. 26, 1987; children: Philip Garland II, Nathalie FitzSimons, Caroline Salley. BA in History, U. S.C., 1977; JD, Yale U., 1980. Bar: S.C. 1980, D.C. 1982. Assoc. Boyd, Knowlton, Tate & Finlay, Columbia, 1980—81, Dewey, Ballantine, Bushby, Palmer & Wood, Washington, 1981—85; spl. counsel to asst. atty. gen. Civil Rights Divsn. U.S. Dept. Justice, Washington, 1985—86, dep. asst. atty. gen. for jud. selection, Office of Legal Policy, 1986—88; exec. asst. to U.S. Atty. Gen., 1988; mem. Haynsworth Sinkler Boyd, PA, Columbia, 1988—, mng. ptnr., 2001—08; nominated by pres. Bush 4th Cir. Ct. of Apeals, 2007. Sec. Landmark Legal Found., 2003—07; chair Gov.'s Edn. Reform Coun., SC, 2005—06. Mem. Federalist Soc., Nat. Assn. Bond Lawyers (bd. dirs. 1995-96), Am. Coll. Bond Counsel (bd. dirs. 1995-99), Collegiate Network, Inc. (chmn. bd. dirs.), 1995-2007, Am. Intellectual Property Law Assn., SC Ind. Colls. and Univs. (bd. dirs.), 2004-07, Phila. Soc., St. Andrews Soc. Columbia, Jr. Achievement (bd. dirs.), 2004-07, SC Govs. Sch. Sci. Maths. Found.(bd. dirs. 2009-). Office: Haynsworth Sinkler Boyd PA 1201 Main St Fl 22 Columbia SC 29201-3226 Office Phone: 803-779-3080. Business E-Mail: smatthews@hsblawfirm.com.

MATTHEWS, THOMAS J., game company executive; BS in Fin., U. So. Calif., 1986. From pres. to pres., CEO, COO Global Gaming Distributors Inc. (acquired by Anchor Gaming), Reno; pres., CEO, chmn. Anchor Gaming (acquired by Internat. Game. Tech.), 1994—2001; COO Internat. Game Tech., 2001—03, pres., CEO, COO, 2003—05, chmn., pres., CEO, COO, 2005—. Office: International Game Technology 9295 Prototype Dr Reno NV 89521-8986

MATTHEWS, WAIDE KAREEM, librarian; b. Pitts., Mar. 9, 1972; s. Waide David and Bonita Adria Matthews; m. Roxanne Hoy, May 5, 2000; children: Peri Madison, Chelsea Leigh. BA, U. Pitts. Libr. technician U. Pitts., 1995—.

MATTHEWS, WYHOMME S., retired music educator, academic administrator; b. Battle Creek, Mich., July 22, 1948; d. Woodrow R. and LouLease (Graham) Sellers; m. Edward L. Matthews, Apr. 29, 1972; children: Channing DuVall, Triston Curran, Landon Edward, Brandon Graham. AA, Kellogg C.C., 1968; MusB, Mich. State U., 1970, MA, MusM, Mich. State U., 1972. Cert. elem. and secondary tchr. Mich. Tchr., vocal music dir. Benton Harbor (Mich.) Pub. Schs., 1971-72, dir. vocal music, 1972; dir. edn. head start program Burlington (N.J.) County, 1972-73; pvt. music tchr., 1973-89; tchr. Southeastern Jr. H.S., 1986-87, W.K. Kellogg Jr. H.S., 1987-89; chair visual and performing arts dept. Kellogg C.C., Battle Creek, Mich., 1989-99, dir. Eastern acad. Ctr., 1999—2003, ret., 2003. Part-time instr. Kellogg C.C., 1973—, dir. Eclectic Chorale, 1973-2005, dir., organizer Kellogg C.C. Eclectic Chorale Sacred Cultural Festival, 1979—, judge various contests; artistic dir. Battle Creek Sojourner Truth Monument Presentation Day, 1999; presenter in field. Pres. Dudley Elem. Sch., 1981-85; active Battle Creek Pub. Schs. PTA, Pennfield Pub. Schs. PTA, Mt. Zion African Meth. Episc. Ch.; v.p. Life Care Amb. Bd., 1990-2008; bd. dirs. Leila Aboretum Soc.; mem. Battle Creek Cmty. Found., Glen Cross Arts and Infrasture Fund, CEO, pres., 2007, dir. cmty. choir; artistic dir. Battle Creek Dr. Martin Luther King Cmty. Celebration, 2003. Recipient Outstanding Cmty. Svc. award, 1975, Sojourner Truth award, 2000, George award, City of Battle Creek, 2000; fellow, Mich. State U., 1971. Mem. Mich. Music Tchr. Assn., Nat. Music Tchrs. Assn., Battle Creek Music Tchrs. Assn., Battle Creek Morning Music Club (bd. dirs.), Nat. Leadership Acad., Battle Creek Cmty. Concert Assn. Home: 466 Alton Ave Battle Creek MI 49017-3212 Home Phone: 269-964-2228. Personal E-mail: wmatth5278@aol.com.

MATTHIES, FREDERICK JOHN, civil and environmental engineer; b. Omaha, Oct. 4, 1925; s. Fred. J. and Charlotte Leota (Metz) M.; m. Carol Mae Dean, Sept. 14, 1947; children: John Frederick, Jane Carolyn Matthies Goding BSCE, Cornell U., 1947; postgrad., U. Nebr., 1952-53. Bd. cert. Am. Acad. Environ. Engrs.; registered profl. engr., Nebr. Civil engr. Henningson, Durham & Richardson, Omaha, 1947-50, 52-54; sr. v.p. devel. Leo A. Daly Co., Omaha, 1954-90; cons. engr., 1990—. Lectr. in field; mem. dist. export coun. U.S. Dept. Commerce, 1981-83. Contbr. articles to profl. jours. Mem. Douglas County Rep. Cen. Com., Nebr., 1968-72; bd. regents Augustana Coll., Sioux Falls., S.D., 1976-89; bd. dirs. Orange County Luth. Hosp. Assn., Anaheim, Calif., 1961-62, Nebr. Humanities Coun., 1988-94, Omaha-Shizuoka City (Japan) Sister City Orgn.; trustee Luth. Med. Ctr., Omaha, 1978-82; mem. adv. bd. Marine Mil. Acad., Harlingen, Tex. 1st lt. USMCR, 1943-46, 50-52, Korea. Fellow ASCE, Instn. Civil Engrs. (London), Euro Engr. European Econ. Commn.; mem. NSPE, Am. Water Works Assn. (life), Air Force Assn., Am. Legion, VFW. Home: 950 Southridge Greens Blvd # 15 Fort Collins CO 80525-6726

MATTHIESEN, LEROY THEODORE, bishop emeritus; b. Olfen, Tex., June 11, 1921; s. Joseph A. and Rosa (Englert) Matthiesen. BA, Josephinum Coll., Columbus, Ohio, 1942; MA, Cath. U., Washington, 1961; LittD, Register Sch. Journalism., Denver, 1962. Ordained priest Diocese of Amarillo, Tex., 1946, editor, West Tex. Cath., 1948—, bishop, 1980—97, bishop emeritus, 1997—; prin. Alamo Cath. HS, 1969—; pastor St. Francis Parish, 1972—; ordained bishop, 1980. Roman Catholic. Office: Diocese of Amarillo 1800 N Spring St PO Box 5644 Amarillo TX 79107-5644

MATTHIESSEN, PETER, author; b. NYC, May 22, 1927; s. Erard A. and Elizabeth (Carey) Matthiessen; m. Patricia Southgate, Feb. 8, 1951 (div.); m. Deborah Love, May 8, 1963 (dec. Jan. 1972); children: Lucas, Sara, Rue, Alexander; m. Maria Eckhart, Nov. 28, 1980. BA, Yale U., New Haven, 1950; degree (hon.), Yale U., 2007. Co-founder The Paris Review, 1953. Author: (fiction) Race Rock, 1954, Partisans, 1955, Raditzer, 1961, At Play in the Fields of the Lord, 1965, Far Tortuga, 1975, On the River Styx and Other Stories, 1989, Killing Mister Watson, 1990, Lost Man's River, 1997, Bone By Bone, 1999, Shadow Country, 2008 (Nat. Book award for fiction, 2008), (non-fiction) Wildlife in America, 1959, The Cloud Forest: A Chronicle of the South American Wilderness, 1961, Under the Mountain Wall: A Chronicle of Two Seasons in the Stone Age, 1962, The Shorebirds of North America, 1967, Oomingmak, 1967, Sal Si Puedes: Cesar Chavez and the New American Revolution, 1969, Blue Meridian. The Search for the Great White Shark, 1971, The Tree Where Man was Born, 1972, The Snow Leopard, 1978 (Nat. Book award, 1980), Sand Rivers, 1981, In the Spirit of Crazy Horse, 1983, Indian Country, 1984, Nine-headed Dragon River: Zen Journals 1969-1982, 1986, Men's Lives: The Surfmen and Bayen of the South Fork, 1986, African Silences, 1991, Baikal: Sacred Sea of Siberia, 1992, East of Lo Monthang: In the Land of Mustang, 1995, The Peter Matthiessen Reader: Nonfiction, 1959-1961, 2000, Tigers in the Snow, 2000, The Birds of Heaven: Travels With Cranes, 2001, End of the Earth: Voyages to Antarctica, 2003. Trustee NY Zool. Soc., 1965—78. Named Offl. State Author of NY, NY State Writers Inst., 1995—97. Mem.: AAAL, AAAS.

MATTICE, DEBORA J., special education educator, consultant; b. Concord, Calif., June 21, 1959; d. Fred Alexander and Sarah Elizabeth Elder; m. Galen Donald Mattice, July 24, 1993; 1 child, Paul Daniel Reininger. AS, Monroe C.C., 1990; BS, SUNY, Brockport, 1990; MS, Nazareth Coll., 1995; postgrad., Cumberland U., 2002. Cert. profl. tchg. State Dept. Edn., Tenn., permanent tchg. State of N.Y. Tchr. Rochester City Sch., 1993—94, spl. edn. tchr., 1995—96, Dede Wallace Sch., Nashville, 1996, Stones River Acad., Murfreesboro, Tenn., 1996—97, Metro Nashville Sch., 1997—. Notary pub., Tenn. Foster parent Dept. Children's Svcs., Davidson County. Mem.: Assn. Supr. and Curriculum Design, Christian Educators Assn., Nat. Geographic, Smithsonian Instn.,

Davison County Foster and Adoptive Care Assn. (sec. 2000—06), Am. Civil Liberties Union, Kappa Delta Epsilon Phi, Kappi Delta Pi. Democrat. Presbyterian. Avocations: reading, crafts, writing. Home: 5020 Sunshine Dr Antioch TN 37013 Office: John F Kennedy Middle School 2087 Hobson Pike Antioch TN 37013-1119 Office Phone: 615-941-7515 ext. 1216, 615-501-7900 ext. 1136. Business E-Mail: missman@comcast.net.

MATTICE, HARRY SANDLIN, JR., federal judge, former prosecutor; b. Chattanooga, Tenn., Mar. 10, 1954; s. Harry Sandlin Sr. and Kathryn (McCoy) M.; m. Janet Lynn LeVan, Jan 4, 1975; children: Harry Sandlin III, Bryan Christopher, Kevin LeVan. BS, U. Tenn., Chattanooga, 1976; JD, U. Tenn., 1981. Bar: Tenn. 1981, US Dist. Ct. (ea. dist.) Tenn. 1981, US Ct. Appeals (6th cir.) 1984, US Tax Ct. 1984, US Claims Ct. 1984, US Dist. Ct. (we. dist.) Tenn. 1989. Staff acct. Deloitte, Haskins & Sells, Chattanooga, 1976-78; from assoc. to ptnr. Miller & Martin, Chattanooga, 1981—2000; shareholder Baker, Donelson, Bearman & Caldwell, Chattanooga, 2000—01; U.S. atty. (ea. dist.) Tenn. US Dept. Justice, 2001—05; judge US Dist. Ct. (ea. dist.) Tenn., Chattanooga, 2005—. Pres. Chattanooga Tax Practitioners, 1987-88; sr. counsel U.S. Senate Com. on Govtl. Affairs, Spl. Investigation, 1997. Asst. to pres. Chattanooga Goodwill Industries, 1988-92; chmn. Hamilton County Rep. Party, 1993-95. Mem. Order of Coif, Rotary Club Chattanooga, Tenn., Phi Kappa Phi. Republican. Episcopalian. Home: 609 Marr Dr Signal Mountain TN 37377-2280 Office: US Dist Ct Rm 104 900 Georgia Ave Chattanooga TN 37402

MATTICE, HOWARD LEROY, education educator; b. Roxbury, NY, Sept. 23, 1935; s. Charles Pierce and Loretta Jane (Ellis) M.; m. Elaine Grace Potts, Feb. 4, 1956 (dec. Jan. 2002); children: Kevin, Stephen. BA, King's Coll., 1960; MA, L.I. U., 1965, NYU, 1969; cert., CUNY, 1972; EdD, NYU, 1978. Cert. tchr. N.Y., clin. educators trainer, Fla. Dept. Edn. Social studies tchr. NYC Bd. Edn., 1961-90, mid. and jr. HS asst. prin., 1970-72, 73-75; assoc. prof. edn. and history Clearwater Christian Coll., Fla., 1990-92, chmn. divsn. edn., prof. edn. and history, 1992-99, prof. edn. and history, 2002—; social studies curriculum writer Accelerated Christian Edn., 2003. Adj. lectr. history SI CC, CUNY, 1969-75; curriculum writer NYC Bd. Edn., 1985, Accelerated Christian Edn., Largo, Fla., 2003—; program reviewer Fla. Dept. Edn., Tallahassee, 1994—; item writer GED Testing Svc., Washington, 1988-92; mem. So. Assn. Colls. and Schs. Accreditation Team HS, 1995—; adj. prof. DeVry U., Tampa, Fla. 2004-06; adj. prof. Derry U., 2004-2006; conversational English tchr., Chengdu, China, 2006. Chmn. bd. New Dorp Christian Acad., S.I., 1973-90; chmn. bd. deacons New Dorp. Bapt. Ch., S.I., 1981-90. Mem. Assn. Tchr. Educators, Nat. Coun. Social Studies, So. Assn. Colls. and Schs. (h.s. accreditation review team 1995—). Avocations: reading, travel, gardening. Office Phone: 727-726-1153 ext. 259. Business E-Mail: howardmattice@clearwater.edu.

MATTILA, EDWARD CHARLES, music educator; b. Duluth, Minn., Nov. 30, 1927; s. Edward H. and Ellen M. (Matson) M.; m. Nancy Ann Norton, Oct. 12, 1956; children: Amy Lara, Edward Norton. BA in Music, U. Minn., 1950, PhD in Music Theory and Composition, 1963; MMus, New Eng. Conservatory, 1956. Instr. Concordia Coll., St. Paul, 1958-62; asst. prof. Bishop Coll., Dallas, 1962-64; faculty U. Kans., Lawrence, 1964—, prof. music, 1975—, producer, host program contemporary music Sta. KANU, 1971—. Served with Signal Corps, U.S. Army, 1952-53. Grantee in field. Mem. Am. Soc. Univ. Composers, Coll. Music Soc., Am. Music Ctr. Composer: Symphony No. 1, Theme and Variations for 2 pianos, Partitions for String Orch., 6 arrays for piano, Repercussions for Tape, Movements for Computer and Dancers, Six by Six, Seaborne for Solo Dancer & Tape, Pelagos, Caracole, Primordius, Dreaming up the Cosmos, Proa, (cd recordings) View from the Keyboard, Extended Resources, Electrophonic Means. Office: U Kans Sch Fine Arts Lawrence KS 66045-0001 Personal E-mail: edmattila@comcast.net.

MATTINGLY, MACK FRANCIS, former ambassador, Former United States Senator, Georgia, entrepreneur; b. Anderson, Ind., Jan. 7, 1931; m. Carolyn Longcamp, 1957 (dec.); children: Jane, Anne; m. Leslie Ann Davisson, 1998. BS, Ind. U., 1957. Acct. supr. IND, Arvin, Ind., 1957-59; mktg. rep. IBM, Ga., 1959-79; owner, pres. M's Inc., Ga., 1975-80; U.S. senator from Ga., 1981-87; asst. sec. gen. def. support NATO, Brussels, 1987-90; amb. to Seychelles Dept. State, 1992-93. Spkr./author econ., def., fgn. policy, entrepreneur, 1993—; mem. U.S. Senate Com. Appropriations, chmn. legis. and mil. constrn. subcoms.; mem. energy and water devel., agt. rural devel., treasury, postal svc. and gen. govt., mil. constrn. legis. subcoms., U.S. Senate com. Banking, Housing and Urban Affairs, chmn. rural housing, econ. policy subcoms.; mem. select com. ethics, 1981-83, joint econ. com., 1983-87; chmn. Rep. Com. on Coms., mem. Rep. Senate Leadership, 1985-87, Holocaust Comm.; U.S. del. GATT, Geneva, 1982; bd. dirs. CompuCredit Corp.; hon. co-chmn. GMACC, Hemisphere, Inc. Author 40 U.S. Sen. Bills, Amendments and Resolutions. Sgt.-at-arms, Rep. Nat. Convs., del. Georgian Rep. Party Convs., 1964-90; chmn. 8th Dist. Goldwater for Pres., 1964, Ga. 8th Congl. Dist., Cand. U.S. Congress, 8th Dist., 1966; mem. Ga. Rep. Ctrl. Com.; mem. Ga. Exec. Com., vice chmn., 1968-75; chmn. Ga. Rep. Party, 1975-77; elected 1st Rep. U.S. Senator from Ga. since 1871, 1980; bd. dirs. NOVECON, Cumberland Preservation Soc., Inst. for Global Econ. Growth, Ga. Ports Authority; hon. bd. dirs. M.L. King Jr. Fed. Holiday Commn., Brunswick Golden Isles C. of C. Staff sgt. USAF, 1951-55. Recipient S.E. Father of Yr. award 1984, Ga. Wildlife Fed. Conservationist of Yr. award 1985, Selective Svc. System Dist. Svc. Gold medal 1985, Watchdog of Treasury award 1981-86, Nat. Taxpayers Union Taxpayers Best Friend award 1981-86, NFIB's Guardian of Small Bus. award 1981-86, Am. Security Coun. award 1981-86, Sec. Def. medal for Outstanding Pub. Svc. 1988. Episcopalian.

MATTIODA, ANDREW LIGE, chemist, researcher, space scientist; b. Hartshorne, Okla., Jan. 20, 1967; s. Tony and Gloria (Ranallo) Mattioda. AS, Ea. Okla. State Coll., Wilburton, 1987; BSc, East Ctrl. U., Ada, Okla., 1989; MSc in Chemistry, U. Okla., Norman, 1993, DSc in Chemistry, 1995. Cert. open water diver Profl. Assn. Diving Instrs., 1994, lic. pvt. pilot FAA, 2004. Environ. chemist US Army Corps. Engrs., Tulsa, Okla., 1995—99; vis. prof. U. Tulsa, 1999—2000, Rogers State U., Tulsa, 1999—2000; NRC fellow Ames Rsrch. Ctr. NASA, Moffett Field, Calif., 2000—03; rsch. scientist, prin. investigator Ames Astrochemsitry Lab. SETI Inst. NASA, Mountain View, Calif., 2003—07; rsch. scientist, space scientist NASA, Moffett Field, 2007—. Spkr. in field; lectr. in field. Contbr. articles to profl. jours. Coord. Mountain View Cath. Singles, Calif., 2000—02. Recipient Superior Performance Award, U.S. Army Corps. Engrs., 1996, Spl. Svc. Achievement award, 1997, Performance Evaluation award, 1997, 1998, Ark. Traveler award, Gov. Mike Huckabee, Ark., 2004, Safety award, NASA, 2007; fellow Karcher Fellowship, U. of Okla., 1989, Nat. Rsch. Coun., 2000—03. Mem.: AAAS, Am. Chem. Soc. (chmn. organizing annual chemistry day Tulsa chpt. 1997—98, co-chmn. environ. chemistry symposia), Profl. Assn. Diving Instrs., Nat. Italian Am. Found., Planetary Soc., Nat. Space Soc., Aircraft Owners and Pilots Assn. Roman Catholic. Achievements include identifying the possibility that polycyclic aromatic nitrogen heterocycles are present in interstellar space; research in molecular spectroscopy of interstellar polycyclic aromatic hydrocarbons and lunar dust. Avocations: hiking, travel, scuba diving, flying, cooking. Office: NASA MS245-6 Moffett Field CA 94035 Personal E-mail: andrew@mattioda.com. Business E-Mail: andrew.mattioda@nasa.gov.

MATTIS, DANIEL CHARLES, physicist, researcher; b. Brussels, Sept. 8, 1932; came to US, 1941; s. Joseph and Lucie (Applebaum) M. BS, MIT, Cambridge, 1953; MS, U. Ill., Urbana, 1954, PhD, 1957. Mem. rsch. staff IBM, NYC, 1959—65; prof. Belfer Grad. Sch. Yeshiva U., NYC, 1965—78; Thomas Potts prof. Polytech. U., NYC, 1978—80; prof. U. Utah, Salt Lake City, 1980—. Wei-Lun vis. prof. Chinese U. Hong Kong, 1997. Author: Theory of Magnetism, Vol. 1, 1981, Vol. 2, 1985, Many Body Theory, 1994, 2009, Statistical Mechanics Made Simple, 2003, 2nd edit., 2008, Theory of Magnetism Made Simple, 2006; mem. editl. bd. Internat. Jour. Modern Physics; contbr. articles to profl. jours. Fellow: Am. Phys. Soc. Achievements include 4 patents. Office: U Utah Dept Physics Salt Lake City UT 84112 Office Phone: 801-581-3690. Business E-Mail: mattis@physics.utah.edu.

MATTIS, JAMES N., career military officer; b. Seattle, 1950; Grad., Amphibious Warfare Sch., Command and Staff Coll., Nat. War Coll. Commd. 2d lt. USMC, 1972, advanced through grades to gen., 2007, rifle & weapons platoon comdr., 3rd Marine divsn., bn. landing team asst. ops. officer 1st Marine Brigade, asst. divsn. ops. officer, exec. officer, 7th Marines Regiment, commdr. 1st bn. 7th Marines Rgt. Saudi Arabia, comdr. 7th Marines Rgt., 1994-96; exec. sec. US Dept. Def., Washington, 1996-98, sr. mil. asst. to dep. sec.; dir. manpower plans & policy divsn. USMC, Washington, comdr. 1st Marine Expeditionary Brigade Afghanistan, comdr. Task Force 58, comdt. 1st Marine divsn., 2003—04, comdr. USMC Combat Devel. Command, dep. comdt. for combat devel., 2004—06, commdg gen. USMC I Marine Expeditionary Force, comdr USMC Forces Ctrl. Command Camp Pendleton, Calif., 2006—07; comdr. US Joint Forces Command (USJFCOM), Norfolk, Va., 2007—; supreme allied comdr. for transformation NATO, Brussels, 2007—. Decorated Def. Disting. Svc. award with oak leaf cluster, Navy Disting. Svc. medal, Def. Superior Svc. medal, Legion of Merit, Bronze Star with Combat V, Meritorious Svc. medal with 2 Gold award stars, Navy & Marine Corps Achievement medal, Combat Action Ribbon, Presdl. Unit Citation, Joint Meritorious Unit award, Navy Unit Commendation, Navy & Marine Corps Meritorious Unit Commendation, Marine Corps Expeditionary medal, Nat. Def. Svc. medal (with 2 Bronze Svc. stars), Southwest Asia Svc. medal (with 2 Bronze Svc. stars), Afghanistan Campaign medal, Iraq Campaign medal, Global war On Terror Expeditionary medal, Global War on Terrorism Svc. medal, Humanitarian Svc. medal, Sea Svc. Deployment Ribbon (with Bronze Svc. star), Marine Corps Recruiting Svc. Ribbon (with Bronze Svc. Star) Kuwait Liberation medal (Saudi Arabia), Kuwait Liberation medal (Kuwait) Achievements include serving in Operation Desert Storm, Operation Enduring Freedom and Operation Iraqi Freedom. Office: US Joint Forces Command (USJFCOM) 1562 Mitscher Ave Ste 200 Norfolk VA 23551*

MATTISON, PRISCILLA JANE, lawyer; d. Verne Sylvester and Virginia M.; m. Bernard M. Resnick, Aug. 4, 1995. Student in Comm., Technical U. Berlin, 1982—83; BA, Yale U., 1982; cert. in producing, Am. Film Inst., LA, 1987; JD, U. Pa., 1997; student of, Jeff Corey, Malibu, Calif., 1989, Judish Weston, LA, 1994, Don Richardson, Ron Richards, Westwood, Calif., 1989. Bar: Pa. 1997, D.C. 1999. Distbn. dir. Michael Blackwood Prodns., NYC, 1985-86; dir. devel., head of casting/head of overseas prodn. Concorde Pictures, LA, 1987-90; ind. filmmaker LA, 1990-94; assoc. Harkins Cunningham, Phila., 1997—2000; staff atty. Clean Air Coun., Phila., 2000—02; assoc. atty. Bernard M. Resnick Esq. PC, 2000—08; of counsel to Bernard M. Resnick, Esq., P.C., 2008—. Instr. bus. law Art. Inst. Phila., 2000; instr. bus. mgmt., music KAJEM recording arts program Cabrini Coll., 2002—05; invited spkr. in field. Dir., assoc. prodr. numerous films, 1987-90; screenwriter, 1988-94; songwriter, 1983—; photographer; author numerous poems. Sec. Penn Valley Civic Assn., Pa., 1998-2006, mem. Natural Lands Trust Phila Zoo. Named Pa. Rising Star, Super Lawyers Mag., 2005, 06, 07; Merit scholarship RCA, 1978-81, Fulbright grantee, 1982-83. Mem. Phila. Bar Assn., Fulbright Alumni Assn. (bd. dirs. Delaware Valley chpt. 1997-2002), BMI, NY Women in Film and T.V., Rec. Acad. (assoc.), Internat. Assn. Entertainment Lawyers, Nature Conservancy, PennFuture, Lower Merion Conservancy, Bridlewild Trails Assn., Pa. Horticultural Soc., Internat. Documentary Assn. Avocations: travel, photography, writing, songwriting, hiking. Office: Bernard M Resnick Esq PC Two Bala Plaza Ste 300 Bala Cynwyd PA 19004 Office Phone: 610-660-7774. Personal E-mail: smattison@aol.com.

MATTNER, JOCHEN, medical educator, researcher; s. Gerhard and Heidi Mattner; m. Elizabeth Araujo, July 28, 2007. MD, U. Erlangen, Germany, 2001. Rsch. assoc. U. Chgo., 2003—05, rsch. asst. prof., 2006—07; asst. prof. CCHMC, Cin., 2008—. Organisator, Cin., 2008. Recipient Fritz and Ursula Melchers Price, European Socs. Immunology, 2006. Achievements include discovery of characterization of first endogenous and microbial antigens of NKT cells. Office: CCHMC 3333 Burnet Ave Cincinnati OH 45229 Business E-Mail: jochen.mattner@cchmc.org.

MATTOO, AADITYA, economist; PhD in Economics, Kings Coll., Cambridge, 1990. Counsellor World Trade Orgn., Geneva, 1991—99; lead economist World Bank, Washington, 1999—. Office: World Bank 1818 H Street NW Washington DC 20433 Office Fax: 202-522-1159. Business E-Mail: amattoo@worldbank.org.

MATTOON, DANIEL J., lobbyist; m. Jane Mattoon. Congl. aide US Congressman Tom Corcoran, 1977—84, US Congressman John Grotberg, 1985—86; v.p. Congl. affairs BellSouth Corp., 1986—2001; dep. chmn. Nat. Rep. Congl. Com., 1999—2000; polit. and strategic legis. counsel US House and Senate Republicans; co-founder, co-chmn. PodestaMattoon, Washington, 2001—06; founder, pres. Mattoon & Assocs., Washington, 2006—. Named one of Fabulous Fifty, Roll Call, Top Hired Guns, The Hill. Office: Mattoon & Assocs 660 Pennsylvania Ave SE Ste 301 Washington DC 20003 Office Phone: 202-544-9760. Office Fax: 202-544-9764.*

MATTOON, PETER MILLS, lawyer; b. Bryn Mawr, Pa., Oct. 22, 1931; s. Harold Gleason and Marguerite Jeanette (Mills) M.; m. Mary Joan Henley, June 27, 1953; children: Pamela M. Zisselman, R. Stephen, Peter H., Philip P. AB, Dartmouth Coll., 1953; LLB, Harvard U., 1959; LLD (hon.), Widener U., 2001. Bar: Pa. 1960. Assoc. Ballard Spahr Andrews & Ingersoll, Phila., 1959-67; ptnr. Ballard Spahr Andrews & Ingersoll, LLP, Phila., 1967—2001, sr. counsel, 2002—. Emeritus trustee Episcopal Acad., Merion, Pa., 1970—, past chmn.; trustee, v.p. Widener Meml. Found., Lafayette Hill, Pa., 1972—; trustee, Thomas Jefferson U., Phila., 1989—; overseer Widener U. Law Sch., Wilmington, 1979—. Lt. USN, 1953-56. Office: Ballard Spahr Andrews & Ingersoll LLP 1735 Market St Fl 51 Philadelphia PA 19103-7599 Business E-Mail: mattoon@ballardspahr.com.

MATTOON, SCOTT ALEXANDER, private school educator; b. NYC, May 12, 1969; s. David Scott and Diana Mattoon; m. Dawn Rachel Gray, July 6, 1996; children: Ryland David, Avery Rachel. BA, Trinity Coll., 1991; MA, UCLA, 1994. Tchr. St. Mark's Sch. Tex., Dallas, 1991—92, UCLA, 1992—94, Collegiate Sch., NYC, 1997—2000; tchr., head lang. dept. Webb Sch. Calif., Claremont, 1994—97; tchr. Choate Rosemary Hall, Wallingford, Conn., 2000—08, head lang. dept., 2006—08; outreach coord. Oreg. Roadmap to Lang. Excellence, Ctr. Applied 2nd Lang. Studies U. Oreg., 2009—. Vis. evaluator Chase Collegiate Acad., Waterbury, Conn., 2004; mem. evaluation com. New Eng. Assn. Schs. and Colls., 2006. Recipient Excellence in Tchg. award, Webb Sch., 1996, Collegiate Sch., 1998—99; NEH ind. study grantee, Coun. Basic Edn., 1996. Mem.: Alliance Francaise, Am. Assn. Tchrs. French (chmn. nat. French contest 1997—2000). Business E-Mail: smattoon@choate.edu.

MATTOX, CLAUDE, councilman; m. Sherri Mattox. V.p. Nat. Western Vistas Real Estate; owner Desert Sun Enterprises; councilman, Dist.5 Phoenix City Coun., 2000—; vice mayor City of Phoenix, 2002. Chmn. Natural Resources, Pub. Safety & Vets. Coms.; mem. Transp. & Infrastructure, Econ., Commerce & Sustainability Coms. Chmn. Nat. League Cities EENR Steering & Policy Com.; exec. com. & bd. mem. Western Maricopa Coalition; bd. mem. Gomper's Habilitation Ctr., West Phoenix Bus. Alliance, Maryvale U.N.I.T.E., Phoenix Econ. Devel. Task Force; chmn. Maryvale Village Planning & Desert West Park Planning Coms., West Phoenix Cactus League Spring Baseball Coalition, Phoenix Surface Transp. Adv. Com., Maricopa Neighbors Airport Noise & Safety Com.; mem. Valley of the Sun West Phoenix Branch YMCA Founders Com., Desert Sky YMCA Ext. Adv. Com.; founding mem. Maryvale Citizens for Arts Programming Com. Mem.: Ariz. Mcpl. Water Users Assn. (bd. mem. & treas.). Office: 200 W Washington St 11th Fl Phoenix AZ 85003 Office Phone: 602-262-7446. Office Fax: 602-495-0628. Business E-Mail: council.district.5@phoenix.gov.*

MATTOX, JOHNNY LYNN, biologist, educator; b. Corinth, Miss., Apr. 13, 1951; s. Oliver Lee Mattox Jr. and Margaret Joyce Mills; m. Glenda Jean Eaton, Aug. 11, 1973; children: Jason Lynn, Jenny Amanda, Julia Elizabeth. AA, NE Miss. C.C., Booneville, 1971; BA Edn., U. Miss., Jackson, 1973, MCS, 1974, PhD, 1979. Tchr. sci. Kossuth HS., Miss., 1973—74; instr. sci. Itawamba CC, Fulton, Miss., 1975—80; instr. Biology NE Miss. CC, Booneville, 1981—2005; HEADWAE faculty rep. Blue Mountain Coll., Miss., 2008—09, assoc. prof. Biology, 2005—. Adj. asst. prof. Miss. U. Women, Columbus, 1984—2000, U. Miss., University, 1991—93, 1996—, U. Tenn. Martin, Selmer, 2000—; chair dept. math. and natural scis. Blue Mountain Coll., 2007—; vice chair, sci. edn. div. Miss. Acad. Scis. Chmn. Sci. Edn. divsn. Miss. Acad. Sci., 1980—81, vice chmn. sci. edn. dvsn., 2008—09; deacon Union Bapt. Ch., Kossuth, 1963—, treas., 1963—, organist, 1963—. Recipient HEADWARE Faculty award, Blue Mountain Coll., 2009; named Outstanding Coll. Sci. Tchr., MS Sci. Tchrs. Assn., 2008. Mem.: NSTA, SAR (Booneville chpt.), Assn. Southeastern Biologists, Miss. Acad. Scis., Miss. Sci. Tchrs. Assn. (Outstanding Coll. Sci. Tchr. award 2008—09), Nat. Assn. Biology Tchrs., Alcorn County Hist. Soc. (pres. 1982—83), Kossuth Hist. Soc. (pres. 1996—98), Kappa Delta Pi, Phi Theta Kappa (advisor 1979—2005), Phi Kappa Phi. Baptist. Home Phone: 662-462-5637; Office Phone: 662-685-4771 ext. 164. Business E-Mail: jmattox@bmc.edu.

MATTOX, SHARON M., lawyer; b. Wichita Falls, Tex., Oct. 4, 1952; BA, Emporia State U., 1974; JD, U. Tex., 1974, PhD, 1978. Ptnr. Vinson & Elkins LLP, Houston, environ. law sect. Fellow: Tex. Bar Found. Office: Vinson & Elkins LLP First City Tower 1001 Fannin St, Ste 2300 Houston TX 77002 Office Phone: 713-758-4598. E-mail: smattox@velaw.com.

MATTRAN, DONALD ALBERT, management consultant, educator; b. Chgo., July 8, 1934; s. George Charles and Lucille Alice (Boule) M.; m. Betty Elena Flores, July 18, 1953 (div. Mar. 1988); children: Donald, Julie, Kimberly, Guy, Christy; m. Rose Lynn Castellano, May, 1988. B.Mus., U. Mich., 1957, M.Mus., 1960. Tchr. Van Buren Schs., Belleville, Mich., 1957-61; asst. prof. U. N.H., Durham, 1961-65, Boston U., 1965-66; assoc. prof. Hartt Sch. Music, West Hartford, Conn., 1966-82, dean, 1971-80; dir. Syracuse U. Sch. Music, NY, 1982-83; dean Sch. Fine and Performing Arts Montclair State Coll, Upper Montclair, NJ, 1983-87; pres. Sales Consultants of Sarasota (Fla.) Inc., 1987—. Cons. Music div. Kaman Corp., Bloomfield, Conn.; cons., evaluator Nat. Assn. Schs. of Music and Joint Commn. Theater and Dance Accreditation; guest condr. Hartford Symphony Orch., Hartt Opera Theatre, All-State Festivals, 1976-83, Soc. New Music, Syracuse, N.J. Sch. Arts Orch., 1985-87. Co-author: (with Mary Rasmussen) A Teacher's Guide to the Literature of Woodwind Instruments, 1966; condr.: rec. Concerto for Cello and Jazz Band, 1972. Chmn. adv. com. Prodigy Inc., Syracuse, 1982-86; trustee Conn. Opera Assn., 1977-80; bd. advs. Watkinson Sch. Creative Arts Program, Hartford, 1977-80; mem. humanities adv. com. N.J. Dept. Higher Edn., 1984—; mem. multi-disciplinary panel N.J. State Council on Arts, 1985-87; mem. adv. com. on auditions Met. Opera Nat. Council, 1984-87; mem. adv. com. Frank and Lydia Bergen Found., 1986-87; grants panelist, Sarasota County Arts Coun., 2005-; bd. mem. WUSF Ptnrs., 2006-; pres. Condo on the Bay Tower 1 Assn., 2007-; v.p. Condo on the Bay Mgmt. Corp., 2007-. Mem. Nat. Assn. Schs. Music (exec. bd., sec. 1978-81). Avocations: yachting, auto racing. Home: Apt 204 888 Boulevard Of The Arts Sarasota FL 34236-4827 Office: 1343 Main St Ste 600 Sarasota FL 34236-5630 Home Phone: 941-952-0639; Office Phone: 941-365-5151. Business E-Mail: dmattran@scsarasota.com.

MATTRICK, DONALD A., computer software company executive; Founder, chmn. Distinctive Software Inc. (acquired by Electronic Arts in 1991), 1982—91; sr. v.p. N.Am. Studios, exec. v.p., gen. mgr. EA Canada, v.p. Electronic Arts, Inc., 1991—96, exec. v.p. N.Am. Studios, 1996—97, pres. Worldwide Studios, 1997—2006; external advisor, entertainment & devices divsn. Microsoft Corp., 2007, sr. v.p., interactive entertainment bus., entertainment & devices divsn., 2007—. Office: Microsoft Corp One Microsoft Way Redmond WA 98052-7329*

MATTSON, HAROLD FRAZYER, JR., mathematics professor; s. Harold Frazyer and Jane (Reynolds) M.; m. Jeanette Asare, Oct. 2, 1966; children: David Frazyer, Jennifer. AB magna cum laude, Oberlin Coll., Ohio, 1951; PhD, MIT, Cambridge, 1955; Docteur Honoris Causa, U. Paul Sabatier, Toulouse, France, 1992. Mathematician AF Cambridge Rsch. Ctr., Bedford, Mass., 1955-60; mathematician Applied Rsch. Lab. GTE Sylvania, Waltham, Mass., 1960-69, Needham, Mass., 1969-71; owner Frazyer Rsch. Co., Syracuse, NY, 1971—; prof. Syracuse U., 1971-94, rsch. prof., 1994—2005, emeritus prof., 1994—. Mem. conf. bd. Applied Algebra and Error-Correcting Codes Symposia, 1986—91, 1997; sci. dir. Applied Algebra and Error-Correcting Codes 7, Toulouse, 1989; sci. co-chair Applied Algebra and Error-Correcting Codes 9, New Orleans, 1991, Applied Algebra and Error-Correcting Codes 12, Toulouse, 1997; cons. in field of discrete math. Author: Discrete Mathematics, 1993; mem. editl. bd. Applicable Algebra in Engring., Comm. and Computing, 1990-2007, co-editor-in-chief, 2007-08, mem. mng. bd.,

2009-, others; contbr. articles to profl. jours. Founding pres. S.E. Univ. Neighborhood Assn., Syracuse, 1973. Fellow IEEE (life); mem. Am. Math. Soc., Math. Assn. Am. Office Phone: 315-443-3046. Business E-Mail: hmattson@syr.edu.

MATTSON, INGRID, theology studies educator, religious organization administrator; married; 2 children. BA, U. Waterloo, 1987; PhD in Islamic Studies, U Chgo., 1999. Prof. Islamic studies, dir. Islamic chaplaincy Macdonald Ctr for Islamic Studies and Christian-Muslim Relations, Hartford Seminary, Conn., 1998—. Dir. Projects for Afghan Refugee Women, 1987—98; advisor to Afghan delegation UN Commn. on the Status of Women, 1995; vis. prof. Osgoode Law Sch., Toronto, 2003; spkr. in field. Advisor to PBS film project Muhammad: Legacy of a Prophet, 2001—02, assoc. editor The Muslim World; contbr. articles to profl. jours.; author: (book) The Story of the Qur'an (Blackwell), 2007. Bd. dirs. Nawawi Found., Chgo., 2000—. Mem.: Am. Acad. Religion, Middle East Studies Assn., Islamic Soc. N.Am. (v.p. 2001—06, pres. 2006—), Middle East Medievalists. Office: Hartford Seminary Duncan Black Macdonald Ctr 77 Sherman St Hartford CT 06105 also: Islamic Soc NAm PO Box 38 Plainfield IN 46168 Office Phone: 860-509-9531, 317-839-8157. Office Fax: 860-509-9539. Business E-Mail: imattson@hartsem.edu, isnapresident@isna.net.

MATTSON, JAMES STEWART, lawyer, environmental scientist, educator; b. Providence, July 22, 1945; s. Irving Carl and Virginia (Lutey) M.; m. Carol Sandry, Aug. 15, 1964 (div. 1979); children: James, Birgitta; m. Rana A. Fine, Jan. 5, 1983. BS in Chemistry, U. Mich., 1966, MS in Environ. Health Scis., 1969, PhD in Water Resources Scis., 1970; JD with honors, George Washington U., 1979. Bar: D.C. 1979, Fla. 1983, U.S. Dist. Ct. D.C. 1979, U.S. Dist. Ct. (so. dist.) Fla. 1984, U.S. Ct. Appeals (D.C. cir.) 1979, U.S. Ct. Claims 1985, U.S. Supreme Ct. 1985, U.S. Ct. Appeals (11th cir.) 1985, U.S. Ct. Appeals (5th cir.) 1987, U.S. Ct. Appeals (fed. cir.) 1990. Staff scientist Gulf Gen. Atomic Co., San Diego, 1970-71; dir. R & D Ouachita Industries, Inc., Monroe, La., 1971-72; asst. prof. chem. oceanography Rosenstiel Sch. Marine & Atmospheric Sci., U. Miami, Fla., 1972-76; phys. scientist NOAA, Washington, 1976-78; mem. profl. staff & congl. liaison Nat. Adv. Commn. on Oceans and Atmosphere, 1978-80; ptnr. Mattson & Pave, Washington, Miami, Key Largo, 1980-86, Mattson & Tobin, Key Largo, 1987-2000; founder/CEO Great House of Wine, Inc, Ft. Lauderdale, Fla. and Napa, Calif., 1997—2003; sole practitioner Key Largo, Fla., 2000—. Adj. prof. law U. Miami, 1983-93; cons. Alaska Dept. Environ. Conservation, 1981-91, cons. oil and hazardous material spills, natural res. damage assessment. Author: (with H.B. Mark) Activated Carbon: Surface Chemistry and Adsorption from Solution, 1971; editor (with others): Computers in Chemistry and Instrumentation, 8 vols., 1972-76; (with P.L. Grose) The Argo Merchant Oil Spill: A Preliminary Scientific Report, 1977, (with H.B. Mark) Water Quality Measurement: Modern Analytical Techniques, 1981; contbr. articles to profl. jours. Candidate dist. 120 Fla. Ho. of Reps., 1994. Fellow Fed. Water Pollution Control Adminstrn., 1967-68; recipient Spl. Achievement award U.S. Dept. Commerce, 1976-77; Regents Alumni scholar U. Mich., 1963. Mem. ABA, Am. Chem. Soc. (chmn. Symposium on Oil Spill Indentification 1971), Order of Coif. Avocations: photography, hiking, sailing, scuba diving, fishing. Address: PO Box 586 Key Largo FL 33037-0586 Home Phone: 305-451-3951; Office Phone: 305-451-3951. Personal E-mail: mattsonj@bellsouth.net. Business E-Mail: jmattson@mattsonlaw.com.

MATULICH, ERIKA, marketing educator; b. Sacramento, Sept. 14, 1963; d. Serge and Margarete (Manderscheid) M.; m. John H. Porter, 1995. BBA, Tex. Christian U., 1984, MBA, 1986; PhD, U. Wis., 1994. Profl. cert. marketer. Ops. officer M Bank Dallas, 1986-87; ops. analyst Bell Helicopter, Textron, Ft. Worth, 1987-89; teaching asst. U. Wis., Madison, 1989-92; instr. Tex. Christian U., Ft. Worth, 1986-89, asst. prof. mktg., 1993-98; assoc. prof. mktg. U. Tampa, Fla., 1998—. Market researcher All Saints Epis. Hosp., Ft. Worth, 1984, Shakespeare in the Park, Ft. Worth, 1985, Informart, Dallas, 1985; strategic planner Williamson-Dickie, Ft. Worth, 1985; presenter at confs. Editor: Pets.com, 1999—2000. Mem. Am. Mktg. Assn. (bd. dirs.), Soc. Mktg. Advances (Tchg. Champion 2001), Acad. Mktg. Sci., Ferret Lovers' Club Tex. (pres. 1996-98), Beta Gamma Sigma. Avocations: carriage driving, computers, ferrets, drawing. Office: U Tampa Box O 401 W Kennedy Blvd Tampa FL 33606-1450 Office Phone: 813-253-6221 3187. Business E-Mail: ematulich@ut.edu.

MATULICH, SERGE, accounting educator, writer; b. Split, Croatia, June 8, 1933; came to U.S., 1946; s. Daniel M. and Josephine (Schuster) Raseta; m. Margarete Manderscheid, Dec. 7, 1957; children: Alexander Matulich, Erika Matulich. BS in Acctg. with honors, Calif. State U., Sacramento, 1964; PhD in Bus., U. Calif., Berkeley, 1971. CPA, Fla.; cert. cost analyst. Grad. asst. U. Calif., Davis, 1964-65; asst. prof. Calif. State U., Hayward, 1966-67; assoc. in acctg. U. Calif., Berkeley, 1968-71, vis. asst. prof., 1974-75; asst. prof. Sch. Bus. Ind. U., 1971-76; assoc. prof. acctg. Sch. Bus. Tex. Christian U., 1976-84; vis. prof. U. North Tex., spring 1983; prof. Crummer Grad. Sch. Bus. Rollins Coll., Winter Park, Fla., 1984—2001, prof. emeritus, 2002—. Bd. dirs. Marconi Med. Ctr., Inc., Sacramento, 1967-71, Bazeghi Corp., Oakland, Calif., 1968-71, Crescent Gen. Corp., 1969-71 (also v.p.), Fin. Floorplans, Inc., Ft. Worth, 1980-2003, Way To Go, Inc., Orlando, Fla., 1988-2000, Unicorn Rsch. Corp., Orlando, 1989—, Global Ptnrs. Corp., Orlando, 1994-2000 (also sec.). Author number of fin. acctg., mgmt. acct., cost acctg. textbooks, study guides; contbr. many articles to profl. jours. With U.S. Army, 1956-58. Recipient U. Pitts. BEFEE grant, 1993, 94, Ernst & Ernst Acctg. Achievement award, 1967, EMBA Outstanding Prof. award Class of 1986, 88, Delta Sigma Pi Scholarship key, 1964; Fulbright fellowship, 1999; Fulbright Alumni Initiatives Awards program grant, 2000-02. Mem. AICPA, Am. Acctg. Assn., World Future Soc., Fulbright Assn. (founding mem., treas. mid-Fla. chpt. 2002--), Beta Alpha Psi, Beta Gamma Sigma. Avocations: classical music, travel. Home: 4621 N Landmark Dr Orlando FL 32817-1235 Office: Crummer Grad Sch Bus Rollins Coll 1000 Holt Ave Winter Park FL 32789-4499 Home Phone: 407-657-4974. Personal E-mail: serge@unicorn.us.com. Business E-Mail: serge@rollins.edu.

MATUS, KRISTI ANN, insurance company executive; B, U. Wis., Oshkosh. Product devel. actuary Thrivent Fin. Bank, Wis., Medicare supplement actuary, product mgr. Wis., exec. v.p., COO Wis.; with USAA (United Svcs. Automobile Assn.), San Antonio, 2002—, v.p. products and regulatory mgmt. Life Ins. Co., pres. Life Ins. Co., 2004—08, CFO, 2008—. Bd. dirs. Am. Coun. Life Insurers. Fellow: Soc. Actuaries; mem.: Am. Acad. Actuaries. Office: USAA 9800 Fredericksburg Rd San Antonio TX 78288 Office Phone: 210-498-8222.

MATUS, WAYNE CHARLES, lawyer; b. NYC, Mar. 10, 1950; s. Eli and Alma (Platt) M.; children: Marshall Scott, Scott Adam. BA, Johns Hopkins U., 1972; JD, NYU, 1975. Law clk. Superior Ct. D.C., 1975-76; assoc. Marshall, Bratter, Greene, Allison and Tucker, NYC, 1976-79, Christy & Viener, NYC, 1979-83, ptnr., 1984—98, Salans Hertzfeld Heilbronn Christy & Viener, NYC, 1999—2001, Leboeuf Lamb Greene & MacRae, NYC, 2001—04, Mayer, Brown, Rowe & Maw LLP, NYC, 2004—06, Pillsbury Winthrop Shaw Pittman, 2006—. Faculty ABA-Am. Law Inst., 1988; neutral mediator comml. divsn. 1st jud. dist. Supreme Ct. State of NY Unified Ct. Sys., 1997—. Assoc. editor Nanotechnology Law and Bus. Jour., mem. editl. bd. ABA Model Jury Instructions for Trademarks, Trade Dress and Copyright; contbg. editor: Commercial Corporate Strategies for Drafting and Negotiating. Recipient Burton award for disting. legal writing, 2009. Mem. Assn. Bar City of NY (com. on computer law 1985-88, chmn. com. on state cts., subcom. on motion practice 1982-84, com. product liability 1994-97, com. on privacy 2003—), NY State Bar Assn. (com. on class actions and complex civil litigation comml. fed. litigation sect. 1990-99, com. on Internet and litigation 2000-02, lectr.), N.Y. Litigators Club (steering com. 1985—), Johns Hopkins U. Alumni Assn. (bd. dirs. met. NY chpt., v.p. 1988—2002, nat. alumni counsel 1996-2002, pres. 2002-06, mem. The Sedona Conf. 2003-). Office: Pillsbury Winthrop Shaw Pittman 1540 Broadway New York NY 10036 Office Phone: 212-858-1774.

MATUSCHAK, MARK G., lawyer; b. 1959; AB cum laude, Dartmouth Coll., 1981; JD, Columbia U., 1984. Bar: Mass., US Dist. Ct. (Mass. dist.), US Ct. Appeals (1st, 2d, 3d & Fed. cir.). Law clk. Judge Neil L. Lynch, Supreme Judicial Ct. Mass., 1984—85; assoc. to sr. ptnr. Wilmer Cutler Pickering Hale & Dorr, Boston, 1985—, vice chmn. Litigation dept. & mem. Intellectual Property Litigation group. Mem.: Dartmouth Lawyers Assn., Boston Coll. Law Sch. Intellectual Property Am. Inn of Ct., Boston Bar Assn., Am. Intellectual Property Law Assn. Office: Wilmer Cutler Pickering Hale & Dorr 60 State St Boston MA 02109 Office Fax: 617-526-6559, 617-526-5000. Business E-Mail: mark.matuschak@wilmerhale.com.

MATUSEVICH, YELENA, artist, educator; d. Vladislav Davidovich and Alla Borisovna Mazur; life ptnr. Sean Russell Bledsoe; children: Yan, Vadim Samuel Bledsoe. MA, U. Okla., Norman, 1993; PhD, U. Ill., Urbana Champaign, 1998. Cert. tchr. Herzen Inst., 1989. Instr. Vanderbilt U., Nashville, 1997—98; assoc. prof. U. Alaska Fairbanks, 1998—. Rsch. fellow CNRS, Paris, 2003; vis. faculty Jawaharlal Nehru U., New Dehli, 2005, Portland State U., Oreg., 2008—. One-man shows include exhbn. Personal Show. Donor Inst.Theology and Philosophy, St. Petersburg, 2005—08, sponsor, 2005—08. Recipient Tchg. Excellence award, UAF, 2002, Outstanding Advisor award, 2003, Usibelli Excellence Tchg. award, 2007; Coolidge fellowship, Assn. Religion and Intellectual Life, NY, 2008. Mem.: Internat. Gerson Soc. (pres. 2008—). Avocation: dancing. Office: UAF Gruening 609 Fairbanks AK 99775-6440 Office Fax: 907-474-5344.

MATUSIAK, FREDERICK, military analyst, educator; BA in History, Iona Coll., 1967; MA, U. Nebr., 1970, PhD, 1992. Tchg. asst. U. Nebr., Lincoln, 1970—71; instr. Humboldt State U., Arcata, Calif., 1971—73; asst. prof. US Air Force Acad., Colorado Springs, 1982—84, 1989—93; lectr. Col State U., Pveblo, 1994—; analyst, briefer Strategic Air Command, 1979—82; chief Indications and Warning Ctr., Osan Air Base, Republic of Korea, 1998. Recipient David H. Zook award, 1990. Mem.: Springs Ranch Homeowners Assn. (pres. cascades), Military Officer Assn. Am., Air Force Assn., World History Assn., Am. Hist. Assn., Am. Legion, Disabled Am. Vets.

MATUSZAK, ALICE JEAN BOYER, pharmacy educator; b. Newark, Ohio, June 22, 1935; d. James Emery and Elizabeth Hawthorne (Irvine) Boyer; m. Charles Alan Matuszak, Aug. 27, 1955; children: Matthew, James. BS summa cum laude, Ohio State U., 1958, MS, 1959; postgrad., U. Wis., 1959-60; PhD, U. Kans., 1963. Registered pharmacist, Ohio, Calif. Apprentice pharmacist Arensberg Pharmacy, Newark, 1953-58; rsch. asst. Ohio State U., Columbus, 1958, lab. asst., 1958-59; rsch. asst. U. Wis., Madison, 1959-60, U. Kans., Lawrence, 1960-63; asst. prof. U. of the Pacific, Stockton, Calif., 1963-67, assoc. prof., 1971-78, prof., 1978—2000, prof. emerita, 2000—; order of Pacific, 2000. Vis. fgn. prof. Kobe-Gakuin U., Japan, 1992. Contbr. articles to profl. jours. Mem. rev. bd. U.S. Adopted Names Commn. Recipient Disting. Alumna award Ohio State U. Coll. Pharmacy, 1994, Profl. Frat. Assn. Career Achievement award, 2000, Order of Pacific award U. of Pacific, 2000; NIH grantee, 1965-66. Fellow Am. Pharm. Assn. (chmn. basic scis. 1990); mem. Am. Assn. Colls. of Pharmacy (chmn. chemistry sect. 1979-80, bd. dirs. 1993-95), Am. Inst. History of Pharmacy (exec. coun. 1984-88, 90-92, 92-95, chmn. contributed papers 1990-92, pres.-elect 1995-97, pres. 1997—99, cert. of commendation 1990), Am. Chem. Soc., Internat. Fedn. Pharmacy, Acad. Pharm. Rsch. Sci. (pres. 1993-94), Coun. Sci. Soc. Pres., U.S. Adopted Names Coun. Review Bd., U.S. Pharmacopeial Conv., Clan Irwin Assn., Donald Salvatori Calif. Pharmacy Mus., Sigma Xi, Rho Chi, Phi Lambda Sigma, Phi Kappa Phi, Kappa Epsilon (Unicorn award, award of merit 1995, Merck Vanguard leadership award 2000), Lambda Kappa Sigma, Delta Zeta. Democrat. Episcopalian. Avocation: collecting pharmacy artifacts. Home: 1130 W Mariposa Ave Stockton CA 95204-3021 Office: U Pacific Sch Pharmacy Stockton CA 95211-0001 E-mail: amatuszak@pacific.edu.

MATUSZEK, JOHN MICHAEL, JR., environmental scientist, educator, consultant; b. Worcester, Mass., Apr. 16, 1935; s. John Michael and Felicia Martha (Shandruk) M.; m. Roberta Eva Coonan, Nov. 30, 1957; children: Debra-Jane Y., John Michael III, Kevin P., Jennifer R. BS in Chemistry with distinction, Worcester Poly. Inst., 1957; PhD in Nuclear Chemistry, Clark U., 1962. Dept. mgr. Teledyne Isotopes, Westwood, NJ, 1964-71; rsch. scientist in nuclear chemistry, radioactive waste mgmt., radiological health, environ. radioactivity and radiation N.Y. State Health Dept., Albany, 1971-2000; cons., owner JMM Cons. Svcs., Delmar, NY, 1992—. Adj. prof. Rensselaer Poly. Inst., Troy, N.Y., 1977-2003; prof. SUNY, Albany, 1996-99. Lt. comdr. USPHS, 1962-64. Mem.: Internat. Commn. Radionuclide Metrology. Avocations: skiing, music. Home and Office: JMM Cons Svcs 10 Fieldstone Dr Delmar NY 12054

MATUSZKO, ANTHONY JOSEPH, research chemist, administrator; b. Hadley, Mass., Jan. 31, 1926; s. Joseph Anthony and Katherine (Narog) M.; m. Anita Colley, Oct. 26, 1956; children— Martha, Mary, Stephen, Richard. BA, Amherst Coll., 1946; MS in Chemistry, U. Mass., 1951; PhD in Chemistry, McGill U., 1953. Demonstrator in chemistry McGill U., Montreal, Que., Can., 1950-52; from instr. to assoc. prof. chemistry Lafayette Coll., Easton, Pa., 1952-58; head fundamental process div. Naval Propellant Lab., Indian Head, Md., 1958-62; program mgr. in chemistry Air Force Office Sci. Research, Washington, 1962-89; rsch. steering com. Dept. Def. Biotech., 1986-89; cons., Annandale, Va., 1989—. Contbr. articles to tech. jours. Patentee in field. Pres. Forest Heights PTA, Md., 1967. Served with U.S. Army, 1946-48. Named Hon. Fellow in Chemistry, U. Wis.-Madison, 1967-68, recipient Superior Performance award USAF, Outstanding Career Svc. award U.S. Govt. Fellow AAAS, Am. Inst. Chemists (life); mem. Am. Chem. Soc., Cosmos Club, Sigma Xi. Home: 4210 Elizabeth Ln Annandale VA 22003-3654

MATVEEVA, ELENA ALEKSANDROVNA, microbiologist, biochemist, educator; b. St. Peterburg, Russia, Sept. 11, 1962; arrived in US, 1996, naturalized, 2002; d. Aleksander Ivanovich Kochergin and Ludmila Aleksandrovna Kochergina; m. Sergey Valentinovich Matveev, Oct. 1, 1992; m. Gregory Nikolaevech Filatov, June 30, 1985 (div. Aug. 25, 1992); children: Diana Grigorievna Palmer, Elina Sergeevna, Faina Sergeevna. BS in Biochemistry, St. Petersburg U., Russia, 1984; PhD in Biophysics, Russian Acad. Sci., Moscow, 1992. Biologist and Biochemist Russian Acad. Sci., 1992. Postdoc. fellow Inst. Biophysics, Pushchino, Russia, 1992—96; postdoc. fellow dept. biochemistry U. Ky., Lexington, 1997—99, rsch. assoc. dept. molecular and cellular biochemistry, 1999—. Adj. faculty Bluegrass Cmty. and Tech. Coll., Lexington, Ky., 2004—; presenter in field. Contbr. articles to profl. pubs. Recipient Soros Travel award, 1996. Mem.: Nat. Geog., Broadway Christian Ch. Democrat. Mem. Christian Ch. (Disciples Of Christ). Avocations: piano, mystery books. Office: U Ky 741 S Limestone Lexington KY 40536 Office Fax: 859-257-2283. Business E-Mail: elmatva@uky.edu.

MATVEEVA, EVGENIA, chemist; b. Russia; m. Mikhail Matveev; 1 child, Maria. PhD (hon.), Moscow Lomonosov State U., Russia. Rsch. asst. prof. UNTHSC, Fort Worth, Tex., 2005—. Mem.: Am. Chem. Soc. Office: UNT HSC Dept Mol Biol & Immunol 3500 Camp Bowie Blvd Fort Worth TX 76107 Business E-Mail: ematveev@hsc.unt.edu.

MATYJASZEWSKI, KRZYSZTOF, chemist, educator; b. Konstantynow, Poland, Apr. 8, 1950; arrived in U.S., 1985; s. Henryk and Antonina (Styss) M.; m. Malgorzata Kowalska, July 15, 1972; children: Antoni, Maria. BS, MS, Tech. U., Moscow, 1972; PhD, Polish Acad. Scis., Lodz, 1976; DSc, Lodz Poly., 1985, degree, 2006, degree, 2007; degree (hon.), U. Ghent, Belgium, 2002, Russian Acad. Sci., 2006; degree, U. Athens, Greece, 2009, Inst. Poly., Toulouse, France, 2009. Postdoctoral fellow U. Fla., 1977-78; rsch. assoc. Polish Acad. Scis., 1978-84, CNRS, France, 1984-85; asst. prof. chemistry Carnegie Mellon U., Pitts., 1985-89, assoc. prof., 1989-93, prof., 1993—, head dept. chemistry, 1994-98, J.C. Warner prof., 1998—, univ. prof., 2004—. Invited prof. U. Paris, 1985; vis. prof. U. Freiburg, 1988, U. Paris, 1990, 97, 98, 06, U. Bayreuth, 1991, U. Strasbourg, 1992, U. Bordeaux, 1996, 04, U. Ulm, 1999, U. Pisa, 2000; adj. prof., U. Pitts., 2000-, Polish Acad. Sci., 2000-; cons. Dow Corning, Midland, Mich., 1988-89, Arco, Phila., 1990-92, GE, Schenectady, 1992-00, Amoco, Naperville, Ill., 1994-97, Reilly Ind., Indpls., 1994—, Air Products, Allentown, Pa., 1994-97. Author 10 books; mem. editorial bd. Macromolecules, Macromolecular Synthesis, Jour. Polymer Sci., Jour. Macromolecular Sci.-Pure and Applied Chemistry, Jour. Inorganic and Organometallic Polymers, Polymer, others; editor Progress Polymer Sci., Ctrl. European Jour. Chemistry; contbr. chpts. to books, more than 600 articles to profl. jours.; 31 U.S. and 78 internat. patents in field. Recipient award Polish Chem. Soc., 1980, Polish Acad. Sci., 1981, Presdl. Young Investigator award NSF, 1989, Humboldt award for Sr. US Scientists, 1999, Pitts. award, 2001, Polish Sci. Found. prize, 2004, UK Macro Group medal, 2005; Presdl. Green Chemistry award, 2009. Fellow: Internat. Union Pure and Applied Chemistry (corr. mem. polymer nomenclature), Polymer Materials Sci. Engring., Am. Chem. Soc. (Carl S. Marvel award 1995, Polymer Chemistry award 2002, Coop. Rsch. award 2004, Hermann F. Mark Sr. Scholar award 2007); mem.: NAE, Polish Acad. Scis. (fgn. mem. 2005), French Acad. Sci. (Elf chair 1998). Achievements include research in synthesis of well defined macromolecules via living and controlled polymerizations; organometallic polymers. Office: Carnegie Mellon U 4400 5th Ave Pittsburgh PA 15213-2617 Home: 307 S Negley Ave Pittsburgh PA 15232 Business E-Mail: matyjaszewski@yahoo.com.

MATZ, ALISON ADLER, publishing executive; married; 2 children. BS, Syracuse U., NY. With Self mag. Condé Nast Publs., 1988—93; advt. dir. Mirabella mag.; advt. dir. Country Home mag. Meredith Corp.; assoc. pub. US Weekly Wenner Media LLC; assoc. pub. House & Garden mag. Condé Nast Publs., assoc. pub. Teen Vogue, assoc. pub. Glamour mag., pub. Brides mag., 2008—. Office: Brides 750 Third Ave New York NY 10017 Office Phone: 212-630-3976. Business E-Mail: Alison_Matz@condenast.com.*

MATZ, JAMES RICHARD, municipal official; BA with honors, U. Tex., 1961; postgrad., Mexico city Coll., 1961-62. Mktg. exec. Fluor Corp.; mem. diplomatic corps Dept. of State; commr. City of Harlingen, Tex., Cameron County. Mem. Pres.'s Exec. Interchange Program, Bank of Am.; mayor Palm Valley, Tex. Contbr. articles to profl. jours. Founder Harlingen Proud; founder, chmn. Valley Proud Environ. Coun., 1990; mem. citizen's exec. adv. coun. Rio Grande State Mental Health and Retardation Ctr.; bd. dirs. Harlingen, South Padre Island, San Benito Emergency Med. Svcs.; chmn. Tex. Reg. Cmty. Devel. Grant Rev. Com.; mem. Met. Planning Orgn., Cameron County; mem. exploration com. World Birding Ctr.; bd. dirs. Tex. Urban Forestry Coun.; mem. Tex. Energy Coord. Coun., Govt. Adv. Com. to U.S. Rep. to N.Am. Commn. for Environ. Coop.; past vice chmn. legis. policy com. on utility regulation and environment Tex. Mcpl. League; past chmn. City of Harlingen Utility Rate Rev. Bd., pub. works com. Harlingen Capital Improvement Adv. Bd.; past. bd. dirs. Rio Grande basin Sustainable Devel. Initiative, Border Trade Alliance, Area Health Edn. Ctr. South Tex., Keep Tex. Beautiful; former commr. Cameron County; past exec. com. Rio Grande Valley Emergency Mgmt. Coord. Coun., numerous others. Recipient Dist. Svc. award Rotary Found., 1990, Svc. Above Self award Harlingen Rotary, 1991, Tex. Urban Forestry Individual Accomplishment award, 1992, Harlingen Proud, Chairman's award, 1992, Outstanding Dist. Gov., Keep Tex. Beautiful, 1995, Leadership award, 1995, Pres.'s Nat. Svc. award, 1995, Outstanding tex. Urban Forester award, 1996, State of Tex. Senate Resolution #989, 1995, Joint Resolution of Appreciation, San Benito City Commn. and San Benito Area C. of C., 1997, Tex. Environ. Excellence award Tex. Commn. Environ. Quality, 2004, Gulf Guardian award, 2004, Tex. Gov.'s Lonestar Cmty. Svc. award, 2005, Lone Star Land Steward award Tex. Parks and Wildlife Dept., 2006, Frederick Law Olmsted award Nat. Arbor Day Found., 2006, One Nation award Valley Morning Star Newspaper. Mem. Harlingen Area C. of C. (past dir.), Assn. for Local Control of Utility Rates (past officer, dir.). Office: 900 Palm Valley Dr W Harlingen TX 78552

MATZ, JOSEPH S., computer software company executive; BS in Economics, Georgetown U., 1987; MBA, U. Chgo. Joined Microsoft Corp., Redmond, Wash., 1993, asst. treas., corp. v.p. worldwide licensing and pricing. Recipient Gold Alexander Hamilton award for Fin. Risk Mgmt., 2003. Office: Microsoft Corp One Microsoft Way Redmond WA 98052-6399*

MATZ, SEAN CORMICK, electrical engineer; b. Fullerton, Calif., July 31, 1959; s. Joseph Albert and Audrey Margaret Matz. BS in Math., U. Calif., Irvine, 1981, MS in Math., 1983, PhD in Elec. Engring., 2000; MSEE, Calif. Poly. U., Pomona, 1985. Mem. of the tech. staff Hughes Aircraft Co., Fullerton, Calif., 1986—88; staff engr. Walter Dorwin Teague Assoc., Pomona, Calif., 1989—92; engr./scientist The Boeing Co., Seal Beach, Calif., 2000—. Fellow Calif. Microelectronics and Computer Sci. fellow, U. of Calif., Irvine, 1993—94, Regents' fellow, 1996. Mem.: Math. Assn. of Am., IEEE. Independent-Republican. Roman Catholic. Avocations: reading, music, mathematics, computers. Home: 313 South Poinsettia Ave Brea CA 92821 Office: The Boeing Company 2800 Westminster Blvd Seal Beach CA 90740 Personal E-mail: smatz@att.net. Business E-Mail: sean.c.matz@boeing.com.

MATZIORINIS, KENNETH N., economist; b. NYC, May 4, 1954; s. Neocles N. and Popi (Gregoratos) Matziorinis; m. Catherine Marina Astrakianakis, July 27, 1985; children: Anna Maria, Angela Ellen Fylitsa. BA, McGill U., 1976, MA, 1979, PhD, 1988. Cert. mgmt. cons. Asst. economist Nat. Bank Greece (Can.), Montreal, 1978-81; adj. prof. economics McGill U., Montreal, 1977—; prof. econs. John Abbott Coll., Montreal, 1981—. Pres. Canbek Econ. Cons., Inc., Montreal, 1983—; econs. adviser to bd. dirs. Internat. Orgn. Psychophysiology, 1982-89; bd. dirs. Nat. Bank Greece, Can., 1991-2006; dir. Hellas Capital, Inc., Can., 2001—. Author: Introduction to Macro Economics: An Applied Approach, 5th edit., 2007, Business Economics: Theory and Practice, 5th edit., 2008; editor: Vital Graphs of Canadian Economy, 1984; contbr. articles to profl. jours. V.p. Westmount Liberal Riding Assn., Montreal, 1975-77; bd. govs. McGill U., 1978-81, John Abbott Coll., 1988-91; chmn. bd. dirs. Cmty. Svc. Ctr. St. Louis, Montreal, 1978-80; bd. trustees Trafalgar Sch. for Girls, 2002—; pres. Mount Royal chpt. CJF AHEPA, 2009-. Recipient Distinguished Tchg. award McGill U., 1993, 2006. Mem. Am. Econ. Assn., Am. Hellenic Ednl. and Progressive Assn., Can. Assn. Bus. Economists, Can. Econ. Assn., Que. Inst. Cert. Mgmt. Cons., Nat. Assn. Bus. Economists. Greek Orthodox. Home: 4862 Felix-Mclernan Pierrefonds Montreal PQ H8Y 3KI Canada Business E-Mail: canbekeconomics@videotron.ca.

MATZKIN, ROSA LILIANA, economics professor; d. Jose and Paulina (Rosemberg) M.; m. Jorge T. Lapsenson, June 5, 1996. BS in Mgmt. and Econs. cum laude, Israel Inst. Tech., Haifa, 1981; PhD in Econs., U. Minn., 1986. Rsch. asst. dept. of banks regulation Bank of Israel, Jerusalem, 1980; tchg. asst., assoc. U. Minn., Mpls., 1981-84; asst. prof. econs. Yale U., New Haven, 1986—91, assoc. prof. econs., 1991—92, Northwestern U., Evanston, Ill., 1992—95, prof. econs., 1995—. Econ. cons. The Brattle Group, 2003—04. Grantee U. Tel Aviv, Israel, 1982-83, grantee Nat. Sci. Found., 1987—1999, 2003-, Sloan Found. U. Minn., 1984-85. Fellow Econometric Soc.; Phi Kappa Phi. Office: Northwestern U Dept Econs 2003 Sheridan Rd Evanston IL 60208-0826 Home Phone: 312-751-9128; Office Phone: 847-491-8220. Business E-Mail: matzkin@northwestern.edu.

MAU, BOB, statistician, evolutionary biologist; b. Sheboygan, Wis., Sept. 1, 1950; s. Robert W. Mau and Lydia Welsch; m. Lynn Ellen Deschler, Sept. 29, 1979. BA, Lawrence U., Appleton, Wis., 1973; PhD, U. Wis., Madison, 1996. Mgr. rsch. program Wis. Survey Rsch. Lab., Madison, 1980—90; sr. scientist U. Wis., Madison, 1996—. Contbr. articles to profl. jours. Postdoctoral fellow Computational Molecular Biology, Sloan Found. / DOE, 1999—2001. Fellow: Royal Statis. Soc.; mem.: Soc. Molecular Biol. Evolution, Inst. Math. Stats., Am. Statis. Soc. Achievements include research in the identification of genomic rearrangements using Markov chain Monte Carlo; Bayesian phylogenetic inference using Markov chain Monte Carlo; genome-wide detection of allelic substitution. Home: 207 E Racine Jefferson WI 53549 Office: U Wis Madison 425 Henry Mall Madison WI 53706 Business E-Mail: bobmau@biotech.wisc.edu.

MAU, LISA ANNE, special education educator; b. Niskayuna, NY, Jan. 13, 1966; d. Joanne Elizabeth and William DiCaprio; m. Matthew Walter Mau, July 1, 1989; 1 child, Joshua Matthew. AA in Early Childhood Edn. with high honors, SUNY, Cobleskill, 1986; BS in Spl. Edn. magna cum laude, Coll. St. Rose, Albany, 1988, M with honors, 1993. Cert. Tchr. NY Dept. Edn., 1993. Spl. edn. tchr. grades 3-5 Middleburgh Elem., NY, 1988—. Wilson reading tchr. Middleburgh Elem., 2002—. Home: 405 Glen Ave Scotia NY 12302 Office: Middleburgh Elem Sch 245 Main St Middleburgh NY 12122

MAUCEC, MARKO, nuclear engineer, researcher; b. Murska Sobota, Slovenia, Nov. 22, 1967; s. Matija Maucec and Angela Recek-Maucec; m. Branka Maucec, Oct. 7, 1989; children: Jernej, Jan, Katja. BSEE, U. Ljubljana, Slovenia, 1993; PhD in Nuclear Engring., U. Ljubljana, 1999; MSc in Nuclear Engring., U. Maribor, Slovenia, 1996. Rsch. asst., young rschr. fellow of MST Slovenia Jozef Stefan Inst., Ljubljana, 1993—99; vis. rschr., Fulbright fellow Claremont (Calif.) Grad. U., CRIAMS, 1999—2000; postdoctoral assoc. Jozef Stefan Inst., Ljubljana, 1999—; rschr., Marie Curie fellow Kernfysisch Versneller Inst., Groningen, Netherlands, 2000—04; sr. engr. HOLTEC Internat., Marlton, NJ, 2005—06; rsch. geophysicist Shell Internat. E&P, Houston, 2006—08; tech. rsch. fellow Halliburton-Landmark, Highlands Ranch, Colo., 2008—. Presenter in field. Contbr. articles to profl. jours. Recipient Young Investigator grad. position, Ministry of Sci. and Tech., 1993—99, Best Paper award, 1997, 1998, Marie Curie Individual fellowship, European Union, 2001—03; fellow Fulbright fellowship, Inst. of Internat. Edn., 1999—2000. Mem.: AAAS, Marie Curie Felllows Assn. (hon.), Soc. Exploration Geophysicists (assoc.), Soc. Petroleum Engrs. (assoc.), European Fedn. Non-destructive Testing (assoc.), Internat. Soc. Neutron Capture Therapy (assoc.), Nuc. Soc. Slovenia (assoc.), European Nuc. Soc. (assoc.), Am. Nuc. Soc. (assoc.), Fulbright Assn. Slovenia (hon.). Achievements include development of non-destructive pulse neutron multiple detector tool (NuPulse) for use in environmental, hydrocarbon and mineral exploration work; Monte Carlo perturbation/sensitivity techniques for determination of geological formations by natural gamma-radiation; irradiation facilities for Boron Neutron Capture Therapy (BNCT) at TRIGA reactor in Ljubljana; Monte Carlo perturbation and nuclear techniques for characterization of non-metallic land-mines by Thermal Neutron Backscattering; gamma-ray spectrometry techniques for detection of radioactive particles (Cs-137) in offshore environments; Bayesian methods for dynamic data integration in geophysical exploration; multi-step Markov chain Monte Carlo code for streamline-assisted automated history matching of well-production data; methods for estimation of orientation and local anisotropy in geological structures. Office: Halliburton-Landmark Geol & Geophys Techs 1805 Shea Center Dr Highlands Ranch CO 80129 Office Phone: 303-803-0327. Personal E-mail: marko_maucec@yahoo.com. Business E-Mail: marko.maucec@halliburton.com.

MAUCH, ROBERT CARL, energy and financial services executive; b. Cleve., Dec. 7, 1939; AMP, Harvard U., 1983; MS, U. Calif., Berkeley, 1965; BSChemE, Cleve. State U., 1962. V.p., gen. mgr., LP gas divsn. Amerigas Inc., Valley Forge, Pa., 1978-83; v.p. UGI Corp., Valley Forge, 1978-87, sr. v.p., 1987-90; dir. Ansutech, Inc., Valley Forge, 1981-82, Matheson Gas Products, Inc., Valley Forge, 1981-82; pres., dir. AP Propane Inc., Valley Forge, 1983-90, Amerigas Propane, Valley Forge, 1983-96; pres., CEO, dir. AmeriGas Inc., Valley Forge, 1991-96, Petrolane, Inc., Valley Forge, 1993-96, Amerigas, Inc. subs. UGI Corp., Valley Forge, 1990-96, AmeriGas Propane Inc. (gen. ptnr. AmeriGas Ptnrs. L.P.); chmn., CEO Anthem Holdings Corp., Valley Forge, 1997-98, AllianceOne Inc., Exton, 1998—2006. Bd. govs. Pa. Economy League, Phila., 1985-91; mem. World Affairs Coun., Phila., 1980-95. Mem.: Propane Vehicle Coun. (chmn. 1994—), Waynesborough C. of C., Nat. Propane Gas Assn. (pres. 1978—, bd. dirs., exec. com.). Lutheran. Avocations: tennis, reading, yoga, opera, weight training.

MAUCHER, HELMUT OSWALD, food products executive; b. Eisenharz, Germany, Dec. 9, 1927; BA in Bus. Adminstrn. and Economy, Frankfurt U., Germany; D (hon.), Autonomous U. Guadalajara, Mexico, 1989, European Bus. Sch., Oestrich-Winkel, Germany, 1997, Technical U., Munich, 1998. Various mgmt. positions Nestlé Co., Germany, 1964-80; pres., CEO Nestlé Gruppe Deutschland GmbH, Frankfurt, 1975-80; exec. v.p., mem. exec. com. Nestlé S.A., Vevey, Switzerland, 1980-81, CEO, 1981—90, chmn. bd. dirs., 1990—97, chmn. bd., 1997—2000, hon. chmn. bd., 2000—. Chmn. bd. trustees Stiftung Demoskopie Allensbach, Frankfurt Inst. Advanced Studies,; Germany mem. adv. coun. Author: (book) Leadership in Action, Management Brevian. Recipient Gold medal, Fortune Mag., 1984, Leadership award, Internat. Inst. Mgmt. Devel., 1993, award, Appeal of Conscience Found., NY, 1995, INTERNORGA prize, Hamburg, 1996, Scopus award, Hebrew U., Jerusalem, 1999, Social Market Economy prize, Konrad-Adenauer Found., 2004; named Maucher Nestlé Chair, Internat. Inst. Mgmt. Devel., 1993; named to Order El Aguila Azteca, Mexico, 1993, Bus. Hall Fame, Mgr. Mag., 1997. Office: Nestlé Haus Lyoner Strasse 23 Frankfurt 60528 Germany

MAUCKER, EARL ROBERT, editor, publishing executive; b. St. Louis, Sept. 20, 1947; s. Robert Buffem and Linette (Meloy) M.; m. Betsy Ann Johnson, May 21, 1977; children: Eric Robert, Michael Earl. BA in Mass Communications, So. Ill. U., 1972. Reporter Alton Telegraph, Ill., 1969-73; reporter, city editor, news editor, asst. mng. editor Rockford Morning Star, 1973-79; mng. editor Springfield Daily News, Mo., 1979-80, Ft. Lauderdale Sun-Sentinel, 1990-95, v.p. editorial, 1995—2001, editor & sr. v.p., 2001—. Sgt. SUAF, 1966-69. Named Editor of Yr., Editor & Pub., 2007. Mem. Am. Soc. Newspapers Editors, Fla. Soc. Newspapers Editors, Associated Press Mng. Editors Assn. (bd. dirs. 1989-93). Office: Sun-Sentinel 200 E Las Olas Blvd Fort Lauderdale FL 33301-2293 Office Phone: 954-356-4600. E-mail: emaucker@sun-sentinel.com.*

MAUER, JOE, professional baseball player; b. St. Paul, Apr. 19, 1983; Catcher Minn. Twins, 2004—. Recipient Silver Slugger award, 2006, 2008, Gold Glove award, 2008; named to Am. League All-Star Team, Maj. League Baseball, 2006, 2008, 2009. Achievements include leading the American League in: batting average, 2006, 2008; becoming the first American League catcher to win a batting title, 2006. Mailing: c/o Minn Twins Metrodome 34 Kirby Puckett Pl Minneapolis MN 55415*

MAUGANS, JOHN CONRAD, lawyer; b. Miami County, Ind., May 10, 1938; s. Willis William and Evelyn Jeannette (Mills) M.; m. Judith M. Gallagher, Jan. 24, 1960 (dec. June 1984); children: Lisa Denise, Stacy Erin, Kristen Cherie; m. Jo Ella Middlekauff, June 7, 1985. AB, Manchester Coll., 1960; LLB with distinction, Ind. U., 1962, JD, 1969. Bar: Ind. 1962. Assoc. Barnes, Hickam, Pantzer & Boyd, Indpls., 1962-63; pvt. practice Kokomo, Ind., 1966—; ptnr. Bayliff, Harrigan, Cord, Maugans & Cox, Kokomo, 1969—. Guest lectr. Coll. Bus. Manchester Coll., 1966-80 Contbr. articles to profl. jours. Chmn. Howard fund dr. Manchester Coll., 1971; bd. dirs. Tribal Trials coun. Girl Scouts U.S.A., 1977-85, Vols. in Cmty. Svc., 1978-84, Home Health Care of Ctrl. Ind., Inc., 1983-89; bd. mgrs. Woodhaven Homeowners Assn., 2002-; trustee Western Sch. Corp., 1986—, pres., 1991-93, 2003-2005, 2007-09; bd. dirs. Kokomo Park Band, Inc., 1989—; chmn. Christian Edn. com., Main St. Christian Ch., 1993—; mem. asset devel. and mktg. com. Cmty. Found. Howard County, Inc., 2000-05, mem. profl. adv. com., 2006—. Capt. AUS, 1963-66. Fellow Am. Trial Lawyers Assn. (Roscoe Pound Found. chpt.), Ind. Bar Found.; mem. Ind. Bar Assn., Howard County Bar Assn. (pres. 1989), Ind. Trial Lawyers Assn., Manchester Coll. Alumni Assn. (chmn. area chpt. 1970, 88, 89, 90, 91), Manchester Coll. M. Alumni Assn. (pres. 1972), Am. Legion, Order of Coif, Phi Delta Phi. Home: 3274 Woodhaven Trl Kokomo IN 46902-5062 Office: PO Box 2249 123 N Buckeye St Kokomo IN 46904-2249 Office Phone: 765-459-3941. Business E-Mail: connie.maugans@bhcmlaw.com.

MAUGER, JOHN W., dean, pharmacy educator; BS, Albany Coll. Pharmacy, NY, 1965; MS in Pharmaceutics, U. RI, 1968, PhD, 1971. Former faculty mem. U. Nebr. Med. Ctr., W.Va. U. Coll. Pharmacy; prof. dept. pharmaceutics & pharm. chemistry, dean U. Utah Coll. Pharmacy, Salt Lake City, 1994—. Bd. trustees US Pharmacopeia Conv. (USP), Washington, chmn. bd. trustees, 2005—09; USP rep. European Directorate Quality of Medicines, Strasbourg, France, 2007, World Health Professions Alliance, Geneva, 2008. Mem. editl. bd. Pharm. Devel. & Tech.; contbr. articles to profl. jours., chapters to books. Fellow: AAAS; mem.: Am. Coun. Pharm. Edn. (past pres.). Office: U Utah Coll Pharmacy 30 S 2000 E Salt Lake City UT 84112 Office Phone: 801-581-6731. Office Fax: 801-581-3716.*

MAUGERE, DENNIS PAUL, historian, educator; b. Newark, Sept. 3, 1946; s. William John and Virginia Webb Maugere; m. Joanne Maria Cella, Sept. 21, 1974; children: Lisa Marie, Anthony Paul, Lauren Michelle. AS cum laude in History and Polit. Sci., Broward Jr. Coll., 1966; BA in hist., polit. sci., U. Fla., 1969, MA in tchg., am. hist., polit. sci., social founds. of edn., 1976. Cert. profl. social studies educator State Dept. Edn., Fla and NY. Human rels. specialist Broward County Commn. Govt., Ft. Lauderdale, Fla., 1977—80, Broward Employ. Tng. Admin., 1981—82; adj. prof., hist. govt. Broward CC, Pembroke Pines, Fla., 1984—99; hist. prof. Cooper City (Fla.) HS, 1984—. Chmn. Broward County Adv. Bd. for Disabled, Ft. Lauderdale, 1979—81; keynote spkr. South Fla Second Conf. on Handicapped, Hollywood, Fla., 1979. Author: (social studies course) The Warren Commission Report and The Assassination of President John F. Kennedy, 1998; performer: (talk show host) Concerns of the Disabled, Sta. WAVC-TV, 1977, Hotline for the Disabled, Sta. WKID-TV, 1978. Guest spkr. various comm. functions for handicapped issues. Recipient Citation of Merit award, Muscular Dystrophy Assn., Inc., 1978, Physically Handicapped, Inc., 1978, Award of Excellence, Nat. Assn. County Organ., 1978, Three Presdl. Invitations for Ann. Meeting Pres.'s Com. Employment of Handicapped, Pres. Carter Adminstrn., 1978—80, US Citizen Ambassador, Hist. Edn. Del. to Russia and Latvia selectee, Ariz. State U., 1993, honoree, Cmty. Leader's Banquet, Tamarac, Fla., 1993, Tchrs. Making a Difference award in the Lives of Fla. Children, Fla. Devel. Disabilities Coun., 2005; named Leadership Coun. Wall of Tolerance Honoree, So. Poverty Law Ctr., 2005. Mem.: Southern Poverty Law Ctr., Am. Hist. Assn., Phi Alpha Theta, Internat. Roman Catholic. Achievements include co-founder South Florida's 1st annual conference on the handicapped; development of numerous county ordinances for the rights of the handicapped. Office: Cooper City HS Wendy Doll Principle 9401 Stirling Rd Cooper City FL 33328 Office Phone: 754-323-0200. Office Fax: 754-323-0330. Personal E-mail: maugered@aol.com.

MAUL, KEVIN JAY, financial consultant, economist; BA, Shippensburg U., 1990; MA, U. Va., 1992. Economist USDA Econ. Rsch. Svc., Washington, 1991-92; fin. cons. Pricewaterhouse Coopers LLP, Washington, 1992-99, Resources Connection, McLean, Va., 1999-2000, Deloitte & Touche LLP, Washington, 2000—03, Callaway Ptnrs., LLC, Reston, Va., 2005—. Author: The Handbook of Mortgage Banking, 1993. Mem. Am. Econ. Assn., Mortgage Bankers Assn. Am. Lutheran. Avocations: music, travel, gardening, stamp collecting/philately.

MAULA, MOHAMMAD MOJIBUL, biology professor; s. Abdul Majid and Rokea Khatun; m. Rokea Akhtar, July 2, 1967; children: Ruhul Amin, Inamul. PhD, U. Md., Coll. Pk., 1993. Reader zoology Surendranath Coll., Kolkata, West Bengal, India, 1965—85; assoc. prof. zoology Voorhees Coll., Denmark, SC, 1994—95; biologist Am. Type Culture Collection, Rockville, Md., 1996—97; dir., cell biology & embryology lab, dept biology U. Md., 1997; prof. biology HACC, Ctrl. Pa.'s Comm., Lancaster, 1997—. Coun. mem. United Islamic Assn., Lancaster, 1999—2004. Islam. Avocation: travel. Office: HACC Lancaster Campus 1641 Old Phila Pike Lancaster PA 17602 Office Fax: 717-358-2259. Business E-Mail: mmmaula@hacc.edu.

MAULDIN, JOHN INGLIS, public defender; b. Atlanta, Nov. 6, 1947; s. Earle and Isabel (Inglis) M.; m. Cynthia Ann Balchin, Apr. 15, 1967 (div. Dec. 1985); children: Tracy Rutherford, Abigail Inglis; m. Linda W. Farmer, Nov. 7, 1998. BA, Wofford Coll., 1970; JD, Emory U., 1973. Bar: S.C. 1974, U.S. Ct. Appeals (4th cir.) 1974, U.S. Dist. Ct. S.C. 1975, U.S. Supreme Ct. 1978. Asst. pub. def. Defender Corp. Greenville County, S.C., 1974-76; ptnr. Mauldin & Allison, Greenville, 1977-92; pub. defender Greenville County, SC, 1992—2008, 13th judicial cir. pub. defender SC, 2008—. Chair S.C. Commn. on Indigent Def., 1993-96. Bd. dirs. Speech Hearing and Learning Ctr., Greenville, 1977-90, pres., 1982; bd. dirs. Def. Corp. Greenville County, 1979-92, Save Our Sons, 1995-2006, Palmetto Innocence Project, 2002—. Named SC Atty. Yr. ACLU, SC, 1986. Mem.: SC Pub. Defender Assn. (bd. dirs. 1992—2006, SC Atty. of Yr. 2006), SC Assn. Criminal Def. Lawyers (bd. dirs. 1997—99), SC Trial Lawyers Assn., Nat. Legal Aid and Defender Assn. (defender policy group 1999—2007, bd. dirs. 2002—07), Nat. Assn. Criminal Def. Attys., Rotary, Sigma Delta Phi. Democrat. Methodist. Office: PO Box 10264fs Greenville SC 29603 Office Phone: 864-467-8522.

MAULE, JAMES EDWARD, law educator; b. Phila., Nov. 26, 1951; s. Edward Randolph George and Jennie Elisabeth (Zappone) M.; m. Susan Margaret Noonan, June 26, 1982 (div. May 1988); children: Charles Edward, Sarah Margaret; m. Susan K. Garrison, Apr. 7, 1990 (div. 1991). BS cum laude, U. Pa. Wharton Sch., 1973; JD cum laude, Villanova U., 1976; LLM with highest honors, George Washington U., 1979. Bar: Pa. 1976, US Tax Ct. 1986. Atty.-adv. Office Chief Counsel to IRS Legis. and Regulations Divsn., Washington, 1976-78; atty.-adv. judge US Tax Ct., Washington, 1978-80; asst. prof. law Dickinson Sch. Law, 1981-83, lectr. and tax program chmn. continuing legal edn., 1981-83; assoc. prof. Villanova Sch. Law, 1983-86, prof., 1986—. Lectr. continuing legal edn. Pa. Bar Inst., Harrisburg, Continuing Legal Edn. Satellite Network, Inc., 1988; lectr. state and local taxes Georgetown U. Law Ctr. Inst., 1992; sr. tax and tech. ptnr. Ctr. Info. Law and Policy, 1993—99; owner JEMBook Pub. Co., TaxJEM Inc.; co-owner Starjem LLC, 2001—04; lectr. continuing legal edn. Phila. Tax Conf., 1996, 2001. Author: Cases and Materials in Federal Income Taxation, 1981, 26th edit., 2006, 27th edit., 2007, 28th edit., 2008, Materials in Partnership Law and Taxation, 1985, 6th edit., 1991, Materials in Partnership Taxation, 1987, 31th edit., 2008, 32nd edit., 2008, 33rd edit., 2009, Materials in Introduction to Taxation, 1987, Cases and Materials in Introduction to the Taxation of Business Entities, 1992, 16th edit., 2008, 17th edit., 2009, Materials in Taxation of Fundamental Wealth Transfers, 1986;: 2d edit., 1988, Materials in Tax Consequences of Disposition of Property, 1983, Materials and Problems in Taxation of Property Disposition I, 1987, Materials in Tax Planning for Real Estate, 1986, Materials in Estate and Gift Tax, 1983;: 3d edit., 1985, Materials in Taxation of Real Estate Transactions, 1986, 3d edit., 1992, Taxation of Residence Transactions, 1985, S Corporations: State Law and Taxation, 1989, (supplemental edits.), 1989, 1990, 1991, 1992, 1993, Materials and Problems in Computer Applications in the Law, 1990, 6th edit., 1995, Materials in Tax Policy, 1990, Materials in Digital Legal Practice Skills, 1996, Materials and Problems in Computer Applications in Tax Law, 1991, 8th edit., 1998, Better That 100 Witches Should Live, 1995, Materials in Decedents Estates and Trusts, 1997, 11th edit., 2008; co-author (with A. Clay): Preparing the 1065 Return, 1992, 1993; author: Continuing Legal Edn. Publs., 1981—; contbg. author: Federal Tax Service, 1989, Tax Practice Series, 1989—, Center for Computer-Assisted Legal Instruction, 2005—07; contbr. articles to profl. jours., chapters to books, monographs; author, developer: Computer Assisted Legal Edn. Programs in Taxation, owner, author, editor: computer assisted tax law instruction TaxJEM Inc., cons., prin. author: ABA Section of Taxation Model S Corporation Income Tax Act and Commentary, 1989, author, editor: Report of the Subcommittee on Comparison of S Corporations and Partnerships, 1990, 1991, case and comment editor: Villanova Law Rev., 1975—76, columnist, mem. editl. bd.: S Corps. Jour., 1987—91, Jour. of Ltd. Liability Cos., 1994—98, BNA Tax Mgmt., 1994—. Recipient Disting. Author award, BNA Tax Mgmt., 1993; Nat. Merit scholar, 1969—73. Mem. ABA (chair and reporter phaseout Elimination Project, Tax Simplification and Restructuring Com., sect. of taxation, cons., ex-officio mem. subcom. on state law, S Corp. com., chmn. subcom. on comparison of partnerships, mem. task force on pass-through entities, tax sect., former chmn. subcom. manuscripts and unpublished tchg. material, com. tchg. tax), Phila. Bar Assn. (lectr. tax sect. state and local tax CLE program 1991, fed. income taxes 1992—), Ctr. Info. Law and Policy, Order of Coif, Friars Sr. Soc. (Phila), Beta Alpha Psi. Office: Villanova U Sch Law Rm 12 299 N Spring Mill Rd Villanova PA 19085 Home: 219 Comrie Dr Villanova PA 19085-1402 Home Phone: 610-527-5144. Business E-Mail: maule@law.villanova.edu.

MAULL, GEORGE MARRINER, conductor, educator; b. Phila., Oct. 14, 1947; s. Frederick Dunlap and Helen Norbury (Jordan) M.; m. Marcia Eileen Korn, Aug. 13, 1984. MusB, U. Louisville, Ky., 1970, MusM, 1972; postgrad., Juilliard Sch. Music, 1976-78. Condr. Louisville Ballet Co., 1971-75; asst. condr. Opera Orch. NY, NYC, 1976-78, NJ Symphony Orch., Newark, 1979-80; music dir., condr. Bloomingdale Chamber Orch., NYC, 1980-83, NJ Youth Symphony, Summit, 1979—97, Philharm. Orch. NJ, Warren, 1987—2006; Condr. Laureate NJ Youth Symphony, 1997; founder, artistic dir. The Discovery Orch., 2006—. Conductor: Carnegie Hall, NYC, 1989, Lincoln Ctr., NYC, writer, host, condr.: Philharmonic Orch. of NJ, Discovery Concert Bach to the Future, Am. Pub. TV, 2003 (Emmy nomination, 2004), Polish Nat. Radio Symphony Orch., 2001—02 (CD recs. with); writer, host, condr. Sono Lumina, 2006; featured in WNET mini-documentary: Art Effects: Young and Noteworthy, 1988. Named Disting. Alumnus, U. Louisville, 1994. Mem. Am. Fedn. Musicians, Am. Symphony Orch. League (conducting fellow 1978, Nat. Cert. Merit 1980), Condr's. Guild. Episcopalian. Office: The Discovery Orch PO Box 4064 Warren NJ 07059-0064

MAUMBE, BLESSING MUKABETA, finance educator; s. Enock Chiyangwa and Violet Maumbe; m. Kudzayi Chitiyo, Dec. 23, 1995; children: Amanda Chido, Wayne Violet, Samantha Rufaro, Michael Rufaro, Victoria Taonanyasha. BSc, U. Zimbabwe, Harare, 1988; MSc,

Sokoine U. Agr., Morogoro, Tanzania, 1992; PhD in Agrl. Economics, Mich. State U., East Lansing, 2001. Cert. in online tchg. Mich. Virtual U., 2001. Economist Head Office, Ministry of Agr., Harare, 1989—90; lectr., agribus. studies coord. Africa U., Mutare, Zimbabwe, 1993—2002; sr. lectr. U. Ft. Hare, Alice, South Africa, 2004—05; assoc. prof. Cape Peninsula U. Tech., Cape Town, South Africa, 2005—07, Eastern Ky. U., Richmond, 2007—. Author, report devel. pvt. univs. in Africa Mich. State U., 2003. Contbr. articles to profl. jours. Advocacy Africa U., East Lansing. Fellowship, WK Kellogg Found., 1996—2001. Mem.: Internat. Assn. Agribus. Mgmt. Home: 131 Alycia Dr #4 Richmond KY 40475 Office: Eastern Ky Univ 521 Lancaster Ave Richmond KY 40475-3102 Office Fax: 859-622-6676. Personal E-mail: maumbebl@msu.edu. Business E-Mail: blessing.maumbe@eku.edu.

MAUNDER, ADDISON BRUCE, agronomic research company executive; b. Holdrege, Nebr., May 13, 1934; s. Addison Haynes and Marie Sophia (Luebs) M.; m. Katherina Marlene Blum, Sept. 8, 1978; children: Lynda Diane, Christopher Allen. B.Sc., U. Nebr., 1956; M.Sc., Purdue U., 1958, PhD, 1960; DSc (hon.), U. Nebr., 1991; DAgr (hon.), Purdue U., 2003. With DeKalb AgResearch, Inc., Lubbock, Tex., 1960-96, sorghum breeder, 1960-61, dir. sorghum research, 1961-76, v.p. sorghum research, 1976-78, v.p. rsch., 1978-82; v.p. DeKalb-Pfizer Genetics, DeKalb, Ill., 1982-89; v.p. agronomic research DeKalb Plant Genetics, DeKalb, Ill., 1989-91; sr. v.p. DeKalb Genetics Corp., DeKalb, Ill., 1991-96; rsch. advisor Nat. Grain Sorghum Prodrs. Assn., 1997—; with Lubbock Water Adv. Commn., 2008—. Bd. dirs. Diversity Mag., Washington, 1984-95; adj. prof. Tex. Tech. U., 1992—; pres. Nat. Grain Sorghum Prodrs. Found., 2004— Contbr. articles to profl. jours., chapters to books. Mem. deans adv. com. Tex. Tech. U., Lubbock, 1983-86; chmn. external rev. INTSORMIL of U.S. AID, Lincoln, Nebr., 1980-2001; bd. dirs. Tex. Tech. U. Rsch. Found., 1986-92; mem. Nat. Plant Genetic Resources Bd., 1991-92, Nat. Plant Variety Protection Bd., 1991-94; mem. World Food Prize Com., 1997-2003. Recipient Gerald Thomas award Tex. Tech. U., 1974, Prodn. award Grain Sorghum Producers Assn., 1985, Genetics and Plant Breeding award for Industry, 1987, Indsl. Agronomy award, 1988, Purdue Disting. Alumni award, 1997, Monsanto Crop Sci. Disting. Career award, 2000, Pres.'s Disting Svc. award Am. Seed Trade Assn., 2001; Henry Beachell Disting Alumni award, U. Nebraska, 2007. Fellow AAAS, Am. Soc. Agronomy (bd. dirs. 1991-92), Crop Sci. Soc. Am. (bd. dirs. 1991-92, pres. 1995-96); mem. Am. Seed Trade Assn., Sigma Xi, Alpha Zeta. Republican. Achievements include development of plant products (150 hybrids) emphasizing yield, improved drought and insect resistance as well as nutritional quality. Office Phone: 806-749-3478. Personal E-mail: texasgreenbug@aol.com.

MAUNER, CLAUDIA ANNE, design educator; d. George L. and Marianne Mauner; 1 child, Zoé Sophia. BA, Vassar Coll., Poughkeepsie, NY, 1983; BFA, Sch. Visual Arts, NYC, 1986; MFA, Yale Sch. Art, New Haven, 1992. Prin. Artbox Studios, NYC, 1995—; tchr., graphic design & history Sch. Visual Arts, NYC, 2007—. Author, illustrator Chronicle Books, San Francisco, 2003—06. Author and illustrator (children's book) Zoe Sophia's Scrapbook: An Adventure in Venice (awards, Art Dirs. Club, Switz, Print's European Regional Design Ann., 1998, Gold award, U. Continuing Edn. Assn., Starred Review from Publisher's Weekly, 2000); author (illustrator): (children's book) Zoe Sophia in New York: The Mystery of the Pink Phoenix Papers; Puffin Post. Liberal. Achievements include design of private collection of Merrill C. Berman. Business E-Mail: cmauner@artboxstudios.com.

MAUNEY, BRANDI SAVAGE, special education educator; b. Miami, Mar. 5, 1976; d. Victor Martin and Yvonne Marie Savage; m. John David Mauney, Mar. 30, 1975. B in Psychology, Ga. Coll. and State U., 1999, M in Spl. Edn., 2004; student in Child, Youth and Human Svcs., Nova Southeastern U., 2005—. Cert. tchr. Profl. Stds. Commn. in Ga. Spl. edn. tchr. Henry County Bd. of Edn., McDonough, Ga., 2002—04, spl. edn. liason/diagnostician, 2004—. Spl. edn. homebound tchr. for medically fragile Henry Count Bd. of Edn., McDounough, 2004—. Mem.: Collaboration Team: Direct On-going Tng. of Adminstrn. and Staff, State Monitoring Com. (assoc.), Continuous Improvement Monitoring Com. (assoc.), Interagency Child Coun. (assoc.; com. chair 2005—05), Sigma Alpha Iota (life; v.p. 1995—97). Republican. Baptist. Achievements include research in effects of Child-Find and Early Intervention. Avocations: music, swimming, yoga, travel, bicycling. Office: Henry County Bd Edn 33 N Zack Hinton Pkwy Mcdonough GA 30253 Personal E-mail: brandisavage@yahoo.com. E-mail: bmauney@henry.k12.ga.us.

MAUNEY, GARY VANCE, lawyer; b. Tampa, Fla., May 14, 1965; s. Vance Carroll and Barbara Callahan Mauney; m. Anna White Ferguson, Feb. 6, 2004. BA in Econs., NC State U., Raleigh, 1983—88, BA in Bus. Mgmt., 1983—88; JD, Am. U., DC, 1992—95. Bar: NC 1995, US Dist. Ct. (ea., mid. and we. dists.), NC 1997, US Ct. Appeals (4th cir.) 2004, US Supreme Ct. 1997. Law clk. to Hon. Donald L. Smith and Jack Cozort NC Ct. Appeals, Raleigh, 1995—97; ptnr. Law Offices William F. Maready, PLLC, Winston-Salem, NC, 1997—2001, Lewis & Roberts, PLLC, Charlotte, NC, 2002—. Contbr. articles to profl. jours. Pres. Univ. NC Assoc. Student Govts., Chapel Hill; student body pres. NC State U. Fellow: NC Inst. Polit. Leadership; mem.: ABA, NC State U. Alumni Assn., NC Bar Assn., NC Acad. Trial Lawyers, Am. Trial Lawyers Assn. (chair abusive tax shelter litig. com. 2005—08), NC Bar Assn. (com. chair 2004—05), Wolfpack Club, Charlotte City Club, Am. Mensa (life). Office: Lewis & Roberts PLLC 5960 Fairview Rd Ste 102 Charlotte NC 28210 Office Fax: 704-347-8929. Business E-Mail: garymauney@lewis-roberts.com.

MAUNG, KHIN MAUNG, physics professor; b. Lashio, Shan State, Burma, Sept. 24, 1951; s. TaungNyo TinTin Than and Than Than Thwai, Maung Maung (Stepfather) and Yi Yi (Stepmother); m. Vickie A. Chiodo; children: Khin Thitsa, Khin Su Myat, Alexander Raymond, Emily Suzanne, Shela Elizabeth. BSc, Rangoon Atrs & Sci. U., Burma, 1973; PhD, Kent State U., Ohio, 1985. Postdoc. assoc. U. Idaho, Moscow, 1985—86, NASA Langley, Hampton, Va., 1986—90, Old Dominion U., Norfolk, Va., 1986—90; rsch. asst. prof. Hampton U., Va., 1990—92, asst., assoc. & prof. physics, 1992—2005; prof. & chair physics & astronomy U. Southern Miss., Hattiesburg, Miss., 2005—. Home: 105 Hickory Cir Petal MS 39465 Office: UnivSouthern Miss 118 Coll Dr #5046 Hattiesburg MS 39406 Business E-Mail: khin.maung@usm.edu.

MAUPIN, ELIZABETH THATCHER, theater critic; b. Cleve., Oct. 21, 1951; d. Addison and Margaret (Thatcher) M.; m. Jay Yellen, Dec. 29, 1995. BA in English, Wellesley Coll., Mass., 1973; M in Journalism, U. Calif., Berkeley, 1976. Editorial asst. Houghton Mifflin Co., Boston, 1973-74; reporter, movie critic Times-Standard, Eureka, Calif., 1976-78; theater and movie critic Chronicle-Telegram, Elyria, Ohio, 1978-79; movie critic Ledger-Star, Norfolk, Va., 1979-82; feature writer Va.-Pilot and Ledger-Star, Norfolk, 1982-83; sr. theater critic Orlando (Fla.) Sentinel, 1983—. Fellow Nat. Arts Journalism program Columbia U., 1995-96. Fellow Nat. Critics Inst.; mem. Am. Theatre Critics Assn. (exec. com. 1993-99, 05-06, chair 1996-99). Office: Orlando Sentinel 633 N Orange Ave Orlando FL 32801-1349

MAUPIN, KARIN LOUISE, secondary school educator; d. Alfred Bertil and Kathryn Louise (Snapp) Swanson; m. Bernard Kent Fredrick Maupin, Aug. 11, 1973; children: Kristin Louise, Kevin Alfred. BA in Anthropology, Northwestern U., 1970, tchg. cert., 1972; postgrad., U. Ill., 1972—73, Aquinas Coll., 1994—95; M in Spl. Edn. and Learning Disabilities, Calvin Coll., 1998. Commodities trading asst. E.F. Hutton & Co., Chgo., 1972—73; comml. paper trader Montgomery Ward Credit Corp., Chgo., 1973—77; tchr. Creative Learning Ctr., Grand Rapids, Mich., 1982—83; program dir. Alternative Methods for Internat. Stability/Trees Corps., 1989—; tutor SLD Ctr., Grand Rapids, 1995—98; substitute tchr. Forest Hills Pub. Schs., Grand Rapids, 1996—97, tchr., 1997—. Odyssey of the Mind coach Forest Hills No. Middle Sch., Grand Rapids, 1995; adult sponsor F.O.M.E. Environ. Club Forest Hills No. H.S., 1995—98. Contbg. editor: mag. Our Children, 1991—93. Tutor Head Start Program, Grand Rapids, Mich., 1966, James Taylor Sch., Chgo., 1971, Cabrini Green Housing Project, 1976—77; vol. curator Field Mus. Natural History, Chgo., 1978—80; vol. curator, docent Grand Rapids Pub. Mus., 1981—83; bd. mem. Summerfest Ballet Sch., 1983—85; pres. Kent County Med. Soc. Aux., 1984—85; coord. Citizens Liability Action Com., 1984—87; legis. chmn. Mich. State Med. Soc. Aux., 1985—87; pres. Coffinberry Archaeol. Soc., 1988; bd. mem. Children's Inter-active Sci. Ctr., 1995—99, SLD Learning Ctr. Western Mich., 1995—99; rep. Northwestern U. Alumni, 1996—; mem. edn. com. Frederik Meijer Gardens, 1997—2001. Recipient Cert. Appreciation, Mich. State Med. Soc., 1987, AMA, 1987, Letter Appreciation for environ. stewardship, Former Pres. Gerald R. Ford, 1989, Achievement award, Global Releaf, 1990, Letter Appreciation for environ. stewardship, Pres. George Bush, 1992, Cert. Appreciation, Gov. Engler, Mich. Office of Governor, 1992, Cmty. Svc. award, Mich. Forestry & Park Assn., 1992, State Winner, Pres. Bush's Take Pride in Am., 1992, Nongovtl. Agy. award for environ. stewardship, Mich. Audubon Soc., 1993, Letter Appreciation, Kent County Commrs., 1994, Cert. Appreciation, Grand Rapids Pub. Schs., 1994, Pres. Clinton's Coun. on Sustainable Development, 1997. Avocations: travel, gardening, tennis, bicycling, golf. Office: Forest Hills Pub Schs 6590 Cascade Rd SE Grand Rapids MI 49506 E-mail: amistrees@aol.com.

MAUPIN, MICHAEL DENNIS, quality assurance professional; Cert. in Aviation Maintenance Technician, Sacramento City Coll., 1975. Inspector aviation components E.F. Felt Co., San Leandro, Calif., 1977—88; supr. Turbine Engine Shop Associated Aerospace Activities, Inc., San Leandro, 1983—87; dir. quality assurance WECO Aerospace Sys., Inc., Lincoln, Calif., 1988—; facilities mechanic Target Corp., Woodland, Calif.; owner Mikes Aircraft Parts & Svc. Achievements include electrical generator installation for helicopters for law enforcement and emergency medical ships. Avocations: home brewing, gardening, fishing, hiking, camping.

MAURER, CHERYL, lab administrator, researcher; d. R. Chris and Carol Houck; m. David Maurer; children: Sharilyn, Derrick, Darryl, Colby, Alisa. BS in Microbiology, Pa. State U., Univ Pk; MS in Instrnl. Leadership, Robert Morris U., Moon Township, Pa., MS in Engring. Mgmt. Cert. audiometric technician CAOHC, 1997. Ops. mgr. ASI Health Svcs., Pitts., 1997—2004; lab. scientist Robert Morris U., 2005—, mem., Lab. Safety Subcom., 2005—, mem., Hazardous Materials & Waste Subcom., 2005—. Mem. Environ. Adv. Coun., Moon Township, 2007—09. Mem.: Penn State Alumni Assn., Alpha Chi, Alpha Phi Omega. Office: Robert Morris Univ 6001 Univ Boulevard Moon Township PA 15108 Business E-Mail: maurer@rmu.edu.

MAURER, CHRISTOPHER HERMAN, foreign language educator; b. Abington, Pa., Oct. 21, 1949; s. Herman H. and Neva (Kerr) M.; m. Maria Estrella Iglesias, Mar. 2, 1977; children: Daniel, Pablo. BA, Columbia U., 1977; MA, U. Pa., 1980, PhD, 1982. Tchg. fellow Spanish U. Pa., 1977-82; asst. prof. Spanish Harvard U., Cambridge, Mass., 1982-85, assoc. prof. Spanish, 1985-90; prof. Spanish, chair dept. Spanish and Portuguese Vanderbilt U., Nashville, 1990—. Author: Obra y vida de Francisco de Figueroa, 1988; co-author: (textbook) Temas: Invitación a la literatura hispánica, 1993; editor, translator: The Poetical Works of Federico Garcia Lorca, 1988-95, The Art of Worldly Wisdom, 1991, A Pocket Mirror for Heroes, 1996; editor: Epistolario, 1995; mem. editl. bd. FGL Boletin de la Fundación Federico Garcia Lorca, 1988—, Cuadernos Cervantes, 1994—; contbr. articles to profl. jours. Fellow Fulbright Commn., Madrid, Spain, 1981-82; annual rsch. grantee Clark Fund, Harvard U., 1982-90; rsch. grantee Com. on Cultural Cooperation Between Spain's Ministry of Culture and U.S. Univs., 1988; grantee Gen. Book and Libr. Divsn. of the Spanish Ministry of Culture and from Whitehead Found., 1990; Univ. Rsch. Coun. grantee Vanderbilt U., 1993; Travel to Collections grantee NEH, summer 1993, others. Mem. MLA. Democrat. Roman Catholic. Avocation: music. Office: Vanderbilt Univ Dept Spanish & Portuguese PO Box 1617B Nashville TN 37202-1617 Home: 83 Coolidge St Brookline MA 02446-5805

MAURER, DAVID LEO, lawyer; b. Evansville, Ind., Oct. 31, 1945; s. John G. Jr. and Mildred M. (Lintzenich) M.; m. Diane M. Kaput, Aug. 11, 1973; children: Eric W., Kathryn A. BA magna cum laude, U. Detroit, 1967, Cert. in Teaching, 1971; JD, Wayne State U., 1975. Bar: Mich., U.S. Dist. Ct. (ea. and we. dist.) Mich., U.S. Ct. Appeals (6th cir.) Cin. Law clk. Mich. Ct. Appeals, Detroit, 1976, Supreme Ct. Mich., Lansing, 1977-78; asst. U.S. atty. civil div. U.S. Dept. Justice, Detroit, 1978-81; assoc. to ptnr. Butzel, Long, Gust, Klein & Van Zile, Detroit, 1981-85; ptnr. Pepper Hamilton LLP), Detroit, 1985—2007. Guest lectr. Practicing Law Inst., 1988-2007, Nat. Bus. Inst., 1989—, U. Mich. Law Sch., U. Detroit Law Sch., 1990, Hazardous Waste Super Conf., 1986-87. Co-author: Michigan Environmental Law Deskbook, 1992; contbr. articles to profl. jours. and chpts. in books. Mem. Energy & Environ. Policy Com., 1988—, chairperson, 1989-90; mem. Great Lakes Water Resources Commn., 1986. Mem. State Bar Mich. (environ. couns. 1986-91, sec., treas., chairperson-elect, chairperson 1991-93). Office: 941 Sunningdale Dr Grosse Pointe MI 48236 Office Phone: 313-393-7448. Personal E-mail: maurerdavidl@comcast.net.

MAURER, DONALD EUGENE, mathematician; b. Denver, Aug. 21, 1942; s. Edward Michael and Dorothy (Wootton) M.; m. Ann Lucille Outhwaite, May 31, 1975; children: Stephanie Lynn St. John, Laura Ann. BA, U. Colo., 1964; PhD, Calif. Inst. Tech., 1969. Asst. prof. Tufts U., Medford, Mass., 1968-75; vis. mathematician Inst. for Def. Analyses, Princeton, N.J., 1975-77; ops. analyst Ctr. for Naval Analyses, Alexandria, Va., 1978-82; mathematician, principal profl. staff Johns Hopkins U. Applied Physics Lab., Laurel, Md., 1982—; reviewer Math. Revs., 1975—, asst. sect. supr., 1994—; tech. advisor U.S. Navy, 80-81. Contbr. articles to profl. jours. Invention: a distance sorting algorithm. NSF fellow, 1964-68, Merle A. Tuve fellow, 1989-90; recipient Tufts U. Faculty Rsch. award, 1972, Hart prize, John Hopkins U., 2003. Mem. Am. Math. Soc., N.Y. Acad. Sci., Am. Assn. for Advancement of Sci., Sigma Xi. Avocations: hiking; painting. Office: Johns Hopkins U Applied Physics Lab Johns Hopkins Rd Laurel MD 20723-6099 Office Phone: 240-228-4714. Business E-Mail: donald.maurer@jhuapl.edu.

MAURER, FRANK W., JR., land trust administrator; b. Boston, Aug. 25, 1941; s. Frank W Sr. and Elizabeth M. Maurer; m. Lenora Ann Timm, Apr. 19, 1985; children from previous marriage: Pierre Crispin, Basil Gavin. *Father and namesake, Frank W Maurer, Sr., having a background in both engineering and physiology, was asked to work in secret at the beginning of WWII to design and produce high-altitude breathing equipment for Allied pilots to over-fly the Axis pilots with their then superior equipment. At the conclusion of the war, he returned all patents to the federal government, saying he could not profit from such a horrible event. For the rest of his life he was an inventor and designer. The family likes to think that his creative and social sensibilities live on in his children and grandchildren. Mother, Elizabeth M. Maurer, was always a free thinker, having voted for socialist, Norman Thomas, in her first presidential election. During my childhood, she was open minded in her approach to raising me and my siblings. Her role modeling allowed me to be the free thinker I became.* BA in Biology, Antioch Coll., Yellow Springs, Ohio, 1964; PhD in Vertebrate Zoology and Ecology, Cornell U., Ithaca, NY, 1968. Lic. vessel operator Calif. Asst. prof. biology U. Bosphorus, Istanbul, Turkey, 1968—71; lectr. zoology Nat. U. Lesotho, 1971—76; rsch. assoc. Swedish U. Agrl. Scis., Uppsala, 1977; interviewer 13 countries in Asia, 1978; owner, operator, dir. Rsch. Farm, Davis, Calif., 1978—; organic farmers' market prodr., 1978—; exec. dir., pres. Quail Ridge Wilderness Conservancy, Davis, 1989—, Environ. Edn. Farm Found., Davis, 1993—. Lectr. in field; cons. on openspace and conservation models for small landowners, Wyo., 2004—, Nev., 2007—; owner Deer Canyon Preserve, N.Mex., 2006—. *Always among his goals are human rights, education, promoting environmental and open space programs, interwoven with artistic expression. In addition to starting an educational teaching farm in Davis, CA in 1978, he and his wife worked over 24 years to create a 2000 acre native habitat and wildlife reserve in Napa County by purchasing, via innovative fundraising strategies, land destined for development. He led the initiative to incorporate this reserve into the University of California's Natural Reserve System. Today's activities focus on public speaking, voting reform, habitat restoration, creating openspace and conservation models for small landowners, and using the art of hand-carved petroglyphs for teaching and commemorations.* Author: (legislation) Calif. State Grass Bill, 2004; author: (facilitator) Wyo. State Grass Bill, 2007; petroglyphs, Calif. State Archives, 2000, 2004, Wash. State Archives, 2002—03, Assembly of Wales, 2003, Coun. of Cornwall, 2003, Parliament of Scotland, 2004, Oreg. State Archives, 2004, Nev. State Libr. and Archives, 2005, Utah State Archives, 2005, Wyo. State Archives, 2005, Idaho State Hist. Soc. - Pub. Archives Rsch. Libr., 2007, Colo. State Archives, 2007, New Mexico State Records Ctr. & Archives, 2007, Mont. Hist. Soc., 2008, Ariz. State Libr. Archives & Pub. Records, 2008; prodr.: (CD) Scottish Poetry, 2003, (ednl. videos) Quail Ridge Reserve, 1998, Reflections, 2000, (photobook) Portraits of a Vanishing Landscape A Pictorial Interpretation of the Western Sagebrush Steppe, 2006; contbr. articles to profl. publs. Registered pacifist US Draft Bd., 1966; activist Ctr. for Voting and Democracy, Takoma Park, Md., 2004—, Californians for Electoral Reform, Sacramento, 2004—. Recipient John Muir award, Davis Farmers Market, 1989, Conservation Achievement recognition, Napa County Land Trust, 1990, Recognition award, U. Calif. Natural Res. Sys., 2009. Mem.: Soc. Conservation Biology (life), Soc. Study of Evolution (life), Am. Soc. Mammalogy (life), Dixon Scottish Cultural Assn., Sacramento Caledonian Club. Green Party. Avocations: travel, hiking, birdwatching. Home: 25344 County Rd 95 Davis CA 95616 Office: Quail Ridge Wilderness Conservancy/ Environ Edn Farm Found 25344 County Rd 95 Davis CA 95616 Office Phone: 530-758-1387. Office Fax: 530-758-1316. Business E-Mail: qualrid@quailridge.org.

MAURER, FREDERIC GEORGE, III, bank executive; b. Grand Rapids, Mich., May 15, 1952; s. Frederic George and Rhea Marie (Annesser) Maurer. BA, St. Louis U., 1974, MBA, 1977. Dir. residence Marguerite Hall St. Louis U., 1977-79; internat. banking analyst Merc. Trust Co., St. Louis, 1979-80, banking rep. Latin Am., 1980-81, internat. officer, 1981-83, asst. v.p., 1983, Union Bank, LA, 1983-86; asst. v.p. internat. sect. Centerre Bank, N.A., St. Louis, 1986-87, asst. v.p. portfolio mgmt. sect., 1987-88; with pvt. banking dept. Boatmen's Nat. Bank, St. Louis, 1988-90, v.p., 1990-97, Nations Bank, St. Louis, 1997-99, Bank Am., St. Louis, 1999-2001, Commerce Trust Co., St. Louis, 2001—06, Bank Midwest, N.A., St. Louis, 2006—, sr. v.p., 2008—. Bd. dirs. Assocs. St. Louis U. Librs., 1975—79, NCCJ, 1992—, Food Outreach, Inc., 2001—, Downtown/Marquette YMCA, 2003—; mem. dir.'s assn. Mo. Bot. Garden, 1986—; bd. dirs. Franciscan Missionary Union, 1996—2001. Internat. Bus. fellow, 1975—77. Mem.: DuBourg Soc., LA English-Speaking Union, Performaing Arts Coun.-In the Wings, Alumni Coun. St. Louis U., Ctr. Internat. Banking Studies, U. Va., Robert Morris Assocs., Opera Guild, St. Louis Club. Home: 849 Aldan Dr Saint Louis MO 63132-3501 Office: 1 N Brentwood Blvd Ste 100 Saint Louis MO 63105 Office Phone: 314-862-4953. Business E-Mail: maurerfg@dfckc.com.

MAURER, GILBERT CHARLES, media specialist; b. NYC, May 24, 1928; s. Charles and Mildred (Petite) M.; m. Ann D'Espinosa. AB, St. Lawrence U., 1950; MBA, Harvard U., 1952. With Cowles Communications, Inc., NYC, 1952-71, Look Mag., 1952-62; pub. Venture mag., 1963-67; pres. Family Circle mag., 1967-69, v.p., dir. corporate planning, exec. com., 1969-71; sr. v.p., dir. F.A.S. Internat., Inc., 1971-73; v.p. mag. div. Hearst Corp., 1973-74, exec. v.p., 1974-76, pres. mag. div., 1976-90, also dir.; exec. v.p. The Hearst Corp., 1985-98, chief operating officer, 1990-98, cons. Mem. NY adv. bd. Salvation Army, 1979—; trustee Whitney Mus. Am. Art, 1983—, pres., 1994-98, trustee Norton Mus. of Art, 1998—; mem. vis. com. Medill Sch. Journalism Northwestern U., 1985-94, chmn., 1989-94; bd. dirs. Boys and Girls Club Am., 1986—, William Randolph Hearst Found., The Hearst Found.; mem. bd. mgrs. NY Bot. Garden, 1989. Mem. Mag. Pubs. Assn. (bd. dirs., chmn. 1979-81) Clubs: Harvard (NYC), Metropolitan (NYC). Office: Hearst 300 W 57th St New York NY 10019.

MAURER, HAROLD MAURICE, pediatrician; b. NYC, Sept. 10, 1936; s. Isador and Sarah (Rothkowitz) M.; m. Beverly Bennett, June 12, 1960; children: Ann Maurer Rosenbach, Wendy Maurer Linsky. AB, NYU, 1957; MD, SUNY, Bklyn., 1961. Diplomate Am. Bd. Pediatrics, Am. Bd. Pediatric Hematology-Oncology. Intern pediatrics Kings County Hosp., NYC, 1961-62; resident in pediatrics Babies Hosp., Columbia-Presbyn. Med. Center, NYC, 1962-64; fellow in pediatric hematology/oncology Columbia-Presbyn. Med. Center, 1966-68; asst. prof. pediatrics Med. Coll. Va., Richmond, 1968-71, asso. prof., 1971-75, prof., 1975—, chmn. dept. pediatrics, 1976-93; dean U. Nebr. Coll. Medicine, Omaha, 1993-98; chancellor U. Nebr. Med. Ctr., Omaha, 1998—. Chmn. Intergroup Rhabdomyosarcoma Study, 1972-98; exec. com. Pediatric Oncology Group. Editor: pediatrics, 1983, Rhabdomyosarcoma and Related Tumors in Children and Adolescence, 1991; mem. editorial bd. Am. Jour. Hematology, Journal Pediatric Hematology and Oncology, Medical and Pediatric Oncology, 1984-99; contbr. articles to profl. jours. Mem. Youth Health Task Force, City of Richmond., Gov.'s Adv. Com. on Handicapped., Gov.'s Homeland Security Policy Group, Nebr., 2002-; mem. coun. biodefense Assn. Academic Health Ctr., 2003—, coun. global health, 2003—, gov.'s homeland security policy group 2002—; mem. nat. com. on childhood cancer Am. Cancer Soc., bd. dirs. Va. divsn.; bd. dirs. Nebr. Med. Ctr., 1997—, Friends of Nat. Inst. Nursing Rsch., 2004-05; adv. com. Lisstratcom, 2004—. Served to lt. comdr. USPHS, 1964-66. Recipient Midlander of Yr., Omaha World Herald Newspaper, 2004, Face on the Barroom Floor award, Omaha Press Club, 2007, honor, Omaha, 2008; named Ak-Sar-Ben King C IX, 2005; named to Hall of Fame, 2009; grantee, NIH, 1974—98. Mem. Am. Acad. Pediatrics (com. oncology-hematology), Am. Soc. Hematology, Soc. Pediatric Rsch., Am. Pediatric Soc., Va. Pediatric Sic. (exec. com.), Assn. Med. Sch. Pediatric Dept. Chmn., Internat. Soc. Pediatric Oncology, Am. Soc. Clin. Oncology, Va. Hematology Soc., Am. Assn. Cancer Rsch., Am. Cancer Soc., Am. Soc. Pediatric Hematology-Oncology (v.p. 1990-91, pres. 1991-93, Lifetime Achievement award children's oncology group 2003), Sigma Xi, Coun. Deans AAMC, Gov.'s Blue Ribbon Commn., Alpha Omega Alpha. Republican. Jewish. Home: 9822 Ascot Dr Omaha NE 68114-3848 Office: U Nebr Med Ctr 986605 Nebraska Med Ctr Omaha NE 68198-6605 Business E-Mail: hmmaurer@unmc.edu.

MAURER, LAWRENCE MICHAEL, retired acting school administrator, educator; b. Bklyn., Oct. 2, 1935; s. Charles and Ethel (Ryan) M.; married Mar. 20, 1970 (div. 1971); 1 child, Lalaine; m. Carol Schneider, July 27, 1971. B of Vocat. Edn., San Diego State U., 1976; MS in Sch. Adminstrn., Nat. U., 1981. Cert. sch. adminstr., tchr., c.c. educator, Calif. Commd. ensign USN, 1953; advanced through grades to chief, 1969; ret., 1972; tchr. San Diego County Office Edn., 1972—2008, acting vice prin., 1989—2008. Bd. dirs. Multi-cultural Affairs Com., San Diego, 1991—, Self Esteem Devel. C.C., San Diego, 1990—, Sch. to Career Commn., San Diego, 1986—; cons. Vocat. Edn. in Ct. Schs., San Diego, 1986—; adj. prof. U. Calif., San Diego, Nat. U.-Violence Prevention in Sch.; mentor tchrs. in tech. San Diego Office Edn., 1996-2008. Contbr. articles to profl. jours. Organizer Dem. party. Named Excellent Tchr. of Yr. Corp. for Excellence in Pub. Edn., 1992, mentor Tchr.-Tech., 1996; vocat. grantee, 1988. Mem. ASCD (bd. dirs.), Nat. Vocat. Educators, Calif. Reading Assn., Calif. Ct. Sch. Adminstrs. Avocation: civil rights activist. Office: San Diego County Office Edn 6401 Linda Vista Rd San Diego CA 92111-7319 Home: 10442 Ken Ln Santee CA 92071 Home Phone: 619-448-9440; Office Phone: 619-991-4433. Personal E-mail: lmaurer3@yahoo.com, lmaurer2@cox.net.

MAURER, RICHARD MICHAEL, investment company executive; b. Bethlehem, Pa., June 4, 1948; s. Richard Thomas and Anna Theresa (Bold) M.; m. Karen Coe, June 13, 1970; children: Christopher Coe, Mark Emerson. Student, Pa. State U., 1966-68; BS, Point Park Coll., 1971; MBA, U. Pitts., 1982. CPA Pa. Staff acct. Price Waterhouse, Pitts., 1972-74, tax acct., 1974, sr. tax acct., 1974-77, tax mgr., 1977-78; dir. taxes The Hillman Co., Pitts., 1978-85; pres. Maurer Ross & Co., Inc., Pitts., 1985—; co-mng. ptnr. Wesmar Ptnrs., Pitts., 1985—; mng. dir. Source Cos., LLC, Pitts., 2006; pres. Arrow Capital Advisors, LLC, Pitts., 2007—. Bd. dirs. Women's Golf Unltd., Inc., Maurer Ross & Co., Inc., Maurer & Ross, Inc. Mem. AICPA, Assn. Corp. Growth, Pa. Inst. CPAs, Rotary (past dir., past pres.), Oakmont Country Club, Duquesne Club. Office: 1606 Carmody Ct Ste 300 Sewickley PA 15143 E-mail: maurer.rick@gmail.com.

MAURER, ROBERT DISTLER, retired industrial physicist; b. St. Louis, July 20, 1924; s. John and Elizabeth J. (Distler) M.; m. Barbara A. Mansfield, June 9, 1951; children: Robert M., James B., Janet L. BS, U. Ark., 1948, LLD, 1980; PhD, MIT, 1951. Mem. staff MIT, 1951-52; with Corning Glass Works, NY, 1952-89, mgr. physics research, 1963-78, research fellow, 1978-89. Contbr. articles to profl. jours., chpts. to books; patentee in field. Served with U.S. Army, 1943-46. Decorated Purple Heart; recipient Indsl. Physics prize Am. Inst. Physics, 1978, L.M. Ericsson Internat. prize in telecommunications, 1979, Indsl. Rsch. Inst. Achievement award, 1988, Optical Soc. Am./IEEE Leos Tyndall award, 1987, Disting. Alumni award U. Ark, 1994, Am. Innovator award U.S. Dept. Commerce, 1995, Nat. Medal of Technology, 2000, C&C prize Japanese NEC Found, 2007. Fellow IEEE (Morris N. Liebmann award 1978), Am. Ceramic Soc. (George W. Morey award 1976), Am. Phys. Soc. (New Materials prize 1989); mem. NAE (Charles Draper prize 1999), Nat. Inventors Hall of Fame. Home: 2572 W 28th Ave Eugene OR 97405

MAURER, VIRGINIA GALLAHER, law educator; b. Shawnee, Okla., Nov. 7, 1946; d. Paul Clark Gallaher and Virginia Ruth (Watson) Abernathy; m. Ralph Gerald Maurer, July 31, 1971(dec. May12, 2006); children: Ralph Emmett, William Edward. BA, Northwestern U., 1968; MA, Stanford U., 1969, JD, 1975. Bar: Iowa 1976. Tchr. social studies San Mateo H.S. Dist., Calif., 1969—71; spl. asst. to pres. U. Iowa, Iowa City, 1976—80, adj. asst. prof. law, 1979—80; affiliate asst. prof. law U. Fla., Gainesville, 1981, asst. prof. bus. law, 1980—85, assoc. prof., 1985—93, prof., 1993—, Huber Hurst prof., 1997—. Dir. Poe Bus. Ethics Ctr., 1998—, MBA program U. Fla., 1987, chair dept. mgmt., 1994-2003; vis. scholar Wolfson Coll., Cambridge, 1994; vis. prof. SDA Bocconi U., Milan, 1994-96, Helsinki Sch. Econs. and Bus., 1998, U. Catania, Sicily, 1999, 2002-03; cons. Gov.'s Com. on Iowa 2000, Iowa City, 1976-77, Fla. Banker's Assn., Gainesville, 1982, various law firms, 1995—. Contbr. articles to profl. jours.; jr. editor Am. Bus. Law Jour., 1989-90, mng. editor, 1990-91, editor-in-chief, 1992-94 Bd. dirs. Gainesville Chamber Orch., 1990-93; fundraising com. Pro Arte Musica, Gainesville, 1980-84; sr. warden, vestry Holy Trinity Episc. Ch., 1991-93, 99-2004, jr. warden, 2000-02, 2007-; bd. dirs. Holy Trinity Found., Gainesville, 1991-93; com. charter and canon law Episc. Diocese Fla., 1994-96; bd. dirs. Samaritan Ctrs. of North Ctrl. Fla., Inc., 1995-97, Early Childhood Learning Coalition Alachua County, Fla., 2007-09. Named Fla. Blue Key Disting. Faculty mem., 2004, Woman of Distinction, Alachua County, 2005. Fellow Soc. Advanced Legal Studies (UK); mem. ABA, AAUW, Acad. Legal Studies in Bus. (ho. of dels. 1989-90, exec. com. 1992, 98—, sec.-treas. 1998-99, v.p. 1999-2000, pres-elect 2000-01, pres. 2001-02, exec. com. 2002-), Southeastern Bus. Law Assn. (proc. editor 1984-87, treas. 1985-86, v.p. 1986-87, pres.-elect 1987-88, pres. 1988-89), Iowa Bar Assn., LWV, U. Fla. Athletic Assn. (bd. dirs. 2004-, v.p. chmn. fin. com. 1982-88), Gainesville Womens' Forum (bd. dirs. 1988-91), Fla. Women' Network (bd. dirs. 1995-99), Univ. Woman's Club (Gainesville, Fla.), Rotary (bd. dirs. 1989-91, dist. scholarship com. 1997-99, regional scholarship com. 2000, chair 2001), Ctr. Applied Psychological Type, Gainesville, Fla.(bd. dir. 2008-),Beta Gamma Sigma, Kappa Alpha Theta, Delta Sigma Pi. Home: 2210 NW 6th Pl Gainesville FL 32603-1409 Office: U Fla Grad Sch Bus Gainesville FL 32611 Office Phone: 352-392-1048. Business E-Mail: virginia.maurer@cba.ufl.edu.

MAURICE, PAUL, professional hockey coach; b. Sault Ste. Marie, Ont., Canada, Jan. 30, 1967; m. Michelle Maurice; children: Sydney, Jake, Luke. Asst. coach Detroit Jr. Red Wings, 1988-93, head coach, 1993-94, Hartford Whalers, 1995—97, Carolina Hurricanes, 1997—2003, 2008—, Toronto Marlies, 2005—06, Toronto Maple Leafs, 2006—08. Asst. coach NHL All-Star Game, 1997. Named runner up Coach of Yr. nominamtion OHL, 1995. Mem. Compuware Hockey Orgn. Office: Carolina Hurricanes Hockey Club RBC Ctr 1400 Edwards Mill Rd Raleigh NC 27607*

MAURIN, JAMES E., real estate executive; Grad. in Aerospace Engring., La. State U., 1970; MBA, Tulane U., 1972. Acct. Ernst and Ernst, New Orleans; mng. ptnr. Maurin-Ogden Properties, Covington, La., 1975—; chmn. Stirling Properties, Covington, La., 1975—. Mem. bus. sch. coun. Tulane U., La. State U.; bd. dirs., chmn., exec. com. Ochsner Found. Hosp. Mem.: LSU Tiger Athletic Found. (pres. elect., exec. com., bd. chair.), Northshore Arena Found. (bd. dirs., bd. mem.), Blueprint La. (founding trustee), Internat. Coun. Shopping Ctrs. (chmn. exec. com. 2004—05), World Pres.'s Orgn. (chmn. La. chpt. 2005), Urban Land Inst. (chmn. La. dist. coun. 2002—04). Office: Stirling Properties 109 Northpark Blvd Covington LA 70433-5005 Office Phone: 985-898-2022. Business E-Mail: jmau@stirlingprop.com.

MAURIOCOURT, GREGORY, history professor; b. Cleve., Dec. 15, 1963; s. Flory Eugene and Anne Marie Mauriocourt; m. Nicole Mauied, May 16, 2009; children: Stephen Gregory, Randall Flory. BA, Hiram Coll., Ohio, 1986; MA, Cleve. State U., 1990. Adj. faculty Cuyahoga CC, Cleve., 1993—98; history instr. Tech. Coll. Lowcountry, Beaufort, SC, 1998—. Advisor Phi Theta Kappa, Jackson, Miss., 2007—. Active precinct cmty., Maple Heights, Ohio, 1995—97. Nominee, SC Tech. Edn. Assn., 2002—03. Independent. Methodist. Avocations: tennis, Bocce. Home: 803 Battery Creek Rd Beaufort SC 29902 Office: Tech Coll Lowcountry 921 Ribaut Rd Beaufort SC 29901 Business E-Mail: gmaurio@tcl.edu.

MAURO, MICHAEL ANTHONY, Secretary of State, Iowa; b. Sept. 29, 1948; m. Dorothy Fischer; children: Steven, Nick, Michael. Grad., Drake U., Des Moines, 1970. Lic. real estate broker, cert. elections/registration adminstr. 2003. HS govt. tchr., coach, referee; election dir. Polk County, Iowa, 1984—96, auditor Iowa, 1997—2007; sec. state State of Iowa, Des Moines, 2007—. Mem. I-VOTERS Standards com. Polk County, mem. HAVA State Plan Adv. Com., mem. Voting Equipment Users Grp., mem. Deferred Compensation Bd. Democrat. Office: Office Sec State State Capitol Rm 105 1007 E Grand Ave Des Moines IA 50319

MAURO, RICHARD FRANK, retired lawyer, investment company executive; b. Hawthorne, Nev., July 21, 1945; s. Frank Joseph and Dolores D. (Kreimeyer) M.; m. LaVonne M. Madden, Aug. 28, 1965; 1 child, Lindsay Anne. AB, Brown U., 1967; JD summa cum laude, U. Denver, 1970. Bar: Colo. 1970. Assoc. Dawson, Nagel, Sherman & Howard, Denver, 1970-72, Van Cise, Freeman, Tooley & McClearn, Denver, 1972-73, ptnr., 1973-74, Hall & Evans, Denver, 1974-81, Morrison & Forester, Denver, 1981-84; of counsel Parcel & Mauro, P.C., Denver, 1984—; pres. Parcel, Mauro & Hultin, P.C., Denver, 1988-90; of counsel Parcel, Mauro P.C., Denver, 1992-99; pres. Sundance Oil Exploration Co., 1985-88; exec. v.p. Castle Group, Inc., 1992-97, pres., 1998—, Richard F. Mauro, P.C., 1999—; ptnr. Moye, Giles, O'Keefe, Vermeire & Gorrell, 1999—2003, ret., 2003. Adj. prof. U. Denver Coll. Law, 1981-84. Symposium editor: Denver Law Jour., 1969-70; editor: Colorado Corporation Manual; contbr. articles to legal jours. Pres. Colo. Open Space Coun., 1974; mem. law alumni coun. U. Denver Coll. Law, 1988-91. Francis Wayland scholar, 1967; recipient various Am. jurisprudence awards Mem. ABA, Colo. Bar Assn., Denver Bar Assn., Colo. Assn. Corp. Counsel. (pres. 1974-75), Am. Arbitration Assn. (comml. arbitrator), Order St. Ives, Denver Athletic Club (bd. dirs. 1986-89). Home: 2552 E Alameda Ave Unit 128 Denver CO 80209-3330 Office: 1225 17th St Fl 29 Denver CO 80202-5534 Personal E-mail: dick.mauro@comcast.net.

MAU-SHIMIZU, PATRICIA ANN, lawyer; b. Jan. 17, 1953; d. Herbert G. K. and Leilani (Yuen) Mau; 1 child, Melissa Rose. BS, U. San Francisco, 1975; JD, Golden Gate U., 1979. Bar: Hawaii 1979. Law clk. State Supreme Ct., Honolulu, 1979-80; atty. Bendet, Fidell & Sakai, Honolulu, 1980-81; legis. atty. Honolulu City Coun., 1981-83, House Majority Staff Office, Honolulu, 1983-84, dir., 1984-93; chief clk. Hawaii Ho. of Reps., 1993—. Mem. Hawaii Bar Assn., Hawaii Women Lawyers, Jr. League Hawaii. Democrat. Roman Catholic. Home: 7187 Hawaii Kai Dr Honolulu HI 96825-3115 Office: State House Reps 415 S Beretania St Rm 027 Honolulu HI 96813-2407 Office Phone: 808-586-6127.

MAUSKOPF, ROSLYNN R., federal judge, former prosecutor; b. Washington, 1957; d. Barry and Regina Mauskopf. BA, Brandeis U., 1979; JD, Georgetown U., 1982. Asst. dist. atty. NY County Dist. Atty.'s Office, 1982—95, dep. chief spl. prosecution bur., 1992, chief frauds bur., 1993; insp. gen. State of NY, 1995—2002; US atty. (ea. dist.) NY US Dept. Justice, Bklyn., 2002—07; judge US Dist. Ct. (ea. dist.) NY, 2007—. Chair Moreland Commn. N.Y.C. Schs., 1999. Office: US Dist Ct 225 Cadman Plz E Brooklyn NY 11201

MAUSKOPF, SEYMOUR HAROLD, history professor; b. Cleve., Nov. 11, 1938; s. Philip and Dora (Trompeter) M.; m. Josephine Mary Album, Aug. 9, 1964; children: Deborah, Philip, Alice. AB, Cornell U., 1960; PhD, Princeton U., 1966. Instr. history Duke U., Durham, NC, 1964-66, asst. prof., 1966-72, assoc. prof., 1972-80, prof., 1980—, dir. program in sci. tech. and human values, 1979-84, dir. Focus Interdisciplinary programs, 1995—2003; resident dir. U. Mich.-U. Wis.-Duke U. Program, Florence, Italy, 2008. Author: Crystals and Compounds, Molecular Structure and Composition in Nineteenth Century French Science, 1976, (with M.R. McVaugh) The Elusive Science; Origins of Experimental Physical Research, 1915-1940, 1980; editor: The Reception of Unconventional Science by the Scientific Community, 1979, Chemical Sciences in the Modern World, 1993. Recipient Dexter award for outstanding achievement in history of chemistry, 1998, award Sci. and Religion Course Program, Ctr. Theology and the Natural Scis., 2002, Alumni Disting. Undergraduate Tchg. award Duke U., 2006; NSF postdoctoral fellow, 1971-72, Charles Price fellow Chem. Heritage Found., 2000; NSF grantee, 1974, 92-93; Am. Philos. Soc. travel grantee, 1979; Nat. Endowment for Humanities summer stipend, 1982; Edelstein internat. fellow in history chem. scis. and tech. Beckman Ctr. U. Pa. and Hebrew Univ., Jerusalem, 1988-89. Mem. History Sci. Soc. (exec. com. treas. 1979-83, coun. 1993-95). Jewish. Office Phone: 919-684-2581. E-mail: shmaus@duke.edu.

MAUZERALL, DENISE L., science educator; b. NYC; d. David and Miriam Jacob Mauzerall; m. Kenneth Duell, June 28, 2003; 1 child, Leala Duell. BS, Brown U., Providence, 1985; MS, Stanford U., Palo Alto, Calif., 1988; PhD, Havard U., Cambridge, Mass., 1996. Assoc. prof. Princeton U., NJ, 2006—, asst. prof. Office: Princeton Univ Woodrow Wilson Sch Princeton NJ 08544

MAVERAKIS, EMANUAL, dermatologist, educator; b. Calif. s. Nick H. and Maria Maverakis; m. Dalila Maverakis; 1 child, Natalia. BS with Summa Cum Laude, U. Calif., Los Angeles, 1995; MD with Summa Cum Laude, Harvard Med. Sch., Boston, 2003. Cert. internal medicine internship Beth Israel Deaconess Med. Ctr., Harvard Med. Sch., 2004. Rschr. tech. III La Jolla Inst. Allergy & Immunology, Calif., 1997—98; chief resident U. Calif. Davis, Sacramento, 2006, resident dermatology, 2007, asst. prof., 2008. Recipient Career award, Burroughs Wellcome Fund, 2007—, Physician Scientist Early Career award, Howard Hughes Med. Inst., 2007—, Young Investigators award, Am. Acad. Dermatology, 2009. Avocation: running. Office: Univ Calif Davis 3301 C St Ste 1400 Sacramento CA 95816

MAVERICK, ANDREW WILLIAM, chemistry educator, researcher; b. LA, Mar. 21, 1955; s. Andrew L. and Emily (Fisch) M.; m. Anne Beattie, Aug. 13, 1983; children: James B., Emily E. BA, Carleton Coll., 1975; PhD, Calif. Inst. Tech., 1982. Asst. prof. chemistry Washington U., St. Louis, 1981-87, La. State U., Baton Rouge, 1987-90, assoc. prof., 1990-99, prof., 1999—, chair dept. chem., 2006—, west prof. chem., 2008—. Guest contbr. Chemtracts-Inorganic Chemistry, Pasadena, Calif., 1990—2006; contbr. articles to profl. jours. Vol. Peace Corps, Ghana, 1975-77. Recipient Charles E. Coutes award, Am. Chem. Soc., Baton Rouge, 1999. Mem. AAUP, Am. Chem. Soc., Materials Rsch. Soc. Home: 834 Bourbon Ave Baton Rouge LA 70808-4817 Office: La State U Dept Chemistry Baton Rouge LA 70803-0001 Office Phone: 225-388-4415. Business E-Mail: maverick@lsu.edu.

MAVES, MICHAEL DONALD, medical association executive; b. East St. Louis, Ill., Oct. 14, 1948; BS, U. Toledo, Ohio, 1970; MD, Ohio State U., 1973; MBA, U. Iowa, 1988. Diplomate Am. Bd. Otolaryngology, lic. physician Iowa, Mo., Ill., DC. Rsch. fellow Ohio State U. Coll. Medicine, Columbus, 1977; head & neck surgery fellowship Columbia-Presbyn. Med. Ctr., NYC, 1978, U. Iowa Hosp. & Clinics, Iowa City, 1980-81, asst. prof. otolaryngology, head & neck surgery, 1984-87, assoc. prof., 1987-88; asst. prof. otolaryngology, head & neck surgery Ind. U. Sch. Medicine, Indpls., 1981-84; chmn. dept. otolaryngology St. Louis U. Sch. Medicine, 1988-94; exec. v.p. Am. Acad. Otolaryngology, Head & Neck Surgery, Alexandria, Va., 1994—2001; pres. Consumer Healthcare Products Assn., Washington, 1999—2001; exec. v.p., CEO AMA, Chgo., 2002—. Contbr. articles to profl. jours. Capt. US Army, 1974—76. Named one of 400 Best Cancer Doctors in America, Good Housekeeping mag., 1992, 1000 Best Physicians in US, 1992, 1994. Fellow: ACS; mem.: Am. Acad. Facial & Plastic Reconstructive Surgery, Am. Cancer Soc. Office: AMA 515 N State St Chicago IL 60654*

MAVILIO, DOMENICO, medical researcher, physician; b. Brindisi, Brindisi, Italy, May 22, 1975; s. Angelo Nicolo' Mavilio and Rosa Capitanio; m. Ivana Matera, Dec. 18, 2005; 1 child, Francesco Angelo. MD, PhD, U. Genova, Italy, 2006. Lic. Italian Bd. Med. Drs. Italy, 1998. Resident U. Genova, 1998—2002; rsch. fellow LIR/NIAID/NIH, Bethesda, 2002—. Achievements include research in clinical immunology. Home: 4201 Wexford DR Kensington MD 20895-1528

MAVRIDES, ELAINE, retired mental health services professional, social worker; b. Akron, Ohio, July 24, 1936; d. Paul A. and Clara Regas Mavrides; children: Kimberly Ann Morgan, Patty Blower, Denise M. Riegler. BA, U. Akron, Ohio, 1970, MEd, 1980. Elem. tchr. Cath. Diocese Cleve., 1966—76; psychiat. social worker Western Res. Human Svcs., Stow, Ohio, 1976—88; counselor, case mgr. Cmty. Support Svcs., Akron, 1988—2003; psychiat. screener Psychiat. ER Svcs., 1988—98; ret., 2003. Family therapist Barberton Citizens Hosp., Ohio, 1988; adv. bd. Summit County Homeless, 1989—90; organizer First Link Family Support Group Families Emotionally Ill Summit County, 1980—88. Citizens adv. bd. Summit County Bd. Mental Retardation, Akron, 1990; treas., pres. Ohio Mental Health Counselors, Columbus, 1990—91. Recipient Excellence cert., Ohio Dept. Mental Health, 1988, Case Mgr. of Yr. award, 1989, award, Summit County Mental Health Assn., 1990, Past Pres.'s award, Ohio Mental Health Counselor's Assn., 1992, award, Am. Mental Inst. Mem.: Nat. Health and Wellness Club, Nat. Gerontology Honor Soc., Sigma Phi Omega. Democrat. Avocations: reading, walking, bicycling, movies, swimming. Home: 76 Emerald Woods Dr L9 Naples FL 34108

MAVROMATIS, JOHN, psychology professor; b. Bklyn., May 16, 1944; PhD, U. Pitts., 1970. Prof. St. John Fisher Coll., Rochester, NY, 1970—. Office: Saint John Fisher Coll 3690 East Ave Rochester NY 14618-0265 Business E-Mail: jmavromatis@sjfc.edu.

MAVROUDIS, JOHN M., lawyer; b. NYC, July 24, 1947; s. Michael and Anna (Hariton) Mavroudis; m. Anne Drogaris; children: Michael, Lauren. JD cum laude, Syracuse Coll. Law, 1972. Bar: Fla. 1972, N.Y. 1973, N.J. 1975. Assoc. Patterson, Belknap & Webb, NYC, 1972—74; sole practice NYC, 1974—77; CEO Rio Vista Cos., 1977—; sr. ptnr. Nicolette & Mavroudis, P.A., Hackensack, NJ, 1978—83, Klinger, Nicolette, Mavroudis & Honig, P.A., 1984—89, Mavroudis & Rizzo, 1990—. CEO Rio Vista Group, 1977—. Editor: Syracuse Law Rev., 1972. Trustee The Greek Orthodox Cathedral of St. John the Theologian, NJ, Hellenic Coll. and Holy Cross Greek Orthodox Sch. Theology, Brookline, Mass., 1987—91; gen. counsel Greek Orthodox Archdiocese Am., 1997—2000; bd. advisors Syracuse Coll. Law, 2005—. Served to capt. USAR. Recipient Ellis Island Medal of Honor, 1999; Archon of the Ecumenical Patriarchate Constantinople. Mem.: Bar Assn. City N.Y., Justinian Soc. Office: 690 Kinderkamack Rd # 300 Oradell NJ 07649-1524 Office Phone: 201-262-3000.

MAVROVIC, PAUL J., information technology executive; s. Ivo and Erna Mavrovic. BS in Bus. Mgmt., U. Hartford, Conn., 1987—91. Cert. Info. Sys. Security Profl. Internet Info. Sys. Security Certification Consortium, 2005. Dir., info. tech. svcs. Urea Technologies Inc., Hackensack, NJ, 1991—99; pres. Pm Tech Inc, Hackensack, 1999—. 2nd v.p. Edgewater Apts Inc., New York, NY, 2000—04. Mem.: ISC2. Office: Pm Tech Inc 1 University Plz Ste 304 Hackensack NJ 07601-6205 Office Fax: 201-488-1062. Business E-Mail: paul@pmtechinc.net, mavrovic@pmtechinc.net.

MAWAE, KEVIN JAMES, professional football player; b. Savannah, Ga., Jan. 23, 1971; s. David Mawae; m. Tracy Mawae; children: Kirkland, Abigail. Grad., La. State U.; M in Sport's Mgmt., Adelphi U., Garden City, NY, 2006; attended NFL's bus. program, Wharton Bus. Sch., Pa., 2006, Stanford Grad. Sch. Bus., Calif., 2008. Guard, ctr. Seattle Seahawks, 1994—99; ctr. NY Jets, 1998—2005, Tenn. Titans, 2006—. Player rep. NFL Players Assn., 1999—2001, mem. exec. com., 2002—07, pres., 2008—; mem. NFL Diversity Com., 2003. Active Children's Cup Internat. Relief, Mercy Ministries; founder Kevin Mawae First and Goal Challenge; vol. football coach Grassland Athletic Assn., Williamson County, Tenn.; co-founder Touchdowns for Spl. Kids; spokesman David Ctr. Autism Rsch. Recipient Marty Lyons award for cmty. svc., NY Jets; named Two-time Man of Yr., 1st Team All-Pro, AP, 1999, 2001, 2008, Titans Cmty. All-Star, 2007, Titans Neighborhood MVP, The Home Depot, 2007; named to Am. Football Conf. Pro Bowl Team, NFL, 1999—2004, 2008, La. State U. Hall of Fame, 2007, Sr. Bowl Hall of Fame, 2008. Avocations: golf, bowling, hunting, fishing. Office: Tenn Titans LP Field One Titans Way Nashville TN 37213*

MAWARDI, OSMAN KAMEL, retired plasma physicist; b. Cairo, Dec. 12, 1917; arrived in U.S., 1946, naturalized, 1952; s. Kamel Ibrahim and Marie (Wiennig) M.; m. Betty Louise Hosmer, Nov. 23, 1950. BS, Cairo U., 1940, MS, 1945; A.M., Harvard U., 1947, PhD,

1948. Lectr. physics Cairo U., 1940-45; asst. prof. Mass Inst. Tech., 1951-56, assoc. prof., 1956-60; prof. engring., dir. plasma research program Case Inst. Tech., Cleve., 1960-88; dir. Energy Research Office, Case Western Res. U., 1977-82; ret., 1988. Pres. Collaborative Planners, Inc.; mem. Inst. Advanced Study, 1969-70; also cons. Contbr. articles to profl. jours. Past trustee Print Club Cleve., Cleve. Inst. Art. Recipient Biennial award Acoustical Soc. Am., 1952; CECON medal of achievement, 1979 Fellow AAAS, Acoustical Soc. Am., IEEE (Edison lectr. 1968-69, Centennial award 1984, Cleve. sect. Engr. of Yr. 1994); mem. N.Y. Acad. Scis., Sigma Xi, Eta Kappa Nu. Home: 8505 Woodfield Crossing Blvd Ste 104 Indianapolis IN 46240 *I never cease to be amazed that the goals I really believe in invariably materialize.*

MAX, CLAIRE ELLEN, physicist; b. Boston, Sept. 29, 1946; d. Louis William and Pearl (Bernstein) M.; m. Jonathan Arons, Dec. 22, 1974; 1 child, Samuel. AB, Harvard U., 1968; PhD, Princeton U., 1972. Postdoctoral rschr. U. Calif., Berkeley, 1972-74; physicist Lawrence Livermore (Calif.) Nat. Lab., 1974—; dir. Livermore br. Inst. Geophysics and Planetary Physics, 1984-93, dir. univ. rels., 1993-2000; prof., astronomer U. Calif., Santa Cruz, dir. Ctr. for Adaptive Optics, 2005—. Mem. Math.-Sci. Network Mills Coll., Oakland, Calif.; mem. com. on fusion hybrid reactors NRC, 1986, mem. com. on internat. security and arms control NAS, 1986-89, mem. com. on phys. sci., math. and applications NRC, 1991-94, mem. policy and computational astrophys. panels, astron. and astgrophys. survey NRC, 1989-91; mem. sci. steering com. W.M. Keck Obs., 1992-96, mem. adaptive optics sci. team, 1994—; mem. vis. com. Space Telescope Sci. Inst., 1996-2000, Hubble Space Telescope Second Decade Com., 1998-2000. Editor: Particle Acceleration Mechanisms in Astrophysics, 1979; contbr. numerous articles to sci. jours. Recipient E.O. Lawrence award, US Dept. Energy, 2004. Fellow AAAS (coun. rep. physics sect. 2001—), Am. Phys. Soc. (exec. com. divsn. plasma physics 1977, 81-82) Am. Acad Arts and Scis.; mem. Am. Astron. Soc. (exec. com. divsn. high energy astrophysics 1975-76), Am. Geophys. Union, Internat. Astron. Union, Phi Beta Kappa, Sigma Xi. Achievements include rsch. on adaptive optics and laser guide stars for astronomy; astrophys. plasmas. Office: U Calif Santa Cruz Ctr for Adaptive Optics 1156 High St Santa Cruz CA 95064 Business E-Mail: max@ucolick.org.

MAX, EDWARD ELLIS, molecular biologist; married. BA, Harvard Coll., Cambridge, Mass., 1967; MD, U. Pa., Phila., 1974, PhD, 1976. Assoc. dir., rsch. OBP CDER, FDA, Bethesda, Md., 1998—. Site mgr. Adventure Sci., Bethesda, 1993—2009. Office: FDA CDER HFD-122 29 Lincoln Dr Bethesda MD 20892

MAX, ELIZABETH, english language educator; b. Ft. Worth, Oct. 9, 1924; d. Frederick Ward and Alice Louise (Matthews) Maxwell; m. Herbert Jones McCorkle, Sept. 22, 1945 (div. Oct., 1969); children: Anne McCorkle Moore, Louise Kate McCorkle, Bruce Ward McCorkle, Sallie Matthews McCorkle. BS, Tex. Woman's U., 1944; MSLS, U. North Tex., 1966; EdD, Okla. State U., 1974. Cert. secondary, elementary tchr., Tex., Okla.; cert. sch. librarian, Tex., Okla. Copy clerk, beginning writer UPI, NBC, NYC, 1944—45; tchr. elem. and secondary various schs., Tex., 1950—69; instr. libr. sci. We. Ill. U., Macomb, 1969—70; asst. prof., fine arts libr. & architecture Okla. State U., Stillwater, 1970—72, asst. prof., coord. Libr. Sci. Dept., 1972—76, assoc. prof., 1976—82, prof. emerita, 1990—, supr. English Edn., 1982—90. Cons. Skelly Oil Co., Tulsa, Okla., 1976, The Ctr. for Local Govt. Tech., 1983-84, media reviewer Previews; book revs. Sch. Libr. Jour., 1976-77. Author (with others): Teaching the Short Story, 1996; mem. reader panel New York Times, 1996—2001, mem. New York Times Online Panel, 2002—; contbr. articles to profl. jours. Pres. Meml. Soc. Central Pa., 1994, 96-99; vol. Nat. Disaster Relief, ARC, 1991-96; mem. Dem. Nat. Com.; women's rights activist. Mem. NEA, ALA, Nat. Women's Studies Assn. (founder), Okla State U. Women's Coun. (founder, 2d chair), Okla. Adult and Continuing Edn., Nat. Collegiate Players, Stillwater Okla. Writer's Club (pres., 1985-89), Greek Sabbatical, Nat. Coun. Tchrs. of English (comparative and world lit. com. 1990-97), Gen. Soc. Mayflower Descs. Richard Warren Parents and Friends of Lesbians and Gays, Emily's List, NARAL, ACLU, Phi Delta Kappa, Phi Kappa Phi, Beta Phi Mu. Home and Office: 2414 North Glenwood Dr Stillwater OK 74075 Personal E-mail: elizabethmax@earthlink.net.

MAXA, RUDOLPH JOSEPH, JR., journalist; b. Cleve., Sept. 25, 1949; s. Rudolph Joseph and Christine Marie (Kimpel) Maxa; m. Kathleen Ann Zolciak, June 19, 1971 (div. 1988); children: Sarah Lynn, Alexander. BS in Journalism, cum laude, Ohio U., 1971. Reporter, columnist Washington Post, 1971-83; sr. writer, columnist The Washingtonian, 1983-92; daily commentator Cable News Network, 1980-82; chief Washington bur. Spy mag., 1992-94; weekly travel columnist Am. On-Line, 1995-96. Weekend morning talk show host Sta. WRC-AM, NBC Radio, Washington, 1982—84; travel commentator bus. show 'Marketplace' Pub. Radio Internat., 1991—, co-founder, host weekend show 'The Savvy Traveler', 1995—2000; columnist Ocean Drive mag., 1993—97, Spectrum Mag., 1996—97, MSNBC.com, 1998—2001. Author: Dare To Be Great, 1976, Public Trust, Private Lust, 1977; editor: (newsletter) Rudy Maxa's Traveler, 1998—2004; co-editor: Worth Mag., 1995—98; contbr. P.O.V. mag., 1997—99, Forbes mag., 1999—2000, host to exec. prodr. (pub. TV show) Rudy Maxa's World, 2008— (CINE Golden Eagle award, EMM award, 2008, Telly award, 2008), other shows include Smart Travels: Europe with Rudy Maxa, Smart Travels: Pacific Rim with Rudy Maxa; contbg. editor: National Geographic Travelers' 'Walks of a Lifetime', 2000—. Recipient John Hancock award for Excellence in Bus. & Fin. Writing, 1972, Writing Excellence award, Fla. Mag. Assn., 1995, L.J. Hortin Disting. Alumnus award, E.W. Scripps Sch. Journalism, 2002, Am. Pub. TV Programming Excellence award, 2007, Lowell Thomas Bonze award for Excellence in Travel Writing (2). Office: PO Box 65066 Saint Paul MN 55165

MAXFIELD, GUY BUDD, lawyer, educator; b. Galesburg, Ill., May 4, 1933; s. Guy W. and Isabelle B. Maxfield; m. Carol Tunick, Dec. 27, 1970; children: Susan, Stephen, Karen. AB summa cum laude, Augustana Coll., 1955; JD, U. Mich., 1958. Bar: NY 1959. Assoc. White & Case, NYC, 1958—63; prof. law NYU Sch. Law, NYC, 1963—; sr. counsel Fox Rothschild LLP. Author: Tennessee Will and Trust Manual, 1982, Federal Estate and Gift Taxation, 8th edit., 2002, Florida Will and Trust Manual, 1984, Tax Planning for Professionals, 1986; contbr. articles to law jours. Trustee Acomb Found., Newark, 1974—. With U.S. Army, 1958-64. Fellow Am. Coll. Tax Counsel; mem. ABA, Am. Law Inst., NY State Bar Assn., Order of Coif, Phi Beta Kappa. Office: NYU Sch Law 40 Washington Sq S New York NY 10012-1099

MAXFIELD, JOHN EDWARD, retired university dean; b. LA, Mar. 17, 1927; s. Chauncey George and Rena Lucile (Cain) M.; m. Margaret Alice Waugh, Nov. 24, 1948; children— Frederick George (dec.), David Glen, Elaine Rebecca, Nancy Catherine, Daniel John. BS, Mass. Inst. Tech., 1947; MS, U. Wis., 1949; PhD, U. Oreg., 1951. Instr. U. Oreg., 1950-51; mathmatician U.S. Naval Ordnance Test Sta., China Lake, Calif., 1949-56, head computing br., 1956-57, head math. div., 1957-60; lectr. UCLA, 1951-60; head prof. dept. math. U. Fla., 1960-67; prof., chmn. dept. math. Kans. State U., 1967-81; dean Grad. Sch. and univ. research La. Tech. U., 1981-92, dean emeritus, 1992—; ret. La. Tech. U., 1992. Mem. Am. Math. Soc., Math. Assn. Am., Sigma Xi. Home: 3380 Blairs Ln #108 Placerville CA 95667-5804

MAXFIELD, LORI ROCHELLE, education educator; b. Denver, Jan. 16, 1959; d. Lawrence Wesley and Caroline Kay (Gideon) M. BS in Edn., U. Nebr., Lincoln, 1983, MEd, 1991; PhD in Ednl. Psychology, U. Conn., Storrs, 2000. Recreation aide Lincoln Parks and Recreation, Nebr., 1976-84; tchr. Harding County Pub. Schs., Reva, Buffalo, SD, 1984-89; rsch. assoc. U. Nebr., 1990-91, asst. project coord., 1991-92; sch. enrichment coord. Sch. Dist. 145, Waverly/Eagle, Nebr., 1992-94, future problem solving coach, Invent America! coord., 1992-94; rsch. assoc. U. Conn., 1994-96, lectr., 1995-97, instr. CONFRATUTE, 1995-97; asst. prof. Mankato State U., Minn., 1997—98; state staff develop coord. Minn. Dept. Children, Families, Learning, 1998—99; program dir. under grad. edn. program Coll. St. Catherine, 2000—05, asst. prof. edn., 2000—07, assoc. prof. edn., 2007—, undergrad. program dir., 2000—05, program dir. undergrad. & grad. edn. programs, 2005—07, social studies coord., 2007—, stem minor coord., 2008—, globe tng. coord., 2008—, sci., tech., engring. and math. coord., 2008—. Adv., coach Nat. History Day Harding County Pub. Schs., Reva, 1987-89; coach Odyssey of the Mind, 1986, 93; head coach Jr. High Sch. girls basketball, 1988; asst. coach varsity track, 1989. Field reviewer: Gifted Child Today, 2003—. Youth advisor Slim Buttes Luther League, Reva, 1988-89; ptnr. Spl. Olympics, 1992-94. Recipient Outstanding Youth award Nebr. Coun. for Youth and Children, 1977, Outstanding Leadership award Elks, 1977, Golden Apple award Harding County Tchrs., Buffalo, S.D., 1988, Nebr. Ednl. Tech. Assn. grant, 1993. Mem. ASCD, Am. Ednl. Rsch. Assn., Northeastern Ednl. Rsch. Assn. (Lorne H. Wollatt Disting. Paper of Yr. award 1995), Nebr. Assn. for Gifted (adv. bd. 1991-93, bd. dirs. 1993-94, mem. editl. bd. 1992-94, Disting. Svc. award 1994), Nebr. U. Alumni Assn. (life), Wilson Ctr. Assocs., Nat. Assn. for Gifted Children Outstanding Doctoral Student award 1997), Nat. Mid. Sch. Assn., Nat. Coun. Social Studies, Nat. Sci. Tchrs. Assn., Am. Assn. Univ. Women Profs., Am. Soc. Engring. Edn., Am. Assn. Colls. and Univs. (assoc.), So. Poverty Law Ctr. (leadership counsel, named to Wall Tolerance 2007), Nat. Women's History Mus., Phi Delta Kappa, Phi Lambda Theta. Democrat. Lutheran. Avocations: gardening, hiking. Home: 766 Curfew St Saint Paul MN 55114-1045 Office Phone: 651-690-8898. Business E-Mail: lrmaxfield@stkate.edu.

MAXFIELD, LOUISE FONDA GRIBBLE, executive secretary; b. Waco, Tex., Sept. 27, 1924; d. Theodore Miles and Louise Irwin Gribble; m. Jack G.S. Maxfield, July 21, 1951 (dec.); children: Martha Woodson Maxfield Cottingham, Elizabeth Fonda. BA, Randolph-Macon Woman's Coll., Lynchburg,Va., 1945; M Liberal Arts, So. Meth. U., Dallas, 1982. Editor, indsl. house organ Gen. Tire & Rubber Co., Waco, Tex., 1945—51; bus. mgr. Maxfield Clin./Hosp., Dallas, 1976—84, Covenant Presbyn. ch., Carrollton, Tex., 1984—99. Named Woman of Yr., Carrollton, Tex., 2004; Paul Harris fellow, Rotary Internat. Home: 139 Estrella Xing Unit 318 Georgetown TX 78628-7056

MAXFIELD, MAX R., Secretary of State, Wyoming; b. Wis., 1945; m. Gayla Y. Maxfield; 4 children. Student, U. Wis. Dir. Wyo. Recreation Commn., 1987—89, Wyo. Dept. Commerce, 1989—94; state auditor State of Wyo., Cheyenne, 1995—2006, sec. state, 2007—. Mem. state loan and investment bd. State of Wyo., mem. bd. land commrs., mem. state bldg. commn., mem. state canvassing bd., chmn. state fin. adv. com. Dir. YMCA. Republican. Office: Office of State Auditor State Capitol Bldg Rm 114 Cheyenne WY 82002 Office Phone: 307-777-7831. Office Fax: 307-777-6983. E-mail: mmaxfi@state.wy.us.

MAXFIELD, PETER CHARLES, state legislator, lawyer, educator; b. 1941; AB, Regis Coll., 1963; JD, U. Denver, 1966; LLM, Harvard U., 1968. Bar: Colo. 1966, Wyo. 1969. Trial atty. Dept. Justice, 1966-67; assoc. Hindry, Erickson & Meyer, Denver, 1968-69; asst. prof. U. Wyo. Coll. Law, 1969-72, assoc. prof., 1972-76, prof., 1976-96, dean, 1979-87, prof. emeritus, 1996—. Vis. assoc. prof. U. N.Mex., 1972-73; Raymond F. Rice Disting. prof. U. Kans., 1984; Chapman Vis. Disting. prof., U. Tulsa, 1987; vis. prof. U. Utah, 1992. Author: (with Garr Houghton) Cases and Materials on the Taxation of Oil and Gas and Natural Resources Transactions, 1990, (with Allen and Houghton) Taxation of Mining Operation, 1981, 97, 2002; (with Trelease and Dietrich) Natural Resources Law on American Indian Lands, 1977. Coord. Wyo. State Planning 1988-89; spl. asst. Gov. Wyo. 1989-90; Dem. nominee U.S. Ho. Reps., 1990; mem. Wyo. Environ. Quality Coun., 1991-93; mem. Wyo. Senate, Laramie, 1993-97; counsel Gov. Wyo., 2006. Mem. Omicron Delta Kappa, Pi Delta Phi, Order of the Coif (faculty). Home: 1159 Escalera St Laramie WY 82072-5020 Office: PO Box 100 Laramie WY 82073 Business E-Mail: petemaxfield@earthlink.net.

MAXFIELD, ROSE MARY, retired government official; b. Shelbyville, Ill., Mar. 23, 1918; d. Claude Fielding Stiarwalt and Nina Eugenia Whitlock; m. Orville Eldred Maxfield, June 6, 1941; children: Mary Patricia, Mary Constance, Marilyn Joan. BS, U. Ill., Champaign-Urbana, 1939, Sparks Coll., Shelbyville, 1940. Cert. esteem Dept. Def., 1953. Adminstrv. asst. U.S. Treasury Dept., Washington, 1942—73; ret., 1973. Author: (chpt.) Amy White of the Old 300, 1986, Biography for New Texas Handbook, 1996. Mem. Sam Houston Regional Libr. and Rsch. Ctr., Tex., Va. Ctr. Civil War Studies, Atascocito Hist. Soc., Liberty, Tex., Shelby County Hist. and Geneal. Soc, Nat. Geneal. Soc. Recipient Meritorious Svc. award, U.S. Treasury Dept., 1967, Sec.'s Cert., 1969, Albert Gallatin award, 1973, Spl. Achievement award, 1973. Mem.: Nat. Soc. DAR, Wharton County Hist. Mus., Glover Park Citizens Assn., Friends of Folger Libr., So. Relief Soc. D.C., Nat. Soc. Sons. and Daus. of the Pilgrims, Soc. Descs. of Austin's Old 300, Nat. Soc. Col. Dames 17th Century, Treasury Hist. Assn. (charter mem. 1968), Flagon and Trencher (life), Assn. for Preservation of Va. Antiquities (life), Soc. Descs. of Colonial Clergy (life), U. Ill. Alumni Assn. (life), Nat. Soc. U.S. Daus. of 1812, United Daus. Confederacy, Daus. of Republic of Tex., Nat. Soc. Daus. of Colonial Wars, Nat. Mus. Women in Arts (charter mem.), Swiss Club Washington, Delta Zeta. Avocations: reading, genealogy, needlecrafts, travel, musical performances. Home: 218 Mayfair Cir Wharton TX 77488 Personal E-mail: msmaxfield@sbcglobal.net.

MAXIN, DANIEL, mathematics professor; s. Alixandru and Evdochia Maxin. BS, Dunarea Jos U., Galati, 1997; MS, Purdue U., West Lafayette, Ind., 2005, PhD, 2007. HS tchr. math. & computer sci. V. Alecsandri HS, Galati, 1997—2001; grad. instr. Purdue U., 2001—07; asst. prof. math. Valparaiso U., Ind., 2001—. Contbr. articles to profl. jours. Ensign Romanian Navy, 1998, Constanta, Romania. Mem.: SMB, MAA, AMS. Office: Valparaiso Univ 1900 Chapel Dr Valparaiso IN 46383

MAXMAN, SUSAN ABEL, architect; b. Columbus, Ohio, Dec. 30, 1938; d. Richard Jack Abel and Gussie (Brenner) Seiden; m. Rolf Sauer; children: Andrew Frankel, Thomas Frankel, Elizabeth Frankel, Melissa, Abby, William Jr., Madeleine Sauer. Student, Smith Coll., 1960; MArch., U. Pa., 1977; HHD, Ball State U., 1993, U. Detroit Mercy, 1997. Registered profl. arch. Pa., Mich., NH, Nat. Coun. Archtl. Registration Bds. Project designer Kopple Sheward & Day, Phila., 1978-80; ptnr. Maxman & Sutphin, Phila., 1980-83; prin. Susan Maxman & Ptnrs., Phila., 1984—. Mem. bd. overseers Grad. Sch. Fine Arts U. Pa., mem. corp. vis. com. MIT; mem. Planning and Design Commn., Ga. Inst. Tech. Works include design of Women's Humane Soc. Animal Shelter, Bensalem, Pa. (Northeastern Sustainable Energy Assn.'s Comml. Bldg. award, 1994, Metal Constrn. Assn. award 1995, Gov.'s Award for Environ. Excellence 1997, AIA Pa. Hon. award 1997), Camp Tweedale-Freedom Valley Girl Scouts USA (AIA Honor award, 1991), Cusano Environ. Edn. Ctr. at John Heinz Nat. Wildlife Refuge at Tinicum, Phila. (US Dept. Energy Fed. Energy Saver Showcase award, US Dept. Interior Environ. Achievement award, Top Ten Green Bldg. award AIA 2003, AIA Cote Top Ten Green Buildings award, 2003), Robert Lewis House (McArthur award 1985), Phila., Restoration Pennock Farmstead (Grand Prize Nat. Trust Hist. Preservation 1995), Canaan Valley Inst. Hdqs., Renovation of Second Bank of US, Phila., Navy Yard Bldg. 10 (Honor award, AIA, Phila. chpt., 2004, citation of merit, PA Historic Presercation award), Natural Lands Trust Hdqs. Expansion, Media, Pa. (N.E. Sustainable Energy Assn. Bldg. award 2004, Exemplary Sustainable Bldgs. Industry Coun. award 2005), Kutztown U., Pa. Sisters Servants of the Immaculate Heart of Mary Renovation of the Motherhouse (Mich. Hist. Preservation Network Bldg. award 2003, Top Ten Green Bldg. award AIA 2006), Renovation of U. Pa. Nursing Edn. Bldg., Phila., Barbara C. Harris Camp and Conf. Ctr., Greenfield, NH, Chestnut Hill Nat. Bank, Phila., Somerset (Pa.) Hist. Ctr., Seneca Rocks Visitor Ctr., Seneca Rocks, W.Va., Fort Necessity/Nat. Rd. Interpretive Edn. Ctr., Farmington, Pa., The Woods Residence Hall at Pa. State-Berks, Reading, Roberts Hall Renovation and Addition U. Pa. Law Sch., others. Mem. Eco-Efficiency Task Force Pres. Coun. Sustainable Devel.; past chair Environ. Coun., Urban Land Inst.; mem. trustee's coun. for Pa. Women, U. Pa. Recipient Disting. Dau. Pa. award Gov. Tom Ridge, 1995, Excellence citation Engring. News Record, Shattering the Glass Ceiling award Women's Nat. Dem. Club, Mayor's commendation City Phila., citation Pa. Ho. Reps., Gov.'s award Environ. Excellence, 1997, Pa. Hist. and Mus. Commn. Preservation Achievement award Preservation Alliance Greater Phila.; named to Pa. Honor Roll of Women, Pa. Commn. for Women, 1996, named 1 of Pa.'s Best 50 Women in Bus. 1996. Mem. AIA (nat. pres. 1993), Pa. Women's Forum, Forum Exec. Women, Carpenter's Co. Phila. Avocation: sailing. Office: SMP Architects 1600 Walnut St 2nd Fl Philadelphia PA 19103-5405 Office Phone: 215-985-4410. Business E-Mail: smp@smparchitects.com.

MAXMEN, MIMI (MARY ELIZABETH MAXMEN), costume and scenic designer; b. Mpls., May 12, 1945; d. Edward Jacob and Sarah Faye (Arenson) Berman; m. Jerrold Samuel, Dec. 18, 1966. BA with honors, U. Mich., 1967. Resident costume designer Roundabout Theater, NYC, 1969-74; costume designer Dayton (Ohio) Ballet, 1980-88. Vis. lectr. U. Mich. MFA Seminar, Ann Arbor; vis. instr. SUNY, Geneseo; instr. Parson's Sch. Design, 1994—. Costume designer (films) Muse, Women Without Implants, The Coming Round Fairy Tale of New York, The War's Over, (ballets) The Sleeping Beauty, (scenery and costumes), Random Dances, (Joffrey Ballet), Jubilee!, (N.Y.C. Ballet), La Dame Aux Camelias, (Ballet de Santiago de Chile), (plays) The Play's Thing, (Obie award), Inadmissible Evidence, (with Nicol Williamson), Vieux Carré, (off-Broadway revival), A Shayna Maidel, (original N.Y. prodn.), A Piece of My Heart, (N.Y. prodn.), (mus.) A...My Name Is Alice, (original N.Y. prodn.), (opera) Ariadne Auf Naxos, (Santa Fe). Mem. United Scenic Artist. Avocations: music, theater, travel. Address: 30 5th Ave Apt 6E New York NY 10011-8807 Also: PO Box 93021 Los Angeles CA 90093-0021

MAXSON, LINDA ELLEN, biologist, educator; b. NYC, Apr. 24, 1943; d. Albert and Ruth (Rosenfeld) Resnick; m. Richard Dey Maxson, June 13, 1964; 1 child, Kevin. BS in Zoology, San Diego State U., 1964, MA in Biology, 1966; PhD in Genetics, San Diego State U./U. Calif., Berkeley, 1973. Instr. biology San Diego State U., 1966-68; tchr. gen. sci. San Diego Unified Sch. Dist., 1968-69; instr. biochemistry U. Calif., Berkeley, 1974; asst. prof. zoology, dept. genetics and devel. U. Ill., Urbana-Champaign, 1974-76, asst. prof. dept. genetics, devel. and ecology, ethology & evolution, 1976-79, assoc. prof., 1979-84, prof., 1984-87, prof. ecology, ethology and evolution, 1987-88; prof., head dept. biology Pa. State U., State College, 1988-94; assoc. vice-chancellor acad. affairs/dean undergrad. acad. affairs, prof. ecology and evolutionary biology U. Tenn., Knoxville, 1995-97; dean Coll. Liberal Arts & Scis., prof. biol. scis. U. Iowa, Iowa City, 1997—. Exec. officer biology programs Sch. Life Scis., U. Ill., 1981-86, assoc. dir. acad. affairs, 1984-86, dir. campus honors program, 1985-88; vis. prof. ecology and evolutionary biology U. Calif., Irvine, 1988; mem. adv. panel rsch. tng. groups behavioral biol. scis. NSF, 1990-94; rsch. assoc. Smithsonian Instn. Author: Genetics: A Human Perspective, 3d edit., 1992; mem. editl. bd. Molecular Biology Evolution; exec. editor Biochem. Sys. & Ecology, 1993-2001; contbr. numerous articles to scientific jours. Recipient Disting. Alumni award, San Diego State U., 1989, Disting. Herpetologist award, Herpetologists' League, 1993. Fellow: AAAS; mem.: Soc. Molecular Biology and Evolution (treas. 1992—94, sec. 1992—95), Soc. Study Evolution, Soc. for Study of Amphibians and Reptiles (pres. 1991), Am. Men and Women in Sci., Phi Beta Kappa. Office: U Iowa 240 Schaeffer Hall Iowa City IA 52242-1409 Business E-Mail: linda-maxson@uiowa.edu.

MAXSON, ROBERT E., biology professor; b. San Francisco, June 12, 1951; s. Robert E. and Helen D. Maxson; m. Margaret J. Yost, June 28, 2007; children: Rachel E., Thomas C. PhD, U. Calif., Berkeley, 1978. Asst. prof. U. Southern Calif. Keck Sch. Medicine, Dept. Biochemistry and Molecular Biology, LA, 1983—99, assoc. prof., 1983—99, prof., 1999—. Home: 2870 White Ridge Pl #27 Thousand Oaks CA 91362 Office: Univ Southern Calif Norris Cancer Hosp 1441 Eastlake Ave Los Angeles CA 90033 Office Fax: 323-865-0098. Business E-Mail: maxson@usc.edu.

MAXSTADT, JOHN M., librarian; b. Royal Oak, Mich., June 4, 1958; s. Donald F. and Martha K. Maxstadt. BA, Wabash Coll., Crawfordsville, Ind., 1980; MA in Tchg., Fairleigh Dickinson U., Teaneck, NJ, 1982; MLS, Ball State U., Muncie, Ind., 1983. Reference libr. La. State U., Baton Rouge, 1984—88; instrn. coord. U. Ark., Fayetteville, 1988—91; pub. svcs. libr. Lamar U., Orange, Tex., 1991—95; head pub. svcs. Tex. A&M Internat. U., Laredo, 1995—. Named Tchr. of Yr., Tex. A&M Internat. U., 2007. Mem.: ALA, Tex. Faculty Assn., Tex. Libr. Assn., Assn. Coll. and Rsch. Librs., Phi Kappa Phi (sec. local chpt. 2007—), Phi Delta Kappa (pres. local chpt. 2008—). Avocations: theater, gardening. Office: Texas A&M International Univ 5201 University Blvd Laredo TX 78041

MAXTED, LAWRENCE RICHARD, librarian; b. Erie, Pa., Feb. 21, 1954; s. George Lawrence and Clara emelia Maxted; m. Regina Marie Gapinski, Aug. 5, 1995; 1 child, Emma Lauren. BA, Oberlin Coll., Ohio, 1976; MA, U. Chgo., 1980. Reference libr. U. Denver, 1979—80; computer support specialist Mace Electronics, Erie, 1981—87; periodicals libr. Gannon U., Erie, 1987—93, collection devel. libr., 1993—. Reviewer Libr. Jour., NYC, 1996—. Contbr. articles. Named Video Reviewer of Yr., Libr. Jour., 2006. Office: Gannon Univ 109 University Sq Erie PA 16541-0001

MAXWELL, ANDERS JOHN, investment banker; b. San Francisco, Oct. 3, 1946; s. John L. and Deborah A. Maxwell; m. Carlene S. Maxwell, 2000; children from previous marriage: Lauren A., Colin A., Ian W., Erin C., Ryan N. BArch, U. Calif., Berkeley, 1969; MBA, U. Pa., 1971. Analyst GE, 1971-73; v.p. GE Credit Corp., Stamford, Conn., 1973-83; mng. dir. Dean Witter Reynolds Inc., NYC, 1983-87; v.p. Kidder Peabody & Co., Inc., NYC, 1987-88; prin. L.F. Rothschild & Co., NYC, 1988; v.p. Smith Barney, Harris Upham & Co., Inc., 1989-91, Lazard Frères & Co., NYC, 1991-92; ptnr. Benedetto, Gartland & Greene, NYC, 1992-94; v.p., gen. mgr. GE Capital Corp., Stamford, Conn., 1994-96; dir. Salomon Smith Barney Inc., NYC, 1997-98; mng. dir. Barington Capital Group, NYC, 1998; mng. dir., ptnr. Peter J. Solomon Co., NYC, 1999—. Capt. US Army, 1971. Office: Peter J Solomon Co 520 Madison Ave New York NY 10022 Home Phone: 201-612-0744; Office Phone: 212-508-1683. Business E-Mail: amaxwell@pjsolomon.com.

MAXWELL, BARBARA RUTH, not-for-profit developer; b. Madison, Wis., Oct. 30, 1953; d. Bertram L. Ellenbogen and Ruth Elizabeth Hill. BA in Elem. Edn. III A, U. Minn., Mpls., 1976, MALS, 1985. Libr. Ind. State Libr., Indpls., 2003—05; vice pres. adminstrn. MDAA, Alexandria, Va., 2006—. Classifier, rschr. Star Tribune, Minneapolis, Minn., 1978—85; reference libr. Domino's Pizza, Ann Arbor, Mich., 1986—88, USA Today, Arlington, Va., 1988—90, libr. dir., McClean, Va., 1990—2003. Author: (book) Butterflies and Other Fanciful Thoughts, S.I.G.E. Mem.: Friend Alexandra Pub. Libr., Spl. Libraries Assn., King St. Cats, Alexandria Animal Rescue League, No. Va. Land Trust, Nature Conservancy. Avocations: exercise, travel, writing.

MAXWELL, CAROLE ANN, director; b. Phila., Sept. 10, 1944; d. Frank J. and Ruth M. (Steck) Coyne; m. Richard A. Nuzzo, Jan. 10, 1998; 1 child, Courtney Ruth. BA, Immaculata Coll., Pa., 1967; M in Music Edn., Temple U., Phila., 1972; D in Sacred Music, Grad. Theol. Inst., South Bend, Ind., 2003. Dir. choral and liturgical music Fairfield U., Conn., 1980—; artistic dir., conductor Mendelssohn Choir of Conn., Fairfield, 1984—. Guest conductor Westchester County HS All State Choir, 1999, So. Conn. Region HS All State Choir, 2005. Chorusmaster Conn. Grand Opera and Orch., Stamford, 1990—, Yale Opera Co., New Haven, 1997—2002, Bridgeport Symphony, Conn., 1999—, Norwalk Symphony, Conn., 2002—; guest conductor Gregg Smith Singers/Adirondack Music Festival, 1989; prin. conductor Nat. Pastoral Musicians Conv., 1997, 2006; guest conductor Messiah Sing-in Lincoln Ctr., NYC, 2004—06; hunger clean-up Fairfield U., 1987—; bd. dirs. Mendelssohn Choir Conn., 1984—, Fairfield County Children's Choir, 1996—. Recipient Humanicare award, Oxford Ins., 2000; named Disting. Music Alumnae, Immaculata Coll., 1992, Woman of Substance, Conn. Post, 1994, Woman of Yr., Fairfield U. Women's Study, 2000. Mem.: Music Educators Nat. Conf., Am. Choral Dirs. Assn., Phi Kappa Lambda. Avocations: reading, travel. Home: 39 Regency Cir Trumbull CT 06611 Office: Fairfield Univ North Benson Rd Fairfield CT 06824

MAXWELL, CHARLES THOBURN, energy analyst; b. Bryn Mawr, Pa., Oct. 26, 1931; s. Charles Thoburn and Genevieve Sarilda (McNellis) Maxwell; m. Virginia Carden Dorr, Sept. 9, 1977; children: Bruce, Christiane, Stephen, Brandon, Virginia, Russell, Peter. BA cum laude, Princeton U., 1953; BA (Marshall scholar), St. Johns Coll., Oxford U., 1957, MA, 1963. With Mobil Oil Corp., 1957—68, dist./regional mgr. Kaduna, Nigeria, 1964—67, exec. Middle East affairs NYC, 1967—68; energy analyst Cyrus J. Lawrence Inc., NYC, 1968—80, vice chmn., sr. energy analyst, 1980—97, dir., exec. v.p., 1997; sr. energy analyst Weeden & Co., Greenwich, Conn., 2000—. Spkr. at internat. energy and monetary confs.; assoc. mem. NY Stock Exchange. Contbr. articles to profl. jours. Mem.: Soc. Security Analysts. Office: Weeden & Co 145 Mason St Greenwich CT 06830 Office Phone: 203-861-7600. Office Fax: 203-861-7701. E-mail: maxwell@weeden.com.

MAXWELL, DIANA KATHLEEN, primary school educator; b. Seminole, Okla., Dec. 16, 1949; d. William Hunter and ImoJean (Mahurin) Rivers; m. Clarence Estel Maxwell, Jly 3, 1969; children: Amanda Hunter, Alexandra Jane. BS, U. Md., 1972; M of Secondary Edn., Boston U., 1974; PhD, U. Md., 1980. Cert. tchr., counselor, Tex. Tchr. Child Garden Presch., Adelphi, Md., 1969-71; tchr., dir. PREP Edn. Ctr., Heidelberg, Germany, 1972-74; tchr. N.E. Ind. Schs. Larkspur, San Antonio, 1974-77, 89-90, Headstart, Boyds, Md., 1978; tchg. asst. Coll. Edn. U. Md., College Park, 1978—80; dir., founder First Bapt. Child Devel. Ctr., Bryan, Tex., 1982-84; instr. English lang. Yonsei Med. Ctr., Seoul, Republic of Korea, 1985-87; asst. prof. Incarnate Word Coll., San Antonio, 1987-89; tchr. kindergarten Fairfax County Pub. Schs., Kings Park, Va., 1990-94; tchr. Encino Park, San Antonio, 1994-95; lectr. U. Tex., San Antonio, 1995-96; multi-age tchr., theater arts tchr. 4th grade & 5th grade sci. Ft. Sam Houston Elem. Sch., San Antonio, 1996—. Cons. Sugar N'Spice Child Devel. Ctr., Kilgore, Tex., 1980—90; trainer region XX Tex. Edn. Assn., 2000—03. Contbr. articles to newspapers. Block chair March of Dimes, 1991-93, 2000-08, Am. Heart Assn., Fairfax, Va., 1991, 92, San Antonio, 2000-08, Am. Diabetes Assn., Fairfax, 1992, San Antonio, 1996-2008; judge speaking com. Burke Optomists, 1992-93; judge writing competition N.E. Ind. Sch. Dist., 1996; judge speech/debate competition Tex. Forensics League, MacArthur HS, 2003-08; sec. Cole H.S. Cougar Club, Ft. Sam Houston, San Antonio, 1996-97, v.p., 1997-2002, chair project graduation, 2002-03; Bible tchr. 1st Bapt. Ch., Alexandria, Va., 1993-95; tchr. kindergarten Trinity Bapt. Ch., San Antonio, 1995-99, 2005, tchr. 1st grade, 2001-05; Region XX TEA TOPP trainer, 2001-03. Named one of Outstanding Young Women of Am., 1983; Md. fellow State of Md., 1978, 79; Tech. grantee Tex. Edn. Agy., San Antonio, 1990, State of Va. and Fairfax County, Springfield, 1991; recipient Yellow Rose of Tex. vol. award Gov. of Tex., 1996, Dean's Outstanding Tchg. award U. Tex., San Antonio, 1995-96, Ft. Sam Houston Hero award, 2001, 02. Mem. ASCD, Assn. Profl. Tchr. Educators, Nat. Coun. Tchrs. Math., Nat. Sci. Tchrs. America. Avocations: oriental brush painting, singing, collecting butterflies, children/teacher advocate. Home: 2602 Country Square St San Antonio TX 78209-2235 Office: Ft Sam Houston Elem Sch 3370 Nursery Rd San Antonio TX 78234-1479 Business E-Mail: kmaxwell@fshisd.net.

MAXWELL, GEORGE PATRICK, plastic surgeon; b. Selma, Ala., July 15, 1946; married; 1 child. MD, Vanderbilt U., Nashville, 1972. Cert. Am. Bd. Plastic Surgery, 1981. Intern gen. surgery Johns Hopkins Hosp., Balt., 1972—73, resident plastic surgery, 1973—76, resident microsurgery, 1976—79; fellow Davis Med. Ctr., San Francisco, 1975; with Baptist Hosp., Nashville; asst. clin. prof. Vanderbilt U.; founder Inst. Aesthetic and Reconstructive Surgery, Nashville, 1989; with Nashville Plastic Surgery. Med. advisor Inamed Corp., Santa Barbara, Calif.; founder, chmn. Inamed Acad.; co-founder, exec. v.p., chief surg. officer Diversified Specialty Insts.; founder, bd. mem. Aspen Ctr. Integrative Health. Contbr. articles to med. jours.; featured: newspapers New York Times, magazines Departures, 1997, Town & Country, 1999, Good Housekeeping, 1999, W, 2000, 2001, Redbook, 2001, New York Times Mag., 2005, More. Mem.: Southeastern Soc. Plastic Surgeons, Am. Soc. Aesthetic Plastic Surgery (Walter Scott Brown award), Am. Assn. Plastic Surgeons (James Barrett Brown award), Am. Soc. Plastic Surgeons (Presdl. award 2005, Robert H. Ivy Soc. award), Am. Coll. Surgeons, South African Soc. Plastic Surgery (hon.), Japanese Soc. Plastic Surgery (hon.), Can. Soc. Plastic Surgery (hon.). Achievements include patents in field.

MAXWELL, JACK ERWIN, manufacturing executive; b. Cleve., July 17, 1926; s. Fred A. and Gertrude F. (Haug) M.; m. Martha Jane Miller, Dec. 28, 1966; children by previous marriage: Laura Jane, Fredric, Elizabeth Grant, Carla Moore, Linda Hanson. BS, Case Inst. Tech., 1949; MBA, Harvard U., 1952. Indsl. engr. Lincoln Electric Co., Cleve., 1952—53; mgr. purchase analysis Ford Motor Co., Dearborn, Mich., 1953—57; v.p. Booz, Allen & Hamilton, Inc., Detroit, 1957—69; v.p. corp. devel. Am. Motors Corp., Detroit, 1969—71, v.p. adminstrn., 1967—76, v.p. non-automotive subsidiaries, 1976—79, v.p. diversified ops., 1979—80; chmn., pres. Wheel Horse Products, Inc., South Bend, Ind., 1974—80; chmn., CEO Ingersoll Products Corp., Chgo., 1980—86; pres. Wellmax, Inc., 1976—. Served with USNR, 1944-46. Mem. Case Inst. Tech. Alumni Assn., Harvard Bus. Sch. Alumni Assn., Detroit Athletic Club, Detroit Econ. Club, Chgo. Club, Old Club, Tau Beta Pi, Theta Tau. Address: Ste 105-37 1000 S Old Woodward AVe Birmingham MI 48009 Home Phone: 248-669-5235; Office Phone: 248-646-3554. Personal E-mail: wellmaxx@earthlink.net.

MAXWELL, JEROME EUGENE, corporate executive; b. Princeton, Ill., June 2, 1944; s. Emmett Eugene and June (Erickson) M.; m. Cynthia Jane O'Connell, July 30, 1977; children: Eric Vaughn, Christina Dawn, Jeremy Emmett, Jason Daniel, Nicholas Mark. BSEE, So. Meth. U., 1967, MSEE, 1971. Maintainability engr. product support divsn. Collins Radio Co., Richardson, Tex., 1965-67, jr. engr. computer sys. divsn., 1967-70; sr. engr. TRW Electronics Products, Inc., Colorado Springs, Colo., 1970-73, mgr. engring., 1973-79, mgr. program mgmt. office, 1979-81, gen. mgr. space electronics mfg. divsn., 1981-86; pres., CEO G&S Sys., Inc., Bedford, Mass., 1986-87, Atec, Inc., Houston, 1987-91; v.p., divsn. dir. Nat. Sys. & Rsch. Co., Colorado Springs, 1992-94; pres., chmn. bd. dirs. Tech. Assocs. of Colo., Inc., Colorado Springs, 1994-96; pres., CEO Advanced Profl. Tng., Inc., Colorado Springs, 1996—. Patentee in field. Mem. adv. coun. U. Colo., Colorado Springs, 1973-86, U. So. Colo., Pueblo, 1974-78; Webelo leader, asst. pack leader Boy Scouts Am., 1976-77; fin. chmn. Ascension Luth. Ch., 1981-86; cons. to cmty. edn. coord. for computer sys. and equipment, 1980-86; mem. Soli Deo Gloria Choir, 1999—. Fellow: Nat. Assn. of Ch. Bus. Adminstr.; mem.: AIAA (sr.), Mesa Sertoma (charter, bd. dirs.), Assn. Old Crows (pres. space chpt.). Republican. Personal E-mail: president@yourtraining.net.

MAXWELL, MARY BETH, labor advocate; b. Omaha, May 22, 1965; 1 adopted child, Coleman Charles. BA in English, Philosophy and Polit. Sci. with honors, Marquette U., Milw. Field dir. US Student Assn., 1989—92; dep. field dir. Nat. Abortion and Reproductive Rights Action League, 1992—96; nat. field dir. Jobs with Justice, 1996—2003; founding exec. dir. Am. Rights at Work, Washington, 2003—. Co-author (with Bruce Nissen): Some of Them Are Brave: The Unfulfilled Promise of American Labor Law; contbr. columns in newspapers. Active Human Rights Coun., Family Equality Coun., Sacred Heart Cath. Parish, Washington; bd. dirs. Partnership for Working Families, Discount Found. Roman Catholic. Office: Am Rights at Work 1100 17th St Ste 950 Washington DC 20036 Office Phone: 202-822-2127. Office Fax: 202-822-2168.*

MAXWELL, RICHARD ANTHONY, retail executive; b. NYC, Apr. 1, 1933; s. Arthur William and Mary Ellen (Winestock) M.; m. Jacqueline Ann Creamer, Oct. 27, 1962. Student, NYU, 1957-58, Acad. Advanced Traffic, 1959. Import ops. mgr. Associated Merchandising Corp., NYC, 1950-52, 56-65; v.p. Associated Dry Goods Corp., NYC, 1965-86, sr. v.p. mktg., 1980-82, exec. v.p. mktg., 1982-86; pres. A.D.G. Export Mktg., Florence, Italy, 1982-86, Associated Dry Goods Ltd., Hong Kong, 1983-86, Inter Textyle Corp., 1987-89; with Matol Botanical Internat. Ltd.; exec. v.p. Matol World Corp., Montreal, Que., Canada, 1992-94; dir. Matol Botannical New Zealand, 1994-96; v.p. internat. ops. L'Aprina Internat. Inc., 1994-96; chief internat. officer Camelot Concept Co., Montreal, 1995-96; CFO Showcase Prodns., Phoenix, 1996; exec. v.p. Harmony House Internat., Phoenix, 1996-97, IGW Trust, Phoenix, 1997-99, Pre-Paid Legal Svcs., Inc., 1999—; pres. Team 39, Inc., Dunedin, Fla., 2000-2001; dir. Presley Promotions Inc., Memphis, 2001—02; pres., COO Home Farms Techs. Inc., Brandon, Man., Canada, 2002—08. Mem. industry sector adv. com. Dept. Commerce, 1984-93; mem. shippers adv. com. Nat. Maritime Coun. Served with USAF, 1952-56. Recipient Silver medal for contbns. to trade expansion, Republic of China, 1980; apptd. to rank of comdr. in Order of Merit in recognition of improvement of trade between Italy and U.S., Republic of Italy, 1985. Mem. Am. Assn. Exporters and Importers (past pres., dir.), Shippers Conf. Greater N.Y. (past pres., dir.), Nat. Retail Mchts. Assn. (vice chmn. fgn. trade com.), Nat. Com. Internat. Trade Documentation (past vice chmn. gen. bus. com.), Transp. Assn. Am., Italy-Am. C. of C. (past pres., dir.), Am. Soc. of Italian Legion of Merit (dir.). Home: 2408 Stag Run Blvd Clearwater FL 33765-1832 Office Phone: 727-791-8885.

MAXWELL, RICHARD CALLENDER, retired lawyer, educator; b. Mpls., Oct. 7, 1919; s. Bertram Wayburn and Blossom (Callender) M.; m. Frances Lida McKay, Jan 27, 1942; children: Richard Callender, John McKay. BSL, U. Minn., 1941, LLB, 1947; LLD (hon.), Calif. Western U., 1983; LLD, Southwestern U., 1993. Assoc. prof. U. ND, 1947-49, U. Tex., 1949-51, prof., 1951-53; counsel Amerada Petroleum Corp., 1952-53; prof. UCLA, 1953-81; dean UCLA Sch. Law, 1959-69, Connell prof., 1979-81, Connell prof. emeritus, 1981—; Chadwick prof. Duke U. Sch. Law, 1981-89, Chadwick prof. emeritus, 1989—. Vis. prof. Columbia U., 1955; vis. Alumni prof. U. Minn., 1970-71; Fulbright lectr. Queen's U., No. Ireland, 1970; vis. Ford Found. prof. U. Singapore, 1971; Thompson prof. U. Colo., 1982; vis. prof. Hastings Coll. Law, 1976, Duke U., 1979-80, U. Tex., 1985; pres. Minn. Law Rev., 1946; chmn. Coun. Legal Edn. Opportunity, 1971-72; pres. Assn. Am. Law Schs., 1972; chmn. adv. com. law Fulbright Program, 1971-74, chmn. adv. com. U.K., 1974-77; mem. com. on gas prodn. opportunities NRC, 1977-78; mem. law sch. editl. and adv. bd. West Pub. Co., 1971-94. Author: (with S. A. Riesenfeld) Cases and Materials on Modern Social Legislation, 1950, (with H.R. Williams and C.J. Meyers) Cases on Oil and Gas Law, 1956, 8th edit., (with Patrick H. Martin, Bruce M. Kramer), 2007, (with S.A. Riesenfeld) California Cases on Security Transactions, 1957, 4th edit. (with S.A. Riesenfeld, J.R. Hetland, W.D. Warren), 1991; West Coast editor Oil and Gas Reporter, 1953-. Mem. LA Employee Rels. Bd., 1971-74; bd. dirs. Constl. Rights Found., 1963-81; trustee Calif. Western U., 1979-81; bd. visitors Duke U. Sch. Law, 1973-79, chmn. bd. Pvt. Adjudication Ctr., 1984-89; bd. visitors Southwestern U. Sch. Law, 1981-90. Served to lt. comdr. USNR, 1941-46. Recipient Clyde O. Martz Tchg. award Rocky Mountain Mineral Law Found., 1994, Disting. Tchg. award, UCLA, 1977, Duke Law Sch., 1986, UCLA medal, 1982. Mem. ABA (com. on youth edn. for citizenship 1975-79, spl. com. on pub. understanding about the law 1979-84), Order of Coif. (nat. exec. com. 1980-86). Office: Duke U Sch Law Durham NC 27708-0362 Personal E-mail: rcmaxwell@mindspring.com.

MAXWELL, ROBERT EARL, federal judge; b. Elkins, W.Va., Mar. 15, 1924; s. Earl L. and Nellie E. (Rexstrew) M.; m. Ann Marie Grabowski, Mar. 29, 1948; children— Mary Ann, Carol Lynn, Ellen Lindsay, Earl Wilson. LLD (hon.), Davis and Elkins Coll., 1984; LLB, W.Va. U., 1949. Bar: W.Va. 1949. Practiced in, Randolph County, 1949; pros. atty., 1952-61; U.S. atty. for No. Dist. W.Va., 1961-64; judge US Dist. Ct. (no. dist.) W.Va., Elkins, 1965—94, sr. judge, 1994—; judge Temp. Emergency Ct. of Appeals, 1980-89. Past chmn. budget com. Jud. Conf. US; former mem. exec. com. Nat. Conf. Fed. Trial Judges; former mem. adv. bd. W.Va. U. Mem. bd. advisors W.Va. U., past chmn.; bd. advisors Mary Babb Randolph Cancer Ctr. Recipient Alumni Disting. Svc. award Davis and Elkins Coll., 1969, Religious Heritage Am. award, 1979, Outstanding Trial Judge award W.Va. Trail Lawyers Assn., 1988, Order of Vandalia award W.Va. U., Outstanding Alumnus award, 1992, Tenured Faculty Mem. Recognition award Bd. Govs., Def. Trail Coun., W.Va., 1992, Cert. of Merit, W.Va. State Bar, 1994, Justitia Officium award Coll. of Law, W.Va. U., 1994, award of merit W.Va. Bar Assn., 2004, Lawyer Citizen of Yr. award, 2005, Humanitarian award Odd Fellows, 2005; fellow W.Va. Bar Found., 1999; Melvin Jones fellow Lions Internat. Found., 2001. Mem. Nat. Conf. Federal Trial Judges, Dist. Judges Assn. 4th Cir. (past pres.), Moose (life), Lions (life), Beta Alpha Beta (merit award), Elkins-Randolph County C. of C. (citizen of yr. 1994). Office: US Dist Ct No Dist PO Box 1275 Elkins WV 26241-1275 E-mail: judge_maxwell@wvnd.uscourts.gov.

MAXWELL, ROBERT WALLACE, II, lawyer; b. Sept. 6, 1943; s. Robert Wallace and Margaret Maxwell; m. Mamie Lee Payne, June 18, 1966; children: Virginia, Robert, William. BS magna cum laude, Hampden-Sydney Coll., 1965; JD with honors, Duke U., 1968. Bar: Ohio 1968. Assoc. Taft, Stettinius & Hollister, Cin., 1968—75, ptnr., 1975—88, Keating, Muething & Klekamp, Cin., 1988—. Instr. U. Cin. Sch. Law, 1975—76. Elder Knox Presbyn. Ch.; bd. dir. Contemporary Arts Ctr. of Cin., Cin. Ballet Co. Mem.: ABA, Am. Assn. Mus. Trustees. Republican. Home: The Ascent Unit 503 One Roebling Way Covington KY 41011 Office: Keating Muething & Klekamp 1 E 4th St Ste 1400 Cincinnati OH 45202-3752 Office Phone: 513-579-6594. E-mail: rmaxwell@kmklaw.com.

MAXWELL, SARZ, psychiatrist, educator; b. Des Moines, Iowa, Sept. 22, 1954; d. Helen Travis Maxwell. MD, Loyola U. Stritch Sch. Medicine, Maywood, Ill., 1984. Cert. Am. Soc. Addiction Medicine, 1994. Founder & med. dir. Behavioral Medicine Unit, St. Francis Hosp., Maryville, Mo., 1988—92; pvt. practice Chgo., 1989; rsch. dir. Ctr. Addictive Problems, Chgo., 1993—2002; med. dir. Chgo. Recovery Alliance, 1999—; founder & med. dir. Mobile Opiate Substitution Treatment, Chgo., 2004—07. Dir. dual diagnosis edn. Ill. Dept. Mental Health, Chgo., 1996—2000; lectr. & cons. Midwest AIDS Tng. & Edn., Chgo., 2000—; lectr. Genessee County Bd. Health, Flint, Mich., 2007—; cons. WHO, Phnom Penh, Cambodia, 2008; vol. med. mentor Family Health Internat., Hanoi, 2008. Contbr. scientific papers. Vol. homeless addicts Cmty. Outreach, Chgo., 1992—2007; pres. Ill. Soc. Addiction Medicine, Chgo., 2004—06; vol. Obama for America. Recipient Harm Reduction Adv. of Yr., Chgo. Recovery Alliance, 2001, Alumnus Hall of Fame, Ill. State U., 2009. Fellow: Am. Soc. Addiction Medicine; mem.: Assn. Clinicians for Underserved. Avocations: crafts, reading, needlecrafts. Home: 1020 W Ardmore Ave 2M Chicago IL 60660 Home Fax: 773-561-2499. Personal E-mail: sarzmaxmd@yahoo.com.

MAXWELL, SOPHENIA (SOPHIE), city supervisor; b. San Francisco; Supr., Dist. 10 San Francisco Bd. Supervisors, 2001—, chair land use & econ. devel. com., vice-chair pub. safety com., mem. govt. audit & oversight com., Transp. Authority. Founder, chair San Francisco Recreation Coun.; chair Bayview Project Area Com.; rep. League Calif. Cities, Peninsula Corridor Study Joint Powers Bd.; mem. San Francisco Bay Conservation & Devel. Com.; past mem. Southeast Alliance Environ. Justice, Third St. Light Rail Adv. Com., Southern Water Front Adv. Com. Vol. Neighborhood Emergency Response Team (NERT), San Francisco; bd. dirs. Bayview-Hunters Point Ctr. Arts & Tech., San Francisco. Mem.: San Francisco League Women Voters (past v.p.). Office: 1 Dr Carlton B Goodlett Pl Rm 244 San Francisco CA 94102-4689 Office Phone: 415-554-7670. Fax: 415-554-7674. E-mail: Sophie_Maxwell@ci.sf.ca.us.*

MAXWELL, W(ILBUR) RICHARD, retired management consultant; b. Troy, Ohio, June 20, 1920; s. Wilbur D. and Gertrude (McDowell) M.; m. Roberta Mae Kennedy, June 29, 1942 (dec.); children: Douglas R., Jean Ann. Student, Ohio Wesleyan U., 1938-41; BS, Richmond Profl. Inst. of Coll. William and Mary, 1955. Sec. Troy C. of C., 1948-50, Va. C. of C., 1950-55; asst. to pres./chmn. bd. Reynolds Metals Co., 1955-64; v.p., dir. Reynolds Fgn. Sales Inc., 1964-68; pres. Nat. Better Bus. Bur., 1968-70; pres., chief exec. officer Jr. Achievement, Inc., Stamford, Conn., 1970-82. Instr. Richmond Profl. Inst., part-time 1955-57; sponsor-trustee U. Va. Grad. Bus. Sch., 1963-72. Pres. Lancaster County Libr., 1984-85, Rappahannock Gen. Hosp. Found., 1988-90, Northern Neck Vocat.-Tech. Edn. Ctr., 1991-93; bd. dirs. Rappahannock Gen. Hosp., 1988-90, Richmond (Va.) Cmty. H.S., 1989-91; chmn. Northumberland County (Va.) Econ. Devel. Commn., 1994-97. Civilian specialist USAAC, USN, 1942-46. Recipient Albert Schweitzer award Hugh O'Brien Youth Fedn., 1982; named to Jr. Achievement Profl. Hall of Fame, 1986. Mem. Indian Creek Yacht and Country Club (v.p., 1991-93, bd. dirs. 1991-93).

MAXWELL, WILLIAM HALL CHRISTIE, civil and environmental engineer, educator; b. Coleraine, No. Ireland, Jan. 25, 1936; came to U.S., 1958, naturalized, 1967; s. William Robert and Catherine Dempsey (Christie) M.; m. Mary Carolyn McLaughlin, Sept. 28, 1960; children: Katrina, Kevin, Wendy, Liam. BSc, Queen's U., Belfast, No. Ireland, 1956; MSc, Queen's U., Kingston, Ont., Can., 1958; PhD, U. Minn., 1964. Registered profl. engr., Ill. Site engr. Motor Columbus AG, Baden, Switzerland, 1956; tchg. asst. Queen's U., Kingston, 1956-58; from rsch. asst. to instr. U. Minn., Mpls., 1959-64; asst. prof. civil engring. U. Ill., Urbana, 1964-70, assoc. prof., 1970-82, prof., 1982-96, prof. emeritus civil and environ. engring., 1997—. Chmn. program com. 1st Internat. Conf. on New/Emerging Concepts for Rivers, Chgo., 1996. Editor: Water Resources Management in Industrial Areas, 1982, Water for Human Consumption, Man and His Environment, 1983, Frontiers in Hydrology, 1984, New/Emerging Concepts for Rivers, 1996. Vestryman Emmanuel Meml. Episcopal Ch., Champaign, Ill., 1977-80; state exhibitor Ministry Edn., Stormont, No. Ireland, 1953-56. Queen's U. Found. scholar, Belfast, 1954-56, R.S. McLaughlin travel fellow Queen's U., Kingston, 1958-59. Fellow ASCE (com. chmn. 1982-83), Internat. Water Resources Assn. (editor-in-chief Water Internat. 1986-93, sr. editor 1994-98, mem. publs. com. 1980-98, v.p. U.S. geog. com. 1986-91, chmn. awards com. 1995-97, bd. dirs. 1995-97, Editl. award

1994); mem. Am. Geophys. Union, Internat. Assn. for Hydraulic Rsch., Nat. Assn. Scholars. Avocations: home construction, painting. Home: 1210 Devonshire Dr Champaign IL 61821-6527 Office: U Ill Dept Civil and Environ Engring 205 N Mathews Ave Urbana IL 61801-2350 Business E-Mail: wmaxwell@illinois.edu.

MAXWELL, WILLIAM LAUGHLIN, retired industrial engineering educator; b. Phila., July 11, 1934; s. William Henry and Elizabeth (Laughlin) M.; m. Judith Behrens, July 5, 1969; children: Deborah, William, Judith, Keely BMechE, Cornell U., 1957, PhD, 1961. Andrew Schultz Jr. prof. dept. indsl. engring. Cornell U., Ithaca, NY, 1961-98. Author: Theory of Scheduling, 1967. Recipient Disting. Teaching award Cornell Soc. Engrs., 1968, Ralph S. Watts Tchg. award, 1997. Fellow Informs, Inst. Indsl. Engrs.; mem. Nat. Acad. Engring. Home: 106 Lake Ave Ithaca NY 14850-3537

MAXWELL, WILLIAM STIRLING, retired lawyer; b. Chgo., May 2, 1922; s. W. Stirling and Ethel (Bowes) Maxwell Reineke. AB with distinction, U. Mich., 1947, postgrad., 1946-49, JD, 1949. Bar: Ill. 1949, U.S. Ct. Mil. Appeals 1951, U.S. Supreme Ct. 1952. Assoc. Sidley & Austin, Chgo., 1949-60, 61, ptnr., 1962-84; now ret.; sr. legis. counsel U.S. Treasury, Washington, 1960-61. Trustee Mid-North Animal Shelter Found., Chgo., 1971—. Mem. Order of Coif, Phi Beta Kappa Clubs: Lawyers Club. Republican. Episcopalian. Home: PO Box 1839 Brookings OR 97415-0048

MAXWELL DIAL, ELEANORE, foreign language educator; b. Norwich, Connecticut, Feb. 21, 1929; d. Joseph Walter and Irene (Beetham) Maxwell; m. John E. Dial, Aug. 27, 1959. BA, U. Bridgeport, Conn., 1951; MA in Spanish, Mexico City Coll., 1955; PhD, U. Mo., 1968. Mem. faculty U. Wis., Milw., 1968—75, Ind. State U., Terre Haute, 1975—78, Bowling Green State U., Ohio, 1978—79; asst. prof. dept. fgn. lang. and lit. Iowa State U., Ames, 1979—85, assoc. prof., 1985—96, emerita assoc. prof., 1996—. Cons. pub. companies; participant workshops; del. First World Congress Women Journalists and Writers, Mex., 1975, mem. edn. commn. Contbr. articles, anthologies, and reviews to scholarly journals. Active governor's commn. on fgn. lang. and internat. studies, 1988-95. NDEA grantee, 1967, Ctr. Latin Am. grantee, 1972, NEH summer seminar UCLA, 1981, U. Calif., Santa Barbara, 1984. Mem. MLA, Am. Assn. Teachers Spanish and Portuguese, Midwest MLA, N. Ctrl. Coun. Latin Americanists, Midwest Assn. Latin Am. Studies, Clermont County Geneal. Soc., Ohio Geneal. Soc., Story County Iowa Geneal. Soc., Caribbean Studies Assn., P.G. Wodehouse Soc., Phi Beta Delta, Phi Sigma Iota, Sigma Delta Pi. Home: 190 North St Batavia OH 45103-2911 Office: Iowa State U Ames IA 50011-0001

MAXWELL-JOLLY, DAVID, state agency administrator, public health service officer; BA in History and Polit. Sci., Ind. U., Bloomington; MPH, U. Mich.; PhD in Pub. Policy, Frederick S. Pardee RAND Grad. Sch. Project analyst Kaiser Permanente Med. Care Program; supervising analyst Office of the Calif. Legis. Analyst, 1982—86; prin. cons. health and human services issues Calif. State Senate, 1986—99; dep. sec. Calif. Health and Human Services Agency, Sacramento, 1999—2002, project dir., Calif. Child Support Automation Sys., 2002—04, chief dep. dir., dept. child support services, 2005—07, dir., dept. child support services, 2007—08, dir., dept. health care services, 2008—. Democrat. Office: Calif Health and Human Services Agency Dept Health Care Services 1600 Ninth St Rm 460 Sacramento CA 95814-7413 Office Phone: 916-445-4171.*

MAXWORTHY, TONY, mechanical and aerospace engineering educator; b. London, May 21, 1933; came to U.S., 1954, naturalized, 1961; s. Ernest Charles and Gladys May (Butson) M.; m. Emily Jean Parkinson, June 20, 1956 (div. 1974); children: Kirsten, Kara; m. Anna Barbara Parks, May 21, 1979 BS in Engring. with honors, U. London, 1954; MSE, Princeton U., 1955; PhD, Harvard U., 1959. Rsch. asst. Harvard U., Cambridge, Mass., 1955-59; sr. scientist, group supr. Jet Propulsion Lab., Pasadena, Calif., 1960-67; assoc. prof. U. So. Calif., LA, 1967-70, prof., 1970—, Smith Internat. prof. mech. and aero. engring., 1988—, chmn. dept. mech. engring., 1979-89; cons. BBC Rsch. Ctr., Baden, Switzerland, 1972-82, J.P.L., Pasadena, Calif., 1968-80; lectr. Woods Hole Oceanographic Inst., Mass., summers 1965, 70, 72, 83. Forman vis. prof. aeronautics Technion Haifa, 1986; vis. prof. U. Poly., Madrid, 1988, Inst. Superiore Tech., Lisbon, 1988, Swiss Fed. Inst. Tech., Lausanne, 1989-95; assoc. prof. IMG, U. Joseph Fourier, Grenoble, 1980—, Ecole Superieure Physics and Indsl. Chemistry, Paris, 1995—; Shimizu vis. prof. Stanford U., 1996—, U. Canterbury, New Zealand, 2005—. Mem. editorial bd. Geophys. Fluid Dynamics, 1973-79, 88-96, Dynamic Atmospheric Oceans, 1976-83, Phys. Fluids, 1978-81, Zeitschrift fuer Angewandte Mathematik und Physik, 1987-96; contbr. articles to profl. jours. Recipient Humboldt Sr. Scientist award, 1981-93, G.I. Taylor medal Soc. Engring. Sci., 2003; life fellow Clare Hall, Cambridge U., 1974, 93—, Australian Nat. U., 1978, Nat. Ctr. Atmospheric Rsch., 1976, Glennon fellow U. Western Australia, 1990, F.W. Mosey fellow, 1993, Sr. Queen's fellow in marine scis. Commonwealth of Australia, 1984; sr. visitor DAMTP, Cambridge U., 1975—. Fellow: Am. Phys. Soc. (chmn. exec. com. fluid dynamics divsn. 1974—79, Otto Laporte award 1990), Am. Acad. Arts and Scis.; mem.: NAE, Oceanography Soc., European Geophys. Soc., Am. Geophys. Union. Office: U So Calif Dept Aerospace & Mech Engr Exposition Park Los Angeles CA 90089-1191 Business E-Mail: maxworth@usc.edu.

MAY, AVIVA RABINOWITZ, music educator, musician, linguist; b. Tel Aviv; naturalized, 1958; d. Samuel and Paula Pessia (Gordon) Rabinowitz; children: Chelley Mosoff, Alan May, Risa McPherson, Ellanna May/Gassman. AA, Oakton C.C., 1977; BA in Piano Pedagogy, Northeastern Ill. U., 1978. Folksinger, educator, musician Aviva May Studio/Piano and Guitar, 1948—; Sunday sch. dir. Canton Synagogue, Ohio, 1952-54; nursery sch. tchr. Allentown Jewish Cmty. Ctr., Pa., 1954—62; Hebrew music tchr. Brith Shalom Cmty. Ctr., Bethlehem, Pa., 1958—62; Hebrew tchr. Beth Hillel Congregation, Wilmette, Ill., 1962—78, Anshe Emet Day Sch., 1989—97, West Suburban Temple Har Zion, Oak Park, Ill., 1983—99; tchr. B'nai Mitzva, 1972—81; music dir. McCormick Health Ctrs., Chgo., 1978-79, Cove Sch. Perceptually Handicapped Children, Evanston, 1978-79; prof. Hebrew and Yiddish, Spertus Coll. Judaica, Chgo., 1980-89; music studio tchr. Cosmopolitan Sch., Chgo., 1992—. Tchr. continuing edn. Niles Twp. Jewish Congregation, 1993—97, also Jewish Cmty. Ctrs., 1972-78, Northeastern Ill. U., 1978-84; translator Office Spl. Investigations, Dept. Justice, Washington, 1978-88; music dir. Temple Emanuel Rosenwald Sch., 1989-1992. Composer classical music for piano, choral work, folk songs; developer 8-hour system for learning piano or guitar; contbr. articles to profl. jours. Recipient Magen David Adom Pub. Svc. award 1973; grantee Ill. State, 1975-79, Ill. Congressman Woody Bowman, 1978-79. Mem. Music Tchrs. Nat. Assn., Ill. Music Tchrs. Assn., Organ and Piano Tchrs. Assn., Am. Coll. Musicians, Ill. Assn. Learning Disabilities, North Shore Music Tchrs. Assn. (charter mem., co-founder), Sherwood Sch. Music, Friends of Holocaust Survivers, Nat. Yiddish Book Exch., Yiddish Book Exch. Ctr., Nat. Ctr. for Jewish Films, Chgo. Jewish Hist. Soc., Oakton C.C. Alumni Assn., Northeastern Ill. U. Alumni Assn. Office: Aviva May Studio 410 S Michigan Ave Ste 920 Chicago IL 60605-1471 Office Phone: 773-271-7765.

MAY, BARBARA, social sciences educator; d. Lawrence and Susan May; children: Adam, Courtney Kulick, Sasha Kulick. AGS, Montgomery County Cmty., Bluebell, 1972; BA in History, Gwynedd Mercy, Pa., 1974; MA in Philosophy, Villanova U, Pa., 1977; JD, Widener U Law, Brandywine, Del, 1981. Tchr. North Penn Sd, Lansdale, Pa., 1974—83; law clk. Superior Ct., Norristown, Pa., 1983—84; adj. instr. Villanova U, Pa., 1985—93, MCCC, Bluebell, Pa., 1984—; with ctrl. bucks hs CBSD, Doylestown, Pa., 1993—. Mem.: Montg Bar. Conservative. Roman Catholic. Home: 672 Godshall Rd Telford PA 18969 Office: Montgomery County CC 340 Dekalb Pike Blue Bell PA 19422 Personal E-mail: hrmbarbara@verizon.net. Business E-Mail: bmay@mc3.edu.

MAY, CECIL RICHARD, JR., academic administrator; b. Memphis, June 13, 1932; BA in Biblical Langs. magna cum laude, Harding U., MA in New Testament, MTh; LLD (hon.), Freed-Hardeman U., 1984. Min., Holly Springs, Miss., 1954-57, Ripley, Miss., 1957-59, Pine Bluff Ch., Ctrl. Acad. Ch., Miss., 1959-60; dist. scout exec. Yocona Area Coun. Boy Scouts Am., Oxford, Miss., 1959-60; min. Ashland, Miss., 1961, Fulton, Miss., 1962-67, Eastside Campus Ch., Portland, Oreg., 1967-69; Bible tchr. Columbia Christian Coll., Portland, 1967-69; min. Vicksburg, Miss., 1969-76; dean Internat. Bible Coll., Florence, Ala., 1977-80; pres. Magnolia Bible Coll., Kosciusko, Miss., 1980-97; dean bibl. studies Faulkner U., Montgomery, Ala., 1998—, dir. annual Bible lectureship. Lectr. in field. Editor: Preacher Talk; assoc. editor: Magnolia Messenger; contbr. articles to profl. jours. Elder Vicksburg Ch., Miss., 1971-76, South Huntington St. Ch., Kosciusko, 1981-97, U. Ch., Montgomery, 2003—; active Boy Scouts Am., 1954-76; com. chair Kosciusko-Attala County C. of C., 1992; bd. dirs. Am. Cancer Soc., 1971-74, fin. campaign chmn., 1971; bd. dirs. Miss. Econ. Coun., 1985-86, 89-92, area vice-chmn., 1991-92; chmn. Attala County Med. Study Task Force, 1991-92; mem. Evang. Theol. Soc. Recipient Disting. Christian Svc. award, Harding U., 2003, Tower of Strength award, Cloverdale Ctr. Family Strengths, Faulkton U., Montgomery, Ala., 2009. Mem.: Evangelical Theol. Soc. Achievements include Classroom Building at Magnolia Bible College named Cecil May Jr. Classroom Building, 1997. Office: Faulkner Univ 5345 Atlanta Hwy Montgomery AL 36109-3390 Office Phone: 334-386-7154. Business E-Mail: cmay@faulkner.edu.

MAY, DARLENE RAE, language educator; b. Akron, Ohio, Feb. 13, 1947; d. James Alva May and Bertha Hannah Graham; m. Abdulrahman Ahmed Abdullah, Aug. 31, 1974; children: Muhammad Abdulrahman Abdullah, Mustafa Abdulrahman Abdullah. Degree, Instituto Caro y Cuervo, Bogota, Colombia, 1967; BA, Ind. U., Bloomington, 1968, MA, 1971, PhD, 1978. Asst. prof. arabic & islamic studies Rhodes Coll., Memphis, 1973—81; adj. assoc. prof. arabic Elon U., NC, 2005—07, Wake Forest U., Winston-Salem, NC, 2005—07, vis. assoc. prof. arabic, 2007—. Dir. arabic study abroad program fes, morocco Wake Forest U., 2005. Contbr. articles to profl. jours., chapters to books. Mem. Cmty. Mosque, Winston-Salem, NC, 2005—09. Scholarship, Nat. Merit Scholarship Corp., 1964—68, Ford Found. Asian Studies fellowship, 1969—70, Arabic Study Abroad fellowship, CASA, Am. U., Cairo, 1970—71, fellow, Mid. East Studies Assn., 1979, Transl. Rsch. grant, Nat. Endowment Humanities, 1980—81. Mem.: Am. Assn. Tchrs. Arabic (exec. bd. 1975—76), Phi Beta Kappa (pres., gamma chpt. Tenn. 1979—80). Office: Wake Forest Univ PO Box 7343 Winston Salem NC 27109 Business E-Mail: maydr@wfu.edu.

MAY, DONALD ROBERT LEE, ophthalmologist, educator, academic administrator, farmer; b. Spring Valley, Ill., Nov. 26, 1945; BS in Liberal Arts and Scis. with high honors and distinction, U. Ill., 1968, MD, 1972. Diplomate Am. Bd. Ophthalmology, Nat. Bd. Med. Examiners. Rsch. fellow dept. ophthalmology U. Ill. Eye and Ear Infirmary, Chgo., 1971—72; intern Northwestern U. Sch. Medicine Meml. Hosps., Chgo., 1972—73; resident in ophthalmology U. Ill. Eye and Ear Infirmary, Chgo., 1973—76, instr. dept. ophthalmology, 1974—77, attending surgeon dept. ophthalmology, 1976—77, fellow in diabetic retinopathy study, diabetic retinopathy vitrectomy study, and retina and vitreous surgery, 1976—77; founder, dir. retina svc., dept. ophthalmology Wilford Hall USAF Med. Ctr., San Antonio, 1977—79; asst. prof. ophthalmology, founder, dir. Retina/Vitreous/Ocular Trauma Svc. U. Calif. Davis Sch. Medicine, Calif., 1979—81; assoc. prof., dir. retina, vitreous and ocular trauma svc. U. Calif. Sch. Medicine, Davis, 1981—84; prof. ophthalmology Tulane U. Sch. Medicine, New Orleans, 1984—89, dir. med. student edn. dept. ophthalmology, 1985—89, dir. ophthalmology Charity Hosp., 1985—89; prof. Tex. Tech U. Health Scis. Ctr., Lubbock, Tex., 1989—2001, chmn. dept. ophthalmology and visual scis., 1989—94, prof. dept. health orgn. mgmt., 1993—2001, assoc. dean Sch. Medicine, 1994—96; del. 19th Congaessional Dist. to Repulican Nat. Convention, Tex. Co-investigator in the intraocular gentamicin prophylaxis study Govt. Erskine Hosp., Madurai, India, 1975, Dept. Ophthalmology, Audie Murphy VA Hosp., San Antonio, 1977—79, Martinez VA Hosp., Calif., 1979—84, VA Hosp., New Orleans, 1984—89, VA Med. Ctr., Big Spring, Tex., 1989—93, 1996—2001, VA Ctr., Lubbock, Tex., 1989—92, Lubbock, 1996—2001; vis. prof., Germany, 1984, Switzerland, 87; pres. US Eye Injury Registry, 1994—96; founder, med. dir. Tex. Eye Injury Registry, 1991—2001; cons. in field; co-owner Fullanime Cos., Lubbock, Tex., Selenium Ltd. Concert Lighting Internat., Compliance Svcs. Group Internat. Contbg. editor: Outcome/Fragmatome Newsletter, 1978—81; assoc. editor: Vitreorentinal Surgery and Tech., 1989—98, mem. editl. bd.: Jour. Eye Trauma, 1996—2001; contbr. articles to profl. jours.; appeared in numerous TV and radio programs. Com. mem. Sch. Medicine U. Calif., Davis, Tulane U. Sch. Medicine, New Orleans, Sch. Medicine Tex. Tech. U. Health Scis. Ctr.; bd. dirs. Lubbock Internat. Cultural Ctr., Inc., 1997—, pres. bd. dirs., 2005—07; planning com., chmn. medicine and history com., liaison Vatican Mus. Exhbn. Found., 2001—02; bd. trustees Nat. Exhibits Assn. Mus., Post, Tex., 2007—; Tex. del. 19th Congl. Dist. to Rep. Nat. Convention, 2008. Maj. USAF, 1973—80. Decorated Air Force Commendation medal. Mem.: AMA, ACS, Mil. Officers Assn. of Am., Mil. Officers Assn. Am. (bd. dirs. Greater Lubbuck chpt. 2007—), Ill. Farm Bur., Ill. Agrl. Assn., Am. Farm Bur. Fedn., Soc. Med. Cons. Armed Forces, Vitreous Soc. (charter), Retina Soc., Schepens Internat. Soc., Tex. Tech. Rsch. Found. (bd. dirs. 1993—96), Tex. Ophthal. Assn. (chair edn. com. 1990—93, coun. 1990—93, nominating com. 1991—93), So. Retina Study Group, Tex. Med. Assn. (com. continuing edn. 1993—96, bd. dirs. TEXPAC 2000—02), So. Med. Assn. (vice-chmn. sec. ophthalmology 1995—96, chmn. sec. ophthalmology 1996—97), Christian Med. Assn., Assn. Rsch. Vision and Ophthalmology (pub. rels. com. 1997—2000), Am. Acad. Ophthalmology (bylaws and rules com. 1990—95, com. internat. ophthalmology 1991—95), Lubbock C. of C., Am. Legion, Sigma Xi (sec. Tex. Tech. chpt. 1990—91, v.p., pres.-elect 1999—2000, pres. 2000—01). Republican. Lutheran. Avocations: travel, photography, bicycling, hiking. Office: PO Box 1678 Lubbock TX 79408-1678 *If we are to survive as a free society, we must each accept responsibility. The individual must function on the premise that personal rewards come with the investment of hard, honest work and not as a right mediated by government at the expense of others. Our legislative bodies must enact laws for the common good and not for individual self-interest. Our judicial systems must provide for the just enforcement of our laws. Our leadership must be the watchdog to ensure the indivdual has the opportunity to life without unreasonable danger, the freedom to follow one's dreams, and the ability to pursue happiness through individual achievement. Security comes with the contribution of all who are able.*

MAY, ERNEST DEWEY, academic administrator, musician; b. Jersey City, May 8, 1942; s. Ernest Max and Harriet Elizabeth (Dewey) May; m. Eileen Marie Mayhew, Jan. 29, 1963 (div. 1984); children: Ernest Jr., Elizabeth May Goodell, Katherine May Waite, Caroline, Christopher, Abigail May Robles, Deirdre May Maitre; m. Mary L. Milkey, June 29, 1985. AB, Harvard U., Cambridge, Mass., 1964; MFA, Princeton U., NJ, 1968, PhD, 1975. Asst. prof. music Amherst Coll., Mass., 1969-75; from asst. prof. to prof. music dept. music and dance U. Mass., Amherst, 1976-88, prof. music, chmn. dept. music and dance, 1988-2000, presiding officer faculty senate, 1997-2000, sec. faculty senate, 2000—. Faculty rep. bd. trustees U. Mass., 1988-97; chair Intercampus Faculty Coun., 2001—; organist, dir. mus. South Congl. Ch., Springfield, Mass., 1983-05. Rec.: Music for Trumpet and Organ, 1979, 2001; co-editor: J.S. Bach: Neve Ausgabe Samtlicher Werke Vol. I/20, 1986, J.S. Bach as Organist, 1986; contbr. New Harvard Dictionary of Music, 1986. Mem.: Am. Musicological Soc. (pres. New Eng. chpt. 1988—90), Am. Guild Organists. Home: 44 Amherst Rd Pelham MA 01002-9700 Office: U Mass Faculty Senate Amherst MA 01003 Business E-Mail: secretary@senate.umass.edu.

MAY, GARY STEPHEN, electrical engineer; b. St. Louis, May 17, 1964; s. Warren and Gloria (Hunter) M.; m. LeShelle; c. Simone Imani, Jordan Amani May BEE, Ga. Inst. Tech., 1985; MEE and Computer Science, U. Calif., Berkeley, 1987, PhD in Electrical Engring. and Computer Sci., 1991. Tutor Ga. Inst. Tech., 1982-84, rsch. asst., 1985; joined Sch. Electrical and Computer Engring., the microelectronics group Ga. Inst. Tech, 1991, Motorola Found. prof., 2001—05, assoc. chair., sch. electrical and computer engring., 2001—05, exec. asst. to pres., 2002—05, prof., Steve W. Chaddick Sch. Electrical and Computer Engring. chair, 2005—; coop. edn. staff McDonnell-Douglas Corp., 1982-84; mem. tech. staff AT&T Bell Labs., summers 1985-86; rsch. asst. U. Calif., Berkeley, 1989-90, grad. student instr.; 1988—91. Founder, dir. Summer Undergraduate Rsch. Engring./Sci. Prog. (SURE), Ga. Inst. Tech., 1992—, Facilitating Academic Careers in Engineering and Science (FACES), Ga. Inst. Tech., 1998—; served on Congl. Commn. on the Advancement of Women and Minorities in Sci., Engring., and Tech., NSF Com. on Equal Opportunity in Sci. and Engring., chair, 2000—01; spkr. in field. Editor-in-chief IEEE Transactions on Semiconductor Manufacturing, 1997—2001 (Oustanding Paper award, 1998, 2000); contbr. articles to profl. jours. NSF fellow, AT&T Bell Lab. Fellow; recipient Outstanding Young Alumnus, Ga. Inst. Tech., 1993, AT&T Info. Systems award, Eso-Systems award, GE Latimer Achievement award, Martin Luther King Jr. Svc. award., Giant of Sci. award, Quality Edn. for Minorities Network, 2002, Wickenden award for Outstanding Paper, Journal of Engring. Edn., 2003, Minorities in Engring. award, 2004, 2006 AAAS Mentor award, 2007; named Nat. Young Investigator, 1993-98; selected by the NAE to Participate in Frontiers of Engineering Conference as one of the nation's top 100 engineers between the ages of 30-45, 2000. Fellow IEEE; mem. Nat. Soc. Black Engrs. (nat. chmn. emeritus, nat. chmn. 1987-89, editorial bd. 1985-, mem. nat. adv. bd., Outstanding Leadership award, 1988, 89, Golden Torch Award: Janice A. Lumpkin Educator of Yr., 2006, Nat. Action Coun. for Minorities in Engring., NAACP, Ga. Inst. Tech. Exec. Roundtable, Phi Eta Sigma (Dorothy C. Yancy Incentive award), Lambda Sigma, Eta Kappa Nu, Briarean Soc., Eta Kappa Nu, Omicron Delta Kappa, Phi Kappa Phi, Tau Beta Pi, Anak. Avocations: art, reading, music, football, tennis. Office Phone: 404-894-2902. Office Fax: 404-894-4641. E-mail: gary.may@ece.gatech.edu.

MAY, GITA, literature educator; b. Brussels, Sept. 16, 1929; came to U.S., 1947, naturalized, 1950; d. Albert and Blima (Sieradska) Jochimek; m. Irving May, Dec. 21, 1947. BA magna cum laude, CUNY-Hunter Coll., 1953; MA, Columbia U., 1954, PhD, 1957. Lectr. French CUNY-Hunter Coll., 1953—56; from instr. to assoc. prof. Columbia U., NYC, 1956—68, prof., 1968—, chmn., 1983—93, mem. senate, 1979—83, 1986—88, chmn. Seminar on 18th Century Culture, 1986—89. Lecture tour English univs., 1965. Author: Diderot et Baudelaire, critiques d'art, 1957, De Jean-Jacques Rousseau à Madame Roland: essai sur la sensibilité préromantique et révolutionnaire, 1964, Madame Roland and the Age of Revolution, 1970 (Van Amringe Disting. Book award), Stendhal and the Age of Napoleon, 1977, French Women Writers, 1991, Encyclopedia of Aesthetics, 1998, Dictionnaire de Diderot, 1999, The Feminist Encyclopedia of French Literature, 1999, Elisabeth Vigée Le Brun: The Odyssey of an Artist in an Age of Revolution, 2005; co-editor: Diderot Studies III, 1961; mem. editl. bd. Romanic Rev., 1959—, 18th Century Studies, 1975—78, French Rev., 1975—86, 1998—, Women in French Studies, 2000—; contbg. editor: Oeuvres complètes de Diderot, 1984—, 1995—; gen. editor The Age of Revolution and Romanticism: Interdisciplinary Studies, 1990—, extensive essays on Diderot and George Sand in European Writers, 1984, 1985, and on Rebecca West, Anita Brookner and Graham Swift in British Writers, 1996, 1997, 1999, Bayle, Fontenelle and Fénelon in Dictionary of Literary Biography, 2003, Voltaire's Candide (in Barnes and Noble Classics), 2003; contbr. articles and revs. to profl. jours. Decorated chevalier and officier Ordre des Palmes Acad.; recipient award Am. Coun. Learned Socs., 1961, award for outstanding achievement CUNY-Hunter Coll., 1963; Fulbright rsch. grantee, 1964-65; Guggenheim fellow, 1964-65, NEH fellow, 1971-72. Mem. AAUP, MLA (del. assembly 1973-75, com. rsch. activities 1975-78, exec. coun. 1980-83), Am. Assn. Tchrs. French, Am. Soc. 18th Century Studies (pres. 1985-86, 2d v.p. 1983-84, 1st v.p. 1984-85, One of Gt. Tchrs. award 1999), Soc. Française d'Etude du Dix-Huitième Siècle, Soc. Diderot, Am. Soc. French Acad. Palms, Soc. des Etudes Staëliennes, N.Am. Soc. for Study of Jean-Jacques Rousseau, Soc. des Professeurs Français et Francophones d'Amérique, Phi Beta Kappa. Office: Columbia U Dept French/Romance Philol 516 Philosophy Hall MC4918 New York NY 10027 Business E-Mail: gm9@columbia.edu.

MAY, HAROLD LOUIS, retired surgeon, not-for-profit developer; s. Arthur Earnest and Margaret Jestina May; m. Agnes Martens, Apr. 26, 1960; children: Jeannette Elizabeth, Alison Gabrielle, Margaret May Jenkins. MD, Harvard Med. Sch., Boston, 1951, MPH, 1974. Lic. physician Mass., 1959, diplomate Am. Bd. of Surgery, 1965. Med. intern U. Minn. Hosps., Mpls., 1951—52; med. asst. resident Boston City Hosp., 1952—53; surg. resident Mass. Gen. Hosp., Boston, 1953—59; chief of surgery Albert Schweitzer Hosp., Deschapelles, Haiti, 1960—70; dir. Divsn. Cmty. Health and Med. Care Peter Bent Brigham Hosp., Boston, 1970—75; assoc. surgery Peter Bent Brigham Hosp. and Brigham and Women's Hosp., Boston, 1970—94; asst. prof. surgery Harvard Med. Sch., 1970—94; dir. med. svcs. Wrentham (Mass.) Devel. Svcs., 1975—94, ret., 1994. Exec. com. Boston-Brookline (Mass.) Health Resources Orgn., 1970—73; chmn. Region VI Emergency Med. Svcs. Com., Mass., 1972—74. Editor (author): Emergency Medicine,

1984; editor: Emergency Procedures, 1984; editor in chief: Emergency Medicine, 2d edit., 1992. Founder and pres. FAMILY, Inc., Boston, 1997; co-founder Ecole La Providence Primary Sch., Deschapelles, Haiti, 1962; founder Family Inst. Artibonite Valley, Haiti, 2009. Aviation cadet US Army Air Corps, 1945. Recipient Excellence in Tchg. Faculty prize, Harvard Med. Sch., 1987, 1992, Congl. Gold medal, Tuskegee Airmen, 2008, Living Legends award, Tuskegee Airman, Mus. African Am. History, Boston. Fellow: ACS; mem.: MGH Surg. Soc., Tuskegee Airmen, Boston Surg. Soc. Avocations: music, painting. Home and Office: FAMILY Inc 80 Waban Hill Road Newton MA 02467 Business E-Mail: haroldmay@familysystem.net.

MAY, INGRID BARBARA, elementary school educator; d. Pedro B. and Maria B. Luna; m. Fred L. May, Aug. 13, 1977; 1 child, Rebecca S. BA, Oklahoma City U., 1971; MA, So. Nazarene U., Bethany, Okla., 1975. Reading cert. Okla., 1975, nat. bd. cert. Nat. Bd. for Profl. Tchg. Stds., 2005. Educator third grade Ctrl. Elem. Sch., 1972—75, Overholser Elementary Sch., Oklahoma City, 1976—, Overholser Elem. Sch., Bethany, 1976—; mem. reading com. Putnam City Sch. Dist., 1974—, report card com., 2007—08; mem. Putnam City Sch. Reading Coun., Oklahoma City, 1972—82, treas., 1974—79, pres., 1980—81; chmn. Overholser Reading Com., Bethany, 1980—, Overholser Social Studies Com., 1999—2005; mem. Title I, Bethany, 2004—, Overholser Prin.'s Adv. Comm., 2005—07. Accompanist Silver Strings of Putnam City, Oklahoma City, 2000—05; mem. Title I. Bethany, 2004—08. Dir. Adopt-a-Grandparent Project, Bethany, 2004—; tchr. MPACT A Chance to Change Found., 2006—. Named Tchr. of Yr., Overholser Elem. Sch., 1980—81, 2005—06; scholar Nat. Bd. Certification, Edn. Leadership Okla., 2005, Gt. Expectations, Okla. State Reading Orgn., 2006—. Mem.: NEA (assoc.), Putnam City Assn. Classroom Tchrs. (assoc.), Okla. Edn. Assn. (assoc.). Republican. Nazarene. Avocations: handbell choir, piano, singing, gardening, sewing.

MAY, JAMES HARVEY, communications educator; s. Rhoudy and Ruby Mae May; m. Margit Röder, June 10, 1967; children: James Richard, Anika Nikol; 1 child, Tanja Babette Youngs. BS, Stanford U., 1958; MBA, Harvard U., 1964; certificate in radio and TV, NYU, 1966; DLS, Columbia U., 1973—78, advanced certificate in librarianship, 1977. Econ. engr. Gilbert Associates, Inc., NYC, 1964—67; v.p., treas. Pandex, Macmillan Info. Corp., NYC, 1967—72; dir., ctr. comm. and info. rsch. U. Denver, 1972—74; assoc. libr. dir., acting libr. dir. Sonoma State U., Rohnert Pk., Calif., 1974—83; vice provost info. resources Calif. State U., Chico, 1983—94; prof. comm. sci. and tech. Calif. State U. Monterey Bay, Seaside, 1994—, founding dean instrn., 1994—96, asst. to the pres., 1996—98. Ofcl. historian, bd. mem. Soc. Computer Simulation, 1991—97; panelist with US v.p. Al Gore Unity '99, Seattle, 1999; treas. Calif. Faculty Assn., 1999—2003, chpt. pres., 1998—2001, 2004—05; ednl. effectiveness panel Am. Distance Edn. Consortium, 2000—; keynote spkr. Open Learning 2000, Brisbane, Queensland, Australia, 2000; bd. dir. Am. Indian Sci. and Engring. Soc., 2002—; co-chair, vice chair, bd. mem. Native Am. Pub. Telecom.; chmn. bd. Native Am. TV. Contbr. articles to jour. and chpt. to books. Lt. JG USN, 1959—62, Las Vegas and No. Ireland. Recipient outstanding leadership in libr. services for Am. Indian People and founding the Am. Indian Libr. Assn., Am. Indian Libr. Assn., 1994, Svc. to Am. Indians in Field of Tech., Stanford U. Am. Indian Alumni Assn., 1995, Union Mem. Yr., Monterey Ctrl. Labor Coun., AFL-CIO, 2000, Trade Unionist Yr., Monterey Bay Ctrl. Labor Coun., AFL-CIO, 2002. Mem.: Am. Indian Sci. and Engring. Soc. (life; bd.dir. 2002—, Ely S. Parker Medal 2000), United Keetoowah Band of Cherokee Indians (life). Achievements include created first computerized bibliographic database. Office: Calif State Univ Monterey Bay 100 Campus Ctr Seaside CA Home: 3704 Clubside Ln Sacramento CA 95835 E-mail: jameshmay@yahoo.com.

MAY, JAMES WARREN, JR., plastic surgeon; b. Lexington, Ky., 1943; MD, Northwestern U., 1969. Cert. gen. surgery Am. Bd. Surgery, 1975, plastic surgery Am. Bd. Plastic Surgery, 1977. Intern gen. surgery Mass. Gen. Hosp., Harvard Medical Sch., 1969, surg. resident Boston, 1969—74; resident plastic surgeon Harvard Medical Sch., 1974—75; fellow, hand and Microsurgery U. Louisville, 1975, U. Melbourne, Australia, 1975—76; assoc. prof. clin. surgery Harvard Med. Sch., Boston; chmn. Am. Bd. Plastic Surgery; chief, plastic, reconstructive surgery Mass. Gen. Hosp. Cancer Ctr., Boston; prof. surgery Harvard Medical Sch.; chmn. plastic and Reconstructive Surgery Mass. Gen. Hosp., 1982—. Named one of Top Cancer Specialists for Women, Good Houskeeping mag., 1999, Top Breast Cancer Doctors, Redbook mag., 2002, Boston's Top Doctor's, Boston mag., 2006. Mem.: Royal Coll Physicians and Surgeons (hon. fellow 2008), Am. Assn. Plastic Surgeons (pres. 2007), Am. Assn. Hand Surgery (pres. 1996), Am. Assn. Acad. Chmn. Plastic Surgery (pres. 1995), Am. Bd. Plastic Surgery (chmn. 1992), New England Soc. Plastic Surgeons (pres. 1990), Northeastern Soc. Plastic Surgeons (pres. 1990), Plastic Surgery Rsch. Coun. (chmn. 1987), Mass. Soc.Plastic Surgeons (pres.), Am. Assn. Plastic Surgeons (pres.-elect 2006, pres. 2007). Office: MA Gen Hosp Divsn Plastic Surgery WACC 435 55 Parkman St Boston MA 02114-3117

MAY, JANET SUE, playwright, lyricist; b. Bloomington, Ill., Dec. 24, 1946; d. James Woolston and Josephine Elisabeth (Ferguson) Grubb; children: John, Darbi, Heather, Brandy. Student, Lincoln Coll., 1965, Wabash Coll., 1965, St. Joseph's Hosp., 1966, Indian River C.C., 1983, Bloomington Sch. Practical Nursing, 1984; cert. in food svc. sanitation, Ill. State U., 1988. Chem. lab. tech. Eureka Williams, Bloomington, 1966; histology tech. St. Joseph's Hosp., Bloomington, 1966—67; activity dir. McLean County Nursing Home, Normal, Ill., 1968—70; rsch. asst. U. Fla. Med. Entomology Lab., Vero Beach, Fla., 1984—85; asst. libr. condemned unit Pontiac Prison, Ill., 1974—75; activity dir., meal supr. Bloomington Housing Authority, 1987—89; pub. rels. mgr. Miracle Ear, Peoria, Ill., 1990—92. Author: (children's poetry books) Winston-Smythe Worm, Prissy Penelope Grasshopper Presents, (children's books) Four Little Creatures; co-author (with James Kitzmiller): Patronymics of Mosquitoes, 2d edit., 1986; playwright: More Than Just A Man, 2001; playwright (musical) A Christmas Forgotten, 2007; songwriter: Ice Age; author: (musical) Abraham's House, 2005. Achievements include co-inventor, tissue vacuum pump; invention of jeweled perfumed hair tie; blinking hair tie. Avocations: art, poetry, singing. Personal E-mail: lgrubworm@aol.com.

MAY, JOSEPH LESERMAN (JACK MAY), retired lawyer; b. Nashville, May 27, 1929; s. Daniel and Dorothy (Fishel) M.; m. Natalie McCuaig, Apr. 12, 1957 (dec. May 1990); children: Benjamin, Andrew, Joshua, Maria; m. Lynn Hewes Lance, June 10, 1994. BA, Yale U., New Haven, Conn., 1951; JD, NYU, 1958; postgrad., Harvard Bus. Sch., Cambridge, Mass., 1969. Bar: Tenn. 1959. Prodr. Candied Yam Jackson Show, 1947-51; with CIA, 1951-55; pres. Nuweave Socks, Inc., NYC, 1955-59, May Hosiery Mills, Nashville, 1960-83, Athens Hosiery Mills, Tenn., 1966-83; v.p. Wayne-Gossard Corp., Chattanooga, 1972-83; dir. pvt. practice law Nashville, 1984—; ret., 2004. Dir. Merrill Lynch Investment Mgmt., 1987—2002; mem. adv. bd. Asian Strategies Group, 1994; chmn. Guardianship and Trust Corp., 1994—96; founding dir. Nashville Bank and Trust Co., 2003. Author: (book) Walking Around the House, 2007, A Confetti of Papers, 2008. Bd. dirs. Vanderbilt Cancer Ctr., 1994-99; pres. Jewish Cmty. Ctr., 1969; chmn. Campus for Human Devel., 2000-02; mem. Collectors Cir., Frist Art Mus., 2004—; With USN, 1947-53, US Army, 1954. Mem. Tenn. Bar Assn., Nashville Bar Assn., Am. Arbitration Assn. Panel of Neutrals, Tenn. Hist. Soc. (trustee, pres. 2000-02), Eagle Scout Assn., Belle Meade Country Club, Shamus Club, Old Oak Club, Old Goats, Zodiac, Group of Six, Yale Club NY, Rotary (pres. Nashville 1971). Republican. Jewish. Home: 133 Abbottsford Nashville TN 37215-2442

MAY, KENNETH AUSTIN, former consumer products company executive; b. Memphis, Nov. 14, 1960; s. Forrest Sherman and Elizabeth (Austin) M. Degree in real estate, Memphis State U., 1983; MBA, U. Tenn., 1994. Supr. United Parcel Svc., Memphis, 1979-82; sr. mgr. Federal Express Corp., Memphis, 1982-90, mng. dir. Miami, 1990-96, v.p. Memphis, 1996—2004; exec. v.p., CEO FedEx Kinko's Inc., Dallas, 2004—06, pres., CEO, 2006—08. Trustee March of Dimes Birth Defects Found., White Plains, NY. Republican. Baptist. Avocations: water-skiing, skiing, basketball, golf, fishing. Home: 5139 Palomar Ln Dallas TX 75229-6407

MAY, KENNETH NATHANIEL, retired food industry consultant; b. Livingston, La., Dec. 24, 1930; s. Robert William and Mary Hulda (Caraway) M.; m. Patsy Jean Farr, Aug. 4, 1953; children: Sherry Alison (dec.), Nathan Elliott. BS in Poultry Sci., La. State U., 1952, MS in Poultry Sci., 1955; PhD in Food Tech., Purdue U., 1959, DAgr, 1988. Asst. prof. U. Ga., Athens, 1958-64, assoc. prof., 1964-67, prof., 1967-68, Miss. State U., State College, 1968-70; dir. rsch. Holly Farms Poultry, Wilkesboro, N.C., 1970-73, v.p., 1973-85, pres., 1985-88, chmn., CEO, 1989—89, ret., 2005. Adj. prof. N.C. State U., 1975. Contbr. over 60 articles to profl. jours.; patentee treatment of cooked poultry. Bd. trustees Appalachian State U., 1987-94, chmn., 1989-90. Recipient Industry Service award Poultry and Egg Inst. Am., 1971, Meritorious Service award, Ga. Egg Commn., 1964, Disting. Service award Agribus. N.C., 1986; named to Am. Poultry Hall of Fame, 1992. Fellow Poultry Sci. Assn. (Disting. Poultry Industry Career award 2007); mem. Nat. Poultry Hist. Soc. (bd. dirs. 1982-83), Inst. Food Technologists. Methodist. Avocations: reading, stained glass.

MAY, MATTHEW P., chemist; b. Calif. s. Buddy G. and Jean M. May; m. Shannon K. Fee, Sept. 18, 1999. MS, U. Calif., Davis, 1999. Sr. assoc. rsch. chemist Dade Behring MicroScan, West Sacramento, Calif., 2000—01; rsch. chemist Idaho State U., Pocatello, 2002—. Treas. Sunrise Thereputics, Boisie, Idaho, 2008—. Achievements include research in anti-cancer drug discovery. Office: Idaho State Univ 1651 Alvin Ricken Dr Pocatello ID 83201

MAY, RABBI MEYER H., museum director; b. 1952; MS in guidance and counseling, Nova U., 1976; attended, UCLA. Ordained by Rabbi Isaac Elchanan Theological Seminary, Yeshiva U., NY, 1977. Joined Simon Wiesenthal Ctr. and Mus. of Tolerance, LA, 1978—, exec. dir. Pres. Rabbinical Coun. Calif.; bd. mem. Artscroll's Mesorah Heritage Found., Yeshiva of LA, Young Israel of Hancock Park, LA. Office: Simon Wiesenthal Ctr and Mus Tolerance 1399 South Roxbury Los Angeles CA 90035

MAY, MICHAEL, chemistry professor; married. PhD, U. Ala. Prof. chemistry Darton Coll., Albany, Ga., 1987—. Office: Darton Coll 2400 Gillionville Rd Albany GA 31707

MAY, PHILIP ALAN, sociologist, educator; b. Bethesda, Md., Nov. 6, 1947; s. Everette Lee and Marie (Lee) M.; m. Doreen Ann Garcia, Sept. 5, 1972; children: Katrina Ruth, Marie Ann. BA in Sociology, Catawba Coll., 1969; MA in Sociology, Wake Forest U., 1971; PhD in Sociology, U. Mont., 1976. NIMH predoctoral fellow U. Mont., Missoula, 1973-76; dir. health stats. and rsch. Navajo Health Authority, Window Rock, Ariz., 1976-78; from asst. prof. to prof. U. N.Mex., Albuquerque, 1978—89, prof., 1989—, from dir. Ctr. on Alcoholism, Substance abuse and Addictions to sr. rsch. scientist, 1990—2000, sr. rsch. scientist Ctr. on Alcoholism, Substance abuse and Addictions, 2000—, assoc. dir. Ctr. on Alcoholism, Substance abuse and Addictions, 2002—04, interim dir. Ctr. on Alcoholism, Substance abuse and Addictions, 2004. Fetal alcohol syndrome study com. Inst. Medicine of NAS, 1994-96; dir. Nat. Indian Fetal Alcohol Syndrome Prevention Program, Albuquerque, 1979-85; adv. bd. Nat. Orgn. on Fetal Alcohol Syndrome, Washington, 1990—; rsch. assoc. Nat. Ctr. for Am. Indian and Alaska Native Mental Health Rsch., 1986—; mem. U.S. Surgeon Gens. Task Force on Drunk Driving, 1988-89; prin. investigator fetal alcohol syndrome epidemiology rsch. in South Africa, 1997—; com. on pathophysiology and prevention of adolescent and adult suicide Inst. Medicine of NRC, NAS, 2000-02; cons. in field. Contbr. chpts. to books, articles to profl. jours. V.p. Bd. Edn., Laguna Pueblo, N.Mex., 1998—2002, pres., 2002—08; mem. N.Mex. Indian Edn. Adv. Coun., 2006—, N.Mex. Gov.'s Commn. on Compulsive Gambling, 2006—; bd. mem. Laguna Pueblo Edn. Found., 2009—. Lt. (s.g.) USPHS, 1970—73. Recipient Spl. Recognition award U.S. Indian Health Svc., 1992, award Navajo Tribe and U.S. Indian Health Svc., 1992, Human Rights Promotion award UN Assn., 1994, Program award for Contbns. to Mental Health of Am. Indians, U.S. Indian Health Svc., 1996, O.B. Michael Outstanding Alumnus award Catawba Coll., 2000, Wayne S. Fenton award, NIMH, 2007. Mem. APHA, Am. Sociol. Assn., Am. Assn. Suicidology, Population Ref. Bur., Coll. on Problems of Drug Dependence, Rsch. Soc. Alcoholism. Methodist. Home: 4610 Idlewilde Ln SE Albuquerque NM 87108-3422 Office: U NMex CASAA 2650 Yale Blvd Albuquerque NM 87106-3202 Home Phone: 505-266-0781; Office Phone: 505-925-2307. Business E-Mail: pmay@unm.edu.

MAY, PHYLLIS JEAN, financial executive; b. Flint, Mich., May 31, 1932; d. Bert A. and Alice C. (Rushton) Irvine; m. John May, Apr. 24, 1971 (dec. 1997). Grad., Dorsey Sch. Bus., Detroit, 1957; cert., Internat. Corr. Schs., 1959; MBA, Mich. U., Ann Arbor, 1970; cert., Nat. Tax Inst., NYC, 1978. Registered real estate agt; lic. life, auto and home ins. agt. Office mgr. Comml. Constrn. Co., Flint, 1962-68; bus. mgr. new and used car dealership Flint, 1968-70; contr. various corps., 1970-75; fiscal dir. Rubicon Odyssey Inc., Detroit, 1976-87, Wayne County Treas.'s Office, 1987-93; exec. fin. officer Grosse Pointe Meml. Ch., Mich., 1993—. Acad. cons. acctg. Detroit Inst. Commerce, 1980-81; pres. small bus. specializing in adminstrv. cons. and acctg., 1982—; supr. mobile svc. stat., upholstery and home improvement businesses; owner retail bus. Pieces and Things. Pres. PTA Westwood Heights Schs., 1972; vol. Fedn. of Blind, 1974-76, Probate Ct., 1974-76; mem. citizens adv. bd. Northville Regional Psychiat. Hosp., 1988, sec., 1989-90; pres. La Renaissance Condominium Assn., Atlantic City, 1996-2000, sec., 2000-02, treas., 2004—. Recipient Meritorious Svc. award Genesee County for Youth, 1976, Excellent Performance and High Achievement award Odyssey Inc., 1981. Mem. NAFE (bd. dirs.), Am. Bus. Women's Assn. (treas. 1981, rec. sec. 1982, v.p. 1982-83, Woman of Yr. 1982), Womens Assn. Dearborn Orch. Soc., Dearborn Cmty. Art Ctr., Mich. Mental Health Assn., Internat. Platform Assn., Guild of Carillonneurs in N.Am., Pi Omicron (officer 1984-85, treas. 2002-05, state treas. 2004-06, dist. treas. 2005-06, nat. treas. 2006). Presbyterian. Avocations: music, piano, dollhouses. Business E-Mail: pmay@gpmchurch.org.

MAY, RICHARD B., psychology professor; b. Seattle, Dec. 20, 1938; s. Louie B. and Ruby J. (Simmons) M.; m. Marjorie Ann Stevenson, Aug. 25, 1962; children: Robert Tobyn, Richard Forrest. BA, Whitman Coll., 1961; MA, Claremont Grad. Sch., 1963, PhD, 1966. Asst. prof. U. Victoria, B.C., Can., 1966-71, assoc. prof. B.C., 1971-81, prof. psychology, 1981-96, prof. emeritus, 1996—; rsch. assoc. Oxford U., England, 1972-73; vis. scholar U. Utah, Salt Lake City, 1995—96. Cons. Victoria Sch. Dist., 1971-72, Dept. Human Resources, Victoria, 1974-75. Author: Application of Statistics in Behavioral Research, 1990; contbr. articles to profl. jours., chpt. to book. Mem. foster care rev. bd. State of Utah, 1997-2001; gen. mgr. RMAY Investments LLC, 2001—. Fellow Social Scis. and Humanities Rsch. Coun., 1972-73, 79-80, 86-87, USPHS, 1962-66; rsch. grantee Nat. Sci. and Engrig. Coun. Rsch., 1969-71, 71-74, 74-77. Avocations: investing, reading, internet, card games. Home: 2072 S Parkwood Cir Spokane WA 99223-5037 Personal E-mail: rb.may@comcast.net.

MAY, RICHARD LEE, biologist, educator; b. Houston, Apr. 21, 1967; s. Dan and Pamela Sue Mayfield. Asst. prof. biology Morningside Coll., Sioux City, Iowa, 1997—2001; assoc. prof. biology Southern Oreg. U., Ashland, 2001—. Office: Southern Oregon Univ 1250 Siskiyou Blvd Ashland OR 97520 Business E-Mail: mayr@sou.edu.

MAY, ROBERT E., history professor; b. Brklyn., July 6, 1943; s. Edna L. May; m. Jill Powell, June 10, 1967; children: Heather R., S. Beth. PhD, U. Wis., Madison, 1969. Assoc. prof. history Purdue U., 1975—86, prof. history, 1986—. Historian-in-residence Monmouth Plantation, Natchez, Miss., 1988; exec. com. mem. Ind. Assn. Historians, Indpls., 1989—90; bd. govs. Tippecanoe County Hist. Assn., Lafayette, Ind., 1995—2002; Francis B. Simkins award com. Southern Hist. Assn., 1996—97; Merle Curti award intellectual history com. mem. Orgn. Am. Historians, Bloomington, Ind., 2001—03; english 12 end-of-course assessments team mem. Ind. Dept. Edn., Indpls., 2003, CORE-40 US history assessment com. mem., 2003—04. Author: (history book) Manifest Destiny's Underworld: Filibustering in Antebellum America, 2002 (Choice Outstanding Academic Title, 2003), John A. Quitman: Old South Crusader (McLemore Prize, 1986), The Southern Dream of a Caribbean Empire; contbr. articles to profl. jours. (Willie D. Halsell prize, Miss. Hist. Soc., 1989). Pres., program chair West Lafayette Sagamore Lions Club, Ind., 1978—2006. Recipient MCL Excellence in Tchg. award, Sch. Humanities, Social Sci., and Edn., Purdue U., 1979—80, Grant-in-Aid, Am. Coun. Learned Socs., 1980, Outstanding Undergraduate Tchg. award, Purdue U., 2007; Frederick W. Beinecke Fellowship in Western Americana, Yale U., 1997—98, Fletcher Jones Found. Fellow, Huntington Libr., San Marino, Calif., 2004. Office: Dept History Purdue Univ 672 Oval Dr West Lafayette IN 47907 Office Fax: 765-496-1755. Business E-Mail: mayr@purdue.edu.

MAY, ROBERT MCCREDIE (LORD MAY OF OXFORD), biology educator; b. Sydney, Jan. 8, 1936; s. Henry W. and Kathleen (McCredie) M.; m. Judith Feiner, Aug. 3, 1962; 1 child, Naomi Felicity. BSc, Sydney U., 1956, PhD, 1959; DSc (hon.), City U. London, 1989, Uppsala U., 1990, Yale U., 1993, Heriot-Watt U., 1994, U. Edinburgh, 1994; DSC (hon.), U. Sydney, 1995. Gordon Mackay lectr. applied math Harvard U., Cambridge, Mass., 1959—61, mem. vis. faculty, 1966; theoretical physics lectr. Sydney U., 1962—64, reader, 1964—69, personal chair, 1969—73; prof. biology Princeton U., NJ, 1973—88; Royal Soc. rsch. prof. U. Oxford, England, 1989—, fellow Merton Coll., 1989—. Vis. faculty Calif. Inst. Tech., 1967; vis. prof. UKAEA Culham Lab., 1971, Magdalen Coll., 1971, Imperial Coll., England, 1975—95; chief sci. adviser to U.K. Govt., head U.K. Office Sci. and Tech., 1995—2000. Editor: Stability and Complexity in Model Ecosystems, 1973, Population Biology of Infectious Diseases, 1982, Theoretical Ecology: Principles and Applications, 1976, Perspectives in Ecological Theory, 1989, Infectious Diseases of Humans: Dynamics and Control, 1991, Extinction Rates, 1995. Trustee Nuffield Found., Cambridge U. Gates Trust; chmn. emeritus bd. trustees Natural History Museum; bd. mem. UK Sport Institute. Decorated Order of Australia, Knighthood; recipient MacArthur award, 1984, Linnean Medal, Linnean Soc., 1991, Christian Marsh prize, 1992, Frink medal, 1995, Crafoord prize, Royal Swedish Acad. Scis., 1996, Balzan prize, 1998, Blue Planet prize, Asahi Glass Found., 2001, Life Peerage, Ho. of Lords Appointments Commn., 2001, Order of Merit, 2002. Fellow Royal Soc. (pres. 2000-2005, Copley medal, 2007), Am. Acad. Arts and Scis.; mem. NAS, Athenaeum Club. Office: The Royal Society 6-9 Carlton House Terrace SW1Y 5AG London England E-mail: robert.may@zoo.ox.ac.uk.

MAY, RONALD ALAN, lawyer; b. Waterloo, Iowa, Sept. 8, 1928; s. John W. and Elsie (Finlayson) M.; m. Naomi Gray, Aug. 18, 1950 (div. Feb. 1974); children: Sarah, Jonathan, Andrew, Rachel; m. Susan East Gray, May 9, 1975. BA, U. Iowa, 1950; LL.B., Vanderbilt U., 1953. Bar: Ark. 1953. Atty. Daggett & Daggett, Marianna, 1953-57, Wright, Lindsey & Jennings LLP, Little Rock, 1957-84, sr. ptnr., 1984-96; of counsel Wright, Lindsey & Jennings, LLP, 1996—. Editor: Automated Law Research, 1972, Sense and Systems in Automated Law Research, 1975; contbg. editor Fifty State Construction Lien and Bond Law, 1992, Fifty State Public Construction Contracting, 1996; assoc. editor Jour. Irreproducible Results. Pres. Spl. Com. on Pub. Edn., Ark. Assn. for Mental Health, Friends of Library, Central Ark. Radiation Therapy Inst.; chmn. Ark. Cancer Research Ctr., 1990-92; bd. dirs. Nat. Assn. for Mental Health, Ark. State Hosp., Gaines House, State Bd. Architects; bd. dirs. State Bd. Bar Examiners, chmn. 1987-88, Ark. ethics com., 1991-93; trustee Mus. Sci. and Natural History, Little Rock, chmn., 1973; mem. profl. adv. bd. sch. architecture U. Ark., 1990-96, mem. profl. adv. bd. sch. urban studies and design, 1993—; mem. instl. rev. bd. U. Ark. for Med. Scis., 2000—. Served with AUS, 1946-47. Mem. ABA (chmn. sci. and tech. sect. 1975-76), Ark., Pulaski County Bar Assns., Internat. Assn. Def. Counsel, Am. Inns of Ct. (Master of the Bench), Assn. for Computing Machinery, Order of Coif, Phi Beta Kappa. Episcopalian. Home: 821 Ash St Little Rock AR 72205-2051 Office: Wright Lindsey & Jennings LLP 200 W Capitol Ave Ste 2300 Little Rock AR 72201-3699 Office Phone: 501-371-0808. Business E-Mail: rmay@wlj.com.

MAY, S. BETH, music educator, composer; b. Lafayette, Ind., Aug. 13, 1974; d. Robert E. and Jill P. May; m. K. Dennis Smith, July 5, 2003. BMus, U. Ill., Urbana-Champaign, 1996; MMus, Yale U., New Haven, 1998; DMA student, U. Tex., Austin. Lower primary tchr. trainer US Peace Corp., Omuntele, Namibia, 1998—2000; ednl. skills specialist NW Vista Coll. Writing Ctr., San Antonio, 2002—06. Composer: (string quartet) Witch Hunt (Judith Lang Zaimont Award, 2008); author: (textbook) Music Fundamentals: An Introduction. Mem.: ASCAP, SCI, Am. Music Ctr., Composers Alliance San Antonio. Office: NW Vista Coll 3535 N Ellison Dr San Antonio TX 78251 Office Fax: 210-486-4036. Business E-Mail: smay8@mail.accd.edu.

MAY, SHELDON W., chemistry professor; married. PhD, U. Chgo., 1970. Regents' prof. chemistry & biochemistry Ga. Inst. Tech., Atlanta, 1974—. Editor-in-chief Enzyme & Microbial Tech., Amsterdam, 1980—. Contbr. scientific papers to numerous publs. Sr. scholarship, Fulbright Found., 1985—87, Fellowship, NSF, 1966—70, Alfred P.

Sloan Found., 1979—83. Mem.: AAAS, Am. Soc. Biochemistry & Molecular Biology, Am. Chem. Soc. Office: Sch Chemistry & Biochemistry Georgia Inst Tech Atlanta GA 30332

MAY, STEPHEN, writer, federal official, historian; b. Rochester, NY, July 30, 1931; s. Arthur J. and Hilda (Jones) M. Grad., Wesleyan U., 1953; LLB, Georgetown U., 1961. Bar: NY 1963. Exec. asst. to Rep. and Senator Kenneth B. Keating, 1955-64; assoc., mem., then ptnr. Branch, Turner & Wise, Rochester, 1965-81; city councilman-at-large Rochester, 1966-73; mayor, 1970-73; chmn. and commr. N.Y. State Bd. Elections, Albany, 1975-79; asst. sec. for legis. and Congl. rels. Dept. Housing and Urban Devel., 1981-88; ind. historian, writer, lectr. for mags. and newspapers, 1988—. Vice chmn. Temporary State Commn. on Powers of Local Govt., 1970-73; mem. 20th Century Fund Task Force on Future of N.Y.C., 1979, Nat. Adv. Commn. Higher Edn. for Police Officers, 1977-79, Joint Com. Assn. Bar City N.Y. and Drug Abuse Coun. on N.Y. Drug Law Evaluation, 1977-78; chmn. Rochester Interfaith Com. on Israel, 1973-81; del.-at-large Rep. Nat. Conv., 1972; mem. N.Y. State Crime Control Planning Bd., 1970-73; historian, writer and lectr. on art, culture, historic preservation and travels, 1988—. Bd. dirs. Police Found., 1970-81, Nat. Com. for Labor Israel, 1977-81, Empire State Report, 1974-81, Inst. Mediation and Conflict Resolution, 1973-81. Served with U.S. Army, 1953-55. Mem. Phi Beta Kappa. Home and Office: 4101 Cathedral Ave NW Washington DC 20016-3585 also: 270 Mt Pleasant Rd Union ME 04862-3003 Office Phone: 202-362-2399, 207-785-4178. Personal E-mail: stephenmay4@yahoo.com.

MAY, STEPHEN JAMES, communications educator, writer; b. Toronto, Ont., Can., Sept. 10, 1946; s. Thomas and Claire (Thompson) M.; m. Caroline Casteel, Sept. 27, 1947; children: Trevor. BA, Calif. State U., Carson, 1975; MA, Calif. State U., LA, 1977; DLitt, Internat. U., London, 1990. Prof. and chair dept. of Englist and Lit. Pikes Peak C.C., Colorado Springs, Colo., 1980-91; prof. Colo. N.W. C.C., Craig, 1992-98; chair dept. of English and Lit. Pikes Peak C.C., Colorado Springs, Colo., 1998—2001; vis. prof. U. No. Colo., 2001—; prof. English Front Range CC, Ft. Collins, Colo., 2001—06. Advisor Internat. Biog. Ctr., Cambridge, Eng., 1989-95; vis. prof. U. Colo., Greeley, Colo., 2000—; spl. cons. James A. Michener Art Mus., 2006-, James A. Michener Libr. Author: Pilgrimage, 1987, Fire From the Skies, 1990, Footloose, 1993, Zane Grey, 1997, Maverick Heart, 2000, Rascals, 2002, Michener: A Writer's Journey, 2005, American Heritage; contbr. articles to profl. jours. including SouthWest Art, Ohio Review, Texas Highways, 20th Century Fox, Hawaii Mag. Mem. Western Writers Am., Colo. Authors League, Zane Grey Soc., Soc. S.W. Authors, C.C. Humanities, James A. Mitchener Soc. Avocations: travel, writing, drawing. Home: 731 Peregrine Run Fort Collins CO 80524 Personal E-mail: stepkm@msn.com.

MAY, STERLING RANDOLPH, biology professor, department chairman; b. Muskogee, Okla., Dec. 27, 1946; s. William Sterling and Mary Catherine (Griffith) May. BA with honors, U. Kans., 1968; MS, U. Mich., 1969, PhD, 1977; M in Bus., Johns Hopkins U., 1995, MBA, 2000. Coord. Skin Bank St. Agnes Med. Ctr., Phila., 1977-79, assoc. dir. Burn Rsch., 1980, dir. Burn Rsch., 1981-83; dir. Southeastern Burn Rsch. Inst., Augusta, Ga., 1983-87; v.p. LifeCell Corp., The Woodlands, Tex., 1987-91; chief oper. officer ARC Nat. Hdqs., Arlington, Va., 1991-2000; pres. Health Care Rsch., Arlington, 2000—04; assoc. prof. biology and genetics, chmn. dept. math. and sci. Brenau U., Gainsville, Ga., 2004—09; prof. biology and genetics, Richard & Phyllis Leet disting. chair, biol. sci., dir. Anna Thomas Biosci. Ctr., 2009—. Rsch. asst. prof. Hahnemann U. Sch. Medicine, Phila., 1979-82, rsch. assoc. prof., 1983; assoc. clin. prof. Med. Coll. Ga., 1984-87; adj. prof. U. Tex. Med. Sch., Houston, 1987-91. Editor: Care of the Burn Wound, 1985; author 84 published articles in biomed. lit., 1974—; mem. editorial bd. Jour. Burn Care and Rehab., 1982-90, Burns, 1985-92, Cryobiology, 1987-93. Mem. Soc. for Cryobiology (pres. 1989-91, chmn. 23d ann. meeting, 1986), Am. Burn Assn. (chmn. rsch. com. 1998-2000), Internat. Soc. For Burn Injuries (mem. gen. coun. 1982-90), Am. Assn. Tissue Banks (sec. 1991-93, v.p. 1993-95, pres. 1995-97, bd. govs. 1989-93), Sigma Xi, Phi Kappa Phi (chartered mem., founding mem. Brenau U. chpt.). Avocations: antique furniture, music. Home: 2318 River Cliff Dr Gainesville GA 30501-1685 Office: Dept Math and Sci Brenau Univ 500 Washington St NE Gainesville GA 30501 Home Phone: 770-536-9171; Office Phone: 770-534-6278. Business E-Mail: rmay@brenau.edu.

MAY, THOMAS J., electric company executive; BS, Stonehill Coll.; MS in Fin., Bentley Coll. Various positions Boston Edison Co., 1976-90, exec. v.p., 1990-93, pres., CEO, 1993-94, chmn., CEO, 1994-99, NStar, Boston, 1999—2002, chmn., pres., CEO, 2002—. Office: NStar MSC P 1600 800 Boylston St Boston MA 02199

MAY, TIMOTHY JAMES, lawyer; b. Denver, Aug. 3, 1932; s. Thomas Henry and Helen Frances (O'Conner) M.; m. Monica Anita Gross, Aug. 24, 1957; children: Stephanie, Maureen, Cynthia, Timothy, Anthony. BA, Cath. U. Am., 1954; LLB, Georgetown U., 1957, LLM, 1960. Bar: D.C. 1957, US Ct. Appeals (Armed Forces, DC, 2d, 3d cir.), U.S. Supreme Ct. 1961. Law clk. to judge U.S. Ct. Appeals, D.C. Cir., 1957-58; assoc. Covington & Burling, Washington, 1958-61; cons. Exec. Office of Pres. U.S., Washington, 1961-62; chief counsel subcom. on stockpile Armed Svcs. Com., U.S. Senate, Washington, 1962-63; mng. dir. Fed. Maritime Commn., Washington, 1963-66; gen. counsel U.S. Post Office Dept., Washington, 1966-69; ptnr., Postal Policy & Regulation, Legis. Affairs practices, Patton Boggs LLP, Washington, 1969—, mem. exec. com. Bd. dirs. Legal Aid Soc. DC, 1984—; pres. Holy Family of Bethlehem Found., 1997-99, Coun. for Ct. Excellence, Washington, 1999-2005, Marine Corps Law Enforcement Found., 1996-2003; chmn. bd. regents Cath. U. Am., 1988-93, trustee, 1993-2005, trustee emeritus, 2005—. Recipient Servant of Justice award Legal Aid Soc. D.C., 1997, St. Elizabeth Ann Seton award SOAR!, 1998, Caritas award Archdiocese D.C., 1998, Presdl. Award for Pub. Adminstrn., Jump Mem. Award. Fellow Am. Bar Found. (life); mem. ABA (ho. of dels.), Fed. Bar Assn., Bar Assn. of DC (pres. 1991-92, Lawyer of Yr. award 1999), Congl. Country Club (bd. govs. 1992-98, sec. 1994-97), Nat. Christian Leadership Conf. for Israel (exec. com. 1992-2003), Met. Club, Indian Creek Country Club (bd. dirs. 1999—, pres. 2005—07), Fed. City Coun., Econ. Club DC (bd. dirs. 2001—08), Knight of Malta, Constantinian Order St. George (knight). Democrat. Roman Catholic. Home: 3828 52nd St NW Washington DC 20016-1924 Office: Patton Boggs LLP 2550 M St NW Washington DC 20037-1350 Home (Winter): 286 Bal Bay Dr Miami FL 33154 Office Phone: 202-457-6050. Office Fax: 202-457-6315. Business E-Mail: tmay@pattonboggs.com.

MAY, WALTER GRANT, chemical engineer, educator; b. Saskatoon, Sask., Can., Nov. 28, 1918; came to U.S., 1946, naturalized, 1954; s. George Alfred and Abigail Almira (Robson) M.; m. Mary Louise Stockan, Sept. 26, 1945 (dec. 1977); children: John R., Douglas W., Caroline O; m. Helen Dickerson, 1988. BSc, U. Sask., Saskatoon, 1939, MSc, 1942; ScD, MIT, 1948. Chemist Brit. Am. Oil Co., Moose Jaw, Sask., 1939-40; asst. prof. U. Sask., 1943-46; with Exxon Rsch. & Engring. Co., Linden, NJ, 1948-83, sr. sci. adv., 1976-83; prof. U. Ill., 1983-90, prof. emeritus, 1990—. With Advanced Research Projects Agy., Dept. Def., 1959-60; industry based prof. Stevens Inst. Tech., 1968-74, Rensselaer Poly. Inst., 1975-77 Recipient Process Indsl. Div. award ASME, 1972 Fellow AIChE (Chem. Engring. Practice award 1989); mem. Nat. Acad. Engring. Office: U Ill Dept Chem and Biochem Engring 1209 W California Ave Urbana IL 61801-3705 Home: 401 Burwash Ave 127 Savoy IL 61874 Home Phone: 217-356-1820. Business E-Mail: w-may@uiuc.edu.

MAY, WILLIAM FREDERICK, manufacturing executive; b. Chgo., Oct. 25, 1915; s. Arthur W. and Florence (Hartwick) M.; m. Kathleen Thompson, June 14, 1947; children: Katherine Hartwick (Mrs. Edward W. Bickford), Elizabeth Shaw. BS, U. Rochester, 1937; grad. Advanced Mgmt. Program, Harvard U., 1950; D in Engring., Clarkson U.; LLD, Okla. Christian Coll.; LHD, Livingstone U.; LLD, Lafayette U. Rsch. worker E.I. Du Pont de Nemours Co., 1937-38; with Am. Can Co., Greenwich, Conn., 1940-80, mgr., 1957-58, v.p., 1958-64, exec. v.p., 1964-65, vice chmn. bd. dirs., 1965, chmn. bd. dirs., CEO, 1965-80, mem. exec. com., 1960—. Dean Grad. Sch. Bus. Adminstrn., NYU, 1980-84; chmn. and CEO Statue of Liberty Found., 1984—. Bd. dirs. Lincoln Ctr.; trustee Am. Ditchley Found., Am. Mus. Natural History, Columbia-Presbyn. Hosp., U. Rochester; mem. corp. Poly. Inst. N.Y.; chmn. pub. policy coun. Advt. Coun. Mem. Nat. Order of Merit (France, officier), Econ. Club, Round Hill Club, Megunticook Golf Club, Indian Harbor Yacht Club, Camden Yacht Club, Phi Beta Kappa, Alpha Delta Phi. Episcopalian. Home: 84 Indian Harbor Dr Greenwich CT 06830-7148 Personal E-mail: wkmay@aol.com.

MAYBERG, HELEN SUSAN, neurologist, educator; b. Orange, Calif., Jan. 2, 1956; BA in psychobiology, UCLA, 1976; MD, U. Southern Calif., 1981. Cert. Neurology, 1987. Resident in medicine LA County-U. Southern Calif. Med. Ctr., LA, 1981—82; resident in neurology Columbia-Presbyn. Med. Ctr., NYC, 1982—85; fellow in nuclear medicine Johns Hopkins Med. Inst., Balt., 1985—87, staff, 1987—91; asst. prof. neurological psychiatry Johns Hopkins Sch. Medicine, Balt., 1987—91; assoc. prof. U. Tex. Health Sci. Ctr., San Antonio, 1991—98; prof. psychiatry and neurology U. Toronto, 1999—2003, Sandra Rotman chair neuropsychiatry; staff Baycrest Hosp., Toronto, 1999—2004; prof. psychiatry, behavioral sciences, and neurology Emory U. Sch. Medicine, Atlanta, 2003—, Dorothy C. Fuqua chair psychiatric neuroimaging and therapeutics. Recipient Arnold Pfeffer prize, Jour. Neuropsychoanalysis, 2001. Fellow: Royal Coll. Physicians of Can.; mem.: NARSAD (Young Investigator award 1991, Independent Investigator award 1995, Disting. Investigator award 2002, Falcone prize for Outstanding Achievement in Mood Disorders Rsch. 2007), Inst. Medicine, Am. Coll. Neuropsychopharmacology, Am. Neurological Assn., Alpha Lambda Delta. Office: Emory U Sch Medicine WMB 4313 101 Woodruff Cir Atlanta GA 30322 Office Phone: 404-727-6740. Office Fax: 404-727-6743. E-mail: helen.mayberg@emory.edu.*

MAYBERRY, SHAWNA, preventive medicine physician, educator; b. Jan. 1944; d. Marsha (Wong) and John Mayberry; m. Alfred Stein; children: Charlotte Mayberry-Stein, Cy Mayberry-Stein, William Mayberry-Stein. BS in Biology, U. Minn., 1966, MS in Alternative Medicine, 1967, MD, 1971. Cert. in alt. medicine Minn., 1968, lic. Minn., 1971. Intern U. Minn. Hosp., 1972—75, resident, 1975—79; alt. medicine dept. physician Minn. State Hosp., 1980—95; physician, cons. Meriks Eastern Med. Ctr., Richfield, Minn., 1996—2000, v.p., 2000—. Asst. U. Minn. biology dept., 1965—67; adj. prof. U. Minn. Sch. Medicine, 1992—. Author: The Alternative Route to Health, 2001. Conservative. Greek Orthodox. Avocations: video games, quilting, lacrosse. Office: Meriks Eastern Medical Ctr 2200 W 66th St #190 Richfield MN 55423-2196

MAYDWELL, ROBERT MASON, JR., social sciences educator; b. Bronx, NY, July 6, 1962; s. Robert Mason Maydwell, Sr.; children: Kristy Lynn, Kelly Ann, Ethan Robert. M, Ft. Hays State U., Kans., 1999. Social sci. and human svcs. instr. Iowa Western C.C., Council Bluffs, 2005—. Grants mgmt. asst. Nat. Pk. Svc., Omaha, 2005. With USN, 1983—87. Decorated Expeditionary medal US Navy-Submarine Svc.; Viva Stimits Meml. scholar, Ft. Hays State U., 1997. Mem.: Am. Legion, Phi Alpha Theta (life; historian, pres. 1994—96). Office: Nat Pk Svc 601 Riverfront Dr Omaha NE 68102 Home: 2631 Sewell St Lincoln NE 68502-4035 Personal E-mail: rmaydwell@iwcc.edu. Business E-Mail: robert_maydwell@nps.gov.

MAYEAUX, ANNE RUSSELL, education educator; b. Meridian, Miss., Aug. 27, 1943; d. Constant Hyacinth and Laura Archer Mayeaux. BA, St. Xavier U., 1961—65; PhD, Emory U., 1968—75. Dir. World Peace Ctr., Chgo., 1967—68; postdoctoral fellow and adj. faculty Candler Sch. of Theology, Atlanta, 1975—81. Exec. dir. Ga. Endowment for the Humanities, 1979—81; faculty and pres. Aquinas Ctr. of Theology at Emory U., Atlanta, 1983—90; vis. scholar in ethics and soc. Harvard Div. Sch., Cambridge, Mass., 1990—91; assoc. prof. Siena Heights U., Adrian, Mich., 1991—96; rschr. Inst. for Social Rsch., U. of Mich., 1996—99; chair, theology dept., and faculty St. Joseph, Madison, Miss., 1999—; adj. faculty Hinds C.C., Jackson, Miss., 2000—. Contbr. articles to jours. Pres. Las Casas, Nat. Ministry among the Native Americans, Clinton, Okla., 1989—93; bd. dirs. Nat. Assembly of Religious Women, Chgo., 1991—94; sec./treas. Internat. Found. for Scholarly Exch., Atlanta, 1988—94. Recipient Human Rights Citation, Dominican Justice Promoters of N.Am., 1991, Outstanding Tchg. of the Yr., Siena Heights U., 1992—93, Internat. Del. of Scholars to Russia and the Ukraine, People to People and Am. Acad. of Religion, 1993, Outstanding Tchg., Archdiocese of Atlanta, 1983—84, Catharine of Siena award, St. Catharine's Dominican Congregation, 1990, Citation for Courage for Human Rights Work in Gulf War, U.S. Dominican Leadership Conf., 1991; Catherine McAuley scholar, St. Xavier U., 1965, Raskob Found. grant, Raskob Found., 1992—94, N.E.H. Landmarks of Am. History: Summer Inst., Nat. Endowment for the Humanities, 2004, grant, 2002, Fulbright Scholar, U. of Tuebingen, German, Fulbright Commn., 1966—67. Mem.: AAUP (v.p., siena heights u. chpt. 1995), Am. Acad. of Religion (chair, program sect., s.e. region 1975—91). Democrat-Npl. Roman Catholic. Home: 217 Melrose Dr Jackson MS 39211

MAYEED, MOHAMMED, engineering educator, researcher; PhD, U. Tokyo, Japan, 2002. Vis. asst. prof. Wayne State U., Detroit, 2005—08, rsch. asst. prof., 2008—. Contbr. articles to profl. jours. Recipient Dr. Rashid Gold medal, Bangladesh U. Eng. & Tech., 1998; JSPS Postdoc. fellowship, Japan Soc. Promotion Sci., 2002—03. Mem.: ASME. Office: Wayne State Univ 5050 Anthony Wayne Dr Detroit MI 48202 Home Phone: 313-549-6366. Personal E-mail: mayeed3@yahoo.com, mmayeed@hotmail.com. Business E-Mail: mayeed@wayne.edu.

MAYER, ALISANDE FOUNTAIN, media specialist; d. Fritz and Marie Fountain; m. David Edward Mayer. MEd, Valdosta State U., Ga., 2002. ESOL tutor Lowndes County Sch., Valdosta, 1999—2002; media specialist Moulton Br. Elem., Valdosta, 2002—. Author: (article) Christmas Miracle (Valdosta Daily Times Writing Contest winner, 2000). Grant, Valdosta State U., 1999—2000. Mem.: Ga. Libr. Media Assn.

MAYER, ALLAN, public relations executive, consultant; b. NYC, Mar. 15, 1950; s. Theodore H. and Phyllis (Zwick) M. BA, Cornell U., 1971. Staff reporter Wall Street Jour., NYC, 1972-73; assoc. editor, gen. editor Newsweek mag., NYC, 1973-77, fgn. corr. London, 1977-80, sr. editor NYC, 1980-82; editl. dir. Arbor House Pub., NYC, 1986-88; sr. editor Simon & Schuster, NYC, 1988-89; editor-in-chief Buzz mag., LA, 1990-95, editor-in-chief, pub., 1996; sr. ptnr. Sitrick and Co., LA, 1997—2004, mng. dir., 2004—06; ptnr. 42 West LLC, LA, 2006—. Bd. dir. Am. Apparel Inc., Film Ind. Author: Madam Prime Minister, 1980, Gaston's War: A True Story of a Hero of the Resistance in World War II, 1987; co-author: (with Michael S. Sitrick) Spin: How to Turn the Power of the Press to Your Advantage, 1998. Recipient award Overseas Press Club, 1974, Nat. Mag. award Am. Soc. Mag. Editors, 1978, William Allen White award City and Regional Mag. Assn., 1995-96. Personal E-mail: allan.mayer@42west.net.

MAYER, ANTHONY JOHN, investment company executive; b. Milw., Apr. 21, 1936; s. Anton J. and Mary (Plensk) Mayer. BS in Bus., Marquette U., 1958, advanced degree in Bus., 1965. Registered investment adv., 1994; cert. nutritionist 2000. Adminstrv. mgr. Marquette U., 1960—63, US Navy, 1962; ins. claims exec., 1962—65; founder Fixed Income Mutual Fund, Milw., 1968—; motel exec., 1968—80; retail exec., 1973—75; pvt. investor, 1968—; pres. Anthony J. Mayer, Inc., Milw., 1994—, Tunica Southern Belle Project, 1995—98; v.p. Banc One Investment Mgmt. Group, Chgo., 2001—07. Founder Fixed Income Fund, Milw., 1968—; chmn. Westridge Investors, 1998—2007, New Berlin Investors, 1998—2007, Millionaire Investor Entities Guidance-.Com, 2000—07, Hungarian Investors Com., 2003; Philanthropist country music seminar host, 1995; reporter Election Ctrl., 1973. Anthony J. Mayer Investment Parables, 1995, Anthony J. Mayer Investment Advisory Book, 2003; author, editor, newsletter: Anthony J. Mayer Investment Bible, 1995; columnist: Alaska newspapers, 1959—60; investment radio personality, 1990—93, Recorded music historian, 1980—2008; prodr.: (plays) Surviving Without Love, 2001; contbr. articles to profl. jours. Vol. ARC, 1961—62; del. Adv. Coun. Nat. Rep. Congl. Com., 2001—08; mem. Rep. Nat. Com., 2005—09; chmn. adv. bd. Nat. Rep. Party, 2004—08; hon. sponsor Pres. Bush victory dinner, 2001; grassroots leader Rep. Campaign, 2004; primary election candidate for gov. Wis., 2006; election candidate West Allis Mayer, 2008; active Heritage Inner Cir., 1999—; bd. dirs. West Allis Food for Milw., 1997—2007, First Mcpl. Credit Union, 1996—2001, Mukwonago State Bank, Wis., 2006—08; pres. Pub. Lands Decor Classics, 2000—07; trustee Jesuit Ptnrs., 1998—. With US Army, 1958—60. Recipient VIP award, Speedway-Super Am., 1995, Cleve. Meadows Achievement award, 1998, VIP award, Speedway-Super Am., 2000, Commendation cert., State of Wis., 2002, Animal Stewardship award, 2002, Cmty. Svc. award, Jerusalem Christian, 2003; named Successful Investor of Yr., Sta. WGN, 1996, Notable Pulaskian, Milw. Pub. Sch. Sys., 1999, Hon. Regional Chmn., Nat. Rep. Com., 2007. Mem.: N.Am. Investors Alliance, Milw. County Vets. Plz. Honor, West Allis Vets. Memorial Honor, West Allis Memorial Walkway Friends, Liberty Olympic Hiking Club, West Allis Century Club. Roman Catholic. Avocation: reading. Office Phone: 414-321-7126.

MAYER, CARL JOSEPH, prosecutor, lawyer, educator; b. Boston, Apr. 23, 1959; s. Arno Joseph and Nancy Sue (Grant) M. AB magna cum laude, Princeton U., 1981; JD, U. of Chgo., 1986; LLM, Harvard U., 1988. Bar: NJ 1986, Mass. 1988, NY 1989, DC 1989. Writer for Ralph Nader, Washington, 1981-83; law clk. to presiding justice US Dist. Ct., Wilmington, Del., 1986-87; prof. law Hofstra Law Sch., Hempstead, NY, 1989-94; atty. Milberg, Weiss, Bershad, Hynes and Lerach, NYC, 1995-96; spl. counsel NY State Atty. Gen.'s Office, NYC, 1999—2000; pvt. practice Mayer Law Group, LLC, 2000—. Cons. US Senate Com., Washington, 1988-89. Author: Shakedown, 1998; co-author: Public Domain, Private Dominion, 1985; contbr. articles to profl. jours. Town committeeman, Princeton, NJ, 1995-98. NYU fellow, 1988-89. Mem. ABA, NY Bar Assn., NJ Bar Assn., Mass. Bar Assn. Avocations: running, squash, tennis. Home: 58 Battle Rd Princeton NJ 08540-4902 Office: Mayer Law Group LLC 1040 Ave of Americas Ste 2400 New York NY 10018 Office Phone: 212-382-4686. Business E-Mail: carlmayer@carlmayer.com.

MAYER, CHRISTOPHER, lawyer; b. Phila., Feb. 21, 1946; BA, Princeton U., 1968; JD, Columbia U., 1974. Bar: N.Y. 1975. Assoc. Davis Polk & Wardell, NYC, 1974—82, ptnr., 1982—, mem. firm mgmt. com., 1992—2005. Mem. ABA, N.Y. State Bar Assn., Assn. of Bar of City of N.Y. Office: Davis Polk & Wardwell 450 Lexington Ave New York NY 10017-3982 Office Phone: 212-450-4338. Office Fax: 212-701-5338. Business E-Mail: chris.mayer@davispolk.com.

MAYER, FRANK CHARLES, math/science educator; b. Lafayette, Ind., Dec. 13, 1955; s. James Walter and Elizabeth Billmire Mayer; m. Kimberly Ruth Cook, Mar. 23, 1996; children: James Gillam, Matthew Ross. BS in Conservation Edn., Colo. State U., Ft. Collins, 1981; MS in Environ. Sci., U. Colo., Denver, 1991. Cert. in secondary tchg. Colo. Dept. Edn., 1981. Tchr. Littleton Pub. Schs., Colo., 1985—86, 1989—2003, HS girl's basketball coach, 1994—2001, HS football asst. coach, 1995—98; tchr., mid. sch. basketbal and football coach Steamboat Springs Schs., Colo., 1986—88, tchr., 2004—, Douglas County Sch., Castle Rock, Colo., 1988—89. Faculty assoc. Ariz. State U., Tempe, 1994—. Youth soccer coach Littleton Soccer Club, 1990—95; youth basketball coach Gold Crown Sports, Littleton, 1990—95; bd. mem. Mayer Sch., Ithaca, NY, 1981—83, Ithaca Sci. and Discovery Ctr., 1981—83, North Routt Early Learning Ctr., Clark, Colo., 2008—. Tchg., Rsch. grant, Colo. State U., 1994, Cocoa Cola Tech. grant, Littleton Pub. Schs., 1996. Achievements include assisted in the creation, implementation and instruction of one of the first online science courses at Arizona State University. Avocation: carpentry. Home: PO Box 807 54750 Routt Co Rd #62 Clark CO 80428 Personal E-mail: frank.mayer@asu.edu.

MAYER, GEORGE, materials scientist, chemist, consultant; b. Györ, Hungary, Feb. 10, 1934; came to U.S., 1939; s. Eugene and Eleanor (Fürst) M.; m. Mavis Margaret Tanner, Sept. 23, 1961 (div. 1990); 1 child, Peter; m. Jane Ellen Tusch, Mar. 1, 1990. BS in Aero. Engring., Boston U., 1957; M Metall. Engring., U. Okla., 1963; PhD in Metallurgy, MIT, 1967. Registered profl. engr., Mass., aero. rsch. engr. Allied Rsch. Assocs., Boston, 1957. Test and devel. engr. Chrysler Corp., Warren, Mich., 1957-58; project mgr. Ilikon Corp., Natick, Mass., 1961-63; staff mem. MIT, Cambridge, 1963-67; sr. rsch. scientist Monsanto Rsch. Corp., Everett, Mass., 1966-68; dir. materials div. U.S. Army Rsch. Office, Research Triangle Park, N.C., 1968-88; staff scientist Inst. for Def. Analyses, Alexandria, Va., 1988-92; assoc. dir. materials rsch. ctr. U. Pitts., 1992—. Mem. adv. bd. Materials Processing Ctr., MIT, 1984—, Light Metals Ctr., U. Va., Charlottesville, 1986—, Ctr. for Applied Polymer Rsch., Case Western Res. U., 1988—. Contbr. articles to profl. jours., chpts. to books. Bd. dirs. Troy House, youth half-way house, Durham, N.C., 1975-78; scoutleader Boy Scouts Am., Durham, 1982-85; founder, bd. dirs. Durham Youth Vol. Program, Durham, 1983-87. Capt. USAF, 1958-61. Recipient outstanding performance award U.S. Army, 1974, 76, 77, 82, spl. achievement award 1987, Meritorious Civilian Svc. medal, 1988; Order of Long Leaf Pine, Gov.

State of N.C., 1982, Outstanding Vol. award, 1989. Fellow Am. Inst. Chemists; mem. Rotary, Sigma Xi. Achievements include development of methods for solid state single crystal growth and deformation processing of polymers; discovery of failure mechanisms in metal-matrix composites. Office: U Pitts 231 Benedum Hall Pittsburgh PA 15261-2202

MAYER, GERARD J., physician; b. Buenos Aires, Nov. 8, 1942; Came to the U.S., 1968. s. Ludwig and Yvonne (Moritz) M.; m. Nicole Paulette Wolf, July 23, 1971; children: Daniella, Marc. BA, Saint Andrews Scots Sch., Olivos, Argentina, 1960; MD, U. Buenos Aires, 1967. Diplomate Am. Bd. Pediatrics. Intern pediatrics Michael Reese Hosp., Chgo., 1968-69, resident in pediatrics, 1969-70, Montefiore Med. Ctr., Bronx, NY, 1970-71, Strong Meml. Hosp., U. of Rochester, NY, 1971-72; fellow in pediatrics St. Christopher's Hosp. for Children, Phila., 1972-74; attending physician Montefiore Hosp., Bronx, 1974—, North Central, Bronx, 1976-98; pvt. practice Yorktown Heights, NY, 1985—; head pediatric emergency Montefiore-NCB, Bronx, 1978-83; head pediatric primary care North Central Bronx Hosp., 1978-85; attending physician No. Westchester Hosp., Mount Kisco, NY, 1986—. Fellow Am. Acad. Pediatrics. Home: 60 Old Aspetong Rd Katonah NY 10536-3845 Office: 1880 Commerce St Yorktown Heights NY 10598 Office Phone: 914-962-5556.

MAYER, HALDANE ROBERT, federal judge; b. Buffalo, Feb. 21, 1941; s. Haldane Rupert and Myrtle Kathleen Mayer; m. Mary Anne McCurdy, Aug. 13, 1966; children: Anne Christian, Rebecca Paige. BS, US Mil. Acad., 1963; JD, Coll. William and Mary, 1971. Bar: Va. 1971, DC 1980, US Ct. Appeals (4th cir.) 1972, US Dist. Ct. (ea. dist.) Va. 1972, US Ct. Mil. Appeals 1973, US Supreme Ct. 1977, US Ct. Claims 1984. Law clk. US Ct. Appeals (4th cir.), Richmond, Va., 1971—72; atty. McGuire Woods & Battle, Charlottesville, Va., 1975—77; spl. asst. to chief justice US Supreme Ct., Washington, 1977—80; atty. Baker & McKenzie, Washington, 1980—81; acting spl. counsel US Merit Systems Protection Bd., Washington, 1981—82; judge US Claims Ct., Washington, 1982—87, US Ct. Appeals (Fed. cir.), Washington, 1987—, chief judge, 1997—2004. Adj. prof. U. Va. Sch. Law, 1975—77, 1992—94, George Washington U. Law Sch., 1992—96. Bd. dirs. William and Mary Law Sch. Assn., 1979—85. Maj. US Army, 1963—75, ret. lt. col. USAR. Decorated Bronze Star. Mem.: West Point Soc. DC, Army Athletic Assn., West Point Assn. Grads., Omicron Delta Kappa. Office: US Ct Appeals for Fed Cir 717 Madison Pl NW Washington DC 20439-0002 Office Phone: 202-633-6556.*

MAYER, JAMES HOCK, lawyer, mediator; b. Neptune City, NJ, Nov. 1, 1935; s. J. Kenneth and Marie Ruth (Hock) M.; m. Carol I. Keating, Sept. 20, 1958 (div. Feb. 1981); children: Craig, Jeffrey; m. Patrisha Renk, Mar. 28, 1981 (div. July 2001); m. Judith Courtemanche, Mar. 23, 2004. AB with distinction, Dartmouth Coll., 1957; JD, Harvard U., 1964. Bar: Calif. 1965, US Dist. Ct (no. dist., so. dist.) Calif. 1965, US Ct. Appeals (9th cir.) 1965, US Supreme Ct. 1974. Assoc. Pillsbury, Madison & Sutro, San Francisco, 1964—72, ptnr., 1973—; ind. mediator, 1992—. Rear adm. USNR, 1957-93. Rufus Choate scholar Dartmouth Coll., 1956-57. Mem. Newcomen Soc., Navy League, Naval Order of US, Naval War Coll. Found. (regional v.p.), Harvard Club, La Jolla Country Club, La Jolla Beach and Tennis Club. Office: Mayer Mediation Svcs 7924 Ivanhoe Ave Ste 3 La Jolla CA 92037 Home: 2370 Avenida de La Playa La Jolla CA 92037 Office Phone: 858-551-5525. Business E-Mail: just-results@msn.com.

MAYER, JAMES JOSEPH, retired corporate lawyer; b. Cin., Nov. 27, 1938; s. Cletus Joseph and Berna Mae (Schroeder) M.; m. Margaret Ann Hobbs, Oct. 24, 1964; children: Kimberly, Susanne, Terri. BEE, U. Cin., 1961; JD, No. Ky. U., 1969. Registered profl. engr., Ohio. Bar: Ohio 1969, Ky. 1975. Engr. Cin. Gas & Electric Co., 1961-69, atty., 1969-85, gen. counsel, 1986-91, v.p., gen. counsel, 1991-95, ret., 1995; of counsel Taft, Stetinius & Hollister, Cin., 1995—. With USAFR, 1961-64. Mem. Ohio Bar Assn., Ky. Bar Assn., Cin. Bar Assn., Heritage Palms Country Club. Republican. Roman Catholic. Avocations: home remodeling, sports, golf. Office Phone: 513-381-2838. Business E-Mail: mayer@taftlaw.com.

MAYER, JANE, journalist; b. NYC, 1955; Grad., Yale U., New Haven, 1977; student, Bedales Sch., Eng., Oxford U. Met. reporter Washington Star, Md.; reporter Wall Street Journal, NYC, 1982—84, White House corr., 1984—94; staff writer The New Yorker mag., 1995—. Author: The Dark Side: The Inside Story of How the War on Terror Turned into a War on American Ideals, 2008; co-author: Landslide: The Unmaking of the President 1984—1988, 1989, Strange Justice: The Selling of Clarence Thomas, 1994; contbr. NY Review of Books, Am. Prospect mag. Office: New Yorker Condé Nast Pubs 4 Times Square New York NY 10036*

MAYER, JOHN, musician; b. Bridgeport, Conn., Oct. 16, 1977; Student, Berklee Coll. Music. Singer: (albums) Inside Wants Out, 1999, Room for Squares, 2001, Any Given Thursday, 2003, Heavier Things, 2003, As/is, 2004, Continuum, 2006 (Best Pop Vocal Album, Grammy Awards, 2007); musician Where the Light Is, 2008; singer (with John Mayer Trio) Try! John Mayer Trio Live In Concert, 2005; singer: (songs) Your Body is a Wonderland (Grammy award for Best Male Pop Vocal Performance, 2002), Daughters (Grammy award for Song of Yr., 2005), Waiting on the World to Change (Grammy award for Best Male Pop Vocal Performance, 2007), Say (Grammy award for Best Male Pop Vocal Performance, 2009), Gravity (Grammy award for Best Solo Rock Vocal Performance, 2009); composer: (films) Serendipity, 2001, Vanilla Sky, 2001, How to Deal, 2003, Win a Date with Tad Hamilton!, 2004; exec. prodr.: (TV series) John Mayer Has a TV Show, 2004; monthly columnist Esquire mag., 2004—. Named one of The World's Most Influential People, TIME mag., 2007. Office: Creative Artists Agy c/o Scott Clayton 3310 West End Ave 5th Fl Nashville TN 37203*

MAYER, JOHN WILLIAM (BILL MAYER), lawyer; b. Houston, Nov. 17, 1941; s. Maurice William and Julie Eldee (Borodofsky) Mayer; m. M. Ann Jodoin, July 30, 1972; children: Norbert, Kristin, Mara. BA in Econs., Vanderbilt U., 1963; JD, U. Chgo., 1966; postgrad., Armed Forces Staff Colls., 1977, Nat. Jud. Coll., 1984—85, Nat. Def. Coll., 1986. Bar: Ill. 66 2007, Colo. 87 2007, Ala. 87, US Ct. Mil. Appeals 71. Assoc. Lorenz & Stamler, Newark, 1963—66; estate tax atty. IRS, Chgo., 1966—67; commd. 1st lt. USAF, 1967, advanced through grades to lt. col., 1980, judge advocate, 1967—87, RAN pilot, Area Def. Counsel Program, George AFB, 1973, trial counsel, def. counsel, mil. judge, chief mil. justice, chief utilities negotiator, HQ TAC, chief circuit counsel, 1980—83, circuit mil. judge, 1983—86, ret., 1987; dep. dist. atty. 15th Jud. Dist. Ala., Montgomery, 1987—90, chief dep. dist. atty., 1991—98; dep. atty. gen. State of Ala., 1990—91; pvt. practice, 1998—2007. Adj. prof. Jones Coll. Law, 1995—2007. Chief Ala. Utilities Divsn., Pub. Svc. Comm.; chmn. Arthritis Found. Com. Ctrl. Ala., 1988—91; primary asst. Dist. Atty. Decorated Bronze Star; recipient 3 Meritorious Svc. medals, 4 Air Force Commendation medals, Nat. Pub. Defenders award, Chgo., 1966; Nat. Honor scholar, U. Chgo., 1963. Mem.: ATLA, ABA (chmn. mil. judges com. 1984—85, elec. military judges 1986), Phi Delta Phi (magister), Zeta Beta Tau. Jewish.

MAYER, JOYCE HARRIS, artist; b. NYC, May 7, 1935; d. Harold and Dorothy Harris; m. Bernard Charles Mayer, Mar. 15, 1969; 1 child, Robert Charles. AAS, Inst. of Applied Art and Sci., NYC, 1957. Sketcher Merrylen Cartooning Studio, 1952. Client contact, layout artist, Haire Publ., NYC, 1957-59; art dir., Real Estate Forum, NYC, 1959-60; Denhard and Stewart, NYC, 1960-67; Herb Lubalin Graphic Art Award, 1964; self employed NYC, 1967-71; co curator, New Orleans Mus. of Art, 1985. Among first women to have work pub. in Art Direction, 1964, exhibitions include NY Inst. of Applied Arts and Sci., New Orleans Mus. of Art, 2003, Horizon Gallery, Royal Typographers, NY, Nat. Arts Club, Tulane Univ., Dominican Coll., Robinson Gallery, Mario Villa and Arthur Roger, New Orleans, TWEED Gallery, Plainfield, N.J., Barbara Gillman Gallery, Miami, Contemporary Art Ctr., New Orleans, Bruce Mus., Conn., Historic New Orleans Collection, N.C. Mus. Art, LBI Found. Arts and Sci. NJ, Cheltenham Art Ctr., Pa., Long Beach Island Nat. Exhbn., 2004, NJ Print Coun. Traveling Internat. Competition, 2005, 2009, AIR Gallery, Chelsea, NY, 2009, Spring Bull Gallery, Newport, RI, 2006, Ctr. Contemporary Printmaking, Conn., Monroe Ctr. for Arts, NJ, Plastic Club, Pa., Represented in permanent collections paintings, mono prints, and digital art in numerous collections in Europe and. U.S., Digital La., Contemporary Art Ctr., New Orleans, 2002, Biennale Internazionale dell Arte Contemporanea, Florence, Italy, 2003, NC Mus. Art, numerous others, Winds of My Mind, 2008. Mem. Bd. Edn., Greenwich, Conn., 1978; art advisor Freeport McMoRan Art Collection, New Orleans, 1985; curator Mario Villa Gallery, New Orleans, 1989; juror Arts Coun., New Orleans, 1990. Recipient Chiam Gross sculpture award, 1967, N.Y. Graphic Soc. award, 1976, medal in new media, Florence Biennale, 2003, Otis B. Morse Meml. award, Am. Coll., Pa., 2005, Silicon Gallery Fine Art award, 2006, Stella Drabkin Meml. award, 2007, Gladys B. Blum Meml. award, 2007, award, Photo Review Competition Winners, 2008, Manmouth Mus. Competition Exhbn., 2008, NAWA Penn State Exhbn., 2009, Honor, NAWA, 2008, medal, Minds Eye New, New Orleans Mus. Art, 2009, Urban legends, Bonita Mus., Calif., 2008, NY Hall of Sci., Art Envisions Sci., 2008. Mem. Am. Color Print Soc., The Print Ctr., Nat. Assn. Women Artists, Coll. Art Assn. Avocations: reading, theater, ballet, birdwatching. Studio: 8 Golfview Dr Medford NJ 08055 Office Phone: 609-953-2390. E-mail: joycehmayer@aol.com.

MAYER, KIT, scenic designer, director; s. Fred C. and Elinor Mayer; m. Kathryn L. Mayer; children: Emily Pilmonas, Anne Pilmonas, Caitlin, Amelia, Scout. BA, U. Wis., Lacrosse, 1987. Designer St. Mary's U. Minn., Winona, 1998—, instr., tech. dir. Designer, founding mem. Fairbanks Shakespeare Theatre, Alaska, 1994—. Designer (scenery & lighting theatre). Office: Saint Mary's Univ Minn 700 Ter Heights Winona MN 55987 Business E-Mail: kmayer@smumn.edu.

MAYER, MARGARET ANN, environmentalist, educator; b. Pottsville, Pa., Nov. 23, 1948; d. Harry William Mayer and Signe Margaret Paris. BA in Fine Arts, Painting, U. Colo., Boulder, 1970; MS in Botany, U. RI, North Kingston, 1974. Instr. Seattle Ctrl. CC, 1975—79; lectr. Eastern Ct. St. U., Willimantic, Conn., 1979—80; with Conducted Landscape Ecology Co. & Alpine Flora, Austria Sch. Field Studies, 1983—87; tchr./chair art dept. Fryeburg Acad., Maine, 1985—90; botanist, cons. Critical Areas Program, Augusta, Maine, 1986—92; interpreter naturalist NPS (Olympic Nat. Pk.), Forks, Wash., 1987, NPS Acadia NP, Bar Harbor, Maine, 1991—92; instr. Wildlands Studies, Cazadero, Calif., 1992, U. New Eng., Biddeford, Maine, 1995—98; tchr. Elan Sch., Poland, Maine, 2001—05; instr. Dine Coll., Tsaile, Ariz., 2006—. Dir. life sci. internships U. New Eng., Biddeford, Maine, 1995—98. Author: (bot. surveys) Bot. Survey Vernon Walker Refuge; contbr. articles to numerous profl. jours. Grant, RISE, Am. Natural History Mus., 2006—07. Mem.: Nat. Conservation Edn. Program, ESA. Achievements include development of green club and recycling on campus; mentor water quality research of unregulated water sources of Navajo nation with summer interns and resource management in Canyon de Chelley; rescue dogs on Naviojo rez. Avocations: travel, reading, painting, reading, hiking. Home: PO Box 143 Tsaile AZ 86556 Office: Dine Coll 1 Cir Dri Tsaile AZ 86556 Office Fax: 928-724-6821; Home Fax: 927-724-6821. Business E-Mail: mmayer@dinecollege.edu.

MAYER, MARGARET ELLEN, medical coding specialist; d. Theodore Robert and Doris Jane Mayer; children: J. Bradford Bellamy, Christian D. Bellamy, Stephen J. Bellamy. Student, Towson U., Md.; AA, Essex CC, Balt., 1990. Coding and data mgr. Union Hosp. Cecil County, Elkton, Md.; coding specialist Johns Hopkins Bayview Med. Ctr., Balt., Greater Balt. Med. Ctr., Towson. Cons. Receivables Out-Sourcing, Inc., Tominium, Md., FMAS Corp., Columbia, Md., Quadra Med. Corp., Bethlehem, Pa. Docent Md. Zoo, Balt., 2005; mem. gov.'s team Md. Rep. Party, 2006. Mem.: Am. Health Info. Mgmt. Assn. (cert. coding specialist), Phi Theta Kappa. Republican. Methodist. Avocations: equestrian events, painting, history, wildlife conservation, beekeeping. Office: Union Hosp Cecil County 106 Bow St Elkton MD 21921

MAYER, MARGERY WEIL, publishing executive; b. Beaufort, SC, Feb. 11, 1952; d. Warren Burke Weil and Elise Jean (Schiff) Rubel; m. Theodore Van Huysen Mayer, Dec. 28, 1975; children: Lily, Henry. BA, Middlebury Coll., Vt., 1974; MS, MIT, 1976. Planning analyst Digital Equipment Corp., Maynard, Mass., 1976-77; editor-in-chief sch. pub. sect. Holt, Rinehart & Winston, NYC, 1977-87; pres. Ginn div. Silver, Burdett & Ginn, Needham, Mass., 1987-90; exec. v.p. Scholastic Inc., NYC, 1990—. Editor: Sloan Mgmt. Rev., 1975—76. Mem. rev. panel US Dept. Edn. Sch. Recognition Prog.; trustee Read With Me prog., Dedham, Mass., 1989. Mem.: Phi Beta Kappa. Office: Scholastic Inc 555 Broadway New York NY 10012-3919

MAYER, MARISSA ANN, information technology executive; b. Wausau, Wis., May 30, 1975; BS in Symbolic Sys., with honors, Stanford U., MS in Computer Sci. With UBS rsch. lab, Zurich, Switzerland, SRI Internat., Menlo Park, Calif.; programmer, software engr. Google Inc., 1999, dir. consumer web products Mountain View, v.p. search products & user experience. Tchr. computer programming Stanford U. Recipient Centennial Tchg. award, Stanford U., Forsythe award; named a Maverick, Details mag., 2008; named one of 25 Masters of Innovation, BusinessWeek, 2006, America's Top Women in Bus.-Game Changers, Pink mag. & Forté Found., 2007, 50 Most Important People on the Web, PC World, 2007, 50 Most Powerful Women in Bus., Fortune mag., 2008, Most Influential Women in Technology, Fast Company, 2009. Office: Google Inc 1600 Amphitheatre Pky Mountain View CA 94043 Office Phone: 650-253-0000. Office Fax: 650-253-0001. E-mail: marissa@google.com.*

MAYER, MICHAEL FREDERICK, chemistry professor; b. Milwaukee, Wis., June 28, 1971; s. Frederick Charles and RoseMary Mayer; m. Fay Lynn Marchese, Apr. 17, 1999; children: Annabelle Fe, Leopold Anton, James David. BS, U. Wis. Oshkosh, 1994; PhD, U. Wis. Milwaukee, 2000. Postdoc. rsch. assoc. U. Ill., Urbana, 2001—04; asst. prof. Tex. Tech U., Lubbock, 2004—. Contbr. articles to profl. jours. Recipient Ruth L. Kirschstein Nat. Rsch. Svc. award, NIH, 2002—04; grantee, Tex. Higher Edn. Coordinating Bd., 2008—; Petroleum Rsch. Fund Starter grant, Am. Chem. Soc., 2005—07, Advanced Rsch. Project grant, Tex. Higher Edn. Coordinating Bd., 2006—08, Rsch. Grant, Welch Found., 2006—. Mem.: AAAS, Am. Chem. Soc. Achievements include development of ring-opening polymerization of catenanes. Office: TX Tech Univ Box 41061 Lubbock TX 79409-1061 Business E-Mail: mf.mayer@ttu.edu.

MAYER, SISTER PATRICIA E., retired elementary school educator; b. Union City, NJ, Dec. 20, 1929; d. Joseph Victor and Johanna Bruns Mayer. BA, Coll. St. Elizabeth, Convent Station, NJ, 1964. Joined Sisters of Charity Roman Cath. Ch., 1948; cert. tchr. Alaska. Tchr. 1st grade St. Aloysius Sch., Jersey City, 1949—50, St. Andrew's Sch., Westwood, NJ, 1950—51; tchr. 4th grade St. Rose of Lima Sch., Short Hills, NJ, 1951—53; tchr. 5-6th grade St. Michael's Sch., Union City, NJ, 1953—59; tchr. 4th grade St. Nicholas Sch., Passaic, NJ, 1959—60; tchr. 3rd, 6-7th grades St. Bridget Sch., Jersey City, 1960—70; tchr. 7-8th grade St. Paul of Cross Sch., Jersey City, 1970—83, Immaculate Conception/Monroe Cath. HS, 1983—2007, Monroe Cath. Jr./Sr. HS, 2007—08; ret., 2008. Spkr. in field. Bd. dirs. Monroe Found., 2004—. Recipient Appreciation cert., Alaska Interagy. Coord. Ctr., 2004. Avocations: bowling, tennis, cooking, baking, sewing.

MAYER, RAYMOND RICHARD, business administration educator; b. Chgo., Aug. 31, 1924; s. Adam and Mary (Bogdala) M.; m. Helen Lakowski, Jan. 30, 1954; children: Mark, John, Mary, Jane. BS, Ill. Inst. Tech., 1948, MS, 1954, PhD, 1957. Indsl. engr. Standard Oil Co., Whiting, Ind., 1948-51; orgn. analyst Ford Motor Co., Chgo., 1951-53; instr. Ill. Inst. Tech., Chgo., 1953-56, asso. prof., 1958-60; asst. prof. U. Chgo., 1956-58; Walter F. Mullady prof. bus. adminstrn. Loyola U., Chgo., 1960—. Author: Financial Analysis of Investment Alternatives, 1966, Production Management, 1962, rev. edit., 1968, Production and Operations Management, 1975, rev. edit., 1982, Capital Expenditure Analysis, 1978. Served with USNR, 1944-46. Ingersoll Found. fellow, 1955-56; Machinery and Allied Products Inst. fellow, 1954-55; Ford Found. fellow, 1962 Mem. Acad. Mgmt., Am. Econ. Assn., Am. Statis. Assn., Am. Inst. for Decision Scis., Nat. Assn. Purchasing Mgmt., Polish Inst. Arts and Scis. in Am., Alpha Iota Delta, Alpha Kappa Psi, Beta Gamma Sigma. Home: 730 Green Bay Rd Winnetka IL 60093-1912 Office: 820 N Michigan Ave Chicago IL 60611-2147 Office Phone: 312-915-6595.

MAYER, REINHARD ALBERT, language educator; b. Pforzheim, Germany, Aug. 1, 1942; s. Roman and Wally Mayer; 1 child, Shantia. PhD, Northwestern U., Evanston, Ill., 1972. Cert. translator Am. Translators Assn., 1995. Asst. prof. German Carthage Coll., Kenosha, Wis., 1969—70, Kendall Coll., Evanston, 1970—73; prof. German Bennington Coll., Vt., 1973—94; vis. assoc. prof. Skidmore Coll., Saratoga Springs, NY, 1996—2004, Wheaton Coll., Norton, Mass., 2004—. Translator in numerous fields. Scholarship, Fulbright Program, 1964—66. Mem.: AAUP, MLA, Am. Brecht Soc., Am. Assn. Tchrs. German, Am. Coun. Tchg. Fgn. Lang. (OPI tester 1996), ALTA, Am. Translators Assn. Office: Wheaton Coll E Main St Norton MA 02766

MAYER, RICHARD EDWIN, psychology professor; b. Chgo., Feb. 8, 1947; s. James S. and Bernis (Lowy) M.; m. Beverly Linn Pastor, Dec. 19, 1971; children: Kenneth Michael, David Mark, Sarah Ann. BA with honors, Miami U., Oxford, Ohio, 1969; MS in Psychology, U. Mich., 1971, PhD in Psychology, 1973. Vis. asst. prof. Ind. U., Bloomington, 1973-75; asst. prof. psychology U. Calif., Santa Barbara, 1975-80, assoc. prof., 1980-85, prof., 1985—, pres., chmn. dept., 1987-90. Vis. scholar Learning Rsch. and Devel. Ctr., U. Pitts., 1979, Ctr. for Study of Reading, U. Ill., 1984. Author: Foundations of Learning and Memory, 1979, The Promise of Cognitive Psychology, 1981, Thinking, Problem Solving, Cognition, 1983, 2d edit., 1992, BASIC: A Short Course, 1985, Educational Psychology, 1987, The Critical Thinker, 1990, 2d edit., 1995, The Promise of Educational Psychology, Vol. I, 1999, Vol. II, 2002, Multimedia Learning, 2001, Learning and Instruction, 2003, (with R. Clark) E-Learning and the Science of Instruction, 2004, Cambridge Handbook of Multimedia Learning, 2005; editor: Human Reasoning, 1980, Teaching and Learning Computer Programming, 1988; editor jours. Instructional Sci., 1983-87, Educational Psychologist, 1983-89. Sch. bd. officer Goleta (Calif.) Union Sch. Dist., 1981—. Grantee, NSF, 1975—88, 1991—. Fellow APA (divsn. 15 officer 1987—, G. Stanley Hall lectr. 1988, E.L. Thorndike award 2000), Am. Psychol. Soc.; mem. Am. Ednl. Rsch. Assn. (divsn. C officer 1986-88, 2007-), Psychonomic Soc. Democrat. Jewish. Avocations: computers, hiking, bicycling, reading, dogs. Office: U Calif Dept Of Psychology Santa Barbara CA 93016 Home Phone: 805-964-5936. Business E-Mail: mayer@psych.ucsb.edu.

MAYER, ROBERT J., oncologist, gastroenterologist, educator; MD, Harvard Med. Sch., 1969. Fellow Nat. Cancer Inst., Dana Farber Cancer Inst.; dir. Ctr. for Gastrointestinal Oncology Dana-Farber Cancer Inst., dir. Partners CancerCare's Fellowship Training Program in Hematology & Medical Oncology, vice chmn. acad. affairs dept. medical oncology; prof. medicine Harvard Med. Sch.; sr. physician Beth Israel Deaconess Med. Ctr.; attending physician MGH Cancer Ctr. Mass. Gen. Hosp. Mem.: Am. Soc. Clinical Oncology (pres. 1997). Office: Dana-Farber Cancer Institute 44 Binney St Dana 1602 Boston MA 02115 Office Phone: 617-632-3474. Office Fax: 617-632-2260.*

MAYER, RONALD WESLEY, psychology professor; b. Clyde, Ohio, July 3, 1928; s. Sidney Arnold Mayer and Dorothy Ellen Mead; life ptnr. Allen Chapman Fuller. BA, Ohio Wesleyan U., Delaware, 1951; MA, Ohio State U., Columbus, 1952, PhD, 1959. Res. dir. students in mental hosps. Am. Friends Svc. Com., Columbus, 1952; asst. instr. Ohio State U., 1956—58; instr., acting jr. counselor Wash. State U., Spokane, Wash., 1955—56; assoc. prof. Auburn U., Auburn, Ala., 1958—63; asst. prof. San Francisco State U., 1963—67, assoc. chair psychology dept., 1967—68, assoc. prof., 1967—72, prof., 1972—. Pres. singles club Auburn U., 1960—63; cons. Office Vocat. Rehab., State of Ala., 1960—63, Lee County Mental Health Clinic, Ala., 1960—69, Electronics for Edn., Md., 1962—63, Southern Telephone and Telegraph, Atlanta, 1963; mem. com. on tng. and standards sch. psychologists Ala. Psychol. Assn., 1961—62; alt. del. Am. Assn. State Psychology Bds., 1962; presenter Ala. Ednl. TV, 1962. Co-editor: History of Psychology Newsletter, 1962—66; actor: Spokane, Wash. Civic Theater, 1956—58; chief of staff: San Francisco Gay Men's Chorus, 1984—85. Office mgr. Pioneer Youth Am., Inc., 1948; chmn. cmty. self-study Auburn, Ala., 1961—63; bd. mem. Ala. Coun. Human Rels., 1963; docent, asst. to dir. Calif. Hist. Soc., 1969—70; pres. Ohio Methodist Youth, 1946—47; alt. del. World Conf. Christian Youth, Oslo, 1947. Pvt. 1st class US Army, 1954—56, Spokane Examining Station. Mem.: AAUP (sec. Calif. conf. 1972—73), APA (life), AAAS (life), APA Divsn. 26 History Psychology (chair organizing com. 1964—65, sec.-treas. 1987—93, elections com. 1966—67, membership com. 1967—79), Western Psychol. Assn. (bd. dirs., sec.-treas. 1969—73, convention mgr. 1967), Am. Assn. Lit. Critics (life), Phi Delta Theta. Democrat. Methodist. Home: 30 Lopez Ave San Francisco CA 94116 Office: San Francisco State Univ 1600 Holloway Ave San Francisco CA 94132 Office Fax: 415-338-2398; Home Fax: 415-681-4997. Business E-Mail: mayer@sfsu.edu.

MAYER, ROSEMARY, artist; b. Ridgewood, NY, Feb. 27, 1943; d. Theodore Albert and Marie Anne (Stumpf) M. AB magna cum laude, U. Iowa, 1964; postgrad., Bklyn. Mus. Art Sch., 1964—65, Sch. Visual Arts, NYC, 1967—69. Model Raphael Soyer, NYC, 1968—74; writer Arts Mag., NYC, 1972—75, Art in Am., NYC, 1974—75. Vis. artist many schs. including Hartwick Coll., Oneonta, N.Y., 1976, Art Inst., Chgo., 1974; guest artist Nat. Endowment Workshop, Tyler Sch. Art, Phila., Mpls. Acad. Art and Design, 1981; adj. lectr. La Guardia C.C., CUNY, 1992—; adj. prof. L.I. U., 1988—; writer, speaker A.I.R. Gallery, N.Y.C., 1972-74. Translator: Pontormo's Diary 1983; author: Swatches, 1969, Surroundings, 1977. Grantee numerous orgns. including NEA, CAPS, 1976—. Democrat. Home: 55 Leonard St New York NY 10013-2928

MAYER, SUSAN E., dean, political science professor; BA, Ind. U., 1974, MA in Sociology, 1981; PhD in Sociology, Northwestern U., 1986; LLD (hon.), Lake Forest Coll., 2007. Instr. Dept. Sociology Ind. U., 1975—76; equal rights specialist Office of Civil Rights US Dept. Health and Human Svcs., 1980—81; rsch. assoc. Ctr. for Urban Affairs and Policy Rsch. Northwestern U., 1986—89, vis. prof., 1996—97; asst. prof. Irving B. Harris Grad. Sch. Pub. Policy Studies, U. Chgo., 1989—96, assoc. prof., 1996—2003, dean, 2002—, prof., 2003—; dir. Northwestern U. / U. Chgo. Joint Ctr. for Poverty Rsch., 1997—2000, dep. dir., 2000—. Office: Harris Sch Pub Policy Studies U Chgo 1155 E Sixtieth St Chicago IL 60637 Office Phone: 773-702-9623. E-mail: s-mayer@uchicago.edu.*

MAYER, SUSAN MARTIN, art educator; b. Atlanta, Oct. 25, 1931; d. Paul McKeen and Ione (Garrett) Martin; m. Arthur James Mayer, Aug. 9, 1953; 1 child, Melinda Marilyn. Student, Am. U., 1949-50; BA, U. N.C., Greensboro, 1953; postgrad., U. Del., 1956-58; MA, Ariz. State U., 1966. Artist-in-residence Armed Forces Staff Coll., Norfolk, Va., 1968-69; mem. art faculty U. Tex., Austin, 1971—2003; ret., 2002. Co-editor: Museum Education: History, Theory and Practice, 1989; author various mus. publs.; contbr. articles to profl. jours. Recipient award Austin Ind. Sch. Bd., 1985. Mem. Nat. Art Edn. Assn. (bd. dirs. 1983-87, award 1987, 91), Tex. Art Edn. Assn. (mus. edn. chair 1982-83, Mus. Educator of Yr. 1986), Tex. Assn. Mus. (mus. edn. chair), Austin Visual Arts Assn., Am. Assn. Mus. Home Phone: 512-327-1716. Business E-Mail: susanm@mail.utexas.edu.

MAYER, THEODORE V.H., lawyer; b. Waltham, Mass., Sept. 30, 1952; s. Jean and Elizabeth (Van Huysen) M.; m. Margery Weil, Dec. 28, 1975; children: Lily, Henry. BA, Yale U., 1974; JD, Harvard U., 1977. Bar: NY 1978, Mass. 1989, US Ct. Appeals 2nd, 3rd, 7th, Fed. Circuits, US Dist. Ct. So., Ea., We. Districts NY, US Dist. Ct. Dist. Ariz. Assoc. Hughes, Hubbard & Reed LLP, NYC, 1978-85, ptnr., 1985—, exec. com. mem., 1996—, chair lit. dept., 2008—. Co-author (with Robb Patryk): Product Liability, 1998; contbr. articles to profl. jours. Bd. dirs. New Media Repertory Co., NYC, 1991—, chair, 1996-2006; adv. bd. mem. Inst. Global Leadership, Tufts U., 2005—. Mem. Assn. Bar City NY (chair com. product liability 2002-05). Office: Hughes Hubbard & Reed LLP One Battery Pk Plz New York NY 10004-1482 Office Phone: 212-837-6888. Office Fax: 212-422-4726. E-mail: mayer@hugheshubbard.com.

MAYER, VICTOR JAMES, geologist, educator; b. Mayville, Wis., Mar. 25, 1933; s. Victor Charles and Phyllis (Bachhuber) M.; m. Mary Jo Anne White, Nov. 25, 1965; children: Gregory, Maribeth. BS Geology, U. Wis., 1956; MS Geology, U. Colo., 1960, PhD Sci. Edn., 1966. Tchr. Colo. Pub. Schs., 1961—85; asst. prof. SUNY, Oneonta, 1965—67, Ohio State U., Columbus, 1967—70, assoc. prof., 1970—75, prof. ednl. studies, geol. scis. and natural resources, 1975—95, prof. emeritus, 1995—; affiliate prof. U. Northern Colo., 2005—. Co-organizer symposa 29th and 31st Internat. Geol. Congresses; internat. sci. edn. assistance to individuals and orgns. in Japan, Korea, Taiwan, Russia, and Venezuela; dir. NSF Insts., program leadership Earth Sys. Edn., 1990-95; dir. Korean Sci. Tchrs. Insts., 1986-88, 95, 2005-08; co-convenor Second Internat. conf. Geosci. Edn., Hilo, Hawaii, 1997; disting. vis. prof. SUNY, Plattsburg, 1994; vis. rsch. scholar Hyogo U., Japan, 1996; sr. Fulbright rschr. Shizuoka U., Japan, 1998; vis. prof. Korea Nat. U. Edn., 2000; Fulbright prof. Pusan Nat. U. Korea, 2003-04, spkr. in field. Author, editor: books Global Science Literacy, 2002, Implementing Global Science Literacy, 2003, with Jeonghee Nam and Hyonyong Lee The Earth System Approach to Integrated Science (in Korean), 2006; contbr. articles to profl. jours. With USAR. Recipient Lifetime Disting. Svc. award Internat. Earth Sci. Edn. Cmty., 1997; named Disting. Investigator Ohio Sea Grant Program Fellow AAAS (chmn. edn. 1988-89), Ohio Acad. Sci. (v.p. 1978-79, exec. com. 1993-94, Outstanding univ. educator 1995); mem. NSTA (bd. dirs. 1984-86), Sci. Edn. Coun. Ohio (pres. 1987-88), Sigma Xi, Phi Delta Kappa Roman Catholic. Avocation: photography. Home and Office: 8483 Sand Dollar Dr Windsor CO 80528 Personal E-mail: mayer.4@osu.edu.

MAYER, WILLIAM EMILIO, investor; b. NYC, May 7, 1940; s. Emilio and Marie Mayer; m. Katherine Mayer, May 16, 1964; children: Kristen Elizabeth, William Franz. BS, U. Md., 1966, MBA, 1967. Pres., CEO First Boston Corp., NYC, 1967-91; dean Coll. Bus. and Mgmt. U. Md., College Park, 1992-96; ptnr. Devel. Capital, 1996-99, Park Ave. Equity Ptnrs., 1999—. Bd. dirs. Lee Enterprises, Inc., Black Rock/Kelso, Columbia Fund Group. Chmn. bd. U. Md.; chmn. bd. trustees Aspen Inst. 1st lt. USAF, 1961—65. Mem. Annapolis Yacht Club, Manhasset Bay Club (NY), Wilson Cove Yacht Club, Univ. Club (NYC), Mashomack Fish and Game Club, Met. Club (Washington). Home: 172 Long Neck Point Rd Darien CT 06820-5816 Office: 12 E 49th St 40th Fl New York NY 10017 Office Phone: 212-430-0160.

MAYER, WILLIAM P., lawyer; AB summa cum laude, Dartmouth Coll., 1973; MS, U. Dar es Salaam, Tanzania, 1974; JD, U. Va. Law Sch., 1977. Bar: DC 1978, Mass. 1984. Law clerk, Hon. William H. Timbers US Ct. Appeals (2nd cir.), 1977—78; ptnr., bus. law dept., mem. fin. svcs. dept. Goodwin Procter LLP, Boston. Editor: Va. Law Rev.; lectr. in field. Bd. adv. Morin Ctr. Banking and Fin. Law Studies, Boston Univ. Office: Goodwin Procter LLP Exchange Pl 53 State St Boston MA 02109 Office Phone: 617-570-1534. Office Fax: 617-523-1231. Business E-Mail: wmayer@goodwinprocter.com.

MAYERS, DANIEL KRIEGSMAN, lawyer; b. Scarsdale, NY, July 10, 1934; s. Chauncey Maurice and Helen P. (Kriegsman) M.; m. Karen E. Silverman, Sept. 30, 1956, children: Peter D., Leslie H. Shroyer. AB, Harvard U., 1955, LLB, 1960. Bar: D.C. 1961, U.S. Supreme Ct. 1961. Law clk. to Justice Felix Frankfurter, U.S. Supreme Ct., Washington, 1960-61; spl. asst. U.S. Dept. Justice, Washington, 1961-62; assoc. Wilmer Cutler & Pickering, Washington, 1962-65, ptnr., 1967-99, of counsel, 2000—; exec. asst. to undersec. U.S. State Dept., Washington, 1965-66. Vis. com. Harvard Law Sch., Cambridge, Mass., 1982-89, chmn., 1986-89; chmn. Legal Action Ctr., N.Y.C., 1998—, chmn. Washington Ednl. TV Assn., 1993-97, chmn. Survivors Fund for Pentagon Victims, 2001, 08. Pres. Nat. Symphony Orch., Washington, 1987-89; chmn. Sidwell Friends Sch., Washington, 1979-81; mem. Ams. for Peace Now, 1991—, Fed. City Coun., Washington, 1981—; chmn. Cmty. Found. for Nat. Capital Area, 2008—; dir. Internat. Sr. Lawyers' Program, 2004-; counsel, dir. Ctr. for Nat. Policy, Washington, 1984-93. With U.S. Army, 1955-57. Recipient Sears prize Harvard Law Sch., 1959 Mem. ABA, Met. Club, Burning Tree Woodstock Country Club. Democrat. Jewish. Avocations: tennis, fishing. Home: 3222 Woodland Dr NW Washington DC 20008-3547 Personal E-mail: dan@dmayers.com.

MAYERS, STANLEY PENROSE, JR., public health service officer, educator; b. Phila., Nov. 9, 1926; s. Stanley Penrose and Margaret Amelia (Thorpe) M.; m. Virginia Lee Lytle, Aug. 25, 1951 (dec. Oct. 1990); children: Douglas Lytle, Kenneth Stanley, Daniel John, Andrew William; m. Patricia Ann Harne Hulsey, Mar. 6, 1993. BA, U. Pa., 1949, MD, 1953; MPH, Johns Hopkins U., 1958. Diplomate Am. Bd. Preventive Medicine. Intern Phila. Gen. Hosp., 1953-54; resident Arlington County Health Dept., Va., 1954-55; health dir. Henry-Martinsville-Patrick Health Dist., Martinsville, Va., 1955-57; regional dir. Va. State Health Dept., Richmond, 1958-59; dist. state health officer N.J. State Dept. of Health, Trenton, 1959-62; asst. prof. and asst. dean Johns Hopkins Sch. Hygiene and Pub. Health, Balt., 1962-65; dir. Arlington County Dept. of Human Resources, Arlington, Va., 1965-71; prof. health policy and adminstrn. Pa. State U., University Park, 1971-97, prof. emeritus, 1997—, chmn., 1979-88, assoc. dean undergrad. studies Coll. Health and Human Devel., 1989-92, assoc. dean acad. studies Coll. Health and Human Devel., 1992-95, assoc. dean emeritus, 1997—. Interim dir. internat. edn. programs and studies Pa. State U., 2000-2001; faculty assoc. Johns Hopkins U. Sch. Hygiene and Pub. Health, Balt., 1965-75; clin. assoc. prof. Georgetown U. Sch. Medicine, Washington, 1965-71; cons. VA, 1985—. Contbr. articles to profl. jours. Pres. Arlington Optimist Club, 1970-71; bd. dirs. Centre County Family Planning Svcs., Bellefonte, Pa., 1972-79, vice chmn., Ctr. County Hosp. Commn., 2005-; With USN, 1945-46. Recipient Outstanding Achievement award Dept. Community Medicine, Georgetown U. Sch. Medicine, 1968, Saubel award Coll. of Human Devel., Pa. State U., 1985, Pioneer Achievement award Frankford H.S., Phila., 1999. Fellow Am. Coll. Preventive Med., APHA (chmn. membership com. health officer's sect. 1968-70, mem. nominating com. health adminstrn. sect. 1970-72, chmn. com. to draft a statement on local health agy. responsibilities 1973-74); mem. AMA, Arlington County Med. Soc. (Wellborn award 1971), Centre County Med. Soc. (pres. 1978), Med. Soc. Va., Met. Washington Health Officers Assn. (sec. 1967-71), Am. Assn. Pub. Health Physicians (pres. Va. chpt. 1970-71), Pa. Med. Soc. (mem. Ho. of Dels. for Centre County 1974-76, 81-97, treas. 1973-74, 85—, sec. 1974-76, v.p. 1976, pres. elect 1977, pres. 1978), Mt. Nittany Soc., Univ. Club (State College, Pa.), Phi Beta Kappa. Episcopalian. Avocations: fishing, boating, hiking. Home: 648 Wiltshire Dr State College PA 16803-1450 Office: Pa State U Human Devel Bldg Rm 115 University Park PA 16802 Business E-Mail: spm1@psu.edu. *Never attempt to promote something or someone that you do not believe in yourself.*

MAYES, MICHELE COLEMAN, insurance company executive, lawyer; b. LA, July 9, 1949; BA, U. Mich., 1971, JD, 1974. Bar: Mich. 1974, US Dist. Ct. 1974, Ea. Dist. Mich. 1976, Ill. 1980, US Supreme Ct. 1988, Pa. 1988. Asst. US atty. US Dept. Justice, Detroit, Bklyn., 1976—82; mng. atty. Burroughs Corp.; staff v.p., assoc. gen. counsel worldwide litig. Unisys Corp.; v.p., asst. gen. counsel Colgate-Palmolive Co., NYC, 1992—93, v.p. human resources & legal, N. Am., v.p., dep. gen. counsel, asst. sec., v.p. legal, asst. sec., 2001—03; sr. v.p., gen. counsel Pitney Bowes Inc., Stamford, Conn., 2003—07, The Allstate Ins. Co., Northbrook, Ill., 2007—; v.p., gen. counsel The Allstate Corp., Northbrook, Ill., 2007—. Adj. prof. Wayne State U., 1981—87; bd. mem. Legal Momentum, 1996—2006, chair, 2001—06; bd. dirs. Assurant Corp. Recipient Margaret Brent award, ABA Commn. on Women in the Profession, 2003, Trailblazer award, Minority Corp. Counsel Assn. Mem.: ABA (mem. commn. on women in the profession 1992, co-chair, arbitration com. 1990—92). Office: The Allstate Corp 2775 Sanders Rd Northbrook IL 60062*

MAYES, WENDELL WISE, JR., former broadcasting company executive; b. San Antonio, Mar. 2, 1924; s. Wendell Wise and Dorothy Lydia (Evans) M.; m. Mary Jane King, May 11, 1946; children: Cathey, Sarah, Wendell Wise, III. Student, Schreiner Inst., 1941-42, U. Tex., 1942, Daniel Baker Coll., 1946; BS, Tex. Tech. Coll., 1949; BA summa cum laude, St. Edward's U., 2002, MLA, 2005, MBA, 2006. Program dir., sta. mgr. Sta. KBWD, Brownwood, Tex., 1949-57; mgr. Sta. KCRS, Midland, Tex., 1957-63, pres., 1965-84, chmn., 1984-96; pres. Sta. KNOW, Austin, Tex., 1970-81, Stas. KVIC and KAMG, Victoria, Tex., 1970-84, chmn., 1984-98, Sta. KCRS-FM, Midland, 1984-96; pres. Sta. KCSW, San Marcos, 1976-81; sec.-treas. Sta. KSNY-AM-FM, Snyder, 1952-94; mem. bd. mgrs. Sta. KLBJ/KHHT-AM-FM, Austin, 1991-97. Bd. advisors Patton Med. Devices, 2006—08; lectr. Coll. Comm., U. Tex., Austin, 1978—81. Chmn. bd. Am. Diabetes Assn., 1974—77; mem. Nat. Diabetes Adv. Bd., 1977—84; v.p. Internat. Diabetes Fedn., 1980—88, pres.-elect, 1988—91, pres., 1991—94, hon. pres., 1997—; pres. Tex. Broadcast Edn. Found., 1973—76, dir., 2002—; mem. Tex. Diabetes Coun., 1983—86, chmn., 1983—86, exec. dir., 1999; bd. regents Tex. Tech U., 1985—91, chmn., 1987—88; bd. dirs., treas. Writer's League Tex., 2005—08. With USNR, 1943—46. Recipient Addison B. Scoville award, Am. Diabetes Assn., 1977, first Wendell Mayes Jr. award, 1986, Josiah K. Lilly award, 1991, Harold Rifkin award, 1994, Masaji Takeda medal, Kobe, Japan Colloquium Med. Sci., 1994; named Disting. Alumnus, Tex. Tech U., 1981, Disting. Engr., 1985, Disting. Alumnus, Schreiner U., 2006; named to Tex. Tech. Mass Comm. Hall of Fame, 1978, Hall of Fame Tex. affiliate, Am. Diabetes Assn., 1994, Tex. Radio Hall of Fame, 2002. Mem. Tex. Assn. Broadcasters (pres. 1964, named Pioneer Broadcaster of Year 1978), Nat. Assn. Broadcasters (dir. 1969-72), Am. Council on Edn. in Journalism (dir. 1977-80), Broadcast Edn. Assn. (dir. 1973-77), AP Broadcasters (bd. dirs. 1988-91), Tex. Tech. Elec. Engring. Acad. Episcopalian (vestryman 1966-69, 86-88; sr. warden 1988). Home: 2834 Montebello Rd Apt 1 Austin TX 78746-6820 Office: 1907 N Lamar Blvd 200 Austin TX 78705-4992

MAYEUX, RICHARD, hospital administrator, neurologist; b. New Orleans, 1946; MD, U. Okla., 1972. Diplomate Am. Bd. Psychiatry and Neurology. Intern Boston City Hosp., 1972—73, resident in internal medicine, 1973—74; resident in neurology Columbia Presbyn. Med. Ctr., NYC, 1974—77; fellow in neurology Boston U., 1977—78; neurologist Sergievsky Ctr., NYC; staff neurologist Columbia Presbyn. Med. Ctr., NYC; prof. Columbia Coll. Physicians and Surgeons, NYC; dir. Taub Inst., NYC; Gertrude H. Sergievsky prof. neurology, psychiatry & epidemiology Columbia Univ., dir. Gertrude H. Sergievsky Ctr.; mem. Aging Rev. Com. NIH, mem. Epidemiology of Chronic Disorders Com.; med. & scientific adv. bd. Alzheimer's Assn. Robert Aird visiting prof. U. Calif. San Francisco; Emanuel Goldberg visiting prof. U. Rochester; J.L. Silversides visiting prof. U. Toronto. Recipient Leadership & Excellence in Alzheimer's Disease award, Nat. Inst. Aging, 1992, MERIT award, 2004, Dean's Disting. Clin. Scientist award, Columbia U., Rita Hayworth award, Alzheimer's Assn. Fellow: Am. Acad. Neurology (Potamkin prize 2007); mem.: AAP, Soc. for Neuroscience, Soc. Epidemiologic Rsch., Am. Neurological Assn., NY Acad. Sci., Am. Epidemiological Soc., Assn. Rsch. Nervous & Mental Disease (ARNMD), Inst. of Medicine of NAS. Office: Coll Physicians and Surgeons Columbia U 630 W 168th St New York NY 10032 Office Phone: 212-305-2391. Office Fax: 212-305-2518. E-mail: rpm2@columbia.edu.

MAYFIELD, JEREMY (ALLEN), race car driver; b. Owensboro, Ky., May 27, 1969; m. Shana Mayfield. Profl. race care driver NASCAR Cale Yarborough Motorsports, 1995—96, Kranefuss-Haas Racing, 1997, Penske-Kranefuss Racing, 1998—2000, Penske Racing, 2001, Evernham Motorsports, 2002—06, Bill Davis Racing, 2007, Haas CNC Racing, 2007—. 2nd pl. Calif. 500 Calif. Speedway, 1998, 1st pl. NAPA Auto Parts 500, 2000; 1st pl. Pocono 500 Pocono Raceway, 1998, 2000, 2nd pl. Pocono 500, 04; 2nd pl. TranSouth Fin. 400 Darlington Raceway, 1999; 2nd pl. UAW-GM Quality 500 Lowe's Motor Speedway, 2000; 2nd pl. Checker Auto Parts/Dura Lube 500 Phoenix Internat. Raceway, 2000; 2nd pl. Pennzoil 400 Homestead-Miami Speedway, 2000; 2nd pl. UAW-Daimler Chrysler 400 Las Vegas Motor Speedway, 2002; 2nd pl. Chevy Rock and Roll 400 Richmond Internat. Raceway, 2003, 1st pl. Chevy Rock and Roll 400, 04; 2nd pl. Dover 400 Dover Internat. Speedway, 2003; 2nd pl. Golden Corral 500 Atlanta Motor Speedway, 2004; 1st pl. GFS Marketplace 400 Mich. Internat. Speedway, 2005. Mailing: c/o Haas CNC Racing 6001 Haas Way Kannapolis NC 28081 Office Phone: 704-652-4227.

MAYFIELD, MAX (BRITT MAYFIELD), meteorologist; b. Okla. City, Sept. 19, 1948; m. Linda C. Mayfield; 3 children. BS in Math., U. Okla., 1970; MS in Meterology, Fla. St. U., 1987. With NOAA/Nat. Weather Svc., Miami, 1972—2007, hurricane forecaster, 1988—90, sr. forecaster, 1990—98, dep. dir. Nat. Hurricane Ctr., 1998—2000, acting dir., 2000, dir., 2000—07; hurricane specialist WPLG-TV Local 10, Miami, 2007—. Chmn. regional assn. IV hurricane com. World Meterological Orgn.; chmn. office of fed. coord. Meteorology Working Group on Hurricanes; spkr. in field. Contbr. articles to profl. jours. Recipient Francis W. Reichelderfer award, Am. Meterological Soc., 1996, Outstanding Achievement award, Nat. Hurricane Ctr., 2000, Richard Hagemeyer award, Interdepartmental Hurricane Conf., 2004, Emmy award, 2004, Presdl. Rank award for Meritorious Svc., 2005, NOAA Bronze medal, US Dept. Commerce. Mem.: Nat. Weather Assn., Am. Meteorological Soc. Office: WPLG-TV 3900 Biscayne Blvd Miami FL 33137

MAYFIELD, PEGGY LEE, counselor, educator; d. Ralph Russel Horn and Dorothy Fae Reid; m. Jack Lynn Mayfield. AS in Biology, Richland C.C., Decatur, Ill., 1988; BA in Psychology, U. Ill., Springfield, 1993, MA in Counseling, 1996. Cert. nat. counselor Nat. Bd. Cert. Counselors, 1996. Child and adolescent therapist Decatur Mental Health Ctr., Ill., 1994—95, intensive family therapist, 1995—96; foster care supr., therapist Cath. Social Svcs., Bloomington, Ill., 1996—97, foster care supr., 1997—2000; lic. clin. profl. counselor Decatur, 2000—; adj. human devel. instr. U. Ill., Springfield, 1998—, accredition documentation coord., 2002—06, chair alumni coun. Coll. Edn. and Human Svcs., 2004—06, dir. accreditation documentation, 2006—, immediate past chair, 2006—, adj. instr., tchr. edn. program, 2007—. Human devel. counseling program adv. bd. U. Ill., Springfield, 1996—, mem. coll. edn. & human svc. coun. on profl. edn., 2001—, mem. coll. edn. & human svc. unit assessment adv. team, 2001—; compassion fatigue trainer, Decatur, 1996—; trainer Lips Are Sealed Syndrome, 1997—; comm. skills trainer, Decatur, 1998—2000. Recipient Loyalty award, U. Ill. Springfield Alumni Assn., 2005; named Alumni of Yr., Human Devel. Counseling Program, 1998. Mem.: U. Ill. Alumni Assn. (Loyalty award 2005), U. Ill. Coll. of Edn. Human Svcs. Alumni Coun. (chair 2004—06, immediate past editor 2006—), Chi Sigma Iota. Home: 2155 W Center St Decatur IL 62526 Office Phone: 217-206-7583. Personal E-mail: mayfield.peggy@uis.edu.

MAYFIELD, ROBERT CHARLES, academic administrator, geographer, educator; b. Abilene, Tex., Oct. 15, 1928; s. Percy Anderson and Fay (Hicks) M.; m. Loraine Poindexter, Sept. 3, 1952; children: Julie Barnes, Jennifer Manley, Mark Stanley, Malcolm Randall. BA, Tex. Christian U., 1952; MS, Ind. U., 1953; PhD, U. Wash., 1961. Chmn. geography dept. Tex. Christian U., Ft. Worth, 1960-64, U. Tex., Austin, 1968—71, Boston U., 1971—84, acad. v.p. external programs, 1977-83, provost, 1979-84. Cons. Coun. for Econ. Action, Boston, 1980—; adj. prof. U. Tex., Austin, 1987—; lectr. U.S. Info. Svc., Bangladesh, 1994; seminar dir. U. Tex. Seminars for Adult Growth and Enrichment, 1995—; mem. faculty rev. bd. Bangladesh U. Engring. and Tech., Dacca, 1996—. Editor, contbg. author: Man, Environment and Space, 1972. With USAF, 1946-49. Rsch. fellow Nat. Acad. Sci. No. India, 1957-58, Fulbright-Hays fellow Office Edn., Bangalore, Mysore, India, 1966-67; Rsch. grant Agrl. Devel. Coun., 1968. Mem. Assn. Am. Geographers. Business E-Mail: rmayfield7@austin.rr.com.

MAYFIELD, SANDRA J., literature and language professor; d. Emery Jack and Elizabeth Malin; m. Tommy Grant Mayfield, Dec. 23, 1971 (div. Dec. 1973). BA, Okla. Bapt. U., Shawnee, 1964; MA, U. Okla., Norman, 1969, PhD, 1976. Cert. in tchr. edn. Okla., 1965, English tchr. State Okla., 1965. Asst. prof. English Okla. Bapt. U., 1976—80; cons., dept. edn. Okla. State, Okla. City, 1980—85; prof. English U. Ctrl. Okla., Edmond, 1985—. Contbr. encyclopedia. Southwestern regent Sigma Tau Delta Internat., DeKalb, Ill., 2001—04, dir., leadership workshop, 2004—08; pres. Edmond Cambridge Club, 1998—99; mem. Delta Kappa Gamma, Edmond, 1995—2008, Westminster Presbyn. Ch., Okla. City; mem., exec. bd. Edmond Arts and Humanities Coun., Edmond, Okla., 2001—03. Recipient Outstanding Tchr. award, Student selection, UCO, 2001, Excellence award, Okla. Bapt. U., 2005; fellowship, Nat. Endowment Humanities, 1998. Mem.: AAUP (pres. 2001—02, Outstanding Svc. award 2004), AAUW. Presbyterian.

MAYFIELD-CLARKE, ANN BERNADETTE, speech, language pathologist; d. Bobby Clarence and Johnnie Lee Mayfield; m. Don Lazaro Clarke, June 24, 1989. BSc, Marquette U., Milw., 1976; MSc, Howard U., Washington, 1978, PhD, 1998. Cert. in clin. competence Am. Speech Lang. Hearing Assn., Md., 1983. Spl. edn. program specialist DC Pub. Schs. State Edn. Agy., Washington, 1986—88; speech lang. pathologist Morena Valley Pub. Sch. Sys., Calif., 1988—89, Locomotion Therapy Co., San Gabriel, Calif., 1992—94, Suzanne Barnes & Assocs., Sierra Madre, Calif., 2000—02; instr. Calif. State U. Northridge, 1994—96, clin. faculty supr., 1994—96, adj. prof., 1998—99, asst. prof., 1999—2002; contractor, speech lang. pathologist Berman Peverley & Assocs., Silver Springs, Md., 1996—98, Posh Rehab. U. South Calif. Hosp., LA, 1998—2002; dir., speech lang., pathology & audiology Therapeutic Comprehensive Svcs., Mission Hills, Calif., 1998—2000; assoc. prof. NC A & T State U., Greensboro, 2002—, program dir., 2002—. Contbr. scientific papers. Adv. bd. mem. State Employees Credit Union Stoney Creek, Stoney Creek, NC, 2005—09. Recipient Outstanding Svc. award, NC A & T State U., 2003—08. Fellow: Am. Speech Lang. Hearing Assn. (Continuing Edn. award 2003—09); mem.: Nat. Acad. Pre-profl. Programs Comm. Disorders, Southeastern U. Clin. Educators, Coun. Academic Program Comm. Scis. & Disorders (Diversity Incentive award 2006), Nat. Black Assn. Speech Lang. & Hearing (bd. dirs. 2005—, convention program chair 2005—07), Phi Kappa Phi (com. mem. bylaws 2005), Delta Sigma Theta. Personal E-mail: bc62489@sbcglobal.net.

MAYHALL, CLIFFORD WESLEY, lawyer; b. Birmingham, Ala., Aug. 23, 1972; s. Clyde Wesley and Pamela Hayes Mayhall. BA in Govt. and English, Coll. William and Mary, Williamsburg, Va., 1994; MA in Polit. Sci., U. Fla., Gainesville, 1996; JD, Fla. State U., Tallahassee, 2000. Bar: Fla. 2000, US Dist Ct. (no. dist.) Fla. 2002, US Dist. Ct. (so. dist.) Fla. 2002, US Dist. Ct. (mid. dist.) Fla. 2005, US Ct. Appeals (11th cir.) 2005, US Supreme Ct. 2005. Rsch. asst. Reubin Askew Inst., Gainesville, 1994—96; staff aide US Senator Bob Graham, Tallahassee, 1995; rsch. specialist Legis. Com. on Intergovtl. Rels., Tallahassee, 1996—98; jud. clk. Sr. US Dist. Judge Maurice Paul, Gainesville, 2000—01; atty. Katz, Kutter, Alderman & Bryant, PA, Tallahassee, 2001—04, Akerman Senterfitt, Tallahassee, 2004—08; regulatory counsel Home Shopping Network, St. Petersburg, 2008—. Legis. editor Fla. State U. Law Rev., 2000. Sec., past pres. Tree House Children's Shelter, Tallahassee, 2001—08; mem. rector search com. St. John's Episcopal Ch., Tallahassee, 2006—08; bd. dirs. So. Shakespeare Festival, Tallahassee, 1998—2002. Mem.: FBA, ABA, Fla. Bar, Emerge Tallahassee, Emerge Fla., Capital Tiger Bay Club, Order of Coif. Office: Home Shopping Network Legal Dept 1 HSN Dr Saint Petersburg FL 33729 Office Phone: 727-872-7787. Office Fax: 727-872-6066. Personal E-mail: cwmayhall@yahoo.com.

MAYHAR, ARDATH FRANCES (FRANK CANNON, JOHN KILLDEER, FRANCES HURST), writer; b. 1930; Ind. book cons., 1979—99; dairyman, 1947—57; prin. East Tex. Bookstore, Nacogdoches, 1958—62; proofreader Capital Jour., Salem, Oreg., 1968—75; chicken farmer, 1976—78; proofreader Daily Sentinel, Nacogdoches, 1979—82; writer, 1982—99; co-mgr. View From Orbit Bookstore, Nacogdoches, 1984—99; writing instr. Writer's Digest, 1982—2005. Author: How the Gods Wove in Kyrannon, 1979, The Seekers of Shar Nuhn, 1980, Soul Singer of Tyrnos, 1981, Warlock's Gift, 1982, Khi to Freedom, 1982, Runes of the Lyre, 1982, Golden Dream, 1983, Lords of the Triple Moons, 1983, Exile on Vlahil, 1984, The Saga of Grittel Sundotha, 1985, The World Ends in Hickory Hollow, 1985, Medicine Walk, 1985, Carrots and Miggle, 1986, The Wall, 1987, Makra Choria, 1987, Feud at Sweetwater Creek (as Frank Cannon), 1988, A Place of Silver Silence, 1988; (collaboration with Marylois Dunn) The Absolutely Perfect Horse, 1983; (collaboration with Ron Fortier) Trail of the Seahawks, 1987, Monkey Station, TSR, 1989; (as John Killdeer) Wild Country, The Untamed, Wilderness Rendezvous, Blood Kin, People of the Mesa, 1992, Island in the Lake, 1993, Towers of the Earth, 1994, Passage West, 1994, Far Horizons, 1994, Hunters of the Plains, 1995, (as Frances Hurst) High Mountain Winter, 1996, Riddles and Dreams, 2003, (with Ron Fortier) Witchfire, 2007, elec. edits., 2004-05, 50 out-of-print paperback reprints, 2007. Mem.: Sci. Fiction/Fantasy Writers Am. (chosen author emeritus 2008). Home: 533 CR 486 Chireno TX 75937 Office Phone: 936-362-2913. E-mail: ardathm@netdot.com.

MAYHEW, DAVID RAYMOND, political science professor; b. Putnam, Conn., May 18, 1937; s. Raymond William and Jeanie (Nicholson) M. BA, Amherst Coll., 1958; PhD, Harvard U., 1964. Tchg. fellow Harvard U., 1961-63; from instr. to asst. prof. polit. sci. U. Mass., Amherst, 1963-67; vis. asst. prof. Amherst Coll., 1965-66; faculty Yale U., 1968-77, prof. polit. sci., 1977—, chmn. dept., 1979-82, Alfred Cowles prof. govt., 1982-98, Sterling prof. polit. sci., 1998—. Olin vis. prof. Am. Govt. Nuffield Coll., Oxford (Eng.) U., 2000-01; vis. prof. Govt. Harvard U., 2008. Author: Party Loyalty Among Congressmen, 1966, Congress: The Electoral Connection, 1974 (Washington Monthly ann. polit. book award 1974), Placing Parties in American Politics, 1986, Divided We Govern, 1991 (Richard E. Neustadt prize, 1992), America's Congress, 2000, Electoral Realignments, 2002, Parties and Policies, 2008. Recipient James Madison Career award, 2002, Yale Grad. Student Mentor award, 2002, Samuel J. Eldersveld award, 2004; Woodrow Wilson fellow, 1958-59, vis. fellow Nuffield Coll., Oxford, 1978, Guggenheim fellow, 1978-79, Hoover Nat. fellow, 1978-79, Sherman Fairchild fellow, 1990-91, fellow Ctr. for Advanced Study in Behavioral Scis., 1995-96. Fellow Am. Acad. Arts and Scis.; mem. Am. Polit. Sci. Assn. (nat. council 1976-78, Congl. fellow 1967-68), Am. Philos. Soc., So. Polit. Sci. Assn., New Eng. Polit. Sci. Assn. Home: 100 York St Apt 5C New Haven CT 06511-5611 Office: Yale U Polit Sci Dept Box 208301 New Haven CT 06520-8301 Office Phone: 203-432-5237. Business E-Mail: david.mayhew@yale.edu.

MAYHEW, ERIC GEORGE, medical researcher, educator, consultant; b. London, June 22, 1938; came to U.S., 1964; s. George James and Doris Ivy (Tipping) M.; m. Barbara Doe, Sept. 28, 1966 (div. 1976); 1 child, Miles; m. Karen Caruana, Apr. 1, 1978 (div. 1994); children: Ian, Andrea; m. Ludmila Khatchatrian, June 29, 1995. BS, U. London, 1960, MS, 1963, PhD, 1967, DSc, 1993. Rsch. asst. Chester Beatty Rsch. Inst., London, 1960—64; cancer rsch. scientist Roswell Pk. Meml. Inst., Buffalo, 1964—68, sr. cancer rsch. scientist, 1968—72, assoc. cancer rsch. scientist, 1979—83, dep. dir. exptl. pathology, 1988—93; prin. scientist The Liposome Co., Princeton, NJ, 1993—99, May Pharm Consulting, 2000—. Assoc. rsch. prof. SUNY, Buffalo, 1979-93; ad-hoc mem. NIH study sects., 1982-94; cons. to industry, 2000-. Editor jour. Selective Cancer Therapeutics, 1989-91; contbr. articles to Jour. Nat. Cancer Inst., Cancer Rsch. and many other profl. jours. Grantee NIH, Am. Heart Assn., and pvt. industry, 1972-93. Mem. Am. Assn. Cancer Rsch., N.Y. Acad. Sci. Achievements include development of liposomes for drug delivery and patents for new chemical entities and liposome delivery. Office: May Pharm Consulting 1782 S Seaview Ave Coupeville WA 98239 Home Phone: 360-678-2175.

MAYHEW, KARIN D., health and medical products executive; BA, Fordham U., NY; M, Wesleyan U., Middletown, Conn.; grad. Smith Coll. Mgmt. Program, U. Mich. Advanced Human Resources Exec. Program. Sr. v.p. orgn. devel. So. New Eng. Telecom. Corp.; with Health Net, Inc., Woodland Hills, Calif., 1999—, sr. v.p. orgn. effectiveness. Lectr. Babson Coll. Ctr. Exec. Edn., Wellesley, Mass. Office: Health Net Inc 21650 Oxnard St Woodland Hills CA 91367 Office Phone: 818-676-6000.

MAYHEW, KENNETH EDWIN, JR., retired transportation executive; b. Shelby, NC, Sept. 27, 1934; s. Kenneth Edwin and Evelyn Lee (Dellinger) M.; m. Frances Elaine Craft, Apr. 7, 1957 (dec. 2005); m. Darlene Burgess Randall, Jan. 7, 2006; 1 dau., Catherine Lynn Prince. AB, Duke U., 1956. CPA NC. Sr. auditor Arthur Andersen & Co., Atlanta, 1956-58, 60-63; controller Trendline, Inc., Hickory, NC, 1963-66; with Carolina Freight Corp., Cherryville, 1966-93, treas., 1969-74; v.p. Carolina Freight Carriers Corp., Cherryville, 1971-72, exec. v.p., 1972-85, pres., COO, 1985-89, dir., 1968-93, chmn., pres., CEO, 1989-93; ret., 1993. Pres., dir. Robo Auto Wash Shelby Inc., 1967-73, Robo Auto Wash Cherryville, Inc., 1968-73; dir. Cherryville Nat. Bank. Mem. Bus. Adv. Bd., Fuqua Sch. Bus., Duke U.; bd. dirs., vice-chmn. Gaston Meml. Hosp.; trustee Pfeiffer U. With AUS, 1958-60. Mem. AICPA, Am. Trucking Assn. (dir., v.p.), N.C. Trucking Assn. (dir., chmn.), Gaston County C. of C. (v.p. pub. affairs), Lions Club (pres. Cherryville 1972-73), Phi Beta Kappa, Omicron Delta Kappa, Phi Eta Sigma. Methodist. Home: 507 Spring St Cherryville NC 28021-3540

MAYHEW, MARTIN R., professional sports team executive, retired professional football player; b. Daytona Beach, Fla., Oct. 8, 1965; m. Sabrina Mayhew; children: Sierra, Ryan, Justin. BS in Bus. Mgmt., Fla. State U., Tallahassee, 1988; JD, Georgetown U. Law Ctr., Washington, 2000. Bar: Fla. Corp. trainee First Union Nat. Bank, Charlotte, NC, 1988; cornerback Buffalo Bills, 1988, Washington Redskins, 1989—92, intern, pro pers. dept., 1999; cornerback Tampa Bay Bucaneers, 1993—96; intern, labor ops. and legal depts. NFL; legal asst. Akin, Gump, Strauss, Hauer & Feld; dir. football adminstrn. XFL; sr. dir. football adminstrn., staff counsel Detroit Lions, 2001—03, sr. v.p. football, legal affairs, 2003—04, sr. v.p., asst. gen. mgr., 2004—08, gen. mgr., 2009—. Spokesman United Way, 1995—96. Recipient Chelo Huerta Cmty. Svc. award, 1993; nominee True Value Man of Yr., 1994. Mem.: ABA, Sports Lawyers Assn. Achievements include member of Super Bowl XXVI Championship winning Washington Redskins, 1992. Office: Detroit Lions 222 Republic Dr Allen Park MI 48101*

MAYHUE, RICHARD LEE, dean, minister, writer; b. Takoma Park, Md., Aug. 31, 1944; s. J. Richard Mayhue and Myrtle Lorraine (Hartsell) Lee; m. Lois Elaine Nettleingham, June 18, 1966; children: Lee, Wade. BS, Ohio State U., 1966; MDiv, Grace Theol. Seminary, 1974, ThM, 1977; ThD, Grace Theol. Seminary, Winona Lake, Ind., 1981. Ordained pastor. Asst. pastor Grace Brethren Ch. of Columbus, Ohio, 1975—77; asst. prof. New Testament and Greek, Grace Theol. Seminary, Winona Lake, Ind., 1977—80; assoc. pastor Grace Cmty. Ch., Sun Valley, Calif., 1980—84, 1989—2004; sr. pastor Grace Brethren Ch., Long Beach, Calif., 1984—89; sr. v.p., dean, prof. systematic theology and pastoral mins. The Master's Seminary, Sun Valley, 1989—; sr. v.p., provost The Master's Coll., Santa Clarita, Calif., 2000—08. Bd. dirs. Grace Theol. Sem., 1987-89. Author: The Biblical Pattern for Divine Healing, 1979, 2002, Snatched Before the Storm, 1980, 2002, Divine Healing Today, 1983, How to Interpret the Bible for Yourself, 1986, A Christian's Survival Guide, 1987, Unmasking Satan, 1988, 2d edit., 2001, Spiritual Intimacy, 1990, Spiritual Maturity, 1992, The Healing Promise, 1994, What Would Jesus Say About Your Church?, 1995, 2d edit., 2001, Fight the Good Fight, 1999, 2d edit., 2006, 1 and 2 Thessalonians, 1999, Seeking God, 2000, Practicing Proverbs, 2003; contbr., co-editor: Rediscovering Expository Preaching, 1992, rev. edit., 2005, Rediscovering Pastoral Ministry, 1994, rev. edit., 2005, The Master's Perspective on Pastoral Ministry, 2002, The Master's Perspective on Biblical Prophecy, 2002; contbr., assoc. editor MacArthur Study Bible, 1997, Think Biblically!, 2003; editor MacArthur Bible Commentary, 2005, assoc. editor: Counseling: How to Counsel Biblically, 2005; contbr. articles to profl. jours., chpts. to books. Bd. dirs. Capitol Ministries, 1996-2005, Slavic Gospel Assn, 1993-2002; bd. elders Grace Cmty. Ch., 1989-2004; mem. bd. of ref. Coun. on Bibl. Manhood and Womanhood, 1991—. Recipient Bronze Star with Combat V USN, 1969. Mem. Evang. Theol. Soc., Nat. Fellowship Grace Brethren Ministers (pres. 1988), Far West Region Evang. Theol. Soc. (pres. 1995), Evang. Homiletics Soc. Avocations: n-gauge model railroading, U.S. stamp collecting. Office: The Master's Seminary 13248 Roscoe Blvd Sun Valley CA 91352-3739 Business E-Mail: rmayhue@tms.edu.

MAYLAND, KENNETH THEODORE, economist; b. Miami, Fla., Nov. 17, 1951; s. Herbert and Vera (Bob) M; m. Gail Fern Bassok, Apr. 14, 1984. BS, MIT, Cambridge, Mass., 1973; MS, U. Pa., Phila., 1976, PhD, 1979. Cons. economist Data Resources, Inc., Lexington, Mass., 1973; economist, then chief economist First Pa. Bank, Phila., 1973-89; sr. v.p., chief economist Soc. Nat. Bank, Cleve., 1989-94; sr. v.p., chief fin. economist Key Corp., Cleve., 1994-96, sr. v.p., chief economist, 1996-2000; pres. ClearView Econs., LLC, 2000—. Econs. instr., Chartered Fin. Aanalysts Assn., Phila, 1984—; econ. adv. com. Phila. Econ. Devel. Coalition, 1984-86; chmn. econ. adv. com. Pa. Bankers Assn., Harrisburg, 1982-84; mem. Gov.'s Econ. Adv. Com., Ohio, 1989—. Contbr. semi-monthly periodical Money Markets, 1981-85, quar. periodical Regional Report, 1980-89, EconViewpoint/KeyViewpoint biweekly periodical, 1989-2000, Regional Rev. quar. periodical, 1989-94, ClearView on the Economy, 2000—. Mem. curriculum adv. com. Widener U., 1986-89. Recipient Lawrence R. Klein award, 2007; named 2d Best Forecaster for 2003, USA Today survey panel, Top Forecaster mid-2003 to mid-2004, Bloomberg Mag., 2004, #1 Most Accurate Forecaster, BusinessWeek, 2006. Mem. Am. Bankers Assn. (econ. adv. com. 1990-93), Internat. Econ. Roundtable (vice chmn. 1987-88, chmn. 1988-90), Nat. Assn. Bus. Economists (New Face for the Eighties award 1979), Phila. Coun. Bus. Economists (pres. 1982-84), Cleve. Bus. Economist Club (sec.-treas. 1990-91, v.p. 1991-92, pres. 1992-93). Avocations: fishing, badminton, gardening, camping. Office: 3237 Fox Hollow Dr Cleveland OH 44124-5426 Office Phone: 216-595-9931.

MAYMAN, TODD A., publishing executive, lawyer; BA, Swarthmore Coll.; JD, Boston Univ. Bar: DC 1988. Assoc. Arent, Fox, Kintner, Plotkin & Kahn, Washington, 1988—93; asst. gen. counsel through assoc. gen. counsel & sec. Gannett Co., McLean, Va., 1993—2009, sr. v.p., sec., gen. counsel, 2009—. Office: Gannett Co 7950 Jones Branch Dr Mc Lean VA 22107-0910*

MAYNARD, CHARLES DOUGLAS, radiologist; b. Atlantic City, Sept. 11, 1934; m. Mary Anne Satterwhite; children: Charles D., Deanne, David. BS, Wake Forest U., 1955, MD, 1959. Diplomate Am. Bd. Radiology (trustee 1987-99, sec.-treas., v.p. 1992-94, pres. 1994-96, guest examiner). Intern U.S. Army Hosp., Honolulu, 1959—60; resident N.C. Baptist Hosp., 1963—66; dir. Nuclear Medicine Lab., 1966—77; asst. dean admissions Bowman Gray Sch. Medicine, 1966—71, asso. dean student affairs, 1971—75, prof. radiology, chmn. dept., 1977—2000. Mem. Am. Bd. Med. Specialists; acting dean Wake Forest U. Sch. Medicine, 2001—02. Author: Clinical Nuclear Medicine, 1969; mem. editl. bd.: Yearbook of Diagnostic Radiology, Contemporary Diagnostic Radiology. Mem. Leadership Winston-Salem, Triad Leadership Network; bd. dirs. Downtown Devel. Corp., 1995—2000, Winston-Salem Bus., Inc., 1995—99, Forsyth Tech. CC, 1997—2005, pres., 2004—05; bd. dirs. Va. Tech. Coll. Engring., 2002—06, Wake Forest U. Health Scis., 2003—. Mem.: AMA, Greater Winston-Salem C. of C. (bd. dirs.), Acad. Radiology Rsch. (pres. 1999—2001), Soc. Chairmen Radiology Depts. (past pres.), Assn. Univ. Radiologists, Radiol. Soc. N.Am. Rsch. and Edn. Found. (chmn. bd. 1999), Radiol. Soc. N.Am. (pres. 1999—2000), Am. Coll. Radiology (past bd. chancellors, past chmn. commn. on nuc. medicine), Soc. Nuc. Medicine (past pres.). Office: Wake Forest U Sch Medicine Dept Radiology Medical Center Blvd Winston Salem NC 27157-1088

MAYNARD, HUGH M., lawyer; b. Bethesda, Md., Mar. 29, 1949; BA math., Carleton Coll., 1971; JD, Harvard U., 1975. Bar: Minn. 1975, Maine 1980. Ptnr. Leonard, Street and Deinard P.A., Mpls., shareholder. Former staff mem. Harvard Civil Rights-Civil Liberties Law Review. Mem. ABA (property sect.), Minn. Bar Assn., Hennepin County Bar Assn. (real property sect.), Phi Beta Kappa, Sigma Xi, Pi Mu Epsilon, Sensible Land Use Coalition. Office: Leonard Street & Deinard PA 150 S 5th St Ste 2300 Minneapolis MN 55402-4223 Office Phone: 612-335-1562. Office Fax: 612-335-1657. Business E-Mail: hugh.maynard@leonard.com.

MAYNARD, JAMES HAROLD, chemistry professor; s. Dale Eugene and Barbara Ruth Maynard; m. Sharon Marie Lewis, Nov. 8, 1991; 1 child, Sebastian James Beaureguard. BS in Chemistry, U. Wis., Madison, 2000. Electrician's US Navy, San Diego, 1985—89; faculty asst. U. Wis., 2000, instrnl. specialist, 2001—. Contbr. columns in newspapers. Vol., Madison, Wis., 2006—08. Petty Officer 1st Class USN, 1983—89, San Diego. Decorated Good Conduct medal US Navy; Profl. Devel. grant, UW Profl. Devel. and Recognition Com., 2004. Mem.: Am. Chem. Soc., Alpha Chi Sigma (chpt. advisor 2006—08). Independent. Office: Univ Wis 1101 University Ave Madison WI 53706 Office Fax: 608-265-9858; Home Fax: N/A. Personal E-mail: maynard@uwalumni.com. E-mail: maynard@chem.wisc.edu.

MAYNARD, JOHN RALPH, lawyer; b. Mar. 5, 1942; s. John R. Maynard and Frances Jane (Mitchell) Maynard Kendryk; m. Meridee J. Sagadin, Sept. 11, 1995; children: Bryce James, Pamela Ann. BA, U. Wash., 1964; JD, Calif. Western U., San Diego, 1972; LLM, Harvard U., 1973. Bar: Calif. 1972, Wis. 1973. Assoc. Whyte & Hirschboeck, Milw., 1973-78, Minahan & Peterson, Milw., 1979-91, Quarles & Brady, Milw., 1991-2000, Davis & Kuelthau, Milw., 2000—05, Maynard, McIlnay, Schmitt & Button, Grafton, Wis., 2005—. Bd. dirs. Transitional Living Svcs., Inc., 1999—2003; pres. Milw. Chamber Orch., 2000—02; mem. Wis. Adv. Coun. to U.S. SBA, 1987—89; bd. dirs. Am. Heart Assn., 1979—82, Found. Internal Medicine Exchange, 2004—, Bel Canto Chorus, 2004—. Mem.: ABA, Harvard Club (Wis.). Office: Maynard McIlnay Schmitt & Button 1150 Washington St Grafton WI 53024 Home Phone: 414-840-2818; Office Phone: 262-387-4980. Business E-Mail: jmaynard@runbox.com.

MAYNARD, JOHN ROGERS, language educator; b. Williamsville, NY, Oct. 6, 1941; s. Atherton Rogers and Olive (Fisher) M.; m. Florence Michelson, July 1, 1967 (div. 1980); 1 child, Alex Stevens; m. Ursula Krammer, Oct. 17, 1992 (div. 1995). BA, Harvard U., 1963, PhD, 1970. Asst. prof. Harvard U., Cambridge, Mass., 1969-74, NYU, NYC, 1974-76, assoc. prof., 1976-84, prof. English, 1984—, chmn. English dept., 1983-89. Chmn. Faculty Council NYU, 1983-84; vis. prof. U. Venice, Italy, 1991; co-dir. Biography Seminar, 2004—. Author: Brownings Youth, 1977 (Wilson prize 1977), Charlotte Bronte and Sexuality, 1984, Victorian Discourses on Sexuality and Religion, 1993, Browning Re-Viewed, 1998, Literary Inteution Literacy Interpretation and Readers, 2009; editor: Literature and Sexuality, 1991-2004; series of books on sexuality and lit.; co-editor: (with Lockridge and Stone) Nineteenth Century Lives, 1989, (with Bloom) Shankman's Anne Thackeray Ritchie: Journals and Letters, (with Munich) Victorian Literature and Culture, 1991—, Tennyson: Poetry for Young People, Blake: Poetry for Young People. Organizer Concord Sq. Assn., Boston, 1972—74. NEH grantee, 1972-73; Guggenheim fellow, 1979-80. Mem. IAUPE, MLA, PEN, Browning Inst. (bd. dirs.), Signet Soc., Fly Club, Andiron Club (pres. 1983-84), Brooklyn Heights Assn. Democrat. Avocation: bicycling. Office: NYU Dept of English 5th Fl 19 University Pl New York NY 10003-4556

MAYNARD, KENNETH DOUGLAS, architect; b. Hackensack, NJ, Aug. 16, 1931; s. Douglas Harry and Eva (Whiting) M.; m. Myrna Myrtle James, Feb. 4, 1956; children: Colin, Vivien Noll. Cert. in Architecture, U. Natal, Durban, Republic of South Africa, 1958. Registered arch. 1964. Draftsman Morross & Graff, Johannesburg, Republic of South Africa, 1950-51, Anglo-Am. Corp., Johannesburg, Republic of South Africa, 1951-54, Moir & Llewellyn, Empangeni, Zululand, Republic of South Africa, 1955-57; architect Pearse Aneck-Hahn & Bristol, Johannesburg, 1957-60, Manley & Mayer, Anchorage, 1960-61, FAA, Anchorage, 1961-62, Crittenden Cassetta Wirum & Jacobs, Anchorage, 1962-65; prin. Schultz & Maynard, Anchorage, 1965-68, Kenneth Maynard Assocs., Anchorage, 1968-78; pres. Maynard & Partch, Anchorage, 1978-96; prin. USKH, Inc., Anchorage, 1996—. Active Western Alaska Coun. Boy Scouts. Am., Anchorage, 1965-84; bd. dirs. Salvation Army Adv. Bd., Anchorage, 1981-87, Anchorage Mus. Assn., 1969-86, Anchorage Opera Co., 1983-90; chmn. Mayor's Comprehensive Homeless Program Strategy Group, 1992-94. Fellow: AIA (pres. Alaska chpt. 1969, NW regional rep. for nat. com. on design 1976—89, nat. bd. 1999—2001); mem.: Constrn. Specification Inst. (pres. Cook Inlet chpt. 1993—94). Republican. Avocations: reading, travel. Home: 2237 Forest Park Dr Anchorage AK 99517-1324 Office: USKH 2515 A St Anchorage AK 99503-2776 Business E-Mail: kmaynard@uskh.com.

MAYNARD, KENNETH IRWIN, pharmaceutical executive, medical educator, researcher; b. San Fernando, Trinidad, Jan. 17, 1963; Student, Howard U., 1982; BSc with honors, Univ. Coll., London, 1986, MSc, 1987, PhD, 1991. Cert. design and conduct of clin. trials. Postdoctoral rsch. assistantship Univ. Coll., London, 1991; postdoctoral rsch. fellow Stroke Rsch. Lab. Neurosurg. Svc. Mass. Gen. Hosp., Harvard Med. Sch., Boston, 1991—93, postdoctoral rsch. fellow neurophysiology lab. Neurosurg. Svc., 1993—97; tchg. fellow dept. neurobiology Harvard Med. Sch., Boston, 1992, instr. in surgery, 1995—98, asst. prof., 1998—2001; asst. neuroscientist Mass. Gen. Hosp., 1998—2001; section head, cerebrovascular disorders Aventis Pharms., Inc., 2000—02, prin. sci., 2002—04; project dir. Sanofi-Aventis, Inc., 2005—. Ad hoc reviewer Jour. Vascular Rsch., 1991, Neurosci. Letters, 1995, Vision Rsch., 1996, Neurosurgery, 1998, others; presenter in field; tutor dept. of neurobiology, 1998—2000; asst. prof. surgery, 1998; steering com. Boston Area Neurosci. Group, 1998—2000; ad hoc reviewer Ministry of Health, Internal Grant Agy., Czech Republic, 1998; med. rsch. grant program Jewish Hosp. Found., 2000; cons. neurosurgery Mass. Gen. Hosp., 2001—02; lectr. Harvard U. Med. Sch., 2001—02. Contbr. articles to med. jours. including Neurosci. Letters, articles to med. jours. including Stroke, articles to med. jours. including Exptl. Neurology, articles to med. jours. including Jour. Neurol. Rsch. Mem. parish pastoral coun. St. Joseph's Cath. Ch., Boston, 1992—95, chmn. stewardship commn., 1997; advisor regional com. ctrl. region on stewardship Archdiocese of Boston, 1995—97. Recipient Travel fellowship for minority neuroscientists, Nat. Inst. Neurol. Disease and Stroke, 1995, travel award, FASEB MARC, 1998; scholar, Autumn Sch. Caen France, 1996, Tokyo, 1998. Fellow: Am. Heart Assn. (minority scientist devel. award 1996, nat. affiliate brain/stroke study sect. 1999—, stroke coun. 2002, minority affairs com.); mem.: AAAS, Am. Acad. Neurology, Internat. Soc. Cerebral Blood Flow and Metabolism (Young Scientist Bursary award 1993), Congress of Neurosurg. Surgeons, Am. Assn. Neurosurg. Surgeons (adj. assoc. mem. joint sect. on cerebrovascular surgery 1995), Soc. for Neurosci. (minority neurosci. fellowship program 2000—02, minority edn., tng. and profl. advancement com. 2000—03, membership com. 2002—07, fin. com. 2007—), N.Y. Acad. Sci., Am. Stroke Assn. (affiliate brain rsch. peer rev. group 1999—2003). Roman Catholic. Office: Sanofi Aventis Inc 200 Crossing Blvd BX2-309A Bridgewater NJ 08807 Office Phone: 908-304-6352. Business E-Mail: kenneth.maynard@sanofi-aventis.com.

MAYNARD, NATALIE RYSHNA, pianist, educator; b. Phila., Aug. 21, 1930; d. George Thomas Hook and Helen Agatha Reese; m. Harry Edgar Maynard, Jan. 30, 1960; children: Melanie Dawn, Amie Anne. Degree in piano performance, Juilliard Graduate Sch. Music, NYC, 1952. Concert pianist Columbia Artists Mgmt., tours in U.S. and Europe, 1963-94; rec. artist Contemporary Records and Ambiphon Records, 1957-75; pvt. piano instr., 1985—; project dir. Title III and State Urban Edn. program N.Y.C. schs. Founder, chmn. edn. com. Sta. WNET/13-TV, NYC, 1973—77; pres. Performers Conn., Westport, 1985—91, bd. dirs., 1982—; exec. dir. R. B. Fisher Found. Composer Awards, 1986—96; v.p. ednl. outreach Friends of Music Fairfield County, 1995—99. Apptd. to arts adv. com. Town of Westport, 1998—2000, 2000—09, co-chair town millenium edn. com., 1998; mem. adv. bd. Stamford Symphony Orch., 2004—07; bd. dir. Friends of Channel 13 Nat. Friends Pub. Broadcasting, 1971—82. Recipient Outstanding Women Conn. award, Lt. Gov. Conn., 2003. Mem.: Conn. State Music Tchrs. Assn., Nat. Music Tchrs. Assn., Schubert Club. Office Phone: 203-226-7309. Business E-Mail: nmyn123@aol.com.

MAYNARD, VIRGINIA MADDEN, foundation administrator; b. New London, Conn., Jan. 29, 1924; d. Raymond and Edna Sarah (Madden) Maynard. BS, U. Conn., 1945; postgrad., Am. Inst. Banking, 1964—66, Cornell U., 1975. With Nat. City Bank (now Citibank), NYC, 1954—79, asst. cashier, 1965—69, asst. v.p., 1969-74, v.p. internat. banking group, 1974-76, comptroller's div., 1976-79; v.p. First Women's Bank, NYC, 1979-80; rep. Internat. Fedn. Univ. Women UN, 1982—2003. Trustee fellowships endowment fund AAUW Ednl. Found., Washington, 1977—80, Va. Gildersleeve Internat. Fund Univ. Women, Inc., pres., 1987—93, bd. dirs., 1994—2000, rep. UN, 1997—2008, chair nominating com., 2008—09; bd. dirs. Conf. Nongovtl. Orgns. Found., Inc., 1997—2008, treas., 1999—2008. Mem.: AAUW (fin. chmn. N.Y.C. br. 1976—79, bylaws chmn. 1979—83, adminstr. Meml. Fund 1983—92, bd. dirs. 1992—94, 1996—99, adminstr. Meml. Fund 2000—08, Woman of Achievement 1976). Republican. Congregationalist. Home: 601 E 20th St New York NY 10010-7622

MAYNE, ALFRED R., research scientist; b. Oamaru, South Island, New Zealand, Aug. 14, 1937; s. Alfred and Rhoma Mayne; children: Paul, Tracy. Student, Christchurch Tech. Coll., New Zealand, 1951; PhD (hon.), ABI, 2008, IBC, 2009. Dir. Split Cycle Technology. Lectr. in field, 1990—2003. Recipient Am. medal of Honor, 2007. Mem.: Soc. Automotive Engrs. Am. Australia (assoc.). Achievements include invention of the split cycle engine and related research and development. Home and Office: Diablo Pty Ltd 191 Nerang St Southport 4215 Australia Office Fax: 0755310618.

MAYNE, LUCILLE STRINGER, finance educator; b. Washington, June 6, 1924; d. Henry Edmond and Hattie Benham (Benson) Stringer; children: Pat A., Christine Gail, Barbara Marie. BS, U. Md., College Park, 1946; MBA, Ohio State U., Columbus, 1949; PhD, Northwestern U., Evanston, Ill., 1966. Instr. fin. Utica Coll., 1949-50; lectr. fin. Roosevelt U., 1961-64, Pa. State U., 1965-66, asst. prof., 1966-69, assoc. prof., 1969-70; assoc. prof. banking and fin. Case-Western Res. U., 1971-76, prof., 1976-94, prof. emerita, 1994—, grad. dean Sch. Grad. Studies, 1980-84. Sr. economist, cons. FDIC, 1977-78; cons. Nat. Commn. Electronic Fund Transfer Sys., 1976; rsch. cons. Am. Bankers Assn., 1975, Fed. Res. Bank of Cleve., 1968-70, 73; cons. Pres.'s Commn. Fin. Structure and Regulation, 1971, staff economist, 1970-71; analytical statistician Air Materiel Command, Dayton, Ohio, 1950-52; asst. to promotion mgr. NBC, Washington, 1946-48; expert witness cases involving fin. instns. Assoc. editor: Jour. Money, Credit and Banking, 1980-83, Bus. Econs., 1980-85; contbr. articles to profl. jours. Vol. Cleve. Soc. for Blind, 1979-2004, Benjamin Rose Inst., 1995-2005; mem. policyholders nominating com. Tchrs. Ins. and Annuity Assn./Coll. Retirement Equities Fund, 1982-84, chair com., 1984; bd. dirs. Women's Cmty. Found., 1994-96. Grad. scholar, Ohio State U., 1949, doctoral fellow, Northwestern U., 1963—65. Mem. LWV (bd. dirs. Shaker Heights chpt. 1999--), Midwest Fin. Assn. (pres. 1991-92, bd. dirs. 1975-79, officer 1988-93), Phi Kappa Phi, Beta Gamma Sigma. Episcopalian. Home: 3723 Normandy Rd Cleveland OH 44120-5246 Office: Case Western Res U Weatherhead Sch Mgmt U Circle Cleveland OH 44106-7235

MAYNE, THOM, architect; b. Waterbury, Conn., Jan. 19, 1944; s. Walter and Bernice (Gornall) M.; m. Susan Burnham, Sept. 10, 1964 (div. 1970); 1 child, Richard; m. Blythe Alison Mayne, Aug. 8, 1981; children: Sam, Cooper. BArch, U. So. Calif., 1968; MArch, Harvard U., 1978. Mem. faculty UCLA Sch. Art and Architecture, Santa Monica, Calif., 1972—; bd. dirs. So. Calif. Inst. Architecture, Santa Monica, Calif., 1983—; architect Morphosis, Santa Monica, Calif. Adj. prof. UCLA, 1993; mem. vis. faculty Calif. State Coll., Pomona, 1971, Miami U., Ohio, 1982, Washington U., St. Louis, 1984, U. Tex., Austin, 1984, U. Pa., 1985, Columbia U., NYC, 1986, Harvard U., 1988, Clemson U., 1991, Yale U., 1991, UCLA, 1986, 92, U. Ill., Urbana-Champaign, 1992-93, Tech. U., Vienna, Austria, 1993, Berlage Inst., Amsterdam, 1993, Hochschule für Andgewandt Kunst, Vienna, 1991, 93; lectr. in field; adjudicator numerous awards. Archtl. one-man exhbns. include 2 AES Gallery, San Francisco, 1988, Cheney Cowles Mus., Spokane, Wash., 1989, Walker Arts Ctr., Mpls., 1989, Gallery of Architecture, LA, 1989, Contemporary Arts Ctr., Cin., 1989, San Francisco Mus. Modern Art, 1990, Graham Found., Chgo., 1990, Aedes Galerie and Architecture Forum, Berlin, 1990, Fenster Architekturgalerie, Frankfurt, Germany, 1990, Gallery MA, Toyko, 1990, Laguna (Calif.) Art Mus., 1991, G201 Gallery, Ohio, 1991, 1-Space Gallery, Chgo., 1992, Sadock & Uzzan Galerie, Paris, 1992, Diane Farris Gallery, 1993; group exhbns. include Umwelt Galerie, Stuttgart, Germany, 1978, The Archtl. Gallery, Venice, Calif., 1979, La Jolla (Calif.) Mus. of Contemporary Art, 1982, Inst. Contemporary Arts, London, 1983, Archtl. Assn., London, 1983, NAD, NYC, 1983, 88, Mus. Modern Art, San Francisco, 1983, Calif. Mus. Sci. and Industry, 1984, G.A. Gallery, Tokyo, 1985, 87, 90, Max Protech Gallery, NYC, 1985, 86, I.D.C., NYC, 1986, Axis Gallery, Tokyo, Milan, Paris, 1988, Pacific Design Ctr., LA, 1988, Australia Ctr. for Contemporary Arts, Victoria, 1988, Cooper-Hewitt Mus., NYC, 1988, Aedes Galerie für Architektur und Raum, Berlin, 1988, Kirsten Kiser Gallery, 1988, 89, Visual Arts Ontario, Toronto, 1988, Gallery Functional Art, Santa Monica, Calif., 1989, Deutsches Architektur Mus., Frankfurt, 1989, USIA, Moscow, 1989-90, Lameier Sculpture Park, St. Louis, 1989, Gwenda Jay Gallery, Chgo., 1990, Sadock & Uzzan Galerie, 1991, Bannatyne Gallery, Santa Monica, 1991, ROM Galleri for Arkitektur, Oslo, 1992, 65 Thompson Street Gallery, NYC, 1992; archtl. projects include Sequoyah Edn. and Rsch. Ctr., Santa Monica, 1977 (Progressive Architecture award 1974), Flores Residence, 1979 (Progressive Architecture award 1980), Sedlak Residence, 1980 (AIA award 1981), Western Melrose Office Bldg, 1981 (Progressive Architecture award 1982), Hermosa Beach Ctrl. Bus. Dist. (Progressive Architecture award 1984), 72 Market Street Restaurant, 1983 (AIA award 1985, CCAIA award 1986), Bergren Residence, 1984 (AIA award 1985, CCAIA award 1986, Nat. AIA award 1986), Cedar Sinai Comprehensive Cancer Ctr., L.A., 1988 (Progressive Architecture award 1987, AIA award 1988, CCAIA award 1989), Arts Park Performing Pavilion, 1988, (Progressive Architecture award 1989), Leon Max Showroom, LA, 1988 (CCAIA award 1990, Archtl. Record Interior award 1990), Club Post Nulear, Laguna Beach, Calif., 1988, Berlin Wall Competition, 1988, Expo '90 Folly, Osaka, Japan, 1989, The Emery Ctr. Performing Arts, 1989, Temple U. CCC, Phila., 1989, Politix, 1990 (AIA award 1990), Salick Health Care Corp. Hdqs., 1990 (AIA award 1992, CCAIA award 1993), Visual Performing Arts Sch. at Thomas More Coll., Crestview, NY, 1990, MTV Studios, LA, 1990, Higashi Azabu Tower, Tokyo, 1991, Yuzen Vintage Car Mus., LA, 1991 (AIA award 1993), Disney Inst. and Town Ctr. Competition, Orlando, Fla., 1991, Cranbrook Acad. Gatehouse Competition (Pilkington Planar prize 1993), Spreebogen Master Plan, Berlin, 1993, Check Point Charlie Office Bldg., Berlin, 1993; contbr. articles to profl. jours. Rome Prize fellow Am. Acad. Rome, 1987; recipient Architecture award Am. Acad. Arts and Letters, 1992, Pritzker Architecture prize Hyatt Found., 2005. Fellow Am. Acad. Arts and Sciences; mem. AIA, Am. Acad. Design. Democrat. Avocations: skiing, travel. Office: Morphosis Architecture 2041 Colorado Ave Santa Monica CA 90404-3415 Office Phone: 310-570-0123. Business E-Mail: t.mayne@morphosis.net.

MAYO, CALVIN JAY, engineering executive; b. Washington, NC, Aug. 10, 1960; s. Jesse Jay Mayo and Doris Elizabeth Davenport; m. Vivian Lee Dorsey, Dec. 14, 1980; 1 child, Amanda Lee. AAS, Pitt CC, Greenville, NC, 1999. Tool and die maker Mestek Inc., Farmville, NC, 1980—2000; chair machining tech. Pitt CC, Winterville, NC, 2000—. Mem.: Exptl. Aircraft Assn. Office: Pitt CC 1986 Pitt Tech Rd Winterville NC 28590 Office Fax: 252-321-4409. E-mail: cmayo@email.pittcc.edu.

MAYO, CLYDE CALVIN, psychologist, educator; b. Robstown, Tex., Feb. 2, 1940; s. Clyde Culberson and Velma (Oxford) Mayo; m. Jeanne Lynn McCain, Aug. 24, 1963; children: Brady Scott, Amber Camille. BA, Rice U., Houston, 1961; BS, U. Houston, 1964, PhD, 1972; MS, Trinity U., 1966. Lic. psychologist Tex., La. Mgmt. engr. LWFW, Inc., Houston, 1966-72, sr. cons., 1972-78, prin., 1978-81; ptnr. Mayo, Thompson, Bigby, Houston, 1981-83; founder Mgmt. and Pers. Systems, Houston, 1983—. Counselor Interface Counseling Ctr., Houston, 1976—79; dir. Mental Health HMO Group, 1985—87; instr. St. Thomas U., Houston, 1979—90, U. Houston Downtown Sch., 1972, 2002—06, U. Houston, Clear Lake, 1983—88, U. Houston-Ctrl. Campus, 1984—; dir. mgmt. devel. insts. U. Houston Woodlands and West Houston, 1986—91; adj. prof. U. Houston, 1991—. Author: LWFW Annual Survey of Manufacturers, 1966—81, Bi/Polar Inventory of Strengths, 1978. Coach, mgr. Meyerland Little League, 1974—78, So. Belles Softball, 1979—80, S.W. Colt Baseball, 1982—83, Friends of Fondren Libr. Rice U., 1988—; charter mem. Holocaust Mus. Mem.: APA, Rice U. Hist. Soc., Houston Area Indsl. Orgnl. Psychologists (bd. dirs. 1989—92), Am. Psychol. Soc., Tex. Psychol. Assn., Houston Psychol. Assn. (membership dir. 1978, sec. 1984), Tex. Indsl. Orgnl. Psychologists (founder, bd. dirs. 1995—, pres. 1999—2002), Soc. Indsl. Orgn. Psychologists, Found. Contemporary Theology (bd. dirs. 2005—, chair youth recruitment com. 2006—), Meyerland Club (bd. dirs. 1988—92, pres. 1991), Forum Club. Home: 8723 Ferris Dr Houston TX 77096-1409 Office: Mgmt and Personnel Systems 4545 Bissonnet St Bellaire TX 77401-3121 Office Phone: 713-667-9251. Personal E-mail: mpsmayo@aol.com.

MAYO, CORA LOUISE, educator; b. Chgo., Oct. 31, 1925; d. Charles Amos and Mary (Elder) Scott; m. Marion Wesley Mayo, July 21, 1948; children: Lynne, Charles (dec.), Janice (dec.), Jo Ann, Thomas. BS, U. Ill.-Urbana, 1949, advanced degree in adminstrn. and supervision, 1973; MA, U. Chgo., 1961; PhD, Heed U., Fla., 1981. Program facilitator Chgo. Bd. Edn., 1955—; owner/pres. From the Black Experience, Inc., Chgo., 1979—; dir. pub. relations Afro-Am. Pub. Co., Chgo., 1972-73; ednl. cons. Ednl. Leadership Inst., Chgo., 1976-78; cmty. prof. Govs. State U., Park Forest, Ill., 1975—83. Author: Developmental Skills Activities Guide, 1982; columnist Teaching Black Positively; editor Human Relations Digest; author/pub.: (early childhood learning kit) Mwenzi Compañeros, 1982. Bd. dirs. Woodson Delany Ednl. Fund, Chgo., 1975—77, House of the Black Madonna, Chgo., 1978—80; cons. Head Start, St. Stephen's Ch., Chgo., 1982-83; organizer Women for Washington, 1982-83, Women for Jackson, 1984; vol. instr. parenting House of the Black Madonna; proposals cons. Du Sable Mus. Afro-Am. History, Chgo. Recipient Leadership award Boy Scouts Am., 1971; named Outstanding Educator of Yr., Woodson-Delany Ednl. Fund, 1976, Sr. Citizen of Yr, Chgo. Dist., 1994; others. Mem. Assn. for Study of Ancient Classical African Civilizations (bd., elder), Nat. Assn. Media Women (pres., fin. sec. 1983—, sec. chpt. 1982—, v.p. 1973), Nat. Hook Up of Black Women, Women in Comm., Friends of Amistad (bd. dirs.), Alpha Gamma Pi (v.p., corres. sec.), Delta Sigma Theta, Phi Delta Kappa. Democrat. Congregationalist. Club: Debonnettes (pres. 1984) (Chgo.). Home: 1618 E 85th Pl Chicago IL 60617-2235 Fax: 773-374-6749.

MAYO, DANA WALKER, chemistry professor; b. Bethlehem, Pa., July 20, 1928; s. Dana Harrat Nickerson and Ethel Marie (Chapman) M.; m. Odile Jeanne d'Arc Mailhiot, Jan. 12, 1962; children: Dana Lawrence, Chapman Scott, Sara Walker. BS, MIT, 1952; PhD, Ind. U., 1959. Asst. prof. chemistry Bowdoin Coll., Brunswick, Maine, 1962-65, assoc. prof. chemistry, 1965-68, prof. chemistry, 1969-70, Charles Weston Pickard prof. chemistry, 1970-91, Charles Weston Pickard rsch. prof. chemistry, 1991—2007, Charles Weston Pickard prof. chemistry emeritus, 2007—. Pres. Microscale Organic Lab. Co., New Castle., N.H., 1985-2007. Author: Microscale Organic Laboratory, 1986, 2d edit., 1989, 3d. edit., 1994, 4th edit., 2000, Microscale Techniques for the Organic Laboratory, 1991, 2d edit., 2001, Course Notes on the Interpretation of Infrared and Raman Spectra, 2004; patentee microscale spinning band distillation column. Capt. USAF, 1956-61. Fellow MIT, 1959-62; recipient Charles A. Dana Found. award, N.Y.C., 1986, John A. Timm award New Eng. Assn. Chemistry Tchrs., 1987, Catalyst nat. award Chem. Mfr. Assn., Washington, 1989. Fellow AAAS, mem. Nat. Inst. Chemists (cert.), Am. Chem. Soc. (health and safety award 1987, James Flack Norris award New Eng. sect. 1988, chair Maine sect. 1971-72), Soc. Applied Spectroscopy, Coblentz Soc. (bd. dirs. 1977-79). Avocations: book collecting, genealogy, forest management, swimming. Personal E-mail: dmayo@bowdoin.edu.

MAYO, GEORGE WASHINGTON, JR., lawyer; b. Waycross, Ga., Dec. 23, 1946; s. George Washington and Perrie R. (Ling) M.; m. Katherine Louise Boland, Nov. 15, 1977; children: Regan L.B., Taylor L.B. BA, Emory U., 1967; JD, U. Va., 1973. Bar: Va. 1973, DC 1974. Assoc. Hogan & Hartson, Washington, 1973—80, ptnr., 1980—, mng. ptnr.-ops. Contbr. articles. Bd. dirs. Vietnam Vets Meml. Fund, Inc., 1978—, Earth Conservation Corps, 1990—; bd. dirs. coll. coun. advisors Emory U., 1994—; bd. dirs. Deafness Rsch. Found., 1997—2001. 1st lt. US Army, 1969—71, Vietnam. Mem.: ABA, DC Bar Assn., Congl. Country Club (Washington), City Club (Washington), Met. Club (Washington), Order of the Coif. Democrat. Methodist. Home: 26 Holly Leaf Ct Bethesda MD 20817-2652 Office: Hogan & Hartson 555 13th St NW Ste 800E Washington DC 20004-1161 Office Phone: 202-637-5679. Office Fax: 202-637-5910. Business E-Mail: gwmayo@hhlaw.com.

MAYO, JEROD, professional football player; b. Feb. 23, 1986; Student in sports mgmt., U. Tenn., 2004—08. Linebacker New Eng. Patriots, 2008—. Named First Time All-SEC, 2007, Defensive Rookie of Yr., AP, 2008. Office: New Eng Patriots One Patriot Pl Foxboro MA 02035*

MAYO, JOHN ARTHUR, microbiologist, researcher, educator; b. Mpls., Feb. 7, 1941; s. Gerald Snow and Mary-Louise Mayo; m. Sylvia Darlene Breland, Feb. 26, 1982; children: Jennifer Snow, Mary Harriet. BA, U. Minn., 1963, MS, 1967; PhD, U. N.Mex., 1971. Rsch. assoc. U. Minn., Mpls., 1970—71; asst. prof. U. New Orleans, 1971—76; rsch. assoc. LSU Health Sciences Ctr., New Orleans, 1976—77, asst. prof., 1977—81, assoc. prof., 1981—94, prof., 1994—99, clin. prof., 1994—99, prof. emeritus, 1999—; rsch. scientist U. Ga., Athens, 2000—06. Cons. Internat. Com. Taxonomy Viruses, 1978—87, Am. Assn. Dental Schools, 1991, Am. Dental Assn./Joint Commn. Nat. Dental Examinations, 1991—96, NIH, 1989—98, EPA, 2002—03; mem., editl. bd. The Open Dental Jour., 2007—; vis. scientist Pub. Health Lab. Svc., Salisbury, England, 1983—84, Inst. Dental Rsch., Sydney, 1993—94; adj. prof. La. State U., Baton Rouge, 1996—2000, U. Ga., Athens, Ga., 2007—. Elder Lakeview Presbyn. Ch., New Orleans, Ctrl. Presbyn. Ch., Athens, Ga. Grantee, The Wellcome Trust, 1981; fellow, NIH, 1968—70, Fogarty Internat. Ctr., 1983—84. Mem.: Orgn. Safety and Asepsis Procedures, Soc. Gen. Microbiology, Internat. Assn. Dental Rsch., Am. Soc. Microbiology, Sigma Xi. Achievements include patents for a multi-component safe biocidal complex. Office: U Ga Dept Biochemistry Athens GA 30602-7229 Business E-Mail: jmayo@uga.edu.

MAYO, JOHN W., finance educator; BA in Econs., Hendrix Coll.; MA in Econs., PhD in Econs., Washington U., St. Louis. Chief economist US Senate Small Bus. Com.; mem. faculty Washington U., U. Tenn., Va. Tech.; prof. McDonough Sch. Bus., Georgetown U., 1997—, sr. assoc. dean, 1999—2001, acting dean, 2002—04. Adv., cons. pub. and pvt. agys. including U.S. Dept. Justice, Fed. Trade Commn., Tenn. Valley Authority, U.S. Dept. Energy, Oak Ridge Nat. Lab.; former chief economist U.S. Senate Small Bus. Com. Co-author (with David L. Kaserman): Government and Business: The Economics of Antitrust and Regulation, 1995; contbr. numerous articles to profl. jours. Zaeslin Fellowship in law and econs., U. Basel, Switzerland. Mem.: Antitrust Law and Economics Assn., We. Econ. Assn., So. Econ. Assn., Am. Econ. Assn. Office: Georgetown U McDonough Sch Bus 37th and O Sts NW Washington DC 20057 Office Phone: 202-687-6972. Business E-Mail: mayoj@georgetown.edu.

MAYO, LOUIS ALLEN, policy management counseling company executive; b. Durham, NC, Nov. 27, 1928; s. Louis Allen and Amy Earl (Overton) M.; m. Emma Jean Minshew, Oct. 31, 1953 (div.); children: Louis Allen III, Robert Lawrence, Carolyn Jean; m. Myrna Ann Smith, Feb. 16, 1980 (div.). Student, Calif. State Poly. Coll., 1948—50; BA in Criminology, Calif. State Coll., Fresno, 1952; MA in Pub. Adminstrn., Am. U., 1960, PhD in Pub. Adminstrn., 1983; postgrad., U. So. Calif., 1960—62. Spl. agt. U.S. Secret Svc., Treasury Dept., LA, 1956-58, 60-63, White House, Washington, 1958-60, 63-66; program mgr. law enforcement Office Law Enforcement Assistance, Justice Dept., 1967-68; acting chief Rsch. Ctr., rsch. program mgr. Nat. Inst. Law Enforcement and Criminal Justice, 1968-74; alternate assoc. mem. Fed. Coun. on Sci. and Tech., White House, 1973-74; dir. tng. and testing divsn. Nat. Inst. Justice, 1975—87; pres. Mayo, Mayo & Assocs., Alexandria, Va., 1987—. Lectr. criminology Armed Forces Inst. Tech., 1954-55; professorial lectr. Am. U., 1974-82; adj. prof. August Vollmer U., 1990-95. 2d lt. to 1st lt. USAF, 1952-56. Mem. Police Assn. Coll. Edn. (exec. dir., founder), Internat. Assn. Chiefs of Police, ASPA (nat. chmn. sect. on criminal justice adminstrn. 1975-76), Acad. Criminal Justice Scis., Police Exec. Rsch. Forum, Soc. Police Futurists Internat., Pi Sigma Alpha. Methodist. Home: 63 Lake Forest Dr Mineral VA 23117 Home Phone: 540-894-8781; Office Phone: 540-894-8781. Personal E-mail: loumayo@police-association.org, louisamayo@hotmail.com.

MAYO, NED HENDERSON, retired physics professor; b. Pitts., Feb. 24, 1936; s. Robert S. Mayo and Ruth A. Henderson; m. Janet Marie Smith; children: John Henderson, Jennifer Lynn Burrough, Cynthia Marie Lindsay. BS in Physics, Ga. Tech., Atlanta, 1958; MS in Physics, Naval Postgrad. Sch., Monterey, Calif., 1969; Grad. with Distinction, Naval War Coll., Newport, RI, 1977; Grad., Def. Sys. Mgmt. Coll., Fort Belvoir, Va., 1986. Cert. instrument rated comml. pilot FAA, 1996, physics prof. Pensacola Jr. Coll., 1998. Naval officer US Navy, Norfolk, Va., 1958—60, capt., 1965—88, program mgr. Washington, 1986—88; rsch. physicist Armstrong World Industries, Lancaster, Pa., 1960—64. Commdg. officer USS Glover, Frigate, Norfolk, 1975—77. Contbr. scientific papers. Lay mem. Fla. Bar Grievance Com., Pensacola, Pa. Decorated Legion of Merit awards US Navy. Mem.: Aircraft Owners and Pilots Ass'n. Conservative. Anglican. Achievements include patents for automatic freeness tester. Avocations: flying, sailing, skiing. Office: Pensacola Junior Coll 1000 College Blvd Pensacola FL 32500 Business E-Mail: nmayo@pjc.edu.

MAYO, PAULA, museum director; BFA, Hunter; BA, Carnegie Mellon; MBA, Columbia. Dir. ops. South Street Seaport Mus., NYC, dir. mus. programs, v.p. mus. programs and devel., acting exec. dir., 2004, exec. dir. Office: South Street Seaport Mus 12 Fulton St New York NY 10038-2106 Office Phone: 212-748-8681. Office Fax: 212-748-8610. Business E-Mail: pmayo@southstseaport.org.

MAYO, ROBERT N., computer science researcher; b. Washington, Aug. 23, 1959; s. Robert P. and Marian A. Mayo. BS in Computer Sci., Washington U., St. Louis, 1981; MS in Computer Sci., U. Calif., Berkeley, 1983, PhD of Computer Sci., 1987. Asst. prof. U. Wis., Madison, 1988; staff Digital Equipment Corp./Compaq Computer/Hewlett Packard, Palo Alto, Calif., 1989—2006; cons., 2007—. Mem. IEEE, Assn. Computer Machinery. Home: 2800 Elliott Ave Apt 624 Seattle WA 98121

MAYO, ROBERT RAYMOND (BOB MAYO), university librarian; AA, Acad. Aeronautics; BA, SUNY, Plattsburgh; MLS, SUNY, Geneseo. Worked with sys. test, cost engring., and market devel. IBM Corp.; adminstrv. libr. Rensselaer Poly. Inst., Troy, NY, 2001—06, acting dir. rsch. libraries, 2006—. Office: Research Libraries Rensselaer Poly Inst 110 8th St Troy NY 12180 Office Phone: 518-276-8300. Office Fax: 518-276-2044. Business E-Mail: mayor@rpi.edu.

MAYOPOULOS, TIMOTHY J., lawyer, mortgage company executive; b. Reading, Pa., Mar. 7, 1959; s. Harry B. and Eleanor Ida (Raifsnider) M.; m. Amy F. Lefkof, Apr. 28, 1990; 1 child, Philip Alexander. AB with distinction, Cornell U., 1980; JD cum laude, NYU, 1984. Bar: NY 1985, US Dist. Ct. (so. and ea. dists. NY) 1987, US Ct. Appeals (2nd cir.) 1993, Supreme Ct., 1993, US Dist. Ct. (ea. and we. dists. Ark.) 1994, US Ct. Appeals (8th cir.), 1995. Law clk. to Hon. William C. Conner US Dist. Ct. (so. dist. NY), NYC, 1984-86; assoc. Davis, Polk & Wardwell, NYC, 1986—94; assoc. ind. counsel Office Ind. Couns. Kenneth Starr, 1994—96; assoc. gen. counsel Donaldson,

Lufkin & Jenrette, 1996; mng. dir., sr. dep. gen. counsel, Americas Credit Suisse First Boston; mng. dir., gen. counsel, corp. investment bank, Americas Deutsche Bank AG, 2002—04; exec. v.p., gen. counsel Bank of America Corp., Charlotte, NC, 2004—08; exec. v.p., gen. counsel, corp. sec. Fannie Mae, Washington, 2009—. Mem. Fed. Bar Coun., Assn. of Bar of City of NY, NY State Bar Assn., Securities Industry Assn., Order of the Coif. Office: Fannie Mae 3900 Wisconsin Ave NW Washington DC 20016-2892*

MAYORA, EDUARDO A., lawyer, educator, author; b. Guatemala, Apr. 20, 1957; s. Eduardo Alfredo Mayora-Dawe and Adelaida (Alvarado) De Mayora; m. Alicia Bascunana, June 18, 1983; children: Javier Eduardo, Santiago, Jose Andres, Sebastian. JD, U. Rafael Landivar, Guatemala, 1980; LLM, Georgetown U., U.S.A., 1982; Diploma (2) in Principles Econ. Sci., U. Francisco Marroquin, Guatemala, 1991, LLD, 1997; D in Pluralist, Pub. and Pvt. Law, M in Pluralist, Pub. and Pvt. Law, U. Autonoma Barcelona, 2004. Bar: Guatemala, 1980; cert. notary. Assoc. Mayora & Mayora, Guatemala, 1980-81, ptnr., 1982—, mem. tax adminstrn. bd., 1998-2000; prof. bus. law and principles of law U. Francisco Marroquin, Guatemala, 1984-87, prof. bus. law and principles of law Sch. of Econs., 1986-88, prof. constitutional law, dean Sch. of Law, 1989-2000, prof. principles of pvt. and pub. law, 1993; bd. dirs. Financiera de Inversion, S.A., Guatemala, 1988-96. Alt. dir. Seguros Alianza S.A., Guatemala, 1988-94; trustee U. Francisco Marroquin, 1989—; vis. prof. Pontificia U. Catolica, Porto Alegre, Brazil, 1994, Montpellier U. Sch. Law, France, 1995. Co-author: El Desafio Neoliberal, 1992; author: Teoría Constitucional para una sociedad libre Fundación República para una nueva generación, 1997, El Imperio Del Derecho Y El Contencioso Administrativo En El Derecho Guatemalteco Comparado, 2005; (essay) El Drama De La Arena Movedisa, 1993 (Charles Stillman award 1993); contbr. to profl. jours. Mem. Guatemala Bar Assn. (author articles Bar Law Jour. 1990—m v.p. ethics bd. 1985-86), Assn. De Amigos Del Pais, Fundacion Para La Cultura (v.p. 1994), Inst. Guatemalteco De Derecho Notarial, Phi Delta Phi, Guatemala Country Club. Roman Catholic. Avocations: reading, sailing, golf. Office: Mayora & Mayora15 Calle 1-04 Plz Centrica 3er Nivel #301 Zona 10 Guatemala City Guatemala also: PO Box 661447 Miami FL 33266-1447 Home Phone: 502-369-7979; Office Phone: 502-223-6868. Business E-Mail: emayora@mayora-mayora.com.

MAYORKAS, ALEJANDRO N., federal agency administrator, lawyer; b. Havana, Cuba, 1959; BA in History, U. Calif., Berkeley, 1981; JD, Loyola U., 1985. Bar: Calif. With Patterson, Belknap, Webb & Tyler, LA, 1986-89; asst. US atty. US Dept. Justice, 1989-99, chief gen. crimes sect., 1996-98, US atty. (ctrl. dist.) Calif., 1999—2001; ptnr. O'Melveny & Myers LLP, L.A., 2001—09; dir. US Citizenship & Immigration Services (USCIS) US Dept. Homeland Security, Washington, 2009—. Tchr. trial advocacy Loyola Law Sch., 1997—98. Bd. chmn. Bet Tzedek Legal Services; bd. dirs. United Friends of Children. Named one of The 50 Most Influential Minority Lawyers in America, The Nat. Law Jour., 2008. Office: US Citizenship & Immigration Services (USCIS) US Dept Homeland Security 20 Massachusetts Ave NW Washington DC 20529 Office Phone: 213-430-6363. Business E-Mail: amayorkas@omm.com.*

MAYOR ZARAGOZA, FEDERICO, biochemistry educator; b. Barcelona, Jan. 27, 1934; s. Federico Mayor and Juana Zaragoza; m. Maria Angeles Menéndez, 1956; 3 children. B in Pharmacy, U. Madrid, 1956; PhD in Pharmacy, 1958, doctorates (hon.). Prof. biochemistry, Faculty Pharmacy Granada (Spain) U., 1963-73, rector, 1968-72; prof. biochemistry, Faculty Sci. Autonomous U., Madrid, 1973, dir. Molecular Biology Ctr., Higher Council for Sci. Rsch., 1974-78; under-sec. Ministry for Edn. and Sci. Govt. of Spain, 1974—75; chmn. adv. com. sci. and tech. rsch. Prime Min.'s Office, Madrid, 1977-78; mem. Cortes for Granada, 1977-78; dep. dir.-gen. UNESCO, 1978-81; minister for edn. and sci. Govt. of Spain, 1981-82; spl. adviser to dir. gen. UNESCO, 1983-84; Spanish mem. European Parliament, Strasbourg, France, 1987; dir. gen. UNESCO, 1987-99; founder, chmn. Found. for a Culture of Peace, 2000—; chmn. European Rsch. Coun. Expert Group, 2002—03. Vis. prof. Oxford (Eng.) U., 1966-67. Author: Mañana siempre es tarde, 1987, La Nueva Página, 1994, La Mémoire de l'Avenir, 1994, Un mundo nuevo, 2000, Los Nudos Gordianos, 2000, (poetry) Patterns, 1994, Terral, 1999; contbr. sci. articles to profl. jours. Recipient decorations various countries. Mem. AAAS, Am. Chem. Soc., European Acad. of Arts, Scis. and Lit. (founding), Royal Soc. Chemistry (U.K.), Royal Acad. Fine Arts San Fernando (Spain), Internat. Brain Rsch. Orgn., Internat. Cell. Rsch. Orgn., World Acad. Art and Sci., Spanish Soc. Biochemistry (chmn. 1970-74), Spanish Royal Acad. Pharmacy, Spanish Royal Acad. of Medicine, French Acad. Pharmacy (corr.), Biochem. Soc. (U.K.), Argentinian Acad. Pharmacy and Biochemistry, Academia Europea, Chinese Acad. Scis., Russian Acad. Sci., Am. Acad. Microbiology, Issyk-Kul Forum (founding), Club of Rome, Ateneo Veneto. Avocation: tennis. Office: Fundacion Cultura De Paz c/Velazquez 14-3 28001 Madrid Spain E-mail: fmayor@fundculturadepaz.org.

MAYPOLE, JOHN FLOYD, real estate company executive; b. Chgo., May 17, 1939; s. John James and Althea Floyd M.; m. Anne White, 1961; children: Cynthia, John, Kimberly. BA in Econs, Yale U., 1961. With Arthur Andersen & Co., 1961-62, 65-66; mgr. corp. acctg. Interpace Corp., 1966, asst. treas., 1967-68, treas., 1968-70, treas., controller, 1970-73, v.p. fin., 1973-77, sr. v.p., 1977-80, exec. v.p., 1980-81, pres., 1981-83; pres., chief operating officer Clevepak Corp., 1983—; mng. ptnr. Peach State Real Estate Holding Co., Toccoa, Ga., 1984—. Bd. dirs. Knoll, Inc., Mass. Mut. Fin. Group, Nat. Captioning Inst., Inc. Bd. adjustment Borough of Mountain Lakes, N.J., 1971-81, chmn., 1980-81. Served with USMC, 1962-65. Mem. Yale Club, Ivy League Club (Sarasota), Rockaway River Country Club, Laurel Oak Country Club. Republican. Office: PO Box 1223 Toccoa GA 30577-1421

MAYR, NINA A., medical educator; married. MD, Ludwig Maximilians U. Munich, Germany, 1978—85. Chair, dept. radiation medicine Ohio State U., Columbus, Ohio, 2004—08; prof. Radiation Medicine, Ohio State U., Columbus, Ohio, 2008—. Dir. vice chair dept. radiology U.Okla., 2001—04. Contbr. scientific papers to profl. jours. Bd. examiner Am. Bd. Radiology; dir. Ohio State U., 2005—06. Recipient Merit award, Radiol. Soc. North Am., 1997, 2002; Young Oncologist Travel grant, Am. Radium Soc., 1990, Seed grant, RSNA Rsch. & Edn. Fund, 1995—96. Mem.: AAAS, Am. Assn. Women Radiology, Am. Coll. Physician Execs., Am. Brachytherapy Soc., Am. Soc. Clin. Oncology, Radiol. Soc. North Am., Am. Soc. Therapeutic Radiology and Oncolgy (mem. 2007). Achievements include research in cervical cancer. Home and Office: Ohio State Univ 300 W 10th Ave Columbus OH 43210

MAYR-HARTING, THOMAS, ambassador; b. 1954; married; 3 children. Degree in law, U. Vienna, 1977; student in European law, Coll. Europe, Bruges, Belgium, 1977—78; diploma, The Hague Acad. Internat. Law, 1978. Joined diplomatic svc. Ministry Fgn. Affairs, Austria, 1979, with the Austrian mission to the European Communities Brussels, 1982—86, with Austrian Embassy Moscow, 1986—90, with, pvt. office the Austrian fgn. min., 1991—95, dep. polit. dir., dir. security policy and policy planning, 1995—99, Austrian amb. to Belgium, head Austrian del. to NATO Brussels, 1999—2003, spl. rep., the We. Balkans, 2002—04, dir. gen. polit. affairs, 2003—08, amb., perm. rep. to the UN NYC, 2009—. Former chmn. supr. bd. Austrian Development Agency. Office: Perm Mission Austria to the UN 600 Third Ave 31st Fl New York NY 10016 Office Phone: 917-542-8400. Business E-Mail: austria@un.int.*

MAYRO, KARL R., realtor; b. Drexel Hill, Pa., Apr. 13, 1966; s. Allan Dale and Patricia Mayro. BA in Econs., St. Joseph's U., 1988. Realtor Prudential Fox & Roach, Newtown Square, Pa., 1988—. Bd. mgrs. The Episcopal Acad., Merion, Pa., 2002—. Mem.: Suburban West Realtors Assn., Pa. Assn. Realtors, Nat. Assn. Realtors, World Affairs Coun. Phila., Phila. Mus. Art, Pa. Hort. Soc. Avocations: gardening, classic Cadillacs, golf, photography.

MAYRON, LEWIS WALTER, clinical ecology consultant; b. Chgo., Sept. 20, 1932; s. Max and Florence Minette (Brody) M.; m. Sondra Mayron; children: Leslie Hope Mayron Coff, Eric Brian. BS in Chemistry, Roosevelt U., 1954; MS in Biol. Chemistry, U. Ill., 1955, PhD in Biol. Chemistry, 1959. Rsch. assoc. dept. biochemistry and nutrition U. So. Calif., LA, 1959-61; asst. biochemist dept. biochemistry Presbyn.-St. Luke's Hosp., Chgo., 1961-62; instr. dept. biol. chemistry U. Ill., Chgo., 1961-62; biochemistry group leader Tardanbek Labs., Chgo., 1962-63; sr. devel. chemist Abbott Labs., Chgo., 1963-64; asst. attending physician, mem. spl. staff Michael Reese Hosp. and Med. Ctr., Chgo., 1964-66, rsch. assoc. Dept. Allergy Rsch., 1964-66; asst. prof. in biochemistry and physiology Sch. Dentistry Loyola U., Chgo., 1968-71; guest investigator Argonne (Ill.) Nat. Lab., 1973-79; rsch. chemist V.A. Hosp., Hines, Ill., 1968-79; chief clin. radiobiochemist nuclear medicine svc. V.A. Wadsworth Hosp. Ctr., LA, 1979-83; cons. in clin. ecology, 1980—. Contbr. articles to profl. jours. Mem. AAAS, Am. Assn. Clin. Chemists, Soc. for Exptl. Biology and Medicine, Sigma Xi. Home: 823 S 1850 West Cedar City UT 84720-8237

MAYS, G. LARRY, criminal justice educator; b. Knoxville, Tenn., July 2, 1949; s. Robert Lee and Dorothy Jane Mays; m. Brenda Jane Oliver; children: Gregory Lawrence, Gelaine Leslie Jensen. PhD, U. Tenn., Knoxville, 1979. Police officer Knoxville Police Dept., Tenn., 1971—76; instr. East Tenn. State U., Johnson City, 1975—79; asst. prof. Appalachian State U., Boone, NC, 1979—81; regents prof. N.Mex State U., Albuquerque, 1981—. Author: (textbook) Essentials of Corrections, Making Sense of Criminal Justice, Juvenile Delinquency and Juvenile Justice, Juvenile Justice; editor: Courts and Justice, Gangs and Gang Behavior, Privatization and the Provision of Correctional Services, American Jails. Recipient Donald C. Roush award, N.Mex State U., 1993, Regents Professorship, 2005—; named N.Mex Prof. of Yr., Carnegie Found. Advancement Tchg., 1997. Baptist. Office: N Mex State University 2444 La NE Ste 101 Albuquerque NM 87110 Business E-Mail: glmays@nmsu.edu.

MAYS, GEORGE FRANCIS, small business owner; b. Springfield, Ohio, Feb. 17, 1956; s. Sylvester Francis Mays and Dorothy (Hirsch) Mays Oppie; m. Becky Lou Rollins, Aug. 2, 1979; 1 child, Joseph David. BS, Campbellsville Coll., 1982; MDiv, Ashland Theol. Sem., Ohio, 1989. Ordained to ministry United Ch. Christ, 1990. Pastor Emmanuel Chapel, Wellington, Ohio, 1984-88, First Congl. Chs., Florence-South Amherst, Ohio, 1988-90, First Congl. Ch., Lodi, Ohio, 1990—96; owner karaoke and DJ co., Ohio, 1996—. Com. mem. United Ch. Christ, Canton, Ohio. Vol. Salvation Army. Mem. Rotary. Democrat. Mailing: PO Box 54 Norwalk OH 44857

MAYS, J. C., automotive executive; b. 1955; Grad., Art Ctr. Coll. of Design, 1980. Designer Audi AG, Ingolstad, Germany, 1980—83, BMW, Munich, 1983—84; sr. designer Audi AG, Ingolstad, Germany, 1984—89; chief designer Volkswagon of Am., Simi Valley, Calif., 1989—93; design dir. Audi AG, Ingolstad, Germany, 1993—95; v.p. design devel. SHR Perceptual Mgmt., Scottsdale, 1995—97; v.p. design Ford Motor Co., Dearborn, Mich., 1997—2003, group v.p. design, 2003—, chief creative officer, 2005—. Design (exhibitions) "Retrofuturism: The Car Design of J. Mays", Geffen Mus. Contemporary Art LA, 2002. Recipient Excellence in Design award, Harvard Design Sch., 2002, Don Kubly Profl. Attainment award, 2002; named a Master of Design, Fast Company mag., 2004. Office: Ford Motor Co One American Rd Dearborn MI 48126-1899*

MAYS, JANICE ANN, lawyer; b. Waycross, Ga., Nov. 21, 1951; d. William H. and Jean (Bagley) M. AB (hon.), Wesleyan Coll., Macon, Ga., 1973; JD, U. Ga., 1975; LLM in Taxation, U. Georgetown, 1980. Bar: Ga. 1976. Tax counsel com. on ways and means U.S. Ho. Reps., Washington, 1975-88, chief tax counsel com. on ways and means, staff dir. subcom. select revenue measures, 1988-93, chief counsel, staff dir. com. on ways and means, 1993-95, 2007—, minority chief counsel, staff dir. com. on ways and means, 1995—2006. Recipient Disting. Achievement in Profession Alumnae award Wesleyan Coll., 1998. Mem. Tax Coalition (past chair). Office: Ways & Means Com 1102 Longworth Office Bldg Washington DC 20515-0001

MAYS, KENNETH ROBERT, music educator; b. Ft. Wayne, Ind., Jan. 13, 1939; s. Henry M. and Estella Mays; m. Nita Molly Newbury, July 19, 1980; children: Heather Bellamy, Craig, Kimberly Pavicich. B in Sacred Music, Ft. Wayne Bible Coll., 1960; MusM, Ind. U., Bloomington, 1961, PhD, 1971. Instr. music Ft. Wayne Bible Coll., 1961—64; tchg. asst. in music theory Ind. U., Bloomington, 1964—67; from asst. to assoc. prof. music Wheaton Conservatory Music, Wheaton Coll., Ill., 1964—86; prof. piano and theory The Master's Coll., Santa Clarita, Calif., 1986—. Min. music Ch. of the Canyons, Canyon Country, Calif., 1987—94, Valley Presbyn. Ch., North Hills, Calif., 1994—2004; clinician, adjudicator Music Tchrs. Assn. Calif., Santa Clarita, 1994—. Arranger: Reflection and Praise, 2003. Alumni Faculty Study grantee, Wheaton Coll. Alumni Assn., 1977—78, Sabbatical Study grantee, The Master's Coll., 2000. Mem.: Music Tchrs. Assn. Calif., Nat. Assn. Ch. Musicians. Avocations: golf, travel. Home: 26188 Rainbow Glen Dr Santa Clarita CA 91321 Office: The Master's Coll 21726 Placerita Canyon Rd # 13 Santa Clarita CA 91321 Office Phone: 661-259-3540 ext 3189. Business E-Mail: kmays@masters.edu.

MAYS, L(ESTER) LOWRY, broadcast executive; b. Houston, July 24, 1935; s. Lester T. and Virginia (Lowry) M.; m. Peggy Pitman, July 29, 1959; children: Kathryn Mays Johnson, Linda Mays McCaul, Mark P., Randall T. BS in Petroleum Engring., Tex. A&M U., 1959; MBA, Harvard U., 1962. Comml. recorder, San Antonio; with Sta. KTTU-TV, Tucson, Sta. KOKI/KTFO-TV, Tulsa, Sta. WMPI/WJTC-TV, Mobile and Pensacola, Okla., Sta. WAWS-TV, Jacksonville, Fla., Sta. KSAS-TV, Wichita, Kans., Sta. KLRT/KASN-TV, Little Rock, Sta. WFTC-TV, Mpls., Sta. WFTC-TV, WLMT/WMTU-TV, Memphis, Sta. WXXA, Albany, Sta. WQUE-AM-FM, New Orleans, Clear Channel Sports, Des Moines, Okla. News Network, Oklahoma City, Va. News Network, Stas. KJYO and KTOK, Oklahoma City, Sta. KEBC, Oklahoma City, Sta. WELI, New Haven, Sta. WKCI-WAVZ, New Haven, Sta. KPEZ, Austin, Tex., Stas. KHYS, KALO, KBXX, KMJQ, KPRC, KSEV and KYOK, Houston and Point Arthur, Tex., KMOD & KAKC, Tulsa, KTAM & KORA, Bryan and College Station, Tex., WHAS & WAMZ, Louisville; with radio and TV broadcasting WOAI, KQXT, and KAJA, San Antonio; chmn., CEO Clear Channel Communications Inc., San Antonio, 1975—2004; chmn. C;ear Channel Communications Inc., San Antonio, 2004—. Past chmn. bd. CBS Radio Affiliates Bd. Bd. dirs., trustee Tex. Rsch. Pk.; bd. dirs., mem. exec. com. United Way; chmn. United Way San Antonio and Bexar County, 1995; regent emeritus Tex. A&M U. Sys.; trustee Tex. Rsch. and Tech. Found.; mem. deve. bd. U. Tex. Health Sci. Ctr.; adv. dir. Permanent Univ. Fund Tex. Mem. Nat. Assn. Broadcasters (past chmn. joint bd.), Greater San Antonio C. of C. (past chmn.), Rotary. Home: 400 Geneseo Rd San Antonio TX 78209-6127 Office: Clear Channel Comms Inc PO Box 659512 San Antonio TX 78265-9512

MAYS, MARK PITMAN, communication company executive; b. San Antonio, Aug. 2, 1963; BA in Econs. and Math., Vanderbilt U.; MBA, Columbia U. V.p., treas. Clear Channel Comms., San Antonio, sr. v.p. ops., 1993—96, pres., COO, 1996—2004, interim CEO, 2004, pres., CEO, 2004—06, CEO, 2006—. Bd. dirs. NAB Radio Bd. Bd. dirs. Jr. Achievement San Antonio Chap., Alamo Area Coun. Boy Scouts Am., United Way San Antonio, SW Found. Biomedical Rsch. Office: Clear Channel Comms 200 E Basse Rd San Antonio TX 78209-8328 Fax: 210-822-2299.

MAYS, MARYANN, neurologist; Grad., Marquette U.; MD, Med. Coll Ohio, Toledo, 1993. Cert. clinical neurophysiology. Intern Cleveland Clinic, 1993—97, fellow, staff neurologist, 1998—, dir. neurology residency program, 2005—. Mem.: Assn. U. Professors Neurology, Am. Acad. Neurology, Nat. Headache Found., Am. Headache Soc., Alpha Omega Alpha. Office: Clevland Clinic 9500 Euclid Ave Mail Code S91 Cleveland OH 44195 Office Phone: 216-445-3616.

MAYS, QUINCEY, art educator; b. Jinmachi, Japan, July 21, 1948; s. Joseph Roles and Edna Eilleen Mays; 1 child from previous marriage, Isaac Marshall. B in Mil. Sci., Cameron U., 1971, BA in Math., 1971, BS in Elem. Edn., 1981, BFA, 1984; MEd, U. Okla., 1979. Tchr. Indiahoma (Okla.) HS, 1974—75, Brockland Elem., Lawton, Okla., 1976—81; tchr. art Whittier Elem., Lawton, 1982—93, Pat Henry Elem., Lawton, 1994—97, Lawton HS, 1998—. Adj. prof. Cameron U., Lawton, 1984—96; coach cross country/tennis Lawton HS, 1998—, chmn. curriculum fine arts dept., 1999—; artist-in-residence kindergarten acad. Lawton Pub. Schs., 2002—; instr. Goddard Youth Camp Gifted/Talented, Lake of Arbuckles, Sulpher, 1981—2001; coach cross country MacArthur H.S., Lawton, 2005—. Mem. Arts and Humanities Coun., Lawton, 1995—. Capt. US Army, 1970—74. Recipient numerous Best of Show awards for Visual Art; named Cross Country Coach of Yr., Okla. Secondary Schs. Athletic Assn., 2006—07; grantee, Coll. Bd., 1999. Mem.: Okla. Secondary Schs. Activities Assn., Phi Theta Kappa. Republican. Avocations: running, fishing, art, guitar, tennis. Office: Lawton HS 601 NW Fort Sill Blvd Lawton OK 73507 Home: 7401 NW Willow Creek Dr Lawton OK 73505-4220

MAYS, RANDALL T., communications company executive; b. 1966; married. BA with honors, Univ. Tex., Austin, Tex.; MBA, Harvard Bus. Sch. With Trammell Crow Co. Real Estate Firm, Goldman, Sachs & Co., NY; v.p., treas. Clear Channel Commn., San Antonio, 1993—97, CFO, exec. v.p., 1997—2006, CFO, pres., 2006—; chmn. CCE SpinCo, Inc. Bd. dirs. XM Satelitte Radio. Adv. coun. Univ. Tex McCombs Bus. Sch. Mem.: Broadcast Cable Fin. Mgmt. Assn. (CFO of the Yr. 2002), Nat. Assn. of Broadcasters. Office: CCE Spinco Inc 2000 W Loop South Ste 1300 Houston TX 77027

MAYS, ROGER WILLIAM, theater educator; b. Grand Island, Nebr., Nov. 20, 1953; s. Glenn and Helen Mays; m. Lucinda Wilken, Sept. 12, 1980; 1 child, Walt Henry. BA, U. Nebr., Kearney, 1977; MA, Denver U., CO, 1981; MFA, U. Ga., Athens, 1998. Cert. Actors Equity, NY, 1990. Theatre instr. Coker Coll., Hartsville, SC, 1985—88; assoc. artistic dir. Springer Opera Ho., Columbus, Ga., 1990—95; theatre prof. Chadron State Coll., Nebr., 1998—; acting co. Ga. Shakespeare Festival, Atlanta, 1995—96; intern Cooper Found., 2008. Mng. dir. Post Playhouse, Crawford, Nebr., 2006—08. Dir.: (plays, theatre) Reckless, Picasso at the Lapin Agile, The God of Hell, cyrano; (plays, children's theatre) Treasure Islande; prodr.: (Broadway plays, musical) Guys & Dolls, South Pacific, Oklahoma; dir.: Godspell. Theatre liaison Chadron Libr. Bd., 1999—2008. Conservative. Lutheran. Achievements include development of touring children's theatre program. Avocations: music, fishing. Office: Chadron State Coll 1000 Main St Chadron NE 69337 Office Fax: 308-432-6464. Business E-Mail: rmays@csc.edu.

MAYS, ROY MARK, JR., (MARK MAYS), psychologist, educator; b. Billings, Mont., Apr. 26, 1948; m. Paula Dillon Mays; 5 children. BA in Sociology and Psychology, Austin Coll., Sherman, Tex., 1970; MA in Psychology, U. Tex., Austin, 1972, PhD in Psychology, 1973; JD, Gonzaga U. Sch. Law, Spokane, Wash., 1984. Instr. Gonzaga U. Grad. Sch. Bus.; lectr. in evidence law Gonzaga U. Sch. Law; clin. prof. U. Wash. Sch. Medicine; pvt. practice psychologist, 1980—. Cons. Kellogg Rural Health Project, Prisoner of War Rsch. Project. Founder B.R.I.G.H.T.; bd. trustees Ea. Wash. U. Capt. USAF. Mem.: Wash. State Bar. Democrat. Office: 105 W 8th Ave #7035 Spokane WA 99204 Office Phone: 509-624-4800, 509-624-1216. Business E-Mail: markmays@markmays.com.

MAYS, WILLIE HOWARD, JR., (SAY HEY KID), retired professional baseball player; b. Westfield, Ala., May 6, 1931; s. William Howard and Ann M.; m. Margherite Wendell Chapman, 1956 (div. 1961), 1 adopted son, Michael; m. Mae Louise Allen, Nov. 27, 1971 LHD (hon.), Yale U., 2004. Baseball player Birmingham Black Barons, 1948-50, Trenton Inter-State League, 1950-51, Mpls. Millers, Am. Assn., 1951, N.Y. Giants, 1951-57, San Francisco Giants, 1958-72, N.Y. Mets, 1972-73; pub. rels. exec. San Francisco Giants, 1986-98, retired, 1998. Author: Willie Mays: My Life In and Out of Baseball, 1966, Say Hey: The Autobiography of Willie Mays, 1988. Served with AUS, 1952-54. Named MVP Nat. League, 1954, 65, Player of Yr. Sporting News, 1954, Baseball Player of Decade Sporting News, 1970, Male Athlete of Yr. AP, 1954, NL Rookie of Yr., 1951, Sporting News Player of the Year award, 1954, All-Star Game, 1954-73; recipient Hickok belt, 1954, Golden Bat award to commemorate 600 home runs, Gold Glove award (12 times), 1st Commissioner's award, 1970, Golden Plate awarded to America's Captains of Achievement by Am. Acad. Achievement, 1976, Spirit of Life award City of Hope, 1988, Sportsman of Decade, Cong. Racial Equality, 1991, Legendary Star award HBO Video; inducted into Ala. Sports Hall of Fame, Baseball Hall of Fame, 1979, Black Hall of Fame, 1973, Calif. Hall of Fame, 2007; named to All-Time Rawlings Gold Glove Team, 2007. Achievements include being the holder of 4th place in major league homeruns (660); lifetime batting average of .302; signed lifetime pub. rels. contract with San Francisco Giants, 1993. Office: Baseball Hall of Fame PO Box 590 Cooperstown NY 13326-0590

MAYSILLES, DANIEL BRUCE, pharmaceutical services executive; b. Hamilton, Ohio, May 26, 1952; s. Carl A. and Ella Jean (Thorpe) M.; m. Dawn M. Hamilton, Aug. 9, 1975 (div. May 1989); m. Nancy K. Cragg, Feb. 15, 1992; 1 child, Ryan. AA, U. South Fla., 1972; BS in Pharmacy, U. Fla., 1975. Registered pharmacist. Pharmacist Roscoe's Rexall Drugs, New Port Richey, Fla., 1975-77, Eckerd Drugs, Spring Hill, Fla., 1977-79; staff pharmacist Cmty. Hosp., New Port Richey, 1979-83; assoc. dir. pharmacy HCA New Port Richey Hosp., 1983-85; dir. pharmacy Cmty. Hosp. New Port Richey, 1985—. Pharmacy adv. com. Hosp. Corp. Am., Nashville, 1985—93, tech. adv. com., 1991—93, HPG/PACT adv. com., 2001—; care of the patient chairperson Columbia New Port Richey Hosp., 1994—2003, cons. pharmacist; assoc. prof. Pasco/Hernando C.C., New Port Richey, 1987—88; interim dir. pharmacy HCA Oak Hill Hosp., 2001, Regional Med. Ctr. of Bayonet Point, 2004. Chmn., mem. planning and zoning bd. City of New Port Richey, 1979—, hand devel. rev. bd., 2003-07; sect. chair Acad. Pharmacy Practice Fla. Pharmacy Assn.; mem. pastors coun. Ch. of God, Tarpon Springs, Fla., 1978-88. Regents scholar Bd. Regents, 1970. Mem. Pasco/Hernando Pharmacy Assn. (pres. 1995-96, historian 1993-94, John Dunwoody award 1996, Humanitarian award 1993), Am. Soc. of Health Systems, Rotary Internat., Kappa Psi (Pres. award 1975). Republican. Avocations: golf, tennis, fishing, reading, music. Home: 6134 Oak Ridge Ave New Port Richey FL 34653-4235 Office: Cmty Hosp New Port Richey 5637 Marine Pkwy New Port Richey FL 34652-4316 Office Phone: 727-845-9140. E-mail: gatorx1@msn.com, daniel.maysilles@hcahealthcare.com.

MAYSLES, ALBERT H., filmmaker; b. Boston, Nov. 26, 1926; s. Philip and Ethel (Epstein) M.; m. Gillian Walker, Sept. 14, 1976; children: Rebekah, Philip, Sara. BA, Syracuse U., 1949; MA, Boston U., 1953. Rsch. fellow in anesthesia Mass. Gen. Hosp., Boston, 1951-52; instr. social rels. Boston U., 1953-55; pres. Maysles Films, Inc., NYC, 1962—. Filmmaker, prodr. Psychiatry in Russia, 1955, (with others) Primary, 1960, Showman, 1963, What's Happening: The Beatles in the USA, 1964, Salesman, 1967, Gimme Shelter, 1970, Christo's Valley Curtain, 1974, (Blue Ribbon award 1975, Acad. award nomination), Grey Gardens, 1976, Running Fence, 1978 (Blue Ribbon award 1978), Ozawa, 1985, Vladimir Horowitz: The Last Romantic, 1985, Islands, 1986 (Blue Ribbon award, Emmy award), Horowitz Plays Mozart, 1987, Christo in Paris, 1990, Soldiers of Music: Rostropovitch Returns to Russia, 1990 (Emmy award), Abortion: Desparate Choices, 1995 (Peabody award), Letting Go, A Hospice Journey, 1996 (Ace Cable award), Concert of Wills: The Making of the Getty Art Center, 1997; LaLee's Kin, 2000, The Gates, 2007, The Reales of Grey Gardens, 2006. Served as pvt. U.S. Army, 1944-46. Recipient Career Achievement award, Internat. Documentary Assn., 1994, John Grierson award for Documentary, SMPTE, 1997, Pres.'s award, Am. Soc. Cinematographers, 1998, Vision award, The Boston Film and Video Found., 1998, The Doubletake Career Achievement award, 1998, Lifetime Achievement award, Toronto's Hot Docs, 1999, Flaherty award, 1999, award for documentaries, Sundance Film Festival Cinematography, 2001, Dupont award, 2004, Medal of Honor for Theatre, Nat. Arts Club, 2007; named one of 100 World's Finest Cinematographers, Eastman Kodak, 1999; Guggenheim fellow, 1965. Mem. The Reality Club (Charter Guggenheim award, 2009). Home: 21 W 122nd St New York NY 10027-5602 Office: 343 Lenox Ave New York NY 10027 Office Phone: 212-582-6050. E-mail: amaysles@mayslesfilms.com.

MAY-TREANOR, MISTY, Olympic athlete; b. LA, July 30, 1977; d. Robert "Butch" May; m. Matt Treanor. Majored in Kinesiology & Physical Ed., Long Beach State U. Mem. U.S. National Indoor Team, 1998, 1999; player FIVG Internat. Tour; beach volleyball player, Team USA Sydney Olympic Games, 2000, Athens Olympic Games, 2004, Beijing Olympic Games, 2008. Performer: (TV series) Dancing with the Stars, 2008. Recipient Honda Broderick NCAA Athlete of Yr. award, 1998, Gold medal, beach volleyball, Athens Olympic Games, 2004, Beijing Olympic Games, 2008; named First-Team All-Am., NCAA, 1996—98, Nat. Player of Yr., AVCA, 1997, 1998, BVA Rookie of the Yr., 2000, AVP Team of Yr. (with Kerri Walsh), 2003—07, AVP Best Offensive Player, 2004, 2006—07, AVP MVP, 2006—07, Crocs Cup Champion (with Kerri Walsh), 2006—07, Most Outstanding Player, FIVB, 2006, Best Offensive Player, 2006, Sportswoman of Yr., 2007, Female Beach Volleyball Player of Yr., USA Volleyball, 2007. Achievements include being a member of NCAA national championship winnning Long Beach State University, 1998; winning FIVB World Championships (with partner Kerri Lee Walsh), 2003, 2005, 2007; becoming the first repeat gold medalist in Olympic women's beach volleyball history (with Kerri Lee Walsh), 2004, 2008; having the most all-time tournament wins in women's beach volleyball history (108). Office: c/o USOC One Olympic Plz Colorado Springs CO 80909

MAYWEATHER, FLOYD, JR., retired professional boxer; b. Grand Rapids, Mich., Feb. 24, 1977; s. Floyd Mayweather, Sr.; 3 children. Profl. boxer, 1996—2008; ret., 2008. Winner world title vs. Genaro Hernandez by tech. knockout, superfeatherweight divsn. World Boxing Coun., 1998, winner world title def. vs. Angel Manfredy by tech. knockout, superfeatherweight divsn., 98, winner world title def. vs. Carlos Rios by unanimous decision, superfeatherweight divsn., 99, winner world title def. vs. Justin Juuko, superfeatherweight divsn., 99, winner world title def. vs. Carlos Gerena by tech. knockout, superfeatherweight divsn., 99, winner world title def. vs. Goyo Vargas by unanimous decision, superfeatherweight divsn., 2000, winner world title def. vs. Diego Corrales by tech. knockout, superfeatherweight divsn., 01, winner world title def. vs. Carlos Hernandez by unanimous decision, superfeatherweight divsn., 01, winner world title def. vs. Jesus Chavez by tech. knockout, superfeatherweight divsn., 01, winner world title vs. Jose Luis Castillo by unanimous decision, lightweight divsn., 02, winner world title def. vs. Jose Luis Castillo by unanimous decision, lightweight divsn., 02, winner world title def. vs. Victoriano Sosa by unanimous decision, lightweight divsn., 03, winner world title def. vs. Phillip Ndou by tech. knockout, lightweight divsn., 03, winner world title eliminator vs. Demarcus Corley by unanimous decision, superlightweight divsn., 04, winner world title eliminator vs. Henry Bruseles by tech. knockout, light welterweight divsn., 05, winner world title def. vs. Arturo Gatti by tech. knockout, light welterweight divsn., 05, winner world title vs. Carlos Manuel Baldomir by unanimous decision, welterweight divsn., 06, winner world title vs. Oscar De La Hoya by split decision, light middleweight divsn., 07, winner world title def. vs. Ricky Hatton by tech. knockout, welterweight divsn., 07. Performer: Dancing With the Stars, 2007. Recipient Bronze medal, 125 pound divsn., Olympics Games, Atlanta, 1996, ESPY award, Best Fighter, ESPN, 2008; named Fighter of Yr., The Ring Mag., 1998. Achievements include being a five-time US national amateur champion; being the former World Boxing Council's super featherweight champion with eight successful title defenses; being the World Boxing Council's emeritus Lightweight Champion of the World.

MAYYAS, MOHAMMAD A., mechanical engineer, researcher; b. Al-Ramtha, Jordan, Mar. 1978; s. Abdullah Ayed Mayyas and Taraky Zubi. BS in Mech. Engring., Jordan U. Sci. & Tech., Irbid, 2001; MS in Mech. Engring., U. Tex., Arlington, 2004; PhD in Mech. Engring., U. Tex., 2007. Cert. mech. engr., Jordan Assn. Engring., 2001. Lectr. Jordan U. Sci. & Tech., 2001—03; tchg. asst. U. Tex., Arlington, 2003—04; rsch. assoc. Automation & Robotics Rsch. Inst., Ft. Worth, 2005—, rsch. scientist, 2009—. Recipient Best Symposium Paper award, Nano & Micro-Smart Sys. Symposium, 2006, Best Conf. Paper, TEXMEMS VII. Mem.: Am. Soc. Mech. Engring. (corr.). Achievements include development of novel designs of electrothermal microgrippers; patents for selective detethering of MEMS; research in micro and nanotechnologies. Avocation: travel. Office: Univ Tex Arlington 7300 Jack Newell Blvd S Fort Worth TX 76118 Home: 1601 Stoneleigh Ct 3131 Arlington TX 76011 Personal E-mail: mayyas2@yahoo.com, mmayyas@gmail.com. Business E-Mail: mohammad@arri.uta.edu.

MAZAK, ARLENE PATRICIA, marriage and family therapist; d. John Andrew Mazak and Irene Kraszewski. BA in Liberal Arts, Sarah Lawrence Coll., Bronxville, NY, 1967; MA in Counselling, U. San Francisco, Calif., 1992; MA & PhD in South Asian Langs. and Civilization, U. Chgo., Ill., 1994. Cert. orgnl. devel. and transformation specialist Calif. Inst. Integral Studies, 1993, lic. marriage and family therapist Calif. Core faculty Calif. Inst. Integral Studies, San Francisco, 1986—93; tng. dir. Spiritual Emergence Network, Menlo Park, Calif., 1990—91; core faculty Inst. Transpersonal Psychology, Palo Alto, Calif., 1993—2000; adj. faculty gerontology Coastline C.C., Fountain Valley, Calif., 2001—06; marriage and family therapist, life coach and spiritual dir. Innercall: Transpersonal Healing and Devel. Svcs., Fountain Valley and Encinitas, Calif., 2001—; adjunct faculty, transpersonal psychology San Diego U. Integrative Studies, 2001—04. Recipient Dean's prize, Calif. Inst. Integral Studies, 1993; Fulbright Hays fellow, India, 1971—72, NDEA Title IV fellow, U. Chgo., 1967—70, NDFL Title VI fellow, 1970—71. Personal E-mail: arlene@innercall.net.

MAZANKOWSKI, DONALD FRANK, Canadian government official; b. Viking, Alta., Can., July 27, 1935; s. Frank and Dora (Lonowski) M.; m. Lorraine Poleschuk, Sept. 6, 1958; children: Gregory, Roger, Donald. Student, pub. schs., 1987; PhD in Engring (hon.), N.S. Inst. Tech.; LLD (hon.), U. Alta., 1993. MP Ho. of Commons, 1968—, chmn. com. transp., 1972-74, mem. com. govt. ops., 1976-77, mem. com. trans. and communication, 1977-79; min. of transp., min. responsible for Can. Wheat Bd. Govt. of Can., 1979-80, min. of transp. (re-drafted Nat. Transp. Act), 1984-86, dep. prime min., 1986—, govt. house leader, 1986-88, pres. Privy Coun., 1986-91, pres. Treas. Bd., 1987-88, min. responsible for privatization and regulatory affairs, 1988-91, min. of agriculture, 1988-91, min. of fin., 1991-93; former chmn. Inst. Health Econs. Former mem. bd. govs. U. Alta; bd. dirs. Power Corp. Can., Power Fin. Corp., Great West Life Assurance, The Investors Group, Can. Oilsands Trust, ATCO Ltd., London Life Ins., Yellow Pages Group; former chmn. Can. Genetic Diseases Network.; sr. advisor Gowlings Lafleur Henderson, LLP. Apptd. chmn. Premier's Adv. Coun. on Health. Decorated officer Order of Can., Alta. Order of Excellence; recipient Alta. Centennial medal, 2005; Paul Harris fellow Rotary Internat., 2002; honoree Pub. Policy Forum Can., 2003; named one of Alta.'s 50 Most Influential People, 2002. Mem. Royal Can. Legion (life). Clubs: Vegreville Rotary (past dir.). Lodges: KC, Prime Ministers Adv. Com. Pub. Svc.(co-chair, 2006). Roman Catholic. Office Phone: 780-410-0728. E-mail: donmaz@shaw.ca.

MAZER, MIKE, cardiologist, retired nephrologist, artist; b. Boston, May 17, 1936; s. Louis and Belle Mazer; m. Marilyn Wood, Feb. 26, 1987; children: Mark, Pamela. BS cum laude, Boston U., Mass., 1958; MD, U. Cin., 1962. Diplomate in internal medicine Am. Bd. Internal Medicine, 1970, in nephrology Am. Bd. Nephrology, 1978, in cardiology Am. Bd. Cardiology, 1979. Fellow gastrointestinal disease U. Cin., 1962—64; fellow renal and metabolic studies Med. Ctr. Boston U., 1964—65; fellow cardiovasc. disease West Roxbury VA Hosp., Boston, 1967—68; dir. acute hemodialysis Goddard Meml. Hosp., Stoughton, Mass., 1968—90, chief Echocardiography and Noninvasive Vascular Lab, 1977—94, chief cardiology, 1986—94; chief of nephrology Cardinal Cushing Hosp., Brockton, Mass., 1968—94; pvt. practice Bridgewater Goddard Pk. Med. Assocs., Mass., 1968—98; co-dir. Brockton-Goddard Hemodialysis Unit, Brockton, 1992—97; chief cardiology Good Samaritan Med. Ctr., Brockton, 1994—97, chief Echocardiography and Noninvasive Vascular Lab, 1994—97; med. dir. Pk. Cardiographics, Taunton, Mass.; dir. Cardiac Ultrasonography and Transtelephonic Monitoring Nat. Med. Co, Taunton; dir. Cardiac Rehab. Ctr. Striar Jewish Cmty. Ctr., Stoughton, 1994—97; artist Mattapoisett, Mass., 1997—. Splash 9: Watercolor Secrets, 2006, Solo New Bedford Art Mus., Mass., 2006, Splash 10: Passionate Brush Stations, 2008, Contemporary American Marine Art, 2003—04; co-author: Principles of Interpretation in Echocardiography, 1985; editor: Jour. Diagnostic Med. Sonography, 1985—87; over 400 exhbns. & 90 awards, collections, US Coast Guard, Wash., Tabor Acad., Marion, Mass., New Bedford Free Pub. Lib., Commonwealth Mass, Dept. Environ. Protection, Lakeville, Mass., Marion Art Ctr., exhibitions include Zeeland Maritime Mus., Vlissingen, 2009, internat. exhbn., Maritime Mus., Vlissingen, Holland, one-man shows include New Bedford Art Mus., 2006, Cape Cod Art Museum, Dennis, Mass., 2009, Represented in permanent collections Cape Cod Mus. Art, New Bedford Whaling Mus. Recipient Top Money Water Media award, Am. Artists Profl. League, Grand Nat. Exhibitions, 1999, 2004, Best in Show award, Stoughton Art Assn., 2002, 2004, Miss. Grand Nat. Exhbn., 2003; named Top 100, Paint America Exhbn., 2007; nominee Top 100 award, 2008. Fellow: Am. Artists Profl. League; mem.: Nat. Watercolor Soc., Phila. Watercolor Soc., New Eng. Watercolor Soc. (pres. 2004—07), Canton (Mass.) Art Assn. (dir. edn. 1997—2007), Coast Guard Artist Program, Cape Cod Art Assn., Audubon Artists, Inc, Allied Artists of Am., Academic Artists Assn., Am. Soc. of Marine Artists, R.I. Watercolor Soc. (Best in Show award 2004), North Shore Arts Assn., Phila. North East Watercolor Soc., Tex. Watercolor Soc., Pa. Watercolor Soc., Nat. Soc. of Artists, Mo. Watercolor Soc., Internat. Guild of Realism (assoc.), Miss. Watercolor Soc., Mont. Watercolor Soc., Internat. Soc. of Marine Painters, Hudson Valley Art Assn., Ga. Watercolor Soc., The Salmagundi Club, Alpha Omega Alpha, Watercolor U.S.A. Honor Soc. Achievements include development of the first acute hemodialysis on the South Shore of Massachusetts, 1968; discovery of a Left Ventricular Myxoma by ultra sonography, 1984. Home: 7 Holly Woods Rd Mattapoisett MA 02739

MAZER, ROSLYN A., federal official, lawyer; BA magna cum laude, Syracuse U., NY; JD, Cath. U. America, Washington, 1975. Bar: DC 1976. Atty. Dickstein Shapiro; spl. counsel intellectual property US Dept. Justice, Washington, assoc. dep. atty. gen., spl. investigation counsel Office of Insp. Gen., 2002—09; chair Interagency Security Classification Appeals Panel, 1996—2000; insp. gen. Office of Dir. Nat. Intelligence, Washington, 2009—. Recipient Disting. Svc. Award, Atty. Gen., 2007, Award for Excellence, Pres.'s Coun. Integrity & Efficiency in Govt., 2007, Award of Merit, US Dept. Justice Office of Insp. Gen., 2007. Mem.: Phi Beta Kappa. Office: Office of Dir Nat Intelligence Washington DC 20511*

MAZHER, WASEEM, special education educator; b. Dhaka, Bangladesh, Nov. 17, 1969; s. Mazharul Haque and Ehsan Jahan; m. Khaleda Akhter, July 7, 2000; 1 child, Joshua. MA, U. Southern Miss., Hattiesburg, 1995; attending, Tchrs. Coll., Columbia U., NYC, 2009. Cert. in spl. Edn. Miss., 1997. Tchr. spl. edn. East Side Elem. Sch., Picayune, Miss., 1995—99, Lafayette Elem., New Orleans, 1999—2000. Adj. prof. U. Southern Miss., 2006—07. Contbr. articles to profl. jours. Home: 13 Sharmont Dr Hattiesburg MS 39402 Business E-Mail: waseem.mazher@usm.edu.

MAZIARZ, RICHARD THOMAS, hematologist, educator; b. New London, Conn., Oct. 30, 1953; m. Margaret Retondo, June 12, 1988; children: Jonathan Walter, Steven Richard. MD, Harvard Med. Sch., Boston, 1979. Diplomate internal medicine, hematology, med. oncology Am. Bd. Internal Medicine. Med. dir., adult bone marrow transplant program Oreg. Health and Sci. U., Portland, 1994—, prof. medicine, 1999—. Mem.: Am. Soc. Blood and Marrow transplantation. Achievements include research in bone marrow transplantation immunology. Office: Oreg Health and Sci Univ 3181 SW Sam Jackson Pk Rd Portland OR 97201 Office Fax: 503-494-1552. Business E-Mail: maziarzr@ohsu.edu.

MAZIE, DAVID A., lawyer; b. NYC, Nov. 17, 1961; BA, Rutgers U., New Brunswick, NJ, 1983; JD, George Washington U., Washington, 1986. Bar: N.J. 1986, D.C. 1988, cert.: N.J. Supreme Ct. (trial atty.), Nat. Bd. Trial Advocacy (civil trial atty.). Assoc. Stern Steiger, Paramus, NJ, 1986—88; ptnr. Mazie Slater Katz & Freeman and predecessor firms, Roseland, NJ, 1988—. Named Lawyer of Yr., NJ Law Jour., 2005, Top NJ Super Lawyer, 2005, 2007. Mem.: ABA, ATLA, N.J. Bar Assn. Office: Mazie Slater Katz & Freeman 103 Eisenhower Pkwy Roseland NJ 07068 Office Phone: 973-228-9898. Business E-Mail: dmazie@mskf.net.

MAZLACK, LAWRENCE JOSEPH, science educator; b. Toronto, Ind., Can. s. Samuel Joseph and Ann Mary Mazlack; life ptnr. Annette Stowasser; 1 child, Nadja Stowasser. BS, Marquette U., Milw., 1964; MS, DSc, Wash. U., St. Louis, 1973. Mgr. IBM, White Plains, NY, 1965—68; prof. U. Guelph, Ont., Canada, 1972—78, U. Cin., 1978—. Contbr. numerous articles to publs. Multiple Rsch. grants, NSF, USAF, Corps. Mem.: Can. Soc. Computational Studies Intelligence, BISC Spl. Interest Group Database Mining, Inst. Elec. and Electronic Engrs., Cognitive Sci. Soc., Can. Man Computer Comm. Soc., Can. Image Processing and Pattern Recognition Soc., Assn. Computing Machinery (spl. interest group chmn.), Assn. Computational Linguistics, Am. Assn. Artificial Intelligence, Omega Rho. Office: Applied Artificial Intelligence Lab Univ Cin Cincinnati OH 45221 Business E-Mail: mazlack@uc.edu.

MAZLEN, ROGER GEOFFREY, internist, pharmacologist; b. Bklyn., Nov. 23, 1937; s. Henry Gershwin and Ann Kurland (Shapero) M.; m. Sandra Phyllis Kuritzky, Aug. 7, 1960; children: James Edward, Vivien Gayle. BS in Biology, Rensselaer Poly. Inst., 1959; MD, SUNY, Bklyn., 1963. Intern maimonides Med. Ctr., Bklyn., 1963-64, resident in medicine, 1964-65; rsch. assoc. NIH, Bethesda, Md., 1965-67; resident in med. ophthalmology Mt. Sinai Med. Ctr., NYC, 1967-69; assoc. med. dir. Pfizer Inc., NYC, 1970-71; asst. dir. clin. rsch. Ayerst Labs., NYC, 1971-75; assoc. dir. clin. rsch. Schering Corp., Bloomfield, NJ, 1975-78; adj. asst. prof. medicine N.Y. Med. Coll.; sr. clin. asst. prof. Mt. Sinai Sch. Medicine; sr. faculty, sr. attending div. endocrinology and metabolism Mt. Sinai Med. Ctr. Mem. cons. Profl. Children's Sch.; cons. in clin. nutrition and metabolism South Oaks Hosp; chief sci. officer Biomelecular Sci., Inc., 2000-07. Author: A New Manifesto for Middle America, 1972; author: (with others) Nutrition and Health Care; contbr. (chpt.) Quick Reference to Clinical Nutrition, mem. editl. staff Jour. of the Chiropractic Coun. on Nutrition. Founder, chmn. Queens County (N.Y.) Common Cause, 1972—75, vice chmn. for N.Y. State, 1974—75; bd. dirs. Bayside Hills Civic Assn., 1970—80; adv. mem. bd. dirs. U.S.A., Inc., 1970—72; chmn. hyperalimentation com. Astoria (N.Y.) Gen. Hosp.; former dir. Clin. Rsch. N. Am. Immunatee Ltd., Montreal; nutrition dir. Cernitin Am. Nutritional, 1983—88, also mem. eating disorder adv. bd. With USPHS, 1965—67. Fellow: Am. Coll. Nutrition (chmn. coun. on nutrition and cardiovasc. diseases 1976—85, sec.-treas.); mem.: N.Y. State Soc. Internal Medicine, Soc. for Natural Immunity, Am. Coll. Cardiology (constituent mem. N.Y. State chpt.), Am. Soc. Clin. Pharmacology and Therapeutics, Muhammad Ali Internat. Sport Youth Athletic Found. Inc. (bd. dirs.). Republican. Office: 30 Middledeck Rd Roslyn NY 11576 Home Phone: 718-631-4908; Office Phone: 516-869-0717. Personal E-mail: rgm1@aol.com.

MAZLISH, BRUCE, historian, educator; b. NYC, Sept. 15, 1923; s. Louis and Lee (Reuben) M.; m. Neva Goodwin, Nov. 22, 1988; children from previous marriage: Cordelia, Peter, Anthony, Jared. BA, Columbia U., 1944, MA, 1947, PhD, 1955. Instr. history U. Maine, 1946-48, Columbia U., 1949- 50, Mass. Inst. Tech., 1950-53; dir. Am. Sch. in Madrid, Spain, 1953-55; from mem. faculty to prof. emeritus Mass. Inst. Tech., 1955—2004, prof. emeritus, 2004—. Vis. prof. Harvard U., Cambridge, Mass., 2001—02; scholars coun. Libr. of Congress, 2001—04. Author: (with J. Bronowski) The Western Intellectual Tradition, 1960, The Riddle of History, 1966, In Search of Nixon, 1972, James and John Stuart Mill: Father and Son in the 19th Century, 1975, 2d edition, 1988, The Revolutionary Ascetic, 1976, Kissinger, The European Mind in American Policy, 1976, The Meaning of Karl Marx, 1984, A New Science: The Breakdown of Connections and the Birth of Sociology, 1989, The Leader, the Led and the Psyche, 1990, The Fourth Discontinuity: The Co-Evolution of Humans and Machines, 1993, The Uncertain Sciences, 1998, Civilization and Its Contents, 2004, (with Alfred Chandler) Leviathans, The Multinational Corporations and New Global History, 2005, (with Akira Iriya) The Global History Reader, 2005, The New Global History, 2006, The Idea of Humanity in a Global Era, 2009; Editor: Psychoanalysis and History, 1963, rev. edit., 1971, The Railroad and the Space Program: An Exploration in Historical Analogy, 1965, (with Ralph Buultjens) Conceptualizing Global History, 1993, (with Leo Marx) Progress: Fact or Illusion, 1996; contbr. articles to profl. jours. Bd. dirs. Rockefeller Family Fund, 1987-97; v.p. Mount Desert Festival of Chamber Music, 1985—; bd. dirs. Toynbee Prize Found., 1992—, pres., 1997—2006; mem. gov. bd. Rockefeller Archives Ctr., 1999-2005. Served with inf. and OSS, AUS, 1943-45. Recipient Toynbee prize, 1986-87. Fellow Am. Acad. Arts and Scis. Clubs: Cambridge Tennis, Badminton and Tennis; Harbor (Seal Harbor, Maine). Home: 11 Lowell St Cambridge MA 02138-4725 Office: MIT 77 Massachusetts Ave Cambridge MA 02139-4307 Business E-Mail: bmazlish@mit.edu.

MAZO, MARK ELLIOTT, lawyer; b. Phila., Jan. 12, 1950; s. Earl and Rita (Vane) M.; m. Fern Rosalyn Litman, Aug. 19, 1973; children: Samantha Lauren, Dana Suzanne, Ross Elliott, Courtney Litman. AB, Princeton U., 1971; JD, Harvard U., 1974. Bar: DC 1975, US Dist. Ct. DC 1975, US Claims Ct. 1975, US Ct. Appeals (DC cir.) 1976, US Supreme Ct. 1979. Ptnr. Hogan & Hartson, LLP, Washington, Paris, Abu Dhabi, United Arab Emirates, 1990—. Contbr. articles to profl. jours. White House intern Exec. Office of Pres., Washington, 1972. Capt. USAR, 1971-79. Mem. ABA, Harvard Law Sch. Assn., DC Bar Assn., Columbia Country Club, Princeton Club (NYC), Colonial Club, City Club, Nassau Club, Timbers Club, Phi Beta Kappa. Republican. Home:

3719 Cardiff Rd Chevy Chase MD 20815-5943 Office: Hogan & Hartson LLP 555 13th St NW Washington DC 20004 Office Phone: 202-637-5673, 33 0 1 55 73 23 00. Business E-Mail: memazo@hhlaw.com.

MAZO, ROBERT MARC, retired chemistry professor; b. Bklyn., Oct. 3, 1930; s. Nathan and Rose Marion (Mazo) M.; m. Joan Ruth Spector, Sept. 5, 1954; children: Ruth, Jeffrey, Daniel. BA, Harvard U., 1952; MS, Yale U., 1953, PhD, 1955. Rsch. assoc. U. Chgo., 1956-58; asst. prof. Calif. Inst. Tech., 1958-62; assoc. prof. U. Oreg., Eugene, 1962-65, prof. chemistry, 1965-95, prof. emeritus, 1996, head chemistry dept., 1978-81, dir. Inst. Theoretical Sci., 1964-67, 84-87, assoc. dean Grad. Sch., 1967-71; program dir. NSF, 1977-78. Alfred P. Sloan fellow, NSF Sr. Postdoctoral fellow, vis. prof. U. Libre de Bruxelles, Belgium, 1968-69; vis. prof. Technische Hochschule Aachen, Weizmann Inst., Rehovoth, Israel, 1981-82, U. New South Wales, Australia, 1989. Author: Statistical Mechanical Theories of Transport Processes, 1967, Brownian Motion, 2002, also rsch. articles. NSF Postdoctoral fellow U. Amsterdam, Netherlands, 1955-56. Fellow Am. Phys. Soc. Home: 2460 Charnelton St Eugene OR 97405-3214 Office: U Oreg Inst Theoretical Sci Eugene OR 97403 Home Phone: 541-344-0807; Office Phone: 541-346-5224. Business E-Mail: mazo@uoregon.edu.

MAZON, MARGARET FAUSOLD, language educator; b. Windber, Pa., Dec. 26, 1946; d. George McLelland and Ann (Shank) Fausold; m. José Antonio Mazón, Apr. 21, 1973 (div. June 1985); children: David José Mazón, Daniel Eladio Fausold Mazón. Student, U. Valladolid, 1967; BS in Spanish Edn., Ind. U. Pa., 1968; MA in Spanish, W.Va. U., 1973, EdD, 1992. Permanent state tchg. cert., Spanish N-12 NY. Tchr. Spanish McGuffey Sr. Jr.-Sr. H.S., Claysville, Pa., 1968—70; tchr. ESL Briam Inst., Madrid, 1970—71; adj. prof., asst. prof. St. Bonaventure U., Olean, NY, 1979—2002, assoc. prof., Dept. Chair, 2002—06, assoc. prof., 2006—, advocacy officer, 2006—. Contbr. articles to profl. jours.; translator: Olean Gen. Hosp., 2000—. Vol. Interfaith Caregivers, Olean, 1999—. Recipient Fr. Joe Doino award, Olean Area Unity award, 2009. Mem.: Modern Lang. Assn. Democrat. Avocations: swimming, bicycling, cooking, gardening. Office: Modern Lang Dept St Bonaventure Univ Saint Bonaventure NY 14778 Office Phone: 716-375-2468. Business E-Mail: mmazon@sbu.edu.

MAZRUI, ALI AL'AMIN, political science professor, researcher; b. Mombasa, Kenya, Feb. 24, 1933; came to U.S., 1960; s. Al'Amin Ali and Safia (Suleiman) M.; m. Molly Vickerman, 1962 (div. 1982); children: Jamal, Al'Amin, Kim Abubakar; m. Pauline Uti, Oct. 1991; children: Farid Chinedu, Harith Ekenechukwu. BA with distinction, U. Manchester, Eng., 1960; MA, Columbia U., 1961; DPhil, Oxford U., 1966. Lectr. Makerere U., Kampala, Uganda, 1963-65, prof. polit. sci., head dept. polit. sci., 1965-73; dean faculty social scis. Faculty Social Scis., Makerere U., Kampala, Uganda, 1967-69; prof. polit. sci. U. Mich., Ann Arbor, 1974-91, prof. Ctr. Afroam. and African Studies, dept. polit. sci., 1974-91; Andrew D. White prof.-at-large Cornell U., Ithaca, 1986-92; research prof. polit. sci. U. Jos, Nigeria, 1981-86; Albert Schweitzer prof. humanities SUNY, Binghamton, 1989—; Albert Luthuli prof.-at-large U. Jos (Nigeria), 1991—; sr. scholar, Andrew D. White prof.-at-large emeritus Cornell U, Ithaca, 1992—; dir. Inst. Global Cultural Studies SUNY, Binghamton, 1991—; chancellor Jomo Kenyatta Univ. Agrl. and Tech., Kenya, 2003—. Ibn Khaldun prof.-at-large Sch. Islamic and Social Scis., Leesburg, Va., 1997-2000; Reith lectr. BBC, London, 1979; vis. prof. various univs. including U. London, U. Chgo., Oxford U., U. Pa., Ohio State U., Manchester U., Harvard U., Nairobi U., UCLA, Northwestern U., U. Singapore, Colgate Coll., U. Australia, Stanford U., U. Cairo, Sussex U., U. Leeds, Internat. Islamic U., Malaysia, 1965—; mem. bank's coun. African advisers, World Bank, Washington, 1988-91; Walter Rodney disting. prof. U. Guyana, Georgetown, 1997-98. Author: Towards A Pax Africana: A Study of Ideology and Ambition, 1967, The Anglo-African Commonwealth: Political Friction and Cultural Fusion, 1967, On Heroes and Uhuru-Worship: Essays on Independent Africa, 1967, Violence and Thought: Essays on Social Tensions in Africa, 1969, Cultural Engineering and Nation-Building in East Africa, 1972, World Culture and the Black Experience, 1974, The Political Sociology of the English Language: An African Perspective, 1975, Soldiers and Kinsmen in Uganda: The Making of a Military Ethnocracy, 1975, Euro-Jews and Afro-Arabs: The Great Semitic Divergence in World History, Washington, 2008; co-editor: (with Robert I. Rotberg) Protest and Power in Black Africa, 1970, (with Hasu Patel) Africa in World Affairs: The Next Thirty Years, 1973; editor: The Warrior Tradition in Modern Africa, 1978, Africa since 1935 Volume III Unesco General History of Africa, 1973-93, (with Alamin M. Mazrui) The Political Culture of Language: Swahili, Society and the State, 1996—99, (with Alamin M. Mazrui) The Power of Babel: Language and Governance in Africa's Experience, 1998; sr. editor: (with T.K. Levine) The Africans: A Reader, 1986; author: The Trial of Christopher Okigbo, 1971, A World Federation of Cultures: An African Perspective, 1976; Africa's International Relations: The Diplomacy of Dependency and Change, 1977, Political Values and the Educated Class in Africa, 1978, The African Condition: A Political Diagnosis, 1980, (with Michael Tidy) Nationalism and New States in Africa, From About 1935 to the Present, 1984; narrator, presenter: The Africans: A Triple Heritage, 1986, Cultural Forces in World Politics, 1990, A Tale of Two Africas, 2006, Islam Between Globalization and Counterterrorism, 2006; mem. editl. bd. various profl. jours., 1963—; contbr. articles to profl. publs. Fellow Ctr for Advanced Study in Behavioral Scis., Palo Alto, Calif., 1972-73; sr. fellow Hoover Instn. on War, Revolution and Peace, Stanford, Calif., 1973-74, Mich. Soc. Fellows, 1978-82; Commander of the Burning Spear award, Kenya, 2005, ECOWAS award of Living Legend, 2007, South African award of Grand Companion of Oliver Tambo, 2007, Image of Africa prize, Friends Africa Internat., NY, 2008. Fellow Internat. Assn. Mid. Ea. Studies, Ghana Acad. Arts and Scis. (hon.); mem. African Studies Assn. (exec. bd. 1975-80, pres. 1978-79, Disting. Africans award 1995), Internat. Congress African Studies (v.p. 1978-85), Internat. Polit. Sci. Assn. (v.p. 1970-73), World Order Models Project (dir. African sect. 1968-83), Royal African Soc. (v.p.), Royal Commonwealth Soc., United Kenya Club (Nairobi), Athenaeum Club (London), Assn. Muslim Social Scientists (Washington) (elected pres. 2007-). Office: SUNY Inst Global Cultural Studies Off Schweitzer Chair PO Box 6000 Binghamton NY 13902-6000 Office Phone: 607-777-4494. E-mail: amazrui@binghamton.edu.

MAZUR, ALLAN CARL, sociologist, educator; b. Chgo., Mar. 20, 1939; s. Joseph and Esther (Markowitz) M.; m. Minnette Albrecht, Jan. 21, 1968; children— Julie Elizabeth, Rachel Lee. BS, Ill. Inst. Tech., Chgo., 1961; MS, UCLA, 1964; PhD, Johns Hopkins U., Balt., 1969. Rsch. engr. North Am. Aviation Co., Los Angeles, 1961-64; instr. polit. sci. Mass. Inst. Tech., 1966-67; ops. rsch. analyst Lockheed Missile & Space Corp., Sunnyvale, Calif., 1967-68; asst. prof. sociology Stanford U., 1968-71; mem. faculty Syracuse U., NY, 1971—, prof. pub. affairs NY, 1992—. Author: Dynamics of Technical Controversy, 1981, Global Social Problems, 1991, 2005, A Hazardous Inquiry: The Rashomon Effect at Love Canal, 1998, True Warnings and False Alarms, 2004, A Romance in Natural History: The Lives and Works of Amadeus Grabau and Mary Antin, 2004, Biosociology of Dominance and Deference, 2005, Global Social Problems, 2007, Implausible Beliefs in the Bible, Astrology and UFOs, 2008-, The Female Nude In Westren Art, 2009; co-author: Biology and Social Behavior, 1972; contbr. articles to profl. jours. Fellow AAAS. Jewish. Office: Syracuse U 400 Eggers Maxwell Sch Syracuse NY 13244 Home Phone: 315-445-1970; Office Phone: 315-443-9310. Business E-Mail: amazur@syr.edu.

MAZUR, EDWARD JOHN, JR., financial planner; b. Lowell, Mass., Mar. 5, 1948; s. Edward John Sr. and Mary Annette (Terry) M.; m. Sheila MacDonald, Dec. 13, 1969 (div. Nov. 1984); 1 child, Kristen Leigh; m. Anna Maria Maia, May 18, 1985; children: Edward John III, Kara Maia Mazur. BA in History, U. Mass., 1969. CLU, Chartered Fin. Cons., Life Underwriters Tng. Coun. Fellow. From agt. to dir. agys. John Hancock Mut. Life Ins. Co., Boston, 1973—84, gen. agt. Hartford, 1984-89; founder Mazur Fin., Farmington, Conn., 1990—2000, Profl. Investors Exch., LLC, Farmington, 2000—05, Profl. Investor's Life and Annuity LLC, 2005—. Team coord. Team Conn., 1998—. Recipient Raymond T. Wilbur award, Mass. Jaycees, 1982-83; named President of Yr., Mass. Jaycees, 1982-83, Outstanding Young Men of Am., Mass. Jaycees, 1984. Mem. Million Dollar Round Table, Nat. Assn. Ins. and Fin. Advisors (pres. Conn. chpt. 2000-01), Hartford Life Underwriters Assn. (pres. 1995-97), US Racquetball Assn. (pres. jr. coun. 2005—07), Conn. Racquetball Assn. (pres. 1985-94). Avocations: racquetball, coaching, hiking. Home: 48 Knollwood Ln Avon CT 06001-2701 Office Phone: 860-678-7806. Personal E-mail: mazurfin@aol.com.

MAZUR, JOHN M., orthopedist, educator; m. Susan Beck; children: John, Julie. MD, U. Pitts. Sch. Medicine, 1970. Cert. orthop. surgeon Am. Bd. Orthop. Surgery, 1979. Affiliated clin. prof. U. Fla. Coll. Medicine Jacksonville Program, 1989—; staff physician Nemours Children's Clinic, Jacksonville, 1989—; prof. Mayo Clinic, Jacksonville, 1994—. Orthop. surgeon Mission Trips, Haiti, 2005—08, Spinal Defects Clinic, Jacksonville, 2005—08. Lt. comdr. US Dept. Health Edn., 1972—74, Washington. Named Pediat. Surg. Specialist of Yr., NE Fla. Pediat. Soc., 2007. Mem.: ACS, Am. Acad. Cerebral Palsy and Devel. Medicine, Southern Orthop. Assn., Duval County Med. Assn., Pediat. Orthop. Soc. N.Am., Fla. Med. Assn., Am. Orthop. Assn., Fla. Orthop. Soc., Southern Med. Assn., Soc. Internat. de Chirurgie Orthop. Traumatologie, Am. Acad. Pediat. Office: Nemours Children's Clinic 807 Children's Way Jacksonville FL 32207

MAZUR, THOMAS A., music educator; b. Newark, Nov. 10, 1945; s. Richard C. and Leocadia Mazur; m. Faith Frankel, Mar. 29, 1975; 1 child, Joy; m. Jacqueline Mazur, Dec. 30, 2004. BA in Music, Rutgers U., 1989; M in Music Edn., NJCU, 2004. Vocal music tchr. Long Branch (N.J.) H.S., 1990—95, Roosevelt Mid. Sch., West Orange, NJ, 1995—. Recipient Excellence in Tchg. award, N.J. Symphony Orch., Newark, 1996—97. Mem.: Kappa Delta Pi. Avocation: mountain climbing. Home: 708 Buckland Ct Denville NJ 07834 Office: N Plainfield HS 34 Wilson Ave Plainfield NJ 07060 Personal E-mail: tmazur@woboe.org.

MAZUREK, MONICA ANN, engineering educator; d. Eugene Theodore and Emily Lucia Mazurek; m. Gary Lee Taghon, Dec. 31, 1998; children: Max Edward Taghon, Meredith Marie Taghon. PhD in Geochemistry, U. Calif., LA, 1985. Coord. program devel. sci., math., engrng. Office v.p. for undergrad. edn. Rutgers U., Piscataway, NJ, 1988—2000, dir. academic initiatives, Sch. Engrng., 2000—02, asst. prof., 2002—08, assoc. prof., 2008—. Chemist, environ. chemistry divsn. Brookhaven Nat. Lab., 1989—95; assoc. program dir. atmospheric chemistry program NSF, Arlington, Va., 1996—98. Recipient Haagen-Smit award, 2001, 2007. Mem.: United Nations Intergovtl. on Climate Change (Nobel Peace prize 2007), Am. Soc. Engrng. Edn., Air Waste Mgmt. Assn., Am. Assn. Aerosol Rsch., Am. Chem. Soc. Achievements include patents for efficient synthesis of iodomethyl methyl ether. Office: Rutgers Univ CEE Dept 100 Brett Rd Piscataway NJ 08854-8058

MAZURKEWYCZ, CHRISTINE A., literature and language professor; d. Lubomir Mazurkewycz. BA in English & Psychology, U. Kans., Lawrence, 1997; MA in English Lit., Purdue U., West Lafayette, Ind., 2002; attending, U. Iowa, 2009. Tchg. U. Iowa, purdue U. Presdl. fellowship, U. Iowa, 2003. Home: 421 S Lucas St Iowa City IA 52240 Business E-Mail: christine-mazurkewycz@uiowa.edu.

MAZUSKI, JOHN EDWARD, surgeon, researcher; b. Fresno, Calif., Nov. 23, 1951; s. Paul G. and Ruth L. (Likely) M.; m. Clemencia Montoya, June 30, 1979; children: Maria Andrea, Paul Edward, Cristina Nora, Richard John. BA in Zoology, Calif. State U., 1973; MS in Biochemistry, U. Wis., 1975; MD, U. Calif., 1981; PhD in Biochemistry, U. Minn., 1993. Diplomate Am. Bd Surgery. Resident in surgery U. Minn., Mpls., 1981-90, fellow in surg. critical care, 1990-91; asst. prof. surgery St. Louis U., 1991-97, assoc. prof. surgery, 1997—. Dir. surg. ICU, dir. nutrition support svc. VA Med. Ctr., St. Louis, 1991—. Contbr. articles to profl. jours., chpt. in book. Fellow Am. Coll. Surgeons; mem. AAAS, Soc. Critical Care Medicine, Surgical Infection Soc., Assn. Acad. Surgery, Assn. VA Surgeons, Phi Kappa Phi, Alpha Omega Alpha. Office: St Louis Univ Surgery Dept 3635 Vista Ave Saint Louis MO 63110-2539

MAZZA, DAVID S., pediatric allergist, immunologist; b. Burlington, Vt., Dec. 10, 1947; s. Frank, Jr. and Margret Alice (Fuller) Mazza. BA, U. Vt., Burlington, 1969, MA in Math., 1971; MD, U. Vt. Coll. Med., Burlington, 1977. Diplomate Am. Bd. Pediats., lic. NY. Resident pediats. NYU-Bellevue Hosp., NYC, 1977—80, fellow in ambulatory pediats., 1980—82, attending staff emergency svc., 1982—. Instr. NYU, 1982—84; dir. ambulatory svcs. Booth Meml. Med. Ctr., NYC, 1982—, dir. fellowship program, 1985; attending staff North Shore U. Hosp., NY, 1985—, Cornell U., 1985—. Campaign vol. City Coun., NYC, 1985. Mem.: AAAS, NY Acad. Sci., Am. Acad. Pediats., Nature Conservancy Group, Defenders of Wildlife, Sierra Club. Democrat. Avocations: swimming, bicycling, travel. Office: David S Mazza MD 7 Lexington Ave #3 New York NY 10010 Office Phone: 212-677-7170.

MAZZA, DOMENICO, orthodontist; b. Rimini, Italy, Nov. 16, 1935; s. Dino and Flora (Morri) M.; m. Valeria Berger, July 30, 1970; children: Maddalena, Francesco, Stefano. MD, U. Bologna, 1960, DDS, 1964. Pvt. practice dentistry, Rimini, 1964—. Med. dental cons. City Ct., Rimini, 1970-71. Translator: (book) Biomechanics in Orthodontics, 1993; contbr. articles to profl. jours. Mem. W.W.F., Rimini, 1970-72, Movement for Earth Conservation, Rimini, 1972-74. Lt. Italian Mil. Corps, 1961-62. C.H. Tweed Internat. Found. for Orthodontic Rsch. fellow, 1970-74. Fellow Italian Dental Assn., Italian Assn. Orthodontists; mem. Rotary. Achievements include development of a highly non-linear software for the calculation of ortodontic springs; Identification of a general procedure for clinical application of calculated springs in edgewise orthodontics. Avocations: swimming, canoeing, reading. Home: Via C Colombo 6 Rimini RN47900 Italy Office: Via Tempio Malatestiano 12 Rimini RN 47900 Italy Office Phone: 39 541 22902. Office Fax: 39 541 23563.

MAZZAFERRI, ERNEST LOUIS, endocrinologist, educator; b. Cleve., Sept. 27, 1936; s. Joseph and Nanetta (Marinelli) M.; m. Florence Mildred Marolt, Nov. 23, 1957; children: Patricia Marie Atchison, Michael Louis, Sharon Lynne Brown, Ernest Louis. BS cum laude, John Carroll U., 1958; MD, Ohio State U., 1962. Diplomate Am. Bd. Internal Medicine. Intern Ohio State U. Hosps., Columbus, 1962-63, resident, 1963-64, 66-68; asst. prof. medicine Ohio State U., 1968-70, assoc. prof., 1973-76, prof., 1976-79, dir. div. endocrinology and metabolism, 1975-78; acting dean U. Nev., Reno, 1979-81, prof., chmn. dept. medicine, 1978-84, prof. physiology, 1982-84; prof., chmn. dept. medicine, prof. physiology Ohio State U., Columbus, 1984-99, prof. emeritus, 1999—; pres. Dept. of Medicine Found., 1986-99; chmn. bd. Ohio State Practice Group, 1996-99; clin. prof. medicine U. Fla., Gainesville, 2001—. Bd. dirs. The Ohio State U. Hosps., 1997—99; mem. com. on exposure of Am. people to I-131 from Nev. atomic bomb tests Nat. Acad. Sci. Inst. of Medicine, 1997—99, mem. com. on health effects assoc. with exposures experienced during the Gulf War, 1999—2000; mem. com. guidelines for thyroid cancer screening Inst. Medicine, 1997—99; chmn. Nat. Cancer Ctr. Network Com. on Thyroid Cancer Guidelines; mem. com. on health effects associated with exposures during the Gulf War Inst. of Medicine Nat. Academies of Sci., 1999—2000. Author: Endocrinology Case Studies, 3d edit., 1985, Internal Medicine Pearls, 1993; editor: Textbook of Endocrinology, 3d edit., 1986, Contemporary Internal Medicine, 1988, 3d edit., 1990, Advances in Endocrinology and Metabolism, Vol. 6, 1995, Endocrine Tumors, 1993, Morning Report, 1999, Yearbook of Endocrinology, 1999—; Endocrine editor Yearbook of Medicine, 1999—; editor: Practical Management of Thyroid Cancer: A Medical Disciplinary Approach, 2005, Essentials of Thyroid Cancer Management, Kluwer Acad. Publishers, 2005-; editor-in-chief: Clinical Thyroidology; mem. sci. adv. bd. Western Jour. Medicine, 1993; mem. editl. bd. Jour. Lab. Clin. Medicine, 1987-97, Hosp. Practice, Jour. of Clin. Endocrinology and Metabolism, Thyroid, 1999—; contbr. articles to profl. jours. Chmn. Gov.'s Com. on Radiation Fallout in Nev., 1980-84, hosp. ethics com. Ohio State U., 1994-98; mem. Sec. of Energy Dose Assessment Adv. Com., 1980-84, Agy. for Health Care Policy, Rsch. Cataract Guideline Com., 1991-92, Inst. of Medicine Guideline for Thyroid Cancer Screening com., 1997-99; mem. rsch. coun. com. on expense of Am. People to I-131 from Nev. Atomic Bomb Tests: Implications for Public Health, 1997-99,editor in chief Clin. Thyroidology. Capt. USAF, 1964, maj. USAF, 1968, lt. col. USAF, 1968—73, col. USAR, 1984—91. Recipient Earl N. Metz Disting. Physician award, Ohio State U., 1998, Light of Life award, Light of Life Found. N.Y., 1999, Graves' award, Thyroid Soc. for Rsch. and Edn., 2001, Disting. Svc. award, Ohio State U., 2009. Master: ACP (gov. for Nev. 1984—85, chmn. clin. efficacy assessment program com. 1992—95, edn. policy com. 1992—95, mem. health and pub. policy com.); mem.: AMA, Ohio State U. (Disting. Svc. award), Am. Coll. Clin. Endocrinology (bd. dis. 1995—96, Disting. Clinician award 2002), Ctrl. Soc. Clin. Rsch., Am. Clin. and Climatol. Assn., Endocrine Soc. (Disting. Educator award 2005), Am. Diabetes Assn. (pres. Ohio affiliate 1988—89), Am. Thyroid Assn. (pres.-elect 2004—05, pres. 2005—, Paul Star award, Disting. Svc. award), Am. Bd. Internal Medicine (chmn. Endocronology and Metabolism 1999—2003, bd. dirs. 1999—2003, cert. in endocrinology and metabolism, gen. internal medicine, cert. in geriatrics, continuous profl. devel.), Alpha Omega Alpha. Roman Catholic. Achievements include research in thyroid cancer. Home: 4020 SW 93rd Dr Gainesville FL 32608-4653 *Success, like every other human experience, is relative, measured against shifting standards and subject to the scrutiny of time. One must strike a fine balance— self certainty against external review— that permits the full expression of new ideas enriched by the best and time-worn thoughts of others.*

MAZZAFERRO, JAMES JOSEPH, music educator; b. San Francisco, Calif., Apr. 19, 1956; s. James John and Marilyn Jean Mazzaferro; m. Anita Marie Piccone, Nov. 27, 1976; children: Cherylyn, Joseph, Jeanette. Bachelors Music Edn., San Francisco State U., San Francisco, CA, 1978; Masters in Music Conducting, Calif. State U., Sacramento, 1995. San Francisco Archdiocese Archbishop Riordan HS, San Francisco, 1979—89; tchr. music Florin H.S. Elk Grove Unified, Sacramento, 1989—97, Sacramento City Coll. Los Rios CC, Sacramento, 1997—2001, Sheldon HS Elk Grove Unified, Sacramento, 1997—, Cosumnes River Coll. Los Rios CC, Sacramento, 1999—. Bd. directors Cazadero Performing Arts, Cazadero, Calif., 1995—2001, Calif. Band Directors, Fresno, Calif., 1999—2001. Mem.: Calif. Music Educators Assn. (band rep. 1994—98), Musician's Union Local 6, Music Educators Nat. Conf., Phi Kappa Lambda (hon.), Phi Kappa Phi (hon.). Avocation: music performance. Home: 9068 Shetland Court Elk Grove CA 95624 Office: Sheldon High School 8333 Kingsbridge Drive Sacramento CA 95829 Personal E-mail: jmazz1@surewest.net.

MAZZE, EDWARD MARK, marketing educator, consultant; b. NYC, Feb. 14, 1941; s. Harry Alan and Mollie (Schneider) M.; m. Sharon Sue Hastings, Sept. 9, 1967; children: Candace, Thomas. BBA, City U. NY, 1961, MBA, 1962; PhD, Pa. State U., 1966. Lectr. bus. adminstrn. CCNY, 1961-62; bus. cons., 1961—; instr. bus. Pa. State U., 1963-66; assoc. prof. mktg. U. Detroit, 1966-68; assoc. prof., dir. spl. programs W.Va. U., 1968-70; prof. bus. adminstrn., coordinator mktg. program Va. Poly. Inst. and State U., Blacksburg, 1970-75; v.p. adminstrv. services, dean Sch. Bus., Seton Hall U., South Orange, NJ, 1975-79; dean sch. bus. adminstrn. Temple U., Phila., 1979-86, prof. mktg. and internat. bus., 1979-93; dean Belk Coll. Bus. Adminstrn., prof. mktg. U. NC, Charlotte, 1993-98, co.-dir. Frank Hawkins Kenan Inst. Pvt. Enterprise, 1997—98; dean Coll. Bus. Adminstrn., Alfred J. Verrecchia-Hasbro Inc. Leadership chair in bus. U. RI, Kingston, 1998—2006, disting. univ. prof. bus. adminstrn., 2006—. Chmn. bd. William Penn Bank, Phila., 1985-87; bd. dirs. Technitrol, Inc., Washington Trust Bancorp, Inc., Barrett Growth Fund, Ocean State Bus. Devel. Authority; mem. dist. export coun. US Dept. Commerce, 1978-80, 83-93; mem. panel chpt. 7 trustees US Dept. Justice, 1984-96, 2005; adv. bd. McGettigan Ptrns., 1997-99, Radiator Specialty Co., 1997-99, Piedmont Venture Ptrns., 1997-98; mem. faculty master liberal arts in mgmt. program Harvard U., 2003, 06-07. Author: International Business: Articles and Essays, 1963, Readings in Organization and Management, 1963, Marketing in Action, 1963, Case Histories in Sales Management, 1965, Sales Management: Theory and Practice, 1965, International Marketing Adminstration, 1967, Introduction to Marketing, 1970, Marketing in Turbulent Times: The Challenges and the Opportunities, 1975, Personal Selling: Choice Against Chance, 1976, The Food Marketing Wars: Marketing Triumphs and Blunders, 1998, Specialty Retailers: Marketing Triumphs and Blunders, 2001, Lifestyle Marketing: Reaching the New American Consumer, 2003, The Affluent Consumer: Marketing and Selling the Luxury Lifestyle, 2006; mem. editl. bd. Jour. Econs. and Bus., 1976-80, Indsl. Mktg. Mgmt., 1977-2006, Jour. Internat. Bus. Studies, 1978-82, Jour. Acad. Mktg. Sci., 1980-91, Jour. Mktg. Edn., 1985-94, Jour. Global Mktg., 1987-2006; contbr. articles to profl. jours. Trustee Phila. Home Care, 1984-89, Manor Coll., 1985-92, Thomas A. Edison State Coll. Found., 1987-89, Delaware Valley Coll. Sci. and Agr., 1991-97, Pa. Inst. Tech., 1992-93; chmn. econ. devel. adv. com. Village South Orange, 1977-80, Town Narragansett, 2009-; mem., vice-chmn. Bd. Suprs. Doylestown Twp., 1980-81. Ford. Found. fellow, 1962-63 Mem. Acad. Internat. Bus.,New Eng. Economic Partnership (co-forecast mgr. 2005-),

Nat. Assn. Corp. Dirs., Acad. Mktg. Sci., Beta Gamma Sigma, Pi Kappa Alpha. Home: 52 Horizon Dr Saunderstown RI 02874-2402 Office: U RI Coll Business 304 Ballentine Hall Kingston RI 02881 Home Phone: 401-295-5802; Office Phone: 401-874-4308. Personal E-mail: emazze@cox.net.

MAZZILLI, LEE, sportscaster, former professional baseball manager; b. Bklyn., Mar. 25, 1955; s. Libero Mazzilli; m. Dani Mazzilli; children: Jenna, Lee Jr., Lacey. Profl. baseball player NY Mets, 1976—81, 1986—89, Tex. Rangers, 1982, NY Yankees, 1982, Pitts. Pirates, 1983—86, Toronto Blue Jays, 1989; coach Tampa (Fla.) Yankees, 1997—98, Norwich (Conn.) Yankees, 1998—2000; first base & outfield coach NY Yankees, 2000—03, bench coach, 2006; mgr. Balt. Orioles, 2004—05; lead studio analyst SportsNet NY, 2006—. Named to Nat. League All Star Team, 1979.

MAZZIO-MOORE, JOAN L., retired radiology educator, physician; b. Belmont, Mass., Oct. 26, 1935; d. Frank Joseph and Maria L. Mazzio; children: Hon James Thomas Moore, Edwin Stuart Moore. BA in Chemistry and Theology, Emmanuel Coll., 1957; MA in Genetics and Physiology, Wellesley Coll., Mass., 1961; PhD student in Genetics, Bryn Mawr Coll., Pa.; grad., Phila. Coll. Medicine, 1977, MSc in Radiology, 1981. Instr. organic chemistry Gwynedd Mercy Coll., 1962—64; instr. in genetics Holy Family Coll., Phila., 1964—65; instr. in anatomy Phila. Coll. of Medicine, 1971—77, assoc. prof., 1977—84; prof. W.Va. Sch. of Medicine, 1984—2003, ret., 2004; rotating intern Phila. Coll. of Medicine Hosp., 1977—78, resident in radiology and radiation therapy, 1978—81, mem. hosp. staff, 1981—84; consulting radiologist Bgnd Clinic, Lewisburg, W.Va., 1984—2004; med. dir. Anthony Correctional Ctr., 1986—99; pvt. practice, 1986—2004. Author (with Dr. DiVirgilito): Essentials of Neuropathology, 1974. Treas. Hist. Soc. of Frankford, Phila., 1968—75, Sch. Mother's Assn., Devon, Pa., 1980—81; vol. mem. Ct. Appts. Spl. Adv. for Children, 2000—; parlamentarian Greenbrier Com. on Aging, 2000—07; bd. trustees Lake Erie Coll. Medicine and Pharmacy, Erie, Pa., Bradenton, Fla.; organist Ch. of Incarnation, W.Va., St. Charles Borromeo Ch., White Sulphur Springs, W.Va., 2001—; lector St. Ann's Cath. Ch., Phoenixville, Pa., 1981—84. Lt. col. MC USAR, 1984—2002. Mem. AAUP, Am. Assn. Women Radiologists, Am. Med. Women's Assn., Am. Osteo. Coll. Radiology (life), Am. Soc. Clin. Oncology, Am. Soc. Therapeutic Radiologists, Hist. Soc. Lewisburg (life), Pa. Osteo. Med. Assn., Radiol. Soc. N.Am., Radiation Rsch. Soc., Res. Officers Assn. (life), W.Va. Soc. Osteo. Medicine, Greenbrier Valley Med. Soc., NRA (life). Home: PO Box 97 Frankford WV 24938 Home Fax: 304-497-2752. Personal E-mail: drjoanlmoore@yahoo.com.

MAZZO, KAY, ballet dancer, educator; b. Evanston, Ill., Jan. 17, 1946; d. Frank Alfred and Catherine M. (Hengel) M.; m. Albert C. Bellas, 1978; children: Andrew, Kathryn. Student, Sch. Am. Ballet, 1959-61. Co-chair faculty Sch. Am. Ballet. Profl. debut in ballets U.S.A. 1961, touring Europe with co., performing for Pres. Kennedy at White House, 1961, joined N.Y.C. Ballet, 1962-80, soloist, 1965-69, prin. ballerina, 1969-80, prin. roles in world premiere of ballets including Tschaikowsky Suite No. #3, 1970, PAMTGG, 1971, Stravinsky Violin Concerto, 1972, Scherzo A La Russe, 1972, Duo Concertant, 1972, Sheherazade, 1975, Union Jack, 1976, Vienna Waltzes, 1977, Davidsbundlertanze, 1980; ballet tchr. Sch. Am. Ballet, 1980—; appeared as guest artist in leading roles with numerous cos. including Boston Ballet, Washington Ballet, Berlin Ballet, Geneva Ballet; appeared on TV in U.S., Can., Fed. Republic Germany. Recipient Mademoiselle Merit award 1970 Office: Sch Am Ballet 70 Lincoln Center Plz New York NY 10023-6548

MAZZOCCA, AUGUSTA D., surgeon; s. Augustus D. and D'Ann Mazzocca; m. Jennifer Mazzocca; children: Augustus III, Jillian, Nicolo. MS, U. Conn. Sch. Medicine, Farmington, MD, 2001. Cert. in sports medicine Am. Bd. Orthop. Surgeons, 2008. Assoc. prof. U. Conn. Health Ctr. & Sch. Medicine, 2002—, asst. dir. orthop. surgery residency program, 2003—. Contbr. articles to profl. jours. (Gaspari award, 2001). Grants., Arthrex Inc., 2002—08. Fellow: Am. Acad. Orthop. Surgery. Office: Univ Conn Health Ctr 263 Farmington Ave MARB 4 Farmington CT 06034-4037 Business E-Mail: mazzocca@uchc.edu.

MAZZOLA, ANTHONY THOMAS, editor, graphics designer, consultant, curator; b. Passaic, NJ, June 13, 1923; s. Thomas and Jennie (Failla) M.; m. Michele Morgan, Nov. 18, 1967; children: Anthony Thomas II, Marc Eden, Alisa Morgan. Grad., Cooper Union Art Sch., NYC, 1948. Art dir. Street & Smith Publs., NYC, 1948, Town and Country mag. (pub. by Hearst Corp.), NYC, 1948-65, editor-in-chief, 1965-72, Harpers Bazaar, 1972-92; editor-in-chief, pres. Anthony Mazzola Design Corp., NYC, 1963—; creative cons. Hearst Corp., 1992—. Editl. dir. 125 Great Moments of Harper's Bazaar, 1991—94, Town & Country 150th Anniversary, 1994—; curator fine arts Hearst Corp., 2001—; cons. designer UN Childrens' Fund, Assn. Jr. Leagues Am., Columbia Pictures Corp., Sells Spltys., Gen. Foods, Paramount Pictures, Princess Marcella Borghese, Inc., Huntington Hartford Ltd., NY World's Fair, 1965 Exhibited, Art Dirs. Club NY, ann. exhbns., 1948—. Exhibited, Art Dirs. Club. N.Y., ann. exhbns., 1948—. Served with AUS, 1943-46. Decorated Bronze Star, Knight Officer of Order of Merit Italy; recipient Cert. of Merit awards N.Y. Art Dirs. Club; medal Art Dirs. Club N.Y.C., 1955. Office: Hearst Corp 300 W 57th St New York NY 10019

MAZZOLA, CHRIS, dentist; DDS, Loyola U. Intern Pub. Health Svc., BC Coll. of Dental Surgeons; pvt. practice cosmetic dentistry Ketchum, Idaho. Featured on The Cutting Edge-Cosmetic Surgery, Discovery Channel, The Learning Channel; spkr. in field. Fellow Internat. Acad. Dental-Facial Esthetics, 2002—03. Mem.: Am. Acad. Cosmetic Dentistry (bd. dirs. 1996—2000, accredited mem. 1990). Office: 181 First Ave N Box 1222 Ketchum ID 83340 Office Phone: 208-726-4711.

MAZZOLA, JOHN WILLIAM, retired performing company executive, consultant; b. Bayonne, NJ, Jan. 20, 1928; s. Roy Stephen and Eleanor Burton (Davis) M.; m. Sylvia Drulie, Mar. 7, 1959; children: Alison, Amy. AB, Tufts U., 1949; LLD, Fordham U., 1952. Bar: N.Y. 1956. Mem. firm Milbank, Tweed, Hadley & McCloy, NYC, 1952-64; sec., exec. v.p. Lincoln Center for Performing Arts, NYC, 1964-68, gen. mgr., chief exec. officer, 1968—70, mng. dir., chief exec. officer, 1970-77, pres., chief exec. officer, 1977-84; exec. v.p. Embassy Pictures, 1984—86. Cons. performing arts ctrs. in U.S. and abroad, also motion pictures, non-profit orgns. Bd. dirs. various charitable orgns.; mem. adv. bd. Santa Fe Symphony. With Air Force USN, 1945—46, with CIC US Army, 1953—55. Decorated cavaliere ufficiale Ordine al Merito della Repubblica Italiana; Ordre des Arts et des Lettres France; Benjamin Franklin fellow Royal Soc. Arts. Mem. Watch Hill Yacht Club, Misquamicut Club (R.I.). Episcopalian. Home: 12 Beekman Pl New York NY 10022-8059 Office Phone: 212-755-5117. Personal E-mail: johnwmazzola@aol.com.

MAZZOLA, MARJORIE ELLEN, humanities educator; BA, Mundelein Coll., Chgo., 1968; MA, NYU, NYC, 1980. Cert. in primary and secondary tchg. Ill. Adj. instr. St. Xavier U., Chgo., 1989—; English instr. Mother McAuley Liberal Arts HS, Chgo., 1992—. Mem.: Friends Libr. Orgn.

MAZZOLI, LINDA FABRIZIO, personal trainer, consultant, marketing professional; BS in Student Design, Athletic Tng., West Chester U., Pa., 1990; AS in Phys. Therapy Asst., Harcum Coll., Bryn Mawr, Pa., 1994; MS, Calif. U. Pa., 2004. Mgr. clin. NovaCare, Breemall, Pa., 1993—94, regional dir. athletic tng. cert. svcs. Exton, Pa., 1994—97, nat. dir. King of Prussia, Pa., 1997—2000, dir. program devel., 1998—2000; pres. QuinTech Health Svcs., LLC, Essington, Pa., 2000—02; v.p. clin. svcs. Benchmark Med. Inc., Malvern, Pa., 2002—04; dir. mktg. & profl. devel. Cooper Univ. Hosp., Camden, NJ, 2004—. Cons., 2004—06; adj. prof. Eastern U., Wayne, Pa., 2005—06; bus. adv. bd. Harcum Coll., Bryn Mawr, 2005—06. Mem.: Am. Phys. Therapy Assn., Athletic Trainers Soc. NJ (bd. dirs. 2006), Nat. Athletic Trainers Assn. (Dist. II liaison to COR 2001—06, BOC), Pa. Athletic Trainers Soc. (bd. dirs. 1997—2001, athletic trainer cert., Svc. award 2005). Republican. Roman Cath. Avocations: gardening, reading, golf. Home: 3828 Marsh Rd Boothwyn PA 19061 Office: Cooper Bone and Joint Inst 3 Cooper Plz Ste 411 Camden NJ 08103

MAZZOLLA, D. PATRICK, healthcare services executive; b. Trenton, Pa., Mar. 23, 1947; s. Dan D. and Marguerite D. (Fox) M.; m. Georgia Lee Swartley, May 27, 1972; 1 chld, John Patrick. BS, Pa. State U., University Park, 1969; M Adminstrn., Pa. State U., Harrisburg, 1976. With mgmt. svcs. York Hosp., Pa., 1970-73, chief info. officer, 1973-77; mgmt. cons. Pa. Hosp. Svcs. Assn., Camp Hill, 1978-81; v.p. Hosp. Assn. Pa., Camp Hill, 1982-83, sr. v.p., 1983-86; pres., CEO Hapsco Group, Inc., 1986-93, Allhealth, Harrisburg, Pa., 1994—2006; mng. dir. Remuda Mgmt. Consulting, LLC, 2006—. Chmn. Assn. Health Care Enterprises, 1988-89, bd. dirs., 1984-91, 96-99; bd. dirs. Pa. Hosp. Svcs. Assn., 1983-98; adj. faculty York Coll. Pa., 1976-77. Corr. editor York County Med. Soc. newsletter, 1972-74. Chmn. non-profit divsn. United Way, Harrisburg, Pa., 1987, chmn. healthcare divsn., 1992; bd. dirs. Pa. Joint Underwriters Assn., Phila., 1983-87, Pa. C. of C. Edn. Found., 1995-01; mem. adv. coun. Pa. State U. Harrisburg Sch. Bus., 2002-; bd. dirs. Smeal Sch. Bus. Alumni Soc., 2004-. Avocations: fly fishing, target shooting, photography, reading. Home: 2640 Waterford Camp Hill PA 17011

MAZZOTTI, JOSÉ ANTONIO, humanities educator, researcher; PhD, Princeton U., NJ, 1993. Assoc. prof. Harvard U., Cambridge, Mass., 1997—2005; prof. and chair Tufts U., Medford, Mass., 2005—. Pres. Internat. Assn. Peruvianists, Medford, 1996—2008. Author: (poetry) Sakra Boccata. Grant, NEH, 2004—05. Mem.: Latin Am. Studies Assn. Office: Tufts Univ Olin Ctr 180 Packard Ave Medford MA 02155 Business E-Mail: jose.mazzotti@tufts.edu.

MAZZUCELLI, COLETTE GRACE CELIA, author, educator; b. Bklyn., Nov. 26, 1962; d. Silvio Anthony and Adeline Marie De Ponte. BA, U. Scranton, 1983; MALD in Law and Diplomacy, Fletcher Sch., Tufts U., 1987; PhD, Georgetown U., 1996; post grad., Columbia U., 2003—. Asst. ratification process Treaty European Union German Fgn. Ministry, 1992—93; lectr. U.S. Info. Svc. Spkrs. Program, Europe, 1994; dir. internat. programs and lectr. Budapest Inst. Grad. Internat. and Diplomatic Studies, 1995—97; instr. in-ho. tng. negotiations Hungarian Fgn. Ministry, 1996—97; del. to NATO accession talks Hungarian Ministry Def., 1997; advisor to bd. dirs. Transatlantic Info. Exch. Svc., 1997—98; founding dir., internat. peace and conflict resolution grad. program, asst. prof. polit. sci. Arcadia U., 1998—2000; chair Transatlantic internet multimedia seminar S.E. Europe (TIMSSE) ScPo, Paris, 2000—03; fellow EastWest Inst., 2001; program officer, edn. NGO rep. UN Carnegie Coun. Ethics and Internat. Affairs, 2001—02; program devel. assoc. Tchrs. Coll. Columbia U., 2002—04; faculty John C. Whitehead Sch. Diplomacy and Internat. Rels. Seton Hall U., 2005—06; asst. prof. dept. history and polit. sci. Molloy Coll., Rockville Centre, 2006—09. Rsch. fellow Inst. Europaeische Politik, Deutsche Gesellschaft Auswaertige Politk, Bonn, Deutsch-Franzoesisches Inst., Ludwigsburg; instr. Georgetown U., Washington, 1990, 96; adj. asst. prof. MS program global affairs Sch. Continuing and Profl. Studies NYU, 2005—; mem. tech. master plan steering com. Molloy Coll., 2007—08, mem. enrollment and finance task force, middle state period review, 2008, rep., academic integrity ctr., 08; adj. assoc. prof. polit. sci. Hofstra U., 2009—. Author: Monnet Case Studies in European Affairs, 1995, France and Germany at Maastricht Politics and Negotiations to Create the European Union, 1997, paperback 2d edit., 1999, Web Commentaries Aices Advisor, Libertas, Conversations on Diplomacy and Power Politics, Enquaring America; asst. editor: The Evolution of an International Actor: Western Europe's New Assertiveness, 1990; co-editor: Ethics and Global Politics: The Active Learning Sourcebook, 2004, Leadership in the Big Bangs of European Integration, 2007; contbr. articles to profl. jours.; chpts. to books. Mem. founding cabinet World Peace and Diplomacy Forum, 2003—; adv. group UN Chronicle, 2006—; v.p. recognition World Congress Arts, Scis. and Comm., 2007; pub. affairs spkr. Molloy Inst. Lifelong Learning, 2007—. Named Internat. Educator of Yr., 2003, Da Vinci Laureate, 2004, Pirate of Yr., 2006; recipient citation Nat. Women's Conf., 2006, Fgn. Affairs Faculty Spotlight Profile, 2009; grantee Swiss U., 1984-85, Profl. Devel. NYU, 2006, Fulbright Found., 2007, Coun. Fgn. Rels., NYC, Website Listing; scholar Pi Gamma Mu, 1985, Rotary Grad. scholar, 1987-88, Fulbright scholar, 1991, 07; fellow Jean Monnet Coun., 1991, European Commn., 1992, Robert Bosch Found., 1992-93, Salzburg Seminar, 1997, 21st Century Trust fellow Merton Coll., Oxford U., Eng., 2001, Bosch Pub. Policy fellow Am. Acad., Berlin, Aspen Inst., Berlin, 2001, Wilton Park Conf. fellow, Poland, 2007. Mem.: AAUW, Salzburg Global Seminar, Fgn. Policy Rsch. Inst., Women's Foreign Policy Group, Wilton Park Internat. Assn., Carnegie Coun. Ethics and Internat. Affairs, Fgn. Policy Assn., Robert Bosch Found. Alumni Assn. (mem. exec. com. 1994—96, 1997—98, co-pres. 1999—2000), European Union Studies Assn., Am. Coun. Germany, Am. Assn. Advancement Slavic Studies, Am. Polit. Sci. Assn., Rotary Club Metro N.Y., The Fletcher Club of N.Y. (v.p. 1998), Delta Tau Kappa, Alpha Mu Gamma, Pi Sigma Alpha, Phi Alpha Theta, Phi Sigma Tau (founder Scranton chpt.), Pi Gamma Mu (chpt. sec. 1982—84, Frank C. Brown scholarship medal 1984), Alpha Sigma Nu (student pres. 1984). Avocations: chess, swimming, creative writing, astrology, Tae Kwon Do. Home: 1864 74th St Brooklyn NY 11204-5752 Office: Ctr Global Affairs NY Univ Wool Worth Bldg 15 Barclay St New York NY 10007 Office Phone: 646-372-4396. E-mail: cm@americanacademy.de.

M. B. SAHANA, materials scientist, researcher; d. Bheema Moodakere Bhat and Lalitha Moodakare Bhat; m. Sudakar Chandran; 1 child, Ananya Sudakar. PhD, Indian Inst. Sci., 2004. Postdoc. fellow Stockholm U., 2004—05, Wayne State U., Detroit, 2006—, rschr. Achievements include research in transition metal oxide. Office: Wayne State Univ 666 W Hancock Detroit MI 48201 Personal E-mail: sahanamb@gmail.com.

MBAH, EMMANUEL MBAH, history professor; b. Mamfe, Cameroon, Jan. 4, 1970; s. Levi Tibong and Theresia Mbibabo Mbah; m. Ndah Njohjam. AAS in Computer Info. Sys., South Plains Coll., Levelland, Tex., 2001; PhD, U. Tex., Arlington, 2006. Cert. in internet South Plains Coll., Levelland, 2001. Grad. tchg. asst. U. Tex., Arlington, 2004—05, instr. history, 2005—06; asst. prof. history CUNY, Coll. SI, NY, 2006—. Author: (book) Land/Boundary Conflict in Africa: The Case of Former British Colonial Bamenda, Present-day North-West Province of the Republic of Cameroon, 1916-1996. Grant, Rsch. Found. CUNY, 2007—08. Independent. Avocations: travel, photography, movies. Office: CUNY Coll SI 2800 Victory Blvd Staten Island NY 10314 Office Fax: 718-982-2875.

M'BAYE, BABACAR, black literature educator; s. Moussa Mbaye and Fatou Wade; married. Degree, U. Gaston Berger, St. Louis, 1995; MA in Am. Studies, Pa. State U., Middletown, 1998; PhD in Am. Studies, Bowling Green State U., Ohio, 2002. Asst. prof. African Am. & African diasporan studies Evergreen State Coll., Olympia, Wash., 2002—06; asst. prof. pan-African lit. & culture Kent State U., Ohio, 2006—. Author: (book) The Trickster Comes West; contbr. articles to profl. jours., chapters to books. Mem.: AAUP (Kent State Chpt.), MLA, Senegalese Academic Soc. (founding mem.), Pan African Faculty & Staff Assn., African Cultures & Policy Studies Inst. (founding mem., dir. 1999—), Am. Studies Assn. Office: Dept English Kent State Univ Kent OH 44242 Office Phone: 330-672-1742. Business E-Mail: bmbaye@kent.edu.

MBULAITEYE, SAM, medical researcher; s. Daniel F. and Elizabeth S. Mbulaiteye; m. Annet N Nagadya; children: Daniel E., Delma E., Donna E. MB, Makerere U. Kampala, Uganda, 1990; MPhil in Epidemiology and Biostatistics, U. Cambridge, England, 1994; M.Med, Makerere U., 1996. Lic. med. practice Uganda Med. and Dental Practitioners Coun., 1991. Intern med. officer St. Mary's Hosp. Lacor, Gulu, Uganda, 1990—91; med. officer Mulago Hosp., Kampala, 1991—92, sr. ho. officer, 1993—96; med. officer, spl. grade Uganda Cancer Inst., Kampala, 1996—98; project leader Uganda Virus Rsch. Inst. Med. Rsch. Coun., Entebbe, 1998—2000; rsch. fellow Nat. Cancer Inst., Bethesda, Md., 2000—05, prin. investigator, 2005—. Dir., cmty. svcs. Rotaract Club Mengo, Kampala, 1992—96. Promoter Uganda Cancer Rsch. Found., 2007. Recipient Dir's Intramural Innovation award, Nat. Cancer Inst., 2008, Individual Merit award, NIH, 2008, Elective Bursary, Common Wealth Trust, 1989. Fellow: Darwin Coll. Soc., Cambridge Common Wealth Trust; mem.: Uganda Acad. Scis., Uganda Med. Assn., African Orgn. Rsch. and Tng. Cancer. Independent. Achievements include research in significant declines in HIV incidence; risk of transmission of human herpesvirus 8 with history of blood transfusion; mother-to-child transmission of human herpesvirus 8 infection within families; first to feasibility of using registry record-linkage methods to study HIV/AIDS-associated cancers; research in extremely high levels of Epsterin-Barr virus, linked to Burkitt lymphoma, in the saliva and peripheral blood of children and their mothers. Avocations: travel, jogging, bicycling, water-skiing.

MCABEE, THOMAS ALLEN, psychologist; b. Spartanburg, SC, Mar. 31, 1949; s. Thomas Walker and Doris Lee (Gillespie) McA. Student, Ga. Inst. Tech., 1967-69; BA, Furman U., 1971; MA, U. SC, 1975, PhD, 1979. Clin. counselor Adolescent Inpatient Svc. William S. Hall Psychiat. Inst., Columbia, SC, 1971-73; counselor children's therapeutic camp Columbia Area Mental Health Ctr., 1974; co-dir. cmty. problems survey Eau Claire Cmty. Project, Columbia, 1975; asst. aging svcs. planner Ctrl. Midlands Regional Planning Coun., Columbia, 1976; instr. U. SC, 1976; NSF intern SC State Legislature, 1978; rsch. dir. SC Legis. Gov.'s Com. Mental Health and Mental Retardation, Columbia, 1979-80; co-dir. TV project "Feelings Just Are" Columbia Area Mental Health Ctr., 1980-89; psychologist SC Dept. Mental Retardation, 1982-93, SC Dept. Disabilities and Spl. Needs, 1993—2003, SC Vocat. Rehab. Dept., 2004—. Cons. SC Protection and Advocacy System for Handicapped Citizens, 1980, 81, SC Dept. Mental Health, 1981; mem. deinstitutionalization task force SC Developmental Disabilities Coun., 1979-80; mem. subcom. State Commr.'s Ad Hoc Com. to Study and Develop Work/Lodge System for SC, SC Dept. Mental Health, 1979-80; mem. Media Task Force of Gov.'s Adv. Com. on Early Childhood Devel. and Edn., 1980-81; chmn. primary prevention public media com. SC Dept. Mental Health, 1979-81; adj. faculty U. SC, Spartanburg, 2003; treas. Direct Client Svcs. Divsn. SC Vocat. Rehab. Assn., 2006-08; chmn. Workforce Readiness Com., Spartanburg Human Resources Assn., 2008-2009; pres. Victor Mill Cmty. Assn., 2009. Recipient Palmetto Pictures Photography award, 1977; NIMH fellow, 1976-77. Mem. APA, SC Psychol. Assn., Zoning Appeals Bd., City of Greer, SC. Home: 310 Snow St Greer SC 29651-4006 Office Phone: 864-585-3693. Business E-Mail: tmcabee@scvrd.state.sc.us.

MCADAM, DOUGLAS JOHN, sociologist, educator, director; s. Donald Neer McAdam and Patricia Tapscott; m. Tracy Lee Stevens, Feb. 20, 1988; children: Taylor, Molly. BA, Occidental Coll., 1973; MA, SUNY, Stony Brook, 1977, PhD, 1979. From asst. prof. to prof. sociology U. Ariz., Tucson, 1983, prof. sociology, Stanford (Calif.) U., 1998—, dir. Ctr. Advanced Study in Behavioral Scis., 2001—05. Mem. adv. bd. Inst. Social Rsch., Ann Arbor, Mich., 2001—04; trustee Social Sci. Rsch. Coun., NYC, 2002—06. Author: Political Process and the Development of Black Insurgency, 1982, Freedom Summer, 1988 (C. Wright Mills award, 1990), Dynamics of Contention, 2001. Fellow, Ctr. for Advanced Study in the Behavioral Scis., 1991—92, 1997—98; Fellowship, Guggenheim Found., 1984—85. Mem.: Am. Acad. Arts and Scis. Office: Dept Sociology Stanford Univ Stanford CA 94305

MCADAM, LOWELL C., telecommunications industry executive; b. May 28, 1954; B in Engring., Cornell U.; MBA, U. San Diego. EIT. With Pacific Bell, 1983—93, v.p., Bay Area Mktg., gen. mgr., South Bay customer services; exec. dir. internat. applications and ops. AirTouch Commn., 1993, v.p. internat. ops.; COO PrimeCo Personal Commn., pres., CEO; exec. v.p., COO Verizon Wireless, pres., CEO, 2007—. Vice chmn., bd. dirs. CTIA. Mem., Engr. USN. Office: Verizon Wireless 1 Verizon Way Basking Ridge NJ 07920*

MCADAMS, JOHN POPE, lawyer; b. Phila., June 5, 1949; s. Eugene P. and Mary (Miller) McA.; m. Anne Christina Connelly, Sept. 5, 1970; children: Emily Lane, Anne Connelly. BA, U. NC, 1971; JD, Wake Forest U., 1976. Bar: Fla. 1976, NC 1976, US Dist. Ct. (mid. dist.) Fla. 1977. Assoc. Carlton Fields, Tampa, Fla., 1976-82, ptnr., 1982—2007, of counsel, 2007—. Contbg. editor: The Developing Labor Law, 1983, Employee Duty of Loyalty, 1995; contbr. articles to profl. jours. Pres. Hillsborough Cmty. Mental Health Ctr., Tampa, 1983; trustee City of Temple Terrace Pension Plan, Fla., 1985-89; pres. Hyde Park Preservation, Inc., Tampa, 1993; bd. dir., pres. Child Abuse Coun., Inc., Tampa Lighthouse Blind. Mem. ABA, ABA Equal Rights & Responsibilities Com., Fla. Bar Assn. (exec. coun. labor sect. 1987-89). Democrat. Episcopalian. Home: 820 S Delaware Ave Tampa FL 33606-2915 Office: Carlton Fields PO Box 3239 Tampa FL 33601-3239 Office Phone: 813-223-7000, 813-229-4320. Business E-Mail: jmcadams@carltonfields.com.

MCADAMS, RACHEL, actress; b. London, Ont., Can., Oct. 7, 1976; d. Lance and Sandy McAdams. BFA with honors, NYU. Actor: (films) My Name is Tanino, 2002, Perfect Pie, 2002, The Hot Chick, 2002, Mean Girls, 2004, The Notebook, 2004, Wedding Crashers, 2005, Red-Eye, 2005, The Family Stone, 2005, Married Life, 2007, The Lucky Ones, 2008, State of Play, 2009, The Time Traveler's Wife, 2009; (TV films) Guilt by Association, 2002; (TV series) Shotgun Love Dolls, 2001, Slings and Arrows, 2003. Named Choice Movie Actress: Comedy, Teen Choice awards, 2006. Office: The Gersh Agy 232 N Canon Dr Beverly Hills CA 90210 Office Phone: 310-274-6611.

MCADARAGH, RAYMON MICHAEL, aerospace engineer, researcher; b. Springfield, Ohio, Feb. 19, 1951; s. Bernard E. and Joan Patricia McAdaragh; m. Carol Ann Reese, Jan. 23, 1988; children: Jeffrey, Eric; 1 child from previous marriage, Sandra. BS, Christopher New Port U., 1980; BS in Aerospace Tech., Thomas A. Edison State Coll., 1990; M in Aerospace, Embry/Riddle Aero. U., 1994; PhD, U. Fla., 1999. Electrician Newport News (Va.) Ship Bldg. Co., 1974—78; wastewater treatment plant operator Hampton Rds. Sanitation Dist., Williamsburg, Va., 1980, lab. technician, 1981; air traffic control specialist FAA, Williamsport, Pa., 1982—88, Gainesville, Fla., 1988—99, aero. engring. rsch. psychologist Hampton, Va., 1999—. Cons., rschr. NASA, Hampton, 1999—2004; initiator, dir. human factors rsch. coordination NASA/FAA, Hampton, 2002—04, mem. weather tech. integration team, Washington, 2005—, mem. vision team, 2005—; chmn. SAE G-10 aerospace behavioral engring. tech. Weather Info. Subcom., 2006—08. Writer, musician, singer: albums Midnight on the Water, 2001, East Virginia Bound, 2001, New World Destiny, 2005, Pleromatic Journey, 2006, Destination Mars, 2008. Vol. curriculum devel. team Poquoson Sch. Bd., Va., 2001. With US Army, 1969—74. Recipient 1st degree black belt, Shorin-Ken Karate, brown belt, Shorin-Ryu Karate, orange belt, Judo, Outstanding Contbns. to Aviation Weather Info. Rsch. award, NASA, 2002, Avaiation Safety Program award, 2004. Mem.: Tidewater Human Factors and Ergonomic Soc., Aerospace Human Factors Assn., Aerospace Med. Assn., Theosophical Soc. Am., Masons (3d degree, 32d degree Scottish Rite). Avocations: fishing, boating. Home: 40 Lodge Rd Poquoson VA 23662 Office: FAA NASA Langley Rsch Ctr Hampton VA 23681 Office Phone: 757-864-1941. Business E-Mail: raymon.mcadaragh@nasa.gov.

MCAFEE, DIANA MAE, media specialist, music educator; b. Charlestown, Ind., Oct. 24, 1951; d. Robert E. and Dorothy N. Williams; m. John J. McAfee, May 27, 1972; children: Michelle Renee McAfee Logan, Jennifer Melynne. B in Music Edn., Evangel U., Springfield, Mo., 1973; MusM, Pittsburg State U., Kans., 1977. Libr. cert. Mo. Piano instr. Evangel U., Springfield, 1971—73; piano tchr., judge Nat. Piano Guild, Carthage, Mo., 1975—; tchr. Carthage R-9 Schs., 1986—94, libr. media coord., 1995—99, libr. media specialist, 1999—. Adj. prof. Crowder Coll., Neosho, Mo., 1995—97; chairperson Career Ladder Carthage Schs., 2003—05. Choir dir. 1st Assembly God, Carthage, 1974—94. Mem.: Mo. Assn. Sch. Librs., Mo. State Tchrs. Assn. Avocations: travel, reading, movies. Home: 17184 Hawthorne Rd Carthage MO 64836 Office: Fairview Elem Sch 1201 E Fairview Carthage MO 64836 Business E-Mail: mcafeed@carthage.k12.mo.us.

MCAFEE, LARRY W., chemistry educator; b. Oklahoma City, Okla., Oct. 20, 1946; s. Mv and Margaret McAfee; m. Donna Sigwart, Aug. 7, 1971; children: Joy Kiser, Hope Morgan. BA, U. N.C., Charlotte, 1965—69, MA, 1975—80. Chemistry tchr. South Cobb HS, Austell, Ga., 1969—71; sci. tchr. Coulwood Jr. HS, Charlotte, NC, 1971—74; chemistry tchr. East Mecklenburg HS, Charlotte, 1974—. Cross country/track coach South Cobb HS, 1969—71; track coach Coulwood Jr. HS, 1971—74; cross country/track coach East Mecklenburg HS, 1974—2003. State meet dir., cross country N.C. HS Athletic Assn., Charlotte, 1980—2001, state meet dir., indoor track Chapel Hill, 1990—2000; asst. regional coord. Foot Locker Cross Country Championships, Charlotte, 1982—2006; asst. coord. Foot Locker Nat. Cross Country Championships, San Diego, Calif., 1982—2006. Recipient Country Achievement award, Nat. Assn. Counties, Wash. D.C., 1981, Outstanding Achievement, N.C. HS Athletic Assn., 1992, N.C. Chemistry Tchr. of Yr., Ciba Chem., N.C. State U., 1993, Star Tchr. award, Time-Warner, 1997, Oustanding Svc., N.C. HS Athletic Assn., 1999, Track Coach of Yr., 2000, Merit award, Foot Locker Cross Country Championships, 2005; grantee Summer Tchr. Rsch. Program, Hoechst Celanese, 1992, Sandoz Chem., 1994. Mem.: State Employees Assn. N.C. Avocations: photography, travel. Office: E Mecklenburg HS 6800 Monroe Rd Charlotte NC 28212

MCAFEE, NOELLE CLAIRE, philosopher, educator; b. Tagiura, Libya, Nov. 25, 1960; d. Horatio Paul and Marika Chaniotakis McAfee; m. David G Armstrong, Aug. 8, 1992; children: Guthrie McAfee Armstrong, Eliza Dorothy Armstrong. BA in hist., U. of Tex. at Austin, 1986; MA in pub. policy, Duke U., 1987; MA in Philosophy, U. of Wis. at Madison, 1990; PhD, U. of Tex. at Austin, 1998. Lectr. in polit. theory U. Tex., Dept. of Govt., 1998—99; asst. prof. philosophy U. Mass., 1999—2003, assoc. prof. philosophy, 2003—06; vis. assoc. prof. philosopy George Mason U., 2005—08, assoc. rsch. prof., 2008—. Dir. honors program U. Mass., 2004—; vis. prof. philosophy Brandeis U., Waltham, Mass., 2004. Assoc. editor Kettering Review, 1991—; author: Habermas, Kristeva and Citizenship, 2000, Julia Kristeva, 2003, Democracy and the Political Unconscious, 2008; editor: Standing with the Public, 1997; contbr. chapters to books, articles to profl. jours. Office Phone: 978-934-3912. Business E-Mail: noelle_mcafee@mac.com.

MCAFEE, ROBERT ELWOOD, retired surgeon; b. Portland, Maine, Aug. 25, 1935; BS Biology, Bates Coll., 1956; MD, Tufts U., 1960. Diplomate Am. Bd. Surgery. Intern Maine Med. Ctr., Portland, 1960-61, resident in gen. surgery, 1961-65, mem. staff, 1965-96; assoc. prof. surgery U. Vt., Burlington, 1965-96; ret., 1996. Sr. cons. Am. Med. Accreditation Program. Mem.: AMA (pres. 1994—95), ACS, New Eng. Cancer Soc., New Eng. Surg. Soc. Home: 158 Clinton St Portland ME 04103-3228 Personal E-mail: rmcafee1@maine.rr.com.

MC AFEE, WILLIAM, government official; b. Port Royal, Jan. 25, 1910; s. French and Willietta (Anderson) McA. BA, Coll. of Wooster, 1932; MA in Am. History, Pa. State U., 1941; student, Oxford, Eng., summer 1937. Wooster in India rep. on faculty Ewing Christian Coll., Allahabad, India, 1932-35; tchr. pub. high schs. and prep. sch. Pa., 1935-42; joined State Dept., 1946; country specialist (Office Chinese Affairs), 1946-50; coordinator current intelligence (Bur. Intelligence and Research), 1950-56, spl. asst. to dir., 1956-60, dir. ops. staff, 1960-66, asst. dep. dir. coordination, 1966-72, dep. dir. coordination, 1972-80, dep. asst. sec. intelligence coordination, 1980—; dir. (Office of Intelligence Liaison), 1981-86, ret. Adviser Griffin Econ. Aid Mission to S.E. Asia, 1950 Served to lt. col. AUS, 1942-46, CBI. Decorated Legion of Merit; Order Brit. Empire; Precious Tripod Chinese Nationalist Govt.; recipient Superior Honor award State Dept., 1964, Disting. Honor award, 1980 Mem. Am. Fgn. Service Assn., Delta Sigma Rho. Home: 3050 Military Rd NW Apt 212 Washington DC 20015-1374

MCALEXANDER, MELISSA, chemistry professor, researcher; Cmty. partnerships mgr. Tech. Mus. Innovation, San Jose, Calif., 2001—07; asst. prof. Notre Dame Namur U., Belmont, Calif., 2007—.

MCALISTER, MICHAEL H., architect; b. Calif. s. Doyle R. and Mary E. McAlister. AA, Bakersfield Coll.; BArch, Calif. Poly. U., N.L.C. Sch. Ministry. Planning technician Bakersfield (Calif.) City Hall, 1963; carpenter Del Webb Corp., Kern City, Calif., 1964; archtl. draftsman Goss & Choy Archs., Bakersfield, 1965-67; arch., v.p. D.G.C. & Assocs., Bakersfield, 1971-80; dir. architecture, v.p. N.B.A. & Assocs., Archs., Bakersfield, 1980-83; arch. Michael H. McAlister, A.I.A., Bakersfield, 1983—. Nepthrology design cons. for various treatment groups and hosps., 1987—. Commr., archtl. advisor Hist. Preservation Commn., Bakersfield, 1986-87; bd. dirs. Camp Fire Coun., Kern County, Calif., 1980-84 Recipient Archtl. Pub. Bldg. Hist. award Beautiful Bakersfield Com., City of Bakersfield's City Coun. and Hist. Preservation Commn., 1985, 87, Exterior Environ. Design Excellence Bakersfield C. of C., 1988, Comml. Design Excellence award, 1984, Design Excellence and Beautification award City of Taft, Calif., 1989, Design Excellence award State of Nev., 1992, Beautiful Bakersfield Archtl. Comml. Remodel award, 2003 Mem. AIA (Calif. Coun., Golden Empire chpt.). Avocation: religious architecture and art. Office: 1302 Ironstone Dr Studio 201 Bakersfield CA 93312-4668

MCALLISTER, BRUCE RICHARD, art educator; b. Stanford, Calif., Feb. 25, 1964; s. Mark Marion McAllister and Ruth Cannon Lee; m. Katherine Reed, Apr. 10, 1993; children: Cameron Dale, Eric Reed. BFA, U. Calif., Irvine, 1989; MFA, Calif. Coll. of the Arts, San Francisco, 1993—95. Art instr. Pacific Art League, Palo Alto, Calif., 1991; adj. art instr. City Coll. of San Francisco, 1998; art instr. Antelope Valley Coll., Lancaster, Calif., 2000—, LA Pierce Coll., Woodland Hills, Calif., 2001—; adj. art instr. Glendale C.C., Calif., 2003—; art instr. Moorpark Coll., Calif., 2004—. Muralist, prop designer, builder Ahrens Studios, Novato, Calif., 1995—97, Club Ed, Lancaster, 1999—2002; creator storyboard for film The Big E Oaf Prodns., Glendale, Calif., 1999; web site developer Strategic Internet Sollutions, Lancaster, 1999—2001, bkmdesign.com, Quartz Hill, Calif., 2001—; juror Antelope Valley Union HS Dist. Art Show, Lancaster City Gallery and Mus., 2001. One-man shows include Pamela Skinner Gallery, Sacramento, 2004, 2005 (Critic's Pick, Sacramento Bee, 2005), 2006, B. Sakata Garo Gallery, Sacramento, 2004 (Critic's Pick, Sacramento Bee, 2004), exhibited in group shows at Fed. Bldg. Towers, Oakland, Calif., 1994, Palo Alto Cmty. Ctr., 1995, Andrea Schwartz Gallery, San Francisco, 1995, Weintraub Thomas Gallery, Sacramento, 1997, Lancaster City Gallery and Mus., Calif., 2001, Julie Baker Fine Art Gallery, Grass Valley, Calif., 2003—04, O'Hanlon Ctr., Calif., 2004, Solaris Gallery, West Hollywood, Calif., 2005, Pierce Coll., Woodland Hills, Calif., 2005, contemporaryquarterly.com, 2006, Roshambo Winery Gallery, Healdsburg, Calif., 2006, Pamela Skinner Gallery, 2006, Calif. Coll. of Arts 100th Anniversary Exhbn., San Francisco, 2007, Calif. Coll. of the Arts Alumni Exhbn., 2007, represented in numerous pvt. collections, one-man shows include Evtempore Three Person Show Moov Park Coll. Woorpark Calif., 2008. Recipient Gold Key Nat. Honor Soc., U. of Calif. at Irvine, 1988. Home: 4803 W Ave L 14 Quartz Hill CA 93536 Personal E-mail: bruce@brucemcallister.com.

MCALLISTER, DEUCE (DULYMUS JENOD MCALLISTER), professional football player; b. Lena, Miss., Dec. 27, 1978; s. Carl and Cornelia McAllister. Attended, U. Miss., 2000—01. Running back New Orleans Saints, 2001—09; owner Deuce McAllister Nissan, Jackson, Miss. Founder Catch 22 Found., 2003—. Recipient Conerly Trophy, 1999; named to Nat. Football Conf. Pro Bowl Team, NFL, 2002, 2003. Office: Deuce McAllister Nissan 905 I-20 S Frontage Rd Jackson MS 39204*

MC ALLISTER, GERALD NICHOLAS, retired bishop, minister; b. San Antonio, Feb. 23, 1923; s. Walter Williams and Leonora Elizabeth (Alexander) McA.; m. Helen Earle Black, Oct. 2, 1953; children—Michael Lee, David Alexander, Stephen Williams, Elizabeth. Student, U. Tex., 1939-42, Va. Theol. Sem., 1948-51, DD (hon.), 1977. Ordained to ministry Episcopal Ch. as deacon, 1953, as priest, 1954. Rancher, 1946-48; deacon, priest Ch. of Epiphany, Raymondville, Ch. of Incarnation, Corpus Christi, St. Francis Ch., Victoria, Tex., 1951-63; 1st canon Diocese of West Tex., 1963-70; rector St. David's Ch., San Antonio, 1970-76; consecreated Episcopal bishop of Okla., Oklahoma City, 1977-89, ret., 1989; bishop-in-residence Episcopal Theol. Sem., Austin, Tex., 1990-93. Trustee Episcopal Theol. Sem. of S.W., 1961-2000, adv. bd., 1974—; mem. Case Commn. Bd. for Theol. Edn., 1981-82; pres. Tex. Council Chs., 1966-68, Okla. Conf. Chs., 1980-83; bd. dirs. Presiding Bishop's Fund for World Relief, 1972-77, Ch. Hist. Soc., 1976—; chmn. Nat. and World Mission Program Group, 1973-76; mem. Structure of Ch. Standing Commn., 1979, mem. standing com. on Stewardship/Devel., 1979-85; founder Chaplaincy Program, Bexar County Jail, 1968; mem. governing bd. nat. council Ch. of Christ, 1982-85; chmn. standing commn. on stewardship Episcopal Ch., 1983-85; v.p., trustee The Episc., Episc. Theol. Sem. of Southwest, 1987-93, chmn. bd. trustees, 1993-97. Author: What We Learned from What You Said, 1973, This Fragile Earth Our Island Home, 1980. Bd. dirs. Econ. Opportunity Devel. Corp., San Antonio, 1968-69; mem. exec. com. United Way, 1968-70, vice-chmn., 1970. With U.S. Mcht. Marines, 1942; to 1st lt. USAAF, 1942-45. Recipient Agudas Achim Brotherhood award, 1968. Mem.: Alumni Coun. Va. Theol. Sem. Episcopalian. Address: 507 Bluffestates San Antonio TX 78216-7930

MCALLISTER, JAMES ANTHONY, literature and language professor; s. William Hershel and Dian D. McAllister. BA in Spanish; MA in Romance Lang. Spanish, U. New Orleans, 1996, MA in Romance Lang. French, 2000, MA, 2004, MS in Acctg. and Taxation, 2004. Instr. U. New Orleans, 2006—. Recipient Stewart George Wolf award, U. New Orleans, 2003. Mem.: Am. Assn. Tchrs. Spanish and Portuguese, La. Tchrs. English Speakers to Other Lang., Am. Assn. Tchrs. Italian, Am. Assn. Tchrs. French., Golden Key Nat. Honor Soc., Omicron Delta Kappa. Honor Soc., Phi Beta Delta. Honor Soc., Beta Gamma Sigma. Internat., Pi Gamma Mu. Internat. Honor Soc., Gamma Theta Epsilon. Internat. Geography Honor Soc. Office: Univ New Orleans 2000 Lakeshore Dr New Orleans LA 70115 Business E-Mail: jmcallis@uno.edu.

MC ALLISTER, LESTER BELDEN, economics professor; b. Chgo., Feb. 21, 1921; s. Lester Belden and Bertha (Wulpi) McA.; m. Elaine Schneider, Feb. 17, 1945; 1 child, Margaret. BA, Coe Coll., 1942; MA, Northwestern U., 1947; PhD (Carnegie fellow 1950-52), U. Oreg., 1953. Instr. econs. Coe Coll., 1947-50, Oreg. State Coll., 1952-53; mem. faculty Beloit Coll., 1953-91, prof. econs., 1959-91, prof. emeritus, 1991—, chmn. dept. econs. and bus., 1960-74. Cons.-examiner, 1974-91; vis. prof. econs. U. Wis., 1968; prof. fgn. affairs Nat. War Coll., 1961-62; mem. Wis. Banking Rev. Bd., 1974-79, Beloit Bd. Edn., 1955-58 Author articles, essays. Served to maj. USAAF, 1942-46. Ford Found. fellow U. Wis., 1957 Mem. Phi Beta Kappa. Home: 1400 N Drake Rd Apt 255 Kalamazoo MI 49006-3918

MCALLISTER, TODD, biomedical engineer; PhD in biomedical engring., U. Calif., San Diego. Co-founder Cytograft Tissue Engring., Inc., Novato, Calif.; co-dir. Ctr. Regenerative Medicine St. Joseph's Translational Rsch. Inst., Atlanta. Achievements include development of Lifeline vascular graft. Office: Cytograft Tissue Engring Inc Ste 220 3 Hamilton Landing Novato CA 94949 also: Ctr Regenerative Medicine St Josephs Translational Rsch Inst 5673 Peachtree Dunwoody Rd NE Ste 675 Atlanta GA 30342 Office Phone: 415-506-0260, 678-843-6500. E-mail: contact@cytograft.com.*

MCALLISTER, WILLIAM HOWARD, III, newspaper reporter, columnist, public affairs consultant; b. Durham, NC, Nov. 6, 1941; s. William Howard, Jr. and Dorothy Fisk (Tillett) McA.; m. Rena Catherine Farrell, June 13, 1965; children: William Howard IV, Christopher F., Jonathan T., Benjamin J. BA in Polit. Sci, U. NC, Chapel Hill, 1964, MA in Journalism, 1966. Cecil Prince research asst. U. NC, 1965; reporter The Virginian-Pilot, Norfolk, 1964-67; reporter, city editor Virginian-Pilot, 1972-75; reporter Wall St. Jour., San Francisco, 1968-72, Washington Post, 1975-78, Va. editor, 1978-86, nat. reporter, 1986-99, columnist stamp and coin sect., 1987-99, lobbying columnist, 1997-99; Washington bur. chief Denver Post and MediaNews Newspapers, 1999—2003; Washington corr. Linn's Stamp News, 1997—. TV cons. Ford Found., 1969-72; cons. The Newseum, Arlington, Va., 2003-06. Capt. USNR, 1966-93. Decorated Navy Commendation medal, Meritorious Svc. medal, Gold Star; recipient Lidman prize for philatelic writing, 1990. Mem. Am. Soc. Newspaper Editors, Kappa Tau Alpha, Nat. Press Club. Presbyterian. Home and Office: 10121 Ratcliffe Manor Dr Fairfax VA 22030-2427 Personal E-mail: bmcallister@cox.net. Business E-Mail: whmcallister@verizon.net.

MCALPIN, KIRK MARTIN, lawyer; b. Newark, Sept. 14, 1923; s. Aaron Champion and Margaret (Martin) McAlpin; m. Sarah Frances Morgan, Dec. 14, 1951; children: Kirk Martin Jr., Philip Morgan, Margaret Champion Margeson. LLB, U. Ga., 1948; postgrad., Columbia U., 1949. Bar: Ga. 1949. Asst. solicitor gen. Ea. Jud. Cir. Ct. Ga., 1951; assoc. Bouhan, Lawrence, Williams, Levy & McAlpin, Savannah, Ga., 1952-53, ptnr., 1954-63; sr. ptnr. King & Spalding, Atlanta, 1963-86; pvt. practice Savannah, 1987—97, Atlanta, 1998—. Chmn. Inst. Continuing Legal Edn., 1980-81, Inst. Continuing Jud. Edn. in Ga., 1981-84, Jud. Council Ga., 1979-82. Pres. Atlanta Legal Aid Soc., 1971. Fellow Am. Bar Found., Am. Law Inst., Am. Coll. Trial Lawyers, Internat. Acad. Trial Lawyers, Internat. Soc. Barristers; mem. ABA (Jr. Bar Conf. chmn. 1958-59, chmn. gen. practice sect. 1972-73, chmn. sr. lawyers div. 1986-87, ho. of dels. 1960-90, state del. 1970-90, bd. govs. 1973-76), State Bar Ga. Assn. (chmn. Young Lawyers 1953-54, bd. govs. 1953-63, pres. 1979-80), Atlanta Bar Assn., Savannah Bar Assn. (v.p. 1960-61), Nat. Conf. Bar Pres. (exec. com. 1981-83), Ga. Def. Lawyers Assn., Am. Judicature Soc., Assn. R.R. Trial Counsel, Soc. of Cin., Sons Colonial Wars, St. Andrews Soc., Capital City Club, Piedmont Driving Club, Oglethorpe Club, Phi Delta Phi, Sigma Alpha Epsilon. Episcopalian. Office: The Paces 352 77 E Andrews Dr NW Atlanta GA 30305-1392 Home Phone: 404-467-8307; Office Phone: 404-467-8307. Office Fax: 404-467-0619. Personal E-mail: kmcasratty@mindspring.com, kirksratty@mindspring.com.

MCALWEE, MARTIN FREDERICK, lawyer; b. Washington, Oct. 4, 1943; s. Robert Walter and Norma Jean McAlwee; m. Maryann Sharma Siuda, Apr. 21, 2000; children from previous marriage: Gerald Steven, Jennifer Anne, Geoffrey Patrick. BA in Govt. and Polit., U. Md., Coll. Pk., 1966; JD, Cath. U., Washington, 1969; MSc in Acquistion and Contract Mgmt., Fla. Inst. Tech., 1982. Bar: DC 1969, Fla. 1982, Fla. Supreme Ct., US Ct. Appeals (DC cir.), US Dist. Ct. DC. Judge advocate USAF, 1970—74; trial atty. Fed. Maritime Commn., Washington, 1974—79; contract mgmt. position Harris Corp., 1979—88; atty. advisor Office Staff Advocate 45th Space Wing, Patrick AFB, Fla., 1988—. Adj. prof. AF Inst. Tech., Wright-Patterson AFB, Ohio. Leader Boy Scouts Am. Ret. col. USAFR, 1999. Decorated Legion of Merit medal USAF, Bronze Star medal, Civil Svc. Meritorious Svc. medal; recipient James O. Wrightson award, 2000, Outstanding Civilian Atty., USAF Space Command, 1994, AF Space Command, 1998. Fellow: Nat. Contract Mgmt. Assn.; mem.: ABA, DC Bar Assn., Fla. Bar Assn. Avocations: golf, fishing. Office: 45th Space Wing Office Staff Judge Advocate 642 O Malley Rd Patrick AFB FL 32925-3329

MCAMIS, EDWIN EARL, retired lawyer; b. Cape Girardeau, Mo., Aug. 8, 1934; s. Zenas Earl and Anna Louise (Miller) McAmis; m. Malin Eklof, May 31, 1959 (div. 1979); 1 child, Andrew Bruce; life ptnr. Gerson Gonzalez. AB magna cum laude, Harvard U., 1956, LLB, 1959. Bar: NY 1960, US Dist. Ct. (so. dist.) NY 1962, US Supreme Ct. 1965, US Ct. Appeals (2d and 3d cirs.) 1964, US Ct. Appeals (DC cir.) 1981. Assoc. law firm Webster, Sheffield & Chrystie, NYC, 1959-61, Regan Goldfarb Powell & Quinn, NYC, 1962-65, Lovejoy, Wasson, Lundgren & Ashton, NYC, 1965-69, ptnr., 1969-77, Skadden, Arps, Slate, Meagher & Flom, NYC, 1977-90, spl. ptnr., pro bono, 1990-93; adj. prof. law Fordham U., 1984-85, Benjamin N. Cardozo Sch. Law, NYC, 1985-90. Bd. dir. Lambda Legal and Edn. Fund, 1991—95; bd. dirs. Aston Magna Found. Music, Inc., 1982—93, Cmty. Rsch. Initiative N.Y., 1988—89. With US Army, 1961—62. Mem.: ABA, Selden Soc.

MCANALLY, MAC, musician, songwriter; b. Belmont, Miss., July 1, 1959; Mem. Jimmy Buffett's Coral Reefer Band; session artist and songwriter for numerous musicians. Musician: (albums) Mac McAnally, 1977, Finish Lines, 1978, Cuttin' Corners, 1980, Nothin' But the Trugh, 1989, Simple Life, 1990, Live and Learn, 1992, Knots, 1994, Word of Mouth, 1999, No Problem Here, 1999, Semi-True Stories, 2004; composer: (songs) I Need You Tonight, It's a Crazy World, It's My Job, Old Flame, When the Coast is Clear, Crime of Passion, Back Where I Come From, It's a Precious Thing, The Trouble With Diamonds, Junk Cars. Recipient Musician of Yr. award, Country Music Assn., 2008; named to Nashville Songwriters Hall of Fame, 2007. Office: TKO Artist Mgmt 1107 17th Ave S Nashville TN 37212 E-mail: mac@macmcanally.com.*

MCANDREW, FRANCIS THOMAS, psychology professor; b. Augsburg, Germany, Jan. 27, 1953; came to U.S., 1953; s. John Francis Paul and Jane Ann (Tuman) McA.; m. Maryjo Ann McCarthy, July 29, 1978; children: Timothy Ned, Maura Jill. BS in Psychology, King's Coll., 1974; PhD in Exptl. Psychology, U. Maine, Orono, 1981. Cornelia H. Dudley prof. psychology Knox Coll., Galesburg, Ill., 1979—2002, chair dept. psychology, 1993—2002. Head wrestling coach Knox Coll., Galesburg, 1985-89, 92-2000, program chair environ. studies, 1993-2001; vis. prof. U. Pretoria, South Africa, 1996; cons. C.E., U.S. Army. Author: Environmental Psychology, 1993; reviewer NSF, profl. jours.; contbr. articles to prol. jours. and mags. Fellow U. Maine, Orono, 1974-75. Fellow Assn. for Psychol. Sci.; mem. Midwestern Psychol. Assn., Internat. Soc. for Human Ethology, Soc. for Personality and Social Psychology, Coun. Undergrad. Tchrs. of Psychology, Human Behavior and Evaluation Soc. Home: 733 Bateman St Galesburg IL 61401-2822 Office: Dept Psychology Knox Coll Galesburg IL 61401-4999 Office Phone: 309-341-7525. Business E-Mail: fmcandre@knox.edu.

MCANDREW, MARK S., insurance company executive; Mgmt. positions with Torchmark Corp., McKinney, Tex., 1980—; pres. Globe Life & Accident Ins. Co., 1991—2005, CEO, 1999—2005; pres. United Am. Ins. Co., 1991—2004, CEO, 1999—2004; pres., CEO Am. Income Life Ins. Co., 1999—2003; bd. dir. Torchmark Corp., 1998—, exec. v.p., 1999—2003, chmn. ins. ops., 2003—05, CEO, 2005—06, chmn., CEO, 2006—. Office: Torchmark Corp 3700 S Stonebridge Dr PO Box 8080 Mc Kinney TX 75070-8080

MCANDREW, THOMAS JOSEPH, lawyer; b. Providence, Oct. 19, 1945; s. Joseph L. and Amelia L. (Bonhotel) McA.; children: John Maxwell, Mercedes, Hope, Marya, Cornelia. BA, Providence Coll., 1968; JD, Georgetown U.-Am. U.-George Washington U., 1971; LLM, Georgetown U., 1973. Bar: RI, 1971, US Dist. Ct. RI, 1972, DC 1972, US Ct. Claims, 1972, US Tax Ct., 1971, US Custom and Patent Ct., 1971, US Ct. Mil. Appeals, 1971, US Ct. Appeals (1st cir.), 1971, US Ct. Appeals (DC), 1971, US Ct. Appeals (4th cir.), US Supreme Ct., 1974, Commonwealth Mass., 1985. Trial atty. Civil Aeros. Bd., Washington, 1971-72; legal asst. to John H. Fanning NLRB, Washington, 1972-73; labor rels. officer dept. edn. State of RI, Providence, 1973-74, dep. asst. commr. edn., 1974-79, adminstr. labor rels., 1979-80; ptnr. Powers & McAndrew, Inc., Providence, 1980-87; pvt. practice Thomas J. McAndrew & Assocs., Providence, 1987—. Adj. prof. law U. RI, Kingston, 1976; lectr. in field. Contbr. articles to profl. jours. Treas., trustee John E. Fogarty Found., Providence, 1974—; mem. Providence Com. on Fgn. Rels., Providence. Mem. ABA (com. on labor law) FBA, ATLA, Am. Arbitration Assn. (adv. coun.). Avocations: golf, tennis, walking. Home: 6 Wingate Rd Providence RI 02906-4910 Office: Ste 205 One Turks Head Place Providence RI 02903 Office Phone: 401-455-0350. Fax: 401-455-0882. Business E-Mail: tmcandrew@tjmcandrewlaw.com.

MCANDREWS, BRIAN PATRICK, venture capitalist, former computer software company executive; AB in Economics, Harvard U., Cambridge, Mass.; MBA, Stanford U. Grad. Sch. Bus., Calif. Product mgr. Gen. Mills, Inc., 1984—89; exec. positions at ABC Sports, ABC Entertainment and ABC TV Network including exec. v.p. and gen. mgr. of ABC Sports ABC, 1990—99; CEO, bd. dirs. aQuantive, Inc. (acquired by Microsoft Corp.), Seattle, 1999—2007, pres., 2000—07; sr. v.p., advertiser and publisher solutions (APS) group aQuantive, Inc. (a wholly owned subs. Microsoft Corp.), Seattle, 2007—08; mng. dir. Madrona Venture Group, Seattle, 2009—. Bd. dirs. Blue Nile, Inc., 2004—, Advt. Rsch. Found., Whitepages.com, Inc., aQuantive, Inc., 1999—, Fisher Comm., 2006—. Named Digital Exec. of Yr., Advt. Age, 2008; named one of 50 Who Matter Now, CNNMoney.com Bus. 2.0, 2006, 2007. Mem.: Nat. Assn. Corp. Dirs. (bd. dirs Seattle-N.W. chpt.). Office: Madrona Venture Capital 1000 Second Ave Ste 3700 Seattle WA 98104 Office Phone: 206-674-3000. Office Fax: 206-674-8703.*

MCANDREWS, JAMES PATRICK, retired lawyer; b. Carbondale, Pa., May 11, 1929; s. James Patrick and Mary Agnes (Walsh) McA.; m. Mona Marie Steinke, Sept. 4, 1954; children: James P., George A., Catherine McAndrews Hazel, Joseph M., Anne Marie, Michael P., Edward R., Daniel P. BS, U. Scranton, 1949; LL.B., Fordham U., 1952; grad., Real Estate Inst., NYU, 1972. Bar: N.Y. 1953, Ohio 1974. Assoc. James F. McManus, Levittown, NY, 1955; atty. Emigrant Savs. Bank, NYC, 1955-68; counsel Tchrs. Ins. and Annuity Assn., NYC, 1968-73; assoc. Thompson, Hine & Flory, 1973-74, ptnr. Cleve., 1974-84, Benesch, Friedlander, Coplan & Aronoff, Cleve., 1984-94. Mem. law faculty Am. Inst. Banking, N.Y.C., 1968-69; mem. faculty Lakeland C.C., 1995-97. Author: Commercial Real Estate Law Practice Manual with Forms, 2001, 2nd edit., 2009. 1st lt. USAF, 1952-54. Fellow Am. Bar Found. (life); mem. Am. Coll. Real Estate Lawyers (gov. 1983-86, treas. 1986-88, chmn. membership devel. com. 1985-87), Ohio Land Title Assn. (life, trustee 1985-88), Bar Assn. Greater Cleve. (hon. life; past chmn. real estate sect.), Ohio State Bar Assn. (hon. life). Roman Catholic. Home: 12568 Summit Manor Dr Apt 118 Fairfax VA 22033-5719 Home Phone: 703-537-0867. Personal E-mail: jpmmnn@cox.net.

MCANDREWS, LAWRENCE A., medical association administrator; married; 2 children. BA in psychology, Vanderbilt U.; Master's in health adminstrn., George Washington U. V.p. professional affairs Lafayette Gen. Hosp., La.; adminstrv. asst. MacNeal Meml. Hosp., Berwyn, Ill.; adminstr. Inst. Psychiatry Northwestern Meml. Hosp., Chgo., adminstr. Prentice Women's Hosp.; pres., CEO Children's Mercy Hosp., Kansas City, Mo., 1986—92, Nat. Assn. Children's Hospitals and Related Institutions, Alexandria, Va., 1992—. Vice-chair Generations United. Fellow: Am. Coll. Health Care Executives; mem.: Am. Hosp. Assn. Office: Nat Assn Childrens Hosps and Related Instns 401 Wythe St Alexandria VA 22314 E-mail: lmcandrews@nachri.org.*

MCANDREWS, LAWRENCE JOHN, history professor; b. Phila. s. John Patrick and Margaret Ellen McAndrews. BA in History, U. Notre Dame, 1977; MA in History, Millersville U., Penn., 1981; PhD, Georgetown U., Washington, 1985. History educator York Catholic HS, Pa., 1977; vis. history prof. Georgetown U., 1990, U. Philippines, Diliman, 2001—02, U. San Francisco, 2002; history prof. St. Norbert Coll., Wis., 1985—. Mem. Big Brother, Wis., 1987—95, Youth Sports, Wis., 1997. Recipient Outstanding Tchr. award, St. Nobert Coll., 1990, Outstanding Scholar award, 1997, Outstanding Educator award, 2001. Roman Catholic. Avocations: running, skiing, reading, sports.

MCANDREWS, ROBERT KIERNAN, lawyer, social work educator; b. NYC, June 5, 1948; s. Philip and Kathleen McAndrews; m. Edy McAndrews, Oct. 18, 1987; children: Sara, Daniel. BS, SUNY, Oneonta, 1971; MSW, Syracuse U., NY, 1977, PhD, 1985; JD, New Eng. Sch. Law, Boston, 2002. Bar: Mass. 2003. Prof. sociology C. W. Post campus LI U., Brookville, NY, 1984—92; prof. social work Salem State Coll., Mass., 1992—; sole practice law Marblehead, Mass., 2003—. Pro bono mediator North Shore Cmty. Mediation, Beverly, Mass., 1995—; pro bono atty. Polytical Asylum and Immigration Representation Project, Boston, 2003—; pres. bd. dirs. Holocaust Ctr. North Shore, Inc., Peabody, Mass., 1998—. Mem.: ABA, Nat. Lawyers Guild, Am. Immigration Lawyers Assn. Democrat. Jewish. Avocations: swimming, kayaking, skiing, hiking, guitar. Home: 6 Dunns Ln Marblehead MA 01945 Office Phone: 978-542-6815.

MCANIFF, NORA P., former publishing executive; b. NY, Oct. 14, 1958; BA, Baruch Coll., 1980. From mktg. info. mgr. to pres. People Mag. Time Inc., NYC, 1982—98, pub. Life Mag., 1992—93, pub. Teen People, 1997—98, pres. People Mag., 1998—2001, group pres. People Mag. Group, 2001—02, exec. v.p., women's entertainment & luxury group, 2002—05, co-COO, 2005—07. Pres. Advt. Women of NY, 1997—99; bd. dirs. Saks Inc., 2002—, Michael J. Fox Found. for Parkinson's Rsch.

MCANIFF, RICHARD, computer software company executive; married; 5 children. BS in Economics, U. Mass. Amherst, 1971, M in Resource Economics, 1976; M in Systems and Indsl. Engring., U. Ariz. Mem. tech. staff Sandia Nat. Laboratories, Albuquerque; joined Microsoft Corp., Redmond, Wash., 1987, sr. prog. mgr. Access 1.0 database, group prog. mgr. LAN Mgr. group, head FoxPro Database Product Unit, gen. mgr. Visual Basic devel. system, corp. v.p. Microsoft Office; exec. v.p., chief devel. officer VMware, Inc., Palo Alto, Calif., 2009—. Exec. alumnus U. Mass./Microsoft Partnership. Avocations: snowboarding, windsurfing, rock climbing. Office: VMware Inc World Hdqs 3401 Hillview Ave Palo Alto CA 94304*

MCANINCH, JACK WELDON, urological surgeon, educator; b. Merkel, Tex., Mar. 17, 1936; s. Weldon Thomas and Margaret (Canon) McA.; m. Barbara B. Buchanan, Dec. 29, 1960 (div. Aug. 1972); m. Burnet B. Sumner, Dec. 29, 1987; children: David A., Todd G., Brendan J. BS, Tex. Tech U., 1958; MS, U. Idaho, 1960; MD, U. Tex., 1964. Diplomate Am. Bd. Urology (trustee 1991-97, pres. 1996-97). Commd. capt. U.S. Army, 1964-66, advanced through grades to col., 1977, ret., 1977; col. USAR; intern then resident Letterman Army Med. Ctr., San Francisco, 1964-69; chief urol. surgery San Francisco Gen. Hosp., 1977—; prof. urol. surgery U. Calif., San Francisco, 1977—. Editor: Urogenital Trauma, 1985, Urologic Clinics of North America, 1989, Smith's gen. Urology, 1995; section editor: Early Care of Injured Patient, 1990, Traumatic and Reconstructive Urology, 1996. Col. US Army, 1964-72. Recipient Disting. Alumnus award Tex. Tech U., 1994; named Disting. Alumnus U. Idaho, 1997. Fellow ACS (govt. 1992-97, regent 1998—); mem. Am. Urol. Assn. (pres. we. sect. 1992-93, bd. dirs. 1990—, pres. 1996-97), Genitourinary Reconstructive Surgeons (pres.), Am. Assn. Surgery Trauma (v.p.), Soc. U. Urologists, Am. Bd. Urology (pres. 1996-97). Office: San Francisco Gen Hosp Dept Urology 1001 Potrero Ave San Francisco CA 94110-3594 Home Phone: 415-282-1149; Office Phone: 415-476-3372. Business E-Mail: jmcaninch@urology.ucsf.edu.

MCANUFF, DES, artistic director; b. Princeton, Ill., June 19, 1952; s. John Nelson and Ellen Boyd; m. Susan Berman, Jan. 1, 1984; 1 child, Julia Violet. Artistic dir. La Jolla Playhouse, Calif., 1994—2007, artistic dir. emeritus Calif., 2007—. Founding mem. Dodger Prodns.; former faculty Julliard Sch.; now adj. prof. theatre U. Calif. San Diego. Dir.: (Broadway plays) Big River (Tony award 1985), A Walk in the Woods (San Diego Critics Circle award), Tommy (Tony award 1993), How to Succeed in Business Without Really Trying (Tony nomination 1995), Dracula, the Musical, 2004, 700 Sundays, 2004, Jersey Boys, 2005, The Farnsworth Invention, 2007, Guys and Dolls, 2009; (off-Broadway prodns.) Gimme Shelter (Soho Arts award 1979), The Crazy Locomotive, Chelsea Theatre Ctr., Mary Stuart, How It All Began, Henry IV Part One, The Death of Von Richthofen as Witnessed from Earth (Villager award 1982), NY Shakespeare Festival, A Mad World My Masters, Romeo & Juliet, As You Like It (San Diego Critics Circle award), The Sea Gull, Shout Up A Morning, Gillette, The Matchmaker, Two Rooms, 80 Days, Down The Road, Macbeth, The Three Sisters, A Funny Thing Happened on the Way to the Forum, Twelfth Night, La Jolla Playhouse, Macbeth, Stratford Festival Can., Palm Beach: The Screwball Musical, 2005; others; prodr.: A Walk in the Woods, My Children! My Africa!; playwright Leave it to Beaver is Dead (Soho Arts award), The Death of Von Richthofen as Witnessed from Earth (Villager and Bay Area Circle Critics awards), Troll, A Lime in the Morning, Silent Edward; contbg. editor Am. Theatre Mag. Can. Council grantee, Rockefeller grantee. Mem. Theatre Communications Group (past bd. dirs.), Soc. of Stage Dirs. and Choreographers.*

MCANULTY, WILLIAM E., JR., former state supreme court justice; m. Kristi W. McAnulty; 4 children. Grad., Ind. U.; MAT, JD, U. Louisville. With Jefferson County Juvenile Ct., Ind., 1975—83; judge Jefferson Dist. Ct., 1978—83, Jefferson Circuit Ct., 1984—90; atty., priv. practice Ind., 1990—93; judge Jefferson Circuit Ct., 1993—98, chief judge, 1998; judge Ky. Ct. of Appeals, 1998—2006; justice Ky. Supreme Ct., 2006—08. Recipient Thomas C. Simons Disting. Leadership award, Leadership Louisville Foundation. Mem.: Ky. Trial Attorneys Assn. (Henry V. Pennington Outstanding Judge of Yr. 1997), Ky. Bar Assn., Louisville Bar Assn.

MCARTHUR, JANET DAVIS PENLAND, literature and language educator; b. Charleston, Sc, Sept. 23, 1953; d. William Ames Davis, Jr. and Bernice Janene Noffsinger; m. James Matthew McArthur III, Jan. 6, 2001; m. David Reagan Penland, Sept. 22, 1973 (div. May 21, 1997); children: Holly Ann Penland Clark, Nathaniel Glen Penland. BA, Jacksonville State U., Alabama, 1999, MA, 2000. Numerous cert. Delgado CC. Adj. instr. English Delgado CC, New Orleans, 2001—02, instr. English, 2002—06, presenter, online tech. devel. software com., 2003, adj. mentor, 2003, divsn. web designer comm. divsn., 2003—, sec. English 102 Adv. Bd., 2003—04, faculty advisor images lit. and visual arts mag., 2004—08, chair, campus ministry com., 2005—07, chair, English online com., 2005—06, asst. prof. English, 2006—, dept. chair English, French, and Spanish, 2007—; adj. instr. English and speech Gadsden State CC, Anniston, Ala., 2000. Presenter in fields. Author: (play) The J Murder; actor(historical interpretor): (historical interpretation) Roanoke Island Festival Park Museum - Vivian Myddleton; dir.: (play) The J Murder. Soloist and choir mem. Calhoun County Chorale, Anniston, Ala., 1997—2000; sunday sch. supt. Etowah United Meth. Ch., Etowah, NC, 1978—80; sunday sch. tchr. Ft. McClellan, Anniston, Ala., 1980—83; bible sch. coord. Ferris Barracks Chapel, Erlangen, Bavaria, Germany, 1983—86; children's choir dir. Ft. Irwin, Ft. Irwin, Calif., 1990—93; pres. Protestant Women Chapel, Ft. McClellan, Ala., 1996—97, Ladies of the Chapel, Erlangen, Bavaria, Germany, 1983—86; vol. Army Cmty. Svc., Annniston, Ala., 1980—83. Named Order of St. Joan D'Arc, Ready First Combat Team, Butzbach, Germany, 1995. Mem.: NCTE, Alpha Psi Omega, Sigma Tau Delta. Methodist. Avocations: history, travel, reading, sewing, gardening. Office: Delgado CC 615 City Park Av New Orleans LA 70119 Office Fax: 504-483-1953.

MCARTHUR, JOHN HECTOR, business educator; b. Vancouver, BC, Can., Mar. 31, 1934; came to U.S., 1957; s. Hector and Elizabeth Lee (Whyte) McA.; m. Netilia Ewasiuk, Sept. 15, 1956; children: Jocelyn Natasha, Susan Patricia. B in Commerce, U. B.C., 1957, LLD (hon.), 1995; MBA, Harvard U., 1959, DBA, 1962; LLD (hon.), Simon Fraser U., 1982, Queens U., 1985, Middlebury Coll., 1988, U. Navarra, Spain, 1989, U. Western Ont., 1992. Prof. bus. adminstrn. Harvard U., Cambridge, Mass., 1962—79, Sylvan C. Coleman prof. fin. mgmt., 1972—80, George F. Baker prof. bus. adminstrn., 1980—96; dean Harvard Bus. Sch., 1980-96; sr. advisor to pres. World Bank Group, Washington, 1995—2005. Bd. dirs., chmn. Asia Pacific Found. Can., AES Corp., Bell Can., Bell Can. Enterprises, Inc., Duke U. Health System, KOC Holdings A.S., Nat. Healthcare Coalition, Reuters Founders Share Co. Ltd., Telsat Can., Devel. Gateway Found.; cons. numerous cos. and govt. agys. in Can., Europe, Asia and U.S. Recipient Harvard Statesman award, HBS Club, NYC, Mgmt. Achievement award, McGill U., Can. Bus. Leadership award, HBS Clubs of Can., Lifetime Achievement award, Nat. Assn. Corp. Dirs., 2007; named Hon. Citizen, Remauville, France, McArthur Hall in his honor, Harvard Bus. Sch., 1999, John H. McArthur Can. Fellowship program in his honor, 2002, Dir. of Yr., Nat. Assn. Corp. Dirs., 2007; John and Natty McArthur Univ. chair established at, Harvard U., 1997. Mem. Harvard Club, Links Club, Comml. Club, Somerset Club, Willowbend Club, Varsity Club. Home: 140 Old Connecticut Path Wayland MA 01778-3202 Office: Harvard Univ Sch Bus Adminstrn Boston MA 02163

MCARTHUR, JOHN R., utilities executive, lawyer; b. Rock Hill, SC, Jan. 5, 1956; BA cum laude, Davidson Coll., 1977; JD with honors, Univ. So. Carolina, 1981. Bar: NC 1982. Law clk. Judge Sam. J. Ervin III, US Ct. Appeals, 4th cir., 1981—82; assoc. to ptnr. Hunton & Williams, Raleigh, NC, 1982—92; chief counsel NC Atty. Gen. Office, NC, 1993—97; sr. advisor NC Gov., Mike Easley, NC, 1998—2001; v.p., pub. affairs Progress Energy Inc., Raleigh, NC, 2001—02, sr. v.p., corp. rels., 2002—, gen. counsel, corp. sec., 2004—08, exe. v.p., corp. sec., 2008—. Editor Law Rev. U.S.C.; law clerk Hon. Sam J. Ervin III US Ct. Appeals Fourth Cir. Mem.: NC Bar Assn., Order of the Coif, Wig & Robe. Office: Progress Energy Inc 410 S Wilmington St Raleigh NC 27601-1551 Office Phone: 919-546-4070. Business E-Mail: john.mcarthur@pgnmail.com.

MCARTHUR, STEVEN B., Internet company executive; BS, Queen's U., Belfast; MBA, Harvard Bus. Sch. Strategy cons. Bain & Co., founder Toronto office; with Maple Leaf Foods; pres., CEO AOL Can. AOL, exec. v.p. web properties; pres. North Am. Travel Group Expedia Inc.; pres. Classmates Online United Online, 2007, pres. Classmates Media segment. Office: Classmates Online 21301 Burbank Blvd Woodland Hills CA 91367-6677

MCARTHUR, STEVEN FRANCIS, psychologist, educator; b. Grand Rapids, Mich., Aug. 12, 1954; s. George Harold and Evelyn Theresa McArthur; m. Barbara Louise Duch, Oct. 18, 1975; children: Ryan, Alan. BA in Psychology, Aquinas Coll., Grand Rapids, 1975; PhD in Psychology, So. Ill. U., 1990. Lic. psychologist, Mich. Staff psychologist St. John Hosp. and Med. Ctr., Detroit, 1990-95, Henry Ford Ctr. Human Sexuality, West Bloomfield, Mich., 1991-95, John D. Dingell Va. Med. Ctr., 2008; asst. prof. dept. psychiatry and behavioral neuroscis. Wayne State U. Sch. Medicine, 1995—2008. Mem. rev. panel behavior and performance NASA, Washington. Mem. APA, Nat. Register Health Svc. Providers Psychology, Mich. Psychol. Assn., N.Y. Acad. Scis. Office: John D Dingell VA Med Ctr 4646 John R Rd Detroit MI 48201 Business E-Mail: steven.mcarthur@va.gov.

MCARTHUR, TILLIAN (TILLY MCMAC), freelance/self-employed music educator, small business owner; b. Sept. 1975; adopted d. Imgram and Julio Syers; m. Mark McArthur; children: Sandy, Danny, Angie. MusB, U. Kans., 1997, MusM, 1998. Cert. in music edn. Kansas, 1998. Asst. composer Lawrence City Orch., 1999—2003, composer, 2003—05, dir., sr. composer, 2006—; co-owner McMac & Meriks Music Montage, Wichita, Kans., 2007—. Intern U. Kans. musical dept. orch., Kans., 1995—97. Composer: (Operas) over 30 operas, 1999—; dir.: (plays);, author Broadway plays. Vol. dir. Wichita high school, 2003—. Green Party. Baptist. Avocations: music box collecting, fantasy football, harpsichord. Office: McMac & Meriks Music Montage 2250 N Rock Rd #118-269 Wichita KS 67226-2304

MCATEE, DAVID RAY, lawyer; b. Rosebud, Tex., Nov. 20, 1941; s. Lee Ray and Florine (Davis) McAtee; m. Carole Kay Pendergraft, Jan. 28, 1967; children: David Ray, Kristin Carole. BBA with honors, Baylor U., 1964; LLB, U. Tex., 1967. Bar: Tex. 1967, US Dist. Ct. (no. dist.) Tex. 1968, US Dist. Ct. (so. dist.) Tex. 1994, US Dist. Ct. (ea. dist.) Tex. 1996, US Ct. Appeals (5th cir.) 1969, US Ct. Appeals (11th cir.) 1981, US Tax Ct. 1993. Briefing atty. Supreme Ct. Tex., Austin, 1967—68; ptnr. Thompson & Knight, Dallas, 1968—90, Gibson, Dunn & Crutcher, Dallas, 1990—95; with Akin Gump Strauss Hauer & Feld LLP, Dallas, 1995. Mem. City of Dallas Plan Commn., 1979—83, vice chmn., 1981—83; chmn. City of Dallas Thoroughfare Com., 1979—81; mem. City of Dallas Citizens Safety Adv. Com., Goals for Dallas Com.; founder, bd. dirs. No. Hills. Neighborhood Assn., 1974—76; pres., bd. dirs. Montessori Sch. of Park Cities, 1975—76; chmn. bd. dirs. Dallas Area Rapid Transit, 1992; bd. dirs. Friends of the Katy Trail, 2005—06. Mem.: Tex. Bar Found. (trustee 2005—), ABA (antitrust sect.), Tex. Bar Assn. (legal ethics com. 1975—81), Dallas Bar Assn., U. Tex. Law Alumni Assn. (exec. com. 2003—08). Democrat. Methodist. Office: Akin Gump Strauss Hauer & Feld LLP 1700 Pacific Ave Ste 4100 Dallas TX 75201-4675

MCAULIFFE, DANIEL JOSEPH, lawyer; b. NYC, Mar. 27, 1945; s. Daniel Joseph and Ethel Louise (Dierks) McA.; m. J. Wyn Drake, May 20, 1972 (div. Sept. 1977); 1 child, Kelly Elizabeth McAuliffe; m. Shirley J. Wahl, Apr. 8, 2006. BA, Fordham U., 1966; JD, Harvard U., 1969. Bar: DC 1969, Ariz. 1973, Supreme Ct. Ariz., Calif., Nev., Supreme jud. Ct. Mass., US Supreme Ct., US Cts. Appeals (9th & 10th cir.), US Dist. Ct., Dist. Ariz., US Dist. Ct. Dist. Nev. Trial atty. U.S. Dept. Justice, Washington, 1969-71, Dep. Asst. Atty. Gen., 1971-73; atty. Snell & Wilmer, Phoenix, 1973-77, ptnr., 1977—. Mem. Ariz. Commn. on Judicial Qualifications, Task Force Ariz. Commn. on Courts, Ariz. Bar Found. Fellows (vice chmn.). Author/editor: Arizona Legal Forms Vols. 1 and 2, 1988. Chmn. Phoenix Human Rels. Commn., 1974-79; bd. dirs. Phoenix Symphony Assn., 1989—, Phoenix Symphony Coun., 1987—. Mem. ABA, State Bar Calif., Fed. Bar Assn., Am. Judicature Soc., Am. Law Inst., Ariz. State Bar Assn. (chmn. civil practice & procedure com. 1984-91; bd. govs. 1991-1999 & 2002-2003; chmn. professionalism course com. 1994; exec. coun. appellate practice sect. 1995, task force tech. 1995; 2nd v.p. 2004, pres. 2007-08). Avocations: tennis, reading. Office: Snell & Wilmer One Ariz Ctr Phoenix AZ 85004-0001 Office Phone: 602-382-6272, 602-382-6000. Office Fax: 602-382-6070. E-mail: daniel.mcauliffe@azbar.org.

MCAULIFFE, JANE DAMMEN, academic administrator, religious studies and Islamic studies educator; BA in Classics and Philosophy, Trinity Coll., 1968; MA in Religious Studies, U. Toronto, 1979, PhD in Islamic Studies, 1984. Asst. prof. dept. religious studies U. Toronto, 1981-86, assoc. to full prof. dept. Middle East and Islamic studies, dept. study religion, 1992-99, chair dept. study of religion, dir. Ctr. Study of Religion, 1992-97; from asst. prof. to assoc. prof. history of religions and Islamic studies Candler Sch. Theology Emory U., Atlanta, 1986-92, assoc. dean Candler Sch. Theology, 1990-92; prof. Dept. for the Study of Religion, 1997-99; dean, prof. history and Arabic Georgetown Coll. Georgetown U., Washington, 1999—2008; pres. Bryn Mawr Coll., 2008—. Appointed Vatican Commn. for Religious Rels. with Muslims, 1994. Author: Qur'anic Christians: An Analysis of Classical and Modern Exegesis, 1991, 'Abbasid Authority Affirmed: The Early Years of al-Mansur, vol. 28, 1995; editor: Encyclopaedia of the Qur'an, 2001—; contbr. articles to profl. jours. Danforth Found. fellow, 1976-80, NEH Summer fellow, 1979-80, Charles Gordon Heyd fellow, 1980-81, Social Scis. and Humanities Rsch. Coun. doctoral fellow, 1981-84, Postdoctoral fellow, 1984-86, CASA II fellow, 1986, NEH Summer Faculty Travel fellow, 1989, NEH Rsch. fellow, 1992, Mellon fellow, 1994, Guggenheim fellow, 1996. Mem. Am. Soc. Study of Religion, Am. Acad. Religion, Am. Oriental Soc., Can. Soc. Study of Religion, Mid. East Studies Assn. (Thesis award 1985), Soc. Values in Higher Edn. Office: Bryn Mawr Coll 101 N Merion Ave Bryn Mawr PA 19010-2899 Office Phone: 610-526-5000.*

MCAULIFFE, ROSEMARY, lawyer; b. New Rochelle, NY, May 24, 1927; d. William J. and Rose B. (Payne) McA. BA, Regis Coll., 1949; JD, New Eng. Sch. Law, 1954; MEd, Boston State Coll., 1971, Cert. advanced grad studies, 1981; LLD (hon.), New Eng. Sch. Law, Boston, 2002. Bar: Mass. 1956, U.S. Dist. Ct. Mass. 1957, U.S. Supreme Ct. 1961. Pvt. practice law, Boston, 1956—. Tchr. City of Boston, 1965-93. Prodr. (weekly TV show) The Legal Line, Boston Pub. Access Answer Channel. Active World Affairs Coun., Boston 1980-95; sec. Italian Hist. Assn. Mass., 1988—. Mem. Mass. Bar Assn., Am. Acad. Trial Lawyers, Mass. Assn. Women Lawyers. Home and Office: 61 Prince St Boston MA 02113-1829

MCAULIFFE, TERRY (TERENCE RICHARD MCAULIFFE), former political organization administrator; b. Syracuse, NY, Feb. 9, 1957; s. Jack and Millie McAuliffe; m. Dorothy Swann, 1988; children: Dori, Jack, Mary, Sally, Peter. BA in Polit. Sci., Cath. U., 1979; JD, Georgetown U., 1984. Fin. chmn. Gephardt for Pres. Campaign Com., 1988; amb., commr. gen. Internat. Expo., 1993; chmn. Dem. Bus. Coun., 1993; fin. chmn. Dem. Nat. Com., 1994, Bill Clinton/Al Gore Election Campaign, 1996; co-chair Presdl. Inaugural Com., 1997; chmn. Dem. Nat. Conv., LA, 2000, Dem. Nat. Com., 2001—05. Author: What A Party: My Life Among Democrats: Presidents, Candidates, Donors, Activists, Alligators, and Other Wild Animals, 2007. Democrat.*

MCAULIFFE-CURNIAS, SUSAN EILEEN, secondary school educator; b. Hartford, Conn., June 28, 1951; d. Daniel Joseph and Shirley Anne (Pierce) McAuliffe; m. James Michael Curnias, Aug. 16, 1985; 1 child, Christina McAuliffe Curnias. BS in health and physical edn., Southern Conn. State U., 1973; MS, Ctrl. Conn. State U., 1976. Cert. tchr./coach. Tchr./coach West Hartford Bd. Edn., Conn., 1973—. Roman Catholic. Avocation: cooking. Home: 37 Summerfielde Dr Wethersfield CT 06109 Office: William Hall HS West Hartford 975 W Main St West Hartford CT 06117 Personal E-mail: macurn@sbcglobal.net.

MCAVEY, MARION SHEILA, college professor, editor; d. Donald Francis and Frances Margaret McAvey; m. Daniel James Rose, Aug. 10, 1997. MA, Syracuse U., NY, 1974; PhD, U. Mass., Amherst, 1983. Cert. in Software Tech. Writing Middlesex CC, 2001, in Reader, GRE Analytical Essay Ednl. Testing Svc., 2002, in Reader, SAT Essay Pearson Edn. Pub., 2005. Asst. editor Am. Antiquarian Soc., Worcester, Mass., 1983—91; prof. English Becker Coll., Worcester, 1992—. Contract editor, Mass., 1987—. Contbr. articles to profl. publs. Reviewer, sec. Shrewsbury Cultural Coun., Mass., 2002—08. Mem.: MLA, Irish-Am. Cultural Inst., Popular Culture Assn., Am. Conf. Irish Studies. Office: Becker Coll 61 Sever St Worcester MA 01609

MCAVITY, JOHN GILLIS, museum director, association executive, museologist; b. St. John, NB, Can., Oct. 30, 1950; s. J. Patrick H. and Catharine A. (McNeill) McA. BA, U. N.B., 1972; LLB (hon.), U. New Brunswick, LLD, 2007. Cert. assn. exec. Asst. curator Kings Landing Mus., Fredericton, N.B., Can., 1972-73; provincial mus. adviser N.B. Mus., St. John, Can., 1973-76; exec. dir. Ont. Mus. Assn., Toronto, Canada, 1976—81, Can. Mus. Assn., Ottawa, Ont., Canada, 1981—; hon. ambassador U. New Brunswick, 2008. Bd. dirs. Internat. Mus. Mgmt. Com., Internat. Coun. Mus., Paris, chair; sec. treas. Intercom, 2001—. Editor INTERCOM News, 1997—. V.p. St. John Heritage Trust, 1974-76; exec. com. Can. Club, St. John, 1975, English Speaking Union, St. John, 1974-76; vol. fundraiser Kidney Found., Can.; bd. dirs. Centretown Citizens Corp.; founding dir. Mus. Found. Can., 1994—. Recipient Queen's Jubilee medal, 2002. Mem.: Internat. Coun. Museums (task force, legal affairs com. 2002—), Shefford Heritage Co-op (membership chair 1992—95, 2000—), Can. Art Mus. Dirs. Orgn., Can. Soc. Assn. Execs. (bd. dirs. 1993—96, Long Svc. Achievement award 2002), Can. Soc. Copyright Consumers, Ont. Assn. Art Galleries (bd. dirs. 1986—90), Nat. Mus. Assn. (chair internat. com. 2000—), Assn. Museums N.B. (founding), Tourism Industry Assn. Can. (bd. dirs.), Quaco Hist. and Libr. Soc. (hon. life), Assn. Cultural Execs. (bd. dirs. 1988—92, apptd. to senate 1995), Inst. Assn. Execs. (chmn. postal com., cert., bd. dirs. Ottawa chpt.), Mus. Found. Can. (founding dir. 1994—), Am. Assn. State and Local History (awards com. 1981—84, nominations com. 1985), Am. Assn. Museums. Anglican. Home: 300 Cooper St Apt 41 Ottawa ON Canada K2P 0G7 Home (Summer): 29 Kingshurst Ln Rothesay NB Canada E2H 1T3 E-mail: jmcavity@museums.ca.

MCAVOY, BRUCE RONALD, engineer, consultant; b. Jamestown, NY, Jan. 30, 1933; s. George Harold and Agda Amelia (Martinson) McA. BS in Physics, U. Rochester, 1954. Jr. engr. Westinghouse Air Arm Div., Balt., 1956-57, assoc. engr., 1957-58; rsch. engr. Westinghouse Rsch. Ctr., Pitts., 1958-69; sr. rsch. engr. Westinghouse R & D Ctr., Pitts., 1969-78, fellow engr., 1978-84, adv. scientist, 1984—. Mem. adv. bd. Nat. Ctr. Phys. Acoustics, U. Miss., 1987—88; lectr. elect. engring. dept. Carnegie Mellon U., 1968—70. Editor spl. issue IEEE Trans. Microwave Theory Tech., Ultrasonics Symposium procs., 1976-96; mem. editl. bd. jour. Microwave and Guided Wave Letters, 1990. With U.S. Army, 1954-56. Fellow IEEE (life, awards and recognition com. 1989—, def. R&D policy com. 1989-91, Centennial medal 1984, tech. program com. Internat. Microwave Symposium 1986-99); mem. DAV (life), Ultrasonic, Ferroelectric and Frequency Control Soc. of IEEE (pres. 1986-87, Disting. Svc. award 1999), Electromagnetics Acad., Microwave Theory and Techniques Soc. (chmn. microwave acoustics tech. com. 1988-99). Republican. Lutheran. Home: 926 Ivy St Pittsburgh PA 15232-2651 Home Phone: 412-621-2791; Office Phone: 412-621-2791. E-mail: brmcavoy@comcast.net.

MCAVOY, JAMES ANDREW, actor; b. Glasgow, Scotland, Apr. 21, 1979; m. Anne-Marie Duff, 2006. Actor: (films) The Near Room, 1995, Regeneration, 1997, The Pool, 2001, Bollywood Queen, 2002, Bright Young Things, 2003, Strings, 2004, Wimbledon, 2004, Inside I'm Dancing, 2004, The Chronicles of Narnia: The Lion, the Witch and the Wardrobe, 2005, The Last King of Scotland, 2006 (Best Actor, Brit. Acad. Film and TV Arts, 2007), Penelope, 2006, Starter for 10, 2006, Becoming Jane, 2007, Atonement, 2007, Wanted, 2008; (TV films) An Angel Passes By, 1997, Lorna Doone, 2000, White Teeth, 2002, Macbeth, 2005; (TV series) Early Doors, 2003, State of Play, 2003, Shameless, 2004—05; (TV miniseries) Children of Dune, 2003. Recipient Chopard trophy, Cannes Film Festival, 2007, Rising Star award, Brit. Acad. Film and TV Arts, 2006, Best Actor award, Elle Mag., 2008. Office: PFD Drury House 34-43 Russell St London WC2B 5HA England

MCAVOY, JOHN MARTIN, plastic surgeon; b. White Plains, NY, Jan. 8, 1947; s. Joseph Patrick and Claire Margaret (Boucher) McAvoy; m. Laurel Ann Streeter, June 21, 1969; children: Holly, Ian. BS in Biology, Tufts U., Medford, Mass., 1968; MD, Tufts U., Boston, 1972. Cert. Am. Bd. Surgery, Am. Bd. Plastic Surgery, Nat. Bd. Med. Examiners, ACLS. Resident dept. surgery UCLA Med. Ctr., 1972—77, chief resident dept. surgery, 1976—77; resident plastic surgery U. Colo. Med. Ctr., Denver, 1977—79, chief resident plastic surgery, 1978—79; chief plastic surgery Santa Rosa Meml. Hosp., Calif., 1986—91; pvt. practice Santa Rosa, Calif., 1979—. Presenter in field. Contbg. editor: Hosp. Physician mag., 1976—81; contbr. articles to profl. jours. Youth baseball coach Santa Rosa Babe Ruth Rincon Valley Little League, 1992—96. Reinach-Turnesia Caddie scholar, Westchester County, 1964. Fellow: ACS; mem.: Am. Soc. Plastic Surgeons (membership com.), Calif. Soc. Plastic Surgeons (ins. mediation com.), Am. Soc. for Aesthetic Plastic Surgery. Avocations: woodworking, gardening, poetry. Office: 4773 Hoen Ave Santa Rosa CA 95405 Office Phone: 707-526-2276. Personal E-mail: dr.jmcavoy@yahoo.com. Business E-Mail: jmcavoy@sonic.net.

MCAVOY, SUSAN A., legislative staff member; b. Alexandria Bay, NY, July 10, 1953; BA in Polit. Sci., U. Tex., Arlington, 1987, MA in Urban Affairs, 1989. Adminstrv. asst. for Rep. Martin Frost US House of Reps., Washington, chief of staff for Rep. Emanuel Cleaver, 2005—06, legis. dir., chief of staff and comm. dir. for Rep. Leonard L. Boswell, 2006—; dep. press sec. US Dept. Agr., 1999—2001; sr. policy adviser US House Dem. Caucus, 2001—02. Avocations: gardening, walking. Office: Office of Congressman Leonard L Boswell 1427 Longworth House Office Bldg Washington DC 20515 Office Phone: 202-225-3806. Business E-Mail: susan.mcavoy@mail.house.gov.*

MCBEE, CHRISTY DAWN, art educator; b. Tullahomo, Tenn., Nov. 15, 1974; d. Larry Wayne and Dorothy Jean McInturff; m. Michael Scott McBee, June 26, 2004; children: Stacy Carol, Mitchell Larry. BSc, Mid. Tenn. State U., Murfreesboro, 1997. Art endorsement Arrowmont Sch. Arts & Crafts, 2002, registered visual arts tchr. Tenn., 2002. Tchr. 3rd grade Broadview Elem. Sch., Winchester, Tenn., 1997—98; Sparks grant tchr. Warren County Schs., McMinnville, Tenn., 1998—2000; tchr. art Woodland Elem. Sch., Woodbury, Tenn., 2000—03, Cascade H.S., Shelbyville, Tenn., 2003—04, Crab Orchard & Pineview Elem. Schs., Crossville, Tenn., 2004—; mktg. Village Advocate, 2008—09. Head fine arts dept. Cascade H.S., Pineview; mem. spl. concerns com. Crab Orchard Elem. Sch., Crossville, 2003—06, chmn. flower com., 2006—. Contbr. poetry to Anthology of American Poetry, 1997. Sponsor Awana Internat. Worldwide Missions, 2005—06, Habitat for Humanity, Warren County, 1997—2006, Jesus Film Project Worldwide Missions, 2005—06. Recipient Awana Achievement award, Morrison 1st Bapt. Ch., 2005; nominee 10 Yr. Svc. award, Cumberland County Schs., Crossville, 2006; Sparks grant, Warren County Schs., 1998—2000. Mem.: Tenn. Edn. Assn., Nat. Tchrs. Edn. Assn. Democrat. Southern Bapt. Achievements include leading a student to receive statewide recognition for winning the My Home Is Tennessee Art Contest in Nashville. Avocations: reading, poetry, painting, music, birdwatching. Office: Crab Orchard Elem Sch 240 School Rd Crab Orchard TN 37723 Office Phone: 931-474-3939. Business E-Mail: mcbee@cumberlandcountyk-12.com, vadvocate@blomand.net.

MCBEE, MARY LOUISE, state legislator, academic administrator; b. Strawberry Plains, Tenn., June 15, 1924; d. John Wallace and Nina Aileen (Umbarger) McB. BS, East Tenn. State U., 1946; MA, Columbia U., 1951; PhD, Ohio State U., 1961. Tchr. East Tenn. State U., Johnson City, 1947-51; asst. dean of women, 1952-56, 57-60; dean of women, 1961-63, U. Ga., Athens, 1963-67; world campus afloat adminstr., 1966-67; assoc. dean of students, 1967-72; dean of students, 1972-74; asst. v.p. acad. affairs, 1974-76; assoc. v.p. acad. affairs, 1976-86; v.p. acad. affairs, 1986-88; ret., 1988; state rep. Clarke County Ga. Gen. Assembly, 1991—2004. Author: College Responsibility for Values, 1980; co-author: The American Woman: Who Will She Be?, 1974, Essays, 1979, 2d edit. 1981. Bd. dirs. Salvation Army, Athens, 1978—, United Way, Athens. Fulbright scholar, The Netherlands, 1956-57. Mem. Athens C. of C. (bd. dirs.). Democrat. Methodist. Avocations: gardening, tennis, hiking. Home: 145 Pine Valley Pl Athens GA 30606-4031 Personal E-mail: louisemcbee@charter.com.

MCBEE, STEVE, lobbyist; b. Wash. m. Jennifer McBee; children: Brody, Finn. Attended, Western Wash. U., Bellingham. Staff mem. US Congressman Al Swift; legis. aide US Congresswoman Maria Cantwell, US Congressman Norm Dicks; COO Denny Miller McBee Assocs., 1999—2002; pres., CEO McBee Strategic Consulting, LLC, 2002—. Named one of Best in the Bus., The Hill. Avocations: snowboarding, hiking, mountain biking. Office: McBee Strategic Consulting 601 Pennsylvania Ave NW Ste 800 N Bldg Washington DC 20004 Office Phone: 202-234-1224. Office Fax: 202-234-1223.

MCBEE, SUSANNA B., freelance journalist; b. Santa Fe, N.Mex., Mar. 28, 1935; d. Jess Stephen and Sybil Elizabeth (Barnes) McBee; m. Paul H. Recer, July 2, 1983. AB, U. So. Calif., 1956; MA, U. Chgo., 1962. Staff writer Washington Post, 1957-65, 73-74, 77-79, asst. nat. editor, 1974-77; asst. sec. pub. affairs HEW, 1979; articles editor Washingtonian mag., 1980-81; assoc. editor U.S. News & World Report, 1981-86; news editor Washington Bur., Hearst Newspapers, 1987-89, asst. bur. chief, 1990—2003, ret., 2003; Washington corr. Life mag., 1965—69; Washington editor McCall's mag., 1970—72. Bd. dirs. Washington Press Club Found., 1992-95. Recipient Penney-Missouri mag. award, 1969, Hall of Fame award, Soc. Profl. Journalists, 1996, Sigma Delta Chi Pub. Svc. award, 1969, Hearst Eagle award, 1994. Mem. Nat. Press Club, Cosmos Club. Home: 5190 Watson St NW Washington DC 20016-5329

MCBRAYER, SANDRA L., educational director, homeless outreach educator; AA, San Diego Mesa Coll., 1981; BA in Applied Arts and Scis., San Diego State U., 1986, MA in Edn., 1990. Cert. presch.-kindergarten, grs. 1-12, adult edn., Calif. Tchr. asst. group homes Oz, The Bridge, Gatehouse, 1984-87; tchr. Hillcrest Receiving Home, 1987-88, Juvenile Hall, 1987-88, Comprehensive Adolescent Treatment Ctr., 1987-88; head tchr. the Monarch HS, 1988-96; CEO The Children's Initiative, San Diego. Lectr., cons. Ctrs. Careers Edn., Sch. Tchr. Edn. San Diego State U., 1990—; collaborator sch. dists. State Dept. Edn., Equity/Homeless Office, 1992—; staff devel. tng.; adj. prof. Coll. Edn., San Diego (Calif.) State U. Recipient award Exceptional Vols. Svc. Family Care Ctr., 1988, San Diego's 10 Leadership award Sta. KGTV, 1991, Celebrate Literacy award Internat. Reading Assn., 1992, Women of Vision in Edn. award LWV San Diego, 1992, Disting. Alumna of Yr.-Edn. award San Diego State U., 1992, Golden Bell award Calif. Sch. Bds. Found., 1992, Coun. of State Sch. Officers Nat. Tchr. of Yr. award 1994; named San Diego County Tchr. of Yr. by San Diego County Office of Edn., 1993, Calif. Tchr. of Yr. by State Dept. Edn., 1993, Nat. Tchr. of Yr., Pres. Clinton, 1994, Tech. Tchr. of Yr., Coun. on Tech. Tchr. Edn., 1994, Exceptional Svc. award Calif. State PTA, Humanitarian award Youth Advocacy Assn., Living Legacy award Internat. Women's Ctr.; recognized by local and nat. news media. Mem. NEA, Calif. Tchrs. Assn., Assn. Educators, Nat. Dropout Prevention Network, Calif. Homeless Coalition, Phi Kappa Phi. Office: The Childrens Initiative 4438 Ingraham St San Diego CA 92109

MCBRIDE, ANGELA BARRON, nursing educator; b. Balt., Jan. 16, 1941; d. John Stanley and Mary C. (Szczepanska) Barron; m. William Leon McBride, June 12, 1965; children: Catherine, Kara. BS in Nursing, Georgetown U., Washington, 1962; MS in Nursing, Yale U., New Haven, Conn., 1964; PhD, Purdue U., West Lafayette, Ind., 1978; doctorate of Pub. Svc. (hon.), U. Cin., 1983; LittD (hon.), Purdue U., 1998; LLD (hon.), Ea. Ky. U., 1991; LHD (hon.), Georgetown U., 1993; DSc (hon.), Med. Coll. Ohio, 1995; LHD (hon.), U. Akron, 1997. Asst. prof., rsch. asst. inst. Yale U., New Haven, 1964-73; assoc. prof., chairperson Ind. U. Sch. Nursing, Indpls., 1978-81, 80-84, prof., 1981-92, assoc. dean rsch., 1985—91, interim dean, 1991—92, univ. dean, 1992—2003, disting. prof., 1992—2005, disting. prof., univ. dean emerita, 2006—; sr. v.p. acad. affairs, nursing Clarian Health Ptnrs., 1997—2003; Am. Acad. Nursing, Am. Nurses Found. scholar-in-residence Inst. Medicine, 2003—04; Helene Denne Schulte vis. prof. U. Wis., Madison, 2006; cons. prof. Duke U. Sch. Nursing., 2008—09. Mem. Nat. Adv. Mental Health Coun., 1987—91; adv. com. NIH Office of Women's Health Rsch., 1997—2001, NIH Office of Women's Health Rsch. Specialized Ctrs. Rsch. on Sex and Gender Factors, 2003—06; coun. mem. Yale U. Coun., 1999—2005; ext. acad. advisor Sch. Nursing, Hong Kong Poly. U., 2000—06; adv. bd. Meth. Health Found., 2000—; advisor U. Hong Kong, 2004—06, Hong Kong Acad. Nursing, 2004—; appointed to Old Master Program Purdue U., 2007. Author: The Growth and Development of Mothers, 1973 (Best Book award 1973), Living with Contradictions, A Married Feminist, 1976, How to Enjoy A Good Life With Your Teenager, 1987; editor: Psychiatric-Mental Health Nursing: Integrating the Behavioral and Biological Sciences, 1996 (Best Book award 1996); compiler: Nursing and Philanthropy, 2000. Adv. bd. Women's Fund Indpls., 2000—05; chair Nat. Adv. Com. Nurse Faculty Scholars Program Robert Wood Johnson Found., 2007—09; bd. dirs. United Way of Ctrl. Ind., 2002—06, Clarian Health Ptnrs., 2004—, chair quality and patient safety com.; mem. Yale U. Sch. Nursing Adv. Bd., 2006—, chair, 2007—09. Recipient Disting. Alumna award Yale U., Disting. Alumna award Purdue U., Univ. Medallion, U. San Francisco, 1993, Hoosier Heritage award, 2000, Disting. Nurse Educator award Coll. Mt. St. Joseph, Cin., 2000, Ross Pioneering Spirit award Am. Assn. Critical-Care Nurses, 2004, Lifetime Achievement award Assn. Fundraising Profls., Ind., 2005, Woman of Achievement award, Ball State U., 2005 Torchbearer award Ind. Commn. for Women, 2005, Melva Jo Hendrix Leadership award Internat. Soc. Psychiat. Nursing, 2006; named Influential Woman in Indpls., Indpls. Bus. Jour./Ind. Lawyer, 1999, HealthCare Hero Indpls. Bus. Jour., 2003, Adele Herwitz Disting. scholar Commn. Fgn. Nursing Schs., 2005, Harold Burdette award Behavioral Coop. Oncology Group, 2007; Kellogg nat. fellow; Am. Nurses Found. scholar, Salute to Women award Indpls. YMCA, 1999, Sagamore of Wabash, 1999, medal Yale Sch. Nursing, named to Hall of Fame, 2008. Fellow: Nat. Acads. Practice, Am. Acad. Nursing (dir. leadership devel. bldg. acad. geriatric nursing capacity program 2000—, past pres., Living Legend 2006), APA (Nursing and Health Psychology award divsn. 38 1995); mem.: MNRS Found. (trustee 2007—09), Soc. for Women's Health Rsch. (bd. mem. 2007—), Nat. Acad. Scis., Inst. of Medicine (mem. bd. health policy ednl. programs and fellowships 2006—), Soc. for Rsch. in Child Devel., Midwest Nursing Rsch. Soc. (Disting. Rsch. award 1985), Sigma Theta Tau (past pres., Mentor award 1993, disting. lectr 1995—99, Melanie Dreher award for contbns. as a dean 2001), Chi Eta Phi (hon.). Home: 744 Cherokee Ave Lafayette IN 47905-1872 Home Phone: 765-474-9187; Office Phone: 317-278-9076. Business E-Mail: amcbride@iupui.edu.

MCBRIDE, ANITA BEVACQUA, former federal official; b. Bridgeport, Conn., 1959; m. Timothy J. McBride; children: Andrew, Giovanna. BA in Internat. Studies, U. Conn., 1981; student in Internat. Rels., Am. U.; student, U. Florence. Dir. pers. The White House, 1987—92, spl. asst. to Pres. for White House mgmt.; dir. spkrs. bur. US Info. Agy.; sr. adv. to sec. & White House liaison US Dept. State, 2001—03, sr. adv. Bur. Internat. Orgns., 2004; dep. asst. to Pres., chief of staff to First Lady Laura Bush The White House, 2005—06, asst. to Pres., chief of staff to First Lady Laura Bush, 2006—09. Mgmt. cons. Am. Automobile Manufacturers Assn.; exec. recruiter J. Naylor Cope Co.; project mgr. flagship philanthropic program Smith Kline Beecham Found. Parent vol. Dept. Def. Sch., Stuttgart, Germany. Recipient Patriot award, Nat. Guard and Res., 2006.*

MCBRIDE, ANTHONY, pharmaceutical executive; b. Houston; married; 2 children. BA in Psychology, U. Tex., Austin; MA in Indsl. Orgnl. Psychology, PhD in Indsl. Orgnl. Psychology, Tex. A&M U. Cons. Personnel Decisions Inc., NYC; assoc. dir. human resources devel., worldwide medicines Bristol-Myers Squibb Co., various leadership positions including dir. leadership devel., v.p. in Europe, internat. medicines and US pharm., v.p. worldwide pharm. comml. ops., sr. v.p. human resources, 2008—. Avocations: photography, music, travel. Office: Bristol Myers Squibb Co 311 Pennington Rocky Hill Rd Pennington NJ 08534 Office Phone: 609-818-3000.

MCBRIDE, DANNY R., actor; b. Statesboro, Ga., Dec. 29, 1976; Attended, NC Sch. of Arts. Night mgr. Holiday Inn, Burbank, Calif. Actor: (films) All the Real Girls, 2003, Hot Rod, 2007, The Heartbreak Kid, 2007, Drillbit Taylor, 2008, Pineapple Express, 2008, Tropic Thunder, 2008, Land of the Lost, 2009; actor, writer (films) The Foot Fist Way, 2006, guest appearances include (TV series) Late Night with Conan O'Brien, 2008, Jimmy Kimmel Live!, 2008. Office: c/o Gotham Group Inc 9255 Sunset Blvd Ste 515 Los Angeles CA 90069

MCBRIDE, GUY THORNTON, JR., college president emeritus; b. Austin, Tex., Dec. 12, 1919; s. Guy Thornton and Imogene (Thrasher) McB.; m. Rebekah Jane Bush, Sept. 2, 1942 (dec. Aug. 1998); children: Rebekah Ann, William Howard, Ellen M. Alsobrooks; m. Cordelia D. Rush, Aug. 7, 1999. BS in Chem. Engring., U. Tex., 1940; Sc.D., MIT, 1948; D.P.S. (hon.), Regis Coll., 1979; D.Engring. (hon.), Colo. Sch. Mines, 1984. Registered profl. engr., Tex. La., N.Y., Colo. Instr. chem. engring. Mass. Inst. Tech., 1942-44, research assoc., 1946-48; job engr. Standard Oil Co. Calif., 1944-46; asst. prof. chem. engring Rice Inst., 1948-55, assoc. dean students, 1950-57, dean, 1957-58, assoc. prof., 1955-58; cons. Tex. Gulf Sulphur Co., 1950-58, asst. mgr. research dept., 1958-59, mgr., 1959-60, v.p., mgr. research, 1960-63; v.p. Tex. Gulf Sulphur Co. (Phosphate div.), 1963-70, gen. mgr., 1966-70; pres. Colo. Sch. Mines, Golden, 1970-84; ret. Dir. Halliburton Co., Kerr-McGee Corp., Hercules, Inc.; hon. dir. Texasgulf Inc. Fellow Am. Inst. Chem. Engrs.; mem. Am. Chem. Soc., Nat. Soc. Profl. Engrs., Sigma Xi, Phi Lambda Upsilon, Tau Beta Pi. Clubs: Mile High (Denver). Home: 2615 Oak Dr Apt 13 Lakewood CO 80215-7182

MCBRIDE, JANET MARIE, small business owner; b. Ft. Wayne, Ind., Nov. 21, 1948; d. Robert W and Helen F Plasterer; m. Joey W McBride, July 26, 1976; children: Kenneth Schortgen, Jr., Christian Schortgen, Dawna McBride Ross, Brand. Grad., Phoenix Coll., 1995. Feng Shui practitioner Western Sch. of Feng Shui, Calif., 2000. Dod ednl. exec asst DOD Schools-Europe, Madrid, 1979—82; engring. project adminstr. Honeywell, Inc., Tempe, 1987—95; cons., coach Young Living, Salt Lake City, 2000—. Singer (songwriter/producer): (spiritual songs) Irish Girl with the Heart of a Jew; singer: (musician/producer) (messianic hymns) Irish Girl with Heart of a Jew; author: Scriptural Essence; Radio Health Talk Personality, Feng Shui, God's Way, 2008. Home: 500 N Estrella Pky Ste B2-440 Goodyear AZ 85338 Personal E-mail: womanscents@cox.net.

MCBRIDE, JOHN KUHNS, lawyer; b. Cin., Jan. 15, 1943; s. Leland Dale and Mary Huggins McBride; m. Prella Philips McBride, Aug. 20, 1966; children: John Scott, Daniel Philips, Rebecca M. Klepser. AB, Denison U., Ohio, 1965; JD, U. Cin., 1968. Assoc. Ball Egglestr Bumble

Burg, Lafayette, Ind., 1968—71; ptnr. Ball Egglestr PC, Lafayette, 1971—. Pres. Tippecanoe County Bar Assn., 1992—93. Bd. mem., pres., campaign chair United Way, 1983—89; pres. Lafayette Home Hosp., 1992—93; bd. mem., chmn. North Ctrl. Health Svc., 1999—2002; with Ctr. Lafayette Mem. Art Bd., 1993—98; bd. mem. Lafayette Symphony Found., 2005—, Bank One, Lafayette, 1992—97; bd. mem., sec. treas. Lafayette Union Railway Campaign, 1980—; chmn. North Ctrl. Health Svc., 2002—04; bd. mem. Lafayette Symphony Orchestra, 1999—2003. Mem.: Ind. Commn. Continuing Legal Edn. (chmn. 1997), Am. Bar Assn., Ind. Bar Assn., Tippecanoe Bar Assn. Avocations: travel, tennis, numismatics. Office: Ball Eggleaton PC 701 Mam St Ste 810 P O Box 1535 Lafayette IN 47902

MCBRIDE, JONATHAN EVANS, governance consultant, director; b. Wash., June 16, 1942; s. Gordon Williams and Martha Alice (Evans) McBride; m. Emilie Evans Dean, Sept. 5, 1970; children: Webster Dean, Morley Evans. BA, Yale U., New Haven, Conn., 1964. Account exec. Merrill Lynch & Co., Washington, 1968—72; v.p. dept. mgr. Lionel D. Edie & Co., NYC, 1972—76; v.p. and exec. search cons. Simmons Assoc., Inc., Washington, 1976—79; pres. McBride Assoc., 1979—. Bd. dir. Yale U. Alumni Fund, 1974—79; trustee Sidwell Friends Sch., Washington, 1996—2004, vice chair, 2002—04. To lt. USNR, 1964—68. Mem.: Chevy Chase (Md.) Club, Met. Club (Washington), Yale Club (NYC). Office: 1701 Pennsylvania Ave NW Ste 300 Washington DC 20006 Office Phone: 202-349-3663. Personal E-mail: hearthunt@aol.com.

MCBRIDE, MARTINA, singer; b. Medicine Lodge, Kans., July 29, 1966; d. Daryl and Jeanne Schiff; m. John McBride, May 15, 1988; children: Delaney Katherine, Emma Justine, Ava Rose Kathleen. Vocalist Schiffters, 1975-86, assorted bands, Wichita, Kans.; backup singer Garth Brooks, 1992—93. Singer: (albums) The Time Has Come, 1992, The Way That I Am, 1993, Wild Angels, 1995, Evolution, 1997, Martina McBride Christmas, 1998, Emotion, 1999, White Christmas, 1999, Greatest Hits, 2001, Martina, 2003, Timeless, 2005, Waking Up Laughing, 2007, Martina McBride: Live In Concert, 2008, Shine, 2009, (albums with various artists) Girls Night Out, 1999. Recipient Breakthrough Artist Video for "My Baby Loves Me", Music Row Ind. Summit Award, 1994, Music Video Yr. for "Independence Day", Country Music Assn. Awards, 1994, Best Video Yr. for "Independence Day", Gt. Brit. Music Awards, 1994, Video Yr. for "Independence Day", Nashville Music Awards, 1995, TNN Music City News Award, 1995, Gold Clio for Country Music Video Yr. for "Independence Day", Clio Awards, 1995, Best Southern Gospel, Country Gospel or Bluegrass Gospel for "Amazing Grace - A Country Salute To Gospel", Grammy Awards, 1995, Country Album Yr. for "Wild Angels", Nashville Music Awards, 1996, Video Yr. for "Safe In The Arms of Love", 1996, Female Video Yr. for "Blessed", CMT Flameworthy Awards, 2002, Female Video Yr. for "Concrete Angel", CMT Flameworthy Award, 2003, Top Female Vocalist, Acad. Country Music, 2002, Acad. Country Music award, 2003, 2004, Female Vocalist Yr., Country Music Assn. Award, 2002, Female Vocalist Yr. award, Country Music Assn., 2003, 2004, Country Female Artist Yr., Billboard Music Award, 2002, Best Female Artist, Country Radio Music Awards, 1996, Favorite Female Artist, Country, Am. Music Awards, 2003, Favorite Female Artist, Country Weekly, 2003; nominee Best Country Song for "Independence Day", Grammy, 1994, Video Yr. for "Independence Day", Acad. Country Music, 1994, Best Country Collaboration with Vocals for "Own My Own" with Reba McEntire, Linda Davis, and Trisha Yearwood, Grammy, 1995, Vocal Event Yr. for "On My Own" with Reba McEntire, Linda Davis, and Trisha Yearwood., Country Music Assn., 1996, Album Yr. for "Wild Angels", 1996, Best Country Female Vocal Performance for "Safe In The Arms of Love", Grammy, 1995, Vocal Event Yr. for "Still Holding On" with Clint Black, Country Music Assn., 1997, Best Country Collaboration with Vocals for "Still Holding You" with Clint Black, Grammy, 1997, Video Yr. for "A Broken Wing", Country Music Assn., 1998, Single Yr. for "A Broken Wing", 1998, Acad. Country Music, 1999, Song Yr. for "A Broken Wing", 1999, Video Yr. for "A Broken Wing", 1999, Best Country Female Vocal Performance for "I Love You", Grammy, 1999, Single Yr. for "Blessed", Country Music Assn., 2002, Best Female Country Vocal Performance for "Blessed", Grammy, 2002, Video Yr. for "Concrete Angel", Country Music Assn., 2003, Top Female Vocalist, Acad. Country Music, 1993, 1998, 2000, 2001, Horizon award, Country Music Assn., 1994, Female Vocalist Yr., 1996, 1998, 1999, 2001, Am. Music Awards, 2003. Office: RCA Records 1400 18th Ave S Nashville TN 37212-2809

MCBRIDE, MILDRED MAYLEA, retired elementary school educator; b. Bowerston, Ohio, Oct. 7, 1922; d. Harry Scott and Mary McGary (Mowl) McB.; 1 adopted child, Marjorie Mi Sang McBride. BS in Music, Baldwin-Wallace Coll., 1944; MA, Columbia U., NYC, 1949. Cert. tchr., Ohio, Hawaii. Traveling music tchr. Tuscarawas County Sch., 1944-45; tchr. elem. music Parma (Ohio) Schs., 1945-48, tchr. jr. h.s. music, 1946-48; tchr. h.s. gen. music, chorus Kamehameha Sch. for Girls, Honolulu, 1949-59; tchr. elem. music Tempe (Ariz.) Schs., 1959-60, Hawaii Pub. Sch. Sys., 1960-86, ret., 1986. Co-founder Elem., Intermediate, Gen. Music Interest Group, Honolulu, 1969-79. Author, editor: Meg!, 1996, Three Women of Kintail, 2001, Lady Janet, Genny MacKenzie and Her Bairns, 2003, The Troubled Child, Angus and Margaret Moira, 2004, Two Brothers, 2006, Travel with MiSong, The Family Visit Paris; writer mus. plays. Helper Bowerston Pub. Libr., 1939, 48, 97—; bd. dirs.; mem. Honolulu Symphony Chorus; soup kitchen, vol. Harris United Meth. Ch., Honolulu, 1990-96, mem. choir, 1975-96. Mem.: Knights. Avocations: golf, travel, singing, cooking, enjoying daughter.

MCBRIDE, SUSAN ALYSE, interior designer, consultant; b. Watsonville, Calif., Sept. 24, 1948; d. Allan Edwin and Jeanne Marie Petersen; BA, Ariz. State U., 1970. Prin. designer Susan Alyse Enterprises, Watsonville, Calif., 1980—. Sales mgr. Andrew Morgan Collection, Bklyn., 2001—. Mem.: SFDC, HIA, NEWH (assoc.). Roman Catholic. Avocations: travel, art history, architecture, swimming, sculpting. Home: 100 Via Del Sol Watsonville CA 95076 Office: Andrew Morgan Collection Mount Vernon NY 10550 Home Fax: 831-768-1878. E-mail: susanalyse@aol.com.

MCBRIDE, TAMERA SHAWN DEW, geologist; d. Lawrence Bernard Dew, Jr. and Daris Virginia Hutchinson Dew; m. William Scott McBride, June 6, 1998; children: Alynaza Isabella, Rastus. BA cum laude, Rollins Coll., 1993; MS, U. So. Fla., 1995. Cert. radon measurement technician Fla. Dept. Health, Divsn. Environ. Health, 1997, profl. geologist Fla. Dept. Bus. and Profl. Regulation, 2002. Phys. sci. technician U.S. Geol. Survey, Ocala, Fla., 1991—94; scientist Environ. Resources Mgmt., Inc., Tampa, Fla., 1995—2000; planner S.W. Fla. Water Mgmt. Dist., Brooksville, Fla., 2000—04, profl. geologist, 2004—. Acting ex-officio mem. Ctrl. Fla. Regional Planning Coun., Bartow, Fla., 2000—04. Soloist St. Catherine (Fla.) United Meth. Ch., 1975—, mem. choir, 2001—, vice chair com. lay leadership, 2005; asst. sec. S.W. Fla. Water Mgmt. Dist. Employee Com., 2003—04, vice-chair, 2004—06, Fla., 2007—. Mem.: U. South Fla. Geology Alumni Soc. (bd. dirs. 1998—2000), Fla. Assn. Profl. Geologists, Chronic Fatigue and Immune Dysfunction Syndrome Assn. of Am., Phi Eta Sigma. Avocations: fishing, travel, dance. Home: PO Box 1223 Bushnell FL 33513 Office: Southwest Florida Water Mgmt Dist 2379 Broad St Brooksville FL 34604 Business E-Mail: tamera.mcbride@swfwmd.state.fl.us.

MCBRIDE, TIMOTHY J., lobbyist; B in Bus. Adminstrn., Eastern Mich. U. Asst. to pres., dir. White House Mgmt. and Adminstrn. The White House, Washington, sr. advisor on policy initiatives and polit. agenda to pres., asst. sec. commerce for trade devel.; dir. comm. Sun Company, Inc.; dir. fed. lobbying, v.p. external affairs/pub. policy DaimlerChrysler; sr. v.p. govt. rels. Freddie Mac, 2005—. Bd. dirs. Discovery Creek Children's Mus. Office: Freddie Mac 8200 Jones Branch Dr Mclean VA 22102-3110*

MCBRIDE, TODD, biology professor, department chairman; b. Seattle, Apr. 13, 1963; m. Rhonda Farrell, Dec. 31, 1988. PhD, U. Calif., Davis, 1988. Prof. biology Calif. State U., Bakersfield, 1996—, chair, 1996—. Office: Calif State Univ 9001 Stockdale Hwy Bakersfield CA 93311

MC BRIDE, WILLIAM LEON, philosopher, educator; b. NYC, Jan. 19, 1938; s. William Joseph and Irene May (Choffin) McB.; m. Angela Barron, July 12, 1965; children: Catherine, Kara. AB, Georgetown U., Washington, DC, 1959; postgrad. (Fulbright fellow), U. Lille, 1959-60; MA (Woodrow Wilson fellow), Yale U., New Haven, Conn., 1962, PhD (Social Sci. Rsch. Coun. fellow), 1964. Instr. philosophy Yale U., New Haven, 1964-66, asst. prof., 1966-70, assoc. prof., 1970-73; lectr. Northwestern U., Evanston, Ill., summer 1972; assoc. prof. Purdue U., West Lafayette, Ind., 1973-76, prof., 1976-2001, Arthur G. Hansen disting. prof., 2001—. Senate chmn. Purdue U., 2004-05; lectr. Korcula Summer Sch., Yugoslavia, 1971, 73; Fulbright lectr. Sofia U., Bulgaria, 1997. Author: Fundamental Change in Law and Society, 1970, The Philosophy of Marx, 1977, Social Theory at a Crossroads, 1980, (with R.A. Dahl) Demokrati og Autoritet, 1980, Sartre's Political Theory, 1991, Social and Political Philosophy, 1994, Philosophical Reflections on the Changes in Eastern Europe, 1999, From Yugoslav Praxis to Global Pathos, 2001; editor: (with C.O. Schrag) Phenomenology in a Pluralistic Context, 1983, Sartre and Existentialism, 8 vols., 1997, (with M.B. Matustik) Calvin O. Schrag and the Task of Philosophy after Postmodernity, 2002, The Idea of Values, 2003, Social and Political Philosophy, 2006. Decorated chevalier Ordre des Palmes Académiques. Mem. AAUP (pres. Purdue chpt. 1983-86, pres. Ind. conf. 1988-89), Am. Philos. Assn. (chmn. com. on internat. coop. 1992-95, bd. dirs. 1992-95), N.Am. Soc. for Social Philosophy (v.p. 1997-2000, pres. 2000-05), Am. Soc. Polit. and Legal Philosophy, Soc. Phenemonology and Existential Philosophy (exec. co-sec. 1977-80), Sartre Soc. N.Am. (chmn. bd. dirs. 1985-88, 91-93), Am. Soc. Philosophy in the French Lang. (pres. 1994-96), Fed. Internat. Soc. Philosophie (steering com. 1998—, sec. gen. 2003—08, pres. 2008-). Home: 744 Cherokee Ave Lafayette IN 47905-1872 Office: Purdue U Dept Philosophy 100 N Univ St West Lafayette IN 47907-2098 Office Phone: 765-494-4285. Business E-Mail: wmcbride@purdue.edu.

MCBRIDE, WILLIAM R., legislative staff member; b. Oct. 18, 1953; BA, Mich. State U., East Lansing, 1974; MA, George Mason U., Fairfax, Va., 1992. Staff mem. Mich. Senate, 1974—76; adminstrv. asst. for Rep. Carl D. Pursell US House of Reps., Washington, 1977—93, dep. chief of staff for Mich. Gov. John Engler, 1993—95, chief of staff for Rep. Vernon J. Ehlers, 1995—; staff dir. Joint Com. on Libr. Congress. Office: Office of Congressman Vernon J Ehlers 2182 Rayburn House Office Bldg Washington DC 20515 Office Phone: 202-225-3831. Business E-Mail: william.mcbride@mail.house.gov.*

MCBROOM, JAMES RANDY, sociologist, educator; b. Bonham, Tex., Nov. 17, 1951; s. James Denzil and Shirley Elizabeth McBroom; m. Dana Jo Denton, Jan. 11, 1996; children: Chad Edward Burns, James Joshua, Jennifer L Stevens, Mark Thomas, Raven Scott Stevens, Stetson Cole Robinson. BS in Spl. Edn. & Sociology, East Tex. State U., Commerce, 1983, MS in Sociology, 1986; PhD, U. North Tex., Denton, 1989. Assoc. prof. dept. sociology & criminal justice Tex. A & M U., Commerce, 1994—, asst. to the pres. planning, 2003—, assoc. v.p. academic affairs, 2009—; bd. mem. Tex. A & M-Commerce Alumni Assn., 1997. Bd. mem. Bonham Ind. Sch. Dist., Tex., 2007; pastor Bethel Bapt. Ch., Whitewright, Tex., 2008; bd. mem. Valley Caddo Mus., Tex., 2008. Mem.: Am. Assn. Higher Edn. Baptist. Avocations: music, fishing, horseback riding, motorcycling. Home: 2229 FM 2815 Bonham TX 75418 Office: Tex A & M Univ Commerce PO Box 3011 Commerce TX 75429 Office Fax: 903-886-5019. Personal E-mail: jrmcbroom@peoplepc.com. Business E-Mail: randy_mcbroom@tamu-commerce.edu.

MCBRYDE, JOHN HENRY, federal judge; b. Jackson, Oct. 9, 1931; m. Betty Vinson; children: Rebecca, Jennifer, John Blake. BS in Commerce, Tex. Christian U., 1953; LLB, U. Tex., 1956. Bar: Tex. 1956, U.S. Ct. Appeals (5th cir.) 1958, U.S. Dist. Ct. (no. dist.) 1958, U.S. Dist. Ct. (ea. dist.) 1989, U.S. Supreme Ct. 1972. Assoc. Cantey, Hanger, Johnson, Scarborough & Gooch, Ft. Worth, 1956-62; ptnr. Cantey & Hanger and predecessor firm, Ft. Worth, 1962-69, McBryde, Bennett and predecessor firms, Ft. Worth, 1969-90; judge U.S. Dist. Ct. (no. dist.) Tex., Ft. Worth, 1990—. Fellow Am. Bar Found. (life), Tex. Bar Found. (life), Am. Coll. Trial Lawyers. Office: US Dist Ct US Courthouse 501 W 10th St Ste 401 Fort Worth TX 76102-3642

MCBRYDE, NEILL GREGORY, lawyer; b. Durham, NC, Jan. 11, 1944; s. Angus M. and Priscilla (Gregory) McBryde; m. Margaret McPherson, Aug. 1, 1970; children: Margaret Courtauld McBryde Young, Neill Gregory Jr. AB cum laude, Davidson Coll., 1966; JD with high honors, U. N.C., 1969. Bar: N.C. 1969., Ga. 1972. Assoc. King & Spalding, Atlanta, 1971-76; ptnr. Fleming, Robinson, Bradshaw & Hinson, Charlotte, NC, 1977-81, Helms, Mulliss & Johnston, Charlotte, 1981-86, Smith Helms Mulliss & Moore, Charlotte, 1986-90, Moore & Van Allen PLLC, Charlotte, 1990—. Lectr. in field; condr. workshops in field; chair, bd. dirs. Crossroads Corp. Affordable Housing & Cmty. Devel. Inc., 2008-; dir. Residential & Support Svcs. Inc., 2008-. Author, editor: First Union National Bank of North Carolina Will Book, 1986; contbr. articles to profl. jours. Elder and Deacon Myers Park Presbyn. Ch., Charlotte, 1980-86, 92-95, 2001-04, 05—; bd. dirs., sec. Presbyn. Home for Aged, Charlotte, 1978-82; trustee Charlotte Latins Schs., Inc., 1980-86, 87-93; past chmn., past trustee Mint Mus. Charlotte. Fellow Am. Coll. Trust and Estate Counsel (past mem. bd. regents, past pres.), Am. Coll. Tax Counsel; mem. ABA, Ga. Bar Assn., NC Bar Assn. (probate and fiduciary law sect.), So. Fed. Tax Inst. (trustee 1999—, pres. 2005-06), Order of Coif, Phi Beta Kappa, Omicron Delta Kappa. Avocations: tennis, golf, fishing. Office: Moore & Van Allen PLLC Bank of Am Corp Ctr 100 N Tryon St Fl 47 Charlotte NC 28202-4003 Office Phone: 704-331-1094.

MCBURNEY, CHARLES WALKER, JR., state representative, lawyer; b. Orlando, Fla., June 6, 1957; s. Charles Walker McBurney and Jeane (Brown) Chappell; children: Katherine Turpin, Madeline. BA, U. Fla., 1979, JD, 1982. Bar: Fla. 1982, US Dist. Ct. (mid. dist.) Fla. 1983, US Ct. Appeals (11th cir.) 1984. Assoc. Mathews, Osborne, McNatt, Gobelman & Cobb, Jacksonville, Fla., 1982-84; asst. state's atty. State's Atty.'s Office, Jacksonville, 1984-90, civil atty., 1987-88, sr. trial atty., 1988-90; dir. Serious or Habitual Juvenile Offender Program, 1986; ptnr. Fischette, Owen, Held & McBurney, Jacksonville, 1990—2004; pvt. practice Law Office Charles W. McBurney Jr., Jacksonville, 2004—; mem. Dist. 16 Fla. House of Reps., Tallahassee, 2007—. Mem. adv. coun. Mandarin Oaks Elem. Sch., vice chmn., 2003—04, chmn., 2004—06; mem. Mayor's Bicentennial Constnl. Commn., 1989—91; chmn. com. congl. campaigns Jacksonville, 1982, 1984, 1988; deacon South Jacksonville Presbyn. Ch., 2003—; bd. dirs. Civic Round Table, 1988—92, treas., 1988—89, pres., 1989—90; dir. Internat. Devel. Commn. for Jacksonville, 1993—2003, treas., 1995—97; chmn. S.E. Citizens Planning Adv. Com., 2005—07; bd. dirs. Am. Heart Assn. N.E. Fla., 1990—92. Mem.: ABA, Comml. Law League (So. region exec. coun. 1998—, treas. 2000—), Jacksonville Bankruptcy Bar Assn. (bd. dirs. 1999—2004, treas. 2003—04), Jacksonville Bar Assn. (chmn. bankruptcy sect. 1998—2000, 2002—03), Duval County Rep. Party (treas. 2002—07), Jacksonville Hist. Soc., First Coast Tiger Bay Forum (bd. dirs. 2001—07, Leadership award 2004), Jacksonville C. of C. (bd. govs. 1987, govtl. affairs com. 1998—2007), Fla. Jaycees (legal counsel 1987—88, Most Outstanding Local Pres. award 1987), Jacksonville Jaycees (pres. 1986, Jaycee of yr. 1984, Businessperson of Yr. 2006), Summit Civitan (judge adv. 1991—93, 2001—02), James Madison Inst., Southside Bus. Men's Club (v.p. 2003—04, parliamentarian 2006—07), Bull Snort Club (pres. 1995—96, chmn. bd. 1996—99, pres. 1999—2000), Masons, N.E. Fla. Phi Beta Kappa Alumni Assn. (v.p. 1998—2000, 2003—04). Republican. Presbyterian. Office: Dist Office 76 S Laura St Ste 590 Jacksonville FL 32202 also: 214 House Office Bldg 402 S Monroe St Tallahassee FL 32399-1300 Office Phone: 850-488-4171.

MCBURNEY, ELIZABETH INNES, dermatologist, physician, educator; b. Lake Charles, La., Dec. 24, 1944; d. Theodore John and Martha (Caldwell) Innes; divorced, 1980; children: Leanne Marie, Susan Eleanor. BS, U. Southwestern La., 1965; MD, La. State U., 1969. Diplomate Am. Bd. Internal Medicine, Am. Bd. Dermatology. Intern Pensacola (Fla.) Edn. Program, 1969-70; resident in internal medicine Boston U. and Carney Hosps., 1970-72; resident in dermatology Charity Hosp., New Orleans, 1972-74; staff physician Ochsner Hosp., New Orleans, 1974-80; assoc. head of dermatology Ochsner Clinic, New Orleans, 1974-80; clin. asst. prof. La. Health Scis., New Orleans, 1976-79, clin. assoc. prof., 1979-90, clin. prof., 1990—; clin. asst. prof. Tulane Health Scis., New Orleans, 1976-88, clin. assoc. prof., 1988-91, clin. prof., 1991—. Courtesy staff Northshore Regional Med. Ctr., Slidell, La., 1985—; staff Slidell Meml. Hosp., 1988—; chmn. CME courses, 1988—, pres.-elect med. staff, 2000-01, pres., 2001—02; regional dir. Mycosis Fungoides Study Group, Balt., 1974-94. Contbr. articles to profl. jours. Bd. dirs. Slidell Art Coun., 1988—, Camp Fire, New Orleans, 1979-83, Cancer Assn. New Orleans, 1978-83; juror Art in Pub. Places, Slidell, 1989; councilman St. Tammany Art Coun., 2003-06. Recipient Disting. Woman Physician award AMA, 1999, Thomas Pearson edn. meml. award, 2004. Fellow ACP; mem. Am. Soc. Dermatologic Surgery (treas. 1991-94, bd. dirs. 1988-91, pres. elect 1995-96, pres. 1996-97), Women's Dermatol. Soc. (pres. 2006—07, Samuel Stegman award 2000, Pub. Svc. award, 2001), Am. Acad. Dermatology (bd. dirs. 1994-98), Am. Bd. Laser Medicine and Surgery (bd. dirs. 1991-96), La. Dermatologic Soc. (pres. 1989-90), Am. Dermatologic Soc. (pres. 2007-08), St. Tammany Med. Soc. (pres. 1988), Phi Kappa Phi, Alpha Omega Alpha. Avocations: reading, gardening, fine art, music, films. Office: 1051 Gause Blvd Ste 460 Slidell LA 70458-2985 Office Phone: 985-649-5880.

MCBURNEY, MARGOT B., retired librarian; b. Lethbridge, Alta., Can. d. Ronald Laurence Maness and R. Blanche (Lott) Hart; children: Margot Elisabeth McBurney Lane, James Ronald Gordon. BA with honours, Principia Coll., 1953; M.Sc. in L.S, U. Ill., 1969. Sec. Marshall Brooks Library, Principia Coll., Elsah, Ill., 1966-69, reference librarian, 1969-70; systems analyst trainee in library systems U. Alta. Library, Edmonton, 1970-71, undergrad. reference librarian, 1971-72, editor periodicals holdings list, 1972-73, serials catalogue, 1973-74, head acquisitions div., 1974-77; chief librarian Queen's U. Library, Kingston, Ont., Canada, 1977-90; distbr. Pharmanex, 2005—06. Chmn. Friends of Perth & Dist. Libr., 2006—. Editor: Am. Soc. Info. Sci. Western Can. chpt. Proceedings, 1975, 76. Mem. Am. Soc. Info. Sci. (councilor-at-large 1976-79, past chmn. chpt.), Assn. Research Libraries (dir. 1978-81, chmn. task force on library edn. 1980-83), Can. Assn. Info. Sci., Can. Assn. Research Libraries, Can. Library Assn., Council on Library Resources (PETREL com. 1981-84), Phi Alpha Eta, Beta Phi Mu, Friends of Perth Literacy(chmn. 2004-07) Home Phone: 613-267-4280. E-mail: mbm33@sympatico.ca.

MCCABE, BRIAN, political strategist; m. Loren McCabe; children: Claire, Colin. Grad., U. NH, 1991. Congl. staff mem. for Congressman Bill Zeliff; exec. dir. for Senator Bob Dole's NH Primary Campaign; founder McCabe Consulting Group, 1996; mng. ptnr. DCI Group, LLC, Washington; exec. CustomScoop, Concord, NH. Former pres. Progress for America. Office: DCI Group, LLC 1828 L St, NW, Ste 400 Washington DC 20036 Office Phone: 202-546-4242.*

MCCABE, BROOKS FLEMING, JR., state legislator; b. Charleston, W.Va., Jan. 19, 1949; s. Brooks F. Sr. and Jane (Mason) McC.; m. Barbara Given McCabe; 1 child, Katherine Jane. BS in Mgmt. Engring., MEd in Adminstrn., U. Vt., Burlington, 1972; EdD in Admin., W.Va. U., 1975. Asst. to dir. Gov.'s Office Fed. and State Rels., Gov.'s Office Fed. and State Rels., Charleston, 1975-77; gov.'s housing coord. State of W.Va., Charleston, 1977-79; comml. real estate salesperson Home Finders, Inc., Charleston, 1979-80; comml. real estate brokerage & devel. McCabe Hanley LP, Charleston, 1980—2008; mng. mem., broker W.Va. Comml. LLC, 2009—; gen. ptnr. McCabe Land Co. LP, Charleston, 1987—; mem. Dist. 17 W.Va. State Senate, Charleston, 1998—. Bd. dirs. Charleston Renaissance Corp., 1995-02; pres., bd. dirs. Silver Creek Properties, Inc., Slaty Fork, W.Va., 1988-92. Pres. Cmty. Coun. of Kanawha Valley, Charleston, 1987-89; campaign chmn. United Way of Kanawha Valley, Charleston, 1988; trustee U. Vt., Burlington, 1976-82, The Gow Sch., South Wales, NY, 1988-97, W.Va. Wesleyan Coll., Buchanon, 2000-02; bd. dirs. Greater Kanawha Valley Found., 1988-91, Charleston Area Med. Ctr. Found., 1992-98, W.Va. State Coll. Found., Inc., 1994-98; bd. trustee Nature Conservancy, W.Va., 2009-. Named Vol. of the Yr., United Way of Kanawha Valley, 1986-87. Mem. Am. Inst. Cert. Planners, W.Va. Planning Assn., Kanawha Valley Bd. Realtors, W.Va. Assn. Realtors, Urban Land Inst., Nat. Trust Hist. Preservation, W.Va. Roundtable. Democrat. Episcopalian. Avocations: reading, history, gardening. Office: W Va Comml Real Estate 107 Capitol St Charleston WV 25301-2609 Address: WVa State Senate 1900 Kanawha Blvd E Rm 441M Bldg 1 Charleston WV 25305-0009 Office Phone: 304-347-7500, 304-357-7990. Business E-Mail: brooks.mccabe@wvsenate.gov, bmccabe@wv-commercial.com.

MCCABE, DAVID J., lawyer; b. New Rochelle, NY, Aug. 16, 1958; BA, Iona Coll., 1980; JD, Fordham U., 1983. Bar: NY 1984. Sr. ptnr. Pvt. Clients Group Willkie Farr & Gallagher LLP, NYC. Mem. estate planning and taxation com. Trusts and Estates Mag.; lectr. in field. Co-author: New York Limited Liability Companies: A Guide to Law and Practice, 1995; contbr. articles for mags. Co-founder Huguenot Children's Libr., pres., 1993—98, dir., 1993—2002; mem. adv. bd City Harvest, Inc., 1989—93, bd. dirs., 1993—96, mem. exec. com., sec., 1994—96; mem. Profl. Adv. Com. Mus. Arts and Design, NYC, 2003—; mem. Profl. Adv. Coun. Lincoln Ctr. for Performing Arts, NYC, 2003—; bd. dirs., v.p., co-counsel Boys and Girls Club, New Rochelle, 2002—; bd. dirs. New Rochelle Humane Soc., New Rochelle, 2002—05, Ursuline Sch., 2004—; bd. legal trustees Iona Coll., New Rochelle, 2006—. Fellow: Am. Coll. Trusts and Estate Counsel; mem.: Assn. Bar City NY (chair com. trusts, estates and surrogate cts. 2005—, judiciary com. 2005—), NY State Bar Assn. (trusts and estates law sect., vice chmn. com. estate and trust adminstrn. 1996—99, ad hoc com. liaison to legis. adv. com.). Office: Willkie Farr & Gallagher LLP 787 Seventh Ave New York NY 10019 Office Phone: 212-728-8723. Office Fax: 212-728-9723. Business E-Mail: dmccabe@willkie.com.

MCCABE, EDWARD R. B., hospital administrator, educator, physician; b. Balt., Mar. 26, 1946; BA in Biology, Johns Hopkins U., 1967; PhD in Pharmacology, U. So. Calif., 1972, MD, 1974. Diplomate Am. Bd. Pediatrics. Resident in pediatrics U. Minn. Hosps., Mpls., 1974—76; pediatric metabolism fellow Sch. Medicine U. Colo., Denver, 1976—78, instr., asst. prof., assoc. prof. pediatrics Sch. Medicine, 1978—86; from assoc. prof. to prof. genetics, pediatrics Baylor Coll. Medicine, Houston, 1986—94; exec. prof., chmn. dept. pediatrics David Geffen Sch. Medicine UCLA, 1994—. Physician-in-chief Mattel Children's Hosp. UCLA, 1995—; mem. med. genetics residency rev. com. Accreditation Coun. Grad. MEd. Edn., 1993—97; chmn. conf. gaucher disease NIH, Bethesda, Md., 1994—96; mem. NICHD Coun., 1995—99. Editor: Biochem. and Molecular Medicine, 1990—97, Molecular Genetics and Metabolism, 1998—. Chair sci. adv. bd. HEreditary Disease Found., LA, 1998—99; chmn. Basil O'Connor award March Dimes, White Plains, NY, 1997—99. Mem.: Inst. Medicine, Soc. Pediatric Rsch. (E. Mead Johnson award 1993), Am. Coll. Med. Genetics (chair sec.'s adv. com. genetics, health and society 2002—, maternal and child health bur. 1999—2000, pres. 2001—02, co-chair newborn screening screening task force), Am. Soc. Biochem. and Molecular Biology, Am. Pediatric Soc., Am. Fedn. Clin. Rsch., Am. Soc. Human Genetics, Am. Bd. Med. Genetics (bd. dirs. 1992—97, pres. Bethesda 1995—96, diplomate), Am. Acad. Pediatrics (chmn. com. genetics Elk Grove Village, Ill. 1987—91, co-founder, chmn. sect. genetics Elk Grove Village 1990, 1993—95), Alpha Omega Alpha, Sigma Xi, Phi Kappa Phi. Achievements include First to describe the Continguous Gene Syndrome Complex Glyverol Kinase Deficiency; first to extract DNA from blood in newborn screening blotters; first to set up molecular genetic diagonosis for sickle cell disease as part of newborn screening; development of concept of molecular genetic triage of bacterial infection. Office: UCLA Pediatrics Box 951752 22-412 MDCC Los Angeles CA 90095 Office Phone: 310-825-5095. E-mail: emccabe@mednet.ucla.edu.*

MCCABE, EUGENE, information technology executive; Various positions in network and sys. product design and field engrng. support Digital Equipment Corp., v.p. mfg. Alpha Systems and Mfg. Tech.; with Compaq, Sun Microsystems, Inc., Santa Clara, Calif., 1999—, v.p. high end ops., exec. v.p. worldwide ops., 2006—. Office: Sun Microsystems Inc 4150 Network Cir Santa Clara CA 95054 Office Phone: 650-960-1300.

MC CABE, GERARD BENEDICT, retired library administrator; b. NYC, Jan. 22, 1930; s. Patrick Joseph and Margaret Irene (McDonald) McC.; m. Jacqueline L. Maloney, Aug. 3, 1963 (dec. 1987); children: Theresa Marie, Rebecca Mary. BA in English, Manhattan Coll., 1952; A.M. in Library Sci. (scholar), U. Mich., 1954; MA in English, Mich. State U., 1959. Asst. acquisitions dept. U. Nebr. Library, Lincoln, 1954-56; chief bibliog. acquisitions dept. Mich. State U. Library, East Lansing, 1956-58; librarian Inst. Community Devel. and Service, Mich. State U., 1958-59; acquisitions librarian U. S. Fla., Tampa, 1959-66, asst. dir. planning and devel., 1967-70; assoc. dir. U. Ark. Library, Fayetteville, 1966-67; dir. univ. libraries Va. Commonwealth U., Richmond, 1970-82; dir. libraries Clarion U. of Pa., 1982-95; ret., 1995. Libr. cons., Wilmington, NC, 1995—. Editor: The Smaller Academic Library: A Management Handbook, 1988, Operations Handbook for Small Academic Library, 1989, Academic Libraries in Urban and Metropolitan Areas, 1992; co-editor ann. pub. Advances in Libr. Adminstrn. and Orgn., vols. 1-12, Insider's Guide to Libr. Automation: Essays of Practical Experience, 1993, Acad. Librs.: Their Rationale and Role in Am. Higher Edn., 1995, Introducing and Managing Academic Library Automation Projects, 1996, Leadership for Academic Librarians, 1998, Planning for a New Generation of Public Library Buildings, 2000, Planning the Modern Public Library Building, 2003, It's All About Student Learning, 2006, Our New Public, A Changing Clientele: Bewildering Issues or New Challenges for Managing Libraries, 2008; contbr. articles to profl. jours. Mem. ALA, Southeastern Libr. Assn. Home and Office: 201 Crain Hwy N Apt 3B Glen Burnie MD 21061-3375 Home Phone: 410-302-5911; Office Phone: 410-302-5911. Personal E-mail: bldlib@comcast.net. *Consideration for others is a guiding principle for my personal and professional behavior. I, as a librarian, must have concern for those I serve. Their needs are my first and only interest, not success, not notoriety, only their service and their satisfaction.*

MCCABE, JAMES J., lawyer; b. May 8, 1929; s. James J. and Marie D. (Seitz) McCabe; m. Dolores A. Ruane, Sept. 17, 1954 (dec.); children: Deirdre McCabe Affel, Judith Ann McCabe Jarvis, James J. III; m. Rosemarie T. Smith, June 29, 1984. AB, LaSalle Coll., Phila., 1951; JD, Temple U., Phila., 1955. Bar: Pa. 1956, US Dist. Ct. (ea., mid. and we. dists.) Pa. 1956, US Ct. Claims, US Ct. Appeals (3rd cir.), Supreme Ct. Pa., US Supreme Ct. 1971. Adjuster, investigator Mfrs. Casualty Ins. Co., Phila., 1951—55; assoc. Duane Morris LLP, Phila., 1955—64, ptnr., 1964—94, of counsel, 1995—, chmn. litig. dept., 1984—95. Adj. prof. family medicine Thomas Jefferson Med. Coll., Phila. Contbr. articles to profl. jours. Fellow: Am. Coll. Trial Lawyers, Pa. Bar Found. (life; chmn. lawyers assistance com. 1980—82); mem.: Def. Rsch. Inst. (Pa. chmn. 1973—77, atlantic region v.p. 1977—80, dir. 1980—83, mem. law institutes com. 1983—92), Am. Bd. Profl. Liability Attorneys (chmn. third cir.), Assn. Ins. Attorneys, Internat. Assn. Ins. Counsel (chmn. advocacy com. 1985), Am. Coll. Legal Medicine (assoc.), Phila. Assn. Def. Counsel (past pres.), Am. Bd. Trial Advocates (mem. nat. exec. com. 1985—91, pres., founder Pa. chpt.), Phila. Bar Assn., Pa. Bar Assn., Temple Inn of Ct., St. Thomas More Soc. Phila. (past pres.). Office: Duane Morris LLP 30 S 17th St Philadelphia PA 19103 Office Phone: 215-979-1000. Office Fax: 215-689-3601. Business E-Mail: mccabe@duanemorris.com.*

MCCABE, JIM, Internet company executive; BA in Polit. Sci., Hartwick Coll., Oneonta, NY. Rsch. analyst Ogilvy & Mather Advertising; mgr. mktg. sales Forbes; with The New Republic; pub. Worth mag., Fast Company mag.; publ., v.p. Fast Company/Inc. mags.; v.p., pub. PC mag. Ziff Davis Publs., 2005; v.p. sales Terra Networks, Miami, Fla., 2008—. Office: Terra Networks 130 W 42nd St New York NY 10036 Office Phone: 212-503-3500. Office Fax: 212-503-5799. E-mail: jim_mccabe@ziffdavis.com.*

MCCABE, JOHN B., emergency physician, health science association administrator; MD, SUNY Upstate Medical Coll., Syracuse, NY, 1979. Cert. American Bd. Emergency Medicine. Resident emergency medicine Wright State U. Sch. Medicine, Dayton, Ohio; prof., founding chair dept. emergency medicine SUNY Upstate Medical U., Syracuse, NY, 1991—, interim CEO, sr. v.p. clinical affairs, 2009—. Mem.: American Bd. Emergency Medicine (trustee), American Bd. Medical Specialties (vice chair). Office: SUNY Upstate 911 Jacobsen Hall 750 E Adams St Syracuse NY 13210*

MCCABE, JOHN L., lawyer; b. Chgo., Oct. 17, 1941; BA, U. Notre Dame, 1963; LLB, Harvard U., 1966. Bar: Ill. 1967, Colo. 1967. Ptnr. Davis Graham & Stubbs LLP, Denver. Office: Davis Graham & Stubbs LLP 1550 Seventeenth St Ste 500 Denver CO 80202 Office Phone: 303-892-9400. Business E-Mail: john.mccabe@dgslaw.com.

MCCABE, LINDA JEAN, elementary school educator; d. Francis E. and Virginia M. Brazes; m. Robert D. McCabe. BA, U. No. Colo., Greeley, 1969. Lic. profl. tchr. State of Colo., 1969, cert. tchr. Tex. Edn. Agy., 1981, profl. edn. State of Wash., 2000. Tchr. Pub. Schs., Colo., 1969—76, tchr., coach k-12 phys. edn., 1971—79, tchr. elem. sch. Tex., 1980—97, Colo., 1997—2001, Wash., 2001—. Com. mem. Develop Comprehensive Math Model OSPI, Wash., 2004—05; trainer and facilitator cert. Project Wild, PLT, WET, FLP, Colo.; math modules trainer Tex. Edn. Agy., Tex. Amateur radio operator lic.; fire fighter US Forest Svc.; vol. fire fighter Maybell Fire Dept., Colo., 1999—2001. Recipient Outstanding Rural Educator, Moffat County Edn. Assn., 1998, John Irwin award, Colo. Dept. Edn. Mem.: Nat. Sci. Tchr. Assn., Nat. Coun. Tchrs. Math., Internat. Reading Assn. Avocations: outdoor activities, travel, music.

MCCABE, LOUISE BEACHBOARD, language educator; b. NYC, Apr. 11, 1941; d. Walter William and Harriet Wood (Colby) Beachboard; m. James Laws McCabe, June 8, 1974; children: Sarah Beachboard, William Laws. BA, Smith Coll., 1963; MAT, Yale U., 1966; PhD, Harvard U., 1978. Instr. Italian, Harvard U., 1969-70, Harvard U., 1971-72, Yale U., New Haven, 1974-75, Tyler Art Sch. Temple U., Elkins Park, Pa., 1984-87, Villanova U., Pa., 1987-91; Latin tchr. Roxbury Latin Sch., Mass., 1970-71; tchr. ESOL, Sch. Dist. Phila., 1992-93, Inst. Italian and French Holy Family Coll., 1999-2002, Ctrl. HS, Phila., 2002-04; adj. prof. Italian, St. Joseph's U., Phila., 1993; instr. Pa. State U., 2003-05. Asst. editor Chilton Books, Phila., 1963-65.; contbr. articles to profl. jours. Founding mem. Somerville Police Cmty. Rels. Com., Mass., 1973. Mem. Colonial Dames Am., Internat. Womens Club Phila., Acorn Club (Phila.), Smith Coll. Club (bd. dirs. 1989-91). Republican. Episcopalian. Avocation: genealogy Home: 701 Williamson Rd Bryn Mawr PA 19010-1830 Personal E-mail: whatisthis@erols.com.

MCCABE, MARY F., marketing professional; d. Frank Camarda and Inez Cunningham; children: Vincent Joseph Papile, Kristin Julia Papile. BA, Smith Coll., 1982, MA, 1983; MFA, Yale U., 1994. Co-founder, mng. dir. Children's Theatre of Mass., Springfield, 1980—91; assoc. mng. dir. Yale Repertory Theatre; mng. dir. Nat. Playwrights Conf., O'Neill Ctr., 1994—2001; assoc. mktg. solution Lehman Bros., 2001—. Strategic planning com. O'Neill Theater Ctr., 1997—2000, transition com. to identify exec. dir., 1999—2000. Edn. task force Springfield Schs., 1987—99; liaison for Yale Repertory Theatre Spl. Olympic World Games, 1993; mem. Coast Guard Auxiliary, 1997—; bd. advisors Seven Devils Playwrights Festival, Boise, Idaho, 2000—. Recipient regional award for artistic achievement, New England Theater Conf. (NETC), 1990. Democrat. Roman Catholic. Home: 95 Cabrini Blvd Apt 3-L New York NY 10033 Office: Lehman Bros 745 7th Ave 30th Fl New York NY 10033 Personal E-mail: acthuman@aol.com. Business E-Mail: mmccabe@lehman.com.

MCCABE, ROBERT HOWARD, college president; b. Dec. 23, 1929; s. Joseph A. and Kathryn (Greer) McC.; m. Arva Moore Parks, June 1992. BEd, U. Miami, 1952, LLD (hon.), 1992; MS, Appalachian State U., Boone, NC, 1959; PhD, U. Tex., 1963; LLD (hon.), Barry U., 1986, Fla. Internat. U., 1990. Asst. to pres. Miami Dade C. of C., Fla., 1963-65, v.p. Fla., 1965-67, exec. v.p. Fla., 1967—80, pres. Fla., 1980—95, Essex County Coll., Newark, 1967-69; sr. fellow League for Innovation in the C.C., 1995—; Disting. fellow Edn. Commn. of the States, 2000—; exec. dir. Nat. Alliance Cmty. & Tech. Colls., 2004—. Exec. com. So. Regional Edn. Bd., Atlanta, 1981-83; trustee Coll. Bd., chmn., 1988-90; vice chair The Miami Coalition for a Drug-Free Cmty., 1989-94, chair, 1991—; dir. The Bridge Partnership, 2002-. Author: Man and Environment, 1971, No One to Waste, 2000, Yes We Can, 2002, several monographs; editor: Jour. Environ. Edn.; cons. editor Change Mag., 1980—; contbr. articles to profl. jours. Bd. dirs. Nat. Ctr. Pub. Policy and Higher Edn., 1998—. Recipient Disting. Svc. award Fla. Congl. Del., 1983, Spirit of Excellence award The Miami Herald, 1988, Harold W. McGraw Jr. prize in Edn., 1991, The Coll. Bd. medal, 1995; named Outstanding Grad., Coll. Edn., U. Tex., 1982, named one of the 18 Most Effective Chief Exec. Officers in Am. Higher Edn. Bowling Green U., 1988; Disting. Svc. award Dade County, Fla., 1983; Kellogg fellow, 1962-63, MacArthur sr. fellow John D. and Catherine T. MacArthur Found., 1992. Fellow League for Innovation in the C.C. (sr. fellow, dir. exec. com. 1985—, Disting. Svc. award 1995); mem. Am. Assn. C.C. (bd. dirs. 1991—, Disting Svc. award 1995), Am. Assn. Higher Edn. (dir. on Higher Edn. Issues, Higher Edn. Consortium), Am. Coun. Edn. (dir. 1973-75), Am. Assn. for Environ. Edn. (pres. 1970-73), Am. Coun. on Edn. (bd. dirs. 1983-85, 92—), Southeast Fla. Edn. Consortium (chmn. bd. 1981-83). Episcopalian. Home: 1601 S Miami Ave Miami FL 33129-1103 Office Phone: 305-854-4428. Personal E-mail: rmccabe@bellsouth.net.

MCCAFFERTY, LEO RAYMOND, plastic surgeon; b. Pitts., Nov. 24, 1953; s. Leo Garvey and Virginia Catherine (Ballard) McC.; m. Susan Mary Kimball, July 31, 1992; children: Leo Thomas, Kristin Rae, Kimberly Lynn. BS, Pa. State U., 1975; MD, Temple U., 1981. Diplomate Am. Bd. Plastic Surgery. Resident in gen. surgery Cedars-Sinai Med. Ctr., LA, 1981-85; resident in plastic surgery Jackson Meml. Hosp. U. Miami (Fla.), 1985-87, asst. prof. plastic surgery, 1987-90; pvt. practice, vol. asst. prof. Plastic Surgery U. Pitts., Pitts., 1990—. Asst. clin. prof. Plastic Surgery U. Pitts. Sch. Medicine, Pitts., 1990—. Contbr. articles to profl. jours. Med. practitioner Govt. Jamaica, Jamaica, 1987. State Sen. scholar Temple U., 1977-78, Measey scholar Temple U., 1977-78. Mem. Am. Soc. Plastic Surgeons, Am. Soc. Maxillofacial Surgeons, Am. Cleft Palate Assn., Am. Burn Assn., Greater Pitts. Plastic Surgery Soc. Avocations: athletics, art, music. Office: Plastic Surgery 211532 S Aiken Ave Pittsburgh PA 15232

MCCAFFERY, FRAN, men's college basketball coach; b. Phila., May 23, 1959; m. Margaret McCaffery; children: Connor, Patrick, Jonathan, Marit. Attended, Wake Forest U., Winston-Salem, NC, 1977—78; BS, U. Pa. Wharton Sch. Fin. and Commerce, Phila., 1982; MEd, Lehigh U., Bethlehem, Pa., 1985. Asst. varsity coach, head sub-varsity coach U. Pa. Quakers, 1982—83; asst. coach, recruiting coord. Lehigh U. Engineers, 1983—85, head basketball coach, 1985—88; asst. coach U. Notre Dame Fighting Irish, 1988—99; head basketball coach U. NC Greensboro Spartans, 1999—2005, Sienna Coll. Saints, 2005—. Active Coaches vs. Cancer. Office: Siena Coll Athletics 515 Loudon Rd Loudonville NY 12211-1462 Office Phone: 518-783-2551. Business E-Mail: fmccaffery@siena.edu.*

MCCAFFERY, SEAMUS P., state supreme court justice; b. Belfast, Northern Ireland, June 3, 1950; m. Lisa Rapaport; children: Sean, Jim, Brian. B, La Salle U.; JD, Temple U. Sch. Law. Bar: Pa., NJ, Washington DC. Patrolman to supr. Phila. Police Dept., 1970—89; litig. assoc. Lavin, Coleman, Finarelli & Gray, 1989—93; trial judge Phila. Mcpl. Ct., 1993—2001, adminstrv. judge, 2001—03; appellate judge Pa. Superior Ct., Phila., 2003—08; justice Pa. Supreme Ct., 2008—. Emergency preparedness liaison, Pa. Dept. Homeland Security. Creator Nuisance Night Court, 1996, Eagles Court, 1998; adv. mem. Phila. Civil War and Underground Railroad Mus.; bd. mem. Vietnam Vets. Meml. Com., Pa. March Dimes. Capt. USMC Res., col. USAFR, 1985—, Langley AFB. Decorated 5 Meritorious Svc. Medals, War on Terrorism Svc. Medal; recipient Disting. Pa. award, Pa. Air Force Assn., 1996; named Squadron Comdr. Yr., USAFR, 1995. Democrat. Office: Supreme Ct Pa 1400 Spring St Philadelphia PA 19130 Office Phone: 215-560-3082.*

MCCAFFREE, MARY ANNE WIGHT, pediatrician, neonatal-perinatal specialist, educator; b. Guatemala City, June 30, 1945; m. Robert McCaffree; 2 children. MD, U. Okla. Coll. Medicine, 1971. Cert. Pediat., 1976, Neonatal-Perinatal Medicine, 1977. Intern, pediat. Bethesda Nat. Naval Med. Ctr., 1971—72; resident, neonatal perinatal medicine Children's Hosp. Nat. Med. Ctr., 1972—74, fellow, 1973—75; prof. pediat. U. Okla. Health Sciences Ctr.; co-dir., Infantile Apnea Diagnostic Ctr. Children's Hosp. Okla. Named Physician of Yr., U. Okla. Coll Medicine, 1996, Alumnus of Yr., 2006. Mem.: AMA (mem. Commn. on Unity 1998—2000, bd. trustee 2008—, chair, Coun. on Sci. and Pub. Health, mem. pediat. sect. coun., alternate delegate and delegate, House of Delegates), Okla. State Med. Assn. (pres. 1998—99, Ed. L. Calhoon MD Leadership in Medicine award 2005, Women in Medicine award 2007), Am. Acad. Pediat. (chair, com. on fed. govt. affairs, Abraham Jacobi award (first Oklahoman and first neonatologist to receive the award) 2005). Office: U Okla Childrens Physicians PO Box 26307 Oklahoma City OK 73126

MCCAFFREY, BARRY RICHARD, consulting firm executive, retired military officer; b. Taunton, Mass., Nov. 17, 1942; s. William Joseph and Mary Veronica (Curtin) McC.; m. Jill Ann Faulkner, June 8, 1964; children: Sean, Tara, Amy. BS, U.S. Mil. Acad., 1964; MA, Am. U., 1971; postgrad., Command and Gen. Staff Coll., Ft. Leavenworth, Kans., 1976, Army War Coll., Carlisle Barracks, Pa., 1982. Commd. 2d lt. U.S. Army, 1964, advanced through grades to gen., 1994; ret., 1996; co.-comdr. 7th Cavalry Divsn., Vietnam, 1968-69; assoc. prof. dept. social sci. US Mil. Acad., West Point, NY, 1972-75; from chief ops. br. to comdr. 2d battalion 3d Inf. Divsn., Germany, 1976-81; from chief staff to comdr. 3d brigade 9th Inf. Divsn., Ft. Lewis, Wash., 1982-86, comdr. 3d brigade, 1984-86; asst. comdt. US Army Inf. Sch., Ft. Benning, Ga., 1986-88; dep. U.S. mil. rep. NATO, Brussels, 1988-89; div. comdr. 24th Inf. Divsn., Ft. Stewart, Ga., 1990-92; asst. to Chmn. Joint Chiefs of Staff US Dept. Def., Washington, 1992-93, dir. strategic plans and policy directory, The Joint Staff, 1993-94; comdr. US So. Commd. (USSOUTHCOM), Quarry Heights, Panama, 1994-96; dir. Office Nat. Drug Control Policy (ONDCP), Washington, 1996—2001; pres. B.R. McCaffrey Associates, LLC, Alexandria, Va., 2001—; mil. analyst NBC News. Bradley Disting. prof. nat. security studies US Mil. Acad., 2001—05, adj. prof. internat. affairs, 2005—; bd. dirs. HNTB Corp., 2008—, DynCorp Internat., CRC Health Corp/, McNeil Technologies, The Wornick Co. Contbr. articles to mil. publs. Bd. advisors Nat. Infantry Found.; sr. exec. assoc. Army Aviation Assn. America; chmn. advisory bd. Vietnam Veterans Meml. Edn. Center. Decorated: D.S.C. with oak leaf cluster (2), D.M.S. with oak leaf cluster, Silver Star with oak leaf cluster, Def. Superior Svc. medal, Purple Heart with two oak leaf clusters; recipient: Health & Human Services Lifetime Achievement award for Extraordinary Achievement in the Field of Substance Abuse Prevention, 2004, Superior Honor award for Strategic Arms Limitation Talks, US Dept. State, CIA Great Seal Medallion, US Coast Guard Disting. Pub. Svc. award, NAACP Roy Wilkins Renown Svc. award, Norman E. Zinberg award, Harvard Med. Sch., Fed. Law Enforcement Found. Nat. Svc. award, Lifetime Achievement award, The Cmty. Anti-Drug Coalitions of America, Golden Eagle award, The Soc. Am. Mil. Engineers, 2007, W. Stuart Symington award, Air Force Assn., 2008; named one of The 500 Most Influential People in Am. Fgn. Policy, World Affairs Councils Am., 2004; named to The US Army Ranger Hall of Fame, 2007 Mem. NAACP, Assn. of U.S. Army, Coun. of Fgn. Rels., Inter-Am. Dialogue, Legion of Valor of U.S., CSIS US-Mexico Bilateral Coun.; prin. Coun. Excellence in Govt. Democrat. Avocations: hunting, reading. Office: BR McCaffrey Associates LLC 2900 S Quincy St Arlington VA 22206-2231

MCCAFFREY, EDMUND F., abbot emeritus; b. Savannah, Ga., Jan. 9, 1933; AB, Belmont Abbey, 1955, STB, 1959; MA, Cath. U. of Am., 1963, PhD, 1969. Ordained priest Order of Saint Benedict, 1959; abbot Territorial Abbey of Belmont-Mary Help of Christians, NC, 1970—75, abbot emeritus, 1975—; founder polit. sci. dept. Belmont Abbey Coll., NC. Priest, retreat master, lectr. Diocese of Charleston, SC; pres. Eternal Life, Bardstown, Ky. Recipient Pro Fidelitate et Virtute award, Inst. on Religious Life, Chgo., 2003. Mem.: Equestrian Order of Holy Sepulcher (knight comdr.), KC (fourth degree). Roman Catholic. Office: PO Box 70548 Myrtle Beach SC 29572-0028 Office Phone: 843-213-0528.

MCCAFFREY, JUDITH ELIZABETH, lawyer; b. Providence, Apr. 26, 1944; d. Charles V. and Isadore Frances (Langford) McC.; m. Martin D. Minsker, Dec. 31, 1969 (div. May 1981); children: Ethan Hart Minsker, Natasha Langford Minsker. BA, Tufts U., 1966; JD, Boston U., 1970; grad. in pastry arts, French Culinary Inst., 2004. Bar: Mass. 1970, D.C. 1972, Fla. 1991, NY, 2005. Assoc. Sullivan & Worcester, Washington, 1970-76; atty. FDIC, Washington, 1976-78; assoc. Dechert, Price & Rhoads, Washington, 1978-82, McKenna, Conner & Cuneo, Washington, 1982-83; gen. counsel, corp. sec. Perpetual Savs. Bank, FSB, Alexandria, Va., 1983-91; ptnr. Powell, Goldstein, Frazer & Murphy, Washington, 1991-92, McCaffrey P.A., 1992—2006, McCaffrey PLLC, 2006—. Contbr. articles to profl. jours. Mem. Leadership Collier, 1998. Mem. ABA (chair subcom. thrift instns. 1985-90), D.C. Bar Assn. (bd. govs. 1981-85), Fla. Bar Assn. (chmn. fin. svcs. com. 1999-2000, exec. coun. bus. law sect. 1998-2005), Women's Bar Assn. D.C. (pres. 1980-81), Collier County Women's Bar Assn. (pres. 1997-98), Gulf

Coast Venture Forum (pres. 2001-03), Burleith Citizens Assn. (dir. 2006—08). Episcopalian. Avocations: travel, reading, martial arts, Spanish. Home: 177 Avenue B Apt 2b New York NY 10009-3632

MCCAFFREY, ROBERT HENRY, JR., retired manufacturing company executive; b. Syracuse, NY, Jan. 20, 1927; s. Robert Henry and May Ann (McGuire) McC.; m. Dorothy Anne Evers, Sept. 22, 1956; children: Michael Robert, Kathleen Mary. BS, Syracuse U., 1949. Sales asst. Sealright Corp., Fulton, NY, 1949-50; with TEK Hughes div. Johnson & Johnson, Metuchen, NJ, 1950-67, gen. sales mgr., 1958-59, v.p. sales, 1959-62, pres., 1962-67; gen. mgr. med. div. Howmet Corp., NYC, 1967-70; group v.p. Howmedica, Inc., 1970-73, sr. v.p., 1973-74, exec. v.p., also bd. dirs., 1974-76; pres., CEO C.R. Bard, Inc., Murray Hill, NJ, 1976-78, chmn. bd. dirs., CEO, 1978-89, chmn. bd., 1989-91, also bd. dirs., chmn. exec. com., 1991—99. Bd. dirs. Summit and Elizabeth Trust, Summit Bancorp, Thomas & Betts Corp. Trustee Found. for Univ. Medicine and Dentistry N.J., 1987-90, Syracuse U., 1979-04, chmn. corp. adv. council, 1974-75. With AUS, 1945-46. Mem. Orthopedic Surg. Mfrs. Assn., Health Industry Mfrs. Assn. (bd. dir., chmn. 1982-83), N.Y. Sales Execs. Club, Sigma Chi. Republican. Roman Catholic. Avocations: reading, skiing, golf. Office: C R Bard Inc 730 Central Ave New Providence NJ 07974

MCCAGHY, CHARLES HENRY, retired social sciences educator; b. Eau Claire, Wis., Apr. 29, 1934; s. Elmer and Anna Josephine (Soha) McC.; m. M. Dawn Ysebaert, June 10, 1961 BBA, U. Wis., 1956, MS, 1962, PhD, 1966. Instr. sociology U. Conn., 1964-66; asst. prof. sociology Case Western Res. U., Cleve., 1966-70; assoc. prof. sociology Bowling Green State U., Ohio, 1970-76, prof. Ohio, 1976-94, prof. emeritus Ohio, 1994—; ret., 1994. Vis. scholar Australian Inst. Criminology, 1984 Author: Deviant Behavior: Crime, Conflict and Interest Groups, 1976, 7th edit., 2006, 8th edit., 2007, Crime in American Society, 1980, 2d edit., 1987. Lt. (j.g.) USN, 1956-59 Mem. Am. Soc. Criminology (treas. 1978-82). Home: 221 Williams St Bowling Green OH 43402-3259 Business E-Mail: cmccagh@bgsu.edu.

MCCAHILL, BARRY WINSLOW, public relations executive; b. Glen Ridge, NJ, May 25, 1947; s. William Francis and Frances (Elliott) McC.; m. Margaret Anne Bonnes, Feb. 8, 1980; children: Jennifer, Kimberly, Erin, Meghan. BA in English, U. Va., 1969, postgrad., 1974-76. USCG lic. master. Account exec. Whyte Berry Price, Advt. & Pub. Rels., Washington, 1967-69; publs. mgr. Nat. Telephone Coop. Assn., Washington, 1972-74; visual info. specialist U.S. Customs Svc., Washington, 1974-76; pub. affairs specialist IRS, Washington, 1976-79; mgr. radio and TV news Nat. Hwy. Traffic Safety Adminstrn., U.S. Dept. Transp., Washington, 1979-85, dep. dir. Office Pub. and Consumer Affairs, 1985-96; ret., 1996; sr. counselor Strat@Comm, Inc., Washington, 1996-99; exec. dir. Ams. for Respon. Alcohol Access, Washington, 1997—2000; pres. McCahill Comms. Inc., 1999—, Sports Utility Vehicle Owners of Am., Inc., 2004—08. Co-creator Vince & Larry crash dummies pub. svc. campaigns The Ad Council. Loaned exec. Combined Fed. Campaign United Way, Washington, 1983; mem. nat. bd. Voice of the Retarded, 1999-2008, adv. bd. 2008-. 1st lt. U.S. Army, 1969-72. Recipient Blue Pencil award Nat. Assn. Govt. Communicators, 1975, 88, Adminstrs. award for exceptional achievement Nat. Hwy. Traffic Safety Adminstrn., 1983, Adminstr.'s Leadership award, 1995, Sec.'s Honor award Sec. of Treasury, 1983, Sec.'s award for meritorious achievement Sec. of Transp., 1985, Spl. Recognition awards, 1995, 96, Sec. Transp. Way To Go awards, 1995, 96, Disting. Career Svc. award, 1996. Mem. Washington Automotive Press Assn., Cobbosseecontee Yacht Club (Manchester, Maine), Pi Kappa Alpha, ADA County Hwy Dist. Capital Investment Citizens (adv. com.). Avocations: boating, motorcycling. Home: 424 E Connemara Ln Eagle ID 83616-6091 Home Phone: 208-938-2314; Office Phone: 208-938-9994.

MCCAIN, BETTY LANDON RAY, political party and state official; b. Feb. 23, 1931; d. Horace Truman and Mary Howell (Perrett) Ray; m. John Lewis McCain, Nov. 19, 1955; children: Paul Pressly III, Mary Eloise. Student, St. Mary's Jr. Coll., Raleigh, NC, 1948—50; AB in Music, U. N.C., Chapel Hill, 1952, LLD (hon.), 1998; MA, Columbia U., NYC, 1953; LittD (hon.), U. N.C., Wilmington, 1997; LLD (hon.), Wake Forest U., Winston-Salem, NC, 1999, Barton Coll., Wilson, NC, 1999; DHL (hon.), U. NC, Greensboro, 2007. Courier, European tour guide Ednl. Travel Assocs., Plainfield, NJ, 1952-54; asst. dir. YWCA, U. N.C., Chapel Hill, 1953-55; chmn. N.C. Dem. Exec. Com., 1976-79; mem. Dem. Nat. Com., 1971-72, 76-79, 80-85, chmn. sustaining fund NC, 1981, 88-91, mem. com. on presdl. nominations (Hunt Commn.), 1981-82, mem. rules com., 1982-85, mem. cabinet Gov. James B. Hunt, Jr., 1993-2001, sec. dept. cultural resources, 1993-2001; mem. State Dem. Exec. Com., 1971—99, 2001—. Mem. Winograd Commn., 1977-78; pres. Dem. Women of N.C., 1971-72, dist. dir., 1969-72; pres. Wilson County Dem. Women, 1966-67; precinct chmn., 1972-76; del. Dem. Nat. Conv., 1972, 88; mem. Dem. Mid-Term Confs., 1974, 78, mem. jud. coun. Dem. Nat. Com., 1985-89; dir. Carolina Tel. & Tel. Co. (now Embarq), 1981-97 (1st woman); bd. trustees U. N.C.-TV, 2002—, vice chmn., 2006—, chair, 2008-; interim chair McCain Internat. Empowerment Project, 2001—. Contbg. editor: History of N.C. Med. Soc. Treas. Wilson on the Move, 1990—92, mem., 2007—, Coun. on State Goals and Policy, 1970—72, Gov.'s Task Force on Child Advocacy, 1975—78; chmn. Wilson-Greene Morehead scholarship com., 1986—89; mem. career and personal counseling svc. adv. bd. St. Andrews Coll.; charter mem. Wilson Edn. Devel. Coun.; active Arts Coun. of Wilson, Inc.; pres. Wilson County Mental Health Assn., bd. dirs., legis. chmn.; bd. govs. U. N.C., 1975—81, 1985—93, pers. and tenure com., 1985—91, chmn. budget and fin. com., 1991—93; bd. regents Barium Springs Home for Children, chair Founds. com. Capital Campaign, 2003—; bd. dirs. N.C. Mus. History Assocs., 1982—83, pres., 1982—83, membership chair, 1987—88; co-chmn. Com. to Elect Jim Hunt Gov., 1976, 1980, co-chmn. senatorial campaign, 1984; mem. N.C. Adv. Budget Com. (1st woman), 1981—85; chmn. State Employees Combined Campaign N.C., 1993; bd. visitors Peace Coll., Wake Forest U. Sch. Law, 1980—83, U. N.C., Chapel Hill; co-chmn. fund dr. Wilson Cmty. Theater; v.p. Wilson County Hist. Assn., 2004—; chmn. devel. com., bd. visitors Lineberger Comprehensive Cancer Ctr., 2006—, vice chmn. bd. visitors, 2007—, chmn., 2009—; chmn. centennial Am. Lung Assn., NC, hon. chmn. hist. observance centennial N.C., 2006—07; Sunday sch. tchr. 1st Presbyn. Ch., Wilson, 1970—71, 1986—88, 1990—92, mem. chancel choir, 1985—, deacon, 1986—92, chmn. fin. com., 1990—91, chair, 1992—93, Pastor Nominating Com., 2008; elder 1st Presbyn. Ch., 1992—98, 2006—09; N.C. state bd. dirs. Am. Lung Assn., state bd. dirs., 1985—88; bd. dirs. Roanoke Island Commn.; mem. battleship commn. USS/NC, 1993—2001; bd. dirs. Wilson Rose Garden, 2002—. Recipient state awards N.C. Heart Assn., 1967, Easter Seal Soc., 1967, Cmty. Svc. award Wilson Downtown Bus. Assocs., 1977, award N.C. Jaycees, 1979, 85, Women in Govt. award N.C. and U.S. Jaycettes, 1985, Alumni Disting. Svc. award U. N.C., Chapel Hill, 1993, Flora Mac Donald Scottish Heritage award, 1995, Carpathian award N.C. Equity, 1995, Pinnacle award, 1997, 1st winner Holderness-Weaver award U. N.C., Greensboro, 1999, Citizen of Yr. award Wilson C. of C., 2001, Ruth Coltrane Cannon award for hist. preservation Preservation N.C., 2000, N.C. State U. Sch. of Design award, 2000, The North Caroliniana award, 2006; named to Order of Old Well and Valkyries, U. N.C., 1952; named Dem. Woman of Yr., N.C., 1976, Internat. Founders award Eta State Delta Kappa Gamma Soc., 2005; named Outstanding Wilson Citizen of Yr., Wilson Red Cross, 2004. Mem.: DAR, UDC (former historian John W. Dunham chpt.), UNC-TV (chair, bd. trustees 2009—), Peace Coll. Found. (chair 2009—), Carolinas Ctr. Med. Excellence (bd. dir. 2008—), Rotary Internat. (Paul Harris fellow 2003), N.C. Inst. Medicine (bd. dirs. 1993—2005), N.C. Sch. Arts (trustee 1993—2001), N.C. Equity (bd. dirs.), N.C. Soc. Internal Medicine Aux. (pres.), N.C. Symphony (trustee 1993—2001, 2002—05), Info. Resources Mgmt. Commn. N.C. (bd. dirs. 1993—2001), N.C. Agy. Pub. Telecom. (bd. dirs. 1993—2001, 2009), N.C. Found. for Nursing (bd. dirs. 1989—92), St. Mary's Alumni Assn. (regional v.p., Most Disting. Alumna 2005), U. N.C. Chapel Hill Alumni Assn. (chmn. 2001—02, bd dir.), Nat. Soc. Colonial Dames Am. NC (sec. local com., program co-chmn.), AMA Alliance (dir., nat. vol. health svcs. chmn., aux. liaison rep. AMA Coun. on Mental Health, aux. rep. Counsel on Vol. Health Orgns.), N.C. Art Soc., N.C. Lit. and Hist. Assn., Wilson Sertoma Club (Svc. to Mankind award 2006), The Book Club (past pres.), Little Book Club, Wilson Country Club, Pi Beta Phi. Home: 1134 Woodland Dr NW Wilson NC 27893-2122 Home Phone: 252-243-4248. Home Fax: 252-243-4248.

MCCAIN, CINDY (CINDY LOU HENSLEY MCCAIN), philanthropist, wholesale distribution executive; b. Phoenix, May 20, 1954; d. James and Marguerite Hensley; m. John Sidney McCain III, May 17, 1980; 1 adopted child, Bridget children: Meghan, Jack, Jimmy. BA in Edn., U. So. Calif., LA, 1976, MA in Spl. Edn., 1978. Tchr. Agua Fria HS, Phoenix, 1979—83; founder Am. Vol. Med. Team, 1988—95, Hensley Family Found., 1995—; v.p., dir., vice chair Hensley & Co., Phoenix, chmn., 2000—. Chairwoman, Ariz. delegation Republican Nat. Convention, 2000; bd. trustees HALO Trust; bd. dirs. Operation Smile, CARE USA. Mem.: Kappa Alpha Theta. Office: Hensley & Co 4201 N 45th Ave Phoenix AZ 85031 also: John McCain 2008 PO Box 16118 Arlington VA 22215 Office Phone: 703-418-2008, 602-264-1635. Office Fax: 623-247-7094.

MCCAIN, JOHN (JOHN SIDNEY MCCAIN III), United States Senator from Arizona; b. Canal Zone, Panama, Aug. 29, 1936; s. John Sidney and Roberta (Wright) McCain; m. Carol Shepp, July 3, 1965 (div. Apr. 2, 1980); 1 child, Sidney Ann stepchildren: Douglas, Andrew; m. Cindy Lou Hensley, May 17, 1980; 1 adopted child, Bridget children: Meghan, Jack, Jimmy. Grad. US Naval Acad., 1958; grad., Nat. War Coll., 1973-74; degree (hon.), Johns Hopkins U., 1999, Colgate U., 2000, U. Penn., 2001, Wake Forest U., 2002, U. So. Calif., 2004. Dir. Navy Senate Liaison Office, Washington, 1977-81; mem. US Congress from 1st Ariz. Dist., 1983—86; US Senator from Ariz., 1987—; ranking mem. US Senate Armed Services Com., 2009—; mem. US Senate Energy & Nat. Resources Com., 2009—, US Senate Health, Edn., Labor & Pensions Com., 2009—, US Senate Homeland Security & Governmental Affairs Com., 2009—, US Senate Indian Affairs Com., chmn., 1995—97, 2005—07, US Senate Commerce Sci. & Transp. Com., 1997—2001, 2003—05. Bd. dirs. Nixon Ctr. for Peace & Freedom, Cmty. Assistance League, Phoenix, 1981—; chmn. Internat. Republican Inst., 1993—; candidate for Republican presdl. nomination, 2000, 08; Republican presdl. nominee, 08; mem. Commn. on Intelligence Capabilities of US Regarding Weapons of Mass Destruction, 2004; speaker Republican Nat. Convention, NYC, 2004. Co-author (with Mark Salter): Faith of My Fathers, 1999, Worth the Fighting For: What I Learned from Mavericks, Heroes, and Politics, 2002, Why Courage Matters: The Way to a Braver Life, 2004, Character Is Destiny: Inspiring Stories Every Young Person Should Know and Every Adult Should Remember, 2005, Hard Call: Great Decisions and the Extraordinary People Who Made Them, 2007. Served in USN, 1958—81, prisoner of war, 1967—73, Vietnam, became captain USN, 1977. Decorated Legion of Merit, Silver Star, Bronze Star, Purple Heart, Disting. Flying Cross, Vietnamese Legion of Honor; recipient Excellence in Pub. Svc. award, Am. Acad. Pediat., 1999, Friendship award, League Latin Am. Citizens, 1999, Freedom award, Intrepid Mus. Found., 1999, John F. Kennedy Profile in Courage award, John F. Kennedy Library Found., 1999, Paul H. Douglas Ethics in Govt. award, U. Ill. Inst. Govt. & Pub. Affairs, 2000, William Penn Mott Jr. Park Leadership award, Nat. Parks Conservation Assn., 2001, Citizen Patriot award, Citizen Patriot Orgn., 2003, Arthur T. Marix Congl. Leadership award, Mil. Officers Assn. America, 2004, Econ. Patriot award, Concord Coalition, 2004, Evelyn F. Burkey award, Writers Guild America East, 2004, Disting. Leadership award, Am. Ireland Fund, 2005; named Cancer Survivor of Yr., Cancer Rsch./Treatment Fund, 2004; named one of The 25 Most Influential People in America, TIME mag., 1997, The 100 Most Influential People in the World, 2006, 2008, 10 People Who Mattered, Newsweek, 2008. Mem.: VFW, Soc. of the Cin., Am. Legion. Republican. Baptist. Office: US Senate 241 Russell Office Bldg Washington DC 20510 also: District Office Ste 105 5353 North 16th St Phoenix AZ 85016-3282 Office Phone: 202-224-2235, 602-952-2410. Office Fax: 202-228-2862, 602-952-8702.*

MCCALEB, GARY DAY, university official; b. Anson, Tex., Nov. 2, 1941; s. Victor Earl and Vivian (Day) McC.; m. Sylvia Ravanelli, June 5, 1964; children: Cara Lee Cranford, Bryan Day. BA, Abilene Christian Coll., 1964; MBA, Tex. A&M U., 1975, PhD, 1979. Asst. dir. alumni rels. Abilene (Tex.) Christian U., 1964-65, dir. alumni rels., 1965-69, dir. coll. rels., 1969-73, asst. acad. dean, 1978-80, v.p. pub. rels., 1980-83, v.p., dean campus life, 1983-91, v.p., 1991—, exec. dir. Ctr. for Bldg. Cmty., 1999—; asst. dir. devel. Tex. A&M U., Bryan, 1973-75. Leader internat. travel and goodwill groups; U.S. rep. to world exec. com. Internat. Union Local Authorities, 1996-99. Author: Community, The Gift of Community. Coun. mem. City of Abilene, 1985-90, mayor, 1990-99; bd. dirs. Taylor County Am. Cancer Soc., 1972-73; mem. adv. bd. United Way of Abilene, 1979-83, dir. pub. svc. divsn., 1987, chmn. consortium on drug and alcohol abuse, 1989; bd. dirs. Civic Abilene, Inc., 1981-83; treas. Abilene Task Force on Drug and Alcohol Abuse, 1984-86; active March of Dimes; mem. Tex. Sci. and Tech. Coun., 1997-2000. Recipient Polit. Courage award John Ben Shepperd Pub. Leadership Forum, Austin, Tex., 1993, Tex. Urban Leadersip award U. Tex.-Arlington Sch. Urban and Pub. Affairs, 1995. Mem. Nat. League Cities (nat. steering com. on fin., adminstrn. and intergovtl. rels. 1989-90, adv. bd. 1994, bd. dirs. 1992-94), U.S. Conf. Mayors, Internat. Mcpl. Consortium (chmn. 1994-95), Tex. Mcpl. League (legis. policy com. Houston 1986, resolutions com. Dallas 1988, v.p. region 6 1988-89, bd. dirs. 1989-90, pres. 1992), Abilene C. of C. (aviation com. 1981, 94). Republican. Mem. Ch. of Christ. Avocations: art, baseball, jogging. Office: Abilene Christian Univ PO Box 29136 Abilene TX 79699-0001 E-mail: mccalebg@acu.edu.

MCCALEB, JOE WALLACE, lawyer; b. Nashville, Dec. 9, 1941; s. J.W. McCaleb and Majorie June (Hudson) DePriest; m. Glenda Jean Queen, June 26, 1965. BA, Union U., 1964; JD, Memphis State U., 1970; MSEL cum laude, Vt. Law Sch., 1995. Bar: Tenn. 1971, US Dist. Ct. (mid. dist.), Tenn., 1977, US Ct. Appeals (6th cir.) 1984, US Supreme Ct. 1978, US Dist. Ct. (ea. dist.) Tenn. 2001, US Dist. Ct. (west dist.) Tenn., 2007. Law clk. to presiding justice Tenn. Supreme Ct., Memphis, 1970-71; staff atty. Tenn. Dept. of Pub. Health Bur. Environ. Svcs., Nashville, 1971-77; pvt. practice Hendersonville, Tenn., 1977—94, 1996—2009. Chmn. Hendersonville Recycling Com., 1990-91; adv. coun. Indian affairs State of Tenn., 2005—, chair, 2009. Mem.: League Women Voters Hendersonville, Tenn. (bd. dirs., chmn. environ. com. 2007—), Tenn. Bar Assn., Native Am. Indian Assocs. Tenn. (Aniyaweya Nation Eagle award 2001), Alliance Native Am. Indian Rights, Tenn. Clean Water Network (pres. 2001—03), Tenn. Environ. Coun. (v.p. 1987—88, conservation advocate 1991—92), Sierra Club (chmn. local chpt. 1980—81, chmn. mid-Tenn. group 1989—90, 1993—94, chmn. water quality com., co-chmn. forestry com.). Democrat. Avocations: wilderness backpacking, photography, forestry, environmental protection. Home: 100 Colonial Dr Hendersonville TN 37075-3205 Office: 315 W Main St Ste 112 Hendersonville TN 37075 Office Phone: 615-826-7245. Personal E-mail: jeremyah@bellsouth.net.

MCCALL, ANTHONY, filmmaker, conceptual artist; b. London, Apr. 14, 1946; BA with first-class honors, Ravensbourne Coll. Art and Design, Bromley, 0196. Founder Anthony McCall Associates, 1979; founder & mng. ptnr. Narrative Rooms LLC, 1996. Instr. London Coll. Printing, 1970—71; vis. lectr. avant-garde film theory NYU Dept. Cinema Studies, 1977. Flim, Line Describing a Cone, 1973; author: (article) Visitors Online: Designing a Virtual Art Mus., 1996; Represented in permanent collections, Mus. Modern Art, NY, Whitney Mus. Am. Art, Centres Georges Pompidou, exhibited in group shows, Edinburgh Internat. Film Festival, 1980, Carnegie Mus. Art, Pitts., Australian Nat. Gallery, Whitney Biennial, Whitney Mus. Am. Art, 2001, 2004, Tate Modern, London, 2002, Gagosian Gallery, London, 2004, Sean Kelly Gallery, NYC, 2007. Recipient Marie-Josi prize, 5th Internat. Experimental Competition, Knokke, Belgium, 1975; fellow John S. Guggenheim Meml. Found., 2008; Creative Artists prog. svc. grant, 1976, Film Prodn. grant, NY State Coun. Arts, 1981. Studio: 11 Jay St New York NY 10013 Office Phone: 212-334-0976. Office Fax: 212-925-5821.

MCCALL, ANTHONY LEO, medical educator, researcher; b. Rockville Ctr., NY, Oct. 16, 1946; s. Raymond Joseph and Mary Elizabeth McCall; m. Madelyn Frances Wessel, Oct. 3, 1983; children: Christopher Evan, Jonathan Stuart. MD, Med. Coll. Wis., Milw., 1972; PhD, MIT, Cambridge, Mass., 1981. Diplomate Am. Bd. Internal Medicine, 1975, in endocrinology, diabetes & metabolism 1981. Prof. medicine Oreg. Health & Sci. U., Portland, 1989—2001; James M. Moss prof. diabetes U. Va. Sch. Medicine, Charlottesville, 2001—. Fellow: ACP; mem.: Endocrine Soc., Am. Diabetes Assn. Office: Univ Va Health Sys 450 Ray C Hunt Dr Rm 1213 Charlottesville VA 22903

MCCALL, BRIAN DAVID, history educator, political science educator; MA History, Ctrl. Mich. U., Mount Pleasant, 1994. History/ polit. sci. instr. Interlochen Arts Acad., Mich., 1998—.

MCCALL, CHARLES BARNARD, retired health facility administrator; b. Memphis, Nov. 2, 1928; s. John W. and Lizette (Kimbrough) McCall; m. Carolyn Jean Rosselot, June 9, 1951 (dec. Feb. 2002); children: Linda, Kim, Betsy, Cathy; m. Ernestine Mann, Jan. 5, 2004. BA, Vanderbilt U., 1950, MD, 1953. Diplomate Am. Bd. Internal Medicine, Am. Bd. Pulmonary Diseases. Intern Vanderbilt U. Hosp., Nashville, 1953-54; clin. assoc., sr. asst. surgeon USPHS, Nat. Cancer Inst., NIH, 1954-56; sr. asst. resident in medicine U. Ala. Hosp., 1956-57, chief resident, 1958-59; fellow chest diseases Nat. Acad. Scis.-NRC, 1957-58; instr. U. Ala. Med. Sch., 1958-59; from asst. prof. to assoc. prof. medicine U. Tenn. Med. Sch., 1959-69, chief pulmonary diseases, 1964-69; mem. faculty U. Tex. Sys., Galveston, 1969-75, prof. med. br., 1971-73; assoc. prof. medicine Health Sci. Ctr., Southwestern Med. Sch., Dallas, 1973-75, also assoc. dean clin. programs, 1973-75; dir. Office Grants Mgmt. and Devel., 1973-75; dean, prof. medicine U. Tenn. Coll. Medicine, 1975-77, Oral Roberts U. Sch. Medicine, Tulsa, 1977-78; interim assoc. dean U. Okla. Tulsa Med. Coll., 1978-79; clin. prof. medicine U. Colo. Med. Sch., Denver, 1979-80; prof. medicine, assoc. dean U. Okla. Med. Sch., 1980-82; exec. dean and dean U. Okla. Coll. Medicine, 1982-85; v.p. patient affairs, prof. medicine U. Tex. M. D. Anderson Cancer Ctr., 1985-94; chief of staff VA Med. Ctr., Oklahoma City, 1980-82; ret., 2004. Exec. dir. Worldwide Healthcare Svcs., Inc., Waco, Tex., 1998—2002; clinic dir. Claremore Family Medicine, 2002—04, cons., 2002; bd. dirs. Amigos Internacionales, Inc. Contbr. articles to med. jours. Fellow: ACP, Am. Coll. Chest Physicians; mem.: AMA, Am. Fedn. Clin. Rsch., So. Thoracic Soc. (pres. 1968—69), Am. Thoracic Soc., Sigma Xi, Alpha Omega Alpha. Baptist. Home: 1392 Forest Lake Dr Branson West MO 65737 Personal E-mail: mccallcharles@centurytel.net.

MCCALL, ELIZABETH KAYE, columnist, consultant, writer; b. Columbus, Ohio, Mar. 18, 1951; d. Frank and Patricia J. McCall. BA in Sociology, Miami U., Oxford, Ohio, 1973; MBA, Ryokan Coll., 1985. Writer horse industry, travel, entertainment, bus. and various spiritual publs., Malibu, Calif., 1981—; cons. Elizabeth Kaye McCall & Assocs., Malibu, 1989—; pres. Magic Horse Prodns., Malibu, 1991—. Pub. rels. advisor Equestrian Edn. Ctr. Pepperdine U., Malibu, 1986—2001, Inner City Slickers, LA, 1997—; mktg. and pub. rels. cons. Horse Industry Liaison, Cavalia, Montreal, 2004—06. Author: The Tao of Horses: Exploring How Horses Guide Us on Our Spiritual Path, 2004; contbr. chapters to books. Mem.: Am. Horse Publs., Am. Horse Coun. (affiliate mem.). Avocations: horseback riding, travel, drawing, perfume, films. Office: PO Box 2102 Malibu CA 90265-7102 Office Phone: 310-720-4096. E-mail: elizmccall@earthlink.net.

MCCALL, GENE WILLIAM, conservator, sculptor, artist, furniture designer; s. Joseph Frederick and Verna Irene McCall; m. Sandra Ann Andreassi, Apr. 21, 1982; children: Kate, Taylor. Student, Keystone Coll., 1969—71, Elizabethtown Coll., 1971—73, Nat. Acad. Design/Sch. Fine Arts, 1981—82, SUNY, Purchase, 1983—84. Restorer/furniture maker Brumble's Antiques, Richmond, Va., 1973—75; owner McCall's Antiques, Richmond, 1975—78; conservator/furniture designer Reese's Antique Co., Richmond, 1978—79, Antique Furniture Workroom (formerly Stair & Co.), NYC, 1979—82; owner McCall & Co., Mahopac, NY, 1983—91; pres. Gene McCall Conservation & Restoration Inc., Englewood, Fla., 1991—. Instr. wood sculpture Ringling Sch. Art and Design, Sarasota, Fla., 1992—93; judge fine furniture competition Fla. State Fair, Tampa, 1995—2003; guest expert Antiques Roadshow (PBS), Tampa, 1999; spkr. in field; cons. in field. Author: Best of Fine Woodworking (Tables and Chairs), 1995; sculpture, City of Joy (Best of Show, 1993), exhibitions include Ringling Mus. Art, 1998, Kristofer Lindsay Gallery; prodr.: (video series (episode 1) The Art of Gold Leafing with Gene McCall, 2004. Co-founder/bd. mem. Englewood (Fla.) Cmty. Alliance, 2004—05; pres. bd. Olde Englewood Village Assn., 2005. Recipient Outstanding Achievement award, Tampa/Hillsborough Planning Commn., 1999; fellow Conservation grantee, Hillsborough County Pub. Arts Commn., 2004. Mem.: Nat. Sculpture Soc., Am. Inst. for Conservation Hist. and Artistic Works (assoc.), Sierra Club, Environ. Def.,

OxFam Am. Achievements include patents for new type of extensible furniture. Avocations: photography, kayaking. Office: Conservation & Restoration Inc 860-D South River Rd Englewood FL 34223 Personal E-mail: gmccall@ewol.com.

MCCALL, H. CARL, financial services firm executive, former state official; b. Boston, Oct. 17, 1935; m. Joyce F. Brown; 1 child, Marci. BA, Dartmouth Coll., 1958; student, Andover Newton Theol. Sch., U. Edinburgh. Mem. NY State Senate, 1975—79; dep. amb. to UN US Dept. State, NYC, 1979—82; commr. NY State Divsn. Human Rights, Albany, 1983—84, Port Authority NY & NJ, 1984—89; v.p. Citicorp/Citibank, 1984—93; pres. N.Y.C. Bd Edn., 1991—93; comptr. State of NY, Albany, 1993—2003; vice chmn., mng. dir. HealthPoint, LLC, 2003—04; prin. Convent Capital, LLC, NYC, 2004—. Bd. dirs. NY Stock Exch., 1999—2003, Tyco Internat. Ltd., 2003—, TAG Entertainment Corp., 2005—, Ariel Mutual Fund. Bd. trustees SUNY, 2007—. Recipient Nelson A. Rockefeller Disting. Public Service award, Rockefeller Coll. Pub. Affairs & Policy, U. Albany, 2002. Mem.: Coun. Fgn. Rels. Democrat. Office: Convent Capital LLC One Penn Plz Ste 1703 New York NY 10119*

MCCALL, JENNIFER JORDAN, lawyer; b. NYC, Feb. 15, 1956; m. James W. McCall; children: Caroline, Hillary. BA cum laude in English Lit., Princeton U., 1978; JD, U. Va. Sch. Law, 1982; LLM in Taxation, NYU, 1988. Bar: N.Y. 1983, Calif. 2002. Assoc. Lord Day & Lord, NYC, 1982-92; ptnr. Lord Day & Lord, Barrett Smith, NYC, 1992-94; ptnr. Pvt. Client Group Cadwalader, Wickersham & Taft, NYC, 1994—2003; ptnr. Pillsbury Winthrop, LLP, NYC & Palo Alto, Calif., 2003—05; ptnr., co-chmn. Wealth Mgmt. & Individual Client practice Pillsbury Winthrop Shaw Pittman, NYC & Palo Alto, Calif., 2005—. Trustee Charitable Founds. and Trusts and advisor to numerous high net worth individuals; spkr. in field on estate and tax planning and adminstrn. Co-author: Estate Planning for Authors and Artists, 1998; contbr. chpt. to Estate Tax Techniques. Steering com., Planned Giving Adv. Com., The Mus. of Modern Art; mem. Profl. Advisor's Coun., Lincoln Ctr., Inc.; trustee League for the Hard of Hearing, N.Y.C., 1992-2003, East Side House Settlement, Bronx, N.Y., 1995-2002, Chapin Sch., N.Y.C., 1998-2001; chairperson Ethel Gray Stringfellow Art Case Com., N.Y.C.; bd. trustees San Francisco Ballet. Fellow Am. Coll. Trust and Estate Counsel; mem. ABA (real property, probate and trust law sects.), N.Y. State Bar Assn. (com. on trusts and estates adminstrn.; chairperson subcom. on proposed legislation on executor's commns.), Calif. State Bar Assn. Office: Pillsbury Winthrop Shaw Pittman 2470 Hanover St Palo Alto CA 94304-1114 also: Pillsbury Winthrop Shaw Pittman 1540 Broadway New York NY 10036 Office Phone: 650-233-4020. Office Fax: 650-233-4545. Business E-Mail: jenniferjordan.mccall@pillsburylaw.com.

MCCALL, JOHN CLARK, JR., interior designer; b. Vidalia, Ga., Sept. 6, 1949; s. John Clark McCall and Carolyn Elizabeth Kay. BA, Ga. State U., 1972, MPA, 1980. Program coord. dept. music Ga. State U., Atlanta, 1972-73, adminstrn. supr. dept. music, 1973-78, asst. to dir. office acad. assistance Coll. Arts and Scis., 1978-81; dir. Ctr. for Career Devel. Winthrop U., Rock Hill, S.C., 1981-83, dir., founder Office Campus Planning and Design, 1983-85, asst. prof. interior design, 1985-89; pres. John Clark McCall, Jr. Design Cons., Inc., Rock Hill, S.C., Hahira, Valdosta, Moultrie, Ga., 1983—. Acting chair dept. interior design Winthrop U., Rock Hill, 1985-86. Author: (foreword) Frank McCall: A Complete Designer in the Class Tradition, 1985, (monograph) Atlanta Fox Album: Mecca on Peachtree Street, 1975; contbr.: The Alabama Theatre: Showplace of the South, 2002; designer interiors for residential and non-residential projects; Artist: (cd recordings) A Paramount Idea, 2003, A Capital Idea, 2006, Alabama Album, 2008. Dir. Friends of Albany (Ga.) Theatre, 1998-99; bd. trustees Valdosta (Ga.) Symphony Orch.; vol. Save the Atlanta Fox, 1974-80; project dir. Rylander Theatre Moller Pipe Organ Donation, Americus, Ga., 1998-99. Mem. Am. Soc. Interior Designers (allied mem., D. Brahms H. Presv. award 1985, Pres.'s award 1987), Am. Theatre Organ Soc., Theatre Hist. Soc., Found. for Interior Design Edn. Rsch. (bd. visitors), Packard Club. Episcopalian. Avocations: antique automobiles, theater and theater organ history and research, watercolor painting. Office: John Clark McCall Jr Design Cons Inc 1415 Crescent Dr Moultrie GA 31768 Business E-Mail: jcmdc@windstream.net.

MCCALL, JOHN PATRICK, college president, educator; b. Yonkers, NY, July 17, 1927; s. Ambrose V. and Vera E. (Rush) McC.; m. Mary-Berenice Morris, June 15, 1957; children: Claire, Anne, Ambrose, Peter. AB, Coll. of Holy Cross, 1949; MA, Princeton U., 1952, PhD, 1955; DHL, Knox Coll., Galesburg, Ill., 1993. Instr. Georgetown U., 1955-57, asst. prof. English, 1957-62, assoc. prof., 1962-66; prof. U. Cin., 1966-82, head dept. English, 1970-76, sr. v.p., provost, 1976-82; pres. Knox Coll., 1982-93, pres. emeritus and prof. emeritus English, 1993—; vol. Peace Corps, Turkmenistan, 1993-95. Vis. prof. Turkmen State U., 1994-95; vice chmn. Gov.'s Task Force on Rural Ill., 1986; pres. Associated Colls. Ill., 1986-88; chmn. Associated Colls. of M.W., 1991-92; mem. edn. com. Ill. Bd. Higher Edn., 1985, 90; mem. rural libr. panel, State of Ill., 1992. Author: Chaucer Among the Gods: the Poetics of Classical Myth, 1979; contbr. articles to profl. jours.; research in medieval lit. and Chaucer's poetry. Exec.-in-residence Xavier U. La., 1997—. With Signal Corps, U.S. Army, 1952-54. Am. Coun. Learned Socs. fellow, 1962-63; John Simon Guggenheim Meml. Found. fellow, 1975; Fulbright grantee, 1962. Mem. Medieval Acad. Am. MLA, AAUP, World Affairs Coun. New Orleans, Order of St. Louis, Archdiocese of New Orleans. Democrat. Roman Catholic. Home: 1750 St Charles Ave #317 New Orleans LA 70130 Office Phone: 504-520-6795. Business E-Mail: jmccall@xula.edu.

MC CALL, JULIEN LACHICOTTE, banker; b. Florence, SC, Apr. 1, 1921; s. Arthur M. and Julia (Lachicotte) McC.; m. Janet Jones, Sept. 30, 1950; children: Melissa, Alison Gregg, Julien Lachicotte Jr. BS, Davidson Coll., 1942, LLD (hon.), 1983; MBA, Harvard U., 1947. With First Nat. City Bank, NYC, 1948-71, asst. mgr. bond dept., 1952-53, asst. cashier, 1953-55, asst. v.p., 1955-57, v.p., 1957-71; 1st v.p. Nat. City Bank, Cleve., 1971-72, pres., 1972-79, chmn., 1979-85, chief exec. officer, from 1979, also bd. dirs.; pres. Nat. City Corp., 1973-80, chmn., chief exec. officer, 1980-86, also bd. dirs., cons. Mem. fed. adv. coun. Fed. Res. Bd., 1984-87. Trustee St. Luke's Found., United Way Services, Boy Scouts Am., Playhouse Sq. Found., Cleve. Mus. Natural History. To 1st lt. Ordinance Corps US Army, 1942—46, Aftrica, ETO. Mem. Pepper Pike Club, Chagrin Valley Hunt Club, Mountain Lake Club (Lake Wales, Fla.) Episcopalian. Home: Mountain Lake PO Box 832 Lake Wales FL 33859

MCCALL, LAURA, education educator, writer; b. Ill., Nov. 8, 1951; d. Richard Joseph and Corinne (Durava) McC. Cert. in French Lang. and Lit., U. Geneva, 1971; BA in History, Northwestern U., Evanston, Ill., 1973; MA in History, U. Mich., 1980, PhD, 1988. History tchr., womens basketball coach Shattuck Prep. Sch., Faribault, Minn., 1976-78; tchr. Gunnison (Colo.) H.S., 1979-86; history teaching fellow U. Mich., Ann Arbor, 1980-82, history instr. Dearborn, 1980-82; from instr. to asst. prof. history Western State Coll., Gunnison, 1982-90, asst. chair dept. history, politics and econs., 1987-90, chair dept., 1990; prof. history Met. State Coll., Denver, 1990—. Chair athletic coun. Met. State Coll., Denver, 1991—, promotion and tenure com. history dept., 1990—, com. on internat. edn., 1991—; chair dept. history, politics and econ. Western State Coll., Colo., 1990, asst. chair, 1987-90, chair Livermore Scholarship, 1988-90, student adv. corps., gen. edn. com., 1989-90; faculty athletic rep. NCAA, Denver, 1993—; adj. prof. liberal arts and internat studies Colo. Sch. Mines, Golden, spring 1992. Mem. editorial bd. Jour. of the Early Republic, 1988-95, 96-98; contbr. articles to profl. jours. Host, lectr. for advanced placement history students Adams County H.S., 1991; Arbor Day participant Lake Elem. Sch., 1990; pub. sch. vol. Blackstocks Elem. Sch., 1989-90; Colo. Knowledge Bowl sponsor Gunnison H.S., 1985-86. Namaed Tchr. of Yr., Golden Key Nat. Honor Soc., 1995-96; Teaching fellow U. Mich., 1980-82, John D. Pierce fellow, 1982, Program in Am. Instn. fellow, 1986-87, Newberry Libr. Chgo. fellow, 1986-87; NEH grantee, 1989. Mem. Soc. for Historians the Early Republic, Orgn. Am. Historians, Rocky Mountain MLA, Colo. History Group, Northwestern Alumni Assn., Sierra Club, World Wildlife Fund, Nature Conservancy, Phi Beta Kappa, Phi Alpha Theta (host, organizer Regional Conf. 1988, faculty sponsor 1987-90, Best Chpt. award 1991, Best Sponsor award 1995), Alpha Lambda Delta, Delta Kappa Gamma. Office: Met State Coll PO Box 173362 Denver CO 80217-3362

MCCALL, LOUISE CALLAHAM, psychologist; d. Roy Pickens and Dorothy Wynne Callaham; m. Charles Ellis McCall, June 1, 1968 (div. June 13, 1979); children: Renee Louise Callaham, Michelle Charlene Murray. BA in Fine Arts, Winthrop U., Rock Hill, SC, 1960; MEd, Clemson U., SC, 1972; degree in Psychology, U. SC., Columbia, 1974. Diplomate in psychol. edn. State Bd. Doctors, Clinicians, & Psychologist, 2000; cert. State Dept. Edn., 1960. Psychologist Anderson Sch. Dist. Five, SC, 1968—76, Dept. Exceptional Children, Florence Sch. Dist. One, SC, 1979—89, Lawton Pub. Schs., 2001—; dir., exceptional children's programs Lexington Sch. Dist. 3, Batesburg, SC, 1976—78; pvt. practise, 1990—2000; pres. Pee Dee Assn. Sch. Pay, 1980—84; mem. NC Crisis Team; NC sch. psychologist Foster County Schs., 2001—. Mem.: NC Sch. Psychology Assn. Home: 4521 Hood Dr Charlotte NC 28213 Office: Dept Exceptional Children 215 West 13th St Gastonia NC 28052 Home Phone: 704-200-6899. Personal E-mail: nannylouise@hotmail.com.

MCCALL, MAXINE COOPER, publisher, minister, educator, writer; d. Lloyd Edison and Minnie Belle (Rector) Cooper; m. Donald Jackson McCall, Oct. 15, 1960. BS in English magna cum laude, Appalachian State U., 1960, MA in English, 1965. English tchr. Appalachian State U., Boone, NC, 1959—60; tchr., adminstr. Burke County Pub. Schs., Morganton, NC, 1960—90; English tchr. gifted programs Valdese and Drexel HS, 1960—71; coord. grades K-12 Burke Schs. Coord. for Lang. Arts, Fgn. Lang., Gifted Programs, 1972—90; adj. faculty English dept. Western Piedmont CC, Morganton, NC, 1990—; owner C&M Resources, Drexel, NC, 1997—. Ednl. cons. grades K-12 Burke County Pub. Schs., Morganton, NC, 1960—90; Christian edn. cons., conf. leader Ch. of God Ministries, Anderson, Ind., 1982—; cons. ch. growth and planting Bd. of Ch. Extension, Anderson, Ind., 1990—2001; bd. dirs. Warner Press, 2008. Author: (book) They Won't Hang a Woman, 1972, What Mean These Stones?, 1993 (History Book award from N.C. Soc. of Historians, 1993, Willie Parker Peace History Book award, 2008); author: (graphic designer) Guidebook to the Trail of Faith, 1998; author, graphic designer They Wont Nang A Woman, 2008 (Barrenger award, NC Soc. Historians, 2008), (book) Etched in Granite, 1999 (Pres. award NC Soc. Historians, 2005); co-author (graphic designer, publ.): (book) Posthumorously Berk, 2000; editor (graphic designer, pub.): Silver Wings and a Gold Star, 2003; editor: A Handful of Stars, 1996, author. Guest spkr. various ch. and civic orgns. in Burke County, NC, 1971—; co-founder, facilitator Christians Broadcasting Hope Nat. Bible Conf. in Western N.C., 1981—; chairperson Area Adminstr. Assn. Ch. of God, 1988, sec., 1984—87, state rep., cons. long-range planning, 1984, governance and policy task force and implementation team, 1988—93, task force implementation team, 1997—98; bd. trustees Anderson U., Ind., 1988—2003; bd. dirs. The History Mus. of Burke County, Morganton, NC, 2003—. Mem.: NC Soc. Historians (bd. dir. 2007—), Delta Kappa Gamma (sec. 2004—08, pres. 2008—). Mem. Ch. Of God (Anderson, Ind.). Avocations: travel, theater, films, antiques, history. Office: C & M Resources PO Box 487 Drexel NC 28619

MCCALL, SHEDRICK DWIGHT, psychologist; b. Richmond, Va., Apr. 24, 1970; s. Roslyn Annette and Shedrick Dwight McCall; m. Nancy Adelle Swann, July 25, 1992. B, Maryville Coll., 1995; M, Liberty U., 2000; D, Argosy U., 2005. Ceo Youth Pathways, LLC, Richmond, Va., 2000—. Mem. NCAAP, Chesterfield, Va., 1997. Minority scholarship, Maryville Coll., 1989—95. Mem.: Kappa Alpha Psi (assoc.; asst. keeper of exchequer 2004—). Office: Youth Pathways LLC PO Box 34003 Richmond VA 23234 Home: Po Box 75054 Richmond VA 23236-0018 Office Fax: 804-674-1021; Home Fax: 804-674-1021. Personal E-mail: shedrickmccall@verizon.net.

MCCALLIE, JOANNE P., women's college basketball coach; m. John McCallie; children: Madeline, John (Jack) Wyatt. BA in Polit. Sci., Northwestern U., 1987; MBA, Auburn U., 1990. Asst. basketball coach Auburn U. Tigers, 1988—92; head women's basketball coach U. Maine Black Bears, 1992—2000, Mich. State U. Spartans, 2001—07, Duke U. Blue Devils, 2007—. Recipient Nat. Coach. of Yr., AP, 2005; named to Maine Sports Legends Hall of Fame, 2005. Office: Duke Athletics 118 Cameron Indoor Stadium Durham NC 27708*

MCCALLISTER, BEN D., internist, cardiologist, educator; b. Fort Worth, Tex., 1932; s. Clarence Dee and Agnes (Horton) McC.; m. Virginia McCallister, Aug. 20, 1956; children: Ben Jr., Scott, John, Tom, Katherine. BA, U. Kans., 1954; MD, U. Kans., Kansas City, 1957. Intern Tripler Army Hosp., Honolulu, 1957-58; resident cardiology and internal medicine Mayo Clinic, Rochester, Minn., 1960-65, cons., 1965-70, St. Lukes Hosp., Kansas City, 1970—; dir. cardiovasc. rsch., endowed chair Mid-Am. Heart Inst., Kansas City, 1996—2007, dir. emeritus, CV rsch.; emeritus prof. medicine Univ. Mo.-Kans. City Sch. Medicine; mentor Am. Coll. Cardiology, 2007. Prof. medicine U. Mo., Kansas City. Recipient Nobel award for leadership potential, Mayo Found., 1965, W.F. Yates Medallion for Disting. Svc. in Medicine, William Jewell Coll., 1989, named a Kans. City Super Doctor, Kans. City mag., 2007. Fellow ACP, Am. Coll. Cardiology (treas., bd. trustees), Clin. Coun. Cardiology, Soc. Cardiac Angiography & Intervention; mem. AMA., Am. Heart Assn., Kans. City Heart Assn., Mo. Heart Assn., Am. Fedn. Clin. Rsch., Ctrl. Soc. Clin. Investigation, Met. Med. Assn. Kans. City, SW Clin. Soc., Mo. Med. Assn., Phi Beta Kappa, Sigma Xi, Office: MidAm Heart Inst 4401 Wornall Rd Kansas City MO 64111-3220

MCCALLISTER, CAROLYN G., secondary school educator; b. Warren, Ark., Oct. 26, 1955; d. Richard Gillespe, III and Julia Maia (Reaves) Garison; m. Bobby Alan McCallister, July 5, 1986; 1 child, Courtney Jean stepchildren: Leah S., Jason Alan. BS, U. Ark., Monticello. Advanced placement cert. English tchr. Humnoke HS, Ark., 1976—79, Wilmar HS, Ark., 1979—84, Perryville HS, Ark., 1984—. Mem. Ark. State Book Adoption Com., Little Rock. Methodist. Avocations: sewing, camping. Home: 1725 Hwy 10 W Adona AR 72001 Office: Perryville HS 325 Houston Ave Perryville AR 72126-9056 Office Phone: 501-889-2326. E-mail: mcadona@tcworks.net.

MCCALLISTER, MICHAEL B., insurance company executive; b. Indpls., May 27, 1952; m. Charlene Gray, 1985; children: Megan, Ryan. BA, La. Tech. U., 1974; MBA, Pepperdine U., 1983. Fin. specialist Humana Inc., Louisville, 1974—75, exec. dir. fin. Cmty. Hosp. Springhill, La., 1975; exec. dir. Humana Hosps. in, Huntington and West Anaheim, Calif., 1978—85, Humana Hosp. West Hills, Canoga Park, Calif., 1985—88; pres. Humana Hosp. Phoenix, 1988—89; v.p. Humana Health Care Plans, Phoenix, 1989—92, San Antonio, 1992—96, pres. divsn. 1 with responsibility for Tex., Fla. and P.R., 1996—97; sr. v.p. health sys. mgmt. Humana Inc., Louisville, 1997—99, sr. v.p., office chmn., 1999—2000, pres., CEO, 2000—. Recipient Tower Medallian Award, La. Tech., 2003. Mem.: Am. Assn. Health Plans (bd. dirs.). Office: Humana Inc 500 W Main St Ste 300 Louisville KY 40202-4268*

MCCALLISTER, RICHARD ANTHONY, business consulting company executive; b. Newark, Ohio, Apr. 10, 1937; s. Ward C. and LeDema Mc.; m. Trina D. Gordon, Sept. 1, 1979; children: Todd, Mark. BS, Ill. State U., 1960; postgrad., U. So. Calif., 1960-62. Indsl. cons. Sci. Rsch. Assocs., 1964-66; v.p. Mgmt. Psychologists, Inc., Chgo., 1966-68; dir. Price Waterhouse & Co., Chgo., 1968-75; pres. William H. Clark Assocs., Inc., Chgo., 1975-89; sr. v.p., dir. Boyden Internat., Chgo., 1989-91; mng. dir. Boyden Midwest, Chgo., 1991—. Chmn. bd. DH2O, 2004—; chmn. WHCA Ptnrs., 1986—; bd. dir. Spirian Techs., Boyden World Corp., mng. dir.; bd. dir. Mid Am., sec., treas.; mem. adv. bd. Fiduciary Management, Inc., Lionheart Trust Co., 1988—93; bd. dirs. Opencel, LLC, 2005—. Former pres. Dist. 113 Bd. Edn., Deerfield, Ill.; bd. dirs., exec. com. Grant Hosp., Chgo., House of Vision, 1975-82. Mem. Glen View Club, Racquet Club, Chgo. Club, Mid-Am. Club (bd. dirs., treas., pres. 1998—). Office: 180 N Stetson Ave Chicago IL 60601-6710 Office Phone: 312-565-1300.

MCCALLUM, BENNETT TARLTON, economist, educator; b. Poteet, Tex., July 27, 1935; s. Henry DeRosset and Frances (Tarlton) McCallum; m. Sally Jo Hart, June 3, 1961. BA, Rice U., 1957, BSChemE, 1958, PhD, 1969; MBA, Harvard U., 1963. Chem. engr. Petro-Tex Chem. Corp., Houston, 1958-61; lectr. U. Sussex, England, 1965-66; asst. prof. to prof. U. Va., Charlottesville, 1967-80; prof. econs. Carnegie-Mellon U., Pitts., 1981-86, H. J. Heinz prof. econs., 1986—. Cons. Fed. Res. Bd., Washington, 1974—75; adviser Fed. Res. Bank, Richmond, Va., 1981—; rsch. assoc. Nat. Bur. Econ. Rsch., Cambridge, Mass., 1979—; mem. Shadow Open Market Com., 2000—; hon. advisor Inst. Monetary Econ. Studies, Bank Japan. Author: (book) Monetary Economics, 1989, International Monetary Economics, 1996; co-editor: Am. Econ. Rev., 1988—91, Carnegie-Rochester Conf. series pub. policy, 1995—; contbr. articles to profl. jours. Vis. scholar, IMF, Washington, 1989—90, Bank Japan, 1993, Victoria U. Wellington and Res. Bank New Zealand, 1995; NSF grantee, 1977—86. Fellow: Econometric Soc.; mem.: Am. Econ. Assn. Home: 219 Gladstone Rd Pittsburgh PA 15217-1111 Office: Carnegie-Mellon U Tepper Sch 256 Pittsburgh PA 15213

MC CALLUM, CHARLES ALEXANDER, academic administrator; b. North Adams, Mass., Nov. 1, 1925; s. Charles Alexander and Mabel Helen (Cassidy) McC.; m. Alice Rebecca Lasseter, Dec. 17, 1955; children: Scott Alan, Charles Alexander III, Philip Warren, Christopher Jay. Student, Dartmouth Coll., 1943-44, Wesleyan U., Middletown, Conn., 1946-47; DMD, Tufts U., 1951; MD, Med. Coll. Ala., 1957; DSc (hon.), U. Ala., 1975, Georgetown U., 1982, Tufts U., 1988, Chulalongkorn U., Thailand, 1993, U. Medicine and Dentistry, NJ, 1993. Diplomate Am. Bd. Oral Surgery (pres. 1970). Intern oral surgery Univ. Hosp., Birmingham, Ala., 1951-52, resident oral surgery, 1952-54, intern medicine, 1957-58; mem. faculty U. Ala. Sch. Dentistry, 1956-96, prof., chmn. dept. oral surgery, 1959-65, dean sch., 1962-77; prof., dept. surgery U. Ala. Sch. of Medicine, 1965-96; v.p. for health affairs, dir. U. Ala. Med. Center, Birmingham, 1977-87; pres. U. Ala., Birmingham, 1987-93, chief sect. oral surgery Sch. Dentistry, 1958-65, 68-69; prof., 1959-93; disting. prof., 1992-2000; disting. prof. emeritus, dean emeritus, 2000—. Mem. nat. adv. dental rsch. coun. NIH, 1968-72; mem. Joint Commn. on Accreditation of Hosps., 1980-91, vice chmn., 1985, chmn., 1986-88. Fellow Am. Coll. Dentists, Internat. Coll. Dentists; mem. ADA (council on dental edn. 1970-76), Am. Assn. Dental Schs. (pres. 1969), Ala. Acad. of Honor, AMA, Am. Soc. Oral Surgeons (trustee 1972-73, pres. 1975-76), Southeastern Soc. Oral Surgeons (pres. 1970), Inst. of Medicine of Nat. Acad. of Scis., Assn. Acad. Health Ctrs. (chmn. bd. dirs. 1984-85), Omicron Kappa Upsilon, Phi Beta Pi. Home: 2328 Garland Dr Birmingham AL 35216-3002 Home Phone: 205-822-8445. Personal E-mail: cmccallum@charter.net.

MCCALLUM, CHARLES EDWARD, lawyer; b. Memphis, Mar. 13, 1939; s. Edward Payson and India Raimelle (Musick) McC.; m. Lois Ann Gowell Temple, Nov. 30, 1985; children: Florence Andrea, Printha Kyle, Chandler Ward, Sabra Nicole Temple. BS in Math., MIT, 1960; JD, Vanderbilt U., 1964. Bar: Mich., Tenn. 1964. Assoc. Warner Norcross & Judd LLP, Grand Rapids, Mich., 1964-69, ptnr., 1969—2008, mng. ptnr., 1992-97, of counsel, 2009—. Rep. assemblyman State Bar Mich., 1973-78; chmn. Rsch. and Tech. Inst. West Mich., 1989-91; lectr. continuing legal edn. programs; mem. West Mich. World Trade Week Com., 1988-99, chmn., 1990-91; mem. Mich. Dist. Export Coun., 1990-99, chmn., 1992-97; chmn., CEO TerraLex, 2006-. Chmn. Grand Rapids Area Transit Authority, 1976-79, mem., 1972-79; regional v.p. Nat. Mcpl. League, 1978-86, mem. coun., 1971-78; pres. Grand Rapids Art Mus., 1979-81, 96-98, trustee, 1976-83, 94-99; chmn. Butterworth Hosp., 1979-87, trustee, 1977-87; chmn. Butterworth Health Corp., 1982-89, dir., 1982-97, vice chmn., 1989-91, sec., 1991-97; chmn. Priority Health, 1995-2004, bd. dirs., 1995-2006. Woodrow Wilson fellow, 1960-61; Fulbright scholar U. Manchester, Eng., 1960-61. Fellow Coll. Law Practice Mgmt.; mem. ABA (chair bus. law sect. 2007-08, chair standing com. on ethics and profl. responsibility 2004-05, mem. com. multijurisdictional practice 2000-02, mem. task force on corp. responsibility, 2001-03, editor-in-chief Bus. Lawyer 2005-06), Am. Bar Found., Am. Law Inst., Tenn. Bar Assn., Mich. Bar Assn. (mem. coun. bus. law sect., sect. chmn. 1988-89), Grand Rapids Bar Assn., Internat. Bar Assn., Grand Rapids C. of C. (pres. 1975, bd. dirs. 1970-76), Univ. Club, Order of Coif, Sigma Xi. Office: Warner Norcross & Judd LLP 900 Fifth Third Ctr 111 Lyon St NW Grand Rapids MI 49503 Home (Summer): 265 Clear Ridge Dr Healdsburg CA 95448 Home: Plz Tower Apts 201 W Fulton #1012 Grand Rapids MI 49503 Office Phone: 616-752-2104.

MCCALLUM, GERALD CHRISTOPHER, clinical psychologist; s. William Robert and Helen Frances (Kaullen) McCallum. BS in Psychology, U. Ill., Champaign, 1984; MS in Clin. Psychology, U. Memphis, 1991, PhD in Clin. Psychology, 1992. Lic. clin. psychologist Ill. Technician Forest Hosp., Des Plaines, Ill., 1983—86; clin. therapist, rschr., instr. U. Memphis, 1986—91; clin. intern Ark. Children's Hosp., U. Ark. Med. Scis., Little Rock, 1991—92; postdoctoral fellow U. Tenn.,

Memphis, 1992—93; clin. psychologist, program coord. Alexian Bros. Med. Ctr., Elk Grove, Ill., 1993—98; instr. Chgo. Sch. Profl. Psychology, 1995; clin. psychologist DuPage Psychol. Assocs., Naperville, Ill., 1995—. Mem.: APA, Ill. Psychol. Assn., Nat. Register Health Svc. Providers in Psychology. Roman Catholic. Avocations: reading, gardening, woodworking, travel, running. Home: PO Box 4345 Naperville IL 60567 Office: DuPage Psychol Assocs 1112 S Washington St Ste 217 Naperville IL 60540 Office Phone: 630-355-4070.

MCCALLUM, ROBERT DAVIS, JR., former ambassador; b. Memphis, Jan. 30, 1946; s. Robert D. McCallum Sr. and Virginia Blackwell Jett McCallum; m. Mary Rankin Weems, 1969. BA, Yale U., 1968, JD, 1973; MA, Oxford U., 1971. Spl. asst. atty gen. State of GA, Atlanta, 1979—87; assoc. Alston & Bird LLP, Atlanta, 1973—79, ptnr., 1973—2001; asst. atty. gen. civil divsn. US Dept. Justice, Washington, 2001—03, assoc. atty. gen., 2003—06, acting dep. atty. gen., 2003—06; US amb. to Australia US Dept. State, Canberra, 2006—09. Scholar Rhodes scholar, 1971. Republican.*

MCCALLUM, SCOTT, not-for-profit developer, former governor; b. Fond du Lac, Wis., May 2, 1950; m. Laurie McCallum; children: Zachary, Rory, Cara. BA, Macalester Coll., 1972; MA in Internat. Studies, Johns Hopkins U., 1974. Property developer, Fond du Lac; mem. Wis. State Senate, 1976-87; lt. gov. State of Wis., 1987-2001, gov., 2001—03; pres., CEO Aidmatrix Found. Dir. Workplace Child Care Clearinghouse; chair Repeat Offenders Task Force State of Wis., Trauma and Injury Prevention Task Force; coord. Gov.'s Conf. on Small Bus.; presdl. appointee to Internat. Trade Policy Adv. Com.; past chair Nat. Conf. of Lt. Govs.; gov.'s appointee to Nat. Aerospace States Assn. Republican. Office: Aidmatrix Found 11701 Luna Rd Dallas TX 75234 Office Phone: 469-357-3791. E-mail: scott_mcCallum@aidmatrix.org.

MCCALLY, CHARLES RICHARD, construction company executive, consultant, mathematician, educator; b. Dallas, Oct. 5, 1958; s. Richard Holt and Elizabeth Ann (Webster) McC.; m. Shirley Elizabeth Avant, Aug. 18, 1979 (div.); children: Charles Richard Jr., Meredith Holt; m. Judy Lynn Tackett, June 24, 1993. BSME, So. Meth. U., 1981; MS in Higher Edn. and Math. summa cum laude, Tex. A&M U., 2003. Engr. McCally Co., Dallas, 1977-83; owner, v.p. DRT Mech. Corp., Dallas, 1983-95; owner McCally Svc. Co., Inc., Dallas, 1995-97; pres. C.R. McCally & Assocs., Inc., Dallas, 1997—. Prof. math. Navarro Coll., Corsicana, Tex., 1999—; cons. McCally Group, Inc., Lewisville, Tex., 2002—05; mech. group mgr. Hidalgo Internat. Svcs., Inc., 2005—. Active Young Reps., Dallas, 1980—. Mem. NSPE, ASME, ASHRAE, Am. Soc. Plumbing Engrs. (membership com. 1983-89), Tex. Soc. Profl. Engrs., So. Meth. U. Alumni Assn., SMU Mustang Club, Bent Tree Country Club (Dallas), Oaktree Country Club (Garland, Tex.) (bd. dirs. 1986-89), Sigma Chi. Avocations: tennis, boating, travel, camping. Home: 203 Chinaberry Way Coppell TX 75019-2961 E-mail: rick@mccally.com, rmccally@hidalgoindustrial.com.

MCCAMBRIDGE, JOHN JAMES, retired civil engineer; b. Bklyn., Oct. 27, 1933; s. John Joseph and Florence Josita (McDonnell) McC.; m. Dorothy Antoinette Cook, Mar. 17, 1962; children: Sharon J., John S., Patrick J., Kathleen C. BCE, Manhattan Coll., 1955; MS, Vanderbilt U., 1958; postgrad., UCLA, 1963—66. Civil engr. Raymond Concrete Pile Co., NYC, 1955; commd. 2d lt. USAF, 1955, advanced through grades to col., 1972; exec. sec. Def. Com. On Rsch., Washington, 1971-73, DOD-NASA Supportive Rsch. Tech. Panel, Washington, 1972-74; asst. dir. Def. Rsch. and Engring. (for Environ. and Life Scis.) Office Sec. Def., Washington, 1974-75; dir. Air Force Life Support Systems Program Office, Wright Patterson AFB, Ohio, 1975-79; ret. USAF, 1979; prin. Booz, Allen & Hamilton, Inc., Bethesda, Md., 1979-86; v.p. Espey, Huston & Assoc., Inc., Falls Church, Va., 1986-90; mng. prin. JMC Cons. Group, McLean, Va., 1990—2005; ret., 2006. Chmn. air panel on NBC Def., NATO, Evere, Belgium, 1970-71; def. dept. rep. to physics survey com., NAS, Washington, 1971. Contbr. articles to profl. jours. Decorated Legion of Merit with oak leaf cluster; named John J. McCambridge Rsch. grant in his honor, Inst. Hazardous Materials Mgmt., 2006. Fellow Aerospace Med. Assn. (exec. coun. 1972-73), Inst. Hazardous Materials Mgmt. (Disting. Diplomate, dir. 1984—2005, chmn. 1988-94, Lifetime Achievement award 2005, Founding Father award 2005); mem. Coun. Engring. and Sci. Splty. Bds. (dir., exec. com. 1995—2005, v.p. 2000, pres. 2001), Acad. Cert. Hazardous Materials Mgrs. (pres. 1984-86), Survival and Flight Equipment Assn. (nat. sec. 1977-78), Air Force Ret. Officers' Cmty. (dir. 1997-2003), The Washington Assembly (treas. 2002-03, vice chmn. 2003-05, chmn. 2005-06), Black Tie Club (treas. 2002-03, v.p. 2003-04, pres. 2004-05, 2008-09), Dwight D. Eisenhower Soc. (trustee 2006-, treas., 2009-), Tower Club, KC, Sigma Xi, Chi Epsilon. Republican. Roman Catholic. Personal E-mail: jjmccambridge@earthlink.net.

MC CAMERON, FRITZ ALLEN, retired university administrator; b. Nacogdoches, Tex., Oct. 8, 1929; s. Leland Allen and Gladys (Turner) Mc C.; m. Jeannine Young, June 11, 1957; 1 child, Mary Hartley. BBA, Stephen F. Austin State Coll., 1950, MA, 1951; PhD, U. Ala., 1954. C.P.A., La. Asso. prof. La. State U., 1959-62, prof., 1962-67, chmn. dept. accounting, 1967-71, asst. vice chancellor, 1971-73, dean continuing edn., 1973-95; ret., 1995. Cons. in field. Author: FORTRAN Logic and Programming, 1968, Cobol Logic and Programming, rev. edit, 1970, 5th edit., 1985, FORTRAN IV, 1970, rev. edit., 1974, 3d edit., 1977. Mem. numerous civic and charitable bds. including Salvation Army, Womens Hosp., Computer Rehab. Tng. and others. Mem. Am. Inst. C.P.A.'s, La. Soc. C.P.A.'s, Am. Accounting Assn. Home: 930 Rodney Dr Baton Rouge LA 70808-5867

MCCAMMON, HOLLY, sociologist, educator; b. Lafayette, Ind., Nov. 13, 1959; d. Jack Stark and Rebecca Vincent; m. John McCammon, Apr. 11, 1981; children: Seth, Hadley. PhD, Ind. U., Bloomington, 1990. Asst. prof. sociology Vanderbilt U., Nashville, 1990—97, assoc. prof. sociology, 1997—2004, assoc. dean, grad. studies, 2006—08, prof. sociology, 2004—. Contbr. articles to profl. jours. Recipient Carrie Chapman Catt prize, Iowa State U., 1998; grants, NSF, 1996—98, 2004—06, Postdoc. fellowship, AAUW, 2003—04. Mem.: Am. Sociol. Assn. (collective behavior and social movements sect. chair 2007—08). Office: Vanderbilt Univ Dept Sociology Box 351811 Nashville TN 37235 Office Fax: 615-322-7505.

MCCAMMON, JAMES ANDREW, chemistry professor; b. Lafayette, Ind., Feb. 8, 1947; s. Lewis Brown and Jean Ann (McClintock) McC.; m. Anne Elizabeth Woltmann, June 6, 1969. BA magna cum laude, Pomona Coll., 1969; MA, Harvard U., 1970, PhD, 1976. NSF/NIH postdoctoral research fellow Harvard U., Cambridge, Mass., 1976-78; asst. prof. chemistry U. Houston, 1978-81, full prof., 1981, M.D. Anderson prof. chemistry, 1981-94, dir. Inst. for Molecular Design, 1987-94, prof. biochemistry, 1989-94; Joseph E. Mayer chair theoretical chemistry U. Calif. San Diego, 1995—; prof. pharmacology U. Calif. San Diego Sch. Medicine, 1995—; investigator Howard Hughes Med. Inst., 2000—. Adj. prof. molecular physiology and biophysics Baylor Coll. Medicine, Houston, 1986-94, adj. prof. biochemistry, 1992-94; cons. to Sterling-Winthrop Pharma., Stardent Computers, Rhone-Poulenc, Accelrys, Kimberly-Clark, DuPont-Merck Pharm., Merck — Co., and Bristol-Myers Squibb; mem. adv. bd. NAS, NSF, NIH and other agencies. Author: Dynamics of Proteins and Nucleic Acids, 1987; contbr. articles to profl. jours. Recipient Tchr.-scholar award Camille and Henry Dreyfus Found., 1982-87, NIH Rsch. Career Develop. award, 1980-85, George H. Hitchings award for Innovative Methods in Drug Design, Burroughs-Wellcome Fund, 1987, Smithsonian award for Breakthrough Computational Sci., 1995, Chancellor's Associates award for Rsch., 2002, Am. Chem. Soc. Natl. award, Computers Chem. & Pharm. Rsch. 2008; named Alfred P. Sloan Rsch. fellow, 1980-84, Centennial lectr., U. Chgo., 1991 Fellow AAAS, Am. Phys. Soc., Biophys. Soc., Am. Acad. Arts & Sciences; mem. Am. Chem. Soc., Protein Soc., Phi Beta Kappa. Achievements include development of the molecular dynamics simulation method for proteins and nucleic acids, of the thermodynamic cycle perturbation method for studying molecular recognition, and of the Brownian dynamics method for simulating diffusion-controlled reactions. Office: U Calif San Diego Dept Chemistry La Jolla CA 92093-0365 E-mail: jmccammon@ucsd.edu.

MCCAMPBELL, ROBERT GARNER, lawyer, former prosecutor; b. Oklahoma City, Nov. 23, 1957; s. Stanley Reid and Joan Fontane (Garner) McC. BA in History with honors, Vanderbilt U., 1980; JD, Yale U., 1983. Bar: Okla. 1983. Assoc. Crowe & Dunlevy, Oklahoma City, 1983-87, dir., 1994—2001, 2005—; asst. US atty. (we. dist.) Okla. US Dept. Justice, 1987-94, chief fin. fraud unit (we. dist.) Okla., 1990-94, Us atty. (we. dist.) Okla., 2001—05. Dir. Ctr. for Advancement of Sci. and Tech., 1995, chmn., 1999—2001; chmn. sub-com. sentencing Atty. Gen., 2004—05. Mem. ABA, Nat. Assn. Former U.S. Attys., Phi Beta Kappa. Republican. Episcopalian. Office: Crowe & Dunlevy 20 N Broadway Ste 1800 Oklahoma City OK 73102 Office Phone: 405-235-7700. Business E-Mail: mccampbr@crowedunlevy.com.

MCCAMY, CALVIN SAMUEL, retired optics scientist; b. St. Joseph, Mo., Sept. 22, 1924; s. Benjamin Samuel and Della Emma (Cervenka) McC.; m. Mabel Alice Bellerud, Nov. 4, 1945; children: Susan, Nicholas, Carter. BSChemE, U. Minn., 1945, M in Physics, 1950. Instr. math. U. Minn., Mpls., 1947-50; instr. physics Clemson U., SC, 1950-52; chief image optics and photography Nat. Bur. Stds., Gaithersburg, Md., 1952-70; v.p. for rsch. Macbeth, Newburgh, NY, 1970-89; pvt. practice cons. in color sci. Edgewater, Md., 1990—. Leader in nat. and internat. standardization; adj. prof. chemistry Rensselaer Poly. Inst., Troy, NY, 1980-85; mem. adv. bd. Munsell Color Sci. Lab., Rochester (NY) Inst. Tech., 1985—; pres. Kollmorgen Found., Hartford, 1979-89; photog. analyst Ho. of Reps. investigation of shooting of Pres. John F. Kennedy, Washington, 1978. Editor: Papers on Image Optics from National Bureau of Standards, 1973; contbr. over 100 articles to profl. jours., books and encys. Lt. (j.g.) USN, 1943-47. Fellow Optical Soc. Am. (chmn. color com. 1978), Soc. Photographic Scientists and Engrs. (v.p. sci. 1968-72, vis. lectr. 1986), Royal Photographic Soc. Gt. Britain, Soc. Motion Picture and TV Engrs., Washington Acad. Scis., NY Acad. Scis., Inter-Soc. Color Coun.(hon. mem.). Achievements include improving Munsell color system; development of new principle of absolute radiometry, the compensated variable aperture; discovery of cause of redox blemishes threatening federal microfilm records; design of color test chart used internationally; discovery of visual effects of dotforms on colored grounds. Home: 617 Barton Rd Edgewater MD 21037 Personal E-mail: csmccamy@comcast.net.

MCCAMY, SHARON GROVE, English educator; b. Fredericksburg, Va., May 31, 1961; d. Howard E. and Vivian R. Grove; m. Michael D. McCamy, Jan. 10, 1986; 1 child, Katherine Howard. BA in English, U. Va., 1983; MA in English, George Mason U., 1994. Devel. asst. Corcoran Gallery of Art, Washington, 1983-84; coord. individual giving Nat. Parks Conservation Assn., Washington, 1984-87; dir. devel. Piedmont Environ. Coun., Warrenton, Va., 1991-94; lectr. in English Mary Washington Coll., Fredericksburg, Va., 1996-99; head Divsn Arts and Scis. No. Va. Campus ECPI Coll. Tech., 2005—, dir. edn. No. Va. Campus, 2006—, provost, No. Va. campus, 2006—08, provost cmty. relations, 2008—, bus. development mem., 2008—; assoc. dean gen. studies ITT Tech. Inst., 2009—. Mem. Fauquier County Bd. Suprs., 2000—03; mem. bd. Fauquier County Water and Sewer Authority, 2000—03; mem. Fauquier County Soc. Svcs.Bd., 2004—07; vice chair Fauquier County Social Svcs. Bd., 2007—; mem. com. Fauquier Rep. Com., 1997—; bd. dirs. Fauquier County Pub. Libr., Warrenton, 1996—2000, Libr. Va., 1998—2003, Libr. Va. Found., 1999—2003, Va. Ctr. Book, 2000—03. Mem.: Fauquier County Social Svcs. Bd. (vice chair 2007—08, chair 2008—), Piedmont Rep. Women's Club (sec. 1998—2000, v.p. 2004—06). Home: PO Box 10 Sumerduck VA 22742 Personal E-mail: sharonmccamy@hughes.net.

MCCANCE, SEAN E., orthopedist; b. NYC, July 3, 1965; m. Zsuzsanna Boros; children: Matthew, John, Brian; 1 child, Daniel. MD, Columbia Coll. Physicians & Surgeons, NY, 1991. Diplomate Am. Bd. Orthop. Surgery, 2001, Am. Bd. Spine Surgery, 2006. Coord. spine edn. Lenox Hill Hosp., NYC, 1997—2006, attending surgeon, dept. orthopedics, 1997—, Mt. Sinai Sch. Medicine, NYC, 2000; Co-dir. spine surgery Mt. Sinai Hosp., NCY, 2000—, clin. assoc. attending, 2001—08, clin. assoc. prof., dept. orthopaedics, 2008—; dir. Spine Assocs., NYC, 2006—. Clin. asst. prof. NY U. Sch. Medicine, NYC, 2000—. Recipient Resident-Fellow Rsch. award, Eastern Orthop. Assn., Americas Top Physician award, 2005, 2006. Mem.: AMA, Med. Soc. State NY, Am. Acad. Orthop. Surgeons, North Am. Spine Soc., Scoliosis Rsch. Soc. Office: Spine Assocs 1155 Pk Ave New York NY 10128

MCCANDLESS, BRUCE, II, aerospace engineer, retired astronaut; b. Boston, June 8, 1937; s. Bruce and Sue McCandless; m. Alfreda Bernice Doyle, Aug. 6, 1960; children: Bruce III, Tracy. BS, U.S. Naval Acad., 1958; MSEE, Stanford U., 1965; MBA, U. Houston, Clear Lake, 1987. Commd. ensign USN, 1958, advanced through grades to capt., 1979, naval aviator, 1960, with Fighter Squadron 102, 1960-64; astronaut Johnson Space Ctr., NASA, Houston, 1966-90; mem. Skylab 1 backup crew Johnson Space Center, NASA, Houston, mem. STS-11 shuttle crew, mem. STS-31 Hubble Space Telescope deployment crew; ret. USN, 1990; prin. staff engr. Lockheed Martin Astronautics, Denver, 1990-97, chief scientist Advanced Space Transp. Sys. Co., 1997—2005, prin. staff scientist civil space, 2005—. Mem. Hubble salvage strategy panel NASA. Decorated Legion of Merit; recipient Def. Superior Service medal, NASA Exceptional Service medal, NASA Spaceflight medal, NASA Exceptional Engring. Achievement medal, Collier Trophy, 1985, Haley Space Flight award AIAA, 1991; named to Astronaut Hall Fame, 2005. Fellow Am. Astron. Soc.; mem. U.S. Naval Inst., Nat. Audubon Soc., Houston Audubon Soc. (past pres.) Episcopalian. Achievements include executing 1st untethered free flight in space using Manned Maneuvering Unit. Home: 21852 Pleasant Park Rd Conifer CO 80433-6802 Office: Lockheed Martin Space Sys Co Sensing & Exploration Sys Product Area PO Box 179 Denver CO 80201-0179 Office Phone: 303-971-6308. Personal E-mail: bruce2mc@logcabin.com.

MCCANDLESS, CAROLYN KELLER, retired human resources executive; b. Patuxent River, Md., June 6, 1945; d. Stevens Henry and Betty Jane (Bethune) Keller; m. Stephen Porter McCandless, Apr. 22, 1972; children: Peter Keller, Deborah Marion. BA, Stanford U., Calif., 1967; MBA, Harvard U., Cambridge, Mass., 1969. Fin. analyst Time Inc., NYC, 1969-72, mgr. budgets and fin. analysis, 1972-78, asst. sec., dir. internat. adminstrn., 1978-85, v.p., dir. employee benefits, 1985-90; v.p human resources and adminstrn. Time Warner, Inc., NYC, 1990—2001; ret., 2001. Bd. dirs., treas. FTRIA; bd. dirs., v.p., mem. exec. com. Svc. Program Older People, Inc.; chmn. investment com., trustee Annie Eaton Soc.; bd. dirs. Time-Life Alumni Soc. Democrat. Unitarian. Avocations: reading, travel, theater.

MCCANLESS, ROSS WILLIAM, lawyer, retail executive; b. 1957; BS in Acctg., Univ. N.C., 1979; JD cum laude, Wake Forest Univ., 1982. CPA. Pvt. practice, 1982—89; various positions, CEO, vice chmn. FoodLion, Delhaize Am., Inc., 1989—2003; sr. v.p., gen. counsel, sec. Lowe's Cos. Inc., Mooresville, NC, 2003—. Mem.: Am. Corp. Counsel Assn., Rowan County Bar Assn., Am. Bar Assn., N.C. State Bar Assn. Office: SVP & General Counsel Lowe's Companies Inc 1000 Lowe's Blvd Mooresville NC 28117 Office Phone: 704-758-1000.

MCCANN, BIFF (RAYMOND BIFF MCCANN), plastic surgeon; b. Fayetteville, Ark., Dec. 24, 1966; BS (cum laude) in Natural Scis., U. Ark., Fayetteville, 1989; MD, U. Ark. for Med. Scis., Little Rock, 1993. Intern, gen. surgery U. Ark. for Med. Scis., Little Rock, 1993—94, resident, gen. surgery, 1994—96; fellow, plastic surgery Scott & White Clinic, Temple, Tex., 1996—98; staff plastic surgeon U. Med. Ctr., Las Vegas, Nev., Mountain View Hosp., Las Vegas, Nev., Sunrise Hosp., Las Vegas, Nev.; chief, plastic surgery Valley Hospital, Las Vegas, Nev.; private practice Ctrl. Tex. to practice in Las Vegas, Nev., 1998—. Guest appearances on Plastic Surgery Before and After. Recipient Best Scientific Presentation by Resident Candidate, Am. Soc. for Aesthetic Plastic Surgery Ann. Mtg., NYC, 1997, Am. Soc. for Aesthetic Plastic Surgery Ann. Mtg., Dallas, Tex., 1999; named one of Las Vegas Top 10 Plastic Surgeons. Mem.: Golden Key, Gamma Beta Phi, Alpha Epsilon Delta. Office: 241 N Buffalo Dr Las Vegas NV 89145 Office Phone: 702-360-9500.

MCCANN, BRIAN MICHAEL, professional baseball player; b. Athens, Ga., Feb. 20, 1984; s. Howard McCann. Catcher Atlanta Braves, 2005—. Mem. US nat. team World Baseball Classic, 2009. Recipient Silver Slugger award, 2006, 2008; named to Baseball Am. All-Rookie Team, 2005, Topps' All-Rookie Team, 2005, Nat. League All-Star Team, 2006—09. Achievements include being the third catcher in Brave's franchise history to have 58 extra-base hits in 2006; having a five game home run streak in 2006, the longest streak by a catcher since Sandy Alomar in 1997. Office: Turner Field 755 Hank Aaron Dr Atlanta GA 30315 Office Phone: 404-522-7630.*

MCCANN, CLIFTON EVERETT, lawyer; b. Des Moines, July 11, 1950; s. George Lockhart and Evelyn Elizabeth (Miller) McC.; m. Marcia Ellen Morrow, Feb. 19, 1984; children: Gregory Lockhart, Jeanna Lauren. BA in Psychology, No. Ill. U., 1972; JD, Columbus Sch. Law, 1977; LLM in Intellectual Property, George Washington U., 1985. Bar: Va. 1978, US Patent Office 1980, US Ct. Appeals (fed. cir.) 1982, US Supreme Ct. 1983, DC 1984. Assoc. Beveridge, DeGrandi & Kline, Washington, 1978-83; ptnr. Lane, Aitken & McCann, Washington, 1983-2000; ptnr., intellectual property litig. Venable LLP, Washington, 2000—. Counsel intellectual property Am. Mensa, Ltd., Fort Worth, 1984—. Mem.: ABA (chair fed. litigation sub-com. on patent claim interpretation 1996—99, chair com. on intellectual property litigation 1999—2001), Am. Intellectual Prperty Law Assn., Bar Assn. DC (mem. steering com. patent, trademark, copyright sect. 1984—, chair 1996—97), DC Bar Assn. (chmn. trademark com. of the patent, trademark and copyright sect. 1985—89), Va. Bar Assn., Patent Lawyers Club (Washington), Delta Theta Phi. Office: Venable LLP 575 7th St NW Washington DC 20004

MCCANN, ELIZABETH IRELAND, theater, television and film producer; b. NYC, Mar. 29, 1931; d. Patrick and Rebecca (Henry) McC. BA, Manhattanville Coll., 1952, PhD hon., 1983; MA, Columbia U., 1954; LLD, Fordham U., 1966; ArtsD (hon.), Manhattanville Coll., 1987; LitD (hon.), Marymount Coll., 1993. Bar: N.Y. 1966. Assoc. firm Paul, Weiss, Rifkind, Wharton & Garrison, NYC, 1965-66; assoc. numerous theater mgmts. Robert Joffrey, Hal Prince, Saint Suber, Maurice Evans, 1956-68; mng. dir. Nederlander Orgn., NYC, 1968-76; pres. McCann & Nugent Prodns., Inc., NYC, 1976-86; mng. prodr. Tony Awards, NYC, 2001—. Bd. dirs. City Ctr. Music and Dance, Marymount Coll. Prodr.: (play) My Fat Friend, 1975, Dracula (Tony award for most innovative prodn. revival, 1978), The Elephant Man, 1978 (Tony award for best play, 1979, Drama Critics award, 1978, Drama Desk award, 1978, Outer Critics Circle award 1978, Obie award 1978), Night and Day, 1979, Home, 1980 (Adelco award, 1980), Morning's at Seven, 1980 (Tony award for reproduction play/musical, 1980), Amadeus, 1980 (Tony award for best play, 1981, Drama Desk award, 1980), The Philadelphia Story, 1980, Piaf, 1981, Rose, 1981, The Dresser, 1981, Mass Appeal, 1981, Macbeth, 1981, The Floating Light Bulb, 1981, The Life and Adventures of Nicholas Nickleby, 1981 (Tony award for best play, 1982, Drama Critics Circle award, 1981), Good, 1982, All's Well That Ends Well, 1983, The Glass Menagerie, 1983, Total Abandon, 1983, Painting Churches, 1983, The Lady and the Clarinet, 1983, Cyrano de Bergerac/Much Ado About Nothing, 1984, Pacific Overtures, 1984, Leader of the Pack, 1985, Les Liaisons Dangereuses, 1987 (Drama Critics Circle award, 1987), Stepping Out, 1987, Orpheus Descending, 1989, Nick & Nora, 1991, Three Tall Women, 1995, A Midsummer Night's Dream, 1995, In the West End with Robert Fox, Ltd., 1996, Who's Afraid of Virginia Woolf?, 1996, A Delicate Balance, 1997, A View from the Bridge, 1998 (Tony award for best revival play, 1998), The Unexpected Man, 1998, A View from the Bridge (Tony award), 1999, Copenhagen, 2000 (Tony award for best play, 2000), Cobb, 2000, The Play About the Baby, 2001, Tuesdays with Morrie, 2002, The Goat, or Who is Sylvia?, 2002 (Tony award for best play, 2002), The Smell of the Kill, 2002, Beckee/Albee, 2003, Well-, 2005, Who's Afraid of Virginia Woolf?, 2005; Butley, 2006; The Lady from Dubuque, 2007, Passing Strange, 2008, Equals, 2008; TV show Piaf, 1981, Morning's at Seven, 1982, Pilobolus Dance Theatre, 1982; assoc. prodr. Orpheus Descending, 1990. Recipient Entrepreneurial Woman award Women Bus. Owners of N.Y., 1981, 82, James J. and Jame Hoey award for Interracial Justice, 1981, Spl Drama League award for co-producing the Life and Adventures of Nicholas Nickleby on Broadway, 1982, Dr Louis M. Spadero award Fordham Grad. Sch. Bus., 1982, named one of The 100 Most Influential Women in NYC Bus., Crain's NY Bus., 2007, Drama Desk award, 2008, OBIE award, 2008.

MCCANN, GAIL ELIZABETH, lawyer; b. Boston, Aug. 25, 1953; d. Joseph and Ruth E. McC.; m. Stanley J. Lukasiewicz. AB, Brown U., 1975; JD, U. Pa., Phila., 1978. Bar: RI 1978, Mass. 1984, US Dist. Ct. RI 1978, US Dist. Ct. Mass. 1990. Ptnr. Edwards Angell Palmer & Dodge LLP, Providence, 1978—. Bd. dirs. Caritas House, Inc.; mem. R.I. adv. coun. New Eng. Legal Found. Mem.: Am. Coll. Mortgage

Attys. (RI state chair), RI Bar Assn., Brown U. Alumni Assn. (past pres.). Avocations: hiking, travel, yoga. Office: Edwards Angell Palmer & Dodge LLP 2800 Financial Plz Providence RI 02903 Office Phone: 401-274-9200.

MCCANN, JEAN FRIEDRICHS, artist, educator; b. NYC, Dec. 6, 1937; d. Herbert Joseph and Catherine Brady (Ward) Friedrichs; m. William Joseph McCann, May 14, 1960; children: Kevin, Brian, Maureen McCann Breslin, William, James, Denis Gerard, Kathleen. Student, Caton-Rose Inst. Fine Arts, 1955—57; AAS, SUNY, Farmingdale, 1959; BS, SUNY-Empire State U., Binghamton, 1986; MA summa cum laude, Marywood U., 1987, MFA in Art summa cum laude, 1989; completed Kellogg Leadership Program, Sch. Mgmt., SUNY, Binghamton, 1992; PhD, Nova U., 1995. Designer Patton Corp., NYC, 1959—66; sub. art tchr. Owego-Apalachin Sch. Dist., 1968—88; tutor, evaluator Empire State U. SUNY, 1987—; dir. ArtSpace Gallery, Owego, NY, 1992—94. V.p. bd. dirs. Tioga County Coun. on Arts, 1990—91, pres., 1992—95; demonstrator for various schs., ednl. TV and county museums. One-woman shows include IBM, Owego, 1972, Tioga Hist. Soc. Mus., 1975, Nat. Hist. Ct. House, 1982, Visual Arts Ctr., Scranton, Pa., 1989—90, ArtSpace, Owego, NY, 1991, MacDonald Art Gallery, Coll. Misericordia, Dallas, Pa., 1992, Plaza Gallery, Binghamton, 1992, Krembs Gallery, 1993, 2000, 2003, Wilson Gallery, Johnson City, N.Y., 1994, 2001, 2003, Countryside Gallery, Owego, 1996, 2002, Meml. Gallery, SUNY, Farmingdale, 1998, juried group shows, Roberson Mus., Binghamton, N.Y., 1972, Arnot Art Mus., Elmira, NY, 1974, 1989, 1992, Arena Nat. Exhibits, Binghamton, 1974—76, Pennino's Gallery, Burlington, Vt., 1975—77, Riise Gallery, St. Thomas, 1975—78, Grand Concourse Gallery, Albany, 1987, Schweinfurth Meml. Art Ctr., Auburn, NY, 2002, Link Gallery, Rochester, NY, 2006, 2007, 2008, 2009, numerous pvt. and pub. collections. Bd. dirs. Birthright of Owego, 1993—2003. Recipient NY State Artisans award, 1982, Nat. Strathmore award, 1989, 1st pl. in Graphic Arts award Jericho Arts Coun., 1994. Mem. Nat. Mus. Women in Arts (charter), Kappa Pi (pres. Zeta Omicron chpt. 1987-89, life), Artists Guild. Avocations: travel, reading. Home: 1776 Atwater Ct Kissimmee FL 34746 also: 6431 Francis Dr Victor NY 14564

MCCANN, JIM (JAMES F. MCCANN), consumer products company executive; b. July 28, 1951; married; 3 children. BS in Psychology, John Jay Coll., 1974. Creator chain of 14 flower shops, NYC; chmn., CEO 1-800-FLOWERS.COM, 1987—. Bd. dirs. PETCO, Inc., 1997- Office-Max, Inc., 2001-, Nat. Retail Fedn., Very Spl. Arts., Gtech Holdings, Boyd's Bears Author: Stop and Sell the Roses, 1998. Bd. dirs. Hofstra U., Winthrop-Univ. Hosp. Named Entrepreneur of Yr., Merrill Lynch and Inc. Mag., Retailer of Yr., Ernst & Young and L.I. Assn., One of Top 100 Bus. Men, Irish Am. Mag., Direct Marketer of Yr., Direct Mktg. Day N.Y., 1996, Outstanding Bus. Spkr., Toastmaster Internat., 1997. Office: 1 800 Flowers.com Inc 1 Old Country Rd Ste 500 Carle Place NY 11514-1847

MCCANN, JOHN JOSEPH, research scientist, consultant; b. Boston, Mass., July 1, 1942; s. John Joseph McCann and Gertrude Rita Martin McCann; m. Mary A. Conlin; children: Sarah Ann Herlihy, John Joseph children: Martha Mary Carnman. AB, Harvard Coll., Cambridge, Mass., 1964. Sr. lab. mgr. Polaroid Vision Rsch. Lab., Cambridge, 1961—96; cons. McCann Imaging, Belmont, Mass., 1996—. Pres. Artist Found., Boston. Fellow: Optical Soc. Am., Soc. Imaging Sci. Tech. (pres. 1992—95, Recipient Edwin H. Land medal 2002). Achievements include research in capturing scene information and calculating human color appearance. Home: 161 Claflin St Belmont MA 02478 Personal E-mail: mccanns@tiac.net.

MCCANN, JOHN MICHAEL, performing arts company professional; b. London, Mar. 29, 1952; s. Tom W. and Nora (Power) McC.; m. Christine Ioele, July 30, 1990. BFA, U N.C., 1979; MFA, Va. Tech. U., 1986. Film/TV producer Dept. of Def., Thailand/Vietnam, 1970-72; prodn. mgr. WWWC Radio Sta., Wilkesboro, N.C., 1973-74; news dir. WIFM Radio St., Elkin, N.C., 1974-75; gen. mgr. Lakeside Amphitheatre, Wilkesboro, 1980-81; mng. dir. Jenny Wiley Theatre, Prestonsburg, Ky., 1981-83; exec. dir. San Diego Repertory Theatre, San Diego, 1983-86; pres. Ptnrs. in Performance, Washington, 1987—. Cons. in field. Contbr. articles to profl. jours. Founder McCann Family Found., chmn. Sgt. U.S. Army. Democrat. Avocations: billiards, sailing, sky diving, pilot. Office: Ptnrs in Performance 301 13th St SE # 201 Washington DC 20003-2211

MCCANN, JOSEPH LEO, lawyer, former government official; b. Phila., Aug. 27, 1948; s. Joseph John and Christina Mary (Kirwan) McCann; m. Aida Laico Kabigting, Dec. 6, 1986; 1 child, Angela Kathleen. BA, St. Charles Sem., Phila., 1970, postgrad., 1970-71; MA, Temple U., 1975, JD, 1977. Bar: Pa. 1977, U.S. Dist. Ct. (ea. dist.) Pa. 1977, U.S. Dist. Ct. (mid. dist.) Pa. 1978, U.S. Ct. Appeals (3d cir.) 1978, D.C. 1986, U.S. Supreme Ct. 1986, Md. 1987, U.S. Ct. Appeals (Fed. cir.) 1988, U.S. Ct. Internat. Trade 1988. Law clk. to chief justice Pa. Supreme Ct., Phila., 1977-78; dep. atty. gen. Pa. Dept. Justice, Harrisburg, 1978-80; sr. atty. U.S. GAO, Washington, 1980-96; sr. asst. gen. counsel GSA, Washington, 1996-99; pres., counsel, headmaster The Kabigting-Kirwan Meml. Nonprofit Corp., 1997-2000; atty., 2001—. Mem. Pa. Bar Assn., Phila. Bar Assn., Md. State Bar Assn. Roman Catholic. Home and Office: 204 Bookham Ln Gaithersburg MD 20877-3789 Office Phone: 301-330-1585. Personal E-mail: ajmccann1@msn.com.

MCCANN, LAWRENCE ALTON, music educator; b. Sikeston, Mo., Jan. 11, 1951; s. William Alton and Billie Sue (Thomas) McC.; m. Vickie Dean Brown, Apr. 14, 1979; children: Luke Adam, Mollie Elizabeth. B Music Edn., Southeast Mo. State U., 1976; M Ednl. Adminstrn., William Woods U., 2003. Cert. vocal music K-12 tchg. Interstate Sch. Leaders Licensure Consortium, k-8 sch. prin. Music/youth dir. First Bapt. Ch., Gideon, Mo., 1974-77, Red Star Bapt. Ch., Cape Girardeau, Mo., 1977-78; news dir., announcer KPBM-FM, Poplar Bluff, Mo., 1979; elem. music tchr. Doniphan (Mo.) Elem. Sch., 1979—; pvt. guitar tchr. Three Rivers C.C., Poplar Bluff, 1979-86; music/youth dir. Calvary Bapt. Ch., Dexter, Mo., 1982-87; music dir. Temple Bapt. Ch., Poplar Bluff, 1987—. Profl. devel. chmn. Doniphan R-I Sch. Dist., 1993-2005; owner Luke and Mollie Music. Composer, lyricist: Mo. Conservation Melodies, 1982, Opus One, 1988, Choral Praise, 1989, Mo. State Tchrs. Assn., 1992, Sacred Music Quarterly/Hong Kong, 1993, Luke and Mollie Music, Dare to Live, 1993. Commr. planning and zoning, City of Poplar Bluff, 1982; team coach/youth soccer Optimist Soccer League, Poplar Bluff, 1988-96; team coach/youth baseball, Park and Recreation Dept., Poplar Bluff, 1993; bicentennial choir dir., Gideon (Mo.) Bicentennial Com., 1976. Recipient Cmty. Svc. award Mo. N.G., 1991; Outstanding Contbr. DARE and Drug Consortium, Ripley County, Mo., 1993. Mem. ASCAP, ASCD, Mo. State Tchrs. Assn. (state exec. bd. 1994-2000, pres. S.E. dist. 1992-93, CTA pres. 1984-85, 91-92, 2004-05, Medium Sized Sch. Outstanding Leadership award for state, dist. and local svc., SE Region meritorious svc. edn. award 2001), Music Educators Nat. Conf., Mo. Music Educators Assn., Nat. Staff Devel. Coun., Mo. Staff Devel. Coun., Nashville Songwriters Assn. Internat., Rec. Acad., Gospel Music Assn. Baptist. Avocations: photography, sports card collecting, record collecting, ornament collecting. Office: Doniphan Elem Sch 603 E Summit St Doniphan MO 63901-1142 also: Temple Baptist Ch 1813 Barron Rd Poplar Bluff MO 63901 Home Phone: 573-785-4836; Office Phone: 573-996-3523. Personal E-mail: lamc1969@hotmail.com.

MCCANN, MARTIN BRUCE, civil engineer; s. Robert Bruce and Margaret Ann McCann; m. Lynnette Sage, Aug. 12, 1984; children: Kari, Kelly, Kevin. PhD in Civil Engring., U. Nev., Reno, 2001. Cert. profl. engring, Wash., 1985. Lead engr. Western Rsch. Inst., Laramie, Wyo., 2001—04; hwy. engr. US Forest Svc., Atlanta, 2004—. Tech. mgr. Corps Engrs., Walla Walla, Wash., 1985—98. Home: 10645 Avian Dr Alpharetta GA 30022 Office: US Forest Svc 1720 Peachtree Rd NW Atlanta GA 30309

MCCANN, MELINDA CAMILLE, agricultural professional; d. Charles Edward and Eugenia Gaye Fleisher; children: Samantha Lynn, Rebecca Danielle. BS in Chemistry, U. Mo., St. Louis, 1992, MS in Biology, 2004. Quality assurance technician United Techs. Automotive, St. Louis, 1993—94; rsch. technician Today's Temp., St. Louis, 1994—96; rsch. chemist Monsanto Co., St. Louis, 1996—2000, analytical biochemist, 2001—05, regulatory affairs mgr., 2005—. Contbr. articles to numerous profl. jours. Office: Monsanto Co 800 N Lindbergh Blvd Saint Louis MO 63167

MCCANN, PETER PAUL, biology researcher, educator; s. Peter F. and Kathleen (Burnett) McC.; m. Danielle Soury, July 31, 1971. AB in Zoology, Columbia U., 1965; PhD, Syracuse U., 1970. Fellow NIH, Bethesda, Md., 1970-73; sr. scientist Ctr. of Rsch. Merrell Internat., Strasbourg, France, 1973-79; sr. biochemist Merrell Dow Rsch. Ctr., Cin., 1979-82; rsch. assoc. scientist Merrell Dow Rsch. Inst., Cin., 1982-84, dir. scientific and acad. liaison, 1984-90, dir. sci. adminstrn., 1988-90; prof. U. Cin. Coll. Medicine, 1981—; sr. dir., ctr. dir. Marion Merrell Dow Inc., Indpls., 1990-93; pres. Brit. Biotech Inc., Annapolis, Md., 1993-98; interim pres. U. Md. Biotech. Inst., College Park, Md., 1998-99; pres., CEO Oncostasis, Inc., 1999—2001, Mymetics Corp., 2001—03; GG; ptnr. Profl. Fin. Assoc., 2004—07; registered rep. MetLife, 2008—. Co-vice chmn. Gordon Rsch. Conf. on Polyamines, 1987, co-chmn., 1989. Chief editor, co-author Inhibition of Polyamine Metabolism, 1987; co-editor, co-author: Enzymes as Targets for Drug Design, 1989; contbr. articles to profl. jours. Mem. Am. Soc. Cell Biology, Am. Soc. Tropical Medicine and Hygiene, Am. Soc. Biochemistry and Molecular Biology, Biochem. Soc. (editl. adv. bd. 1986-92, editor 1992-99), Soc. Protozoologists (editl. bd. reviewers 1989-95), Am. Philat. Congress, Inc. (pres. 1990-95), Am. Philat. Soc. (v.p. 1995-99, pres. 1999-2003, Fédération Internat. De Philatélie (v.p. 2004—). Achievements include patents for method of inhibiting the growth of protozoa, method of controlling phytopathogenic fungus. Personal E-mail: p103226706@cs.com.

MCCANN, RENETTA, former advertising executive; b. Chgo., Dec. 8, 1956; d. Aditha Lorraine Collymore Walker; married; 2 children. BS in Speech, Northwestern U., 1978. Client svc. trainee Starcom, 1978, v.p., 1988, media dir., 1989, sr. v.p., 1995; CEO Starcom N.Am., Chgo., 1999—2004; CEO Americas Starcom MediaVest Group, 2004—08. Bd. mem. Audit Bur. Circulations Northwestern U., mem. adv. bd. Media Mgmt. Ctr.; bd. mem. Chgo. United. Spkr. in field. Recipient Outstanding Women in Comm. award, Ebony, Vanguard award, Chgo. Mags. Assn., Media Strategies award, Bus. Week, Matrix award for Advt., NY Women in Comm. Inc., 2006; named Media Maven, Advt. Age, 2001, Corp. Exec. of Yr., Black Enterprise, 2002, Advt. Woman of Yr., Women's Advt. Club Chgo., 2002; named a Woman to Watch, Crain's Chgo. Bus., 2007; named one of 50 Women Who Are Changing the World, Essence, 2003, 50 Women to Watch, Wall Street Journal, 2005, Most Influential Black Americans, Ebony mag., 2006, Next 20 Female CEOs, Pink Mag. & Forté Found., 2006, 100 Most Powerful Women, Forbes mag., 2007; named to Power 150, Ebony mag., 2008. Mem.: Am. Advt. Fedn. (mem. multicultural bus. practices leadership coun.), Am. Assn. Advt. Agys. (chair media policy com.).

MCCANN, ROBERT JAMES, former diversified financial services company executive; b. 1958; m. Cindy McCann; 2 children. BA, Bethany Coll., 1980; MBA, Tex. Christian U., 1982; grad. from advanced mgmt. prog., Harvard Bus. Sch. Assoc. MBA sales and trading prog. Merrill Lynch & Co., Inc., 1982, head US Equities divsn., 1995—98, COO corp. & instl. client group (now global markets and investment banking), 2000—01, head global securities rsch. & economics, 2001—03, exec. v.p., vice chmn. wealth mgmt. group, 2003—05, exec. v.p., vice chmn. & pres. global wealth mgmt. (formerly pvt. client group), 2005—08. Bd. dirs. Am. Ireland Fund. Recipient Annie Moore award, Irish Am. Cultural Inst.*

MCCANN, S. ANTHONY, financial management consultant, former federal agency administrator; b. Washington, Sept. 9, 1943; s. Harry A. and Anita P. McC.; m. Jo Ann Miller, Aug. 27, 1966; children: Spencer A., Catherine E. BA, Lake Forest Coll., 1966; MA, Syracuse U., 1969, postgrad. Grad. asst. Maxwell Sch. Syracuse U., 1968-72, instr., 1972; govtl. researcher Office of the City Exec., Onondaga County, Syracuse, N.Y., 1972-73; research assoc. and project dir. Nat. Assn. of Counties, Washington, 1973-79; vis. prof., assoc. dir. Office Personnel Mgmt., Washington, 1979-81; legis. analyst U.S Senate Com. on the Budget, Washington, 1981-85, sr. analyst human resources, 1985-86; asst. sec. mgmt. and budget U.S. Dept. Health and Human Services, Washington, 1986—89; asst. sec. mgmt. & budget U.S. Dept. Veterans Affairs, Washington, 1989—93; dep. dir. Am. Internat. Health Alliance, 1993—95; staff dir. subcommittee on Labor, Health & Human Svcs. U.S. Ho. Reps., Washington, 1995—2001; dir. fin. affairs Smithsonian Inst., Washington, 2001—04; sec. Md. Dept. Health & Mental Hygiene, Balt., 2004—07; CFO HHS Health Resources & Services Adminstrn., 2007—09; mem. adv. com. Fin. Mgmt. Services, Inc., Rockville, Md., 2009—. Mem. steering com. Nat. Health Policy Forum, Washington; commr. Pres. Task Force to Improve Health Care Delivery for Veterans, 2001-03. Contbr. articles to profl. jours. Pres. Indian Spring Civic Assn., Silver Spring, Md., 1980-83. Republican. Avocations: woodworking, bicycling, exercising, gardening. Office: c/o Fin Mgmt Services Inc 15200 Wycliffe Ct Rockville MD 20853 Office Phone: 301-929-3042. Office Fax: 301-929-1158.*

MCCANN, TIM, legislative staff member; Grad., Georgetown U., Washington, 2004. Polit. assoc. Sutter's Mill Fund Raising & Strategy, 2002—05; dep. campaign mgr. Chris Bell's Gubernatorial Campaign, Tex., 2005—06; campaign mgr. Sam Coats' Mayoral Campaign, Dallas, 2007; social media mktg. mgr. Revolution Health, 2007—08; campaign mgr. Frank Kratovil's Congl. Campaign, 2008; chief of staff to Rep. Frank Kratovil US House of Reps., Washington, 2009—. Democrat. Office: 314 Cannon House Office Bldg Washington DC 20515 Office Phone: 202-225-5311. Office Fax: 202-225-0254.*

MCCANNELL, CHRISTOPHER, legislative staff member; Grad., Fordham U., NYC, 1991. Fin. asst. Fraioli & Assoc., Washington, 1994; regional field coord. Nat. Assn. Letter Carriers, 1994—96; press sec. to rep. Paul Kanjorski, 1996—98, to rep. Steny Hoyer, 1997—99; chief of staff to congressman Joseph Crowley US House of Reps., Washington, 1999—2007, chief of staff to congressman Michael E. McMahon, 2009—; dir. Quinn Gillespie & Assoc. LLC, Washington, 2007—08. Democrat. Mailing: US House Reps 323 Cannon House Office Bldg Washington DC 20515 Office Phone: 202-225-3371, 202-225-1272.*

MCCANN-LAWSON, KIM, theater educator, director; b. Joplin, Mo., Dec. 8, 1954; d. James Cleland McCann and Mary Earline (Campbell) Kelley; m. Mark A. Lawson, Feb. 15, 2003; children: Mark Lawson Jr., Marcus Lawson. AA in Drama, Diablo Valley Coll., 1974; BA in Theater, Calif. State U., 1976; MFA in Drama, U. Calif., Davis, 1981. Cert. adult spl. edn. credential. Artist, instr. Short Ctr. South, Sacramento, 1982—2004, asst. program dir., 2004—06, program dir., 2006—; theater, film lectr., resident dir. Sacramento City Coll., City Theatre and Sacramento Shakespeare Festival, 1984—. Chair bd. dirs. City Theatre Sacramento Shakespeare Festival, 1995—; mem. theatre alumni chpt. bd. Calif. State U., Sacramento, 2003—, pres., 2005—06. Dir. Twelfth Night, Love's Labour's Lost, Hamlet, Cyrano DeBergerac, Measure for Measure, Midsummer Night's Dream, Three Musketeers, Much Ado About Nothing, Twelfth Night, Shrew, Equus, As You Like It, Blood Wedding, Romeo & Juliet, Comic Potential, MacBeth and 60 others; actor in over 150 prodns. including Mother Courage, Top Girls, Dancing at Lughnasa, Our Town, Hay Fever, Midsummer Night's Dream, The Matchmaker, Merry Wives, Winter's Tale, others. Recipient 5 Elly awards, Sacramento Area Regional Theatre Alliance, Chesley award, Woodland Opera House. Mem.: Sacramento State U. Theatre, Dance Alumni Chpt., U. Calif. Davis Alumni Chpt. Avocations: music, reading, films. Office: Sacramento City College ACTH 3 3835 Freeport Blvd Sacramento CA 95822-1386 Business E-Mail: mccannk@scc.losrios.edu.

MCCANNY, JOHN VINCENT, engineering educator, executive; b. Ballymoney, Northern Ireland, June 25, 1952; s. Patrick Joseph and Kathleen Brigid (Kerr) McC.; m. Maureen Bernadette, Mellon, July 1979; children: Damian Patrick, Kathryn Louise. BSc in Physics with honors, U. Manchester, 1973; PhD, U. Ulster, 1978; DSc, Queen's U. Belfast, 1998. Chartered physicist, engr. Higher sci. officer RSRE, Malvern, England, 1979—80, sr. sci. officer, 1981—83, prin. sci. officer, 1983—84; lectr. Queen's U., Belfast, Northern Ireland, 1984—87, reader, 1987—88, prof. microelectronics engring., 1988—, dir. Inst. Electronics, Comm. Info. Tech., 2004—, head Sch. Electronics, Elec. Engring. and Computer Sci., 2005—. Dir. Audio Processing Tech., Ltd., Belfast, 1988—96, CTO Amphion Semiconductor Ltd., Belfast, 1990—2004; mem. U.K. Engring. and Phys. Scis. Rsch. Coun., 1992—98, strategic advisory, 2006—; mem. Royal Acad. Engring. Policy Com., 1999—2002, U.K. Foresight Panel Info., Comm. and Media Panel, 2001—02. Author 6 electronics rsch. books and 330 sci. articles; patentee in field. Named a Commander of the Order of the British Empire by Queen Elizabeth II, 2002. Fellow: IEEE (tech. com. design and implementation of signal processing sys. 1992—, chair tech. com. design and implementation of signal processing sys. 1999—2001, 3rd Millennium medal 2000), Royal Soc. (chair sect. com. 4 2004—05, fellowships com. chems. and engring., Irish Times Boyle medal 2003), Royal Soc. Encouragement Arts, Mfg. and Commerce, Inst. Elec. Engrs., Royal Acad. Engring. (Silver Medal 1996), Inst. Physics; mem.: Irish Acad. Engring., European Acad. Scis., Brit. Computer Soc. (IT Profl. of Yr. award 2004), Royal Dublin Soc., Royal Irish Acad., Clandeboye Golf Club. Avocations: golf, swimming, photography, sports, music. Office: Queens U Belfast Inst Electronics Comms and Info Tech Belfast BT3 9DT Northern Ireland Office Phone: 44 2890 971800. Business E-Mail: acit@qub.ac.uk.

MCCANTS, WILLIAM DAVID, lawyer, writer; s. John Gordon and Gwendolyn Patricia McCants; m. Anne Elizabeth Conger, June 30, 1984; children: Thomas Edward, James Douglas. BA in History, U. Calif., LA, 1983; degree in Psychology, Harvard U., Cambridge, Mass., 1994; MS in Criminal Justice, N.E. U., Boston, 1997; JD, Harvard U., Cambridge, Mass., 2000. Law clk. Mass. Supreme Jud. Ct., Boston, 2000—01; assoc. environ. law Goodwin Procter LLP, Boston, 2001—02; liaison pub. sch. U.S. Dept Edn., Malden, Mass., 2002—03, atty. Office for Civil Rights Boston, 2003—. Moot ct. judge Harvard Law Sch. Author: Anything Can Happen in High School and It Usually Does, 1993, Much Ado About Prom Night, 1995 (Two awards ALA, 1996, Young Adult's Choice award Internat. Reading Assn., 1997, award ALA, 2000). Tchr. Sunday sch. Plymouth Congl. Ch., Belmont, Mass., 2003—06. Mem.: ABA. Avocation: sailing. Personal E-mail: wmccants@post.harvard.edu.

MCCARBERG, BILL HAROLD, physician; b. Seattle, Apr. 4, 1948; s. Harold Carl and Elizabeth Ann Mehlberg; m. Peggy J. McCarthy McCarberg. BA summa cum laude, U. Calif., Berkeley, 1972; MD, Northwestern U., 1976. Diplomate Am. Bd. Family Practice, Am. Coll. Pain Medicine; cert. in geriatrics. Residency Highland Hosp., Rochester, NY, 1979; physician in charge Kaiser Permanent, Escondido, Calif., 1982—2003; asst. clin. prof. U. Calif. Sch. Medicine, San Diego, 1983—; coord. pain svcs. Kaiser Permanent, San Diego, 1974—2002, dir. chronic pain mgmt. program, 1984—2003; founding mem. managed care task force Am. Pain Soc., 1990—. Author: (monograph) Chronic Pain Management: Perspective for Primary Care Physicians, 1998, (book chpt.) A Sample of Existing Managed Care Organizations Pain Programs, 1999; contbr. articles to profl. jours. Recipient K Star for Outstanding Svc., Kaiser Permanente, San Diego, 1985, 92, Award of Excellence Southern Calif. Cancer Pain Initiative, L.A., 1999. Mem. Am. Acad. Pain Medicine, Am. Pain Soc. (chair managed care com. 2000—, bd. dirs., Elizabeth Narcessian award 2003), Western Pain Soc. (chair program 1999—, pres. 1998-), Appraisal Physician Svcs., Phi Beta Kappa. Avocations: running, guitar, golf. Office: Kaiser Permanente 732 N Broadway Escondido CA 92025

MCCARDELL, JAMES ELTON, retired naval officer; b. Daytona Beach, Fla., Jan. 22, 1931; s. J. Elton and Margaret Almira (Payne) McC.; m. Nancy Ann Chandler, July 9, 1955; children: Jenise, Patrick. Student, U. Fla., Gainesville, 1948-50; BA, US Naval Postgrad. Sch., 1965. Commd. ensign USN, 1952, advanced through grades to rear adm., 1980; exec. officer USS Forrestal, 1972-73; dep. chief of staff Air Readiness Staff, Chief Naval Res., New Orleans, 1973-76; comdg. officer NAS, Key West, Fla., 1976-78; chief of staff Staff of Chief Naval Res., New Orleans, 1978-80; def. and naval attache US Embassy, Brasilia, Brazil, 1981-83; dir. Inter-Am. Def. Coll., Fort L.J. McNair, Washington, 1983-85; ret., 1985. Decorated Legion of Merit with cluster, Bronze Star medal, Air medal with 12 clusters, Def. Disting. Service medal, Def. Superior Performance medal Republican. Roman Catholic. Home: PO Box 719 Pass Christian MS 39571-0719 *The absolute measure of successful leadership has always been reflected by performance of subordinates in the achievement of unit goals.*

MCCAREY, WILMA RUTH, retired lawyer; b. St. Louis, Dec. 7, 1943; d. Ferdinand Martin and Ruth Anna Cora Kisro; m. Michael Carl McCarey, Aug. 21, 1965; children: Darren Michael, David Brian. BS in Math. with honors, Valparaiso U., Ind., 1965; JD with honors, George Washington U., 1978. Bar: DC, Va., U.S. Dist. Ct. Md., U.S. Dist. Ct. DC, U.S. Ct. Appeals (DC cir.), U.S. Ct. Appeals (4th cir.). Computer sys. analyst Tech. Ops., Inc., Rosslyn, Va., 1965—66, Kroger Co., Cin., 1966—69; rsch. asst. govt. contracts George Washington Nat. Law Ctr., 1976—78; atty. C&P Telephone/Bell Atlantic (now Verizon), 1978—83; sr. atty. AT&T Corp. Mid Atlantic Region, 1983—85, gen. atty., 1985—95, v.p. govt. affairs, pres. atty. comm. Va., Md., W.Va. and DC, 1995—2001; ret., 2001. Bd. dirs. Fairfax Edn. Found., Fairfax C. of C., Fairfax Symphony, Juvenile Diabetes Rsch. Found., No. Va. Luth. Campus Ministries, Va. Econ. Bridge, Vol. Fairfax, Character Counts; mem. adv. bd. Women Execs. in State Govt. Mem.: Va. Telephone Industry Assn. (treas. exec. bd.). Lutheran. Avocations: sailing, golf, travel, exercise, volunteering.

MCCARRICK, EDWARD R., publishing executive; married; 2 children. Grad., Manhattan Coll., Riverdale, NY, 1971. Sales rep. TIME Mag., Boston, Mpls., 1973—77, sr. sales rep., 1977—80, automotive category supr., 1980, divsn. sales mgr. Boston, 1981—85, advt. sales dir. NYC, 1985—86, assoc. pub., internat. advt. sales dir., 1986—91; sales dir. Life Mag., NYC, 1988—91, pub., 1993—99; pub. US TIME Mag., NYC, 1999—2003, worldwide pub., 2003—08, pres. NYC, 2005—08; exec. v.p. account mgmt. and media partnerships ICON Internat., Inc., Stamford, Conn., 2009—. Vol. Cath. Charities; bd. dirs. Concern Worldwide, First Tee of Conn., YMCA/YWCA. Avocations: golf, squash, tennis. Office: ICON International Inc 4 Stamford Plz 15th Fl 107 Elm St Stamford CT 06902 Office Phone: 212-522-3273. E-mail: ed_mccarrick@timeinc.com.*

MCCARRICK, THEODORE CARDINAL, cardinal, archbishop emeritus; b. NYC, July 7, 1930; s. Theodore Egan and Margaret (McLaughlin) McCarrick. AB, St. Joseph's Sem., 1954, AM, 1958; MA, Cath. U., 1960, PhD, 1963. Ordained priest Archdiocese of NY, 1958, assoc. dir. edn., 1969—71, sec. to archbishop, 1971—77, aux. bishop, 1977—81; asst. chaplain Cath. U. America, Washington DC, 1959—61, dean students, 1961—63, asst. to rector, dir. devel., 1963—65, instr. dept. sociology, 1961—65; domestic prelate, 1965; pres. Cath. U. PR, 1965—69; ordained bishop, 1977; first bishop Diocese of Metuchen, 1982—86; archbishop Archdiocese of Newark, 1986—2000, Archdiocese of Washington DC, 2001—06, archbishop emeritus, 2006—; elevated to cardinal, 2001; cardinal-priest Ss. Nereo ed Archilleo, 2001—. Mem. Fed. Commn. for Study of Migration and Econ. Devel., 1989; policy bd. Washington Consortium, Peace Corps, 1962—63, Pontifical Commn. for Migrants and Refugees, 1987; chmn. US Bishops Com. on Migration, 1986—89, 1992—95, Gov.'s Commn. for Higher Edn. in P.R., 1968, PR Adv. Coun. on Tech. and Vocat. Edn., 1968—69; with US Sec. of State's Adv. Com. on Religious Freedom Abroad, 1996—99, US Com. Internat. Religious Freedom, 1999—2001, Synod for Am. and Post Synod Coun.; Episcopal promoter Apostleship of the Sea, 1989—92; chmn. Com. Aid to Ch. in Ctrl. and Ea. Europe, U.S. Conf. of Cath. Bishops, 1992—96, chmn. internat. policy com., 1996—99, chmn. domestic policy com., 2002—05. Sec.-treas. Papal Found., 1988—96, pres., 1997—. Decorated officer, knight grand cross Holy Sepulchre, Order of Cedars of Lebanon; recipient Global Citizen award, Whitehead Sch. Diplomacy & Internat. Rels., Seton Hall U., 2007. Mem.: Knights Malta (chaplain 1978—82). Roman Catholic. Office Phone: 301-927-0278.

MCCARRON, DOUGLAS J., labor union administrator; b. LA, Sept. 23, 1950; Construction worker, mem. Local 1506 United Brotherhood Carpenters, LA, 1968; pres. So. Calif. Conf. Carpenters, 1982, LA County Dist. Coun. Carpenters, 1983; sec.-treas. So. Calif. Coun. Carpenters, 1987; v.p. United Brotherhood Carpenters & Joiners of America, 1994—95, gen. pres. Washington, 1995—. Trustee So. Calif. Pension Fund, 1984—; former mem. bd. dirs. Union Labor Life Ins. Co. (ULLICO). Office: UBC 101 Constitution Ave NW Washington DC 20001-2133 also: 1221 Massachusetts Ave Washington DC 20005 Office Phone: 202-589-0520.*

MCCARRON, JOHN FRANCIS, editor; b. Providence, Jan. 20, 1949; s. Hugh Francis and Katherine Anne (Brooks) McC.; m. Janet Ann Velsor, Sept. 3, 1971; children: Veronica, Catherine. BS in Journalism, Northwestern U., 1970, MS in Journalism, 1973. Gen. assignment reporter Chgo. Tribune, 1973-80, urban affairs writer, 1980-91, fin. editor, 1991-92, editorial bd. columnist, 1992-2000; v.p. strategy and comms. Met. Planning Coun. Chgo., 2000—02; adj. prof. Medill Sch. Journalism Northwestern U., 2002—; cons. Local Initiatives Support Corp., 2003—. Contbr. to Planning Mag., World Book Ency., Preservation Mag., Land & People Mag. Lt. USNR, 1970-72. Recipient Editors award AP, 1983, 84, Ann. Journalism award Am. Planning Assn., 1983, Heywood Broun award Am. Newspaper Guild, Washington, 1989, Peter Lisagor award Soc. Profl. Journalists, 1994, Nat. Journalism award Lambda Alpha Internat., 2007. Mem.: Lambda Alpha Internat. Home: 1425 Noyes St Evanston IL 60201-2639 E-mail: j.mccarron@att.net.

MC CARTAN, PATRICK FRANCIS, lawyer; b. Cleve., Aug. 3, 1934; s. Patrick Francis and Stella Mercedes (Ashton) Mc Cartan; m. Lois Ann Buchman, Aug. 30, 1958; children: M. Karen, Patrick Francis III. AB magna cum laude, U. Notre Dame, 1956, JD, 1959. Bar: Ohio 1960, US Ct. Appeals (6th cir.) 1961, US Ct. Appeals (3rd cir.) 1965, US Ct. Appeals (DC cir.) 1980, US Ct. Appeals (5th cir.) 1981, US Ct. Appeals (4th cir.) 1989, US Ct. Appeals (7th cir.) 1992, US Supreme Ct. 1970. Law clk. to Hon. Charles Evans Whittaker, U.S. Supreme Ct., 1959; assoc. Jones Day, Cleve., 1961—65, ptnr., 1966—93, mng. ptnr., 1993—2002, sr. ptnr., 2003—. Trustee U. Notre Dame, 1989—, chair, 2000—07; trustee Cleve. Clinic Found.; standing com. on rules of practice and procedure Jud. Conf. of US. Fellow: Internat. Acad. Trial Lawyers, Am. Coll. Trial Lawyers; mem.: ABA, Bar Assn. Greater Cleve. (pres. 1977—78), Ohio Bar Assn., 6th Cir. Jud. Conf. (life), U.S.-Japan Bus. Coun., Coun. on Fgn. Rels., Greater Cleve. Growth Assn. (chmn. 1997—2000). Roman Catholic. Office: Jones Day North Point 901 Lakeside Ave E Cleveland OH 44114-1190 Office Phone: 216-586-3939, 216-586-7272. Business E-Mail: pmccartan@jonesday.com.

MCCARTER, CHARLES CHASE, lawyer; b. Pleasanton, Kans., Mar. 17, 1926; s. Charles Nelson and Donna (Chase) McC.; m. Clarice Blanchard, June 25, 1950; children: Charles Kevin, Cheryl Ann. BA, Principia Coll., 1950; JD, Washburn U., 1953; LLM, Yale U., 1954. Bar: Kans. 1953, U.S. Supreme Ct. 1962, Mo. 1968. Asst. atty. gen. State of Kans., 1954-57; lectr. law sch. Washburn U., 1956-57; appellate counsel FCC, Washington, 1957-58; assoc. Weigand, Curfman, Brainerd, Harris & Kaufman, Wichita, 1958-61; gen. counsel Kans. Corp. Commn., 1961-63; ptnr. McCarter, Frizzel & Wettig, Wichita, 1963-68, McCarter & Badger, Wichita, 1968-73; pvt. practice law St. Louis, 1968-76; ptnr. McCarter & Greenley, St. Louis, 1976-85; mng. ptnr. Gage & Tucker, St. Louis, 1985-87, Husch and Eppenberger, St. Louis, 1987-89, McCarter & Greenley, LLC, St. Louis, 1990—. Prof. law, assoc. dir. law sch. Nat. Energy Law and Policy Inst. Tulsa U., 1977-79; prof. law, coach nat. moot ct. coll. of law Stetson U. Coll., St. Petersburg, Fla., 1980-84; mem. govtl. adv. coun. Gulf Oil Corp., 1977-81; legal com. Interstate Oil Compact Commn.; mem. adv. bd. Allegiant Bank, 1997—. Co-author: Missouri Lawyers Guide; assoc. editor Washburn U. Law Rev., 1952-53; contbr. articles to profl. jours. Chmn. Wichita Human Rels. Devel. Adv. Bd., 1967-68; bd. dirs. Peace Haven Assn.; active St. Louis Estate Planning Coun., 1987—; mem. bequests and endowment com. Salvation Army, 1995—; mem. YMCA endowment com., 1996—; mem. gifts and endowment bd. TV Channel 9, KETC, St. Louis, 2004—. With USNR, 1944-46. Recipient Excellent Prof. award U. Tulsa, 1979; vis. scholar Yale U., 1980 Mem. ABA (sect. real property, probate and trust law, bus. law sect.), Kans. Bar Assn., Mo. Bar Assn. (probate and trust com., tax com.), Am. Legion, VFW, Native Sons and Daus. Kans (pres. 1957-58), Kappa Sigma, Delta Theta Phi, Principia Dads Club (bd. dirs.) Republican. Office: One Metropolitan Sq Ste 2100 Saint Louis MO 63102-2751 Office Phone: 314-436-2100 ext. 107. Business E-Mail: cmccarter@mccartergreenley.com.

MC CARTER, JOHN WILBUR, JR., museum executive; b. Oak Park, Ill., Mar. 2, 1938; s. John Wilbur and Ruth Rebecca McC.; m. Judith Field West, May 1, 1965; children: James Philip, Jeffrey John, Katherine Field. AB, Princeton U., 1960; postgrad., London Sch. Econs., 1961; MBA, Harvard U., 1963. Cons., assoc., v.p. Booz Allen and Hamilton, Inc., Chgo., 1963-69; White House fellow Washington, 1966-67; dir. Bur. Budget and Dept. Fin., State of Ill., Springfield, 1969-73; v.p. DeKalb AgResearch, Ill., 1973-78, dir. Ill., 1975-86, exec. v.p. Ill., 1978-80, pres. Ill., 1981-82; pres., chief exec. officer DeKalb-Pfizer Genetics, 1982-86; pres. DeKalb Corp., 1985-86; sr. v.p. Booz Allen & Hamilton Inc., 1987-97; pres., CEO Field Mus., Chgo., 1996—. Bd. dirs. Divergence Inc., W.W. Grainger, Inc., Janus. Trustee Chgo. Pub. Television, 1973—, chmn., 1989-96, trustee Princeton U., 1983-87, U. Chgo., 1993—. Office: Field Museum 1400 S Lake Shore Dr Chicago IL 60605-2496

MCCARTER, KATHERINE SAUTER, association executive; b. Nov. 12, 1942; d. William Charles and Josephine RFosina (Schoenie) Sauter; m. Robert James McCarter, Dec. 6, 1969; 1 child, Emily Katherine. BA in Biology, Cedar Crest Coll., Allentown, Pa., 1964; MHA (EPA trainee), Johns Hopkins U., 1973. Chmn. sci. dept. Arundel (Md.) Jr. H.S., 1964—68; assoc. career devel. program Am. Lung Assn., NYC, 1968; air conservation cons. Mass. Lung Assn., 1968—69; exec. dir. Met. Boston Citizen's Coalition Clean Air, 1968—69; cmty. health educator Environ. Health Adminstrn., Md. Dept. Health, 1971—76; dir. govt. rels. APHA, Washington, 1976—80, asst. exec. dir., 1980—83, assoc. exec. dir., 1984—97; exec. dir. Ecol. Soc. Am., Washington, 1997—, pub., 2006—. Mem. nat. air pollution manpower devel. adv. com. EPA, 1973—76. Mem. editl. adv. bd.: The AIDS Reference Guide, 1987. Bd. dirs. Nat. Coalition Health and Environment, 1980—82, Coalition for Health Funding, 1983—, treas., 1983—86, v.p., 1987—88, pres., 1989—94, past pres., 1994—97. Mem.: APHA, Coun. Engring. and Sci. Soc. Execs. (bd. dirs. 2003—, sec. 2007—08, v.p. 2008—09, pres. 2009—). Home: 9027 Billow Row Columbia MD 21045-2343 Office: 1990 M St NW Ste 700 Washington DC

MCCARTER, SHARONDIA RENEE, elementary school educator; b. Dublin, Miss., Jan. 25, 1970; d. Jesse McCarter and Deltora Wilson. BA, Rutgers U., New Brunswick, NJ, 1988—93. Tchr. math & sci. Bridgeton Bd. Edn., NJ, 2001—06; substitute tchr. Vineland Pub. Schs., NJ, 2006—. Tutoring co-coord. Union Bapt. Temple, Bridgeton, 2002—. Recipient 3d Place Features award, Garden State Assn. Black Journalists, 1994. Mem.: Nat. Coun. Tchrs. Math. D-Conservative. Home: 9138 Edmonston CT Apt 304 Greenbelt MD 20770-4550 Personal E-mail: msrmccarter@msn.com.

MCCARTER, THOMAS NESBITT, III, investment company executive, consultant; b. NYC, Dec. 16, 1929; s. Thomas N. Jr. and Suzanne M. (Pierson) McCarter. Student, Princeton U., 1948-51. Chartered investment counselor. Sales exec. Mack Trucks, Inc., NYC, 1952—59; ptnr. Kelly, McCarter, D-Arcy Investment Counsel, NYC, 1959—62; v.p., sec., dir. D-Arcy McCarter & Chew, NYC, 1962—66; v.p., dir. Trainer, Wortham & Co., Inc., NYC, 1967—71, exec. v.p., 1971—75; chmn. bd., dir. Island Security Bank Ltd., 1976—78; pres. Knottingham Ltd., NYC, 1976—84; gen. ptnr. W.P. Miles Timber Properties, New Orleans, 1974—; exec. v.p., dir. Yorke McCarter Owen & Bartles, Inc., NYC, 1985—89. Cons. Laidlaw Holdings, Inc., 1990—92; pres. Mentor Mgmt. Group, Inc., NYC, 1986—90; chmn. bd. dirs. Ramapo Land Co., Sloatsburg, NY, 1990—, Stillrock Mgmt., Inc., NYC, 1992—96, Pendragon Tech., 1996—98, Dir Anker Coal Group Inc., Hyseq, Inc., Nuvelo, Inc.; bd. advisors Knowledge Delivery Sys. Inc.; vice chair Runnymede Capital Mgmt., 1997—2002; adv. dir. Runnymede Capital Mgmt., Inc.; bd. dirs. Inst. Scientific Investment and Governance KCK Tokyo, So. Union Co. Chmn. bd. trustees Christodora Found., Inc., NYC, 1970-93; charter trustee Dalton Sch., NYC, 1969-76, v.p., 1972-76; pres., trustee Civil War Libr. and Mus., Phila., 1985-92; chmn. bd. trustees ASPCA, 1984-95; chmn. loyal Legion Found., NYC; trustee Children's Aid Soc. NYC, 1973-94, Joffrey Ballet, Found. for Am. Dance, 1973-77; pres., trustee NYC Marble Cemetery Assn., 1990-2002; mem. Nat. Com. for Preservation of US Treasury Bldg., 1988-92; trustee Nat. Symphony Orch., Washington, 1990-94; chmn. Gibraltar Am. Coun., 1998-2002; bd. assocs. Whitehead Inst., Cambridge, Mass., 2000—09. Mem. Loyal Legion US (comdr. NY State 1964-66, nat. comdr. in chief 1977-81), Brook Club, Links Club, River Club, St. Nicholas Soc., Pilgrims of US (NYC), Meadow Club (Southampton, NY), Ivy Club (Princeton, NJ), Moorings Club (Vero Beach, Fla.), Everglades Club (Palm Beach, Fla.). Republican. Office: PO Box 2380 Palm Beach FL 33480 Office Phone: 772-696-3025.

MCCARTHY, ANDREW, actor; b. NYC, Nov. 29, 1962; m. Carol Schneider, Oct. 9, 1999 (div. 2005); 1 child, Sam; 1 child, (with Dolores Rice), Willow. Represented by Internat. Creative Mgmt., Beverly Hills, Calif. Actor: (films) Class, 1983, The Beniker Gang, 1985, Heaven Help Us, 1985, St. Elmo's Fire, 1985, Pretty in Pink, 1986, Waiting for the Moon, 1987, Mannequin, 1987, Less Than Zero, 1987, Kansas, 1988, Fresh Horses, 1988, Weekend at Bernie's, 1989, Jours tranquilles à Clichy, 1990, Dr. M, 1990, Year of the Gun, 1991, Only You, 1992, Weekend at Bernie's II, 1993, The Joy Luck Club, 1993, Night of the Running Man, 1994, Getting In, 1994, Dead Funny, 1994, Mrs. Parker and the Vicious Circle, 1994, Dream Man, 1995, Mulholland Falls, 1996, Everything Relative, 1996, Stag, 1997, I Woke Up Early the Day I Died, 1998, Bela Donna, 1998, I'm Losing You, 1998, A Twist of Faith, 1999, New World Disorder, 1999, New Waterford Girl, 1999, Nowhere in Sight, 2000, Diggity: A Home at Last, 2001, Standard Time, 2002, 2BPerfectlyHonest, 2004, The Orphan King, 2005, The Spiderwick Chronicles, 2008, The Good Guy, 2009; (TV films) Common Pursuit, 1992, The Courtyard, 1995, Hostile Force, 1996, The Christmas Tree, 1996, Escape Clause, 1996, A Father for Brittany, 1998, Perfect Assassins, 1988, A Storm in Summer, 2000, Jackie Bouvier Kennedy Onassis, 2000, The Secret Life of Zoey, 2002, Straight from the Heart, 2003, Crusader, 2004, The Way, 2006; (TV series) Kingdom Hospital, 2004, E-Ring, 2005; actor, dir. (TV series) Lipstick Jungle, 2008—09; actor(guest appearances): (TV series) Law & Order: Special Victims Unit, 2000, Law & Order, 2003, The Twilight Zone, 2003, Monk, 2003, Law & Order: Criminal Intent, 2007, Gossip Girl, 2009; writer, prodr. News for the Church, 2004. Office: c/o One Entertainment Penthouse 12 West 57th St New York NY 10019*

MCCARTHY, APRIL C., elementary school educator; d. James B. and Dorothy Seto; m. Gary W. McCarthy, July 5, 1975; children: Michael, Gregory. BS in Art Edn., SUNY, Buffalo, 1975; MS in Elem. Edn., SUNY, Brockport, 1988, cert. advanced study in ednl. adminstrn. Cert. in reality therapy William Glasser Inst., in schs. attuned All Kinds Minds Inst., herbal cons. Elem. tchr. Medina Ctrl. Sch. Dist., NY, 1988—. Mem.: ASCD, NY State Reading Assn., Niagara Frontier Reading Coun. (dir. membership 2004—07).

MCCARTHY, BRIAN NELSON, real estate developer; b. Detroit, May 24, 1945; s. Andrew Nelson and Ruth Elizabeth (Hill) McC.; children: Amanda Lang, Kelly Elizabeth, Meghan Virginia, Connor Michael; m. Valerie Reiheld, 1997. BS in Engring. Sci., Oakland U., 1966; MBA, Harvard U., 1972. Engr. Gen. Motors Corp., Pontiac, Mich., 1965-67; co-owner Sound Wave Systems, Costa Mesa, Calif., 1971-78; CFO, controller A&W Gershenson Co., Farmington, Mich., 1972-75; pres. Devel. Group, Inc., Southfield, Mich., 1975—81; CEO Brichard & Co., San Francisco, 1982-87; pres. Watermark Corp., Sausalito, Calif., 1987—92, Indian Wells Water Co., Inc., Sausalito, 1993—2000; dir. Co-Investor Group, Sonoma, Calif., 2000—01; chmn., pres. Southfork Devel. Group, El Dorado Hills, Calif., 2002—06; CEO Watermark Property Group, Balt., 2008—. Rear adm. USNR, 1966-96, res. Recipient Navy Achievement medal, Navy Commendation medal with gold star, Joint Commendation medal, Navy Meritorious Svc. medal with 2 gold stars, Joint Meritorious Svc. medal with oak leaf cluster, others. Mem. Navy Supply Corps Assn. (bd. dirs. 1987-96). Republican. Office: 1800 2nd St Ste 705 Sarasota FL 34236-5961 Office Phone: 941-350-9026, 941-870-7910, 410-982-0602. Personal E-mail: bnmccarthy@gmail.com. Business E-Mail: brian.mccarthy@watermarkpg.com.

MCCARTHY, CAROLYN, United States Representative from New York; b. Bklyn., Jan. 5, 1944; m. Dennis McCarthy (dec. Dec. 1993); 1 child. LPN, Glen Cove Nursing Sch., NY, 1964. LPN St. Francis and Winthrop Hosp., 1964—93; gun safety activist, 1994—97; mem. US Congress from 4th NY dist., 1997—. Mem. edn. & labor, fin. svcs. com., US Congress; chairwoman subcommittee on healthy families and communities. Recipient numerous awards including being honored by the US Women's Soccer Team and Oprah Winfrey; named one of 100 LI Influentials, Newsday, 50 Most Effective Legislators in Congress, Congl. Quar., Nine Mothers and Shakers, Redbook mag., America's 100 Most Important Women, Ladies' Home Jour.; named to Most Impact by Women, Advertising Age mag., 1999. Mem.: New Yorkers Against Gun Violence, NYC Stop the Violence Campaign, Guns for Goods, Ams. Against Gun Violence (hon.). Democrat. Roman Catholic. Office: US House Reps 106 Cannon House Office Bldg Washington DC 20515-3204 Office Phone: 202-225-5516.*

MCCARTHY, CONNIE KEARNS, university librarian; BA, Rosary Coll., Ill., 1968; MSLS, Catholic U., 1972. Past cataloger Folger U. Shakespeare Libr.; asst. univ. libr. for collections George Washingtn U.; assoc. univ. libr. William R. Perkins Libr. Duke U.; dean univ. libr. Coll. William and Mary, 1997—. Chair steering com. Virtual Libr. of Va.; chair edtl. bd. CHOICE jour. Mem.: ALA. Office: Earl Gregg Swem Libr Coll William and Mary PO Box 8794 Williamsburg VA 23187-8794 Office Phone: 757-221-3055. Office Fax: 757-221-2635. E-mail: ckmcca@wm.edu.

MCCARTHY, CORMAC (CHARLES JOSEPH MCCARTHY), writer; b. Providence, July 20, 1933; s. Charles Joseph and Gladys (McGrail) McCarthy; m. Lee Holleman, 1961 (div.); 1 child, Cullen; m. Anne DeLisle, 1967 (div. 1981); m. Jennifer Winkley; 1 child, John Francis. Author: (novels) The Orchard Keeper, 1965 (William Faulkner Found. award, 1965), Outer Dark, 1968, Child of God, 1974, Suttree, 1979, Blood Meridian, or The Evening Redness in the West, 1985, All the Pretty Horses, 1992 (Nat. Book award for fiction, 1992, Nat. Book Critics Circle award for fiction, 1993), The Crossing, 1994, Cities of the Plain, 1998, No Country for Old Men, 2005, The Road, 2006 (James Tait Black Meml. Prize for fiction, 2006, Pulitzer Prize for fiction, 2007, Quill Book award for gen. fiction, 2007), (screenplays) The Gardener's Son, 1976, (plays) The Stonemason, 1995, The Sunset Limited, 2006. Served in USAF, 1953—57. Recipient Jean Stein award, AAAL, 1991; named a Traveling fellow, 1965—66, Guggenheim fellow, 1976; grantee for creative writing, Ingram-Merrill Found., 1960, Rockefeller Found., 1966, MacArthur Found., 1981. Mailing: c/o Amanda Urban ICM 40 W 57th St New York NY 10019

MCCARTHY, DANIEL ANTHONY, biology professor; s. Frederick John and Milagros McCarthy; m. Heather Picot Walton, Oct. 14, 2001; children: Jelena Tatem, Calypsa Milagros, Marina Mercer. PhD, U. London, 2001. Comdr. USNR, 1999—2006; asst. prof. biology and marine sci. Jacksonville U., Fla., 2004—; rsch. assoc. Smithsonian Instn., Washington, 2004—. Recipient Faculty award, Jacksonville U., 2007—08. Office: Jacksonville Univ 2800 University Blvd North Jacksonville FL 32211 Business E-Mail: dmccart1@ju.edu.

MCCARTHY, DANIEL WILLIAM, management consultant; b. Syracuse, NY, Apr. 15, 1952; s. William Cornelius and Ruth Francis (Geller) McC.; m. Mary Coleen Kisil, Jan. 17, 1987; children: Katherine M., Kevin D., Patrick W. BA in Polit. Sci., SUNY, Geneseo, 1974; MBA, NYU, 1982. Asst. buyer Abraham & Straus, Bklyn., 1976—78; buyer Lord & Taylor, NYC, 1978—80; cons. Touche Ross, Newark, 1982—87; sr. mgr. Deloitte & Touche, NYC, 1987—93; dir. Coach Leatherware, NYC, 1993—94; prin. Greenvale Consulting Group, Poughkeepsie, NY, 1994—2000; pres. Retex Cons. Group, NYC, 2000—02, Greenvale Cons. Group, LLC, NY, 2002—03; dir. spl. projects Island Pacific, Inc., 2003—06; prin. Greenvale Cons. Group, 2006—07; ops. mgr. N.Am. Wipro Retail, 2007—. Author: Point of Sale - Current Trends and Beyond, 1986; contbr. articles to profl. jours. Mem. Town of Poughkeepsie Hist. Planning Commn. Named Open Foil Champion, North Atlantic Veterans, 2000, 2001, 2004. Mem. Nat. Retail Fedn., Inst. Mgmt. Cons. Roman Catholic. Avocations: wine collecting, ballet, fencing, architecture, investing. Personal E-mail: danmcd@msn.com.

MCCARTHY, DAVID BRUCE, minister; b. Owatonna, Minn., Mar. 8, 1955; s. Harold Charles and Barbara Susan (Kaercher) McC.; m. Joan Christina LaFollette, Oct. 12, 1986. BA cum laude, Carleton Coll., 1977; AM, Duke U., 1979; MDiv with distinction, Harvard U., 1985; PhD, Duke U., 2003. Ordained to ministry Presbyn. Ch., 1986. Pastor John Hus Presbyn. Ch., Binghamton, N.Y., 1986-93; mem. staff Grad. Inst. Duke U., 1993-2000; interim pastor Cross Roads Presbyn. Ch., 1994-96; asst. prof. religion, chaplain to coll. Hastings (Nebr.) Coll., 2001—06; assoc. prof. religion, chaplain Hastings Coll., Nebr., 2006—. Mem. 1st

Ward Clergy, Binghamton, 1986-93, convener, 1987-89; dir. Metro Interfaith, 1988-93; moderator Broad Ave.-North Presbyn. Ch., Binghamton, 1989-91; moderator Permanent Jud. Commn., Presbytery of Susquehanna Valley, 1986-92, mem. com. on preparation for ministry, 1986-92, bills and overtures com., 1988-91, presbytery coun., 1990-91; mem. ecumenical and worship com. Broome County Coun. Chs., N.Y., 1989-92; mem. planning, evaluation and rev. com. Synod of N.E., 1990-91, presbytery rep. synod mission coun., 1990-91, commr., 1990, mem. synod permanent jud. commn., 1992-98; mem. faculty Ghost Ranch, Abiquiu, N.Mex., 1991, 96; vis. instr. Duke U., 1999-2001. Editor Report from Susquehanna Valley Presbytery, 1989-90; contbr. author: The Organizational Revolution, 1991, Concise Encyclopedia of Preaching, 1995, Dictionary of Heresy Trials in American Chrisianity, 1997, Encyclopedia of Religious Controversies in the United States, 1997, American National Biography, 1999, African American National Biography, 2007. Capt. Unitd Way Appeal, Broome County, 1990—91; chair CPM Presbytery of Ctrl. Nebr., 2001—03, 2009—; moderator PJC Presbyn. of Ctrl. Nebr., 2001—05, vice moderator, 2007; mem. presbytery coun. Presbytery of Ctrl. Nebr., 2001—07, 2008—09. Mem. Am. Soc. Ch. History, Am. Acad. Religion, Soc. for Scientific Study Religion, Witherspoon Soc. (editorial asst. 1989-93), Presbyn. Hist. Soc. Office: Hastings Coll 710 Turner Ave Hastings NE 68901

MCCARTHY, DENIS M., medical educator; b. Galway, Ireland, July 16, 1938; s. Michael Denis and Mary Beatrice McCarthy; m. Sallie Susan Schirmer; children: Michael, Kevin, Anne, Brian, Jessica, Ben. MB BCh, BAO, U. Coll. Dublin, Ireland, 1962, MD, 1970; BSc in Physiology and Biochemistry with 1st Class honors, U. Coll. Cork, Ireland, 1963, MSc in Physiology, 1965. Cert. E.C.F.M.G. Exam., 1970, bd. eligible ABIM, 1973, in FLEX exam. State Bd., Md., 1974; gastroenterologist Md., 1975, registered Eng., 1963, Ireland, 1963, Calif., 1976, Washington, 1977, Va., 1977, lic. N.Mex., 1980. Attended U. Coll. Dublin, Med. Sch., 1956—62; med. internship Mater Misericordial Hosp., Dublin, 1962—63, sr. med. registrar, gastroenterology, 1969—70; asst. lectr. physiology U. Coll. Cork, 1963—65; med. residency London U., Royal Postgrad. Med. Sch. Fedn., Hammersmith, Dept. Gastroenterology, 1966—69, Brompton Hosp. Diseases Chest, Cardio-Pulmonary and Pediat. Cardiology Dept., London, 1966—69, Royal Free Hosp., Gastroenterology Dept., London, 1967—69; postdoc. rsch. fellow, biochemistry and gastroenterology U. Calif. Med. Ctr., San Francisco, 1970—74, asst. prof. medicine, gastroenterology, Vet. Adminstrn. Hosp., 1973—74; vis. scientist NIH, Bethesda, Md., 1974—77, attending physician, clin. ctr., 1974—80, supr., clin. rsch. digestive diseases, 1974—80, sr. investigator, Digestive Disease Br., 1977—80, capt., USPHS, 1977—80, dir., 2006; prof. medicine, GI U. N.Mex., Sch. Med., Albuquerque, 1980—, adj. prof. biochemistry, adv. com., NIH clin. rsch., exec. com., chief gastroenterology, 1988—2000, dir., GI fellowship tng. program, 1988—2001; chief gastroenterology Vets. Adminstrn. Health Care Svc., N.Mex. Regional Fed. Med. Ctr., 1980—2002, hepatologist, 2007, adj. prof., sect. gastroenterology and hepatology. Mem. US Food and Drug Adminstrn., cons., gastrointestinal and arthritis adv. com., 1985—92. Contbr. scientific papers to profl. med. jours., chapters to books. Recipient Leonard prize, Mater Hosp., Dublin, 1962, Gold medal, 1962, Irish Nat. Maternity Hosp., 1962; named one of Am. Top Physicians, Consumer Rsch. Coun. America, 2007. Master: RCP (fellow specialty bds., Ireland 1975, fellow specialty bds., London 1998); fellow: ACP; mem.: Am. Digestive Disease Soc. (exec. com. 1975—80, v.p. 1978—80, bd. mem. 1980—84), NY Acad. Scis., Western Assn. Physicians, NY Acad. Scis., Western Soc. Clin. Investigation, Brit. Soc. Gastroenterology, Gastroent. Rsch. Group, Am. Gastroent. Assn. (fellow 2006—, Disting. Mentorship award, Am. Digestive Health Found. 2005). Democrat. Roman Catholic. Avocations: music, history, travel, mountain climbing, skiing. Office: NM Vets Adminstrn Health Care Svc Med Ctr 111F Dept Vet Affairs 1501 San Pedro Blvd SE Albuquerque NM 87108 also: Univ NM HSC Divsn Gastroenterology MSC10 5550 Albuquerque NM 87131 Home: 3012 Don Quixote Dr NW Albuquerque NM 87104-3036 Office Fax: 505-256-2803; Home Fax: 505-256-5751. Business E-Mail: denis.mccarthy2@med.va.gov, bmccarthy@salud.unm.edu.

MCCARTHY, DENNIS M., federal agency administrator, retired military officer; b. Cleveland, Ohio, Feb. 1, 1945; m. Rosemary McCarthy; children: Sean, Michael. BA, U. Dayton, 1967; JD, Capital U. Law Sch., 1975. Advanced through ranks to lt. gen. USMC, 2001, ret., 2005; communications officer 1st Battalion 13th Marines, Vietnam, 1968-69; asst. ops. officer Schs. Demo. Troops, Quantico, Va.; judge advocate, military judge Camp Lejeune, N.C., 1978; pvt. practice law Columbus, Ohio, 1979—; dir. tactical exercise evaluation, control group Marine Corps. Air Ground Combat Ctr., 29 Palms, Calif.; commanding gen. Marine Corps. Res. Support Command, 1993-95, IMACE, 1995-97, 3d Marine Divsn., 1997; deputy dir. Ops. U.S. Atlantic Command, 1997-99, dir., 1999; dir. reserve affairs USMC, Quantico, Va., 2000—01; comdr. Marine Forces Reserve, New Orleans, 2001—05; asst. sec. for reserve affairs US Dept. Def., Washington, 2009—; exec. dir. Reserve Officers Assn., 2005—09; chmn. Medifast, Inc. Served US Marine Corps. Office: US Dept Def Reserve Affairs 1500 Defense Pentagon Washington DC 20301*

MCCARTHY, DOROTHY A. (LANDERS), educator; d. Dorthy Landers; m. Philip Francis McCarthy; children: Colleen, Timothy, Kevin, Shawn. BA, Elms Coll., Chicopee, Mass., 1971; MEd, Nat. Louis U., Heidelberg, Germany, 1990. Tchr. Rochester Cath. Sch., NH, 1979—80, Dept. Defense Schs., Wuerzburg, Germany, 1980—83, Vogelweh, 1983—86, Ramstein, 1986—90, Naples, Italy, 1990—2004, Ft. Stewart, Ga., 2004—. Adv., students of Dept. Def. Schs. Nat. Honor Soc., Italy & Germany, 1980—2004; social studies task mem. Dept. Def. Schs.; visitation team mem. North Ctrl. Accreditation; coord. global svc. and humanitarian projects NCAA. Mem. Italia chpt. Phi Delta Kappa, 1992—. Mem.: Nat. Coun. Social Studies, Fed. Edn. Assn. Avocation: travel. Office: Brittin Elem Sch 2772 Hero Rd Fort Stewart GA 31313 Office Phone: 912-368-3324.

MCCARTHY, EDITH A., pediatrician, educator; b. Elizabeth, NJ, Sept. 22, 1964; BA in biology with honors, NYU; MD, U. Medicine and Dentistry NJ, Robert Wood Johnson Med. Sch., 1992. Cert. Pediat., 1997, Neonatal-Perinatal Medicine, 2005. Resident pediat. Cornell Med. Ctr.-NY Hosp., 1992—95, fellowship neonatology, 1997—2000, instr. pediat., child protection rep., clin. dir. Children's Advocate Ctr. of Manhattan; pvt. practice Watchung Pediat., NJ, 1996—97; asst. prof. pediat. to clin. asst. prof. NYU Sch. Medicine; attending NYU Med. Ctr.; mem. NYU Neonatology Assocs.; staff Bellevue Hosp. Ctr.; founder Care Intensive Pediatrics, PLLC, NYC. Contbr. articles to med. jours. Office: Care Intensive Pediat 244 E 32nd St New York NY 10016 Office Phone: 212-726-0005. Office Fax: 212-726-9073. E-mail: info@careintensivepediatrics.com.

MC CARTHY, EDWARD, JR., retired lawyer; b. Jacksonville, Fla., Jan. 17, 1931; s. Edward and Margaret R. (Durkee) McC.; m. Julie Beville Fant, May 18, 1962; children: Mitchell Fant, Beville Durkee, Edward III. AB, Princeton U., 1953; LLB, U. Colo., 1956. Ptnr. firm Strang & McCarthy, Montrose, Colo., 1956-59, McCarthy, Adams & Foote, Jacksonville, 1959-68, Freeman, Richardson, Watson, Slade, McCarthy & Kelly, P.A., Jacksonville, 1968-80; pvt. practice, 1980—96. Past pres. Riverside Hosp. of Jacksonville; trustee Edna Sproull Williams Found., Eunice Pitt Odom Semmes Found., Jess & Brewster J. Durkee Found. Mem. ABA, Fla. Bar Assn., Jacksonville Bar Assn., Timuquana Country Club, Univ. Club Republican. Episcopalian. Home: 4401 Lakeside Dr Apt 804 Jacksonville FL 32210-3362 also: PO Box 2257 Highlands NC 28741-2257

MC CARTHY, FRANK MARTIN, oral surgeon, educator; b. Olean, NY, Aug. 27, 1924; s. Frank Michael and Joan (Quinn) McC.; m. Julia Richmond, Nov. 24, 1949; children: Robert Lee, Joan Lee. BS, U. Pitts., 1943, DDS, 1945, MD, 1949; MS in Oral Surgery, Georgetown U., 1954; ScD (hon.), St. Bonaventure U., 1956. Med. intern Mercy Hosp., Pitts., 1949-50; practice oral surgery LA, 1954-75; tchg. fellow Georgetown U., 1952-53; rsch. fellow NIH, 1953-54; prof. oral surgery U. So. Calif. Sch. Dentistry, 1966-75, prof., chmn. sect. anesthesia and medicine, 1975-90, prof. emeritus, 1990—, chmn. dept. surg. scis., 1979-84, assoc. dean adminstrv. affairs, 1977-79, asst. dean hosp. affairs, 1979-84. Dir. anesthesiology U.So. Calif. oral surgery sect. L.A. County Hosp., 1958-89; clin. supr., lectr. dental hygiene program Pasadena City Coll., 1992—; v.p. Am. Dental Bd. Anesthesiology, 1984-89; lectr. in field; mem. adv. panel on dentistry sect. anesthesizing agts. Nat. Fire Protection Assn., 1971-79; mem. Am. Nat. Stds. Com., 1974-86, 95—; cons. in field. Author: Emergencies in Dental Practice, 1967, rev., 1972, 79, Medical Emergencies in Dentistry, 1982, Safe Treatment of the Medically Compromised Patient, 1987, Essentials of Safe Dentistry for the Medically Compromised Patient, 1989; mem. editorial bd.: Calif. Dental Assn. Jour; contbr. articles to profl. publs. Bd. councilors Sch. Dentistry, U. So. Calif., 1972-75. Served as lt., M.C. USNR, 1950-52. Recipient Lifetime Achievement award, So. Calif. Orofacial Acad., Palm Springs, Calif., 2006. Fellow Internat. Assn. Oral Surgeons (founder), Am. Coll. Dentists, Internat. Coll. Dentists; mem. ADA (editl. bd. jour.), Am. Dental Soc. Anesthesiology (Heidbrink award 1977), Am. Assn. Oral-Max Surgeons (chmn. anesthesia com. 1971), So. Calif. Soc. Oral Surgeons (pres. 1974), Calif., L.A. County Dental Assns., Delta Tau Delta, Psi Omega, Phi Rho Sigma, Omicron Kappa Upsilon. Home and Office: 480 S Orange Grove Blvd Apt 11 Pasadena CA 91105-1720

MCCARTHY, G. DANIEL, lawyer; b. Butte, Mont., Mar. 23, 1949; s. George Denis and Mary Agnes (Kiely) McC.; m. Carolyn M. Scully, June 19, 1976; children: Brendan, Katie, Kelly, Sean. BA, U. Dayton, 1971; JD, U. Notre Dame, 1974; AMP, Harvard U., 1994. Bar: Md. 1974, D.C. 1975, U.S. Ct. Appeals (D.C. cir.) 1976, Pa. 1977, N.Y. 1985, U.S. Ct. Appeals (10th cir.) 1985. Assoc. Bilger & Blair, Washington, 1974-77, 79-80; asst. U.S. atty. U.S. Dist. Ct. (ea. dist.) Pa., Phila., 1977-78; assoc. Abourezk, Shack & Mendenhall, Washington, 1980-83; atty. AT&T, NYC, 1983-85; v.p., gen. counsel and sec. AT&T Credit Corp., Morristown, NJ, 1985-89; sr. v.p., gen. counsel, sec., chief risk mgmt. officer, AT&T Capital Corp., Morristown, NJ, 1990-96; v.p., gen. counsel, sec. Compaq Fin. Svcs. Corp., Murray Hill, NJ, 1996—2002; v.p. govt. affairs, dep. gen. counsel Compaq Computer Corp., Houston, 2001—02; v.p., gen. counsel, sec. Hewlett-Packard Fin. Svcs. Co., Murray Hill, NJ, 2002—. Vis. lectr. Marymount Coll., Arlington, Va., 1979-83; mem. adv. coun. U. Dayton, Coll. of Arts and Scis., 1993-97, chmn., 1994-96; bd. dirs. Hewlett-Packard Europe Fin., Ltd., HP Fin. Svcs. Internat. Holdings Co., Hewlett-Packard Internat. Bank PLC. Mem.: DC Bar Assn., Fairmount Country Club (Chatham, NJ) (bd. dirs. 2002—07). Avocations: golf, fly fishing. Office: HP Fin Svcs Co 420 Mountain Ave New Providence NJ 07974-0006 Office Phone: 908-898-4003. Business E-Mail: dan.mccarthy@hp.com.

MCCARTHY, HAROLD CHARLES, retired insurance company executive; b. Madelia, Minn., Dec. 5, 1926; s. Charles and Merle (Humphry) McC.; m. Barbara Kaercher, June 24, 1949; children: David, Susan. BA, Carleton Coll., Northfield, Minn., 1950; postgrad. With Federated Mut. Ins. Co., Owatonna, Minn., 1950-67; with Meridian Mut. Ins. Co., Indpls., 1967-91, exec. v.p., then exec. v.p., gen. mgr., 1972-75, pres., 1975-90, bd. dirs., past chmn. bd., 1990-91; past pres. North Meridian Bus. Group; past pres., chmn. bd. Meridian Ins. Group, Inc. Chmn. bd., dir. Meridian Life Ins. Co.; past chmn., exec. com., bd. dirs. Ind. Ins. Inst.; mem. adv. bd. Harbor Fed. Savs. Bank. Former mem. Metl. Devel. Commn., Corp. Cmty. Coun.; bd. dirs. Meth. Health Found., Family Services Assn., Boy Scouts Am., Indian River Symphony Assn.; trustee Butler U. With USNR, 1944-46. Named Sagamore of the Wabash. Mem. Skyline Club (Indpls.), Indian River Golf Club. Republican.

MCCARTHY, IAN J., construction executive; BS, City U., London. Chartered civil engr. With Kier Ltd., 1980—81; pres., CEO Beazer Homes USA, Inc., Atlanta, 1989—, bd. dirs., 1994—. Dir. Beazer Far East, 1981—91; bd. dirs. Builder Homesite, Inc. Chmn. HomeAid's Nat. Adv. Bd.; trustee Woodruff Arts Ctr., Atlanta; bd. dirs. Metro Atlanta C. of C. Named to Calif. Bldg. Industry Hall of Fame, 2004. Office: Beazer Homes 1000 Abernathy Rd Ste 1200 Atlanta GA 30328-5606 Office Phone: 770-829-3700. Office Fax: 770-481-2808.

MCCARTHY, J. THOMAS, lawyer, educator; b. Detroit, July 2, 1937; s. John E. and Virginia M. (Hanlon) McC.; m. Nancy Irene Orrell, July 10, 1976 BS, U. Detroit, 1960; JD, U. Mich., 1963. Bar: Calif. 1964. Assoc. Julian Caplan, San Francisco, 1963—66; prof. law U. San Francisco, 1966—; counsel Morrison and Foerster, 2001—. Founding dir. McCarthy Inst. Intellectual Property and Tech. Law; mem. Trademark Rev. Commn., 1986—88; cons. in field. Author: McCarthy on Trademarks and Unfair Competition, 7 vols., 4th edit., 1996, McCarthy on Rights of Publicity and Privacy, 1987, 2d edit., 2000, McCarthy's Desk Encyclopedia of Intellectual Property, 3d edit., 2004. Recipient Jefferson medal N.J. Intellectual Property Assn., 1994, Ladas award Brand Names Ednl. Found., 1997, Pattishall medal Brand Names Found., 2000, Pres.'s award Internat. Trademark Assn., 2003. Mem. IEEE, Am. Intellectual Property Law Assn. (Watson award 1965, Centennial award in Trademark law 1997), Am. Law Inst. (adv. com. on restatement of law of unfair competition).

MCCARTHY, JEANNE, literature and language professor; PhD, U. Tex., Austin, 2000. Vis. asst. prof. Oglethorpe U., Atlanta, 2000—. Business E-Mail: jmccarthy@oglethorpe.edu.

MCCARTHY, JENNY, actress; b. Chgo., Nov. 1, 1972; m. John Mallory Asher, Sept. 11, 1999 (div. 2005); 1 child, Evan Joseph Asher. Student Sch. Nursing, So. Ill. U. Spokeswoman Jose Cuervo Tequilla. Appeared in films Things to Do in Denver When You're Dead, 1995, The Stupids, 1996, BASEketball, 1998, Diamonds, 1999, Scream 3, 2000, Thank Heaven, 2001, The Perfect You, 2002, Scary Movie 3, 2003, Dirty Love, 2005 (also writer, prodr.), John Tucker Must Die, 2006, Witless Protection, 2008; TV films Python, 2000, Honey Vicarro, 2001, Lingerie Bowl, 2006, Santa Baby, 2006; TV shows The Jenny McCarthy Show, 1997, Jenny, 1997-98, The Bad Girl's Guide, 2005; host game show Singled Out, MTV, 1995-96, Party @ the Palms, 2005; guest appearances Silk Stalkings, 1994, Mr. Show with Bob and David, 1995, Baywatch, 1996, Wings, 1996, Home Improvement, 1999, Going to California, 2001, Drew Carey Show, 2002, Fastlane, 2003, Just Shoot Me! (3 episodes 2000-03), Charmed, 2003, Wanda at Large, 2003, Less Than Perfect, 2003, Wild Card, 2004 All About the Andersons, 2004, One on One (4 episodes 2003-04), Hope & Faith, 2004, What I Like About You, 2005, Stacked, 2005, My Name is Earl, 2006; featured photographs in Playboy mag., 1993-96, 98, 05, including as Miss Oct. 1993, then as Playmate of Yr., 1994; author Jen-X, 1997, Belly Laughs: The Naked Truth About Pregnancy and Childbirth, 2004 (NY Times Bestseller list, 2004), Baby Laughs: The Naked Truth About the First Year of Mommyhood, 2005 (NY Times Bestseller list, 2005), Louder Than Words: A Mother's Journey in Healing Autism, 2007. Named one of 50 Most Beautiful People in the World, People mag., 1996. Avocation: kickboxing. Address: c/o United Talent Agy 9560 Wilshire Blvd Ste 500 Beverly Hills CA 90212-2427

MCCARTHY, JOHN, computer scientist, educator; b. Boston, Sept. 4, 1927; s. Patrick Joseph and Ida McCarthy; children: Susan Joanne, Sarah Kathleen, Timothy Talcott. BS in Math., Calif. Inst. Tech., 1948; PhD in Math., Princeton U., 1951; Degree (hon.), Linkoping U., Sweden, Polytechnic U., Madrid, Colby Coll., Dublin and Concordia U., Montreal. Procter Fellow Princeton U., 1950—51, Higgins Rsch. instr. in math., 1951—53; acting asst. prof. math. Stanford U., 1953—55; asst. prof. math. Dartmouth Coll., 1955—58; asst. prof. comm. sciences MIT, Cambridge, 1958—61, assoc. prof. comm. sciences, 1961—62; prof. computer sci. Stanford U., 1962—2001, Charles M. Pigott prof. Sch. Engring., 1987—94, prof. emeritus computer scis., 2001—. Academic advisor Nat. Legal Ctr. for Pub. Info., 1976—80; fellow Ctr. for Advanced Study in the Behavioral Sciences, 1979—80; Bobby R. Inman prof. computer sci. U. Tex., 1987; bd. dir. Info. Internat., Inc., 1962—95, Inference Corp., 1983—91, Mad Intelligent Systems, 1987—91. Contbr. articles to profl. jours.; mem. editl. bd. Artificial Intelligence Jour., 1975—. Served with AUS, 1945-46. Recipient first Rsch. Excellence award, Internat. Joint Conf. on Artificial Intelligence, 1985, Kyoto prize, Inamori Found., 1988, Nat. Medal of Sci., NSF, 1990, Fellow award, Computer History Mus., 1999; named Disting. Alumnus, Calif. Inst. Tech.; Sloan Fellow in Phy. Sci., 1957—59. Fellow: Am. Assn. Artificial Intelligence (pres. 1983—84); mem.: NAE, NAS, AAAS, Am. Math. Soc., Assn. for Computing Machinery (A.M. Turing award 1971), Am. Acad. Arts and Scis., Sigma Xi. Achievements include invention of LISP programming language in 1958; circumscription method of non-monotonic reasoning in 1978; coined the term Artifical Intelligence in 1955. Home: 885 Allardice Way Stanford CA 94305-1050 Office: Stanford U Rm 208 Gates Bldg 2A Computer Sci Dept Stanford CA 94305-9020 Office Phone: 650-723-4430. Office Fax: 650-725-7411. Business E-Mail: jmc@cs.stanford.edu. E-mail: mccarthy@stanford.edu.

MCCARTHY, JOHN EDWARD, bishop emeritus; b. Houston, June 21, 1930; s. George Gaskell and Grace Veronica (O'Brien) McCarthy. Attended, St. Mary's Sem., Houston, 1949-56; MA, St. Thomas U., Houston, 1979. Ordained priest Archdiocese of Galveston-Houston, 1956; served various Houston Cath. parishes; exec. dir. Nat. Bishops Com. for Spanish speaking, 1966-68; asst. dir. Social Action Office, US Cath. Conf., 1967-69; exec. dir. Tex. Cath. Conf., Houston, 1973-79; ordained bishop, 1979; aux. bishop Diocese of Galveston-Houston, 1979—85; bishop Diocese of Austin, Tex., 1986—2001, bishop emeritus, 2001—. Bd. dirs. Nat. Center for Urban Ethnic Affairs, Mexican-American Cultural Ctr., Sisters of Charity of the Incarnate Word, Houston, 1981-, St. Thomas U., Houston, 1980—. Mem. Cath. Conf. for Urban Ministry. Democrat. Roman Catholic. Office: Chancery PO Box 13327 Austin TX 78711-3327

MCCARTHY, JONATHAN PAUL, economist; b. Britt, Iowa, Dec. 8, 1957; s. Henry Felix and Lucille McC.; m. Diana Marie Shaw, Aug. 23, 1997. BS summa cum laude, U. Wis., Parkside, 1980, MS, 1991; PhD, U. Wis., Madison, 1992. Tchg. asst. U. Wis., Madison, 1986-87, rsch. asst., 1987-90, lectr. Whitewater, 1990-91; economist Fed. Res. Bank, NYC, 1992—2004; sr. economist Fed. Res. Bank N.Y.C., 2004—. Vis. economist Bank Internat. Settlements, Basel, Switzerland, 1997-98 Contbr. articles to profl. jours. Mem. Am. Econ. Assn., Nat. Assn. Bus. Economists. Avocations: running, softball. Home: 288 Burns St Forest Hills NY 11375 Office: Fed Res Bank 33 Liberty St New York NY 10045-1003 Home Phone: 718-544-8043; Office Phone: 212-720-5645.

MCCARTHY, JOSEPH D., advertising agency executive; b. Salem, Mass., Oct. 16, 1955; s. James J. and Delia D. (O'Donnell) McCarthy. BA, Lake Forest Coll., 1978. Various positions to sr. v.p., mgmt. supr. Saatchi & Saatchi DFS, NYC, 1980—93; head global advt. Nike, Inc., 1993—2001; founding ptnr. advt. agy. McCarthy Mambro Bertino, Boston, 2001; v.p. worldwide advt. Johnson & Johnson, 2005—08; CEO Publicis Worldwide, NY, 2008—. Mem.: St. Nick's Hockey Club, Essex Hunt Club. Roman Catholic. Office: Publicis USA 4 Herald Sq 950 6th Ave New York NY 10001

MCCARTHY, JOSEPH GERALD, plastic surgeon, educator; b. Lowell, Mass., Nov. 28, 1938; s. Joseph H. and Eva (Murphy) McC.; m. Karlan von L. Sloan, June 6, 1964; children: Cara, Stephen. AB, Harvard U., 1960; MD, Columbia U. Coll. Physicians and Surgeons, 1964. Diplomate: Am. Bd. Surgery, Am. Bd. Plastic Surgery. Intern, gen. surgery Columbia-Presbyn. Med. Ctr., 1964—65, resident, plastic surgery, 1967—71, NYU Med. Ctr., NYC, 1971—73, dir., Inst. Reconstructive Plastic Surgery; Lawrence D. Bell prof. plastic surgery NYU Sch. Medicine, NYC, 1981—; attending physician Univ. Hosp.; vis. plastic surgeon Bellevue Hosp.; attending surgeon Manhattan Eye, Ear and Throat Hosp., N.Y.C. VA Hosp. Editor: Symposium on Diagnosis and Treatment of Craniofacial Anomalies, 1979, Plastic Surgery, 1990; assoc. editor Reconstructive Plastic Surgery, 1977, Jour. Plastic and Reconstructive Surgery, Jour. Craniofacial, Genetics and Developmental Biology; contbr. several articles to peer-reviewed jours.; cotbr. chpts. to books. Bd. trustee Nat. Found. for Facial Reconstruction; founding chmn. med. adv. bd. Smile Train. Lt. comdr. USPHS, 1965—67. Recipient Joseph Garrison Parker prize Columbia U., 1964, 1st prize Plastic Surgery Edn. found., 1980, James Barret Brown prize, 1991, 1st prize Am. Soc. Maxillofacial Surgeons, 1991, 93, 94, Surgical Pioneer award, U. Zurich, 2003, Clin. Excellence award, Castle Connolly Med. Ltd., 2007; Am. Cancer Soc. fellow Presbyn. Hosp., N.Y.C., 1969-70, prin. investigator NIH, 1974. Fellow ACS; mem. Am. Soc. Plastic and Reconstructuve Surgeons, Assn. Acad. Chairmen Plastic Surgery (pres. 1988-89), N.Y. Regional Soc. Plastic and Reconstructive Surgeons (pres. 1984-85), Am. Assn. Plastic Surgeons (historian 1990-93), Internat. Soc. Craniomaxillofacial Surgeons (pres. 1989-91), Northeastern Soc. Plastic Surgeons. Achievements include first to the concept of craniofacial distraction. Mailing: NYU Langone Med Ctr TCH 1 148 550 1st Ave New York NY 10016 Office: 722 Park Ave New York NY 10021 Office Phone: 212-263-5208. Office Fax: 212-988-7230.

MC CARTHY, JOSEPH MICHAEL, historian, educator; b. Lynn, Mass., Oct. 2, 1940; s. Joseph Donald and Josephine Johanna (Downing) Mc C.; m. Kathleen Theresa Wright, July 30, 1966; children: Joanna, Kristenmarie, Erika, Joseph Michael. AB, St. Johns Sem., 1961, AM candidate, 1961—63; AM, Boston Coll., 1968, PhD, 1972. Tchr. Bishop

Fenwick H.S., Peabody, Mass., 1964-67; fin. adminstr. Boston Coll., 1967-71, lectr. edn., 1971-74; prof. history and edn., dir. leadership programs Suffolk U., Boston, 1973—2006, prof. emeritus, 2006—. Vis. prof. Boston Coll., 1990; adj. lectr. Merrimack Coll., 1975, Boston U., 1973; prin. Ednl. Mgmt. Svcs., 1976—; gen. editor Garland Pub., 1979-92; bd. dirs. Inst. for Study of Academia, 1992-94. Author: An International List of Articles on the History of Education, 1977, Guinea-Bissau and Cape Verde Islands, 1977, Humanistic Emphases in the Educational Thought of Vincent of Beauvais, 1976, Pierre Teilhard de Chardin, 1981; assoc. editor The Urban and Social Chage Rev., 1969-72, asst. editor The Bureaucrat, Inc., 1974-76; contbr. articles to profl. jours. Pres. N.E. region Popular Culture Assn./Am. Culture Assn., 1998-99. Hearn scholar, 1959-61, fellow, 1961-63. Mem. Am. Cath. Hist. Assn., Soc. for Medieval and Renaissance Philosophy, Soc. Romanian Studies, Soc. Mil. History, East European Rsch. Inst., Phi Alpha Theta, Phi Delta Kappa. Home: Knockglen Farm 103 Fuller St Middleboro MA 02346-1700 Office: Suffolk U Beacon Hill Boston MA 02108 Office Phone: 617-573-8261. Business E-Mail: jmccarth@suffolk.edu.

MCCARTHY, KAREN P., former congresswoman, state legislator; b. Mass., Mar. 18, 1947; BS in English, Biology, U. Kans., 1969, MBA, 1985; MEd in English, U. Mo., Kansas City, 1976. Tchr. Shawnee Mission (Kans.) South High Sch., 1969-75, The Sunset Hill (Kans.) Sch., 1975-76; mem. Mo. House of Reps., Jefferson City, 1977-94; cons. govt. affairs Marion Labs., Kansas City, Mo., 1986-93; mem. U.S. Congress from 5th Mo. dist., Washington, 1995—2005; mem. commerce com.; mem. Ho. Select Com. on Homeland Security. Rsch. analyst pub. fin. dept. Stearn Bros. & Co., 1984-85, Kansas City, Mo.; rsch. analyst Midwest Rsch. Inst., econs. and mgmt. scis. dept., Kansas City, 1985-86. Del. Dem. Nat. Conv., 1992, Dem. Nat. Party Conf., 1982, Dem. Nat. Policy Com. Policy Commn., 1985-86; mem. Ho. Commerce Com. Energy and Power, Telecom., Trade and Consumer Protection; co-chair Dem. Caucus Task Health Care Reform. Recipient Outstanding Young Woman Am. award, 1977, Outstanding Woman Mo. award Phi Chi Theta, Woman of Achievement award Mid-Continent Coun. Girl Scouts U.S., 1983, 87, Annie Baxter Leadership award, 1993; named Conservation Legislator of Yr., Conservation Fed. Mo., 1987. Fellow Inst. of Politics; mem. Nat. Inst. of Politics; mem. Nat. Conf. on State Legis. (del. on trade and econ. devel. to Fed. Republic of Germany, Bulgaria, Japan, France and Italy, mem. energy com. 1978-84, fed. taxation, trade and econ. devel. com. 1986, chmn. fed. budget and taxation com. 1987, vice chmn. state fed. assembly 1988, pres.-elect 1993, pres. 1994), Nat. Dem. Inst. for Internat. Affairs (instr. No. Ireland 1988, Baltic Republics 1992, Hungary 1993). Democrat.

MCCARTHY, KATHLEEN JANE, law educator, school librarian; b. Lansing, Mich., Sept. 17, 1953; d. Robert John and Marthena DuBois McCarthy. BSEd with distinction, U. Mich., Ann Arbor, 1975; JD, Wayne State U., Detroit, 1987; MLS, Rutgers U., New Brunswick, NJ, 1989. Bar: NJ Bd. Bar Examiners (atty.) 2007. Assoc. prof. Seton Hall U. Sch. Law, Newark, 2001—, reference libr. Fulbright sr. specialist US Dept. State Bur. Edn. and Cultural Affairs, Washington, 2003—07; specialist ABA Rule of Law Initiative, Washington, 2007. Mem.: NJ Law Librs. Assn., Am. Assn. Law Librs. (West Pub. Co. award 1998), U. Mich. Women's Athletic Assn. Avocations: swimming, reading, travel, fly fishing. Office: Seton Hall Univ Sch Law One Newark Ctr Newark NJ 07102 Office Fax: 973-642-8748. Business E-Mail: mccartka@shu.edu.

MCCARTHY, KEVIN, United States Representative from California, former state legislator; b. Bakersfield, Calif., Jan. 26, 1965; m. Judy McCarthy; children: Connor, Meghan. Student, Bakersfield Coll.; BS in Bus. Adminstrn., Calif. State U., Bakersfield, 1989, MBA, 1994. Owner Bakersfield Batting Range, Kevin O's Deli; dist. dir. to Rep. Bill Thomas US Congress; mem. Calif. State Assembly, 2002—07, minority leader, 2004—06; mem. US Congress from 22nd Calif. dist., 2006—, asst. whip, 2006—, mem. agrl com., house adminstrn. com., joint com. on printing. Chmn. Young Republican Nat. Fedn., 1999—2001; bd. dirs. Kern Econ. Opportunity Corp. Trustee dist. bd. Kern C.C., 2000—02; exec. dir. McCarthy Found., 2000—; coach YMCA, 1999—; mem. Kern County Rep. Ctrl. Com., 1992—; bd. dirs. First Book, 2001—, Head Start, Kern County Food Bank. Mem.: Rotary. Republican. Baptist. Office: 1523 Longworth House Office Bldg Washington DC 20515 also: 4100 Empire Dr Ste 150 Bakersfield CA 93309*

MCCARTHY, KEVIN BART, lawyer; b. Washington, May 7, 1948; s. Frank Jeremiah and Frances Patricia (Bilderback) McC.; m. Patrice Borders, Apr. 3, 1971; children: Kevin Patrick, Charles Ryan, Molly Virginia, Bridget Louise, Moira Patrice. BBA, U. Notre Dame, 1970; JD, Ind. U., Indpls., 1973; diploma, U. St. Thomas Aquinas, Rome, 2008. Bar: Ind. 1973, U.S. Dist. Ct. (so. dist.) Ind. 1973, U.S. Ct. Appeals (7th cir.) 1974, Ill 1976, U.S. Dist. Ct. (cen. dist.) Ill. 1985, U.S. Ct. Appeals (6th cir.) 1985. Bail commr. Mcpl. Ct. Marion County, Indpls., 1972-73; asst. regional counsel Fed. Hwy. Adminstrn., Homewood, Ill., 1973-75; 1st asst., chief counsel Ill. Dept. Transp., Springfield, 1975-77; counsel com. on interstate and fgn. commerce, subcom. on transp. and commerce Ho. Reps., Washington, 1977-79, asst. counsel com. on pub. works and transp., 1979-82, counsel com. on pub. works and transp., 1982; pvt. practice law Springfield, 1982-87; acting U.S. trustee Dept. Justice, Springfield, 1987-88, U.S. trustee Indpls., 1988—. Pvt. practice Indpls. and Springfield. Mem. Ill. State Bd. Agrl. Advisors, 1987-88. Home: 5619 Surrey Hill Rd Indianapolis IN 46226-1561

MCCARTHY, MARK FRANCIS, lawyer; b. Boston, July 8, 1951; s. William Alfred and Martha Louise (Blodgett) McC.; m. Karen Marie Umerley; children: Kevin Francis, Daniel Henry. AB in Theology, Georgetown U., 1973, JD, 1976. Bar: Ohio 1976. Assoc. Sweeney, Mahon, & Vlad, Cleve., 1976-80; ptnr. Arter & Hadden, 1980—2003, Tucker Ellis & West LLP, Cleve., 2003—. Atty. asst. to bd. pres. Bd. Cuyahoga County Commrs., Cleve., 1976-80; adj. prof. Case Western Reserve Law Ctr., Cleve., 1986-. Active Greater Cleve. Growth Assn. Leadership Cleve., 1979-80; chmn. Parmadale, Parma, Ohio; trustee Western Res. Hist. Soc., 1978-80, Cath. Charities Found.; chmn. Cath. Charities Svcs. Corp.; trustee, sec. Cath. Cmty. Connection, Inc.; founder, sec., gen. counsel St. Martin De Porres HS, Cleve. Mem. Ohio Assn. Civil Trial Attys. (chmn. product liability sect. 1989—), Fedn. Ins. & Corp. Counsel, Ct. of Nisi Prius, Rowfant Club. Democrat. Roman Catholic. Avocations: book collecting, fly fishing, upland shooting. Home: 363 Britannia Pky Avon Lake OH 44012-2180 Office: Tucker Ellis & West LLP 1150 Huntington Bldg 925 Euclid Ave Cleveland OH 44115-1475 Home Phone: 440-930-2707; Office Phone: 216-696-3290. Business E-Mail: mfm@tuckerellis.com.

MCCARTHY, MARY ANN, counselor, educator; b. Barstow, Calif., Jan. 16, 1954; d. Thomas Edward and Helen C. (Krutell) McC. BA in Psychology, San Francisco State U., 1975; MS in Counseling, Calif. State U., Fullerton, 1995. Cert. pupil pers. svcs., 1995. Br. mgr., asst. v.p. Great American First Savings, Orange County, Calif., 1981-88, dist. mgr., v.p., 1988-90; dir. re-entry ctr. Saddleback Coll., Mission Viejo, Calif., 1995; intern coord. Orange Coast Coll., Costa Mesa, Calif., 1995—2000, adj. counselor, 2006—; assoc. prof. counseling, counselor Saddleback Coll., Mission Viejo, 1996—, Irvine Valley Coll., Calif., 2004—05; assoc. prof. Mid. Coll. HS. Vol. Beverly Manor Convalescent Hosp., Laguna Hills, Calif., 1989-94, Mission Viejo Animal Shelter, 1996-97, Big sister Big Bros./Big Sisters Am., Mission Viejo, 1980-83; vol. and cmty. rep. Trauma Intervention Program, 2002-2004, Am. Red Cross, 2007-, disaster svcs.; mem scholarship and ednl. coms. Saddleback Valley C. of C., Laguna Hills, 1982-86; spkr. local schs. Saddleback Valley Vol. Network, Mission Viejo, 1982-86; scholarship com Orange Coast Coll., 1997—. Recipient Outstanding Young Woman Am. award, 1983, Outstanding Part-time Faculty Orange Coast Coll., 2005-06; named Saddleback Valley Young Careerist, Bus. and Profl. Women, 1983, Outstanding Orange Coast Coll. Part Time Faculty, 2005-06. Mem. AAUW (past pres., editor, scholarship chair, pub. info. officer, sec. 1996-97), Am. Counseling Assn., Am. Coll. Counseling Assn., Calif. C.C. Counselor Assn., Calif. Assn. Counseling and Devel. Avocations: reading, travel. Home: 5 Martinique St Laguna Niguel CA 92677-5804 Office: Orange Coast Coll 2701 Fairview Rd Costa Mesa CA 92626-5563 also: Saddleback Coll 28000 Marquerite Pkwy Mission Viejo CA 92692

MCCARTHY, MICHAEL, military officer; s. Roger D. McCarthy and Mary Margret McGinn; m. Doreen Moore. BS, Mass. Maritime Acad., Buzzards Bay, 1997; MS, Nat. Grad. Sch., Falmouth, Mass., 2003; MBA, Averett U., Danville, Va., 2008. Cert. master instructor USCG, 2008. Lt. US Coast Guard, 1999—; maritime tech. safety advisor Sunoco Inc., Phila., 2003—06; instr. sch. chief US Coast Guard, Yorktown, Va., 2006—. Fin. mgmt. cons. Clean Harbors; B-120 Oil Spill, Buzzuards Bay, Mass., 2003. Contbr. articles to profl. jours. Active mem. Boy Scouts America, Suffolk, Va., 2006—09. Lt. / o3 U.S. Coast Guard, 1999—2009, Maine, Maryland; Virginia. Decorated Achievement medals US Coast Guard, Mil. Volunteerism medal US Mil., Armed Forces Svc. medal - Hurricane Katrina Dept. Def. Mem.: Am. Soc. Safety Engrs., SAR, Nat. Honor Soc., Eagle Scout Assn. Conservative. Roman Catholic. Avocations: travel, flute, woodworking. Personal E-mail: macanddoreen@verizon.net. Business E-Mail: michael.f.mccarthy@uscg.mil.

MCCARTHY, MICHAEL E., protective services official, director; MS in Human Resource Devel., St. John Fisher Coll., Rochester, NY, 2002. Police officer Rochester Police Dept., 1972—92; security dir. St. John Fisher Coll., 1998—. Bd. dirs. NE Coll. and U. Security Assn., 2003—08. Contbr. articles to profl. publs. 1st v.p. Assn. Rochester Police and Area Law Enforcement Retirees, 1999—2007. Recipient Pres. award, NE Coll. and U. Security Assn., 2007. Office: Saint John Fisher Coll 3690 E Ave Rochester NY 14618 Business E-Mail: mmccarthy@sjfc.edu.

MCCARTHY, MICHAEL SCOTT, biology professor, publishing executive; b. Joliet, Ill., Mar. 8, 1950; s. John Vernon and June Clara McCarthy; m. Barbara Arviso, Apr. 22, 1979; children: Kimberly Ann Kemper, Joseph Michael Shay, Kelly Louise Featherman, Adam Matthew Shay, Sarah Turner. MS, Ariz. State U., Tempe, 1986. Am. sign lang. cert. State CC Bd., 1995. Instrnl. coord. Rio Salado CC, Phoenix, 1988—91; dir. Frank X. Gordan Literacy Program, Mesa, Ariz., 1991—95; prof. Ea. Ariz. Coll., Thatcher, Ariz., 1995—, biology dept. head, 1999—. Owner Waterwheel Publs. LLC, Thatcher, 2003—. Author: (non-fiction - sci.) A Deeper Understanding of Life, (book) A Basic Understanding of the Body Anatomy & Physiology Lab Book, 2007. Scout leader Cub Scouts Am., Thatcher, 1998—2000; bd. mem. Discovery Park, Safford, Ariz., 1998—2004. Recipient Gov.'s Pride in Ariz. award, Ariz. Clean and Beautiful, 2003, Faculty Recognition award, Ea. Ariz. Coll., 1997, ASEAC Faculty Mem. of Yr., 2005—06, Nat. Literacy award, White Ho., 1991. Independent. Mem. Lds Ch. Avocation: travel. Home: PO Box 445 Thatcher AZ 85552 Office: Eastern Arizona Coll 615 N Stadium Thatcher AZ 85552 Business E-Mail: mike.mccarthy@eac.edu.

MCCARTHY, MIKE, professional football coach; b. Pitts., Oct. 10, 1963; Grad., Baker U., 1986. Grad. asst. Fort Hays State, 1987—88; quarterbacks, wide receivers coach U. Pitts., 1989—92; offensive asst. Kans. City Chiefs, 1993—94, quarterbacks coach, 1995—98, Green Bay Packers, 1999, head coach, 2006—; offensive coord. New Orleans Saints, 2000—04, San Francisco 49ers, 2005. Named Nat. Football Conf. Asst. Coach of Yr., NFL, 2000, Motorola NFL Coach of Yr., 2007, NFL Coach of Yr., NFL Alumni, 2007. Office: Green Bay Packers Lambeau Field 1265 Lombardi Ave Green Bay WI 54307*

MCCARTHY, PATRICIA ANNE, reading educator; d. John Donald and Ruth Catherine McCarthy; m. Moses Samuel Schanfield, Aug. 16, 1998; 1 stepchild, Amanda P. Schanfield; children: Stephanie Anne Murdock, Karin Joann Plotkin. BS, Le Moyne Coll., 1969; MA, Marquette U., 1971, PhD, 1999. Adj. asst. prof. Cardinal Stritch U., Milw., 1988—98; dir. Early Literacy Intervention Program, Wauwatosa, Wis., 1988—98; asst. prof. SUNY, Geneseo, 1999—2002, Hood Coll., 2003—04, Loyola Coll. in Md., Balt., 2004—08, Towson U., 2008—. Scholar Milw. Area Tchrs. Assn., 1988—98, Marquette U. Edn. Dept., 1994—95. Mem.: ASCD, Nat. Reading Conf., Internat. Reading Assn., Phi Delta Kappa. Avocations: travel, art collecting, reading, walking. Office: Towson Univ Hawkins Hall 8000 York Rd Baltimore MD 21252 Business E-Mail: pamccarthy@tawson.edu.

MCCARTHY, PATRICK M., surgeon; s. Martin Joseph and Margaret Anne McCarthy; m. Michelle M. Despres, June 20, 1978; children: Daniel, Elizabeth. BA, U. Notre Dame, Ind.; MD, Loyola U. Stritch Sch. Medicine, Maywood, Ill., 1980. Cert. Am. Bd. Surgery, 1987, Am. Bd. Thoracic Surgery, 2000. Residency in gen. surgery Mayo Clinic, Rochester, Minn., 1980—85, residency in thoracic & cardiovascular surgery, 1985—88, fellowship, 1988, Stanford U., Palo Alto, Calif., 1989; dir. heart transplantation Kaufman Ctr. Heart Failure, George M. and Linda H. Kaufman endowed chair Cleve. Clinic Found., 1990—2004; chief cardiothoracic surgery, co-dir. Bluhm Cardiovasc. Inst. Northwestern U., Chgo., 2004—, Heller-Sacks prof. surgery, Feinberg sch. medicine, 2006—. Cons. Edwards Lifescis., LLC, Irvine, Calif., AtriCure, West Chester, Ohio. Fellow: Am. Coll. Cardiology; mem.: AMA, Heart Failure Soc. Am., Flagship Healthcare Mgmt., Chgo. Cardiothoracic Surg. Soc. (dir.), Cardiac Surgery Biology Club, Am. Soc. Transplant Surgeons, Am. Heart Assn. (coun. mem.), Priestley Soc., Internat. Soc. Heart and Lung Transplant (com. mem.), Internat. Acad. Cardiology (internat. sci. adv. bd.), Heart Valve Soc. Am. (coun. mem.), Am. Assn. Thoracic Surgery. Independent. Achievements include invention of valve rings for mitral & tricuspid repair. Office: Northwestern University 201 E Huron Galter 10-105 Chicago IL 60611 Office Fax: 312-695-0178.

MCCARTHY, PAUL, artist; b. Salt Lake City, 1945; Attended, U. Utah, 1966—68; BFA, San Francisco Art Inst., 1969; MFA, U. Southern Calif., 1973. One-man shows include Mus. Modern Art, NYC, 1995, Blum & Poe, Santa Monica, 1995, 1999, Galerie Hauser & Wirth, Zurich, Switzerland, 1997, 2001, 2002, 2007, Mus. Contemporary Art, LA, 2000, Deitch Projects, NYC, 2001, New Mus. Contemporary Art, 2001, Kunstverein Hamburg, Germany, 2001, Nat. Mus. Contemporary Art, Oslo, Norway, 2003, Tate Modern, London, 2003, Whitechapel, 2005, Moderna Museet, Stockholm, Sweden, 2006, Whitney Mus. Am. Art, NYC, 2008, exhibited in group shows at Venice Biennale, 1993, 1995, 1999, 2001, Whitney Biennial, 1995, 1997, 2004, Tate Gallery, London, 2000, Mus. Modern Art, NYC, 2000, 2005, 2006, 2007, Walker Art Ctr., Mpls., 2001, 2002, 2005, Harvard U. Art Mus., 2001, Inst. Contemporary Art, London, 2003, 2004, 2006, New Mus. Contemporary Art, NYC, 2004, Internat. Ctr. Photography, 2004, Pompidou Ctr., Paris, 2005, 2006, Reina Sofia, Madrid, 2005, Barbican Ctr., London, 2007, 2008, White Columns, NYC, 2008. Recipient Skowhegan Medal for Sculpture, Skowhegan Sch Painting & Sculpture, 2009. Mailing: c/o 1301PE 6150 Wilshire Blvd 8 Los Angeles CA 90048*

MCCARTHY, PAUL FENTON, aerospace transportation executive, retired military officer; b. Boston, Mar. 3, 1934; s. Paul Fenton and Jane Gertrude (O'Connor) McC.; m. Sandra Williams, June 20, 1959; children: Paul Fenton III, Susan Stacy. BS in Marine and Elec. Engring., Mass. Maritime Acad., 1954; MS in Mgmt., U.S. Naval Postgrad. Sch., 1964; D of Pub. Adminstrn. (hon.), Mass. Maritime Acad., 1987. Commd. ensign U.S. Navy, 1954, advanced through grades to vice adm., 1985; 7 command tours have included Aircraft Carrier USS Constellation, Carrier Group One, Task Force Seventy-seven; commdr. U.S. 7th Fleet, 1980-82; dir. R & D USN, Washington, 1980-83; negotiator Naval Air, Incidents at Sea Agreement, Moscow, 1980; ret., 1990; cons. in field Alexandria, Va., 1990-92; pres. McCarthy and McCarthy, Ltd.; v.p., chief engr., dep. gen.mgr. McDonnell Douglas Aerospace/Boeing, St. Louis, 1992-95; v.p. processes and sys. integration McDonnell Douglas Aerospace, St. Louis, 1995-97, dir. naval systems integration, 1997-2000; vis. disting. prof. Peter Conrad chair Naval Post Grad. Sch., 2000-02; sr. ptnr. McCarthy and McCarthy, LLC, 2002—; sr. lectr. grad studies U. San Diego, 2005—. Decorated D.S.M., Legion of Merit, D.F.C., also by govts. of South Vietnam, Korea, Japan. Mem.: Mass. Maritime Acad. Alumni Assn. Episcopalian. Avocations: development and acquisition, aircraft and missile systems, financial management. Home Phone: 619-435-1012; Office Phone: 619-922-9494. Personal E-mail: mcandmc@yahoo.com.

MCCARTHY, REGINA (GINA MCCARTHY), federal agency administrator; married; 3 children. BA in Social Anthropology, U. Mass., Boston; MS in Environ. Health Engring., Planning and Policy, Tufts. U., Medford, Mass. Part-time staff Bd. Health, Stoughton, Mass.; mem. Hazardous Waste Facility Site Safety Coun., Mass. Exec. Office Environ. Affairs, 1985—90, appt. coun. chair, 1990—94, exec. dir. adminstrv. coun., 1994—99, asst. sec. pollution prevention, environ. bus. & tech., 1999—2003, undersec. for policy, 2003; dep. sec. ops. Mass. Office. Commonwealth Devel., 2003—04; commr. Conn. Dept. Environ. Protection, 2004—09; asst. adminstr. for air & radiation EPA, Washington, 2009—. Chair bd. dirs. The Climate Registry. Office: EPA Ariel Rios Bldg 1200 Pennsylvania Ave NW Washington DC 20460 Office Phone: 202-272-0167.*

MCCARTHY, ROBERT EMMETT, lawyer; b. Bklyn., May 26, 1951; s. John Joseph and Leona Mary (Hart) McC.; m. Elizabeth Anne Naumoff, May 20, 1978; children: John Philip, Emily Jane. BS in Fgn. Studies, Georgetown U., 1973, MS in Fgn. Studies, JD, 1978. Bar: NJ 1978, US Dist. Ct. (ea. and so. dists.) NY 1979. Assoc. Patterson, Belknap et al, NYC, 1978-84; gen. counsel MTV Networks Inc., NYC, 1984-86; v.p., counsel/communications Viacom Internat., NYC, 1986-87; exec. v.p. Nelson Vending Tech., Ltd., NYC, 1987-89; exec. v.p., gen. counsel Cateret Savs. Bank FA, Morristown, N.J., 1989-91; cons. McCarthy Comms., Elizabeth, N.J., 1991-95; sr. v.p., gen. counsel Time, Inc., NYC, 1996—. Cons. UN Ctr. on Transnat. Corps., NYC, 1979; exec. dir. Spl. Master Reapportionment of NY, 1982; term mem. Council Fgn. Relations, NYC, 1980-84. Founder, pres. Elizabeth (NJ) Dem. Assn., 1980; coordinator Florio for Gov., Union County, NJ, 1981. Mem. ABA, NY State Bar Assn., NJ State Bar Assn., Assn. Bar City NY Roman Catholic. Home: 3 Woods Ln Chatham NJ 07928-1760 Office: Time Inc 33rd Fl 1271 Avenue Of The Americas New York NY 10020-1300 E-mail: RobertMcCarthy1@aol.com.

MCCARTHY, SHERRI NEVADA, psychologist, educator, educational consultant; b. Topeka, June 2, 1958; d. Wallace Gene and Lois Elaine (McDyson) McCarthy; m. Scott Newlin Tucker, Feb. 14, 1983 (div. Feb. 2001); children: Colin Apollo, Chrysallis Altair; m. Brian David Ewing, Feb. 5, 2006. AA in Liberal Arts, Phoenix Coll., 1981; BA in Psychology, Ariz. State U., 1984, BEd in English Lit., 1985, MA in Spl. Edn., 1987, PhD in Ednl. Psychology, 1995. Cert. kindergarten -12 spl. edn., ESL tchr., Ariz. Mng. editor Scottsdale (Ariz.) Free Press, 1977-78; instr. English Skills Ctr. Phoenix C.C., 1978-80; spl. instr. Title I Creighton Sch. Dist., Phoenix, 1980-81; lit. instr. CTY program Johns Hopkins U., 1985; gifted specialist Fountain Hills (Ariz.) Schs., 1985-87; writing instr. Ariz. State U. Ctr. Acad. Precocity, 1986; tchr. ESL Chandler-Gilbert C.C., Chandler, Ariz., 1986-87; tchr. of gifted Chandler (Ariz.) Unified Schs., 1987-90; psychology tchr., cons. Maricopa County C.C., Tempe, Ariz., 1988-96; prof. ednl. psychology No. Ariz. U., Yuma, 1993—. Freelance writer, 1974—; spl. edn. tchr. Hawaii Dept. Edn., 1990-91; faculty assoc. ednl. psychology Ariz. State U., Phoenix, 1992-96; tchr. English Mesa (Ariz.) C.C., 1993-96; advisor, asst. honors coord. Phi Theta Kappa, 1994-96; gifted ednl. specialist Kyrene Pub. Schs., Chandler, Ariz., 1995-96; vis. prof. adolescent psychology Fed. U., Porto Alegre, Brazil, 2002-06, U. Malaya, 2008-; sr. lectr., rschr. Vologola State U., Russia, 2003-04. Author: Metamorphosis-A Collection of Poems, 1975, Speed Communication, 1979, A Matter of Time, 1980, A Death in the Family, 1988, Coping with Special Needs Classmates, 1993, Preventing Adolescent Aggression, 2005, Tchg. Psychology Around World, 2007; staff writer: Ariz. Hwy. Patrolman mag., Phoenix, 1979-82; newsletter editor: Ednl. Opportunity Ctr., Tempe, Ariz., 1982-83; contbr. articles to profl. jours. Bd. dirs. Young Astronauts, Fountain Hills, 1985-87. US Fulbright scholar, US State Dept. to Russian Fedn., 2003—04, Rsch. scholar, U. Fed. Rio Grande do Sul, 2004—06. Fellow APA (CIRP liaison 1992—), Internat. Coun. Psychologists (bd. dirs. 1998—), Internat. Coun. Psychology Educators (conf. organizer 2000—), Asian Psychol. Assn (bd. dirs. 2006-); mem. Ariz. Ednl. Rsch. Orgn. (bd. dirs. 1997—), Ariz. English Tchrs. Assn. (bd. dirs. 1998—), Odyssey of the Mind (mem. bd. govs. 1987-89, Creativity award 1986, 87). Democrat. Roman Catholic. Avocations: writing, guitar, camping, travel, piano. Office: No Ariz U PO Box 6236 Yuma AZ 85366-6236 Business E-Mail: sherri.mccarthy@nau.edu.

MCCARTHY, THOMAS GREGORY, theater educator; s. Robert Kenneth and Ruth Janet McCarthy; m. Patti J. Hynes-McCarthy; children: Christopher Thomas, Jonathon Gregory, Josephine, Josephine Mae. BA, St. Mary's U., Winona, Minn., 1980; MA, ND State U., Fargo, 1982; PhD, U. St. Thomas, St. Paul, 1997. Tchg. prof. Anoka Ramsey CC, Coon Rapids, Minn., 1982—. Office: Anoka Ramsey CC 11200 Miss Blvd Coon Rapids MN 55433 Business E-Mail: thomas.mccarthy@anokaramsey.edu.

MCCARTHY, THOMAS JAMES, JR., lawyer; b. Pulaski, Va., Nov. 24, 1943; s. Thomas James and Jane (Osborne) McC.; m. Sally Stockdale, July 25, 1987. BA in Econs., Washington and Lee U., 1967; JD, U. Va., 1970. Bar: Va. 1970, U.S. Dist. Ct. (we. dist.) Va. 1974, U.S. Supreme Ct. 2000. Assoc. Gilmer, Sadler, Ingram Sutherland & Hutton, Pulaski, 1970-75, ptnr., 1975—; county atty. Pulaski County, Pulaski, 1983—. Adminstrv. hearings officer Commonwealth of Va., 1983—; commr. of accts. Pulaski County, 1989—. Bd. dirs. Va. Coun. Sch. Attys., 2005—, chair, 2008; bd. dirs. New River CC, 1980—88, 1996—2004, vice-chair, 1981—88, 2000—02, chair, 2002—04, found. bd., 1989—91, 2004—05. Col. JAGC USAR, 1997, ret. Decorated Legion of Merit, Meritorious Svc. medal, Army Commendation medal. Mem. Va. Bar Assn., 27th Jud. Cir. Bar Assn. (pres. 1978-81), Pulaski County Bar Assn.; fellow Va. Law Found., Sigma Chi, Phi Alpha Delta. Democrat. Episcopalian. Home: PO Box 818 Pulaski VA 24301-0818 Office: Gilmer Sadler et al 65 E Main St Pulaski VA 24301-0878 Office Phone: 540-980-1360 x33.

MCCARTHY, VINCENT PAUL, lawyer; b. Boston, Sept. 25, 1940; s. John Patrick and Marion (Buckley) McC.; children: Vincent, Sybil, Hope. AB, Boston Coll., 1962; JD, Harvard U., 1965. Bar: Mass. 1965. Ptnr. Hale and Dorr LLP, Boston, 1965—; sr. ptnr. Hale and Dorr, Boston, 1976—2003; counsel Wilmer Cutler Pickering Hale & Dorr LLP, 2004—. Co-founder, bd. dirs., sec. Robert F. Kennedy Action Corps, Inc.; mem. Mass. Gov.'s Adv. Coun. on Alcoholism, Boston, 1984-94, Gov.'s Jud. Nominating Com., 1991-96; chmn. Mass. Housing Partnership Fund, 1991-2003; past chmn. Boston Ctr. for Arts; mem. adv. coun. Harvard Internat. AIDS Inst.; trustee, sec. Franklin Square House; past pres. Mass. Assn. for Mental Health; bd. dirs., past sec.-treas. Human Rights Campaign Found.; chmn. Gov.'s Commn. on Gay and Lesbian Youth, 2001-2003. Recipient Vols. of Am. Outstanding Svc. award, 1989. Mem.: ABA (Pro Bono Publico award 1987), Boston Bar Assn. (Pub. Svc. award 1995), Mass. Bar Assn. Home Phone: 617-783-2134; Office Phone: 617-526-6933. Business E-Mail: vincent.mccarthy@wilmerhale.com.

MC CARTHY, WALTER JOHN, JR., retired utilities executive; b. NYC, Apr. 20, 1925; s. Walter John and Irene McC.; m. Linda Lyon, May 6, 1988; children by previous marriage: Walter, David, Sharon, James, William. B.M.E., Cornell U., 1949; grad., Oak Ridge Sch. Reactor Tech., 1952; D.Eng. (hon.), Lawrence Inst. Tech., 1981; D.Sc. (hon.), Eastern Mich. U., 1983; LHD, Wayne State U., 1984; LLD, Alma Coll., Mich., 1985. Engr. Public Service Electric & Gas Co., Newark, 1949-56; sect. head Atomic Power Devel. Assos., Detroit, 1956-61; gen. mgr. Power Reactor Devel. Co., Detroit, 1961-68; with Detroit Edison Co., 1968-90, exec. v.p. ops., 1975-77, exec. v.p. divs., 1977-79, pres., chief operating officer, 1979-81, chmn., chief exec. officer, 1981-90. Author papers in field. Past chmn., bd. dirs. Inst. Nuc. Power Ops., Detroit Econ. Growth Corp., Detroit Symphony Orch., Monterey County Symphony Orch., Detroit Area Coun. Boy Scouts of America, Am. Cranbrook Inst. Sci.; bd. dirs. Fed. Mogul Corp., Comerica Bank, Perry Drugs, Wolverine Aluminium Corp. Fellow Am. Nuc. Soc., Engring. Soc. Detroit; mem. ASME, NAE. Methodist.

MCCARTIN, JOSEPH T., bank executive; BSEE, Worcester Poly. Inst., Mass.; M in Sys. Tech., Naval Postgraduate Sch.; MBA, U. Notre Dame, Ind. Chief info. officer Banc One Mortgage, Indpls., 1993—97; v.p., chief info. officer GE Capital Mortgage Svcs., Cherry Hill, NJ, 1997—98; chief info. officer Fleet Mortgage Group, Columbia, SC, 1998—2002; cons. Feld Group, 2002—03; sr. v.p., chief info. officer Nat. City Corp., Cleve., 2003—. Served in USAF, 1984—93. Named one of Premier 100 Info. Tech. Leaders, Computerworld, 2006. Office: Nat City Corp Nat City Ctr 1900 E 9th St Cleveland OH 44114-3484 Office Phone: 216-222-2000.

MCCARTNEY, DAVID FARNHAM, archivist, educator; b. Charles City, Iowa, May 29, 1956; s. Ralph Farnham and Rhoda Mae Huxsol McCartney; life ptnr. James Anthony Petersen. BA, U. Wis., 1979; MA, MLS, U. Md., 1998. Cert. Acad. Cert. Archivists, 2000. Archives technician Nat. Archives and Records Adminstrn., College Park, Md., 1994—98; records officer IMF, Washington, 1998—99; archives asst. Nat. Pub. Broadcasting Archives, College Park, 1995—2000; archives cons. History Assoc., Inc., Rockville, Md., 1999—2000; archivist U. Iowa, Iowa City, 2001—, adj. prof., 2002—. Nat. adv. bd. Iowa Broadcasting Archives, Waverly, Iowa, 2004—; bd. dirs. Nat. Collaborative for Women's History Sites, Chgo., 2004—07. Contbr. chapters to books. Donor, scholarship fund Midwest Archives Conf., Milw., 2005—; donor, vol. web mgr. Floyd County Hist. Soc., Charles City, 1998—; donor Englert Civic Theater, Iowa City, 2002. Grantee, Nat. Film Preservation Found., 2002, 2003, 2005, Nat. TV and Video Preservation Found., 2004; fellow, Richard Eaton Found., 1996—98; scholar, H.W. Wilson Co., U. Md., 1996; Frank G. Burke fellow in Archives Studies, U. Md., 1998. Mem.: Soc. Am. Archivists (steering com. coll. and u. archives sect. 2004—06, donor scholarship fund), Midwest Archives Conf. (sec. 2007—09), Iowa Conservation and Preservation Consortium, Consortium Iowa Archivists, Com. Instl. Coop. U. Archivists Group (chair 2008—), Assn. Moving Image Archivists, Nat. 19th Amendment Soc. (adv. bd. 1991—), Nat. Collaborative for Women's History Sites, Beta Phi Mu. Avocations: reading, bicycling, hiking. Home: 1302 Muscatine Ave Iowa City IA 52240 Office: Dept Special Collections 100 Main Library Iowa City IA 52242-1420 Office Fax: 319-335-5900. Personal E-mail: dfmcc@yahoo.com. Business E-Mail: david-mccartney@uiowa.edu.

MCCARTNEY, DAVID L., ophthalmologist, department chairman; MD, U. Tex., San Antonio, 1982. Cert. Am. Bd. Ophthalmology, 1987. Chair med. sch. dept. Tex. Tech. U. Health Sci. Ctr., Lubbock, 1994—. Business E-Mail: david.mccartney@ttuhsc.edu.

MCCARTNEY, MARTHA ROGERS, physics professor; d. William Loveland and Dolores Stack Rogers; children: Patricia Olivia, Melissa Lee. BS, Evergreen Coll., 1983; PhD, Ariz. State U., Tempe, 1989. Postdoc. rsch.assoc. Ariz. State U., 1989—92, rsch. scientist, 1993—94, assoc. rsch. scientist, 1994—2009, sr. rsch. scientist, 1999—2005, assoc. prof., 2005—, prof., 2009—. Contbr. 11 book chpts., over 100 articles to profl. jours. Mem.: Material Res. Soc., Microscopy Soc. Am., Am. Phys. Soc. Office: Ariz State Univ Dept Physics Tempe AZ 85287-1504 Office Phone: 480-965-4558. Business E-Mail: molly.mccartney@asu.edu.

MCCARTNEY, SIR PAUL (JAMES PAUL MCCARTNEY), musician; b. Liverpool, Eng., June 18, 1942; s. James and Mary Patricia (Mohin) McC.; m. Linda Eastman, Mar. 12, 1969 (dec. April 17, 1998); children, James, Stella, Mary, Heather; m. Heather Mills, June 11, 2002 (div. May 12, 2008); 1 child, Beatrice. Degree, Univ. Sussex, Brighton, 1988; MusD (hon.), Yale U., 2008. Singer, guitarist various groups including Quarrymen, Johnny and the Moondogs, Silver Beatles, 1956—62; singer guitarist The Beatles, 1962—70; solo artist, 1970—. Singer, guitarist: (albums with The Beatles) Meet the Beatles, 1964, The Beatles '65, 1964, Hard Day's Night, 1964, Help!, 1965, Rubber Soul, 1965, Revolver, 1966, Sgt. Pepper's Lonely Hearts Club Band, 1967, Magical Mystery Tour, 1967, The Beatles (The White Album), 1968, Yellow Submarine, 1969, Abbey Road, 1969, Hey Jude, 1970, Let It Be, 1970; (solo albums) McCartney, 1970, Ram, 1971, Red Rose Speedway, 1973, Band on the Run, 1973, Venus and Mars, 1975, Wings Over America, 1975, Wings at the Speed of Sound, 1976, London Town, 1978, Wings Greatest, 1978, Back to the Egg, 1979, McCartney II, 1980, Tug of War, 1982, Press to Play, 1986, All the Best, 1987, Flowers in the Dirt, 1989, Jet, 1989, Tripping the Live Fantastic, 1990, Unplugged/The Official Bootleg, 1991, Off the Ground, 1993, Paul is Live, 1993, Flaming Pie, 1997, Run Devil Run, 1999, Driving Rain, 2001, Chaos and Creation in the Backyard, 2005, Memory Almost Full, 2007; (albums with The Firemen) Electric Arguments, 2008; composer The Liverpool Oratorio, 1991; animator, composer Paul McCartney: The Music and Animation Collection, 2004; film appearances include: A Hard Day's Night, 1964, Help!, 1965, Let It Be, 1970, Give My Regards to Broad Street, 1984, Get Back, 1991; TV appearances include Doctor Who, 1965, Magical Mystery Tour, 1967, The Morecambe & Wise Show, 1968, Frost on Sunday, 1968, James Paul McCartney, 1973, Wings Over the World, 1979, Bread, 1986, (voice) The Simpsons, 1995, Saturday Night Live, 1998, V.I.P., 2000; videos include The Beatles: The First U.S. Visit, 1994, Paul McCartney: In the World Tonight, 1997, Twentieth Century Blues: The Songs of Noel Coward, 1998; producer animated film The Oriental Nightfish, 1978; author, Each One Believing: Paul McCartney On Stage, Off Stage, and Backstage, 2004; (children's book) High in the Clouds, 2005. Decorated Order of Brit. Empire (OBE), 1965, Knight Comdr. (KBE), 1997; recipient Acad. award (with Beatles) for Best Original Song Score, Let It Be, 1970, 5 Grammy awards with Beatles, 2 solo, 1 with Wings, Ivor Novello award for outstanding services to Brit. music, 1989, (with Linda McCartney) Lifetime Achievement award People for the Ethical Treatment of Animals, 1996; named to The Rock and Roll Hall of Fame (as a mem. of The Beatles), 1988, Lifetime Achievement award, 1990. Fellow Royal Coll. Music.

MCCARTNEY, ROBERT CHARLES, retired lawyer; b. Pitts., May 3, 1934; s. Nathaniel Hugh and Esther Mary (Smith) McC.; m. Janet Carolyn Moore, June 16, 1956; children: Ronald K., Sharon S., Carole J. AB, Princeton U., 1956; JD, Harvard U., 1959. Bar: D.C. 1959, Pa. 1960, U.S. Dist. Ct. (we. dist.) Pa. 1960, U.S. Ct. Appeals (3d dist.) 1960, U.S. Supreme Ct. 1966. Assoc. Eckert Seamans Cherin & Mellott, LLC, Pitts., 1959—64, ptnr., 1965—93, mem. exec. com., 1991—93, of counsel, 1993—. Sec., gen. counsel Ryan Homes, Inc., 1969-93; bd. dirs. United Meth. Found. of Western Pa., 1971— v.p., 1981-85, chmn., 1985-86; sec., gen. counsel Rimoldi of Am., Inc., 1989-99. Solicitor North Pitts. Cmty. Devel. Corp., 1968-76, alt. dir., 1968-80; mem. McCandless Twp. Govt. Study Commn., 1973-74, Princeton U. Leadership Devel. Coun., 2002-06; solicitor, asst. sec. McCandless Indsl. Devel. Authority, 1972-98; exec. com. Princeton U. Alumni Coun., 1966-70, 76-85, vice-chmn., 1981-83, chmn., 1983-85, co-chair spl. com. 250th Anniversary Princeton U., 1994-97, nat chmn. class planned giving program, 2002—, mem. planned giving adv. com., 2002-, mem. steardship adv. coun., 2004—; trustee Otterbein Coll., 1975-83, Pa. S.W. Assn., 1992-96; bd. dirs. Pitts. Cultural Trust, 1992-99; chmn. conf.-wide endowment program United Meth. Conf. We. Pa., 1985-87; bd. dir. Pitts. Civic Light Opera Assn., 1984—, v.p., 1987-92, pres., 1992-99; dir. The Ireland Inst. Pitts., 1991-2004, vice-chmn., 1996-2004; mem. No. Ireland Partnership, 1991—; bd. dir. Pitts. Concert Chorale, 1997-2003, Pitts. Irish and Classical Theater, 2000-05. Princeton fellow Harvard U., 1956-59. Mem. Princeton U. Alumni Assn. West Pa. (pres. 1976-78), Duquesne Club, Princeton Club of NY, Nassau Club. Republican. Home: 9843 Woodland Rd N Pittsburgh PA 15237-4347 Office: Eckert Seamans 600 Grant St Ste 44th Fl Pittsburgh PA 15219-2703

MCCARTNEY, SCOTT, travel editor, columnist; AB in Pub. Policy Studies, Duke U., 1982. Former writer AP; joined Wall St. Jour., 1993, former staff writer, now travel editor, columnist The Middle Seat. Co-author: Trinity's Children: Living Along America's Nuclear Highway, 1991; author: Defying the Gods, 1994, ENIAC: The Triumphs and Tragedies of the World's First Computer, 1999; chair alumni network The Chronicle, Duke U. Recipient George Polk Award, 2000, Online News Assn. award, 2003. Office: Wall St Jour 200 Liberty St New York NY 10281 Office Phone: 212-416-2000. E-mail: middleseat@wsj.com.

MCCARTNEY, STELLA, apparel designer; b. London; Creative dir. Chloe, Paris, 1997; head designer, owner Stella McCartney fashion house, London, 2001—; designer Stella perfume, 2003, Stella In Two perfume, 2006, CARE skinline, 2007. Recipient Woman of Courage award, Unforgettable Evening event, 2003, Glamour award for Best Designer of Yr., London, 2004, Organic Style Woman of Yr. award, 2005, Elle Style award for Best Design of Yr., 2007, Green Designer of Yr. award, Accessories Coun. Excellence Awards, 2008; named Designer of Yr., VH1/Vogue Fashion and Music Awards, 2000, Best Designer of Yr., Brit. Style Awards, 2007, Spanish Elle Awards, 2008; named one of The World's Most Influential People, TIME mag., 2009. Office: 429 W 14th St New York NY 10014*

MCCARTT, DEBRA, Mayor, Amarillo, Texas; BS in Health & Phys. Edn., U. Tex., Arlington. Former mem. Amarillo Econ. Devel. Corp.; sr. dir. cmty. rels. Tex. Tech Sch. Med.; mayor City of Amarillo, 2006—. Alumnus Leadership Tex., Leadership Amarillo. Regional rep. Tex. Mcpl. League; bd. mem. Dept. Info. Resources. Office: City Hall 509 S E Seventh Ave PO Box 1971 Amarillo TX 79105-1971 Office Phone: 806-378-3000. Fax: 806-379-9394. Business E-Mail: Mayor@ci.amarillo.tx.us.*

MCCARTY, DARREN, professional hockey player; b. Burnaby, BC, Can., Apr. 1, 1972; children: Griffin, Emerson, Avery, Gracyn. Right wing Detroit Red Wings, 1993—2005, 2008—, Calgary Flames, 2005—07, Grand Rapids Griffins (Am. Hockey League), 2008. Recipient NHL Found. Player Award, 2003. Achievements include being a member of Stanely Cup Champion Detroit Red Wings, 1997, 1998, 2002, 2008. Office: Detroit Red Wings Joe Louis Arena 600 Civic Center Detroit MI 48226*

MCCARTY, FREDERICK BRIGGS, electrical engineer, consultant; b. Dilley, Tex., Aug. 11, 1926; s. John Frederick Briggs and Olive Ruth (Snell) Briggs McCarty; m. Doris Mary Cox, May 3, 1950 (div. 1970); children: Mark Frederick, David Lambuth, Jackson Clare; m. Nina Lucile Butman, Aug. 17, 1973. BSEE, U. Tex., 1949. Design engr. GE, Schenectady, NY, 1949-51; sr. design engr. Convair, Ft. Worth, 1951-55; sr. engr. Aerojet Gen., Azusa, Calif., 1955-61; sr. engring. specialist Garrett Corp., Torrance, Calif., 1961-91; v.p., founder Patio Pacific, Inc., Torrance, 1973-84; owner, operator Textiger Co., Torrance, 1980-91; cons., 1991—. With USNR, 1944—46, PTO. Mem.: IEEE (sr.), Eta Kappa Nu, Tau Beta Pi. Democrat. Achievements include patents in field; design of superconducting acyclic motor for USN and high speed elec. machines for aerospace and transp. Home and Office: 1366 Stonewood Ct San Pedro CA 90732-1550

MCCARTY, MARY COLLEEN, legislative staff member; B, Towson U., Md., 1973. Exec. asst./caseworker to congressman Alan Mollohan US House of Reps., Washington, 2000—02, chief of staff, 2002—, asst. to ranking mem., House Standards Ofcl. Conduct Com., 2003—05. Democrat. Mailing: US House Reps 2302 Rayburn House Office Bldg Washington DC 20515 Office Phone: 202-225-4172. Office Fax: 202-225-7564. Business E-Mail: colleen.mccarty@mail.house.gov.*

MCCARTY, PERRY LEE, civil and environmental engineering educator; b. Grosse Pointe, Mich., Oct. 29, 1931; m. Martha Davis Collins, Sept. 5, 1953; children: Perry Lee, Cara L., Susan A., Kathleen R. BSCE, Wayne State U., Detroit, 1953; MS in San. Engring., MIT, Cambridge, 1957, ScD, 1959; DEng (hon.), Colo. Sch. Mines, Golden, 1992. Field engr. Edwin Orr Co., Dearborn, Mich., 1951-52; engr. Pate & Hirn, Detroit, 1952-53; field engr. Hubbell, Roth & Clark, Detroit, 1953; instr. civil engring. Wayne State U., 1953-54; field engr. George Jerome & Co., Detroit, 1954; engr. Civil Engrs., Inc., Detroit, 1956; assoc. Rolf Eliassen Assocs., Winchester, Mass., 1958-61; asst. prof. san. engring. MIT, 1958-62; faculty Stanford U., Calif., 1962—, prof. civil engring., 1967-75, Silas H. Palmer prof., 1975-99, Silas H. Palmer prof. emeritus, 1999—, chmn. dept. civil engring., 1980-85; chair prof. environ. sci. and engring. Tsinghua U., 2004—07. Chmn. Gordon Rsch. Conf. Environ. Scis., 1972; vice chmn. environ. studies bd. NRC-NAS, 1976-80, mem. com. on phys. scis., math. and resources, 1985-88, bd. on radioactive waste mgmt., 1989-96, mem. com. geoscis., environment, resources, 1994-97. Co-author: Chemistry for Environmental Engineering and Science, 5th edit., 2003, Environmental Biotechnology Principles and Applications, 2001. Served with AUS, 1954-56. Recipient Tyler Prize for Environ. Achievement, 1992, Clarke Prize Outstanding Achievement Water Sci. and Tech., 1997, Stockholm Water prize, 2007; NSF faculty fellow, 1968-69. Fellow AAAS, Am. Acad. Microbiology, Am. Acad. Arts and Scis.(Named to Hall of Fame Water Industry, 2009.); mem. ASCE (Walter L. Huber Rsch. prize 1964, Simon W. Freese Environ. Engring. award 1979, James R. Croes medal 1995), NAE, Am. Water Works Assn. (hon., life, chmn. water quality divsn. 1972-73, trustee rsch. divsn. 1980-85, Best Paper award 1985, A.P. Black Rsch. award 1989), Am. Soc. for Microbiology, Water Environment Fedn. (hon. 1989, Harrison P. Eddy award 1962, 77, Thomas Camp award 1975), Assn. Environ. Engring. Sci. Profs. (Disting. Faculty award 1966, Oustanding Publ. award 1985, 88, 98, 2003, Founders award 1992), Am. Soc. Engring. Edn.(vice-chmn. environ. engring. divsn. 1968-69), Sigma Xi, Tau Beta Pi (fellow 1957-58), Am. Acad. Environ. Engrs., 2009 Home: 823 Sonoma Ter Stanford CA 94305-1024 Office: Stanford U Civil Environ Enging Dept Stanford CA 94305-4020 Office Phone: 650-723-4131. Business E-Mail: pmccarty@stanford.edu.

MCCARTY, RICHARD CHARLES, psychology professor, dean; b. Portsmouth, Va., July 12, 1947; s. Constantine Ambrose and Helen Marie (Householder) McC.; m. Sheila Adair Miltier, July 15, 1965; children: Christopher Charles, Lorraine Marie, Ryan Lester, Patrick James. BS in Biology, Old Dominion U., 1970, MS in Zoology, 1972; PhD in Pathobiology, Johns Hopkins U., 1976. Rsch. assoc. NIMH, Bethesda, Md., 1976-78; asst. prof. U. Va., Charlottesville, 1978-84, assoc. prof., 1984-88, prof., 1988-2001, chair psychology, 1990-98, chair Coun. of Grad. Depts. Psychology, 1996-97; exec. dir. sci. directorate APA, Washington, 1998-2001; dean arts and sci. Vanderbilt U., Nashville, 2001—08, provost, 2008—. Mem. editl. bd. Behavioral and Neural Biology, 1985—90, Physiology and Behavior, 1989—2007, editor-in-chief Stress, 1995—99; editor: Am. Psychologist, 2000—01. Lt. comdr. USPHS, 1976—78. Recipient Rsch. Scientist Devel. award, NIMH, 1985—90; sr. fellow, Nat. Heart Lung Blood Inst., NIH, 1984—85. Fellow AAAS, APA, Assn. Psychol. Sci. Roman Catholic. Office: Office of the Provost Vanderbilt Univ 205 Kirkland Hall Nashville TN 37240 Business E-Mail: richard.mccarty@vanderbilt.edu.

MCCARTY, SHIRLEY CAROLYN, retired aerospace executive; b. Minot, ND, May 2, 1934; d. Harry and Cecelia Marie (Engene) Wolhowe; m. John Myron McCarty, Apr. 3, 1958. BSBA, U. ND, Grand Forks, 1958. Mem. tech. staff Douglas Aircraft, El Segundo, Calif., 1960-62, The Aerospace Corp., El Segundo, 1962-72, mgr., 1972-73, dir., 1973-79, prin. dir., 1979-89, gen. mgr., 1989—96; ret., 1996; pres. Shamrock Consulting, 1996—. Mem. adv. coun. Calif. State U., Northridge, 1979-01, chmn., 1984-86; mem. indsl. adv. bd. Purdue U. Soc. Women Engrs., West Lafayette, Ind., 1979-82, 85-; mem. adv. bd. Calif. Acad. Math. and Sci., 1991-96; apptd. mem. aerospace safety adv. panel NASA, 1998, chair, 2002-03; spkr. in field. Named Woman of Yr. The Aerospace Corp., 1976, Pres.'s award, 1987; named to Hall of Fame Women in Tech. Internat., 2003; recipient Spl. Judges Award for Leadership, Los Angeles YWCA, 1977, Sioux Alumni Award, U. N.D, 1982, Achievement award Los Angeles County Commn. for Women, 1987. Fellow Soc. Women Engrs.; mem. IEEE, Assn. for Computing Machinery, Soc. Women Engrs., Bus. and Profl. Women (Woman of Achievement 1984, Golden Nike award 1985), Women in Bus.(corp. achievement award, 1987), Women in Computing (founding mem., bd. dirs.). Avocations: raising and training siberian huskies, travel, writing, architecture. Office Phone: 310-351-1619.

MCCARTY, TODD C., publishing executive, former retail executive; BBA, U. Minn. Positions including divsn. employment supr. Quaker Oats Co., Chgo., 1989—92; positions including human resources mgr., dir. human resources North Am. ops. and v.p. human resources Frito-Lay Can. PepsiCo, Inc., 1992—2000; sr. v.p. human resources N.Am. Starwood Hotels and Resorts Worldwide, 2000—05; sr. v.p. human resources Rite Aid Corp., Camp Hill, Pa., 2005—08; sr. v.p. global human resources The Reader's Digest Assn., Inc., Pleasantville, NY, 2008—. Office: The Reader's Digest Association Inc Reader's Digest Rd Pleasantville NY 10570 Office Phone: 717-761-2633.

MCCARTY, V. K., publishing executive, chaplain, librarian, editor; b. Boston, June 26, 1948; d. Charles Osner and Dorothy June (McAlister) Long. MusB, Mich. State U., 1969; MusM, U. Louisville, 1972; cert. in theatre arts, U. London, 1972; intern in clin. pastoral edn., St. Luke's Roosevelt Hosp., 1989, resident in clin. pastoral edn., 1995; student, Congl. Devel. Inst. Tng., Diocese of Newark, 2003. Advt. asst. Lansing (Mich.) State Jour., 1968-69; market rsch. cons. Sta. WKLO, Louisville, 1969-70; libr. Louisville Free Pub. Libr., 1970-72; v.p. assoc. pub. Gen. Media Inc., NYC, 1979-2000; acquisitions libr. Gen. Theol. Sem. St. Mark's Libr., NYC, 2000—; part-time acquisitions libr. Union Theol. Sem. Burke Libr., NYC, 2001—02; dir. Christian Formation, St. Paul's Ch., Chatham, NJ, 2002—03. Bd. dirs. B.F.T., Inc., NYC. Dance editor Saturday Review Mag. Online, 1993-95. Master of ceremonies St. Ignatius of Antioch, N.Y.C., 1984-98; chaplaincy coord. St. Luke's Roosevelt Hosp., N.Y.C. Mem. N.Y. Liturgical Music Found. (steering com. 1982-84), N.Y. Ch. Club. Avocations: Biblical languages, riding, ballet, preservation of Benedictine monasticism, Byzantine art. Office: Gen Theol Sem St Mark's Libr 175 9th Ave New York NY 10011-4977

MCCARTY, WENDY LYNETTE, education educator; d. Roland and Lois Going; married; children: Benjamin, Andrew, Tyler. EdD, U. Nebr., Lincoln, 2003. Supervisory & tchg. cert. Nebr. Project coord. Ctrl. Nebr. Coun. Alcoholism & Addictions, Grand Island, 1986—2002.

MCCARTY-PUHL, J-PETRINA, chemistry educator; BS in Botany, Univ. Nev., Reno; MA in Curriculum and Instruction, Nova Southeastern Univ.; Crime Investigator Technician Degree, Kaplan Coll., 2005. Cert. Nat. Bd. Tchg. Standards, 2001. Tchr. Washoe County Sch. Dist., 1987—; chemistry, forensics tchr. Robert McQueen H.S., Reno. Recipient Outstanding H.S. tchr. award, Ariz.-Nev. Acad. Sci., 2003, Presdl. Excellence award for Secondary Sci. Tchr., Best of Edn. award, Subaru Sci. award for Excellence in Tchg., We. Region, The I CAN Learn-NEA Found. awards for Tchg. Excellence, 2007; named Nev. Tchr. of Yr., 2006; grantee Brandywine Fellowship. Office: Robert McQueen High Sch 6055 Lancer St Reno NV 89523 Business E-Mail: pmccarty@washoe.k12.nv.us.

MCCARUS, ERNEST NASSEPH, retired language educator; b. Charleston, W.Va., Sept. 10, 1922; s. Nasseph Mitchell and Della (Saad) McC.; m. Adele Najib Haddad, Sept. 10, 1955; children: Peter Kevin, Carol Ann. Student, Morris Harvey Coll., 1939-40; AB, U. Mich., 1945, MA, 1949, PhD, 1956. Translation team capt. Allied Translators and Interpreters' Service, Allied Hqrs., Tokyo, 1946-47; mem. English Lang. Inst. staff U. Mich., 1948-52, mem. univ. expdn. to Near East, 1951, instr. univ., 1952-56, asst. prof. Arabic, 1956-61; dir. Fgn. Service Inst. Field Sch. Arabic Lang. and Area Study, U.S. Dept. State, Beirut, 1958-60; assoc. prof. Arabic and Kurdish, dept. Near Ea. studies U. Mich., 1961-67, prof., 1967-95, chmn. dept., 1969-77, dir. Ctr. for Arabic Study Abroad, 1974-83, dir. U. Mich. Center for Middle Eastern and North African Studies, 1983-92, prof. emeritus, 1995—, vis. prof., 2008—09, 2008—09. Author: Grammar of Kurdish of Sulaimania, Iraq, 1958, (with H. Hoenigswald, R. Noss, J. Yamagiwa) A Survey of Intensive Programs in the Uncommon Languages, 1962, (with A. Yacoub) Elements of Contemporary Arabic, 1962, 3d edn., 1966, (with Raji Rammuny) First Level Arabic: Elementary Literary Arabic for Secondary Schools, 1964, Teacher's Manual to Accompany First Level Arabic, 1964, (with Jamal J. Abdullah) Kurdish Basic Course - Dialect of Sulaimania, Iraq, 1967, Kurdish Readers, Vol. I Newspaper Kurdish, Vol. II. Kurdish Essays, Vol. III Kurdish Short Stories, 1967, A Kurdish-English Dictionary, 1967, (with P. Abboud) Elementary Modern Standard Arabic, 1983, (with R. Rammuny) Word Count of Elementary Modern Literary Arabic Textbooks, 1969, (with P. Abboud, E.T. Abdel-Massih, S. Altoma, W. Erwin, R. Rammuny) Modern Standard Arabic Intermediate Level, 1971, (with R. Rammuny) A Programmed Course in Modern Literary Arabic Phonology and Script, 1974; editor: Language Learning, Vol. VII, 1956-57, Language Learning, Vol. XIII, 1963, An-Nashra, 1967-74, Contemporary Arabic Readers, Vols. I-V, 1962-66, The Development of Arab-American Identity, 1994, English Grammar for Students of Arabic, 2006; contbr. articles to scholastic jours. Served with US Army, 1942-46. Recipient Lifetime Contbn. award CASA, 2004, Middle East Studies Assoc. North America/Bacharach Svc. award, 2005; Rockefeller fellow, 1951. Mem. Mich. Linguistic Soc. (pres. 1962-63), Am. Assn. Tchrs. Arabic (pres. 1973, exec. coun. 1979-81, 89-92, lifetime svc. award, 2007), Middle East Studies Assn. (bd. dirs. 1973-75), Linguistic Soc. Am., Am. Oriental Soc., Linguistic Circle N.Y., Arabic Linguistic Soc. (pres. 1992). Home: 1400 Beechwood Dr Ann Arbor MI 48103-2940 E-mail: enm@umich.edu.

MCCASH, JUNE HALL, writer, retired language educator; b. Newberry, SC, June 8, 1938; d. James DeLeon and Williemaye Stone Hall; m. Marvin Hampton Martin (div. June 1971); children: Michael Hall Martin, Christopher Brenden Martin; m. William Barton McCash, July 3, 1974 (dec. Feb. 1991); m. Richard Douglas Gleaves, Jr., May 21, 1994. BA, Agnes Scott Coll., 1960; MA, Emory U., 1963, PhD, 1967. Instr. dept. romance langs. Emory U., Atlanta, 1964—66; from asst. to assoc. prof. Mid. Tenn. State U., Murfreesboro, 1967—70, from assoc prof. to prof., 1970—75, founding dir. honors program, 1973—80, prof. dept. fgn. langs., 1975—2004, chair dept. fgn. langs., 1980—92, grad. dir. dept. fgn. langs. and lits., 1996—2004, prof. emerita, 2004—. Presenter in field; fellow Am. Coun. Edn., 1986—87; elderhostel instr. W. Ga. Coll., 1992; interpreter for vis. French del. C. of C., Murfreesboro, 1992; exec. bd. Tenn. Humanities Coun., 1987—89, chair grant program com., 1987—88, vice-chair, 1988—89, chair, 1990—96, So. Humanities Media Fund, 1989—91, Tenn. Humanities Coun., 1989—91, exec. bd., 1991—92; local coord. ESL Inst. Tenn. Dept. Edn., 1992; coord. various profl. workshops. Author: Love's Fools: Aucassin, Troilus, Calisto and the Parody of the Courtly Lover, 1972, The Jekyll Island Cottage Colony, 1998, Jekyll Island's Early Years: From Prehistory through Reconstruction, 2005; co-author: Jekyll Island Club Historic District 100 Years, 1986, The Jekyll Island Club: Southern Haven for America's Millionaires, 1989, The Life of Saint Audrey: A Text by Marie de France, 2006; editor: The Cultural Patronage of Medieval Women, 1996; contbr. articles to profl. jours.; mem. editl. bd. Le Cygne: A Jour. on Marie de France. Hon. life mem. Jekyll Island Mus. Assocs., Friends of Linebaugh Libr.; trustee Jekyll Island Found., 2000—; layreader St. Paul's Episcopal Ch., Murfreesboro; chair adv. bd. So. Festival Books, 1988—92, mem. author's com., 1988—94; disting. mem. honors coll. bd. MTSU, 2007—. Recipient awrds for poetry, non-fiction novel and juvenile fiction, Southeastern Writers Assn., 2006, Novel award, 2006, 2008, Juvenile Writing award, 2009, Smith Moseley Poetry award, 2006, Daphne Cantrell Chambless Juvenile Fiction award, 2006, Josephine Mellichamp Nonfiction award, 2008, Poetry award, By-Line Mag., 2007; fellow, Nat. Humanities Coun., 1975; Young Humanists fellow, NEH, 1975, Mellon grantee for workshop on medieval culture, Vanderbilt U., 1982, Am. Coun. Edn. fellow, 1986—87. Mem.: AAUP (chair com. on status of women 1969—70, sec. MTSU chpt. 1970—71, mem. exec. com. 1970—74, v.p. 1971—72), Medieval Acad. Am., Internat. Marie de France Soc. (mem. exec. bd. 1993—95, mem. adv. coun. 2001—07), Southeastern Medieval Assn. (mem. exec. com. 1991—94, v.p. 1995—97, pres. 1997—99,), Internat. Courtly Lit. Soc. (internat. treas. 1980—86, v.p. N.Am. br. 1990—92, pres. N.Am. br. 1992—95, internat. v.p. 2001—04, internat. pres. 2004—07, hon. pres. 2007—), Soc. Rencesvals, Phi Sigma Iota, Phi Kappa Phi (pres. elect 1997—98, pres. 1998—99, MTSU chpt.), Alpha Mu Gamma. Democrat. Avocations: painting, photography, reading. Personal E-mail: jmccash9@gmail.com.

MCCASKEY, RAYMOND F., retired health insurance company executive; b. 1944; m. Judy McCaskey. With Continental Assurance Co., Chgo., 1963-73; assist v.p. Health Care Service Corp., 1973—79, chief actuary, 1979—82, CFO, 1982—91, pres., COO, 1991—98, pres., CEO, 1998—2008. Bd. dirs. Health Care Service Corp. Former bd. chmn. Lincoln Found. for Bus. Excellence.*

MCCASKILL, CLAIRE C., United States Senator from Missouri; b. Houston, July 25, 1953; d. William Y. and Betty Anne McCaskill; m. David Exposito (div. 1995); children: Austin, Maddie, Lily; m. Joseph Shepard, 2002; stepchildren: Benjamin, Carl, Marilyn, Michael. BS in Polit. Sci., U. Mo., Columbia, 1975, JD, 1978. Law clk. Mo. Ct. Appeals (we. dist.), Kansas City, 1978—79; asst. prosecutor County of Jackson, Mo., county prosecutor Mo., 1993—99; mem. Mo. Ho. of Reps., 1982—88; auditor State of Mo., Jefferson City, 1999—2007; US Senator from Mo., 2007—. Democrat. Office: US Senate 825A Hart Senate Office Bldg Washington DC 20510 Office Phone: 202-224-3121. Fax: 573-751-6539.*

MCCASLIN, ELIZABETH ANN, athletic trainer; b. Murfreesboro, Tenn., May 12, 1979; d. James Donald and Edwina Hassell McCaslin. BS in Athletic Tng., East Tenn. State U., Johnson City, 2001; postgrad., U. SC, Columbia, 2006—. Cert. athletic trainer Nat. Athletic Trainers' Assn. Head camp mgr. Universal Cheerleaders Assn., Memphis, 2000—01; athletic tng. fellow Steadman Hawkins Clinic, Vail, Colo., 2002—03; clin. coord., 2003—05; athletic trainer, med. asst. Moore Orthopedic Clinic, Columbia, SC, 2006—. Contbr. articles to profl. jours. Mem.: US Tennis Assn. (vol. 2006), SE Athletic Trainers Assn., SC Athletic Trainers Assn., Nat. Athletic Trainers Assn. (cert.). Avocations: tennis, golf, skiing, travel. Office: Moore Orthopedic Clinic 14 Medical Park Ste 200 Columbia SC 29203 Home: 2157 Seven Springs Rd Cookeville TN 38506-6233 Personal E-mail: lizatc01@msn.com.

MCCASLIN, LATANYA, art educator; d. Frank and Eloise McCaslin. Student, U. Ala., Birmingham, 1987—92. Art lectr., amb. Birmingham Mus. Art, 1992—; cultural arts dir. Sparkle Arts and Computers, Fairfield, Ala., 1992—. Mem. Friend of U. Ala. Art Dept.; active Dem. Nat. Com., Washington, Dem. Congl. Campaign Com., Washington. Mem.: Coll. Art Assn., Am. Assn. Mus., Amnesty Internat. Home: 113 60th St Fairfield AL 35064 Office Phone: 205-785-3636. Personal E-mail: dartagnan@wwisp.com.

MCCASLIN, RICHARD BRYAN, history educator; b. Atlanta, Feb. 21, 1961; s. Jerry L. and Ann Elizabeth (Sharman) McCaslin; m. Jana Dawn Maryovich, Apr. 5, 1979; 1 child, Christina Michele. BA, Delta State U., 1982; MA, La. State U., 1983; PhD, U. Tex., 1988. Tchg. asst. La. State U., 1982-83, grad. asst. La. Bus. Rev., 1983; tchg. asst. U. Tex., Austin, 1983-87, rsch. assoc., 1984-87; rsch. asst. prof. U. Tenn., Knoxville, 1988-90; asst. prof. High Point U., 1990-94, assoc. prof., 1994-2000, prof., 2000—04; assoc. prof. U. N. Tex., Denton, 2004—07, prof., 2007—. Instr. Pellissippi State CC, 1988—89, Roane State CC, 1989; adj. prof. Corpus Christi State U., Tex., 1989, Hawaii Pacific U., 2003—; lectr. E. Tenn. Hist. Soc., 1990; rsch. cons. Tex. Senate, 1986—89, Nat. Pk. Svc., 1989—90, Tex. State Hist. Assn., 2000—; assoc. historian Futurepast: History Co., Spokane, Wash., 1987—89; presenter Southwestern Social Sci. Assn., AAAS, Soc. Mil. History. Author (with Earnest F. Gloyna): Commitment to Excellence: One Hundred Years of Engineering Education at the University of Texas at Austin, 1986; author: Andrew Johnson: A Bibliography, 1992, Portraits of Conflict: A Photographic History of South Carolina in the Civil War, 1994, Tainted Breeze: The Great Hanging at Gainesville, Texas, October 1862, 1994 (Tullis prize Tex. State Hist. Assn., commendation Am. Assn. State and Local History), Remembered Be Thy Blessings: High Point University - The College Years, 1924-1991, 1995, Portraits of Conflict: A Photographic History of North Carolina in the Civil War, 1997, Lee in the Shadow of Washington, 2001 (Slatten award Va. Hist. Soc., Laney prize Austin Civil War Roundtable), The Last Stronghold: The Fort Fisher Campaign, 2003, Portraits of Conflict: A Photographic History of Tennessee in the Civil War, 2007, At the Heart of Texas: One Hundred Years of the Texas State Historical Association, 2007; co-author: 100 Years of Science and Technology in Texas: A Sigma Xi Centennial Volume, 1986; columnist: Greensboro News and Record, 1993—94; referee Southwestern Hist. Quar., La. State U. Press, U. Nebr. Press, U. S.C. Press, Tex. A&M U. Press, U. N. Tex. Press, Tex. State Hist. Assn.; from asst. editor to assoc. editor: Papers of Andrew Johnson, U. Tenn., 1988—90; contbr. articles and book revs. to profl. publs.; editor: A Soldier's Letter to Charming Nellie, 2008. Recipient Freeman award, MOSB, Merit award, Tex. Philos. Soc.; Dissertation fellow, U. Tex., 1987—88, Clara H. Driscoll fellow, Daus. Republic of Tex., 1985—87, James H. and Minnie M. Edmonds Ednl. Found. scholar, 1983—85, Colonial Dames Am. grad. scholar, 1987. Fellow: Tex. State Hist. Assn. (presenter); mem.: Am. Hist. Assn., E. Tex. Hist. Soc. (presenter), Soc. Civil War Historians (presenter), So. Hist. Assn. (presenter). Episcopalian. Home: 1321 East Windsor Dr Denton TX 76209 Office: Univ North Tex Dept History PO Box 310650 Denton TX 76203-0650 Office Phone: 940-565-4207. Business E-Mail: mccaslin@unt.edu.

MCCASLIN, SHARON, librarian; b. Clay Center, Kans., Feb. 27, 1948; d. Stephen Merle and Goldie Gentry; m. Stanley John McCaslin, May 20, 1972; children: Heather Megargee, Stephen. BA, Kans. State U., Manhattan, 1970; ML, Emporia State U., Kans., 1971; PhD, U. Nebr., Lincoln, 1987. Tech. svcs. libr. Peru State Coll., Nebr., 1971—99; serials libr. Longwood U., Farmville, Va., 1999—2005; libr. Fontbonne U., St. Louis, 2005—. Pres. Nebr. Libr. Assn., Lexington, 1990—93; coun. mem. Va. Libr. Assn., Richmond, 2000—01; exec. com. mem. MOBIUS, Columbia, Mo., 2006—08; treas. Mo. Libr. Network Corp., St. Louis, 2007—. First v.p. Homestead Girl Scout Coun., Lincoln, 1996—98; trainer Commonwealth Girl Scout Coun., Mechanicsville, Va., 2002—04. Recipient Disting. Svc. award, Coll. & U. Sect., NE Libr. Assn., 1997. Mem.: ALA, Mo. Libr. Assn. (pres. 2009—), Libr. Adminstrn. and Mgmt. Assn., ALA Intellectual Freedom Round Table (edn. liaison 2006—), Assn. Coll. and Rsch. Librs., Westminster Handbell Choir, P.E.O. (chpt. NB, Mo.) (pres. 2008—), Beta Phi Mu, Phi Kappa Phi (charter pres. 2006—08). Office: Fontbonne Univ Libr 6800 Wydown Blvd Saint Louis MO 63105 Office Fax: 314-719-8040. Business E-Mail: smccaslin@fontbonne.edu.

MCCASLIN, TERESA EVE, human resources specialist; b. Jersey City, Nov. 22, 1949; d. Felix F. and Ann E. (Golaszewski) Hrynkiewicz; m. Gary A. McCue. BA, Marymount Coll., 1971; MBA, L.I. U., 1981. Adminstrv. officer Civil Service Commn., Fed. Republic Germany, 1972-76; personnel dir. Oceanroutes, Inc., Palo Alto, Calif., 1976-78; mgr., coll. relations Continental Grain Co., NYC, 1978-79, corp. personnel mgr., 1979-81, dir. bus. redesign, internal cons., 1981-84; dir., human resources Grow Group, Inc., NYC, 1984-85, v.p. human resources, 1985-86, v.p. adminstrn., 1986-89; corp. v.p. human resources Avery Dennison Corp., Pasadena, Calif., 1989-94; v.p. human resources Monsanto Co., St. Louis, 1994-97; sr. v.p. human resources, mem. mgmt. com. Continental Grain Co., NYC, 1997—, exec. v.p. human resources & info. supreme, 1999. Bd. dirs. Am. Arbitrator Assn., 2005; bd. trustees, Thunderbird Grad. Sch. Internat. Mgmt., 2008. Mem. Am. Mgmt. Assn. (chair bd. trustees, fin. and exec. com., compensation com.), Human Resources Coun. Roman Catholic. Avocations: skiing, travel, golf. Office: Continental Grain Co 277 Park Ave New York NY 10172-0003 Business E-Mail: teri.mccaslin@conti.com.

MCCAUGHEY, BETSY (ELIZABETH P. MCCAUGHEY), health policy advocate, former lieutenant governor; b. Oct. 20, 1948; d. Albert Peterkin; m. Thomas McCaughey, 1972 (div. 1994); children: Amanda, Caroline, Diana; m. Wilbur Ross, 1995 (div. 1998) BA, Vassar Coll., 1970; MA, Columbia Univ., 1972, PhD, 1976. Sr. scholar Ctr. for the Study of the Presidency, 1989—92; lt. gov. State of NY, Albany, 1995—99; sr. fellow Hudson Inst., 1999—2001; founder, chmn. Com. to Reduce Infectious Deaths (RID), 2004—. Vis. asst. prof. Vassar Coll., 1977-78; lectr., Columbia U., 1979-1980, asst. prof., 1981-83; guest curator, The NY Historical Soc., 1986-88; chmn. Governor's Medicaid Task Force, 1994; adj. fellow, Hudson Inst., 1999- Author: From Loyalist to Founding Father: The Political Odyssey of William Samuel Johnson, 1980, Government By Choice: Inventing the United States Constitution, 1987; also articles including an article in The New Republic (Nat. Mag. award for Pub. Policy 1995). Recipient Bancroft Dissertation award, Richard B. Morris prize, H.L. Mencken award; Woodrow Wilson fellow, Herbert H. Lehman fellow, Honorary Vassar fellow, John Jay fellow, Post Doctoral Rsch. fellow NEH, 1984, John M. Olin fellow Manhattan Inst., 1993-94, sr. fellow Ctr. Study of the Presidency. Republican. Office: Committee to Reduce Infectious Deaths (RID) 185 E 85th St Ste 35B New York NY 10028 Office Phone: 212-534-3047. E-mail: Betsy@hospitalinfection.org.*

MCCAUL, JOSEPH PATRICK, chemical engineer; b. NYC, May 11, 1952; s. Joseph and Marion (Sheehan) McCaul; m. Kathleen Anne Crowley, Aug. 3, 1974 (div.); children: Kenneth, Christine; m. Nancy Marie Powell, May 28, 2000. BSChemE, Poly. Inst. Bklyn., 1973, M in Polymer Sci. and Engring., 1977; MBA, Case Western Res. U., 1987. Registered ofcl. baseball umpire Ill. H.S. Assn., cert. bus. intermediary 2005, master intermediary 2006. Prodn. supr. Mobay Chem. Corp., Bayonne, NJ, 1973—77; process engr. Borg Warner Chems., Parkersburg, W.Va., 1977—78, process control engr. Ottawa, Ill., 1978—79, process control mgr. Linmar plant, 1979—82; mgr. tech. svc. Std. Oil Co., Cleve., 1982—87; mgr. internat. sales and tech. svc. Barex Group BP Chems., Cleve., 1987—96, dir. sales and licensing, 1996—98; group v.p. sales and mktg. EVAL Co. Am., Lisle, Ill., 1998—2001, v.p. rsch. and bus. devel., 2001; founder, pres. Joseph Assoc. Internat., Inc., Chgo., 2002—; bd. dirs. Corecon Inc. Bd. dirs. U. Chgo. Booth Sch. Bus. Entrepreneurial Roundtable, 2008—. Contbr. articles to profl. jours., mags., ency. Exec. bd. dirs. Mentor Lake Area Baseball, Mentor on the Lake, Ohio, 1988—89; pres. Mentor McMinn Area Baseball League, 1989—91; trustee Pinegate Homeowners Assn., Mentor, Ohio, 1988—89. Recipient award, Soc. Plastics Engrs., 1987, Ann. award for bus. excellence, Bus. Ledger, 2006. Mem.: U. Chgo. Booth Sch. Bus. Entrepreneurial Roundtable (bd. dirs. 2008—), Midwest Bus. Brokers and Intermediaries (bd. dirs. 2005—06, Collaboration award 2005, 2006, 2008), Internat. Bus. Brokers Assn., DuPage Exec. Network (bd. dirs. 2004—06), Am. Mensa, Naperville C. of C. (com. chair, mem. spkrs. bur. 2004), Union League Club Chgo., World Trade Ctr. Ill. (bd. dirs. 2007—08). Achievements include patents in field. Avocations: fishing, boating, exercise, baseball, travel. Office: Chgo Bd of Trade Bldg 141 W Jackson Blvd Ste 3420 Chicago IL 60604 Office Phone: 312-212-8046. Business E-Mail: jmccaul@brokerchicago.com.

MCCAUL, MICHAEL T., United States Representative from Texas; b. Dallas, Jan. 14, 1962; m. Linda McCaul; children: Caroline, Jewell, Lauren, Michael, Avery. BS, Trinity U., 1984; JD, St. Mary's U., 1987; sr. exec. fellow, Harvard U. John F. Kennedy Sch. Govt. Asst. atty. gen., Austin, Tex., 1987—90; atty. US Dept. Justice Criminal divsn., Washington, 1990—99; spl. asst. atty. gen. State of Tex., 1999—2000, dep. atty. gen. for criminal justice, 2000—02; chief Terrorism & Nat. Security sect. US Dept. Justice, U.S. Atty. we. dist. Tex., 2002; mem. US Congress from 10th Tex. dist., 2005—, mem. homeland security com., chmn. investigations subcommittee, mem. internat. rels. com., mem. sci. com. Mem. Com. Fgn. Affairs, Ho. Rep. Policy Com.; vice chmn. US-Mex. Inter-Parliamentary Group, 2005. Republican. Roman Catholic. Office: US House Reps 131 Cannon House Office Bldg Washington DC 20515-4310 Office Phone: 202-225-2401.*

MCCAULEY, ANN, lawyer, retail executive; b. Washington, July 28, 1950; BA, Clark U., 1972; JD, Columbia U., 1978. Bar: NY 1979, US Dist. Ct. (so. dist. NY) 1979. Assoc. Cadwalader, Wickersham & Taft, NYC, 1978—80; atty. Port Authority of NY & NJ, 1980—83, TJX Cos., Framingham, Mass., 1985, v.p. legal, 1992—2004, sr. v.p. legal, 2004—07, chief corp. gen. counsel Framingham, Mass., 2005—07, exec. v.p., gen. counsel, sec., 2007—. Mem.: New Eng. Corp. Counsel Assn., NY State Bar Assn. Office: TJX Cos Inc 770 Cochituate Rd Framingham MA 01701 Office Phone: 508-390-1000. Office Fax: 508-390-2457. E-mail: ann_mccauley@tjx.com.*

MCCAULEY, BRUCE GORDON, financial consultant; b. St. Louis; s. William Maurice and Evylin Adele (Halbert) McC.; m. Barbara Allen Stevens, Mar. 16, 1945 (dec.); children: David S., Sharon; m. Gwen Crumpton Cummings, Nov. 25, 1967. Student, U. Mo., 1939-41, Yale U., 1944; BS in Engring., U. Calif., Berkeley, 1948, MBA, 1949, MS in Indsl. Engring., 1952. Registered profl. engr., N.Y., Calif., Hawaii. Asst. purchasing agt. Curtis Mfg. Co., St. Louis, 1941—43; teaching asst. U. Calif., Berkeley, 1948—49, asst. prof. mech. engring., 1950—56, chmn. indsl. engring. inst., 1954—55; design engr. Standard Oil Co. of Calif., 1949—50; sr. ptnr. McCauley & Dunmire, San Francisco, 1952—56; v.p. Shand & Jurs Co., Berkeley, 1956—58, exec. v.p., 1958—60; asst. to pres. Honolulu Star-Bulletin, 1960—62; gen. mgr. Christian Sci. Pub. Soc., Boston, 1962—69; gen. mgr., sec. N.Y. Daily News Inc., NYC, 1969—74, v.p., 1971—73, sr. v.p., 1973—75, asst. to pres., 1974—75, dir., 1971—75; v.p. Daseke & Co. Inc., Westport, Conn., 1975—77, sr. v.p., 1977—86, mgr. West Coast office, 1978—86; vis. scholar Principia Coll., Elsah, Ill., 1988—91; pres. Rossmoor Mut. 48 Corp., Walnut Creek, 1994—97. Bd. dirs. Better Bus. Bur., N.Y.C., 1973-77, N.Y.C. Conv. and Visitors Bur., 1974-77, Albert Baker Found., 1979-90, Asher Found., 1983-93, Sopac Energy Corp., 1986-92. Capt. USAAF, 1943-46, PTO. Mem. ASME (life), NSPE (life), Am. Inst. Indsl. Engrs. (life), Nat. Assn. Accts. (life), U. Calif. Alumni Assn., Principia Alumni Assn., Rossmoor Golf Club, Masons (32 degree), Kiwanis, Sigma Xi, Tau Beta Pi, Beta Gamma Sigma, Pi Mu Epsilon. Christian Scientist. Home: 3266 Ptarmigan Dr Apt 3B Walnut Creek CA 94595-3149

MCCAULEY, CLEYBURN LYCURGUS, lawyer; b. Houston, Feb. 8, 1929; s. Reese Stephens and Elizabeth Ann (Burleson) McCauley; m. Elizabeth Kelton McKoy, June 7, 1950; children: Stephens Francis, Lillian Elizabeth, Cleyburn, Lucy Annette. BS, US Mil. Acad., 1950; MS in Engring. Econ., Statistical Quality Control and Indsl. Engring., Stanford U., 1959; JD, Coll. William and Mary, 1970. Bar: DC 1971, Va. 1970, Tex. 1970, US Ct. Claims 1971, US Tax Ct. 1971, US Supreme Ct. 1973. Commd. 2d lt. USAF, 1950, advanced through grades to lt. col., 1971; ret., 1971; pvt. practice law Washington, 1975—. Mem.: AIAA, IEEE, Am. Soc. Quality Control, DC Bar Assn., Tex. Bar Assn., Va. Bar Assn., Fed. Bar Assn., Phi Alpha Delta. Home: 402 S 3rd St Wilmington NC 28401-5102

MCCAULEY, DAN PAUL, dentist; b. Pittsburg, Tex., Nov. 13, 1949; s. Loyd Cecil McCauley and Claudia Aletha Moore; m. Sandra Scott Kraemer, Sept. 14, 1974; children: Jennifer, Rebecca, Crissy. BA in Psychology, So. Meth. U., 1974; DDS, U. Tex., 1977. Pvt. practice, Mt. Pleasant, Tex., 1977—. Sec. N.E. Tex. CC, 1994—2001. Active Boy Scouts Am., 1977—; trustee N.E. Tex. C.C., 1989—, pres., 1989—2001, pres. found., 1994—2005; bd. dirs. Red River Girl Scouts, 1986—89; pres. Tex. Acad. Gen. Dentistiny, 2009—; chmn. bd. trustees Northeast Tex. Cmty Coll., 2009—; regent Pierre Fauchard Acad., 2009—; chmn. Titus county Reps., Mt. Pleasant, 1980; deacon First Bapt. Ch., Mt. Pleasant, 1977—; bd. dirs. N.E. Tex. C.C., 1989—. Recipient Fraternal Achievement award, Psi Omega Dental Fraternity, 1976, Sandy Niforus Humanitarian award, Ralph Waller Lifetime Achievement award, Optimist Internat., 2004; named one of Am. Top Dentists, Rsch. Coun. Am., 2009, Super Dentist of Tex., 2004—09. Fellow: Am. Acad. Gen.

Dentistry, Internat. Coll. Dentists, Am. Coll. Dentists, Pierre Fauchard Soc.; mem.: ADA, Acad. Gen. Dentistry (state dir. 2005—09), 1st Dist. Dental Soc. (pres. 1986—87, 2001—02, v.p. 2002, dir. 2002—), Tex. Dental Assn. (del. 1995—, dir. 2002—, sr. dir. 2003—04, v.p. 2004—), N. Tex. Optimists (gov. 1985—86, Optimist Lifetime Achievement 1995). Republican. Baptist. Avocations: tennis, travel, skiing. Home: 1403 S Florey Ave Mount Pleasant TX 75455-5813 Office: 1603 N Jefferson Ave Mount Pleasant TX 75455-2366 Office Phone: 903-572-3981. Personal E-mail: drdansmu@hotmail.com.

MCCAULEY, GERARD FRANCIS, literary agent; b. Pitts., Apr. 9, 1934; s. John Edward and Beatrice (McNally) McCauley; m. Kerstin E. Borg, Apr. 24, 1965; children: Peter, Brian. BA, U. Pitts., 1956. Editor Alfred A. Knopf Publishing, NYC, 1961—62, Little Brown, Boston, 1962—63; literary agt. Curtis Brown Ltd., NYC, 1964—70, Gerard McCauley Agy., Katonah, NY, 1970—2003. Editor: (book) Playing Around, 1973. Petty officer 3d class USN, 1956—58, Key West, Fla. Mem.: Orgn. of Am. Historians, Assn. of Authors Reps., Dutch Treat Club. Democrat. Episcopalian. Home: 7 Outpost Rd Katonah NY 10536

MCCAULEY, LINDA A., dean, nursing educator; BSN, U. NC; Master's in child health nursing, Emory U., 1979; PhD in environ. health and epidemiology, U. Cin., 1988. Nightingale prof. nursing U. Pa. Sch. Nursing, Phila., assoc. dean rsch.; dean Nell Hodgson Woodruff Sch. Nursing Emory U., Atlanta, 2009—. Fellow: Am. Acad. Nursing; mem.: ANA, Inst. Medicine, Am. Coll. Occupational and Environ. Medicine, Internat. Soc. Environ. Epidemiology, Am. Assn. Occupational Health Nurses, Am. Pub. Health Assn., Sigma Theta Tau. Office: Nell Hodgson Woodruff Sch Nursing Emory U 1520 Clifton Rd NE Atlanta GA 30322-4207 Office Phone: 404-727-7976. Office Fax: 404-727-9800. E-mail: dean@nursing.emory.edu.*

MC CAULEY, R. PAUL, criminologist, educator; b. Highspire, Pa., Jan. 13, 1943; s. Paul Herbert and Frances Vaden (Harper) McC.; m. Gail Lee Gummo, Jan. 30, 1965; 1 child, Brent Clayton. A.S., Harrisburg Area Community Coll., 1968; BS, Va. Commonwealth U., 1969; MS, Eastern Ky. U., 1971; PhD (fellow), Sam Houston U., 1973; certificate Home Office Detective Tng. Course, Eng., 1967. Diplomate Am. Coll. Forensic Examiners, Am. Bd. Law Enforcement Experts. Police officer Highspire Police, 1964-69; adminstr. Burns Internat. Security Services Inc., 1969-71; prof. police sci. and adminstrn., dir. grad. studies in adminstrn. of justice U. Louisville, 1973-82; prof., chmn. dept. criminology Indiana U. of Pa., 1982—; co-founder Sempas Security and Safety Technologies, 1980; advisor Reagan Presdl./Congressional Task Force on Criminal Justice, 1980; mem. staff So. Police Inst., 1973-82, Nat. Crime Prevention Inst., 1973-82. Researcher, ptnr. McShan Assocs., 1974-85; cons. U.S. Congress Com. on Emergency Communications, 1967. Co-author: The Criminal Justice System, 1976, 3d edit., 1984; co-founder, editor: Criminal Justice Policy Rev., 1984-86; contbr. chpts. to books, articles to profl. jours.; patents. Active Metro Child Abuse Program, Crime Clinic of Greater Harrisburg, 1965-74; mem. Lower Swatara Twp. Police Civil Service Commn., 1967-69. Served with USMC, 1962-66 Recipient Mayor's Citation, City of Louisville, 1982, Gold medal Educator of the 1980's; honoree Silliman Coll., Yale U., 1984; Fulbright scholar, lectr., Australia, 1987. Mem. Acad. Criminal Justice Scis. (exec. bd. 1980-83, pres. 1985), Navy League (award for disting. community service) Home: 4620 Lucerne Rd Indiana PA 15701-6003 Office: Ind U Pa 209 Wilson Hall Indiana PA 15705-0001 Office Phone: 724-349-9676. Business E-Mail: mccauley@iup.edu. *One's philosophy, spirit, and drive contributes more to his relative success than do economic resources, social position, planning, or timing.*

MCCAUSLAND, PETER, technology company executive; b. 1950; BA, U. S.C.; JD, Boston U. Bar: Pa. 1974. Gen. counsel MG Industries, Inc.; founder, chmn., CEO Airgas, Inc., Radnor, Pa., 1982—. Bd. dirs. Metrocall, Inc. Dir. Fox Chase Cancer Center, Independence Seaport Museum, Internat. Oxygen Manufacturers Assoc., Inc. Fax: 610-687-1052.

MCCAUSLAND, THOMAS JAMES, JR., retired brokerage house executive; b. Cleve., Nov. 27, 1934; s. Thomas James and Jean Anna (Hanna) McC.; m. Kathryn Margaret Schacht, Feb. 9, 1957; children: Thomas James III, Andrew John, Theodore Scott. BA in Econs., Beloit Coll., Wis., 1956. V.p. A.G. Becker & Co., Inc., Chgo., 1959-74; v.p. The Chgo. Corp., 1974-76, sr. v.p., dir., 1976-83, exec. v.p., 1983-90, vice chmn., 1991-96; pres. The Chgo. Corp. Internat., 1990-96; ret., 2000. Treas. The LaSalle St. Coun., Chgo., 1990-95. V.p. Hospice the North Shore, Evanston, Ill., 1986-90; bd. dirs. McCormick Theol. Sem., Chgo., 1971-79, Presbyn. Home, Evanston, 1968-74; trustee Beloit Coll., 1987-90. Lt. USN, 1956-59. Mem. United Presbyn. Found. (trustee, vice-chmn. 1980-86), Skokie Country Club (bd. dirs. 1983-85, pres. 1993), Pelican Bay Club (Naples, Fla.)(chmn. 2001-03), Forum Club of Naples (bd. dirs.), Royal Poinciana Golf Club (Naples), Old Elm Club (Ill.). Republican. Avocations: travel, golf, history.

MCCAW, CRAIG OLIVER, communications executive; b. Centralia, Wash., Aug. 11, 1949; s. John Elroy and Marion (Oliver) McCaw; m. Wendy McCaw, 1974; m. Susan Rasinski, 1998; 3 children. BA in History, Stanford U., 1973. Pilot; chmn., CEO McCaw Comm., 1968-88, McCaw Cellular Comm., Inc. (acquired MCI's cellular and paging ops. in 1986 sold to AT&T in 1994), Kirkland, Wash., 1982-94; founder, chmn., CEO Eagle River Investments, LLC, Kirkland, Wash., 1993; chmn., CEO XO Communications, Inc. (formerly NEXTLINK Communications, Inc.), 1994—97; chmn. Clearwire Corp., 2003—, CEO, 2003—06, co-CEO, 2006—07. Bd. dirs. Nextel Communications, Inc., 1995—2003, XO Communications, Inc. (formerly NEXTLINK Communications, Inc.), 1997—2002, ICO Global Communications Holdings Ltd., 2000—, Clearwire Corp., 2003—, ICO North America, Inc., 2004—, RadioFrame Networks, Inc., China Unicom Ltd., 2000—, non-exec. dir., 2002—; mem. Nat. Security Telecom. Adv. Com. Named one of 400 Richest Ams., Forbes mag., 2006; named to Gallery of Achievers Hall of Bus., 1989, Horatio Alger Assn. of Disting. Ams., 1999. Republican. Avocation: boating. Office: Clearwire Corp 3525 E Post Rd Ste 210 Las Vegas NV 89120 also: 5808 Lake Washington Blvd NE Ste 300 Kirkland WA 98033

MCCAW, JOHN ELROY, JR., investment company executive, professional sports team executive; s. John Elroy McCaw; married; 4 children. Grad., U. Wash. Co-founder McCaw Cable Vision, McCaw Cellular Comm., Orca Bay Ptnrs., Vancouver, BC; former chmn. Orca Bay Sports and Entertainment; chmn. Orca Bay Capital Corp.; former chmn., gov. Vancouver Canucks; owner, bd. dirs. Seattle Mariners, 1992; co-founder Tahoma Fund. Bd. dirs. Kistler Aerospace Corp. Bd. mem. Conservation Internat. Office: Orca Bay Ptnrs 1301 First Ave Seattle WA 98101

MCCAW, ROBERT BRUCE, lawyer; b. Durham, NC, Dec. 24, 1943; s. Robert Hall and Patricia Louise (McKean) McC.; m. Susan Leland Wood, June 15, 1968 (dec. June 2002); children: Anne Meredith, Benjamin Hugo. BS in Math., Georgetown U., 1965; JD, U. Va., 1970. Bar: Va. 1970, U.S. Dist. Ct. D.C. 1971, U.S. Ct. Appeals (10th cir.) 1974, U.S. Supreme Ct. 1974, U.S. Ct. Appeals (7th cir.) 1987. Law clk. to assoc. justice Hugo L. Black U.S. Supreme Ct., Washington, 1970-71; assoc. Wilmer, Cutler & Pickering, Washington, 1971-78, ptnr., 1978—2004; ptnr., co-chmn. Securities dept., office sr. ptnr. Wilmer Cutler Pickering Hale & Dorr, NYC, 2004—. Adj. prof., lectr. securities regulation George Washington U., Washington, 1980-83. Editor-in-chief Va. U. Law Rev., 1969-70; contbr. articles to profl. jours. 1st lt. U.S. Army, 1965-67. Mem. Order of Coif. Presbyterian. Office: WIlmer Cutler Pickering Hale & Dorr LLP 399 Park Ave New York NY 10022 Office Phone: 212-230-8810. Office Fax: 212-230-8888. Business E-Mail: robert.mccaw@wilmerhale.com.

MCCAW, ROBERT JOHN, language educator; b. Palo Alto, Calif. life ptnr. John Mendenhall. BA, U. Calif., Berkeley, 1989; PhD, Princeton U., NJ, 1994. Instr. Spanish Ohio State U., Columbus, 1994—96; vis. asst. prof. Spanish SUNY Buffalo, 1996—99; asst. prof. Spanish U. Montevallo, Ala., 1999—2001, U. Wis. Milw., 2001—05, 2005. Office: Univ Wisconsin Milwaukee PO Box 413 Milwaukee WI 53201

MCCAW, SUSAN RASINSKI, former ambassador; b. Orange City, Calif., 1962; m. Craig Oliver McCaw, 1998; 3 children. BA, Stanford U.; MBA, Harvard U., 1988. Bus. analyst McKinsey & Co., NY, Hong Kong; assoc. Robertson Stephens' Venture Capital Group; principal Robertson Stephens & Co., San Francisco; pres. COM Investments, Wash.; mng. ptnr. Eagle Creek Capital; US amb. to Austria US Dept. State, Vienna, 2005—07. Mem. exec. bd. Stanford Alumni Assn.

MCCAWLEY, AUSTIN, psychiatrist, educator; b. Greenock, Scotland, Jan. 17, 1925; arrived in U.S., 1954; s. Austin and Anna Theresa (McBride) McC.; m. Gloria Klein, Feb. 15, 1958; children: Joseph, Tessa. MBCHB, U. Glasgow, 1948. Diplomate Am. Bd. Psychiatry and Neurology; DPM Royal Coll. London. Intern Glasgow Royal Infirmary, Scotland, 1948; resident Inst. Living, Harford, Conn., 1954-57, clin. dir., 1960-66; med. dir. Westchester br. St. Vincent's Hosp., NYC, 1966-72; dir. psychiatry St. Francis Hosp., Hartford, 1972-88; prof. psychiatry U. Conn. Med. Sch., Farmington, 1983-93; pvt. practice, West Hartford, Conn., 1988—. Dir. psychiatry Kaiser Permanente of Conn., 1996-99. Author: A Comb for a Bald Man: A Psychiatrist Experience, 2009; co-author: The Physician, 1983; contbr. articles to profl. jours. Chmn. Bd. Mental Health, State of Conn., 1981-84, Search Com. for Commr. Mental Health, Conn., 1981; mem. Gov.'s Spl. Task Force on Mental health Policy, Conn., 1982. With RAF, 1948-50. Fellow: Am. Coll. Psychiatry (charter fellow, founder), Am. Psychiat. Assn.; mem.: Conn. Psychiat. Soc. (pres. 1978—79, Disting. Life fellow). Democrat. Roman Catholic. Avocation: music. Home and Office: 20 Worthington Dr Farmington CT 06032 Home Phone: 860-677-0109. Business E-Mail: amccawley@oliviasar.com.

MCCELLON-ALLEN, VENITA, utilities executive; B in journalism, Tex. A&M Univ. Cert. Profl. in HR Soc. Human Resource Mgmt. Mgmt. positions SW Elec. Power, 1983—95, v.p. corp. services Dallas, 1995—96, sr. v.p. corp. develop., 1996—98, sr. v.p. corp. develop. & customer rels., 1998—2000; sr. v.p. HR Baylor Health Care Sys., Dallas, 2000—04; sr. v.p. shared services Am. Elec. Power, Columbus, Ohio, 2004—06; pres., COO SW Elec. Power, 2006—08; exec. v.p. AEP West Utilities Am. Elec. Power, 2008—. Office: Am Elec Power 1 Riverside Plz Columbus OH 43215-2372

MCCHESNEY, JEAN ANGELINE, community health nurse; b. Abington, Pa., Apr. 1, 1937; d. M. Luther and Jane Ann (Pratt) Kauffman; m. Richard W. McChesney, July 9, 1960; children: Kevin R., Darrell O. BS, Columbia U., 1960. Cert. case mgr. Clin. instr. RN program Pikes Peak Commun. Coll., Colorado Springs, Colo.; case mgr. Genex Svcs. Inc., Colorado Springs. Instr. Basic Aid Tng. ARC; instr. cert. nursing asst. program Pikes Peak C.C., clin. supr. area vocat.-tech. program; rater State Cert. of Nurse Aides; massage therapist. Mem. Non-Practicing and Part-Time Nurses Assn. Home: 1522 Auburn Dr Colorado Springs CO 80909-2625

MCCHESNEY, ROBERT MICHAEL, SR., retired academic administrator; s. J.D. and Helen Grace (Russell) McC.; m. Laraine Freestone Freeman, Aug. 28, 1965; children: Robert M. Jr., Todd Patrick, Jennifer Laraine Turner, Grant Russell, Brent Steven. BA, U. La., Lafayette, 1964; MA, U. Va., 1967, PhD, 1969. Asst. instr. U. Va., Charlottesville, 1967-68; chmn. dept. polit. sci. U. Ctrl. Ark., Conway, 1971-76, dean coll. scis. and humanities, 1976-82, v.p. for acad. affairs, 1982-89, disting. prof., 1989-90; provost U. Montevallo, Ala., 1990-92, pres., 1992—2006, emeritus pres., 2006—. V.p. Survey Rsch., Inc., Conway, 1989-92; spl. cons. U. Ark. System, Little Rock, 1989. Mem. Carmichael Found., Conway, 1975-79; exec. bd. Quapaw coun. Boy Scouts Am., Little Rock, 1982-88; Greater Ala. Area Coun., 1995-2006; chair Ala. Coun. Univ. Pres., 1994-96, Ala. Higher Edn. Partnership, Pres. Adv. Coun., 1999-2001. Capt. med. svcs. US Army, 1969—71. Grantee, State Justice Inst./Adminstrv. Office of Cts., Ark., 1989. Mem. Ala. Coun. Univ. and Coll. Pres. (chmn. 1993-95, vice chmn. 2005-06), So. Com. Colls. and Schs. (exec. coun. 1996-99), Birmingham C. of C. (met. devel. bd. mem.), Montevall C. of C., Rotary (pres. Conway Club 1987-88, Paul Harris fellow 1986), Phi Beta Kappa, Phi Kappa Phi, Alpha Chi, Golden Key, Phi Alpha Theta, Phi Eta Sigma, Blue Key. Mem. Lds Ch. Avocations: hunting, fishing, golf. Home: 402 Norwick Cir Alabaster AL 35007 Personal E-mail: rmcchesney@gmail.com.

MCCHRYSTAL, STANLEY A., career military officer; b. Aug. 14, 1954; s. Herbert J. McChrystal; m. Annie McChrystal. BS, US Mil. Acad., 1976; MA in Nat. Security & Strategic Studies, US Navel War Coll.; MS in Internat. Rels., Salve Regina U.; Student, Spl. Forces Officer Course, Spl. Forces Sch., Ft. Bragg, NC, 1978—79, Infantry Officer Advanced Course, Ft. Benning, GA, 1980—81, Command & Staff Course, US Naval War Coll., Newport, RI, 1989—90. Advanced through grades to gen. US Army, 2009; weapons platoon leader C Co., 1st Bn., 504th Parachute Inf. Regiment, 82nd Airborne Divsn, Ft. Bragg, NC, 1976—78; rifle platoon leader C Co., 1st Bn., 504th Parachute Inf. Regiment, 82nd Airborne Divsn., Ft. Bragg, NC, 1978, exec. officer, 1978—79; comdr., Detachment A, A Co. 7th Spl. Forces Group, Ft. Bragg, NC, 1979—80; S-2/S-3 (intelligence, ops.) UN Command Support Group-Joint Security Area, Republic of Korea, 1981—82; training officer Directorate Plans & Training, Headquarters Command, Ft. Stewart, Ga., 1982; comdr. A Co. 3rd Bn., 19th Infantry, 24th Infantry Divsn. (Mechanized), Ft. Stewart, Ga., 1982—84, S-3 (ops.), 1984—85; liaison officer 3rd Bn., 75th Ranger Regiment, Ft. Benning, Ga., 1985—86, 1987—88, comdr. A Co., 1986—87, S-3 (ops.), 1988—89; Army spl. ops. action officer (J-3) Joint Spl. Ops. Command (JSOC), Ft. Bragg, NC, 1990—93; comdr. 2d Bn., 504th Parachute Infantry Regiment, 82d Airborne Divsn., Ft. Bragg, NC, 1993—94, 2d Bn., 75th Ranger Regiment, Ft. Lewis, Wash., 1994—96; sr. svc. coll. fellow John F. Kennedy Sch. Govt., Harvard U., Cambridge, Mass., 1996—97; comdr. 75th Ranger Regiment, Ft. Benning, Ga., 1997—99; mil. fellow Coun. on Fgn. Rels., NYC, 1999—2000; asst. divsn. comdr. (ops.) 82d Airborne Divsn., Ft. Bragg, NC, 2000—01; also comdr. Combined Joint Task Force-Kuwait, Camp Doha, 2000—01; chief staff XVIII Airborne Corps and Fort Bragg, Ft. Bragg, NC, 2001—02; also chief of staff Combined Joint Task Force-180, OPERATION ENDURING FREEDOM, Afghanistan, 2001—02; vice dir. ops. (J-3) The Joint Staff, US Dept. Def., Washington, 2002—03, dir., 2008—09; commdg. gen. Joint Spl. Ops. Command (JSOC), Ft. Bragg, NC, 2003—06; comdr. Joint Spl. Ops. Command (JSOC) and Joint Spl. Ops. Command Forward, US Spl. Ops. Command (USSOCOM), Ft. Bragg, NC, 2006—08, US Forces Afghanistan (USFOR-A), Kabul, 2009—; comdr., Internat. Security Assistance Force (ISAF) NATO, Kabul, 2009—. Decorated Def. Disting. Svc. medal, Def. Superior Svc. medal with oak leaf cluster, Legion of Merit with 2 Oak Leaf Clusters, Bronze star, Meritorious Svc, medal with 3 oak leaf clusters, Army Commendation medal, Army Achievement medal, Expert Infantryman Badge, Master Parachutist Badge, Ranger Tab, Spl. Forces Tab, Joint Chiefs of Staff Identification Badge. Office: ISAF-Kabul (AFG) Pub Info Office Feldpost 64298 Damsatadt Germany*

MCCLAIN, CINDY DUNSTAN, music educator; d. Kenneth Warren and Janet Lou Dunstan; children: Melinda Wrye Washington, John Michael Kritos. MusB in Vocal and Instrumental Edn. K-12, Lincoln U. of Mo., Jefferson City, 1977; MA in Piano performance, Ctrl. Mo. State U., 1995. Dir., coord. music, adjudicator State Fair Coll., Sedalia, Mo., 1988—2003; dir. music, coord. fine arts Westminster Coll., Fulton, Mo., 2003—. Dir. Jefferson City (Mo.) Cantorum. Recipient Governor's award for excellence in tchg., State of Mo., 2000. Mem.: Mo. Assn. Dept. Schs. of Music, Mo. C.C. Assn., Music Educators Nat. Conf., Am. Choral Dirs. Assn. Office: Westminster Coll 501 Westminster Ave Fulton MO 65251 Personal E-mail: cmcclain@socket.net. E-mail: mcclaic@westminster_mo.edu.

MCCLAIN, GEORGE NELSON, economist, lawyer; b. New Haven, Aug. 20, 1962; s. James and Trina. BS in Econs., U. Conn., 1975; JD, Yale U., 1978. Pres. McClain Internat., Washington, 1990—. Office: 6923 Storck CIR Lanham MD 20706-2129

MCCLAIN, JOHN T., corporate financial executive; BS, Lehigh Univ. CPA NJ. Audit mgr. Arthur Andersen; asst. controller, dir. acctg. ITT Corp.; v.p., chief acctg. officer Sirius Satellite Radio, 1998—99; sr. v.p. fin., controller Cendant Corp., 1999—2006; sr. v.p., chief acctg. officer Avis Budget Group Inc., Parsippany, NJ, 2006—07; CFO Jones Apparel Group Inc., Bristol, Pa., 2007—. Office: Jones Apparel Group PO Box 728 Bristol PA 19007-0728

MCCLAIN, LE'RON DE'MAR, professional football player; b. Ft. Wayne, Ind., Dec. 27, 1984; B in Human Environ. Sci., U. Ala., 2007. Fullback Balt. Ravens, 2007—. Named 1st Team All-Pro, AP, 2008; named to Am. Football Conf. Pro Bowl Team, NFL, 2008. Office: Balt Ravens M&T Bank Stadium 1101 Russell St Baltimore MD 21230*

MCCLAIN, LENA ALEXANDRIA, protective services official; b. Toledo, Ohio, Aug. 15, 1966; d. Lee Earl McClain, Mattie May Roberts-McClain; m. David Angelo Neyland, Aug. 4, 1990 (div. July 1995). AAS in Criminal Justice Adminstrn., Pikes Peak C.C., Colorado Springs, Colo., 1994; postgrad., U. Colo., 1994—95; BS in Criminology, U. So. Colo., 1996; postgrad., Spring Arbor U., Mich., 2001—02; postgrad. in Social Work, Lourdes Coll., Toledo, OH, 2003—. Corrections officer Colo. Dept. Corrections, Colorado Springs, 1994—96, sgt., 1996—97, case mgr./lt., 1997—99; sr. resident specialist coord. NW Cmty. Corrections Ctr., Bowling Green, Ohio, 1999—2000; shift supr. Lucas County Dept. Wk. Release, Toledo, 2000—. Employee counsel, bd. dirs. Delta Correctional Ctr., 1998—99. Mem. Colo. Grievance Team, 1998; trio mem. Townsend Learning Ctr.; bd. dirs. Pub. Arts Commn., Delta, Colo., 1999; bd. dirs., liaison Nat. Assn. Blacks in Criminal Justice, Delta, 1998. With US Army, 1987—90. Mem.: Am. Correctional Assn., Correctional Peace Officers Found., Social Work Nat. Honor Soc., Phi Theta Kappa. Democrat. Avocations: golf, basketball, softball, chess, writing. Office Phone: 419-213-6051. Business E-Mail: brealis@toast.net. E-mail: brealis37@aol.com.

MCCLAIN, MICHAEL H., writer; b. Middletown, Ohio, Aug. 30, 1940; s. Thomas H. and Blanche (Hamilton) McC. BA in History, U. Miami, Ohio, 1962; MA in History, U. Granada, Spain, 1973. Staff columnist El Correo Gallego, Santiago de Compostela, Spain, 1974-84; scholarly pubs. various countries English & Spanish. Spkr. in field. Author: Persian Traditions in Spain; contbr. articles to profl. jours. With U.S. Army, 1963-67. Mem. Nat. Assn. Scholars, Nat. Alumni Forum, Art History, Caths. United for the Faith (sec. Dayton chpt. 1990—), Coun. of Shia Islamic Orgn., Valaam Soc. Am., Ameer Khusro Soc. Am., Assn. Literary Scholars and Critics, Great War Soc., Am. Tradition Family and Property, The 1745 Assn., Order of the White Rose, Archconfraternité du Archange St. Michel, Comunión Tradicionalista, Mensa, Alliance for Separation Sch. and State, NRA, Cardinal Newman Soc., Islamic Soc. N.Am., Miami Alumni Assn., Kateri Tekakawitha League, Sierra Club, Islamic Soc. N.Am., Sons Confederate Vets., Civil War Preservation Trust. Avocations: hunting, fishing, travel. Home: 4518 Bonita Dr Apt 130 Middletown OH 45044-6759 Office Phone: 513-423-8862.

MCCLAIN, PAULA DENICE, political scientist, educator; b. Louisville, Jan. 3, 1950; d. Robert Landis and Mabel (Molock) McC.; stepdau. of Annette Williams McClain; m. Paul C. Jacobson, Jan. 30, 1988; children: Kristina L., Jessica A. BA, Howard U., Washington, 1972; MA, Howard U., 1974, PhD, 1977; postgrad., U. Pa., 1981—82. Asst. prof. dept. polit. sci. U. Wis., Milw., 1977-82; assoc. prof. and prof. pub. affairs Ariz. State U., Tempe, 1982-91; prof. govt. and fgn. affairs U. Va., Charlottesville, 1991-2000, chair govt. and fgn. affairs, 1994-97; prof. dept. polit. sci. Duke U., Durham, NC, 2000—. Co-author: Can We All Get Along? Racial and Ethnic Minorities in American Politics, 1995, 4th edit. 2006, Race, Place and Risk: Black Homicide in Urban America, 1990; editor: Minority Group Influence, 1993; co-editor: Urban Minority Administrators, 1988. Mem. Nat. Conf. Black Polit. Scientists (pres. 1989-90), Am. Polit. Sci. Assn. (exec. coun. 1985-87, v.p. 1993-94), So. Polit. Sci. Assn. (exec. coun. 1992-95, v.p. 2002-03, pres. elect 2004, pres. 2005), Internat. Polit. Sci. Assn. (exec. com. 1997-2003, v.p. 1997-2003), Midwest Polit. Sci. Assn. (v.p. 2002-04). Office: Duke U Dept Polit Sci Perkins Libr PO Box 90204 Durham NC 27708-0204 Office Phone: 919-660-4303. E-mail: pmcclain@duke.edu.

MCCLAIN, SHAWN, chef; Grad., U. Miami Ohio, School of Culinary Arts Kendall Coll., 1988—90. Chef Les Plumes, Prairie Restaurant, Boulevard Restaurant, Hotel Intercontinental, Chgo., sous chef; chef Betise, Wilmette, Ill., 1992—94; line cook Trio, Evanston, Ill., 1993—94, sous chef, 1994—95, chef de cuisine, 1995, exec. chef Evanston, Ill.; owner, exec. chef Spring Restaurant, Chgo., 2000—, Green Zebra, Chgo., 2004—, Custom House, Chgo., 2005—. Recipient Chef of Yr. award, Esquire Mag., 2001, Best chef: Midwest award, James Beard Found., 2006; named Rising Star Chef of Yr., Jean Banchet Awards for Culinary Excellence, 2002, 40 Under 40, Crain's Chgo. Bus., 2002; named one of Chgo.'s Rising Stars, StarChefs.com, 2008. Office: Spring Restaurant 2039 W N Ave Chicago IL 60647

MCCLAIN, TIM S., lawyer; b. 1948; m. Lynn Hollyfield; children: Scott, Brendan. Grad., U.S. Naval Acad., 1970; JD, Calif. We. Sch. Law, San Diego, 1978. Bar: Calif., DC, US Supreme Ct. Commd. Navy JAG Corps USN, ret., 1990, mil. def. counsel Navy Legal Svc. Office San Diego, head claims officer Navy Legal Svc. Office, head legal assistance officer Navy Legal Svc. Office, staff judge adv. for the commanding officer Naval Air Station Miramar, 1981—83, dept. head, instr. Naval Justice Sch. Newport, RI, 1981—86, gen. court-martial mil. judge Navy-Marine Trial Judiciary, S.W., 1986—90; with litigation law firm, San Diego, 1990—96; joined internat. mgmt. cons. firm, dir. opers., 1996—99; pvt. practice Principi and McClain, La Jolla, Calif., 1999—2001; gen. counsel US Dept. Vets. Affairs, Washington, 2001—06, acting asst. sec. for human resources & adminstrn., 2004; mem. Womble Carlyle Sandridge & Rice PLLC, Washington, 2007—; CFO, chief procurement exec., agency environ. exec. Vets. Affairs, 2005; pres., CEO Humana Inc., 2009—. Office: Humana Inc 500 W Main St Louisville KY 40202 Office Phone: 502-580-1000. Office Fax: 502-580-3639.

MCCLAIN, WILLIAM ANDREW, lawyer; b. Sanford, NC, Jan. 11, 1913; s. Frank and Blanche (Leslie) McClain; m. Roberta White, Nov. 11, 1944. AB, Wittenberg U., 1934; JD, U. Mich., 1937; LLD (hon.), Wilberforce U., 1963, U. Cin., 1971; LHD, Wittenberg U., 1972. Bar: Ohio 1938, U.S. Dist. Ct. (so. dist.) Ohio 1940, U.S. Ct. Appeals (6th cir.) 1946, U.S. Supreme Ct. 1946. Mem. Berry, McClain & White, 1937—58; dep. solicitor City of Cin., 1957—63, solicitor, 1963—72; mem. Keating, Muething & Klekamp, Cin., 1972—73; gen. counsel Cin. br. SBA, 1973—75; judge Hamilton County Common Pleas Ct., 1975—76, Mcpl. Ct., 1976—80; of counsel Manley, burke, Lipton & Cook, Cin., 1980—. Adj. prof. U. Cin., 1963—72, Salmon P. Chase Law Sch., 1965—72. Mem. exec. com. ARC, Cin., 1978—; bd. dirs. NCCJ, 1975—. 1st lt. JAG US Army, 1943—46. Decorated Army Commendation medal; recipient Nat. Layman award, A.M.E. Ch., 1963, Alumni award, Wittenberg U., 1966, Nat. Inst. Mcpl. Law Officers award, 1971, Ellis Island Medal of Honor, 1997. Fellow: Am. Bar Found.; mem.: ABA, Nat. Bar Assn., Ohio Bar Assn., Cin. Bar Assn., Am. Judicature Soc., Fed. Bar Assn., Bankers Club, Friendly Sons St. Patrick, Masons (32d degree), Sigma Pi Phi, Alpha Phi Alpha. Republican. Methodist. Home: 2101 Grandin Rd Apt 904 Cincinnati OH 45208-3346 Office Phone: 513-721-5525.

MCCLANAHAN, DAVID M., energy executive; B in Math., U. Tex.; MBA, U. Houston. Various exec. capacities Reliant Energy, 1986—; pres., COO electric utility divsn. Reliant Energy HL&P, 1997—99; pres., COO delivery group Reliant Energy, 1999—2000, vice-chmn., 2000—02; pres., CEO, dir. CenterPoint Energy, Houston, 2002—. Chmn. bd. dirs. ERCOT; bd. dirs. Edison Electric Inst., Am. Gas Assn., Interstate Natural Gas Assn. Am. Chmn. bd. Univ. St. Thomas. Office: CenterPoint Energy PO Box 4567 Houston TX 77210-4567

MCCLANAHAN, RUE (EDDI-RUE MCCLANAHAN), actress; b. Healdton, Okla., Feb. 21, 1934; d. William Edwin and Dreda Rheua-Nell (Medaris) McC.; m. Tom Bish, 1958; 1 child, Mark Thomas Bish; m. Norman Hartweg; m. Peter DeMaio; m. Gus Fisher, 1976; m. Tom Keel, 1984 (div. 1985); m. Morrow Wilson, 1997. BA in German & Theatre Arts cum laude, U. Tulsa, 1956. Appearances include (theatre) Lottice and Lovage, Vienna, 1993, Harvey (London); (Broadway) Jimmy Shine, 1968-69, Sticks and Bones, 1972, California Suite, 1977, After-Play, 1995, The Women, 2002, Wicked, 2005, (autobiography) My First Five Husbands, 2007; (TV series) Maude, 1973-78, Apple Pie, 1978, Mama's Family, 1982-84, Golden Girls, 1985-92, Golden Palace, 1992-93, Safe Harbor, 1999, Sordid Lives, Logo Channel, 2008-; (TV movies) Having Babies III, 1978, Sgt. Matlowch vs. the U.S. Air Force, 1978, Rainbow, 1978, Topper, 1979, The Great American Traffic Jam, 1980, Word of Honor, 1981, The Day the Bubble Burst, 1982, The Little Match Girl, 1987, Liberace, 1988, Take My Daughters Please, 1988, Let Me Hear You Whisper, 1988, To the Heroes, 1989, After the Shock, 1990, Children of the Bride, 1990, To My Daughter, 1990, The Dreamer of Oz, 1990, Baby of the Bride, 1991, Mother of the Bride, 1993, Danielle Steele's Message from Nam, 1993, Burning Passion: The Margaret Mitchell Story, 1994, Nunsense, 1995, A Holiday to Remember, 1995, Columbo: Ashes to Ashes, 1998; (films) The People Next Door, 1970, They Might Be Giants, 1971, The Pursuit of Happiness, 1971, Modern Love, 1990, This World, Then the Fireworks, 1996, Dear God, 1996, Out to Sea, 1997, Rusty: A Dog's Tale, 1997, Starship Troopers, 1997, Border to Border, 1998, Columbo: Ashes to Ashes, 1998, A Saintly Switch, 1999, The Moving of Sophia Miles, 2000, (off-Broadway prodn.) The Vagina Monologues, 2001, (mini-series) Innocent Victims, 1995. Recipient Obie award for leading off-Broadway role in Who's Happy Now, 1970; Emmy award Best Actress in a comedy, 1987; named Woman of Yr., Pasadena Playhouse, 1986; Spl. scholar Pasadena (Calif.) Playhouse, 1959, Phi Beta Gamma scholar, 1955. Mem. Actors Studio, Actors Equity Assn., AFTRA, Screen Actors Guild. Office Phone: 212-372-1270.

MCCLANE, ROBERT SANFORD, entrepreneur, bank executive; b. Kenedy, Tex., May 5, 1939; s. Norris Robert and Ella Addie (Stockton) McC.; m. Sue Nitschke, Mar. 31, 1968; children: Len Stokes McClane Brown, Norris Robert. BS in Bus. Adminstrn., Trinity U., San Antonio, 1961. With Ford Motor Co., Detroit, 1961-62; with Frost Nat. Bank, San Antonio, 1962-97; exec. v.p. Cullen/Frost Bankers, Inc., 1976—85, pres., 1985-97, dir., 1985—, Benefit Planners, Inc., 1997-2001; advisor, dir. Ellison Grandchildren Trust, 1996—; pres., owner McClane Ptnrs., LLC, 1997—; dir., vice chmn. Tobin Internat., 1998—2003. Bd. dirs. Frost Nat. Bank, San Antonio, 1987-, Princeton eCom., 1999-2006, CCI Telecom, Inc., 2004-06, CareNet, 2005—. Crusade chmn. Bexar County chpt. Am. Cancer Soc., 1974; bd. dirs. Bexar County ARC, 1969-72; sr. warden St. Luke's Episopal Ch., San Antonio, 1980; trustee Alamo Pub. Telecomms. Coun., San Antonio, 1981-88; chmn. San Antonio Econ. Devel. Found., 1987-89, exec. com. 1985-91; bd. trustees Trinity U., 1990—, chmn., 2001-04 Mem. Greater San Antonio C. of C. (chmn. leadership San Antonio 1975-76, bd. dirs. exec. com. 1994-97, chmn. 1996), Trinity U. Alumni Assn. (pres. 1968-69, disting. alumnus 1987), Free Trade Alliance San Antonio (bd. dirs., 1997—, chmn. 1998-2000), Southwest Rsch. Inst. (trustee 1997—), San Antonio German Club, Order Alamo, Tex. Cavaliers, Argyle Club, Club Giraud, Plaza Club (bd. dirs. 1973-92). Episcopalian. Office Phone: 210-220-5353.

MCCLARD, JACK EDWARD, lawyer; b. Lafayette, La., May 13, 1946; s. Lee Franklin and Mercedes Cecile (Landry) McClard; m. Marilyn Kay O'Gorman, June 3, 1972; 1 child, Lauren Minton. BA in History, Rice U., 1968; JD, U. Tex., 1974. Bar: Va. 1974, U.S. Dist. Ct. (ea. and we. dists.) Va. 1974, U.S. Ct. Appeals (4th cir.) 1978, DC 1981, U.S. Dist. Ct. DC 1981, U.S. Ct. Appeals (DC cir.) 1981, N.Y. 1985, U.S. Dist. Ct. (so. and ea. dists.) N.Y. 1985, U.S. Ct. Appeals (5th cir.) 1993, Tex. 1996, U.S. Dist. Ct. (ea. dist.) Tex. 1998, U.S. Ct. Appeals (7th cir.) 2001. Assoc. Hunton & Williams, Richmond, Va., 1974-81, ptnr., 1981—2006, sr. counsel, 2006—. Contbr. articles to profl. jours., chapters to books. Served to lt. (j.g.) USN, 1968—71. Mem.: Lewis F. Powell, Jr. Inns Ct. (exec. com. 2003—07), 5th Cir. Bar, Richmond Bar Assn. Democrat. Episcopalian. Avocations: bridge, gardening, wine. Home: 100 Trowbridge Rd Richmond VA 23238 Office: Hunton and Williams Riverfront Plz E Tower 951 E Byrd St Richmond VA 23219-4074 Home Phone: 804-740-0898; Office Phone: 804-788-8490. Business E-Mail: jmcclard@hunton.com.

MCCLATCHY, J. D., editor, writer, educator; b. Bryn Mawr, Pa., Aug. 12, 1945; s. J. Donald and Mary Jane (Hayden) McC. BA summa cum laude, Georgetown U., 1967; PhD, Yale U., 1974. Instr. English dept. LaSalle Coll., Phila., 1968-71; asst. prof. English dept. Yale U., New Haven, 1974-81, lectr. English dept., 1983, 86-87; writer-in-residence CCNY, 1982; writer-in-residence Poetry Ctr. 92d St. YMCA, NYC, 1983-84, workshop leader Poetry Ctr., 1982-91; lectr. Creative Writing program, English dept. Princeton U., 1981-87, 89-93; editor The Yale Rev., New Haven, 1991—; prof. English Yale U., 2001—. Poet-in-residence Southampton Writers Conf., 1988; lectr. MFA Parsons/New Sch., 1989, English dept. Rutgers U., 1989, writing divsn. Columbia U., 1989, 92; vis. prof. English dept. UCLA, 1990, 92; selection com. Conn. Poetry Cir. Author: (poetry) Scenes from Another Life, 1981, (London 1983), Lantskip, Platan, Creatures Ramp'd, 1983, Stars Principal, 1986, Kilim, 1987, The Rest of the Way, 1990, Ten Commandments, 1998, Hazmat, 2002, Mercury Dressing, 2009; librettist: A Question of Taste, 1989, Mario and the Magician, 1994, Orpheus Decending, 1994, Emmeline, 1996, revised edition, 2005; editor: The Yale Review, 1991—, (books) Anne Sexton: The Artist and Her Critics, 1978, For James Merrill: A Birthday Tribute, 1986, Recitative: Prose by James Merrill, 1986, Poets on Painters: Essays on the Art of Painting by Twentieth Century Poets, 1988, The Vintage Book of Contemporary American Poetry, 1990, Woman in White: Selected Poems of Emily Dickinson, 1991, The Vintage Book of Contemporary World Poetry, 1996, Twenty Questions, 1998, Christmas Poems, 1999, On Wings of Song, 2000, The Magic Flute (translation) 2000, Longfellow, Selected Poetry and Prose, 2000, Poems of the Sea, 2001, Love Speaks its Name, 2001, Bright Pages: Yale Writers, 1701-2001, 2001, James Merrill: Collected Poems, 2001, James Merrill: Collected Novels and Plays, 2002, Horace: The Odes, 2002, Division of Spoils, 2002, James Merrill Collected Prose, 2004, Poets of the Civil War, 2005; translator Carmen, 2001; assoc. editor Four Quarters, 1968-71; contbg. editor Am. Poetry Review; poetry editor The Yale Review, 1981-91; trans. articles, contbr. poems, stories, articles, reviews to various jours. Recipient gold medal Vergilian Acad., 1967, O. Henry award, 1972, prize Am. Acad. Poets,1972, Chase Going Woodhouse Poetry prize, 1976, Michener award, 1982, Gordon Barber Meml. award Poetry Soc. Am., 1984, Eunice Tietjens Meml. prize Poetry Mag., 1985, Witter Bynner Poetry prize Am. Acad. and Inst. Arts and Letters, 1985, award in lit., 1991, Oscar Blumenthal prize Poetry Mag., 1988, Levinson prize, 1990, Melville Cane award Poetry Soc. Am., 1991, Literary Lion N.Y. Pub. Libr., 1992; grantee Ingram Merrill Found., 1979, Conn. Commn. Arts, 1981; fellow NEA, 1987, John Simon Guggenheim Meml. Found., 1988; fellow lit. Acad. Am. Poets, 1991; artist resident Djerassi Found., 1988; Woodrow Wilson fellow 1967-68; Yale U. fellow, 1971-72; Ethel Boise Morgan fellow, 1972-74; artist's fellow N.Y. Found. Arts, 1986; artist resident Yaddo, 1991, MacDowell Colony, 1991. Fellow Am. Acad. Arts and Sciences; mem. AAAL (pres. 2009—), Acad. Am. Poets (chancellor 1996-2003, bd. dirs. 2003—), Phi Beta Kappa, Alpha Sigma Nu. Home: 15 Grand St Stonington CT 06378-1340 Office: The Yale Review Yale Univ PO Box 208243 New Haven CT 06520-8243 also: AAAL 633 W 155 St New York NY 10032*

MCCLATCHY, KEVIN S., professional sports team executive; b. Sacramento, Jan. 13, 1963; Diploma in Polit. Sci., U. Calif., Santa Barbara. Sport prodr. WPLG-TV, Miami; mktg. profl. Knight-Ridder Newspapers; nat. sales mgr. Newspaper Network (subs. McClatchy Newspapers); bus. ops. mgr. Amador Ledger-Dispatch, Calif., 1990; CEO, mng. gen. ptnr., owner Pitts. Pirates, 1996—2007. Co-owner Modesto A's, Oakland Athletics. Trustee Trinity-Pawling H.S., Pawling, N.Y., U. Calif. Santa Barbara; active United Way, Roberto Clemente Found., Extra Mile Found., U. Pitts. Cancer Inst., also Catholic charities.

MCCLAUGHERTY, JOE L., lawyer, educator; b. June 1, 1951; s. Frank Lee and Elease (Terrell) McClaugherty. BBA with honors, U. Tex., 1973, JD with honors, 1976. Bar: Tex. 1976, N.Mex 1976, U.S. Dist. Ct. N.Mex 1976, U.S. Ct. Appeals (10th cir.) 1976, U.S. Supreme Ct. 1979, Colo. 1988. Assoc. Rodey, Dickason, Sloan, Akin & Robb, P.A., Albuquerque, 1976-81, ptnr., dir., 1981-87, resident ptnr. Santa Fe, 1983-87, mng. ptnr., 1985-87; ptnr. Kemp, Smith, Duncan & Hammond, P.C., 1987-92, mng. ptnr., 1987-92; ptnr. McClaugherty & Silver, P.C., Santa Fe, 1992—. Adj. prof. law U. N.Mex, Albuquerque, 1983—; faculty Nat. Inst. Trial Advocacy, So. Meth. U. Law Sch., 1983—, Hastings Ctr. Trial and Appellate Advocacy, 1985—, U. Denver Law Sch., 1986—, U. Colo. Law Sch., 1987; bd. dirs. MCM Corp., Brit.-Am. Ins. Co., Ltd., Nassau, 1985—91. Mem.: N.Mex Assn. Def. Lawyers (pres. 1982—83, bd. dirs. 1982—85), N.Mex Bar Assn. (bd. dirs. trial practice sect. 1976—85, chairperson 1983—84, dir. young lawyers divsn. 1978—80). Office: McClaugherty & Silver PC PO Box 8680 Santa Fe NM 87504-8680 Office Phone: 505-988-8804.

MCCLAY, WILFRED MARK, history educator, writer; b. Champaign, Ill., Dec. 7, 1951; s. Clarence Harvey and Mary Rosalie (Bear) McC.; m. Julie Louise Holt, July 8, 1983; children: Mark, Barbara. BA cum laude, St. John's Coll., 1974; MA, John's Hopkins U., 1982, PhD, 1987. Legis. aide Md. Gen. Assembly, Annapolis, 1974-75; tchr. St. Mary's H.S., Annapolis, 1975-76; editor U.S. Naval Inst., Annapolis, 1976-78; dir. pubs. Folger Shakespeare Libr., Washington, 1978-80; vis. instr. history Towson (Md.) State U., 1985-86; asst. prof. history U. Dallas, Irving, Tex., 1986-87, Tulane U., New Orleans, 1987-93, assoc. prof. history, 1993—; Royden B. Davis chair in interdisciplinary studies Georgetown U., Washington, 1998—. Author: The Masterless: Self and Society in Modern America, 1994 (Merle Curti award Orgn. Am. Historians 1995); mem. editl. bd. Continuity: A Journal of History, 1995—. Mem. exec. bd. Crescent City Youth for Christ, New Orleans, 1995—. Danforth fellow Danforth Found., 1980-84, Richard Weaver fellow Intercollegiate Studies Inst., 1982-83, Spencer postdoct. fellow Nat. Acad. Edn. Stanford U., 1993-94, Howard fellow Howard Found. Brown U., 1993-94, fellow Woodrow Wilson Internat. Ctr. for Scholars, Washington, 1997-98, Univ. fellow NEH, 1997-98; named to Templeton Honor Rolls, John Templeton Found., 1997. Mem. Am. Hist. Assn., Orgn. Am. Historians, Social Sci. History Assn., Hist. Soc. Presbyterian. Avocation: music. Office: Tulane U Dept History New Orleans LA 70118

MCCLEA, ROBIN MUSE, museum director, painter; BFA, U. Arts, Phila.; M in Mus. Edn., Bank St. Coll. of Edn., NYC. Dir. edn. Barnes Found., Merion, Pa., 1999—2005; dir. Appleton Mus. Art, Ocala, Fla., 2005—. Office: Appleton Mus of Art 4333 E Silver Springs Blvd Ocala FL 34470 Office Phone: 352-291-4455. Office Fax: 352-291-4460. Business E-Mail: mcclear@cf.edu.

MCCLEAN, MURRAY R., metal products executive; Mng. dir. Commercial Metals Co., Sydney, 1985—93, pres. internat. div., 1993—99, pres. mktg. & dist. segment Irving, Tex., 1999—2004, exec. v.p., COO, 2004—06, pres., COO, 2006, pres., CEO, 2006—08, chmn., pres., CEO, 2008—. Office: Commercial Metals Co Ste 800 6565 N MacArthur Blvd Irving TX 75039

MCCLEARY, BERYL NOWLIN, volunteer, travel company executive; b. Ft. Worth, Feb. 22, 1929; d. Henry Bryant and Phyllis (Tenney) Nowlin; m. Henry Glenn McCleary, May 29, 1950; children: Laura Gail, Glenn Nowlin, Neil Ray, Paul Tenney. BS in Zoology, Tex. Tech U., 1950. Owner, mgr. Beryl McCleary Travels, Chicago, 1975-81, Denver, 1981-84. Treas. Kappa Alpha Theta Ednl. Found., Tex. Christian U., Ft. Worth, 1958-61; pres. study club Jr. Woman's Club, Ft. Worth, 1959-60; pres. Symphony League, Ft. Worth, 1961-62; v.p., dir. Ft. Worth Symphony Orch. Assn. Inc., 1961; treas. Jr. Pro-Am Tarrant County, 1961-62; corr. sec. Ft. Worth Children's Mus. Guild, 1961; sec. Tarrant County (Tex.) Democratic Exec. Com., 1956-62; pres. guild, bd. dirs. Maadi Community Ch., Cairo, 1964-66; mem. women's bd. Lincoln Park Zool. Soc., Chgo, 1976-81; mem. Episcopal Ch. Women's Diocesan Bd., Chgo., 1976-79; pres., charter mem. Rainbow Investment Club, London, 1970-71, travel dir. Over the Hill Gang Ski Team Internat., Denver, 1982-84. Mem. AAAS, DAR, Geol. Geophys. Aux., Service Club Chgo., Jr. League Denver, Denver Symphony Guild, Central City Opera Guild, Houston Symphony League, Alpha Epsilon Delta, Kappa Alpha Theta (charter mem. Gamma Phi chpt. 1953). Home: Apt F209 2501 Westerland DR Houston TX 77063-2276 Home Phone: 713-464-4374. Personal E-mail: berylmcc@sbcglobal.net.

MCCLEARY, LLOYD E(VERALD), education educator; b. Bradley, Ill., May 10, 1924; s. Hal and Pearl McC.; m. Iva Dene Carter, June 13, 1971; children: Joan Kay, Victoria Lea, Karen Ann. Student, Kans. U., 1941—42; BS, U. Ill., 1948, MS, 1950, EdD, 1956; postgrad., Sorbonne U., Paris, 1946. Tchr., asst. prin. Portland (Oreg.) Pub. Schs., 1949-51; asst. prin. Univ. H.S., Urbana, Ill., 1951-52, prin., 1953-56; asst. supt. Evanston Twp. (Ill.) H.S., 1956-60; assoc. Roosevelt U., 1957-69; mem. faculty U. Mich., summers, 1958-59; prof. ednl. adminstrn. U. Utah, 1969—, chmn. dept., 1969-74. Assoc. CFK Ltd. Found., 1971-76; dir. projects in L.Am. for AID, World Bank, Ford Found., Bolivian Govt.; dir. Nat. Sch. Prin. Study, 1976-79, 86-89, res. project Families in Edn., 1992-94; edn. rep. to Utah People to People Program; keynoter Asian Conf. Edn., 1985; edn. adviser Office of the Queen, Jordan, 1985-86; advisor Nat. Commn. on Stds. in the Principalship; U.S. del. Conf. on Status Children, Senegal, 1992, Yr. of the Family, Malta, 1993; J. Lloyd Trump lectr., New Orleans, 1994. Author: Organizational Analysis X-Change, 1975, Politics and Power in Education, 1976, The Senior High School Principalship, 1980, Educational Administration, Today, 1984, High School Leaders and Their Schools, vols. 1 and 2, 1990, Leadership, 1996; editor Western Hemisphere Edn. Sch. Orgn., 1989—. Served with inf. AUS, 1941-46. Decorated Bronze Star with oak leaf cluster, Army Commendation medal; S.D. Shankland fellow, 1956; grantee Ford Found., 1968, 72, AID, 1966, 67, 70, 72, 74, 76, CFK Ltd., 1970-74, Rockefeller Family Found., 1979-80, U.S. Dept. State, 1981, 86-87, U.S. Dept. Def., 1986—; recipient Hatch Prize, 1988-89. Mem. Nat. Assn. Secondary Sch. Prins. (cert. of merit 1978, scholar-in-residence fall 1989, grantee 1969, 77, 86—), Assn. Supervision and Curriculum Devel., Nat. Assn. Elem. Sch. Prins., Phi Delta Kappa, Kappa Delta Pi. Methodist. Home: 1470 Wilton Way Salt Lake City UT 84108-2549 Office: U Utah 339 MBH Salt Lake City UT 84112 E-mail: www.birdsphoto@aol.com.

MCCLEERY, WINSTON THEODORE, information technology executive; b. Mobile, Ala., Sept. 6, 1935; s. Robert Alton and Theadora K. (Kiebel) McC.; m. Sandra Thoss, Dec. 28, 1958; children: Winston T., Jacqueline McCleery McNeely. BS, Springhill Coll., 1957; postgrad., U. Ala., 1957-58. Logic design engr. Autonetics N.Am. Aviation, Anaheim, Calif., 1960—65; dir. info. sys. Litton Industries, LA, 1965—69; founder, owner Winston T. McCleery, Cons., 1969—; pres., CEO Mgmt. Software Systems, Inc., Mobile, 1979—. Patentee in field. With U.S. Army, 1958-60. Recipient Cert. for Heroism, Boy Scouts Am., 1949, Collifontanum award, Spring Hill Coll., 2006. Mem. Data Processing Mgmt. Assn., Assn. Computer Machinery, Am. Mgmt. Assn., Ind. Computer Cons.'s Assn., Optimists (pres. 1972). Republican. Achievements include contributions to the design and development of the U.S. Army Field Artillery's first digital fire direction computer; member of design team of the centaur missile's guidance system that made the first soft landing on the moon; design and development of seamless, integrated, on-line and instant-time computer application system for main frame class computers; inventor computer power and temperature enviroment control system, development of automatic documentation system used to document computer programs written in the Cobol language. Home: 5213 Janekyn Dr Mobile AL 36693-4142 Office: PO Box 9365 Mobile AL 36691-0365 Office Phone: 251-345-9960.

MCCLELLAN, EDWIN, literature educator; b. Kobe, Japan, Oct. 24, 1925; came to U.S., 1952; s. Andrew and Teru (Yokobori) McC.; m. Rachel Elizabeth Pott, May 28, 1955; children: Andrew Lockwood, Sarah Rose. MA, U. St. Andrews, Scotland, 1952; PhD, U. Chgo., 1957. Instr. English, U. Chgo., 1957-59, asst. prof. Japanese lang. and lit., 1959-63, assoc. prof., 1963-65, prof., 1965-70, Carl Darling Buck prof., 1970-72, chmn. dept. Far Eastern langs. and civilizations, 1966-72; prof. Japanese lit. Yale U., New Haven, 1972-79, Sumitomo prof. Japanese studies, 1979-98, Sterling prof. Japanese lit., 1998-2000, Sterling prof. emeritus Japanese lit., 2000—, chmn. dept. East Asian langs. and lits. New Haven, 1973-82, 88-91, chmn. council humanities, 1975-77, chmn. council East Asian studies, 1979-82. Vis. lectr. Far Eastern langs. Harvard U., spring 1965; mem. adv. coun. dept. Oriental studies Princeton U., 1966-71; mem. Com. to Visit East Asian Studies, Harvard U., 1982-88; mem. Am. adv. com. Japan Found., 1985-95; mem. bd. Coun. for Internat. Exch. Scholars, 1981-84. Translator: Kokoro (Natsume Soseki), 1957, Grass on the Wayside (Soseki), 1969, A Dark Night's Passing (Naoya Shiga), 1976, Fragments of a Past (Eiji Yoshikawa), 1992; author: Two Japanese Novelists: Soseki and Toson, 1969, Woman in the Crested Kimono, 1985; mem. bd. editors Jour. Japanese Studies, 1986-99; contbr. articles to profl. jours. Liason intelligence officer Royal Air Force, Washington, 1945-47; bd. trustees Society Japanese Studies U. Wash., 1992-99. With Royal Air Force, 1944—48. Recipient Kikuchi Kan prize for contbn. to study of Japanese lit., Tokyo, 1994, Noma Lit. Translation prize, 1995, Order of the Rising Sun, Gold Rays with Neck Ribbon, Japanese Govt., 1998, Dist. Contributions to Asian Studies award Assn. Asian Studies, 2005 Fellow Am. Acad. Arts and Scis. Home: 641 Ridge Rd Hamden CT 06517-2516

MCCLELLAN, MARK B., former federal agency administrator; b. Austin, Tex., June 26, 1963; m. Stephanie McClellan; 2 children. BA, BS, U. Tex., Austin, 1985; MA, MPA, Harvard U., 1991, MD, 1992; PhD in economics, MIT, 1993. Resident in internal medicine Brigham and Women's Hosp., Boston; cons. The Rand Corp., Santa Monica, Calif., 1989—91; rsch. assoc. Harvard Med. Sch. Dept. of Health Care Policy, Boston, 1991—95; attending physician Stanford U. Health Services; assoc. prof. economics Stanford U., 1995—99; assoc. prof.

medicine Stanford Med. Sch., dir. program on health outcomes rsch.; dep. asst. sec. for econ. policy US Dept. Treasury, Washington, 1998—99; mem. Coun. Econ. Advisors Exec. Office of the Pres., Washington, 2001—02; commr. FDA, Rockville, Md., 2002—04; adminstr. Centers for Medicare & Medicaid Services US Dept. Health & Human Services, Washington, 2004—06; sr. rsch. fellow Am. Enterprise Inst.-Brookings Joint Ctr. for Regulatory Studies, Washington, 2006—. Recipient Kenneth J. Arrow award for Outstanding Rsch. In Health Economics. Mem.: Inst. Medicine. Office: AEI Brookings Joint Ctr 1150 Seventeenth St NW Ste 1100 Washington DC 20036 Home: 4900 Chesapeake St NW Washington DC 20016-4335*

MCCLELLAN, MARY ANN, pediatric nurse practitioner; b. Mar. 29, 1942; BS, Tex. Woman's U., 1964; MN, U. Wash., 1968-69; cert., U. Tex., Arlington, 1997. Cert. family life educator, CPNP, pediatric nurse practitioner; advanced RN practitioner, Okla. Charge nurse Baylor U. Med. Ctr., Dallas, 1964—65; pub. health staff nurse Dallas County Health Dept., Dallas, 1965—68; supervising nurse Okla. State Dept. Health, Oklahoma City, 1969—70, maternal-child health nurse cons., 1971; asst. prof. U. Okla. Coll. Nursing, Oklahoma City, 1971—72; from instr. to asst. prof. Harris Coll. Nursing Tex. Christian U., Ft. Worth, 1972—75; asst. prof. continuing edn. U. Okla. Coll. Nursing, Oklahoma City, 1976—79, asst. prof. baccalaureate program, 1979—96, mem. grad. faculty, 1991—. Cons. and lectr. in field. Contbr. chpts. to books, articles to profl. jours. Mem. Nat. Coun. on Family Rels., Okla. Family Resources Coalition, Nat. Assn. Pediatric Nurse Assocs. and Practitioners, Assn. Faculty of Pediat. Nurse Practitioner Programs, Okla. Coun. on Family Rels., Sigma Theta Tau., Phi Kappa Phi. Office: U Okla Coll Nursing PO Box 26901 Oklahoma City OK 73126-0901

MCCLELLAN, ROGER ORVILLE, toxicologist; b. Tracy, Minn., Jan. 5, 1937; s. Orville and Gladys (Paulson) McC.; m. Kathleen Mary Dunagan, June 23, 1962; children: Eric John, Elizabeth Christine, Katherine Ruth. DVM with highest honors, Wash. State U., 1960; M of Mgmt., U. N.Mex., 1980; DSc (hon.), Ohio State U., 2005. Diplomate Am. Bd. Vet. Toxicology, Am. Bd. Toxicology. From biol. scientist to sr. scientist Gen. Electric Co., Richland, Wash., 1957-64; sr. scientist biology dept. Pacific N.W. Labs., Richland, Wash., 1965; scientist med. rsch. br. divsn. biology and medicine AEC, Washington, 1965-66; asst. dir. rsch., dir. fission product inhalation program Lovelace Found. Med. Edn. and Rsch., Albuquerque, 1966-73; v.p., dir. rsch. adminstrn., dir. Lovelace Inhalation Toxicology Rsch. Inst., Albuquerque, 1973-76, pres., dir., 1976-88; chmn. bd. dirs. Lovelace Biomed. and Environ. Rsch. Inst., Albuquerque, 1988-96; pres., CEO Lovelace Respiratory Rsch. Inst., Triangle Park, NC, 1988-99; pres. emeritus Hamner Inst. Health Sci., Triangle Park, NC, 1999—; pvt. advisor Toxicology and Human Health Risk Analysis, 1999—. Mem. rsch. com. Health Effects Inst., 1981-92, mem. future techs. com., 2000—; bd. dir. Toxicology Lab. Accreditation Bd., 1982-90, treas., 1984-90; adj. prof. Wash. State U., 1980-95, U. Ark., 1970-88; clin. assoc. U. N.Mex., 1971-85, adj. prof. toxicology, 1985—; adj. prof. toxicology and occupl. and environ. medicine Duke U., 1988—; adj. prof. toxicology U. N.C., Chapel Hill, 1989-2000; adj. prof. toxicology N.C. State U., 1991-2008; cons. faculty Colo. State U., 2002—; regents lectr. UCLA, 1999-2000; mem. dose assessment adv. group U.S. Dept. Energy, 1980-87, mem. health and environ. rsch. adv. com., 1984-85, 1999-2004; mem. exec. com. sci. adv. bd. EPA, 1974-95, mem. environ. health com., 1980-83, chmn., 1982-83, chmn. radionuclide emissions rev. com., 1984-85, chmn. Clean Air Sci. Adv. Com., 1987-92, Diesel Exhaust Panel, 1996-2001, chmn. rsch. strategies adv. com., 1992-94, mem. Particulate Matter Panel, 1993-97, 99-2006; mem. com. toxicology NAS-NRC, 1979-87, chmn., 1980-87; mem. com. risk assessment methodology for hazardous air pollution NAS-NRC, 1991-94, com. biol. effects of Radon NAS NRC, 1994-98, com. rsch. priorities airborne particulate matter, 1998-2004; mem. Environ. Roundtable, Inst. Medicine, 1998-2002; mem. com. on environ. justice Inst. of Medicine, 1996-99, trustee toxicology excellence in risk assessment, 2000-07, chmn. bd. trustees, 2002-04, mem. coord. com. strengthening sci.-based decision making, 2002—; pres. Am. Bd. Vet. Toxicology, 1970-73; mem. adv. coun. Ctr. for Risk Mgmt., Resources for the Future, 1987-2001; mem. Nat. Coun. Radiation Protection Measurements, 1970-2001, disting. emeritus fellow, 2002—; bd. dirs. NC Assn. Biomed. Rsch., 1989-91, N.C. Vet. Med. Found., 1990-95, pres., 1993-94; bd. govs. Rsch. Triangle Inst., 1994-2001; mem. adv. com. alternative toxicol. methods Interagy. Ctr. Evaluation Alternative Methods, Health and Human Svcs., 1998-2001, mem. sci. adv. com. on Alternative Toxic and Logical Methods Nat. Inst. Environ. Health Scis., 2006-; mem. sci. adv. bd. strategic environ. rsch. strategies program Dept. Def./Dept. Energy/EPA, 1997-99; mem. adv. com. Ctr. for Environ. Health, Agy. for Toxic Substances and Disease Registry, CDC, 2002-04, lunar dust toxicity panel NASA, 2005—; mem. bd. sci. counselors Ctr. for Environ. Health/Agy. Toxic Substances Disease Registry, 2004-06; mem. sci. adv. com. alternative toxicol. methods Nat. Inst. Environ. Health Scis., 2006-08. Jour. Toxicology, 1984—89, assoc. dir., 1987—89; editor: Critical Revs. in Toxicology, 1987—; mem. editl bd.: Regulatory Toxicology and Pharmacology, 1993—, Risk Analysis, 1998—, Ullman's Ency. of Indsl. Chemistry, 1999—2008, Non-Linearity in Biology-Toxicology-Medicine, 2003—08; contbr. articles to profl. jours. Trustee Wash. State U. Found., 2001—; mem. bd. of vis. Wash. State Univ., Coll. Sci., 2002—; mem. dean's adv. coun. Coll. Vet. Medicine Wash. State U., 2003—, chair dean's adv. coun., 2003—05. Recipient Herbert E. Stokinger award Am. Conf. Govtl. Indsl. Hygienists, 1985, Alumni Achievement award Wash. State U., 1987, Disting. Assoc. award Dept. Energy, 1987, 88, Arnold Lehman award Soc. Toxicology, 1992, Disting. Vet. Medicine Alumnus award Wash. State U., 1999, Regents Disting. Alumnus award, 2008, N.Mex. Disting. Pub. Svc. award, 2006; co-recipient Frank R. Blood award Soc. Toxicology, 1989, Merit award Soc. Toxicology, 2005, Founders award, 2009, Disting. Pub. Svc. award N.Mex., 2006,; named Robert Leader Meml. lectr. Mich. State U., 1999, H.M. Parker Meml. lectr. H.M. Parker Found., 1999; named to Hall of Fame Robert O. Anderson Schs. of Mgmt., U. N.Mex., 2002; fellow Internat. Aerosol Rsch. Assembly, 1998. Fellow: AAAS, Acad. Toxicol. Sci., Gesellschaft fur Zerosol Forschung, Health Physics Soc. (chmn. program com. 1972, fellow 1997, Elda E. Anderson award 1974), Soc. Risk Analysis (fellow 1992), Am. Vet. Med. Assn., Am. Acad. Vet. and Comparative Toxicology; mem.: Internat. Soc. Aerosols in Medicine (Thomas Mercer Joint prize for Aerosol Rsch. 1997), Am. Assn. Aerosol Rsch. (bd. dir. 1982—94, treas. 1986—90, v.p. to pres. 1990—93, fellow 2008), Toxicology Edn. Found. (founding pres. 1990—91), Internat. Congress Toxicology VII (treas. 1995), Soc.Toxicology (chmn. 1983—85, inhalation splty. sect. v.p. to pres. 1983—86, bd. publs. 1983—86, v.p.-elect to pres. 1987—90, Amb.mid-Atlantic chpt. 1995, founding chair endowment fund bd. 2006—09), Am. Conf. Govtl. Indsl. Hygienists, Internat. Regulatory Pharmacology and Toxicology (Internat. Achievement award 1999), Am. Assn. Cancer Rsch., Am. Thoracic Soc., Radiation Rsch. Soc. (chmn. fin. com. 1979—82, sec.-treas. 1982—84), Inst. Medicine (elected mem. 1990, chair other health professions sect. 1999—2001), Am. Chem. Soc., Phi Zeta, Phi Kappa Phi, Sigma Xi. Republican. Lutheran. E-mail: roger.o.mcclellan@att.net.

MCCLELLAN, SCOTT, consulting company executive, former White House press secretary; b. Austin, Tex., Feb. 14, 1968; s. Barr McClellan and Carole Keeton Strayhorn; m. Jill Martinez, Nov. 2003. BA, U. Tex., Austin, 1991. Campaign mgr. for Carole Keeton Strayhorn Tex. Comptroller, 1998; dep. comm. dir. to Gov. State of Tex., 1999—2000; traveling press sec. Bush-Cheney Presdl. Campaign, 2000; dep. press sec. The White House, Washington, DC, 2001—03, asst. to Pres., press sec., 2003—06; sr. v.p. corp. & govt. affairs HHB Inc., Washington, 2007—. Mem. Internat. Advisory Coun. APCO Worldwide, 2008—. Author: What Happened: Inside the Bush White House and What's Wrong with Washington, 2008. Recipient Outstanding Young Tex. Ex Award, 2005. Republican. Office: HHB Inc 816 Connecticut Ave 5th Fl Washington DC 20006

MC CLELLAN, WILLIAM MONSON, retired library director; b. Groton, Mass., Jan. 7, 1934; s. James Lewis and Ruth Caldwell (Monson) McC.; m. Jane Muir, Sept. 3, 1955; children— Jennifer, Anne, Margaret, Amy. BA, Colo. Coll., 1956, MA, 1961; A.M. in L.S, U. Mich., Ann Arbor, 1959. Music librarian U. Colo., Boulder, 1959-65; dir. Music Library, U. Ill., Urbana, 1965-97. Cons. music library resources and services to colls. and univs.; co-dir. Inst. Music Librarianship, Kent State U., 1969 Editor: Music Library Assn. Notes, 1977-82; Contbr. articles to profl. jours. Council on Library Resources fellow, 1976-77 Mem. Internat. Assn. Music Librs., Music. Libr. Assn. (pres. 1971-73, conf. panelist, chmn. stats. subcom. 1990-93). Home: 1212 Raintree Dr Apt I175 Fort Collins CO 80526 Home Phone: 970-266-0284. Personal E-mail: muirmack@frii.com. *To commit myself daily to giving and opening myself to others in all professional and other contexts.*

MCCLELLAND, HELEN, music educator; b. Chgo., Dec. 5, 1951; d. Leon Leroy and Willie Jo (Darnell) McC.; (div. Sept. 1981); 1 child, Tasha Renee. Diploma in arts, Kennedy-King Coll., 1971; cert. in voice, Sherwood Music Coll., 1971-73; BS, Chgo. State U., 1975, MA in Adminstrn., 1983; D in Adminstrn. and Supervision, U. Calif., 1993. Tchr. Faulkner Sch., Chgo., 1975-78; tchr. music Harvey (Ill.) Pub. Sch. Dist. 152, 1978—. Dir. music Pleasant Green Missionary Bapt. Ch., Chgo., 1971—; mem. sch. bd. New World Christian Acad., Chgo., 1988—; bd. dirs. South Shore Drill Team, Chgo. Author: operetta So You Want to Be a Star, 1987. Cmty. worker People United to Save Humanity, Chgo., 1973, Harold Washington Orgn., Chgo., 1987; cmty. educator Chgo. Planned Parenthood, 1988; cmty. counselor Lincoln Cmty. Ctr., Chgo., 1975; mem. sch. bd. Dist. 160, 1994, now v.p.; mem. Ill. State Sch. Bd., 1997-98; bd. dirs. Operation P.U.S.H.; vice chmn. Ill. Assn. Sch. Bds., Ill. State Assn. Bd.; bd. dirs. Ill. State Assn. Bd., So. Cook Div., 2003-; v.p. Sch. Dist. #160; mem. Grace M.B. Ch. Named Tchr. of the Yr., Faulkner Sch., 1976; recipient Nat. Sch. Bd. award for Disting. Svc., Ill. State Assn. Bd., 2003. Mem. Ill. Edn. Assn., NEA, Harvey Edn. Assn., Tennis Club, Traveling Club, Phi Delta Kappa, Pi Lambda Theta. Democrat. Baptist. Avocations: singing, bowling, piano. Home: 18029 Ravisloe Ter Country Club Hills IL 60478-8442

MCCLELLAND, JAMES LLOYD, psychologist, educator, cognitive neuroscientist; b. Cambridge, Mass., Dec. 1, 1948; s. Walter Moore and Frances (Shaffer) McClelland; m. Heidi Marsha Feldman, May 6, 1978; children: Mollie S., Heather Ann. BA in Psychology, Columbia U., 1970; PhD in Cognitive Psychology, U. Pa., 1975. Asst. prof. dept. psychology U. California, San Diego, 1974-80, assoc. prof., 1980-84, Carnegie-Mellon U., Pitts., 1984-85, prof. psychology, 1985—2006, co-dir. Ctr. for Neural Basis of Cognition, 1994—2006, univ. prof., 2001—06, Walter Van Dyke Bingham chair in psychology and cognitive neurosci., 2002—06; prof. psychology, dir. Ctr. Mind, Brain and Computation Stanford U., Calif., 2006—. Rev. panel for cognition, emotion and personality NIMH, 1983-87, Cognitive Functional Neurosci., 1995-99, chair 1997-99; mem. Nat. Adv. Mental Health Coun., 2000-2003. Author: (with others) Parallel Distributed Processing: Explorations in the Microstructure of Cognition, Vols. I, II, 1986; co-author: A Handbook of Models, Programs, and Exercises, 1988, Semantic Cognition: A Parallel-Distributed Processing Approach, 2004; contbr. numerous articles, reports, book chpts. to profl. publs.; sr. editor Cognitive Sci., 1988-91; sect. editor (Cognitive Neuroscience), Internat. Ency. of The Social and Behavioral Sciences; mem. numerous jour. edit. bds. Recipient William W. Cumming prize, Columbia U., 1970, Rsch. Scientist Career Devel. award, NIMH, 1981—86, 1987—97; co-recipient Grawemeyer prize in psychology, 2002; grantee, NSF, 1976—79, 1980—84, 1986—87, 1988—, Office Naval Rsch., 1982—87; fellow, NSF, 1970—73. Fellow: APA (Disting. Sci. Contbn. award 1996), AAAS, Am. Psychol. Soc. (William James Fellow award 2003—04); mem.: NAS, Fedn. Behavioral Psychol. and Cognitive Scis. (pres. elect 2008—), Soc. Exptl. Psychologists (Warren medal 1993), Internat. Assn. for Study Attention and Performance (lectr. 1986, governing bd. 1986—94), Psychonomics Soc., Cognitive Sci. Soc. (governing bd. 1988—93, chmn. 1991), Phi Beta Kappa. Office: Stanford Univ Dept Psychology Jordan Hall Bldg 420 450 Serra Mall Stanford CA 94305-2130 Business E-Mail: mcclelland@stanford.edu.

MC CLELLAND, ROBERT NELSON, surgeon, educator; b. Gilmer, Tex., Nov. 20, 1929; s. Robert Hilton and Verna Louise (Nelson) McC.; m. Connie Logan, May 5, 1958; children: Robert Christopher, Alison, Julie. BA, U. Tex., Austin, 1952; MD, U. Tex., Galveston, 1954. Diplomate Am. Bd. Surgery. Rotating intern U. Kans. Med. center, 1954-55; resident in gen. surgery Parkland Hosp., Dallas, 1957-59, 60-62; instr. surgery Southwestern Med. Sch., U. Tex., Dallas, 1962-63, asst. prof., 1963-67, asso. prof., 1967-71, prof., 1971—, Alvin Baldwin prof. surgery, 1977—. Examiner Nat. Bd. Med. Examiners Editor Audio Jour. Rev. Gen. Surgery, 1971-82, Selected Readings in Gen. Surgery, 1974—; contbr. numerous articles to profl. jours., chpts. to books. Served to capt. M.C. USAF, 1955-57. Fellow ACS (mem. grad. edn. com.); mem. AMA, Am. Surg. Assn., Western Surg. Assn., Soc. Surgery of Alimentary Tract, Am. Gastroent. Assn., Southwestern Surg. Soc., So. Surg. Assn., Dallas Soc. Gen. Surgeons (pres. 1987-88), Tex. Surg. Soc., Tex. Med. Assn., Dallas Country Med. Soc., Soc. Internatale de Chiurgie (bd. dirs. Am. chpt.), Phi Beta Kappa, Alpha Omega Alpha. Republican. Methodist. Home: 3601 Potomac Ave Dallas TX 75205-2110 Office: 5323 Harry Hines Blvd Dallas TX 75390-7208

MCCLELLAND, SHEARWOOD, III, physician; b. NYC, May 24, 1978; s. Shearwood J. McClelland and Yvonne S. Thornton. Artium Baccalaureus, Harvard Coll., Cambridge, Mass., 2000; MD, Columbia U. Coll. of Physicians and Surgeons, NYC, 2004. Extramural post-doc. rsch. fellow NIH, NYC, 2004—05; physician U. Minn., Mpls., 2006—. Recipient Life Chess Master, US Chess Fedn., 1996, Nat. Scholar-Chessplayer award, 1996, US Jr. Open Chess Champion, 1997, NJ State Chess Champion, NJ State Chess Fedn., 1997—98, Wilbert C. Jordan Clin. Sci. Rsch. award, Student Nat. Med. Assn., 2004, Young Investigator award, Am. Epilepsy Soc., 2006, Cone Pevehouse award, Am. Assn. Neurol. Surgeons, 2008. Mem.: US Chess Fedn., World Soc. Stereotactic and Functional Neurosurgery, Am. Soc. Stereotactic and Functional Neurosurgery, Congress Neurol. Surgeons (Life Chess Master award 1996, Nat. Scholar-Chessplayer award 1996, Jr. Open Chess Champion winner 1997), Am. Assn. Neurol. Surgeons. Democrat. Mem. Christian Ch. Achievements include first to examine the efficacy of hemispherectomy in adult patients with intractable epilepsy; first African-American to win multiple national chess championships; most national chess championships by an African-American. E-mail: drwood@post.harvard.edu.

MCCLELLAND, SHEARWOOD JUNIOR, orthopaedic surgeon; s. Shearwood and Zenobia McClelland; m. Yvonne Shirley Thornton, 1974; children: Shearwood III, Kimberly. AB, Princeton U., 1969; MD, Columbia U., 1974, MPH, 1996. Diplomate Am. Bd. Orthopaedic Surgery., Nat. Bd. Med. Examiners, 1975. Intern St. Luke's Hosp., NYC, 1974—75; resident St. Luke;s Hosp., 1975—76; asst. resident in orthop. surgery N.Y. Orthop. Hosp., 1976—79; lt. comdr. USNR, 1979—82; staff orthop. surgeon Nat. Naval Med. Ctr., Bethesda, Md., 1979—82; asst. prof. surgery Uniformed Svcs. U. Health Scis., 1980—82; acting chief orthop. surgery Harlem Hosp. Ctr., 1983—84, assoc. dir. orthop. surgery, 1985—92, acting dir., 1992—94, dir., 1994—; asst. prof. clin. orthop. surgery Columbia U., 1983—94, assoc. prof. clinic, 1994—. Oral examiner Am. Bd. Othopaedic Surgery, 1993—; mem. N.Y. State Bd. of Profl. Med. Conduct, 1989-98. Annie C. Kane fellow in orthopaedic surgery, 1978-79; fellow in total joint implant surgery Ohio State U., 1982. Recipient Alumni Fedn. medal, Columbia U., 2005, P&S Gold medal, 2006, Am. Leading Dr., Black Enterprise Mag., 2001; named America's Leading Physician, 2001, 2008; fellow, Nat. Assn. Pub. Hosps., 2005. Fellow ACS, AMA, Am. Acad. Orthop. Surgeons, N.Y. Acad. Medicine, Nat. Assn. Pub. Hosps.; mem. Assn. Mil. Surgeons U.S., Am. Coll. Phys. Execs., N.Y. Orthop. Hosp. Alumni Assn., Mensa, No. N.J. Princeton Alumni Assn., Columbia P&S Alumni Assoc. (pres. 2002-04, Alumni Fedn. medal 2005) Office: Harlem Hosp Ctr Dept Orthopaedic Surgery 506 Lenox Ave New York NY 10037-1802 Office Phone: 212-939-3510. E-mail: sjm2@columbia.edu.

MCCLENDON, AUBREY K., energy executive; m. Kathleen Byrns. Graduate, Trinity Coll. Duke Univ., 1981. Independent producer of oil & gas, 1982—89; co-founder, chmn., CEO Chesapeake Energy Corp., Okla. City, 1989—. Mem. bd. vis. Fuqua Sch. Bus., Duke Univ., Fuqua Sch. Bus. Duke Univ. Named one of Forbes' Richest Americans, 2006. Office: Chesapeake Energy Corp PO Box 18496 Oklahoma City OK 73154-0496

MC CLENDON, WILLIAM HUTCHINSON, III, retired lawyer; b. New Orleans, Feb. 19, 1933; s. William H. and Eleanor (Eaton) McC.; m. Eugenia Mills Slaughter, Feb. 6, 1960; children: William Hutchinson, IV, Virginia Morris, Eleanor Eaton, Bryan Slaughter. BA, Tulane U., 1956, LLB, 1958. Bar: La. 1958, US Supreme Ct. 1964. Atty. Humble Oil & Refining Co., 1958-60; with firm Taylor, Porter, Brooks & Phillips, Baton Rouge, 1960—, ptnr., 1966-2001, mem. exec. com., 1987-2001; mediator, assoc. Mediation Arbitration Profl. Sys., Inc., 1999—2001. Instr. comml. law and negotiable instruments Am. Inst. Banking, 1963-74; lectr. movable Property La. Bar Assn. Bridging the Gap Inst., 1965; lectr. La. State U. LAw Sch. and Real Estate Seminar chmn., 1972, 74, 76, 80, 82, 85, 87, 95, La. Soc. of Profl. Surveying, 1989, La. Soc. CPA's, 1991, Banking Seminar, 1995; adj. prof. La. State U. Legal Negotiation, 1983—, U. Tenn., 2003-, Western Carolina U., 2003-; mem. faculty Profl. Edn. Group, Inc. Author: Negotiate Effectively The Art of Persuasion Using Timeless Values; Contbr. articles to legal jour. Bd. dir. Cancer Soc. Baton Rouge, 1968-71; trustee Episcopal HS, 1976-78; mem. Dean's council Tulane U. Law Sch., 1984-88. Served to capt. AUS. Recipient Preservation award Found. for Hist. La., 1997 Mem. ABA, Am. Judicature Soc., La. Bar Assn. (chmn. sect. trust estates, probate and immovable property law 1969-70, Meml. award article 1987), Baton Rouge Bar Assn. (chmn. title standards com. 1968-69), Tulane Alumni Assn. Greater Baton Rouge (pres. 1968-69), Baton Rouge Green (bd. dir. 1991-93), Hilltop Aboretum (bd. dir. 1993-95), La. Civil Svc. League (pres. 1992-94), La. Tulane Law Alumni (treas., 2d v.p. 1964-65), Baton Rouge Assembly (treas. 1983, ball chmn. 1997, chmn. 1999), Toastmasters (pres. 1970), Pickwick Club, Rotary (bd. dir. Baton Rouge club 1972), Kappa Alpha, Baton Rouge Symphony (bd. dir. 2001-02). Republican. Episcopalian (vestry, sr. warden 1975, 81, 84, diocesan standing com. 1985-89). Personal E-mail: wh.mcclendoniii@verizon.net.

MCCLENNEN, MIRIAM J., former state official; b. Seattle, Sept. 16, 1923; d. Phillip and Frieda (Golub) Jacobs; m. Louis McClennen, Apr. 25, 1969; stepchildren: Adams Peter, James C.A., Helen, Persis, Crane, Emery. BA, U. Wash., 1945; MBA, Northwestern U., 1947. Exec. trainee Marshall Field & Co., Chgo., 1945-47; buyer Frederick & Nelson (subs. of Marshall Field), 1949-57, Goldwaters, Phoenix, 1963—67; adminstrv. asst. to pres. Ariz. State Senate, Phoenix, 1973-76; dir. publs. Office of Sec. of State, Phoenix, 1976-87. Chairwoman legis. subcom. adminstrv. procedure Ariz. State Legislature, Phoenix, 1984-85. Original compiler, codifier, editor publ. Ariz. Adminstrv. Code, 1973-87, Ariz. Adminstrv. Register, 1976-87. Mem. Cape Mus. Fine Arts, 1996—2007; commr. Ariz. Commn. on Arts, 1989—96; bd. dirs., mem. exec. bd. Phoenix Symphony Guild, 1969—88; bd. dirs., mem. Phoenix Art Mus. League, 1972—90; bd. dirs. Phoenix Art Coun., 1973—78; bd. dirs., sec. Advisory Bd. Combined Met. Phoenix Arts and Scis., 1974—95; bd. dirs. Master Apprentice Programs, 1980—83; bd. dirs., mem. exec. bd. life trustee Heard Mus., 1982—; mem. adv. bd. Ariz. State Hist. Records, 1987—90, Combined Met. Phoenix Arts and Scis., 1990—95; bd. dirs. Arizonans for Cultural Devel., 1996—2002; mem. Phoenix Symphony Bd. Overseers, 2007—. Recipient Disting. Svc. award Atty. Gen. Ariz., 1987, Outstanding Svc. to People, Ariz. State Senate, 1987, Nat. Assn. Secs. of State award, 1987. Mem.: Ballet Ariz., Univ. Club, Ariz. Club, Phoenix Country Club, Charter 100 (bd. dirs. 1981—85). Personal E-mail: mjmlm@cox.net.

MCCLINTOCK, ANNE, literature and language professor; d. Eric and Carmella McClintock; life ptnr. Robert Donald Nixon. PhD, Columbia U., NY, 1987. Asst. prof. English Columbia U., 1987—98; prof. English & women's studies U. Wis., Madison, 1999—. Author: (book) Imperial Leather (MacArthur Found. Peace & Security fellowship, 1991); contbr. articles to profl. jours. Recipient award, Am. Coun. Learned Soc., 2005. Business E-Mail: rdnixon@wisc.edu.

MCCLINTOCK, JESSICA, fashion designer; b. Frenchville, Maine, June 19, 1930; d. Rene Gagnon and Verna Hedrich; m. Frank Staples (dec. 1964); 1 child Scott. BA, San Jose State U., 1963. Elem. sch. tchr., Marblehead, Mass., 1966-68, Long Island, N.Y., 1968, Sunnyvale, Calif., 1964-65, 68-69; fashion designer Jessica McClintock, Inc., San Francisco, 1969—. Active donor, AIDS and Homeless programs; scholarship sponsor Fashion Inst. Design and Merchandising. Recipient Merit award Design, 1989, Dallas Fashion award, 1988, Tommy award, 1986, Pres. Appreciation award, 1986, Best Interior Store Design, 1986, Calif. Designer award, 1985, Earnie award, 1981, numerous others. Mem. Coun. Fashion Designers of Am., Fashion Inst. Design & Merchandising (adv. bd. 1979—), San Francisco Fashion Industry (pres. 1976-78, bd. dirs. 1989). Office: Jessica McClintock Inc 1400 16th St San Francisco CA 94103-5181*

MCCLINTOCK, KENNETH D. (KENNETH D. MCCLINTOCK-HERNANDEZ), Puerto Rican secretary of state, former state legislator; b. London, Jan. 19, 1957; arrived in PR, 1957; s. George Davison and Nivea M. (Hernández) McClintock; m. María E. Batista, 1994; children: Kevin, Stephanie. Attended, U. PR, San Juan, 1974-77; JD, Tulane U., 1980. Staff dir. consumer affairs com. PR House Reps., San Juan, 1977, legis. asst., 1978-80; legis. cons. PR House Reps./Senate, San Juan, 1981-92; city councilman San Juan City Coun., 1991-92; senator PR Senate, San Juan, 1993—2008, chmn. govtl. & fed. affairs com.; sec. state Commonwealth of PR, San Juan, 2009—; co-chair Hillary Clinton Puerto Rico Campaign. Mem., Pres. Carter appointee Nat. Adv. Com. on Juvenile Justice, Washington, 1978-81; pres. Parliamentary Conf. America, 2000 Mem.-at-large Dem. Nat. Platform Com.; chmn. Dems. for Statehood, San Juan, 1989-93; exec. dir. PR State Dem. Com., San Juan, 1984-88; co-chair New Progressive Party Platform Com., 1996; vice chmn. Coun. State Govts., 1996-97, chmn.-elect, 1997-98, chmn., 1998; bd. dirs. Washington Ctr. for Internships. Recipient Inst. TV and Radio Ethics award PR TV and Radio Inst., 1989, 90, State Legislator of Yr. award, The Washington Ctr., 2008; named one of Outstanding Young Men, Jaycees, 1984. Mem.: PR 2000, Puerto Ricans in Civic Action, Inter-Am. Acad. PR, PR Statehood Student's Assn. Democrat. Episcopalian. Avocations: numismatist, reading, swimming. Office: PR Dept State Box 9023271 San Juan PR 00902 Office Phone: 787-722-4010. Personal E-mail: kenneth.mcclintock@yahoo.com.

MCCLINTOCK, MARGARET ELEANOR, finance educator; d. Florence Martin Rabon; children: Roseanne Marie Gwin, Larisa Ann Ritchie, Monica Lynn Ritchie, Vanessa Lee Ritchie. BS in Info. Sys. Mgmt., San Diego State U., 1971; MBA, Ohio U., Athens, 1986, PhD, 1996. CDP Inst. Cert. Computer Profls., 1986, Ic3 Certiport in Miss., 2005. MIS dir. Fisherman's Hosp., Marathon, Fla., 1973—77; sys. analyst Ohio U., Athens, 1978—82; MIS instr. Miami U. & Hocking Coll., Ohio, 1982—87; MIS dir. Yuma County Govt., Ariz., 1987—91, Shawnee State U., Portsmouth, Ohio, 1991—96; dept. chair acctg. and MIS, prof. MIS Miss. U. Women, Columbus, Miss., 1996—. Geneal. rschr. Monroe County Pub. Libr., Key West, 2005—; bahamian rsch. U. Fla., Gainesville, 2005—. Contbr. scientific papers (3 Disting. Paper awards, 1998, 2000, 2002). Rschr. and hist. records transcription Various Chs. And Libr., Key West, 2005—. Hist. Rsch. grant, U. Fla., 2006—08, Miss. U. Women, 2007. Mem.: Beta Gamma Sigma. Achievements include websites on bahamian records. Avocation: genealogy. Office: Miss Univ Women Coll of Business Box W940 Columbus MS 39701 Business E-Mail: maggiem@bu.muw.edu.

MCCLINTOCK, PETER L., federal agency administrator; b. NY, 1948; BS, Wagner Coll., Staten Island, 1970; MBA, George Mason U., Fairfax, Va., 1976. Cert. Govt. Fin. Planner. With US Dept. Housing & Urban Devel. (HUD), US Dept. Commerce; dep. inspector gen. US Small Bus. Adminstrn. (SBA), 1999—, acting inspector gen., 2008—. Office: US Small Bus Adminstrn 409 3rd St SW Washington DC 20416 Office Phone: 202-205-6586. Business E-Mail: OIG@sba.gov.*

MCCLINTOCK, RICHARD POLSON, dermatologist; b. Lancaster, NH, Dec. 16, 1933; s. Richard P. and Dorothy Grace McClintock; m. Barbara Wyatt, June 1959 (div. Mar. 1970); children: Peter, Pamela; m. Mary Joy Fitzgerald, Mar. 21, 1970; children: Wayne, Patrick. BA, Dartmouth Coll., 1956; MD, Harvard U., 1960. Diplomate Am. Bd. Dermatology, Am. Bd. Dermatopathology. Intern in medicine U. N.C., Chapel Hill, 1960-61; resident in dermatology Stanford U., Palo Alto, Calif., 1964-67; pvt. practice Ukiah, Calif., 1967—; clin. instr. dermatology Stanford U., Palo Alto, 1967-78, clin. asst. prof., 1978-86, assoc. clin. prof., 1986-92, lectr., 1992-98, assoc. clin. prof., 1998—. Mem. hosp. staff Ukiah Valley Med. Ctr., chief of staff, 1974. Contbr. articles to profl. jours. Trustee Found. for Med. Care for Mendocino and Lake Counties, 1990-2008, pres., 1992-94. Lt. Med. Corps, USN, 1961-64. Mem. San Francisco Dermatol. Soc. (Practitioner of Yr. 2004), Pacific Dermatol. Assn., Am. Acad. Dermatology, Calif. Med. Soc., Mendocino Lake County Med. Soc., Internat. Soc. Dermatopathology. Office: 723 S Dora St Ukiah CA 95482-5335 Office Phone: 707-462-1401. E-mail: fitzmac@pacific.net.

MCCLINTOCK, STUART, language educator; married. BA, Williams Coll.; MA, NYU; D in Modern Langs., Middlebury Coll. Assoc. prof. French Midwestern State U., Wichita Falls, Tex., 1993—. Office: Midwestern State Univ 3410 Taft Blvd Wichita Falls TX 76308

MCCLINTOCK, TOM (THOMAS MILLER MCCLINTOCK II), United States Representative from California, former state senator; b. Bronxville, NY, July 10, 1956; s. Thomas Miller and Marianne (Christy) McClintock; m. Lori McClintock; children: Justin, Shannah. BA, UCLA, 1978. Chief of staff to Senator Ed Davis Calif. State Senate, 1980—82; mem. Calif. House of Reps. from Dist. 28, 1982—92, Calif. House of Reps. from Dist. 38, 1996—2000, Republican whip, 1984—89; mem. Calif. State Senate from Dist. 19, 2000—09, vice chmn. transp. & housing com., mem. revenue & taxation com., pub. employment & retirement com., com. on legis. ethics, joint com. on rules, joint legis. audit com.; mem. US Congress from 4th Calif. Dist., 2009—. Mem. housing and cmty. devel. Calif. Ho. of Reps. Recipient Benjamin Franklin award, Calif. Printing Industry, Medal of Merit, Ventura County Peace Officers Assn. Republican. Office: US Congress 508 Cannon House Office Bldg Washington DC 20515-0504 also: Dist Office 4230 Douglas Blvd Ste 200 Granite Bay CA 95746 Office Phone: 202-225-2511, 916-786-5560. Office Fax: 202-225-5444, 916-786-6364.*

MCCLINTON, DONALD GEORGE, retired diversified holding company executive; b. Pitts., June 30, 1933; s. Donald K. and Ethel M. McC.; m. Jane Ann Knoebel, Apr. 12, 1958; children: Catherine, D. Scott. BS, Miami U., Oxford, Ohio, 1955. Audit mgr. Arthur Andersen & Co., Cleve., 1955-62; mgr. accounting E. Ohio Gas Co., Cleve., 1962-66; exec. v.p. Nat. Industries, Inc., Louisville, 1966-79; pres. Yellow Cab Co., Louisville, 1979-94; owner, chmn. bd. Interlock Industries, Inc., 1982-94; pres. Skylight Thoroughbred Tng. Ctr., Inc., 1994—2002. Bd. dirs. Almost Framily, Clifton Ctr., MidAm. Bancorp, 1980—2002; trustee Jewish Hosp. Health Care Systems, Inc., 1983—2004, 2006—. Mem. Louisville-Jefferson County Bicentennial Commn., 1976-77; mem. coun., treas. Old Kentucky Home. coun. Boy Scouts Am., 1976-94; mem. Citizens at Large Jefferson County Budget Com., 1978-84; bd. overseers Bellarmine Coll., 1978-84; bd. dirs. Ky. Derby Festival, 1978—, Jewish Hosp., Louisville, 1978-83; trustee Spalding U., 1985-91. Mem.: Fin. Execs. Inst. Personal E-mail: dmcclinton502@aol.com. Business E-Mail: dmcclinton@insight.bb.com.

MCCLINTON, JOANIE, elementary and secondary school educator; b. Dec. 3, 1964; BA in Spanish, U. Memphis, Tenn., 1988, MA in English, ESL, 2003. Tchr. Memphis Pub. Schs., 1989—. Author: Gift of Devotion, 1992. Mem.: Zeta Phi Beta (2d v.p. 2006—). Home: 3358 Wesfield Dr Memphis TN 38115-4234 E-mail: mcclintonjoanie@mcsk12.net.

MCCLISH, RICHARD R., transportation executive; B in Mech. Engring., U. Akron. Sr. mgr. Gen. Electric Plastics; chief process officer, interim chief info.officer R.R. Donnelly & Sons; v.p., continuous improvement Union Pacific RR Co., 2004—. Bd. dirs. Past bd. dirs. YMCA. Office: Union Pacific Corp 1400 Douglas St Omaha NE 68179 Office Phone: 402-544-5000. Office Fax: 402-501-0011.*

MCCLISTER, MICHAEL, writer; b. Bristol, Va., July 9, 1941; s. Cecil McClister and Pauline McNeil; divorced; children: Porter, Jennifer. BA, U. N.C., Chapel Hill, 1962; MA, Rutgers U., New Brunswick, NJ, 1963. Author: Campaign Manual Series -- Democratic National Committee, 1976, Grassroots Campaigning -- National Education Association, 1981, Victim's Choice, 1999, Double Deal, 2000. Mem.: Phi Beta Kappa. Home: PO Box 3279 Placida FL 33946-3279 Home Phone: 941-716-0273. Home Fax: 941-697-1868. Personal E-mail: mcclister123@comcast.net.

MCCLOSKEY, DEIRDRE NANSEN, economics and history educator; b. Ann Arbor, Mich., Sept. 11, 1942; s. Robert Green and Helen (Stueland) McC.; m. J. Comi, June 19, 1965 (div. 1995); children: Daniel Robert, Margaret Anne. BA, Harvard U., 1964, PhD, 1970. Mem. faculty U. Chgo., 1968-80, assoc. prof. econs., 1973-80, assoc. prof. history, 1979-80; prof. econs. and history U. Iowa, Iowa City, 1980-99; Disting. Prof. Econs., History, English, and Comm. U. Ill., Chgo., 1999—. Vis. prof. Erasmus U. Rotterdam, Stanford U., Austrialian Nat. U., U. York, U. Manchester, U. London, U. Free State, South Africa. Author: Economic Maturity and Entrepreneurial Decline, 1973, Enterprise and Trade in Victorian Britain, 1981, The Applied Theory of Price, 1986, The Rhetoric of Economics, 1986, If You're So Smart, 1990, Knowledge and Persuasion in Economics, 1994, The Vices of Economists, 1996, Crossing: A Memoir, 1999, How to Be Human Though an Economist, 2001, Bourgeois Virtues: Ethic for an Age of Commerce, (with S. Ziliak) The Cult of Statistical Significance, 2008; editor: Jour. Econ. History, 1980-85. Fellow Guggenheim, 1983, Inst. for Advanced Study-Princeton, N.J., 1983-84 Mem. Am. Econ. History Assn. (pres. 1996-97), Social Sci. History Assn. (pres.), Midwest Econ. Assn. (pres. 1992), Ea. Econ. Assn. (pres. 2003). Home: 720 S Dearborn St Apt 206 Chicago IL 60605-1820 Office: Dept Economics U Ill 601 S Morgan 210UH M/C 144 Chicago IL 60607 Office Phone: 312-996-3913. Office Fax: 312-996-3344. E-mail: deirdre2@uic.edu.

MCCLOSKEY, J(OHN) MICHAEL, retired environmental policy organization manager; b. Eugene, Oreg., Apr. 26, 1934; s. John Clement and Agnes Margaret (Studer) McC.; m. Maxine Mugg Johnson, June 17, 1965 (dec. 2006); stepchildren: Claire, Laura, James, Rosemary Johnson. BA, Harvard U., 1956; JD, U. Oreg., 1961. N.W. rep. Sierra Club, Eugene, 1961-65, asst. to pres. San Francisco, 1965-66, conservation dir., 1966-69, exec. dir., 1969-85, chmn. Washington, 1985-99, acting exec. dir., 1986-87; vice-chmn. Commn. on Environ. Law and Policy (Internat. Union for Conservation of Nature), Gland, Switzerland, 1978-88; mem. Pres.'s Commn. on Agenda for 1980's, Washington, 1979-80; co-chmn. OSHA-Environ. Conf., Washington, 1983-87; vice chmn. Am. Com. on Internat. Conservation, 1988-90; mem. Internat. Union Conservation of Nature World Commn. Protected Areas, 1988—; ret.; with urban forestry commn. City of Portland, 2005—; chmn. Portland Heritage Tree Com. Mem. adj. faculty Sch. Natural Resources, U. Mich., 1988—2000; chmn. Mineral Policy Ctr., 1998-2001, Nat. Resources Coun. of Am., 1992-93; co-chmn. environ. policy task force Pres.'s Coun. Sustainable Devel., 1997-99; pres. Fedn. of Western Outdoor Clubs, 2000-03. Contbr. articles to profl. jours. Bd. dirs. Nat. Resources Coun. Am., 1988-94, vice chmn., 1989-91, chmn., 1992-93, chmn. Advocacy Forum, 1989-91; bd. dirs. Ind. Sector, 1990-96, Mineral Policy Ctr., 1988-2001, Coalition for Environmentally Responsible Economies, 1989-99, OMB Watch, 1998-2004; bd. trustees Sierra Club Found., 2000—; mem. steering com. Blueprint for Environ., 1987-88; nominated candidate Oreg. Ho. of Reps., 1962. Recipient award Calif. Conservation Coun., 1969, John Muir award Sierra Club, 1979, UN Environ. Program Global 500 award, 1992, Lifetime Achievement award Wild Found., 1998, Honor award Natural Resources Coun. Am., 1999, Packard award Internat. Union for Conservation of Nature Parks Commn., 2003, Conservation award Fedn. of Western Outdoor Clubs, 2004, Lifetime Achievement award Pub. Land Law Conf., 2006. Mem. Explorers Club (NYC). Democrat. Personal E-mail: jmmccloskey@aol.com.

MCCLOSKEY, MICHAEL, social sciences, psychology, and sociology educator; AB with honors, U. Scranton, Pa., 1965; MA, Loyola U., Chgo., 1969, PhD, 1974; MDiv, Cath. Theol. Union Chgo., 1987. Ordained Roman Cath. deacon Holy Name Cathedral, Chgo. Asst. prof. Benedictine U., Lisle, Ill., 1970—74; prof. social sci., psychology, sociology Harry S. Truman City Coll., Chgo., 1974—. Recipient Grad. medal, Loyola U. Chgo., 1970, Centennial medallion, 1970; Arthur J. Schmitt scholar, Schmitt Found., 1969—70. Mem.: Religious Rsch. Assn. (mng. editor 1972—78), Assn. for Sociology Religion, Am. Sociol. Assn. Office: Harry S Truman City College 1145 W Wilson Ave Chicago IL 60640-6063

MCCLOSKEY, PETE (PAUL NORTON MCCLOSKEY JR.), lawyer, former congressman; b. San Bernardino, Calif., Sept. 29, 1927; s. Paul Norton & Vera McNabb McCloskey; m. Caroline Wadsworth, 1949 (div.); children: Nancy, Peter, John, Kathleen; m. Helen Virginia Hooper, 1982 AB, Stanford, 1950, LL.B., 1953; JD, Santa Clara Law Sch., 1974. Bar: Calif., 1953. Dep. dist. atty. Alameda County, Calif., 1953-54; mem. firm McCloskey, Wilson, Mosher & Martin, Palo Alto, 1956-67; mem. US Congress from 11th Calif. Dist., 1967-83; ptnr. Brobeck Phleger & Harrison, 1983-89; counsel McClung & Davis, Laguna Hills, Calif.; founder, ptnr. Law Office of Paul McCloskey; ptnr. McCloskey, Hubbard, Ebert & Moore, LLP; prin. Cotchett, Pitre & McCarthy, San Francisco, 2008—. Del. UN Law of Sea Conf.; lectr. in law Stanford Law Sch., 1964-67, Santa Clara Law Sch., 1964-67; co-chair, Earth Day, 1970; mem., US Commn. on Nat. & Cmty. Svc., 1990-92 Author: Guide of Professional Conduct for New Practitioners, 1961, Text on the US Constitution, 1961, Truth and Untruth: Political Deceit in America, 1972, The Taking of Hill 610, 1992 Served with USN, 1945-47, to col. USMC, 1950-52. Decorated Navy Cross, Silver Star, Purple Heart; named Young Man of Yr. Palo Alto Jr. C. of C., 1961; recipient Edgar Wayburn award, Sierra Club, 2006 Mem. ABA, Palo Alto Bar Assn. (pres. 1960-61), Santa Clara County Bar Assn. (trustee 1965-67), State Bar Calif. (pres. conf. barristers 1961-62), Family Svc. Assn., Phi Delta Phi. Democrat. Presbyterian. Achievements include co-authoring the 1973 Endangered Species Act. Office: Cotchett Pitre & McCarthy San Francisco Airport Ctr 840 Malcolm Rd Burlingame CA 94010*

MCCLOUD, ANECE FAISON, retired academic administrator; b. Dudley, NC, May 29, 1937; d. J.D. Faison and Nancy Jane (Simmons) Faison-Cole; m. Verable Lancaster McCloud, June 1, 1959; children: Aja Siobhan, Carla Danette. BS, Bennette Coll., Greensboro, NC, 1959; MA, U. Nebr., Omaha, 1989; Basic Mediations Skills, Ea. Mennonite Coll., 1994. Tchr. Lincoln Jr. HS, Greensboro, NC, 1959-60, Woodbridge Airforce Base, England, 1961-62; resident advisor and ednl. coord. Child Saving Inst., Omaha, 1967-71; asst. registrar for acad. records U. Nebr. Med. Ctr., Omaha, 1972-76, first dir. minority student affairs, 1976-85; assoc. dean of students Washington and Lee U., Lexington, Va., 1985—99. Cons. Deans Forum on Revitalizing Health Profl. Edn., Dept. of Health and Human Svcs., 1985, Campus Alcohol Initiative, N.C. Gov.'s Inst. Alcohol and Substance Abuse, 1999, Peer Rev., Health Careet Opportunity Program, 1982, 1984; cons. on simulated minority admissions Assn. Am. Med. Colls., Washington, 1979. Bd. mem., v.p. Rockbridge Area Housing Corp., Lexington, 1988—90; mem. Va. adv. com. US Commn. on Civil Rights, 1995—99; mem. Va. Identification Program for Advancement of Women in Higher Edn., 1995—96; treas. Mayor's Commn. on Status of Women, Omaha, 1977—78. Recipient Plaque for Outstanding Svc. to Washington and Lee Cmty., 1994, Cert. Acknowledgement of Contbn. to Edn., Omaha Pub. Schs., 1984, Cert. Black History Month Spkr., VA Hosp., Omaha, 1977; grantee Health Career Opportunity, Disadvantaged Assistance Office, HHS, 1976, 1980, 1983; Anece F. McCloud Excellence in Diversity award established in her honor, Washington and Lee U., 2001. Mem. Am. Assn. for Higher Edn., Nat. Assn. For Women in Edn., Am. Coll. Personnel Assn., Assn. of Am. Med. Colls., Am. Assn. of Counseling and Devel., Nebr. Assn. for Non-White Concerns, Nebr. Assn. of Collegiate Registrars and Admissions Officers (chairperson sub.-com. on minority affairs 1978-84), Nat. Assn. of Med. Minority Educators (vice coord. 1982-83). Democrat. Avocations: social research, writing, interior decorating.

MCCLOUD, MELODY T., obstetrician, gynecologist, surgeon, media consultant, health care strategist; BA, Boston U., 1977, MD, 1981. Intern Emory U. Affiliated Hosps., Atlanta, 1981-82, resident in ob-gyn., 1982-85; pres., founder, CEO Atlanta Women's Health Care, 1985—. Bd. dirs. Vis. Nurses Health Sys., Atlanta; spkr. Nat. Dental Assn.-Atlanta Bus. League, 1995, Speaking of Women's Health, Universal Sisters, Nat. Coalition 100 Black Women, Congl. Black Caucus-Women, others; cons. health WXIA-TV, Atlanta, 1995, 99; owner McCloud Renaissance, LLC, pres., med. editor Nat. Orgn. African-Am. Women Author: Medical Bloopers!! Amusing, Amazing Stories, 1994, The Health Diary for Women, 1999, Blessed Health, 2003, Melodies of the Heart, 2004; med. advisor Body and Soul, 1994. Med. support group Com. Olympic Games, Atlanta, 1996; chair selection com. YWCA Acad., Atlanta, 1992 Inductee Leadership Atlanta, YWCA Acad. for Women Achievers; named Bus. Woman of Yr. Am. Bus. Women's Assn., Atlanta's Top 100 Black Women of Influence Atlanta Bus. League, 2008; recipient Cmty. Health Svc. award Black Pages. Mem. Med. Assn. Ga., Ga. Ob-Gyn Soc., Med. Assn. Atlanta, Atlanta Med. Assn., Soc. Laparoendoscopic Surgeons. Baptist. Avocations: tennis, bowling, water sports, theater, travel. Office: Melody T McCloud MD PO Box 344 Roswell GA 30077-0344 Office Phone: 770-921-6038. E-mail: mtm@drmccloud.com.

MCCLOUGHAN, SCOT G., professional sports team executive; b. San Leandro, Calif., 1971; s. Kent McCloughan; m. Kelli A. McCloughan; children: Caden, Adison, Avery. Attended, Wichita State U. Minor league baseball player St. Catharines Blue Jays; scout Green Bay Packers, 1994—97; dir., coll. scouting Seattle Seahawks, 2000—04; v.p, pro personnel San Francisco 49ers, 2004—07, gen. mgr., 2008—. Office: c/o San Francisco 49ers Marie P DeBartolo Sports Ctr 4949 Centennial Blvd Santa Clara CA 95054*

MCCLOY, SHIRLEY, adapted physical education specialist; b. Riverton, Utah, May 30, 1972; d. Ronald J. and LaFawn Stepan; m. Scott Alexander McCloy, May 14, 1994; children: Makenna, Tamika. AA, Coll. So. Idaho, Twin Falls, 1993; BS, U. Utah, Salt Lake City, 2005, MS, 2006. Cert. tchr. Utah, adapted phys. educator 2006. Coach Globe Unified Sch. Dist., Ariz., 1995—96, Jordan Sch. Dist., Salt Lake City, 1997—98; claims processor Unibase, Salt Lake City, 1999—2000; referee Tooele Jr. Jazz, Utah, 2000; stocker/receiver Maceys Grocery, Tooele, 2000—02; coach Tooele Sch. Dist., 2000—03; asst. coord. UFIT U. Utah, Salt Lake City, 2006; tchr. health, phys. edn. Tooele Jr. High Sch., 2007—08; adapted phys. educator Tooele County Sch. Dist., 2008—, girls basketball coach head, Tooele HS, 2009—. Lic. foster care parent Utah Foster Care, Divsn. Child Family Svcs., 2002—. Mem.: AAHPERD, Nat. Fedn. State HS Assns., Utah Golf Assn. Mem. Lds Ch. Avocations: golf, camping, hiking, basketball, boating, snowboarding. E-mail: macnstep@comcast.net.

MCCLUGGAGE, KERRY, film and television executive; Studied broadcasting and film, U. So. Calif., 1976; MBA, Harvard U., 1978. With MCA/Universal, 1979—90; chmn. Paramount TV Group, Viacom, 1991—2002; founder, independent prodr., CEO Craftsman Films, 2002—; acquired with Jeff Sagansky, also co-chmn. Ardustry Home Entertainment, Woodland Hills, Calif., 2005—. Co-founder UPN Network, 1995. Supervised and developed programs such as: The A-Team, Coach, Deadwood, The Equalizer, Frasier, JAG, Northern Exposure, Law & Order, Miami Vice, Murder She Wrote, Quantum Leap and a few Star Trek Series. Address: Ardustry Home Entertainment 21250 Califa St Ste 102 Woodland Hills CA 91367

MCCLUNG, A(LEXANDER) KEITH, JR., retired lawyer; b. Gallipolis, Ohio, Sept. 13, 1934; s. Alexander Keith and Florence (Juhling) McC.; m. Sandra B. Foley, Aug. 17, 1957; children: Alexander Keith III, Martha E. AB, W.Va. U., 1956; JD, Harvard U., 1959. Bar: W.Va. 1959, Md. 1970, Mich. 1972. Assoc. Jackson, Kelly, Holt & O'Farrell, Charleston, W.Va., 1959-69; assoc. counsel Comml. Credit Corp., Balt., 1969-70; v.p., counsel McCullagh Leasing, Inc., Roseville, Mich., 1970-73, Comml. Credit Corp., Balt., 1973-82, gen. atty., 1982-85; sr. gen. atty. Comml. Credit Co., Balt., 1985-89, sr. v.p., gen. counsel, 1989-98. Bd. dirs. Travelers Bank; trustee Roland Park Found.; mem. adv. coun. Coll. Arts and Sci., W.Va. U. Capt. USAR. Mem. ABA (subcom. uniform comml. code, com. equipment leasing), Soc. Colonial Wars in the State of Md., St. George Soc. Md. Democrat. Home: 13 Devon Hill Rd Baltimore MD 21210-1044 E-mail: campussandy@aol.com.

MCCLUNG, GWENDOLYN, soil microbiologist; b. Takoma Pk., Md., Sept. 5, 1956; d. Lowell Neal and Margaret May (Whaley) McC.; m. Guy Alan Athey; children: John Carl, Elaine Ashley Athey. BS in Agronomy, U. Md., 1977, MS in Soil Microbiology, 1981; PhD in Soil Microbiology, U. Calif., Riverside, 1986. Student lab. technician dept. agronomy U. Md., College Park, 1974-77, faculty rsch. asst., 1977-81; grad. rsch. and tchg. asst. dept. soil and environ. scis. U. Calif., Riverside, 1981-86; postdoctoral fellow dept. agronomy Ohio State U., Wooster, 1987-88; postdoctoral fellow Belts Agrl. Rsch. Ctr., USDA, Beltsville, Md., 1988-90; microbiologist, ecol. hazard assessor, risk assessor of genetically engineered microorganisms U.S. EPA, Washington, 1990—. Contbr. articles to profl. jours. Pres. postdoctoral fellow Ohio State U., Wooster, 1986-87, Kinney postdoctoral fellow Beltsville Agrl. Rsch. Ctr., USDA, 1988-90. Mem. Am. Soc. Microbiology, Am. Soc. Agronomy, Soil Sci. Soc. Am. Achievements include research on plants and soil science and microbiology. Office: US EPA 1200 Pennsylvania Ave NW Washington DC 20460-0002 Office Phone: 202-564-8911. E-mail: mcclung.gwendolyn@epa.gov.

MCCLUNG, J(AMES) DAVID, corporate executive, lawyer, academic administrator; b. Lamesa, Tex., July 16, 1943; s. Jack Weldon Sr. and Ruby (Brown) McC.; m. Linda Nelson, Feb. 12, 1966; children: LeEtta McClung Felter, Dennis, Pamela McClung Frazier, Jennifer McClung Kearns. Student, N.E. La. State Coll., 1961-62, McNeese State Coll., 1963; BSBA cum laude, Bethany Nazarene Coll., 1965; postgrad., U. Okla., 1967-68; JD cum laude, Baylor U., 1973. Bar: Tex. 1973, U.S. Dist. Ct. Northern Dist. Tex. 1975, U.S. Ct. Appeals (5th cir.) 1974. Assoc. Jackson & Walker, Dallas, 1973-76; exec. v.p. Austin Industries, Inc., Dallas, 1976-88; pres., chief exec. officer, chmn. bd. Green Internat., Inc., Denver, 1988—93; owner NazNet.Com, 1999—. Arbitrator Am. Arbitration Assn., 1978—; bd. dirs. Green Holdings, Inc., Denver; chmn. bd. Green Construction Co., Green Mining, Inc., Green Alaska, Inc., GEM Investors, Inc., Green Overseas Corp., Northland Maintenance Co., Northland Alaska, Inc., Green Investments, Inc., Denver, 1988-93; pres. Triton Marine Cons., 1994-2000; chmn. Triton Marine Cons., 2000—; pres. Ea. Nazarene Coll., 2002—2005.chmn. ePD Svcs. Inc., 2008-. Contbr. articles to profl. jours. Trustee So. Nazarene U., Bethany, Okla., 1978-2003; mem. gen. bd. Ch. of the Nazarene, Kansas City, 1985-89, sec. Commn. Report, 1989. Capt. USAF, 1965-71, Vietnam. Decorated 6 Air medals; recipient Young Grads. award of merit Baylor U., 1983, Outstanding Alumni award So. Nazarene U., 1989, Disting. Svc. award Ch. of the Nazarene, 1989. Mem. ABA, Tex. Bar Assn., The Beavers. Republican. Avocations: digital photography, hiking. Home: 3504 C St NW Gig Harbor WA 98335-7801 Home Phone: 253-853-2041; Office Phone: 253-853-2041. E-mail: mcclung@naznet.com.

MCCLUNG, JOHN ARTHUR, cardiologist; b. Oneonta, NY, Mar. 18, 1949; s. Charles Harvey and Ruth Steiner (Voegtly) McC.; m. Jane Giles, June 29, 1985; children: Daniel James, Timothy John. AB, Johns Hopkins U., 1971; MD, N.Y. Med. Coll., 1975. Diplomate Am. Bd. Internal Medicine with specialties in cardiovascular disease, critcal care medicine, Nat. Bd. Echocardiography. Instr. in clin. medicine NY Med. Coll., Valhalla, 1979-82, asst. prof. medicine, 1982-89, assoc. prof. medicine, 1989—2006, prof. medicine, 2006—, founder, divsn. clin. ethics, 1990—, dir. Inst. Human Values Med. Ethics, 1993-98, dir. cardiovascular fellowship program, 2001—; chief critical care sect. Westchester Med. Ctr., Valhalla, 1982—, asst. dir. cardiac catheterization lab., 1987—99; dir. Noninvasive Cardiology Lab., 2006—, Westchester Med. Ctr. Regional corr. Soc. Bioethics Consultants, Cleve., 1992-94; dir. cardiovasc. fellowship program NY Med. Coll., 2001—. Contbr. articles to profl. jours. Fellow: Soc. Cardiac Angiography and Interventions, Am. Heart Assn. (coun. clin. cardiology), Am. Coll. Physicians, Am. Coll. Cardiology, Am. Soc. Echocardiography; mem.: Alpha Omega Alpha (N.Y. Iota chpt.). Episcopalian. Office: Westchester Med Ctr 19 Bradhurst Ave Ste 700 Hawthorne NY 10532-2140 Office Phone: 914-593-7800.

MCCLUNG, PATRICIA BEATRICE, special education educator; d. Earnest Harold and Marjorie Beatrice Lee; m. Alan Greg McClung, Sept. 11, 1982; 1 child, Alexandra Enetha. EdD, U. East Anglia, Eng., 2006. Lic. tchr. Tenn., 1996. Tchr. & coord., spl. edn. Bradley County Schs., Cleve., Tenn., 1993—2002, ednl. surrogate parent, state custody children, 2002—09; asst. prof., spl. edn. Lee U., Cleve., 2002—, dir. & tchr., summer study, 2002—08. Contbr. articles. Com. mem., distbn. funds United Way, Cleve., 2008—09. Recipient Excellence Edn. Tchg. award, State Tenn. Spl. Edn., 1999; named Tchr. of Yr., Bradley County Schs., 1999. Mem.: Coun. Exceptional Children, Kappa Delta Pi. Avocation: travel. Home: 430 26th St NW Cleveland TN 37312 Office: Lee Univ Ocoee St Cleveland TN 37320 Office Fax: 423-614-8180. Business E-Mail: pmcclung@leeuniversity.edu.

MCCLUNG, PHIL ORAN, psychology professor; s. Basil McClung Jesse and Virginia Pearl McClung; m. Mary Denise McClung, Sept. 14, 1979; children: Dustin Chad, Donovan Shane. BA in Psychology, W.Va. U., Morgantown, 1970, MS in Indsl. Rels., 1974, EdD, 1993. Cert. counselor NBCC, 1984, lic. practical counselor W.Va. Bd. Examiners Counseling, 1988. Dir. W.Va. U., 1970—90, prof., 1970—2007. Cons. W.Va. U. Mgmt. Inst., Parkersburg, 1975—2007; adj. prof. Marshall U. Grad. Sch., Charleston, W.Va., 2000—03. Author: (books) Desulfurization Technology, 1975, Potential Waste Products from Coal, 1975. Bd. mem. Sharpe Hosp., Weston, W.Va., 2000—07, W.Va. Alliance Mentally Ill, Charleston, 2000—07, Transitional Living Facility, Weston, 2007. Recipient Outstanding Staff Support Person award, W.Va. UP Student Body, 1976—77, 1980, W.Va. Prof. of Yr. award, Nat. Merit Found., 2007, Prof. of Yr. award, W.Va. UP Student Body, 2006; finalist W.Va. Prof. of Yr. award, Nat. Merit Found., 2006. Mem.: W.Va. Career Counseling Assn. (assoc.; pres. 1979—80), W.Va. Alliance Mentally Ill (assoc.; dir. 2000—07). Democrat-Npl. Achievements include development of an environmental psychology program. Avocations: tennis, volleyball, golf, badminton, table tennis. Home: 136 Whispering Pines Rd Davisville WV 26142 Office: WVa Univ 300 Campus Dr Parkersburg WV 26104 Office Fax: 304-424-8315; Home Fax: 304-424-8315. Personal E-mail: philwvup@gmail.com. Business E-Mail: phil.mcclung@mail.wvu.edu.

MCCLURE, ALVIN BRUCE, watchmaker; b. Cin., Mar. 2, 1953; s. Alphonso Bruce McClure and Jewel Lee (Smith) Yates; m. Katherine Shenkar, Nov. 7, 1979; children: Jaina, Randi; m. Penny Bliss, July 7, 2000. Student, U. Mich., 1971-73, 76-77, Fanshawe Coll., London, Ont., Can., 1974-75, Coll. of St. Thomas, 1989-91, St. Paul Coll., 2005—06. Programmer Mfg. Data Systems, Ann Arbor, Mich., 1978-79; systems software specialist Mpls. Star and Tribune, 1979-81; systems analyst NCR COMTEN, Inc., Roseville, Minn., 1981-84; software systems support programmer INTRAN Corp., Bloomington, Minn., 1984-85; programmer/analyst Minn. Dept. Natural Resources, St. Paul, 1985-97; local area network adminstr. Minn. Pollution Control Agy., St. Paul, 1997-98; network mgr. Minn. Dept. Health, Mpls., 1998; info. sys. mgr. Van Wagenen Co., Eden Prairie, Minn., 1998-99; sr. tech. cons. Database/Network/WEB Lawson Software, St. Paul, 1999-2000; tech. cons. Productive Solutions Group, Mpls., 2000—01; pres. Reality Bytes, Inc., Elk River, 2001—; data mgmt. engr. Kroll Ontrack, Inc., Eden Prairie, 2002—03; watchmaker Ben Bridge Jewelers, Edina, Minn., 2007—09. Mem. mgmt. info. svcs. tech. com. St. Paul, Miss., 1987—97. Mem. cmty. adv. bd. Sta. WCAL-FM, 1988-90; mem. Otsego Police Commn., 2003-05, program adv. comm. mem. St. Paul Coll. Mem. IEEE, AWI, Am. Inst. Physics, Audio Engring. Soc., Internat. Platform Assn., Mgmt. Info. Svcs., Am. Watchmakers-Clockmakers Inst., Nat. Assn. Watch and Clock Collectors, Aikido Yoshinkai Mpls.-St. Paul (5th degree black belt, head instr.). Avocations: chess, photography, audiophile, sailing, aquaria. Home: 14348 96th St NE Elk River MN 55330-7376 Office: Reality Bytes Inc 14348 96th St NE Elk River MN 55330-7376 Office Phone: 763-360-6097. Personal E-mail: alvin@heisei.com. E-mail: alvin.mcclure@otsegomn.net.

MCCLURE, BROOKS, management consultant; b. NYC, Mar. 8, 1919; s. Walter Harsha and Angelica (Mendoza) McClure; m. Olga Beatrice Gallik, Oct. 15, 1949; 1 child, Karen (dec.). AB summa cum laude, U. Md.; disting. grad., U.S. Naval War Coll. N.Y. corr. Western Press Ltd., Australia, 1939-42; copy editor Washington Eve. Star, 1946-51; joined State Dept. Fgn. Service, 1951; information officer, attache embassy Copenhagen, 1951-53; press attache embassy Vienna, 1953-55; information officer, attache embassy Cairo, 1956—57, Seoul, 1957-60, Bonn, 1960-63; policy officer Europe USIA, 1963-66; pub. affairs officer 1st sec. embassy, Copenhagen, 1967-72; spl. asst. policy plans and nat. security council affairs, internat. security affairs Dept. Def., 1972-76; internat. security adviser USIA, 1976-77; program coordinator Crisis Assessment Staff, Dept. Commerce, 1977-78; dir. ops. Internat. Mgmt. Analysis and Resources Corp., 1978-81, v.p., 1982—2007, ind. cor. cons., 2008—; sec. Cross-Continent Assocs. Ltd., 1994-99; pvt. practice, 2008—. Various spl. assignments Europe, Mid. East, Asia, Africa; detailed to Vietnam, 1967; mem. working group Cabinet Com. to Combat Terrorism, 1973—77; lectr. FBI Acad., Fgn. Svc. Inst., Inter-Am. Def. Coll., Army War Coll., Navy War Coll., NJ Police Acad., NY State Police Acad. Contbg. author: book Modern Guerrilla Warfare, 1962, International Terrorism in Contemporary World, 1978, Corporate Vulnerability and How to Assess it: Political Terrorism and Business, 1979, Business and the Middle East, 1981, Political Terrorism and Energy, 1981; author (treatise) Dynamics of Terrorism, Internat. Assn. Chiefs Police, 1977; contbr. articles to profl. jours.; author: report to Senate Judiciary Com. on internat. terrorism and hostage def. measures; testifier on internat. security, hostage behavior, def. of Alaskan pipeline, FBI charter U.S. Senate, 1975—79. With AUS, 1942—46, ETO. Recipient Presdl. medal, Slovak Republic, 2002. Mem.: DACOR, Nat. Press Club, Assn. Diplomatic Studies, Am. Fgn. Svc. Assn., Alpha Sigma Lambda, Phi Kappa Phi. Home: 6204 Rockhurst Rd Bethesda MD 20817-1756 E-mail: b-kmcclure@mindspring.com.

MCCLURE, CHARLES G., automotive executive; BS in Mech. Engring., Cornell U.; MBA, U. Mich. Heavy truck sales engr., product engr. Ford Motor Co.; v.p., gen. mgr. automotive sys. groups for the Ams. Johnson Controls, Inc., pres., Detroit Diesel Corp., 1997—2003, CEO, 1999—2003; CEO, pres. Federal-Mogul Corp., 2003—04; chmn., pres., CEO ArvinMeritor Inc., Troy, Mich., 2004—. Mem. Bus. Roundtable; bd. dir. NAM, R.L. Polk and Co., Intermet Corp., Motor & Equip. Mfr. Assn. Bd. dir. Detroit Renaissance, Detroit Regional C. of C., Horizons Upward Bound; mem. exec. com. A World in Motion. Lt. (j.g.) USN, 1975—79. Office: ArvinMeritor Inc 2135 W Maple Rd Troy MI 48084

MCCLURE, CHARLES RICHARD, retired superintendent of schools; b. Morgantown, W.Va., Apr. 8, 1935; s. C.W. and Alta M. (Cale) McC.; BA, W.Va. U., 1957, MA, 1960; m. Shirley Pat Tallman, July 11, 1964; children: Marilyn, Scott, Mary, Marlin. Tchr., Preston County Schs., W.Va., 1957-60, supr., personnel dir. fed. programs, 1960-67; program coordinator N. Ctrl. W.Va., Dept. Edn., 1967-73; adminstrv. asst. Harrison County Schs., Clarksburg, W.Va., 1974, supt., 1974—98, ret. 1998. Mem. exec. bd. Harrison County United Way. Mem. Am. Assn. Sch. Adminstrs., Nat. Sch. Bd. Assn., Nat. Assn. Supervision and Curriculum Devel., W.Va. Assn. Sch. Adminstrs. (Service award 1979), W.Va. U. Alumni Assn., W.Va. Univ. Emeritus Club, W.Va. Sch. Bd. Assn., W.Va. Assn. Supervision and Curriculum Devel., Clarksburg C. of C. (edn. com.), Phi Delta Kappa, Phi Mu Alpha Sinfonia. Methodist. Clubs: Clarksburg Lions, Clarksburg Elks Club, Kingwood Rotary, Masons, Shriners. Author papers in field. Home: 402 James St Bridgeport WV 26330-1336

MCCLURE, CHARLES ROBERT, library and information science educator, consultant; b. Syracuse, NY, May 24, 1949; s. Robert C. and Doris C. (Gordon) McC.; m. Victoria A. Jones, Dec. 30, 1971; 1 child, Gwendolyn A. BA in Spanish, Okla. State U., 1971, MA in History, 1972; MLS, U. Okla., 1973; PhD in Info. Studies, Rutgers U., 1977. Head govt.-history dept. U. Tex. Libr., El Paso, 1972-73; instr. Sch. Libr. and Info. Scis., Rutgers U., New Brunswick, NJ, 1974-76; prof. Sch. Libr. and Info. Scis., U. Okla., Norman, 1977-86, Sch. Info. Studies, Syracuse U., 1986—94, disting. prof., 1994—99; pres. Info. Mgmt. Cons. Svcs. Inc., 1986—; Francis Eppes prof. info. studies Coll. Info., Fla. State U., Tallahassee, 1999—, dir. Info. Use Mgmt. and Policy Inst. Cons. US Govt. Printing Office, Washington, 1989-90, US Congress Office Tech. Assessment, Washington, 1990-91; assoc. Rsch. Librs., NC State Libr., Am. Libr. Assn., 2005, Cornell U. Libr., 2007. Author: Federal Information Policies in the 1980s, 1988 (Best Book of Yr. Am. Soc. Info. Sci.), Public Access to Government Information, 1989, Stats. and Performance Measures for Pub. Librs., Evaluating Networked Svcs., 2002, Librs. Connect Cmtys., 2007, Pub. Libr. Svc. Roles, 2008. Named Disting. Rschr. Nat. Commn. Librs. and Info. Sci., 1993, Disting. Prof. Syracuse U., 1996, Francis Eppes Prof. Fla. State U., 1999 Mem. ALA (cons. 1986-), Am. Soc. for Info. Sci., Assn. Libr. and Info. Sci. Educators. Office: Coll Info Fla State U Louis Shores Bldg Rm 226 Tallahassee FL 32306-2100 Office Fax: 850-644-9763.

MCCLURE, DONALD E., mathematics professor, mathematical society executive; AB in Math., U. Calif., Berkeley, 1966; PhD in Applied Math., Brown U., 1970. Instr. Brown U., 1969—70, asst. prof., 1970—75, assoc. prof., 1975—82, divsn. chair, 1985—88, 1994—96, prof., divsn. applied math., 1982. Assoc. dir. Brown-Harvard-MIT Center for Intelligent Control Systems, 1986—2000. Contbr. several articles to profl. jours. Mem.: Am. Math. Soc. (bd. trustee 1995—2000, assoc. treas. 2003—09, exec. dir. 2009—). Office: Am Math Soc 201 Charles St Providence RI 02904 also: Divsn Applied Math Brown U 182 George St Providence RI 02912 Office Phone: 401-455-4000, 401-863-1496. Office Fax: 401-863-2353. Business E-Mail: donald.mcclure@brown.edu.*

MCCLURE, FREDERICK DONALD, lawyer; b. Ft. Worth, Feb. 2, 1954; s. Foster Donald and Mayme Nell (Barnett) McClure; m. Harriet Elizabeth Jackson, Dec. 17, 1977; children: Lauren Elizabeth, Frederick Donald. BS in Agrl. Economics, summa cum laude, Tex. A&M U., 1976; JD, Baylor U., 1981. Bar: Tex., 1981, DC, US Dist. Ct. So. Dist. Tex., 1982, US Ct. Appeals 5th Cir., 1982. Agrl. asst. to Senator John Tower, US Senate, Washington, 1977-79, legis. dir., 1983-84; assoc. Reynolds, Allen & Cook, Houston, 1981-83; assoc. dep. atty. gen. US Dept. Justice, Washington, 1984-85; spl. asst. for legis. affairs to Pres. The White House, Washington, 1985-86; v.p. govt. affairs Tex. Air. Corp., 1986—89; asst. for legis. affairs to Pres. The White House, Washington, 1989-92; mng. dir. First S.W. Co., Dallas, 1992-94, Pub. Strategies, Inc., 1995—2001; mng. shareholder Winstead Sechrest & Minick, Washington, 2001—04; ptnr., pub. law & policy strategies group Sonnenschein Nath & Rosenthal LLP, Washington, 2004—, mng. dir. Washington DC Office, 2007—. Mem. State of Tex. Inaugural Com., 1994, Bush-Cheney Transition Com., 2001; mem. transition com. Gov. Rick Perry, Tex., 2001; mem. Sec. Energy Adv. Bd.; bd. dirs. Alex Lee, Inc. Mem. bd. visitors US Naval Acad., 1992-95, chmn., 1994; bd regents Tex A&M U. Sys., 1995-2001. Recipient Jimmy Williams Disting. Svc. Award, Dallas A&M Club, 2002; named Disting. Alumnus, Baylor U., 1991; named a Tex. A&M Disting. Alumni, Assn. Former Students & Tex. A&M U., 1991; named one of Am.'s 50 most promising leaders age 40 and under, Time mag., 1994. Mem. State Bar Tex., Former Students Assn. of Tex. A&M (v.p. 1985-89, 93-95), Future Farmers Am. (nat. sec. 1973-74), Tex. Future Farmers Am. (state pres. 1972-73), Cotton Bowl Athletic Assn. (chmn. 1998—2002), Phi Alpha Delta, Phi Kappa Phi, Alpha Zeta (dir. 1985-93), Alpha Gamma Rho. Republican. Baptist. Office: Sonnenschein Nath & Rosenthal LLP Ste 600, E Tower 1301 K St NW Washington DC 20005 Office Phone: 202-408-3235. Office Fax: 202-408-6399. Business E-Mail: fmcclure@sonnenschein.com.

MCCLURE, HAL H., film producer; b. Indpls. s. Harold Alonzo and Betty (Zemah Hays) McClure; m. Dorothea Vernell Millar, Jan. 15, 1949 (dec. 1994). AA, L.A. City Coll., 1941. Journalist various newspapers, Calif., 1949-56; newsman AP, LA, 1956-58, NYC, 1959-60, fgn. corr. S.E. Asia and Mid. East, 1961-76, bur. chief N.J. Newark, 1976-77; prin., travel film prodr. Hal McClure Prodns., Laguna Woods, Calif., 1978—. Adj. asst. prof. journalism Seton Hall U., South Orange, NJ, 1976—77. Co-author: (book) Lighting Out of Israel, 1967; co-editor: Fire Over Suez, 1971; prodr.: (films) Istanbul-Travels in Turkey, 1990, Land of Legend-England Scotland and Wales, 1993, Adventure Holland, 1994, Mystery Tales of Europe, 1996, Dracula-Travels in Transylvania, 1997, Story Book England, 1999, Magic of Malaysia, 2001, Casablanca-Travels in Morocco, 2003, Echo of Hoofbeats - the Pony Express Story, 2005; editor, co-owner Travel Adventure Cinema mag., 1978—, leader in move to digital prodn. travel film field. Capt. USAFR, 1942—56. Recipient Rising Star award, 1978, Lifetime Achievement award, Travel Adventure Cinema Soc., 2008; named to Travelogue Hall of Fame, 1994; Ogden Reid Found. fellow, 1959. Mem.: Travel Adventure Cinema Soc. Home and Office: 686 Avenida Sevilla # C Laguna Woods CA 92637-3838

MCCLURE, HOWARD JEAN, JR., advocate; b. High Point, NC, June 15, 1959; s. Howard Jean McClure Sr. and Mary Elizabeth McClure. Author: Conflict Of Interest, 1999. Chmn. polit. action com. Carolina Advocates for Legal Reform, Charlotte, NC, 2001—02, v.p., 2001—02; mem. Charlotte Mecklenburg Cmty. Rels. Com., 2002—07; chmn. membership and cmty. rels. com. Western Region NC Black Leadership Caucus, 2003—05; active Black Polit. Caucus Charlotte-Mecklenburg, 1998—2004, Robert F. Kennedy Meml., 2005—07; founder Citizens Coun. for Equal Opportunity, 2003; mem. Nat. Campaign for Tolerance; vice chmn. 29th precinct Mecklenburg County Dem. Party, 2004—07. Recipient Outstanding Svc. award, Black Polit. Caucus of Charlotte Mecklenburg, 2003, Appreciation award, 2004, Chmn.'s Dem. of Month award, Mecklenburg County Dem. Party, 2004, Advocacy award, Nat. Assn. Human Rights Workers, 2005, Award of Recognition, 8th Dist. Black Leadership Caucus, 2008. Mem.: NAACP (mem. legal redress com. 1999—, edn. com. 2001—, labor and industry com. 2003—). Conservative. Avocations: music, writing, fishing, travel, football, coin collecting/numismatics. Office: Citizens Coun Equal Opportunity PO Box 18812 Charlotte NC 28218 Home: APT 1B 6402 English Hills DR Charlotte NC 28212-7903 Office Phone: 704-531-3543. Personal E-mail: theebonysaint@webtv.net, theebonysaint2@msn.com.

MCCLURE, JAMES FOCHT, JR., federal judge; b. Danville, Pa., Apr. 6, 1931; s. James Focht and Florence Kathryn (Fowler) McC.; m. Elizabeth Louise Barber, June 14, 1952; children: Holly McClure Kerwin, Kimberly Ann Pacala, Jamee McClure Sealy, Mary Elizabeth Hudec, Margaret McClure Persing. AB, Amherst Coll., 1952; JD, U. Pa., 1957. Bar: D.C. 1957, Pa. 1958, U.S. Dist. Ct. D.C. 1957, U.S. Dist. Ct. (ea. and mid. dist.) Pa. 1958, U.S. Ct. Appeals (3d cir.) 1959. Atty., advisor Dept. State, Washington, 1957-58; assoc. Morgan, Lewis & Bockius, Phila., 1958-61; atty. Merck & Co., Inc., NYC, 1961-65; ptnr. McClure & McClure, Lewisburg, Pa., 1965-77, McClure & Light, Lewisburg, 1978-84; pres., judge Ct. Common Pleas, 17th Jud. Dist. Pa., Lewisburg, 1984-90; sr. dist. judge U.S. Dist. Ct. (mid. dist.) Pa., Williamsport, Pa., 1990—. Dist. atty. Union County, Lewisburg, 1974-75. Pres. bd. sch. dirs. Lewisburg Area Sch. Dist., 1969-74. Cpl. U.S. Army, 1952-54. Mem. Pa. Bar Assn., Union County Bar Assn., Bucknell U. Golf Club, Order of Coif, Phi Beta Kappa. Republican. Presbyterian. Office: US Dist Ct 240 W 3rd St Ste 320 Williamsport PA 17701-6466 Home Phone: 570-524-7341; Office Phone: 570-323-9772.

MCCLURE, JAMES JULIUS, JR., lawyer, former city official; b. Oak Park, Ill., Sept. 23, 1920; s. James J. and Ada Leslie (Baker) McC.; m. Margaret Carolyn Phelps, Apr. 9, 1949; children: John Phelps, Julia Jean, Donald Stewart. BA, U. Chgo., 1942, JD, 1949. Bar: Ill. 1950. Ptnr. Gardner, Carton & Douglas, Chgo., 1962-91, of counsel, 1991—2007; drinker biddle gardner, carton of counsel, 2007—08; of consel Drinker Biddle & Reath, 2008—; mem. Oak Park Plan Commn., 1966-73, Northeastern Ill. Planning Commn., 1973-77, pres., 1975-77, Village of Oak Park, 1973-81, Oak Park Exch. Congress Inc., 1978—2002. Mem. Bus. Leaders for Transp., 1998—. Pres. United Christian Cmty. Svcs., 1967-69, 71-73, Erie Neighborhood House, 1953-55, Oak Park-River Forest Cmty. Chest, 1967; moderator Presbytery Chgo., 1969; mem. Gov.'s Spl. Com. on MPO, 1978-79; bd. dirs. Leadership Coun. of Met. Open Cmtys., 1981-2002, sec., 1990-98; bd. dirs. Met. Planning Coun., 1982-93, hon. dir., 1993—; bd. dirs. Cmty. Renewal Soc., 1982-91, v.p., 1984-88, treas. 1988-91; bd. dirs. Christian Century Found., 1972—, chmn., 1981-2008; trustee McCormick Theol. Sem., 1981—, chmn. bd. 1987-90. hon. trustee, 1990—; mem. vocation agy., 1973-82; mem. ch. vocations unit, 1987-92, vice chair 1990; mem. gen. assembly coun. Presbyn. Ch. U.S.A., 1987-90, mem. gen. assembly Permanent Jud. Commn., 1997-2003; bd. dirs. Oak Park Edn. Found., 1991-96, Oak Park River Forest Cmty. Found., 1991-2002; mem. Vision 2000 (Oak Park) Coordinating Com., 1995. With USNR, 1942-46, CD 1944 USS SE 1025, CD 1944, 1943-1944, USS Weber APP75, 1945-1946, exec. officer, 1946. Recipient Disting. Citizen award Oak Park, 1976; Silver Beaver award; Disting. Eagle Scout award Boy Scouts Am., Carl Winters Cmty. Svc. award Oak Park Rotary Club, 1996, William Staczak award Oak Park Edn. Found., 1997, Rita Johnson award Oak Park Family Svc. and Mental Health Ctr., 1997, Public Svc. award U. Chgo. Alumni Assn., 1997, Tradition of Excellence award Oak Pk. River Forest H.S., 1998, Alumni Svc. medal, Chgo. Alumni Assn., 2003, Gutenberg Award Chgo. Bible Soc., 2003; named one of 100 disting. Oak Parkers for Millenium, Wed Jour., 2002. Mem. ABA, Am. Coll. Trust and Estate Counsel, Ill. State Bar Assn., Chgo. Bar Assn., Am. Law Inst., Order of the Coif, Lambda Alpha. Clubs: Univ. (Chgo.). Office: Drinker Biddle & Reath 191 N Wacker Dr Chicago IL 60606-4719 *Love of God, love of family, awareness of both the uniqueness and the contribution of every other human being, a sense of the wholeness of life with my religious faith, my profession of law, my family and my community service each playing an important part and complimenting each other.*

MCCLURE, MARGARET MCNAMARA, psychologist, educator; b. NYC, Aug. 27, 1977; d. William Joseph and Agnes Theresa McNamara; m. Neil M. McClure, July 28, 2001; children: Liam M., Maeve A., Aidan N. PhD, Fordham U., Bronx, NY, 2005. Lic. psychologist NY State, 2007. Dir., psychology fellowship Vets. Affairs, Bronx, NY, 2007—; asst. prof. Mt. Sinai Sch. Medicine, NYC, 2008—. Contbr. articles to profl. jours. Advanced Psychology fellowship, Mt. Sinai Sch. Medicine, 2005—07. Mem.: APA. Achievements include research in cognitive abnormalities of schizophrenia spectrum disorders. Office: James J Peters VAMC 00MH 130 W Kingsbridge Rd Bronx NY 10458

MCCLURE, MATTHEW K., secondary school educator; b. Anderson, Ind., Sept. 20, 1963; s. M. Kenneth and Noma Joan (Prince) McC.; m. Nancy Lee Waymire, July 14, 1984; children: Katherine, Maggie. BS, Ball State U., 1984; CAS, U. Chgo., 1985, MA, 1986; MS, Northwestern U., 1987. Cert. educator K-12. Social sci. Maine H.S. Dist. 207, Park Ridge, Ill., 1987—. Edn./tech. cons. Motorola, Schaumburg, Ill., 1994—; co-chair Writing Across the Curriculum Dist. 207, 1989-92, social science audio-visual libr., 1987—, staff devel., tech., 1997—. Contbr. articles to ednl. jours. Mem. ASCD, Coun. for Am. Studies Edn., Phi Delta Kappa. Avocations: photography, model railroading, politics. Office: Maine West HS 1755 S Wolf Rd Des Plaines IL 60018-1923

MCCLURE, R. DALE, physician; b. Jan. 4, 1943; MD, U. Western Ontario, Can., 1968. Prof. urology U. Wash. Sch. Medicine, 1991—. Fellow: RCS; mem.: Pacific Coast Reproductive Soc., Am. Soc. Reproductive Medicine (mem. exec. bd. 2004—, pres. elect, pres. 2008—09). Office: Virginia Mason Med Ctr 1100 9th Ave Seattle WA 98101-2756 Office Phone: 206-311-1326.

MCCLURE, ROGER JOHN, lawyer; b. Cleve., Nov. 22, 1943; s. Theron R. and Colene (Irwin) McClure. BA, Ohio State U., 1965, JD cum laude, 1972; MA, Northwestern U., 1966. Bar: Va. 1973, Md. 1973, U.S. Ct. Appeals (D.C. cir.) 1974, U.S. Supreme Ct. 1978, Ohio, U.S. Ct. Appeals (4th, 5th & 10th cirs.). Asst. atty. gen. State of Ohio, Columbus, 1972; trial atty. FTC, Washington, 1972-76; sr. assoc. Law Offices of A.D. Berkeley, Washington, 1976-81; pvt. practice Alexandria, Va., 1981—; pres. Wash. Wealth Counsellors, McLean, 1987—; del. Va. Gen. Assembly, 1992—2002, co-chmn. militia and police com., 1998—2002; dean Bus. Coll. Nat. Network Estate Planning Attys., 2003—. Adj. prof. Acad. Multidisciplinary Practice Mich. State U., Lansing, 2001—; host talk show Sta. WRC Radio, 1987—93, 1999—2001, Sta. WPGC, 1993—94. Co-author: (book) Winning the Syndication Game, 1988, Advanced Estate Planning in Virginia, 2001, Virginia Elder Law, 1988, Asset Protection in Virginia, 1999, Estate and Wealth Strategies Planning, 2000, Choice of Entity in Virginia, 2000, Business Succession and Sale of Businesses, 2003, (book) Family Limited Partnerships and LLCS, 2005; contbg. reviewer; contbr. articles to profl. jours. Mem. No. Va. Transp. Commn., 2001, commr.; adv. bd. dirs. No. Va. Cmty. Found., 1995—. With US Army, 1967—69. Decorated Bronze Star; fellow Masters, Espertis Peterson Inst., 1996—. Mem.: Dulles Area Transp. Assn. (bd. dirs.), Nat. Network Estate Planning Attys., No. Va. Apt. Assn. (bd. dirs. 1988—92, 1st v.p. 1987—88, pres. 1988—89), D.C. Bar Assn. (real estate steering com. 1982—84, chmn. antitrust divsn. 1975—76), Wolf Trap Found. (adv. coun.). Avocation: sailing. Office: NNEPA 1355 Beverly Rd Ste 225 Mc Lean VA 22101 Mailing: 1355 Beverly Rd Ste 225 Mc Lean VA 22101 Home Phone: 703-968-8348; Office Phone: 571-633-0330. E-mail: rmcclure@ix.netcom.com.

MCCLURE, TERI PLUMMER, lawyer, delivery service executive; b. Kansas City, Dec. 31, 1963; m. Roderick McClure; 2 children. BS, BA, Washington U., 1985; JD, Emory U., 1988. Bar: Ga. 1988. Employment counsel United Parcel Svc. Inc., 1995—98, coord. labor and practice group, 1998—2003, mgr. ctrl. Fla. dist., 2003—05, gen. counsel, sr. v.p. legal, compliance & pub. affairs, corp. sec., mgmt. com. mem., 2005—. Bd. dirs. Jr. Achievement Ga., Anne E. Casey Found., UPS Found., Ctr. for Working Families. Mem.: Nat. Employment Law Counsel (mem. coord. com.), State Bar Ga. (mem. labor and employment law sect.), Am. Corp. Counsel Assn., Atlanta Bar Assn. Office: United Parcel Svc Inc 55 Glenlake Pkwy NE Atlanta GA 30328*

MCCLURE, THOMAS EDWARD, lawyer; b. Urbana, Ill., Nov. 8, 1954; s. William Leslie McClure and Carolyn Jean McClure Byrnes; m. Karen Leah Zinn, Dec. 14, 1985. BS, Ill. State U., 1976; JD, DePaul U., 1979; MS, Ill. State U., 2001. Bar: Ill. 1979, US Dist. Ct. (no. dist.) Ill. 1979, US Ct. Appeals (7th cir.) 1980, US Dist. Ct. (cen. dist.) Ill. 1983, US Dist. Ct. (no. dist.) Ind. 1991, US Supreme Ct. 1993. Law clk. to presiding justice Ill. Ct. Appeals (1st dist.), Chgo., 1979-81; assoc. Elliott & McClure, Bourbonnais and Momence, Ill., 1981-88; ptnr. Elliott & McClure P.C., Bourbonnais and Momence, Ill., 1988—2006, of counsel, 2007—. Legal counsel Ill. Jaycees, 1985-86, individual devel. v.p., 1987-88, regional dir., 1988-89; atty. Village of Bourbonnais, 1989-93, Village of Chebanse, 1993-97, Village of Manteno, 1999-2001; bd. mem. Bourbonnais Elem. Sch. Dist., 2001-05, pres., 2003-2004; adj. instr. Ill. State U., 2003—, asst. prof., dir. legal studies, 2007-. Editor DePaul Law Rev., 1978-79; contbr. articles to profl. jours. Recipient Outstanding Instrn. award Dale Carnegie & Assocs., 1982, 83, Dennis Hamilton Meml. award US Jaycees, 1988. Mem. ABA, Ill. Bar Assn. (cert. of recognition 1983), 7th Cir. Bar Assn. (cert. of recognition 1994), Chgo. Bar Assn., Kankakee County Bar Assn., Appellate Lawyers Assn., Ill. Jaycees (individual devel. v.p. 1987-88, Outstanding Local Pres. 1985, Outstanding Local Dir. East Region 1984, Outstanding Portfolio V.P. 1987-88, Outstanding Regional Dir. 1988-89), Kankakee Jaycees (pres. 1984-85, bd. dirs. 1983-86), Ill. Jaycees Charitable Found., Inc. (bd. dirs., mem. and legal counsel 1986-89), Ill. Jaycees Charitable Camp, Inc. (bd. dirs., legal counsel 1989-91). Office: Elliott & McClure 18 Briarcliff Prof Ctr Bourbonnais IL 60914-1775

MCCLURE, WILLIAM PENDLETON, lawyer; b. Washington, May 25, 1925; s. John Elmer and Helen Newsome (Pendleton) McC.; children: Marilyn Alexander, Helen Pendleton, Elizabeth Ruffin, Melinda Geoghegan. BS, U. Pa., 1949; JD, George Washington U., 1951, LLM, 1954; postgrad., The Hague Acad. Internat. Law, Netherlands, 1952. Bar: D.C. 1951. Sr. ptnr. McClure & Trotter, Washington, 1952-91, McClure, Trotter & Mentz, Washington, 1991-93, McClure, Trotter & Mentz, chartered, Washington, 1993-95; of counsel White & Case, Washington, 1995—. Chmn. DC div. Crusade Against Cancer, Am. Cancer Soc., 1966, 67, ptnr. Served from pvt. to 1st lt., inf. US Army, 1943—46, PTO. Mem. Am. Bar Assn., Bar Assn. D.C., Am. Judicature Soc., Order of Coif, Phi Delta Phi, Phi Delta Theta. Clubs: Metropolitan (Washington), Columbia Country (Washington). Office: 701 13t St NW Washington DC 20005

MCCLUSKEY, STEPHEN C., retired history professor; s. Stephen C. and Mary J. McCluskey; m. Constance Hopkins, June 14, 1969; children: Thomas J., Rose C. BS in Physics, Ill. Inst. Tech., Chgo., 1961; PhD in History Sci., U. Wis., Madison, 1974. Vis. asst. prof. U. Kans., Lawrence, 1974—75, U. Notre Dame, 1975—76; prof. history W.Va. U., Morgantown, 1976—2006. Author: (book) Astronomies and Cultures in Early Medieval Europe. Lt. USN, 1961—67. Mem.: Internat. Soc. Archaeoastronomy and Astronomy in Culture (pres. 2005—08), Am. Astron. Soc. (chair working group on preservation of astron. heritage 2007—08), Am. Hist. Assn., History Sci. Soc., Mediaeval Acad. America. Avocations: hiking, travel. Office: W Va Univ Dept History Morgantown WV 26506 Business E-Mail: stephen.mccluskey@mail.wvu.edu.

MC COIN, JOHN MACK, social worker; b. Sparta, NC, Jan. 21, 1931; s. Robert Avery and Ollie (Osborne) McC. BS, Appalachian State Tchrs. Coll., Boone, NC, 1960; MS in Social Work, Richmond Profl. Inst., Va., 1962; postgrad., U. NC, 1959—60; PhD, U. Minn., 1977. Lic. master social worker; cert. social worker, NY. Social svc. worker Broughton State Hosp., Morganton, NC, 1958-59, John Unstead State Hosp., Butner, NC, 1960-61; clin. social worker Dorothea Dix State Hosp., Raleigh, NC, 1962-63; child welfare case worker Wake County Welfare Dept., Raleigh, 1963-64; psychiat. social worker Toledo Mental Hygiene Clinic, 1964-66; sr. psychiat. social worker NY Hosp.-Cornell U. Med. Ctr. Westchester divsn., White Plains, 1966—68; social worker VA Hosp., Montrose, NY, 1968-73; also vol. mental health worker Westchester County Mental Health Assn. and Mental Health Bd., White Plains; seminar instr. Grad. Sch. Social Work U. Minn., Mpls., 1973-74; social worker F.D.R. VA Health Care Facility, Montrose, 1975-77; asst. prof. social work U. Wis., Oshkosh, 1977-79, chmn. dept. cmty. liaison com., 1978-79; assoc. prof. social work Grand Valley State Colls., Allendale, Mich., 1979-81; social worker VA Med. Ctr., Battle Creek, Mich., 1981-83, supr. social worker dept. Leavenworth, Kans., 1983-94. Cons. 44th Gen. Hosp., USAR, Menasha, Wis., 1978-79, 5540th Support Command, USAR, Grand Rapids, Mich., 1979-83; cons. in field; adj. faculty social scis. dept. Kansas City CC, 1985-89, St. Mary Coll., 1984, Kellogg CC, Battle Creek, 1981-83; adj. faculty sch. social welfare U. Kans., Lawrence, 1992; presenter in field. Author: Adult Foster Homes: Their Managers and Residents, 1983; founder (with Human Scis. Press), editor Adult Foster Care Jour., 1987-88, Adult Resdl. Care Jour., 1989-91, ind. jour., 1992-96; contbr. articles to profl. jours. With USMC, 1948-52, USMCR, 1957-72; lt. col. USAR, 1972-91. Recipient Outstanding Performance award VA, 1971, 83, Superior Performance award, 1982; grantee NIMH, 1974. Mem. NASW (social action com. West Mich. br. 1980-81), Alpha Delta Mu. Democrat. Baptist. Avocations: golf, jogging, genealogy, military history. Home and Office: 4913 Colonial Way Lawrence KS 66049-3599 Office Phone: 785-842-1386.

MCCOLGAN, ELLYN A., diversified financial services company executive; b. Jersey City, Jan. 16, 1954; BA in Psychology, Montclair State Coll., NJ, 1975; MBA, Harvard Bus. Sch., 1983; LLD, Babson Coll., 2005. With Shearson Lehman Bros., NYC, 1983, Bank of New Eng., Fidelity Investments, 1990—2007; pres. Fidelity Investments Tax-Exempt Svcs. Co., 1996—2000, Fidelity Investments Institutional Retirement Group, 2000—01, Fidelity Fin. Intermediary Svcs., 2001—02, Fidelity Brokerage Co., 2002—07; pres. distbn. & ops. Fidelity Investments, 2007; pres., COO Global Wealth Mgmt. Grp. Morgan Stanley, 2008—. Co-chmn. Securities Industry & Fin. Markets Assn., 2006—07. Trustee Mus. Fine Arts, Boston. Named one of 50 Most Powerful Women in Bus., Fortune mag., 2006—07. Office: Morgan Stanley 1585 Broadway New York NY 10036

MCCOLLAM, MARION ANDRUS, consulting firm executive, educator; b. New Orleans, Feb. 8, 1931; d. Gerald Louis and Lucile Gordon (Isacks) Andrus; m. Andrew McCollam, Jr., Jan. 29, 1955 (div. 1978); children: Andrew III, Gerald Andrus, Marion Cage. BA, Tulane U., 1952; M. Urban and Reg. Planning, U. New Orleans, 1978. Human affairs coord. Office of the Mayor, City of New Orleans, 1978, arts coord., 1978-80; dir. planning, prin. cons. Duncan Plaza Design Project, New Orleans, 1978-80; dir. planning Downtown Devel. Dist., New Orleans, 1980-81; pres. Andrus and Roberts Inc., Phoenix, New Orleans, 1980-84; exec. dir. Arts Coun. New Orleans, 1981-90, Cultural Arts Coun. of Houston and Harris County, 1991-98; pres. McCollam Cons., LLC, 1998—. Adj. instr. Goucher Coll. Master's Program in Arts Adminstrn., 1999—2004, mem. nat. adv. com., 2004—08; mem. nat. adv. bd. Newcomb Art Gallery, Tulane U., 2005—; cons. in field. Mem. nat. adv. com. Working Capital Fund, Mpls., 1995-99, Nat. Arts Stabilization, Balt., 1998—; adv. panel design Nat. Endowment for the Arts, Washington, 1995, adv. and chair local arts agencies, 1992-94; bd. dirs., sr. fellow Am. Leadership Forum, Houston, 1994-; mem. cmty. assessment com. United Way of Tex. Gulf Coast, 1995-99; bd. dirs. Urban League of New Orleans, 1984-89; pres. Jr. League of New Orleans, 1969-70. Recipient Arts Adminstr. of Yr. award Arts Mgmt. Inst./Nat. News Svc., 1987, Award for Sustained Mgmt. Excellence, Greater New Orleans Found., 1989. Mem. Am. Inst. Cert. Am. Inst. Certified Planners, 1978-, AIA (hon.), Am. Leadership Forum (mem. curriculum com. 2006-), U.S. Urban Arts Fedn. (pres. 1988), Nat. Assembly of Local Arts Agencies (vice chmn. bd. dirs. 1988-94, Chairman's award 1992), Newcomb Art Gallery (mem. nat. adv. bd. 2007-). Avocations: music, art, reading, travel. Office: 1914 Bissonnet St Houston TX 77005-1645

MCCOLLAM, SHARON L., retail executive; b. 1962; BS in Acctg., U. Ctrl. Okla. CPA. Acctg. Ernst & Young; v.p., CFO fresh vegetables divsn. Dole Food Co., Inc., 1996—2000; v.p. fin. Williams-Sonoma, Inc., San Francisco, 2000, sr. v.p., CFO, 2000—03, exec. v.p., CFO, 2003—06, exec. v.p., CFO, COO, 2006—. Bd. dirs. Del Monte Foods Co., 2007—. Office: Williams-Sonoma Inc 3250 Van Ness Ave San Francisco CA 94109

MCCOLLISTER, CHRISTOPHER MICHAEL, forester; b. Jackson, Wyo., Nov. 30, 1969; s. Michael Joseph McCollister and Jean Elizabeth Dilley. BS in Biology, U. Calif., San Diego, 1993; MS in Geography, Mont. State U., Bozeman, 2004. Avalanche forecaster Bridger-Teton Nat. Forest, Jackson, Wyo., 2001—. Contbr. scientific papers. Bd. mem. Avalanche Ctr. Support Org., 2003—08. Mem.: Am. Avalanche Assn. Home: PO Box 412 Teton Village WY 83025 Personal E-mail: chrismccollister@yahoo.com.

MC COLLISTER, JOHN CHARLES, writer, minister, educator; b. Pitts., June 1, 1935; s. John Charles and Caroline Jesse (Hall) Mc C.; m. Beverly Ann Chase, Aug. 6, 1960; children: Beth Ann, Amy Susan, Michael John. BA, Capital U., 1957; MDiv, Luth. Theol. Sem., Columbus, Ohio, 1961; PhD, Mich. State U., 1969. Ordained to ministry Luth. Ch., 1961. Pastor Zion Luth. Ch., Freeland, Mich., 1961-65, Bethlehem Luth. Ch., Lansing, Mich., 1965-71; prof. religion and Greek Olivet (Mich.) Coll., 1970-74; prof. religion and philosophy Bethune-Cookman Coll., Daytona Beach, Fla., 1974-76, Embry-Riddle Aero. U., 1976-82, dir. profl. programs, 1979-80, cons. to pres., 1980-82. Pres. Wright Advt. Co., Daytona Beach, 1975-76; CEO New Arran Prodns., Inc., Daytona Beach, 1993—, Yongestreet Prodns., Ormond Beach, Fla., 1986; arbitrator Fed. Mediation and Conciliation Svc., 1978; spl. master Fla. Pub. Employees Rels. Commn., 1975—; mgmt. cons. Hoover Ball and Bearing, Charlotte, Mich.; pres. Am. Writers Inst., 1982—. Host Open Phone Forum, radio sta. WROD, Daytona Beach, 1974—76; author: A Philosophy of Flight, 1981, So Help Me, God, 1981, The Christian Book of Why, 1983; Problem Solving for Executives, 1984; author: The Sky is Home, 1986; co-author: The Sunshine Book, 1979, Day by Day, 1990; editor and compiler A Child is Born, 1972, Portraits of the Christ, 1974, Writing for Dollars, 1995, The Story of the Pittsburgh Pirates, 1998, The Tigers and Their Den, 1999, The Best Baseball Games Ever Played, 2002, Tales from the Pirates Dugout, 2003, Tales from the Cockpit, 2003, Echoes from the Smithsonian, 2004; editor and compiler: Tales From The 1979 Pittsburgh Pirates, 2005, God and the Oval Office, 2005; editor and compiler The Good, The Bad and The Ugly, 2008; contbr. articles to various mags. Vol. probation officer, Mich., 1961-71, hearing officer, 1970-74; commr. Mich. Dept. Commerce, 1969-72; speaker Nat. Lincoln Day Observance, Washington, 1982; internat. adviser Han Nam U., Taejon, Republic of Korea, 1989. Recipient Outstanding Am. award Daytona Beach Jaycees, 1974. Mem. Am. Arbitration Assn. Home and Office: 26 Lazy Eight Dr Port Orange FL 32128-6775

MCCOLLOUGH, CHERIE A., science educator; b. Hampton, Va. d. Edwin F. and June E. Phillips; children: Jennifer Elaine, Andrew Scott, Anne Marie. Degree in Summa Cum Laude, Baylor U., 1994; BS in Edn., Baylor U., Waco, Tex., 1994, MS, 1999; PhD, U. Tex., Austin, 2005. Lic. sci. tchr. State Bd. Edn., Tex., 1994. Sci. tchr. Temple Ind. Sch. Dist., Tex., 1994—98; biology faculty Ctrl. Tex. Coll., Killeen, 1999—2000; adminstr. Schleicher County Ind. Sch. Dist., Eldorado, 2000—01; asst. prof. Tex. A&M Corpus Christi, 2005—. Rsch. asst. U. Tex., 2001—05. Contbr. articles to profl. jours. Recipient Grad. Rsch. award, Baylor U., 1995. Fellow: Tex. A&M U. Corpus Christi; mem.: Assn. Supervision Curriculum Devel., Nat. Biology Tchrs. Assn., Am. Ednl. Rsch. Assn., Nat. Sci. Tchrs. Assn., Tex. Coastal Bend Audubon Soc. (sec. 2008—), Tri Beta, Alpha Chi, Kappa Delta Pi, Sigma Xi Sci., Golden Key. Office: Tex A&M Univ Corpus Christi 6300 Ocean Dr Unit 5800 ST 310A Corpus Christi TX 78412-5800 Business E-Mail: cherie.mccollough@tamucc.edu.

MCCOLLOUGH, NEWTON CLARK, III, orthopaedic surgeon; b. Butler, Pa., July 17, 1934; s. Newton C. and Margaret Elizabeth (Mattocks) McC.; m. Mary Eva Semanski, Feb. 22, 1968; children: Peter Scott, Amy Marie. BA, Duke U., 1956; MD, U. Pa., 1959. Diplomate: Am. Bd. Orthopaedic Surgery. Intern Jackson Meml. Hosp., Miami, Fla., 1959-60, resident in orthopaedic surgery, 1960-64; dir. orthopaedic resident edn. Orange Meml. Hosp., Orlando, Fla., 1965-66; asst. prof. orthopaedics and rehab. U. Miami Sch. Medicine, 1968-72, assoc. prof., 1972-76, prof., vice chmn. dept., 1976-78, prof., chmn. dept., 1978-86; dir. rehab. Jackson Meml. Hosp., Miami, 1972-82, chief orthopedics and rehab., 1978-86; dir. med. affairs Internat. Shriners Hosps. Children, Tampa, Fla., 1986-2001, 2001—, mem. med. adv. bd., 2001—, dir. med. affairs emeritus, 2001—, med. adv. bd., 2001—. Dir. Am. Bd. for Certification in Prosthetics/Orthotics, 1974-77; mem. Health Planning Council So. Fla. Task Force on Long Term Patient Care, 1974-77; asst. med. dir. Div. of Children's Med. Services, State of Fla., 1975-86; chmn. Statewide Com. for Spinal Cord Injury, 1976-78 Trustee Jour. Bone and Joint Surgery, 1992-98, vice chmn., 1996-98; contbr. articles to med. jours. Served to lt. comdr. M.C. USNR, 1966-68. Decorated Legion of Merit. Mem. ACS, AMA, Am. Acad. Orthopaedic Surgeons (bd. dirs. 1978-79, 87-92, 2d v.p. 1987-88, 1st v.p. 1988-89, pres. 1989-90), Am. Burn Assn. (Disting. Achievement award 2001), Fla. Orthopaedic Soc. (mem. exec. com. 1978-79), Miami Orthopaedic Soc. (v.p. 1978-79), Am. Acad. Orthotists and Prosthetists (hon.), Fla. Med. Soc. Hillsborough County Med. Assn., Am. Congress Rehab. Medicine, Nat. Rehab. Assn., Scoliosos Rsch. Soc., Internat. Soc. Prosthetics and Orthotics, Am. Orthopaedic Assn., Orthopaedic Rsch. and Edn. Found. (trustee 1991-97, sec. 1995-97), Internat. Soc. Prosthetics and Orthotics (dir. 1980-83), Assn. Children's Prosthetic and Orthotic Clinics (pres. 1983-84), Rehab. Engring. Soc. N.Am. (dir. 1980-83), Am. Spinal Injury Assn., Internat. Med. Soc. Paraplegia, Pediatric Orthopaedic Soc. (dir. 1983-84, pres. 1984-85, Disting. Achievement award 2000), 20th Century Orthopaedic Assn. (treas. 1984-89), Am. Acad. Pediatrics, Phi Beta Kappa, Alpha Omega. Republican. Lutheran. Office: 602 Juan Anasco Dr Longboat Key FL 34228 Office Phone: 941-383-6146. Personal E-mail: newt3md@aol.com.

MCCOLLUM, BETTY, United States Representative from Minnesota; b. Mpls., July 12, 1954; m. Douglas McCollum; 2 children. BS in Edn., Coll. St. Catherine, 1987. Retail store mgr., Minn.; mem. Minn. Ho. Reps., 1992-2000, mem. edn. com., environ. and natural resources com., mem. gen. legis. com., vet. affairs and elections com., mem. transportation and transit com., asst. majority leader, chair legis. commn. on econ. status of women, mem. rules and adminstrv. legis. com.; mem. U.S. Congress from Minn. 4th Dist., Washington, 2001—; mem. edn. and workforce com., resources com.; mem. Com. on Internat. Relations. Mem. St. Croix Valley Coun. Girl Scouts. Mem.: Am. Legion Aux., VFW Aux. Dfl. Office: US Ho Reps 1029 Longworth Ho Office Bldg Washington DC 20515-2304*

MCCOLLUM, BILL (IRA WILLIAM MCCOLLUM JR.), state attorney general, former congressman; b. Brooksville, Fla., July 12, 1944; s. Ira William and Arline Gray (Lockhart) McCollum; m. Ingrid Mary Seebohm, Sept. 25, 1971; children: Douglas Michael, Justin Randolph, Andrew Lockhart. BA, U. Fla., 1965, JD, 1968. Bar: Fla. 1968, DC 2002. Ptnr. Pitts, Eubanks & Ross, P.A., Orlando, Fla., 1973-80; mem. US Congress from 5th Fla. dist., 1981-92, US Congress from 8th Fla. dist., 1993-2001, vice chmn. banking/fin. svcs. com., chmn. judiciary subcommittee on crime, mem. select com. on intelligence; ptnr. Baker & Hostetler, L.L.P., Orlando, Fla. and Washington, DC, 2001—06; atty. gen. State of Fla., 2007—. Vice chair House Rep. Conf. 101st-103d Congresses. Chmn. Rep. Exec. Com. Seminole County, Fla., 1976-80; county chmn.'s rep. 5th Dist. Fla. State Rep. Exec. Com., 1977-80; co-chmn. rep. platform com., 1992. Served in USN, 1969—72, comdr. Judge Adv. Gen.'s Corps USNR, 1973—92. Mem. Fla. Bar, Naval Res. Assn., Res. Officers Assn., Orange County Bar Assn. (exec. coun. 1975-79), Am. Legion, Mil. Order World Wars, Fla. Blue Key, Phi Delta Phi, Omicron Delta Kappa, Kiwanis. Republican. Episcopalian. Office: Office of Atty Gen The Capitol PL-01 Tallahassee FL 32399-1050 Office Phone: 850-245-0222.*

MCCOLLUM, CLIFFORD GLENN, college dean emeritus; b. South Gifford, Mo., May 12, 1919; s. William Henry and Aultie V. (Westfall) McC.; m. Alice Elizabeth Erickson, Aug. 18, 1940; children: Eric Edward, Lisa Buren. Student, Central Coll., 1935-37; BS, U. Mo., 1939, MA, 1947, EdD, 1949. Tchr. pub. schs., Monett, Mo., 1938-39, Poplar Bluff, Mo., 1939-41, Boonville, Mo., 1941-42; asst. prof. sci. U. No. Iowa, 1949-55, assoc. prof., 1956-59, prof., 1959-84, prof. emeritus, 1984—, head dept. sci., 1957-68; dean U. No. Iowa (Coll. Natural Scis.), 1968-84, dean emeritus, 1984—. Prof. State U. N.Y. at Oneonta, 1955-56; Dir., instl. rep. Central States Univs., Inc.; cons. Coronet Instrnl. Films; cons. on sci. curricula to pub. schs. and colls.; speaker in field. Contbr. articles to profl. jours. Served with USAAF, 1943-46. Sci. Bldg. at U. Norther Iowa named in his honor, upon retirement. Fellow AAAS (nat. committeeman 1964-67), Iowa Acad. Sci. (pres. 1979-80); mem. Am. Inst. Biol. Scis., Nat. Assn. Biology Tchrs. (regional dir. 1963-65), Nat. Assn. Research in Sci. Teaching, Nat. Sci. Tchrs. Assn., Sigma Xi, Phi Delta Kappa. Home: 8559 N Line Creek Pky Apt 352 Kansas City MO 64154-2131 Personal E-mail: cmccollum1@kc.rr.com, amccollum@kc.rr.com. *My personal response to the philosophical conditions in which we live today is one of preparing to live rather consistently with crises. It is my conviction that the mood of our time is toward a growing pessimism, and much of this is associated with the concomitants of a galloping technology. Yet we are not willing at this point to give up our human condition to the natural evolution that would result from basic environmental mechanisms. We will still try to condition that destiny.*

MCCOLLUM, DELORES LARHEINE, secondary school educator; b. Sept. 5, 1951; BA in History, Spelman Coll., 1973; MA in History, Cleve. State U., 1977. Tchr. social studies Cleve. Pub. Schs., 1973—2005; ret., 2005; owner event planning and coord. svc. Majestic Butterfly. Author: (essays) The Black Family, 1984, Reflections, 1985; creator (project picture) Happy Birthday Dr. King!, 1986, Ann. Dr. Martin Luther King Jr. Holiday Breakfast Celebration, 2001; author: (guide book) Bible Studies In Joahn's Headlines. Vol. McMickle for Congress campaign, Cleve., 1998; chair, trustee Antioch Bapt. Ch., 1996; vol. Bethany Bapt. Ch. Food Bank Ministry; mem. YWCA of Cleve Fulbright scholar, 1984, Armonk Inst. scholar, 1992, Ednl. Exec. award, Ohio Dr. Martin Luther King, Jr. Holdan Commn, 2008. Home: 4266 E 170th Pl Cleveland OH 44128-3306 Office Phone: 216-283-5209. Personal E-mail: info@majesticbutterfly.com.

MCCOLLUM, JAMES FOUNTAIN, lawyer; b. Reidsville, NC, Mar. 24, 1946; s. James F. and Dell (Frazier) McC.; m. Susan Shasek, Apr. 26, 1969; children: Audra McCollum Bowers, Amy McCollum Sullivan. BS, Fla. Atlantic U., Boca Raton, 1968; JD, Fla. State U., Tallahassee, 1972. Bar: US Ct. Appeals (5th cir.) 1973, Fla. 1972, US Ct. Appeals (11th cir.) 1982, US Supreme Ct. 2006. Assoc. Kennedy & McCollum, 1972-73; prin. McCollum & Rinaldo, PA, 1973-77, McCollum & Oberhausen, PA, 1977-80, McCollum, Oberhausen & Tuck, LLP (and predecessor firm), Sebring, Fla., 1977—. Bd. dirs. Comml. Bancorp, Inc., Comml. Bank Highlands County; pres. Highlands Devel. Concepts, Inc., Sebring, 1982—; sec. Focus Broadcast Comm., Inc., Sebring, 1982-87; mng. ptnr. Highlands Investment Service; pres. Am. Svc. Title & Escrow, Inc., 2001— Treas. Highlands County chpt. ARC, 1973-76; vestryman St. Agnes Episcopal Ch., 1973—, chancellor, 1978—; mem. Fla. Sch. Bd. Atty.'s Assn., 1974-2001, bd. dirs., 1989-97, pres., 1995-96; mem. Com. 100 of Highlands County, 1975-83, bd. dirs., 1985-87, chmn., 1991-92; chmn. Highlands County High Speed Rail Task Force; chmn. bd., treas. Ctrl. Fla. Racing Assn., 1976-78; chmn. Leadership Sebring: life mem., past pres. Highlands Little Theatre, Inc.; bd. dirs. Palms of Sebring Nursing Home, 1988-90, Palms Estate Mobile Home Park, Sebring Airport Authority, 1988-90, treas., 1988, chmn. indsl. com., 1988, vice-chmn., 1989-90, chmn., 1990-91, Highlands County High Speed Rail Task Force, 1986-89, Highlands County Family YMCA, 1985-93, pres. Sebring br., 1992-93, chmn. bldg. com., 1992-94, Good Shepherd Hospice, Inc., v.p., 2000—, chmn. bd. dirs., 2003-05, Primal Connection, Inc., 2006—; commr. Sebring Redevel. Agy., 2006—, chmn. March Dine Celebrity Chef's Auction, 2009; campaign chmn. Jeb Bush for Gov., Highlands County, 1994, 1998, 2002, George W. Bush for President, 2000, 04. Recipient ARC citation, 1974, Presdl. award of appreciation Fla. Jaycees, 1980-82, 85, Outstanding Svc. award Highlands Coun. of 100, 1988, Most Valuable Player award Highlands Little Theatre, Inc., 1986, Zenon Significant Achievement award, 1991, Best Set award, 2002; named Jaycee of Year, Sebring Jaycees, 1981, Outstanding Local Chpt. Pres., US Jaycees, 1977, Citizen of Yr., United Way Ctrl. Fla., 2004, Highlands Counties Best Lawyer, Highlands Today and News Sun newspapers, 2003, 05, 06, 07, 08, 09. Mem. ABA, ATLA, Comml. Law League Am., Am. Arbitration Assn. (comml. arbitration panel), Nat. Assn. Retail Credit Attys., Fla. Bar (jour. com.), Highlands County Bar Assn. (past chmn. legal aid com.), Fla. Sch. Bd. Attys. Assn. (bd. dirs. 1989-97, v.p. 1993-94, pres. 1994-95), Greater Sebring C. of C. (dir. 1982-89, pres. 1986-87, chmn. transp. com. 1986—, Most Valuable Dir. award 1986-87), Fla. Jaycees (life, internat. senate 1977—), Lions (bd. dirs. 1972-73, v.p. 1994-95, Disting. award 1984). Republican. Episcopalian. Office: 129 S Commerce Ave Sebring FL 33870-3602 Office Phone: 863-385-5188. Personal E-mail: jim@jimmccollum.com.

MCCOLLUM, JOHN MORRIS, tenor; b. Coalinga, Calif., Feb. 21, 1922; s. Fay James and Ingabord Telette (Mason) McC.; m. Mary Margaret Wilson, Jan. 23, 1944; children: Kristi Elizabeth, Timothy James. Student, Coalinga Coll., 1939—40; BA in Journalism, U. Calif., Berkeley, 1947; student, Am. Theatre Wing, 1951—53. Reporter, city editor Coalinga Record, 1947-50; editor agrl. news U. Calif. Coll. Agr., 1950-51. Prof. music and chmn. voice faculty U. Mich.; dir. U. Mich. div. Nat. Music Camp; faculty Aspen Music Festival and School, 1963-76 Concert and opera singer, 1951—, soloist, Fifth Ave. Presbyn. Ch., NYC, 1953-56, debut, Town Hall, NYC, 1952, with, Boston Symphony Orchestra, Tanglewood, Mass., 1952, engagements with Symphony Orchestras in, N.Y.C., Chgo., Phila., San Francisco, Cleve., Washington, St. Louis, Detroit, New Orleans, Toronto, London, Mexico; with opera companies of, Boston, Washington, Toronto, Ft. Worth, Central City, Colo., NBC-TV, music festivals and oratorio societies, European debut, Festival of Two Worlds, Spoleto, Italy, summer 1958, Santa Fe Opera Co., leading tenor, NYC Opera Co., performing mem., Music Assos. of Aspen. (Recipient award Atwater Kent Auditions 1950, Am. Theatre Wing award 1952). Mem. Rep. Ctrl. Com., Fresno County, Calif., 1950; pres. Ann Arbor Civic Theatre, 1987-88; mem. Sarasota County Rep. exec. com.; mem., bd. dirs. Sarasota Concert Assn.; bd. dirs. Univ. Mich. Alumni Club. Served with U.S. Navy, 1942-49. Mem. U. Calif. Alumni Assn., Nat. Assn. Tchrs. Singing, Am. Acad. Tchrs. Singing, Alpha Tau Omega, Sigma Delta Chi, Pi Kappa Lambda. Episcopalian (lay reader). Clubs: Rotary (pres. 1977, Paul Harris fellow), Ann Arbor Golf and Outing (pres. 1979), The Meadows Country Club (Sarasota, Fla.). Home: 3380 W Chelmsford Ct Sarasota FL 34235-0947

MCCOLLUM, MARIANNE, pharmacist, educator, medical researcher; d. Victor Joseph and Marianne McCollum. BA in Molecular, Cellular and Developmental Biology, U. Colo., Boulder, 1983; BS, in Pharmacy, U. Colo. Health Scis. Ctr., Denver, 1989, PhD in Pharm. Outcomes Rsch., 1999. Cert. pharmacotherapy specialist Am. Pharm. Assn., 1995, Board Certified Pharmacotherapy Specialist (Recertified) Am. Pharm. Assn., Wash., DC, 2002, Registered Pharmacist State of Colo., 1989. Asst. prof. Sch. Pharmacy U. Colo. Health Scis. Ctr., Denver, 2000—; asst. chief inpatient pharmacy mgr. Denver Vets. Affairs Med. Ctr., 2001—06. Pres. Symmetry Enterprises, Inc., Boulder, 2004—. Contbr. articles to profl. publs., chpt. to book. Vol. Boulder County AIDS Project, 1989—96; mem. friends of flock ATL Found., Denver, 2000—06. Pre-doctoral fellow, Am. Found. Pharm. Edn., 1998—99. Mem.: Am. Diabetes Assn., Internat. Soc. Pharmacoeconomics and Outcomes Rsch., Am. Assn. Colls. Pharmacy, Am. Coll. Clin. Pharmacy (chmn. outcomes and economics practice and rsch. network 2006—, Investigator Devel. award 2004—05, Career Devel. award 2005—), Phi Lambda Sigma (life), Rho Chi Soc. (life; pres. 1988—89). Avocations: golf, fishing, boating. Office: U Colo Health Scis Ctr 4200 East 9th Ave Box C-238 Denver CO 80262

MCCOLLUM, MARK A., oil industry executive; BBA, Baylor U., Waco, Tex. CPA Tex. Assoc. Arthur Andersen, 1980—91, audit and bus. adv. ptnr., 1991—94; v.p. fin. analysis and planning, corp. controller Tenneco Inc., v.p. corp. devel.; sr. v.p., CFO Tenneco Automotive, 1999—2003; sr. v.p., chief acctg. officer Halliburton, Houston, 2003—07, dir., KBR, Inc., 2006—07, exec. v.p., CFO, 2008—. Mem. exec. com. Halliburton. Bd. dirs. Exterran Partners; bd. trustees Found. for the Retarded, Star of Hope Mission, Houston. Mem.: Fin. Execs. Internat., Inst. Mgmt. Accountants, Tex. Soc. CPA's, Am. Inst. CPA's. Office: Halliburton 5 Houston Ctr 1401 McKinney Ste 2400 Houston TX 77010-4008 Office Phone: 713-759-2600.

MCCOMAS, DAVID JOHN, science administrator, space physicist; b. Milw., May 22, 1958; s. Harrold James and Hazelyn (Melconian) McC.; m. Richelle Wolff, May 30, 1981; children: Random A., Koan I., Orion G. BS in Physics, MIT, Cambridge, 1980; MS in Geophysics and Space Physics, UCLA, 1985, PhD in Geophysics and Space Physics, 1986. Mem. staff Los Alamos Nat. Lab., N.Mex., 1980-91, sect. leader space plasma and planetary physics N.Mex., 1991-92, group leader for space and atmospheric scis. N.Mex., 1992-98, founding dir. Ctr. for Space Sci. and Exploration, NASA program N.Mex., 1998—2000; exec. dir. space sci. and engring. divsn. S.W. Rsch. Inst., San Antonio, 2000—03, sr. exec. dir., 2004—. Strategic planning com. earth and space scis. divsn. Los Alamos Nat. Lab, 1986; advanced composition explorer phase A study team NASA, 1988-89, space physics data system steering com., 1990-91, inner magnetosphere imaging study team, 1991-94, prin. investigator Interstellar Boundary Explorer, Ulysses Solar Wind Observations Over the Poles of the Sun Experiment, Two Wide-Angle Imaging Neutral-Atom Spectrometers, Explorer Mission-of-Opportunity, Solar Wind Electron Proton Alpha Monitor (instrument on the Advanced Composition Explorer, co-investigator Medium Energy Neutral Atom instrument on IMAGE Midsized Discovery Mission, plasma instrument for Cassini mission to Saturn, GENESIS Discovery mission, ISTP Polar Spacecraft's Thermal Ion Dynamics Experiment, Cluster plasma electron instrument, team New Millennium Plasma Experiment for Planetary Exploration, Space Sci. Adv. Com., chmn. Sun-Earth Connections Adv. Subcom., Solar Probe Sci. and Tech. Definition Team, NASA, 2004-05; com. solar-terrestrial rsch. Nat. Rsch. Coun., 1991-94, com. space sci. tech. planning Aeronautics and Space Engring. Bd./space studies bd., 1992, task group rsch. prioritization future space sci. space studies bd., 1994—; former prin. investigator series of 10 magnetospheric plasma analyzer instruments at geosynchronous orbit Dept. Energy; com. mem., panelist Nat. Acad. Sci.'s Nat. Rsch. Coun., U. Calif., State of N.Mex., others; adj. prof. dept. physics and astronomy U. Tex., San Antonio. Assoc. editor Jour. Geophys. Rsch.-Space Physics, 1993-94; contbr. articles to profl. jours. Grad. fellow Inst. Geophysics and Planetary Physics, 1983-84. Fellow AAAS, Am. Geophys. Union (James B. Macelwane award 1993). Achievements include patents in field. Office: SW Rsch Inst PO Drawer 28510 San Antonio TX 78228-0510

MCCOMB, DAVID GLENDINNING, history professor; b. Kokomo, Ind., Oct. 26, 1934; s. John Floyd and Jennie (Glendinning) McC.; m. Mary Alice Collier, Sept. 6, 1957; children: Katherine, Susan, Joseph. BA, So. Meth. U., 1956; MBA, Stanford U., 1958; MA, Rice U., 1962; PhD, U. Tex., 1968. Purchasing agt. McRan Co., Houston, 1958-60; instr. South Tex. Jr. Coll., Houston, 1962, U. Houston, 1966-68; asst. prof. San Antonio Coll., 1962-66; rsch. assoc. U. Tex., Austin, 1968-69; asst. prof. history Colo. State U., Ft. Collins, 1969-72, assoc. prof., 1972-77, prof., 1977—2002, chmn. dept., 1975—80, emeritus prof., 2002—. Interviewer, dir. Oral History of Colo. Project, 1973—77, Big Thompson Disaster Oral History, 1976—78, Olympic Tng. Ctr. Oral History, 1983—87. Author: Houston, a History, 1969, rev. edit., 1981 (Tullis award 1969), Galveston, a History, 1986 (Tex. history 1987), Texas, a Modern History, 1989, Texas, an Illustrated History, 1995, Historic Seacoast of Texas, 1999, Travels with Joe, 2001, Sports in World History, 2004, Spare Time in Texas, 2008, also others; editor: World History Ann. Edits., 1987, 89, 92, 96, 98, 2000, 01; contbr. articles to hist. jours. Recipient award of merit Am. Assn. for State and Local History, 1980, Disting. Svc. award Colo. State U., 1986; Danforth Found. grantee, 1978, Sigma Xi, 2001, also others, 1966-85. Fellow Tex. Hist. Assn.; mem. Oral History Assn. (program chmn. 1980), N.Am. Assn. for Sports History, World History Assn. (exec. coun. 1997-99), Western History Assn. (program chmn. 1979), Rocky Mountain World History Assn. (chmn. 1988-92). Democrat. Unitarian Universalist. Avocation: master swimming competition. Office: Colo State U Dept History Fort Collins CO 80523-0001 Office Phone: 970-491-6335. Business E-Mail: david.mccomb@colostate.edu.

MCCOMB, WILLIAM L., apparel company executive; b. Columbia, Mo., Dec. 29, 1962; m. Marianne D. McComb; 2 children. BA in Economics, Miami U. of Ohio, 1984; MBA in Mktg. and Fin., U. Chgo., 1987. With Leo Burnett advertising firm, 1989—92; asst. product dir. consumer products Johnson & Johnson, 1992—93, product dir. consumer products, 1993—94, group product dir. consumer products, 1995, v.p. Johnson & Johnson Merck, 1996—97, v.p. new markets, Johnson & Johnson Professional Markets, 1997—98, v.p. mktg. McNeil Consumer Healthcare, 1999—2001, pres. McNeil Consumer & Specialty Pharmaceuticals, 2001—05, pres. Ortho Women's Health and Urology, 2004—05, group chmn. orthopaedics and neurologics, worldwide franchise chmn., mem. J&J medical device and diagnostics group operating com., 2005—06; CEO Liz Claiborne Inc., NYC, 2006—. Bd. dirs. Liz Claiborne Inc., 2006—. Office: Liz Claiborne Inc 1441 Broadway New York NY 10018 Home: 141 Hodge Rd Princeton NJ 08540*

MCCONAUGHEY, MATTHEW, actor; b. Uvalde, Tex., Nov. 4, 1969; s. Jim and Kay McConaughey; 1 child (with Camila Alves), Levi Alves. Grad., U. Tex., Austin, 1993. Actor: (films) My Boyfriend's Back, 1993, Dazed and Confused, 1993, The Return of The Texas Chainsaw Massacre, 1994, Angels in the Outfield, 1994, Submission, 1995, Judgement, 1995, Boys on the Side, 1995, Lone Star, 1996, A Time to Kill, 1996, Larger than Life, 1996, Glory Daze, 1996, Scorpion Spring, 1997, Amistad, 1997, Contact, 1997, The Rebel, 1998, The Newton Boys, 1998, Making Sandwiches, 1998, South Beach, 1999, Last Flight of the Raven, 1999, Edtv, 1999, U-571, 2000, The Wedding Planner, 2001, Thirteen Conversations About One Thing, 2001, Frailty, 2001, Reign of Fire, 2002, How To Lose a Guy in 10 Days, 2003, Tiptoes, 2003, Two for the Money, 2005, Failure to Launch, 2006, We Are Marshall, 2006, Fool's Gold, 2008, Surfer, Dude, 2008, Ghosts of Girlfriends Past, 2009; actor, exec. prodr.: Sahara, 2005; actor: (TV films) Absolute Evel: The Evel Knievel Story, 2005; (TV appearances) Unsolved Mysteries, 1992, (voice) King of the Hill, 1999, Sex and the City, 2000; (TV series) Freedom: A History of Us, 2003 Recipient Favorite Male Action Star, People's Choice Award, 2006; named Sexiest Man Alive, People mag., 2005.

MCCONKEY, JAMES RODNEY, literature and language educator, writer; b. Lakewood, Ohio, Sept. 2, 1921; s. Clayton Delano and Grace (Baird) McC.; m. Gladys Jean Voorhees, May 6, 1944; children: Lawrence Clark, John Crispin, James Clayton. BA, Cleve. Coll., 1943; MA, Western Res. U., 1946; PhD, U. Iowa, 1953. Teaching fellow, instr. Cleve. Coll., 1945-46; teaching asst. U. Iowa, Iowa City, 1949-50; asst. prof. Morehead State Coll., Ky., 1950-54, assoc. prof. Ky., 1954-56; asst. prof. Cornell U., Ithaca, N.Y., 1956-62, assoc. prof., 1962-67, prof., 1967-87, Goldwin Smith prof. English lit., 1987-92; Goldwin Smith prof. emeritus, 1992—. Dir. Morehead Writers Workshop, 1951-56, Antioch Seminar in Writing and Pub., Yellow Springs, Ohio, 1957-59 Author: The Novels of E.M. Forster, 1957, Night Stand, 1965, Crossroads, 1968, Journey to Sahalin, 1971, The Tree House Confessions, 1979, Court of Memory, 1983, To a Distant Island, 1984, Kayo: The Authentic and Annotated Autobiographical Novel From Outer Space, 1987, Rowan's Progress, 1992, Stories From My Life With the Other Animals, 1993, The Telescope in the Parlor, 2004; editor: The Structure of Prose, 1963, Chekhov and Our Age, 1984, The Anatomy of Memory, 1996. Served with U.S. Army, 1943-45. Guggenheim fellow, 1970; Eugene Saxton Meml. Trust Fund fellow, 1962; recipient Nat. Endowment of Arts essay award, 1968, Am. Acad. and Inst. Arts and Letters award in lit., 1979 Democrat. Home: 402 Aiken Rd Trumansburg NY 14886-9733 Office: Cornell Univ Goldwin Smith Hall Dept English Ithaca NY 14853 E-mail: jrm9@cornell.edu.

MCCONKIE, GEORGE WILSON, education educator; b. Holden, Utah, July 15, 1937; s. G. Wilson and Mabel (Stephenson) McC.; m. Orlene Carol Johnson, Sept. 6, 1962; children: Lynnette Mooth, Heather Usevitch, April Rhiner, Faline Coffelt, George Wilson, Bryce Johnson, Camille Howard, Elissa, Esther Ostler, Bryna Fisher, Ruth Olson, Anna May Cooke, Cynthia Lau, Thomas Oscar. AA, Dixie Jr. Coll., 1957; BS, Brigham Young U., 1960, MS, 1961; PhD, Stanford U., 1966. Missionary LDS Ch., 1957-59; asst. prof. edn. Cornell U., 1964-70, asso. prof., 1970-75, prof., 1975-78, chmn. dept. edn., 1977-78; prof. U. Ill., Champaign, 1978—2003, chmn. dept. ednl. psychology, 1993-94, 95-97, prof. emeritus, 2003—. Sr. scientist Ctr. for Study of Reading, 1978-95, Beckman Inst., 1989-2004; rsch. fellow Cath. U. Louvain, Belgium, 1991-92; vis. prof. Nat. Yang Ming U., Taiwan, 1998, Beijing Normal U., 1999. Contbr. articles to profl. jours. Recipient Outstanding Sci. Contbn. award Soc. for Sci. Study of Reading, 1995; NIMH spl. fellow, 1971-72, NIH Fogarty Internat. fellow, 1991-92; grantee U.S. Office Edn., 1970-73, Nat. Inst. Edn., 1974-77, NIMH, 1974-84, NICHHD, 1983-89, 91-95, AT&T, 1986-89, NSF, 1989-91, 2000-03, CIA, 1991-97, Army Rsch. Lab., 1996-2001, Yamaha Motor Corp., 1997-99, GM, 2002-04; Fulbright scholar, Taiwan, 1998, Sr. scholar Chiang Chung Kuo Found., 1998-99. Mem. Lds Ch. Home: 2605 Berniece Dr Champaign IL 61822-7225 Office: Coll Education Dept Educational Psych 1310 S Sixth St Champaign IL 61820 Business E-Mail: gmcconk@illinois.edu.

MCCONLOGUE, TERENCE R., protective services official; b. Easton, Pa., Sept. 6, 1960; s. Thomas John and Mildred Christine McConlogue; children: Kevyn Britton, Coleman Quinn. BA, Moravian Coll., Bethlehem, 1983; MEd, Lehigh U., Bethlehem, 1984; PhD, Temple U., Phila., 2002. Cert. firefighter I & II, Nat. Pro Bd., 2002. Counselor Temple U., 1991—2009, Family Enrichment Ctr., Easton, 2002—; firefighter hazmat technician Us Dod, Bagdad, Iraq, 2008—09. Firefighter Palmer Mcpl. Fire Dept., Easton, 2001—09; firefighter, emt Nancy Run Fire Dept., Bethlehem, Pa., 2009. Author: (psychological test) Cognitive Risk Taking Scale. Active Am. Assn. Fire Chaplains, Washington, 2007—09. Independent. Avocations: swimming, bicycling, music. Home and Office: 18 Middle Ct Easton PA 18045 Business E-Mail: trmcc27@gmail.com.

MCCONNAUGHAY, PHILIP J., dean, law educator; BA, Ill. U., 1975, JD, 1982. Bar: Ill. 1978, Calif. 1979, DC 1983. Clk. to Hon. A.Y. Kirkland US Dist. Ct., No. Dist., Ill., 1978—79; assoc. Morrison & Foerster, San Francisco, 1979—83, ptnr. Washington, DC, Tokyo, Hong Kong, 1985—95; spl. dep. gen. counsel EEOC, Washington, DC, 1983—84; assoc. prof. U. Ill. Coll. Law, 1996—2001, prof., 2001—02; dean, Donald J. Farage prof. law Pa. State U., Dickinson Sch. Law, Carlisle, Pa., 2002—. Office: Dickinson Sch Law Pa State U 150 S Coll St Carlisle PA 17013 Office Phone: 814-863-1521. E-mail: pjm30@psu.edu.*

MCCONNAUGHEY, FLIP, legislative staff member; BA, MA, U. Wyo. Asst. city mgr., Casper, Wyo.; city adminstr. Gillette, Wyo., 1975—80; city mgr. Laramie, Wyo., 1981—96; chief of staff Senator Michael B. Enzi, Washington, 1997—. Office: Office of Senator Michael B Enzi 379A Senate Russell Office Bldg Washington DC 20510-5004 Office Phone: 202-224-3424. E-mail: Flip_McConnaughey@enzi.senate.gov.*

MCCONNAUGHEY, GEORGE CARLTON, JR., retired lawyer; b. Hillsboro, Ohio, Aug. 9, 1925; s. George Carlton and Nelle (Morse) McC.; m. Carolyn Schlieper, June 16, 1951; children: Elizabeth, Susan, Nancy. BA, Denison U., 1949; LLB, Ohio State U., 1951, JD, 1967. Bar: Ohio 1951. Sole practice, Columbus; ptnr. McConnaughey & McConnaughey, 1954-57, McConnaughey, McConnaughey & Stradley, 1957-62, Laylin, McConnaughey & Stradley, 1962-67, George, Greek, King, McMahon & McConnaughey, 1967-79, McConnaughey, Stradley, Mone & Moul, 1979-81, Thompson, Hine & Flory (merger McConnaughey, Stradley, Mone & Moul with Thompson, Hine & Flory), 1981—92, ret. ptnr., 1992—. Bd. dirs. N.Am. Broadcasting Co. (Sta. WMNI, WRKZ and WTDA Radio); asst. atty. gen. State of Ohio, 1951-54. Pres. Upper Arlington (Ohio) Bd. Edn., 1967-69, Columbus Town Meeting Assn., 1974-76; chmn. Ohio Young Reps., 1956; U.S. presdl. elector, 1956; trustee Buckeye Boys Ranch, Columbus, 1967-73, 75-81, Upper Arlington Edn. Found., 1987-93; elder Covenant Presbyn. Ch., Columbus. With U.S. Army, 1943-45, ETO. Fellow Am. Bar Found., Ohio Bar Found., Columbus Bar Found.; mem. ABA, Ohio State Bar Assn., Columbus Bar Assn., Scioto Country Club, Athletic Club, Rotary, Masons. Home: 1993 Collingswood Rd Columbus OH 43221-3741 Office Phone: 614-469-3224.

MCCONNAUGHEY, JAMES WALTER, economist; b. Washington, May 8, 1951; s. William Eugene and Eunice (Ensor) McC.; m. Rosemarie Fuchs, June 23, 1984. BS in Econs. with high honors, U. Md., 1973; MA in Econs., George Washington U., 1979; MPA with high honors, Harvard U., 1992. Industry economist FCC Common Carrier Bur., Washington, 1973-80, sr. economist, 1981-83; sr. assoc. Bolter and Nilsson, Bethesda, Md., 1983; mgr. rsch. studies div. Bethesda Rsch. Inst., 1983-89; sr. economist office policy analysis and devel. U.S. Dept. Commerce Nat. Telecommunications and Info. Adminstrn., Washington, 1989—2005, sr. econ. advisor, 2005—06, chief economist, 2007—. Mem. rsch. bd. advisors Am. Biographical Inst., 1994—; presenter in field of telecomms. policy. Author: (with others) Telecommunications Policy for the 1980's: The Transition to Competition, 1984, Telecommunications Policy for the 1990's and Beyond, 1990, U.S. Telecommunications in a Global Economy: Competitiveness at a Crossroads, 1990, Telecommunications in the Age of Information, 1991, NII Field Hearings on Universal Service and Open Access: America Speaks Out, 1994, Falling Through the Net and a Nation Online: Reports on the "Digital Divide," 1995, 1998-2004, (with others) Structure of American Industry, 2000, 3rd edit., 2008. Campaign worker, contbr. nat. and local elections; coach Bowie (Md.) Boy's Club; mem. Neighborhood Open Space Com.; worker, contbr. numerous environ. and consumer orgns.; awards evaluator Ford Found./Harvard U. Recipient certs. of appreciation for leadership Prince George's County (Md.) Pub. Sch. System, 1986, Nat. Found. Cancer Rsch., 1990, U.S. Dept. Commerce Gold medal, 1998, 2000, Silver medal for leadership/excellence, 2000, 2001, Robert Seamans tech. fellow, Lucius Littauer fellow John F. Kennedy Sch. Govt., Harvard U., 1991-92. Mem. Am. Econ. Assn. (pub. utilities group), Ea. Econ. Assn., So. Econ. Assn., Soc. Govt. Economists, Indsl.

Orgn. Soc., DAV Comdrs. Club, Phi Eta Sigma, Omicron Delta Epsilon, Beta Gamma Sigma, Phi Kappa Phi. Avocations: hiking, reading, travel. Home: 8380 Sweet Cherry Ln Laurel MD 20723-1062 Office Phone: 202-482-1880.

MCCONNELL, ALBERT LYNN, dean of education; b. Springfield, Ohio, Oct. 20, 1946; s. Jack Pershing and Betty Ann (Venema) McConnell; m. Rannette Oledge, Dec. 21, 2001; 1 child, Ciara Lynn 1 stepchild, Joshua Hooper. BA, Ctrl. State U., 1969; MA, Webster U., 1983; MS, USACGSC, 1984. Commd. 2d. lt. U.S. Army, 1969, advanced through grades. to maj., 1980; ret., 1989; served as inf. bn. intelligence officer Schofield Barracks, Hawaii, 1970-71; inf. co. comdr., asst. ops. officer, inf. bn., 1971; intelligence analyst and briefer U.S. Mil. Assistance Command, Schofield Barracks, 1972-73; instr. U.S. Army Intelligence Sch., Ft Huachuca, Ariz., 1973-77; served in 3rd Armored Divsn., Frankfurt, Germany, 1980-81; project officer Combined Arms Ctr., Ft. Leavenworth, Kans., 1981-83, comdr. spl. security detachment, 1981-83; dir. intelligence, asst. chief staff for intelligence U.S. Army South, Ft. Clayton, Panama, 1984-85, mng. exec. officer Ft. Davis, Panama, 1985-86; tactical intelligence officer, chief adminstrv. svcs. U.S. Army Air Def. Arty. Sch., Ft. Bliss, Tex., 1986-87, dep. directorate chief, 1987-88, sr. intelligence officer, dept. divsn. chief, 1988-89; ops. analyst RAM Inc., Sierra Vista, Ariz., 1989-92; prof. bus. adminstrn. and mgmt. So. Ohio Coll., Columbus, 1992, Bliss Coll., Columbus, 1993; store mgr. Circle K Corp., Yuma, Ariz., 1993-94; tchr. Glendale (Ariz.) Union HS, 1994-95; mgr. Dexter Book Store, 1995-96; dean students Ariz. Inst. Bus. and Tech., Phoenix, 1996-98, 2002—04, campus dir. Mesa, Ariz., 1998-2000, prof. Phoenix, 2002—03; dir. edn. High Tech Inst., Phoenix, 2000—02; dean students Internat. Inst. Ams., Phoenix, 2003—05, campus dir., 2005—, Met. Coll., Phoenix, 2005. Adj. prof. Chapman U., Sierra Vista, 1990—92; tax preparer H&R Block, Sierra Vista, 1990—92; br. mgr. Jackson Hewitt Tax Svc. Met. Ctr., Phoenix, 2002—. Voter registration ofcl. Maricopa County, Ariz., 2001—02; treas. Antioch Missionary Bapt. Ch., Huachuca City, Ariz., 1991—92. Decorated Bronze Star. Mem.: Assn. Old Crows, Ret. Officers Assn., Assn. U.S. Army, Air Force Assn., Scabbard and Blade, Iota Beta Sigma, Phi Alpha Theta. Republican. Baptist. Avocations: photography, reading, coaching youth football and baseball. Office: Apollo Coll 2701 W Bethany Home Rd Phoenix AZ 85017 Office Phone: 602-433-4702. Personal E-mail: azlynnmac@hotmail.com. Business E-Mail: amcconnell@apollo.edu.

MCCONNELL, BRIGHT, III, orthopaedic surgeon; b. Augusta, Ga., Mar. 3, 1953; s. Bright McConnell, Jr. and Elizabeth Custer McConnell; m. Pam Hollings, Oct. 14, 1978; children: Elizabeth Anne, Bright McConnell, IV, Ian Deryck. BS, Davidson Coll., NC, 1971—75; MD, Med. Coll. Ga., Augusta, 1975—79. Lic. orthopaedic surgeon Am. Bd. Orthopaedic Surgery, 1987, cert. clin. densitometrist Internat. Soc. Clin. Densitometry, 2001. Residency in orthopaedic surgery U. Fla., 1984; fellowship in sports medicine Kerlan-Jobe Orthopaedic Clinic & Nat. Athletic Health Inst., 1985; orthopaedic surgeon, ptnr. Orthopaedic Specialists of Charleston, SC, 1985—2002; CEO Prevecare, Charleston, 2002—05; pvt. practice Daniel Island, SC, 2005—. Bd. dir. Internat. Ctr. Birds of Prey, Awendaw, SC, 2000—. Named to Best Doctors in Am., 2006. Fellow: Am. Acad. Orthopaedic Surgery; mem.: Charleston County Med. Soc., Am. Orthopaedic Soc. Sports Medicine, Aircraft Owners & Pilots Assn. Avocations: aerobatics, fishing, flying. Home: 8863 Hwy 17N Mc Clellanville SC 29458 Office: 900 Island Park Dr Ste 105 Charleston SC 29492 Office Fax: 843-284-5201. Personal E-mail: makaira1@aol.com. Business E-Mail: drbrightmcconnell@yahoo.com, pmcconnell@charlestonsportsmed.com.

MCCONNELL, CHARLES PRESCOTT, retired science educator; b. Wayne, Nebr., Mar. 3, 1942; s. Charlie Irving and Truma McConnell; m. Cathie Dianne Harris, Aug. 22, 1964; children: Stefanie Michele, John Edward. BS, U. Nebr., 1964, MS, 1967. Tchr. Fresno Unified Sch. Dist., Calif., 1967—2001. Active Boy Scouts Am. Recipient Silver Beaver award. Mem. NEA (life), Calif. Tchr. Assn., Fresno Tchr. Assn. (life), Calif. Retired Tchr. Assn., Quarter Century Wireless Assn. (life), Am. Radio Relay League (life, sect. mgr. 1976-89, 2002-09, vice dir. Pacific div. 1988-90, dir. 1990-93), Sigma Xi (assoc.). Republican. Lutheran. Avocation: amateur radio. Home: 1658 W Mesa Ave Fresno CA 93711-1944 E-mail: w6dpd@arrl.org.

MCCONNELL, DAVID KELSO, lawyer; b. NYC, July 12, 1932; s. David and Caroline Hanna (Kelso) McC.; m. Alice Schmitt, Dec. 26, 1953; children: Elissa Anne McConnell Henebry, Kathleen Anne, David Willet. BCE, CCNY, 1954; LLB, Yale U., 1962. Bar: Conn. 1962, US Dist. Ct. Conn. 1963, US Ct. Appeals (2d cir.) 1964, US Ct. Appeals (3d cir.) 1966, US Sup. Ct. 1970, US Dist. Ct. (ea. dist.) Pa. 1971, Pa. 1975, NY 1986. Asst. counsel N.Y.N.H. & H. R.R., New Haven, 1962-65, counsel, 1966-68; asst. atty. gen. U.S. V.I., 1965-66; asst. gen. atty. Pa. Cen. Transp. Co., New Haven, 1969-70, asst. gen. counsel Phila., 1970-71, sr. reorganization atty., 1971, adminstrv. officer, spl. counsel to trustees, 1971-76, gen. atty., 1977-78; asst. to chmn., CEO The Penn Cen. Corp., NYC, 1979-80, corp. sec., 1980-82; v.p., gen. counsel Gen. Cable Co., Greenwich, Conn., 1982-85; pvt. practice Stamford, Conn., 1985-86, Pelham, NY, 1989-91, Greenwich, Conn., 1991-98. Of counsel McCarthy, Fingar, Donovan, Drazen & Smith, White Plains, NY, 1986-89. Dep. supr., councilman Town of Pelham, NY, 1986—90, budget officer; dep. mayor, trustee Village of Pelham, 1992—95, village atty., 1995—96; clk. of session, elder, trustee, deacon Huguenot Meml. Ch., Pelham; pres., bd. dirs. Newport Rotary Charities Fund, 2005—. With USN, 1954—59, with USNR, 1959—79. Mem.: ACLU, Common Cause, Mil. Officers Assn., Navy League, Yale Law Sch. Assn. (exec. com. 1988—91, dir. New Eng. 2001—), Assn. Bar City NY, NY Bar Assn., Conn. Bar Assn., Quindecim, St. Andrews Soc. NY (chmn. bd. mgrs. 1988—89, bd. mgrs. 1996—99), The Corinthians (mem. afterguard, dir. The Corinthians Assn., fleet capt. New Eng. fleet, trustee, pres., treas., sec. The Corinthians Endowment Fund), Little Ship Club, Newport Sail and Power Squadron (Squadron Edn. Officer 2006—08), Newport Rotary Charitable Found. (trustee, pres. 2005—), Rotary Club of Newport RI (dir. 2001—06), Rotary Club of The Pelhams NY (pres. 1993—94). Home: 68 1/2 Roseneath Ave Newport RI 02840-3849 Personal E-mail: dkmcconnell@cox.net.

MCCONNELL, E. HOY, II, advertising and public policy executive; b. Syracuse, NY, May 14, 1941; s. E. Hoy and Dorothy R. (Schmitt) McC.; m. Patricia Irwin, June 26, 1965; children: E. Hoy, III, Courtney. BA in Am. Studies magna cum laude with high honors, Yale U., 1963; MBA in Mktg, Harvard Bus. Sch., 1965. With Foote, Cone & Belding, Chgo., 1965-76, v.p. account supr., 1971—76; with D'Arcy-MacManus & Masius, Chgo., 1976-85, sr. v.p., dir. client services, then vice chmn., 1978-80, pres., 1980-84, chmn., 1984-85; mng. dir. D'Arcy Masius Benton & Bowles, Chgo., 1986-96, also bd. dirs.; sr. v.p., account dir. Leo Burnett Co., Chgo., 1996-98; exec. dir. Bus. and Profl. People for the Pub. Interest, 1999—. Bd. dirs. Evanston (Ill.) United Way, 1980-83, Evanston Youth Hockey Assn., 1980-89, pres. 1981-83; bd. dirs. Off-the-Street Club, 1980-90, Bus. Profl. People for Pub. Interest, 1981-, v.p. 1984-89, pres. 1990-95; co-chair Housing Ill., 2002-; bd. dirs. Harvard Bus. Sch. Club, 1990-92; bd. dirs. The Cradle Soc., 2000-07, mem. exec com., 2004-07, sec, 2004-05, treas., 2005-07; mem. Chgo. Coun. on Fgn. Rels., 1989-95, Wayfarers Club, 2001-. Mem. Am. Assn. Advt. Agys. (gov.-at-large Chgo. coun. 1984, sec. 1986, vice chmn. 1987, chmn. 1988-89), Glen View Country Club (bd. dirs. 1992-96), Dairymen's Country Club, Yale Club Chgo. (bd. dirs. 1996-99). Democrat. Unitarian Universalist. Home: 2703 Colfax St Evanston IL 60201-2035 Office: BPI 25 E Washington St Ste 1515 Chicago IL 60602-1804 Office Phone: 312-759-8259. Business E-Mail: hmcconnell@bpichicago.org.

MCCONNELL, EDWARD BOSWORTH, legal association administrator, lawyer; b. Greenwich, Conn., Apr. 3, 1920; s. Raymond Arnott and Anna Bell (Lee) McC.; m. Jeanne M. Rotton (dec. 1984); children: Annalee, Marilyn, Edward (dec. 1994), Barbara, William; m. Florence M. Leonard, (dec. 1991); stepchildren: Susan L. Little, William R. Leonard, Molly M. Leonard. AB, U. Nebr., 1941, LLB, 1947; MBA with distinction, Harvard U., 1943. Bar: Nebr. 1947, NJ 1950. Mem. faculty Rutgers U. Sch. Bus. Adminstrn., Newark, 1947-53; assoc. firm Toner, Speakman and Crowley, Newark, 1949-50; adminstrv. asst. and law sec. to Chief Justice of NJ, 1950-53; adminstrv. dir. Cts. of NJ, Trenton, 1953-73; also standing master Supreme Ct., 1953-73; pres. Nat. Center for State Cts., Williamsburg, 1973-90, bd. dirs., 1980-90, pres. emeritus, 1990—, cons. on ct. mgmt., 1990—92. Mem. US Dept. Justice Coun. on Role of Cts. in Am. Soc., 1978-83; mem. adv. com. Dispute Resolution Policy Study, Social Sci. Rsch. Inst., U. So. Calif., 1975-79, Civil Litigation Rsch. Project, U. Wis. and U. So. Calif., 1979-83, nat. judge edn. program to promote equality for men and women in the cts., 1980-92; mem. Nat. Inst. Criminal Justice Task Force, Urban Consortium, 1979-83; participant Access To Justice Colloquium, European Univ. Inst., Florence, Italy, 1979; nat. adv. coun. Ctr. Adminstrn. Justice, Wayne State U., 1973-77; nat. project com. State Jud. Info. Sys. Project SEARCH Group, 1973-76; lectr. Inst. of Local and State Govt. Wharton Sch. U. Pa., 1955-65, Appellate Judges Seminar, Inst. Jud. Adminstrn., NYU, 1962-75; vis. expert UN Asia and Far East Inst., Tokyo, 1971; mem. Cts. Task Force Nat. Adv. Commn. Criminal Justice Standards and Goals, 1971-73; nat. adv. com. DC Ct. Mgmt. Project, 1966-70; trustee Inst. Ct. Mgmt., 1969-73, 84-86; chmn. Nat. Conf. Ct. Adminstrv. Officers, 1956; mem. nat. task force on gender bias in cts. Nat. Assn. Women Judge's 1985-90; mem. adv. bd. Nat. Ctr. for Citizen Participation in Adminstrn. of Justice, 1984-90; mem. Nat. Commn. Trial Ct. Performance Standards, 1991-95. Mem. adv. com. on article III Commn. on the Bicentennial of the Constitution, 1989-91; adv. com. Judicary Leadership Coun., 1990-95. Maj. C.E., AUS, 1943-46, European Theater, 1944-46. Decorated Bronze Star medal; recipient Warren E. Burger award for greatest contbn. to improvement of ct. adminstrn. Inst. for Ct. Mgmt., 1975, Herbert Lincoln Harley award for efficient adminstrn. justice Am. Judicature Soc., 1973, Glenn R. Winters award for outstanding service in jud. adminstrn. Am. Judges Assn., 1974, Tom C. Clark award for outstanding contbns. to field of ct. adminstrn. Nat. Conf. Met. Cts., 1983, Award of Merit Nat. Assn. Ct. Mgmt., 1987, Spl. award, Nat. Assn. Women Judges, 1989, Paul C. Reardon award for disting. svc. Nat. Ctr. for State Cts., 1991, Alumni Achievement award U. Nebr., 1991, Robert B. Yegge award ABA Jud. Divsn. Lawyers Conf., 1997. Fellow Nat. Acad. Pub. Adminstrn. (mem. panel on evaluation budget decentralization project of fed. cts. 1989-91, chmn. panel long range planning in fed. cts. 1991-92, mem. panel for study of fed. trial ct. adminstrv. structure 1995-96); mem. ABA (fellow-at-large, coun. mem. 1960-66, 71-80, house of dels., 1977-80, chmn. com. on oversight and goals 1975-76, chmn. com. on jud. compensation jud. adminstrn. div. 1984-89, chmn. jud. adminstrn. div. 1976-77, sect. of litigation task force on excess litigiousness in Am. 1986-88, task force on reduction of litigation cost and delay, jud. adminstrn. dir. 1984-94, chmn. 1991-94, mem. long range planning com. 1989-94), N.J. Bar Assn., Nebr. Bar Assn., Fellows of Am. Bar Found. (life), Warren E. Burger Soc., Kingsmill (Va.) Golf Club, Kingsmill Tennis Club (pres. 2001), Kingsmill Yacht Club, Order of Coif (hon.), Delta Upsilon, Sigma Delta Phi, Phi Delta Phi. Office Phone: 757-220-3012. Personal E-mail: ebm80@aol.com.

MCCONNELL, JOHN, environmental activist, founder of Earth Day; b. Davis City, Iowa, Mar. 22, 1915; V.p. Nobell Rsch. Found., Calif., 1939; publisher Toe Valley View, NC, 1956, Mountain View, Calif., 1959; dir. No. Calif. Meals for Millions, 1962; founder Minute for Peace, 1963, World Equality Inc., 1968; proposed & organized Earth Day, 1969; founder Earth Soc., 1973. Author: Earth Charter, 1979, 77 Theses on the Care of Earth, 1985, Earth Magna Carta, 1995. Mailing: 4924 E Kentucky Cir Denver CO 80246 E-mail: trusteeone@aol.com.

MCCONNELL, JOHN EDWARD, retired electrical engineering company executive; b. Minot, ND, July 28, 1931; s. Lloyd Waldorf and Sarah McConnell; m. Carol Claire Myers, July 4, 1952 (dec. Feb. 1989); children: Kathleen Anne, James, Amy Lynn; m. Heidi Banziger, Sept. 29, 1990. BSME, U. Pitts., 1952; MS, Drexel Inst. Tech., 1958. Registered profl. engr., Pa. With mktg. and design depts. for turbomachinery Westinghouse Electric Corp., Lester, Pa., 1954-60, 63-67, Pitts., 1960-63; mgr. power generation equipment activities in U.S. ASEA, Inc., White Plains, NY, 1967-79, regional mgr. power equipment activities Middle Atlantic and Southeastern U.S. regions, 1967-79, mgr. turbine generator dept., 1979-83, mgr. internat. ops. Power Sys. divsn., 1983-84, mgr. transmission substas. dept., 1984-85; mgr. Ea. U.S. ops. ASEA Power Sys., Inc., 1985-86, mgr. ea. ops. measurement divsn. GEC, 1986-91; mgr. ea. region Protection and Control divsn. GEC Alsthom T&D Inc., 1991-98; prin. JEMTECH, 1998—2005; v.p. ATG Exodus, 2000—02. Adviser U.S. Congress 1968-74; spkr. in field Contbr. articles on energy and electric power to profl. jours. 1st lt. C.E., U.S. Army, 1952-54. Mem. IEEE (life, sr., energy com., past chmn. subcom. energy conservation and cogeneration, hon. mem. power sys. relay com.), IEEE Power Engring. Soc. (sr., past chmn. chpts. pub. affairs subcom.). Republican. Achievements include development of analytical techniques for power systems performance characteristics and economics of cogeneration sys. Office: JEMTECH PO Box 229 Ridgefield CT 06877-0229 Home: Apt E197 200 Laurel Lake Dr Hudson OH 44236-2167 Personal E-mail: j.e.mcconnell@ieee.org. *1) If it doesn't produce revenue, is it worthwhile? 2) Problem solving begins with careful listening. 3) Keep people informed. If they don't know, they'll assume the worst. 4) The truth is the most credible explanation you'll find.*

MCCONNELL, JOHN P., metal products executive, professional sports team executive; s. John Henderson McConnell and Margaret Jane Rardin; married; 4 children. With Worthington Industries, Columbus, Ohio, 1975—, v.p., gen. mgr., 1985, dir., 1990—, vice chmn., 1992—96, CEO, 1993—, chmn., 1996—; maj. owner, gov. Columbus Blue Jackets, 2008—. Bd. dir. Alltel Corp., The Wilds. Office: Worthington Industries 200 Old Wilson Bridge Rd Columbus OH 43085 also: Columbus Blue Jackets Nationwide Arena 200 W Nationwide Blvd, Ste Level Columbus OH 43215

MCCONNELL, MATTHEW STEPHEN, composer, educator; b. North Adams, Mass., Dec. 1, 1980; s. Stephen Earl and Patricia Ann McConnell. BA in Music, Bennington Coll., 2003; MusM in Composition, New England Conservatory, 2005, MusD, 2009. Organist St. Andrew's Epsicopal Chapel, North Adams, Mass., 1996—2003; organist, choir dir. 1st Bapt. Ch., Cheshire, 1998—99; asst. instr. composition Bennington Coll., Vt., 2002; music copyist Ricky Ian Gordon, 2002—04; tchg. fellow New Eng. Conservatory Music, 2006—; min. music Good Shepherd United Meth. Ch., Malden, Mass., 2008—. Pvt. tutor, Boston, 2003—; freelance organist, 2003—; co-founder, performer The Toyland Band, Boston, 2004—. Composer: Sonata for Solo Viola, 2003, Piano Trio No. 1, 2004, Concerto for Toy Piano & Chamber Orch., 2004. Benefit concert organist Salvation Army, North Adams, Mass., 1999, Berkshire Food Project, 2000, C.O.D.Y. Youth Project, 2001. Grantee, Wolley Fund Composition, 2003; scholar, Berkshire AGO, 1993—94, The Conducting Inst., 2001. Mem.: Am. Guild Organists. Episcopalian. Home: 39 Williams St North Adams MA 01247

MCCONNELL, MICHAEL ARTHUR, lawyer; b. Ft. Worth, Jan. 15, 1947; BA, Loyola U., New Orleans, 1969; JD, U. Tex., 1975. Bar: Tex. 1976, U.S. Dist. Ct. (no. dist.) Tex. 1976, U.S. Dist. Ct. (ea. dist.) Tex. 1981, U.S. Dist. Ct. (we. dist.) Tex. 1982, U.S. Dist. Ct. (so. dist.) Tex. 1989, U.S. Ct. Appeals (5th cir.) Tex. 1980, U.S. Ct. Appeals (10th cir.) 1987. Briefing atty. U.S. Dist. Ct. Hon. Eldon B. Mahon, Ft. Worth, 1976-77; assoc. atty. Cantey, Hanger, Gooch, Munn and Collins, Ft. Worth, 1977-81, ptnr., 1981-83; judge no. dist. U.S. Bankruptcy Ct., Ft. Worth, 1983-86; ptnr. Jackson Walker LLP, Ft. Worth, 1988—95, McConnell & Assocs., Ft. Worth, 1995—2000, Winstead Sechrest & Miniak P.C., Ft. Worth, 2000—06, Kelly Hart & Hallman LLP, Ft. Worth, 2006—. Trustee Am. Inns of Ct. Nat. Found. Sgt. USAF, 1969—73. Fellow: Am. Coll. Bankruptcy; mem.: Am. Law Inst. Office: Kelly Hart & Hallman LLP 201 Main St Ste 2500 Fort Worth TX 76102 Office Phone: 817-332-2500. Business E-Mail: michael.mcconnell@khh.com.

MCCONNELL, MICHAEL W., federal judge, law educator; b. Louisville, Ky., May 18, 1955; m. Mary Cargill Norton McConnell; 3 children. BA, Mich. State U., 1976; JD, U. Chgo., 1979. Bar: DC 1981. Law clk. to Hon. J. Skelly Wright US Ct. Appeals (DC cir.), 1979-80; law clk. to Hon. William J. Brennan Jr. US Supreme Ct., Washington, 1980-81; asst. gen. counsel US Office of Mgmt. and Budget, Washington, 1981-83; asst. to the solicitor gen. US Dept. Justice, Washington, 1983-85; asst. prof. U. Chgo., 1984-89, prof., 1989—92, William Graham prof. law, 1992—96; Presdl. prof. U. Utah Coll. Law, 1997—2002; vis. prof. Harvard Law School, 1999; special consultant Mayer, Brown & Platt, 1989—2002; judge US Ct. Appeals (10th cir.), 2002—. Mem. Am. Acad. Arts and Scis., Order of Coif, Phi Beta Kappa, Phi Kappa Phi. Office: 10th Circuit Ct Appeals 125 S State St # 6404 Salt Lake City UT 84138*

MCCONNELL, MIKE (JOHN MICHAEL MCCONNELL), former Director of National Intelligence, retired military officer; b. Greenville, SC, July 26, 1943; s. Harold Eddie and Dorothy Beatrice (Cassell) Mc.; children from previous marriage: Susan Erin McConnell, Jennifer Michelle McConnell; m. Mary Theresa Wagner, Jan. 29, 1988; children: Mark Richard Sentner, Christine Marie Sentner; 2 stepchildren BA in Econs., Furman U., 1966; MPA in Govt./Pub. Adminstrn., George Washington U., 1986; grad., Nat. Def. U., 1986; PhD in Strategic Intelligence (hon.), Def. Intelligence Coll., 1992. Advanced through ranks to vice admiral USN, 1992, ret., 1996; asst. engr., damage control officer USS Colleton, Mekong Delta, Vietnam, 1967-68; counterintelligence analyst Naval Investigative Svc., Yokosuka, Japan, 1968-70; analyst and supr. CNO Undersea Warfare Intelligence Watch, Washington, 1971-74; force intelligence officer Commdr. Middle East Force Persian Gulf, Indian Ocean, 1974-76; ops. officer Fleet Ocean Surveillance Info. Facility, Rota, Spain, 1976-79; intelligence analyst CNO Intelligence Staff, Washington, 1979-81; intelligence officer Commdr. in Chief Pacific Fleet, Honolulu, 1981-83; fleet intelligence officer Commdr. Seventh Fleet Western Pacific, 1983-85; exec. asst. to dir. Office Naval Intelligence, Washington, 1985-86; chief naval forces divsn. Nat. Security Agy., Ft. Meade, Md., 1987-88; asst, chief staff/intelligence Commdr. in Chief Pacific Fleet, Honolulu, 1988-90; dir. intelligence, The Joint Staff The Pentagon, Washington, 1990-92; dir. Nat. Security Agy., Ft. Meade, Md., 1992—96; sr. v.p. Booz Allen Hamilton, McLean, Va., 1996—2006; dir. Office Nat. Intelligence, 2007—09. Bd. dirs. CompuDyne Corp., 2004—07. Recipient Navy Unit Commendation Sec. Navy, 1968, Presdl. Unit Citation Combat Action ribbon CINC-PACFLT, Navy Achievement medal Sec. Navy, 1974, Navy Commendation medal w/Combat V, 1968, Navy E ribbon Sec. of the Navy, 1984, Nat. Defense Svc. medal with 1 Bronze star, Vietnam Svc, medal with 2 Bronze Stars, Humanitarian Svc. medal, Sea Svc. Deployment ribbon, Navy & Marine Corps Overseas Svc. ribbon, Rep. Vietnam Meritorious Unit Citation Civil Actions Color, Campaign medal Rep. Vietnam, Meritorious Svc. medal with 2 Gold Stars Sec. Navy, 1981, 85, Legion of Merit with 2 Gold Stars, 1985, 87, 90, Defense Superior Svc. medal, 1988, Defense Dist. Svc. medal, 1992. Avocations: world affairs, foreign policy, reading.*

MCCONNELL, MITCH (ADDISON MITCHELL MCCONNELL), United States Senator from Kentucky, lawyer; b. Tuscumbia, Ala., Feb. 20, 1942; s. Addison Mitchell and Julia (Shockley) McC.; m. Elaine Lan Chao, Feb. 6, 1993; children: Eleanor Hayes, Claire Redmon, Marion Porter. BA with honors, U. Louisville, 1964; JD, U. Ky., 1967. Bar: Ky. 1967. Chief legis. asst. to Senator Marlow Cook, Washington, 1968-70; pvt. law practice Louisville, 1970-74; dep. asst. atty. gen. US Dept. Justice, Washington, 1974-75; judge Jefferson County, Louisville, 1978-85; US Senator from Ky., 1985—; asst. majority leader (majority whip), 2002—07; minority leader, 2007—. Mem. US Senate Agrl., Nutrition, & Forestry Com., US Senate Appropriations Com., US Senate Rules & Adminstrn. Com. Chmn. Jefferson County Republican Com., 1973-74; co-chmn. Nat. Child Tragedies Coalition, 1981; chmn., founder Ky. Task Force on Exploited and Missing Children, 1982; mem. Pres.'s Partnership on Child Safety. Recipient commendation, Nat. Trust on Hist. Preservation in US, 1982, Conservationist of Yr. award, League Ky. Sportsmen, 1983, cert. of appreciation, Am. Correctional Assn., 1985, Golden Plow award, Am. Farm Bur. Fedn., 1996, Freedom award, Nat. Coun. Union Burma, 1999, Sam Rainsy Pary Freedom award, 2002, Ky. Warbler Migratory Songbird Conservation award, US Fish and Wildlife Svc., Ky. Dept. Fish and Wildlife Resources, 2002, Defender of Freedom award, James Madison Ctr. Freedom Speech, 2002, Disting. Svc. award, Am. Farm Bur., 2002; named one of the 50 Most Powerful People in DC, GQ mag., 2007. Mem. Ky. Assn. County Judge Execs. (pres. 1982), Nat. Inst. Justice (adv. bd. 1982-84) Republican. Baptist. Avocations: fishing, cooking. Office: US Senate 361-A Russell Office Bldg Washington DC 20510-0001 also: Gene Snyder US Courthouse Rm 630 601 West Broadway Louisville KY 40202-2228 Office Phone: 202-224-2541, 502-582-6304. Office Fax: 202-224-2499, 502-582-5326.*

MCCONNELL, NICHOLAS STILLWELL, lawyer; b. Chgo., May 25, 1946; s. James Millholland and Emily (Robinson) McC.; m. Nancy Haines Fifield, Dec. 14, 1968; children: Abigail Haven, Rebecca Fifield. BA, Bowdoin Coll., 1968; JD, George Wash. U., 1972. Bar: Va. Supreme Ct. 1972, U.S. Supreme Ct. 1973, U.S. Ct. Appeals D.C. 1973, D.C. Ct. Appeals 1973, U.S. Dist. Ct. D.C. 1973, Md. Ct. Appeals 1978, US Ct. Claims, 1991, US Ct. Appeals (11th cir), 1996, US Dist. Ct., Md.,

2001. Assoc. Jackson, Gray & Laskey, Washington, 1972-78; prin. Jackson & Campbell, P.C., Washington, 1978—. Mem. faculty Nat. Inst. Trial Advocacy, South Bend, Ind., 1984-95; dir. Sauls Lithograph Co., Inc., Washington, 1986—, Am. Hospice Found., 1997-2003. Pres., dir. Combined Health Appeal Nat. Capital Area, Washington, 1980-93; dir. Combined Health Appeal Am., Atlanta, 1993-94; pres. Albert L. and Elizabeth T. Tucker Found, 1996-; dir. Am. Hospice Found., 1997-2003. With U.S. Army, 1969-71. Recipient Young Lawyer of Yr. award Bar Assn. D.C., 1982. Fellow Am. Coll. Trial Lawyers; mem. Am. Health Lawyers Assn., D.C. Def. Lawyers, Def. Rsch. Inst., Barristers (pres. 1998), Counsellors, Bar Assn. D.C. (pres.-elect 2002-03, pres. 2003-04), Am. Bar Assn. (house of dels., 2003-2004)9+, Cosmos Club, Lawyers Club Congregationalist. Avocations: tennis, squash, golf, sailing. Home: 5004 Warren St NW Washington DC 20016-4370 Office: Jackson & Campbell PC 1 Lafayette Ctr 300 S Tower 1120 20th St NW Washington DC 20036-3437 Office Phone: 202-457-1628. E-mail: nmcconnell@jackscamp.com.

MCCONNELL, SCOTT RUSHTON, educational psychology educator; b. Sacramento, Calif., Apr. 21, 1955; s. Howard Rushton and Babbette Lenore (Halleck) McC.; m. Ann Johnson, Aug. 17, 1988; children: Nora McConnell-Johnson, Reid McConnell-Johnson. BS, Portland State U., Oreg., 1978; MS, U. Oreg., 1980, PhD, 1982. Rsch. assoc. U. Pitts., 1982-84, asst. prof. child psychiatry, 1984-86; asst. prof. ednl. psychology U. Minn., Mpls., 1986-88, assoc. prof. dept. ednl. psychology, 1988—; assoc. prof. child psychology, 1992—. Dir. Inst. on Community Integration, 1991—. Co-editor: Social Competence..., 1991; contbr. articles to profl. jours. Grant U.S. Dept. Edn., 1982. Mem. Assn. for Behavior Analysis, Nat. Assn. Sch. Psychologists, Am. Psychol. Soc., Coun. Exceptional Children (div. for early childhood). Avocation: skiing. Office: U Minn N548 Elliott Hall 102 Pattee Hall Minneapolis MN 55455

MCCONNELL, STEPHEN JOHN, lawyer; b. Oakland, Calif., Sept. 15, 1959; s. Francis Xavier McConnell and Anna Krystyna Hinck, adopted s. Douglas Frederick and Florence Estelle Van Horn; children: Kristin Chandler, Daniel Austin. AB in Govt., Harvard U., Cambridge, Mass., 1981; JD, U. Chgo., 1985. Bar: Pa. 1997, DC 1989, Calif. 1987. Fed. prosecutor US Attys.'s Office, LA, 1992—97; ptnr. Dechert LLP, Phila., 1997—. Dep. gen. counsel Kolts Commn., LA, 1991—92; counsel Christopher Commn., LA. Contbr. articles to legal jours. Bd. dirs. Villanova U. Ctr. Mktg. and Pub. Rsch., Pa., 2005—. Named one of Best Lawyers in Am., Woodward/White, 2008, Legal 500. Office: Dechert LLP 2929 Arch St Philadelphia PA 19104-2808 Office Fax: 215-994-2222. Business E-Mail: stephen.mcconnell@dechert.com.

MCCONNELL, WILLIAM F., JR., medical products executive; b. LaGrange, Ill. BS in sys. analysis, Miami U., Oxford, Ohio, 1971. CPA. Staff mem. Arthur Andersen LLP, Indpls., 1971—75, mgr., 1975—81, ptnr., 1981—83, mng. ptnr., bus. cons., 1983—89, rejoined, 1997; CFO Resort Condo. Internat., 1989—90, COO, 1990—96, info. officer, worldwide, 1996—97; v.p., COO Guidant Corp., Indpls., Ill., 1998—2006; sr. v.p. adminstrn. Boston Scientific Corp., Natick, Mass., 2006—. Bd. dir. Global Healthcare Exchange, Vesalius Ventures. Former chmn. Children's Mus. of Indpls., Am. Red Cross of Greater Indpls., Red Cross of Conner Prairie; former bd. mem. Acordia Personal Ins. Svcs.; hon. trustee Children's Mus. of Indpls.; bd. gov. Nat. Am. Red Cross; chmn. bd. trustee Trustee Leadership Development; bd. mem., info. tech. com. Cmty. Hosp. of Indpls., Inc., Ind. U. Info. Tech. Advancement Coun. Office: Boston Scientific Corp One Boston Scientific Pl Natick MA 01760*

MCCONNELL, WILLIAM STEWART, application developer; b. Munich, June 30, 1955; s. William Marion and Mary Catherine McConnell; m. Lisa Ann Fuller, July 17, 2004; children: Elizabeth Ann Sammulia, Stephan Anthony, Margrette Catherine, Ashley Marie Fuller, Brian Daniel Fuller, Caleb Matthew Fuller Whiteside. AS in Aerospace Control Sys., C.C. USAF, 1983; AS in Computer Info. Sys., George C. Wallace State C.C., 1995; BS in Computer Info. Sys., Troy State U., 1998; MS in Computer Info. Sys., U. Phoenix, 2005. Commd. lt. USAF, 1974, advanced through grades to MSGT, 1974—87, non-commissioned officer various assignments, 1977—93, ret., 1994; warehouse mgr. The Barn, Ozark, Ala., 1993—98; software designer Grossman and Assocs., Savoy, Ill., 1998—. Dist. leader Boy Scouts Am., Del Rio, Tex., 1989—92. Decorated Commendation medal USAF, Meritorious Svc. medal, Achievement medal. Avocations: music, ballroom dancing. Home: 1353 Abram Dr Rantoul IL 61866 Office: Grossman and Assocs 710 N Neil St Champaign IL 61820-3013 Personal E-mail: stew_mcconnell@hotmail.com. Business E-Mail: smcconnell@gman.com.

MCCONNELL, WILLIAM THOMPSON, bank executive; b. Zanesville, Ohio, Aug. 8, 1933; s. William Gerald and Mary Gladys McC.; m. Jane Charlotte Cook, Aug. 25, 1956; children: Jennifer Wynne, William Gerald. BA, Denison U., 1955; MBA, Northwestern U., 1959. Pres. Park Nat. Bank, Newark, Ohio, 1979-83, pres., chief exec. officer, 1983-93, chmn., chief exec. officer, 1993-98, also bd. dirs., chmn., 1999—2004; pres., chief exec. officer Park Nat. Corp., Newark, 1987-94, chmn., CEO, 1994-98, chmn., 1999—2004, chmn. exec. com., 2005—. Mem. Newark Area C. of C. (past pres., dir. 1977-83), Ohio Bankers Assn. (pres., chmn. 1981-83), Am. Bankers Assn. (pres. 1997-98). Office: Park Nat Bank PO Box 3500 Newark OH 43058-3500

MCCONVILLE, EDWARD PATRICK, lawyer; b. Albany, NY, Nov. 5, 1932; s. Edward Patrick McConville and Anne Dolores Leonard; m. Lois Anne Bessette, June 30, 1956 (div. Aug. 1982); 1 child, Stephen Patrick; m. Michelle Cristin Coderre, Mar. 17, 1984; 1 child, Collin William. BA, U. Notre Dame, 1954; JD, Union U., 1956. Bar: NY, INd., DC, US Supreme Ct. Investigator US Civil Svc. Commn., NYC, 1958—59; asst. divsn. counsel bowling divsn. Am. Machine and Foundry Co., NYC, 1959—63; asst. counsel Lincoln Nat. Life Ins. Co., Ft. Wayne, Ind., 1963—66; asst. chief counsel US Dept. Commerce, Econ. Devel. Adminstrn., Portland, Maine, 1966—67, Washington, 1967—68; v.p. First Nat. Bank, Washington, 1968—70, sr. v.p., 1970—73, exec. v.p., 1973, Cmty. State Bank, Albany, NY, 1973—75, Union Nat. Bank, Albany, 1975—77; sr. v.p. Maney McConville & Liccardi, P.C., East Greenbush, NY, 1977—, ptnr. Valatie, NY, 1977—; pres. People Comml. Bank, Albany, 1984—86; hearing officer NYS Dept. Agr. and Markets, 2006—. Instr. Hudson Valley CC, 1978—85, 1992; lectr. fin. Siena Coll., 1989; instr. bus. law and internat. bus. St. Rose Coll., 1991—98; chmn. bd. Evergreen Bank, Albany, NY, 1991—92; counsel NY State Senate Banking Com., 2009—. Vol. probation officer Albany County Probation Dept., 1981; dir. Cath. Youth Orgn., Washington, 1971—73; bd. dirs. Model Cities Econ. Devel. Corp., Washington, 1972—73. With US Army, 1956—58, with USAR, 1958—60. Mem.: N.Am. Curragh Assn. (pres. 1988—89), Old Chatham Hunt Club (pres. 1981—85), Albany Curragh Rowing Club (dir. 1987—). Democrat. Roman Catholic. Avocations: rowing, horseback riding. Home: 55 Fordham Rd Valatie NY 12184 Office: Maney McConville and Liccari 22 Troy Rd East Greenbush NY 12061 Home Phone: 518-758-6517; Office Phone: 518-477-7951. Business E-Mail: edmcconville@mmlesq.com, ed@mmlesq.com.

MCCONVILLE, JUDY ALLEN, social studies educator; d. Edwin Frederick and Bertha Herdegen Allen; m. James McConville, June 25, 1978; children: Catherine Margarethe, Elizabeth Allen. BA in History, Randolph-Macon Woman's Coll., Lynchburg, Va., 1968; MA in Tchg. Govt., U. Va., Charlottesville, 1972. Tchr. Alexandria City Pub. Schools, Va., 1971—98, curriculum specialist for social studies, 1998—. Chmn. Va. Conf. for Social Studies Educators, Norfolk, 2004, World History Stds. of Learning Revision Com., Richmond, Va., 2000—01; mem. Mgmt. Com. History and Social Sci. Stds. of Learning, Richmond, Va., 2000—01. Edn. com., sub com. co-chair coll. student outreach Annandale United Meth. Ch., Va., 1998—2004. Mem.: NEA, Nat. Social Studies Suprs. Assn., Nat. Coun. for the Social Studies, Va. Conf. for Social Studies Educators (treas. 2005—), Va. Consortium of Social Studies Specialists and Coll. Educators (pres. 2003—04), Nat. Coun. for History Edn., Va. Edn. Assn., Edn. Assn. Alexandria, Alpha Delta Kappa (pres. 1988—90, pres. chpt. 1996—98). Methodist. Avocations: reading, needlecrafts. Office: Alexandria City Pub Schools 2000 N Beauregard St Alexandria VA Office Fax: 703-370-7704. E-mail: jmcconvi@acps.k12.va.us.

MCCOOK, JACQUELINE K. HESLOP, food products executive; B in Internat. Rels., Stanford U., Calif.; MBA, Harvard Bus. Sch. Gen. mgr. Taco Bell Internat.; v.p. mktg. PepsiCo Restaurants Internat. (now YUM! Brands); sr. v.p. worldwide strategic planning & branding Burger King; pres., CEO McCook Group, 2000—06; chief growth officer, exec. v.p. internat. ConAgra Foods, Inc., Omaha, 2006—. Bd. dirs. Pasha's Restaurants, Inc. Office: ConAgra Foods Inc 1 ConAgra Dr Omaha NE 68102-5001 Office Phone: 402-595-4000.

MCCOOL, FRANKLIN DENNIS, pulmonologist, researcher; b. Clinton, Mass., Oct. 3, 1950; s. Frank and Mary McCool; m. Jacqueline M. Savoie, Dec. 23, 2005. MD, St. Louis U., Mo., 1976. Cert. pulmonary critical care ABIM, 1981. Prof. medicine Brown U., Providence, 1981—; rsch. assoc. Harvard Sch. Pub. Health, Boston, 1987—97; chief pulmonary critical care Meml. Hosp., Pawtucket, RI, 2001—. Editor in chief lung Springer Pub., NYC, 2003—. Contbr. articles to profl. jours. Recipient Trudeau Scholar award; grantee, NIH Funding; fellow, Electric Power Rsch. Inst. Fellow: Am. Coll. Chest Physicians; mem.: Phi Beta Kappa, Alpha Omega Alpha, Am. Lung Assn., Am. Thoracic Soc. Achievements include research in applied respiratory physiology and chest wall disease and respiratory muscles. Office: Memorial Hosp RI 111 Brewster St Pawtucket RI 02860

MCCORD, ARLINE FUJII, retired university administrator, educator; b. Nahcotta, Wash., May 16, 1935; d. George and Mary (Murakami) Fujii; m. Ted T. Sakuma, Nov. 10, 1952 (div. Dec. 1970); m. William McCord, May 8, 1971; children: Karen, Ted, Michael, William, Elinor. BA, U. Wash., 1960, MA, 1965, PhD, 1968. High sch. tchr. Seattle Pub. Schs., 1960-63; asst. prof. Calif. State Univ., Fullerton, 1967-68, Syracuse Univ., NY, 1968-71; asst. to assoc. prof. Hunter Coll., NYC, 1971-85, chair dept., 1983-85; prof. and dean social scis. CCNY, 1985—89; assoc. provost Yale Univ., New Haven, 1989—99, assoc. dir. Ctr. Comparative Studies, 1999—2003; ret., 2003. Researcher, cons. Eisenhower Commn. on Causes and Prevention of Violence, Washington, 1968-69. Co-author: Black Students on White College Campuses, 1972, Urban Social Conflict, 1977, American Social Problems, 1977, Power and Equity, 1977, Paths to Progress, 1986. Cons. Edn. Policy Rsch. Ctr., Syracuse (N.Y.) Univ., 1968-69; dir. Rosenberg/Humphrey Inst. Pub. Affairs, 1985-89, Bus. and Internat. Edn. Program, CCNY and Harlem Third World Trade Inst., 1987-89. Personal E-mail: amccord@att.net.

MCCORD, CLINTON D., JR., oculoplastic surgeon; b. Dec. 10, 1935; married; 2 children. BA, Emory U., Ga., 1957; MD, Emory Sch. Medicine, 1961; MS in Physiology, Emory U., Ga., 1963. Cert. Am. Bd. Ophthalmology, diplomate Am. Acad. Ophthalmology, lic. Ga. Resident, ophthalmology Emory U., Ga., 1963—66; Heed fellowship, oculoplastic Manhattan Eye and Ear Hosp., 1966—67; mem. USAF Keesler AFB (Biloxi, Miss.) & Andrews AFB (Washington, DC), 1967—69; private practice Atlanta, 1969—79; chief of staff Metropolitan Eye and Ear Hosp., 1974; prof., ophthalmology Emory U. Sch. Medicine, Ga., 1979—80, assoc. clin. prof., plastic surgery Ga., 2002—; private practice Paces Plastic Surgery, Atlanta, 1980—; clin. prof., ophthalmology Emory U., 1980—2002. Invited spkr. in field; vis. professorship at nat. universities and institutions. Contbr. chapters to books, several articles to profl. jours.; co-author: (textbooks) Optical Techniques, 1971; author: Oculoplastic Surgery, 1981, Oculoplastic Surgery, 2nd edit., 1987, Oculoplastic Surgery, 3rd edit., 1994, Eyelid Surgery, Standard and Advanced, 1996; co-author: Color Atlas of Cosmetic Oculofacial Surgery, 2004. Med. missions Interplast Mission Nicaragua (Managua)- Oculoplastica Jornada, 2003, Tanzanian Project (Moshi, Tanzania) Surgical Lectures-Surgical Demonstrations, Kilimanjari Christian Med. Ctr., 2007. Recipient Montague Boyd award, Best Physician Book award, Piedmont Hosp., Atlanta, Oculoplastic Surgery-2nd edit., 1988, Best Clin. Paper of the Yr.-Midfacial Rejuvenative Surgery, Am. Soc. Aesthetic Surgery, NYC, 1997; co-recipient Best Resident's Paper (with Hisham Seify)-Quantitating Ptosis Surgery, 2007; named one of Best Doctors in US, 1979, 1981, The Doctor's Doctors, Atlanta Mag., 1988, Top Docs, Atlanta's most trusted specialists, 2005, Outstanding Med. Specialists in the US, Town and Country Mag., 1989, Best Doctors in America, 1992, Best 200 Ophthalmologist in America, Ophthalmology Times, 1996; named to Guide to the 1,500 Best Doctors in America, Town and Country Mag., 1984, America's Top Doctors, Castle Connolly Med. Inc, 2004, NY Times Beauty Supplement Edit., Best Three Cosmetic Eyelid Surgeons in US, 2005. Fellow: ACS (program chmn. 1975); mem.: Med. Assn. Atlanta, Med. Assn. Ga., Internat. Orbital Soc., Am. Acad. Ophthalmology (Ednl. Honor award 1980), Atlanta Ophthal. Soc. (pres. 1978), Ga. Soc. Ophthamology (program chmn. 1978, coun. mem. 1983—87), Am. Soc. Ocularists (program chmn. 1978), Am. Soc. Ophthalmic Plastic Surgery and Reconstructive Surgery (program chmn. 1982, pres. 1989, chmn. adv. bd. 1990, mem. adv. bd. 1991—99, with Am. Acad. Ophthalmology, Wendell Hughes Lecture Coun. 1995—2000, Lester Jones Surgical Anatomy award, Best Clin. Presentation of Anatomy 1984), Byron Smith Study Club. Avocations: hiking, mountaineering. Office: Paces Plastic Surgery 3200 Downwood Cir Ste 640 Atlanta GA 30327 Office Phone: 404-351-0051. Office Fax: 404-351-0632.

MCCORD, GUYTE PIERCE, JR., retired judge; b. Tallahassee, Sept. 23, 1914; s. Guyte Pierce and Jean (Patterson) McC.; m. Laura Elizabeth Mack, Dec. 1, 1939 (dec. Oct. 8, 2000); children: Florence Elizabeth, Guyte Pierce III, Edward LeRoy; m. Elizabeth Rogers Green, May 24, 2002. Student, Davidson Coll., 1933-34; BA, JD, U. Fla., 1940. Bar: Fla. 1940. Summer ranger Yosemite Nat. Park, 1936-39; rsch. aide Fla. Supreme Ct., summer 1940; pvt. practice Tallahassee, 1940-48; dep. commr. Fla. Indsl. Commn., 1946-47; pros. atty. Leon County, 1947-48; asst. gen. counsel Fla. Pub. Svc. Commn., 1949-60; judge 2d Jud. Cir. Fla., Tallahassee, 1960-74, Ct. Appeals 1st Dist. Fla., 1974-83, chief judge, 1977-79; ret., 1979. Mem. Fla. Senate Pres.'s Council on Criminal Justice 1972; mem. appellate ct. rules com. Fla. Supreme Ct., 1977-78, mem. appellate ct. structure commn. 1978-79. Pres. Murat House Assn., Inc., 1967-69; bd. dirs. Fla. Heritage Found., 1969-70, mem. exec. com., 1965-69; mem. Andrew Jackson staff of Springtime Tallahassee, 1973-74, 84-86, Andrew Jackson, 1987. Commdr. USNR, 1942—64, WWII, Korea. Mem. ABA, Mil. Officers Assn. Am., Fla. Bar, Fla. Conf. Cir. Judges (sec.-treas. 1970, chmn. 1972), Fla. State U. Pres. Club, Kiwanis (dir. 1958-59), Sigma Alpha Epsilon, Phi Delta Phi. Presbyterian (elder 1960—, ch. trustee 1981-86). Home: 2718 Timbertrail Cir Tallahassee FL 32308-5745

MCCORD, ROBERT M., state treasurer; b. Mar. 5, 1959; m. Leigh McCord; 2 children. BA, Harvard U.; MBA, Wharton Sch. U. Pa. CEO Congl. Inst. for the Future, Washington; sr. exec. Safeguard Scientifics, 1994—98; founder Eastern Tech. Fund; co-founder & mng. dir. Pa. Early Stage Partners; chmn. Eastern Tech. Coun., 1996—2007; treas. Commonwealth of Pa., Harrisburg, 2009—. Sr. fellow, adj. faculty mem. Wharton Sch., U. Pa., Phila., Haverford Coll., Pa. Office: Pa Treasury Dept 129 Finance Bldg Harrisburg PA 17120 Office Phone: 717-787-2465.*

MCCORISON, MARCUS ALLEN, librarian, cultural organization administrator; b. Lancaster, Wis., July 17, 1926; s. Joseph Lyle and Ruth (Mink) McCorison; m. Janet Buckbee Knop, June 10, 1950 (dec. 1998); children: Marcus Allen II, Judith McCorison Gove, Andrew Buckbee, Mary McCorison Rosenbloom(dec.), James Rice, Peter Gardner; life ptnr. Carolyn K. Dik. AB, Ripon Coll., 1950; MA, U. Vt., 1951, LittD (hon.), 1992; MS, Columbia U., 1954; LittD (hon.), Assumption Coll., Worcester, Mass., 1987; LHD (hon.), Coll. of the Holy Cross, 1992; LittD (hon.), Clark U., 1992. Librarian Kellogg-Hubbard Library, Montpelier, Vt., 1954-55; chief of rare books dept. Dartmouth Coll. Library, Hanover, NH, 1955-59; head spl. collections dept. State U. Iowa Libraries, 1959-60; libr. Am. Antiquarian Soc., Worcester, Mass., 1960-91, editor Procs., 1960-67, dir., 1967-89, pres., 1989-92, pres. emeritus, 1993—; cons. Christie, Manson & Woods, Internat., 1993-96, N.Y. Hist. Soc., 1994-95, Libr. Congress, Hist. Soc. of Pa., 1996, U. Kans., 1998-99. Mem. N.Am. steering com. 18th Century Short Title Catalogue, 1977—; mem. Com. for a New Eng. Bibliography, 1968-90, treas., 1970-77; mem. adv. com. Eleutherian Mills-Hagley Found., 1971-74, 87-89; chmn. Ind. Rsch. Librs. Assn., 1972-73, 78-80; mem. adv. coun. Princeton U. Libr., 1988-92; bd. govs. Rsch. Librs. Group, 1980-91, chmn. preservation com., 1982-85, chmn. governance com., 1989-91, chmn. Writings of James Fenimore Cooper, 1991-2002. Author: Vermont Imprints 1778-1820, 1963, The 1764 Catalogue of the Redwood Library, 1965; contbr.: The Pursuit of Knowledge in the Early American Republic, 1976, Publishing and Readership in Revolutionary France and America, 1993; editor: History of Printing in America by Isaiah Thomas, 1970. Trustee Fruitlands Mus., 1978-89, Old Sturbridge Village, 1981-92, Hist. Deerfield, Inc., 1991-2002, Newberry Libr., 1995—2008, life trustee, 2008-; mem. bd. mgrs. Lewis Walpole Libr., Yale U., 1995—2009; mem. Cultural Commn. City Worcester, Mass., 1999-2004, Mass. Hist. Commn., 1999-2007; mem. com. mgmt. Wm. L. Clements Libr., U. Mich., 2001—. Recipient Samuel Pepys medal Ephemera Soc., London, 1980, Disting. Alumni award Ripon Coll., 1989, Columbia U. Sch. Libr. Svc., 1992. Rickards medal Ephemera Soc. Am., 2000. Mem. Am. Antiquarian Soc., Coll. and Rsch. Librs. Assn. (chmn. rare books sect. 1966-67), Bibliog. Soc. Am. (pres. 1980-84, del. to ACLS 1985—2002), Am. Printing Hist. Assn. (trustee 1998—2004, laureate 1998), Vt. Hist. Soc. (trustee 1956-66), Worcester Hist. Mus. (exec. com. 1967-80), Ctr. for Rsch. on Vt. (assoc.), N.E. Am. Soc. 18th Century Studies (pres. 1978-79), Colonial Soc. Mass., Club of Odd Vols., Grolier Club (councillor 1979-82, 83-84), Zamorano Club (hon.), Roxburghe Club, Century Assn. Democrat. Home and Office: 101 Greenwich Ct Worcester MA 01609-1159 Home Phone: 508-791-3668.

MCCORKINDALE, DOUGLAS HAMILTON, publishing executive; b. NYC, June 14, 1939; s. William Douglas and Kathleen (Miles) McC.; m. Nancy Walsh, Dec. 24, 1991; children by previous marriage: Laura Ann, Heather Jean. BA, Columbia U., 1961, LLB cum laude (Harlan Fiske Stone scholar), 1964. Bar: N.Y. 1964. Assoc. Thacher Proffitt & Wood, NYC, 1964-70, ptnr., 1970-71; gen. counsel, sec. Gannett Co., Inc., Arlington, Va., 1971-72, v.p., gen. counsel, sec., 1972-77, sr. v.p. fin. and law, 1977-79, sr. v.p., chief fin. officer, 1979-83, pres. diversified media div., 1980-83, exec. v.p., 1983, vice chmn., 1985—2001, CFO, 1985—97, chief adminstrv. officer, 1986—97, pres., 1997—2005, CEO, 2000—05, chmn., 2005—06. Bd. dirs. Continental Airlines Inc., Lockheed Martin Corp. Mem. ABA, Newspaper Assn. Am., Pine Valley Golf Club, Mid Ocean Club, Burning Tree Club. Office: Gannett Co Inc 7950 Jones Branch Dr Mc Lean VA 22102

MCCORKLE, ANNE FRANCES, social studies educator; married. MA, Colo. State U., Ft. Collins, 2004. Cert. teacher Colo. Dept. Edn., 2008. Adj. history instr. Mesa State Coll., Grand Junction, Colo., 2004—; secondary social studies tchr. Mesa County Sch. Dist. 51, Grand Junction, 2008—. Office: Mesa County Sch Dist 51 1102 Wildcat Ave Fruita CO 81521 Office Fax: 970-858-9661. Business E-Mail: amccorkl@mesa.k12.co.us.

MCCORKLE, ROBERT ELLSWORTH, agribusiness educator; b. Salinas, Calif., Apr. 3, 1938; s. Stanley Harold and Muriel Eugenia (Vosti) McC.; m. Mary E. McCorkle, June 26, 1965; children: Bonnie Kathleen, Robyn Krystyna. BSc in Farm Mgmt., Calif. Poly. State U., San Luis Obispo, 1960; MSc in Agrl. Econs., U. Calif., Davis, 1962; postgrad., U. Wis., 1969, Oreg. State U., 1966. Rsch. statistician U. Calif., Davis, 1960-62; asst. prof. agrl. bus. Calif. Poly. State U., San Luis Obispo, 1962-66, dir. internat. edn., 1970-74, assoc. prof. agrl. mgmt., 1969-76, prof. agribus., 1976—; chief farm mgmt. officer Ministry Agr., Lusaka, Zambia, 1967-69; dir., owner McCorkle Farms, Inc., Willows, Calif., 1970—. Vis. prof. Mich. State U., U.S. AID, Washington, 1984-85; dir., owner McCorkle Trucking, Glenn, Calif., 1988—; agrl. economist U.S. AID-Redso ESA, Nairobi, Kenya, 1984-85. Author: Guide for Farming in Zambia, 1968. Pres. Cabrillo Property Owners Assn., Los Osos, Calif., 1976-78; vol. Atty. Gen.'s Adv. Com., Calif., 1972-74. U.S. Peace Corps strategy grantee, Washington, 1976-. Mem. Am. Agrl. Econs. Assn., Am. Soc. Farm Mgrs. and Rural Appraisers, Western Agrl. Econs. Assn., Calif. Poly. Farm Mgmt. Club, Calif. Farm Bur., Calif. Poly. Alumni Assn., Blue Key, Alpha Zeta (sr. advisor Calif. Delta chpt., nat. high coun. chronicler, sec.-treas., bd. dirs., Centennial Honor Roll), Nat. Alpha Zeta Found. (bd. dirs.), Golden Key. Republican. Episcopalian. Avocations: hunting, fishing. Home Phone: 805-528-3729; Office Phone: 805-756-5024. Business E-Mail: rmccorkl@calpoly.edu.

MC CORMAC, JOHN WAVERLY, judge; b. Zanesville, Ohio, Feb. 8, 1926; s. Samuel D. and Phyllis (Murray) McC.; m. Martha Ann Cunningham, June 22, 1952; children: Michael Paul, John Mark, James Samuel. BS, Muskingum Coll., 1951; JD, Capital U., 1961. Bar: Ohio 1961. Fire protection engr. Ohio Insp. Bur., 1951—60; pvt. practice Columbus, 1961—65; prof. law Capital U., Columbus, 1965-66, 71-74, dean Law Sch., 1966—71; judge 10th Dist. Ct. Appeals, 1975—92; prof. law Ohio State U., Columbus, 1993—2001. Mem. staff cons. rules adv. com. Supreme Ct. Ohio; chmn. adv. bd. Vols. in Probation, 1972-74; chmn. ohio Jud. Conf., 1982-84; commr. Ohio Dispute Resolution Com., 1989-96, chmn., 1993-95; chief justice Ohio Ct. Appeals Assn., 1989-91. Author: Ohio Civil Rules Practice, 1970, 2nd edit., 1992, Anderson's Ohio Civil Practice, Vol. 1, 1971, Vol. 2, 1976, Vol. 3, 1977, Wrongful Death in Ohio, 1982. Served with USNR, 1943-46. Fellow Ohio Bar Assn. Found.; mem. League Ohio Law Schs. (pres. 1969-70), ABA, Ohio Bar Assn. (council of dels. 1973-77), Columbus Bar Assn. (bd. govs. 1968-72, sec.-treas. 1973-74, pres. 1975-76), Am. Judicature Soc., Phi Alpha Delta. Clubs: Masons (33 deg.). Republican. Home: 395 Longfellow Ave Columbus OH 43085-3024 E-mail: johnmccormac46@hotmail.com.

MCCORMACK, DAVID RICHARD, lawyer; b. Macon, Ga., Apr. 19, 1945; s. Richard and Margaret Helen (Pivarnik) McC. BA, Yale U., 1967; MA, Northwestern U., 1969; JD, So. Meth. U., 1976. Bar: Tex. 1977, Ariz. 1977, US Dist. Ct. Ariz. 1977, US Dist. Ct. (no. dist.) Tex. 1977, US Dist. Ct. (so. dist.) Tex. 1987, US Dist. Ct. (east dist.) Tex. 2004, US Ct. Appeals (5th cir.) 1989; diplomate Am. Bd. Forensic Examiners. Outreach dir. Planned Parenthood, Benton Harbor, Mich., 1971-72; exec. dir. Am. Cancer soc., St. Joseph, Mich., 1973-74; asst. atty. gen. Ariz. Atty. Gen., Phoenix, 1979-84; trial atty. U.S. Dept. Justice, Dallas, 1984-85; assoc. Bruner, McColl, McCulloch & McCurley, Dallas, 1985-86; pvt. practice Houston/Galveston, 1986—. Registered arbitrator Am. Registry of Arbitrators, 1994—; lectr. Tex. Assn. Lic. Investigators; cons. and expert witness. Author: RICO, 2 vols., 1988, Extraneous Offenses, 1986; contbr. articles to profl. publs. Vol. VISTA, Crawfordville, Ga., 1969; Dem. candidate from 4th dist. Mich. for US House of Reps., 1970, from 44th dist. for Mich. State House of Reps., 1972; Dem. del. from Mich. to Nat. Convention, 1972; party chmn. Mich. Dem. Party, 1971-73; mem. Am. for Democratic Action, Am. United for Separation Ch. and State, NAACP Legal Defense Fund, Amnesty Internat. Mem. ACLU, Am. Coll. Forensic Examiners, Assn. Cert. Fraud Examiners (cert., lectr. 1991-99), Cajun French Music Assn., Northwestern U. Wildcat Fund., Internat. Nat. Assn. Investigative Specialist, Human Rights Watch, Northwestern U. Leadership Ctr. Office Phone: 409-740-2680. Personal E-mail: davidrmccormack@comcast.net.

MCCORMACK, DONALD PAUL, newspaper consultant; b. Brockton, Mass., Jan. 15, 1926; s. Everett G. and Esther (Lufkin) McC.; m. Petronella Ruth Seger, Apr. 28, 1951; 1 son, Christopher Paul. BA, U. Pitts., 1949. Corr. U.P.I., 1949-52; asst. city editor Pitts. Sun-Telegraph, 1952-56; pub. relations exec., 1956-64; copy reader N.Y. News, 1964-67, editorial writer, 1967-72, chief editorial writer, 1972-82; cons., 1982—. With USAAF, 1944-46, Pa. N.G., 1952-57. Home and Office: PO Box 3539 Westport CT 06880-8539

MC CORMACK, FRANCIS XAVIER, lawyer, former oil company executive; b. Bklyn., July 9, 1929; s. Joseph and Blanche V. (Dengel) Mc C.; m. Margaret V. Hynes, Apr. 24, 1954; children: Marguerite, Francis Xavier, Sean Michael, Keith John, Cecelia Blanche, Christopher Thomas. AB cum laude, St. Francis Coll., Bklyn., 1951; LLB, Columbia U., 1954. Bar: N.Y. 1955, Mich. 1963, Calif. 1974, Pa. 1975. Assoc. Cravath, Swaine & Moore, NYC, 1956-62; sr. atty. Ford Motor Co., 1962-64, asst. gen. counsel, 1970-72; v.p., gen. counsel, sec. Philco-Ford Corp., 1964-72; v.p., gen. counsel Atlantic Richfield Co., 1972-73, sr. v.p., gen. counsel, 1973-94. Editor Columbia U. Law Rev., 1954. Decorated commendatore Ordine al Merito (Italy); Stone scholar Columbia U., 1954. Mem. Calif. Club, Chancery Club, Annandale Golf Club.

MCCORMACK, JOHN BRENDAN, bishop; b. Winthrop, Mass., Aug. 12, 1935; s. Cornelius and Eleanor (Noonan) McCormack. Attended, Cardinal O'Connell Sem. Coll., Brighton, Mass., St. John's Sem.; MSW, Boston Coll., 1969. Ordained priest Archdiocese of Boston, 1960, cabinet sec., vicar for religious and priests, 1984-94, aux. bishop, 1995, regional bishop, south region, 1995—98; assoc. pastor St. James Parish, Salem, Mass.; exec. dir. North Shore Cath. Charities Ctr., Peabody, Mass., 1967-81; pastor Immaculate Conception Parish, Malden-Medford, Mass., 1981—85, St. Francis Xavier Parish, South Weymouth, Mass., 1995; ordained bishop, 1995; bishop Diocese of Manchester, NH, 1998—. Roman Catholic. Office: PO Box 310 153 Ash St Manchester NH 03105

MCCORMACK, JOHN JOSEPH, JR., insurance company executive; b. Morristown, NJ, Aug. 22, 1944; s. John Joseph and Marion Loretta (Smith) McC.; m. Judith Gail Harvey, July 20, 1968; children: Brendan, Matthew, Margaret. BBA, St. Bonaventure U., 1966. From group underwriter to exec. v.p. Tchrs. Ins. and Annuity Assn.-Coll. Retirement Equities Fund, NYC, 1966-98; pres. TIAA-CREF Enterprises, 1998-99, group pres., 1999-2001; chmn. McCormack's Retirement and Fin. Svcs. Cons., 2001—. Trustee Am. Psychol. Assn. Ins. Trust, Washington, 1980-90, chmn., 1985-86, trustee investment com., 1990-98, 2001—; trustee Employee Benefit Rsch. Inst., Washington, 1983—, treas., 1986-90, vice-chmn., 1997-98, chmn., 1999-2001; mem. adv. bd. Andrew W. Mellon Found., N.Y.C., 1997-2001. Pres.'s coun. St. Bonaventure U., 1986—, chmn., 1986-89, trustee, 1996—, chmn. investment com., 1999-2003, vice chmn. bd. trustees, 2003—; bd. visitors Ctr. for Study Future Mgmt. U. Md., 1987-92; trustee Coll. and Univ. Pers. Assn. Found., 1992-94; bd. govs. Investment Co. Inst., 1994-2000; trustee Fenimore Asset Mgmt. Funds, 2004-. Roman Catholic. Office: PO Box 432 New Vernon NJ 07976-0432 Office Phone: 908-415-0104. Personal E-mail: jmccsbu@aol.com.

MCCORMACK, LOWELL RAY, oil industry and corporate financial executive, consultant; b. Ladonia, Tex., Oct. 26, 1925; d. Lowell and Orianna (McDonnold) Coney; m. Paul H. McCormack, June 4, 1948; children: Sharron Ann, Lowell Henry. At, Rutherford Met. Coll., Dallas, 1962, U. Tex., Arlington and Dallas, Eastfield Coll., Dallas, Cooke County Coll., Gainesville, Tex., 1989—; AA, Wm. Alexander Art, 1991. Master graphoanalyst Internat. Graphoanalysis Soc. Bookeeper Jot-Em-Down Gin Corp., Pecan Gap, Tex., 1947, Shedd-Bartush Foods, Dallas, 1948—52; v.p. and sec.-treas. Safari Oil Co., 1954—88, pres., 1989—; acct. and credit mgr. J. P. Ashcraft Co., Inc., 1956—65; v.p., sec.-treas. and CFO Dallas Title Co., 1965—83; treas. First Nat. Bank, Cooper, Tex., 1986—87; pres. Scorpio Oil Co., 1987—. Treas. Butterfield Stage, Gainesville, Tex.; acctg. cons. to atty.; lectr. in field. Author: Stories of Growing Up in the Coney Family, 2005; featured writer Tex. State Hist. Assn. Web Site, 2005; contbr. articles to profl. jour.; co-author (with Lincecum Renshaw): Cancer Changes Lives; author: Taking Care of Each Other. Troop leader Girl Scouts USA, 1955—65; founder Yarn Spinners, Gainesville, Tex., 1988; mem. Newcomers Club, 1986—, pres., 1989—92; columnist Cooke County Leader, 1988; founding mem. Gainesville Area Visual Arts; assoc. arts dir. Cooke County Coll., 1992; mem. Baptist Choir, Centennial Cir.; asst. sunday sch. tchr., 2007—. Mem.: Internat. Platform Assn., North Tex. Oil and Gas Assn., Internat. Graphoanalysis Soc. (life; v.p. Tex. chpt. 1978, pres. 1979, Graphoanalyst of Yr. 1987, keynote spkr. 1987, Okla. seminar leader 1990), Red Hat. Soc., Crosstimbers Geneal. Soc., Gainesville C. of C., Cooke County Heritage Soc., Kiwanis (one of 1st women mems. Gainesville chpt. 1988, v.p. 1990—91, pres. 1991—92), Zonta Club (co-chmn. fin. com. 1982, dir. and 2d v.p. 1983—84), Soroptimist Club, Toastmistress (pres. 1981, com. chmn. internat. conv 1984), Phi Theta Kappa (treas. Psi Iota chpt. 1990, acad. all-Am. 3d team for cmty. tech. and jr. colls. 1992). Baptist. Home: 631 S Lindsay St Gainesville TX 76240-5336

MCCORMACK, MICHAEL, state supreme court justice; b. Omaha, July 20, 1939; JD, Creighton U., 1963. Asst. pub. defender, Douglas County, Nebr., 1963-66; pvt. practice Omaha, 1966-97; justice Nebr. Supreme Ct., 1997—. Fellow: Internat. Soc. Barristers; mem.: Sarpy County Bar Assn., Omaha Bar Assn., Colo. Bar Assn., Nebr. State Bar Assn. Office: State Capitol Bldg Rm 2218 Lincoln NE 68509 also: PO Box 98910 Lincoln NE 68509*

MCCORMACK, MIKE, former congressman; b. Basil, Ohio, Dec. 14, 1921; s. Henry Arthur and Nancy (Jenkins) McCormack; m. Margaret Louise Higgins, June 21, 1947; children: Mark Alan, Steven Arthur, Timothy Arnold. BS, Wash. State U., 1948, MS in Chemistry, 1949; postgrad. studies in law, Gonzaga U., 1965—66; DEng (hon.), Stevens Inst. Tech., 1976; LLD (hon.), Salisbury State Coll., 1981. Instr. U. Puget Sound, 1949—50; chemist, engr. supr. Hanford plant GE, 1950—64; rsch. scientist Battelle-Northwest Lab., Richland, Wash., 1965—70; nuclear energy cons. Wash. Assn. Pub. Utility Dists., 1970; mem. Wash. Ho. of Reps., 1955—60, Wash. State Senate from Dist. 16, 1960—70, chmn. natural resources com., 1961, 1963, mem. edn. com., 1965, mem. revenue and taxation com., 1967—70; mem. US Congress from 4th Wash. Dist., 1971—81, mem. pub. works, transp., sci. and tech. com., chmn. energy rsch., prodn. subcom., chmn. Dem Freshman caucus; pres. McCormack Assocs., Inc., 1982—90, Chelan Assocs., Washington, 1985—89; dir. Inst. Sci. & Soc., Elleneburg, Wash., 1990—2000. Dir. engring. and sci. policy seminars Sch. Engring. and Applied Sci., George Washington U., 1984; dir. Universal Voltronics Corp., Mt. Kisco, NY; dir., sci. policy advisor Council of Sci. Soc. Pres., Washington. Advisor youth groups Wash. YMCA, Boy Scouts Am., Little League, Campfire Girls; mem. Wash. State Higher Edn. Bd, 1994—97. Served as First Lt. US Army, 1943—46, World War II. Recipient Charles Lathrop Parsons award, Am. Chemical Soc., 1999, Disting. Pub. Svc. award, IEEE, 1980; named Solar Energy Man of Yr., Solar Energy Industry Assn., 1975; named one of The Top 100 Innovators in the World, Tech. mag., 1981. Mem.: AAAS (former dir.), Am. Chem. Soc. (Charles Lathrop Parsons award 1999), Am. Nuclear Soc. (nat. com. pub. info.), Masons, Am. Legion, VFW. Democrat.

MCCORMACK, RICHARD THOMAS FOX, diversified financial services company executive, former ambassador; b. Bradford, Pa., Mar. 6, 1941; s. C.H. and Ruth N. (Fox) McC.; m. Karen L. Hagstrom, Oct. 18, 1980; children: Charlotte Louise, Justin Randall, Elizabeth Caroline. BA, Georgetown U., 1963; PhD, U. Fribourg, Switzerland, 1966. With Peace Corps, 1966-67; sr. staff mem. Pres.' Adv. Council on Exec. Orgn., White House, Washington, 1969-71; with Am. Enterprise Inst., 1975-77; dep. asst. sec. for internat. econ. affairs US Dept. Treasury, 1974; mem. staff U.S. Senate, 1979-81; asst. sec. state for econ. and bus. affairs U.S. Dept. State, Washington, 1982-85, US amb. to OAS, 1985-89, under sec. for econ. affairs, 1989-91; sr. advisor Ctr. Strategic Internat. Studies, Washington, 2004—06; vice chmn. Merrill Lynch & Co., Inc., NYC, 2006—. Candidate in primary elections for U.S. Congress, 1972, 74; cons. Office Telecommunications Policy, 1971, Coun. on Internat. Econ. Policy, 1972, Office Spl. Trade Rep., 1975, Exec. Office of the Pres., White House, Washington; guest scholar Woodrow Wilson Ctr. Smithsonian Instn., Washington, 1991-92; bus. advisor Am. companies, cons. U.S. Govt. on Internat. Econ. Affairs, 1992-2005. Author: Asians in Kenya, 1971, The Twilight War, 1979, Microeconomic Reforms for Israel, 1991, Managing Japan's Financial Crisis, 1992, Vulnerabilities in the Global Economy: Looking Forward in War Time, 2005. Recipient Superior Honor award Dept. State, 1987, Sec. of State's Disting. Svc. award, 1991; decorated Legion of Honor (France). Mem. Econ. Club NY, Coun. Am. Ambs.,counsil Am. Bd. Mem.,Coun. Fgn. Rels. Republican. Office: Bank of America Tower One Bryant Park 36th Fl New York NY 10036 Office Phone: 212-449-9300.

MCCORMACK, SEAN IAN, former federal agency administrator; b. 1964; BS in Economics, Colby Coll., 1986; MA, U. Md., 1990. Analyst Meridian Corp.; with Fgn. Svc., 1995—99; Farsi-speaking officer consular sect. U.S. Embassy, Ankara, 1996—98, econ. reporter on consular issues Algiers, 1998—99; with ops. ctr. US Dept. State, Washington, 1999, with exec. secretariat staff; dep. press sec. for fgn. policy The White House, Washington; spl. asst. to Pres., spokesman NSC, Washington, 2001—05; asst. sec. for pub. affairs, dept. spokesman US Dept. State, Washington, 2005—09.*

MCCORMACK, TERRY R., automotive executive; BS in Pyschology, Ball State U., Muncie, Ind. Sales trainee Dana Corp., 1973, pres. Aftermarket Group, 2000—04; pres., CEO Affinia Group Intermediate Holdings, 2004—. Bd. dirs. Motor & Equipment Mfrs. Assn. Bd. dirs. U. NC Charlotte Belk Coll. Sch. Bus. Mem.: Automotive Presidents' Group. Office: Affinia Group Inc 1101 Technology Dr Ann Arbor MI 48108 Office Phone: 734-827-5400.

MCCORMACK, THOMAS JOSEPH, retired publishing executive, playwright; b. Boston, Jan. 5, 1932; s. Thomas Joseph and Lena Carolyn (Allen) McC.; m. Sandra Harriet Danenberg, Aug. 21, 1964; children: Daniel Aaron, Jed Charles (dec.), Jessie Ann. Student, U. Conn., 1950-51; AB summa cum laude (James Manning scholar), Brown U., 1954; postgrad. (G.H. Palmer scholar, Woodrow Wilson fellow), Harvard U., 1956. Writer radio news WSTC, Stamford, Conn., 1957-59; editor Doubleday & Co., Inc., NYC, 1959-64, Harper & Row, NYC, 1964-67; edn. editor New Am. Library, NYC, 1967-69; dir. trade dept. St. Martin's Press, NYC, 1969-70, pres., 1970-87, chief exec. officer, editorial dir., 1970-96, chmn., 1987-97. Pres., chmn. bd. St. James Press, Ltd., London, 1973-79; v.p., treas. Sandra D. McCormack, Inc. (Interior Designer.); chmn., chief exec. officer Tor Books, NYC, 1987-96; exec. com. Holtzbrinck GmbH, Stuttgart, Germany, 1995-97. Author: Afterwords, Novelists on Their Novels, 1969, The Fiction Editor, the Novel and the Novelist, (plays) American Roulette, 1969, Endpapers, 2002; columnist: The Cheerful Skeptic, 1997—99. Mem. Play Devel. Coun., Manhattan Theater Club, 1995-2001, Dramatists Gild, 1997—. With AUS, 1954-56. Mem. Assn. Am. Pubs. (dir. 1973-76, freedom to read com. 1974-77, Curtis Benjamin award 1997, LMP Lifetime Achievement award 1997), Phi Beta Kappa. Clubs: The Players (NYC), Century Assn. (NYC). Home: 50 Central Park W New York NY 10023-6028 E-mail: cheerskep@aol.com.

MCCORMACK, WILLIAM J., bishop emeritus; b. NYC, Nov. 24, 1924; Attended, Christ the King Sem., St. Bonaventure U. Ordained priest Archdiocese of NYC, 1959, aux. bishop, 1986—2001, aux. bishop emeritus, 2001—; ordained bishop, 1987. Nat. dir. Soc. for Propagation Faith, 1980. Roman Catholic. Office: 142 E 29th St New York NY 10016-8102

MCCORMICK, DAVID ARTHUR, venture capitalist; b. McKeesport, Pa., Oct. 26, 1946; s. Arthur Paul and Eleanor Irene (Gibson) McC. BA, Westminster Coll., 1967; JD, Duquesne U., 1973, U. Pa., 1975. Bar: Pa. 1973, D.C. 1978, U.S. Ct. Appeals (3d cir.) 1977, U.S. Ct. Appeals (4th and D.C. cirs.) 1980, U.S. Supreme Ct. 1980. Asst. commerce counsel Penn Ctrl. R.R., Phila., 1973—76; assoc. labor counsel Consol. Rail Corp., Phila., 1976—78; atty. Dept. Army, Washington, 1978—2007; pres. Gibsondale Corp., Pa., 2007—. Author: various geneal. and hist. works; contbr. articles to profl. jours. Mem. Pa. Bar Assn., Phila. Bar Assn., DC Bar Assn., Am. Assn. for Justice, Assn. Transp. Law Profls., Soc. Petroleum Engrs., Soc. Cin., SAR, Am. Legion, Res. Officers Assn., Masons, Phi Alpha Delta, Theta Chi. Presbyterian.

MCCORMICK, DAVID HAROLD, federal agency administrator; b. Washington, Pa., Aug. 17, 1965; s. James Harold and Maryan (Garner) McCormick; m. Amy Frances Richardson, May 30, 1999; children: Elizabeth Cora, Tess Ann, Ava Garner. BS in Mech. Engring., US Mil. Acad. West Point, 1987; MPA, Princeton U., 1994, PhD, 1996. Mgmt. cons. McKinsey & Co., Inc., 1996—99; gen. mgr. core bus. markets FreeMarkets, Inc., 1999—2001, v.p., 1999—2000, sr. v.p., 2000—01, exec. v.p., 2001—02, pres., 2002—04, CEO, 2003—04; pres. Ariba, Inc., 2004—05; under sec. for industry & security US Dept. Commerce, Washington, 2005—06; dep. asst. to Pres., dep. nat. security adv. for internat. econ. affairs NSC, Washington, 2006—07; under sec. for internat. affairs US Dept. Treasury, Washington, 2007—. Bd. mem. Pitts. Tech. Coun., 2004—05, Allegheny Conf. on Cmty. Devel., 2004—05. Author: (chapt.) From Peacekeeping to Peacebuilding: Restructuring Military and Policy Institutions in El Salvador in Keeping the Peace: Multidimensional UN Operations, (book) The Downsized Warrior: America's Army in Transition. Bd. mem. Pitts. Parks Conservancy, 2001—05, Manchester Bidwell Corp., Pitts., 2000—05. Served in US Army, 1987—92, Ft. Bragg, NC, 1st Gulf War. Decorated Bronze Star; recipient Young Leader award, French-Am. Found., 1999; fellow, Earhart Found., 1996; Henry Crown Fellow, Aspen Inst., 2003. Fellow: Henry Crown Fell. Peace Corps, 2003. Office: US Dept Treasury 1500 Pennsylvania Ave Rm 4440 Washington DC 20220*

MCCORMICK, DAVID LOYD, toxicologist, researcher, educator; b. Abington, Pa., Jan. 19, 1953; s. Robert Lee and Mary Jane (Gehres) McC.; m. Marion B. Adler, Sept. 3, 1978; 1 child, Michael. AB, Middlebury Coll., Vt., 1974; MS, NYU, 1976, PhD, 1979. Diplomate Am. Bd. Toxicology. Asst. rsch. scientist NYU Med. Ctr., Tuxedo, N.Y., 1977-79; assoc. physiologist Ill. Inst. Tech. Rsch. Inst., Chgo., 1979-80, rsch. physiologist, 1980-82, sr. physiologist/toxicologist, 1982-90, mgr. rsch., head toxicology and environ. health, 1990-94, head pathophysiology, 1992-94, head toxicology and carcinogenesis, 1994-97, assoc. dir. dept. life scis., 1997-98, head exptl. toxicology and carcinogenesis, 1997-99, asst. v.p., 1998-99, v.p., dir. life scis. rsch., 1999—; prof. Ill. Inst. Tech., 1997—; sr. v.p., dir. IIT Rsch. Inst., 2004—. Adj. assoc. prof. Ill. Inst. Tech., 1982-98, adj. prof., 1998—; bd. dirs. Ill. Cancer Ctr., Chgo. Contbr. articles to profl. jours.; contbg. author books/abstracts in field. Mem. AAAS, N.Y. Acad. Sci., Bioelectromagnetics Soc., Am. Assn. Cancer Rsch., Soc. Exptl. Biology and Medicine, Internat. Assn. Breast Cancer Rsch., Soc. Toxicology (councilor Midwest regional chpt. 1991-94, treas. Midwest regional chpt. 1997-99, councilor carcinogenesis splty. sect. 1994-95). Office: IIT Rsch Inst 10 W 35th St Chicago IL 60616-3799

MCCORMICK, DONALD BRUCE, retired biochemist, educator; b. Front Royal, Va., July 15, 1932; s. Jesse Allen and Elizabeth (Hord) McC.; m. Norma Jean Dunn, June 6, 1955; children: Susan Lynn, Donald Bruce, Michael Allen. BA, Vanderbilt U., Nashville, Tenn., 1953, PhD, 1958. Postdoctoral fellow U. Calif., Berkeley, 1958—60; asst. prof. Cornell U., 1960-63, assoc. prof., 1963-69, prof. nutrition, biochemistry and molecular biology, biol. scis., 1969-79, Liberty Hyde Bailey prof. nutritional biochemistry, 1978-79; chmn. dept. biochemistry Emory U., Atlanta, 1979-94, Fuller E. Callaway prof. biochemistry, 1979-99, prof. emeritus, 1999—; exec. assoc. dean sci. Emory U. Sch. Medicine, 1985-89. Vis. lectr. U. Ill, 1963; Wellcome vis. prof. U. Fla., 1986, Med. Coll. Pa., 1989; Hurley lectr. U. Calif., Davis, 1992; O'Dell lectr. U. Mo., Columbia, 1993; biochem. cons. Interdepartmental Com. on Nutrition for Nat. Def., Spain, 1958; mem. and chmn. nutrition study sect. NIH, 1977-81; mem. diet and health com., dietary guidelines implementation com., vice chmn. food and nutrition bd. NRC, Inst. Medicine of NAS; exec. com., chmn. dept. med. biochemistry, Coun. Acad. Soc., Am. Assn. Med. Colls., 1984-87; mem. biology panel U.S. Civilian R&D Found., 1998-2001. Author: (with others) Spain: Nutrition Survey of the Armed Forces, 1958, Molecular Associations in Biology, 1968, Flavins and Flavoproteins, 1968, 71, 76, 80, 84, 87, 91, Comprehensive Biochemistry, Vol. 21, 1971, Riboflavin, 1974, Metal Ions in Biological Systems, Vol. 1, 1974, Present Knowledge in Nutrition, 1976, 2006, Natural Sulphur Compounds, 1979, Vitamin B6, Metabolism and Role in Growth, 1980, Ann. Rev. of Nutrition, Vol. 1, 1981, Vol. 9, 1989, Vol. 24, 2004, Mechanisms of Enzymatic Reactions: Stereochemistry, 1986, Chemical and Biological Aspects of Vitamin B6 Catalysis, Part A, 1984, Biochemistry of Vitamin B6, 1987, Biochemistry and Molecular Biology of Vitamin B6 and PQQ-Dependent Proteins, 2000, Tietz Textbook of Clinical Chemistry, 1986, 99, Fundamentals of Clinical Chemistry, 1987, 2000, Vitamins and Biofactors in Life Science, 1992, Encyclopedia of Food Science, 1993, 2003, Encyclopedia of Life Sciences, 1999, Encyclopedia of Molecular, Biology and Molecular Medicine, 1996, 2003, McGraw-Hill Encylopedia of Science and Technology, 2006, Modern Nutrition in Health and Disease, 1988, 2006, New Trends in Biological Chemistry, 1990, Chemistry and Biochemistry of Flavins, 1991, Encyclopedia of Human Biology, 1991, 97, Liver, 1994, Molecular Biology and Biotechnology, 1995, Biochemical and Physiological Bases of Human Nutrition, 2000, 2006, Nutrition in Space Flight and Weightlessness Models, 1999, Molecular Nutrition, 2003, Encyclopedia of Dietary Supplements, 2005; editor: Vitamins and Hormones, Vitamins and Coenzymes, Ann. Rev. of Nutrition, Handbook of Vitamins. Recipient award Bausch and Lomb, 1950, award Mead Johnson, 1970, award Osborne and Mendel, 1978, award Ga. Nutrition Coun., 1989, award Bristol-Myers Squibb/Mead Johnson, 1999; Westinghouse Sci. scholar, 1950; fellow NIH, 1957-58, 58-60; Guggenheim fellow, 1966-67. Fellow AAAS, Am. Inst. Nutrition (now Am. Soc. Nutrition, pres. 1991); mem. Am. Soc. Biochemistry and Molecular Biology, Soc. Exptl. Biology and Medicine, Am. Chem. Soc., Am. Inst. Biol. Sci., Biophysics Soc., Fedn. Am. Socs. Exptl. Biology (bd. dirs., LSRO sci. steering group), Microbiol. Soc., Photobiol. Soc., N.Y. Acad. Sci., Protein Soc., Sigma Xi. Office Phone: 770-270-5508. Business E-Mail: biocdbm@emory.edu.

MCCORMICK, FRANK, research scientist, biology professor; BSc in Biochemistry, U. Birmingham, Eng., 1972; PhD in Biochemistry, U. Cambridge, Eng., 1975. Postdoc. fellow SUNY, Stony Brook, 1975—78, Imperial Cancer Rsch. Fund, London, 1978—81; dir. molecular biology Cetus Corp., 1981—90, v.p. rsch., 1990—91, Chiron Corp., 1991—92; founder, chief sci. officer Onyx Pharm., 1992—96; prof. dept. microbiology & immunology U. Calif., San Francisco, 1997—, David A. Wood disting. prof. tumor biology & cancer rsch., E. Dixon Heise disting. prof. oncology, dir. UCSF Cancer Rsch. Inst., 1997—2009, assoc. dean, dir.

UCSF Helen Diller Family Comprehensive Cancer Ctr., 1997—. Mem. sci. adv. bd. Iconix Pharm. Contbr. articles to profl. jours. Recipient G.H.A. Clowes Meml. award, Am. Assn. Cancer Rsch., 2002, Novartis Drew award in Biomed. Rsch., 2002, Shubitz award, U. Chgo. Cancer Rsch. Ctr., 2003. Fellow: Royal Soc.; mem.: Inst. Medicine. Office: UCSF Comprehensive Rsch Ctr Box 0128 San Francisco CA 94143-0128 Office Phone: 415-502-1710. Office Fax: 415-502-1712. Business E-Mail: director@cc.ucsf.edu.*

MCCORMICK, HUGH THOMAS, lawyer; b. McAlester, Okla., Nov. 24, 1944; s. Hugh O. and Lois (McGucken) McC.; m. Suzanna G. Weingarten, Dec. 5, 1975; 1 child, John B. BA, U. Mich., 1968; JD, Rutgers U., 1977; LLM in Taxation, Georgetown U., 1980. Bar: N.Y. 1977, D.C. 1979, Maine 1981. Atty. office chief counsel interpretative divsn. IRS, Washington, 1977-81; assoc. Perkins, Thompson, Hinkley & Keddy, Portland, Maine, 1981-83, LeBoeuf, Lamb, Leiby & MacRae, NYC, 1983-88, counsel, 1989-91; ptnr. LeBoeuf, Lamb, Greene & MacRae, L.L.P., NYC, 1992—2005; exec. v.p. Scottish Re Group, Ltd., Hamilton, Bermuda, 2005—. Dir. Ins. Tax. Conf., 1993-04, pres., 2002-04. Mem. bd. contbrs. and advisors Jour. of Taxation of Investments; contbr. articles to profl. jours. Trustee U.S. Team Handball Found., N.J., 1985-95. Fellow Am. Bar Found.; mem. ABA (chmn. com. on taxation of ins. cos. 1989, chmn. subcom. sect. of taxation 1989-96, mem. torts and ins. practice sect., sect. on taxation), D.C. Bar Assn. Democrat. Office: Scottish Re Group Ltd Crown House 4 Par La Ville Rd 3rd Flr Hamilton HM MX Bermuda Office Phone: 441 298 4397. Business E-Mail: hugh.mccormick@scottishre.com.

MCCORMICK, JAMES HAROLD, academic administrator; b. Ind., Pa., Nov. 11, 1938; s. Harold Clark and Mary Blanche (Truby) McCormick; m. Maryan Kough Garner, June 7, 1963; children: David Harold, Douglas Paul. BS, Indiana U. of Pa., 1959; MEd, U. Pitts., 1961, EdD, 1963, postdoctoral, 1966, Columbia U., U. Mich., 1966-67, Harvard U., 1982. Tchr. Punxsutawney (Pa.) Area Joint Sch. Dist., 1959-61; adminstr. Baldwin-Whitehall Schs., Pitts., 1961-64; grad. asst. U. Pitts., 1962-63; asst. supt. instrn. Washington (Pa.) City Schs., 1964-65; prof. dept. edn. and psychology, asst. dean acad. affairs, acting dean acad. affairs, acting dean tchr. edn., asst. to pres., v.p. adminstrn. and fin. Shippensburg (Pa.) U., 1965-73; pres. Bloomsburg (Pa.) U., 1973-83, pres. emeritus, 1983—; founding chancellor Pa. State Sys. Higher Edn., Harrisburg, 1983—2001, Pa. chancellor emeritus, 2009; chancellor Minn. State Colls. and Univs., 2001—. Falk intern in politics, 1959; mem. adv. bd. Pa. Ednl. Policy Seminar; mem. Gov.'s Econ. Devel. Partnership Bd.; mem. higher edn. adv. coun. Pa. State Bd. Edn.; past commr. Edn. Commn. of the States; past chmn. Midwestern Higher Edn. Compact; bd. mem. Great North Alliance, Minn. Job Skills Partnership; founder, mem. Minn. P-16 Edn. Partnership; active Govs. Edn. Coun.; mem. postsecondary edn. and workforce devel. adv. com. Edn. Comm. States. Contbr. articles profl. jours. Named One of 10 Outstanding Young Men of Yr., Pa. Jr. C. of C., Disting. Friend of Higher Edn., Assn. Pa. State Coll. & U. Faculties, 2005; recipient Young Leader in Edn. award Phi Delta Kappa, 1981, Disting. Alumnus award Indiana U. Pa., 1981, Outstanding Alumni award Bloomsburg U., 1984, Outstanding Alumnus award U. Pitts., 1985, Adler award Pa. Edn. Assn., 1992, selected CIVITAS Prague mission, 1995, Presdl. Lectures, Kuwait U., 1993, Svc. award Coll. and Univ. Pub. Rels., Assn. Pa., 1999, Disting. Svc. award Pa. Assn. Couns. Trustees, 1998, Minn. Assn. Sch. Adminstrs., 2009, Alumni Assn. Leadership award Bloomsburg U., 1999, Disting. Svc. award Minn. Assn. Sch. Administrators, 2009; McCormick Human Svcs. Ctr. named in his honor Bloomsburg U., 1983; McCormick House named in his honor Dixon U., 1994, Accreditation Team Negotiator US Dept. Edn., 2007. Mem. Am. Assn. State Colls. and Univs. (Pa. state rep. 1988-93, former chmn. acad. and student pers. com., mem. com. on state rels. and task force on ednl. equity, chmn. policies and purposes com., mem. Internat. Edn.), Am. Coun. on Edn. (commn. on women in higher edn.), Nat. Assn. Sys. Heads, (exec. com., past pres.), Commn. State Colls. and Univs. (mem. and past chmn. govt. rels. and student rels. coms.), Assn. Governing Bds. (coun. pres., 2008, adv. coun.), Am. Assn. for Affirmative Action, Am. Assn. Higher Edn., Am. Assn. Sch. Adminstrs., Am. Assn. Univ. Adminstrs. (Tosney Leadership award 1993), Pa. Assn. Colls. and Univs. (bd. dirs., chair 1982), Natl. Ctr. for the Study of Sport in Soc., Pa. Black Conf. on Higher Edn., State Higher Edn. Exec. Ofcrs. (exec. com., chair Fed. Relations Com.), Pers. Assn., Bloomsburg Area C. of C. (pres. 1983), Harrisburg Rotary (bd. dirs. to 1992), St. Paul Rotary (bd. dir. to 2007), Phi Delta Kappa. Office: Wells Fargo Pl 30 7th St East Ste 350 Saint Paul MN 55101 Home: 10560 Pinnacle Way Woodbury MN 55129 Office Phone: 651-296-7971.

MCCORMICK, JOHN OWEN, retired comparative literature educator; b. Thief River Falls, Minn., Sept. 20, 1918; s. Owen Charles and Marie Antoinette Beauchemin (Smith) McC.; m. Helen Manuel, 1942; m. Mairi Clare MacInnes, 1954; children: Jonathan, Peter, Antoinette, Fergus. BA magna cum laude, U. Minn., 1941; MA, Harvard U., 1947, PhD, 1951. Dean, lectr. Salzburg Seminar in Am. Studies, 1951-52; lectr., prof. Free U., Berlin, 1952-59; prof. comparative lit. Rutgers U., 1959-87, prof. emeritus, 1987—. Vis. prof. Nat. U. Mexico, 1961-62, Hachioji (Tokyo) seminar, 1979; Christian Gauss Seminar lectr. Princeton, 1969; resident fellow Sch. Letters of Ind. U., 1970 Author: The Middle Distance: A Comparative History of American Imaginative Literature, 1919-32, 1971, The Complete Aficionado, 1967, 2d edit., 1998, (with Mairi MacInnes McCormick) Versions of Censorship, 1962, Der moderne amerikanische Roman, 1960, Amerikanische Lyrik, 1957, Catastrophe and Imagination, 1957, 2d edit., 1998, Fiction as Knowledge, 1975, 2d edit., 1999, George Santayana: A Biography, 1987, 2003, Wolfe, Malraux, Hesse, 1987, American and European Literary Imagination: 1919-1932, 2000; editor: (with G. Core) Sallies of the Mind: Essays of Francis Fergusson, 1998, Seeking Gossage: Essay-Memoirs, 2000, Another Music, 2008. With USNR, 1941-46. Recipient prize for non-fiction Longview Found., 1960, Am. Acad. and Inst. Arts and Letters award, 1988; Gugenheim fellow, 1964-65, 79-80, Bruern fellow Leeds (Eng.) U., 1975-76, NEH fellow, 1983-84, hon. fellow U. York, 1992. Mem. Taurino Club (London), Harvard Club (NYC)

MCCORMICK, JOSEPH B., healthcare educator; b. Knoxville, Tenn., Oct. 16, 1942; s. Jewell I. Gibson; m. Susan P. Fisher-Hoch, Mar. 17, 1992; children: Christopher R., Peter J., Anne S. BS, Fla. Southern Coll., Lakeland, Florida, 1964; MS, Harvard Sch. Pub. Health, Boston, 1970; MD, Duke U., Durham, NC, 1971. Resident pediat. Children's Hosp. Phila., 1971—73; chair, cmty. health scis. Aga Khan U., Karachi, Pakistan, 1993—97; chief epidemiology Inst. Pasteur, Paris, 1997—99; EIS officer Centers Disease Control, Atlanta, chief, spl. pathogens br.; dean and prof. UT Sch. Pub. Health, Brownsville Campus. Author: (book) Level 4: Virus Hunters of the CDC; contbr. scientific papers. Capt. US Pub. Health Svc., 1973—95, CDC, Atlanta. Avocations: piano, winemaking, hiking, skiing, backpacking. Business E-Mail: jxsmccormk@aol.com.

MCCORMICK, MARIE CLARE, pediatrician, educator; b. Winchester, Mass., Jan. 7, 1946; d. Richard John and Clare Bernadine (Keleher) McC.; m. Robert Jay Blendon, Dec. 30, 1977. BA magna cum laude, Emmanuel Coll., 1967, LHD (hon.), 2006; MD, Johns Hopkins U., 1971, ScD, 1978; MA, Harvard U., 1991; D of Humane Letters (hon.), Emmanuel Coll., Boston, 2006. Diplomate Am. Bd. Pediat. Pediatric resident, fellow Johns Hopkins Hosp., Balt., 1971-75, rsch. fellow, 1972-75; asst. prof. U. Ill. Schs. Medicine & Pub. Health, Chgo., 1975-76; pediat. instr. Johns Hopkins Med. Sch., Balt., 1976-78; asst. prof. healthcare orgn. Johns Hopkins Sch. Hygiene & Pub. Health, 1978-81; asst. prof. pediat. U. Pa., Phila., 1981-86, assoc. prof. pediat., 1986-87, Harvard Med. Sch., Boston, 1987-91, prof. pediat., 1992—, 1st Sumner and Esther Feldberg prof. maternal/child health, 1996—; prof. Harvard Sch. Pub. Health, Boston, 1992—2003, chair maternal and child health, 1992—2003, prof. Soc., Human Devel. and Health, 2003—. Adj. assoc. prof. pediat. U. Pa., 1987-92; active attending physician, Johns Hopkins Hosp., 1976-81, asst. physician Children's Hosp. Phila., 1981-84, assoc. physician, 1984-86, sr. physician, 1986-87, assoc. pediatrician Brigham & Women's Hosp., 1987—; sr. assoc. in medicine Children's Hosp., 1987—; sr. assoc. in pediat. Beth Israel Deaconess Med. Ctr., 1987—; vis. prof. Wash. U., St. Louis, 1993; editl. bds. Health Svcs. Rsch., 1985-94, Pediat. in Rev., 1986-91, Pediat., 1993-99; assoc. editor Jour. Ambulatory Pediatric Assn., 1999—; adv. coun. Ctr. Perinatal & Family Health Brigham & Women's Hosp., 1991—; cons. to numerous coms., orgns. and bds. Contbr. articles to profl. jours. Adv. The David and Lucile Packard Found., 1993-95; bd. dirs. Family Planning Coun. S.E. Pa., 1984-87; chair com. child health Mayor's Commn. Phila., 1982-83. Recipient Johns Hopkins U. Soc. Scholars award, 1995, award, Nat. Assn. of Nat. Acads., 2001, David Rall award, Inst. Medicine, 2005, Knisely Lecture award, U. Pa., 2008; named Henry Strong Denison scholar, Johns Hopkins Sch. Medicine, 1971, Leonard Davis Inst.; Health Econs. fellow, U. Pa., 1984. Fellow Am. Acad. Pediat.; mem. AAAS, Inst. Medicine of NAS, Ambulatory Pediat. Assn. (Rsch. award 1996), Soc. Pediatric Rsch. (sr., Douglas K. Richardson award 2006), Am. Pediatric Soc., Am. Pub. Health Assn., Internat. Epidemiol. Assn., Assn. Health Svcs. Rsch., Ea. Soc. Pediatric Rsch., Soc. Pediatric Epidemiologic Rsch., Assn. Tchrs. Maternal and Child Health, Mass. Med. Soc., Mass. Med. Soc.(Henry Bowditch Pub. Health award, 2008), Norfolk Dist. Med. Soc., Mass. Pub. Health Assn., Johns Hopkins U. Soc. Scholars, Nat. Vaccine Adv. Com. (safety subcom., 2008-). Office: Harvard Sch Pub Health 677 Huntington Ave Boston MA 02115-6096 Business E-Mail: mmccormi@hsph.harvard.edu.

MCCORMICK, RICHARD LEVIS, academic administrator; b. New Brunswick, NJ, Dec. 26, 1947; s. Richard Patrick and Katheryne Crook (Levis) McCormick; m. Joan C. Barry, July 22, 2006; children: Elizabeth, Michael. BA in Am. Studies, Amherst Coll., 1969; PhD in History, Yale U., 1976. From asst. prof. to prof. Rutgers U., New Brunswick, NJ, 1976—92, dean Faculty Arts and Scis., 1989—92; exec. vice chancellor, provost, vice chancellor acad. affair U. N.C., Chapel Hill, 1992—95; pres. U. Wash., Seattle, 1995—2002, Rutgers U., New Brunswick, NJ, 2002—. Author: From Realignment to Reform: Political Change in New York State 1893-1910, 1981, The Party Period and Public Policy: American Politics from the Age of Jackson to the Progressive Era, 1986. Fellow, Am. Coun. Learned Socs., 1978—79, John Simon Guggenheim Meml. Found., 1985. Mem.: Phi Beta Kappa. Office: Rutgers Univ New Brunswick NJ 08901 Office Phone: 732-932-7454. E-mail: rlm@rutgers.edu.*

MCCORMICK, ROBERT JUNIOR, former federal agency administrator; b. Boone, Iowa, Aug. 1929; s. Ivyl Robert and Darlene Adel (Bowes) McC.; m. Shirley May Zerbe, Dec. 24, 1950; children: Elaine McCormick Newland, Kathleen, Michael, Tara McCormick Wieting, Tammy McCormick Kirby. Grad., Flying Sch., Williams Field, Ariz., 1951, Parachute Jump Sch., 1964, Armed Forces Staff Coll., Norfolk, Va., 1966, Def. Systems Mgmt. Coll., Ft. Belvoir, Va., 1975; BS in Mech. Engring., Tex. Tech. U., 1963; cert., Harvard U. Def. Studies Program, 1984. Served as enlisted man USAF, 1948—51, commd. 2d lt., 1951, advanced through grades to col., 1971, pilot U.S., Japan, Europe, Vietnam, fighter pilot Korean War, 1951—52; exec. officer to Gen. George Brown 7th Air Force, Saigon, Vietnam, 1969—70; mil. asst. to asst. sec. of Air Force for research and devel. USAF, Washington, 1970—74, ret., 1975; exec. officer NASA, Washington, 1976—80; adminstrv. asst. to sec. of Air Force USAF, Washington, 1980—94; mem. U.S. Sr. Exec. Service, 1979—94; pres. McG, Ltd., Fairfax, Va. Mem. Pres.'s transition team Dept. of Def., 2001. Decorated Air Force Legion of Merit, Bronze star, Air medal, Meritorious Svc. medal, Air Force Exceptional Civilian Svc. medal, NASA Exceptional Svc. medal, 1980; recipient Presdl. Meritorious Rank, 1989, Disting. Civilian Svc. medal Dept. Def., 1994, Commendation medal State of Calif., 2001. Mem. ASME, DAV, Air Force Assn., Nat. Def. Indsl. Assn., Order of Daedalians, St. Andrews Soc. Washington, Mil. Order of Carabao, Chevaliers du Testevin. Clubs: Army-Navy Country (Fairfax, Va.). Personal E-mail: mcgltd1@aol.com.

MCCORMICK, STEVEN J., foundation administrator; BS in Agrl. Econ., with honors, U. Calif., Berkeley, 1973; JD, U. Calif. Hastings Coll. Law, 1976. Western regional legal counsel The Nature Conservancy (TNC), 1976, pres., CEO, 2001—07; ptnr. Resources Law Group, Sacramento, 2000—01; bd. trustee, pres. Gordon & Betty Moore Found., San Francisco, 2008—. Mem. adv. bd. U. Calif. Berkeley Coll. Natural Resources, Harvard Bus. Sch. Social Enterprise Initiative. Office: Gordon and Betty Moore Found 1661 Page Mill Rd Palo Alto CA 94304-1209 Office Phone: 415-561-7700.

MCCORMICK, WALTER BERNARD, JR., trade association administrator; b. Kansas City, Mo., Feb. 8, 1954; s. Walter Bernard and Dorothy Ann (Power) M.; m. Mary Lou Edlefsen, Jan. 3, 1987; children: Walter Patrick, Megan Boutin. Student, Georgetown U., 1975; BJ, U. Mo., 1976, JD, 1979. Bar: Mo. 1979, D.C. 1980. Assoc. Leighton, Conklin, Lemov & Jacobs, Washington, 1980-81, Pepper, Hamilton & Scheetz, Washington, 1981-82; legis. asst. US Senate, Washington, 1982-84; gen. counsel US Senate Com. Commerce, Sci. and Transp., Washington, 1985-87, minority chief counsel, staff dir., 1988-92; gen. counsel US Dept. Transp., Washington, 1992-93; ptnr. Bryan Cave LLP, Washington, 1993—98; pres., CEO Am. Trucking Assns., 1998—2001, US Telecom Assn., 2001—. Mem. City Club, Washington, 1993—. Republican. Roman Catholic. Office: US Telecom Assn 607 14th St NW Ste 400 Washington DC 20005 Office Phone: 202-326-7300.*

MCCORMICK, WILLIAM PAUL, United States Ambassador to New Zealand and Samoa; b. Providence, Aug. 18, 1939; m. Gail McCormick; 6 children. Attended, Roger Williams Jr. Coll., Boston U. With Conn. Gen. Life Ins. Co., San Francisco, 1963—65; co-owner Refectory Internat. Inc.; co-founder, pres. McCormick & Schmick's Seafood Restaurants, Inc., 1972—94, chmn., 2003—04, chmn. emeritus, 2004—05; U.S. amb. to New Zealand and Samoa US Dept. State, Wellington, 2005—. Served with Army Res. Mil. Police. Recipient Secretary's award, US Dept. Veteran's Affairs. Office: 4360 Wellington Pl Washington DC 20521*

MCCOSHAM, JOYCE L., retired secondary school educator; b. Norwood, Ohio, Dec. 25, 1927; d. Stanley James and Mary Emily Chambers; m. William Duncan McCosham, June 12, 1948 (dec.); children: Lynn Colleen Hamberg, Kyle Maureen Hellman. BS in Edn., U. Cin., 1948, MEd, 1972. Lic. profl. counselor Ohio, 1986. Instr. water safety, cmty. ctr. leader Cin. Recreation Commn., 1948—74; tchr. phys. edn., health, coach North College Hill Schs., 1948—52; tchr., coach Bethesda Hosp. Sch. Nursing, Deaconess Hosp. Sch. Nursing; tchr. phys. edn., health, coach, athletic dir., counselor, asst. prin. Mother of Mercy High Sch. and Acad., 1952—92; counselor Divorce Groups for Aring Inst., 1972—92; instr., tchr. edn. Edgecliff Coll., 1959—74; counselor Oak Hills High Sch., 1992—99, ret., 1999. Elder Mt. Auburn Presbyb. Ch., Cin., 1965—, recreation program, 1965—70. Recipient cert. of Merit, Ohio Counseling Assn., 1999; named Disting. Alumni, U. Cin. Coll. Edn., 1998, in her honor Joyce McCosham Day, Mayor Roxanne Qualls, Cin., 1999; named to Ath. Hall Fame, Mother of Mercy HS, 1987. Mem.: Southwestern Ohio Edn. Assn., Mother of Mercy Athletic Hall of Fame (selection com.), Oak Hills Ret. Tchrs. Assn., Mercy Ret. Tchrs. Assn., Ohio Edn. Assn., Nat. Edn. Assn., Hamilton County Ret. Tchrs. Assn., Greater Cin. Counseling Assn. (pres., v.p., sec.-treas. 1972—99, Mary Corre Foster award 1994), Nat. Hole-in-One Assn., U. Cin. Golden Bearcat Club, Kappa Delta Pi. Avocations: boating, water-skiing, golf, bowling, travel.

MCCOTTER, THADDEUS GEORGE, United States Representative from Michigan; b. Livonia, Mich., Aug. 22, 1965; s. Dennis and Joan McCotter; m. Rita Michel; children: George, Timothy, Emilia. BA in Polit. Sci., summa cum laude, U. Detroit, 1987, JD, 1990. Bar: Mich. 1991. Trustee Schoolcraft C.C., 1989; commr. Wayne County, Mich., 1992-98; mem. Mich. State Senate from Dist. 9, Lansing, 1998—2002, US Congress from 3rd Mich. Dist., 2003—, US House Financial Services Com.; chmn. US House Republican Policy Com., 2007—. Rep. precinct del., 1986; chair Wayne County Rep. com. Recipient Outstanding Michigander award, Mich. Jaycees, 2001, Legis. of Yr., Police Officers Assn. of Mich., 2002. Republican. Roman Catholic. Office: US Congress 1632 LHOB Washington DC 20515-2211 also: District Office 17197 N Laurel Pk Dr Ste 533 Livonia MI 48152-7908 Office Phone: 202-225-8171, 734-632-0314. Office Fax: 202-225-2667, 734-632-0373.*

MCCOURT, JAMIE, professional sports team executive; b. Baltimore, Md., 1953; d. Jack and Jean Luskin; m. Frank McCourt, 1979; children: Drew, Travis, Casey, Gavin. BS in French, Georgetown U., 1975; diploma, La Sorbonne U. Paris; JD, U. Md., 1979; MBA, MIT, 1994. Bar: NY, Mass. Atty. specializing in internat. and securities law, NYC, 1979; atty. private practice, Boston; v.p., general counsel McCourt Co., Boston, 1994—; vice chmn., pres. LA Dodgers, 2004—. Visiting prof. UCLA. Bd. dirs. LA Sports Coun.; mem. Calif. Governor's Coun. Physical Fitness and Sports; Leadership Council Literacy Network Greater LA; bd. dirs. Dodgers Dream Found. Recipient Scopus award, Am. Friends Hebrew U.; named one of 100 Women Who Run This Town, Boston mag., 2003, 20 Most Influential Women in Sports Bus., Street & Smith, 2005, 10 Women to Watch, Jewish Woman mag., 2007, 50 Women to Watch, Wall St. Journal, 2007. Mem.: LA INC. The Convention & Visitors Bureau (bd. dirs.), LA Bus. Coun. (bd. dirs.), LA area C. of C. (exec. com., bd. dirs.), LA Rotary Club (hon.). Jewish. Avocation: swimming. Office: Dodger Stadium 1000 Elysian Park Ave Los Angeles CA 90012

MCCOWAN, OTIS BLAKELY, mathematics professor; b. Monterey, Tenn., June 17, 1934; s. Burton and Martha Catherine (Phipps) McC. BS, Tenn. Tech. U., 1959; MA, La. State U., 1966; PhD, Vanderbilt U., 1975. Mathematician Missile Devel. Ctr., Holloman AFB, N.Mex., 1962-63; math. tchr. Rhea Ctrl. H.S., Dayton, Tenn., 1963-65; math. instr. Kilgore (Tex.) Coll., 1966-67; asst. prof. math. Belmont U., Nashville, 1967-72, assoc. prof. math., 1972-75, prof. math., 1975—2004, Chaney disting. prof., 1981, prof. emeritus, 2004—. With U.S. Army, 1959-62. Named Outsting Young Educator in Rhea County, Dayton C. of C., 1964. Mem. Nat. Coun. Tchrs. Math., Math. Assn. Am., Kappa Delta Pi, Kappa Mu Epsilon, Pi Mu Epsilon, Omicron Delta Kappa, Alpha Chi (Region III v.p. 1980-82, pres. 1982-84, nat. v.p. 1991-93). Democrat. Baptist. Avocations: travel, gardening, reading, attending concerts and theatre. Office: Belmont Univ Dept Math and Computer Sci Nashville TN 37212 Home: 210 E Hoyt Ave Monterey TN 38574 Business E-Mail: mccowano@mail.belmont.edu.

MCCOWN, GEORGE E., venture banking company executive; b. Portland, Oreg., July 1, 1935; s. Floyd Conly and Ada Elizabeth (Stephens) McC.; m. Karen Stone, Mar. 22, 1986; children: Taryn, Daniel, David; stepchildren: Bryan, Norman, Mark, Amy. BSME, Stanford U., 1957; MBA, Harvard U., 1962. Assoc. Am. Rsch. & Devel. Corp., 1962-63; from asst. to the pres. to sr. v.p. Boise (Idaho) Cascade, 1963-80; pres. Boise Cascase Home & Land Corp., 1974-80; chmn. Sequoia Corp., Boise, 1981—. Co-founder, mng. gen. ptnr. McCown De Leeuw & Co., Foster City, Calif., 1984—; chmn. bd. BMC West Corp., Vans, Inc.; bd. dirs. Specialty Paperboard Inc., Fitness Holding Inc. Trustee Stanford U., chmn. fin. com. and investment policy subcom., 1980-85; dir. Packard Childrens Hosp. Ctr. Econ. Policy Rsch., Stanford; trusteeNeuva Learning Ctr., Pacific Crest Outward Bound Sch.; chmn. bd. govs. Wyo. Centennial Everest Expdn.; mem., past chmn. policy adv. bd. Harvard Joint Ctr. Housing Studies, Ctr. Real Estate and Urban Econs., U. Calif. Berkeley; chmn. World Bus. Acad.; overseer Hoover Inst. War, Revolution and Peace. Capt. USAF, 1957-60. Mem. Harvard Bus. Assn. No. Calif. (chmn.), Chief Execs. Orgn., World Pres. Orgn., Explorers Club, Bus. Execs. Nat. Security, Bohemian Club. Republican. Avocations: classical piano, mountain climbing, adventure travel, aviation, tennis, skiing. Home: 250 Greer Rd Woodside CA 94062-4206 Personal E-mail: gmccown@aimlp.com. E-mail: gmccown@mdcpartners.com.

MCCOY, AMY L., special education educator; d. Robert and Barbara McCoy. BA in Counseling, Bob Jones U., Greenville, SC, 2001, MA in Tchg. Spl. Edn., 2003. Cert. tchr. SC, 2004. Tchr. emotionally disabled, self-contain tchr. Slater-Marietta Elem., Marietta, SC, 2004; tchr. learning disabledes, resource Cherrydale Elem., Greenville, 2004—. Co-chmn. United Way, Greenville, SC, 2005—. Mentor Hampton Pk. Bapt. Ch., Greenville, SC, 1999—2001. Mem.: Internat. Reading Assn., Coun. Exceptional Children. Home: 2320 Northway Denton TX 76207

MCCOY, BERNARD ROGERS, television anchor; b. Cortland, NY, Dec. 24, 1955; s. Donald Richard and Vivian Alicia (Rogers) McC.; m. Joanne Louise Lohr, Apr. 29, 1989; children: Emily Louise, Marian Alicia. BS in Journalism, U. Kans., 1979; M in Telecomm. Mgmt., Mich. State U., 1996. Mgmt. trainee Garney Constrn. Co., Kansas City, Mo., 1979-80; reporter, anchor Sta. WIBW-AM-FM-TV, Topeka, 1979-80, Sta. KCTV-TV, Kansas City, 1980-89; anchor Sta. WKBD-TV, Detroit, 1989-93, Sta. WILX-TV, NBC, Lansing, Mich., 1993-99, Sta. WBNS-TV, CBS, Columbus, Ohio, 1999—. Chmn. Earthwork Environ. Adv. Bd., Southfield, Mich., 1989—. Bd. dirs. Judson Ctr.; celebrity fundraiser Salvation Army, Detroit, 1989, March of Dimes, Detroit, 1989, hon. co-chair Mid-Mich. WalkAmerica, 1996; celebrity fundraiser

Cancer Soc., Detroit, 1989, The Sanctuary, Royal Oak, Mich., 1989; mem. YMCA, 1991—; mem. Sparrow Hosp. Children's Miracle Network Com., 1996, Mid-Mich. Environ. Action Coun., 1996; project coord. News-10 Computer Edn., 1996. Recipient Spot News awards Mo. Broadcasters Assn., 1987, Kansas City Press Club, 1987, Kans. Broadcasters Assn., 1987, Disting. Environ. Reporting awards Detroit Audubon Soc., 1991, Mich. Audubon Soc., 1992, Ben East award Mich. United Conservation Clubs, 1991, 93, Mich. Outstanding Individual Reporting award UPI, 1991, Emmy award for Outstanding Reporting in Mich., 1994, Gen. Excellence in TV Reporting award Mich. AP, 1999, Disting. Svc. medal Mich. Dept. Mil. Affairs, Wolverine Guard award for media excelence Mich. N.G. Mem. Nat. Acad. of TV Arts and Scis. (bd. dirs. Mich. chpt., Dising. Svc. award 1997), Nat. Geo. Soc., Soc. Environ. Journalists (charter, planner nat. conf.). Avocations: backpacking, golf, fishing, tennis, running. Office: WBNS-TV 770 Twin Rivers Dr Columbus OH 43215 E-mail: rmc@wbnslotv.com.

MCCOY, DUSTAN ELWOOD, manufacturing executive, lawyer; b. Ashland, Ky., July 16, 1949; s. Elwood and Mary Anna (Mullins) McC.; m. Rebecca Lancashire, Feb. 28, 1970; children: Dustan Chad, Drew Christopher. BA, Eastern Ky. U., 1971; JD, No. Ky. U., 1978. Bar: Ky. 1978. Atty. Ashland Oil Inc., Ky., 1973-83, sr. atty. Ky., 1983-85, gen. atty. Ky., 1985, assoc. gen. counsel Ky.; sr. v.p., gen. counsel, corp. sec., exec. v.p. Witco Corp.; v.p., gen. counsel Brunswick Corp., 1999—2000, pres. Brunswick boat group, 2000—05, chmn., CEO, 2005—. Bd. dirs. La.-Pacific Corp. Local bd. mem. U.S. SSS, 1987; mem. law bd. visitors No. Ky. U. Mem. ABA, Ky. Bar Assn. Avocations: jogging, hunting, fishing. Office: Brunswick Corp 1 N Field Ct Lake Forest IL 60045-4811 Office Phone: 847-735-4700. Office Fax: 847-735-4765.

MCCOY, GORDON R., minister; s. Herman G. and Dorothy McCoy; life ptnr. Eugene M. Thomas. BA, Macalester Coll., St. Paul, 1961; MDiv, McCormick Theol. Sem., Chgo., 1964. Ordained to ministry Presbyn. Ch., 1965. Pastor First Presbyn. Ch. West Unity and Kunkle, Ohio, 1965—66; grants adminstr. Ill. Dept. of Mental Health and Devel. Disabilities, Chgo. and Elgin, 1972—84, Ctr. on Deafness, Northbrook, Ill., 1984—97, dir., cmty. outreach programs, 1997—99; sr. pastor Ch. of the Resurrection MCC, Chgo., 1984—97; pastor Met. Cmty. Ch. of the Fox Valley, Elgin, Ill., 2002—05; dir. program devel. Mental Health & Deafness Resources, Inc., Northbrook, Ill., 2000—03, 2008, Pastoral Care Team A Churlitte MCC, Chgo., 2008—. Faculty Samaritan Theol. Inst., 1990—92; adj. faculty McCormick Theol. Sem., Chgo., 1993—94. Dir. at large Nat. Assn. Railroad Passengers, 2004—09, rep. coord., 2009—; editor Ill. Railgram, 2004—05; bd. dirs. Mental Health and Deafness Resources, Inc., 2005—; west area coord. Gt. Lakes Dist., UFMCC, Chgo., 1998—2002; cluster team leader Metro Politan Cmty. Chs., 2009—; regional dir. Nat. Assn. R.R. Passengers, Washington, 2002—; bd. dirs. Ill. Assn. R.R. Passengers, Chgo., 2001—05. Named Clergyperson of the Yr., Gt. Lakes Dist., Met. Cmty. Chs., 1994. Avocations: travel, reading. Personal E-mail: grmchitown@aol.com.

MCCOY, J. KELLY, biology professor; s. Clarence John and Patsy Ruth McCoy; m. Therese Marie Wasielewski, Oct. 19, 1984; children: Kelly Marie, Margaret Mae, William Patrick. PhD in Zoology, Okla. State U., Stillwater, 1995. Prof., head dept. biology Angelo State U., San Angelo, Tex., 1996—. Editor: (book) Lizard Social Behavior. Office: Biology Dept Angelo State Univ San Angelo TX 76909 Business E-Mail: kelly.mccoy@angelo.edu.

MCCOY, JEANIE SHEARER, analytical chemist, consultant; b. Mancelona, Mich., May 27, 1921; d. Theophil R. and Goldie Margaret (Halladay) Schroeder; m. Theodore R. Shearer, June 14, 1958 (div. 1964); 1 child, Blair Barnett; m. George Altha McCoy, July 23, 1966. AA, North Park Coll., 1941; BS, Northwestern U., 1944; MS, No. Ill. U., 1970. Jr. analytical chemist Buick Motor divsn. GM, Melrose Park, Ill., 1944—45; asst. rsch. chemist Hodson Oil Corp., Chgo., 1945—47; asst. analytical chemist Internat. Harvester Co., Melrose Park, 1947—49, analytical chemist, 1949—60, prin. chemist, 1961—74, supr. metal process control, 1974—82; cons. cutting fluid mgmt. divsn. JMT, Inc., Lombard, Ill., 1983—2003; cons. Jeanie McCoy Cutting Fluid Mgmt., Lombard, 2004—06. Editor: Lubrication Engring. Mag., 1979—2000; contbr. chapters to books. Recipient P. M. Ku award, 1991, Internat. award, 2000. Fellow: Soc. Tribologists and Lubrication Engrs. (Allan Mantafel award Chgo sect. 1987); mem.: AAUW, Soc. Mfg. Engrs., Am. Chem. Soc., Soc. Automotive Engrs. Avocations: seashell collecting, stamp collecting/philately, fitness activities. Home and Office: 654 N West Rd Lombard IL 60148-1547 Home Phone: 630-627-2379; Office Phone: 630-627-2721. Personal E-mail: j10mccoy@aol.com.

MCCOY, JERRY JACK, lawyer; b. Pitts., Aug. 4, 1941; s. Norris and Martha (Jack) McC.; m. Alexandra Armstrong; children: MadeleineRena, Allison Norah, Jonathan Howard. BS, W.Va. U., 1963; LLB, Duke U., 1966; LLM in Taxation, N.Y.U., 1967. Bar: D.C. 1968, N.Y. 1967. Assoc. Silverstein & Mullens, Washington, 1968-72, ptnr., 1973-92; of counsel Reid and Priest, NYC, Washington, 1992-94; sole practitioner Washington, 1994—. Adj. law faculty U. Miami, Fla., 1983—, Law Ctr. Georgetown U., 1996—. Exec. editor Tax Management, Estates Gifts and Trusts series, Washington, 1972—92, co-founder, co-editor Charitable Gift Planning News, Dallas, 1983—, Family Foundation Advisor, 2002—; contbr. articles to profl. jours. Mem. ABA, Am. Law Inst., Am. Coll. Trust and Estate Counsel (past chair com. on charitable planning and exempt orgns.), Am. Coll. Tax Counsel. Home: 3560 Winfield Ln NW Washington DC 20007-2368 Office: PO Box 66491 Washington DC 20035-6491 Business E-Mail: jjm@mccoylaw.com.

MCCOY, JOHN BONNET, retired bank executive; b. Columbus, June 11, 1943; s. John Gardner and Jeanne Newlove (Bonnet) McC.; m. Jane Deborah Taylor, Apr. 21, 1968; children: Tracy Bonnet, Paige Taylor, John Taylor. BA, Williams Coll., Williamstown, Mass., 1965; MBA, Stanford U., Calif., 1967; LLD (hon.), Williams Coll., 1991; D of Bus. Adminstrn. (hon.), Ohio State U., Columbus, 1993; LLD (hon.), Kenyon Coll., Gambier, Ohio, 1994. With Banc One Corp., Columbus NA, Columbus, Ohio, 1970—, banking officer, 1970-73, v.p., 1973-77, pres., 1977-83, Bank One Trust Co., 1979—81; pres., COO Banc One Corp., Columbus, Ohio, 1983-84, pres., CEO, 1984-87, chmn., CEO, 1987-99. Bd. dirs. Cardinal Health, Inc., Fed. Home Loan Mortgage Corp., 1990-2005, Ameritech Corp., 1991-99, AT&T Inc. (formerly AT&T Corp.), 1999-, Cardinal Health, Inc., 1996-, Choice Point, Inc., 2003-, Onex Corp.; mem. fed. adv. coun. Fed. Res. Sys., 1991-93. Trustee, chmn. bd. dirs. Kenyon Coll., 1992-95; trustee Stanford U., 1986-96, Williams Coll., 1996-2001, Battelle Meml. Inst.; bd. dirs., chmn. bd. PGA Tour; past pres. Columbus Area Growth Found.; chmn. Capitol South Urban Redevel. Corp., 1975-2007. Capt. USAF, 1967-70. Recipient Ernest C. Arbuckle award Stanford U., 1994. Mem. Columbus C. of C. (past chmn., trustee), Am. Bankers Assn., Bankers Roundtable (bd. dirs. 1989-94), Assn. Bank Holding Cos., Young Pres. Orgn. (chmn. Columbus chpt. 1982-83), Cypress Point Club, Seminole Golf Club, Links Club N.Y.C. Episcopalian. Office: Banc One Corp 191 W Nationwide Blvd Ste 625 Columbus OH 43215

MCCOY, JOSEPH G., oil industry executive; V.p. global products supply and trading Chevron Corp., 2001—05, v.p. trading capability, 2005—07; sr. v.p. supply and optimization Tesoro Corp., San Antonio, 2008—. Office: Tesoro Corp 300 Concord Plz Dr San Antonio TX 78216 Office Phone: 210-828-8484.*

MCCOY, LILYS D., lawyer; b. San Diego, Sept. 23, 1967; d. Walter Lee, Jr. and Leoné Doris McCoy; children: Joshua Thomas Moses-McCoy, Jonathan Lee Moses-McCoy. BA with distinction, U. Calif., San Diego, 1987; JD, U. Ariz., Tucson, 1991. Of counsel Law Offices of Frederick Meiser, San Diego, 1992—94; assoc. Law Offices of Gregory Jon Anthony, San Diego, 1994—96; of counsel Barmick, Rutherford and Scott, San Diego, 1996—99; assoc. Rosner Law and Mansfield, San Diego, 1999—2003; shareholder McCoy, Turnage & Robertson APLC, San Diego, 2003—. Pres. Lawyers Club of San Diego, 2002—03, adv. bd., 2002—, judicial endorsements, 2002—, chair, 2005. Named one of Top Attys., San Diego Daily Transcript, 2006. Mem.: Conf. of Delegates (bd. mem. 2004—), Tom Homann Law Assn. (co-pres. 2005—). Democrat. Episcopalian. Office: McCoy Turnage & Robertson APLC 5469 Kearny Village Rd #206 San Diego CA 92123 Home: 9252 Samantha Ct San Diego CA 92129-2121 Office Phone: 858-300-1900. Business E-Mail: ldm@mtrlaw.com.

MCCOY, LOIS CLARK, retired social services administrator, county official, editor; b. New Haven, Oct. 1, 1920; m. Herbert Irving McCoy, Oct. 17, 1943; children: Whitney, Kevin, Marianne, Tori, Debra, Sally, Daniel. BS, Skidmore Coll., 1942; student, Nat. Search and Rescue Sch., 1974. Asst. buyer R.H. Macy & Co., NYC, 1942-44, assoc. buyer, 1944-48; instr. Mountain Medicine & Survival, U. Calif., San Diego, 1973-74; cons. editor Search & Rescue Mag., 1975, Rescue Mag., 1988-97, editor, 1992-94, Press On Newsletter, 1992—2000. Coord. San Diego Mountain Rescue Team, La Jolla, Calif., 1973-75; disaster officer San Diego County, 1980-86, Santa Barbara County, 1985-91, ret.; pres. Nat. Inst. Urban Search & Rescue, Inc., 1987—; assoc. dir. Armed Forces Commns. and Electronics Assn., 2003—; mem. project info. techs. to enhance disaster mgmt., NAS, 2005, group using info. tech. to enhance crisis preparedness and response, Nat. Rsch. Coun., 2005; lectr. in field. Author: Search and Rescue Glossary, 1974, The Last Desperado, 2005, Kiss, Shoot, Aim, 2006, Max's Story, 2006, Unspoken Words, 2007; contbr. editor Rescue Mag., 1989-97; editor-in-chief Response! mag., 1982-86; editor Press On! Electronic mag., 1994-2001; adv. bd. Hazard Monthly, 1991-99; contbr. articles to profl. jours. Cons. law enforcement divsn. Calif. Office Emergency Svcs., 1976-77; pres. San Diego Com. for LA Philharm. Orch., 1957-58; bd. dirs. Search and Rescue of the Californias, 1976-77; exec. sec. Nat. Assn. for Search and Rescue, Inc., Nashville, La Jolla, 1975-80, comptr., 1980-82, bd. dirs., 1980-87, pres., 1985-87, trustee, 1987-90, mem. Calif. OES strategic com., 1992-96; CEO Nat. Inst. for Urban Search, 1989—; mem. Gov.'s Task Force on Earthquakes, 1981-82, Earthquake Preparedness Task Force, Seismic Safety Commn., 1982-85, Army Sci. and Tech. Commn., 2003; adv. coun. Nat. Meml. Inst. for the Protection from Terrorism; named to NSF Project Info. Tech. to Enhance Disaster Mgmt., 2005. Recipient Hall Foss Outstanding Svc. to Search and Rescue award, 1982, Diamond Safety award, 1996, Superior Performance award AFCEA, 2004, Rep. Senatorial Freedom medal, 2004, Congl. Order merit Rep. Congl. Del., 2005; named to The Fed. 100, 2002, Sec. Def. medal, 2009, award, Office of Sec. Def. Med. Exceptional Pub. Svc., 2009. Mem.: IEEE, Armed Forces Comm. and Electronics Assn. (named to Army Sci. and Tech. com. for Homeland Def. 2003—04, bd. dirs. 2003—), San Diego Mountain Rescue (life), Nat. Assn. Search and Rescue (life Svc. award 1985, 2002), Santa Barbara Amateur Radio Club. Episcopalian. Office: PO Box 91648 Santa Barbara CA 93190-1648 Office Phone: 800-767-0093. Personal E-mail: niusr@cox.net.

MCCOY, MARY NELL, music educator; d. James Albert Swope Jr. and Marjorie Gayle Swope; m. Gary Wayne McCoy, Nov. 28, 1968; children: Amy Annelle, Jason Todd, Joyce Elaine. MusB in Edn., Ctrl. Mo. State U., 1968; M in Ch. Music, S.W. Bapt. Theol. Sem., 1972. Cert. crosscultural, lang. and academic devel. State of Calif., 2000. Elem. music tchr. Knob Noster (Mo.) Elem. Sch., 1968—70; music cons. Internat. Mission Bd., Richmond, 1974—91; elem. music tchr. Bay Elem. Sch. San Lorenzo United Sch. Dist., Calif., 1995—; co-chair San Lorenzo United Sch. Dist., 2006—. Support provider for new tchrs. Beginning Tchr. Support and Assessment, San Lorenzo, 2001—; mentor tchr. Peer Assessment and Rev., San Lorenzo, 2001—; rep. Gifted and Talented Program, San Lorenzo, 2000—; adj. prof. Golden Gate Bapt. Theol. Sem., Mill Valley, Calif. Min. music First Bapt. Ch., Novato, Calif., 1992—96; interim min. music Petaluma (Calif.) Valley Bapt. Ch., 1997—99; children's choir leader Concord Korean Bapt. Ch., Martinez, Calif., 2000—03. Mem.: Calif. Tchrs. Assn. (assoc.), Calif. Music Educator's Conv. (assoc.), Music Educator's Nat. Conv. (assoc.), Calif. Parents, Tchrs. Assn., Phi Kappa Lambda. Democrat. Baptist. Home Phone: 510-639-7005. Personal E-mail: marynell.mccoy@comcast.net.

MCCOY, MICHAEL, economics professor; b. Jal, N.Mex., Dec. 5, 1952; s. Murl and Rosie McCoy; m. Debbie Hall., Oct. 6, 1979; children: Kristan, Rachael. MA, Tex. Tech U., Lubbock, 1987. Economics instr. Weatherford Coll., Tex., 2004—08; dir. distance learning Vernon Coll., Tex., 2008—. Mem. Optimist Club, Vernon, Tex., 1998—2000. Named Outstanding Grad. of Divsn. of Bus. and Economics, Midwestern Stat U., 1975. Office: Vernon Coll 4400 College Dr Vernon TX 76384 Office Fax: 940-552-9759. Business E-Mail: mmccoy@vernoncollege.edu.

MCCOY, MICHAEL D., lawyer; b. Joliet, Ill., Apr. 8, 1950; BSEE with honors, U. Ill., 1972; JD with honors, Chgo.-Kent Coll. Law, 1975. Bar: Ill. 1975, NC 1983, US Patent and Trademark Office. Ptnr. and coord. intellectual property law practice Alston & Bird LLP, Charlotte, NC. Mem. panel patent dispute arbitrators Am. Arbitration Assn. Contbr. articles to profl. jours. Named one of Best Lawyers in Am., 2005—. Mem.: ABA, Licensing Exec. Soc. Office: Alston & Bird LLP Bank of Am Plz Ste 4000 101 S Tryon St Charlotte NC 28280-4000 Office Phone: 704-444-1011. Office Fax: 704-444-1111. Business E-Mail: mike.mccoy@alston.com.

MCCOY, R. WESLEY, biology educator; b. Augusta, Ga., Sept. 20, 1954; s. Roger and Frances (Amick) McC.; m. Deborah Stringer, June 16, 1984. BS in Biology, Ga. State U., 1975; MEd in Sci. Edn., U. Ga., 1977; PhD, Ga. State U. Tchr. North Cobb High Sch., Kennesaw, Ga., 1978-83, sci. dept. chmn., 1987—, tchr., Biology, Genetics, and Astronomy; edn. specialist NASA, Kennedy Space Ctr. (Fla.), 1983-87; tchr. Ga. Govs. Honors Program, Dahlonega, 1981-82. Adj. asst. prof. Okla. State U., Stillwater, 1983-87; mem. NSF DNA literacy program, Cold Spring Harbor Lab, NOAA Nat. Undersea Rsch. Program Marine Biology Workshop; del. leader People to People Youth Sci. Exch. to Soviet Union; Fulbright tchr. exch. to U.K.; vice-chair, Ga. Citizens for Integrity in Sci. Edn. Christa McAuliffe fellow, 1992, SCI-MAT fellow, NSF, 1992, Ga. Sci. Tchr. of Yr., GTE G.I.F.T. fellow, 1993, Tandy scholar 1994; recipient Presdl. Award for Excellence in Sci. and Math. Teaching, 1996, Outstanding Biology Tchr. for Ga., Evolution-Education award, Found. for the Furure, 2003, 2006 AAAS Award for Scientific Freedom and Responsibility, 2007. Mem. NSTA, Vice Pres. Presbyn. Assn. for Sci., Tech. and Christian Faith, Ga. Sci. Tchrs. Assn., Fulbright Assn., Phi Delta Kappa. Presbyterian. Office: North Cobb High Sch 3400 Old Highway 41 Kennesaw GA 30144-1072

MCCOY, SHERILYN S., pharmaceutical executive; b. 1958; married; 3 children. BS in Textile Chemistry, U. Mass., 1980; MChemE, Princeton U., 1982; MBA, Rutgers U., 1988. Various positions from assoc scientist through v.p. Johnson & Johnson, New Brunswick, NJ, 1982—96, v.p. R&D, 1996—2000, v.p. mktg. skin care franchise, 2000—02, global pres. baby & wound care franchises New Brunswick, NJ, 2002—05, group chmn. & worldwide franchise chmn. Ethicon & med. devices & diagnostics, 2005—08, worldwide chmn. surgical care group., mem. exec. com., 2008, worldwide chmn. pharm. divsn., 2009—. Bd. dirs. FIRST; mem. president's' bus. leaders cabinet Rutgers U.; v.p. Montgomery Twp. Edn. Found. Named one of The 50 Most Powerful Women in Bus., Fortune mag., 2008, 100 Most Powerful Women, Forbes mag., 2009. Office: Johnson & Johnson 1 Johnson & Johnson Plz New Brunswick NJ 08933*

MCCOY, SUE, retired surgeon, biochemist, bioethicist; b. Charlottesville, Va., Nov. 14, 1935; d. Hulburt Christopher and Evelyn (Savage) McC. AB, Radcliffe Coll., 1957; PhD, Johns Hopkins U., 1964; MD, U. Va., 1980, postgrad., 2001—. Diplomate Am. Bd. Surgery. Fellow in physiol. chemistry Johns Hopkins U., Balt., 1964-67; asst. prof. chemistry U. South Fla., Tampa, 1967-69; asst. prof. orthopedics U. Va., Charlottesville, 1969-73, asst. prof. surgery, 1973-78; resident in surgery Hosp. U. Pa., Phila., 1980-83; resident in surgery Cooper Hosp. Rutgers U. Med. Sch., Camden, N.J., 1983-85, asst. prof. surgery, 1985-86, East Tenn. State U., Johnson City, 1986-91, assoc. prof., 1991-2000, prof., 2000—01; ret., 2001. Fellow: ACS; mem.: Assn. for Women Surgeons, Southeastern Surg. Congress, Shock Soc., Assn. for Acad. Surgery, Royal Soc. Chemistry, N.Y. Acad. Sci., Am. Chem. Soc., Sigma Xi. Achievements include research in hemorrhagic shock, aging, oxygen transport. Home: 8658 Batesville Rd Afton VA 22920

MCCOY, THOMAS M., information technology executive; BA in History, Stanford U.; JD, U. So. Calif. Law clk. US Ct. Appeals (9th cir.); assoc. to ptnr, O'Melveny and Meyers, 1977—95; gen. counsel Advanced Micro Devices, Sunnyvale, Calif., 1993—95, sec., 1995—2003, sr. v.p., gen. counsel, 1998—2003, exec. v.p. legal affairs, chief adminstrv. officer, 2003—. Office: Advanced Micro Devices One AMD Pl PO Box 3453 Sunnyvale CA 94088-3453

MC COY, TIDAL WINDHAM, former government official; b. Gainesville, Fla., Apr. 25, 1945; Grad., U.S. Mil. Acad., 1967; MA in Bus. Fin, George Washington U., 1975. Officer U.S. Army, 1967-72; mem. long-range planning and net assessment group Office of Sec. Def., Washington, 1972-73; mem. staff Nat. Security Council, 1973; staff asst. and then dep. asst. to Sec. Def., 1973-77; sci. asst. to asst. sec. for research, engring. and systems Dept. Navy, 1977-78; dir. policy research, office of under sec. for policy Dept. Def., 1978-79; asst. for nat. security affairs to Sen. Jake Garn, 1979-81; asst. sec. for manpower, res. affairs and installations Dept. Air Force, Washington, 1981-87; asst. sec. for readiness support USAF, Washington, 1987-88, acting sec. and undersec., 1981-88; sr. assoc. Hecht, Spencer & Assocs., 1988-89; v.p. govt. rels. Thiokol Corp., 1989—2002; chmn., CEO Washington Capital Ptnrs., 1998—. Chmn. Washington Capital Ptnrs., 1998—. Recipient DOD Outstanding Civil Svc. medal, USAF Exceptional Civilian Svc. medal. Mem. Space Transp. Assn. U.S.A. (dir., chmn. 1996—), Def. Forum Found. (vice-chmn.).

MCCOY, WESLEY LAWRENCE, musician, educator, conductor; b. Memphis, Jan. 27, 1935; s. Harlan Eftin and Gladys (Coggin) McC.; m. Carolyn June Noble, Aug. 26, 1960; children: Jill Laurene McCoy Kurtz, Scott Edward. B of Music Edn., La. State U., 1957, PhD, 1970; M of Music Edn., U. Louisville, 1958; M of Sacred Music, So. Bapt. Theol. Sem., 1960. Min. of music Beechmont Bapt. Ch., Louisville, 1959-62; also instr. music So. Bapt. Theol. Sem., Louisville; asst. prof. music, dir. bands Carson Newman Coll., Jefferson City, Tenn., 1962-67; asst. prof. music U. S.C., Columbia, 1969-72; assoc. prof. music U. Ark., Little Rock, 1972-77, prof., 1977-80, asst. dean for pub. svc. Coll. Fine Arts, 1978-79; condr. Wind Ensemble, River City Cmty. Band, 1972-80, Oklahoma City Youth Symphony, 1985—87; chmn. dept. music Phillips U., Enid, Okla., 1980-82, chmn. fine arts divsn., 1982-84; music tchr. Bishop Sullivan H.S., 2003—04; supr. Baton Rouge Recreation Dept., 2004—; asst. conductor Baton Rouge Concert Band, 2008—. Choral dir. 1st United Meth. Ch., Edmond, Okla., 1983-2000; owner WJ Travel, Oklahoma City, 1985-2002 French horn player, Knoxville (Tenn.) Symphony Orch., 1962-67, Columbia Philharm. Orch., 1969-72, Ark. Symphony Orch., 1972-80, Enid-Phillips Symphony, 1980-84; contbr. to Ch. Musician, 1974-76, 85-86. Co-chmn. Jefferson County (Tenn.) Com. for Goldwater for Pres., 1962; mem. Pulaski County (Ark.) Rep. Com., 1977-81; mem. Oklahoma County Rep. exec. Com., 1995-97; pres. Ctrl. Okla. La. State U. Alumni, 1997-98; choir dir. First United Meth. Ch., Hammond, La., 2004—; asst. dir. Baton Rouge Concert Band, 2007-. Mem. S.C. Music Educators Assn. (pres. coll. divsn. 1971-73), Ark. Music Edn. Assn. (chmn. rsch. 1975-80), Phi Mu Alpha, Pi Kappa Lambda, Phi Delta Kappa, Alpha Tau Omega. Republican. Baptist. Home and Office: 8548 Kaylynn Ave Baton Rouge LA 70810 Personal E-mail: wesleymccoy@yahoo.com.

MCCRACKEN, EUGENE LUKE, lawyer; b. Savannah, Ga., Aug. 9, 1932; s. John and Estelle (Powers) McCracken; m. Helen Kelly Morekis, May 9, 1964. AA, Armstrong State Coll., 1952; BA, Mercer U., Macon, Ga., 1954; LLB, U. Ga., Athens, 1957. Bar: Ga. 1958, US Dist. Ct. (so. dist.) Ga. 1959, US Ct. Appeals (11th cir.) 1961, US Supreme Ct. 1978. Assoc. Brannen, Clark & Hester, Savannah, 1958—64; sole practice Savannah, 1964—; asst. dist. atty. Chatham County, Ga., 1963—64; asst. city atty. City of Savannah, 1970—74. Judge pro temJuvenile Ct. Chatham County, Ga., 1963—64; asst. city atty. City of Savannah, 1970—74; judge pro tem Juvenile Ct. Chatham County, 1974—80. Mem. Chatham County Zoning Bd. Appeals, 1967—70; bd. dirs. United Way Savannah, 1973—74; chmn. Chatham County Reps., 1985—87; chmn. 1st congl. dist. Ga. Rep. Party, 1987—89. Recipient Named Savannah's Outstanding Young Man of Yr., Jaycees, 1966, Sword of Hope award, Am. Cancer Soc., 1968. Mem.: St. Andrews Soc. Savannah, Hibernian Soc. Savannah (pres. 2004—05), Armstrong State Coll. Alumni Assn. (pres. 1973, 1983), Savannah (Ga.) Bar Assn., State Bar of Ga. Roman Catholic. Home: 16 Brightwater Dr Savannah GA 31410-3301 Office: 223 W York St Savannah GA 31401-3636 Home Phone: 912-897-2373. Business E-Mail: legalmetts@aol.com.

MCCRACKEN, HARRY, journalist; b. Boston; s. Samuel and Natalie (Jacobson) McC. BA in History, Boston U., 1986. Editor Animato Mag., Cambridge, Mass., 1987-91; sr. editor CorpTech, Woburn, Mass., 1987-91; reviews editor Computer Buying World Mag., Wakefield, Mass., 1991-92; features editor Infoworld Direct mag., Boston, 1992-94; sr. assoc. editor PC World mag. and pcworld.com, 1994—2000, exec. features editor, 2000—02, editor, 2002—04, editor-in-chief, 2004—, v.p, 2004—. Chmn. Jesse H. Neal award competition Am. Bus. Media,

2007—. Contbg. editor: Multimedia World Mag., San Francisco, 1994-96; mem. editl. bd. Am. Bus. Media; contbr. articles to profl. jours. Office: PC World Communications 501 Second Street San Francisco CA 94107

MCCRACKEN, MARK B., county official; b. Clearfield, Pa., Nov. 27, 1963; s. Blair McCracken; m. Kelly McCracken; 1 child, Amanda. Attended, ICM Sch. Bus., Pitts. Data systems programmer North Am. Refractories Co., 1983—88; dir. info. tech. Clearfield County Govt., 1988—2004, commr., 2004—. Mem. Clearfield Area Sch. Dist. Bd. Dirs., 1993—2003; chmn. Pa. Counties Health Ins. Purchasing Co-op, 2005—; tech. com. chmn. County Commissioners Assn. Pa. Bd. mem. Clearfield United Way, Am. Red Cross Clearfield Chpt., Ctrl. Pa. Cmty. Action, Clearfield County Area Agency on Aging, Penn-AG Democrats, 2004—, Clearfield County Econ. Devel. Corp, 2004—08. Mem.: Sons the Am. Legion. Democrat. Office: Clearfield County Commrs 230 E Market St Clearfield PA 16830 Office Phone: 814-765-2641.

MCCRACKEN, PETER H., librarian; b. 1969; BA in English, Oberlin Coll.; MLS, U. N.C., Chapel Hill; MA in Maritime History, U. N.C. Reference libr. East Carolina U., Greenville, NC, 1999—2000; reference libr., coord. for collection devel. U. Wash., Seattle; co-founder, dir. electronic content mgmt. Serial Solutions, Seattle, 2000—. Mem. coun. advocates U. Wash. Libraries, Seattle; mem. bd. visitors Sch. Info. & Library Sci., U. N.C., Chapel Hill. Office: Serial Solutions 501 N 34th St #400 Seattle WA 98103

MC CRACKEN, PHILIP TRAFTON, sculptor; b. Bellingham, Wash., Nov. 14, 1928; s. William Franklin and Maude (Trafton) McC.; m. Anne MacFetridge, Aug. 14, 1954; children— Timothy, Robert, Daniel. BA in Sculpture, U. Wash., 1954. Asst. to Henry Moore, England, 1954. One-man shows: Willard Gallery, N.Y.C., 1960, 65, 68, 70, Seattle Art Mus., 1961, Wash. State Capitol Mus., Olympia, 1964, Art Gallery of Greater Victoria, B.C., 1964, LaJolla (Calif.) Mus. Art, 1970, Anchorage Hist. and Fine Arts Mus., 1970, Tacoma Art Mus., 1980, Kennedy Galleries, N.Y.C., 1985, Lynn McAllister Gallery, Seattle, 1986, 89, Valley Mus. N.W. Art, La Conner, Wash., 1993, Whatcom Mus., Bellingham, Wash., 1994, Schneider Mus. Art, 1994, So. Oreg. State Coll., 1994, Monterey Mus. Art, 1999, Mus. N.W. Art, La Conner, 2004, others; group shows include: Mus. Art, Ogunquit, Maine, 1957, Chgo. Art Inst., 1958, Detroit Inst. Arts, 1958, Pa. Acad. Fine Arts, 1958, Contemporary Art Gallery, Houston, 1958, DeYoung Meml. Mus., San Francisco, 1960, L.A. Mcpl. Art Mus., 1960, Galerie Claude Bernard, Paris, 1960, Phillips Gallery, Washington, 1966, Corcoran Gallery, 1966, Mus. Art, Akron, 1967, Finch Coll., N.Y.C., 1968, Rutgers U., 1968, Whitney Mus. Art, 1978, Portland Art Mus., 1976, Mont. State U., Bozeman, 1979, Brigham Young U., 1980, Bellevue (Wash.) Art Mus., 1986, Lynn McAllister Gallery, 1986, Am. Acad. Arts and Letters, N.Y.C., 1986, Schmidt Bingham Gallery, N.Y.C., 1987, Wash. State Capital Mus., 1987, 89, Cheney-Cowles Mus., Spokane, Wash., 1988, Smithsonian Instn., 1991—, Nat. Mus., Ottawa, Can., 1991-92, Gallery Three-Zero, N.Y.C., 1993, Seattle Art Mus., 1994, SA Gallery Christ Ch., New Zealand, 1996, Art and Cultural Ctr., Fallbrook, Calif., 2002, Port Angeles Fine Art Ctr., Wash., 2007, John Sisko Gallery, Seattle, 2008, others; sculptures represented: Norton Bldg., Seattle, Kankakee (Ill.) State Hosp., Swinomish Indian Tribal Center, LaConner, UN Assn., N.Y.C., King County King Dome, Seattle, City Hall, Everett, Wash., Bartlett Square, Tulsa, 2005, others. Recipient numerous art awards. Address: 5029 Guemes Island Rd Anacortes WA 98221-9039

MCCRACKEN, RICHARD JOSEPH, English educator, college administrator; b. Mineola, N.Y., Dec. 29, 1938; d. Clarence Aloysius and Margaret Elise (Dowling) McC. B.A., St. John's U., 1962, M.A., 1966; postgrad. U. Tex., 1968; LHD (hon.) U. Incarnate Word, 2005. Grad. asst. St. John's U., Jamaica, N.Y., 1962-64; asst. prof. English, Incarnate Word Coll., San Antonio, 1964—, dir. pub. relations, 1966-82, asst. to pres., 1982-86, dean alumni relations and planned giving, 1987-2005, dean emeritus, 2005; bd. govs. St. Peter's-St. Joseph's Children's Home, San Antonio, 1983—, pres. 1987-88; task force target 90 City San Antonio, 1984; mem. San Antonio Estate Planners Council, 1987—. Coordinator United Way Bexar County, San Antonio, 1972-80. Recipient 40 Yr. Service medal U. Incarnate Word, 1989; McCracken scholar U. Incarnate Word. Mem. Council for Advancement and Support Edn. (past officer, competition coordinator, Appreciation award SW dist. 1983-84), Nat. Soc. Fund Raising Execs., Southland Corp. Pilot Scholarship Program (task force, 2004. Independent. Roman Catholic. Avocations: gourmet cooking; gardening; art; writing. Home: 122 Burr Rd Apt 217 San Antonio TX 78209-6273 Home Phone: 210-826-6280; Office Phone: 210-829-6073. Business E-Mail: dickm@uiwtx.edu.

MCCRACKEN, THOMAS JAMES, JR., lawyer; b. Chgo., Oct. 27, 1952; s. Thomas J. Sr. and Eileen (Brophy) McC.; children: Catherine, Michael, Amanda, Quinn. BA, Marquette U., 1974; JD, Loyola U., 1977. Bar: Ill. 1977, U.S. Dist. Ct. (no. dist.) Ill., U.S. Ct. Appeals (7th cir.) 1984. Asst. state's atty. DuPage County State's Atty.'s Office, Wheaton, Ill., 1977—81; assoc. atty. McCracken & Walsh, Chgo., 1981—84, ptnr., 1984—2007; prin. Thomas J. McCracken Jr and Assoc., Chgo., 2007—. Commr. Nat. Conf. of Commns. on Uniform State Laws, 1989-. Contbr. articles to profl. jours. State rep. Ill. Gen. Assembly, Springfield, Ill., 1983-93, state senator, 1993; chmn. Regional Trans. Authority, Chgo., 1993-2004 Named Top Ten Legislators Chgo. Mag., 1990. Mem.: Chgo. Bar Assn., Ill. State Bar Assn. Avocations: skiing, hunting, golf. Office: Thomas J McCracken Jr and Assoc 161 N Clark St Chicago IL 60601 Office Phone: 312-346-0800. Business E-Mail: tjm@mcclawassociates.com.

MCCRACKEN, WILLIAM E., information technology executive; Various positions including gen. mgr. mktg., sales and distbn. IBM PC Co. and pres. Europe, Mid. East and Africa and Asia PC Co. IBM, mem. chmn.'s worldwide mgmt. coun. and gen. mgr. printing divsn.; bd. dirs. CA, Inc., 2005—, chmn. spl. litig. com., chmn., 2007—; pres. Exec. Consulting Group, LLC. Dir. IKON Office Solutions. Past pres. Plainfield Habitat for Humanity; bd. chmn. Luth. Social Ministries NJ. Mem.: NJ State Anti-Poverty Network. Office: CA Inc One CA Plz Islandia NY 11749

MCCRACKEN, WILLIAM HENRY, retired mining executive; b. Johnstown, Pa., Dec. 3, 1923; s. William Henry and Bernice (Johnson) McCracken; m. Juana Edelmira Pascarella, Oct. 3, 1959; children: William Henry, Derek James, David Andrew, Susan Linda. BS in Mining Engring., Pa. State U., 1944, MS in Mining Engring., 1947. Profl. engr., Pa. Field engr. Harbison-Walker Refractories Co., Pitts., 1947-57; mng. dir. Refractarios Peruanos SA, Lima, Peru, 1957-72; mgr. raw materials Harbison-Walker Refractories Co., Pitts., 1972—85; tech. dir. minerals and ores F&S Internat., Inc., Pitts., 1985-98; ret., 1998. Lt. (j.g.) USNR, 1944—46. Named William Tredennick award, The Refractory Inst. Fellow: Am. Ceramic Soc.; mem.: AIME (legion of honor mem.), ALAFAR (hon.), UNITECR (life), Pa. Ceramic Assn. (dir. emeritus). Home: 2219 Alnwick Dr Duluth GA 30096-2212

MCCRADY, BARBARA SACHS, psychologist, educator; b. Evanston, Ill., May 7, 1949; d. James Frederick and Margaret Maxine (Miller) Sachs; m. Dennis D. McCrady, June 13, 1969; 1 child, Eric Paul. BS, Purdue U., 1969; PhD, U. R.I., 1975. Lic. clin. psychologist. Clin. project evaluator Butler Hosp., Providence, 1974-75, chief psychol. assessment program, 1975-76, chief problem drinkers' project, 1976-83; assoc. prof. psychology Rutgers U., Piscataway, NJ, 1983-89, prof. psychology, 1989-2000, prof. II, 2000—07. From instr. to assoc. prof. psychiatry Brown U., Providence, 1975—83; reviewer Nat. Inst. on Alcohol Abuse and Alcoholism, Washington, 1979—82, extramural sci. adv. bd., 1989—93; cons. Inst. Medicine, Washington, 1988—89; acting dir. Rutgers Ctr. Alcohol Studies, Piscataway, 1990—92, dir. clin. tng. dept. psychology, 1993—2005, chair dept. psychology, 2005—07; dir. Ctr. on Alcoholism, Substance Abuse, and Addictions U. N. Mex., Albuquerque, 2007—, prof. dept. psychol., 2007—. Author: The Alcoholic Marriage, 1977; editor: Marriage and Marital Therapy, 1978, Directions in Alcohol Abuse Treatment Research, 1985, Research on Alcoholics Anonymous: Opportunities and Alternatives, 1993, Addictions: A Comprehensive Guidebook, 1999. Grantee Nat. Inst. on Alcohol Abuse and Alcoholism, 1979-83, 1988—. Fellow Am. Psychol. Assn. (past pres. divsn. addictions); mem. Assn. for Advancement Behavior Therapy, Rsch. Soc. on Alcoholism (bd. dirs., 1999-2003). Avocations: horseback riding, skiing, piano. Office: Univ N Mex CASAA 2560 Yale Blvd SE MSCII 6280 Albuquerque NM 87106 Home Phone: 505-856-1161; Office Phone: 505-925-2388. Business E-Mail: bmccrady@unm.edu.

MCCRADY, JAMES DAVID, veterinarian, educator; b. Beaumont, Tex., June 26, 1930; s. James Homer and Lucyle (Ward) McCrady; m. Mary Elizabeth McDougald, Sept. 8, 1951; children: David, Diane, Darla. BS, Tex. A&M U., 1952, DVM, 1958; PhD, Baylor U., 1965. From instr. to asst. prof. Tex. A&M U., 1958- 62, mem. faculty, 1964—, prof., head dept. vet. physiology and pharmacology, 1966-90, prof., dir. spl. programs, 1990—; dir. animal rsch., instr. Baylor U. Coll. Medicine, 1962-64. Dir. Russian-Am. Tng. Partnership, 1995—; adj. prof. Baylor Coll. Medicine, M.D. Anderson Hosp., Tumor Inst. With USAF, 1952—54. Mem.: AVMA, Am. Physiol. Soc., Tex. Acad. Sci., Sigma Xi, Phi Zeta, Phi Kappa Phi. Achievements include research in comparative cardiovascular and respiratory physiology. Home: 511 Olive St Bryan TX 77801-3506 Office: Tex A&M U College Station TX 77843-0001 Office Phone: 979-845-7261. Business E-Mail: jd-mccrady@tamu.edu.

MCCRANK, LAWRENCE J., dean, university librarian; b. Fargo, ND, Apr. 17, 1945; s. James F. McCrank and Florence Kloeckner; m. Ruth D. Madson; children: Kirstin L., Jaime L. BA, Minn. State U., Moorhead, 1967; MA, U. Kans., 1969; PhD, U. Va., 1974; MLS, U. Oregon, 1975. Asst. prof. libr. and info. sci. U. Md., College Park, 1976—82; dept. head rare books and spl. collections Ind. State U., Terre Haute, 1982—84; dean librs. Auburn U., Montgomery, Ala., 1984—88, Ferris State U., Big Rapids, Mich., 1988—95; dir. librs. ITT Tech. I, Grand Rapids, Mich., 1996—97, Davenport U., Grand Rapids, Mich., 1998—99; dean libr. and instrn. svcs. Chgo. State U., 2000—. Author: Historical Information Science, 2002, History Under Debate, 2004; contbr. articles to profl. jours. Fellow: Royal Archeol. Soc. Tarragona, Soc. Am. Archivists. Avocations: medieval history, Frontier studies. Office: Chgo State Univ 9501 S King Dr Chicago IL 60628-1598 Office Phone: 773-995-2253. Office Fax: 773-995-3772. Business E-Mail: lmccrank@csu.edu.

MCCRARY, CHARLES D., utilities executive; b. 1951; BS in Mech. Engring., Auburn U., Ala.; JD, Birmingham Sch. Law. Asst. project planning engr. Ala. Power Southern Co., 1973, various exec. positions Ala. Power and Southern Nuc., chief prodn. officer, exec. v.p. external affairs Ala. Power, 1994—98, pres. Southern Co. Generation and Energy Mktg., 1998—2001, v.p., 1998—2001, pres., COO Ala. Power, 2001, pres., CEO Ala. Power, 2001—, exec. v.p., 2002—. Bd. dirs. Amsouth Bancorporation, 2001—, Protective Life Corp., 2005—, Mercedes-Benz US Internat., Inc. Office: Southern Co 30 Ivan Allen Jr Blvd NW Atlanta GA 30308 Office Phone: 404-506-5000.*

MCCRARY, EUGENIA LESTER (MRS. DENNIS DAUGHTRY MCCRARY), civic worker, writer; b. Annapolis, Md., Mar. 23, 1929; d. John Campbell and Eugenia (Potts) Lester; m. John Campbell Howard, July 15, 1955 (dec. Sept. 1965); m. Dennis Daughtry McCrary, June 28, 1969; 1 child, Dennis Campbell. AB cum laude, Radcliffe Coll.-Harvard U., 1950; MA, Johns Hopkins U., 1952; postgrad., Harvard U., 1953, Pa. State U., 1953—54, Drew U., 1957—58, Inst. Study of USSR, Munich, 1964. Grad. asst. dept. Romance langs. Pa. State U., 1953—54; tchr. dept. math. The Brearley Sch., NYC, 1954—57; dir. Sch. Langs., Inc., Summit, NJ, 1958—69, trustee, 1960—69. Co-author: Nom de Plume: Eugenia Campbell Lester, (with Allegra Branson) Frontiers Aflame, 1987; film script adaptation (with John Gallagher) Frontier, 1998. Dist. dir. Ea. Pa. and NJ auditions Met. Opera Nat. Coun., NYC, 1960-66, dist. dir. publicity, 1966-67, nat. vice chmn. publicity, 1967-71, nat. chmn. public rels., 1972-75, hon. nat. chmn. pub. rels., 1976-99; bd. govs., chmn. Van Cortlandt House Mus., 1985-90 Mem. Nat. Soc. Colonial Dames Am. (bd. mgrs. NY 1985-90), Met. Opera Nat. Coun., Soc. Mayflower Descs. (former bd. dirs. NY soc., chmn. house com. 1986-89), Soc. Daus. Holland Dames (bd. dirs. 1982-87, 96—, 3d directress gen. 1987-92, directress gen. 1992-96), L'Eglise du St.-Esprit (vestry 1985-88, sr. warden 1988-90), Huguenot Soc. Am. (governing coun. 1984-90, 2000-03, 2004-05, asst. treas. 1990-91, sec. 1991-95, 2d v.p. 1995-2000), Colonial Dames Am., Daus. of Cin., Colony Club (bd. govs. 1988-96), Causeries du Lundi, The Hereditary Order Descendants of Colonial Govs. Republican. Episcopalian. Home: 24 Central Park S New York NY 10019-1629 Home Phone: 212-755-4988. Personal E-mail: d-emccrary@hotmail.com.

MCCRARY, VICTOR R., JR., engineering company executive; BA in Chemistry, Cath. U. America, 1973—78; PhD in Chemistry, Howard U., 1978—85; MS in Engring. Mgmt., U. Pa., 1993—95. Mem. tech. staff Bell Labs, Murray Hill, NJ, 1985—95; divsn. chief Nat. Inst. Standards and Tech., 1995—2003; bus. exec. sci. and tech. Johns Hopkins U. Applied Physics Lab.; asst. dept. head Milton Eisenhower Rsch. Ctr. Mem. nat. digital strategy adv. bd. Libr. Congress; adj. lectr. exec. masters tech. mgmt. prog. U. Pa. Recipient Gold medal, Dept. Commerce, 2000, Percy Julian award for Lifetime Achievement in Sci. and Engring., 2002, 2004 Emerald Honors, Sci. Spectrum mag. & US Black Engr. & Info. Tech. mag.; named to Power 150, Ebony mag., 2008. Mem.: Sigma Xi (mem. disting. lecturers com.), Nat. Org. Prof. Advancement Black Chemists and Chem. Engrs. (pres.), IEEE.

MCCRAVEN, EVA STEWART MAPES, health service administrator; b. LA, Sept. 26, 1936; d. Paul Melvin and Wilma Zech (Ziegler) Stewart; m. Carl Clarke McCraven, Mar. 18, 1978; children: David Anthony, Lawrence James, Maria Lynn Mapes. ABS magna cum laude, Calif. State U., Northridge, 1974; MS, Cambridge Grad. Sch. Psycholoy, 1987, PhD, 1991. Dir. spl. projects Pacoima Meml. Hosp., 1969—71, dir. health edn., 1971—74; asst. exec. dir., v.p. Hillview Cmty. Mental Health Ctr., Lakeview Terrace, Calif., 1974—99, exec. dir., 1999—2004, CEO and pres., 2004—. Past dir. dept. consultation and edn. Hillview Ctr., developer, mgr. long-term residential program, 1986-90; former program mgr. crisis residential program, transititional residential program and day treatment program for mentally ill offenders, past dir. mentally ill offenders svcs.; former program dir. Valley Homeless Shelter Mental Health Counseling Program; dir. Integrated Svcs. Agy., Hillview Mental Health Ctr., Inc., 1993-98, dir. clin. programs, 1996-99, exec. dir. 1999— Former pres. San Fernando Valley Coordinating Coun. Area Assn., Sunland-Jujunga Coordinating Coun.; bd. advisors Pacoima Sr. Citizens Multi-Purpose Ctr.; bd. dirs. N.E. Valley Health Corp., 1970-73, Golden Gate Cmty. Mental Health Ctr., 1970-73 Recipient Resolution of Commendation State of Calif., 1988, Commendation award, 1988, Spl. Mayor's plaque, 1988, Cmty. Svcs. Commendation awards City of L.A., 1989, County of Los Angeles, 1989, Calif. Assembly, 1989, Calif. Senate, 1989, award Sunland-Tujunga Police Support Coun., 1989 Mem. Health Svcs. Adminstrn. Alumni Assn. (past v.p.), Sunland-Jujunga Bus. and Profl. Women (Women of Achievement award 1990), LWV, Valley Philharm. Soc Office: Hillview Cmty Mental Health Ctr 11500 Eldridge Ave Lake View Terrace CA 91342-6523 Office Phone: 818-896-1161 ext. 211. Business E-Mail: esm@hillviewmhc.org.

MCCRAW, MICHAEL, music educator; MusB, NC Sch. Arts, Winston-Salem, 1969; MA, City Coll. NY, 1972. Prin. bassoonist Tafelmusik Baroque Orch., Toronto, Ontario, Canada, 1991—2001; prof. music Ind. U. Sch. Music, Bloomington, 2004—. Dir. early music inst. Ind. U. Sch. Music. Musician: more than 150 recordings. Hon. fellow, Acad. St. Cecilia, 2007. Mem.: Early Music America (bd. dirs. 2008—). Avocation: cooking. Office: Indiana Univ Sch Music 1201 E 3d St Bloomington IN 47405 Home: 824 W Fourth St Bloomington IN 47404 Business E-Mail: mmccraw@indiana.edu.

MCCRAY, DORIS RAINES, minister; b. Petersburg, Va., July 1, 1940; d. Linwood and Florence Raines; m. John McCray, Aug. 29, 1958; children: Ronald, Deborah Ramsey, Wayne, Donald. Student, Va. State U., 1980; BA, Richmond Va. Sem., 1986, MDiv, 1988. Notary pub. Va. Assoc. min. Met. Ch., Petersburg, Va., 1982—84, 1990—2000; assoc. pastor Good Shepherd Ch., 1985—86, asst. pastor, 1986—87, interim pastor, 1987—90; assoc. pastor Olive Br. Ch., Dinwiddle, 2000—. Counselor Southside Mental Health, Petersburg, 1984—90, Southside Area Family Counseling, 1984—90; chaplain Southside Regional Hosp., 1983—95. Sr. citizen mem. Sr. Adv. Com., Richmond, Va., 2002; ct. apptd. spl. advocate, 2001—; counselor Contact Tri-City Teleministry, 1978—87; mem. Am. Baptist Churches, 1983—91, Min. Coun., 1989, Petersburg Area Clergy, 1982—2004, pres., 1989; founder, advisor Cmty. Out-Reach Mighty Ministerial Advocacy, 2000—04. Mem.: AARP, Nat. Notary Assn., Nat. Women's History Mus. (charter mem.), U. Va. Alumni Assn. (assoc.). Democrat. Baptist. Avocations: reading, travel. Home: 1712 W Clara Dr Petersburg VA 23803 Office: Olive Br Ch 11119 Bovdton Plank Rd Dinwiddie VA 23841 Personal E-mail: preacherdot@hotmail.com, preachendozt@aol.com.

MCCRAY, NIKKI KESANGAME, women's college basketball coach, former professional basketball player; b. Collierville, Tenn., Dec. 17, 1971; BA in Sports Mktg. and Edn., U. Tenn., 1995. Basketball player USA Women's Nat. Team, 1996; guard Washington Mystics WNBA, 1998—2001, Ind. Fever WNBA, 2003, Phoenix Mercury WNBA, 2004, San Antonio Silver Stars WNBA, 2005, Chgo. Sky WNBA, 2006; asst. coach Western Ky. U. Hilltoppers, 2006—08, U. SC Gamecocks, 2008—. Recipient Gold Medalist, Atlanta Olympic Games, 1996, Sydney Olympic Games, 2000. Achievements include a park named in her honor in hometown of Colliersville, Tenn. Avocation: singing. Office: U SC c/o Dept Athletics Roost Bldg B 1322 Heyward St Columbia SC 29208

MC CRAY, RONALD DAVID, lawyer, apparel executive; b. Bronx, NY, July 2, 1957; s. Sylvester David and Vivian Marie (Bethea) McCray; m. Monica Ann Simon, Sept. 28, 1985; children: Morgan Marie, Adriane Michelle, Jordan Ellyse. BA, Cornell U., Ithaca, NY, 1979; JD, Harvard U., 1983. Bar: NY 1984, Tex. 1994. Assoc. Weil, Gotshal & Manges, NYC, 1983-85, Jones, Day, Reavis & Pogue, Dallas, 1985-87; sr. atty. Kimberly-Clark Corp., Dallas, 1987—93, sr. counsel, 1993—96, v.p., chief counsel, 1996—99, v.p., sec., 1999—2001, v.p., assoc. gen. counsel, sec., 2001—03, sr. v.p. law and govt. affairs, 2003—08, chief compliance officer, 2004—08; v.p., chief adminstrv. officer Nike Inc., Beaverton, Oreg., 2008—. Bd. dirs. Knight-Ridder Inc., 2003—. Editor: Pattern Discovery: Anti-Trust, 1982, Harvard CR/CL Law Rev., 1981-82. Trustee The Hockaday Sch., Dallas. Mem. ABA (wire payment systems subcommittee 1988—), NY Bar Assn., Tex. Bar Assn. (comml. code com. 1989-93), Dallas Bar Assn., Tex. Bus. Law Found. (bd. dirs. 1990-93), Nat. Assn. Securities Profls., Am. Corp. Counsel Assn., Coun. Fgn. Rels. Roman Catholic. Avocations: reading, sports, music. Office: Nike Inc 1 Bowerman Dr Beaverton OR 97005-6453

MCCREA, MARSHALL S., III, energy executive; Joined Energy Transfer Ptnrs., LP, Dallas, 1997, sr. v.p. bus. devel. and prodr. svcs., 1997, sr. v.p. comml. devel., 2004, pres. midstream ops., 2005—08, pres., COO, 2008—. Office: Energy Transfer Company 3738 Oak Lawn Ave Dallas TX 75219-4333 Office Phone: 214-981-0700. Office Fax: 214-981-0703.

MCCREADY, SAM, theater educator and director, actor; b. Belfast, No. Ireland, Nov. 22, 1936; s. David James and Sarah Elizabeth (Howlett) McC.; m. Joan Carslake, Mar. 16, 1962; children: Marcus Diarmuid Julian, Richard Alastair. MA, U. N. Wales, UK, 1976. Advt. mgr. Berkshire Internat., Ireland, 1961-63; head dept. theatre Orangefield Boys Sch., Belfast, Ireland, 1963-67, head English dept., 1967-69; lectr. U. North Wales, Bangor, England, 1969-78; artistic dir. Lyric Theatre, Belfast, Ireland, 1980-81; head dept. theatre Stranmillis Coll., Belfast, Ireland, 1978-83; assoc. prof. theatre U. Md., Catonsville, 1984-99, prof., 1999—2001; artistic dir. Shakespeare On Wheels, 1985-96. Examiner Guildhall Sch. Music and Drama, London, 1969—; trustee Lyric Theatre, Belfast, 1978-82; adjudicator Hong Kong Speech and Drama Festival, 1980, 84, 87, 93, 96, 2001, 04, 06, 08, 09; actor Tartuffe, Md. Stage Co., Ctr. Stage, Balt., 1997, 98, Serebriakov, Round House Theatre, Washington, 1997, Songs of Wandering Aengus, NYC, Sligo, Ireland, 1999, 2000, Krapp's Last Tape, Trinity Coll., Hartford, Conn., 1999, That Time, 2000, Early Memories, NY, 2001; The Great Yeats, 2002, Elizabeth the Queen, Folger Theatre, Washington, 2003; Heartbreak House, Roundhouse, DC, 2003, Table Seventeen, Crossroads Theatre Co., 2007, Purgatory, PWT, 2008; lectr. Yeats Internat. Summer Sch., Sligo, Ireland, 1998, 99, 2000, 2003-. Author: Theatre in the North of Ireland, 1969-99, 2000, Lucille Lortel: The Queen of Off-Broadway, 1993, Yeats Encyclopedia, 1997, Coole Lady, 2005, Baptism by Fire, 2007, New York State of Mind, 2007; adaptor, dir. play: Spring's Awakening, 1987 (Best Dir. award 1987), No Country for Old Men, 1985, Picture of Dorian Gray, 1988, Salome, 1989, The Tutor, 1992, The Widening Gyre, 1994, The Shadow of a Gunman, 1995, Diary of a Scoundrel, 1996 (Best Dir. award 1997), On the Verge, 1997, Deirdre, 1997, What the Butler Saw, 1998, Yerma, 2000, Macbeth, 2001, The Belfast Carmen, 2002, Death of Cuchulain, Sligo, 2003, Coole Lady (Irish tour), 2004, (off Broadway) Sword Against the Sea (Terre Haute and Irish tour), 2005, Two By Yeats, 2006, Philadelphia, Here I Come!, 2007, Three Irish Plays, 2008, A Time To Speak, 2008, contbr. articles to profl. jours. Named Outstanding Dir. Am. Coll. Theatre Festival, 1986, 87, 93, 97. Mem. Brit. Actors Equity, Am. Actors Equity, East Ctrl. Theatre Conf., Am. Conf. Irish Studies, Phi Kappa Phi. Episcopalian. Avocations: painting, music, photography, reading, gardening. Personal E-mail: akwadux@yahoo.com.

MCCREARY, FRANK E., III, retired lawyer; b. Santa Monica, Calif., Mar. 25, 1943; s. Frank Elijah and Irma (Holland) McC.; m. Jacqueline Moehlman, Feb. 15, 1969; children: Jennifer Claire, Frank Ward. BA, Cornell U., 1965; LLB with honors, U. Tex., 1968. Bar: Tex. 1968. Ptnr. Vinson & Elkins, Houston, 1970—2006. Trustee United Way Tex. Gulf Coast, Houston, 1988-90; bd. dir. Vol. Ctr., Houston, 1987-99. Capt. US Army, 1968-70, Vietnam. Mem. Nat. Assn. Bond Lawyers, Tex. Law Rev. Assn., Houston Bar Found. Office: Vinson & Elkins Ste 2500 First City Tower 1001 Fannin St Houston TX 77002-6760 Office Phone: 713-758-2440. Office Fax: 713-615-5256. E-mail: fmccreary@velaw.com.

MC CREARY, JAMES FRANKLIN, lawyer, mediator; b. Farmington, Mo., June 15, 1942; s. Frank J. and Bernice E. (Dugal) McCreary; m. Martha Jean Tucker, June 30, 1962; children: James Franklin, III, Jason Tucker, Josh Adam. BSBA, U. Evansville, 1964; JD, Nashville Law Sch., 1969; MBA, Vanderbilt U., 1980. Bar: Tenn. 1969, rule 31 listed mediator: Tenn. With Old Nat. Bank, Evansville, Ind., 1960-64; with First Am. Corp., Nashville, 1972-80, exec. v.p., corp. sec., gen. counsel, 1974-80; with First Am. Nat. Bank Nashville (N.A.), 1964-72, 80-86, exec. v.p., 1980-86; ptnr. Borod & Huggins Attys., Memphis, 1986-87, Gerrish McCreary Smith PC, Memphis, 1988, of counsel, 1988—92, dir., 1993—. Pres. Met. Fed. Bank, 1988-91; vis. prof. bus. law David Lipscomb U., 1975-77; instr. law and banking Am. Inst. Banking, 1969-75. Recipient Mid South Superlawyer award, 2006—09; named one of Best Lawyers in America, 2005—09. Mem. Am. Arbitration Assn., Beta Gamma Sigma Mem. Ch. of Christ. Office: Gerrish McCreary Smith PC 700 Colonial Rd Memphis TN 38117 E-mail: fmccreary@gerrish.com.

MCCREARY, PATRICK, theater educator, director; b. Kingston, Pa., Apr. 22, 1949; s. Thomas F. and Esther L. McCreary; m. Mary E. Koetje; children: Sara Zebrowski, Katherine. MFA, Rutgers U. Mason Gross Sch. Arts, NB, NJ, 1979. Lic. journeyman electrician Vt. Dept. labor and Industry, 1984, cert. vari lite technician Genlyte, 2008. Tech. dir. Livingston Coll. Theater Program, Piscataway, NJ, 1971—77; staff carpenter Mason Gross Sch. Arts, NB, 1977—79; faculty tech. dir., drama and dance Bennington Coll., Vt., 1979—83; faculty tech. dir. Ind. U. Pa., 1983—. Theater cons. New Freedom Theater, Phila., 1992—95. Cons. Ind. Players, 2000—08. Specialist Army Corps. Engrs., 1969—70, Stuttgart, Germany. Recipient Tech. Direction, Kennedy Ctr., Am. Coll. Theater Festival, 1984, 1987, 1993, 2006. Mem.: US Inst. Theatrical Tech. Office: Ind Univ Pa 401 S 11th St Indiana PA 15705

MCCREARY, ROBERT J., legislative staff member; White House appointee US Dept. Labor; dep. comm. dir., spokesman Pentagon Base Realignment Commn.; chief of staff to Rep. Doug Lamborn US House of Reps., Washington, 2007—. Served with USAF. Republican. Office: 437 Cannon House Office Bldg Washington DC 20515 Office Phone: 202-225-4422. Office Fax: 202-226-2638.*

MCCREDIE, JAMES ROBERT, fine arts educator; b. Chgo., Dec. 31, 1935; s. William and Mareta (Black) McC.; m. Marian Lucille Miles, Sept. 3, 1960; children: Miles William, Meredeth Black Winter. AB in History and Literature summa cum laude, Harvard U., 1958, AM, 1961, PhD, 1963; student, Am. Sch. Classical Studies, Athens, Greece, 1958-59, 61-62; LittD (hon.), U. Athens, 2004. Instr. NYU, 1963-64, asst. prof., 1965-66, assoc. prof., 1967-70, prof., 1970, 78-88, Sherman Fairchild prof. fine arts, 1988—2002, Sherman Fairchild prof. emeritus fine arts, 2002—, dep. dir. Inst. Fine Arts, 1967-69, acting dir., 1982-83, dir., 1983—2002, trustee, 2003—, asst. field dir. Excavations in Samothrace, 1962, field dir., 1963-65, dir. excavations, 1966—. Dir. Am. Sch. Classical Studies at Athens, Greece, 1969—77, chmn. mng. com., 1980—90, trustee, 1980—, pres., 2001—; vis. mem. Inst. Advanced Study, Princeton, NJ, 1977—78; mem. vis. com. dept. classical and Near Ea. archaeology Bryn Mawr Coll., 1982; mem. vis. com. dept. European paintings Met. Mus. Art, 1983—2003; mem. vis. com. Ctr. Old World Archaeology and Art Brown U., Providence, 1985; mem. adv. bd. Alexander S. Onassis Ctr. for Hellenic Studies NYU, 1990—97; cons. in field. Author: Fortified Military Camps in Attica, Hesperia, 1966, Samothrace, 7, The Rotunda of Arsinoe, 1992; mem. adv. bd. Am. Jour. Archaeology, 1969-81; contbr. articles to prof. jours. Bd. dirs. Hellenic-Am. Union, Athens, 1973-77, vice chmn., 1974-77, U.S. Ednl. Found., Greece, 1969-75; active Pres. Adv. Com. on Cultural Property, 1992-95. Charles Norton fellow, 1961-62; named hon. citizen Community of Samothrace, 1976. Mem. Am. Philos. Soc., Archaeol. Inst. Am. (life, trustee 1972-75, mem. exec. com. 1978-81), Archaeol. Soc. Athens (hon.), Deutsches archaeologisches Inst. (corr.). Home: 30 Battle Rd Princeton NJ 08540-4902 also: Palaiopolis GR-680 02 Samothrace Greece Office: NYU Inst Fine Arts 1 E 78th St New York NY 10021-0119 Business E-Mail: jrm1@nyu.edu.

MCCREE, PAUL WILLIAM, JR., systems design and engineering company executive; b. St. Louis, Oct. 27, 1926; s. Paul William and Hazel Elfrieda (Wilson) McC.; m. Carolyn Williams, Sept. 7, 1955; children: Brian, Paula, Ross. BS in Biochem. Scis., Harvard U., 1950. Mem. tech. staff System Devel. Corp., Santa Monica, Calif., 1956-62, Mitre Corp., Bedford, Mass., 1966-67; prin. engr. equipment divsn. Raytheon Co., Sudbury, Mass., 1963-66, 67-72; mem. tech. staff MIT Lincoln Labs., Lexington, Mass., 1972-76; mgr. Aerospace Systems divsn. Input Output, Waltham, Mass., 1976-79, tech. dir., 1979-80; mem. tech. staff Mitre Corp., Bedford, Mass., 1980-82; founder, pres. BPR Co., Profl. Cons. Svcs., 1981—. Sr. mem. tech. staff, mgr. subsystem design and devel. dept. GTE Strategic Systems Divsn., 1982-84; tech. dir. HH Aerospace and Design Co. Inc., Bedford, 1984-85; prin. engr., mem. tech. staff Raytheon equipment divsn. Software Sys. Lab., Sudbury, 1985-86; v.p. HH Aerospace and Design Co. Inc., Bedford, 1986-91. Mem. NAACP, Urban League. Served with U.S. Army, 1944. Recipient Black Achiever award, Greater Boston YMCA, 1977. Mem. AAAS, IEEE, Math. Assn. Am., Am. Math. Soc., N.Y. Acad. Scis., Harvard Inst. Learning in Retirement. Democrat. Home: 173 Goodman's Hill Rd PO Box 77 Sudbury MA 01776-0077 Office Phone: 978-440-9268. Personal E-mail: pmccree@att.net.

MCCREEDY, EDWIN JAMES, lawyer; b. Atlanta, Dec. 29, 1939; m. Linda Jandora, Mar. 20, 1965; children: James M., Matthew B. BA, Columbia Coll., 1961; JD, Fordham U., 1968. Bar: N.J. 1968, U.S. Supreme Ct. 1982, cert. civil trial atty. N.J. Supreme Ct. 1982. Ptnr. McCreedy & Cox, Cranford, NJ, 1984—. Pres. Richard J. Hughes Inn of Court, 1991-92; mem. civil practice com. Supreme Ct. N.J., 1985-96. Capt. USMC, 1961—65. Fellow ABA, Internat. Soc. Barristers, Internat. Acad. Trial Lawyers, Am. Coll. Trial Lawyers (chair state com, 1995-97); mem. N.J. State Bar Assn. (trustee 1997-2001, chmn. jud. adminstrn. com. 1994-96, treas. 2001, 1st v.p. 2002, pres. elect 2002-03, pres. 2004-05), Trial Attys. N.J. (trustee), Union County Bar Assn. (pres. 1987). Avocations: golf, travel. Office: McCreedy & Cox 6 Commerce Dr Ste 13 Cranford NJ 07016-3551 Home Phone: 732-946-2693; Office Phone: 908-709-0400. Personal E-mail: edjmccr@aol.com.

MCCREIGHT, LOUIS, retired materials scientist; b. Nov. 26, 1922; s. Ralph and Phronia (Benckendorf) McC.; m. Malvina Eloris Smith, Oct. 15, 1949; children: Brian R., Barbara L. BS in Ceramic Engring., U. Ill., 1946, MS, 1949. Rsch. asst., rsch. assoc. U. Chgo. and MIT Ceramic Group for Manhattan Project, 1944—45, U. Ill., Urbana, 1945-49; ceramic engr. Knolls Atomic Power Lab., Schenectady, NY, 1949-55; mgr. materials rsch. and devel. Gen. Electric Missiles and Space Divsn., Phila., 1955-81; dir. materials sci. lab. Aerospace Corp., El Segundo, Calif., 1981-84, sr. engr., engring. divsn., 1984-92, ret., 1992. Mem. rsch. adv. com. on materials NASA, Washington, 1959-69, chmn., 1965-67; mem. Nat. Materials Adv. Bd., NRC, 1966-70. Co-author: Ceramic and Graphite Fibers and Whiskers, 1965, 2d edit., 1968; contbr. articles to profl. jours.; patentee in field. Pres. Chester County coun. Boy Scouts Am., 1979-81; v.p. Upper Main Line YMCA, 1973-81. Fellow Am. Ceramic Soc. (officer); mem. ASTM (rsch. com. 1963-70), Materials Rsch. Soc. Republican. Presbyterian. Home: 101 Cresta Verde Dr Rolling Hills Estates CA 90274-5477

MCCRERY, JIM (JAMES OTIS MCCRERY), lobbyist, former United States Representative from Louisiana; b. Shreveport, La., Sept. 18, 1949; m. Johnette Hawkins, Aug. 3, 1991; children: Claiborne Scott, Otis Clark. BA in English & History, La. Tech. U., 1971; JD, La. State U., 1975. Bar: La. 1975. Pvt. practice, Leesville, La., 1975-78; asst. city atty. City of Shreveport, 1979-80; staff mem. to Rep. Buddy Roemer US Congress, 1981-84; regional mgr. Ga.-Pacific Corp., 1984-88; mem. US Congress from 4th La. dist., 1988—93, 1997—2009, US Congress from 5th La. dist., 1993-97. US House Ways & Means Com., 1993—2008, ranking mem., 2007—08; ptnr. Capitol Counsel LLC, Washington, 2009—. Vice chmn. Nat. Republican Congressional Com. (NRCC), 1998—2004. Republican. Methodist. Office: Capitol Counsel LLC 900 19th St Ste 800 Washington DC 20006 Office Phone: 202-861-3200. Office Fax: 202-861-3219.

MCCRIE, ROBERT DELBERT, prison reformer, editor, educator; b. Sarnia, Ont., Can., Oct. 8, 1938; s. Robert Newton and Evelyn May (Johnston) McC.; m. Fulvia Madia, Dec. 22, 1965; children: Carla Alexandra McAuley, Mara Elizabeth Kellan. BA, Ohio Wesleyan U., 1960; MS, U. Toledo, 1964; postgrad., U. Chgo., 1962-63; MA, Hunter Coll., 1994; MPhil, CUNY, 1994, PhD, 1995. Cert. protection profl. Rschr. Connective Tissues Rsch. Lab., Copenhagen, 1963; copywriter numerous advt. agys., 1965-70; owner, editor Security Letter, NYC, 1970—; editor, pub. HBJ Publs., NYC, 1973-76; pres. Mags. for Medicine, Inc., NYC, 1972-81. Faculty John Jay Coll. Criminal Justice, 1985—, adj. to full prof., chair Law, Police Sci. and Criminal Justice Adminstrn., 1997—2003, Protection Mgmt., 2008-; cons. in field; spkr. at numerous meetings. Author: Security Operations Management, 2001, rev. edit., 2007, Readings in Security Management, 2002; editor: Security Letter Source Book, 1983—, Behavioral Medicine, 1978—81, Security Jour., 1989—98; contbr. books and articles on security and urban crime and policing; editor: Security Letter, 1970—. Recipient Eugene Fink award, Associated Lic. Detectives NY State, 2008. Mem.: AAUP, Am. Soc. Criminology, Am. Correctional Assn., Acad. Criminal Justice Sci., Accolade, Internat. Assn. Profl. Security Cons. Disting. Svc., Internat. Security Mgmt. Assn. (Brennan award 1993), Nat. Coun. Investigation and Security Svcs. (Duffy Meml. Achievement award 1992), ASIS Internat. (pres.'s cert. of merit 1990), Correctional Edn. Assn., Urban History Assn. (life), Union League Club, Pi Delta Epsilon, Delta Sigma Rho, Alpha Tau Omega. Presbyterian. Home: 49 E 96th St New York NY 10128-0782 Office: 166 E 96th St New York NY 10128-2565 also: John Jay Coll Criminal Justice 899 10th Ave New York NY 10019-1069 Office Phone: 212-237-8386. Personal E-mail: rmccrie@verizon.net. Business E-Mail: rmccrie@jjay.cuny.edu.

MCCRIGHT, PAUL R., engineer, educator; b. Texarkana, Ark., Sept. 16, 1949; s. Ray and Marguerite (Ross) McC. BS in Indsl. Engring., Tex. Tech. U., 1971; MS in Engring., Ariz. State U., 1973; PhD, Stanford U., 1987. Safety engr. U.S. AEC, Golden, Colo., 1973-76; weapons engr. U.S. Energy R & D Adminstrn., Albuquerque, 1976-78; contract adminstr., then energy mgmt. specialist U.S. Dept. Energy, Las Vegas, Nev., 1978-80; grad. rsch. asst. Stanford (Calif.) U., 1980-81, 83-87; sr. facility planning engr. Salt River Project, Tempe, Ariz., 1981-83; exec. v.p., ptnr. Solutions for Mgmt., Mountain View, Calif., 1985-87; asst. prof. engring. Kans. State U., Manhattan, 1987—. Cons. Solutions for Mgmt., 1985-87, Farm Bur. Kans., Manhattan, 1990, Am. Inst. Banking, Manhattan, 1992. Mem. Inst. Indsl. Engrs., Soc. Engring. Mgmt. Systems (bd. dirs. 1992), Am. Soc. Engring. Mgmt., Am. Soc. Engring. Educators, Human Factors Soc., Phi Kappa Phi, Alpha Pi Mu. Office: Kans State Univ Dept Indsl Engring Manhattan KS 66506

MCCRIMMON, BARBARA SMITH, writer, librarian; b. Anoka, Minn., May 3, 1918; d. Webster Roy and Jessie (Sargeant) Smith; m. James McNab McCrimmon, June 10, 1939; Children: Kevin Mor, John Marshall. BA, U. Minn., Mpls., 1939; MSL.S., U. Ill., Champaign-Urbana, 1961; PhD, Fla. State U., Tallahassee, 1973. Asst. librarian Ill. State Nat. Hist. Survey, Champaign, Ill., 1961-62; research assoc. Bur. Community Planning, U. Ill., Champaign, 1962-63; librarian Ill. Water Survey, Champaign, 1964-65, Am. Meterol. Soc., Boston, 1965-67; edit. asst. Jour. Library History, Tallahassee, 1967-69, 73-74. Adj. asst. prof. Sch. Library Sci., Fla. State U., Tallahassee, 1976-77. Author: Power, Politics and Print, 1981, Richard Garnett: The Scholar as Librarian, 1989; editor: American Library Philosophy, 1975; contbr. articles to profl. jours. Mem. ALA, Pvt. Libraries Assn., Beta Phi Mu, Manuscript Soc. Democrat. Home: The Colonnades C30 2600 Barracks Rd Charlottesville VA 22901 Home Phone: 434-244-0636.

MCCRIMMON, MILES, educator; b. San Antonio, Sept. 2, 1963; s. Joseph Paxton and Mary Rennie McCrimmon; m. Catherine Ingrassia, June 22, 1990; children: Sophia, Paul. BA, Tex. A & M, Coll. Sta., 1985; MA, La. State.U., Baton Rouge, 1987; PhD, U. Tex., Austin, 1992. Prof. J. Sargeant Reynolds CC, Richmond, Va., 1992—. Home: 9244 Old Ivy Trace Mechanicsville VA 23116 Office: J Sargeant Reynolds CC PO Box 85622 Richmond VA 23285-5622 Business E-Mail: mmccrimmon@reynolds.edu.

MCCRODDEN, BRUCE A., bank executive; B in Engring., U. Del., Newark, 1969. With pub. and govt. sectors and various bus. lines BP, Cleve., NYC, London and Washington; with Nat. City Corp., Cleve., 1999—, sr. v.p. corp. pub. affairs. Bd. dirs. ARC, Ctr. for Families and Children, Ohio C. of C. Office: Nat City Corp Nat City Ctr 1900 E Ninth St Cleveland OH 44114-3484 Office Phone: 216-222-2000.

MCCRONE, ALISTAIR WILLIAM, retired academic administrator; b. Regina, Can., Oct. 7, 1931; BA, U. Sask., 1953; MSc, U. Nebr., 1955; PhD, U. Kans., 1961. Instr. geology NYU, 1959-61, asst. prof., 1961-64, assoc. prof., 1964-69, prof., 1969-70, supr. Rsch. Ship Sea Owl on L.I. Sound, 1959-64, asst. dir. univ. program at Sterling Forest, 1965-66, resident master Rubin Internat. Residence Hall, 1966-69, chmn. dept. geology, 1966-69, assoc. dean Grad. Sch. Arts and Scis., 1969-70; prof. geology, acad. v.p. U. Pacific, 1970-74, acting pres., 1971; prof. geology, pres. Calif. State U. Sys. Humboldt State U., Arcata, 1974—2002. Exec. coun. Calif. State U. Sys., 1974-2002, acad. senate Humboldt State U., 1974-2002, chancellor's com. on innovative programs, 1974-76, trustees' task force on off-campus instrn., 1975-76, exec. com. Chancellor's Coun. of Pres., 1976-79, Calif. state del. Am. Assn. State Coll. and Univ., 1977-80; mem. Commn. on Ednl. Telecomm., 1983-86; chair Calif. State U. Statewide Task Force on Earthquake and Emergency preparedness, 1985-88, 95-97; chmn., accreditation teams Western Assn. Sch. and Coll.; chair com. on energy and environ. Am. Assn. State Coll. and Univ., 1980-84; chair program com. Western Coll. Assn., 1983-84, panelist, 1983. Contbr. articles to profl. jour.; lectr. on geology Sunrise Semester program CBS Nat. Network, 1969-70; various appearances on local TV stas. Bd. trustees Presbyn. Hosp.-Pacific Med. Ctr., San Francisco, 1971-74; mem. Calif. Coun. for Humanities, 1977-82; mem. local campaign bd. United Way, 1977-83; mem. Am. Friends Wilton Park, 1980—; bd. dirs. Humboldt Convention and Visitors Bur., 1980-87, Redwood Empire Assn., 1983-87; bd. dirs. Calif. State Automobile Assn., 1988-2007, Am. Automobile Assn., 1990-93; bd. trustees Calif. State Parks Found., 1994-2000. Recipient Erasmus Haworth Disting. Alumnus award U. Kans., 2000; Shell fellow in geology U. Nebr., 1954-55; Danforth assoc. NYU, 1964. Fellow Calif. Acad. Sci.; mem. AAAS, Geol. Soc. Am., Am. Assn. U. Adminstrs. (nat. bd. 1986-89, 96-99, 2001-2002), Assn. Am. Coll. (bd. dir. 1989-92, chair 1991), St. Andrews Soc. NY (life), Rotary, Sigma Xi (pres. NYU chpt. 1967-69), Phi Kappa Phi. Avocation: golf. Office: Humboldt State U Univ Campus Arcata CA 95521 Office Phone: 707-826-5074. Business E-Mail: mccrone@humboldt.edu.

MCCRORY, JOHN BROOKS, retired lawyer; b. St. Cloud, Minn., Oct. 23, 1925; s. John Raymond and Mary Lee (Rutter) McC.; m. Margaret Joan Dickson, Sept. 4, 1954 (dec. Apr. 1957); 1 child, William B.; m. Elizabeth Ann Quick, June 27, 1959; children: John B., Ann Elizabeth. BA, Swarthmore Coll., Pa., 1948; JD, U. Pa., Phila., 1951. Bar: N.Y. 1952, D.C. 1985. Assoc. Donovan, Leisure, Newton, Lumbard & Irvine, NYC, 1951-52, Nixon, Hargrave, Devans & Doyle, Rochester, NY, 1952-62, ptnr., 1963-92; ret., 1992. Author: Constitutional Privilege in Libel Law, 1977-90. Served to lt. comdr. USNR, 1943—47, PTO. Fellow Am. Coll. Trial Lawyers; mem. ABA, Monroe County Bar Assn., N.Y. State Bar Assn., D.C. Bar Assn. Democrat. Mem. Soc. Of Friends. Address: 25 Kendal Dr Kennett Square PA 19348-2321 Office: Nixon Peabody LLP Clinton Sq PO Box 31051 Rochester NY 14603-1051 Office Phone: 585-263-1000.

MCCRORY, PATRICK, Mayor, Charlotte, North Carolina; b. Columbus, Oct. 17, 1956; m. Ann Gordon McCrory. BA in Polit. Sci. and Edn., Catawba Coll., 1978, doctorate (hon.), 2001. With Duke Energy Corp., NC, 1978; at-large rep. Charlotte City Coun., NC, 1989—95; mayor protem City of Charlotte, 1993-95, mayor, 1995—. Co-chmn. Charlotte's Fighting Back Commn.; mem. Children Svcs. Network; hon. chmn. Cystic Fibrosis Found., Arthritis Found.; former chmn. United Way Corp. Campaign; former mem. U. NC-Charlotte Bus. Adv. Com., Charlotte Bond Campaign, ARC Pers. Recruitment Com.; HS basketball ofcl.; former bd. dirs. Drug Free Workplace Alliance Com.; founder Uptown Crime Prevention Coun., Mayor's Mentoring Alliance, 1995; leader Homeland Security; mem. adv. coun. President's Homeland Security; pres. Republican Mayors and Local Ofcls.; bd. dir. US Conf. of Mayors, chair, Hosing and Cmty. Develop. Com.; chair NC Metropolitan Coalition; hon. chair Charlotte chpts., Alzheimer Found., Cystic Fibrosis Found., Arthritis Found. Recipient Governor's Outstanding Local Ofcl. award, 2001. Mem.: Mayor's Mentoring Alliance (founder 1995), Republican Mayors and Local Ofcls. Orgn. (pres.), U.S. Conf. Mayors. Office: Office of the Mayor Govt Ctr 600 E 4th St Charlotte NC 28202-2816 Business E-Mail: mayor@ci.charlotte.nc.us.*

MCCRYSTAL, ANN MARIE, community health nurse, administrator; b. Jersey City, Jan. 5, 1937; d. Robert W. and Sybilla M. (Koenig) Bouse; m. Hugh K. McCrystal, Sept. 14, 1963; children: Carolyn, Hugh K., Kelly Ann. BSN, U. Miami, 1959. Office mgr., sec.-treas. Indian River Urology Assocs., P.C., Vero Beach, Fla.; chmn. bd. Vis. Nurse Assn. of the Treasure Coast, Vero Beach. Chmn. Vis. Nurse Assn. Treasure Coast Found., 1991, adv. coun. Vis. Nurse Assn. of Am., 1994; chmn. bd. dirs. Vis. Nurse Assn./Hospice Found. Named Indian River County Woman of Distinction, Girl Scouts Am., 1998, Vol. Fundraiser of Yr., Treasure Coast Nat. Soc. Fundraising Execs., 1999, Book of Golden Deeds award Exch. Club Vero Beach, 2000; recipient C. of C. Cmty. Svc. award, 2000, Nat. award for Cmty. Svc., Nat. Soc. Colonial Dames VXII Cadbury, 2005. Mem. Fla. Nurses Assn. (Dist. 17 Nurse of Yr. 2004), Am. Urol. Assn. Allied, Am. Cancer Soc. (life hon.), Vis. Nurse Assn. Am. (chmn. bd. dirs. 1995—, adv. coun., edn. com., Vol. of Yr. 1991), Sigma Theta Tau. Home: 511 Bay Dr Vero Beach FL 32963-2163 Office Phone: 772-567-5551. Personal E-mail: ammccrystal@yahoo.com.

MCCRYSTAL, JENNIFER CROSS, elementary school educator; b. Sarasota, Fla., Dec. 11, 1970; d. J. Walter and Frances Marie Cross; m. Michael John McCrystal, Mar. 12, 1994; children: Mary Kathryn, Benjamin Thomas. BS, Fla. So. Coll., Lakeland, 1992; M in Ednl. Leadership, U. South Fla., Tampa, 2006. Cert. profl. educator Fla., 2004. Asst. prin. elem. instr., tchr. Buckhorn Elem. Sch., Valrico, Fla. Author: (character edn. program) Captain Character (What's Right with Tampa Bay, 1999), The Friendship Company (Drum Maj. in Edn. Award Nominee, 1999); contbr. chapters to books. Coord. donations The Friendship Co., Valrico, 1998—2006; vol. First United Meth. Music Ministry, Brandon, Fla., 1995—2009, First United Meth. Student Ministry, Brandon, 1998—2009; sec. United Meth. Women/Daughters of the Son, Brandon, 1999—2009. Named Tchr. of Yr., Valrico Elem. Sch., 2006—07; finalist, Hillsborough Sch. Dist., 2006—07. Mem.: Hillsborough County Coun. Internat. Reading Assn., Literacy Coaches Assn. Fla. Methodist. Avocations: reading, travel, cooking. Office: Buckhorn Elem Sch 2420 Buckhorn Sch Ct Valrico FL 33594

MCCUAN, WILLIAM PATRICK, philanthropist, real estate company executive; b. Muskogee, Okla., Oct. 28, 1941; s. Lee L. and LaRee A. (Beverage) McC.; m. Jill Pamela Thomas, May 5, 1982; children: LaRee, Megan. Student, U. Tulsa, 1961—62; BA Psychology, Baylor U., 1965; MRE, So. Sem., Louisville, 1967; MS, U. Louisville, 1969; postgrad., U. Md., 1971—73; AA (hon.), Howard Cmty. Coll., Columbia, Md., 2008. Employment prof., asst. dean grad. sch. U. Md., Balt., 1969—73; lobbyist and cons. Washington, 1973—76; CEO KMS Group, Inc., Columbia, Md., 1976—84, MDG Cos. Md., 1984—, MDG-Capital Corp., Naples, Fla., 1992—, MDG Cos. W.Va., 1991—, McCuan Family Found., 1997—, McCuan Farms, LLC, 2005—. Adj. prof. Cmty. Coll., Balt., 1969-72, U. Md. College Park, 1969-71; lectr. Univ. Coll.-U. Md., Balt., 1970-71, Howard C.C., Columbia, 1987-88; CEO Pet Holiday, Inc., Toledo, 1973-94; CEO Uniglobe Columbia Travel Ctr. Cmty. & Profl., 1986-94; non-lawyer mem. Md. Atty.

Grievance Commn., 1990-96. Contbr. articles to numerous publs. Chmn., bd. dir. Concert Soc. Md., 1988-98; chmn. United Way, Howard County, Md., 1984, Am. Presdl. Inaugural Com., Md., 1988, 2004, Howard County Cmty. Partnerships, 2004; fin. chmn. Rep. Ctrl. Com., Howard County, 1988-92; trustee Columbia Found., 1980-82; mem. Pres.'s Commn. on Food, Nutrition and Health, Washington, 1970, Howard County Environ. Affairs Bd.; mem. bus. adv. coun. Howard C.C.; bd. dir. Congl. Commn. on Mental Health of Children, Washington, 1973-75, Human Svcs. Inst. Children and Families; pres., 1973-75, chmn. & trustee McCuan Family Found., 1997—, Nat. Rep. Com. Eagles, Team 100, 2002-08; bd. govs. St. Margaret's Sch., 2003-07/ Recipient Alumni Fellows award, U. Louisville, 1996; named Nation's Top Philanthropist, Coun. Resource Devel., 2007. Mem. Nat. Assn. Home Builders (bd. dir. 1979-87, fed. govt. affairs com.), Md. Builders Assn. (pres. 1981-82), Home Builders Assn. Md. (bd. dir. 1977-82, Award of Honor 1979, Award of Excellence 1980, Presdl. award 1982), Howard County Home Builders Assn. (pres. 1978-80), Howard County C. of C. (pres. bd. dir. 1984-86), BB&T Bank Corp. (regional bd. mem. 2008-). Home: 4256 Snowberry Ln Naples FL 34119-8513 Office: MDG Corp Ctr I Ste 400 8850 Columbia 100 Pky Columbia MD 21045 Office Phone: 410-730-9091. Personal E-mail: pmccuan@aol.com. Business E-Mail: pmccuan@mdgcompanies.com.

MCCUE, DAVID J., information systems specialist, entrepreneur; b. Phila., Mar. 28, 1956; s. Earl E. and A. Kathleen McCue; m. Nicole E. Schumacher, Aug. 16, 1981; 1 child, Christopher D. BSc, Rider U., 1978; MBA, NYU, 1980. Cons. Human Sys. Inc., New Vernon, NJ, 1980-81; from cons. to regional dir. tech. Andersen Consulting, NJ, 1981-93; chief info. and resource officer Am. Practice Mgmt., Inc., NYC, 1993-96; chief info. officer Computer Scis. Corp., NYC, 1996-2001; corp. dir. global applications Computer Scis. Corp. Worldwide, NYC, 2001—03; v.p. applications portfolio mgmt. Computer Scis. Corp., Falls Church, Va., 2003—06, chief info. officer, 2006—. Mem. adv. bd. Coll. Edn., Rider U., Lawrenceville, N.J., 1997-99. Mgr. Somerset County 4-H Fair, 1998—99; mem. Air Safety Found.; bd. dirs. Rider U. Alumni Assn., 1984—. Mem. Inst. Mgmt. Cons. (cert.), Assn. MBA Execs., Am. Prodn. and Inventory Control Soc. (cert. prodn. and inventory mgr.). Am. Soc. Indsl. Security, Aircraft Owners and Pilots Assn., Exptl. Aircraft Assn., NRA, NRCC (bus. adv. coun.). Republican. Roman Catholic. Avocations: aviation, horseback riding. Home: PO Box 909 21580 Lower Woodchuck Rd Florence MT 59833-0909 Office: CSC Corp Office VTC-C 630 MC 320 3170 Fairview Park Dr Falls Church VA 22042 Office Phone: 706-641-3076. Business E-Mail: djmccue@mccue.org.

MCCUE, JUDITH W., lawyer; b. Phila., Apr. 7, 1948; d. Emanuel Leo and Rebecca (Raffel) Weiss; m. Howard M. McCue III, Apr. 3, 1971; children: Howard, Leigh. BA cum laude, U. Pa., Phila., 1969; JD, Harvard U., Cambridge, Mass., 1972. Bar: Ill. 1972, U.S. Tax Ct. 1984. Ptnr. McDermott Will & Emery LLP, Chgo., 1995—. Dir. Schawk, Inc., Des Plaines, Ill.; past pres. Chgo. Estate Planning Coun. Trustee Chgo. Symphony Orch., 1995—, vice chmn., 1998—2001, 2005—. Mem.: Chgo. Bar Assn. (chmn. probate practice com. 1984—85, chmn. estate and gift tax divsn. of fed. tax com. 1988—89), Am. Coll. Trust and Estate Counsel (com. chmn. 1991—94, regent 1993—2000, com. chmn. 1998—2001, pres. 2005—06). Office: McDermott Will & Emery LLP 227 W Monroe St Ste 3100 Chicago IL 60606-5096 Business E-Mail: jmccue@mwe.com.

MCCUE, SUSAN M., communications executive; b. NJ, 1965; BS in Economics & Journalism, Rutgers U., New Brunswick, 1987. Chief of staff to Senator Harry Reid US Senate, 1998—2006; founding pres, CEO ONE, 2006—; founder, pres. Message Global LLC, 2008—. Trustee Third Way; lead cons. Rock and Roll Forever Found., 2008—; bd. dirs. Global Action for Children, 2009—. Creator: (TV series) Staffers, 2004. Named one of The 100 Most Powerful Women in Washington, Washingtonian mag., 2006, The 50 Most Powerful People in DC, GQ mag., 2007. Democrat. Office: ONE Ste 601 1400 Eye St NW Washington DC 20005*

MCCUEN, JOHN JOACHIM, columnist, educator, US military counterinsurgery and hybrid war consultant; b. Washington, Mar. 30, 1926; s. Joseph Raymond and Josephine (Joachim) McCuen; m. Gloria Joyce Seidel, June 16, 1949; children: John Joachim Jr., Les Seidel. BS, U.S. Mil. Acad., 1948; M of Internat. Affairs, Columbia U., 1961; grad., U.S. Army War Coll., 1968. Commd. 2d. lt. US Army, 1948, advanced through grades to col., 1969; dir. internal def. and devel. US Army War Coll., Carlisle Barracks, Pa., 1969—72; chief US Def. Liaison Group, Jakarta, Indonesia, 1972—74; chief field survey office US Army Tng. and Doctrine Command, Ft. Monroe, Va., 1974—76; ret. US Army, 1976; cons. to US Govt. on nuclear security, 1976—77; mgr. tng. Chrysler Def., Center Line, Mich., 1977—82; mgr. modification ctr. Land Sys. divsn. Gen. Dynamics, Sterling Heights, Mich., 1982—83, mgr. field ops. Warren, Mich., 1983—94; pres. Mich. Econ. Devel. Corp., Birmingham, Mich., 1994—, The Magic Christmas Tree, Inc., Birmingham, 1994—; pres., CEO Laminar, Inc., Southfield, Mich., 1996—; owner Adventure and Exotic Travel Outfitters, Inc., Birmingham, 1995—; past pres. First Internat. Corp., Birmingham, 1995—97; chmn., CEO Multi-Nat. Tooling LLC, Birmingham, 2005—; cons. US Mil. Counterinsurgency Ops. & Hybrid War, 2006—. Ptnr. East West Connection, Birmingham; past pres. Energy Resource Mgmt. Sys., Inc., Birmingham; armor advisor 3d Royal Thai Army, 1957—58; gen. staff Dept. of Army, Washington, 1961—64; chief tng. US Army Europe, Heidelberg, Germany, 1964—66; US rep. users' com. NATO Missile Firing Installation Crete, Paris, 1964—66; squadron comdr. 8th Cavalry, Manheim, Germany, 1966—67; advisor Vietnamese Nat. Def. Coll., Saigon, 1968—69; spkr., writer terrorism, counterinsurgency & hybrid war; lectr. in field. Author: The Art of Counter Revolutionary War-The Strategy of Counter Insurgency, Faber, 1966, Stackpole, 1967, Circulo Militar, 1967, Hailer, 2005 (Book now designated by Army and Marines as a "classic" on counterinsurgency); columnist: Army Times, 2002—. Bd. dirs. Troy and Mt. Clemens Cmty. Concert Assn., Mich., 1982—2006, pres., 1985—2006; past pres. Mich. Oriental Art Soc., Birmingham; pres. Grander View Found. Sr. Housing and Nursing, Milford, Mich., 1984—89; past chmn. region VI NE unit Detroit United Way Campaign; 1st reader First Ch. of Christ Scientist, Birmingham, 1989—92, chmn. bd. dirs., 2000—01. Mem., dept. def. & state consortium complex ops., mem. Warlord Loop US Army. Mem.: Nat. Mgmt. Assn., Soc. Logistics Engrs., Oriental Art Soc., Assn. U.S. Army. Republican. Avocations: oriental antiques, writing. Home: 1530 Northlawn Blvd Birmingham MI 48009 Office: Consultancy Counterinsurgency & Hybrid War 1530 Northlawn Blvd Birmingham MI 48009 Home Phone: 248-644-7426; Office Phone: 248-644-3485. Personal E-mail: jjmccuen@aol.com.

MCCUEN, MAUREEN E., history educator; b. Fairfax, Va., July 24, 1972; d. John M. and Mary Anne McGovern; m. Jeffrey P. McCuen, Apr. 25, 1998; children: Elizabeth K., Patrick R. BA, James Madison U., Harrisonburg, Va., 1989—93. Cert. Secondary Composite Social Studies Tchr. Tex. Bd. Edn., 1998. Social studies tchr. Potomac Sr. HS, Prince William County Pub. Schs., Dumfries, Va., 1995—98, Travis Jr. HS, Paris Ind. Sch. Dist., Tex., 1998—2002; AP/honors. US history tchr. Paris HS, Paris Ind. Sch. Dist., 2002—08; global studies I tchr. Carolina HS and Acad., 2008—. Acad. decathlon coach Paris HS, 2003—05, future problem solving coach, 2006—07. Mem.: Nat. Coun. Social Studies, Assn. Supervision and Curriculum Devel. Avocations: camping, running, violin, theater. Home: 10 Groveview Trl Mauldin SC 29662-3023 Office: Carolina HS and Acad 2725 AnderRd Greenville SC 29611 Business E-Mail: mmccuen@greenville.k12.sc.us.

MCCUISTION, PEG OREM, retired health facility administrator; b. Houston, July 28, 1930; d. William Darby and Dorothy Mildred (Beckett) Orem; m. Palmer Day McCuistion, Sept. 4, 1949 (div. 1960); 1 child, Leeanne E. BBA, Southwest Tex. State, 1963; MBA, George Washington U., 1968; EdD, Wayne State U., 1989. Patient care adminstr. Holy Cross Hosp., Silver Spring, Md., 1968-79; exec. dir. Hospice of S.E. Mich., Southfield, 1979-86, Hospice Austin, Tex., 1987-94; CEO EMBI, Inc., Arlington, Tex., 1994—98; gen. mgr. Hospice Home Care, San Antonio, 2001—04, ret., 2004. Bd. dirs. Cmty. Home for the Elderly, Austin, 1989-92. Fellow Am. Coll. Health Care Execs. (membership com.); mem. Internat. Hospice Inst. (assoc.), Nat. Hospice Orgn. (chair standards and accreditation com.), Tex. Hospice Orgn. (pres. 1993-94), exec. com., standards and ethics com., edn. com., chair legis. com.), Mich. Hospice Orgn. (chair edn. com., bd. dirs.). Personal E-mail: pegomc@txwinet.com.

MCCUISTION, ROBERT WILEY, hospital administrator, management consultant, lawyer; b. Wilson, Ark., June 15, 1927; s. Ed Talmadge and Ruth Wiley (Bassett) McC.; m. Martha Virginia Golden, June 11, 1949 (dec. Nov. 1991); children: Beth, Dan, Jed.; m. Sudola M. Getz, Feb. 12, 1994. AB in History, Hendrix Coll., Conway, Ark., 1949; JD, U. Ark., 1952. Bar: Ark. 1952, U.S. Dist. Ct. (we. dist.) Ark. 1953. Practice in, Dermott, Ark., 1952-57; dep. pros. atty. 10th Jud. Dist. Ark., 1952-57; bus. mgr. St. Mary's Hosp., Dermott, 1953-56, asst. adminstr., 1956-57; adminstr. Stuttgart (Ark.) Meml. Hosp., 1957-60, Forrest Meml. Hosp., Forrest City, Ark., 1960-68; assoc. adminstr. St. Edward Mercy Hosp., Ft. Smith, Ark., 1968-70; pres. Meml. Med Center, Corpus Christi, Tex., 1970-79; adminstr. Methodist Hosp., Mitchell, SD, 1979-85, cons., 1985-86; mgmt. cons., owner Creative Leadership Concepts, Arlington, Tex., 1985—; adminstr. Cen. United Meth. Ch., Fayetteville, 1986-91. Sec. Ark. Hosp. Adminstrs. Forum, 1958-59, pres., 1959-60; pres. Ark. Hosp. Assn., 1964-65, Areawide Health Planning, 1970; pres. Ark. Conf. Cath. Hosps., 1970; chmn. Twin City Hosp. Coun. West Ark., 1968; v.p. Ark. Assn. Mental Health, 1966-70. Feature writer, make up editor, editor Wiesbaden Post, Germany, 1946—47; editor: Air Force Publ. Div. chmn. Forrest City United Cmty. Svcs., 1961, Corpus Christi United Way Cmty. Svcs., 1972, DeSoto coun. Boy Scouts Am., Explorer advisor, 1954-57; vice-chmn., sec. ofcl. bd. Meth. Ch., 1957, lay del. S.D. ann. conf., 1980-85, cert. lay spkr., 1960—; trustee Midwest Hosp. Conf., Kansas City, Mo., 1964-1966. With USAAF, World War II. Recipient Eminent Leadership award DeSoto Area council Boy Scouts Am., 1956 Mem. Am. Assn. Hosp. Accts. (pres. Ark. chpt. 1957), S.D. Hosp. Assn. (dist. chmn. 1980-81), Am. Coll. Health Execs. (life), Rotary (pres. Forrest City 1964-65, Internat. Order of St. Luke (grief counselor, Stephen min.). Home and Office: 2401 St Gregory St Arlington TX 76013 Home Phone: 817-275-8378. Personal E-mail: sudobobm@tx.rr.net.

MCCULLAGH, GRANT GIBSON, retired architect; b. Cleve., Apr. 18, 1951; s. Robert Ernest and Barbara Louise (Grant) McC.; m. Suzanne Dewar Folds, Sept. 13, 1975; children: Charles Weston Folds, Grant Gibson Jr. BArch, U. Ill., 1973; MArch, U. Pa., 1975; MBA, U. Chgo., 1979. Registered architect, Ill. Dir. mktg. The Austin Co., Chgo., 1977-83, asst. dist. mgr., 1983-84, dist. mgr., 1984-88, v.p., 1987-88; chmn., CEO McClier Corp., Chgo., 1988—98; chmn. Holmes & Narver, Orange, Calif., 1997-2001; exec. v.p. AECOM, LA, 2000—03, vice chmn., 2003—04; chmn., CEO Global Integrated Bus. Solutions, Inc., 2004—; CEO The Facility Group, 2006—07. Contbr. articles to various indsl. publs. Trustee Newberry Libr., Brookfield Zoo/Chgo. Zool. Soc., 2004—, Chgo. Pub. Libr. Found.; council trustee Nat. Trust for Historic Preservation. Fellow: AIA; mem.: Design/Build Inst. Am., Calif. Club, Comml. Club, Indian Hill Country Club, Univ. Club, Casino Club, Chgo. Club, Econ. Club. Republican. Episcopalian. Home: 43 Locust Rd Winnetka IL 60093-3725 Office: 181 W Madison St Ste 3900 Chicago IL 60602 E-mail: grant.mccullagh@gibscorp.com.

MC CULLOCH, ERNEST ARMSTRONG, internist, educator; b. Toronto, Ont., Can., Apr. 27, 1926; s. Albert E. and Letitia (Riddell) McC.; m. Ona Mary Morganty, 1953; children: James A., Michael E., Robert E., Cecelia E., Paul A. MD with honors, U. Toronto, 1948, DSc (hon.), 2004. Intern Toronto Gen. Hosp., 1949-50, sr. intern, 1951-52; NRC fellow dept. pathology U. Toronto, 1950-51; asst. resident Sunnybrook Hosp., Toronto, 1952-53; pvt. practice specializing in internal medicine Toronto, 1954-67; clin. tchr. dept. medicine U. Toronto, Toronto, 1954-60, asst. prof. dept. med. biophysics, 1959-64, assoc. prof., 1964-66, prof., 1966, asst. prof. dept. medicine, 1967-68, assoc. prof., 1968-70, prof., 1970—, Univ. prof., 1982-91, Univ. prof. emeritus, 1991—; mem. grad. faculty U. Toronto (Inst. Med. Sci.), 1968—, dir., 1975-79; asst. dean Sch. Grad. Studies U. Toronto, 1979-82. Physician Toronto Gen. Hosp., 1960-67; sr. scientist, sr. physician Ont. Cancer Inst., 1957-91, head divsn. biol. rsch., 1982-89, head divsn. cell and molecular biology, 1989-91, sr. scientist emeritus, 1991-93; vis. prof. U. Tex. Med. Ctr. Anderson Cancer Ctr., Houston, 1992-93, adj. prof., 1993-98; cons. Nat. Cancer Plan, 1972—; mem. standing com. on health rsch. and devel. Ont. Coun. Health, 1974-82. Author numerous articles on rsch. in hematology; mem. editl. bd.: Blood, 1969-80, Biomedicine, 1973, Clin. Immunology and Immunopathology, 1972-76; assoc. editor: Jour. Cellular Physiology, 1966-68; editor, 1968-91. Trustee Banting Rsch. Found., 1975-84, hon. sec.-treas., 1958-74, v.p., 1977-79. Decorated officer Order of Can., 1988; recipient William Goldie prize U. Toronto, 1964, Gairdner award Internat. Gairdner Found., 1969, Starr Medallist award Dept. Anatomy U. Toronto, 1957; Thomas W. Eadie Medal, 1991, Royal Soc. Canada, Nat. Cancer Inst. Can. fellow, 1954-57, Albert Lasker award for Basic Med. Rsch., Lasker Found., 2005; named to Can. Med. Hall of Fame, 2004. Fellow Royal Soc. Can. (pres. Nat. Acad. Sci. 1987-90, Thomas W. Eadie Medal 1991, Golden Jubilee Medal), Royal Coll. Physicians and Surgeons Can., Royal Soc. London, Can. Acad. Sci.; mem. Am. Soc. Exptl. Pathology, Am. Assn. Cancer Rsch., Can. Soc. Cell Biology, Can. Soc. Clin. Investigation, Am., Internat. Socs. Hematology, Internat. Soc. Exptl. Hematology, Inst. Acad. Medicine (charter mem.), Badminton Club, Racquet Club. Home: 480 Summerhill Ave Toronto ON Canada M4W 2E4 Home Phone: 416-767-4812. E-mail: mcculloch@uhnres.utoronto.ca. *Research success depends on associating with agreeable and talented people.*

MCCULLOCH, LINDA HARMAN, state official, former school system administrator; b. Mont., Dec. 21, 1954; m. Bill McCulloch, 1978. BA in Elem. Edn., U. Mont., 1982, MA in Elem. Edn., 1990. Pub. sch. tchr., Ashland, Missoula, Bonner, Mont., 1978—95; mem. Dist. 70 Mont. House of Reps., 1995—2001; supt. pub. instrn. State of Mont., 2002—09, sec. state, 2009—. Faculty affiliate U. Mont., 1995—2000; mem. judiciary, highways & transportation, local govt. edn. and house rules committees Mont. House Reps., 1997, interim com. assignments included juvenile justice & mental health, Indian Affairs, and edn. & local govt.; minority caucus leader House Reps., Helena, Mont., 1999; vice chair edn. com. Mont. House Reps., 1999. Mem., officer PTA Assn., Helena, 1985; bd. dirs. Missoula Developmental Services. Corp.; mem. adv. com. Missoula Youth Homes Foster Care; bd. mem. Pub Edn., Bd. Reagents, Mont. Libr. Commn. and Land Board, N.W. Regional Ednl. Lab., Mont. Heritage Project, Profl. Tchg. Found. Recipient Mike and Maureen Mansfield Libr. scholaship, 1981, J.C. Penny Vol. Program award, 1998. Mem.: AAUW, LWV, Five Valleys Reading Assn., Mont. State Reading Coun., Mont. Fedn. Tchrs., Mont. Ednl. Assn., Mont. Libr. Assn. (Legislator of Yr. award 1997), Mont. Family Union, Mont. Dem. Womens Club. Democrat. Methodist. Office: Office Sec State State Capital Rm 260 PO Box 202801 Helena MT 59620 Office Phone: 406-444-2034. Office Fax: 406-444-3976. Business E-Mail: sos@mt.gov.*

MCCULLOCH, RACHEL, economist, educator; b. 1942; m. Gary Edward Chamberlain; children: Laura Chamberlain Gehl, Neil Dudley Chamberlain. BA in Math., U. Pa., Phila., 1962; MA in Math. Tchg., U. Chgo., 1965, MA in Econs., 1971, PhD in Econs., 1973; student, MIT, 1966—67. Economist Cabinet Task Force on Oil Import Control, Washington, 1969; instr., then asst. prof. Grad. Sch. Bus. U. Chgo., 1971-73; asst. prof., then assoc. prof. econs. Harvard U., Cambridge, Mass., 1973-79; assoc. prof., then prof. econs. U. Wis., Madison, 1979-87; prof. Brandeis U., Waltham, Mass., 1987—, Rosen Family prof., 1989—, dir. Lemberg Program in Internat. Econs. and Fin., 1990-91, dir. PhD program Internat. Bus. Sch., 1994—2001, chair dept. econs., 2006—09. Mem. Pres.'s Commn. on Indsl. Competitiveness, 1983-84; mem. adv. coun. Office Tech. Assessment, U.S. Congress, 1979-88; cons. World Bank, Washington, 1984-86, 2004-05; mem. com. on internat. rels. studies with People's Republic of China, 1984-91; rsch. assoc. Nat. Bur. Econ. Rsch., Cambridge, 1985-93; mem. adv. com. Peterson Inst. for Internat. Econs., Washington, 1987—; faculty Advanced Mgmt. Network, La Jolla, Calif., 1985-92; mem. com. examiners econs. test Grad. Record Exam. Ednl. Testing Svc., 1990-96, chair, 1992-96; mem. discipline adv. com. for Fulbright scholar awards in econs. Coun. Internat. Exch. Scholars, 1991-93, chair, 1992-93; mem. adv. com. for Fulbright Chairs Program, 1997; cons. Global Economy Project, Edn. Film Ctr., 1993-94; mem. study group on pvt. capital flows to developing and transitional economies Coun. Fgn. Rels., 1995-96, acad. adv. panel, Fed. Reserve Bank of Boston, 1999—; faculty assoc. Harvard Inst. for Internat. Devel., 1997-2000; fellow Internat. Leadership Forum, 2001-; AGIP prof. internat. econs. Sch. Advanced Internat. Studies, Bologna Ctr., Johns Hopkins U., 2004-05, cons. Asian Devel. Bank, 2007. Author: Research and Development as a Determinant of U.S. International Competitiveness, 1978; contbr. articles to profl. jours. and books. Grantee NSF, 1975-79, Hoover Inst., 1984-85, German Marshall Fund of US, 1985, Ford Found., 1985-88, US Dept. Edn., 1990-91, Schulhof Found., 2001-02; recipient John R. Commons award Omicron Delta Epsilon, 2007. Mem. Am. Econ. Assn. (dir. summer program for minority students 1983-84, mem. executive com., 1997-2000), Internat. Trade and Fin. Assn. (bd. dirs. 1993-95). Office: Brandeis U Dept Econs MS 021 PO Box 549110 Waltham MA 02454-9110 Business E-Mail: mcculloch@brandeis.edu.

MC CULLOCH, SAMUEL CLYDE, history professor; b. Ararat, Australia, Sept. 3, 1916; came to U.S., 1936, naturalized, 1944; s. Samuel and Agnes Almond (Clyde) McC.; m. Sara Ellen Rand, Feb. 19, 1944; children: Ellen (Mrs. William Henry Meyer III), David Rand, Malcolm Clyde. AB with highest honors in History, UCLA, 1940, MA (grad. fellow history), 1942; PhD, U. Calif. at Los Angeles, 1944. Asst. U. Calif. at Los Angeles, 1943-44; instr. Oberlin Coll., 1944-45; asst. prof. Amherst Coll., 1945-46; vis. asst. prof. U. Mich., 1946-47; mem. faculty Rutgers U., 1947-60, prof. history, assoc. dean arts and scis., 1958-60; dean coll., prof. history San Francisco State Coll., 1960-63; dean humanities, prof. history U. Calif. at Irvine, 1963-70, prof., 1970-87, prof. emeritus, 1987—, coordinator Edn. Abroad Program, 1975-85, dir. Australian Study Ctr., 1986, 87. Vis. summer prof. Oberlin Coll., 1945, 46, U. Calif. at Los Angeles, 1947, U. Del., 1949; Fulbright Research prof. Monash U., Melbourne (Australia) U., 1970; Am. Philos. Soc. grantee, 1970 Author: British Humanitarianism, 1950, George Gipps, 1966, River King: The Mc Culloch Carrying Company and Echura, 1865-1898, 1986, Instant University: A History of U.C.I., 1957-1993, 1995, William McCulloch, 1932-1909, 1997, A Collection of Book Reviews, 1948-93, 2000; contbr. numerous articles, revs. to profl. jours.; assoc. editor Jour. Brit. Studies, 1960-68, bd. advisors, 1968-70; bd. corrs. Hist. Studies: Australia and New Zealand, 1949-83. Mem. Calif. Curriculum Commn., 1961-67, Highland Park (N.J.) Bd. Edn., 1959-60. Grantee Am. Philos. Soc., Social Sci. Rsch. Coun. and Rutgers U. Rsch. Coun. to Australia, 1951; Fulbright rsch. fellow U. Sydney, Australia, 1954-55; grantee Social Sci. Rsch. Coun. to Eng., summer 1955 Fellow Royal Hist. Soc.; mem. Am. Hist. Assn., Church, Royal Australian Hist. Socs., A.A.U.P., N.Am. Conf. Brit. Studies (exec. sec. 1968-73, pres. 1975-77, Liftime Disting. Contbns. Brit. Studies award 1995), English Speaking Union (pres. New Brunswick 1957-59), Phi Beta Kappa, Pi Gamma Mu; Clubs: Univ. Club Irvine (forum moderator 1981-2008). Episcopalian (vestry). Home: 2121 Windward Ln Newport Beach CA 92660-3820

MCCULLOH, THAYNE MARTIN, university administrator, consultant; b. LA, Aug. 20, 1964; m. Julie Ann Lopach, July 24, 1993; children: Kathryne Angela, Anne Elizabeth, Emily Clara. BA in Psychology, Gonzaga U., 1989; PhD in Exptl. Social Psychology, Oxford U., 1998. Test adminstr. Pearn Kandola Downs Occupl. Psychologists, Oxford, England, 1989—90; coord. residence life Gonzaga U., Spokane, 1990—92, dir. housing, 1993—95, asst. dean students, 1995—96, dean student acad. svcs., 1996—98, dean student fin. svcs., 1998—2002, assoc. acad. v.p., 2002—04, v.p. adminstrn. and planning, 2004—. Tutor in social psychology Oxford U., England, 1989—93; accreditation evaluator N.W. Commn. Coll. and U., Redmond, Wash., 1997—; cons. enrollment mgmt. and fin. aid, Spokane, 2000—. Mem. Human Rights Commn., Spokane, 2005—06. Sgt. US Army, 1983—86. Decorated Army Achievement medal U.S. Army, Army Commendation medal; recipient Sr. award, Gonzaga U. Alumni Assn., 1989; scholar, Chancellors and Prin., U.K., 1989—93. Mem.: APA, Citibank Ednl. Leadership Financing Coun., Nat. Assn. Student Fin. Aid Adminstrs., Nat. Assn. Student Pers. Adminstrs. (New Profl. of Yr., region V 1995). Roman Catholic. Achievements include research in mentoring and its relationship to leadership succession planning. Office: Gonzaga Univ 502 E Boone Ave Spokane WA 99258-0086 Home: 1716 W 15th Ave Spokane WA 99203-1017 Office Fax: 509-323-6288.

MCCULLOUGH, ANDREW RICHARD, physician; b. Orleans, France, Oct. 2, 1952; s. Madeleine and Clarence Prentiss McCullough; children: Jason Andrew, Christopher Brendan, Dylan Kent, Alicia Gabrielle Fine-McCullough. BA, The Johns Hopkins U., Balt., 1974; MD, U. Md., 1978. Cert. in Urology Residency The Johns Hopkins U., Balt., 1983, lic. NY State, 1994. Instr. urology The Johns Hopkins U. Hosp., 1983—84, Yale U. Urology, New Haven, 1984—93; assoc. prof. NYU, New York, NY, 1994—. Contbr. articles to med. jours. Fellowship, Am. Cancer Soc., 1981. Mem.: Am. Urol. Assn. Office: NYU Urology 150 East 32 St New York NY 10016 Office Fax: 646-825-6397. Business E-Mail: andy.mccullough@nyumc.org.

MCCULLOUGH, DAVID, writer; b. Pitts., July 7, 1933; s. Christian Hax and Ruth (Rankin) McC.; m. Rosalee Ingram Barnes, Dec. 18, 1954; children: Melissa, David, William Barnes, Geoffrey Barnes, Doreen Kane. BA, Yale U., 1955; LHD, Skidmore Coll., 1983, Rensselaer Poly. Inst., 1983; LHD (hon.), Wesleyan U., Middletown, Conn., 1984, Colo. Coll., 1985, U. N.H., 1993, Chatham Coll., 1994, Beloit Coll., 1996, Georgetown U., 1995, Coll. William and Mary, 1996, Grinnell Coll., 1997, Dickinson Coll., 1998, Northeastern U., 2002, Brandeis U., 2003, OH State U., 2003; DEng (hon.), Villanova U., 1984; doctorate (hon.), Worcester Poly. Inst., 1984, U. Miami, 1996, Grand Valley State U., 1997, Yale U., 1998, Brown U., 2000, Tufts U., 2001, U. Del., 2001; LittD (hon.), Allegheny Coll., 1984, Middlebury Coll., 1986, Indiana U. at Pa., 1991, U. S.C., 1993, U. Pitts., 1994, Union Coll., 1994, Washington Coll., 1994, Hamilton Coll., 1996, SUNY, 1999, U. Conn., 1999, U. Vt., 2002, Dartmouth Coll., 2003; LLD (hon.), Lafayette Coll., 1995, U. Mass., 1998, Wheaton Coll., 2002. Writer, editor Time, Inc., NYC, 1956-61, USIA, Washington, 1961-64, Am. Heritage Pub. Co., NYC, 1964-70; sr. contbg. editor Am. Heritage mag.; free-lance author, 1970—. Newman vis. prof. American civilization, Cornell U., fall 1989; mem. Bennington (Vt.) Coll. Writers Workshop, 1978-79; scholar-in-residence U. N. Mex., 1979, Wesleyan U. Writers Conf., 1982, 83; mem. adv. bd. Ctr. for the Book, Libr. of Congress; past vis. prof. Dartmouth Coll., Wesleyan U.; spkr. and lectr. in field. Author:The Johnstown Flood, 1968, Great Bridge: The Epic Story of the Building of the Brooklyn Bridge, 1972, The Path Between the Seas: The Creation of the Panama Canal, 1870—1914, 1977, Mornings on Horseback: The Story of an Extraordinary Family, a Vanished Way of Life and the Unique Child Who Became Theodore Roosevelt, 1981, Brave Companions: Portraits in History, 1992, Truman, 1992 (Pulitzer Prize for biography 1993), John Adams, 2001 (Pulitzer Prize for biography 2002), 1776, 2005 (Quills award for best history/current events/politics, 2005, #1 on Publishers Weekly Bestseller list, 2005); host: (TV series) Smithsonian World, 1984-88, The American Experience, 1988—; narrator: (TV documentaries) Huey Long, 1985, The Shakers: Hands to Work, Hearts to God, 1985, The Civil War, 1990, LBJ: A Biography, 1991, The Donner Party, 1992, Degenerate Art, 1993, Eisenhower, 1993, Battle of the Bulge, 1994, Brooklyn Bridge, 1995, The Statue of Liberty, 1996, Secrets of a Master Builder, 2000, Napoleon, 2000, Abraham & Mary Lincoln: A House Divided, 2001; (films) Seabiscuit, 2003; appearances: (documentaries) David McCullough: Painting with Words, 2008 Mem. Harry S. Truman Centennial Commn.; trustee Nat. Trust Hist. Preservation, Harry S. Truman Libr. Inst., Hist. Soc. Western Pa., Jefferson Meml. Found., Boston Pub. Libr.; hon. trustee Carnegie Inst.; founding mem. Protect Hist. Am. Guggenheim fellow, 1986; recipient N.Y. Diamond Jubilee award, 1973, cert. of merit Mcpl. Art Soc. N.Y., 1973, Nat. Book award for history, 1978, Francis Parkman prize, 1978, 93, Samuel Eliot Morison award, 1978, Cornelius Ryan award, 1978, Civil Engring. History and Heritage award, 1978, L.A. Times prize for biography, 1981, Am. Book award for biography, 1982, Harry S. Truman Pub. Svc. award, 1993, St. Louis Lit. award, 1993, Pa. Gov.'s award for excellence, 1993, Pa. Soc. Gold Medal award, 1994, Charles Frankel prize contributions to humanities Endowment Humanities and U.S. Govt., 1995, Disting. Contbns. to Am. Letters award. Nat. Book Found., Lit. Lion award N.Y. Pub. Libr., 1981, Emmy award for work in pub. TV, 1985, Gold medal Pa. Soc., Carl Sandburg Lit. award, 2000, Am. Revolution Round Table Book award, 2001, LA Pub. Libr. Lit. award, 2002, William Bradford award, Pilgrim Soc., 2002, Christopher award, 2002, Robin Winks award, Nat. Pks. Conservation Assn., 2003, Presdl. Medal of Freedom, The White House, 2006. Fellow Soc. Am. Historians (pres.); mem. ASCE (hon.), Am. Acad. Arts and Scis., Am. Acad. Arts and Letters, Soc. Am. Historians (pres. 1991—). Avocations: travel, reader, landscape painter, sunday night spaghetti chef. Office: Janklow & Nesbit Associates 445 Park Ave # 13th New York NY 10022-2606

MCCULLOUGH, EDWARD L., artist, educator; b. Danville, Ill., Sept. 18, 1934; s. Fred and Helen McCullough; m. Gale Carter, Dec. 15, 1954; children: Scott, Reggie Johnson, Allison McClendon. BA, Ill. State U., 1962, MA, 1966. Assoc. prof. of art Ill. Wesleyan U., Bloomington, 1966—80; adj. prof. of art Columbia Coll., Chgo., 1990—. Sculpture, Meridian III, Ea. Ill. U., 1998, VISION, Fed. Res. Bank Chgo., 1999, Meridian VII, Chgo. Pub. Art Program, 2002, Meridian VI, Ctrl. Ill. Regional Airport, Bloomington, Ill., 2002, sculptue, Enigma Variation #1, Spring Arbor U., Spring Arbor, Mich., 2005, Enigma Variation #2, So. Ill. U. Sch. Medicine, Springfield, Ill., 2005, Meridian VIII, Dominican U., River Forest, Ill., 2006, Meridian II, Luther Coll., Decorah, Iowa, 2008, Meridian IX, State of Ill. for Kankakee Cmty. Coll., Kankakee, Ill., 2009. Petty officer 2nd class submarine svc. USN, 1955—59. Fellow Artist in Residence Program, Nat. Endowment of the Arts, 1980, 1981; Project Completion grant, Ill. Arts Coun., 1985. Mem.: Chgo. Sculpture Soc., Internat. Sculpture Soc., Chgo. Artists Coalition (assoc.). Home: 421 N First St Cissna Park IL 60924-9789 Home Fax: 815-457-3010.

MCCULLOUGH, EILEEN (EILEEN MCCULLOUGH LEPAGE, ELLI MCCULLOUGH), financial consultant, writer, editor, educator; b. Phila., Oct. 16, 1946; d. Charles Norman and Marie Teresa (Inglesby) McCullough; m. Clifford Bennett LePage Jr., Mar. 6, 1970; children: Clifford Bennett III, Alexander Pierce. BA in English and Secondary Edn., George Washington U., DC, 1969; MEd in Spl. Edn., Temple U., Phila., 1972. Cert. secondary sch. tchr.; registered securities rep. Record-keeper child growth and devel. program Children's Hosp. of Phila., 1965; with advt. dept. Phila. Inquirer, 1966-67; with ops. control U.S. Civil Svc. Commn., Washington, 1967-69; mgr. N.J. Bell Telephone, Trenton, 1969; rschr. Temple U., Phila., 1969-71; tchr. Wyomissing, Pa., 1972-77; fin. cons. various orgns., 1984-93; cons. EMLC, Reading, 1994—. Adj. instr. Reading (Pa.) Area C.C., 1978-81; lectr. English Albright Coll., Reading, 1981-84; founding mem. Common Cents Investment Club, 1983-93; founding and mng. ptnr. Klein LePage McCullough Partnership, Ocean City, N.J., 1982-96; presenter in field. Author: The Clue in the Snow, 1959; editor: 1st Complete Pocket Guide to Atlantic City Casinos, 1984, The Autobiography of Capt. Michael Kevolic, 1986; photographer Cherry Hill Mtg. Bd. dirs. Nat. Found. March of Dimes, Reading, 1969-75, chmn., 1974-75; bd. sch. dirs. Wyomissing Area Sch. Dist., 1984-92; bd. dirs. Wyomissing Pub. Libr., Reading, 1980-85; asst. chmn Region 8 Pa. Sch. Bds. Assn., 1989-91; dir. Saturday Morning Sch., Assn. for Children with Learning Disabilities, Reading, 1970; acting sec. Berks County Commn. for Women, Reading, 1993; active Reading Community Players, 1980; past bd. mem. Berks Ballet Theatre; past vol. Berks C. of C.; vol. mus. guide Reading Pub. Mus. and Art Gallery, 1999-2002, Berks County Chpt Am. Red Cross, 1997; presenter Green Circle, Reading Berks Human Rels. coun., Reading Pub. Schs., 1998-99. Fellow Pa. writing project; mem. AAUW (life; topic chmn.), Am. Assn. Individual Investors (life), Internat. Platform Soc., Women's Internat. Fedn. for World Peace. Avocations: dance, singing. Home and Office: EMLC 10 Phoebe Dr Reading PA 19610-2857 E-mail: emlco@comcast.net.

MCCULLOUGH, GARY E., education company executive; BS, Wright State Univ.; MBA, Northwestern Univ. Mgmt. positions Procter & Gamble, 1987—95, mktg. dir., 1995—98, gen. mgr. No. Am. home care, 1998—2000; sr. v.p. Americas Wm. Wrigley Jr. Co., 2000—03; pres. Ross products div. Abbott Laboratories, 2003—07; pres., CEO Career Edn. Corp., Hoffman Estates, Ill., 2007—. Bd. dir. Sherwin Williams Co. Served 5 years to capt. US Army. Decorated Meritorious Service Medal; named one of 75 Most Powerful African Americans in bus., Black Enterprise Mag., 2005. Office: Career Edn Corp 2895 Greenspoint Pkwy Hoffman Estates IL 60169

MCCULLOUGH, JAMES P., JR., psychology professor; b. Baton Rouge, Oct. 13, 1936; s. James P. and Willie Howell R. McCullough; m. Rosemary F. Fleming, Jan. 17, 1964; children: Michael J., John P., Kristin R. PhD, U. Ga., Athens, 1970. Cert. in clin. psychology Va. Bd. Psychology, 1974. Prof. psychology & psychiatry Va. Commonwealth U., Richmond, 1972—. Contbr. scientific papers. 2nd lt. Arty., 1954—55. Recipient Disting. Scholar award, Coll. Humanities & Sci., 2006. Fellow: APA. Home: 512 Glendale Dr Richmond VA 23229-7228 Office: Virginia Commonwealth Univ 806 W Franklin St Richmond VA 23284-2018 Home Phone: 804-740-7646. Office Fax: 804-740-0305. Business E-Mail: jmccull@vcu.edu.

MCCULLOUGH, JOSEPH, retired academic administrator; b. Pitts., July 6, 1922; s. Joseph Phillip and Margaret (List) McC.; m. Elizabeth Cramer, Mar. 31, 1945; children— Marjorie Ann, Warren BFA, Yale U., 1949-50, MFA, 1951; Diploma, Cleve. Sch. Art, 1948; DFA (hon.), U. Evansville, Ind., 1980; DA (hon.), Cleve. Inst. Art, 1996. Instr. San Jose State Coll., Calif., 1948-49; asst. instr. Yale U., New Haven, 1949-51; asst. dir. Cleve. Inst. Art, 1952-54, dir., 1954-74, pres., 1974-88. Artist paintings, nat. regional and local exhbns., 1948— Chmn. Fine Arts Adv. Com., Cleve. Planning Commn., 1963-91; trustee Mpls. Coll. of Art and Design, 1988-98, Sculpture Ctr. Cleve., 1990-98; trustee, sec. Access to the Arts, Cleve., 1991-95. Capt. USAAF, 1943-46, ETO. Recipient Cleve. Arts prize Women's City Club, 1971, Centennial medal John Carroll U., 1987, medal for excellence Cleve. Inst. of Art, 1997. Mem.: Coll. Art Assn. ((past dir.)). Home: 20101 North Park Blvd Cleveland OH 44118-5006

MCCULLOUGH, LAURENCE BERNARD, medical educator, consultant; b. Phila., Aug. 2, 1947; s. Henry Joseph and Marie J. (Burns) McC.; m. Linda Jean Quintanilla, May 14, 1977. AB, Williams Coll., 1969; PhD, U. Tex., 1975. Postdoctoral fellow Hastings Ctr., Hastings-on-Hudson, N.Y., 1975-76; Asst. prof. med. humanities and philosophy Tex. A&M U., College Station, 1976-79; from asst. prof. to prof. cmty. and family medicine Georgetown U., Washington, 1979-88; prof. medicine and med. ethics Baylor Coll. Medicine, Houston, 1988—, Dalton Tomlin chair med. ethics & health policy, 2008—. Adj. prof. ethics in ob-gyn. and pub. health Weill Med. Coll., Cornell U., N.Y.C., 1988—. Co-author: Ethics in Obstetrics & Gynecology, 1994, Medical Ethics, 1984, Spanish transl., 1987, Japanese transl., 1992; author: Leibniz on Individuals and Individuation, 1996, John Gregory and the Invention of Professional Medical Ethics and the Profession of Medicine, 1998; co-editor: Surgical Ethics, 1998, The Cambridge World History Med. Ethics, 2009. Office Phone: 713-798-3505. Business E-Mail: mccullou@bcm.edu.

MCCULLOUGH, MARY T. (TERRI MCCULLOUGH), legislative staff member; m. Howard Wolfson; 2 children. Statutory US House of Reps., Washington, 2003, advisor, chief of staff to Rep. Nancy Pelosi, 2003—. Fellow, Stennis Ctr. Pub. Svc. Leadership. Democrat. Office: 235 Cannon House Office Bldg Washington DC 20515 Office Fax: 202-225-4965.*

MCCULLOUGH, RALPH CLAYTON, II, law educator; b. Daytona Beach, Fla., Mar. 28, 1941; s. Ralph C. and Doris (Johnson) McCullough; m. Elizabeth Grier Henderson, Apr. 5, 1986; children: Melissa Wells, Clayton Baldwin. BA, Erskine Coll., 1962; JD, Tulane U., 1965. Bar: La. 1965, SC 1974. Assoc. Baldwin, Haspel, Maloney, Rainold and Meyer, New Orleans, 1965-68; from asst. prof. law to prof. U. SC, Columbia, 1968—2002, disting. prof., 2002—03; mng. dir., prof. Charleston Sch. Law, 2005—. Asst. dean U. SC Sch. Law 1970-75, Disting. prof. law, 2001, Disting. prof. law emeritus, 2003—; of counsel Finkel & Altman, 1978-; adj. prof. medicine Med. U. SC, 1984-, adj. prof. pathology, 1985—, mem. bd. vis.; mem. adv. com. rules and procedures US Ct. Appeals (4th cir.), 2001—, chair, 2006—. Author: (with J.L. Underwood) The Civil Trial Manual, 1974, 7th supplement, 1987, The Civil Trial Manual II, 1984, 87, (with Myers and Felix) New Directions in Legal Education, 1970, (with Finkel) S.C. Torts II, 1986, III, 1990, IV, 1995; co-reporter S.C. Criminal Code, 1977, S.C. Study Sentencing, 1977. Mem. bd. visitors Med. U. SC, 2006—. Mem. ATLA, ABA, La. Bar Assn., SC Bar (sec. 1975-76, exec. dir. 1972-76, award of service 1978), New Orleans Bar Assn., Am. Law Inst. (life), Am. Coll. Trial Lawyers, Southeastern Assn. Am. Law Schs. (pres.), SC Trial Lawyers Assn. (bd. govs. 1984-88), Forest Lake Club, Phi Alpha Delta. Republican. Episcopalian. Home: PO Box 939 Charleston SC 29402 Office: 414 King St Charleston SC 29402 Office Phone: 843-329-1000 ext. 2426. Business E-Mail: rmccullough@charlestonlaw.edu.

MCCULLOUGH, RICHARD LAWRENCE, advertising executive; b. Chgo., Dec. 1, 1937; s. Francis John and Sadie Beatrice McCullough; m. Julia Louise Kreimer, May 6, 1961; children: Stephen, Jeffery, Julie. BS, Marquette U., 1959. Commd. U.S. Army, 1959, advance through grades to sgt., 1966; account exec. Edward H. Weiss Advt., Chgo., 1960-66; account supr. Doyle Dane Bernbach, NYC, 1966-68; sr. v.p. J. Walter Thompson Co., Chgo., 1969-86; pres. E.H. Brown Advt., Chgo., 1986-97; exec. v.p. Space-Time Media Mgmt., Chgo., 1997—; ptnr. Callahan Group, Chgo., 2000—05. Developer Mktg. with Country Music nat. seminar, 1996; chmn. J. L. McCullough Advertising and Pub. Rels., Evanston, Ill., 2004—. Author: Building Country Radio, 1986, A New Look at Country Music Audiences, 1988, (video) Country Music Marketing, 1989. Bd. dirs. Gateway Found., Chgo., 1976—, chmn., 1988-91; bd. dirs., chmn. mktg. com. Cath. Charities, Chgo. Recipient Nat. Cmty. Svc. award, Gateway Found., 2002, Dennis Kelly Honor award, Cath. Charities, 2002. Mem. Country Music Assn. (Nashville bd. dirs. 1979-2004, pres. 1983-85, Pres.'s award 1987, elector Country Music Hall of Fame), NARAS (Nashville and Chgo. chpt.), North Shore Country Club (Glenview, Ill.), Dairymen's Country Club (Boulder Junction, Wis.). Roman Catholic. Home: 2720 Lincoln St Evanston IL 60201-2043 Office: Space-Time Media Mgmt Inc 35 E Wacker Dr Chicago IL 60601-2103 Home: 2720 Lincoln St Evanston IL 60201-2043 E-mail: dick@spacetimemedia.com, relchar@aol.com.

MCCULLOUGH, ROBERT DALE, II, osteopath; b. Tulsa, June 2, 1937; s. Robert Dale and Roberta Maud (Purdy) McC.; m. Lindell Arlene Wilcox, Sept. 28, 1963; children: Robert Mark, Lori Lindell. Student, Wheaton Coll., Ill., 1955-57; BS, N.E. Mo. State U., 1958; DO, Kans. City Coll. Osteopathy, Mo., 1958-62. Diplomate in internal medicine and med. oncology Am. Osteo. Bd. Internal Medicine. Gen. practice McCullough Clinic, Tulsa, 1963-68; internal medicine resident Detroit Osteo. Hosp., 1968-71; internal medicine Baker-Todd-McCullough-Sutton, Tulsa, 1971-74; fellow med. oncology M.D. Anderson Hosp., Houston, 1974-75; internal medicine-med. oncology Baker-Todd-McCullough-Sutton, Tulsa, 1975-90; pvt. practice Tulsa, 1990-93; attending staff mem. VA Outpatient Clinic, Tulsa, 1993-94; assoc. med. dir. Blue Cross/Blue Shield of Okla., Tulsa, 1994—2005. Trustee Tulsa Regional Med. Cttr., 1983-88, 90-93; bd. dirs. Okla. Blue Cross Blue Shield, Tulsa, 1983-92, vice chmn., 1991-92; mem. adv. coun. Okla. State U. Coll. Osteo. Medicine, 1988-94, chmn., 1988-90; part-time worker VA and Indian Health Svc. Mem. bd. editors Patient Care Magazine, Montvale, N.J., 1988-93. Mem. Okla. State Bd. Health, Oklahoma City, 1983—87, Tulsa City/County Bd. Health, 1988—95, chmn., 1993; bd. mem. Cmty. Health Found., 1997—, chmn., 2003—05. Mem. Nat. Osteo. Found. (trustee 1993-00, treas. 1998-00), Am. Osteo. Assn. (vice speaker Ho. of Dels. 1986-92, trustee 1993-00), Am. Coll. Osteo. Internists, Okla. Osteo. Assn. (pres. 1982-83), Tulsa Downtown Lions Club, Soc. for Preservation and Encouragement of Barbershop Quartet Singing in Am. Republican. Southern Baptist. Avocation: barbershop quartets. Home: 5803 E 75th Pl Tulsa OK 74136-7255 Home Phone: 918-481-8725. Personal E-mail: RMccull207@aol.com.

MCCULLOUGH, THERESA MARIE, pharmacist, director; b. Springfield, Ill., Nov. 10, 1978; d. James A. and Nita L. Jansen. BS, St. Louis Coll. Pharmacy, 2002, PharmD, 2003. Registered pharmacist Ill. Dept. Profl. Regulation, cert. Am. Pharmacists Assn., 2007, in therapy mgmt. 2008. Clin. and staff pharmacist Meml. Med. Ctr. Inpatient Pharmacy, Springfield, 2002—06; asst. dir. experiential edn. SIUE Sch. Pharmacy, Edwardsville, Ill., 2007—. Contbr. articles to profl. jours. Mem.: Ill. Pharmacist Assn., Am. Assn. Colls. Pharmacy, Ill. Coun. Health Sys. Pharmacist, Metro East Pharmacist Assn. (bd. mem. 2007). Office: SIUE Sch Pharmacy 200 Univ Pk Dr Ste 220 Edwardsville IL 62026 Business E-Mail: thmccul@siue.edu.

MCCULLY, THOMAS RICHARDSON, lawyer; b. Rushville, Ind., Mar. 10, 1941; s. Kenneth Brody and Frances (Richardson) McCully; m. Susan C. McCully, Dec. 5, 1998; children: Julie A., Thomas R. II, Michael G. stepchildren: Keith W. Long, Thomas Long. BA Polit. Sci., Philosophy, Wabash Coll., Crawfordsville, Ind., 1963; JD with distinction, Ind. U., Bloomington, 1966. Bar: Ind. 1966, U.S. Dist. Ct. (So. Dist.) Ind. 1966, U.S. Dist. Ct. (No. Dist.) Ind. 1968, U.S. Ct. Appeals (7th cir.) 1973, U.S. Supreme Ct. 1973. Assoc. Stuart & Branigin, LLP, Lafayette, Ind., 1966—71, ptnr., 1971—. Guest lectr. Purdue U., Lafayette, Ind.; frequent speaker, author Ind. Continuing Legal Edn. Forum, Lohrman Bus. Ctr., Lafayette; speaker Greater Lafayette Small Bus. Devel. Ctr.; bd. dirs. LSB Fin. Corp. and Lafayette Savings Bank, Ind., 1999—. Pres. Highland Sch. PTA; exec. com. Gus Macker, Lafayette, 1997—2001; Elder Ctrl. Presbyn. Ch., Lafayette; bd. dirs. Ctrl. Presbyn. Found., Lafayette, Legal Aid Corp., Tippecanoe County, Ind., 1974—96, pres., 1987—89; bd, visitors Ind. U. Sch. Law, Bloomington, Ind., 1994—; bd. dirs. Jr. Achievement of Greater Lafayette, 1994—, Harrison Trails and Sagamore Couns., Boy Scouts Am. (past), Lafayette, Vol. Bur. Tippecanoe County (past). Recipient Pro Bono Publico award, Ind. Bar Found., 1995; named one of Best Lawyers in Am., 1987—. Master: Ind. Bar Found. (fellow); mem.: ABA, Am. Health Lawyers Assn., Ind. State Bar Assn. (mem. spl. com. to revise Ind. Zoning Laws 1982—88, chmn. land use and zoning sect. 1992—94, chmn. health law sect. 2006—07), Tippecanoe County Bar Assn., John Purdue Club, Lafayette Country Club (legal counsel 1977—), Ind. U. Varsity Club, Elks Lodge 143, Phi Delta Phi. Office: Stuart & Branigin LLP 300 Main St Ste 900 Lafayette IN 47902 Home Phone: 765-447-7181; Office Phone: 765-423-1561. Office Fax: 765-742-8125. Business E-Mail: trm@stuartlaw.com.

MCCUNE, BRENDA L., lawyer; BS, Western State Univ., 1994, JD, 1995. Bar: Calif. 1996. Atty. McCune Family Law, Yorba Linda, Calif. Contbr. articles to profl. jours. Named a Rising Star, So. Calif. Super Lawyers, 2004—06. Mem.: ABA, State Bar Calif., Orange County Bar Assn. (dir. family law sect. 2001—04), Peter M. Elliott Inns of Ct. Office: McCune Family Law Ste 206 4676 Lakeview Ave Yorba Linda CA 92886 Office Phone: 714-695-0502. Office Fax: 714-695-0568. Business E-Mail: brenda@bmccunefamilylaw.com.

MCCUNE, PHILIP SPEAR, lawyer; b. Spokane, Wash., Sept. 14, 1965; s. Calmar A. McCune and Katrina Y. Spear; children: Emma Sophia, Jackson Spear. BA magna cum laude, Dartmouth Coll., 1987; JD cum laude, U. Mich., 1991. Bar: Wash. 1991, US Dist. Ct. (we. dist.) Wash. 1991, US Dist. Ct. (ea. dist.) Wash. 1996, US Ct. Appeals (9th cir.) 1991, US Dist. Ct. (no. dist.) Utah 1996, US Supreme Ct. 2004. Law clk. Hon. John C. Coughenour U.S. Dist. Ct. (we. dist.) Wash., Seattle, 1991—93; with Heller, Ehrman, White and Maculliffe, Seattle, 1993—97; ptnr., founder Summit Law Group, Seattle, 1997—. Author: The Forest Practices Act, Washington Environmental Law and Practice; sr. editor U. Mich. Jour. Law Reform; contbr. articles to profl. jours. Bd. dirs. Friends of Ind. Schs. and Better Edn., Seattle Repertory Theater, Am. Friends St. Michael's U. Sch. Recipient Rising Star and Super Lawyer awards, Wash. Law and Politics Mag., Outstanding Wash. Bus. Litigator, Benchmark Publs.; fellow, Litigation Counsel America, 2008. Mem. ABA, Wash. State Bar Assn., King County Bar Assn., Wash. Athletic Club, U. Mich. Law Sch. Barristers, Fed. Bar Assn. Avocations: hiking, running. Office: Summit Law Group 315 Fifth Ave S Ste 1000 Seattle WA 98104-2682 Office Phone: 206-676-7038. E-mail: philm@summitlaw.com.

MCCUNNEY, ROBERT JOSEPH, physician; b. July 4, 1948; s. Robert H. McCunney; m. Marilyn Stanton, Nov. 7, 1987; children: Robby, Kelsey. BSCE, Drexel U., 1971; MS in Environ. Health, U. Minn., 1972; MD, Jefferson Med. Coll., 1976; MPH in Occupl. Health, Harvard U., 1981. Intern, resident Northwestern U. Med. Ctr., Chgo., 1976-78; occupl. medicine fellow Harvard Sch. Pub. Health, Boston, 1979-81; emergency rm. physician Choate Meml. Hosp., Woburn, Mass., 1979-80, Sancra Maria Hosp., Cambridge, Mass., 1979-80; med. dir. occupl. health svc. Sturdy Meml. Hosp., Attleboro, Mass., 1981-83; med. dir. Goddard Occupl. Health Svcs., Stoughton, Mass., 1982-90; chief occupl. & environ. medicine, dir. occupl. med. residency program Boston U. Med. Ctr., 1983-94; corp. med. dir. Cabot Corp., Boston, 1983—; dir. environ. med. svc. med. dept. MIT, Cambridge, 1994—. Instr. anatomy Thomas Jefferson U., 1973; instr. medicine Brown U., Providence, 1982-85; adj. asst. prof. pub. health Boston U., 1983—; clin. asst. prof. Med. Coll. Wis., Milw., 1989—; lectr. medicine Harvard Med. Sch., Boston; staff physician Mass. Gen. Hosp., Boston. Editor: Handbook of Occupational Medicine, 1988, A Practical Approach to Occupational and Environmental Medicine, 1994, A Manager's Guide to Occupational Health Services, 1995, Occupl. & Environ. Medicine Report, Medical Center Occupational Health and Safety, 1999, Occupational and Environmental Medicine Self Assessment Guide, 1998; co-editor Health & Safety Manual, 1992; contbr. chpts. to books and articles to profl. jours. Fellow Am. Occupl. Medicine Assn., Am. Coll. Preventive Medicine; mem. AMA, APHA, Am. Conf. Govtl. Indsl. Hygienists, Am. Coll. Occupl. & Environ. Medicine (bd. dirs. 1991-94, 95—, chair pubs. com. 1985-88, house dels. 1983-89, govt. affairs com. 1989-93, past pres. New Eng. chpt. 1984-86, dir. residency sect. 1988-93), Tau Beta Pi, Phi Beta Upsilon. Roman Catholic. Avocations:

athletics, photography, boating. Office: MIT Dept Biol Engring 77 Massachusetts Ave 16-771 Cambridge MA 02139-4307 Office Phone: 617-258-5650. E-mail: mccunney@mit.edu.

MCCURDY, DAVID KEITH, trade association administrator, former congressman; b. Canadian, Tex., Mar. 30, 1950; s. Thomas L. and Aileen (Geis) McC.; m. Pamela Mary Plumb, Aug. 14, 1971; children: Josh, Cydney, Shannon. BA, U. Okla., 1972, JD, 1975; postgrad., U. Edinburgh, Scotland, 1977-78. Bar: Okla. 1975. Asst. atty. gen. State of Okla., 1975-77; assoc. Luttrell, Pendarvis & Rawlinson, Norman, Okla., 1978-79; pvt. practice Norman, 1979-80; mem. US Congress from 4th Okla. dist., Washington, 1981—95; mem. armed svcs. com., sci., space and tech. com.; chmn., CEO McCurdy Group LLC; pres. Electronic Industries Alliance, Arlington, Va., 1998—2007, Alliance Automobile Manufacturers, Inc., Washington, 2007—. Chmn. Nat. Dem. Leadership Coun. Fellow Internat. Rotary Club; recipient Disting. Svc. award U. Okla., 1991. Mem. Okla. State Bar Assn., Norman C. of C., Omicron Delta Kappa, Rotary. Office: Alliance Automobile Manufacturers Inc 1401 I St NW Ste 900 Washington DC 20005

MCCURDY, DEBORAH K., pediatric rheumatologist; MD, Hahnemann U. Sch. Medicine, 1976. Cert. Am. Bd. Pediat., 1982, in pediatric rheumatology Am. Bd. Pediat., 2007. Internship in pediat. La. State U. Sch. Medicine, New Orleans, 1976—77; residency in pediat. Hosp. Sick Children Rsch. Inst., 1977—80, fellowship in immunology, 1981—82; fellowship in pediatric rheumatology Children's Hosp. LA, 1983—86; assoc. prof. pediat. UCLA David Geffen Sch. Medicine, assoc. clin. prof. pediatric immunology, allergy and rheumatology; physician UCLA Children's Health Ctr. Office: UCLA Children's Health Ctr Peter Morton Med Bldg Ste 265 200 UCLA Medical Plz Los Angeles CA 90095 also: UCLA Med Ctr UCLA David Geffen Sch Medicine 10833 Le Conte Ave Los Angeles CA 90095 Office Phone: 310-825-6481, 310-206-1826. Business E-Mail: dmccurdy@mednet.ucla.edu.

MCCURDY, HARRY WARD, otolaryngologist; b. Branchton, Pa., Aug. 15, 1918; s. Adam Oscar and Sarah Fern (Hindman) McC.; m. Joan Jacqueline Talty, Dec. 10, 1955; children: Bridget Elizabeth, Peter Adam. AB, Allegheny Coll., 1940; MD, U. Pa., 1943. Diplomate Am. Bd. Otolaryngology. Intern Geisinger Meml. Hosp., Danville, Pa., 1944, resident in otolaryngology, 1944-45, 48-49; resident in pathology Hamot Hosp., Erie, Pa., 1945-48; mem. staff Geisinger Med. Center, Danville, 1948-50; commd. 2d lt. U.S. Army, 1945, advanced through grades to col., 1962-74; mil. cons. Surgeon Gen., U.S. Army, 1964-74; ret., 1974; exec. v.p. Am. Acad. Otolaryngology-Head and Neck Surgery, Washington, 1974-84; mem. staff Walter Reed Army Hosp. Resources coun. Gallaudet Coll., 1975-80; nat. adv. coun. Sertoma Found., 1976-84; chmn. FDA Panel on Otolaryngologic Med. Devices, 1974-78, cons., 1978-84 Mem. ACS, AMA, Royal Soc. Medicine (U.K.), Am. Acad. Otolaryngology, Mil. Surgeons Assn., Am. Soc. Assn. Execs., Soc. Med. Consultants to Armed Forces, AAAS, Am. Soc. Facial Plastic Surgery, Soc. Mil. Otolaryngologists, Am. Acad. Facial Plastic and Reconstructive Surgery, Am. Laryngol., Rhinol. and Otol. Soc., Anglo-Am. Med. Soc., Am. Audiology Soc., Royal Soc. Health, Osler Med. Soc., Acad. Medicine, Soc. Univ. Otolaryngologists, Am. Council Otolaryngology, Pan-Am. Soc. Bronchoesophagology., Internat. Fedn. Otolaryngol. Socs. (sec. gen. 1981—), Soc. Mil. Cons. to Armed Forces (sec. 1993—). Clubs: Army Navy, Press, Mil. Attaches of London, Les Chevaliers du Tastevin. Republican. Methodist. Home and Office: 6006 Dellwood Pl Bethesda MD 20817-3812 Home Phone: 301-229-5388.

MCCURDY, HOWARD EARL, educator; b. Atascadero, Calif., Dec. 18, 1941; s. Howard Earl and Jo Janeleen (Test) McC.; m. Margaret Mary Hurley, June 27, 1970. BA, U. Wash., 1962, MA, 1965; PhD, Cornell U., 1969. Legis. aide Washington State Legislature, Olympia, 1963-65; mgmt. analyst Office of Mgmt. & Budget, Washington, 1966-67; prof. Am. U., Washington, 1968—, dir. pub. adminstrn. programs, 1976-81. Fulbright-Hays lectr. U.S. Govt., U. Zambia, Lusaka, 1978; mem. history adv. com. NASA, Washington, 1990-92. Author: Public Administration, 1977, The Space Station Decision, 1990, Inside NASA, 1993; contbr. articles to profl. jours. V.p. Brookmont (Md.) Civic Assn., 1977-78, mem. exec. bd., 1981-88. Mem. Am. Soc. Pub. Adminstrn., Canoe Cruisers Assn. Roman Catholic. Avocations: canoeing, hiking, farming, gardening. Home: RR 2 Box 438 Purcellville VA 20132-9802

MCCURDY, KAREN, human development professor; b. Evanston, Ill. d. John Casey and Patricia McCurdy; m. Frank Karpowicz; children: Kristin Karpowicz, Jacqueline Karpowicz. BA in Polit. Sci., Stanford U., Palo Alto, Calif., 1982; MS in Human Devel. & Social Policy, Northwestern U., Evanston, 1987, PhD in Human Devel. & Social Policy, 1997. Legislative aide Mass. State Legislature, State Rep. Barbara Gray, Boston, 1984—85; dir. Spl. Commn. Relative Divorce, Mass. State Legislature, Boston, 1985—87; sr. rsch. assoc. Prevent Child Abuse Am., Chgo., 1987—95, dep. dir. rsch., 1996—98; asst. prof. dept. human devel. & family studies U. RI, Kingston, 1999—2005, assoc. prof. dept. human devel. & family studies, 2005—. Editor APSAC Advisor, Chgo., 1998—2001; editl. bd. Child Abuse & Neglect: The Internat. Jour., Denver, 2006—; bd. mem. RI Inter Agency Coordinating Coun., Providence, 2009—. Author: (book) Supporting Families: Lessons from the Field; contbr. articles to numerous profl. jours., chapters to books. Chair sch. improvement team South Rd. Elem. Sch., Wakefield, RI, 2005—06; chair elem. sch. improvement team West Kingston Elem. sch., Wakefield, 2006—08; family ptnr. South County Habitat Humanity, Charlestown, RI, 2004; grant reviewer United Way RI, Providence, 2004—05. Grant, William T. Grant Found., 2000—03, Annie E. Casey Found., 2000, Ctr. Urban Studies and Rsch., U. RI, 2008. Mem.: Nat. Coun. Family Rels., Soc. Rsch. Child Devel. Avocations: swimming, skiing. Office: Univ RI 2 Lower Coll Kingston RI 02881 Business E-Mail: kmccurdy@uri.edu.

MCCURDY, LARRY WAYNE, automotive parts company executive; b. Commerce, Tex., July 1, 1935; s. Weldon Lee and Eula Bell (Quinn) McC.; m. Anna Jean Ogle, June 2, 1956; children: Michael, Kimberly, Laurie. BBA, Tex. A&M U., 1957. Jr. acct. Tenneco Inc., Houston, 1958-60; sr. acct. Tenneco Oil Co., Houston, 1960-64; acctg. supr. Tenneco Chems., Houston, 1964-69, from divsn. controller to v.p. fin. Saddle Brook, NJ, 1970-78; sr. v.p. fin. Tenneco Automotive, Deerfield, Ill., 1978-80; pres. Walker Mfg. Co., Racine, Wis., 1980-81; exec. v.p. N.Am. ops. Tenneco Automotive, Deerfield, 1981-82; v.p. fin. Echlin Inc., Branford, Conn., 1983; pres., COO Echlin, Inc., Branford, Conn., 1983-85, pres., 1997—; pres., CEO Moog Automotive Inc., St. Louis, 1985-94; exec. v.p. ops. Cooper Industries, Houston, 1994-97; chmn. bd., pres., CEO Echlin, Inc., Branford, Conn., 1997-98; pres. Dana Automotive Aftermarket Group, 1998-2000; ret., 2000. Bd. dirs. Lear Corp., Mohawk Industries, Inc., Gen. Parts, Inc., Affinia Group Inc. Trustee Somerset County Coll., Somerville, N.J., 1974-78, Millikin U., Decatur, Ill., 1991-97, St. Raphaels's Hosp., New Haven, Conn., 2002—; former mem. bd. dirs. Jr. Achievement, Chgo.; bd. dirs. Sam Houston coun. Boy Scouts Am., 1995-97; mem. adv. coun. Tex. A&M U. Engring. Sch., 1995-97; dir. New Haven Symphony Orch., 2002—. Mem. Fin. Execs. Inst., Nat. Assn. Accts., Motor Equipment Mfrs. Assn. (chmn. bd. dirs. 1989). Personal E-mail: larrywmccurdy@aol.com.

MCCURDY, LAYTON, medical educator; b. Florence, SC, Aug. 20, 1935; m. Gwendolyn A. McCurdy, 1958; children: Robert Jr., David Barclay. BS, U. NC, 1956; MD, Med. U. SC, 1960. Resident in psychiatry NC Meml. Hosp., Chapel Hill, 1961—64; with psychiatry tng. br. NIMH, Bethesda, Md., 1964—66; asst. prof. dept. psychiatry Sch. Medicine Emory U., Atlanta, 1966—68; prof., chmn. dept. psychiatry and behavioral scis. Med. U. SC, 1968—82, v.p. med. affairs, dean, 1990—2001, dean emeritus, disting. prof., 2001—; prof. psychiatry Sch. Medicine U. Pa., Phila., 1982—90; psychiatrist-in-chief Inst. of Pa. Hosp., Phila., 1982—90. Vis. colleague Inst. Psychiatry, U. London, 1974—75; nat. adv. mental health coun. NIMH, 1980—83; apptd. Pa. Adv. Com. for Mental Health and Mental Retardation, 1984—87. Recipient Disting. Alumnus award, Med. U. SC, 1988, Earl B. Higgins Diversity Achievement award, 1999, Disting. Alumnus award, George C. Ham. Soc., 1990, Humanatati award, La Soc. Francaise, 2002. Fellow: Am. Coll. Psychiatrists (pres. 1993—94, Bowis award 1997); mem.: Am. Bd. Psychiatry and Neurology (pres. 1993), Assn. Academic Psychiatry (pres. 1970—71), SC Commn. on Higher Edn. (chmn. 2005—), Royal Coll. Psychiatrists (UK), Am. Psychiat. Assn. (joint commn. pub. affairs 1981—84, chmn. com. on diagnosis and assessment 1988—94), Cosmos Club. Office: Med Univ SC Inst Psychiatry PO Box 250861 Charleston SC 29425 Home Phone: 843-723-1186; Office Phone: 843-792-2084. Business E-Mail: mccurdy@musc.edu.

MCCURDY, MICHAEL CHARLES, illustrator, author; b. NYC, Feb. 17, 1942; s. Charles Errett and Beatrice (Beatson) McC.; m. Deborah Lamb, Sept. 7, 1968; children: Heather, Mark. BFA, Tufts U., 1964, MFA, 1971. Dir. Penmaen Press, Lincoln, Mass., 1968-85; instr. Concord (Mass.) Acad., 1972-75, Wellesley (Mass.) Coll., 1976. Illustrator: The Man Who Planted Trees, 1985, American Tall Tales, 1991, American Buffalo, 1992, The Way West: Journal of a Pioneer Woman, 1993, Giants in the Land, 1993, The Gettysburg Address, 1995, The Seasons Sewn, 1996, American Fairy Tales, 1996; author, illustrator: Hannah's Farm, 1988, Trapped by the Ice, 1997, The Sailor's Alphabet, 1998, An Algonquian Year: The Year According to the Full Moon, 2000, So Said Ben, 2007, War and the Pity of War, 1998, Tarzan, 1999, The Wizard of Oz, 1999, Iron Horses, 1999, The Signers: The 56 Stories Behind the Declaration of Independence, 2002, Walden by H.D. Thoreau, 2004, Tales of Terror, 2004, The Founders: The 39 Stories Behind the U.S. Constitution, 2005; editor, illustrator: Escape From Slavery: The Boyhood of Frederick Douglass in His Own Words, 1994. Mem. Great Barrington (Mass.) Housing Authority, 1990-93. Small press grantee Nat. Endowment Arts, 1978, Mass. Arts and Humanities, 1978. Mem. Soc. Printers, St. Botolph Club. Democrat. Episcopalian. Office Phone: 413-783-3614. Personal E-mail: michaelmccurdy@verizon.net.

MC CURDY, PATRICK PIERRE, editor; b. Angers, France, Sept. 14, 1928; s. Joseph Alexander and Constance Yolande (Hillairet de Boisferon) McC.; m. Eiko Yamada, May 30, 1953; children: Alan J., Wendy C., Alec J., Jeffrey R. BS in Chem. Engring., Carnegie Inst. Tech., 1949. Chem. engr. tech. service dept. Humble Oil & Refining Co., Baytown, Tex., 1949-50; chem. engr. Callery Chem. Co., Pa., 1954-56; sr. chem. engr. U.S. Army Engr. R & D Labs., Ft. Belvoir, Va., 1956-60; asst. editor Chem. & Engring. News, Washington, 1960-61, NYC, 1961-62, bur. head Frankfurt, Germany, 1962-64, Tokyo, 1964-67, mng. editor Washington, 1967-69, editor, 1969-73; editor in chief Chemical Week, 1973-80, 84-87, editor-in-chief, assoc. pub., 1987-88; dir. communications Am. Chem. Soc., 1988-91, dir. industry rels., 1991-93, founding editor Today's Chemist at Work, 1989-97; cons. American Chemical Soc., 1993-97; pub. issues mgr. Dow Chem. Co., Midland, Mich., 1980-82, dir. tech. communications, 1982-84. Cons. in field, 1997—; editl. cons. Chem. Heritage mag., 1997—. Served U.S. Coast Guard, Great Lakes, 1945, first lt. C.E. AUS, 1950-54. Recipient Jesse H. Neal award, 1979, finalist 1985; recipient Carnegie Mellon Univ. Alumni Merit award, 1988. Mem.: Societe de Chimie Industrielle (past pres. Am. sect.), Chemists Club, Fgn. Corrs. Club Japan, Am. Chem. Soc., Tokyo Am. Club, Tau Beta Pi, Phi Kappa, Theta Tau, Phi Kappa Phi. Home and Office: 11717 Chauncey Ln Mason Neck VA 22079-4140 Personal E-mail: mccurdypp@aol.com.

MCCURLEY, MARY JOHANNA, lawyer; b. Baton Rouge, Oct. 3, 1953; d. William Edward and Leora Elizabeth (Block) Trice; m. Carl Michael McCurley, June 6, 1983; 1 stepchild, Melissa Reneé McCurley. BA, Centenary Coll., 1975; JD, St. Mary's U., 1979. Bar: Tex. 1979; cert. family law. Assoc. Martin, Withers & Box, Dallas, 1979-82, Raggio & Raggio, Inc., 1982-83; ptnr. Bruner, McColl, McColloch & McCurley, 1983-87; assoc., ptnr. Selligson & Douglass, 1987-90; jr. ptnr. Koons, Fuller, McCurley & VandenEykel, 1990—92; ptnr. McCurley, Orsinger, McCurley,. Nelson & Downing, 1992—. Contbr. articles to profl. jours. Adv. Women's Service League, Dallas, 1993—. Master: Annette Stewart Am. Inn Ct. (sec.-treas. 2003—04); mem.: Dallas Bar Assn., Tex. Acad. Family Law Specialist, Tex. State Bar Assn. (sec. 2001, vice-chair 2001, treas. 2001, chair 2003, family law coun. 1987), Dallas Bar Assn. (chair family law sect. 1985), Am. Acad. Matrimonial Lawyers (treas. Tex. chpt. 1993—95, sec. 1995—96, pres. 1997, pres. Tex. chpt. 1997—98, bd. govs. 2000, nat. sec. 2000—02, nat. v.p. 2002—, nat. bd. dirs.). Methodist. Avocations: golf, travel, jogging, horseback riding. Home: 4076 Hanover Ave Dallas TX 75225-7009 Office: McCurley Orsinger McCurley Nelson & Downing LLP 5950 Sherry Ln Ste 800 Dallas TX 75225-6533 Office Phone: 214-273-2400.

MCCURLEY, ROBERT LEE, JR., lawyer, educator; b. Gadsden, Ala., Sept. 7, 1941; s. Robert Lee and Nellie Ruth McC.; m. Barbara; 1 child, Allison Leah. BS, U. Ala., 1963, JD, 1966. Bar: Ala. 1966, D.C. 1973, U.S. Ct. Mil. Appeals 1966, U.S. Supreme Ct. 1970, U.S. Ct. Appeals (5th cir.) 1972, U.S. Ct. Appeals (11th cir.) 1973, U.S. Ct. Appeals (fed. cir.) 1981. Asst. to dir. Fed. Savs. & Loan Ins. Corp., Washington, 1966-67; partner firm Rains, Rains, McCurley & Wilson, Gadsden, Ala., 1967-75; city judge Southside, Ala., 1970-75; dir. Ala. Law Inst., 1975—; assoc. dir. U. Ala. Center Public Law and Service, 1981-82; asst. dean Sch. Law U. Ala., 1978-81. Panelist White House Conf. on Volunteerism; pres. Gadsden Jaycees, 1972; mem. White House Fifty States Project; adj. prof. Ala. Sch. Law, 1975-2006, Cumberland Sch. Law, 2005-07. Editor: Divorce, Alimony and Child Support Custody, 4th edit., 2005, Land Laws of Alabama, 9th edit. rev., 2007, The Legislative Process, 9th edit., 2007, Alabama Law Office Practice Deskbook, 10th edit., 2007, Federally Mandated State Legislation, 1990, Alabama Legislation, Cases and Statutes, 6th edit., 2007, Alabama Election Handbook, 13th edit., 2008. Pres. Gadsden Boys Club, 1971, Kiwanis Internat. Found., 1998—2000; mem. Nat. Dem. Charter Commn., 1974. Recipient Svc. award, Ala. Bar Commr., 2004, Gewin award, Ala. State Bar, 2000, Bar Commnrs. award, 2004, Roger Sayers Disting. Svc. award, U. Ala., 2005; Henry Toll fellow, Coun. State Govt., 1992. Fellow ABA, Ala. Bar Assn., mem. Am. Law Inst. (life), Order of Coif, Scribes, Farrah Law Soc., Commn. Uniform State Laws, Kiwanis (pres. Tuscaloosa club 1976, gov. Ala. dist. 1984, 91-92, v.p. 1998-2000, Internat. Found. pres.), Indian Hills County Club, Univ. Club. Presbyterian. Office Phone: 205-348-7411.

MCCURN, NEAL PETERS, federal judge; b. Syracuse, NY, Apr. 6, 1926; LL.B., Syracuse U., 1952, JD, 1960. Bar: N.Y. 1952. Ptnr. Mackenzie Smith Lewis Mitchell & Hughes, Syracuse, 1957-79; judge U.S. Dist. Ct. (no. dist.) N.Y., 1979-88; chief judge U.S. Dist. Ct. (no. dist.), NY, 1988-93; sr. judge, 1993—. Del. N.Y. State Constl. Conv., 1976; mem. 2d Cir. Jud. Council, 1987-93. Pres. Syracuse Common Coun., 1970-78. Mem. ABA, N.Y. State Bar Assn. (chmn. state constn. com.), Onondaga County Bar Assn. (past pres.), Am. Coll. Trial Lawyers, Am. Judicature Soc. (bd. dirs. 1980-84). Office: US Dist Ct 100 S Clinton St Rm 344 Syracuse NY 13261-6100 Office Phone: 315-234-8590. Business E-Mail: neal_mccurn@nynd.uscourts.gov.

MCCURRY, MARGARET IRENE, architect, furniture and interior designer, educator; b. Chgo., Sept. 26, 1942; d. Paul D. and Irene B. McC.; m. Stanley Tigerman, Mar. 17, 1979. BA, Vassar Coll., 1964. Registered arch., Ill., Mass., Mich., Tex., Wis., Pa., Ind., Fla.; registered interior designer, Ill. Design coord. Quaker Oats Co., Chgo., 1964-66; sr. interior designer Skidmore, Owings & Merrill, Chgo., 1966-77; pvt. practice architect Margaret I, Chgo., 1977-82; ptnr. Tigerman McCurry Archs., Chgo., 1982—. Vis. studio critic Art Inst. Chgo., 1985-86, 88, 98, lectr., 1988, 98; vis. studio critic U. Ill., Chgo., Miami U., Oxford, Ohio, 1990; juror Internat. furniture awards Progressive Architecture mag., NYC, 1986, advt. awards, 1988; juror design grants Nat. Endowment for Arts, Washington, 1983; NEA Challenge Design Rev., 1992; peer reviewer design excellence program GSA, 1992—; juror, Wis., Minn., Calif., Va., Washington, Pitts., Ky., Ga. Conn. Soc. Archs., Detroit, NYC, Memphis, Austin, LA, Toledo, Jacksonville chpts. AIA, Am. Wood Coun., AIA Students Design Competition, 1993. Author: Margaret McCurry: Constructing 25 Short Stories, 2000; contbr. Chgo. Archtl. Club Jour.; designer, contbr. archtl. exhibit Art Inst. Chgo., 1983-85, 93, 99, 2005, Chgo. Hist. Soc., 1984, Gulbenkian Found., Lisbon Portugal, 1989, Chgo. Athenaeum, 1990, Gwenda Jay Gallery, 1992, Women of Design Traveling Exhbn., 1992-96; archtl. drawings and models in permanent collection Art Inst. Chgo. and Deutsches Architektur Mus., Frankfurt. Chmn. furniture sect. fundraising auction Sta. WTTW-TV, PBS, Chgo., 1975-76; mem. Chgo. Beautiful Com., 1968-70; pres. alumni coun. Grad. Sch. Design, Harvard U., 1997-2000; bd. dirs. Architecture and Design Soc. Art Inst. Chgo., 1988-97, mem. textile adv. bd. textile dept. Loeb fellow Harvard U., 1986-87; recipient Builders Choice Grand award Builders Mag., 1985, Interior Design award Interiors Mag., 1983, Dean of Architecture award Chgo. Design Source and the Mdse. Mart, 1989, Designer of Distinction award ASID, 2002; named a Dean of Design, Archtl. Digest, 2005, AD 100 award, 2007; inducted into Interior Design Hall of Fame, Interior Design Mag., 1990, Best of Year Interior Design Magazine, Ill., 2006, Best of Show ASID Chpt., 2008, Design Excellence award, 2008. Fellow AIA (mem. coll. fellows, v.p. bd. dirs. Chgo. chpt. 1984-89, nat. design com., chair 1993, lectr. Colo. chpt. 1985, nat. conv. 1988, 97-98, Monterey Design Conf. 1989, Washington Design Ctr. 1989, Nat. Honor award 1984, Nat. Interior Architecture award 1992, 98, Disting. Bldg. award Chgo. chpt. 1984, 86, 91, 94, 99-2000, Disting. Interior Architecture award 1981, 83, 88, 91, 97, product display Neocon award 1985, 88, Gold award best of Neocon 1998, Associated Lic. Archs. Silver Medal Design award 2003), Internat. Interior Design Assn., Chgo. Network, Am. Soc. Interior Designers (v.p. bd. dirs. Chgo. chpt., Nat. Design award 1992, 94, Ill. chpt. Excellence Design award 1994, 2005,2008, Design Excellence award in hist. preservation, 2005, in corp. interiors, 2005), Chgo. Archtl. Club, Arts Club Chgo., Harvard Alumni Assn. (dir. 2000-06, v.p. Chgo., 2004-06, pres. 2006-), Harvard Club of Chgo. Harvard Club Chgo(v.p. 2004-06, pres. 2006-08). Episcopalian. Avocations: drawing, writing, travel, golf, gardening. Office: Tigerman McCurry Archs 444 N Wells St Ste 206 Chicago IL 60654-4501 Home Phone: 312-944-5418; Office Phone: 312-644-5880. E-mail: mimccurry@tigerman-mccurry.com.

MCCUTCHAN, GORDON EUGENE, retired lawyer, insurance company executive; b. Buffalo, Sept. 30, 1935; s. George Lawrence and Mary Esther (De Puy) McC.; m. Linda Brown; children: Lindsey, Elizabeth. BA, Cornell U., 1956, MBA, 1958, LLB, 1959. Bar: N.Y. 1959, Ohio 1964. Pvt. practice, Rome, NY, 1959-61; atty., advisor SEC, Washington, 1961-64; ptnr. McCutchan, Druen, Maynard, Rath & Dietrich, 1964-94; mem. office of gen. counsel Nationwide Mut. Ins. Co., Columbus, Ohio, 1964-94, sr. v.p., gen. counsel, 1982-89, exec. v.p., gen. counsel, 1989-94; exec. v.p. Law and Corp. Svcs., Nationwide Ins. Enterprise, 1994-98; ret., 1998. Trustee, bd. govs. Franklin U., 1992-97; trustee Ohio Tuition Trust Authority, 1992-97. Mem. Columbus Bar Assn., Ohio Bar Assn., Am. Corp. Counsel Assn., Assn. Life Inst. Counsel (bd. govs. 1990-94), Fedn. Ins. and Corp. Counsel, Am. Coun. Life Ins. (chair legal sect. 1992-93). Home: 2376 Oxford Rd Columbus OH 43221-4011 E-mail: tunkpa@columbus.rr.com.

MCCUTCHEN, TAMMY DEE, lawyer, former federal agency administrator; b. Kewanee, Ill., Oct. 20, 1965; BA, Western Ill. U., 1987; JD, Northwestern U., 1990. Clk. US Ct. Appeals (7th Cir.), 1991—92; assoc. Skadden, Arps, Slate, Meagher and Flom, Chgo., 1992—95, Matkov, Salzman, Madoff anf Gunn, 1995—99; sr. counsel Hershey Foods Corp., 1999—2001; adminstr. wage & hour divsn. US Dept. Labor, Washington, 2001—04; ptnr. Dickstein Shapiro LLP, Washington, 2004—07; shareholder Littler Mendelson, P.C., Washington, 2007—. Mem.: ABA, DC Bar Assn., Ill. Bar Assn., The Federalist Soc. Office: Littler Mendelson PC 1150 17th St NW Ste 900 Washington DC 20036 E-mail: tmccutchen@littler.com.

MCCUTCHEON, ALLAN LEE, statistics educator; b. Clarinda, Iowa, Mar. 15, 1950; s. Merle Marvin and Margaret Lucille (Larabee) McC.; m. Nancy Ann Cooper, June 13, 1970 (div. May 1975); 1 child, Jennifer; m. Elisabeth Jean Crockett, May 25, 1985. BS, Iowa State U., 1972; MA, U. Chgo., 1977, PhD, 1982. Asst. prof. sociology U. Del., Newark, 1982-88, assoc. prof. sociology, 1988-96, assoc. chair dept. sociology, 1989-95; Donald O. Clifton chair survey rsch. U. Nebr., Lincoln, 1996—, dir. Gallup Rsch. Ctr., 1996—; sr. scientist Gallup Orgn., 1996—. Cons. Disaster Rsch. Ctr., Newark, 1986-88; vis. scientist Max Planck Inst., Freiburg, Germany, 1988-89; dozent U. Cologne (Germany), 1989, 96, 2001, 07; instr. European Consortium for Polit. Rsch. U. Essex (Eng.), 1990—; mem. sci. adv. coun. German Ctr. for Survey Rsch. and Methodology, 1998-2004. Author: Latent Class Analysis, 1987; editor (with J. Hagenaars): (book) Applied Latent Class Analysis, 2002 (newsletter) States and Societies, 1988-95; contbr. articles to profl. jours. Resource cons. Leadership Del. United Way, Wilmington, 1991-92. U. Chgo. rsch. fellow, 1974-77; Deutscher Akademischer Austauschdienst scholar, 1990; Fulbright scholar, The Netherlands, 1995-96. Fellow Am. Statis. Assn.; mem. World Assn. for Pub. Opinion Rsch. (sec.-treas. 2000-2004, gen. sec. 2004—), Coun. for European Studies, Am. Assn. for Pub. Opinion Rsch., Midwest Assn. for Pub. Opinion Rsch. (v.p. 2002-2003, pres. 2003-2004), Am. Sociol. Assn., Sigma Xi. Avocations: German culture, literature. Office: Univ Of Nebraska Gallup Research Ctr 201 N 13th St Lincoln NE 68508-1505 E-mail: AMcCutcheon1@unl.edu.

MCCUTCHEON, DEBRA, school librarian; m. David McCutcheon; 1 child, Reid. MS, Southern Ill. U., Carbondale. Cert. tchr. Nat. Bd. Profl. Tchg. Standards, 2008. Libr. tchr. Red Bud HS, Ill., 1984—. Mem.: ALA, Internat. Reading Assn., Ill. Sch. Libr. Media Assn., Ill. Edn. Assn. (regional coun. sec. 2006—08).

MCCUTCHEON, STEVEN CLIFTON, ecological and environmental engineer, hydrologist; b. Decatur, Ala., Oct. 29, 1952; s. Bernard Clifton and Rosa May (Askenburg) McC.; m. Sherry Lynn Sharp; children: Michael Ian, Alexander Tavis. BS, Auburn U., 1975; MS, Vanderbilt U., 1977, PhD, 1979. EIT Ala., 1975, diplomate, Am. Acad. Water Resources Engrs., 2005, registered civil and environ. engr., La., 2004, profl. engr., Miss., 2007. Hydrologist US Geol. Survey, Bay St. Louis, Miss., 1977-86; sr. environ. engr. US EPA, Athens, Ga., 1986—. Instr., asst. Vanderbilt U, 1977-79; adj. asst. prof. Tulane U., New Orleans, 1984-85; cons., expert witness in field, 1985—; panel mem. Nat. Rsch. Coun., Washington, 1989-92; adj. prof. forestry, mem. faculty engring., affiliate ecology U. Ga., Athens, 1989—; asst. prof. Clemson U., SC, 1990-97; program evaluator Accreditation Bd. Engring. & Tech., 1992—; sci. oversight panel, Interagency Fla. Bay Sci. Program, 1996-; MS com. Fla. Internat. U. Dept. Civil Engring., 1998; reader U. Roorkee, India, 2001-02; prof. U. Parma, Italy, 2004; U. Miss. PhD com., 2004-06; reader U. Ctrl. Queensland, Australia, 2005-06; temp mem. grad. faculty U. Ala., Tuscaloosa, 2005-08. Author: Water Quality Modeling, vol. 1, 1989, Water Quality, Handbook of Hydrology, 1993; editor and author (with others): Manual for Performing Estuarine Waste Load Allocations, 1990, Hydrodynamics and Transport for Water Quality Modeling, 1999, editor and author: Phytoremediation, 2003; editor Jour. Environ. Engring., 1992—94, mem. editl. bd. Ecol. Engring., 1995—, Hazardous Toxic and Radioactive Waste Mgmt., 1996—97, Internat. Jour. Phytoremediation, 2000—, mem. editl. bd., adv. bd. (book series) Science, Education, Innovations, 2004—, co-editor Environ. Sci. and Pollution Rsch., 2003—05, assoc. editor, 2005—06, assoc. subject editor, 2006—07, advisor, 2008—; contbr. chapters to books, articles to profl. jours. Mem. Zoning Commn., St. Tammany Parish, La., 1984-85; vice=chmn. Planning Adv. Bd., St. Tammany Parish, 1985; asst. den leader Cub Scouts Am., Athens, pack 83, 1991-92, pack 96, 1998-99, den leader, 1999-2001; mem. Am. Inst. Architects Recon. Team, Sri Lanka, 2005; originator Hurricane Relief Fund Am. Soc. Civil Engrs. Found., 2005-07. Recipient medal and plaque, Korea Soc. Water Pollution Rsch. and Control, Seoul, 1986, Engr. of Yr. award in EPA, NSPE, 1992, Engr. of Yr. in Govt. award, Ga. Engr. Week Com., 2004, Performance award, EPA, 1986—99, Spl. Svc. award, 1990, 1991; co-recipient EPA Sci. Achievement award in waste mgmt., Air and Waste Mgmt. Assn., 1995, EPA Sci. Achievement award in Chemistry, Am. Chem. Soc., 1997, Sci. and Tech. Achievement award, EPA, 1999, 2006, Bronze medal, 2001, 2002; grantee Tewkesbury fellowship, U. Melbourne, Australia, 2004. Mem.: ASCE (br. pres. 1983—84, sect. dir. 1984—85, 1995—2001, sect. v.p. 2001—03, sect. pres.-elect 2003—04, rep. Dist. 14 coun. 2003—04, sect. pres. 2004—05, nat. dir. Dist. 14, Region 5 2004—07, exec. com. 2006—07, chair bd. govs. region 5 2006—07, Young Civil Engr. of Yr. award 1984, Richard R. Torrens award 1994, Govt. Civil Engr. of Yr. award 2004, Outstanding Membership Chair 2004, Environ. Engring. Divsn. Service award 1995, Louisiana Sect. Svc. award 2006), Internat. Soc. Phytotechnologies (charter), Am. Acad. Water Resources Engrs. (elected charter diplomate 2005), Water Environ. Fedn., Internat. Assn. Hydrologic Scis., Internat. Water Assn., Internat. Soc. Environ. Ethics (charter), Am. Geophys. Union, Am. Ecol. Engring. Soc. (chair com. registration and certification 2001—04, v.p., pres.-elect 2004—05, pres. 2005—06, past pres. 2006—07, charter), Phi Theta Kappa, Phi Kappa Phi, Sigma Xi (chpt. sec. 1982—84, membership com. 1984—85). Achievements include pioneering research in phytoremediation and ecological engring. to clean up federal facilities and response to Exxon Valdez oil spill. Avocations: travel, reading, history. Home: 147 Spalding Ct Athens GA 30605-3716 Office: U Ga Faculty of Engring Driftmier Engring Ctr Athens GA 30602 Home Phone: 706-543-6972; Office Phone: 706-542-1455. Personal E-mail: EnvironHyd@aol.com. Business E-Mail: StevenMc@uga.edu.

MCDADE, JAMES RUSSELL, management consultant; b. Dallas, Jan. 15, 1925; s. Marion W. and Jeannette (Reneau) McD.; m. Elaine Bushey, Sep. 10, 1955. BSEE, So. Meth. U., Dallas, 1947; MBA, Northwestern U., Evanston, Ill., 1950. Asst. to pres. Davidson Corp., Chgo., 1951-52, Mergenthaler Linotype Co., Bklyn., 1952-53, comml. works mgr., 1953-56; chief indsl. engr. Tex. Instruments, Inc., Dallas, 1956-57, product gen. mgr., 1958-60, v.p., 1961-64; chmn. bd. McDade Properties Co., Aspen (Colo.), Denver, Dallas, 1964—. Bd. dirs. Pitkin County Bank, Aspen; chmn. bd. dirs. Harley-Davidson Tex., Westec Security of Aspen, Aspen Security, Inc. Founding mem. Aspen Art Mus., 1980; mem. Ballet Aspen, 1980—; pres. club Aspen Valley Hosp., 1984—. Served to 1st lt. USAF, 1943-46. Mem.: Presidents Assn., Am. Mgmt. Assn., Rep. Senatorial Inner Circle. Avocations: skiing, horseback riding, camping, swimming. Personal E-mail: jrmco@jrmco.com.

MCDADE, ROBERTA CLARK, secondary school educator; b. Balt., Dec. 19, 1951; d. Joseph Thomas and Esther Claire Clark; children: Edward Matthew Day, Rebecca Marie Day. BA in English and Elem. Edn., Salisbury State Coll., Md., 1973; MEd in Secondary Math., U. Del., Newark, Del., 1976. Lic. profl. tchr. Colo. Dept. Edn., 2002. Resident asst. Salisbury State Coll., Md., 1971—73; tchr. Kent County Pub. Schs., Chestertown, Md., 1973—76; home daycare provider Chestertown, Md., 1976—82; instr. math. Chesapeake Coll., Wye Mills, Md., 1982—83; tchr. Anne Arundel County Pub. Schs., Annapolis, Md., 1983—87; substitute tchr. Colo. Springs, 1987—88; instr. Basic Skills Edn. Program, Fort Carson, Colo., 1989; tchr. Colo. Springs Dist. 11, Colo., 1990—. Mem. com. Md. State Dept. Edn., Balt., 1980—83; participant step program NASA, Houston, 1996. Coach baseball Severna Pk. (Md.) Little League, 1986; coach wrestling Severna Pk. (Md.) Parks and Recreation, 1985—86; sec. Boy Scouts Am., Cape St Claire, Md., 1986—87, mem. troop com. Pikes Peak Coun. Colo. Springs, 1989—2006; leader Girl Scouts Am., Arnold, Md., 1986—87, leader wagon wheel coun. Colo. Springs, 1992—97; host parent Am. Field Svc., Colo. Springs, 1991—2000; adv. youth Sr. H.S. Chapel at Peterson AFB, Colo. Springs, 1987—89, Asbury United Meth. Fellowship, Salisbury, Md., 1970—73; tchr. christian edn. St Francis Assisi Ch., 1994—97, coord. christian edn., 1998—2001, mem. discernment com., 2005—06. Home: 1811 Summernight Terr Colorado Springs CO 80909-2725 Office: Sprng Creek Youth Svcs Ctr 3190 E Las Vegas St Colorado Springs CO 80906 Personal E-mail: beccyesmom@hotmail.com. Business E-Mail: ackerrc@d11.org.

MCDADE, SANDY D., lawyer, paper company executive; BA, Whitman Coll., 1974; JD cum laude, Seattle U., 1979. Mem. law dept. Weyerhaeuser Co., Federal Way, Wash., 1980—2000, corp. sec., 1993—2000, v.p. strategic planning, 2000—03, sr. v.p. Can., 2003—05, sr. v.p., indsl. wood products and internat. bus., 2005—06, sup. gen. counsel, 2006—. Mem.: World Trade Ctr. (bd. of governors, Seattle), Bd. of Arts Fund, Wash. State Bar Assn. (past chmn. corp. law dept. sect.). Office: Weyerhaeuser Co PO Box 9777 Federal Way WA 98063-9777

MCDADE, SEAN, market research company executive; BAA, Temple U., 1990, PhD in Bus. Mgmt., 1996. With Gallup Orgn.; dir. rsch. LRA Worldwide, founder, pres. PeopleMetrics, Inc., 2000—. Named one of 40 Under 40, Phila. Bus. Jour., 2006. Office: PeopleMetrics, Inc Ste 3220 1717 Arch St Philadelphia PA 19103 Office Phone: 215-979-8030, 215-979-8031. Office Fax: 215-979-8049.

MCDAID, JIM, government official; b. Termon, Ireland, Oct. 3, 1949; div.;5 children. Student, U. Coll., Galway, Ireland; MB, Bel B.A.O. Surg. H.O., 1974-79. Sr. surg. ho. officer Letterkenny Gen. Hosp., 1974-79; gen. practice, 1980-97; founder, chmn. Donegal Hospice Movement, Fianna Fáil Teachta Dála, Donegal North East, 1988—; min. Dept. Tourism & Trade, Dublin, 1997—2002; min. state Dept. Transport, 2002—04. Office: Dept Tourism Sport & Rec Kildare St Dublin 2 Ireland

MCDANIEL, A. STEPHEN, lawyer; b. Memphis, Nov. 13, 1946; BBA, U. Memphis, 1968, JD, 1973. Bar: Tenn. 1973, Mo. 1975, cert.: Tenn. Commn. Continuing Legal Edn. and Specialization (estate planning specialist). Estate and gift tax atty. US Treasury Dept., 1973—75; positions up to mng. ptnr. Williams, McDaniel, Wolfe & Womack, P.C., Memphis, 1975—. Instr. estate planning and estate & gift tax U. Memphis Sch. Law, 1990—2000. Contbr. articles to profl. jours. Named one of Top 100 Attys., Worth mag., 2006—08. Fellow: Am. Coll. Trust and Estate Counsel; mem.: Tenn. Bar Assn., Memphis Bar Assn. Office: Williams McDaniel Wolfe & Womack 5521 Murray Ave Memphis TN 38119 Office Phone: 901-767-8200. E-mail: sMcDaniel@wmww.com.

MCDANIEL, CHARLES J., art educator; b. Chgo., Dec. 6, 1959; s. John William and Betty Anne McDaniel; m. Debra Lynn Riley, June 17, 1989. BA in Art Edn., Morehead State U., Ky., 1983, MA in Studio Art, 1993. Provisional cert. Ky., 1982, cert. EMT Ky., 1988, firefighter Ky., 1993. Tchr., coach Knott County Ctrl. HS, Hindman, Ky., 1989—93, Jenkins Mid./HS, Ky., 1993—94, E. Carter HS, Grayson, Ky., 1998—; tchr. Cordia Sch., Lotts Creek, Ky., 1989—93, W. Brown HS, Mt. Orab, Ohio, 1994—97. Firefighter, EMT 1st responder Rt. 377 Vol. Fire Dept., Ky., 1998—. Mem.: NEA. Avocations: Civil War reenactment, travel, blacksmith. Home: 471 Rockfork Rd Morehead KY 40351 Office: E Carter HS 405 Hitchins Rd Grayson KY 41143-1423

MCDANIEL, DUSTIN, state attorney general; b. Fayetteville, Ark., Apr. 29, 1972; m. Amanda Miller; 1 child, Emma Grace. BA in Pub. Adminstrn., U. Ark., Fayetteville, 1994; JD, U. Ark. Law Sch., 1998. Patrol officer Jonesboro Police Dept., 1994—96; legal counsel Craighead County Dem. Ctrl. Com.; ptnr. McDaniel & Wells, Jonesboro, Ark.; mem. Ark. Ho. Reps. from dist. 75, Little Rock, 2005—06; atty. gen. State of Ark., Little Rock, 2007—. Named Outstanding State Legislator, Ark. Mcpl. League; named one of 10 Best Legislators, Ark. Dem. Gazette, 2005. Mem.: Craighead County Bar Assn., Ark. Trial Lawyers Assn. (mem., Bd. Governors), Ark. Bar Assn. (chairman, Civil Litig. Sect. 2002—03, chair, Consumer Law Handbook Com., Golden Gavel award, Disting. Svc. award). Democrat. Office: Office of Atty Gen 200 Tower Bldg 323 Center St Little Rock AR 72201-2610 Office Phone: 501-376-1500, 800-482-8982. Office Fax: 501-376-1507.*

MCDANIEL, JAMES ALAN, lawyer; b. St. Joseph, Mo., June 10, 1953; s. John Redmond and Mary Jane (Chiles) McD.; m. Margaret L. Randle, Sept. 22, 1990; children: Susan (dec.), John. AB with distinction, Stanford U., 1975; JD, Harvard U., 1978. Bar: Mass. 1978, U.S. Dist. Ct. Mass. 1979, U.S. Ct. Appeals (1st cir.) 1979. Assoc. Choate, Hall & Stewart LLP, Boston, 1978-85, ptnr., 1986—, chmn. bus. dept., 1993-96, mem. firm mgmt. com., 1998-2000, chmn. gen. corp. and securities group, 2001—04. Co-founder, editor-in-chief Harvard Environ. Law Rev., 1976-77. Bd. dirs. DARE Family Svcs., Inc., chmn. bd. dir., 2003—. Fellow Am. Coll. Investment Counsel; mem. ABA, Boston Bar Assn. (chmn. banking law com. 1996-98, bus. law sect. 1999-2001), Soc. Corp. Secs. Governance Profls., Jamestowne Soc., Somerset Chpt. Magna Charta Barons, Plantagenet Soc., Harvard Club Boston, Boston Athenaeum, St. Peter's Episcopal Ch. (mem. vestry 2001—07), Phi Beta Kappa. Democrat. Episcopalian. Home: 326 Highland St Weston MA 02493-2626 Personal E-mail: jmdaniel@choate.com.

MCDANIEL, JAMES EDWIN, lawyer; b. Dexter, Mo., Nov. 22, 1931; s. William H. and Gertie M. (Woods) McD.; m. Mary Jane Crawford, Jan. 22, 1955; children: John William, Barbara Anne. AB, Washington U., St. Louis, 1957, JD, 1959. Bar: Mo. 1959. Assoc. firm Walther, Barnard, Cloyd & Timm, 1959—60, McDonald, Barnard, Wright & Timm, 1960—63, ptnr., 1963—65, Barnard, Timm & McDaniel, St. Louis, 1965—73, Barnard & Baer, St. Louis, 1973—82, Lashly & Baer, St. Louis, 1982—2002, of counsel, 2002—; pros. atty. Glendale, Mo., 1968—2008. City atty. City of Glendale, Mo., 1996-2009; bd. dirs. Eden. Theol. Sem., 1995-2007; lectr. Latvian U., Riga, Inst. Fgn. Rels., Banking in Am., 1992-93. Leader legal del. Chinese-Am. Comparative Law Study, China, 1988, Russian-Am. Comparative Law Study, Russia, 1990; trustee, past chmn., past treas. 1st Congl. Ch. St. Louis. With USAF, 1951-55. Fellow Am. Bar Found. (life), St. Louis Bar Found. (life; bd. dirs. 2005-, pres. 2007—09); mem. ABA (bd. govs. 1997-2000, ho. of dels. 1976-80, 84-92, 97-2000, state del. 1986-92, chmn. lawyers conf., jud. adminstrn. divsn. 1992-95, 8th cir. rep. standing com. on fed. jud. 1995-98, mem. standing com. on jud. qualification, tenure and compensation 1996-97, adv. com. law and nat. security 1999-2008), The Mo. Bar (pres. 1981-82, bd. govs. 1974-83), Mo. Assn. Def. Counsel, Bar Assn. Met. St. Louis (pres. 1972), Internat. Assn. Ins. Counsel, Assn. Def. Counsel St. Louis (past pres.), Phi Delta Phi. Home: 767 Elmwood Ave Saint Louis MO 63122-3216 Office: Lashly & Baer 714 Locust St Saint Louis MO 63101-1699 Office Phone: 314-621-2939. Personal E-mail: jemglendale@earthlink.net. Business E-Mail: jemcdaniel@lashlybaer.com.

MCDANIEL, JARREL DAVE, lawyer; b. Clovis, N.Mex., Oct. 17, 1930; s. Raymond Lee and Blanch McD.; m. Anne Louise McAllister; children: Jarrel Dave Jr., Julia Anne. AA, Riverside Coll., 1951; BA, U. Tex., 1956, LLB, 1957. Bar: Tex. 1957. Assoc. Vinson & Elkins, Houston, 1957-69, ptnr., 1969-96; of counsel Sheinfeld, Maley & Kay, Houston, 1997-2001; sr. counsel Akin Gump Strauss Hauer & Feld LLP, Houston, 2001—06; counsel King & Spalding, LLP, Houston, 2007—. Author, lectr. in field. Served with USAF, 1950-54. Mem.: ABA, Am. Bankruptcy Inst., State Bar Tex., Am. Coll. Bankruptcy, Houston Club. Roman Catholic. Home: 1217 Potomac Dr Houston TX 77057-1919 Office: King & Spalding LLP 1100 Louisiana Ste 4000 Houston TX 77002-5213 Office Phone: 713-751-3251. Business E-Mail: jmcdaniel@kslaw.com.

MCDANIEL, MILDRED GAGE, elementary school educator; b. Marion, NC, June 6, 1938; d. William James and Nellie Ruth (Davis) Ledbetter; m. Keith S. Gage, June 13, 1959 (dec. May 1976); children: Wendy Carver, Tammy Butler; m. William Royce McDaniel, Apr. 23, 1983 (dec. July 2005). BS, Towson U., 1960; masters equiv., Johns Hopkins U., U. Md., 1972. Tchr., grade 6 Balt. (Md.) County Bd. Edn., 1960-66, reading tchr., 1968-73, reading specialist, 1974—98. Recipient Vol. Svc. award Gov. of Md., 1988, Thanks to Tchrs. Excellence award, 1990. Mem. Internat. Reading Assn., Women Educators Baltimore County, Vol. Network (mem. vol. adv. com. 1994-2003, chmn. vol. partnership adv. com. Baltimore County Bd. Edn. 2001-03) Baptist. Home: 22 Dihedral Dr Baltimore MD 21220-4611

MCDANIEL, MYRA ATWELL, lawyer, former state official; b. Phila., Dec. 13, 1932; d. Eva Lucinda (Yores) Atwell; m. Reuben Roosevelt McDaniel Jr., Feb. 20, 1955; children: Diane Lorraine, Reuben Roosevelt III. BA, U. Pa., 1954; JD, U. Tex., 1975; LLD, Huston-Tillotson Coll., 1984, Jarvis Christian Coll., 1986. Bar: Tex. 1975, U.S. Dist. Ct. (we. dist.) Tex. 1977, U.S. Dist. Ct. (so. and no. dists.) Tex. 1978, U.S. Ct. Appeals (5th cir.) 1978, U.S. Supreme Ct. 1978, U.S. Dist. Ct. (ea. dist.) Tex. 1979. Asst atty. gen. State of Tex., Austin, 1975-81, chief taxation div., 1979-81, gen. counsel to gov., 1983-84, sec. of state, 1984-87; asst. gen. counsel Tex. R.R. Commn., Austin, 1981-82; gen. counsel Wilson Cos., San Antonio and Midland, Tex., 1982; assoc. Bickerstaff, Heath & Smiley, Austin, 1984, ptnr., 1987-96; mng. ptnr. Bickerstaff, Heath, Smiley, Pollan, Kever & McDaniel, Austin, Tex., 1996—2000, of counsel, 2003, Bickerstaff, Heath, Delgado, Acosta LLP, Austin, Tex., 2007. Mem. asset. mgmt. adv. com. State Treasury, Austin, 1984-86; mem. legal affairs com. Criminal Justice Policy Coun., Austin, 1984-8, Inter-State Oil Compact, Oklahoma City, 1984-86; bd. dirs. Austin Cons. Group, 1983-86; mem. Jud. Efficiency Coun., Austin, 1995-96; lectr. in field. Contbr. articles to profl. jours., chpts. to books Del. Tex. Conf. on Librs. and Info. Sci., Austin, 1978, White House Conf. on Librs. and Info. Scis., Washington, 1979; mem. Libr. Svcs. and Constrn. Act Adv. Coun., 1980-84, chmn., 1983-84; mem. long range plan task force Brackenridge Hosp., Austin, 1981; clk. vestry bd. St. James Episcopal Ch., Austin, 1981-83, 89-90; bd. visitors U. Tex. Law Sch., 1983-87, vice chmn., 1983-85; bd. dirs. Friends of Ronald McDonald House Ctrl. Tex., Women's Advocacy, Inc., Capital Area Rehab. Ctr.; trustee Episcopal Found. Tex., 1986-89, St. Edward's U., Austin, 1986—, chmn. acad. com., 1988-2002, vice chair, 2002-04, chmn. 2004—; chmn. divsn. capital area campaign United Way, 1986; active nat. adv. bd. Leadership Am.; trustee Episcopal Sem. S.W., 1990-96, Assn. Governing Bds. Univs. and Colls., Leadership Edn. Arts Program, 1995-2004; adv. bd. mem. Women Basketball Coaches Assn., 1996-99; bd. dirs. U.Tex. Law Sch. Found., 1997-98, Wells Fargo Cmty. Bd., Ctrl. Tex., 2000-03; trustee Episcopal Health Charities, 1997—. Recipient Tribute to 28 Black Women award Concepts Unltd., 1983; Focus on women honoree Serwa Yetu chpt. Mt. Olive grand chpt. Order of Eastern Star, 1979, Woman of Yr. Longview Metro C. of C., 1985, Woman of Yr. Austin chpt. Internat. Tng. in Communication, 1985, Citizen of Yr. Epsilon Iona chpt. Omega Psi Phi, Lone Star Girl Scout Coun. Women of Distinction, 1997, Profiles in Power Austin Bus. Jour., 1999, Silent Samaritan award Samaritan Counseling Ctr., 2000, Sandra Day O'Connor award Tex. Ctr. Legal Ethics professionalism, 2006. Master Inns of Ct.; mem. ABA, Am. Bar Found., Tex. Bar Found. (trustee 1986-89), Travis County Bar Assn., Travis County Women Lawyers' Assn., Austin Black Lawyers Assn., State Bar Tex. (chmn. Profl. Efficiency & Econ. Rsch. subcom. 1976-84), Golden Key Nat. Honor Soc., Longhorn Assocs. for Excellence in Women's Athletes (adv. coun. 1988—), Order of Coif (hon. mem.), Omicron Delta Kappa, Delta Phi Alpha. Democrat. Office: Bickerstaff Health Delgado Acosta LLP 1700 First Bank Plz 816 Congress Ave Austin TX 78701-2443 Office Phone: 512-472-8021. Business E-Mail: mmcdaniel@bickerstaff.com.

MCDANIEL, NORWOOD ALLAN, insurance broker; b. Pitts., Dec. 16, 1928; children: Norwood Jr., Cherie Suzanne, Thomas Cavin. Student, Washington and Lee U., 1948-50; PhD (hon.), C.C. Allegheny County. Gen. ins. broker, Pitts., 1949—. Adv. bd. Union Nat. Bank, Pitts. Asst. treas. C.C. Allegheny County, 1980-90. Recipient citation Pa. Senate, 1987, Pa. Ho. of Reps., 1987, tribute Congl. Record, Pres. Ronald Reagan, 1987; inducted into Pa. Sports Hall of Fame, 1973. Mem. Fellows Club (pres.), City Club, Ins. Club Pitts., Profl. Ins. Agts. Assn., Amen Corner (pres.), Masons, Shriners (potentate Syria Temple Shrine 1978), Variety Club (chief barker), The Shrine Treas. Assn. N.Am. (sec.-treas. 1985-98). Home and Office: 26319 Feathersound Dr Punta Gorda FL 33955 Personal E-mail: woodymcdaniel@embarqmail.com.

MCDANIEL, RANDALL CORNELL, substitute teacher, retired professional football player; b. Phoenix, Dec. 19, 1964; m. Marianne McDaniel. BPE, Ariz. State U., 1988. Offensive guard Minn. Vikings, 1988-98, Tampa Bay Buccaneers, 1998—2002; ret., 2002; substitute tchr. Robbinsdale Area Schools, Minn. Vol. YMCA; founder, Team McDaniel Sandburg Mid. Sch., Minn., 2005—. Named 1st Team All-Pro, AP, 1990, 1992—96, 1998; named to Nat. Football Conf. Pro Bowl Team, NFL, 1989—2000, Pro Football Hall of Fame, 2009. Office: Robbinsdale Area Schs 4148 Winnetka Ave N New Hope MN 55427*

MCDANIEL, RAYMOND W., JR., financial information company executive; b. 1958; BS in Polit. Sci., Colgate U.; JD, Emory U., 1983. Bar: NY 1984. Joined Moody's Corp., 1987, sr. analyst asset securitization dept., mng. dir. internat., 1996—2000, sr. v.p. internat., 2000—01, sr. v.p. global ratings and rsch., 2001—03, exec. v.p. global ratings and rsch., 2003—04, pres., COO, 2004—05, chmn., CEO, 2005—; sr. mng. dir. global ratings & rsch. Moody's Investors Svc., 2001, pres., 2001—05, 2008—. Bd. dirs. John Wiley & Sons, Inc., 2005—, Moody's Corp., 2008—, Nat. Coun. Econ. Edn. Mem.: Fixed Income Analysts Soc. Office: Moody's Corp 7 World Trade Ctr 250 Greenwich St New York NY 10007 Office Phone: 212-553-1658. Office Fax: 212-553-0882. E-mail: raymond.mcdaniel@moodys.com.*

MCDANIEL, SUE POWELL, writer; b. Jefferson City, Mo., Mar. 13, 1946; d. Ernest Gayle and Ruth Angeline (Raithel) Powell; m. Walter Lee Zimmerman, Aug. 14, 1966 (div. 1980); m. Olin Cleve McDaniel, June 23, 1985 (div. 2002). BS in Edn., U. Mo., 1968, MEd in Edn., 1977, EdS, 1980, PhD, 1985. Cert. tchr., Mo. Tchr. Jefferson City Pub. Schs., 1968-80; fiscal assoc. Mo. Coordinating Bd. for Higher Edn., Jefferson City, 1980-90; exec. dir. Mo. Women's Coun., Jefferson City, 1990-99; exec. dir. Skillpath Seminars, 2000—03; pres. Alternatives, Jefferson City, Mo., 1999—2009; dir. Heisinger Hope Found., 2004—07, U. Mo., 2008—09. Author: (with C. Dixon) Learning, Changing, Leading: Keep to Success in the 21st Century, 1998, Missouri Women Today, 1993, Status of the Women, 1994, I.M. Heart, 2007. Mem. Zonta Internat. Avocations: reading, music, drawing, flower garden, writing. Home: 1907 Limestone Columbia MO 65203

MCDANIELS, DARRYL (D.M.C.), rap artist; b. Queens, NY, May 31, 1964; m. Zuri L. McDaniels, Sept. 28, 1992; 1 child, Darryl M. Jr. Founding mem. Run-D.M.C., 1982. Albums include Run-D.M.C., 1984, King of Rock, 1985, Raising Hell, 1986, Tougher Than Leather, 1988, Back From Hell, 1990, Down With The King, 1993, Crown Royal, 2001, (solo album) Checks Thugs and Rock N Roll, 2006; singles include It's Like That/Sucker MCs, 1983, Can You Rock It Like This, 1985, Walk This Way, 1986, Rock Box, King of Rock, Beats To The Rhyme, Pause, What's It All About; author: King of Rock: Respect, Responsibility, and My Life with Run-D.M.C., 2001; actor (films) Tougher Than Leather, 1988, Who's the Man?, 1993, Roll Bounce, 2005; appeared in (documentary) D.M.C.: My Adoption Journey, 2006 (Emmy award for Outstanding Arts & Culture Programming, 2007). Recipient Congl. Angels in Adoption award, Congl. Coalition on Adoption Inst., 2006; inducted into Rock & Roll Hall of Fame as member of Run-D.M.C., 2009. Office: ME-DMC 4 Brussles St Worcester MA 01610*

MCDANIELS, JOHN LOUIS, retired mathematics professor; b. Alton, Ill., Oct. 3, 1933; s. John Clarence and Carrie Elizabeth (Kortkamp) McD.; m. Betty Lou Verble, June 20, 1964. BS, U. Mo., Rolla, 1960; MS, So. Ill. U., 1977. Registered profl. engr., Ill., Mo. Engr. McDonnell Douglas Corp., St. Louis, 1960-74; prof. Lewis and Clark Community Coll., Godfrey, Ill., 1975-96. Dist. TEAMS competition coord. Ill. Jr. Engring. Tech. Soc., Lewis and Clark C.C., 1987-96, pre-engring. coord., 1975-96, water tech. coord., 1975-92. Bd. dirs. Alton (Ill.) Mus. History and Art, 1984-86. With U.S. Army, 1954-56. Recipient Man Distinction award, YWCA, 2008. Mem. Ill. Math. Assn. Cmty. Colls., Kiwanis (Alton-Godfrey pres. 1989-90, Alton-Godfrey sec. 1997—, Disting. Pres. award 1990), Service Corps of Ret. Execs., Sigma Pi Sigma, Tau Beta Pi, Kappa Delta Pi. Presbyterian. Home: 3208 Greenwood Ln Godfrey IL 62035-1815 Personal E-mail: jlmcdaniels@charter.net.

MCDANIELS, JOSH, professional football coach; b. Barberon, Ohio, Apr. 22, 1976; s. Thom McDaniels; m. Laura McDaniels; children: Jack Thomas, Maddie. Grad., John Carroll U., University Heights, Ohio. Grad. asst. Mich. State U. Spartans, 1999—2000; pers. asst. New Eng. Patriots, 2001, defensive coaching asst., 2002—03, quarterbacks coach, 2004—06, offensive coord., quarterbacks coach, 2006—09; head coach Denver Broncos, 2009—. Achievements include member of Super Bowl championship winning New England Patriots, 2004, 2005. Office: Denver Broncos 13655 Broncos Pky Englewood CO 80112*

MCDANIELS, WILLIAM E., lawyer; b. Needham, Mass., July 1, 1941; BA, Williams Coll., 1963; JD, Georgetown U., 1966. Bar: D.C. 1967, Md. 1983. Grad. fellow criminal law, litigation U. Pa., Phila., 1966-68; pub. defender Phila. Pub. Defender's Office, 1966-68; adj. prof. evidence, criminal law, advanced criminal procedure Georgetown U. Law Ctr., Washington, 1970-87; mem. Williams & Connolly LLP, Washington, 1968—. Instr. Nat. Inst. Trial Advocacy, 1975—. Fellow Am. Coll. Trial Lawyers; mem. ABA, Md. State Bar Assn, D.C. Bar. Office: Williams & Connolly LLP 725 12th St NW Washington DC 20005-5901 Office Phone: 202-434-5055. Business E-Mail: wmcdaniels@wc.com.

MCDAVID, GEORGE EUGENE (GENE), retired newspaper executive; b. McComb, Miss., June 30, 1930; s. O. C. and Inez S. McDavid; m. Betty Ernestine Tinsley, Sept. 24, 1949; children: Carol, Martha Gene Newman. BBA cum laude, U. Houston, 1965. Owner, pub. Wilk Amite Record, Gloster, Miss., 1949-58; with Houston Chronicle, 1958—, prodn. mgr., 1967-74, v.p. ops., 1974-85, v.p., gen. mgr., 1985-90, pres., 1990-98, ret., 1998. Mem. adv. bd. Am. Press Inst.; past pres., bd. dirs. S.W. Wch. Printing Mgmt. Chmn. Greater Houston chpt. ARC, 1st vice-chmn.; pres.'s counsel Houston Bapt. U; vice-chmn. Sam Houston Boy Scouts Am., United Negro Coll. Fund, Asia Soc. Goodwill Industries, YMCA; chmn. Houston Forum, Houston region Am. Cancer Soc., bd. regents, 1997—; spl. deacon Second Bapt. Ch., Houston.; bd. dirs. Nat. Conf. Christians and Jews; nat. bd. govs. Greater Houston chpt. ARC; bd. dirs. Greater Houston Partnership; bd. dirs., pres. Houston Symphony; bd. dirs., v.p. Books of the World; vice-chmn. devel. bd. U. Houston, chair bd. regents, 2003; sec. U. Houston Found., bd. dirs. Recipient Franklin award, U. Houston, 1961, Disting. Alumnus award, 1990, 1997, Taggart award, Tex. Newspaper, 1992, Man of Yr. award, NCCJ, 1993, named Outstanding Ex-Citizen Gloster, 1973, Hon. Father of Yr., 1996, named to Miss. Jour. Hall of Fame, 2002. Mem.: So. Newspaper Pubs. Assn. (pres.), Am. Newspaper Pubs. Assn. (chmn. tech. com.), Pine Forest Country Club, Houston C. of C. (Houston Citizen's Cmty. Svc. award 1993, named Houston Cultural Leader of Yr. 1998), Tex. Daily Newspaper Assn. (pres.), Crown Colony Country Club, Beta Gamma Sigma, Phi Kappa Phi. Address: 403 Hunters Park Ln Houston TX 77024-5438 Personal E-mail: gene.mcdavid@chron.com.

MCDAVID, JANET LOUISE, lawyer; b. Mpls., Jan. 24, 1950; d. Robert Matthew and Lois May (Bratt) Kurzeka; m. John Gary McDavid, June 9, 1973; 1 child, Matthew Collins McDavid. BA, Northwestern U., 1971; JD, Georgetown U., 1974. Bar D.C. 1975, U.S. Ct. Appeals (fed. cir.) 1975 (D.C. cir. 1976), U.S. Supreme Ct. 1980, U.S. Ct. Appeals (5th cir.) 1983, (9th cir.) 1986. Assoc. Hogan & Harston, Washington, 1974-83, ptnr., 1984—. Gen. counsel ERAmerica, 1977-83; mem. antitrust task force Dept. Defense, 1993-94, 96-97; mem. antitrust coun. U.S. C. of C., 1994—; advisor Bush adminstrn. transition team, 2001. Contbr. articles to profl. jours. Participant Obama, Clinton and Bush adminstrn. transition team FTC. Mem. ABA (antitrust sect., vice chmn. civil practice com. 1986-89, sect. 2 com. 1989-90, chmn. franchising com. 1990-91, coun. mem. 1991-94, program officer 1994-97, vice chair 1997-98, chair-elect 1998-99, chair 1999-2000, immediate past chair, governing com. of forum on franchising 1991-97), ACLU, U.S. C. of C. (antitrust coun. 1995—), Washington Coun. Lawyers, D.C. Bar Assn., Fed. Bar Assn., Womens Legal Def. fund. Democrat. Office: Hogan & Hartson 555 13th St NW Washington DC 20004-1109 Office Phone: 202-637-8780. Business E-Mail: jlmcdavid@hhlaw.com.

MCDAVID, JOHN SANFORD, lawyer; b. New Orleans, June 19, 1958; s. John Land and Sylvia (Sanford) McD.; m. Mary Beth Waggener, July 31, 1982; children: Patrick Sanford, Jason Harkins. BBA in Mgmt., U. Miss., 1981, JD, 1984. Bar: Miss. 1984, La. 1984. Ptnr. McDavid Noblin & West PLLC, Jackson, Miss., 1984—2003, Young Williams PA, 2003—. Mem. ABA, La. State Bar, Miss. Bar (chmn. sect. real property 2000-01), Miss. Oil and Gas Lawyers Assn. (pres. 1999-00), Tri-County Real Estate Attys. Assn. (pres. 2007), Hinds County Bar Assn., Univ. Club. Home: 112 Woodbury Park Pl Madison MS 39110 Home Phone: 601-790-4042; Office Phone: 601-360-9014. Business E-Mail: jmcdavid@youngwilliams.com.

MCDAVID, SARA JUNE, librarian; b. Atlanta, Dec. 21, 1945; d. William Harvey and June (Threadgill) McRae; m. Michael Wright McDavid, Mar. 20, 1971. BA, Mercer U., 1967; MLS, Emory U., 1969. Head librarian Fernbank Sci. Ctr., Atlanta, 1969-77; dir. rsch. libr. Fed. Res. Bank of Atlanta, 1977-81; mgr. mem. services SOLINET, Atlanta, 1981-82; media specialist Parkview High Sch., Atlanta, 1982-84; ptnr. Interncontinental Travel, Atlanta, 1984-85; librarian Wesleyan Day Sch., Atlanta, 1985-86; mgr. info. svcs. Internat. Assn. Fin. Planning, Atlanta, 1986-90; dir. rsch. Korn Ferry Internat., Atlanta, 1990-95; Atlanta rsch. coord. Lamalie Amrop Internat., Atlanta, 1995-98; dir. practice splty. teams LAI Ward Howell, 1998; prin. McDavid Rsch. Assocs., Atlanta, 1998-99; lead rschr. The Boston Consulting Group, Atlanta, 1999—. Bd. dirs. Southeastern Library Network, Atlanta, 1977-80, vice chmn. bd., 1979-80. Contbr. articles to profl. jours. Pres., mem. exec. com. Atlanta Humane Soc., 1985-86, bd. dirs. aux., 1978-90. Mem. Ga. Libr. Assn. (v.p. 1981-83), Spl. Librs. Assn. (treas. libr. mgmt. divsn. 1998-2000, editor Libr. Mgmt. Quar. 1996-98, 2002). Home: 1535 Knob Hill Dr NE Atlanta GA 30329-3206 Office: Boston Consulting Group Inc 600 Peachtree St NE Ste 3800 Atlanta GA 30308-2218 Office Phone: 404-877-5200. Business E-Mail: mcdavid.sara@bcg.com.

MCDAVIS, RODERICK J., academic administrator; b. Dayton, Ohio, Oct. 17, 1948; m. Deborah Moses; children: Ryan, Tony. BS in Social Scis. in Secondary Edn., Ohio U., 1970; MS in Student Pers. Adminstrn., U. Dayton, 1971; PhD in Counselor Edn., U. Toledo, 1974. Asst. prof. edn. grad. divsn. Siena Heights Coll., Adrian, Mich., 1973—74; asst. prof. edn. dept. counselor edn. Coll. Edn. U. Fla., Gainesville, 1974—79, assoc. prof. edn. dept. counselor edn. Coll. Edn., 1979—82, prof. edn. dept. counselor edn. Coll. Edn., 1982—89, acting asst. dean for grad. studies Grad. Sch., 1984—85, assoc. dean Grad. Sch. and Minority Programs Grad. Sch., 1986—89, prof. edn. dept. counselor edn. Coll. Edn., 1994—99, dean Coll. Edn., 1994—99; prof. counselor edn. dept. edn. leadership, counseling and founds. Coll. Edn. U. Ark., Fayetteville, 1989—94, dean Coll. Edn., 1989—94; prof. edn. divsn. ednl. studies Sch. Edn. Va. Commonwealth U., Richmond, 1999—2004, provost, v.p. acad. affairs, 1999—2004; pres. Ohio U., Athens, 2004—. Vis. prof. edn. dept. counselor edn. and human svcs. Grad. Sch. Edn. U. Dayton, 1979—83, 1992. Recipient Disting. Svc. award for cmty. outreach through TV media, Fla. Assn. for Counselor Edn. and Supervision, 1978, Key to the City, City Commn., Gainesville, 1995, Outstanding Alumnus award, Ohio U. Coll. Edn., 1996, Black Achiever's award in edn., Fla. Conf. Black State Legislators, Tallahassee, 1997; named Person of Yr. in Edn., The Gainesville Sun, 1995. Mem.: Nat. Alliance Black Sch. Educators, Am. Coll. Pers. Assn., Phi Kappa Phi, Phi Delta Kappa (Post-secondary Outstanding Educator award North Ctrl. Fla. chpt. 1996). Office: Office of the Pres 108 Cutler Hall Athens OH 45701 Home: 29 Park Pl Athens OH 45701 Office Phone: 740-593-1804. E-mail: mcdavis@ohio.edu.*

MCDERMID, MARGARET E. (LYN MCDERMID), information technology executive, engineer; b. 1948; B in bus., Mary Baldwin Coll.; MBA, U. Richmond. With Stone and Webster Engring. Corp.; joined Va. Power, 1982, various positions engring. & construction dept., 1982—86, dir. adminstrv. svcs., 1986—98; v.p. info. tech., CIO Dominion Resources Inc., 1998—2000, sr. v.p. info. tech., CIO, 2000—. Mem. apptd. by Gov. Gilmore CIO Adv. Bd., 2000; bd. dirs. Fed. Res. Bank, Richmond, 2007—. Active with United Way, Big Brothers, Big Sisters; bd. trustees Mary Baldwin Coll.; found. bd. J. Sargeant Reynolds Cmty. Coll.; bd. dirs. Greater Richmond Tech. Coun., Children's Mus. Richmond Bus. Com., CIO Forum; mem. Va. Rsch. and Tech. Adv. Coun. Achievements include first woman to enter the Apprentice Program at Newport News Shipyard where she completed the Patternmaker's program. Office: Dominion Resources Inc 120 Tredegar St Richmond VA 23219 Office Phone: 804-819-2000.

MCDERMOTT, AGNES CHARLENE SENAPE, philosophy educator; b. Hazelton, Pa., Mar. 11, 1937; d. Charles G. and Conjetta (Ranieri) Senape; children: Robert C., Lisa G., Jamie C. BA, U. Pa., Phila., 1956, PhD, 1964; postgrad., U. Calif., Berkeley, 1960—61, U. Amsterdam, Netherlands, 1965, U. Wis., 1967—69. Instr. math. Drexel Inst. Tech., Phila., 1962-63; asst. prof. philosophy SUNY-Buffalo, 1964-65, Hampton Inst., Va., 1966-67; asst. prof. U. Wis.-Milw., 1967-70; assoc. prof. philosophy U. N.Mex., Albuquerque, 1970-80, prof., dean grad. studies, 1981-86; dean in residence Coun. of Grad. Schs., Washington, 1985-86; provost, v.p. acad. affairs CUNY, 1986-89, prof. philosophy, 1986-91; dean for acad. and student affairs, cons. Albuquerque Acad., 1991-93; ind. cons. Corrales, N.Mex., 1993—. Vis. assoc. prof. U. Wash., Seattle, 1974, U. Calif.-Berkeley, 1973-74, U. Hawaii, Honolulu, 1975; vis. prof. U. Calif.-Berkeley, 1980; vis. prof. Semester at Sea, U. Pitts., fall 1994; bd. dir. Juvenile Diabetes Rsch. Found.; lectr., panelist in field. Author: An Eleventh Century Buddhist Logic of 'Exists', 1969, Boethius' Treatise on the Modes of Signifying, 1980; compiler, editor anthology: Comparative Philosophy: Selected Essays, 1983; rev. editor Phil. East West, 1986—; contbr. articles and stories to profl. and literary jours. Bd. mem. Peanut Butter & Jelly Found.; mem. lay rsch. rev. com. Juvenile Diabetes Rsch. Found., N.Mex. AAUW postdoctoral fellow, 1965-66; NEH Younger Humanist fellow, 1971-72; faculty rsch. fellow U. N.Mex., 1978, 79, 80; U. Pa. grad. fellow, 1961-62; S. Fels Found. fellow, 1963-64; U. Pa. tuition scholar; Pa. Hist. Soc. scholar Mem. NY Acad. Scis., Am. Philos. Soc., Am. Philos. Assn. (exec. com. 1977-80), Assn. Asian Studies (exec. com. 1977-80), Am. Oriental Soc., Western Assn. Grad. Schs. (pres. 1986-87), Phi Beta Kappa, Pi Mu Epsilon. Democrat. Avocations: skiing, fly fishing. Personal E-mail: mcdercott@msn.com.

MCDERMOTT, ALICE, writer; b. Bklyn., June 27, 1953; married; 3 children. BA, SUNY, Oswego, 1975; MA, U. N.H., 1978. Instr. U. Calif., San Diego, Am. U., Washington; lectr. in English U. N.H.; writer-in-residence Lynchburg Coll., Va., Hollins Coll., Va.; prof. The Writing Seminars Johns Hopkins U., Balt. Author: A Bigamist's Daughter, 1982, That Night, 1987 (Pulitzer Prize finalist, Nat. Book Award finalist, L.A. Times Book Prize finalist, PEN Faulkner award finalist), At Weddings and Wakes, 1992 (Pulitzer prize finalist), Charming Billy, 1998 (Nat. Book Award), Child of My Heart, 2002, After This, 2006 (Pulitzer prize finalist); contbr. short stories to numerous profl. publs. Recipient Whiting Writers award. Office: Farrar Straus and Giroux 18 W 18th St New York NY 10011-4607 Office Phone: 212-838-7777.

MCDERMOTT, DREW VINCENT, computer science educator; b. Madison, Wis., Dec. 27, 1949; s. James Kenneth and Lucy Lea (Hurt) McD.; m. Judith Claire Rosenbaum, July 22, 1974; children: Noel Timothy, Katherine Anne. SB, SM, MIT, 1972, PhD, 1976. Asst. prof. computer sci. Yale U., New Haven, 1976-83, prof., 1983—, chmn. dept., 1991-96. Co-author: Introduction to Artificial Intelligence, 1985, Artificial Intelligence Programming, 1987. Fellow Am. Assn. for Artificial Intelligence; mem. Assn. for Computing Machinery. Roman Catholic. Avocations: philosophy of mind, chess. Office: Yale Univ Dept of Computer Sci PO Box 2158 New Haven CT 06520

MCDERMOTT, DYLAN, actor; b. Waterbury, Conn., Oct. 26, 1961; s. Richard "Mac" and Diane McDermott; m. Shiva Rose Afshar, Nov. 19, 1995 (div. Dec. 2, 2008); children: Colette, Charlotte Rose. BA in Drama, Fordham U., 1983. Actor: (films) Hamburger Hill, 1987, Twister, 1988, Steel Magnolias, 1989, In The Line Of Fire, 1993, The Cowboy Way, 1994, Miracle on 34th Street, 1994, Destiny Turns On The Radio, 1995, Home For The Holidays, 1995, 'Til There Was You, 1996, Three to Tango, 1999, Texas Rangers, 2001, Party Monster, 2003, Wonderland, 2003, Edison, 2005, The Tenants, 2006, Unbeatable Harold, 2006, The Messengers, 2007; (TV films) The Neon Empire, 1989, Into the Badlands, 1991, The Fear Inside, 1992, A House Divided, 2006; (TV series) The Practice, 1997-2003, The Grid, 2004; (TV appearances) Ally MacBeal, 1997, Tales from the Crypt, Will & Grace, 2003; stage The Treatment, 2006. Recipient Golden Globe award, 1999. Address: William Morris Agy 151 El Camino Dr Beverly Hills CA 90212

MCDERMOTT, FRANCIS OWEN, retired lawyer; b. Denver, Feb. 25, 1933; s. Paul Harkins and Agnes (Clark) McD.; divorced; children: Diana, Daniel, Christopher, Anthony, Justine; m. Estella Marina Idiaquez, June 6, 1986; stepchildren: Bernard, Michael, Nicole, Marie, Steven. JD, Am. U., 1960. Bar: D.C. 1960, U.S. Dist. Ct. D.C., 1960, U.S. Ct. Appeals (D.C. cir.) 1960, u.S. Tax Ct. 1961, U.S. Supreme Ct. 1964. Trial atty. office regional counsel IRS, Washington, 1961-65; mem. profl. staff com. on fin. U.S. Senate, Washington, 1965-68; tax counsel Assn. Am. R.R.s, Washington, 1968-73; assoc. Hopkins & Sutter, Washington, 1973-76, ptnr., 1976-98, ret., 1999; ret. ptnr. Foley & Lardner, Washington, 2001—. Gen. counsel Inst. Ill., Washington, 1987-96. Mem. ABA, Fed. Bar Assn., Nat. Def. Transp. Assn. (v.p., gen. counsel 1974—). Roman Catholic. Avocation: tennis. Home: 1 S Montague St Arlington VA 22204-1007 Office Phone: 202-945-6092. E-mail: fmcdermott@foley.com.

MCDERMOTT, JAMES A., United States Representative from Washington, psychiatrist; b. Chgo., Dec. 28, 1936; m. Therese Hansen; 2 children. BS, Wheaton Coll., Ill., 1958; MD, U. Ill. Med. Sch., Chgo., 1963. Intern Buffalo Gen. Hosp., 1963-64; resident adult psychiatry U. Ill. Hosps., Chgo., 1964-66; resident child psychiatry U. Wash. Hosps., Seattle, 1966-68; asst. clin. prof. dept. psychiatry U. Wash., Seattle, 1970-83; mem. Wash. State House Reps. from 43rd Dist., 1971-72, Wash. State Senate, 1975-87; regional med. officer US Fgn. Svc., 1987-88; mem. US Congress from 7th Wash. dist., 1989—, mem. ways and means com., ranking minority mem. human resources subcommittee. Mem. exec. and edn. com. Nat. Conf. State Legislatures, chair ethics com.; co-chmn. Congl. task force internat. HIV/AIDS, Congl. Caucus on India and Indian Ams., Africa Trade and Investment Caucus, Congl. Kidney Caucus. Mem. Wash. State Arts Commn., Wash. Coun. for Prevention Child Abuse and Neglect; Dem. nominee for gov., 1980. Lt. comdr. M.C. USN, 1968—70. Mem. Am. Psychiat. Assn., Wash. State Med. Assn., King County Med. Soc. Democrat. Episcopalian. Office: US House Reps 1035 Longworth House Office Bldg Washington DC 20515 Office Phone: 202-225-3106.*

MC DERMOTT, JOHN FRANCIS, psychiatrist, physician; b. Hartford, Conn., Dec. 12, 1929; s. John Francis and Camilla R. (Cavanaugh) McD.; m. Sarah N. Schemm, Dec. 27, 1958; children: Elizabeth C., John Francis III. AB, Cornell U., 1951; MD, N.Y. Med. Coll., 1955. Diplomate in psychiatry and child psychiatry Am. Bd. Psychiatry and Neurology. Intern Henry Ford Hosp., Detroit, 1955-56; resident in psychiatry U. Mich. Med. Center, 1956-58, resident in child psychiatry, 1960-62; practice medicine, specializing in psychiatry and child and adolescent psychiatry Honolulu, 1969-95; instr., asst. prof., asso. prof. psychiatry U. Mich. Sch. Medicine, 1962-69; prof., chmn. dept. psychiatry U. Hawaii Sch. Medicine, 1969-95, prof. emeritus, 1995—; scholar-in-residence Rockefeller Found. Study Ctr., Bellagio, Italy, 1985, 92. Chmn. com. cert. in child psychiatry Am. Bd. Psychiatry and Neurology, 1974-78, bd. dirs., 1983-91, chmn. R&D com., 1985-91; sr. vis. scientist dept. exptl. psychology Oxford (Eng.) U., 1993; sr. vis. fellow Inst. Criminology Cambridge U., Eng., 1998, 2000; vis. prof. numerous univs.; cons. in field. Author: Psychiatry for the Pediatrician, 1970, Childhood Psychopathology, 1972, Mental Health Education in New Medical Schools, 1973, Roles and Functions of Child Psychiatrists, 1976, Psychiatric Treatment of the Child, 1977, New Directions in Childhood Psychopathology, vol. I, 1980, vol. II, 1982, Raising Cain (and Abel Too), 1980: People and Cultures of Hawaii, 1980, Culture Mind and Therapy: An Introduction to Cultural Psychiatry, 1982, Japanese edit., 1984, The Complete Book on Sibling Rivalry, 1987, German edit., 1991; editor Jour. Am. Acad. Child and Adolescent Psychiatry, 1987-97; contbr. over 150 articles to profl. jours.; mem. editorial bds. numerous psychiat. jours. Served with USN, 1958-60. Named Disting. Alumnus N.Y. Med. Coll., 1976. Fellow Cambridge Univ. Clare Hall (Eng.) (life), Am. Psychiat. Assn. (disting. life, Agnes Purcell McGavin award 1998), Am. Orthopsychiat. Assn. (life), Am. Acad. Child and Adolescent Psychiatry (life)(Jeanne Spurlock award and Lectr. for Culture and Diversity, 2008), Am. Coll. Psychiatrists, World Psychiat. Assn. (chmn. child and adolescent psychiatry 1977-89), Benjamin Rush Soc. (sec.-treas. 2000-02, v.p. 2002-04, pres. 2004-06), Cosmos Club, Outrigger Canoe Club, Waialae Country Club.

MCDERMOTT, JOHN H., lawyer; b. Evanston, Ill., June 23, 1931; s. Edward Henry and Goldie Lucile (Boso) McD.; m. Ann Elizabeth Pickard, Feb. 19, 1966; children: Elizabeth A., Mary L., Edward H. BA, Williams Coll., 1953; JD, U. Mich., 1956. Bar: Mich. 1955, Ill. 1956. Assoc. McDermott, Will & Emery, Chgo., 1958-64, ptnr., 1964-99, of counsel, 2000—. 1st lt. USAF, 1956-58. Mem. ABA, Chgo. Bar Assn. Clubs: Commerical of Chgo., Econ. of Chgo., Legal Chgo. (pres. 1981-82), Law Chgo. (pres. 1986-87). Home: 330 Willow Rd Winnetka IL 60093-4130 Office: McDermott Will & Emery 227 W Monroe St Ste 4400 Chicago IL 60606-5096 Home Phone: 847-446-2022; Office Phone: 312-984-7562. Personal E-mail: johnhmcdermott@comcast.net.

MCDERMOTT, KATHLEEN E., lawyer, corporate executive; b. July 1949; BS in fgn. svc., Georgetown U., JD. Bar: 1975. Assoc. Collier, Shannon, Rill & Scott, Washington DC, 1975—80, ptnr., 1981—93, 2000—01; exec. v.p., chief legal officer Am. Stores Inc. (now Albertson's Inc.), Salt Lake City, 1993—99; sr. v.p., gen. counsel Nash Finch Inc., Mpls., 2002—06. Mem.: FTC Com. (chair), ABA (former vice chair corp. counseling com. antitrust sect.). Home: 29 E Churchhill Dr Salt Lake City UT 84103-2267 Office Phone: 801-703-1143. Personal E-mail: mcdermott.kathleen@gmail.com.

MCDERMOTT, KEVIN R., lawyer; b. Youngstown, Ohio, Jan. 26, 1952; s. Robert J. and Marion D. McD.; m. Cindy J. Darling, Dec. 11, 1976; children: Ciara, Kelly. AB, Miami U., Oxford, Ohio, 1974; JD, Ohio State U., 1977. Bar: Ohio 1977, US Dist. Ct. (so. dist.) Ohio 1978, US Dist. Ct. (no. dist.) Ohio 1988, US Dist. Ct. (we. dist.) Mich. 1993, US Supreme Ct. 1990, US Ct. Appeals (3rd cir.) 1996, US Ct. Appeals (6th cir.) 1988. Assoc. ptnr. Murphey Young & Smith, Columbus, Ohio, 1977-88; ptnr. Squire Sanders & Dempsey, Columbus, Ohio, 1988-90, Schottenstein Zox & Dunn, Columbus, Ohio, 1990—. Adv. bd. mem. Capital U. Legal Asst. Program, Columbus, Ohio, 1988—. Bd. pres. Easter Seal Soc. Ctrl. Ohio, Columbus, 1992-94, bd. mem. 1988-92; pres. Upper Arlington Civic Svc. Commn., Columbus, Ohio, 1988-93. Office: Schottenstein Zox & Dunn 250 West St Columbus OH 43215 Office Phone: 614-462-5001. Business E-Mail: kmcdermott@szd.com.

MCDERMOTT, RAYMOND, JR., physician; b. Chgo., Apr. 20, 1924; s. Raymond A. and Helen (Furlong) M.; m. Audrey H. Bergt, Feb., 1995; children: Kathy, Mary Anne, Raymond III, Thomas, Laura, Sharon, Jean, Michael, Trish. MD, Loyola U., 1947. Bd. cert. Obstertrics and Gynocology. Assoc. attending Cook County Hosp., Chgo., 1954-61; asst. prof. obgyn. Northwestern U. Med. Sch., Chgo., 1958—; med. reviewer Healthcare Compare, Oakbrook, Ill., 1978-88, CIMRO, Champaign, Ill., 1988—2003; med. dir. Wellmark (Health Network), Oakbrook, 1992—2002. Staff pres. Grant Hosp. Chgo., 1976-78, staff v.p., 1974-76. Lt. U.S. Navy, 1941-53. Avocation: sailing. Home: 3950 W Bryn Mawr Ave Chicago IL 60659-3156 Office Phone: 312-346-6330.

MCDERMOTT, ROBERT J., commissioner; b. Bklyn., Sept. 5, 1944; AB, Georgetown U., 1966; JD cum laude, NYU, 1970, LLM in Taxation, 1974. Bar: NY 1971. Commr. tax appeals tribunal NY State,

2005—. Mem. ABA, NY State Bar Assn. (exec. com., tax sect. 1980-91), Assn. of Bar of City of NY, Order Coif. NY State Bar Found. (life fellow), NYU Law Alumni Assn. (pres. 1989-91) Office: Divsn Tax Appeals Riverfront Pro Tower 500 Federal St Troy NY 12180 Office Phone: 518-266-3000. Office Fax: 518-272-5178.

MCDERMOTT, SANDRA, national park administrator; d. Joseph McDermott and Julia Ferrari; children: Jennifer Faulkner, Benjamin Faulkner. BA in Psychology, U. Alaska, 1975, BA in History, 1980; MA in History, U. Oreg., 1984. Grad. tchg. fellow U. Oreg., 1982—84; adj. faculty U. Alaska, 1984—97; acting asst. supt. Joshua Tree Nat. Pk., Twenty-Nine Palms, Calif., 2004; hist. preservation program mgr. Nat. Pk. Svc., Anchorage, 1987—92, regional historian, 1992—2004, asst. regional dir. intermountain region Denver, 2004—; acting supt. Bighorn Canyon Nat. Recreation Area, 2008. Assoc. Dir. Nat. Cultural Resourse Adv. Group, Nat. Pk. Svc., Washington, 2000—; instr., Alaska nat. interest conservation act US Dept. of Interior U., 2003; spkr. Alaska Humanities Forum Speakers Bur., 1996—98. Book reviewer (professional journal) Journal of Public History; contbr. articles to profl. jours. Co-chair Alaska at War Internat. Conf., 1993; pres. Nat. History Day in Alaska, 1989—2004, Alaska Hist. Soc., 1992—98; chair, publs. com. Cook Inlet Hist. Soc., Anchorage, 1997—2000; mem. program com. Western Mus. Assn., Alaska, 1997—98. Recipient President's award, Alaska Hist. Soc., 1989, Fed. Employee of the Yr., Team Leader award, Fed. Employees Assn., 1996, Spl. Svc. Act award, Nat. Pk. Svc., 1997, 2007, Nat. Partnership award, Hon. Mention, Nat. Pk. Found., 2001, Cert. of Appreciation, Nat. Coun. for History Edn., 2003, Spl. award for Contributions to Alaska History, Alaska Hist. Soc., 2004, Cert. of Merit in Hist. Preservation, Alaska State Hist. Preservation Office, 2004, Lifetime Achievement award, Nat. History Day in Alaska, 2004, STAR award, NPS-Cultural Resource Adv. Coun., 2004, Superior Svc. award, Dept. Interior, 2007. Mem.: Am. Hist. Assn. (assoc.). Avocation: music. Office: Nat Pk Svc PO Box 25287 Denver CO 80225-0287

MCDERMOTT, THOMAS JOHN, JR., lawyer; b. Santa Monica, Calif., Mar. 23, 1931; s. Thomas J. Sr. and Etha Irene (Cook) McD.; m. Yolanda Amante Jatap; children: Jodi Friedman, Kimberly E., Kish S. BA, UCLA, 1953, JD, 1958. Bar: Calif. 1959. Ptnr. Gray, Binkley and Pfaelzer, LA, 1964-67, Kadison, Pfaelzer, Woodward, Quinn and Rossi, LA, 1967-87, Rogers & Wells, LA, 1987-93, Bryan Cave, LA, 1993-95, Manatt, Phelps & Phillips, LLP, LA, 1995-99, Shanks and Herbert, San Diego, 1999—2003. Served with U.S. Army, 1953-56, Korea, 1999-2003. Fellow Am. Coll. Trial Lawyers; mem. ABA, Assn. Bus. Trial Lawyers (pres. 1980-81, mem. exec. com. 9th cir. jud. conf. 1993—, chair 1997), State Bar Calif. (chair litigation sect. 1993-94), UCLA Law Alumni Assn. (pres. 1961-62), Order of Coif. Office: Law Offices Thomas J McDermott 74-770 Hwy 111 Ste 201 Indian Wells CA 92210 Office Phone: 760-779-5800. Business E-Mail: tmcdermott@mcdelaw.com.

MCDERMOTT, WILLIAM R., information technology executive; b. 1962; BS, Dowling Coll.; MBA, Northwestern Univ. Regional sales and customer ops. positions Xerox Corp., 1983-97, pres., corp. officer, 1997-2000, head Global Document Solutions Group, 1999-2000; pres. Gartner Inc., Stamford, Conn., 2000—01; exec. v.p. worldwide sales ops. Siebel Systems, 2001—02; pres., CEO SAP Americas SAP AG, Newtown Sq. Pa., 2002—. Mem. U.S. C. of C., Enterprise Software Roundtable; bd. dir. PAETEC Communications, Under Armour. Bd. dirs. Welfare to Work Partnership, Students in Free Enterprise; mem. adv. bd. Villanova Univ.; mem. nat. adv. bd. Knowledge Is Power Program; trustee Dowling Coll.; vice chmn. ed. & workforce task force, Bus. Roundtable; mem. adv. council Hands On Network. Named Entrepreneur of the Yr., applied tech., Ernst & Young, 2005. Office: SAP Americas 3999 West Chester Pike Newtown Square PA 19073 Fax: (203) 316-1100.

MCDEVITT, CHARLES FRANCIS, retired judge, lawyer; b. Pocatello, Idaho, Jan. 5, 1932; s. Bernard A. and Margaret (Hermann) McDevitt; m. Virginia L. Heller, Aug. 14, 1954; children: Eileen A., Kathryn A., Brian A., Sheila A., Terrence A., Neil A., Kendal A. LLB, U. Idaho, 1956. Bar: Idaho 1956. Ptnr. Richards, Haga & Eberle, Boise, 1956-62; gen. counsel, asst. sec. Boise Cascade Corp., 1962—68; mem. Idaho State Legislature, 1963-66; sec., gen. counsel Boise Cascade Corp., 1965-67, v.p. sec., 1967-68; pres. Beck Industries, 1968-70; group v.p. Singer Co., NYC, 1970-72, exec. v.p., 1973-76; pub. defender Ada County, Boise, 1976-78; co-founder Givens, McDevitt, Pursley & Webb, Boise, 1978-89; justice Idaho Supreme Ct., Boise, 1989-97, chief justice, 1993-97; ptnr., founder McDevitt & Miller, LLP, Boise, 1997—. Served on Gov.'s Select Com. on Taxation, Boise, 1988-89; mem. State Select Com. on Campaign Ethics and Campaign Finances, State Select Com. on Legis. Compensation. Chair Idaho Jud. Coun., 1993-97, Cts. Advisors Coun., 1994-98; mem. Multi-State Tax Com. Recipient Legal Merit award, Univ. of Idaho, 2002, Professionalism award, Idaho State Bar, 2005. Home: 4940 Boise River Ln Boise ID 83716-8816 Office: McDevitt Miller 420 W Bannock Boise ID 83702-6034 Office Phone: 208-343-7500. Business E-Mail: chas@McDevitt-Miller.com.

MCDEVITT, JAMES A., prosecutor, lawyer; b. July 1943; B, U. Wash.; MBA, JD, Gonzaga U. Asst. atty. gen. State of Wash., Office of Atty. Gen., 1975—77; from sr. ptnr. to mng. ptnr. Reed & Geisa, Spokane, Wash., 1977—94; ptnr. Preston, Gates & Ellis, Spokane, Wash., 1994—2002; US atty. (ea. dist.) Wash. US Dept. Justice, 2002—. With USAF, 1965—71, brig. gen. Wash. Air Nat. Guard, ret. Office: US Attys Office PO Box 1494 Spokane WA 99210 Office Phone: 509-353-2767.

MCDEVITT, JOHN, delivery service executive; b. Upper Darby, Pa., Aug. 15, 1958; m. Lori McDevitt; children: Kelly, Tara, Shannon, John. BS in Polit. Sci., Rutgers U., 1980; grad., U. Mich., 1999. Part-time loader UPS, Edison, NJ, 1976—77, part-time supr. Bound Brook, 1977—80, package car driver, 1980—81, supr., 1981—84, mgr. Parsippany, 1984—87, divsn. mgr. Meadowlands, 1987—92, dist. mgr. East Long Island, NY, 1992—94, West Long Island, 1994—96, v.p. corp. compliance Atlanta, 1996—98, mgr. corp. labor rels., 1998—99, v.p. air ops., 1999—2003, sr. v.p. strategic integration, 2003—05, sr. v.p. global transp. services, 2005—. Office: UPS 55 Glenlake Kwy NE Atlanta GA 30328*

MCDEVITT, SHEILA MARIE, retired lawyer, energy executive, business consultant; b. St. Petersburg, Fla., Jan. 15, 1947; d. Frank Davis and Marie (Barfield) McD. AA, St. Petersburg Jr. Coll., 1966; BA in Govt., Fla. State U., 1968, JD, 1978. Bar: Fla. 1978. Rsch. asst. Fla. Legis. Reference Bur., Tallahassee, 1968-69; adminstr., research assoc. Constitution Revision Commn. Ga. Gen. Assembly, Atlanta, 1969-70; adminstrv. asst., analyst Fla. State Sen., Tallahassee, Tampa, 1970-79; assoc. McClain, Walkley & Stuart, P.A., Tampa, Seminole, Fla., 1979-81; govtl. affairs counsel Tampa Electric Co., 1981-82, corp. counsel, 1982-86; sr. corp. counsel TECO Energy, Inc., Tampa, 1986-89, asst. v.p., 1989-92, v.p., asst. gen. counsel, 1992-99, corp. compliance officer, 1993-99, v.p., gen. counsel Tampa, 1999—2001, sr. v.p., gen. counsel, chief legal officer, 2001—. Mem. Worker's Compensation adv. coun. Fla. Dept. Labor, Tallahassee, 1984-86; trustee St. Leo U., 1999—, vice chair, 2001-2005, chair 2005-; mem. bd. visitors Fla. State U. Coll. Law, 1996—, chmn., 2003-2005; mem. bd. advisors The Centre for Women, 1998—, Met. Ministries, 1996-99; mem. ethics adv. bd. U. Tampa Ctr. for Ethics, 1997-99; mem. jud. nominating commn. 13th Jud. Cir., 2001-2003; mem. Fla. bd. govs. State Univ. sys., 2003, vice chair, 2006-. Mem. Fla. Rep. Exec. Com., Tallahassee, 1974-75, Hillsborough County Rep. Exec. Com., 1974-75, Fed. Jud. Adv. Commn., 1989-93, Fla. Humanities Coun., 2000-2004, WW Women's Leadership, 2004—; bd. dirs. Vol. Ctr. Hillsborough County, Tampa, 1984-85, Hillsborough County Easter Seal Soc., 1994-95, Fla. Aquarium, 1999-2000, Lowry Park Zoo Soc., 1999-2004, chmn., trustee, 1986-94, also legal advisor; mem. transition team for Fla. Gov. Bob Martinez, 1986-87; trustee St. Leo U., 1999, vice chair, 2001-05, chair, 2005-07; trustee Fla. Orch., 2004—. Recipient Spl. Contbn. award for pioneering efforts in bus. ethics, U. Tex. Ctr. for Ethics, 2007; named Alumni of Yr., Fla. State U. Coll. Law, 2006. Mem ABA, Fla. Bar (vice chmn., then chmn. energy law com. 1984-87, jud. nominating procedures com. 1986-91, jud. adminstrn. selection and tenure com. 1991-93), Hillsborough Bar Found. (trustee 2002-), Hillsborough County Bar Assn. (chmn. law week com. 1990, corp. counsel com. 1986-87, internat. law com. 1994-95, Corp. Counsel of Yr. award 2003), Am. Corp. Counsel Assn. (bd. dirs. Ctrl. Fla. chpt. 1986-87), Hillsborough County Bar Found., Tampa Club, Tiger Bay Club, Tampa Yacht and Country Club. Roman Catholic. Avocations: bicycling, reading. Office: TECO Energy Inc PO Box 111 702 N Franklin St Fl 5 Tampa FL 33602-4440 Business E-Mail: smmcdevitt@tecoenergy.com.

MCDIARMID, LUCY, literature educator, writer; b. Louisville, Mar. 29, 1947; BA, Swathmore Coll., Pa., 1968; MA, Harvard U., 1969, PhD, 1972. Asst. prof. Boston U., 1972-74; from asst. prof. to assoc. prof. Swarthmore Coll., 1974-81; asst. prof. U. Md. Baltimore County, Balt., 1982-84; prof. Villanova (Pa.) U., 1984—; Marie Frazee Baldassarre chair English Montclair State U., 2009—. Vis. prof. English Princeton U., 1995; Carole and Gordon Segal vis. chair Irish lit. Northwestern U., 2005; mem. exec. com. Am. Conf. for Irish Studies, 1987-91, v.p., 1995-97, pres., 1997-99, past pres., internat. rep., 1999—2001; first Sara and Jess Cloud vis. prof. of English Coll. William and Mary, 2008. Author: Saving Civilization: Yeats, Eliot and Auden Between the Wars, 1984, Auden's Apologies for Poetry, 1990, The Irish Art of Controversy, 2005; co-editor: Selected Writings of Lady Gregory, 1995, High and Low Moderns: Literature and Culture, 1889-1939, 1996; contbr. articles to profl. jours. ACLS grantee, 1976; NEH fellow, 1981-82, Bunting Inst. fellow, 1981-82, Guggenheim fellow, 1993-94, vis. fellow N.Y. Inst. Humanities, 1993-95, fellow Dorothy and Louis B. Cullman Ctr. Scholars and Writers, NY Pub. Libr., 2005-06. Mem. MLA (exec. com. Twentieth Century Lit. divsn.), Internat. Assn. for Study Anglo-Irish Lit. (Am. sec.-treas. 1994-96), Phi Beta Kappa.

MCDIARMID, ROBERT CAMPBELL, lawyer; b. NYC, July 13, 1937; s. Norman Hugh and Dorothy (Shoemaker) McD.; m. Ruth Sussman, 1963 (div. 1996); children: Jennifer, Alexander Samuel; m. Frances Enseki Francis, 1996. BS in Mech. Engring., Swarthmore Coll., 1958; MS in Engring. Physics, Cornell U., 1960; LLB, Harvard U., 1963. Bar: DC 1964, Va. 1964, US Supreme Ct. 1967, US Ct. Appeals (4th, 6th and 9th cirs.) 1965, US Ct. Appeals (3d, 5th and 10th cirs.) 1966, US Ct. Appeals (7th, 8th and DC cirs.) 1967, US Ct. Appeals (2d cir.) 1970, US Ct. Appeals (1st cir.) 1979, US Ct. Appeals (11th cir.) 1981. Assoc. Weaver & Glassie, Washington, 1963-64; trial atty. civil divsn. appellate sect. Dept. Justice, Washington, 1964-68; asst. to gen. counsel Fed. Power Commn., Washington, 1968-70; assoc. Law Office of George Spiegel, Washington, 1970-73; ptnr. Spiegel & McDiarmid, Washington, 1973—. Mem. alumni coun. Swarthmore Coll., 1986-89. Mem. ABA, Va. State Bar, Bar Assn. DC, DC Bar, Energy Bar Assn. (exec. com. 1982-83, bd. dirs. 1997-2000). Democrat. Mem. Soc. Of Friends. Home: 3625 Fulton St NW Washington DC 20007-1452 Office: Spiegel & McDiarmid 1333 New Hampshire Ave NW Washington DC 20036 Office Phone: 202-879-4040. Business E-Mail: robert.mcdiarmid@spiegelmcd.com.

MCDONALD, ANDREW J., bishop emeritus; b. Savannah, Ga., Oct. 24, 1923; s. James Bernard and Theresa (McGrael) McDonald. AB, St. Mary's Sem., Balt., 1945, STL, 1948; JCB, Cath. U. Am., 1949; JCD, Lateran U., Rome, 1951. Ordained priest Diocese of Savannah, Ala., 1948, chancellor Ga., 1952-68, vicar gen. Ga., from 1968, vice oficialis Ga., 1952-57, oficialis Ga., 1956-72; curate Port Wentworth, Ga., 1952-57; pastor Blessed Sacrament Ch., Savannah, 1963-72; bishop Diocese of Little Rock, 1972-2000, bishop emeritus, 2000—. Named Papal Chamberlain, Roman Cath. Ch., 1956, Domestic Prelate, 1959. Roman Catholic. Home: 80 W Northwest Hwy Palatine IL 60067-3582

MCDONALD, ANGUS WHEELER, farmer; b. Washington, Apr. 21, 1927; s. John Yates and Dorothy Helen (Bosworth) McD.; m. Mary Joan Montgomery, May 8, 1952 (div. Sept. 1958); children: Mary Ann Hetzer, Paul Yates. BA, Columbia Union Coll., 1974. Farmer, owner Pleasant View Farm, Charles Town, W.Va., 1953—. Presdl. candidate Democratic Party, 1987-88, 92, 2000. With U.S. Army, 1946-47. Mem. AARP, Jefferson County Farm Bur., W.Va. State Hort. Soc., No. W.Va. Automobile Club, Am. Legion, The Moose. Avocations: photography, travel, attending historical events. Home and Office: Pleasant View Farm 2225 Flowing Springs Rd Charles Town WV 25414-9413

MCDONALD, ANNE LEGGETT, mathematics professor; b. Columbus, Ohio, May 28, 1947; d. Ernest William Leggett and Esther Irene Wilson; m. Gerard McDonald, Jan. 9, 1982. BA, Ohio State U., 1969; PhD, Yale U., 1973. Instr. MIT, Cambridge, 1973-75; asst. prof. U. Tex., Austin, 1975-79; assoc. prof. Western Ill. U., Macomb, 1979-83, Loyola U., Chgo., 1983—. Author: Complexities: Women in Mathematics, 2005; contbr. articles to profl. jours. Recipient Jesuit Book award Alpha Sigma Nu Nat., 2006; NSF fellow, 1974-76. Mem. Assn. for Women in Math. (newsletter editor 1977—, editor 150th issue 2003, Award for Disting. Svc. 1993, Book award 2005). Democrat. Avocations: genealogy, computer multimedia, scrapbooks. Office: Math Dept Loyola Univ 6525 N Sheridan Rd Chicago IL 60626-5344 Office Phone: 773-508-3554. E-mail: amcdona@luc.edu.

MCDONALD, APRIL D., writer; d. Butler Cassell William, Jr. and Veronica Denise McDonald. Degree in Journalism, No. Va. Coll., 2003. Cert. A+ NOVA, 2001. CEO ADM Publishing LLC, Nocross, Ga. Author: Sex, Lies & Consequences, 2005. Mentor Big Sister program, Atlanta, 2005—. Independent. Avocations: travel, jet skiing, writing, public speaking. Business E-Mail: aprilmcdonaldinc@yahoo.com.

MCDONALD, AUDRA ANN, actress, vocalist; b. Berlin, July 3, 1970; d. Stanley and Kathryn McDonald; m. Peter Donovan, Sept. 10, 2000; 1 child, Zoe Madeline Donovan. BFA in Voice, Juilliard Sch., 1993; attended, Sch. Arts., Calif. Stage appearances include (operas) La Voix Humaine/Send, 2006, Rise and Fall of the City of Mahogany, 2007 (Grammy awards for best classical album and best opera recording, 2009); (regional plays) Man of La Mancha, Evita, The Wiz, A Chorus Line, Grease, Anything Goes, The Real Inspector Hound, Anyone Can Whistle, 2005; (Broadway plays) The Secret Garden, Man of La Mancha, 1989, Carousel, 1994 (Tony award best featured actress in a musical, 1994, Outer Critics Circle award outstanding actress in a musical, 1994), Master Class, 1995-97 (Tony award best featured actress in a musical, 1996, LA Ovation award best featured actress in a musical, 1996), Ragtime, 1998-99 (Tony award for best featured actress in a musical, 1998), Sweeney Todd, 2000, A Raisin in the Sun, 2004 (Tony award best featured actress in a play, 2004, Drama Desk award best featured actress in a play, 2004), See What I Wanna See (formerly titled R Shomon), 2005, 110 in the Shade, 2007 (Drama Desk award outstanding actress in a musical 2007); (TV series) Bill Cosby pilot, 1996, Mister Sterling, 2003, The Bedford Diaries, 2006, Kidnapped, 2006-07, Private Practice, 2007-; (TV Movies) Having Our Say: The Delaney Sisters' First 100 Years, 1999, Annie, 1999, The Last Debate, 2000, Wit, 2001 (Emmy award nom. best supporting actress, 2001), A Raisin in the Sun, 2008; (films) Seven Servants, 1996, The Object of My Affection, 1998, Cradle Will Rock, 1999, It Runs in the Family, 2003, The Best Thief in the World, 2004; concert performances include S'Wonderful, Some Enchanted Evening, Christa Ludwig and James Levine Recital, Revelation in Courthouse Park, Requiem Canticles; singer: (albums) Leonard Bernstien's New York, 1996, Sings Rodgers & Hart, 1996, George & Ira Gershwin: Standards & Gems, 1998, George Gershwin: 100th Birthday Celebration, 1998, Broadway in Love, 2000, Marie Christine: A New Musical, 2000, Broadway Cares: Home for the Holidays, 2001, Dreamgirls in Concert, 2002, (solo albums) Way Back to Paradise, 1998, How Glory Goes, 2000, Happy Songs, 2002, Build a Bridge, 2006. Recipient Theatre World award, 1994, Drama League award for distinguished achievement in musical theatre, 2000. Office: Gersh Agency Inc 41 Madison Ave Fl 33 New York NY 10010-2210*

MCDONALD, BERNARD ROBERT, retired federal agency administrator; b. Kansas City, Nov. 17, 1940; s. Bernard Luther and Mabel McD.; m. Jean Graves, June 7, 1963 (div. 1996); children: Aaron Michael, Elizabeth Kathleen; m. Joann Huffaker, Aug. 2, 1997. BA in Math., Park Coll., Parkville, Mo., 1962; MA in Math. and Physics, Kans. State U., 1964; PhD in Math., Mich. State U., East Lansing, 1968. Prof. dept. math. U. Okla., Norman, 1968—83, chmn. dept. math., 1981—83; program dir. div. math. scis. NSF, Washington, 1983—86, program dir. spl. projects, 1986—88, dep. dir. div. math. scis., 1988—2004; ret., 2004. Author: R-linear Endomorphism, 1983, Geometric Algebra, 1976, Finite Rings, 1974, Ring Theory III, 1980. Recipient Meritorious Svc. award, NSF, 1995, Disting. Svc. award, 1999. Mem. AAAS, Am. Math. Soc., Math. Assn. Am., Soc. Ind. and Applied Math., Assn. Women Math., Sigma Xi. Home: 5016 35th St N Arlington VA 22207-2816 Personal E-mail: math1940@aol.com.

MCDONALD, BRADLEY G., lawyer; m. Ann Gilbert, Sept. 3, 1964; 1 child, Perry. BA, U. Okla.; JD, Georgetown U., 1961. Bar: D.C. 1961, U.S. Ct. Appeals (D.C., 11th and 4th cirs.), U.S. Supreme Ct. With McDonald & Karl, Washington. Guest lectr. Wash. Coll. of Law, Am. Univ., Washington. Mem. nat. alumni adv. coun. U. Okla; mem. Arlington Com. of 100; bd. dirs gen. counsel, sec. Close Up Found.; trustee Randolph Macon Acad.; bd. dirs. Montessori Sch. of McLean. 1st lt. USMC, 1956-58. Recipient 1st Regent's Alumni award U. Okla. Mem. Sigma Nu (trustee Ednl. Found.). Office Phone: 202-293-3200.

MCDONALD, CAMILLE ANN, retail executive; b. Springfield, Mass., May 3, 1953; d. George Francis and Theresa Margaret (Disabella) McD. BA, Smith Coll., 1975. Mktg. rep. children's wear Monsanto Textiles Co., NYC, 1975-78; mgr. mktg. mass fragrances Charles of Ritz, NYC, 1979-81, dir. mktg., 1981-83; dir. mktg. fragrances Revlon Internat., NYC, 1983-84; dir. mktg. DFD-women's fragrances Cosmair Inc., NYC, 1984-86, v.p. mktg. DFD-Ralph Lauren; v.p. mktg. Parfums Phenix, Avon Co., NYC, 1987-88; exec. v.p. merchandising & brand devel. Bath & Body Works, Inc., Reynoldsburg, Ohio, 2004—07, pres. brand devel. & merchandising, 2007—. Bd. dirs. Timex Group B.V., 2008—. Mem. Cosmetic Exec. Women, Fragrance Found. (best popular fragrance award 1981, best packaging and advt. award 1984, best ltd. distbn. fragrance award 1987, best advt. award 1987). Roman Catholic. Office: Bath & Body Works Inc 7 Limited Pkwy E Reynoldsburg OH 43068*

MCDONALD, CAPERS WALTER, biomedical engineer, manufacturing executive, entrepreneur, educator; b. Georgetown, SC, Nov. 29, 1951; s. WalBern and Cecilia (Lockwood) McD.; m. Marion Elizabeth Kiper, Aug. 23, 1975; 1 child, Adam Capers. BS in Engring. magna cum laude, Duke U., 1974; MS in Mech. Engring., MIT, 1976; MBA, Harvard Bus. Sch., 1983. Dir. mktg. Becton Dickinson Co., Sunnyvale, Calif., 1978-81; cons. Booz, Allen & Hamilton, San Francisco, 1982-84; v.p. Siegen Corp., Mountain View, Calif., 1984, HP Genenchem, South San Francisco, Calif., 1984-87; bio-analytic systems mgr. Hewlett-Packard Corp., Palo Alto, Calif., 1986—87; v.p. Orion Instruments, Inc., Redwood City, Calif., 1987-89, Spectroscopy Imaging Systems Corp., Fremont, Calif., 1989-90, pres., bd. dirs., 1991—92; pres., CEO, bd. dirs. BioReliance Corp., Rockville, Md., 1992—2004; pres., CEO Magenta Corp., Rockville, 1993—2000; chmn., dir. Magenta Svcs., Ltd., Stirling, Scotland, 1994-2000; dir. BioReliance Holdings GmbH, Heidelberg, Germany, 1996—2004, Q-One Biotech Group Ltd., Glasgow, Scotland, 2003—04; exec. in residence, faculty mem. Johns Hopkins U., 2004—. Bd. dirs. Expion, Inc., Olney, Md.; bd. visitors U. Md. Biotech Inst., 1996-00, Duke U. Sch. Engring., 2001—, chmn. edn. and student affairs com., 2005-; bd. advisors Md. Partnership for Workforce Quality, 1996-98, Washington Bus. Jour., 2003-05; vice chmn. High Tech. Coun. Md., 1998-01; chmn. Tech. Coun. Md., 2001-04; mem. industry adv. bd. Chesapeake Bay Area chpt. ISPE, 1998-2000; mem. mfg. extension partnership nat. adv. bd. US Dept. Commerce, 2007—, mem. MBA exec. bd., Carey Bus. Sch. Johns Hopkins U., 2007-; lectr. in field. Contbr. chpts. to books; patentee flow microfluorometer; contbr. articles to profl. jours. Asst. scoutmaster Boy Scouts Am., Georgetown, SC, 1965-66; trustee Bethesda Acad. Performing Arts, 1998-01; mem. oversight bd. advanced tech. consortium Montgomery Coll., 1998-01; mem. steering com. Biotech. Industry Orgn., 2003 Ann. Meeting, 2002-03; mem. econ. adv. coun. Montgomery County, 1998-05; mem. founding exec. bd. Greater Washington Regional Partnership, 1998-01; mem. leadership coun. Treatment and Learning Ctrs., 1998-2000; with Capstone Co., Johns Hopkins U., 2003-04; mem. Md. Advanced Tech. Bus. Devel. Commn., 2003; state planning com. for postsecondary edn. Md. Higher Edn. Commn., 2004; chmn. Md. Adv. Tech. del. to Peoples Republic China, 2004; chmn. Eagle Career Day, Greater Washington, 2002-03. Angier B. Duke Scholar, Duke U., 1970-74, MIT scholar, 1974-76; hon. fellow NSF, 1974; recipient Leadership in Tech. award Md. High Tech. Coun., 1996, Employer of Yr. award Md. Pvt. Industry Coun., 1996, Region's Most Admired Bosses award Washington Techway Mag., 2000, Good Scout award Nat. Capital Area Coun., 2000, Nat. Disting. Eagle Scout award Boy Scouts Am., 2001, Export award Scottish Coun. Devel. and Industry, 2001, Stevie award Am. Bus. Awards, 2003, Disting. Alumnus award Pratt Sch. Engring., Duke U., 2005, Endowed Ann. award, Excellence in Mentoring and Advising, 2005; named Greater Washington Entrepreneur of Yr. in Life Scis., 2002. Mem. AAAS, ASME, Acad. Mgmt., Biomed. Engring. Soc., NC Acad. Sci., Md. C. of C. (bd. dirs.

1996-00), Soc. Cin. (endowment com., lib. com. 2008-), Order Founders and Patriots Am., St. Andrews Soc. of Washington, Order Magna Charta, First Families SC, Hugnenot Soc. SC, Gen. Soc. Colonial Wars, Soc. Sons Am. Revolution, Harvard U. Alumni Assn., Duke U. Alumni Assn., MIT Alumni Assn., Johns Hopkins Club, Iron Dukes, Congl. Country Club, Sigma Xi, Tau Beta Pi (chpt. pres. 1973-74, nat. fin. devel. com. 2007-), Phi Eta Sigma, Pi Mu Epsilon. Methodist. Avocations: fishing, travel. Office: Johns Hopkins Univ 9601 Med Ctr Dr Rockville MD 20850 Home Phone: 301-299-6504. Business E-Mail: capersmcd@jhu.edu.

MC DONALD, CHARLES J., dermatologist, educator; b. Tampa, Fla., Dec. 6, 1931; s. George B. and Bertha C. (Harbin) McDonald; m. Maureen McDonald; children: Marc S. McDonald, Norman D. McDonald, Eric S. McDonald. BS magna cum laude, A and T Coll., NC, 1951; MS, U. Mich., 1952; MD with highest honors, Howard U., Washington, DC, 1960. Diplomate Am. Bd. Dermatology. Rotating intern Hosp. St. Raphael, New Haven, 1960-61, asst. resident in medicine, 1961-63; asst. resident, dermatology Yale U., 1963-65, spl. USPHS rsch. fellow, chief resident dermatology, 1965-66, instr. medicine, pharmacology, 1966-67, asst. prof. medicine, pharmacology, 1967-68; asst. prof. med. sci. Brown U., Providence, 1968-69, assoc. prof., 1969-74, prof., 1974—, dir. dermatology program, 1970-74, head subsect. dermatology, 1974-82, dir. divsn. dermatology, 1982—96, chair dept. dermatology, 1996—; dir. dermatology Roger Williams Gen. Hosp., 1968-97; physician in chief, dept. dermatology RI Hosp., 1989—. Mem. com., task force, chmn. task force minority affairs Am. Acad. Dermatology, 1975—80; mem. dermatology adv. panel Fed. Drug Adminstrn., 1975—78, cons., 1978—; chmn. com. pub. edn., dir., v.p. RI divsn. Am. Cancer Soc., 1978—83, bd. dir. nat. soc., 1983—90, nat. dir. at large, 1990—95, mem. nat. exec. com., 1991—99, nat. officer, 1995—2001, pres. elect, 1997—98, pres., 1998—99; mem. pharm. scis. rev. commn. NIH, 1979—83; mem. residency rev. com. dermatology ACGME, 1992—97, mem. bd. accreditation appeals dermatology, 1999—; vice chmn. RRC dermatology, 1996—97; mem. adv. com. Arthritis, Muscular, Skeletal, Skin Disease Inst., NIH, 1993—95. Editor: Post Grad. Med. Jour., 1970—85; mem. editl. bd.: Jour. of Am. Acad. Dermatology, 1981—86; contbr. numerous articles to med. publs. Bd. trustees Citizens Bank of RI, 1975—97, chair cmty. reinvestment com., 1991—97; trustee Howard U., 1993—, chair health affairs com., 1994—98, mem. exec. com., 1994—98; chair adv. bd. Howard U. Cancer Ctr., 2005—; chair bd. advisors Sch. Medicine, 1998—2005; founding mem., bd. dirs. Providence Health Care Found., 1968—76, chmn. mem. adv. com., 1976—87; bd. dirs. Providence Fund for Edn., 1986—90; mem. bd. dirs. Providence Pub. Libr., 1971—2000, sec., 1977—2000; bd. dirs. R.I. Cancer Coun., 1999—2001; mem. bd. dirs. Lifespan Hosp. Consortium, RI, 2001—; mem. R.I. State Bd. Edn., 1970—72. Maj. USAF, 1952—56. Recipient Disting. Svc. award, Hosp. Assn., RI, 1971, Disting. Alumni award, Howard U. Coll. Medicine, 1983, St. George medal, Nat. Divsn. award, Am. Cancer Soc., 1992, WW Keen award, Brown Med. Alumni, 2002, Candle award, Morehouse Coll., 2005, Disting. Alumni award for medicine and cmty. affairs, Howard U., 2005, Cmty. Svc. and Medicine award, RI Black Heritage Soc., 2005. Mem.: Assn. Profs. Dermatology (bd. dirs. 1991—94), Dermatology Found. (chmn. sci. com. 1972—76), New Eng. Dermatology Soc., Am. Soc. Clin. Oncology, Nat. Med. Assn. (chmn. sect. dermatology 1973—75), Am. Acad. Dermatology (bd. dirs. 1987—91), Am. Fedn. Clin. Rsch., Soc. Investigative Dermatology, Noah Worcester Dermatol. Assn. (bd. dirs. 1983—86), RI Dermatol. Assn., Am. Cancer Soc. New Eng. (Lifetime Achievement award 2007), New Eng. Dermatol. Soc. (v.p. 1983—84, pres. 1984—85), Am. Dermatol. Assn. (bd. dirs. 1995—2000, pres elect 2002, pres. 2003—04), AAAS, Beta Kappa Chi, Alpha Kappa Mu, Alpha Omega Alpha, Sigma Xi. Democrat. Office: RI Hosp Dept Dermatology 593 Eddy St Providence RI 02903-4971 Office Phone: 401-444-7137. Business E-Mail: cmcdonald@lifespan.org, charles_mcdonald@brown.edu.

MCDONALD, CHRISTIE ANNE, literature and language professor, writer; b. NYC, May 4, 1942; d. John Denis and Dorothy (Eisner) McD.; m. Eugene Augustus Vance, June 11, 1965 (div. June 1986); children: Adam Vance, Jacob Vance; m. Michael David Rosengarten, Dec. 4, 1987. AB, Mt. Holyoke Coll., 1964; PhD, Yale U., 1969; MA (hon.), Harvard Coll., 1994. Acting instr. Yale U., New Haven, 1968-69; asst. prof. French U. Montreal, Que., Canada, 1969-77, assoc. prof. French Que., 1977-83, prof. Que., 1983, 86-93; prof. modern langs. Emory U., Atlanta, 1984-86; prof. romance langs. and lits. Harvard U., Cambridge, Mass., 1994—, chmn. romance langs. and lits., 2000—06. Author: The Dialogue of Writing, 1985, Dispositions, 1986, The Proustian Fabric, 1991; editor: The Ear of the Other, 1988, The Extravagant Shepherd, 1993, 2nd edit., 2007, Transpositions, 1994, Images of Congo, 2005, Painting My World, 2008. Decorated chevalier Order Palmes Academiques; recipient Clifford prize, Am. Assn. 18th-Century Studies, 1994—95. Mem.: Royal Soc. Can. Office: Harvard U 431 Boylston Hall Cambridge MA 02138

MCDONALD, DAVID EUGENE, transportation operator; b. Decatur, Ill., July 6, 1956; s. Robert Alexander McDonald and Ida Jane (Varvil) Crowell; m. Lynda Jean Christensen McDonald, Apr. 23, 1983; children: Melanie Ann, Joshua Glen and Jordan David (twins). BS in History, Ill. State U., Normal; student, Parkland C.C., Champaign, Ill. Asst. mgr. Gen. Cinema Corp., Decatur, Champaign, Chgo., 1978-81; mgr. Classic Cinemas, Elmhurst, Ill., 1981-83, World Mgmt. Inc., Downers Grove, Ill., 1983-87; driver UPS, Addison, Ill., 1987—. Active Jr. Achievement, 1971-75, Dupage County Rep., Wheaton, Ill., 1993-2002; treas. Local Luth. Laymans League, 2000—. Named Mr. Exec. Jr. Achievement, Decatur, Ill., 1975; recipient Internat. Literary award Manuscripts Internat., Dayton, Wash., 1988. Republican. Lutheran. Avocations: politics, photography, reading, writing. Home: 841 Prospect Ave Elmhurst IL 60126-4862 Office: UPS 150 S Lombard Rd Addison IL 60101-3020

MCDONALD, DAVID MICHAEL, church administrator; b. Springfield, Ill., June 13, 1964; s. John Joseph McDonald and Lavena Pauline Smith; m. Jennet Ruth Shepherd, Dec. 31, 1986; children: Julia Rose, Cullen Read, Rachel Leigh. BA, Beloit Coll., Wis., 1986; MDiv, Eden Theol. Sem., St. Louis, 1993; DMin, Christian Theol. Seminary, Indpls., 2009. Cert. in ordained minister United Ch. Christ, 1993; Bd. Certification Genealogists, 2004. Pastor Immanuel United Ch. Christ, Peotone, Ill., 1997—2001; sr. pastor Windsor United Ch. Christ, Wis., 2001—. Sec. Ill. Conf., UCC, Westchester, 1994—2000; moderator SW Assn., Wis. Conf. UCC, Madison, 2008—. Contbr. articles to profl. jours. Trustee Bd. Certification Genealogists, Washington, 2008. Mem.: Nat. Geneal. Soc. (bd. dirs. 2008), Wis. State Geneal. Soc. (jour. editor 2007—08), Madison, Priory St. John Bapt., SMOTJ, Phi Kappa Psi (nat. chaplain 1992). Liberal. Home: P O Box 144 De Forest WI 53532 Office: Windsor United Ch Christ P O Box 187 Windsor WI 53598 Business E-Mail: office@windsorucc.org.

MCDONALD, DENNIS, rancher, political organization administrator; b. Salina, Kans, 1944; m. Sharon McDonald; children: Kelly, Courtney, Casey, Clay. JD, San Francisco Law Sch. Owner, operator Open Spear Ranch; chmn. Mont. State Dem. Party, 2005—. Former mem. Agrl. Trade Adv. Com. for Livestock. Co-founder R-CALF. Mem.: US Cattlemen's Assn. (interim dir. Region VI), Mont. Cattlemen's Assn. (former pres.). Democrat. Office: Mont Dem Party PO Box 802 Helena MT 59624 also: Open Spear Ranch 856 Tony Creek Rd Melville MT 59055 Office Phone: 406-537-2333. Office Fax: 406-537-2334. E-mail: mcdonald@mcn.net.*

MCDONALD, DOUGLAS ROBERT, retired non profit agency executive; b. San Francisco, May 27, 1949; s. Robert Angus and Shirley Anne (Beine) McD.; m. Karen Bachanas, June 24, 1978; children: Jennifer, Cameron. AB, Stanford Univ., 1971; MBA, Santa Clara Univ., 1974. Dist. exec. Boy Scouts Am., San Mateo, Calif., 1971-74, exec. Palo Alto, Calif., 1974-76; regional sales mgr. Baron Data Systems, San Leandro, Calif., 1976-81; field dir., COO Boy Scouts Am., San Mateo, Calif., 1981-86, assoc. reg. dir. Sunnyvale, Calif., 1986-88, scout exec., CEO Stockton, Calif., 1988-92, San Jose, Calif., 1992-99, Sacramento, 1999—2003, scout exec., COO Redlands, Calif., 2003—08. Active 1910 Soc. Boy Scouts Am. Recipient Paul Harris fellow Rotary Internat., 1990, St. George award Roman Cath. Diocese of Sacramento, 2000; James E. West fellow Boy Scouts Am., 1993, Asian AM. Spirit of Scouting award, 2009, Cliff Dochterman award 2009. Mem. Am. Fundraising Profls., Sigma Alpha Epsilon, Alpha Phi Omega, Rotary Internat., Scouting Heritage Soc., KC. Republican. Roman Catholic. Avocations: travel, computers, investments. Home: 19698 Explorer Dr Penn Valley CA 95946 Home Phone: 530-432-2726. Personal E-mail: drmcdon@aol.com.

MCDONALD, DOUGLASS WAYNE, museum administrator; b. Marshalltown, Iowa, July 22, 1953; s. Wayne Eldon and Miriam Gertrude (Thurber) McD.; m. Kay Louise Stangeland, Sept. 14, 1974; 1 child, Timothy. BA, William Penn Coll., 1974. Pastor Friends Ch., Indpls., 1974-83; dir. of ops. Conner Prairie, Indpls., 1983-95; pres., CEO Genesee Country Village & Mus., Rochester, NY, 1995-99, Cin. Mus. Ctr., 1999—. Presenter seminars Mus. and Entrepreneurial Endeavors, 1996, Codes of Ethics, 1993. Mem. City Coun., Noblesville, Ind., 1980-95; bd. govs. Legacy Fund, Carmel, Ind., 1991-95. Mem. Am. Assn. Mus. (v.p. 1992-95), Mid-Atlantic Assn. Mus. (bd. dirs. 1996-99), Mid-West Mus. Conf. (life, exec. v.p. 1994-95). Mem. Soc. Of Friends. Office: Cin Mus Ctr 1301 Western Ave Cincinnati OH 45203-1130 Home: 7660 Overlook Hills Ln Cincinnati OH 45244-3285 Office Phone: 513-287-7006. E-mail: dmcdonald@cincymuseum.org.

MCDONALD, ED, legislative staff member; b. Balt., Jan. 13, 1955; BS in mass comm. and history, Towson State U., 1978. Clk. A&P Food Stores, 1972—79; reporter WDOS-AM and WSRK-FM, Oneonta, NY, 1979—81, WRQK-FM and WPET-AM, Greensboro, NC, 1981—84; adminstrv. asst. for Rep. Howard Coble, US House of Reps., chief of staff, press sec., 1997—2003, 2004—; dep. chief of staff for Gov. Bob Ehrlich, Md., 2003. Avocations: swimming, baseball, basketball, football. Office: Office of Congressman Howard Coble 2468 Rayburn House Office Bldg Washington DC 20515-3306 Office Phone: 202-225-3065. Office Fax: 202-225-8611. E-mail: ed.mcdonald@mail.house.gov.*

MCDONALD, FRANK G., lawyer, energy executive; BA, JD, Tex. Tech U. Sr. counsel Grace Energy Corp.; sr. v.p., gen. counsel, asst. sec. XTO Energy, 1993—. Shareholder Kliewer and Hood, P.C. Office: XTO Energy Inc 810 Houston St Fort Worth TX 76102-6298 Office Phone: 817-870-2800.

MC DONALD, GAIL FABER, musician, educator; b. Jersey City, Oct. 24, 1917; d. Samuel and Jennie (Weiss) Faber; m. George Walther, Nov. 17, 2000; children from previous marriage: Lora McDonald Ferguson, Charles McDonald, Henry McDonald. Diploma, Mannes Music Sch., NYC, 1938; BA, U. Md., 1962; MusM, Cath. U., 1968; DMus Arts, U. Md., 1977. Legis. asst. Capitol Hill, 1943-46; pvt. tchr. piano and music theory Washington and Md., 1950—. Piano soloist Nat. Gallery Art, 1977; rec. artist Educo Records; lectr., performer Bach Sinfonias and Mendelssohn's Complete Songs Without Words; recorded complete solo piano works of Daniel Gregory Mason. Author: Muzio Clementi and the Gradus Ad Parnassum, 1968. Mem. D.C. Music Tchrs. Assn., Md. Music Tchrs. Assn. (pres. 1977-1981), D.C. Fedn. Music Clubs, Nat. Guild Piano Tchrs. (adjudicator 1972-2005), Friday Morning Music Club (performing mem.). Home: 900 N Taylor St Apt 1026 Arlington VA 22203-1869 E-mail: gailmcdonald@comcast.net.

MCDONALD, GARY C., mathematics professor; s. Guy F. and Louise J. McDonald; m. Jeanne E. Darr; children: Darryl D., Christopher M., Kevin M. BA, St. Mary's U. Minn., Winona, 1964; MS; PhD, DSc, Purdue U., W. Lafayette, Ind., 1969. Dir., enterprise sys. lab. Gen. Motors R & D Labs., Warren, Mich., 1998—2002; adj. prof. math. & stats. Oakland U., Rochester, Mich., 2002—. Contbr. scientific papers. Mem. & chmn. Mathcounts Found., Alexandria, Va., 1992—2006. Fellow: AAAS; mem.: Inst. Math. Statistics, Am. Statis. Assn. (Founders award 2007). Office: Oakland Univ Dept Math & Stat Rochester MI 48309-4485 Office Fax: 248-370-4184. Business E-Mail: mcdonald@oakland.edu.

MCDONALD, JOHN GREGORY, financial investment educator; b. Stockton, Calif., 1937; m. Melody McDonald. BS, Stanford U., 1960, MBA, 1962, PhD, 1967. Mem. faculty Grad. Sch. Bus. Stanford U., Calif., 1968—, now The Stanford Investors prof. fin. Grad. Sch. Bus. Vis. prof. U. Paris, 1972, Columbia Bus. Sch., 1975, Harvard Bus. Sch., 1986; gov., vice-chmn., bd. govs. NASD/NASDAQ Stock Market, 1987—90; mem. adv. bd. InterWest Venture Capital; bd. dirs. Growth Fund of Am., New Perspective Fund, Inc., Plum Creek Timber Co., EuroPacific Growth Fund, Scholastic Corp., 1985—. Contbr. articles to profl. jours. Bd. overseers vis. com. Harvard U. Bus. Sch., Cambridge, Mass., 1994-2000. Fulbright scholar, Paris, 1967—68. Office: Stanford U Grad Sch Bus 518 Memorial Way Stanford CA 94305 also: Scholastic Corp 557 Broadway New York NY 10012*

MCDONALD, JOHN J., JR., lawyer; b. St. Paul, Dec. 12, 1954; BA, Univ. St. Thomas, 1977; JD, Creighton Univ., 1981. Bar: Minn. 1982, Wis., US Dist. Ct. (Minn., Wis., ND dist.), US Ct. Appeals (1st, 7th, 8th cir.), US Supreme Ct. Ptnr., comml. litigation, mem. mgmt. com. Meagher & Geer PLLP, Mpls. Named a Minn. Super Lawyer, Minn. Law & Politics, 2000—04. Mem.: ABA, Am. Bd. Trial Advocates, Internat. Assn. Def. Counsel, Def. Rsch. Inst., Minn. State Bar Assn., Wis. State Bar Assn. Office: 33 S 6th St Ste 4400 Minneapolis MN 55402-3720 Office Phone: 612-347-9120. Office Fax: 612-338-8384. Business E-Mail: jmcdonald@meagher.com.

MC DONALD, JOHN RICHARD, lawyer; b. Connersville, Ind., Aug. 8, 1933; s. Vernon Louis and Thelma (Venham) McD.; m. Mary Alice Boyd, Aug. 17, 1957; children: Anne Elizabeth, John Richard, Colleen Lynn. BA, U. Ariz., 1957, LL.B., 1960. Bar: Ariz. 1960. Since practiced in, Tucson; assoc. Richard N. Roylston, 1961-62; pvt. practice, 1963-65; ptnr. McDonald & Rykken, 1965-68, DeConcini & McDonald (now DeConcini, McDonald, Yetwin, Lacy, and Richardson P.C.), 1968—. Mem. adv. bd. Dependable Nurses, Inc., 1994—. Mem. Ariz. Law Rev. Pres., bd. dirs. emeritus Comstock Children's Hosp. Found.; v.p. Ariz. Sch. Bds. Assn., 1979, pres., 1981; v.p. All Ariz. Sch. Bd., 1981; v.p., bd. dirs. Tucson Assn. for Blind, 1966-86; trustee Catalina Foothills Sch. Dist., 1976-82; bd. dirs. Tucson Unified Sch. Dist. Ednl. Enrichment Found., 1994-2003, Ariz. Acad., 1981-89, Tucson Symphony Soc., 1997-2003, Catalina Foothills Sch. Dist. Found., 1998-2004, Grand Canyon Music Festival, 2003—. Recipient Outstanding Svc. in Sch. Law award, Ariz. Sch. Bds. Assn., 2006. Mem. Ariz. Bar Assn., Ariz. Law Rev. Assn. (pres. 1994), Pima County Bar Assn. (dir. 1978-86, pres. 1984-85), Nat. Coun. Sch. Attys. (dir. 1992-96), Delta Chi. Independent. Presbyterian. Home: 6151 N Camino Almonte Tucson AZ 85718-3729 Office: 2525 E Broadway Blvd Tucson AZ 85716-5398 Home Phone: 520-299-9077; Office Phone: 520-322-5000. Personal E-mail: mjm85718@aol.com. Business E-Mail: jmcdonald@dmyl.com. E-mail: mjm@aol.com.

MCDONALD, JOHN W., oil industry executive; b. Ont., Can., 1951; BS in Geophysics, U. Western Ont., 1975. Geophysicist to various positions of increasing responsibility Texaco, Calgary, Alta., Canada, 1975—91, strategic adviser, asst. to chmn., 1992—94; asst. divsn. mgr. Texaco Exploration and Prodn., New Orleans, 1994—96, v.p. exploration and prodn. offshore divsn., 1996—98; v.p. prodn. Texaco Internat., London, 1998—99; mng. dir. Texaco Ltd., 1998—2001, ChevronTexaco Upstream Europe, Aberdeen, Scotland, 2001—02; v.p. strategic planning ChevronTexaco Corp., San Ramon, Calif., 2002—08, v.p., chief tech. officer, 2008—. Mem.: U.K. Industry/Govt. Forum, U.K. Offshore Operators Assn. (past pres, exec. officer), Soc. Exploration Geophysicists, Am. Assn. Petroleum Geologists. Office: ChevronTexaco Corp 6001 Bollinger Canyon Rd San Ramon CA 94583-2324*

MC DONALD, JOHN WARLICK, diplomat; b. Coblenz, Germany, Feb. 18, 1922; s. John Warlick and Ethel Mae (Raynor) McD.; m. Barbara Jane Stewart, Oct. 23, 1943 (div.); children: Marilyn Ruth, James Stewart, Kathleen Ethel, Laura Ellen; m. Christel Meyer, Oct. 24, 1970. AB, U. Ill., 1943, JD, 1946; PhD (hon.), Mt. Mercy Coll., 1989, Teikyo Marycrest U., 1991, Salisbury State U., 1993; JD (hon.), St. John's U., 2007. Bar: Ill. 1946, U.S. Supreme Ct. 1951. With legal div. Office Mil Govt., Berlin, 1947; asst. dist. atty. U.S. Mil. Govt. Cts., Frankfort, Germany, 1947-50; with Allied High Commn., Bonn, Germany, 1950-52; U.S. mission to NATO and OEEC, Paris, 1952-54; fgn. affairs officer Dept. State, Washington, 1954-55; exec. sec. to dir. ICA, Washington, 1955-59; U.S. econ. coord. for CENTO affairs Ankara, Turkey, 1959-63; chief econ. and comml. sect. Am. Embassy, Cairo, 1963-66; student Nat. War Coll., Washington, 1966-67; dep. dir. office econ. and social affairs Bur. Internat. Orgn. Affairs, Dept. State, 1967-68, dir., 1968-71; coord. UN Multilateral Devel. Programs, Dept. State, 1971-74, acting dep. asst. sec. econ. and social affairs, 1971, 73; dep. dir. gen. ILO, Geneva, 1974-78; pres. INTELSAT Conf. Privileges and Immunities, 1978; U.S. coord. Tech. Coop. among Developing Countries, 1978; rep. with rank of amb. to UN Conf., 1978—83. Sec. gen. 27th Colombo Plan Ministerial Meeting, 1978; U.S. coord. UN Decade on Drinking Water and Sanitation, 1979; U.S. coord., amb. Third World Conf. on Indsl. Devel., 1979, World Assembly on Aging, 1980-82; chmn. fed. inter-agy. com. Internat. Yr. of Disabled Persons, 1980-81; U.S. rep. Internat. Youth Yr., 1981-83; coord. multilateral affairs Ctr. Study of Fgn. Affairs, 1983-87; profl. lectr. in law George Washington U. Nat. Law Ctr., 1987-88, lectr. in conflict resolution, multilateral diplomacy and art of negotiation; pres. Iowa Peace Inst., Grinnell, 1988-92; prof. polit. sci. Grinnell Coll., 1989-92; Disting. vis. prof. George Mason U., Fairfax, Va., 1992-93; chmn., CEO Inst. for Multi-Track Diplomacy, Wash, DC, Arlington, Va, 1992—; mem. Fgn. Affairs Res. Corps., 1993—; adj. prof. Union Inst., 1993-94, 97-98; adj. prof. conflict resolution, 1998-01, 05-06, George Mason U., 2008-09. Author: The North-South Dialogue and the UN, 1982, How to Be a Delegate, 1984, 2nd edit., 1994, Conflict Peacebuilding: Stories & Lessons, 2008; co-editor: International Negotiation, 1985, Perspectives on Negotiation, 1986, Conflict Resolution: Track Two Diplomacy, 1987, 2nd edit., 1995, U.S. Soviet Summitry, 1987, US Bases Overseas: Negotiations with Spain, Greece and The Philippines, 1990, Multi-Track Diplomacy, 1991, 2nd edit., 1993, 3rd edit., 1996, Chinese edit., 2006, Defining A U.S. Negotiating Style, 1996, The Shifting grounds of conflict and Peacebuilding, 2008, paperback, 2009, Conflict Resolution & Peacebuilding-The Role of NGO's in Historical Reconciliation & Twintorial Issue,2009; contbr. articles on aging, terrorism, water and conflict resolution; featured in exhibit Va. Hist. Soc., 2006, The Role of NGOs in Historical Re Peacebuilding,2009 Bd. dirs. Global Water, 1982-, chair, 1982—1984, Touchstone Theatre, 1982-88, World Com.-UN Decade of Disabled Persons, 1983-1992, Countdown 2001, 1987-93, People-to-People Com. on Disability, 1987—2003, Am. Impact Found., 1987-89, chmn. bd., 1988-89; dir. Am. Assn. Internat. Aging, 1983—2003, chmn., 1983—2003; v.p. nat. capital area UN Assn., 1993-98, mem., 1978—. Recipient Superior Honor award, State Dept., 1972, Presdl. Meritorious Svc. award, State Dept., 1984, Peace Builders award Search for Common Ground Internat., 2005, Alumni Achievement award U. Ill. Sch. Liberal Arts and Sci., 2004, Alumni of Yr. award U. Ill., 2006; named Patriot of Yr., Kansas City, 1987; nominee Nobel Peace prize, 1994. Mem. ABA, Am. Fgn. Svc. Assn., U.S. Assn. for Club of Rome (chair 2002-05), People to People Internat. (bd. trustees 2003-), Soc. Profls. in Dispute Resolution, Consortium of Peace Rsch., Edn. and Devel., USA Club Rome (Donella Meadows award 2006), Cosmos Club, Delta Kappa Upsilon, Phi Delta Phi. Office: IMTD 1901 Fort Myer Drive Ste 405 Arlington VA 22209 Home Phone: 703-525-9755; Office Phone: 703-528-3863. Business E-Mail: jmcdonald@imtd.org.

MCDONALD, JOSEPH LEE, insurance broker; b. Bremerton, Wash., Aug. 15, 1931; s. Joseph Okane and Ida Elizabeth (Finholm) McDonald; m. Glorietta Maness, Jan. 22, 1954 (dec. 1984); children: Holly Ann Chaffin, Andrew Lee; m. Beverly Mae Falkner, June 22, 1986 (div. Nov. 2005). BS, U. Wash., 1954. Various mgmt. positions AT&T, 1956-62; broker, ptnr. McDonald & McGarry Co., Seattle, 1962-84; ptnr., exec. McDonald Ins. Group, Kirkland, Wash., 1984—. V.p., bd. dirs. Chimayo Inc., Seattle, 1990—94, Santa Fe Food Corp., Seattle, 1991—96. Commr. Water Dist. # 97, Bellevue, 1967—71, Lake Hills Sewer Dist., Bellevue, 1965—71; pres. Wash. State Assn. Sewer Dists., Seattle, 1969; city councilman City of Bellevue, Wash., 1971—75. With US Army, 1954—56. Mem.: Apt. Assn. Seattle and King County, Seattle Master Builders Assn., Ind. Ins. Agts. Assn., Western Assn. Ins. Brokers, Nature Conservancy, Nat. Wildlife Fedn., Roche Harbor Yacht Club, Overlake Golf and Country Club, Coll. Club Seattle, Chi Phi. Avocations: skiing, sailing, tennis. Office: McDonald Ins Group 416 6th St S Kirkland WA 98033-6718 Home: 7235 91st Pl SE Mercer Island WA 98040 Home Phone: 425-585-0501; Office Phone: 425-827-7400. E-mail: bevnjoe@comcast.net.

MCDONALD, JOSEPH VALENTINE, neurosurgeon; b. NYC, June 7, 1925; m. Carolyn Alice Patricia Petersen, Apr. 30, 1955; 5 children. AB, Coll. Holy Cross, 1946; MD, U. Pitts., 1949. Intern St. Vincent's Hosp., NYC, 1949-50; rsch. fellow neuroanatomy Vanderbilt U., 1950-51; gen. surgery asst. resident Cushing VA Hosp., Boston, 1951-52; neurology extern Lenox Hill Hosp., 1952; asst. resident neurosurgery

Johns Hopkins Hosp., 1953-55, resident neurosurgeon, 1955-56; practice medicine specializing in neurol. surgery Rochester, NY, 1956—; emeritus prof. neurosurgery U. Rochester Med. Sch. Mem. Soc. Neurol. Surgeons, A.C.S., Am. Assn. Neurol. Surgeons, Congress Neurosurgeons. Home: 800 Allens Creek Rd Rochester NY 14618-3412

MCDONALD, KELLY KRISTIN, engineering educator; b. Nashville, Aug. 1, 1971; d. Maurice and Patricia McDonald; m. Stephen Nowicki, May 15, 1999. PhD, U. Fla., Gainesville, 1998. Sr. scientist, project mgr. Applied Biosys., Foster City, Calif., 2003—05; NSF bioinformatics coord., adj. prof. Am. River Coll., Sacramento, 2005—08; lectr. Biotech Primer, Towsen, Md., 2009—. Coach Spl. Olympics, Davis, Calif., 2002—; sec. Team Davis Local Support Fund, Davis, Calif., 2008—; competitive cyclist Touchstone Climbing Cycling Team, Berkeley, Calif., 2006—. Recipient Fleet Feet Cmty. Svc. award, Golden Valley Harriers, 2005, award, USA Triathlon, 2003, Med. Guild Rsch. award, U. Fla. Coll. Medicine, 1998. Mem.: NSTA, AAAS, SCST, NABT, Phi Kappa Phi. Office: Am River Coll 4700 Coll Oak Dr Sacramento CA 95841

MCDONALD, L. CLIFFORD, epidemiologist; Epidemiologist CDC Divsn. Healthcare Quality Promotion. Office: 1600 Clifton Rd Atlanta GA 30333 Office Phone: 404-639-3311.*

MCDONALD, MALCOLM WILLIS, retired real estate company executive; b. Mpls., Nov. 17, 1936; s. Malcolm Blanchard and Ruth Virginia (Stees) McD.; m. Judy Glynn Ballard, Aug. 22, 1959 (dec. 2003); children: Malcolm Scott, Margaret Alice, Philip Brian; m. Patricia Kathleen Condon, Oct. 8, 2005. BA magna cum laude with high honors and high orations, Yale Coll., 1958; MBA, Harvard U., 1960. V.p. First Nat. Bank of St. Paul, 1960-77; dir., sr. v.p., trustee Space Center, Inc., St. Paul, 1977—2002. Adj. prof. grad. programs in mgmt. U. St. Thomas, St. Paul, 1975—94; bd. dirs. Scherer Bros. Lumber Co., Mpls., 1988—, HMN Fin., Inc., 2004—; mem. adv. bd. Firstar Bank of Minn., St. Paul, 1999—2001; vice chair adv. com. Minn. State Bd. of Investment, St. Paul, 1982—; mem. adv. bd. Sherbrooke Capital, 2002—, Hill Monastic Manuscript Libr., St. John's U., Collegeville, Minn., 1980—97. Mem. North Oaks Home Owners Assn. Bd., 1996; trustee, sec., chmn. audit com., investment com. Amherst H. Wilder Found., St. Paul, 1971—; trustee Bigelow & FR Bigelow Found., St. Paul, 1967-98, Lee and Rose Warner Found., 1990-2002, Manitou Fund, 1990-2002, Adelaide and Harry G. McNeely Found., St. Paul, 1980-98; trustee Minn. State Fair Found., 2002—, chmn., 2006-08; trustee Episcopal Diocese Minn., 2004-, v.p., 2004-09; trustee Grotto Found., St. Paul, 1980—, 2d v.p., 2005—; trustee Way to Grow, 2006—, MBR bd. dirs., 2009-; pres. Minn. Taxpayers Assn., 1994-96; former bd. dirs. Guthrie Theater, Minn. Orchestral Assn.; chmn. Minn. Landmark, Minn. Kids First, 2004—08; bd. dir. Ready 4 K, 2009-, Star Base Inc. Mem. Mpls. Club (bd. govs. 2002-06), North Oaks Golf Club, St. Paul C. of C. (Bravo awards), Colony Found., Phi Beta Kappa, Phi Gamma Delta, Fellow. Phi Beta Kappa. Republican. Episcopalian. Avocations: physical fitness, gardening, travel, encouraging 3, 4 and 5 yr. olds to want to read. Home: 21 E Oaks Rd North Oaks MN 55127-2527 Office Phone: 651-484-7714. Personal E-mail: malcolmmcdonald@comcast.net.

MCDONALD, MARIANNE, classicist; b. Chgo., Jan. 2, 1937; d. Eugene Francis and Inez (Riddle) McD.; children: Eugene, James, Bryan, Bridget, Kirstie (dec.), Hiroshi. BA magna cum laude, Bryn Mawr Coll., 1958; MA, U. Chgo., 1960; PhD, U. Calif., Irvine, 1975; doctorate (hon.), Am. Coll. Greece, 1988; diploma (hon.), Am. Archaeol. Assn.; DLitt (hon.), U. Athens, 1994, U. Dublin, 1994, Aristotle U., 1997, U. Thessalonika, 1997, Nat. U. Ireland, 2001. Instr. Greek, Latin, English, mythology, cinema U. Calif., Irvine, 1975-79; founder, rsch. fellow Thesaurus Linguae Graecae Project, 1975-97. Tchg. asst. U. Calif., Irvine, 1972-74; vis. prof. U. Ulster, Ireland, 1997, U. Dublin, 1990—, Univ. Coll. Dublin, 1999, 2002, U. Cork, 1999-; adj. prof. theatre U. Calif., San Diego, 1992-94, prof. theatre and classics, 1994—; bd. dirs. Centrum. Author: (novels) Semilemmatized Concordances to Euripides' Alcestis, 1977, Semilemmatized Concordance to Euripides Cyclops, 1978, Terms for Happiness in Euripides, 1978, Cyclops, Andromache, Medea, 1978, Heraclidae, Hippolytus, 1979, Hecuba, 1984, (play) And Then He Met A Woodcutter, 2005 (San Diego Critics Cir. award for best play, 2005), (critical works) Hercules Furens, 1984, Electra, 1984, Ion, 1985, Trojan Women, 1988, Iphigenia in Taurus, 1988, Euripides in Cinema: The Heart Made Visible, 1983, The Living Art of Greek Tragedy, 2003; translator: The Cost of Kindness and Other Fabulous Tales (Shinichi Hoshi), 1986, Views of Clytemnestra, Ancient and Modern, 1990, Classics and Cinema, 1990, Modern Critical Theory and Classical Literature, 1994, A Challenge to Democracy, 1994, Ancient Sun/Modern Light: Greek Drama on the Modern Stage, 1990, Star Myths: Tales of the Constellations, 1996, Sole Antico Luce Moderna, 1999, Mythology of the Zodiac: Tales of the Constellations, 2000, Antigone by Sophocles, 2000, Mythology of the Zodiac, 2000, Sing Sorrow: Classics, History, Heroines in Opera, 2001; translator: (with Michael Walton) Euripides Andromache, 2001; translator: Euripides' Electra, 2004, Euripides' Hecuba, 2005; editor (with M. McDonald and Michael Walton): Six Greek Tragedies, 2002; editor: (with Michael Walton) Amid Our Troubles: Irish Versions of Greek Tragedy, 2002, Canta la tua Pena, 2002; contbr. chapters to books, articles in field to profl. jours., reviews. Bd. dirs. Am. Coll. of Greece, 1981-90, Scripps Hosp., 1981, Am. Sch. Classical Studies, 1986-; mem. bd. overseers U. Calif., San Diego, 1985-; nat. bd. advisors Am. Biog. Inst., 1982—; pres. Soc. for the Preservation of the Greek Heritage, 1990-, Asian Am. Repertory Theatre, 2003; founder Hajime Mori Chair for Japanese Studies, U. Calif., San Diego, 1985, McDonald Ctr. for Alcohol and Substance Abuse, 1984, Thesaurus Linguarum Hiberniae, 1991-, Hiroshi McDonald Mori Performing Arts Ctr. Recipient Ellen Browning Scripps Humanitarian award, 1975, Disting. Svc. award U. Calif., Irvine, 1982, 2001, Irvine medal, 1987; named one of the Cmty. Leaders Am., 1979-80, Philanthropist of Yr., 1985, Headliner San Diego Press Club, 1985, Philanthropist of Yr. Honorary Nat. Conf. Christians and Jews, 1986, Woman of Yr. AHEPA, 1988, San Diego Woman of Distinction, 1990, Woman of Yr. AXIOS, 1991; recipient Bravissimo gold medal San Diego Opera, 1990, Gold Medal Soc. Internationalization of Greek Lang., 1990, Athens medal, 1991, Piraeus medal, 1991, award Desmoi, 1992, award Hellenic Assn. of Univ. Women, 1992, Acad. of Achievement award AHEPA, 1992, Woman of Delphi award European Cultural Ctr. Delphi, 1992, Civis Universitatis award U. Calif., San Diego, 1993, Hypatia award Hellenic U. Women, 1993, Am.-Ireland Fund Heritage award, 1994, Contbn. to Greek Letters award Aristotle U. Thessaloniki, 1994, Mirabella Mag. Readers Choice One of 1000 Women for the Nineties, 1994, citations from U.S. Congress and Calif. Senate, Alexander the Gt. award Hellenic Cultural Soc., 1995, made hon. citizen of Delphi and gold medal of the Amphiktuonon, Del. Bus. award for Fine Arts San Diego Bus. Jour., 1995, Vol. of Decade Women's Internat. Ctr., 1994, 96, Gold Star award San Diego Arts League, 1997, Golden Aeschylus award Inst. Nat. Drama Antkg. Siracusa, 1998, Women Who Mean Bus., Fine Arts award San Diego Bus. Jour., 1998, Fulbright award, 1999, Ellis Island award, 1999, Spirit of Scripps award 1999; Theatre Excellence award KPBS Patte, 2001, Laud and Laurels, U. Calif. Disting. Alumni award Hellenic Cultural Soc. San Diego, 2003, Sledgehammer Theatre award, 2003, New Path award, 2003, Egeria award Women's Internat. Ctr., 2004, Billie award, 2004, Patté award, 2004. Mem. MLA, AAUP, Am. Philol. Assn. (disting. svc. award 1999), Soc. for the Preservation of the Greek Heritage (pres.), Libr. of Am., Am. Classical League, Philol. Assn. Pacific Coast, Am. Comparative Lit. Assn., Modern and Classical Lang. Assn. So. Calif., Hellenic Soc. (coun. award 2000), Calif. Fgn. Lang. Tchrs. Assn., Internat. Platform Assn., Royal Irish Acad., Greece's Order of the Phoenix (comdr. 1994), KPBS Prodrs. Club, Hellenic Univ. Club (bd. dirs.). Avocations: Karate, harp (medieval), skiing, diving. Home: PO Box 929 Rancho Santa Fe CA 92067-0929 Office: U Calif at San Diego Dept Theatre La Jolla CA 92093 Office Phone: 858-481-0107. E-mail: mmcdonald@ucsd.edu.

MCDONALD, MARY BETH, academic administrator; d. John and Muriel McDonald. MA in Tchg., Wayne State U., Detroit, 1972. Instr. Cuyahoga CC, Cleve., 1972—76; reading instr. Cleve. State U., 1976—2005, acad. advisor, 2005—. Home: Cedarwood Dr Westlake OH 44145 Office: Cleve State Univ Euclid at East 22 St Cleveland OH 44115 Business E-Mail: m.mcdonald@csuohio.edu.

MCDONALD, PATRICK ALLEN, lawyer, educator, arbitrator; b. Detroit, May 11, 1936; s. Lawrence John and Estelle (Maks) Mc D.; m. Margaret Mercier, Aug. 10, 1963; children: Michael Lawrence, Colleen Marie, Patrick Joseph, Timothy, Margaret, Thomas, Maureen. PhB cum laude, U. Detroit, 1958, JD magna cum laude, 1961; LLM (E. Barrett Prettyman Trial scholar, Hugh J. Fegan fellow), Georgetown U., 1962. Bar: D.C. 1961, Mich. 1961, Colo. 1993. Case worker Dept. Pub. Welfare, Detroit, 1958; field examiner NLRB, Detroit, 1961; practiced in Washington, 1961-62; trial cons. NIH, Bethesda, Md., 1962; staff judge adv. USAF, France, 1962-65; prtnr. Monagham, LoPrete, Mc Donald, Yakima & Grenke, Detroit, 1965—2006, Law Offices of Patrick McDonald, 2006—. Bd. dirs., past chmn. Delta Dental Plan Mich.; past chmn. Delta Dental Plan Ohio; bd. dirs., chmn. Guest House, Lake Orion, Mich., Rochester, Minn., Detroit Athletic Club, Brighton Hosp.; instr. polit. sci. and law U. Md., 1963-65, U. Detroit Law Sch., adj. prof., 1965-2004; adj. prof. Ave Maria Law Sch., 2003—. Co-author: Law and Tactics in Federal Criminal Cases, 1963; author magnet plans for schs., Detroit, Boston. Mem. Nat. Acad. Arbitrators, Detroit Bd. Edn., 1966-76, pres.; sec., trustee Mt. Elliott Cemetary Assn.; mem. U. Detroit Sports Hall of Fame; mem. adv. bd. Providence Hosp., Southfield, Mich.; exec. bd. U. Detroit Pres.'s Cabinet. Named one of Five Outstanding Young Men of Mich., Outstanding Young Man of Detroit. Mem. ABA, Detroit Bar Assn., State Bar Mich. (commr.), U. Detroit Alumni Assn. (bd. dirs.), Mensa, Blue Key, Alpha Phi Omega (pres. Eta Pi chpt. 1955), Alpha Sigma Nu (v.p. 1960), Nat. Acad. Arbitrators. Home: 13066 Lashbrook Ln E Brighton MI 48114-6002 Office: 134 N First St Brighton MI 48116 Office Phone: 810-220-3444. Office Fax: 248-642-9460. Personal E-mail: pmcd101@sbcglobal.net. *In the field of law, as an attorney, professor and arbitrator, I have prayed and attempted to be able in argument, accurate in analysis, correct in conclusion, candid with clients, honest with adversaries, and responsible for obligations assigned to me. I have advocated moderation in all things with the exception of my love for Him who created me.*

MCDONALD, PETER D., air transportation executive; m. Diane McDonald; children: Megan, Katie. BA, Judson Coll., 1976. Mng. dir. L.A. Metro Area UAL Corp., 1995—99, v.p., op. services, 1999—2001, sr. v.p. airport ops., 2001—02, exec. v.p. ops., 2002—04, exec. v.p., COO, 2004—08, exec. v.p., chief adminstrv. officer, 2008—. Bd. dirs. United Airlines Inc. Bd. dirs. Children's Meml. Hosp., Chgo. Symphony Orch. Office: UAL Corp PO Box 66100 Chicago IL 60666

MCDONALD, PEYTON DEAN, brokerage house executive; b. Kansas City, Kans., Feb. 6, 1936; s. Charles H. and Myra (Miller) McD.; m. Frances B. Beighley, June 14, 1958; children: Peyton D., Todd B. BS, Bucknell U., 1958. Sales rep. Sprout Waldron and Co., Inc., Muncy, Pa., 1958-67; v.p. Blair & Co., Williamsport, Pa., 1967-69; v.p., mgr. Hugh Johnson, Williamsport, 1969-77, E.F. Hutton & Co. Inc., Williamsport, 1977-87; sr. v.p. Smith Barney, Williamsport, 1987—2006; v.p. Merrill Lynch, 2006—, Bank America, 2009. Pres. Hope Enterprizes. Pres. United Way, Williamsport, 1977-80, Pa. Coll. Found., 1985-86; campaign chmn. Heinz for Senator, Lycoming County, Pa., 1978, 96; bd. dirs., treas. Divine Providence Hosp., chmn.; mem. Susquehanna Health Care Bd. 1st lt. U.S. Army, 1958-59. Mem. Ross Club, Williamsport Country Club, Farmington Country Club, Masons. Republican. Presbyterian. Avocation: golf. Home: 1545 Grampian Blvd Williamsport PA 17701-1917

MCDONALD, R. BRUCE, manufacturing executive; b. 1960; B Commerce, McMaster U., Hamilton, Ont. With Ernst & Young, Lucas Varity plc, 1987—98; v.p. fin. legal & info. tech. LucasVarity Automotive, Livonia, Mich.; v.p., fin. TRW Inc.; corp. controller Johnson Controls Inc., Milw., 2001—02, corp. v.p., corp. controller, 2002—04, corp. v.p., asst. CFO, 2004—05, corp. v.p., CFO, 2005—06, exec. v.p., CFO, 2006—. Treas. Columbia St. Mary's Found. Office: Johnson Controls Inc 5757 N Green Bay Ave Milwaukee WI 53201*

MCDONALD, RICHARD BLAISE, literature and language professor; b. NYC, Feb. 21, 1966; s. John Joseph and Ruth Irene McDonald; m. Jennifer Lowry Marren; children: Nicholas Blaise, Zoe Marren. MA, U. South Fla., Tampa, 1993, PhD; MEd, U. Fla., Gainesville, 1989. Assoc. prof. Utah Valley U., Orem, 1998—. Contbr. articles to profl. jours. Recipient Faculty Excellence award, Utah Valley U., 2002, 2008. Mem.: SE Medieval Assn. Office: Utah Valley Univ 800 W University Pky Orem UT 84058 Business E-Mail: mcdonari@uvu.edu.

MCDONALD, ROBERT ALAN (BOB MCDONALD), consumer products company executive; b. Gary, Ind., June 20, 1953; s. Ray Wellington and Froso (Manolios) McD.; m. Diane Janine Murphy, Dec. 31, 1977; children: Jennifer Elizabeth, Robert Wade. BS in Engring., U.S. Mil. Acad., 1975; MBA, U. Utah, 1978. Asst. Solo brand Procter & Gamble, Cin., 1980-81, asst. mgr. Dawn brand, 1981-82, asst. mgr. Cascade brand, 1982-83, mgr. Cascade brand, 1983-84, mgr. Tide brand, 1984—86, assoc. advt. mgr., 1986—89, mgr. laundry prod. P&G Canada, 1989—91, gen. mgr. P&G Far East, 1991—94, v.p., gen. mgr. P&G Far East, 1994—96, regional v.p. Japan, P&G Asia, 1996—99, v.p. NE Asia, 1999, pres. NE Asia, 1999—2001, pres. global fabric care & home care, 2001—04, vice chmn. global ops., 2004—07, COO, 2007—09, pres., CEO, 2009—. Instr. economics, Meth. Coll., Golden Gate U., Campbell U., Fayetteville, N.C., 1979-80; bd. dirs. Xerox Corp., 2005-, The Procter & Gamble Co., 2009-. Deacon Knox Presbyn. Ch., Cin., 1982-85, Mt. Washington Presbyn. Ch., Cin., 1986; mem. bd. vis. Fuqua Sch. Bus., Duke Univ.; mem. bd. adv. Northwestern Integrated Mktg. Communications. Advanced through grades to capt. US Army, 1975—80. Fellow Royal Soc. of Arts of London (Silver medal 1975); mem. Phi Kappa Phi, Beta Gamma Sigma, Commonwealth Club. Republican. Avocations: reading, running, painting. Office: Procter & Gamble 1 Procter And Gamble Plz Cincinnati OH 45202-3393 Mailing: Procter & Gamble PO Box 599 Cincinnati OH 45201-0599 Office Phone: 513-983-1100. Office Fax: 513-983-4381.*

MC DONALD, SHIRLEY PETERSON, social worker; b. Indpls., July 7, 1934; d. Harry Angen and Marcella Iona (Kober) Peterson; B.A., Denison U., 1956; teaching credentials Chgo. State U., Nat. Coll. Edn., Prairie State U.; M.S.W., U. Ill., 1976; LCSW; cert. mediator ednl. disputes, Ill. State Bd. Edn.; m. Stanford Laurel McDonald, Apr. 26, 1964; children— Stacia Elizabeth Virginia, Jeffrey Jared Stern, Kathleen Shirley, Patricia Marie. Tchr., Chgo. Public Schs., 1962-64, Flossmoor, Ill., 1972-74; communication devel. program social worker S. Met. Assn., Harvey, Ill., 1976-79; sch. social worker S.W. Cook County Coop. Spl. Edn., Oak Forest, Ill., 1979-87; prof., field liaison Jane Addams Coll. of Social Work, U. Ill. at Chgo., 1987-2000, clin. assoc. prof. emeritus, 2000—, pvt. clin. practice, Park Forest, Ill., 1980—. Cons. sch. social work issues, practice & litigation; supr. candidates for lic. in clin. social work; trainer & presenter, peer meditation Elem. and HS, 1987-2007, Editor: School Social Work: Practice, Policy and Research Perspectives, 2d through 7th edits.; editor Sch. Social Work Jour., 1998-2002, religious edn. dir. Unitarian Universalist Cmty. Ch., Park Forest, 1975-79, bd. dirs., 1978-81, chmn. bldg. feasibility com., 1981, chmn. bldg. com., 1981-82, also adv. to bd. Mem. Acad. Cert. Social Workers, Nat. Assn. Social Workers, Ill. Assn. Sch. Social Workers (area rep.; mem. com. consultation service, program com. state conf. 1981, adv. 1981-83, pres.-elect 1982-83, pres. 1983-84, Lifetime Achievement award, 2001), Kappa Kappa Gamma, Women's Internat. League Peace and Freedom (past chpt. pres.), Pi Sigma Alpha. Personal E-mail: smcdo12602@ameritech.net.

MCDONALD, SUSANN HACKETT, music educator; b. Rock Island, Ill., May 26, 1935; d. George Hobart and Catherine Reid (Hackett) McD. Student, Ecole Normale Superieur de Musique, Paris, 1954; Premier Prix, Paris Conservatory, 1955. Prof. music U. Ariz., Tucson, 1963-79; head harp dept. Juilliard, NYC, 1975-85; chmn. harp dept. Ind. U., Bloomington, 1980—, disting. prof. music. Lectr. Cal. State U., LA, 1965-79, U. So. Calif., LA, 1967-79; artistic dir. World Harp Congress, Inc., Washington, 1983—; founder, mus. dir. USA Internat. Harp Competition, Inc., Bloomington, 1987. Editor (music) Harp Sonatas, Rossetti; musician numerous recs.; composer (music) Haiku for the Harp, Harp for Today, Universal Harp Method, 2008; author (book) Praise the Local with the Harp, 2007. Mem. Nat. Soc. Arts and Letters, Am. Harp Soc., Assn. Internat. de la Harpe (hon. pres.). Presbyterian. Office: Ind U Sch Music Bloomington IN 47401 also: 2208 E Covenanter Dr Bloomington IN 47401-6133 Office Phone: 812-855-9733.

MCDONALD, THERESA BEATRICE PIERCE (MRS. OLLIE MCDONALD), church official, minister; b. Vicksburg, Miss., Apr. 11, 1929; d. Leonard C. Pierce and Ernestine Morris Templeton Pierce; m. Ollie McDonald, Apr. 23, 1966. Student, Tougaloo Coll., 1946-47, U. Chgo. Indsl. Rels. Ctr., 1963-64; BA in Sociology with deptl. honors, Roosevelt U., 1997; student, Chgo. Theol. Sem., 1997—. Ordained to Gospel Ministry, 1997. Vol. rep. Liberty Bapt. Ch., Am. Legion Aux., VA West Side Hosp., Chgo., 1971-73; nat. instr. ushers dept. Prog. Nat. Bapt. Conv. Inc., Washington, 1973-75, nat. sec. ushers dept., 1975-76, v.p. at large, 1980-82, chmn. pers. com., 1982-84; mem. faculty Congress of Christian Edn., 1978-85; mem. pub. rels. staff Liberty Bapt. Ch., Chgo., 1973-79, trustee, 1987-91; asst. Christian edn. dir. Maryland Ave. Bapt. Ch., Chgo., 1995-99; assoc. min. Md. Ave. Bapt. Ch., Chgo., 1997—; Tchr. Tng. Instr., 1998, 2000; dir. Christian edn. Md. Ave. Bapt. Ch., Chgo., 2000—02. Cons., lectr. in field; Sunday ch. sch. tchr.; bible class instr.; guest speaker TV and radio programs. Participant White House Regional Confs., 1961. Recipient Christian Svc. award Prog. Nat. Bapt. Conv. Inc., 1986, 92, 94, Disting. Svc. award, 1990-94, Dedicated Svc. award, 1998. Mem. VFW (life mem. Hunt aux. 2024), Bethlehem Bapt. Dist. Assn. Chgo. (asst. sec. 1982-84), Ch. Women United in Greater Chgo. (Ecumenical Actions com. 1981-83), Am. Legion (Outstanding Svc. award 1972, 73), Bapt. State Conv. Ill. (life), Order Ea. Star. Address: 9810 S Calumet Ave Chicago IL 60628-1432

MCDONALD, THOMAS ALEXANDER, lawyer; b. Chgo., Aug. 20, 1942; s. Owen Gerard and Lois (Gray) McD.; m. Sharon Diane Hirk, Nov. 25, 1967; children: Cristin, Katie, Courtney, Thomas Jr. AB, Georgetown U., Washington, DC, 1965; JD, Loyola U., Chgo., 1968. Bar: Ill. 1969, US Dist. Ct. (no. dist.) Ill. 1969. Ptnr. Clausen Miller, PC, Chgo., 1969—2001, McDonald & McCabe, LLC, Chgo., 2001—. Mem.: ABA, Chgo. Bar Assn., Ill. Bar Assn. Office: McDonald & McCabe LLC 225 S Wacker Dr Ste 2100 Chicago IL 60606-1299 Office Phone: 312-845-5190. Business E-Mail: tmcdonald@mcdonaldmccabe.com.

MCDONALD, WARREN GEORGE, accountant, mortage company, savings and loan association executive, consultant; b. Oakland, Calif., Feb. 14, 1939; s. George Daniel and Barbara (Sainsot) McD.; m. Roberta Anne Peterson, Apr. 27, 1968; children: Edward Bruce, Deborah Lynn. BA, San Francisco State Coll., 1962. CPA, Calif. Ptnr. Main Lafrentz & Co., CPAs, San Francisco, 1969-74; v.p., treas. Imperial Corp. Am., San Diego, 1975-80; v.p. fin. No. Calif. Savs. & Loan, Palo Alto, 1980-82; sr. v.p. fin. Unified Mortgage Co., Santa Clara, Calif., 1982-85; pres. Saratoga Savs., 1985-89; pvt. practice cons. San Francisco, 1989—2003; ret., 2003. Co-author: Power Above The Law, 1990. Served to capt. USCGR. Mem. AICPA, Calif. Soc. CPAs, Inst. Mgmt. Accts., Res. Officers Assn., Naval Inst., Navy League, Mil. Officers Assn. Am. (nat. bd. dirs. 2004—). Home: 1430 Wendy Way Menlo Park CA 94025-6022 Personal E-mail: mcdcpa@gmail.com.

MCDONALD, WESLEY S., retail executive; b. 1962; B cum laude, Bucknell U., Lewisburg, Pa.; MBA, Wharton Sch., Phila., 1988. Various fin. positions Target Corp., 1988—2000; v.p., CFO Abercrombie & Fitch, New Albany, Ohio, 2000—03; exec. v.p., CFO Kohl's Corp., Menomonee Falls, Wis., 2003—. Office: Kohls Corp N56 W17000 Ridgewood Dr Menomonee Falls WI 53051-5660 Office Phone: 262-703-7000.

MCDONALD, WILLIAM HENRY, venture capitalist; b. Ottawa, Ont., Can., Sept. 8, 1924; s. Joseph and Constance Mary (Gordon) McD.; m. D. Gwen Selkirk, July 8, 1950; 1 child, Barbara Elaine. Grad. high sch. Credit and operating mgr. B.F. Goodrich Co., Winnipeg, Man., Canada, 1945-49; fin. adminstrn. officer Govt. Can., Ottawa, 1949-55; asst. gen. mgr. mortgages Bank of N.S., 1955-66; mng. dir. Boyd Stott & McDonald Ltd., Toronto, Ont., 1966-79; exec. v.p., dir. Morguard Trust Co., 1966-74; chmn. bd. Can. Comml. Bank, Toronto, 1976-81, chmn. exec. com., 1981-84; chmn. bd. Can. Comml. Bank Mortgage Investment Corp., 1983-84; pres., CEO, dir. Boyd Stott and McDonald Techs., Ltd., 1984—2003. Pres. Thornton McDonald Assocs., Inc. Mem. bd. govs. J. Douglas Ferguson Hist. Research Found., 1971—. Served with RCNVR, 1943-45. Mem. Can. Paper Money Soc. (hon. pres.), Internat. Bank Note Soc. (life), Can. Credit Inst., Classical & Medieval Numismatic Soc. (exec. sec.). Conservative. Anglican. E-mail: billmcdo@sympatico.ca.

MCDONALD TERLAJE, PATRICIA, counselor; b. Tamuning, Mar. 16, 1962; d. Charles H. and Lucia G. McDonald; m. Paul J. Terlaje, Jan. 11, 2001; children: Pedro C. Lizama, Allen M. McDonald, Trinity E. Terlaje. BA in Secondary Edn. English (hon.), U. Guam, Mangilao,

1985, MA in Counseling, 2001. Tchr. English Guam Pub. Sch. Sys., Hagatna, Guam, 1985—99; counselor Acad. Our Lady Guam, 2000—01, Guam C.C., Mangilao, 2002—. Career resource network counselor U.S. Dept. Edn. Perkins Act, Mangilao, 2002—03. Mem.: Am. Coll. Counseling Assn., Guam Sch. Counselor Assn., Am. Sch. Counselor Assn., Am. Counseling Assn. Home: 557 Chalan Macajna Agana Heights GU 96910 Office: Guam CC PO Box 23069 Barrigada GU 96921 Office Fax: 671-734-5238; Home Fax: 671-734-5238. Business E-Mail: pterlaje@guamcc.edu.

MCDONALD-WEST, SANDI MACLEAN, director, consultant; b. Lowell, Mass., May 8, 1930; d. Walter Allan and Celina Louise (Lalime) MacLean; m. Thomas D. McDonald, Sept. 8, 1951 (div.); children: Todd F., Brooke Goodfriend, Ned M., Reid A., Heather McDonald McLean. BA, DePauw U., 1951; MA, Fairleigh Dickinson U., 1966; MEd, North Tex. State U., 1980. Cert. in Montessori teaching. Tchr., adminstr. Hudson (Ohio) Montessori Sch., 1966-68, Berea (Ohio) Montessori Sch., 1968-70, Creative Learning Ctr., Dallas, 1970-71; tchr., head of lower sch. The Selwyn Sch., Denton, Tex., 1971-83; tchr., headmaster Cimarron Sch., Enid, Okla., 1983-87; cons. Corpus Christi (Tex.) Montessori Sch., 1987-89, Azlann-Eren Horn Montessori Sch., Denton, 1989-95, Highland Meadow Montessori Acad., Southlake, Tex., 1994-2001, various pub. and pvt. Montessori Schs., 1999—. Ednl. dir., pres. Southwestern Montessori Tchg. Ctr., Inc., Denton, 1974—; adj. prof. North Tex. State U., Denton, 1979-80; cons., lectr. Am. Montessori Soc., N.Y.C., 1970—, Japanese Montessori Soc., 1978—, also pub. and pvt. schs., 1972—; chair commn. for accreditation Montessori Accreditation Coun. Tchr. Edn., 1991-97, chair emerita, 1997—; cons. Public Montessori Programs, 1995-. Developer various Montessori materials; contbr. articles to profl. jours. Mem. AAUW, No. Ohio Montessori Assn. (pres. 1968-70), Assn. Montessori Internat., N.Am. Montessori Tchrs. Assn Avocations: ecology, golf, reading, travel. Home: 2005 Marshall Rd Denton TX 76207-3316 Personal E-mail: swest4smtc@aol.com.

MCDONELL, TERRY, publishing executive, writer, editor; b. Santa Cruz, Calif. m. Joanie McDonell; children: Robert Nicholas, Thomas Hunter. Attended, U. Calif., Berkeley/Irvine. Worked on film in Tehran, Iran; began career in journalism as freelance photographer; writer, photographer NY Associated Press, 1971; founder, writer, editor Outside, 1977, Rocky Mountain, 1979; mng. editor Rolling Stone, 1981—83; asst. mng. editor Newsweek, 1983—88; founder, pres., editor Smart, 1988—90; editor-in-chief Esquire, 1990—93; editor-in-chief, publishing editor Sports Afield, 1993—97, publishing/editorial dir., 1997; editor Men's Jour., 1997—99, editor-in-chief, 1999—2000, Us Weekly, 2000—02; mng. editor Sports Illus. Time Inc., 2002—06, editor Sports Illus. Grp., 2006—. Author: California Bloodstock, 1980; screenwriter: TV series Miami Vice, China Beach. Avocations: painting, surfing. Office: Sports Illustrated 1271 Ave of Americas New York NY 10020 Office Phone: 212-522-1650. Office Fax: 212-522-7117. E-mail: Terry_McDonell@simail.com.*

MCDONNELL, BOB (ROBERT FRANCIS), former state attorney general, state legislator; b. Phila., June 15, 1954; m. Maureen Patricia Gardner; children: Jeanine, Cailin, Rachel, Robert, Sean. BBA in Mgmt., U. Notre Dame, 1976; MBA, Boston U., 1980; MA, JD, Regent U., 1989. Various positions Am. Hosp. Supply Corp., 1981—85; policy intern, Rep. Policy Com. US Ho. Reps, 1988; law clk. Office Commonwealth's Atty., Chesapeake, 1989, asst. Commonwealth atty. Virginia Beach, 1990—91; mem. Va. State Legis., 1992—2006, asst. majority leader, 2002—06, mem. cts. of justice com., mem. edn. com., mem. health welfare & insts. com., mem. Chesapeake and its tributaries com.; ptnr. Huff, Poole & Mahoney, P.C., Virginia Beach, 1992—2006; atty. gen. State of Va., Richmond, 2006—09. Served in US Army, 1976—81 USAR, 1981—97. Named Legislator of Yr., Network of Victims of Crime, 1996, Family Found., 1998, 2001, Nat. Legislator of Yr., Nat. Child Support Enforcement Assn., 1998, Legislator of Yr., Va Sheriff's Assn., 2005. Republican. Roman Catholic. Office: 2819 N Parham Rd Ste 210 Richmond VA 23294 Office Phone: 804-786-2071.*

MCDONNELL, CHARLES JAMES, bishop emeritus; b. Queens, NY, July 7, 1928; Ordained priest Archdiocese of Newark, 1954, aux. bishop, 1994—2004, aux. bishop emeritus, 2004—; ordained bishop, 1994. Roman Catholic. Home: 34 Maple Ave Hackensack NJ 07601-4502 Office: Archdiocese of Newark PO Box 9500 171 Clifton Ave Newark NJ 07104-0500

MCDONNELL, ERIN M., lawyer; BA, Hunter Coll., MA in Comm.; JD, U. Notre Dame. Counsel US Small Bus. Adminstrn.; sr. investigative atty. NY State Investigations Commn.; asst. dist. atty. King's County Atty.'s Office, NY; assoc. spl. counsel for legal counsel and policy US Office Spl. Counsel. Office: US Office Spl Counsel 1730 M St NW Ste 218 Washington DC 20036*

MCDONNELL, JOSEPH B., lawyer; b. Salina, Kans., Nov. 20, 1935; s. John Francis and Edith (Engle) McD.; m. Betty E. Marlin, Nov. 27, 1965 (dec.); children: Jean Elizabeth, Jennifer Ann. BS in Govt., St. Louis U., 1958, LLB, 1960. Bar: Ill. 1960, Mo. 1960, U.S. Ct. Appeals (7th cir.) 1973. Law clk. U.S. Dist. Ct., Springfield, Ill., 1960-61; assoc. Pope & Driemeyer, East St. Louis, Ill., 1961-66; ptnr. Dixon & McDonnell, Belleville, Ill., 1966-75, 1975—98, Churchill, Nester & McDonnell, Belleville, 1998—. Mem. character and fitness com. Ill. Supreme Ct., 1978-83. Committeeman St. Clair County Democratic Party, 1974. With USAR, 1953-61. Fellow Ill. Bar Found.; mem. ABA, Ill. Bar Assn., St. Clair County Bar Assn. (pres. 1977-78, del. assembly 1986-92), Acad. Ill. Laureates. Roman Catholic. Home Phone: 618-394-0526; Office Phone: 618-257-7353. Personal E-mail: jbm@greensfelder.com.

MCDONNELL, PATRICIA JOAN, museum director; b. Mpls., Mar. 30, 1956; d. Robert Frances and Joan Ruth (Fortune) McD.; 1 child, Kate Marie Pluth. BA in German Studies cum laude, Mills Coll., 1978; MA in Art History, Brown U., 1985, PhD in Art History, 1991. Profl. tng. coord. Art Mus. Assn. Am., San Francisco, 1978-83; asst. to dir. Mus. of Art, R.I. Sch. Design, Providence, 1984; curator Frederick R. Weisman Art Mus., U. Minn., Mpls., 1991—2002; chief curator Tacoma Art Mus., 2002—06; dir. Ulrich Mus. Art, Wichita State U., 2007—. Author: Dictated by Life: Marsden Hartley's German Paintings and Robert Indiana's Hartley Elegies, 1995, Marsden Hartley: American Modern, 1997, Painting Berlin Stories: Oscar Bluemner, Marsden Hartley and the First American Avant-Garde in Expressionist Berlin, 2003, On the Edge of Your Seat: Populat Theater & Film in Early 20th-Century American Art, 2002; contbr. articles to profl. jours. Teaching fellow Brown U., 1984-87, Dissertation fellow Deutscher Akademischer Austauschdienst Freie U. Berlin, 1987, Smithsonian Inst., Hirshhorn Mus., 1988-90, Samuel H. Kress Found., 1990; fellow J. Paul Getty Trust, 1992, Nat. Endowment Humanities, 1993; Smithsonian Inst. Mus. Res. fellow, 1998, 2000; grantee U. Minn. Inst. Internat Studies, 1999. Mem. Coll. Art Assn., Assn. Art Mus. Curators, Assn. Historians of Am. Art. Office: Ulrich Mus Art Wichita State U 1845 Fairmount St Wichita KS 67260-0046 Home Phone: 316-440-4698; Office Phone: 316-978-3664. Office Fax: 316-978-3898. E-mail: patricia.mcdonnell@wichita.edu.

MCDONNELL, THOMAS A., information technology executive; b. Kansas City, Mo. BSBA in Acctg., Rockhurst Univ., 1966; MBA, Univ. Pa., 1968. With DST Systems, Inc., 1969—, pres., 1973—84, 1987—, treas., 1973—95, vice chmn., 1984—95, CEO, 1984—. Bd. dir. DST Systems Inc., 1971—; bd. dirs. Blue Valley Ban Corp., 1996—2009; bd. dir. BHA Group Holdings Inc., Commerce Bancshares Inc., Computer Sci. Corp., Euronet Worldwide Inc., Garmin Ltd., Janus Capital Corp., Ascential Software Inc., Asurion. Trustee Ewing Marion Kauffman Found., 2003—; chmn. Greater Kansas City C. of C., 1994, Civic Coun. Greater Kansas City, 1999—2001; bd. dir. Greater Kansas City Cmty. Found., Midwest Rsch. Inst., Harry S Truman Libr. Inst.; trustee Rockhurst Univ. Office: DST Systems 333 W 11th St Kansas City MO 64105 Office Phone: 816-435-1000.*

MCDONNELL, TIMOTHY ANTHONY, bishop; b. NYC, Dec. 23, 1937; s. John J. and Margaret (Looney) McDonnell. AB in Philosophy, St. Joseph's Sem., Yonkers, NY, 1959; MS in Edn., Iona Coll., New Rochelle, NY, 1970; attended sabbatical prog., North Am. Coll., Vatican City, 1999. Ordained priest Archdiocese of NYC, 1963, aux. bishop, 2001, vicar gen., 2002—04; faculty mem. Maria Regina High Sch., Hartsdale, NY, 1963—69; assoc. pastor Our Lady of Perpetual Help Parish, Ardsley, NY, 1963—70; asst. dir. Archdiocesan Office for Christian and Family Devel., 1970—77; resident chaplain Cardinal McCloskey Sch. and Home, White Plains, 1971—77; dir. Archdiocesan Soc. for Propagation of Faith, 1977—80; vice-chancellor, sec. Archdiocesan Bd. Consultors, 1980—84; pastor Holy Trinity Parish, NYC, 1984—90; episcopal vicar of West Manhattan, 1989—90; acting dep. pres., dep. CEO Covenant House, 1990; pastor St. John, St. Mary Parish, Chappaqua, NY, 1993—2002; COO Cath. Charities of Archdiocese of NY, 1990—93; ordained bishop, 2001; titular bishop of Semina, 2001; bishop Diocese of Springfield, 2004—. Roman Catholic. Office: Diocese Of Springfield 65 Elliot St Springfield MA 01105-1713

MCDONOUGH, DENIS, federal official; b. Stillwater, Minn., Dec. 2, 1969; married; 3 children. Grad. summa cum laude, St. John's U., Collegeville, Minn., 1992; M, Georgetown U., Washington, 1996. Staff Internat. Rels. Com. US House of Reps., Washington, 1996—99; fellow Robert Bosch Found., Stuttgart, Germany, 1999—2000; sr. fgn. policy adv. to Senator Tom Daschle US Senate, 2000—04, legis. dir. to Senator Ken Salazar; sr. fellow Ctr. Am. Progress, Washington, 2004—06; fgn. policy coord. Dem. Presdl. Campaign, 2008; staff mem. Obama-Biden Transition Project, Washington, 2008—09; dir. strategic comm. NSC, Washington, 2009—. Democrat. Office: National Security Council 1600 Pennsylvania Ave NW Washington DC 20500 Office Fax: 202-456-2461.*

MCDONOUGH, JOHN F., professional sports team executive; b. 1953; m. Karen McDonough; 3 children. BA, St. Mary's Coll., 1975. Dir. sales and promotions Chgo. Cubs, 1983—87, mktg. dir., 1987—91, v.p. mktg. and broadcasting, 1991—94, sr. v.p. mktg. and broadcasting, 2004—06, interim pres., 2006, pres., 2006—07, Chgo. Blackhawks, 2007—. Named one of Top 10 mktg. execs., Promo Mag., 1997. Office: Chgo Blackhawks 1901 W Madison St Chicago IL 60612-2459

MCDONOUGH, JOHN PATRICK, Secretary of State, Maryland; b. 1950; m. Mary Lou McDonough, 1972; children: Emily, Caitlin, Aisling. BA, Johns Hopkins U.; JD, U. Md. Bar: Md. 1977. Legis. aide Prince George County Coun.; atty., v.p. Md. C. of C.; sec. state State of Md., 2008—. Mem. Governor's Exec. Coun., 2008, Governor's Commn. on Md. Mil. Monuments, 2008—, Bd. State Canvassers, 2008—; chair Governor's Subcabinet for Internat. Affairs, 2008—; mem. President's Roundtable, Greater Wash. Bd. Trade. Bd. visitors U. Md. Sch. Law. Democrat. Office: Secretary of State Jeffrey Bldg 16 Francis St Annapolis MD 21401

MCDONOUGH, KENNETH LEE, pharmaceutical company medical administrator; b. Buffalo, Apr. 7, 1953; s. Sidney Lee and Jeanne Francis (Sheets) McD.; children: Jameson, Laurel, Meghan; m. Connie Kay Staley; stepchildren: Audrey, Kelsie. BS, U. Minn., 1975, MD, 1979, MS, 1986. Diplomate Am. Bd. Quality Assurance and Utilization Rev. Physicians. Resident in occupl. medicine U. Calif., San Francisco, 1984; v.p. Indsl. Health and Hygiene Group, Mpls., 1982-86; pvt. practice occupl. medicine, 1985—92; v.p. Am. Gen. Ins., Dallas, 1986-88, Mut. of Omaha Ins., Omaha, 1988-91, sr. v.p., 1991-95; med. dir. Stuart Disease Mgmt. Svcs. Inc., Wilmington, Del., 1995-98; asst. clin. prof. dept. preventive medicine and pub. health Creighton U. Sch. Medicine, 1994—; med. dir. AstraZeneca Pharms., Wilmington, Del., 1998—2009; instr. Monmouth (NJ) U., 2004—; payer rels. dir. Bristol-Myers Squibb, 2009—. Instr. nursing Gustavus Adolphus Coll. Nursing, St. Paul, 1984-86; instr. astronomy Met. State U., St. Paul, 1982-83; prin. rsch. into cost effectiveness of Dr. Dean Ornish's coronary reversal program in collaboration with Harvard Med. Sch., 1992-95. Author and designer of computer software. Instr. Sci. Mus. of Minn., St. Paul, 1982. Recipient Design Excellence award Seako, Inc., 1987, 3M Creativity award Minn. Mining & Mfg., 1971; recipient acad. scholarships. Mem. Am. Coll. Med. Quality, Am. Coll. Occupl. and Environ. Medicine, Nat. Assn. Managed Care Physicians, Gt. Plains Occupl. Medicine Assn. (nominating com. 1990-91), Am. Lung Assn. Nebr. (bd. dirs. 1995—), Disease Mgmt. Assn. Am. (bd. dirs. 2005—), Phi Kappa Phi. Avocations: genealogy, travel, astronomy, medical informatics, ancient history. Home: 9 Devonshire Ct Greenville DE 19807-2572 Office: Bristol Meyers Squibb 9 Devonshile Ct Greenville DE 19807 Business E-Mail: kenneth.mcdonough@bms.com, rumster@verizon.net.

MCDONOUGH, RAENELL, musician, educator; b. Amarillo, Tex., Aug. 19, 1946; d. Ray Sam and Doris Winnie (Williams) Roberts; m. Jerome F. McDonough, Dec. 21, 1978 (dec.); 1 child, Brian Christopher. BA in Music Edn., W. Tex. State U., Canyon, 1968, MEd, 1971. Music edn. cert., elem. edn. cert. Music educator Amarillo Ind. Sch. Dist., 1968—73; music educator, piano accompanist, performer W. Tex. State U., Canyon, 1973—89; pianist Amarillo Opera, 1989—; coach, accompanist, instr. music theory and organ Amarillo Coll., 2000—. Mem. textbook com. Amarillo Ind. Sch. Dist., 1970. Mem. W. Tex. State U. Friends Fine Arts Assn., 1980—, Amarillo Little Theatre Guild, 1980—, Friends Aeolian Skinner, Amarillo, 2004—, Amarillo United Citizens Forum, 2006, W. Tex. A&M U. Found., Canyon, Amarillo Youth Choir Orgn., Sta. KACV-TV PBS Orgn., Amarillo; mem., sec. exec. bd., trustee Amarillo Opera, 2006—; organist, music coord. St. Paul Meth. Ch., Amarillo, 1968—. Recipient Bill and Louise Dee Vol. award, Amarillo Opera, 1997—98; named Outstanding Young Women Am., 1980. Mem.: Amarillo Symphony Guild, Tex. CC Tchrs. Assn., Amarillo Art Force (sec. exec. bd. 2006—), Am. Guild Organists (sub-dean 1990—95). Avocations: travel, crafts, reading, theater. Home: 6106 Dartmouth Amarillo TX 79109

MCDONOUGH, RICHARD MICHAEL, philosophy educator; b. Pitts., Jan. 29, 1950; s. Walter and Marilyn (Duman) McD.; m. Mary Lau, July 26, 1991. BA summa cum laude, U. Pitts., 1971; MA, Cornell U., 1974, PhD, 1975. Asst. prof. philosophy Bates Coll., Lewiston, Maine, 1975-82; sr. lectr. Nat. U. Singapore, 1982-91; asst. prof. philosophy U. Tulsa, 1991—; assoc. prof. philosophy, psychology U. Putra Malaysia, Selangor, 1997-98; prof. philosophy Overseas Family School: The College, Republic of Singapore, 1999—2005; assoc. lectr. philosophy PSB Acad., 2005—07. Lectr. philosophy Arium Acad., 2005—, lectr. physics, 2008—; lectr. math. dept. U. Md., 2005—07, lectr. philosophy and psychology, 2005—07; assoc. lectr. James Cock U., Singapore Campus, 2009—. Author: The Argument of the Tractatus, 1986, Martin Heidegger's Being and Time, 2006; editor: Wittgenstein and cognitive sci. spl. issue Idealistic Studies, 1999; contbr. articles to profl. jours. Woodrow Wilson fellow, 1971-72, NSF fellow, 1971-74; postdoctoral rsch. grantee NEH, Ind. U., 1980-81. Mem. Australasian Debating Fedn. (hon. life, adjudicator 1991—), Phi Kappa Phi. Achievements include prodn. of original interpretation of Wittgenstein's logical-metaphys. sys., original application Kantian Copernican Revolution to philosophy of lang.; significant interdisciplinary work logic, linguistics, psychology & philosophy. Personal E-mail: richmary@pacific.net.sg, wittgensteins_poker2007@yahoo.com.

MCDONOUGH, RUSSELL CHARLES, retired state supreme court justice; b. Glendive, Mont., Dec. 7, 1924; s. Roy James and Elsie Marie (Johnson) McD.; m. Dora Jean Bidwell, Mar. 17, 1946; children: Ann Remmich, Michael, Kay Jensen, Kevin, Daniel, Mary Garfield. JD, George Washington U., 1949. Bar: Mont. 1950. Pvt. practice, Glendive, Mont., 1950-83; judge Gen. Jurisdiction State of Montana, Glendive, 1983-87; justice Mont. Supreme Ct., Helena, 1987-93, ret., 1993. City atty. City of Glendive, 1953-57; county atty. Dawson County, Mon., 1957-63; del. Mont. Constl. Conv., Helena, 1972. 1st lt. USAAF, 1943-45, ETO. Decorated DFC. Mem. Mont. Bar Assn. Roman Catholic. Home: 210 Gresham St Glendive MT 59330 Personal E-mail: swedemc@yahoo.com.

MCDONOUGH, WILLIAM ANDREWS, architect, former dean; b. Tokyo, Feb. 20, 1951; s. James Edwin and Sara (Andrews) McDonough; m. Elizabeth Demetriades, May 30, 1981. BA magna cum laude, Dartmouth Coll.; MArch, Yale U.; AB, Dartmouth Coll., 1973; postgrad. in Art Studies, Yale U., 1973—76, MArch, 1976. Registered architect, NY. Photographer Kilkenny Design Workshop, Ireland, 1974; architect, builder William A. McDonough, Cork, 1974—77; architect Davis, Brody & Assocs., NYC, 1977—81; prin. Mad River Hydro, Warren, Vt., 1981—, McDonough, Rainey Architects, NYC, 1981—85, McDonough Nouri Rainey & Assocs., Inc., 1985—. Cons. Inst. for Indsl. Rsch. and Stds., Dublin, 1975—77; founder Solar Energy Soc. Ireland, Dublin, 1976, McDonough Braungart Design Chemistry, 1995—; dir. North Wind Power Co., Inc., Moretown, Vt., 1982, Am. Residential Architecture Found., NYC, 1983—; founding ptnr. William McDonough & Ptnrs.; dean sch. architecture U. Va., Charlottesville, 1994—99. Author (with Michael Braungart): Hannover Principles: Design for Sustainability, 1992; author: Cradle to Cradle: Remaking the Way We Make Things, 0202. Recipient Presdl. award for Sustainable Devel., 1996, Design of Yr. award, Bus. Wk. & Archtl. Record mags., 1997, Presdl. Green Chemistry award, 2003, Nat. Design award, 2004; named one of 50 Who Matter Now, CNNMoney.com Bus. 2.0, 2006. Mem.: AIA, Yale Club NYC. Office: William McDonough & Ptnrs 700 E Jefferson St Charlottesville VA 22902

MCDONOUGH, WILLIAM J., diversified financial services company executive; b. Chgo., 1934; married. BS, Coll. of Holy Cross, 1956; MA, Georgetown U., 1962. With Dept. of State, 1961-67, 1st Nat. Bank of Chgo., 1967-89, asst. v.p. internat. banking dept., 1967-70, v.p., gen. mgr. Paris, 1970-72, area head, Europe, Mid. East and Africa, 1972-73, sr. v.p., head internat. banking dept., 1973-75, exec. v.p., 1975-86, CFO, 1982-89, chmn. asset and liability mgmt. com., until 1989; vice chmn. 1st Chgo. Corp. and 1st Nat. Bank Chgo., 1986-89; exec. v.p., head markets group Fed. Res. Bank of N.Y., NYC, 1992-93, pres., CEO, 1993—2003; chmn. Pub. Co. Acctg. Oversight Bd., Washington, 2003—05; vice chmn. Merrill Lynch & Co., Inc., NYC, 2006—. Bd. dirs. N.Y. Philharm. Orch.; chmn. investments com. joint staff pension fund UN. Home Phone: 212-838-1188; Office Phone: 212-449-0871. Business E-Mail: william_mcdonough@ml.com.

MCDORMAND, FRANCES, actress; b. Chgo., June 23, 1957; m. Joel Coen, 1984; 2 children. BA, Bethany Coll., 1979; MFA, Yale U. Sch. Drama, 1982. Stage appearances include Awake and Sing!, NYC, 1984, Painting Churches, NYC, 1984, The Three Sisters, Mpls., 1985, NJ, 1991, All My Sons, New Haven, 1986, A Streetcar Named Desire, NYC, 1988, Moon for the Misbegotten, 1992, Sisters Rosensweig, NYC, 1993, The Swan, NYC, 1993, To You, the Birdie!, 2002, Far Away, 2002, The Country Girl, NYC, 2008; (films) Blood Simple, 1984, Crime Wave, 1986, Raising Arizona, 1987, Mississippi Burning, 1988 (Best Supporting Actress Nat. Bd. Review, 1988, Acad. award nominee, Best Supporting Actress Chgo. Film Critics Assn., 1989, Best Supporting Actress Kansas City Film Critics Cir., 1989), Chattahoochee, 1990, Darkman, 1990, Miller's Crossing, 1990, Hidden Agenda, 1990, The Butcher's Wife, 1991, Passed Away, 1992, Short Cuts, 1993 (Golden Globe for Best Ensemble Cast, 1994, Volpi Cup for Best Ensemble Cast, 1993), Beyond Rangoon, 1995, Plain Pleasures, 1996, Fargo, 1996 (Best Actress San Diego Film Critics Soc., 1996, Best Actress Nat. Bd. Review, 1996, Acad. award for Best Actress in a Leading Role, 1997, Am. Comedy award for Funniest Actress in Motion Picture, 1997, Best Actress Broadcast Film Critics Assn., 1997, Best Actress Chgo. Film Critics Assn., 1997, Chlotrudis award for Best Actress, 1997, Empire award for Best Actress, 1997, Best Actress Fla. Film Critics Cir., 1997, Best Female Lead Ind. Spirit award, 1997, Best Actress Kansas City Film Critics Cir., 1997, Actress of Yr. London Critics Cir., 1997, Golden Satellite award, 1997, Outstanding Performance by Female Actor in Leading Role SAG, 1997, Best Actress Southeastern Film Critics Assn., 1997), Lone Star, 1996, Primal Fear, 1996, Palookaville, 1996, Paradise Road, 1997, Johnny Skidmarks, 1998, Madeline, 1998, Talk of Angels, 1998, Wonder Boys, 1999, Almost Famous (Acad. award nominee, Brit. Acad. award nominee, Golden Globe nominee, SAG nominee, Best Supporting Actress Boston Soc. Film Critics, 2000, Best Supporting Actress San Diego Film Critics Soc., 2000, Best Supporting Actress Broadcast Film Critics Assn., 2001, Blockbuster Entertainment award for Favorite Supporting Actress - Drama/Romance, 2001, Best Supporting Actress Chgo. Film Critics Assn., 2001, Best Supporting Actress Fla. Film Critics Cir., 2001, Best Supporting Actress LA Film Critics Assn. 2001, Best Ensemble Performance Online Film Critics Soc., 2001, Best Supporting Actress, Phoenix Film Critics Soc., 2001, Best Supporting Actress Southeastern Film Critics Assn., 2001), Man Who Wasn't There, 2001, City by the Sea, 2002, Laurel Canyon, 2002 (Gijon Internat. Film Festival award, 2003), Something's Gotta Give, 2003, Last Night, 2004, North Country, 2005 (Best Supporting Actress Las Vegas Film Critics Soc., 2005), Aeon Flux, 2005, Friends With Money, 2006 (Best Supporting Female Ind. Spirit award, 2007), Miss Pettigrew Lives for a Day, 2008, Burn After Reading, 2008; (TV movies) Scandal Sheet, 1985, Vengeance: The Story of Tony Cimo, 1986, Crazy In Love, 1992, Good Old Boys, 1995, Hidden in America, 1996, (narrator) Precinct Hollywood, 2005; (TV appearances) The Twilight Zone, 1986, The Equalizer, Spencer: For Hire, Hill Street Blues, 1985, Hunter, 1985,

Legwork, 1986-87, State of Grace, 2001 Recipient Tribute to Ind. Vision award, Sundance Film Festival, 1998, Gotham award, 1998. Office: c/o PMK/HBH 700 San Vicente Blvd Ste G 910 West Hollywood CA 90069*

MCDOUGAL, STUART YEATMAN, comparative literature educator, author; b. LA, Apr. 10, 1942; s. Murray and Marian (Yeatman) McDougal; m. Menakka Weerasinghe, Apr. 29, 1967 (div. 1977); children: Dyanthe Rose, Gavin Rohan; m. Nora Gunneng, Aug. 4, 1979; children: Angus Gunneng, Tobias Yeatman. BA, Haverford Coll., 1964; MA, U. Pa., 1965, PhD, 1970. Lectr. U. Lausanne, Switzerland, 1965-66; asst. prof. Mich. State U., East Lansing, 1970-72; from asst. prof. to prof. English, comparative lit. and film /video U. Mich., Ann Arbor, 1972-85; dir. program in comparative lit. U. Mich., Ann Arbor, 1981-97, asst. to dean spl. projects, 1997-98; Dewitt Wallace prof. English, chair English Dept. Macalester Coll., St. Paul, 1998—2005; vis. scholar Cornell U., 2006—; co-founder Assn. Program and Depts. Comparative Lit. Vis. prof. film Aegean Inst., Greece, 1994; vis. scholar Senapulli, Brazil, 1996. Author: Ezra Pound and the Troubadour Tradition, 1972 (Bredvold prize 1973), 1973; Made into Movies: From Literature to Film, 1985, Korean edit., 2002; editor: Dante Among the Moderns, 1985; co-editor: Play It Again, Sam: Retakes on Remakes, 1998; editor: Stanley Kubrick's A Clockwork Orange, 2003; contbr. articles to profl. jours.; commentator: (dvd) Sclockwork Orange, Eyes Wide Shut. Am. Council of Learned Socs. fellow, 1974-75; U. Mich. Rackham Research grantee, 1975-76; Fulbright Assn. sr. lectr., Italy, 1978; recipient Faculty Recognition award, U. Mich., 1987. Fellow Dirs. Guild Am. (summr workshop, 1993); mem. MLA, Am. Comparative Lit. Assn. (sec.-treas. 1983-89, v.p. 1989-91, pres. 1991-93), Internat. Comparative Lit. Assn., 7th Art, Ithaca, NY (bd. mem. 2007-), Ithaca Motion Picture Project. Democrat. Home: 916 Stewart Ave Ithaca NY 14850 Business E-Mail: mcdougal@macalester.edu, sym23@cornell.edu.

MCDOUGAL, WILLIAM SCOTT, urology educator; b. Grand Rapids, Mich., 1942; s. William Julian and Verna Wilma (Pasma) McD.; m. Mary Stuart Logan, Sept. 19, 1992; 1 child, Molly Katherine. AB, Dartmouth Coll., 1964; MD, Cornell U., 1968. Intern in surgery U. Hosps., Cleve., 1968-69, resident in surgery, 1969-75, attending urologist, 1977-80; postdoctoral fellow in physiology Yale U., New Haven, 1971-72; postdoctoral fellow in surgery Case-Western Res. U., Cleve., 1972-75; chief, burn study div. Inst. Surg. Rsch. Brooke Army Med. Ctr., Ft. Sam Houston, 1975-77; instr. surgery U. Tex., San Antonio, 1975-77; asst. prof. urology Case Western Res. U., Cleve., 1977-78, assoc. prof., 1978-80, Dartmouth Coll., Hanover, NH, 1980-84, chmn. dept. urology, 1982-84; prof., chmn. dept. urology Vanderbilt U., Nashville, 1984-90; Walter S. Kerr Jr. prof. urology Harvard Med. Sch., 1996—; chief urology Mass. Gen. Hosp., Boston, 1990—. Office: Mass Gen Hosp Dept Urology Fruit St Boston MA 02114

MCDOUGALL, DONALD BLAKE, retired provincial official, librarian; BA, BEd, U. Sask., 1966; BLS, U. Toronto, 1969; MLS, U. Alta., 1983, cert. pub. adminstrn., 1990. Classroom tchr. Regina Bd. Edn., Sask., 1960-63, vice prin., 1963-68; asst. chief libr. Stratford Pub. Libr., Ont., Canada, 1969, chief libr., 1970-72; supr. info. svcs. Edmonton Pub. Libr., Alta., Canada, 1972, head pub. svcs., 1973-74; legislature libr. Legis. Assembly Alta., Edmonton, 1974-87, asst. dep. min., legis. libr., 1987—93; ret., 1993. Editor microfilm: Alberta Scrapbook Hansard, 1906-1964, 1976; editor: A History of the Legislature Library, 1979; author: Princess Louise Caroline Alberta, 1988, Premiers of the Northwest Territories and Alberta, 1876-1991, 1991; co-author, editor: Lieutenant-Governors of the Northwest Territories and Alberta, 1876-1991; (pamphlet) Canadian Parliamentary Libraries, 1989. Govt. Sask. scholar, 1965; recipient Queen's Silver Jubilee medal Govt. Can., 1977; named Hon. Clk.-At-The-Table, Legis. Assembly Alberta, 1987-93. Mem. Alta. Govt. Librs. Coun. (chmn. 1975), Assn. Parliamentary Librs. in Can. (pres. 1980-82), Greater Edmonton Libr. Assn., Hist. Soc. Alta. (v.p. Edmonton chpt. 1987), Libr. Assn. Alta., Can. Libr. Assn., Edmonton Jazz Soc., Can. Vintage Motorcycle Assn., Beta Phi Mu. Presbyterian.

MCDOUGALL, DUANE C., manufacturing executive; Grad., Ohio State U. With Willamette Industries, exec. v.p. bdlg. materials group, pres., COO, pres., CEO, 1998—2002; chmn., CEO Boise Cascade Holdings, LLC, 2008—09, chmn., 2009—. Bd. dir. Boise Cascade Holdings LLC, Cascade Corp., InFocus Corp., The Greenbrier Cos., West Coast Bancorp. Past pres. Portland Rotary Charitable Trust Found.; vice chmn. Oreg. Symphony Office: Boise Cascade Holdings LLC Ste 300 1111 W Jefferson St Boise ID 83702-5389 Office Phone: 208-384-6161.*

MCDOUGALL, RODERICK GREGORY, lawyer; BBA in Econs., U. Ariz., JD. Bar: Ariz. 1965, U.S. Ct. Claims 1965, U.S. Supreme Ct. 1970, U.S. Dist. Ct. Ariz. 1972, U.S. Ct. Appeals (9th cir.) 1972. Law clk. Ariz. Supreme Ct., 1964, Ariz. Ct. Appeals, 1965; dep. county atty. Maricopa County, 1965-67; staff atty. Ariz. State Senate, 1967; asst. atty. gen., 1967-74; chief asst. Atty. Gen., Ariz., 1974-84; city atty. City of Phoenix, 1984-2000; pvt. practice, 2000—. Advisor Ariz. Supreme Ct. Mem. ABA, Internat. Mcpl. Lawyers Assn. (bd. dirs. 1994-2000), Ariz. Bar Assn., Maricopa County Bar Assn. E-mail: rodmcdougall@cox.net.

MCDOWELL, BETSY M., critical care nurse, educator; d. James S. and Betty W. Mickey; m. Fred H. McDowell, Aug. 31, 1996; 1 child, Thomas Scott Barnes. BSN, U. SC, Columbia, 1971; PhD, U. SC, 1997; MSN, U. NC, Chapel Hill, 1975. Cert. critical-care nurse, Am. Assn. Critical-Care Nurses, 1977. Staff nurse Self Meml. Hosp., Greenwood, SC, 1971—89; nursing faculty Lander U., Greenwood, SC, 1971—2007; head nurse pediat. Self Meml. Hosp., 1973—73; staff nurse NC Meml. Hosp., Chapel Hill, 1973—75; staff nurse picu/piicu Children's Hosp. Palmetto Health Richland, Columbia, 1988—2002; staff nurse nicu Self Regional Healthcare, Greenwood, 2002—; prof. and chair nursing Newberry Coll., SC, 2007—. Cons. Newberry Coll., 2006—07. Editl. bd. mem., chair SC Nurse Jour., Columbia, 1987—2004; contbr. articles to profl. jours. Weekly children's support grp. facilitator to domestic violoence shelther MEG's Ho., Greenwood, 1998—2007; mentor Maternal Child Leadership Acad., Indpls., 2006—07. Recipient Excellence in Maternal Child Health Nursing Practice award, SC Nurses Assn., 2002, President's award, 2003—04, Excellence in Tchg. award, SC League for Nursing, 2005, Nursing Excellence award, 2005, Palmetto Gold award, SC Nurses Found., 2006. Master: Neuman Sys. Model Internat. (trustee, treas. 2002); mem.: Jour. Specialists in Pediatric Nursing (editl. bd. mem. 2001), Am. Assn. Critical-Care Nurses (work grp. mem. 2005—06), High Noon Sertoma Club (officer 1997—2007), Sigma Theta Tau Internat. (mentor 2006—07). Achievements include research in examining pain perceptions and responses of acutely and critically ill pediatric and adult patients undergoing procedures; home apnea monitoring, family functioning, concerns and coping. Avocations: reading, crossword puzzles, sudoko. Home: 131 Annie Dr Ninety Six SC 29666 Office: Newberry Coll 2100 College St Newberry SC 29108 Business E-Mail: betsy.mcdowell@newberry.edu.

MCDOWELL, CHARLES EAGER, lawyer, retired military officer; b. Manchester, NH, Sept. 9, 1923; s. Joseph Curry and Mildred (Eager) McD.; m. Carolyn A. Gibbons, June 21, 1947; children— Robin, Patricia. AB, Dartmouth Coll., 1947; JD, U. Va., 1950. Bar: Tex. 1950, Va. 1981, D.C. 1981. With land div. Shell Oil Co., Houston, 1950; commd. lt. (j.g.) USN, 1951, advanced through grades to rear adm., 1976; staff legal officer Comdr. Service Force, U.S. Pacific Fleet; staff judge adv., head internat. law div. Naval War Coll., 1963-66; staff legal officer, comdr. 7th Fleet, 1966-68; sr. Navy mem. ad hoc com., dep. asst. judge adv. gen. Office Judge Adv. Gen. Dept. Def., Washington, 1968-72; staff judge adv. on staff comdr. in chief U.S. Naval Forces, Europe, London, 1972-75; comdg. officer Naval Justice Sch., Newport, RI, 1975-76; dep. judge adv. gen. Navy Dept., Washington, 1976-78, judge adv. gen., 1978-80; pvt. practice Dumfries, Va., 1981-96. Served to 2d lt. AUS, 1943-46. Decorated D.S.M., Bronze Star, Joint Service Commendation medal, Navy Commendation medal with Combat V, Purple Heart, Combat Inf. badge. Mem. FBA, Tex. Bar Assn., Va. Bar Assn., Judge Advs. Assn., Order of Coif, Chi Phi, Square Dancer Club. Methodist. Home: 1106 Croton Dr Alexandria VA 22308-2008

MCDOWELL, DAVID LYNN, mechanical engineering educator; b. Red Oak, Iowa, Dec. 20, 1956; s. Leland Lee and Wilma McDowell; m. Kathryn M. McDowell, May 26, 1979; children: Matthew Todd, Andrew Joel, James Neal. BSME, U. Nebr., Lincoln, 1979; PhDME, U. Ill., Champaign, 1983. Asst. prof. mech. engring. Ga. Inst. Tech., Atlanta, 1983-87, assoc. prof., 1987-92, prof., 1992—, regents prof., 1996—, Carter N. Paden Jr. Disting. chair in metals processing, 1998—. Dir. Mech. Properties Rsch. Lab., 1992—; presenter in field. Mem. editl. bd. Internat. Jour. Plasticity, Fatigue and Fracture of Engring. Material Structure, Internat. Jour. Damage Mechs., Jour. Multiscale Computational Engring., Mechanics Advanced Materials and Structures; co-editor, Internat. Jour. Fatigue; contbr. over 300 articles to profl. jours. and confs. Recipient Alfred Noble prize ASCE, 1986, Ralph R. Teetor award Soc. Automotive Engrs., Outstanding Young Faculty award Dow Chem. Soc., 1990, Presdl. Young Investigator award NSF, 1986. Fellow ASME (Henry Hess award 1988, Nadai award 1997, editor Jour. Engring. Material Tech. 1997-2002), ASM Internat., Soc. Engring. Sci.; mem. ASTM (ann. fatigue lectr., 2002), Materials Rsch. Soc., TMS, Am. Acad. Mechanics, Am. Soc. for Engring. Edn., Soc. Engring. Sci. (v.p. 2001, pres. 2002), Khan Internat. (Medal Plasticity, 2008). Office: Ga Inst Tech GWW Sch Mech Engring Atlanta GA 30332-0405

MCDOWELL, DAVID MICHAEL, psychiatrist, educator, researcher; b. Middletown, Conn., Mar. 16, 1963; s. Arthur Vanall and Jacqueline Larson McDowell. MD, Columbia Coll. Physicians and Surgeons, 1989. Bd. cert. psychiatry Am. Bd. Psychiatry and Neurology, 1993, cert. addiction psychiatry Am. Bd. Psychiatry and Neurology, 1996. Fellow in addiction psychiatry NYU Med. Ctr., NYC, 1993—95; instr. psychiatry Bellevue Hosp./NYU Med. Ctr., NYC, 1995—; asst. prof. clin. psychiatry Columbia U. Coll. Physicians and Surgeons, NYC, 1995—; dir. buprenorphine program Columbia U.; founder, med. dir. STARS the Substance Treatment and Rsch. Svc. Columbia U., NYC, 1997—. Cons. Malinkrodt Pharmaceuticals, St. Louis, 2002—; cons. psychiatrist The Actors Fund. Author: (textbook) Substance Abuse: From Principles to Practice; contbr. chapters to books, articles to profl. jours. Bd. mem. The Three Dollar Bill Theater Co., NYC, 1995—99. Named one of Best Dr.'s in Am.; grantee, NIH/Nat. Inst. on Drug Abuse, 2000—. Fellow: APA (sr. disting.), Am. Psychiat. Assn. (vice chair sci. program com. 2000—, disting.); mem.: Charaka Club. Achievements include Advisor for Creative work including the Golden Globe Award winning film Quills, and other plays and film scripts. Avocations: cooking, singing. Office: 37 West 57th St 6B New York NY 10019 Home: 160 W 86th St # 6 B New York NY 10027 Office Phone: 212-750-7801. Personal E-mail: drdave@bway.net.

MCDOWELL, DONNA SCHULTZ, lawyer, educator; b. Cin., Apr. 23, 1946; d. Robert Joseph and Harriet (Parronchi) Schultz; m. Dennis Lon McDowell, June 20, 1970; children: Dawn Megan, Donnelly Lon. BA in English with honors, Brandeis U., Waltham, Mass., 1968; MEd, Am. U., Washington, DC, 1972; C.A.S. with honors in Reading, Johns Hopkins U., Balt., 1979; JD with honors, U. Md., 1982, postgrad.; MS, Hood Coll., Frederick, Md., 1995. Bar: Md. 1982; cert. tchr. reading K-12, D.C.; advanced prof. cert. in English, law, biology, reading, Md. Instr. Anne Arundel & Prince George's C.C., Severna Park and Largo, Md., 1977-78; coll. adminstr. Bowie State Coll., Md., 1978—79; assoc. Miller & Bortner, Lanham, Md., 1982-83; pvt. practice Lanham, 1983—87, Gaithersburg, Md., 1987—; sci. tchr. DC Pub. Schs., Washington, 1999-2000; chair dept. English Montgomery County Pub. Schs., Md., 2000—, English lit. tchr. Md., 2002—03, lit. lead tchr. Md., 2003—05, instrnl. specialist Md., 2005—06, lit. coach, devel. curriculum literacy and law Md., 2006—. Ednl. cons.; presenter in field. Mem. Solid Waste Adv. Com., Montgomery County, Md.; election judge; presenter in field. Recipient Am. Jurisprudence award U. Md., 1981; Michael Jordan grantee, 2000, D.C. Pub. Schs. grantee. Mem. Phi Kappa Phi. Democrat. Avocations: gardening, reading, bluebirds, movies. Home: 24308 Hipsley Mill Rd Gaithersburg MD 20882-3132 Personal E-mail: donnasmcd@aol.com.

MCDOWELL, ELIZABETH MARY, retired pathology educator; b. Kew Gardens, Surrey, Eng., Mar. 30, 1940; arrived in U.S., 1971; d. Arthur and Peggy (Bryant) McD. B Vet. Medicine, Royal Vet. Coll., London, 1963; BA, Cambridge U., 1968, PhD, 1971. Gen. practice vet. medicine, 1964-66; Nuffield Found. tng. scholar Cambridge (Eng.) U., 1966-71; instr. dept. pathology U. Md., Balt., 1971-73, asst. prof., 1973-76, assoc. prof., 1976-80, prof., 1980-96, ret., 1996. Co-author: Biopsy Pathology of the Bronchi, 1987; editor: Lung Carcinomas, 1987; contbr. over 120 articles to sci. jours., chpts. to books. Rsch. grantee, NIH, 1979—92. Avocations: conservation education, gardening, swimming.

MCDOWELL, JENNIFER, sociologist, composer, playwright; b. Albuquerque; d. Willard A. and Margaret Frances (Garrison) McD.; m. Milton Loventhal, July 2, 1973. BA, U. Calif., 1957; MA, San Diego State U., 1958; postgrad., Sorbonne, Paris, 1959; MLS, U. Calif., 1963; PhD, U. Oreg., 1973. Tchr. English Abraham Lincoln H.S., San Jose, Calif., 1960-61; free-lance editor Soviet field, Berkeley, Calif., 1961-63; editor, pub. Merlin Papers, San Jose, 1969-80, Merlin Press, San Jose, 1973—; rsch. cons. sociology San Jose, 1973—; music pub. Lipstick and Toy Balloons Pub. Co., San Jose, 1978—, Abbie & Dolley Records, 2003—; composer Paramount Pictures, 1982-88. Tchr. writing workshops; poetry readings, 1969-73; co-producer radio show lit. and culture Sta. KALX, Berkeley, 1971-72. Author: (with Milton Loventhal) Black Politics: A Study and Annotated Bibliography of the Mississippi Freedom Democratic Party, 1971 (Smithsonian Inst. 1992), Contemporary Women Poets, Anthology of California Poets, 1977; co-author: (plays off Broadway) Betsy and Phyllis, 1986, Mack the Knife Your Friendly Dentist, 1986, The Estrogen Party To End War, 1986, The Oatmeal Party Comes to Order, 1986, (plays) Betsy Meets the Wacky Iraqi, 1991, Bella and Phyllis, 1994; author numerous poems; contbr. articles and short stories to profl. jours, local newspapers; writer: (songs) Money Makes a Woman Free!, 1976, 2004; 3 songs featured in Parade of Am. Music, 1976-77; co-creator mus. comedy Russia's Secret Plot To Take Back Alaska, 1988; (Cassingle) Intern Girl, 1998, Smithsonian, 2002; (CDs) Our Women Are Strong, 2000, 02, The Wearing of the Green Burkas, 2003; (musical revs., CD) She, A Tapestry of Women's Lives, 2004. Recipient 8 awards Am. Song Festival, 1976-79, Service to Poetry award, 1977, Bill Casey Award in Letters (Soviet Studies), 1980, SHE award, Calif. State U.-ERFA Found., 2004, collected by Nobel Inst. for 2003 Nobel Peace Prize laureate Shirin Ebadi, award USA Songwriting Competition, 2006; doctoral fellow AAUW, 1971-73; grantee Calif. Arts Coun., 1976-77. Mem. AAUW, Am. Assn. for Advancement of Slavic Studies, Soc. Sci. Study of Religion, Am. Sociol. Assn., Dramatists Guild, Phi Beta Kappa, Sigma Alpha Iota, Beta Phi Mu, Kappa Kappa Gamma. Democrat. Office: care Abbie and Dolley Records PO Box 5602 San Jose CA 95150-5602 Office Phone: 800-889-8305. Business E-Mail: jeditorphd@earthlink.net.

MC DOWELL, JOHN BERNARD, bishop emeritus; b. New Castle, Pa., July 17, 1921; s. Bernard A. and Louise M. (Hannon) Mc Dowell. BA, St. Vincent Coll., 1942, MA, 1944, Catholic U. Am., 1950, PhD, 1952; LittD (hon.), Duquesne U., 1962; grad., St. Vincent Sem., Latrobe, Pa. Ordained priest Diocese of Pitts., 1945, asst. supt. schs., 1952-55, supt. schs., 1955-70, aux. bishop, 1966—96, vicar for edn., 1970-85, aux. bishop emeritus, 1996—; ordained bishop, 1966; asst. pastor St. Irenaeus Ch., Oakmont, 1945-49; vicar gen.; pastor Epiphany Parish, Pitts., 1969-96. Papal chamberlain to Pope Pius XII, 1956, to Pope John XXIII, 1958; domestic prelate to Pope Paul VI, 1964; chmn. ad hoc com. on moral values in our soc. Nat. Conf. Cath. Bishops, from 1973, Bishops Com. for Pastoral on Moral Values, from 1976; mem. Internat. Council for Catechesis, from 1975 Author: Water, Death and Grace: The Life of Hugh C. Boyle, 6th Bishop of Diocese of Pittsburgh, 1999, Catholic Schools, Public Education, and American Culture, 2000, Giants Were On the Earth in Those Days, The Life of John Francis Regis Canevin, 5th Bishop, Diocese of Pittsburgh, 2000, Blessed Are the Poor in Spirit, For Theirs is the Kingdom of Heaven, the Life of Vincent Martin Leonard, the 9th Bishop of Diocese of Pittsburgh, 2001, I Am Going To Tell You A Mystery, the life of the fourth Bishop, Diocese of Pitts., 2002, To Dwell in the House of the Lord All the Days of My Life, the life of Father Charles Bonaventure Maguire, O.F.M., 2003, Reflections on the Life of John Cardinal Wright, S.T.D. Eighth Bishop of Pittsburgh, 2003; co-author: elem. sch. religions series, JHS lit. series, elem. sci. series and elem. reading series; contbr. ednl. articles to various publs.; former editor: Cath. Educator Mag. Bd. dir. Allegheny County Community Coll.; bd. dir. Western Pa. Safety Council, Duquesne U. Named Man of Yr. in Religion Pitts., 1970, 93, Educator of Yr., United Pvt. Acad. Schs. Assn., 1978, Man of Yr., Pitts. chpt. KC, 1989. Mem. Nat. Cath. Ednl. Assn., Cath. Ednl. Assn. Pa., Omicron Delta Kappa Gamma Circle (hon.) Roman Catholic. Address: Chancery Office 111 Blvd Of The Allies Pittsburgh PA 15222-1613

MCDOWELL, JOHN HENRY, JR., lawyer; b. Las Cruces, N.Mex., June 1, 1957; s. John H. and Jacqueline (O'Sullivan) McD.; 1 child, Michal Jillian. BA in Econs., Stanford U., 1979; JD, U. Va., 1982. Bar: Tex. 1983, US Dist. Ct. (no. dist. Tex.) 1983, US Dist. Ct. (ea. dist. Tex.) 1985, US Dist. Ct. (we. dist. Tex.) 1987, US Dist. Ct. (so. dist. Tex.) 1995. Ptnr. Hughes & Luce, LLP, Dallas. Spkr. in field. Named one of Best Lawyers in Dallas, D Mag., 2005. Fellow: Dallas Bar Found., Tex. Bar Found., Dallas Assn. Young Lawyers Found. (life; chair fellows prog. 2004); mem.: Am. Intellectual Property Law Assn. (antitrust com.), Dallas Assn. Young Lawyers (pres. 1991), Tex. State Bar Assn. (long range planning com. 1990—91), Tex. Young Lawyers Assn. (bd. dir. 1991—93, Award of Achievement 1990), Dallas Bar Assn. (bd. dir. 1990—91), ABA (antitrust com. litig. sect., litig. and antitrust sect. Award of Achievement 1990). Office: Hughes & Luce LLP 1717 Main St Ste 2800 Dallas TX 75201 Office Phone: 214-939-5413. Office Fax: 214-939-5849. E-mail: john.mcdowell@hughesluce.com.

MCDOWELL, LAURA ONEITA, secondary school educator; b. Erick, Okla., Jan. 21, 1929; d. Roy Marion and Sybil Faye (Tapley) Carr; m. Billy Gene McDowell, Aug. 15, 1954; children: Darwin, Deonn, Dwila, Donnette, Deylan, Devin. Student, Jacksonville Coll., Tex., 1948-49; BA, Wayland Bapt. U., Plainview, Tex., 1950-54; MA, West Tex. U., 1954-57; postgrad., U. Ariz. Cert. tchr., Ariz; lic. minister Assembly of God Ch. English tchr. Kress (Tex.) Ind. Sch. Dist., 1954-60, Ea. Ariz. Coll., Clifton, 1965-72; substitute English tchr. various high schs., Clifton, Morenci, Ariz., 1973-78; English and typing tchr. Bowie (Ariz.) High Sch., 1979-80; bus. and publs. tchr. San Simon (Ariz.) High Sch., 1980-87, English and Spanish tchr., 1987—92; pastor Oakwood Assembly of God, Oakwood, Tex., 1995—99; adult Sunday sch. tchr. Buffalo Assembly of God, Buffalo, Tex., 1999—2002; sub. adult Sunday sch. tchr. Chapel of the Hills, Centerville, Tex., 2002—08. Evaluator computer software Ariz. State Dept. Edn., Phoenix, 1984-86. Author: Your Identity in Christ, 2002. Vol. Clifton Pub. Schs., 1972-73; adult sunday sch. tchr. Assembly of God Ch., Willcox, Ariz., 1980-92. Mem. Delta Kappa Gamma Soc. Internat. (pres. alpha lambda chpt. 1984-86, sec. 1982-84, newsletter editor 1984-86). Mem. Pentecostal Church. Avocations: reading, studying theology, cooking, poetry, bowling.

MCDOWELL, MALCOLM, actor; b. Leeds, Eng., June 13, 1943; m. Mary Steenburgen, 1980 (div.); 2 children; m. Kelley Kuhr, 1991; children: Beckett Taylor, Finnian Anderson; m. Margot Dullea (div.). Began career with: Royal Shakespeare Co., Stratford, Eng., 1965-66; early TV appearances include: role of Dixon of Dock Green in Z Cars, British TV; other TV appearances: Little Red Riding Hood, Faerie Tale Theatre, Showtime TV, 1983, Gulag, HBO, 1985, Tales From the Crypt, 1989, Spider-Man, 1995, Our Friends in the North, 1996, Lexx: The Dark Zone, 1996, The Great War, 1996, Captain Simian and The Space Monkeys, 1996, The Little Riders, 1996, Superman, 1996, Pearl, 1996-97, Nazis: The Occult Conspiracy, 1998, Beings, 1998, Ruby, 1999, (voice) South Park, 2000, Entourage, 2005-06, Heroes, 2007, Metalocalypse, 2007-; stage appearance: Look Back in Anger, N.Y. Stage, 1980, In Celebration, N.Y.C., 1984, Hunting Cockroaches, L.A. Stage, 1987, Another Time - Stage, 1993; films include: Poor Cow, 1967, If..., 1969, Figures in a Landscape, 1970, The Raging Moon, 1971, A Clockwork Orange, 1971, O Lucky Man, 1973, Royal Flash, 1975, Aces High, 1976, Voyage of the Damned, 1977, Caligula, 1977, The Passage, 1978, Time After Time, 1979, Cat People, 1981, Britannia Hospital, 1984, Blue Thunder, 1983, Get Crazy, 1983, Cross Creek, 1983, Sunset, 1987, Buy and Cell, 1989, Class of 1999, 1989, Assassin of the Tsar, 1990, Bopha!, 1993, Milk Money, 1994, The Caller, Star Trek: Generations, 1997, Tank Girl, 1995, Yesterday's Target, 1996, Where Truth Lies, 1996, Asylum, 1996, Superman, 1996, Mr. Magoo, 1997, Hugo Pool, 1997, 2103 The Deadly Wake, 1997, The Gardener, 1998, Beings, 1998, World of Moss, 1998, Y2K, 1999, Southern Cross, 1999, My Life So Far, 1999, Love Lies Bleeding, 1999, Gangster #1, 2000, Island of the Dead, 2000, Just Visiting, 2001, Dorian, 2001, Between Strangers, 2001, I Spy, 2002, I'll Sleep When I'm Dead, 2003, Tempo, 2003, The Company, 2003, Red Roses and Petrol, 2003, Bobby Jones, Stroke of Genius, 2004, (voice) Pinocchio 3000, 2004, (voice) Dinotopia: Curse of the Ruby Sunstone, 2004, Halloween, 2007, Doomsday, 2008, (voice) Bolt, 2008, (voice) Delgo, 2008, Halloween II, 2009*

MCDOWELL, MARY, bank executive; b. Cameron, Tex. BBA Summa cum Laude, Tex. A&M U. CPA; Chartered Fin. Cons., Chartered Life Underwriter. With Ernst & Young; CFO Am. health and life Citigroup Inc., 1991, CFO CitiFinancial, CFO CitiFinancial Mortgage Co., CFO Citicorp Trust Bank, pres. CitiFinancial Auto, 2003—06, pres., COO CitiFinancial North America, 2006—07, pres., CEO CitiFinancial North America, 2007—. Chairwoman Citi's Tex. Leadership Coun.; chmn. CitiFinancial Credit Co.; co-chair Citi's Md. Leadership Coun.; mem. bd. dirs. Living Classrooms Found., Tex. Bus. and Edn. Coalition; bus. sponsor Citi's Women's Network - Baltimore/Washington. Mem.: Consumer Bankers Assn. (mem. fin. adv. bd.), Am. Fin. Svcs. Assn. (mem. exec. com., mem. bd. dirs., mem. fin. adv. bd.). Office: Citigroup Inc 399 Park Ave New York NY 10043*

MCDOWELL, MICHAEL J., literature and language professor; married. AB, Stanford U., Palo Alto, Calif., 1973; MA, U. Va., Charlottesville, 1975; PhD, U. Oreg., Eugene, 1992. Instr. Portland CC, Oreg., 1976—. Contbr. articles. Office: Portland CC 12000 SW 49th Ave Portland OR 97219

MCDOWELL, ROBERT MALCOLM, commissioner; b. 1963; s. Herbert K. and Martha Louise (Shea) McDowell; m. Jennifer McDowell; 2 children. AB cum laude, Duke U., 1985; JD, Coll. William and Mary. Bar: Va. 1990, US Dist. Ct. (ea. dist.) Va., US Ct. Appeals DC (1st, 4th, and 5th cir.), US Supreme Ct. Chief legis. aide Va. Ho. of Delegates; with Arter & Hadden, Washington; exec. v.p., gen. coun. Am. Carriers Telecomm. Assn.; sr. v.p., asst. gen. counsel COMPTEL, 1999—2006; commr. FCC, 2006—. Mem. North Am. Numbering Coun.; bd. dirs. North Am. Numbering Plan Billing and Collection, Inc. Mem. gov.'s advisory bd. Safe and Drug-Free Va., Va. Bd. Contractors; chmn. bd. McLean Project for Arts; counsel Bush-Cheney Fla. Recount Team, 2000. Republican. Office: FCC 445 12th St SW Washington DC 20554*

MCDOWELL, WILBUR BENEDICT, retired chemist consultant; b. Omaha, Feb. 27, 1920; s. Samuel Brownlee and Rose Gwendolen (Benedict) McDowell; m. Jean Erskine Clapp, Aug. 9, 1947 (dec. Aug. 1996); children: Linda Jane, Wendy Sue, Bruce Benedict. BSc, Ohio State U., 1941, MSc, 1942, PhD, 1944. Asst. Ohio State U., Columbus, 1942—43, tchg. fellow, 1943—44; rsch. assoc. The Squibb Inst., New Brunswick, NJ, 1944—52, section head, 1953—58, sr. rsch. assoc., 1958—66; mgr. prof. svc. dept. Squibb Corp., NYC, 1966—69, Princeton, NJ, 1970—85; ret., 1985. Cons., archivist Squibb Corp., 1985—89, Bristol-Myers Squibb Co., Princeton, 1989—99, New Brunswick, NJ, 2000—. Mem., v.p., pres. BOE, East Brunswick, NJ, 1957—65. Fellow: AAAS; mem.: Soc. Nuclear Medicine, Am. Chem. Soc., Sigma Xi. Achievements include wartime research on penicillin; 8 patents in field of manufacturing processes for phamaceuticals. E-mail: benmcdowell@prodigy.net.

MCDOWELL-CRAIG, VANESSA DENNISE, supervisor, consultant; b. Washington, Dec. 9, 1954; d. John David and Ossie Ola McDowell; m. John Maurice Craig, May 19, 1984. BS, U. DC, 1995; MEd, Trinity U., Washington, 2000; postgrad., Gallaudet U., 2001—. Cert. mgmt. change leadership Gallaudet U., elem. edn. DC, emergins leaders program DC, ednl. rsch. and dissemination program Am. Fedn. Tchrs. Tng. instr. Blue Cross - Blue Shield, Washington, 1980—87; claims supr. Mut. Omaha, Washington, 1987—88, Health Plus, Riverdale, Md., 1988—89; supr., team mgr. Humana Group Health Plan, Washington, 1989—93; elem. tchr. grades 1-6 DC Pub. Sch. Sys., 1993—2001, instrnl. facilitator, supr., 2002—, program coord., supr., cons. Cons. TechAgility LLC, Washington, 2004—. Mem.: ASCD (assoc.), Assn. Childhood Edn. Internat. (assoc.), Internat. Reading Assn. (assoc.; corr. sec. DC reading coun. 1999—2002), Delta Sigma Theta (life). Democrat. African Methodist Episcopal. Avocations: travel, reading, bicycling, singing, dance. Home: 7134 Marbury Court District Heights MD 20747 Home Phone: 301-736-5912; Office Phone: 202-907-7927. Office Fax: 202-442-5517, 202-442-5518; Home Fax: 301-736-2365. Personal E-mail: vannettie@aol.com. Business E-Mail: vanessa.craig@dc.gov.

MCDUFFIE, KEITH A., literature educator; b. Spokane, Wash., Feb. 12, 1932; s. Clair L. and Helen Marie (Yaeger) McD.; m. Helen E. Ferry, June 5, 1965 (div. July 1995); children: Anne Leslie, Andrew Keith; m. Pamela Philips Bacarisse, Aug. 10, 1995 (dec. Mar. 1996). BA in English, Gonzaga U., Spokane, 1954; MA in Spanish, Middlebury Coll., Vt., 1960, Univ. Complutense, Madrid, Spain, 1960; PhD in Hispanic Lit., U. Pitts., 1969. Prof. U. Mont., 1969-74; Mellon postdoctoral fellow U. Pitts., 1974, prof., chair dept. Hispanic lit., 1975-92, prof. Hispanic lit., 1975-99, ret., 1999. Editor Revista Iberoamericana, Pitts., 1991-96; pres. Univ. Senate, 1995-97. Co-author: Co-Textes: Cesar Vallejo, 1987; co-editor: Texto y Contexto-Actas 19 Congreso del IILI, 1980, En Este Aire de America: Homenaje a Alfredo Roggiano, 1990. With U.S. Army Security Agy., 1954-56. Mellon Predoctoral fellow U. Pitts., 1965, Title VI fellow U.S. Govt., 1966; Spanish Govt. scholar Spanish Govt., 1959-60. Mem. Instituto Internacional de Literatura Iberoamericana (contbg., bd. dirs. 1991-96, exec. dir. 1991-96). Democrat. Home: 220 N Dithridge St Apt 1001 Pittsburgh PA 15213-1425 E-mail: kamcd@pitt.edu.

MCDYESS, ANTONIO KEITHFLEN, professional basketball player; b. Quitman, Miss., Sept. 7, 1974; m. Liara McDyess. Attended, U. Ala., Tuscaloosa. Forward Denver Nuggets, 1995—97, 1998—2002, 2008, Phoenix Suns, 1997—98, NY Knicks, 2003—04, Phoenix Suns, 2004, Detroit Pistons, 2004—08, 2008—. Mem. US nat. team Summer Olympic Games, Sydney, 2000. Recipient Gold medal, men's basketball, Sydney Olympic Games, 2000, Sportsmanship award, NBA, 2008; named to All-Rookie First Team, 1995—96, We. Conf. All-Star Team, 2001. Avocations: bowling, rhythm and blues. Office: San Antonio Spurs 1 AT&T Center Pky San Antonio TX 78219*

MCEACHEN, RICHARD EDWARD, banker, lawyer; b. Omaha, Sept. 24, 1933; s. Howard D. and Ada Carolyn Helen (Baumann) McE.; m. Judith Ann Gray, June 28, 1969; children: Mark E., Neil H. BS, U. Kans., Lawrence, 1955; JD, U. Mich., 1961. Bar: Mo. 1961, Kans. 1982; cert. trust and fin. advisor Inst. for Cert. Bankers, 1991. Assoc. Hillix, Hall, Hasburgh, Brown & Hoffhaus, Kansas City, Mo., 1961-62; sr. v.p. First Nat. Bank, Kansas City, Mo., 1962-75; exec. v.p. Commerce Bank Kansas City, Mo., 1975-85, Centerre Bank of Kansas City N.A., 1985-87, Security Bank Kansas City, Kans., 1987-88; exec. v.p., trust officer UMB Overland Park Bank, 1988-93; atty. Ferree, Bunn, O'Grady & Rundberg, Chartered, Overland Park, 1994—2005. Gov. Am. Royal Assn., Kansas City, Mo., 1970-2002, amb., 1980-2004, com. mem., 1995-2005; bd. dirs. Harry S. Truman Med. Ctr., Kansas City, 1974-86, mem. fin. com., 1975-86, treas., 1979-84, bd. govs., 1986-2002, mem. bldg. and grounds com., 1993-2002, mem. pension com., 1976-93, 96-2000; trustee Clearinghouse for Midcontinent Founds., 1980-87; bd. dirs. Greater Kansas City Mental Health Found., 1963-69, treas., 1964-69, v.p., 1967-69; adv. bd. urban svcs. YMCA, Kansas City, 1976-83; cubmaster Kanza dist. Boy Scouts Am., 1982-83, dist. vice chmn., 1982-83, troop com., 1983-90, treas., 1986-88; bd. dirs. Scout Booster Club, Inc., 1989-94; mem. planned gift com. William Rockhill Nelson Gallery Art, Children's Mercy Hosp. Planned Gift Coun., 1991-; mem. adv. com. Legal Assistance Program Avila Coll., 1978-80, adv. coun. Future Farmers Am., 1972-82; mgr. Oppenstein Bros. Found., 1979-85; trustee Village Presbyn. Ch., 1987-90, chmn., 1989-90, elder, 1994-97, Golf Classic Com., 2005-; found. com. Am. Royal Charitable Found., 1995-2005; bd. dirs. Village Presbyn. Ch. Found., 1987-89, 94-97, chmn., 1996-97, mem. adv. bd., 1997-2001; bd. dirs. Estate Planning Coun., 1984-86; mem. Kansas City Fed. Estate Planning Symposium Com., 1992-98; bd. dirs. Shawnee Mission Med. Ctr. Found., 1988—, fin. com., 1989-92, 2002—, mem. planned giving com., 1996-, mem. investment com., 2000—; mem. adv. coun. Shawnee Mission Edn. Found., 2003. Recipient Eagle Scout, Boy Scouts Am., 1948. Mem. Nat. Assn. Securities Dealers Inc. (bd. arbitrators 1994—2004), Am. Arbitration Assn. (panel arbitrators 1994-96), Estate Planning Soc. Kansas City, Mo. Bar Assn., Kans. Bar Assn., Johnson County Bar Assn., Estate Planning Assn. (pres. 1974-75), Kansas City Jr. C. of C. (v.p. 1964-66), Ea. Kans. Estate Planning Coun., 40-Yrs. Ago Column Club (program com. 1999-2000, pres. 2001, 2009, trustee 2001-04), Indian Hills Club, Delta Tau Delta Alumni (v.p. Kansas City chpt. 1978-80, Hibbs Scholarship Com., 2007-), Kans. City Srs. Golf Assn. (bd. dirs. 2009-) Republican. Home: 9100 El Monte St Shawnee Mission KS 66207-2627

MCEACHERN, WILLIAM ARCHIBALD, economics educator; b. Portsmouth, NH, Jan. 4, 1945; s. Archibald Duncan and Ann Teresa (Regan) McE.; m. Patricia Leonardo, Aug. 18, 1973. AB in Econs., Holy Cross Coll., 1967; MA in Econs., U. Va., 1969, PhD in Econs., 1975. Asst. prof. U. Conn., Storrs, 1973-78, assoc. prof., 1978-84, prof. econs., 1984—, dir. grad. studies, 1981-87. Econ. cons. U.S. Dept. Labor, 1977-79, FTC, 1979-82, Conn. Conf. on Municipalities, New Haven, 1975-76, 87-88; dir. Bipartisan Commn. on Conn. Finances, Hartford, 1982-83. Author: Managerial Control and Performance, 1975, Economics: A Contemporary Introduction, 8th edit., 2008, Contemporary Economics, 2nd edit., 2007, MicroECON, 2009, MacroECON, 2009; founding editor Quarterly Rev. on Conn. Economy, The Teaching Economist; contbr. articles to profl. jours. 1st lt. U.S. Army, 1969-71. Nat. Def. fellow U. Va., 1967-69, 72-73. Mem. Am. Econ. Assn., Northeast Bus. and Econs. Assn. (founder, assoc. editor 1978-81, adv. bd. 2008—). Office: U Conn Dept Econs 341 Mansfield Rd Storrs Mansfield CT 06269

MCELDOWNEY, NANCY EILEEN, United States Ambassador to Bulgaria; b. Fla., 1958; m. Tim Hayes; 2 children. BA, New Coll., Sarasota, 1980; degree, Columbia U., NYC, Nat. Def. U. With Office of Sec. Def. US Dept. Def.; with Office Dep. Sec. US Dept. State, mem. European Bur. front office, mem. Office European Security Affairs, mem. Office Soviet Affairs, fgn. svc. assignments, US Embassy Bonn, Germany, Cairo, dep. chief of mission, US Embassy Baku, Azerbaijan, dep. chief, chargé d'affaires, US Mission Ankara, Turkey, 2005—08, US amb. to Bulgaria Sofia, 2008—; dir. European affairs Nat. Security Coun., Washington. Recipient Disting. Writing award, Nat. War Coll., Sinclair Linguistic award, Superior Honor award, US Dept. State. Office: DOS Amb 5740 Sofia Pl Washington DC 20521-5740 also: US Embassy 16 Kozyak St 1407 Sofia Bulgaria*

MC ELHANEY, JOHN HESS, lawyer; b. Milw., Apr. 16, 1934; s. Lewis Keck and Sara Jane (Hess) McE.; m. Jacquelyn Masur, Aug. 4, 1962; children— Scott, Victoria. BBA, So. Meth. U., 1956, JD, 1958. Bar: Tex. bar 1958. Pvt. practice law, Dallas, 1958—; pntr. Locke, Liddell & Sapp, L.L.C., Dallas, 1976—. Lectr. law So. Meth. U., 1967-76 Contbr. articles to legal jours. Trustee St. Mark's Sch. Tex., 1980-86. Fellow Am. Coll. Trial Lawyers; mem. Am. Bd. Trial Advs., ABA, Tex. Bar Assn., So. Meth. U. Law Alumni Assn. (pres. 1972-73, dir. 1970-73), Town and Gown Club (pres. 1981-82). Presbyterian. Home: 5340 Tanbark Dr Dallas TX 75229-5555 Office: Locke Liddell & Sapp 2200 Ross Ave Ste 2200 Dallas TX 75201-6776 Home Phone: 214-363-7700.

MCELHENY, JOSIAH G., sculptor; b. Boston, 1966; BFA, Rhode Island Sch. Design, 1989. Apprentice to master glassblower Jan-Erik Ritzman, 1989—91, Sven-Ake Carlsson, 1989—91, Lino Tagliapietra, 1992—97; artist-in-residence Isabella Stewart Gardner Mus., 1998, U. Nev., Las Vegas, 2000; vis. critic Yale U. Sch. Art, 2001—03. Spkr. in field. One-man shows include Henry Art Gallery, Seattle, Isabella Stewart Gardner Mus., Boston, 1999, Johnson County CC, Overland Park, Kans., 2001, Art Inst. Chgo., Centro Galego de Arte Contemporanea, Spain, 2002, Brent Sikkema, NYC, 2000, 2003, Donald Young Gallery, Chgo., 1995, 1997, 2000, 2004, others, exhibited in group shows at Site Santa Fe, N.Mex., Whitney Biennial, Whitney Mus. Am. Art NYC, 2000, The Saatchi Gallery, London, Nordic Inst. Contemporary Art. Recipient award, Louis Comfort Tiffany Found., 1995, Bagley Wright Fund award, Seattle, 1998, 15th Rakow Commission, Corning Mus. Glass, Corning, NY, 2000; MacArthur Fellow, John D. and Catherine T. MacArthur Found., 2006. Office: c/o Donald Young Gallery 224 S Michigan Ave Ste 266 Chicago IL 60604-2534

MCELHINNEY, JAMES LANCEL, artist, educator; b. Abington, Pa., Feb. 3, 1952; s. James and Joan Howland (Carpenter) McE.; m. Victoria Maria Dávila, Sept. 12, 1981 (div.), m. Katherine E. Menthorne, Aug. 22, 2006. Scholarship student, Skowhegan Sch. Painting and Sculp, Maine, 1973; BFA, Temple U., 1974; MFA, Yale U., 1976. Asst. prof. Moore Coll. Art, Phila., 1977-78, Skidmore Coll., Saratoga Springs, NY, 1979-87; instr. Milw. Inst. Art and Design, 1991-93; vis. artist East Carolina U., Greenville, NC, 1994-98; head painting and drawing program visual arts dept. U. Colo., Denver, 1998—2003; vis. assoc. prof. Pratt Inst., NYC, 2004—. Adj. instr. UCLA, 1983, Moore Coll. Art, 1983, Tyler Sch. Art, Phila., 1983—86, U. Arts, 1985—89; artist in residence Harper's Ferry Nat. Hist. Pk., 1999; dir. study abroad program Feltre, Veneto, Italy, 2000—02; lectr. USAF Acad., 2001; faculty Art Students League NY, 2005—, coord. apprentice program, 2007; lectr. in field; lectr. NY Hist. Soc., 2006, Nat. Acad. Design; vis. lectr. Ctrl. Mich. U., NY Hist. Soc., 2007, Hudson River Sch. Painting, 2007, U. Iowa Grad. Sch. Art, 2008. Exhibited in group shows at Chrysler Mus., Norfolk, Va., 1999, Allen Sheppard Gallery, NYC, 1999, Ucross Found., 2000, Nicolaysen Mus., 2000, Newarts Gallery, Litchfield, Conn., 2005, Kent Gallery, Conn., 2005, Reinstallation Hamilton Wing, Inst. Western Art, Denver Art Mus., 2006, one-man shows include Peninsula Ctr. for Fine Arts, Newport News, Va., 1993, Danville Mus., Va., 1993, Second St. Gallery, Charlottesville, Va., 1995, F.A.N. Gallery, Phila., 1995, 1998, Greenville Mus. Art, NC, 1996, Lee Hansley Gallery, Raleigh, NC, 1996, 1998, 1999, Asheville Art Mus., NC, 1996, William Havu Gallery, Denver, 2001—02, Mus. of SW, Midland, Tex., 2003, William Havu Gallery, 2001, Letterkenny Arts Ctr., Donegal, Ireland, 2003, The Painting Ctr., NYC, 2005, one-woman shows include New Arts Gallery, Litchfield, Ct., 2008, Represented in permanent collections Chrysler Mus. Art, Denver Art Mus., Asheville Art Mus.; author: (manual) The Instruction of Civil War Pioneer Troops, 2004; web editor (drawing and edn.) Newington Cropsey Study Ctr., NY; contbr. articles to various profl. mag.; contbr., editor: articles to profl. jours.; interviewer (oral history program) Archives of Am. Art, Smithsonian Instn., broadcast interviewer Newington Cropsey Cultural Studies Ctr. Vol. Richmond (Va.) Nat. Battlefield Park, 1991—, Frontier Army Living History Corps of Discovery, U.S. Army C.E. Lewis and Clark Bicentennial, Topog. eng. 1st Divsn. Staff, Hdqs. A.N.V (U.S.C.W.). Grantee painting, NEA, 1987—88, Ptnrs. in Arts, Richmond Arts Coun., 1995; rsch. grant, U. Colo., 2000, Faculty Devel. grant, 2003. Mem. Coll. Art Assn., SAR, Civil War Preservation Trust, Met. Mus. Art, Foote Family Assoc. Office: Art Students League of NY 215 W 57th New York NY 10019 Personal E-mail: mcelhinney@aol.com.

MCELHINNY, WILSON DUNBAR, banker; b. Detroit, July 27, 1929; s. William Dunbar and Elizabeth (Wilson) McE.; m. Barbara Cheney Watkins, June 6, 1952 (dec.); children: David Ashton, Ward Cheney, Edward Wilson, William Dunbar; m. Lisa Lesher, Mar. 27, 1993. BA, Yale U., 1953. With Union and New Haven Trust Co., 1952-63, Reading Trust Co., Pa., 1963-68, pres., 1968-70, Nat. Ctrl. Bank (formerly Reading Trust Co.), Pa., 1970-79, CEO, 1975-79; chmn. bd. dirs., pres., CEO Hamilton Bank (formerly Nat. Ctrl. Bank), Lancaster, Pa., 1979-81, chmn. bd. dirs., CEO, 1981-83, chmn. bd. dirs., 1981-90; pres. CoreStates Fin. Corp., Phila., 1983-86, vice chmn., 1986-90; pres., chmn. Hamilton Bank, Lancaster, 1988-90. Bd. dirs. chmn. Sun Valley Bank, 1st Bank Idaho, SIGCO, Portland, Maine. Mem. Sun Valley Summer Symphony Bd. Mem. Pa. C. of C. (chmn. 1990-92), Yale Club N.Y., The Valley Club, Franklin & Marshall Coll. (bd. visitors). Home and Office: PO Box 3070 Ketchum ID 83340-3070

MCELIECE, MICHELLE, biology professor; married. PhD, Lehigh U. Assoc. prof., biology Gwynedd-Mercy Coll., Gwynedd Valley, Pa., 2003—; adj. faculty Arcadia U., Glenside.

MCELIGOT, ARCHANA JAISWAL, epidemiologist, educator; d. Indravadan Jayaswal and Jyotsna Jaiswal; m. Jeremy McEligot, July 20, 1996; children: Lee, Rohan. BS, MS, U. Calif., San Diego, PhD, 2001. Asst. prof. U. Calif., Irvine, 2002—; assoc. prof. Calif. State U., 2006—. Grantee, Tobacco Related Disease Rsch. Program, 2000—02, U. Calif. Irvine, 2003—04, Nat. Cancer Inst., 2005—. Mem.: Cancer Family Registry (co-chair 2002—03), Am. Soc. Nutrition. Office: University of California Irvine/CSUF 224 Irvine Hall Irvine CA 92697-7555 Business E-Mail: mceligot@uci.edu.

MC ELRATH, RICHARD ELSWORTH, retired insurance company executive; b. Thompsontown, Pa., Oct. 11, 1932; s. Clayton Ellsworth and Jane Elizabeth (Shoop) McE.; m. Donna Gail Booher, Aug. 18, 1952; children: Leslie Jo, Jennifer Jo, Josie Arlene Elizabeth, Rebekah Clare. BS cum laude, Elizabethtown Coll., Pa., 1955; MBA cum laude, Harvard U., 1961. Research asst. Harvard U., 1961-62; asst. to pres. Callaway Mills Co., LaGrange, Ga., 1963-65; with Irving Trust Co., NYC, 1965-73, v.p., 1969-73; treas. Tchrs. Ins. Annuity Assn. and Coll. Retirement Equities Fund, 1973-81; v.p. Met. Life Ins. Co., 1982-95. Pres., dir. MetLife Funding, Inc., MetLife Credit, Inc., 1984-95. Author articles, case studies. Trustee Elizabethtown Coll.; mem. Society Valley Hosp., Ridgewood, N.J.; mem. Boston Rep. Com., 1961-63, Troup County (Ga.) Rep. Com., 1964-65; bd. dirs. Family Counseling Svc., Ridgewood, 1986-92. Lt. comdr. USNR, 1956-59. Mem. Assn. Gov. Bds. Univs. and Colls. Clubs: Harvard (N.Y.C.). Methodist. Home: 17 Cedar St Glen Rock NJ 07452-1608

MCELROY, JEROME LATHROP, economics professor; b. St. Louis, Sept. 14, 1937; s. King Gerard and Audrey (Lathrop) McE.; m. Birdie Maria Rossow; children: Jacqueline, Christopher. BA, St. Louis U., 1961, PhL, 1962, MA in Econs., 1965; PhD in Econs., U. Colo., 1972. Instr. St. John's Coll., Belize City, Belize, 1962-65; grad. assoc. U. Colo., Boulder, 1971-72; asst. prof. econs. Coll. of V.I., St. Thomas, 1972-75, assoc. prof. econs., 1975-79; dir. planning Govt. of V.I., St. Thomas, 1979-80; assoc. prof. econs. U. Notre Dame, Ind., 1980-82, St. Mary's Coll., South Bend, Ind., 1982-86, prof. econs., 1986—, chmn. dept. bus. and econs., 1990-93. Rsch. fellow Island Resources Found., Washington, 1980—; expert adv. panel Office Tech. Assessment, U.S. Congress, 1985-86; econ. cons. U.S. AID, 1987-89, Govt. V.I., 1974-79, 89; editl. bd. mem. Annals Tourism Rsch.; founding mem. Island Studies Jour. Author: Consumer Expenditure Patterns, 1980, USVI Status Options, 1989, Secret Seams, 2007, Sacred Traces, 2008, Sparks of Eden, 2009; numerous poems; contbr. articles to profl. jours. Mem. adv. bd. Ea. Caribbean Ctr., U. V.I., 1993-95. Recipient Maria Pieta Tchr. award, St. Mary's Coll., 1989, Tchr. of the Yr., Coll. of V.I., 1973, Spes Unica Svc. award, 1997. Mem. Am. Econ. Assn., Caribbean Studies Assn., So. Reg. Sci. Assn., Midwest Assn. Latin Americanists, Internat. Small Islands Studies Assn., Internat. Sci. Coun. for Island Devel. (founding mem.), Inst. for Devel. of Insular Economies and Socs. (founding mem.), Island Environ. Inst. (founding mem.). Democrat. Roman Catholic. Avocations: swimming, poetry. Home: 2036 Portage Ave South Bend IN 46616-2033 Office: Saint Mary's Coll 363 Spes Unica Notre Dame IN 46556 Home Phone: 574-234-2827; Office Phone: 574-284-4488. Business E-Mail: jmcelroy@saintmarys.edu.

MCELROY, LINDA SUE, retired elementary school educator; b. Stephenville, Tex., Sept. 14, 1945; d. E. J. McElroy Sr. and Margaret Walsworth McElroy. BME, Tarleton State U., Stephenville, Tex., 1974, MEd, 1980. Cert. English as Second Lang. 1992, Elem. Edn. 1980. With Evant Ind. Sch. Dist., Tex., 1978—80, tchr. k-2, 1979—80; tchr. 1st and 2nd grade Lingleville Ind. Sch. Dist., Tex., 1981—85; elem. music tchr. Granbury Ind. Sch. Dist., Granbury, Tex., 1985—86; spl. edn. tchr. Mineral Wells Ind. Sch. Dist., Mineral Wells, Tex., 1987—88; tchr. ESL and music Huckabay Ind. Sch. Dist., Stephenville, 1988—2003; mgr. Stephenville Mus., 2003—. Sec./treas. Tex. State Gospel Singing Conv., 1984—2003. Mem.: AAUW (pres. 1988), Assn. Tex. Profl. Educators. Methodist. Avocations: singing, reading. Home: 2643 W Washington Stephenville TX 76401 Office: Stephenville Mus 525 E Washington Stephenville TX 76401

MCELROY, MICHAEL, physicist, researcher, educator; b. Shercock, County Cavan, Ireland, May 18, 1939; married, 1963. BA, Queen's U., Belfast, Ireland, 1960; PhD in Math., Belfast, Ireland, 1962. Project assoc. Theoretical Chemistry Inst., U. Wis., 1962-63; from asst. physicist to physicist Kitt Peak Nat. Obs., 1963-71; physicist Ctr. Earth and Planetary Physics Harvard U., Cambridge, Mass., 1971—, now Abbott Lawrence Rotch prof. atmospheric sci., chmn. Dept. Earth and Planetary Scis., 1986—. Mem. Mars panel Lunar and Planetary Missions Bd., NASA, 1968-69, Stratospheric Research Adv. Com., Space and Terrestrial Applied Adv. Com., Com. Atmospheric Sci., Nat. Acad. Sci. Space Sci. Bd.; chmn. Com. Planetary and Lunar Exploration Recipient James B. Macelwane award Am. Geophys. Union, 1968; recipient Newcomb Cleve. prize AAAS, 1977, Pub. Service medal NASA, 1978 Fellow AAAS, Am. Geophys. Union, Internat. Acad. Aeronautics and Astronautics, Am. Acad. Arts and Scis. Office: Harvard U Dept Earth and Planetary scis 20 Oxford St Cambridge MA 02138-2902

MCELROY, MICHAEL ROBERT, lawyer; b. Providence, Feb. 7, 1951; s. Gerald Robert and Jeannette (Belanger) McE.; m. Christine Anne O'Donnell, June 5, 1976; children: Brian Robert, Dianne Elizabeth, Erin Christine. BA with highest distinction, U. RI, 1973; JD cum laude, Boston U., 1976; MS in Taxation cum laude, Bryant U., 1985.

Bar: Tenn. 1976, Mass. 1985, U.S. Dist. Ct. (ea. dist.) Tenn. 1977, U.S. Ct. Appeals (5th cir.) 1977, U.S. Supreme Ct. 1979, U.S. Ct. Appeals (6th cir.) 1980, R.I. 1981, U.S. Dist. Ct. R.I. 1981, U.S. Ct. Appeals (1st cir.) 1981, U.S. Dist. Ct. Mass. 2000. Staff atty. TVA, Knoxville, 1976-81; counsel RI Pub. Utilities Commn., Providence, 1982-83; spl. asst. atty. gen. Office Atty. Gen., Providence, 1982-83; ptnr. O'Leary & McElroy, Providence, 1981-85, Schacht & McElroy, Providence, 1987—; sole practice Providence, 1985-87. Pres. Utility Cons., Inc., Providence, 1983; ptnr. McElroy, Lawrence, Edge & Assocs., Providence, 1983-85. Legal counsel for candidate Congl. campaign, Providence, 1982; chief speech writer for candidate gubernatorial campaign, R.I., 1984; chief legal counsel for candidate gubernatorial campaign, R.I., 1988, Gov. Bruce Sundlun's successful gubernatorial campaign, 1990; legal counsel to R.I. Pers. Appeal Bd., 1991—; arbitrator Superior Ct. R.I., 1992—; spl. master/commr., 1993—; mediator Superior Ct., 1999—; spl. legal counsel to R.I. Ethics Commn., 2000-02. Danforth Found. hon. fellow, 1973; Rhodes scholar nominee, 1973; honoree for life-saving CPR, TVA, 1980; nominated for judgeship Jud. Nom. Commn. Superior Ct., 1994; elected fellow RI Bar Found., 2007. Mem.: Am. Assn. for Justice, Million Dollar Advs. Forum, RI Assn. for Justice, RI Bar Assn. (fed. ct. com. 1983—, mem. superior ct. Bench/Bar coms. 1983—, mem. Supreme Ct. com. 2002—, chmn. Superior Ct. Bench/Bar com. 2003—06, exec. com. ho. of dels. 2006—, treas. 2008—09, sec. 2009—). Roman Catholic. Office: PO Box 6721 Providence RI 02940-6721 Office Phone: 401-351-4100. Business E-Mail: michael@mcelroylawoffice.com.

MCELROY, TUCKER SPRAGYE, mathematician, consultant, statistician; b. Boston, Aug. 26, 1974; s. Paul Tucker and Linda Sprague McElroy; m. Autumn Lyn Dennison, July 7, 2001. BA, Columbia U., 1996; PhD in Math., U. Calif., San Diego, 2001—01. Faculty fellow U. Calif., San Diego, 2001—03; prin. rschr. US Census Bur., 2003—. Mem.: Am. Statis. Assn. (publs. officer, B & E sect. 2008—). Republican. Presbyterian. Achievements include invention of analytical methodology for rater reliability. Avocation: rock climbing. Office: US Census Bur 4600 Silver Hill Rd Washington DC 20233-0002 Office Phone: 301-763-3227. Personal E-mail: tsm2@columbia.edu. Business E-Mail: tucker.s.mcelroy@census.gov.

MCELVAIN, DAVID PLOWMAN, retired manufacturing, finance company executive; b. Chgo., Oct. 16, 1937; s. Carl R. and Ruth P. (Plowman) McE.; m. Mary Rosalind Hysong, Dec. 20, 1961; children: Jana, Jodi. BBA, U. Ariz., 1961, MBA, 1962. Cert. mgmt. acct. Consolidation acct., exec. divsn. Dresser Industries, Inc., Dallas, 1962-67, corp. fin. controller, 1973-76, dir. fin. svcs., 1976-78, staff v.p. fin. svc. and risk mgmt., 1978-82, exec. v.p. fin. svcs. group, 1982-83, pres. fin. svcs. group, 1984-86, v.p. fin., CFO, 1987-93; owner McElvain Oil Co., Dallas, 1993—. Controller crane, hoist & tower div., Muskegon, Mich., 1967-73. Mem. Nat. Assn. Accts., Beta Gamma Sigma, Phi Delta Theta. Episcopalian. Home: 14828 Bellbrook Dr Dallas TX 75254-7647 Personal E-mail: mcelvaincl@msn.com.

MCELVANY, ROCKY, state agency administrator; BS in Chemistry, U. Ctrl. Okla., Edmond; MS in Environ. Sci., U. Okla., Norman. Lab. analyst Okla. State Environ Lab., supr., environ. monitoring lab.; svc. chief Okla. Occupl. Licensing and Consumer Health Services; dep. commr., protective health svc. Okla. State Dept. Health, 2004—06, COO, 2006—, interim commr. health, 2009—. Okla. dept. health rep. Okla. Emergency Mgmt. Divsn. Named Lloyd Pummill Sanitarian of Yr., 1986. Mem.: Okla. Soc. Environ. Health Profls., Okla. Pub. Health Assn. (chmn., environ. sect.). Office: Okla State Dept Health 1000 NE 10th St Rm 305 Oklahoma City OK 73117-1299 Office Phone: 405-271-5600.*

MCELVEEN, JOSEPH JAMES, JR., journalist, writer, newscaster, educator; b. Sanford, Fla., Feb. 23, 1939; s. Joseph James Sr. and Genevieve (Stoll) McE.; m. Mary Louise Young, Aug. 18, 1979; 1 child, Ryan Leighton. BA, Furman U., 1961, MA, U.S.C., 1968. Editor, pub. West Ashley News, Charleston, SC, 1951-57; reporter, photographer Charleston Post, 1955-57; tchr. English and journalism St. Andrew's Parish High Sch., Charleston, 1961-65; dir. info., prof. journalism Columbia Coll., SC, 1965-68; prof. journalism U. S.C., Columbia, 1968-79; sr. pub. affairs specialist FCC, Washington, 1979-81; dir. pub. affairs adminstrn. Nat. Cable TV Assn., Washington, 1981-87; dir. internal communications Corp. for Pub. Broadcasting, Washington, 1987-92, dir. program adminstrn., 1992-96, sr. program officer, 1996-99; media/comms. cons. Vienna, Va., 1999—; tchr. English, Fairfax County Pub. Schs., Vienna, Va., 2002—. Ombudsman, columnist Alexandria Gazette, Va., 1981—88; pres. McElveen Seminars, Vienna, 2000—. Author: Introduction to Creative Writing, 1963, Modern Communications, 1964; contbr. chpt. to Dictionary of Literary Biography (Mencken), 1986, Words, Words, Words: A Journalist's Memoir, 1997, Effective Writing and Editing, 2000, 1940s: Decade on the Threshold, 2000. Mem. Orgn. of News Ombudsmen, Soc. Profl. Journalists, Mencken Soc. Episcopalian. Avocations: photography, reading, desktop pub. Office: 1807 Hursley Ct Vienna VA 22182-2105 Home Phone: 703-281-4237. Personal E-mail: jjmcelveen@aol.com.

MCELVEEN, JUNIUS CARLISLE, JR., lawyer; b. Rogersville, Tenn., Feb. 17, 1947; s. Junius Carlisle and Martha Kathleen (Harrison) McE.; m. Mary Wallace Pyles, Sept. 22, 1973; children: Kathryn Carlisle, Sarah Elizabeth. BA cum laude, U. Va., 1969, JD, 1972. Bar: Va. 1972, Calif. 1975, US Dist. Ct. (ea. dist.) Va. 1976, DC 1978, US Ct. Appeals (4th cir.) 1978, US Ct. Appeals (Fed. cir.) 1986, US Ct. Appeals (11th cir.) 1990. Rsch. assoc. Atlantic Richfield, Washington, 1972; assoc. Pender & Coward, Norfolk, Va., 1976-77; from assoc. to ptnr. Seyfarth, Shaw, Washington, 1977—83; ptnr. Jones Day, Washington, 1983—. Mem. adv. com., reproductive hazards in the workplace Office of Tech. Assessment, Washington, 1984-86; mem. adv. council Ctr. Environ. Health, U. Conn., 1986-95; mem. editorial bd. The Occupational and Environ. Medicine Report, 1986—2000, Human and Ecol. Risk Assessment, 1998—. Contbr. articles to legal jours. Elder Kirkwood Presbyn. Ch., Springfield, Va., 1984-86, Old Presby. Meeting House, Alexandria, Va., 2009-; docent Folger Shakespeare Libr., 2009-. Served as lt. USN, 1972-75, bd. dir. Wash. Map. Soc., 2005-, elder Old Presbyn. Meeting House, Va., 2009- Mem. ABA, Va. State Bar, State Bar Calif., Folger Shakespeare libr.(docent), Phi Beta Kappa, Phi Delta Phi (sec. local chpt. 1971-72, Outstanding Grad. award 1972). Home: 2121/2 S Pitt St Alexandria VA 22314 Office: Jones Day 51 Louisana Ave NW Washington DC 20001 Home Phone: 703-299-1719; Office Phone: 202-879-3726. Business E-Mail: jcmcelveen@jonesday.com.

MCELVEEN, WILLIAM LINDSAY, broadcast executive, educator; b. Columbia, SC, Sept. 20, 1950; s. Henry Moody and Dorothy Butler (Sligh) McE.; m. Laurie Wells Boyle, Sept. 8, 1969 (div. 1976); 1 child, Earle Sligh; m. Catharine Elizabeth McCaslin, Aug. 13, 1992; 1 child, Kerry Elizabeth McCaslin. BA in English, U. of South, 1972. Acct. exec. Stas. WNOK-FM, Columbia, SC, 1972-73, mng. dir., 1973-79; v.p., gen. mgr. Stas. WNOK-AM-FM, Columbia, 1979-84; pres. Audubon Broadcasting Co., Columbia, 1984-89, Radio South Carolina, Columbia, 1989—. Exec. dir. Bloomington Broadcasting Corp., 1998-2000; lectr. Internat. Media Fund, Washington, 1993—; v.p. s.e. region Citadel Broadcasting, 2000—. Chmn. bd. dirs. Columbia Urban League, 1983-85; bd. dirs. Crimestoppers of Midlands, 1984-88, S.C. Law Inst., Columbia, 1985-88, Helpline of Midlands, 1986-90, U. S.C. Coll. Journalism Partnership, 1996—, Greater Columbia C. of C., 2002-04, Children's Hosp. SC, 2006—; gen. campaign chair United Negro Coll. Fund, Columbia, 1985-86; mem. exec. com. United Way of Midlands, Columbia, 1987-88. Mem. Nat. Assn. Broadcasters (bd. dirs. 1988-92, 96—2000, 2008-, v.p. 1997-98, chmn. 1998-2000), S.C. Broadcasters Assn. (exec. com., bd. dirs. 1980-87, pres. 1985-86, Hall of Fame inductee 1996), Columbia Advt. Fedn. (pres. 1980-81), Media Club of Columbia (bd. dirs., pres. 1983-84). Presbyterian. Avocations: golf, tennis, travel. Office: Radio SC 1801 Charleston Hwy Cayce SC 29033-2019 Home: 23 Cedarwood Ln Columbia SC 29205-1925 Office Phone: 803-796-7600. Business E-Mail: bill.mcelveen@citcomm.com.

MCELVEEN-HUNTER, BONNIE, international relief organization executive; b. SC, Jan. 1945; m. Bynum Merritt Hunter, Sr.; 1 child, Bynum Merritt Hunter Jr. Grad., Stephens Coll., Columbia, Mo., 1972; LHD (hon.), NC State U., 2006; LLD (hon.), Pepperdine U., Graziadio Sch. Bus. and Mgmt., 2008. Founder, pres., CEO, owner Pace Mag. (now Pace Comm.), Greensboro, NC, 1973—; US amb. to Finland Dept. of State, Helsinki, 2001—03; nat. chair Am. Red Cross, Washington, 2004—. Chmn. Alexis de Tocqueville Soc., United Way Greater Greensboro, NC; bd. mem. United Way Am., chair nat. women's leadership giving campaign; chair Women in Philanthropy Summit, Washington; internat. bd. mem. Habitat for Humanity; bd. mem. Internat. Women Build Habitat for Humanity, Habitat for Humanity First Ladies Build; founder $1 Billion dollar Women's Leadership Initiative. Recipient Dr. Carl--Christian Rosenbröijer award, Woman Entrepreneur of the Yr. award, Nat. Found. for Women Legislatures, Nat. Athena award for bus. and civic contbn., US C. of C., Trailblazer of the Yr. award, Women Leaders Forum, Outstanding Bus. Leader award, Northwood U., Nat. Alexis de Tocqueville Soc. award, United Way, 2004, Ellis Island Medal of Honor, 2005, Appeal Conscience award Pub. Svc. award, 2006; named Comdr. Grand Cross Order of Lion, Pres. of Finland; named to Jr. Achievement Bus. Hall of Fame, 2004. Achievements include being the first woman to be selected as Chairman to the American Red Cross in it's 126-year history. Office: American Red Cross National Headquarters 2025 E St NW Washington DC 20006 also: Pace Comm 1301 Carolina St Greensboro NC 27401 Office Phone: 202-737-8300.

MCELVY, JAMES DOUGLAS, lawyer; BS, U. Ala., JD, 1971; student, St. Bernard Coll. Cert.: mediator, Am. Acad. of Atty. Mediators. Of counsel Azar & Azar LLC, Montomery, Ala. Bd. dir. Univ. Ala. Law Sch. Found.; trustee Ala. Law Found.; former chmn. Tuscaloosa Coalition for Character; former adj. prof. of law Univ. Ala. Sch. of Law; former prof., alternative dispute resolution Oak Brook Coll. of Law and Govt. Policy. Christian Legal Soc.; former deacon First Baptist Ch. of Tuscaloosa; former v.p. bd. dir. YMCA Metro. Mem.: Ala. State Bar Assn. (mem. bd. of bar commrs.-3 terms, exec. coun.-4 terms, v.p. 2002—03, pres.-elect 2003—04, pres. 2004—05), Tuscaloosa County Bar Assn. (sec. treas. 1989, pres.-elect 1990, pres. 1990—91, exec. com.). Office: Azar & Azar LLC Floor 4 2740 Zelda Rd Montgomery AL 36106 Office Phone: 334-265-8551. Office Fax: 334-261-3489. Business E-Mail: dmcelvy@azarlaw.com.

MCELWEE, ANDREW ALLISON, JR., insurance company executive; b. Dover, NJ, Apr. 10, 1955; s. Andrew Allison and Grace Lloyd (Lloyd) M.; m. Connie Chapman, May 24, 1980; children: Alexandra Chapman, Andrew Allison III. BA magna cum laude, Davidson Coll., NC, 1977; JD, U. Va., Charlottesville, 1980. Bar: NY 1981, NJ 1981, US Dist. Ct. (ea. and so. dists. NY). Assoc. Dewey, Ballantine, Bushby, Palmer & Wood, NYC, 1980-83, Morgan Stanley & Co. Inc., NYC, 1984-85; v.p. fin. Bellemead Devel. Corp., Roseland, NJ, 1985, exec v.p., 1995; sr. v.p. mergers and acquisitions Chubb Corp., 1997, internat. field ops. mgr., 2000—02, exec. v.p., mng. dir. Chubb & Son, COO Chubb Personal Ins., 2002—. Bd. dirs. Lamont Fin. Svcs., Inc., Essex Fells, NJ. Bd. dirs. World Impact, Inc., Newark, 1986; elder First Presbyn. Ch., Caldwell, NJ, 1983-87. Mem. ABA, NJ Bar Assn., NY Bar Assn. Office: Chubb Corp 15 Mountain View Rd Warren NJ 07059 Office Phone: 908-903-2000. Office Fax: 908-903-2027.

MCELWREATH, SALLY CHIN, corporate communications executive; b. NYC, Oct. 15, 1940; d. Toon Guey and Jean B. (Wong) Chin; m. Joseph F. Callo, Mar. 17, 1979; 1 child, R.J. McElwreath III. BA, Pace Coll., 1963; MBA, Pace U., 1969. Copywriter O.E. McIntyre, NYC, 1963-65; editl. asst. Sinclair Oil Corp., NYC, 1966-70; account exec. Muller, Jordan & Herrick, NYC, 1970-71; regional mgr. pub. rels. United Airlines, NYC, 1971-79; dir. corp. comm. Trans World Airlines, NYC, 1979-86; v.p. pub. rels. TWA Mktg. Svcs., Inc. The Travel Ch. Divsn., NYC, 1986-88; ptnr. The Comm. Group, NYC, 1988-90; gen. mgr. corp. comm. Ofcl. Airline Guides, 1990-91; v.p. corp. comm. Macmillan, Inc., 1991-93; cons. NYC, 1993-94; sr. v.p. corp. comm. Aquila Inc., 1994—2005; dir. USS New York Commn. Com., 2006—. Pub. affairs officer USNR, 1973-2000. Ret. Capt. Named Woman of Yr., YWCA, 1980, Alumnus of Yr., Pace U., 1976. Mem. N.Am. Pub. Rels. Assn. (vice chair 2003—), Wings Club (N.Y.C.) Nat. Press Club, Am. Friends Royal Naval Mus. (trustee). Personal E-mail: sallymc79@aol.com.

MCELYA, JAMES S., automotive executive; Student, West Chester U., Pa. Pres. Siebe Automotive Worldwide Invensys, PLC; various exec. mgmt. positions including pres. Automotive and corp. v.p. Handy & Harman; corp. v.p. Cooper Tire & Rubber Co.; pres. Cooper-Std. Automotive; pres., CEO Cooper-Std. Holdings, chmn., CEO, 2006—08, 2009—, exec. chmn., 2008—09. Bd. mem. Original Equipment Suppliers Assn., Rubber Mfrs. Assn.; adv. Nat. Alliance for Accessible Golf. Office: Coop-Std Holdings 39550 Orchard Hill Pl Novi MI 48375 Office Phone: 248-596-5900. Office Fax: 248-596-6535.*

MCENROE, JOHN PATRICK, JR., retired professional tennis player; b. Wiesbaden, Fed. Republic Germany, Feb. 16, 1959; s. John Patrick and Kathy McEnroe; m. Tatum O'Neil, Aug. 1, 1986 (div. 1994); children: Kevin, Sean, Emily; m. Patty Smyth, 1997; children: Anna, Ava 1 stepchild, Ruby. Grad., Trinity Sch., NYC, 1977; student, Stanford U. Winner numerous U.S. jr. singles and doubles titles; winner jr. titles French Mixed Doubles, 1977, French Jr. Singles, 1977; winner Nat. Coll. Athletic Assn. Intercollegiate U.S. Men's Singles title, 1978; professional tennis player, 1978-93; played on victorious U.S. Davis Cup Team, 1978, 79, 81, 82, 92; winner Grand Prix Masters Tournament, NYC, 1979, U.S. Open Men's Singles Championship, 1979, 80, 81, 84, World Championship Tennis Championship, 1979, 83, Wimbledon Singles, 1981, 83, 84, Tournament of Champions, 1981, 83, Wimbledon Doubles, 1992; winner (with Jonas Bjorkman) Doubles Title SAP Open, 2006; tennis sportscaster USA Network, 1993; host The Chair, 2002, McEnroe, 2004. Owner John McEnroe Gallery. Co-author (with James Kaplan): (autobiography) You Cannot Be Serious, 2000; author: Serious, 2003. Inducted, Tennis Hall of Fame, 1999. Mem: Men's Seniors' Tour Circuit, 1994. Achievements include winner 21 Singles Titles, Sr. Champions Tour, 1998-2005.

MCENROE, PATRICK, former professional tennis player, sports commentator; b. Manhasset, NY, July 1, 1966; s. John Patrick Sr. and Katy McEnroe. Grad., Stanford Univ. Doubles winner French Open, 1989; winner ATP tournament, Sydney, Australia, 1995. Mem. US Davis Cup team, 1993, 94, 96, captain, 2001—04; commentator CBS Sports and ESPN, 1998—; bd. dir. US Tennis Assn, 1999—2000; player, partial owner NY Sportimes, World Team Tennis; US Olympics Men's Tennis coach, Athens, Greece, 2004; guest host Pardon the Interruption, ESPN; analyst ESPN First Take. Author: (books) Tennis for Dummies, 1998. Achievements include ranked 12th, US Tennis Assn., 1991; ranked 664th, 1999. Office: Sportime at Harbor Island PO Box 783 Mamaroneck NY 10543

MCENTEE, GERALD W., labor union administrator; b. Phila., Jan. 11, 1935; m. Barbara McEntee; 4 children. B in Econs., LaSalle U., Phila., 1956; student, Temple U., Phila.; grad. trade union prog., Harvard U. Labor leader AFSCME, Pa., 1957, exec. dir. Dist. Coun. 13 Harrisburg, Pa., 1973, internat. v.p., mem. exec. bd., 1974, internat. pres. Washington, 1981—. V.p., mem. exec. coun., chair polit. edn. com. AFL-CIO; co-founder, chmn. Econ. Policy Inst., Washington; mem. Presdl. Adv. Commn. Quality & Consumer Protection in Health Care Industry, 1997. Contbg. writer Huffington Post. Mem. Dem. Nat. Com. Recipient Hubert H. Humphrey award, Leadership Conf. on Civil Rights, 2004. Office: AFSCME 1625 L St NW Washington DC 20036-5687 Office Phone: 202-429-1000. Office Fax: 202-429-1293. Business E-Mail: gmcentee@afscme.org.*

MCEVOY, SHARLENE ANN, law educator; b. Derby, Conn., July 6, 1950; d. Peter Henry Jr. and Madaline Elizabeth (McCabe) McE. BA magna cum laude, Albertus Magnus Coll., 1972; JD, U. Conn., West Hartford, 1975; MA, Trinity Coll., Hartford, 1980, UCLA, 1982, PhD, 1985. Bar: Conn., 1975. Pvt. practice, Derby, 1984—; asst. prof. bus. law Fairfield (Conn.) U. Sch. Bus., 1986—92; adj. prof. bus. law, polit. sci. Albertus Magnus Coll., New Haven, 1978-80, U. Conn., Stamford, 1984-86; acting chmn. polit. sci. dept. Albertus Magnus Coll., 1980; assoc. prof. law Fairfield U., 1992-98, prof. bus. law, 1998—. Chmn. Women's Resource Ctr., Fairfield U., 1989-91. Staff editor Jour. Legal Studies Edn., 1989-94; reviewer Am. Bus. Law Assn. jour., 1988—, staff editor, 1995—; sr. articles editor N.E. Jour. Legal Studies in Bus., 1995-96; editor-in-chief N.E. Jour. Legal Studies, 2003—. Active Derby Tercentennial Commn., 1973—74; justice of the peace City of Derby, 1975—83; alt. mem. Parks and Recreation Commn., Woodbury, 1995—99; v.p. N.E. Acad. Legal Studies in Bus., 2001—02, 2006—, pres., 2003—04, pres, 2008—09, program chair, 2007—08; treas. Woodbury Dem. Town Com., 1995—96, corr. sec., 1996—98; bd. dirs. Valley Transit Dist., Derby, 1975—77. Recipient Best Paper award N.E. Regional Bus. Law Assn., 1990, Best Paper award Tri-State Regional Bus. Law Assn., 1991; Fairfield U. Sch. Bus. rsch. grantee 1989, 91, 92, Fairfield U. rsch. grantee, 1994. Mem. ABA, Conn. Bar Assn., Acad. Legal Studies in Bus., Mensa (coord. SINISTRAL spl. interest group 1977—). Democrat. Roman Catholic. Avocations: sailing, tennis, swimming. Office: 198 Emmett Ave Derby CT 06418-1258 Office Phone: 203-254-4000 ext. 2836. Business E-Mail: samcevoy@mail.fairfield.edu.

MCEWEN, ALEXANDER CAMPBELL, legal association administrator, consultant, cadastral studies educator, former Canadian government official, land use planner; b. Ryde, Isle of Wight, Eng., Aug. 22, 1926; emigrated to Can., 1949; s. Walter Scott and Florence Lilian (Goodall) McE.; m. Patricia Stuart Richards, July 27, 1956 (div. 1988); m. Sherry Lee Wilson, June 13, 1993; children: Ann Florence, Sheila Jean, Laura Susan. LL.B., U. London, 1966, PhD, 1979; LL.M., U. East Africa, 1970. Survey adviser Govt. Can., Jesselton, 1954-56; tech. expert UN, Victoria, Seychelles, 1958-61; sr. surveyor H. Wheeler Assocs., Toronto, Ont., Can., 1961-62; sec. treas. Assn. Ont. Land Surveyors, Toronto, 1963-64; prin. Survey Tng. Centre, Dar es Salaam, Tanzania, 1964-70; survey cons. Ottawa, Ont., Can., 1970-72; dir. lands and surveys Govt. Nfld., St. John's, 1972-76; commr. Internat. Boundary Commn., Ottawa, Ont., 1976-90; survey adviser Govt. Can., Lagos, Nigeria, 1989-90; prof. cadastral studies dept. geomatics engring. U. Calgary, Alta., Canada, 1991—96; survey cons. Can. Exec. Svc. Orgn., La Paz, Bolivia, 2002—03; pvt. practice Calgary, Canada, 2004—. Cons. in field. Author: International Boundaries of East Africa, 1971 In Search of the Highlands, 1988; contbr. articles to profl. jours. Served with Royal Armoured Corp., NW Europe, 1943-45, Palestine, 1945-47. Mem. Can. Inst. Geomatics (mem. coun. 1977-81, 97-2002, Jim Jones award 1967, 83, 90, 99, 2006, Presdl. citation 1981), Western Can. Bd. Examiners for Land Surveyors (registrar, bd. dirs. 1991-96), Assn. Ont. Land Surveyors (sec.-treas. 1963-64), Assn. Nfld. Land Surveyors (bd. examiners 1975-76). Home: 2129 2d Ave NW Calgary AB Canada T2N OG8 Office Phone: 403-283-9087. Personal E-mail: amcewen@telusplanet.net.

MCEWEN, DORIS ANN, education educator; b. Oxford, Miss., Aug. 6, 1950; d. Earnest Jr. and Mildred (Blackmon) McEwen; m. Grady Walker Jr., June 19, 1971 (div. Aug. 1990); children: Maleika René, Cheo Da'Mu; m. Jerry E. Harris, Aug. 26, 2006. BS, No. Mich. U., 1971; MS, Mich. State U., 1975, PhD, 1981. Cert. tchr. 7-12, secondary adminstr. 5-12, supt. endorsement, Mich.; tchr., adminstr., Nev.; secondary adminstr., supt., Ind., Wash. Tchr. Flint (Mich.) Sch. Dist., 1972; tchr., sch. adminstr. Lansing (Mich.) Sch. Dist., 1973-86; prof. U. Nev., Reno, 1986-88, 96—; asst. prin. Waverly H.S., Lansing, 1988-91; prin. East Lansing (Mich.) H.S., 1991-94; assoc. prof. Ind. U., South Bend, 1994-96; asst. supt. Edmonds Sch. Dist. 15, Lynnwood, Wash., 1996—; supt. Clover Pk. Sch. Dist., Lakewood, Wash., 2000—. Edn. cons. Nev. State Dept. Edn., Carson City, 1986-88 Contbr. articles to profl. jours. Bd. dirs. Lansing Art Gallery, Neutral Zone, Wash., YWCA Pathways for Women, South Bend (Ind.) Meml. Hosp., Spice of Life, Ind.; past advisor Boy Scouts Am.; cadette leader Mich. Capitol Girl Scouts; mem. nominating bd. YWCA; trustee meml. Hosp.; mem. urban youth adv. bd. YMCA. Mem. ASCD, NAACP, Nat. Assn. Secondary Sch. Prins., Nat. Alliance Black Sch. Educators, Am. Assn. Sch. Adminstrs., Mich. Assn. Secondary Sch. Prins., Ind. Assn. Secondary Sch. Prins., Optimist Club, Clover Pk. Rotary, Phi Delta Kappa, Delta Sigma Theta. Avocations: reading, computers, multimedia. Home: 12775 Gravelly Lake Dr SW Lakewood WA 98499-1459 E-mail: mcewendoris@hotmail.com.

MCEWEN, LAURA ELLEN, publishing executive; b. 1959; d. Robert and Roslyn Farbman; m. James Wallace McEwen; 1 child, Sean. BA in Media Studies, Fordham U., NY. Advt. dir. to assoc. pub. New Woman mag.; pub. Snow Country mag.; sr. pub. Family Circle mag. Meredith Corp.; v.p., assoc. pub. Harpers Bazaar Hearst Corp.; pub. YM mag., 2000—03; v.p., pub. dir. Readers Digest, 2003—06; advt. dir. beauty Vogue Condé Nast Publs., 2006—08, assoc. pub., 2008, pub. Teen Vogue, 2008—. Mem. planning com. Mag. Pub. America, 2003. Mem.:

Fragrance Found., NY Advt. Club, Advt. Women NY, Fashion Grp. Internat. (bd. dirs.), Cosmetic Exec. Women (bd. dirs.). Office: Teen Vogue 4 Times Sq New York NY 10036 Office Phone: 212-286-7694.*

MCEWEN, MEGAN, research scientist; d. William and Florence McEwen; m. Thomas Moran; 1 child, Luna Moran. PhD, La. State U., Baton Rouge, 2007. Rsch. asst. La. State U., 1999—2007; postdoc. rsch. assoc. U. Alcala Henares, Madrid, Spain, 2007—. Contbr. articles to profl. jours. Achievements include research in the origins of ultra-high energy cosmic rays.

MCFADDEN, CORI ERIN, psychotherapist, educator; b. Woodbury, NJ, Feb. 25, 1975; d. John Thomas and Linnea Maska McFadden; m. Paul Edward McMahon, June 14, 2003. MA in clin. Counseling Psychology, La Salle U., Phila., 2001; PsyD in Clin. Psychology, La Salle U., 3Phila., 2003. Staff clinician, psychotherapist Cmty. Treatment Solutions, Moorestown, NJ, 2003—05, interim dir., 2005; psychotherapist Friends Hosp., Phila., 2005; psychology prof. - part time La Salle U., Phila., 2002—, adj. faculty psychology. Assessment lab coord.; admissions counselor. Mem. Rebuilding Together of Gloucester County, NJ; alumni coun. chairperson Friends Sch., Mullica Hill, NJ, 2004—06. Recipient Grad. Student of the Yr., La Salle U. Dept. of Grad. Psychology, 2001. Mem.: APA (assoc.), Pa. Psychol. Assn. (assoc.), Assn. for Behavior and Cognitive Therapy (assoc.), Rotary Internat. Wooddbury Breakfast Club, Psi Chi (life). Independent. Avocations: travel, art museums, bicycling. Office: La Salle University 1900 West Olney Ave Philadelphia PA 19141 Personal E-mail: coridoc@aol.com. E-mail: mcfadden@lasalle.edu.

MCFADDEN, DANIEL LITTLE, economist, educator; b. Raleigh, NC, July 29, 1937; s. Robert S. and Alice (Little) McFadden; m. Beverlee Tito Simboli, Dec. 15, 1962; children: Nina, Robert, Raymond. BS in physics, U. Minn., 1957, PhD in econs., 1962; LLD, U. Chgo., 1992; degree (hon.), U. Coll. London, 2003; PhD in Sci. (hon.), No. Carolina St. Univ., 2006. Asst. prof. econs. U. Pitts., 1962-63, U. Calif., Berkeley, 1963—66, assoc. prof. econs, 1966—68, prof., 1968—79, E. Morris Cox Chair, prof. econs. Coll. Letters & Sci., 1991—, dir. Econometrics Lab., 1991—95, 1996—, chmn. dept. of econ., 1995—96; vis. assoc. prof. U. Chgo., 1966—67; Irving Fisher research prof. Yale U., New Haven, 1977—78; prof. econs. MIT, Cambridge, Mass., 1978—91, James R. Killian Chair, 1984—91, dir. Stats. Rsch. Ctr. Cambridge, Mass., 1986—88; Sherman Fairchild Disting. Scholar Calif. Inst. Tech., 1990. Mem. econs. adv. panel NSF, 1969—71, Univs. Nat. Bur., 1974—77; chmn. NSF-NBER Conf. Econs. of Uncertainty, 1970—; bd. dirs. Nat. Bur. Econ. Rsch., 1976—77, 1980—83; mem. book com. Sloan Found., 1977—79; mem. rev. com. Calif. Energy Com. Forecasts, 1979; chmn. awards com. AEA, 1981—84. Editor: Jour. Statis. Physics, 1968—70, Econometric Soc. monographs, 1980—83; mem. bd. editors Am. Econ. Rev., 1971—74, Jour. Math. Econs., 1973—77, Transp. Rsch., 1978—80; assoc. editor: Jour. Econometrics, 1977—78; adv. com. Jour. Applied Econs., 1996—; co-editor: Essays on Economic Behavior Under Uncertainty, 1974, Production Economics, Vols. I and II, 1978, Structural Analysis of Discrete Data with Econometric Applications, 1981, Preferences, Uncertainty, and Optimality, 1990, Handbook of Econometrics Vol. IV, 1994; co-author: Urban Travel Demand: A Behavioral Analysis, 1975, Microeconomic Modeling and Policy Analysis, 1984. Mem. adv. com. Transp. Models Project, Met. Transp. Commn., 1975, City of Berkeley Coordinated Transit Project, 1975—76. Recipient Outstanding Tchr. Award, MIT, 1981, Nobel Prize in Econs., 2000, Nemmers prize in Econs., Northwestern U., 2000, Richard Stone prize in Applied Econs., Jour. Applied Econmtrics, 2000—01; Ford Found. Behavioral Sci. Fellow, 1958—62, Earhart Fellow, 1960—61, Mellon Post-Doctoral Fellow, 1962—63, Ford Faculty Rsch. Fellow, 1966—67. Mem.: NAS (mem. com. basic rsch. social scis. 1982—87, mem. com. energy demand modelling 1983—84, mem. commn. behavioral and social scis. and edn. 1989—94, mem. commn. sci. engring., pub. policy 1995—, chair sect. 54 econ. scis. 2003—, chair com. forecasting demand/supply of doctoral scientists and engrs. 1997—2000), Am. Phil. Soc., Transp. Rsch. Bd. (mem. exec. com. 1975—78), Math. Assn. Am., Am. Statis. Assn., Econometrics Soc. (Fisher-Schultz lectr. 1979, mem. exec. com. 1983—86, v.p. 1984, pres. 1985, fellow 1969, Frisch Medal 1986), Am. Econ. Assn. (mem. exec. com. 1985—87, v.p. 1994, pres.-elect 2004, John Bates Clark Medal 1975), Am. Acad. Arts and Scis. Democrat. Avocations: bicycling, tennis, squash, sailing, skiing. Office: U Calif Berkeley Dept Econs 549 Evans Hall # 3880 Berkeley CA 94720-3880 Office Phone: 510-643-8428. Office Fax: 510-642-0638. Business E-Mail: mcfadden@econ.berkeley.edu.*

MCFADDEN, DARREN, professional football player; b. North Little Rock, Ark., Aug. 27, 1987; s. Graylon McFadden and Mini Muhammad. Student, U. Ark., 2005—08. Running back Oakland Raiders, 2008—. Featured on the covers of Sports Illus. and ESPN Mag. Recipient Doak Walker award, 2006, 2007, Walter Camp Player of Yr. award, 2007; named SEC Offensive Player of Yr., 2006, 2007, Nat. Player of the Yr., The Sporting News, 2007, First Team All-American, AP, 2007. Achievements include being the first sophomore to win the Doak Walker award; becoming only the second two-time winner of the Doak Walker award, joining Ricky Williams; becoming only the second running back in the Razorbacks' history to rush for 1,000 yards or more in three consecutive years; becoming the all-time rusher in the University of Arkansas' history with 4,485 yards. Office: Oakland Raiders 1220 Harbor Bay Pkwy Alameda CA 94502*

MCFADDEN, DENNIS, psychologist, educator; b. Oakland, Calif., Oct. 2, 1940; s. Samuel John and Evelyn (Dinnerson) McF.; m. Nancy L. Wilson, Dec. 28, 1960; children: Tracie Ann, Devin James. BA, Sacramento State Coll., 1962; PhD, Ind U., 1967. Asst. prof. U. Tex., Austin, 1967-72, assoc. prof., 1972-77, prof., 1977—, Piper prof., 1987, Ashbel Smith prof., 1998—. Contbr. articles to profl. jours. Recipient Jacob K. Javits Neurosci. Investigator award, NIH, 1984-89, Claude Pepper award of Excellence, 1989-91; NIH grantee. Fellow AAAS, Acoustical Soc. Am., Am. Psychol. Soc.; mem. Assn. for Rsch. in Otolarynology, Com. Hearing, Bioacoustics and Biomechanics (NAS-NRC com. on hearing, bioacoustics and biomechanics), Soc. Neurosci., Soc. for Behavioral Neuroendocrinology, Internat. Acad. for Sex Rsch., Orgn. for Study of Sex Differences. Avocations: jogging, bicycling, birdwatching, travel. Office: U Tex Dept Psychology 1 University Station Seay Bldg A 8000 Austin TX 78712-0187 Business E-Mail: mcfadden@psy.utexas.edu.

MCFADDEN, FRANK HAMPTON, lawyer, former judge; b. Oxford, Miss., Nov. 20, 1925; s. John Angus and Ruby (Roy) McF.; m. Jane Porter Nabers, Sept. 30, 1960; children— Frank Hampton, Angus Nabers, Jane Porter. BA, U. Miss., 1950; LL.B., Yale U., 1955. Bar: N.Y. 1956, Ala. 1959. Assoc. firm Lord, Day & Lord, NYC, 1955-58, Bradley, Arant, Rose & White, Birmingham, Ala., 1958-63, partner, 1963-69; judge U.S. Dist. Ct. No. Dist. Ala., Birmingham, 1969-73, chief judge, 1973-81; sr. v.p., gen. counsel Blount, Inc., Montgomery, Ala., 1982-91, exec. v.p. adminstrn. and govt. affairs, 1991, exec. v.p. legal affairs, 1991-93, exec. v.p., gen. counsel, 1993-95; mem. Capell & Howard, P.C., Montgomery, 1995—. Chmn. Blount Energy Resource Corp., Montgomery, 1983-88. Mem. jud. panel CPR Inst. for Dispute Resolution, 1985—. Served from ensign to lt. USNR, 1944-49, 51-53. Fellow Am. Coll. Constrn. Lawyers; mem. Am. Corp. Counsel Assn. (bd. dirs. 1984-93, chmn. 1989). Office: Capell & Howard PC 150 S Perry St Montgomery AL 36104-4227 Home Phone: 334-241-3700; Office Phone: 334-241-8041. Business E-Mail: fhm@chlaw.com.

MC FADDEN, GEORGE LINUS, retired army officer; b. Sharon, Pa., Oct. 16, 1927; s. George Linus and Frances Jane (Byrne) McF.; m. Floretta Theresa McFadden, Nov. 20, 1948; children: Kenneth William, Mark Edward (dec.), Mary Kathleen, Robert Bernard, George Linus, William. BE, U. Omaha, Nebr., 1961; MS, George Washington U., Washington, 1967; grad., Advanced Mgmt. Program Harvard U., Cambridge, Mass., 1971. Pvt. U.S. Army, 1946, advanced through grades to maj. gen., 1976; comdg. officer (7th inf. div. arty.), Korea, 1969-70; dep. comdg. gen. U.S. Army Security Agy., Arlington, Va., 1972-74; dep. dir. for field mgmt. and evaluation, dep. chief central security service Fort George G. Meade, Md., 1975-78; dep. dir. ops. Nat. Security Agy., 1978-79; comdg. gen. U.S. Army So. European Task Force, Vicenza, Italy, 1979-82; corp. v.p. CompuDyne Corp., 1986-89; sr. v.p. The Abbott Group, Inc., Annapolis, Md., 1989-90; dir. Washington Studies and Analysis Group McDonnell Douglas Corp., 1985-86; dir. security affairs Dept. Energy, 1990-97, cons., 1999—. Pres., chmn. bd. Met. Washington chpt. Arthritis Found., 1986-95. Decorated D.F.C., D.S.M., Silver Star, Bronze Star, Purple Heart, others. Roman Catholic. Personal E-mail: mcfaddengl@verizon.net.

MCFADDEN, JOHN VOLNEY, retired manufacturing company executive; b. NYC, Oct. 3, 1931; s. Volney and Mary Lucile (McConkie) McF.; m. Marie Linstead, June 27, 1953; children— Deborah, John Scott, David. BS in Commerce and Fin, Bucknell U., 1953; JD, Detroit Coll. Law, 1960. Pres., vice chmn. MTD Products, Inc., Cleve., 1960-92; pres. MTD Products Inc., Cleve., 1980-91, vice chmn., 1990-92; gen. ptnr. Camelot Ptnrs., Cleve.; pres. Parkside Acquisition Ptnrs. Ltd., Cleve., 1997—. Bd. dirs. Fusion Inc., Flambeau Corp., Hinkley Lighting, Inc., SGS Tool Co.; past chmn. financing adv. bd. State of Ohio Devel.; past pres. Cleve. World Trade Assn. Trustee Cleve. Eye Bank, former trustee Fairview Health Svcs, Cleve. Clinic. Lt. Supply Corps, USN. Mem. Cleve. Yachting Club. Office: Parkside Acq Ptnrs Ltd 20160 Parkside Dr Cleveland OH 44116-1347

MC FADDEN, JOSEPH MICHAEL, historian, educator; b. Joliet, Ill., Feb. 12, 1932; s. Francis Joseph and Lucille (Adler) McF.; m. Norma Cardwell, Oct. 11, 1958; children: Timothy Joseph, Mary Colleen, Jonathan Andrew. BA, Lewis Coll., 1954; MA, U. Chgo., 1961; PhD, No. Ill. U., 1968. Tchr. history Joliet Cath. High Sch., 1957-60; mem. faculty history dept. Lewis Coll., Lockport, Ill., 1960-70, asso. prof., 1967-70, v.p. acad. affairs, 1968-70; prof. history, dean sch. Nat. and Social Sci., Kearney (Nebr.) State Coll., 1970-74; prof. history, dean Sch. Social and Behavioral Scis., Slippery Rock (Pa.) State Coll., 1974-77; pres. No. State Coll., Aberdeen, SD, 1977-82, U. S.D., Vermillion, 1982-88, U. St. Thomas, Houston, 1988-97, pres. emeritus, prof. history, 1997—2007. Served with USNR, 1954-56. Roman Catholic. Office Phone: 713-942-5905. Business E-Mail: mcfadden@stthon.edu.

MCFADDEN, JOSEPH PATRICK, bishop; b. Phila., May 22, 1947; BS, St. Joseph's U., 1969; MDiv, St. Charles Borromeo Sem., 1981. Ordained priest Archdiocese of Phila., 1981, aux. bishop, 2004—; deacon Our Lady of Fatima Parish, Secane, Pa.; parochial vicar St. Laurence Parish, Highland Park, Pa., 1981—82; adminstrv. sec. to Cardinal Krol, 1982—93; pres. Cardinal O'Hara HS, Springfield, Pa., 1993—2001; pastor St. Joseph. Parish, Downinggtown, 2001—04; ordained bishop, 2004. Tchr., basketball coach West Cath. HS, Phila., 1969—76. Roman Catholic. Office: Archdiocese of Phila 222 N 17th St Philadelphia PA 19103-1299 Office Phone: 215-965-8280. Office Fax: 215-965-8283. E-mail: bjmcfadd@adphila.org.

MCFADDEN, LEE VERNON, religious organization administrator; b. Manning, SC, Jan. 5, 1968; s. Daisy Rena and Aaron McFadden; m. Landa LaYota Montgomery, July 22, 2001; children: Ricky Antonio Montgomery-McFadden, Lee Vernon Jr., Aliaya Chanell, Destiny Le'anda. B in Bus. Adminstrn., Trinity U., Sioux Falls, SD, 1999. Founder, CEO Youth Ministry Tng. Corps, Sumter, SC, 1996—. Prodr.(composer,musician,choreographer): Testimony. Musician St. Mark Bapt. Ch., Silver, SC, 2006—06. Recipient Dedication and Leadership to Youths award, 2005. Mem.: Alpha Phi Omega.

MCFADDEN, MARY JOSEPHINE, fashion industry executive; b. NYC, Oct. 1, 1938; d. Alexander Bloomfield and Mary Josephine (Cutting) McF.; m. Philip Harari; 1 child, Justine. Student, Sorbonne, Paris, Traphagen Sch. Design, 1957, Columbia, 1959-62; DFA, Internat. Fine Arts Coll., 1984. Pub. rels. dir. Christian Dior, NYC, 1962—64; merchandising editor Vogue South Africa, 1964—65, editor, 1965—69; polit. and travel columnist Rand Daily Mail (South Africa), 1965—68; founder sculptural workshop Vukutu, Zimbabwe, 1968—70; spl. projects editor Vogue U.S.A., 1973; pres. Mary McFadden, Inc., NYC, 1976—; ptnr. MMcF Collection by Mary McFadden, 1991—; with Isate U. Archeology Penn. U., 2009. Bd. dirs., advisor Sch. Design and Merchandising Kent State U., Eugene O'Neill Meml. Theatre Ctr.; mem. profl. com. Cooper-Hewitt Mus., Smithsonian Inst., Nat. Mus. of Design; designer Collection by Mary McFadden, 2000, Mary McFadden Collection, 2003, Earth-BOUND, N.Y.C., 2003; dir. Musical Festival Ancient Instruments Mahaswhar, Indore, India, 2002-09; lectr. U. Phila., 2004, Dept. Ancient Near Eastern Art, Met. Mus. Art, 2004, Sackler Mus., Japan Soc., 2004, U. Archeology and Anthropology, Pa., 2005, Newark Mus., 2005, Freer Gallery, 2006, RMA, N.Y., 2006, Parrish Mus., 2006, CUNY Grad. Sch., 2006, Phipps Westbury Gardens, 2006, Rubin Mus., Queens Coll., NYC, Preservation Soc., Newport, RI, 2007; lectr. Bing Auditoriam LACMA, LA. Fashion and jewelry designer, 1973—; maj. retrospective of fashion, textiles and jewels at Allentown (Pa.) Art Mus., 2004, Ursuline Coll., 2007; author introduction Mary McFadden High Priestess of High Fashion, 2004; artist (exhbn.) Allentown Mus., 2005, Dixon Mus. and Garden, Memphis, 2005, 06, Retrospective More Coll. Art, Phila., 2008, Retrospective show, Gold Collection Exhibited Ancient Textiles Collection, Nat. Womens Museum Arts Wash., DC, 2009. Advisor Nat. Endowment for Arts; active local Police Athletic League, We Care About N.Y., CFDA-Vogue Breast Cancer Initiative, Beth Israel Hosp., The Chemotherapy Found.; curator emeritus Lannan Found., 1973-85; founding trustee Robert Redford's Sundance Inst., 1978-83; trustee Devi Ahilya Bai Holkal Meml. Charitable Trust, Maheshwar, Indore, India. Recipient Am. Fashion Critics award-Coty award, 1976, 78, 79, Audemars Piguet Fashion award, 1976, Rex award, 1977, award More Coll. Art, 1977, Pa. Gov.'s award, 1977, Roscoe award, 1978, Pres.'s Fellows award RISD, 1979, Neiman-Marcus award of excellence, 1979, Design Excellence award Pratt Inst., 1993, award N.Y. Landmarks Conservancy, 1994, NU Breed Fashion award, 1996, Marymount Coll. Fashion award, 1996, Legends award N.Y., 2001, Lifetime Achievement award South Am. Press Assn., Miami, Fla., 2002, Pratt Legions award, 2002, Spirit of Design award Phila. U., 2004, Visionary Woman award More Coll., Phila., 2008; named to Fashion Hall of Fame, 1979; fellow RISD. Mem. Fashion Group (bd. dirs. 1981-82), Council of Fashion Designers Am. (past pres., I Can award). Office: Mary McFadden Inc 525 E 72nd St New York NY 10021

MCFADDEN, NANCY ELIZABETH, utilities executive; b. Wilmington, Del., Oct. 20, 1958; d. William P. and Mary Elizabeth (Adams) McF. BA, San Jose State U., Calif., 1984; JD, U. Va., Charlottesville, 1987. Jud. clk. to Hon. John P. Wiese US Claims Ct., Washington, 1987-88; atty. O'Melveny & Myers, Washington, 1988-91; deputy comm. dir. Office of Pres.-Elect, Washington, 1992-93; asst. atty. gen. US Dept. Justice, Washington, 1993, prin. dep. assoc. atty. gen., 1993-95; gen. counsel Dept. Transp., Washington, 1996—2000; dep. chief of staff V.P. Al Gore, Washington; sr. advisor, dep. chief of staff Gov. Gray Davis Adminstrn., Calif.; with Gov. Arnold Schwarzenegger Adminstrn., Calif.; sr. v.p. pub. affairs PG&E Corp., San Francisco. Nat. dep. polit. dir. Clinton for Pres. Campaign, 1992, nat. surrogate dir. Clinton-Gore for Pres. Campaign, 1992; bd. trustees Calif. Mus. for History, Women and the Arts. Named one of 40 Best Lawyers Under 40, Washingtonian mag. Office: PG&E Corp One Market Spear Tower Ste 2400 San Francisco CA 94105-1126 Office Phone: 415-267-7070. Office Fax: 415-267-7268.

MCFADDEN, P. MICHAEL, physician, surgeon; b. Hobbs, N.Mex., June 16, 1946; s. Paul Marion and Venita Lenora (Bowen) McF.; m. Jennifer Marie James, Apr. 8, 1990; children: Heather Anne, Jennifer Suzanne, Bryn Ellen, Callan Michael. BS, La. State U., 1968; MD, Tulane U., 1974. Diplomate Am. Bd. Surgery, Am. Bd. Thoracic Surgery. Surg. intern, resident Tulane U. Sch. Medicine, New Orleans, 1974-79, instr. surgery, 1974-79, clin. prof. surgery, 1991—; resident in thoracic surgery Ochsner Clinic, New Orleans, 1979-81, cardiovascular and thoracic surgeon, 1991—2006, surg. dir. lung transplantaion, 1991—2006, dir. thoracic surgery program, 1998—2006; cardiovascular and thoracic surgeon Stanford U. Hosp., Calif., 1981-91; chief cardiovascular surgery Palo Alto Med. Clinic, Calif., 1983-91; prof. cardiothoracic surgery, surg. dir. lung transplantation Keck Sch. Medicine, U. So. Calif., 2006—. Contbr. articles to profl. jours. Bd. dirs. YMCA, Palo Alto area, 1988-91; bd. dirs. U. Tulane Health Svcs., 2006—. Capt USNR, 1984-94. Fellow ACS, Am. Coll. Cardiology, Am. Coll. Chest Physicians; mem. AMA, Alton Ochsner Surg. Soc., Am. Assn. for Thoracic Surgery, Am. Soc. Vascular Surgery, Am. Soc. Transplant Surgeons, Am. Heart Assn. (coun. on cardiovascular surgery), Assn. Mil. Surgeons U.S., Internat. Soc. for Cardiovascular Surgery, Internat. Soc. for Heart and Lung Transplantation, Norman E. Shumway Surg. Soc., Pacific Coast Surg. Assn., So. Surg. Assn., So. Thoracic Surg. Assn., Thoracic Surgery Found., Tulane Surg. Soc., Tulane U. Med. Alumni Assn., Western Thoracic Surg. Assn., Alpha Omega Alpha, Alpha Epsilon Delta, Nu Sigma Nu, Kappa Alpha. Republican. Presbyterian. Office: Dept Cardiothoracic Surgery U So Calif Keck Sch Medicine 1520 San Pablo St Ste 4300 Los Angeles CA 90033 Office Phone: 323-442-5849. Business E-Mail: mmcfadden@surgery.usc.edu.

MCFADDEN, PETER WILLIAM, retired mechanical engineering educator; b. Stamford, Conn., Aug. 2, 1932; s. Kenneth E. and Marie (Gleason) McF.; children: Peter, Kathleen, Mary. BSME, U. Conn., 1954, MS, 1956; PhD, Purdue U., 1959. Registered profl. engr., Ind. Asst. instr. U. Conn., 1954-56, prof. mech. engring., 1971-98, dean Sch. Engring., 1971-85, dir. devel., 1985-88, provost, v.p., 1988, exec. asst. to pres., exec. sec. to bd. trustees, 1989-98; mem. faculty Purdue U., 1956-71; prof. mech. engring., head Purdue U. (Sch. Mech. Engring.), 1965-71; postdoctoral research Swiss Fed. Inst., Zurich, 1960-61. Cons. to industry, 1959-98. Achievements include research in cryogenics, heat transfer, mass transfer.

MCFADDEN, ROBERT DENNIS, reporter; b. Milw., Feb. 11, 1937; s. Francis Joseph and Violet (Charleston) McF.; m. Judith Marian Silverman, June 20, 1971; 1 son, Nolan Seth. BS cum laude, U. Wis., 1960. Reporter Wis. Rapids Daily Tribune, 1957-58, Wis. State Jour., Madison, 1958-59, Cin. Enquirer, 1960-61; sr. writer, reporter New York Times, 1961—. Mem. adv. coun. St. John's U. dept journalism, 1996-. Co-author: No Hiding Place, 1981, Outrage: The Story Behind the Tawana Brawley Hoax, 1990. With US Army, 1960—61, with USAR, 1961—68. Recipient Pulitzer Prize for Spot News Reporting (N.Y. Times team), 1994, (individual) 1996; Byline award N.Y. Press Club, 1973, 74, 80, 87, 89, 92, Page One award Newspaper Guild N.Y., 1978, Spot News award Uniformed Firemen's Assn., 1967, Spot News award L.I. Press Club, 1984, 95, Chancellor's award for Disting. Svc. U. Wis., 1987, Man of Yr. award Alumni N.Y., 1997, Excellence in Local Reporting award N.Y. Newpaper Publishers Assn., 1988, Spot News award N.Y. Newspaper Publishers Assn., 1988, Spot News award N.Y. State Associated Press, 1989, 91, Continuing Coverage award, 1995, 99, In Depth Reporting award, 1989, 91, Feature Writing award, 1996, Ochs Prize in Journalism, 1989, Best News/Feature Story award Internat. Assn. Fire Fighters, 1991, Nat. Spot News award Asian-Am. Journalists Assn., 1994, Comprehensive Reporting award, N.Y. Uniformed Fire Officers Assn., 1995. Mem. N.Y. Soc. Silurians (Spot News Story award 1977, 2001, Peter Kihss award 1987, Investigative reporting award 1989, Excellence in Journalism award 1994, President's award, 2006, gov. 1988—). Office: New York Times 620 8th Ave New York NY 10018

MCFALL, DONALD BEURY, lawyer; b. Charleston, W.Va., Aug. 2, 1941; s. Henry Tucker and Elizabeth Katharine (Beury) McF.; m. Donna Glenn Binion, May 27, 1972; children: Katharine Atkinson, Mary Crawford. BA, Washington and Lee U., 1964, JD, 1969. Bar: Va. 1969, Tex. 1969, U.S. Supreme Ct. 1979, U.S. Dist. Ct. (we., no., so. and ea. dists.) Tex. 1969. Asst. U.S. atty. U.S. Dept. Justice, Houston, 1970-71; assoc. Butler & Binion, Houston, 1971-77, ptnr., 1977-85, McFall, Sherwood & Sheehy, Houston, 1985-2000; shareholder McFall, Breitbeil & Shults P.C., Houston, 2000—. Trustee Humana Hosp.-Sharpstown, Houston, 1984—85, Southmore Med. Ctr., Houston, 1994—98; bd. dirs. Planned Parenthood Houston and S.E. Tex., 1978—88; trustee Woodberry Forest Sch., Orange, Va., 1984—90, Washington and Lee U., 1997—2006. Lt. US Army, 1964—66. Named Super Lawyer, Tex. Monthly Mag., 2003—, Houston's Top Lawyers, Houston Tex. Mag., 2004—. Fellow: Internat. Soc. Barristers, Am. Coll. Trial Lawyers, Houston Bar Found., Tex. Bar Found.; mem.: Def. Rsch. Inst., Tex. Assn. Def. Counsel, Am. Judicature Soc., Am. Bd. Trial Advocates (nat. bd. dirs. 1996—2000), Fedn. Def. and Corp. Counsel, Tex. State Bar Assn., Va. State Bar Assn., Internat. Assn. Def. Counsel, Garland Walker Inn, Am. Inns of Ct. Office: McFall Breitbeil & Shults PC 1250 Four Houston Ctr 1331 Lamar St Houston TX 77010-3027 Office Phone: 713-590-9300. Personal E-mail: dbmcf@aol.com. Business E-Mail: dmcfall@mcfall-law.com.

MCFALL, JOHN, performing company executive; b. Kansas City, Mo. Studies with Tatiana Dokoudovska, Conservatory of Music; student, San Francisco Ballet Sch., 1964-65. Formerly with San Francisco Ballet, prin. dancer, 1969; artistic dir. BalletMet, Columbus, Ohio, 1986-94; artistic dir., CEO Atlanta Ballet Co., 1994—. Choreographer Nat. Ballet Can., Am. Ballet Theatre, Dance Theatre Harlem, San Francisco, Hubbard St. Dance Co., Atlanta Ballet, for other artists, including

Mikhail Baryshnikov, Cynthia Gregory. Choreographer Commd. 2 world premieres for 1996 Olympic Arts Festival; recently staged: 10 Atlanta prodns., including The Nutcracker. Ford Found. scholar San Francisco Ballet Sch., 1964, Nat. Endowment for Arts fellow, 1978, 1980, 1985. Office: Atlanta Ballet 1400 W Peachtree St Atlanta GA 30309-2906 E-mail: jmcfall@atlantaballet.com.

MCFALLS, JAMES C., trombonist and music educator; b. Columbia, Pa., Jan. 5, 1960; s. James and Etta McFalls; m. Barbara L. Mann, Oct. 21, 1978. BS in Psychology, Calif. Coast U., Anaheim, 1996. Lead trombonist US Army Jazz Ambs., Washington, 1981—98; asst. dir. jazz studies Shepherd U., Shepherdstown, 1998—99; jazz faculty Towson U., Md., 1999—; dir. group sales Balt. Symphony Orch., 1999—2000; jazz trombone prof. U. Md., Coll. Pk., Md., 2004—06, Peabody Inst., 2004—06; edn. specialist and designer Antoine Courtors Brass, Paris, 2006—. Jazz artist Buffet Crampon, Paris, 2006—; edn. specialist Antoine Courtois Brass, Paris, 2006—, designer, 2006. Decorated Mil. Retirement US Army. Office: Towson Univ Dept Music 8000 York Rd Towson MD 21252 Business E-Mail: mjim@towson.edu.

MCFALLS, TIFFANY BETH, biology professor; d. Jerry Lee and Lynn Padgett McFalls; m. James Paul Smith, May 13, 2001; 1 child, Jayme Alysann Smith. BS in Wildlife Mgmt., Eastern Ky. U., Richmond, 2001; MS in Biol. Scis., Southeastern La. U., Hammond, 2004. Rsch. mgr. Southeastern La. U., 2004—06, instr., 2006—. Outreach specialist Lake Pontchartrain Basin Rsch. Program, Hammond, 2006—08. Com. mem. Tangi Clean, Amite, La., 2008—09. Rsch. & Edn. grant, LOSCO, 2008—09. Mem.: La. Sci. Tchrs. Assn., NSTA, La. Acad. Scis., Soc. Wetland Scientists. Office: Southeastern La Univ Hammond LA 70402 Office Fax: 985-549-3851. Business E-Mail: tiffany.mcfalls@selu.edu.

MCFARLAND, ANN LOUISE, music educator; b. Danville, Pa., Aug. 3, 1953; d. Robert E. and Jane F. Montague; m. James R. McFarland, June 3, 1972; children: Ailie S. Herr, Kevin S., Jennie E., Grant R. MusB, Susquehanna U., Selinsgrove, Pa., 1975; MusM, Temple U., Phila., 1978; PhD in Music Edn., Temple U., 2006. Cert. music and movement tchr. level III Am. Orff Schulwerk Assn., 1999, movement tchr. High Scope, 2005. Tchr. Hempfield Sch. Dist., Lancaster, Pa., 1991—92, Conestoga Valley Sch. Dist., Lancaster, 1992—99; asst. prof. music edn. West Chester U., Pa., 1999—. Presenter in field. Contbr. articles to profl. jours. Mem.: Internat. Soc. Music Edn., Soc. Ethnomusicology, Am. Orff Schulwerk Assn., Music Educators Nat. Conf. Office: West Chester Univ Sch Music 817 South High St West Chester PA 19383 Personal E-mail: annmcfarland@juno.com. Business E-Mail: amcfarland@wcupa.edu.

MCFARLAND, DAVID ALEXANDER, literature and language professor; b. Shelbyville, Tenn., Apr. 29, 1948; s. Charles Douglas and Sue M. McFarland; m. Julie Ann Coyne, Sept. 26, 1983; children: Alexander Franklin, Camille Elizabeth. BA in English, U. Ala., Huntsville, 1980; MFA in Fiction, U. Iowa, 1984. English prof. Scott CC, Bettendorf, 1987—, Black Hawk Coll., Moline, Ill., 2000—. Age group swimming referee Ill. Swimming, Rock Island, 1988—2008. Sgt. USAF, 1969—73, Fla. Independent. Avocations: reading, fishing. Office: Black Hawk Coll 6600 34th Ave Moline IL 61265

MCFARLAND, DOUGLAS C., muscle biologist, educator; b. Stamford, Conn., June 21, 1948; s. Claude B. McFarland and Gladys J. (Hitt) McFarland; m. Sandra Yooko Ishimaru, July 13, 1985; children: Nathan K., Ian K. BA in Biology, Southern Conn. State U., New Haven, 1971; MS in Chemistry, Wash. State U., Pullman, 1975, PhD in Nutrition, 1984. Asst. prof. SD State U., Brookings, 1986—92, assoc. prof., 1992—97, prof., 1997—2007, disting. prof., 2007—. Active Masonic Frat., Brookings, SD; boy scout leader Boy Scouts Am., Brookings, SD. Recipient Outstanding Rschr. award, Gamma Sigma Delta, 2002. Master: Brookings Masonic Lodge #24 (master 1998—99); mem.: NC-1131 Muscle Rsch. Independent. Achievements include research in the role of growth factors in avian skeletal muscle development. Avocations: bagpiping, american history, freemasonry, reading. Office: SD State U ASC 101; Box 2170 Brookings SD 57007 Business E-Mail: douglas.mcfarland@sdstate.edu.

MCFARLAND, EDWARD T., lawyer; b. Lufkin, Tex., Oct. 15, 1923; s. Tommy Otis McFarland and Lucy Barker. BA, Southwestern U., Georgetown, Tex., 1947; JD, U. Tex., Austin, 1950. Bar: Tex., US Dist. Ct. (ea. dist.), US Ct. Appeals. Judge Angelina County, Lufkin, 1955—59; pvt. practice Lufkin, 1959—. Capt. USMC, 1951—53. Mem.: Angelina County Bar Assn., Lufkin Masonic Lodge. Democrat. Methodist. Home and Office: 303 E Groesbeck Lufkin TX 75901

MC FARLAND, H. RICHARD, food products executive; b. Hoopeston, Ill., Aug. 19, 1930; s. Arthur Bryan and Jennie (Wilkey) McF.; m. Sarah Forney, Dec. 30, 1967. BS, U. Ill., 1952. With Campbell Soup Co., Camden, NJ, 1957-67, mgr. purchasing, 1961-67; dir. procurement Keebler Co., Elmhurst, Ill., 1967-69; v.p. purchasing and distbn. Ky. Fried Chicken Corp., Louisville, 1969-74, v.p. food svcs., sales and distbn., 1974-75; pres., dir. Mid-Continent Carton Co., Louisville, 1974-75, Ky. Fried Chicken Mfg. Corp., Nashville, 1974-75; owner, pres., dir. McFarland Foods Corp., Indpls., 1975—. Chmn. processed foods com. World's Poultry Congress, 1974; mem. exec. coun., nat. franchise coun. Ky. Fried Chicken, 1979-85; dir. nat. advt. coun. Ky. Fried Chicken, 1985-91, exec. com., 1988-90, chmn., 1989-90; mem. devel. com. U. Ill., 1989—. Mem. U. Ill. Found., 1992—, bd. dirs., 1993-05, life bd. dirs., 2005—, vice chmn., 2001-05, Ind. U. President's Cir., 2005-; chmn. U. Ill. Nat. Advocates, 1992-2001; life pres. U. Ill. Sr. Class of '52; bd. dirs. Ind. Fedn. Children and Youth, 1983-84; Ind. bd. dirs. Fellowship Christian Athletes, 1997-98, Ind. bd. advisors, 1998-2007; chmn. campaign Ind. Ky. Fried Chicken March of Dimes, 1978-87; nat. trustee McCormick Theol. Sem., 1993-97, mem. adv. coun., 1998-2002; trustee Hanover Coll., 2004—; life trustee Indpls. Mus. Art, 2005—; bd. dirs. U. Ind. Cancer Ctr. Devel., 2004—, Ind. Ovarian Cancer Orgn., 2003—. 1st lt. USAF, 1952-54, Korea. Recipient Award of Merit U. Ill. Coll. Agr., 1988, Achievement award U. Ill. Alumni Assn., 1996, Disting. Hoosier State Ind., 2007, Disting. Citizen City of Indpls., Office of Mayor, 2007. Mem. Ky. Restaurant Asns. (bd. dirs. 1970-75), Nat. Broiler Coun. (bd. dirs. 1971-74), Ind. Restaurant Assn., Am. Shorthorn Breeders Assn., Great Lakes Ky. Fried Chicken Franchise Assn. (bd. dirs. 1975-91, 1st v.p. 1978-79, pres. 1979-80), Delta Upsilon. Clubs: Main Line Ski (Phila.) (pres. 1964); Hillcrest Country. Presbyterian. Home: 10720 Compass Ct Indianapolis IN 46256-9532 Office Phone: 317-842-4532.

MCFARLAND, JAMES WILLIAM, real estate company executive, consultant; b. Montgomery, Ala., Sept. 7, 1948; s. Ward Wharton and Frances Adelia (Morrow) McFarland; m. Miriam Melinda Webster, Feb. 20, 1971 (div.); children: James William, Mimi Morrow. BS, U. Ala., University, 1971. Dir. real estate Ky., Ind. and Tenn. Winn-Dixie Stores, Inc., Louisville, 1970—72; v.p. Ward McFarland, Inc., Tuscaloosa, Ala., 1972—. Dir. Ward McFarland, Inc., Tuscaloosa, Ala.; charter investor chair of real estate U. Ala. Mem. Coun. Devel. of French in La., 1976—, Friends of Libr., 1975—; commr. Dept. Mental Health, Ala., 1987—89; Rep. nominee US Congress Ala. 7th Dist., 1986; chmn. Ala. Rapid Rail Transit Commn.; vice chmn. La.-Miss.-Ala. Rapid Rail Transit Commn., 1983—84, chmn., 1984; state advisor Congl. Adv. Com., Am. Security Coun.; mem. Rep. State Exec. Com., 1991—; chmn. Tuscaloosa County Reps., 1991—; young churchmen adviser Episcopal Diocese Ala., 1976, conv. del.; sr. warden Christ Episc. Ch., 1984; bd. dir. Tuscaloosa Kidney Found. Named hon. citizen of Mobile and New Orleans, hon. mem. mayor's staff, Mobile, Ala. Mem.: Nat. Small Bus. Assn., Tuscaloosa Bd. Realtors, Nat. Assn. Realtors, USCG Aux. (flotilla comdr. and dist. pub. affairs officer 1997, flotilla staff officer 1994—, dist. staff officer 1997—), U. Ala. Alumni Assn., U. Ala. Commerce Execs. Soc., Ala. Assn. R.R. Passengers (pres. 1982, 1990, 1991), Nat. Assn. R.R. Passengers, Kiwanis (Greater Tuscaloosa chpt.), North River Yacht Club, Delta Sigma Pi. Office: 325 Skyland Blvd E Tuscaloosa AL 35405-4030 Office Phone: 205-759-5161.

MCFARLAND, MICHAEL C., academic administrator; b. Boston, 1948; AB in Physics, Cornell U., 1969; M in Elec. Engring., Carnegie M in Elec. Engring., PhD in Elec. Engring., Carnegie Mellon U.; MDiv, Weston Sch. Theology, ThM in Social Ethics. Ordained to ministry Jesuits, 1984. Cons. AT&T Bell Labs., 1985—86; assoc. prof. computer sci. Boston Coll., 1986—96, dept. chair; prof. computer sci., dean Coll. Arts and Scis. Gonzaga U., Spokane, 1996—2000; pres. Coll. of the Holy Cross, Worcester, Mass., 2000—. Bd. dir. Worcester Mcpl. Rsch. Bur., Worcester Cath. Charities; bd. dirs. U. Scranton. Avocation: running. Office: Coll of the Holy Cross 1 College St Worcester MA 01610-2395 Office Phone: 508-793-2525.*

MCFARLAND, NORMAN FRANCIS, bishop; b. Martinez, Calif., Feb. 21, 1922; Attended, St. Patrick's Sem. Ordained to ministry Cath. Ch., 1946, consecrated bishop Cath. Ch., 1970. Ordained priest Archdiocese of San Francisco, 1946, aux. bishop, 1970—74; ordained bishop, 1970; apostolic adminstr. Diocese of Reno, 1974—76; bishop Diocese of Reno-Las Vegas, 1976—87, Diocese of Orange, Calif., 1987—98, bishop emeritus, 1998—. Roman Catholic. Office: 200 W La Veta Ave Orange CA 92866-1936

MCFARLAND, ROBERT BRUCE, physician; b. Ames, Iowa, Sept. 18, 1929; s. Julian Ecwart and Winnie Florence (Goering) McF.; m. Zoë Euphrosyne Bucuvalas, June 1, 1958; children: Laura Ann, Bruce Damon. BA, Kenton Coll., 1950; MD, U. Iowa, 1954. Intern San Francisco Gen. Hosp., 1955; house officer Mass. Gen. Hosp., Boston, 1957-59; asst. resident U. Colo. Med. Ctr., Denver, 1959-61; physician pvt. practice, Boulder, Colo., 1961-76, 78-93; prof. U. Mo., Kansas City, 1976-78. Contbg. editor Jour. Psychohistory, 1996—; contbr. articles to profl. jours. Vestryman St. John's Episcopal Ch., Boulder, 1966-69; jail physician Boulder County, Kansas City, 1972-75, 76-78; co-founder Parenting Place, Boulder, 1984-2001; cons., bd. health No. Cheyenne Tribe, Lame Deer, Mont., 1976-84. Comdr. USNR-R, 1955-78. Avocations: hiking, reading. Home: 2300 Kalmia Ave Boulder CO 80304-1931 E-mail: mcfarland73@msn.com.

MCFARLAND, RONALD GEORGE (RON), composer, music educator, musician; b. San Bernardino, Calif., Apr. 20, 1928; s. George Millard McFarland and Anna Belle Hagy. Student, Arnold Schoenberg Studio, Brendwood, Calif., 1946—48, Carpenter Music Studio, San Bernardino, 1944—48, Leginska Piano Studio, Hollywood, Calif., 1945—52, Sheinfeld Studio, San Francisco, 1969—71, San Francisco State U., 1961—66. Prin. instr. McFarland Piano Studio, Tiburon, Calif., 1962—; piano tchr., composer-in-residence San Domenico Sch., Fairfax, Calif., 1966—72. Mem. artist adv. com. Old First Concerts, San Francisco, 1994—. Musician: (profl. debut) Leginska Symphony Orch., Wilshire Ebell Theatre, 1948—49; soloist: Arensky's Piano Concertro in F Minor, Hollywood Bowl Symphony Orchestra, Hollywood Bowl, LA, 1948, Beethoven's Piano Concerto in C Major, Tulare County Symphony Orch., 1963, Carnegie Hall, 1983, composer numerous works for piano, voice, violin, orch., opera, ballet. Bd. dirs., founding mem. Composers, Inc., San Francisco, 1984—88. Recipient 1st prize, Composers Today Competition, 1984, Std. award, ASCAP, 1996—2006, Honors, McFarland Musical Retrospective, 1998, 2008. Mem.: Music Tchrs. Assn. Calif. (registered tchr. piano and composition, chmn. music competition 1970—72, 1st prize 1975, 1988, 1981, 1982, 1985), Landmark Soc., Belvedere-Tiburon Libr. Soc. Avocations: swimming, gardening, travel, reading, architecture. Home and Studio: 765 Tiburon Blvd Belvedere Tiburon CA 94920 Home Phone: 415-435-1657. Home Fax: 415-789-1339. E-mail: mcfar9@pacbell.net.

MCFARLAND, STEPHEN GEORGE, United States Ambassador to Guatemala; Grad., US Air War Coll., Yale U., New Haven, Colegio Roosevelt, Lima, Peru; attended, Marine Corps Platoon Leaders Course. Joined US Fgn. Svc., 1977; fgn. svc. post US Dept. State, Maracaibo, Venezuela, polit. counselor El Salvador, Bolivia, Peru, desk officer Nicaragua, polit. officer Ecuador, Peru, dep. chief of mission, chargé d'affaires Paraguay, Guatemala, dep. chief of mission Venezuela, dir. Cuban affairs Washington, dir. stability ops. tng., Fgn. Svc. Inst., US amb. to Guatemala, 2008—. Mem. interim cease-fire monitoring group on the Peru-Ecuador border, 1995; head civilian-mil. provincial reconstrn. team Marine Corps Regimental Combat Team, 2007. Office: DOS Amb 3190 Guatemala Pl Washington DC 20521-3190*

MCFARLAND, THOMAS, English literature educator; b. Birmingham, Ala., Sept. 13, 1926; s. Thomas Alfred McFarland and Lucile Sylvester. AB, Harvard U., 1949; AM, Yale U., 1951, PhD, 1953; postgrad., Eberhard-Karls-Universität, Tübingen, Germany, 1953—54; MA (hon.), Oxford U., Eng., 1986. Instr. in English Oberlin Coll., 1954-56, U. Va., 1956-58; asst. prof. Western Res. U., Cleve., 1958-62, assoc. prof., 1962-64, prof., 1964-67, Grad. Ctr. CUNY, 1967-73, disting. prof. English lit., 1973-78; prof. Princeton (NJ) U., 1978-81, Murray prof. English lit., 1981-89; Murray prof. English lit. emeritus Princeton U., 1989—. Vis. prof. U. Colo., 1968, U. Va., 1972, Yale U., 1975; vis. fellow All Souls Coll., U. Oxford, Eng., 1986-87, Humanities Rsch. Ctr., Australian Nat. U., Canberra, 1992, Lechter Inst. for Lit. Rsch., Bar-Ilan U., Ramat Gan, Israel, 1989, U. Otago, Dunedin, New Zealand, 1992; adv. bd. Bull. Rsch. in Humanities, 1978—, Studies in Romanticism, 1982—, Nineteenth-Century Lit., 1986—, Works of Thomas De Quincey, 1990, Romanticism, 1995—; hon. fellow Ctr. for European Romanticism, Glasgow, 1997—; mem. supervising com. English Inst., 1971-74, chmn. 1974; assoc. trustee The Dove Cottage Trust, The Lake Dist., Eng., 1982—; bd. advisors Milton and the Romantics, 1975—; seminar assoc. Columbia U., 1971—; pres. com. English dept. Harvard U., 1987-88; lectr. in field. Author: Tragic Meanings in Shakespeare, 1966, Coleridge and the Pantheist Tradition, 1969, Shakespeare's Pastoral Comedy, 1972, Romanticism and the Forms of Ruin: Wordsworth, Coleridge and Modalities of Fragmentation, 1981, Originality and Imagination, 1985, Shapes of Culture, 1987, Romantic Cruxes: The English Essayists and the Spirit of the Age, 1987, William Wordsworth; Intensity and Achievement, 1992, Romanticism and the Heritage of Rousseau, 1995, Paradoxes of Freedom; The Romantic Mystique of a Transcendence, 1996, The Masks of Keats: The Endeavor of a Poet, 2000; editor: The Opus Maximum of Samuel Taylor Coleridge, 2002; mem. editl. bd. Comparative Criticism, 1977—, European Romantic Rev., 1989—, Festschrift: the Coleridge Connection: Essays for Thomas McFarland, 1990; contbr. 52 articles to scholarly jours. Fulbright scholar, 1953-54; fellow Guggenheim Found., 1964-65, 74-75, Am. Coun. Learned Socs., 1973-74, Ctr. for Advanced Study in Behavioral Scis., Stanford, Calif., 1981-82, NEH, 1981-82, 86-87. Mem. MLA (exec. com. English 9 1970-73, chmn. 1974), Sydney Soc. for Lit. and Aesthetics (hon. life). Home: 1046 Cornwall C Boca Raton FL 33434

MCFARLAND, WILLIAM JOSEPH (JOE), academic administrator; b. Sterling, Kans., July 25, 1929; s. Armour James and Sylvia Jane Louise (Hutcheson) McF.; m. Mary Roberta Dill, Dec. 21, 1951; children: William Joseph, Kathryn Ann, Matthew Curtis. BA, Sterling Coll., 1951; MA, U. No. Colo., 1957; EdD, Ind. U., 1966; PhD (hon.), Sterling Coll., 1992, Geneva Coll., 2001. Cert. tchr. and adminstr., pilot. Elem. prin., coach, tchr., supt. schs. Turon Pub. Schs., Kans., 1953-59; assoc. prof. edn., dir. student teaching, head edn. dept. Emporia State U., Kans., 1959-68; assoc. exec. sec. Kans. NEA, Topeka, 1968-71; dir. acad. affairs Kans. Bd. Regents, Topeka, 1971-84; pres. Geneva Coll., Beaver Falls, Pa., 1984-92; cons., scholar in residence Christs Coll., Taipei, Taiwan, 1992—2002; headmaster Am. Acad. Nicosia, Cyprus, 2002—03. Chmn. scholarship selection com. Beech Aircraft Co., Wichita, Kans., 1979-84; pres. coun. Nat. Assn. Intercollegiate Athletics, Kansas City, Kans., 1984-92. Author: (autobiography) My Time on the Clock: The Shaping of a College President, 2008; contbr. articles to profl. jours. Pres. Topeka Fellowship, Inc., 1977-84; mem. exec. coun., v.p. Boy Scouts Am., Emporia and Topeka, 1963-83; legis. liason person NEA, Topeka, 1968-71; chmn. Kans. Commn. on Aerospace Edn., 1971-83, Gov's. Commn. on Sch. to Work, 1995-2001; trustee Sterling Coll., Kans., 1971-84, Geneva Coll., 1973-84; sec. Pa. Found. Ind. Colls.; bd. dirs. United Way, Beaver County, Pa., 1985-92, ARC of Beaver County, 1985-92, Beaver Valley C. of C., 1985-88; mem. Christian Coll. Coalition, 1984-92. With U.S. Army, 1951-53, Korea. Recipient Lieber Meml. Teaching award Ind. U., Bloomington, 1966; Disting. Service award Sterling Coll., 1983; VIP award Sta. WREN, Topeka, 1971; 50 Yr. Recognition award Kansas State H.S. Activities Assn., 2005. Mem. Assn. Governing Bds. (exec. com.), Pa. Assn. Colls. and Univs., Nat. Assn. Ind. Colls. and Univs., Beaver Valley C. of C., ARC (pres. local chpt.), Knife and Fork Club (bd. dirs. 1979-84, Rotary (life, pres. 1986-87, Paul Harris fellow 1988, chmn. scholarship selection com. Rotary Found.), Phi Delta Kappa (v.p. 1969-73) Republican. Presbyterian. Avocations: flying, football officiating, golf, hunting. Home and Office: 2709 SW Boswell Ave Topeka KS 66611-1604 E-mail: joromcf@sbcglobal.net.

MCFARLAND LORD, JENNA, set designer, educator; b. Dallas, Feb. 20, 1975; d. Fred Huey and Scotta Edelen McFarland; m. Andrew James Lord, Sept. 15, 2006; 1 child, Evelyn Scotta Lord. MA, Emerson Coll., Boston, 1999. Resident set designer Gloucester Stage Co., Mass., 2003—; set design tchr. Boston Arts Acad., 2007—. The Mousetrap (ADDISON award, 2006). Office: Boston Arts Acad 174 Ipswich St Boston MA 02215 Personal E-mail: infinitedrama@yahoo.com.

MCFARLANE, BETH LUCETTA TROESTER, retired mayor; b. Osterdock, Iowa, Mar. 9, 1918; d. Francis Charles and Ella Carrie (Moser) Troester; m. George Evert McFarlane, June 20, 1943 (dec. May 1972); children: Douglas, Steven(dec.), Susan, George. EdB, U. No. Iowa, Cedar Falls, 1962, MEd, 1971. Cert. tchr. Tchr. rural and elem. schs., Iowa, 1936-50, 55-56; elem. tchr. Oelwein Cmty. Schs., Iowa, 1956-64, jr. high reading tchr., 1964—71, 1983; city council Oelwein, 1981-82; mayor of Oelwein, 1982-89; ret. Evaluator N. Ctrl. Accreditation Assn. Ednl. Programs; mem. planning team confs. Iowa cities N.E. Iowa, 1985; v.p. N.E. Iowa Regional Coun. Econ. Devel., 1986—89; mem. area econ. devel. com. N.E. Iowa, 1985, mem. legis. interim study com. rural devel., 1987—88; mem. policy com. Iowa League Municipalities, 1987—88. V.p. Fayette County Tourism Coun., 1987—88; mem. Iowa State steering com. road use tax financing, 1988—89; chmn. bd. govs. Oelwein Cmty. Ctr., 1990—94, bd. govs., 2001—; chmn. bldg. and fin. com. Cmty. Christ Ch., 1990—2007; dist. ch. fin. com. Reorganized LDS/Cmty. Christ Ch., 1992—2001, dist. ch. revolving loan com., 1982—2000. Recipient Outstanding Contbn. to Reading Coun. Acitivities award, Internat. Reading Assn. N.E. Iowa, 1978, State of Iowa's Gov.'s Leadership award, 1988; named Iowa Reading Tchr. of Yr., Internat. Reading Assn. Iowa, 1978. Mem.: Oelwein Bus. and Profl. Women (Woman of Yr. 1983), MacDowell Music and Arts Orgn. (pres. 1978—80), N.E. Iowa Reading Coun. (pres. 1975—77), Area Univ. Women (pres. 1999—2000), Oelwein Area Ret. Sch. Pers. (pres. 1994—96), Oelwien Area C. of C. (bd. dirs. 1986—89, Humanitarian award 1987), Delta Kappa Gamma (pres. 1980—82). Republican. Mem. Cmty. Of Christ Ch. Avocations: hiking, refinishing antiques, gardening, walking, creative sewing. Home: 512 7th Ave NE Oelwein IA 50662-1326

MCFARLANE, DONOVAN ANTHONY, finance educator, consultant; b. Manchester, Jamaica, Apr. 19, 1978; arrived in US, 1997; s. Merceline A. Wright. Cert., deCarteret Coll., Jamaica, 1995, Church Tchrs. Coll., 1997; PhD in Parapsychic Sci., Am. Inst. Theology, 2003; diploma in fitness and nutrition, Harcourt Learning Direct, Scranton, Pa., 1999; diploma in mgmt. restaurant and hotel, Profl. Career Devel. Inst., Atlanta, 2000; diploma in bus. mgmt. with highest honor, Stratford Career Inst., Washington, 2000; diploma in small bus. mgmt., Lifetime Career Sch., Archbald, Pa., 2000; BS in Geog. Sci., Bernadean U., North Hollywood, Calif., 2000; PhD in Metaphysics, Am. Coll. Metaphys. Theology, Golden Valley, Minn., 2000, PhD in Comparative Religion, 2002; cert. in paralegal studies, Blackstone Sch., 2002; BS in Parapsychic Sci., Am. Inst. Holistic Theology, 2003, MS in Parapsychic Sci., 2002; MBA, Frederick Taylor U., 2002; MBA in Mgmt., Barrington U., 2003; BSBA, Nova Southeastern U., Fla., 2003; diploma in writing, Inst. Childrens Lit., 2003; B in Metaphys. Sci., U. Metaphysics, Calif., 2003; diploma, U. Metaphysics, 2003; cert. metaphysical practitioner, U. Metaphysics Sem., 2003; MSc in Metaphys. Sci., D in Metaphys. Sci., U. Metaphysics, Sedona, 2003; MBA, Nova Southeastern U., 2005; D in Metaphys. Psychology, U. Sedona, Ariz., 2007; grad. cert. in Internat. Bus., St. Thomas U., Miami Gardens, Fla., 2007; D in Bus. Adminstrn., Calif. Pacific U., Escondido, 2008; M in Internat. Bus., St. Thomas U., Miami Gardens, 2008; MS in Religious Studies, Nations U., West Monroe, La., 2009. Bd. cert. holistic health practitioner Am. Assn. Drugless Practitioners, 2005, bd. cert. alternative med. practitioner Am. Alternative Med. Assn., 2005; cert. in secondary edn. Tchr. trainee in Spanish and social studies Comprehensive HS, Jamaica, 1997; tutor gen. sci. Church Tchrs. Coll., Jamaica; curriculum planner pvt. orgn., Fla., essayist Fla., cons. Lauderdale Lakes, Fla., 1998—; clk. Phillips and Phillips, Ft. Lauderdale, Fla., 1997—98; supr. inventory and warehouse Lord's Supermarket, Oakland, Fla., 1999; with Corp. Edu. Rsch., 2001—; prof. bus. studies U. Ft. Lauderdale, 2005—, City Coll. Ft. Lauderdale, 2005; univ. tutor Lynn U., Boca Raton, Fla., 2007. Prefect emeritus DeCarteret Coll., Manchester, Jamaica, 1997; adj. instr. bus. studies City Coll., Ft. Lauderdale, Fla., 2005—; founder, chief preceptor, chancellor Donovan Soc., LLC, Ft. Lauderdale, 2006; adv. dir. peer-rev. jours. Franklin Pub. Co., Arlington, Tex., 2008. Author: (book) The

Insights of Donovan A. McFarlane, 2008, numerous poems; editor: 21st Century Leadership Strategies: An Anthology of Selected Articles and Book Reviews, 2008; contbr. scientific papers to profl. jours.; author: (book) From Saddam Hussein To Barack Hussein: The Story of Change, Legacy and Ascendency, 2009. Recipient cert. excellence in Spanish, social studies, geography, math., history, cert. diligence in Spanish, religious edn., cert. outstanding achievement in social studies, cert. outstanding achievement in Spanish, Internat. Poet of Merit award, 2002, Outstanding Achievement in Poetry Silver award, 2003, Commemorative award, 2003; named hon. alumni, Oglata Lakota Coll., S.D., 2000. Mem.: Joseph Campbell Found., Nat. Honor Scholars Soc., Am. Alternative Med. Assn., Am. Assn. Drugless Practitioners, Ctr. Rsch. in Values and Philosophy, Internat. Libr. Poetry (laureate cert. 2002), Internat. Soc. Poets (Editor's Choice award 1998), Nat. Libr. Poetry (Disting. Membership cert. and plaque 1998), Sigma Beta Delta (Outstanding Scholastic Achievement 2005). Avocations: dance, oratory, martial arts, singing, writing.

MCFARLANE, JOANNA, chemist, researcher; d. Clare Elizabeth Bradley and John Elwood McFarlane; m. Stephen Edward Oliver, Dec. 27, 1985; children: Hilde Oliver, Rachel Oliver. PhD, U. Toronto, Ont., Can., 1989. Chemist Atomic Energy Can. Ltd., Pinawa, Man., Canada, 1989—2001, Oak Ridge Nat. Lab., Tenn., 2001—. Mem.: Am. Chem. Soc. Office: Oak Ridge Nat Lab Bldg 4500N MS6181 Oak Ridge TN 37831-6181

MCFARLANE, SETH WOODBURY, television producer, animator; b. Kent, Conn., Oct. 26, 1973; s. Ron and Perry McFarlane. Grad., RI Sch. Design. Animator Hanna-Barbera Prodns. (now Cartoon Network Studios); writer Walt Disney Animation, Fox Broadcasting Co. Writer, dir. (TV series) Shnookums and Meat Funny Cartoon Show, 1993, writer, dir., actor The Life of Larry, 1995, Larry & Steve, 1996, writer Dexter's Laboratory, 1996—, Jungle Cubs, 1996—98, Ace Ventura: Pet Detective, 1996, Cow and Chicken, 1997—2001, Johnny Bravo, 1997—, writer, dir. Zoomates, 1998, exec. prodr., writer, creator, actor Family Guy, 1999—, cons. prodr. The Pitts, 2003, exec. prodr., writer, dir., actor American Dad!, 2005—.

MCFARLANE, WALTER ALEXANDER, lawyer, educator; b. Richlands, Va., May 4, 1940; s. James Albert and Frances Mae (Padbury) McF.; m. Judith Louise Copenhaver, Aug. 31, 1962. BA, Emory and Henry Coll., 1962; JD, U. Richmond, 1966. Bar: Ba. 1966, U.S. Supreme Ct. 1970, U.S. Ct. Appeals (4th cir.) 1973, U.S. Ct. Appeals (D.C. cir.) 1977, U.S. Dist. ct. (ea. dist.) Va. 1973. Asst. atty. gen. Office Va. Atty. Gen., Richmond, 1969-73, dep. atty. gen., 1973-90; exec. asst., chief counsel, dir. policy Gov.'s Office Commonwealth of Va., 1990-94, supt. Dept. Correctional Edn., 1994—. Acting dir. Dept. Juvenile Justice, 1997, State Bd. Dept. Criminal Justice Svcs., 1994—; prof. adj. staff U. Richmond, 1978—, A.L.Philpott disting. prof. T.C. Williams Sch. Law, 2003; chmn. transp. law com. Transp. Rsch. Bd., Nat. Rsch. Bd. Nat. Acads. Sci. and Engring., Washington, 1977-85, 88-94, chmn. legal affairs com., 1978-85, chmn. environ., archeol. and hist. com., 1985-90; mem. State Water Commn., 1994-96, mem., Coun. of State Govts. Henry Toll Fell., 1988, Legal Task Force, 1988-2002. Contbr. articles to profl. jours. Exec. com., bd. govs. Emory and Henry Coll., 1985-98; pres. Windsor Forest Civic Assn., Midlothian, Va., 1975-76; bd. dirs. Greater Midlothian Civic League, 1980-86, v.p., 1980; instr. water safety ARC, 1962-87; chmn. bldg. com. Mt. Pisgah United Meth. Ch., 1980-85, pres. men's club, 1980-81; bd. dirs. ctrl. Va. chpt. Epilepsy Assn. Va., 1988-91. Capt. JAGC, USAF, 1966-69. Recipient J.D. Buscher Disting. Atty. award Am. Assn. State Hwy. and Transp. Ofcls., 1983, John C. Vance legal writing award Nat. Acads. Sci. and Engring., 4th ann. outstanding evening lectr. award Student Body, U. Richmond, 1980. Mem. Chesterfield Bar Assn., Richmond Bar Assn. (bd. dir. 1989-93), Richmond Scottish Soc. (bd. dirs. 1980-82), Va. Correctional Assn. (pres.-elect 2004-06, pres. 2007—09, Lifetime Achievement award 2004), Am. Correctional Assn. (gen. assembly 2002-06, bd. govs. 2006—), Woodland Pond Civic Assn. (bd. dirs. 2005—08), Emory and Henry Coll. Alumni Assn. (chpt. pres. 1971-73, regional v.p. 1974-77, pres. 1981-83), Meadowbrook Country Club (bd. dir. 2001-04). Home: 9001 Widgeon Way Chesterfield VA 23838-5274 Office: 101 N 14th St Richmond VA 23219-3684 Business E-Mail: wamcfarlane@dce.state.va.us.

MCFARLIN, BRIAN KEITH, medical educator, researcher; b. Richardson, Tex., Oct. 2, 1975; s. Keith L. and Debbie Mayer McFarlin; m. Meredith Ann Lewis, Dec. 9, 1977; 1 child, Michael Keith. PhD, Purdue U., West Lafayette, Ind., 2003. Postdoctoral fellow Purdue U., West Lafayette, 2003—04; asst. prof. U. of Houston, 2004—. Recipient GEAR award, U. Houston Rsch. Coun., 2005—06. Mem.: Am. Coll. of Sports Medicine (assoc.). Republican. United Methodist. Avocation: running. Office: U Houston 3855 Holman St Houston TX 77204-6015 Office Fax: 713-743-9860. Business E-Mail: bmcfarlin@uh.edu.

MCFARLIN, DIANE HOOTEN, publisher; b. Lake Wales, Fla., July 10, 1954; d. Ruffie Denton Hooten and Anna Loraine (Peeples) Huff; m. Henry Briggs McFarlin, Aug. 28, 1976 (div. 1993). BS, U. Fla., 1976. Reporter Sarasota (Fla.) Jour., 1976-77, asst. news editor, 1977-78, city editor, 1978-82; asst. mng. editor Sarasota (Fla.) Herald Tribune, 1983-84, mng. editor, 1985-87; exec. editor Gainesville (Fla.) Sun, 1987-90; from exec. editor to assoc. publ. Sarasota Herald-Tribune, 1990-99, publ., 1999—. Adv. bd. U. Fla. Coll. Journalism and Comm., 1987—; Pulitzer juror Columbia U., 1995-96, 2001-02, 2007-08. Mem. accrediting coun. Edn. in Journalism and Mass Comms., 1994-96. Recipient Alumna of Distinction award U. Fla., 1999. Mem. Am. Soc. Newspaper Editors (com. chair 1992, 94, 96, 2000, bd. dirs. 1994—, treas., sec., v.p. 2001, pres. 2002), Fla. Soc. Newspaper Editors (sec.-treas. 1993, v.p. 1994, pres. 1995). Office: Sarasota Herald-Tribune PO Box 1719 Sarasota FL 34230-1719: 1741 Main St Sarasota FL 34236-7824

MCFARLING, USHA LEE, journalist; b. Landstuhl, West Germany, June 28, 1967; m. Michael Dickinson; children: Phoebe, Peter. BA in Biology, Brown U., 1988; MA in Biol. Psych., U. Calif., Berkeley, 1998. Sci. reporter Brown Daily Herald, RI, 1988—89; asst. city editor & med. writer San Antonio Light, 1990—92; hlth. & sci. writer Boston Globe, 1994—95; freelance writer, 1995—98; former reporter with Washington bur. Knight Ridder, 1998—2000; sci. writer planetary and earth scis. LA Times, 2001—07. Mem. sci. and soc. journalism awards com. Nat. Assn. Sci. Writers, Inc.; mem. judging com. Wistar Inst., 2004—; spkr. in field; freelance journalist. Recipient award, Wistar Inst., 2004; co-recipient John B. Oakes award for Outstanding Environmental Journalism, Columbia U. Grad. Sch. Journalism, 2006, George Polk award for Environmental Reporting, 2006, Walter Sullivan award for Excellence in Sci. Journalism, Am. Geophys. Union, 2007, Pub. Comm. award, Am. Soc. Microbiol., 2007, Print Media award, Am. Inst. Biol. Scis., 2007, Pulitzer Prize for Explanatory Reporting, 2007; fellow Knight Sci. Journalism, MIT, 1992—93.

MCFARLIN-KOSIEC, BARBARA ANN, elementary school educator, secondary school educator, literature and language professor, small business owner; b. Lamesa, Tex., Oct. 4, 1937; d. Roy W. and Laura Corine (Daniel) McFarlin; m. Leonard E. Kosiec; 1 child, James Daniel. BA in Spanish, Tex. Christian U., Ft. Worth, 1960; attended, Instituto Tecnologico and Estudios Superiores Monterrey, Mex., 1961, Instituto Tecnologico and Estudios Superiores Monterrey, 1962, Pan Am. Coll., Edinburgh, Tex., 1962, Ea. Wash. State U., Cheney, 1963, attended, 1972, attended, 1974, attended, 1977, attended, 1989, Ctrl. Washington State U., Ellensburg, 1971, attended, 1973, attended, 1976, attended, 1977, attended, 1987, attended, 1988, U. of Ams., Mex. City, Mex., 1966, U. San Carlos, Guatemala City, Guatemala, 1967; MA in Spanish, Tex. Christian U., Ft. Worth, 1964; PhD in Leadership in Edn., Gonzaga U., Spokane, Wash., 1985. Tchr. 2d grade Mercedes (Tex.) Pub. Schs., 1962; tchr. English Instituto Tecnologico and Estudios Superiores Monterrey, Mexico, 1962; tchr. Spanish, English and social studies Dayton (Wash.) HS, 1963—65; tchr. Spanish, Mexican and Latin Am. history Peninsula CC, Port Angeles, Wash., 1965-68; tchr. grades 4-12 Spanish, English and social studies Burbank (Wash.) Pub. Schs., 1968-73; tchr. Spanish, ESL and multicultural rels. evening staff mem. Columbia Basin CC, Pasco, 1973—80; tchr. 1st, 2d, 3d, 4th, 5th and 6th grades, bilingual and migrant edn. programs Pasco (Wash.) Pub. Schs., 1973-82, 1993—95; tchr. Tex.-Wash. migrant edn. program Pasco HS, 1975—77; sub. tchr. Fernie Pub. Schs., East Kootenay CC, BC, Canada, 1982—85, Fernie Pub. Schs., 1990—92; tchr. grade 3 bilingual edn. Othello Pub. Schs., Wash., 1985—93; pres. McFarlin-Kosiec Enterprises, Fernie, 1986—; tchr. Spanish grades 1-8 St. Joseph Sch., Kennewick, Wash., 1995—96; tchr. Spanish, history and psychology Mt. Baker Secondary Sch. Southeast Kootenay Sch. dist. 5, Cranbrook, Canada, 1997—2004. Instr. English as second lang. Inst. Tech. y de Estudios Superios de Monterrey, Mex., 1962, Spanish Big Bend CC, Moses Lake, Wash., 1986-87, Seattle Pacific U., 1986, Columbia Bain CC, Pasco, Wash., 1973-80, 87-89; edn. editor El Sol newspaper, Pasco; writer Temos, Buenos Aires; cons. in field; freelance writer Fernie Free Press; adj. prof. second lang. and culture Seattle Pacific U., 1980; mem. Tri-Cities Higher Edn. Orgn., 1987-88, Kennewick Schs. Facilities Com., 1990-96; activist State Com., Wash., 1995-96; del. ann. gen. meeting BC Tchrs.' Fedn., 2002; labour affiliation rep. Cranbrook Dist. Tchrs.' Assn., 2001-02, rep. Cranbrook Tchrs. Assn. to BC Fedn. Labour Capilano Coll. Labour studies program, 2002; mem. Growth Mgmt. Act Com., Kennewick, 1990-96; rschr. maternity care experiences women Elk Valley and South Country Health Care Coalition, 2004-06, v.p., 2004-05, pres., 2005-09; com. mem. Can. Day, Fernie; rschr. rural maternity care rsch. dept. family practice U. BC; guest spkr. and cons. in field. Performer: Recess; choreographer, dir. Phantom of the Opera Ballet Lutacoga Modern Dance Troup, 1991, Hook, 1992; choreographer: Desert, Art of Noise, Water, Fire, Rejoice, Autumn Leaves, Sunday in the Parkm Military Celebration, Snow, Meet Me in St. Louis, 1993; artistic dir.: Desert Storm Charity Show, Pasco, 1991; exhbns. include The US Bank, Othello, 1992, City Hall, Othello, 1993, Mark Twain Elem. Sch., Pasco, 1993, The Fernie Arts Co-op; writer, prodr. actor (play) Windows on Women, Fernie, BC, 2007; contbr. articles to profl. jours.; contbr. short stories various programs. Bd. dirs. Mid Columbia Regional Ballet Co., Richland, Wash.; precinct com. mem. Cen. Com., Benton County, 1991—; del. Benton County and Washington State Dem. Convs., 1988, 92, 94, 96, 04; active various Rep. convs.; deaconess Disciples of Christ Ch., Richland; mem. Columbia Chorale, Kennewick, Wash.; mem. negotiations com. Othello Sch. Dist., 1990—; artistic dir. benefit show Persian Gulf War Vets, UNICEF, 1991, Lutacaga Modern Dance Troupe, 1991—, founder; mem. Arts Coun., Fernie, BC, 1991, Writers' Guild Fernie, 1991; facility com. Kennewick Schs., Kennewick, Wash., 1989—; media and urban design planning commr. Kennewick, Wash., 1991—; parks and rec. commn. Kennewick, Wash., 1991—; active mem. Wash. Recreation and Park Assn, 1993—; pianist, organist, vocalist, dancer, performer Not For Profit Theater; organist Christ Ch. (Anglican), Fernie, 2004-09; precinct committeewoman Dem. Party, 1988-06; mem. Electoral Coll., Wash., 1996, Washington Assn. Fgn. Lang. Tchrs., 1962-90; commr. Parks and Recreation, Kennewick, 1990-96; vol. costumes Royal Winnipeg Balley Key City Theater, Cranbrook, 2000; scrutineer East Kootenay Electoral Dist., 2001, 05; sec. East Kootenay constituency exec. com. New Dem. Party, 2002-06, alt. del. provincial coun., 2002-03, del., 2003, chair nomination conv., 2005, master of ceremonies fundraiser, 2005; master of ceremonies fundraiser Elk Valley and South Country Health Care Coalition, 2005; coord. dance divsn. Performing Arts Festival 2001-05, presenter awards, 2001-06, sec., 2002-04, mem. bd., 2005; dir. Fernie Arts Coop., 2005-07, Soc. Restoration Fernie Heritage Cemetry, 2009; mem. Royal Can. Legion, Fernie, 2004, 09; vol. The Can. Cancer Soc., 2005, 09; mem. Fernie Arts Coun., 2006-09, Columbia Chorale, Kennewick, 1990-93; mem. Allied Arts Gallery, Richland, Wash.; pres. Fernie Nordic Soc., 2006-07. Honored Spanish Embassy rsch. Lope de Vega, 1962; recipient Helen Gibbs award most talented Miss Walla Walla, 1965, award Assn. Quality Participation, 1989, 90, 91, 92, award Rainbow Rockers to Lutacaga Dance Troupe, Othello, 1992, Recognition award Mayor of Othello, Recognition award Othello City Libr., Recognition award Columbia Basin CC. Mem. AAUW (scholarship, legis. conf. 1977), NEA, Wash. Edn. Assn. (exec. bd. 1992—), Pasco Edn. Assn. (grievance rep. 1975-77, bldg. rep. 1980), Columbia Edn. Assn. (legis. com. 1968-73), Peninsula CC Edn. Assn. (profl. rights and negotiations com. 1966-68), Can. Fedn. U. Women, Internat. Platform Assn., Assn. Quality and Participation (chmn. edn. com. 1991, mem. awards com., v.p. 1996-97), Dance Educators Assn. Washington, Tri Cities Higher Edn. Orgn. (bd. dirs. 1987), Provintial Intermediate Tchr.'s Assn., Tchrs.' Fedn. and Coll. of Tchrs. (chmn. unemployed tchrs. Fernie dist. 1984-85, activist sub. tchrs.), BC Ret. Tchrs.'s Assn., Writer's Guild. Achievements include research in advanced statistics and research design. Avocations: arranging solo piano music, teaching modem dance. Home and Office: PO Box 1275 Fernie BC Canada V0B 1M0 E-mail: bkosiec@telus.net.

MCFARREN, LELAND CULLEN, educational association administrator, educator; b. Navarre, Ohio, Nov. 13, 1923; s. Cullen Perry and Clara Caroline (Agler) McFarren; m. Beatrice Virginia German, Dec. 21, 1947; children: Michael Leland, Lynne Caroline Morris. BE, Kent State U., Ohio, 1949, MEd, 1952, postgrad., 1952—55, Case Western Res. U., Cleve., 1960. Cert. supt. East Ctrl. Ohio Tchr.'s Assn., 1970. Bricklayer apprentice Timken Roller Bearing, Canton, Ohio, 1941—43; tchr. Plain Local Schs., Canton, 1949—53, prin., 1953—62, asst. supt., 1963—77, supt., 1978—79. Stark County rep. East. Ctrl. Ohio Tchrs. Assn., 1965—69. Contbr. articles to profl. jours. Pres. Otis German Shopping Ctr. Platoon sgt., tank comdr. US Army, 1943—46. Decorated Silver Star medal US Army, Purple Heart, European Theatre medal with three stars, Good Conduct medal, Am. Theatre medal, Victory medal; recipient Disting. Alumni award, Timken H.S., 2006; named to Hall Distinction, Plain Local Schs., 2001, Ohio Mil. Hall Fame for valor, 2006. Mem.: DAV (life), Order Ky. Cols., Stark County Golf Assn. (past pres., dir.), Stark County Fast Pitch Assn. (Hall of Fame), Stark County Mental Health Soc. (bd. dirs.), East Ctrl. Ohio Tchrs. Assn., Buckeye Assn. Sch. Adminstrs., Stark County Elem. Prins. Assn. (pres. 1953—60, past. pres.), Timken HS Alumni Assn. (life disting. alumni 2006), Plain Local Alumni Assn. (life), Order Purple Heart (life), Ft. Lauderdale Country Club, Dapper Dan Club Akron, Willowbrook Lions Club, Canton Rotary Club, Pro Football Hall Fame Luncheon Club (past pres., dir.), Alliance County Club, North Canton Elks, Phi Delta Kappa. Avocations: golf, reading, sports. Home: 1130 Brushmore Ave NW Canton OH 44720 Home (Winter): 2320 Terra Ceia Blvd #401 Palmetto FL 34221 Home Phone: 330-499-6692, 941-729-9590.

MCFATE, PATRICIA ANN, foundation executive, science educator; b. Detroit, Mar. 19, 1936; d. John Earle and Mary Louise (Bliss) McF.; m. Sidney Norman Graybeal, Sept. 10, 1988. BA (Alumni scholar), Mich. State U., 1954; MA, Northwestern U., 1956, PhD, 1965; MA (hon.), U. Pa., 1977. Assoc. prof. English, asst. dean liberal arts and scis. U. Ill., Chgo., 1967-74, assoc. prof. English, assoc. vice chancellor acad. affairs, 1974-75; assoc. prof. folklore Faculty Arts and Scis., U. Pa., Phila., 1975-81; prof. tech. and soc. Coll. Engring. and Applied Sci., 1975-81, vice provost, 1975-78; dep. chmn. Nat. Endowment for Humanities, Washington, 1978-81; exec. v.p. Am.-Scandinavian Found., NYC, 1981-82, pres., 1982-88; sr. scientist Sci. Applications Internat. Corp., Mc Lean, Va., 1988—, program dir. Ctr. for Nat. Security Negotiations, 1988—; cons. UN, 1994-95. Vis. assoc. prof. dept. medicine Rush U., Chgo., 1970-85; bd. dirs. First Union Corp.; mem. sr. adv. panel Dept. Def., 1998—. Author: The Writings of James Stephens, 1979, Uncollected Prose of James Stephens, 1983; exec. producer Northern Stars, 1985, Diego Rivera: I Paint What I See, 1989, The Bear in the Skies, 1998; contbr. articles in fields of sci. policy and lit. to various jours. Mem. Arms Control and Non-Proliferation Adv. Bd., Dept. of State, 1995-2001; mem. disting. adv. panel Sandia Nat. Labs.; bd. dirs. Raoul Wallenberg Com. of U.S., Swedish Coun. Am., Santa Fe Cmty. Found., Santa Fe Opera, Lensic Performing Arts Ctr. Decorated officer Order of Leopold II Belgium, comdr. Order Icelandic Falcon, comdr. Royal Order of Polar Star (Sweden), comdr. Order of Lion (Finland), comdr. Royal Norwegian Order Merit, Knight 1st class Royal Order Dannebrog (Denmark); U. Ill. Grad. Coll. faculty fellow, 1968; Swedish Bicentennial Fund grantee, 1981 Fellow N.Y. Acad. Scis.; mem. AAAS (chmn. com. on sci., engring. and pub. policy 1984-87, com. on sci. and internat. security 1976-79, 88-93), Coun. on Fgn. Rels., Acad. Scis. Phila. (founding mem., corr. sec. 1977-79), Theta Alpha Phi, Omega Beta Pi, Delta Delta Delta. E-mail: patricia.a.mcfate@saic.com.

MCFAUL, DANIEL F., legislative staff member; b. Poughkeepsie, NY, July 31, 1972; BA, U. Fla., Gainesville, 1994; MPA, U. West Fla., Pensacola, 1999. Dir. mktg. First Nat. Life Ins. Co., 1994—96; sr. field analyst Nat. Rep. Congl. Com., 1998, sr. legis. asst., 1997—2000; dep. chief of staff, legis. dir. for Rep. Joe Scarborough US House of Reps., Washington, 2000—01, chief of staff for Rep. Jeff Miller, 2001—; campaign mem. Miller for Congress, 2001. Mem.: Fla. State Soc., Fla. Cicerones, Coll. Reps., Alpha Tau Omega. Roman Catholic. Office: Office of Congressman Jeff Miller 2205 Rayburn House Office Bldg Washington DC 20515 Office Phone: 202-225-4136. Business E-Mail: dan.mcfaul@mail.house.gov.*

MCFAYDEN, SHANNON W., bank holding company executive; b. Sept. 21, 1960; BA in psychology, Davidson Coll. Head human resources Fla. Bank (merged with Wachovia); with Wachovia Corp., 1982—, dir. human resources client svc., 1998—2001, dir. cmty. affairs, 2001—04, sr. v.p., 2004—, head corp. and cmty. affairs, 2004, sr. exec. v.p. HR & corp. rels., 2004—. Mem. steering com. Bus. Strengthening Am. Bd. dirs. United Way Capital Campaign Planning, KinderMourn, Cmty. Sch. Arts and Child Care Resources, Charlotte -Mecklenburg Pub. Schs. Found. Named one of 25 Most Powerful Women in Banking, US Banker, 2006. Mem.: Davidson Coll. Alumni Assn. Office: Wachovia Corp 1 Wachovia Ctr Charlotte NC 28288 E-mail: shannon.mcfayden@wachovia.com.

MCFEATTERS, ANN CAREY, journalist; b. Colorado Springs, Colo., June 27, 1944; d. Norman Cromer and Mildred Harriet Carey; m. Dale B. McFeatters, Sept. 27, 1969; children: Dale C., Matthew C., Kirsten C. BA, Marquette U., 1966. Reporter Evansville (Ind.) Press, 1966-68, Pitts. Press, 1969, Washington Daily News, 1969-70, Scripps Howard News Svc., Washington, 1970-99; Washington bur. chief Pitts. Post-Gazette and Toledo Blade, Washington, 1999—2006; polit. columnist Scripps Howard News Svc., 2006—. Author: Sandra Day O'Connor: Justice In The Balance, 2006. Named to Hall of Fame Soc. Profl. Journalists, 1998; recipient Disting. Svc. award Scripps Howard News Svc., 1999. Mem. Nat. Press Found. (chmn. 1996-98), Washington Press Club (pres. 1980-81), The Gridiron Club. Home Phone: 301-229-4999. Personal E-mail: amcfeatters@hotmail.com.

MCFEE, ARTHUR STORER, physician; b. Portland, Maine, May 1, 1932; s. Arthur Stewart and Helen Knight (Dresser) McF.; m. Iris Goeschel, May 13, 1967. BA cum laude, Harvard U., Cambridge, Mass., 1953, MD, 1957; MS, U. Minn., Mpls., 1966, PhD, 1967. Diplomate: Am. Bd. Surgery. Intern U. Minn. Hosp., 1957-58, resident in surgery, 1958-65; asst. prof. surgery U. Tex. Med. Sch., San Antonio, 1967-70, asso. prof., 1970-74, prof., 1974-2001, ret., 2001, prof. emeritus, 2001—. With Univ. Health Sys., Bexar-County, 1968-2003; spl. cons. on emergency med. care text to AAOS. Contbr. articles to profl. jours. Served with USNR, 1965-67. Fellow ACS; mem. AMA, Am. Assn. History of Medicine, Assn. Acad. Surgery, Tex. Med. Assn., Bexar County Med. Soc., Tex. Surg. Soc., Western Surg. Assn., San Antonio Surg. Soc., Soc. Surgery Alimentary Tract, So. Med. Assn., N.Y. Acad. Scis., Royal Soc. Medicine, So. Surg. Assn., Internat. Surg. Soc., Halsted Soc., J. Bradley Aust Surg. Soc., Am. Surg. Assn. Home: 131 Brittany Dr San Antonio TX 78212-1721 Office: MC 7842 7703 Floyd Curl Dr San Antonio TX 78229-3900 Office Phone: 210-567-2164. Business E-Mail: mcfee@uthscsa.edu. *Most of my life has been spent in training surgeons. It has been an informative experience.*

MCFEE, RICHARD, electrical engineer, physicist; b. Pitts., Jan. 24, 1925; s. William and Beatrice (Allender) McF.; m. Anne Stauffer, June 26, 1947 (div. 1960); m. 2d., Joanellen Lewis, Dec. 31, 1974. BEE, Yale U., 1947; MS in Physics, Syracuse U., 1949; PhDEE, U. Mich., 1955. Rsch. asst. Syracuse U. Med. Sch., 1947-48; instr. Syracuse U. elec. engring. dept., 1948-49; rsch. assoc. U. Mich. Med. Sch., 1949-51; engr. Electro-Mech. Rsch. Inc., Ridgefield, Conn., 1951-52; mem. tech. staff Bell Tel. Labs., Whippany, NJ, 1952-57; prof. elec. engring. Syracuse U., 1957-82; ind. rschr. Union Springs, NY, 1982—86, Hawi, Hawaii, 1986—. Contbr. articles on electronics, electrocardiography, magnetocardiography, superconductivity, circuit theory, thermodynamics, elec. measurements; patentee in field. Sgt. U.S. Army, 1943-46. Sci. Faculty fellowship NSF, Stanford U., 1970. Fellow IEEE; mem. AAAS, Sigma Xi. Home and Office: PO Box 989 Kapaau HI 96755-0989

MCFEELY, WILLIAM DRAKE, publishing company executive; b. Port Chester, NY, July 15, 1954; s. William Shield and Mary (Drake) McF.; m. Karen Gail Eliason, Aug. 12, 1978; children: Matthew Bensen, Eric Daniel, Laura Mae. BA cum laude, Amherst Coll., 1976. Coll. traveler W.W. Norton & Co., Inc., NYC, 1976-80, asst. sales mgr., 1980-82, editor, 1982—, v.p., 1990-94, bd. dirs., 1990—, pres., 1994—, chmn., 2000—. Dir. W.W. Norton & Co., Ltd.; trustee Princeton Univ. Press, chmn., 2004-, Ithaka Harbors, Inc. Mem. Assn. Am. Book Pubs.,

Nat. Book Found., Pubs. Lunch Club (pres. 1998-99), Seven Bridges Field Club (pres. 1989). Home: 106 Seven Bridges Rd Chappaqua NY 10514-1121 Office: WW Norton & Co 500 5th Ave Fl 6 New York NY 10110-0054

MC FERON, DEAN EARL, mechanical engineer, educator; b. Portland, Oreg., Dec. 24, 1923; s. Wallace Suitor and Ruth Carolyn (Fessler) McF.; m. Phyllis Grace Ehlers, Nov. 10, 1945; children: David Alan, Phyllis Ann, Douglas Dean, Donald Brooks. Student, Oreg. State Coll., 1942-43; BSME with spl. honors, U. Colo., 1945, MSME, 1948; PhD, U. Ill., 1956. Instr. U. Colo., Boulder, 1946-48; assoc. prof. U. Ill., 1948-58; rsch. assoc. Argonne (Ill.) Nat. Lab., 1957-58; prof. mech. engring., assoc. dean U. Wash., Seattle, 1958-82, prof. emeritus, 1983—. Cons. to industry, 1959-80. Served with USNR, 1942-46, to comdr. Res., 1946-72. Co-recipient Outstanding Tech. Applications Paper award ASHRAE, 1974; Ednl. Achievement award Soc. Mfg. Engrs., 1970; NSF faculty fellow, 1967-68 Mem. ASME, Am. Soc. Engring. Edn., U.S. Naval Inst. (life), Sigma Xi (nat. dir. 1972-80, nat. pres. 1978), Tau Beta Pi, Sigma Tau, Pi Tau Sigma. Office: U Wash Dept Mech Engring Seattle WA 98195-0001 Home: Heartstone Apt 1027 6720 E Green Lake Way N Seattle WA 98103-5458 Home Phone: 206-774-4315. *What matters most in life is what you can do for others.*

MCG, (JOSEPH MCGINTY NICHOL), television producer, film director; b. Kalamazoo, Mich., Aug. 9, 1968; BA in Psychology, U. Calif.-Irvine. Dir.: (videos) Korn: Who Then Now?, 1997, Sublime: Sublime, 1997, Cypress Hill: Still Smokin', 2001, The Offspring Complete Music Video Collection, 2005; (films) Charlie's Angels, 2000, Charlie's Angels: Full Throttle, 2003, We Are Marshall, 2006, Terminator Salvation, 2009; prodr.: (music videos) Smashmouth's Walking on the Sun, 1997 (Pop Video of Yr. award, Billboard Awards, 1997); prodr., co-writer (music videos) Sugar Ray's Fly, 1997 (Pop Video of Yr. award, Music Video Prodn. Assn., 1997), dir., exec. prodr. (TV series) Dan Finnerty & the Dan Band: I Am Woman, 2005, writer, exec. prodr. Fastlane, 2002—03; exec. prodr.: (TV films) The Dan Show, 2003, The Danny Comden Project, 2006, Jump, 2006, Skyler's Revolution, 2007, Spaced, 2008, (TV series) The O.C., 2003—07, The Mountain, 2004—05, Supernatural, 2005—09, The Pussycat Dolls Present: Search for the Nest Doll, 2007, Chuck, 2007—09, Pussycat Dolls Present: Girlicious, 2008, Sorority Forever, 2008, Exposed, 2008; prodr.: (films) Stay Alive, 2006. Recipient Hollywood Breakthrough award, Hollywood Film Festival, 2002. Office: c/o Mgmt 360 9111 Wilshire Blvd Beverly Hills CA 90210*

MCGAFFEY, JERE D., retired lawyer; b. Lincoln, Nebr., Oct. 6, 1935; s. Don Larsen and Doris McG.; m. Ruth S. Michelsen, Aug. 19, 1956; children: Beth, Karen. BA, BSc with high distinction, U. Nebr., 1957; LLB magna cum laude, Harvard U., 1961. Bar: Wis. 1961. Mem. firm Foley & Lardner LLP, Milw., 1961—2004, ptnr., 1968—2004. Dir. Wis. Gas Co., 1978-00, Smith Investment Co., 1973-2009, Northwestern Mut. Trust Co., 2000-06, Lord Balt. Corp.; mem. take-over adv. com., Gov. Wis., 1988-89, commn on state/local partnerships 21st century 2000-01. Author works in field. Chmn. bd. dirs. Helen Bader Found.; former vice chmn. legis. Milw. Met. Assn. Commerce, 1984—2003; former chmn. Wis. Taxpayers Alliance, sec.-treas., 1994—; bd. dirs. Aurora Health Care, 1986—, chmn., 1986—90; chmn. bd. advisors U. Wis. Nursing Sch., Milw. Mem. ABA (chmn. tax sect. 1990-91, ho. dels. 1995-2000, Sect. Taxation Disting. Svc. award 2005), AICPA, Wis. Bar Assn., Wis. Inst. CPAs, Am. Coll. Tax Counsel (chmn. 1996-98), Am. Coll. Trust and Estate Counsel (chmn. bus. planning com. 1994-97, regent 2000-06), Am. Law Inst., Univ. Club, Milw. Country Club, Harvard Club, Phi Beta Kappa, Beta Gamma Sigma, Delta Sigma Rho. Home: 12852 NW Shoreland Dr Mequon WI 53097-2304 Office: Foley & Lardner 777 E Wisconsin Ave Ste 3600 Milwaukee WI 53202-5302 Home Phone: 262-242-1766. Business E-Mail: jmcgaffey@foleylaw.com.

MCGAGH, WILLIAM GILBERT, financial consultant; b. Boston, May 29, 1929; s. Thomas A. and Mary M. (McDonough) McG.; m. Sarah Ann McQuigg, Sept. 23, 1961; children: Margaret Ellen, Sarah Elizabeth. BSBA, Boston Coll., 1950; MBA, Harvard U., 1952; MS, MIT, 1965. Fin. analyst Ford Motor Co., Dearborn, Mich., 1953-55; mem. staff treas. office Chrysler Corp., Detroit, 1955-64, compt., treas. Canadian divsn. Windsor, 1965-67, staff exec.-fin. Latin Am. ops. Detroit, 1967-68, asst. treas., 1968-75, treas., 1975-76, v.p., treas., 1976-80; sr. v.p. fin., dir. Northrop Grumman Corp., LA, 1980-88. Mem. adv. bd. Santa Monica-UCLA and Orthopaedic Hosp. Mem. bd. regents Mt. St. Mary's Coll.; bd. dirs. L.A. Orthop. Hosp.; bd. dirs. John Tracy Clinic. Sloan fellow MIT, 1965. Mem. Fin. Execs. Inst. (pres. Detroit chpt. 1979-80), L.A. Country Club, Calif. Club (L.A.), Eastward Ho Country Club (Chatham, Mass.). Home: 2189 Century Hill Los Angeles CA 90067 Home Phone: 310-557-0992; Office Phone: 310-248-4395. Personal E-mail: wgm9601@aol.com.

MCGAHEE, WILLIS ANDREW, professional football player; b. Miami, Fl, Oct. 20, 1981; s. Willis McGahee and Jannie Jones. Student, U. Miami, 1999—2003. Running back Buffalo Bills, 2004—07, Balt. Ravens, 2007—. Named to Am. Football Conf. Pro Bowl Team, NFL, 2007. Office: Balt Ravens 1101 Russell St Baltimore MD 21230*

MCGAHN, DONALD F., II, commissioner, lawyer; b. Atlantic City, 1968; Attended, US Naval Acad., Annapolis, Md.; BA in History, U. Notre Dame, Ind., 1991; JD, Widener U. Sch. Law, 1994; attended, Georgetown U. Law Ctr. Bar: DC 1994. Law clerk to Hon. Charles R. Alexander Ct. Common Pleas, Clarion, Pa.; cert. legal intern Lebanon County Dist. Atty., Pa.; atty., litig. group Patton Boggs LLP, Washington; atty., head McGahn & Associates, PLLC, Washington; gen. counsel Nat. Republican Congl. Com., Washington, 1999—; counsel Ill. Republican Party, 2005—; commr. Fed. Election Commn., Washington, 2008—, chmn., 2008—. Republican. Avocation: guitar. Office: McGahn & Associates PLLC 509 7th St NW Washington DC 20004 also: Fed Election Commn 999 E St NW Washington DC 20463 Office Phone: 202-694-1000, 202-654-7035. Office Fax: 202-654-7033.*

MCGAHREN, EUGENE DEWEY, III, surgeon; b. NYC, Aug. 24, 1958; MD, U. Va., 1984. Diplomate Am. Bd. Surgery. Intern U. Va., Charlottesville, 1984-85; resident in pediatric surgery Childrens Hosp., Seattle, 1990-92; asst. prof. pediat., pediatric surgery U. Va., 1992—. Mem. Am. Coll. Surgeons, Assoc. Acad. Surgery, Va. Med. Soc., Va. Surg. Soc. Office: Univ Va Health Sci Ctr PO Box 800709 Charlottesville VA 22906-0109

MCGANN, C. STEVEN, United States Ambassador to Fiji, Nauru, Kiribati and Tonga and Tuvalu; BA, Claremont McKenna Coll., Calif., 1973; grad. studies in comparative govt., Cornell U., Ithaca, NY, 1975—78; MS, Nat. Def. U. Indsl. Coll. the Armed Forces, 2003; participant Fourth Joint Force Maritime Comdr. component course, Naval War Coll., 2007. Fgn. svc. assignments US Dept. State, Taiwan, Zaire, South Africa, Australia, Kenya, with US mission to the UN, 1998—2000, dep. dir. South Asia Bur., 2000—02, dir. Asia and Near East, Bur. Population, Refugees and Migration, 2003—05, sr. adviser, Bur. East Asian and Pacific Affairs, dir. office Australian, New Zealand and Pacific Island affairs, Bur. East Asian and Pacific Affairs, US amb. to the Republics of Fiji, Nauru, Kiribati and the Kingdom of Tonga and Tuvalu Suva, 2008—. Office: DOS Amb 4290 Suva Pl Washington DC 20521-4290*

MCGANN, JEROME JOHN, language educator; b. NYC, July 22, 1937; s. John Joseph and Marie Violet (Lecouffe) McG.; m. Anne Patricia Lanni, July 26, 1938; children: Geoffrey, Christopher, Jennifer. BS, Le Moyne Coll., 1959; MA, Syracuse U., 1962; PhD, Yale U., 1966; LHD (hon.), U. Chgo., 1996. From asst. prof. to prof. U. Chgo., 1966-75; prof. Johns Hopkins U., Balt., 1975-80; Dreyfuss prof. humanities Calif. Inst. Tech., Pasadena, 1980-86; John Stewart Bryan univ. prof. U. Va., Charlottesville, 1987—. Author: Swinburne: An Experiment in Criticism, 1972 (Melville Cane award 1972), The Romantic Ideology, 1983, The Beauty of Inflections, 1985, Social Values and Poetic Acts, 1987, Towards a Literature of Knowledge, 1989, The Textual Condition, 1991, Black Riders: The Visible Language of Modernism, 1993; editor: The New Oxford Book of Romantic Period Verse, 1993, Poetics of Sensibility: A Revolution in Literary Style, 1996, Byron: Complete Poetical Works, 7 vols., 1980-93, Dante Gabriel Rossetti and the Game That Must Be Lost, 2000, The Complete Writings and Pictures of Dante Gabriel Rosetti: A Hypermedia Research Archive, 2000—, Radiant Textuality, Literature after the World Wide Web, 2001, Byron and Romanticism, 2002, D.G. Rossetti. Collected Poetry and Prose, 2003, Swinburne, Selected Poetry and Prose, 2004, The Scholar's Art: Literary Studies in a Managed World, 2006, The Point Is To Change It, Literature in the Continuing Present, 2007; author Are the Humanities Inconsequent?, Byron's Manfred, Black Riders: And Other Lines, 2009, editor 27 scholarly books and 5 poetry books. Recipient Mellon Achievement award, 2003, Richard Lyman award, 2002, James Russell Lowell award, 2002; Fulbright fellow, Fels Found. fellow, Eng., 1965-66; Guggenheim fellow, Eng., 1970-71, 74-75; NEH fellow, Eng. and Europe, 1975-76, 87-88, 2003—. Fellow: Am. Acad. Arts and Scis.; mem.: MLA. Address: English Department Bryan Hall U VA Charlottesville VA 22903 Office Phone: 434-924-4064. Business E-Mail: jjm2f@virginia.edu.

MCGANN, LISA B. NAPOLI, language educator; b. West Hartford, Conn., Sept. 07; d. James Napoli; m. Edward Harrison McGann, Jr. BA, Vassar Coll., 1980; MA, Columbia U., 1983, postgrad., 1991-95; MA, Middlebury Coll., 1987. Cert. tchr. French, ESL and Italian, Conn. Cmty. English program coord. Tchrs. Coll. Columbia U., NYC, 1982-83; mgr. English tchg. com. Jr. League N.Y., NYC, 1983-84; asst. dir. ESL Fordham U., NYC, 1988-89; ESL instr. Laguardia C.C., CUNY, Long Island City, NY, 1983—, Columbia U., 1983-96. ESL instr. Yale U., 1988, 89; ESL specialist, tchr. UN, NYC, 1990. Big sister Highland Hts., New Haven, 1976-77; ESL tchr. Boys and Girls Club, Astoria, NY, 1992. Recipient awards and scholarships. Mem. Nat. TESOL Soc., Italian-Am. Hist. Soc., Nat. Italian Am. Found. (coun.), The Statue of Liberty-Ellis Island Found., Inc. Roman Catholic. Avocations: ballet, reading, travel, real estate, tennis.

MCGARITY, ARTHUR EDWIN, engineering educator, researcher; b. Chgo., Apr. 2, 1951; s. Owen and Lois Thomas McGarity; m. Jane Ellen Ziegler, June 11, 1977; children: Kate McGarity Woodruff, Owen Carlos, Samuel Arthur, Micajah Ziegler. BS, Trinity U., San Antonio, 1973; MSE, Johns Hopkins U., Balt., 1978, PhD, 1979. Asst. prof. Swarthmore Coll., Swarthmore, 1978—84, assoc. prof., 1984—93, prof., 1993—, Henry C. and J. Archer Turner prof. engring., 2000—, coord. environ. studies, 2000—05; vis. asst. prof. Johns Hopkins U., 1981; scientist residence Argonne Nat. Lab., Ill., 1981—82; vis. fellow Princeton U., NJ, 1985—86; fulbright sr. lectr. Krakow U. Tech., Poland, 1989—90, 1998, hon. prof., 2005—. Founder and chair Crum Creek Watershed Partnership, Swarthmore, 1999—2004. Contbr. scientific papers. Trustees Swarthmore United Meth. Ch., Swarthmore, Pa., 2005—08; bd. mem. Swarthmore Swim Club, Swarthmore, Pa., 2001—05; mem. Chester Ridley Crum Watersheds Assn., Media, Pa., 1995—2001. Growing Greener grant, Pa. Dept. Environ. Protection, 2002—04, grant, US EPA, 2005—06, Coastal Zone Rsch. grant, Pa. Dept. Environ. Protection, 2003—05, 2007—. Mem.: ASCE, INFORMS, Am. Water Resources Assn. Achievements include research in analytical simulation method for solar energy system design; storm WISE method for optimal investments in stormwater management. Avocations: amateur radio, lap swimming, football. Office: Swarthmore Coll 500 College Ave Swarthmore PA 19081

MCGARR, FRANK JAMES, retired federal judge, consultant; b. Feb. 25, 1921; married; 6 children. BA cum laude, Loyola U., Chgo., 1942, JD, 1950, degree (hon.), 2002. Bar: Ill. 1950. Assoc. Dallstream Schiff Stern & Hardin, Chgo., 1952—54; asst. U.S. atty., chief criminal divsn. No. dist. of Ill., 1954—55, first asst. U.S. atty., 1955—58; ptnr. McKay Solum & McGarr, Chgo., 1958—68; first asst. atty. gen. State of Ill., 1969—70; judge U.S. Dist. Ct. for No. Ill., 1970—88, chief judge, 1981—86, sr. judge, 1986—88; of counsel Phelan Cahill & Quinlan, Chgo., 1988—96, Foley & Lardner, Chgo., 1996—2001; arbitration and medication pvt. practice, 2001—. Instr. Eng. and pub. speaking Loyola U., 1946—48, administrv. asst. to pres., 1948—52; instr. law Loyola U. Law Sch., 1950—52, instr. criminal law, 1953—57, prof. admiralty and maritime law, 1953—57; instr. legal ethics John Marshal Law Sch., 1985—86. Chmn. law observance com. Chgo. Crime Comm., v.p., bd. dirs.; chmn. Law Enforcement Week Com.; pres. Constl. Rights Found., 1994; chmn. Ill Gov.'s Comm. on Death Penalty, 2000. With USN, 1942—45, Pacific Fleet. Recipient Alumni Medal of Excellence, Loyola Law Alumni, 1964, Mother Cabrini award, Columbus-Cuneo-Cabrini Med. Ctr., 1978, Dei Gloriam award, St. Ignatius Coll. Prep, 1984, Disting. Jurist award, Loyola U. Law Sch., Chgo.; named Man of Yr., Cath. Lawyers Guild Chgo., 1985. Fellow: Am. Coll. Trial Lawyers; mem.: Soc. Trial Lawyers, Chgo. Bar Assn., Fed. Bar Assn. (pres. chgo. chpt. 1962—63, mem. exec. com.), 7th Cir. Bar Assn. Office: 4146 Venard Rd Downers Grove IL 60515-1908 Office Phone: 630-960-4655, 630-960-0985.

MCGARRELL, JAMES, artist, educator; b. Indpls., Feb. 22, 1930; s. James and Gretchen (Heermann) McG.; m. Anna (Harris), June 24, 1955; children: Andrew Rider, Flora Raven. BA, Ind. U., 1953; MA, U. Calif. at Los Angles, 1955. Artist in residence Reed Coll., Portland, Oreg., 1956—59; prof. fine arts, dir. grad. painting Ind. U., Bloomington, Ind., 1959—80; prof. fine arts Washington U., St. Louis, 1981—93, prof. emeritus, 1993—; artist in residence Dartmouth Coll., 1993, Roswell, N. Mex. Found., 1999. Exhibitions include Frumkin, Adams Gallery, N.Y.C., 1961, 1964, 1966, Gallery Claude Bernard, Paris, 1967, Gallery Il Fante de Spade, Rome and Milan, 1967, Frumkin, Adams Gallery, N.Y.C., 1968, Gallery Claude Bernard, Paris, 1970, Gallery Il Fante de Spade, Rome and Milan, 1971, Frumkin, Adams Gallery, N.Y.C., 1971, Gallery Il Fante de Spade, Rome and Milan, 1972, Utah Mus. Art, Salt Lake City, 1972, Frumkin, Adams Gallery, N.Y.C., 1973, Gallery Il Fante de Spade, Rome and Milan, 1974, Gallery Claude Bernard, Paris, 1974, Gallery Il Fante de Spade, Rome and Milan, 1976, Frumkin, Adams Gallery, N.Y.C., 1977, Gallery Il Fante de Spade, Rome and Milan, 1979, Frumkin, Adams Gallery, N.Y.C., 1980, Galeria Gian Ferrari, Milan, 1981, Art Mus. Univ. N.Mex., Albuquerque, 1982, Gallery Gian Ferrari, Milan, 1983, Frumkin, Adams Gallery, N.Y.C., 1984, St. Louis Art Mus., 1985, Frumkin, Adams Gallery, N.Y.C., 1986, More Gallery, Phila., 1987, Frumkin, Adams Gallery, N.Y.C., 1988, 1988, Struve Gallery, Chgo., 1988, Frumkin, Adams Gallery, N.Y.C., 1989, Gallery Simonne Stern, New Orleans, 1989, Frumkin, Adams Gallery, N.Y.C., 1989, More Gallery, Phila., 1989, Frumkin, Adams Gallery, N.Y.C., 1990, Struve Gallery, Chgo., 1990, Printworks Gallery, 1990, Gallery Simonne Stern, New Orleans, 1991, Frumkin, Adams Gallery, N.Y.C., 1991, 1993, More Gallery, Phila., 1994, Gallery Simonne Stern, New Orleans, 1994, Frumkin, Adams Gallery, N.Y.C., 1995, Gallery Simonne Stern, New Orleans, 1995, George Adams Gallery, N.Y.C., 1997, Gallery Simonne Stern, New Orleans, 1998, The Art Gallery Univ. N.H., Durham, 1998, Art Mus. U. Ariz., Tucson, 1998, Printworks Gallery, Chgo., 1999, Gallery Simonne Stern, New Orleans, 2000, George Adams Gallery, N.Y.C., 2000, Sonia Zaks Gallery, Chgo., 2001, 2003, Heriard Cimino Gallery, New Orleans, 2003, Roswell (NM) Mus. Art Ctr., 2004, Brattleboro Art Mus., Brattleboro (VT), 2005, Jane Haslem Gallery, Wash., DC, 2008, Represented in permanent collections Mus. Modern Art, N.Y.C., Met. Mus. Art, Whitney Mus. Am. Art, Pa. Acad., Phila., Santa Barbara Mus. Art, Calif., San Francisco Art Mus., Art Inst., Chgo., Joseph Hirshborn Mus., Washington, St. Louis Art Mus., Hamburg Mus. Art, Germany, Centre Georges Pompidou, Paris, Rose Art Mus., Brandeis U. Bd. gov. Skowhegan Sch. Painting and Sculpture. Recipient Am. Acad. Arts and Letters Lifetime Achievement award, 1995, Oscar Williams amd Gene Derwood award, 2008; Fulbright Fellow, 1955-56; Guggenheim Found. Fellow, 1965; Nat. Endowment for Arts grantee, 1967, 85; Bogliasco Found. Fellow, 2003; Rockerfeller Found. Bellagio Ctr. Fellow, 2005. Mem. Coll. Art Assn. (bd. dir. 1969-73), Academie des Beaux Arts de L'Institut de France, Nat. Acad. Design. Home: PO Box 39 Newbury VT 05051-0039 Office Phone: 802-866-5447. E-mail: bluedeuce@charter.net.

MCGARRY, FREDERICK JEROME, civil engineering educator; b. Rutland, Vt., Aug. 22, 1927; s. William John and Ellen (Dunn) McG.; m. Alice M. Reilly, Oct. 7, 1950 (dec. Jan. 1971); children: Martha Ellen, Alice Catherine, Joan Louise, Carol Elizabeth, Susan Elizabeth, Janet Marian. AB, Middlebury Coll., Vt., 1950; S.B., MIT, 1950, S.M., 1953. Faculty MIT, 1950—2002, prof. civil engring., 1965—2002, prof. materials sci. and engring., 1974—2002, head materials divsn., 1964—2002, dir. materials rsch. lab., 1964—2002, assoc. dir. inter-Am. program civil engring., 1961—2002, dir. summer session, 1983—2002; ret., 2002. Contbr. numerous articles to profl. jours. Recipient Best Paper award Soc. Plastics Industry, 1968, 91. Mem. AAAS, ASTM, Soc. Rheology, Soc. Plastics Engrs., Am. Soc. Metals, Sigma Xi. Office: MIT Rm 8-209 77 Massachusetts Ave Cambridge MA 02139-4301 Mailing: PO Box 446 Weston MA 02493

MCGARRY, MARCIA, retired community service coordinator; b. Washington, Dec. 9, 1941; d. Emil Sylvester and Bernice B. (Bland) Busey. BS, Morgan State U., 1964. Cert. tchr., law enforcement officer, Fla. Payroll clk., jr. acct. U.S. Dept. Labor, Washington, 1964-65; English tchr. Taiwan, 1968-70; tchr. Monroe County Sch. Bd., Key West, Fla., 1971-81; exec. dir. Monroe Assn. Retarded Citizens, Key West, 1977-79; dep. sheriff Monroe County Sheriff's Dept., Key West, 1979-83, 86-90; probation/parole officer Fla. State Dept. Corrections, Key West, 1983-91; law enforcement instr. Fla. Keys C.C., 1983-91; cmty. svc. coord. City of Bradenton, 1991-2000; domestic violence specialist II Broward County Sheriff Dept., 2001—06. Mem. judicial nom. commn. Fla. Gov. Lawton Chiles, 1994—96; former mem. rev. bd. Bradenton Police Dept., mem. cmty. rels. com., 1996—2000; mem. adv. bd. Manatee County Sheriff's Dept., mem. eligibility bd., 1996—2000; mem. Mayor's adv. bd. City of Bradenton, 1999—2000. Active local polit. campaigns; co-founder day schs. for under-privileged children; former mem. Big Bros./Big Sisters Am., mem. com., 1985-86, former bd. dirs., Spouse Abuse, former bd. dirs.; bd. dirs. Adv. Coun. Orange-Ridge Elem., 1991-93; bd. dirs. mayor's com., chmn. task force Drug Free Cmtys., 1991-94, bd. dirs., 1996-2001; bd. dirs. Human Rels. Commn., 1991-93, Drug Free Schs. and Cmty. Adv. Coun., 1991-98, T.O.T.S. (These Our Tots), Inc., 1998-2000; former mem. adv. coun. Byrd Edn. Found., Sweet Adelines Internat., 1992-94, commr. 12th Jud. Nominating Commn., 1992-99, cons., facilitator Cultural Diversity Conflict Resolution Workshops, Manatee County High Schs. and Bradenton Police Dept.; attendance adv. com. Bayshore High, 1993, multicultural com., 1994, former rep. Women's Forum; former dir. choir Luth. Ch.; founding mem. Comprehensive Neighborhood Support Network; charter mem. Women's History Month Mus., Nat. Womens Hist. Mus. Recipient Appreciation cert., Lions Club, 1978, 1979, Career Week award, Harris Elem. Sch., 1981, Glynn Archer Elem. Sch., 1989, Trainers award, Probation/Parole Acad., 1987, Cert. of Acknowledgement for Cmty. Svc., AAUW, 1995, awadrd, Vol. Army for the War on Drugs, 1989. Mem.: Delta Sigma Theta (v.p. 1990—91, corr. sec. 1993—95). Republican. Lutheran. Avocations: reading, travel, musuems. Personal E-mail: marciadnc@aol.com.

MCGARVA, ANDREW ROBERT, psychology professor; b. Buffalo, Nov. 7, 1968; s. Mary Ann and William Nmi McGarva; m. Kay Lynn Hoff, July 25, 2000; children: Lexi Katherine, Keely Elizabeth. PhD, U. NH, Durham, 1997. Cert. in cognate coll. tchg. NH, 1997. Prof. psychology Dickinson State U, ND, 1997—. Coach Dickinson Hockey Club, ND, 1998—2008. Mem.: Sigma Xi. Democrat. Episcopal. Achievements include research in factors underlying driver aggression. Avocations: skiing, golf, sailing, hockey, hiking. Home: 1252 1st St West Dickinson ND 58601 Office: Dickinson State Univ Campus Dr Dickinson ND 58601 Business E-Mail: andrew.mcgarva@dsu.nodak.edu.

MCGARVEY, DANIEL JOHN, ecologist, educator; b. Seoul, Republic of Korea, Sept. 7, 1975; adopted s. Gary McGarvey and Christine Smith; m. Angela Obery, June 30, 2007. BA, Wittenberg U., Springfield, Ohio, 1997; MS, Pa. State U., University Pk., 2001; PhD, U. Ala., Tuscaloosa, 2007. Stream ecologist Nat. Coun. Air and Stream Improvement, Anacortes, Wash., 1999—2002; instr. Oreg. State U., Dept. Fisheries and Wildlife, Corvallis, Oreg., 2006; fisheries ecologist Ind. Multidisciplinary Sci. Team, Corvallis, 2007; postdoc. rsch. assoc. US EPA, Athens, Ga., 2007—. Instr. U. Ga., Athens, 2008—09. Contbr. articles to profl. jours. Fellowship, US EPA, 2005—07. Mem.: Soc. Conservation Biology, N.Am. Benthological Soc. (President's award 2005), Ecol. Soc. Am., Am. Fisheries Soc. Avocations: rock climbing, bicycling.

MCGARY, CARL THOMAS, pathologist; s. Thomas E. and Nellie C. McGary; m. Maureen C. Lowe, Mar. 1, 1997; children: Margaret A., Elizabeth C. BS in Biology, Slippery Rock U. Pa., 1983; PhD, U. Tex. Med. Br. Sch. Biomed. Scis., Galveston, 1988; MD, Pa. State U. Coll. Medicine, Hershey, 1990. Diplomate in anatomic pathology Am. Bd. Pathology, 1995. Resident and fellow anatomic pathology Pa. State U. Coll. Medicine, 1990—95; asst. prof. pathology U. Rochester Sch. Medicine, NY, 1995—2001; pathologist and ptnr. Ctrl. Regional Pathology, Woodbury, Minn., 2001—. Cytology, histology med. dir. Health-East Care Sys., St. Paul, 2003—08. Office: Ctrl Regional Pathology 1875 Woodwinds Dr Ste 220 Woodbury MN 55125-2502 Business E-Mail: cmcgary@healtheast.org.

MCGAUGHEY, CHARLES GILBERT, retired biochemist; b. San Diego, Sept. 8, 1925; s. Gilbert Arthur and Louisa Ellen (Inskeep) McG. BA, U. Calif., Berkeley, 1950; MA, U. So. Calif., 1952. Diplomate Am. Inst. Oral Biology. Scientist radiol. hazards evaluation U.S. Naval Radiol. Def. Lab., San Francisco, 1952; rsch. biochemist VA Med. Ctr., Long Beach, Calif., 1953-81; prin. investigator studied dental caries, plaque and oral cancer Oral Diseases Rsch. Lab., 1978-81. Contbr. articles to profl. jours. Grantee Nat. Inst. Dental Rsch., 1965. Mem. AAAS. Home: 337 N Winnipeg Pl Long Beach CA 90814-2564

MCGAVIN, JOHN DAVID, lawyer; b. Washington, Apr. 15, 1957; s. Thomas A. and Jane Louise (Haupt) McG.; m. Linda Judith Peele, Oct. 6, 1984. BA with distinction, U. Va., 1979; JD, Coll. William and Mary, 1982. Bar: Va. 1982, U.S. Dist. Ct. (ea. dist.) Va. 1983, U.S. Ct. Appeals (4th cir.) 1983, U.S. Dist. Ct. (we. dist.) Va. 1985, U.S. Supreme Ct., 1995, DC, US DC Circuit, 2004. Law clk. to presiding justice U.S. Dist. Ct. (ea. dist.) Va., Alexandria, 1982-83; assoc. Lewis, Tydings, Bryan & Trichilo, P.C., Fairfax, Va., 1983-87; ptnr. Trichilo, Bancroft, McGavin, Horvath & Judkins, P.C., Fairfax, 1988—. Recipient NICB award, 2004, DRI award, 2005, Furniss award, Va. Assn. Def. Attys., 2006, Best Lawyer award, Wash. Mags.; named Super Lawyer, Va., 2007—, Washington, 2007—. Fellow Va. Law Found., Am. Coll. Trial Lawyers (Va. state com. mem. 2009); mem. Va. Bar Assn. (cir. rep. young lawyers conf. 1988), Fairfax Bar Assn. (chmn. law and medicine com. 1988), No. Va. Young Lawyers Assn (sec. 1986, pres. 1987), Va. Assn. Def. Attys. (pres. 2004-05), Boyd-Graves Conf., US Dist. Ct. Judicial Selection Com. Ea. Dist. 7, Va., 21st Century Va. Ct., River Bend Golf and Country Club, Martindale Hubbell. Republican. Methodist. Avocations: tennis, golf. Home: 10004 Park Royal Dr Great Falls VA 22066-1847 Office: 3920 University Dr Fairfax VA 22030-2514 Home Phone: 703-759-6432; Office Phone: 703-385-1000. Business E-Mail: jmcgavin@tbmhjlaw.com.

MCGAVRAN, FREDERICK JAEGER, lawyer; b. Columbus, Ohio, Apr. 24, 1943; s. James Holt and Marion (Jaeger) McG.; m. Elizabeth Dowlig, Jan. 5, 1980; children: Sarah Ann, Marian Katherine. BA, Kenyon Coll., 1965; JD, Harvard U., 1972. Bar: Ohio 1972, U.S. Supreme Ct. 1984, Ky. 1992. With Kyte, Conlan, Wulsin & Vogeler, Cin., 1972-78, Frost & Jacobs, Cin., 1978-2000, Frost, Brown & Todd, LLC, Cin., 2000—. Editor-in-chief Sixth Circuit Federal Practice Manual, 1999. Lt. USN, 1965—69. Mem. Fed. Bar Assn. (pres. Cin. chpt. 1984-85, mem. exec. com. Cin. chpt. 1985—), Ohio State Bar Assn. (chmn. com. on fed. cts. 1982-85), Univ. Club of Cin., The Literary Club (trustee). Home: 3528 Traskwood Cir Cincinnati OH 45208 Office: Frost Brown & Todd LLC 2200 PNC Ctr 201 E Fifth St Cincinnati OH 45202 Home Phone: 513-871-4840; Office Phone: 513-651-6940. Business E-Mail: fmcgavran@fbtlaw.com.

MCGEARY, BARBARA JOYCE, artist, educator; b. Ellwood City, Pa., June 26, 1932; d. Harold Raymond and Helma Joyce Conner; m. Clyde Mills McGeary, Aug. 25, 1954; children: Melinda, Martha, Marilee, Clyde. BS, Ind. U. Pa., 1954; postgrad., U. Pitts., 1962—64, Temple U., 1975—77, Pa. Dept. Edn., 1978. Cert. tchr. art, supr. Pa. Tchr. secondary art North Allegheny Schs., Pitts., 1954—55; supr. art Laurel Joint Schs., New Castle, Pa., 1955—56, New Kensington, Arnold Schs., Pa., 1963; instr. U. Manitoba, Winnipeg, Canada, 1965; thcr. art Harrisburg Schs., Harrisburg, Pa., 1970—72; tchr. art Mechanicsburg Schs., Pa., 1967—69; dir. Arts Magnet Sch., Harrisburg Schs., Pa., 1972—89, supr. arts, 1974—89. Assoc. McGeary Consulting Group, Camp Hill, Pa., 1988—93; spl. advisor/cons. Pa. Dept. Edn., Harrisburg, 1989. Co-author (text series): My World of Art, 1963, Learning Through Art, 1972. Chmn. judges Scholastic Arts, Harrisburg, Pa., 1975—90; mem. edn. com. Susquehanna Art Mus., Harrisburg, Pa., 1995—2005; co-chair fine arts Cumberland County 250th, Carlisle, Pa., 2000; pres. Hist. Soc. of Camp Hill, 2008—; ruling elder Camp Hill Presbyn. Ch., 1970—76. Recipient Disting. Svc. in the Arts award, Harrisburg Theatre Assn., 1995; named one of Outstanding Women Who Work, Harrisburg Patriot-News, 1980. Mem.: Pa. Art Edn. Assn., Nat. Art Edn. Assn., Cosmopolitan Internat. (founding mem., Capital region pres. 1995—96), Tuscarora Forest Property Owners Assn. (1st female pres. 2001—03). Republican. Presbyterian. Avocations: historic preservation, environmental projects, gardening, interior decorating, landscape design. Home: 248 Willow Ave Camp Hill PA 17011 Office: McGeary Assocs 248 Willow Ave Camp Hill PA 17011 Personal E-mail: cbmcgeary@verizon.net.

MCGEE, HAROLD JOHNSTON, former academic administrator; b. Portsmouth, Va., Apr. 13, 1937; s. Harold Valentine McGee and Clara Mae (Johnston) Webber; m. Mary Frances Eure, Mar. 22, 1959; children: Harold Johnston, Mary Margaret, Matthew Hayden; m. Linda Gayle Stevens, Apr. 3, 1976; 1 child, Andrew Meade. BS, Old Dominion U., 1959; MEd, U. Va., 1962, EdD, 1968; HumD, James Madison U., 1999. Tchr. Falls Church (Va.) City Schs., 1959-62; asst. dean, then dean of admissions Old Dominion U., Norfolk, Va., 1962-65; field rep., program officer, sr. program officer U.S. Office Edn. Bur. Higher Edn., Charlottesville, 1965-70; provost Tidewater Community Coll., Portsmouth, 1970-71; founding pres. Piedmont Va. Community Coll., Charlottesville, 1971-75; various offices including dean grad. sch., asst. to pres., v.p. student affairs, v.p. adminstrv. affairs, sec. bd. visitors James Madison U., Harrisonburg, Va., 1975-86; pres. Jacksonville (Ala.) State U., 1986-99, pres. emeritus, 1999—. Bd. dirs. Gulf South Conf., chmn., 1990—92, Ala. Coun. Univ. Pres., 1991—92; bd. dirs. Trans America Athletic Conf., chmn., 1998—99. Author: Impact of Federal Support, 1968, The Virginia Project, 1976. Mem. United Way Calhoun County Ala., 1986—92, Leadership Ala.; bd. dir. Ala. 529 Fund Savs. Bd., 2009—, Ala. Prepaid Coll. Tuition Bd., 2004—09. Mem.: NCAA (coun. 1991—95), Phi Delta Kappa. Episcopalian.

MCGEE, HENRY ALEXANDER, JR., academic administrator; b. Atlanta, Sept. 12, 1929; s. Henry Alexander and Arrie Mae (Mallory) McG.; m. Betty Rose Herndon, July 29, 1951; children: Henry Alexander, Charles Nelson, Kathy Nan. BChemE, Ga. Inst. Tech., 1951, PhD, 1955; postgrad., U. Wis., 1955-56. Rsch. scientist Army Rocket and Guided Missile Agy. and NASA, Huntsville, Ala., 1956-59; from assoc. prof. to prof. chem. engring. Ga. Inst. Tech., Atlanta, 1959-71; prof. Va. Poly. Inst. and State U., Blacksburg, 1971-94, head dept. chem. engring., 1971-82; assoc. provost for engring. Va. Commonwealth U., Richmond, 1994-95, founding dean engring., 1995-99, founding dean emeritus, prof. chem. engring., 1999—; asst. to dean engring. and mfg. techs. J. Sargeant Reynolds C.C., 2006—. Vis. prof. Calif. Inst. Tech., 1984; dir. chem. and transport sys. div. NSF, Washington, 1990-93; cons. in field. Author: Molecular Engineering, 1991; editorial adv. bd.: Chemical Abstracts; contbr. numerous articles to profl. publs. Bd. dirs. Greater Richmond Tech. Coun., Math. Sci. Innovation Ctr. Recipient Cmty. Svc. award Richmond Joint Engrs. Coun., 2000, Leadership award Greater Richmond Tech. Coun., 2002; Rsch. grantee NSF, NASA, Air Force Office Sci. Rsch.; named one of five Outstanding Young Men of Yr. Atlanta, 1964, Acad. Disting. Engring. Alumni, Ga. Tech., 1994; Danforth assoc.; named to Hall of Fame, Ga. Tech., 2006. Fellow AIChE (chmn. nat. program com., mem. editl. bd. jour), AAAS (chmn. sect. on engring. 1985-86); mem. Am. Chem. Soc.; mem. Sigma Xi. Republican. Home: 6 River Court Ln Richmond VA 23238-5581 Office Phone: 804-754-5576. Business E-Mail: hmcgee@vcu.edu.

MCGEE, HUGH E., III, investment company executive; BS summa cum laude, Princeton Univ., 1981; JD with honors, Univ. Tex., 1984. With Lehman Bros. Holdings, NYC, 1993—, mng. dir., mem. exec. com., head investment banking div., 2002—. Office: Lehman Bros Holdings 745 Seventh Ave New York NY 10019 Office Phone: 212-526-2863. Business E-Mail: hmcgee@lehman.com.

MCGEE, HUMPHREY GLENN, retired architect; b. June 26, 1937; s. James Gladney and Elizabeth Adams (Williams) McG. BArch, Clemson U., 1960. Designer Clark, McCall & Leach, Hartsville-Kingstree, S.C., 1961; designer prodn. A. G. Odell & Assocs., Charlotte, N.C., 1962; chief designer Clark, McCall & Leach, Hartsville-Kingstree, 1963; sr. designer LBC & W, Inc., Columbia, SC, 1965—76, sr. v.p. client svcs. and design, 1976; pres. CEDA, Inc., Columbia, S.C., 1976-86; pres., treas. McGee-Howle & Assocs., Vero Beach, Fla., 1986—2002; pvt. practice Indian River Shores, Fla., 2002—05, Chattanooga, 2002—05; ret., 2005. Pub.: Who's Who in Interior Design, 1993-95; cited in 100 Designer's Favorite Rooms, 1993, 94, 95. With USAR, 1961-67. Mem. AIA, Nat. Soc. Interior Designers (award 1972), Am. Soc. Interior Designers (chmn. S.C. chpt. com. on Found. Interior Design Edn. and Rsch. 1976). Personal E-mail: hglennmcgee@aol.com, hglennmcgee@comcast.net.

MCGEE, JAMES D., United States Ambassador to Zimbabwe; b. Chgo., 1949; m. Shirley Jean French. Grad., Ind. U.; grad. in Vietnamese Lang. Studies, Def. Lang. Inst., Monterey, Calif. With US Fgn. Svc., 1981—82, third sec., vice consul, US Embassy Lagos, Nigeria, 1982—84, adminstrv. officer, Am. Consulate Gen. Lahore, Pakistan, 1984—86, second sec., supervisory gen. svcs. officer, Am. Embassy The Hague, Netherlands, 1986—89, adminstrv. officer, Am. Consulate Gen. Bombay, adminstrv. counselor, Am. Embassy Bridgetown, Barbados, 1992—95, Kingston, Jamaica, 1995—98, Abidjan, Cote d'Ivoire, 1998—2001; spl. asst., bur. fin. and mgmt. policy US Dept. State, 1991—92, US amb. to Swaziland, 2002—04, US amb. to Madasgascar, 2004—07, US amb. to Comoros, 2006—07, US amb. to Zimbabwe, 2007—. With USAF, 1968—74, Vietnam. Decorated Three Disting. Flying Crosses. Office: DOS Amb 2180 Harare Pl Washington DC 20521-2180 also: Consular Sect the US Embassy 172 Herbert Chitepo Ave Harare Zimbabwe Office Phone: 263-4-250593/4. Office Fax: 263-4-796488.*

MCGEE, JAMES M., federal agency administrator; Pres. Nat. Alliance Postal and Fed. Employees. Named one of Most Influential Black Americans, Ebony mag., 2006; named to Power 150, 2008. Office: Nat Alliance Postal Federal Employees 1628 11th St NW Washington DC 20001 Office Phone: 202-939-6325. E-mail: JMcGee@NAPFE.ORG.

MCGEE, JAMES SEARS, historian, educator; b. Houston, July 12, 1942; s. William Sears and Mary Elizabeth (Peterson) McG.; m. Mary Arnall Broach, Aug. 20, 1966; children: Elizabeth, Claude. BA, Rice U., 1964; MA, Yale U., 1966, M in Philosophy, 1968, PhD, 1971. Asst. prof. Ga. So. Coll., Statesboro, 1969-71; asst. prof. history U. Calif., Santa Barbara, 1971-78, assoc. prof., 1978-84, prof., 1984—, chmn. dept., 1990-95, 2006—07. Pres. Pacific Coast Conf. on Brit. Studies, 1998-2000. Author: The Godly Man in Stuart England, 1976; co-author: The West Transformed, 2000; editor: The Miscellaneous Works of John Bunyan, Vol. 3, 1987. Named Disting. Tchr. in Soc. Scis., U. Calif., Santa Barbara, 1989; fellow Abraham Found., 1962-63; Woodrow Wilson fellow, 1964-65; recipient summer stipend NEH, 1975. Fellow Royal Hist. Soc.; mem. Am. Soc. Ch. History, Am. Hist. Assn., N.Am. Conf. on Brit. Studies. Democrat. Episcopalian. Avocation: gardening. Office: U Calif Dept History Santa Barbara CA 93106

MCGEE, JANE MARIE, retired elementary school educator; b. Paducah, Ky., Nov. 3, 1926; d. William Penn and Mary Virginia (Martin) Roberts; m. Hugh Donald McGee, Oct. 11, 1946; children: Catherine Jane McGee Bacon, Nancy Ann McGee McManus. BS in Elem. Edn., Murray State U., 1948; cert. in gifted edn., Nat. Coll. Edn., 1976. Tchr. Hazel Pub. Schs., Ky., 1948—49, Pittsford Pub. Schs., Mich., 1949—50, Leal Elem. Sch., Urbana, Ill., 1950-53, Cleveland Elem. Sch., Skokie, Ill., 1953-57; pvt. tutor, pre-sch. tchr., 1953-61; tchr. Woodland Park Elem. Sch., Deerfield, Ill., 1968-83; ret., 1983. Beauty and skin care cons. Mary Kay Cosmetics, Gunnison, Colo., 1984—2002, seller, Sequim, Wash., 2002, beauty and skin care cons., 2002—; co-owner Eagles Nest B&B, 1996—2002. Soprano Western State Coll. and Cmty. Chorus, Gunnison, 1986-02, European concert tour, 1990. Mem. AAUW, Top World Garden Club (sec. 1984-2002, winner first place at numerous garden club shows). Baptist. Avocations: flower arranging, crafts, knitting, bird watching, rock collecting. Office Phone: 360-582-0917. Personal E-mail: jmcgee@surfmk.com.

MCGEE, LIAM E., former bank executive; b. County Donegal, Ireland, 1955; BA, U. San Diego, 1976; MBA, Pepperdine U., Malibu, Calif.; JD, Loyola Marymount U. Law Sch., LA. With Wells Fargo and Co., Security Pacific Corp.; head Calif. Consumer Bank, corp. tech. & ops. Bank of America Corp., 1990, pres. So. Calif., 1998—2000, pres. Calif., 2000—01, pres. global consumer banking, 2001—04, pres. global consumer & small bus. banking Charlotte, NC, 2004—09. Bd. dirs. Fed. Res. Bank, San Francisco; mem. risk and capital com., mgmt. operating com. Bank of America Corp. Bd. trustees Nat. Urban League; bd. dirs. Arts and Sci. Coun., Charlotte; chmn. bd. trustees U. San Diego; chmn. United Way Greater LA. Recipient Arthur E. Hughes Career Achievement award, U. San Diego, 2008.*

MCGEE, MEGAN E., coach, consultant; BS in Animal Sci., Calif. Poly., San Luis Obispo, 1983. Cert. eventing and dressage steward Fedn. Equestrian Internat., 1995. Head coach equestrian team S.D. State U., Brookings, 2004—; registered eventing judge USEF, 2005; reining chief steward FEI, 2007; exec. dir. Equestrian Coaches Assn., 2007—. Office: SD State Univ HPER Box 2820 Brookings SD 57007-1497 E-mail: megan.mcgee@sdstate.edu.

MCGEE, PATRICK EDGAR, postal service clerk; b. Chgo., Jan. 13, 1944; s. Ralph and Minnie Odelia (Crutcher) McG. Machine clk. U.S. Postal Svc., Chgo., 1977—. Author of poems. Mem. The Art Inst. Chgo., Mus. Sci. & Industry, Chgo. Mem. Internat. Soc. Poets. Democrat. Roman Catholic. Avocations: painting, jazz, walking, jogging.

MCGEE, ROBERT MERRILL, oil industry executive; b. Laramie, Wyo., Dec. 15, 1946; s. Gale William and Loraine (Baker) McG.; m. Mary Louise Lehman, July 26, 1969; children: Kirk Lehman, Scott Baker. BA in Polit. Sci., Allegheny Coll., 1969. Bus. assoc. B.F. Goodrich Co., Akron, Ohio, 1969-70; dir. of info. Nat. Petroleum Coun., Washington, 1970-73; asst. dir. pub. rels. Occidental Internat. Corp., Washington, 1973-74, exec. asst. to pres., 1974-76, v.p., 1976-78, exec. v.p., 1978-82, sr. exec. v.p., 1982-91, pres., 1991—2008; v.p. Occidental Petroleum Corp., 1994—2008. Mem. Pres.'s Commn. on White House Fellowships, Washington, 1993—2001, Meridian Internat. Ctr., Washington, 1994—98; mem. bd. advisors Pan Am. Devel. Found., Washington, 1985—2007, pres., 1991—93; bd. govs. Ford's Theatre, Washington, 1991—2007; bd. govs. Karl Landegger Program in internat. bus. diplomacy Sch. Fgn. Svc., Georgetown U., Washington, 1991—2000; bd. dirs. Decatur House, Washington, 1998, vice chmn. bd., 2000, chmn. bd. dirs., 2001—04. Mem. The Econ. Club of Washington, Met. Club Washington, Nat. Press Club.

MCGEE, STACIE, social worker, educator; m. Jon McGee, May 28, 1994; children: Jake, Hannah. BA, Tex. State U., San Marcos, BSW, 1992; LMSW, Our Lady Lake U., San Antonio, 1994. Adj. faculty Tex. State U., 2006—. Vice chair City San Marcos Youth Commn., 2007—. Mem.: Nat. Assn. Social Workers. Home Phone: 512-353-1807.

MCGEE, WILLIAM HOWARD JOHN, retired library director; b. Rochester, NY, May 15, 1942; s. William Peter and Cecilia Matilda (Kuhn) McG.; m. Sheila Anne Drumm, Sept. 4, 1965; children: Kathleen Moira, Margaret Frances. BA with honors, U. Toronto, Ont., Can., 1965; MEd, U. Toronto, 1973; MLS, U. Western Ont., London, 1980. Tchr. Mimico (Ont.) High Sch., 1966-67; tchr., libr. Applewood Secondary Sch., Mississauga, Ont., 1967-71; libr. Crestwood Secondary Sch., Peterborough, Ont., 1971-74; libr. cons. Cayman Islands Edn. Dept., Grand Cayman, B.W.I., 1975-79; adminstrv. asst. Lake Erie Regional Libr., London, Ont., 1980-83; chief libr. Ft. Erie (Ont.) Pub. Libr., 1983-86; asst. dir. McAllen (Tex.) Pub. Libr., 1986-89; coord. Hidalgo County Libr. System, McAllen, 1989—2001; libr. br. mgr. Lark Cmty. Ctr. Library, McAllen, 2001—08. Cons. Grand Ct. Libr., Grand Cayman, 1974-79; mem. Tex. State Libr. Task Force, Austin, Tex., 1991-93; adv. coun. Libr. Svcs. Tech. Act, Austin, 1993—. Editor InTraLogue jour., 1980-83; assoc. editor Can. Jour. Info. Sci., 1980. Bd. dirs. C-ME-CU Credit Union, 1994-99, chmn., 1999. Mem. ALA, Ont. Libr. Assn., Tex. Libr. Assn. (chmn. dist. 4 1994-95, 96-97, intellectual freedom com. 1995-96, profl. rights, responsiblities, and recruitment, 1996—, centennial celebration com. 2000—), Bibliothecaires Francophones Internat. Roman Catholic. Avocations: gourmet cooking, music, travel, reading. Office: Lark Community Center P R PO Box 220 Mcallen TX 78505-0220 Personal E-mail: liam_mcgee@hotmail.com.

MCGEE, WILLIAM TOBIN, internist; b. Port Chester, NY, May 23, 1957; s. James R. and Mary (Delzotto) McG.; m. Sarah McGrath; children: Erin, Kelly, Mary, Kate. BA in Physics, Dartmouth Coll., 1979; MD, N.Y. Med. Coll., 1983; M in Health Adminstrn., Clark U., 1997. Diplomate Am. Bd. Internal Medicine with spl. qualifications in Critical Care. Resident in internal medicine Baystate Med. Ctr., Springfield, Mass., 1983-86, intensivist, acting dir. surg. ICU, 1990-95; fellow in critical care St. Louis U./St. John's Mercy Med. Ctr., St. Louis, 1986-88; intensivist critical care divsn. Baystate Med. Ctr., Springfield, Mass., 1990-98, dir. ICU quality improvement, 1998—. DeWitt Wallace fellow rehab. medicine Rusk Inst. NYU Med. Ctr. Fellow Coll. Chest Physicians (Cecile Lehman Mayer award 1993); mem. AMA, Soc. Critical Care Medicine (presdl. citation 2000, internal medicine specialty award 2000), Am. Soc. Parenteral and Enteral Nutrition. Roman Catholic. Avocations: skiing, biking, hiking, sailing, windsurfing. Office: Baystate Med Ctr 759 Chestnut St Springfield MA 01199-1001

MCGEER, EDITH GRAEF, retired neurological science educator; b. NYC, Nov. 18, 1923; d. Charles and Charlotte Annie (Ruhl) Graef; m. Patrick L. McGeer, Apr. 15, 1954; children: Patrick Charles, Brian Theodore, Victoria Lynn. BA, Swarthmore Coll., 1944; PhD, U. Va., 1946; DSc (hon.), U. Victoria, 1987, U. B.C., 2000; DSc, Shiga U., 2006. Rsch. chemist E.I. DuPont de Nemours & Co., Wilmington, Va., 1946—54; rsch. assoc. divsn. neurol. sci. U. B.C., Vancouver, Canada, 1954-74, assoc. prof., 1974—76, prof., acting head, 1976—83, prof., head, 1983—89, prof. emerita, 1989—. Author: (with others) Molecular Neurobiology of the Mammalian Brain, 1978, 2d edit., 1987; editor: (with others) Kainic Acid as a Tool in Neurobiology, 1978, Glutamine, Glutamate, and GABA, 1983; contbr. articles to profl. jours. Decorated officer Order of B.C., Order of Can.; recipient citation, Am. Chem. Soc., 1958, Rsch. award, Clarke Inst., 1992, Lifetime Achievement award, Sci. Coun. B.C., 1995, Hon. Alumnus award, 1996, cert., Internat. Sci. Inst., 2001, medal of svc., Dr. Cam Coady Found., 2003, Lifetime Achievement award, U. B.C. Med. Faculty, 2006. Fellow Can. Coll. Neuropsychopharmacology, Royal Soc. Can.; mem. Can. Biochem. Soc., Internat. Brain Rsch. Orgn., Internat. Soc. Neurochemistry, Soc. Neurosci., Am. Neurochem. Soc. (councilor 1979-83), North Pacific Soc. Neurology and Psychiatry (hon. fellow), Lychnos Soc., Sigma Xi, Phi Beta Kappa. Office: U BC Divsn Neurol Sci 2255 Wesbrook Mall Vancouver BC Canada V6T 1Z3 Business E-Mail: mcgeer@interchange.ubc.ca.

MCGEGAN, NICHOLAS, conductor; b. Eng., Jan. 14, 1950; Studied piano, Trinity Coll. Music, London; BA, Corpus Christi Coll., Cambridge U., 1972; MA, Maagdalen Coll., Oxford U., 1976. Prof. Baroque flute Royal Coll. Music, London, 1973—79, dir. early music, 1973—80, prof. music hist., 1975—79; music dir. Philharmonia Baroque Orch., San Francisco, 1985—2001, music dir. laureate, 2001—; prin. guest condr. Scottish Opera, Glasgow, 1992-98; prin. condr. Drottningholm Theatre, Sweden, 1993-95; Baroque series dir. St. Paul Chamber Orch., 1999—2004, artistic ptnr., 2004—09; music dir. Irish Chamber Orch., Limerick, 2002—05. Artist-in-residence Washington U., St. Paul, 1979—85, Milw. Symphony Orch., 2003—06; artistic cons. Santa Fe Chamber Music Festival, 1990—92; artistic dir. Göttingen Händel Festival, Germany, 1991—; founder, artistic dir. chamber music group Arcadian Acad., San Francisco, 1992—. Condr. (Operas) Mostly Mozart Festival, NYC, 2003. Recipient Handel Music prize, Germany, 1993. Office: Philharmonia Baroque Orch 180 Redwood St Ste 200 San Francisco CA 94102*

MC GEHEE, H. COLEMAN, JR., (HARRY COLEMAN MCGHHE), retired bishop; b. Richmond, Va., July 7, 1923; s. Harry Coleman and Ann Lee (Cheatwood) McG.; m. June Stewart, Feb. 1, 1946; children: Lesley, Alexander, Harry III, Donald, Cary. BS, Va. Poly. Inst., 1947; JD, U. Richmond, 1949; MDiv, Va. Theol. Sem., 1957, DD, 1973. Bar: Va. 1949, U.S. Supreme Ct. 1954; ordained to ministry Episcopal Ch., 1957. Spl. counsel dept. hwys. State of Va., 1949-51, gen. counsel employment svc., 1951, asst. atty. gen., 1951-54; rector Immanuel Ch.-on-the-Hill, Va. Sem., 1960-71; bishop Diocese of Mich., Detroit, 1971-90. Adv. bd. Nicaraguan Network, Ctr. for Peace and Conflict Studies, Wayne State U.; bd. dirs. Mich. Religious Coalition for Abortion Rights, 1976-84; trustee Va. Theol. Sem., 1978-93; pres. Episc. Ch. Pub. Co., 1978-85. Columnist Detroit News, 1979—85, weekly commentator pub. radio sta. WDET-AM, Detroit, 1984—90. Mem. Gov.'s Commn. on Status of Women, 1965-66, Mayor's Civic Com., Alexandria, 1967-68; sponsor Nat. Assn. for ERA, 1977-85; pres. Alexandria Legal Aid Soc., 1969-71; bd. dirs. No. Va. Fairhousing

Corp., 1963-67; pres. Mich. Coalition for Human Rights, 1980-89 (Humanitarian award 2001); chmn. Citizens' Com. for Justice in Mich., 1983-84; sponsor Farm Labor Orgn. for Children, 1983-85; bd. dirs. Pub. Benefit Corp., Detroit, 1988-90, Mich. Citizens for Personal Freedom, 1989-92, Poverty and Social Reform Inst., Detroit, 1989—, Bread for the World, 1990-94, Ams. United for Separation of Ch. and State, 1990, ACLU Oakland County, Mich., 1991-94; co-chair Lesbian-Gay Found. Mich., 1991—. 1st lt. C.E., U.S. Army, 1943-46. Named Feminist of Yr., Detroit NOW, 1978, Person of Yr., Econ. Justice Commn. Mich., 1997; recipient Humanitarian award Detroit ACLU, 1984, Phillip Hart medal Mich. Women's Studies Assn., 1984, Sayre award for justice and peace Episc. Peace Fellowship, 1988, Spirit of Detroit award, 1989, Archbishop Romero award Mich. Labor Com., 1990, Brotherhood award AME Ch., Detroit, 1993, Ira Jayne award Detroit br. NAACP, 1993, Martin Luther King, Jr. award United Ch. of Christ, 1995, William Scarlett award Episc. Ch. Pub. Co., 1997, Humanitarian award Mich. Coalition for Human Rights, 2001. Mem.: Detroit Econ. Club (bd. dirs.). Episcopalian. Home: 1496 Ashover Dr Bloomfield Hills MI 48304-1215

MCGEHEE, LARRY THOMAS, retired academic administrator; b. Paris, Tenn., May 18, 1936; s. George Eugene and Margaret Elizabeth (Thomas) McG.; m. Elizabeth Hathhorn Boden, Aug. 26, 1961; children: Elizabeth Hathhorn, Margaret Thomas. BA, Transylvania Coll., 1958; BD, Yale U., 1963, MA, 1964, PhD, 1969. Dir., asst. v.p. for univ. relations U. Ala., 1966-68, exec. asst. to pres., 1968-69, exec. v.p., 1969-71; lectr., assoc. prof. dept. Am. studies, 1969-71, acad. v.p., 1971; chancellor U. Tenn., Martin, 1971-79; spl. asst. to pres. U. Tenn. Sys., Knoxville, 1979—82; v.p. coll., prof. religion Wofford Coll., Spartanburg, SC, 1982—2005; emeritus prof. religion, 2005—. Syndicated columnist Southern Seen, 1982—. Danforth fellow Yale U., 1960-66. Home: 1047 Woodburn Rd Spartanburg SC 29302-2867 Office: Wofford Coll 429 N Church St Spartanburg SC 29303-3663 Office Phone: 864-597-4197. E-mail: mcgeheelt@wofford.edu.

MCGEORGE, DON W., retail executive; Joined Kroger Co., Cin., 1977, sr. v.p., 1997—2000, former pres., Tex. Divsn., exec. v.p., 2000—03, pres., COO, 2003—. Office: Kroger Co 1014 Vice St Cincinnati OH 45202-1100*

MCGETTIGAN, CHARLES CARROLL, JR., investment banker; b. San Francisco, Mar. 28, 1945; s. Charles Carroll McGettigan and Molly (Fay) McGettigan Pedley; m. Katharine Havard King, Nov. 1, 1975 (div. 1981); m. Meriwether Lewis Stovall, Aug. 6, 1983; 1 child, Meriwether Lewis Fay. AB in Govt., Georgetown U., Washington, DC, 1966; MBA in Fin., U. Pa., Phila., 1969. Assoc., asst. v.p., v.p. Blyth Eastman Dillon, NYC, 1970-75, 1st v.p., 1975-78, sr. v.p. San Francisco, 1978-80, Dillon, Read & Co., San Francisco, 1980-83; gen. ptnr. Woodman Kirkpatrick & Gilbreath, San Francisco, 1983-84; prin. corp. fin. Hambrecht & Quist, Inc., San Francisco, 1984-88; mng. dir., founder McGettigan, Wick & Co., Inc., San Francisco, 1988—; gen. ptnr., founder Proactive Ptnrs., L.P., San Francisco, 1990—, Proactive Investment Mgrs., L.P., San Francisco, 1991—. Gen. ptnr. Fremont Proactive Ptnrs., 1991—2001; bd. dirs. Cuisine Solutions, Inc., Alexandria, Va.; chmn. Trader Vic's Mgmt. Corp., Emeryville, Calif., Modtech, Inc., Perris, Calif., Onsite Energy Corp., Carlsbad, Calif., Popco Entertainment Ltd, Hong Kong, Tanknology, Inc., Austin, Tex.; adv. dir. Chesapeake Ventures, Balt., 1984—94. Trustee St. Francis Meml. Hosp., San Francisco, 1980-86, dir. Wm. H. Adams Found. ALS Rsch.; mem. United San Francisco Rep. fin. com., 1983—, steering com., 1986—; adv. bd. dirs. Leavey Sch. Bus. Adminstrn., Santa Clara U., Calif., 1984-90. With USN, 1966. Mem. The Brook, Racquet and Tennis Club (NY), The Pacific Union Club, Bohemian Club (San Francisco), San Francisco Golf Club, Burlingame Country Club (Hillsborough, Calif.), Boston (New Orleans), White's (London), Royal St. Georges Golf Club (Sandwich Kent, Eng.). Republican. Roman Catholic. Home: 3375 Clay St San Francisco CA 94118-2006 Office: McGettigan Wick & Co Inc 50 Osgood Pl San Francisco CA 94133-4622 Office Phone: 415-986-4433. Business E-Mail: Chas@McGettigan-Wick.com.

MCGETTRICK, MARK F., energy executive; V.p. customer svc. and mktg. Dominion, sr. v.p. customer svc. and metering, sr. v.p., chief adminstrv. officer, 2002, pres. Dominion Resources Svcs. Inc., 2002—03, pres., CEO generation Va. Power, 2003—06, exec. v.p., 2006—, pres., COO generation Va. Power, 2006—. Bd. dirs. Nuc. Energy Inst. Office: Dominion PO Box 26532 Richmond VA 23261-6532

MC GHAN, WILLIAM FREDERICK, pharmacist, educator; b. Sacramento, July 6, 1946; s. Roy William and Nelleen (Zischang) McG.; children: Monica, Matthew, Brian, Brent; m. Marilyn Dix Smith. Pharm.D., U. Calif., San Francisco, 1970; PhD, U. Minn., 1979. Clin. intern U. Calif. Med. Center, San Francisco, 1969-70, clin. resident, 1970-71; pharmacy coordinator Appalachian Student Health Project, 1970; staff dir. Student Am. Pharm. Assn., Washington, 1971-74, chmn. community health, 1969-70; staff dir. Project SPEED, nat. drug edn. program, 1971-73; assoc. dir., 1973-74; staff dir. Acad. Pharm. Scis., Washington, 1974-76, mem. pub. policy com., 1974-78, chmn. publs. com., 1975-76; grad. fellow, instr. Coll. Pharmacy, U. Minn., 1976-78; asst. prof. Sch. Pharmacy, U. So. Calif., 1978-82; prof., coord. div. adminstrv. and behavioral scis. Coll. Pharmacy U. Ariz., Tucson, 1982-89; founder, sr. rschr. Inst. for Pharm. Econs., 1989—2000; prof. Phila. Coll. Pharm., 1989—, dir. pharmacy adminstrn. grad. program, 1990—. With membership com. Nat. Coord. Coun. for Drug Edn., 1974-75; mem. steering com. Am. Pharm. Assn. Drug Interactions Program, 1973-76; Acad. Pharm. Scis. liaison to NAS-NRC, 1975-76. Editor Student Am. Pharm. Assn. News, 1971-74; editor Acad. Reporter, 1974-76; contbr. over 200 profl. articles and book chpts. Recipient Archambault award Am. Soc. Cons. Pharm., 1987; cmty. scholar, Jackson, Calif., 1964. Fellow Am. Found. for Pharm. Edn., Am. Assn. Pharm. Sci. (chmn. econs. sect. 1988); mem. Am. Pharmacy Assn., Acad. Pharm. Rsch. and Sci. (chmn. econ., social and adminstrv. scis. sect. 1987-88, pres. 1988), Am. Soc. Hosp. Pharmacists, Am. Assn. Colls. Pharmacy (bd. dirs. 1995-97, chmn. pharm. adminstrn. sect. 1989-90, chmn. coun. of faculties 1995-96, co-recipient Lyman award 1989), Internat. Soc. Pharmacoecons. and Outcomes Rsch. (founding trustee; founding pres. 1995-96), Delta Sigma Phi, Rho Chi, Phi Kappa Phi, Sigma Xi Office: Phila Coll Pharmacy Univ of the Scis 600 S 43rd St Philadelphia PA 19104-4418 Business E-Mail: w.mcghan@usp.edu. *Through creativity, integrity, dedication, and compassion, we must all be the instruments for improving the welfare of mankind and the environment.*

MCGHEE, CARL ANDREW, lawyer; b. Lewistown, Pa., Jan. 17, 1954; s. Carl Richard and Virginia McGhee; m. Rebecca Rush, Dec. 6, 1980; children: Anna Rush, Nathaniel McClellan. BA, Washington & Jefferson Coll., Washington, Pa., 1976; JD, U. Va., Charlottesville, 1979. Bar: Pa. 1979, US Dist. Ct. (we. dist.) Pa. 1979, US Ct. Appeals (3d cir.) 1994. Assoc. Tucker, Arensberg, Pitts., 1979—82; ptnr. Rose, Schmidt, Hasley & DiSalle, Pitts., 1983—98; asst. gen. counsel Dollar Bank, FSB, Pitts., 1998—2005, v.p., gen. counsel, 2006—. Bd. dirs., exec. com. Wilkinsburg Cmty. Ministry, Pa., 1994—2001. Mem.: ABA, Assn. Corp. Counsel, Allegheny Bar Assn. (bd. dirs. bus. law sect.), Pa. Bar Assn., Genesis of Pitts. Inc. Office: Dollar Bank FSB 3 Gateway Ctr 7-W Pittsburgh PA 15222

MCGHEE, CARLA RENEE, women's college basketball coach, retired professional basketball player; b. Peoria, Ill., Mar. 6, 1968; B in Sports Mgmt. with honors, U. Tenn., 1990. Forward Germany, France, Turkey, South Korea, Spain, Italy and Greece, Atlanta Glory, 1996—99, Orlando Miracle, 1999—2002; asst. coach Temple U. Owls, 2003—04, Auburn U. Tigers, 2004—06; amb., cons. Atlanta Dream, 2007; asst. coach U SC Gamecocks, 2008—. Mem. USA Women's Nat. Team, 1996. Recipient Gold medal, Olympic Games, Atlanta, 1996. Achievements include being a member of two Tennessee Lady Volunteers NCAA Women's National Basketball Championship teams, 1987, 1989. Office: U SC c/o Dept Athletics Roost Bldg B 1322 Heyward St Columbia SC 29208

MCGHEE, DIANE BAUMANN, dance instructor, consultant; b. Salem, NJ, 1954; d. Nelson Paul and Alice Elizabeth Baumann; children: Christine, Jonathan, Michael Porcaro. BS, Madison Coll., 1972—76; MS, James Madison U., 1976—78. Phys. edn. and dance instr. Salisbury State Coll., Md., 1978—82; resident choreographer; booking and tour mgr. Mandala Folk Ensemble, Boston, 1984—88; dir. of sch. outreach programs and tchr. MJT Dance Co., Boston, 1988—94; sr. tchr. Boston Renaissance/Edison Project Partnership Sch., 1994—97; dir. SE Ctr. for Dance Edn., Columbia Coll., 1997—2000; assoc. prof. Dept. of Theatre and Dance, Winthrop U., Rock Hill, SC, 2000—02; dir., arts for children interdisciplinary program; assoc. prof. of dance SUNY Coll. at Brockport, Brockport, NY, 2002—. Steering and coordinating committees Arts in Basic Curriculum Project, cons., arts edn. leadership inst.; adv. bd. and cons. Am. Dance Legacy Inst.; edn. cons. NY State Summer Sch. of the Arts Sch. of Dance; dir. Etudes Ednl. Project; exec. bd. Project U.N.I.Q.U.E., arts learning lab; art edn. roundtable Greater Rochester Arts and Cultural Coun. Author: (dance education lesson studies) Roots & Branches: Exploring an Evolving Dance Legacy, (dance unit of study) Civil War to Civil Rights: A Lesson in Humanity, Making Connections: Technology, Education, and Dance, American Indian Dance; A Celebration of Survival and Adaptation, Structuring Time and Space: A Dance Hypothesis. Recipient Presdl. Leadership award in Dance, SC. Dance Assn., 1998, Contbn. to Dance Edn., Fidelity Investments (Am. Ballet Gala, Boston), 1999, Artistic Vision, Comittment to Children, Dedication to Dance Edn., MJT Dance Co., 1994. Mem.: Internat. Assn. for Health, Phys. Edn., Recreation, Sport and Dance, SC Dept. Edn. (co-chair, arts tech. standards com., mem. task force, visual and performing arts curricular standards, arts report card task force, SAT improvement com.), Nat. Dance Edn. Org. (exec. bd. and charter mem.). Office: SUNY Brockport 350 New Campus Dr Brockport NY 14420 Home: 369 Dumbarton ST NW Concord NC 28027-5346 Business E-Mail: dmcghee@brockport.edu.

MCGHEE, JAMES HAMILL, theatre director, teacher, poet; b. Summit, NJ, Jan. 28, 1935; s. Terence and Teresa McGhee; m. Kirstin Kaye Gross, May 31, 1985; children: India Jean, Kieran Elizabeth, Lillia Rosalee. PhD, Bowling Green U., Ohio, 1977—80. Assoc. prof. York Coll. Pa., 1983—, dir. theatre, 1983—. Home: 2825 Loman Ave York PA 17402 Office: York Coll Pa 441 Country Club Rd York PA 17403 Business E-Mail: jmcghee@ycp.edu.

MCGHEE, LAURA L., molecular biologist, researcher; d. Monford Donald and Beverly Ann McGhee. PhD, La. State U. Health Sci. Ctr., Shreveport, LA, 2004. Postdoc. fellow La. State U. Health Sci. Ctr., 2004—06; project area mgr., battlefield pain control US Army Inst. Surg. Rsch., Fort Sam Houston, Tex., 2006—. Cons. Constella Group, Fort Detrick, Md., 2007. Cpt. US Army, 2006—, Fort Sam Houston. Recipient Jason A. Cardelli award, La. State U. Health Sci. Ctr., Cancer Ctr., 2002. Achievements include research in determined that Gfi-1 associates with the leukemia associated transcription factor ETO and represses transcription in an HDAC dependent manner.

MCGIFFERT, MICHAEL, retired historian; b. Chgo., Oct. 5, 1928; s. Arthur Cushman and Elisabeth (Eliot) McG.; m. Genevieve White Mischel, Aug. 13, 1960 (dec. Mar. 15, 2007); m. Elizabeth Eastman, June 19, 1949 (div. 1960). BA, Harvard Coll., 1949; B.D., Yale U., 1952, PhD, 1958; postgrad., Union Theol. Sem., NYC, 1949-50. Instr. history Colgate U., Hamilton, NY, 1954-55, 56-60, U. Md., College Park, 1955-56; asst. prof. history U. Denver, 1960-64, assoc. prof., 1964-69, prof. history, 1969-74; editor William and Mary Quar., Inst. Early Am. History and Culture, prof. history, Coll. William and Mary, Williamsburg, Va., 1972-97; ret. Author: The Higher Learning in Colorado, 1964; editor: The Character of Americans, 1964 (rev. edit.), 1969, Puritanism and the American Experience, 1969, (with Robert A. Skotheim) American Social Thought, 1972, God's Plot: The Paradoxes of Puritan Piety, 1972, God's Plot: Puritan Spirituality in Thomas Shepard's Cambridge, 1994. Faculty rsch. grantee U. Denver, 1970, Coll. William and Mary, 1981-82, 89; rsch. fellow NEH, 1977-78. Mem. Am. Hist. Assn., Orgn. Am. Historians, Confr. of Hist. Jours. (pres.1987-89), Am. Antiquarian Soc., Mass. Hist. Soc. Home: 102 Old Glory Ct Williamsburg VA 23185-4914 Personal E-mail: mcgiff@widomaker.com.

MCGIHON, ANNE LEE, state legislator, lawyer; b. Newport, RI, June 1, 1957; d. Robert Sidney and Clara Lee (Denman) McG. BA, McGill U., 1978; MSW, Fla. State U., 1980, JD with honors, 1984. Bar: Fla. 1984, US Dist. Ct. (mid. dist.) Fla. 1984, US Ct. Appeals (11th cir.) 1984, US Ct. Claims 1986, US Supreme Ct. 1988, US Dist. Ct. (DC) 1987, Colo. 1990. Social worker Tallahassee Meml. Regional Med. Ctr., Fla., 1980-81; assoc. Akerman, Senterfitt & Eidson, Orlando, Fla., 1984-86, Kirkpatrick & Lockhart, Washington, 1987-89, Holland & Hart, Denver, 1989-93, McGihon's Assoc., LLC, Denver, 1993—; mem. Dist. 3 Colo. House of Reps., Denver, 2003—. Contbr. articles to profl. jours. Vol. Fla. Dem. Com., Orlando, 1986, Dem. Nat. Com., Nat. Lawyers Coun., 1987-88. Mem. ABA (litig. and bus. law sect. 1989-91, apptd. to banking com. 1991-96), Fla. Bar Assn. (vice chmn. out of state practitioners com. 1989-91, bus. law sect., vice chmn. fin. instns. com. 1989-90, comml. litig. com.), DC Bar Assn. (litig. and corp. sect.) Democrat. Episcopalian. Office: Dist Office 837 Sherman St Denver CO 80203-2943 also: Colo State Capitol 200 E Colfax Denver CO 80203 Office Phone: 303-866-2921. Business E-Mail: anne.mcgihon.house@state.co.us.*

MCGILL, DAN MAYS, insurance business educator; b. Greenback, Tenn., Sept. 27, 1919; s. John Burton and Jane (Mays) McG.; m. Elaine Kem, June 22, 1952; children: Douglas Russell, Melanie Mays BA, Maryville Coll., 1940, LLD (hon.), 1982; MA, Vanderbilt U., 1941; PhD, U. Pa., 1947. Assoc. prof. fin. U. Tenn., Knoxville, 1947-48; Julian Price assoc. prof. ins. U. NC, Chapel Hill, 1948-51; assoc. prof. ins. U. Pa., Phila., 1952-56, Frederick H. Ecker prof. life ins., 1959-90, chmn. ins. chpt., 1965—89. Trustee NW Mut. Life Ins. Co., Milw., 1978-90; bd. dirs. NRG Life Reassurance Corp., Phila., 1984-94, Phila. Reins. Corp., 1990—, Independence Blue Cross, 1990—; exec. dir. S.S. Huebner Found., 1954-75, 78-86, chmn., 1965-94; dir. rsch. Pension Rsch. Coun., 1952-90; chmn., mem. governing bd. Leonard Davis Inst. Health Econs., 1967-90; 1st chmn. adv. commn. Pension Benefit Guaranty Corp., 1975-78, mem. 1978-81. Author: An Analysis of Government Life Insurance, 1949, The Fundamentals of Private Pensions, 8th edit., 2005, Legal Aspects of Life Insurance, 1959, Fulfilling Pension Expectations, 1962, Life Insurance, 1967, Preservation of Pension Benefit Rights, 1972, others; editor: (with others) World Insurance Trends, 1959, others. Trustee Presbyn. Med. Ctr., Phila., 1987—96; chmn. Boettner Inst. Fin. Gerontology, 1993—2002; mem. retirement bd. Mass. Bay Transp. Authority, 1980—96; chmn. bd. pensions Presbyn. Ch. USA, 1977—88; trustee Presbyn. Found. for Phila., 1996—2001. Maj. USAF, 1942—46, Maj. USAF, 1951—52. Recipient Disting. Alumni award Maryville Coll., 1962, Huebner Gold medal award Am. Coll., 1977, Gold medal Internat. Ins. Soc., 1987. Mem.: Am. Risk and Ins. Assn. (pres. 1959, Elizur Wright award 1955, 1981), Merion Cricket Club, Union League. Republican. Presbyterian. Avocations: music, travel, sports.

MCGILL, GEORGIA, theater educator, director; d. George McGill and Gloria Salvitti-McGill; m. Peter James Houle, June 2, 1979 (dec.); children: Amanda Leigh Houle, Rachel Nicole Houle. MA, LI U., Brookville, 1987; PhD, CUNY, New York. Dir.: (theater) Modern Theatre of Myth. Mem.: ATHE (coll.-festival coord. 2009—), Kennedy Ctr. Am. Coll. Theatre Festival (nat. mem. large-playwriting 2009—, Kennedy Ctr. Gold medallion 2000). Office: Queensborough CC 222-05 56th Ave Oakland Gardens NY 11364

MCGILL, HENRY COLEMAN, JR., pathologist, educator, researcher; b. Nashville, Oct. 1, 1921; s. Henry Coleman and Thursa (Lowry) McG.; m. Cloace Laurite Ferguson, Sept. 12, 1945; children: Margaret Ann, Laurilynn, Elizabeth Gail. BA, Vanderbilt U., 1943, MD, 1946. Intern Vanderbilt Hosp., Nashville, 1946-47; asst. prof. pathology La. State U. Med. Ctr., New Orleans, 1950-55, assoc. prof., 1955-61, prof., chmn. dept., 1961-66; prof. pathology U. Tex. Health Sci. Ctr., San Antonio, 1966-92, chmn. dept., 1966-72; sci. dir. S.W. Found. for Biomed. Rsch., San Antonio, 1978-92, sr. scientist, 1992-96, sr. scientist emeritus, 1996—. Contbr. articles to med. jours. Capt. M.C., U.S. Army, 1948-50. Mem. Phi Beta Kappa, Sigma Xi, Alpha Omega Alpha. Home: 4102 Fawnridge Dr San Antonio TX 78229-4212 Office: PO Box 760549 San Antonio TX 78245-0549 Business E-Mail: hmcgill@sfbr.org.

MCGILL, JOHN KNOX, lawyer; b. Charlotte, NC, Aug. 25, 1956; s. John Charles and Mabel (Hamilton) Mc. BS in Bus. cum laude, Erskine Coll., 1978; MBA, JD, U. N.C., 1982. Bar: NC 1983; CPA, NC. Ptnr., tax atty. Garland & Alala, P.A., Gastonia, NC, 1982—86, McGill & Hassan, P.A., Charlotte, 1999—; CEO John K. McGill & Co. Inc., Charlotte, NC. Chmn., bd. dirs. Select Cons. Inc., Charlotte; bd. dirs., founder, Advanced Pension Systems, Inc., Charlotte. Tax editor: Dental Economics Mag., 1982—; editor-in-chief newsletter The McGill Advisory; contbg. editor: (textbook) Contemporary Marketing, 4th edit., 1983. Trustee Erskine Coll., 1998-04; treas. 1st Assoc. Reformed Presbyn. Ch., Gastonia, NC, 1989-94, deacon, 1989-94, elder, 1995-04. Recipient Tax Law scholarship, Touche, Ross & Co., CPA's, 1982. Mem. ABA, NC Bar Assn., Am. Inst. CPA's, NC Assn. CPA's, Sertoma Club (Disting. Svc award, Kings Mt. NC, 1983). Republican. Avocations: jogging, basketball, baseball, skiing, card/stamp collecting. Home: 2236 Lake Ridge Dr Belmont NC 28012 Office: Lake View Profl Bldg 8816 Red Oak Blvd Ste 240 Charlotte NC 28217 Office Phone: 704-424-9780.

MCGILL, LISA M., semiconductor engineer; d. Stephen McGill and Karen Milgate McGill; m. Matthew Borthwick, Oct. 7, 2001. BA, Cornell U., Ithaca, NY, 1997; PhD, MIT, Cambridge, 2004. Sr. process engr. Intel Corp., Hillsboro, Oreg., 2004—. NDSEG Fellowship, US DOD, 1997—2000. Mem.: Isshinryu Karate-do Hillsboro (instr., second-degree black belt 2006—08). Personal E-mail: lmm9_97@yahoo.com.

MCGILL, MAURICE LEON, corporate financial executive; b. Malden, Mo., Aug. 22, 1936; s. William Howard and Iris (Phillips) McG.; m. Wanda Coral Wirt, Feb. 2, 1957; children— Melany, Melinda, William Shannon BS, U. Mo., 1958, MA, 1959. C.P.A., Mo., Iowa, Ariz. Mgr. Touche, Ross, Bailey & Smart, Kansas City, Mo., 1959-64; fin. v.p., treas. Iowa Beef Packers, Inc., Dakota City, Nebr., 1964-69; exec. v.p., treas. Spencer Foods, Inc., Iowa, 1969-71, also dir. Iowa; sr. v.p. Diamond Reo Trucks, Inc., Lansing, Mich., 1971-72; fin. v.p. Ariz. Colo. Land & Cattle Co., Phoenix, 1972-75; ptnr. Touche Ross & Co., Phoenix, 1975-81; exec. v.p. fin. and adminstrn., treas., bd. dirs. IBP, Inc., Dakota City, Nebr., 1981-89; pres., bd. dirs. Wirmac Corp., Garland, Tex., 1989—. Mem.: AICPA. Home: 1406 O Shannon Ln Garland TX 75044-3510 E-mail: mandwmcgill@msn.com.

MCGILL, ROBERT M., lawyer; s. Frederick Charles McGill and Patricia Irene McGill Ek. JD, Boston Coll. Law Sch., Chestnut Hill, Mass., 2005. Lic.: Mass. Bd. Bar Overseers 2005. Rsch. analyst Mass. State Legislature, Boston, 1997—99; found. and govt. support coord. Boston Symphony Orch., Boston, 1999—2000; paralegal Hill & Barlow, P.C., Boston, 2000—02; law clk. Justices Mass. Superior Ct., Boston, 2005—06; assoc. Sherin and Lodgen LLP, Boston, 2006—. Mem.: ABA, Boston Bar Assn. Roman Catholic. Avocation: music.

MCGILLICUDDY, JOAN MARIE, psychotherapist, consultant; b. Chgo., June 23, 1952; d. James Neal and Muriel (Joy) McG. BA, U. Ariz., 1974, MS, 1976; PhD, Walden U., 1996. Cert. nat. counselor. Counselor ACTION, Tucson, 1976; counselor, clin. supr. Behavioral Health Agy. Cen. Ariz., Casa Grande, 1976-81; instr. psychology Cen. Ariz. Coll., Casa Grande, 1978-83; therapist, co-dir. Helping Assocs., Inc., Casa Grande, 1982—, v.p., sec., 1982—; cert. instr. Silva Method Mind Devel., Tucson, 1986—. Active Mayor's Com. for Handicapped, Casa Grande, 1989-90, Human Svcs. Planning, Casa Grande, 1985-95, Pinal Gila Srs. Coun. Found., 2005—. Named Outstanding Am. Lectr. Silva Mind Internat., 1988-99; recipient Gov. Special Recognition award, 2006. Mem. ACA. Avocations: jogging, singing. Office: Helping Assocs Inc 1901 N Trekell Rd Casa Grande AZ 85222-1706 Office Phone: 520-421-1029. Business E-Mail: jmcgillicuddy@helpingassociates.com.

MCGILLIGAN, PATRICK MICHAEL, writer, editor; b. Madison, Wis., Apr. 22, 1951; s. William Anthony and Marion Elizabeth (Schubert) McG.; m. Tina E. Daniell; 3 children. BA, U. Wis., 1973. Staff writer The Boston Globe, 1973-76; arts editor The Real Paper, Boston, 1978-80; contbr. editor Am. Film, Washington, 1979-81; sr. editor Playgirl mag., Los Angeles, 1980-86; book editor TSR Inc., Lake Geneva, Wis., 1986—; adj. asst. prof. Marquette U., Milkw., Wis., 1997—; film series advisor U. Wis. Pres., Madison, Wis., 2000—, U. Ky. Pres., Lexington, Ky., 2006—. Unit pub. One From the Heart, Los Angeles, 1981, Let's Spend the Night Together, LA, 1982. Author: Cagney: Actor as Auteur, 1975, 2d rev. edit. 1982, Ginger Rogers, 1977; editor: Backstory: Interview with 1930's Screenwriters, 1986 and many others, contbr. to anthologies & ency. Fellow Niemen Found., 1973; scholar Fullbright. Home: 2746 N Frederick Ave Milwaukee WI 53211-3631 Personal E-mail: pat.mcgilligan@gmail.com.

MC GIMSEY, CHARLES ROBERT, III, anthropologist; b. Dallas, June 18, 1925; s. Charles Robert, Jr. and Ellen Randolph (Parks) McG.; m. Mary Elizabeth Conger, Dec. 20, 1949; children— Charles Robert, Brian Keith, Mark Douglass. Student, Vanderbilt U., 1942-43, U. of South, 1943-44; BA, U. N.Mex., 1949; MA, Harvard U., 1954, PhD, 1958. Instr. U. Ark., Fayetteville, 1957, asst. prof., 1958-62, assoc. prof., 1962-67, prof. anthropology, 1967-90, prof. emeritus, 1990—, chmn. dept., 1969-72; asst. curator U. Ark. Mus., 1957-59, dir., 1959-83, Ark. Archeol. Survey, 1967-90, dir. emeritus, 1990—. Cons. archeology U.S. GAO, 1979-87, U.S.-Internat. Com. on Monuments and Sites; Rep. to Internat. Com. on Archeol. Heritage Mgmt., 1988-95. Author: (with G.R. Willey) Monagrillo Culture of Panama, 1954, Mariana Mesa, 1980, Indians of Arkansas, 1969, Public Archeology, 1972, Archeology and Archeological Resources, 1973, (with H.A. Davis) The Management of Archeological Resources, 1977, CRM on CRM, 2004; assoc. editor Am. Antiquity, 1972-80; Co-editor (with H. A. Davis) Southeastern Museums Conf., 1964-73; Contbr. articles to profl. jours. Mem. Ark. Rev. Com., Historic Preservation Program, 1968-76; collaborator Nat. Park Service, 1971-74, adviser, 1974-77; mem. Com. on Recovery Archeol. Remains, 1971-78; mem. adv. bd. dirs. Red River Mus., 1975-76; mem. adv. bd. Am. Indian Archeol. Inst., 1975-80, Ark. Natural and Cultural Heritage Dept., 1976-90. Served to lt. (j.g.) USNR, 1943-47. Recipient Cert. Recognition State of Ark., 1990; rsch. grantee Am. Philos. Soc., Am. Acad. Arts and Scis., Andean Rsch. Inst., Nat. Park Service, NSF, Smithsonian Instn., Wenner-Gren Found.; rsch. fellow dept. archaeology U. Cambridge, 1985-86, assoc. mem. Darwin Coll., 1985— Fellow: Am. Anthrop. Assn.; mem.: Archeol. Inst. Am. (Conservation and Heritage Mgmt. award 2006), Register Profl. Arch., Am. Assn. State and Local History (award of merit 1985), Am. Assn. Mus., Soc. Profl. Archeologists (founder, bd. dirs. 1976—79, pres. 1983—84, emeritus, life, Seiberling 1989, presidential recognition award 1997), Am. Soc. Conserv. Archeology (founding, outstanding contrib. 1980), Southeastern Mus. Conf. (coun. 1962—71, editor 1964—77), Ark. Archeol. Soc. (editor 1960—83, Preservationist 1989), Soc. Am. Archeology (pres. 1974—75, Distinguished Serv. 1975, excellence in cultural resource mgt. 1995), Register of Profl. Archeologists (Disting. Svc. award 2005). Office: Ark Archeol Survey 2475 N Hatch Ave Fayetteville AR 72704-5590 Home: 3646 N Brodie Sta Fayetteville AR 72703-3104

MCGINLEY, JOHN C., actor; b. NYC, Aug. 3, 1959; m. Lauren Lambert, 1997 (div. 2001); 1 child, Max; m. Nichole Kessler, Apr. 7, 2007; 1 child, Billie Grace. Attended, Syracuse U.; MFA, NYU. Ptnr. McGinley Entertainment Inc. Actor: (TV series) Another World, 1985—86, Scrubs, 2001—; (films) Sweet Liberty, 1986, Platoon, 1986, Wall Street, 1987, Shakedown, 1988, Talk Radio, 1988, Prisoners of Inertia, 1989, Suffering Bastards, 1989, Lost Angels, 1989, Fat Man and Little Boy, 1989, Born on the Forth of July, 1989, Highlander II: The Quickening, 1991, Point Break, 1991, Article 99, 1992, A Midnight Clear, 1992, Little Noises, 1992, Hear No Evil, 1993, Car 54, Where Are You?, 1994, On Deadly Ground, 1994, Mother's Boys, 1994, Surviving the Game, 1994, Wagons East, 1994, Born to Be Wild, 1995, Se7en, 1995, Nixon, 1995, Psalms from the Underground, 1996, Hollywood Boulevard, 1996, The Rock, 1996, Mother, 1996, Set It Off, 1996, Johns, 1996, Flypaper, 1997, Truth or Consequences, 1997, Nothing to Lose, 1997, Office Space, 1999, Three to Tango, 1999, Any Given Sunday, 1999, Get Carter, 2000, The Animal, 2001, Crazy as Hell, 2002, Highway, 2002, Stealing Harvard, 2002, Identity, 2003, (voice) Lil' Pimp, 2005, A.W.O.L., 2006, Two Tickets to Paradise, 2006, Puff, Puff, Pass, 2006, American Crude, 2007, Wild Hogs, 2007, Are We Done Yet?, 2007; (TV films) Clinton and Nadine, 1988, Cruel Doubt, 1992, Long Island Fever, 1995, The Return of Hunter, 1995, Intensity, 1997, Target Earth, 1998, The Pentagon Wars, 1998, Sole Survivor, 2000; actor, prodr. (films) Watch It, 1993, Colin Fitz, 1997, actor, exec. prodr. (TV films) The Jack Bull, 1999; actor: (TV appearances) Spenser: For Hire, 1988, The Practice, 1997, Spider-Man, 2003, (voice only) Kim Possible, 2003, Justice League, 2003—05, American Dragon: Jack Long, 2005; prodr.: (films) Sex & the Other Man, 1995. Nat. spokesperson Nat. Down Syndrome Soc.'s Buddy Walks. Office: c/o Innovative Artists 1505 10th St Santa Monica CA 90401

MCGINLEY, MARK ALAN, biology professor; b. Corpus Christi, Tex., Apr. 28, 1958; s. Pat H. and Jonila Graves McGinley. BS in Zoology, U. Calif., Santa Barbara, 1980; MS in Biology, Kans. State U., Manhattan, 1983; PhD in Biology, U. Utah, Salt Lake City, 1989. Master scuba diver trainer PADI, 2001. Asst. prof., dept. biol. scis. Tex. Tech U., Lubbock, 1991—97, assoc. prof., dept. biol. scis., 1997—2004, assoc. prof., honors coll. and dept. biol. scis., 2005—. Scuba instr., marine biologist Odyssey Expdns., Clear River, Fla., 2003—08; mem., stewardship com. Environ. Info. Coalition, Washington, 2006—; topic editor, author Ency. of Earth, Boston, 2006—. Author: (textbook) The Process of Science. Recipient Pres.'s Excellence Tchg. award, Tex. Tech U., 1998; named Elected Tchg. Acad., 2000, Honors Coll. Prof. of Yr., 2005. Mem.: World Conservation Union. Achievements include development of natural history and humanities degree and multidisicplinary science masters for in-service high school teachers at Texas Tech University. Avocations: scuba diving, travel, music. Office: Honors Coll Tex Tech Univ MS 1017 Lubbock TX 79409-1017 Business E-Mail: mark.mcginley@ttu.edu.

MCGINLEY, MATTHEW S., legislative staff member; Legis. asst., legis. counsel, dep. chief of staff, legis. dir., Rep. Brian Kerns US House of Reps., Washington, 2002, legis. dir., Rep. Patrick Kennedy, 2003, chief of staff to Rep. Tom Price, 2005—. Republican. Office: 424 Cannon House Office Bldg Washington DC 20515 Office Phone: 202-225-4501. Office Fax: 202-225-4656.*

MCGINN, BERNARD JOHN, theologian, educator; b. Yonkers, NY, Aug. 19, 1937; s. Bernard John and Catherine Ann (Faulds) McG.; m. Patricia Ann Ferris, July 10, 1971; children: Daniel, John. BA, St. Joseph's Sem., Yonkers, NY, 1959; Licentiate in Sacred Theology, Gregorian U., Rome, 1963; PhD, Brandeis U., 1970. Diocesan priest Archdiocese N.Y., NYC, 1963-71; prof. U. Chgo., 1969—, Naomi Shenstone Donnelly prof., 1992—2003, emeritus, 2003—. Program coord. Inst. for Advanced Study of Religion, Divinity Sch., U. Chgo., 1980-92. Author: The Calabrian Abbot, 1985, Meister Eckhart, 1986, Foundations of Mysticism, 1991, Growth of Mysticism, 1994, Antichrist, 1994, Flowering of Mysticism, 1998, Harvest of Mysticism,; editor: (series) Classics of Western Spirituality, 1978, (book) God and Creation, 1990. Fellow Medieval Acad. Am., Am. Acad. Arts and Scis. Home: 5701 S Kenwood Ave Chicago IL 60637-1718 Office: U Chgo Divinity Sch 1025 E 58th St Chicago IL 60637-1509 Business E-Mail: bmcginn@uchicago.edu.

MCGINN, EILEEN, public health service officer, researcher; b. Phila., Mar. 29, 1947; BA cum laude, CUNY, 1968; MPH, U. Pitts., 1974. Cert. aging Brookdale Ctr. Hunter Coll., CUNY, 2007. Tchr. English Peace Corps, Dogondoutchi, Niger, 1968-70; tchr. sci. Diocese of Bklyn., 1971-72; clinic dir. Monsour Med. Ctr., Jeannette, Pa., 1974-76; grants officer Assn. for Voluntary Surg. Contraception, NYC, 1976-79; program officer Planned Parenthood Fedn., NYC, 1979-81; chief of party USAID/Zaire, Kinshasa, 1983-85; dep. chief of party John Snow, Inc., Nepal, Kathmandu, 1986-89; program mgr. Asia Assn. Voluntary Surg. Contraception, NYC, 1989-92; cons., 1992—. Cons. Ctr. Devel. and Pop. Activities, Washington, 1985, Population Svcs. Internat., Washington, 1985, Assn. Voluntary Surg. Contraception, Kenya and Tanzania, 1982, Bangladesh, 1989, USAID, Togo, 1993, John Snow/Svc. Expansion and Tech. Support, Papua New Guinea, 1994; Nathan Kline Inst. 2009-; 1996-99; founding bd. dirs., treas. N.Y. Fibromyalgia Connection, 1996-99. Author: Field Worker's Manual, 1989, Nurse's Manual, 1989; contbr. articles to profl. jours. Mem. docent Mus. for African Art, 2000-02; chair, bd. dirs. Neighborhood Adv. Bd. Manhattan #6, 1994-2000; mem. cmty. action bd. NYC Dept. Youth and Cmty. Devel., 2000-05; English conversation ptnr. Internat. Ctr. and Manhattan Comprehensive Day and Night H.S., 2005-; vol., Upwardly Global, 2007-. N.Y.S. State Regents scholar, 1964-68, NYU scholar, 1982; USPHS grantee, 1972-73. Avocations: reading, writing, sewing. Office: 210 E 15th St New York NY 10003-3922 Office Phone: 212-982-4348.

MCGINN, KEVIN B., insurance company executive; BA, Fordham U., Bronx; MA, Fordham U. V.p. Marine Midland Bank, head European multi-nat. bus. unit, v.p. L.Am.; sr. v.p. Bank Austria NY, chief credit officer, head lending; credit mgr. enterprise risk mgmt. unit Am. Internat. Group, Inc. (AIG), 1999, credit exec. internat. credit, 2003—04, chief credit officer, 2004—, v.p., 2006—. Vol. US Peace Corps, Nicaragua, Guatemala. Office: Am Internat Group Inc (AIG) 70 Pine St New York NY 10270*

MCGINN, MAX DANIEL, lawyer; b. Lexington, NC, July 30, 1942; s. Max Terry and Ethel Mae (Peck) McG.; m. Judith Eaton McBee, June3, 1965; children: Brian, Tracie. BA magna cum laude, Wake Forest U., 1964, JD cum laude, 1967. Bar: US Dist. Ct. (mid. dist.) NC 1971, US Supreme Ct. 1977, US Ct. Appeals (4th cir.) 1976, US Dist. Ct. (we. and ea dists.) NC 1979. Atty. NLRB, Winston-Salem, NC, 1967, 1970; ptnr. Brooks, Pierce, McLendon, Humphrey & Leonard, Greensboro, NC, 1971—. Lt., atty. Judge Adv. Gen.'s Corps, USN, 1967-70. Fellow Am. Coll. of Trial Lawyers; mem. ABA, NC Bar Assn. (chmn. Labor and Employment Law sect. 1989). Presbyterian. Avocations: tennis, sports, reading. Office: Brooks Pierce McLendon Humphrey & Leonard 230 N Elm St Greensboro NC 27401-2436 Home: 400 Rockford Rd Greensboro NC 27408-5026

MCGINNIES, ELLIOTT MORSE, psychologist, educator; b. Buffalo, Sept. 19, 1921; BA, SUNY, Buffalo, 1943; MA, Brown U., 1944; PhD, Harvard U., 1948. Tchg. fellow Harvard U., 1944—47; asst. prof. U. Ala., 1947—52; from assoc. prof. to prof. U. Md., 1952—70; prof., chmn. Dept. Psychology American U., Washington, 1970—86, prof. emeritus, 1987. Vis. prof. U. Calif., Berkeley, 1987—88; Fulbright prof. Nat. Taiwan U. Author: Social Behavior: A Functional Analysis, 1970, The Reinforcement of Social Behavior, 1971, Attitudes, Conflict and Social Change, 1972, Perspectives on Social Behavior, 1994. Fellow: Am. Psychol. Assn.; mem.: Psychonomic Soc., Eastern Psychol. Assn., Harvard Club DC, Nat. Press Club, Sigma Xi.

MCGINNIS, ARTHUR JOSEPH, JR., public relations executive; b. Jersey City, Mar. 12, 1952; s. Arthur Joseph and Roselind (Diskon) McG.; m. Kim Elizabeth Midgarden; children: Kirsten Elizabeth, Ashley Alexandra. BS, Siena Coll., 1975. Mgr. trainee Lebhar-Friedman, NYC, 1975-76; regional sales mgr. Simmons-Boardman Pub. Corp., Chgo., 1976-77; pub. Plant Location Mag., Simmons-Boardman, NYC, 1977-89; v.p. mktg. Railway Div., Simmons-Boardman, NYC, 1978-88; exec. v.p., sec. Simmons-Boardman Pub. Co., NYC, 1987-88; pres., pub. Simmons-Boardman Pub. Corp., NYC, 1988—; chmn. bd. Simmons-Boardman Pub. Co., NYC, 1991—; pres. Simmons-Boardman Books, Omaha, 1989—, chmn. bd., 1992—96. Bd. dirs. Am. Bus. Press; chmn. bd. dirs. McGinnis Corp.; adv. bd. United Publ., Inc., 2000—, Davison Pub. Co., LLC, Orlando, 2006—, pres., 2006. Home: 35 Cheston Ct Belle Mead NJ 08502-4907 Office: Simmons Boardman Pub Corp 345 Hudson St New York NY 10014-4502 Office Phone: 212-620-7200.

MCGINNIS, CHARLES IRVING, civil engineer; b. Kansas City, Mo., Jan. 31, 1928; s. Paul Sherman and Sidney (Bacon) McG.; m. Shirley Ann Meyer, Nov. 5, 1955; children: Gail B., Ann K., James P. BS, Tex. A & M Coll., 1949, M.Engring., 1950; grad., Army Engr. Sch., 1955, Command and Gen. Staff Coll., 1959, Armed Forces Staff Coll., 1962, Army War Coll., 1969. Registered profl. engr., Tex., Mo. Enlisted as pvt. U.S. Army, 1945, advanced through grades to maj. gen., 1976; area engr. Ethiopia and Somalia, 1962-65; dist. engr. St. Paul, 1969-71; dir. engring. and constrn. bur. Panama Canal Co., 1971-72, v.p., 1972-74; lt. gov. C.Z., 1972-74; div. engr. southwestern div. C.E., Dallas, 1974-77; dir. civil works Office Chief of Engrs. U.S. Army, Washington, 1977-79; civil engr., 1979—; exec. v.p. Fru-con Corp.; pres. Fruco Engrs., Inc., 1983-87; assoc. dir. Constrn. Industry Inst. U. Tex., Austin, 1987-93, sr. lectr. civil engring. dept., 1992-97; vice chmn. chem. weapons stockpile com. NRC, 2000—04. Vis. com. dept. civil engring. MIT, 1978-81; mem. Mississippi River Commn., 1975-77, Bd. Engrs. for Rivers and Harbors, 1975-77; chmn. water policy task force NSPE, 1979-81. Chmn. Combined Fed. Campaign coordinating com., C.Z., 1972-74; pres. C.Z. coun. Boy Scouts Am., 1973-74, exec. bd. St. Louis area coun., 1983-87, Capitol Area coun., 1987-90, Stonewall Jackson Area coun., 1999-2006; com. mgmt. Balboa YMCA, 1973-74; trustee C.Z. United Way, 1972-74. Decorated D.S.M., Legion of Merit with oak leaf cluster, Joint Svcs. Commendation medal, U.S. Army Commendation with oak leaf cluster, Chuong My medal 1st class Vietnam; named Disting. Grad. Civil Engring. Dept., Tex. A&M U., 2002. Fellow ASCE, Soc. Am. Mil. Engrs. (past pres. Twin Cities post and Panama post); mem. Assn. U.S. Army, Mil. Order of the World Wars, Nat. Acad. Constrn. (charter), Tau Beta Pi, Chi Epsilon. *The simple four-part philosophy that has well served three generations of my family requires an uncompromising commitment to honesty in all things, industry, concentration on the job and on personal objectives, and economy of all resources, both natural and man-made.*

MCGINNIS, CHRISTOPHER, travel correspondent, editor; b. Atlanta; Grad., U. Colo., Boulder; MA, Gavin Sch. Internat. Mgmt., Phoenix. With mgmt. cons. co.; bus. travel columnist Atlanta Jour.-Constn., Atlanta Bus. Chronicle; travel adv. columnist CNN.com; travel corr. Weather Channel, 1998—2000, CNN Headline News, 1995-1998, 2001-2005; dir. Travel Skills Group, Inc. Author: (books) 202 Tips Even the Best Business Travelers May Not Know, 1994, The Unofficial Business Traveler's Pocket Guide, 1998; editor: Expedia Travel Trendwatch; editor: (pub.) (travelers newsletter) The Ticket; contbr. articles on bus. travel for Entrepreneur, Fortune, Conde Nast Traveler, Travel & Leisure. Mailing: c/o Christopher McGinnis 12 Chattanooga St San Francisco CA 94114 Office Phone: 415-550-4104. Business E-Mail: chris@travelskills.com.

MCGINNIS, JAMES LANDON, lawyer; b. St. Louis, May 10, 1954; s. Robert Delmar (Stepfather) and Rosalind Appel Ritchie; children: Lorna Rose, Rowan Grace. BA in History, Yale U., 1976; JD, U. Calif., Berkeley, 1979. Bar: Pa. 1979, Calif. 1980. Assoc. Morgan, Lewis & Bockius, Phila., 1979—80, Jackson, Tufts, Cole & Black, San Francisco, 1980—84; asst. US atty. Ea. and Ctrl. Districts of Calif., Fresno, LA, 1984—88; ptnr. Morgenstein & Jubelirer, San Francisco, 1988—2002, Sheppard, Mullin, Richter & Hampton, San Francisco, 2002—. Author: (article-Nat. Law Jour.) The Impact of Booker on Sentencing in Criminal Antitrust Cases. Mem.: San Francisco Bar Assn., Calif. Bar Assn., ABA. Avocations: weightlifting, tennis, guitar, motorcycling. Office: Sheppard Mullin 17th Fl Four Embarcadero Ctr San Francisco CA 94111 Home: 375 N Ferndale Ave Mill Valley CA 94941-3423 Office Fax: 415-434-3947. Business E-Mail: jmcginnis@sheppardmullin.com.

MCGINNIS, JAMES MICHAEL, physician; b. Columbia, Mo., July 12, 1944; s. Leland Glenn and Lillian Ruth (Mackler) McG.; m. Patricia Anne Gwaltney, Aug. 4, 1978; children— Brian, Katherine AB, U. Calif., Berkeley, 1966; MA, MD, UCLA, 1971; M.P.P., Harvard U., 1977. House officer in internal medicine Boston City Hosp., 1971-72; internat. med. officer HEW, 1972-74; dir. Office for Asia and Western Pacific, 1974-75; state coordinator smallpox eradication program WHO, India, 1974-75; fellow Harvard Center for Community Health and Med. Care, Boston, 1976-77; cons. to sec. HEW, Washington, 1977, dep. asst. sec. for health, dir. office disease prevention, 1977-95, asst. surgeon gen., 1980-95, acting dir. office of rsch. integrity, 1992-93; scholar-in-residence NAS, Washington, 1995-99; sr. cons. Robert Wood Johnson Found., Princeton, 1996—99, sr. v.p., dir. Health Grp., 1999—2004, counselor to pres., 2004—05; sr. scholar, Inst. Medicine NAS, 2005—. Instr. medicine George Washington U. Med. Sch., 1973-75; adj. prof. pub. policy Duke U., 1979-81, 99—; chair, sec. task force on smoking and health; chair exec. com. HHS Environ. Health Policy Com.; mem. U.S. Japan Leadership program; chair World Bank/European Commn. Task Force on Reconstrn. of Health Sector, Bosnia, 1996-97; sr. scholar Assn. of Acad. Health Ctrs., 1997-99. Mem. editl. bd. Jour. Med. Edn., 1975-78, Jour. Preventive Medicine, 1987—, Jour. Health Promotion, 1992-98; editor-in-chief: Healthy People, Healthy People 2000, Surgeon General's Report on Nutrition and Health, Determining Risks to Health, Food Marketing to Children and Youth. Bd. dirs. United Way of Nat. Capital, Nemours Found. With USPHS, 1972—75, with USPHS, 1977—95. Recipient Arthur S. Flemming Pub. Svc. award, 1979, USPHS Disting. Svc. medal, 1989, Surgeon Gen.'s medallion, 1995, Fed. Profile in Leadership award, 1989, Wilbur Cohen award, 1995, award for excellence APHA, 1995, Health Leader of Yr. award, 1996. Fellow Am. Coll. Epidemiology, Am. Coll. Preventive Medicine; mem. Inst. Medicine/NAS. Office: 500 5th St NW Washington DC 20001 Office Phone: 202-334-3963. Business E-Mail: mcginnis@nas.edu.

MCGINNIS, PATRICIA GWALTNEY, non-profit organization executive; b. Goldsboro, NC, July 19, 1947; d. Thomas McKim Gwaltney and Patricia Anne (Watkins) Schools; m. James Michael McGinnis, Aug. 4, 1978; children: J. Brian, Katherine B. BA, Mary Washington Coll., 1969; MPA, Harvard U., 1975. Dir. spl. studies U.S. Dept. Commerce, Washington, 1975-76; prof. staff mem. U.S. Senate Budge Com., Washington, 1976-77; dep. assoc. dir. U.S. Office Mgmt. and Budget, Washington, 1977-81; sr. cons. Cresap, McCormick and Paget, Inc., Washington, 1981-82; prin. The FMR Group, Inc., Washington, 1982-94; pres., CEO Coun. for Excellence in Govt., Washington, 1994—; mem., dean's alumni coun. Harvard Kennedy Sch. Environment, 2005—; mem. steering com. Homeland Soc. Policy Inst., Washington, 2006—. Mem. exec. alumni coun. Kennedy Sch. Govt., Harvard U., Cambridge, Mass., 1992-96; dir. Primark Corp., Waltham, Mass., 1995-2000; mem. assoc. coun. George Washington Sch. Bus. and Pub. Adminstrn., 1996-99; bd. dirs. Brown Shoe Co., St. Louis, Imagitas, Inc., Newton, Mass.; bd. visitors U. Md. Sch. Pub. Affairs; dir. Logistics Mgmt. Inst., McLean, Va. Contbr. articles to profl. jours. Fellow: Nat. Acad. Pub. Adminstrn. Office: Coun for Excellence in Govt 1301 K St NW Ste 450W Washington DC 20005-3397

MCGINNIS, ROBERT E., lawyer; b. Caldwell, Ohio, May 1, 1931; s. Earl Peregoy and Mary Ethel (Richner) McG.; m. Jane Ann Lindenmeyer, Sept. 12, 1953; children: Sharon Ann, David E. BA, Ohio Weslayan U., 1952; JD summa cum laude, Ohio State U., 1954. Bar: Ohio 1954, Calif. 1956. Asst. judge advocate USAF, 1954-56; sr. ptnr. Luce, Forward, Hamilton, & Scripps, San Diego, 1956—. Counsel to pub. utilities, pub. agys., savs. and loan instns., ins. cos. and contractors. Trustee Wesley Meth. Ch., San Diego, Fine Arts Soc., First Meth. Ch., La Mesa, Calif.; counsel Kensington Community Ch.; dir. San Diego Opera Assn., corp. sec., v.p. Mem. Order of Coif. Republican. Mem. United Ch. Christ. Office: Luce Forward Hamilton & Scripps 600 W Broadway Ste 2600 San Diego CA 92101-3372

MCGINNIS, TAMMY MARIE, health services manager; b. Dover, Ohio, Sept. 2, 1958; d. Lindy Luck and Rita Marie Williams; life ptnr. James Gordon Geerts; 1 child, Shaun Michael. Cert. office software profl. Bus. & Industry Inst./OSU & COTC, 1999; nat. cert. med. asst. Nat. Ctr. for Compentency Testing, 1997, cert. instr. ARC, 2000; food protection mgr. Nat. Restaurant Assn. Edn. Found., 2003, child devel. assoc. The Coun. for Early Childhood Profl. Recognition, 1995. Health services mgr. Kno Ho Co Ashland Head Start, Coshocton, Ohio, 1990—. Birth-five health & social services com. pres. Kno Ho Co Ashland Head Start, Glenmont, 2000—05; early intervention collaborative pres. Early Intervention Help Me Grow, Coshocton, 2003—05. Recipient Ohio Head Start Assn. award of Excellence, Ohio Head Start Assn., 2002—05, Colgate-Palmolive award of Excellence, Nat. Head Start Assn., 2004—05, Samuel Harris award, ADA, 2004—06; named Top Med. Sec., Coshocton County Joint Vocat. Sch., 1997. Mem.: Kno Ho Co Ashland Head Start Birth to Five Yr. Old Health & Social Services Com. (corr.), Holmes County Dept. of Jobs and Family Services Work Force Devel. Com. (corr.), Holmes County Tng. Ctr. Dental Adv. Bd. (corr.), Help Me Grow (corr.), Ashland Dental Clinic Collaborative (assoc.). Democrat. Roman Catholic. Office: Kno Ho Co Ashland Head Start 120 N 4th St Coshocton OH 43812 Office Fax: 330-377-4595; Home Fax: 330-377-4595. Personal E-mail: tmcginnis2@adelphia.net.

MC GINTY, JOHN MILTON, architect, consultant; b. Houston, Apr. 24, 1935; s. Milton Bowles and Ruth Louise (Dreaper) McG.; m. Juanita Jones, May 4, 1957; children: Christopher Harold, Jacqueline Ruth McGinty Carlson. BS, Rice U., 1957; M.F.A., Princeton U., 1961. With archtl. firm Barnes, Landes & Goodman, Austin, Tex., 1957-58, Ingram & Harris, Beaumont, Tex., 1958-59; prin. McGinty Partnership, Architects, Inc., Houston, 1961-89, City Assos., Inc., 1979-91, Bovay-McGinty, Inc., engrs. & architects, Houston, 1989-91; founder, pres. Am. Constrn. Investigations Inc., Houston, 1991-2000, McGinty Archtl. Consultants, LLP, Houston, 2001—. Instr. archtl. design U. Houston, 1965-67; White House fellow, asst. to Sec. of Interior, 1967-68; vis. prof. architecture Rice U., 1969-70 Named Disting. Alumnus Rice U., 1986. Fellow AIA (mem. U.S. delegation to USSR 1972, pres. Houston chpt.

1973, nat. pres. 1977) Office: McGinty Archtl Cons LLP 602 Sawyer St Ste 740 Houston TX 77007 Home: 3614 Montrose Blvd #607 Houston TX 77006 Office Phone: 713-868-7021. Personal E-mail: jmginty@arch.com.

MCGIRR, DAVID WILLIAM JOHN, pharmaceutical executive; b. Glasgow, Scotland, May 19, 1954; arrived in US, 1991, naturalized, 2004; s. Edward McCombie and Diane Curzon (Woods) McG.; m. Margaret Joslin Richardson, May 9, 1981; children: William David, Katherine Joslin, Lucy Ann, Elizabeth Margaret. BSc (hon.), U. Glasgow, 1976; MBA, U. Pa., 1978. Assoc. S.G. Warburg & Co. Ltd., London, 1978—80, exec. dir., 1981—86; mng. dir. S.G. Warburg & Co. Inc., NYC, 1991—95, CFO, 1992—95; assoc. Warburg Paribas Becker Inc., NYC, 1980—81; exec. dir. S.G. Warburg Securities, London, 1986—87; CEO S.G. Warburg Securities Ltd., Toronto, Ont., Canada, 1987—89; COO, CFO Bunting Warburg Inc., Toronto, 1989—91; pres. GAB Robins North Am. Inc., Parsippany, NJ, 1996—99, CEO, 1997—99; COO hippo, Inc., New Haven, 1999—2002, pres., 2001—02; sr. v.p., CFO Cubist Pharm., Inc., Lexington, Mass., 2002—, treas., 2002—03. Selection com. Thouron Scholarship, 1989-2009 Bd. dirs. Friends of Glasgow U., Inc., 2003—08; bd. dirs., chmn audit com. Lifecell Corp., 2007—08. Thouron scholar, 1976-78. Mem. Apawamis Club (Rye, N.Y.). Avocations: collecting cars, golf, classic wooden boats. Office: 65 Hayden Ave Lexington MA 02421 Home Phone: 203-629-5607; Office Phone: 781-860-8526. Business E-Mail: david.mcgirr@cubist.com.

MCGIVNEY, JOHN JOSEPH, lawyer; b. Boston, Oct. 31, 1956; s. William A. and Mary Angela (Wall) McG. AB magna cum laude, Boston Coll., 1978, JD cum laude, 1981. Bar: Mass. 1981, U.S. Dist. Ct. Mass. 1982, U.S. Ct. Appeals (1st cir.) 1983, U.S. Supreme Ct. 1990. Assoc. Burns & Levinson, Boston, 1981-87, ptnr., chief appellate sect., 1988-96; ptnr. Rubin and Rudman, Boston, 1997—. Sec. Lynnfield (Mass.) Dem. Town Com., 1974-75, chmn., 1976-77. Mem. Mass. Acad. Trial Attys., Mass. Def. Lawyers Assn. (bd. dirs.), Algonquin Club of Boston. Home: 47 Doncaster Cir Lynnfield MA 01940-2255

MCGLADE, JOHN E., chemicals executive; b. Bethlehem, Pa., 1954; BS, Lehigh U., 1976, MBA, 1981. Mgmt. positions Air Products & Chemicals Inc., Allentown, Pa., 1976—94, gen. mgr. chem. & process ind. div., 1994—96, v.p., chem. & process ind. div., 1996—98, v.p., gen. mgr., chem. & process ind. & energy systems, 1998—2001, v.p., gen. mgr. performance materials div., 2001—03, v.p. chemicals group, 2003, group v.p. chemicals group, 2003—06, pres., COO, 2006—07, pres., CEO, 2007—08, chmn., pres., CEO, 2008—. Mem.: Nat. Petroleum Refiners Assn. (mem. petrochemical com.), Soc. Chem. Industry. Office: Air Products & Chemicals Inc 7201 Hamilton Blvd Allentown PA 18195-1501 E-mail: mcgladje@airproducts.com.

MCGLASHAN, THOMAS HAMEL, psychiatrist, educator; b. Rochester, NY, Oct. 20, 1941; m. Patricia L. Gwiazdowski, 1964; children: Lara, Jennifer. BA in Chemistry magna cum laude, Yale U., 1963; MD, U. Pa., 1967. Diplomate in psychiatry Am. Bd. Psychiatry and Neurology. Intern Mary Hitchcock Meml. Hosp., Hanover, NH, 1967-68; resident, chief resident psychiatry Mass. Mental Health Ctr., 1968-71; officer in psychiatry, sr. asst. surgeon USPHS, 1971-73; chief clin. rsch. unit psychiat. assessment sect. NIMH, Adult Psychiatry Br., Bethesda, Md., 1973-75; staff psychiatrist Chestnut Lodge, Rockville, Md., 1975-90, dir. adult studies Rsch. Inst., 1977-81, dir. rsch., 1982-90; prof. dept. psychiatry Yale U. Sch. Medicine, 1990—; exec. dir. Yale Psychiat. Inst., New Haven, 1990-2000. Spl. and invited faculty, supr. Washington Sch. Psychiatry, 1978, 81, 82, 83; instr. Washington Psychoanalytic Inst., 1982-89, Western New Eng. Psychoanalytic Inst., 1992-93; clin. assoc. prof. dept. psychiatry Uniformed Svcs. U. of the Health Scis., 1983-88, clin. prof. dept. psychiatry, 1988-90; rsch. prof. dept. psychiatry U. Md. Sch. Medicine, 1986-90; bd. dirs. Parents Found. for Transitional Living, 1991-97; cons. and grant cons. in field; presenter in field; many others. Author: The Documentation of Clinical Psychotropic Drug Trials, 1973, The Borderline: Current Empirical Research, 1985, Schizophrenia: Treatment, Process and Outcome, 1989. Early Intervention in Psychosis, 2001, A Developmental Model of Borderline Personality Disorder, 2003; editl. cons.: Schizophrenia Bull., 1980-82, 84—, Archives of Gen. Psychiatry, 1982—, Am. Jour. Psychiatry, 1982—, Hosp. and Cmty. Psychiatry, 1984—, Jour. Personality Disorders, 1987—, Schizophrenia Rsch., 1987—, Acta Psychiatrica Scand., 1999—, Jour. Abnormal Psychology, 1988, Psychiatry Rsch., 1988—, others; mem. editl. bd.: Jour. Personality Disorders, 1989—, Schizophrenia Bull., 1989—; contbr. chpts. to books, over 200 articles to profl. jours. Recipient Gary Morris Rsch. award Washington Psychoanalytic Soc., 1980, Presdl. award for rsch. Nat. Assn. Pvt. Psychiat. Hosps., 1988, Silvano Arieti award Am. Acad. Psychoanalysis, 1990, Psychiat. Inst. Am. Found. award for rsch. devel. in hosp. psychiatry, 1990, Alexander Granlick award Am. Psychiat. Found., 1997, Established Investigator award Nat. Alliance Rsch. Schizophrenia & Depression, 1997-98; grantee Fund for Psychoanalytic Rsch. Am. Psychoanalytic Assn., 1978, 79, NIMH, 1996—, Norwegian Rsch. Coun., 1997—. Fellow Am. Psychiat. Assn., Am. Psychopathol. Assn.; mem. Western New Eng. Psychoanalytic Inst. and Soc., Soc. for Psychotherapy Rsch., Assn. for Clin. Psychosocial Rsch., Psychiat. Rsch. Soc., Internat. Soc. Study Personality Disorders, Internat. Early Psychosis Assn. Business E-Mail: thomas.mcglashan@yale.edu.

MCGLATHERY, JAMES MELVILLE, retired foreign language educator; b. New Orleans, Nov. 22, 1936; s. Samuel Lyon and Mary Jackson (Garrott) McG.; m. Nancy Judith Beyer, June 1, 1939; children: Samuel Lyon, Daniel Beyer, Andrew James, Benjamin Kim. AB, Princeton U., 1958; AM, Yale U., 1959, PhD, 1964. Instr. German Phillips Andover (Mass.) Acad., 1959-60; lectr. German Harvard U., 1963-64, instr. German, 1964-65; from asst. prof. to assoc. prof. U. Ill. at Urbana-Champaign, 1965-84, prof. German, 1984-2000, prof. emeritus, 2000—, acting dept. head, spring 1985, dept. head, 1985-95. Instr. Colby Coll. Summer Lang. Sch., 1964, Harvard U. Summer Lang. Sch., 1965-66, 70, U. Ill., Urbana-Champaign, 1972, 74, 76, 78, 80, 82, 87, 90, U. Göttingen, Germany, 1993-94, 2001; lectr., presenter in field. Author: Mysticism and Sexuality: E. T. A. Hoffmann, Part One: Hoffmann and His Sources, 1981, Desire's Sway: The Plays and Stories of Heinrich von Kleist, 1983, Mysticism and Sexuality: E. T. A. Hoffmann, Part Two: Interpretations of the Tales, 1985, Fairy Tale Romance: The Grimms, Basile, Perrault, 1991, Grimms' Fairy Tales: A History of Criticism on a Popular Classic, 1993, E.T.A. Hoffmann, 1997, Wagner's Operas and Desire, 1998; editor: German Source Readings in the Arts and Sciences, 1974, Journal of English and Germanic Philology, 1976, The Brothers Grimm and Folktale, 1988, 91, Music and German Literature: Their Relationship since the Middle Ages, 1992; contbg. author: Reader in German Literature, 1969, Molière and the Commonwealth of Letters: Patrimony and Posterity, 1975, Fairy Tales as Ways of Knowing: Essays on Märchen in Psychology, Society, and Literature, 1981, Reflection and Action: Essays on the Bildungsroman, 1991, A Companion to the Nibelungenlied, 1998, A Companion to Wagner's Parsifal, 2005; mng. editor: Jour. English and Germanic Philology, 1972-00; contbr. articles and book revs. to profl. jours. Princeton U. scholar, 1954-58; undergrad. rsch. assistantship Princeton U., 1956-58; Woodrow Wilson Nat. fellow Yale U., 1958-59, Jr. Sterling fellow Yale U., 1960-61, Nat. Def. Edn. Act fellow in Russian, Yale U., 1961-63; grad. rsch. bd. grantee U. Ill. Urbana-Champaign, 1975, 79-80, 86, 89, 92. Mem.: N.Am. Heine Soc. Home: 1204 Thomas Dr Champaign IL 61821-1632 Home Phone: 217-352-6902. Business E-Mail: mcglath@uiuc.edu.

MCGLOTHLEN, JOHN M., librarian; s. Gary and Barbara (Myers) McGlothlen; m. Angela Wells, Aug. 17, 1991; children: Emily, Ethan. BS, Charter Oak State Coll., 1995; MA, U. Iowa, 1998. Assoc. libr. Iowa Wesleyan Coll., Mount Pleasant, Iowa, 1998—2000; electronic svcs. libr. Sioux City Pub. Libr., Sioux City, Iowa, 2000—01; libr. The Gazette, Cedar Rapids, Iowa, 2001—. Editor: (web site) The Bible as Music (http://bibleasmusic.com). Mem.: SLA. Avocation: music.

MCGLOTHLIN, MICHAEL GORDON, lawyer; b. Richlands, Va., Oct. 31, 1951; s. Woodrow Wilson and Sally Ann (Cook) McGlothlin; m. Sandra Lee Keen McGlothlin, Oct. 1, 1983; children: Michael Alexander, Robert Aaron. BA, U. Va., 1974; JD, Coll. William & Mary, 1976. Bar: Va. 1977, US. Dist. Ct. (we. dist.) Va. 1978. Ptnr. McGlothlin, McGlothlin & McGlothlin, Grundy, Va., 1977—79, McGlothlin & Wife, Grundy, 1984—; commonwealth atty. Buchanan County, Grundy, 1980—83, atty., 1984—89; bd. dirs. Gt. Southwest Home Commn., vice chmn., 1983—. Mem. adv. bd. Clinch Valley Coll.; sec. Buchanan County Dem. Party. Mem.: ABA, Kiwanis (sec. Buchanan County Dem. Com.), Buchanan County Bar Assn. (pres. 1984), Va. State Bar Assn., Phi Sigma Kappa, Phi Alpha Delta. Presbyterian. Home and Office: PO Box 810 Grundy VA 24614-0810

MCGLYNN, ELIZABETH A., health policy analyst; PhD, RAND Grad. Sch., 1988; MPP, U. Mich. Assoc. dir. RAND Health, Santa Monica, Calif.; dir. Ctr. Rsch. on Quality in Health Care, Santa Monica, Calif. Adv. com. Nat. Com. for Quality Assurance (NCQA), Nat. Quality Forum (NQF), Coun. Accountable Physician Practices, Am. Med. Group Assn.; editorial bd. Health Svcs. Rsch., Milbank Meml. Fund Quarterly. Mem.: Inst. Medicine. Achievements include development of QA Tools. Office: RAND Health Communications PO Box 2138 1776 Main St Santa Monica CA 90407-2138

MCGLYNN, MARY ASPINWALL, artist, juror instructor; d. William E. Aspinwall and Frances P. Sedore; m. Joseph Michael McGlynn, June 29, 1963; children: Patrick, James, Joseph. Degree, Nat. Acad. Design, NYC, 2004—. Bd. dir. Salmagundi Club, NYC, 2003—, dir. chairman, 2004—. Exhibitions include Zeeuws Maritiem, Vlissingen, Holland, Noyes, Hiram Blauvelt, Fraunces Tavern Fed. Hall, Jasper Cropsey Tavern, US Customs House, Treasure Island. Judge North Shore Art Assn., Mass., 1996—2003, Washington Sq., NYC, Blauvelt Mus. Internat., Olo Greenwich, Salmagundi Club, North Shore Arts, 2003—04. Recipient Nordhausen award, Salmagundi Club, 2006, White award, 2004, J & D Salomon award, Pastel Soc. Am., 2002, Schumaker award, Hudson Valley Art Assn., 1998, Steinschneider award, 1999—2000, Van Steen award, 1995, US Coast Guard George Gray award, 1995, Pres. award, Johnson & Johnson Gallery, 2002; named Best Show, Barrons Art Ctr., 1999. Mem.: Nat. Mus. Women Arts, Artists Fellowship, Artists Equity, Portrait Soc. America, Internat. Soc. Marine Painters, North Shore Art Assn., Am. Artist Profl. League. Avocation: paleontology. Office: 737 Greentree Ln Oradell NJ 07649-1413 Office Phone: 201-265-4437. Business E-Mail: prestigeart@verizon.net.

MC GLYNN, SEAN PATRICK, physical chemist, educator; b. Dungloe, Ireland, Mar. 8, 1931; arrived in U.S., 1952, naturalized, 1957; s. Daniel and Catherine (Brennan) Mc Glynn; m. Helen Magdalena Salacz-von Dohnanyi, Apr. 11, 1955 (div.); children: Sean Ernst, Daniel Julian, Brian Charles, Sheila Ann, Alan Patrick; m. Maureen G. Potts, Oct. 23, 1985; children: Shane Joseph, Brennan John, Colin Michael. BS, Nat. U. Ireland, 1951, MS, 1952; PhD, Fla. State U., 1956. Fellow Fla. State U., 1956, U. Wash., 1956-57; mem. faculty La. State U., 1957—, prof. chemistry, 1964—, Boyd prof. chemistry, 1967—, dean Grad. Sch., 1981-82, vice chancellor rsch., 1981-91. Assoc. prof. biophysics Yale U., 1961; Humboldt prof. physics U. Bonn, Germany, 1979—80; cons. to pvt. cos. Author (with others): (book) Molecular Spectroscopy of the Triplet State, 1969, Introduction to Applied Quantum Chemistry, 1971, Photophysics and Photochemistry in the Vacuum Ultraviolet, 1985, The Geometry of Genetics, 1988; editor: Wiley-Interscience Monographs in Chem. Physics; contbr. articles to profl. jours., chapters to books. Recipient award, Baton Rouge Coun. Engring. and Sci. Socs., 1962—63, Sr. Scientist award, Alexander von Humboldt Found., 1979, Disting. Rsch. medal, U. Bologna, Italy, 1979; fellow, Rsch. Corp., 1960—63; Sloan fellow, 1964—68. Mem.: AAAS, Am. Phys. Soc., Am. Chem. Soc. (S.W. Regional award 1967, Fla. sect. award 1970, Coates award 1977). Achievements include research in molecular electronic spectroscopy; electronic structure; energy transfer; molecular genetics; bioenergetics; mathematical biology; optoaccoustics; optogalvanics. Home: 12048 Pecan Grove Ct Baton Rouge LA 70810-4835 Office Phone: 225-578-3392. Business E-Mail: chspm@lsu.edu. E-mail: maureenpotts@cox.net.

MCGOLDRICK, JOHN LEWIS, medical products executive, lawyer; b. Plainfield, NJ, Mar. 2, 1941; s. John Leslie and Sarah (Walker) McGoldrick; m. Ann Chapman Puffer, Oct. 1, 1966; children: Scott Runyon, Jennifer Winslow. BA cum laude, Harvard U., 1963, LLB, 1966. Bar: N.J. 1966, N.Y. 1985. Assoc. McCarter & English, Newark, 1966-73, ptnr., 1974-95; sr. v.p., gen. counsel Bristol-Myers Squibb Co., NYC, 1995—98, sr. v.p., gen. counsel, pres., Med. Devices Group, 1998—2000, exec. v.p., 1995—2006, gen. counsel, 2001—06; sr. v.p. Internat. AIDS Vaccine Initiative, 2006—. Vice-chmn., bd. dirs. N.J. Transit Corp., Newark, 1979—2005; bd. dir. Bristol-Myers Squibb Found., Zimmer Holdings, Inc., non-exec. chmn., 2007—; bd. dir. HealthCare Inst. N.J., Regional Plan Assn., N.J. Network Found. Trustee Essex-Newark Found. Legal Svcs. N.J. Montclair State U.; mem. com. to visit The Coll., mem. com. to visit Sch. Pub. Health Harvard U.; mem. Harvard Malaria Initiative Adv. Coun. Fellow: Am. Acad. Appellate Lawyers, Am. Bar Found., Am. Coll. Trial Lawyers; mem.: ABA, Am. Arbitration Assn., Nat. Panel Arbitrators, Aspen Inst. World Economy, Coun. Chief Legal Officers (Conf. Bd. Inc.), Assn. Gen. Counsel, Am. Law Inst., Assn. Fed. Bar N.J. (former pres.), Assn. Bar City of N.Y., N.Y. Bar Assn., N.J. Bar Assn., Legal Svcs. N.J. (bd. dirs.), World Econ. Forum, Coun. U.S. and Italy, Harvard Law Sch. Assn. N.J. (former pres.). Office: Zimmerman Holdings Inc 345 E Main St Warsaw IN 46580

MCGOLDRICK, KATHRYN ELIZABETH, anesthesiologist, educator, writer; b. Worcester, Mass., 1946; MD, Cornell U., NYC, 1970. Diplomate Am. Bd. Anesthesiology. Intern N.Y. Hosp.-Cornell Med. Ctr., 1970—71; resident anesthesiology Peter Bent Brigham Hosp., Boston, 1971—73; fellow pediat. anesthesiology Children's Hosp. Med. Ctr., Boston, 1973—74; prof. anesthesiology Yale U., New Haven, 1992—2001; prof., chmn. dept. anesthesiology N.Y. Med. Coll., Valhalla, 2001—. Med. dir. ambulatory surgery Yale-New Haven Hosp., 1991—2001; bd. dirs. Found. Anesthesia Edn. and Rsch., 2005—. Editor-in-chief Survey of Anesthesiology, 1995—. V.p., trustee Wood Libr.-Mus. Anesthesiology, 1998—2001, pres., 2001—04. Fellow Am. Coll. Anesthesiology; mem. AMA, Am. Soc. Anesthesiologists, Conn. State Soc. Anesthesiologists (pres. 1998-2000), Assn. Univ. Anesthesiologists, Acad. Anesthesiology (v.p., 2008-), Soc. Ambulatory Anesthesia (pres-elect 2003, pres. 2004-05), NY State Soc. Anesthesiologists. Office: Dept Anesthesiology NY Med Coll Valhalla NY 10595

MCGONAGLE, DUNCAN FRANCIS, mental health nurse, substance abuse counselor; b. Bklyn., May 6, 1939; s. John and Kathleen (Rooney) McGonagle; m. Gloria Maria Carrubba, Dec. 5, 1987. AA, Allan Hancock, 1964; AAS in Nursing, CUNY, 1992. Cert. psychiat. and mental health nurse, addictions RN. Substance abuse counselor Pritikin Longevity Ctr., Santa Monica, Calif., 1978-84; paramedic N.Y.C. Emergency Med. Svc., 1987-92; psychiatric nurse Bellevue Hosp. Ctr., NYC, 1992-99; adminstr. Methadone Maintenance Treatment Program, St. Barnabas Hosp., Bronx, NY, 1999—2001; nurse mgr. Methadone Maintenance Treatment Program, Beth Israel Med. Ctr., NYC, 2001—. Founder Methadone Anonymous, N.Y. Aux. police officer N.Y.C. Police Dept., 1985—. With USN, 1956-60, 1961-62, Vietnam. Recipient Nat. award for Clin. Excellence in Nursing, Nat. Nurses Soc. on Addictions, 1995. Mem. Blue Knights, Knights of Life, Rolls Royce Owners Club, Harley Owners Group. Roman Catholic. Avocations: computers, sailing, motorcycling, antique autos. Home: 73 Verona St Brooklyn NY 11231-1612 Office: Beth Israel Med Ctr 160 Water St New York NY 10038-4922 E-mail: duncan73@aol.com.

MCGONIGLE, TERRY L., theater educator, consultant; b. Wichita, Kans., Aug. 17, 1951; s. Arthur Glen and Betty Ruth McGonigle; 1 child, Tiffani Dawn Black. MA, Emporia State U., Kans., 1974. Cert. tchr. Ga., 1994. Theatre arts tchr. Forsyth County Schs., Cumming, Ga., 2002—04; tchr. tech. theatre studies Grayson Sch. Tech., Loganville, 2004—. Costume designer: Ragtime. Maj. contbr. Broadway Cares / Equity Fights AIDS, NYC, 2000. Named to Hall of Fame, Kans. Thespian Soc., 2005, Ga. Theatre Hall of Fame, 2006. Mem.: Ednl. Theatre Assn. (life; internat. student officer adult liaison 2006). Office: Grayson HS 50 Hope Hollow Rd Loganville GA 30052 also: 330 S 7TH St Apt 411 Las Vegas NV 89101-5829 Personal E-mail: tmcgoni817@yahoo.com. E-mail: terry_mcgonigle@gwinnett.k12.ga.us.

MCGOON, MICHAEL DOUGLAS, cardiologist, educator; b. Balt., Nov. 29, 1950; s. Dwight Charles and Betty Lou Hall McGoon; m. Bonnie Kay Kruger, Aug. 7, 1992; children: Alana Moran, Brenna Paulson, Megan Lohr, Joe. BA, Harvard, Cambridge, Mass., 1973; MD, Johns Hopkins, Balt., 1977. Cert. in internal medicine ABIM, 1977, cardiologist 1983. Cons., cardiovasc. diseases Mayo Clinic, Rochester, Minn., 1983—, prof. medicine, 1999—. Chair, sci. leadership coun. Pulmonary Hypertension Assn., 2002—04, chair, bd. trustees, 2006—08; fellow Am. Coll. Cardiology, Am. Coll. Chest Physicians. Mem., regional adv. com. Planned Parenthood Minn. Office: Mayo Clinic 200 1st St SW Rochester MN 55905

MCGOUGH, DUANE THEODORE, economist, consultant, retired federal official; b. Rice Lake, Wis., Aug. 3, 1932; s. James Patrick and Josephine Margaret (Huerth) McG.; m. Donna Mae Jones, June 13, 1959 Student, Wis. State Coll., Eau Claire, 1950-52, U. Wis., Madison, 1952-54, 56-60, BS in Light Constrn. Industry, 1959, MBA in Urban Land Econs., 1962; postgrad., U. So. Calif. Urban Planning, LA, 1968-69. Housing mgmt. officer Pub. Housing Adminstrn. Atlanta, 1960-62; program planning analyst Pub. Housing Adminstrn. Phila., 1962-67; program analyst HUD, Washington, 1967-68, 69-70, industry economist, 1970-73, supervisory economist, 1973-77, dir. housing and demographic analysis, 1977-97, govt. tech. rep. ann. housing survey, 1977-83; govt. tech. rep. Am. Housing Survey, 1984-97; acting dep. asst. sec. for econ. affairs (chief economist) HUD, Washington, 1977, 82, 84-85, ret., 1997. US rep housing subcom. UN Econ. Commn. for Europe, Geneva, 1976, 79, Madrid, 1982; HUD rep. Interagy. Com. on Population Rsch., 1978-97, Interagy. Forum on Aging-Related Stats., 1986-97; mem. Fed. Task Force on Household Survey Redesign, 1988-97; mem. policy com. Year 2000 Census; coord. PRSC Ctr. U.S./Mex. Sem. Housing Stats., Mexico City, 1997. Editor: President's Report on Housing Goals, 1974—78, Nat. Housing Prodn. Report, 1980, 1982, US Housing Market Conditions Report, 1994—97, FEMA National Emergency Management Program, 1967—97, Housing Consultant, 1997—; musician (tenor): Washington Choral Ensemble, 2002—06. With US Army, 1954—56, saxophonist 7th Army Band US Army, Stuttgart, Germany. Fellow Nat. Inst. Pub. Affairs, 1969; recipient Outstanding Performance award Pub. Housing Adminstrn., Phila., 1966, HUD, 1984, 92, 97, Career Edn. award Nat. Inst. Pub. Affairs, 1968-69, Cert. Spl. Achievement, HUD, 1978, 83, 84, 96, Cert. Superior Svc., HUD, 1988, 95, Cert. Appreciation, Bur. Census, 1990. Mem. Lambda Alpha Internat. (v.p. programs 1987-89, chmn. real estate and fin. com. George Washington chpt. 1990-92, dir.-at-large 1992-93), Lambda Chi Alpha. Avocations: music, gardening, rockhounding, web-surfing. Personal E-mail: duanetm@aol.com.

MCGOUGH, JAMES JOHN, psychiatrist; m. Jacqueline Ann Axtell, Feb. 13, 1993; children: Caitlin Marie, Daniel Patrick. BA, Gettysburg Coll., Pa., 1979; MD, Duke U. Sch. Medicine, Durham, NC, 1986; MS in Clin. Rsch., UCLA, 2003. Diplomate in psychiatry, child and adolescent psychiatry Am. Bd. Psychiatry and Neurology, 1992, 1996. Asst. clin. prof. UCLA Sch. Medicine, 1994—98, assoc. clin. prof., 1998—2000; assoc. prof. clin. psychiatry David Geffen Sch. Medicine UCLA, 2001—04, prof. clin. psychiatry, 2004—; mem. instl. rev. bd. UCLA, 2004—, chair med. instl. rev. bd., 2008—. Mem. clergy misconduct oversight com. Archdiocese LA, 2002—; mem. psychopharmacology adv. panel US FDA, 2004—06; mem. editl. bd. Jour. ADHD and Related Disorders, 2008—. Grant, NIMH, 2000—05. Mem.: Am. Acad. Child and Adolescent Psychiatry (mem. program com. 2002—, mem. workgroup on rsch. 2005—), Am. Psychiat. Assn. Avocations: running, swimming. Office: UCLA 300 UCLA Med Plz Ste 1414 Los Angeles CA 90095 Business E-Mail: jmcgough@mednet.ucla.edu.

MCGOUGH, WALTER THOMAS, JR., lawyer; b. Pitts., Nov. 7, 1953; s. Walter Thomas and Jane (Fitzpatrick) McGough; m. Rebecca Gai Frazier, June 24, 1978; children: Emily Ann, Walter Thomas III. BA, Princeton U., 1975; JD, U. Va., 1978. Bar: Pa., 1978, DC, US Dist. Ct. We. Dist. Pa. 1980, US Ct. Appeals 3rd cir., 1983, US Ct. Appeals, 6th cir. 1984, Pa. Supreme Ct., 1978, US Supreme Ct., 1983. Law clk. to Hon. Collins J. Seitz U.S. Ct. Appeals 3rd Cir., Wilmington, Del., 1978-79; law clk. to Hon. William H. Rehnquist US Supreme Ct., Washington, 1979-80; asst. US atty. We. Dist. Pa., 1980-82; assoc. Reed Smith LLP, Pitts., 1982-86, ptnr., 1987—, head of litigation dept., 1998—2006, mem. exec. com., 1998—. Assoc. counsel, Sen. Select Com. on Secret Mil. Assistance to Iran and the Nicaraguan Opposition, Washington, 1987; mem. lawyers adv. com. US Ct. Appeals 3d cir., 1987-89, chmn., 1989; mem. appellate rules com. US Jud. Conf., 1998-2005. Co-author: Fed. Appellate Procedure, 3rd Cir., 1996; contbr.

articles to profl. jours. Trustee Sta. WQED, Pitts., 1996-2002, vice chmn, 1997-99, chmn., 1999-2002; mem. 3d Cir. Task Force on Rule 11, 1987-89. Fellow Am. Coll. Trial Lawyers, Am. Acad. Appellate Lawyers; mem. Allegheny County Bar Assn. (ethics com. 1983-86, bd. govs. 1994-2001, pres. 1999-2000), Allegheny County Acad. Trial Lawyers, Duquesne Club, Ross Mountain Club. Office: Reed Smith LLP 225 5th Ave Pittsburgh PA 15222 Office Phone: 412-288-3088. Office Fax: 412-288-3063. Business E-Mail: wmcgough@reedsmith.com.

MCGOVERN, GAIL J., international organization executive, former investment company executive; b. 1952; m. Donald E. McGovern; 1 child. BA in Quantitative Scis., Johns Hopkins U., 1974; MBA, Columbia U., 1987. Computer programmer Bell Telephone Co., Pa., 1974-80; dist. mgr. long range sys. planning AT&T Corp., Basking Ridge, NJ, 1980-84, dist. sales mgr. NYC, 1984-87, br. mgr., 1987, divsn. mgr. industry mktg. Basking Ridge, NJ, 1987-89, v.p. strategic planning for Comm. Svcs. Group, 1993, v.p. gen. mgr. Bus. Services, 1994-96, exec. v.p. Bus. Markets Divsn., 1996-98; pres., distbn. and svcs. Fidelity Investments, Boston, 1998—2001, pres. personal investments, 2001—02; MBA Class of 1966 prof. mgmt. practice Harvard Bus. Sch., Boston, 2002—; pres., CEO Am. Red Cross, Washington, 2008—. Bd. dirs. Hartford Fin. Svcs. Group, 2003—, DTE Energy Co., 2003—, Digitas, Inc., Boston, 2004—. Bd trustees Johns Hopkins U., Teach for Am. Found., Boston Children's Hosp. Named one of 25 Most Influential Working Mothers, Working Mother mag., 1995, 50 Most Powerful Women in Corp. America, Fortune Mag., 2000, 2001; recipient Disting. Alumna award Columbia Grad. Sch. Bus., 1997, Disting. Citizens award Boy Scouts Am., 1997, Alumna award, John Hopkins U., 2000. Office: Harvard Bus Sch Soldiers Field Boston MA 02163 also: American Red Cross 2025 E Street NW Washington DC 20006 Office Phone: 617-495-6394. Business E-Mail: gmcgovern@hbs.edu.

MCGOVERN, GEORGE STANLEY, former United States Senator from South Dakota; b. Avon, SD, July 19, 1922; s. Joseph C. and Frances (McLean) McG.; m. Eleanor Stegeberg, Oct. 31, 1943 (dec. Jan. 25, 2007); children: Ann, Susan, Teresa (dec. Dec. 13, 1994), Steven, Mary. BA, Dakota Wesleyan U., 1945; MA, Northwestern U., 1949, PhD, 1953. Prof. history & polit. sci. Dakota Wesleyan U., 1949-53; exec. sec. S.D. Dem. Party, 1953-55; mem. US Congress from 1st Dist. S.D., 1957—61; spl. asst. to Pres., dir. Food for Peace, 1961-62; US Senator from S.D., 1963-81; chmn. select com. on nutrition and human needs; pres. Middle East Policy Coun.; US amb. to Food & Agrl. Agencies UN, Rome, 1998—2001, Global Amb. on World Hunger, 2001—. Chmn. Ams. for Common Sense, Washington, 1981-82; guest lectr. Northwestern U., Evanston, Ill., Duke U., Columbia U., Cornell U., Munich, Berlin, and numerous others in U.S. and Europe, 1981- Author: The Colorado Coal Strike, 1913-14, 1953, War Against Want, 1964, Agricultural Thought in the Twentieth Century, 1967, A Time of War, A Time of Peace, 1968, An American Journey, 1974, Grassroots: The Autobiography of George McGovern, 1977, Terry: My Daughter's Life-and-Death Struggle with Alcoholism, 1996, The Third Freedom: Ending Hunger in Our Time, 2002, The Essential America: Our Founders and the Liberal Tradition, 2004, Social Security and the Golden Age: An Essay on the New American Demographic, 2005, Abraham Lincoln: The American Presidents Series: The 16th President, 1861-1865, 2008; co-author: (with Leonard Guttridge) The Great Coalfield War, 1972, (with Bob Dole, Donald Messer): Ending Hunger Now: A Challenge to Persons of Faith, 2005, (with William R. Polk) Out of Iraq: A Practical Plan for Withdrawal Now, 2006. Democratic nominee for Pres. U.S., 1972; candidate for presdl. nomination of Dem. Party, 1984 Served in US Army Air Corps, 1942—45. Decorated Disting. Flying Cross; recipient Presdl. Medal of Freedom, 2000, Food for Life award World Food Program, 2000 Mem. Am. Hist. Assn.; Clubs: Mason (33 deg., Shriner), Elk, Kiwanian. Methodist.*

MCGOVERN, JAMES P., United States Representative from Massachusetts; b. Worcester, Mass., Nov. 20, 1959; m. Lisa Murray; children: Patrick George, Molly Ginette. BA, Am. U., 1981, MA in Pub. Administration, 1984. Aide U.S. Senator George McGovern (Dem. South Dakota); spokesman, legis. dir., sr. aide U.S. Congressman Joe Moakley (Dem. South Boston); mem. U.S. Congress from 3rd Mass dist., 1997—; elected regional whip, mem. transp. & infrastructure com., house rules com. Mgr. George McGovern for Pres., 1984; delivered McGovern presdl. nomination speech Dem. Nat. Convention, San Francisco, 1984; leader Congressional Investigation on El Salvador, 1989 Candidate for U.S. Congress, 1996; vol. Mt. Carmel House; bd. dirs. Jesuit Internat. Vols. Democrat. Roman Catholic. Office: US House Reps 438 Cannon House Office Bldg Washington DC 20515-2103 Home: 34 Mechanic St Worcester MA 01608-2424*

MCGOVERN, JAY, aeronautical engineer, consultant; b. Sanford, Fla., Mar. 28, 1961; m. Carolyn McGovern; 2 children. BS in Marine Engring., US Naval Acad., 1983; MS in Aeronautical Engring., US Naval Postgrad. Sch. Registered profl. engr., Fla.; lic. gen. contractor Fla. Officer, pilot USN, 1983—96, officer, 2004—05; engr. Carpco, Inc., 1996—98, Hubbard Construction Co., Winter Park, Fla., 1998—99, McGovern Grp., Jacksonville, Fla., 1999—2002, engring. cons., 2008—; engr. US Dept. Navy, 2006—08. Chmn. Riverside Avondale Devel. Orgn., Inc., 1997—98, Riverside Avondale Preservation, 1999—2001; rehab. dir. Housing Partnership N.E. Fla., Jacksonville, 2002—04. Democrat. Roman Catholic. Achievements include patents for a process & apparatus used in plastics recycling. Office: PO Box 41103 Jacksonville FL 32203 Office Phone: 904-626-9618.*

MCGOVERN, JILLAINE, literature and language educator; b. Mpls., Sept. 30, 1967; BA, Augsburg Coll., Mpls., 1990; MA, U. St. Thomas, St. Paul, Minn., 1992. English tchr. Rosemount HS, Minn., 1992—95, Hastings HS, Minn., 1995—. Grantee, NEH, 2003—04. Mem.: NEA. Office: Hastings High Sch 200 General Sieben Dr Hastings MN 55033 Personal E-mail: jmcgovern@hastings.k12.mn.us.

MCGOVERN, MICHAEL B., lawyer; b. NYC, Mar. 6, 1947; s. Michael Malachy and Annette (Barbot) McG.; m. Christine Anne Beaudet, Sept. 2, 1972; children: Kathleen, Ellen, Maura. AB, Georgetown U., 1969, JD, 1972; LLM in Taxation, George Washington U., 1987. Bar: D.C. 1973, Md. 1978. From assoc. to ptnr. Wilkes & Artis, Washington, 1973-79; sole practice Washington, 1980, 84-87; ptnr. Lambert, Griffin & McGovern, Washington, 1981-84, Venable LLP, Washington, 1987-93, Montedonico, Hamilton & Altman, Washington, 1994-98, Hanson & Molloy, Washington, 1998—. Bd. dirs. Hist. Soc. Washington, 1984-93, Montgomery County Hist. Soc., 1997-2007; co-founder, vice-chair, bd. dirs., mem. Greater Bethesda-Chevy Chase Coalition Inc., 1986—; pres. Westmoreland Citizens Assn. Inc., 1988-90; mem. Leadership Washington, 1987—, Washington Estate Planning Coun. Served to capt. USAFR, 1969—82. Recipient Disting. Svc. award, Fed. Bar Assn., 1978. Mem. Columbia Country Club (Chevy Chase), Met. Club (Washington), Barristers, John Carroll Soc. Republican. Home: 5414 Albemarle St Bethesda MD 20816-1825 Office: Hanson & Molloy 1320 19th St NW Ste 300 Washington DC 20036 Office Phone: 202-833-9300. Business E-Mail: mcgovern@hanson-molloy.com.

MCGOVERN, PATRICK J., communications executive; m. Lore Harp. BA in biophysics, M.I.T., 1959. Founder Internat. Data Corp., Framingham, Mass., 1964, chmn., 1976—; founder IDG Comm. Inc., Framingham, 1987, CEO, 1999. Dir. Info. Inds. Assn., Mag. Publishers Assn., Am. Mgmt. Assn; trustee Mass. Inst. Tech., McGovern Inst. for Brain Rsch., Whitehead Inst. Recipient James Smithsonian Bicentennial Medal, Smithsonian Inst., Entrepreneurial Leadership Award, MIT Enterprise Forum of Cambridge, Inc., The Bus. Pub. of the Year award Delaney Report, The Communicator of the Year award N.Y. Chpt. Bus. Profl. Advertisers Assn., The Entrepreneur of the Year award Ernst & Young, Lifetime Achievement award, Am. Soc. Bus. Publ. Editors, 2004, Top Innovator in Bus. Publishing Award, BtoB Media Bus. mag., 2004, Lifetime Achievement award, Mag. Publishers of Am., 2005; Named one of 25 Entrepreneurs We Love, Inc. mag., 2004, 50 Most Generous Philanthropists, Fortune Mag., 2005, Richest Americans, Forbes, 1999-, World's Richest People, 2001-. Fellow: Am. Acad. of Arts and Sciences. Achievements include providing a $350 mil. endowment to M.I.T. Office: Internat Data Group 1 Exeter Plz Fl 15 Boston MA 02116-2848

MCGOVERN, STEPHEN JOHN, political scientist; b. New York, Nov. 15, 1959; s. John Robert and Sheila McGovern; m. Lisa Baglione, July 19, 1991; children: Jack Anthony, Maria Rose. PhD, Cornell U., Ithaca, NY, 1993; JD, NYU Sch.Law. Cert.: Calif. State Bar Assn. 1987. Prof. Haverford Coll., Pa., 1999—2009. Author: (books) The Politics of Downtown Development; co-author: Urban Policy Reconsidered; contbr. articles to profl. jours. Avocations: swimming, reading, travel. Home: 4 Coll Cir Haverford PA 19041 Office: Haverford College 370 Lancaster Avenue Haverford PA 19041 Office Fax: 610-896-1495.

MCGOVERN-SCATURO, DIANE JOAN, psychotherapist; d. Francis Michael and Joan Veronica (Quinn) McCarthy; m. Thomas Joseph McGovern (dec.); children: Judith Ann McGovern, Robert Thomas McGovern; m. Christopher John Scaturo, Aug. 1, 1992. BA, Trinity U., Washington, 1953; MEd, U. Pitts., 1956; MS in Edn., St. Bonaventure U., NY, 1992. Lic. mental health counselor N.Y. State Edn. Dept., cert. group psychotherapist Nat. Registry Cert. Group Psychotherapists, credentialed Alcoholism and Substance Abuse Counselor N.Y. State Offics Alcoholism Substance Abuse Svcs., cert. rational marriage and family therapists Nat. Assn. Cognitive Behavioral Therapists, rational addictions counselor Nat. Assn. Cognitive Behavioral Therapists. Family svcs. coord. Cattaraugus County Coun. on Alcoholism and Substance Abuse, Olean, 1987—92; behavioral health therapist Charter Behavioral Health Sys. Winston-Salem, NC, 1994—96; behavioral health therapist, group psychotherapist Olean Gen. Hosp. Behavioral Health Unit, 2000—. Oral panel examiner Credentialled Alcoholism Counselor Exam., Credentialling Application Svcs., Albany, NY, 1992. Mem., bd. dirs. Olean Gen. Hosp. Found., 2000—, sec., bd. dirs., 2005—; mem., adv. bd. Salvation Army, Olean, 1959—86, chmn., adv. bd., 1972—77. Fellow: Am. Psychotherapy Assn.; mem.: ACA, Am. Group Psychotherapy Assn. (clin. mem.), Rochester Group Psychotherapy Soc. Avocations: golf, downhill skiing. Office: Olean Gen Hosp Behavioral Health Unit 515 Main St Olean NY 14760

MCGOWAN, ANGELA KAY, public information officer; b. Decatur, Ga., Sept. 6, 1970; d. John E. McGowan, Jr. and Linda Kay (Hudson) McGowan. BA, Coll. William & Mary, 1992; JD, Vanderbilt U., 1995; MPH, Emory U., 1998. Bar: Ga. 1995. Atty. Troutman Sanders, LLP, Atlanta, 1996—97; legal svcs. officer Divsn. Pub. Health Ga. Dept. Human Resources, Atlanta, 1999—2002; epidemic intelligence svc. officer Ctrs. for Disease Control & Prevention, Atlanta, 2002—04, pub. health law analyst, 2004—06, health scientist, 2006—07. Pres. Atlanta chpt. William & Mary Alumni Club, 1999—2000; alumni bd. govs. Rollins Sch. Pub. Health, Emory U., Atlanta, 2004—, pres., 2007—08. Mem.: Ga. Bar Assn., Pub. Health Law Assn., Am. Pub. Health Assn. Home: 2410B Fitlers Walk Philadelphia PA 19103-5562 Office: Robert Wood Johnson Foundation College Rd E Princeton NJ 08540-6672 Office Phone: 770-488-8210. Personal E-mail: angiemcgowan@cs.com, angiemcgowan@gmail.com. Business E-Mail: amcgowan@rwjf.org.

MCGOWAN, FRANCIS X., anesthesiologist, educator; b. Long Beach, NY, Apr. 30, 1959; s. Francis X McGowan and Lorraine Miller. MD, Duke U. Sch. Medicine, Durham, NC, 1983. Diplomate Am. Bd. Anesthesiology, 1990. Pres. Soc. Pediatric Anesthesia, Richmond, Va., 2004—06; prof. Harvard Med. Sch., Boston, 2003—; chief, divsn. cardiac anesthesia Children's Hosp. Boston, 2003—. Contbr. chapters to books, articles to profl. jours. Mem. Outward Bound, Boston, 1998—2002. Grants, NIH, 1995—. Fellow: Am. Acad. Pediat. Office: Childrens Hosp Boston 300 Longwood Ave Boston MA 02115 Business E-Mail: francis.mcgowan@childrens.harvard.edu.

MCGOWAN, MICHAEL JEREMY, lawyer; b. Evanston, Ill., Aug. 28, 1961; s. Melvin Joseph and Lydia Judith McGowan; m. Karen Jean Palmer; children: Genevieve, Quinn, Grace. BA, U. Notre Dame, 1983; JD, Loyola U., 1988. Bar: Ill. States atty. Lake County, Ill. States Atty. Office, Waukegan, 1988—89; assoc. Querrey & Harrow, Ltd., Waukegan, 1989—95, non-equity ptnr. Chgo., 1995—97, O'Hagan, Smith and Amundsen, LLC, Chgo., 1997—2000, equity ptnr., 2000—06, Smith Amundsen LLC, Chgo., 2006—. Trustee St. Martin de Porres HS, Waukegan, 2003—07; mem. Defense Rsch. Inst., Chgo., 2005—, Ill. Ann. Defense Counsel, Chgo., 1995—, U.S. Law Network, 2002—. Named Ill. Super Lawyer, 2006—08. Mem.: Leading Lawyers Network, U. Notre Dame Law Club (bd. dirs. 2001—05). Republican. Roman Catholic. Avocations: history, football, skiing, travel. Office: Smith Amundsen LLC 150 N Michigan Ave Ste 3300 Chicago IL 60601 Home Phone: 847-735-1745; Office Phone: 312-894-3242. Business E-Mail: mmcgowan@salawus.com.

MCGOWAN, SUSAN, gifted and talented educator; b. Alameda, Calif., May 12, 1959; d. Thomas and Gladys Mae (Prutzman) McG.; m. Warren Howard Jones, Oct. 31, 1980 (div.); children: Kelly Hardcastle, Reilly James; m. Barry William McLaughlin, May 22, 2004 (div.). AS in Edn., No. Va. Community Coll., 1988; BA in Russian Area Studies, George Mason U., 1991; MEd, Marymount U., 1994; EdD, Coll. William & Mary, 2007. Cert. in mid. childhood Nat. Bd.; tchr. Va. Data processor Tracor Inc., Va. Beach, 1982-83, data analyst, 1984; systems analyst Advanced Tech., Inc., Va. Beach, 1984-85, computer programmer Reston, Va., 1986-87; tech. writer Swiger Group, Reston, 1987; tchr. 3rd grade Loudoun Country Day Sch., Leesburg, Va., 1991-93; tchr. 4th and 5th grade Loudoun County Pub. Schs., 1994—2000, Va. Beach City Pub. Sch., 2001—03; coord. Gifted Edn. Mecklenburg Co.Pub. Sch., 2006; asst. prof. Longwood U., 2008—. Master tchr. Nat. Tech. Tchr. Inst., WNVT, Fairfax, 1998-99; translation cons. Systems Ctr., Inc., Reston, 1990— Recipient Presdl. award, Va. Gov.'s Sch., 2005, Outstanding Tchg. award, 2007. Mem. AAUW, Golden Key, Phi Theta Kappa, Alpha Chi., Kappa Delta Pi (faculty advisor, 2008-), Alpha Delta Kappa. Office Phone: 434-395-2325. Business E-Mail: jonessm@longwood.edu.

MCGOWEN, LORRAINE S., lawyer; b. Phila., 1960; m. Gailon McGowen; 4 children. BS, Georgetown U., 1983; JD, Columbia U., 1986. Bar: N.Y. 1987, U.S. Dist. Ct., So. Dist. N.Y. 1988, U.S. Dist. Ct., Ea. Dist. N.Y. 1988, D.C. 1994, U.S. Ct. Appeals, Second Cir. 1994. Ptnr. Orrick, Herrington & Sutcliffe LLP, NYC, 1996—, co-chair Bankruptcy and Debt Restructuring Group, 2001—. Mem.: Am. Coll. Investment Counsel, Am. Bankruptcy Inst., DC Bar, Assn. Bar City NY, ABA (bus. law com.). Office: Orrick Herrington & Sutcliffe LLP 666 Fifth Ave New York NY 10103 Office Phone: 212-506-5114. Office Fax: 212-506-5151. Business E-Mail: lmcgowen@orrick.com.

MC GOWIN, WILLIAM EDWARD, artist; b. Hattiesburg, Miss., June 2, 1938; s. William Edward and Emily (Ratliff) Mc G.; m. Claudia DeMonte, May 28, 1977; children: Leah, Jill. BS, U. So. Miss., 1961; MA, U. Ala., 1964. Prof. art SUNY, Old Westbury, 1978—2003, Coll. Old Westbury; mem. faculty Corcoran Gallery Art, 1966-77, head sculpture dept., 1967-74; lectr. in field. One-man shows include Corcoran Gallery Art, Washington, 1962, 71, 75, Martha Jackson Gallery, NYC, 1968, Am. Cultural Ctr., Paris, 1974, Mus. Modern Art, Paris, 1978, Brooks Jackson Gallery, Iolas, NYC, 1978-80, Fendrick Gallery, Washington, 1977-80, U. Colo., New Orleans Contemporary Art Ctr., 1982, Project Studios 1, L.I., NY, Cranbrook Acad., Bloomfield Hills, Mich., 1983, Art Park, Lewiston, NY, 1984, Gracie Mansion Gallery, NYC, 1985-86, 89, Mus. Fine Arts, Miami, Jones, Troyer Gallery, Washington, 1987, 89, 91, Boca Raton (Fla.) Mus., 1991, Margulis-Taplin Gallery, Miami, 1993, Paris-NY-Bangkok Gallery, Bangkok, Thailand, 1994, Grey Art Gallery, NYU, 1995, Siipakorn U., Bangkok, 1997, Genkan Gallery, Tokyo, 1997, Miss. Mus. Art, 2000, Osuna Art, Bethesda, Md., 2005, Mobile Mus. Art., Ala., 2006, PS1 Mus. Modern Art, L.I., 2006, The Ogden Mus., New Orleans, LA, 2007, Flint Inst. Art, Mich., 2008, Tallin Kunsethoone, Tallin Estonia, Jan Colle Gallery Ghent, Belgium, 2008, The Mississippi Mus. Art, 2009, Herron Inst. Art, Indpls., 2009; group shows include Contemporary Mus., Houston, Miss. Mus. Art, Whitney Mus., NYC, Detroit Inst. Art, Guggenheim Mus., Speed Mus., Ky., Cologne (Germany) Art Fair, Zurich Art Fair, Miss. Mus. Art; represented in permanent collections Phillips Collection, Washington, Indpls. Mus. Art, Addison Mus. Art, Andover, Mass, Corcoran Gallery Art, Nat. Collection Fine Arts, Washington, New Orleans Mus. Art, Whitney Mus. Am. Art, NYC, Guggenheim Mus., NYC, Hirshorn Gallery and Sculpture Garden, Ogden Mus. New Oleans, Cabinet des Estampes Musée d'art Eihistoire, Geneva, The Mississippi Story, Jackson Hills, MS Mus., 2007, Sanghai Art Fair, 2008-09.; permanent commn. U.S. Gen. Svc. Adminstrn., 1979, VA, Indpls., 1985, Percent for Art, NYC, 1992, City of Jubai, Saudi Arabia, 1993, Dallas Rapid Transit Authority, 1994, Queens County N.Y. Supreme Ct., 1996, Art in Pub. Places, Socorro, N.Mex., 1997, Met. Transit Authority State NY, Bayside, 1998, Inst. for Internat. Econs., Washington, 2000, St. Marks Gates, Plan de Grass, France, 2002, U. Iowa, Cedar Falls, 2003, Clarette Group, NYC, 2004, N.Mex. Arts Sculpture, Santa Rosa, 2004-05, Broward County (Fla.) Pub. Art Commn., 2006, Ft. Lauderdale Fire Rescue, 2006, Rockville Town Sq., Md., 2007. Recipient Oscar for painting, 1977, Painting prize 9th Internat. Painting Festival, Cagnes-sur-Mer, France, 1977, Miss. Arts and Letters award for visual arts, 1980, Art Commn. Design award N.Y.C., 1998; Nat. Endowment for Arts grantee, 1967-68, 79-80, pub. outdoor sculpture grantee, 1977, Cassandra Found. grantee. Home and Office: 96 Grand St New York NY 10013-2633 Office Phone: 212-966-4496. Personal E-mail: edmcgowin@aol.com.

MCGOWN, JOHN, JR., lawyer; b. Bowling Green, Ky., June 15, 1949; s. John Stanley and Margaret (Deatherage) McG.; m. Mary Grunewald, Apr. 20, 1978; children: Erin Margaret, Brenna Kathryn. BS, U. Ky., Lexington, 1971; JD, U. Colo., Boulder, 1974; LLM in Taxation, U. Denver, 1981. Bar: Colo. 1975, US Tax Ct. 1981, Idaho 1982. Dep. dist. atty. Weld County, Colo., 1974-78; assoc. Montgomery, Little, Young, Campbell, & McGrew, Denver, 1979-80; rschr. appellate divsn. IRS, Denver, 1980-81; mem. staff tax dept. Price Waterhouse, Denver, 1981-82; ptnr. Hawley Troxell Ennis & Hawley, LLP, Boise, Idaho, 1982-99, of counsel, 2000—. Adj. prof. Boise State U., 1983, assoc. prof., 2000-02; guest lecturer U. Idaho Coll. Law, Moscow, 1990, 2003, 04, 05, adj. prof., 06; guest speaker various tax seminars, 1983—. Contbr. over 90 articles to profl. jours. Bd. dirs. Assn. for Retarded Citizens Ada County, Inc., 1987-93, pres. 1991-92, Assoc. Taxpayers Idaho, Inc., 1993-2002, exec. com., 1995-2002; audit review panel United Way Ada County, 1986-91; IRS vol. tax asst. program 1982, 87. Fellow Am. Coll. of Trust and Estate Counsel; mem. ABA (taxation sect.), Idaho State Bar Assn. (chair 2009, taxation probate and trust law sect.), Idaho Soc. CPAs (fed. and state taxation com. 1984-89, bus. legis. com. 1989-91, pers. fin. com. 2000—), Boise Bar Assn., Pioneer Club, Toastmasters (pres. 1991), Beta Gamma Sigma, Sigma Chi. Home: 282 S Mobley Ln Boise ID 83712-8329 Office: Hawley Troxell Ennis & Hawley LLP 877 Main St Ste 1000 Boise ID 83702-5883 Office Phone: 208-344-6000.

MCGRADY, C. NADINE, science educator; children: Aaron John Dolezal, Olen James, Jennifer Carol. MS, Emporia State U., Kans., 1978. Instr. chemistry & earth scis. Western Piedmont CC, Morganton, NC, 1995—, dept. head, sci. and math., 2008—. Recipient Tchg. Excellence award, WPCC, 2005. Office: Western Piedmont CC 1001 Burkemont Ave Morganton NC 28655 Office Fax: 828-448-6175. Business E-Mail: nmcgrady@wpcc.edu.

MCGRADY, CORINNE YOUNG, design company executive; b. NYC, May 6, 1938; d. Albert I. and Reda (Bromberg) Young; m. Michael Robinson McGrady; children: Sean, Siobhan, Liam. Student, Bard Coll., Annandale-on-Hudson, NY, 1960, Harvard U., 1968—69. Founder, pres. Corinne McGrady Designs; designer Corinneware (joint venture Corinne McGrady Designs and Boston Warehouse Trading Corp.), East Northport, NY, 1970—. Exhibited in group shows at Mus. Contemporary Crafts, N.Y.C., 1969—70, Smithsonian Instn., 1970—71, Pompidou Ctr., Paris, 1971, Mus. Sci. and Industry, 1970, exhibitions include Guild Hall Show, Southampton, N.Y., 1968, Hecksher Mus., 1968; patentee cookbook stand. V.p. Women's Internat. League for Peace and Freedom, Huntington, NY, 1971; mem. bldg. com. Timberland Lib Hoodsport, 1996—97. Recipient Design Rev. award, Indsl. Design, 1969, 1970, Instant Supergraphic Indsl. Design Rev. award, 1971. Home and Office: PO Box 27 Lilliwaup WA 98555-0027

MCGRADY, JONATHAN L., lawyer; b. Knoxville, Tenn., Oct. 29, 1969; s. Joseph Harry and Ann Abate McG.; m. Jennifer Blackmon, Aug. 5, 1995. BA, Hampden-Sydney Coll., 1991; JD, Coll. William & Mary, 1995. Bar: Va. 1995, U.S. Dist. Ct. (we. dist.) Va. 1995, U.S. Ct. Appeals (4th cir.) 1995. Ptnr. McGrady & McGrady, LLP, Hillsville, Va., 1996—. Chmn. Carroll County Dem. Party, 1996—; deacon Hillsville Christian Ch; mem. criminal justice svc. bd. Commonwealth of Va.; pres. Twin County Regional. Mem. Va. Trial Lawyers Assn., Va. Bar Assn., Carroll Bar Assn., Hillsville Masonic Lodge, Kazim Shriners. Home: 149 Camelot Ln Hillsville VA 24343-1676 Office: McGrady & McGrady LLP 127 Mill St Hillsville VA 24343-1314 E-mail: mcgradylaw@psknet.com.

MCGRADY, TRACY, professional basketball player; b. Bartow, Fla., May 24, 1979; s. Melanise Williford; m. CleRenda Harris, Sept. 12, 2006; children: Layla Clarice, Laycee Aloe, Laymen Lamar. Forward Toronto Raptors, 1997—2000, Orlando Magic, 2000—04, Houston Rockets, 2004—. Active NBA's Reading Time-Out prog. Named to Eastern Conf. All-Star Team, NBA, 2000—04, Western Conf. All-Star Team, 2005—07, All-NBA 1st Team, 2002, 2003. Achievements include leading the NBA in: points per game, 2003, 2004. Office: c/o Houston Rockets 1510 Polk St Houston TX 77002*

MCGRAIL, JEANE KATHRYN, artist; b. Mpls., May 1, 1947; d. Robert Vern and Mary Virginia (Kees) McGrail. BS, U. Wis.-River Falls, 1970; MFA, Cranbrook Acad. Art, 1972; postgrad., Sch. of Art Inst. of Chgo., 1985, Ill. Inst. Tech., 1993. Tchr. Inst. Contemporary Art. Group exhbns. include Saginaw Art Mus., Mich., 1972, Met. Mus. Art, Miami, Fla., 1974, Lowe Mus. Art, Coral Gables, Fla., 1974, 76, Miller Galleries, Coconut Grove, Fla., 1978, 80, Cicchinelli Gallery, NYC, 1980-82, Harper Coll., 1984, Contemporary Art Ctr. Arlington, Arlington Heights, Ill., 1984, 85, 86, 94, Evanston Art Ctr., 1985, South Shore Cultural Ctr., Chgo., 1990, N.A.M.E. Gallery, 1990, Artemisia Gallery, Chgo., 1991, 92, 93, 94, North Lakeside Art Ctr., Chgo., 1991, 94, 95, Ceres Gallery, NYC, 1992, Harper Coll., Ill., 1993, Environ. Concerns, Chgo., 1993, North Park Coll., Chgo., 1993, Franklin Square Gallery, Chgo., 1994, 95, 96, Space 900 Gallery, Chgo., 1994-2007, Chuck Levitan Gallery, NYC, 1995, Riverwest Art Ctr., Milw., 1995, Nat. Mus. Women in the Arts, Wash., 1996, Gallery 1040, 1997-, "Red", Chgo., 1998, Oakton Coll. Gallery, Ill., 1999-, Women's Works, Woodstock, Ill., 1999, "Paint It Siver", ARC Gallery, Chgo., 1999, Past/Present, Chgo., 1999, "Blue", Northeastern Ill. U., Chgo., 2000, Then and Now, Chgo., 1999, Norris Cultural Ctr., St. Charles, Ill., 1999, others; represented in permanent collections at Chgo. Mus. Sci. and Industry, U. Chgo., Mus. Photography, Chgo., Miami-Dade Pub. Libr., U. Wis.-River Falls, MacGregor Found., Printmakers Workshop, NYC, Norman R. Eppnik Art Gallery Emporia State U., Kans., 2000, Mini Print Internat. Exhbn., Binghamton, NY, 2000, Yale U. Med. Libr., 2000, Columbia U. Med. Ctr., 2000, 08, Mini Print Internat. of Cadaques, Spain, Macy Gallery, Providence, RI, 2000, Brickton Gallery, Park Ridge, Fla., 2001-, Mini Print Internat. of Cadaques, Spain, 2001—, Last of Primaries, Coll. of Lake Co., 2003—, Ukrainian Mus. Contemporary Art, Chgo., 2003, Chautauqua Nat. Exhbn., NY, 2004, Rockford Coll., Ill., 2006, Space 900, Chgo., 2006, Inspiring Change for Global Warming, Chgo., 2007 others; solo exhbns. include Cicchinelli Gallery, 1981, Gallery at the Commons, Chgo., 1982, Truman Coll. Gallery, Chgo., 1991, C.G. Jung Inst., Evanston, Ill., 1992, Carlson Tower Gallery, Chgo., 1994, Olcott Ctr. Gallery, Theosophical Soc. Am., Wheaton, Ill., 2001; pub. "Mosaic", 1992, The Best of Printmaking, 1997; contbr. publ. to profl. jour. Cranbrook Acad. Art scholar, 1971; CAAP grantee Dept. Cultural Affairs City Chgo, 1992; recipient Poster Competition award Vizcaya Mus., 1974; Print award Auction WPBT, 1979, Tchr. Inst. Contemporary Art, Art Inst. Chgo., 2004, Mems. Exhbn. 1st Place prize, The Phipps Ctr. the Arts, Wis., 2007. Mem. Coll. Art Assn., Chgo. Women's Caucus for Art (bd. dirs. 1992-95, sec.), Chgo. Artists Coalition, Sierra Club (sec. chpt. exec. com. 2005-07). Independent. Studio: 1040 W Huron St LL5 Chicago IL 60622-6591 E-mail: whoswho@jeanemcgrail.com.

MCGRATH, J. PAUL, lawyer; b. Rochester, NY, Sept. 9, 1940; s. Thomas E. and Evelyn R. McG.; m. Eileen Robinson, Aug. 29, 1964; children: John P., Patricia, David R., Robyn. AB, Coll. of the Holy Cross, 1962; LL.B., Harvard U., 1965. Mem. firm Dewey, Ballantine, Bushby, Palmer and Wood, NYC, 1965-73, ptnr., 1973-81, 85-92; asst. atty. gen. civil div. Dept. Justice, Washington, 1981-83, asst. atty. gen. antitrust div., 1983-85; v.p., gen. counsel Allied-Signal Inc., 1992—96; sr. v.p., gen. counsel FMC Corp., Chgo., 1996—2000; sr. v.p., gen. counsel, sec. Am. Standard Cos. Inc., Piscataway, 2000—. Fellow Am. Coll. Trial Lawyers. Clubs: Montclair Golf. Republican. Roman Catholic.

MCGRATH, JAMES THOMAS, real estate investment company executive; b. NYC, Nov. 10, 1942; s. Thomas James and Mary Ita (Finnegan) McG.; m. Paulette L. Franck, Aug. 16, 1980; 1 child, Tara (dec.). BS in Acctg., Providence Coll., 1964. CPA, N.Y.; lic. gen. contractor, N.C., 2006. Sr. auditor Coopers & Lybrand, NYC, 1968-72, mgmt. cons., 1972-74; group contr. IU Internat. Corp., Phila., 1974-77; v.p. fin. Taylor Engring. Corp. subs. IU Internat., Detroit, 1977-78; controller Pool Co. subs. Enserch Corp., Houston, 1978-85; sr. v.p. fin., treas. Lone Star Gas Co. subs. Enserch Corp., Dallas, 1985-91; pres. McGrath & Assocs., Inc., Dallas, 1991—. Ct. Apptd. Spl. Advocate. Bd. dirs. ARC, Dallas chpt., 1990-93. Lt. USN, 1964-68. Mem. AICPA, Dallas Athletic Club, St. Vincent de Paul Soc. Libertarian. Roman Catholic. Avocations: golf, cooking, skiing, scuba diving, sailing. Home and Office: 2838 Colleen Dr Garland TX 75043-1215 Office Phone: 972-271-5803. Personal E-mail: pjmcgrath2@yahoo.com.

MCGRATH, JOHN MICHAEL, educator; b. Johnstown, Pa., Aug. 13, 1960; s. John Michael and Margaret Rose McGrath; m. Anne Frances Hafeli, Dec. 29, 1990; children: Maura Clare, Kathleen Margaret. BBA, U. Notre Dame, South Bend, Ind., 1978; MM, Northwestern U., Evanston, Ill., 1990; PhD, Pa. State U., State Coll., 2001. V.p. J. Walter Thompson, Chgo., 1984—94; prof. U. Pitts. Recipient Chancellor's Disting. Tchg. award, Cmty. Svc. Recognition award. Home: 409 Luzerne St Johnstown PA 15905 Office: Univ Pitts Johnstown 250 Schoolhouse Rd Johnstown PA 15904 Business E-Mail: mcgrath@pitt.edu.

MCGRATH, JUDY (JUDITH ANN MCGRATH), broadcast executive; b. Scranton, Pa., July 2, 1952; BA in English Lit., Cedar Crest Coll. Copy chief Glamour mag.; sr. writer Mademoiselle; copywriter Nat. Advt., Phila.; copywriter, on-air promotion Warner Amex Satellite Entertainment Corp. (predecessor to MTV), 1981; editl. dir. MTV, sr. v.p., creative dir., 1988—92, exec. v.p., creative dir., 1992—93, co-pres., creative dir., 1993—94, pres., 1994—96, MTV, MTV2, 1996—2000, pres. MTV Group, chmn. Interactive Music, 2000—02; pres. MTV Networks Music Group, 2002—04, chmn., CEO, 2004—. Hon. chair Cable Positive. Trustee emeritus Nat. Campaign to Prevent Teen Pregnancy; bd. dirs. Rock the Vote, NYC Ballet, McCarton Sch.; mem. adv. bd. LifeBeat. Recipient Cable Ace award, 1993, Founders award, Rock the Vote, 2001, Friend of the Children award, Harlem Children's Zone, 2001; named Humanitarian of Yr., T.J. Martell Found. Leukemia, Cancer and AIDS Rsch., 2003; named one of The 50 Most Powerful Women in Bus., Fortune mag., 1998—2008, The 100 Most Powerful Women in Entertainment, Hollywood Reporter, 2004—07, The 100 Most Powerful Women, Forbes Mag., 2006—09, The 100 Most Influential Women in NYC Bus., Crain's NY Bus., 2007. Office: MTV 1515 Broadway Fl 28 New York NY 10036-8901*

MCGRATH, KATHRYN BRADLEY, lawyer; b. Norfolk, Va., Sept. 2, 1944; d. James Pierce and Kathryn (Hoyle) Bradley; children: Ian M., James D. AB, Mt. Holyoke Coll., 1966; JD, Georgetown U., 1969. Ptnr. Gardner, Carton & Douglas, Washington, 1979-83; dir. div. investment mgmt. SEC, Washington, 1983-90; ptnr. Morgan Lewis, Washington, 1990—2002, Crowell & Moring, LLP, Washington, 2002—05, Mayer, Brown, Rowe & Maw LLP, Washington, 2005—07; sr. v.p. ICMA Retirement Corp., Washington, gen. counsel. Named Disting. Exec., Pres. Reagan, 1987. Mem. ABA, Fed. Bar Assn. (exec. council securities law com.). Office: ICMA Retirement Corp 777 N Capitol St NE Washington DC 20002 Office Phone: 202-962-6910. Business E-Mail: kmcgrath@icmarc.org.

MCGRATH, KEVIN MICHAEL, military analyst, civilian military employee, researcher; b. Huntington, NY, Aug. 7, 1973; s. John Patrick and Michaele Marie McGrath. BA in History, Polit. Sci. summa cum laude, James Madison U, Harrisonburg, Va., 1995; MA in Internat. Rels., U. Md., Coll. Pk., 1998, PhD in Internat. Rels., Nat. Security, 2007—. Intern, Va. Gov.'s fellow Office Sec. Edn., 1995; intern Dept. of State, Wash., DC, 1995, intern Am. Embassy Nicosia, Cyprus, 1996; intern FBI, Wash., DC, 1997; tchg. asst. dept. polit. sci. U. Md., 1997—98, lectr.; fgn. policy analyst Dept. of Def., Wash., DC, 1999—. Assoc. The MASY Group, Global Intelligence and Risk Management Solutions. Author: Sheathing the Sword of Damocles: Assessing Al Qaeda and Devising a US Response, 2007; contbr. articles to profl. jours. Eagle scout Boy Scouts of Am. Recipient Sustained Superior Svc., Dept. Def., 1999, NATO Svc. medal, 2001, Civilian Combat Support award, 2001, 2003, 2005, 2006, Def. Civilian Expeditionary medal for Svc. Afghanistan, 2003—06, SFOR/NATO, Bosnia, 2001. Mem.: Kennedy Ctr., World Affairs Coun., Alpha Phi Omega. Democrat. Catholic. Avocations: sports, theater, travel, languages. Home: 28 Delancey Dr Geneva NY 14456 Office: Dept of Def Washington DC Mailing: 2915 Connecticut Ave NW Apt 307 Washington DC 20008

MCGRATH, MARY HELENA, plastic surgeon, educator; b. NYC, Apr. 12, 1945; d. Vincent J. and Mary M. (Manning) McG.; children: Margaret E. Simon, Richard M. Simon. BA, Coll. New Rochelle, 1966; MD, St. Louis U., 1970; MPH, George Washington U., 1994. Diplomate Am. Bd. Surgery, Am. Bd. Plastic Surgery, lic. physician Calif. Resident in surg. pathology U. Colo. Med. Ctr., Denver, 1970-71, intern in gen. surgery, 1971-72, resident in gen. surgery, 1971-75; resident in plastic and reconstructive surgery Yale U. Sch. Medicine, New Haven, 1976—78, chief resident plastic and reconstructive surgery, 1977-78; fellow in hand surgery U. Conn.-Yale U., New Haven, 1978; instr. in surgery divsn. plastic and reconstructive surgery Yale U. Sch. Medicine, New Haven, 1977-78, asst. prof. plastic surgery, 1978-80; attending in plastic and reconstructive surgery Yale-New Haven Hosp., 1978-80, Columbia-Presbyn. Hosp., NYC, 1980-84, George Washington U. Med. Ctr., Washington, 1984-2000, Children's Nat. Med. Ctr., Washington, 1985-2000, Loyola U. Med. Ctr., 2000—02, Hines VA Hosp., 2001—02, U. Calif., San Francisco, 2003—, San Francisco VA Ctr., 2003—, San Francisco Gen. Hosp., 2003—; asst. prof. plastic surgery Columbia U., NYC, 1980-84; assoc. prof. plastic surgery Sch. Medicine, George Washington U., Washington, 1984-87, prof. plastic surgery, 1987-2000, Loyola U. Med. Ctr., 2000—02, U. Calif., San Francisco, 2003—. Bd. dirs. Am. Bd. Plastic Surgery, 1989-95, historian, 1991-95; examiner certifying exam., 1986—; mem. Residency Rev. Com. Plastic Surgery, 2006—; senator med. faculty senate George Washington U., bd. govs. Med. Faculty Assocs.; presenter, cons. in field. Co-editor: (with M.L. Turner) Dermatology for Plastic Surgeons, 1993; assoc. editor: The Jour. of Hand Surgery, 1984-89, Annals of Plastic Surgery, 1984-87, Plastic and Reconstructive Surgery, 1989-95, Contemporary Surgery, 1999-2006, Archives of Surgery, 2004—; advt. editor Plastic and Reconstructive Surgery, 2003-06; guest reviewer numerous jours.; contbr. chpts. to books and articles to profl. jours Recipient numerous rsch. grants, 1978—. Fellow ACS (DC chpt. program ann. meeting chmn., 1992, pres. 1994-95, bd. govs. 1995-98, exec. com. 1996-97, chmn. adv. coun. plastic surgery 1995-98, regent 1997—2006, vice-chair bd. regents 2005-06, 1st v.p. 2007-08, jt. commr., 2009-); mem. AAAS, Am. Surg. Assn., Am. Assn. Hand Surgery, Am. Assn. Plastic Surgeons (trustee 1997-00), Am. Burn Assn., Am. Soc. for Aesthetic Plastic Surgery, Am. Soc. Maxillofacial Surgeons, Am. Soc. Plastic and Reconstructive Surgery (chmn. ethics com. 1985-87, chmn. device/tech. evaluation com. 1993-94, chmn. workforce task force 1997-00, bd. dirs. 1994-96, chmn. endowment bd. dirs. 2000-04, trustee 2004—07, chmn. bd. trustees 2006-07, ednl. found. bd. dirs. 1985-96, treas. 1989-92, v.p. 1992-93, pres.-elect 1993-94, pres. 1994-95), Am. Soc. Reconstructive Microsurgery (edn. com. 1992-94), Am. Soc. Surgery of Hand (chmn. 1987 ann. residents' and fellows conf. 1986-87, rsch. com. 1988-90), Assn. Acad. Chmn. Plastic Surgery (bd. dirs. 1999—), Assn. Acad. Surgery, Chgo. Soc. Plastic Surgeons (treas. 2001-02), Calif. Soc. Plastic Surgeons, San Francisco Surg. Soc., Chgo. Surg. Soc., Internat. Soc. Reconstructive Surgery, Met. D.C. Soc. Surgery Hand (pres. 1995-97), N.Y. Surg. Soc., Northeastern Soc. Plastic Surgeons (treas. 1993-96, pres. 1997-98), Pacific Coast Surg. Assn., Plastic Surgery Rsch. Coun. (chmn. 1990), Surg. Biology Club III, The Wound Healing Soc Office Phone: 415-353-4389. Business E-Mail: mary.mcgrath@ucsfmedctr.org.

MCGRATH, MICHAEL G., management consulting firm executive; BS in Chemical Engring., U. Wis., MBA in Acctg. With Accenture Ltd., 1973—, consulting mng. ptnr. St. Louis, 1987—89, country mng. ptnr. Italy, 1989—92, mng. ptnr. Practice Process & Quality, London, 1992—97, CFO, 1997—2001, 2004—06, treas., mng. ptnr. corp. matters, 2001, capital risk officer, 2001—02, chief risk officer, 2002—04, internat. chmn., 2006—. Office: Accenture Ltd 1345 Ave of the Americas New York NY 10105 also: 22 Victoria St HM12 Hamilton Bermuda

MCGRATH, MIKE, state supreme court chief justice, former state attorney general; b. Aug. 22, 1947; BS, U. Mont., 1970; JD, Gonzaga U., 1975. Bar: Wash. 75, Mont. 77, U.S. Ct. Appeals (9th cir.) 80, U.S. Supreme Ct. 80. Reginald Heber Smith cmty. lawyer fellow; atty. Washoe County Legal Svcs., Reno, 1975—76; asst. atty. gen. State of Mont., Helena, 1977—82, atty. gen., 2001—09; county atty. Lewis and Clark County, Helena, 1983—2001; chief justice Mont. Supreme Ct., 2009—. Bd. dirs. Mont. Legal Svcs. Assn., 1980—2003, pres., 1984—85, 1995—96; bd. dirs. Mountain chpt. Nat. Com. for Prevention of Child Abuse, 1985—90, Big Bros. Sisters, Helena, 1977—83, Friendship Ctr. Helena, 1989—2003, pres., 1995—97; chmn. Conf. Western Atty. Gens., 2003—04. With USAF, 1970—72. Mem.: Mont. County Attys. Assn. (pres. 1996—97), Nat. Dist. Attys. Assn., Mont. Bar Assn., Rock Mountain Elk Found. Home: 514 Hayes Ave Helena MT 59601-6106 Office: Mont Supreme Ct Justice Bldg - 215 N Sanders PO Box 203001 Helena MT 59620-3001 Office Phone: 406-444-5490.*

MCGRATH, PATRICK, writer; b. London, Feb. 7, 1950; s. Patrick and Helen (O'Brien) McG; m. Maria Aitken. BA with honors, U. London, 1971; student, Simon Fraser U. Mng. editor Speech Tech. mag. Media Dimensions, NYC, 1982-87; freelance writer; with Broadmoor Hosp., England; tchr. BC, Canada. Author: The Lewis and Clark Expedition, 1985, Blood and Water and Other Tales, 1988, The Grotesque, 1989, Spider, 1990 (screenplay 2002), Dr. Haggard's Disease, 1993, Asylum, 1996, Matha Peake, 2000 (Premio Flaiano prize), Port Mungo, 2004, Ghost Town, 2005, Trauma, 2008; editor: (with Bradford Morrow) The New Gothic: A Collection of Contemporary Gothic Fiction, 1991, Picador Book of the New Gothic, 1992; contbg. editor Bomb mag., Conjunctions mag. Mailing: c/o Deborah Rogers Rogers Coleridge & White 20 Powis Mews London W11 1JN England Home: NYC & London England

MCGRATH, PATRICK JOSEPH, bishop; b. Dublin, July 11, 1945; came to US, 1970; Grad., St. John's Coll. Sem., Waterford, Ireland; D in Canon Law, Lateran U., Rome, 1977. Ordained priest Archdiocese of San Francisco, 1970, aux. bishop, 1989-98; rector, pastor St. Mary Cathedral, 1986; ordained bishop, 1989; co-adjutor bishop Diocese of San Jose, 1998-99, bishop, 1999—. Roman Catholic. Office: Diocese San Jose 900 Lafayette St Ste 301 Santa Clara CA 95050-4934

MCGRATH, RAYMOND J., lobbyist, former congressman; b. Valley Stream, NY, Mar. 27, 1942; m. Joanne Coady, 1967; 1 son, Timoth; m. Sheri Peterson; four sons. BS, SUNY, Brockport, 1963; MA, NYU, 1968. Tchr. SUNY, Farmingdale, 1969; lectr. Hunter Coll., NYC, 1969; mem. NY State Assembly, 1976-80; dep. commr. Hempstead Twp. Parks and Recreation; mem. from 5th Dist. NY US Ho. of Reps, 1981—93; mem. ways and means com., 1981; pres. & CEO Beer Inst., Washington, 1993; pres. Downey McGrath Group, Inc., Washington, 1999—. Mem. curriculum adv. coms. Nassau Community Coll., C W Post Coll.; dir., Alcoholic Beverage Med. Rsch. Found.; guest instr., Lobbying Inst., Am. U., Washington, DC, bd. dirs. Ctr. Congl. and Presdl. Studies; bd. dirs., Support Our Aged Religious. Contbr. articles on recreation of handicapped to profl. jours. Named Man of Yr., Nassau Suffolk LI chap., Cystic Fibrosis Found., 1980; named one of 50 Top Lobbyists, Washingtonian mag., 2007. Mem. Ancient Order Hibernians, Naral Club, Elks, Malta, K.C., Holy Name Soc., Am. Irish Congress. Clubs: Ancient Order Hibernians, Elks, KC, Holy Name Soc, Am. Irish Congress, Capitol Hill (pres.). Republican. Office: Downey McGrath Group, LLC 1225 Eye St NW Ste 600 Washington DC 20005 Office Phone: 202-789-1110.*

MCGRATH, RICHARD, lawyer; b. Chgo., Aug. 10, 1929; s. John Francis and Helen Leone (Hoyer) M.; m. Luisa Sacco y Artze, Aug. 12, 1956; children: Lisa, Deborah, Holly. BA magna cum laude, Georgetown U., 1951; JD cum laude, Harvard U., 1954. Bar: NY 1955, Conn. 1960, US Supreme Ct. 1965. Assoc. Hughes, Hubbard, Blair and Reed, 1954-57; corp. counsel Raytheon Co., 1957-60; assoc. Cummings & Lockwood, Stamford, Conn., 1960-63, ptnr., 1963—2003; counsel Murtha Cullina, LLP, Stamford, 2004—. Gen. counsel, corp. sec. Internat. Exec. Svc. Corps, 1990—. Mem. editl. bd. Harvard Law Rev., 1952-54; contbr. articles to profl. jours.; panelist law seminars. Past pres. Fairfield County Coun. Boy Scouts Am. Mem.: Conn. Bar Assn. (fee disputes arbitration com. 1980—84, chmn. corp. law com. 1984—86), Woodway Country Club (Darien, Conn.) (bd. govs., sec. 1986—91, chmn. nominating com. 2000), Stamford Rotary Club (past pres.), Gold Key Soc., Eta Sigma Phi, Pi Gamma Mu. Avocations: golf, trap, chess. Office: Murtha Cullina LLP 177 Broad St Stamford CT 06901 Office Phone: 203-653-5412. Business E-Mail: rmcgrath@murthalaw.com.

MCGRATH, THOMAS JOHN, lawyer, writer, film producer; b. NYC, Oct. 8, 1932; children: Maura Lee, J. Connell; m. Diahn W. McGrath, Sept. 28, 1974; 1 child, Courtney C. BA, NYU, 1956, JD, 1960. Bar: NY 1960. Assoc. Milbank, Tweed, Hadley & McCloy, NYC, 1960-69; ptnr. Simpson, Thacher & Bartlett, NYC, 1970-95; ret., 1995. Lectr., writer Practicing Law Inst., 1976—, Am. Law Inst. ABA, 1976-81. Author: Carryover Basis Under Tax Reform Act, 1977; contbg. author: Estate and Gift Tax After ERTA, 1982; producer: (film) Deadly Hero, 1977. Bd. dirs. NY Philharm.; pres. Am. Austrian Found. With US Army, 1953-54, Korea. Fellow Am. Coll. Trust and Estate Coun.; mem. ABA, NY State Bar Assn., Assn. Bar City NY Office: Simpson Thacher & Bartlett 425 Lexington Ave New York NY 10017-3954 Office Phone: 212-355-2232. Personal E-mail: mcgrathtwf@aol.com.

MCGRATH, WILLIAM ARTHUR, arbitrator, mediator, lawyer, real estate broker; b. Hackensack, NJ, Jan. 31, 1941; s. Donald Marble and Elinor (Peck) McGrath; m. Diane Gurley, Apr. 25, 1965 (div. Nov. 1976); children: Philip M., Christian P.; m. Jackie Wynne, Aug. 10, 2002. BS, Calif. U., Long Beach, 1963; JD, U. Pacific, 1972. Bar: Colo. 1972, US Dist. Ct. Colo. 1972. Pvt. practice, Breckenridge, Colo., 1972—82, Aurora, Colo., 1982—84; ptnr. McGrath & Callan, P.C., Breckenridge, 1975—80, McGrath & Lavenhar, Esq., Denver, 1984—85; prin. William A. McGrath & Assocs., Denver, 1985—88; pvt. practice San Diego, 1988—, Sacramento, 1993—. Vocat. instr. Colo. Mountain Coll., 1972—80; instr. Sacramento City Coll., 2004—. Mem.: ABA, Nat. Assn. Realtors, Calif. Assn. Realtors, Colo. Trial Lawyers Assn. Republican. Episcopalian. Home: 1200 Nevis Court Sacramento CA 95822 Office Phone: 916-447-9852. Personal E-mail: wmcgrathppl@aol.com.

MC GRAW, DARRELL VIVIAN, JR., state attorney general; b. Mullens, W.Va., Nov. 8, 1936; s. Darrell Vivian and Julia (ZeKany) Mc Graw; m. Jorea Marple; children: Elizabeth, Sarah, Darrell, Elliott. AB, W.Va. U., 1961, JD, 1964, MA, 1977. Bar: W.Va. 1964. Gen. atty. Fgn. Claims Settlement Commn., US Dept. State, 1964; counsel to gov. State of W.Va., 1965—68; pvt. practice Charleston, Shepherdstown and Morgantown, 1968—76; judge W.Va. Supreme Ct. Appeals, Charleston, 1977—88, chief justice, 1982—83; atty. gen. State of W.Va., Charleston, 1993—. With US Army, 1954—57. Fellow, W.Va. U., Nat. Ctr. Edn. in Politics/Ford Found. Fellow: Am. Polit. Sci. Assn., Rotary. Democrat. Office: Office of Atty Gen 1900 Kanawha Blvd E Rm E-26 Charleston WV 25305-0009 Office Phone: 304-558-2021.*

MCGRAW, HAROLD W., III, (TERRY MCGRAW), information company executive; b. Summit, NJ, Aug. 30, 1948; s. Harold W. McGraw Jr.; m. Nancy Goodrich, Sept. 22, 1973; children: Harold W. IV, Megan G. BA, Tufts U., 1972; MBA, U. Pa., 1976. Fin. mgmt. staff GTE; asst. v.p. pension investment GTE Mgmt. Corp., McGraw-Hill, Inc., NYC, 1980-83, dir. corp. planning systems, 1983-84, v.p. corp. planning, 1984-85; group v.p., pub. transp. group McGraw-Hill Publs. Co., NYC, 1985-86, group v.p., pub. transp., aerospace and def. group, 1986-87, pres., 1987-88, McGraw-Hill Fin. Svcs. Co., NYC, 1988-89; exec. v.p. McGraw-Hill Cos., NYC, 1989-93, pres., COO, 1993-98, pres., CEO, 1998—, chmn., 1999—. Bd. dirs. ConocoPhillips, United Technologies Corp.; bd. mem., chmn. internat. trade/investment task force Bus. Rountable; chmn. Nat. Coun. Econ. Edn. Chmn. Emergency Com. Am. Trade (ECAT); bd. dirs. NY Pub. Libr., Hartley House, NYC, Nat. Orgn. Disability, Nat. Acad. Found.; bd. trustees Carnegie Hall, NYC. Mem.: Bus. Coun, Assn. Am. Publ. (bd. dirs.). Office: The McGraw Hill Cos Ste C3A 49th Fl 1221 Ave Americas New York NY 10020-1095 Office Phone: 212-512-6206.

MCGRAW, HAROLD WHITTLESEY, JR., publishing executive; b. Bklyn., Jan. 10, 1918; s. Harold Whittlesey and Louise (Higgins) McG.; m. Anne Per-Lee, Nov. 30, 1940; children: Suzanne, Harold Whittlesey III, Thomas Per-Lee, Robert Pearce. AB, Princeton U., 1940. With G.M. Basford (advt. agy.), NYC, 1940-41, Brentano's Bookstores, Inc., 1946; with McGraw-Hill Book Co., Inc., NYC, 1947—, successively promotion mgr., dir. co. advt. and trade sales, 1947-55, dir., v.p. charge trade book, indsl. and bus. book depts., co. advt., 1955-61, sr. v.p., 1961-68, pres., 1968-74, McGraw-Hill, Inc., 1974-81, CEO, 1975-83, chmn., 1976-88; chairman emeritus, 1988—. Bd. dirs. McGraw Hill, Inc., 1954-88. Founder, pres., bd. dirs. Bus. Council Effective Literacy and Bus. Press Ednl. Found. Served as capt. USAAF, 1941-45. Mem.: Wee Burn Club (Darien, Conn.), Blind Brook Club (Purchase, N.Y.). Home: Watch Tower Rd Darien CT 06820 Office: The McGraw-Hill Cos 1221 Avenue Of The Americas New York NY 10020-1095

MCGRAW, LEIGH KYLE, family practice nurse practitioner, researcher; d. Ronald and Cleo Kyle; m. Joseph James McGraw, Oct. 2008; children: KM, TK, SE. PhD, U. Calif., San Francisco, 2008. RN family nurse, Am. Acad. Nurse Practitioners, 1998, ANCC, 1998. Pediat. clin. staff nurse Eisenhower Army Med. Ctr., Ft. Gordon, Ga., 1991—93, Evans Army Cmty. Hosp., Ft. Carson, Colo., 1994—95; lt. col. US Army, Ft. Lewis, Wash., 1991—; staff nurse, newborn nursery clin. 121 Gen. Hosp., Yongsan, Republic of Korea, 1993—94; family nurse practitioner Womack Army Med. Ctr., Ft. Bragg, NC, 1998—2000, Madigan Army Med. Ctr., Tacoma, 2000—03, clin. nurse rschr., 2008—; officer in-charge South Post Health Clinic, Dewitt Army Cmty. Hosp., Ft. Belvoir, Va., 2003—05. Assoc. cons. Duke U. Sch. Nursing, Durham, NC, 2008—. Contbr. articles to profl. jours. Decorated Parachutist Badge US Army, Expert Field Med. Badge, Army Commendation medal, Meritorious Svc. medal, Army Achievement medal; recipient Thelma Ingles award, Duke U., 1998, Best Student Poster award, Western Inst. Nursing, 2008; grant, TriService Nursing Rsch. Program, 1997, Sayer Meml. Fund scholarship, Am. Nurses Found., 2007, Grad. Dean's Health Scis. fellowship, U. Calif., 2007. Mem.: Preventive Cardiovasc. Nurses Assn., Am. Acad. Nurse Practitioners. Conservative. Roman Catholic. Office: Madigan Army Med Ctr 9040A Reid St Tacoma WA 98431 Office Fax: 253-968-2559. Business E-Mail: leigh.mcgraw@us.army.mil.

MCGRAW, MUFFET, women's college basketball coach; b. Pottstown, Pa., Dec. 5, 1955; m. Matt McGraw; 1 child, Murphy. BS in Sociology, St. Joseph's U., 1977. Head coach Archbishop Carroll H.S., Phila., 1977-79; point guard Calif. Dreams, 1979-80; asst. coach St. Joseph's U., 1980-81, Lehigh U., 1982-87, U.S. Olympic Festival, 1993; head coach women's basketball U. Notre Dame, 1987—. Mem. spl. com. on recruiting and access Women's Basketball Coaches Assn., 2004, bd. dirs., 05. Co-author (with P. Gullifor): Coaching Success: Muffet McGraw's Formula for Winning In Sports and In Life, 2003. Named Naismith Women's Coll. Coach of Yr., Atlanta Tipoff Club, 2001, Nat. Coach of Yr., Women's Basketball Coaches Assn., 2001, AP, 2001, Sports Illus. for Women, 2001; named to Women's Basketball Hall of Fame, St. Joseph's U., 1986, Athletics Hall of Fame, 2002, Phila. Big Five Women's Hall of Fame, 1989. Achievements include head coach of NCAA Women's Final Four National Championship winning Univeristy of Notre Dame Fighting Irish, 2001. Office: Univ Notre Dame Women's Athletic Dept Joyce Ctr Notre Dame IN 46556*

MCGRAW, NANCY MCCALL, singer, theater producer; b. Atlanta, Jan. 12, 1948; d. James Ira and Susan (Self) Teat; m. Steve McGraw, Sept. 2, 1991. BMus, Northwestern U., 1970. Mgr., booking agt. Palsson's Supper Club, NYC, 1984-88; owner, mgr., booking agt. Steve McGraw's Supper Club, NYC, 1989—98; owner Triad Cabaret Theatre, NYC, 1995—98. Program dir. Songbook Project. Actor: (plays) Godspell, 1974, The Heebie Jeebies, 1981, Forbidden Broadway, 1985—87; (Broadway plays) Nine, 1982 (Tony award Best Musical); assoc. prodr.: Forbidden Broadway Strikes Back, 1996—; prodr.: (plays) A Couple of Blaguards. Trustee Broadway Cares/Equity Fight AIDS, 1993—99. Mem.: SAG, AFTRA, PEO Sisterhood, NY Marble Collegiate Ch., Actors Equity Assn., Dutch Treat Club. Office: 210 W 70th St Apt 808 New York NY 10023-4311 Office Phone: 212-580-8442. E-mail: nanmcgraw@aol.com.

MCGRAW, PHILLIP CALVIN See DR. PHIL

MCGRAW, TIM, country music singer; b. Delhi, La., May 1, 1967; s. Tug McGraw; m. Faith Hill, Oct. 6, 1996; children: Gracie Katherine, Maggie Elizabeth, Audrey Caroline. Musician: (albums) Tim McGraw, 1993, Not a Moment Too Soon, 1994 (triple-platinum, Album of Yr., Acad. County Music, 1994), All I Want, 1995, Everywhere, 1997 (Album of Yr., Country Music Assn., 1998), A Place in the Sun, 1999 (Album of Yr., Country Music Assn., 1999), Tim McGraw Greatest Hits, 2000, Set the Circus Down, 2001 (Best Country Album, Am. Music Awards, 2002), Tim McGraw and the Dancehall Doctors, 2002, Live Like You Were Dying, 2004 (Most Inspiring Video of Yr., Country Music Television Music award, 2005, Single Record of Yr., Acad. Country Music Awards, 2005, Am. Music Awards Favorite Country Album, 2005), Tim McGraw Reflected Greatest Hits Vol. 2, 2006 (Favorite Country Album Am. Music Awards, 2006), Let it Go, 2007, (single) Welcome to the Club, 1992, It's Your Love, 1997 (Single & Song of Yr., Acad. Country Music, 1998), Grown Men, 2001 (Single of Yr., Radio Music Assn., 2001), Live Like You Were Dying, 2004 (Single & Song of Yr., Country Music Assn., 2004, Song of Yr., Acad. Country Music Awards, 2005), (with Nelly) Over and Over, 2004, (songs) (with Tracy Lawrence & Kenny Chesney) Find Out Who Your Friends Are, 2007 (Musical Event of Yr., Country Music Assn., 2007, Vocal Event of Yr., Acad. Country Music, 2008); vocal collaboration (with Faith Hill) Let's Make Love, 2001 (Grammy award, 2001); actor: (films) Black Cloud, 2004, Friday Night Lights, 2004, Flicka, 2006, Four Christmases, 2008, (TV appearances) The Jeff Foxworthy Show, 1997. Recipient Favorite New Artist, Am. Music Awards, 1995, Favorite Male Country Artist, 2002, 2001, 2003, 2005, 2007, Top Male Vocalist, Acad. Country Music, 1994, 1999, 1998, Vocal Event of Yr., 1997, 1998, Country Music Assn., 1997, Male Vocalist of Yr., 1999, 2000, Entertainer of Yr., 2001, Male Artist of Yr., TNN/Music City News, 1999, Favorite Male Artist, Blockbuster Award, 2001, Country Male Artist, Radio Music Awards, 2003, Favorite Male Musical Performer, People's Choice Awards, 2004, Favorite Male Performer, 2006, Best Country Collaboration With Vocals (with Faith Hill), 2006. Office: care Curb Records 3907 W Alameda Ave Burbank CA 91505-4332

MCGREEVEY, GREG, insurance company executive; BA in Mktg. and Mgmt., U. Portland, Oreg.; MBA, Portland State U., 1991. CFA. Various mgmt. positions Columbia Fin. Svcs., Norwest Corp.; pres., chief investment officer Laughlin Asset Mgmt.; various leadership roles including head proprietary investments, chmn. & exec. v.p. Americas, pres. institutional markets and mem. mgmt. coun. ING Investment Mgmt., 1997—2008; exec. v.p., chief investment officer Hartford Fin. Svcs. Group, Inc., Conn., 2008—; pres. Hartford Investment Mgmt. Co., 2008—. Office: Hartford Fin Svcs Group Inc One Hartford Plz Hartford CT 06155*

MCGREGOR, CHRISTOPHER GEORGE ALOYSIUS, surgeon, educator, consultant; b. Glasgow, Scotland, June 21, 1949; came to U.S., 1983; s. Hugh and Amelia McGregor; m. Diana G. McGregor. MB ChB, U. Glasgow, 1972; cert. higher surg. tng. cardiothoracic surg., Joint Bd. Royal Coll. Surgeons, 1983. Registrar in cardiothoracic surgery Royal Infirm. and Royal Hosp. for Sick Children, Glasgow, 1977-78; lectr. in cardiac surgery Royal Infirm., Edinburgh, 1978-80; sr. registrar in cardiothoracic surgery Papworth Hosp., Cambridge, Eng., 1980-82; Brit. Heart Found.-Am. Heart Assn. Internat. scholarship Stanford (Calif.) U., 1983-84; cons. cardiothoracic surgeon, dir. cardiothoracic transplantation No. Regional Health Authority/Freeman Hosp., Newcastle upon Tyne, Eng., 1985-87; prof. surgery, dir. cardiothoracic transplantation Mayo Clinic, Rochester, Minn., 1987—. Mem. editl. bd. Transplantation, 1994—, Jour. Heart and Lung Transplantation, 1999—, Internat. Jour. Angiology, 1996—; contbr. more than 150 articles to profl. jours. Fellow Royal Coll. Surgeons (Edinburgh), Royal Coll. Surgeons (Glasgow); mem. ACS, Am. Coll. Cardiology, Am. Assn. for Thoracic Surgery, Internat. Soc. for Heart and Lung Transplantation, Soc. Thoracic Surgeons, Xenotransplantation Assn. Office: Mayo Clinic 6-716 Saint Marys Hosp Rochester MN 55905-0001

MCGREGOR, DOUGLAS HUGH, pathologist, educator; b. Temple, Tex., Aug. 28, 1939; s. Harleigh Heath and Joyce Ellen (Lambert) McG.; m. Mizuki Kitani, July 6, 1969; children: Michelle Sakuya, David Kenji. BA, Duke U., 1961, MD, 1966; postgrad., U. Edinburgh, Scotland, 1961-62. Diplomate Am. Bd. Pathology. Intern, chief resident in pathology UCLA Med. Ctr., 1966-68; surgeon, lt. comdr. Atomic Bomb Casualty Commn., Hiroshima, Japan, 1968-71; chief resident in pathology Queens Med. Ctr., Honolulu, 1971-73; asst., assoc. prof. pathology U. Kans. Med. Ctr., Kansas City, 1973-82, prof., 1982—. Dir. anat. pathology VA Med. Ctr., Kansas City, Mo., 1975-94, chief pathology and lab. medicine, 1994-2003, dir. surg. pathology, 2003—. Contbr. numerous articles to profl. jours., chpts. to books. Leader YMCA Indian Princess Program, Overland Park, Kans., 1977-79, Indian Guide Program, 1978-80, Cub Scout Am., Overland Park, 1980-82, Boy Scouts Am., Leawood, Kans., 1982—. Lt. comdr. USPHS, 1968-71, Japan. Grantee Merck, Sharp and Dohme, 1980. Fellow Coll. Am. Pathologists, Am. Soc. Clin. Pathologists; mem. Am. Assn. Pathologists, Internat. Acad. Pathologists, Soc. Exptl. Biology and Medicine, N.Y. Acad. Scis., AAAS, Kansas City Soc. Pathologists (sec.-treas. 1982-83, pres. 1983-84). Achievements include research in ultrastructure and pathobiology of neoplasms, radiation carcinogenesis, and morphogenesis of atherosclerosis. Home: 9400 Lee Blvd Shawnee Mission KS 66206-1826 Office: VA Med Ctr 4801 E Linwood Blvd Kansas City MO 64128-2226 Business E-Mail: douglas.mcgregor@va.gov.

MCGREGOR, EWAN GORDON, actor; b. Crieff, Perthshire, Scotland, Mar. 31, 1971; s. James and Carol McGregor; m. Eve Mavrakis, July 22, 1995; children: Clara Mathilde, Esther Rose; 1 adopted child. LLD, U. Ulster, 2001. Motion picture actor; stage actor; co-founder (with John Lee Miller, Sean Pertwee, Jude Law, Sadie Frost) Natural Nylon (prodn. co.). Actor: (films) Being Human, 1993, Shallow Grave, 1994, The Pillow Book, 1994, Blue Juice, 1995, Emma, 1996, Trainspotting, 1996 (Brit. Actor of Yr., 1996), Brassed Off, 1996, A Life Less Ordinary, 1997, Velvet Goldmine, 1998, Little Voice, 1998, Nora, 1999, Eye of the Beholder, 1999, Star Wars: Episode I-The Phantom Menace, 1999, Moulin Rouge, 2001 (European Film award for Achievement in World Cinema, 2001, Film Actor Award, The Variety Club Showbusiness Awards, 2002), Black Hawk Down, 2001, Star Wars: Episode II-Attack of the Clones, 2002, Down With Love, 2003, Young Adam, 2003, Big Fish, 2003, Star Wars: Episode III-Revenge of the Sith, 2005, The Island, 2005; voice (films) Robots, 2005, Valiant, 2005; actor: (films) Stay, 2005, Cassandra's Dream, 2007, Incendiary, 2008, Deception, 2008, Angels & Demons, 2009; (TV films) Lipstick on Your Collar, 1993, Doggin' Around, 1994, TV guest appearances include Tales from the Crypt, 1989, ER, 1994, Kavanagh QC, 1994; (plays) Guys and Dolls, 2005; actor: (TV films) Motor Bike: Round the World Trip, 2004; (films) The Tourist; (documentaries) Long Way Around, 2004, Long Way Down, 2007. Recipient ALFS award, 1997; named No. 36 on the list "100 Top Movie Stars of All Time", Empire mag. (UK), 1997, No. 4 on the list, "British Culture's Top 50 Movers and Shakers", BBC 3, 2004. Office: care Lindy King Drury House 34-43 Russell St Peters etc London WC2B 5HA England*

MCGREGOR, JOHN M., medical educator; Assoc. prof. neurosurgery Ohio State U., Columbus, 1990—.

MCGREGOR, JUDITH ANN, education educator; b. Pitts., Aug. 24, 1954; d. William James and Jeanne Harris McGregor. BS in Elem. Edn., Fla. State U., 1976, MS in Elem. Edn. with honors, 1977, PhD in Elem. Edn. with honors, 1992. Instr. Devel. Rsch. Sch., Fla. State U., Tallahassee, 1976—77; asst. prof. St. Petersburg Jr. Coll., Clearwater, 1978—80; instr. Fla. State U., 1981—82; asst. prof. Calif. State U., Long Beach, 1983—87, instr. Fullerton, 1990—91, asst. prof., supr. field work Dominguez Hills, 1992—. Pres. Jeanne Harris Entertainment, LA, 2005—; cons. in field of children and family TV and film. Author: Occupational Protrayal in Television: A Comparative Study of Children and Family Programs, 1993, (children's TV series) Whispie and Company (educational toys and goods), 1994. Mem.: NOW, NEA, AAUW, AAUP, Fla. State U. Alumni Assn. Avocations: skiing, rollerblading, kayaking, golf. Office: Brentwood Village 149 S Barrington Ave Ste 182 Los Angeles CA 90049 Office Phone: 310-650-0774.

MCGREGOR, MICHAEL N., writer, educator; b. Seattle, Jan. 23, 1958; s. Norman L. and Doris E. McGregor; m. Sylvia Farkas, Nov. 27, 1993. BA in Journalism, U. Oreg., 1980; MFA in Writing, Columbia U., 1997. Editor World Concern Mag., Seattle, 1981-84, Back Door Travel, Seattle, 1985-88; editor-in-chief Columbia: A Jour. of Lit. and Art, NYC, 1995-96; instr. Columbia U., NYC, 1995-97, asst. to composition dir., 1996-97; lectr. So. Ill. U., Carbondale, 1997-2000; assoc. prof. Portland (Oreg.) State U., 2000—. Judge, Charles Johnson award, Carbondale, 1998-99; lectr., guide, European cultural tours, Europe Through the Back Door, Seattle. Contbr. short stories, poems and essays to profl. publs. Recipient Daniel Curley award for short fiction, 2000; Walden Residency fellow, So. Oreg. U., 2001, Lily Endowment Residency Collegeville Inst., 2009. Mem. MLA, Associated Writing Programs, The Authors Guild. Office: Portland State U Box 751 Portland OR 97207-0751

MCGREGOR, SCOTT A., broadband communications company executive; BS, MS, Stanford Univ. Dir., interactive intelligence group Microsoft; sr. mgmt. Digital Equip. Corp., 1985—90; sr. v.p. & gen. mgr. Santa Cruz Ops., 1990—98; pres. & CEO, semiconductor div. Royal Philips Electronics, 2001—04; pres., CEO, dir. Broadcom Co., Irvine, Calif., 2005—. Office: Broadcom Corporation 5300 California Ave Irvine CA 92617-3038

MCGREGOR, THEODORE ANTHONY, chemical company executive; b. Detroit, Mar. 28, 1944; s. Lorraine Shorrey; m. Bonny-Joan Beach, Sept. 14, 1963; children: Todd, Timothy, Amy. Student, Henry Ford Coll., 1961-63. Mem. sales staff Gen. Binding Corp., GBC Sales and Service, Oak Brook, Ill., 1965-69; with indsl. chem. divsn. Diversey Chem. Corp., Chgo., 1967-69; with Detrex Corp., Detroit, 1969-75, regional mgr. indsl. chem. specialties divsn., 1975-77, asst. gen. mgr., 1977-81, gen. mgr. indsl. chem. specialties divsn., 1981-85, corp. v.p., gen. mgr., 1985-89; group v.p. indsl. chem. specialties divsn. Wayne Chem., RTI, Seibert-Oxidermo, Detroit, 1987-93; exec. v.p., also bd. dirs. Wayne Chem., Detroit; exec. v.p. Asian Rim and Internat. Mktg. Seibert Oxiderno, 1989-90; pres. TAM Consulting Svcs., Redford, Mich., 1993—; exec. v.p. Harbor Group, 1993—; U.S. dir. comm. devel. Novamax Techs., 1994-96; v.p. Automotive Texo Corp., Cin., 1996—2001; pres. IOM Tech., Southfield, Mich., 2001—. Mem. Intergrated Operation Mgmt. (pres. 2001-). Avocations: reading, chess, boating. Office Phone: 586-405-6754.

MCGREW, KELLY CALHOUN, training services executive, systems engineer; b. Tacoma, Wash., Apr. 16, 1954; s. Kenneth Keith and Evelyn Elsie McGrew; m. Tammy Idette Lee, June 14, 1980; 1 child, Duncan Kendrick. BA in Liberal Arts, The Evergreen State Coll., Olympia, Wash., 1981; MBA, City U., Seattle, 1987. Cert. Ccnp Cisco Sys., Inc., 2000, Ccvp Cisco Sys., Inc., 2006. Network mgr. Wash. State Dept. Licensing, Olympia, 1986—89, network team leader, 1989—95; network sys. engr. CompuServe Network Svcs., Inc., Columbus, Ohio, 1995—98; instr., cons. Chesapeake Computer Cons., Inc., Annapolis, Md., 1998—99; program mgr. Microsoft, Inc., Redmond, Wash., 1999; instr. Cisco Sys., Inc., San Jose, Calif., 1999—2000; v.p. Mcgrew.net, Inc., Land O Lakes, Fla., 1999—; instr., cons. CCPrep.com, Tampa, Fla., 2005—07; sr. LAN/WAN engr. CSO/CIS Raytheon, Baghdad, Iraq, 2007—09; sys. engr. Cisco Sys. Inc., San Jose, 2009—. Author: (books) Cisco Voice over Frame-relay, ATM and IP, 2001, Optimizing and Securing Cisco AVVID Applications, 2002, Cisco Network Design Toolkit, 2003. Yn2 USN, 1973—76, USS Barbel, USS Guardfish. Mem.: IEEE (assoc.), Internet Soc., Author's Guild. Avocations: photography, travel, writing. Office: PO Box 1436 Land O Lakes FL 34639-1436

MCGRUDER, LARRY, history professor; b. Rocky Mount, Ga., June 13, 1958; m. Linda Wilkins-McGruder; 1 child, Stephen Alden. EdB, Ft. Valley State U., 1980; MA in History, Miami U., Ohio, 1981, PhD, 1984. Tchg. fellow Miami U., Oxford, Ohio, 1982—84; prof. history Abraham Baldwin Agrl. Coll., Tifton, Ga., 1984—. Mem. chancellor search com. U. Sys. Ga., Atlanta, 1993—94; mem. fund raising com. Friends United for Edn., Tifton, Ga., 1994—95; chairperson Goizueta Found. Scholarship Selection Com., Tifton, 2003—04; mem. several sub-committees Habitat for Humanity, Tifton, 1990—94; chair incentive grants com. Tift County Found. Ednl. Excellence, Tifton, 1996—2005; chair subcommittee Reading Capital of the World, Tifton, 2002—05. Recipient Alumnus of Yr. award, Ft. Valley State U., 1985, Tchg. Excellence award, Phi Theta Kappa, 1993, W. Bruce Donaldson Faculty award, Abraham Baldwin Coll., 2000; named one of Outstanding Young Men of Am., Outstanding Young Americans, 1985—86; fellow, Miami U. Dept. History, 1982—84. Mem.: Alpha Kappa Mu, Phi Alpha Theta. Avocations: researching local history, hiking, travel. Office: Abraham Baldwin Agricultural Coll 2802 Moore Hwy Tifton GA 31793 Business E-Mail: lmcgruder@abac.edu.

MCGUFF, KEVIN, women's college basketball coach; m. Letitia McGuff; children: Kilyn, Keiryn, Lukas. BBA, St. Joseph's Coll., Ind., 1992; MS in Sports Studies, Miami U., Oxford, Ohio. Asst. girls basketball coach Hamilton Badin HS, 1992—93; scouting coord., ops. asst., dir. summer basketball camp Miami U. RedHawks, 1993—96; asst. coach U. Notre Dame Fighting Irish, 1996—2002; head women's basketball coach Xavier U. Musketeers, Cin., 2002—. Office: Xavier Univ Womens Basketball 3800 Victory Pky Cincinnati OH 45207-7530 Office Phone: 513-745-3414. Business E-Mail: maas@xavier.edu.*

MCGUFFEE, JAMES W., engineering educator; b. La., 1970; m. Lynn Barta, Dec. 28, 2005; 1 child, Gage W. BS, La. Tech. U., Ruston, 1989; PhD, La. State U., Baton Rouge, 1994. Asst. prof., computer sci. St. Edward's U., Austin, Tex., 2000—04, assoc. prof., computer sci., 2004—. With, regional steering com. Consortium Computing Scis. Coll., 2000—. Trustee Austin CC Dist., 2006—. Mem.: ACM. Mem. Christian Ch. Office: St Edward's Univ 3001 S Congress Ave Austin TX 78704

MCGUFFEY, CARROLL WADE, JR., lawyer; b. Decatur, Ga., Dec. 1, 1951; s. Carroll Wade and Dorothy (Landers) McG.; m. Virginia Elizabeth Miller, Aug. 12, 1972; children: Carroll Wade, III, Michelle Elizabeth, Jennifer Lanier. BBA, U. Ga., 1973, JD cum laude, 1976. Bar: Ga. 1976, Fla. 1977, U.S. Dist. Ct. (mid. dist.) Ga. 1976, U.S. Supreme Ct. 1980. Capt. Chief Claims Tort Litigation Div. USAF, Eglin AFB, Fla., 1976-80; assoc., ptnr. Savell and Williams, Atlanta, 1980-90; mng. ptnr., CEO Goodman McGuffey Aust & Lindsey LLP, Atlanta, 1990—2003; CEO Goodman McGuffey Lindsey & Johnson, LLP, Atlanta and Orlando, 2003—. Mem. adv. coun. Ga. State Bd. Workers' Compensation, 2005—; lectr. in field. Editor: Employers Guide to Workers Compensation in Georgia, Employee Leasing: An Employer's Guide. Ward capt. Athens Mayoral Campaign (Ga.), 1975; commr., dir. Stone Mountain Dixie Youth Baseball, 1982-87; cubmaster Boy Scouts Am., 1986-88, scoutmaster, 1988-90, troop chmn., 1991-92, dist. chmn., 1993-95; mgr., coach Murphy Candler Girls Softball Assn., 1996-2003; mem. Citizen Dunwoody Cts. Task Force, 2008; chair jud. qualification com. City of Dunwoody, 2008, mem., bd. ethics, 2009-. Recipient Dist. Award of Merit, Boy Scouts Am., 1995. Mem. ABA, Fla. Bar Assn., Atlanta Bar Assn. (workers compensation seminar chmn. 1993, 97, fundraising chmn. Kid's Chance Found. Race, 1992, workers compensation section, bd. dirs. 1994-01, sec.-treas. 1997, chair-elect 1998, chair 1999), Ga. Def. Lawyers Assn. (trial acad. instr. 1987), Def. Rsch. Inst., Ind. Ins. Agts. of Ga. (hon. life, young agents com.), Ga. Mental Health Assn. (bd. dirs. 1987). Clubs: Athens Boat (dir. 1982-90), Lawyers (Atlanta), UGA Pres. Club. Methodist. Office Phone: 404-264-1500. Business E-Mail: wmcguffey@gmlj.com.

MCGUIGAN, MICHAEL DETURCK, research scientist; BS, Carnegie-Mellon U., 1982; MS, Yale U., New Haven; PhD, Rockefeller U., NYC, 1989. Postdoc. assoc. Inst. Advanced Study, Princeton, NJ, 1989—91, U. Fla., Gainesville, 1991—94; asst. editor Am. Phys. Soc., Ridge, NY, 1994—98; computational scientist Brookhaven Nat. Lab., Upton, NY, 1998—. Contbr. articles to profl. jours. Recipient Outstanding Mentor award, Dept. Energy.

MCGUIGAN, STUART M., pharmaceutical executive; BA, Fairfield Univ., 1982; MS, MPhil, Yale Univ., 1986. Assoc. rsch. scientist Honeywell, 1986—88; dir. info. planning Merck & Co., 1988—93; sr. v.p. info. tech. Medco Health Solutions, 1993—2004; sr. v.p., CIO Liberty Mutual Group, 2004—08, CVS Caremark Corp., 2008—. Bd. dir. Netscout Systems Inc. Office: CVS Caremark Corp 1 CVS Dr Woonsocket RI 02895*

MCGUINN, MARTIN GREGORY, retired bank executive, lawyer; b. Phila., Sept. 9, 1942; s. Martin G. and Rita (Horgan) McG.; m. Ann M. Muldoon, Sept. 17, 1977; children: Patrick J., Christopher M. AB, Villanova U., 1964, JD, 1967. Bar: Pa. 1967, NY 1970. Assoc. Sullivan & Cromwell, NYC, 1970-77; mng. counsel The Singer Co., Stamford, Conn., 1977-80; chmn., CEO Mellon Bank, Pitts., 1998—2006; CEO, chmn. Mellon Fin. Corp, Pitts., 1999—2006. Bd. consultors Villanova Law Sch., 1972—, chmn. 1985-87; bd. dirs. U.S.-Japan Bus. Coun., Inc.,

Allegheny Conf. on Cmty. Devel., chmn., 2003-05. Editor in chief Villanova Law Rev., Vol. 12, 1966-67. Bd. dirs. UPMC Health Sys.; trustee Carnegie Mus. of Pitts.; chmn. Hist. Soc. Western Pa., 1997-2002. Mem. The Fin. Svcs. Roundtable (chmn. 2004-05), Fed. Reserve Adv. Bd. (chmn. 2005), Am. Soc. Corp. Secs. (chmn. 1990-91), Celanese Corp. (dir. 2007-), Chubb Corp. (dir. 2008-), CapGen Fin. (adv. bd.). Office Phone: 412-234-4966. Business E-Mail: martin.mcguinn@bnymellon.com.

MCGUINNESS, KEVIN MICHAEL, psychologist, director; s. Donald William and Rita D. McGuinness; m. Maria F. Lira, Apr. 10, 1976; children: Erin Maria, Joshua Cruz, Kieran David. BS, George Wash. U., DC; BS in Physiol. Psychology, George Mason U., Fairfax, VA; MA in Psychology, Calif. Sch. Profl. Psychology, Fresno, PhD in Clin. Psychology; PostDoc. MS in Clin Psychopharmacology, Fairleigh Dickinson U., Teaneck, NJ. Diplomate Am. Bd. Profl. Psychology. Hosp. corpsman third class US Navy, Bethesda, Md., 1973—76; forensic chemist US Drug Enforcement Adminstrn., McLean, Va., 1979; chief, psychol. svcs. USAF Med. Hosp., Riverside, Calif., 1988—92; dir.,clin. health psychology, USPHS, Rockville, 1994—; with USN, 1973—2008, USAF, 1973—2008, USPHS, 1973—2008. Pres. Parents Reaching Out, Inc., Los Lunas, N.Mex., 1998—2000. Contbr. articles to profl. jours. Decorated Multiple Uniformed Svc. Decorations award USN, USAF, USPHS, USDoD; recipient Disting. Svc. award, Sec. Health & Human Svcs., 2003. Mem.: APA (chair 2003—04), Health Psychology Divsn. APA, Am. Soc. Advancement Pharmacotherapy. Achievements include development of co-developer of the Mercy Model, an International Health Diplomacy Model.

MCGUIRE, CHARLES EDWARD, musicology educator; b. Mpls., Nov. 24, 1969; s. Charles Leonard and Rose Marie White McGuire. MusB, BA, Oberlin Coll., Ohio, 1992; PhD, Harvard U., Cambridge, Mass., 1998. Asst. prof. James Madison U., Harrisonburg, Va., 2000—01; assoc. prof. musicology Oberlin Coll. Conservatory Music, 2001—. Author monograph and essays. Mem.: Elgar Soc., Am. Musicological Soc., N.Am. Brit. Music Studies Assn. (v.p. 2003—07). Office: Oberlin Coll Conservatory Music 77 W College St Oberlin OH 44074 Business E-Mail: cmcguire@oberlin.edu.

MCGUIRE, DAVID ROBERT, music educator, composer; s. Robert Bernard and Doris Claire (Brosnan) McGuire; m. Kristen Shiner-McGuire, June 23, 1990. BS in Music Theory and Math, Nazareth Coll., Rochester, 1984; M in Music Theory and Composition, Ariz. State U., Tempe, 1987; PhD in Music Theory, U. Buffalo, 1996. Tchg. artist Aesthetic Edn. Inst., Rochester, 1989—2000; music prof. Finger Lakes CC, Canandaigua, 2000—. Music lectr. Nazareth Coll., 1991—2000; rsch. fellow Bernstein Ctr. Edn. through Arts, Nashville, 1994—98; tchg. artist Wolftrap Inst. for Early Learning, Rochester, 1996—2000; tchg. fellow, cons. Hilton Ctrl. Sch. Classic Project, NY, 1996—97; writing fellow Finger Lakes CC, 2002—03; presenter in field. Composer: (numerous) Group Pieces Percussion Ensemble; composer: (contemporary dance); composer: (choreographer) Electronic; composer: Solo Piano. Mem. ACLU, 2000—, ASPCA, 1997—, Humane Soc., 1997—, NY Civil Liberties Union, 2000—, Metro-Justice, Rochester, 2003—; bd. mem. Pandora's Collective, Vancouver, Canada, 2004—. Recipient SUNY Chancellor's Tchg. Excellence award, Finger Lakes CC, 2006—07; grantee, NY State Found. for Arts, 1992, 1993. Mem.: Nat. Assn. Schs. of Music, Soc. for Music Theory, Pi Kappa Lambda. Avocations: writing, art, coin collecting/numismatics, weightlifting. Home: 106 Lanark Cir Rochester NY 14609 Office: Finger Lakes CC 4355 Lakeshore Dr Canandaigua NY 14424 Office Phone: 585-394-3500 ext. 7385.

MCGUIRE, EDWARD DAVID, JR., lawyer; b. Waynesboro, Va., Apr. 11, 1948; s. Edward David and Mary Estelle (Angus) McG.; m. Karen Elizabeth Jacobson, Dec. 31, 2005; children: Matthew Edward, Kathryn Ann, Georgia Gail. BS in Commerce, U. Va., 1970; JD, Coll. William and Mary, 1973. Bar: Va. 1973, DC 1974, Md. 1990, Pa. 1995, US Dist. Ct. (ea. dist.) Va. 1974, U.S. Dist. Ct. DC 1974, US Dist. Ct. Md. 1990, Ct. Appeals (4th cir.) 1974, US Ct. Appeals (DC cir.) 1974, US Supreme Ct. 1993. Assoc. Wilkes and Artis, Washington, 1973-78; gen. corp counsel Mark Winkler Mgmt., Alexandria, Va., 1978-80; sr. contracts officer Amtrak, Washington, 1980-81; sr. real estate atty., asst. corp. sec. Peoples Drug Stores, Inc., Alexandria, 1981-88; of counsel Cowles, Rinaldi & Arnold, Ltd., Fairfax, Va., 1989-91; sr. assoc. Radigan, Rosenberg & Holmes, Arlington, Va., 1991; pvt. practice Annandale, Va., 1992-97, 2000—05; sr. assoc. Stein, Sperling, Bennett, DeJong, Driscoll, Greenfeig Metro, Rockville, Md., 1997-99; of counsel Hodes, Ulman, Pessin & Katz, P.A., Annandale, 1999-2000; mng. dir., personal trust adminstr. Riggs Bank, N.A., Washington, 2000—03; mng. dir., gen. counsel MFB Holdings, LLC, 2004—. Co-author: Legacy: Plan, Protect and Preserve Your Estate, 1995, Generations: Planning Your Legacy, 1998. Bd. dirs. Dist. XVI Va. Student Aid Found., 1978-85, George Washington dist. Boy Scouts Am., 1986; active William and Mary Law Sch. Assn., bd. dirs., 1983-96, pres., 1987-88, treas., 1990-91. Capt. JAGC, USANG, 1973-79. Mem. ABA, Va. Bar Assn., DC Bar, Md. State Bar Assn., Pa. Bar, William and Mary Alumni Soc. (bd. dirs. DC chpt. treas. 1992-94), U. Va. Club of Washington (schs. com. chmn. 1995—, v.p. outreach 1997-99, pres.-elect 1998-99, bd. dirs. 1996-99), Rotary (treas. Springfield chpt. 1985-86, sec. 1986-87, pres.-elect 1987, chmn. World Affairs Conf. 1985-88, bd. dirs. 1984-88, 96-97, Dist. 7610 youth leadership awards chmn. 1994-97, Outstanding Rotarian award 1985). Greek Orthodox. Avocations: racquetball, coaching youth sports. Office: Nfb Holdings Llc 31 W Myrtle St Alexandria VA 22301-2422 Office Phone: 407-456-3304, 202-246-6370. Personal E-mail: edwmcg31@aol.com.

MCGUIRE, FRANKLIN RILEY, pulmonologist, educator; b. Columbus, Ind., Oct. 26, 1967; s. Henry F. McGuire and Betty L. Riley; m. Amanda Tyler, Aug. 8, 2005; 1 child, Samuel Cotton. MD, U. Ky., Lexington, 1993. Diplomate in pulmonary Am. Bd. Internal Medicine, 2004, cert. in internal medicine Bd. U. NC Sch. Medicine, Greensboro, 2002. Physician Pulmonary Assocs., Harrisonburg, Va., 2004—05; clin. asst. prof. East Carolina U., Greenville, NC, 2005; asst. prof. clin. internal medicine, sch. medicine U. SC, Columbia, 2006—, nodule clinic co-dir., pulmonary and critical care medicine, dir. fellowship rsch., 2007—. Dir. bronchoscopic svcs. Palmetto Health Richland, Columbia, SC, 2006—. Contbr. numerous rsch. articles and poster presentation to profl. publs. Grantee, Am. Cancer Soc., Palmetto Health Found. Mem.: Am. Assn. Bronchology-World Congress Bronchology, Am. Thoracic Soc., Am. Coll. Chest Physicians, Soc. Critical Care Medicine. Home: 316 Lake Front Dr Columbia SC 29212-2425 Office: Univ SC Pulmonary and Critical Care Medicine 8 Medical Pk Ste 410 Columbia SC 29203 Office Fax: 803-454-2699. Business E-Mail: franklin.mcguire@uscmed.sc.edu.

MCGUIRE, JACK (JOHN F. MCGUIRE), international relief organization executive; m. Jane McGuire. BS in Chemistry, Iona Coll., 1968; MBA, Harvard U. With DuPont; mng. dir. UK and Belgium Johnson & Johnson Ortho Diagnostics Inc.; pres., CEO Hemasure Inc., 1997—2001; pres. Waltman PLC N.Am., 2001—04; exec. v.p. biomedical services Am. Red Cross, 2004—, interim pres., CEO, 2005—07. Capt. USMC. Recipient Disting. Svc. award, Am. Assn. Blood Banks, 2000. Avocations: golf, fly fishing. Office: American Red Cross National Headquarters 2025 E St NW Washington DC 20006 Office Phone: 202-303-5646.

MCGUIRE, JAMES HORTON, physics educator; b. NY, June 7, 1942; s. Horton E. and Karolyn W. (Wright) McG.; m. V. Jane Rasmussen, Oct. 10, 1981; children: Carrie Marti, Bruce, Brooke. BS, Rensselaer U., 1964; PhD, Northeastern U., 1969. Asst. prof. Tex. A&M U., College Station, 1969-72; prof. Kans. State U., Manhattan, 1972-91; Murchison-Mallory prof. physics Tulane U., New Orleans, 1991—. Assoc. editor: Encyclopedia Physics; contbr. articles to profl. jours. Recipient Disting. Alumni award in edn. Northeastern U., 1995; grantee NSF, 1992, DOE, 1992. Fellow Am. Phys. Soc. (sec.-treas. divsn. atomic molecular optical physics 1989-92), Internat. Conf. on Physics of Atmoic and Elec. Collisions (sec.); mem. The Nat. Faculty, Am. Chem. Soc., Am. Assn. Physics Tchrs. Democrat. Office: Tulane U Dept Physics New Orleans LA 70118

MCGUIRE, JAMES KAVANAUGH, retired education educator; b. Danville, Ky., July 10, 1938; s. Virgil Leon McGuire and Mary Elizabeth Petrey McGuire; m. Alma Irene Kirkpatrick, Aug. 6, 1960; children: Daron Scott, Deidre Sue. AB, Asbury Coll., 1960; MEd, Xavier U., 1969. Cert. tchr. Ohio. Tchr. social studies Campbell County Schs., Alexandria, Ky., 1960—62; tchr. social studies, dept. head Middletown Madison Local Schs., West Middletown, Ohio, 1962—69; prin. Pkwy. Local Schs., Rockford, Ohio, 1969—70; asst. prin. HS Celina City Schs., Ohio, 1970—71, prin. Jr. H.S., 1974—80; prin. Bellbrook HS, Ohio, 1971—74, Groveport Madison Schs., Ohio, 1980—83; supt. Cedarcliff Local Schs., Cedarville, Ohio, 1983—93; assoc. prof. Circleville Bible Coll., Ohio, 1994—2004; ret., 2004. Presenter in field. Trustee Mt. Vernon Nazarene Coll., Ohio, 1978—80; bd. dirs. Miami Valley Ednl. Computer Assn., Xenia, Ohio, 1990—92. Grantee in history, NDEA, 1967. Republican. Mem. Ch. Of Nazarene. Avocations: golf, volleyball, reading, travel.

MCGUIRE, JOHN ALBERT, dentist; b. Warren, Ohio, June 20, 1950; s. Bernard Leo and Lucille Ann (Guarnieri) McG.; m. Pamela Kay Muter, May 30, 1969; children: John, Jessica. BS, Ohio State U., 1972, DDS, 1975. Dentist, capt. USAF, Bellevue, Nebr., 1975-77; dentist pvt. practice Dayton, Tenn., 1977-83, Knoxville, Tenn., 1983—. Author: (short story) Stirs, 1990, (screenplay) Sonspot, 2000. Mem. Sertoma Club, Knoxville, 1983-86, Jaycees, Dayton, 1978-81; vol. United Meth. Ch., Tilaran, Costa Rica, 1985. Recipient Scholarship, Fred M. Roddy Found., 1990. Mem. Phi Kappa Phi. Avocations: fly fishing, photography, bicycling, music, writing. Home: 301 Grandeur Dr Knoxville TN 37920-6325 Office: Dr John Mcguire PO Box 20548 Knoxville TN 37940-1548

MCGUIRE, JOHN LAWRENCE, pharmaceutical executive; b. Kittanning, Pa., Nov. 3, 1942; s. Lawrence F. and Florence G. (Jones) McG.; m. Pamela Hale, Aug. 2, 1969; children: Megan L., Christa H. BS, Butler U., 1965; MA, Princeton U., 1968, PhD, 1969; postgrad., Columbia Sch. Bus., 1981. Asst. in instrn. Princeton U., 1967-69; pharmacologist Ortho Pharm. Corp., Raritan, NJ, 1969-72, sect. head molecular biology, 1972-75, exec. dir. rsch., 1975-80, v.p. preclin. R&D, 1980-88, bd. dirs., 1988—92; sr. v.p. global rsch. and devel., bd. dirs. R.W. Johnson Pharm. Rsch. Inst., Raritan, 1988-92; corp. v.p. bus. devel., pharm./diagnostics group Johnson & Johnson, New Brunswick, NJ, 1992—2004; pres. Ferring Rsch. Insts., Lausanne, Switzerland, 2004—; exec. com. Ferring Pharm. Corp., Lausanne, 2004—; bd. dirs. Ferring Holding SA, St. Prex, Switzerland, 2005—. Adj. assoc. prof. dept. medicine M.S. Hershey Sch. Medicine Pa. State U., 1978—; adj. prof. dept. animal sci. Rutgers U., 1983-92, ob-gyn. East Va. Med. Sch., 1987—, ob-gyn. and reproductive endocrinology U. Medicine and Dentistry of NJ, 1988—; cons. NASA, 1985-87; cons. Nat. Tech. Transfer Ctr., 1997-2000; bd. dirs. MDAdvantage Ins. Co., Lawrenceville, N.J. Mem. editl. bd. Ullman's Ency. Indsl. Chemistry, 1987—; editor numerous books; contbr. articles to profl. jours.; patentee in field. Trustee Hunterdon Med. Ctr. Found., 1986—, chmn., 2002—; trustee NJ State Hosp. Assn., 2002—, NJ State Theater, New Brunswick, 2002—06, August Found., 1997—, pres., 1997—; trustee Raritan Valley CC, North Branch, NJ, 1986—, vice chmn., 1990—2005, chmn., 2005—; trustee Hunterdon Med. Ctr., Flemington, NJ, 1978—2002, vice chmn., 1984—86, chmn., 1988—98; trustee Hunterdon Health Care Sys., Flemington, NJ, 1986—, chmn., 1989—2002; trustee Atlantic Health Sys., Morristown, NJ, 1991—93, vice chmn., 1992—93; trustee The Pennington Sch., NJ, 1995—, pres., CEO, 1996—; exec. bd. Keystone Area coun. Boy Scouts Am., Harrisburg, Pa., exec. bd. George Washington coun. Trenton, NJ, 1980—86, 1995—99, exec. bd. Ctrl. N.J. coun. Princeton, 1999—, pres., 2000—05, mem. N.E. Region bd., 2004—; bd. dirs. United Way of Hunterdon County, NJ, 1983—97, pres. NJ, 1985—87; bd. dirs. Tri-State United Way, NY, 1987—94, Hunterdon County YMCA, NJ, 1982—87, Mid Jersey Health Corp., 1986—88, chmn., 1986—88; bd. visitors Butler U., Indpls., 2004—. Recipient Silver Beaver award, Boy Scouts Am., 1984, Disting. Eagle Scout award, 2000, Silver Antelope award, 2006, Johnson medal for rsch. and devel., 1990; named NJ Hosp. Trustee of Yr., 2001; Population Coun. fellow, 1969. Mem. Am. Soc. Pharmacology and Exptl. Therapeutics, Soc. Exptl. Biology and Medicine, Am. Physiol. Soc., Endocrine Soc., Am. Coll. Ob-Gyn, Am. Soc. Clin. Pharmacology and Therapetics, Soc. Gynecol. Investigation, Licensing Execs. Soc., Biochemistry Soc. Great Britain, Royal Soc. Medicine (UK), Am. Chem. Soc. Clubs: Princeton (NYC). Home: 10 Club House Dr Whitehouse Station NJ 08889-3378 Personal E-mail: John.McGuire@Ferring.com.

MCGUIRE, JOHN W., SR., advertising executive, marketing professional, writer; b. Chgo., May 12, 1952; s. Eugene H. Sr. and Marjorie (Bolger) McG.; m. Mary Sue Roper, June 17, 1972 (div. 1977); 1 child, John William Jr.; m. Lynn L. Rembos, June 21, 1984 (div. April 1991); children: Kelly Lynn, Ryan Michael. AA, Chgo. City Colls., 1972; BA, Northeastern Ill., Chgo., 1974. Janitor Bd. of Edn., Chgo., 1970-74; sales rep. Motorola Comms., Inc., Schaumburg, Ill., 1974-76, Pattis Group, Chgo., 1976-77; midwest sales mgr. Harcourt Brace Jovanovich Pub. Co., NYC, 1977-79; account sales mgr. Cosmopolitan Mag. Hearst Pub. Co., NYC, 1979-81; midwest acct. mgr. Psychology Today Mag. Ziff-Davis Pub. Co., NYC, 1981-82; midwest regional mgr. Pennwell Pub. Co., Tulsa, Okla., 1982-84; western regional sales mgr. Nursing Mgmt. Mag. SN Pub. Co., West Dundee, Ill., 1984-91; western regional sales mgr., midwest regional sales mgr. U.S. Pharmacist Mag. Jobson Pub. Co., NYC, 1991-98; v.p. SK&A Info. Svcs., Irvine, Calif., 1998-99; assoc. pub. Health Mgmt. Technology Mag. Nelson Pub., Nokomis, Fla., 1999; pres., CEO Blossom Pub. Co., Wasco, Ill., 2000—. Author: (book) One Man's Life: A Poetic Review, 1995; co-author: (with Scott Mennie) The Original Parent and Family Logbook, 2002; singer (cassette tapes), designer (creative posters). With USN, 1970. Mem. VFW, Midwest Healthcare Mktg., Arlington Poetry Project. Republican. Roman Catholic. Avocations: writing, scuba diving, horseback riding, travel, skydiving.

MCGUIRE, KATHLEEN ALISON, conductor; b. Melbourne, Australia, May 22, 1965; d. Frank Leonard McGuire and Jeanette Mary Tilson. MusB, U. Melbourne, 1987; grad. diploma arts in music, Victorian Coll. Arts, U. Melbourne, 1990; grad. diploma in edn., Monash U., Melbourne, 1992; MusM with Distinction, U. Surrey, Guildford, UK, 1995; Dr. in Mus. Arts, U. Colo., 2000. Cert. preparing future faculty U. of Colo. at Boulder, 2000, grad. tchr. cert. U. Colo., Boulder, 2000. Music educator Sacre Coeur Girls' Sch., Melbourne, Victoria, Australia, 1983—86; educator Our Lady of Mercy Coll., 1986; music dir. Mentone Old Time Theatre Soc., Melbourne, Victoria, Australia, 1985—88; educator Killester Coll., Melbourne, Victoria, Australia, 1987; music educator Sacred Heart Regional Girls' Coll., Melbourne, Victoria, Australia, 1988; educator Mentone Girls' Secondary Coll., Melbourne, Victoria, Australia, 1988—89; music tchr. McKinnon Secondary Coll., Melbourne, Victoria, Australia, 1988—90, Mentone Girls' Grammar Sch., Melbourne, Victoria, Australia, 1990—94; dir. of music Sandringham East Primary Sch., Melbourne, Victoria, Australia, 1988—89; condr. Musical Theatre Soc., U. Surrey, Guildford, Sussex, England, 1994—95; asst. condr. Symphony Orch., U. Surrey, Guildford, Sussex, England, 1994—95; condr. Wind Symphony, U. of Surrey, Guildford, Sussex, 1994—95; educator Parkdale Secondary Coll., Melbourne, Victoria, Australia, 1995; music dir. St. Aidan's Episcopal Ch., Boulder, Colo., 1996—2000; asst. condr. U. of Colo. at Boulder Symphony Orch., Boulder, Colo., 1996—2000; assoc. condr. Lakewood Symphony Orch., Denver, 1996—2000; artistic dir./condr. The Rainbow Chorus, Fort Collins, Colo., 1997—2000; asst. condr. Lyric Theatre, U. Colo., Boulder, Colo., 1997—2000; assoc. condr. New Music Ensemble, U. of Colo., Boulder, Colo., 1998—2000; lead grad. tchr. U. of Colo. at Boulder, 1999—2000; assoc. condr. Boulder Youth Symphony, Boulder, Colo., 1999—2000; artistic dir., condr. San Francisco Gay Men's Chorus, 2000—; condr. Opera By the Bay, Marin, Calif., 2001, Cmty. Women's Orch., San Francisco, 2005—; music tchr. Convent of the Sacred Heart H.S., San Francisco, 2004—07; music dir. Melbourne U. Choral Soc., Melbourne, Victoria, Australia, Mordialloc Light Opera Co., Melbourne, Victoria, Australia, Nova Theatre, Melbourne, Victoria, Australia, Whitehorse Mus. Theatre, Melbourne, Victoria, Australia; condr., founder Victorian Women's Orch., Melbourne, Victoria, Australia; condr. Kew Philharm. Orch., Melbourne, Victoria, Australia, Steamboat Springs Cmty. Orch.; music dir. Festival Theatre Co., Melbourne, Victoria, Australia, Renaissance Opera Co., Melbourne, Victoria, Australia, Viola Operatic Soc., Melbourne, Victoria, Australia, Melbourne Opera Co., Melbourne, Victoria, Australia, Melbourne Dancers Co., Melbourne, Victoria, Australia, CLOC Musical Theatre, Melbourne, Victoria, Australia, Gilbert and Sullivan Soc., Melbourne, Victoria, Australia, Melbourne U. Gilbert and Sullivan Soc., Melbourne, Victoria, Australia; asst. condr. St. Aidan's Anglican Ch., Melbourne, Victoria, Australia; music dir. Altona City Theatre, Melbourne, Victoria, Australia, Lyric Opera, Melbourne, Victoria, Australia. Instrumentalist Marie Wilson Band, Melbourne, Victoria, Australia, 1992—94; guest condr. for lighting Guildford Philharm., Guildford, Surrey, England, 1995; guest condr. Rocky Mountain Ctr. Mus. Arts, Boulder, Colo., 1996, Boulder Philharm., Boulder, 1996; condr. & founder Colo. Quilt Chorus, Denver, 1997; guest condr. Golden Gate Opera, San Francisco, 2001, Women's Philharm., San Francisco, 2001—02, Sacramento Ballet & Empyrean Ensemble, Sacramento, 2002, Gay Games & Cultural Festival, Sydney, 2002, Chgo., 06, Goat Hall Prodns., San Francisco, 2002, Cmty. Women's Orch., San Francisco, 2005, Victorian Music Theatre Guild Awards, Melbourne, Victoria, Australia, Royal Women's Hosp. Fundraiser, Melbourne, Fairfield Hosp. Fundraiser, Melbourne, Ann. AIDS Requiem Svcs., Melbourne; asst. condr. Byrd-Cage Singers, Melbourne; cantor Toorak Uniting Ch. Choir, Melbourne; condr. Malvern City Coun. - ann. fundraiser, Melbourne; instrumentalist Frankston City Band, Melbourne, Mordialloc City Band, Melbourne, Moomba Youth Band, Melbourne, Victoria, Australia; asst. condr. Intervarsity Choral Festival, Melbourne; instrumentalist Yamaha Youth Music Festival, Melbourne. Arranger (choral music concert suite) SFGMC Does Queen, (choral music) We Shall Overcome, Turn the World Around by Harry Belafonte, Every Time I Feel the Spirit, Harriet Tubman, Silent Night, Land of the Free, Peace Like a River; editor: (choral music) (by Gareth Valentine) Requiem in Memory of Those Who Have Died of AIDS; contbr. article to profl. jour., CD insert, ednl. pubs., electronic newsletter; prodr.: (comml. compact disc recording) Home for the Holidays (winner, OutMusic award, Outstanding New Choral Recording, 2006), Oh, Happy Day! (finalist OutMusic awards, Outstanding New Recording, choir or chorus, 2005), Closer Than Ever (winner, OutMusic Awards, Outstanding New Recording, choir or chorus, 2005); prodr.: (comml. compact disc recording) Divas' Revenge; prodr.(and arranger): (comml. compact disc recording) SFGMC Does Queen (finalist, Outstanding new choral rec., OutMusic awards, 2002); contbr. comml. compact disc recording (Wash. Area Music award and finalist, Outstanding New Rec., OutMusic awards, 2001); composer: (choral music) Magnificat, On Love, May God Shield You, Don't Ask, Don't Tell; music dir. (comml. compact disc recordings) Beginnings, Five Years for Freedom, St. Aidan's Prayer for Lindisfarne. Mem. Bay Area Cmty. Women, San Francisco; grand marshal San Francisco Pride, 2006; musician City of Refuge United Ch. Christ, San Francisco, 2004—; bd. mem. Gay and Lesbian Assn. Choruses, Washington, 2002—03; ex-officio bd. mem. Golden Gate Performing Arts, Inc., San Francisco, 2000—. Fellow Enrollment Enhancement fellowship, U. of Colo., Coll. of Music, 1996 - 1997; Ambassadorial fellow, Rotary Internat., 1994 - 1995, Writing fellow, Choral Jour., Florence Bradford scholar, U. Melbourne, 1991, Ivy-May Pendlebury scholar, 1985. Mem.: ASCAP, Coll. Music Soc., Am. Choral Dirs. Assn., Gay and Lesbian Assn. Choruses, Inc., Am. Symphony Orch. League, Conductors Guild, Phi Kappa Lambda. Achievements include first appointed woman conductor and artistic director of the world's oldest and largest openly gay men's chorus (founded 1978); was one of the same-sex couples married at San Francisco City Hall, February 23, 2004; conducted the Australian premiere of the rock opera, Metropolis; conducted the U.S. and Australian premieres of the world's first AIDS Requiem (by Gareth Valentine - composed in 1991); conducted the Australian premiere of The Apple Tree by Jerry Bock; arranged for men's chorus and conducted John Rutter's renowned Gloria in honor of the work's 30th anniversary (December, 2004); founder of Australia's first women's orchestra; conducted performances at Carnegie Hall (NY), Kennedy Center (DC), Davies Symphony Hall (San Francisco), Salle Wilfrid Pelletier (Montreal, Canada), Grace Cathedral (San Francisco); conducted the Sacramento Ballet and the Empyrean Ensemble at the inaugural season of the Mondavi Center, Sacramento, CA; conducted a choir of 560 voices at the Sydney Opera House (Australia) for Gay Games VI (November, 2002); opening ceremonies Chgo. Gay Games VII (July 2006); performed with many celebrities, including: Carol Channing, Sir Ian McKellen, Alan Cumming, Joanna Gleason, Sharon Gless, B.D. Wong, Armistead Maupin, Nichelle Nichols, Julie Newmar, Cris Williamson; arranged music that has been performed by premier artists, including: Turtle Creek Chorale, Pot Pourri, Les Ms, Boston Gay Men's Chorus, Men Alive, Metropolitan Community Church Choir of San Francisco; arranged music performed by artists including: San Diego Men's Chorus, Atlanta Gay Men's Chorus, Buffalo Gay Men's Chorus, Seattle Men's Chorus, Houston Gay Men's Chorus, Twin Cities Gay Men's Chorus; arranged music performed by artists including: Lesbian/Gay Chorus San Francisco, Oakland Eastbay Gay Men's Chorus, Phila. Gay

Men's Chorus, Rochester Gay Men's Chorus, Vancouver Men's Chorus; conducted a choir of 80 at Rosie O'Donnell's wedding at San Francisco City Hall, February 2004; completed AIDS Life Cycle V 585 mile bicycle ride from San Francisco to Los Angeles June 2006. Avocations: travel, culinary arts, outdoor sports, crossword puzzles. Office: Golden Gate Performing Arts Inc 1800 Market St PMB 1000 San Francisco CA 94102

MCGUIRE, LILLIAN (ELIZABETH) HILL, historian, researcher, retired education educator, writer; b. Middlesex County, Va., 1928; d. Howard Garfield Hill, Sr. and Malissie O'Neal (Carter) Hill; m. Charles Edward McGuire, Aug. 11, 1957 (dec. July 30, 1997); children: Brenda Colette, Gina Renae, Laura Jane Fortune Battle. Student, Hampton Inst., 1946—48; BS, Morgan State U., 1951. Primary and Secondary Tchg. Cert. Va. Dept. of Edn. Classroom tchr. Richmond County Sch. Sys., Warsaw, Va., 1951—65, Essex County Sch. Sys., Tappahannock, Va., 1965—88; adult edn. tchr. Rappahannock C.C., Warsaw, Va., 1989—94; adult edn. tchr. Essex County Sch. Sys., Tappahannock, 1989—94. Pres. Essex Edn. Assn., Tappahannock, 1982—86, editor-news letter, 1982—88; historian Va. Ret. Tchrs. Assn., Blacksburg, 1995—97. Author: (book) The Vista of a Century: History of the Southside Rappahannock Baptist Association and Allied Bodies, 1977, Our Spiritual Heritage: History of First Baptist Church Tappahannock, VA, 1993, Uprooted & Transplanted: From Africa to America; Focus on African Americans in Essex County, VA, 2000, In Retrospect, 2005, Roots and Branches, Seven Generations Genealogy of the Hill Family of Middlesex County, Va., 2008; curator The Gallery of History, 1st Bapt. Ch., Tappahannock, Va., 2009; contbr. poetry to Twilight Musings, chapters to books. Charter mem. Mid. Peninsula African-Am. Geneaol. and Hist. Soc. Va., 2005—, Essex County Mus., Tappahannock, 1996—2006, mem. bd. dir., 1996—2006; mem. adv. coun. Essex County Mus./Hist. Soc., Tappahannock, 2006—; mem. NAACP Essex County Br., Tappahannock, 1950. Recipient Honor award, Essex Edn. Assn., Tappahannock, 1977, Disting. Svc. award, 1982; named Outstanding Elem. Sch. Tchr. of Am., Bd. of Advisors, Washington, 1974. Mem.: Internat. Soc. Poets, Mid. Peninsula Geneal. and Hist. Soc. Va. (charter mem.), Rappahannock Indsl. Acad. Alumni Assn. (historian 1975), Morgan State U. Nat. Alumni Assn., Dist. A of Va. Ret. Tchrs. (life; historian 1988). Baptist. Avocations: writing, puzzles, travel, exercise. Home: 445 Marsh St PO Box 143 Tappahannock VA 22560

MCGUIRE, MARK M., lawyer, manufacturing executive; b. Lynn, Mass., 1957; BA with distinction in Psychology, George Washington U., 1979; JD, U. Va. Sch. Law, 1983. Assoc. Morgan, Lewis & Bockius, Phila., 1983—85, Powell, Goldstein, Frazer & Murphy, Atlanta, 1985—90, ptnr., 1991—92; assoc. gen. counsel Internat. Paper Co., Stamford, Conn., 1992—2002, gen. counsel Europe, assoc. gen. counsel, v.p., dep. counsel, 2002—05; exec. v.p., gen. counsel Eaton Corp., Cleve., 2005—. J. Hardy Dillard Fellow, U. Va. Sch. Law. Office: Eaton Corp 1111 Superior Ave Cleveland OH 44114-2584 Office Phone: 216-523-4376. E-mail: markmmcguire@eaton.com.*

MCGUIRE, MAUREEN A., marketing executive; b. 1952; Degree in English, French, Spanish Lang. and Lit., U. Glasgow, Scotland, 1974. With IBM Corp., 1975, v.p. worldwide market mgmt. and integrated mktg. comm., 1995—2003, v.p. worldwide strategy and mktg., global svcs., 2003—05, v.p. worldwide strategy and mktg., sys. tech. grp., 2005; exec. v.p., chief mktg. officer Sears Holdings Corp., 2005—08; ind. cons., 2008—09; chief mktg. officer Bloomberg L.P., NYC, 2009—. Bd. advisors Catalyst, Inc.; bd. dirs. Furniture Brands Internat., Inc., 2008—. Named Marketer of Yr., B2B mag., 2002, Communicator of Yr., Bus. Mktg. Assn., 2003; named a Woman to Watch, Advt. Age, 2008. Office: Bloomberg LP 731 Lexington Ave New York NY 10022 Office Phone: 847-286-2500.*

MCGUIRE, MICHAEL FRANCIS, plastic surgeon; b. St. Louis, Oct. 4, 1946; s. Arthur Patrick and Virginia Claribel (Gannon) McG. BA, Columbia U., 1968, MD, 1972. Diplomate Am. Bd. Surgery, Am. Bd. Plastic Surgery. Intern UCLA, 1972-73, resident in gen. surgery, 1973-77, resident in plastic surgery, 1978-80; fellow in plastic surgery rsch. Stanford (Calif.) U., 1977-78; traveling fellow in plastic surgery Gt. Britain, 1980; chief plastic surgery L.A. County-Olive View Med. Ctr., Sylmar, Calif., 1980-85; pvt. practice Santa Monica, Calif., 1980—; chief plastic surgery St. John's Health Ctr., 1990—; asst. clin. prof. surgery UCLA, 1980-97, assoc. clin. prof., 1998—. Bd. dirs. Calif. Med. Rev., Inc., sec.-treas., 1997, v.p., 1997-99, chmn. bd. dirs. 1999-2003; chmn. surg. rev. St. Johns Health Ctr., 1996-98, chief plastic surgery, 1992-; pres. Pacific Coast Plastic Surgery Ctr., 1988—. Charter patron LA Music Ctr. Opera, 1983—; sponsoring patron LA County Art Mus., 1986—2005; patron Colleague Helpers in Philanthropic Svc., Bel Air, Calif., 1987, 93, 95; pres. Found. for Surg. Reconstrn., 1996-2007, LA Philanthropic Com. Arts Bd., 2009, with Nat. Accred Program Breast Ctrs. Bd., 2009-. Fellow ACS, Royal Soc. Medicine; mem. Am. Soc. Plastic Surgeons (membership chmn. 1997-2000, bd. dirs. 2002-05, sec. 2005-2007, v.p. 2007-08, pres.-elect, 2008-, chmn. leadership devel. com. 2004-07), Am. Soc. Aesthetic Plastic Surgery (ethics chmn. 1998-99, bd. dirs. 2004—07, pub. edn. chmn. 2004-05, commr. comm., 2005-2007, publications chair, 2007-), Am. Health Quality Assn. (bd. dirs. 1999—2005), LA County Med. Assn. (v.p. 1995-97, sec.-treas. 1997-99), Calif. Med. Assn. (del., exec. com., splty. delegation 1994-99), Calif. Soc. Plastic Surgery (exec. com., auditor 1988-89, program chmn. 1990, exec. coun. 1991-94, treas. 1994-97, v.p. 1997-98, acting pres. 1997, pres.-elect 1998-99, pres. 1999-2000, nominating com. chmn. 2000-01, strategic planning com. chmn. 2005—), Am. Assn. Accreditation of Ambulatory Surgery Facilities (ops. com. 1995-96, bd. dirs. 1996-, treas. 1996-98, sec. 1998-2000, v.p. 2000-02, pres. 2002-04), Surgery Facilities Resources (founding pres. 2005-07), Alpha Omega Alpha, Am. Mensa Avocations: golf, travel, collecting antique glass, opera, art. Office: 1301 20th St Ste 460 Santa Monica CA 90404-2054 Office Phone: 310-315-0121. Business E-Mail: mmcguire@ucla.edu.

MCGUIRE, MICHAEL JOHN, environmental engineer; b. San Antonio, June 29, 1947; s. James Brendan and Opal Mary (Brady) McG.; m. Deborah Marrow, June 19, 1971; children: David, Anna. BS in Civil Engring., U. Pa., 1969; MS in Environ. Engring., Drexel U., 1972, PhD in Environ. Engring., 1977. Diplomate Am. Acad. Environ. Engring.; registered profl. engr., Pa., N.J., Calif., Ariz., Tex. San. engr. Phila. Water Dept., 1969-73; rsch. assoc. Drexel U., Phila., 1976-77; prin. engr. Brown & Caldwell Cons. Engrs., Pasadena, Calif., 1977-79; water quality engr. Met. Water Dist. of So. Calif., LA, 1979-84, water quality mgr., 1984-86, dir. water quality, 1986-90, asst. gen. mgr., 1990-92; pres. McGuire Environ. Cons., Inc., Santa Monica, Calif., 1992—2005, Michael J. McGuire Inc., LA, 2008—; v.p. Malcolm Pirnie Inc., Santa Monica, 2005—08. Cons. to subcom. on adsorbents, safe drinking water com. Nat. Acad. Scis., 1978-79, NRC, Drinking Water Contaminants (comm. mem.), 1998-99; mem. Water Sci. and Tech. Bd., NRC, 2009-; cons. mem. Techs. Workgroup U.S. EPA, DBP Reg. Neg., 1992-93, 97, 99-2000. Editor: (with I.H. Suffet) Activated Carbon Adsorption of Organics from the Aqueous Phase, 2 vols., 1980, Treatment of Water by Granular Activated Carbon, 1983, (with J.L. McLain and A. Obolensky) Information Collection Rule Data Analysis, 2003; contbr. articles to profl. jours. Recipient Best Paper award, Water Quality Tech. Divsn., 2007. Mem. ASCE, Internat. Water Assn. (specialist group on taste and odor control 1982—, chmn. organizing com. 1991, off-flavor symposium 1987-91), Internat. Ozone Assn. (internat. bd. dirs. 1992-95), Am. Water Works Assn. (Calif.-Nev. sect. chmn. water quality and resources divsn. 1982-83, governing bd. 1984-87, 89-96, exec. com. 1989-96, chmn. 1991-92, nat. edn. divsn. chmn. 1982-83, dir. 1994-96, chair taste and odor com. 1993-98, exec. com. 1994-96, water quality and tech. divsn. trustee 2004—, Acad. Achievement award 1978, Fuller award 1994, Publs. award 2001, George A. Elliot award 2005, Hon. Membership award 2006, WQTD Best Paper award 2007, A.P. Black Rsch. award, 2009), Am. Chem. Soc., Sigma Xi, Sigma Nu, Sigma Tau, Nat. Acad. Engring.

MCGUIRE, MICHAEL K., periodontist; DDS, Emory U., Atlanta, 1979. Diplomate Am. Bd. Periodontology, 1984. Periodontist Perio Health Profls., Houston, 1979—. Office: Perio Health Profls 3400 s Gessner Rd Ste 102 Houston TX 77063

MCGUIRE, PATRICIA A., lawyer, academic administrator; b. Phila., Nov. 13, 1952; d. Edward J. and Mary R. McGuire. BA cum laude, Trinity Coll., 1974; JD, Georgetown U., 1977. Bar: Pa. 1977, D.C. Ct. Appeals 1979. Program dir. Georgetown U. St. Law Clinic, Washington, 1977-82; asst. dean for devel. and external affairs Georgetown U. Law Ctr., Washington, 1982-89; pres. Trinity Coll., Washington, 1989—. Adj. prof. law Georgetown U., 1977-82, Georgetown Law Ctr., 1987—; commr. Mid. States Commn. on Higher Edn., 1991—; bd. dirs. Acacia Group, Elderhostel, Inc. Editor: Street Law Mock Trial Manual, 1984; contbr. articles to profl. jours. Trustee Trinity Coll., 1986—; bd. dirs. Assn. Cath. Colls. and Univs., 1991—, Eugene and Agnes Meyer Found.; mem. adv. bd. Merion Mercy Acad. and Sisters of Mercy, 1990—; bd. dirs. Nat. Assn. Ind. Colls. and Univs.; mem. commn. govt. rels. Am. Coun. Edn.; bd. dirs. Women's Coll. Coalition; adv. bd. Nat. Coll. Access Network; mem. dollar coin design adv. com. U.S. Mint; bd. vis. Joint Mil. intelligence Coll. Recipient Daytime Emmy, TV Acad., N.Y.C., 1979-80. Mem. ABA, Assn. Am. Law Schs. (instl. advancement 1985—), Coun. for the Advancement and Support of Edn., Trinity Coll. Alumnae Assn. (pres. 1986-89) Democrat. Roman Catholic. Office: Trinity Coll Office of the President 125 Michigan Ave NE Washington DC 20017-1091 E-mail: president@trinitydc.edu.

MCGUIRE, PIERRE, sports analyst, former professional hockey coach; b. Aug. 8, 1961; m. Melanie McGuire; children: Justine, Ryan. Asst. hockey coach Hobart Coll., Geneva, NY, 1984; hockey coach Babson Coll., Wellesley, Mass., St. Lawrence U., Canton, NY; scout Pitts. Penguins, 1990—92; asst. coach Hartford Whalers, 1992—93, also asst. gen. mgr., head coach, 1993—94, Baton Rouge Kingfish (East Coast Hockey League), 1996—97; pro scout, asst. coach Ottawa Senators orgn., 1994—96; radio colour commentator Montreal Canadiens, 1997; analyst Habs This Week; hockey analyst TSN (The Sports Network), Toronto, 2000—; colour commentator, studio host NHL on NBC, 2006—. Spl. contbr. Sports Illustrated. Named Best Game Analyst, Gemini Awards, 2007; nominee Gemini Award, 2004. Office: NHL on NBC 30 Rockefeller Plaza New York NY 10112

MCGUIRE, RAYMOND J., diversified financial services company executive; b. Dayton, Ohio, Jan. 23, 1957; AB cum laude, Harvard Coll., 1979; MBA, Harvard Bus. Sch., 1984; JD, Harvard Law Sch., 1984. With Mergers & Acquisitions Group First Boston Corp., 1984—88; joined Wasserstein Perella & Co., 1988, ptnr., mng. dir., 1991—94; mng. dir. Mergers & Acquisitions Group Merrill Lynch & Co., 1994—2000, Morgan Stanley, NYC, 2000—03, global co-head mergers & acquisitions, 2003—05; co-head global investment banking Citi Markets & Banking Instl. Clients Group, NYC, 2005—. Bd. dirs. Wyeth, 2006—. Pres. bd. trustees Internat. Ctr. Photography; trustee Whitney Mus. Am. Art, mem. investment com.; trustee NY Presbyterian Hosp., Enterprise Found.; chmn. Studio Mus. Harlem, bd. dir.; chmn. De LaSalle Acad., bd. dir., The Enterprise Found., Joseph & Claire Flom Found., Howard Gilman Found.; mem. overseers, dirs. nominating com. Harvard U. Recipient Rotary Fellowship, U. of Nice, France, 1980. Office: Citigroup Inc 388 Greenwich St New York NY 10013

MCGUIRE, RICHARD (MICK MCGUIRE), retail executive; b. 1977; B, Princeton U., NJ; MBA, Harvard Bus. Sch. Formerly with J.H. Whitney & Co., Stonington Ptnrs., Inc.; ptnr. Pershing Square Capital Mgmt., L.P., NYC, 2005—09; non-exec. chmn. Borders Group, Inc., 2009—. Bd. dirs. Borders Group, Inc., 2008—. Office: Borders Group Inc 100 Phoenix Dr Ann Arbor MI 48108 Office Phone: 734-477-1100. Office Fax: 734-477-1285.*

MCGUIRE, ROBERT A., economics professor; s. Russell K. and Viola R. McGuire. AA, Rio Hondo Coll., Whittier, CA, 1968; BA, Calif. State U., Long Beach, CA, 1970; MA, U. Wash., Seattle, 1973, PhD, 1978. Asst. prof. Ball State U., Muncie, Ind., 1977—82, assoc. prof., 1982—88; vis. prof. law U. Calif., Berkeley, Calif., 1986, vis. assoc. prof. economics Santa Cruz, Calif., 1986—88, Davis, 1988—90; prof. economics U. Akron, Ohio, 1990—. Contbr. articles to profl. jours.; co-author: (book) Government and the American Economy; author: To Form A More Perfect Union, An Empirical Investigation of Farmers' Behavior Under Uncertainty; reviewer (book) Law and Politics Book Review, The Independent Review, Technology and Culture, Wall Street Review of Books, Jour. Econ. History, Jour. Econ. Lit. Recipient Prin. Investigator, Rsch. Challenge Matching award, Ohio Bd. of Regents, 2000—01, 2007—10; Prin. Investigator, Rsch. grant, NSF, 2000—01, 2007—10. Mem.: Cliometric Soc. (assa program rep. 2008—), Econ. History Assn. (com. rsch. econ. history 2009—), Am. Econ. Assn. Avocations: travel, running, skiing, hiking, wine collecting. Office: The Univ Akron Dept Economics Akron OH 44325-1908 Office Fax: 330-972-5356. Business E-Mail: rmcguire@uakron.edu.

MCGUIRE, SANDRA LYNN, nursing educator; b. Jan. 28, 1947; d. Donald Armstrong and Mary Lue (Harvey) Johnson; m. Joseph L. McGuire, Mar. 6, 1976; children: Matthew, Kelly, Kerry. BSN, U. Mich., 1969, MPH, 1973, EdD, 1988, MSN, 1997. Staff nurse Univ. Hosp., Ann Arbor, Mich., 1969; pub. health nurse Wayne County Health Dept., Eloise, Mich., 1969—72; instr. Madonna Coll., Livonia, Mich., 1973; pub. health coord. Plymouth Ctr. for Human devel., Northville, Mich., 1974—75; asst. prof. cmty. health nursing U. Mich., Ann Arbor, 1975—83; asst. prof. U. Tenn., Knoxville, 1983—88, assoc. prof., 1990—2007, prof., 2007—09, coord. gerontol. nurse practitioners program, 1998—2006, chair MSN program Coll. Nursing, coord. gerontology, 2008—09; asst. dean Lincoln Meml. U. Sch. Nursing, 2009—. Dir. Kids Are Tomorrow's Srs. Program, 1988—; resource person Gov.'s Com. Unification of Mental Health Svcs. in Mich.; spkr. profl. assns. and workshops; mem. Coun. Accreditation Nurse Anesthesia Ednl. Programs, 2007—. Author (with S. Clemen-Stone and D. Eigsti): Comprehensive Community Health Nursing, 1981, Comprehensive Community Health Nursing, 5th edit., 1998, Comprehensive Community Health Nursing, 6th edit., 2002. Bd. dirs. Ctr. Understanding Aging, 1987-93, v.p., 1995; bd. dirs. Mich. chpt. ARC, 1980-83, Knoxville chpt., 1984-85; founder Knoxville Intergenerational Network, 1989; mem. nat. policy coun. AARP, 2006-. Recipient John W. Runyan, Jr. Cmty. Health Nursing award U. Tenn. Memphis, 2002, Outstanding Svc. award U. Tenn. Knoxville Libr. Friends, 2004; USPHS fellow, 1972-73, Robert Woodruff fellow Emory U., 1996-97, Hewlett Innovative Tech. fellow U. Tenn., Knoxville, 1999-00, Profl. Devel. awardee U. Tenn. Knoxville, 1996-97, 99-2000. Mem. ANA, AARP Nat. Policy Coun., Tenn. Nurses Assn., Gerontological Soc. Am., Assn. Gerontology in Higher Edn., Nat. Gerontol. Nursing Assn., Coun. on Accreditation Nurse Anesthesia Ednl. Programs, Mich. Pub. Health Assn. (chmn. mental health sect. 1976, dir., co-chmn. residential svcs. com. 1976-79, chmn. health svcs. 1979-82), Nat. Assn. Retarded Citizens, Mich. Assn. Retarded Citizens, Nat. Coun. on Aging, Ctr. for Understanding Aging (v.p. 1994-95), Plymouth (chmn. residential svcs. com. 1975-77), Tenn. Assn. Retarded Citizens, Sr. Citizens Home Assistance Svcs. (bd. mem. 2008-), Sigma Theta Tau, Pi Lambda Theta, Phi Kappa Phi. Home: 11008 Crosswind Dr Knoxville TN 37934 Office: Cumberland Gap Pky. Harrogate TN 37752 Office Phone: 800-325-0900 x 6324. Business E-Mail: smcguire@utk.edu, sandra.mcguire@lmunet.edu.

MCGUIRE, SARAH LEA, biology professor; married; 1 child. BA, Miss. Coll.; MA, U. So. Miss.; PhD, Baylor Coll. Medicine. Faculty mem. to prof. biology Millsaps Coll., Jackson, Miss., 1995—. Contbr. articles to sci. jours. Recipient US Prof. of Yr. award, Carnegie Found. for Advancement of Tchg. and Coun. for Advancement and Support of Edn., 2006. Mem.: Miss. Acad. Scis. (former pres.). Avocations: rock climbing, trombone, birdwatching. Office: Dept Biology Millsaps Coll 1701 N State St Jackson MS 39210-0001 Office Phone: 601-974-1414. E-mail: mcguisl@millsaps.edu.

MCGUIRE, SHARON, SR., nursing educator; d. Robert John and Jean Elizabeth McGuire. BA, Siena Heights U., Adrian, Mich., 1968; MEd, Wayne State U., Detroit, 1974; BSN, Barry U., Miami Shores, Fla., 1984; MSN, U. Miami, Coral Gables, Fla., 1989; PhD, U. San Diego, 2001. Cert. family nurse practitioner, ANCC, 1990, pediat. nurse practitioner, ANCC, 1998. Fnp Ctr. San Vicente Family Health Ctr., El Paso, Tex., 1989—94; lectr. U. Tex., El Paso, 1992—98; asst. prof. U. San Diego, 2001—07; assoc. prof. nursing Siena Heights U., Adrian, 2008—. Contbr. articles to profl. jours., chapters to books. Founder Quincentennaria Com., El Paso, 1991—92; bd. mem. St. Rose Dominican Hosp., Henderson, Nev., 2003—; adv. bd. mem. UTEP Coll. Nursing Women's Health Care Nurse Practitioner Program, El Paso, 1990—92, Head Start, El Paso, 1994—96. Recipient Svc. award, Cystic Fibrosis Found., 1982, Most Influential Faculty award, RN Students, U. San Diego, 2007, award, Barbara Buchanan Meml. Cmty., Dean's award, Barry U., Impact award, Barbara Buchanan Meml. Cmty. Impact award, U. Miami. Mem.: ANA, Am. Acad. Nurse Practitioners, Transcultural Nursing Soc., Am. Coll. Nurse Practitioners, Nat. Orgn. Nurse Practitioner Faculty, Sigma Theta Tau Internat. Roman Catholic. Avocations: reading, gardening, swimming, bicycling, skateboarding. Office: Siena Heights Univ 1247 E Siena Heights Dr Adrian MI 49221 Office Phone: 517-264-7212. Personal E-mail: smcguireop@yahoo.com.

MCGUIRE, TIMOTHY WILLIAM, economics and management educator, dean, information technology executive; b. Englewood, NJ, Nov. 30, 1938; s. Charles James and Marie (McCarthy) McG.; children: Timothy William Jr., Gretchen Elizabeth, Michael Joseph; m. Nancy Paule Melone, 1991. BS in Indsl. Mgmt., Carnegie Inst. Tech., Pitts., 1960; MS in Econs., Carnegie Inst. Tech., 1961; PhD in Econs., Stanford U., Calif., 1968. Staff mem. Coun. Econ. Advisors, 1963—64; rsch. assoc. econs. Grad. Sch. Indsl. Adminstrn. Carnegie Mellon U., Pitts., 1964—66, asst. prof. econs. Grad. Sch. Indsl. Adminstrn., 1966—69, assoc. prof. Grad. Sch. Indsl. Adminstrn., 1969—75, prof. Grad. Sch. Indsl. Adminstrn., 1975—79, prof. mgmt. and econs. Grad. Sch. Indsl. Adminstrn., 1982—, dep. dean Grad. Sch. Indsl. Adminstrn., 1983—90, prof. social scis. and econs. Dept. Social Scis., 1981—82; prof. econs., chmn. dept. U. Iowa, Iowa City, 1979—80; dean, Harry B. Miller prof. bus. Charles H. Lundquist Coll. Bus. U. Oreg., Eugene, 1994—98; COO, sr. exec. v.p. Mgmt. Sci. Assocs., Inc., Pitts., 1998—2005, chmn., sr. exec. v.p., 2005—07, chief analytics officer, sr. exec. v.p., vice chmn., 2008—. Sr. visitor U. Cambridge, England, 1970; bd. dirs. Mgmt. Sci. Assocs., Inc., Pitts.; bd. visitors Joseph M. Katz Grad. Sch. Bus., U. Pitts. Contbr. articles to profl. jours. Bd. trustees, chmn. acad. and student affairs com. Point Park U.; chmn. corp. adv. bd. Pitts. Ctr. Sports, Arts and Entertainment Mgmt., 2003—07; bd. visitors Katz Grad. Sch. Mgmt, U. Pitts. Fellow, Ford Found., 1962—63, 1970—71; Woodrow Wilson Nat. Hon. fellow, Carnegie Inst. Tech., 1960—61, Stanford U. fellow, 1961—62. Mem.: Soc. Judgment and Decision Making, Omicron Delta Kappa, Tau Beta Pi. Avocations: piano, dogs. Home: 118 Lakeland Dr Mars PA 16046-2114 Office: Mgmt Sci Assocs Inc 6565 Penn Ave Pittsburgh PA 15206-4490 Home Phone: 724-772-0837; Office Phone: 412-362-2000. Business E-Mail: tmcguire@msa.com.

MCGUIRE, VAIL H., literature and language professor; d. Alvah S. Hutson and Dana Hutson Wood; m. John A. McGuire; 1 child, Dana Vail Grilli. PhD, Miami U., Oxford, Ohio, 2008. Adj. instr. English Wright State U., Fairborn, Ohio, 1985—87, Miami-Jacobs Jr. Coll. Bus., 1986—87; prof. English Kettering Coll. Med. Arts, Ohio, 1987—. Youth advisor Westminster Presbyn. Ch., Dayton, Ohio, 1975—2008. Mem.: NCTE. Democrat. Presbyterian.

MCGUIRE, WILLIAM, civil engineer, educator; b. S.I., NY, Dec. 17, 1920; s. Edward Joseph and Phoebe (Sellman) McG.; m. Barbara Weld, Feb. 5, 1944; children: Robert Weld, Thomas Rhodes. BSCE, Bucknell U., 1942; MSCE, Cornell U., 1947. Structural designer Jackson & Moreland (engrs.), Boston, 1947-49; faculty Cornell U., Ithaca, 1949—, prof. civil engring., 1960-90, prof. emeritus of civil engring., 1990—; dir. Cornell U. (Sch. Civil Engring.), 1966-68; vis. prof. civil engring. Asian Inst. Tech., Bangkok, Thailand, 1968-70. Vis. research engr. Nat. Bur. Standards, 1972; Gledden vis. sr. fellow U. Western Australia, 1973; cons. structural engr., 1951—; vis. prof. U. Tokyo, 1979, U. Strathclyde, 1986 Author: Steel Structures, 1967; author: (with R.H. Gallagher and R.D. Ziemian) Matrix Structural Analysis, 1979, 2d edit., 2000. Served to lt. USNR, 1942-45. Recipient Naval Letter of Commendation, award for Outstanding Achievement, Bucknell U., 1987, T.R. Higgins Lectureship award Am. Inst. Steel Constrn., 1992, G. Haaijer awrd Am. Inst. Steel Constrn., 2000, L. Beedle award Structural Stability Rsch. Coun., 2005. Fellow ASCE (pres. Ithaca 1964, Norman medal 1962, 94, Hardesty award 1992, honorary mem. 1994); mem. Internat. Assn. Bridge and Structural Engring., Nat. Acad. Engring., Sigma Xi, Chi Epsilon, Kappa Delta Rho. Congregationalist. Home: 121 Simsbury Dr Ithaca NY 14850-1728 Business E-Mail: wm20@cornell.edu.

MCGUIRE, WILLIAM B(ENEDICT), lawyer; b. Newark, Feb. 14, 1929; children: Joan Ellen, Ralph R., James C., Keith P., Grant W. BS, Fordham U., 1950; JD, Seton Hall U., 1958; LLM in Taxation, NYU, 1963. Bar: NJ 1958, US Dist. Ct. NJ 1958, US Supreme Ct. 1971, US Ct. Appeals (3d cir.) 1980, NY 1982. Chief acct. Hanover Fire Ins. Co., NYC, 1950-58; sr. ptnr. Lum, Blunno & Tompkins, Newark, 1958-83, Tompkins McGuire Wachenfeld & Barry LLP, Newark, 1984—, mng.

ptnr. Asst. prosecutor Essex County, NJ, 1964-65; trustee St. Barnabas Corp. and St. Barnabas Med. Ctr.; mem. Essex County Ethics Com., 1974-77; chair bd. visitors Seton Hall U., Sch. Law, 2004—. Fellow Am. Coll. Trial Lawyers, Am. Bar Found. (state chmn. 1990-95), Am. Bd. Trial Advocates, Internat. Acad. Trial Lawyers, Internat. Soc. Barristers; mem. ABA, NJ State Bar Assn. (trustee 1982-89, sec. 1989-90, treas. 1990-91, 2d v.p. 1991-92, 1st v.p. 1992-93, pres.-elect 1993-94, pres. 1994-95), NJ State Bar Found. (pres. 1988-89), Essex County Bar Assn. (pres. 1975-76), Internat. Assn. Ins. Counsel, Fedn. Ins. Counsel, Def. Rsch. Inst., Maritime Law Assn., Trial Attys. NJ, Assn. Fed. Bar NJ (pres. 1985-88), Essex County Country Club (pres. 1983), Newark Club. Roman Catholic. Office: Tompkins McGuire Wachenfeld & Barry LLP 4 Gateway Ctr 100 Mulberry St Newark NJ 07102-4007 Office Phone: 973-622-3000, 973-623-7750. Office Fax: 973-623-7780. Business E-Mail: wmcguire@tompkinsmcguire.com.

MCGUIRE, WILLIAM DENNIS, healthcare consultant; b. Glen Ridge, NJ, Sept. 24, 1943; s. John William and Kathleen Mary (Sexton) McG.; m. Nancy Katherine Hoyne, Aug. 13, 1966; chldren: Kathleen Anne, Colleen Dempsey. BA, U. Notre Dame, 1965; M.H.A., U. Mich., 1968. Asst. adminstr. U. Wis. Hosps., Madison, 1971-74; adminstr. Children's Med. Ctr., Dayton, Ohio, 1974-79; COO Mercy Cath. Med. Ctr., Phila., 1979-80; CEO Wills Eye Hosp., Phila., 1980-85; pres., CEO Mercy Health Care Sys., Scranton, Pa., 1985-89, Mt. Carmel Health, Columbus, Ohio, 1989-92, Incarnate Word Health Svcs., San Antonio, 1992-95, Cath. Med. Ctrs. of Bklyn. and Queens, NYC, 1996—2000, Kaleida Health, Buffalo, 2002—06; pvt. practice San Antonio, 2000—02, 2006—. Asst. clin. prof. U. Wis., 1971—74, instr., 1972—73; allied health techs. adv. com. Sinclair CC, 1974—79; mem. Dayton Pub. Schs. Lay Adv. Com. on Vocat. Edn., 1974—79; pres. Dayton Area Young Adminstrs. Group, 1977; asst. clin. prof. Wright State U. Sch. Medicine, Dayton, Ohio, 1978—79; asst. prof. Ohio State U., 1990—92; adj. faculty dept health care Trinity U., 1992—95, Harvard Bus. Sch. Club, 2003—06. Trustee Cath. Social Svcs., 1976—79, pres., 1978—79; trustee Cmty. Blood Ctr., 1977—79; pres. elect Greater Dayton Area Hosp. Assn., 1979; mem. Wilkes Coll. Health Adminstrn. Adv. Com., 1988—89; bd. dirs. Coop. Purchasing Corp., 1974—79, Coll. Misericordia Health Care Task Force, 1988—89, Covenant Health Sys., 1992—2003, chmn. fin. com., 2001—03, Fletcher Allen Health Care, 2002—03; consol. Cath. Risk Retention Group, 1992—95, Cath. Charities, 1996—2000, Primary Care Devel. Corp., 1997—2000, Buffalo Niagara Partnership, 2002—06, D'Youville Coll., 2004—06, Hosp. Billing & Collection Svc. Ltd., 2004—, Computer Task Group, 2008—; bd. govs. League Vol. Hosps., 1996—2000, sec., 1997—2000; bd. govs. Fidelis Care NY, 1996—2000, Queensbrook Ins. Ltd., 1996—2000, vice chmn., 1996—97, chmn., 1997—2000; active Health Policy Forum, United Hosp. Fund, United Way, ARC. Fellow Am. Coll. Healthcare Execs. (life), NY Acad. Medicine; mem. Acad. for Cath. Health Care Leadership, Mercy Leadership Group. (nat. commn. Cath. health care ministry), Maj. Cath. Health Alliance (sec. 1990-95, chmn. 1997-99), Health Care Fin. Mgmt. Assn. (advanced mem.), Am. Assn. Univ. Profs. Ophthalmology, Am. Soc. Law and Medicine, Am. Hosp. Assn., Am. Assn. Eye and Ear Hosps. (pres.-elect 1984-85), Health Mgmt. Edn. Assn. (pres. 1987-88), Hosp. Assn. NY State (bd. dirs. 1998-2000, 02-05), Greater NY Hosp. Assn. (bd. govs. 1997-2000, 02-06), Tex. Hosp. Assn., We. NY Hosp. Assn. (bd. dirs. 2002-05), Ohio Hosp. Assn., Hosp. Assn. Pa., Cath. Health Assn., Am. Pub. Health Assn., Pa. Pub. Health Assn., Del. Valley Hosp. Council, Pa. Emergency Health Svcs. Coun., Del. County Emergency Health Svcs. Coun., Nat. Union Hosp. and Health Care Employees (plan trustee), Pa. Hosps. Ins. Co. Adv. Coun., 1988-89. C. of C., U. Notre Dame Alumni Assn., U. Mich. Alumni Assn., Pres.'s Soc., U. Wis. Med. Sch. Alumni Assn., Wills Eye Soc., Sorin Soc., Badin Guild, Notre Dame Club (pres. 1971, v.p. 1983-84), Dominion Country Club, Royal Soc. Medicine Office: 6 Clubhouse Green San Antonio TX 78257 Home: 6 Clubhouse Grn San Antonio TX 78257-1295 Office Phone: 210-698-6543. Personal E-mail: billmcg@together.net.

MCGUIRK, RONALD CHARLES, retired bank executive, economic advisor; b. Balt., Dec. 9, 1938; s. Charles F. and Grace E. (Delcher) McG.; m. Katherine Sauer, Oct. 1, 1960; children: Frank D., Ann E. Student, St. John's Coll., Annapolis, Md., 1956-59. Sr. data processing officer 1st Nat. Bank, Balt., 1966-72, v.p. data processing, 1972-76, v.p. mktg., 1976-80, sr. v.p. mktg., 1980-90, sr. v.p. corp. plan, chief of staff to CEO, 1990-94; sr. v.p., corp. sec. 1st Md. Bancorp, Balt., 1995-99; sr. econ. advisor Anne Arundel County, Md., 1999—2006; ret., 2006. Bd. dirs., v.p., treas. Balto-Washington Med. Ctr., Glen Burnie, Md., 1974—, v.p., 1999—; bd. dirs., treas. Internet, Inc., 1990-95, Glen Burnie Town Ctr. Com., 1995-2006, AACO Conf. and Vis. Bd., 1999-2006, Annapolis Symphony, 1991-92; trustee Mt. Washington Pediat. Hosp., 1997—2004; mem. adv. bd. Hist. Annapolis Found., 1982-85, dir., 1985-90; chmn. Annapolis Boundary Commn., 1983-84; mem. Anne Arundel County Coun., 1974-82, Anne Arundel County Libr. Bd., 1974-84; pres. Anne Arundel County Scholarship for Scholars/Bd. Edn., 1983-85, treas., 1985-88; mem. Anne Arundel County Charter Rev. Commn., 1986, Anne Arundel County Govt. Salary Commn., 1985, 89; chmn. Anne Arundel County Impact Fee Study Task Force, 1987; pres. Anne Arundel County YMCA, 1987-89, bd. dirs., 1982-87, 89-90; mem. Commn. for Ednl. Excellence, 1988-90; vice chmn. Ft. Meade Coordinating Coun., 1989-91; mem. Exec. Com. Md. Bus.-Industry PAC, 1991-99, Anne Arundel County Charter and Orgn. Transition Group, 1991; corp. ptnr. Sch. Bus. and Mgmt. Morgan State U., 1991-92; trustee Md. Hist. Soc., 1995-96; co-chair Anne Arundel County transition fin. com., 1998-99; chair adhoc Fire Dept. Com., 2003-04. Mem. Ctr. Club. Democrat. Roman Catholic. Personal E-mail: rm21061@aol.com.

MCGUIRK, TERRENCE, former broadcasting company executive; b. Bklyn., Apr. 2, 1925; s. William Edward and Loretta Beatrice (Lanigan) McG.; m. Gloria Helen Geoghan, June 17, 1950; children: Terence F., Sara McGuirk Duncan, Susan McGuirk Blank, Elizabeth McGuirk Magee, Melissa McGuirk Bowman, Bryan, Michelle McGuirk O'Connor. BS, Fordham U., 1950. Nat. sales mgr. St. WAGA-TV, Atlanta, 1966-68; mgr. Sta. WAGA-TV, Atlanta, 1970-75; eastern sales mgr. Storer TV Sales, NYC, 1968-70; pres., gen. mgr. Sta. WTEN-TV, Albany, NY, 1976-82; pres. Knight-Ridder Broadcasting, Inc., 1982-85; ret. Assoc. trustee Siena Coll., Loudonville, N.Y., 1979-83; trustee Meml. Hosp. Found., 1980-83; dir. Albany chpt. ARC, 1987-91. Served with U.S. Army, 1943-46. Mem. Babylon Yacht Club (hon.). Home Phone: 772-794-0335.

MCGUIRL, MARLENE DANA CALLIS, law librarian, educator; b. Hammond, Ind., Mar. 22, 1938; d. Daniel David and Helen Elizabeth (Baludis) Callis; m. James Franklin McGuirl, Apr. 24, 1965. AB, Ind. U., 1959; JD, DePaul U., 1963; MALS, Rosary Coll., 1965; LLM, George Washington U., 1978; postgrad., Harvard U., 1985. Bar: Ill. 1963, Ind. 1964, D.C. 1972. Asst. DePaul Coll. of Law Libr., 1961-62, asst. law libr., 1962-65; ref. law librarian Boston Coll. Sch. Law, 1965-66; libr. dir. D.C. Bar Libr., 1966-70; asst. chief Am.-Brit. Law Divsn. Libr. of Congress, Washington, 1970, chief, 1970-90, environ. cons., 1990—; counsel Cooter & Gell, 1992-93; adminstr. Washington Met. Transit Authority, 1994—2004. Libr. cons. Nat. Clearinghouse on Proverty Law, OEO, Washington, 1967-69, Northwestern U. Nat. Inst. Edn. in Law and Poverty, 1969, D.C. Office of Corp. Counsel, 1969-70; instr. law librarianship Grad. Sch. of U.S. Dept. of Agr., 1968-72; adj. asst. prof., 1973-91; assoc. prof. environ. law George Washington U., 1979—; lectr. justice and peace, Georgetown U., Washington, 2007—; judge Nat. and Internat. Law Moot Ct. Competition, 1976-78, 90—; pres. Hamburger Heaven, Inc., Palm Beach, Fla., 1981-91, L'Image de Marlene Ltd., 1986-92, Clinique de Beautè Inc., 1987-92, Heads & Hands Inc., 1987-92, Horizon Design & Mfg. Co., Inc., 1987—; dir. Stoneridge Farm Inc., Gt. Falls, Va., 1984—; lectr. in field. Contbr. articles to profl. jours. Mem. Georgetown Citizens Assn.; trustee D.C. Law Students in Ct.; del. Ind. Democratic Conv., 1964. Recipient Meritorious Svc. award Libr. on Congress, 1974, letter of commendation Dirs. of Pers., 1976, cert. of appreciation, 1981-84. Mem. ABA (facilities law libr. Congress com. 1976-89), Fed. Bar Assn. (chpt. council 1972-76), Ill. Bar Assn., Women's Bar Assn. (pres. 1972-73, exec. bd. 1973-77, Outstanding Contbn. to Human Rights award 1975), D.C. Bar Assn., Am. Bar Found., Nat. Assn. Women Lawyers, Am. Assn. Law Libraries (exec. bd. 1973-77), Law Librarians Soc. of Washington (pres. 1971-73), Exec. Women in Govt. Home: 3416 P St NW Washington DC 20007-2705 Personal E-mail: marlenemcguirl@aol.com.

MCGUNNIGLE, GEORGE FRANCIS, lawyer, judge; b. Rochester, NY, Feb. 22, 1942; s. George Francis and Mary Elizabeth (Curran) McG.; m. Priscilla Ann Lappin, July 13, 1968; children: Cynthia A., Brian P. AB, Boston Coll., 1963; LLB, Georgetown U., 1966; LLM, George Wash. U., 1967. Bar: Conn. 1971, Minn. 1972, US Dist. Ct. DC 1967, US Dist. Ct. Conn. 1971, US Dist. Ct. Minn. 1972, US Ct. Appeals (2d cir.) 1971, US Ct. Appeals (8th cir.) 1977, US Supreme Ct. 1986. Asst. US atty. Office of US Atty., Bridgeport, Conn., 1971-72; assoc. Leonard, Street and Deinard, Mpls., 1972—73, ptnr., 1974—2000; judge Fourth Jud. Dist., Mpls., 2000—. Editor: Business Torts Litigation, 1992. Bd. dirs. Cath. Charities, 1997—2003, North Ctrl. chpt. Arthritis Found., Mpls., 1986-92, 94—2003, mem. exec. com., 1988-92, 2001—03. Lt. JAGC, USN, 1967-71. Recipient Nat. Vol. Svc. citation Arthritis Found., 1992. Mem. ABA (litigation sect., chmn. bus. torts litigation com. 1988-91, divsn. dir. 1991-92, 97-98, coun. 1992-95, sect. of dispute resolution coun. 2000-01). Avocation: reading. Office: Fourth Judicial Dist C-1251 Hennepin County Govt Ctr Minneapolis MN 55487-0422 Office Phone: 612-596-8822.

MCGURK, CHRISTOPHER JAMIE, film company executive; b. 1957; BS, Syracuse U., 1978; MBA, U. Chgo. Various positions including CFO Pepsico, 1982—88; sr. v.p. fin. Walt Disney Studios, 1988-90, exec. v.p., CFO, 1990—94, pres. motion pictures group, 1994—96; various positions including pres., CEO Universal Pictures, 1996—99; vice chmn., COO Metro-Goldwyn-Mayer Inc., 1999—2005; sr. adv. new ventures IDT Entertainment, 2006—; CEO Overture Films, 2006—. Bd. dirs. DivX, Inc., 2006—. Exec. prodr.: (films) The Brothers Grimm, 2005.

MC GURN, BARRETT, communications executive, writer; b. NYC, Aug. 6, 1914; s. William Barrett and Alice (Schneider) McG.; m. Mary Elizabeth Johnson, May 30, 1942 (dec. Feb. 1960); children: William Barrett III, Andrew; m. Janice Ann McLaughlin, June 19, 1962; children: Summers, Martin Barrett, Mark Barrett. AB, Fordham U., 1935, LittD (hon.), 1958. Editor-in-chief Fordham Ram, 1934-35; with N.Y. Herald Tribune, 1935-66, asst. corr. Rome, 1939, bur. chief, 1946-52, 55-62, reporting staff NY, 1935-42, 62-66, bur. chief Paris, 1952—55, acting chief bur. Moscow, 1958; with, assignments in Morocco, Algeria, Tunisia, Hungary (1956 revolution), Egypt, Greece, Yugoslavia, Poland, Cen. Africa, Gaza Strip.; press attache Am. Embassy, Rome, 1966-68, counselor for press affairs Saigon, 1968—69; U.S. consular officer, sec. appointed by Pres., 1969; dir. U.S. Govt. Press Ctr., Vietnam, 1968-69; White House and Pentagon liaison for State Dept. spokesman Washington, 1969-72; World Affairs commentator USIA, 1972-73; dir. pub. info. U.S. Supreme Ct., Washington, 1973-82; dir. communications Cath. Archdiocese of Washington, 1984-87; pres. Carroll Pub. Co. pub. Cath. Standard and El Pregonero, 1987-91; dir. Our Sunday Visitor Pub. Co., 1988-98. Mem. Italian-Am. com. to select Italian fellowship winners for study in U.S., 1950-52; mem. U.S. Nat. Cath. Com. on Comm. Policy, 1970-74, White House Com. on Drug Control Info., 1970-72; interdept. com. on U.S. govt. press info. policy, 1970, interdept. U.S. govt. task force to rescue 100 Ams. kidnapped in Jordan, 1970, one-man U.S. Presdl. mission to Cambodia on media news problems, 1970; archivist John Carroll Soc., Washington, 1990-97. Author: Decade in Europe, 1959, A Reporter Looks at the Vatican, 1962, A Reporter Looks at American Catholicism, 1967, America's Court, The Supreme Court and The People, 1997, The Pilgrim's Guide to Rome, 1999, Yank, Reporting the Greatest Generation, 2004, (one act play) Semper Sistema, Fordham Coll. Stage, 1932; contbg. author: The Best from Yank, 1945, Yank, the GI Story of the War, 1946, Combat, 1950, Highlights from Yank, 1953, Overseas Press Club Cook Book, 1962, I Can Tell it Now, 1964, U.S. Book of Facts, Statistics and Information, 1966, New Catholic Treasury of Wit and Humor, 1967, How I Got that Story, 1967, Heroes for Our Times, 1968, Newsbreak, 1975, Saints for all Seasons, 1978, Informing the People, 1981, The Courage to Grow Old, 1989, Am. Peoples Encyclopedia Yearbook, Close To Glory: Yank Correspondents Untold Stories of World War II, 1992; contbr. articles to profl. jours. Trustee Corrs. Fund, 1965-68; mem. bd. Anglo-Am. Charity Fund in Italy, 1967-68; v.p. Citizens Assn., Westmoreland Hills, Md., 1984-86. Sgt. AUS, 1942-45. Decorated Purple Heart; grand knight Italian Order of Merit; Vietnam Psychol. Warfare medal 1st class; recipient Polk award for outstanding fgn. reporting L.I. U., 1956; named best press corr. abroad Overseas Press Club, 1957; recipient N.Y.C. Fire Dept. Essay Silver Medal, 1924, N.Y. Times Oratorical Contest Bronze Medal, 1930; Christopher award for one of ten most inspiring books of year, 1959; named Man of Year Cath. Inst. Press, 1962, Fordham U. Alumnus of Year in communications, 1963; co-winner ann. Golden Typewriter award N.Y. Newspaper Reporters Assn., 1965, nominated by N.Y. Herald Tribune for Journalism Pulitzer Prize, 1965; outstanding pub. service award N.Y. chpt. Sigma Delta Chi, 1965; recipient Page One award N.Y. Newspaper Guild, 1966, Silurians award, 1966, award N.Y. Newspaper Reporters Assn., 1966, Citation for pub. service N.Y.C. Citizens Budget Commn., 1966, U.S. Govt. medal for civilian svc. in Vietnam, 1969, pres. commendation for Cambodia mission on news problems, 1970, Meritorious Honor award Dept. State, 1972; Lifetime Achievement award Fordham U. Club, Washington, 1986. Mem. Fgn. Press Assn. Italy (v.p. 1951-52, pres. 1961-62), SHAPE Corrs. Assn. Paris (treas. 1955), Authors Guild, Silurians, Am. Fgn. Svc. Assn., Pax Romana Soc. for Cath. Intellectuals, Overseas Press Club (pres. 1963-65), Nat. Press Club, Diplomats and Consular Officers, Ret., Kenwood Club, Cosmos Club, Fordham U. Club Washington (bd. govs. 1980—99). Roman Catholic. Home: 5229 Duvall Dr Bethesda MD 20816-1875 Office Phone: 301-229-7439. Personal E-mail: jmcgurn@erols.com. *Providing information to our democratic public has been the work of my life both as a foreign correspondent, as a government spokesman, and as a lecturer. The newsman and the person who speaks for government share the same objective of explaining government policy. The spokesman has an added responsibility— to help government policy succeed. The reporter and the spokesman sometimes are at war with one another, but it is a war in behalf of the same beneficiary: the people.*

MCGURN, WILLIAM BARRETT, III, lawyer; b. NYC, Apr. 3, 1943; s. Barrett and Mary Elizabeth (Johnson) McGurn; m. Catherine Roche, June 17, 1972; children: Mary Anne, Edward Johnson. BA, Yale U., 1965; JD, Harvard U., 1972. Bar: DC 1973, Paris 1992. Ptnr. Cleary, Gottlieb, Steen & Hamilton LLP, Washington, Paris, Rome, 1972—. Gov. Am. Hosp. Paris, 1991—; pres. Yale Club Italy, 2008—; chmn. Dem. Abroad, France, 1987—89; bd. dirs. Spl. Olympics Italy, 2005—. Lt. USNR, 1967—69. Mem.: ABA, Am. C. of C. France (bd. dirs. 1996—, v.p. 1998—2000, pres. 2000—02). Democrat. Home: via del Piè di Marmo 16 00186 Rome Italy Office: Cleary Gottlieb Steen and Hamilton LLP Piazza di Spagna 15 00187 Rome Italy

MCGURN, WILLIAM JOSEPH, speechwriter, editor; b. Oceanside, Calif., Dec. 4, 1958; s. William A. and Mary S. (Gormley) McG.; m. Julie Ann Hoffman, Apr. 24, 1993; 3 adopted children: Grace, Maisie, Lucy BA in Philosophy, U. Notre Dame, 1980; MS in Comm., Boston U., 1981. Asst. mng. editor The American Spectator, Bloomington, Ind., 1981-83; mng. editor This World mag., NYC, 1983-84; editl. features editor The Wall St. Jour. Europe, Brussels, 1984-86; dep. editl. page editor The Asian Wall St. Jour., Hong Kong, 1987-89; bur. chief Nat. Rev., Washington, 1989-92; sr. editor Far Eastern Econ. Rev., Hong Kong, 1992—98; chief editl. writer The Wall St. Jour., 1999—2003; exec., Office of the Chmn. News Corp., 2004—05; asst. to Pres. for speechwriting The White House, Washington, 2005—. Mem. editl. bd. The Wall St. Jour., 1998—2003. Editor: Basic Law, Basic Questions, 1988; author: Perfidious Albion: The Abandonment of Hong Kong, 1997; co-author: Is the Market Moral: A Dialogue on Religion, Economics & Justice, 2004 Named to Outstanding Young Men of Am., 1991. Mem. Fgn. Corr. Assn., Nat. Press Club, Notre Dame Club of Hong Kong (pres. 1993—). Office: The White House 1600 Pennsylvania Ave Washington DC 20500

MCHALE, DAVID R., utilities executive; b. Thompson, Conn. BS, So. Conn. State Univ., 1982; MBA, Univ. New Haven, 1986. Intern Northeast Utilities Sys., Hartford, Conn., 1981—82, rsch. analyst, 1982—86, fin. analyst, 1986—93, mgr. project & short-term fin., 1993—95, asst. treas., 1995—98, v.p., treas., 1998—2004, v.p. strategic bus. plans, 2004—05, sr. v.p., CFO, 2005—09, exec. v.p., CFO, 2009—. Fellow: Am. Leadership Forum (sr.); mem.: Edison Elec. Inst. Mailing: Northeast Utilities Sys PO Box 270 Hartford CT 06141-0270*

MCHALE, EDWARD ROBERTSON, retired lawyer; b. Chgo., Jan. 24, 1921; s. Edward F. and Martha (Robertson) McH.; m. Helen Louise Lindgren, Aug. 28, 1953; children: Nancy Ellen McHale Kaufman, Sally Jane McHale Cutler, John Robertson. BSS., Northwestern U., 1942; LL.B., Harvard U., 1948. Bar: Calif. 1949. Asst. U.S. atty. U.S. atty. So. Dist. Calif., 1949—61, chief tax div., 1954—61; assoc. Mitchell, Silberberg & Knupp, Los Angeles, 1961—64, ptnr., 1965—86, mgr. litigation dept, 1978—82; pres. Edward R. McHale, P.C., 1979—86; ret., 1986. Lectr. U. So. Calif. Law Center, 1958-61 Co-author: Handling Federal Tax Litigation, 1961. Served to lt. USNR, 1943-46. Mem. Fed. Bar Assn. (past pres. Los Angeles chpt., past nat. v.p. for 9th Circuit), Assn. Bus. Trial Lawyers (bd. govs. 1981-83), State Bar Calif., Delta Sigma Rho. Clubs: South Hills Country (West Covina); Clan Donnachaidh Soc. Lutheran. Home: 1116 S Serena Dr West Covina CA 91791-3754 E-mail: casu8@earthlink.net.

MCHALE, JOHN JOSEPH, JR., major league baseball executive, former professional sports team executive; b. Detroit, 1949; s. John J. and Patricia (Cameron) McH.; m. Sally McHale; children: Duncan, William, Frances. Grad., U. Notre Dame, 1971; JD, Boston Coll., 1975; LLM, Georgetown U., 1982. Lawyer, Denver, 1981-91; chmn. bd. Denver MLB Stadium Dist., 1989-91; exec. v.p. baseball ops. Colo. Rockies, 1991-93, exec. v.p. ops., 1993; pres., CEO Detroit Tigers, 1995—2001; COO Tampa Bay Devil Rays, 2001—02; exec. v.p. adminstrn. MLB, 2002—. Dir. Maj. League Baseball Enterprises; mem. baseball ops. com. Maj. League Baseball. Chmn. Southeast Mich. WalkAm., March of Dimes, 1996, 97; mem. pres. adv. coun. Henry Ford Mus., Greenfield Village; bd. dirs. caring athletes team Children's Hosp., Henry Ford Hosp. Office: Major League Baseball 245 Park Ave 31st Fl New York NY 10165 Fax: 313-965-2138.

MCHALE, JUDITH A., federal agency administrator, former broadcast executive; b. NYC, 1947; m. Michael McHale; 2 children. B in Politics, U. Nottingham, Eng.; JD, Fordham U.Law Sch., 1979. Atty. Battle, Fowler, NYC; gen. counsel MTV Networks, Discovery Comm., Inc., 1987, sr. v.p., gen. counsel, exec. v.p., gen. counsel, pres., COO, 1995—2004, pres., CEO, 2004—06; mng. ptnr. GEF/Africa Growth Fund, 2006—09; under sec. for pub. diplomacy & pub. affairs US Dept. State, Washington, 2009—. Bd. dirs. Polo/Ralph Lauren, 2001—09, Host Hotels & Resorts Inc., 2006—09, DigitalGlobe Inc., 2008—09. Mem. Md. State Bd. of Edn., 1997—2001; bd. dirs. John Hancock Co., Potomac Electric Power Co., Cable in the Classroom, Vital Voices Global Partnership, Africa Soc., Africare, Sister-to-Sister Everyone Has a Heart Found. Office: US Dept State 2201 C St NW Rm 7261 Washington DC 20520*

MCHALE, MAUREEN BERNADETTE KENNY, controller; b. Scranton, Pa., July 2, 1955; d. John Theodore and Ann Marie (Slowey) McH. BFA cum laude, Wilkes Coll., 1977; postgrad., Wilkes Coll., Rome, 1977; MBA in Acctg. with honors, U. Notre Dame, 1984; MST with honors, Kings Coll., 1995. Internal auditor Cen. Tax Bur., Forty Fort, Pa., 1977-82; placement coord. U. Notre Dame, South Bend, Ind., 1983-84; sr. acct. Laventhol and Horwath, Wilkes Barre, Pa., 1984-88; contr. Greco Holdings, Inc., Wilkes Barre, 1988-97; dir. fin. Mercy Health Care Ctr., Nanticoke, Pa., 1997—2000; CFO Little Flower Manor/St. Thérèse Residence, Wilkes-Barre, Pa., 2000—. Founder Entrepreneurship Lecture Series, U. Notre Dame, 1984. Leader Girl Scouts US, Forty Fort, 1977-82; mem. exec. com., bd. dirs. Bishop O'Reilly HS, 1990—; bd. dirs. Northeastern Pa. Choral Soc., 1996-2000, Mercy Ctr.; pres. bd. dirs. St. Michael's Sch., 2005—. U. Notre Dame Scholar, 1984. Mem. Jaycees (bd. dirs. 1987-88), U. Notre Dame Alumni Assn. (bd. dirs., pres. Scranton chpt. 2004—) Democrat. Roman Catholic. Avocations: walking, bicycling, football. Home: 31 Virginia Ter Forty Fort PA 18704-4929 Office: 200 S Meade St Wilkes Barre PA 18702-6221 Office Phone: 570-823-6131. E-mail: mmchale@lfmstr.com.

MCHALE, PAUL F., JR., lawyer, former United States Representative from Pennsylvania; b. Bethlehem, Pa., July 26, 1950; m. Katherine McHale; children: Matthew, Mary, Luke. BA in Govt. sigma cum laude, Lehigh U., 1972; JD, Georgetown U. Law Sch., 1977. Atty., Bethlehem, 1977—82; mem. Pa. House of Reps., 1983—92, US Congress from 15th Pa. dist., 1993—99, Tallman, Hudders and Sorrentino, Allentown, Pa., 1999—2003; asst. sec. for homeland def. & America's security affairs

US Dept. Def., Washington, 2003—09; of counsel McKenna Long & Aldridge LLP, Washington, 2009—. Infantry officer USMC, 1972—74, Okinawa, Philippines, maj. USMCR, 1990—92, Persian Gulf. Decorated Navy Commendation medal; recipient Disting. Pub. Svc. medal, US Dept. Def., Frank M. Tejada Leadership award, Marine Corps. Reserve Officers Assn., 1997, Reserve Officers Assn. Minuteman of the Yr. award, 1998, Baryal medal. Mem.: Phi Beta Kappa. Democrat. Office: McKenna Long & Aldridge LLP 1900 K St NW Washington DC 20006 Office Phone: 202-496-7781. Office Fax: 202-496-7756. E-mail: pmchale@mckennalong.com.*

MCHALE, VINCENT EDWARD, political science professor; b. Jenkins Twp., Pa., Apr. 17, 1939; m. Ann Barbara Cotner, Nov. 8, 1963; 1 child, Patrick James. A.B., Wilkes Coll., 1964; M.A., Pa. State U., 1966, Ph.D. in Polit. Sci., 1969. Asst. prof. polit. sci. U. Pa., Phila., 1969-75, dir. grad. studies, 1971-73; assoc. prof. Case Western Res. U., Cleve., 1975-84, prof., 1984-03, chmn. dept. polit. sci., 1978-03; vis. lectr. John Carroll U., summer 1980, Beaver Coll., 1975; Marcus A. Hanna prof., 2006—. Author: (with A.P. Frognier and D. Paranzino) Vote, Clivages Socio-politiques et Developpement Regional en Belgique, 1974. Co-editor; contbr.: Evaluating Transnational Programs in Government and Business, 1980; Political Parties of Europe, 1983; edtl. adv. bd. Worldmark Ency. of Nations, 1994—. Contbr. chpts. to books, articles to profl. jours. Project cons. Council Econ Opportunity in Greater Cleve., 1978-81; mem. Morris Abrams Award Com., 1977—. Recipient Outstanding Prof. award Lux chpt. Mortar Bd., 1989, 90; named one of Most Interesting People of 1988, Cleve. Mag.; NSF grantee, 1971-72; HEW grantee, 1976-78; Woodrow Wilson fellow, 1968, Ruth Young Boucke fellow, 1967-68; All-Univ. fellow, 1967-68. Mem. Phi Kappa Phi. Home: 3070 Coleridge Rd Cleveland OH 44118-3556 Office: Case Western Res U Cleveland OH 44106 Office Phone: 216-368-2425. Business E-Mail: vem@case.edu.

MCHARD, JAMES LORIN, corporate financial executive, freelance/self-employed composer, writer; b. Bay City, Mich., June 23, 1942; s. James Alvah and Daisy Evelyn McHard; m. Jerilee Miles, June 6, 1964 (div. May 15, 1985); m. Alice Brallie Dekle, May 24, 1997; children: Maureen Day, Clair James Ian. BS, U. Mich., 1964. Cert. secondary sch. tchr. Mich. Engring. fin. analyst Ford Motor Co., Livonia, Mich., 1964—97; pres. J & A Music Enterprises, Mich. Freelance composer, lectr., writer; lectr. music theory. Composer: Tremors, 1991, Virtuals, 1992; editor: Voice of Reason newsletter, 1980—82; author: The Future of Modern Music, 2001, Julio Estrada, Five Years of ONCE, Pape: Cinema Texas, 2002; contbr. articles to profl. jours.; pub.: program notes for premiere of Estrada's opera ISCM New Music Festival. Mem.: Southern Poverty Law Ctr. (name included on Wall of Tolerance), Electronic Music Found., S.E. Mich. Horn Club (assoc.; sec. 1985—88). Home: 28860 Richland Livonia MI 48150 Personal E-mail: release10@sbcglobal.net.

MC HARGUE, CARL JACK, lab administrator; b. Jan. 30, 1926; s. John David and Virginia (Thomas) McH.; m. Edith Trovillion, Aug. 28, 1948; children: Anne Odell McHargue Diegel, Carol Virginia Hornberger, Margaret Katherine McHargue; m. Betty Ford, Sept. 30, 1960. BS in Metall. Engring., U. Ky., 1949, MS, 1951, PhD, 1953. Instr. U. Ky., Lexington, 1949-53; with Oak Ridge Nat. Lab., 1953-90, sect. head, 1960-80, program mgr. for materials scis., 1961-88, sr. rsch. staff, 1980-90; prof. materials sci. and engring. U. Tenn., Knoxville, 1991—, dir. ctr. materials processing, 1991—. Vis. prof. U. Newcastle upon Tyne, Eng., 1987; adj. prof. Vanderfilt U., 1988—; bd. dirs. Accreditation Bd. for Engring. and Tech., 1998—; bd. dirs. The Minerals, Metals and Materials Soc. Contbr. numerous articles in field to profl. jours. With AUS, 1944-46. Recipient Disting. Svc. award The Minerals, Metals and Materials Soc., 2001; named to Engring. Hall of Distinction, U. Ky., 1995. Fellow Metall. Soc. AIME, Am. Soc. for Metals; mem. Materials Rsch. Soc., Sigma Xi, Tau Beta Pi, Accreditation Bd. Engring. Tech. Republican. Presbyterian. Home: 7201 Sheffield Dr Knoxville TN 37909-2414 Office: U Tenn 514 E Stadium Hill Knoxville TN 37996-0750 Office Phone: 865-974-7680. Business E-Mail: crl@utk.edu.

MCHENRY, BARNABAS, lawyer; b. Harrisburg, Pa., Oct. 30, 1929; s. William Cecil and Louise (Perkins) McH.; m. Marie Bannon Jones, Dec. 13, 1952; children: Thomas J.P., W.H. Davis, John W.H. AB, Princeton U., 1952; LLB, Columbia U., 1957. Bar: N.Y. 1957. Assoc. Lord, Day, & Lord, NYC, 1957-62; gen. counsel The Reader's Digest Assn., Inc., NYC, 1962-85; exec. dir. Wallace Funds, NYC, 1985-86; chmn. N.Y. state orgns., 1986—. Trustee, pres. Boscobel Restoration, Inc., 1964; trustee Am. Conservation Assn., 1977; trustee emeritus Met. Mus. Art, 1980; coun. mem. Villa I Tatti, Harvard Sch. Renaissance Studies, 1982; regent emeritus Smithsonian Instn., 1985; commr. Palisades Interstate Park Commn., 1987; chmn. Hudson River Valley Greenway Coun., 1989; co-chair Hudson River Valley Nat. Heritage Assn., 1996.

MCHENRY, BART, academic administrator; MFA, U. Calif., Irvine; BFA in Acting, U. Southern Calif., LA. Chair dept. theater, film and TV Azusa Pacific U., Azusa, Calif., 2006—.

MCHENRY, HENRY MALCOLM, anthropologist, educator; b. LA, May 19, 1944; s. Dean Eugene and Emma Jane (Snyder) McH.; m. Linda Jean Conway, June 25, 1966; children: Lindsay Jean, Annalisa Jane. BA, U. Calif., Davis, 1966, MA, 1967; PhD, Harvard U., 1972. Asst. prof. anthropology U. Calif., Davis, 1971-76, assoc. prof. anthropology, 1976-81, prof. anthropology, 1981—, chmn. dept. anthropology, 1984-88. Fellow AAAS, Am. Anthrop. Assn., Calif. Acad. Sci.; mem. Am. Assn. Phys. Anthropologists (exec. com. 1981-85), Soc. Study Evolution, Soc. Vertebrate Paleontology, Phi Beta Kappa, Phi Kappa Phi. Democrat. Buddhist. Avocation: winemaker. Home: 330 11th St Davis CA 95616-2010 Office: U of Calif Davis Dept Of Anthropology Davis CA 95616 Office Phone: 530-752-1588. Business E-Mail: hmmchenry@ucdavis.edu.

MCHENRY, JANICE, councilwoman; BS, Ind. U., Bloomington; MS, Butler U., Indpls. Elem. sch. tchr. Mill Creek East Elem. Sch., Ind.; councillor, dist. 6 Indpls.-Marion County City-County Coun., Indpls. Precinct committeeman Wayne Twp., Ind., ward chmn.; asst. chmn. Pike Twp., Ind. Vol. Pan Am Games, Police and Fire Games, Red Cross, Taste of Pike; founder, children's book program Wayne Twp. Trustees Office; poor relief com. Wayne Twp., walk coord., 2002, 2004, 2006, Pike Twp., 2006; del., Ind. state convention Rep. Party; cmty. svc. chmn., recording sec., Americanism chmn., dir. GIRWC; cmty. svc. chmn. WINS; mem. adv. bd. Divsn. Equal Opportunity Contract Compliance Com. Mem.: Pike Twp. Rep. Club (corr. sec., v.p., pres.), Wayne Twp. GOP Club (bd. dirs.), Eagle Creek GOP Club (recording sec.). Republican. Office: 7641 Torbay Cir Indianapolis IN 46254 also: Indpls Marion County City County Coun 241 City County Bldg 200 E Washington St Indianapolis IN 46204 Office Phone: 317-298-5285, 317-327-4242. Business E-Mail: jfmchenry@iquest.net.*

MCHENRY, JONATHAN KEITH, artist; BFA, Boston U., 1984. Founder Food Not Bombs, Boston, 1980—, Taos Peace House, N.Mex., 2007—08. Author: (book) Food Not Bombs How to Feed the Hungry and Build Community. Recipient Clio awards, 1984—85. Avocations: swimming, painting, bicycling, drawing. Home: 801 Paseo Del Pueblo Norte Taos NM 87571 Office: Food Not Bombs PO Box 424 Arroyo Seco NM 87514 Business E-Mail: keith@foodnotbombs.net.

MCHENRY, MARTIN CHRISTOPHER, physician, educator; b. Feb. 9, 1932; s. Merl and Marcella (Bricca) McH.; m. Patricia Grace Hughes, Apr. 27, 1957; children: Michael, Christopher, Timothy, Mary Ann, Jeffrey, Paul, Kevin, William, Monica, Martin Christopher. Student, U. Santa Clara, 1950-53; MD, U. Cin., 1957; MS in Medicine, U. Minn., 1966. Diplomate Am. Bd. Internal Medicine. Intern Highland Alameda County (Calif.) Hosp., Oakland, 1957-58; resident, internal medicine fellow Mayo Clinic, Rochester, Minn., 1958-61, spl. appointee in infectious diseases, 1963-64; staff physician Henry Ford Hosp., Detroit, 1964-67, Cleve. Clinic, 1967-72, chmn. dept. infectious diseases, 1972-92, sr. physician infectious diseases, 1992-98. Cons. infectious diseases, 1998—2006; asst. clin. prof. Case Western Res. U., 1970-77, assoc. clin. prof. medicine, 1977-91, clin. prof. medicine, 1991—2006; assoc. vis. physician Cleve. Met. Gen. Hosp., 1970-00; cons. VA Hosp., Cleve., 1973-74. Contbr. more than 100 articles to profl. jours., also chpts. to books. Chmn. manpower com. Swine Influenza Program, Cleve., 1976. With USNR, 1961-63. Named Disting. Tchr. in Medicine, Cleve. Clinic, 1972, 90; recipient 1st ann. Bruce Hubbard Stewart award Cleve. Clinic Found. for Humanities in Medicine, 1985, Nightingale Physician Collaboration award Cleve. Clinic Found. Divsn. Nursing, 1995, Clinician of Yr. award Acad. Medicine of Cleve./No. Ohio Med. Assn., 2002. Fellow ACP, Infectious Diseases Soc. Am. (Clinician award 2000), Am. Coll. Chest Physicians (chmn. com. cardiopulmonary infections 1975-77, 81-83), Royal Soc. Medicine of Gt. Britain; mem. Am. Soc. Clin. Pharmacology and Therapeutics (chmn. sect. infectious diseases and antimicrobial agts. 1970-77, 80-85, dir.). Home: 2779 Belgrave Rd Pepper Pike OH 44124-4601 Office: 9500 Euclid Ave Cleveland OH 44195-0001

MCHENRY, PATRICK TIMOTHY, United States Representative from North Carolina; b. Mecklenburg, NC, Oct. 22, 1975; Attended, NC State U.; BA in Hist., Belmont Abbey Coll., 1999. Exec. DCI/New Media, Inc., Washington; owner & broker McHenry Real Estate, Gastonia, NC; spl. asst. to Sec. Elaine L. Chao US Dept. Labor, Washington, 2000; mem. NC State Ho. Reps., 2003—05, US Congress from 10th NC dist., 2005—. Mem. fin svcs. com. US Congress, 2005—, mem. budget com., mem. oversight and govt. reform com., vice chmn. fin. for exec. com. Nat. Rep. Congl. Com., dep. Rep. whip. Bd. dirs. United Success by Six Youth Prog. Recipient Spirit of Enterprise award, US C. of C.; named a Small Bus. Champion, Small Bus. and Entrepreneurship Coun., Hero of the Taxpayer, Ams. for Tax Reform, Protector of Property Rights, Property Rights Alliance. Mem.: Gaston C. of C., NRA, Gastonia Rotary Club. Republican. Roman Catholic. Office: US House Reps 224 Cannon House Office Bldg Washington DC 20515-3310 Office Phone: 202-225-2576. Office Fax: 202-225-0316.*

MCHOSE, ANDRE H., industrial engineer; b. Bethlehem, Pa., Jan. 30, 1920; s. Howard H. and Hermina (Wiengartner) McH.; m. Joy N. Wirthlin, June 1, 1946; children: Michael, Caryn, Brian, Robert, Marilyn. BSME, Antioch Coll., 1944; MS in Indsl. Engring., Pa. State U., 1959. Registered profl. engr., Pa. Mfg. engr. Dictaphone, Western Electric, Bridgeport, Conn., 1945-58, Allentown, Pa., 1945-58; engring. instr. Pa. State U., Allentown, 1948-50; sr. engr. HRB-Singer, State College, Pa., 1958-61; project mgr. Automation Systems, Stanford, Conn., 1961-65; mgmt. cons. Andre McHose Cons., Ridgefield, Conn., 1965-92. Author: Manufacturing Development Applications, 1992. Mem. Inst. of Indsl. Engrs. (sr. mem., pres. S.W. Conn. chpt. 1957-58). Achievements include co-inventor of automatic sewing method and apparatus. Home: 514 Cushing Rd Newmarket NH 03857-1738 Home Phone: 603-659-4567; Office Phone: 603-659-4567. Personal E-mail: ahmch@comcast.net.

MCHUGH, JAMES JOSEPH, JR., lawyer; b. Phila., Sept. 15, 1961; s. James Joseph and Helene Anne (Kiernan) McHugh; m. Colette Marie McHugh, May 20, 1989; children: Albert Taylor, James Joseph III, Cole Michael, Sophia Kiernan. BSME, Drexel U., 1985; JD magna cum laude, Villanova U., Pa., 1992. Bar: Pa. 1992, N.J. 1992, U.S. Dist. Ct. (ea. dist.) Pa., U.S. Dist. Ct. N.J. Ptnr. McHugh Plumbing & Heating, Phila., 1984-89; project mgr. Fluidics Mech Contractors, Phila., 1989-92; assoc. Pepper, Hamilton & Scheetz, Phila., 1992-94; ptnr. The Beasley Firm, LLC, Phila., 1994—2006, Lopez McHugh LLP, Calif., NJ, Pa., 2006—. Author, editor case notes. Mem. adv. com. Penn Pub. Svc. Program, Sch. Law, U. Pa. Mem. ATLA, ABA, Pa. Assn. Justice, Pa. Bar Assn., Phila. Bar Assn., Order of Coif. Home: 65 Brooks Rd Moorestown NJ 08057-3855 Office: Lopez McHugh LLP 1123 Admiral Peary Way Quarters K Philadelphia PA 19112 Office Phone: 215-952-6910. Business E-Mail: jmchugh@lopezmchugh.com.

MCHUGH, JOHN MICHAEL, United States Representative from New York; b. Watertown, NY, Sept. 29, 1948; s. Donald and Jane (O'Neill) McHugh. BA in Polit. Sci., Syracuse U. Utica Coll., 1970; MPA, SUNY Nelson A. Rockefeller Grad. Sch. Pub. Affairs, 1977. Asst. city mgr., Watertown, NY, 1968-73; confidential asst. to city mgr., 1971-76; chief rsch., liaison with local govts. Staff of NY State Senator H. Douglas Barclay, 1976-84; mem. NY State Senate, 1985—93, chmn. joint legis. commn. on dairy industry devel., 1987-92; mem. US Congress from 23rd NY dist., 1993—, mem. oversight and govt. reform com., mem. armed svcs. com., ranking mem. mil. pers. subcommittee, mem. permanent select com. on intelligence. Recipient Individual Achievement award, NY State Dept. Econ. Devel., George (Buck) Gillespie award, Blinded Am. Vets. Found., 1999, President's award, Nat. Newspaper Assn., 2000, Outstanding Legislator award, Assn. US Army, 2003, Friend of Zion award, Jerusalem Fund, 2004, Pub. Svc. award, Direct Mktg. Assn. Nonprofit Fedn., 2004, Bertrand H. Snell award, Clarkson U., 2005; named Hon. First Citien, City of Watertown, NY, 1976. Mem. Legis. on State Legislators (nat. conf. state legislators), Nat. Conf. State Legislators (vice chmn. agrl. and internat. trade com. State-Fed. Assembly), Am. Soc. Young Polit. Leaders. Republican. Roman Catholic. Avocations: boating, skiing, music. Office: 120 Washington St Ste 200 Watertown NY 13601-3370 also: 2366 Rayburn House Office Bldg Washington DC 20515 Office Phone: 202-225-4611, 315-782-3150. Office Fax: 315-782-1291.*

MCHUGH, MILES WILLIAM, corporate financial executive; b. Evanston, Ill., Sept. 26, 1964; s. Raymond Thomas and Mary Anne Theresa (Murphy) McH.; m. Susan Kay Bogner, Oct. 13, 1990. BS in Accountancy, U. Ill., 1986; MBA, Univ. Chgo., 1993. CPA, Ill. Staff acct. Price Waterhouse, Chgo., 1986-88, sr. acct., 1988-89; asst. v.p. Westpac Banking Corp., Chgo.; asst. contr. Mirant Corp., 2000—02; contr. DPL Inc., 2003; asst. contr. R.R. Donnelley & Sons, Chgo., 2003—04; CFO R.R. Donnelley Logistics, Chgo., 2004—06; sr. v.p., corp. contr. R.R. Donnelley & Sons, Chgo., 2006—07, exec. v.p., CFO, 2007—. Ptnr., treas. Envirogard Rsch. Assocs., Chgo., 1988-90. V.p. ops. Pro-Life Assn. North Side, Chgo., 1989-90. Mem. AICPA, Ill. CPA Soc. Roman Catholic. Avocations: golf, basketball, skiing. Office: RR Donnelley & Sons 111 S Wacker Dr Chicago IL 60606-4301

MCHUGH, PAUL R., psychiatrist, neurologist, educator; b. Lawrence, Mass., May 21, 1931; s. Francis Paul and Mary Dorothea (Herlihy) McH.; m. Jean Barlow, Dec. 27, 1959; children: Clare Mary, Patrick Daniel, Denis Timothy. AB, Harvard U., 1952, MD, 1956. Diplomate: Am. Bd. Psychiatry and Neurology. Intern Peter Bent Brigham Hosp., Boston, 1956-57; resident in neurology Mass. Gen. Hosp., 1957-60, fellow in neuropathology, 1958-59; teaching fellow in neurology and neuropathology Harvard, 1957-60; clin. asst. psychiatry Maudsley Hosp., London, Eng., 1960-61; mem. neuropsychiatry div. Walter Reed Army Inst. Research, Washington, 1961-64; asst. prof. psychiatry and neurology Cornell U., NYC, 1964-68, assoc. prof., 1968-71, prof., 1971; dir. electroencephalography N.Y. Hosp., 1964-68; founder, dir. N.Y. Hosp. Bourne Behavioral Rsch. Lab., 1967-68, clin. dir., supr. psychiat. edn., founder, dir. Weschester divsn. dept. psychiatry, 1968-73; prof., chmn. dept. psychiatry U. Oreg. Health Sci. Center, Portland, 1973-75; Henry Phipps prof. psychiatry Johns Hopkins U. Sch. Medicine, Balt., 1975—2001, chmn. dept. psychiatry, 1975—2001, dir. dept. psychiatry and behavioral sciences, univ. disting. svc. prof. psychiatry, prof. dept. mental hygiene, 1976; psychiatrist-in-chief Johns Hopkins Hosp., 1975—2001, chmn. med. staff, 1983-89, trustee, 1983—89; dir. Blades Ctr. for Clin. Practice and Rsch. in Alcoholism Johns Hopkins Med. Inst., 1992—2001; prof. mental health John Hopkins Bloomberg Sch. Pub. Health. Author: The Perspectives of Psychiatry, 1983, 1998; (with Phillip R. Slavney) Psychiatric Polarities, 1987, Genes, Brain and Behavior, 1990, The Mind Has Mountains: Reflections on Society and Psychiatry, 2006; contbg. author: Cecil-Loeb Textbook of Medicine; mem. editl. bd. Am. Jour. Physiology, Jour. Nervous and Mental Disease, Comprehensive Psychiatry, Medicine, Psychol. Medicine, 1976—, Am. Scholar; contbr. articles to profl. jours. Mem. Md. Gov.'s Adv. Com., 1977—80, U.S. Conf. Cath. Bishops Nat. Rev. Bd. Office of Child and Youth Protection, 2002—07, Pres. Coun. on Bioethics, 2001—; serving on False Memory Syndrome Found.; advisor Assn. for Rsch. in Nervous and Mental Disease. Grantee NIH, 1964-68, 67-70, 70-74, 75-96; recipient William C. Menninger award ACP, 1987. Fellow: Am. Psychiat. Assn., Royal Coll. Psychiatry; mem.: Am. Coll. Psychiatrists (Disting. Svc. award 2002), Pavlovian Soc., Am. Psychopath. Assn. (Joseph Zubin award 1995, Paul Hoch award 2006), Am. Coll. Neuropsychopharmacology (co-chmn., ethics com.), Harvey Soc., Am. Physiol. Soc., Am. Neurol. Assn., Inst. Medicine (Rhonda and Bernard Sarnat Internat. prize in Mental Health 2008), W Hamilton St. Club, Phi Beta Kappa (vis. scholar 2003—04). Home: 3707 St Paul St Baltimore MD 21218-2403 Office: Johns Hopkins Med Insts Meyer 127 615 N Wolfe St Baltimore MD 21205 Office Phone: 410-502-3150. Office Fax: 410-502-3152. Business E-Mail: pmchugh1@jhmi.edu.

MCHUGH, THOMAS EDWARD, state supreme court justice, lawyer; b. Charleston, W.Va., Mar. 26, 1936; s. Paul and Melba McHugh; m. Judith McHugh, Mar. 14, 1959; children: Karen, Cindy, James, John. AB, W.Va. U., 1958, LLB, 1964. Bar: W.Va. 1964. Pvt. practice law, Charleston, 1964-66, 69-74; law clk. to presiding judge Harlan Calhoun W.Va. Supreme Ct. of Appeals, 1966-68; chief judge Cir. Ct. (13th cir.) W.Va., Charleston, 1974-80; justice W.Va. Supreme Ct. of Appeals, Charleston, 1980-97, 2008—, chief justice, 1984, 88, 92; atty, mediation practice Allen Guthrie McHugh & Thomas, PLLC, Charleston, 1997—2003, of counsel, 2003—. Served to 1st lt. U.S. Army, 1958-61. Mem. W.Va. Jud. Assn., W.Va. Bar Assn., Order of the Coif. Democrat. Roman Catholic. Office: Allen Guthrie McHugh & Thomas PLLC PO Box 3394 500 Lee St E Charleston WV 25333-3394 also: WVa Supreme Ct Appeals Capitol Complex Bldg 1 Rm E-308 Charleston WV 25305*

MCHUGHEN, ALAN, geneticist, educator; b. Ottawa, Ontario, Can., Apr. 13, 1954; m. Donna Greschner; children: Stephanie, Nicola. PhD, Oxford U., Eng., 1979. Lectr. Yale U., New Haven, 1979—82; prof. U. Saskatchewan, Canada, 1982—2001; prof., botany and plant scis. U. Calif., Riverside, 2002—. Author: Pandora's Picnic Basket (Book of Yr., Can. Sci.Writers Assn., 2000); contbr. articles to profl. jours. Pres. Internat. Soc. for Biosafety Rsch., Riverside, 1988—2004. Fellow, Am. Coll. Nutrition, 2002, Am. Assn. Advancement Sci., 2009. Fellow: AAAS. Achievements include patents in field, including one of the first for a higher lifeform; development of public sector commercial transgenic and conventional crop cultivars. Office: Univ Calif University Ave Riverside CA 92521-0124 Office Fax: 951-827-5717. Business E-Mail: alanmc@ucr.edu.

MCILROY, ALAN F., manufacturing executive; b. 1950; Internat. contr. Wheelabrator Corp., 1983-87; bus. unit contr. Gen. Chem., 1987-90; sr. v.p. Harris Chem.; head Greenock Group; CFO Dayton Superior Corp., Miamisburg, Ohio, 1997—2007.

MCILROY, M. DOUGLAS, computer scientist, educator; m. Barbara McIlroy. BS, Cornell U., 1958; PhD in Applied Math., MIT, 1959. Lectr. MIT, 1957—58; joined Bell Labs., Murray Hill, NJ, 1958, head Computing Techniques Rsch. Dept., 1965—86, disting. mem. tech. staff Computing Scis. Rsch. Ctr.; adj. prof. Dept. Computer Sci. Dartmouth Coll., Hanover, NH, 1997—. Vis. lectr. Oxford U., 1967—68. Contbr. articles to profl. jours. Mem.: NAE. Office: Dartmouth Coll Dept Computer Sci 6211 Sudikoff Hall Hanover NH 03755 Office Phone: 603-464-1077. E-mail: mcilroy@dartmouth.edu.

MCILVAIN, PETER JAMES, literature and language professor; b. Little Rock, Oct. 17, 1983; d. Richard Lee McIlvain and Sandra Folden Branstiter. MA, U. Memphis, Tenn., 2008. Busboy China Royal, Bartlett, Tenn., 2000—02; package handler Fed. Express, Memphis, 2002—05; tchg. asst. U. Memphis, 2006—08. Independent. Home and Office: Guandong Med Coll Dongguan 523808 China Business E-Mail: pmcilvan@memphis.edu.

MCILVAINE, PATRICIA MORROW, physician; b. Pitts., Feb. 4, 1947; d. James Morrow McIlvaine and Virginia Fuller Tucker. BS in Chemistry, Simmons Coll., 1969; MD, U. Utah, 1984. Rsch. technician Mass. Gen. Hosp., Boston, 1969-70, MIT, Cambridge, 1970-75, Utah State U., Logan, 1975-80; resident in internal medicine U. Mass. Hosp., Worcester, 1984-87; pvt. practice, Monson, Mass., 1987-2001; mem. pvt. group practice Walla Walla (Wash.) Clinic, 2002—. Staff physician Wing Meml. Hosp., Palmer, Mass., 1987-2001. Vol., trainer IRBIS Enterprises, Mongolia, 1998-2004. NFS summer scholar, 1968, Helena Rubinstein scholar Simmons Coll., 1968-69. Mem. ACP/Am. Soc. Internal Medicine, Sigma Xi. Avocations: fiber crafts, international travel, hiking, gardening, sailing. Home: 913 Bonnie Brae Walla Walla WA 99362

MCILVAINE, ROBERT MORTON, literature educator; b. Vernon, Tex., Dec. 28, 1943; s. Paul Morton McIlvaine and Nancy Juanita Wickliffe; m. Martha Briegel McIlvaine, July 27, 1966; children: Jessica, Miranda. BA, Davis & Elkins Coll., W.Va., 1966; MA, U. Pa., 1967; PhD, Temple U., 1972. From asst. prof. to prof. Slippery Rock

(Pa.) U., 1972—83, prof., 1983—. Contbr. articles to profl. jours. Home: PO Box 144 110 McIlvaine Ln Slippery Rock PA 16057 Office: Slippery Rock University 312D Spotts WCB Slippery Rock PA 16057 Office Phone: 724-738-2351. Business E-Mail: robert.mcilvaine@sru.edu.

MCILVANE, EDWARD JAMES, stained glass artist, educator; b. NYC, July 5, 1947; s. Edward James Sr. and Irene (Logue) McI.; m. Rose F. Aloisi, 1970 (div. 1985); children: Jessica, Blake. BS in Edn. and Art Edn., St. John's U., NYC, 1975; MFA, R.I. Sch. Design, 1978. Stained glass craftsman Claude Gaches Studio, LI, 1969-71, The Lamb Studio, N.J., 1971-72, Greenland Studio, NYC, 1972-75, Helmut-Schardt Studio, Northport, N.Y., 1975-78; freelance artist and designer Providence, 1978—. Guest artist Summrvail Workshop for Art, Vail, Colo., 1980, N.Y. Exptl. Glass Workshop, N.Y.C., 1980; program coord. Pilchuck Sch., Stanwood, Wash., 1979; instr. Haystack Mt. Sch. Crafts, Deer Isle, Maine, 1977. Prin. works include Johnson's Wax Co., Rancine, Wis., Temple Beth-El, Prov, R.I., Providence Coll., Bank of Boston, Joseph W. Martin, Jr. Inst. for Law and Soc. Stonehill Coll., North Easton, Mass., Licht residence, Little Compton, R.I., Vinyl Tech. Sch., Middletown, Conn., Presbyn. World Hdqs., Louisville. R.I. State Coun. on the Arts fellow, 1980, 86, Nat. Endowment for the Arts fellow, 1983. Mem. Glass Art Soc. Avocations: tai chi, angling. Home: 329 Pomfret Rd Brooklyn CT 06234 Office Phone: 860-774-4822. Personal E-mail: macdeverre@charter.net.

MCILWAIN, HARRIS H., physician, researcher; s. Cordelia B. McIL-wain; m. Linda Fulghum, June 19, 1970; children: Laura E. McILwain, Kimberly L. McILwain, Michael Fulghum McILwain, Daniel E. McIL-wain, Virginia H. McILwain, Lisa Ann McILwain. MD, Emory U., Atlanta, 1973. Diplomate Am. Bd. Internal Medicine, Am. Bd. Rheumatology, Am. Bd. Geriat. Internal medicine intern Grady Meml. Hosp., Atlanta, 1973—74; resident in internal medicine Emory U., Atlanta, 1974—76, rheumatology fellow, 1976—78; physician Tampa Med. Group, Fla., 1978—. Med. dir. John Knox Village Retirement Ctr., Tampa, 1995—. Contbr. articles to profl. jours. Bd. dirs. Fla. Osteoporosis Bd., Tampa, 1998—2003. Named one of Top Physicians in the US, Town and Country Mag., 1997, Top 100 Physicians in the US, 1998. Mem.: AMA, ACP, Assoc. Profls. in Coll. Pub. Health, Am. Med. Dirs. Assn. (cert.), Fla. Med. Assn., Hillsborough County Med. Assn., Am. Coll. Rheumatology, Alpha Omega Alpha. Avocation: soccer. Office: Tampa Med Group 4700 Habana Ave Ste 303 Tampa FL 33614 Office Phone: 813-875-9742, 813-879-5485. Personal E-mail: hmcil@aol.com.

MC ILWAIN, WILLIAM FRANKLIN, newspaper editor, writer; b. Lancaster, SC, Dec. 15, 1925; s. William Franklin and Docia (Higgins) McI.; m. Anne Dalton, Nov. 28, 1952 (div. 1973); children: Dalton, Nancy, William Franklin III; m. K. L. Brelsford, June 5, 1978 (div. 1983). BA, Wake Forest Coll., 1949; postgrad., Harvard, 1957-58. Various positions with Wilmington (N.C.) Star, 1943, Charlotte (N.C.) Observer, 1945, Jacksonville (Fla.) Jour., 1945, Winston-Salem (N.C.) Jour.-Sentinel, 1949-52, Richmond (Va.) Times-Dispatch, 1952-54; chief copy editor Newsday, Garden City, N.Y., 1954-57, day news editor, 1957-60, city editor, 1960-64, mng. editor, 1964-66, editor, 1967-70; writer-in-residence Wake Forest U., 1970-71; dorm leader Alcoholic Rehab. Ctr., Butner, N.C., 1971; dep. mng. editor Toronto Star, 1971-73; mng. editor The Record, Hackensack, N.J., 1973-77; editor Boston Herald Am., 1977-79; dep. editor Washington Star, 1979-81, exec. mng. editor, 1981; editor Ark. Gazette, 1981-82; founding editor N.Y. Newsday, 1982-84; exec. editor Sarasota (Fla.) Herald-Tribune, 1984-90; sr. editor N.Y. Times Regional Newspaper Group, 1991-92; chmn. Bill Mc Ilwain, Inc., 1993—. Author: The Glass Rooster, 1960, (with Walter Friedenberg) Legends of Baptist Hollow, 1949; collaborator: (with Newsday staff) Naked Came The Stranger, 1969, A Farewell to Alcohol, 1973, Dancing Naked with the Rolling Stones, 2007; contbr. articles to popular mags. including Reader's Digest, Harper's, Esquire, Atlantic Monthly; editor N.C. Writer's Workshop. Mem. Pres. Johnson's Commn. on Civil Rights; adv. bd. Pulitzer Prize, 1982. With USMC, 1944. Named to N.C. Journalism Hall of Fame. Mem. Am. Soc. Newspaper Editors, Soc. Nieman Fellows. Home and Office: 305 N Channel Dr Wrightsville Beach NC 28480-2723 Personal E-mail: bmcilwain77@gmail.com. *As Fats Waller said, "One never knows, do one?".*

MC INDOE, DARRELL WINFRED, retired nuclear medicine physician; b. Wilkinsburg, Pa., Sept. 28, 1930; s. Clarence Wilbert and Dorothy Josephine (Morrow) McIndoe; m. Carole Jean McClain, Aug. 23, 1952; children: Sherri L. McIndoe, Wendy L. McIndoe, Darrell B. McIndoe, Ronald S. McIndoe, Holly B. McIndoe. BS, Allegheny Coll., 1952; MD, Temple U., 1956, MS, 1960. Commd. 2d lt. M.C. US Air Force, 1956, advanced through grades to col., 1971; intern Brooke Army Med. Ctr., San Antonio, 1956-57; resident in medicine Temple U. Med. Ctr., Phila., 1957-60; chief internal medicine and Hosp. svc. Norton AFB, 1960-64; chief internal medicine and hosp. services 7520 U.S. Air Force Hosp., England, 1964-68; vis. rsch. fellow Royal Post Grad. Med. Sch., London, 1968-69; chief endocrinology svcs., chmn. dept. nuc. medicine USAF Med. Ctr., Keesler AFB, Miss., 1969-75; dep. dir. Armed Forces Radiobiology Rsch. Inst., Def. Nuc. Agy., Bethesda, Md., 1975-77, dir., 1977-79; staff physician nuc. medicine br., dept. radiology Nat. Naval Med. Ctr., Bethesda, Md., 1979-82; sr. lectr. mil. medicine Uniformed U. of Health Scis., Bethesda, Md., 1975-80; asst. prof. radiology/nuc. medicine and rsch. program coord. Uniformed U. of Health Sci., 1980-82; assoc. divsn. nuc. medicine St. Joseph Hosp., Towson, Md., 1982-91, dir. divsn. nuc. medicine, 1991—2000; ret, 2000. Med. advisor Nev. ops. office Dept. Energy, Las Vegas; cons. in field. Fellow: Am. Coll. Nuc. Physicians (regent ea. USA), Fellow royal Soc. Medicine; mem.: AMA, Soc. Med. Cons.'s to Armed Forces, Assn. Mil. Surgeons U.S., Health Physics Soc. (dir. Balt., Washington chpt.), Md. Soc. Nuc. Medicine (past pres.), Soc. Nuc. Medicine (ho. of dels.), Uniformed Svcs. Nuc. Medicine Assn. (pres. 1975), Air Force Soc. Physicians (bd. govs. 1973—77), Alexander Graham Bell Soc. Home: 15510 Foxpaw Trail Woodbine MD 21797-8000

MCINERNEY, ELAINE F., medical educator; Physician Pvt. Practice, Calif., 2004—; med. dir. In Time TV.com, Chgo., 2004—; prof. U. Chgo., 2005—. Mem.: Philippine Med. Assn. Business E-Mail: elainemcinerney@gmail.com.

MCINERNEY, JAMES EUGENE, JR., trade association executive; b. Springfield, Mass., Aug. 3, 1930; s. James Eugene and Rose Elizabeth (Adikes) McInerney; m. Mary Catherine Hill, July 17, 1963; children: Anne Elizabeth, James Eugene III. BS, U.S. Mil. Acad., 1952; MS in Engring., Princeton U., 1960; postgrad., Royal Air Force Staff Coll., 1964; MS in Internat. Affairs, George Washington U., 1970. Commd. 2d lt. USAF, 1952, advanced through grades to maj. gen., 1976, fighter pilot Republic of Korea, Japan and Germany, comdr. tactical fighter squadron S.E. Asia Thailand, 1967, tactical fighter wing Germany, 1971; sr. US adviser Turkish Air Force, 1973—75; dir. mil. assistance and sales Hdqrs. USAF, 1975-78; comdt. Indsl. Coll. Armed Forces, 1978-79; dir. programs Hdqrs. USAF, 1979-80, asst. dep. chief of staff for programs and evaluation, 1980; dir. legis. liaison McDonnell Douglas Corp., Washington, 1980-83, dir. internat. affairs, 1983-86; from v.p. to exec. v.p. Am. League for Exports and Security Assistance, 1986-92, exec. v.p., 1989-92; v.p. Am. Def. Preparedness Assn., 1992-97, Nat. Def. Indsl. Assn., 1997—. Decorated Air Force Cross, D.S.M. (2), Silver Star (3), D.F.C. (7), Bronze Star, Air medal (18), Meritorious Svc. medal (2), Air Force Commendation medal, Vietnamese Crosses of Gallantry with palm and star, Republic of Korea Cheongsu medal, comdr. Order of the Brit. Empire (CBE). Mem. Air Force Assn. (citation of honor 1968, Medal of Merit, 2002), Brit.-Am. Bus. Assn.-Washington (pres. 1982-94, chmn. 1994-96), Brit.-Am. Bus. Coun. (chmn. 1996-97), Am.-Air Mus. in Britain (exec. dir. 1984—), The Jefferson Islands Club, Capitol Hill Club, Congl. Country Club. Roman Catholic. Home: 1031 Delf Dr Mc Lean VA 22101-2009 Business E-Mail: jmcinerney@ndia.org.

MCINERNEY, JAY, writer; b. Hartford, Conn., Jan. 13, 1955; s. John Barrett and Marilyn Jean (Murphy) McI.; m. Linda Rositer, 1979 (div. 1979); m. Merry Reymond, June 2, 1984 (div. 1991); m. Helen Bransford, Dec. 27, 1991 (div. 2000); m. Anne Hearst, Nov. 21, 2006. BA in Philosophy, Williams Coll., 1976; postgrad., Syracuse U. Reporter Hunterdon County Democrat, Flemington, NJ, 1977; textbook editor Time Life Pubs., Osaka, Japan, 1978-79; fact checker New Yorker, NYC, 1980; reader Random House Pubs., NYC, 1980-81; instr. English Syracuse U., 1983; writer, 1983—. Author: (novels) Bright Lights, Big City, 1984, Ransom, 1985, Story of My Life, 1988, Brightness Falls, 1992, The Last of the Savages, 1997, Model Behavior: A Novel and 7 Stories, 2000, How It Ended, 2001, The Good Life, 2006, How It Ended: New and Collected Stories, 2009; (non-fiction) Bacchus and Me: Adventures in the Wine Cellar, 2002, A Hedonist in the Cellar: Adventures in Wine, 2006; screenwriter: (films) Bright Lights, Big City, 1988; (TV movies) Gia, 1998; (TV series) Hotel Room, 1993; actor: (TV appearances) Gossip Girl, 2009 Princeton in Asia fellow, 1977. Mem. Authors Guild, PEN, Writers Guild. Home: 25 E 9th St Penthouse New York NY 10003 Home Phone: 631-537-7668; Office Phone: 212-556-5764. Personal E-mail: bitbright@aol.com.

MCINERNEY, THOMAS J., Internet company executive; BA, Yale Univ.; MBA, Harvard Univ. Prin. Morgan Stanley, 1988—99; exec. v.p., CFO Ticketmaster, 1999—2003; CEO retailing sector IAC/Interactive Corp., NYC, 2003—05, exec. v.p., CFO, mem. office of chmn., 2004—. Office: IAC 555 W 18th St New York NY 10011

MCINERNY, RALPH MATTHEW, philosopher, educator, writer; b. Mpls., Feb. 24, 1929; s. Austin Clifford and Vivian Gertrude (Rush) McI.; m. Constance Terrill Kunert, Jan. 3, 1953 (dec. May 2001); children: Cathleen, Mary, Anne, David, Elizabeth, Daniel. BA, St. Paul Sem., 1951; MA, U. Minn., 1952; PhD summa cum laude, Laval U., 1954; LittD (hon.), St. Benedict Coll., 1978, U. Steubenville, 1984; DHL (hon.), St. Francis Coll., Joliet, Ill., 1986, St. John Fisher Coll., 1994, St. Anselm's Coll., NH, 1995, Holy Cross Coll., New Orleans, 2001, Assumption Coll., Worcester, Mass., 2007. Instr. Creighton U., 1954-55; prof. U. Notre Dame, Ind., 1955—, Michael P. Grace prof. medieval studies Ind., 1988—, dir. dept. Ind., 1978-85, dir. Jacques Martin Ctr., 1978—2005. Vis. prof. Cornell U., 1988, Cath. U., 1971, Louvain, 1983, 95; founder Internat. Cath. U.; disting. vis. prof. Truman State U., Mo., 1999; Gifford lectr. Glasgow U., Scotland, 1999-2000, Joseph lectr. Pontifical Gregorian Inst., Rome, 2003; vis. lectr. Pontifical U. of Holy Cross, Rome, 2006, Ctr. of Applied Law, Cath. U. Chile, 2006. Author: The Logic of Analogy, 1961, History of Western Philosophy, vol. 1, 1963, vol. 2, 1968, Thomism in an Age of Renewal, 1966, Studies in Analogy, 1967, New Themes in Christian Philosophy, 1967, St. Thomas Aquinas, 1976, Ethica Thomistica, 1982, History of the Ambrosiana, 1983, Being and Predication, 1986, Miracles, 1986, Art and Prudence, 1988, A First Glance at St. Thomas: Handbook for Peeping Thomists, 1989, Boethius and Aquinas, 1989, Aquinas on Human Action, 1991, The Question of Christian Ethics, 1993, Aquinas Against the Averroists, 1993, The God of Philosophers, 1994, Aquinas and Analogy, 1996, Ethica Thomistica, 1997, Student Guide to Philosophy, 1999, Vernunftgemässes Leben, 2000, Characters in Search of Their Authors, 2001, Conversion of Edith Stein, 2001, John of St. Thomas, Summa Theologiae, 2001, Defamation of Pius XII, 2001, Very Rich Hours of Jacques Maritain, 2003, Aquinas, 2003, Praeambula Fidei, 2005, Nalicanor II: Chi Cosa i andato Shorto?; (novels) Jolly Rogerson, 1967, A Narrow Time, 1969, The Priest, 1973, Gate of Heaven, 1975, Rogerson at Bay, 1976, Her Death of Cold, 1977, The Seventh Station, 1977, Romanesque, 1977, Spinnaker, 1977, Quick as a Dodo, 1978, Bishop as Pawn, 1978, La Cavalcade Romaine, 1979, Lying Three, 1979, Abecedary, 1979, Second Vespers, 1980, Rhyme and Reason, 1981, Thicker than Water, 1981, A Loss of Patients, 1982, The Grass Widow, 1983, Connolly's Life, 1983, Getting Away with Murder, 1984, And Then There Were Nun, 1984, The Noonday Devil, 1985, Sine Qua Nun, 1986, Leave of Absence, 1986, Rest in Pieces, 1985, Cause and Effect, 1987, The Basket Case, 1987, Veil of Ignorance, 1988, Abracadaver, 1989, Body and Soil, 1989, Four on the Floor, 1989, Frigor Mortis, 1989, Savings and Loan, 1990, The Search Committee, 1991, The Nominative Case, 1991, Sister Hood, 1991, Judas Priest, 1991, Easeful Death, 1991, Infra Dig, 1992, Desert Sinner, 1992, Seed of Doubt, 1993, The Basket Case, 1993, Nun Plussed, 1993, Mom and Dead, 1994, The Cardinal Offense, Law and Ardor, 1995, Let's Read Latin, 1995, Aguinas and Analogy, 1996, The Tears of Things, 1995, Half Past Nun, 1997, On This Rockne, 1997, Penguin Classic Aquinas, 1997, The Red Hat, 1998, What Went Wrong With Vatican II, 1998, Lack of the Irish, 1998, Irish Tenure, 1999, Grave Undertakings, 1999, Heirs and Parents, 2000, Shakespearean Variations, 2000, Book of Kills, 2001, Triple Pursuit, 2001, Still Life, 2001, Sub Rosa, 2001, Emerald Aisle, 2001, John of St. Thomas, Summa Theologiae, 2001, Law and Ardor, 2001, As Good as Dead, 2002, Celt and Pepper, 2002, Prodigal Father, 2002, Last Things, 2002, Ablative Case, 2003, Irish Coffee, 2003, Requiem For A Realtor, 2004, Green Thumb, 2004, Blood Ties, 2005, Irish Gilt, 2005, Soul of Wit, 2005, (memoirs) Only I Have Escaped to Tell You, 2006, Prudence of the Flesh, 2006, Perambula Fidei, 2006, The Letter Killeth, 2006, The Widow's Mate, 2007, Irish Alibi, 2007; editor New Scholasticism, 1967-89; editor, pub. Crisis, 1982-96; pub. Catholic Dossier, 1995-2002, Fellowship of Cath. Scholars Quar., 2003—. Exec. dir. Wethersfield Inst., 1989-92; bd. govs. Thomas Aquinas Coll., Santa Paula, Calif., 1993-2001; bd. dirs. Southern Cross Found., 1999—; mem. Pres. Bush's Com. on the Arts and Humanities, 2002—. With USMC, 1946-47. Named to Cath. Edn. Found. Hall of Fame, 2007; recipient Thomas Aquinas medal U. Dallas, 1990, Thomas Aquinas Coll., 1991, St. Thomas Aquinas medal for eminence in philosophy, 1993, Maritain medal Am. Maritain Assn., 1994, P.G. Wodehouse award CRISIS Mag., 1995, Cardinal Journet medal Ave Maria U., Fla., 2007; Fulbright rsch. fellow, Belgium, 1959-60, NEH fellow, 1977-78, NEA fellow, 1983, Catholic Scholars fellow, 1992-95, Oxford fellowship, fellowship, Inst. Psychol. Scis., Blackfriars, Oxford, Eng., 2008; Fulbright scholar, Argentina, 1986, 87, Outstanding Philosophical scholar Delta Epsilon Sigma, 1990; honoree Ralph McInerny Ctr. Thonistic Studies Thomas Internat. U., 2006. Fellow Pontifical Roman Acad. St. Thomas Aquinas; mem. Am. Philos. Assn., Am. Cath. Philos. Assn. (past pres., St. Thomas Aquinas medal 1993), Cath. Acad. Scis., Am. Metaphys. Soc. (pres. 1992), Am. Maritain Assn. (pres. 2004-06), Internat. Soc. for Study Medieval Philosophy, Medieval Acad., Mystery Writers Am. (Lifetime Achievement award 1993), Authors Guild, Fellowship Cath. Scholars (pres. 1992-95, Cardinal Wright award 1996, Premio Roncevalles de Navarre 2002), Christendom Coll., Va. Office: U of Notre Dame Jacques Maritain Ctr 714 Hesburgh Notre Dame IN 46556-5677

MCINNES, DONALD GORDON, rail transportation executive; b. Buffalo, Nov. 6, 1940; s. Milton Gordon and Blanche Mae (Clunk) McI.; m. Betsy Campbell, Mar. 18, 1967 (dec. Feb. 1995); children: Campbell Gordon, Cody Milton; m. Carol Anne Haverty, Oct. 12, 1996; stepchildren: Molly Caroline, Lawrence Joseph. BA, Denison U., 1963; MS, Northwestern U., 1965; Cert. in Transp., Yale U., 1965. Budget mgr. operating AT&SF R.R. Co., Chgo., 1969-71, from asst. trainmaster to sr. v.p., COO, 1971—94; COO Burlington No. Santa Fe Corp., 1995—2000. Bd. dirs. Nocona Athletic Goods Co., Clark Holding Inst.; founding mem. Intermodal Assn. N.Am., 1st chmn., 1991-93. Trustee Vt. Acad., Saxtons River; chair bd. Heritage Mus. and Gardens, Sandwich, Mass. Served to 2d lt. USAF, 1965-67; capt. U.S. Army, 1967-69. Decorated Bronze Star. Mem. Woods Hole Golf Club(Falmouth, Mass.), Falmouth Yacht Club. Home: 75 Waterside Ave Falmouth MA 02540-3825

MC INNES, WILLIAM CHARLES, priest, academic administrator; b. Boston, Jan. 20, 1923; s. William Charles and Mary (Byrne) Mc Innes. BS, Boston Coll., 1944, AB, 1950, MA, 1951; STL, Weston Coll., 1958; PhD, NYU, 1955; degree (hon.), U. Bridgeport, Sacred Heart U., Xavier U., Cin., U. Scranton, Loyola U., Chgo., Fairfield U. Joined Soc. of Jesus, 1946; ordained priest Roman Cath. Ch., 1957; prof. mktg. and bus. ethics Sch. Bus. Adminstrn. Boston Coll., 1959-63, assoc. dean Sch. Bus. Adminstrn., 1961-63, dir. honors program, 1963-64, mem. citizens seminar planning com., 1959-63, dir. Nat. Jesuit Honor Soc., 1997—2003; pres. Fairfield (Conn.) U., 1964-73, prof. urban problems, 1969-72; pres. U. San Francisco, 1972-77, Assn. Jesuit Colls. and Univs., 1977-89; campus min. U. Conn., Storrs, 1990-96. Vis. fellow Woodstock Theol. Ctr., 1990—91; adj. prof. bus. ethics Boston (Mass.) Coll., 1996—. Life mem. United Cerebral Palsy Assn. Fairfield County; adv. com. Conn. Dept. Social Svcs., 1993—96; priest Chaplain Alumni Assn., emeritus priest; chaplain Boston Coll. Alumni Assn., 1997—; past chmn. bd. dirs. ABCD (cmty. action agys.); bd. dirs. Nat. Better Bus. Bur.; past pres. Conn. Assn. Cmty. Action Programs; founder Fairfield County Cmty. Forum Conn. Charter Oak Coll.; vice chmn. Nat. Better Bus. Bur. Found.; chmn. Calif. Coun. Humanities. Served to capt. USAF, 1942—46, CBI. Recipient B.C. Outstanding Alumnus award, 2005, Disting. Svc. award, Carroll Sch., 2008. Mem.: Alpha Epsilon Delta, Phi Kappa Theta, Delta Sigma Pi, Alpha Sigma Nu, Beta Gamma Sigma. Home: Campion Ctr Weston MA 02493 Home Phone: 781-788-4756. Business E-Mail: mcinnewi@bc.edu.

MCINNIS, CAROLYN CRAWFORD, real estate broker; b. Fayetteville, Tenn., Oct. 30, 1937; d. Sidney Johnson and Winnie Grace Jean Crawford; m. Bobby Jack Graben, June 30, 1960 (div. Aug. 1975); children: Niles Crawford, Nancy Carol, Norman Curtis. BS, No. Ala. U., 1960; MA in Edn., Tenn. State, 1972. Real estate agt. McKinney Realty World, Dallas, 1979—80; tchr. Comstock Middle Sch., 1976—82; broker Carolyn McInnis, Inc., Realtors, 1982—. Membership chmn. Buckner Ter. Homeowners Assn., Dallas, 1983, publicity chmn., 1980—81; mem. Economic Devel. City of Dallas, 1985—89; crime reduction chair for neighborhood, 2006; mem. economic devel. Buckner Terrace, 2008; mem. Mayor's Southern Dallas Task Force Area II, 2009—; co-chair SE Dallas Realtors, 2009—; elder Eastminster Presbyn., 2005; v.p., economic devel. East Dallas C. of C., Southeast C. of C., 1985—89. Mem.: Greater Dallas Bd. Realtors, Kappa Omicron Phi. Republican. Presbyn. Home: 6903 Glacier Dr Dallas TX 75227-1763 Office: Carolyn McInnis Properties 6903 Glacier Ave Dallas TX 75227 Office Phone: 214-381-0469. Personal E-mail: carolyn.m@sbcglobal.net.

MCINNIS, RICHARD KAVIN, lawyer; b. Vicksburg, Miss., Sept. 17, 1956; s. Jack Hazzard and Verna Mabel McInnis; m. Anya Elizabeth McInnis, Oct. 24, 1998; children: Thomas Powell, Jack Payton. BBA, U. Miss., University, 1978, JD, 1981. Bar: Miss. 1981, Tex. 1982, US Dist. Ct. (no. dist.) Miss. 1981, US Dist. Ct. (all dists.) Tex., US Supreme Ct., bd. cert. comml. and residential real estate: Tex. Bd. Legal Specialization. Tax staff Arthur Andersen & Co., Houston, 1981—82; from assoc. to ptnr. Fouts & Moore, LLP, Houston, 1982—92; gen. counsel, sec. Champion Realty Co., Houston, 1992—98; of counsel Hoover, Bax & Solvacek, LLP, Houston, 1998—99, Hanson, Lamberth & Kiatta, LLP, Houston, 1999—2000; ptnr. Singleton, Cooksey, Hanson & Lanbarth, LLP, Houston, 2000—02, Berie, Lamberth & McInnis, LLP, Houston, 2002—07, Looper Reed & McGraw, P.C., Houston, 2007—. Mem.: ABA, Houston Bar Assn., Miss. State Bar, State Bar Tex., Briar Club. Episcopalian. Avocations: skiing, water sports, golf, hunting, military history. Home: 2711 Quenby Ave Houston TX 77005 Office: Looper Reed & McGraw P C 1300 Post Oak Blvd Ste 2000 Houston TX 77056

MCINTIER, RUSSELL J., retired writer; s. Ralph E. and Caroline M. McIntier; m. Gladys F. VanZandt, Sept. 12, 1965; children: Debbra F. Burchett, Russell J.(dec.). Airman/sgt. USAF, McConnell AFB, 1955—64; chief, parking missing rebuild and repair sect. US ACRC, Pueblo Army Depot, Colo., 1966—75, team leader, 1975—80; site mgr. US ATSC, Ft. Sill, Okla., 1980—88, br. chief Corpus Christi Army Depot, Tex., 1988—94. Survey officer US ATSC, Corpus Christi Army Depot, Tex., 1990—94. Author: (novel) Hardscrabble, (short story) The Denver City No Girls Club (Cert. Of Exellence, 1997), (book of short stories) Peace Officer: A Collection of Short Stories, (songs) Safe in the Arms of Jesus, 2008, (album) Sing Hallelujah, 2008.

MCINTIRE, JAMES L., state treasurer; b. Bluffton, Ohio, Apr. 9, 1953; m. Regina Cullen (div.); 3 children. BA, Macalester Coll.; MPP, U. Mich.; PhD in Economics, U. Wash. Economist, joint economic com. US Congress, 1977—80; staff, labor and human resources com. US Senate, 1980—81; spl. legislation asst. Congressman Augustus Hawkins, 1981; spl. asst. fiscal policy policy Gov. Booth Gardner, 1985—87; chmn. Wash. State Cmty. Economic Revitalization Bd., 1994—98; mem., steering com., partnership for Washington's Future Children's Alliance, 1996—98; mem. Dist. 46 Wash. House of Reps., 1999—2009, vice chmn., Financial Inst. & Ins. Com., 1999; treas. State of Wash., 2009—. Lectr. U. Wash. Grad. Sch. Public Affairs, 1983—85, sr. lectr., 1987—; rsch. scientist Battelle Human Affairs Rsch. Ctr., 1983—85. Dir. U. Wash. Fiscal Policy Ctr., 1993—98; ruling elder Wedgwood Presbyn. Ch., 1982—85, 1996—; bd. dirs. Common Ground, 1990—96, chmn., 1995—. Democrat. Presbyterian. Mailing: State Treasurer Legislative Bldg PO Box 40200 Olympia WA 98504-0200 Office Phone: 360-902-9000. Office Fax: 360-902-9037. Business E-Mail: watreas@tre.wa.gov.*

MCINTIRE, LARRY VERN, biomedical engineering educator; b. St. Paul, June 28, 1943; s. James Lawrence and Lenore Vineal (Converse) McI.; m. Suzanne G. Eskin, June 27, 1997. BChemE, MS, Cornell U., 1966; MA, Princeton U., 1968, PhD, 1970. Registered profl. engr., Tex. Asst. prof. Rice U., Houston, 1970-74, assoc. prof., 1974-78, prof. chem. engring., 1978—2003, E.D. Butcher prof., 1983—2003, chmn. dept.,

1981-91, chmn. Bioscis. and Bioengring. Inst., 1991—2003, chmn. rsch. coun., 1988-91, dir. biomed. engring. lab., 1980—99, chmn. dept. biomed. engring., 1997—2003; Wallace Coulter prof. Ga. Tech., 2003—. Adj. prof. medicine Baylor Coll. Medicine, Houston, 1982—2007, U. Tex. Med. Sch., Houston, 1982—2007, M.D. Anderson Cancer Ctr., 2001-08; Emory U. Sch. Medicine, 2003-, chmn. blood/materials working group NIH, Bethesda, Md., 1982-85; surgery and bioengring. study sect. NIH, 1984-88, 99-2003; com. bioprocessing NRC, 1991-94; chmn. rheology subcom. Internat. Coun. Thrombosis and Hemostasis, 1985-89; engring. directorate adv. coun. NSF, 2002-05; chmn. Coulter dept. biomed. engring. Gal Tech., 2003-. Editor-in-chief: Annals of Biomed. Engring., 2002—; contbr. over 278 articles to profl. jours. Recipient Merit award NIH, 1989; NSF fellow Cornell U., Princeton U., 1965-69, NATO-NSF postdoctoral fellow Imperial Coll., London, 1976-77. Fellow AAAS, Am. Inst. Med. Biol. Engring. (sec., treas. 1993-96, pres. 1997-98), AICHE (officer local sect. 1980-81, 86, Food Pharm. and Bioengring. divsn. award 1992, divsn. chair 1998), Biomed. Engring. Soc. (bd. dirs. 1992-97, pres. 1995-96, Disting. lectr. 1992, Presdl. award, 2004); fellow Am. Heart Assn.; mem. N.Am. Soc. Biorheology (v.p. 1992-94, pres. 1994-96), N.Y. Acad. Scis., Faculty Club Rice U. (bd. dirs., chmn. 1982-84), Sigma Xi (nat. lectr. 1993-96), Nat. Acad. Engring. (editor-in-chief Annals Biomed. Engring., 2002-). Presbyterian. Avocations: tennis, squash, classical music, hiking. Office: Ga Tech Dept Biomed Engring Atlanta GA 30332-0535 Office Phone: 404-894-5057. Office Fax: 404-385-5028. Business E-Mail: larry.mcintire@bme.gatech.edu.

MCINTOSH, CAROLYN LEIGH, lawyer; b. Boulder, Colo., Dec. 10, 1955; d. Glen Elvis and Alice Joy McIntosh; m. Roger Alan Bucholz, Oct. 4, 1980 (div. Dec. 1998); m. Leland Kioshi Marable, Dec. 11, 1998. BA cum laude, Middlebury Coll., 1978; JD, U. Colo., 1981. Bar: Colo. 1981, U.S. Dist. Ct. Colo. 1981, Mont. 1988 (specially admitted), U.S. Dist. Ct. Mont. 1989, U.S. Ct. Appeals 2000. Rsch. asst. Rocky Mountain Mineral Law Found., Boulder, 1979—80; assoc. Sisk, Foley, Hultin & Driver, Denver, 1981—83, Hultin, Driver & Spaanstra, Denver, 1983—85; asst. atty. gen. Colo. Dept. of Law, Denver, 1986—88; assoc. Cogswell & Wehrle, Denver, 1988—89, shareholder, 1989—90; spl. asst. atty. gen. State of Mont., 1988—90; sr. assoc. Patton, Boggs & Blow, Denver, 1990—92; ptnr. Patton Boggs, LLP, Denver, 1992—, mng. ptnr. Denver office, 1993—2002. Assoc. adj. prof. Colo. Sch. Mines, 1991—2000; mem., atty. program to provide legal svcs. to indigent, Denver, 1982—86; co-chair recruiting com. Colo. Campaign Inclusive Excellence, 2008—; fellow Litig. Coun. America, 2009, U. Colo. Law Alumni Bd., 2009—. Mem. procedural rules subcom. Colo. Air Quality Control Commn., 1983-84; mem. Lafayette Planning Commn., 1986-87, 95-99, Lafayette City Coun., 1987-99, mayor pro tem, 1989-91, mayor, 1995-99; mem. bd. Denver Regional Coun. Govts., 1990-99; mem. Regional Air Quality Coun., 1992-99, mem. exec. com., 1996-99; mem. Colo. Water Conservation Bd., 2001-04, Urban Drainage and Flood Control Bd., 1995-99. Mem. ABA (natural resources sect.), Colo. Bar Assn., Denver Bar Assn. (legal fees arbitration com. 1983-84, 86-87), Alliance Profl. Women (bd. dirs. 1986-90), Internat. Inst. Environ. Risk Mgmt. (bd. govs. 1996—). Office: Patton Boggs 1801 California St Ste 4900 Denver CO 80202 Office Phone: 303-894-6127. Business E-Mail: cmcintosh@pattonboggs.com. *Notable cases include: Environ. Def. Fund vs. Colo. Dept. Health, 1986, defending against unsuccessful challenge to the State of Colo.'s prevention of significant deterioration air quality regulations; State of Colo. vs. Idarado Mine Co., 1989, prosecution of superfund clean up claims against Idarado; Denver vs. Adolph Coons Co., et al, superfund cost recovery action.*

MCINTOSH, CECILIA ANN, biochemist, educator; b. Dayton, Ohio, Apr. 30, 1956; d. Russell Edward McIntosh and Geraldine Rita (Cochran) Slemp; m. Kevin Smith Schweiker, May 28, 1978 (div. Mar. 1989); children: Katrina Lynn McIntosh Schweiker, Rebecca Sue McIntosh Schweiker. BA in Biology cum laude, U. South Fla., 1977, MA in Botany, 1981, PhD in Biology, 1990. Rsch. assoc. U. South Fla., Tampa, 1981-86; sci. mentor Ctr. for Excellence, U. So. Fla., Tampa, 1984-90; tchg. and rsch. asst. dept. biology U. South Fla., Tampa, 1986-90; postdoctoral fellow dept. biochemistry U. Idaho, Moscow, 1990-93; asst. prof. dept. biol. scis. East Tenn. State U., Johnson City, 1993-98, assoc. prof., 1998—2004, prof., 2004—, grad. student coord., 1997—2003, asst. dean Sch. Grad. Studies, 2004—06, dean Sch. Grad. Studies, 2006—; adj. prof. dept. biochemistry and physiology Quillen Coll. Medicine East Tenn. State U., Johnson City, 1995—, adj. prof. physiology, 2007—; metabolic biochemistry program dir. NSF DMCB, 2003—04. Rsch. forum judge Coll. Medicine Rsch. Forum, East Tenn. State U., Johnson City, 1994—; program dir. biomolecular sys. NSF, 2003-04. Contbr. articles to sci. jours. including Plant Sci., Plant Physiology, Archives Biochemistry and Biophysics. Sci. fair judge East Tenn. Regional Sci. Fair, Johnson City, 1994—. Grantee USDA, 1994-96, East Tenn. State U. Rsch. Devel. Coun., 1994-2002, USDA NRI, 1998-2001, 2003-2005, NSF, 2006-; co-grantee Howard Hughes Med. Inst., 2000-2005. Mem. Am. Assn. Women in Sci., Am. Soc. Plant Biologists, Phytochem. Soc. N.Am. (treas. 1998-2002, mem. exec. adv. bd. 2004-), Sigma Xi (sci. fair workshop coord. Appalachian chpt. 1995). Achievements include characterization of new enzyme in plant flavonoid biosynthesis; biochemical characterization of plant mitochondrial membrane tricarboxylate and phosphate transporters and TCA cycle enzymes. Office: East Tenn State U Dept Biol Scis Box 70 703 Johnson City TN 37614-0703 E-mail: mcintosc@mail.etsu.edu.

MCINTOSH, DENNIS KEITH, veterinarian, consultant; b. Glen Ridge, NJ, June 12, 1941; s. Sheldon Weeks and Enid Nicholson (Casey) McIntosh; children: Kevin, Jamie. BS in Animal Sci., Tex. A&M U., College Station, 1963, BS in Vet. Sci., 1967, DVM, 1968. Asst. county agrl. agt., Cleburne, Tex., 1963—65; owner, operator Park North Animal Hosp., San Antonio, 1970—75, El Dorado Animal Hosp., San Antonio, 1973—. Founding mem. and vet. liaison Tex. Assn. Animal Technicians (now TARVT), 1976-81; co-chmn., founding mem. vet. tech. adv. coun. Palo Alto Coll., 1995—, tchr. Animal Health Tech., San Antonio Coll., 1985-95; tchr. ethics for vet. students Tex. A&M U. Coll. Vet. Medicine, 1990-; pres., mgr. Bexar County Emergency Animal Clinic, Inc., 1978-81; cons. vet. practice mgmt., mktg., client rels.; spkr. for vet. meetings, assns.; co-host Ask the Vet, Adopt a Pet, Sta. KENS-TV, 1980-93; vet. mem. Tex. Bd. Health, 1984-89, chmn. disease control com., pers. com.; mem. environ. health, hosps. com. Team capt. Alamo Roundup Club and Pres.' Club of San Antonio C. of C., 1970-75; mem. Guadalupe County Youth Fair Bd., 1978-80. Contbg. author: Mosby's Review Questions and Answers for Veterinary Boards, 1998, Chicken Soup for the Pet Lover's Soul, 1998, Chicken Soup for the Soul: Loving Our Cats, 2008; contbr. articles to profl. jours. With Vet. Corps, USAF, 1968-70. Recipient Alumnus award Guadalupe County 4-H Club, 1979, Outstanding Svc. award San Antonio Coll., 1986-87, Lynn Anderson Outstanding Svc. award San Antonio chpt. Delta Soc., 1990, Outstanding Bus. Ptnrs. award N.E. Ind. Sch. Dist., 1995-96. Mem. AVMA, Tex. Vet. Med. Assn. (pres., chmn. bd. dirs.), Tex. Acad. Vet. Practice (charter mem., pres.), San Antonio C. of C. (life), Tex. County Agrl. Agts. Assn. (4th v.p. 1964), Am. Legion Post 245, Tex. Old Time Fiddler's Assn., Delta Soc. (first pres.and founding mem. San Antonio chpt. 1989-90), Alpha Zeta. Office: 13039 Nacogdoches Rd San Antonio TX 78217-1960 Office Phone: 210-656-1444.

MC INTOSH, JAMES EUGENE, JR., interior designer; b. Dadeville, Ala., Nov. 13, 1938; s. James Eugene and Jessie (Latimer) McI. B.Interior Design, Auburn U., Ala., 1961. Designer contract div. Rich's Dept. Store, Atlanta, 1961-64; assoc. William Trapnell & Assocs., Atlanta, 1964-70; dir. Interior Concepts, Inc., Atlanta, 1970-72; dir. design comml. design div. Rich's Dept. Store, 1972-80; v.p. Comml. Interior Designs, Inc., 1980-82; exec. staff Rollins Inc., 1982—; pres. Gene Mc Intosh & Assocs., 1985—. Fellow Am. Soc. Interior Designers (Presdl. citation 1974); mem. Nat. Trust Hist. Preservation, Ala. Hist. Soc., High Mus. Art Home and Office: 325 W Ponce de Leon #202 Decatur GA 30030 Personal E-mail: cmeneg@earthlink.net.

MCINTOSH, JON CHARLES, illustrator, graphics designer, painter; b. Alliance, Ohio, Aug. 8, 1947; s. John Cowles and Lucile Tipple (Ketcham) McI.; 1 child, Forgan Cowles. Student, Hobart Coll., 1965-67; BFA, R.I. Sch. of Design, 1974. Pres. McIntosh Ink, Inc., Key West, Fla., 1971—; exec. v.p. advt. Chill Internat., Inc., 2004—. Mem. bd. overseers New Eng. Conservatory of Music, Boston, 1989-95; bd. dirs. Sail Martha's Vineyard. Illustrator: (book) The Foolish Dinosaur Fiasco, 1978, The Mysterious Zetabet, 1980, The Doctor's Handbook, 1982, Witch Way to The Country, 1995, Witch Way to the Beach, 1997, The Longest Hair in the World, 1999; author, illustrator: Hooked On Golf, 1986, Fineart: Gallery on Greene, Grannary Gallery, Casa Vieja Gallery, W.H. Patterson Gallery, London. Artwork contbr. Ducks Unltd; art for advt. Bose, Wang, Digital, NASA. Recipient Silver medal V.I. Internat. Film Festival, 1976, Gold medal Soc. of Newspaper Designers, 1985, First place Francis Hatch Advt. Awards, 1987, First place New Eng. Newspaper Awards, 1998, Silver award Soc. Newspaper Designers, 2000. Mem. Soc. of Illustrators (Silver Funny Bone 1991) Republican. Episcopalian. Avocations: musician, ski racing, tennis, fishing, skeet shooting. Office: McIntosh Ink Inc 813 Frances St Key West FL 33040 Office Phone: 305-295-2533.

MCINTOSH, TERRIE TUCKETT, lawyer; b. Ft. Lewis, Wash., July 20, 1944; d. Robert LeRoy and Elda Tuckett; m. Clifton Dennis McIntosh, Oct. 13, 1969; children: Alison, John. BA, U. Utah, 1967; MA, U. Ill., 1970; JD, Harvard U., 1978. Bar: NY 1979, Utah 1980. Assoc. Hughes, Hubbard & Reed, NYC, 1978-79, Fabian & Clendenin, Salt Lake City, 1979-84, shareholder, 1984-86; staff atty. Questar Corp., Salt Lake City, 1986-88, sr. atty., 1988-92, sr. corp. counsel, 1992—. Instr. philosophy Douglass Coll. Rutgers U., New Brunswick, N.J., 1971-72; mem. adv. com. civil procedure Utah Supreme Ct., Salt Lake City, 1987—; mem. jud. nominating com. 5th Cir. Ct., Salt Lake City, 1986-88. Mem. Utah State Bar (ethics and discipline screening panel 1989-96, vice chair ethics and discipline com. 1996-99, 2006—, co-chair law related edn. com. 1985-86, bar examiner rev. com. 2005—), Women Lawyers of Utah (chair exec. com. 1986-87, Woman Lawyer of Yr. award 2005), Salt Lake Legal Aid Soc. (trustee 1999-2008), Harvard Alumni Assn. Utah (bd. dirs. 1987—), Phi Beta Kappa, Phi Kappa Phi Office Phone: 801-324-5532.

MCINTYRE, BRIAN P., sports association executive; married; 2 children. Grad., Loyola U., Chgo. Dir. mktg. and media info. Chgo. Bulls, 1978—81; dir. pub. rels. NBA, NYC, 1981—89, v.p. pub. rels., 1989—97, sr. v.p. basketball comm., 1997—. Mem. FIBA (Internat. Basketball Fedn.) News Coun.; mem. media adv. com. USA Basketball. Named to Loyola Acad. Athletic Hall of Fame, 1999. Achievements include creating numerous awards for the NBA, including the Sixth Man, the Defensive Player and the Most Improved Player. Office: NBA Olympic Tower 645 5th Ave Fl 10 New York NY 10022-5986*

MCINTYRE, EDWARD PATRICK, JR., not-for-profit executive; b. Montgomery, Ala., Aug. 27, 1969; s. Edward Patrick McIntyre Sr. and Mary Kathryn Campbell; m. Ellen Maureen Bowden, Aug. 9, 2003. BA, U. Ala., 1992; MA, U. Miss., 1995. Cert. preservation leadership Nat. Trust Hist. Preservation. Endangered properties coord. Ala. Hist. Commn., Montgomery, 1999—2002; exec. dir. Tenn. Preservation Trust, Nashville, 2002—. Mem. Sec. Interior's Adv. Coun., Selma-Montgomery Nat. Hist. Trail, Montgomery, 1998—2000; bd. dirs. Preservation Action, Washington, 2004—06, Belmont Mansion Assn., Nashville, 2003—06, Ala. Preservation Alliance, Montgomery, 1997—2001; mem. adv. bd. Tenn. Civil War Preservation Assn., Nashville, 2005—06; bd. dirs. Tenn. Conservation Voters, Nashville, 2003—06. Named one of 40 Under 40, Tennessean Newspaper, Nashville, 2004; Group Study Exch. fellow, Rotary Found., 2001. Episcopalian. Avocations: travel, photography, antiques, art. Office: Tenn Preservation Trust Ste 119 315 10th Ave N Nashville TN 37203 Home: 226 Deer Park Cir Nashville TN 37205-3325 E-mail: ellenbowde@aol.com.

MCINTYRE, JAMES G., lawyer; b. 1933; 3 children. BS, Stephen F. Austin State U.; LLB, Miss. Coll. Sch. Law. Bar: 1964. Atty. McIntyre Law Firm, Jackson, Miss., 1964—. Achievements include defense atty. for former Neshoba County Sheriff Lawrence Rainey, who won acquittal in the 1967 federal trial; defense atty. for Edgar Ray Killen, convicted of the 1964 manslaughter of 3 civil rights workers, Andrew Goodman, James Chaney and Michael Schwerner in June 2005. Office: McIntyre Law Firm 828 N State St Jackson MS 39202 Office Phone: 601-355-2481.

MCINTYRE, JERILYN SUE, academic administrator; b. June 24, 1942; d. Frank Otto and Maxine (Ward) McIntyre; m. W. David Smith. Student, Stanford U., Italy, 1962; AB in History with distinction, Stanford U., 1964, MA in Journalism, 1965, cert. Summer Radio-TV Inst., 1965, tchrs. cert., 1968; PhD in Comms., U. Washington, 1973; postgrad. Inst. Ednl. Mgmt., Harvard U., 1993. Corr. World News Bureau McGraw-Hill Pub. Co., LA, 1965-67; asst. prof. dept. mass comm. Chico (Calif.) State Coll., 1968-70; asst. prof. Sch. Journalism U. Iowa, Iowa City, 1973-77; assoc. prof., prof. dept. comm. U. Utah, Salt Lake City, 1977-2000, assoc. dean Coll. Humanities, 1984-88, assoc. v.p. acad. affairs, 1988-90, interim pres., 1997, v.p. acad. affairs, 1990-98; pres. Ctrl. Wash. U., Ellensburg, 2000—. Dir. Wall St. Jour. Publs. Workshop, Chico State Coll., 1968; mem. edn. adv. bd. NFL, 1996; mem. exec. com. coun. acad. affairs Nat. Assn. State Univs. and Land Grant Coll., 1995—98, chair, 1997; mem. steering com. Utah Edn. Network, 1995—98. Editl. asst. Chemical Week Mag., 1965-66, World News Bureau, 1966-67; mem. editl. bd. Journalism History; co-author: Symbols & Society; contbr. articles to profl. jours., chpts. to books. Mem. Utah Women's Forum. Recipient Yesterday's Girl Scout Today's Successful Woman, Utah Girl Scout Coun., 1996, Salt Lake City chpt. Disting. Woman, AAUW, 1994; named a David P. Gardner fellow, 1984. Mem.: Assn. Edn. in Journalism and Mass Comm. Office: 400 E University Way Ellensburg WA 98926-7501 E-mail: mcintyrej@cwu.edu.

MCINTYRE, JERRY L., lawyer; b. Atlantic City, July 1, 1941; AB, Columbia U., 1963; JD, Fordham U., 1969. Bar: N.Y. 1969, R.I. 1970. Mem. McIntyre, Tate & Lynch, Providence, 1993—. Com. mem. Family Ct. Bench/Bar Com., 1985—. Pres. town coun., Town of Jamestown, R.I., 1983-89. Fellow Am. Acad. Matrimonial Lawyers; mem. ABA (sect. family law), N.Y. State Bar Assn. (sect. trusts and estates law), R.I. Bar Assn., R.I. Bar Found. Office: McIntyre Tate & Lynch 321 S Main St Providence RI 02903-7108 Office Phone: 401-351-7700. Business E-Mail: jlm@mtlesq.com.

MCINTYRE, JOHN ARMIN, physics professor; b. Seattle, June 2, 1920; s. Harry John and Florence (Armin) McI.; m. Madeleine Forsman, June 15, 1947; 1 son, John Forsman. BS, U. Wash., 1943; MA, Princeton U., 1948, PhD, 1950. Mem. faculty elec. engring. Carnegie Inst. Tech., Pitts., 1943; radio engr. Westinghouse Elec. Co., Balt., 1944; research asso. Stanford, 1950-57; mem. faculty Yale, 1957-63, assoc. prof., 1960-63; prof. physics Tex. A&M U., College Station, 1963-95, emeritus prof., 1995—; asso. dir. Cyclotron Inst., 1965-70. Mem. council Oak Ridge Asso. Univs., 1964-71 Contbr. articles to profl. jours. Fellow Am. Phys. Soc., Am. Sci. Affiliation (exec. council 1968-73); mem. AAAS. Presbyterian. Achievements include research and publs. on scintillation counters for gamma ray spectroscopy; determination of nuclear charge distbns. by electron scattering; study of nuclear structure by neutron transfer reactions; devel. variable energy gamma ray beams, gamma ray cameras. Home: 2316 Bristol St Bryan TX 77802-2405 E-mail: jmcintyre@physics.tamu.edu.

MCINTYRE, LEE CAMERON, philosophy educator; b. Portland, Oreg., Jan. 2, 1962; s. Frank Pettygrove and Drena Jane McIntyre; m. Josephine Marie Hernández, July 26, 1986; children: Louisa Hernández, James Gabriel. BA with high honors, Wesleyan U., Middletown, Conn., 1984; MA, U. Mich., 1987, PhD in Philosophy, 1991. Rsch. assoc. Ctr. for Philosophy and History of Sci. Boston U., 1991-93; asst. prof. Philosophy Colgate U., Hamilton, N.Y., 1993—; vis. scholar Santa Fe (N.Mex.) Inst., 1997. Vis. lectr. Tufts U., 1992 Coord. editor Founds. Chemistry, 1998—; co-editor: Readings in the Philosophy of Social Science, 1994; author: Laws and Explanation in the Social Sciences, 1996. Recipient Rackham dissertation fellowship U. Mich., Ann Arbor, 1991, Wise prize for philosophy Wesleyan U., Middletown, Conn., 1984. Mem. Am. Philos. Assn., Philosophy of Sci. Assn., N.Y. State Philos. Assn. (sec.-treas. 1995-96), Phi Beta Kappa. Office: Colgate U 13 Oak Dr Hamilton NY 13346-1383 E-mail: LMcIntyre@mail.colgate.edu.

MCINTYRE, MIKE (DOUGLAS CARMICHAEL MCINTYRE II), United States Representative from North Carolina; b. Lumberton, NC, Aug. 6, 1956; s. Douglas Carmichael and Thelma Riley (Hedgpeth) McIntyre; m. Lola Denise Strickland, June 26, 1982; children: Joshua Carmichael, Stephen Christopher. BA, U. NC, 1978, JD, 1981. Bar: NC 1981, US Dist. Ct. (ea. dist.) NC 1984, US Dist. Ct. (mid. dist.) NC 1985., US Ct. Appeals (4th cir.) 1987, US Supreme Ct., 1987. Assoc. Law Office Bruce Huggins, Lumberton, 1981-82, McLean, Stacy, Henry & McLean, Lumberton, 1982-86; ptnr. Price & McIntyre PA, Lumberton, 1987-89; prin. McIntyre Law Firm, PA, Lumberton, 1989-96; mem. US Congress from 7th NC dist., 1997—. Mem. law-focused edn. adv. com. NC Dept. Pub. Instrn., 1986-87; mem. US Ho. Com. on Agr., 1997—, Armed Svcs. Com., 1997—; co-chmn. Coalition Task Force on Edn., 1997-98, Congrl. Task Force on Promotion of Fatherhood, Rural Health Care Coalition, 1999-2002, Dem. Task Force on Children, 1999-2000, Coalition Task Force on Bus. and Tech., Spl. Forces Caucus, 2002—; chmn. U.S. H. Agr. Subcom. on Splty. Crops, Rural Devel. and Fgn. Agr.; mem. Pres.'s Summit on Am.'s Future, 1997. Del. Dem. Nat. Conv., NYC, 1980, NC Dems., Raleigh, 1974—; pres. Robeson County Young Dems., Lumberton, 1982; sec.-treas. 7th Congl. Dist. Young Dems., NC, 1983, chmn., 1984; 2nd vice chmn. 7th Congl. Dist. Dems. So. NC, 1986-89, 1st vice chmn., 1989; mem. state adv. bd. North Carolinians Against Drug and Alcohol Abuse, Raleigh, 1984-85; chmn. Morehead Scholarship Selection Com., Robeson County, 1985-94; deacon, elder, clk. of session Presbyn. Ch.; active Boy Scouts Am., Lumberton, 1983; mem. NC Commn. on Children and Youth, 1987-89, NC Commn. on the Family, 1989-91; mem. Young Life Lumberton com., 1987-89; chmn. Robeson County US Constn. Bicentennial com., 1986-87; mem. lawyers' adv. com. to NC Commn. on Bicentennial of US Constn., 1986-89; bd. dirs. Robeson County Grp. Home, Lumberton, 1984-87, Lumberton Econ. Advancement for Downtown, Inc., 1987-90, pres., 1988-89, 89-90; chmn. legis. affairs com. C. of C., 1991, 92, 93, bd. dirs., 1992-94; mem. NC Mus. Hist. Assocs., 1987-89; mem. regional selection com. Gov.'s Award for Excellence in Tchg. Social Studies, 1991. Morehead Found. scholar, 1974-78; named one of Outstanding Young Men in Am., 1981, 84-85, 88; Outstanding Young Dem. Robeson County Young Dems., 1984-85; one of State's Outstanding Young Dems. Young Dems. NC, 1984-85; recipient Algernon Sydney Sullivan award U. NC, 1978, Outstanding Young North Carolinian award NC Jaycees, 1988, Outstanding Young North Carolinians, Heart Robeson Jaycees, 1988, Nat. Bicentennial Leadership award for Individual Achievement Coun. for Advancement of Citizenship and Ctr. for Civic Edn., Washington, 1987, Gov.'s Outstanding Vol. Svc. award, 1989, Thomas Jefferson award Food Distbrs. Internat., 1998, 2002, Guardian of Small Bus. award, Nat. Fedn. Ind. Bus., 1997-99, Nat. Rural Health Legis. award, 1999, 2003, Outstanding Health Svc. award Cmty. Ptnrs. Health Net, 2000, Spirit of Enterprise award, US C. of C., 1997-98, Super Hero award Nat. Assn. Cmty. Health Ctrs., 2001-05, Internat. Pub. Policy award Internat. Assn. Pers. Employment, 2002, Law Enforcement award, NC Narcotics Officers Assn., 2002, Quality Pub. Svc./Pub. Edn. and Health Care award Am. Fedn. Tchrs., 2001, Charles Dick Medal of Merit Nat. Guard Assn., 2000, Disting. Svc. to Agr. award Robeson County Crop Promotion Assn., 2001, Congrl. Partnership award Nat. Assn. Devel. Orgns., 2002, 2004-05, Nat. Leadership award, 2006, Admiral's Cir. award Nat. Marine Mfrs. Assn., 2004, MVP award Sr. Citizens League, 2004, True Blue Pro-Family award, Family Rsch. Coun., 2006, 07, Disting. Christian Statesman award, 2006, Nat. Lagislator Tr. award, Svc. Agency Employees Assn., 2007, Nat. Assn. County Veterans Svc. Officers, 2008; named to Legis. Honor Roll So. Econ. Devel. Coun., 1997, 2001-06, Beach Preservationist of Yr., Oak Island Preservation Soc., 2005; Nat. Sports Ethics fellow, Positive Coaching Alliance, 2008. Mem. ABA (exec. com. citizenship edn. com. 1985-87, nat. cmty. law week com. 1982-83), Internat. Platform Assn., NC Bar Assn. (chmn. youth edn. and constn. bicentennial com. 1986-87, youth edn. com., exec. coun. young lawyers divsn. 1986-87), Robeson County Bar Assn. (founder, chmn. citizenship edn. com. 1982-94, law day com.), 16th Jud. Dist. Bar Assn., NC Acad. Trial Lawyers, NC Coll. Advocacy, Christian Legal Soc. (state adv. bd. 1986-90, state pres. 1987), Lumberton C. of C. (bd. dirs. 1992-94), Mil. Officers' Assn. (hon. life), Order of Old Well, Lumberton Rotary Club (bd. dirs. 1995-96), Phi Beta Kappa, Phi Eta Sigma. Democrat. Avocations: tennis, skiing, softball, dance, bible study. Office: US House Reps 2437 Rayburn House Office Bldg Washington DC 20515 Office Phone: 202-225-2731. Office Fax: 202-225-5773. E-mail: congmcintyre@mail.house.gov.*

MCINTYRE, OSWALD ROSS, physician; b. Chgo., Feb. 13, 1932; m. Helen Whyte; children: Margaret Jean, Archibald Ross, Elizabeth Geary. AB cum laude, Dartmouth Coll., Hanover, NH, 1953, postgrad, 1953-55; MD, Harvard U., Cambridge, Mass., 1957. Intern U. Pa. Hosp., 1957-58; resident in medicine Dartmouth Med. Sch. Affiliated Hosps., 1958-60; instr. medicine Dartmouth Coll., 1964-66, asst. prof. medicine, 1966-69, assoc. prof., 1969-75, prof., 1976—, James J. Carroll prof. oncology, 1980-95, dir. Norris Cotton Cancer Center, 1975-92, prof. emeritus, 1995—; attending physician VA Hosp., White River Junction, Vt., 1964. Cons. in hematology and oncology; acting chmn. dept. medicine Dartmouth-Hitchcock Med. Ctr., 1987-89; chmn. Cancer and Leukemia Group B.; 1990-95. Mem. Am. Soc. Hematology, Am. Assn. Cancer Rsch., Am. Soc. Clin. Oncology, Assn. Cancer Inst. (pres. 1988-89), New Eng. Cancer Soc. (pres. 1989-90). Home: 34 Lamphire Hill Ln Lyme NH 03768-3109

MCINTYRE, PETER MASTIN, physicist, researcher; b. Clewiston, Fla., Sept. 26, 1947; s. Peter Mastin and Ruby Eugenia (Richaud) McI.; m. Rebecca Biek, June 29, 1968; children: Peter B., Colin H., Jana M., Robert J. AB with honors, U. Chgo., 1967, MS, 1968, PhD, 1973. Asst. prof. Harvard U., Cambridge, Mass., 1975-80; group leader Fermilab, Batavia, Ill., 1978-80; assoc. prof. Tex. A&M U., College Station, 1980-84, prof. physics, 1985—, assoc. dean Coll. of Sci., 1990-92; pres. Accelerator Tech. Corp., Bryan, Tex., 1988—. Dir. Tex. Accelerator Ctr., The Woodlands, 1991—93. Recipient IR-100 award, Indsl. Rch. Mag., 1980; fellow, Sloan Found., 1976—78. Fellow: Am. Phys. Soc. (pres. Tex. sect. 1990—91); mem.: AAAS. Achievements include proton-antiproton colliding beams; E-beam assisted removal of mercury and sub-micron carbon particles from power plant exhausts; electronic pasteurization system for killing bacteria in food and removing organic contaminants in water; tesla superconducting magnets for future hadron colliders; silicon microdevices for DNA sequencing; structured cable using high-temperature superconductors for practical coils; flux-coupled isochronous cyclotron driver for thorium-cycle nuclear fission power; creation of Visual Physics, a new laboratory/problem solving curriculum for first-year college physics; hybrid magnet technology for accelerating dipoles and spectroscopy solenoids to 25 Tesla; polyhedral superconductivity cavity for linac collides; a method by which to steer hurricanes modular emergency wall to protect city blocks from hurricane sea suege; patents for continuous unitized tunneling system, gigatron high power microwave amplifier, microstrip chamber for medical imaging. Home: 611 Montclair Ave College Station TX 77840-2868 Office: Tex A&M U Dept Physics College Station TX 77843-0001 Business E-Mail: p-mcintyre@physics.tamu.edu.

MCINTYRE, ROBERT C., JR., surgeon, critical care consultant; m. Jacquelin Horn; 1 child, Brookmyer. BS, Vanderbilt U., Nashville, 1983; MD, Tulane U., 1987. Prof. surgery U. Colo. Denver Sch. Medicine, 1992—99; assoc. prof. surgery U. Colo. Health Scis. Ctr., Denver, 1999—. Office: U Colo Health Scis Ctr 4200 East 9th Ave Box C313 Denver CO 80262 Address: 12631 E 17th Ave C313 Aurora CO 80045 Office Phone: 303-315-7673. Office Fax: 303-315-5527. Business E-Mail: robert.mcintyre@uchsc.edu.

MCINTYRE, VIRGIE M., retired elementary school educator; b. Chesnee, SC, Feb. 27, 1923; d. Ed Lawson and Etta Rebecca (Jones) Mahaffey; m. Henry Bryson McIntyre, June 8, 1947; children: Teresa, Dawn. BA in edn., Berea Coll., 1945; M in supr. and adminstrn., Western Carolina U., 1964. Cert. advanced standing (reading) Syracuse U., 1968. Elem. tchr. Polk County Pub. Sch., Columbus, NC, 1945—53, 1957—65, Rutherfordton County, Spindale, NC, 1953—56; suprv. Polk County, 1965—67, reading cons., title 1 dir., 1968—70; reading ctr. prof. Western Carolina U., Cullowhee, NC, 1971—84; ret., 1984. Dir. reading conf. Western Carolina U., Cullowhee, NC, 1971—84, reading cons., 1971—84. Author: Reading Strategies and Enrichment Activities for Grades 4-9, 1979, Split Level Christians, 1993; contbr. articles various profl. jours. Vol. Outreach Min., Columbus, NC, 2000, Green Creek Computer Ctr., Tryon, NC, 2002; vol., dir, pianist Ch. Choir, Columbus, NC, 1984—99. Fellowship grant, Syracuse U., 1969. Mem.: Christian Writer's Group, NC Retired Employee Group. Independent. Avocations: painting, travel, swimming, music, volunteerism.

MCIVER, DEBORAH KAY, tax specialist, entrepreneur, small business owner; b. Des Moines, Iowa, May 6, 1948; d. Floyd Malcolm and Nora Marguerite McIver. BS, N.Mex. Inst. Mining and Tech., 1970; MBA, Pepperdine U., 1981; postgrad., U. N.Mex., 1985—87. Chem. control technician McGaw Labs., Glendale, Calif., 1971—72; statistician Northrop Corp., Hawthorne, 1972—73; math. analyst TRW Sys. Group, Redondo Beach, 1973—76; sci. programmer ISS/Sperry Univac, Cupertino, 1976—77; mem. tech. staff TRW Sys. Group, Sunnyvale, 1977—78, ArgoSys., 1978—79; sr. sci. programmer Finnigan-MAT Corp., San Jose, 1979—82; software engr. Ford Aerospace Co., Sunnyvale, 1982—83; v.p. software ops. controller Askeri, Inc., Santa Clara, 1983; owner McIver Enterprises, 1983—86, Deborah K. McIver, MBA, EA, 1990—. Gen. contractor own home, 1994—95. Active Sea Scouts Am., LA, 1975—76; friendly visitor United Way, LA, 1977—79; judge Santa Clara County Sci. and Engring. Sci. Fair, 1980, 1982, 1984; instr., coord. AARP Tax-Aide, 1992—, Colo. state coord., 2004—. Mem.: Soc. Women Engrs. (v.p. San Francisco Bay Area sect. 1980—81, pres. 1981—82, sect. rep. 1982—83), N.Mex. Inst. Mining and Tech. Alumni Assn. (life; pres. No. Calif. chpt. 1980—81). Republican. Home and Office: PO Box 889 Monument CO 80132-0889 Office Phone: 719-488-3022.

MCIVOR, DONALD KENNETH, retired petroleum company executive; b. Winnipeg, Man., Can., Apr. 12, 1928; s. Kenneth MacIver and Nellie Beatrice (Rutherford) McI.; children: Gordon, Deborah, Duncan, Donald, Daniel. BS with honors in Geology, U. Man., 1950; postgrad., Nat. Def. Coll., 1973. Geophysical trainee seismic crew Imperial Oil Ltd., Alta., 1950, various operational and rsch. positions in exploration Alta., 1950-58, held various positions including asst. to exploration mgr., suprv. exploration planning, mgr. exploration rsch. Calgary, 1958-68, with Jersey Prodn. Rsch. Co. Angola, France and Tulsa, Okla.; asst. mgr., mgr. corp. planning Toronto HO, 1968-69, mgr. exploration, 1970-72, sr. v.p., dir., 1973, exec. v.p., 1975; v.p. oil and gas exploration and prodn. Exxon Corp., 1977-81; dep. chmn., dir. Imperial Oil Ltd., 1981, chmn., chief exec. officer, 1982-85; dir., sr. v.p. Exxon Corp., Dallas, 1985-92; with John S. Herold Inc., 2006—. Bd. dirs. Nat. Coun. on Econ. Edn., Internat. Exec. Svc. Corps., N.W. Oil Co. Mem. Can. Soc. Petroleum Geologists, Am. Petroleum Inst. Home: 79 Lukes Wood Rd New Canaan CT 06840-2202 Personal E-mail: mcivordon@aol.com.

MCKAGUE, SHIRLEY, state legislator; b. Nampa, Idaho, Dec. 4, 1935; m. Paul McKague; children: Rhonda, Van, Dan, Randy, Rick, Robert. Legal sec. Carey Nixon, 1964—78; bus. ptnr., book keeper Family Svc. Station, 1969—96; co-owner Paul's Meridian Stinker, 1970; columnist Valley Times, 1980—82; mem. Dist. 14B Idaho House of Reps., Boise, 1997—2003, mem. Dist. 20B, 2003—07; mem. Dist. 20 Idaho State Senate, Boise, 2007—. Mem. Alec Info. Tech. Com., 2007. Mem. Miss Meridian Pageant com., Rep. Precinct Com., 1980—. Mem.: Meridian C. of C., Idaho Farm Bur. Republican. Address: Dist 20 933 East Pine Meridian ID 83642 Office Phone: 208-888-2842. Office Fax: 208-888-3379. Business E-Mail: smckague@senate.idaho.gov.*

MCKALE, MICHAEL, religious studies educator, director; b. Piqua, Ohio; BA, Notredame U., Ind., 1972; MA, Jesuit Sch. Theology, Berkeley, Calif., 1975; PhD, Grad. Theol. Union, Berkeley, 1986. Prof. St. Francis U., Loretto, Pa., 1986—; dir. Inst. Ethics, Loretto, 1993—; rep. Consortium Ednl. Resources Islamic Studies, Pitts., 2002. Recipient Nat. Endowment Humanities award, US Govt., Chgo., 1988; Fulbright Hays grant, US Govt., Egypt, 2007. Mem.: Consortium Ednl. Resource Islamic Studies. Roman Catholic. Avocations: reading, music, travel. Office Phone: 814-472-3396. Business E-Mail: mmckale@francis.edu. E-mail: mmckale@atlanticu.net.

MCKANE, DAVID BENNETT, business executive; b. Salem, Mass., July 10, 1945; s. Vernon Wilson and Barbara Inez (Bennett) McK.; m. Wilson Lineburgh Baldwin, Apr. 16, 1977; adopted daughters, Taylor A., Lee and Paige Baldwin. BA, Dartmouth Coll., 1967; MBA, Amos Tuck Sch., 1969. Product mgr. Church & Dwight Co. Inc. (Arm and Hammer Products), NYC, 1969-72; v.p. NTA Inc. NYC, Nanuet, NY, 1972-75; v.p., exec. asst. to chmn. Schick Inc., Westport, Conn., 1975-77, sr. v.p., 1977-79, COO, exec. v.p., 1979-84, treas., 1980-84; chmn., CEO A.I. Friedman, Inc., NYC, 1985-87; chmn. McKane Robbins & Co. Inc., NYC and Westport, 1986-96; mng. gen. ptnr. Riverland and Indian Sun, L.C., Westport, 1996—. Bd. dirs. Oakhurst Dairy, Portland, Maine, Impax Corp., Westport, Sprout Foods, Inc., NYC, PCC, Inc., Burlington, UT. Bd. trustees Greens Farms (Conn.) Acad., 1991—; bd. overseers Tuck Sch. Bus., Dartmouth Coll., Hanover, NH, 2008-. Mem. New Eng. Soc. in City N.Y., Mass. Mayflower Soc., Union Club (N.Y.C.), Country Club Fairfield, John's Island Club (Vero Beach, Fla.), RedStick Golf Club (Vero Beach, Fla.), Tucker's Point Club (Bermuda). Episcopalian. Home: 48 Owenoke Park Westport CT 06880-6833

MCKAY, DAVID E., mathematics professor; b. Long Beach, Calif., Aug. 4, 1951; s. John James McKay and Belva Jean Leithead. BA, U. Calif., Riverside, 1974; MA, U. Calif., Irvine, 1978. Math. tchr. Orange Coast, Costa Mesa, Calif., Calif. State U., Long Beach, Santiago Canyon Coll., Orange, Calif. Home: 20062 Midland Ln Huntington Beach CA 92646 Home Phone: 714-964-2866. Business E-Mail: dmckay@csulb.edu.

MC KAY, EMILY GANTZ, civil rights and nonprofit professional; b. Columbus, Ohio, Mar. 13, 1945; d. Harry S. and Edwina (Bookwalter) Gantz; m. Jack Alexander McKay, July 3, 1965. BA, Stanford U., 1966, MA, 1967. From pub. info. specialist to rsch. assoc. Cmty. Action Pitts., 1967—70; freelance cons., 1969—70; pub. rels. and materials specialist Met. Cleve. JOBS Coun., 1971—72; rsch. and mgmt. cons. BLK Group, Inc., Washington, 1970—73; dir. tech. products Am. Tech. Assistance Corp., McLean, Va., 1973—74; rsch. and mgmt. cons. CONSAD Rsch. Corp., Pitts., 1974—76, v.p., 1976—78; spl. asst. to pres. for planning and eval. Nat. Coun. La Raza, Washington, 1978—82, v.p. rsch., advocacy & legislation, 1981—88, exec. v.p., 1983—88, cons. to pres., 1988—90, v.p. instl. devel., 1991—93, sr. v.p. instl. devel., 1993—94. Pres. Mosaica: Ctr. for Nonprofit Devel. and Pluralism, 1994—; cons. resource devel. New Israel Fund, 1989-91; cons. City of Cleve., Nat. Assn. Cmty. Devel., Nat. Coun. La Raza, 1975-78, Ford Found., 1989, Nat. AIDS Network, 1988-89, Am. Cultural Ctr., Israel, 1990, Nat. Hispana Leadership Inst., 1993; vol. orgnl. cons. SHATIL, Jerusalem and cmty. based groups in Israel, 1987—; guest faculty Union Inst. Grad. Sch., 1975-78; adj. faculty Sch. Internat. Svc. Am. U., Washington, 1995—; mem. faculty Salzburg (Austria) Seminar on Leadership, 2003. Author orgnl. devel. tng. materials and HIV/AIDS tech. assistance materials. Co-chmn. Citizens Adv. Com. to D.C. Bar, 1986-87; mem. Mayor's Commn. Coop. Econ. Devel., 1981-83; non-lawyer bd. govs. D.C. Bar, 1982-85; exec. com., bd. dirs. Indochina Resource Action Ctr., 1982-92; bd. dirs. exec. com. Southeast Asia Resource Action Ctr., 1993-97; co-chmn. Citizens Commn. Adminstrn. Justice, 1982-84; exec. com. Coalition on Human Needs, 1981-88; Washington area steering com. New Israel Fund, 1989-91; co-chmn. adv. com. to Washington dist. office dir. Immigration and Naturalization Svc., 1984-88; chair Refugee Women in Devel., 1987-90, vice-chair, 1990-94; nat. adv. bd. Project Blueprint United Way of Am., 1992-94, diversity com., 1994-96; vice-chair, treas. Fund for Future of Our Children, 1994—; sec. bd. dirs. New Bosnia Fund, 1995-99, U.S. vice-chair, 1997-99; bd. advisors Internat. Ctr. for Residential Edn., 1994-96; bd. dirs. Mary's Ctr. Maternal and Child Care, 1995-2000, treas., 1996-2000; treas., bd. dirs. AVODAH: The Jewish Svc. Corps., 1996-99; bd. dirs. Acad. of Hope, 2001—; bd. dirs. Nat. Hispana Leadership Inst., 1997-2003, treas., 1998-2003, 2007-, Hispanic Link Journalism Found., Washington, D.C., 2004—; working group Memorandum of Understanding between HHS and Israeli Ministry of Labour and Social Welfare, 1990-94, chair subcom. Youth at Risk, 1992-94; adv. merit sel. panel Superior Ct. D.C., 1987-90; planning task force U.S.-Israel Women to Women, 2000-01. Recipient I. Pat Rios award Guadalupe Ctr., 1988, Milagros Beanfield award Ayuda, 2004; Ford Found. nat. honors fellow, 1966-67. Mem. NAACP, Nat. Coun. La Raza, Phi Beta Kappa. Democrat. Home: 3200 19th St NW Washington DC 20010-1006 Office: 1522 K St NW Ste 1130 Washington DC 20005-1225 Office Phone: 202-887-0620. Business E-Mail: Emily@mosaica.org.

MCKAY, JOANN, retired musician, composer; b. Cin., Feb. 16, 1939; d. Frederic Lawrence Ott and Gladys Leona Phillips; m. John Patrick McKay, Apr. 21, 1961; children: John Philip, Thomas Jeffrey. MusB in Performance, Cin. Coll. Conservatory Music, 1960; postgrad., Union Theol. Sem., NYC, 1960—61; MA in Music, San Francisco State Coll., 1965. Organist St. Martin's Episc. Ch., Pompano Beach, Fla., 1953—56, Faith Meth. Ch., Champaign, Ill., 1998—99; organist, choir dir., recitalist Bethlehem Meth. Ch., Cin., 1958—60, First Congl. Ch., Medford, Mass., 1961—62, St. Peter's Episc. Ch., Oakland, Calif., 1962—65; organist, recitalist First Meth. Ch., Urbana, 1967—74, Wesley Meth. Ch., Urbana, Ill., 1975—89, 2001—04; ret., 2004. Performer Tuesday Morning Musicale, Champaign, 1970—2003. Vol. with prisoners, charitable orgns. Mem.: Am. Guild Organists (registrar 1963—65, sub-dean 1975—76, winner Young Organists competition, San Francisco 1965). Avocation: reading and speaking French. Home: 915 W Charles St Champaign IL 61821

MCKAY, JOHN, law educator, former prosecutor; b. Seattle, June 19, 1956; s. John Larkin and Kathleen (Tierney) M. BA, U. Wash., 1978; JD, Creighton U., 1982. Bar: Wash. 1982, US Dist. Ct. (we. dist.) Wash. 1982, US Supreme Ct. 1990, US Ct. Appeals (9th cir.) 1990, DC 1999. Ptnr. Lane Powell, Seattle, 1982-92, Cairncross & Hempelmann, Seattle, 1992-97; pres. Legal Svcs. Corp., Washington, 1997—2001; US atty. (we. dist.) Wash. US Dept. Justice, 2001—07. Law prof. Seattle U. Law Sch., 2007—. White House fellow, Washington, 1989-90; named Pro Bono Lawyer of Yr. Wash. State Bar Assn., 1995, Assn. Award of Merit, 2001, Courageous Award, 2007 Mem. ABA (bd. govs. 1991-94), Wash. State Bar Assn. (pres. young lawyers divsn. 1988-89). Independent. Roman Catholic. Avocations: soccer, golf. Office: Seattle U Sch Law Sullivan Hall PO Box 222000 901 12th Ave Seattle WA 98122-1090

MCKAY, JOHN PATRICK, history professor; b. St. Louis, Aug. 27, 1938; s. John Price and Eleanor Jeffrey McKay; m. JoAnn Ott, Apr. 21, 1961; children: John Philip, Thomas Jeffrey. BA, Wesleyan U., Middletown, Conn., 1961; MA, Tufts U., 1962; PhD, U. Calif., Berkeley, 1968. From instr. to assoc. prof. history U. Ill., Urbana, 1966-76, prof., 1976-99, prof. emeritus, 1999—. Mem. author's adv. bd. Houghton Mifflin Co., Boston, 1992-94. Author: Pioneers for Profit: Foreign Entrepreneurship and Russian Industrialization, 1885-1913, 1970 (Herbert Baxter Adams prize Am. Hist. Assn. 1970), Tramways and Trolleys: The Rise of Urban Mass Transit in Europe, 1976; co-author: (with B. Hill, J. Buckler, C. Crowston and M. Wiesner-Hanks) A History of Western Society, 1979, 9th edit., 2008, (with B. Hill, J. Buckler, P. Ebrey, C. Crowston, M. Wiesner-Hanks and R. Beck) A History of World Societies, 1983, 8th edit., 2009. Fellow for western Europe, Fgn. Area Program, 1964-66, John Simon Guggenheim fellow, 1970, Internat. Rsch. Exch. fellow, USSR, 1970, fellow NEH, 1984. Mem. Am. Hist. Assn., Econ. History Assn., Bus. History Conf., World History Assn., French Hist. Soc. Avocations: hiking, travel, gardening, cooking. Office: U Ill Dept History 810 S Wright St Urbana IL 61801 Business E-Mail: jpmckay@illinois.edu.

MCKAY, KENNETH GARDINER, retired physicist, electronics company executive; b. Montreal, Quebec, Canada, Apr. 8, 1917; came to U.S., 1946, naturalized, 1954; s. James Gardiner and Margaret (Nicholas) McK.; m. Irene C. Smith, July 25, 1942; children— Margaret Craig, Kenneth Gardiner B.Sc., McGill U., 1938, M.Sc., 1939; Sc.D, MIT, 1941; D.Eng. (hon.), Stevens Inst. Tech., 1980. Research engr. Nat. Research Council Can., 1941-46; with Bell Telephone Labs., 1946-66, 73-80, dir. solid state device devel., 1957-59, v.p. systems engring., 1959-62, exec. v.p. systems engring., 1962-66, exec. v.p., 1973-80; v.p. engring AT&T, 1966-73; chmn. bd. Bellcomm Inc., 1966-73, Charles Stark Draper Lab., 1982-87; ret., 1987. Advisor Min. of Transp. and Comms., Republic of China, 1982-95. Trustee Stevens Inst. Tech., 1974-87; bd. govs. McGill U., 1972-77, N.Y. Coll. Osteo. Medicine, 1980-89; mem. vis. com. for engring. Stanford U., 1974-87; mem. sci. and acad. adv. com. U. Calif., 1980-88; mem. Sci. and Tech. Adv. Group, Republic of China, 1982-96. Fellow IEEE, Am. Phys. Soc., N.Y. Acad. Scis.; mem. NAS, NAE (councillor 1970-73), Century Assn.

MCKAY, KENNETH K., political organization administrator; BS, High Point U., NC, 1991; JD, Roger Williams U. Sch. Law, Bristol, RI, 1996. Bar: RI 1996, US Dist. Ct. (RI dist.) 1996. Atty. Taft & McSally, RI; campaign mgr., chief of staff to Gov. Don Carcieri State of RI, 2002—07; ptnr. Brown Rudnick Berlack Israels LLP, Providence; now pvt. practice atty.; chief of staff Rep. Nat. Com., 2009—. Served in inf. divsn. US Army. Republican. Office: RNC 310 First St Washington DC 20003 Office Phone: 202-863-8500. Office Fax: 202-863-8820.*

MCKAY, LAMAR, oil industry executive; m. Nancy McKay. BS in Petroleum Engring., summa cum laude, Miss. State U.; MBA, Ind. U. Reservoir engr. Amoco Production Co., 1980, various comml. and oper. roles in US, then gen. mgr. Arkoma Basin, 1993—97, bus. unit leader Gulf of Mexico, 1997, (merger with Brit. Petroleum), 1998; head strategy/planning, worldwide exploration & prodn. BP plc, London, 1999—2000, Ctrl. North Sea bus. unit leader Aberdeen, Scotland, 2000, chief of staff worldwide exploration/prodn. London, chief of staff to dep. group chief exec., 2002—03, group v.p. Russia & Kazakhstan upstream/downstream bus. London, 2003—07, sr. group v.p. BP plc, exec. v.p. and COO BP America Houston, 2007—08, exec. v.p. spl. projects, 2008—09, chmn., pres. BP America, 2009—. Bd. dirs. TNK-BP Ltd, 2004—07, vice chmn. remuneration/compensation com.; former mem. adv. coun. Russian Fedn. Fgn. Investors; bd. mem. US-Russia Bus. Coun. Office: BP America Inc 501 Westlake Pk Blvd Houston TX 77079*

MCKAY, LAURA L., bank executive, consultant; b. Watonga, Okla., Mar. 3, 1947; d. Frank Bradford and Elizabeth Jane (Smith) Drew; m. Cecil O. McKay, Sept. 20, 1969; 1 child, Leslie. BSBA, Oreg. State U., 1969. Cert. cash mgr., Assn. Fin. Profls. New br. rsch. U.S. Bank, Portland, Oreg., 1969-80, cash mgmt. officer, 1980-82, asst. v.p., 1982-87, v.p., 1987-94; founder, cons. LLM Cons., Milw., 1994-97; co-founder, mng. ptnr. DMC & Assocs. LLC, Portland, 1997—2001; v.p. treasury mgmt., sales mgr. West Coast Bank, 2000—06, sr. v.p mgr., treasury mgmt., 2006—. Cert. trainer Achieve Global and Edge Learning. Chmn. Budget Com., North Clackamas Sch. Dist., 1982-84. Mem. Assn. for Fin. Profls., Nat. Assn. Bank Women (chmn. Oreg. group 1979-80), Portland Treasury Mgrs. Assn., Portland C. of C. Republican. Office: Ste 100 5000 Meadows Rd Lake Oswego OR 97034 Home Phone: 503-632-3564; Office Phone: 503-603-8052. E-mail: mckayl@wcb.com.

MCKAY, MARGO MARQUITA, lawyer, former federal agency administrator; b. Baltimore, Md., Oct. 9, 1946; d. Gordon and Gary Venetia (Jones) M.; m. James Phillip Allen, Jr., June 10, 1978; children: Marja Allen, Eric Allen, Kaila Allen. BA, Fisk U., Nashville, Tenn., 1968; JD, Georgetown U., DC, 1975. Bar: Penn. 1975, Va. 1982, DC 1992. Trial atty. US Dept. Justice, Washington, 1975-78; atty. Am. Legal Cons., 1979; br. chief Dept. Army US Dept. Def., 1980-81; mng. atty. Legal Serv. No. Va., Alexandria, 1982-83; exec. asst. to vice-chmn., sr. advisor, US Merit Systems Protection Bd., Washington, 1983-91; dep. dir. for ethics US Dept. Housing & Urban Devel. (HUD), Washington, 1990; adminstrv. judge, temp. panel Office Employee Appeals, DC, 1991—92; dir. compliance, assoc. gen. counsel Fannie Mae (Fed. Nat. Mortgage Assn.), 1992—2006; asst. sec. for civil rights USDA, Washington, 2006—09. Author (high sch. textbook): Street Law, 1975. Recipient numerous awards. Mem. ABA, NBA, Federal Circuit Bar Assoc. Personal E-mail: margomckay@aol.com.

MCKAY, MARIE CONYERS, librarian, writer; b. Brumley, Mo., Aug. 18, 1930; d. Raymond Harold Conyers and Nellie Mae Bunch; m. Julius S. McKay, Oct. 19, 1964; children: Michelle Leighanne O'Beirne, Rosemary Susan O'Hern. AA, S.W. Bapt. Coll., Bolivar, Mo., 1948; BA, Okla. Bapt. U., Shawnee, 1950; MA in Libr. Sci., George Peabody Coll. Tchrs. (now Vanderbilt U.), Nashville, 1951; M in Religious Edn., So. Bapt. Theol. Sem., Louisville, Ky., 1959. Libr. cataloger N.E. Mo. State Coll. (now Harry Truman State U.), Kirksville, 1951—53; libr. S.W. Bapt. Coll. (Now U.), Bolivar, Mo., 1953—57; dep. libr. Hong Kong Bapt. U., Kowloon, 1960—64, curator archive on the history of Christianity in China, 1996—98; libr. cataloger Miss. State U., Starkville, 1987—96. Contbr. articles to profl. jours. Missionary So. Bapt. Fgn. Mission Bd., Richmond, Va., 1959—64. Mem.: ALA. Baptist. Home: 108 Kyle Ct Gardendale AL 35071 Personal E-mail: mmckay@bellsouth.net.

MCKAY, MICHAEL DENNIS, lawyer; b. Omaha, May 12, 1951; s. John Larkin and Kathleen (Tierney) McK.; m. Nancie Miller McKay.; children: Kevin Tierney, Kathleen Lindsay, John Larkin. BA in Polit. Sci. with distinction, U. Wash., 1973; JD, Creighton U., 1976. Bar: Wash. 1976, U.S. Dist. Ct. (we. dist.) Wash. 1978, U.S. Dist. Ct. (ea. dist.) Wash. 1982, U.S. Ct. Appeals (9th cir.) 1982, U.S. Supreme Ct. 1993. Sr. dep. pros. atty. King County, Seattle, 1976-81; ptnr. McKay &

Gaitan, Seattle, 1981-89; U.S. atty. we. dist. Wash. Seattle, 1989-93; ptnr. Lane Powell Spears Lubersky, Seattle, 1993-95, McKay Chadwell PLLC, Seattle, 1995—. Bd. dirs. Mental Health North, Seattle, 1982-85, St. Joseph Sch. Bd., 1984-87, Our Lady of Fatima Sch. Commn., 1994-97, stadium adv. bd., Seattle Kingdome, 1987-89; mem. U.S. Atty. Gen. Adv. Com., 1991-93, vice chmn., 1992; mem. Washington Citizens' Commn. on Salaries for Elected Officials, 1997-2001; vice chmn., 1999-2001; vice chmn. Seattle Expert Rev. Panel, 1999; vice chair Washington State George W. Bush Campaign, 2000, 2004; co-chair McCain 2008 Wash. State Steering Com. Recipient Alumni Merit award, Creighton U. Law Sch., 2001. Mem. Creighton U. Alumni Assn. (pres. 1988-90, nat. alumni bd. 1988-92, bd. dirs.), Wash. Athletic Club. Republican. Roman Catholic. Avocations: golf, reading. Office: McKay Chadwell PLLC 600 University St Ste 1601 Seattle WA 98101 Business E-Mail: mdm@mckay-chadwell.com.

MCKAY, MICHAEL I., biologist, researcher; b. Browning, Mont., June 26, 1968; Degree in Biology, Mont. State U., Billings, 2002. Rsch. supr. Blackfeet CC, Browning, 2002—. Home: PO box 1385 Browning MT 59417 Office: Blackfeet CC US Hwy 2 & 89 Browning MT 59417

MCKAY, MICHAEL KEVIN, nurse, priest, chaplain; b. Chgo., Jan. 10, 1952; s. Gilbert Angus Jr. and Winifred Mary (Endebrock) McKay; m. Kathryn Jane Young, July 10, 1976 (div. Apr. 1, 1980). AA, St. Petersburg Coll., Fla., 1974; AS in Paramedic Tech., St. Petersburg Coll., Clearwater, Fla., 1974; AS in Nursing, St. Petersburg Coll., Pinellas Park, Fla., 1985; MDiv in Theology, U. Ministries Sch. Theology, Milford, Mich., 2004. LPN, St. Petersburg Vocat.-Tech. Inst., Fla., 1981, RN Fla., 1985, cert. in acute traumatic stress mgmt., Am. Acad. Experts in Traumatic Stress, 2008, cmty. chaplain, Cmty. Chaplains America, 2008, Christian counselor, Am. Assn. Christian Counselors, 2008, stress and trauma mgmt., Light Univ., Am. Assn. Christian Counselors, 2009; evangelism ministry Mercy St. Ministries, NC, 2006. EMT/paramedic Tarpon Springs, Dunedin, Fla., 1974—80; LPN, critical care nurse Mease Hosp., Dunedin, Fla., 1980—85, RN critical care, emergency dept., 1985—94; RN critical care emergency, rehab. Suncoast Hosp., Largo, Fla., 1994—2000; with Sweetbay Supermarket, Clearwater, Fla., 2000—08; ordained priest Old Cath. Ch., 2004, consecrated Bishop, 2005; pastor, founder Regina Caeli Old Cath. Ministries, Oldsmar, Fla., 2004—; hospice nurse Hernando/Pasco Hospice, New Port Richey, Fla., 2006—08; founder, cleric regular, superior gen. Servants of St. Camillus de Lellis, Oldsmar, 2007—; rehab nurse HCR Manor Care/Dunedin, 2008; registered nurse, chaplain Fla. Dept. Vet. Affairs, Baldomero Lopez State Vets. Nursing Home, Land O Lakes, Fla., 2008—. Critical care and rehab. nurse specialist, 1986—; bishop Old Cath. Ch., Fla., 2005—, cmty. chaplain, Fla., 2006—. Mem. Med. Reserve Corps, Pinellas County, Fla., 2008—; exec. officer Fla. brigade 2nd divsn. US Corps Chaplains, 2003—; mem, chaplain AMVETS Post 67 USS Cole, Clearwater, 2003—; emergency contact vol. Next of Kin Registry, 2008—; mem., chaplain, safety officer, bd. dirs. Tampa Bay REACT, Hillsborough County, Fla., 2008—; mem., chaplain Oldsmar Cmty. Emergency Response Team, Pinellas County, Fla., 2009—; mem. Greater Tampa Cmty. Emergency Response Team, Hillsborough County, Fla., 2009. With USN, 1970—72. Mem.: NRA (life; patron), Am. Assn. Christian Counselors, Am. Acad. Experts in Traumatic Stress (cert. acute traumatic stress mgr. 2008), AMVETS (life). Conservative. Catholic. Office Phone: 727-466-5469. Personal E-mail: fr-nevin-mary@earthlink.net.

MCKAY, MICHAEL WENDELL, lawyer; b. Beaufort, SC, Dec. 14, 1949; s. John W. and Alice (Thornhill) M.; m. Leah H. McKay; children: Wendell, Slater, Watson, Harris. BA, La. State U., Baton Rouge, 1971, JD, 1974. Bar: La. 1974, U.S. Dist. Ct. (mid. dist.) La. 1974, U.S. Dist. Ct. (we. dist.) La. 1976, U.S. Dist. Ct. (ea. dist.) La. 1977, U.S. Ct. Appeals (5th cir.) 1977, U.S. Supreme Ct. 1977, U.S. Ct. Appeals (11th cir.) 1981. Assoc./ptnr. Brewer & McKay, Baton Rouge, 1974-80; ptnr. Roy, Kiesel, Patterson & McKay, Baton Rouge, 1980-84; pvt. practice Baton Rouge, 1984-88; dir. Hoffman Sutterfield, Baton Rouge, 1988-97; of counsel Shows, Cali & Burns, Baton Rouge, 1997-99; ptnr. McKay Williamson Lutgring & Cochran, LLC, Baton Rouge, 1999—2004, McKay Lutgring & Cochran, LLC, Baton Rouge, 2004—. Bd. dirs. Baton Rouge Area Found., 1994-97; treas., bd. dirs. Capital Area Legal Svcs. Corp., Baton Rouge, 1978-83. Mem. ABA, La. State Bar Assn. (bd. govs. 1995-98, treas. 1999-2000, pres., 2004-05, Pres.'s award 1997, Pro Bono Publico award 1994), Baton Rouge Bar Assn. (pres., sec., treas. 1989-93), La. Bar Found. (bd. dirs. 1998-2000), La. Assn. Def. Counsel (bd. dirs. 1999-2001), Am. Inns of Ct., La. Trial Lawyers Assn. (bd. govs. 1980-). Democrat. Episcopalian. Avocation: tennis. Office: McKay Lutgring & Cochran 2431 S Acadian Thruway Ste 290 Baton Rouge LA 70808 Business E-Mail: mike@mlclawyers.com.

MCKAY, MONROE GUNN, federal judge; b. Huntsville, Utah, May 30, 1928; s. James Gunn and Elizabeth (Peterson) McK.; m. Lucile A. Kinnison, Aug. 6, 1954; children: Michele, Valanne, Margaret, James, Melanie, Nathan, Bruce, Lisa, Monroe. BS, Brigham Young U., 1957; JD, U. Chgo., 1960. Bar: Ariz. 1961. Law clk. Ariz. Supreme Ct., 1960-61; assoc. firm Lewis & Roca, Phoenix, 1961-66, ptnr., 1968-74; assoc. prof. Brigham Young U., 1974-76, prof., 1976-77; judge US Ct. Appeals (10th cir.), Denver, 1977-91, chief judge, 1991-94, sr. judge, 1994—. Mem. Phoenix Community Council Juvenile Problems, 1968-74; pres. Ariz. Assn. for Health and Welfare, 1970-72; dir. Peace Corps, Malawi, Africa, 1966-68; bd. dirs., pres. Maricopa county Legal Aid Soc., 1972-74. Served with USMCR, 1946-48. Mem. Ariz. Bar Assn. Mem. Lds Ch. Office: Us Ct Appeals 10th Cir Fed Bldg 125 S State St Ste 6012 Salt Lake City UT 84138-1181*

MCKAY, PATRICIA A., corporate financial executive; CPA. V.p. fin., contr. Dole Food Co., 1993—96; various positions including sr. v.p. fin. AutoNation Inc., 1997—2003; exec. v.p., CFO Restoration Hardware Inc., 2003—05, Office Depot, Delray Beach, Fla., 2005—08.

MCKAY, PAUL PATRICK, healthcare educator; b. Pawtucket, RI, Dec. 18, 1964; s. Kenneth John McKay and Ann Virginia Graham; m. Susan Marie Phelps; children: Kristin Nicole, Alannah Kathryn; m. Tambra Mae Sommer. Dir. N.Am. Brain Tumor Coalition, DC, 2001; pres. Brain Tumor Action Network, Zephyrhills, Fla., 2002—. Founder, pres. Brain Tumor Action Network, Zephyrhills, Fla., 2002; tri-state coord. Fathers 4 Justice. E-4 USAF, 1982—86, Ramstein AFB, W.Germany. Recipient Mgr. of Yr. award, San Diego Bus. Jour., 1997. Mem.: Mensa. Independent. Achievements include having an integral role in passing the Benign Brain Tumor Cancer Registries Amendment Act of 2002. Personal E-mail: pmckay@btan.org.

MCKAY, RENEE, artist; b. Montreal, Que., Can. came to US, 1946, naturalized, 1954; d. Frederick Garvin and Mildred Gladys (Higgins) Smith; m. Kenneth Gardiner McKay, July 25, 1942; children: Margaret Craig, Kenneth Gardner. BA, McGill U., 1941. Tchr. art Peck Sch., Morristown, NJ, 1955-56. One woman shows include Pen and Brush Club, NYC, 1957, Cosmopolitan Club, NYC, 1958; group shows include Weyhe Gallery, NYC, 1978, Newark Mus., 1955, 59, Montclair (NJ) Mus., 1955-58, Nat. Assn. Women Artists, Nat. Acad. Galleries, 1954-78, NY World's Fair, 1964-65, Audubon Artists, NYC, 1955-62, 74-79, NY Soc. Women Artists, 1979-80, Provincetown (Mass.) Art Assn. and Mus., 1975-79; traveling shows in France, Belgium, Italy, Scotland, Can., Japan; represented in permanent collections: Slater Meml. Mus., Norwich, Conn., Norfolk (Va.) Mus., Butler Inst. Am. Art, Youngstown, Ohio, Lydia Drake Libr., Pembroke, Mass., Nat. Arts Club, NYC, Provinceton Mus.- Mass., Provincetown, many pvt. collections. Recipient Jane Peterson prize in oils Nat. Assn. Women Artists, 1954, Famous Artists Sch. prize in watercolor, 1959, Grumbacher Artists Watercolor award 1970, Solo award Pen and Brush, 1957, Sadie-Max Tesser award in watercolor Audubon Artists, 1975, Peterson prize in oils, 1980, Michael Engel prize Nat. Soc. Painters in Casein and Acrylic, 1983. Mem. Nat. Assn. Women Artists (2d v.p. 1969-70, adv. bd. 1974-76), Audubon Artists (pres. 1979, dir. oils 1986-88), Artist Equity (dir. 1977-79, v.p. 1979-81), NY Soc. Women Artists, Pen and Brush, Nat. Soc. Painters in Casein and Acrylic M.J. Kaplan prize 1984, Nat. Arts Club, Provincetown Art Assn. and Mus., Key West Art Assn., Cosmopolitan Club.

MCKAY, RICHARD JAMES, professional sports team executive; b. Eugene, Oreg., Mar. 16, 1959; s. John H. and Nancy Jean (Hunter) McK.; m. Terrin Lea Few, May 19, 1984; children: K. Hunter, John Crosby. BA, Princeton U., 1981; JD, Stetson Coll. Law, St. Petersburg, Fla., 1984. Bar: Fla. 1984, U.S. Dist. Ct. (mid. dist.) Fla. 1984. Law clk. to Hon. William Terrell Hodges U.S. Dist. Ct. (middle dist. Fla.), Tampa, 1984-86; ptnr. Hill, Ward & Henderson, Tampa, Fla., 1986-92; gen. mgr. Tampa Bay Buccaneers, 1993—2003, Atlanta Falcons, 2003—07, pres., 2003—. Adj. prof. Stetson Coll. Law, St. Petersburg, 1989-92; co-chmn. NFL Competition Com., 1994—. Office: Atlanta Falcons 4400 Falcon Pkwy Flowery Branch GA 30542*

MCKAY-WILKINSON, JULIE ANN, minister, marriage and family therapist; b. Washington, Feb. 26, 1953; d. Charles William and Evelyn Loretta (Starr) McKay; m. Grover Gene Wilkinson, Jan. 13, 1990; 1 child, Angela Starr Gotti. AS, Camden County Coll., 1975; BA, Rowan U., 1978; grad., Unity Sch. Christianity, Lee's Summit, Mo., 1997. Cert. pastoral addictions counselor, and lic. addictions counselor, co-dependency counselor. Probation officer York County Probation, Pa., 1983—86; therapist pvt. practice, York, 1985—90, New Insights, York, 1985—87, Clare Ctr., York, 1987—90; founder, min., therapist Unity Christ Ch., Lubbock, Tex., 1997—2003. Host weekly TV program Spiritual Lifelines. Editor: (monthly newsletter) Spiritual Lifelines, 1997—2003. Chairperson Christmas toy dr. Unity Christ Ch., 1997—2003, founder, Christmas bear dr., 2003—. Mem.: Lubbock Ecimenical Orgn. Democrat. Avocations: gardening, music, movies. Office: Unity Ctr Spiritual Living 7300 Mallard Creek Rd Charlotte NC 28262 Home: 2540 Pickway Dr Charlotte NC 28269 Office Phone: 704-599-1180. Personal E-mail: revjulie3@carolina.rr.com.

MCKEAGUE, DAVID WILLIAM, federal judge; b. Pitts., Nov. 5, 1946; s. Herbert William and Phyllis (Forsyth) McKeague; m. Nancy L. Palmer, May 20, 1989; children: Mike, Melissa, Sarah, Laura, Elizabeth, Adam. BBA, U. Mich., 1968, JD, 1971. Bar: Mich. 1971, US Dist. Ct. (we. dist.) Mich. 1972, US Dist. Ct. (ea. dist.) Mich. 1978, US Ct. Appeals (6th cir.) 1988. Assoc. Foster, Swift, Collins & Smith, Lansing, Mich., 1971-76, ptnr., 1976-92, sec.-treas., 1990-92; judge US Dist. Ct., (we. dist.) Mich., Lansing, Mich., 1992—2005, US Ct. Appeals (6th Cir.), Lansing, Mich., 2005—. Adm. prof. Mich. State U. Coll. Law, 1998—. Mem. nat. com. U. Mich. Law Sch. Fund, 1980—92, bd. trustees, 2007—; gen. counsel Mich. Rep. Com., 1989—92; mem. adv. coun. Wharton Ctr. Mich. State U., 1996—2002; adv. bd. Corp. Supportive Housing, 2002—. With USAR, 1969—75. Mem.: FBA (bd. dirs. Western Mich. chpt. 1991—), Federalist Soc. Law and Pub. Studies (lawyers divsn. Mich. chpt. 1996—), Am. Inns Ct. (pres. Mich. State U. Coll. Law chpt. 1999—2001), Mich. Bar Assn., Country Club Lansing (bd. govs. 1988—92; 1995—2001). Roman Catholic. Office: Us Court Of Appeals 315 W Allegan St Rm 213 Lansing MI 48933-1515 Office Phone: 517-377-1563. Business E-Mail: ca06-mckeague_chambers@ca6.uscourts.gov.*

MCKEAN, KEVIN S., publishing executive, writer; b. Ann Arbor, Mich; BA in English cum laude, Yale U., 1974. Police reporter City New Bur. Chgo., 1974; gen. assignment writer, broadcast editor AP, Denver and New Orleans, 1975, nat. sci. writer NY, 1978—81; staff writer, sr. editor Discover mag., 1981—87; sr. editor Money mag., 1987—95; founding editor Money.com, 1995—97; asst. mng. editor bus./fin. Time Inc. New Media, 1997—99; editor at large Mutual Funds mag., 1999; exec. editor Forbes.com, 1999—2000; editl. dir. PC World mag., 2000—03; editorial dir., CEO InfoWorld Media Grp., San Francisco, 2003—05; v.p., editl. dir. Consumer Reports mag. Consumers Union, 2005—. Spkr. in field. Sci. editor (3 hr. WGBH-produced pub. TV spl.) Living Against the Odds, 1991, TV appearances include NBC'S Today show, CBS This Morning, CNN, CNBC; contbr. chapters to books. Named to Power Media 50, B2B Mag., 2005. Office: Consumers Union 101 Truman Ave Yonkers NY 10703-1057*

MCKEAN, ROBERT JACKSON, JR., retired lawyer; b. NYC, Dec. 21, 1925; s. Robert Jackson and Isabel (Murphy) McKean; m. Sally H. Ament; children from previous marriage: Katherine, Douglas, Lauren, Andrew. BA, Amherst Coll., 1950; LL.B., Harvard U., 1953. Bar: NY 1954. Assoc. Simpson Thacher & Bartlett, NYC, 1953-62, ptnr., 1962-85. Life trustee Amherst Coll., Mass.; emeritus trustee Folger Shakespeare Libr., Washington. With US Army, 1944—46, ETO. Recipient medal for eminent svc., Amherst Coll., 1968. Mem.: Phi Beta Kappa. Democrat.

MCKEAN, SHERRY LYNN, neurodiagnostic technologist; b. Owosso, Mich., Mar. 3, 1953; d. William Ash and Myrtle Viola (Darling) Salander; m. Brian Patrick McKean, May 31, 1997; 1 child, Jennifer Lynn Bentley. A, John Wesley Coll., 1979; degree, Calif. Coll. Health Scis., 2002. Registered polysomnographic technologist. Neurodiagnostic supr. Dr. Gary Roat, Flint, Mich., 1978—95; neurodiagnostic tech. Flint Osteo. Hosp., 1993—95, Dr. I. Zachar Dyme, Lansing, 1995—, Meml. Healthcare, Owosso, 1995—. Mem.: Assn. Polysomnographic Technologists. Avocations: hiking, travel, reading, sewing, walking. Office: 826 W King St Owosso MI 48867 Home: 2220 West Mason Rd Owosso MI 48867

MCKEAN, THOMAS WAYNE, retired dentist, military officer; b. Adams County, Ind., May 18, 1928; s. Gorman F. and Elmira B. (Staley) McK.; m. Marilyn Kimberlin, Aug. 9, 1952; children: Thomas Wayne, Randall K., Dana K. D.D.S., Ind. U., 1953; grad., Naval Dental Sch., 1963. Diplomate: Am. Bd. Oral Surgery. Commd. ensign Dental Corps USN, 1949—53, advanced through grades to rear adm., 1980; stationed at Naval Tng. Ctr., Great Lakes, Ill., 1953; dental officer U.S.S. Randall, 1953-56; head dental svc., asst. dental officer U.S. Naval Acad./Naval Hosp., Annapolis, Md., 1956-59; dental officer FASRON III; asst. dental officer U.S. Naval Sta., Bermuda, 1959-63; postgrad. student Naval Dental Sch., Bethesda, Md., 1963-64; resident oral and maxillofacial surgery Naval Hosp., Great Lakes, Ill., 1964-66; dental officer U.S.S. America, 1966-68; chief oral surgery Naval Hosp., Orlando, Fla., 1968-70; dir. oral surgery and gen. practice residency tng. programs Naval Regional Med. Ctr., Great Lakes, 1970-74, chmn. dept. dentistry, 1970-74; cons., lectr. U.S. Army, Fort Sheridan, Ill., 1970-74; dir. oral surgery and gen. practice residency tng. programs Naval Regional Med. Ctr., Oakland, Calif., 1974-78, chmn., dept. dentistry, 1974-78; lectr. oral surgery Letterman Army Med. Ctr., San Francisco, 1974-78; clin. lectr. dept. oral surgery U. of Pacific Sch. Dentistry, San Francisco, 1974-78; comdg. officer Naval Regional Dental Ctr., Pensacola, Fla., 1978-80; lectr. oral surgery Pensacola (Fla.) Jr. Coll., 1978-80; cons., lectr. Dwight D. Eisenhower Army Regional Med. Ctr., Augusta, Ga., 1978-80; insp. gen. dental Bur. Medicine and Surgery, Dept. of Navy, Washington, 1980-81; comdg. officer Naval Regional Dental Ctr., San Diego, 1981-82; insp. gen. Naval Med. Command, Washington, 1983-85; ret., 1985—2008. Contbr. articles to profl. jours. Chmn. bd. trustees UMC, Winter Park, 1992, mem. bd. adminstrs. 1995-98; bd. dirs. Circle of Friends Fla. Hosp. Found., 1989-91, Fla. Hosp. Found., 1991—, chmn. bd., 1995-96; bd. dirs., Fla. Hosp. Found., 1991-, chmn., Ctrl. Fla. Veterans, Inc., 2007-, bd. trustees 2008-; chmn. Fla. Hosp. Shares (Internat. Med. Missions), 1994—; mem. Fla. Hosp. Cmty. Benefits subcom., 1996-, Leadership Coun. FUMC Winter Pk., 2007-09. Decorated Humanitarian Service medal, Legion of Merit with Gold Star, Meritorious Service medal, Nat. Def. Service medal with star, Vietnam Service medal, Republic of Vietnam Campaign medal with device, others; recipient Alumnus of Yr. award Ind. U. Sch.of Dentistry Alumnus Assn., 1988. Fellow Am. Dental Soc. of Anesthesiology, Internat. Coll. Dentists, Am. Coll. Dentists, Internat. Assn. Oral Surgeons; mem. Am. Assn. Oral and Maxillofacial Surgeons, ADA, Western Soc. Oral Surgeons, Assn. Mil. Surgeons U.S. (medal), Fla. Soc. Oral Surgeons, Delta Sigma Delta, Sigma Chi (Significant Sig award 1983). Home: 1309 Temple Grove Ct Winter Park FL 32789-2716 Home Phone: 407-644-9672. Personal E-mail: tmckean1@cfl.rr.com.

MCKEAND, PATRICK JOSEPH, newspaper publisher, educator; b. Anderson, Ind., June 10, 1941; s. William Dale and Iva Pearl (Shaw) McK. BA, Ind. U., 1963; MA, Ball State U., 1983. Staff writer The St. Petersburg (Fla.) Times, 1963; mng. editor The Anderson (Ind.) Herald, 1968-79; adminstr. analyst Ind. Medicaid Program, Indpls., 1980-81; assoc. prof. Defense Info. Sch., Ft. Ben Harrison, Ind., 1981-89; owner p.m. ink!, Indpls., 1989—. Pub. bd. dirs. Student Pub. at Ind. U., Purdue U. at Indpls., 1992-2003; bd. dirs. Miss Ind. Scholarship Pageant, Indpls., 2005—. Capt. U.S. Army, 1964-68. Recipient Ind.'s Sagamore of the Wabash award, 2003; decorated Bronze Star, Army Commendation medal with 1 oak leaf cluster. Mem. Soc. Profl. Journalists (bd. dirs.), Soc. Newspaper Design, Assn. Educators in Journalism and Mass Comm., Associated Press Mng. Editors Assn., Investigative Reporters and Editors, Ind. Collegiate Press Assn. (bd. dirs., exec. dir.), Coll. Media Advisors (Disting. Newspaper Adviser award 1998), Faculty Club IUPUI (bd. dirs. 2002—). Home: 4450 E 56th St Indianapolis IN 46220-5710 E-mail: pmckeand@iupui.edu.

MCKECHNIE, JOHN CHARLES, gastroenterologist, educator; b. Louisville, Feb. 1, 1935; s. Albert Hay and Edna Scott (Johnson) McKechnie; children: Steven Keith, Kevin Stuart. BA, U. Louisville, 1955; MD, Baylor Coll. Medicine, Houston, 1959. Diplomate Am. Bd. Internal Medicine, Am. Bd. Gastroenterology. Intern Jefferson Davis Hosp., Houston, 1959—60; resident internal medicine Baylor Affiliated Program, Houston, 1960—61, 1965—66; gen. practice medicine Benham, Ky., 1964; practice medicine specializing in gastroenterology Houston, 1966—; clin. instr. Baylor Coll. Medicine, Houston, 1966—69, asst. prof., 1969—72, assoc. prof., 1972—77, prof., 1977—. Mem. staff Meth. Hosp., assoc. dir. internal medicine program; cons. Ben Taub Hosp., St. Luke's Episcopal Hosp.; clin. prof. Weill Cornell Med. Coll., NYC. Contbr. articles to profl. jours. Capt. USMC, 1962—64. Fellow: ACP, Am. Coll. Gastroenterology (gov. Tex. chpt. 1979—80, trustee 1981—84); mem.: AMA, Houston Gastroent. Soc. (pres. 1983), Tex. Soc. Gastrointestinal Endoscopy, Am. Soc. Gastrointestinal Endoscopy, Digestive Disease Found., Am. Gastroent. Assn., Tex. Med. Assn., So. Med. Assn., Alpha Omega Alpha. Republican. Presbyterian. Office: 6560 Fannin St Ste 1630 Houston TX 77030-2734 Office Phone: 713-797-0916.

MCKEE, BETTY DAVIS, English language educator; b. St. Pauls, NC, June 30, 1946; d. John Chesley and Ernestene King Davis; m. Danny Lee McKee, July 13, 1980; children: Brooke Elizabeth Burgess, Ginger Rae Fears, Amanda Lea. AA, Chowan Coll., Murfreesboro, NC, 1966; BA, Campbell Coll., Buies Creek, NC, 1968. Cert. Collegiate Profl. Va., 1970. Tchr. Pinkston St. Sch., Henderson, NC, 1968—70, Western Br. Jr. HS, Chesapeake, Va., 1970—71, 1971—73, 1975—91, chair English dept., 1976—80, 1990—91; tchr. Deep Creek Jr. HS, Chesapeake, 1974—75; tchr., chair, team leader Western Br. Mid. Sch., Chesapeake, 1991—2006, internal coord. So. Assn. Colls. and Schs., 2004—, mem. faculty adv. com. Mem. AAUW, Portsmouth, Va., 2001—05; bd. dirs. Campbell U. Alumni Assn., Buies Creek, 1978—94; yearbook sponsor, 1971—85; pres. Tidewater chpt. Campbell U. Alumni Assn., Chesapeake, 1978—98. Named Tchr. of Yr., We. Br. Jr. H.S., 1987. Mem.: NEA, PTA (life), Chesapeake Edn. Assn. (treas. 2000—04), Va. Edn. Assn., Delta Kappa Gamma Beta Iota (assoc.; rec. sec. 2000—02, pres. 2002—04). Avocations: reading, travel.

MCKEE, CATHERINE LYNCH, lawyer, educator; b. Boston, June 7, 1962; d. Robert Emmett and Anne Gayle (Tanner) Lynch; m. Bert K. McKee Jr., Dec. 25, 1990; children: Timothy Kingston, Shannon Lancaster. BA in Biol. Sci., U. Calif. Berkeley, 1984; JD, U. San Diego, 1988. Bar: Calif. 1988, U.S. Dist. Ct. (cen., so. and ea. dists.) Calif. 1989, U.S. Ct. Appeals (9th cir.) 1989. Assoc. Parkinson, Wolf, Lazar & Leo, LA, 1988—89, McCormick & Mitchell, San Diego, 1989—91; prof. Mt. San Antonio Coll., Walnut, 1994—, mock trial coach, 1994—2000, dir. paralegal program, 1999—2003, 2004—05, 2007. Cert. rev. hearing officer, Orange County, 1994-2004; legal counsel Imperial Valley Lumber Co., Valley Lumber and Truss Co., 1998—; coach nat. champion C.C. mock trial team, 2000; mem. acad. senate exec. coun. Mt. San Antonio Coll., 1996-2000, chmn. campus equivalency com., 1999, chair paralegal program adv. com., 1999-2003, 04-05, 07, verifier for cert. of online tchg., 2005—, adv. student club Paralegal Soc., 2006; mem. East San Gabriel Valley regional occupl. program adv. com., 2003—, Faculty Assn. Rep. Five Coun., 2009-. Contbr. weekly newspaper column, 1993-99; prodr., star videos An Attorney's Guide to Legal Research on the Internet, 1998, 99; co-author: Jeff and Catherine's World's Best List of Legal (and Law-related) Internet Sites. Chair scholarship com. U. Calif. Alumni Assn., Berkeley, 1995—; capt. auction team SCATS Gymnastics, 2000—02; sec. bd. dir. AC Alliance Youth Soccer Club, Calif. Polytech. U., Pomona, 2007—08. Named Cmty. Person of Yr., Diamond Bar C. of C., 1995. Mem. NEA, State Bar Calif. (probation monitor 1993—), Ea. Bar Assn. L.A. (trustee 2000—, sec., 2007), Calif. Tchrs. Assn., Am. Inns of Ct., Calif. Assn. Lanterman-Petris-Short Hearing Officers. Avocations: weightlifting, photography, reading. Office: Mount San Antonio Coll 1100 N Grand Ave Walnut CA 91789-1341 Office Phone: 909-594-5611 ext. 4907. Business E-Mail: cmckee@mtsac.edu.

MCKEE, CHRISTOPHER FULTON, historian, educator; b. Bklyn., June 14, 1935; s. William Ralph and Frances McKee; m. Ann Adamczyk, 1993; children: Sharon, David. AB, U. St. Thomas, Houston, 1957; AMLS, U. Mich., 1960. Catalogue libr. Washington and Lee U., Lexington, Va., 1958-62; social sci. libr. So. Ill. U., Edwardsville, 1962-66, book selection officer, 1967-69, asst. dir., 1969-72; libr. of coll. Grinnell Coll., Iowa, 1972—2006, Samuel R. and Marie-Louise Rosenthal prof. Sec. of Navy rsch. chair naval history Naval Hist. Ctr., Washington, 1990—91; trustee Bibliog. Ctr. Rsch., Denver, 1984—88; scholar in res., Obermann Ctr. for Advanced Studies U. Iowa, 2006—. Author: (book) Edward Preble, 1972, A Gentlemanly and Honorable Profession: The Creation of the U.S. Naval Officer Corps 1794-1815, 1991, Sober Men and True: Sailor Lives in the Royal Navy 1900-1945, 2002. Mem. vestry Trinity Episcopal Ch., Iowa City. Recipient U.S. Naval History prize, 1985, John Lyman Book award, N.Am. Soc. Oceanic History, 1991, Samuel Eliot Morison Disting. Svc. award, USS Constn. Mus., 1992; fellow NEH-Newberry Libr., 1978—79, Newberry Libr.-Brit. Acad., 1995—96. Mem.: U.S. Naval Inst., Soc. Historians Early Am. Republic, Orgn. Am. Historians, Soc. Mil. History, Navy Records Soc., Can. Nautical Rsch. Soc., Soc. Nautical Rsch. Democrat. Episcopalian. Home: 2382 Willowbrooke Ln Iowa City IA 52246-1834 Office: Obermann Ctr for Advanced Studies Univ Iowa N103 Oakdale Hall Iowa City IA 52242-5000 Home Phone: 319-351-7594; Office Phone: 319-335-4034.

MCKEE, DAVID CHARLES, neurologist; b. May 19, 1961; m. Marie-Laure Mazquiain, Dec. 29, 1984; children: Tyvand, Camille, Charlotte, Alexanne. BA in Chemistry, Macalaster Coll., 1983; MD, U. Wis., 1987. Diplomate Am. Bd. Psychiatry and Neurology, Am. Bd. Electrodiagnostic Medicine. Resident in neurology Oreg. Health Scis. U., 1987—91; Jeanne Timmins fellow Montreal Neurol. Inst., 1991—92; clin. neurologist Northland Neurology and Myology, Duluth, Minn., 1992—; chief sect. neurology St. Lukes Hosp. and Regional Trauma Ctr., Duluth, 1993—; assoc. prof. neurology Duluth Med. Sch. U. Minn., 1993—; pres. Northland Med. Assocs., 2000—02. Chmn. bd. dirs. Care North Health Sys., 2001—02. Comdr. USNR med. corp., 1998—. Named Best Dr. Am., 2007. Fellow: Am. Assn. Electrodiagnostic Medicine; mem.: European Neurol. Soc., Am. Acad. Neurology, Alpha Omega Alpha, Phi Beta Kappa. Office: 1000 E 1st St Ste 202 Duluth MN 55805-2297 Home: 3500 E Superior St Duluth MN 55804-2009

MCKEE, ELIANE, retired literature and language professor; d. Vaclav Lang and Dagmar Slabova; m. Darrell Dean McKee, Jan. 14, 1961; children: Bryan Vaclav, Russell Wade. PhD, Ohio State U., Columbus, 1980. Prof. emeritus Buffalo State Coll., 1980—. Fgn. lang. methodology courses & French lang. & lit. State U. Coll., Buffalo, 1980—. Author: (book) Le Francais Standard: Prononciation et Orthographe. Bible class tchr. HS girls & seminar presenter Ch. Christ, Jamestown, NY, 2008. Recipient Maryalice Seagrave Outstanding Foreign Langs. Tchr., Outstanding Tchg. award, SUNY Chanceller. Mem.: NNELL, Am. Coun. Tchg. Fgn. Langs., NY State Assn. Fgn. Lang. Tchrs., Western NY Fgn. Lang. Edn. Coun. Avocations: hiking, travel, cooking, writing. Office: SUNY Coll Buffalo 1300 Elmwood Ave Buffalo NY 14222-1095 Business E-Mail: mckeee@buffalostate.edu.

MCKEE, ELLSWORTH R., food products executive; BA in Bus. and Econs., So. Adventist U., 1954; postgrad., Andrews U., 1987. Shipping/receiving clk. Jack's Cookie Co., Charlotte, NC, 1949-50; various positions McKee Foods, Collegedale, 1951-54, v.p. prodn. and fin., 1954-62, exec. v.p., treas., 1962-71, pres., CEO, 1971-96, also bd. dirs., 1954—, chmn. bd. dirs., 1997—. Bd. dirs. So. Adventist U., Collegedale, Andrews U., Berrien Springs, Mich., 1976—2000. Recipient Pvt. Sector Initiative Commendation, Pres. Ronald Reagan, 1988. Office: McKee Foods PO Box 750 Collegedale TN 37315-0750

MCKEE, FRANCIS JOHN, medical association consultant, lawyer; b. Bklyn., Aug. 31, 1943; s. Francis Joseph and Catherine (Giles) McK.; m. Antoinette Mary Sancis; children: Lisa Ann, Francis Dominic, Michael Christopher, Thomas Joseph. AB, Stonehill Coll., 1965; JD, St. John's U., 1970. Bar: N.Y. 1971. Assoc. Samuel Weinberg, Esquire, Bklyn., 1970-71, Finch & Finch, Esquire, Long Island City, NY, 1971-72; staff atty. Med. Soc. of State of NY, Lake Success, NY, 1972-77; with Coun. Suffolk County Med. Soc., Hauppauge, NY, 1977—81; prin. Francis J. McKee Assocs., Clinton, NY, 1984—2001; exec. dir. Suffolk Physicians Rev. Orgn., East Islip, NY, 1977-81, with New Bern, 2005—07; exec. dir. NY State Soc. Surgeons, Inc., Clinton, NY, 1981-2000, NY State Soc. Orthopaedic Surgeons, Inc., Clinton, NY, 1981—2000, Upstate NY chpt. ACS, Inc., Clinton, NY, 1981-2000, NY State Ophthalmol. Soc., 1984-92, NY State Soc. Obstetricians and Gynecologists, 1985-2001, Orthopac of NY, 1986-2000, Nat. Com. for the Preservation Orthopaedic Practice, New Hartford, NY, 1989-2000, L.I. Ophthalmol. Soc., 1994-2000. Mgr. Thomas J. McKee and Assocs., LLC, 2005—08, Michael C. Mckee and Assoc., 2009-. With U.S. Army, 1966-68. Mem.: NY State Bar Assn., Am. Legion, Taberna Country Club, Elks (presiding justice, subordinate order 2007—). Republican. Roman Catholic. Home and Office: 908 Taberna Cir New Bern NC 28562

MCKEE, GEORGE MOFFITT, JR., retired civil engineer consultant; b. Valparaiso, Nebr., Mar. 27, 1924; s. George Moffitt and Iva (Santrock) McK.; m. Mary Lee Taylor, Aug. 11, 1945; children: Michael Craig, Thomas Lee, Mary Kathleen, Marsha Coleen, Charlotte Anne. Student, Kans. State Coll. Agr. and Applied Sci., Manhattan, 1942—43, Bowling Green State U., Ohio, 1943; BSE, U. Mich., Ann Arbor, 1947. Registered profl. civil engr., Kans., Okla., land surveyor, Kans. Draftsman Jackson Constrn. Co., Colby, Kans., 1945-46; asst. engr. Thomas County, Colby, 1946; engr. Sherman County, Goodland, Kans., 1947-51; salesman Oehlert Tractor & Equipment Co., Colby, 1951-52; owner, operator George M. McKee, Jr.; cons. engrs. Colby, 1952-72; sr. v.p. engring. Contract Surety Cons., Wichita, Kans., 1974-2000; engring. cons. Wichita, 2000—05. Adv. rep. Kans State U., Manhattan, 1957-62; adv. com. N.W. Kans. Area Vocat. Tech. Sch., Goodland, 1967-71; chmn. ofcl. bd. Meth. Ch., 1966-67. With USMCR, 1942-45. Mem. Kans. Soc. Profl. Engrs. (pres. N.W. profl. engrs. chpt. 1962-63, treas. cons. engrs. sect. 1961-63), Kans. County Engr.'s Assn. (dist. v.p. 1950-51), N.W. Kans. Hwy. Ofcls. Assn. (sec. 1948-49), Nat. Soc. Profl. Engrs., Kans. State U. Alumni Assn. (life, pres. Thomas County 1956-57), Am. Legion (Goodland 1st vice comdr. 1948-49), Alumni Assn. U. Mich. (life), Colby C. of C. (v.p. 1963-64), Goodland Jr. C. of C. (pres. 1951-52), Masons (32 degree, Shriner), Order of the Ea. Star. Home: 3636 North Ridge Rd Apt 213 Wichita KS 67205-1217

MCKEE, JUDITH NELSON, elementary school educator, educational consultant; b. Iowa Falls, Iowa, Nov. 8, 1939; d. Herbert and Emma (Czako) Nelson; m. Bernard B. McKee, Oct. 20, 1962; children: Susan Jennifer Ziegler, Blair David. BA, U. No. Iowa, 1961; MA, Roosevelt U., 1967; postgrad., Ill. State U., Nat. Louis U. Cert. tchr. K-9, learning disabilities K-12. Tchr. 2d grade Dist. 25 Pub. Schs., Arlington Heights, Ill., 1961-67; itinerant tchr. learning disabilities NW Suburban Spl. Edn. Dist., Palatine, Ill., 1968-72; tchr. Winnetka Pub. Sch. Nursery, Ill., 1974-75; tchr. spl. edn. North Suburban Spl. Edn. Dist., Glenview, Ill., 1975-76; tchr. gifted Worlds of Wisdom and Wonder, Evanston, Ill., 1985-87; instr. astronomy North Cook County Ednl. Svc. Ctr., Glenview, 1987; mem. faculty Nat. Louis U., Evanston, Ill., 1991—2000, DePaul U., Chgo., 2000—01; tchr. primary grades dist. 39 Wilmette, Ill., 1976—99; faculty U. No. Iowa, Cedar Falls, 2002—. Presenter, state, nat. and internat. confs. Co-author: Integrating Instruction: Literacy and Science, 2005; author (with others): Physical Science Activities for Elementary and Middle School, 1987, Fact, Fiction, and Fantasy, 1995; contbr. articles to profl. jours. Named Ill. Honors Sci. Tchr. NSF, Ill. State. U., 1989-91. Mem. Internat. Reading Assn., Nat. Sci. Tchrs. Assn. (ret. adv. bd. 2000-03, chair 2002-03, pre-sch. and elem. tchrs. standing com., 2008), Coun. Elem. Sci. Internat., Ill. Sci. Tchrs. Assn. Presbyterian. Home: 315 Fairview Ave Winnetka IL 60093-4210

MCKEE, KEITH EARL, manufacturing technology executive; b. Chgo., Sept. 9, 1928; s. Charles Richard and Maude Alice (Hamlin) McK.; children: Pamela Ann Houser, Paul Earl. BS, Ill. Inst. Tech., 1950, MS, 1956, PhD, 1962. Engr. Swift & Co., Chgo., 1953-54; rsch. engr. Armour Rsch. Found., Chgo., 1954-62; dir. design and product assurance Andrew Corp., Orland Park, Ill., 1962-67; dir. engring. Rsch. Ctr. Ill. Inst. Tech., Chgo., 1967-80, dir. mfg. prodn. ctr., 1977—. Prof. Ill. Inst. Tech., Chgo., 1979—, dir. indsl. programs, 1994—; coord. Nat. Conf. on Fluid Power, Chgo., 1983-88; mem. com. on materials and processing Dept. Def., Washington, 1986-92. Author: Productivity and Technology, 1988; co-author: Managing Technology Dependence Operation, 2004; editor: Automated Inspection and Process Control, 1987; co-editor: Manufacturing High Technology Handbook, 1987; mng. editor: Manufacturing Competitiveness Frontier, 1977-97. Capt. USMC, 1950-54. Recipient oustanding presentation award Am. Soc. of Quality Control, Milw., 1983. Fellow World Acad. Productivity Scis.; mem. ASCE, Am. Def. Preparedness Assn. (pres. Chgo. chpt. 1972-95), Am. Assn. Engring. Soc. (Washington) (coor. com. on productivity 1978-88), Inst. of Indsl. Engrs., Soc. Mfg. Engrs. (Gold medal 1991), Am. Assn. for Artificial Intelligence, Robotic Industry Assn. (bd. dir. 1978-81), Assn. for Mfg. Excellence, Soc. for Computer Simulation. Democrat. Roman Catholic. Home: Ste 504 3115 S Michigan Ave Chicago IL 60616 Office: Illinois Inst Tech Mfg Productivity Ctr 3424 S State St Ste 4001 S Chicago IL 60616 Office Phone: 312-567-3650. Business E-Mail: mckee@iit.edu.

MCKEE, LYNN B., human resources specialist, food products executive; B in Acctg., St. Joseph's U.; MBA, Drexel U. Various positions including dir. employee rels., dir. human resources and exec. devel. Aramark Corp., Phila., 1980—86, mgr. hqtrs. human resources, 1986—89, dir. human resources, 1989, v.p. exec. devel. and compensation, 1998—2001, sr. v.p. human resources, 2001—04, exec. v.p. human resources, 2004—. Mem. human resources roundtable group; mem. conf. bd. advisory coun. human resources mgmt. Office: Aramark Corp Aramark Tower 1101 Market St Philadelphia PA 19107-2988 Office Phone: 215-238-3000. Office Fax: 215-238-3333.

MCKEE, MARGARET JEAN, federal agency administrator; b. New Haven, June 20, 1929; d. Waldo McCutcheon and Elizabeth McKee. AB, Vassar Coll., 1951. Staff asst. United Rep. Fin. Com., NYC, 1952, N.Y. Rep. State Com., NYC, 1953—55, Crusade for Freedom (name later changed to Radio Free Europe Fund), NYC, 1955—57; researcher Stricker & Henning Rsch. Assocs., Inc., NYC, 1957—59; exec. sec. New Yorkers for Nixon (name later changed to N.Y. State Ind. Citizens for Nixon Lodge), NYC, 1959—60; asst. to Raymond Moley, polit. columnist NYC, 1961; asst. campaign com. Louis J. Lefkowitz for Mayor, NYC, 1961; rsch. programmer, treas. Consensus, Inc., NYC, 1962—67; spl. asst. to U. S. Senator Jacob K. Javits NY, 1967—73; adminstr. asst. NY, 1973—75; dep. adminstr. Am. Revolution Bicentennial Adminstrn., 1976, acting adminstr., 1976—77; chief of staff Perry B. Duryea (minority leader) N.Y. State Assembly, 1978; pub. affairs cons., 1979—80; dir. govt. rels. Gen. Mills Restaurant Group, Inc., 1980—83; exec. dir. Fed. Mediation and Conciliation Svc., 1983—86; mem. Fed. Labor Rels. Authority, 1986—89, chmn., 1989—94; mem. Nat. Partnership Coun., 1993—94; chmn. adv. bd. Workplace Solutions, 1996—98. Bd. mem. Nat. Assn. Olmsted Pks.; mem. US Adv.Commn. on Pub. Diplomacy, 1972—82; dir. scheduling and spkrs.' bur. NY Com. to Re-elect the Pres., 1972; mem. bd. govs. Women's Nat. Rep. Club, NYC, 1963—66; mem. N.Y. State Bingo Control Commn., 1965—72; pres. Bklyn. Heights Slope Young Rep. Club, 1955—56; co-chmn. Bklyn. Citizens for Eisenhower-Nixon, 1956; chmn. 2nd Jud. Dist. Assn. N.Y. State Young Rep. Clubs, Inc., 1957—58, vice chmn., mem. bd. govs., 1958—60, v.p., 1960—62, pres., 1962—64; mem. exec. com. Fedn. Women's Rep. Clubs N.Y. State, Inc., 1960—64; asst. campaign mgr. Kenneth B. Keating for Judge Ct. Appeals, NY, 1965; dir. scheduling Gov. Rockefeller campaign, 1966, Sen. Charles E. Goodell campaign, 1970; dir. planning and strategy Conn. Reagan-Bush campaign, Hartford, 1980; mem annual fund adv. com. Vassar Coll., 1992—96, chmn. 50th Reunion, 2001; trustee Vassar Coll. and Assoc. Alumni, 2005—09. Mem.: Conn. Olmsted Heritage Alliance (treas. 2005—09), Nat. Assn. Olmsted Parks (trustee 2003—), New Eng. Hist. Geneal. Soc. (mem. adv. coun. 2001—03, trustee 2003—06, mem. adv. coun. 2006—09), Nat. Women's Edn. Fund. (former mem. bd.), Exec. Women on Govt. (chmn. 1986), DAR (Lady Fenwick chpt.), Nat. Soc. Colonial Dames, Vassar Club, Am. Newspaper Women's Club, Jr. League of Bklyn. (past bd.). Republican. Episcopalian. also: 3001 Veazey Ter NW Apt 1225 Washington DC 20008-5407 Address: 532 S Brooksvale Rd Cheshire CT 06410

MCKEE, PATRICK ALLEN, physician; b. Tulsa, Apr. 30, 1937; s. Charles and Estelle Marie McK. Student, U. Tulsa, 1955-58; MD, U. Okla., 1962. Intern, resident Duke Hosp., Durham, NC, 1962—63, 1963—64; rsch. fellow cell biology Duke U. Med. Ctr., 1963—64; chief resident U. Okla. Med. Center, Oklahoma City, 1967-68; clin. assoc. Framingham Heart Program, NIH, Framingham, MA, 1965-67; assoc. medicine dept. medicine Duke U. Med. Center, 1969-70, clin. investigator, 1970-71, asst. prof. medicine, 1970-72, asst. prof. biochemistry, 1971-85, assoc. prof. medicine, 1972-75, prof. medicine, 1975—, dir. outpatient clinic, 1975-85, chief div. gen. medicine, 1976-85; chmn. dept. medicine U. Okla., Health Sci. Ctr., 1985-95; Laureate chair in molecular medicine and prof. medicine, sci. dir. W.K. Warren Medical Rsch. Ctr. U. Okla., 1995—. Cons. thrombosis research Nat. Heart and Lung Inst., 1970-71; mem. hematology study sect. NIH, 1973-77, NASA Aerospace Medicine Occupl. Health Adv. Subcom., 1995-2000. Contbr. numerous articles to profl. jours. Trustee Okla. Sch. Math. and Sci., 1986-90; vice chmn. Okla. Ctr. for Advancement Sci. and Tech., 1987-91. NIH grantee U. Okla. Med. Center, 1968-69, 2003-07; NIH grantee Duke U. Med. Center, 1972-85, 2003-07. Mem. US Pharmacop (coun. experts, 1995-), Hematology and Blood Products Com. (chair, coun. experts, 2005-); fellow Am. Heart Assn., ACP; Assn. Am. Physicians, Am. Soc. Clin. Investigation, So. Soc. Clin. Investigation, Cen. Soc. Clin. Investigation, Am. Fedn. Medical Research, Internat. Soc. Thrombosis and Haemostasis, Am. Soc. Hematology, Am. Soc. Biochem. Molecular Biol., Am. Clin. and Climatol. Soc., Am. Bd. Internal Medicine, Am. Soc. Internal Medicine, Sword and Key, Alpha Omega Alpha, Phi Eta Sigma, Sigma Xi. Roman Catholic. Office: PO Box 26901 Oklahoma City OK 73126-0901 Office Phone: 405-271-5645.

MCKEE, RAE ELLEN (RAE ELLEN MCKEE-DOUCETTE), special education educator; b. W. Va. BA in Elem. Edn., Shepherd Coll., Shepherdstown, W. Va., 1979; MA in Clin. Reading, W. Va. Univ., Morgantown, 1983, MA student in Ednl. Supervision. Tchr. remedial reading Slanesville (W.Va.) Elem. Sch.; cons. Barbara Bush Found. for Family Literacy, Houston. Recipient Nat. Tchr. of Yr. award, 1991. Office: Barbara Bush Found Family Literacy Ste 1400 4400 Post Oak Pkwy Houston TX 77027

MCKEE, RICHARD MILES, retired agricultural studies educator; b. Cottonwood Falls, Kans., Oct. 8, 1929; m. Marjorie Fisk, June 22, 1952; children: Dave, Richard, Annell, John. BS in Agriculture, Kans. State Coll. Agriculture and Applied Sci., 1951; MS in Animal Husbandry, Kans. State U., 1963; PhD in Animal Science, U. Ky., 1968. Herdsman Moxley Hall Hereford Ranch, Coun. Grove, Kans., 1951-52, 54-55, Luckhardt Farms, Tarkio, Mo., 1955-58; asst. mgr. L&J Crusoe Ranch, Cheboygan, Mich., 1958-59; asst. instr., cattle herdsman Kans. State U., Manhattan, 1959-65, from asst. prof. to assoc. prof., 1959-65, prof., departmental teaching coord., 1976-99; ret., 2005. Program participant and/or official judge numerous shows, field days including Kans. Jr. Hereford Field Day, Kans. Jr. Shorthorn Field Day, Better Livestock Day, Kans. Jr. Livestock Assn., Am. Jr. Hereford Assn. Field Day, Cheyenne, Wyo., 1973, Kans. Jr. Polled Hereford Field Day, Am. Jr. Shorthorn Assn., Kans. City, Mo., 1965, Am. Internat. Jr. Charolais Assn. Show, Lincoln, Nebr., 1976, Am. Royal 4-H Livestock Judging Contest, Kans. City, 1975, Jr. Livestock Activities various cattle breed assns. nationwide, 1977-81; served on many breed assn. coms.; judge County Fairs; official judge 14 different Nat. Beef Breed Shows U.S. and Can.; conducted 60 livestock judging and showmanship schs. at county level. Contbr. articles to profl. jours. Deacon 1st Presbyn. Ch., Manhattan, 1969-75, Sunday Sch. tchr., Chancel choir, elder; project leader com. mem. 4-H; foster parent Kans. State U. Football Program. Lt. USMC, 1952-54, Korea. Named Hon. State Farmer of Kans.; Hall of Merit Honoree for Edn. by Am. Polled Hereford Assn., 1985; NDEA scholar U. Ky., 1966-67; Miles McKee Student Enrichment Fund established at Kans. State U. Mem. Am. Soc. Animal Sci., Kans. Livestock Assn. (beef cattle improvement com. 1970-78, cow-calf clinic com. 1973, 74, 75, 76, 77, 78), Nat. Assn. Colls. and Tchrs. Agriculture, Block and Bridle Club, Am. Jr. Hereford Assn. (hon.), FarmHouse, Sigma Xi, Phi Kappa Phi, Alpha Zeta, Gamma Sigma Delta, Alpha Tau Alpha (hon.). Home: 901 Juniper Dr Manhattan KS 66502-3148 Office: Dept of Animal Scis & Industry Kansas State U Manhattan KS 66506 Office Phone: 785-532-1237. Personal E-mail: mmckee15@cox.net.

MCKEE, ROGER CURTIS, retired federal judge; b. Waterloo, Iowa, Feb. 11, 1931; s. James A. and Leonace (Burrell) McK.; m. Roberta Jeanne Orvis, Sept. 3, 1954; children: Andrea Jane, Brian Curtis, Paul Robert. BA, State Coll. of Iowa, 1955; MA, U. Ill., 1960; JD, U. San Diego, 1968. Bar: US Dist. Ct. (so. dist.) Calif. 1969, Calif. 1970, US Ct. Appeals (9th cir.) 1971. Telegrapher, agt. Ill. Cen. R.R., 1950-55; tng. asst. No. Ill. Gas Co., Aurora, 1959-60; with indsl. rels. dept. Convair div. Gen. Dynamics Corp., San Diego, 1960-68; contract adminstr. and supr. Datagraphix div. Gen. Dynamics Corp., San Diego, 1968-69, asst. counsel, 1969-70; ptnr. Powell & McKee, San Diego, 1970-75, Millsberg, Dickstein & McKee, San Diego, 1975-83; magistrate judge U.S. Dist. Ct. for So. Dist. Calif., San Diego, 1983-97; presiding magistrate judge, 1993-97. Bd. trustees So. Calif. Presbyn. Homes, LA, 1979-81; moderator Presbytery of San Diego, 1980. Capt. USNR, 1949-85. Mem. Calif. Bar Assn., Fed. Magistrate Judges Assn., Navy League US, Naval Res. Officers Assn., Res. Officers Assn., Dixieland Jazz Soc. (bd. dirs. San Diego chpt. 1984—). Republican. Home Fax: 858-277-0444. Personal E-mail: rcmckee10@aol.com.

MCKEE, TAWNYA CARLENE, research scientist; b. Arcadia, Calif., Dec. 24, 1962; d. John Carlos and Delma Loyce McKee; m. Mark Ricardo Augutus Alexander, May 8, 1998; children: Christian Joseph Mark McKee-Alexander, David Michael John McKee-Alexander. BA, Point Loma Coll., San Diego, 1984; PhD, U. Utah, Salt Lake City, 1990. Postdoc. fellow Lab. Drug Discovery & Devel., Nat. Cancer Inst., Frederick, Md., 1990—92; staff scientist Molecular Target Devel. Program, Ctr. Cancer Rsch., Nat. Cancer Inst., Frederick, 1992—. Mem.: AAUW, Am. Women Sci., Am. Chem. Soc., Am. Soc. Pharmacognosy (Young Investigator's award 1996). Democrat. Episcopal. Achievements include patents for macrocyclic lactones, scytovirins & relared conjugates, fusions, proteins, nucleic acids, vectors, host cells, compositions, antibodies, and methods of using scytovirins. Office: Nat Cancer Inst Frederick 1050 Boyds 562-101 Frederick MD 21702-1201 Office Fax: 301-846-6919. Business E-Mail: mckee@ncifcrf.gov.

MCKEE, THEODORE A., federal judge; b. Rochester, NY, 1947; BA, SUNY, Cortland, 1969; JD magna cum laude, Syracuse U. Coll. of Law, 1975. Dir. of minority recruitment & admissions SUNY, Binghamton, 1969—72; atty. Wolf, Block, Schorr & Solis-Cohen, Phila., 1975—77; asst. US atty., Eastern Dist. Pa., 1977—80; asst. US atty., Eastern Dist. Gen. Crimes Unit, Narcotics and Firearms Unit, then Polit. Corruption Unit; lectr. Rutgers U. Coll. of Law, 1980—91; dep. city solicitor Law Dept., Phila., 1980—83; gen. counsel Phila. Parking Auth., 1983; judge Ct. of Common Pleas, 1st Jud. Dist, Pa., 1984—94, judge major felony program, 1986, judge orphans' ct. divsn., 1992; judge US Ct. Appeals (3d cir.), Phila., 1994—. Bd. dirs. Diagnostic and Rehab. Ctr. of Phila. Trustee Edna McConnell Clark Found.; mem. adv. bd. City Yr. for Phila. Mem.: ABA, Pa. Bar Assoc., Phila. Bar Assoc., Temple Inn of Ct., Barristers' Assn. Phila., Am. Law Inst., Nat. Bar Assn., Crime Prevention Assn. (bd. dirs.). Office: 20614 US Courthouse 601 Market St Philadelphia PA 19106*

MCKEE, THOMAS FREDERICK, lawyer; b. Cleve., Oct. 27, 1948; s. Harry Wilbert and Virginia (Light) McK. BA with high distinction, U. Mich., 1970; JD with high distinction, Case Western Rs. U., 1975. Bar: Ohio 1975, U.S. Dist. Ct. (no. dist.) Ohio 1975, U.S. Supreme Ct. 1979. Assoc. firm Calfee, Halter & Griswold, Cleve., 1975-81, ptnr., 1982—, also co-chmn. exec. com.; bd. dirs. Home Décor, Harden Furniture, Stanton Carpet, Path Trak Internat., Case We. Res.U., Musical Arts Assn. Contbg. editor Going Public, 1985. Mem. ABA (com. fed. regulation securities law sect.), Bar Assn. Greater Cleve., Order of Coif., Union Club, Tavern Club, Country Club, 50 Club, Pepper Pike Club. Office: Calfee Halter & Griswold 800 Superior Ave E Ste 1400 Cleveland OH 44114-2601 Home: 17429 Beech Grove Tr Chagrin Falls OH 44023

MCKEE, TIM, chef; b. 1967; married. Prep cook Azur, Mpls.; exec. chef D'Amico Cucina; co-owner, exec. chef La Belle Vie, Stillwater, Minn., 1998—2005, Mpls., 2005—, Solera, Mpls., 2003—. Named Best New Chef, Food and Wine Mag., 1997, Best Chef: Midwest, James Beard Found., 2009, Best Local Chef, City Pages, 1999—2003, 2006,

Best Overall Chef, Twin City's Taste mag., 2003; nominee Best Chef: Midwest, James Beard Found., 2007. Office: Le Belle Vie 510 Groveland Ave Minneapolis MN 55405 Office Phone: 612-874-6440.*

MCKEE, TIMOTHY CARLTON, taxation educator; b. South Bend, Ind., Mar. 9, 1944; s. Glenn Richard and Laura Louise (Niven) McK.; m. Linda Sykes Mizelle, Oct. 13, 1984; children: Brandon Richard. BS in Bus. Econs., Ind. U., 1970, MBA in Fin., 1973, JD, 1979; LLM in Taxation, DePaul U., 1980. Bar: Ill. 1980, U.S. Dist. Ct. (no. dist.) Ill. 1980; CPA, Va.; cert. govt. fin. mgr. Procedures analyst Assocs. Corp., South Bend, 1969-71; asst. dir. fin. Ind. U., Bloomington, 1971-79; sr. tax mgr. Peat Marwick Mitchell & Co., Chgo., Norfolk, Va., 1979-84; corp. counsel K & K Toys, Norfolk, 1984; assoc. prof. acctg. Old Dominion U., Norfolk, 1985-98, chmn. dept., 1994-95, chmn. acctg., fin. and law dept., 1995, univ. prof. dept. acctg., 1998—. Computer coord. Peat, Marwick, Mitchell & Co., 1982-84; micro computer cons. Old Dominion U., 1985-91. Contbr. articles to profl. jours. Active Friends of Music, Bloomington, 1978, Art Inst., Chgo., 1981; loan exec. United Way, Chgo., 1981; telethon chmn. Va. Orch. Group, Norfolk, 1983. Mem. Assn. Govt. Accts., Am. Acctg. Assn., Am. Assn. Atty. CPAs, Inc., Am. Tax Assn., Fin. Execs. Inst. (pres. 1995-96), Hampton Rds. Tax Forum, Inst. Internal Auditors, Beta Alpha Psi, Beta Gamma Sigma. Home: 412 Rio Dr Chesapeake VA 23322-7144 Office: Old Dominion U Constant Hall Rm 2153 Norfolk VA 23529

MCKEEFRY, MARK, attorney, director; b. NYC, Apr. 8, 1961; m. Susan McKeefry, July 29, 1995; children: Penelope Sky, Jack, Daphne Sage. BS, Carnegie Mellon U., 1984; JD, Fordham Law Sch., NY, 1997. Cert. profl. civil engr., State Calif., 1988; bar: NY (atty.) 1999, Calif. 2000; cert. gen. securities rep., gen. securities prin. US Finra, 2003, registered dir. UK Fin. Svcs. Authority, 2006, prin. US Nat. Futures Assn., 2007, dir. Monetary Authority Singapore, 2006, Swiss Fed. Banking Commn., 2008. Pres., COO & gen. counsel Fairfield Greenwich Advisors LLC, NY, 2003—, Fairfield Heathcliff Capital LLC, NY, 2003—. Dir. Fairfield Greenwich Ltd., Hamilton, Bermuda, 2004—, London, 2006—, Cayman Islands, 2006—, Lion Fairfield Capital Mgmt. Ltd., Singapore, 2006—, Banque Benedict Hentsch Fairfield Partners SA, Geneva, 2008—. Mem.: NY State Bar Assn., Sigma Alpha Epsilon (hon.). Home: 202 Round Hill Rd Greenwich CT 06831 Office: Fairfield Greenwich Advisors LLC 919 Third Ave 39th Fl New York NY 10022 Business E-Mail: mark@fggus.com.

MCKEEL, LILLIAN PHILLIPS, retired education educator; b. Rocky Mount, NC, Aug. 23, 1932; d. Ellis Elma and Lillian Bonner (Archbell) Phillips; m. James Thomas McKeel Jr., July 23, 1955; children: Sarah Lillian McKeel Youngblood, Mary Kathleen McKeel Welch. BA, U. N.C., 1954; MEd, Pa. State U., 1977, DEd, 1993. Tchr. State Coll. (Pa.) Area Schs., 1964-90; instr. Pa. State U., University Park, 1990-93; asst. prof. Shippensburg (Pa.) U., 1993—2001; ret., 2001. Mem. of panel NSTA Book Rev. Panel/Outstanding Sci. Tradebooks for Children, Washington, 1992; faculty sponsor Shippensburg U. Sch. Study Coun., 1993-95. Contbr. articles to profl. jours. Recipient Presdl. award for Excellence in Sci. and Math. Tchng., NSF, Washington, 1990; finalist Tchr. of Yr. program Pa. Dept. Edn., Harrisburg, 1992, cert. Recognition, Hon. Robert Casey/Gov., Harrisburg, Pa., 1991; named Achieving Women of Penn State, Pa. State U., 1993. Mem. Nat. Sci. Tchrs. Assn., Soc. Presdl. Awardees, Assn. Edn. Tchrs. in Sci., Coun. Elem. Sci. Internat., Phi Delta Kappa (Disting. Svc. award 1992), Pi Lambda Theta, Phi Kappa Phi. Avocations: photography, collecting antique toys. Home: 3222 Shellers Bend Unit 230 State College PA 16801-3227 E-mail: lmcke637@aol.com.

MCKEEN, ALEXANDER C., retired engineering executive, foundation administrator; b. Albion, Mich., Oct. 10, 1927; s. John Nisbet and Janet (Callander) McK.; m. Evelyn Mae Feldkamp, Aug. 18, 1951; Jeffrey, Brian, Andrew. BSME, U. Mich., 1950; MBA, Mich. State U., 1968. Registered profl. engr., Mich. From asst. supt. maintenance to supt. final assembly Cadillac Motor Car divsn. GM, Detroit, 1961-69; asst. dir. reliability cadillac motor car divsn. GM, Detroit, 1969-72, exec. engr. product assurance Warren, Mich., 1972-75, from asst. dir. to dir engring. analysis, 1975-87; pres., owner Engring. Analysis Assocs., Inc., Bingham Farms, Mich., 1987-99; cons. Detroit Exec. Svc. Corps, 1999—; pres. McKeen Found., 2002—. Pres. Dells of Bloomfield Home Owners Assn., Bloomfield Hills, Mich., 1987-88; trustee Kirk in Hills, Bloomfield Hills, 1990-93, 2003-06, elder, 1995-97. Mem. Soc. Auto. Engrs., Am. Soc. Quality Control, Econ. Club Detroit, Detroit Athletic Club, Bloomfield (Mich.) Lions Club (pres. 2004-05), Stonycroft Hills Golf Club (treas.), Pelican Nest Golf Club, Beta Gamma Sigma. Avocations: tennis, golf, photography, travel, gardening. Office: Detroit Executive Service Corps 16250 Northland Dr Ste 390 Southfield MI 48075

MCKEEN, ANGELA ANNE, science educator; b. Glen Dale, W.Va., Oct. 1, 1971; d. David Robert and Theresa Jane Beckett; m. Russell John McKeen, June 19, 1993; children: Benjamin Russell, Emma Kathleen, Annie Lachlan. EdD, W.Va. U., Morgantown, 2008. English, sci. tchr. Valley HS, Pine Grove, W.Va., 1995—98; ednl. consultanting editor Inst. History Tech. and Indsl. Archaeology, Morgantown, 2001—02; adj. prof. Fairmont State U., W.Va., 2003—06; liason, wetzel and tyler county W.Va. Geol. and Econ. Survey, Cheat Lake, W.Va., 2003—. Active mem. 4-H, Jacksonburg, W.Va., 1980—2008. Mem.: NSTA, Nat. Assn. Geology Tchrs., Assn. Sci. Tchr. Educators. R-Liberal. Roman Catholic. Home: 115 Brown St Clarksburg WV 26301 Office: Fairmont State Univ 1201 Locust Ave Fairmont WV 26554 Business E-Mail: angela.mckeen@fairmontstate.edu.

MC KEEN, CHESTER M., JR., retired manufacturing executive; b. Shelby, Ohio, Mar. 18, 1923; s. Chester Mancil and Nettie Augusta (Fox) McKeen; m. Alma Virginia Pierce, Mar. 1946 (dec. Feb. 1998); children: David Richard(dec.), Karin, Thomas Kevin; m. Sally Ann Werst, Nov. 1999; 1 stepchild, Stephen Harry Werst. BS in Mil. Sci., U. Md., 1962; MBA, Babson Coll., Wellesley, Mass., 1962. Advanced through grades to maj. gen. U.S. Army, 1942-77; dir. logistics Bell Helicopter Internat., Tehran, Iran, 1977-79; v.p. procurement Bell Helicopter Textron, Ft. Worth, 1979-82, v.p. materiel, 1982-89; pres. Logistics Svcs. Internat., Arlington, Tex., 1990—2002; ret., 2002. Decorated D.S.M., Legion of Merit (3), Commendation medal (3); named to U.S. Army Ordnance Hall of Fame. Mem. Nat. Def. Indsl. Assn., Assn. U.S. Army, Ridglea Country Club, Rotary, Masons (33 degree), Shriners, Sojourners, Sigma Pi. Home: 2310 Woodsong Trail Arlington TX 76016-1037 Personal E-mail: cmmckeen@aol.com. *To live for oneself is to pursue emptiness. To live for others is to insure fulfillment.*

MCKEEVER, JOHN EUGENE, lawyer; b. Phila., Oct. 24, 1947; s. John James and Marie Julia (Supper) McKeever; m. Kathleen Marie Wynne, Dec. 9, 1995; children: John Joseph, Jeannine Marie. BA magna cum laude with distinction, U. Pa., 1969, JD magna cum laude, 1972. Bar: Pa. 1972, U.S. Dist. Ct. (ea. dist.) Pa. 1972, U.S. Dist. Ct. (mid. dist.) Pa. 1977, U.S. Ct. Appeals (3d cir.) 1979, U.S. Ct. Appeals (DC cir.) 1981, U.S. Supreme Ct. 1981. Assoc. Schnader, Harrison, Segal & Lewis, Phila., 1972-80, ptnr., 1980-98, DLA Piper US LLP, Phila., 1998—. Trustee Lawyers Com. Civil Rights Under Law, Washington, 2002, dir., 2003—, mem. exec. com., 2005—, regional vice chair, 2007—; dir. Com. 70, Phila., 2007—; mem. policy comm., 2008—; vice chair, 2009—. Mem. Bus. Leadership organized Cath. Schs., Phila., 1984—87; co-chair Oblates St. Francis De Sales Capital Campaign, 1998—99; capt. spl. gifts com. Cath. Charities Appeal, Phila., 1986—91; bd. dir. Jr. Achievement, Phila., 1986—2006; mem. pres.'s coun. De Sales U., Center Valley, Pa., 1980—; mem. adv. com. De Sales Sch. Theology, Washington, trustee, 1988—91. Mem.: Am. Bar Assn., Phila. Bar Assn., St. Thomas More Soc. (gov. 1979—91, pres. 1981—82), Phi Beta Kappa, Order of Coif, Pi Gamma Mu. Democrat. Roman Catholic. Office: DLA Piper US LLP One Liberty Pl 1650 Market St Ste 4900 Philadelphia PA 19103 Office Phone: 215-656-3310. Business E-Mail: john.mckeever@dlapiper.com.

MCKEEVER, JOSEPH FRANCIS, III, lawyer; b. Weymouth, Mass., July 21, 1950; s. Joseph Francis Jr. and Virginia Agnes McK.; m. Janice Danielle Kearney, Oct. 17, 1970. BA, George Washington U., 1972, JD, 1978. Bar: DC 1978, US Supreme Ct. 1989. Editor Congl. Rsch. Svc. Libr. Congress, Washington, 1974-78; law clk. Honorable Harry Wood US Ct. Claims, Washington, 1978-79, Honorable Wilson Cowen US Ct. Claims, Washington, 1979-80; atty. Sutherland, Asbill & Brennan, Washington, 1980-85; ptnr. Davis & Harman LLP, Washington, 1985—. Author, editor: Annuities Answer Book, 1999; contbr. articles to profl. jours. Mem. ABA (chair sect. on taxation com. on ins. cos. 2000-02); Nat. Assn. for Variable Annuities (chmn., 2002-2003) Avocations: gardening, bicycling. Home: 2812 34th Pl NW Washington DC 20007-1405 Office: Davis & Harman LLP Willard Office Bldg 1455 Pennsylvania Ave NW Washington DC 20004-1008 Office Phone: 202-347-2252.

MCKEEVER-THOMPSON, CLAIRE L., nurse, educator, consultant, human services manager; b. Columbus, Ohio, Sept. 29, 1938; d. Harry Edgar and Clara Etta (Brackenbusch) McKeever; m. Roger Lee Thompson, Dec. 20, 1958 (div. 1988); children: Jeffrey, Michael. Diploma, Bethesda Hosp. Sch. Nursing, Cin., 1959; student, Ball State, 1970, Ind. U., 1981, Purdue U., 1982-83. RN, Ohio, Ind., Calif.; cert. ins. rehab. specialist, case mgr.; cert. health occupl. level tchr., Ind. Oper. rm./emergency rm. nurse Greene Meml. Hosp., Xenia, Ohio, 1959-60; med.-surg. nurse, charge nurse Bethesda Hosp., 1960-64; med.-surg. nurse Porter Meml. Hosp., Valparaiso, Ind., 1965-66; staff and charge nurse Mercy Hosp., Elwood, Ind., 1968-74; gen. practice nurse W. A. Scea, MD, Elwood, 1970-74; exec. dir. Vis. Nurse Assn., Elwood, 1974-78; analyst Blue Cross/Blue Shield of Indpls., 1978; supr. Meth. Hosp. Clinic, Indpls., 1979-80; DON Upjohn Health Care, Indpls., 1980; staff nurse Americana Health Care Ctr., Indpls., 1981; instr. health occups. Washington Twp. Schs., Indpls., 1981-84; br. mgr. health & rehab. Crawford & Co., Indpls., 1984-88, regional med. svcs. advisor western region San Francisco, 1988-92; br. mgr. Crawford & Co., Health Care Mgmt., Modesto, Calif., 1992-94; ret., 1994. Developer in case mgmt. nursing svcs., 1974-94. Founder Meals on Wheels, Elwood, 1975, Vis. Nurses Assn., Elwood, 1976; mem. altar guild, lay eucharist min. Episcopal Ch.; vol. H.E.B. Hosp., 2004-07; vol. adv. Good Shepherd Hosp., 2007—. Mem. NLN, Assn. Rehab. Nurses (pres. Ind. chpt. 1987-88), Nat. Ins. Womens Assn., Case Mgmt. Soc. Am., San Francisco Ins. Womens Assn., Rehab. Ins. Nurses Group. OES Chpt. 1040 and 992, Daughters of Am. Revolution (Barrington, Ill.). Avocations: the arts, photography, collecting antique glass.

MCKELDIN, WILLIAM EVANS, management consultant; b. Richmond, Va., Aug. 14, 1927; s. Robert A.W. and Mary E. (Burk) McK.; children: William Evans, Roberts Evans; m. Phyllis Shellhase, Jan. 23, 1982. BSBA, Temple U., 1951, postgrad., 1951—53, U. Pitts., 1953—54. Various mgmt. positions Westinghouse Corp., Pitts., 1950-62, Farrel Corp., Rochester, NY, 1963-66, Gen. Signal Corp., Norwalk, Conn., and Watertown, N.Y., 1966-71, Copperweld Steel Co., Warren, Ohio, 1971-75, Tenn. Forging Steel, Knoxville, 1975-77, Val Bradley Assocs., West Chester, Pa., 1977-79; pres., owner McKeldin Assocs., West Chester, 1979-95; founder, co-owner McKeldin Group, Bala Cynwyd, Pa., 1995—. Contbr. articles to profl. jours. Bd. dirs. United Fund, YMCA, ARC, Rochester Inst. Tech., Jefferson C.C., Kent State U. With USAAF, 1945—47. Mem. Inst. Mgmt. Cons., Am. Soc. Safety Engrs., Am. Soc. Personnel Adminstrn., C. of C. (bd. dirs.), Masons, Rotary. Republican. Presbyterian. Office: The McKeldin Group 24 Timber Ln Hilton Head Island SC 29926-1002 Home Phone: 843-837-6565; Office Phone: 843-837-6565, Personal E-mail: mckeldin@webtv.net.

MCKELL, CYRUS M., retired dean, range plant physiologist, consultant; b. Payson, Utah, Mar. 19, 1926; s. Robert D. and Mary C. (Ellsworth) McK.; m. Betty Johnson; children: Meredith Sue, Brian Marcus, John Cyrus. BS, U. Utah, 1949, MS, 1950; PhD, Oreg. State U., 1956; postgrad., U. Calif., Davis, 1957. Instr. botany Oreg. State U., Corvallis, 1955-56; range rsch. plant physiologist U. Calif. USDA-Agrl. Research Service, Davis, 1956—61; prof., dept. chmn. U. Calif., Riverside, 1961—69; prof. dept. head., dir. Utah State U., Logan, 1969-80; v.p. research NPI, Salt Lake City, 1980-88; dean Coll. of Sci. Weber State U., Ogden, Utah, 1988-94; pres., prin. Applied Ecol. Svcs. Inc., Logan, Utah, 1995—2008. Cons. Ford Found. 1968-72, Rockefeller Found., 1964-70, 89, UN, 1978, 90, NAS, 1980, 89, 91-93, USAID, 1972, UN Devel. Program, 1989; mem. faculty of sci. adv. bd. UAE Nat. U., 2000-02. Editor: Grass Biology and Utilization, 1971, Useful Wildland Shrubs, 1972, Rehabilitation of Western Wildlife Habitat, 1978, Paradoxes of Western Energy Development, 1984, Resource Inventory and Baseline Study Methods for Developing Countries, 1983, Shrub Biology and Utilization, 1989, Wilderness Issues, Arid Lands of the Western United States, 1992; contbr. over 230 articles to profl. jours. Chmn. Cache County Planning Commn., Logan, 1974-79; mem. Utah Energy Conservation and Devel. Coun., 1976-79, Gov.'s Sci. Adv. Coun., 1988-97, chmn., 1990-91, 96-97; mem. Commn. of the Californias, Riverside, 1965-68; mem. Holladay City Planning Commn., 2003-2009. Recipient Utah Gov.'s Sci. and Tech. medal, 1990, Gardner Prize in Sci., awarded by Utah Acad. Scis., Arts and Letters, 1999; Fulbright scholar Spain, 1967-68; World Travel grantee Rockefeller Found., 1964. Fellow: AAAS (com. chmn. 1979—89, sci. exchange to China grantee 1984—85, 1989, sci. panel U.S.-Chile 1987); mem.: Am. Soc. Agronomy, Soc. Range Mgmt. (pres. Calif. sect. 1965, pres. Utah sect. 1982). Mem. Lds Ch. Avocations: travel, photography, history. Home: 2248 E 4000 S Holladay UT 84124-1864 Home Phone: 801-278-6469.

MCKELLEN, SIR IAN, actor; b. Burnley, England, May 25, 1939; s. Denis Murray and Margery (Sutcliffe) McK.; life partner Sean Mathias. Grad., Cambridge U. Prof. Oxford U., 1990-91. First stage appearance as Roper in A Man for All Seasons, Belgrade Theatre, Coventry, Eng., 1961; numerous other parts include title roles in Henry V, Luther, Ipswich, 1962-63, Aufidius in Coriolanus, Arthur Seaton in Saturday Night and Sunday Morning, title role in Sir Thomas More, Nottingham Playhouse, 1963-64; London debut as Godfrey in A Scent of Flowers, 1964, Claudio in Much Ado About Nothing, Andrew Cobham in Their Very Own and Golden City, 1966; title part in O'Flaherty, V.C. and Bonapart in The Man of Destiny, 1966, (Broadway debut) Leonidik in the Promise, London, 1966-67, Richard II, Edward II, Hamlet, Prospect Theatre Co., 1968-71; Captain Plume in The Recruiting Officer; founder-mem. Actors' Co., Edinburgh Festival, 1972 and touring as Giovanni in Tis Pity She's a Whore, Page-Boy in Ruling the Roost, title role Wood Demon; debut with R.S.C. as Dr. Faustus, Edinburgh Festival, 1974; title role in The Marquis of Keith, Philip the Bastard in King John, 1974-75, Young Vic Colin in Ashes, 1975; Royal Shakespeare Co.: Burglar in Too True to be Good, Romeo, MacBeth, Leontes in the Winter's Tale, Face in the Alchemist, Bernick in Pillars of the Community, Langevin in Days of the Commune, 1976-78, Ivanov in Every Good Boy Deserves Favour, Toby Belch in Twelth Night, Andrei in The Three Sisters, Max in Bent, 1979, Amadeus, N.Y.C., 1980, Iago in Othello, The Other Place, Stratford, 1989; European tour of one-man show Acting Shakespeare, 1983, also L.A., N.Y.C., 1984, one-man show A Knight Out at the Lyceum (devised especially for Gay Games IV U.K. and South Africa tour), 1994, An Enemy of the People, 1997, Peter Pan, 1998, The Seagull, 1998, Present Laughter, 1998, The Tempest, 1999, Dance of Death, N.Y.C, 2001-02, London, 2003, Sydney, 2004, King Lear, 2007, The Seagull, 2007; assoc. dir. Nat. Theatre, London, 1984-86; dir. first prodn. The Prime of Miss Jean Brodie, Liverpool Playhouse, 1969, A Private Matter, 1973, The Clandestine Marriage, 1975; plays include: All in Good Time, 1963, The Alchemist, 1977, Amadeus, 1980, Venice Preserved, Wild Honey (recipient, Laurence Oliver Theatre award for Best Actor in a Revival, 1985), Coriolanus, Duchess of Malfi, The Cherry Orchard, King Lear, Richard III (recipient Laurence Olivier Theatre award for Best Actor (Royal Nat. Theatre), 1991, Acting Shakespeare, Napoli Milionaria, Uncle Vanya, An Enemy of The People, Peter Pan, Aladdin, 2004, and several others; films include Alfred the Great, 1968, A Touch of Love/Thank You All Very Much, 1968, The Promise, 1969, The Keep, 1983, Zina, 1985, Plenty, 1986, Scandal, 1988, I'll Do Anything, 1992, The Ballad of Little Jo, 1992, Last Action Hero, 1993, Six Degrees of Separation, 1993, The Shadow, 1994, Jack and Sarah, 1994, Restoration, 1995, Richard III, 1996 (also exec. prodr., writer), Surviving Friendly Fire, 1997, Bent, 1997, Swept From the Sea, 1997, Apt Pupil, 1998, Gods and Monsters, 1998, X-Men, 2000, Lord of the Rings: The Fellowship of the Ring, 2001 (Outstanding Performance by Male Actor in Supporting Role SAG award 2002, nominee Best Supporing Actor Acad. Award 2002, Best Supporting Actor Saturn award 2002; nominee Best Performance by Actor BAFTA Film award, Empire award, Golden Satellite award, MTV Movie award, and OFCS award 2002), Lord of the Rings: The Two Towers, 2002, X2: X-Men United, 2003, The Lord of the Rings: The Return of the King, 2003, Emile, 2004, The Lord of the Rings: The Third Age (voice), 2004, Eighteen (voice), 2004, The Lord of the Rings: The Battle for Middle-Earth (voice), 2004, Sprung!The Magic Roundabout (voice), 2005, Asylum, 2005, Coronation Street, 2005, Neverwas, 2005, Doogal (voice), 2006, X-Men: The Last Stand, 2006, The Da Vinci Code, 2006, Flushed Away (voice), 2006, Stardust, 2007, The Golden Compass, 2007; TV appearances include: Sunday Out of Season, 1965, The Trial ans Torture of Sir John Rampayne, 1965, David Copperfield, 1966, Hay Fever, 1968, What If It's Just Green Cheese?, 1969, Ross, 1970, The Tragedy of King Richard II, 1970,Edward II, 1970,Keats, 1970, The Last Journey, 1971, Hamlet, 1972, The Recruiting Officer, 1973, Graceless Go I,1973, Hedda Gabler, 1974, Macbeth, 1979, Priest of Love, 1979, Every Good Boy Deserves Favour, 1978, Dying Day, 1980, Loving Walter, 1982, Acting Shakespeare, 1982, The Scarlet Pimpernel, 1982, Walter and June, 1983, Windmills of the Gods, 1988, Othello, 1988, Countdown to War, 1989, Sleepers, 1991 (TV mini series), Tales of the City, 1993 (TV mini series), And the Band Played On, 1993 (Emmy nomination, Supporting Actor, 1993), Cold Comfort Farm, 1994, Rasputin, 1996 (Emmy nomination, Supporting Actor,1996) David Copperfield, 1999, The Simpsons: The Regina Monologues, 2003; (voice) To Die For, 1994, Cirque du Soleil: Journey of Man, 2000. Recipient Clarence Derwent award, 1964, Variety and Plays and Players awards, 1966; Actor of Year, Plays and Players, 1976, Soc. of West End Theatres for Best Actor in Revival award, 1977, for Best Comedy Performance, 1978, for Best Actor in a New Play, 1979, Tony Award for Best Actor, Drama Desk award, Outer Critics Circle award, N.Y. Drama League award, 1981, Performer of the Yr. award Royal TV Soc., 1983, Soc. London Theatre Spl. award, 2006; decorated comdr. Order Brit. Empire, Knight Bachelor. Mem. Brit. Actors' Equity (coun. 1970-71). Office: ICM Oxford House 76 Oxford St London W1D 1BS England

MCKELLIPS, GORDON WAYNE, JR., lawyer, land developer; b. Phoenix, Feb. 6, 1941; s. Gordon Wayne and Eunice J. McK.; m. Joslyn M. Guerin, Aug. 4, 1964; children: Briant W., Eric G. BA, Duke U., 1962; JD, U. Ariz., 1965. Bar: Ariz. 1965, US Ct. Appeals (9th cir.) 1978, US Supreme Ct. 1968. Officer, dir. McKellips Land Corp., Phoenix, 1966—, Gem Land Co., Phoenix, 1982—, Willow Valley Water Co., Inc., Mohave Valley, Ariz., 1966-94, Granite Reef Farms, Inc., Mohave Valley, Ariz., 1966—; assoc. Carson Messinger Elliott Laughlin and Ragan, Phoenix, 1965-70, ptnr., 1971—. Editorial bd. Ariz. Law Rev., 1965. Com. mem. North Phoenix Young Life, 1989—. Fellow Ariz. Bar Found. Republican. Office: Carson Messinger Elliott Laughlin and Ragan PLLC 3300 N Central Ave Ste 1900 Phoenix AZ 85012-2515 Home Phone: 602-997-1946; Office Phone: 602-264-2261. Business E-Mail: wmckellips@carsonlawfirm.com.

MCKELVEY, GREGORY A., food products executive; Cons. Accenture Ltd., 1997—2001; strategy cons. Bain & Co., 2001—05; sr. v.p. strategy/mktg. svcs. WhiteWave Foods divsn. Dean Foods Co., Dallas, 2005—08, exec. v.p., chief strategy & transformation officer, 2008—. Office: Dean Foods Co 2515 McKinney Ave Ste 1200 Dallas TX 75201 Office Phone: 214-303-3415. Business E-Mail: greg_mckelvey@deanfoods.com.*

MCKELVEY, JOHN CLIFFORD, mental health services professional; b. Decatur, Ill., Jan. 25, 1934; s. Clifford Venice and Pauline Lytton (Runkel) McK.; m. Carolyn Tenney, May 23, 1980; children: Sean, Kerry, Tara, Evelyn, Aaron. BA, Stanford U., 1956, MBA, 1958. Rsch. analyst Stanford Rsch. Inst., Palo Alto, Calif., 1959—60, indsl. economist, 1960—64; with Midwest Rsch. Inst., Kansas City, Mo., 1964—2000, v.p. econs. and mgmt. sci., 1970—73, exec. v.p., 1973—75, pres., CEO, 1975—2000, The Menninger Clinic, Topeka, 2001—. Chmn. Trustee Vis. Coms. The Menninger Clinic, Topeka, 1978—86, chmn. bd. dirs., 1988—94; chmn. bd. The Menninger Found., 1994—97. Trustee Rockhurst Coll., 1993, Hoover Presdl. Libr. Assn., West Branch, Iowa, 1997; mem. Civic Coun. of Greater Kansas City; bd. dirs. Yellow Corp., Mid-Am. Mfg. Tech. Ctr., 1991; trustee The Menninger Found., 1975. Mem.: Carriage, Mission Hills. Home: 1156 W 103d St # 232 Kansas City MO 64114-4511 Address: Menningers PO Box 809045 Houston TX 77280

MCKELVY, MICHAEL JOHN, chemist, research scientist; b. Berkeley, Calif., Apr. 19, 1954; s. Andy Milton and Dagmar Marie (Johnson) McK.; m. Margaret Knight Riddall, Aug. 2, 1975; children: Robin, Adam, Evan. BS in Chemistry, U. Calif., Berkeley, 1975; MS in Chemistry, Ariz. State U., 1981, PhD in Chemistry, 1985. Engr. crystal growing lab., ctr. solid state sci. Ariz. State U., Tempe, 1976—82, materials sci. engr. II, 1982—84, rsch. specialist, 1984—90, mgr. materials facility, 1986—94, assoc. rsch. scientist, 1990—99, affiliate assoc. prof. sci. & engring. of materials PhD program, 1993—99, dir. materials facility, 1994—2005, dir. Goldwater materials sci. labs., 1995—2005, acting dir. ctr. solid state sci., 1997, sr. rsch. scientist, 1999—, affiliate prof. sci. and engring. materials grad. program, 1999—2006, mgr. Goldwater materials facilities, 2006—, affiliate prof. Sch. Materials, 2006—. Invited asst. prof. Inst. des Matériaux de Nantes, U. Nantes, France, 1993; dir. Sci. is Fun Program Ariz. State U., Tempe, 1997-; NRC sr. rsch. assoc. Albany (Oreg.) Rsch. Ctr., 2002; proposal reviewer Petroleum Rsch. Fund, Washington, 1992-94, U.S. Dept. Energy, 2000—. Contbr. articles to profl. jours.; manuscript reviewer Chemistry of Materials, 1994-2002, Jour. Physics and Chemistry of Solids, 1995, Jour. Solid State Chemistry, 1996—, Molecular Crystals and Liquid Crystals, 1997-98, Journal of American Chemical Society, 1998-2001, Journal of American Ceramic Society, 2001-02, Environmental Science and Technology, 2003—. Coach Chandler (Ariz.) Youth Baseball, 1988-95, Chandler Am. Little League, 1996-97; com. chmn. cub scouts Boy Scouts Am., Mesa, Ariz., 1992, mem. Boy Scout com., Chandler, 1993-95. Recipient Outstanding Cmty. Impact award, Acad. Cmty. Engagement Svcs., ASU, 2002; rsch. grantee NSF, 1986—, Petroleum Rsch. Fund, 1992-95, Dept. Energy, 1995—; NRC sr. rsch. assoc., 2002. Mem. Am. Chem. Soc., Materials Rsch. Soc., Minerals, Metals and Materials Soc. Democrat. Presbyterian. Achievements include patents for method for detection of chemical components, chemical switch and method for detection of chemical compounds, and chemical switch for detection of chemical components; co-development of atomic-level imaging of lamellar intercalation reaction processes using dynamic high-resolution transmission electron microscopy and scanning tunneling microscopy/spectroscopy; research in new materials synthesis, materials reaction mechanisms, carbon dioxide mineral sequestration, intercalation chemistry, thermal chemistry and analysis, materials sci. edn. Office: Ariz State U LeRoy Eyring Ctr for Solid State Science Tempe AZ 85287-1704 Office Phone: 480-965-4535. Business E-Mail: mckelvy@asu.edu.

MCKENDALL, ROBERT ROLAND, neurologist, virologist, educator; b. Providence, Feb. 18, 1944; s. Benjamin Salvatore and Pauline McK.; m. Joyce Marie Podlesak, Oct. 12, 1973; children: Lauren Patricia, Alexis Victoria. BA, Columbia Coll., NYC, 1965; MD, Tufts U., 1969. Diplomate Am. Bd. Neurology and Psychiatry. Resident in neurology Rush-Presbyn.-St. Lukes Hosp., Chgo., 1970-74; neurovirology fellow U. Calif., San Francisco, 1974-78, asst. prof. neurology, 1981-84, U. Tex. Med. Br., Galveston, 1984-88, assoc. prof. neurology, microbiology, immunology, 1988—. Mem. neurology core com. AIDS Clin. Trials Group of NIH, 1996-2005, Adult Clin. Trials Group of NIH, 1996-2005.; mem. toxicity related clin. diagnostics com., 2001-03. Editor: (textbook) Viral Diseases-Handbood of Clinical Neurology, 1989, Handbook of Neurovirology, 1994; editl. reviewer Neurology, 1990, Annals of Neurology, 1990-96, Jour. Neurol. Scis., 1997-2000; contbr. over 40 articles to profl. jours. Mem. Sch. Dist. Parent Adv. Bd., Dickinson, Tex., 1992—94. Recipient Young Investigator award NIH, 1978-81, Career Devel. award VA Rsch. Svc., 1981-84, Herpes Simplex Infection grant, 1984-86, AIDS Clin. Trials grant NIH, 1992-2004. Mem. Am. Acad. Neurology, Am. Assn. Immunologists. Office: U Tex Med Br Dept Neurology E-39 301 University Blvd Galveston TX 77555-0539 Office Phone: 409-772-5910. Business E-Mail: rmckenda@utmb.edu.

MCKENDRY, JOHN H., JR., lawyer; b. Grand Rapids, Mich., Mar. 24, 1950; s. John H. and Lois R. (Brandel) McK.; m. Linda A. Schmalzer, Aug. 11, 1973; children: Heather Lynn, Shannon Dawn, Sean William. BA cum laude, Albion Coll., Mich., 1972; JD cum laude, U. Mich., Ann Arbor, 1975. Bar: Mich. 1975. Assoc., then ptnr. Landman, Latimer, Clink & Robb, Muskegon, Mich., 1976-85; ptnr. Warner, Norcross & Judd, Muskegon, 1985—. Dir. debate Mona Shores High Sch., Muskegon, 1979-90; adj. prof. of taxation (employee benefits), Grand Valley State U., 1988—; debate instr. Muskegon C.C., 1999-2001. Pres. local chpt. Am. Cancer Soc., 1979; bd. dirs. West Shore Symphony, 1993-00, v.p. 1995-97, pres., 1997-99; bd. dirs. Cath. Social Svcs., 1998-04; chair profl. divsn. United Way, 1994, 98; chair bd. dirs. Deaf Hard of Hearing Connection, 2003-09; bd. dirs. Mona Lake Watershed Coun., 2003-05, Hackley Life Counseling, 2007-; chair Charter Commn. City of Norton Shores, 2003-06. Recipient Disting. Service award Muskegon Jaycees, 1981; named 1 of 5 Outstanding Young Men in Mich., Mich. Jaycees. 1982; named to Hall of Fame, Mich. Speech Coaches, 1986, Diamond Key Coach Nat. Forensic League, 1987. Mem. ABA, Mich. Bar Assn., Muskegon County Bar Assn. (dir. 1992-98, pres. 1996-97), Muskegon C. of C. (bd. dirs. 1982-88), Mich. Interscholastic Forensic Assn. (treas. 1979-86), Optimists (pres. 1992). Republican. Roman Catholic. Home: 1575 Brookwood Dr Muskegon MI 49441-5276 Office Phone: 231-727-2637. Business E-Mail: mckendjh@wnj.com.

MCKENNA, ALVIN JAMES, lawyer; b. New Orleans, Aug. 17, 1943; s. Dixon N. Sr. and Mabel (Duplantier) McK.; m. Carol Jean Windheim, 1963; children: Sara, Alvin James Jr., Martha, Andrea, Erin, Rebecca. AB, Canisius Coll., 1963; JD, Notre Dame U., 1966. Bar: N.Y. 1966, Ohio 1967, U.S. Dist. Ct. (so. dist.) Ohio 1968, U.S. Dist. Ct. (no. dist.) Ohio 1978, U.S. Ct. Appeals (6th cir.) 1969, U.S. Supreme Ct. 1977. Law clk. to judge of U.S. Dist. Ct. (so. dist.), Columbus, Ohio, 1966-68; asst. U.S. atty., 1968-70; ptnr. Porter, Wright, Morris & Arthur, 1970—. Mem. Gahanna (Ohio) City Coun., 1972-80, 82-84; chmn. Gahanna Charter Rev. Commn., 1981, 06; pres. Cmty. Urban Redevel. Corp., Gahanna, 1984-. Named one of Ten Outstanding Young Persons in Columbus, Jaycees, 1974. Mem. ABA, Ohio Bar Assn., Fed. Bar Assn. (pres. Columbus chpt. 1973-74), Columbus Bar Assn. (chair fed. cts. com. 1972-74). Roman Catholic. Home: 202 Academy Ct Columbus OH 43230-2104 Office: Porter Wright Morris & Arthur 41 S High St Ste 2800 Columbus OH 43215-6194 Home Phone; 614-475-1511; Office Phone: 614-227-1945. Business E-Mail: amckenna@porterwright.com.

MCKENNA, ANDREW, JR., political organization administrator, printing company executive; BBA, U. Notre Dame, 1979; MBA, Northwestern U. With strategic planning dept. Kraft Foods; pres. Schwarz Paper Co., Morton Grove, Ill., 1981—; mem. Nat. Security Edn. Bd., 2004—; chmn. Ill. Rep. Party, 2005—. Treas. Kirk for Congress, mem. fin. com., 2000; mem. Vol. Polit. Action Com., 2002; chmn. Ill. Bus. Edn. Coalition, Ill. Bus. Roundtable. Chmn. Chicagoland C. of C., Christmas in April. Republican. Office: Schwarz Paper Source 8338 Austin Ave Morton Grove IL 60053*

MCKENNA, ANDREW JAMES, wholesale distribution, printing company executive, sports association executive; b. Chgo., Sept. 17, 1929; s. Andrew James and Anita (Fruin) McK.; m. Mary Joan Pickett, June 20, 1953; children: Suzanne, Karen, Andrew, William, Joan, Kathleen, Margaret. BS, U. Notre Dame, 1951; JD, DePaul U., 1954. Bar: Ill. Chmn. Schwarz Supply Source, Morton Grove, Ill., 1964—; non-exec. chmn. McDonald's Corp., 2004—. Chmn. Chgo. White Sox, 1975—81, Chgo. Cubs, 1981—84; bd. dir. AON Corp., Chgo. Bears Football CLub, McDonald's Corp., 1991—; bd. dirs. Skyline Corp., 1971—. Trustee, Univ. Notre Dame, chmn. 1992-2000; trustee, past chmn. Mus. Sci. and Industry, Chgo.; bd. dir. Cath. Charities of Chgo., Children's Meml. Med. Ctr. Chgo., Lyric Opera, United Way Metro. Chgo.; founding chmn. Chgo. Metropolis 2020. Mem. Comml. Club Chgo., Econ. Club Chgo., Lyric Opera (bd. dirs.), Execs. Club Chgo., Glenview Golf Club, Old Elm Club, Merit Club, Casino Club, The Island Club. Home: 60 Locust Rd Winnetka IL 60093-3751 Office: McDonald's Corp One McDonald's Plz Oak Brook IL 60523 Office Phone: 630-623-3000. Office Fax: 630-623-5700.

MCKENNA, ANN K., nutritionist, educator; d. Mary Giannavola and Joseph Peter Kupchak; m. Robert William McKenna, Aug. 10, 1963; children: Rodney William, Scot Robert, Stacy McKenna Brazil, Alison McKenna Rothwell, Cynthia McKenna Holmes. BS in Nutrition and Edn., Marywood Coll., Pa., 1959, MS in Nutrition and Dietetics, 1992. Registered Dietitian Am. Dietetic Assn., 1968, Cert.in Family and Consumer Sci. Am. Assn. of Family and Consumer Sci., 1985, lic. Dietitian, Nutritionist Pa., 2002. Adminstrv. dietitian Flower & Fifth Ave. Hosp., NYC, 1959—62; clin. dietitian Moses Taylor Hosp., Scranton, Pa., 1971—82; cons. dietitian, self employed in long term care facilities and home health orgns. Pa., 1982—; nutrition cons. Scranton Head Start Program, Scranton, 1984—; part-time faculty Marywood U., 1984—; clin. dietitian, educator Moses Taylor Hosp. Diabetes Edn. Program, 1998—2004. Bd. mem. NE Pa. Dietetic Assn., Scranton, Wilkes-Barre, Pa., 1995—; health adv. bd. mem. Scranton Lackawanna Head Start Program, Scranton, 1990—; coordinating cabinet mem. Marywood U. Nutrition and Dietetics Program, 1990—. Recipient Kappa Kappa Nu, Honor Soc. for Nutrition Grads. through Marywood Coll., 1992, Anita Owen award for Dietetic Profls., N.E. Pa. Dietetic Assn., 1998, Outstanding Dietetic Educator, Pa. Dietetic Assn., 1999, Dietetic Educators of Am. Dietetic Assn., 1999, Woman Yr., Head Start Program Scranton Lackawanna Human Devel. Agy., 2000. Mem.: Am. Assn. of Family and Consumer Sci. (assoc.), Am. Dietetic Assn. (assoc.), Pa. Dietetic Assn. (assoc.; bd. mem. 1999—2000), NE Pa. Dietetic Assn. (assoc.; career guidance, job referral chair 1996—2005). Avocations: fitness, gourmet cooking, reading. Home: 1329 Electric St Dunmore PA 18509 Office: Marywood Univ Adams Ave Scranton PA 18509 Home Fax: 570-346-6422. Personal E-mail: akmrd@aol.com.

MCKENNA, BARBARA J., clinical pathologist; b. Sept. 21, 1954; BS, Mich. State U.; MD, U. Mich., 1981. Cert. Anatomic Pathology and Clin. Pathology, 1985, Cytopathology, 1996. Resident in anatomic and clin. pathology U. Mich. Med. Sch.; staff physician and assoc. dir. laboratories Saratoga Hosp., NY, 1985—88; dir. laboratories Moses-Ludington Hosp., Ticonderoga, NY, 1985—88; assoc. attending physician St. Peter's Hosp., Albany, 1988—94; joined faculty Albany Med. Coll., 1994—2002; assoc. prof. pathology U. Mich. Med. Sch., 2002—, dir. surg. pathology fellowship prog. Mem.: Am. Soc. Clin. Pathology (pres. 2008—, George F. Stevenson Disting. Svc. award, Commn. on Continuing Edn. 2003), A. James French Soc. Pathology, Coll. Am. Pathology, US and Can. Acad. Pathology. Office: U Mich Med Sch 2G332 UH 1500 E Medical Center Dr Ann Arbor MI 48109-0054 also: Am Soc Clin Pathology Ste 1600 33 W Monroe St Chicago IL 60603 Office Phone: 743-936-6770. Office Fax: 734-763-4095. E-mail: barbmcke@umich.edu.*

MCKENNA, ERIN NICOLE, history professor; b. Taylorville, Ill., Mar. 13, 1981; d. Colette Mavis McKenna and Bradley Roe Weakly (Stepfather); m. Michael David Mignin. MA, Bowling Green State U., Ohio, 2006. Tchg. asst. Bowling Green State U., 2005—07, writing cons., 2006—07, instr., history, 2007—. Recipient Grad. Student Tchg. award, Bowling Green State U., History Dept., 2008. Mem.: Am. Hist. Assn., Phi Alpha Theta. Business E-Mail: emckenn@bgnet.bgsu.edu.

MCKENNA, JEANETTE ANN, archaeologist; b. NYC, Aug. 6, 1953; d. Edward Patrick and Ann Jeanette (O'Brien) McKenna; children: Stephanie Jane, Daniel Glen Edward. AA in Phys. Edn., Mount San Antonio Jr. Coll., 1974; BA in Anthropology, Calif. State U., Fullerton, 1977, MA in Anthropology, 1982; postgrad., Ariz. State U., Tempe, 1981-84, U. Calif., Riverside, 1991-92. Field archaeologist Archaeol. Rsch., Inc., Costa Mesa, Calif., 1976-79; rsch. asst. Calif. State U., 1979; lab. dir. Environ. Rsch. Archaeologists, LA, 1978-79; staff archaeologist Ariz. State U., Tempe, 1979-82; rsch. archaeologist Soil Systems, Inc., Phoenix, 1982-84, Sci. Resource Surveys, Huntington Beach, Calif., 1984-87; co-owner, prin. Hatheway & McKenna, Mission Viejo, Calif., 1987-89; owner, prin. McKenna et al., Whittier, Calif., 1989—; dir. Divsn. Cultural Resource Mgmt. Svcs. EIP Assocs., Chino, Calif., 1996-97. Contbr. numerous articles to profl. jours. and reports. Bd. dirs. Whittier Conservancy, 1987-98, interim treas., 1994, pres., 1994-95, bd. dirs. Residents' Voice, 1998—. Recipient Gov.'s award for Hist. Preservation/Calif., The Whittier Conservancy, 1995, Woman of Achievement award for sci. and rsch. YWCA San Gabriel Valley, 2006. Mem. Soc. Profl. Archaeologists (bd. dirs. 1993-97), Archaeol. Inst. Am., Am. Soc. Conservation Archaeology, Am. Mus. Natural History, Soc. Am. Anthropology, Ariz. Archaeol. Coun., Ariz. Hist. Found., Calif. Hist. Soc., Nat. Arbor Day Found., Nat. Parks and Conservation Assn., Nat. Trust for Historic Preservation, Soc. Calif. Archaeology, Soc. Hist. Archaeology, S.W. Mus. Assn., Wilderness Soc., Whittier Conservancy, Southwestern Anthrop. Assn., Gene Autry Western Heritage Mus. Assn., Nature Conservancy, Smithsonian Assocs., Sierra Club, others. Democrat. Roman Catholic. Avocations: travel, reading, hiking, camping, gardening. Office: McKenna et al 6008 Friends Ave Whittier CA 90601-3724 Home Phone: 562-693-6365; Office Phone: 562-696-3852. Business E-Mail: jmckena@earthlink.net.

MCKENNA, MARGARET ANNE, foundation administrator, former academic administrator; b. RI, June 3, 1945; d. Joseph John and Mary (Burns) McK.; children: Michael Aaron McKenna Miller, David Christopher McKenna Miller. BA in Sociology, Emmanuel Coll., 1967; postgrad., Boston Coll. Law Sch., 1968; JD, So. Meth. U., 1971; LLD (hon.), U. Upsala, NJ, 1978, Fitchburg State Coll., Mass., 1979, Regis Coll., 1982; LLD (hon.), Emmanuel Coll., 2000, Episcopal Divinity Sch., 2005. Bar: Tex. 1971, D.C. 1973. Atty. US Dept. Justice, Washington, 1971-73; exec. dir. Internat. Assn. Ofcl. Human Rights Agys., Washington, 1973-74; mgmt. cons. US Dept. Treasury, Washington, 1975-76; dep. council to Pres. The White House, Washington, 1976-79; dep. under sec. US Dept. Edn., Washington, 1979-81; dir. Mary Ingraham Bunting Inst., Radcliffe Coll., Cambridge, Mass., 1981-85; v.p. program planning Radcliffe Coll., Cambridge, Mass., 1982-85; pres. Lesley U., Cambridge, Mass., 1985—2007, The Wal-Mart Found., Bentonville, Ark., 2007—. Bd. dirs. Dominion Resources, Inc., Cisco Learning Inst. Bd. dirs. Am. Assn. Coll. for Tchr. Edn., Coun. for Higher Edn. Accreditation, Datatel Scholars Found.; chmn. higher edn. task force Clinton Transition, 1992-93; chmn. edn. task force Mayor Thomas Menino Transition Com., 1994; mem. Princeton Adv. Bd. ACE Policy Adv. Com., Campus Compact Policy Com., MassNetworks. Recipient Outstanding Contribution award Civil Rights Leadership Conf., 1978; named Woman of Yr. Women's Equity Action League, 1979, Outstanding Woman of Yr. Big Sister Assn., 1986, Pinnacle award for Lifetime Achievement, Lelia J. Robinson award Women's Bar Assn. Mass., 1996, Valeria Addams Knapp award, The Coll. Club, 1995; named Margaret A. McKenna Day, Gov. DePrete, R.I. Mem. Boys Scouts Am., Big Sisters Ass. Boston, Y.W.C.A. Cambridge, Women's Equity Action League, Nat. Women's Polit. Conf., Nat. Assn. Official Human Rights Agencies. Democrat. Office: The Wal-Mart Found 702 SW 8th St Bentonville AR 72716

MCKENNA, MATTHEW MORGAN, lawyer; b. Apr. 29, 1950; s. James Aloysius and Rebecca (Rial) McK.; m. Nancy Fitzpatrick, Sept. 11, 1976; children: Matthew, James, Christine, Connor. BA, Hamilton Coll., 1972; JD, Georgetown U., 1975, LLM, 1978. Bar: N.Y. 1977. Clk. to Hon. Fred B. Ugast Superior Ct., Washington, 1975—76; assoc. Winthrop, Stimson, Putnam & Roberts, NYC, 1979—83, ptnr., 1984—93; sr. v.p., treas. Pepsi Co., Inc., Purchase, NY, 1998—2001, sr. v.p. fin., 2001—07; pres., CEO Keep America Beautruc. Adj. prof. Sch. Law Fordham U., NYC, 1983—94, NYC, 2002—. Trustee Merrill Lynch Found., 1986—95, Mt. St. Mary's Coll., Emmitsburg, Md., 1994—2002; bd. trustees SUNY, Purchase Found., NY, 2003—, Hamilton Coll., 2003—07. Mem.: ABA (tax sect.), Assn. Bar of City of N.Y., N.Y. State Bar Assn. (chmn. com. on fgn. activities of U.S. taxpayers). Home: 35 Valley Rd Bronxville NY 10708-2226 Office: Keep America Beautruc Stamford CT 06901

MCKENNA, PETER DENNIS, lawyer; b. Amityville, NY, Aug. 15, 1937; s. John Paul and Margaret (Foley) McK.; children: Michael A., Suzanne E. AB cum laude, Coll. of the Holy Cross, Worchester, Mass., 1959; JD cum laude, N.Y.U., 1968. Bar: NY 1968, US Dist. Ct. (so. dist.) NY 1970, US Supreme Ct. 1973, US Ct. Appeals (4th cir.) 1977, US Ct. Appeals (7th cir.) 1979, US Ct. Appeals (2nd cir.) 1983. Assoc. Wachtell, Lipton, Rosen & Katz, NYC, 1968-71, ptnr., 1972-91, of counsel, 1992—2001. Mem. pres.'s coun. NYU, Weinfeld Ptnr. NYU Law Sch.; regent mem. pres.'s coun. Coll. Holy Cross. Editor-in-chief NYU Law Review, 1967-68; contbr. articles to profl. jours. Mem. Cmty. Sch. Bd. Dist. 26, Queens, NY, 1973-77; adv. bd. St. Aloysius Sch. for Cen. Harlem Inner-City Children, 1992—, mem. exec. com., 1994-2001; founding dir. Ctrl. Harlem Initiative for Learning and Devel., 1994—; bd. dirs. Mt. St. Michael Acad., 1994-2001, mem. exec. com., 1994-99. Lt. USN 1959-65. MEM. ABA, Am. Arbitration Assn. (comml. and securities panels), Assn. of Bar of City of NY, Order of Coif. Democrat. Roman Catholic. Avocations: history, public affairs, travel, swimming, golf. Address: 21205 NE 37th Ave Apt 1607 Aventura FL 33180-4056 E-mail: ppeter68@aol.com.

MCKENNA, ROB, state attorney general, former councilman; b. Ft. Sam Houston, Tex., Oct. 1, 1962; m. Marilyn McKenna; children: Madeleine, Katie, Robert, Connor. BA in Econs. and Internat. Studies, 1985; JD, U. Chgo., 1988. Bar: Wash., 9th Cir. US Ct. Appeals, US Supreme Ct. Atty. Perkins Cole, Bellevue, Wash., 1988—95; councilman King County, Wash., 1996—2004; atty. gen. State of Wash., 2005—. Co-founder, bd. mem. Eastside Human Svcs. Forum; bd. mem. Econ. Devel. Coun. of Seattle & King County; mem. Sound Transit Bd., 1996—2001; chair Eastside Transp. Partnership, 1999—2001, Wash. State Transp. Improvement Bd., 2001—03. Mem. King County Open Space Citizens Oversight Com., 1990—94; founder, bd. dirs. Advance Bellevue, 1991—2001; past pres., bd. mem. Bellevue Schs. Found., 1993—2002; mem. Bellevue Rotary, 1993—; bd. mem. King County Open Space Citizens Oversight Com., 1995—98; co-chair City of Hope Walk for Hope to Cure Breast Cancer, 1998, 1999; co-founder, bd. mem. Evergreen Forest Trust, 2000—; bd. mem. Bellevue CC Found., 2000—; mem. steering com. Citizens for Renton Schs., 2002—03; mem. exec. bd. Chief Seattle Coun. Boy Scouts Am., 2003—; mem. St. Louise Cath. Parish, 1977—; Eagle Scout. Recipient Doug Mason Meml. award, Mcpl. League King County, 1991, 40 under 40 award, Puget Sound Bus. Jour., 2000, Advance Bellevue 10th Anniversary Legacy award, 2003; named Elected Ofcl. of Yr., Nat. Assn. Indsl. and Office Properties, 1999; named one of The 25 Smartest People in Wash., Wash. Law & Politics, 2003. Mem.: King County Bar Assn., Wash. State Bar Assn. Republican. Office: Office Atty Gen 1125 Washington St SE PO Box 40100 Olympia WA 98504-0100 Office Phone: 360-753-6200. Business E-Mail: rob.mckenna@atg.wa.gov.*

MCKENNA, STEPHEN JAMES, retired lawyer, corporate executive; b. Islip, NY, Sept. 4, 1940; s. John Paul and Margaret (Foley) McK.; m. Lolita Andrea deLeon, Aug. 24, 1963; children: Stephen Jr., Christopher, Matthew, Andrew. BA magna cum laude, Boston Coll., Chestnut Hill, Mass., 1962; JD, Fordham U., 1965. Bar: N.Y. 1966. D.C. 1970, U.S. Supreme Ct. 1990. Atty. Pan Am. World Airlines, NYC, 1965-67, Ea. Airlines, Washington, 1967-69, Lockheed Aircraft Corp., Washington, 1969-72; pvt. practice law Washington, 1972-73; v.p., assoc. gen. counsel Marriott Corp., Bethesda, Md., 1973-93; v.p., gen. counsel Host Marriott Corp., Bethesda, Md., 1993-95, exec. v.p., gen. counsel, 1995-97, of counsel, 1997-99; ret., 1999. Continuing legal edn. panelist Georgetown U. Law Ctr. Founder, pres. Civic Assn. River Falls, Potomac, Md., 1976; committeeman troop 1427 Boy Scouts Am., Potomac, 1977-93; mem. fin. com. St. Bartholomew's Ch., Bethesda, 1979—, chmn. sch. bd., 1979; bd. trustees Marymount U., Arlington, Va., 1992-97, Gonzaga Coll. H.S., Washington, 1997. Mem. ABA (panelist), Am. Coll. Real Estate Lawyers (panelist), D.C. Bar Assn., Assn. Bar City N.Y., N.Y. State Bar Assn.

MCKENNA, TERENCE PATRICK, retired insurance company executive; b. Oldham, Lancashire, Eng., Sept. 3, 1928; came to U.S., 1929, naturalized, 1939; s. Patrick A. and Mary F. McKenna; m. Patricia Buckley, Aug. 22, 1973 (dec. July 1, 2006); m. Suzanne Caffey, Feb. 17, 2007. Student, St. Thomas Coll., Bloomfield, Conn., 1946—48. With John Hancock Mut. Life Ins. Co., 1951-87, gen. agt. Cherry Hill, NJ, 1963-67, field v.p. gen. agy. dept. Atlanta, 1967-69, field v.p. dist. agy. dept. Boston, 1969-73, 2d v.p. mktg. ops. dept., 1973-74, v.p. dept., 1974-76, sr. v.p. dept., 1976-83, sr. v.p. gen. agy. sales dept., 1983-87; ret., 1987. V.p., also bd. dirs. John Hancock Variable Life Ins. Co.; chmn. bd. mgrs. I.V.A.; bd. dirs. John Hancock Distbrs. Inc., John Hancock Property and Casualty Ins. Co. Served with USMC, 1952-54. Mem.: Am. Soc. CLUs, Am. Coll. Life Underwriters, El Niguel Country Club (Laguna Niguel, Calif.), Woods Hole Golf Club (Falmouth, Mass.). Personal E-mail: tpmckenna@cox.net.

MCKENNA, WILLIAM MICHAEL, academic administrator; b. Washington, Apr. 4, 1951; s. William H. and Betty Ann (Cashin) McK.; m. Lynn Stevenson, Dec. 18, 1976; children: James Langdon, Lee Stevenson. BA, Wesleyan U., 1973; MS in Journalism, Boston U., 1978. V.p., creative dir. Ingalls Quinn & Johnson, Boston, 1981-88; sr. v.p., creative dir. Young & Rubicam, NYC, 1988-94; chief creative officer, exec. v.p. AF GL Internat., NYC, 1994-95; mng. dir., chief creative officer Citigate Albert Frank, NYC, 1996-99; mng. dir., COO, Marsteller, NYC, 1999-2000; pres., CEO Marsteller Advt., NYC, 2000—. V.p. comm. Middlebury Coll., Vt., 2005—. Recipient CLIO, Hatch, N.Y. Film Soc. creative advt. awards, 1982-2005, Telly awards. Home: 869 James Rd Middlebury VT 05753-9538 Office: Middlebury Coll 5 Court St Middlebury VT 05753 Business E-Mail: mmckenna@middlebury.edu.

MCKENNEY, KERRY B., legislative staff member; Grad., U. Del., Newark. Legis. dir., press sec., chief of staff to Rep. Donald Payne US House of Reps., Washington. Democrat. Office: Office of Rep Donald Payne 2310 Rayburn House Office Bldg Washington DC 20515 Office Phone: 202-225-3436. Office Fax: 202-225-4160. E-mail: kerry.mckenney@mail.house.gov.*

MCKENNEY, PAUL E., application developer; b. Port Townsend, Wash., Oct. 31, 1958; s. Edward T. McKenney and Alice Fisher; m. Gloria Wyffels, Nov. 14, 1985; children: Melissa, Sarah, Aaron. BS in Mech. Engrng. and Computer Sci., Oreg. State U., Corvallis, 1981, MS in Computer Sci., 1988; PhD in Computer Sci. and Engrng., OHSU OGI Sch. Sci. and Engrng., Beaverton, Oreg., 2004. Contract Programmer & cons. Paul E. McKenney, Corvallis, 1981—85; sr. sys. programmer SRI Internat., Menlo Pk., Calif., 1986—90; software engr. Sequent Computer Sys., Inc., Beaverton, 1990—2000; disting. engr. IBM Corp., Beaverton, 2000—. Mem. Oreg. State U. Indsl. Adv. Bd., Corvallis, 2006—. Contbr. articles to profl. jours. Mem.: IEEE, ACM. Office: IBM Linux Tech Ctr 15350 SW Koll Pky Beaverton OR 97006 Business E-Mail: paulmck@linux.vnet.ibm.com.

MCKENNEY, RICHARD P., insurance company executive; BS in Mech. Engrng. summa cum laude, Tufts U. Mfg. mgmt. program GE, 1991; various positions in fin. and ops. GE Fin. Assurance Holdings Inc.; sr. v.p., CFO Genworth Fin. Inc, 2004; exec. v.p. Sun Life Fin. Inc., 2006, CFO, 2007; exec. v.p., CFO Unum Group, 2009—. Office: Unum Group 1 Fountain Sq Chattanooga TN 37402 Office Phone: 423-294-1011.*

MCKENNON, KEITH ROBERT, chemical company executive; b. Condon, Oreg., Dec. 25, 1933; s. Russel M. and Lois E. (Edgerton) McK.; m. Patricia Dragon, Sept. 30, 1961; children: Brian, Marc, Kevin. BS, Oreg. State U., 1955. Rsch. chemist Dow Chem. Co., Pittsburg, Calif., 1955—67, sales mgr. Houston, 1967, from research mgr. to exec. v.p. Midland, Mich., 1968—87, bd. dirs., 1983—92, 2003—06, exec. v.p., 1987-92; pres. Dow USA, 1987-90; chmn., chief exec. officer Dow Corning Corp., 1992-94, also bd. dirs.; chmn. PacifiCorp, Portland, Oreg., 1994-99, CEO, 1998-99. Patentee. Recipient Chemical Industry medal Soc. of Chemical Industry, 1994 Republican. Presbyterian. E-mail: kmck96@aol.com.

MCKENRICK, LAURENCE LEE, environmentalist; b. Coulee Dam, Wash., May 23, 1949; s. Thomas Aloyious McKenrick and Bobbie Jean Gable; m. Teresa Joanne Reed, May 21, 1977; children: Thomas Aloysius III, Christopher Laurence, Sabrina Lee. AS in Environ. Tech., Merritt Jr. Coll., Oakland, Calif., 1978; BS in Environ. Health, Ferris State U., Big Rapids, Mich., 1985; MS in Health Care Adminstrn., Ctrl. Mich., Mt. Pleasant, 1988. Registered sanitarian Nat. Environ. Health Assn., 1984. Health & environ. investigator Pub. Health Seattle & King County, 1989—. Chief hosp. man USN, 1986—89, Pearl harbor, Hawaii, chief petty officer USN, 1986—89. Home: 15020 Willow Dr Marysville WA 98271-8134 Office: Public Health Seattle & King County 401 5th Ave Seattle WA 98104 Business E-Mail: larry.mckenrick@kingcounty.gov.

MCKENZIE, BRET, musician, actor; b. New Zealand, June 29, 1976; s. Peter McKenzie. Band mem. The Black Seeds, 1997—; band mem., co-creator (with Jemaine Clement) Flight of the Conchords, 2002—. Musician: (albums) (with The Black Seeds) Keep on Pushing, 2001, Keep on Pushing/Pushed, 2005, Into the Dojo, 2006, On the Sun, 2006, Black Seeds EP, 2007, Good People (Get Together), 2007, (with Flight of the Conchords) Folk the World Tour, 2002, The Distant Future, 2007 (Grammy award, Best Comedy Album, 2008), Flight of the Conchords, 2008; actor: (films) The Lord of the Rings: The Fellowship of the Ring, 2001, The Lord of the Rings: The Return of the King, 2003, Futile Attraction, 2004; writer, actor, composer (TV series) One Night Stand, 2005, exec. prodr., writer, actor The Flight of the Conchords, 2007—. Co-recipient (with Jemaine Clement) Best Newcomer award, Melbourne Internat. Comedy Festival, 2003; named one of Wellingtonians of Yr., Dominion Post, Wellington, New Zealand, 2007.

MCKENZIE, BRIAN BRUCE, finance educator; b. Kelowna, BC, Canada, Nov. 23, 1948; arrived in U.S., 2003; s. Rex Bruce and Dorothy McKenzie; m. Molly Kathleen Farrend, Mar. 21, 1970. BA, U. BC, Vancouver, Can., 1974; MBA, U. Victoria, Can., 1997, PhD, 2003. Cert. qualification - boatbuilding Province of BC, 1990. Pres. Brian McKenzie Boatbuilding, Inc, Victoria, Canada, 1982—97; lectr. U. Victoria, 1997—2002; asst. prof. U. Calif., East Bay, 2003—. Vis. instr. Worcester (Mass.) Poly. Inst., 1999—2000. Contbr. scientific papers, rsch. to profl. jours. Recipient Entrepreneurship Theory and Practice Best Conceptual Paper award, 2004. Fellow: Students Free Enterprise (Sam Walton fellow 2005—06); mem.: Can. Anthrop. Assn., Small Bus. Inst., N.Am. Case Rsch. Assn., Acad. Mgmt. (chair nontraditional academics com.entrepreneurship divsn., Innovations in Pedagogy award 1999), U.S. Assn. Small Bus. and Entrepreneurship (Model Undergraduate Program award 2000), Oral History Assn. Office: Calif State U 25800 Carlos Bee Blvd Hayward CA 94542 Personal E-mail: brian@brian-mckenzie.com. Business E-Mail: brian.mckenzie@csueastbay.edu.

MCKENZIE, JEAN HAZEL, academic librarian; b. Wilkie, Saskatchewan, Canada, Oct. 21, 1949; d. Kenneth John McKenzie and Evelyn Nelson; m. Graham Richard Fleming, Sept. 16, 1977; 1 child, Matthew McKenzie Fleming. BA, U. BC, Vancouver, Can., 1971; MLS, U. Chgo., 1982. Reference libr. U. Chgo. Librs., 1989—97; asst. head libr. Kresge Engring. Libr., U. Calif., Berkeley, 1998—2007, head libr., 2007—. Mem.: Am. Soc. Engring. Edn. Office: Kresge Engring Libr UC Berkeley 110 Bechtel Engring Ctr Berkeley CA 94720-1796

MCKENZIE, KATHLEEN JULIANNA, artist; b. Jan. 20, 1957; Artist, Torrington, Conn., 1987—. Paintings featured in 7th, 9th and 11th Encyclopedia of Living Artist, Internat. Encyclopaedic Dictionary of Modern and Contemporary Art in Casa Editrice Alba. Home: 2493 Poole Rd Greer SC 29651-5046 Office Phone: 864-895-1581.

MCKENZIE, KAY BRANCH, public relations executive; b. Atlanta, Feb. 12, 1936; d. William Harllee and Katherine (Hunter) Branch; m. Harold Cantrell McKenzie, Jr., Apr. 11, 1958; children: Ansley, Katherine, Harold Cantrell III. Student, Sweet Briar Coll., 1955, Emory U., 1956-57. Account exec. Hill and Knowlton Inc., Atlanta, 1979-80, account supr./dir. S.E. govt. rels., 1981-83; ptnr. McKenzie, Gordon & Potter, Atlanta, 1983-85; pres. McKenzie & Assocs. Inc., Atlanta, 1986-89; sr. v.p. Manning Selvage & Lee, Atlanta, 1989-93; v.p. comm. and creative svcs. 1996 Atlanta Paralympic Games, 1993-96; v.p. comm. and devel. US Disabled Athletes Fund, 1997—2004; exec. dir. Southeastern Flower Show, 2004—06. Mem. Commn. on Future of South, 1974; co-chmn. John Lewis for Congress, Atlanta, 1986; regional bd. dirs. Inst. Internat. Edn., 1987-93. Fellow Soc. Internat. Bus. Fellows (bd. dirs. 1983-85, 92-93, v.p. 1986-88), Ga. C. of C. (bd. dirs. 1983-97), Leadership Atlanta, Ga. Internat. Horse Park Found. (bd. dirs. 1993-98), Friends of Ga. State Pks. & Hist. Sites (bd. dir.), Democrat. Episcopalian. Home: 670 Crossfire Ridge Marietta GA 30064 Personal E-mail: kay.mckenzie@comcast.net.

MCKENZIE, KEVIN PATRICK, performing company executive; b. Burlington, Vt., Apr. 29, 1954; s. Raymond James and Ruth (Davison) McKenzie. Grad. high sch., Washington. Mem. corps de ballet Nat. Ballet of Washington, 1972-74; prin. Joffrey Ballet, NYC, 1974-78, Am. Ballet Theatre, NYC, 1979-91; artistic assoc. Washington Ballet, 1991-92; artistic dir. Am. Ballet Theatre, NYC, 1992—; assoc. artistic dir. New Amsterdam Ballet. Pres. bd. dirs. Am. Ballet Theatre Dancers Fund, Inc., 1982—89; founding bd. mem. Kaatsbaan Internat. Dance Ctr., 1991—. Performer: (films) Unicorn, 1971; dancer Houston Ballet, 1978, Spoleto Festival, 1980, 1984, Theatre des Champs Elysees, Paris, 1981, Sadler's Wells Theatre, London, 1981, Asami Maki Ballet Co., Tokyo, 1983, Aspen Festival, 1982; prodr., dir. The Party of the Year, 1982; choreographer Groupo Zambaria Ballet, 1984, Liszt Etudes, 1991, Lucy and the Count, 1992, The Nutcracker, 1993, Don Quixote, 1995; created roles Adrienne Dellos' The Blind Man's Daughter, Seoul, Korea, 1986, Amnon V'Tamar, S.P.E.B.S.Q.S.A., appeared with Martine Van Hamel Swan Lake, Nat. Ballet of Cuba, Havana, 1986, appeared with Merrill Ashley Tchaikowsky Pas de Deux, Bolshoi Theatre, Moscow, 1986; dancer La Bayadere, Carmen, Cinderella, Coppelia, Dim Lustre, Don Quixote, Giselle, The Garden of Villandry, Jardin aux lilas, The Leaves Are Fading, Pillar of Fire, Raymonda, Requiem, Rodeo, Romeo and Juliet, The Sleeping Beauty, Swan Lake, La Sylphide, Paquita, Sylvia Pas de Deux, Theme and Variations. Recipient Silver medal, Varna Internat. Ballet Competition, Bulgaria, 1972, Artistic Achievement medal, Dept. State, U.S. Govt., 1972, Mayor Burlington, Vt., 1984, Performing Arts award, Am. Ireland Fund, 1994; named Kevin McKenzie Day, City of Burlington, 1985. Office: Am Ballet Theatre 890 Broadway New York NY 10003-1211 Fax: 212-254-5938.*

MCKENZIE, LAURIE JANE, medical association administrator; d. Edwin Kent and Dolores Evenson. MD, U. Fla., Gainesville. Med. dir. Houston IVF, 2004—; clin. faculty U. Tex., Houston. Clin. faculty Baylor Coll. of Medicine, Houston. Recipient John Harrington Rsch. award, U. Fla., Rsch. award, Am. Coll. OBGYN, Ortho Pharms. Fellow: Am. Coll. Ob-Gyn.; mem.: AMA, Harris County Med. Soc., Am. Soc. Reproductive Medicine, Alpha Omega Alpha. Office: Houston IVF 929 Gessner Ste 2300 Houston TX 77024 Office Fax: 713-550-1475. Business E-Mail: lmckenzie@houstonivf.net.

MCKENZIE, LAWRENCE J., composition educator; b. Cumberland, Md., Oct. 9, 1970; s. Lawrence J. McKenzie, Sr. and Judith A. Crumbaugh-Erlewine. BA in Philosophy/Religion, U. Charleston, 1994; MA, Meth. Theol. Sch., Delaware, Ohio, 1998. Cert. candidate for ordination W.Va., 1993. Theol. intern/assoc. pastor St. Andrew United Meth. Ch., St. Albans, W.Va., 1993—96; assoc. pastor/cmty. youth dir. Ostrander United Meth. Ch., Ohio, 1994—96; pastor Hyatt's United Meth. Ch., Ohio, 1997—98; instr. of humanities U. Charleston, W.Va., 1998—2000; instrn. of composition/lit. W.Va. State Coll., Institute, 1998—2000; paralegal The Law Office, Parkersburg, W.Va., 2000—01; prof. of composition W.Va. U., Parkersburg, 2000—. Exec. bd. sec., acquisitions editor Mountain State Press, Charleston, W.Va., 2000—05; faculty senate rep. W.Va. U., Parkersburg, 2002—, mem. humanities spkr. series, 2002—, asst. forensic coach, 2003—, mem. internationalization com., 2007—; mem. W.Va. Assn. of Devel. Educators, Institute, 2002—, W.Va. Consortium for Faculty and Course Devel. in Internat. Studies, Morgantown, 2004—; acquisitions editor W.Va. Writers Assn., Inc., Charleston, 2003—. Pres. Cmty. Acres Homeowners Assn., Inc., Davisville, W.Va., 2003—05; assoc./intern United Meth. Ch., Charleston, W.Va., 1987—89; mem. Order of St. Luke, Delaware, Ohio, 1994—98; interim pres. Cmty. Acres Homeowners Assn., Inc., Davisville, W.Va., 2002—03. Recipient Unsung Hero award, W.Va. U., 2003, 5 Yr. Svc. award, 2008; fellow, W.Va. Humanities Coun., 2002. Mem.: MLA, ASCD (hon.), W.Va. Assn. Devel. Educators, Nat. Coun. Tchrs. of English. Achievements include development of Erik J. Bitterbaum Pres.'s Award for Innovation in Tchg; Gear Up For Success (GUS) Innovation in Tchg. Avocations: fly fishing, national/international travel, fiction/non-fiction, academic writing. Office: W Va U 300 Campus Dr Parkersburg WV 26104 Office Fax: 304-424-8315. Business E-Mail: lawrence.mckenzie@mail.wvu.edu.

MC KENZIE, LIONEL WILFRED, economist, educator; b. Montezuma, Ga., Jan. 26, 1919; s. Lionel Wilfred and Lida (Rushin) McK.; m. Blanche Veron, Jan. 2, 1943 (dec. July 1999); children— Lionel Wilfred (dec.), Gwendolyn Veron (dec.), David Rushin. AB, Duke U., 1939; MA, Princeton U., 1946, PhD, 1956; BLitt, Oxford U., Eng., 1949; postgrad., U. Chgo., 1950-51, LLD (hon.), 1991; D of Econs. (hon.), Keio U., Japan, 1998; DPhil (hon.), Kyoto U., Japan, 2004. Asst. economist WPB, 1942; instr. Mass. Inst. Tech., 1946; from asst. prof. to assoc. prof. Duke, 1948-57; prof. econs. U. Rochester, 1957-64, John Munro prof. econs., 1964-67, Wilson prof. econs., 1967-89, Wilson prof. emeritus, 1989—, chmn. dept., 1957-66. Taussig research prof. Harvard U., 1980-81; Mem. math. divsn. NRC, 1960-63, mem. behavioral scis. divsn., 1964-70; mem. math., social scis. bd. Center Advanced Study in Behavioral Scis., Palo Alto, Calif., 1964-70, chmn., 1969-70 Author: Classical General Equilibrium Theory, 2002, Equilibrium Trade & Growth, 2009; assoc. editor Internat. Econs. Rev., 1964-96, Jour. Econ. Theory, 1970-73, Jour. Internat. Econs., 1970-84, Econ. Theory, 1991-95; contbr. articles to profl. jours. Lt. (s.g.) USNR, 1943-45. Recipient Rising Sun award Japan, 1995; Rhodes scholar Oriel Coll. Oxford U., 1939; Guggenheim fellow, 1973-74, fellow Center for Advanced Study in Behavioral Scis., 1973-74. Fellow Econometric Soc. (coun. 1973-78, pres. 1977), Am. Acad. Arts and Scis., Am. Econ. Assn.; mem. NAS, Royal Econ. Soc., Am. Math. Soc., Am. Econ. Assn. (Disting. Fellow 1993), Phi Beta Kappa (chpt. v.p. 1968-70, chpt. pres. 1972-73). Home: 225 Dorchester Rd Rochester NY 14610-1322 Personal E-mail: lionelmck@aol.com.

MCKENZIE, ROBERT ERNEST, lawyer; b. Cheboygan, Mich., Dec. 7, 1947; s. Alexander Orlando and Edna Jean (Burt) McK.; m. Theresia Wolf, Apr. 26, 1975; 1 child, Robert A. BA in Pers. Adminstrn., Mich. State U., 1970; JD with high honors, Ill. Inst. Tech., 1979. Bar: Ill. 1979, US Dist. Ct. (no. dist.) Ill. 1979, US Tax Ct. 1979, US Ct. Appeals (7th cir.) 1979, US Supreme Ct. 1984; lic. pvt. pilot; enrolled agnet with IRS. Revenue officer IRS, Chgo., 1972-78; ptnr. McKenzie & McKenzie, Chgo., 1979-2000, Arnstein & Lehr LLP, 2000—. Author: Representation Before the Collection Divison of the IRS, 1989, 2007; co-author: Representing the Audited Taxpayer Before the IRS, 1990, 2007, Representation Before the US Tax Court, 2006; contbr. articles to profl. jours. Mem. tax adv. com. Nat. Bankruptcy Rev. Commn., 1997; bd. mem. Ctr. for Econ. Progress, 1999-2005; del. Rep. Nat. Conv., Detroit, 1980. 2nd lt. US Army, 1970, capt. US Army, 1978. Recipient scholarship Mich. State U., 1966-70, State of Mich., 1966-70, Silas Strawn scholarship ITT, 1977, 2009, IRS Adv. Coun.; fellow Am. Bar. Fellow Am. Bar Found., mem. ABA (chmn. employment tax com. tax sect. 1992-94, co-chmn. bankruptcy task force 1997-98, coun. tax sect. 1998-2001, vice chmn. tax sect. 2003-05, chmn Pro Bono Com., 2007-), Chgo. Bar Assn. (chmn. com. devel. and tax coms. 1996-97), Am. Coll. Tax Counsel (bd. regents 2007-), Union League Chgo. Avocations: travel, flying. Office: Ste 1200 120 S Riverside Plz Chicago IL 60606 Home Phone: 847-981-1441; Office Phone: 312-876-6927. Business E-Mail: remckenzie@arnstein.com.

MCKENZIE, VASHTI MURPHY, bishop; m. Stan McKenzie; 3 children. Grad., U. Md., Coll. Park; MDiv, Howard U.; D in Ministry, United Theol. Sem., Dayton, Ohio; D (hon.), Howard U., Wilberforce U., Morgan State U., Goucher Coll. Radio program dir.; city desk reporter; staff writer; corp. v.p. programming; pastor Payne Meml. AME Ch., Balt.; chief pastor 18th Episcopal Dist. (Lesotho, Swaziland, Botswana, Mozambique) AME, 2000—04, presiding bishop 13th Episcopal Dist. (Tenn. and Commonwealth Ky.), 2000—, pres. Coun. Bishops. Founding pres., organizer Collective Banking Group Balt.; organizer Ch. Health Coalition; pres. AME Ministerial Alliance. Author: Not without a Struggle, Strength in the Struggle, Journey to the Well. Named one of 15 Greatest African Am. Female Preachers, Ebony mag.; named to Honor Roll of Great Am. Preachers, 1993, 1997, Power 150, 2008. Mem.: NAACP (life), Delta Sigma Theta Sorority, Inc. (nat. chaplain). Achievements include first woman ever to be elected to Bishop and Titular Head of AME. Office: AME 500-8th Ave S Nashville TN 37203 Office Phone: 615-242-6814. Business E-Mail: 13th_episcopal@bellsouth.net.

MCKENZIE, WALTER L., JR., information technology executive, consultant; b. Boston, Mass., Oct. 31, 1960; s. Walter L. McKenzie and Mary D. Golden; m. Carleen R. Fisher; children: Christopher Michael, Mallory Elise. BS in Edn., Ohio State U., 1985; MEd in Instrnl. Tech., George Mason U., 2000. Tchr. Fredericksburg City Schs., Va., 1985—86; tchr./gifted coord. King George County Schs., Va., 1986—95; tchr./trainer Spotsylvania County Schs., Va., 1995—99; sr. tech. tng. specialist Advanced Tech. Sys., McLean, Va., 1999—2000; dept. chair, presenter, course developer Classroom Connect, El Segundo, Calif., 1999—; tech. coord. Arlington Pub. Schs., 2000—03; dir. info. sys. Salem Pub. Schs., Salem, Mass., 2003—05; dir. Tech. Pub. Sch. Northborough and Southborough, Mass., 2005—07; asst. supt. Info. Svcs., Arlington Pub. Sch., Va., 2007—. Webmaster, surfaquarium.com The One and Only Surfaquarium, Amesbury, Mass., 1995—2005, webmaster, multiple intelligence pages, 1996—2005; cons. Surfaquarium, Amesbury, Mass., 1997—2005; editor Innovative Tchg. Newsletter, Amesbury, Mass., 1998—2005; participant, the arts in every classroom Annenberg Project, Washington, 2001—02; participant, changing edn. through the arts Kennedy Ctr., Washington, 2002—03; editor Va. Soc. Tech. Educators Jour., Blacksburg, Va., 2002—; dir. Mass. Computer Using Educators, Wellesley, Mass., 2004—07; editor Digital Dozen Newsletter, Amesbury, Mass., 2004—05. Contbr. articles to profl. jours.; author: (book) Multiple Intelligences and Instructional Technology: A Manual for Every Mind, Standards-Based Lessons for tech-Savvy Students: A Multiple Intelligences Approach; prodr.: (online collaborative project) eIditarod Project, Art & Architecture, Build a Better Mousetrap, 2004 National CyberConvention, The Presidents' Project; editor (contributing author): (book) NETS S Curriculum Series: Social Studies Units for Grades 9—12; editor: Va. Soc. Tech. Educators. Judge ThinkQuest, Mass., 1999; sponsor Ann. Top Ten Online Educators Awards, Amesbury, Mass., 2003—05. Recipient Pathfinder award, MASSCUE, 2006; grantee Instrnl. Devel. Project, Va. Coun. Fine Arts, 2002. Mem.: ASCD, Internat. Soc. Tech. in Edn., MassCUE (dir., webmaster 2003—05). Avocations: writing, music, reading, travel. Office: Arlington Public Sch 1426 N Quincy St Arlington VA 22207 Personal E-mail: walter@surfaquarium.com. E-mail: mckenzie@arlington.k12.va.us.

MCKEON, HOWARD PHILLIP (BUCK MCKEON), United States Representative from California; b. Tujunga, Calif., Sept. 9, 1938; m. Patricia Kunz; 6 children. BS, Brigham Young U., 1985. Mem. Santa Clarita City Council, Calif., 1987—92; mayor City of Santa Clarita, 1987—88; mem. US Congress from 25th Calif. Dist., 1992—; chmn. US House Edn. & Workforce Com., 2006—07; ranking minority mem. US House Armed Services Com., 2009—. Co-owner Howard & Phil's Western Wear, Inc., 1963—; founding dir., chmn. Valencia Nat. Bank, 1987—92; mem. Calif. Rep. State Ctrl. Com., 1988—92. Hon. chmn. Leukemia Soc., 1990, Red Cross Cmty. Support Campaign, 1992; sch. bd. mem., bd. trustees William S. Hart Union HS Dist., 1978—87; active dist. com. Boy Scouts of America, Little League; bd. dirs. Henry Mayo Newhall Meml. Hosp., 1983—88, Santa Clarita Valley Sml. Bus. Devel. Ctr., 1990—92. Recipient Silver Spur award for Outstanding Cmty. Svc., Coll. of Canyons Found., 2000, Robert J. Collier award, Nat. Aeronautic Assn., 2001, Advocacy of Ind. Higher Edn. award, Nat. Assn. Ind. Colls. & Univs., 2002; named Newsmaker of Yr., Santa Clarita Press Club, 1996. Mem.: Nat. Guard & Reserve Components Orgn., Canyon Country C. of C. (bd. dirs. 1988—92). Republican. Mem. Lds Ch. Office: US House Reps 2184 Rayburn House Office Bldg Washington DC 20515-0525 also: 26650 The Old Rd Ste 203 Santa Clarita CA 91381 E-mail: tellbuck@mail.house.gov.*

MCKEON, JOHN JOSEPH, economics professor; b. Mass., Jan. 20, 1945; s. John and Rose McKeon; m. Janet Ann McKeon. MS in Economics, Southern Ill. U., Edwardsville, 1972. Assoc. prof. Fitchburg State Coll., Mass., 1979—. Chpt. pres. Mass. State Coll. Assn. Home: 92 North Row Rd Sterling MA 01564 Office: Fitchburg State Coll 120 Pearl St Fitchburg MA 01420 Personal E-mail: jack.mckeon@comcast.net. Business E-Mail: jmckeon@fsc.edu.

MCKEOUGH, SUSAN ANNE, elementary school educator; d. Richard Blair McKeough and Barbara Jean McKeough. BS, St. Francis Coll., Biddeford, Maine, 1976; MA, Sacred Heart U., Bridgeport, Conn., 1982. Cert. tchr. Conn. Supr. tchr. Child Devel. Ctr., Bellefonte, Pa., 1976—78; tchr. St. Gabriel Sch., Stamford, Conn., 1978—85, Greenwich (Conn.) Cath., 1986—88, Saxe Mid. Sch., New Canaan, Conn., 1988—97, 2001—, Grace Episcopal Sch., Ocala, Fla., 1998—2000. Spl. edn. aide, sub- tchr. Saxe Mid. Sch., New Canaan, 1985—86. Recipient Sci. award, State of Fla., 1998. Home: 3 Valley View Rd #17 Norwalk CT 06851 Office: Saxe Mid Sch 468 South Ave New Canaan CT 06840 Personal E-mail: smckeo2621@aol.com.

MCKEOUGH, WILLIAM DARCY, retired supply company executive; b. Chatham, Ont., Can., Jan. 31, 1933; s. George Grant and Florence Sewell (Woodward) McK.; m. Margaret Joyce Walker, June 18, 1965; children: Walker Stewart, James Grant. BA, U. Western Ont., 1954; LLD (hon.), Wilfred Laurier U., 1980; DDiv, Huron Univ. Coll., 2003. Chmn. McKeough Supply Inc. Bd. dirs. Can. Gen. Tower Ltd.; former chmn. Ridley Coll. Found., Huron Coll. Found. Former mem. exec. com. Anglican Diocese of Huron; former mem. Gen. Synod, Anglican Ch., Can.; mem. Chatham City Coun., 1960-63; also mem. Planning Bd. and Lower Thames Valley Conservation Authority; former mem. Chatham-Kent adv. bd. Can. Nat. Inst. of the Blind; former bd. dirs. Chatham YMCA, Chatham Little Theatre; former chmn. and pres. bd. govs. pres. Ridley Coll.; former bd. govs. Stratford Shakespearian Festival, Wilfrid Laurier U.; former mem. Can. group Trilateral Commn.; mem. Ont. Legislature, 1963-78, minister without portfolio,

1966, minister mcpl. affairs, 1967; treas. and minister of econs., also chmn. Treasury Bd., 1971-72, minister mcpl. affairs, 1972, treas. and minister of econs. and intergovtl. affairs, 1972, parliamentary asst. to premier Ont., 1973, minister of energy, 1973-75, treas. and minister econs. and intergovtl. affairs, 1975-78. Decorated officer of Order of Can. Home and Office: PO Box 940 Chatham ON Canada N7M 5L3 Office Phone: 519-676-0446.

MCKEOWN, JAMES CHARLES, accounting educator, consultant; b. Cleve., Nov. 3, 1945; s. Charles Joseph and Dara Ferrol (Prew) McK.; m. Mary Alinda Park, Jan. 2, 1965 (div. May 1980); children— Jeffrey Charles, Pamela Lynn; m. 2d, Nancy Ann Stratton, Jan. 3, 1981 BS in Math. with high honors, Mich. State U., 1966, PhD in Bus. Adminstrn., 1969. Asst. prof. accountancy U. Ill., Urbana-Champaign, 1968-73, assoc. prof., 1973-76, prof., 1976-80, Weldon Powell prof. accountancy, 1980-83, A.C. Littleton prof. accountancy, 1983-89; disting. prof. acctg. Pa. State U., University Park, 1989-92, Ernst & Young prof. acctg., 1992-99, Mary Jean and Frank P. Smeal chaired prof. acctg., 1999—. Cons. research, computers; expert witness. Editor: Inflation and Current Value Accounting, 1979; author computer-delivered acctg. course PLATO for Elementary Accounting, 1978; contbr. numerous articles to acad. jours. Recipient Instructional award U. Ill., Urbana-Champaign, 1970, Weldon Powell award, 1973; Fred Roedgers Research award U. Ill., 1978; Ford Found. fellow, 1967-68 Mem. Am. Acctg. Assn. (Manuscript award 1970, Outstanding Acctg. Educator 2003), Am. Statis. Assn., Decision Scis. Inst. Republican. Office: Pa State U 314 Business Bldg University Park PA 16802

MCKEOWN, MARY ELIZABETH, retired academic administrator; m. James Edward McKeown, Aug. 6, 1955. BS, U. Chgo., 1946; MS, DePaul U., Chgo., 1953. Supr. h.s. dept. Am. Sch., 1948-68, prin., 1968-99, trustee, 1975—, v.p., 1979, ednl. dir., 1979—2002, exec. v.p., 1992—2002; ret., 2002. Author study guides for algebra, geometry, and calculus. Trustee Am. Sch., 2002—. Home Phone: 708-423-2701.

MCKEOWN, MARY MARGARET, federal judge; b. Casper, Wyo., May 11, 1951; d. Robert Mark and Evelyn Margaret (Lipsack) McKeown; m. Peter Francis Cowhey, June 29, 1985; 1 child, Megan Margaret. BA in Internat. Affairs and Spanish, U. Wyo., 1972; JD, Georgetown U., 1975. Bar: Wash. 1975, DC 1982. Assoc. Perkins Coie, Seattle, 1975—79, Washington, 1979—80; spl. asst. US Dept. Interior, Washington, 1980—81, The White House, Washington, 1980—81; ptnr., mem. exec. com. Perkins Coie, Seattle, 1981—98, mng. dir. strategic planning and client rels., 1990—95; judge US Ct. Appeals (9th cir.), San Diego, 1998—. Trustee The Pub. Defender, Seattle, 1982—85; rep. 9th Cir. Judicial Conf., San Francisco, 1985—89; mem. gender bias task force, 1992—93; jud. conf. Com. on Codes of Conduct, 2001—, chair, 2009—; exec. com. 9th Cir., 2001—04; lect. U. Wash. Law Sch., 2000—01; adj. prof. U. San Diego, 2003—; bd. dirs. RAND Inst. for Civil Justice, 2003—. Author: Girl Scout's Guide to New York, 1990; contbr. chpt. to book and articles to profl. jours. Nat. bd. dirs. Girl Scouts US, NYC, 1976—87; mem. exec. com. Corp. Coun. for the Arts, Seattle, 1988—98; bd. gen. counsel Downtown Seattle Assn., 1986—89; mem. exec. com. Wash. Coun. Internat. Trade; bd. dirs. YMCA Greater Seattle, Family Svcs., Seattle, 1982—84. Recipient Rising Stars of the 80's award, Legal Times Washington, 1983; named one of 100 Young Women of Promise, Good Housekeeping, 1985, Washington's Winningest Trial Lawyers, Washington Jour., 1992, Top 50 Women Lawyers, Nat. Law Jour., 1998; fellow Japan leadership, 1992—93. Fellow: ABA (ho. of dels. 1990—96, Jud. Adv. Com. to Standing Com. on Ethics 2001—05, Joint Commn. to Evaluate Code of Jud. Conduct 2003—07, chair 2004—05, standing com. fed. judicial improvements chair 2006—, mem. Justice Ctr. Coord. Coun. 2006—, com. mem. world justice project 2007—, adv. panel prof. responsibility 2007—); mem.: Louis M. Welsh Chpt. Am. Inns of Ct., Am. Judicature Soc. (bd. dirs. 2001—), Assn. Bus. Trial Lawyers (bd. dirs. 2002—, exec. com. mem. 2007—), Am. Intellectual Property Law Assoc., Am. Law Institute, Nat. Assn. Iolta Programs (bd. dirs. 1989—91), Wash. Women Lawyers (bd. dirs., pres. 1978—79), Legal Found. Wash. (trustee, pres. 1989—90), Seattle-King County Bar Assn. (trustee, sec. 1984—85, Outstanding Lawyer award 1992), Wash. Bar Assn. (chmn. jud. recommendations 1989—90), Fed. Bar Assn. (trustee western dist. Wash. 1980—90), White House Fellows Found. (bd. dirs. 1998—, pres. 2000—01). Avocations: travel, classical piano, hiking, gourmet cooking, tennis. Office: US Ct Appeals 401 West A St Ste 2000 San Diego CA 92101-7908 E-mail: Judge_McKeown@ca9.uscourts.gov.*

MCKEOWN, ROBERT E., epidemiologist, educator; b. Chester, SC, Feb. 19, 1947; s. Melvin Brice and Mary McCluney McKeown; m. Jane Arrington, Apr. 13, 1974; children: Hannah Alice, Sarah Abigail. BS, Furman U., Greenville, SC, 1969; MDiv, Duke U., Durham, NC, 1972, PhD, 1976, U. SC, Columbia, 1991. Pastor United Meth. Ch., Waterloo, SC, 1976—77; asst. prof. religious studies Kans. Wesleyan U., Salina, 1977—80; assoc. pastor Clemson United Meth. Ch., SC, 1980—87; adj. faculty Luth. Theol. Southern Sem., Columbia, 1987—91; asst. prof. epidemiology U. SC, 1990—, assoc. prof. epidemiology, 1990—, prof. epidemiology, 1990—, assoc. dean rsch., Arnold sch. pub. health, 2005—06, dir., health sci. rsch. core, 2006—, liaison Greenville hosp. sys., 2006—, chair, dept. epidemiology & biostats., 2008—. Surveillance subcom. cancer adv. com. mem. Dept. Health & Environ. Control, Columbia, 2002—06; chair, rsch. & planning com. SC United Meth. Conf., Columbia, 1993—96; program svcs. com. mem. Chpt. Mar. Dimes, SC, 2006. Recipient Algernon Sidney Sullivan award, Furman U., 1969, Excellence Tchg. award, Arnold Sch. Pub. Health, 1996, Disting. Alumnus award, 2003, Faculty Svc. award, 2004, Faculty Rsch. award, 2006; Dempster fellow, United Meth. Bd. Higher Edn., 1973—74. Fellow: Am. Coll. Epidemiology (com. chair 2001—, bd. dir. 2001—, chair, ethics and stds. practice 2001—05); mem.: APHA (sect. chair 1997—2005, governing coun. mem. 1997—2005, intersectional coun. mem. 1997—2005, chair, epidemiology sect. 2001—03), Delta Omega (Mu chpt.), Sigma Xi Sci. Rsch. Soc. (U. SC chpt.), Soc. Epidemiologic Rsch. Methodist. Office: Univ SC Arnold Sch Pub Health Columbia SC 29208

MCKEOWN, WILLIAM P., retired lawyer; m. Elizabeth McKeown; 4 children. B Comm., McGill U., Montreal, Que., 1956; LLB, U. Toronto 1959. Queen's counsel Ont. 1983. Counsel Dept. Health, Province Ont., Toronto, 1962-63, McMillan Binch, Toronto, 1963-64, Can. GE, Toronto, 1965-74; dep. dir. investigation and rsch. Bur. Competition Policy, Ottawa, Ont., 1974-77; ptnr. Stephens French McKeown, Toronto, 1977-86; judge Supreme Ct. Ont., Toronto, 1986-90; judge gen. divsn. Ont. Ct. Justice, Toronto, 1990—93; judge trial divsn. Fed. Ct. Can., Ottawa, Canada, 1993—2002; chmn. Competition Tribunal, Ottawa, 1993—2002; sr. counsel Fasken, Martineau, DuMoulin, LLP, Toronto, 2002—06; ret., 2006. Mem. Toronto Lawyers' Club. E-mail: mckeown4575@rogers.com.

MC KEOWN, WILLIAM TAYLOR, magazine editor, author; b. Ft. Collins, Colo., July 4, 1921; s. Stuart Ellison and Eunice Harris (Akin) Mc K.; m. Lorraine Laredo; children: Elizabeth Ellison, Katherine, Suzanne. AB, Bowdoin Coll., 1942; student, Columbia U. Grad. Sch., 1948. Editor Fawcett Library Series, 1953-56; founding editor True's Boating Yearbook, 1955-56, Popular Boating mag., 1956, editor-in-chief, 1956-62; CEO The Mc Keown Co., NYC, 1993—; editl. dir. Computer Travel Info., 1994—. Travel editor Davis Publs.; outdoor/boating/travel editor Popular Mechanics, 1971-82; sr. editor Outdoor Life, 1983-93. Author weekly NEA syndicated newspaper column American Afloat, 1959-65; contbr. fiction, non-fiction to nat. mags., 1947—; author: Boating Handbook, 1956, Boating in America, 1960. Pilot USAAF, WW II, ETO. Mem. Am. Power Boat Assn., U.S. Power Squadrons, 357 FIghter Group Assn., N.Y. Yacht Club, Overseas Press Club, Royal Danish Yacht Club (Copenhagen), Turtles Internat. Avocation: international competitor in power and sail racing events.

MCKEOWN-MOAK, MARY PARK, educational consultant; d. John Paton and Sophie Cichon Park; m. Lynn Martin Moak, Oct. 4, 1997; children: David Lynn Moak, Susan Marie Moak; m. James Charles McKeown, Jan. 2, 1965 (div.); children: Jeffrey Charles McKeown, Pamela Lynn McKeown; m. Kenneth Forbis Jordan, Jan. 2, 1982 (div. Sept. 1993). BA, MA, Mich. State U., East Lansing, 1966; PhD, U. Ill., Urbana-Champaign, 1974. Cert. tchr. Mich., 1966, real estate agent Ill., 1977. Bus. mgr. U. Ill. Found., Champaign, 1974—77; sch. fin. specialist, asst. prof. pub. adminstrn. Ill. Bd. Edn., Sangamon State U., Springfield, 1977—80; assoc. dir. fin. and facilities Md. State Bd. Higher Edn., Annapolis, 1980—87; dir. strategic planning Ariz. State U., Tempe, 1987—94; assoc. exec. dir., sr. fin. officer Ariz. Bd. Regents, Phoenix, 1994—98; sr. ptnr. MGT, Inc., Austin, Tex., 1998—. Pres. Fiscal Issues Spl. Interest Group Am. Edn. Rsch. Assn., Washington, 1990—91, pres., chair Futures Planning Spl. Interest Group, 1992—93; pres. Am. Edn. Fin. Assn., Denver, 1996—97. Contbr. articles to profl. jours. Pres. Coll. Bus. Faculty Wives, Champaign, 1971—73; troop leader Girl Scouts, Boy Scouts, Champaign, 1974—78; treas. Champaign-Urbana PTA Coun., 1978—80; pres. Alameda Estates Homeowners Assn., Tempe, Ariz., 1988—95, v.p., 1988—95, sec., 1988—95. Mem.: Impact Austin, Assn. Inst. Rsch., Soc. Coll. U. Planning, Nat. Assn. Coll. U. Bus. Officers, Travis Audubon Soc., Phi Delta Kappa (sec. Ariz. chpt. 1987—91). Avocations: gardening, travel, birdwatching. Home: 8800 Gallant Fox Road Austin TX 78737 Office: MGT Am Inc 502 E 11th Street Ste 300 Austin TX 78701 Business E-Mail: mmoak@mgtamer.com.

MCKERNS, CHARLES JOSEPH, lawyer; b. Shenandoah, Pa., July 17, 1935; s. Charles Francis and Bridgett Ann (Barrett) McK.; m. Helen Patricia Nott, Feb. 13, 1960; children: Charles J. Jr., Michael H., Patricia B. BS, Georgetown U., 1957, JD, 1960. Bar: DC 1960, US Ct. Appeals (DC cir.) 1961, US Supreme Ct. 1971, Va. 1992. Law clk. to assoc. judge US Ct. Appeals (DC cir), Washington, 1960—61; assoc. Dow, Lohnes & Albertson, Washington, 1961—65, ptnr., 1965—91, of counsel, 1991—95; ptnr. McKerns and McKerns, Heathsville, Va., 1991-96, of counsel, 1996—98. 1st lt. US Army, 1957—59. Mem. ABA, University Club (Washington), Belle Haven Country Club (Alexandria, Va.), Indian Creek Yacht and Country Club (Kilmarnock, Va.). Republican. Roman Catholic. Avocations: hiking, reading, swimming. Home: Windy Blue PO Box 248 Ophelia VA 22530 Office: McKerns Law Office PO Box 220 Heathsville VA 22473-0220 also: Dow Lohnes & Albertson 1200 New Hampshire Ave NW Washington DC 20036-6802 Office Phone: 804-580-8225. Personal E-mail: cmckerns@yahoo.com.

MCKERROW, RAYMIE E., communications educator; m. Gayle D. Neibauer, June 12, 1965; 1 child, Matthew. PhD, U. Iowa, 1973. Prof. U. Maine, Orono, 1976—95, Ohio U., Athens, 1995—. Mem.: Nat. Comm. Assoc. (pres. 1999—2000, C. Woolbert award 2006, Douglas W. Ehninger Disting. Rhetorical award 2006). Home: 11 Cable Ln Athens OH 45701 Office: Sch Comm Studies Ohio Univ 212 Lasher Athens OH 45701 Personal E-mail: ray.mckerrow@gmail.com.

MC KETTA, JOHN J., JR., chemical engineering professor; b. Wyano, Pa., Oct. 17, 1915; s. John J. and Mary (Gelet) McK.; m. Helen Elisabeth Smith, Oct. 17, 1943; children: Charles William, John J. III, Robert Andrew, Mary Anne. BS, Tri-State Coll., Angola, Ind., 1937; BSE., U. Mich., 1943, MS, 1944, PhD, 1946; D.Eng. (hon.), Tri-State Coll., 1965, Drexel U., 1977; Sc.D., U. Toledo, 1973. Diplomate: registered profl. engr., Tex., Mich. Group leader tech. dept. Wyandotte Chem. Corp., Mich., 1937-40, asst. supt. caustic soda div., 1940-41; teaching fellow U. Mich., 1942-44, instr. chem. engring., 1944-45; faculty U. Tex., Austin, 1946—, successively asst. prof. chem. engring., assoc. prof., then prof. chem. engring., 1951-52, 54—, E.P. Schoch prof. chem. engring., 1970-81, Joe C. Walter chair, 1981-94, prof. emeritus, 1994—. Asst. dir. Tex. petroleum research com., 1951-52, 54-56, chmn. chem. engring. dept., mem. bd. regents, Tri State Univ, 56-, disting. service in trusteeship, 2002, 1950-52, 55-63, dean Coll. Engring., 1963-69; exec. vice chancellor acad. affairs U. Tex. System, 1969-70; editorial dir. Petroleum Refiner, 1952-54; pres. Chemoil Cons., Inc., 1957-73; chmn. Tex. AEC, So. Interstate Nuclear Bd., 1963-70; mem. Tex. Radiation Adv. Bd., 1978-84; chmn. Nat. Energy Policy Com., 1970-72, Nat. Air Quality Control Com., 1972-85; mem. adv. bd. Carnegie-Mellon Inst. Research, 1978-84; pres. Reagans's rep. on U.S. Acid Precipitation Task Force, 1982-88; apptd. mem. Nuclear Waste Tech. Rev. Bd., 1992-97. Author: series Advances in Petroleum Chemistry and Refining (10 vols.); Chmn. editorial com.: series Petroleum Refiner; mem. adv. bd.: series Internat. Chem. Engring. mag; exec. editor: series Ency. of Chem. Processing and Design (68 vols.). Recipient Bronze plaque Am. Inst. Chem. Engrs., 1952, Charles Schwab award Am. Steel Inst., 1973, Lamme award as outstanding U.S. educator, 1976, Joe J. King Profl. Engring. Achievement award U. Tex., 1976, Gen. Dynamics Teaching Excellence award, 1979, Triple E award for contbns. to nat. issues on energy, environment and econs. Nat. Environ. Devel. Assn., 1976, Boris Pregal Sci. and Tech. award NAS, 1978, Internat. Chem. Engring. award, Italy, 1984, Pres. Herbert Hoover award for advancing well-being of humanity and developing richer and more enduring civilization Joint Engring. Socs., 1989, Centennial award exceptional contbn. Am. Soc. Engring. Edn., 1993; named Disting. Alumnus U. Mich Coll. Engring., 1953, Tri-State Coll., 1956; fellow Allied Chem. & Dye, 1945-46; named Disting. fellow Carnegie-Mellon U., 1978; Chem. Engring. Dept. at U. Tex. named The John J. McKetta Ctr. for Excellence in Chem. Engring. Edn. in his honor, 1995, Chem. Engring. Dept. at Tri State U. named The Dr. John J. McKetta Chem. Engring. Dept. in his honor, 1998. Mem. Am. Chem. Soc. (chmn. Central Tex. sect. 1950), Am. Inst. Chem. Engrs. (chmn. nat. membership com. 1955, regional exec. com., nat. dir., nat. v.p. 1961, pres. 1962, service to soc. award 1975), Am. Soc. Engring. Edn., Chem. Markets Research Assn., Am. Gas Assn. (adv. bd. chems. from gas 1954), Houston C. of C. (chmn. refining div. 1954, vice chmn. research and statistics com. 1954), Engrs. Joint Council (dir.), Engrs. Joint Countil Profl. Devel. (dir. 1963-85), Nat. Acad. Engring., Sigma Xi, Chi Epsilon, Alpha Psi Omega, Tau Omega, Phi Lambda Upsilon, Phi Kappa Phi, Iota Alpha, Omega Chi Epsilon, Tau Beta Pi, Omicron Delta Kappa. Home: 4100 Jackson Ave Apt 229 Austin TX 78731-6070 Office Phone: 512-451-1501, 512-471-5227. Business E-Mail: mcketta@mail.utexas.edu, mcketta@mail.edu.

MCKETTA, JOHN J., III, lawyer; b. Austin, Tex., May 5, 1948; s. John J. and Helen Elisabeth (Smith) McK.; m. Sallie Martin Sharp, Aug. 6, 1977; children: Elisabeth, Mary Elliott, Sarah, John. BA, Harvard U., 1969; JD, U. Tex., Austin, 1977. Bar: Tex. 1977, D.C. 1978, U.S. Ct. Appeals (D.C. cir.) 1978, U.S. Dist. Ct. D.C. 1978, U.S. Dist. Ct. (we. dist.) Tex. 1982, U.S. Ct. Appeals (5th cir.) 1982. Assoc. Covington & Burling, Washington, 1977-82, Graves, Dougherty, Hearon & Moody, Austin, Tex., 1982-84, ptnr., 1984—, pres., 1998—2008. Fellow: Am. Coll. Trial Lawyers; mem.: Am. Law Inst. (coun. 1998—). Democrat. Episcopalian. Office: PO Box 98 Austin TX 78767-0098 Business E-Mail: mmcketta@gdhm.com.

MCKIBBIN, WILLIAM ALEX, artist; b. Phila., May 7, 1940; s. William A. and Jane Harrison (Pippin) McK.; m. Dorothy K. McKibbin, Jan. 26, 1963; children: Erin P., William Alex IV. Student, Barnes Found., Merion, Pa., 1958-59, 60-61; BFA, Temple U., Phila., 1963; MFA, The Claremont Grad. Sch., 1965; postgrad., U. Hartford, Conn., 1967-68. Instr. Mt. Pleasant Jr. HS, Del., 1965-66, U. Hartford Coll. Basic Studies, 1966-68; instr. evening divsn. Cen. Conn. State Coll., 1967-68; instr. Aegean Sch. Fine Arts, Paros, Greece, summers 1967-68; asst. prof. Western Coll., 1968-74, acting chair, 1968, 69, 70-71; instr. Cin. Art Acad., 1972-74; asst. prof. Miami U., Oxford, Ohio, 1974-77, assoc. prof., 1977-84, full prof., 1984—. Juried various exhbns. throughout US One-man shows at Evansville (Ind.) Mus. Arts and Scis., Main Artist Gallery, 1985, Museum of the Maya Culture, Chetumal, Q.R., Mex., 2002, Casa de la Cultura de Cancun, Mex., 2001, Carrollton Cultural Art Ctr., Ga., 2006, Cultural Arts Coun. Douglasville, Douglas County, Ga., 2006, Rome Gal Carrollton Ga., 2008, Met. Structures One Ill Ctr. Chgo., 1983, Rippon Coll., Harwood Gal Ripon WI74; exhibited in over 200 exhbns. including group shows at East Carolina U., Greenville, NC, 1981, Second Crossing Gallery, Valley City, ND, 1981, 93, Okla. Art Ctr., Oklahoma City, 1981-82, U. ND, Grand Forks, 1982, 85, Art Chgo. Internat. Art Expo, 1982-90, Trenton (NJ) State Coll., 1983, Fort Hays (Kans.) State U., 1984, 88, Owensboro (Ky.) Mus. Fine Arts, 1984, Middletown (Ohio) Fine Arts Ctr., 1985, Cameron U., 1986, Springfield (Mo.) Art Mus., 1978, 2009, La Fond Galleries, Inc., Pitts., 1994, numerous others; represented by Zaks Gallery, Chgo., The Art Exch., Columbus, Boody Fine Arts, Inc., St. Louis, Nancy Mulle Assocs., Cleve., Steinway Gallery, Chapel, NC, Yvonne Rapp Gallery, Louisville, Orbe Gallery, Cancun, Mex., Gallery Henoch, NYC; 27 pub. collections include Pomona Coll., Claremont, Calif., Thomas More Coll., Ft. Mitchell, Ky., The Springfield Mus., Ind. U. East, Richmond, Evansville (Ind.) Mus. Art and Sci., Art Ctr., Inc., South Bend, Ind., Cin. Art Mus., Grinnell (Iowa) Coll., Ft. Hays State U., Hays, Kans., Des Moines Art Ctr., Charles H. MacNider Mus., Mason City, Iowa, Ohio State U., Columbus, Clark State U., Springfield, Ohio, U. NC, Chapel Hill, Ohio State U. Law Sch., So. Alleghenies Mus. of Art, Loretto, Pa., Blanden Meml. Art Mus., Ft. Dodge, Iowa, Ark. Arts Ctr., Little Rock, Taos Art Mus., Taos, N.Mex., Casa de la Cultura de Cancun, Mex., Fitton Ctr. for Creative Arts, Hamilton, Ohio; pvt. collections, 70 corporate collections; reprodns. of work appear in (books) Watercolor Bold and Free, 1980, Figure Drawing, 5th edit., 2000, The Watercolor Solution Book, 1988, Splash I, 1990, The Art of Responsive Drawing, 1992, Splash II, 1993, Watercolor Step-By-Step, 1993, Watercolor School, 1993, Collins' Artist's Manual, 1995, Splash IV, 1995, The Encyclopedia of Watercolour Landscape Techniques, 1996, Painting Shapes and Edges, 1996, North Light Illustrated Book of Watercolor Techniques, Splash VIII, 2004; (mags.) Artist's Mag., The Bull., Jiangsu Pictorial, China, Watercolor Magic, Tropo a la una, Cancun, Mex., Internat. Artist, 2000, Vibrant Watercolours, 2006; work included as cover art on CDs Music for Winds, The Miami Wind Quintet, Vol. 1, 1995, Vol. 2, 1996. Recipient Cert. of Merit Tyler Sch. of Art Temple U., Gen. Alumni Assn., 1991, First State Bank award for watercolor Vechten-Lineberry, Taos Art Mus., 19 cash and purchase awards from various orgns. Home: 199 Berkley Dr Villa Rica GA 30180-2400

MCKIERNAN, DAVID D., retired military officer; b. 1950; m. Carmen D. McKiernan. Grad., Coll. Wiliam and Mary, 1972, D (hon.) in Pub. Svc.; MPA, Shippensburg U., Pa. Commd. 2d lt. US Army, 1972, advanced through grades to gen., 2005, comdr., 1st bn., 35th armor (Iron Knights), 1st armored divsn., 1988—90, dep. chief staff G-2/G-3, Allied Command Europe Rapid Reaction Corps Sarajevo, Bosnia-Herzegovina and Rheindahlen, Germany, 1996—97, asst. divsn. comdr., 1st inf., 1997—98, comdr., 1st brigade (Iron Horse), 1st cavalry divsn., 1993—95, dep. chief staff, ops., hdqs., Europe and 7th Army, 1998—99, comdr., 1st cavalry divsn. Fort Hood, Tex., 1999—2001, comdr., 3rd US Army/Combined Forces Land Component Command Bosnia, Albania and Kosovo, 2002—04, dep. commdg. gen., chief staff, US Army Forces Command, commdg. gen., US Army Europe & 7th Army (USAREUR), 2005—08; comdr., Internat. Security Assistance Force (ISAF) NATO, Kabul, 2008—09; comdr. US Forces Afghanistan (USFOR-A), Kabul, 2008—09. Decorated Bronze Star, Parachutist badge, Ranger tab, Army Disting Svc. medal with oak leaf cluster, Amy Commendation medal with 3 oak leaf clusters, Army Achievement medal with oak leaf cluster, Def. Disting. Svc. medal, Def. Superior Svc. medal, Def. Meritorious Svc. medal, Legion of Merit with 2 oak leaf clusters, Meritorious Svc. medal with 3 oak leaf clusters; named one of The World's Most Influential People, TIME mag., 2009. Office: ISAF-Kabul (AFG) Pub Info Office Feldpost 64298 Damsatadt Germany*

MCKIM, KIM S., biology professor; b. Vancouver, BC, Canada, June 6, 1963; married. PhD, U. BC, Vancouver, 1991. Assoc. prof. Rutgers U., Piscataway, NJ, 1997—. Office: Rutgers Univ 190 Frelinghuysen RD Piscataway NJ 08854 Business E-Mail: mckim@rci.rutgers.edu.

MCKIM, PAUL ARTHUR, management consultant, retired gas industry executive; b. Milford, Conn., Feb. 1, 1923; s. Arthur and Helen Agnes McK.; m. Daisy Flora Brown, June 18, 1945; 1 dau., Meredith Ann. Student, Lamar Inst. Tech., 1940-42; BS in Chem. Engring., La. State U., 1943, MS, 1947, PhD, 1949; grad. Advanced Mgmt. Program, Harvard, 1959; grad. Aspen Inst. Humanistic Studies Exec. Program, 1970. With Ethyl Corp., 1949-62, asst. gen. mgr. research and devel. operations, 1958-62; v.p., gen. mgr. rsch. and devel. Atlantic Refining Co., Phila., 1962-66; v.p. Atlantic Richfield Co., 1966-78; v.p. comml. devel. Arco Chem. Co., 1966-69, v.p. nuclear operations and comml. devel., 1969-73; exec. v.p. Sinclair Koppers Co., 1973; pres. Arco Polymers, Inc., 1974-78; asst. to pres. Tex. Eastern Corp., 1978-80, v.p., 1980-84, sr. v.p., 1985-88. Chmn. US Organizing com. for 12th World Petroleum Congress, Houston, 1987. Past chmn. bd. mgrs. Franklin Inst. Research Labs; past vice chmn. bd. mgrs. Spring Garden Coll., Phila. Coll. Art.; past vice chmn. World Affairs Council of Phila. Served to lt. (j.g.) USNR, 1944-46. Mem. AIChE, Alpha Chi Sigma, Omicron Delta Kappa, Tau Beta Pi, Phi Lambda Upsilon, Phi Kappa Phi, Delta Kappa Epsilon. Home: Sterling Glen of Darien 50 Ledge Rd Apt 252 Darien CT 06820 Personal E-mail: paulmckim@yahoo.com.

MCKIM, RUTH ANN, financial planner; b. Keokuk, Iowa, Nov. 26, 1932; d. Carl Edward and Ruby Irene (Martin) McKim; m. William James Ashbrook, Aug. 15, 1959 (div. 1974); children: Leslie, Diane Hodges. BS, U. Louisville, 1955, MS in Cmty. Devel., 1977. Dir. art therapy Ky. Bapt. Hosp., Louisville, 1955—56; co-dir. art therapy

Norton-Children's Hosps. Inc., 1956—57; dir. art therapy NKC Hosps., 1957—59; rschr. Bd. Aldermen, 1976; pub. rels. staff Dept. Consumer Affairs, 1976—78; realtor assoc. Century 21, 1979—86; fin. planner Nat. Life Vt., 1986—. Tutor Ky. Assn. Specific Perceptual-Motor Disability, Louisville, 1970—74. Author: Banking Survey, 1977. Arts festival com., 1975—77; coord. Louisville Food Day, 1978; vol. and art donor PBS, 1985—88; voter registration canvasser, 1976, 1978, 1982; active Rep. Nat. Com., Rep. Presdl. Task Force, Nat. Rep. Senatorial Com., Nat. Rep. Congl. Com. Com.; sec., treas. St. Francis in the Fields Espicopal Ch., Louisville, 1975—76. Recipient Rep. Presdl. Legion of Merit medal, Order of Merit; scholar Allen R. Hite Art Inst., 1952—54; Bd. Realtors scholar, 1979—. Mem.: Inst. Community Devel. Assn., Ky. Artists and Craftsmen, Louisville Craftsmans Guild (life), U. Louisville Alumni Assn. Republican. Episcopalian. Avocation: oil and acrylic painting. Home: No 43 410 Mockingbird Valley Rd Louisville KY 40207-1318

MCKIM, SAMUEL JOHN, III, lawyer; b. Pitts., Dec. 31, 1938; s. Samuel John and Harriet Frieda (Roehl) McK; children: David Hunt, Andrew John; m. Eugenia A. Leverich. AA cum laude, Port Huron Jr. Coll., 1959; BA cum laude, U. Mich., 1961, JD cum laude, 1964. Bar: Mich. 1965, US Dist. Ct. (so. dist.) Mich. 1965, US Ct. Appeals (6th cir.) 1969, US Supreme Ct. 1994. Assoc. Miller, Canfield, Paddock and Stone, PLC, Detroit, Bloomfield Hills, 1964-71, sr. mem., 1971—2008, mng. ptnr., 1979-85, chmn., mng. ptnr., 1984-85, head state and local tax sect., 1985—2007, chmn. tax dept., 1989-94, of counsel, 2009—. Mem. tax coun. State Bar Mich., 1981-94, chmn. state and local tax com. real property sect., 1982-90; adj. prof. law sch. Wayne State U., 1993-. Assoc. editor Mich. Law Rev. Bd. dirs., past chmn. Goodwill Industries of Greater Detroit, 1970-2000; dir. Goodwill Industries Found., 1982-95, mem. lexington Arts County, 2009-; Stevens min., commd. lay assoc. pastor First Presbyn. Ch., Lapeer, Mich., 2003- Fellow: Am. Coll. Tax Counsel; mem.: ABA, Barrister's Soc., Detroit Bar Assn., Mich. Bar Assn., Mariner Sands Country Club (mem., bd. govs. 2008—), Order of Coif, Phi Delta Phi. Home (Summer): 8351 Lakeshore Rd Lexington MI 48450 Home (Winter): 6403 SE Brandywine Ct # 124 Stuart FL 34994 Office: Miller Canfield Paddock & Stone 150 W Jefferson Ave Ste 2500 Detroit MI 48226-4416 Office Phone: 313-496-7546. Business E-Mail: mckim@millercanfield.com.

MCKINLEY, CAMERON SHARBEL, elementary school educator; married. BA in Corp. Fin., Mktg. magna cum laude, Univ. Ala. Nat. Bd. Cert. Tech. tchr. Riverchase Elem. Sch., Hoover, Ala. Named Ala. Elem. Tchr. of Yr., 2006, Ala. Tchr. of Yr., 2007. Office: Riverchase Elem Sch 1950 Old Montgomery Hwy Birmingham AL 35244 Office Phone: 205-402-0509. Business E-Mail: camruns@gmail.com.

MCKINLEY, CRAIG R., career military officer; BSBA, So. Meth. U., 1974; MS in Mgmt. and Econs., Webster Coll., 1979; postgrad., Squadron Officer Sch., 1984, Air Command and State Coll., 1990; postgrad. in Nat. Security Strategy, Nat. War Coll., 1995; postgrad., Nat. Security Mgmt. Course, Syracuse, NY, 1997, Capstone, Ft. Lesley J. McNair, Washington, 1998, Combined Forces Air Component Comdr. Course, Maxwell AFB, Ala., 2002, US-Russia Security Program, Harvard U., 2004. Commd. 2nd lt. USAF, 1974, advanced through grades to lt. gen., 2006, T-38 instr. pilot Craig AFB, Ala., 1975-77, comdr. air force mil. tng. ctr. Lackland AFB, Tex., 1977-78, T-38 instr. pilot Laughlin AFB, Tex., 1978-80, F-106 alert pilot 125th Fighter Interceptor Group Jacksonville, Fla., 1980-82, F-106 instr. pilot, chief of safety 125th Fighter Interceptor Group, 1982-87, F-16 instr. pilot, chief of standardization/evaluation 125th Fighter Interceptor Group, 1987-88, dep. comdr. ops. 125th Fighter Interceptor Group, 1988-91, group comdr. 125th Fighter Interceptor Group, 1991-94, wing comdr. 125th Fighter Interceptor Wing, 1995-96, vice comdr. Southeast Air Def. Sector Tyndall AFB, Fla., 1996, comdr. Southeast Air Def. Sector, 1996-98; dep. dir. Air Nat. Guard, Arlington, Va., 1998—2001; comdr. Air Nat. Guard Readiness Ctr., Andrews AFB, Md., 1998—2001; dep. insp. gen. USAF, Washington, 2001—02, comdr. 1st Air Force, Air Combat Command, comdr. continental US NORAD region Tyndall, Fla., 2002—04; dir., mobilization & reserve affairs directorate US European Command, Stuttgart-Vaihingen, Germany, 2004—05; asst. dep. chief of staff for plans & programs USAF, Washington, 2005—06; dir. Air Nat. Guard, Arlington, Va., 2006—. Decorated Def. Disting. Svc. medal, Disting. Svc. medal with one oak leaf cluster, Def. Superior Svc. medal, Legion of Merit, Meritorious Svc. medal with two oak leaf clusters, Air Force Tng. Ribbon, Armed Force Res. medal, Air Force Commendation medal with two oak leaf cluster, Air Force Achievement medal with two oak leaf clusters, Air Force Outstanding Unit award, Combat Readiness medal with four oak leaf clusters, Nat. Def. Svc. medal with bronze star, Global War on Terroris, Svc. medal, Humanitarian Svc. medal, Air Force Longvity Svc. award with silver oak leaf cluster, Armed Forces Reserve meal with silver hourglass; Recipient I.G. Brown trophy, 1993, Disting. Alumni award So. Methodist U., 2003, Office: Air Nat Guard 1411 Jefferson Davis Hwy Arlington VA 22202-3231

MCKINLEY, ELLEN BACON, priest; b. Milw., June 9, 1929; d. Edward Alsted and Lorraine Goodrich (Graham) Bacon; m. Richard Smallbrook McKinley, III, June 16, 1951 (div. Oct. 1977); children: Richard, Ellen Graham, David Todd, Edward Bacon. BA cum laude, Bryn Mawr Coll., 1951; MDiv, Yale U., 1976; STM, Gen. Theol. Sem., NYC, 1979; PhD, Union Theol. Sem., NYC, 1988. Ordained deacon Episcopal Ch., 1980, as priest Episcopal Ch., 1981. Intern St. Francis Ch., Stamford, Conn., 1976-77; pastoral asst. St. Paul's Ch., Riverside, Conn., 1979-80, curate, 1980-81; asst. St. Saviour's Ch., Old Greenwich, Conn., 1982-90; interim asst. Trinity Ch., Princeton, NJ, 1990—91; priest assoc. All Saints Ch., Princeton, NJ, 1992—97, St. Christopher's Ch., Chatham, Mass., 1997—. Episc. election com. Diocese of Conn., 1986—87, com. on human sexuality, 1987—90, donations and bequests com., 1987—90; major chpt. mem. Trinity Cathedral, Trenton, NJ, 1992—96; interim rector All Saints Ch., Princeton, NJ, 1993. Sec. Greenwich Com. Drugs, 1970—71; active Episcopal Women's Caucus; bd. dirs. Greenwich YWCA, 1971—72, Chatham Old Village Assn., 1998—2004. Mem.: Colonial Dames Am.

MC KINLEY, JOHN KEY, retired oil company executive; b. Tuscaloosa, Ala., Mar. 24, 1920; s. Virgil Parks and Mary Emma (Key) McK.; m. Helen Grace Heare, July 19, 1946; children: John Key Jr., Mark Charles. BS in Chem. Engring, U. Ala., 1940, MS in Organic Chemistry, 1941, LL.D. (hon.), 1972; grad., Advanced Mgmt. Program, Harvard U., 1962; LL.D. (hon.), Troy State U., 1974. Registered profl. engr., Tex. With Texaco Inc., 1941-86, asst. dir. research Beacon, NY, 1957-59, asst. to v.p., 1959-60, mgr. comml. devel., 1960, gen. mgr. petrochem. dept. NYC, 1960-67, v.p. petrochem. dept., v.p. in charge supply and distbn., 1967-71, sr. v.p. worldwide refining, petrochems., also supply and distbn., 1971, pres., dir., 1971-80, pres., chief operating officer, chmn. exec. com., 1980, chmn. bd., pres., chief exec. officer, 1980-83, chmn. bd., chief exec. officer, 1983-86, ret., 1986. Bd. dirs. emeritus Federated Dept. Stores, Inc. Patentee for chem. processing. Hon. bd. dirs. Met. Opera Assocs.; nat. chmn. Met. Opera Centennial Fund, 1980; bd. dirs. The Ams. Soc.; mem. Bus. Coun. Maj. AUS, 1941-45, ETO. Decorated Bronze Star; recipient George Washington Honor medal Freedoms Found., 1972; Andrew Wellington Cordier fellow Columbia U.; named to Ala. Bus. Hall of Fame, 1982, Ala. Acad. Honor, 1983, State of Ala. Engring. Hall of Fame, 1992. Fellow Am. Inst. Chem. Engrs.; mem. Am. Petroleum Inst. (hon. dir.), Wee Burn Country Club, Brook Club, Augusta Nat. Golf Club, Blind Brook Country Club, North River Yacht, Sigma Xi, Tau Beta Pi, Gamma Sigma Epsilon, Kappa Sigma. Office: 1 Canterbury Grn Stamford CT 06901-2032

MCKINLEY, P. MICHAEL (PETER MICHAEL MCKINLEY), United States Ambassador to Peru; b. Venezuela; m. Fatima Salces Arce; 3 children. Undergrad., grad. studies, UK; PhD, Oxford U. Joined US Fgn. Svc., 1982; fgn. svc. assignments US Dept. State, Bolivia, 1983—85, Washington, 1985—90, London, 1990—94, dep. chief of mission, chargé d'affaires Mozambique, Uganda, Belgium, 1994—2001, dep. asst. sec., Bur. Population, Refugees and Migration, 2001—04, dep. chief of mission, chargé d'affaires, European Union Brussels, 2004—07, US amb. to Peru Lima, 2007—. Author: Pre-Revolutionary Caracas: Politics, Economy, and Society 1777-1811, 1986. Office: DOS Amb 3230 Lima Pl Washington DC 20521-3230*

MCKINLEY-HAAS, MARY, artist; b. St. Louis; d. Lee Carrington and Florence (Dowden) McK.; m. Saul Haas; children: Christopher, Matthew. BA, Smith Coll.; student, Art Students League, 1973—74, Nat. Acad. Design, 1965—66, Studio and Forum Stage Design. Head costume design dept. ABC-TV, NYC, 1968-73. One-woman shows include Tarlowe Gallery, Westhampton Beach, NY, 1974, Fontbonne Gallery, St. Louis, 1977, Gallery Yssa, NYC, 1979, Vered Gallery, East Hampton, NY, 1981, Netherlands Bank & Ludlow-Hyland Gallery, NYC, 1981, U. Tex., Austin, 1988, RVS Fine Art, Southampton, NY, 1990, TSS Gallery, NYC, 1992, U. Tex., Austin, 1992, TAI Gallery, NYC, 1999, Ezair Gallery, NYC, 2007; exhibited in group shows at Guild Hall, East Hampton, 1974-76, 78, 81, 85, 96, Parrish Art Mus., Southampton, 1975-76, 78, 81, Water Mill Mus., 1983, 92, Vared Gallery, East Hampton, 1985, Lincoln Ctr., NYC, 1989-90, Queens Coll. Art Ctr., Flushing, NY, 1991, Dorothy Chandler Pavillion, LA, 1993, Stony Brook U. Art Gallery, NY, 1994, Women in Art and Culture, Beijing, 1995, Elite Gallery, Moscow, 1995, Nat. Mus. Women in Arts, Washington, 1996, Soho 20 Gallery, NYC, 1998—, Canajoharie Libr. and Art Ctr., NY, 2000, Weill Cornell Med. Libr., NYC, 2002, Noho-NY Art Walk, 2004-05, 07, Venezuelan Consulate, NYC, 2006-07, Westbeth Galleny NYC, 2009; others; represented in permanent collections at Nat. Mus. Women in Arts, Washington, Tari Women's Cultural Ctr., Papua, New Guinea, Fontbonne Coll., St. Louis, No. Trust Naples, Fla.; pvt. collections; costume designer for Broadway and network TV shows, Harkness Ballet, Holiday on Ice, others. Mem. United Scenic Artists, Women in the Arts, N.Y. Artists Equity. Office: 284 Lafayette St Loft 5B New York NY 10012-3303 Office Phone: 212-334-8030. Business E-Mail: marymcsaul@aol.com.

MCKINNELL, HANK (HENRY A. MCKINNELL JR.), retired pharmaceutical executive; b. Victoria, BC, Can., Feb. 23, 1943; 4 children. BA, U. BC, 1965; MBA, Stanford U., 1967, PhD in Bus., 1969. Joined Pfizer, Inc., Tokyo, 1971; pres. Pfizer Asia, Hong Kong; CFO, pres. med. technology group Pfizer, Inc., exec. v.p., 1992—99; pres. Pfizer Pharms. Group, prin. oper. divsn., 1997—2001; COO Pfizer, Inc., NYC, 1999—2000, pres., 1999—2001, chmn., CEO, 2001—06, chmn., 2006. Bd. dirs. Moody's Corp., 1997—, Pfizer, Inc., 1997—2006, ExxonMobil Corp., 2002—07, Angiotech Pharmaceuticals Inc., 2008—, Trilateral Commn., Bus. Coun.; chmn. Bus. Roundtable, 2003—06, Accordia Global Health Found. Bd. trustee NY Pub. Libr., NYC Police Found., Econ. Club of NY; chmn. Stanford U. Grad. Sch. Bus. Adv. Coun.; chmn. emeritus, Bus.-Higher Edu. Forum. Recipient Excellence in Leadership award, Stanford Grad. Sch. Bus., 2003; fellow, NY Acad. Medicine.*

MCKINNELL, ROBERT GILMORE, retired zoologist, biology professor, geneticist; b. Springfield, Mo., Aug. 9, 1926; s. William Parks and Mary Catherine (Gilmore) McK.; m. Beverly Walton Kerr (dec.); children: Nancy Elizabeth, Robert Gilmore, Susan Kerr. B in Naval Sci., U. Notre Dame, 1946; AB, U. Mo., 1948; BS, Drury Coll., 1949, DSc (hon.), 1993; PhD, U. Minn., 1959. Rsch. assoc. Fox Chase Cancer Ctr., Phila., 1958-61; asst. prof. biology Tulane U., New Orleans, 1961-65, assoc. prof., 1965-69, prof., 1969-70; prof. zoology U. Minn., Mpls., 1970—76, prof. genetics and cell biology St. Paul, 1976—99, prof. emeritus, 1999—. Vis. scientist Dow Chem. Co., Freeport, Tex., 1976; guest dept. zoology U. Calif., Berkeley, 1979; Royal Soc. guest rsch. fellow Nuffield dept. pathology John Radcliffe Hosp., Oxford U., 1981-82; NATO vis. scientist Akademisch Ziekenhuis, Ghent, Belgium, 1984; faculty rsch. assoc. Naval Med. Rsch. Inst., Bethesda, Md., 1988; secretariat Third Internat. Conf. Differentiation, 1978; organizer, secretariat 6th Internat. Conf. on Pathology of Reptiles and Amphibians, 2001; mem. amphibian com. Inst. Lab. Animal Resources, NRC, 1970-73, mem. adv. coun., 1974; mem. panel genetic and cellular resources program NIH, 1981-82, spl. study sect., Bethesda, 1990. Author: Cloning: Amphibian Nuclear Transplantation, 1978, Cloning, A Biologist Reports, 1979; sr. editor: Differentiation and Neoplasia, 1980, Cloning: Leben aus der Retorte, 1981, Cloning of Frogs, Mice and Other Animals, 1985, (with others) The Biological Basis of Cancer, 1998, 2d edit., 2006, (with D.L. Carlson) Pathology of Reptiles and Amphibians, 2002, Prevention Cancer, 2008, also symposium procs. in field; mem. bd. advisors Marquis Who's Who; contbr. articles to profl. jours. Served to lt. USNR, 1944-47, 51-53. Recipient Outstanding Teaching award Newcomb Coll., Tulane U., 1970; Disting. Alumni award Drury Coll., 1979, Morse Alumni Tchg. award U. Minn., 1992; Rsch. fellow Nat. Cancer Inst., 1956-58, Prince Hitachi award Japanese Found. Cancer Rsch., 1998; Sr. Sci. fellow NATO, 1974. Fellow AAAS, Linnean Soc. (London); mem. Am. Assn. Cancer Rsch. (emeritus), Am. Assn. Cancer Edn. (sr.), Am. Assn. History of Medicine, Indian Soc. Devel. Biology (lifetime emeritus), Internat. Soc. Differentiation (pres. 1994-96), Minn. Acad. Medicine, Gown-in-Town Club, Sigma Xi. Office: 140 Gortner Lab Biochemistry 1479 Gortner Ave Saint Paul MN 55108 Home Phone: 651-646-3690. Business E-Mail: mckin002@umn.edu.

MCKINNEY, BART, orthopedist, researcher; m. Laura McKinney. BS in Chemistry, East Tenn. State U.; PhD, James H Quillen Coll. Medicine, 2003. Orthop. resident SUNY, Stony Brook, 2003—08; sports medicine fellow Andrews Inst., Gulf Breeze, Fla., 2008—. Mem.: Am. Orthop. Soc. Sports Medicine. Independent. Achievements include research in stem cell; knee extensor mechanism ruptures and associated injuries.

MCKINNEY, BRETT, medical educator; b. Tulsa, Okla., Aug. 1, 1974; s. Larry and Elizabeth McKinney; m. Shauna Dick; children: Jackson Cole, Leyton Grey. PhD, U. Okla., Norman, 2003. Asst. prof. U. Ala. Sch. Medicine, Birmingham, 2006—; co-dir., bioinformatics Heflin Ctr., Birmingham, 2008—. Personal E-mail: brett.mckinney@gmail.com.

MCKINNEY, CYNTHIA ANN, former United States Representative from Georgia; b. Atlanta, Ga., Mar. 17, 1955; d. Billy and Leola McKinney; 1 child, Coy Grandison. BA in internat. rels., U. So. Calif., 1978; MA, Tufts U. Fletcher Sch. Law & Diplomacy; postgrad., Ga. State U., U. Wis. Former instr. Clark Atlanta U., Atlanta Met. Coll.; mem. Ga. Ho. Reps., 1988-92, US Congress from 4th Ga. dist., 1993—2003, 2005—07, mem. com. on armed svc., com. on budget. Mem. HIV Health Services Planning Coun., Atlanta, 1991—92; Frank H.T. Rhodes vis. prof. Cornell U., Ithaca, NY, 2003—04. US presdl. candidate Green Party, 2008. Recipient Edgar Wayburn award, Sierra Club, 1998, Outstanding Contribution award, Nat. Orgn. Sierra Leonians in N Am., 2000; named a Diplomatic fellow, Spellman Coll., 1984; named one of Most Influential Black Americans, Ebony mag., 2006. Mem.: Progressive Caucus, Congl. Black Caucus, Agrl. Com., Sierra Club, Nat. Coun. Negro Women, Metro Atlanta, NAACP. Green Party. Roman Catholic. Achievements include the first African American woman elected to Congress from Georgia. Office: Hon Cynthia McKinney 5656 Hunters Chase Dr Lithonia GA 30038-1644 Office Phone: 202-225-1605. Office Fax: 202-226-0691.*

MCKINNEY, DAVID DUANE, museum director, architectural historian; b. Danville, Va., Nov. 14, 1956; s. Lafayette Wadsworth and Katie Jones McKinney. AB in History, Coll. William & Mary, 1979; MA in Archtl. History, U. Va., 1984, PhD in Archtl. History, 1992. Archivist, asst. curator Ash Lawn Coll. William & Mary, Charlottesville, 1981—84; reference staff Alderman Libr. U. Va., Charlottesville, 1984—91; dir. programming Very Spl. Arts, Washington, 1991—95; instrnl. designer, sr. scientist Human Resources Rsch. Orgn., Alexandria, Va., 1995—97; dir. statewide partnerships Va. Mus. Fine Arts, Richmond, 1997—2003; dir. US Dept. of the Interior Mus., Washington, 2003—06; chief cultural resources divsn. Office of Sec., Interior Dept., 2006—. Lectr. archtl. history Goucher Coll., Washington, 1996—97; bd. dirs. Va. Assn. Museums, Richmond, 1998—2005; lectr. art history Va. Commonwealth U., Richmond, 2000—01; mem. steering com. stds. learning devel. Va. State Bd. Edn., 2000—02, mem. governor's adv. bd. on gifted edn., 2001—02. Contbr. dictionary, exhibition catalogue, articles to profl. jours. Fellow Alumni Dissertation fellow, U. Va., 1990—91; scholar, Scottish Rite Order, 1977—79; Governor's scholar, Commonwealth Va., 1981—83, Dewey Lee Curtis scholar, Am. Decorative Arts Trust, 1988, Maverick fellow, Attingham Program, 1988, Resident scholar, Lewis Walpole Libr., Yale U., 1989, Va. Mus. fellow, Va. Mus. Fine Arts, 1989—90, Dumas Malone Meml. Traveling fellow, U. Va., 1989—90, Fiske Kimball Meml. fellow, 1990—91. Mem.: Va. Assn. Museums (dir. art 1998—2005, bd. dirs. 1998—), Am. Assn. Museums. Home: 1239 Vermont Ave NW #409 Washington DC 20005 Office: US Department of the Interior Mail Stop 2266 1849 C Street NW Washington DC 20240 Office Fax: 202-208-1535. Business E-Mail: david_d_mckinney@nbc.gov.

MCKINNEY, DENNIS, state treasurer; b. Coldwater, Kans., Nov. 24, 1960; m. Jean McKinney; children: Kelly, Lindy. BA in Polit. Sci., Wichita State U., MA in Pub. Finance and Adminstrn. Commr. Kiowa County, 1989—92; state rep dist. 116 Kans. House of Reps., 1992—2009, minority leader, 2003—08; treas. State of Kans., 2009—. Comanche Co Farm Bureau (past board member); Kansas Farm Bureau; Kansas Livestock Association. Democrat. Methodist. Office: Office State Treasurer 900 SW Jackson St Ste 201 Topeka KS 66612-1235 Office Phone: 785-296-7658, 785-296-3171. Fax: 785-296-0251; Office Fax: 785-295-7950. Business E-Mail: dennis@treasurer.ks.gov. E-mail: mckinney@house.state.ks.us.*

MCKINNEY, DENNIS KEITH, lawyer; b. Ottawa, Ill., May 12, 1952; s. Robert Keith and Delroy Louise (Clayton) McK.; m. Patricia Jean Boyle, Oct. 4, 1986; 1 child, Geoffrey Edward. BS, Ball State U., 1973; JD, Ill. Inst. Tech., 1976. Bar: Ind. 1977, U.S. Dist. Ct. (so. dist.) Ind. 1977, U.S. Supreme Ct. 1993. Appellate dep. Ind. Atty. Gen, Indpls., 1977-78, trial dep., 1978-79, sr. trial dep., 1979-81, chief real estate litigation sect., 1981-94; clk. to Hon. James S. Kirsch Ind. Ct. Appeals, Indpls., 1994-95; staff atty. Ind. Supreme Ct. Disciplinary Commn., Indpls., 1995—. Author: Eminent Domain, Practice and Procedure in Indiana, 1991, A Guide to Indiana Easement Law, 1995, A Railroad Ran Through It, 1996, Road and Access Law in Indiana, 2002, Indiana Eminent Domain Practice and Procedure, 2003, Boundary Disputes: Resolving Client Conflicts, 2007; contbg. author: Indiana Real Estate Transactions, 1996; contbr. articles to profl. jours. Active Indpls.-Scarborough Peace Games, 1983-84. Avocations: reading, volleyball, wargaming. Office: Ind Supreme Ct Disciplinary Ste 850 30 S Meridian St Indianapolis IN 46204-3420 Office Phone: 317-233-1881.

MCKINNEY, DONALD LEE, magazine editor; b. Evanston, Ill., July 12, 1923; s. Guy Doane and Cora Redfield (Brenton) McK.; m. Mary Frances Joyce, Dec. 14, 1958; children— Jennifer Joyce, Douglas Guy. AB, U. N.C., 1948. Salesman textbooks John Wiley & Sons, NYC, 1949-52; freelance writer mostly comic books with some short articles and fiction, 1952-54; asst. mng. editor True mag., NYC, 1955-62; editor articles Saturday Evening Post, 1962-69; spl. features editor N.Y. Daily News, 1969-70; mng. editor McCalls mag., NYC, 1969-86; Gonzales prof. journalism U. S.C., Beaufort, 1986-90, prof. emeritus, 1990—. Author: Magazine Writing That Sells, 1994; reporter, book reviewer. Served with USNR, 1943-46. Democrat. Home: 1512 Springmoor Giaor Cir Raleigh NC 27615 *I learned early that it is important to speak up if you think you are being treated unfairly; sometimes it's true, and nobody else will complain if you don't. I also learned that in my business, and probably in most others, it is best to always say what you think. Truth is usually more helpful than any assortment of euphemisms, and it also saves a lot of worry over who you have lied to and just what you've said. Truth is not only the best policy— by all odds it's the easiest to keep track of.*

MCKINNEY, DOUG, political organization administrator, urologist; b. Bud, W.Va., Mar. 17, 1943; s. Dewey and Violet Church McKinney; m. Sue McKinney; children: Margaret Weaver, William, Matt, Samuel. MD, W.Va. U., 1967. Pvt. practice, Ashland, Ky., 1978—86, Bridgeport-Clarksburg, 1986—2004; chief urology Clarksburg VAMC. Chair WESPAC, 1992—2002; bd. mem. UROPAC, 2000—. Mem. W.Va. Rep. Exec. Com., 2002, 2006, Harrison County Rep. Exec. Com., 2000—; chmn. W.Va. Rep. Party, 2006—. With USN, 1967—76. Mem.: Am. Urological Assn. (pres.-elect), Am. Assn. Clin. Urologists (bd. mem.), W.Va. Med. Assn. (pres. 2003). Republican. Office: WVa Rep Party PO Box 2711 Charleston WV 25330 Office Phone: 304-768-0493. Office Fax: 304-768-6083.

MCKINNEY, E. KIRK, JR., retired insurance company executive; b. Indpls., Mar. 27, 1923; s. E. Kirk and Irene M. (Hurley) McK.; m. Alice Hollenbeck Greene, June 18, 1949; children: Kirk Ashley, Alan Brooks, Nora Claire McKinney Hiatt, Margot Knight. AB, U. Mich., 1948. Asst. treas. Jefferson Nat. Life Ins. Co., Indpls., 1949-52, asst. to pres., asst. treas., 1952-53, treas., asst. to pres., 1953-55, v.p., treas., 1955-59, pres., 1959-90, chmn. bd., 1970-90; vice chmn. bd. Somerset Group Inc., 1986-89; ret., 1990. Corp. rels. com. U. Mich.; former pres., former CEO, bd. govs., treas., bd. dirs., exec. com. Indpls. Mus. Art; past bd. dirs. (hon.) Greater Indpls. Progress Com.; former vice chmn. Indpls.-Marion County Bd. Ethics; former dir. Park Tudor Sch., Cmty. Svc. Coun. Indpls., Hosp. Devel. Corp., Ind. Repertory Theater; past adv. com. Indpls. Retirement Home; former bd. dirs., and pres. Episcopal

Cmty. Svcs., Inc.; former vice chmn., life trustee Nature Conservancy; mem. adv. bd. Ind. U., Purdue U.; active Indpls. Symphony Orch.; former bd. dirs. Ind. Pub. Broadcasting Soc.; bd. dirs. Civic Thocter, 2001—, former bd. mem., 2008, Athenaeum Found., 2000—. Mem. Life Office Mgmt. Assn. (bd. dirs. 1981-83), Am. Coun. Life Ins. (state v.p. 1973-75, dir., exec. com. 1976-79), Assn. Ind. Life Ins. Cos. (pres. 1969-71), Indpls. C. of C., Sigma Chi. Clubs: Economic of Indpls. (bd. dirs.). Democrat. Home: 250 W 77th St Indianapolis IN 46260-3608 Office: 1330 W 38th St #100 Indianapolis IN 46208-4103 Home Phone: 317-253-0166; Office Phone: 317-925-2223. Personal E-mail: ekirkjr@sbcglobal.net. Business E-Mail: eknkjr@sbcglobal.net.

MCKINNEY, JAMES CLAYTON, electronics executive, electrical engineer; b. Charleston, W.Va., June 3, 1940; s. George Clayton and Leona (Adams) McK. BSE.E., W.Va. Inst. Tech., 1963. Mem. staff Sta. WMON, Montgomery, W.Va., 1961-63; stringer AP, Charleston, W.Va., 1961-63; with FCC, Washington, 1963-87, chief ops. br., 1969-73, chief monitoring div., 1973, chief enforcement div., 1974, dep. chief Field Ops. Bur., 1974-80, chief Field Ops. Bur., 1980-81, chief Pvt. Radio Bur., 1981-83, chief Mass Media Bur., 1983-87; dep. asst. to Pres., dir. White House Mil. Office Washington, 1987-89; chmn. Advanced TV Systems Com., Washington, 1989-96; CEO Model HDTV Sta. Project, Inc., 1996-97. Chmn. U.S. del. UN Conf. on Radio, Geneva, 1986.; mem. U.S. Dels., Geneva, 1978-79, Can., 1984, Italy, 1985, Mexico, 1986, S.Am., 1986, Fed. Republic Germany, 1990; mem. presdl. dels., NATO, UN, Mexico, USSR, Can., Eng., Finland, Econ. Summit, 1987-88; U.S. Spokesman High Definition TV Conf., Geneva, 1989. Author: (with Eliot Maxwell) Future of Electronic Information Handling at the FCC— Blue Print for the 80's, 1980; (with G.A. Fehlner) Direct Broadcast Satellites in the United States, 1985; New Look at AM Radio, 1986, HDTV Approaches the End Game, 1991. Vice chmn. Montreux Medal Award Com., 1990-95; chmn. High Definition TV World Conf., 1990-93; chmn. strategic planning group for Internat. Consultative Com. for Radio, Dept. State, 1990-91; bd. dirs. Bowler Found., 1990-95, PICA Found., Inc., 1996-97; CEO & bd.dirs. HDTV Sta. Project, Inc., 1996-97; bd.dirs. Deercreek Country Club Owners Assn., 2005-08. Recipient Outstanding Fed. Exec. award FCC, 1979, 80, 82, 83, 85, 86; Presdl. Rank award for disting. exec. svc., 1985, Gold medal for disting. fed. svc., 1987, TV Engring. Achievement award, 1992, NAB award of honor, 1996, Broadcast Pioneers' Disting. Svc. award, 1996; W.Va. Broadcasters Disting. West Virginian, 1997. Fellow Radio Club Am., Soc. Broadcast Engrs. (sr.), Broadcast Pioneers, Soc. Motion Picture and TV Engrs. (presdl. proclamation 1991); mem. Fed. Exec. Assn., Cosmos Club of Washington. Episcopalian. Home: 10055 Heather Lake Ct W Jacksonville FL 32256-3595 E-mail: jimmckin@comcast.net.

MCKINNEY, JOHN ADAMS, JR., lawyer; b. Washington, Mar. 10, 1948; s. John A. and Cleo G. (Turner) McK., m. Carol A. Cowen, Dec. 22, 1970; children: John III, Thomas. BA, Principia Coll., 1970; JD, Coll. William and Mary, 1973. Bar: N.J. 1973. Assoc. Mason, Griffin & Pierson, Princeton, NJ, 1973-77; gen. atty. Nabisco, Inc., East Hanover, NJ, 1977-79; asst. counsel Republic Steel Corp., Cleve., 1979-84; atty. and sr. atty. AT&T, Berkeley Heights, NJ, 1984-90; ptnr. McCarter & English LLP, Newark, 1990—2003; mem. Wolff & Samson PC, West Orange, NJ, 2003—. Adj. prof. Sch. of Law, Seton Hall U., 1997—; charter mem., program chair Justice Pollock Environ. Am. Inn of Ct., 2004-08; mem. NJ Historic Sites Coun., 2005-. Co-author: The RCRA Practice Manual, 2d edit., 2004; co-editor: CERCLA Enforcement, 1996. Trustee Hackettstown (N.J.) Free Pub. Libr., 1998—2005, Drumthwacket Found., 2003—. Mem. ABA (vice-chair sect. natural resources energy and environ. law solid and hazardous waste com. 1990-98, chair, teleconf. programs 1994-97), N.J. State Bar Assn. (dir. environ. law sect. 1992-96, chair 1996-97). Office: Wolff & Samson PC One Boland Dr West Orange NJ 07052-3698 Home Phone: 908-850-3336; Office Phone: 973-530-2036.

MCKINNEY, JOSEPH CRESCENT, bishop emeritus; b. Grand Rapids, Mich., Sept. 10, 1928; s. Joseph Crescent and Antoinette (Theisen) McKinney. Attended, Seminaire de Philosophie, Montreal, Can., 1948—50; STL, Collegio di Propaganda Fide, Rome, 1954. Ordained priest Diocese of Grand Rapids, Mich., 1953; high sch. prof. St. Joseph Sem., Grand Rapids, Mich., 1954—62; asst. pastor Sacred Heart Parish, Mt. Pleasant, Mich., 1962—65; pastor St. Francis Parish, Conklin, Mich., 1965—68; asst. chancellor Diocese of Grand Rapids, 1965—68, aux. bishop, 1968—2001, vicar gen., 1968—2001, aux. bishop emeritus, 2001—; pastor St. Andrew Cathedral, Grand Rapids, 1968—69, Our Lady Of Consolation, Rockford, Mich., 1985—98. Adminstr. Sede Vacante, 1969; pastor St. Stephen's Ch., Grand Rapids, 1971—77, Sacred Heart Parish, Muskegon Heights, Mich., 1977—. Roman Catholic.

MCKINNEY, JUDSON THAD, broadcast executive; b. Sacramento, Aug. 21, 1941; s. Judson Bartlet and Mildred Eoline (Taylor) McK. Student, Sacramento State U., 1959-61, Western Bapt. Bible Coll., 1961-62, Am. River Coll., 1962-63. Prodn. dir. Sta. KEBR, Sacramento, 1962-65; prodn. dir. Sta. KEAR, Merced, Calif., 1965-68; sta. mgr. Sta. KAMB, 1968-75, Sta. KEAR, San Francisco, 1975-78, 79-88, WFME, Newark, 1978; western regional mgr. Family Stas. Inc., 1988—. Pres. Abounding Love Ministries, 2000-04; instr.for study of electronic Christian media Grad. Theol. Union. V.p. New Millennium Strings, 2003—04, pres., 2005—; sec., treas. Trinity Lyric Opera, 2005—08; chmn. 1st. Bapt. Ch. San Francisco, 1985—91; recording engr. 1st Bapt. Ch. Los Altos, Calif., 2000—08. Mem. Gideons. Republican. Baptist. Office: Family Stations Inc 290 Hegenberger Rd Oakland CA 94621-1436 Business E-Mail: thad@familyradio.org.

MCKINNEY, LARRY J., federal judge; b. South Bend, Ind., July 4, 1944; s. Lawrence E. and Helen (Byers) McK.; m. Carole Jean Marie Lyon, Aug. 19, 1966; children: Joshua E., Andrew G. BA, MacMurray Coll., Jacksonville, Ill., 1966; JD, Ind. U., 1969. Bar: Ind. 1970, U.S. Dist. Ct. (so. dist.) Ind. 1970. Law clk. to atty. gen. State of Ind., Indpls., 1969-70, dep. atty. gen., 1970-71; ptnr. Rodgers and McKinney, Edinburgh, Ind., 1971-75, James F.T. Sargent, Greenwood, Ind., 1975-79; judge Johnson County Cir. Ct., Franklin, Ind., 1979-87, U.S. Dist. Ct. (so. dist.) Ind., Indpls., 1987—, chief judge, 2001—08. Presbyterian. Avocations: reading, jogging. Office: US Dist Ct 204 US Courthouse 46 E Ohio St Indianapolis IN 46204-1903

MCKINNEY, MARK, educator; Asst. prof. Miami U., Oxford, Ohio, 1994—2000, assoc. prof., 2000—. Office: Miami Univ 500 East High St Oxford OH 45056

MCKINNEY, MEGAN, writer; b. Columbia, Mo., July 11; d. Fred and Margery (Mulkern) McKinney; m. Robert Whitfield, June 6, 1958 (separated 1981); 1 child, Katherine Whitfield. BA, U. Mo., Columbia, 1956. Writer TV Guide, N.Y.C., 1956—58; sr. press rep. CBS TV Network, N.Y.C., 1958—64; v.p. Frank Sullivan Assoc., Chgo., 1979—84; dir. pub. rels. Swedish Covenant Hosp., Chgo., 1985—86; editor Ave. M. Mag., Chgo., 1986—90; freelance columnist, writer, 1990—. Pres. Art Resources in Tchg., Chgo., 1980—82; mem. Womans Bd. Northwestern Meml. Hosp., Chgo., 1979—, pres., 1988—90; mem. gov. bd. English Speaking Union, 1986—2002; chmn. Passavant Cotillion, Chgo., 1983, Ascot Ball, Chgo., 1989; co-chmn. Salute to Mike Wallace Mus. Broadcast Comm., Chgo., 1989, co-chmn. Salute to Betty White, 1990, co-chmn. Salute to A.C. Nielsen Jr., 1991, co-chmn. Salute to Irv Kupcinet, 1994. Mem.: Pi Beta Phi. Episcopal. Home: One East Scott Chicago IL 60610

MCKINNEY, MICHAEL MERRITT, law educator; b. Bitburg, Germany; s. Ethan and Katalin McKinney; m. Jo Clark; 1 child, Michael Merritt McKinney II. BS, MBA, East Tenn. State U., Johnson City; JD, Columbia U., NY. Bar: Tenn. Bar Assn. Asst. dean external programs East Tenn. State U., Coll. Bus. and Tech., Johnson City, assoc. prof. bus. law. With USN. Office: East Tenn State Univ ETSU Box 70613 Johnson City TN 37614 Business E-Mail: mckinney@etsu.edu.

MCKINNEY, SUEANNE E., education educator; b. Portsmouth, Va., Dec. 10, 1959; d. Joseph Edward and Betty Ann McKinney. BA in Elem. Edn., U. NC, Wilmington, 1982; MEd in Adminstrn., Old Dominion U., Norfolk, Va., 1991, PhD in Urban Edn., 2000. Cert. mid. sch. tchr., prin. Va. Tchr. Norfolk Pub. Schs., 1983—97; grad. asst. Old Dominion U., 1998—2003, asst. prof., 2005—, U. NC, Charlotte, 2003—05. Contbr. articles to profl. jours. Named Tchr. of Yr., Norfolk Pub. Schs., 1996, Teletechnet Instr. of Yr., Old Dominion U., 2002. Mem.: Am. Educator Rsch. Assn., Assn. Tchr. Educators, Nat. Assn. Holms Scholars Alumni (membership chmn.). Office: Old Dominion U Hampton Blvd Norfolk VA 23529

MCKINNEY, VIRGINIA ELAINE ZUCCARO, educational administrator; b. San Francisco, Nov. 18, 1924; d. Salvadore John and Elaine Agnes (Shepard) Zuccaro; BA, Calif. State U., LA, 1968; MA, Calif. State U., Northridge, 1969; PhD, Claremont Grad. Sch., 1983; children: Joe, Walter Clifton. Official ct. reporter LA County Superior Cts., 1948-59; tchr. speech-reading, adult edn. LA Bd. Edn., 1966-71; lang., reading specialist Marlton Sch. for the Deaf, LA, 1971-79; founder, pres., dir. communication skills program Ctr. for Communicative Devel., Inc., LA, 1969-; part-time lectr. spl. edn. Calif. State U., LA, 1971-1978; cons. for various univs. and programs for the hearing-impaired; mem. State Ind. Living Coun., 1993-2000, adv. com. for deaf Calif. Dept. Rehab., 1979—1984, Atty.'s Gen. Commn. on Disability, 1987-1990. Recipient Leadership award Nat. Leadership Tng. Program in Area of Deaf, Calif. State U., Northridge, 1974; NEA Project Life grantee, 1970, Gallaudet Coll. Ctr. for Continuing Edn. grantee, 1974. Mem. Calif. Educators for Deaf and Hard of Hearing, Calif. Assn. For Postsecondary Edn. and Disability, Beverly-Hollywood (Calif.) Hearing Soc. (pres. 1967-68). Republican. Presbyterian. Author: The Picture Plus Dictionary, 1997, (CD) Picture Plus Vocabulary, 2000, developer, producer audio-visual media, including 22 films and 4 books, to aid in speechreading and auditory tng., 1963-68; participant research project with Project Life on devel. of communication skills for multiply-handicapped deaf adults, 1970; developer, pub. Toe-Hold Literacy Packet, 1973, Linguistics 36, interactive computer lang. devel. program, 1986. Office: 3460 Wilshire Blvd Ste 200 Los Angeles CA 90010 Office Phone: 213-738-8176. Personal E-mail: ccdcom40@yahoo.com.

MCKINNEY, WILLIAM MARK, retired geology educator; b. Spring Valley, NY, Dec. 26, 1923; s. John and Mabel Genevieve (Munger) McKinney; m. Georgia Anna Coleman, June 2, 1951 (dec. Mar. 23, 2003); 1 child, Mark Warren (dec.). Student, U. NC, Raleigh and Chapel Hill, 1940—42; BA, New Sch. U., NYC, 1948; MA, U. Fla., 1949, PhD, 1958. Cons. Ga. Dept. Pub. Health, Atlanta, 1953—58; asst. prof. So. Oreg. U., Ashland, 1958—63; asst. prof. to prof. U. Wis., Stevens Point, 1963—88; ret., 1988. Guest rschr. Lowell Obs., Flagstaff, Ariz., 1969—78. Contbr. articles to profl. jours., chpts. to books. Pres. Unitarian Soc., Medford, Oreg., 1959—62, Stevens Point, Wis., 1970—73. With USN, 1943. Mem.: Geol. Soc. Am., Phi Kappa Phi. Unitarian Universalist. Avocations: comparative religion, astronomy, railroads. Home: 1540 NW Kings Blvd Corvallis OR 97330 Home Phone: 541-753-3928.

MCKINNIES, RICHARD CHARLES, radiation therapist, assistant professor; b. DuQuoin, Ill., May 2, 1977; m. Jaymee Louise Evans, May 26, 2001; children: Brayden Charles, Aubrey Jean. MS in Workforce Edn., So. Ill. U., Carbondale, 2006. Diplomate ARRT, 2002, IEMA, 2003. X-ray technologist SE Mo. Hosp., Cape Girardeau, 2001—03; radiation therapist So. Ill. Radiation Oncology Ctr., Mt. Vernon, 2003—05; asst. prof. So. Ill. U., 2006—. Consulting radiation therapist St. Mary's Good Samaritan Hosp., Centralia, Ill., 2007—. Contbr. articles to profl. jours. Site visitor Joint Rev. Com. Edn. Radiologic Scis., Chgo., 2007—08. Human Capital Health Care grant, So. Ill. U., 2007. Mem.: Am. Soc. Radiologic Technologists. Office: Southern Ill Univ Engring A 1230 Lincoln Dr Rm 407B Carbondale IL 62901-6615 Business E-Mail: rmck@siu.edu.

MCKINNIS, MICHAEL BAYARD, lawyer; b. St. Louis, May 31, 1945; s. Bayard O. and Doris (Lammert) McK.; m. Patricia Butow, Aug. 24, 1968; children: Scott, Christopher, Elizabeth. BS, Drake U., 1967; JD, U. Mo., 1970. Bar: Mo. 1970, U.S. Dist. Ct. (ea. dist.) Mo. Ptnr. Bryan Cave LLP, St. Louis, gen. counsel. Editor U. Mo. Law Rev., 1969-70. Mem. ABA, Mo. Bar Assn., Order of Coif, Phi Delta Phi. Office: Bryan Cave LLP One Metropolitan Square 211 N Broadway, Ste 3600 Saint Louis MO 63102-2733 Office Phone: 314-259-2000. E-mail: mbmckinnis@bryancave.com.

MC KINNON, CLINTON DAN, aerospace transportation executive; b. San Bernardino, Calif., Jan. 27, 1934; s. Clinton Dotson and Lucille V. McK.; m. Janice Bernard; children: Holly Jean, Sherri Lynn, Clinton Scott, Lisa Caroline BA, U. Mo., 1956; doctorate (hon.), Nat. U., 1987. Page U.S. Ho. of Reps., 1950-52; reporter, photographer, advt. salesman Sentinel Newspaper, San Diego, 1960-62; owner, pres. KSON Radio, San Diego, 1962-85, KSON-FM, San Diego, 1964-85; pub. La Jolla (Calif.) Light Jour., 1969-73; owner House of Hits (book and music pub.), San Diego, 1972—; co-owner KIII-TV, Corpus Christi, Tex., 1964—, KBMT-TV, Beaumont, Tex., 1976—, KUSI-TV, San Diego, 1992—; chmn. CAB, Washington, 1981-84; with spl. projects CIA, 1985-86; founder, chmn., pres. North Am. Airlines, Jamaica, NY, 1989—2005. Author: Bullseye--One Reactor (aka Bullseye Iraq), 1986, The Ten Second Message, 1994, Words of Honor, 1995, Rescue Pilot, 2002, Safe Air Travel Companion, 2002. Chmn. exec. com. Greater San Diego Billy Graham Crusade, 1976, commr., Nat. Guard and Reserves Commn., 2005-08. Served as aviator USNR, 1956—60. Recipient Advt. Man of Year award San Diego Advt. and Sales Club, 1971; Radio Sta. Mgr. of Year award Billboard Mag., 1973; Internat. Pres.'s award Youth for Christ, 1975; Man of Distinction award Mexican-Am. Found., 1976; George Washington Honor medal Freedoms Found., 1976; Headliner of Yr. (govt.), San Diego Press Club, 1985; named to Country Radio Hall of Fame, 2003. Mem. Country Music Assn. (pres. 1977, Pres. award 1980), C. of C. (dir.), Nat. Assn. Broadcasters (bd. dirs. 1970-74), Calif. Broadcasters Assn. (dir.), Navy League (Media Man of Yr. 1980), Wings Club (bd. govs. 1995-2003, pres. 2002-2003), San Diego Rotary, Nat. Guard and Reserves (commr., 2005-08). Achievements include setting Navy helicopter peacetime rescue record of 62 air/sea rescues, 1958; 1st person to close down fed. govt. regulatory agy., CAB, 1984. Office: 1125-101 Pacific Beach Dr San Diego CA 92109

MCKINNON, FLOYD WINGFIELD, textile executive; b. Columbus, Ga., Dec. 1, 1942; s. Malcolm Angus and Sarah C. (Bullock) McK.; m. Barbara Evans Roles, June 18, 1966; children: James Wingfield, Sarah Elizabeth, Robert Kent. AB, Washington and Lee U., 1964. Lic. airplane pilot. Pres. Cotswold Industries, Inc., NYC, 1966—, also bd. dirs.; v.p., corp. sec. Cen. Textiles, Inc., S.C., 1984—, also bd. dirs. S.C. Arbitrator Am. Arbitration Assn., 1983-2001; bd. dirs. Scarsdale Leasing Corp. Pres. Berkley-in-Scarsdale Assn., 1980; admissions rep. Washington and Lee U., 1979-89, 93-99. Mem. Aircraft Owner's and Pilot's Assn., St. Andrews Soc. N.Y., Union League Club N.Y. (bd. govs. 1974-77, 88-91, 97—, sec. 1981-83, chmn. admissions com. 1996, pres. 2005-07), Scarsdale Golf Club (bd. govs. 1983-91, pres. 1990-91) (Hartsdale, N.Y.), Bras Coupe Club (exec. com. 1980—) (Maniwaki, Can.). Republican. Episcopalian. Home: 26 Taunton Rd Scarsdale NY 10583-5610 Office: Cotswold Industries 10 E 40th St Rm 3410 New York NY 10016-0367 Personal E-mail: wink85wm@optonline.net. Business E-Mail: wink@cotswoldindustries.com.

MCKINNON, MARK DAVID, consulting firm executive; b. 1955; m. Annie McKinnon; children: Brita, Kendall. Attended, U. Tex. Austin. Democratic campaign cons., Tex.; media advisor Gov. Ann Richards, Tex., 1990, Pres. George W. Bush, 2000, 2004; founder, pres. Maverick Media, 2004—; vice chmn. Pub. Strategies, Inc., Austin, 2004—; founding mem. hotsoup.com, 2006; media advisor Senator John McCain's Presdl. Campaign, Arlington, Va., 2006—08. Lectr. Harvard U. JFK Sch. Govt.; adj. prof. pub. affairs U. Tex. Austin LBJ Sch. Pub. Affairs, 2007. Former songwriter: Kris Kristofferson. Bd. mem. Lance Armstrong Found. Recipient More than 30 Pollie and Tellie awards. Republican. Office: Public Strategies Inc 98 San Jacinto Blvd Ste 1200 Austin TX 78701 Office Phone: 512-474-8848. Office Fax: 512-474-0120.*

MCKINNON, PAUL, bank executive, human resources specialist; BA, MA, Brigham Young U.; PhD in Orgnl. Studies, MIT. Sr. v.p. human resources Dell; head talent mgmt., human resources Citigroup Inc., 2008—. Former asst. prof. orgnl. behavior Darden Grad. Sch. Bus., U. Va. Fellow: Nat. Acad. Human Resources; mem.: HR Policy Assn. (bd. dirs.). Office: Citigroup Inc 399 Park Ave New York NY 10043*

MCKINNON, RONALD IAN, retired economics professor; b. Edmonton, Alta., Can., July 10, 1935; s. Ian Nicholson and Lois Harrison McKinnon; m. Margaret McQueen Learmonth, Sept. 7, 1957; children: Neil Charles, Mary Elizabeth, David Bruce. BA with honors, U. Alta., Edmonton, 1956; PhD, U. Minn., Mpls., 1961. Instr. bus admin U. Minn., Mpls., 1957—59; lectr. economics Syracuse U., NY, 1960—61; asst. prof. economics Stanford U., Calif., 1961—66, assoc. prof. economics, 1966—69, prof. economics, 1969—2008, prof. economics, emeritus, 2008—. Rockefeller vis. rsch. prof. internat. economics Brookings Instn., Washington, 1970—71; fellow Ctr. Advanced Study Behavioral Scis., Stanford, 1974—75; Frank D. Graham meml. lectr. Princeton U., NJ, 1977; vis. scholar Hoover Instn., Stanford, 1982—83; cons. IMF and World Bank, Washington. Author: (book) Money and Capital in Economic Development, Money and Finance in Economic Growth and Development: Essays in Honor of Edward S. Shaw, Money in International Exchange: The Convertible Currency System, An International Standard for Monetary Stabilization, The Order of Economic Liberalization: Financial Control in the Transition to a Market Economy, The Rules of the Game: International Money and Exchange Rates; co-author (with Kenichi Ohno): Dollar and Yen: Resolving Economic Conflict Between the United States and Japan. Office: Dept Economics Landau Bldg 579 Serra Mall Stanford CA 94305 Office Fax: 650-725-5702. Business E-Mail: mckinnon@stanford.edu.

MCKINNON, RUSSELL F., professional society administrator; b. Springfield, Mass., Feb. 11, 1944; s. John McKinnon and Margret Louise Bates; m. Deborah Oplinger, July 11, 1987; 1 child, John. AB in History, Coll. Holy Cross, 1966; M in Mgmt., George Washington U., 1988. Pres. The Mackinnon Co. LLC, Alexandria, Va., 1972—, Internat. Theos Found., Alexandria, 1998—. Photographer Parade Mag., 1989. Lt. USNR, 1966-72. Mem. Am. Soc. Assn. Execs. (cert.), Assn. Meeting Planners (treas.). Avocations: skiing, golf. Office: PO Box 7361 Alexandria VA 22307-2002 Business E-Mail: russ.mckinnon@verizon.net.

MCKINSTRY, GLENN ALLEN, secondary school educator; b. Pinckneyville, Ill., June 7, 1963; s. George Edgar and Wanda Lee McKinstry. BS in History Edn., So. Ill. U., Carbondale, 1986, BS in Mktg., 1991; MS in Counseling, Ea. Ill. U., Charleston, 2005. Cert. 6-12 tchg. State of Ill., 1986, sch. counseling State of Ill., 2005. Tchr. Pinckneyville Cmty. HS, Ill., 1994—2000; bus. tchr. Grayville HS, Ill., 2000—03; guidance counselor Harrisburg HS, Ill., 2005—. Sunday sch. tchr. First United Presbyn. Ch., Pinckneyville, 1992—97, deacon, 1992—98, elder, 1998—2000. Mem.: Ill. Edn. Assn., Nat. Edn. Assn., Chi Sigma Iota (life), Phi Theta Kappa (life). Presbyterian. Home: 206 N Walnut St Pinckneyville IL 62274 Office: Harrisburg HS 333 W College St Harrisburg IL 62946

MCKINZIE, BARBARA ANNE, educational association administrator; b. Ada, Okla., Jan. 2, 1954; d. Leonard Terry and Johnnie Mae (Moses) Watson. BS, East Cen. U., Ada, Okla., 1976; MA, Northwestern U. Kellogg Sch. Mgmt., Evanston, Ill., 1997; doctorate (hon.), Stillman Coll., Ala., 2006. CPA Ill., Okla. Supr. Touche Ross & Co., Tulsa, 1976-83; mgr. Deloitte Haskins & Sells, Chgo., 1983-85, Coopers & Lybrand, Chgo.; dep. dir. fin. and adminstrn. Chgo. Neighborhood Housing Svcs.; comptroller Chgo. Housing Authority; exec. dir. Alpha Kappa Alpha, Inc., Chgo., 1985-87, internat. treas., 1998—2002, internat. v.p., 2002—06, internat. pres., 2006—. Bd. dirs. Africare, 2005—. Named Woman of Yr., Am. Biographical Inst., 2001; named one of Top 25 Outstanding Bus. Women, NY Network Jour., 2002; named to Power 150, Ebony mag., 2008. Mem.: Am. Arbitration Assn., Ill. Soc. CPA's, Am. Women's Soc. CPA's, Am. Inst. CPA's. Baptist. Avocations: travel, racquetball.

MCKINZIE, CARL WAYNE, lawyer; b. Lubbock, Tex., Dec. 3, 1939; s. J. Clyde and Flora (Cates) McK.; m. Rowena Ann Williams; children: Wayne, Clinton, Morgan (dec.). BBA, Tex. Tech U., 1962, MBA, 1963; JD, So. Meth. U., 1966. From assoc. to ptnr. Nossaman, Guthner, Knox & Elliot, LA, 1966-80; prin. Riordan & McKinzie, LA, 1980—2003; ptnr. Bingham McCutchen (merged with Riordan & McKinzie), 2003—. Bd. dirs., exec. com., Saint John's Health Ctr., Santa Monica, Calif., 2001-2007, 2008-, vice chair, 2002-2003, chair, 2003-2007, trustee, 2007-. Contbr. articles to law jours. Trustee Jaquish Found., 2000-04, Raymond Marshall Found., 1993-2003; bd. visitors Sch. Law So. Meth. U., Dallas, 1979-82, 90—, bd. dirs., 1970-73, 84-89, chmn. exec. com., 1996-98; bd. visitors Ariz State U. Coll. Law, 1990-98; bd. dirs. Riordan Found., 1992—, Rx for Reading, 1992—, The Welk Group, 2004—, Leprechaun Holding Company LLC, 2008-, Corporesano Holding LLC,

2008-; bd. dirs., exec. com. Libr. Found. LA, 2002—08, vice chair, 2003-04; bd. dirs., exec. coun. Pub. Counsel, 1996-99, Calif. Cmty. Found., 1994-98; bd. advisors Coll Law, U. Wyo., 1987-91, 2001—. Recipient disting. alumni award, So. Meth. U., Dallas, 1994. Mem. ABA (chmn. current devel. subcom., com. tax problems 1978-80), Nat. Assn. Real Estate Investment Trusts (bd. govs. 1986-89), Calif. Bar Assn., Los Angeles County Bar Assn., Jonathan Club, L.A. Country Club. Republican. Home: 527 21st Pl Santa Monica CA 90402-3047 Office: Bingham McCutchen 44th Fl 355 S Grand Ave Los Angeles CA 90071-3106 Home Phone: 310-393-3692; Office Phone: 213-229-8484. Business E-Mail: carl.mckinzie@bingham.com.

MCKIRAHAN, RICHARD DUNCAN, classics and philosophy educator; b. Berkeley, Calif., July 27, 1945; s. Richard Duncan and Helen Marion (Hixson) McK.; m. Voula Tsouna, June 3, 1961; 1 child, Helen Hamilton. AB, U. Calif., Berkeley, 1966; BA, U. Oxford, Eng., 1969; MA, Oxford U., Eng., 1979; PhD, Harvard U., 1973. Teaching fellow, tutor Harvard U., Cambridge, Mass., 1971-73; asst. prof. classics and philosophy Pomona Coll., Claremont, Calif., 1973-79, assoc. prof., 1979-87, E.C. Norton prof. classics and philosophy, 1987—, chair dept. classics, 1992—. Author: Socrates and Plato, A Comprehensive Bibliography, 1958-1973, 1978, Plato's Meno, 1986, Principles and Proofs: Aristotle's Theory of Demonstrative Science, 1992, Philosophy Before Socrates, 1994, A Presocratics Reader, 1996, Cicero, De Natura Deorum I, 1997, Simplicius, On Aristotle's Physics, book 8, chpts. 6-10, 2001, Philoponus on Aristotle's Posterior Analytics, Book 1, chpts. 1-8, 2008; contbr. articles on Greek philosophy, math. and scis. Marshall Aid Commemoration Commn. scholar, U. Oxford, 1966-69, Fulbright Sr. scholar, 1999, Overseas Vis. scholar St. John's Coll., Cambridge, 1999; Woodrow Wilson Found. fellow, 1966-67; NEH grantee, 1975, 85, 90, 98, 2004. Mem. Am. Philol. Assn., Soc. Ancient Greek Philosophy, Phi Beta Kappa. Office: Pomona Coll Dept Classics 140 W 6th St Claremont CA 91711-4301 Business E-Mail: rmckirahan@pomona.edu.

MCKISSOCK, DAVID LEE, retired manufacturing company executive; b. Boston, Mar. 27, 1933; s. Allan and Elizabeth (Lee) McK.; m. Diana Parish, Sept. 1, 1956; children: David Lee Jr., Christopher Lee. BA, Middlebury Coll., 1955. Salesman Am. Flange and Mfg. Co., NYC, 1957-62, asst. to v.p. sales Linden, NJ, 1962-64, salesman rip cap closures, 1964-73, v.p. rip cap closures, 1973-89, also bd. dirs. With USNR, 1955-57. Mem. Rumson Country Club, Seabright Lawn Tennis and Cricket Club. Republican. Unitarian Universalist. Avocations: tennis, golf, platform tennis. Home: 20 Hance Rd Fair Haven NJ 07704-3210 Personal E-mail: dlmpaddle@aol.com.

MCKITTRICK, WILLIAM WOOD, lawyer; b. Mt. Carmel, Ill., July 11, 1915; s. Lafe E. and Mary Lynn (Wood) McK.; m. Carolyn Lenne Davis, Dec. 19, 1942; children: Lynn McKittrick Pond, Bruce W. AB, DePauw U., 1936; JD, Northwestern U., 1939. Bar: Ill. Assoc. Pope & Ballard, Chgo., 1939-48, ptnr., 1948-52; atty. Office Gen. Counsel, Panama C.Z., 1942; ptnr. Vedder, Price, Kaufman & Kammholz, Chgo., 1952-95; lectr. on labor law Northwestern U. Sch. Law, Chgo., 1961-62. Case note editor, mem. editorial bd. Ill. Law Rev., 1938-39. Life trustee Orchestral Assn. of Chgo. Symphony Orch., 1980—, Chgo. Symphony Musicians Pension Trust, 1987-98; bd. dirs. Am. Symphony Orch. League, 1986-93, mem. exec. com., 1988-91; trustee Newberry Libr., Chgo., 1984-98, life trustee, 1998—, exec. com., 1989-98; vice chmn. exec. bd. Libr. Coun., Northwestern U., 1984-96; chmn. Friends of Ryerson & Burnham Librs., Art Inst. Chgo., 1988-90, mem. com. on librs., 1982—. Lt. USNR, 1943-45, PTO. Recipient Svc. award Northwestern U., 1968. Mem. ABA, Ill. Bar Assn., Chgo. Bar Assn. (lectr. various programs 1940-70, bd. mgrs. 1961-63), Lawyers Club of Chgo., Univ. Club (Chgo.), Caxton Club of Chgo. (v.p. 1982-83, pres. 1983-85). Home: The Clare At Water Tower Apt 3905 55 EastPearson St Chicago IL 60611 Home Phone: 312-867-0053, 312-867-0035.

MCKIZZIE, ROBERT R., economics professor; s. Robert Lee and Alice Lee McKizzie; m. Barbara M. Monmouth, Aug. 7, 1971; children: Courtney Annise Buzbee, Corey Antoinette. BS, Tex. Wesleyan U., Ft. Worth, 1973; MBA, LeTourneau U., Longview, Tex., 2000; EdD, Nova Southeastern U., Davie, Fla., 2007. Cert. life and health agent Tex., 1980. Coord. economic dept. Tarrant County Coll., 2003—07, pres., 2004, ch. EAP, 2004—08, dept. chair, 2007, prof. economics Arlington, Tex., 2000—, North lake Coll., Irving, Tex., 2004—, Tex. Christian U., Ft. Worth, 2006—. Lead advisor Beta Delta Omicron Chpt.-Phi Theta Kappa Internat. Honor Soc., Arlington, 2003—04; dir. Arlington Ind. Sch. Dist. Edn. Found., 2005—08; mem. cc adv. com. U. North Tex., Dallas, 2006—07. Recipient award, Nat. Inst. Staff and Orgnl. Devel., Austin, Tex., 2006, Nom. Chl. Exem. Tchg. award. Office: Tarrant County Coll-SE 2100 Southeast Pky Arlington TX 76018 Business E-Mail: robert.mckizzie@tccd.edu.

MCKLENSHAW, IRVIN LEE, retired small business owner, advocate; b. Waco, Tex., June 12, 1945; s. Irvin Nicholas McKlenshaw, Jr. and Evelyn Lucile (Maycumber) McKlenshaw.; m. James William Kershaw, Jr., July 1, 2008; children: Michael Boyd, Irvin Lee Jr., Laura Ann, Paul Nicholas, Richard Lester. Attended, El Camino Coll., 1961—63, U. Southern Calif., 1962—66; student, Fullerton Coll., 1998, student, 2004—06; attended in Psychology and Sociology, Orange Coast Coll., 2005; BA in Math., Calif. State U., Fullerton, 1970, postgrad. in Bus. Adminstrn., 1976; postgrad. in Religion, Summit Sch. Theology, Denver, 1982—84. Cert. in nat. security mgmt. Indsl. Coll. Armed Forces, Washington, 1974. Engring. lab. asst. Rockwell Internat. Corp., Anaheim, Calif., 1967-68, test data analyst, 1968-70, mem. tech. staff, 1970-82; sys. programmer A-Auto-trol Tech. Corp., Denver, 1982-84; sr. tech. writer, editor Colo. Data Systems, Inc., Englewood, Colo., 1986-87; sr. tech. writer CDI Corp., Arvada, Colo., 1987-88; staff cons. CAP GEMINI AM., Englewood, 1989; sr. tech./instrnl. writer & editor TTS Inc., Aurora, Colo., 1990-96, sr. multimedia developer, 1996-97; info. processing technician County of Orange, Health Care Agy., Santa Ana, Calif., 1998—2002; vol. The David Bohnett Cyber Ctr., The Ctr. Orange County, Garden Grove, Calif., 2002—04; owner, gen. mgr., writer, editor, proofreader, tutor McClendon Profl. Svcs., Garden Grove, Calif., 2004—06; engring. writer III CalComp subs. Lockheed Co., Hudson, NH, 1987; film crew assoc. AMC 30 Theatres, The Block, Orange, Calif., 2006—; writer Am. Resume Ctr., Northglenn, 1997—98; gen. mgr., chief editor Berkeley Group, LLC, Denver, 1997—99; copy editor Orange County and Long Beach Blade, Laguna Beach, 2003—04; asst. project mgr. Social Sci. Rsch. Ctr. Calif State U., Fullerton, 2005—06. Sec. governing bd. Yorba Linda Libr. Dist., 1973-78; mem. Calif. State U. and Coll. Statewide Alumni Coun., 1976-77, Adams County Rep. Ctrl. Com., 1984-90, Denver County Rep. Ctrl. Com., 1992-95, Men Alive, Orange County Gay Men's Chorus, 2004-06, Soulforce, Orange County, 2004-, Cmty. United Methodist Ch., Huntington Beach, Calif, 2005-; trustee Ch. of God (Seventh Day), Bloomington, Calif., 1979-81, treas., 1980-81; 2d v.p. Orange County chpt. Calif. Spl. Dists. Assn., 1976, pres., 1977; tech. support adviser to chmn. Colo. Rep. Com., 1997-98; tutor English and math. Fullerton Coll.'s Disability Support Svcs., 2004-05; sec. bd. dirs. The Friendly Ctr., Inc., 2005-06; mem.-at-large Calif.-Pacific Ann. Conf. Bd. Church and Soc., 2005-, dist. dir. Santa Ana, 2009 With USAFR, 1967—71. USAF Nat. Merit scholar, 1963-67. Mem. Calif. Assn. Libr. Trustees and Commrs. (exec. bd., Southern Calif. rep. 1976-78), Nat. Eagle Scout Assn. (life), Bible Sabbath Assn. (life), Calif. State U.-Fullerton Alumni Assn. (dir. 1975-77), Parents, Families and Friends of Lesbians and Gays (Orange County chpt., vol. 1988-, vol. panelist, Orange County and Long Beach spkrs. bureau panelist 2001-). Republican. Home Phone: 714-554-2195. Office Fax: 714-554-2274. Personal E-mail: leeingg2@aol.com.

MCKNEELY, JOEY, choreographer; Performer: (Broadway plays) Starlight Express, 1987, Roza, 1987, Carrie, 1988, Jerome Robbins' Broadway, 1989, She Loves Me, 1993; choreographer (Broadway plays) Smokey Joe's Cafe, 1995, The Life, 1997, Twelfth Night, 1998, On the Town, 1998, The Wild Party, 2000, The Boy from Oz, 2003, West Side Story, 2009, (TV films) Far East, 2001, (films) Zoolander, 2001.*

MCKNIGHT, CARL PHILLIP, psychologist; b. Bogota, Colombia, Jan. 20, 1969; (parents Am. citizens); s. Elwin D. and Elsa V. McKnight; m. Susan A. Kasparrow, July 18, 1998; children: Christopher children: Angela. BS, Tex. A&M U., 1991; MA, Stephen F. Austin State U., 1995; PsyD, Pepperdine U., 2000. Lic. psychologist Calif. Bd. Psychology. Pediatric psychologist Children's Hosp. Orange (Calif.) County, 2001—06; project behavioral psychologist Med. Ctr. U. Calif., Irvine, 2003—06; clin. psychologist II L.A. County Dept. Mental Health, 2006—08, sr. cmty. mental health psychologist, 2008—. Cons. St. Joseph's Hosp., Orange, 2005—06. Contbr. columns in mags. Mem. childhood obesity steering com. Children and Families Commn. Orange County, Irvine, Calif., 2002—04. Lt. USAR, 1990—98. Pediatric and Clin. Child Psychology fellow, Children's Hosp. L.A. and U. So. Calif. Sch. of Medicine, 1999—2001. Mem.: APA, Soc. Pediatric Psychology. Achievements include development of pilot psychological screening and treatment program for morbidly obese children and adolescents. Office: Los Angeles County DMH 550 S Vermont Ave 12th Fl Los Angeles CA 90020 Office Phone: 313-738-2866. Business E-Mail: cmcknight@dmh.lacounty.gov.

MCKNIGHT, JOSEPH WEBB, lawyer, educator, historian; b. San Angelo, Tex., Feb. 17, 1925; s. John Banning and Helen Katherine (Webb) McK.; m. Julia Ann Dyer, July 20, 1957 (dec. Jan. 1972); children: John Banton, Joseph Adair; m. Mildred Katherine Virginia Payne, Aug. 9, 1975 BA, U. Tex., Austin, 1947, Oxford U., Eng., 1949, BCL, 1950, MA, 1954; LLM, Columbia U., NYC, 1959. Bar: Tex. 1951, U.S. Ct. Appeals (5th cir.) 1982. Assoc. Cravath, Swaine & Moore, NYC, 1951-55; asst. prof. So. Meth. U., Dallas, 1955-57, assoc. prof., 1957-63, prof. law, 1963—, acad. dean, 1977-80, Larry and Jane Harlan faculty fellow, 1991—. Vis. prof. various univs. Gen. editor Creditors' Rights in Texas, 1963, History of the Texas Supreme Court, 1998—; author: (with William A. Reppy, Jr.) Texas Matrimonial Property Law, 1983, 11th edit. 2007-08; contbr. articles to profl. jours. Pres., Tex. Old Missions and Forts Restoration Assn., 1977-79, 99-2001; bd. dirs. San Jacinto Mus. History Assn., 1976-99; exec. coun. Tex. State Hist. Assn., 1988-91, fellow, 2004; bd. trustees Tex. Supreme Ct. His. Soc., 1990-; dir. History of Tex. Supreme Ct. History Project, 1998-. Lt. USNR, 1942-47 Rhodes scholar, 1947-50; James Kent fellow Columbia Law Sch., 1958-59; Academico, Acad. Mexicana de Derecho Internat., 1988, Hall of Legends, State Bar of Texas Fam. Law Sec., 1997. Fellow, Soc. for Advanced Legal Studies (London), 1998; mem. ABA, State Bar Tex., Dallas Bar Assn., Tex. Bar Found. (v.p. 1959), Nat. Legal Aid and Defenders Assn. (bd. dirs. 1963-66), Selden Soc., Am. Soc. Legal History (v.p. 1967-68, bd. dirs. 1967-75), Inst. Texan Cultures (exec. bd. 1990-95), Oxford and Cambridge Club (London), Sigma Chi. Democrat. Episcopalian. Office: So Meth U Law Sch 3315 Daniel Ave Dallas TX 75275-0116 Home Phone: 214-361-0894; Office Phone: 214-768-2591, 214-768-3851. Business E-Mail: jmcknigh@smu.edu.

MCKNIGHT, LEE HOLLAND, literature and language professor; b. Austin, Tex., Jan. 7, 1940; s. David Nmi and Louise Hewitt McKnight; life ptnr. Yael Banai, Apr. 11, 1962; 1 child, Richard Jonathon Banai. MA, U. Ala., Tuscaloosa, 1977. Instr. to prof. Stillman Coll., Tuscaloosa, 1986—. Vestryman Canterbury Episcopal Chapel, Tuscaloosa, 1986—. Capt. USAF, Key West, Fla., 1963—67, Danang, Vietnam. Mem.: MLA. Democrat. Episcopalian. Business E-Mail: lmcknight@stillman.edu.

MCKNIGHT, PATRICK E., medical educator, consultant; b. Sacremento, July 5, 1966; s. Andrew D. McKnight; m. McKnight M. McGovern, Mar. 15, 1992; 1 child, Patrick A. BS, U. Notre Dame, Ind., 1988; MS, U. Ariz., Tucson, 1991, PhD, 1997. Health svcs. rschr. Puget Sound VA Health Care Sys., Seattle, 1998—2000; rsch. asst. prof. U. Washington, Seattle, 1998—2000, U. Ariz., 2000—05; asst. prof. George Mason U., Fairfax, Va., 2005—. Rsch. cons. Pub. Interest Rsch. Svcs., Fairfax, 1992—. Mem.: AAAS, Assn. Psychol. Sci., Am. Evaluation Assn. Home: 9548 Old Creek Dr Fairfax VA 22032 Office: George Mason Univ 4400 Univ Dr MSN 3F5 Fairfax VA 22030-4444 Business E-Mail: pem@alumni.nd.edu, pmcknigh@gmu.edu.

MCKNIGHT, ROBERT B., JR., sporting goods manufacturing executive; BS, Univ. So. Calif. Co-founder, bd. dir. Quiksilver Inc., Huntington Beach, Calif., 1976—, pres., 1979—91, chmn., CEO, 1991—2008, chmn., pres., CEO, 2008—. Office: Quiksilver Inc 15202 Graham St Huntington Beach CA 92649

MCKONE, BRENDA KAY, elementary school educator, coach; b. Savanna, Ill., May 29, 1958; d. Ronald Allan and Gloria Luane Wilcke; m. Michael William McKone, July 25, 1992; children: Sarah Kaye, Nathan Michael. BA, Loras Coll., Dubuqe, Iowa, 1980; MA, Franciscan U., Clinton, Iowa, 2005. Nat. bd. cert. tchr. Nat. Bd. Profl. Tchg. Stds. Tchr., head volleyball coach E. Ctrl. Cmty. Schs., Miles/Sabula, Iowa, 1980—, tchr. quality com., 2007—, dist. leader, 2008—. Negotiations team E. Ctrl. Edn. Assn., Miles/Sabula, 1985—; mem. tech. com. E. Ctrl. Schs., Miles/Sabula, 1990—, tchr. induction mentor, 2000—. Local coord. Jump Rope for Heart Am. Heart Assn., Sabula, Iowa. Named Volleyball Coach of the Yr., Big East Conf. Coaches, 1985, 2002, Iowa NE Dist. Coach of the Yr., Dist. Coaches, 2001. Mem.: Clinton Country Club Golf. Presbyterian. Avocation: golf. Office: E Ctrl Cmty Sch 706 Broad St Sabula IA 52070 Business E-Mail: bmckone@east-central.k12.ia.us.

MCKONE, TIMOTHY P., lobbyist, telecommunications industry executive; b. Phoenix; m. Joey McKone; children: Ally, Sam, Jack. Dir. govt. affairs Ind. Ins. Agents of America; joined Southwestern Bell, 1993; lobbyist, ptnr. Davis, Manafort & Freedman, Inc., Arlington, Va., 1998—99; lobbyist, sr. v.p. congl. affairs SBC Comm., Inc., 1999—2005; lobbyist, exec. v.p. fed. rels. AT&T Svcs., Inc., 2005—. Dir. congl. rels. presdl. campaign Bob Dole Rep. Nat. Conv., San Diego, 1996. Named one of Best in the Bus., The Hill, 2007. Republican. Office: AT&T Corp Hdqs 175 E Houston San Antonio TX 78205 Business E-Mail: timothy.mckone@att.com.*

MCKOWEN, DOROTHY KEETON, educator, librarian; b. Bonne Terre, Mo., Oct. 5, 1948; d. John Richard and Dorothy (Spoonhour) Keeton; m. Paul Edwin McKowen, Dec. 19, 1970; children: Richard James, Mark David. BS, Pacific Christian Coll., 1970; MLS, U. So. Calif., 1973; MA in English, Purdue U., 1985, PhD, 2003. Libr.-specialist Doheny Libr., U. So. Calif., LA, 1973-74; asst. libr. Pacific Christian Coll., 1974-78; serials cataloger Purdue U. Librs., 1978-88; head children's and young adult svcs. Kokomo-Howard County Pub. Libr., Ind., 1988-89, coord. children's and tech. svcs. Ind., 1989-91; cataloger, network libr. Ind. Coop. Libr. Svcs. Authority, 1991-2001. Mem. adj. faculty Ivy Tech. C.C. of Ind., 2001—; lectr. Purdue U., 2003—. Mem. ALA, MLA, Nat. Coun. Tchrs. English (former mem. soc.), Soc. Early Americanists, Assn. for Libr. Collections and Tech. Svcs. (bd. dirs. 1986-90, 95-96, vice chair, chair-elect coun. of regional groups 1986-88, chair 1988-90, conf. program com. 1986-88, internat. rels. com. 1986-88, micropub. com. 1986-87, subject analysis com., membership com. 1988-90, planning and rsch. com. 1988-90, chair program initiatives com. 1991-93, orgn. and bylaws com. 1991-92, 99-2001), Network OCLC Svc. Mgrs. (MARC Task Force 2000-01), Ind. Coun. Libr. Automation (bibliog. stds. task force), Ind. Libr. Fedn. (chair tech. svcs. divsn. 1984-85), Ohio Valley Group Tech. Svcs. Libr. (chmn. 1985-86). Republican. E-mail: mckowens2@yahoo.com.

MC KOY, BASIL VINCENT CHARLES, theoretical chemist, educator; b. Trinidad, Wis., Mar. 25, 1938; came to U.S., 1960, naturalized, 1973; s. Allan Cecil and Doris Augusta McK.; m. Anne Ellen Shannon, Mar. 18, 1967; 1 son, Christopher Allan. B.Chem., Dalhousie U., 1960; PhD in Chemistry (Univ. fellow), Yale U., 1964. Instr. chemistry Calif. Inst. Tech., 1964-66, asst. prof. chemistry, 1966-69, asso. prof., 1969-75, prof. theoretical chemistry, 1975—, chmn. of faculty, 1985-87. Cons. Lawrence Livermore Lab., U. Calif., Livermore, 1974—, Inst. Def. Analysis, 1984—; vis. prof. Max Planck Inst., Munich, Ger., 1976—, U. Paris, 1968—, U. Campinas, Brazil, 1976—; lectr. Nobel Symposium, Goteborg, Sweden, 1979. Contbr. articles to Jour. Physics, London, chem. Physics Lettters, Phys. Rev., Jour. Chem. Physics; bd. editors; Chem. Physics Jour., 1977-79, mem. adv. editoral bd., 1992—; co-editor: Electron-Molecule and Photon-Molecule Collisions, 1979, 83, Swarm Studies and Inelastic Electron-Molecule Collisions, 1986; co-author: Electron-Molecule Collisions and Photoionization Processes, 1982. Recipient medal Gov.-Gen. Can., 1960; Alfred P. Sloan Found, fellow, 1969-73; Guggenheim fellow, 1973-74 Fellow Am. Phys. Soc. Home: 3855 Keswick Rd La Canada Flintridge CA 91011-3945 Office: Calif Inst Tech Divsn Chemistry Pasadena CA 91125-0001 Office Phone: 626-395-6545. Business E-Mail: mckoy@caltech.edu.

MCKOY, JUNE MARCIA, medical educator, researcher, lawyer; d. Josephine McKoy. MD, So. Ill. U., Springfield, 1989; MBA student, Kellogg Sch. Mgmt. Bar: Ill. Supreme Ct. 2002; lic. in internal medicine Am. Bd. Internal Medicine, 1997, in geriatric medicine Am. Bd. Internal Medicine, 2002. Gen. surgery intern U. Ill., Chgo., 1989—90, gen. surgery resident, 1990—93, internal medicine resident, 1993—95; attending physician Humana Healthcare, Chgo., 1995—98, Adv. Healthcare, Chgo., 1998—99; clin. instr. Northwestern U., Chgo., 2001—04, asst. prof. medicine, 2004—. Clin. cancer rschr. Northwestern U., 2003—. Author: (poetry) The Letter, 2002. Mem. Leadership Greater Chgo., 2005, Housing Opportunities Maintenance for Elderly, Chgo., 2007; mem. pres. circle Chgo. Coun. Global Affairs, 2008. Recipient 2nd Pl. Essay Contest award, DePaul U. Ctr. Black Diaspora, 2001, Excellence award, DePaul U. Coll. Law, 2000, Harold Wash. Profl. Achievement award, Roosevelt U., 2006, Career Devel. award, Nat. Cancer Inst., 2008—; grantee Rsch. grant, 2003—08; fellow Northwestern U., 2000—01; Rsch. fellow, Leadership Greater Chgo., 2005, Reynolds Scholar, Duke U. Divsn. Geriat., 2006, Disability Ethics Scholar, Rehab. Inst. Chgo., 2006—07, Billings fellow, Inst. Medicine Chgo., 2006—. Fellow: Am. Geriatric Soc.; mem.: Robert H. Lurie Comprehensive Cancer Ctr., Leadership Greater Chgo. (life; bd. mem. 2005), Am. Cancer Soc., Delta Omega Honor Soc. Achievements include research in geriatric cancer aimed at decreasing adverse drug events. Office: Northwestern Univ 645 N Michigan Ave Ste 630 Chicago IL 60611 Business E-Mail: j-mckoy@northwestern.edu.

MCKUSICK, VINCENT LEE, retired chief justice, arbitrator, lawyer, mediator; b. Parkman, Maine, Oct. 21, 1921; s. Carroll Lee and Ethel (Buzzell) McK.; m. Nancy Elizabeth Green, June 23, 1951; children: Barbara McKusick Liscord, James Emory, Katherine McKusick Ralston, Anne Elizabeth. AB, Bates Coll., 1943; SB, SM, MIT, 1947; LLB, Harvard U., 1950; LLD, Colby Coll., 1976, Nasson Coll., 1978, Bates Coll., 1979, Bowdoin Coll., 1979, Suffolk U., 1983; LHD, U. So. Maine, 1978, Thomas Coll., 1981. Bar: Maine 1952. Law clk. to Chief Judge Learned Hand, 1950-51; to Justice Felix Frankfurter, 1951-52; partner Pierce, Atwood, Scribner, Allen & McKusick and predecessors, Portland, Maine, 1953-77; chief justice Maine Supreme Jud. Ct., 1977-92; of counsel to Pierce Atwood LLP (formerly Pierce, Atwood, Scribner, Allen, Smith, & Lancaster), 1992—. Mem. adv. com. rules civil procedure Maine Supreme Jud. Ct., 1957-59, chmn., 1966-75, commr. uniform state laws, 1968-76, sec. nat. conf., 1975-77; mem. Conf. Chief Justices, 1977-92, bd. dirs., 1980-82, 91-92, pres.-elect, 1989-90, pres., 1990-91. standing com. past pres., 1992—; dir. Nat. Ctr. for State Ctrs., 1988-89, chmn.-elect, 1989-90, chmn., 1990-91; spl. master U.S. Supreme Ct. Conn. v. N.H., 1992-93, La. v. Miss., 1994-96, Kans. v. Nebr., 1999-2003; spl. master Mass. S.J.C. Liquidation Am. Mutual Liability Ins. Co., 1995-96; leader Am. Judges Del. to China, 1983, USSR, 1988, U.S. State Dept. Rule of Law Del. to Republic of Ga., 1992; mem. permanent com. Oliver Wendell Holmes Devise, 1993-2001. Author: Patent Policy of Educational Institutions, 1947, (with Richard H. Field) Maine Civil Practice, 1959, supplements, 1962, 67, (with Richard H. Field and L. Kinvin Wroth) 2d edit., 1970, supplements, 1972, 74, 77; also articles in legal publs. Trustee emeritus Bates Coll.; mem. adv. com. on pvt. internat. law US State Dept., 1980-85, Fed.-State Jurisdiction com., Jud. Conf. of US, 1987-89. With AUS, 1943-46. Recipient The Maine prize U. Maine Sys., 1993, Benjamin E. Mays award Bates Coll., 1994, Big M award Maine State Soc. Washington, 1995, Paul C. Reardon award Nat. Ctr. for State Ctrs., 1999. Fellow Am. Bar Found. (bd. dirs. 1977-87), Am. Philos. Soc. (coun. 1990-96, 97-02, v.p. 2002-05); mem. ABA (chmn. fed. rules com. 1966-71, bd. editors jour. 1971-80, chmn. 1976-77, mem. study group to China 1978, house dels. 1983-87, coun. sr. lawyers divsn. 1997-01), Maine Bar Assn., Cumberland County Bar Assn., Am. Arbitration Assn. (bd. dirs. 1994-2006), Am. Judicature Soc. (dir. 1976-78, 92-98), Am. Law Inst. (coun. 1968—2008), Maine Jud. Coun. (chmn. 1977-92), Inst. Jud. Adminstrn., Supreme Ct. Hist. Soc. (trustee 1994-2006), Rotary Club (hon., past pres. Portland club), Phi Beta Kappa, Sigma Xi, Tau Beta Pi. Republican. Unitarian Universalist. Home: 1152 Shore Rd Cape Elizabeth ME 04107-2115 Office: 1 Monument Sq Portland ME 04101-1110 Office Phone: 207-791-1100. Personal E-mail: judgemac@maine.rr.com. Business E-Mail: vmckusick@pierceatwood.com.

MCLACHLAN, C. IAN (CHARLES MCLACHLAN), state supreme court justice; b. Norwalk, Conn., June 2, 1942; s. Charles Joseph and Margaret Lynn (Hefferan) McL.; m. Carol Ann Broughton, Apr. 6, 1968 (div. Nov. 1978); children: Andrew J., Karen E., Graham C.; m. Bonnie Louise Morgan, July 7, 1979. BSBA, Georgetown U., 1964; LLB, Fordham Law Sch., 1967. Bar: NY 1967, Conn. 1968. Assoc. Cummings & Lockwood, Stamford, Conn., 1969-76, ptnr., 1976-79, Berkowitz,

Balbirer & McLachlan, Westport, Conn., 1979-83, Cummings & Lockwood, 1983-86, Greenwich, Conn., 1986-89, Hartford, Conn., 1990—96; judge Conn. Superior Ct., 1996—2003, Conn. Appellate Ct., 2003—09; assoc. justice Conn. Supreme Ct., 2009—. Contbr. articles to profl. jours. Pres. Buttonmill Pond Assn., Easton, Conn. Served through sgt. USMC. Mem. ABA (tax sect. domestic rels. 1990-92), Am. Acad. Matrimonial Lawyers (pres. Conn. chpt. 1987-89, gov. Chgo. 1989-93, counsel 1993-94), Conn. Bar Assn. (chmn. family law sect. 1979-81). Avocation: gardening. Office: Conn Supreme Ct 231 Capitol Ave Hartford CT 06106 Office Phone: 860-757-2200.*

MCLACHLIN, BEVERLEY, Canadian supreme court chief justice; b. Pincher Creek, Alta., Can., Sept. 7, 1943; m. Roderick McLachlin (dec. 1988); 1 child, Angus; m. Frank E. McArdle, Feb. 1992. BA, U. Alberta, MA in Philosophy, 1968, LLB, 1968; LLD (hon.), U. Alta., 1991, U. B.C., 1990, U. Toronto, 1995, York U., 1999, Law Soc. Upper Can., 2000, U. Ottawa, 2000, U. Calgary, 2000, Brock U., 2000, Simon Fraser U., 2000, U. Victoria, 2000, U. Alberta, 2000, U. Lethbridge, 2001, Bridgewater State Coll., 2001, Mt. St. Vincent U., 2002, U. PEI, 2002, U. Montreal, 2003, U. Man., 2004, Queen's U., Belfast, 2004, Dalhousie U., 2004, Carleton U., 2004, U. Ft. Kent, Maine, 2005, Ateneo de Manila U., 2006. Bar: Alberta 1969, B.C. 1971. Assoc. Wood, Moir, Hyde and Ross, Edmonton, Alta., Canada, 1969—71, Thomas, Herdy, Mitchell & Co., Fort St. John, B.C., Canada, 1971—72, Bull, Housser and Tupper, Vancouver, 1972—75; from lectr. to prof. U. B.C., 1974—81; appointed to County Ct., Vancouver, 1981; justice Supreme Ct. of B.C., 1981—85, B.C. Ct. of Appeal, Canada, 1985—88; chief justice Supreme Ct. of B.C., Canada, 1988; justice Supreme Ct. Can., Ottawa, Ont., Canada, 1989—2000, chief justice Can., 2000—. Chairperson adv. coun. Order of Canada; chairperson bd. gov. Nat. Judicial Inst.; mem. Privy Coun. Canada. Co-author: B.C. Supreme Court Practice, B.C. Court Forms, Canadian Law of Arch. and Engring.; contbr. articles to profl. jours. Office: Supreme Ct Bldg 301 Wellington St Ottawa ON Canada K1A 0J1 Office Phone: 613-992-6940.

MCLAFFERTY, FRED WARREN, chemist, educator; b. Evanston, Ill., May 11, 1923; s. Joel E. and Margaret E. (Keifer) McLafferty; m. Elizabeth E. Curley, Feb. 5, 1948; children: Sara L., Joel P., Martha A., Samuel A., Ann E. BS, U. Nebr., 1943, DSc (hon.), 1983, MS, 1947; PhD, Cornell U., 1950; DSc (hon.), U. Liege, Belgium, 1987, Purdue U., 1995. Fellow U. Iowa, 1949-50; rsch. chemist, divsn. leader Dow Chem. Co., 1950-56; dir. Eastern Rsch. Lab., 1956-64; prof. chemistry Purdue U., 1964-68, Cornell U., 1968-92, Peter J.W. Debye prof. chemistry emeritus, 1992—. Chem. sci. and tech. bd., numerical data adv. bd., bd. Army sci. tech., bd. radioactive waste mgmt. NRC; chem. co-chmn. World Bank's Chinese Univ. Devel. Project. Author: Mass Spectrometry of Organic Ions, 1963, Mass Spectral Correlations, 2d edit., 1981, Interpretation of Mass Spectra, 4th edit., 1993, Tandem Mass Spectrometry, 1983, Advances in Analytical Chemistry and Instrumentation; (with C.N. Reilley), Vols. 4-7, 1967-70, Index and Bibliography of Mass Spectrometry, (with J. Pinzelik), 1967, Atlas of Mass Spectral Data; (with E. Stenhagen and S. Abrahamsson), 1969, Registry of Mass Spectral Data, 1974; (with D.B. Stauffer) Wiley/NBS Registry of Mass Spectral Data, 1989, Important Peak Index of Mass Spectral Data, 1991; editor: Accounts of Chemical Research, 1986-94; co-editor: (with E. Stenhagen and S. Abrahamsson) Archives of Mass Spectral Data, 1969-72. With AUS, 1942-45, ETO. Decorated Purple Heart, Combat Inf. badge, Bronze Star with 4 oak leaf clusters, Presdl. Unit citation; recipient Pitts. Spectroscopy award Spectroscopy Soc. Pitts., 1975, Gold medal U. Naples, 1989, Robert Boyle Gold medal Royal Soc. Chemistry, 1992, Bijvoet medal U. Utrecht, 1997, W.L. Evans award Ohio State U., 1987, Jaroslav Heyrovsky Gold medal Czech Acad. Scis., 1999, Guilio Natta Gold medal Italian Chem. Soc., 2000, Torbern Bergman medal Swedish Chem. Soc., 2001, Lavoisier medal French Chem. Soc., 2004; John Simon Guggenheim fellow, 1972, Overseas fellow Churchill Coll., Cambridge (Eng.) U., 1979. Fellow: AAAS, NAS, Am. Acad. Arts and Scis., N.Y. Acad. Scis.; mem.: Internat. Assn. Protein Structure and Analytical Proteomics (Pehr Edman award 2006), Italian Nat. Acad. Scis. XL (fgn.), Am. Inst. Chemists (Chem. Pioneer award 1996), Am. Soc. Mass. Spectrometry (founder, sec. 1957—58, Disting. Contbn. in Mass Spectrometry award 2003), Assn. Analytical Chemists (Anachem award 1985), Internat. Spectrometry Orgn. (Sir J.J. Thomson gold medal 1985), Am. Chem. Soc. (chmn. analytical chem. divsn. 1969, chmn. Midland sect. 1956, Northeastern sect. 1964, award chem. instrumentation 1971, award analytical chemistry 1981, Nichols medal N.Y. sect. 1984, Oesper award Cin. sect. 1986, award mass spectrometry 1989), Soc. Analytical Chemists (Pitts. Analytical Chemist award 1987, Pioneer Analytical Instrumentation award 1994), Alpha Chi Sigma, Phi Lambda Upsilon, Sigma Xi. Home: 103 Needham Pl Ithaca NY 14850-2120 Office Phone: 607-255-4699. Business E-Mail: fwm5@cornell.edu.

MCLAIN, CHIPPY A., language educator; b. Kingsport, Tenn., Apr. 7, 1973; s. Billy G. and Anna Louise McLain; m. Tina J. Gibson; 1 child, Ella Grace. MA, Tenn. Technol. U., 2000. Adj. instr. English NE State Tech CC, Blountville, Tenn., 1998—2001; assoc. prof. and head English dept. Walters State CC. Pres. Tenn. Assn. Devel. Edn., 2003—05. Composer (guitarist and vocalist): Bluegrass. Recipient Disting. Faculty Mem. award, Walters State CC, 2005—06. Mem.: TYCA-SE. Avocation: music. Office: Walters State Cmty Coll 500 S Davy Crockett Pkwy Morristown TN 37813 Business E-Mail: chippy.mclain@ws.edu.

MCLAIN, DONALD, engineering educator; b. Montgomery, La., Oct. 7, 1954; s. Richard and Clydel McLain; m. Suzanne Wilby, Aug. 27, 1977; children: Nicole, Angie Seacamp. AS, Grantham Coll. Engring., Slydell, La., 1995; M in Engring., Internat. Code Coun., 2007. Offshore electrician Penrod Drilling, Great Yarmouth, England, 1990—92; elec. supr. Santa Fe Drilling, Ahamd, Kuwait, 1992—2002, Pride Internat., Kome, Chad, 2003—07; instrumentation electronic instr. Victoria Coll., Tex., 2008—. Author: (novel) Bluewater Seven South from Alaska, Bluewater Seven Terror at Sea. Staff sgt. USAF, 1972—76. Office: Victoria Coll 2200 E Red River Victoria TX 77901 Business E-Mail: donald.mclain@victoriacollege.edu.

MCLAIN, PAUL KING, systems analyst; b. Bremerton, Wash., June 10, 1946; s. Paul Gaylon and Frances Marilyn McLain; m. Maureen Elizabeth Miner, Aug. 23, 1969 (div. Dec. 16, 1986); children: Paul Joseph, Andrew John; m. Donna Joan Miller, Nov. 19, 1988. BA in Psychology, U. Wash., 1973, BA in History, 1975; cert. in bus. computing, North Seattle CC, 1979; MDiv, Seattle U., 2002. Ordained min. Universal Life Ch. Warehouse clk. Seattle Transfer and Storage, 1969—70; returns supr. Transcontinental Music Co., Seattle, 1970—71; entry mgr. A. L. Tokin Custom Ho. Broker, Seattle, 1973—74; import adminstr. Eckert Overseas Agy., Seattle, 1974—76; warehouse and container terminal clk. Port of Seattle, 1976—79; sys. analyst Boeing Co., Seattle, 1979—2001; point-of-sale clk. Sinnett's Market Pl., Longview, Wash., 2004—05; sys. analyst Longview Fibre Co., Wash., 2005—. Presenter in field; lectr. in field. Actor: (musical) The Fantastics. Del. Dem. State Conv., Tacoma, 2004; mem. Cowlitz County Dem. Women's Club, 2003—06; treas. Aspire! for Unitarian Universalist Ministerial Candidates, Boston, 2000—01; pres. Saltwater Unitarian Universalist Ch., Kent, Wash., 1993—94; chpt. pres. Toastmasters Internat., Kent, Wash., 1988—89, area gov., 1989—90. With USN, 1965—69. Decorated Navy Unit Commendation (2) USN, Vietnam Svc. Medal (3), Republic of Vietnam Campaign medal Dept. of Def. Mem.: VFW, La. Vol. for Family and Cmty., Red River Jazz Band, Red River Heritage Assn., Dry Prunl Hist. Soc., Carlow Choir, Alexandria Unitarian Universalist Fellowship (pres. 2007—), Mensa. Liberal. Unitarian Universalist. Achievements include reduction of time required for work center loading system; design of webpage timeline. Avocations: digital video, computing, music. Home: PO Box 190 Dry Prong LA 71423-0190 Personal E-mail: uuseeker@earthlink.net.

MCLANE, CHARLES D., JR., metal products executive; b. Richmond, July 15, 1953; m. Betty McLane; 2 children. B in Acctg., Va. Commonwealth U., Richmond, 1978, M in Acctg., 1984. Various fin. positions including divsn. contr. Reynolds Metals, dir. fin. and adminstrn. Global Can bus. unit, 1990—95, asst. contr., 1995—99, asst. treas., 1999—2000; dir. investor rels. Alcoa, Inc., 2000—02, v.p. Bus. Support Svcs., corp. contr. NYC, 2002, CFO, 2007—. Mem. com. on corp. reporting Fin. Execs. Inst. Office: Alcoa Inc 390 Park Ave New York NY 10022 Office Phone: 212-836-2600.

MCLANE, DEREK, set designer; Set designer (Broadway plays) What's Wrong With This Picture?, 1994, Holiday, 1996, Summer and Smoke, 1996, Present Laughter, 1996, Three Sisters, 1997, London Assurance, 1997, Honour, 1998, The Women, 2001, The Look of Love, 2003, I Am My Own Wife, 2003 (Obie award, Village Voice, scenic design, 2004), Little Women, 2005, Barefoot in the Park, 2006, The Pajama Game, 2006, The Threepenny Opera, 2006, Lestat, 2006, Grease, 2007, 33 Variations, 2009 (Tony award, best scenic design of a play, 2009), (off-Broadway) Aunt Dan and Lemon, The Creadeux Canvas, What the Butler Saw, Servicemen, East is East, subUrbia, The Waverly Gallery, Hazelwood Jr. High, Troilus and Cressida, Hello Again, Saturday Night, Captains Courageous, Time and Again, Intimate Apparel (Lucille Lortel award, outstanding scenic design, 2005), Violet, The Voysey Inheritance, 2007 (Lucille Lortel award outstanding scenic design, 2007), (plays) The Rose Tattoo, Drowning Crow, Waiting for Godot, The Caretaker, Heartbreak House, Hedda Gabler, Misalliance, The Homecoming, Twelfth Night, The Father, A Touch of the Poet, Griller, Glengarry Glen Ross, The Libertine, Harmony (Drama-League award, 1997), The Visit, Abigail's Party, 2005, 10 Million Miles, 2007, (tours) South Pacific, Tallulah, Sunset Boulevard. Recipient Obie award, sustained excellence in scenic design, Village Voice, 1997, Michael Merritt award, 2003, Lucille Lortel award, 2004. Office: 306 W 38th St 3d Fl New York NY 10018 Office Phone: 212-629-0295. Office Fax: 212-279-0189. Business E-Mail: mcmcmclane@aol.com.*

MCLANE, FREDERICK BERG, lawyer; b. Long Beach, Calif., July 24, 1941; s. Adrian B. and Arlie K. (Burrell) McL.; m. Lois C. Roberts, Jan. 28, 1967; children: Willard, Anita. BA, Stanford U., 1963; LLB, Yale U., 1966. Bar: Calif. 1967, U.S. Dist. Ct. (cen. dist.) Calif. 1967. Assoc. prof. law U. Miss., Oxford, 1966-68; assoc. O'Melveny & Myers LLP, LA, 1968-74, ptnr., 1975—2005, of counsel, 2005—. Lectr. in field. Pres., bd. dirs. Legal Aid Found., L.A., 1974-83; deacon Congl. Ch., Sherman Oaks, Calif., 1979-83; vice-chair L.A. Music Ctr., Unified Fund, 1992-94; bd. dirs. Calif. Sci. Ctr. Found., 1991-2000. Mem.: ABA (banking com., fed. regulation of securities com.), Calif. Bar Assn. (fin. insts. com., uniform comml. codes), L.A. Country Club, The Quarry at La Quinta, Order of Coif. Avocations: golf, walking, reading. Office: O'Melveny & Myers LLP 1999 Ave of the Stars Los Angeles CA 90067-6035 Office Phone: 310-246-8554. Business E-Mail: fmclane@omm.com.

MCLAREN, BRIAN, pastor, Christian activist; b. 1956; m. Grace McLaren; 4 children. BA in English, U. Md., Coll. Park, 1978, MA in English, 1981; DD (hon.), Carey Theol. Sem., Vancouver, Can., 2004. English tchr., 1978—86; founding pastor Cedar Ridge Cmty. Ch., 1986—2006. Lectr. in field. Author: (novels) The Church on the Other Side, 1998, Finding Faith, 1999, A New Kind of Christian, 2001 (Merit award, Christianity Today, 2002), More Ready Than You Realize: Evangelism as Dance in the Postmodern Matrix, 2002, A Is for Abductive, 2002; co-author Adventures in Missing the Point, 2003, Church in Emerging Culture: Five Perspectives, 2003; author The Story We Find Ourselves In, 2003, A Generous Orthodoxy, 2004, The Last Word and the Word After That, 2005, The Secret Message of Jesus: Uncovering the Truth that Could Change Everything, 2006; contbr. articles to profl. jours including Leadership, Sojourners, Worship Leader, and Conversations. Named one of 25 Most Influential Evangelicals, Time Mag., 2005. Mem.: Orientacion Cristiana, Red Letter Christians, Sojourners/Call to Renewal, international steering team for Emergent Village. Evangelical. Avocations: fishing, art, ecology, hiking, kayaking, song writing, camping, literature. Office: Emergent Village PO Box 390104 Minneapolis MN 55439

MCLAREN, KYLE, professional hockey player; b. Humboldt, Sask., Can., June 18, 1977; m. Helga McLaren; children: Samantha, Madison, Aydan. Defenseman Boston Bruins, 1995—2003, San Jose Sharks, 2003—09, Phila. Flyers, 2009—. Named to All-Rookie Team, NHL, 1996. Office: Phila Flyers Wachovia Ctr 3601 S Broad St Philadelphia PA 19148*

MCLAREN, MARY, film company executive; Dir. fin. internat. video 20th Century Fox, 1991, sr. v.p. fin. and ops., exec. v.p. home entertainment internat., 1999, COO internat. theatrical and home entertainment. Named one of The 100 Most Powerful Women in Entertainment, Hollywood Reporter, 2007. Office: 20th Century Fox Film Corp 10201 W Pico Blvd Los Angeles CA 90064

MCLAREN, RICHARD WELLINGTON, JR., lawyer; s. Richard Wellington and Edith (Gillett) McL.; m. Ann Lynn Zachrich, 1971; children: Christine, Richard, Charles. BA, Yale U., 1967; JD, Northwestern U., 1973. Bar: Ohio 1973, Ill. 1997, US Dist. Ct. (no. dist.) Ohio 1973, US Dist. Ct. (no. dist.) Ill. 1997, US Ct. Appeals (6th cir.) 1978, US Ct. Appeals (7th cir.) 1997, US Ct. Appeals (fed. cir.) 1997, US Supreme Ct. 1981. Assoc. Squire, Sanders & Dempsey, Cleve., 1973-82, ptnr., 1983-87; prin., counsel Ernst & Whinney, Cleve., 1988-89; assoc. gen. counsel Ernst & Young, Cleve., 1989-93; prin. counsel Centerior Energy Corp., Cleve., 1994-96; prin. Welsh & Katz, Ltd., Chgo., 1997—2007; ptnr. Duane Morris, 2007—. 1st lt. US Army, 1967-70. Mem. ABA (litigation, intellectual property and corp. law), FBA, Am. Judicature Soc., Ohio Bar Assn., Ill. Bar Assn. Home: 638 S Monroe St Hinsdale IL 60521-3926 Office: 120 S Riverside Plz Fl 22 Chicago IL 60606-3913 Office Phone: 312-499-6754. Business E-Mail: rwmclaren@welshkatz.com, rwmclaren@doanemorris.com.

MCLARNEY-VESOTSKI, AMBER RENEE, psychology professor; b. NY; married. PhD in Behavioral Sci., U. Toledo, Ohio. Psychology instr. Alpena C.C., Mich., 2003—. Contbr. articles to profl. jour. Recipient Disting. Alumni award, Jamestown C.C., 2004. Mem.: Soc. Personality & Social Psychology. Office: Alpena Cmty Coll 665 Johnson St Alpena MI 49707 Business E-Mail: vesotska@alpenacc.edu.

MCLARNON, MARY FRANCES, neurologist; b. Montreal, Que., Canada, May 13, 1944; came to U.S., 1969; d. John Francis and Patricia Jessica (Dore) McL.; m. Malcolm Weiner, Dec. 21, 1975; m. Lawrence Zingesser, Oct. 12, 1982; children: Andrea, Eliza. BS, McGill U., 1965, MD, 1969. Intern St. Vincent's Hosp., NYC, 1969-70; fellow seizure unit Boston Children's Hosp., 1970-71; resident in neurology Albert Einstein Coll. Medicine, Bronx, N.Y., 1971-73; resident in radiology N.Y. Hosp.-Cornell Med. Ctr., NYC, 1973-76; pvt. practice. Home: 752 Cove Rd Mamaroneck NY 10543-4324 Office Phone: 917-856-8301. Personal E-mail: mmclmd@hotmail.com.

MCLARTY, MACK (THOMAS F. MCLARTY III), leasing company executive, former White House chief of staff; b. Hope, Ark., June 14, 1946; s. Thomas Franklin and Helen (Hesterly) McL.; m. Donna Kay Cochran, June 14, 1969; children: Mark Cochran, Franklin Hesterly BA, U. Arkansas, Fayetteville, 1968. Founder, pres. McLarty Leasing System Inc., Little Rock, 1969-79; pres. McLarty Cos., 1979-83; with Arkla Inc., Shreveport, from 1983, pres., CEO Arkla Gas divsn., 1983; pres., COO Arkla Gas divsn. Arkla, Inc., Shreveport, 1984, chmn., pres., CEO, 1985—93; chief of staff to Pres. The White House, Washington, 1993-94, sr. adv. to Pres., 1994—97, counselor to Pres., spl. envoy for Americas, 1994—97; pres. Kissinger McLarty Assocs., Washington, 1998—; vice chmn. Asbury Automotive Group, 2002—06; sr. adv. The Carlyle Group, Washington, 2003—; chmn. Asbury Automotive Ark. LLC, 2006—. Chmn. Arkla Energy Mktg. Co., Shreveport, La., Arkla Chem. Corp., Shreveport, AER-Ark. Gas Transit Co., Shreveport; chmn., CEO, Miss. River Transmission Corp., St. Louis, MRT Energy Mktg. Co., St. Louis, Ark. La. Fin. Corp., Shreveport; bd. dirs. Union Pacific Corp., 2006- Mem. Ark. Ho. of Reps., 1970-72; chmn. Ark. Dem. Com., 1974-76; treas. David Pryor Gubernatorial Campaign, 1974, Gov. Bill Clinton campaign, 1978; bd. dirs. Hendrix Coll., Conway, Ark.; bd. visitors U. Ark., Little Rock; former chmn. United Negro Coll. Fund Campaign, fund-raising campaign Ark. Symphony Recipient Humanitarian award, Nat. Conf. Christians & Jews, 1991, Fair Share award, NAACP, 1991, DSM, US Dept. State, Order of the Aztec Eagle. Mem. Greater Little Rock C. of C. (pres. 1983) Office: Kissinger McLarty Assocs 900 17th St NW Ste 800 Washington DC 20006-2511 also: The Carlyle Group 1001 Pennsylvania Ave Washington DC 20004

MCLAUCHLIN, VERA ANN, history professor; MA in Ednl. Leadership, Regent U., Virginia Beach, Va.; MA in Adult Edn., U. DC, Washington, 1983; MA in History, Old Dominion U., Norfolk, Va., 1994; EdD, Regent U., Virginia Beach, Va., 2006. Lic. postgrad. profl. Va., 2007, cert. in advanced grad. studies Regent U., Virginia Beach, 2004. Tchr. City Pub. Schs., Virginia Beach, 1985—; assoc. prof., history Tidewater CC, Virginia Beach, 1995—, dir., cmty. based program for tchrs. Dir. Cmty. Based Program Tchrs.; motivational spkr. Tidewater CC, 1996—; with Citywide Sch. Com. Closing Academic Achievement Gap Black Male. Contbr. articles to profl. jours. Recipient award, Oxford Roundtable Symposium on Diversity, 2007. Mem.: Nat. Sorority Phi Delta Kappa, Inc., Assn. Supervision and Curriculum Devel., Order Ea. Star, Zeta Phi Beta. Democrat. Baptist. Avocations: reading, travel.

MCLAUGHLIN, BARBARA LYN, elementary school educator; b. Watseka, Ill., Jan. 18, 1950; d. LaVerne Melvin and Marian Barbara (Borchers) Reitz; m. Steven Joseph McLaughlin, Oct. 7, 1972; children: Laurie Lyn Peterson, Lisa Kay Kolavennu, Angela Marie Erickson. BS in Edn., Ea. Ill. U., 1971; MA in Edn., Olivet Nazarene U., 1999. Std.Spl. Tchg.K-12 Ill., 1971, Std. Elem. Tchg.K-9 Ill., 1971. Kindergarten tchr. Danville Elem. Schs., Ill., 1971—72; first grade tchr. Clifton Elem., Clifton, Ill., 1972—73; substitute tchr. Ctrl. Unit Sch. Dist. 4, 1973—78; spl. edn. tchr. Chebanse Elem., Chebanse, Ill., 1978—. Chair spl. edn. dept. Ctrl. Unit Sch. Dist. 4, Clifton, Ill., 2000—, mentor spl. edn. dept., Chebanse, Ill., 2004—; mem. sch. improvement team Chebanse Elem., Ill., 1990—2002, 2005—, guest tchr., 2003—; online guest tchr. U. Wash., 2004—05. Contbr. chapters to books. Supporter Spl. Olympics. Recipient Disney Am. Tchr. award Honoree, Walt Disney Co., 2002-2003, Disting. Educator award, Ea. Ill. U., 2004;, First of Am. ednl. grantee, 2004, Ednl. scholar, Target, 1998. Mem.: Assn. Supervision and Curriculum Devel., Coun. for Exceptional Children, Pi Lambda Theta, Kappa Delta Pi (hon.), Delta Kappa Gamma (hon.; sec. 2000—04). Lutheran. Avocations: reading, conservation of natural resources, gardening, sports. Home: 440 East 3200 North Rd Clifton IL 60927 Office: Chebanse Elem 475 School Street Chebanse IL 60922 Personal E-mail: grove@dlogue.net.

MCLAUGHLIN, BERNARD JOSEPH, bishop emeritus; b. Buffalo, Nov. 19, 1912; Ordained priest Diocese of Buffalo, NY, 1935, aux. bishop, 1968—88, aux. bishop emeritus, 1988—; pastor Blessed Sacrament Parish, Buffalo; ordained bishop, 1969. Mem. US Conf. Cath. Bishops. Roman Catholic. Address: 1085 Englewood Ave Kenmore NY 14223-1901

MCLAUGHLIN, CALVIN STURGIS, biochemistry professor; b. St. Joseph, Mo., May 29, 1936; s. Calvin Sturgis and Agnes Jane McLaughlin; m. Chin Helen Moy, Sept. 7, 1960; children: Heather Chin Chu, Christine Leng Oy, Andrew Calvin Moy. BS, King Coll., 1958; postgrad., Yale U., 1958-59; PhD, MIT, 1964. Postdoctoral fellow Institut de Biologie Physico-Chimique, Paris, 1964-66; prof. biochemistry U. Calif., Irvine, 1966—, dir. Cancer Rsch. Inst., 1981-83; vis. prof. Sch. Botany Oxford U., Eng., 1976, 80. Mem. peer rev. panels Am. Cancer Soc., NSF, NIH, VA Contbr. numerous articles to profl. jours.; mem. editl. bds. Jour. Bacteriology, 1975-80, Exptl. Mycology, 1980-86; reviewer profl. jours. Bd. dirs. Am. Cancer Soc., Orange County, 1980-89; mem. Traffic Affairs Com., Newport Beach, Calif., 1972-78. Named Outstanding Tchr. U. Calif.-Irvine, 1978, Gabriel Lester Meml. Lectr. Reed Coll., 1979; fellow Rockefeller Found., 1958-59, Upjohn Found., 1959-60, Nutrition Found., 1960-61, NIH, 1961-64, Am. Cancer Soc., 1964-66 Mem.: Am. Soc. Biochemistry and Molecular Biology. Episc. Office: U Calif Irvine Dept Biol Chemistry Irvine CA 92697-1700 Office Phone: 949-824-5325. Business E-Mail: cal@uci.edu.

MCLAUGHLIN, CHARLOTTE, bank executive; 3 children. Mgr. global-rate risk-mgmt. products Mellon Fin. Services; with derivatives and fgn. exch. bus. PNC Fin. Services Group, Pitts., 1996—2002, pres., CEO capital markets, 2002—. Active United Way. Named one of 25 Most Powerful Women in Banking, US Banker mag., 2007, 2008. Office: PNC Fin Services Group USX Tower 600 Grant St Pittsburgh PA 15219*

MCLAUGHLIN, DAVID MICHAEL, lawyer; b. Palo Alto, Calif., May 11, 1961; s. William Thomas and Marlene Carol (Moreno) McL.; m. Tracey Lynn Sumits, Aug. 3, 1996; children: Lauren Nicole, Brendan Lee Adams, Katherine Marlene Jennison. BA in Econs., UCLA, 1983; JD, Santa Clara U., 1987. Bar: Calif. 1987, U.S. Dist. Ct. (no. dist.) Calif. 1987, U.S. Dist. Ct. (ea. dist.) Calif. 1988, U.S. Dist. Ct. (ctrl. dist.) Calif. 1996, U.S. Dist. Ct. (so. dist.) Calif. 2004, U.S. Dist. Ct. Ariz. 1996. Atty. Ropers, Majeski, Kohn & Bentley, Redwood City, Calif., 1988-94; shareholder Ropers, Majesti, Kohn & Bentley, Redwood City, Calif., 1995—. Judge pro tempore, panel arbitrator San

Mateo County Superior Ct., Redwood City, 1993—. Bd. dirs. S.S. Benefit, Saratoga, Calif., 1988-92. Fellow Litig. Counsel America, AV-Rating, Martindale-Hubbell; mem. San Mateo County Bar Assn. Avocations: golf, tennis, skiing, writing, travel. Office: Ropers Majeski Kohn Bentley 1001 Marshall St Redwood City CA 94063-2000 Office Phone: 650-780-1717, 650-364-8200. Office Fax: 650-780-1701. Business E-Mail: DMcLaughlin@rmkb.com. E-mail: dmclaughlin@ropers.com.

MCLAUGHLIN, FRANK E., nursing educator; b. Bklyn., Mar. 27, 1935; s. Edward Patrick and Anna (Barr) McL. BS, Adelphi U., 1959; MA, NYU, 1961; PhD, U. Calif., Berkeley, 1968. Lecturer U. Calif., San Francisco, 1961—64, asst. prof., 1968—72, coord. rsch. grad. programs, 1970—72, asst. clin. prof. Davis, 1972—80, assoc. clin. prof. San Francisco, 1975—2004; assoc. prof. San Francisco State U., 1981—84, prof., 1984—2004, assoc. dir. sch. nursing, 1996—2001, prof. emeritus, 2004—. Vis. prof. European Inst. of Med. and Health Rsch., U. Surrey, Inst. of Nursing, Sch. of Medicine, U. Wales, U.K., 1996. Edn. bd. (internat. jour. evaluation in clin. practice, UK). V.p. bd. trustees Cen. City Hospitality House, San Francisco, 1975-78; chmn. Mental Health Adv. Bd. San Francisco, 1979-85; bd. dirs. San Francisco Mental Health Assn., 1985-88. Recipient Outstanding Nurse Leadership award Golden Gate Nurses Assn., 1986. Fellow Am. Acad. Nursing; mem. ANA, Sigma Theta Tau. Avocations: opera, travel, cooking.

MCLAUGHLIN, GLEN, financial services company executive; b. Shawnee, Okla., Dec. 21, 1934; s. Champe and Mattie Bet (Jenkins) McL.; m. Ellen Marr Schnake, Aug. 29, 1964; children: Helen Elizabeth, Glen Wallace. BBA, U. Okla., 1956; MBA, Harvard U., 1964. Asst. treas. Foremost-McKesson, Inc., San Francisco, 1964-69; exec. v.p., dir. MacFarlane's Candies, Oakland, Calif., 1969-70; dir. fin. and adminstrn. Memorex Corp., London, 1970-71; sr. v.p. fin. Four-Phase Systems, Inc., Cupertino, Calif., 1971-82; pres., chmn. Four-Phase Fin., Inc., Cupertino, 1977-82; chmn. bd. Four-Phase Systems, Ltd., Toronto, Ont., Can., 1977-82, Four-Phase Systems Internat., Inc., 1977-82, DeAnza Ins. Co. Ltd., Cayman Islands, 1979-82; gen. ptnr. Matrix Ptnrs., L.P., San Jose and Boston, 1982-86; chmn. bd. Venture Leasing Assocs., 1986—2003; chmn. bd. dirs. Cupertino Nat. Bank, Calif., 1990-96; dir. Greater Bay Bancorp, E. Palo Alto, Calif., 1996—2007. Author: The Mapping of California as an Island, 1995. Served USAF 1956-62, USAFR 1964-65 (capt. and pilot), pres. Jr. Achievement Santa Clara County, 1978-79, chmn. bd., 1980-81; chmn. bd. Jr. Achievement Found. Santa Clara County, 1980-87; mem. bus. sch. adv. bd. U. Santa Clara, 1981-84; pres. Boy Scouts Am., Santa Clara County, 1986-87, mem. exec. coun., 1982—, pres. No. Calif. Area, 1988-91; pres. Boy Scouts Am. Meml. Found., 1991-95, mem. nat. adv. coun., 2000-06, chmn. 2003-06, nat. exec. bd., 2003-; mem. pvt. sector investment adv. panel City of San Jose, 1984-92; bd. visitors Sch. Acctg., Coll. Bus. Adminstrn., U. Okla., 1991-94, endowed chair in bus. ethics, 1997, bd. advs., 1998—, Regents award, 2001; trustee Gould Acad., Bethel, Maine, 1993-99, O'Connor Hosp. Found., San Jose, 1994-97; bd. dirs. Am. Cancer Soc., Santa Clara County, 1994-98, Libr. Congress Map Divn., Phillips Soc., 1995—, co-chair, 1998-2000; founding angel Band of Angels, Silicon Valley, Calif., 1995-2003. Recipient Silver Leadership award Jr. Achievement, 1981, Silver Beaver award Boy Scouts Am., 1985, Silver Antelope award Boy Scouts Am., 1990, Disting. Eagle Scout award Boy Scouts Am., 1994, Silver Buffalo award, 2003, pub. svc. citations Calif. State Senate, Calif. State Assembly, Santa Clara County Suprs.; named Freeman of London, 2006; Baden-Powell World fellow, 1986; decorated Order of St. John, 1989, admitted to the Livery, Worshipful Co. Glaziers and Painters Glass, 2008; inducted to Jr. Achievement Bus. Hall of Fame, 2003, Disting. Alumni award, Coll. Bus., 2008. Fellow Royal Geog. Soc.; mem. Fin. Execs. Inst., English Speaking Union, Commonwealth Club, Harvard U. Bus. Sch. Club, The Grolier Club, Roxburghe Club, Book Club Calif., Travelers' Century Club (100 Countries Visitor), Beta Gamma Sigma, Sigma Alpha Epsilon. Home: 155 El Pinar Los Gatos CA 95032-1147 Office Phone: 408-741-1607. Personal E-mail: vla@ix.netcom.com.

MCLAUGHLIN, HARRY ROLL, architect; b. Indpls., Nov. 29, 1922; s. William T. and Ruth E. (Roll) McL.; m. Linda Hamilton, Oct. 23, 1954. Registered Ind., Ohio, Ill., cert. Nat. Coun. Archtl. Registration Bds. Past pres. James Assocs. Inc., Indpls. Restorations include Old State Bank State Meml, Vincennes, Ind., Andrew Wylie House, Bloomington, Ind., Old Opera House State Meml, New Harmony, Ind., Old Morris-Butler House, Indpls. (Merit award 1972), Market St. Restoration and Maria Creek Baptist Ch., Vincennes, Benjamin Harrison House, Old James Ball Residence, Lafayette, Ind. (1st Design award 1972), Lockerbie Sq. Master Plan Park Sch., Indpls., Knox County Ct. House, Vincennes, 1972, J.K. Lilly House, Indpls., 1972, Waiting Station and Chapel, Crown Hill Cemetery, Indpls., 1972, Blackford-Condit House Ind. State U., Terre Haute, Indian houses Angel Mounds Archaeol. Site and Interpretative Ctr., Ind.; architect: Glenn A. Black Mus. Archaeology, Ind. U., Bloomington; Restoration Morgan County Ct. House, Indpls. City Market, Hist. Schofield House, Madison, Ind., Ernie Pyle Birthplace, Dana, Ind., Phi Kappa Psi Nat. Hdqrs, Indpls., 1980 (Design award), East Coll. Bldg, DePauw U., Greencastle, Ind., Pres.'s House Restoration, DePauw U., 1992; contbr. articles to profl. jours.; Illustrator: Harmonist Construction. Past chmn. bd., past pres., now chmn. emeritus Historic Landmarks Found., Ind.; bd. dirs., past archtl. adviser, bd. advisers Historic Madison, Inc.; mem. adv. coun. Historic Am. Bldgs. Survey, Nat. Park Svc., 1967-73; past mem. Ind. profl. rev. com. for Nat. Register nominations, 1967-81; past adv. bd. Conner Prarie Mus., Patrick Henry Sullivan Found.; past adviser Indpls. Historic Preservation Commn.; past mem. preservation com. Ind. U.; past mem. Meridian St. Preservation Commn., Indpls., 1971-2001; hon. mem. Ind. Bicentennial Commn.; bd. dirs. Park-Tudor Sch., 1972-85; past nat. bd. dirs. Preservation Action; life bd. dirs. Historic New Harmony; trustee Masonic Heritage Found.; past bd. dirs. Ind. Masonic Home, 1984-91, Inpls. Pub. Libr. Found., treas. 1988, 95—, v.p., 1989, pres. 1990; past trustee Eiteljorg Mus. Western Art, mem. adv. and planning com., 1999; past mem. Hamilton County Tourism Commn., 1989-91. Recipient Gov.'s citation State of Ind., 1967, Sagamore of Wabash award, 1967, 80, 82, Mayor's citation City of Indpls., 1972, Sec. Interior citation U.S. Dept. Interior, 1970, Design and Environ. citation, 1975, Citation of Spl. Merit, Park Tudor Sch., 1993, Disting. Achievement award Ball State U., 2004, Disting. Alumni award Orchard Sch., 2007, Eli Lilly Lifetime Achievement award Ind. Hist. Soc., 2007, Citation Appreciation for Vol. Svc. Indpls. Pub. Libr. Found., 2007. Fellow AIA (nat. com. historic bldgs., chmn. 1970); mem. Ind. Soc. Architects (state preservation coord. 1960-85, Biennial award 1972, Design award 1978), Nat. Trust Historic Preservation (past trustee, bd. advisers), Soc. Archtl. Historians (Wilbur D. Peat award Ctrl. Ind. chpt. outstanding contbns. to understanding and appreciation of archtl. heritage 1993, past bd. dirs., Disting. Achievement in Hist. Preservation award 2005), Indpls. Mus. Art. (trustee, chmn. bldgs. com., bd. govs. 1986-95), Zionsville C. of C. (hon. bd. dirs.), U.S. Capitol (hon. trustee), Ind. Hist. Soc. (pres. 1999, trustee 1989-99, bldg. com.), Marion County Hist. Soc. (past v.p., bd. dirs.), Zionsville Hist. Soc. (hon. life), Navy League U.S. (life), Ind. State Mus. Soc. (life), English Speaking Union (past bd. dirs. Indpls.), Hamilton County Hist. Soc. (life), Woodstock Club (bd. dirs. 1982-86, pres. 1985, ex-officio 1986), Literary Club Found. (trustee 1990-2007), Skyline Club (life), Packard Club, Masons (33 deg.). Home and Office: 950 W 116th St Carmel IN 46032-8864

MCLAUGHLIN, JAMES LEE, musician, director; b. Hillsboro, Ohio, Mar. 27, 1946; s. Robert Barker McLaughlin and Virgie Lee Prine-McLaughlin. BFA, Ohio U., Athens, 1968. Cert. music dir. West Ohio Conf. United Meth. Ch., 1973. Organist Hillsboro Ch. Christ, Ohio, 1960—64, First Christian Ch., Athens, 1964—68; tchr. vocal music Zanesville City Schs., Zanesville, 1968—99, dept. chair vocal music, 1991—99; dir. music Faith United Meth. Ch., 1968—86, Ctrl. Trinity United Meth. Ch., 1986—. Founder and dir. Optimists Boys Club Choir, 1981—92; pres. Thursday Music Club, Zanesville, Ohio, 1984—86, 1994—96, 2002—04; dir. music and condr. Zanesville Civic Chorus, 1993—; mem. and asst. condr. Y-City Barbershop Chorus, 2000—; organ recitalist; coach voice, piano, organ; accompanist. Performer: Robert Shaw Chorus. Advisor Virgie Lee McLaughlin Fund Found. Appalachian Ohio, 2002—; bd. dirs. So. Ohio Symphony Orch., New Concord, Ohio, 1974—76, Zanesville Concert Assn., 1979—, pres., 1981—84, booking agt., 2006—; bd. dirs. Katherine B. Geis Scholarship, 1991—. Named an Outstanding Educator, Phi Delta Kappa, 1999; scholar, Stewart-Glapat Company, 1999, Matha Holden Jennings Found., 1982—83. Mem.: Am. Guild Organists, Fellowship of United Meth. Musicians, Ohio Music Edn. Assn. (adjudicator 1993—, dist. 9 pres. 1988—90). Avocations: travel, philanthropy. Home: 413 Moore Ave Zanesville OH 43701-1234 Office: Ctrl Trinity United Meth Ch 62 S Seventh St Zanesville OH 43701 Office Phone: 740-453-1210.

MCLAUGHLIN, JEFFREY R., orthopedist, director; b. Balt., June 29, 1960; m. Sherri McLaughlin. MD, U. Md., Balt., 1986. Cert. ABOS, Wis., 1995. Dir. Kennedy Ctr. Hip and Knee, Oshkosh, Wis., 1995—. Mem.: AAOS, AAHKS. Office: Kennedy Ctr Hip and Knee 2700 W 9th Ave Ste 125 Oshkosh WI 54904

MCLAUGHLIN, JOHN EDWARD, former federal agency administrator; b. McKeesport, PA, June 15, 1942; married; 2 children. BA, Wittenberg U., 1964; MA, Johns Hopkins U., 1966; postgrad., SAIS Ctr., Bologna, Italy, U. Pa. With CIA, 1972—2004, with US Dept. State, Bur. European & Can. Affairs, 1984—85, deputy dir. Office European Analysis, 1985—89, dir. European analysis, 1989, dir. Slavic and Eurasian analysis, 1989—95, acting chmn. Nat. Intelligence Coun., 1995—97, dep. dir. intelligence, 1997—2000, dep. dir., 2000—04, acting dir., 2004; non-resident sr. fellow Brooking Instn., Washington, 2005—; sr. fellow, Philip Merrill Ctr. for Strategic Studies John Hopkins U., Washington, 2005—; adv. on nat. security CNN, 2005—. With US Army, 1966—69.

MCLAUGHLIN, JOHN F., pediatrician, educator; b. DesMoines, Iowa, Sept. 28, 1944; s. Daniel J. and Genevieve S. McLaughlin; m. Suzanne Rossire; children: Matthew Ian, Emily Margaret. BA, Yale U., New Haven, Conn., 1966; MD, Northwestern U. Med. Sch., Chgo., 1970. Cert. pediatrician Am. Bd. Pediat., 1978, devel. behavioral pediatrician 2002, in neurodevel. disabilities 2002. Asst. prof., pediat. U. Wash., Seattle, 1979—84, assoc. prof., pediat., 1984—95, prof., pediat., 1995—, dir., clin. tng. unit, ctr. human devel. and disability, 1997—. Dir., neurodevel. program Seattle Children's Hosp., 1979—2007, chief, spasticity mgmt. program, 1990—. Contbr. scientific papers (Richmond Cerebral Palsy award, 1996). Maj. Air Force, 1973—75, Edwards AFB. Fellow: Am. Acad. Pediat.; mem.: Assn. U. Ctrs. Disability, Am. Acad. Cerebral Palsy and Devel. Medicine (pres. 1992, Richmond Cerebral Palsy Award 1991, 1998), Soc. Devel. and Behavioral Pediat. Avocation: art. Office: Univ WA Box 357920 1959 NE Pacific St Seattle WA 98195 Business E-Mail: jfmcl@u.washington.edu.

MCLAUGHLIN, JOHN J., broadcast executive, television producer, journalist, political commentator; s. Augustus Hugh and Eva Philomena (Turcotte) McLaughlin; m. Ann Dore Lauenstein, Aug. 23, 1975 (div. 1992); m. Cristina Vidal, June 22, 1997. AB, Boston Coll., 1951, MA in Philosophy, 1952, BDiv, 1959, MA in English Lit., 1961; PhD, Columbia U., NYC, 1967. Ordained priest Roman Catholic Ch., 1960. Mem. Jesuit Order, NE, NY, Washington; resigned order and active ministry, 1975; tchr., dir. comm. Fairfield U. & Preparatory Sch., Conn., 1960-64; assoc. editor America Mag., NYC, 1967-70; speech writer, dep. spl. asst. to Pres. Richard Nixon and Gerald Ford, Washington, 1971-74; pres. McLaughlin & Co. Pub. Policy Cons., Washington, 1975-79; radio talk-show host Sta. WRC-AM, Washington, 1979-82; creator, prodr., host The McLaughlin Group, 1982—, John McLaughlin's One On One, 1984—; host McLaughlin, CNBC, 1989—94. Washington editor, columnist 'From Washington Straight' Nat. Review mag., 1981—89. TV appearances include Cheers, 1990, Murphy Brown, 1995, Lateline, 1998, film appearances: Dave, 1993, Mission Impossible, 1996, Independence Day, 1996, Murder at 1600, 1997, Bulworth, 1998, Shattered Glass, 2005, War, Inc., 2007. Rep. candidate US Senate, RI, 1970. Recipient Excellence in Journalism award, Cath. Press Assn., 1969, News Media award, VFW, 1984. Mem.: NATAS, Screen Actors Guild, Am. Fedn. TV & Radio Artists. Office: 1717 Rhode Island Ave NW Ste 640 Washington DC 20036 Office Phone: 202-457-0870. E-mail: jmclaughlin@mclaughlin.com.*

MCLAUGHLIN, JOHN SHERMAN, lawyer; b. Pitts., Apr. 1, 1932; s. John H. and Dorothy I. (Schrecongost) McL.; m. Suzanne Shaver, June 5, 1971; children: Dorothy, Sarah, Martha. AB, Harvard U., 1954, LLB, 1957. Bar: Pa. 1958, U.S. Supreme Ct. 1967. Assoc. Reed, Smith, Shaw & McClay, Pitts., 1957-71, ptnr., 1971—2002, of counsel, 2002—. Trustee Harmarville Rehab. Ctr., Inc., 1980-87; pres., trustee Western Pa. Sch. for the Deaf, 1985—; pres. Pa. NG Assn., 1976-78; justice of peace Borough of Edgewood, 1963-73; trustee Winchester Thurston Sch., 1987-2002; life trustee Carnegie Libr. of Pitts., Carnegie Inst., 1994—, Carnegie Mus. Art, 1997—; dir. Pitts. Symphony, 1985-95, adv. 1996-99; emeritus coun. mem. Scotch Irish Soc. USA. Lt. col. Air NG, 1957-79. Mem.: Am. Coll. Trust and Estate Counsel, Allegheny County Bar Assn., Am. Law Inst., Duquesne Club. Office: Reed Smith Ctr 225 5th Ave Ste 1200 Pittsburgh PA 15222 Home Phone: 412-731-7195. Business E-Mail: jmclaughlin@reedsmith.com.

MCLAUGHLIN, JOSEPH, lawyer; b. Newark, Aug. 1, 1941; s. Joseph Nicholas and Genevieve Veronica (Lardiere) McL.; m. Elisabeth Lippold, July 31, 1965; children: Elisabeth Rogers, Jessica Lierzer, Emilie McLaughlin AB, Columbia U., 1962, LLB, 1965. With Sullivan & Cromwell, NYC, 1968-76; v.p., gen. counsel Goldman, Sachs & Co., 1976-88, cons., 1988-90; ptnr. Sidley Austin LLP, NYC, 1993—. Adj. prof. law NYU, 1988-92; dir. Am. Coun. on Germany, 2008-; spkr., presenter in field. Author (with C.J. Johnson Jr.): Corporate Finance and the Securities Laws, 4th edit., 2006, Supplement, 2008; contbr. articles to profl. jours. Trustee Greenwich (Conn.) Acad., 1988-2000; treas. Presbyn. Ch. Old Greenwich, 1988-91; bd. dirs. United Way, Greenwich, 1993-97; mem. Rep. Town Com., Greenwich, 1993-96. Jervey fellow Parker Sch. Fgn. Comparative Law, Columbia Law Sch., U. Munich, 1966-68. Mem. ABA (sect. bus. law, fed. regulation securities com., subcom. broker-dealer matters 1985—, subcom. civil litigation and SEC enforcement matters 1989—, chair task force rule 10b-6 1995-97, co-chair task force sellers' due diligence and similar defenses under fed. securities laws 1989-92), Am. Law Inst., Assn. of Bar of City of NY (internat. law com. 1979-84, chair 1981-84, civil rights com. 1984-87, internat. arms control and security affairs com. 1988-90), NY Stock Exch. (legal adv. com. to bd. govs. 1985-88, subcom. corp. governance, subcom. internat. issues 1988—), Securities Industry Assn. (fed. regulations com. 1978-88, chair 1982-84), Nat. Assn. Securities Dealers, Inc. (corp. financing com. 1983-86), Am. Arbitration Assn. (dir. 1986-90). Republican. Congregationalist. Office Phone: 212-839-5312. Business E-Mail: jmclaughlin@sidley.com.

MCLAUGHLIN, JOSEPH MICHAEL, federal judge; b. Bklyn., Mar. 20, 1933; s. Joseph Michael and Mary Catherine (Flanagan) McLaughlin; m. Frances Elizabeth Lynch, Oct. 10, 1959; children: Joseph, Mary Jo, Matthew, Andrew. AB, Fordham Coll., 1954, LL.B., 1959; LL.M., NYU, 1964; LL.D., Mercy Coll., White Plains, NY, 1981; LLD, Fordham U., 1998. Bar: NY 1959. Assoc. Cahill, Gordon, NYC, 1959—61; prof. law Fordham U., NYC, 1961—71, dean Sch. of Law, 1971—81, adj. prof., 1981—90; judge US Dist. Ct. Eastern Dist. NY, Bklyn., 1981—90, US Ct. Appeals (2nd cir.), NYC, 1990—98, sr. judge, 1998—. Adj. prof. St. John's Law Sch., NYC, 1982—97; chmn. NY Law Revision Commn., Albany, 1975—82. Author (with Peterfreund): New York Practice, 1964; author: Evidence, 1979; editor-in-chief: Fed. Practice Guide; contbr. articles to profl. jours. Capt. Corps of Engineers US Army, 1955—57, Korea. Mem.: ABA, NY State Bar Assn., Assn. of Bar of City of NY, Lotos Club. Roman Catholic. Office: US Courthouse US Ct Appeals 40 Foley Sq Rm 2402 New York NY 10007-1502*

MCLAUGHLIN, LAVERNE LANEY, library director; b. Fort Valley, Ga., July 29, 1952; d. John Laney and Gladys Laney (deceased); m. Frederick McLaughlin; 1 child, Frederick Laney. BA, Spelman Coll., Atlanta, 1974; MLS, Atlanta U., 1975; PhD, Kennedy Western U., Thousand Oaks, Calif., 2003. Cert. libr. Ga., 2008. Head tech. svc. libr., assoc. prof. Ga. Southwestern State U., Americus, 1976—98; dir. libr. Albany State U., Albany, Ga., 1998—. Tchr. Byron Elem. Sch., Ga., 1975—76. Author: (book) Service Learning: A Teaching Design, Freshman Seminar & Service to Leadership, Albany State University Life Skills. Steering com. mem. Civil Rights Digital Libr., Athens, 2005—08. Named Outstanding Young Women of Am., 1981—82; fellow, Andrew Mellon Found., 1974—75. Mem.: Nat. Alumnae Assn. Spelman Coll., Beta Phi Mu, Alpha Kappa Alpha, Inc. Home: 536 East Jefferson St Americus GA 31709 Office: Albany State Univ 404 College Dr Albany GA 31705 Office Fax: 229-430-4803. Business E-Mail: laverne.mclaughlin@asurams.edu.

MCLAUGHLIN, LEIGHTON BATES, II, retired journalist, reporter, educator; b. Evanston, Ill., Apr. 10, 1930; s. Leighton Bates and Gwendolyn I. (Markle) McL.; m. Beverly Jean Jeske, May 5, 1962; children: Leighton Bates III, Jeffrey, Steven, Patrick. Student, Kenyon Coll., Gambier, Ohio, 1948-50, Northwestern U., 1951; BA in English Lit., UCLA, 1983; MA in Comms., Calif. State U., Fullerton, 1990. Copyboy, reporter, rewriteman City News Bur., Chgo., 1957-58; reporter, rewriteman Chgo. Sun-Times, 1958-62; rewriteman, asst. city editor Ariz. Jour., Phoenix, 1962; reporter Miami (Fla.) Herald, 1962-64; successively rewriteman, night city editor, 1st asst. city editor, telegraph editor Chgo. Sun-Times, 1964-74; dir. Chgo. Daily News/Sun-Times News Service, 1974-79; editorial coord. electronics newspaper div. Field Enterprises, 1975-79; adminstr. reference libr. and communications ctr. Field Newspapers, 1976-79; editor News Am. Syndicate, Irvine, Calif., 1979-85; mng. editor San Gabriel Valley Daily Tribune, 1986; assoc. prof. journalism Riverside (Calif.) C.C., 1987-96, chmn. performing arts and media dept., 1993-96, coll. publs. editor, ret., 1996-99; lectr. in journalism Calif. State U.-Fullerton, 1984-96. Copy editor The Press-Enterprise, Riverside, Calif., 1988-95; lectr., condr. seminars in field. Author articles in field. Served to 1st lt. USMC, 1951-54. Recipient Stick-o-Type award for best feature story Chgo. Newspaper Guild, 1961, Best News story award Ill. AP and UPI, 1967 Mem. Chgo. Journalists Assn., Verban Soc., Psi Upsilon. *Reporting the news is like any other intellectual activity in that it involves research, verification, organization, and clarity of presentation. But news reporting is unique in that all this is done on a dead run, in time for the day's editions.*

MCLAUGHLIN, MARGARET BROWN, adult education educator, writer; b. Miami Beach, Fla., Aug. 24, 1926; d. J. Clifford and Grace Lindsey (DuPre) Brown; m. Francis Edward McLaughlin, Oct. 30, 1982 (dec.). BA cum laude, U. Miami, 1946; MA, Duke U., Durham, NC, 1949; PhD, Tulane U., New Orleans, 1976. Instr., lectr. in English U. Miami, Coral Gables, Fla., 1946-47, 56-61, 73-91, 2000; English tchr. Narimasu Am. Sch., Tokyo, 1963-65; asst. prof. Manchester Coll., North Manchester, Ind., 1965-67; instr. Miami-Dade C.C., 1977, 81; dir. writing workshop for fgn. students U. Miami Sch. Medicine, 1991-92; adj. prof. English, Asian and liberal studies and Osher Lifelong Learning Inst., Fla. Internat. U., Miami, Fla., 1997—; instr. humanities Barry U., Miami, 2004. Prodr. Dade County Cable TV series Caribbean Writers and Their Art, 1991; prodr., host cable tv series Haiti Cherie, 1993-94. Contbr. articles to popular Japanese and U.S. mags. and newspapers; contbr. play reviews to Internet pub. Trustee Mus. Sci., Miami, 1977-78. Mem. Am. Lit. Assn. (Henry Adams Soc.), Egyptology and Asian Civilizations Soc. Miami (bd. dirs., pres. 1976-78, 83-85), South Fla. Internat. Press Club (bd. dirs., scholarship chmn. 2002—), South Fla. Writers' Assn.(bd. dirs., pub. rels. dir., 2009-). Avocations: writing, travel, editing. Home and Office: 1621 S Bayshore Dr Miami FL 33133-4201 Office Phone: 305-858-7224. Personal E-mail: margaretj711@comcast.net.

MCLAUGHLIN, MARY A., Federal Judge; b. Phila., 1946; BA, Gwynedd-Mercy Coll., Gwynedd Valley, Pa., 1968; MA, Bryn Mawr Coll., Pa., 1969; JD, U. Pa., 1976. Law clk. to Hon. Stanley Brotman US Dist. Ct. NJ, 1976—77; assoc. Arnold & Porter, Washington, 1977—80; asst. US atty. US Atty.'s Office DC, 1980—84; asst. prof. Vanderbilt U. Sch. Law, 1984—86; litig. ptnr. Dechert, Price & Rhoads, Phila., 1986—2000; adj. prof. U. Pa. Law Sch., 1988, Rutgers U. Sch. Law, 1989; chief counsel subcom. on terrorism, tech. and govt., com. on the judiciary US Senate, 1995; judge US Dist. Ct. (ea. dist.) Pa., 2000—. Bd. chair Women's Law Project. Office: US Dist Ct Eastern Dist Pa US Courthouse 601 Market St Rm # 13614 Philadelphia PA 19106-1723*

MCLAUGHLIN, MICHAEL J., lawyer; BA in Polit. Sci., cum laude, Boston Coll., 1994; JD, U. Mich., 1999. Lic. real estate broker Mass. Law clk. Superior Ct. Mass., 1999—2000; atty. Goodwin Procter LLP, Boston, 2000—05; ptnrs. Lerner & Holmes PC, Boston, 2005—. Recipient Golden Hammer award, Habitat for Humanity Greater Boston, Inc., 2003. Office: Lerner & Holmes PC Ste 415 Two Center Plaza Boston MA 02108 Office Phone: 617-443-9470. Office Fax: 617-443-9471. E-mail: mmclaughlin@lh-law.com.

MCLAUGHLIN, PATRICK J., lawyer; b. 1947; BA summa cum laude, U. Minn., 1971, JD magna cum laude, 1975. Bar: Minn. 1975. Ptnr., banking, trial practice groups, chair, corp. trust svcs. group Dorsey & Whitney LLP, Mpls. Gen. counsel Minn. Police Relief Assn. Lectr. in field. Office: Dorsey & Whitney LLP Ste 1500 50 S Sixth St Minneapolis MN 55402-1498 Office Phone: 612-340-2975. Office Fax: 612-340-2643. Business E-Mail: mclaughlin.patrick@dorsey.com.

MCLAUGHLIN, PATRICK MICHAEL, lawyer; b. Monahans, Tex., July 23, 1946; s. Patrick John and Ann (Donnelly) M.; m. Christine Manos, Aug. 21, 1970; children— Brian Patrick, Christopher Michael, Conor Andrew B Gen. Studies, Ohio U., 1972; JD, Case We. Res. U., 1976. Bar: Ohio 1976, U.S. Dist. Ct. (no. dist.) Ohio 1978, U.S. Ct. Appeals (6th cir.) 1979, U.S. Supreme Ct. 1980; U.S. Dist. Ct. (so. dist.) Ohio 1989, U.S. Ct. Appeals (5th cir.). Dir. vets. edn. project. Am. Assn. Cmty. and Jr. Colls., Washington, 1972—73; law clk. Common Pleas Ct., Cleve., 1976—77; law clk. to judge 8th Jud. Dist. Ct. of Appeals, Cleve., 1977—78; asst. U.S. atty. No. Dist. Ohio, Cleve., 1978—82, chief civil divsn., 1982—84, U.S. atty. Cleve., 1984—88; ptnr. Janik & McLaughlin, Cleve., 1988—89, Mansour, Gavin, Gerlack & Manos Co., LPA, Cleve., 1989—97; apptd ind. spl. prosecutor Ohio Attys. Gen., 1993—96; mng. ptnr. McLaughlin & McCaffrey, LLP, Cleve., 1997—. Cons. Nat. League of Cities, U.S. Conf. Mayors, 1971-72; co-creator Opportunity Fair for Veterans Concept, 1971 Editor-in-chief Case Western Res. Jour. Internat. Law, 1975-76 Chmn. North Ohio Drug Abuse Task Force, 1986-88; chmn. Law Enforcement Coordinating Commn., North Ohio, 1985-88; chmn. civil issues subcom. Atty. Gen.'s Adv. Com., 1986-88; exec. v.p. Greater Cleve. Vets. Meml., Inc., 1993, pres., 1994—. Decorated Silver Star, Bronze Star, Purple Heart, Army Commendation medal, Vietnamese Cross of Gallantry with Silver and Bronze Stars; named to Ohio Vets. Hall of Fame, 2003, Ohio Mil.Hallwhi of Fame for Valor, 2004, Best Lawyers in America Comml. Litig. & White Collar Criminal Def., 2007-09, Ohio Super Lawyer, 2004-09, Americas Leading Lawyer Chambers US, 2004-09, award Litig. & White Collar Crime & Govt. Investigations, Ohio, 2008-09. Fellow Am. Coll. Trial Lawyers (Ohio Super Lawyer 2004-08); mem. ABA, FBA, Ohio Bar Assn., Cleve. Bar Assn., Nat. Assn. Former U.S. Attys. (dir. 2006-09), Soc. 1st Divsn., 18th Inf. Regiment Assn., Order of Ahepa, Vietnam Vets. Am., Nat. Vietnam Vets. Network (Disting. Vietnam Vet. award 1985), Nat. Assn. Concerned Vets. (nat. v.p. external affairs 1971-72, exec. dir. 1972-73), Cuyahoga County Vets. (award 1985), Nat. Soc. SAR (law enforcement commendation medal 1989), Judge John Manos Inn of Ct. (master bencher, pres. 2005-), Nat Bd. Trustees, Am. Inns Ct.(trustee) Republican. Roman Catholic. Office: McLaughlin & McCaffrey LLP Eaton Ctr 1111 Superior Ave Ste 1350 Cleveland OH 44114-2500 Office Phone: 216-623-0900. Business E-Mail: pmm@paladin-law.com.

MCLAUGHLIN, PHILIP VANDOREN, JR., mechanical engineering educator, researcher, consultant; b. Elizabeth, NJ, Nov. 10, 1939; s. Philip VanDoren and Ruth Evans (Landis) McL.; m. Phoebe Ann Feeney, Aug. 19, 1961; children: Philip VanDoren III, Patrick Evans, Christi M. Barton. BSCE, U. Pa., 1961, MS in Engring. Mechanics, 1964, PhD in Engring. Mechanics, 1969. Assoc. engr. Boeing-Vertol, Morton, Pa., 1962-63, engr. II, 1963; rsch. engr. Scott Paper Co., Phila., 1963-65, rsch. project engr., 1965-69, sr. rsch. project engr., 1969; asst. prof. theoretical and applied mechanics U. Ill., Urbana, 1969-73, asst. dean engring., 1971-72; project mgr. Materials Scis. Corp., Blue Bell, Pa., 1973-76; assoc. prof. mech. engring. Villanova U., Pa., 1976-81, prof., 1981—2003, prof. emeritus, 2003—. Cons. Naval Air Engring. Ctr., Lakehurst, NJ, 1977-79, US Steel Corp., Trenton, 1980-82, RCA Corp., Moorestown, NJ, 1986, Coal Tech Corp., Merion Station, Pa., Air Products and Chems., Inc., Allentown, Pa., 1988, Aircraft divsn. Naval Air Warfare Ctr., Patuxent River, Md., 1995-96, Christini Technologies, Phila., 1999—, Alpha Sci. Corp., Southeastern, Pa., 2000-01, Materials Rsch. & Design, Inc., Rosemont, Pa., 2002-, DETechs., King of Prussia, Pa., 2002—; vis. prof. dept. engring. U. Cambridge, Eng., 1990-91. Reviewer: for sci. and tech. jours.; contbr. numerous articles to profl. jours. Rsch. grantee NSF, 1970-72, Naval Air Engring. Ctr., 1978-84, Lawrence Livermore Nat. Lab., 1979-81, Naval Air Devel. Ctr., 1985-86, RCA Corp., 1986-87, Materials Scis. Corp., 2003-05; sr. rsch. assoc. NRC, Washington, 1983-84; USN-Am. Soc. for Engring. Edn. sr. faculty fellow, 1995. Mem.: ASME (life; chmn. applied mechanics divsn. Phila. sect. 1981—83, materials divsn. com. on composites 1992—2003), ASCE (life; chmn. engring. mechanics divsn. com. on inelastic behavior 1977—79, assoc. editor Jour. Engring. Mechanics Divsn. 1977—79, aerospace divsn. com. on structures and materials 1986—95), Am. Soc. Composites, Am. Soc. Engring. Edn., Am. Acad. Mechanics, Sigma Xi. Achievements include research and consulting on composite materials and structures, structural analysis and design and inelastic behavior. Office: Villanova U Dept Mech Engring 800 Lancaster Ave Villanova PA 19085-1681 Office Phone: 610-291-2023. Business E-Mail: philip.mclaughlin@villanova.edu.

MCLAUGHLIN, ROBERT S., lawyer; b. NYC, Sept. 15, 1950; s. Robert V. and Marjorie C. McLaughlin; m. Suzan A. Messer, Aug. 19, 1978; children: Christine A., Carolynn E., Courtney M. BA in Biology, Syracuse U., NY, 1972; MS in Biology, SUNY, Buffalo, 1976; JD summa cum laude, Syracuse U., NY, 1978. Bar: DC 1979, NY 1988, US Dist. Ct. (no. dist.) NY. Atty. Kirkland & Ellis, Washington, 1979—80; atty. advisor US EPA, Washington, DC, 1980—88; atty. Bond, Schoeneck & King, PLLC, Syracuse, 1988—92, ptnr., 1992—. Mem.: ABA, Onondaga County Bar Assn., DC Bar Assn., NY State Bar Assn. (mem. exec. com. 1988—98, 2004—, co-chair pesticides com. 1988—93, co-chair hazardous waste and toxic substances regulation com. 1993—98, co-chair internet coordinating com. 2004—). Avocations: photography, hiking, mountain climbing, skiing. Office: Bond Schoeneck & King PLLC One Lincoln Ctr Syracuse NY 13202 Office Phone: 315-218-8100. E-mail: rmclaughlin@bsk.com.

MCLAUGHLIN, SYLVIA CRANMER, volunteer, environmentalist; b. Denver, Dec. 24, 1916; d. George Ernest and Jean Louise (Chappell) Cranmer; m. Donald Hamilton McLaughlin, Dec. 29, 1948; children: Jean Katherine McLaughlin Shaterian, George Cranmer McLaughlin. AB, Vassar Coll., 1939. Co-founder Save San Francisco Bay Assn., Berkeley-Oakland, Calif., 1961-99, pres., 1993-95. Mem. waterfront adv. com. City of Berkeley, Calif., 1964—68; sec., bd. dirs. Resource Renewal Inst., 1989—, Citizens for East Shore State Pks., 1984—2005, Citizens for East Shore Pks., 2005—; founder, bd. dirs. Pub. Trust Group, Oakland, Calif., 1997—; mem. awards com. Berkeley Cmty. Fund, 1998—; mem. adv. bd. Greenbelt Alliance, San Francisco, 1982—; mem. nat. adv. coun. Trust for Pub. Land, San Francisco, 1986—, Ecocity Builders, Berkeley, 1990—; bd. dirs. Ptnrs. for Liveable Cmtys., Washington, 1975—78. Mem. Nat. Aubudon Soc. (bd. dirs. 1970-76), Nat. Recreation and Parks Assn. (bd. dirs. 1974-78), East Bay Conservation Corps (bd. dirs. 1985-97), Student Conservation Assn. (bd. dirs. 1979-84), Nat. Leadership Coun. Trust for Pub. Land, Save Strawberry Canyon (co-founder, bd. dirs. 2008-). Avocations: reading, travel, environmental causes. Home: 1450 Hawthorne Ter Berkeley CA 94708-1804

MCLAUGHLIN, T. MARK, lawyer; b. Salem, Mass., Apr. 20, 1953; s. Terrence E. and Mary E. (Donlon) McL.; m. Sandra L. Roman, Oct. 16, 1982; children: Daniel, Kathleen, Eileen. BA in Econs., U. Notre Dame, 1975, JD, 1978. Bar: Ill. 1978, U.S. Dist. Ct. (no. dist.) Ill. 1978, U.S. Dist. Ct. (cen. dist.) Ill. 1992, U.S. Dist. Ct. (ea. dist.) Wis. 1992, U.S. Ct. Appeals (7th cir.) 1982, U.S. Ct. Appeals (11th cir.) 1982, U.S. Ct. Appeals (8th cir.) 1998. Assoc. Mayer Brown LLP, Chgo., 1978-84, ptnr., 1985—. Adj. faculty law Loyola U., Chgo., 1983, 86-90. Bd. dirs. no. Ill. affiliate Am. Diabetes Assn., Chgo., 1985-94. Mem. ABA (franchising forum com. antitrust law sect.), Phi Beta Kappa. Office: Mayer Brown LLP 71 S Wacker Dr Chicago IL 60606-4637 Home Phone: 708-246-4234; Office Phone: 312-701-7066. Business E-Mail: mmclaughlin@mayerbrown.com.

MCLAUGHLIN, THOMAS KEITH, diversified financial services company executive; BS in Bus., Calif. State U., Northridge. CPA Grant Thornton, 1980—85; fin. analyst Countrywide Fin. Corp., Calabasas, Calif., 1986—87, treas. Countrywide Home Loans, 1989—96, mng. dir. fin., 1997—2000, CFO, 2000—, sr. mng. dir., 2001—. Office: Countrywide Fin Corp 4500 Park Granada Calabasas CA 91302-1613

MCLAUGHLIN, VERONICA, psychologist; d. Russell and Marilyn McLaughlin. PhD, U. Calif., Riverside, 2002. Cert. PPS Calif., 2001. Sch. psychologist CJUSD, Colton, Calif., 2001—07, MVUSD, Moreno Valley, 2007—. Office: Moreno Valley Unified Sch Dist 25634 Alessandro Blvd Moreno Valley CA 92553

MCLAUGHLIN, WILLIAM IRVING, space technical manager, writer; b. Oak Park, Ill., Mar. 6, 1935; s. William Lahey and Eileen (Irving) McL.; m. Karen Bjorneby, Aug. 20, 1960; children: William, Margot, Walter, Eileen. BS with highest honors, U. Calif., Berkeley, 1963, MA, 1966, PhD, 1968. Mem. tech. staff Bellcomm, Inc., 1968-71, Jet Propulsion Lab., Pasadena, Calif., 1971-99. Supr. terrestrial planets mission design group, 1981-83, mission design mgr. for Infrared Astron. Satellite, 1976-83, mgr. flight engring. office for Voyager/Uranus project, 1983-86; mgr. mission profile and sequencing sect., 1986-92; dep. mgr. astrophysics and fundamental physics program office, 1992-96, mgr. mission and syss. architecture sect., 1996-99. Served with USMC, 1957-60. Recipient Apollo Achievement award, 1969, Pioneer 10 Mission Analysis Team Group Achievement award, 1974, Exceptional Svc. medal NASA, 1984, Outstanding Leadership medal NASA, 1986; asteroid 4838 Billmclaughlin named in his honor. Fellow Brit. Interplanetary Soc. (L.J. Carter Meml. lectr. London 2002, Space at JPL, 1982-1996, Space Achievement Bronze medal 1993); mem. Philosophy Sci. Assn., Internat. Acad. Astros., Phi Beta Kappa, Sigma Xi.

MCLAURIN, HUGH MCFADDIN, III, military officer, museum program director; b. Sumter, SC, Jan. 30, 1936; s. Hugh McFaddin and Louise Mellette (Nettles) McL.; m. Virginia Anne Harvin, Aug. 22, 1958; children: Mary Louise, Virginia Harvin, Hugh IV. BS, Clemson U., 1959; grad. (hon.), Command & Gen. Staff Coll., Ft. Leavenworth, Kans., 1978. Commd. 2d lt. U.S. Army, 1958, advanced through grades to col., 1985; exec. officer 151st Field Arty. Brigade, Sumter, 1975-85; dir. pers. S.C. NG, Columbia, 1986-91; comdr., 1985; dir. logistics S.C. NG, Columbia, 1991-95, rank of brig. gen., ret., 1996; owner McLaurin Farms, Wedgefield, SC, 1999—. Cons. S.C. Ednl. TV, Columbia, 1992-93; moderator Nat. Def. Seminar, Washington, 1978. Author: History of South Carolina National Guard and Militia, 1989. Deacon, elder, Presbyn. Ch., Wedgefield, 1961, moderator Presbytery Coun., 2001-04; v.p. Com. for Progress, Sumter, 1963; chmn. bd. dirs. S.C. NG Mus., Columbia, 1982-99; trustee Thornwell Home for Children and Sch. Fellow Coll. Mil. Historians; mem. Field Arty. Soc. S.C. (pres. 1987), SAR (historian), Sumter County Hist. Soc. (dir. 1996-99, pres. 2000), The Sumter Assembly (pres. 1991), Soc. of High Hills of Santee (steward 2002), Hon. Order St. Barbara, Fortnightly Club (pres. 2007-). Avocation: American Revolution research. Home: Stirling Plantation 6380 McLaurin Rd Wedgefield SC 29168-9393

MCLAURIN, LAMBERT PASCHAL, retired medical educator; b. Siler City, Nc, Apr. 21, 1941; s. Lambert and Grace Porter McLaurin; m. Susan Stapleton, Mar. 24, 1979. BA in English, U. Fla., Gainesville, 1962; MD, U. Fla., 1967. Cert. med. doctor NC Med. Bd., 1968. Ptnr. Cardiovasc. Ctr., Newport News, Va., 1985—98; adj. instr. Appalachian State U., Boone, NC, 1999—2008. Contbr. to numerous profl. jours.; photographic exhibition, Eros and Thanatos, Landing in Cuba. Sr. warden Holy Cross Episcopal Ch., Valle Crucis, NC, 2003. Capt. USAF, 1968, Travis AFB, Calif. Spl. Rsch. Fellow, NIH, 1973—74. Mem.: Soc. of Photographic Educators. Liberal. Avocations: photography, travel, reading, writing. Business E-Mail: pac911@charter.net.

MCLAWHON, RONALD WILLIAM, pathology educator, biochemist; b. Chgo., Sept. 10, 1957; s. William Columbus and Esther Shirley (Bukowski) McL. AB in Biol. Scis., U. Chgo., 1979, MS in Biochemistry, 1980, PhD in Biochemistry, 1982; MD, Rush Med. Coll., 1986. Diplomate Am. Bd. Pathology. Rsch. assoc. pediat. Joseph P. Kennedy Jr. Mental Retardation Rsch. Ctr., Chgo.; rsch. assoc. pediatrics U. Chgo. Pritzker Sch. Medicine, 1982-83; resident in pathology Rush-Presbyn.-St. Luke's Med. Ctr., Chgo., 1986-87, pathologist, 1987-88; instr. Rush Med. Coll., Chgo., 1986-87, asst. prof., 1987-88; resident in pathology U. Chgo. Med. Ctr., 1988-90; asst. prof. U. Chgo. Pritzker Sch. Medicine, 1990-96, assoc. prof., 1996—2007; dir. clin. chemistry, attending physician U. Chgo. Med. Ctr., 1990—2007; dir. outreach and clin. support svcs. U. Chgo. Hosps. and Health Sys., 1997—98, dir. regional lab. svcs. and med. dir. of hosp. labs., 1998—2007; prof., head divsn. lab. medicine dept. pathology U. Calif. San Diego Sch. Medicine, 2007—; dir. clin. labs., attending physician U. Calif. San Diego Med. Ctr., 2007—. Contbr. articles to Jour. Biol. Chemistry, Molecular Pharmacology, Jour. Neurochemistry, Jour. Membrane Biology, Procs. of NAS, Am. Jour. Clin. Pathology, Clin. Chemistry. US Pub. Health Predoctoral fellow NIH, 1981-82; James B. Herrick scholar Rush Med. Coll., 1986-87; recipient Young Investigator award Acad. Clin. Lab. Physicians and Scientists, 1990. Fellow: Am. Soc. Clin. Pathologists, Coll. Am. Pathologists, Nat. Acad. Clin. Biochemistry; mem.: AAAS, Am. Soc. Cell Biology, Am. Soc. Biochemistry and Molecular Biology, Am. Soc. Investigative Pathology, Am. Assn. Clin. Chemistry (chair Chgo. sect. 2005, Chgo. Chpt. Past Chmn. award 2006, Albert A. Dietz Svc. award 2008), Fretted Instrument Guild America (v.p. 2006—08, pres. 2008—), Sigma Xi. Achievements include research in biochemistry of cell membrane receptors and signal transduction in the nervous system, molecular pharmacology of opiates and opioid peptides, regulation of complex carbohydrate and lipid metabolism, clinical laboratory automaton and robotics. Office Phone: 619-543-5816. Business E-Mail: rmclawhon@ucsd.edu.

MCLEAN, DAVID J., lawyer; m. Tammy Lynne Ross; children: Emily, Michael. BA summa cum laude, Washington & Lee U., 1978; grad student, U. Edinburg, Scotland, 1979; JD magna cum laude, Geogetown U. Law Ctr., 1982. Bar: Calif. 1982, DC 1991, N.Y. 2004, NJ 2004. Assoc. Latham & Watkins, LA, 1982—89; ptnr., litigation dept. Latham & Watkins LLP, LA, 1989—2003, ptnr. in charge of tng., 1999—2002, office managing ptnr. Newark, 2004—. Bd. govs. Fed. Bar Assn., Commn. on ADR, Washington, 2000—03; exec. comm. CPR Inst. for Dispute Resolution, NYC, 2003—. Trustee San Marino (Calif.) Schs. Found., 1999—2002. Mem.: Visual Arts Ctr. NJ (trustee), ABTL (LA) (alternative dispute resolution section), Internat. Inst. Conflict Presentation and Resolution (standing com. on arbitration resolution), Chancery Club (litig. section). Office: Latham & Watkins LLP One Newark Ctr Newark NJ 07101 Office Phone: 973-639-1234. Business E-Mail: david.mclean@lw.com.

MC LEAN, DONALD MILLIS, microbiologist, educator, pathologist, pediatrician; b. Melbourne, Australia, July 26, 1926; s. Donald and Nellie (Millis) McL.; married. BSc, U. Melbourne, 1947, MB, 1950, MD, 1954. Fellow Rockefeller Found., NYC and Hamilton, Mont., 1955; vis. instr. bacteriology U. Minn., Mpls., 1957; med. officer Commonwealth Serum Labs., Melbourne, 1957; virologist Research Inst., Hosp. for Sick Children, Toronto, Ont., Canada, 1958-67; assoc. prof. microbiology, assoc. in pediatrics U. Toronto Med. Sch., 1962-67; prof. med. microbiology U. B.C. Med. Sch., Vancouver, Canada, 1967-91, prof. emeritus Pathology, 1991—. Author: Virology in Health Care, 1980, Immunological Investigation of Human Virus Disease, 1982, Same-Day Virus Diagnosis, 1984, Virological Infections, 1988, Medical Microbiology Synopsis, 1991, Acute Viral Infections, 1991; contbr. articles to profl. jours. Fellow Royal Coll. Physicians (Can.), Royal Coll. Pathologists; mem. Am. Epidemiological Soc., Am. Soc. Tropical Medicine, Can. Med. Assn., Am. Soc. Virology, Infectious Diseases Soc. Am. Home and Office: 2720 Yukon St Vancouver BC V5Y 3R1 Canada Office Phone: 604-263-9076. E-mail: donaldmclean@shaw.ca.

MCLEAN, IAN P., utilities executive; m. Kathryn McLean; 4 children. BS with honors in Math., Teesside U., Eng. Mng. dir. London trading operation Engelhard Corp., 1985, sr. v.p. USA Group, 1987, group v.p. indsl. commodities mgmt.; sr. v.p., pres. nat. mktg. divsn. PECO Energy Exelon Corp., 1999, pres. Exelon Power Team, 1999—, exec. v.p., 2002—08, exec. v.p. fin. & markets, 2008—. Office: Exelon Corp 10 S Dearborn St 37th Fl PO Box 805398 Chicago IL 60680-5398 Office Phone: 800-483-3220.*

MCLEAN, JAMES ALBERT, artist, educator; b. Gibsland, La., Nov. 25, 1928; s. Charles Edward and Lucille (Bowdon) McL.; m. Ocelia Jo Perkins, Nov. 27, 1954; 1 child: Gregory Scott. BA, Southwestern La. Inst., 1950; BD, So. Meth. U., 1953; MFA, Tulane U., 1961. Meth. student dir. Centenary Coll., Shreveport, La., 1957-59; head art dept. LaGrange (Ga.) Coll., 1964-66; assoc. prof. art Ga. State U., Atlanta, 1967-68, prof. art, 1968-95; ret., 1995. Exhibited in numerous group shows including Brooklyn Mus., 1976-77, Positive/Negative Exhbn., 1988, Siggraph Exhbn. 1988, 89, Clemson U. Nat. Print and Drawing Exhbn., 1989, Purdue U. Small Print Exhbn., 1990. Mem. Siggraph. Avocations: animation, puppetry. Home: 1256 Dunwoody Knoll Dr Atlanta GA 30338-3219 E-mail: mcle231@bellsouth.net.

MCLEAN, JOHN MAC, museum director; b. 1947; Exec. dir. Strategic Air & Space Mus., Ashland, Nebr. V.p. Am. First Communities, Bellevue, Nebr. Pres. bd. dirs. Habitat for Humanity of Sarpy County, Bellevue, Nebr., 2007—. Vice comdr. 55th Wing USAF, Offutt Air Force Base. Office: Strategic Air and Space Mus 28210 West Park Hwy Ashland NE 68003 Office Phone: 402-827-3100 ext. 201. Business E-Mail: jmclean@strategicairandspace.com.

MCLEAN, ROY L., economics professor; b. Fayetteville, NC, July 15, 1965; s. Houston and Gevenieve McLean (Stepmother). PhD, U. SC, 1994. Vis. asst. prof. U. La., Lafayette, 1994—97; asst. prof. U. Ctrl. Ark., Conway, Ark., 1997—2001; assoc. prof. Ferris State U., Big Rapids, Mich., 2001—. Office: Ferris State Univ 119 South State St Big Rapids MI 49307 Business E-Mail: mcleanr@ferris.edu.

MCLEAN, WALTER FRANKLIN, government agency administrator, business consultant, legislator, minister; b. Leamington, Ont., Can., Apr. 26, 1936; s. J.L.W. McL.; m. Barbara Muriel Scott, Aug. 19, 1961; children: Scott, Chima, Ian, Duncan BA, Victoria Coll., U. B.C., 1957; M.Div., Knox Coll., U. Toronto, 1960; LLD (hon.), Wilfrid Laurier U., 1995; DD (hon.), Knox Coll., 2002. Ordained to ministry, Presbyterian Ch. Min. Knox Presbyn. Ch., Waterloo, 1971-79; mem. House of Commons, Ottawa, Ont., Canada, 1979—93, Sec. of State of Can., 1984—85, sworn to Privy Coun., 1984, min. of immigration, 1985—86; min. responsible for status of women Govt. of Can., 1984-86. CUSO, Nigeria coord., 1962-67; chaplain U. Nigeria, 1962-67; dep. dir. Internat. Program Can. Centennial, 1967; exec. dir. Man. Assn. for World Devel., 1968-69; exec. dir. Manitoba Centennial Corp., 1970; past chmn. World Concerns Commn. Canadian Coun. Chs.; Can. del. Gen. Assemblies UN, 1986-93; apptd. prime minister's spl. rep. Commonwealth and African affairs, 1986-93; Can. rep. So. Africa Devel. Coordination Conf., 1987-93; del. Commonwealth Fgn. Mins. Against Apartheid, 1987-93, African Devel. Bank, 1990-91, Assn. West European Parliamentarians Against Apartheid, 1988-89; leader fact finding mission to Mozambique, 1987, LED Can. delegation UN Conf. on Women, Nairobi, 1985; led Parliamentary del. to observe the pre-election process and attended Namibian Indepedence, 1990; chmn. paliamentary Com. on Devel. and Human Rights, 1990-93; Commonwealth observer South African and Sri Lanka elections 1994; pres. Franklin Cons. Ltd., 1993—; chair McLean and Assocs., 2004—; bd. dirs. TAB Internat. Energy Corp., 2005—. Alderman City of Waterloo, Ont., 1976-79; co-founder UN based Parliamentarians Global Action; hon. consul of the Rep. of Namibia, 1994—; convenor Millenium Celebration Presbyn. Ch., 1998-00; prin. The Osborne Group, 2000—; bd. dirs. Toronto Sch. Theology, 2005-09; adv. bd. Royal Rds. U., Victoria BC, 1995—. Chaplain 404 wing RCAF, 1976-03; mem. Ont. Criminal Injuries Compensation Bd., 2000-03. Recipient Can. U. Svcs. Overseas award, 1990, Can. Bur. Internat. Edn. award, 1994, Disting. Alumni award U. Victoria, 2002; Paul Harris fellow, 1984. Fellow: Rotary; mem.: UN Assn. Can. (chair human rights com.). Progressive Conservative. Office Phone: 519-578-5932. E-mail: walter@mcleanandassociates.ca.

MCLEER FREE, LAUREEN DOROTHY, drug development and pharmaceutical professional; b. NYC, Feb. 5, 1955; d. William Myers and Una Lee (Massey) McLeer; m. Martin Kevin Free, Apr. 27, 2007. BS, Columbia U., 1977; MBA, U. London, 1981. RN N.Y., D.C., state reg. nurse, Eng., registered state nurse, Wales. Staff nurse NYU Med. Ctr., NYC, 1977-78; charge nurse Scripps Clinic and Rsch. Found., La Jolla, Calif., 1979-80; clin. rschr. Ayerst Labs., NYC, 1982; sales rep. Pfizer, Inc., NYC, 1983-87, Cahners Pub. Co., NYC, 1988-89; dir. bus. devel. Pro Clinica, NYC, 1990-91; account supr. Salthouse Torre Norton, Inc., Rutherford, N.J., 1992-93; dir. bus. devel. Med. & Tech. Rsch. Assocs., Inc., Wellesley, Mass., 1993-94; sr. project dir. Quiltiles Inc., Arlington, Va., 1994-99; project mgr. product devel. and commercialization Aventis Pharms., Inc., Berwyn, Pa., 1999—2002; clin. trial mgmt. leader AstraZeneca, LP, Wilmington, Del., 2002—, assoc. dir., 2005—08. Mem. com. for healthcare issues and legis. United Hosp. Fund, NYC, 1992—94. Chmn. Help Our Neighbors Eat Yr. 'Round, NYC, 1987—89; trustee Murray Hill Com., NYC, 1988—90; bd. dirs. East Midtown Svcs. for Older People, 1987—94; vol. nurse Whitman Walker Clinic, 1995—99; bd. dirs. Cecil Land Trust, 2002—06, v.p., 2006—08, bd. dirs., 2008—, Eastern Shore Land Conservancy, 2003—, treas., exec. bd. dirs., 2005—08, 2008—. Named Md. Wildlife Farmer of Yr., Md. Dept. Natural Resources, 2004. Mem.: Drug Info. Assn.,

Regulatory Affairs Profl. Soc. Home: PO Box 746 Chesapeake City MD 21915 Office: AstraZeneca LP 1800 Concorde Pike Wilmington DE 19802-4034 Home Phone: 410-885-5255; Office Phone: 302-885-5213. Business E-Mail: laureen.free@astrazeneca.com.

MCLELLAN, THOMAS (ANDREW THOMAS MCLELLAN), federal agency administrator, psychology professor; b. May 29, 1948; BA, Colgate U., Hamilton, NY, 1970; MS, PhD, Bryn Mawr Coll., Pa.; postgrad. tng. in Psychology, U. Oxford, Eng. Co-founder, exec. dir. Treatment Rsch. Inst., Phila., 1991; prof. psychiatry U. Pa., Phila.; dep. dir. Office Nat. Drug Control Policy (ONDCP), Washington, 2009—. Author more than 400 articles and chapters on addiction research. Recipient Life Achievement Award, Am. Soc. Addiction Medicine, 2001, Brit. Soc. Addiction Medicine, 2003, Award for Disting. Contbn. to Addiction Medicine, Swedish Med. Assn., 2002, Italian Med. Assn., 2002, Innovator Award, Robert Wood Johnson Found., 2005. Achievements include having a leading role in the creation of the Addiction Severity Index and the Treatment Services Review. Office: Office of Nat Drug Control Policy (ONDCP) Drug Policy Info Clearinghouse PO Box 6000 Rockville MD 20849-6000*

MCLELLAN, TODD, professional hockey coach; b. Melville, Sask., Can., Oct. 3, 1967; Center Springfield Indians (Am. Hockey League), 1987—89, NY Islanders, 1987—88; head coach North Battleford North Stars (Sask. Jr. Hockey League), 1993—94, Swift Current Broncos (Western Hockey League), 1994—2000, also gen. mgr.; head coach Cleve. Lumberjacks (Internat. Hockey League), 2000—01, Houston Aeros (Am. Hockey League), 2001—05; asst. coach Detroit Red Wings, 2005—08; head coach San Jose Sharks, 2008—. Achievements include being the head coach of Calder Cup Champion Houston Aeros, 2003; being the assistant coach of Stanley Cup Champion Detroit Red Wings, 2008. Office: San Jose Sharks 525 W Santa Clara St San Jose CA 95113

MCLELLON, RICHARD STEVEN, aerospace engineer, consultant; b. Lawton, Okla., May 28, 1952; s. Robert Nelson and Jane (Warriner) McL. BSME, Old Dominion U., 1979. Aerospace engr. Naval Engring. Support Office, Norfolk, Va., 1979-82, U.S. Army Aviation Systems Commd., Ft. Eustis, Va., 1982-86; mission lead dynamicist Astronautics Space Launch Sys., Lockheed Martin Corp., Denver, 1986—2005, stress analyst, loads analyst, Workshare, Tech. Ops., 2005—. Cons. Aircraft Devel., Inc., Littleton, Colo., 1991—.

MCLEMORE, CAROLYN FAYE, elementary school educator; b. Asheville, NC, Apr. 22, 1943; m. Isaac Eugene McLemore, Nov. 30, 1962; children: Isaac Eugene Jr., Tricia Faith Gravel, Felicia Hope Hopkins, Melanie Love Freeman. BA, Maryville Coll., Tenn., 1977; MEd, Lincoln Meml. U., Harrogate, Tenn., 1999. Lic. tchr. Dept. Edn., Tenn., 1977. Tchr. elem. sch. Dept. Def., Landstuhl, Germany, 1981—88; tchr. reading, English Monroe County Schs., Madisonville, Tenn., 1988—90; substitute tchr. Blount County Schs., Maryville, Tenn., 1990—92; tchr. reading, English Carpenters Middle Sch., Maryville, Tenn., 1992—. Mem.: NEA, Tenn. Edn. Assn., Blount County Ednl. Assn., Alpha Delta Kappa (chpt. pres. 2006—, chmn. 2008—). Office: Carpenters Middle Sch 920 Huffstetler Rd Maryville TN 37803

MCLEMORE, JOAN MEADOWS, librarian, consultant; b. Bivens, Tex., Aug. 24, 1929; d. James Leon Jr. and Dell (Crawford) Meadows; m. Kenneth Lyons McLemore, May 6, 1950 (dec.); 1 child, Ken Malcolm. Student, Miss. State Coll. for Women, 1947-49; BS, U. So. Miss., Hattiesburg, 1976, MLS, 1983. Libr. Franklin County Pub. Libr., Meadville, Miss., 1976-90; libr. dir. Copiah-Lincoln C.C., Natchez, Miss., 1990—2003. Story teller, presenter conf. The Delta Kappa Gamma Soc. Internat., Louisville, 1991, Nashville, 1994; internat. spkr. Delta Kappa Soc., Red Deer, Can., 1994; mem. faculty Elderhostel, Natchez, Miss., 1990—; presenter Southeastern Regional Conf., Delta Kappa Gamma Soc. Internat., Charleston, SC, 1997; pres. Franklinc. Mus., 1999-2004, Franklin County Mus., Meadville, Miss., 2002—, Inst. Learning Retirement, 2003—, pres., 2007-. Contbr. articles to profl. jours. Libr. trustee Franklin County, Meadville, 1962-76, Lincoln-Lawrence-Franklin Regional Libr., Brookhaven, Miss., 1971-76; trustee Franklyn County Meml. Hosp., 1997-2001, jury com., 1998-2001; deacon First Presbyn. Ch., 2003-06, elder, 2008—; Miss. com. Humanities Spkrs. Roster, 2004—. Mem. Miss. Libr. Assn. (com. chair, exec. dir. libr. week activities 1989), Colonial Dames (gov. George Harlan chpt., 2nd v.p. 2002-05, parliamentarian 2005—), DAR (Homochitlo River chpt. 1979-1999, Natchez chpt. 2000—), Dames of the Ct. of Honor (treas. 2001-07, chaplain 1999-2003), Mis. Soc. DAMES of the South, Daughters of Soc. of War of 1812 (sec., treas. 2007—09), Natchez Garden Club, Natchez Hist. Soc. (trustee 2005—, sec. 2007—, pres. 2008-), Miss. Hist. Soc., Order of the First Families (chaplain 2002-05, historian 2005-07, dep. gov. gen. 2007—09, govs. gen., 2009-), First Families Twin Territories, Delta Kappa Gamma (pres. 1979-80, 1979-97 Rho chpt.), Progressive Study Club (sec. 2006-), Natchez Women's Book Soc., Friends of Armstrong Libr., Rose Craft Club, Chaplin 2008-, Scottish Heritage Soc., Natchez Retiree Partnership. Avocations: genealogy, reading, baking, historial research, story telling. Home: Apt A 310 S Dr M L King Jr St Natchez MS 39120-3533 Home Phone: 601-446-5147. Personal E-mail: joanmcl1@bellsouth.net.

MCLENDON, BRIAN ANDREW, lab administrator, educator; s. Fredrick Levonne and Peggy Rae McLendon. Student, U. SC, Columbia, 1989—95. Bldg. supr. U. SC, Columbia, 1990—94, alumni fund solicitor, 1994—95; lab technician Eckerd Drug Corp., Columbia, 1996, group leader, 1996, lab supr., 1996—97, lab mgr., 1998, tng. lab. mgr., 1998—. Named Lab Mgr. of Quarter, Eckerd Drug Corp., 2004. Mem.: Soc. Photofinishing Engrs., Photo Mktg. Assn. Internat. (cert. photographic cons. 2001—), Am. Mensa Ltd. Avocations: cabinet making, horology, photography, astronomy. Office: Eckerd Drug Corp 4730 Forest Dr Columbia SC 29206

MCLENDON, ROGER EDWIN, neuropathologist, educator; s. Vivian W. and Harold Edwin Mclendon; m. Patti Swain, 1982; children: Patrick Edwin, Erin Elizabeth, Ryan Hodges. MD, Med. Coll. of Ga., 1983. Diplomate Am. Bd. Pathology, 1987. Prof. Duke Sch. of Medicine, Durham, NC, 1992—; asst clin. prof. pathology Mercer U. Sch. of Medicine, Macon, Ga., 1988—2006. Dir. anatomic pathology, chief of neuropathology Duke Sch. of Medicine, Durham, NC, 2006—. Contbg. editor: Russell And Rubinstein's Pathology of Tumors of The Nervous System, 2000; author: Pathology of Tumors of the Central Nervous System. Scoutmaster Boy Scouts Of Am., Durham, NC, 2000—06. Fellow: Coll. of Am. Pathologists (ednl. com. mem. 2003—06); mem.: Am. Assn. Neuropathology (bd. councilors 2006—), Am. Bd. Pathology (neuropathology com. mem. 1997—2006). Avocations: coaching youth baseball, reading.

MCLENNAN, BARBARA NANCY, tax specialist; b. NYC, Mar. 25, 1940; d. Sol and Gertrude (Rochkind) Miller; m. Kenneth McLennan, Aug. 14, 1962; children: Gordon, Laura. BA magna cum laude, CCNY, 1961; MS, U. Wis., 1962, PhD, 1965; JD, Georgetown U., 1983. Bar: DC 1983, U.S. Ct. Internat. Trade 1988, U.S. Ct. Appeals (DC cir.) 1988, U.S. Supreme Ct. 1988, Va. 1991; cert. accredited valuation analyst Nat. Assn. Cert. Valuation Analysts, 2004. From asst. prof. to assoc. prof. Temple U., Phila., 1965—78; budget analyst Com. Budget, U.S. Ho. of Reps., Washington, 1978—81; legis. asst. fin. and budget Senator Dan Quayle, Washington, 1981—84; internat. tax specialist IRS U.S. Dept. Treasury, Washington, 1984—89; dep. asst. sec. trade, info. and analysis U.S. Dept. Commerce, Washington, 1989—91; prin., atty.-at-law Bitonti and Wilhelm, PC., McLean, Va., 1991—93; staff v.p. govt.-legal affairs consumer electronics group Electronic Industries Assn., Washington, 1993—94, staff v.p. tech. policy, consumer electronics group, 1994—95; v.p. Van Scoyoc Assocs., Washington, 1995—96; cons. on tax related issues in U.S., former Soviet Union, and West Bank and Gaza McLean, Va., 1996—. Adj. prof. Coll. William and Mary, 2005—; sr. polit. scientist SRI-Internat., Arlington, Va., 1971—74; vis. prof. Am. Coll., Paris, 1975—76; cons. UNESCO, Paris, 1977—78. Author: (book) Comparative Political Systems, 1975, Reagains Mandate, 2009; contbr. articles to profl. jours. Mem. parents adv. coun. Randolph-Macon Coll., Ashland, Va., 1989—92. Fellow NDEA, 1962—65. Mem.: ABA, Va. Bar Assn., Fed. Bar Assn., DC Bar Assn., Am. Soc. Assn. Execs., Phi Beta Kappa. Home: 1620 Harbor Rd Williamsburg VA 23185 E-mail: barb.mcl@cox.net.

MCLENNAN, HAMISH, advertising executive; b. Australia; m. Lucinda McLennan; children: Olivia, Ted. Numerous positions George Patterson Bates, 1985—2002, including internat. client svcs. dir. Hong Kong, 1994, mng. dir. Melbourne, nat. mng. dir., 1999; chmn., CEO Young & Rubicam Brands, Australia/New Zealand, 2002—06, global CEO Y&R Advt. NYC, 2006—. Bd. dirs. Advt. Coun., Inc. Office: Y&R Advt 285 Madison Ave New York NY 10017 Office Phone: 212-210-3000. Business E-Mail: hamish.mclennan@gpyr.com.au.*

MCLEOD, BRUCE ROYAL, electrical engineering educator, consultant; b. Greeley, Colo, Jan. 17, 1939; s. Royal and Alma McLeod; m. Peggy Sue Hubbard, Sept. 30, 1961; children: Robert Royal, Cathryn Alaine McLeod. BSEE, Colo. State U., 1961; MSEE, U. Colo., 1965, PhD in Elec. Engring., 1968. Elec. engr. light mil. electronics dept. GE Co., Utica, NY, 1961-64; rsch. engr. Boeing Aerospace Group, Seattle, 1968-70; asst. prof. elec. engring. Mont. State U., Bozeman, 1970-74, assoc. prof., 1974-79; owner, operator Spear Lazy U Ranch, Wilsall, Mont., 1974—; prof. Mont. State U., Bozeman, 1979, 1979-89, 90-96, head dept. elec. engring., 1996—99, dean coll. grad. studies, 1999—2005, prof. elec. and computer engring., 2005—. Pres. Life Resonances Inc., Bozeman, 1987—, cons., 1990—; vis. rsch. scientist Columbia Presbyn. Hosp., N.Y.C., VA Hosp., U. Ky. Med. Ctr., 1981-82; cons. Devel. Tech. Corp., Bozeman, 1972, Infosystems, Bozeman, 1972, La Jolla (Calif.) Tech. Inc., 1983-85, Finnegan, Henderson, Farabow, Garret & Dunner, Washington, 1983, 85-86, IatroMed Inc., Phoenix, 1989-90. Contbr. over 38 articles to profl. jour. and books; presenter over 40 abstracts at nat. & internat. meetings; invited spkr. in field; holder of 27 US patents, 8 Australian patent, 2 Can. patent, 1 Japanese patent. Pres. Park County Legis. Assn., Livingston, Mont., 1988-90. Mem. IEEE (sr., chmn. Mont. sect. 1983-84), AAAS, Bioelectromagnetics Soc. (program com., bd. dirs. 2000-04, pres. 2004-05, tech. program chair 2005-06), Bioelec. Repair and Growth Soc. (program com. 1985-86, chmn. program com. 1988-90, coun. 1986-88, pres. 1991), Nat. Cattleman's Assn., Park County Stockgrowers Assn., Masons, Shriners, Sigma Xi (v.p. Mont. State U. chpt. 1979-80, pres. 1980-81), Sigma Tau, Eta Kappa Nu, Kappa Mu Epsilon, Sigma Xi. Avocations: hunting, fly fishing, woodcarving, trap and skeet clay pigeon shooting. Office: Mont State Univ Dept Elec and Computer Engring Rm 619 Cobleigh Hall Bozeman MT 59717-3780 Office Phone: 406-994-5960. Business E-Mail: mcleod@montana.edu.

MCLEOD, CHANSE L., lawyer; b. Dallas, 1965; BBA with honors in Fin., U. Tex., Austin, 1988; JD, Houston U., 1991. Bar: Tex. 1991. Ptnr., Real Estate Andrews Kurth LLP, Houston. Assoc. editor Houston Law Rev., 1989—91. Mem.: Houston Bar Found., Tex. Bar Found., Houston Bar Assn., Houston Young Lawyers Assn., State Bar Tex., Tex. Young Lawyers Assn., ABA, Phi Delta Phi. Office: Andrews Kurth LLP 600 Travis St Ste 4200 Houston TX 77002-3090 Office Fax: 713-238-7257, 713-220-4020. Business E-Mail: cmcleod@andrewskurth.com.

MCLEOD, E. DOUGLAS, real estate developer, lawyer; b. Galveston, Tex., Aug. 6, 1941; s. Vaughan Watkins McLeod and Dorothy (Milroy) Burton; m. Sarah Jackson Helms, Mar. 20, 1965 (div. 1979); children: Chanse, Alexandra, Lindsey; m. Joan Margaret Williams, Dec. 26, 1979; 1 child, Joanie stepchildren: Meg, Libbie. BBA, U. North Tex., 1965; postgrad., So. Meth. U., 1965-66; JD, South Tex. Coll. Law, 1990; LLM, U. Houston, 1993. Bar: Tex., U.S. Dist. Ct. (so. dist.) Tex.; lic. real estate broker. Pres., owner McLeod Properties & co., Galveston, 1967—; tchr. Galveston Ind. Sch. Dist., 1967-69, pres., trustee, 1969—73; banker W. L. Moody & Co., Galveston, 1969-72; developer, broker McLeod Properties/Builders, Galveston, 1972-82; developer Moody Found., Galveston, 1982—. Bd. dirs. Am. Nat. Ins. Co., Galveston, Nat. Western Life Ins. Co., Austin, Anrem Corp., Galveston, Colonel Inc., Galveston, Moody Gardens Inc., Galveston, chmn., 1984—. Mem. editl. bd.: Currents Internat. Trade Law Jour., 1992—. Mayor pro-tem, mem. city coun. City of Galveston, 1973—76; state legislator Tex. Ho. Reps., Austin, 1976—83; bd. visitors South Tex. Coll. Law, 1990—96, bd. dirs., 2000—; mem. adv. bd. U. Houston, 1986—95; bd. dirs. STCL, Ronald McDonald House, 1986—93, Trinity Episcopal Sch., 1990—96, Galveston Econ. Devel. Partnership, 1998—2002; vestryman, sr. warden, chancellor Episc. Ch. With USMC, 1961—67. Mem.: ABA, Am. Judicature Soc., Galveston County Bar Assn., Tex. Bar Assn., Marine Corps League. Avocations: physical fitness advocate, legal history collector. Home: 53 Cedar Lawn Cir Galveston TX 77551-4631 Office: The Moody Found 2302 Post Office St Ste 704 Galveston TX 77550-1994 Office Phone: 409-797-1521. Business E-Mail: dmcleod@moodyf.org.

MCLEOD, HARRY O'NEAL, JR., retired petroleum engineer, consultant; b. Shreveport, La., Feb. 26, 1932; s. Harry O'Neal Sr. and Odelle Nan (Crow) McL.; m. Sandra Lou Mahaffey, Feb. 6, 1959; children: Kathleen Odelle, Bryan O'Neal. Degree in engring., Colo. Sch. Mines, 1953; MS in Petroleum Engring., U. Okla., 1963, PhD in Engring. Sci., 1965. Prodn. engr. Phillips Petroleum Co., 1953—58; rsch. engr. Jersey Prodn. Rsch. Co., Tulsa, 1963—64; sr. rsch. engr. Dowell divsn. Dow Chem. Co., Tulsa, 1965—69; dir. info. svcs. dept. U. Tulsa, 1969—75; from sr. prodn. engr. to sr. staff engr. Conoco, Inc., Houston, 1975—86, engring. profl., 1986—91, sr. engring. profl., 1992—97; pvt. practice cons. Houston, 1998—2003; ret., 2004. 1st lt. U.S. Army, 1954-56. Mem. Soc. Petroleum Engrs. (Prodn. Engring. award 1989, Disting. Mem. award 1995, disting. author, 1983, disting. lectr. 1987-88, 96-97, Legion of Honor award, 2006), Sigma Xi. Republican. Methodist. Home: 2006 Southwick St Houston TX 77080-6315 E-mail: homcleod@aol.com.

MCLEOD, JOHN EDMOND, history professor; b. Toronto, Mar. 5, 1963; s. Wallace Edmond McLeod and Elizabeth Marion McLeod (nee Staples); m. Mary Frances Hora, June 15, 1991. BA, U. Toronto, 1985, MA, 1986, PhD, 1993. Tchg. asst., then lectr., dept. history U. Toronto, 1987—93; asst. prof. history U. Louisville, 1995—2001, assoc. prof., 2001—08, prof., 2008—, chair dept. history, 2004—09. Bd. dirs. Can. Royal Heritage Trust, Toronto, Canada, 2003—, English-Speaking Union of the US (Ky. Br.), Louisville, 2004—06. Author: (history books) Sovereignty, Power, Control, The History of India; author: (with Kenneth X. Robbins) African Elites in India; contbr. articles to profl. jours. Mem., US dels. to Bangladesh, India, Pakistan, Islamic Life in US & Religion & Soc. Exch. Programs US State Dept., 2004—09. Recipient Pres.s Award for Outstanding Scholarship, Rsch., and Creative Activity, U. of Louisville, 2003, Outstanding Scholarship, Rsch. and Creative Activity Award in the Social Sci., Coll. of Arts and Sci., U. of Louisville, 2002—03, Hon. Rajvanshi Genealogist, Rajkumar Coll. Rajkot (India), 2001; fellow, Royal Asiatic Soc. Gt. Britain and Ireland, 2006; Postdoctoral fellow, Shastri Indo-Canadian Inst., 1993—94, Sr. Short-term Rsch. fellow, Am. Inst. of Indian Studies, 2004. Mem.: Assn. for Asian Studies. Office: ULouisville Dept History Louisville KY 40292 Office Fax: 502-852-0770. E-mail: john.mcleod@louisville.edu.

MCLEOD, MARILYNN HAYES, retired educational administrator, farmer; b. Lake View, SC, Jan. 2, 1924; d. Cary Victor and Benna (Price) Hayes; m. Charles Edward McLeod, Aug. 24, 1947; children: Cary Franklin, Mary Marilynn. BA, Furman U., 1946; MEd, U. SC, 1952, EdD, 1986. Cert. edn. specialist in ednl. admninistrn. 1974. Tchr. Hamer-Kentyre Sch., Hamer, SC, 1944-45, Bennettsville City Schs., SC, 1946-59, Clio Elem. Sch., SC, 1960-63; asst. prof. elem. edn. St. Andrews Presbyn. Coll., Laurinburg, NC, 1964-67; instr. U. SC, Florence, 1971; reading supr., coord. instrn. Marlboro County Sch. Dist., Bennettsville, SC, 1967-86; prin. Marlboro County Child Devel. Ctr., 1986-87; asst. prin. Bennettsville HS, 1987-89, Marlboro County HS, 1989-92; farmer, 1960—; ret. Mem. Marlboro County Sch. Dist. Bd., 1992-96. Author: The History of Education in Marlboro County, South Carolina, 1737-1895, 1988. Adminstrv. bd. Trinity United Meth. Ch., 1982—, chmn. pastor-parish relations com., 1979-98; trustee Trinity United Meth. Ch., 2000-, lay leader, 2008-; pianist Men's Bible Class Trinity, 1948-83; trustee Epworth Children's Home, chmn. personnel com., Columbia, SC, 1982-94, bd. mem. Hospice of Marlboro County, 1992-97; chmn., sec. Trinity Wesleyan Cir., 1992-2007. Mem. NEA (life), Internat. Reading Assn., SC Edn. Assn. (life, Walker E. Solomon Human Rels. award 1984), SC Reading Assn., Assn. Secondary Prins., SC Internat. Reading Assn., Marlboro County Edn. Assn. (Educator of Yr. 1983-84), Pee Dee Internat. Reading Assn., Marlborough Hist. Soc. (mem. bd.), Marlboro Arts Coun., Marlboro County Assn. for Mental Retardation, Dillon County Farm Bur., Clio Federated Women's Club, Palmetto Book Club,Marlboro Arts Coun., Soc. Internat. outstanding women educators, Golden Key Honor Soc., Delta Kappa Gamma. Home: PO Box 38 127 S Main St Clio SC 29525-3004

MCLEOD, MARY S., pharmaceutical executive; B, Loyola U., Chgo.; M, U. Mo. Expatriate assignments Accenture, Brazil, Australia; v.p. human resources Gen. Elec. Co., 1992—97, Cisco Systems, 1999—2001; head human resources, chief of staff to the chief exec. Charles Schwab & Co., 2001—04; head human resources Symbol Technologies, 2005—06; cons. Korn Consulting Group, 2007; sr. v.p. worldwide human resources Pfizer, Inc., 2007—. Bd. dirs. Belden, Inc., 2008—. Office: Pfizer Inc 235 E 42nd St New York NY 10017 Office Phone: 212-733-2323.*

MCLEOD, ROBERT E., lawyer; b. San Diego, Calif., Mar. 22, 1947; Grad., Rutgers Coll., New Brunswick, NJ; JD, Rutgers U. Law Sch., Newark, 1972. Atty. various firms, 1972—2008; mcpl. prosecutor Union Beach Borough, NJ, 1979—80, 2004—08, Highlands Borough, NJ, 1982—83; pvt. practice cert. civil trial atty., 1987—2003; atty. Union Beach Planning and Zoning Bd., 1990—2004; mem. Keyport Borough Coun., 1990—91; mcpl. ct. judge Holmdel Twp. and Keyport Borough, NJ, 1991—2008. Vol. firefighter Engine Co. No. 1 Keyport Fire Dept., lt., capt., sec., life mem.; sec. Keyport Rep. Club, 2008. Republican. Mailing: PO Box 226 Keyport NJ 07735 Office Phone: 732-335-9814.

MCLEOD, WALTON JAMES, III, state legislator, lawyer; b. Walterboro, SC, June 30, 1937; s. Walton James Jr. and Rhoda Lane (Brown) M.; m. Julie Edwina Hamiter, Feb. 15, 1969; 1 child, Walton James IV. BA, Yale U., 1959; LLB, U. S.C., 1964; postgrad., U. Minn., 1972. Bar: SC 1964, US Supreme Ct. 1974. Law clk. to Chief Judge Clement Haynsworth US Ct. Appeals (4th cir.), Richmond, Va., 1964-65; assoc. Pope and Schumpert, Newberry, SC, 1965-67; asst. US Atty. Columbia, SC, 1967-68; gen. counsel SC Dept. Health & Environ. Ctrl., Columbia, 1968-94, spl. counsel, 1994-96; dep. SC atty. gen. Columbia, 1987-88. Magistrate Newberry County, Little Mountain, SC, 1973-81; mcpl. judge Town of Little Mountain, 1981-83, mayor, 1983-89, 93-96; mem. Dist. 40 SC House of Reps., 1996—. Author: Legal Perspectives of Environmental Health, 1973; co-author: Environmental Quality Law, 1975, Hospital Franchising Law and Regulation, 1979. Pres. Newberry (SC) Jaycees, 1967; bd. dirs. SC Housing Fin. & Devel. Authority, Columbia, 1977-96, Newberry County Coun. Aging, 2001—, Newberry Coll. Found., 2005—; chair Ctrl. Midlands Coun. Govts., Columbia, 1981-82, 2001-03; trustee SC State Mus., Columbia, 1981-85. Lt. (j.g.) USN, 1959-61, served to Capt. USNR, 1961-92, ret. Recipient Outstanding Jaycee award Newberry Jaycees, 1967, Howell Excellence award Naval Res. Law Program, Washington, 1991, Outstanding Legislator award Gift of Life Trust Fund, 1999, Legislative Appreciation award SC Assn. Conservation Dists., 2006, Outstanding Svc. award SC Am. Legion, 2006; named Outstanding Freshman Rep. of Yr. Carolina Hist. Found. Soc., Inc., 1997. Fellow SC Bar Found.; mem. SC Magistrates Assn. (pres. 1976-77, Disting. Jud. Svc. award 1975, 77), Judge Advs. Assn. (nat. pres. 1991-92), SC Res. Officers Assn. (state pres. 1981-82, Res. Officer of Yr. 1998), SC Soc. (pres. 1990-93). Democrat. Luth. Avocations: reading, physical fitness. Home: 308 Pomaria St Little Mountain SC 29075-9003 Office: SC House of Reps PO Box 11867 Columbia SC 29211-1867 also: 422B Blatt Bldg Columbia SC 29201 Office Phone: 803-734-3276. Fax: 803-345-0770. Business E-Mail: WJM@schouse.org.*

MCLESKEY, CHARLES HAMILTON, anesthesiologist, educator, pharmaceutical executive; b. Phila., Nov. 8, 1946; s. W. Hamilton and Marion A. (Butts) McL.; m. Nanci S. Simmons, June 3, 1972; children: Travis, Heather. BA, Susquehanna U., 1968; MD, Wake Forest U., 1972. Diplomate Am. Bd. Anesthesiology. Intern Maine Med. Ctr., Portland, 1972-73; resident in anesthesiology U. Wash. Sch. Medicine, Seattle, 1973-76, NIH rsch. trainee, 1974-75; clin. teaching assoc. dept. anesthesiology U. Calif., San Francisco, 1976-78; asst. prof. anesthesiology Wake Forest U. Bowman Gray Sch. Medicine, Winston-Salem, NC, 1978-83, assoc. prof., 1983-84, U. Tex. Med. Br., Galveston, 1985-87; assoc. prof. anesthesiology U. Colo. Health Sci. Ctr., Denver, 1987-91, prof., 1991-93, dir. acad. affairs, 1987-93; prof., chmn. dept. anesthesiology Tex. A&M U., 1993-2000; chmn. dept. anesthesiology, med. dir. perioperative svcs. Scott and White Clin. and Meml. Hosp., Temple, Tex., 1993-2000; assoc. med. dir. Scott and White Health Plan, 1995-2000; sr. dir. clin. devel. Abbott Labs., Abbott Park, Ill., 2000—02, global med. dir., global mktg. dir. anesthesia and sedation, 2002—06; v.p. clin. affairs ZARS, Salt Lake City, 2006—07; leader therapeutic area Global Anesthesia and Critical, Baxter Pharm., New Providence, NJ,

2007—. Cons., lectr. Janssen Pharmaceutica, Piscataway, N.J., 1980-98, Alza Corp., Palo Alto, Calif., 1986-99; cons. Glaxo-Wellcome Co., Research Triangle Park, N.C., Abbott Labs., Chgo., Hoechst, Marion, Roussel, Kansas City, Kans., Aspect Med., Natick, Mass., Baxter Labs., Chgo., Scott Labs., Lubbock, Tex.; lectr. to over 500 nat. and state med. orgns., 1982—; examiner Am. Bd. Anesthesiology; lectr. Ohmeda, Liberty Corner, N.J. Assoc. editor Anesthesiology Rev., Anesthesiology News, Pharmacy Practia News; editor Geriatric Anesthesiology, 1997; contbr. numerous articles to med. jours. Mem. choir Friendswood (Tex.) Meth. Ch., 1985-87; mem. Friendswood Fine Arts Commn., 1985-87; mem. Temple Chamber Arts Adv. Coun., 1997-99. Lt. comdr. M.C., USN, 1976-78. Woodruff-Fisher scholar, 1964-68. Mem.: Temple C. of C., Evergreen Newcomers, Soc. Acad. Anesthesia Chairs (councilman 1996—99), Soc. for Ambulatory Anesthesia (program chair 1999), Internat. Anesthesia Rsch. Soc., Colo. Soc. Anesthesiologists (past pres.), Soc. for Edn. in Anesthesiology (past v.p., past pres., SEA-Duke Edn. prize), Am. Soc. Anesthesiologists (del. 1983—85, 1988—90), Assn. U Anesthestists, Nat. Spkrs. Assn., Internat. Platform Assn., Mensa, Alpha Omega Alpha. Republican. Presbyterian. Avocations: running, fishing, racquetball, squash. Personal E-mail: charles.mcleskey@comcast.net.

MCLEVISH, TIMOTHY R., food products executive; BS in Acctg., U. Minn., 1982; MBA, Harvard U., 1985. CPA. Various mgmt. positions through div. pres. & gen. mgr. Mead Corp., Dayton, Ohio, 1987-99, v.p., CFO, 1999—2002; sr. v.p., CFO Ingersoll-Rand Co. Ltd., 2002—07; exec. v.p., CFO Kraft Foods Inc., Northfield, Ill., 2007—. Bd. dirs. Kennametal Inc., 2009—. Mailing: Kennametal Inc PO Box 231 Latrobe PA 15650-0231 Office: Kennametal Inc 1600 Technology Way Latrobe PA 15650-0231 Office Phone: 724-539-5000.*

MCLIN, RHINE LANA, Mayor, Dayton, Ohio, former state legislator; b. Dayton, Ohio, Oct. 3, 1948; d. C. Josef, Jr. and Bernice (Cottman) McL. BA in Sociology and secondary edn., Parsons Coll., 1969; MEd in guidance counseling, Xavier U., 1972; postgrad. in law, U. Dayton, 1974-76; AA in Mortuary Sci., Cin. Coll., 1988. Lic. funeral dir. Tchr. Dayton Bd. Edn., 1970-72; divorce counselor Domestic Rels. Ct., Dayton, 1972-73; law clk. Montgomery Common Pleas Ct., Dayton, 1973-74; v.p., dir., embalmer McLin Funeral Homes, Dayton, 1972—; mem. Ohio House of Reps. from 36th & 38th dists., Columbus, 1988-94; mem., Dist. 5 Ohio Senate, Columbus, 1994—2002, minority whip, 1994—2001; mem. Ways & Means Com.; controlling bd., ins. commerce comn. ranking mem.; state and local govt. com. Columbus; mayor City of Dayton, Ohio, 2002—. Instr. Central State U., Wilberforce, Ohio, 1982-97; mem. Ohio Tuition Trust Authority. Mem. Dem. Nat. Com., Children's Def. Fund., mem. Mayors Against Illegal Gun Control Toll fellow; Paul Harris fellow; Flemming fellow; BLLD fellow; named Ohio Legislator of Yr., Ohio Social Workers Assn., 1999. Mem. Nat. Funeral Dirs. Assn., Ohio Funeral Dirs. Assn., Montgomery County Hist. Soc., NAACP (life), Nat. Coun. Negro Women (life), Delta Sigma Theta. Democrat. Achievements include being first female mayor of Dayton. Office: City Hall 2nd Fl 101 W Third St Dayton OH 45402 Office Phone: 937-333-3653. Office Fax: 937-333-4299. Business E-Mail: Rhine.McLin@cityofDayton.org, erica.cain@cityofdayton.org.*

MCLIN-BRONSON, HATTIE ROGERS, school system administrator; b. Prentiss, Miss., Dec. 8, 1946; d. Javan Wilson Sr. and Alberta (Davis) Rogers; m. Prentiss McLin, June 29, 1968 (dec.); m. Gus Bronson, Sr.; children: Alberta Marie Detter, Prentiss II, Dawn Javan Wilson. BS, Jackson State U., 1968, MA, 1972, EdS, 1981, EdD, 1987; student, Howard U., Ohio State U., U. Southern Miss., Millsaps Coll., Baylor U. Tchr. Hinds County Pub. Schs., Clinton, Miss.; assoc. prof. edn. Paul Quinn Coll., Waco, Tex.; asst. prin. Jackson Public Separate Sch. Dist., Miss., 1992; prin. Johnson Elem. Sch., Jackson. Adj. prof. Jackson State U., Hinds Community Coll., Jackson; leader of ednl. ministry; prin. coach, 2006-. Sec. Jackson City Planning Bd.; bd. dirs. Nurture for Bapt. Chs., Greater Fairview Bapt. Ch.; mem. PTA., Youth Leadership Jackson C. of C., C. of C. Youth Devel. Named Outstanding Elem. Prin., Miss. Educator of the Yr., Adminstr. of Yr., 2006-07; Levi Strauss grantee, 1985, 86. Mem. ASCD, Miss. ASCD, NEA, Miss. Assn. Educators, Nat. Assn. Young Children, Bus. Profl. Women Orgn., Kappan Honors Orgn., Kappa Pi Honor Soc., Zeta Phi Beta. Office: Johnson Elem Sch 3319 Oak Park Dr Jackson MS 39212-4124 Home: 4052 Rainey Rd Jackson MS 39212-5324 Business E-Mail: hmclin@jackson.k12.ms.us.

MCLORIE, GORDON ARTHUR, urologist, educator; b. St. John, New Brunswick, Can., May 2, 1945; arrived in U.S., 2003; m. Blair Hilton, Dec. 20, 1968; children: Scott, David, Graham, Megan. MD, U. Toronto, Can., 1969. Cert. Am. Bd. Urology, 1982, in pediat. urology Am. Bd. Urology, 2008. Intern Toronto Gen. Hosp., Canada, 1969; resident in urology and renal transplant U. Toronto, Canada, 1971—76; fellowship dept. urology UCLA, 1976—77; fellowship in pediatric surgery Harvard U., Boston, 1981—82; chief pediatric urology Childrens Hosp. Mich., Detroit, 2002—06; prof. pediatric urology Wayne State U., Detroit, 2002—06; chief pediatric urology Wake Forest U., Winston-Salem, NC, 2006—. Fellow: Royal Coll. Physicians and Surgeons Can., Am. Acad. Pediat.; mem.: Am. Urology Assn., Can. Urology Assn. (pres.). Achievements include research in vesicourethral reflux, and reconstructive surgery of infants and children with congenital anomalies of the genitourinary system; invention of special interest in bladder reconstruction and replacement in children. Avocations: skiing, golf. Office: Wake Forest Sch Medicine Medical Center Blvd Winston Salem NC 27157 Personal E-mail: gmclorie@wfubnc.edu.

MCLOUGHLIN, HILARY ESTEY, broadcast executive; B in Broadcasting and Film, Boston U. Rsch. analyst Seltel, Inc, 1984—86, Lorimar-Telepictures, 1986—89; dir. devel. Telepictures Prodns., 1989—92, v.p. devel., 1992, v.p. programming, sr. v.p. programming and devel., 1999—2002, exec. v.p., gen. mgr., 2002—06, pres., 2006—. Exec. prodr.: (TV series) The Rosie O'Donnell Show (Daytime Emmy award for Outstanding Talk Show, 1998, 1999). Named one of The 100 Most Powerful Women in Entertainment, Hollywood Reporter, 2007. Office: Telepictures Prodns 4000 Warner Blvd Burbank CA 91522*

MCLOUTH, NATHAN RICHARD (NATE MCLOUTH), professional baseball player; b. Muskegon, Mich., Oct. 28, 1981; Outfielder Pitts. Pirates, 2005—09, Atlanta Braves, 2009—. Recipient Gold Glove award, 2008. Achievements include leading the National League in: doubles (46), 2008. Office: Atlanta Braves Turner Field 755 Hank Aaron Dr Atlanta GA 30315*

MCLUCAS, WILLIAM ROBERT, lawyer, former federal agency administrator; b. Altoona, Pa., Aug. 12, 1950; s. James Daniel and Ruth Virginia (Sweeney) McL. BA in Polit. Sci. with distinction, Pa. State U., 1972; JD, Temple U., 1975. Bar: Pa. 1975, DC 1998, NY 1999. Atty. Fed. Home Loan Bank Bd., 1975-77; staff atty. through assoc. dir. SEC, Washington, 1977—89, dir., div. of enforcement, 1989—98; ptnr., co-chmn. Securities dept. Wilmer Cutler Pickering Hale & Dorr, Washington. Rsch. editor Temple Law Quar., 1972-75; contbr. articles to profl. jours. Recipient Nat. Pub. Svc. award, Nat. Soc. Pub. Adminstrn., 1996, Tom C. Clark Outstanding Lawyer award, Fed. Bar Assn., 1997; named a Leading Lawyer in securities & corp. governance, Legal Times, 2004; named one of Top 30 Lawyers in Washington, Washingtonian mag., 2004, 100 Most Influential Lawyers in Am., Nat. Law Jour., 1997. Mem. Phi Beta Kappa. Office: Wilmer Cutler Pickering Hale & Dorr 1875 Pa Ave NW Washington DC 20006 Office Phone: 202-663-6622. Office Fax: 202-663-6363. Business E-Mail: william.mclucas@wilmerhale.com.

MC LURE, CHARLES E., JR., economist, consultant; b. Sierra Blanca, Tex., Apr. 14, 1940; s. Charles E. and Dessie (Evans) McL.; m. Patsy Nell Carroll, Sept. 17, 1962. BA, U. Kans., 1962; MA, Princeton U., 1964, PhD, 1966. Asst. prof. econs. Rice U., Houston, 1965-69, assoc. prof., 1969-72, prof., 1972-79, Allyn R. and Gladys M. Cline prof. econs., 1973-79; exec. dir. for research Nat. Bur. Econ. Research, Cambridge, Mass., 1977-78, v.p., 1978-81; sr. fellow Hoover Instn., Stanford U., 1981—, emeritus, 2006; dep. asst. sec. Dept. Treasury, 1983-85. Sr. staff economist Coun. Econ. Advisers, Washington, 1969-70; vis. lectr. U. Wyo., 1972; vis. prof. Stanford U., 1973; cons. U.S. Treasury Dept., Labor Dept., World Bank, UN, OAS, Interam. Devel. Bank, Tax Found., Com. Econ. Devel., IMF, Internat. Tax and Investment Ctr., govts. Can., Colombia, Malaysia, Panama, Jamaica, Bolivia, Indonesia, New Zealand, Brazil, Trinidad and Tobago, Venezuela, Guatemala, Peoples Republic China, Egypt, Malawi, Mex., Bulgaria, Brazil, Russia, Ukraine, Romania, Kazakhstan, South Africa, Vietnam, Chile, Argentina. Author: Fiscal Failure: Lessons of the Sixties, 1972, (with N. Ture) Value Added Tax: Two Views, 1972, (with M. Gillis) La Reforma Tributaria Colombiana de 1974, 1977, Must Corporate Income Be Taxed Twice?, 1979, Economic Perperspectives on State Taxation of Multijurisdictional Corporations, 1986, The Value Added Tax: Key to Deficit Reduction, 1987; co-author: Taxation of Income from Business and Capital in Colombia, 1989; also numerous articles on econs., tax law and public finance. Ford Found. faculty research fellow, 1967-68, Disting. Svc. medal, US Treas. Dept., 1985, Daniel M. Holland medal, Nat. Tax Assn., 2004. Mem. Am. Econ. Assn., Nat. Tax Assn., Beta Theta Pi. Home: 250 Yerba Santa Ave Los Altos CA 94022-1609 Office: Stanford U Hoover Instn Stanford CA 94305-6010 Office Phone: 650-723-2657. Business E-Mail: cmclure@stanford.edu.

MCLURE, HOWARD A., pharmaceutical executive; BBA, Univ. Ga. CPA. Mgmt. positions through sr. v.p., controller Magellan Health Services Inc., 1984—98; sr. v.p. chief acctg. officer Caremark Inc., 1998—2000, exec. v.p., CFO, 2000—05, sr. exec. v.p., COO, 2005—07; exec. v.p., pres. Caremark Pharm. Services CVS Caremark Corp., Woonsocket, RI, 2007—. Mem.: Am. Inst. CPAs. Office: CVS Caremark Corp 1 CVS Dr Woonsocket RI 02895*

MCLURE, JOHN DOUGLAS, management consultant, former Canadian government official; b. Melita, Man., Can., July 10, 1942; s. Malcolm Alexander and Rachel (Simpson) McL.; m. Nicole Lafrance, Aug. 26, 1967. BSc, U. Man., Winnipeg, 1963; Ammunition Tech. Officer, Royal Mil. Coll. Sci., Shrivenham, Wiltshire, Eng., 1964. Program analyst Treasury Bd. Secretariat, Ottawa, Canada, 1975-79, group chief industry and natural resources divsn., 1979-80, dir. industry and natural resources divsn., 1980-82, asst. sec. econ. devel., 1982-84; asst. dep. min. small bus. and spl. projects Dept. Regional Indsl. Expansion, Ottawa, 1984-85, asst. dep. min. crown investments and spl. projects, 1985-86, asst. dep. min. native econ. devel., 1986-87; asst. dep. min. fin., pers., adminstrn. Dept Industry, Sci. & Tech., Ottawa, 1987—89; asst. dep. min. fin. Dept. Nat. Def., Ottawa, 1989—96, assoc. dep. min., 1996; dep. min. Dept. Western Econ. Diversification, Ottawa, 1996—97; sr. v.p. Hill and Knowlton Can. Ltd., Ottawa, 1997—2000, sr. assoc., 2000—. Chmn. bd. Def. Constrn. Can., 2001—08; CEO JDM Consulting Inc., 2000—; mem. internat. audit com. Correctional Svcs. Can., 2006—. Maj. Can. Land Forces, 1960-75. Recipient N.Am. Best Practice recognition, Ctr. Creative Leadership, Greensboro, N.C., 1994, Leadership award, Assn. Profl. Execs., 1995. Mem. Club Link Le Fontainebleau Golf Club, Rideau Club. Avocations: golf, alpine skiing. Office: Hill and Knowlton Can Ltd 55 Metcalfe St Ste 1100 Ottawa ON Canada K1P 6L5 Home: Ste 202-375 Lisgar St Ottawa ON Canada K2P 0E3 Home Phone: 613-612-0070. Business E-Mail: john.mclure@hillandknowlton.ca.

MCLURE, VICTORIA, literature and language professor; b. Houston, June 24, 1961; d. David and Dorothea McLure. PhD, Tex. Tech U., Lubbock, 1999. Cert. Profl. Skaters Assn., 2000. Lectr. English Tex. Tech U., 1985—92; prof. English South Plains Coll., Lubbock, Tex., 1992—. Skating dir. Tex. Tech Hockey, 2007—. Recipient Dir. of Honors award of Merit, Tex. Tech Honors Program, 1985, Interim Healthcare Commitment to Excellence award, Tex. Tech Hockey, 2008. Mem.: US Figure Skating Assn., Profl. Skaters Assn., Austin Figure Skating Club. Avocations: figure skating, reading, travel. Business E-Mail: vmclure@southplainscollege.edu.

MCLURKIN, THOMAS CORNELIUS, JR., lawyer; b. LA, July 28, 1954; s. Thomas Cornelius and Willie Mae (O'Connor) McL.; m. Charmaine Bobo. BA, U. So. Calif., 1976, MPA, 1980, postgrad., 1998; JD, U. LaVerne, 1982. Bar: Calif. 1984, U.S. Dist. Ct. (ctrl. dist.) Calif. 1984, U.S. Dist. Ct. Hawaii 1984, U.S. Ct. Appeals (9th cir.) 1984, U.S. Dist. Ct. (ea., no. and so. dists.) Calif. 1985, U.S. Tax Ct. 1988, U.S. Ct. Mil. Appeals 1989, U.S. Army Ct. Mil. Rev. 1993, U.S. Supreme Ct., 1995. Law clk. dept. water and power City of L.A., 1979-82; jud. clk. cen. dist. U.S. Dist. Ct., LA, 1982-83; law clk. Office City Atty., LA, 1983-84, dep. city atty., 1984—. Author (with others): Facts in American History, 1968, 2nd edit., 1989. Mem. LA World Affairs Coun., 1980—, Smithsonian Assocs.; bd. dirs. LA Area coun. Boy Scouts Am., Hillsides Homes for Children; provisional patron, mem. Tournament of Roses Assn., Pasadena, 1994—; mem. Verdugo Hills Area coun. Boy Scouts Am., Eagle Scout, 1970; pres. Verdugo Hilla Coun.; comdr. 75th Legal Support Orgn. Col. USAR. Mem. ABA, ALA (pres.), ASPA, Los Angeles County Bar Assn., Assn. Trial Lawyers Am., Langston Law Assn. L.A., U. So. Calif. Gen. Alumni Assn. (bd. govs. exec. bd. 1986-90), U. So. Calif. Black Alumni Assn.-Ebonics (pres. 1988-89), U. So. Calif. Pres.'s Cir., Elks, Am. Legion, Phi Alpha Delta, Kappa Alpha Psi. Republican. United Methodist. Avocations: sailing, tennis, volunteer work, American and world history. Office: LA City Atty Office 200 N Main St Ste 600 CHE Los Angeles CA 90012-4110 Home Phone: 818-244-3530; Office Phone: 213-978-6952. Business E-Mail: thomas.mclurkin-jr@lacity.org.

MCLUSKIE, ED, communications educator; s. Clarence Edward and Francis McLuskie, Irma McLuskie (Stepmother); m. Ariel Thomas Haney, Oct. 4, 2004; m. Mary Elizabeth Trapp, Aug. 11, 1974 (div. Jan. 11, 1986); 1 child, Melissa Davis. BA, Mont. State U., Billings, 1970; PhD, U. Iowa, Iowa City, 1975. Prof. U. Wis., Whitewater, 1974—78, Fla. Atlantic U., Boca Raton, 1978—80, Boise State U., 1981—; Fulbright prof. U. Vienna, 1996—97, guest prof., 2002; Fulbright prof. Tbilisi State U., Georgian Inst. Pub. Affairs, Georgia, 2004—05. Contbr. articles to profl. jours., chapters to books. Bd. dirs. Snake River Alliance, Boise, 1987—88; keynote spkr. Leadership Boise, 2005. Grantee, Can. Embassy, 1983; fellow, NEH, 1979, Fulbright Commn., 1996—97, 2004—08. Mem.: Javnost - The Pub. (edtl. bd. mem., Ljubljana 2004), Media & Zeif (edtl. bd. mem., Vienna 1997), Internat. Comm. Assn. (life). Office: Boise State Univ Dept Communication 1910 Univ Dr Boise ID 83725-1920 Personal E-mail: emclusk@gmail.com. Business E-Mail: emclusk@boisestate.edu.

MCLYMAN, MEGHAN, dance professor; b. Honolulu, Apr. 30, 1976; d. Edward and Kim McLyman; m. Eric Fisher, June 23, 2001. BA, Point Pk. U., Pitts., 1998; MA, Am. U., Washington, 2000; candidate, Hollins U., Roanoke, Va., 2007—. Instr. Salem State Coll., Mass., 2006—. Office: Salem State Coll 352 Lafayette St Salem MA 01970

MCMACKIN, GREG, college football coach; b. Springfield, Oreg., Apr. 24, 1949; m. Heather McMackin; 1 child, Shannon. BS, Southern Oreg. Coll., 1969; MEd, U. Ariz., 1970. Grad. asst., offensive backfield coach U. Ariz., 1968—69; asst. coach, head coach Aloha HS, Beaverton, Oreg., 1969—73; defensive coord., recruiting coord. Western Oreg. State, 1973—76; defensive coord., recruiting coord., secondary/linebacker U. Idaho, 1976—78; recruiting coord., secondary San Jose State U., 1978—84; linebackers coach Stanford U., 1984—85; secondary coach Denver Gold, USFL, 1985—86; head coach, asst. athletics dir. Oreg. Tech., 1986—90; defensive coord. U. Utah, 1990—92, Naval Acad., 1992—93, U. Miami., 1993—94, Seattle Seahawks, 1995—98, U. Hawai'i, 1999, 2007, head coach, 2008—; assoc. head coach, defensive coord. Texas Tech. U., 2000—02; assoc. head coach San Francisco 49ers, 2003—05. Author: Coaching the Defensive Backfield, 1992. Named Coach the Yr., Big 12's Top Recruiter, Rivals Web site; named one of Am. Top Coaches, Am. Football Mag.; named to Sports Hall of Fame, Southern Oreg. U. Mem.: Am. Football Coaches. Assn., NFL Coaches Assn. Mailing: U Hawaii 2500 Campus Rd Honolulu HI 96822 E-mail: football@hawaii.edu.

MCMAHAN, ROBERT, pharmacist, director; BS in Biology, Furman U., Greenville, 1996; MBA, Campbell U., Buies Creek, NC, 1999, PharmD, 2000; MS in Theol. Studies, Bethel Sem., St. Paul, Minn., 2006. Cert. ordained min. NC Baptists, 2006. Clin. pharmacy specialist Mayo Clinic, MMSI, Rochester, Minn., 2000—04; medicare pharmacy mgr. Humana Inc., Louisville, 2004—07; dir. pharmacy Fidelis Care NY, Rego Pk., 2007—09; dir. Optan Health, Golden Valley, Minn., 2009—. Bd. dir. AMCP Horizons, LLC, 2007—09, Acad. Managed Care Pharmacy, Alexandria, Va., 2007—; pres. Greater NY Region AMCP Affiliate, NYC, 2008—. Home: 8300 Golden Valley Rd Apt 333 Golden Valley MN 55427 Office: 6300 Olson Meml Hwy Golden Valley MN 55427 Office Phone: 763-797-2426.

MCMAHAN-WONEIS, CELESTINE, integrative medical educator, health psychologist, educator, educational therapist, health psychology educator; b. Denver, Jan. 4, 1948; d. Frank McMahan and Jean Dolores Kauno; m. John Thomas Woneis, Nov. 10, 2001 (dec.). BA in Urban Studies, U. Colo., Boulder, 1976, M in Urban and Regional Planning, 1977; MA in Orgnl. Psychology, Calif. Sch. Profl. Psychology, Berkeley, 1997, PhD in Orgnl. Psychology, 2002; cert. in ednl. therapy, U. Calif., Santa Cruz, 2006; MA, Henan U., China, 2006; postgrad. in Nutrition, Hawthorne U., 2009. Lic. real estate agt. Colo. Floral design cons. Lehr's Flowers and Alpha Floral, Denver, 1967—70; lic. real estate saleswoman, housing sales coord. Gt. Western United, Colorado City, Colo., 1970—73; archtl. project mgr. facilities planning Stanford U., Calif., 1977—80; designer, facilities planner corp. real estate dept. Sacramento Savs. & Loan, 1980—81; archtl. project mgr., corp. real estate dept. Crocker Bank, San Francisco, 1981—82; project mgr. design and constrn. and real estate, corp. real estate dept. Bank of Am., San Francisco, 1982—96; design cons. McLink, San Francisco, 1985—88; team mgr. design and constrn. Bank of Am., 1986—87; project mgr., design and constrn. cons. Grace Cathedral, San Francisco, 1993—96; mgr. design and constrn., cons. Boudin Bakery & Cafe, San Francisco, 1997—98; exec. coach, complimentary and alternative med. educator and practitioner, orgnl. health psychologist, ednl. therapist Wisdom, Wealth & Health, Felton, Calif., 1997—; labyrinth design and constrn. cons. Minn. Hosp., Mpls., 1999, Trinity Cath., Atlanta, 1999, Columbus, Ohio, 2000. Cons. redeployment team Bank of Am., 1995—96; cons. Veriditas, San Francisco, 1998—99, Parents Helping Parents, Santa Clara Staff Tng., Santa Clara, Calif., 2003—04; ednl. therapy cons. Devel. Learning Solutions, Santa Cruz, 2003—; bus. cons. Inner Voyages, Santa Cruz, 2006—; creativity and innovation cons. Mountain Pks. Found., Felton, 2006—; owner, leadership training for young adults, intergenerational and intercultural comm. Quantum Learning Acad., 2006; owner Wisdom and Wealth and Health, 2008. Interim dir. pks. and recreation City of Edgewater, Colo., 1973; cons., mem. com. Colo. Gov. Lamm's Housing Task Force, Denver, 1975—76; co-founder Aurora Devel. Corp., Calif., 1977; mem. Menlo Pk. Beautification Commn., 1978—79; fundraising cons. Friends of the Arts, San Francisco, 1985; cons. Spirit of Peace Conf., Women's Dream Quest Grace Cath., founder Michaelmas Faire, 1986; cons. Founding of the Labyrinth Project, San Francisco, 1996; docent Henry Cowell & Mountain Pks., Felton, 2006—; trustee Grace Cath.; bd. dirs. Friends of the Arts, Calif. Lawyers for the Arts, Inst. for Study of Natural Systems. Named Citizen of Yr., Hutt River Principality, 1995. Mem.: APA, Internat. Mind, Brain, Edn. Soc., Learning Brain Soc., Coun. for Exceptional Children, Optometric Ext. Program Found., Am. Assn. Clin. Nutritionists, Internat. Assn. Clin. Nutritionists, Assn. for Applied Psychophysiology and Biofeedback, Nat. Assn. Nutritional Profls., Assn. Ednl. Therapists, Am. Holistic Med. Assn., Nat. Assn. Neuropsychologists, Am. Assn. Integrative Medicine. Avocations: music, art, reenacting.

MCMAHON, CATHERINE DRISCOLL, lawyer; b. Mineola, NY, Apr. 28, 1950; d. Matthew Joseph and Elizabeth (Driscoll) McM.; m. Gregory Arthur McGrath, Sept. 10, 1977 (div. 1991); children: Elizabeth Driscoll, Kerry Margaret, Michael Riley. BA, Simmons Coll., 1972; JD, Boston Coll., 1975; postgrad., Suffolk U., 1972-73; LLM, NYU, 1980. Bar: NY 1976, DC 1979, US Supreme Ct. 1980, US Tax Ct. 1991. Tax atty. asst. Exxon Corp., NYC, 1975-76, asst. tax atty., 1976-77, sr. tax atty., 1979-81; tax atty. Exxon Internat. Co., NYC, 1977-79; sr. tax counsel Florham Park, NJ, 1990-92, Exxon Co. USA, Houston, 1992—98, Exxon Coal and Minerals Co., Houston, 1998—2002, Exxon Mobil Corp., 2003—. Tax mgr. Exxon Rsch. & Engring. Co., Florham Park, 1981-90. Bd. dirs. S.E. Morris chpt. ARC, Madison, NJ, 1983. Recipient TWIN award YMCA, Plainfield/Westfield, NJ, 1983. Mem. ABA, NY State Bar Assn., DC Bar Assn. Roman Catholic. Office: Exxon Mobil Corp 800 Bell St Houston TX 77002-7497 Business E-Mail: catherine.d.mcmahon@exxonmobil.com.

MCMAHON, DALTON EDWARD, history professor, social sciences educator, department chairman; b. Rapid City, SD, Nov. 12, 1945; s. Dalton William and Rosemary Lucille McMahon; m. Annie Buendia McMahon, Apr. 28, 1972; children: Annie Christina Norman, Dalton Edward Jr. BS in Edn., U. S.D., 1967, MA, 1975; DA, U. N.D., 1986. Social sci. tchr. Newman Grove (Nebr.) H.S., Dept. Def. Overseas Schs., Subic Bay Naval Station, Philippines, 1969—74, Giessen, Germany, 1974—82; grad. tchg. asst. history U. N.D., Grand Forks, 1982—85, instr. history, 1985—86; asst. prof. history Marymount of Kans., Salina,

1986—89; prof. history/social sci. Mayville (N.D.) State U., 1989—, chair liberal arts divsn., 2003—. Mem. coun. coll. faculties N.D. U. Sys., Bismarck, 1991—98, v.p. coun. coll. faculties, pres. coun. coll. faculties, 1994—95; mem. faculty senate Mayville State U., 1994—95, pres. faculty assn., 1995—97; lectr. in field. Judge DAR Outstanding Am. History Tchr. Contest, ND, 2002—03, Voice of Democracy Contest, Mayville, 1997—99; trustee United Ch. of Christ, Mayville, 1999—2003. Named U. N.D.Outstanding Grad. Historian, Phi Alpha Theta, U. N.D., 1985, Outstanding Tchr., Mayville State U., 1996, I.A. O'Shaughnessy Disting. Prof. of Humanities, Marrymount Coll. Kans., 1988—89; Atlantic-Bridges fellow, 2006. Mem.: Phi Alpha Theta. Home: 605 State Ave Portland ND 58274 Office: Mayville State University 330 3rd St NE Mayville ND 58257 Office Phone: 701-788-4808.

MCMAHON, DARRIN MICHAEL, history professor; b. Carmel, Calif., Sept. 27, 1965; m. Courtney Robyn Burke, July 17, 2005; 1 child, Julien Burke. PhD, Yale, 1996. Prof. history Fla. State U., Tallahassee, 2004—. Author: (book) Happiness: A History (Best Books of the Yr., 2006). Office: Dept History Fla Univ 401 Bellamy Tallahassee FL 32306-2200 Office Fax: 850-644-6402. Business E-Mail: dmcmahon@fsu.edu.

MCMAHON, EDWARD RICHARD, lawyer; b. Jersey City, June 7, 1949; s. Edward Barnawall and Jean (Sullivan) McM.; m. Ellen Mary Bosek; children: Meghan Jean, Kerry Eileen, Ryan Edward. AB, Colgate U., 1972; JD, Seton Hall U., 1975. Bar: NJ 1975, US Dist. Ct. NJ 1975, US Ct. of Appeals (3rd circ.) 1980. Law clk. to judge US Dist. Ct., Newark, 1975-77; assoc. Lum, Biunno & Tompkins, Newark, 1977-83; ptnr. Lum, Danzis, Drasco, & Positan, LLC, Roseland, NJ, 1983—. Mem. Essex County Chancery Ct. Mediation Prog., 1992—, Supreme Ct. of NJ Dist. Ethics Com., 1994—97, Supreme Ct. of NJ Dist. Fee Arbitration Com., 2000—; founding mem. and couns. Morris & Essex Inn of Transactional Counsel, 2001—; mem. US Dist. Ct. Arbitration Prog., 2001—, New Jersey Ct. Approved Mediator, 2002—. Mem. Morris County Rep. Com., NJ, 1982-94; mem. Chatham (NJ) Boro Rep. com., 1982-94, chmn., 1986-94; bd. dirs. Madison area YMCA, 1989-95; bd. trustees Richard J. Hughes Found., 2001-; mem. NJ State Rep. Com., 1994-. Mem.: ABA (litigation and banking sects.), Colgate U. Alumni Assn. (class rep. 1993—), 200 Club Morris County, Delbarton Sch. Alumni Assn. (class rep. 1984—), Essex County Bar Assn. (Essex County Chancery Ct. Mediation program 1992—, Supreme Ct. of N.J. dist. ethics com. 1994—97, Supreme Ct. of N.J. dist. fee arbitration com. 2000—, founding mem., counselor Morris & Essex Inn of Transactional Counsel 2001—, U.S. Dist. Ct. Arbitration program 2001—, N.J. Ct. approved mediator 2002—), Morris County Bar Assn., Am. Judicature Soc., Assn. Fed. Bar NJ, NJ Bar Assn., Colgate (No. NJ), Phi Alpha Delta, Delta Upsilon. Republican. Roman Catholic. Home: 150 Van Houton Ave Chatham NJ 07928-1239 Office: Lum Danzis Drasco & Positan LLC 103 Eisenhower Pky Roseland NJ 07068-1029 also: 325 Broadway New York NY 10007

MCMAHON, ELIZABETH WAGNER, mathematician, educator; b. Chapel Hill, NC, Aug. 1, 1953; d. John Alexander and Betty Wagner McMahon; m. Gary P. Gordon, June 27, 1982; children: Rebecca L. Gordon, Hannah R. Gordon. AB summa cum laude, Mt. Holyoke Coll., South Hadley, Mass., 1975; MS in Math., U. Mich., Ann Arbor, 1978; PhD, U. NC, Chapel Hill, 1982. Prof. math. Lafayette Coll., Easton, Pa., 1986—. Recipient James P. Crawford award, Math. Assn. Am. Eastern Pa. Del. Sect., 2005. Achievements include research in combinatorics. Office: Lafayette Coll Dept Mathematics Easton PA 18042 Business E-Mail: mcmahone@lafayette.edu.

MCMAHON, FRANCINE, publishing executive; BA in English, Hofstra U., Hempstead, NY. Formerly with The Weekly Standard, Roll Call, Congl. Quarterly; assoc. pub. The Hill, Capitol Hill Pub. Co. Inc., Washington, 1997—2007, exec. v.p., pub., 2007—. Office: The Hill 1625 K St NW Ste 900 Washington DC 20006 Office Phone: 202-628-8500. Office Fax: 202-628-8503.*

MCMAHON, FRANK V., insurance company executive; m. Vikki McMahon; 3 children. B in Econs., Villanova U., Pa.; MBA, Duke U., Durham, NC. With Merrill Lynch, 1994—99; positions up to mng. dir. Lehman Bros. Holdings, Inc., 1999—2006; vice chmn., CFO First Am. Corp., Santa Ana, Calif., 2006—. Bd. dirs. First Advantage Corp., 2006—. Office: First Am Corp 1 First American Way Santa Ana CA 92707 Office Phone: 714-250-3000.*

MCMAHON, GERALD LAWRENCE, lawyer; b. Youngstown, Ohio, July 16, 1935; s. Lawrence J. and Lee Z. McM.; m. Donna Ghio, June 17, 1956; children: Maria, Michael, Mark, Matthew, Angela. BS cum laude, U. So. Calif., 1956; JD summa cum laude, U. San Diego, 1964. Bar: Calif. 1965, U.S. Dist. Ct. (so. dist. Calif.), U.S. Ct. Claims 1966, U.S. Ct. Appeals (9th cir.) 1966, U.S. Supreme Ct 1966. Chief of contracts Centaur space vehicle program Gen. Dynamics Astronautics, San Diego, 1960-64; from assoc. to chmn. & head litigation dept. Seltzer Caplan McMahon Vitek, San Diego, 1964—. Adj. prof. Univ. San Diego Sch. Law, 1969—72; lectr. Calif. Western Law Sch. Editor: San Diego Law Rev., 1963-64; frequent speaker & legal edn. panelist. Trustee, Sidney Kimmel Cancer Ctr.; chmn. bd. vis., U. San Diego Law Sch., 1979-80, 1996-98. Aviator with USN, 1956-59. Fellow Am. Coll. Trial Lawyers; mem. ABA, San Diego Bar Assn. (vp., dir. 1974-77), State Bar of Calif. (disciplinary referee pro tem 1977-79), Am. Judicature Soc., Am. Bd. Trial Advocates (pres. San Diego chpt. 1981), Calif. Trial Lawyers Assn., Am. Arbitation Assn., Am. Acad. Matrimonial Lawyers, San Diego Inn of Ct. (panelist 1975, dir. 1979), Phi Alpha Delta, Order of the Coif. Republican. Roman Catholic. Avocations: tennis, skiing, lic. pvt. pilot. Office: Seltzer Caplan McMahon Vitek Symphony Towers 750 B St San Diego CA 92101 Office Fax: 619-702-6803. Business E-Mail: mcmahon@scmv.com.

MCMAHON, HARRY THOMAS, investment company executive; b. Chgo., June 1, 1953; s. Harry Thomas Jr. and Elizabeth (Vincent) McM.; m. Jacqueline Patricia McMahon, July 9, 1983; children: Ryan, Charles. BA, Claremont Coll., Calif., 1975; MBA, U. Chgo., 1980. 2d v.p. No. Trust Co., Chgo., 1975-83; v.p. Merrill Lynch Money Markets, Chgo., 1983-85; dir. investment banking div. through co-head corp. fin. group Merrill Lynch, 1985—2003, vice chmn., exec. client coverage group NYC, 2003—. Mem. pres.'s com. Landmarks Preservation Council Ill., Chgo., 1984; bd. dirs. aux. bd. Art Inst. Chgo., 1986, Chgo. Maternity Ctr., 1985. Avocations: golf, skiing, running.

MCMAHON, JAMES BRISLIN, medical researcher; b. Burlington, Vt., Oct. 9, 1950; s. James William and Margaret Joan (McGarry) McM.; m. Laurie Jean Hinds, Oct. 1, 1983; children: Megan, Michael. BA in Chemistry, U. Vt., 1972, PhD in Cell Biology, 1978. Scientist 1 Frederick Cancer Rsch. Ctr., Md., 1978-81, scientist 2, 1981-83; cancer expert Nat. Cancer Inst., Bethesda, Md., 1983-88, rsch. biologist, 1988-90; sr. rsch. biologist Frederick Cancer R&D Ctr., Nat. Cancer Inst., 1990; now dir. Molecular Targets Lab. Ctr. Cancer Rsch., Nat. Cancer Inst., NIH, Frederick. Contbr. articles to profl. jours.; patentee in field. Pres. Frederick County Alzheimer's Assn., 1987-89; mem. Sci. Curriculum Rev. Com., Frederick, 1990-91. Mem. Am. Chem. Soc., Tissue Culture Assn., N.Y. Acad. Scis., Am. Assn. for Cancer Rsch., Sigma Xi. Avocations: skiing, fishing, photography. Office: Nat Cancer Inst - Frederick Molecular Targets Devel Program PO Box B Bldg 1052 Rm 121 Frederick MD 21702-1201 Office Phone: 301-846-5391. Office Fax: 301-846-6919. E-mail: mcmahon@ncifcrf.gov.*

MCMAHON, JAMES CHARLES, lawyer; b. Bklyn., Dec. 4, 1951; s. James Charles and Rosemary Margaret (Gilroy) McM.; m. Nancy M. Neble, Oct. 30, 1984; children: Deirdre Kathleen Wright, Laura Elizabeth, Elizabeth Jane. BA, Boston Coll., 1973; JD, Fordham U., 1977. Bar: NY 1978, Mass. 1996, US Supreme Ct. 1996. Assoc. Winthrop Stimson Putnam & Roberts, NYC, 1977-78, Brodsky, Linett, Altman, Schechter & Reicher, NYC, 1978-82; ptnr. Brodsky, Altman & McMahon, LLP, NYC, 1982—2003, mng. ptnr., 1988—2003, McMahon & Kelly LLP, NYC, 2003—. Exec. sec., counsel NY Movers Tariff Bur., Inc., NYC, 1984-99; gen. counsel Mass. Movers Assn., South Attleboro, 1986—, Movers and Warehousemen's Assn. Greater NY, 1984-98, Met. Moving & Storage Assn., 1979-1998, USA Section of FIDI Inc., 1984—, Commonwealth Transp. Compensation Corp., Andover, Mass., 1992—, Transport Health Plan, Woburn, Mass., 1994-2003, NY State Movers and Warehousemen's Assn., NYC, 1984-2002, Nat. Moving and Storage Assn., Fairfax, Va., 1988-98, Am. Moving & Storage Tech. Found., Alexandria, Va., 1988-2006; adj. prof. bus. law Queens Borough Cmty. Coll., City Univ. NY, 2004-06. Mem. editl. bd. Fordham Urban Law Jour., 1976; author: Warehouseman's Lien & Auctions, 1991. Recipient Disting. Svc. award Mass. Movers Assn., 1992. Mem. NY State Bar Assn. (labor and employment law sect.), Assn. Bar City NY (transp. com. 1997-99), Assn. for Transp. Law, Logistics and Policy, NY Athletic Club. Democrat. Roman Catholic. Home: 196 Pinesbridge Rd Ossining NY 10562-1428 Office: McMahon & Kelly LLP 60 E 42d St Ste 1540 New York NY 10165-1544 also: 55 Donimo Dr Concord MA 01742 Office Phone: 212-986-4444. Business E-Mail: jmcmahon@mcmahonlaw.com.

MCMAHON, JAMES E., lawyer, former prosecutor; b. 1951; m. Kathy McMahon; 3 children. BS, Morningside U.; JD, U. S.D., 1977. Asst. atty. gen. State of SD, 1978—81; ptnr. Boyce, Murphy, McDowell & Greenfield, 1981—2002; pvt. practice Sioux Falls, SD, 2002—; US atty. Dist. SD US Dept. Justice, Sioux Falls, SD, 2002—05. Recipient Trial Lawyer of Yr. award, S.D. Trial Lawyers Assn., 2000.

MCMAHON, JAMES PATRICK, ecologist, consultant; b. Chgo., July 10, 1951; s. James Patrick and Helen Margaret (Walter) McM.; children: J. Emrys, Jacqueline Anne. BS in Ecology, U. Ill., 1974; postgrad., Ctrl. Wash. U., Ellensburg, 1975-76, Naropa Inst., Boulder, 1993-94. Owner Seattle Recycling, Inc., 1976-79; program planner City of Seattle, 1979-80; divsn. mgr. Fibres Internat., Bellevue, Wash., 1980-85; owner Environ. Enhancement Group, Lynnwood, Wash., 1985-88; regional mgr. 20:20 Recycle Ctrs., Inc., LA, 1987-88; nat. mktg. dir. May Mfg., Denver, 1990-94; ptnr. Agua Fria Enterprises, Prescott, Ariz., 1992-98; project dir. Nature Conservancy, 1994-98; dir. of Virgin River Programs Grand Canyon Trust, 1999—2002; CEO Sweetwater, LLC, 2002—. Sr. fellow Independence Inst., Golden, Colo., 1990-93; participant 50 for Colo. leadership program Colo. Assn. Commerce and Industry, 1993; condr. numerous bus. seminars; developer original recycling strategy City of Seattle; expatriot in Saint Martin, French West Indies, 1989. Exec. prodr. (video) Recycling in Washington State, 1985; contbr. many articles on Western pub. lands, natural resources, Philippine Eagle recovery, logging and men's issues to newspapers, mag. and other publs., U.S. and London; frequent radio commentator. Mem. survey and nat. conf. coms. Dept. Ecology, 1985-86; bd. dirs. Nat. Recycling Coalition, 1983-86. Mem. Greater Seattle C. of C., Rocky Mountain Angling Club, Trout Unltd. Avocations: skiing, fly fishing, scuba diving, hiking, camping. Home and Office: 375 Cedar Tree Dr Brookside UT 84782 E-mail: jim@jamespmcmahon.com.

MCMAHON, JOHN ALEXANDER, law educator; b. Monongahela, Pa., July 31, 1921; s. John Hamilton and Jean (Alexander) McMahon; m. Betty Wagner, Sept. 14, 1947 (div. Mar. 1977); children: Alexander Talpey, Sarah Francis, Elizabeth Wagner, Ann Wallace; m. Anne Fountain Willets, May 1, 1977 (dec. June 1996); m. Anne Hall Davis, Apr. 18, 1999. AB magna cum laude, Duke U., 1942; student, Harvard U. Bus. Sch., 1942—43; JD, Law Sch., 1948; LLD, Wake Forest U., 1978; DSc (hon.), Georgetown U. Sch. Medicine, 1985. Bar: N.C. 1950. Prof. pub. law and govt., asst. dir. Inst. Govt. U. N.C., 1948—59; gen. counsel, sec.-treas. N.C. Assn. County Commrs., Chapel Hill, 1959—65; v.p. spl. devel. Hosp. Saving Assn., Chapel Hill, NC, 1965—67; pres. N.C. Blue Cross and Blue Shield, Inc., Chapel Hill, 1968—72, Am. Hosp. Assn., Chgo., 1972—86; chmn. dept. health adminstrn. Duke U., Durham, NC, 1986—92, exec.-in-residence Fuqua Sch. Bus., 1992—2004. Mem. Chapel Hill bd. N.C. Nat. Bank, 1967—72; bd. govs. Blue Cross Assn., 1969—72; mem. Orange County Welfare Bd., 1956—63; chmn. N.C. Comprehensive Health Planning Coun., 1968—72, Health Planning Coun. of Ctrl. N.C., 1963—69; mem. Pres.'s Com. on Health Edn., 1971—72; mem. com. health svcs. industry and health industry adv. com. Econ. Stblzn. Program, 1971—74; mem. adv. coun. Kate Bitting Reynolds Health Care Trust, 1971—95, Northwestern U., 1973—86; mem. med. adv. com. VA, 1975—85; bd. dirs. The Forest at Duke, Durham, NC, 1994—2002, Exec. Svc. Corps of Greater Triangle, 1986—99, mem. adv. bd., 2000—04. Author: North Carolina County Government, 1959, The North Carolina Local Government Commission, 1960; editor: N.C. County Yearbook, 1959—64, Proceedings of the Annual National Forum on Hospital and Health Affairs, 1993—2000. Chmn. bd. trustees Duke U., 1971—83, chmn. emeritus, 1983—; bd. mgrs., mem. exec. com. Internat. Hosp. Fedn., London, 1975—85, pres., 1981—83; mem. Orange County Dem. Exec. Com., also chmn. Kings Mill Precinct, 1964—68; bd. dirs. Rsch. Triangle Found., 1971—83, 1992—2004, Nat. Ctr. for Health Edn., 1974—86. With USAF, 1942—46, col. Res., ret. Recipient Citation Disting. Svc. by Layman, AMA, 1978, Special award, Ill. Hosp. Assn., 1985, Dallas-Fort Worth Hosp. Coun., 1985, many others. Mem.: Inst. Medicine of NAS (Disting. Svc. award 1979), N.C. State Bar, Duke Alumni Assn. (pres. 1968—70, Silver Medal award 1986), Dunes Golf and Beach Club (Myrtle Beach), Hope Valley Country Club (Durham). Presbyterian. Home: 181 Montrose Dr Durham NC 27707-3929

MCMAHON, JOHN P., electronics executive; BS, Mercy Coll.; MS in Human Resource Mgmt., Upsala Coll., East Orange, NJ. Leadership position human resources Raytheon Corp., ITT Corp.; sr. v.p. global human resources Terra Lycos, S.A., Fisher Sci.; sr. v.p., chief human resources officer UMass Meml. Health Care Sys.; sr. v.p. corp. human resources Arrow Electronics, Inc., Melville, NY, 2007—. Office: Arrow Electronics Inc 50 Marcus Dr Melville NY 11747-4210 Office Phone: 631-847-2000.*

MCMAHON, JOSEPH M., economics educator; b. Cape May Court House, NJ, Oct. 25, 1958; s. William F. and Suzanne E. McMahon; m. Judith A. Winterstein, Nov. 29, 1980; children: Carly J. Mailloux, Peter J., Colleen F., Bridget E., Patrick H. BA, SUNY Cortland, 1980, MEd, 1992, CAS, 2004. Adj. instr. Tompkins Cortland CC, Dryden, NY, 1984—2009; social studies dept. leader Cortland City Schs., NY, 1987—2009. Pres. Cortland Fed. Credit Union, 1991—2004. Recipient Eagle Scout award, Boy Scouts America, 1975. Democrat. Roman Catholic. Avocations: swimming, golf, skiing. Home: 3 Ridgeview Ave Cortland NY 13045 Office: Cortland City Schs 8 Valley View Dr Cortland NY 13045

MCMAHON, MICHAEL E., United States Representative from New York, former city councilman; b. Staten Island, NY, Sept. 9, 1957; m. Judith Novellino; children: Joseph, Judith. AA, Heidelberg U., 1983; BA, NYU, NYC, 1980; JD, NY Law Sch., 1985. Aide Councilman Jerome X. O'Donovan; counsel Assemblywoman Elizabeth Connelly, Assemblyman Eric N. Vitaliano; city councilman Dist. 49, Staten Island, NY, 2002—09; ptnr. McMahon & Spero; mem. US Congress from 13th NY Dist., 2009—. Mem. Friends of Allison Pond Pk., Neighborhood Housing Services, Inc., Goodhue Ctr. the Children's Aid Soc., Dr. Theodore Atlas Found.; lector Blessed Sacrament Ch.; mem. Cath. Youth Org.; bd. dirs. Meals On Wheels of Staten Island, Inc.; pres. Randall Manor Residents' Assn. Named Man of Yr., Staten Island Ctr. Ind. Living, 1999. Mem.: Ancient Order Hibernians, Divsn. 3 (Cmty. Svc. award 2000). Democrat. Roman Catholic. Office: US Congress 323 Cannon House Office Bldg Washington DC 20515-3213 also: Dist Office 4434 Amboy Rd 2nd Fl Staten Island NY 10312 Office Phone: 202-225-3371, 718-356-8400. Office Fax: 202-226-1272, 718-356-1928.*

MCMAHON, PATRICK J., orthopedist; MD, Temple U., Phila., 1987. Diplomate Am. Bd. Orthop. Surgery, 1998. Owner McMahon Orthops. & Rehab., Pitts., 2006—. Editor: (book) Current Diagnosis and Treatment, Sports Medicine. Recipient prize, Bucknell U., 1983; grant, Rehab. R & D, Veterans Affairs, 1996—2001, NIAMS, 2004—08. Mem.: Am. Acad. Orthop. Surgeons, Soc. Am. Shoulder & Elbow Surgeons, Phi Beta Kappa. Avocations: fishing, golf, hiking. Office: McMahon Orthops & Rehab 2100 Jane St Pittsburgh PA 15203 Office Fax: 412-431-7341.

MCMAHON, RICHARD A., finance educator; married. DBA, Argosy U., Sarasota, 2007. Maj. USAF, 1970—91; asst. prof. U. Houston-Downtown, 2000—. Author: (textbook) Introduction to Networking. Office: Univ Houston-Downtown 1 Main St Houston TX 77002 Business E-Mail: mcmahonr@uhd.edu.

MCMAHON, ROBERT MATTHEW, corporate financial executive; b. Bronx, NY; s. Robert Patrick and Evelyn (Kaul) McM.; m. Kristin E. Dodge. BA in Econs., Fairfield U., 1987; MBA, Northwestern U. V.p. European Am. Bank, Uniondale, NY, 1987—91, EURAM Mgmt., Inc., Uniondale, 1991; joined structured assets group GE Comml. Fin. GE, 2000, six sigma team leader, GE Capital Funding, sr. v.p. GE Capital Funding, COO comml. & industrial fin. group, 2003—05, mng. dir. restructuring, GE Corp. Lending, 2005—. Mem. Charles F. Dolan Sch. Bus. Advisory Coun. Office: GE Comml Fin 260 Long Ridge Rd Stamford CT 06927*

MCMAHON HAWKINS, PATRICIA, United States Ambassador to Togo; m. Richard S.D. Hawkins; children: Frédéric, Jessica. Attended, Barnard Coll., NYC; BS in Edn., E. Stroudsburg U., Pa.; student in French, Georgetown U., Washington, Université de Dijon, NYU, NYC. Elem. and secondary sch. tchr., France, Pa.; joined US Internat. Comm. Agency (renamed USIA), Washington, 1980, country affairs officer, Francophone West Africa, policy application and coordination officer; asst. info. officer and dep. press attaché US Dept. State, Paris, info. officer Kinshasa, Democratic Republic of Congo, pub. affairs officer Ouagadougou, Burkina Faso, cultural affairs officer Bogotá, Colombia, counselor pub. affairs, acting dep. chief of mission, chargé d'affaires Abidjan, Cote d'Ivoire, counselor pub. affairs Dominican Republic, 2001, policy application and coordination officer, bur. African affairs, career devel. officer, bur. human resources, US amb. to Togo Lomé, 2008—; exec. asst. to the pres. and CEO Otis Elevator Co., Farmington, Conn. Pub. affairs advisor to the US del. CSCE Conf. on the Human Dimension, Paris, 1989. Office: DOS Amb 2300 Lome Pl Washington DC 20521-2300*

MCMANAMAN, KENNETH CHARLES, lawyer; b. Fairfield, Calif., Jan. 25, 1950; s. Charles James and Frances J. (Holys) McM.; m. Carol Ann Wilson, Apr. 15, 1972; children; Evan John, Kinsey Bridget, Klerin Rose. BA cum laude, S.E. Mo. State U., 1972; JD, U. Mo., Kansas City, 1974; grad., Naval Justice Sch., Newport, RI, 1975; MS in Bus. Mgmt. summa cum laude, Troy State U., Montgomery, Ala., 1978; LLM in Advanced Litigation, Nottingham-Trent U., 2004. Bar: Mo. 1975, US Dist. Ct. (we. dist.) Mo. 1975, Fla. 1976, US Dist. Ct. (No. and mid. dists.) Fla. 1976, US Dist. Ct. Mil. Appeals 1977, US Ct. Appeals (5th and 8th cirs.) 1977, US Dist. Ct. (ea. dist.) Mo. 1978, US Supreme Ct. 1978, D.C. 1991; cert. mil. judge spl. 1996, gen. ct. martials 1998; diplomate Am. Bd. Forensic Examiners; cert. Homeland Security, Level III, Am. Coll. Forensic Examiners Internat.; qualified mil. judge gen. ct. martial, Navy-Marine Corps. Prof. bus. law Troy (Ala.) State U., 1976-78, SEMO State U., 1980—; pvt. practice; ptnr. O'Loughlin, O'Loughlin & McManaman, Cape Girardeau, Mo., 1978—2002, Kenneth C. McManaman, Esq., 2002—06, Kenneth C. McManaman, LLC, 2006—; prof. bus. law S.E. Mo. State U., Cape Girardeau, 1978-84, prof. criminal justice, 1998—; prof. leadership Sch. Law William Woods U., 1998—; prof. bus. mgmt. Sch. Law Nat. Inst. Trial Advocacy; adj. prof. SIU Law Sch., 1985—, Nottinham Trent U., Law Sch., 2005—. Mem. Cape Girardeau County Coun. on Child Abuse, 1980—89; membership dir. S.E. Mo. scouting coun. Boy Scouts Am., 1980—82; mem. Cape Girardeau County Mental Health Assn., 1982—92; sponsor drug edn./prevention program in schs.; sec., pres. Jackson Area Soccer Assn., 1987—93; mem. Jackson R-2 Alt. Sch. Bd., 1999—; mem. dept. acctg. and fin. adv. bd. S.E. Mo. State U., 2001—03; active local and state Dem. Party, del. Dem. Nat. Conv., San Francisco, 1984; chmn. County Dem. Com., 1984—96; mem. 8th Congl. Dist. Dem. Com., 1984—86, 27th State Dem. Senatorial Com., 1980—90; ward committeeman Dem. Party, 1984—96; hon. chmn., bus. adv. coun. Nat. Rep. Congl. Com.; bd. dirs. Area-wide Task Force on Drug and Alcohol Abuse, 1984—87, Cape County chpt. Nat. Kidney Found., 1988—93, S.E. Mo. State Alumni Assn., 2006—. Capt. JAGC USNR, 1994—2003. Recipient Robert Chilton award City of Jackson for Leadership, Integrity and Responsibility, 1995-97, Nat. Leadership award, 2006; named One of Outstanding Young Men Am., 1981, 82, 84, 85, Outstanding Pub. Svc. award Cape Girardeau Police Dept. Fellow Am. Bd. Forensic Examiner; mem. ABA (Mo. del. young lawyers divsn. 1982-83), Mo. Bar Assn. (chmn. trial advocacy task force 1983), Mo. Bar (young lawyers sect. coun. rep. dist. 13 1980-85), Fla. Bar Assn., Kansas City Bar Assn., Assn. Trial Lawyers Am., Fed. Bar Assn., Nat. Coll. Dist. Attys., Cape Girardeau County Bar Assn. (founder, pres. young lawyers sect. 1981-82), Cape County Bar Assn. (sec. 1999, treas. 2000, v.p. 2001, 06, pres. 2007), Naval Res. Assn. (v.p. S.E. Mo/So. Ill. chpt. 1980-85, 2001—06), Grand Praetor So. Mo. Province, Order of Constantine, S.E. Mo. State U. Alumni (bd. dirs., mem. coun.), Sigma Chi (numerous awards), Sigma Tau Delta, Pi Delta Epsilon. Roman Catholic. Home: 1162 Trail Ridge Dr Jackson MO 63755-3507 Office: Blattner Bldg Ste One 1028A N Kings Hwy Cape Girardeau MO 63701 Home Phone: 873-845-7829; Office Phone: 573-335-8522. Personal E-mail: kcn@mcmananlaw.com. Business E-Mail: kenmcm@sbcglobal.net.

MCMANIS, DENA EDWY, psychologist, consultant; b. Montreal, Quebec, Can., Sept. 12, 1974; d. Mido and Sue Edwy; m. James McManis, Oct. 18, 2008. BA, U. Ga., Athen, 1996; MA, John Jay Coll. Criminal Jusitice, NYC, 2000; MA EdS, Chapman U., Walnut Creek, Calif., 2006. Substance abuse specialist NYC Bd. Edn., 2000—03; behavior specialist Fred Finch Youth Ctr., Oakland, Calif., 2003—06; sch. psychologist San Francisco Unified Sch. Dist., 2006—. Mem.: NASP. Home: 5484 Taft Ave Oakland CA 94618 Office: San Francisco Unified Sch Dist 555 Portola Dr Rm 244 San Francisco CA 94131 Personal E-mail: denaedwy@yahoo.com.

MCMANIS, JAMES, lawyer; b. Haverhill, Mass., May 28, 1943; s. Charles and Yvonne (Zinn) McM.; m. Sara Wigh, Mar. 30, 1968. BA, Stanford U., Palo Alto, Calif., 1964; JD, U. Calif., Berkeley, 1967. Bar: Calif. 1967, U.S. Dist. Ct. (no. dist.) Calif. 1967, U.S. Ct. Appeals (9th cir.) 1967, U.S. Supreme Ct. 1971. Dep. dist. atty. Santa Clara County Dist. Atty., 1968-71; mem. McManis, Faulkner, San Jose, Calif., 1971—. Spl. master tech. equities litig., 1987-98; spl. examiner State Bar Calif., 1995-98; prof. law Lincoln U. Law Sch., San Jose, 1972-82; lectr. Calif. Continuing Edn. of Bar, 1989-90; instr. U. Calif. Law Sch., 1992-96, Stanford U. Sch. Law, 1994-99. Pres. Santa Clara County Bar Assn. Law Found., 1996, dir., 1987—. Fellow Am. Coll. Trial Lawyers, Internat. Acad. Trial Lawyers, Am. Bar Found.; mem. ABA, State Bar Calif., Calif. Trial Lawyers Assn., Santa Clara County Bar Assn., Boalt Hall Alumni Assn. (pres. 2009). Avocations: history, books, travel, running. Office: McManis Faulkner 50 W San Fernando St 10th fl San Jose CA 95113 Office Phone: 408-279-8700. Fax: 408-279-3244. Business E-Mail: jmcmanis@mcmanislaw.com.

MCMANUS, ALESIA, librarian; BS, U. Calif., 1988; MLS, UCLA, 1991. Med. libr. Cedars Sinai Med. Ctr., LA, 1991—92; sci. reference libr. NC State U., Raleigh, NC, 1992—99; sci. & tech. U. Md., Coll. Pk., 1999—2004; head rsch., info. instrnl. svcs. Binghamton U., 2004—. Fellow, U. Calif., 1989. Mem.: ALA.

MCMANUS, DECLAN PATRICK See **COSTELLO, ELVIS**

MCMANUS, DELANA ANN, elementary school educator; b. Tulsa, Okla., Mar. 9, 1970; d. Richard Lee and Mary Alice Campbell; m. Sean Michael McManus, June 17, 1995; children: Alexandra, Pete. BA in early childhood Edn., Northeastern State U., Tahlequah, Okla., 1993; MS, Okla. State U., Stillwater, 1996; EdD, Okla. State U., 1999. Cert. early Childhood Edn., Reading specialist, Elem. Edn. First grade tchr. Tulsa Pub. Schs., Tulsa, Okla., 1993—97; reading specialist titleI coord. Bixby Pub. Sch., Bixby, Okla., 1997—. Contbr. scientific papers. Mem.: NEA, Bixby Edn. Assn. Republican. Avocations: reading, travel, scrapbooks. Office: Bixby Pub Schs 501 S Riverview Bixby OK 74008 Business E-Mail: dmcmanus@bixbyps.org.

MCMANUS, JAMES WILLIAM, lawyer; b. Kansas City, Mo., Aug. 1, 1945; s. Gerald B. and Mary M. McManus. BA, Rockhurst Coll., 1967; JD, St. Louis U., 1971. Bar: Mo. 1971, U.S. Dist. Ct. (we. dist.) Mo. 1972, U.S. Ct. Appeals (8th cir.) 1974, U.S. Supreme Ct. 1979, U.S. Ct. Appeals (10th cir.) 1984, U.S. Dist. Ct. Kans., 1995. Law clk. to presiding justice U.S. Dist. Ct. (we. dist.) Mo., 1971-73; assoc. Shughart, Thomson & Kilroy, P.C., Kansas City, 1973-76, dir., 1977-94; counsel Dysart, Taylor, Lay, Cotter & McMonigle, P.C., Kansas City, 1994—2002, DeWitt & Zeldin, L.L.C., Kansas City, 2002—04, McManus Law Offices, Kansas City, 2005—. Course lectr. med. jurisprudence U. Health Scis., Coll. Osteo. Medicine, Kansas City, 1994; lectr. in field. Adv. coun. St. Joseph Health Ctr., 1989-2002, modulator, spkr. Auto Accidents, Insurance & Litigation, Mo Bar CLE, 2009. Recipient Best of the Bar, Appeals and Trials, Kansas City Bus. Jour., 2008, Congenial Counselor award, Kansas City Metro Bar Assn., 2003, Exceptional Trial and Appellate atty. award, Mo. Ho. Reps., 2003; named to Best of the Bar, Appeals and Trials, Kansas City Bus. Jour., 2003, 2005, 2006. Fellow Am. Bar Found.; mem. ABA, AAJ (membership com. 2003-), Mo. Bar Assn., Kansas City Lawyers Assn., Kansas City Met. Bar Assn. (chmn. alternate dispute resolution com. 1996-97, vice chmn. 1994-95, chmn. med. malpractice com. 1989, Congenial Counselor award 2003), Mo. Assn. Trial Attys., Nat. Lawyers Assn., St. Louis Alumni Assn. (pres. 1984-92), St. Louis U. Law Sch. Alumni Assn. Home: 6824 Valley Rd Kansas City MO 64113-1929 Office: McManus Law Offices 1111 Main St Ste 700 Kansas City MO 64105 Office Phone: 816-474-3018, 816-835-1850. Personal E-mail: j-w-mcmanus@hotmail.com. Business E-Mail: jamesmcmanus@justice.com.

MCMANUS, JASON DONALD, retired editor-in-chief; b. Mission, Kans., Mar. 3, 1934; s. John Alan and Stella Frances (Gosney) McM.; m. Patricia Ann Paulson, Oct. 18, 1958 (div. Feb. 1966); 1 child, John Alan; m. Deborah Hall Murphy, Dec. 2, 1973; children: Sophie Eleanor, Mage Caroline. BA, Davidson Coll., 1956, Litt.D. (hon.), 1979; M.P.A., Princeton U., 1958; postgrad., Oxford U., 1958-59; LittD (hon.), Monmouth Coll., 1988, U. N.C., 1991, Loyola U., Balt., 1992. Common Market bur. chief Time Mag., Paris, 1962-64, assoc. editor NYC, 1964-68, sr. editor, 1968-75, asst. mng. editor, 1975-78, exec. editor, 1978-83, mng. editor, 1985-87; corp. editor Time Inc., NYC, 1983-85; editor-in-chief Time Warner Inc., NYC, 1987-95; ret. Author: short stories Introduction, 1960. Mem. presdl. adv. commn. Internat. Edn. Exchange, 1982-83. Rhodes scholar, 1958-59. Mem.: Century Assn. (N.Y.C.).

MCMANUS, JOHN COYNE, educator, writer; s. Michael Francis and Mary Jane McManus; m. Nancy Woody McManus. PhD, U. Tenn., Knoxville, 1996. Assoc. prof. U. Mo., Rolla, 2000—. Contbr. monographs.

MCMANUS, PATRICK FRANCIS, editor, educator, writer; b. Sandpoint, Idaho, Aug. 25, 1933; s. Francis Edward McManus and Mabel Delana (Klaus) DeMers; m. Darlene Madge Keough, Feb. 3, 1954; children: Kelly C., Shannon M., Peggy F., Erin B. BA in English, Wash. State U., 1956, MA in English, 1962, postgrad., 1965-67. News reporter Daily Olympian, Olympia, Wash., 1956; editor Wash. State U., Pullman, 1956-59; with Ea. Wash. U., Cheney, 1959—; ret., 1983; news reporter Sta. KREM-TV, 1960-62; assoc. prof. Ea. Wash. U., Cheney, 1971-74, prof., 1974-83, prof. emeritus, 1983—. Author: A Fine and Pleasant Misery, 1978, Kid Camping from Aaaaiii! to Zip, 1979, They Shoot Canoes, Don't They?, 1981, Never Sniff a Gift Fish, 1983, The Grasshopper Trap, 1985, Rubber Legs & White Tail-Hairs, 1987, The Night The Bear Ate Goombaw, 1989, Whatchagot Stew, 1989, Real Ponies Don't Go Oink!, 1991, The Good Samaritan Strikes Again, 1992, How I Got This Way, 1994, Never Cry "Arp!" and Other Great Adventures, 1996, Into the Twilight, Endlessly Grousing, 1997, The Deer on a Bicycle, Excursions Into the Writing of Humor, 2000, The Bear in the Attic, 2002, The Blight Way, 2006, Avalanche, 2007, Kerplunk!, 2007, The Double Jack Murders, 2009; (stage play) A Fine and Pleasant Misery: The Humor of Patrick F. McManus, 1994, Misery II: McManus In Love, 1995, Pat McManus, Endlessly Grousing, 1997, Pott's Luck, 1999, Poor Again--Dagnabbit!, 2009; assoc. editor Field & Stream mag., 1977-81; editor-at-large Outdoor Life, 1981—2009. Recipient Booksellers award P.N.W. Booksellers, 1983, Trustees medal EWU, 1984, Gov.'s award Wash. State Libr., 1985, Excellence in Craft award OWAA, 1986, Disting. Achievement award WSU, 1994, Founder's Day award EWU, 1994, Disting. alumni Series award, 2003; Circle of Honor award The Outdoor Channel, 2004; named to Idaho's Hall of Fame Assn. Outstanding Achievement, 1995, Legendary Communicator, Nat. Fresh Water Fishing Hall Fame, 2004, OWAA Legends, 2007. Mem.: Mystery Writers America, Outdoor Writers Am. (bd. dirs. 1981—84, Excellence award 1986), Authors Guild. Roman Catholic. Avocations: outdoor sports, woodworking.

MCMANUS, RICHARD PHILIP, lawyer, agricultural products executive; b. Keokuk, Iowa, Oct. 20, 1929; s. Edward William and Kathleen (O'Connor) M.; m. Marjorie Theresa Mullaney, Nov. 5, 1955; children: Michael L., Mark J., Matthew A. BA, St. Ambrose U., Davenport, Iowa, 1949; JD, U. Mich., 1952; MBA, Roosevelt U., Chgo., 1965. Bar: Calif. 1982, Ill. 1958, Iowa 1952. Ptnr. McManus & McManus, Keokuk, 1953-63; div. counsel USN Facility Engring. Command, Great Lakes, Ill., 1963-66; v.p., dir. law Household Fin. Corp., Chgo., 1966-81; exec. v.p., sec. Security Pacific Fin. Svcs., Inc., San Diego, 1981-91, gen. counsel, 1982—91; exec. v.p./sec. Bank Am. Fin. Svcs., San Diego, 1991-92, gen. counsel, 1991—92; pres., chmn. bd. dirs. Mosamac Co., Inc., 1992—. Mem. gen. com. Conf. Consumer Fin. Law, Chgo., 1975-92; mem. adv. bd. Hostler Inst. Internat. Affairs, San Diego State U., 2005-08. Contbr. articles to profl. jours. Bd. dir., treas., atty. Tijuana/San Diego Habitat for Humanity, Inc., 1992-95; trustee Village of Lake Bluff, Ill., 1974-78; bd. dir. Charles Hostler Inst. World Affairs, San Diego State U., 2004-07. Recipient San Diego Vol. Lawyer Disting. Svc. award, 1995-, Pres. Calif. Bar Pro Bono Svs. award, 1998; named San Diego Pro Bono Atty. of Yr., 2005. Mem. Calif. Bar Assn., San Diego Bar Assn., Calif. Fin. Svcs. Assn. (chmn. law com. 1981-92), Am. Fin. Svcs. Assn. (chmn. law forum 1980-81, Disting. Svc. award 1990), Lions, Elks, KC, Beta Gamma Sigma. Democrat. Roman Catholic. Avocations: golf, flying, sailing, woodworking. Personal E-mail: mcman1000@gmail.com.

MCMANUS, ROBERT JOSEPH, bishop; b. Providence, July 5, 1951; s. Edward W. and Helen F. (King) McManus. BA, MA, Cath. U. Am., Washington; MDiv, Toronto Sch. Theology; DST, Pontifical Gregorian U., Rome. Ordained priest Diocese of Providence, 1978, aux. bishop, 1999—2004; asst. chaplain St. Joseph Hosp., 1978; assoc. pastor St. Matthew Parish, Cranston, RI, 1978—81, St. Anthony Parish, Providence, 1981—82; Cath. chaplain Cmty. Coll. RI, Warwick, 1982—84; dir. Diocesan Office of Ministerial Formation, 1986; diocesan vicar edn., 1987; resident St. Luke Parish, Barrington, RI, 1987; named monsignor, 1997; rector Our Lady of Providence Sem., 1998—2004; ordained bishop, 1998; bishop Diocese of Worcester, Mass., 2004—. Theological cons., editl. writer The Providence Visitor newspaper; chmn. com. on edn. US Conf. Cath. Bishops. Roman Catholic. Office: Diocese of Worcester 49 Elm St Worcester MA 01609-2597 Business E-Mail: rmcmanus@worcesterdiocese.com.

MCMANUS, SEAN JOSEPH, broadcast executive; b. Feb. 16, 1955; s. James Kenneth and Margaret Dempsey McManus; m. Tracy Lynne Torre, May 23, 1998. BA in English & History, cum laude, Duke U., 1977. Prodn. asst. to assoc. prodr. ABC Sports, NYC, 1977—79; assoc. prodr. to prodr. NBC Sports, NYC, 1979—81, v.p. planning, devel., 1981—87; sr. v.p. US TV sales, programming Trans World Internat. (TV divsn. IMG), NYC, 1987—96; pres. CBS Sports, NYC, 1996—, CBS News, NYC, 2005—. Dir. CBS SportsLine, 1997—. Named one of The Most Influential People in the World of Sports, Bus. Week, 2007, 2008. Office: CBS TV 51 W 52 St New York NY 10019

MCMANUS, WILLIAM PAUL, police chief; married; 3 children. Bachelor's degree, Villanova U.; MS, Johns Hopkins U. Police officer Met. Police Dept., Washington, asst. police chief, 1998—2001; police chief City of Dayton, Ohio, 2001—03, City of Mpls., 2004—06, City of San Antonio, 2006—.

MCMARTIN, JOHN, actor; b. Warsaw, Ind., 1929; children: Kathleen Alice, Susan Helen. Actor: (Broadway plays) The Conquering Hero, 1961, Blood, Sweat and Stanley Poole, 1961, Children From Their Games, 1963, A Rainy Day in Newark, 1963, Sweet Charity, 1966 (Tony award nomination best featured actor in a musical, 1966), Follies, 1971, The Great God Brown, 1972—73 (Drama Desk award outstanding performance, 1973), Don Juan, 1972 (Drama Desk award outstanding performance, 1973, Tony award nomination best featured actor in a play, 1973), Sondheim: A Musical Tribute, 1973, The Visit, 1973, Chemin de Fer, 1973—74, Love for Love, 1974, The Rules of the Game, 1974, Happy New Year, 1980, Solomon's Child, 1982, A Little Family Business, 1982, Artist Descending a Staircase, 1989, Show Boat, 1994 (Tony award nomination best actor in a musical, 1995), High Society, 1998 (Drama Desk award nomination outstanding featured actor in a musical, 1998, Tony award nomination best featured actor in a musical, 1995), Into the Woods, 2002 (Tony award nominaton best actor in a musical, 2002), Passion, 2004, (off-Broadway) Little Mary Sunshine, 1959—60 (Theatre World award, 1960), The Misanthrope, 1977, Too Much Johnson, 1985, Henry IV, 1985, Julius Caesar, 1988, Grey Gardens, 2006 (Drama Desk award nomination outstanding featured actor in a musical, 2006), Indian Blood, 2006; (films) A Thousand Clowns, 1965, What's So Bad About Feeling Good?, 1968, Sweet Charity, 1969, All the President's Men, 1976, Thieves, 1977, Brubaker, 1980, Blow Out, 1981, Pennies from Heaven, 1981, Dream Lover, 1986, Legal Eagles, 1986, Native Son, 1986, Who's That Girl?, 1987, Little Sweetheart, 1989, A Shock to the System, 1990, Three Businessmen, 1998, The Dish, 2000, Kinsey, 2004; (TV films) Ride with Terror, 1963, Out of the Blue, 1968, Ritual of Evil, 1970, God Bless Mr. Ferguson, 1971, The Rules of the Game, 1975, Fear on Trial, 1975, The Fatal Weakness, 1976, The Defection of Simas Kudirka, 1978, Butterflies, 1979, The Greatest Man in the World, 1980, Looking Back, 1981, Private Contentment, 1982, The Last Ninja, 1983, Concealed Enemies, 1984, Murrow, 1986, Lincoln, 1988, Roots: The Gift, 1988, Day One, 1989, Separate But Equal, 1991, Citizen Cohn, 1992, H.U.D., 2000. Mem.: The Players (N.Y.C.). Office: The Artists Agy 1000 Santa Monica Blvd North Hollywood CA 91601

MCMASTER, BELLE MILLER, religious organization administrator; b. Atlanta, May 24, 1932; d. Patrick Dwight and Lila (Bonner) Miller; m. George R. McMaster, June 19, 1953; children: Lisa McMaster Stork, George Neel, Patrick Miller. BA, Agnes Scott Coll., 1953; MA, U. Louisville, 1970, PhD, 1974. Assoc. corp. witness Presbyn. Ch. USA, Atlanta, 1974-77, dir. corp. witness, 1977-81, dir. div. corp. and social mission, 1981-87, dir. social justice and peacemaking unit Louisville, 1987-93; acting dir. program women in theology and ministry Candler Sch. Theology Emory U., 1993-96, dir. advanced studies Candler Sch. Theology, 1995—2003. Vice-moderator chs. commn. internat. affairs World Coun. Chs., 1984-91, mem. justice, peace and creation commn., 1991-99; chair commn. internat. affairs Nat. Coun. Chs., NYC, 1986-89, v.p., 1990-95, exec. bd., 1986-2003, chair ch. world svc. and witness unit com., 1990-2003; chair fin. com. Ch. World Svc. and Witness Unit Com., NC, 1997-99, bd. dirs., 1995-2003. Author: Witnessing to the Kingdom, 1982, book columnist "What I Have Been Reading" in Church and Society Magazine, 1993-2001; contbr. articles to profl. jours. Pres. League of Women Voters, Greenville, S.C., 1963-64; bd. dirs. Interfaith Housing, Atlanta, 1975-81. Danforth fellow, 1969-74. Mem.: MLA, Soc. for Values in Higher Edn., Acad. Am. Religion, Phi Beta Kappa. Presbyterian. Business E-Mail: bmcmast@emory.edu.

MCMASTER, BRIAN JOHN, artistic director; b. May 9, 1943; With internat. artists dept. EMI, 1968-73; contr. opera planning English Nat. Opera, 1973-76; mng. dir. Welsh Nat. Opera, Cardiff, 1976-91; dir. Edinburgh Internat. Festival, Scotland, 1991—2006; artistic dir. Vancouver Opera, BC, Canada, 1983-89. E-mail: brian.mcmaster@hotmail.co.uk.

MCMASTER, GLORIA (GLORIA BUGNI JUHN), mezzo-soprano, educator; b. Montreal, Wis., Oct. 22, 1926; d. Anton George and Rose (Gatto) Bugni; m. Chester L. McMaster (dec. 1972); children— Chester Anthony, Raymond Dale, Brian Monroe, Maureen Anne, Heather Lynn; m. Martin Juhn, July 30, 1977. Student U. Minn.; B.S., Juilliard Sch. Music, NYC; postgrad. Columbia U., U. Detroit, SUNY-Brockport; Mus.M., Eastman Sch. Music, U. Rochester. Prin., voice instr. McMaster Music Studios, Rochester and Dansville, NY, 1987—. Performed in concert, oratorio, opera throughout US, including solo appearances with Juilliard Opera Theater, Chautauqua Opera Assn., Rochester Opera Theater; appeared as soloist with Mpls. Symphony, Rochester (NY) Philharm. Buffalo Philharm. Music Theater of Rochester, Eastman Rochester Symphony, Rochester, Hornell (NY) Symphony, Sarasota Opera, 2003—; recitals at Youngstown, Ohio, Ironwood, Mich., Hornell, Alfred U., and Rochester, NY; concerts Nazareth Art Ctr., Nat. Opera Assn., New Orleans, Sarasota, Fla.; dir. Dansville Music Theater; asst. prof. Youngstown State U., State U. Coll., Geneseo, NY; prof. Houghton (NY) Coll; judge scholarship com. Sarasota Opera, Artist Series, Fla. Soloist Republican Nat. Convention, Miami; appeared in title role Nat. Edn. Television prodn. The Medium; appeared in plays by Phil Gelb, Sarasota, 1986-87. Mem. pres.'s leadership council U. Rochester. Mem. AAUW (past pres. Dansville area br.), AAUP (past chpt. exec. bd.), Nat. Opera Assn., Nat. Assn. Tchrs. Singing, Juilliard Alumni Assn., Eastman Alumni Assn., NY Music Tchrs. Assn. Address: 3830 Glen Oaks Manor Dr Sarasota FL 34232 Home Phone: 941-365-2178; Office Phone: 585-335-3786. Personal E-mail: gloriajuhn@comcast.net.

MCMASTER, HENRY DARGAN, state attorney general; b. Columbia, SC, May 27, 1947; s. John Gregg and Ida Bacot (Dargan) McM.; m. Peggy Jean McAbee, Mar. 18, 1978 BA, U. SC, 1969, JD, 1973. Bar: SC, US Dist. Ct. SC, US Ct. Claims, US Ct. Appeals (4th cir.), US Supreme Ct. Atty., legis. asst. US Senator Strom Thurmond, Washington, 1973-74; ptnr. Tompkins & McMaster, Columbia, SC, 1974—81, 1985—2003; US atty. Dist. SC, Columbia, 1981-85; atty. gen. State of SC, 2003—. Mem. US Atty. Gen.'s adv. com. of US Attys., Washington, 1981-83; chmn. Com. on Ct. Rules and Legislation, Washington, 1983-85. Contbr. articles to legal publs. Mem. region IV youth adv. bd. EPA, Atlanta, 1972; mem. SC Commn. on Higher Edn., 1991-94; chmn. SC Rep. Party, 1993-2002; bd. dirs. SC Policy Coun., 1991-2003; atty. gen. SC, 2003-. Mem. Richland County Bar Assn. (prog. com. 1978), SC Bar, ABA, Nat. Assn. R.R. Trial Counsel, Def. Rsch. Inst., Centurian Soc., Caroliniana Ball Club, St. Andrew's Soc. (Columbia), Phi Delta Phi, Blue Key, Kappa Alpha (dep. province comdr. 1974-75, province comdr. 1975-91). Republican. Presbyterian. Office: 1731 Senate St Columbia SC 29201 also: Office of Atty Gen Rembert C Dennis Office Bldg PO Box 11549 Columbia SC 29211-1549 Office Phone: 803-734-3970.*

MCMASTER, JULIET SYLVIA, English language educator; b. Kisumu, Kenya, Aug. 2, 1937; emigrated to Can., 1961, naturalized, 1976; d. Sydney Herbert and Sylvia (Hook) Fazan; m. Rowland McMaster, May 10, 1968; children: Rawdon, Lindsey. BA with honors, Oxford U., Eng., 1959; MA, U. Alta., Can., 1963, PhD, 1965. Asst. prof. English U. Alta., Edmonton, Canada, 1965—70, assoc. prof., 1970—76, prof. English, 1976—86, univ. prof., 1986—2000, prof. emeritus, 2000—. Author: Thackeray: The Major Novels, 1971, Jane Austen on Love, 1978, Trollope's Palliser Novels, 1978; author: (with R.D. McMaster) The Novel from Sterne to James, 1981; author: Dickens the Designer, 1987, Jane Austen the Novelist, 1995, Reading the Body in the Eighteenth Century Novel, 2004, Woman Behind the Painter: The Diaries of Rosalie, Mrs. James Clarke Hook, 2006; co-editor: Jane Austen's Business, 1996, Cambridge Companion to Jane Austen, 1997, The Child Writer From Austen to Woolf, 2005; gen. editor: Juvenilia Press, 1993—2002, illustrator/editor: children's picture book (by Jane Austen) The Beautifull Cassandra, 1993, 2007; contbr. articles to profl. jours. Fellow Can. Coun., 1969-70, Guggenheim Found., 1976-77, Killam Found., 1987-89; recipient Molson prize in Humanities for Outstanding Contbn. to Canadian Culture, 1994, Alberta Centennial medal, 2005. Fellow Royal Soc. Can.; mem. Victorian Studies Assn. Western Can. (founding pres. 1972), Assn. Can. Univ. Tchrs. English (pres. 1976-78), MLA, Jane Austen Soc. N.Am. (dir. 1980-91). Business E-Mail: juliet.mcmaster@ualberta.ca.

MCMATH, ELIZABETH MOORE, graphic artist; b. Iredell, Tex., Feb. 20, 1930; d. Fred William and Elizabeth Carol (Smith) Moore; m. Charles Wallis McMath, Jan. 16, 1978 (dec. Dec. 1990); children: Charles Wallis, John Seals. BA, BS in Advt. Design, Tex. Woman's U., Denton, 1951; grad. gemologist, Gemol. Inst. Am., LA, 1977. Layout artist Leonard's Dept. Store, Ft. Worth, Tex., 1951-52; artist/bookkeeper Bud Biggs Studio, Dallas, 1953; sec./artist Squire Haskins Studio, Dallas, 1953-54; artist/art dir. Dowdell-Merrill, Inc., Dallas, 1954-58; owner/artist Moore Co., Dallas, 1958-90. Mem. Stemmons Corridor Bus. Assn., Dallas, 1988-89. Mem. Dallas/Ft. Worth Soc. Visual Comm. (founder), Tex. Woman's U. Nat. Alumnae Assn., Greater North Tex. Orchid Soc. (treas. 1987), Daylily Growers of Dallas (sec. 1989-90, 1st v.p. and program chmn. 1992), Internat. Bulb Soc., Native Plant Soc. Tex. (publicity chmn. Trinity Forks chpt. 1991-02, pres. 1998, sec. 1999-2005, Tex. Master Naturalist, Elm Fork Chpt. (hon., life 1998-2008), Fort Worth Orchid Soc., Presbyn. Women's Assn. (hon., life). Presbyterian. Avocations: ranching, horticulture, plant propagation, lost wax casting, gemstone cutting. Home: PO Box 1068 Denton TX 76202-1068 Home Phone: 940-365-2838. E-mail: elizabeth.mcmath@sbcglobal.net.

MCMATH, LULA WRAY, retired elementary school educator, realtor; b. Grenada, Miss., Apr. 27, 1933; d. Alva and Augusta McMath; m. Jesse C. Terry; 1 child, Damita. BS in Edn., Chgo. State U., 1971, MS in Urban Edn., 1972, MS in Corrections, 1974. Lic. realtor Chgo. (Ill.) Bd. Realtors, 1986. Seamstress Hart Schaffner and Marx, Chgo., 1952—65; tchr. Chgo. (Ill.) Bd. Edn., 1965—93; realtor Ronald Waters, Chgo.,

1986—. Author: How 8th Grade Students View Discipline, 1973, Places I Have Visited, 1994, My Lovely Garden, 1994. Vol. gardener City of Chgo., 1989; vol. literacy educator Roosevelt U., Chgo., 1993; ballot giver Dem. Party, Chgo., 1988, poll watcher, 1984, judge, 1990, registrar, 1988. Recipient Valuable Svc. award, Faith Temple Ch., 1975, Meritorious award, United Negro Colls., 1991. Mem.: Am. Fedn., Ret. Tchrs. Avocations: gardening, singing, dance, interior decorating. Home: 10621 S Wood St Chicago IL 60643-2717

MCMECHAN, GEORGE, science educator; b. Vancouver, B.C., Canada, Aug. 21, 1947; BASc, U. BC, Vancouver, Can., 1970; MS, U. Toronto, 1971; BS, U. Victoria, Can., 1983. Registered profl. engr., B.C. Prof. geosci. U. Tex. at Dallas, Richardson, 1983—, dir. Ctr. for Lithospheric Studies, 1985—. Rsch. scientist Pacific Geosci. Ctr., Sidney, BC, 1972—82. Contbr. articles to profl. jours. Mem.: Seismol. Soc. Am., Am. Geophys. Union, Soc. Exploration Geophysicists (Virgil Kauffman Gold medal 1997). Avocations: physical fitness, movies. Office: Univ Tex Dallas 800 W Campbell Rd Richardson TX 75080 Business E-Mail: mcmec@utdallas.edu.

MCMEEKIN, DOROTHY, botanist, plant pathologist, educator; b. Boston, Feb. 24, 1932; d. Thomas LeRoy and Vera (Crockatt) McM. BA, Wilson Coll., 1953; MA, Wellesley Coll., 1955; PhD, Cornell U., 1959. Asst. prof. Upsala Coll., East Orange, NJ, 1959-64, Bowling Green State U., Ohio, 1964—66; prof. natural sci. Mich. State U., East Lansing, 1981—99, emeritus prof. botany, plant pathology, 1997—. Author: Diego Rivera: Science and Creativity, 1985; contbr. articles to profl. jours. Mem. Am. Phytopath. Soc., Mycol. Soc. Am., Soc. Econ. Bot., Mich. Bot. Soc. (former bd. dirs.), Mich. Women's Studies Assn., Sigma Xi, Phi Kappa Phi. Avocations: gardening, sewing, travel, drawing. Home: 1055 Marigold Ave East Lansing MI 48823-5128 Office: Mich State U Dept Botany-Plant Pathology 100 N Kedzie Hall East Lansing MI 48824-1031 E-mail: mcmeekin@msu.edu.

MCMEEKIN, THOMAS OWEN, dermatologist; b. Shelby, Nebr., Apr. 17, 1945; s. Wallace Walton and Evajane (Taber) McM.; m. Dale Goodwin, 1999(Div. Aug. 15, 2008); children: Michele, Sean. BA with distinction, Stanford U., 1967; MD with honors, U. Rochester, 1971. Intern Beth Israel Hosp., Boston, 1971-72; resident U. Rochester (N.Y.), 1974-76, Mass. Gen. Hosp., Boston, 1976-78; clin. prof. depts. medicine, pediatrics, dermatology U. Rochester Sch. Medicine, 1978—; dermatologist pvt. practice, Rochester, 1978—; clin. asst. prof. SUNY, Buffalo, 1997—. Pres. Geneese Valley Laser Ctr., Rochester, 1990—. Capt. USPHS, 1972—74. Kohn fellow U. Rochester, 1980-81; recipient Doren J. Stephens Alumni award U. Rochester, 1971, Brian Flanagan Teaching Svc. award, 1995, 2003. Fellow Am. Acad. Dermatology (Svc. award 1993), Am. Bd. Internal Medicine, Am. Soc. LAser MEdicine (co-chmn. 1993-94), Am. Soc. Dermatologic Surgery (edn. com. 1983—); mem. N.Y. State Dermatological Soc. (v.p. 1993, treas. 1992), Buffalo Rochester Dermatological Soc. (pres. 1990), Rochester Dermatological Soc. (pres. 1980-89), Alpha Omega Alpha. Avocations: golf, tennis, computers. Office: 300 White Spruce Blvd Rochester NY 14623-1606 Office Phone: 585-424-6770. Personal E-mail: 041745@msn.com.

MCMEEKING, ROBERT MAXWELL, mechanical engineer, educator; b. Glasgow, Scotland, May 22, 1950; came to U.S., 1972; s. Robert Maxwell and Elizabeth Higginson (Craighead) McM.; m. Norah Anne Madigan, Sept. 4, 1976; children: Gavin Robert, Anne Catherine. BSc with 1st class honors, U. Glasgow, 1972; MS, Brown U., 1974, PhD, 1977. Acting asst. prof. Stanford (Calif.) U., 1976-78; asst. prof. U. Ill., Urbana, 1978-82, assoc. prof., 1982-85; prof. U. Calif., Santa Barbara, 1985—, chmn. mech. and environ. engring., 1992—95, 1999—2003; sixth century prof. Engring. Materials, U. Aberdeen, Scotland, 2007—; vis. prof. materials engring. U. Saarland, Germany, 2008—; external mem. Leibniz Inst. New Materials, Germany, 2008—. Cons. in field. Co-editor Intermetallic Matrix Composites, 1990; assoc. editor Jour. Applied Mechanics, 1987-93; editor Jour. Applied Mechanics, 2002—; contbr. articles to profl. jours. Recipient Alexander von Humboldt Rsch. award for Sr. U.S. Scientists, 2004, Alumni medal Brown Engring., 2007, Arthur Newell Talbot Lectr. award U. Ill., 2007; vis. fellow Cambridge U., 1983, 95-96. Fellow ASME, Am. Acad. Mechanics; mem. AAAS, NAE, Inst. Sci. Info. (Highly Cited Rschr. award) Sigma Xi. Office: U Calif Materials Dept Mech Engring Dept Santa Barbara CA 93106 Office Phone: 805-893-8434.

MCMEEN, ELMER ELLSWORTH, III, lay minister, musician, retired lawyer; b. Lewistown, Pa., June 3, 1947; s. Elmer Ellsworth II and Frances Josephine McM.; m. Sheila Ann Taenzler, July 31, 1971; children: Jonathan Ellsworth, Daniel Biddle, James Cunningham and Mary Josephine (twins). BA cum laude, Harvard U., 1969; JD cum laude, U. Pa., 1972. Bar: 1973, U.S. Ct. Appeals (2nd cir.) 1973, U.S. Dist. Ct. (so.and ea. dists.) NY 1975. Assoc. Cravath, Swaine & Moore, NYC, 1972-75, LeBoeuf, Lamb, Greene & MacRae, LLP, NYC, 1975-78, ptnr., 1979-99, of counsel, 2000, retired, 2001. Lectr. Editor U. Pa. Law Rev., 1970-72. Author guitar books, Celtic Treasures for String Trio, Pocket Gospel Guide A; musician: (solo instrnl. audio, guitar artistry and DVD lessons and performance DVDs) Stefan Grossman's Guitar Workshop, Virgin, Shanachie Entertainment, Rounder Records; co-author: The Passion Dialogues, 2006, musician numerous solo guitar recordings; contbr. articles to legal jours. Chmn. N.Y.C. regional com. U. Pa. Law Sch., 1984-86; class sec. Northfield Mt. Hermon Sch. Class of 1965, Mass., 1984-91. Named a Musician of Yr., Internat. Biography Ctr., Cambridge, Eng., 2003. Mem.: Lake Mohawk Golf Club, Rockaway River Country Club. Office: 34 Angelo Dr Sparta NJ 07871 E-mail: mcmeen_el@yahoo.com.

MCMEEN, SHEILA TAENZLER, retired lawyer; b. Morristown, NJ, Aug. 26, 1946; d. William Paul and Mary Cunningham Taenzler; m. E. Ellsworth McMeen, III, July 31, 1971; children: Jonathan, Daniel, James, Mary. AB summa cum laude, Muhlenberg Coll., Allentown, Pa., 1968; JD cum laude, U. Pa., 1971. Bar: N.Y. 1972, U.S. Supreme Ct. 1979. Assoc. Davis Polk & Wardwell, NYC, 1971—80; ret. Editor: U. Pa. Law Rev. Deacon First Presbyterian Ch., Sparta, NJ, 2003—; pastoral care vol. staff Andover (N.J.) Rehab Ctr., 2004—07; mem. Bd. of Edn., Mountain Lakes, NJ, 1993—2001, Sussex County Child Placement Rev. Bd., Newton, NJ, 2003—, mcpl. mediator, 2008—; mem. First Presbyn. Ch., 2007—. Mem.: Phi Beta Kappa. Avocations: needlework, cryptic puzzles, reading. Home: 34 Angelo Dr Sparta NJ 07871 E-mail: elmcmeen@ptd.net.

MCMENAMIN, SARAH KELLY, biologist, educator; b. Santa Barbara, Calif., May 29, 1982; d. Mark McMenamin and Dianna Schulte McMenamin. BA, Mt. Holyoke, South Hadley, 2004; attending, Stanford U., Palo Alto, Calif., 2004—. Rsch. assoc. NASA Ames Rsch. Ctr., Mountain View, Calif., 2002—03; faculty instr. San Francisco Art Inst., 2009—. Fellow, Gifford Endowment Fund, 2008—09. Mem.: Leonardo Scientists, Ecol. Soc. America, Soc. Study Amphibians & Reptiles, NY Acad. Scis., Sigma Xi.

MCMICHAEL, DONALD EARL, lawyer; b. Denver, Aug. 8, 1931; s. Earl L. and Charlotte F. McM.; m. Zeta Hammond, July 6, 1955; children: Lauren A. McMichael Burnett, Thomas D., Susan E. McMichael Markle. AB, Dartmouth Coll., 1953; LLB, U. Colo., 1956. Bar: Colo. 1956, U.S. Dist. Ct. Colo. 1956, U.S. Ct. Appeals (10th cir.) 1956. Assoc. Holme Roberts & Owen, 1956-58; pres. Corp. Ins. Assocs., 1958-70; dir. trust devel. Ctrl. Bank Denver, 1970-72; ptnr. Brenman, Sobol & Baum, Denver, 1972-74, McMichael, Benedict, Multz & Lipton, Denver, 1974—99; of counsel Schmidt & Horen, Denver, 2000—02; pvt. practice, 2002—. Chmn. Denver Ctrl. YMCA, 1971-73. Capt. USAR, 1956—64. Named Layman of Yr. Denver Ctrl. YMCA, 1973, named to Denver Metro YMCA Hall of Fame, 1989. Mem. Colo. Bar Assn., Denver Bar Assn., Denver Estate Planning Coun. (sec. 1971-73). Republican. Methodist. Office: 6325 W Mansfield Ave Unit 234 Denver CO 80235-3015 Home Phone: 303-987-0543; Office Phone: 303-716-8406. E-mail: dmcmic@aol.com.

MCMILLAN, CHARLES WILLIAM, consulting company executive; b. Ft. Collins, Colo., Feb. 9, 1926; s. Charles and Margaret (Jennings) McM.; m. Jardell Hollier, Feb. 12, 1951; children: Brett W., Kurt C., Scott P. BS, Colo. State U., 1948. Asst. 4-H agt., Denver, 1948; county agrl. agt. LaJara, Colo., 1949-50, Julesburg, 1950-53; faculty Colo. State U., 1954; div. head, agrl. research dept. Swift & Co., Chgo., 1954-59; exec. v.p. Am. Nat. Cattlemen's Assn., 1959-77; v.p. Nat. Cattlemen's Assn., 1977-81; asst. sec. for mktg. and inspection services USDA, Washington, 1981-85; pres. McMillan and Farrell Assocs., Inc., Washington, 1985-94, C.W. McMillan Co., Alexandria, Va., 1994—. Served to lt. (j.g.) USNR, World War II. Mem. Sigma Alpha Epsilon. Home: 4003 Pine Brook Rd Alexandria VA 22310-2144 Office: PO Box 10009 Alexandria VA 22310-0009

MC MILLAN, GEORGE DUNCAN HASTIE, JR., lawyer, former state official; b. Greenville, Ala., Oct. 11, 1943; s. George Duncan Hastie and Jean (Autrey) McM.; m. Ann Louise Dial, Nov. 20, 1971; children: George Duncan Hastie, III, Ann Dial. BA magna cum laude, Auburn U., 1966; LL.B. (Southeastern Regional scholar), U. Va., 1969. Bar: Ala. bar 1969. Research asst. dept. agronomy Auburn U., summers 1963-65; law clk. firm Lange, Simpson, Robinson & Somerville, Birmingham, Ala., summers 1967-68; law clk. to judge U.S. Dist. Ct. No. Dist. Ala., 1969-70; instr. U. Ala. Law Sch., 1969-70; individual practice law Birmingham, 1970-71; ptnr. firm McMillan & Spratling, Birmingham, 1971-86; of counsel Haskell, Slaughter, Young and Lewis, 1986; ptnr. McMillan, Jones and Assocs., 1987-90; pres. McMillan Assocs., 1990—; mem. Ala. Ho. of Reps., 1973, Ala. Senate, 1974-78; lt. gov. Ala., 1979-83. Vice-chmn. Nat. Conf. Lt. Govs., 1980-82; mem. Permanent Study Commn. on Ala.'s Jud. System, 1975-79 Chmn. Ala. Film Commn., 1976-83; mem. Arts Task Force, Nat. Conf. State Legislatures, 1978-80, Multi-State Transp. Adv. Bd., 1974-79; mem. exec. com. So. Growth Policies Bd., 1974-83, vice chmn., 1981-83; bd. dirs. Campfire, Inc., 1975-82, Met. YMCA, Birmingham, Boys and Girls Ranches, Ala., Positive Maturity, 1987—; chmn. bd., pres. Birmingham Cultural and Heritage Found., 1988—; pres., bd. dirs. Birmingham Repertory Theatre, 1989—; exec. prodr. City Stages, 2003—; chair Black Belt Cmty. Found. Served to lt. USAR, 1969. Recipient award Ala. Nurses Assn., 1975; named Legislator of Yr. Ala. Forestry Assn., 1978; Hardest Working Senator Capitol Press Corps, 1976; 1 of 4 Outstanding Young Men Ala. Jaycees, 1977; 1 of 10 Most Outstanding State Legislators Assn. Govtl. Employees, 1978; award Birmingham Emancipation Assn., 1977; award Ala. Hist. Commn., 1978; James Tingle award, 1979, Citizen of Yr. award City of Birmingham, 1990. Mem. Birmingham Bar Assn., Ala. Bar Assn., Am. Bar Assn., Birmingham Jaycees, Ala. Jaycees (dir. 1970-72), Birmingham Urban League, United Negro Coll. Fund. Democrat. Mem. Ch. of Christ. Club: Rotary (Birmingham). Office: Mc Millan Assocs Ste 900 1929 3rd Ave N Birmingham AL 35203 Home Phone: 305-871-7462; Office Phone: 205-324-6881. Business E-Mail: george@mcmillan-associates.com.

MCMILLAN, JULIA A., pediatrician, educator; b. Pinehurst, NC, July 10, 1946; m. Jed Dietz; children: Edith Root, Robert Grant, Elihu Root. BA in English Lit., U. NC, Chapel Hill, 1969, M in Tchg., 1971; MD, SUNY, Syracuse, 1976. Diplomate Nat. Bd. Med. Examiners, 1977, cert. Am. Bd. Pediat., 1981. Intern SUNY Health Sci. Ctr., Syracuse, 1976—77, resident pediat., 1977-78, 79-80, fellow in pediat. infectious diseases, 1979-81, physician co-dir. Pediat. Nurse Practitioner Program, 1978—79, asst. prof. infectious disease sect., 1981—87, asst. prof. Dept. Pathology, 1982—87, co-dir. Univ. Hosp. Virology Lab., 1984—90, residency program dir., 1985—90, assoc. prof. Dept. Pediat. and Pathology, 1987—90; assoc. prof. pediat. John Hopkins U. Med. Sch., Balt., 1991—2001, dep. dir. Dept. Pediat., 1991—95, dir., 1995—, vice chair Edn. and Residency Program, 1995—, prof., 2001—, acting divsn. chief gen. pediat., 2001—02, assoc. dean. grad. med. edn., designated institutional official, 2004—. Lectr. in field. Co-author: The Whole Pediatrician Catalog: A Compendium of Clues to Diagnosis and Management, 1977, The Best of the Whole Pediatrician Catalogs, I-III, 1984, The Portable Pediatrician, 1992, Blueprints in Pediatrics, 1998, Oski's Pediatrics: Principles and Practice, 3d edit., 1999; editor-in-chief Contemporary Pediatrics; contbr. articles to med. jours. Recipient Alexander Schaffer Award, 1999, Walter W. Tunnessen, Jr. MD Award, 2007. Mem.: Am. Pediat. Soc., Infectious Diseases Soc. Am., Pediat. Soc. Onondaga County, Am. Soc. Microbiology, Am. Acad. Pediat., Am. Bd. Pediat. (assoc.). Office: Johns Hopkins Hosp Dept Pediatrics 600 N Wolfe St Baltimore MD 21287-3224 Office Phone: 410-955-2727. Office Fax: 410-955-9850. E-mail: jmcmill@jhmi.edu.

MCMILLAN, L. LONDELL, lawyer; b. Bklyn., Aug. 5, 1966; BS with honors, Cornell U., 1987; JD, NYU, 1990. Bar: N.Y. 1991, Conn. 1992. Sports agt. Athletes and Artists, Inc.; atty. LeBoeuf, Lamb, Greene & MacRea, LLP; entertainment lawyer Gold, Farrell & Marks; pres, CEO L. Londell McMillan, PC, NYC, 1997—2007, NorthStar Bus. Enterprises, Inc., NYC, 1997—; ptnr., head entertainment, media & sports Dewey & LeBoeuf LLP, NYC, 2007—. Faculty mem. Practicing Law Inst., 2003—05; guest commentator Oprah Winfrey Show. Exec. pub.: Source Mag.; contbr. articles to profl. jours. Alumni counsel bd. trustee Cornell U.; co-founder, gen. counsel Artist Empowerment Coalition, 2004—07; gen. counsel NAACP, Bklyn., 2006—07. Recipient Alumni Svc. award, NYU Sch. Law, Innovator of Yr. award, Nat. Rainbow Coalition, 2000, Navigator of Yr. award, Direction for Our Youth, Inc., 2001, Haywood W. Burns Lawyer of the Yr. award, MBBA, 2001, Founder's award, Mercedes Benz, 2004, Lifetime Achievement award Medgar Evers Coll., 2005, Corp. award, NY State Assn. Black and Puerto Rican Legislators, Inc., 2005; named one of America's Top Black Lawyers, Black Enterprise mag., 2003, Best & Brightest Under 40, 2003, 100 Most Powerful Leaders, Crain Mag., 2003, 50 Most Influential Minority Lawyers in America, Nat. Law Jour., 2008; named to NY Super Lawyers, entertainment law, 2007. Mem.: ABA, NY City Bar Assn., Assn. Bar City of NY, NY State Bar Assn., Internat. Bar Assn., Red Key, Quill and Dagger. Office: L Londell Mcmillan PC 156 W 56th St Fl 10th Fl New York NY 10019-3877*

MCMILLAN, LEE RICHARDS, II, lawyer, mining executive; b. New Orleans, Aug. 26, 1947; s. John H. and Phoebe (Skillman) McM.; m. Lynne Clark Pottharst, June 27, 1970; children: Leslie Clark, Hillary Anne, Lee Richards III. BS in Commerce, Washington and Lee U., 1969; JD, Tulane U., 1972; LLM in Taxation, NYU, 1976. Bar: La. 1972. Assoc. Jones, Walker, Waechter, Poitevent, Carrere & Denegre, New Orleans, 1976-79, ptnr., 1979—2007, sect. head, corp. and securities sect., 1987—90, 1994—2002, exec. com., 1990—94, 1996—99, 2001—02, chmn. exec. com., 1991—94, 1996—98, 2001—02; sr. v.p., gen. counsel Freeport-McMoRan Copper & Gold Inc., Phoenix, 2007—. Vice chmn. Mech. Equipment Co., Inc., New Orleans, 1980—86, chmn. bd., 1986—, pres., 1989—99; mem. The Bus. Coun. Greater New Orleans, 1998—, exec. com., 1999—; bd. dirs. The Chamber/New Orleans and the River Region, 1996—98; trustee Alton Ochsner Med. Found., 1995—2003. Trustee New Orleans Mus. Art., 1989-95; bd. dirs. Bur. Govt. Rsch. New Orleans, 1987-93, Louise S. McGehee Sch., New Orleans, 1982-88, co-chmn. capital fund dr., 1984-86, pres. bd. dirs., 1986-88; bd. govs. Isidore Newman Sch., New Orleans, 1991-95. Lt. JACG USNR, 1972-75. Mem. ABA (com. on negotiated acquisitions 1986-94), La. State Bar Assn. (chmn. corp. and bus. law sect. 1985-86, mem. com. on bar admissions 1986-87), Young Pres. Orgn., Washington and Lee U. Alumni Assn. (bd. dirs. 1995-99). Republican. Episcopalian. Avocation: sailing. Office: Freeport McMoRan 1 N Ctrl Ave Phoenix AZ 85004

MCMILLAN, MARY BIGELOW, retired minister, volunteer; b. St. Paul, July 30, 1919; d. Charles Henry and Allison (McKibbin) Bigelow; m. Richard McMillan, June 26, 1943; children: Richard Jr., Charles B., Douglas D., M. Allison, Anne E. BA, Vassar Coll., 1941; MDiv, United Theol. Sem. Twin Cities, 1978, DDiv (hon.), 1989. Ordained to ministry Presbyn. Ch., 1978. Asst. min. House of Hope Presbyn. Ch., St. Paul, 1978-82; interim pres. United Theol. Sem. Twin Cities, New Brighton, Minn., 1982-83, ret., 1987. Contbg. author The Good Steward, 1983. Regional dir. Assn. Jr. Leagues, NYC, 1959—61, pres. St. Paul chpt., 1957—59; vice chair Ramsey County Welfare Bd., St. Paul, 1962—66, St. Paul Health and Welfare Planning Coun., 1964—70, F.R. Bigelow Found., St. Paul, 1988—95, also 1st vice chair; 1st vice chair, trustee Wilder Found., 1973—89; active Presbyn. Homes Found., 1996—; trustee Minn. Ch. Found., Mpls., 1984—99, United Theol. Sem. Twin Cities, 1977—89, also chmn. bd. trustees; bd. dirs. Collegeville Inst. Ecumenical and Cultural Rsch., Minn., 1982—2003. Recipient award for cmty. planning United Way, 1965, also for yr. round leadership, 1973, Leadership in Cmty. Svc. award YWCA, 1980, Sisterhood award NCCJ, Mpls., 1989, Outstanding Vol. Fundraiser award Minn., 2005; named Disting Alumna, St. Paul Acad. and Summit Sch., 1988 Mem.: New Century Club. Avocations: bridge, reading. Home: 2925 Lincoln Dr #713 Roseville MN 55113

MCMILLAN, MICHAEL REID, retired orthopedic surgeon; b. Conway, SC, Aug. 28, 1941; s. Hoyt and Sara Best (Sherwood) McM.; BS, Citadel, 1963; MD, Duke U., 1967. Diplomate Nat. Bd. Med. Examiners, Am. Bd. Orthopedic Surgery; lic. physician, 1971-2001, SC; Intern in medicine Balt. City Hosps., 1967-68; fellow in medicine Johns Hopkins Hosp., Balt., 1967-68; resident in orthopedic surgery Greenville Hosp. Sys. and Greenville Shriners Hosp., 1971-75; practice medicine specializing in orthopedic surgery, Conway, 1975—2000, ret. 2000; Mem. staff Conway Hosp., 1975—2000, chief orthopedics, 1975-82; bd. dirs. Burroughs and Chapin Co., 1990-96, Burroughs Co., Snow Hill Co., Conway. Trustee Burroughs Found., Conway, 1979—. Served to lt. comdr. MC, USN, 3d marine divn., 1968-69; Vietnam. Mem. AMA, NRA, SC Orthopedic Assn., Horry County Med. Soc., Citadel Alumni Assn., Stelling Soc. Bapt., Forest Landowners Assn., Pres.'s Club Heritage Found., Pres.'s Coun. Brookgreen Gardens, Nat. Trust, SC Hist. Soc., Found. Ecn. Edn., Save-the-Redwoods-League, Am. Legion, Civil War Preservation Trust, Third Bn. Third Marines RVN Assn., Horry County Citadel. Republican. Home: 1400 9th Ave Conway SC 29526-4106

MCMILLAN, NATHANIEL (NATE MCMILLAN), professional basketball coach; b. Raleigh, NC, Aug. 3, 1964; m. Michelle McMillan; children: Jamelle, Brittany Michelle. Student, Chowan Coll., Murfreesboro, NC, 1982—84, NC State U., 1984—86. Player Seattle SuperSonics, 1986—98, asst. coach, 1998—2000, interim head coach, 2000—01, head coach, 2001—05, Portland Trail Blazers, 2005—. Asst. coach US Men's Sr. Nat. Basketball Team, Beijing, 2008. Named to All-NBA Defensive Second Team, 1994, 1995, Nat. Jr. Coll. Men's Basketball Coaches Assn. Hall of Fame, 2001. Achievements include holding the NBA single-game record for rookie assists. Avocation: football. Office: Portland Trail Blazers Rose Garden One Center Ct Portland OR 97227

MCMILLAN, ROBERT RALPH, lawyer; b. NYC, May 21, 1932; s. Harry and Vivian (Beatty) McM.; m. Phoebe Parker Bunn, Nov. 2, 1996; children: Robin, Karen, Kenneth. Student, Adelphi U., 1951-52, 55-56; JD, Bklyn. Law Sch., 1960. Bar: N.Y. 1960. Spl. asst. staff of Richard M. Nixon, NY., Washington, 1960, 64-65; counsel Senator Kenneth B. Keating, Washington, 1960-62; govt. rels. advisor Mobil Oil Co., NYC, 1962-63, 65-68; v.p. Avon Products, NYC, 1973-78, 79-85; sr. v.p. A&S Dept. Stores, NYC, 1978-79; counsel Rivkin, Radler, Bayh, Hart & Kremer, Uniondale, NY, 1986-91; ptnr. McMillan, Rather, Bennett & Farinoci, P.C., Melville, NY, 1991—2003, Fischbein Badillo Wagner Harding, Melville, 2003—05, Bee Ready Fishbein Hatter & Donovan LLP, Melville, 2005—. Chmn. Panama Canal Commn., 1993-94; mem. nat. adv. coun. FannieMae, 1998-2000, co-hosts Face-Off, PBS, NY. News commentator Sta. WLIW-TV, 1993-2007; columnist, Anton Community Newspapers, Long Island; occasional columnist for Newsday. Trustee Adelphi U., 1984-89; bd. dirs. L.I. (N.Y.) Assn.; chmn. L.I. Housing Parntership, 1988-2002. 1st lt. U.S. Army, 1952-54. Decorated Bronze Star; recipient Excellence in Leadership award, Helen Keller Services for the Blind, Humanitarian award, Alzheimer's Assn. Mem.: AMA (bd. trustees 2002—08), Suffolk County Bar Assn., Nassau County Bar Assn. Republican. Avocations: golf, fishing. Home Phone: 516-746-1193; Office Phone: 516-746-5599. E-mail: mcmillanr@aol.com.

MCMILLAN, TERRY L., writer, educator; b. Port Huron, Mich., Oct. 18, 1951; d. Edward McMillan and Madeline Washington Tillman; m. Jonathan Plummer, 1998 (div. 2005). BA in Journalism, U. Calif., Berkeley, 1979; student, Columbia U., NYC. Instr. U. Wyoming, Laramie, 1987-88; assoc. prof. U. Ariz., Tucson, 1988-91. Vis. prof. Stanford U. Author: (novels) Mama, 1987 (Nat. Book award, Before Columbus Found.), Disappearing Acts, 1989, Waiting to Exhale, 1992 (NY Times bestseller), How Stella Got Her Groove Back, 1996, A Day Late & A Dollar Short, 2001, The Interruption of Everything, 2005 (NY Times bestseller, Publishers Weeklt bestseller), It's Ok If You're Clueless, 2006, (screenplays) Waiting to Exhale, 1995, How Stella Got Her Groove Back, 1998, Disappearing Acts, 2000; editor: Breaking Ice: An Anthropology of Contemporary African-American Fiction, 1990. Recipient Lifetime Achievement award, Essence mag., 2007; grantee NY Found. for Arts fellowship, 1986, Nat. Endowment for Arts fellowship, 1988. Mailing: c/o Viking Penguin 375 Hudson St New York NY 10014-4201 E-mail: fanmail@terrymcmillan.com.

MCMILLEN, MARIETA LOUISE, art educator; b. Kansas City, Kans., May 2, 1937; d. John Sanford and Dorothy Louise Spurgeon; adopted children: Jon Jason(dec.), Wayne Carey. EdB, Kans. U., 1964, M in Art Edn., 1964; postgrad., Art Inst., Kansas City, Mo., 1973—75. Artist Hallmark Cards, Kansas City, Mo., 1955—58; H.S. art tchr. Unified Sch. Dist. 500, Kansas City, Kans., 1962—65, elem. and secondary sch. art tchr., 1971—95; jr. and sr. H.S. art tchr. Unified Sch. Dist. 458, Basehor, Kans., 1966—71; adj. prof. Davis Coll., Johnson City, NY, 2001—. Infant and toddler tchr. U. Mo. Berkeley Ctr., Kansas City, 1960—99; asst. to phys. therapy Presbyn. Manor, Kansas City, Kans., 1971—72. Author: (novels) Death is Belligerent, 2004, Death is Compulsive, 2005. Adoptive parent Kansas City Kans. Black Adoption Agy., 1973, 1980; foster parent Kansas City Kans. S.S., 1985—95; acdtive fgn. exch. students Am. Field Svc., Kansas City, Kans., 1989—91; art tchr. Home Schoolers, Johnson City, 2004—06; active Bethel Bapt. Ch. Scholar, David Nance S. Found., 1958—62, Maude Ellsworth S. Found., 1961—62. Republican. Avocations: creative writing, camping, fishing, fossil records. Office: Davis College 400 Riverside Dr Johnson City NY 13790

MCMILLIN, DAVID ROBERT, chemistry professor; b. East St. Louis, Ill., Jan. 1, 1948; s. Robert Cecil and Clara Rose McMillin; m. Nicole Wilson, Nov. 3, 1974; children: Robert Stephen, Andrew Wilson. BA, Knox Coll., 1969; PhD, U. Ill., 1973. Postdoctoral fellow Calif. Inst. Tech., Pasadena, 1974; asst. prof. chemistry Purdue U., West Lafayette, Ind., 1975-80, assoc. prof., 1980-85, prof., 1985—. Contbr. articles to profl. jours. Recipient F.D. Martin Teaching award Purdue U., 1975. Mem. Am. Chem. Soc., Inter-Am. Photochem. Soc. (sec. 1986-90, v.p. 1994-96, pres. 1996-98), Phi Beta Kappa, Sigma Xi. Methodist. Avocations: sports, reading. Office: Purdue U Dept Chemistry 560 Oval Dr West Lafayette IN 47907-2084 Home Phone: 764-463-4815. E-mail: mcmillin@purdue.edu.

MCMILLIN, JAMES CRAIG, lawyer; b. Oklahoma City, June 27, 1949; s. Lawrence Harold and Rose Lee (Jeffrey) McM. BA, U. Okla., 1971; JD, NYU, 1976. Bar: N.Y. 1977, Okla. 1997, U.S. Dist. Ct. (so. and ea. dists.) N.Y. 1977, D.C. 1979, U.S. Supreme Ct. 1980, U.S. Dist. Ct. (no. dist.) Calif. 1981, U.S. Dist. Ct. (we. dist.) Okla. 1996, U.S. Dist. Ct. (no. dist.) Okla. 2000, U.S. Dist. Ct. (ea. dist.) Okla., 2004, U.S. Ct. Appeals (2d cir.) 1981, U.S. Ct. Appeals (7th cir.) 1982, U.S. Ct. Appeals (11th cir.) 1993, U.S. Ct. Appeals (10th cir.) 2005. Assoc. Donovan, Leisure, Newton & Irvine, NYC, 1976-79; ptnr. Liddle, McMillin & Henze, NYC, 1979-80, Werbel, McMillin & Carnelutti PC, NYC, 1981-96; shareholder McAfee & Taft, P.C., Oklahoma City, 1996—. With US Army, 1971—73. Root-Tilden scholar, 1971, 73-76. Mem. ABA, NY State Bar Assn., Okla. State Bar Assn., DC Bar Assn., Assn. Bar City NY, William J. Holloway, Am. Inn of Ct. Democrat. Office: McAfee & Taft 211 N Robinson Ave Ste S-1000 Oklahoma City OK 73102-7103 Home: 5824 N Barnes Cir Oklahoma City OK 73112-7330 Office Phone: 405-552-2280. Business E-Mail: james.mcmillin@mcafeetaft.com.

MCMILLIN, STEPHEN SCOTT, former federal official; b. Sacramento, July 5, 1966; m. Dawn Michele McMillin; children: Spencer, Christian. BA, U. Tex., Austin, 1989. Staff intern to Representative Dick Armey US Congress, 1989—90; legis. correspondent & staff asst. to Senator Phil Gramm US Senate, 1991, legis. asst. to Senator Phil Gramm, 1991—99; financial economist US Senate Com. on Banking, Housing & Urban Affairs, 1999—2001; legis. dir. to Senator Phil Gramm US Senate, Washington, 2001; assoc. dir. gen. govt. programs Office Mgmt. & Budget, Exec. Office of the Pres., 2001—05, counselor to dir., 2006, dep. dir., 2006—09; dep. asst. to Pres., adv. to chief of staff The White House, 2005—06.*

MCMILLION, MARGARET KIM, foreign service officer; b. New Brighton, Pa., Nov. 4, 1951; d. Theodore M. and Margaret Jane (Houlette) McM. BA, Eisenhower Coll., 1973; MPIA, U. Pitts., 1975; cert., Nat. War Coll., 1990. Analyst, intern Gulf Oil Corp., Pitts., 1974; polit. and consular officer U.S. Embassy, Kigali, Rwanda, 1975-77, consular officer Taipei, Taiwan, 1977-79; travel svcs. officer Am. Inst. in Taiwan, Taipei, 1979; desk officer Office of West African Affairs U.S. Dept. of State, Washington, 1979-81; with tng. dept. Fgn. Svc. Inst., Washington, 1981—82; polit. officer. U.S. Embassy, Pretoria, South Africa, 1982—85; with Thai lang. tng. dept., Washington, 1985-86; prin. officer U.S. Consulate, Udorn, Thailand, 1986—89; asst. dir. Office of Korean Affairs, Washington, 1990—91; spl. asst. under sec. for polit. affairs U.S. Dept. State, Washington, 1991—92; polit. counselor U.S. Embassy, Bangkok, 1992—95; dep. chief Mission in Vientiane, Laos, 1996—99; dir. Office for Analysis of Africa, Bur. Intelligence and Rsch., 1999—2001; U.S. amb. to Rwanda, 2001—04; dep. comdr. internat. affairs U.S. Army War Coll., 2004—06; ret. State Dept., 2006; adj. prof. Webster U., Thailand, 2008, coord., MA Internat. Affairs Program, 2009. Presbyterian. Achievements include speaks French, Afrikaans, Thai and Lao. Avocations: swimming, hiking, music, reading. Office: 191 Surawangse Rd Bangkok 10500 Thailand Office Phone: 66-861-07-3260. Personal E-mail: mkmcmillion@gmail.com.

MCMILLON, DOUG (CARL DOUGLAS MCMILLON), retail executive; b. 1966; m. Shelley McMillon; 2 children. BA in Bus. Adminstrn., U. Ark.; MBA in Fin., U. Tulsa. Buyer trainee in sporting goods Wal-Mart Stores, Inc., 1984—91, sr. v.p., gen. merchandise mgr., 1999—2002, exec. v.p., 2005—09; exec. v.p. merchandising & replenishment Sam's Club Divsn., 2002—05, pres., CEO, 2005—09, Wal-Mart International, 2009—. Corp. bd. advisors Nat. Coun. La Raza; mem. exec. bd. Ctr. Retailing Excellence, U. Ark.; dir. emeritus The Sunshine Sch., Bentonville, Ark. Office: Wal-Mart Stores Inc 702 SW Eighth St Bentonville AR 72716*

MCMINN, J. B., retired philosophy educator, composer; b. Pt. Neches, Tex., Nov. 12, 1922; s. Joe Byron and Mary Thelma (Odom) McMinn; m. Dorothy Louise Smith, Aug. 31, 1944 (div. May 15, 1969); children: Jan Branton, Robert Errol. BA in English and Religious Studies, La. Coll., 1943; ThM in Hellenistic Greek, So. Sem., 1946, PhD in Hellenistic Greek, 1951; postgrad., La. State U., 1948; MA in Classical Greek and Philosophy, Tulane U., 1960, postgrad., 1968, U. Athens, 1970, postdoctoral in Modern Greek, 1979. Asst. prof. English La. Coll., 1948—51; tchg. asst. in classics Newcomb Coll., 1951—52, Tulane U., 1952—54, asst. prof. classics, 1953—58; from asst. prof. philosophy to prof. philosophy U. Ala., 1960—87. Vis. prof. philosophy Miles Coll., 1990; vis. assoc. prof. philosophy and classics Tulane U., 1960, 61; spkr., lectr., presenter in field. Contbr. spirit song for Million Dollar Band, U. Ala. Fight On to Victory, 1987, poetry to anthologies;, composer piano and vocal pieces; author: (book of poetry and songs) Une Petite Ménagerie, 1997, (plays) Waiting for Gotdough, 1995, (book) Mythtaken: Le Mot de L' Énigme, 2002; contbr. articles to profl. jours. Rep. commr., New Orleans, 1956—60; mem. So. Soc. Christian Leadership Conf., New Orleans, 1954—60. Cadet officer USNR, 1941—42. Recipient Merit award, U. Ala. Band Assn., 1991, VIP award, Internat. Soc. Poets, 1996, Fulbright Adj. Lectr. award., 1972, West Germany Lectr. award, 1973, Merit award, Internat. Poet., 1996. Mem.: ASCAP, Poetry Soc. Am., Acad. Am. Poets, Nat. Acad. Popular Music-Songwriters Hall of Fame, Internat. Soc. Poets (life), Eta Sigma Phi. Home: 311 W 4th St Odessa TX 79761-5058

MCMORRIS, JERRY, transportation company, sports team executive; Past CEO NW Transport Svc, Denver; chair, pres., CEO Colorado Rockies, Denver, 1993—. Office: 4765 Oakland St Denver CO 80239-2717

MCMORRIS-RODGERS, CATHY, United States Representative from Washington; b. Salem, Oreg., May 22, 1969; m. Brian Rodgers, Aug. 5, 2006; 1 child, Cole McMorris. BA in Pre-Law, Pensacola Christian Coll., Fla., 1990; MBA, U. Wash., 2002. Mem. Wash. State House Reps. from 7th Dist., 1994—2004, minority leader, 2002—03; mem. US Congress from 5th Wash. Dist., 2005—; vice chair US House Republican Conf., 2009—; mem. US House Armed Services Com., US House Edn. & Labor Com., US House Nat. Resources Com. Recipient Cornerstone award, Assn. Wash. Bus., 1995—96, Sentinal award, Wash. State Law Enforcement Assn., 1996, Guardian of Small Bus. award, Nat. Fedn. Ind. Bus., 1996, Gold Medal, Ind. Bus. Assn., 1996. Mem.: Wash. Women for Survival of Agr., Wash. Rural Health Assn., Wash. State Farm Bur. (Legislator of Yr. 1997), Wash. State Cattlemen's Assn., N.E. Wash. Women in Timber. Republican. Office: US Congress 1323 Longworth House Office Bldg Washington DC 20515-4705 also: 10 N Post 6th Fl Spokane WA 99201 Office Phone: 202-225-2006.*

MCMULLAN, PATRICK, photographer; b. NY; Studied bus., NYU. Columnist, Party Lines NY mag.; columnist Allure, Interview, Hamptons, Ocean Drive and Gotham. Contbr. editor Vanity Fair, British Elle, and Men's Health; contbr. photographs to NY Times mag., Vogue, internat. editions of Harper's Bazaar, Details, Tatler and Out; author: (books) Men's Show, 2000, Secrets of the Riviera: A Photo Essay, 2000, So '80s: A Photographic Diary of a Decade, 2003, InTents, Kiss Kiss, Glamour Girls, 2007; exhibitions include Homer Gallery, NYC, 2000, Tony Shafrazi Gallery, 2001, Steuben Corning Gallery, 2002, Alpan Gallery, Huntington, NY, 2002, Spike Gallery, NYC, 2003. Named one of 25 Most Important Photographers, Am. Photo. Studio: 321 W 14th St #B New York NY 10014 Office Phone: 646-638-2000. Office Fax: 646-638-2224. Business E-Mail: info@patrickmcmullan.com.

MCMULLAN, PAUL, cardiologist; Consulting physician cardiology Ochsner St. Anne Gen. Hosp. Office: Ochsner Hospital 1514 Jefferson Hwy New Orleans LA 70121 Office Phone: 985-537-3712. Office Fax: 985-537-3396.*

MCMULLAN, WILLIAM PATRICK, III, investment banker; b. Newton, Miss., Dec. 29, 1952; s. William Patrick Jr. and Rosemary (Lyons) McM.; m. Rachel Smylie McPherson, Oct. 16, 1982. BA, Vanderbilt U., 1974; MBA, U. Pa., 1976. V.p. Lehman Bros. Kuhn Loeb, NYC, 1976-82; assoc. dir. Prudential-Bache Securities, NYC, 1982-85; mng. dir. Donaldson, Lufkin & Jenrette Securities Corp., NYC, 1985-2000; mng. dir., chmn. global health care Credit Suisse First Boston, NYC, 2000—03; sr. mng. dir., co-head global healthcare Bear, Stearns & Co., NYC, 2003—08; head global healthcare Barclays Capital, 2008—. Bd. dirs. Scenic Hudson, Lar Lubovitch Dance Co., Consolidated Corp. Fund, Lincoln Ctr., Good Dog Found. Mem. Met. Club, Mashomack Fish and Game Club, Confrerie des Chevaliers du Tastevin. Home: 607 6th St Brooklyn NY 11215-3701 Office: Barclays Capital 745 7th Ave New York NY 10019 Business E-Mail: pat.mcmullan@barcap.com.

MCMULLEN, CURTIS T., mathematics professor; b. May 21, 1958; BA, Williams Coll., 1980; PhD, Harvard U., 1985. Faculty MIT, Cambridge, Mass., 1985, MSRI, 1986, Inst. Advanced Study, Princeton, NJ, 1986—87, Princeton U., NJ, 1987—90; prof. U. Calif., Berkeley, 1990—97, Harvard U., Cambridge, Mass., 1997—. Author: Logic Minimization Algorithms for VLSI Synthesis, 1984, Complex Dynamics and Renormalization, 1994, Renormalization and 3-Manifolds which Fiber over the Circle, 1996, (course notes) Riemann surfaces, dynamics and geometry, 1998, Hyperbolic manifolds, discrete groups and ergodic theory, 1996, Complex Manifolds, 1996, Complex Analysis, 1993, 1995, Theichmuller Theory, 1993; contbr. articles to profl. jours. Recipient Fields medal, 1998; grantee Guggenheim Fellowship, 2004. Mem.: AAAS, NAS, Am. Acad. Arts & Sci. (elected mem. 1998). Office: Mathematics Dept Harvard U One Oxford St 523 Science Center Cambridge MA 02138-2901 Office Phone: 617-495-0396. Office Fax: 617-485-5132.

MCMULLEN, MELODY MAE, music educator; b. Garland, Tex., Mar. 1, 1976; d. James Harold and Shirley Mae Wright; m. Jerry Clint McMullen, July 20, 2002. MusB, Stephen F. Austin State U., Nacogdoches, Tex., 1999. Cert. in Tchr. Tex. State Bd. Edn., 2000. Asst. choir dir. Cypress Creek HS, Houston, 2002—06; cons. Arbonne Internation Swiss Skin Care, Longview, Tex., 2006—08; dir., choral activities Pine Tree Ind. Sch. Dist., Longview, 2006—08. Singer: (opera) Houston Grand Opera Chorus Mem. (Chorister, 2002-06). Region vocal chair elect TMEA Region 4 Vocal Divsn., Longview, 2007—08. Recipient Gov.'s Recognition, Tex. Gov. Rick Perry, 2003, UIL Sweepstacks Choirs, Tex. U. Interscholastic League, 2004—08. Mem.: Tex. Choral Dirs. Assn., Tex. Music Educators Assn. Home: 1308 Willow Oak Longview TX 75601 Office: Pine Tree HS PO Box 5878 Longview TX 75608 Office Fax: 903-295-5029. Business E-Mail: mmcmullen@ptisd.org.

MCMULLEN, RONALD, United States Ambassador to Eritrea; b. Iowa; B, Drake U., Des Moines; M, U. Minn.; PhD, U. Iowa. Intern US Dept. State, 1982, dep. prin. officer Cape Town, South Africa, econ. officer Libreville, Gabon, polit. officer Colombo, Sri Lanka, vice consul Santo Domingo, Dominican Republic, dep. chief of mission, charge d'affaires Fiji, 1999—2002, dep. chief of mission Rangoon, Myanmar, 2002—05, assoc. dean, Fgn. Svc. Inst. Sch. Leadership and Mgmt., dir. office Afghanistan and Pakistan, Bur. Internat. Narcotic and Law Enforcement Affairs, US amb. to Eritrea Asmara, 2007—. Vis. prof. in internat. rels. and comparative politics US Mil. Acad., West Point, NY, 1990—93. Contbr. articles to profl. jours. Recipient Superior Honor Award, US Dept. State. Office: DOS Amb 7170 Asmara Pl Washington DC 20521-7170*

MCMULLEN, W. RODNEY, financial officer; BS in Acctg., U. Ky., 1981, BBA in Fin., 1981, MS in Acctg., 1982. CPA. Fin. analyst The Kroger Co., Cin., 1985-88, asst. treas., 1988-90, v.p. planning and capital mgmt., 1990-93, v.p. fin. svcs. and control, 1993-95, group v.p., chief fin. officer, 1995-97, chief fin. officer, sr. v.p., 1997-2000, exec. v.p. strategy, planning and fin., 2000—03, vice chmn., 2003—09, pres., chief operating offices, 2009—. Dir. Cin. Fin. Corp. Office: The Kroger Co 1014 Vine St Cincinnati OH 45202-1100

MCMULLIAN, ANKE HILDE, agricultural studies educator; 1 child, Jennifer Leila. PhD, U. Fla., Gainesville, 1986. Cert. in horticulture profl. Fla. Nursery, Growers & Landscape Assn., 2001. Instr. Chipola Jr. Coll., Marianna, Fla., 1988—90; prof. Indian River State Coll., Ft. Pierce, Fla., 1990—. Recipient Excellence award, Nat. Inst. Staff and Orgnl. Devel., 1994; grantee Banack Family Partnership Endowed Tchg. Chair Agr., Indian River State Coll. Found., 2006—08. Mem.: Landscape Maintenace Assn., Fla. Nursery, Growers & Landscape Assn. Office: Indian River State Coll 3209 Virginia Ave Fort Pierce FL 34981 Business E-Mail: amcmulli@irsc.edu.

MCMULLIN, ERNAN VINCENT, retired philosophy educator; b. Donegal, Ireland, Oct. 13, 1924; came to U.S., 1954; s. Vincent Paul and Carmel (Farrell) McM. BSc, Maynooth Coll., Ireland, 1945, BD, 1948; postgrad. theoretical physics, Dublin Inst. Advanced Studies, 1949-50; BPh, U. Louvain, Belgium, 1951, LPh, 1953, PhD, 1954; DLitt (hon.), Loyola U., Chgo., 1969, Nat. U. Ireland, 1990; PhD (hon.), Maynooth Coll., Ireland, 1995; D Lang. Arts (hon.), Stonehill Coll., 2000; DLaws (hon.), U. Notre Dame, 2002. Ordained priest Roman Catholic Ch., 1949; faculty U. Notre Dame, 1954-57, 59—, assoc. prof. philosophy, 1964, prof. philosophy, 1966-94, prof. emeritus, 1994—, chmn. dept., 1965-72, O'Hara prof. philosophy, 1984-94. Postdoctoral fellow Yale U., 1957-59; vis. prof. U. Minn., 1964-65, U. Cape Town, summers 1972-73, UCLA, 1977, Princeton U., 1991, Yale U., 1992; Cardinal Mercier lectr. U. Louvain, Belgium, 1995, U. Oslo, 1997; mem. exec. bd. Coun. Philos. Studies, 1970-75; chmn. philosophy of sci. div. Internat. Congress Philosophy, 1968, 73; chmn. U.S. Nat. Com. for History and Philosophy of Sci., 1982-84, 86-87. Author: Newton on Matter and Activity, 1978, The Inference That Makes Science, 1992; editor: The Concept of Matter, 1963, Galileo, Man of Science, 1967, The Concept of Matter in Modern Philosophy, 1978, Death and Decision, 1978, Issues in Computer Diagnosis, 1983, Evolution and Creation, 1985, Construction and Constraint: The Shaping of Scientific Rationality; co-editor: (with J.T. Cushing) The Philosophical Consequences of Quantum Theory, 1989, The Social Dimensions of Science, 1992, The Church and Galileo, 2005; cons. editor Studies History and Philosophy of Science, 1970-75, 1983—, Brit. Jour. Philos. Sci., 1988—, Perspectives on Science, 1992—, Ency. of the Scientific Revolution, 1994, Oxford Companion to the History of Science and its Uses, 1998. Named Romanell-Phi Beta Kappa Prof. Philosophy; rsch. grantee, NSF, Yale U., 1957—59, Cambridge U., 1968—69, hon. fellow, St. Edmund's Coll., Cambridge. Fellow Am. Acad. Arts and Scis., Internat. Acad. History Sci.; mem. AAAS (chmn. sect. L 1977-78), Am. Cath. Philos. Assn. (pres. 1966-67, Aquinas medal 1981), Philosophy of Sci. Assn. (governing bd. 1969-73, pres. 1980-82), Metaphys. Assn. Am. (exec. coun. 1968-72, pres. 1973-74, Founder's medal 1997), Am. Philos. Assn. (exec. coun. 1977-81, pres. western divsn. 1983-84), History of Sci. Soc. (exec. coun. 1988-92). Address: 2370 Lexington Ave Apt 306 Mendota Heights MN 55120 E-mail: mcmullin.1@nd.edu.

MCMULLIN, RUTH RONEY, retired publishing executive; b. NYC, Feb. 9, 1942; d. Richard Thomas and Virginia (Goodwin) Roney; m. Thomas Ryan McMullin, Apr. 27, 1968; 1 child, David Patrick. BA, Conn. Coll., 1963; M Pub. and Pvt. Mgmt., Yale U., 1979. Market rschr. Aviation Week Mag., McGraw-Hill Co., NYC, 1962-64; assoc. editor, bus. mgr. Doubleday & Co., NYC, 1964-66; mgr. Natural History Press, 1967-70; v.p., treas. Weston (Conn.) Woods, Inc., 1970-71; staff assoc. GE, Fairfield, Conn., 1979-82; mng. fin. analyst GECC Transp., Stamford, Conn., 1982—84; credit analyst corp. fin. dept. GECC, Stamford, Conn., 1984-85; sr. v.p. GECC Capital Markets Group, Inc., NYC, 1985-87; exec. v.p., COO, CEO, John Wiley & Sons, NYC, 1987—90, pres., CEO; CEO Harvard Bus. Sch. Pub. Corp., Boston, 1991-94; mem. chmn.'s com., acting CEO UNR Industries Inc., Chgo., 1991-92, also bd. dirs.; mgmt. fellow, vis. prof. Sch. Mgmt. Yale U., New Haven, 1994-95; chairperson trustees Eagle-Picher Personal Injury Settlement Trust, 1996—; chairperson Claims Procesing Facility, Inc., 1998—. Bd. dirs. Bausch & Lomb, Rochester, NY, 1987-2007; vis. prof. Sch. Mgmt., Yale U., New Haven, 1994-95. Mem. dean's adv. bd. Sch. Mgmt. Yale U., 1985—92; bd. dirs. Yale U. Alumni fund, 1986—92, Yale U. Press, 1988—99, Math. Scis. Edn. Bd., 1990—93; bd. dirs., treas. Mighty Eighth Air Force Heritage Mus., 2000—; chmn. Mighty Eighth Found., 2003—; bd. dirs. Savannah Symphony, 1999—2003, The Landings Club, 2002—04. Mem. N.Y. Yacht Club, Yale Club, Landings Club. Avocations: sailing, skiing, golf, tennis. Home: 8 Breckenridge Ln Savannah GA 31411-1701 Office: Eagle Picher Trust 30 Garfield Pl Ste 730 Cincinnati OH 45202 Personal E-mail: rrmcmullin@aya.yale.edu. Business E-Mail: ruthmcmullin@mac.com.

MCMURPHY, MICHAEL ALLEN, energy company executive, lawyer; b. Dothan, Ala., Oct. 1, 1947; s. Allen L. and Mary Emily (Jacobs) McM.; m. Maureen Daly, Aug. 8, 1970; children: Matthew, Kevin, Patrick. BS, USAF Acad., 1969; MA, St. Mary's U., San Antonio, 1972; JD, U. Tex., 1975. Bar: Tex. 1975, U.S. Supreme Ct. 1977, U.S. Ct. Mil. Appeals, D.C. 1978, U.S. Ct. Appeals (fed. cir.) 1982. Commd. 2d lt. USAF, 1969, advanced through grades to capt.; instr. Air U., Ala., 1975-79; resigned USAF, 1979; atty., advisor Oak Ridge (Tenn.) ops. U.S. Dept. Energy, 1979-83; gen. counsel COGEMA, Inc., Washington, 1983-87, v.p., 1987-88, pres., CEO, Bethesda, Md., 1988—; pres. Areva T&D, Inc., 2005—. Pres., CEO Va. Fuels, Inc., Lynchburg, 1987-92; co-CEO AREVA Enterprises, Inc., Washington, DC, 2002-03, vice chmn., pres., 2003—; bd. dirs. Soc. Gen. Techs. Nouvelles, S.A., St. Quentin, France, Transnuclear, Inc., Columbia, Md., Canberra Industries, Meriden, Conn., Cogema Resources, Inc, Casper, Wyo., Areva, Inc., Lynchburg, Va. and Richland, Wash.; bd. govs. Duke Cogema Stone & Webster, LLC, Charlotte, N.C., 1998—; pres. Uranium Producers Am., 1991-92 Mem. editorial bd. Air Force Law Rev., 1977-79. Lt. col. USAFR ret., 1992. Decorated chevalier Nat. Order of Merit (France). Avocation: skiing. Home: 9324 Garden Ct Potomac MD 20854 Office: COGEMA Inc 1 Bethesda Ctr 4800 Hampden Ln Ste 1100 Bethesda MD 20814 Business E-Mail: mcmurphy@cogema-inc.com.

MCMURRAY, CLAUDIA ANNE, federal agency administrator, lawyer; d. Raymond D. and Sally Kathryn (Martin) McM.; m. Donald V. Moorehead, June 6, 1987. AB with honors, Smith Coll., 1980; JD, Georgetown U., 1984. Bar: D.C. 1985. Legis. asst. to Rep. Bill Emerson US Ho. Reps, Washington, 1980-81; law clk. Office of Counsel to the Pres. The White House, Washington, 1983-84; atty. Patton, Boggs & Blow LLP, 1984-87, Kirkland & Ellis LLP, 1987-89; legis. counsel to Senator John W. Warner US Senate, 1989-90, minority counsel Com. on Environment and Pub. Works, 1991—95, gen. counsel to Senator Fred Thompson, 1996—98; v.p. Van Scoyoc Associates, Inc., 1998—2000; assoc. dep. adminstr. & chief of staff to dep. adminstr. EPA, 2000—03; dep. asst. sec for environ., Bur. Oceans & Internat. Environ. & Sci. Affairs US Dept. State, Washington, 2003—06, asst. sec. for oceans, internat. environ., & scientific affairs, 2006—. Editor The Tax Lawyer. Office: US Dept State Harry S Truman Bldg 2201 C St NW Rm 7831 Washington DC 20520*

MCMURRAY, JAMES SCOTT, pediatric otolaryngologist; b. Houston, July 17, 1964; s. James Edward and Sheila Frances (Murphy) McM.; m. Jane Howard Suker, May 29, 1993; 1 child, Mary Grace Chilton. BS with honors, U. Wash., 1986, MD, 1990. Diplomate Am. Bd. Otolaryngology. Resident Northwestern U.-Northwestern Meml. Hosp., Chgo., 1990-95; fellow in neurology Johns Hopkins U. Hosp.,

Balt., 1995-96; fellow in pediatric otolaryngology Children's Hosp. Md. Ctr., Cin., 1996—. Office: Childrens Hosp Med Ctr Dept Otolaryngology 3335 Burnet Ave Dept Cincinnati OH 45229-3026

MCMURRY, JAMES FINLEY, JR., endocrinologist, researcher; b. Sentinel, Okla., Aug. 25, 1940; s. James Finley and Anna Jo McMurry; m. Rebecca L. Lomax, May 21, 1987. MD, U. Okla., 1965. Diplomate Am. Bd. Internal Medicine. Chief, med. services USAF Hosp., Dover, Del., 1969—71; endocrinologist Scott and White Clinic, Temple, Tex., 1972—81; assoc prof., internal medicine Tex. A & M U., Temple, 1979—81; asst prof. internal medicine U. Ky., Lexington, 1981—84, Georgetown U., Washington, 1984—87; pvt. practice Rockville, Md., 1984—. Editor: Jefferson, Callender and the SALLY Story, 2000; co-author: Anatomy of a Scandal: Thomas Jefferson and the SALLY Story, 2002. Capt. USAF, 1969—71. Fellow: ACP; mem.: Montgomery County Med. Assn., Md. (com. chmn. 1987—89), Am. Diabetes Assn. (pres. South Tex. chpt. 1980—81, pres. DC chpt. 1986—87, chmn. Ky. affiliate 1983—84), Endocrine Soc. Independent. Avocations: history, photography, gardening. Office: 11119 Rockville Pike Ste 409 Rockville MD 20852-3143 Office Phone: 301-468-1820.

MCMURTRY, LARRY JEFF, writer; b. Wichita Falls, Tex., June 3, 1936; s. William Jefferson and Hazel Ruth (McIver) McM.; m. Josephine Ballard, July 15, 1959 (div. 1966); 1 child, James. BA, N. Tex. State Coll., 1958; MA, Rice U., 1960. Instr. Tex. Christian U., Ft. Worth, 1961-62; lectr. in English and creative writing Rice U., Houston, 1963-69; co-owner Booked Up Book Store, Washington, from 1970. Vis. prof. George Mason Coll., 1970, Am. U., 1970-71. Author: (novels) Horseman, Pass By, 1961 (Jesse H. Jones award Texas Inst. of Letters 1962), Leaving Cheyenne, 1963, The Last Picture Show, 1966, Moving On, 1970, All My Friends Are Going to be Strangers, 1972, Terms of Endearment, 1975, Somebody's Darling, 1978, Cadillac Jack, 1982, The Desert Rose, 1983, Lonesome Dove, 1985 (Pulitzer prize for Fiction 1986), Texasville, 1987, Anything for Billy, 1988, Some Can Whistle, 1989, Buffalo Girls, 1990, The Evening Star, 1992, Streets of Laredo, 1993, The Late Child, 1995, Dead Man's Walk, 1995, Comanche Moon, 1997, Duane's Depressed, 1999, Boone's Lick, 2000, Sin Killer: The Berrybender Narratives Book One, 2002, The Wandering Hill: The Berrybender Narratives Book Two, 2003, By Sorrow's River: The Berrybender Narratives Book Three, 2003, Folly and Glory: The Berrybender Narratives Book Four, 2004, Loop Group, 2004, Telegraph Days, 2006, When the Light Goes: A Novel, 2007; Co-author (with Diana Ossana) Zeke and Ned, 1997, Pretty Boy Floyd, 1994; Author: (non-fiction) Walker Benjamin at Dairy Queen, 1999, Roads: Driving America's Great Highways, 2000, Paradise, 2000, Sacagawea's Nickname: Essays on the American West, 2001, The Colonel and Little Missie: Buffalo Bill, Annie Oakley, and the Beginnings of Superstardom in America, 2005, Oh What a Slaughter: Massacres in the American West: 1846-1890, 2005, Books: A Memoir, 2008; (essays) In a Narrow Grave: Essays on Texas, 1968, It's Always We Rambled: An Essay on Rodeo, 1974, Film Flam: Essays on Hollywood, 1987; screenwriter: (with Peter Bogdanovich) The Last Picture Show, 1971 (Academy award nomination best adapted screenplay 1971), Texasville, 1990, Montana, 1990, Falling From Grace, 1992, (with Cybill Shepard) Memphis, 1992, Brokeback Mountain, 2005 (best screenplay-motion picture Hollywood Fgn. Press Assn., Golden Globe award, 2006, British Acad. Film & TV Arts award for adapted screenplay, 2006, Adapted Screenplay, Acad. Motion Pictures Arts & Sciences, 2006); also articles, essays, book revs. in N.Y. Times, Saturday Rev., Washington Post, Am. Film, others. Wallace Stegner fellow, 1960, Guggenheim fellow, 1964; recipient Barbara McCombs/Lon Tinkle award Texas Inst. of Letters, 1986. Mem. Tex. Inst. Letters (Jesse H. Jones award 1962). Mailing: Author Mail Simon & Schuster 1230 Ave of the Americas New York NY 10020-1586

MCMURTRY, R. CODY, physical education educator; b. Tullahoma, Tenn., Apr. 13, 1978; s. Ken and Iris McMurtry; m. Ashley N. Marine, Dec. 20, 2008. BS, Newberry Coll., SC; MA, Tenn. Tech. U., Cookeville, 2001. Asst. prof. Newberry Coll., Afghanistan, 2002—. Asst. prof., Ala., Afghanistan, 2009—. Business E-Mail: cody.mcmurtry@newberry.edu.

MCMURTRY, R. ROY, federal judge; b. Toronto, Ont., Can., May 31, 1932; s. Roland Roy and Doris Elizabeth (Belcher) McM.; m. Ria Jean Macrae, Apr. 18, 1957; children: Janet, James, Harry, Jeannie, Erin, Michael. BA with honors, U. Toronto, 1954; LLB, Osgoode Hall Law Sch., 1958; LLD (hon.), U. Ottawa, 1983, Leeds U., UK, 1988, York U., 1991, U. Toronto, 1998. Bar: Called to bar 1958, created Queen's counsel 1970. Partner firm Benson, McMurtry, Percival and Brown; mem. Provincial Parliament for Eglinton, 1975-85; atty. gen. for Ont., 1975-85; solicitor gen. for Ont., 1978-82; high commnr. for Can. to Gt. Brit. and No. Ireland, 1985-88; ptnr. Blaney, McMurtry Stapells, Toronto, 1988-91; chmn. Can. Football League, 1989-91; assoc. chief justice Ont. Ct. Justice, Toronto, 1991-94, chief justice, 1994-96; chief justice of Ont. Ont. Ct. of Appeal, Toronto, 1996—2007; counsel Gowling Lafleur Henderson LLP, Toronto, Ont., 2007. Freeman of City of London, 1986. Mem. United Ch. of Can. Office: Gowling Lafleur Henderson LLP Ste 1600 100 King St W Toronto ON M5X 1G5 Canada Office Phone: 416-862-5793. Business E-Mail: roy.mcmurtry@gowlings.com.

MCNABB, DAVID E., educator, author; b. LA, Nov. 29, 1932; s. Jay B. McNabb and Josephine P. Recagno; m. Janet C. Lagerquist, June 12, 1962; children: Meghan, Michael, Sara. BA, Calif. State Coll., Fullerton, 1965; MA, U. Wash., Seattle, 1968; PhD, Oreg. State U., Corvallis, 1980. Prof. Pacific Luth. U., Tacoma, 1979—; vis. prof. UMUC-Europe, Heidelberg, Germany, 1997—98, The Evergreen State Coll., Olympia, Wash., 1998—2000, Stockholm Sch. Econs., Riga, Latvia, 2000—07. Vis. scholar Thunderbird Internat. U., Phoenix, 1990. Author: Research Methods for Public Administration, 2002, 2008, Research Methods for Political Science, 2004, 2009, Public Utilities: Management Challenges, 2005, Knowledge Management In The Public Sector, 2006, The New Face of Government, 2009. Served with USN, 1952—54. Mem.: ASPA, AMA, APSA, Acad. Polit. Sci., Acad. Mgmt., Rotary. Home: 605 E Barbary Rd Shelton WA 98584 Business E-Mail: mcnabbde@plu.edu.

MCNABB, DONOVAN, professional football player; b. Chgo., Nov. 25, 1976; s. Samuel and Wilma McNabb; m. Raquel Nurse, 2003. Grad. in Speech Comm., Syracuse U., NY, 1998. Backup guard, basketball team Syracuse U. Orange, 1995—97; quarterback Phila. Eagles, 1999—. Co-host (with Beasley Reece) The Donovan McNabb Show. Mem. Life as a Rookie panel Rookie Symposium, 2000; program sponsor Am. Diabetes Assn.; founder Donovan McNabb Found., 2000, Donovan McNabb Diabetes Camp for Kids; hon. co-chair Phila. Am. Diabetes Assn.'s Walk for Diabetes, 2001. Named NFL Player of Yr., CBS Radio, 2000, Nat Football Conf. Offensive Player of Yr., NFL, 2004; named to Nat. Football Conf. Pro Bowl Team, 2000—04, All Madden Team, 2000. Achievements include becoming the Philadelphia Eagles all-time franchise leader in pass attempts and passing yards, 2008. Office: Phila Eagles One NovaCare Way Philadelphia PA 19145*

MCNABB, DUNCAN J., career military officer; b. Shaw AFB, SC, Aug. 8, 1952; BS, USAF Acad., 1974; MS in Internat. Rels., U. Southern Calif., LA, 1984. Commd. 2d lt. USAF, 1974, advanced through grades to gen., 2005; instr. navigator 14th Mil. Airlift Wing Squadron, Norton AFB, Calif., 1978-79, instr., pilot, chief pilot, 1980-83; gen.'s aide Air Force Inspection and Safety Ctr., Norton AFB, 1983-84; chief plan integration br. Hdqrs. Mil. Airlift Command, Scott AFB, Ill., 1984-86; aide to the comdr. in chief U.S. Transp. Command and Mil. Airlift Command, Scott AFB, 1986-88; chief pilot to ops. officer 17th Mil. Airlift Squadron, Charleston AFB, S.C., 1988-90; comdr. 41st Mil. Airlift Squadron, Charleston AFB, 1990-92; dep. group comdr. 437th Ops. Group, Charleston AFB, 1992; chief Logistics Readiness Ctr. the Joint Staff, Logistics, the Pentagon, Washington, 1993-95; comdr. 89th Ops. Group, Andrews AFB, Md., 1995-96, 62nd Airlift Wing, McChord AFB, Wash., 1996-97, Tanker Airlife Control Ctr., Hdqrs. Air Mobility Command, Scott AFB, 1997—99; dep. dir. programs, Office of Dep. Chief of Staff for Plans & Programs USAF, Washington, 1999, dir. programs, 1999—2002, dep. chief of staff plan & programs, 2002—04; dir. logistics (J-4) The Joint Staff, Washington, 2004—05; comdr. Air Mobility Command, Scott AFB, Ill., 2005—07; vice chief of staff USAF, Washington, 2007—08; comdr. US Transp. Command (USTRANSCOM), 2008—. Decorated Def. Superior Svc. medal, Def. Meritorious Svc. medal, Meritorious Svc. medal with oak leaf cluster, Joint Svc. Commendation medal, Air Force Commendation medal with oak leaf cluster, Air Force achievement medal, Combat Readiness medal with oak leaf cluster, Nat. Def. Svc. medal, Legion of Merit with oak leaf cluster, Armed Forces Expeditionary medal, Southwest Asia Svc. medal with two bronze stars, Humanitarian Svc. medal, Kuwait Liberation medal (Kingdom of Saudi Arabia), Kuwait Liberation medal (Kingdom of Kuwait); recipent Orville Wright award Order of Daedalians. Office: US Transp Command (USTRANSCOM) Scott AFB Scott Air Force Base IL 62225*

MCNABB, F. WILLIAM, III, (BILL MCNABB), investment company executive; b. 1957; BA, Dartmouth Coll., 1979; MBA, U. Pa. Joined The Vanguard Group, Inc., 1986, mng. dir. client-relationship group, mng. dir. institutional and internat. bus., pres., CEO, 2008—. Office: Vanguard Group Inc 100 Vanguard Blvd Malvern PA 19355

MCNABB GOODWIN, CAROL, music educator; DMA in Bassoon Performance, U. Ariz., Tucson, 1996. Assoc. prof. music U. Tex., Brownsville, 1999—. Recipient Excellence award, NISOD, 2003. Mem.: Tex. Music Educators Assoc. (regional coll. v.p. 2006—08), Coll. Music Soc. Achievements include development of new method of teaching harmonic dictation. Office: Univ Tex Brownsville 80 Fort Brown Brownsville TX 78520

MCNAIR, JOHN WILLIAM, JR., civil engineer; b. Asheville, NC, June 17, 1926; s. John William and Annie (Woody) McN.; m. June Clemens Kratz; children: Jeffry, Marsha, Cathy. BS in Forestry, Pa. State U., 1950; BSCE, Va. Poly Inst. State U., 1955; postgrad., U. Va., 1957—2004. Registered profl. engr., Va., NC, Md., W.Va., Pa., NY, Ky. Forester U.S. Forest Svc., Flagstaff, Ariz., 1950, U.S. Gypsum Co., Altavista, Va., 1951; mem. engring. faculty U. Va., Charlottesville, 1955—58; prin. John McNair & Assocs., Waynesboro, Va., 1958—; owner Brucheum Group, Waynesboro, 1983—; chmn., CEO Info. Systems Support, Inc., Waynesboro, 1998—2007. With Va. Bd. Architects, Profl. Engrs. and Land Surveyors, 1969-79, v.p., 1977-78, pres., 1978-79. Author numerous engring. and land mgmt. study reports. Mem. Waynesboro City Coun., 1968-72, vice mayor, 1970-72; chmn. Waynesboro Indsl. Devel. Authority, 1984-2000. Capt. AUS, 1944-46, 51-53, France, Okinawa. Recipient Disting. Svc. cert. Va. Soc. Profl. Engrs., 1971. Fellow ASCE; mem. Am. Acad. Environ. Engrs. (bd. cert. environ. engr.), Rotary, Rappahannock River Yacht Club (founding mem.). Republican. Presbyterian. Home Phone: 540-949-6261; Office Phone: 540-942-1161. Business E-Mail: jmcnair@brucheum.com.

MCNAIR, MARCIA L., language educator, writer, editor; BA in English, Dartmouth Coll., Hanover, 1980; MA in Writing, NYU, NYC, 1989. Asst. editor Essence Mag., NYC, 1980—83; program coord. NYU, NYC, 1984—87; program coord., adj. lectr. CUNY, NYC, 1987—94; asst. prof. English Nassau CC, Garden City, NY, 1995—. Adj. prof. Molloy Coll., Rockville Center, NY, 2002—; ednl. cons. African Am. Mus., Hempstead, NY, 2005—; workshop facilitator Nassau CC, 2005, lectr., 06. Contbr. essays; creative dir.: Diary of a Mad Black Feminist; author: E-males; editor (arts and entertainment): Lakeview Cmty. News, 2006—. Coord. Nassau Cmty. Co. Nat. African Am. Read In, Garden City, NY, 2002—. Recipient Hon. Mention, New Millenium Writers Creative Non-Fiction Contest, 2002; grantee, LI Coun. Arts, 2006. Mem.: Schomburg Ctr. Rsch. Black Culture, Assn. Black Women Higher Edn., LI Writers Guild, Sigma Delta Chi. Office: Nassau CC English Dept One Education Dr Garden City NY 11530

MCNAIR, RUSSELL ARTHUR, JR., lawyer; b. Detroit, Dec. 2, 1934; s. Russell Arthur and Virla (Standish) McN.; m. Rosemary M. Chesbrough, Apr. 6, 1957; children: Julie McNair Schwerin, Russell Arthur III, Douglas S. AB in Econs. cum laude, Princeton U., 1956; JD with distinction, U. Mich., 1960. Bar: Mich. 1960, Fla. 2001. Assoc. Dickinson, Wright, Moon, Van Dusen & Freeman (now Dickinson Wright PLLC), Detroit, 1960-67, ptnr., 1968-98, chmn., 1994-98, cons. mem., 2007—. Adj. prof. U. Detroit Sch. Law, 1968-72; mem. adv. bd. Fin. Transactions Inst., 1984-94; adj. prof. Wayne State U. Law Sch., 1994-96; spkr. in field. Trustee Children's Home, Detroit, 1975-95, pres. 1986-87, hon. trustee 1995—; mem. community leaders coun. United Way, 1994-98; dir. Mich. Jobs Commn., 1995-98, TED Ctr., Delray Beach, Fla., 2006—. Mem.: Mich. Bar Found., Am. Coll. Real Estate Lawyers, Am. Law Inst., Fla. Bar Assn., Mich. Bar Assn. Republican. Presbyterian. Avocations: golf, tennis, platform tennis. Home: 4148 Gleneagles Dr Boynton Beach FL 33436-4802 Office: PO Box 243351 Boynton Beach FL 33424-3351 Home Phone: 561-740-1037; Office Phone: 313-223-3511. Personal E-mail: mcnairs47@comcast.net.

MCNALL, BRUCE, film producer, former professional sports team executive; b. Arcadia, Calif., Apr. 17, 1950; m. Jane Cody; children: Katie, Bruce. Student, UCLA. Founder, chmn. bd. Numismatic Fine Arts, Inc., LA; owner, chmn. bd. Summa Stable, Inc.; chmn. bd. Gladden Entertainment Corp.; former ptnr. Dallas Mavericks; co-owner LA Kings, 1986—87, owner, 1988—94, co-owner, 1994; owner Toronto Argonauts, 1991; co-chair A-Mark Entertainment, 2004—. Chmn. NHL Bd. Govs., 1993—94. Prodr.: (films) The Sicilian, 1987, Gleaming the Cube, 1989; prodr.: (films) Millennium, 1989, Camille, 2007, Timber Falls, 2007, Autopsy, 2008, Night Train, 2009; exec. prodr.: (films) Weekend at Bernie's, 1989, Short Time, 1990, Asylum, 2005, Next Day Air, 2009; author: Fun While It Lasted: My Rise and Fall in the Land of Fame and Fortune, 2003. Named NHL Exec. of Yr., Sporting News, 1989. Office: A-Mark Entertainment 233 Wilshire Blvd Ste 200 Santa Monica CA 90401*

MCNALL-KNAPP, RENÉ YVONNE, pediatrician, educator; b. Pensacola, Fla., Oct. 28, 1968; d. Lynn Tracy and Ann Sherrie McNall; m. Ryan Robert Knapp, May 16, 1998; children: Cooper McNall Knapp, Jordan Howard McNall Knapp, Carter McNall Knapp. BA, Vanderbilt U., Nashville, 1990; MD, U. Tenn., Memphis, 1994. Diplomate Am. Bd. Pediat., 1997, in hematology/oncology Am. Bd. Pediat., 2002. Resident pediat. Children's Mercy Hosp., Kansas City, Mo., 1994—97; fellow pediatric hematology/oncology St. Jude Children's Rsch. Hosp., Memphis, 1998—2001; asst. prof. U. Okla. Coll. Medicine, 2001—08, assoc. prof., 2008—. Med. advisor coun. mem. Children's Miracle Network, Okla. City, 2004; mem. 363 Group, Okla. City, 2006; bd. mem. Children's Med. Rsch. Inst., Okla. City, 2004—08, med. advisor, 2004—08. Fellow: Am. Acad. Pediat.; mem.: Am. Soc. Pediatric Hematology/Oncology. Democrat. Mem. Christian Ch. Office: Univ Okla Health Scis C 940 NE 13th Rm 3B3308 Oklahoma City OK 73104 Office Fax: 405-271-3756. Business E-Mail: rene-mcnall@ouhsc.edu.

MCNALLY, ALAN G., retail executive; b. Quebec, Can., Nov. 3, 1945; m. Ruth; 2 children. BSc., M Eng., Cornell U., 1967; Internat. MBA, York U., Can. With Aluminum Co. of Can.; vice chmn. personal & commercial fin. services Bank of Montreal Group, 1975-93; CEO, vice chmn. Harris Bank and Haris Bankcorp Inc., 1993-1995, chmn. bd., CEO, 1995—2004; chmn. Harris Financial Corp., 2004—06, spl. adv., 2007—; chmn. Walgreen Co., Deerfield, Ill., 2008—, acting CEO, 2008—09. Bd. dirs. Harris Financial Corp., 2006, Walgreen Co., 2008-; bd. trustees DePaul U., adv. bd. mem. Northwestern U. J.L. Kellogg Grad. Sch. Mgmt., bd. mem. Evenston Northwestern Healthcare, mem. bd. govs. York U., dir. Canadian Coun. for Aboriginal Bus. Gen. chair United Way/Crusade of Mercy fundraising campaign, 1996, dir. Chgo. Youth Ctrs., treas. Queen Elizabeth Hosp. Found., dir. Kid's Help Phone. Recipient Americanism award Anti-Defamation League, Community Builder award Christian Insudtrial League, Outstanding Exec. Leadership award York U. Schulich Sch. Bus., Toronto, Prime Movers award. Bd. dirs. Econ. Club Chgo., Chgo. Club, civic com. Commercial Club Chgo., Executive's Club Chgo., Glen View Club. Office: Walgreen Co 200 Wilmot Rd Deerfield IL 60015*

MCNALLY, ANDREW, IV, publishing executive, director; b. Chgo., Nov. 11, 1939; s. Andrew and Margaret C. (MacMillin) McN.; m. Jeanine Sanchez, July 3, 1966; children: Andrew, Carrie, Ward BA, U. NC, 1963; MBA, U. Chgo., 1969. Bus. mgr. edn. divsn. Rand McNally & Co., Chgo., 1967—70, exec. v.p., sec., 1970—74, pres., 1974—97, CEO, 1978—97, also chmn. bd. dirs., 1993—97; ptnr. McNally Investments, Chgo., 1998—. Bd. dirs. Hubbell Inc., Boyt Harness, Qualis. Trustee Newberry Libr.; bd. dirs. Children's Meml. Hosp. With Air Force N.G., 1963-69. Mem. Chgo. Club, Saddle and Cycle Club, Commonwealth Club, Racquet Club. Office: 333 N Michigan Ave Ste 2200 Chicago IL 60601-4104

MCNALLY, MARK THOMAS, history professor; PhD, UCLA, 1998. Assoc. prof. U. Hawaii, Honolulu, 1999—. Author: (book) Proving the Way: Conflict and Practice in the History of Japanese Nativism. Fulbright fellow, US Dept. State, 2005, Postdoc. fellowship, Reischauer Inst., Harvard U. Mem.: Assn. Asian Studies.

MCNALLY, REGINA C., marketing educator; b. Chgo., Mar. 7, 1960; d. John F. and Rita A. McNally; m. Aidan M. Brodie, July 23, 1999; 1 child, Benjamin M. Brodie. BA in Spanish, Bradley U., Peoria, Ill., 1984, BS in Mech. Engring., 1984; PhD, U. Ill., Urbana-Champaign, 2002; MBA, Ill. Inst. Tech., Chgo., 1995. EIT Ill., 1984. Mfg. engr. Packard Electric, Warren, Ohio, 1984—86, Sgt. Welch Sci. Co., Skokie, Ill., 1986—88, Tellabs, Lisle, Ill., 1988—92, product mgr., 1992—93, Shannon, Ireland, 1993—95, mktg. mgr. Bolingbrook, Ill., 1995—98; grad. asst. U. Ill., Champaign, 1998—2002; asst. prof. Mich. State U., East Lansing, 2002—. Contbr. articles to numerous profl. jours. Recipient Seymour Sudman Tchg. Excellence award, Coll. Bus., U. Ill., 2001, John D. and Dortha J. Withrow Emerging-Scholar award, Mich. State U., 2008, Rsch. Conf. Best Paper award, Product Devel. Mgmt. Assn., 2008; named Excellent Tchrs. List, U. Ill., 1999; Rsch. grant, Teradata Ctr. Customer Relationship Mgmt., Duke U., 2004, Eli Broad Coll. Bus., Mich. State U., 2007—08. Mem.: Acad. Mgmt., Product Devel. and Mgmt. Assn., Mktg. Sci. Inst., Am. Mktg. Assn. Roman Catholic. Avocation: travel. Office Phone: 517-432-6378. Personal E-mail: mcnally@bus.msu.edu.

MCNALLY, RICHARD JAMES, clinical psychologist, educator; b. Detroit, Apr. 17, 1954; s. George Vincent and Marjorie Frances (Tobin) McN.; m. Margaret Cain, Aug. 16, 1985 (div. 2005). BS in Psychology, Wayne State U., 1976; MA in Clin. Psychology, U. Ill., Chgo., 1980, PhD in Clin. Psychology, 1982. Clin. psychology intern dept. psychiatry Temple U. Med. Sch., Phila., 1982-83, postdoctoral fellow dept. psychiatry, 1983-84; from asst. prof. to assoc. prof. dept. psychology U. Health Scis., Chgo. Med. Sch., North Chicago, Ill., 1984-91; assoc. prof. dept. psychology Harvard U., Cambridge, Mass., 1991-95, prof., 1995—, clin. dir., 2003—. Assoc. editor Behavior Therapy, 1992-95; author: Panic Disorder: A Critical Analysis, 1994, Remembering Trauma, 2003; contbr. articles to Psychol. Bull., Psychol. Rev. Recipient Disting. Scientist award, Soc. for the Sci. of Clin. Psychology, 2005; rsch. grantee NIMH Fellow Assn. for Psychol. Sci.; mem. APA (mem. DSM-IV task force 1989-94), Assn. for Behavior and Cognitive Therapies. Democrat. Office: Harvard U Dept Psychology 33 Kirkland St Cambridge MA 02138-2044 Office Phone: 617-495-3853. Business E-Mail: rjm@wjh.harvard.edu.

MCNALLY, TERRENCE, playwright; b. St. Petersburg, Fla., Nov. 3, 1939; s. Hubert Arthur and Dorothy Katharine (Rapp) McNally. BA, Columbia U., 1960. Stage mgr. Actors Studio, NYC, 1961, tutor, 1961-62; film critic The Seventh Art, 1963-65; asst. editor Columbia Coll. Today, NYC, 1965-66. Author: (plays) The Lady of the Camellias, 1963, And Things That Go Bump in the Night, 1964, Apple Pie and Last Gasps, 1966, Sweet Eros, Witness, Tour, Cuba Si!, Noon, 1968, Next, 1969, Where Has Tommy Flowers Gone?, Botticelli, Bringing It All Back Home, 1971, Bad Habits, 1971 (Obie award, 1971), Whiskey, 1973, The Tubs, 1974, The Ritz, 1975 (Obie award best play, 1974), The Golden Age, 1975, Broadway, Broadway, 1979, The Five Forty-Eight, 1974, It's Only a Play, 1982, The Rink, 1984, Frankie and Johnny in the Clair de Lune, 1988, The Lisbon Traviata, 1989, Up in Saratoga, 1990, Kiss of the Spider Woman, 1990 (Tony award best book of a musical, 1993), Andre's Mother, 1990 (Emmy award), Preludes, Fuges & Rifts, Lips Together, Teeth Apart, 1991, (screenplay) Frankie and Johnny, 1991, A Perfect Ganesh, 1993 (Pulitzer prize for drama nomination, 1994), Kiss of the Spiderwoman, 1993, Love! Valour! Compassion!, 1994 (Outer Critics' Circle award best Broadway play, 1995, N.Y. Drama Critics Best Am. play, Tony award for Best Play), Master Class, 1994, Ragtime, 1997 (Tony award Best Book of a Musical Corpus Christi, 1998), The Full Monty, 2000, The Visit, 2001, Frankie and Johnny in the Clair de Lune, 2002, Chita Rivera: The Dancer's Life, 2005, Deuce, 2007, Some Men, 2007. Recipient Dramatists Guild Hull-Warriner award, 1973, 1988, 1990; Guggenheim fellow, 1966—69. Mem.: Am. Acad. Arts and Letters, Dramatists Guild (v.p. 1981—98). Office: care Peter Franklin William Morris Agy 1325 Avenue Of The Americas New York NY 10019-6026

MCNALLY, VINCENT JOSEPH, historian, educator; b. Phila., Feb. 6, 1943; s. Joseph Edward and Dorothy Elizabeth (Connor) McNally. PhD, Univ. of Dublin, Trinity College, Dublin, Ireland, 1971—77. Prof. ch. history Sacred Heart Sch. of Theology, Hales Corners, Wis., 1992—; asst. prof. history Simon Fraser U., Burnaby, B.C., Canada, 1987—92. Author: (Book) Education Facsimiles 241-260: Catholic Emancipation, 1793-1829, 1976, A History of the Roman Catholic Diocese of Victoria, B.C., 1990, Reform, Revolution and Reaction: Archbishop John Thomas Troy and the Catholic Church in Ireland, 1787-1817, 1995, The Lord's Distant Vineyard: A History of the Oblates and the Catholic Community in British Columbia, 2000, "Hope for the Future: the Church's Challenges of the New Millennium", 2000, (book) Christianity and Native Cultures: Christian and Native Spiritualities in British Columbia: The Historic Struggle to Respect Diversity and Ambiguity, 2004, (Journal: Historical Studies) Challenging the Status Quo: An Examination of the History of Catholic Education in British Columbia, 1999, (Journal: Western Oblate Studies) "Fighting for a Foundation: Oblate Beginnings in Far Western Canada, 1847-1864, 1996, (Journal: Canadian Church Historical Soci) "Fighting City Hall: The Church Tax Exemption Battle Between the City and Roman Catholic Diocese of Victoria", 1992, (Journal of Church and State) "Church-State Relations and American Influence in British Columbia before Confederation", 1992, (Catholic Historical Review) "Archbishop John Thomas Troy and the Establishment of St. Patrick's, Maynooth, 1791-1795", 1981, (Research Project) Practicing What We Preach: Testing and Publishing a Guide for Implementing a Pastoral Theology of Acceptance and Reconciliation in Northern Ireland", 2001 (Assoc. of Theological Schools in US and Canada: Lilly Research Award, 2001), (Research Project:) "Challenging Prejudice: Creating a Theology of Acceptance and Reconciliation in the Schools of Northern Ireland, 2000 (Pew Charitable Trusts, 2000), (Research Award) Researching, Writing and Publishing of a survey history: Irish Catholics: The Catholic Church in Ireland from the Reformation to the Present, 1999 (Eli Lilly Fellowship, 1999), Developing Healthy Theological Imaginations, 1998 (Lilly Endowment Fellowship for Teaching and Learning in Theology and Religion, 1998), Challenging Ourselves: A Practical Guide for Moving Beyond Prejudice in the Schools of Northern Ireland, 2004, The Artifact Paper: Challenging Moral Dualism, 2007, Answering God's Call: 1932-2007: A History of the Priests of the Sacred Heart and Their 75 Years of Seminary Education Culminating in the Sacred Heart School of Theology, 2007. Recipient Rsch. award, NEH, 2004, fellowship U. Chgo., 2005.; American Catholic Historical Society (Peter Guilday Prize 1981). Avocations: drawing, harpsichord, painting, travel. Office: Sacred Heart School of Theology PO Box 429 Hales Corners WI 53130 Home Phone: 262-797-6521; Office Phone: 414-425-8300 ext. 181. Office Fax: 414-529-6999. Business E-Mail: vmcnally@shst.edu, vmcnally@execpc.com.

MCNAMARA, BRENDA NORMA, retired secondary school educator; b. Blackpool, Lancashire, Eng., Aug. 8, 1945; arrived in U.S., 1946; d. Milford Hampson and Nola (Welsby) Jones; m. Michael James McNamara, July 19, 1969. BA in History, Calif. State U., Long Beach, 1967; postgrad., Calif. State U., various campuses, 1967—. Cert. secondary tchr. and lang. devel. specialist Calif. Tchr. history West HS, Torrance, Calif., 1968—, dept. chair, 1989-99, 2000—04; ret., 2004. Cons. Golden State Exam. in History Calif. State Dept. Edn., 1998; state del. NEA Annual Meeting, 2000, 02, local del., 03, 04; cons. in field. Co-author: (book) World History, 1988. Western Internat. Studies Consortium grantee, 1988. Mem.: NEA (retired 2004), NEA/CTA, Bay Valley (sec., treas. 2007—, treas. 2007—), Am. Hist. Assn., Nat. Coun. Social Studies, So. Calif. Coun. Social Studies, Torrance Tchrs. Assn. (bd. dirs. 1992—2004), Calif. Coun. Social Studies, Calif. Tchrs. Assn. (retired 2004). Avocations: travel, theater, mystery reading, gourmet cooking. E-mail: brenmcnamara@cox.net.

MCNAMARA, DENNIS K., art educator; children: Lionel C., Timothy J., Olivia K. MFA, U. Minn., Mpls., 1979. Lead instr., art Triton Coll., River Grove, Ill., 1997—. Office: Triton Coll 2000 Fifth Ave River Grove IL 60171 Business E-Mail: dmcnama2@triton.edu.

MCNAMARA, FRANCIS JOSEPH, JR., retired foundation executive, lawyer; b. Boston, Nov. 30, 1927; s. Francis Joseph and Louise (English) McN.; m. Noreen E. O'Connor, June 18, 1953 (dec. Feb. 1984); children: Francis Joseph III, Moira Patricia (Mrs. Lance F. James), John Allen, Kathleen Louise (Mrs. Robert J. Hugin), Martha Jeanne (Mrs. James R. Bordewick), Mark Jeffrey; m. Lois L. Magner, Jan. 17, 1986. AB, Georgetown U., 1949, LLB, 1951; LLD, Fairfield U., 1983. Bar: Conn. 1952. Assoc. firm Pullman, Comley, Bradley & Reeves, 1953; asst. U.S. Atty., dist. Conn., 1953-57; assoc. firm Cummings & Lockwood, Stamford, Conn., 1957-59, ptnr., 1959-91. Guest lectr. Salzburg (Austria) Seminar, 1981; chmn. grievance com. U.S. Dist. Ct. Conn., 1983-89; mem. panel comml. arbitrators Am. Arbitration Assn., Ctr. Dispute Resolution. Trustee Fairfield (Conn.) U., 1968-80, trustee emeritus, 1980—; trustee Charles E. Culpeper Trust, 1968-2001; chmn. bd. Charles E. Culpeper Found., 1968-99, pres., 1991-99. With USNR, 1946, 51-53. Fellow Am. Bar Found., Am. Coll. Trial Lawyers (state com. 1985-91, state chmn. 1989-90); mem. U.S. Supreme Ct. Hist. Soc. (Conn. state chmn. 1989-91, trustee 1992-2000), Navy League U.S., Knight of Holy Sepulchre, Knight of Malta, Knight of St. Gregory the Great, Wee Burn Country Club (Darien, Conn.), Orchid Island Golf and Beach Club (Vero Beach, Fla.). Republican. Roman Catholic. Home: 110 Island Plantation Terrace #302 Vero Beach FL 32963-5000 Personal E-mail: lolommac@aol.com.

MCNAMARA, J. DONALD (JOHN DONALD MCNAMARA), retired lawyer, business executive; b. Bridgeport, Conn., Feb. 28, 1924; s. John T. and Agnes (Keating) McN.; m. Shirley Addison Holdridge, Nov. 5, 1960. BA, Dartmouth Coll., 1945; MA in Govt., Harvard U., 1947, LLB, 1950. Bar: NY 1951, Conn. 1951. Assoc. Hall, Haywood, Patterson & Taylor, NYC, 1951-53, 55-56; asst. U.S. Atty. So. Dist. N.Y., 1953-55; assoc. Wickes, Riddell, Bloomer, Jacobi & McGuire, NYC, 1956-57; assoc., then ptnr. Nottingham & McEniry (and successor), NYC, 1957-59; sec., gen. counsel Interpub. Group of Cos., Inc., NYC, 1960-79, dir., 1965-85, sr. v.p., 1966-73, exec. v.p., 1973-79, pres., 1980-85; ret., 1985. Chmn. U.S. Nat. Tennis Championships, 1965. Served to lt. (j.g.) USNR, 1943-46 Mem. Am. Ceramic Cir., The Silver Soc. (London), River Club, Univ. Club, Met. Opera Club (bd. dirs. 1999-2006, pres. 2004-06), Ekwanok Country Club (bd. govs. Manchester, Vt. 1991-95), Dorset (Vt.) Field Club (bd. govs. 1996-99, pres. 1997-98), West Side Tennis Club (pres. Forest Hills, N.Y. 1964-66, 79-80) Home: 350 E 57th St New York NY 10022-2953 also: River Rd Manchester VT 05254

MCNAMARA, JOHN J(OSEPH), advertising executive, writer; b. Yonkers, NY, Mar. 7, 1934; m. Patricia A. Widmann, Sept. 14, 1963; children: Mary, John. BS, Yale U., 1956; MBA, NYU, 1963. Pres. Young & Rubicam Inc., from 1982; later pres. McCann Erickson Worldwide, ret., 1990. Cons. in field. Author: Advertising Agency Management, 1989; columnist: Gulf Stream mags. Pres. Pelham United Way, NY; chmn. Pelham Manor Planning Bd.; trustee Village of Pelham Manor, mayor, 1989—90; pres. Boys and Girls Club, Indian River County, Fla.; pres., bd. dirs. John's Island Property Owners Assn. Mem.: John's Island Club (bd. dirs.), Winged Foot Club, Pelham Country Club (pres.). Office: 6001 N A1A PMB 8204 Vero Beach FL 32963

MCNAMARA, JOHN PATRICK, nutritionist, educator; s. Raymond Edmund and Alice Virginia McNamara; m. Susan Mary Seniw, Aug. 7, 1976; children: Anne Megan, Daniel Mark, Michael Thomas. BS in Agrl. Scis., U. Ill., Urbana, 1976, MS in Dairy Sci., 1978; PhD in Human Foods & Nutrition, U. Ga., Athens, 1982. Scientist & prof. animal scis. & nutrition Wash. State U., Pullman, 1983—. Contbr. scientific papers to profl. jours. Scoutmaster Boy Scouts Am., Pullman, 2000—08. Recipient ADSA Agway Young Scientist award, 1992, Silver Beaver award, Boy Scouts Am., 1992—2008; named Tchr. of Yr., Wash. Sci. Tchrs. Assoc. Higher Edn., 2001. Mem.: Lions Club (Pullman) (v.p., pres. 2002—08). Home: 510 SouthEast South St Pullman WA 99163 Office: Wash State Univ 116 Clark Hall Pullman WA 99164 Office Fax: 509-335-4246. Business E-Mail: mcnamara@wsu.edu.

MCNAMARA, JOHN REGIS, psychology educator; b. Binghamton, NY, May 27, 1941; s. Regis Charles and Jane (Bradley) McN.; m. Lucille J. Martel, Dec. 5, 1972; children: Brian, Paul. BA, U. Notre Dame, 1963; MA, Xavier U., 1967; PhD, U. Ga., 1972. Diplomate Am. Bd. Profl. Psychology. Asst. prof. psychology and medicine U. Mo., Kansas City, 1971-72; prof. clin. psychology Ohio U., Athens, 1972—. Cons. U.S. Army, Panama Canal Zone, 1972, U.S. Gen. Acctg. Office, Washington, 1977-81; trainer U.S. AID-Mideast, Athens, 1994. Author: Overcoming Dating Anxiety, 1991; editor: Behavioral Approaches to Medicine, 1979, Critical Issues, Developments and Trends in Professional Psychology, Vol. 1, 1982, Vol. 2, 1984, Vol. 3, 1987. Fellow APA, Sigma Xi. Home: 23 Coventry Ln Athens OH 45701-3718 Office: Ohio U Porter Hall Dept Psychology Athens OH 45701 Home Phone: 740-592-4588; Office Phone: 614-593-1707. Business E-Mail: mcnamara@ohio.edu.

MCNAMARA, JOHN STEPHEN, artist, educator; b. Cambridge, Mass., Feb. 16, 1950; s. John Stephen and Mary (Adams) McN, BFA in Painting, Mass. Coll. Art, Boston, 1971, MFA in Painting, 1977. Tchr. Mus. Fine Arts Sch., Boston, 1983, 90-92; undergrad. and grad. painting tchr. Mass. Coll. Art, Boston, 1988; undergrad. painting tchr. Boston Archtl. Ctr., Boston, 1977; color fundamentals tchr. Mass. Coll. Art, Boston, 1987, undergrad. drawing and painting, 1975-88. Vis. lectr. San Francisco Art Inst., 1992, 93, U. Calif., Berkeley, 1993—. One-man shows include The Exhbn. Space at 112 Greene St., N.Y.C., 1982, Stavaridis Gallery, Boston, 1983-85, 86-89, Bess Cutler Gallery, N.Y.C., 1984, 85, 86, 88, Mass. Coll. Art, 1986, Honolulu Acad. Fine Art, 1987, Nielsen Gallery, 1990, 92, Miller Block Gallery, Boston, 1995, Ebert Gallery, San Francisco, Clark Gallery, Lincoln, Mass., 2002, Humanities, Townsgurd Ctr., U. Calif., Berkeley, 2008,others; exhibited in group shows at Boston Collects, Mus. Fine Arts, Stavaridis Gallery, 1986, Bess Cutler Gallery, N.Y.C., 1987, Am. Painters and Sculptors, Met. Mus. Art, N.Y.C., 1988, Resonant Abstraciton, Fuller Mus. Art, Brockton, Mass., 1989-90, Tucson Mus. Fine Art, 1996, DeCordova Mus., Lincoln, Mass., 2002, Painting in Boston, 1950-2000, Honolulu Acad. Fine Arts "Decades Abstraction", 2008-09. Recipient Outstanding Alumnus award, Mass. Coll. Art, 1986, Faculty Outstanding Mentorship award, Grad. Student Instr., U. Calif., Berkley, 2005; grantee, Mass. Arts and Humanities Grant, 1980, 1983, 1986, 1989, Equitable Life and the Rockefeller Found. Awards in the visual arts, 1982, Equitable Life and the Rockefeller Found., 1983, 1986, 1989, Nat. Endowment Arts, 1981; McDowell Colony fellow, Peterborough, NH, 1985. Home: 1501 Park Ct Novato CA 94945-1472 Office Phone: 510-642-2582. Business E-Mail: namara@berkeley.edu.

MC NAMARA, JOSEPH DONALD, researcher, retired protective services official; b. NYC, Dec. 16, 1934; s. Michael and Eleanor (Shepherd) McN.; divorced; children: Donald, Laura, Karen. BS, John Jay Coll., 1968; fellow, Harvard Law Sch., 1970; DPA (Littauer fellow), Harvard U., 1973. Served to dep. insp. Police Dept., NYC, 1956-73; police chief Kansas City, Mo., 1973-76, San Jose, Calif., 1976-91; rsch. fellow Hoover Instn., Stanford U., 1991—. Adj. instr. Northeastern U., 1972, John Jay Coll., 1973, Rockhurst Coll., 1975-76, San Jose State U., 1980; cons. U.S. Civil Rights Commn., 1978; lectr., appearances on nat. TV; apptd. nat. adv. bd. U.S. Bur. Justice Stats., 1980, U.S. Drug Control Policy Office, 1993; commentator Pub. Broadcasting Radio. Author: (non-fiction) Safe and Sane, 1984, (novel) The First Directive Crown, 1985, Fatal Command, 1987, The Blue Mirage, 1990, Code 211 Blue, 1996; contbr. articles to profl. publs. Bd. dirs. Drug Policy Found., Washington; active NCCJ. Served with U.S. Army, 1958-60. Named one of 200 Young Am. Leaders Time mag., 1975; recipient disting. alumni award John Jay Coll., 1979, Pres.'s award Western Soc. Criminology1979, Morrison Gitchoff award Western Soc. Criminology, 1992, H.B. Spear award Drug Policy Found., 1992; Kansas City police named Best in Country by Nat. Newspaper Enterprises, 1974, San Jose Police Dept. named Nat. Model U.S. Civil Rights Commn., 1980; named Law Enforcement Officer of Yr., Calif. Trial Lawyers Assn., 1991. Mem. Internat. Assn. Chiefs of Police, Calif. Police Chiefs Assn., Calif. Peace Officers Assn., Major Cities Police Chiefs Assn., Police Exec. Research Forum (dir.) Office: Hoover Instn Stanford CA 94305 Office Phone: 650-723-1475. Business E-Mail: mcnamara@hoover.stanford.edu. *In our country, social mobility is possible for people from even the most humble backgrounds. Despite problems, our nation has provided more liberty and dignity for the common individual than any other civilization in history. Continuation of our free society depends upon how successful we are in teaching each new generation an appreciation of our precious freedoms and the patience to achieve progress within our democratic process.*

MCNAMARA, KRISTIN TARA, literature and language educator, small business owner; b. Walnut Creek, Calif., May 4, 1980; d. James Richard and Bonnie Lee McNamara. BA in English, Calif. Poly. State U., San Luis Obispo, 2002, MA in English, 2006. Owner, mgr., CFO SLO Op Climbing LLC, San Luis Obispo, Calif., 2006—; lectr. Allan Hancock Coll., Santa Maria, Calif., 2006—. Mem.: Nat. Coun. Tchrs. English, Australian Shepherd Club Am. (dir., treas., com. mem. 1996—2009). Green Party. Avocations: rock climbing, dog training, writing, film, music.

MCNAMARA, MICHAEL, electronics executive; BS, Univ. Cinn.; MBA, Santa Clara Univ. Prin. Pittiglio Rabin Todd & McGrath; v.p. mgr. ops. Anthem Electronics; v.p. No. Am. ops. Flextronics Internat., 1994—97, pres. Americas' ops., 1997—2001, COO Singapore, 2002—05, CEO, 2006—. Office: Flextronics Internat 2 Changri S Lane Singapore 486123 Singapore

MCNAMARA, MICHAEL T., lawyer, lobbyist; b. Kansas City, Mo., June 26, 1969; AB summa cum laude, Duke U., 1990; JD magna cum laude, Harvard U., 1996. Bar: Md. 1996, DC 1997. Economist US Dept. Commerce, Washington; with Arent Fox Kintner Plotkin & Kahn, Washington; ptnr. Sonnenschein Nath & Rosenthal LLP, Washington, 2002—. Office: Sonnenschein Nath & Rosenthal LLP Ste 600, E Tower 1301 K St NW Washington DC 20015 Office Phone: 202-408-6477. Office Fax: 202-408-6399. Business E-Mail: mmcnamara@sonnenschein.com.*

MCNAMARA, THOMAS EDMUND (TED), federal official, former ambassador; b. New Haven, Sept. 16, 1940; s. Joseph Michael and Anne Marie (Meehan) McN.; m. Emma Julia Fonseca, June 11, 1966; children: David Fonseca, Michelle Anne. BA, Manhattan Coll., 1962, LLD (hon.), 1991; MA, Notre Dame U., 1964. Joined fgn. svc. State Dept., 1965; 2nd sec. Am. Embassy, Paris, 1967-69; BENELUX desk officer European bur. US Dept. State, 1969-71; consul Am. Consulate, Lubumbashi, Zaire, 1971-72, Bukavu, Zaire, 1972-73; with Armed Forces Staff Coll., Norfolk, Va., 1973-74; internat. affairs officer Arms Control & Disarmament Agy., 1974-75; chief external divsn., polit. sect. Am. Embassy, Moscow, 1976-78; office dir., polit.-mil. bur. US Dept. State, Washington, 1978-80; dep. chief of mission Am. Embassy, Kinshasa, Democratic Republic of Congo, 1980-83; dept. asst. sec., bur. polit.-mil. affairs US Dept. State, Washington, 1983-86; sr. seminar Fgn. Svc. Inst., Washington, 1986-87; dir. counterterrorism and narcotics Nat. Security Coun., 1987-88; US amb. to Colombia US Dept. State, Bogota, 1988-91; special asst. to the Pres. for nat. security affairs The White House, Washington, 1991-92; coord. for counter-terrorism US Dept. State, Washington, 1992-93, prin. dep. asst. sec., bur. polit.-mil. affairs, 1993-94, asst. sec., bur. polit.-mil. affairs, 1994—98; spl. negotiator for Panama; pres., CEO Am. Soc. & Coun. Americas, NYC, 1998—2001; sr. adv. for counter-terrorism & homeland security US Dept. State, Washington, 2001—04; program mgr. Program Mgr. Info. Sharing Environ., Washington, 2006—. Adj. prof. Eliott Sch. Internat. Affairs George Washington U. Contbr. articles to profl. jours. Recipient LA Gran Cruzde Boyacr, Govt. of Colombia, 1991, Disting. Honor award, 1998, Superior Honor award US Dept. State, 1980, 84, 86. Mem. Am. Fgn. Service Assn., Coun. of Fgn. Rels., Latin Am. Studies Programs Am. U., Cosmos Club.*

MCNAMARA CORLEY, KELLY, lawyer; b. Salt Lake City, Utah; m. Monty McNamara Corley; 1 child. BA in Polit. Sci., U. So. Calif., 1982; JD, George Mason U. Sch. Law, 1989. Bar: Ill., Va. With govt. affairs dept. Sears, Roebuck & Co.; asst. v.p. Dean Witter Reynolds, 1989, v.p. fed. govt. affairs, 1989—94; sr. v.p. govt. & cmty. affairs Dean Witter, Discover & Co., 1994—97; mng. dir. global govt. rels. & cmty. affairs Morgan Stanley, 1997—99; sr. v.p., gen. counsel, sec. Discover Financial Services LLC, 1997—2007, exec. v.p., gen. counsel, 2008—. Bd. dirs. The History Makers. Mem.: Am. Fin. Svcs. Assn. (bd. mem.). Office: Discover Financial Services LLC 2500 Lake Cook Rd Riverwoods IL 60015 Office Phone: 224-405-1747.*

MCNAMEE, BRIAN, medical products executive; B in Journalism, St. Bonaventure U., NY; M in Indsl. and Labor Rels., Cornell U., Ithaca, 1987. Various human resources positions GE, 1988—99; sr. v.p. human resources NBC, 1998—99; v.p. human resources Dell Computer Corp., 1999—2001; sr. v.p. human resources Amgen, Inc., Thousand Oaks, Calif., 2001—. Office: Amgen Inc One Amgen Center Dr Thousand Oaks CA 91320-1799 Office Phone: 805-447-1000. Office Fax: 805-447-1010.

MCNAMEE, SISTER CATHERINE, educator; b. Troy, NY, Nov. 13, 1931; d. Thomas Ignatius McNamee and Kathryn McNamee Marois. BA, Coll. of St. Rose, 1953, DHL (hon.), 1975; MEd, Boston Coll., 1955, MA, 1958; PhD, U. Madrid, 1967. Grad. asst. Boston Coll., 1954-55, asst. registrar Grad. Sch., 1955-57; mem. faculty Coll. St. Rose, Albany, NY, 1960-65, acad. v.p., 1968-75; dir. liberal arts Thomas Edison Coll., Trenton, 1975-76; pres. Trinity Coll., Burlington, Vt., 1976-79, Coll. St. Catherine, St. Paul, 1979-84; dean Dexter Hanley Coll., U. Scranton, Pa., 1984-86; pres. Nat. Cath. Ednl. Assn., Washington, 1986-96; sr. scholar Ctr. for Cath. Studies, U. St. Thomas, St. Paul, 1996-2000; prof. U. Catolica, Talca, Chile, 2000—05; disting. vis. scholar Coll. St. Catherine, St. Paul, 2005—. Hispanic ministry team mem. Archdiocese St. Paul, Mpls., 2005—08; congl. leadership team Sisters St. Joseph Carondelet, 2008—. Trustee assoc. Boston Coll. Spanish Govt. grantee, 1965-67; OAS grantee, 1967-68; Fulbright grantee, 1972-73 Mem. Inter-Am. Confedn. Cath. Edn., Internat. Orgn. Cath. Edn., Nat. Cath. Ednl. Assn., Internat. Fedn. Cath. Univs., Delta Epsilon Sigma. Roman Catholic. Home and Office: Congregational Ctr 2311 S Lindbergh Blvd Saint Louis MO 63131 Personal E-mail: cmncsj@hotmail.com.

MCNAMEE, KATHLEEN METZGER, academic administrator; b. Balt., June 3, 1947; d. Thurl D. and Ruth Landis Metzger; m. Alan H. McNamee, June 24, 1972; children: Kevin Metzger, Nathan Metzger. BA in History, Manchester Coll., Ind., 1969; MBA, Old Dominion U., Norfolk, Va., 1976. HS history instr. Allen County, Ft. Wayne, Ind., 1970—72; acctg. instr. Elon Coll., NC, 1982—86; divsn. chair U. Ark. CC, Batesville, 1998—. Bd. dirs. Big Bros./ Big Sisters, Batesville, 2007. Home: 1517 Chadwick Dr Batesville AR 72501 Office: Univ Ark CC 2005 White Dr Batesville AR 72501

MCNAMEE, LAWRENCE ROSS, JR., manufacturing executive; b. Gary, Ind., June 7, 1931; s. Lawrence Ross and Pearl Agnes (Heyburn) McNamee; m. Mary Ann Youlden, 1956; children: Lawrence R. III, Catherine Ann, John Charles. BA, Claremont McKenna Coll., 1957; MBA, Claremont Grad. U., 1958; postgrad., UCLA. Supr. Gen. Dynamics, Pomona, Calif., 1958-61; mem. staff Arthur D. Little, Inc., LA, 1961-65; dir. Booz Allen & Hamilton, LA, 1965-70; gen. mgr. Hydril Co., LA, 1970-76; pres. Diogenes Group, LA, 1976-91; chmn., CEO Radiant Tech. Corp., Fullerton, Calif., 1991—2005, GreenBridge Tech., Inc., Fullerton, 2006—. With U.S. Army, 1952-54. Mem.: Ops. Rsch. Soc. Am., Turn Around Mgmt. Assn., Semiconductor Equipment and Materials Internat., Malibu Orchid Soc. (pres. 2003), Getty Villa Coun., Calif. Yacht Club. Avocations: sailing, fishing, photography, art collecting.

MCNAMEE, PATRICK, health products executive; Chief info. officer, gen. mgr. e-Bus. GE Transp. Systems, 1999—2001; sr. v.p., chief info. officer, chief quality officer NBC, 2001—02; pres. GE OEC Med. Systems, 2002—03; pres., gen. mgr. Physician Systems Misys Healthcare Systems, 2003—05; sr. v.p., chief info. officer Express Scripts, Inc., Md. Heights, Mo., 2005—07, sr. v.p. ops. & tech., 2007, exec. v.p. ops. & tech., 2007—. Office: Express Scripts Inc 13900 Riverport Dr Maryland Heights MO 63043 Office Phone: 314-770-1666.

MCNAMEE, STEPHEN M., federal judge; b. 1942; BA, U. Cinn., 1964; MA, U. Ariz., 1967, JD, 1969. Atty. legal & fin. dept. Florsheim Shoe Co., 1969—71; asst. US atty. Dist. Ariz., US Dept. Justice, 1971—79, 1st asst. US atty., 1980, chief asst. US atty., 1981—85, US atty. Phoenix, 1985-90; judge US Dist. Ct. Ariz., Phoenix, 1990—2006, chief judge, 1999—2006, sr. judge, 2007—. Lectr. U. Ariz. Coll. Bus., 1975—79. Office: US Dist Judge Sandra Day O'Connor US Ct 401 W Washington St SPC 60 Phoenix AZ 85003-2158 Office Phone: 602-322-7555.

MCNARON, TONI A.H., literature and language educator, director; b. Birmingham, Ala., Apr. 3, 1937; PhD, U. Wis., Madison, 1964. Prof. emeritus U. Minn., Mpls., 1964—2001, dir., coll. schs. lit., 1997—. Author: (book) I Dwell in Possibility. Grant, NEH, U. Minn., 1982, 1990. Mem.: MLA. Dfl. Roman Catholic. Avocations: walking, gardening. Home: 3512 Holmes Ave S Minneapolis MN 55408 Business E-Mail: mcnar001@umn.edu.

MCNATTY, DANNY, pharmacist; b. Buffalo, Oct. 29, 1981; s. Daniel Patrick and Margaret Ann McNatty; m. Andrea Lynn Rokicki, June 23, 2007. PharmD, SUNY, Buffalo, SUNY, Amherst, 2005. Registered pharmacist Tex., Ariz., 2005, cert. pharmacotherapy specialist Bd. Pharm. Specialties, 2006. Pharmacotherapy splty. resident Tex. Tech. U. Health Scis. Ctr., Lubbock, 2005—07; asst. prof. - pharmacy practice Midwestern U. Coll. Pharmacy, Glendale, Ariz., 2007—. Mem.: Am. Soc. Health-Sys. Pharmacy, Am. Coll. Clin. Pharmacy, Am. Assn. Colls. Pharmacy, MENSA, Rho Chi, Phi Lamda Sigma, Kappa Psi Internat. Pharm. Frat. Avocations: golf, poker, volleyball. Office: Midwestern Univ Coll Pharmacy Glendale 19555 N 59th Ave Glendale AZ 85308 Business E-Mail: dmcnat@midwestern.edu.

MCNAUGHTON, WILLIAM JOHN, bishop emeritus; b. Lawrence, Mass., Dec. 7, 1926; s. William John and Ruth Irene (Howe) McNaughton. BA, SUNY, Ossining, 1948, B of Sacred Theology, 1953; M in Religious Edn., Maryknoll Sem., Ossining, 1953. Ordained priest Cath. Fgn. Mission Soc. of America, 1953; pastor Pouk Moun Ro Cath. Ch., Republic of Korea, 1955-57, Nae Duk Dong Cath. Ch., 1957-60; consultor Chong Ju Diocese, 1958-59, vicar gen., 1959-60; ordained bishop, 1961; bishop Diocese of Incheon, 1962—2002, bishop emeritus, 2002—. Roman Catholic. Address: 39 Woodburn Dr Methuen MA 01844-2812 Home Phone: 978-682-9755. E-mail: wjmcn53@comcast.net.

MCNEAL, JANE ERSKINE, musician, educator; b. Somers Point, NJ, Oct. 29, 1958; d. James Kelley and Jane Emma McNeal. BA Psychology, Stockton State Coll., 1983; music studies, Wheaton Coll., Ill., 1976—78; Kindermusik Cert., Westminster Choir Coll., Princeton, NJ, 1997; Crescendo Music Tng., Acad. Cmty. Music, Ft. Washington, Pa., 2005. Choir dir., NJ, 1991—95; piano instr. NJ, 1975—; vocal instr., 1999—; profl. accompanist NJ, 1976—; ch. and synagogue organist NJ, 1983—; organ and piano recitalist NJ, 1989—. Advocate for mentally ill. Scholar Nat. Merit Corp. Scholarship, Sun Shipbuilding, Chester, Pa., 1976—78; music scholar, Wheaton Coll., 1976. Fellow: Internat. Biog. Assn. (Cambridge, Eng.); mem.: Am. Biog. Inst. (NC), Internat. Biog. Ctr. (Cambridge, Eng.), Am. Fedn. Musicians, Am. Guild Organists (mem. rep. nat. com.), Psi Chi. Avocations: walking, classical music, jazz, reading, cooking. Home: 2112 Newcombtown Rd Millville NJ 08332 Office: St Vincent de Paul Cath Ch 114 Rt 50 Mays Landing NJ 08330 Office Phone: 609-625-2124.

MCNEAL, LYLE GLEN, science educator, rancher, consultant; b. Glendale, Calif., May 16, 1942; s. Darrell Glenn and Elizabeth Bessie McNeal; m. Nancy Coles Wilkie, Aug. 10, 1962; children: Tamara A., Sean E., Joshua M., Travis G., Susannah R., Jenny L., Ian B., Ilene L. BS in Animal Husbandry, Cal Poly Coll., 1964; MS in Animal Breeding, U. Nev., 1966; PhD in Reproductive Physiology, Utah State U., 1978. Shepherd Cal Poly Coll., Pomona, 1962—64; prof. animal sci. Cal Poly State U., San Luis Obispo, Calif., 1969—79; grad. rsch. asst. U. Nev., Reno, 1964—66, extension agt. Minden, 1966—69; rsch. scientist U.S. Sheep Experiment Sta., Dubois, Idaho, 1972—77; founder, exec. dir. Navajo Sheep Project, Logan, Utah, 1977—2002; prof. animal sci. Utah State U., Logan, 1979—. Ranch hand Bar Lazy B Ranch, Ronan, Mont., 1959—61; asst. ranch mgr. Hidden Trails Ranch, Agoura, Calif., 1960—61; Arabian horse showman Kellogg Arabian Horse Ranch, Pomona. Author: Small Ruminant Production Medicine, 2002; contbr. chapters to books. 1st lt. USAF, 1959—61, Norton AFB. Recipient award, NHL, 1994, Nat. Camptender award, Am. Sheep Industry Assn.; named Tchr. of Yr, U.S.D.A., 1969—94. Mem.: Am. Livestock Breeds Conservancy (Conservation Breeder of Yr. 1996), Soc. Range Mgmt., Am. Soc. Animal Sci. (mem. tchg. com. 1972—77, Nat. Tchr. of Yr. 1996), Am. Sheep Ctr. (mem. founding bd. 1999—), Navajo-Churro Sheep Assn. (life; hon. 1986—), Dine' be'iina (life; hon. 1991—). Achievements include rescued from extinction the first domestic sheep brought to North America by the Spanish conquistadores; saved and bred back this famous Navajo-Churro sheep for the benefit of Navajo and Hispanic cultures, 1977-2002. Avocations: horseback riding, fly fishing, piloting aircraft, history, reading. Home: 85 Quarter Circle Dr Logan UT 84321 Office: Animal & Vet Dept Utah State U 4815 Old Main Hill Logan UT 84322-4815 E-mail: sheepman@cc.usu.edu.

MCNEAL, MARY KAY, secondary school educator; b. Denver, June 28, 1957; d. Elizabeth Ann and Charles Edwin Willis (Stepfather); m. Johnny Ray McNeal, Feb. 17, 1978; children: Joshua Allen, Sarah Nicole. BA in History and Edn., Augusta State U., Ga., 1986; MA in Tchg. and Learning, Nova Southeastern U., Orlando, Fla., 2002. Nat. bd. cert. tchr. 1999. Tchr. Greenwood Lakes Mid. Sch., Lake Mary, Fla., 1986—90, Rock Lake Mid. Sch., Longwood, Fla., 1991—92, Indian Trails Mid. Sch., Winter Springs, Fla., 1992—. Fundraiser Southeastern Guide Dogs, Inc., Palmetto, Fla., 1990—2006; women's leader Dorcus, Sanford, Fla., 1996—97. With US Army, 1976—79. Named Indian Trails Mid. Sch. Tchr. of Year, 1996, Indian Trails Mid. Sch. Social Studies Tchr. of Year, 2000, Orlando Sentinel Tchr. of Week, 2001. Mem.: NEA (assoc.), Fla. Geog. Alliance (assoc.), Nat. Coun. for the Social Studies (assoc.). Republican. Lutheran. Avocations: reading, gardening. Home: 105 Garden Ct Sanford FL 32771 Office: Indian Trails Middle School 415 Tuskawilla Rd Winter Springs FL 32708 Personal E-mail: mmcneal728@aol.com. Business E-Mail: mary_mcneal@scps.k12.fl.us.

MCNEAL, MONICA MALONE, medical educator, director; b. Cin., Dec. 19, 1952; d. Sidney Martin and Dorothy Marie Malone; m. Donald Kelley McNeal; 1 child, Caitlin Dawn Malone. BS, U. Dayton, Ohio, 1974; MS, U. Cin., 1981. Rsch. asst. La. State Med. Sch., New Orleans, 1979—85; sr. rsch. assoc. James N Gamble Inst. Med. Rsch., Cin., 1985—95; sr. rsch. asst. Cin. Children's Hosp., 1995—2001, rsch. assoc., 2001—06, assoc. dir., 2006—, instr., 2008—. Adj. instr. Union Inst., Cin., 1998—2006. Contbr. articles and sci. papers to profl. jours. Achievements include development of animal model to study rotavirus immunology and vaccine.

MCNEAL, PHYLLIS PAULETTE, parole agent; d. Earline Brown. BA in Psychology, Calif. State U., Long Beach, 1982; MSW, Calif. State U., San Bernardino, 2003. Mental health intern Jenesse Domestic Violence Ctr., LA, 2001—01, Los Padrinos Juvenile Hall, Downey, Calif., 2002—03; group supr. Calif. Youth Authority, Norwalk, 1981—84, youth counselor Ontario, 1984—89; parole agt. I parole and cmty. svcs. divsn. Calif. Dept. Corrections, Inglewood, 1989—99, asst. unit supr. LA, 1999—. Sponsor Calif. Youth Authoity, Ontario, 1986—89; small group tng. instr. Calif. Youth Authority, Onartio, 1986—89; founder, CEO Straight Talk Program, Inc., Corona, Calif., 1990—; coll. internship coord. parole and cmty. svcs. divsn. Calif. Dept. Corrections, Ingelwood, 1990—98, defensive tactics instr., LA, 1991—99. Author: Corrections in America an Introduction, 9th edit. (Correctional Champions, 2001); editor: Corrections Today Mag. (Best in the Bus., 1998). Prison min. Abundant Living Family Ch., Rancho Cucamonga, Calif., 2003—05; prison com. mem. Nat. Assn. Equal Justice in Am., Compton, Calif., 2002—05; bd. dirs. Cornerstone Accelerated Learning Acad., LA, 2001—05. Recipient Cmty. Stars award, Staples, 1999, award, Freedom Jour., 2000, Trailblazer Award, First AME Ch., 2004, amb. of Progress, Blackwall St., 2005, Local Heroes Neighborhood Excellence award, Bank of Am., 2005; named Parole Agt. of the Yr., Calif. Probation, Parole, and Correctional Assn., 1998, Citizen of the Week, KNX Newsradio CBS, 1998, Hero Of the Week, UPN Channel 13, 1998. Mem.: Save Our Sons (assoc.; publicity com. mem. 2000—05), Black Women 's Network (assoc.), Delta Sigma Theta (life; dean pledge 1980). Office: Straight Talk Program Inc PO Box 5693 Norco CA 92860 Business E-Mail: straighttalkprogram@charter.net.

MCNEAL, RALPH LEROY, SR., management consultant, financial executive; b. London, Ohio, Sept. 8, 1935; s. Walter McKinley and Mary Marie Brown; m. Shirley Jane Lowery, Nov. 15, 1957; children: Ralph LeRoy, Scott Damon, Erika Marie. BS, Cen. State U., Wilberforce, Ohio, 1957; postgrad., Seton Hall U., 1965-66, Rutgers U., 1967-68. Field agt. IRS, Cleve., 1957-58; officer 3rd Armored Cavalry Regiment, 1957—60; acct., hearing examiner N.J. Pub. Utilities Commn., Newark, 1961-62; budget examiner City of Newark, 1962-65; budget coord., ops. analyst Schering-Plough Internat., Bloomfield, NJ, 1965-67; corp. budget mgr. Wakefern Food Corp., Elizabeth, NJ, 1967-69; dir. fin. City of Englewood, NJ, 1969-71; prin. mgmt. analyst Offtrack Betting Corp., NYC, 1970—72; pres. Coalition Venture Group, NYC, 1972-76, Ralph L. McNeal & Co. Mgmt. Cons., NYC, 1976-78, pres., chief exec. officer Newark, 1989—, mgmt. cons., 2001—; pres., COO, North Street Capital Corp. subs. Gen. Foods Corp., White Plains, NY, 1978-88; ptnr. McNeal, Janniere and Co., East Elmhurst, NY, 1983—; pres., chief exec. officer West Mich. Bidco Capital, Muskegon, 1988-89; bus. devel. officer Valley Nat. Bank, NJ, 1998—2001. Cons. Newark Coalition Small Bus. Devel. Corp., Inc., All States Transworld Van Lines, Inc., St. Louis, Leeper Labs., Summit, N.J.; prin. MCJAN Securities Co., N.Y.C., 1984—; chmn. bd. govs., chief exec. The Small Bus. Stock Exch. Am., Inc., N.Y.C., 1986—; chmn. bd. dirs. The Asbex Devel. Corp., Balt., 1987—; county adminstr. Essex County, N.J., 1990-91; ptnr. Butts, Gates, McNeal, Riggs and Moaney, 1991; dir. Small Bus. Devel. Ctr., 2000-01, arbitrator 2001-07, pres., 2007; pres. arbitrator Financial Industry Regulatory Authority; small bus. and tax cons. Ralph L. Mccall and Co. Author: Sleeper Cell, 2009, The Venture Capitalist, 2009, The Knuckleballer, 2009. Commr., treas. Newark Housing and Redevel. Authority, 1986-89; mem. dean's adv. com. sch. bus. Ctrl. State U. With US Army, 1958-60. Recipient Outstanding Profl. Achievement award sch. bus. Ctrl. State U., 1979-80, Nat. Kool's Achiever award Brown & Williamson Tobacco Co., 1991; named Alumnus of Yr., Ctrl. State U., 1989, US Small Bus. Adminstrn. State of NJ Advocate of Yr., 2000. Mem.: SCORE, Counselors America's Small Bus. (pres. 2001—). Home: 511 Hidden Garden Pl Henderson NV 89012-4577 Personal E-mail: rmcnealsr@gmail.com.

MCNEALEY, BILLIE, psychologist; d. Larrie Geib and Georgie Wallace; married. PhD in Psychology, Antioch New Eng. Grad. Sch., Keene, NH, 1995. Cert. in autism spectrum disorders Antioch New Eng. Grad. Sch., 2006, diplomate in sch. neuropsychology Am. Bd. Sch. Neuropsychology, 2007. Sch. psychologist Am. Sch. Deaf, West Hartford, Conn., 1986—2001; psychologist Simsbury Pub. Schs., Conn., 2001—.

MCNEALEY, ERNEST, college president; m. Earnestine Green; children: Ernest II, David. BS, Ala. State U.; MAT, Ind. U.; PhD, Ohio State U. V.p. acad. affairs undergrad. acad. affairs Claflin (S.C.) U.; assoc. provost, dean of undergrad. acad. affairs SUNY, Stony Brook; pres. Stillman Coll., Tuscaloosa, Ala., 1997—. Office: Stillman Coll PO Box 1430 Tuscaloosa AL 35403-1430 E-mail: emcnealey@stillman.edu.

MCNEALEY, J. JEFFREY, lawyer, corporate executive; b. Cin., Feb. 8, 1944; s. J. Lawrence and Louise McNealey; m. Sara Wilson, Sept. 24, 1988; children: Anne Elizabeth, John Alexander. BA, Cornell U., 1966; JD, Ohio State U., 1969. Ptnr. Porter, Wright, Morris & Arthur, Columbus, Ohio, 1969—. Bd. dirs. TRC Cos., Windsor, Conn., 1985—; sec., bd. dirs. The Smoot Corp., Columbus, 1972—. Trustee Columbus Cancer Clinic, 1972—, past pres.; trustee German Village Soc., Columbus, 1986—, past pres.; bd. dirs. Columbus chpt. ARC, 1983-86, Columbus Urban League, 1984-90; active Union League Chgo., 1981—, Columbus/Dresden Sister City, Inc., 1996—; mem. vestry Trinity Episcopal Ch., 2000—. Mem. ABA, Ohio State Bar Assn. (past chmn. environ. com. 1978-84), Columbus Bar Assn., Columbus Country Club, Capital Club of Columbus, Cornell Club of Ctrl. Ohio (trustee 1978—, past pres.). Episcopalian. Avocations: flying, racquetball, woodworking, fly fishing. Office: Porter Wright Morris & Arthur 41 S High St Ste 30 Columbus OH 43215-6101

MCNEALY, SCOTT GLENN, information technology executive; b. Columbus, Ind., Nov. 13, 1954; s. Raymond William and Marmaline McNealy; m. Susan Ingemanson, 1994; 4 children. BA, Harvard U., Cambridge, Mass., 1976; MBA, Stanford U., Calif., 1980. With Rockwell Internat. Corp., Troy, Mich., 1976-78, sales engr.; staff engr. FMC Corp., Chgo., 1980-81; dir. ops. Onyx Systems, San Jose, Calif., 1981-82; co-founder Sun Microsystems, Inc., Santa Clara, Calif., 1982, v.p. ops., 1982—84, COO, 1984, pres., 1984—99, 2002—04, CEO, 1984—2006, chmn., 1984—. Bd. dirs. Sun Microsystems, Inc., 1982—. Named one of World's Richest People, Forbes Mag., 400 Richest Ams., Am.'s Most Powerful People. Avocation: hockey. Office: Sun Microsystems Inc 4150 Network Cir Santa Clara CA 95054 Office Phone: 650-960-1300.

MCNEELY, JAMES LEE, lawyer; b. Shelbyville, Ind., May 4, 1940; s. Carl R. and Elizabeth J. (Orebaugh) McN.; m. Rose M. Wisker, Sept. 5, 1977; children: Angela, Susan, Meg, Matt. AB, Wabash Coll., 1962; JD, Ind. U., 1965. Bar: Ind. 1965, U.S. Dist. Ct. (so. dist.) Ind. 1965, U.S. Ct. Appeals (7th cir.) 1970. Assoc. Pell & Matchett, Shelbyville, 1965-70; ptnr. Matchett & McNeely, Shelbyville, 1970-74; sole practice Shelbyville, 1974-76; sr. ptnr. McNeely & Sanders, Shelbyville, 1976-86, McNeely, Sanders & Stephenson, Shelbyville, 1986-89, McNeely, Sanders, Stephenson & Thopy, Shelbyville, 1989-96, McNeely, Stephenson, Thopy & Harrold, Shelbyville, 1997—. Guest lectr. Franklin Coll., Ind., 1965-72; judge Shelbyville City Ct., 1967-71. Chmn. Shelbyville County Rep. Cen. Com., 1968-88; bd. dirs. Ind. Lung Assn., 1972-75, Crossroads Council Boy Scouts Am., 1982; trustee Wabash Coll., 2004—; bd. dirs., pres. Shelbyville Girls Club. Named Sagamore of the Wabash, Gov. Ed Whitcomb, 1971, Gov. Otis Bowen, 1977, Gov. Robert Orr, 1986, 88, Gov. Evan Bayh, 1996, Gov. Frank O'Bannon, 1999; recipient Lifetime Citizenship award for growth Shelby County C. of C., 2003. Fellow Ind. Bar Found. (patron, sec. 1999-2000, chair elect 2000-01, chmn. 2002-03); mem. ABA, Ind. Bar Assn. (sec. 1985-87, bd. dirs. 1976-78, chair-elect Ho. Dels. 1994-95, chair 1995-96, v.p. 1996-97, pres.-elect 1997-98, pres. 1998-99), Shelby County Bar Assn. (pres. 1975), Ind. Lawyers Commn. (pres., dir.), Fed. Merit Selection Commn. (adv. mem. 1988-92, chmn. 2001—), Shelbyville Jaycees (Distinguished Service award 1969, Good Govt. award 1970), Wabash Coll. Nat. Assn. Wabash Men (dir. 1983-89, sec. 1989-91, v.p. 1991-93, pres. 1993-95, Man of Yr. 1995), Kappa Sigma Alpha Pi chpt. (Hall of Fame 1995). Lodges: Lions, Elks, Eagles. Methodist. Avocations: golf, travel. Home: 1902 E Old Rushville Rd Shelbyville IN 46176-9569 Office Phone: 317-825-5110. Business E-Mail: jlmneely@msth.com.

MCNEELY, JASON BRYAN, research scientist; b. New Orleans, La., July 17, 1978; s. Larry LuDell and Jane Elizabeth McNeely. BS in Elec. Engring., U. La. Lafayette, 2001, MS in Computer Engring., 2003. Tchg. asst. UL Lafayette, 2002—03, 2007—, tchg. lab asst., 2004—07. Contbr. articles to rsch. jours. Bible study tchr. First Bapt. Ch., Lafayette, La., 2008—08; reading tutor Bridge Ministries, Lafayette, La., 2007. Finalist Student Paper Contest, Ctr. Advanced Computer Studies, UL Lafayette, 2007. Mem.: IEEE (chair Student Chpt., Outstanding Chpt. award 2007). Independent. Home: 201 Azalea Dr Waggaman LA 70094 Office: UL Lafayette PO Box 40666 Lafayette LA 70504 Personal E-mail: jason.mcneely@gmail.com.

MCNEESE, BEVERLY DIANE, language educator; b. Turlock, Calif., Apr. 4, 1952; d. Jesse Audry and Willie Jean Doty; m. Timothy Dean McNeese; children: Noah Michael, Summer Elizabeth. AA, York Coll., Nebr., 1973, BA in English, 1995; MA in Edn., Drury U., Springfield, Mo., 2003. With White County Libr., Searcy, Ark., 1974—75; presch. tchr. East Grand Ch. of Christ, Springfield, Mo., 1976—91; learning disabilities paraprofessional Strafford Pub. Schs., Mo., 1991—92; libr. aide Levitt Libr., York Coll., Nebr., 1992—94; adj. faculty dept. English, York Coll., 1995—2002, asst. prof. English, 2003—. Mem.: Kappa Omicron Nu, Sigma Tau Delta (York Coll. chpt. pres. 1995—96, York Coll. chpt. faculty sponsor 1998—2006). Republican. Mem. Ch. Of Christ. Avocations: refinishing antiques, reading, travel. Office: York Coll Dept English 1125 E Eighth St York NE 68467 Home: 26 Eastridge Ave York NE 68467-3939 Office Phone: 402-363-5690. Office Fax: 402-363-5699. E-mail: bdmcneese@york.edu.

MCNEESE, ROSE MARIE, retired education educator; b. Angie, La., Aug. 12, 1949; d. Nadine and James W. Freeman; m. George William McNeese, Jr., Nov. 26, 1971; 1 child, Christopher Matthew. BS, U. So. Miss., Hattiesburg, 1971, MS, 1981; EdS, Ga. State U., Atlanta, 1992, PhD, 1997. Lic. edn. adminstr. Miss. Dept. Edn., 2003, cert. edn. tchr. Tchr. Dexter Attendance Ctr., Tylertown, Miss., 1971—72, Lumberton Line Consol. Sch. Dist., Miss., 1972—74, Cobb County Sch. Dist., Marietta, Ga., 1974—87, asst. prin., 1987—92, sch. prin., 1993—2002, curriculum dir., 2002—03; prin. Walthall County Sch. Dist., Tylertown, Miss., 2003—05; grad. rsch. asst. U. Southern Miss., 1978—79, asst. prof., 2005—. Cons. Ga. Dept. Edn., Atlanta, 1998—2001, Kennesaw State U., Ga., 2000—03, Miss. Dept. Edn., Jackson, 2007—. Mem. Rotary Club, Austell, Ga., 1993—2000, Optimist Club, Kennesaw, 1998—2003, Hattieburg Civic Light Orgn., 2005—, Walthall County Arts Alliance, Tylertown, 2007—; choir mem. Carson Springs Bapt. Ch., Sandy Hook, Miss., 2003—; mem. Wieuca Rd. Bapt. Ch., Atlanta, 1987—, edn. com. mem., 2000—03; nat. NCATE accreditation lead reviewer Nat. Coun. Accrediation Tchr. Edn., Washington, 2007—; edn. com. mem. Cobb County C. of C., Marietta, Ga., 1988—2003; silver level contbr. U. Southern Miss. Olgetree Hist. House Restoration Project, 2007—. Recipient State Ga. Drug Free Edn. Program award of Yr., Gov.'s Office, Atlanta, 1989; named Tchr. of Yr., 1985. Mem.: Mid-South Ednl. Rsch. Assn., Assn. Supervision and Curriculum Devel., Nat. Assn. Secondary Sch. Prins., Nat. Coun. Coll. Profs. Assn. (Miss. del. 2007—), Ga. PTA. Baptist. Achievements include research in effective practices and programs for reducing violence in schools. Avocations: gardening, travel, walking. Home: 351 Vincetown Rd Sandy Hook MS 39478 Office: Univ Southern MS 118 College Dr Hattiesburg MS 39406-0001 Office Fax: 601-266-5141; Home Fax: 601-264-0427.

MCNEIL, BARBARA JOYCE, radiologist, educator; b. Cambridge, Mass., Feb. 11, 1941; d. Archibald Pius and Katherine (Joyce) McNeil. AB, Emmanuel Coll., 1962; MD, Harvard U., 1966, PhD, 1972. Diplomate Am. Bd. Nuc. Medicine. Intern Mass. Gen. Hosp., Boston, 1966—67, resident in nuclear medicine, 1971—73; radiologist nuclear medicine Brigham and Women's Hosp., 1974—, Dana-Farber Cancer Inst., Boston, 1976—; prof. radiology and clin. epidemiology Harvard Med. Sch. and Brigham & Women's Hosp., Boston, 1983—88, dir. ctr. for cost effective care, 1980—93; chmn. Dept. Health Care Policy Harvard Med. Sch., 1988—, Ridley Watts prof. health care policy, 1990—, acting dean, 2007. Chmn. Blue Cross-Mass. Hosp. Assn. Fund for Coop. Innovation, 1981—87; mem. Prospective Payment Assessment Commn., 1983—91; mem. nat. adv. coun. Agy. for Health Care Policy, Rsch. and Evaluation, 1991—96; mem. med. adv. com. Blue Cross Blue Shield, 1993—; mem. coverage adv. com. Medicare, 2001—. Contbr. articles to profl. jours. Recipient Rsch. Career Develop. award, Nat. Inst. Health, 1976—81. Fellow: AAAS, Am. Coll. Nuc. Physicians (Presdl. award 1995); mem.: Soc. Nuc. Medicine, Am. Coll. Radiology, Inst. Medicine (coun. 1991—97), Am. Acad. Arts and Scis. Office: Harvard Med Sch Dept Health Care Policy 180 Longwood Ave Rm 202-A Boston MA 02115-5821 Office Phone: 617-432-1909. Business E-Mail: mcneil@hcp.med.harvard.edu.

MCNEIL, BARRY, lawyer; b. Lubbock, Tex., June 29, 1944; BA, Tex. Tech U., 1966; JD, U. Tex., 1969. Bar: Tex. 1969, admitted to practice: US Supreme Ct. 1969, Tex. Supreme Ct., US Dist. Ct. (Ea. Dist.) Tex., US Dist. Ct. (So. Dist.) Tex., US Dist. Ct. (No. Dist.) Tex., US Dist. Ct. (We. Dist.) Tex., US Ct. Appeals (5th Cir.), US Ct. Appeals (8th Cir.). Trial atty. antitrust divsn. Dept. Justice, 1970-75, chief Dallas office antitrust divsn., 1975-79; ptnr. & head Antitrust & Securities Group Haynes and Boone LLP, Dallas. Co-editor: Internal Corp. Investigations (3rd edit.). Fellow: Am. Coll. Trial Lawyers; mem.: ABA (chmn. Litig. Sect. 1996—97). Office: Haynes and Boone LLP 2323 Victory Ave Dallas TX 75219-7657 Office Phone: 214-651-5580. Office Fax: 214-200-0535. Business E-Mail: barry.mcneil@haynesboone.com.

MCNEIL, EDWARD WARREN, real estate company executive; b. Alhambra, Calif., Jan. 5, 1942; s. Murray Charles and Helen Katherine (Curtis) McN.; m. Jutta Bocking, Apr. 1, 1941; children: Anja Britt, Bradley Stuart. Student, U. Calif., Berkeley, 1960-63. Structures engr. Peter Kiewit Sons Co., various cities, Calif., 1961-63; project engr. Huntington Harbour, Sunset Beach, Calif., 1963-64; project supt. Coordinated Realty, Inc., Anaheim, Calif., 1964-65; field ops. mgr. Lear Siegler, Saigon, Vietnam, 1965-67; project engr. Constructora Emkay, Rio Blanco, Chile, 1968-69; ptnr. The Pyramid Cos., Syracuse, NY, 1969-75, The Pioneer Group, Syracuse, 1975-95, ret., 1995. Past chmn., bd. dirs. Crouse Irving Meml. Hosp. Found., Syracuse, 1986—2005; emeritus bd. dirs. Crouse Iving Meml. Hosp. Found., Syracuse, 2005—; trustee, past vice-chmn. Everson Mus. Art, Syracuse, 1981—94; past chmn., vice-chmn., bd. dirs. Syracuse Stage, 1981—93; chmn. Adirondack chpt. Nature Conservancy, 1994—2001, trustee, 2002—, trustee NY state bd., 1998—; trustee Adirondack Land Trust, 1990—2002, chmn., 1994—2001; trustee Manlius Pebble Hill Sch., 1984—86,

1994—99, emeritus, 1999—; chmn. Sea Plane Pilots Found., 2009—. Recipient award for svc. to the arts, Cultural Resource Coun., Syracuse, 1987. Mem. Seaplane Pilots Assn., Slocum Soc., Lake Amphibian Flyers Club, Warbirds of Am., No. Lake Flyers Club. Avocations: sailing, fly fishing, seaplane flying, aviation writing, filmmaking.

MCNEIL, PAUL JOSEPH, JR., financial analyst; b. Winthrop, Mass., Oct. 11, 1941; s. Paul Joseph Sr. and Helen Margaret (Carr) McN. Cert. in ins., U. R.I., 1965; cert. in travel agts., Travel Sch. of Am., 1968; cert., Labor Sch. of Boston, 1976, Labor Studies Inst., 1989. Field investigator R.I. Food Stamp Unit, Providence, 1965-68; cmty. rels. Coordinator Ecology Action for Rhode Island, 1970-71; sec. and rsch. asst. R.I. Worker Assn., 1973-74; enumerator R.I. Polk & Co., Providence, 1970-83; sr. employment security interviewer R.I. Dept. Employment Tng., Providence, 1984-96; sr. employment & tng. interviewer R.I. Dept. Labor & Tng., Providence, 1996—2003, benefits claims specialist, 2003—04; bd. trustees Warwick Pub. Libr., 2003—, vice chair bd. trustees, 2006—. Rec. sec. Local 189 New Eng. chpt., Boston, 1973-76, treas., 1989—; mem. bd. dirs. of R.I. Workers Assn., 1973-74, 75-76, census enumerator U.S. Census Bur., Providence, 1990; mail handler U.S. Post Office, Providence, 1980; claims interviewer R.I. Dept. Employment Security, Providence, 1979-84; rec. sec. R.I. Employment Security Alliance, Providence, 1980-90; v.p. Community Econs. Edn. Ctr., Providence, 1988-91. Exec. com. R.I. State Employees Assn., 1966-68, Community Labor Organizing Com., Providence, 1983-89, Sane Freeze, Washington, 1989-90; shop steward Local 401 SEIU, Providence, 1990-92, 1st v.p., 1992-96; rec. sec. R.I. Sane Freeze, Providence, 1988-94; mem. Nat. Com. Peace Action, 1993—; v.p. Peace Action R.I., 1994-95, pres., 1995—; coord. R.I. Nation Readers Group, 1995—; state committeeman Amvets Dept. R.I., 1965-69, 96—, adj. posts, 1965-68, trustee post 6, 1995-96; v.p. Labor Party R.I., 1994-97, treas., 1997-, pres., 1999, chmn., 1999; exec. bd. R.I. Coalition for Consumer Justice, 1997-2006, v.p., 2006; bd. dirs. Injured Workers R.I., 1996—, Warwick Cmty. Action, 1967-69, R.I. Legal Svcs., 1967-69; founder East Greenwich Dem. Youth Club, 1959; co-chmn. Human Rights Action Coun., Warwick, 1968-70; del. R.I. Dem. State Conv., 1976, 78; mem. R.I. Dem. State Com., 1980-86, bd. dirs., 1985-87; mem. Third Rep. Com., 1976-86, Dem. Study Group R.I., 1986-88, Warwick Democratic City Com., 2000-; organizer United Farm Workers, 1968-71; mem. Fox Point Neighborhood Housing Corp. Dirs., 1980-87, pres., 1981-83, sec., 1983-87; pres. Coalition Consumer Justice, 2000-05. With U.S. Army, 1960-63, ETO. Mem. Internat. Assn. Pers. in Employment Security (R.I. chpt. bd. dirs. 1989-93, sec. 1991-93), Greater R.I. Indsl. Rels. Rsch. Assn., R.I. ACLU (bd. dirs. 1974-80, bd. sec. 1975-77, exec. com. 1979-80), Union of Peace Profls. (exec. bd. 1988-90), Nat. Writers Union, R.I. Cen. Am. Network, Cath. Peace Fellowship, Pax ChristiAncient Order, Order of Hibernians (rec. sec. Providence chpt. 1990-91, 97-98, v.p., 1998-2003, pres. 1991-92, state sec. 1993-96, 99-2005, state pres. 1996-99, state organizer, 2001-03, sec. Providence County 2003—), K. of C., Sierra Club, Newport Mus. Irish History, Am. Irish Hist. Soc., R.I. Hist. Soc., R.I. Labor History Soc., Gaspee Days Com., Americans for Dem. Action, Debs Found., Edward Bellamy Meml. Assn., R.I. Irish Famine Meml. Com., Am. Legion, Indsl. Rels. Rsch. Assn., Assn. Can.-Am., Am. French Geneal. Soc., Irish Nat. Caucus, Am. Irish Polit. Edn. Com., Friendly Sons of St. Patrick (East Greenwich, R.I.), Progressive Democrats of Am. Democrat. Avocation: writing. Home: 155 Hilton Rd Warwick RI 02889-2932

MCNEIL, SHEILA D., Councilwoman; BA in Social Work, MA in Pub. Adminstrn. Self-employed contractor; former aide San Antonio City Coun., councilwoman, Dist. 2, 2007—. Chmn. San Antonio-Bexar County Regional Met. Planning Org., City Coun. Infrastructure & Growth Com., Inner-City Tax Increment Refinance Zone 11; mem. Internat. Affairs, Econ. Devel. & Intergovernmental Rels. coms., Police & Fire Pension Fund, Martin Luther King Commn., Mil. Transformation Task Force; alt. mem. Com. Six. Founder East San Antonio Crime Prevention Coalition. Mem.: Nat. League Cities (Nat. Black Caucus Local Elected Officials), Nat. Forum for Black Pub. Adminstrs., NAACP. Democrat. Office: City Hall PO Box 839966 San Antonio TX 78283-3966 also: Sterling Bank 403 S WW White Ste 300 San Antonio TX 78219 Office Phone: 210-207-7278, 210-333-4286. Business E-Mail: district2@sanantonio.gov.*

MCNEILL, DAN K., retired military officer; b. NC, July 23, 1946; m. Maureen McNeill; 1 child, Dan. BS in Agr. and Forestry, NC State U., 1968; grad., US Army War Coll., 1989; attended, Inf. Officer Basic and Advanced Cources, US Army Command and Gen. Staff Coll.; degree (hon.), NC State U., 2003. Advanced through grades to gen. US Army, 2004, commd. 2nd lt., 1968, sr. aide-de-camp to commdg. gen., 1st Inf. Divsn. (mechanized) Fort Riley, Kans., 1971—72, fixed wing avaitor, later asst. ops. officer, later ops. officer, 55th Aviation Co., 52d Aviation Bn., Korea, 1972—73, asst. S-3 (ops.) (air), 2d Bn. (airborne), 505th Inf., 82 Airborne Divsn. Fort Bragg, NC, 1974, commdr., combat support co., 2d Bn. (airborne), 505th Inf., 82 Airborne Divsn., 1974—76, commdr., E Co., 2d Bn. (Airborne), 505th Inf., 82d Airborne Divsn., 1977—78, sec. to gen. staff, US Army So. European Vicenza, Italy, 1984—85, exec. officer, 1st Bn., 509th Inf., later renamed 4th Bn., 325th Inf., 1982—84, commdr.,1st Bn., 325th Inf., 82d Airborne Divsn. Fort Bragg, NC, 1986—88, asst. chief of staff, G-3 (Ops.), 82d Airborne Divsn., Operation Just Cause, Panama and Operation Desert Shield/Storm, Saudi Arabia, 1989—91, commdr., 3d Brigade, 82d Airborne Corps, 1991—93, asst. S-3 (Ops.), later S-3 (Ops.), 3d Brigade, 82d Airborne Divsn., 1976—77, asst. chief of state, G-3 (Ops.), XVIII Airboboure Coprs., 1993—95, asst. divsn. commdr., 2d Inf. Divsn, Korea, 1995—96, chief of staff, XVIII Airborne Corp. Fort Bragg, NC, 1996—97, dep. commdg. gen., I Corps and Fort Lewis Wis., commdg. gen. 82d Airborne Divsn. Fort Bragg, NC, 1998—2000, commdg. gen., combined joint task force-180 Afghanistan, 2000—03, commdg. gen., XVIII Airborne Corps and Fort Bragg, NC, 2000—03; dep. commdg. gen., chief of staff US Army Forces Command, Fort McPherson, Ga., 2003—04, commdg. gen., 2004—07; comdr., Internat. Security Assistance Force (ISAF) NATO, Afghanistan, 2007—08. Asst. prof. mil. sci., first reserve officer tng. corps region Ga. Mil. Coll., Milledgeville, Ga., 1978—80; doctrine author, dept. tactics US Army Command and Gen. Staff Coll., Fort Leavenworth, Kans., 1981—82. Decorated Defense Superior Svc. medal, Legion of Merit with 2 Oak clusters, Bronze Star medal with 2 oak leaf clusters, Meritorious Svc. medal with 3 Oak Clusters, Army Commendation medal with 2 Oak Leaf Clusters, Army Achievement medal, Expert Infantryman badge, Army Avaitor badge, Master Parachutist badge with Bronze star, Spl. Forces Tab.

MCNEILL, DANIEL RICHARD, writer; b. San Francisco, June 1, 1947; s. Daniel Harry and Maureen Evangeline (Sherriff) McN.; m. Rosalind Deborah Gold, Dec. 20, 1984. AB, U. Calif., Berkeley, 1975; JD, Harvard U., 1982. Author: Fuzzy Logic, 1993 (L.A. Times Book prize in sci. and tech. 1993), The Face, 1998. Mem. Authors Guild. Avocations: photography, bodybuilding. Home and Office: 8110 Redlands St #306 Playa Del Rey CA 90293

MCNEILL, G. DAVID, psychologist, educator; b. Santa Rosa, Calif., Dec. 21, 1931; s. Glenn H. and Ethel G. (Little) McN.; m. Nobuko Baba, Dec. 17, 1957; children: Cheryl, Randall L.B. AB, U. Calif., Berkeley, 1953, PhD, 1962. Research fellow Harvard U., 1962-65; asst. prof. psychology U. Mich., 1965-66, assoc. prof., 1966-68; prof. psychology and linguistics U. Chgo., 1969—2001, chmn. dept. psychology, 1991-97, prof. emeritus, 2001—. Vis. fellow Ctr. for Humanities, Wesleyan U., Middletown, Conn., 1970; mem. Inst. Advanced Study, Princeton, 1973-75; fellow Netherlands Inst. for Advanced Studies, 1983-84; visitor Max Planck Inst. for Psycholinguistics, Nijmegen, Netherlands, 1998-99 Author: The Acquisition of Language, 1970, The Conceptual Basis of Language, 1979, Psycholinguistics: A New Approach, 1987, Gengo Shinrigaku, 1991, Hand and Mind: What Gestures Reveal about Thought, 1992, Gesture and Thought, 2005; editor: Language and Gesture, 2000. Recipient Faculty Achievement award, 1991, Ann. Excellence in Pub. award Assn. Am. Pubs., Gordon G. Laing prize U. Chgo. Press, 1995; Guggenheim fellow, 1973-74; grantee NSF, 1983-89, 97—, Spencer Found., 1979-82, 89-92, 95-99, NIDCD, 1992-96, Advanced Rsch. and Devel. Agy., 2003—. Fellow AAAS, Am. Psychol. Soc.; mem. Internat. Soc. Gesture Studies (v.p. 2002-05, hon. pres. 2007—), Cognitive Sci. Soc., Linguistic Soc. Am., Violoncello Soc., Phi Beta Kappa, Sigma Xi Office: U Chgo Dept Psychology 5848 S University Ave Chicago IL 60637-1515 Business E-Mail: dmcneill@uchicago.edu.

MCNEILL, JOHN HUGH, pharmaceutical sciences educator; b. Chgo., Dec. 5, 1938; s. John and Agnes Margaret (McLean) McN.; m. Sharon Keneffly, July 27, 1963; children: Sandra, Laurie. BS, U. Alta., Can., 1960, MS, 1962; PhD, U. Mich., 1967. Lectr. pharmacy Dalhousie U., 1962-63, U. Alta., 1963; research assoc. U. Mich., Ann Arbor, 1963-65, teaching fellow, 1965-66; asst. instr. Mich. State U., East Lansing, 1966-67, asst. prof., 1967-71; assoc. prof. U. B.C., 1971-72, assoc. prof., chmn. div. pharmacology and toxicology, 1972-75, dir. rsch. and grad. studies Faculty Pharm. Scis., 1977-78, prof. Faculty Pharm. Scis., 1975—2004, dean Faculty Pharm. Scis., 1985-96, asst. dean, 1978-81, Med. Rsch. Coun. rsch. prof., 1981-82, prof., assoc. dean rsch. and grad. studies, 1982-84, prof. and dean emeritus, 2004—. Contbr. more than 800 tech. articles to profl. jours. Fellow Royal Soc. Can., Internat. Acad. Cardiovasc. Scis., Can. Acad. Health Scis., Am. Coll. Nutrition; mem. Pharm. Soc. Can. (various coms. 1974-88, coun. 1977-83, v.p. 1979, pres. 1980-81), Am. Soc. for Pharm. and Therapeutics (J.J. Abel award com. 1981, Upjohn award com., 1978-80, chmn. mem. com. 1983-86), Western Pharm. Soc. (coun. 1977-81, pres. 1979-80, past pres. 1980-81), N.Y. Acad. Scis., Internat. Soc. for Heart Rsch. (coun. 1986-95), AAAS, B.C. Coll. Pharms. (coun. 1985-96), Internat. Union Pharmacologists (Can. rep. 1982-88), Am. Pharm. Assn. Office: Univ BC Fac Pharm Scis 2146 East Mall Vancouver BC Canada V6T 1Z3 Office Phone: 604-822-9373. E-mail: jmcneill@interchange.ubc.ca.

MCNEILL, JOSEPH PEELE, librarian; b. Galveston, Tex., Feb. 27, 1947; s. Joseph Peele and Christine Adele (Evans) M.; m. Linda Ann Hartshorn, Aug. 30, 1980; 1 dau., Mary Lin. B.A., Austin Coll., Sherman, Tex., 1970; postgrad. U. Ams., Puebla, Mex., 1970-71; M.S.L.S., East Tex. State U., Commerce, 1972; M.L.S., La. State U., Baton Rouge, 1976. Catalog librarian Wiley Coll., Marshall, Tex., 1972-74; tech. services librarian Austin Coll., 1976-79; catalog librarian Midwestern State U., Wichita Falls, Tex., 1979-84; head cataloguer McNeese State U., Lake Charles, La., 1985—; reference asst. cen. library br. Calcasieu Parish Pub. Library System, Lake Charles, 1987—; RECON project cons. Calcasion Parish Pub. Libr. System, 1988-89. Co-editor: Periodicals in Library and Information Sciences, prepared for Union List, 1976. Bd. dirs. Sherman Hist. Mus., Tex., 1978-79; pres. bd. dirs. Henry Heights Elem. PTA. Mem. ALA, La. Library Assn., Librs. S.W., S.W. La. Hist. Assn., Beta Phi Mu. Republican. Baptist. Home: 917 Cherryhill St Lake Charles LA 70607-4909 Office: McNeese State U Frazar Meml Library Ryan St Lake Charles LA 70609-0001 Office Phone: 318-475-5720. Business E-Mail: jmcneill@mcneese.edu.

MCNEILL, ROBERT PATRICK, investment advisor; b. Chgo., Mar. 17, 1941; s. Donald Thomas and Katherine (Bennett) McN.; m. Martha Stephan, Sept. 12, 1964; children— Jennifer, Donald, Victoria, Stephan, Elizabeth BA summa cum laude (valedictorian), U. Notre Dame, 1963; M.Letters, Oxford U., 1967. Chartered investment counselor. Assoc. Stein Roe & Farnham, Chgo., 1967-72, gen. ptnr., 1972-77, sr. ptnr., 1977-86, exec. v.p., 1986-89; pres., mng. dir. Stein Roe Internat., Chgo., 1989—. Underwriting mem. Lloyds of London, 1980—; dir. Comml. Chgo. Corp.; vice chmn. bd. Hill Internat. Prodn. Co., Houston, 1982—; dir., adv. bd. Touche Remnant Investment Counselors, London, 1983—; dir. TR Worldwide Strategy Fund, Luxembourg, Konrad Adenauer Fund for European Policy Studies, Fed. Republic Germany. Voting mem., sec Ill. Rhodes Scholarship Selection Com.; voting mem. Ill. rep. Great Lakes Dist. Rhodes Scholarship Selection Com.; bd. dirs. Kennedy Sch. for Retarded Children, Palos Park, Ill., 1972—, Winnetka United Way, Ill., 1984—, Division St. YMCA, Chgo., 1972—; assoc. Rush-Presbyterian-St. Lukes Med. Ctr., Chgo., 1975—; mem. leadership com. Rush Alzheimer's Disease Ctr. Rhodes scholar, 1963 Fellow Fin. Analysts Fedn.; mem. Chgo. Council on Fgn. Relations (bd. dirs., treas. 1975—), Inst. European Studies (bd. govs., vice-chmn. 1981—), Investment Analysts Soc. Chgo. (chgo. com., com. on fgn. affairs, com. on internat. and domestic issues), Assn. for Investment Mgmt. and Rsch., Chgo. Soc. Clubs, Econ. Club of Chgo, Sunset Ridge Country (bd. dirs. Northfield, Ill., 1983—). Avocations: coin collecting/numismatics, bridge, golf, skiing, art. Office Phone: 312-368-7684. Personal E-mail: rmcneill@atlantictrust.com. Business E-Mail: rmcneill@sric.net.

MCNEILL, THOMAS RAY, lawyer; b. Pitts., June 2, 1952; s. Thomas William McNeill and Mary (Shiveley) Hiss; m. Patsy Lynch, June 25, 1977; children: Elizabeth, Kathleen, Thomas. BSBA, U. Fla., 1974; JD, Emory U., 1977. Bar: Ga. 1977, U.S. Dist. Ct. (no. dist.) Ga. 1977. Assoc. Powell Goldstein LLP, Atlanta, 1977-84, ptnr., 1984—2008, mgr. corp. dept., 1993-95, bd. ptnrs., 1998—2004, leader Bus. Transactions Group, 2005—08, mng. ptnr., 2008; ptnr. Bryan Cave Powell Goldstein, 2009—; Atlanta mng. ptnr. mgmt. com. Bryan Cave and Powell Goldstein. Mem. ABA (mem. com. on corp. laws 2007-), Ga. Bar Assn. (exec. com. bus. law sect., 2001-, chmn. 2008), Emory U. Alumni Assn. (pres. exec. com. 1988-89, Law Sch. coun. 1990-2000, 2003—, chmn. 2005-07), Soc. of Internat. Bus. Fellows, Beta Gamma Sigma. Office: Bryan Cave Powell Goldstein 1201 W Peachtree St NW 14th Fl Atlanta GA 30309-3488 Office Phone: 404-572-6681. Business E-Mail: tom.mcneill@bryancave.com.

MCNEILL, WILLIAM, environmental scientist; b. Evanston, Ill., Jan. 1, 1930; s. John and Ebba Katrina (Hansen) McNeill; m. Caryl Mook, June 15, 1951 (dec. 1969); children: Elizabeth Marie, Charles Craig, Margaret Ruth; m. Caecilia Cinquanto, Oct. 10, 1970. BA, Colgate U., 1951; MA, Temple U., 1955, PhD, 1961. Chief phys. chemistry br. Frankford Arsenal U.S. Army, Phila., 1959-70, dir. applied sci., 1970-75, chief scientist, environ. mgr. Rocky Mountain Arsenal Denver, 1975-80, dir. tech. ops., 1980-85; gen. mgr. Battelle Denver Ops., 1985-88; sr. tech. adviser Sci. Applications Internat. Corp., Golden, Colo., 1989-92, dir. tech. devel. Oak Ridge, Tenn., 1992-93. Mem. materials adv. bd. ceramics NAS/NRC, Washington, 1966; mem. Gov.'s Task Group Rocky Mountain Arsenal, 1976, Colo. Pollution Prevention Adv. Bd., Denver, 1991—99; developer environ. programs U.S. Army; expert witness in field. Contbr. articles to profl. jours. Mem.: Nat. Groundwater Assn., Air and Waste Mgmt. Assn., Hazardous Material Control Rsch. Inst., Am. Chem. Soc. Achievements include 11 patents for electrochemical processes; patents for inorganic materials synthesis; electrical-optical devices; others; research in narrow-band optical absorbers for laser protection. Home: 319 Cliffrose Ct Lafayette CO 80026-9391 Office Phone: 303-604-1035. Personal E-mail: wzmcn@indra.com.

MCNEILL, WILLIAM HARDY, retired historian, writer; b. Vancouver, BC, Can., Oct. 31, 1917; s. John Thomas and Netta (Hardy) McN.; m. Elizabeth Darbishire, Sept. 7, 1946; children: Ruth Netta, Deborah Joan, John Robert, Andrew Duncan. BA, U. Chgo., 1938, MA, 1939; PhD, Cornell U., 1947; 20 hon. degrees. Faculty U. Chgo., 1947-87, prof. history, 1957-87, Robert A. Millikan Disting. Svc. prof., 1969-87, prof. emeritus, 1987—, chmn. dept., 1961-67; pres. Demos Fund, 1968-80; chmn. bd. Demos Found., 1980-86. George Eastman vis. prof. Oxford (Eng.) U., 1980-81 Author: Greek Dilemma, War and Aftermath, 1947, Report on the Greeks, 1948, History Handbook of Western Civilization, 1948, rev. and enlarged 6th edit., 1986, America, Britain and Russia, Their Cooperation and Conflict, 1941-46, 1953, Past and Future, 1954, Greece: American Aid in Action, 1947-56, 1957, Rise of the West: A History of the Human Community, 1963, 9th edit., 1991 (Nat. Book award, Gordon J. Laing prize), Europe's Steppe Frontier, 1500-1800, 1964, A World History, 1967, 4th edit., 1998, The Contemporary World, 1967, 2d edit., 1975, The Ecumene: Story of Humanity, 1973, Venice, the Hinge of Europe, 1081-1797, 1974, The Shape of European History, 1974, Plagues and Peoples, 1976, revised edit., 1998, Metamorphosis of Greece since World War II, 1978, The Human Condition, An Ecological and Historical View, 1980, Pursuit of Power, 1982, The Great Frontier, 1983, Mythistory and other Essays, 1986, A History of the Human Community, 1986, 6th edit., 1998, Polyethnicity and National Unity in World History, 1987, Arnold J. Toynbee: A Life, 1989, Population and Politics Since 1750, 1990, Hutchins' University: A Memoir of the University of Chicago 1929-50, 1991, The Global Tradition: Conquerors, Catastrophies and Community, 1992, Keeping Together in Time: Dance & Drill in Human History, 1995, Colebrook: An Historical Sketch, 1996, De excentriciteit van het wiel en audere wereld-historische essays, 1996, The Disruption of Traditional Forms of Nurture, 1998; (with J.R. McNeill) The Human Web: A Birdseye View of World History, 2003, The Pursuit of Truth: A Historian's Memoir, 2005, Summers Long Ago on Grandfather's Farm and in Grandmothers Kitchen, 2009; editor: Lord Acton, Essays in the Liberal Interpretation of History, 1967, (with others) Readings in World History, Vols. I-X, 1968-73, Human Migration, 1978, Jour. Modern History, 1971-79, Jour. Modern Greek Studies, 1983-85, Berkshire Ency. World History, 2005; mem. editl. bd. Ency. Brit., 1981-98; contbr. articles to profl. jours., chpts. to books. Trustee Athens Coll., 1970-88; vice chmn. Christopher Columbus Quincentenary Jubilee Commn., 1985-93; co-chair curriculum task force Nat. Commn. on Social Studies, 1987-89; mem. Bradley Commn. on the Teaching of History, 1986-89; vice chmn. Nat. Coun. for History Edn., 1990-94, Nat. Coun. for History Standards, 1992-94. Fulbright Rsch. scholar Royal Inst. Internat. Affairs, Eng., 1950-51; Rockefeller grantee, 1951-52, 76; Carnegie grantee, 1957-62, 63-64, Josiah H. Macy grantee, 1973-74; Ford Faculty fellow, 1954-55, Guggenheim fellow, 1971-72, 86-87; recipient Erasmus prize, 1996 Fellow Am. Philos. Soc., Am. Acad. Arts and Scis., Brit. Acad. Arts and Scis. (corr.), Royal Hist. Soc. (corr.); mem. Am. Hist. Assn. (council, del. Am. Council Learned Socs., pres. 1985) Office: PO Box 45 Colebrook CT 06021-0045

MCNEILL-MURRAY, JOAN REAGIN, volunteer, consultant; b. Atlanta, July 8, 1936; d. Arthur Edward and Annie May (Busby) Reagin; children: Thomas Pinckney, Clyde Reagin. Student, U. Louisville, 1955-57; BA, U. Tenn., Chattanooga, 1976; D of Music Mgmt. (hon.), Kharkov Philharm. Inst. Music, 2002. Founding pres. Family and Children's Svcs. Assocs., Chattanooga, 1987-88, bd. dirs., 1996-2005; bd. dirs. Chattanooga Symphony and Opera Assn., 1984-88, 99—2008, pres., 1984-87, 2005-07; bd. dirs. U. Chattanooga Found., 1986-89, A.I.M. Ctr. of Chattanooga, 1997-04, Eos Orch., N.Y.C., 1998-04, Chattanooga Little Theater, 2003—08, 09-; v.p. devel. Chattanooga Cares, 1997-04; chair Spl. Needs and Svcs. for the Elderly of Chattanooga, 1997-04; mem. bd. dirs. Hosanna House, 2001-2004; mem. vol. coun. bd. dirs. Am. Symphony Orch. League, N.Y.C., 1986-96; pres.-elect, 1992-93, pres., 1993-95; bd. dirs. Hosanna House of Chattanooga, pres., 2002-06; pres. and dir. Internat. Conducting Competition, 2002—, Vakhtang Jordania Music Found., 2003—, U.S., 2006—; judge Internat. Music Competition, Ibla, Sicily, 2004-06, Ibla Grand Prize. Recipient Outstanding Svc. award U. Tenn., Chattanooga, 1988, Most Outstanding Greek Alumna, 1988-90, 2006-08; named Chattanooga's Disting. Woman, 1999. Mem. U. Tenn. Chattanooga Alumni Assn. (pres. 1985-86), Chattanooga Ballet Assn. (pres. 1986-88, 2007-), Golden Key, Order of Omega, Alpha Psi Omega-Nat. Hon. Drama Fraternity, Sigma Kappa Found. (trustee 1992-98, sec. 1993-94, pres. 1994-98, Colby award for volunteerism 1990), U. Louisville Sigma Kappa Residence (named Nev., 2008). Republican. Episcopalian. Office: 7457 Preston Cir Chattanooga TN 37421-1839 Personal E-mail: clownjoni@aol.com.

MCNELLEY, TERRY R., engineering educator; s. Theodore T. and Norma K. McNelley; m. Susan A. McNelley, 1946; children: Jeffrey T., Ryan S., Erin E. BSMetE, Purdue U., West Lafayette, Ind., 1967; PhD, Stanford U., Calif., 1972. Capt. US Army, 1970—90; asst. prof. U. Wyo., Laramie, 1972—76; disting. prof. Naval Postgrad. Sch., Monterey, Calif., 1976—. Fellow: Am. Soc. Metals Internat. Achievements include research in deformation processing and microstructure property relationships. Office: Naval Postgradu Sch 700 Dyer Rd Monterey CA 93943 Business E-Mail: tmcnelley@nps.edu.

MC NELLY, FREDERICK WRIGHT, JR., psychologist; b. Bangor, Maine, Apr. 14, 1947; s. Frederick Wright and E. Frances (Cutter) McNelly; 1 adopted child, Roger McNelly foster children: Joseph, Ronald, Michael, Jeffrey, Jeremy. BA magna cum laude, U. Minn., 1969; MA, U. Mich., 1971, PhD, 1973. Registered clin. psychologist Ill., cert. profl. qualification, state and provincial bds. of psychology, early intervention program provider Ill., 2007. Rsch. coord. NSF project U. Minn., Morris, 1968-69, lab. instr., 1969, trainee USPHS, 1969-70, 72; teaching fellow psychology U. Mich., Ann Arbor, 1970-72; ednl. examiner Ann Arbor Pub. Schs., 1971; dir. psychol. svcs. Children Devel. Ctr., Rockford, Ill., 1972-82, program dir., 1982-86; cons. psychologist, 1986—2000. Lectr. Rock Valley Coll., Rockford, 1974—75; part-time pvt. practice psychology, Rockford and Belvidere, Ill., 1980—86, Beloit, Wis., 1985—86; full time, 1986—; mental health cons. Rockford Head Start, 1982—, United Cerebral Palsy, Blackhawk Region, 1986—, Access Svcs., Mendota, Ill., 1992—2000; mem. health svcs. adv. com. human resources dept. City of Rockford, 1985—; presenter state and regional workshops and confs. Contbr. articles to profl. jours. Active Boy Scouts Am., 1978—83, Big Bros./Big Sisters; chmn. spl. edn. regional adv. com. Bi-County Office Edn., Rockford,

1976—78; mem. Nat. and Ill. Com. Child Abuse, 1975—85; co-chmn. Winnebago County Child Protection Assn., 1980; elder Willow Creek United Presbyn. Ch., Rockford, 1980—83; mem. stronghold renovation session com. Presbytery Blackhawk, Oregon, Ill., 1985. Named U.S. Jaycees Outstanding Young Man of 1977. Mem.: Ill. Assn. Infant Mental Health, No. Ill. Alliance Mentally Ill, Nat. Assn. Mentally Ill, Nat. Assn. Disability Examiners, State Provincial Bds. Psychology, Nat. Register Health Svc. Providers Psychology, Coun. Exception Children, No. Ill. Pvt. Practice Mental Health Assn. (v.p. 1993, pres. 1994—95), No. Ill. Psychol. Assn., Ill. Psychol. Assn. Home: 11591 Beverly Ln Belvidere IL 61008-8708

MCNELLY, JOHN TAYLOR, retired journalist, educator; b. Lancaster, Wis., Oct. 2, 1923; s. Stephen Sumner and Caroline Hurd (Taylor) McN.; m. Pamela Edith Thompson, Dec. 20, 1952; children: Barbara, Duncan. BA, U. Wis., 1946, MA, 1957; PhD, Mich. State U., 1961. Reporter AP, Milw., 1948-52, Reuters, London, 1952-53; news editor U. Wis. News Service, Madison, 1957; instr., then assoc. prof. Mich. State U., East Lansing, 1957-66; assoc. prof., then prof. U. Wis., Madison, 1966-82, Evjue-Bascom prof., 1982-88, prof. emeritus, 1988—. Asst. dir. Inter-Am. Mass Communications Program, San Jose, Costa Rica, 1961-62; vis. prof. Berlin Inst. Mass. Communication in Developing Nations, W.Ger., 1965, Agrarian U., Lima, Peru, 1968-69; communication cons. UNESCO, Latin Am., 1970-75; lectr. USIA, Latin Am., 1968, 74, 80 Co-author: Communication and Social Change in Latin America, 1968; assoc. editor: Journalism Quar., 1975-77; contbr. monographs and articles to communication publs. Served with USAF, 1942-43. Fulbright-Hays Faculty fellow Lima, Peru, 1968-69 Home and Office: 134 Larkin St Madison WI 53705-5116 Business E-Mail: dtmcnelly@facstaff.wisc.edu.

MCNERNEY, JAMES, JR., (W. JAMES MCNERNEY), aerospace transportation executive, former manufacturing executive; b. Providence, Aug. 22, 1949; m. Haity McNerney, 1987; 3 children. BA in American Studies, Yale U., 1971; MBA, Harvard U., 1975. Brand mgr. Proctor & Gamble, 1975—78; sr. mgr. McKinsey & Co., 1978—82; gen. mgr., GE Mobile Communications GE Co., 1982—86; pres. GE Info. Svcs., Rockville, Md., 1988—89; exec. v.p. GE Fin. Services and Capital, Stamford, Conn., 1989—91; pres., CEO GE Elec. Distribution and Control, Plainville, Conn., 1991—92, GE Lighting, Cleveland, Ohio, 1995—97; pres. GE Asia-Pacific, Hong Kong, 1993—95; pres., CEO GE Aircraft Engines, Cin., 1997—2000; chmn., CEO 3M Co, St. Paul, 2001—05; chmn., pres., CEO The Boeing Co., Chgo., 2005—. Bd. dir. The Boeing Co., 2001—, Proter & Gamble Co.; bd. trustee World Bus. Coun. for Sustainable Develop., Bus. Roundtable, Bus. Coun.; mem. spl. programs com. The Boeing Co. Dir. Greater Twin Cities United Way; bd. trustee Northwestern U. Named one of 25 Most Powerful People in Bus., Fortune Mag., 2007. Fellow: Am. Acad. Arts & Scis. Office: The Boeing Co 100 N Riverside Plz Chicago IL 60606-1596*

MCNERNEY, JERRY (GERALD M. MCNERNEY), United States Representative from California, engineer; b. Alburquerque, June 18, 1951; m. Mary McNerney; children: Michael, Windy, Gregory. Attended, US Mil. Acad., West Point, NY; BS, U. N.Mex., 1973, MS, 1975, PhD in Engring. and Math., 1981. Contractor Sandia Nat. Labs., Kirkland Air Force Base; sr. engr. US Wind Power/Kenetech Inc., 1985—94; energy cons. various cos. PG&E, FloWind, Electric Power Rsch Inst., 1994—98; sr. engr., field mgr. Wind Turbine Co., 1999—2003; CEO Hawt Power Inc., 2003—04; founder, CEO pvt. manufacture of wind turbines, 2004—; mem. US Congress from 11th Calif. dist., 2007—, mem. vets affairs com., transp. & infrastructure com., sci. & tech. com., select com. on energy independence & global warming. Mem.: Am. Math. Soc., Am. Soc. Mech. Engineers. Democrat. Roman Catholic. Avocations: reading, hunting, running, hiking. Office: 312 Cannon House Office Bldg Washington DC 20515 also: 5776 Stoneridge Mall Rd Ste 175 Pleasanton CA 94588*

MCNEVIN, CHRISTOPHER J., lawyer; b. Davenport, Iowa, Sept. 6, 1958; BS summa cum laude, U. Miami, 1979; JD, Stanford U., 1983. Bar: Calif. 1983, Calif. Supreme Ct., US Dist. Ct. (all Calif. dist., we. dist. Pa.), US Ct. Appeals (3d, 9th cir.). Ptnr. Pillsbury Winthrop Shaw Pittman, LA. Spl. counsel Orange County Water Dist.; co-leader environ. litig. team Pillsbury Winthrop Shaw Pittman, LA. Contbr. articles to profl. jours. Named a So. Calif. Super Lawyer, LA Mag., 2004, 2005, 2006. Office: Pillsbury Winthrop Shaw Pittman LLP 725 S Figueroa St Ste 2800 Los Angeles CA 90017-5406 Office Phone: 213-488-7507. Office Fax: 213-629-1033. Business E-Mail: chrismcnevin@pillsburylaw.com.

MCNEW, BENNIE BANKS, retired finance educator; b. Greenbrier, Ark., Nov. 12, 1931; s. Roland H. and Stella (Avery) McNew; m. Bonnie Lou Stone, Mar. 31, 1956; children: Bonnie Banks, Mary Kathleen, William Michael. BS, Ark. State Tchrs. Coll., 1953; MBA, U. Ark., 1954; PhD, U. Tex., 1961. Asst. nat. bank examiner, 1954-56; indsl. specialist Indsl. Rsch. and Ext. Ctr. U. Ark., 1956-59; lectr. finance U. Tex., 1959-61; prof. banking U. Miss., University, 1961-65, dean Sch. Bus. Adminstrn., 1965-79; dean Sch. Bus. Mid. Tenn. State U., Murfreesboro, 1980-88; prof. econs. and fin. U. Ctrl. Ark., Conway, 1988-98; ret., 1998. Asst. dir., v.p. Grad. Sch. Banking La. State U., 1966—97. Author (with Charles L. Prather): (book) Fraud Control for Commercial Banks, 1962; co-author: Money and Banking Casebook, 1966, The Bankers Handbook, 1966, A History of Mississippi, 1973. Pres. Faulkner County Singing Conv., Ark., 2002—04. With US Army, 1950—51. Named Disting. Undergraduate Alumnus, Sch. Bus. Adminstrn., U. Ctrl. Ark., 2002. Mem.: Ward Family Singers and Gospel Music. Soc. (pres. 2002—03), Lions (pres. Oxford, Miss. 1964—65, Edward Dalstrom Disting. Svc. award 2002, Melvin Jones fellow 2003). Home: 12 Bainbridge Dr Conway AR 72034-7217

MCNICHOLS, GERALD ROBERT, consulting company executive; b. Cleve., Nov. 21, 1943; s. Charles Wellington and June Beatrice (Kalal) McN.; m. Paula Kay Austin, Dec. 26, 1964; children: G. Robert Jr., Katherine Lynn Loftis, Melissa Sue Cardon. BS with honors, Case-Western Res. U., 1965; MS, U. Pa., 1966; ScD, George Washington U., 1976. Cert. cost estimator/analyst. Sr. ops. analyst Office of Sec., Dept. of Def., Washington, 1970-76; v.p. GenTech, Inc., Bethesda, Md., 1976-77, J. Watson Noah, Inc., Falls Church, Va., 1977-78; pres., chief exec. officer Mgmt. Cons. and Rsch., Inc., McLean, Va., 1978-99; sr. v.p. GRC Internat. (acquired Mgmt. Cons. and Rsch., Inc.), 1999-2000, also bd. dirs.; CEO McNichols & McNichols, Inc., Middleburg, Va., 2000—. Pres. McNichols Family Found., 2000—; bd. dir. Ordia Solution Inc., Aframe Digital Inc., Wide area Sys., Inc.; mem. bd. advisors The Baldwin Group; vice chmn. com. arts Kennedy Ctr., Wash., 2005—08, also bd. dirs. Co-author: Operations Research for Decision Making, 1975; contbg. author: Software Reliability, 1986, Software System Design Methods, 1986, Electronic Systems Effectiveness and Life Cycle Costing, 1983; editor Cost Analysis, 1984; contbr. articles to profl. jours. Pres. Rondelay Civic Assn., Fairfax Sta., Va., 1985-87; bd. dirs. Kennedy Ctr. Cir., 1995-2000; vice chmn. Washington Com. on the Arts, 2006-08; bd. dirs.VSA Arts, 2007-, Columbia Lighthouse for Blind, 2008-, Capt. USAF, 1967-70; USAF Reserve 1970-82. Recipient Meritorious Achievement award, Case Western Res U., 1995, Engr. Alumni Achievement award, George Washington U., 1989. Mem. Assn. for Corp. Growth; Potomac Officers Club; Inst. Cost Analysis (pres. 1985-88), Internat. Soc. Parametric Analysts (bd. dirs. 1982-84, Frieman Lifetime Achievement award 1990), Ops. Rsch. Soc. Am. (chmn. mil. applications sect.), Assn. for Small Rsch., Engring., and Tech. Svcs. Cos. (pres.), Mil. Ops. Rsch. Soc. (sec., treas. 1986-87, v.p. adminstrn. 1987-88, bd. dirs. 1985-88, 92-96), Soc. Cost Estimating and Analysis (bd. dirs. 1990-93, Lifetime Achievement award 2000), Century Club George Mason Univ. (bd. dirs. 1997-2000). Home: 23349 Parsons Rd Middleburg VA 20117-2817 Office: McNichols & McNichols Inc PO Box 2226 Middleburg VA 20118-2226 Business E-Mail: drmcnichols@mcnichols.org.

MCNICOL, DAVID LEON, retired federal official, researcher; b. South Gate, Calif., May 18, 1944; s. Charles D. and Mary W. (Heisel) McN.; m. Lore Anne Long, Mar. 25, 1967; children: Katharine Anne, Elizabeth Mary. BA magna cum laude, Harvard U., 1966; MS, MIT, 1968, PhD, 1973. Asst. prof. econs. U. Pa., Phila., 1971-75; sr. staff economist Pres.'s Coun. of Econ. Advisors, Washington, 1976; vis. assoc. prof. econs. Calif. Inst. Tech., Pasadena, 1976-77; sr. economist Office of the Sec., U.S. Dept. of Treasury, Washington, 1977-79; dir. Office of Econ. Analysis U.S. Dept. Energy, Washington, 1980-81, dep. asst. adminstr. Office of Applied Analysis, 1981-82; dir. Econ. Analysis and Resource Planning Divsn. Office of Sec. of Def., Office of Program Analysis and Evaluation, Washington, 1982-88, dep. asst. sec., dep. dir., 1988—2002, chmn. cost analysis improvement group, 1988—2002; sr. fellow, mem. rsch. staff, dir., cost analysis and rsch. divsn. Inst. for Def. Analyses, Alexandria, Va., 2002—. Author over 20 publs. on commodity markets, regulatory econs., energy issues and econ. aspects of the U.S. def. program. Recipient Spl. Svc. award Dept. Energy, 1981, Presdl. Rank award U.S. Govt., 1988, 93, 96, 2001, Disting./Meritorious Civilian Svc. medal Dept. Def., 1988, 91, 93, 96, 97, 2001, 2002. Home: 6901 Pineway University Park MD 20782-1163 Office: Inst for Defense Analyses 4850 Mark Center Dr Alexandria VA 22311-1882 Office Phone: 703-573-4991. Business E-Mail: dmcnicol@ida.org.

MCNICOL, EWAN, medical educator, director; b. Glasgow, Oct. 29, 1967; BSc Pharmacy, Strathclyde U., Scotland, 1988; Masters in Pain Rsch. Edn. & Policy, Tufts U. Sch. Medicine, Boston, 2001. Asst. prof. anesthesiology Tufts U. Sch. Medicine, 2007—. Course dir. Tufts U., 2004—; editor Cochrane Collaboration Pain, Palliative & Supportive Care Group, Oxford, 2008—. Mem.: Internat. Assn. Study Pain. Office: Tufts Med Ctr 800 Washington St Box 420 Boston MA 02111 Office Fax: 617-636-4633. Business E-Mail: emcnicol@tuftsmedicalcenter.org.

MCNIEL, ELIZABETH ANN, veterinarian, educator; b. Dallas, Feb. 3, 1965; d. James Samuel McNiel Jr. and Marie H. McNiel. BS, U. Tex., 1988; DVM, Tex.A&M U., College Station, TX, 1992; MS, Colo. State U., 1996, PhD, 2000. Diplomate oncology Am. Coll. Vet. Internal Medicine. Intern in gen. medicine and surgery Angell Meml. Animal Hosp., Boston, 1992—93; resident in med. oncology Colo. State U. Vet. Tchg. Hosp., Ft. Collins, 1993—96; rsch. assoc. Colo. State U., Ft. Collins, 2000—01; asst. prof. U. Minn., St. Paul, 2001—02. Recipient Mentored Clin Scientist award, Nat. Cancer Inst., 2001—06. Mem.: AAAS, Vet. Cancer Soc. (Robert S. Brodey award for excellence in clin. rsch. 1995), Am. Assn. for Cancer Rsch. (Travel award 1998), Am. Vet. Med. Assn., Am. Coll. Vet. Internal Medicine, Radiation Rsch. Soc. (Travel award 1998, 1999). Office: U Minn 1352 Boyd Ave Saint Paul MN 55108 Business E-Mail: mcnie001@umn.edu.

MCNIEL, ROBYN E., psychologist; b. Witchita, Kans., July 23, 1976; d. Robert J. and Barbara E. Perry; m. Benjamin M. McNiel, Aug. 10, 2001. BA, Ind. U., Pa., 1999, MEd in Ednl. Psychology, 2000. Ednl. specialist Ind. U., 2002, lic. in pupil pers. svcs. Commonwealth of Va., 2007. Sch. psychologist Campbell County Pub. Schs., Rustburg, Va., 2002—. Home: 450 Addie Way Lynchburg VA 24501 Office: Altavista Combined Sch 904 Bedford Ave Altavista VA 24517

MCNISH, SUSAN KIRK, retired lawyer; b. San Jose, Calif., Nov. 4, 1940; d. Wallace Garland and Dorothy (Kirk) Shaw; m. Thomas A. McNish, May 12, 1989 (dec. Dec. 2001); children: Jenifer, Michael. BA, U. Calif., 1962; JD, U. Santa Clara, Calif., 1981; postgrad., Stanford U., 1979, U. Mich., 1981. Bar: Mich. 1981, U.S. Dist. Ct. (ea. dist.) Mich. 1981. Various positions Stanford (Calif.) U., 1968-79; law clk. U.S. Dist. Ct. (no. dist.) Calif., San Francisco, 1979; atty. Consumers Power Co., Jackson, Mich., 1981-88; v.p., gen. counsel, corp. sec. Mich. Consol. Gas Co., Detroit, 1988-98; ret. Mem. clin. svcs. adv. bd. Detroit Med. Ctr., Wayne State U.; dir. Vista Maria Corp., Dearborn Heights, Mich. Mem. Am. Arbitration Assn. (arbitrator, Mich. adv. panel). Home: 1809 Bay Meadow Ct Raleigh NC 27615-5482 E-mail: susankmcnish@yahoo.com.

MCNITT, WILLARD CHARLES, food products executive; b. Chgo., June 6, 1920; s. Willard C. and Louise (Richardson) McN.; m. Charlotte D. Boyd, Sept. 14, 1946; children: Willard Charles, James D., Peter B. McNitt. BA, Amherst Coll., 1942; A.M., Harvard Grad. Sch. Bus. Adminstrn., 1942; student, Northwestern Grad. Sch. Bus. Adminstrn., U. Chgo. Sch. Bus. Adminstrn., 1947. Asst. market planning and research Foote, Cone & Belding Co., Chgo., 1946-47; asst. sales promotion and advt. Bell & Gosset Co., Morton Grove, Ill., 1947-48; v.p. sales and mktg. Bowes Industries, Inc., Chgo., 1948-54; gen. mgr. sales and mktg. Clayton Mark & Co., Evanston, Ill., 1954-58; pres., dir. Bowey's, Inc., Chgo., 1958-62; pres., dir., mem. exec. com. H.M. Byllesby Co., Chgo., 1962-63; group v.p., dir. Consol. Foods Corp., Chgo., 1963-67; exec. v.p. consumer products group W.R. Grace & Co., NYC, 1967-72; exec. v.p., dir., mem. exec. com. Ward Foods, Inc., Wilmette, Ill., 1972-73, chief operating officer, pres., dir., mem. exec. com., 1973-76; pres., chief exec. officer, dir. Westgate-Calif. Corp., and Sun Harbor Industries, San Diego, 1977-80; pres., chief exec. officer Nalley's Fine Foods, Tacoma, 1980-83; chmn., dir. Joseph Magnin Inc., 1982-85; chmn. Blue Moon Cheese Co., Thorpe, Wis., 1983—; operating ptnr. Wallner & Co., La Jolla, Calif.; vice chmn., pres., CEO, dir., exec. com. Foremost Dairies, Inc., San Francisco, 1983—85. Chmn. Epcom; bd. dirs. ATI, NCIC, Blue Moon Cheese, Del. Lightweight. Troop head local Boy Scouts Am., 1957-67. Lt. (s.g.) USNR, 1942-46. Mem. Execs. Club (Ch, Amherst Club, Harvard Bus. Sch. Club (Chgo., NYC), Indian Hill Country Club (Winnetka), Dairymen's Club (Boulder Junction, Wis.), Chi Psi. Republican. Congregationalist. Home Phone: 847-657-0662.

MCNULTY, CARRELL STEWART, JR., retired manufacturing executive, architect; b. Newark, Dec. 4, 1924; s. Carrell Stewart and Marjorie (Yaegerlehner) McN.; m. Barbara Brokaw, June 21, 1952 (dec. Oct. 31, 2003), m. Miitie Brown, May 27, 2005; children: Peter Carrell, Susan Abigail. Student, Emory U., 1941-43, U. NC, 1943-44; BArch, Columbia U., 1950, MS in Urban Planning, 1963. Registered architect, Conn. Assoc. SMS Architects, Stamford, Conn., 1950-58, gen. ptnr., 1958-73; pvt. practice architecture Weston, Conn., 1973-76; pres. CMW Co., Weston, 1975-77, NB Products, Inc., Horsham, Pa., 1976-94, NB Instruments, Inc., Horsham, 1979-93, Environ. Svcs. and Products, Inc., Horsham, 1994-96; ret. Mem. Conn. Soc. Architects, 1963-73, sec., 1964-67, pres., 1969-70. Chair S.W. Regional Planning Agy., Norwalk, Conn., 1967-71; mem. Gov.'s Com. on Environment, New Haven, 1970, chair Gov.'s Task Force on Housing, Norwalk, 1972; bd. dirs., sec. Habitat for Humanity of Greater Bucks, Doylestown, Pa., 1990-97; pres. Ctrl. Bucks Crossroads, 1995-96. Lt. (j.g.) USNR, 1943-46; PTO. Recipient citation Am. Assn. Sch. Adminstrs., 1960, 6th Biennial Design award HUD, 1973; grantee HUD, Housing Rsch., 1970. Fellow AIA (mem. urban design com. 1963-73, chmn. 1971); mem. Bucks County Choral Soc., Sigma Nu. Democrat. Mem. United Ch. of Christ (deacon 1965-71, elder 1989-92). Avocations: computers, watercoloring, choral music. Home: 14179 SE 88th Ct Summerfield FL 34491 Personal E-mail: llerracm@embarqmail.com.

MCNULTY, JAMES FRANCIS, engineering executive; b. New Bedford, Mass., July 16, 1929; s. Francis and Mary (Cantwell) McN.; m. Pauline Antoinette Gillotti, Dec. 15, 1962; children: Diana Valencia, Kevin, Irene, James, Theresa. AE in Elec. Engring., Jersey City Tech. Inst.; student, MIT. Supr. Raytheon R&D Lab., Waltham, Mass., 1952-59; elec. engr. Sperry Products, Danbury, Conn., 1959-62; elec. engr. A6A Aircraft Grumman Aircraft, Bethpage, NY, 1963-66; exec. v.p. Adtech Power, Inc., Anaheim, Calif., 1973-80; dir. engring. Datapower, Inc., Santa Ana, Calif., 1980-85; mfg. ops. mgr. Pacific Power Source, Huntington Beach, Calif., 1985-88; v.p., gen. mgr. Powerstar, Inc., Irvine, Calif., 1988-89; dir. engring. and ops. On-Line Power, City of Commerce, Calif., 1989-92; v.p. ops. Tasertron, Corona, Calif., 1992—2001. Cons. On-Line Power, 1993-94, Seimelweis Corp., Bloomington, Calif., 1997, Len Gordon Co., Las Vegas, 1998, Vogt & Resnick Law Corp., Newport Beach, Calif., 1998. Contbr. articles to profl. jours. Sgt. U.S. Army. Mem. VFW. Achievements include patent for ultrasonic testing apparatus and method, patent for control of filament current and voltage, patent for shockley diode pulser, patent for the only non-lethal alternative to the deadly anti-personnel landmine, others. Office: 1731 W Medical Center Dr Apt 213 Anaheim CA 92801-1840 Office Phone: 714-774-4529. Personal E-mail: jfmcnult@yahoo.com.

MCNULTY, JAMES FRANCIS, JR., lawyer, consultant; s. James Francis, Sr. McNulty and Anna Mae Fiorenza; m. Be Thi Tu, Dec. 19, 1986; 1 child, Thomas Vi. Cert. in Elec. Tech., Santa Ana Coll., 1981, AA, 1982; BA in Sociology, Calif. State U., Fullerton, 1990; JD, Glendale U., 1991; MA in Mgmt., Claremont Grad. U., 2002; AS in Microbiology, Crafton Hills Coll., Calif., 2002. Cert. engring. graphics, Riverside Coll., Calif., 2003; bar: Calif. 1993. Assoc. quality engr. Allen Bradley - West, Fullerton, Calif., 1981—83; plant ops. mgr. Taser Industries, Inc., Monrovia, Calif., 1983—86; CEO E.I.D. Labs, Sierra Madre, Calif., 1986—90; v.p. mktg. and product devel. Tasertron, Newport Beach, Calif., 1990—91; atty. pvt. practice, Calimesa, Calif., 1993—2004; atty., mkt. rsch., product designer Def. Tech. Corp., an Armor Holdings, Inc. Co., 2004—06; atty. Law Enforcement Assoc., Inc., a Sirchie Affiliate, 2004—06; v.p. in ho. counsel Atelier McA'Nulty Designs, Inc., 2006—. Mem.: Mensa, Phi Theta Kappa, Alpha Gamma Sigma, Alpha Kappa Delta, Delta Theta Phi. Republican. Achievements include patents in field. Avocations: bicycling, drafting and designing, scientific and technical illustrating. Home and Office: 5020 Indian River Dr Unit 421 Las Vegas NV 89103 Personal E-mail: macslaw2000@yahoo.co.in.

MCNULTY, JAMES J., futures exchange executive; BA, U. Ill., 1973; MA, U. Coll. Dublin, 1974. Ptnr. O'Connor & Assocs., 1989—93; mng. dir., co-head corp. analysis & structuring team Warburg Dillon Read, 1993—2000; pres., CEO Chgo. Mercantile Exch., 2000—03, Chgo. Mercantile Exch. Holdings Inc., 2001—03; chmn. NYSE Liffe LLC, 2008—. Bd. dirs. Chgo. Mercantile Exch., 2002—03, Chgo. Mercantile Exch. Holdings Inc., 2002—03, ICAP plc, 2004—, Archipelago Holdings, Inc., 2004—06, NYSE Euronext, Inc., 2006—. Bd. dirs. Children's Meml. Hosp., 2005—. Office: NYSE Liffe LLC 11 Wall St New York NY 10005 Office Phone: 212-656-3000.*

MCNULTY, JOHN KENT, lawyer, educator; b. Buffalo, Oct. 13, 1934; s. Robert William and Margaret Ellen (Duthie) McN.; m. Linda Conner, Aug. 20, 1955 (div. Feb. 1977); children: Martha Jane, Jennifer, John K. Jr.; m. Babette B. Barton, Mar. 23, 1978 (div. May 1988). AB with high honors, Swarthmore Coll., 1956; LLB, Yale U., 1959. Bar: Ohio 1961, U.S. Supreme Ct. 1964. Law clk. Justice Hugo L. Black US Supreme Ct., Washington, 1959—60; vis. prof. Sch. Law U. Tex., 1960; assoc. Jones, Day, Cockley & Reavis, Cleve., 1960—64; prof. law U. Calif., Berkeley, 1964—91, Roger J. Traynor prof. law, 1991—2002, Roger J. Traynor prof. emeritus, 2002—. Of counsel Baker and McKenzie, San Francisco, 1974-75; acad. visitor London Sch. Econs., 1985, Cambridge U., 1994, U. Edinburgh, 1994; vis. fellow Wolfson Coll., Cambridge, 1994, U. Innsbruck, 1996, Trinity Coll., Dublin, 1997; vis. prof. Yale U., U. Tex., U. Leiden, U. Tilburg, U. Tokyo, U. San Diego, Hastings, Vienna Econ. U., Cologne, others; lectr. in field; mem. adv. bd. Tax Mgmt. Author: Federal Income Taxation of Individuals, (with Lathrope) 7th edit., 2004, Federal Estate and Gift Taxation, (with McCouch) 6th edit., 2003, Federal Income Taxation of S Corporations, 1992; (with A. Kragen) Federal Income Taxation of Business Enterprises, 1995, 2d edit., 1999, (with A. Kragen) Federal Income Taxation (Individuals, Corporations, Partnerships) 4th edit.; mem. bd. overseers Berkeley Jour. Internat. Law. Guggenheim fellow, 1977 Mem. ABA, Am. Law Inst. (life), Internat. Fiscal Assn. (coun. U.S. br.), Order of Coif, Phi Beta Kappa. Home: 1176 Grizzly Peak Blvd Berkeley CA 94708-1741 Office: U Calif Sch Law 463 Boalt Hl Berkeley CA 94720-7200 Home Phone: 510-549-1750; Office Phone: 510-642-1928. Business E-Mail: jmcnulty@law.berkeley.edu.

MCNULTY, KATHLEEN ANNE, social worker, consultant, psychologist; b. Hackensack, NJ, Oct. 6, 1958; d. Alfred Edward and Gertrude Natalie (Currie) McN.; m. Henry Stanislaw Kowal, Sept. 16, 1988. BA, Rutgers U., 1980; MSW, Smith Coll., 1984; postgrad, Fielding Grad. Inst., 2001—09. Lic. marriage and family therapist; lic. clin. social worker; lic. psychologist. Mental health aide Belleville Mental Health Clinic, NJ, 1980-82; clin. social worker Albert Einstein Coll. Medicine, Bronx, NY, 1984-86, Family Guidance Bergen, Hackensack, 1986-87, Cliffwood Mental Health Ctr., Englewood, NJ, 1986-87; pvt. practice Rutherford, NJ, 1987-99, Ridgewood, NJ, 1999—. Cons. Meadowlands Weight Control, Rutherford, 1988—, St. Lukes-Roosevelt Hosp. Ctr., NYC, 1988. Contbr. articles to profl. jours. Mem. Am. Orthopsychiat. Assn., Acad. Cert. Social Workers (cert.), Nat. Assn. Social Workers. Avocations: painting, singing, sports, poetry. Office Phone: 201-444-4010. Personal E-mail: kam1058@aol.com, relationsconnect@aol.com.

MCNULTY, MICHAEL ROBERT, former United States Representative from New York; b. Troy, NY, Sept. 16, 1947; s. John J. and Madelon McNulty; m. Nancy Ann Lazzaro; children: Michele, Angela, Nancy, Maria. Grad., St. Joseph's Inst., Barrytown, NY, 1965, Loyola U. Rome Ctr., 1968, Hill Sch. Ins., NYC, 1970; BA in Polit. Sci., Coll. Holy Cross, Worcester, Mass., 1969; LHD honoris causa (hon.), Coll. St. Rose, Albany, NY, 1991; LLD honoris causa (hon.), Siena Coll.,

Loudonville, NY, 1993, Rensselaer Poly. Inst., Troy, NY, 1995, Excelsior Coll., Albany, NY, 2000. Town supr., Green Island, NY, 1969-77; mayor, 1977-81; mem. NY State Assembly from 106th dist., 1982-88, mem. adminstrv. regulations rev. commn., 1983-88; mem. US Congress from 23rd NY dist., 1989-92, US Congress from 21st NY dist., 1993—2009, at-large whip, mem. ways and means com., ranking mem. select revenue measures subcommittee. Chmn. United Way campaign, 1982 Mem. staff com. on edn. NY State Constl. Conv., 1967; campaign mgr. John J. McNulty Jr. for Sheriff of Albany County, NY, 1973; participant 1974 polit. campaign mgmt. inst. Kent State U., Ohio Recipient Freedom award, Armenian Nat. Com., 1996. Democrat. Roman Catholic.*

MCNULTY, PAUL J., lawyer, former federal agency administrator; b. Pitts., Jan. 21, 1958; m. Brenda Millican; 4 children. BA, Grove City Coll., 1980; JD, Capital U., 1983. Counsel US House Com. on Standards of Official Conduct, Washington, 1983—85; dir. congl. affairs Legal Svcs. Corp., Washington, 1985—87; minority counsel US House Judiciary Subcommittee on Crime, 1987—90, chief counsel, 1995—99; dep. dir. Office Policy Devel., dir. Office Policy and Comms. US Dept. Justice, Washington, 1990—93, prin. assoc. dep. atty. gen., 2001, US atty. (ea. dist.) Va. Alexandria, Va., 2001—06, acting dep. atty. gen. Washington, 2005—06, dep. atty. gen., 2006—07; counsel Shaw Pittman LLP, 1993—95; chief counsel, dir. legis. ops. to majority leader US House Reps., Washington, 1999—2001; ptnr. Baker & McKenzie LLP, Washington, 2007—. Office: Baker & McKenzie LLP 815 Conecticut Ave NW Washington DC 20006 Office Phone: 202-835-1670. E-mail: Paul.J.McNulty@bakernet.com.*

MCNULTY, TERENCE PATRICK, metallurgist, consultant; b. Los Angeles, Nov. 24, 1938; s. John Lambert McNulty and Nelle Mae (Kearney) Knaebel; m. Carol Susan Couch, Oct. 1, 1976; children: Darcy, Dan, Lisa, Peter; children from previous marriage: Tracy, John. BSChemE, Stanford U., 1961; MS in Metall. Engring., Mont. Sch. Mines, 1963; PhD in Metall. Engring., Colo. Sch. Mines, 1967. Registered profl. engr., Colo. Rsch. engr. The Anaconda Co., Anaconda, Mont., 1960-65, sr. rsch. engr. Tucson, 1967-70; concentrator supt. Anaconda Can. Ltd., Bathurst, N.B., 1970-72; supr. process engring. The Anaconda Co., Tucson, 1972-74, dir. metall. rsch. Tucson, Denver, 1974-79; v.p. tech. ops. Kerr-McGee Chem. Corp., Oklahoma City, 1979-83; pres. and chief exec. officer Hazen Rsch. Inc., Golden, Colo., 1983-88; pres. T.P. McNulty and Assocs. Inc., 1989—. Bd. dirs. Hazen Internat. Inc., Golden, Colo., Hazen-Quinn Process Equipment Co., Denver, Hazen Rsch., Inc., Golden, USMX, Denver, Iron Carbide Devel. Corp., Denver. Author 29 tech. papers, 1963-91; patentee in field of mineral processing tech. Trustee, v.p. Colo. Innovation Found., Golden, 1987—; trustee Colo. Sch. Mines, Golden Colo.; bd. dirs. Nat. Mining Mus., Leadville, Colo., 1988-91; chmn. Mines Alumni Ann. Fund., Golden, 1985-88; accreditation visitor Accreditation Bd. for Engring. and Tech., 1977—. Mem. NAE, The Metall. Soc. (Henry Krumb Traveling Lectr. in Metallurgy 1989), Soc. Mining Engrs., Mining and Metall. Soc. Am., Northwest Mining Assn., Colo. Mining Assn., Mining Club of the Southwest (Tucson). Republican. Episcopalian. Avocations: hiking, photography, woodworking. Office: T P McNulty and Assocs Inc 4550 N Territory Place Tucson AZ 85750 Office Phone: 520-529-3355. Office Fax: 520-529-3943. E-mail: Tpmacon1@aol.com.

MCNUTT, JAMES CHARLES, museum director; BA in English cum laude, Harvard U., 1972; MA in English, U. Tex., 1977, PhD in Am. Civilization, 1982. Asst. instr. U. Tex., Austin, 1978-82, rsch. assoc. Inst. Texan Cultures San Antonio, 1982-85, dir. rsch., 1985-86, dir. rsch. and collections, 1986-93, asst. exec. dir. for planning, 1993-95; dir. NC Mus. History, Raleigh, 1995—99; pres., exec. dir. Witte Mus., San Antonio, 1999—2006; pres., CEO Nat. Mus. Wildlife Art, Jackson Hole, Wyo., 2006—. Adj. asst. prof. dept. history N.C. State U., Raleigh, 1995—; lectr. in field; site reporter Nat. Endowment for Arts; advisor Sta. KSTX-FM. Contbr. numerous articles to profl. jours. Grantee Tex. Com. for Humanities, 1984, Nat. Endowment for Arts, 1986, L.J. Skaggs and Mary C. Skaggs Found., 1984, Inst. Mus. Svcs., 1990, Sprint, Inc., 1997. Mem. Am. Assn. Mus. (bd. dirs.), Am. Folklore Soc., Am. Studies Assn., Tex. Folklore Soc. (councilor 1986-88, bd. dirs. 1989-90), NC Folklore Soc., NC Literacy and Hist. Assn. Office: Nat Mus Wildlife Art 2820 Rungius Rd Jackson Hole WY 83001 Mailing: Nat Mus Wildlife Art PO Box 6825 Jackson Hole WY 83002 Office Phone: 307-733-5771. Office Fax: 307-733-5787.

MCNUTT, JOHN GLENN, educator; b. Trenton, NJ, Oct. 31, 1951; s. John Harris and Joan R. McNutt; m. Marcia Fern Barron, Aug. 13, 1978. BA in Psychology, Mars Hill Coll., NC, 1974; MSW, U. Ala., Tuscaloosa, 1978; PhD in Social Work, U. Tenn., 1991. Asst. social and behavioral sci. dept. Mars Hill Coll., 1972-73; pre-trial release counselor VISTA, Birmingham, Ala., 1975-76; grad. asst. nat. criminal justice vol. resource svc. U. Ala., Tuscaloosa, 1977-78; social worker III, child welfare worker Etowah County Dept. Pensions and Security, Gadsden, Ala., 1979-80; asst. prof. social welfare, dir. U. Va. Clinch Valley Coll., Wise, 1980-82; asst. prof. social svcs. Tusculum Coll., Greenville, Tenn., 1982-86; asst. prof. social work James Madison U., Harrisonburg, Va., 1986-89; asst. prof. sociology Lindsey Wilson Coll., Columbia, Ky., 1989-90; dir. tri-coll. social work program Loras Coll., Dubuque, Iowa, 1990—. Human svcs. cons., 1976—; mem. adj. faculty MSW program Va. Commonwealth U., Harrisonburg, 1986-89; conf. participant, coord., presenter. Contbr. articles and book revs. to profl. jours. Mem. bd. dirs. Gemeinschaft House, Harrisonburg, 1986-89; mem. assessment and allocation com. Rockingham County United Way, Harrisonburg, 1988, 89, co-chmn. needs assessment com., 1988-89. Mem. NASW (treas. Upper-East Tenn. chpt. 1982-83, coord. Greeneville area 1983-84), Acad. Cert. Social Workers, Coun. on Social Work Edn., Assn. for Community Orgn. and Social Adminstrn., Am. Evaluation Assn. Office: University of Delaware Schl of Urban Affairs & Public Policy Newark DE 19716 Home: 386 South College Ave Newark DE 19711 Office Phone: 302-831-0765. Business E-Mail: mcnuttjg@udel.edu.

MCNUTT, MONA BELLE, retired clinical social worker; b. Rogers, Ark., Aug. 21, 1934; d. John Harmon McNutt and Effie Eliza Bell. BS in Edn., U. Ark., Fayetteville, 1955; MA in Social Group Work, Scarritt Coll. for Christian Workers, Nashville, 1961; MS in Social Work, U. Tenn., Nashville, 1975. Diplomate Am. Bd. Clin. Social Workers; LCSW Tenn. Social group worker Bethlehem Bd. Missions of Meth. Ch., Spartanburg, SC, 1955—57; cmty. social worker Bethlehem Ctr., Spartanburg, SC, 1961—63, Bethlehem Ctr., Nat. Bd. Missions, Nashville, 1963—70; vocat. rehab. counselor Mid. Tenn. Mental Health Inst., State Tenn. Dept. Edn., Nashville, 1970—74; psychiatric social work supr. Mid. Tenn. Mental Health Inst. State Tenn. Dept., Nashville, 1975—98; dir. social work svc. Mid. Ten. Mental Health Inst., State Tenn. Dept., Nashville, 1998—2000; ret., 2000—. Deaconess United Meth. Ch., 1961—; chief trustee Glendale United Meth. Ch., Nashville, 2000—06, coord. older adult ministries, 2007—. Mem.: Nat. Alliance Mentally Ill, Nat. Assn Deaconesses and Home Missioners. Democrat. Avocations: travel, crafts, photography, gardening, reading. Home: 5041 Kingsview Ct Nashville TN 37220 Home Phone: 615-833-5646.

MCNUTT, RICHARD HUNT, manufacturing executive; b. Princeton, NJ, 1943; s. John and Dorothy Elizabeth (Hunt) McN. Student, Delaware Vly. Coll. Sci./Agr., 1965-68, Temple U., 1978-81; BS in Indsl. Engring., Shelbourn U., 1986. Cert. in vocat. edn.; cert. mfg. engr. Diemaker Custom Tool Co., 1964-67; toolmaker Penn Engring., 1967-69; machine shop mgr., R&D engr. Inertial Motors Corp., 1969-73; machinery design engr. Phila. Rivet Co., Doylestown, Pa., 1973-76; R&D mgr. PHL, Inc., Doylestown, 1976-82; asst. chief engr. PHL Inc./Levr/Air Inc., Prefco Products Inc., 1982-85, chief engr., 1985-86, v.p. ops., 1986-89, dir. engring., 1989—2003; owner Sunrise Solar Heat Co.; cons. Pipersville, Pa.; ptnr. Mediation Assocs., 1990—; R&D engr. fire/smoke divsn. Perfect Air Control, Inc., Pipersville, 2003—04; engring. dir. PHL, Inc., 2004—07. Founder: Gateway Tidal River Jour., 2007—. Exec. v.p. Del. Water Study Citizens Group for Sound Resource Mgmt.; councillor Probational Vol. Svcs.; founding bd. dirs. Del-Aware Unltd., Inc., Del-Art Inc., Ctr. for Performing Arts, Bucks County, Pa., Del. River Greenway Partnership, Inc.; mem. Environ. Polit. Action Com.; founder AWARE, Montgomery County, 1985—, STAND, Bucks County, 1986—, Holicong CSA; mem. exec. bd. Earth Day, 1990, Earth Days Alliance, Bucks County Conservation Dist., 1993—, Del. River Sojourn Steering Com., 1994-, Del. River Greenway, 1994-96, vice chmn., 1995-96, chmn., 1996-98; v.p. Del. River Greenway Partnership Inc., 1998-99, pres., 1999-2004; mem. econ. devel. com. Del. River Wild and Scenic Study Commn., Dept. Interior Nat. Park Svc., 1994-96; founder Solebury Forum, Bucks County, Environ. Party Com.; mem. Plumstead Twp. Pks. and Recreation Commn., sec., 1992-97, vice chmn., 1997-98, chmn., 1998—2004, 2007-; chmn. Plumstead Twp. Pks. & Recreation, 2008-, vice chmn. Plumstead Twp. Shade Tree Commn., NJ, 1992—; planning commn. tech. adv. com. Cape May County, 2001—04, Cape May 400 Anniversary Com., 2008-; founding ptnr. Rising Nation, Native Am. Cultural Heritage Project, 2000-; mem. Lenape Indian Coun., Lenape Nation of Pa., 2003—, NJ Am. Indian Alliance, 2006-, Rising Nations Hon. Journey, 2009-, co-found NJ Am. Indian Alliance, 2006-; founder Tidewaters Gateway Partnership, Inc., 2004—, pres. 2005-; founder Cape May Sunset Beach Amphi Theater Project, 2007-. Served with USMC, 1960-64; designer tidewater trail, NJ Dept. Coastal Zone Mgmt. Office, 2007—. Recipient Hollywood Tech. Achievement Acad. award, 1973. Mem. ASHRAE, NRA (life), UVA, DAV (life), Soc. Mfg. Engrs., Bucks County Assn. Corrections and Rehab., Am. Legion (life), Vietnam Vets. Am. (life), Ctrl. Bucks County C. of C. (environ. and govt. com. 1986—), Internat. Air Movement and Control Assn. (mem. code rev. com., fire-smoke engring. com.), Nat. Fire Protection Assn., Underwriters Lab. (internat. standards com.). Republican. Zen Buddhist. Office: Tidewaters Gateway Partnership Inc 5556 Stump Rd Pipersville PA 18947-1090

MCNUTT, SUZANNE MICHAELENE, music educator; b. Detroit, Mich., Feb. 20, 1952; d. Orville James Cort and Annie Angeline Mikolayek; m. Robert Wayne McNutt, Nov. 21, 1987; 1 child, Christopher Robert Cort-McNutt. BA, Wayne State U., Detroit, 1979. Piano and organ tchr., Detroit, 1970—; pianist, organist various churches, Detroit, 1970—; substitute tchr. Southwestern City Schools, 2004—; pianist Big Bands & Smaller Bands. Accompanist Kinderchor, Westerville, Ohio, 2003—05; piano judge OMEA, Ohio, 2001—; judge piano competition Roscoe Village, Ohio, 1998—2005. Mem. Leadership in Coshocton County, 1998, Lewis Ctr., United Meth. Ch., Ohio. Mem.: Pianist & Accompanist Riverside Bible Ch. Worthington, Ohio Music Tchr. Assn., Am. Guild Organists, Ohio Music Educators Assn., Accompanist Germania Club Colombus. Avocations: travel, walking, music. Home: 5946 Groff Ct Hilliard OH 43026

MCPARLAND, JEFFREY J., energy executive; Various engring. and fin. positions with power generation & engring. and constrn. companies; sr. v.p., CFO, treas. PG&E Gas Transmission, 1999—2000; sr. v.p. fin. Dynegy, Inc., 2000—02; energy industry cons., 2003; sec. Targa Resources, Inc., 2004, exec. v.p., CFO, 2004—. Office: Targa Resources Inc 1000 Louisiana Ste 4300 Houston TX 77002 Office Phone: 713-584-1000. Office Fax: 713-584-1100.*

MCPARLAND, ROBERT PATRICK, literature educator, writer; b. Mar. 7, 1958; BA, Fordham U.; MA, St. John's U., 1996, Montclair State U., 1997; MPhil, Drew U., 2004, PhD, 2005. Assoc. prof., chair English Felician Coll., Lodi/Rutherford, NJ, 1997—. Author: The Speech of Angels, 2003, In the Nick of Time, 2004, Music and Literary Modernism, 2005, Dickens and Melodrama, 2006, Charles Dickens's American Audience, 2009, Writing About Joseph Conrad, 2009; contbr. chapters to books. Home: 39 Rosedale Ave Elmwood Park NJ 07407-3033 Office: Dept English 262 S Main St Lodi NJ 07644 Office Phone: 201-559-6105. Business E-Mail: mcparlandr@felician.edu.

MCPARTLAND, JAMES, research scientist; AB in Psychology, Harvard U., Cambridge, Mass., 1996; PhD in Child Clin. Psychology, U. Wash., Seattle, 2005. Mgr., statistical programming and tech. reports Human Services Rsch. Inst., Cambridge, Mass., 1997—98; grad. rsch. asst. U. Wash., Seattle, 1998—2004; intern, psychology, autism Yale Child Study Ctr., New Haven, 2004—05, post-doctorate, 2005—06, assoc. rsch. scientist, 2006—. Editl. asst. Mental Health Services Research Journal, 1997—98, Ad-hoc reviewer Journal of the International Neuropsychological Society, 2004—, Journal of Child Psychology and Psychiatry and Allied Disciplines, Cognitive Brain Research, 2005—, European Journal of Neuroscience, Journal of International Neuropsychological Society, 2006—, American Journal of Psychiatry, 2007—; contbr. articles. Mem.: APA, Internat. Soc. for Autism Rsch., Soc. Clin. Child and Adolescent Psychology, Soc. for Rsch. in Child Develop., Autism Soc. Am. Office: Yale Ctr for Clinical Investigation 2 Church St South New Haven CT 06519*

MCPARTLAND, JAMES MICHAEL, academic administrator; b. NYC, Sept. 26, 1939; s. James J. and Helen M. (Leddy) McP. BS, Cornell U., 1961, MS, 1963; PhD, Johns Hopkins U., 1968. Rschr. U.S. Office Edn., Washington, 1965-67, U.S. Commn. Civil Rights, Washington, 1967-68; asst. dir. Ctr. Social Orgn. Schs., Johns Hopkins U., Balt., 1968-75, co-dir., 1976-94, dir., 1994—. Co-author: Equality of Educational Opportunity, 1966, Encyclopedia of Educational Research, 1992, Review of Research in Education, 1993; co-editor: Violence in Schools, 1977, Comprehensive Urban School Reform, 2002. Mem. Am. Ednl. Rsch. Assn., Am. Sociol. Assn., Am. Statis. Assn. Democrat. Roman Catholic. Avocation: music. Home: 1102 S Streeper St Baltimore MD 21224-4873 Office: Johns Hopkins U CSOS 3003 N Charles St Ste 200 Baltimore MD 21218-3888 Office Phone: 410-516-8803. E-mail: jmcpartland@csos.jhu.edu.

MCPEAK, MERRILL ANTHONY, retired military officer, investor, company director; b. Santa Rosa, Calif., Jan. 9, 1936; s. Merrill Addison McPeak and Winifred Alice (Stewart) McPeak Bendall; m. Elynor Fay Moskowitz, Nov. 10, 1956; children— Mark Allen, Brian David. AB in Econs., San Diego State Coll., 1957; MS in Internat. Relations, George Washington U., Washington, 1974. Commd. 2d lt. USAF, 1957, advanced through grades to gen., 1988; pilot USAF Thunderbirds, Nellis AFB, Nev., 1966-68; comdr. Misty Forward Air Controllers, Phu Cat, Republic of Vietnam, 1969, 20th Tactical Fighter Wing RAF, Upper Heyford, England, 1980-81, Twelfth Air Force, Bergstrom AFB, Tex., 1987-88; comdr.-in-chief Pacific Air Forces, Hickam AFB, Hawaii, 1988-90; chief of staff USAF, Washington, 1990-94; co. dir., cons., 1994—. Chmn. ECC Internat., 1997-2003, Ethicspoint, 2003-. Decorated DSM, Silver Star, Legion of Merit, DFC. Mem. Air Force Assn., Coun. Fgn. Rels., Daedalians, Sigma Chi. Home: 123 Furnace St Lake Oswego OR 97034 also: 8758 Cliff Swallow Dr Redmond OR 97756 E-mail: mamcpeak@comcast.net.

MCPETERS, SHARON JENISE, artist, writer; b. San Bernardino, Calif., Oct. 17, 1951; d. Cecil L. and Mary I. (Tanner) McPeters; 1 child, Angela M. Degree, Ventura Coll., 1971, writing apprenticeship, 1984; BA in Journalism and English, U. So. Calif., 1981. My Professors, 1993, Interpretations, 1994, The Thoughts of Socrates, 1995, Self Portrait, 1995, Happiness, 1996, My True Self, 1998, Czechoslovakia 1923, 1999, Liszt, 1999, Portrait of Ten Artists, 2000; author: (autobiography) A Human Mind, 1997, (novels) Domestic Symphonies, 1986, The Broken Heart of the World, 1999, An Illuminated Manuscript, 1994, (short stories) The Library of Heaven, 2000, A Girl Without A Name, 2001, A Sanctified Heart, Selected Poems, 1974-2002, 2003, An Intellect's Goodness, 2004, Professor Scapegoat Speaks, 2006, The Hardest Lesson, 2008, Professor Scapegoat's Coworkers, 2009, Ideas, 2008, Three One-Act Plays, 2009. Avocations: piano, philosophy.

MCPHADEN, MICHAEL JAMES, oceanographer, educator; b. Buffalo, Oct. 22, 1950; s. William Francis and Irene (Scholl) McP.; m. Elisabeth Boice, Aug. 14, 1982; 1 child, Megan Boice. BS magna cum laude, SUNY, Buffalo, 1974; PhD in Phys. Oceanography, U. Calif., San Diego, 1980. Postdoctoral fellow Nat. Ctr. for Atmospheric Rsch., Boulder, Colo., 1980-82; rsch. asst. prof. Sch. Oceanography U. Wash., Seattle, 1984-86, from affiliate asst. prof. to affiliate assoc. prof., 1988-93, affiliate prof., 1993—; oceanographer NOAA-Pacific Marine Environ. Lab., Seattle, 1986—; dir. Tropical Atmosphere Ocean Array project office, Seattle, 1992—. Vis. rsch. scientist Joint Inst. Study of Atmosphere and Ocean U. Wash., 1982-84; mem./chmn. various nat. and internat. sci. coms. overseeing ocean climate rsch. Contbr. numerous sci. articles to profl. publs. Recipient Gold medal Dept. of Commerce, 1997. Mem. Am. Geophys. Union, Am. Meteorol. Soc., The Oceanography Soc., Phi Beta Kappa. Office: Pacific Marine Environ Lab 7600 Sand Point Way NE Seattle WA 98115-6349

MCPHAIL, JOANN WINSTEAD, writer; b. Trenton, Fla., Feb. 17, 1941; d. William Emerson and Donna Mae (Crawford) Winstead; m. James Michael McPhail, June 15, 1963; children: Angela C. Morris, Dana Denise Gaizutis, Whitney Gold. Student, Fla. So. Coll., 1959—60, St. John's River Jr. Coll., Palatka, Fla., 1960—61, Houston C.C. With Jim Walter Corp., Houston, 1961—62; receptionist, land lease sec. Oil and Gas Property Mgmt. Inc., Houston, 1962—63; sec. to mng. atty. State Farm Ins. Co., Houston, 1963—64; saleswoman, decorator Oneil-Anderson, Houston, 1973; sec. Law Offices of Ed Christensen, Houston, 1980—82; advt. mgr. Egalitarian Houston C.C. Sys., 1981; fashion display artist, 1985—86; entrepreneur, writer, art agt. Golden Galleries and Antiques, Houston, 1990—95; owner, property mgr. APT Investments, 1994—98; lyricist, pub. Anna Gold Classics, 1995—, writer song lyrics, 1996—. Freelance writer, photographer: Elegance of Needlepoint, 1970, S.W. Art Mag., A Touch of Greatness, 1973, Sweet 70's Anthology, The Budding of Tomorrow, 1974 (award); columnist, photographer: Egalitarian: Names Can be Symbols, Design Your Wall Covering, Student Profile, 1981, National Library of Poetry, Fireworks (award), 1995; contbr. poetry various publs.; playwright, 1993—; screenwriter, 1996—; writer, pub. The Missing Crown, religious drama World Wide Christian Radio, Sta. KCBI-FM, KYND-AM, and other radio stas., 1996—, baby publ. Hello...World...Hello, 1997; author: (poetry) The Budding of Tomorrow, 1997; music pub., 1999-, lyrics writer. Vol. PTO bd. Sharptown Middle Sch. Mem. ASCAP (Outstanding People of 20th Century), Manuscriptors Guild, Mus. Fine Arts Houston Methodist. Avocations: antiques, art. Home: 361 N Post Oak Ln Apt 333 Houston TX 77024-5950 Personal E-mail: joannmcphail@yahoo.com.

MCPHAIL-GEIST, KARIN RUTH, secondary school educator, musician; b. Urbana, Ill., Nov. 23, 1938; d. Wilber Harold and Bertha Amanda Sofia (Helander) Tammeus; m. David Pendleton McPhail, Sept. 7, 1958 (div. 1972); children: Julia Elizabeth, Mark Andrew; m. John Charles Geist, June 4, 1989 (div. 1995). BS, Juilliard Sch. Music, 1962; student, Stanford U., L'Academia, Florence and Pistoia, Italy, Calif. State U., U. Calif., Berkeley. Cert. tchr., Calif.; lic. real estate agt., Calif. Tchr. Woodstock Sch., Musoorie, India, 1957, Canadian, Tex., 1962-66, Head Royce Sch., Oakland, Calif., 1975-79, 87—, Sleepy Hollow Sch., Orinda, Calif., 1985-2001; realtor Freeholders, Berkeley, Calif., 1971-85, Northbrae, Berkeley, Calif., 1985-92, Templeton Co., Berkeley, 1992—99. Organist Kellogg Meml., Musoorie, 1956-57, Mills Coll. Chapel, Oakland, 1972—; cashier Trinity U., San Antonio, 1957-58; cen. records sec. Riverside Ch., NYC, 1958-60; sec. Dr. Rollo May, NYC, 1959-62, United Presbyn. Nat. Missions, NYC, 1960, United Presbyn. Ecumenical Mission, NYC, 1961, Nat. Coun. Chs., NYC, 1962; choral dir. First Presbyn. Ch., Canadian, Tex., 1962-66; assoc. in music Montclair Presbyn. Ch., Oakland, 1972-88; site coord., artist, collaborator Calif. Arts Coun. Artist; cons. music edn. videos and CD Roms Clearvue EAV, Chgo., 1993—. Artist: produced and performed major choral and orchestral works, 1972-88; prodr. Paradiso, Kronos Quartet, 1985, Magdalena, 1991, 92, Children's Quest, 1993—. Grantee Orinda Union Sch. Dist., 1988. Mem. Berkeley Bd. Realtors, East Bay Regional Multiple Listing Svc., Calif. Tchrs. Assn., Commonwealth Club (San Francisco). Democrat. Home: 7360 Claremont Ave Berkeley CA 94705-1429 Personal E-mail: karinmcphail@sbcblobal.net.

MCPHEARSON, GERALDINE JUNE, retired medical/surgical nurse; b. Red Bud, Ill., June 3, 1938; d. Arthur and Viola (Liefer) Althoff; children: Deborah, Michael, Belinda, Sabrina. Diploma, Evang. Deaconess Hosp. Sch. Nursing, St. Louis, 1959. RN. Sch. nurse San Antonio Ind. Sch. Dist.; head nurse Bethesda Gen. Hosp., St. Louis; supr. Am. Blood Components, Inc., St. Louis; nurse mgr. Meml. Hosp., Belleville, Ill.; ret., 2005. Coord. arthritis svc. staff Meml. Hosp. Mem. Nat. Assn. Orthopaedic Nurses (1st pres., sec., v.p., organizer Ill. chpt.).

MCPHEE, GEORGE, professional sports team executive; b. Guelph, Ont., Can., July 2, 1958; BA in Bus., Bowling Green State U., 1982; JD, Rutgers U., 1992. Foward Guelph Platers, 1978, Bowling Green State U., 1978—82, NY Rangers, 1982, NJ Devils; v.p., dir. hockey ops. Vancouver Canucks, 1992—97, alt. gov., 1992—; gen. mgr., v.p Washington Capitals, 1997—. Recipient Hobey Baker Meml. award, 1982. Office: Washington Capitals 627 N Glebe Rd Arlington VA 22203-2110

MCPHEE, JANCY CRANE, aerospace scientist; b. Tokyo, July 8, 1962; d. Raymond Hunter and Elaine Sandra McPhee; m. Stanley Glen Love, June 24, 1995; children: Gavin Christopher Love, Alexander James Love. BA in Neurobiology and Behavior, Cornell U., Ithaca, Ny, 1984; PhD in Biophysics, Brandeis U., Waltham, Mass., 1991. Postdoc. rsch. fellow U. Wash., Seattle, 1991—95, Calif. Inst. Tech., Pasadena, 1995—98; lectr. U. So. Calif., LA, 1997—98, Calif. Inst. Tech., Pasadena, 1997—98; instr. San Jacinto Coll., Pasadena, 2001; rsch.

analysis & planning-asst. prof. Nat. Space Biomedical Rsch. Inst.-Baylor Coll. Medicine, Houston, 2001—04; assoc. program scientist U. Space Rsch. Assn., Houston, 2004—, space life sci. rsch. coord., 2001—; Life sci. commn. mem. Internat. Acad. Astronautics, Paris, 2005—, internat. astronautical congress planning com. mem., 2005—. Actor: (theater) Rumors, Pippin, Hello Dolly, Peter Pan. Children's cmty. theater vol. Upstage Arts, Webster, Tex., 2007—09. Grantee Individual Nat. Rsch. Svc. award, Nat. Inst. Neurol. Disorders & Stroke, 1993—95; fellow Predoc. fellowship, NIH, 1985—89. Mem.: AAAS, Phi Beta Kappa. Avocations: singing, theater, running, aerobics, tennis. Office: NASA-Johnson Space Ctr 2101 NASA Pky MC SK Houston TX 77058 Office Fax: 281-483-2888. Business E-Mail: jancy.c.mcphee@nasa.gov.

MCPHEE, JOHN ANGUS, writer; b. Princeton, NJ, Mar. 8, 1931; s. Harry Roemer and Mary Ziegler McPhee; m. Pryde Brown, Mar. 16, 1957; children: Laura, Sarah, Jenny, Martha; m. Yolanda Whitman, Mar. 8, 1972; stepchildren: Cole Harrop, Andrew Harrop, Katherine Harrop, Vanessa Speir. AB, Princeton U., 1953; postgrad., Magdalene Coll., Cambridge U., Eng., 1953-54; LittD (hon.), Bates Coll., 1978, Colby Coll., 1978, Williams Coll., 1979, U. Alaska, 1980, Coll. William and Mary, 1988, Rutgers U., 1988; LittD, Yale U., 2009; ScD, Maine Maritime Acad., 1992. TV playwright for Robert Montgomery Presents, NYC, 1955-56; contbg. editor, assoc. editor Time mag., 1957-64; staff writer The New Yorker mag., 1965—; Ferris prof. journalism Princeton U., 1975—. Author: A Sense of Where You Are, 1965, The Headmaster, 1966, Oranges, 1967, The Pine Barrens, 1968, A Roomful of Hovings, 1968, Levels of the Game, 1969, The Crofter and the Laird, 1970, Encounters with the Archdruid, 1971, The Deltoid Pumpkin Seed, 1973, The Curve of Binding Energy, 1974, Pieces of the Frame, 1975, The Survival of the Bark Canoe, 1975, The John McPhee Reader, 1976, Coming into the Country, 1977, Giving Good Weight, 1979, Basin and Range, 1981, In Suspect Terrain, 1983, La Place de la Concorde Suisse, 1984, Table of Contents, 1985, Rising from the Plains, 1986, The Control of Nature, 1989, Looking for a Ship, 1990, Assembling California, 1993, The Ransom of Russian Art, 1994, The Second John McPhee Reader, 1996, Irons in the Fire, 1997, Annals of the Former World, 1998, The Founding Fish, 2002, Uncommon Carriers, 2006. Recipient award in lit., Am. Acad. and Inst. Arts and Letters, 1977, Woodrow Wilson award, Princeton U., 1982, Journalism award, Am. Assn. of Petroleum Geologists, 1982, 1987, John Wesley Powell award, US Geol. Survey, 1988, John Burroughs medal, 1990, Walter Sullivan award, Am. Geophys. Union, 1993, Heritage award, Deerfield Acad., 1995, James H. Shea award, Nat. Assn. Geology Tchrs., 1995, award for Outstanding Achievement, Am. Inst. Petroleum Geologists, 1997, award of merit, Field Mus. Natural History, 1998, Pulitzer Prize for Gen. Non-Fiction, Annals of the Former World, 1999, Pres.'s award for disting. tchg., Princeton U., 1999, Pub. Svc. award, Geol. Soc. Am., 2002, Gold medal for Distinction in Natural Art, Acad. Natural Scis., George Polk Career award, 2007. Fellow Geol. Soc. Am.; mem. Am. Acad. Arts and Letters.

MCPHEE, KATHARINE HOPE, singer; b. Sherman Oaks, Calif., Mar. 25, 1984; d. Peisha Burch and Daniel McPhee; m. Nick Cokas, Feb. 2, 2008. Contestant & second-place winner American Idol, 2006; signed to 19 Recordings Ltd./RCA Records, 2006—. Singer: (singles) Somewhere Over the Rainbow/My Destiny, 2006, (albums) Katharine McPhee, 2007; actor: (plays) Annie Get Your Gun, The Ghost & Mrs. Muir, 2005; (films) Crazy, 2006, House Bunny, 2008. Office: 19 Entertainment Ltd 33 Ransomes Dock 35-37 Parkgate Rd London SW11 4NP England Office Phone: 818-788-3056.

MCPHEE, MARK STEVEN, gastroenterologist, educator; b. Kansas City, Mo., Nov. 8, 1951; s. William Robert and Mary Kay (Paige) McP.; m. Christina Marie Luebke, July 14, 1974; children: Molly Amanda, Ian Andrew. BA magna cum laude, Pomona Coll., Claremont, Calif., 1973; MD summa cum laude, U. Kans., Kansas City, 1976. Diplomate Nat. Bd. Med. Examiners; diplomate in internal medicine and gastroenterology Am. Bd. Internal Medicine. Intern, resident, fellow Harvard U. Med. Sch., Boston, 1976-80; dir. gastrointestinal endoscopy unit Kans. U. Med. Ctr., Kansas City, 1980-85; chief sect. gastroenterology St. Luke's Hosp., Kansas City, Mo., 1988-93, chair dept. medicine, 1992-97, assoc. dir. med. edn., 1995-97, dir. med. edn., 1997—; assoc. dean U. Mo.-Kansas City Med. Sch., 1997—. Asst. prof. medicine U. Kans., KansasCity, 1980-85, assoc. prof., 1985; clin. prof. medicine U. Mo., Kansas City, 1970-97, prof. medicine, 1997—. Author: Annotated Key References in Gastroenterology, 1982; contbr. chpts. to textbook, articles to profl. jours. Bd. dirs. St. Luke's Hosp., Kansas City,Mo., 1993—, Am. Digestive Health Found., Bethesda, Md., 1996—. Fellow ACP, Am. Coll. Gastroenterology; mem. Am. Gastroent. Assn. (mem. governing bd., treas.), St. Lukes Hosp. Physicians Assn. (bd. dirs.), HealthNet Physician Ptnrs. (bd. dirs.), Alpha Omega Alpha. Episcopalian. Avocations: poetry, hiking/camping, golf, tennis, sporting clay target shooting. Office: St Lukes Hosp Dept Med Edn 44th and Wornall Rd Kansas City MO 64111

MCPHEE, NORMA HOWATT, publishing executive, author; b. Dunkirk, NY, June 24, 1928; d. Walter Bruce and Hattie Calista (Holcomb) Howatt; m. Richard Samuel McPhee, Jan. 5, 1951; children: Julia Ellen, Jonathan Bruce, James Robert, Keith Richard. BS in Music Edn., SUNY, Fredonia, NY, 1950, student, 1966, Immaculata Coll., Media, Pa., 1988, U. Pa., Phila., 1988. Music edn. Lake Shore Ctrl. Sch., Angola, NY, 1951—52; pvt. music tchr. Oxford, NY, 1956—59, New Britain, Conn., 1959-63; chapel musician USAF, 1963-85; chapel, ch. drama, program dir., 1957—; free lance writer, 1963—; founder, CEO Jason & Nordic Pub., Hollidaysburg, Pa., 1988—. Vol. music edn., therapy staff The Children's Ctr., Montgomery, Ala., 1984-85, Old Forge Sch., Middletown, Pa., 1986-91. Author: Danny and The Merry Go Round, 1988, How About a Hug, 1988, Patrick and Emma Lou, 1989, Andy Opens Wide, 1990, Sarah's Surprise, 1990, A Smile From Andy, 1990, Andy Finds a Turtle, revised 1998, Leah's Night of Wonder, 1999, Of Easter Eggs and Things, 2000, Fair and Square, 2003, Sensitivity and Awareness, 2004. Mem.: AAUW, Authors League, The Authors Guild, Inc. Republican. Protestant. Avocations: swimming, theater arts, camping, reading, sewing. Home: 424 N Montgomery St Hollidaysburg PA 16648-1432 Office: Jason & Nordic Publishers PO Box 441 Hollidaysburg PA 16648-0441 Business E-Mail: mail@jasonandnordic.com. E-mail: turtlbks@jasonandnordic.com.

MCPHEETERS, EDWIN KEITH, architect, educator; b. Stillwater, Okla., Mar. 26, 1924; s. William Henry and Eva Winona (Mitchell) McP.; m. Patricia Ann Foster, Jan. 29, 1950 (div. 1981); children: Marc Foster (dec.), Kevin Mitchell, Michael Hunter; m. Mary Louise Marvin, July 21, 1984. BArch, Okla. State U., 1949; MFA, Princeton U., 1956. Instr. architecture U. Fla., 1949-51; asst. prof. Ala. Poly. Inst., Auburn (Ala.) U., 1951-54; fellow Princeton U., 1955, 81; from asst. prof. to prof. U. Ark., 1956-66; prof. Rensselaer Poly. Inst., 1966-69, dean, 1966-69; prof. Auburn U., 1969-89, dean Sch. Architecture and Fine Arts, 1969-88, dean, prof. emeritus, 1989—. Mem. Ala. Bd. Registration for Archs., 1978-87; profl. adviser South Ctrl. Bell Tel. Co., 1977-79, So. Co., 1979-81, Ala. Power Co., 1979-81, Okla. State U., 1983, Ala. Sch. Fine Arts, 1985-86; cons. Taliesin Archs., 1988-92, adj. prof. Frank Lloyd Wright Sch. of Architecture, 1992-94. Served to 2d lt. USAAC, 1943-45; capt. USAFR 1945-57. Recipient Disting. Arch. award Ala. Archtl. Found., 2001. Fellow AIA (pres. Ala. coun. 1978, Merit award 1976, East Ala. Design awards 1986, 87, 90, 92); mem. Assn. Collegiate Schs. Arch. (bd. dirs. 1970-77, Disting. Prof. 1989), Blue Key, Kappa Sigma, Omicron Delta Kappa, Kappa Kappa Psi, Tau Sigma Delta, Rotary; signature mem. Watercolor Soc. Ala. (pres. 2000—). Episcopalian. Office Phone: 334-887-8779.

MCPHERSON, ALICE RUTH, ophthalmologist, educator; b. Regina, Sask., Can., June 30, 1926; came to U.S., 1938, naturalized, 1958; d. Gordon and Viola (Hoover) McP. BS, U. Wis., 1948, MD, 1951, DSc (hon.), 1997. Diplomate Am. Bd. Ophthalmology. Intern Santa Barbara (Calif.) Cottage Hosp., 1951-52; resident anesthesiology Hartford (Conn.) Hosp., 1952; resident ophthalmology Chgo. Eye, Ear, Nose and Throat Hosp., 1953, U. Wis. Hosps., 1953-55; ophthalmologist Davis and Duehr Eye Clinic, Madison, Wis., 1956-57; clin. instr. U. Wis., 1956-57; fellow retina svc. Mass. Eye and Ear Infirmary, 1957-58; ophthalmologist Scott and White Clinic, Temple, Tex., 1958-60; practice medicine specializing in ophthalmology and retinal diseases Houston, 1960—. Staff Meth., St. Luke's, Tex. Children's Hosps., Harris County Hosp. Dist., Houston; clin. asst. prof. Baylor Coll. Medicine, Houston, 1959-61, asst. prof. ophthalmology, 1961-69, clin. assoc. prof., 1969-75, clin. prof., 1975-98, prof., 1998—; cons. retinal diseases VA Hosp., Houston, 1960—, Ben Taub Hosp., Houston, 1960—; mem. adv. com. for active staff appt. sect. ophthalmology Meth. Hosp., 1986-91, mem equipment com., 1993-95, mem. grievance panel, 1997; vol. clin. faculty appts. and promotions com., 1993; bd. dirs. Highlights of Ophthalmology; v.p. N.Am. Highlights of Ophthalmology Internat. Editor: New and Controversial Aspects of Retinal Detachment, 1968, New and Controversial Aspects of Vitreoretinal Surgery, 1977, Retinopathy of Prematurity: Current Concepts and Controversies, 1986. Amb. Houston Ballet, mem. Houston Ballet Found.; mem. pres.'s coun. Houston Grand Opera; condrs. cir. Houston Symphony, mem. Houston Symphony Soc.; mem. campaign for 80s Baylor Coll. Medicine; mem. Assn. for Cmty. TV, BBB, Physicians' Benevolent Fund, South Tex. Diabetes Assn. Inc., Jr. League Houston; bd. dirs. U. Wis. Found., Madison; mem. Bd. Internat. Coun. Ophthalmology Found., 2008. Recipient Award of appreciation KT Eye Found., 1978, Woodlands Medal for Outstanding Contbn. to the Econ. Devel. of Cmty., 1988, spl. recognition award Assn. for Rsch. in Vision in Ophthalmology, Crystal award Recognizing Generous Support-Ptnrs. with an Eye for Vision Found. Am. Acad. Ophthalmology, 2000, Benjamin Boyd Humanitarian award Pan Am. Assn. Ophthalmology, 2001, Philip Corboy Meml. award Disting. Svc. Ophthalmology, 2002, Women of Vision Houston Delta Gamma Found., 2002; Alice R. Mc Pherson Lab. for Retina Rsch. dedicated Baylor Ctr. for Biotech., 1988; Alice R. Mc Pherson Day proclaimed in her honor Mayor of City of Houston, Mar. 12, 1988. Fellow: ACS (credentials and Tex. credentials com., com. on applications), Am. Acad. Ophthalmology (2nd v.p. 1979, vice chmn. program devel. found. bd. trustees 1993—, nominating com. subspecialty/specialized sect. of coun. 2001, com. for pub. and profl. rels., bd. dirs. opthalmology ednl. trust fund found., laureate award selection com., mem. coun. representing PAAO, honor award 1956, sr. honor award 1986, guest of honor 1998 meeting, Visionary Soc. Gold Mem.); mem.: AMA, Internat. Coun. Ophthal. Found. (bd. dirs. 2006—), Highlights Ophthal. Internat., Schepens Internat. Soc. (sec. 1986—93, v.p. 1993—95, pres. 1995—97), U. Wis. Ophthal. Alumni Assn. (founding pres. 1990—93, founded Alice R. McPherson lectureship 1994), Assn. Rsch. Surgeons, Pan Am. Assn. Ophthalmology Found., Tex. Ophthal. Assn., So. Med. Soc., Rsch. to Prevent Blindness, Pan Am. Assn. Opthalmology (v.p. 1991—92, pres. elect 1992—95, AJO lectr. 1993, pres. 1995—97, pres. found. 1997, bd. dirs., membership com., Benjamin Boyd Humanitarian award 2001), Macula Soc. (credentialing com. 1992), Internat. Soc. Eye Rsch. (credentials com. 1992), Houston Ophthal. Soc. (pres. 1990—91, credentials com.), Harris County Med. Soc., Am. Bd. Laser Surgery, Am. Soc. Contemporary Ophthalmology (Charles Schepens Hon. award), Internat. Coll. Ocular Surgeons (vice regent 1991), Retina Soc. (v.p. 1976—77, pres. 1978—79, credentials com.), Am. Med. Women's Assn., Internat. Coll. Surgeons (vice regent 1991—), Tex. Med. Assn., Vitreous Soc., Jules Gonin Club. Achievements include research in vision and ophthalmology. Office: Tex Med Ctr 7200 B Cambridge Houston TX 77030 E-mail: alicem@bcm.tmc.edu.

MCPHERSON, CRAIG A., cardiologist, educator; s. Lester F. and Gloria K. Mcpherson; m. Anita K. Kerbeshian, 1948; children: Marianne E., Christina R. AB, Columbia U., NYC, 1972; MD, Tufts U., Boston, 1976. Lic. internal medicine Am. Bd. of Internal Medicine, cardiovasc. diseases Am. Bd. of Internal Medicine, cardiac electrophysiology Am. Bd. of Internal Medicine, Am. Bd. of Internal Medicine. Asst. prof. of medicine Yale U., New Haven, Conn., 1984—89, assoc. prof. of medicine, 1989—2006, clin. prof. of medicine, 2006—. Dir. cardiac electrophysiology Bridgeport Hosp., Conn., 1992—, dir. cardiology tng., 1995—. Recipient Hands and Heart award, Dept. of VA, 1989; named Tchr. of the Yr., Bridgeport Hosp., 1995, 2005. Fellow: Am. Coll. of Cardiology; mem.: ACP, Am. Heart Assn., Heart Rhythm Soc., Alpha Omega Alpha. Office: Bridgeport Hosp Yale Univ 267 Grant St Bridgeport CT 06610 Business E-Mail: pcmcph@bpthosp.org.

MCPHERSON, DAVID D., cardiologist, educator; b. Canada; MD, U. Alta., Edmonton, 1978. Lic. Medical Coun. Canada, cert. Nat. Bds. Examinations, diplomate Am. Bd. Medicine Chgo., Am. Bd. Internal Medicine, Am. Bd. Echocardiography Chgo. Med. resident Dalhousie U., Halifax, Nova Scotia, 1979—81, fellow, cardiology medicine, 1981—83; asst. prof. Foothills Hosp. U. Calgary, Canada, 1986—88; fellow assoc. U. Iowa Hosps. & Clinics, 1983—84, assoc. mem. cardiology medicine, 1984—86; assoc. prof. Northwestern U., 1986—89, 1994—96, prof., cardiology medicine, 1996—2006; prof. dir. cardioogy medicine U. Tex. Health Sci. Ctr., 2006—; chmn. dept. internal medicine U. Tex. Health Sci. Ctr. Houston, 2008—; exec. dir. ctr. clincal and translational scis. U. Tex. Health Sci. Ctr., Houston, 2008—. Asst. prof. Foothills Hosp., U. Calgary, 1986—88; assoc. prof. Northwestern U., Chgo., 1988—94, dir. rsch., divsn. cardiology, 1989—2006, associated prof., 1994—96, prof. dept. internal medicine, 1996—2006, faculty, 1999—2006; prof. dept. inernal medicine U. Tex. Health Sci. Ctr., 2006—; faculty, dept. bimed. engring. U. Tex., 2007—; assoc.mem. divsn. cardiology U. Iowa Hosps. & Clinic. Contbr. chapters to books. Recipient Jr. Faculty Rsch. award, Northwestern U., 1988, Rsch. award, Northwestern Meml. Hosp., 1995, award, Houston Am. Heart Assn., 2007—; grantee grant, NIH -RFP, 1999—; fellowship, Can. Heart Found., 1981, 1983, 1984, Med. Rsch. fellowship, Alta. Heritage Found., 1984, 1985, Regulare Rsch. grants, NIH, 2004—08, Regualr Rsch. grant, grant, 2003—07, UT Biomed. Engring. Seed Grant Program, 2007—08, Nat. Scientist Devel. grant, Am. Heart Assn., 2007—, grant, NIH, 2008—, Rsch. grant, 2009—. Fellow: Am. Coll. Cardiology, Am. Heart Assn.; mem.: ACP, Internat. Soc. Adult Congenital Heart Disease, Am. Soc. Echocardiography, Am. Physiol. Soc., Am. Fedn. Clin. Rsch., Am. Soc. Echocardiography, Can. Med. Assn., Cardiovasc. Sys. Dynamics Soc., Am. Inst. Ultrasound Medicine, Can. Cardiovasc. Soc., Am. Med. Assn. Chgo. Medial Soc., Cresent Countries Found., Ctrl. Soc. Clin. Rsch., Assn. Profs. Cardiology. Office: Univ Health Sci Ctr 6431 Fannin St Houston TX 77030 Office Fax: 713-500-6556.

MCPHERSON, DONALD PAXTON, III, lawyer; b. Balt., Aug. 9, 1941; s. Donald Paxton Jr. and Janet Lewis Russell McPherson; m. Anna Mary Teaff; children: David Russell, Cynthia Quandt. AB, Princeton U., 1963; LLB, Columbia U., 1966. Bar: Md. 1966, U.S. Dist. Ct. Md. 1967, U.S. Ct. Appeals (4th cir.) 1967. Assoc. Piper & Marbury, Balt., 1966-74, ptnr., 1974-98, head real estate dept., 1980-94, of counsel, 1998—. Mem. ABA, Md. Bar Assn. Democrat. Presbyterian. Avocations: swimming, bicycling, hiking. Office: DLA Piper US LLP 6225 Smith Ave Baltimore MD 21209-3600

MCPHERSON, DONALD SCOTT, labor and employment arbitrator/mediator; b. Sharon, Pa., June 11, 1947; s. Donald McMillan and Lily (Smith) McP.; m. Linda Jo Leighty, Aug. 16, 1969; 1 child, Kimra Leigh. BA, Indiana U. of Pa., 1969, MA, 1971; PhD, U. Pitts., 1977. Dir. residence life Indiana U. of Pa., 1969-77, prof. employment rels., 1977-93, chmn. dept., 1977-87, disting. univ. prof., 1993—2004, disting. univ. prof. emeritus, 2005—. Pres. Assn. Pa. State Coll. and Univ. Faculty, Indiana U. Pa. chpt., 1980. Author: Resolving Grievances, 1983; contbr. articles to profl. jours. Elder Calvary Presbyn. Ch., 1983—; sec. St. Andrew's Soc. of Indiana, 1991-94. Recipient disting. faculty award for svc., Commonwealth of Pa., 1983, Outstanding Alumni award, Indiana U. of Pa., 1983. Mem. Nat. Acad. Arbitrators (mng. editor Chronicle, 2005-08, bd. govs. 2008-), Labor and Employment Rels. Rsch. Assn. (exec. dir. Western Pa. chpt. 1982-89), Found. for Ind. U. of Pa. (bd. dir. 1977-82), Ind. Coun. on the Arts, Ind. U. of Pa. Alumni Assn. (pres. 1975-79), Clan MacPherson Assn. (life), Phi Kappa Phi. Democrat. Presbyterian.

MCPHERSON, GAIL, publishing and real estate executive; b. Ft. Worth; d. Garland and Daphne McP. Student, U. Tex.-Austin; BA, MS, CUNY. Advt. sales exec. Harper's Bazaar mag., NYC, 1974—76; sr. v.p., fashion mktg. dir. L'Officiel USA mag., NYC, 1976—80; fashion mgr. Town & Country Mag., NYC, 1980—82; v.p. advt. and mktg. Ultra mag., NYC, Tex., 1982—84; fragrance, jewelry and imported automotive mgr. M. Mag., NYC, 1984—85; sr. real estate sales exec. Fredric M. Reed & Co., Inc., NYC, 1985—88; AT&T security system rep. Home-Watch Inc., Amarillo, Tex., 1989—92; sales rep. Universal Comm., Dallas, 1992—94; acct. exec. Corp. Mktg., Inc., Dallas, 1994—98; sales rep. Pub. Concepts, Dallas, 1998—2006; investor, cons. Dallas, 2006—. NY sponsor Southampton Hosp. Benefit Com.; jr. com. Mannes Sch. Music, NYC, Henry St. Settlement; jr. com. mem. Dallas Mus. Art League. Mem. Fashion Group NY, Advt. Women NY, Real Estate Bd. NY, U. Tex. Alumni Assn. of NY (v.p.), Corviglia Club (St. Moritz, Switzerland), Doubles, El Morocco Club (jr. com.), Le Club. Presbyterian. Home: 17850 Sunmeadow Dr #2009 Dallas TX 75252-5382

MC PHERSON, HARRY CUMMINGS, JR., lawyer; b. Tyler, Tex., Aug. 22, 1929; s. Harry Cummings and Nan (Hight) McP.; m. Clayton Read, Aug. 30, 1952 (div.); children: Courtenay, Peter B.; m. Mary Patricia DeGroot, Oct. 17, 1981; 1 child, Sam B. BA, U. South, Sewanee, Tenn., 1949, DCL (hon.), 1965; student, Columbia U., NYC, 1949—50; LLB, U. Tex., Austin, 1956. Bar: Tex. 1955, DC 1969. Asst. gen. counsel Democratic policy com. US Senate, 1956-59, asso. counsel, 1959-61, gen. counsel, 1961-63; dep. under sec. internat. affairs Dept. Army, 1963-64; asst. sec. ednl. and cultural affairs Dept. State, 1964-65; spl. asst. and counsel to Pres. Johnson, 1965-66, spl. counsel, 1966-69; sr. ptnr. Verner Liipfert Bernhard McPherson & Hand, Washington, 1969—2002; counsel, Fed. Affairs & Legis., Govt. Affairs practices DLA Piper, Washington, 2002—. Chmn. task force on domestic policy Dem. Adv. Coun. Elected Ofcls., 1974-76; mem. Pres.'s Commn. on Accident at Three Mile Island, 1979; vice chmn. John F. Kennedy Ctr. for Performing Arts, 1969-76, gen. counsel, 1977-91; bd. dirs. Woodrow Wilson Internat. Ctr. for Scholars, 1969-74; pres. Fed. City Coun., 1983-88; apptd. vice chmn. U.S. Internat. Cultural and Trade Ctr. Commn., 1988-93. Author: A Political Education, 1972, 88, 95. Mem. US Base Closure and Realignment Commn., 1993. 2d lt. USAF, 1950-53. Recipient Disting. Civilian Svc. award Dept. Army, 1964, Arthur S. Flemming award, 1968, Judge Learned Hand Human Rels. award Am. Jewish Com., 1994, Lifetime Achievement award, The Am. Lawyer mag., 2008 Mem. DC Bar Assn., NY Council on Fgn. Relations (dir. 1974-77), Econ. Club. Washington (pres. 1992-99). Democrat. Episcopalian. Home: 10213 Montgomery Ave Kensington MD 20895-3325 Office: 500 Eighth St NW Washington DC 20036-2412 Office Phone: 202-799-4138. Office Fax: 202-689-8570. Business E-Mail: harry.mcpherson@dlapiper.com.

MCPHERSON, JAMES ALAN, writer, educator; b. Savannah, Ga., Sept. 16, 1943; s. James and Mable (Smalls) McP.; 1 dau., Rachel Alice. BA, Morris Brown Coll., 1965; LLB, Harvard, 1968; MFA, U. Iowa, 1971. Asst. prof. lit. U. Calif., Santa Cruz, 1969-71, Morgan State U., 1975-76; assoc. prof. English U. Va., Charlottesville, 1976-81; prof. English U. Iowa, 1981—. Mem. lit. panel Nat. Endowment for Arts, 1977-80; lectr., Japan, 1989-90; vis. scholar Yale Law Sch., 1978-79. Author: Hue and Cry, 1969, Railroad, 1976, Elbow Room, 1977 (Pultizer prize 1978), A World Unsuspected, 1987, The Prevailing South, 1988, Confronting Racial Differences, 1990, Lure and Loathing, 1993, Crossings, 1993, Crab Cakes, 1998, Fathering Daughters, 1998, The View From Exile, 2000; editor Double Take Mag., 1995—; contbr. editor Atlantic Monthly, Boston, 1969. Atlantic grantee, 1968; Guggenheim fellow, 1972-73, Ctr. Behavioral Studies fellow, Stanford, Calif., 1997-98, 2002-03; Recipient award in lit. Nat. Inst. Arts and Letters, 1970, MacArthur Found. award, 1981, Excellence in Tchg. award U. Iowa, 1991, Green Eyeshades award Soc. So. Journalists, 1994; stories selected for O'Henry Collection and Best American Short Stories, 1969, 73, Best Am. Short Stories of the 20th Century, Best Am. Essays various Norton Anthologies, 1990, 93, 94, 95, Pushcart prize, 1995, 96, award Cannon Found., 2002. Mem. ACLU, NAACP, P.E.N., Am. Acad. Arts and Scis. (elected mem. 1995), Authors League. Home Phone: 319-338-3136; Office Phone: 319-335-0416.

MCPHERSON, JAMES E., legal association administrator, former judge, retired military officer; b. Calif., 1953; m. Jennifer L. McPherson. B in Pub. Adminstrn., San Diego U., 1977, JD, 1981; grad., Naval Justice Sch., 1982; LLM in Mil. Law, Judge Advocate Gen. Sch., 1991. Bar: U.S. Supreme Ct., Calif. Enlisted mil. police USAR; commd. ensign JAGC USNR, 1979, intern Naval Legal Svc. Office San Diego, 1979, asst. force judge advocate comdr. staff U.S. Naval Air Force, U.S. Atlantic Fleet, 1982—83, with Naval Legal Svc. Office Norfolk, 1983—85, judge advocate Naval Air Sta. Cubi Point, Philippines, 1985—88, command judge advocate USS Theodore Roosevelt, 1988—91, sr. def. counsel Naval Legal Svc. Office, 1991—92, sr. trial counsel, 1992—94, asst. legal and legis. matters to chief naval ops., 1995—97, spl. counsel to chief naval ops., 1997—2000, comdr. Trial Svc. Office East, 2000—02, dep. JAG, 2002—04, comdr. Navy Legal Svc. Command, 2002—04, JAG, 2004—06; gen. counsel Counterintelligence Field Activity US Dept. Def., 2006—08; exec. dir. Nat. Assn. Atty. Gen., Washington, 2008—. Decorated Legion of Merit (two awards), Meritorious Svc. Medal (four awards), Army Commendation Medal, Navy Achievement Medal (two awards). Office: Nat Assn Atty Gen 2030 M St NW Eight Fl Washington DC 20036

MC PHERSON, JAMES MUNRO, history professor; b. Valley City, ND, Oct. 11, 1936; s. James Munro and Miriam (Osborn) McPherson; m. Patricia Rasche, Dec. 28, 1957; 1 child, Joanna Erika. BA, Gustavus Adolphus Coll., 1958; PhD, Johns Hopkins U., 1963. From mem. faculty to prof. Princeton U., 1962—91, George Henry Davis '86 prof. Am. history, 1991—2004, prof. emeritus, 2004—. Jefferson lectr., 2000. Author: Struggle for Equality, 1964 (Ainsfield-Wolf award race rels., 1965), The Negro's Civil War, 1965, Marching Toward Freedom: The Negro in the Civil War, 1968, Blacks in America: Bibliographical Essays, 1971, The Abolitionist Legacy: From Reconstruction to the NAACP, 1975, Ordeal by Fire: The Civil War and Reconstruction, 1981, 1992, Battle Cry of Freedom: The Civil War Era, 1988 (Pulitzer prize for History, 1989), Abraham Lincoln and the Second American Revolution, 1991, Images of the Civil War, 1992, What They Fought For 1861-1865, 1994, The Atlas of the Civil War, 1994, Drawn With the Sword: Reflections on the American Civil War, 1996, For Cause and Comrades: Why Men Fought in the Civil War, 1997 (Lincoln prize, 1998), Lamson of the Gettysburg: The Civil War Letters of Lt. Roswell H. Lamson, U.S. Navy, 1997 (Theodore and Franklin D. Roosevelt prize in naval history, 1998), Is Blood Thicker than Water? Crisis of Nationalism in the Modern World, 1998, Writing the Civil War: The Quest to Understand, 1998, To the Best of My Ability, 2000, The American Presidents, 2000, Days of Destiny, 2001, Crossroads of Freedom: Antietam, 2002, Hallowed Ground: A Walk at Gettysburg, 2003, Illustrated Battle Cry of Freedom, 2003, This Mighty Scourge: Perspectives on the Civil War, 2007, Tried By War: Abraham Lincoln as Commander in Chief, 2008 (Lincoln prize, 2009), Abraham Lincoln, 2009. Recipient Pritzker Mil. Library Lit. award, 2007; fellow, Huntington-Nat. Endowment for Humanities, 1977—78, Behavioral Scis. Ctr., Stanford U., 1982—83, Huntington-Seaver Inst., 1987—88; Danforth fellow, 1958—62, Guggenheim fellow, 1967—68. Mem.: Am. Acad. Arts & Scis., Soc. Am. Historians (pres. 1999—2000), Orgn. Am. Historians, So. Hist. Assn., Am. Hist. Assn. (pres. 2003—04), Am. Philos. Soc., Phi Beta Kappa (Jefferson lectr. 2000). Home: 15 Randall Rd Princeton NJ 08540-3609 Office Phone: 609-258-4173. Business E-Mail: jmcphers@princeton.edu.

MCPHERSON, LARRY EUGENE, photographer, educator; b. Newark, Ohio, May 1, 1943; s. Eugene Edward and Ethel Grace (Lehman) McP. BA, Columbia Coll., Chgo., 1976; MA, No. Ill. U., 1978. Instr. Columbia Coll., 1971-76; assoc. prof. photography U. Memphis, 1978—. Instr. Sch. of Art Inst. Chgo., spring 1972; workshop instr. Ohio State U., Columbus, summer 1980, VSW Summer Inst., Rochester, N.Y., summer 1988. One-man shows include Art Inst. Chgo., 1969, 78, 81, Dayton Art Inst., 1992; exhibited in group shows at Mus. Modern Art, N.Y.C., 1978, Corcoran Gallery Art, Washington, 1982, George Eastman House, Rochester, N.Y., 1982, New Orleans Mus. Art, 1992, Milw. Art Mus., 1996, Birmingham Mus. Art, 1996, Art Inst. Chgo., 1997; represented in permanent collections Mus. Modern Art, Art Inst. Chgo., George Eastman House, New Orleans Mus. Art, Mus. Fine Arts, Houston, Memphis Brooks Mus. Art, The Dayton Art Inst., Birmingham Mus. Art, Milw. Mus. Art, Ogden Mus. So. Art; author: "Memphis", Santa Fe, NM: Center for American Places, 2002, Beirut City Center, 2006, The Cows, 2007. Faculty Devel. grantee U. Memphis, 1983, 92, 99; grantee-fellow Nat. Endowment for Arts, 1975, 79; Guggenheim fellow, 1980. Mem. Soc. Photog. Edn. Home: 7725 Shadow Bend Ln Arlington TN 38002-8051 Office: U Memphis Dept Art Memphis TN 38152-0001 Office Phone: 901-678-2122. Business E-Mail: lmcphrsn@memphis.edu.

MCPHERSON, MARY PATTERSON, charitable foundation executive; b. Abington, Pa., May 14, 1935; d. John B. and Marjorie Hoffman (Higgins) McP. AB, Smith Coll., 1957, LL.D., 1981; MA, U. Del., 1960; PhD, Bryn Mawr Coll., 1969; LLD (hon.), Juniata Coll., 1975, Smith Coll., 1981, Princeton U., 1984, U. Rochester, 1984, U. Pa., 1985; LittD (hon.), Haverford Coll., 1980; L.H.D. (hon.), Lafayette Coll., 1982; LHD (hon.), U. Pa., 1985, Med. Coll. Pa., 1985; LHD (hon.), Swarthmore Coll., 1990, Coll. Holy Cross, 1997, Brion Coll., 1997, Mt. Holyke Coll., 2000, Amherst Coll., 1999, U. Hartford, 2000, DePavar U., 2004, Middlesury Coll., 2005, Robert & William Smith Coll., 2006, Pomana Coll., 2007, U. Del., 2009. Instr. philosophy U. Del., 1959-61; asst., fellow and lectr. dept. philosophy Bryn Mawr Coll., 1961-63, asst. dean, 1964-69, assoc. dean, 1969-70; dean Bryn Mawr Coll. (Undergrad. Coll.), 1970-78, assoc. prof., from 1970; acting pres. Bryn Mawr Coll., 1976-77, pres., 1978-97, pres. emeritus, 1997—; v.p. The Andrew W. Mellon Found., 1997—2007. Bd. dirs. Agnes Irwin Sch., 1972-90, Shipley Sch., 1972-90, Phillips Exeter Acad., 1973-76, Wilson Coll., 1976-79, Greater Phila. Movement, 1973-77, Internat. House of Phila., 1974-76, Josiah Macy, Jr. Found., 1977—, Carnegie Found. for Advancement Teaching, 1978-86, Univ. Mus., Phila., 1977-79, University City Sci. Center, 1979-85, Brookings Inst., 1984-90, Phila. Contributionship, 1985—, Carnegie Corp. N.Y., 1985-94, Nat. Humanities Ctr., 1986-91, Amherst Coll., 1986-98, Humanity in Action, Inc., 1997—, Goldman Sachs Asset Mgmt., 1997—2008, The Spencer Found., 1993—, Am. Sch. Classical Studies, 1996—, Bank St. Coll., 1998—2003, Smith Coll., 1998—2008. Mem. Am. Philos. Soc., Am. Acad. of Arts and Scis., Cosmopolitan Club. Office: The Andrew W Mellon Found 140 E 62nd St New York NY 10021-8124 also: Am Philosophical Soc 104 S Fifth St Philadelphia PA 19106 Office Phone: 212-838-8400.

MCPHERSON, NAEMI TANAKA, language educator; MA student, Columbia U., NY, 2008—. Tchr. Boston Japanese Lang. Sch., Medford, Mass., 2003—; asst. dir. Wheaton Coll., Norton, Mass., 2005—08, Japanese instr., 2006—.

MCPHERSON, PETER (M. PETER MCPHERSON), educational association administrator, former publishing executive; b. Grand Rapids, Mich., Oct. 27, 1940; s. Donald and Ellura E. (Frost) McP.; m. Joanne McPherson; 4 children. BA in Polit. Sci., Mich. State U., 1963; MBA, Western Mich. U., 1967; JD, Am. U., 1969; LLD (hon.), Mich. State U., 1984; LHD (hon.), Va. State U., Mt. St. Mary's Coll., 1996. Tax law specialist IRS, 1969—75; spl. asst. to Pres. Ford, dep. dir. presdl. pers. The White House, Washington, 1975—77; ptnr. Vorys, Sater, Swymour & Pease, Washington, 1977—80; adminstr. US Agy. for Internat. Devel. (USAID), 1981—87; dep. sec. US Dept. Treasury, Washington, 1987—89; group exec. v.p. Bank of America Corp., 1989—93; pres. Mich. State U., East Lansing, 1993—2004, pres. emeritus, 2004—; co-chair, founder Partnership to Cut Hunger and Poverty in Africa, 2005—; pres. Nat. Assn. State Universities & Land-Grant Colleges, 2006—; chmn. Dow Jones & Co., NYC, 2007. Chmn. bd. Overseas Pvt. Investment Corp., 1981—87; dir. econ. policy Coalition Provisional Authority, Baghdad, Iraq, 2003. Vol. Peace Corps, Peru, 1964—65; gen. counsel Reagan-Bush Transition, 1980—81. Recipient Humanitarian of Yr. award, Am. Lebanese League, 1983, Jewish Nat. Fund Tree of Life award, 1998, UNICEF award for outstanding contributions to child survival, Disting. Svc. award, US Dept. Treasury, 2004, US Presdl. Certificate of Outstanding Achievement, Sec. State's Disting. Leadership award. Mem. DC Bar Assn., Mich. Bar Assn. Republican. Methodist. Office: NASULGC 1307 New York Ave NW Ste 400 Washington DC 20005-4722 also: 499 South Capitol St SW Ste 500B Washington DC 20003 E-mail: pmcpherson@nasulgc.org.*

MCPHERSON, SHERRY LYNN, social worker; b. Bklyn., Mar. 8, 1969; d. George Cephano and Mary Sue McPherson. BA, Hofstra U., Hempstead, NY, 1992; MSW, Adelphi U., Garden City, NY, 1996. Cert. sch. social worker. Program coord. Colonial Youth and Family Svcs., Mastic, NY, 1993; sch. social worker Cmty. Counseling Ctr., Franklin Square, NY, 1996—97; cons. Elmont Pre-Kindergarten, NY, 1997, Glen Cove Child Day Care, NY, 1997—98; sch. social worker Patchogue-Medford Schs., NY, 1997—. Bd. dirs., sec. Pronto LI; liaison coord. tobacco free schs. grant NY State, NY, 2007. Sec. sub com. youth criminal justice, dept. health risk com. Criminal Justice Coordinating Counsel Suffolk County, 2007; mem. site based mgmt., faculty chair Patchogue-Medford High, 2005—09; mem. St. Gerard Majella Cmty. Summit Com., 2009, Suffolk County At Risk Youth Com., 2009. Grantee, MidEast Suffolk Tchrs. Ctr., 2007. Mem.: NASW, Sch. Social Work Assn. Am., Nat. Assn. Black Social Workers (treas. 2002—04), Black/Hispanic Alumni Assn. Hofstra U., Lupus Alliance. Roman Catholic. Avocations: travel, baseball. Office: Patchogue Medford Sch Sys 241 S Ocean Ave Patchogue NY 11772 Personal E-mail: ssenigma8@aol.com.

MCPHERSON, STEPHEN, broadcast executive; b. Pitts., Oct. 28, 1967; BA in Polit. Sci., Cornell U., 1986. Fgn. exchange trader Commodities Corp., NYC, 1986—91; dir. devel. Witt-Thomas Prodns., LA, 1991—93; dir. current programming Fox Broadcasting Co., LA, 1993—94; sr. v.p. creative affairs ABC Prodns., Burbank, Calif., 1994—95; v.p. Primetime Series NBC, Burbank, 1995—98; exec. v.p. Buena Vista Prodns. Walt Disney Co., 1998—2000, pres. Touchstone TV, 2000—04, pres. ABC Primetime Entertainment, 2004—. Recipient Diversity award, Director's Guild America, 2005; named a Maverick, Details mag., 2007. Office: ABC Entertainment 500 S Buena Vista St Burbank CA 91521

MCQUADE, EUGENE M. (GENE MCQUADE), diversified financial services company executive; b. Jan. 31, 1949; m. Peggy McQuade; 3 children. BA in Acctg., St. Bonaventure U., 1971. CPA. With Peat Marwick Mitchell & Co., until 1980; dep. contr. Mfrs. Hanover Trust Co., 1980-85, sr. v.p., 1982—85, contr., 1985; sr. v.p., contr. Mfrs. Hanover Corp., 1985—92; joined Fleet Boston Fin. Group, 1992, CFO, 1993—2002, vice-chmn., 1997—2002, pres.,COO, 2002—04; pres. Bank of America Corp., 2004; pres., COO Fed. Home Loan Mortgage Corp. (Freddie Mac), 2004—07; vice-chmn., pres. banking ops. Merrill Lynch & Co., Inc., NYC, 2008—09; CEO Citibank N.A. Citigroup Inc., NYC, 2009—. Bd. trustees St. Bonaventure U., 1998—; dir. XL Capital Ltd. With USAR. Republican. Office: Citigroup 399 Park Ave New York NY 10043*

MCQUADE, J. MICHAEL, manufacturing executive; BS in Physics, MS in Physics, Carnegie Mellon U., Pitts., PhD in Exptl. High-Energy Physics, 1983. Various positions R & D and tech. mgmt. Med. Imaging Bus. 3M, 1982, v.p. med. divsn., head med. health care bus., 2002—06; gen. mgr. med. imaging sys. bus. Imation Corp., 1996; pres. health imaging bus., sr. v.p. Eastman Kodak, Rochester, NY; sr. v.p. sci. & tech. United Techs., Hartford, Conn., 2006—, head UTC Power, 2009—. Bd. observer GMP Cos.; mem. bd. dirs. AdvaMed. Mem. sr. adv. com. Yale U. Sch. Engring. & Applied Sci.; mem. bd. trustees Conn. Sci. Ctr., Hartford, Ctr. Excellence in Edn.; mem. adv. bd. U. Conn. Sch. Engring.; mem. bd. dirs. Conn. Tech. Coun., Project Hope, United Hosp. St. Paul. Mem.: Am. Phys. Soc. Office: United Techs Corp United Techs Bldg Hartford CT 06101

MC QUADE, LAWRENCE CARROLL, lawyer, investment company executive; b. Yonkers, NY, Aug. 12, 1927; s. Edward A. and Thelma (Keefe) McQuade; m. Morrissey de Rosset Parker, Aug. 3, 1968 (dec. Oct. 1978); 1 child, Andrew Parker McQuade; m. Margaret Osmer, Mar. 15, 1980. BA with distinction, Yale U., 1950; BA, Oxford U., Eng., 1952, MA, 1956; LLB cum laude, Harvard U., 1954; MA (hon.), Colby Coll., 1981. Bar: N.Y. 1955, DC 1968. Assoc. Sullivan & Cromwell, NYC, 1954-60; spl. asst. to asst. sec. internat. security affairs U.S. Dept. Def., Washington, 1961-63; dep. asst. sec. U.S. Dept. Commerce, Washington, 1963-64, asst. to sec., 1965-67, asst. sec., 1967-69; pres. Procon Inc., Des Plaines, Ill., 1969-75, CEO, dir., 1969-75; v.p. Universal Oil Products Co., 1972-75, W.R. Grace & Co., NYC, 1975-78, sr. v.p., 1978-83, exec. v.p., 1983-87, also bd. dirs.; vice chmn. Prudential Mut. Fund Mgmt., NYC, 1988-95; mng. dir. Prudential Securities Inc., 1988-92; chmn. Qualitas Internat., 1994—. Chmn., CEO Universal Money Ctrs., 1987—88; co-chmn. River Capital Internat., 1997—; expert advisor commn. on transnat. corps. UN, 1989—93; bd. dirs. Quixote Corp., Oxford Analytica; chmn. NNRF, Inc., 2007—09. Author (with others): The Ghana Report, 1959; contbr. articles to profl. jours. Dir. Paul and Daisy Soros Fellowships New Ams., 1998—; bd. dirs. Fgn. Bondholders Protective Coun., NYC, 1978—85, Am. Forum, 1985—96, Am. Coun. on Germany, 1985—94, Asian Programs Found., 2006—; trustee Colby Coll., 1981—89, trustee emeritus, 1989—; dir. Czech and Slovak Am. Enterprise Funds, 1994—96, chmn., 1995—96. Rhodes scholar, Oxford U., 1952. Mem.: Pres.'s Cir. NAS, Overseas Devel. Coun. (bd. dirs. 1974—87), Mgmt. and Devel. Inst. (bd. dirs. 1970—99), Atlantic Coun. U.S. (bd. dirs. 1969—99), Nat. Fgn. Trade Coun. (bd. dirs. 1979—87), Chgo. Coun. Fgn. Rels. (bd. dirs. 1969—75), Coun. Fgn. Rels., N.Y., Met. Club (Washington), Century Club, Harvard Club, Phi Beta Kappa. Office Phone: 212-973-9800. Business E-Mail: lmcquade@rivercapital.com.

MCQUAID, JANET, lawyer; BS in Chem. Engring., U. Pitts., 1978; MBA, Houston Bapt. U., 1989; JD, U. Tex., Austin, 1992. Bar: Tex., Colo. Engr. Exxon Co. USA, Houston, 1978—89; assoc. atty. Fulbright & Jaworski LLP, Austin, 1992—2000, ptnr., 2001—07, Smith-Robertson LLP, 2008; sr. counsel El Paso Corp., 2008—. Sec., treas. Paramount & State Theatres, Austin, 2006—08; prog. chair Air & Waste Mgmt. Assn., 2004—06; vol. Therapy Pet Pals Tex. Mem.: Coll. State Bar Tex. (assoc.). Office: El Paso Corp PO Box 2511 Houston TX 77252 Office Fax: 713-445-8804. Business E-Mail: janet.mcguaid@elpaso.com.

MCQUAID, KIM, historian, educator, writer; b. Norwalk, Conn., Nov. 2, 1947; s. Francis Walter McQuaid and Margaret Fitzgerald Phelan. BA, Antioch Coll., Yellow Springs, Ohio, 1970; MA, Northwestern U., Evanston, Ill., 1973, PhD, 1975. Asst. prof. dept. history Lake Erie Coll., Painesville, Ohio, 1977—83, assoc. prof., 1983—89, prof., 1989—. Mary Ball Washington vis. prof. U.S. History U. Coll. Dublin, 1985—86; Fulbright lectr. U. Sci. Malaysia, 1995—96. Co-author: (book) Creating the Welfare State, 1980, 1994; author: Big Business and Presidential Power, 1982, A Response to Industrialism: Liberal Businessmen and The Evolving Spectrum of Capitalist Reform 1886-1960, 2d edit., 2003, The Anxious Years: America in the Vietnam-Watergate Era, 1989, Uneasy Partners: Big Business in American Politics, 1945-1990, 1994, Chapter in NASA History Offices Societal Impact of Spaceflight Volume, 2007, The Real & Assumed Personalities of Famous Men;Rafael De Nogales T.E. Lawrence, & The Birth of The Modern Era, 1914—37; contbr. to profl. jours. Woodrow Wilson fellow, 1970. Green Party. Avocations: wilderness hiking, art. Home: Apt 208 686 E Erie St Painesville OH 44077 Office: Lake Erie Coll 391 W Washington St Painesville OH 44077 Office Phone: 440-375-7173. E-mail: mcquaid@lec.edu.

MCQUEARY, CHARLES E. (CHUCK MCQUEARY), federal agency administrator; MS in Mech. Engring., U. Tex., PhD in Engring. Mechanics, 1966. Head of dept. Missile OPs. Dept. Bell Labs., AT&T Corp., 1971—73, dir. Undersea Systems Devel. Lab., 1983—87, v.p. Fed. Systems Advanced Technology Divsn., 1987—93; pres., v.p. bus. units AT&T, Lucent Techs., 1994—97; pres. Gen. Dynamics Advanced Tech. Sys., Greensboro, NC, 1997—2002; under sec. for sci. & tech. US Dept. Homeland Security, Washington, 2003—06; dir. operational test & evaluation US Dept. Def., Washington, 2006—. Chair bd. dirs., campaign chair United Way, Greensboro; trustee N.C. Agrl. and Tech. State U.; mem. pres. CEO adv. com. Guilford Tech. C.C.; bd. mem. World Trade Ctr. N.C.; chair Action Greensboro Pub. Edn. Initiative; bd. mem. Guilford County Edn. Network. Named Disting. Engring. Grad., U. Tex., 1997. Office: US Dept Def 1700 Def Pentagon Rm 3A1075 Washington DC 20301*

MCQUEEN, JUSTICE ELLIS (L. Q. JONES), actor, television director; b. Beaumont, Tex., Aug. 19, 1927; s. Justice Ellis and Pat (Stephens) McQ.; m. Sue Helen Lewis, Oct. 10, 1950 (dec.); children: Marlin Randolph, Marilyn Helen, Steven Lewis. Student, Lamar Jr. Coll., 1944, Lon Morris Coll., 1949, U. Tex., 1950-51. Actor, writer, dir.: motion picture films including A Boy and His Dog, 1975 (Hugo award, Sci. Fiction Achievement award for dramatic presentation, Golden Boot award, Internat. Star award, Reel Cowboys Silver Spur award, Western Walk of Fame); actor White Line Fever, 1975, Mother, Jugs & Speed, 1976, Winterhawk, 1976, Fast Charlie, The Moonbeam Rider, 1979, Timerider: The Adventures of Lyle Swann, 1982, The Beast Within, 1982, Sacred Ground, 1983, Lone Wolf McQuade, 1983, Bulletproof, 1988, River of Death, 1989, The Legend of Grizzly Adams, 1990, Lightning Jack, 1994, The Friends of Harry, 1995, Casino, 1995, Ben Johnson: Third Cowboy on the Right, 1996, The Edge, 1997, The Patriot, 1998, The Mask of Zorro, 1998, Route 666, 2001, Prairie Home Companion, 2006, numerous others; tv movies include The Sacketts, 1979, Tornado!, 1996, In Cold Blood, 1996, The Jack Bull, 1999, numerous others; appeared in tv series including Gunsmoke, 1955, Alias Smith and Jones, 1971, Cannon, 1971, Cade's County, 1971, Kung Fu, 1972, Matt Helm, 1975, Charlie's Angels, 1976, Columbo: The Conspirators, 1978, The Dukes of Hazzard, 1979, The Fall Guy, 1981, The Yellow Rose, 1983, The A-Team, 1983, Walker, Texas Ranger, 1993, numerous others; producer The Big Thickett, Come In, Children, The Witchmaker; author, prodr.: The Brotherhood of Satan, 1971; dir., prodr. The Devil's Bedroom, 1964, (tv series) The Incredible Hulk, 1978. Served with USNR, 1945-46. Nominee 4 Emmy awards. Mem. Screen Actors Guild, Dirs. Guild Am. Republican. Methodist. Home and Office: 2144 1/2 N Cahuenga Blvd Los Angeles CA 90068-2708 Office Phone: 323-465-4201, 325-465-4426. *Contribute to a space that no one can or will fill.*

MCQUEEN, KEVEN DARRYL, literature and language educator; b. Richmond, Ky., Sept. 9, 1967; s. Charles Darrell McQueen and Nadine Casteel, Swecia Webb McQueen (Stepmother). BA in English, Berea Coll., Ky., 1989; MA in English, Eastern Ky. U., Richmond, 1991. Instr. Dept. English & Theatre Eastern Ky. U., 1989—. Author: (book) Murder in Old Kentucky, Forgotten Tales of Kentucky, Cruelly Murdered, Kentucky Book of the Dead, Forgotten Tales of Indiana. R-Conservative. Baptist. Avocations: travel, history. Home: 225 Baldwin St Berea KY 40403 Office: Dept English & Theatre 467 Case Annex Eastern Ky Univ Richmond KY 40475 Business E-Mail; keven.mcqueen@eku.edu.

MCQUEEN, LYNN, public health service officer, information scientist, administrator; m. Hal Van Gieson; children: Cara Van Gieson, Skye Van Gieson children: Julia Van Gieson, Elizabeth Van Gieson. B in Nursing, U. Calgary, Can., 1983; MS, Johns Hopkins U., Balt., 1986, MPH, 1989; D in Pub. Health, U. NC, Chapel Hill, 1998. RN Va., 1985. Dir., queri rsch. program Dept. Vets. Affairs, Washington, 1998—2002, dir., risk mgmt., 2002—08, dir. sci. collaborations, 2009—. Faculty Johns Hopkins U., Balt., 2000—03; cons. Rand, Inc, Santa Monica, Calif., 1998—99; presenter in field. Contbr. articles to profl. pubs. Legislative coord. Amnesty Internat., Gaithersburg, Md., 1992—96; vol. Regional Inst. for Children and Adolescents, Md., 1992—96; sci. reviewer, advisor Can. Stroke Network, Ottowa, Ontario, Canada, 2002—05. Recipient Outstanding Cmty. Svc. award, Maryland, 1986, Outstanding Young Woman award, Jaycees Am., 1987, Surgeon Gen.'s award, C. Everett Koop, 1988, vol. awards, Reg. Inst. Children Adolescents, 1993—96, Internat. Nursing Leadership award, Sigma Theta Tau, 2002. Mem.: Sigma Theta Tau Intenat., Acad. for Health Services Rsch. (sci. reviewer 2003—). Achievements include research in developed research methodologies and scientific review processes; development of health care software; scientific reviewer, non-profits, journals, government; development of an educational program in evidenced based practice at Johns Hopkins University. Office: Dept Vets Affairs OQP 810 Vermont Street NW (10Q) Washington DC 20420 Business E-Mail: lynn.mcqueen@va.gov.

MCQUEEN, REGENIA, writer; b. Summerville, SC, Oct. 29, 1945; d. William and Mary (Stoutamire) McQueen; m. John Ray Sanders Teasley, Oct. 11, 1961; children: John Ray Sanders Teasley, Tonya Teasley, Ieishia Teasley, Nairobi Teasley, Rhodesia Teasley, Donnish Lindsey Teasley, DeJong Lindsey Teasley. A, Cin. Tech. Coll., 1985; cert., Blackstone Sch. of Law, Dallas, 2000; BA, No. Ky. U., 2005. Clk. Western-So. Life Ins., Cin., 1967-72, IRS, Covington, Ky., 1985-87. Author: Regenia McQueen: Born to Search, 2000, Nairobi Teasley: 1-1/2 Hour Defenseless Lamb, 2001, Witnesses to the Impossible Dreams, 2002, Regenia McQueen: Life Stolen, Name, Land, City Government and History Theft in South Carolina, 2003, Regenia McQueen's Documents, Name, Land, Oil, Government and History Theft of William McQueen in South Carolina vol. 1-4, 2004, John Teasley and Nairobi Teasley: Unlawfully Made Guilty until Lawfully Proven Innocent vol. 1 and 2, 2004, Regenia McQueen, One of the Richest Women in the World yet, I Have Not a Dime to Spend, 2006, Regenia McQueen A Queen that Lives in the Ghetto, 2006, A Vision from God Concerning the Virginia Company.Join the Search, 2008. V.p. 13th St. Tenant Assn., 1979—85; Rosa Parks co-chmn.; trustee Owning the Realty, 1983—85. Recipient Achievement award, Ho. of Reps., Ohio, 2000, Wall of Tolerance award, Nat. Campaign Tolerance, 2002. Avocation: researching. E-mail: rteasley@zoomtown.com.

MCQUEEN, SCOTT ROBERT, broadcast executive; b. Peekskill, NY, June 30, 1946; s. Robert Charles and Donna Marie (Ikeler) McQ.; children: Geoffrey Scott, Mallory Morgan, Brian Daniel; 1 child, by previous marriage, Tasha Lea. BA, Dartmouth Coll., 1968. Founder

Sconnix Radio Ent., Inc., Laconia, NH, 1968, Sconnix Radio Ent., Inc. (became Sconnix Group Broadcasting, Inc.), 1971, pres., 1971—; chmn. Bluewater Broadcasting Co., 2003—. Pres. Charisma Ventures, Ltd., 1995—. Chmn. bd. advisors Pine Crest Sch., Boca Raton, Fla., 2000-02, chmn. bd. trustees, 2003-05. With N.H. N.G., 1968-69. Mem. Nat. Assn. Broadcasters, Nat. Radio Broadcsters Assn., Lakes Region C. of C. (dir. 1977-81),Royal Palm Yacht and Country Club. Home: 431 E Coconut Palm Rd Boca Raton FL 33432-7915

MCQUERRY, PATRICIA ANN, painter, retired secondary school educator; b. Long Beach, Calif., Dec. 8, 1934; d. Jack Wendell and Estella Woodford (Atkinson) M.; m. stepmother Hazel Parnell (dec. 1968); m. stepmother Mary Noble M. (dec. 2006). BA in Art, North Tex. U., 1955; postgrad. in History, U. Ariz., Tucson, 1961-65; postgrad., Stanford U., Calif., 1962-63; diploma in econs., Tex. A&M U., 1974. Tchr. art and social studies Roswell (N.Mex.) Ind. Sch. Dist., 1955-59; grad. asst. history dept. U. Ariz., Tucson, 1959-65; tchr. remedial English, Salpointe Cath. Sch., Tucson, 1961-62; hostess Sequoia-Kings Canyon Nat. Park, 1963; tchr. art Poly. H.S., Ft. Worth, 1966-88; tchr. history Western Hill H.S., Ft. Worth, 1988; tchr. Vision Quest, Elfrida, Ariz., 1991. Counsellor Camp Cruces Episc., Tex., 1968. Author: (plays) New World Playhouse, 1981, Larkenportal, 1993; one-woman show Com. for Artist's Ctr., Ft. Worth, 1990 (citation 1990). Eyewitness U.S.-Mex. Border Patrol; mem. Sky Island Alliance; hon. mem. Az. Cochise County, Attys. Sheriff's Assoc.; mem. Scotsdale Mus. Contemp Art, 2009; mem. youth criminal justice subcom. Suffolk County Criminal Justice Coord. Com., 2006—. Recipient various art awards; Fredrich Usher History scholar U. Ariz., 1964. Mem.: Phi Alpha Theta, Alpha Rho Tau. Home Phone: 520-458-4220.

MCQUILLAN, LAURENCE JOSEPH, communications consultant, educator; b. Bridgeport, Conn., Aug. 4, 1945; s. John Osborne and Mary Catherine McQuillan; m. Geraldine Marie Kenny, Apr. 8, 1972; 1 child, Sean Patrick. BS in Journalism, St. Bonaventure U., 1969; MA in Polit. Sci., SUNY, Albany, 1975. White House corr. UPI, Washington, 1976—80; asst. Washington bur. chief N.Y. Daily News, Washington, 1980—82; Washington corr. San Francisco Examiner, Washington, 1982—84; news editor Scripps Howard News Svc., Washington, 1984—86; dir. of pub. rels. Am. Fedn. of Tchrs., Washington, 1986—87; sr. White House corr. Reuters News Svc., Washington, 1987—99; White House corr. USA Today, Washington, 1999—2004; spokesman, media cons. U.S. Commn. on the Intelligence Capabilities of the U.S., Washington, 2004—05; dir. of comm. Am. Insts. for Rsch., Washington, 2004—. Adj. prof. Sch. of Comm., Am. U., Washington, 2005—06. With US Army, 1969—71, Vietnam. Mem.: White Ho. Corr.'s Assn. (hon.; pres., bd. of dirs. 1993—2004), Gridiron Club of Washington, D.C. (assoc.). Roman Catholic. Office: Am Insts for Rsch 1000 Thomas Jefferson St NW Washington DC 20007 E-mail: lmcquillan@air.org.

MCQUILLAN, MARK K., state official, school system administrator; married; 3 children. BA, U. Calif., Berkeley; EdD, Harvard U. Asst. supt., Beverly, Mass., 1986—91; supt. Andover, Mass., 1991—94, Lincoln, Mass., 1994—2002; dep. commr., chief operational officer Mass. Dept. Edn., Malden, 2002—04; exec. dir., pres. EDCO Collaborative /Edn. Collaborative for Greater Boston, Waltham, 2004—07; commr. edn. Conn. Dept. Edn., Hartford, 2007—. Office: Conn State Dept Edn 165 Capitol Ave Hartford CT 06106 Office Phone: 860-713-6543.*

MCQUILLEN, DANIEL PAUL, infectious diseases physician, medical educator; b. Feb. 28, 1959; s. Michael P. and Louise (Devlin) McQ. BS in Biology magna cum laude, Georgetown U., 1981; MD, Med. Coll. Wis., 1985. Diplomate Nat. Bd. Med. Examiners, Am. Bd. Internal Medicine; bd. cert. internal medicine & infectious diseases. Intern and resident dept. medicine Med. Coll. Wis. Affiliated Hosps. Inc., Milw., 1985-88; clin. fellow in infectious diseases Boston U. Sch. Medicine, 1988-89, instr. in medicine, 1991, asst. prof. medicine, 1992-99; rsch. fellow in infectious diseases Maxwell Finland Lab. Infectious Diseases, Boston City Hosp., 1988-92; staff physician Dept. Veterans Affairs Med. Ctr., Boston, 1990-2001, Deaconess Glover Hosp., 1990—, Beth Israel Deaconess Med. Ctr., 1999—. Staff physician Boston Medical Ctr., 1992—; instr. medicine Harvard Med. Sch., 1999—. Contbr. articles to profl. jours. Recipient Physician Scientist award NIH/Nat. Inst. Allergy & Infectious Diseases, 1991, Trainee Investigator award Am. Fedn. Clin. Rsch., 1992, Maxwell Finland Young Investigator award Mass. Infectious Diseases Soc.; Dr. Henry R. Viets Med. Student Rsch. fellow Myasthenia Gravis Found., 1980, 81, Eli Lilly Co. fellow in infectious diseases Nat. Found. Infectious Diseases, 1990. Mem. Am. Coll. Physicians, Am. Soc. Microbiology, Infectious Diseases Soc. Am., Mass. Med. Soc., Mass. Infectious Diseases Soc. Office: Lahey Clinic 41 Mall Rd Burlington MA 01805 Business E-Mail: daniel.p.mcquillen@lahey.org.

MCQUILLEN, JEREMIAH JOSEPH, distribution executive; b. Buffalo, Jan. 7, 1941; s. Joseph Bernard and Marca Rita (Ammerman) McQ.; m. Maureen Elaine Brett; children: Michael, Karen, Kathleen. BS, Canisius Coll., 1962. Nat. sales mgr. Birge Wallcoverings, Buffalo, 1973-74, v.p., gen. mgr., 1976-79; v.p. mktg. Reed Decorative Products, Toronto, 1974-76, exec. v.p. Atlanta, 1979-81, Northeastern Wallcoverings, Boston, 1981-88, pres., 1989-91; pres. comml. wallcoverings Forbo Wallcoverings Inc., 1991-92; exec. v.p. Hytex Industries, Randolph, Mass., 1992-98, pres., CEO, 1998—. Served to 1st lt., U.S. Army, 1962-64. Mem. Wallcovering Distbrs. Assn. (sec., treas. 1987—, v.p. 1988, pres. 1989-90), Wallcovering Info. Bur. (pres. 1980), Wallcovering Mfg. Assn. (v.p. 1980), Di Gamma (life). Republican. Roman Catholic. Avocations: tennis, racquetball. Home: 3 Nauset St Medfield MA 02052-3006 Office Phone: 781-963-4400. Personal E-mail: jjmhytex@aol.com.

MCQUILLEN, MICHAEL J., Councilman; married. BA in Polit. Sci., U. Indpls., 1987. Owner PoliticalParade.com; councillor, dist. 12 Indpls.-Marion County City-County Coun., 2007—, majority whip. Ward chmn. Lawrence Twp., Ind., former asst. twp. chmn.; former mem., pres. Lawrence Twp. Bd. Fin.; chmn. mcpl. corps. com. Indpls.-Marion County City-County Coun. Mem. Pub. Housing Adv. Coun., Marion County Sheriff's Citizen Adv. Bd., Lawrence Twp. Sch. Com., Citizen's Sch. Org. Republican. Mailing: 9130 Prairie Ridge Ct Indianapolis IN 46256 Office: 241 City-County Bldg 200 E Washington St Indianapolis IN 46204 Office Phone: 317-374-1481, 317-327-4242. Office Fax: 317-327-4230. Business E-Mail: mike@mikemcquillen.com.

MCQUILLEN, MICHAEL PAUL, neurologist, educator; b. NYC, Sept. 9, 1932; s. Paul and Dorothy Marian (Moore) McQ.; m. Louise Devlin; children: Daniel, Thomas, Patrick, Kathleen. BA cum laude, Georgetown U., 1953, MD, 1957; MA, U. Va., 1994. Diplomate Am. Bd. Psychiatry and Neurology (bd. dirs. 1991-95, exec. com. 1995), added qualification in clin. neurophysiology. Rotating intern Royal Victoria Hosp., Montreal, Que., Canada, 1957—58; resident in neurology Georgetown U. Med. Center, 1958—60; fellow in physiology Johns Hopkins U. Med. Sch. and Hosp., 1960—62, instr. medicine, 1962—65; mem. faculty U. Ky. Med. Center, 1965—74, prof. neurology, 1972—74, prof., chmn. neurology, 1987—93; prof. neurology, chmn. dept. Med. Coll. Wis., Milw., 1974—87; clin. faculty mem. dept. neurology U. Va. Health Sci. Ctr., Charlottesville, 1993—94; prof. neurology U. Rochester, NY, 1995—2005; clin. prof. neurology and neurol. scis. Stanford (Calif.) U., 2006—. Vis. sci. Inst. Neurophysiology U. Copenhagen, 1971-72; vis. prof. U. Ky. Med. Ctr., 1978, Royal Coll. Surgeons, Ireland, 1983. Contbr. articles to profl. jours. Mem. Cath. Commn. on Intellectual Affairs. Recipient Neurology medal Georgetown U. Med. Sch., 1957; Clin. Teaching award Med. Coll. Wis., 1976; Disting. Service award N.Y. Med. Coll., 1983; named to Johns Hopkins Soc. Scholars, 1981 Fellow Am. Acad. Neurology; mem. AMA, Royal Acad. Medicine Ireland, Nat. Myasthenia Gravis Found. (chmn. 1981-83), Am. Neurol. Assn., Wis. Neurol. Assn. (pres. 81-82), Alpha Omega Alpha. Office: Stanford Univ 300 Pasteur Dr Rm H3152 Stanford CA 94305 Home: 3611 Louis Rd Palo Alto CA 94303 Office Phone: 650-723-5297. Personal E-mail: michael_mcquillen@comcast.net. Business E-Mail: mmcquillen@stanfordmed.org.

MCQUILLIN, RICHARD ROSS, management consultant; b. Elyria, Ohio, Oct. 15, 1956; s. Wayne Rupp and Frana Rose (Romp) McQuillin; m. Riko Koga; children: Richard K., Sean K. BS, Ohio State U., 1979; MS, U. So. Calif., LA, 1983; MBA, UCLA, 1990. Sr. staff mem. TRW Inc., Redondo Beach, Calif., 1979-88; sr. cons. Deloitte & Touche, LA, 1990-91; cons. mgr. NetBase Computing, El Segundo, Calif., 1993-2000; chief tech. officer When2Click.com, El Segundo, Calif., 2000—04, Casting Networks, Inc., Hollywood, 2004—. Treas., contr. Patio Creek Homeowners Assn., Torrance, Calif., 1986—91, pres., 1991—, TRW Investment Club, Redondo Beach, 1984—87. UCLA fellow, 1989. Mem.: IEEE, Beta Gamma Sigma. Home: 1281 Tennyson St Manhattan Beach CA 90266-6956 Business E-Mail: marquis@mcqcorp.com.

MCQUISTON, ROBERT EARL, lawyer; b. Pitts., Feb. 4, 1936; s. Theodore O. and Bertha L. (Kegley) McQ.; m. Mary Hope Missimer, June 30, 1962; children: Mary Hope, Elizabeth Ann. BA magna cum laude, Yale U., 1958; JD cum laude, Harvard U., 1961. Bar: Pa. 1962. Ptnr. Ballard, Spahr, Andrews & Ingersoll, LLP, Phila., Balt., Denver, Washington, Salt Lake City, 1969—2001, sr. counsel, 2001—. Mem. Nat. Adv. Group Commr. IRS, Washington, 1985-87, US Treas. Dept. Taxpayer Advocacy Panel, 2008-; lectr. in law Temple U., 1968-69, also various tax insts.; bd. dirs. Macromedia Inc., Hackensack, N.J., Gateway Communications, Inc., Binghamton, N.Y. Contbr. articles to profl. jours. Mem. Rep. Fin. Com., Harrisburg, Pa., 1983-86; trustee Am. Soc. Hypertension, 1992-98. Mem. ABA (active numerous coms. sect. taxation 1969—, including coun. mem. 1979-85, vice chmn., sec. 1982-85), Phila. Bar Assn. (bd. govs. 1978-80, mem. coun. 1969-84, sec. treas sect. on taxation 1973-75, vice chmn. 1976-78, chmn. 1978-80), Am. Coll. Tax Counsel (charter, regent 1990-98, vice chmn. 1993-94, chmn. 1994-96), Am. Tax Policy Inst. (trustee 1996-2003, pres. 2001-03), Nat. Conf. Lawyers and CPAs, Exec. Svc. Corps (exec. com. 2005-07), Merion Cricket Club, Yale Club N.Y.C., IRS Nat. Advocacy Panel 2007-, Episcopalian. Home: 1218 Round Hill Rd Bryn Mawr PA 19010-1938 Office: Ballard Spahr Andrews et al 1735 Market St Ste 5100 Philadelphia PA 19103-7599 Office Phone: 215-864-8327.

MCQUOWN, JUDITH HERSHKOWITZ, writer, consultant, financial planner; b. NYC, Apr. 8, 1941; d. Frederick Ephraim and Pearl (Rosenberg) H.; m. Michael L. McQuown, Jan. 13, 1969 (div. 1980); m. Harrison Roth, Dec. 8, 1985 (dec. 1997); m. Harold Allen Lightman, Jan. 2, 2005 (dec. 2007). AB, Hunter Coll., 1963; postgrad., N.Y. Inst. Fin., NYC, 1965-67. Chief underwriting div. mcpl. securities City of N.Y., 1972-73; CEO Judith H. McQuown & Co., Inc., NYC, 1973—. Author: Tax Shelters That Work for Everyone, 1979, The Fashion Survival Manual, 1981, Playing the Takeover Market, 1982, How to Profit After You Inc. Yourself, 1985, Keep One Suitcase Empty: The Bargain Shopper's Guide to the Finest Factory Outlets in the British Isles, 1987, Keep One Suitcase Empty: The Bargain Shopper's Guide to the Finest Factory Outlets in Europe, 1988, Use Your Own Corporation to Get Rich, 1991, Inc. Yourself: How to Profit by Setting Up Your Own Corporation, 10th edit., 2002, 1,001 Tips for Living Well with Diabetes: Firsthand Advice That Really Works, 2004; contbg. editor: Boardroom Reports, Physician's Fin. News, Physician's Guide to Money Mgmt.; contbr. seminars The Learning Annex, seminars The Discovery Ctr., seminars Boston Ctr. for Adult Edn., seminars First Class, seminars Learning Connection, seminars Knowledge Network. Mem. Am. Soc. Journalists and Authors. Home and Office: One Gracie Ter Apt 9C New York NY 10028

MCRAE, HAMILTON EUGENE, III, lawyer; b. Midland, Tex., Oct. 29, 1937; s. Hamilton Eugene and Adrian (Hagaman) McR.; m. Betty Hawkins, Aug. 27, 1960; children: Elizabeth Ann, Stephanie Adrian, Scott Hawkins BSEE, U. Ariz., 1961; student, USAF Electronics Sch., 1961-62; postgrad., U. Redlands, Calif., 1962-63; JD with honors and distinction, U. Ariz., 1967; LHD (hon.), Sterling Coll., 1992; vis. fellow, Darwin Coll. and Martin Ctr., Cambridge U., Eng., 1996-97. Bar: Ariz. 1967, U.S. Supreme Ct. 1979; cert. real estate specialist, Ariz. Elec. engr. Salt River Project, Phoenix, 1961; assoc. Jennings, Strouss & Salmon, Phoenix, 1967-71, ptnr., 1971-85, chmn. real estate dept., 1980-85, mem. policy com., 1982-85, mem. fin. com., 1981-85, chmn. bus. devel. com., 1982-85; ptnr. and co-founder Stuckey & McRae, Phoenix, 1985—; co-founder, chmn. bd. Republic Cos., Phoenix, 1985—. Magistrate Paradise Valley, Ariz., 1983-85; juvenile referee Superior Ct., 1983-85; pres., dir. Phoenix Realty & Trust Co., 1970—; officer Indsl. Devel. Corp. Maricopa County, 1972-86; instr. and lectr. in real estate; officer, bd. dirs. other corps.; adj. prof. Frank Lloyd Wright Sch. Architecture, Scottsdale, Ariz., 1989—; instr. Ariz. State U. Coll. Architecture and Environ. Design; lead instr. ten-state-bar seminar on Advanced Real Estate Transactions, 1992; evaluation com. for cert. real estate specialist Ariz. Bar, 1994-96; mem. real estate adv. commn. Ariz. Bar, 1996—. Author: Development in Third World Countries, 2002; exec. prodr. film documentary on relief and devel. in Africa, 1990; contbr. articles to profl. jours. Elder Valley Presbyn. Ch., Scottsdale, Ariz., 1973-75, 82-85, 96-98, chair evangelism com. 1973-74, corp. pres., 1974-75, 84-85, trustee, 1973-75, 82-85, chmn. exec. com., 1984, mem. mission com. 1993—, chmn. 1998; trustee Upward Found., Phoenix, 1977-80, trustee, Valley Presbyn. Found., 1982-83, Ariz. Acad., 1971—; trustee, mem. exec. com. Phi Gamma Delta Ednl. Found., Washington, 1974-84; trustee Phi Gamma Delta Internat., 1984-86; bd. dirs. Archon, 1986-87, Hall of Fame Ariz., 1999; founder, trustee, pres. McRae Found., 1980—; bd. dirs. Food for Hungry Inc. (Internat. Relief), 1985-95, exec. com., 1986-95, chmn. bd. dirs., 1987-92; chmn. bd. dirs. Food for Hungry Internat., 1993-95, pres. adv. coun., 1995—, mem. building com., 1999—; trustee, mem. exec. com. Ariz. Mus. Sci. and Tech., 1984—, 1st v.p., 1985-86, pres., 1986-88, chmn. bd. dirs., 1988-90, exec. com. 1984-90, exhibits com. 1990—, strategic planning com., 1999—, svc. recognition 1999; Lambda Alpha Internat. Hon. Land Econs. Soc, 1988-98; sec.-treas. Ariz. State U. Coun. for Design Excellence, 1989-90, bd. dirs. 1988-99, pres. 1990-91, trustee 1999—; mem. Crisis Nursery Office of the Chair, 1988-89, Maricopa C.C. Found., 1988-2002, bd. dirs., 1988-2002, sec. 1990-91, 2d v.p. 1993-94, 1st v.p. and pres. elect 1994-95, pres. 1995-96, mem. Elsner scholarship com., 1999—, web site com., 1999, capital campaign cabinet, 1995-96, 98-99, mem. of chair, 1998-99, mem. nominating com., 1997—, deferred gifts com., 1999—, strategic planning com., 2000—, mem. adv. bd., 2002--; mem. Phoenix Cmty. Alliance, 1988-90, Interchurch Ctr. Corp., 1987-90, Western Art Assocs., bd. dirs., 1989-91, Phoenix Com. on Fgn. Rels., 1988-99, U. Ariz. Pres.'s Club, 1984—, chmn., 1991-92; bd. dirs. Econ. Club of Phoenix, 1987—, sec.-treas., 1991-92, v.p., 1992-93, pres. 1993-94; bd. dirs. Ctrl. Ariz. Shelter Svcs., 1995—, bd. dir., Ariz. Cmty. Found., 1996—, invest. com., 1996—, chair, 2000-, exec. com. 1997—, treas. 1997—, chair nominating com. 1997-98, vice chair bd. dirs., 1999—, chair devel. com., 1999—, advancement com., 1999-2000, chair, 1999—, fin. and adminstrn. com. 1999—; founding mem. Alliance linking poverty and homelessness, 1996-98, bd. dirs., 1996-98, mem. exec. com., 1996-98, co-chair long range planning com., 1997-98; mem. adv. bd. Help Wanted USA, 1990-92; vol. fund raiser YMCA, Salvation Army, others; bd. dirs. Frank Lloyd Wright Found., 1992—, chair fin. com. 1997-98, chmn. bd. dirs., 1998—; mem. Taliesin Coun., 1985—; bd. dirs. Taliesin Arch., 1992-98, Taliesin Conservation Com. (Wis.), 1992—; founding mem. Frank Lloyd Wright Soc., 1993—; mem. fin. com. Kyl for Congress, 1985-92, bd. dir. campaign bd. Kyl for U.S. Senate, 1993-94, 99—; Senator Kyl Council, 1995-98; campaign com. Symington for Gov. '90, 1989-90, mem. gubernatorial adv. bd., 1990-91; mem. Gov.'s Selection Com. for State Revenue Dir., 1993; mem. bond com. City of Phoenix, 1987-88; mem. Ariz. State U. Coun. of 100, 1985-89, investment com., 1985-89; bd. govs. Twelve Who Care Hon Kachina, 1991; mem. adv. coun. Maricopa County Sports Authority, 1989-93; mem. Ariz. Coalition for Tomorrow, 1990-92; founding mem., bd. dirs. Waste Not Inc., 1990-94, pres., 1990-92, chmn., 1992-94, adv. bd. 1996—; bd. dirs. Garden Homes at Teton Pines Home Owners Assn., 1996—, v.p., 2000-04, pres., 2004—; selected as bearer for the Olympic Torch Relay Team, 1996; adv. bd. KAET TV PBS (Channel 8) 1999-2000. 1st lt. USAF, 1961-64. Recipient various mil. awards; 1st place award Ariz. Bar exam, 1967; named to Ariz. Hall of Fame, 1999. Mem. ABA, AIEE, AIME, Ariz. Bar Assn., Maricopa County Bar Assn., U. Ariz. Alumni Assn., Nat. Soc. Fund Raising Execs. (Philanthropy award Ariz. chpt. 1991, 97), Clan McRae Soc. N.Am. Phoenix Exec. Club, Internat. Platform Assn., Am. Friends of the U. Cambridge (Eng.), Jackson Hole Racquet Club, Teton Pines Country Club, Tau Beta Pi. Republican. Address: Republic Cos 11811 N Tatum Blvd Ste 1005 Phoenix AZ 85028-1617 Home Phone: 480-991-0603; Office Phone: 602-494-0202. Personal E-mail: repcos@aol.com, hemcrae3@aol.com.

MCRAITH, JOHN JEREMIAH, bishop; b. Hutchinson, Minn., Dec. 6, 1934; s. Arthur Luke and Marie (Hanley) McR. BA, Loras Coll., Dubuque, Iowa, 1956. Ordained priest Diocese of New Ulm, Minn., 1960; assoc. pastor St. Mary's Ch., Sleepy Eye, Minn., 1960—64, 1968—71; pastor St. Michael's Ch., Milroy, Minn., 1964—67, St. Leo's Ch., St. Leo, Minn., 1967—68; dir. Nat. Cath. Rural Life, Des Moines, 1971—78; vicar gen. Diocese of New Ulm, Minn., 1978—82; ordained bishop, 1982; bishop Diocese of Owensboro, Ky., 1982—2009, bishop emeritus Ky., 2009—. Roman Catholic. Home: 501 W 5th St Owensboro KY 42301-0765 Office: 600 Locust St Owensboro KY 42301-2130 Office Phone: 270-683-1545 ext 339.*

MCREYNOLDS, MARY ARMILDA, lawyer; b. Carthage, Mo., Sept. 2, 1946; d. Allen and Virginia Madeliene (Hensley) McR. BA, Mt. Holyoke Coll., South Hadley, Mass., 1968; JD, Georgetown U., Washington, DC, 1971; LLM, Harvard U., Cambridge, Mass., 1973. Bar: DC 1971, US Ct. Appeals (DC cir.) 1971, US Ct. Appeals (2d cir.) 1975, US Ct. Appeals (4th cir.) 1979, US Ct. Appeals (1st, 5th, 6th, 9th 10th cirs.) 1980, US Supreme Ct. 1980, US Ct. Appeals (11th cir.) 1981, US Ct. Appeals (3rd, 7th, 8th cirs.) 1983, US Ct. Appeals (fed. cir.) 1988. Law clk. U.S. Ct. Appeals for D.C. cir., 1971-72; assoc. Wilmer, Cutler & Pickering, Washington, 1973-77; sr. trial atty. civil divsn. fed. program br. U.S. Dept. Justice, 1977-79, mem. appellate staff, 1979-81; ptnr. McReynolds & Mutterperl, Washington, 1981-83, Wilner & Scheiner, Washington, 1983-89, Haley, Bader & Potts, 1989-92; pvt. practice Washington, 1992—. Bd. dirs., gen. counsel Washington Bach Consort, 1977-81, 1985-92, pres. 1981-82, 89-90; pres. bd. dirs., ArtsAm., 1993—; chancellor, All Sts. Ch., Charg Chase, Md., 2006-09; sec., mem. synod coun. Anglican Dist. Va., 2007-, bd. dirs. Am. Anglican Coun, 2008-. Contbr. articles to profl. jours. Chancellor, sec., vestry mem. All Saints' Ch., Chevy Chase, Md., 2006—. Mem. ABA, Kenwood Club, City Tavern Club. Anglican. Home: 2101 Connecticut Ave NW Apt 26 Washington DC 20008-1754 Office: 10th Fl 1050 Connecticut Ave NW Washington DC 20036 Office Phone: 202-429-1770. Business E-Mail: marymcreynolds@mac.com.

MCREYNOLDS, NEIL LAWRENCE, management consultant; b. Seattle, July 27, 1934; s. Dorr E. and Margaret (Gillies) McR.; m. Nancy Joyce Drew, June 21, 1957; children: Christopher, Bonnie. BA in Journalism, U. Wash., 1956, postgrad. bus. and fin., 1973-76. Assoc. editor Bellevue (Wash.) Am., 1956-60, editor, 1960-67; press sec. to Gov. Dan Evans State of Wash., Olympia, 1967-73; N.W. regional mgr. for pub. rels. and pub. affairs ITT Corp., Seattle, 1973-80; v.p. corp. rels. Puget Sound Power & Light, Bellevue, 1980-87, sr. v.p., 1987-95; prin. McReynolds Assocs., Seattle, 1995-97; v.p. external affairs Kaiser/Group Health, Seattle, 1997-99; pres. McReynolds Assocs., Inc. (Donworth/McReynolds), Seattle, 1999—; strategic dir. Buerk Dale Victor, Seattle, 2002—. Bd. dirs. HomeStreet Bank, Seattle, 1986—2009, Eastern Wash. U., Cheney, 2000—; chmn. exec. adv. com. Edison Electric Inst., 1984—88; rsch. adv. coun. Electric Power Rsch. Inst., 1989—90; adj. prof. Grad. Sch. Bus. U. Wash., 2002—. Nat. pres. Electric Info. Coun., 1988; chmn. bd. trustees Bellevue CC, 1976—77; chmn. bd. dirs. Leadership Tomorrow, Seattle, 1987, Fred Hutchinson Cancer Rsch. Ctr., 1993—95, Seattle-King County Econ. Devel. Coun., 1994, Eastside Bus. Roundtable, Bellevue, 2003—04; pres. Seattle Ctr. Found., 1979—80, Horizon House, Seattle, 2007—09; bd. dirs. Seattle Symphony, 1980—89, Ind. Colls. of Wash., 1984—95, Corp. Coun. for Arts, 1985—94, Mus. History and Industry, 1995—2006, Wash. Nat. Pks. Fund, 1995—2000, Seattle Repertory Theatre, 1996—2002, Wash. Dental Svc. Found., 2002—, United Way of King County, 2002—08; state chmn. Nature Conservancy, 1988—90; chmn. King County 2000, 1988—90; mem. Wash. State Commn. on Trial Cts., 1990; chair U. Wash. Bus. and Econ. Devel. Ctr., 1996—98. Named Citizen of Yr., Bellevue, One of Wash. State's Three Outstanding Young Men; recipient Pres. medal Pacific Luth. U. Mem. Pub. Rels. Soc. Am. (accredited; lifetime achievement award, 2003), N.W. Elec. Light and Power Assn. (pres. 1982-83), Greater Seattle C. of C. (officer 1979-81), Soc. Profl. Journalists, Rainier Club (trustee 1995-01, v.p. 1997-98, pres. 1999-2000), Heritage Soc. (pres. 2004-05, 2007-08), Overlake Golf and Country Club (trustee 1993-96), Rotary (pres. Downtown Seattle Club 1991-92). Episcopalian. Avocations: golf, hiking, skiing, photography, mountain climbing. Home: 14315 SE 45th St Bellevue WA 98006 Office Phone: 206-621-7272. Personal E-mail: nmcreyolds@seanet.com.

MCREYNOLDS, PATRICIA RANDOLPH, retired education educator; d. Florence Ann Randolph; m. Stephen Jay Randolph, Dec. 21, 1974; children: Stephanie Ann, Sara McReynolds Payne. BS in Edn., U.

Mo., Columbia, 1970; MS, Western Ill. U., Macomb, 1971. Asst. prof. Culver-Stockton Coll., Canton, Mo., 1971—77; adaptive phys. edn. Pike-Lincoln Co. Coop., Eolia, Mo., 1981—82, spl. edn. tchr., 1984—87; edn. resource tchr. Pike Co. R-II Sch. Dist., Louisiana, Mo., 1982—84; ednl. diagnostician Ft. Zumwalt Sch. Dist., O'Fallon, Mo., 1987—2005; adj. prof. Lindenwood U., St. Charles, Mo., 1998. Trustee Heritage House Corp., St. Louis, 2005—08. State bd. dirs. Mo. Nat. Edn. Assn., Jefferson City, 2002—05. Avocations: travel, sports, reading. Home: 1244 Creve Coeur Mill Rd Saint Louis MO 63146 Personal E-mail: mcrmom7780@yahoo.com. Business E-Mail: pmcreynolds@lindenwood.edu.

MCREYNOLDS, STEPHEN PAUL, lawyer; b. Sacramento, Oct. 16, 1938; s. Leslie N. and Mary C. McR.; m. Chodi D. Greeno, Sept. 29, 1970. AB, U. Calif., Davis, 1969; JD, U. Calif., 1972. Bar: Calif. 1972. Sole practice, Sunnyvale, Calif., 1972—. With USN, 1956—62. Mem.: Mensa Internat. Office: 1111 W El Camino Real # 329 Sunnyvale CA 94087-1056

MCROBBIE, MICHAEL ALEXANDER, academic administrator, computer scientist, educator; b. Melbourne, Australia, Oct. 11, 1950; s. Alexander Hewitt and Joyce Victoria (Gair) McRobbie; m. Andrea Shirley Gibson, Dec. 22, 1973 (dec. 2003); children: Josephine Elizabeth Joyce, Lucien Richard Vernon, Arabella Diana Grace; m. Laurie Lucile Burns Gray, Aug. 7, 2005; children: Carol Charles Burns Gray, Margaret Burns Gray. BA with honors I, U. Queensland, 1974; PhD, Australian Nat. U., 1979; DSc (hon.), U. Queensland, 2007. Rsch. fellow La Trobe U., Melbourne, 1979-81, U. Melbourne, 1981-83, Australian Nat. U., Canberra, ACT, 1983-87; head Automated Reasoning Project, 1985-91; reader, exec. dir. Ctr. for Info. Sci. Rsch., 1987-90, prof., exec. dir., 1990-96; CEO CRC for Advanced Computational Systems, 1992-96; v.p. info. tech., chief info. officer Ind. U., Bloomington, 1997—2006, prof. computer sci., philosophy, informatics, cognitive sci., 1997—, v.p. rsch., 2003—06, interim provost, v.p. academic affairs, 2006—07, pres., 2007—; prof., computer tech. Ind. U.-Purdue U. Indpls., 1997—, prof., philosophy, 2007—; sr. advisor, networking Chinese Acad. Sci., 2000—. Vis. prof. U. Kaiserlautern, Germany, 1987; Fulbright sr. fellow Argonne Nat. Lab., 1988. Co-author: (book) Automated Theorem Proving in Non-Classical Logics, 1986; author, co-author, editor: over 100 papers, articles, reports and books. Recipient Tech. Trailblazer award, Tech-Point, 2004, 10th Anniversary award, APAN, 2006, Sagamore of Wabash award, 2007. Mem.: IEEE (hon.), Australian Acad. Humanities (hon. fellow 2007), Assn. Computer Machinery, Skyline Club, Columiba Club, Commonwealth Club, Univ. House. Avocations: art, book collecting, weightlifting, cricket. Office: Office of Pres Ind U 107 S Indiana Ave Bloomington IN 47405 Office Phone: 812-855-4613. Business E-Mail: iupres@indiana.edu.*

MC ROSTIE, CLAIR NEIL, economics professor; b. Owatonna, Minn., Dec. 16, 1930; s. Neil Hale and Myrtle Julia (Peterson) McR.; m. Ursula Anne Schwieger, Aug. 29, 1968. BSBA cum laude, Gustavus Adolphus Coll., 1952; MA in Mktg., Mich. State U., 1953; PhD in Fin., U. Wis., 1963; postgrad., U. Minn., 1971-72, Am. Grad. Sch. Internat. Mgmt., 1980-81; cert., Coll. for Fin. Planning, 1990. Cert. fin. planner. Faculty Gustavus Adolphus Coll., St. Peter, Minn., 1958-96; emeritus prof., 1996—; chmn. dept. econs. and bus. Gustavus Adolphus Coll., 1967-83, chmn., mem. various coms., 1971-96; teaching asst. Sch. Commerce, U. Wis., 1960-62. Rsch. fellow Fed. Res. Bank, Chgo., 1962—63; lectr. European divsn. U. Md., 1966—67; vis. prof. Am. Grad. Sch. Internat. Mgmt., 1980—81; pres. Minn. World Trade Week, Inc., 1987; bd. dirs. Rite Care Childhood Lang. Clinic. Editor: Global Resources: Perspectives and Alternatives, 1978, The Future of the Market Ecomomy, 1979. Congregation pres. First Luth. Ch., St. Peter, Minn., 1972-73, 93, chmn. pastoral call com., 1968-69, chmn. staffing com., 1975, mem. ch. council, 1968-74, 89-93; chmn. social ministry com. Minn. Synod, Luth. Ch. Am., 1975, mem. long range planning com. Southwestern Minn. Synod; chmn. Rep. council arts professions, scis., Minn., 1968-70, co-chmn. state task force on Vietnam, 1968; mem. adv. commn. Minn. Dept. Manpower Services, 1967-71; mem. North Central Regional Manpower Adv. Com.; bd. dirs. Midwest China Resource Study Center; del. White House Conf. Aging, 1971. Served with U.S. Army, 1954-56. Recipient Leavey Found. award Freedoms Found., Valley Forge, Pa.; rsch. fellow Fed. Res. Bank Chgo., 1962-63. Mem. Fin. Execs. Inst., Fin. Planners Assn., Minn. Econs. Assn. (bd. dirs. 1974-75, 79-80), Masons (master, Royal Arch chpt., commandry Zuhrah Shrine Temple, Scottish Rite, Knight Commdr. Court Honor), Royal Order Scotland, Alpha Kappa Psi, Iota Delta Gamma, Sigma Epsilon. Lutheran. Avocations: bird watching, backpacking, fitness and health. Home: 1208 Pine Pointe Curv Saint Peter MN 56082-1344

MCSAVANEY, RAYMOND S., photojournalist; Co-founder Owens Valley Photog. Workshops, 1975—91; founder McSavaney Photo Workshops, 1991—; also instr. The Ansel Adams Gallery Photography Workshops and the John Sexton Workshops. Books: Explorations, 1992 (named One of 50 Best Books of Yr., Am. Inst. Graphic Arts), (with John Sexton, Arthur Ollman) Recollections: Three Decades of Photography, 2006; photos pub. in West of Eden: A History of the Art and Literature of Yosemite, View Camera, Outdoor Photographer and numerous other publications. Office: Ray McSavaney Photo Workshops Studio 402 1984 N Main St Los Angeles CA 90031-2491 Office Phone: 323-225-1730.

MCSHAN, WILLIAM MICHAEL, medical educator; s. Chester Lee and Oleta McShan; m. Carolyn Ann McCullough; 1 child, Katharine Elizabeth. PhD, Baylor Coll. Medicine, 1988. Asst. prof. U. Okla. Health Scis. Ctr., 2003—05, assoc. prof., 2008—. Office: Univ Okla Coll Pharmacy 1110 N Stonewall Ave Oklahoma City OK 73117 Business E-Mail: william-mcshan@ouhsc.edu.

MCSHANE, IAN, actor; b. Blackburn, Lancashire, Eng., Sept. 29, 1942; s. Harry McShane; m. Ruth Post (div. 1976); m. Suzan Farmer, 1965 (div. 1968); m. Gwen Humble, 1981; children: Kate, Morgan. Actor: (films) The Pleasure Girls, 1965, Sky West and Crooked, 1966, If It's Tuesday, This Must Be Belgium, 1969, Battle of Britain, 1969, Pussycat, Pussycat, I Love You, 1970, Tam Lin, 1970, Villain, 1971, Freelance, 1971, Sitting Target, 1972, Left Hand of Gemini, 1972, The Last of Sheila, 1973, Ransom, 1975, Journey Into Fear, 1975, The Fifth Musketeer, 1979, Yesterday's Hero, 1979, The Great Riviera Bank Robbery, 1979, Cheaper to Keep Her, 1980, Exposed, 1983, Torchlight, 1984, Ordeal by Innocence, 1984, Too Scared to Scream, 1985, Grand Larceny, 1987, Con Man, 1992, Sexy Beast, 2000, Bollywood Queen, 2002, Agent Cody Banks, 2003, Nemesis Game, 2003, Nine Lives, 2005, Scoop, 2006, We Are Marshall, 2006, The Golden Compass, 2007, (voice only) Kung Fu Panda, 2008, Death Race, 2008, (voice only) Coraline, 2009,: (TV series) You Can't Win, 1966, Wuthering Heights, 1967, Bare Essence, 1983, Lovejoy, 1986, Dallas, 1989, Madson, 1996, Deadwood, 2004—06 (Golden Globe award for Best Actor TV series - drama, 2005), Kings, 2009—; (TV miniseries) Roots, 1977, Jesus of Nazareth, 1977, Life of Shakespeare, 1978, Disraeli, 1979, Marco Polo, 1982, Evergreen, 1985, A.D., 1985, War and Remembrance, 1988, Trust, 2003; (TV films) The Wild and the Willing, 1962, Funny Noises with Their Mouths, 1963, Funeral Games, 1968, Whose Life Is It Anyway?, 1972, The Lives of Jenny Dolan, 1975, Code Name: Diamond Head, 1977, The Pirate, 1978, High Tide, 1980, The Letter, 1982, Grace Kelly, 1983, Braker, 1985, Rocket to the Moon, 1986, The Murders in the Rue Morgue, 1986, The Great Escape II: The Untold Story, 1988, Young Charlie Chaplin, 1989, Dick Francis: Twice Shy, 1989, Dick Francis: In the Frame, 1989, Dick Francis: Blood Sport, 1989, Perry Mason: The Case of the Desperate Deception, 1990, Columbo: Rest in Peace, Mrs. Columbo, 1990, White Goods, 1994, Soul Survivors, 1995, Babylon 5: The River of Souls, 1998, D.R.E.A.M. Team, 1999, Man and Boy, 2002. Office: Internat Creative Mgmt 76 Oxford St London W1N 0AX England*

MCSHANE, JOSEPH MICHAEL, academic administrator, priest; b. NYC, June 19, 1949; s. Owen Patrick and Catherine Veronica (Shelley) McS. AB, AM, Boston Coll., 1972; MDiv, STM, Jesuit Sch. Theology, Berkeley, Calif., 1977; PhD, U. Chgo., 1981. Ordained priest Roman Cath. Ch., 1977. English tchr. Canisius H.S., Buffalo, 1972-74; asst. prof. religious studies LeMoyne Coll., Syracuse, NY, 1982-87, assoc. prof. religious studies, 1987-91, prof., 1991-92, chairperson, 1991-92; dean Fordham U., Bronx, NY, 1992-98, prof. theology, 1992-98, pres., 2003—; pres., prof. theology U. Scranton, 1998—2003. Vis. prof. history Loyola House, Berkley, Mich., 1986—87. Author: Sufficiently Radical: Catholicism, Progressivism and the Bishops' Program of 1919, 1986; author chpt. to book; creator video: The Pilgrimage of the People of God: An Introduction to the Study of Church History, 1991; contbr. articles to profl. jours. Bd. dirs. U. Scranton, Pa., Scranton Prep. Sch., Pa., Fordham U., NYC, Fordham Prep. Sch., Bronx, NY, Regis H.S., NYC, Canisius Coll., Buffalo, St. Joseph's Prep. Sch., Phila. Recipient First prize, Cath. Press Assn., 1992. Mem.: Am. Soc. Ch. History, Am. Cath. Hist. Assn., Phi Beta Kappa. Democrat. Roman Catholic. Office: Office of Pres Fordham U Bronx NY 10458 Office Phone: 718-817-3000. Business E-Mail: jmcshane@fordham.edu.

MCSHANE, SYBIL BRIGHAM, retired library director, librarian; Dir. reference & law svcs. Vt. Dept. Librs., Montpelier, info. systems dir., state libr., 1997—2008. Mem.: ALA, Vt. Libr. Assn., Chief Officers of State Libr. Agencies (legis. com. 2004—06). Office: Vt Dept Libraries Pavillion Office Bldg 109 State St Montpelier VT 05609 Office Phone: 802-828-3265. Office Fax: 802-828-2199. E-mail: sybil.mcshane@dol.state.vt.us.

MCSHEFFERTY, JOHN, retired research executive personal care, industry executive consultant; b. Akron, Ohio, Mar. 14, 1929; s. John and Jean McS.; m. Glenna Gloria Childs, Apr. 18, 1959; children: John III, Amy Childs. BSc, U. Glasgow, 1953, PhD, 1957. Various rsch. positions Sterling Winthrop Rsch. Inst., Rensselaer, NY, 1957-62; dir. pharm. devel. Ortho Pharm. Corp. divsn. Johnson and Johnson, Raritan, NJ, 1962-75; dir. rsch. Janssen R & D, Inc. divsn. Johnson & Johnson, Piscataway, NJ, 1975-77; v.p. R & D family products Internat. Playtex, Paramus, NJ, 1977-79; pres. Gillette Rsch. Inst., Gaithersburg, Md., 1979-97; ret., 1997. Cons. in field. Fellow Royal Pharm. Soc. of Gt. Britain; mem. Indsl. Rsch. Inst. (bd. dirs. 1988-92, emeritt com. 1998—), Am. Acad. Dermatology, Am. Mgmt. Assn. (bd. dirs. 1994-97), Am. Chem. Soc., Am. Pharm. Assn., N.Y. Acad. Scis., Soc. Cosmetic Chemists, Dirs. Indsl. Rsch., Assn. Rsch. Dirs., Rotary, Sigma Xi. Personal E-mail: jmcs2@roadrunner.com.

MC SHEFFREY, GERALD RAINEY, architect, educator, city planner, author; b. Belfast, Ireland, Aug. 13, 1931; s. Hugh and Jane (Piggot) McS.; m. Norma Isabella Lowry, June 4, 1956; children: Laurence, Niall, Aidan. Student, Belfast Coll. Tech., 1950-56; Diploma in Architecture, Univ. Coll., U. London, 1959; Diploma in Civic Design, U. Edinburgh, Scotland, 1963. Archtl. asst. various archtl. firms, Belfast, 1950-57; design architect Munce and Kennedy, Belfast, 1957-62; architect/planner Liverpool (Eng.) City Planning Dept. and Livingston New Town, 1963-65; asso. partner James Munce Partnership, Belfast, 1965-68; prin. planning officer (design) Belfast City Planning Dept., 1968-71; prof. architecture U. Kans., 1971-73, dir. archtl. studies, 1976-79; Belfast regional architect, dir. devel. No. Ireland Housing Exec., 1973-76; prof. architecture, dean Coll. Architecture, Planning and Design, Ill. Inst. Tech., 1979-82; dean Coll. Architecture and Environ. Design Ariz. State U., Tempe, 1982-86, prof. architecture, 1988-98; v.p. Ariz. State U., West Campus, Phoenix, 1985-88; prof. and dean emeritus, 1998—. Vis. fellow Princeton (N.J.) U., 1989; external examiner in urban design and landscape studies U. Edinburgh, 1973-76 Author: (with James Munce Partnership) Londonderry Area Plan, 1968, Planning Derry: Planning and Politics in Northern Ireland, 2000. Fulbright award, 1965 Fellow Royal Inst. Brit. Architects, Royal Town Planning Inst.; mem. AIA. Episcopalian.

MCSHERRY, J. PATRICE, political science professor; d. William P. and Bobette H. McSherry; m. Raúl Molina Mejía. PhD, Grad. Sch. and U. Ctr., CUNY. Asst. prof. polit. sci. and internat. rels. SUNY, New Paltz, 1994—97; prof. polit. sci. LI U., Bklyn., 1997—, dir. Latin Am. & Caribbean studies program, 1998—. Assoc. editor Jour. Third World Studies, Ga., 1999—; editl. adv. bd. Social Justice Jour., San Francisco, 2004—. Author: (non-fiction book) Predatory States: Operation Condor and Covert War in Latin America (Choice award, 2006), Incomplete Transition: Military Power and Democracy in Argentina. Recipient David Newton award Excellence Tchg., 2008; fellowship, Fulbright Com., Argentina, 1992, Fulbright Com., Uruguay, 2005. Mem.: Am. Polit. Sci. Assn., Latin Am. Studies Assn. Office: Long Island Univ 1 University Plz Brooklyn NY 11201 Office Fax: 718-488-1086. Business E-Mail: pmcsherr@liu.edu.

MCSHERRY, WILLIAM JOHN, JR., lawyer, consultant; b. NYC, Oct. 28, 1947; s. William John Sr. and Mary Elizabeth (Dunphy) McS.; m. Elizabeth Ann Crosby, June 8, 1974; children: Brendan, Sean, Rory. AB cum laude, Fordham U., 1969; JD cum laude, Harvard U., 1973. Bar: N.Y. 1974, U.S. Dist. Ct. (so. dist.) N.Y. 1975, U.S. Ct. Appeals (2d cir.) 1977. Assoc. Spengler, Carlson, Gubar, Brodsky & Frischling, NYC, 1973-78, ptnr., 1979-88, Bryan, Cave, McPheeters & McRoberts, NYC, 1989-91, Battle Fowler LLP, NYC, 1991—2000. Exec. dir. U.S. Football League, N.Y.C., 1985-86; chmn. litigation dept. Battle Fowler, 1992-96, Arent Fox LLP, 2000-06, Crowell & Moring, 2006-; chmn. Arent Fox L.t. Dept., 2004-06, exec. com., 02-06; pres., bd. dirs. Playtex Mktg. Corp.; bd. dirs. Questron Tech., Inc. Author: (with others) Tender Offer Regulation: The Federal SEC's Challenge and New York State's Response. Derivatives Risk and Responsibility, 1996, Attorney Client Privilege in tge Second Circuit, 1998. Mem. Zoning Bd. Appeals, Village of Larchmont, N.Y., 1988-91, dep. mayor, 1992-98, bd. trustees, 1991-98. Served with USAR, 1970-75. Mem. ABA (litigation, antitrust, entertainment and sports, corp. banking and bus. law sects., subcom. litigation 1940 Act; vice-chair com. alt. dispute resolution), Assn. of Bar of City of N.Y. (mem. 1979-82 com. state cts. superior jurisdiction, 1987-90, com. arbitration and alternative dispute resolution, mem. sports law com. 1998—), Fed. Bar Council, Council N.Y. Law Assocs. (bd. dirs., treas. 1975), Phi Beta Kappa. Roman Catholic. Avocations: community involvement, sports, writing. Home: 2 Summit Ave Larchmont NY 10538-2930 Home Phone: 914-834-7309; Office Phone: 212-895-4207.

MCSLARROW, KYLE E., lobbyist, former federal agency administrator; b. Va., 1960; m. Alison H. McSlarrow. BA, Cornell U., 1982; JD, U. Va., 1985. Asst. to gen. counsel Dept. Army, US Dept. Def., 1985—89; assoc. Hunton & Williams LLP, Washington, 1989—95; dep. chief of staff, chief counsel to majority leaders Bob Dole and Trent Lott US Senate, 1995—97, chief of staff to Senator Paul Coverdell, 1997—2000; nat. chmn. Quayle 2000 Presdl. Campaign, 1998—2000; v.p. polit. and govt. affairs, lead Washington office Grassroots.com, 2000—01; chief of staff to sec. Spencer Abraham US Dept. Energy, Washington, 2001—02, dep. sec., 2002—05; pres., CEO Nat. Cable & Telecom. Assn., Washington, 2005—. Co.-chmn. US-Russia Energy Working Group, 2002—05; mem. Arlington County, Va. Planning Commn., Nat. Security Telecommunications Advisory Com., 2007. Democrat. Office: Nat Cable & Telecom Assn 1724 Massachusetts Ave NW Washington DC 20036 Office Fax: 202-222-2514.

MCSORLEY, RITA ELIZABETH, adult education educator; b. Baraboo, Wis., Feb. 13, 1947; d. Charles Gervase and Bertie Ellen (Baker) Collins; m. William David McSorley III, June 6, 1967; children: William David IV, Kathryn Rita, Stephen Charles, Matthew Thomas. B Liberal Studies, Mary Washington Coll., Fredericksburg, Va., 1988; MEd, U. Va., Charlottesville, 1994. Adult edn. instr. Waipahu (Hawaii) Cmty. Sch. for Adults, 1989-91, literacy coord., 1990-91; dir. religious edn. Marine Meml. Chapel, Quantico, Va., 1992-94; adult edn. instr. Prince William County Schs., Quantico, 1992-93; coord. computer assisted lang. learning project Literacy Coun. No. Va., Falls Church, 1995-96; ednl. cons. Fairfield Lang. Techs., Harrisonburg, Va., 1996-97; adult edn. coord. N.E. Ind. Sch. Sys., San Antonio, 2000—06; ret., 2006; part-time gt. ctr. tng. staff Tex. Ednl. Svc. Ctr. Region XX, 2004—. Lectr. in field. Mem. sch. bd. Quantico Dependent Schs., 1980-82; vol. Boy Scouts Am., Quantico and Pearl City, Hawaii, 1985-97. Mem. TESOL, Commn. on Adult Basic Edn., Daus. Union Vets. Civil War, U. Va. Alumni Assn. Roman Catholic. Avocations: quilting, genealogy, travel.

MC SWAIN, ANGUS STEWART, JR., retired law educator; b. Bryan, Tex., Nov. 26, 1923; s. Angus Stewart and Lois (Pipkin) McS.; m. Betty Ann McCartney, June 3, 1956 (dec. May 30, 2002); 1 child, Angus Earl. BS in Civil Engring., Tex. A. and M. U., 1947; LLB, Baylor U., 1949; LL.M., U. Mich., 1951. Bar: Tex. 1949. Mem. faculty Baylor U. Law Sch., 1949—, prof. law, 1956—, dean, 1965-84, ret., 1994. Mem. panel arbitrators Fe. Mediation and Conciliation Service. Author: (with Wendorf) Cases and Materials on Texas Trusts and Probate, 1965, Supplementary Cases and Materials on Property, 1965, 78, (with Norvell and Simpkins) Cases and Materials for Texas Land Practice, 1968. Served to 1st lt., C.E. AUS, 1943-46. Mem. ABA, Tex.Bar Assn. (chmn. family law sect. 1967-69, chmn. com. on standards of admission 1972-73, 77-79), Tau Beta Pi, Phi Alpha Delta Home: 4600 Kenny Ln Waco TX 76710-2059

MCSWAIN, BYRDIE ENGLE, laboratory scientist, immunohematologist; b. Ethel, Ark., Oct. 13, 1939; d. James Marvin and Katherine Engle (Martin) McSwain. BS, U. Ark., 1968; BS in Med. Tech., U. Ark. Sch. Medicine, 1969; MS, U. Ctrl. Ark., 1973; Specialist in Blood Banking, U. Ark. Med. Scis., 1976. Cert. in regulatory affairs (RAPS). Supr. blood bank Univ. Ark. Med. Scis., Little Rock, clin. instr.; dir. tech. svcs., dir. product mgmt. ARC Blood Svcs., dir. transplantation svcs., dir. regulatory affairs, South Ctrl. area dir. tech. and regulatory svcs., acting area dir. quality assurance. Contbr. 13 articles to profl. jours. Grad. scholar Am. Soc. Med. Tech.; recipient Omicron Sigma award, Am. Soc. for Med. Tech., Outstanding Svc. award, Disting. Alumni award U. Ark. for Med. Scis. Mem. Ark. Soc. Clin. Lab. Scientists (Med. Technologist of Yr.), Am. Assn. Blood Banks, South Ctrl. Assn. Blood Banks (pres., author, editor), Am. Soc. Clin. Lab. Scientists, Clin. Lab. Mgmt. Assn. (pres. Ark. chpt.), Am. Soc. Clin. Pathologists, Regulatory Affairs Profl. Soc., Am. Soc. Quality Assurance, Phi Beta Kappa.

MCSWAIN, ROBERT G., former federal agency administrator; m. June C. McSwain; children: Kristin Ruud, Elizabeth. BSBA, Calif. State U., Fresno, 1969; MPA, U. So. Calif., 1986. Program dir. Ctrl. Valley Indian Health, Inc., Clovis, Calif., 1971—74; exec. dir. Calif. Rural Indian Health Bd., Inc., 1974—76; dir. Calif. Area Office Indian Health Svc. (IHS), US Dept. Health and Human Svc., 1976—84, spl. asst. to dir., 1984, dir. Divsn. Health Manpower and Training, Office Health Programs Rockville, Md., 1984, dep. assoc. dir. Office Adminstrn. and Mgmt., mgmt. analysis officer Office of Dir., acting assoc. dir. Office of Human Resources, 1992—97, dir. Office Mgmt. Ops., 1997, acting dep. dir., 2004—05, dep. dir. health policy, dep. dir. policy Office of Dir., 2005—07, acting dir., 2007—08, dir., 2008—09. Recipient Pres.'s Rank Award for Meritorious Svc., 2002, Pres.'s Rank Award for Disting. Svc., 2006. Mem.: North Fork Rancheria of Mono Indians of Calif.*

MCSWEENEY, FRANCES KAYE, psychology professor; b. Rochester, NY, Feb. 6, 1948; d. Edward William and Elsie Winifred (Kingston) McSweeney. BA, Smith Coll., 1969; MA, Harvard U., 1972, PhD, 1974. Lectr. McMaster U., Hamilton, Ont., Canada, 1973—74; asst. prof. Wash. State U., Pullman, 1974—79, assoc. prof., 1979—83, prof. psychology, 1983—2004, Regents prof. psychology, 2004—, chmn. dept. psychology, 1986—94, vice provost for faculty affairs, 2003—. Cons. in field. Contbr. articles to profl. jours. Woodrow Wilson fellow, Sloan fellow, 1968—69, NIMH fellow, 1973. Fellow: APA, Assn. Behavior Analysis (pres. 2005—06), Assn. for Psychol. Sci.; mem.: Psychonomic Soc., Phi Kappa Phi, Sigma Xi, Phi Beta Kappa. Home: 860 SW Alcora Dr Pullman WA 99163-2053 Office: Wash State U Dept Psychology Pullman WA 99164-4820 Home Phone: 509-332-2320; Office Phone: 509-335-2738. Business E-Mail: fkmcs@wsu.edu.

MCSWEENEY, J. EMMETT, library director; b. Syracuse, NY, Mar. 10, 1955; s. James J and Barbara Thompson McSweeney; m. Moira A Murphy, June 12, 1993; children: Connor G Downing, James P, Liam D. BA in History, LeMoyne Coll., Syracuse, 1977; MLS, SUNY, Buffalo, 1978. Refernce libr. SUNY, NY, 1980—81; humanities libr. Utica Coll., NY, 1981—86; reference cons. Mid-York Libr. Sys., Utica, 1986—87; pub. svc. libr. Post Coll., Waterbury, Conn., 1987—90; circulation divsn. head Silas Bronson Libr., Waterbury, Conn., 1990—2004, libr. dir., 2004—. V.p. Msgr Slocum Divsn. 1 Ancient Order Hibernians, Waterbury, 1994—2008; pres. Waterbury Day Shelter, 1994—95. Roman Catholic. Office: Silas Bronson Libr 267 Grand St Waterbury CT 06702

MCSWEENY, AUSTIN JOHN, psychology educator; b. Berwyn, Ill., May 2, 1946; s. Austin John and Erna Eleanor (De Sollar) McS.; m. Jane Marilee Erickson, Sept. 28, 1968; children: Andrew John, Patrick Michael. BA with honors, U. Wis., 1969; MA, No. Ill. U., 1974, PhD, 1975. Diplomate Am. Bd. Clin. Neuropsychology (examiner cadre 1995—, bd. dirs. 2000—), Am. Bd. Profl. Psychology. Lectr., fellow Northwestern U., Evanston, Ill., 1975-78; asst. prof. W.Va. U., Morgantown, 1978-81; assoc. prof. Med. Coll. Ohio, Toledo, 1981-94, prof. psychiat. and neurology, 1995—, pres. faculty senate, 1999-2001, bd. dirs. Ctr. for Successful Aging, 2000—. Cons. Kennedy Ctr., Morgantown, 1980-81, Toledo VA Med. Ctr., 1981—, Fulton County Health Ctr., Wauseon, Ohio, 1984—; adj. assoc. prof. U. Toledo, 1984; vis. prof. U. Toledo, 1987—, adj. prof., 1995—; cons. editor Jour. Cons. and Clin.

Psychology, 1986-88, Clin. Neuropsychologist, 1987-94, Forensic Neuropsychology, 1997—. Editor: Practical Program Evaluation, 1982, Chronic Obstructive Pulmonary Disease: A Behavioral Perspective, 1988; editor spl. sect. Clin. Neuropsychooogist, 1995—; contbr. articles to profl. jours. Bd. dirs. Presbyn. Youth Home, Clarksburg, W.Va., 1979-81, Apple Tree Nursery Sch., Toledo, 1985-86, Toledo Hearing and Speech Ctr., 1986-87. Leslie Holmes fellow, 1972. Fellow APA (divsn. 40 on computer use, chmn. divsn. 40 ethics com., program com.), Nat. Acad. Neuropsychology (com. on assessment); mem. Am. Acad. Clin. Psychology, N.W. Ohio Soc. Profl. Psychology (pres. 1985-87), N.W. Ohio Psychol. Assn. (pres. 1986-87, Disting. Mem. award 1990), Ohio Acad. Neuropsychologists (pres. 1983-84), Internat. Neuropsychol. Soc. (program com.). Avocations: reading, music, flying, travel. Home: 4146 Northmoor Rd Toledo OH 43606-2231 E-mail: jmcsweeny@mco.edu, jmcsweeny@cs.com.

MCSWEENY, DOROTHY PIERCE, art association administrator; b. Montgomery, Ala., Apr. 17, 1940; d. George Everill and Mary Dorothy Goodrich Pierce; m. William Francis McSweeny, Jan. 20, 1969; children: Ethan Madden Maverick, Terrell Pierce. BA, Brown U., Providence, 1962. Exec. tng. program US Treasury Dept., Washington, 1962—64; officer Agy. Internat. Devel. US Overseas Mission, Saigon, Vietnam, 1964—65; edn. writer The Boston Globe, 1965—67; presdl. oral historian The White Ho., Washington, 1967—69; Lyndon Johnson oral history project U. Tex., Austin, 1969—70; spl. counsel to spkr. US Ho. Reps., Washington, 1970—72; cons. oral historian, 1972—90; vice chair & chair DC Commn. on Arts & Humanities, Washington, 1996—2007, chair emerita, 2008—; chair, vice chair Mid. Atlantic Arts Found., Balt., 1999—. Presdl. trustee John F Kennedy Ctr. Performing Arts, Washington, 1976—81; trustee and v.p. Nat. Symphony Orch., 1981—; founder, trustee and chair Washington Episcopal Sch., Bethesda, Md., 1985—; dir., vice chair Washington Ballet, 1986—; founder and vice chair Discovery Creek Children's Mus., 1993—2008; dir. Nat. Assembly State Art Agencies, Washington, 2002—05; dir., DC chair Nat. Mus. Am. Indian, Washington, 2002—06, DC cultural del., Senegal, 2006—, Ghana, 2006—, South Africa, 2006—, Flag Design Adv. Commn. DC Govt., 2003, John A. Wilson Bldg. Hist. Task Force DC Govt., 2003; dir. Americans for Arts, 2008. Founding dir. Nat. Race for the Cure, 1989—; founding mem. and mem. women's com. Nat. Mus. Women in the Arts, Washington, 1986—2006; co-chair Lombardi Cancer Rsch. Ctr. Georgetown U. Hosp., Washington, 1994—96; inaugural com. Nat. Coun. Negro Women, Washington, 1996—2000; adv. coun. Katzen Arts Ctr. Am. U., 2003—06; bd. dir. Boston U. Sch. Medicine, 1988—2000; founding mem. Lady Bird Johnson Wildflower Rsch. Ctr., Austin, Tex., 1988—2006; founder, chair, vice chair EnvironMentors Nat. Environ. Edn. and Tng. Found., Washington, 1993—2006. Recipient Outstanding Cmty. Svc. award, Boston U., Sch. Medicine, 1995, Founders award, Washington Episcopal Sch., 1999, Lifetime Achievement award, DC Youth Orch., 1999, Patron of the Arts award, Cultural Alliance of Greater Washington, 2000, Laura Phillips Angel of the Arts award, Cathedral Choral Arts Soc., 2004, Lifetime Achievement Art award, Mayor, Washington, 2007; named Outstanding Fundraising Vol., Nat. Capital Philanthropy, 2002, Washingtonian of the Yr., Washingtonian Mag., 1995. Mem.: Fed. City Coun. (trustee 2000—), DC C. of C. (trustee 2000—05), Women's Nat. Dem. Club (life), Order St. John of Jerusalem (comdr. 1987), Internat. Neighbors Club III (pres. and v.p. 1993—). Episcopalian-Eucharistic Lay Minister. Avocations: scuba diving, skiing, hiking, reading, tennis, travel. Home: 5021 Millwood Lane NW Washington DC 20016 Office: DC Commn Arts & Humanities 1371 Harvard St NW Washington DC 20009-4903

MCSWEENY, WILLIAM FRANCIS, petroleum company executive, author; b. Haverhill, Mass., Mar. 31, 1929; s. William Francis and Mary Florence (Doyle) McS.; m. Dorothy Pierce, Jan. 20, 1969; children: William Francis III, Cathy Ann, Ethan Madden Maverick, Terrell Pierce. Reporter, columnist, fgn. corr. Hearst Newspapers, 1943—67; dep. chmn., dir. pub. affairs Dem. Nat. Com., 1967—68; spl. asst. to White House Chief Staff, 1968—69; from sr. exec. v.p. to pres. Occidental Internat. Corp., LA, 1969—91; from exec. v.p. to cons. to chmn. Occidental Petroleum Corp., LA, 1984—91; bd. dirs. Chevy Chase FSB, 1985—2009; dir. Chevy Chese Trust Co., 2005—. Mem. Lloyd's of London; pres.'s envoy to USSR, 1979; mem. Pres.'s Inaugural Com., 1980, 84, 92; Presdl. spl. amb. to Oman, 1980, Bolivia, 1982; Pres.'s com. Korean War Meml., 1987; Pres.'s commr. Exec. Exch., 1976-81; Pres.'s trustee The Kennedy Ctr., 1995—, Pres.'s rep. to Korea, 2000; mem. N.E. White Ho. Fellows Bd.; dir. Collaborative Initiatives MIT; mem. U.S. Com. UNESCO; co-chair NATO 50th Summit; spl. counsel spkr. Ho. of Reps., 1971-72; chmn. Maverick-McSweeny Cattle Co. Author: Go Up for Glory, 1965, Violence Every Sunday, 1966, The Impossible Dream, 1967; contbr. articles to profl. jours Bd. overseers Fletcher Sch. Law and Diplomacy, Tufts U.; bd. advisors Karl F. Landegger Program Internat. Bus. Diplomacy, Sch. Fgn. Svc., Georgetown U.; trustee, pres. Holton Arms; chmn. Washington Episc. Sch., Meridian House Internat., life trustee; mem. World Affairs Coun.; bd. dir. The Atlantic Coun., Overseer Exec. Coun. Fgn. Diplomats, Dept. of State, The Brookings Instn. Coun., 1991-98; vice chmn. Sec. State Fine Arts Commn.; chmn. Ford's Theatre, 1988-95, life trustee; bd. dir. Very Spl. Arts, Arena Stage, Corcoran Gallery Art, Africare, Fed. City Coun., Washington Opera, Folger Shakespeare Theater, Cities in Schs. Nat. Learning Ctr., USO, Arms Control Assn., Nat. Assn. So. Poor, Duke Ellington Sch., Washington Ednl. TV, 1989-95; v.p. Ct. Mary Rose, Portsmouth, Eng.; pres. Commn. to Preserve U.S. Cultural Heritage Abroad; co-chmn. State Dept. diplomatic rooms endowment; chmn. Lombardi Cancer Ctr. Coun., Georgetown U. Med. Ctr.; pres. Ams. Internat. Insts. Advanced Studies; vice-chmn. Kennedy Ctr. Cmty. Bd., 1991-92; trustee V.P. Residence Found., Lyndon Baines Johnson Sch. Pub. Affairs, U. Tex., Cork U., Ireland, 1993-99, Washington Coll., 1995-2005; juror The Heinz Found., 1995-2000; chmn. Chevy Chase Cmty. Com., Coun. Ct. Excellence, 1996-99. Maj. inf. U.S. Army, 1950-53 Decorated Combat Inf. badge; recipient Outstanding Young Man award, Boston Jaycees, 1961, W.R. Hearst for best US reporting, 1964, US Disting. Svc. award, The White House, 1968, US Outstanding Spl. Svc. award, 1969, DC Disting. Citizen award, Mayor, 1981, Paul Hill award, Kennedy Ctr., 1983, DC Cultural award, Arts Commn., 1983, Earthquake Hero medal, Govt. Armenia, 1989, Lincoln medal, Ford's Theatre Soc., 1991, Helen Hayes award, Helen Hayes Theatre Soc., 1991, Washingtonian of Yr. award, Washingtonian Mag., 1995, Golden Plate award, Am. Acad. Achievement, 1999, Cultural Leader award, Cultural Alliance, 2000, Torch of Liberty award, Anti Defamation League, 2001, Angel of Arts award, Cathedral Choral Soc., 2004. Mem. Smithsonian Instn. (nat. adv. com. Kellogg Project), Mus. Native Ams. (dir.), Alfalfa Club, Cosmos Club, 1925 F St. Club (trustee), Internat. Club (trustee) Office Phone: 240-497-7323.

MCTAGGART, TIMOTHY ROBERT, state agency administrator, lawyer; b. Phila., May 6, 1960; s. James Francis and Patricia Ann (Berry) McT. AB cum laude, Harvard U., 1982, JD, 1985. Bar: Mass. 1985, D.C. 1987. Atty. gen. counsel's office Bd. Govs. FRS, Washington, 1985-87; assoc. Morrison & Foerster, Washington, 1987-89, Fried, Frank, Harris, Shriver & Jacobson, Washington, 1989-91; counsel U.S. Senate Banking Com., 1991-94, Del. Bank Commr., 1994-98; ptnr. Nixon Peabody LLP and predecessor firm, Washington, 1999—2003, Willkie Farr & Gallagher, 2003—07, Pepper Hamilton LLP, 2007—. Mem. ABA, Mass. Bar Assn., D.C. Bar Assn. Avocations: reading, basketball, movies. Home Phone: 301-913-5404; Office Phone: 202-220-1210. Business E-Mail: mctaggartt@pepperlaw.com.

MCTAGUE, JOHN J., history professor; b. Albany, NY, Dec. 30, 1944; s. John J. and Eileen M. McTague. PhD, SUNY, 1974. Instr. history SUNY, Buffalo, 1974—76; prof. St. Leo U., Fla., 1976—. Mem.: Am. Hist. Assn. Avocations: bicycling, travel, music. Home: PO Box 1025 12314 Magnolia St San Antonio FL 33576 Office: St Leo Univ Hwy 52 Box 6665 Saint Leo FL 33574 Office Fax: 352-588-8300. E-mail: jack.mctague@saintleo.edu.

MCTAGUE, JOHN PAUL, materials scientist, educator, chemist, researcher; b. Jersey City, Nov. 28, 1938; s. James Aloysius and Teresa Eugenia (Hanley) McT.; m. Carole Frances Reilly, Dec. 30, 1961 (dec. Jan. 1997); children: Kevin W., Catherine E., Margaret A., Maureen E.; m.Margaret Ann Danna, Oct. 15, 2004. BS in Chemistry with honors, Georgetown U., 1960; PhD in Phys. Chemistry, Brown U., 1965, DSc (hon.), 1997. Mem. tech. staff N.Am. Rockwell Sci. Ctr., Thousand Oaks, Calif., 1964—70; prof. chemistry, mem. Inst. Geophysics and Planetary Physics UCLA, 1970—82; chmn. Nat. Synchrotron Light Source Dept. Brookhaven Nat. Lab., 1983; dep. dir. Office Sci. and Tech. Policy, Exec. Office of Pres., Washington, 1983—86, acting sci. advisor to Pres. Reagan, 1986; v.p. rsch. Ford Motor Co., Dearborn, Mich., 1986—90, v.p. tech. affairs, 1990—99; v.p. lab. mgmt., Office of Pres. U. Calif., Oakland, 2001—03, prof. materials Santa Barbara, 2001—. Adj. prof. chemistry Columbia, U., 1982-83. Mem. Pres.'s Coun. Advisors on Sci. and Tech., 1990-93; mem. adv. bd. Sec. Energy, 1990—; chmn. bd. overseers Fermilab, 1994-99. Alfred P. Sloan Research fellow, 1971-73; NATO sr. fellow, 1973; John Simon Guggenheim Meml. fellow, 1975-76. Fellow AAAS, Am. Phys. Soc. (George E. Pake prize 1998), Calif. Coun. Sci. and Tech.; mem. Am. Chem. Soc. (Calif. sect. award 1975), Nat. Acad. Engring., Sigma Xi. Personal E-mail: jmctague1@aol.com.

MCTEER, JANET, actress; b. York, England, 1961; Appeared in (Broadway plays) A Doll's House, 1997 (Tony award 1997, Drama Desk award, Outer Critics Cir. award, Theatre World award, Olivier award, London Critic's award, Time Out award), Mary Stuart, 2009 (Drama Desk award for Outstanding Actress, 2009); (regional plays) Vivat! Vivat! Regina!, Simpatico, The Grace of Mary Traverse (Olivier nomination), Much Ado About Nothing, Uncle Vanya (Olivier nomination), As You Like It, Cumbeline, The Three Sisters, Mary Stuart, 2005; (TV shows) Precious Bane, 1989, Potrait of a Marriage, 1990, Yellowbacks, 1990, A Masculine Ending, 1992, Don't Leave Me This Way, 1993, Black Velvet Gown, 1993, The Governor, 1996, The Amazing Mrs. Pritchard, 2006, Psychoville, 2009; (films) Half Moon Street, 1986, Hawks, 1989, I Dreamt I Woke Up, 1991, Prince, 1991, Wuthering Heights, 1992, Carrington, 1995, Saint-Ex, 1997, Velvet Goldmine, 1998, Tumbleweeds, 1999, Waking the Dead, 1999, Songcatcher, 2000, The King is Alive, 2000, The Intended, 2002, Tideland, 2005, As You Like It, 2006; (TV miniseries) Five Days, 2007, Sense & Sensibility, 2008. Office: Icm Artists 470 Park Ave S New York NY 10016-6819*

MCTIERNAN, CHARLES E., JR., lawyer, energy executive; b. Aug. 1944; m. Barbara K. Farrell; children: Michael, Christopher, Stephen. BA, Coll. St. Thomas, Minn.; JD cum laude, Bklyn. Law Sch. Bar: NY 1972, US Dist. Ct. (ea. and so. dists. NY) 1972, US Ct. Appeals (2nd cir.) 1972, US Ct. Appeals (4th cir.) 1990. Law clk. Hon. Charles D. Breital, NY, 1970—72; assoc. Wickes, Riddell, Blomer, Jacobi & McGuire, 1972—76, Kelley, Drye & Warren, 1976—81; atty. Consol. Edison Inc., NYC, 1981—85, assoc. gen. counsel comml. litig., 1985—2002, gen. counsel, 2003—. Mem. Gen. Counsel Roundtable; mem. litig. adv. com. Edison Electric Inst. Editor (mng.): Bklyn. Law Rev. Office: Consol Edison Inc 4 Irving Pl New York NY 10003*

MCTIGUE, MAURICE P., director; b. Methven, New Zealand, 1940; Ed., St. Bede's Coll., Christchurch, New Zealand, 1958. Cabinet min., mem. parliament, New Zealand, 1985—97; dir. govt. accountability project Mercatus Ctr., George Mason U., Arlington, Va. Spkr. in field; mem. bd. Performance Mgmt. Adv. Com. Contbr. articles numerous prof. jours. Recipient Queen's Svc. Order, Queen Elizabeth II, 1999; scholar disting. vis. scholar, George Mason U. Office: 3301 N Fairfax Dr Arlington VA 22201-4433 Office Phone: 703-993-4930.

MCVEY, DAVID SCOTT, veterinarian, director; b. Bridgeport, Ala., May 5, 1955; s. Chesil Horton and Ruth Ella McVey; m. Diane Bohannon, June 12, 1976; children: Joshua Thomas, Caleb Scott, David Edgar, John Paul Robert. DVM, U. Tennesse, Knoxville, 1980; PhD, Tex. A & M U., College Sta., 1986. Diplomate Am. Coll. Vet. Microbiology, 1989. Vet. McVey Vet. Svc., Athens, Tenn., 1980—83, cons. Beatrice, 2006—; postdoc. rsch. assoc. Tex. A & M U., 1983—86; assoc. prof. infectious disease Kans. State U., Manhattan, 1986—95; R & D scientist Rhone Merieux, Athens, Ga., 1995—98; dir. lab. sci. Pfizer Animal Health, Groton, Conn., 1998—2006; prof. vet. microbiology U. Nebr., Lincoln, 2006—, dir. nebr. vet. diagnostic ctr., 2008—. Pres. Am. Coll. Vet. Microbiology, 2002—04. Contbr. scientific papers, chapters to books. Bioshield adv. panel mem. Homeland Security, Washington, 2002—03. Recipient Beecham award, Kans. State Coll. Vet. Medicine, 1992, Disting. Alumni, U. Tenn. Coll. Vet. Medicine, 2007, Jack Delaplane award, Tex. A & M U., 1986. Mem.: AVMA, Am. Soc. Microbiology, Nebr. Vet. Med. Assn., Am. Barbershop Harmony Soc. Home: 28952 S First Rd Beatrice NE 68310 Office: Nebraska Veterinary Diagnostic Ctr E Campus Loop Lincoln NE 68583-0907

MCVEY, DIANE ELAINE, accountant; b. Wilmington, Del., Apr. 20, 1953; d. C. Granville and Margaret M. (Lindell) McV. AA in Acctg., Goldey Beacom Coll. (Del.), 1973, BS in Acctg., 1980; MBA in Mgmt., Fairleigh Dickinson U., 1985. Acct. Audio Visual Arts, Wilmington, Del., 1973; cost acct. FMC Corp., Kennett Square, Pa., 1973-75; asst. acct. NVF Corp., Kennett Square, 1978—80; staff analyst GPU Nuclear, Parsippany, NJ, 1980—93, staff acct., 1993—95, GPU Svc., Morristown, 1995—2000, Reading, Pa., 2000—, FirstEnergy, 2001—04, sr. accountant, 2004—. Owner, Demac Cons., Dover, N.J., 1988-2000, Reading, 2000—. Elder First Presbyn. Ch., Rockaway, N.J., 1986—, session mem., 1986-91; commr. to bd. adjustment, Dover, N.J., 1994-2000. With U.S. Army, 1975-78. Mem. Assn. MBA Execs. Republican. Presbyterian. Avocations: reading mystery books, writing and performing music, needlecrafts. Office: 2800 Pottsville Pike Reading PA 19601 Office Phone: 610-921-6560. E-mail: dmcvey@firstenergycorp.com.

MCVEY, HENRY HANNA, III, retired lawyer; b. Richmond, Va., Aug. 12, 1935; s. Henry Hanna Jr. and Eva Lawson (Jennings) McVey; m. Reba Jean Robinson, Dec. 12, 1964; children: Margaret Anne McVey Singleton, Lewis Lawson, Ian Douglas. BS, BA magna cum laude, Hampden-Sydney Coll., Va., 1957, LLD (hon.), 2008; LLB, U. Va., Charlottesville, 1960. Bar: Va. 1960, U.S. Dist. Ct. (ea. dist.) Va. 1960, U.S. Ct. Appeals (4th cir.) 1965, U.S. Supreme Ct. 1970, cert.: Hampden Sydney Coll. (honary doc. law) 2008. Assoc. Battle, Neal, Harris, Minor & Williams, Richmond, 1960-66; ptnr. McGuireWoods LLP and predecessor firms, Richmond, 1966—99; ret., 1999. Mem. adv. group under Civil Justice Reform Act of 1990 U.S. Dist. Ct. (ea. dist.) Va. Trustee Hampden-Sydney Coll., 1989—94, 1995—2001, vice chair, 2001—03, chair bd. trustees, 2003—08; mem. Commn. on Archtl. Rev. City of Richmond, 1985—95; mem. Planning Commn. Gloucester County, 2001—, vice chmn., 2006; bd. dirs. Richmond Symphony, 1977—86, 1987—99, v.p., 1979—81, exec. v.p., 1981—83, pres., 1983—85, chmn. bd. dirs., 1985—87, pres. Symphony Coun., 1999—2001; bd. dirs. Carpenter Ctr. for Performing Arts, 1982—89, Rosewell Found., 1999—2004, pres., 2001—02, v.p., 2002—03. Recipient Algernon Sydney Sullivan medallion for svc. to coll., Hampden Sydney Coll., 2001, Alumni Citation for loyal Svc., Hampden-Sydney Coll., 2002, Excellence in Civil Litigation award, Va. Assn. Defense Attys., 2006. Fellow: Am. Bar Found., Am. Coll. Trial Lawyers; mem.: Gloucester Cmty. Found., Va. Bar Assn., Va. Assn. Def. Attys. (v.p. 1981—83, treas. 1983—84, pres.-elect 1984—85, pres. 1985—86), Ware River Yacht Club (bd. dirs. 2000—05). Presbyterian. Home: PO Box 8 Ware Neck VA 23178 Home Phone: 804-694-0994, 804-694-0992. Personal E-mail: hmcvey@cox.net.

MCVEY, WALTER LEWIS, retired lawyer, educator; b. Independence, Kans., Feb. 19, 1922; s. Walter Lewis and Nona (Inge) McV.; m. Rose Mary Ayers, Oct. 28, 1944 (div. Oct. 1962); children: Walter Lewis III (dec.), David Ayers; m. Velma Graham Hulett, Apr. 3, 1964 (dec. Aug. 7, 1998). BA, U. Kans., 1947, JD, 1948; MA, Ga. State U., 1976. Bar: Ga. 1965. Lawyer McVey, McVey & McVey, Independence, 1948-61; rep. U.S. Congress, Washington, 1961-63; sole practice law Atlanta, 1965-95; ret. State rep. Kans. State Legislature, Topeka, 1949-52; judge Ct. Independence, 1952-56; state senator Kans. Legislature, Topeka, 1957-61; adj. prof. Ga. State U., 1968-73, Mercer U., Atlanta, 1971-74, DeKalb Coll., Ga., 1968-93; trustee IRS, Montgomery County, Kans., 1954-55; mgm. cons., 1968-98; evening dean DeKalb Coll. North, Dunwoody, Ga., 1996-98, Ga. Perimeter Coll., Dunwoody, 1998-2001; writer, 2001—. Republican. Methodist. Home: 12824 S Twilight Dr Olathe KS 66062-1785

MCVICKER, CHARLES TAGGART, artist, educator; b. Canonsburg, Pa., Aug. 31, 1930; s. Carl Walter and Mary Ruth (Washabaugh) McV.; m. Lucy Claire Graves, Mar. 20, 1954; children— Lauri, Bonnie, Heather. BA, Principia Coll., Elsah, Ill., 1952; BFA, Art Center Coll. Design, LA, 1957. Staff artist Alexander Chaite Studios, 1957-58; freelance illustrator and painter, 1958—. Asst. prof. Pratt Phoenix Sch. Art, NYC, 1979-84, Coll. of NJ, 1985—2003. One-man shows include Thompson Gallery, NYC, 1967, Capitol Hill Club, Washington, 1988, (retrospective exhibit) Coll. NJ, 2006; represented in permanent collections US Capitol, Am. Hist. Assn., Soc. Illustrators, USAF, Princeton U., DuPont Corp., Zimmerli Art Mus. at Rutgers U., Home Life Ins. Co., Wang Corp. With US Army, 1952—54. Recipient Ralph Fabri award Nat. Audubon Artists Ann. Juried Show, 1986, Ralph Fabri medal Nat. Soc. Painters in Casein and Acrylic, 1991, Michael Engel Meml. award Nat. Audubon Artists, 1992; named Best in Show Ellarslie Mus., 2005. Mem. Soc. Illustrators (exec. com. 1972-74, pres. 1976-78), Am. Watercolor Soc., Graphic Artists Guild (v.p. nat. exec. com. 1978-79), Audubon Artists, Princeton Artists Alliance (pres. 1989-92), Am. Artists Profl. League, Garden State Watercolor Soc. (pres. 2006-07, Best in Show 2007). Home: 26 Old Orchard Ln Princeton NJ 08540-1939

MCVICKER, JEANETTE, literature and language professor; BA in English, Purdue U., West Lafayette, Ind., 1981; MA in Philosophy, Binghamton U., NY, 1986, PhD in Comparative Lit., 1988. Prof. English SUNY, Fredonia, 1988—, dir., women's studies program, 1996—2000, coord., interdisciplinary program, journalism, 2002—08, chairperson, English, 2005—07. Mem. LWV, Chautauqua County, NY. Recipient Pres. award for Excellence in Tchg., SUNY, 2008; Fulbright Tchg. fellowship, CIES-Fulbright Commn., 1991—92, Jeanette McVicker Women's Studies scholarship, SUNY, 2000. Mem.: Katharine Anne Porter Soc., Assn. Educators Journalism and Mass Comm., Modernist Studies Assn., MLA, Va. Woolf Soc. Office: SUNY Dept English 241 Fenton Hall Fredonia NY 14063 Office Phone: 716-673-3861. Office Fax: 716-673-4661.

MCVISK, WILLIAM KILBURN, lawyer; b. Chgo., Oct. 8, 1953; s. Felix Kilburn and June (DePear) Visk; m. Marlaine Joyce McDonough, June 20, 1975. BA, U. Ill, 1974; JD cum laude, Northwestern U., 1977. Bar: Ill. 1977, Ind. 1999, U.S. Dist. Ct. (no. dist.) Ill. 1977, U.S. Ct. Appeals (7th cir.) 1978, U.S. Dist. Ct. (no. and so. dists.) Ind. 1999, U.S. Ct. Appeals (10th cir.) 2001. Assoc. Jerome H. Torshen, Ltd., Chgo., 1977-80, Silets & Martin, Chgo., 1980-81, Peterson & Ross, Chgo., 1981-85, ptnr., 1985-95, Johnson & Bell Ltd., Chgo., 1995—. Contbr. articles to profl. jours. Mem.: Ill. Assn. Def. Trial Lawyers (chmn. ins. coverage com. 1999—2003, bd. dirs. 2008—, ed. in chief IDC quar. 2009—), Ill. Assn. Hosp. Attys. (bd. dirs. 1997—2003, pres. 2002), Am. Health Lawyers Assn., Def. Rsch. Inst. Office: Johnson & Bell 33 W Monroe St Ste 2700 Chicago IL 60603-5713 Home Phone: 708-771-5421; Office Phone: 312-984-0229. Business E-Mail: mcviskw@jbltd.com.

MCWETHY, PATRICIA JOAN, educational association administrator; b. Chgo., Feb. 27, 1946; d. Frank E. and Emma (Kuehne) McW.; m. H. Frank Eden; children: Kristin Beth, Justin Nicholas. BA, Northwestern U., 1968; MA, U. Minn., 1970; MBA, George Washington U., 1981. Geog. analyst CIA, McLean, Va., 1970-71; rsch. asst. NSF, Washington, 1972-74, spl. asst. to dir., 1975, assoc. program dir. human geography and regional sci. program, 1976-79; exec. dir. Assn. Am. Geographers, Washington, 1979-84, Nat. Assn. Biology Tchrs., Reston, Va., 1984-95, Nat. Sci. Edn. Leadership Assn., Arlington, Va., 1995-97; edn. dir. Nat. Alliance for Mentally Ill, Arlington, 1998-99. Prin. investigator grant on biotech. equipment ednl. resource partnership NSF, 1989-93, NSF funded internat. symposium on Basic Biol. Concepts: What Should the World's Children Know?, 1992-94; co-prin. investigator NSF grant, 1995-97; mem. chmn.'s adv. com. Nat. Com. Sci. Stds. and Assessment, 1992-95; mem. Commn. for Biology Edn., Internat. Union Biol. Sci., 1988-97; mem. exec. com. Alliance for Environ. Edn., 1987-90, chmn. program com., 1990; condr. seminars in field; lectr. in field. Author monograph and papers in field; editor handbook. NSF grantee, 1989-93, 95-97; NSF fellow, 1968-69; recipient Outstanding Performance award, NSF, 1973. Mem. Phi Beta Kappa.

MCWHINNEY, DEBORAH DOYLE, diversified financial services company executive; b. 1955; married; 2 children. BA, U. Mont., 1977; Grad., Pacific Coast Banking Sch. With consumer electronic banking divsn. Bank of America Corp., 1978—95; exec. v.p. bus. planning and strategy Visa Internat., 1995—99; group pres. Engage Media Svc., 1999—2001; pres. Charles Schwab Institutional, 2001—07; pres., CEO Dennis & Phyllis Washington Found., 2007—09; head Citi Personal Wealth Mgmt., NYC, 2009—. Bd. dirs. Securities Investor Protection Corp. (SIPC), 2002—; exec. advisor to bd. and exec. team Hitachi Data Sys. and Hitachi Ltd., 2003; bd. dirs. Novadigm, Inc., PLUS Sys., Touch Am. Holdings, Inc. Trustee Calif. Inst. Tech., 2007—. Recipient Movers

& Shakers award Fin. Planning, 2004; named one of The 100 Most Influential Women in Bay Area Bus., San Francisco Bus. Times, 2002, 2003, 2004, The 25 Most Influential People in Planning Profession, Investment Advisor List, 2004. Office: Citigroup Inc 399 Park Ave New York NY 10022 Office Phone: 800-854-3322.*

MCWHINNEY, EDWARD WATSON, Canadian government legislator; b. Sydney, May 19, 1924; s. Matthew and Evelyn Annie (Watson) McW.; m. Emily Ingalore Sabatzky, June 27, 1951. LLB, U. Sydney, 1949; LLM, Yale U., 1951, D Juridical Sci., 1953; diploma, Acad. de Droit Internat., The Hague, 1950; LLD, U. Thessaloniki, Greece, 1998. Bar: called to Australian bar 1949, apptd. Queen's counsel, Can 1967. Crown prosecutor, Sydney, 1949-50; lectr., then asst. prof. Law Sch. and Grad. Sch., Yale U., 1951-55; prof. law, mem. Centre Russian Studies, U. Toronto, Ont., Canada, 1955-66; prof. law, dir. Inst. Air and Space Law, McGill U., Montreal, Que., Canada, 1966-71; prof. law, dir. internat. and comparative legal studies U. Ind., Indpls., 1971-74; disting. prof. Simon Fraser U., Burnaby, BC, 1974—93, prof. emeritus, 1992; mem. Permanent Ct. Arbitration, The Hague, 1985-91; Paul Martin prof. U. Windsor, Canada, 1986; pres., dir. Found. Internat. and Comparative and Fed. Law, 1996—; M.P. Ho. of Commons, Ottawa, Ont., Canada, 1993-2000; co-chmn. joint standing com. Senate and Ho. of Commons, Ottawa, Ont., Canada, 1993-95, parliamentary sec. (fisheries and oceans), 1996-97, parliamentary sec. (fgn. affairs), 1997-2000; fed. govt. rep. nat. unity commn. Govt. of B.C., 1997-98. Vis. prof. Ecole Libre des Hautes Etudes, 1952, Heidelberg and Max-Planck-Inst., 1960-61, 90, NYU, 1954, Faculté Internat. de Droit Comparé, Luxembourg, 1959-60, U. San Antonio, 1963, U. Laval, Que., 1967, U. Paris, 1968, U. Madrid, 1968, U. Aix-Marseille, 1969, U. Nat. Autónoma de México, 1965, Inst. U. Luxembourg, 1972, 74, 76, Acad. Internat. Law, The Hague, 1973, 90, 2002, Aristotelian U., Thessaloniki, Greece, 1974, 78, 85, 96, 2003, U. Nice, 1976-77, Jagellonian U., Cracow, Poland, 1976, U. Paris I (Sorbonne), 1982, 85, Coll. de France, Paris, 1983, Meiji U., Tokyo, 1987, Inst. Internat. Relations, Bejing, 1987, 92, Sch. Internat. Rels., Tehran, 2003; legal cons. UN, 1953-54; cons. Japanese Commn. Constn., mem. prime minister Ont. Adv. Com. Confedn., 1964-71; cons. U.S. Naval War Coll., 1961-68; legal cons. Ministère de la Justice, Que., 1969-70; 74-75; constl. adviser to prime minister of Que., 1974-75; royal commr. Commn. Lang. Rights, Que., 1968-72; cons. U.S. Senate select com. presdl. campaign activities, 1973; spl. commr. inquiry Legislature B.C., 1974-75; chief adv. Fed. Govt.'s Task Force on Nat. Unity, 1978; commr. of enquiry, City of Vancouver, 1979; constl. adv. Fedn. Can. Municipalities, 1978-82; spl. advisor Can. del. UN Gen. Assembly, ann. sessions, 1981-83, 96; constl. adviser Indian Nations (Treaties 6-9), Can., 1980-82; mem. Assoc. de l'Inst. de Droit Internat., 1967, membre titulaire, 1975, pres. 1999-2001; mem. Assoc. de l'Acad. Internat. de Droit Comparé, Paris, 1986, mem. titulaire, 2002-- Author: Judical Review, 4th edit, 1969, Canadian Jurisprudence, 1958, Föderalismus und Bundesverfassungsrecht, 1961, Constitutionalism in Germany, 1962, Comparative Federalism, 2d edit, 1965, Peaceful Coexistence and Soviet-Western International Law, 1964, Law Foreign Policy and the East-West Détente, 1964, Federal Constitution- Making for a Multi-National World, 1966, International Law and World Revolution, 1967, Conflit idéologique et ordre public mondial, 1970, (with M.A. Bradley) The Freedom of the Air, 1968, New Frontiers in Space Law, 1969, The International Law of Communications, 1970, Aerial Piracy and International Law, 1971, (with Pierre Pescatore) Federalism and Supreme Courts and the Integration of Legal Systems, 1973, Parliament and Parliamentary Power Today, 1976, The Executive and Executive Power Today, 1977, (with J-D Gendron and others) La situation de la lanque françaisé au Québec (3 vols.), 1973, The Illegal Diversion of Aircraft and International Law, 1974, Parliamentary Privilege and the Broadcasting of Parliamentary Debates, 1975, The International Law of Detente, 1978, The World Court and the Contemporary International Law-making Process, 1979, Quebec and the Constitution, 1979, Municipal Government in a New Canadian Federal System, 1980, Conflict and Compromise: International Law and World Order in a Revolutionary Age, 1981, Constitution-Making: Principles, Process, Practice, 1981, Canada and the Constitution, 1982, United Nations Law Making, 1984, Supreme Courts and Judicial Law-Making, 1986, Les Nations-Unies et la Formation du Droit, 1986, Aerial Piracy and International Terrorism, 1987, The International Court of Justice and the Western Tradition of International Law, 1987, (with Nagendra Singh) Nuclear Weapons and Contemporary International Law, 1988, Judicial Settlement of International Disputes, 1990, (with G.I. Tunkin and V.S. Vereshchetin) From Coexistence to Cooperation: International Law and Organisation in the Post-Cold War Era, 1991, (with J. Zaslove and W. Wolf) Federalism-in-the-Making, Contemporary Canadian and German Constitutionalism, National and Trans-national, 1992, Judge Shigeru Oda and the Progressive Development of International Law, 1992, Judge Manfred Lachs and Judicial Law-Making, 1994, The United Nations and a New World Order for a New Millennium, 2000, (with N. Ando and R. Wolfrum) Liber Amicorum Judge Shigeru Oda, 2002, Self-Determination of Peoples and Plural-Ethnic States. Secession and State Succession and the Alternative, Federal Option, 2003, Chretien and Canadian Federalism, Politics and the Constitution, 1993-2003, 2003, The September 11 Terrorist Attacks and Invasion of Iraq in Contemporary International Law, 2004, The Governor General and the Prime Ministers, 2005, (with Mariko Kawano) Judge Shigeru Oda and the path to judicial wisdom, 2006, Self-Determination of Peoples and Plural- Ethnic States in Contemporary Internat. Law, 2007, (with Sienho Yee & Jacques Yuan Morin) Multiculturism and Internat. Law Essays in Honor of Edward McWhinney, 2009; bd. editors Australian Quar., 1949-50, Can. Yearbook of Internat. Law, 1963—, Jour. Media Law and Practice, 1980-85, Annuaire International de Justice Constitutionnelle, 1987—; editl. adv. com. Ency. Brit., 1985—; mem. bd. adv. Chinese Jour. Internat. Law, 2002—; contbr. to Ency. Brit. Served as officer Australian Air Force, 1943-45. Recipient Aristotle medal, Govt. of Greece, 1997, Queen's Golden Jubilee medal, 2002; Carnegie Endowment fellow, 1951, Fulbright fellow, 1950-51, Sterling fellow Yale, 1950-51, Rockefeller fellow, 1960-61, 66-68, Can. Coun. fellow, 1960-61, fellow Am. Soc. Internat. Law, 1962-63, Marco Polo fellow Xi'an Jiaotong U., China, 2007-, Hon. fellow U. Sydney, 2008. Mem. Australian Inst. Polit. Sci. (dir.), Internat. Law Assn. (pres. Toronto br. 1964-66, pres. Montreal br. 1970-71, chmn. exec. com. Canadian br. 1972-75), Canadian Bar Assn. (council Ont. 1956-58), Yale Law Sch. Assn. (pres. Can. 1964-69), Canadian Civil Liberties Assn. (v.p. 1965-67), Am. Soc. Internat. Law (coun. 1965-68, patron 2002—), Am. Fgn. Law Assn., Inst. interamericano de Estudios Juridicos Internacionales (dir. 1965—), Inst. Grand-Ducal de Luxembourg, Internat. Commn. Jurists (mem. coun. Can. br. 1988—), German Soc. for Völkerrecht (hon.), Knights of Mark Twain (U.S., hon.). Home: 1949 Beach Ave Ste 402 Vancouver BC Canada V6G 1Z2

MCWHINNEY, MADELINE H. (MRS. JOHN DENNY DALE), economist, director; b. Denver, Mar. 11, 1922; d. Leroy and Alice (Houston) McW.; m. John D. Dale, June 23, 1961; 1 child, Thomas Denny. BA, Smith Coll., 1943; MBA, NYU, 1947. Economist Fed. Res. Bank, NYC, 1943-73, chief fin. trade statis. divsn., 1955-59, mgr. market stats. dept., 1960-65, asst. v.p., 1965-73; pres. First Women's Bank, NYC, 1974-76, Dale, Elliott & Co., Inc., Red Bank, NJ, 1977-97. Trustee Retirement System Fed. Res. Bank, 1955-58; vis. lectr. NYU Grad. Sch. Bus., 1976-77; mem. NJ Casino Control Commn., 1980-82, Women's Econ. Round Table, 1978-89, chmn. 1987-88; bd. govs. Am. Stock Exch., 1977-81; trustee Monmouth Mus., 1995-2009, Vis. Nurse Assn. Ctrl. Jersey, 1995-2004, Planned Parenthood Ctrl. Jersey, 1995-2003, Carnegie Corp. NY, 1974-82, Central Savs. Bank NY, 1980-82, Monmouth Conservatory Music, 2002-09; trustee Charles F. Kettering Found., 1975-93, chmn. 1987-91; trustee Inst. Internat. Edn., 1975-, Investor Responsibility Rsch. Ctr., Inc., 1974-81; asst. dir. Whitney Mus. Am. Art, 1983-86; dir. Atlantic Energy Co., 1983-93; trustee Mgrs. Funds, 1983-2004; mem. adv. com. profl. ethics NJ Supreme Ct., 1983-98. Recipient Smith Coll. medal, 1971, Alumni Achievement award NYU Grad. Sch. Bus. Adminstrn. Alumni Assn., 1971, NYU Crystal award, 1982. Mem. Am. Fin. Assn. (past dir.), Money Marketeers (v.p. 1960, pres. 1961-62), Alumni Assn. Grad. Sch. Bus. Adminstrn. NYU (dir. 1951-63, pres. 1957-59), Soc. Meml. Ctr., Phi Beta Kappa Fellows (v.p. 1979-87). Office: PO Box 458 Red Bank NJ 07701-0458 Home: 192 Heritage Court Little Silver NJ 07739 Personal E-mail: mdale38569@comcast.net.

MCWHIRTER, BRUCE J., retired lawyer; b. Chgo., Sept. 11, 1931; s. Sydney and Martha McWhirter; m. Judith Hallett, Apr. 14, 1960; children: Cameron, Andrew. BS, Northwestern U., 1952; LLB, Harvard U., 1955. Bar: DC 1955, Ill 1955, US Ct Appeals (7th cir) 1963, US Supreme Ct. Assoc. Lord, Bissell & Brook, Chgo., 1958-62; from assoc. to sr. ptnr. Ross & Hardies, Chgo., 1962-95, of counsel, 1996—2003. Editor: Donnelley SEC Handbook, 1972—87; contbr. articles to profl jours. With US Army, 1955—57. Mem.: ABA, Harvard Law Soc Ill., Chgo. Bar Assn., Harvard Club (N.Y.C.), Lawyers Club Chgo., Phi Beta Kappa. Democrat. Home: 111 Sheridan Rd Winnetka IL 60093-4223 Personal E-mail: jbmcw@aol.com.

MCWHIRTER, GLENNA SUZANNE (NICKIE), retired columnist; b. Peoria, Ill., June 28, 1929; d. Alfred Leon and Garnet Lorene (Short) Sotier; m. Edward Ford McWhirter (div.); children: Suzanne McWhirter Orlicki, Charles Edward, James Richard. BS in English Lang. and Lit., U. Mich., postgrad., 1960-63. Editl. asst. McGraw-Hill Pub. Co., Detroit, 1951-54; staff writer Detroit Free Press, Inc., Detroit, 1963-70, asst. city editor, 1971-77, columnist, 1977-88, Detroit News Inc., Detroit, 1988-97; advt. copy writer Campbell-Ewald Co., Detroit, 1967-68; ret., 1997. Author: Pea Soup, 1984 Winner 1st Place Commentary award UPI, Mich., 1979; 1st Place Columns AP, Mich., 1978, 81; 1st Place Columns Detroit Press Club Found., Mich., 1978; Disting. Service award State of Mich., 1985 Mem. Women in Comm. (Headliner award 1978), Alpha Gamma Delta. Avocations: flower gardening, interior design. Home: 495 Lake Shore Ln Grosse Pointe Woods MI 48236 Personal E-mail: nickiemcwhirter@earthlink.net.

MCWHIRTER, JAMILA LEANN, choral conductor; d. John Robert and Lenora Evelyn Lucy; m. R. Mark McWhirter, Oct. 27, 1995. MusB, S.W. Bapt. U., Bolivar, Mo., 1989; MA, Ctrl. Mo. State U., Warrensburg, 1995; PhD, U. Mo., 2005—. Cert. tchr. elem. and secondary edn. Mo. Choral music tchr. Plato R-V Sch. Dist., Mo., 1989—92; fine arts dept. chair Morgan County R-2 Sch. Dist., Versailles, Mo., 1992—2002; choral dir. Stephens Coll., Columbia, Mo., 2002—; choral dir./music educator U. Mo., Columbia, 2002—; adj. faculty Ctrl. Mo. State U., Warrensburg, 1995—2000; excel adj. faculty Mo. Bapt. Coll., St. Louis, 1997—2002; asst. prof. choral music edn. Mid. Tenn. State U., 2005—. Adjudicator/clinician Mo. Music Educator's Assn., Mo., 1989—, Mo. Choral Dirs. Assn., Mo., 1989—; choral dir. Ctrl. Mo. State U. Summer Music Camp, Warrensburg, Mo., 1997—2000; applied voice instr., Mo., 1989—; panelist Nat. Piano Pedagogy Rev., 2006; faculty advisor Collegette Nat. Assn. Music Educators, 2005—, Collegette Am. Choral Dirs. Assn., 2005—; presenter nat. convention Nat. Assn. Music Educators, 2006; guest condr. Tenn. Mid-State Women's Choir, 2007; clinician Tri-County Chorus Clinic, 2008; adjudicator Middle Tenn. Vocal Assn. Regional Choral Festival, 2006—08, Middle Tenn. Vocal Assn. Solo & SMall Ensemble Festival, 2007; coll. chair Middle Tenn. Vocal Assn., 2008—, guest educator Middle Sch. Mass Choir, 2008; founder and organizer First Tenn. All-Collegiate Choir, 2009. Dir.: (numerous choral performances), (musical) Camelot, Annie Get Your Gun; singer: (musicals) Oklahoma, Wizard of Oz, Anything Goes; dir.: (yuletide feasts); contbr. articles to profl. jours. including Jour. Rsch. in Music Edn. Dir. Versailles Cmty. Chorus, Versailles, Mo., 1992—94; musical dir./bd. advisor Royal Theater Arts Coun., Versailles, 1992—2001; mentor Tenn. Music Educators Assn.; min. of music Second Bapt. Ch., Lebanon, Mo., 1989—92; asst. min. of music Trinity So. Bapt. Ch., Versailles, 1992, chair pers. com., 1999—2003. Recipient Tom Mills Choral award, U. Mo., Columbia; Regents scholar, Ctrl. Mo. State U., S.W. Bapt. U. scholar, Vocal Performance scholar, S.W. Bapt. U. Mem.: Tenn. Choral Dirs. Assn., Tenn. Music Educators Assn. (presenter 2006—08, state advisor 2007—, higher edn. chair 2008—, chair 2008—), West Ctrl. Mo. Music Educators Assn. (jr. high choral v.p. 1996—98, dist. pres. 2002—04), Classroom Tchrs. Assn. (v.p. 1994—95), Mo. State Tchrs. Assn., West Ctrl. Mo. Choral Dirs. Assn. (dist. rep. 1998—2000), Mo. Music Educators Assn. (Selected for Choral Performance at State Conv. 1999), Mo. Choral Dirs. Assn. (state treas. 2000—04), Sigma Alpha Iota, Pi Kappa Lambda. Avocations: horseback riding, reading, swimming, fishing, hiking.

MCWHORTER, DIANE, writer; b. Tupelo, Miss., Nov. 1, 1952; BA in Comparative Lit., Wellesley Coll. Writer, NYC. Author: Carry Me Home: Birmingham, Alabama,The Climactic Battle of the Civil Rights Revolution, 2001 (Pulitzer prize for gen. nonfiction, 2002, named NY Times Notable Book, winner, Southern Book Critics Circle award, 2001, J. Anthony Lukas Book prize, 2002, English Speaking Union Amb. award, 2002, Sidney Hillman Found. award, 2002), A Dream of Freedom: The Civil Rights Movement from 1954 to 1968, 2004 (NY Times Notable Children's Book, 2004, USA Today Best Children's History, 2004, on ALA Best New Book for Young Adults list, 2004); contbr. articles to newspapers, chapters to books. Recipient Clarence Cason award, 2003. Personal E-mail: dmcwhorter@earthlink.net.

MCWHORTER, HOBART AMORY, JR., lawyer; b. Birmingham, Ala., Dec. 24, 1931; s. Hobart Amory and Marjorie (Westgate) McW.; remarried Feb. 1, 1997; children: Margaret G., Marjorie W. BA, Yale U., 1953; LLB, U. Va., 1958. Bar: Ala. 1958. Ptnr. Bradley Arant Rose & White, Birmingham, 1958—. 1st lt. U.S. Army, 1953-55. Fellow Am. Coll. Trial Lawyers; mem. Internat. Assn. Ins. Counsel, Nat. Assn. r.R. Counsel. Republican. Presbyterian. Office: Bradley Arant Rose & White One Federal Pl 1819 Fifth Ave N Birmingham AL 35203-2104 Office Phone: 205-521-8241. Business E-Mail: hmcwhorter@bradleyarant.com.

MCWHORTER, SHARON LOUISE, engineering executive, inventor, consultant; b. Feb. 22, 1951; d. Leroy Byron Harris Jr. and Josiebell (Richards) Harris Aaron; m. Abner McWhorter II, Mar. 15, 1969 (div. Aug. 1974); 1 child, Abner III. BA, Wayne State U., 1988; cert., SBA, Detroit, 1978; cert. in sound engring., Detroit Rec. Inst., Warren, Mich., 1982. Directory asst. Mich. Bell Telephone Co., Detroit, 1969; quality control clk. Chevrolet Gear & Axle, Detroit, 1971-74; circulation clk. Wayne County C.C., Detroit, 1977-85, mem. libr. standing com. and open house com., 1983-84; pres. Galactic Concepts & Designs, Detroit, 1977-88, cons., 1983—. Gen. ptnr., mgr. S.M.J. Corridor Devel., Detroit, 1982—, hist. rschr., 1982; del. Small Bus. Conf., 1981; ad hoc mem. Minority Tech. Coun., 1981-82; elected alt. Mich. del. White House Conf. on Small Bus., Washington, 1985-86; lectr., cons. Author, editor: Creative Dilemma newsletter, 1985—; co-patentee cup holding apparatus. Vol. counselor Barat House/March of Dimes, Detroit, 1977; active Concerned Citizens Cass Corridor, Detroit, 1982-87, Cass Corridor Citizen's Patrol, Detroit, 1983-84, Empowerment Zone Devel. Corp., Detroit, 1996—, bd. dirs., corp. chair, 1997—; pres. Wayne County chpt. MADD, Mich., 1987-88; apptd. citizen rev. com, 1988—; mem. adv. bd. Neighborhood Family Initiative, Southeastern Cmty. Found.; pres. Am. Res. Tng. Sys., Inc., 1990—. Recipient Hist. Landmark award Dept. Interior, 1983, cert. appreciation Tri-County Substance Abuse Awareness Com., 1984. Mem. Inventors Coun. Mich. (bd. dirs. 1985-88), Black Women in Bus. (sec. 1984-85), Greater Detroit C. of C., South Cass Bus. Assn. (v.p. 1987-88, pres. 1988-89), Detroit Econ. Club. Democrat. Methodist. Avocations: photography, filmmaking. Office: SMJ Corridor Devel Co 453 Myrtle St Ste 102 Detroit MI 48201-2311

MCWILLIAMS, C. PAUL, JR., engineering executive; b. Louisville, June 4, 1931; s. Cleo Paul and Audrey Dora (Hale) McW.; m. Barbara Ann Sparks, Feb. 22, 1950 (div. 1962); children: Bruce Kevin, Craig Tinsley; m. Barbara Ann Heintz, Apr. 25, 1980; 1 stepchild, Kimberly Jean Moorhouse Beaumont. B Chem. Engring., U. Louisville, 1954, M Engring., 1972. Lic. profl. engr., N.Y., N.C., Pa. Sr. process devel. engr. Olin Mathieson Chem. Corp., Brandenburg, Ky., 1958-66, Rochester, NY, 1958-66; sr. chem. engr. GTE Sylvania, Seneca Falls, NY, 1966-74, Eastman Kodak Co., Rochester, 1974-81; prin., treas. Flint & Sherburne Assocs., P.C., Rochester, 1981-89; project engr. Roy F. Weston, Inc., Rochester, 1989-92; engring. mgr. ECCO, Inc. (Environ. Cons. Co., Inc.), Buffalo, 1992-94; pres. ECCO Engring., Buffalo, 1993-94; staff engr. Environ. Products & Svcs., Inc., Rochester, NY, 1994-96; pvt. cons. engr. Webster, NY, 1996—. Cons. water tech. Water Tech. Corp., Tonawanda, N.Y., 1973-76; product rsch. panel Chem. Engring. Mag., 1982-83. Author: Waste Disposal Manual, 1976. Life mem. Rep. Presdl. Task Force, Webster, N.Y., 1986—; mem. Rep. Nat. Com., Webster, 1991-92. 1st lt. USAF, 1954-58, ret. lt. col. USAF, 1982. Decorated Meritorious Svc. medal. Mem. NSPE, AIChE, Soc. Am. Mil. Engrs., Res. Officers Assn. (life), Monroe Profl. Engrs. Soc. (environ. com. 1972-75, chmn. 1973-75, bd. dirs. 1982-84, program chmn. 1984), Cons. Engrs. Coun. N.Y. State (program chmn. Rochester chpt. 1986-87, sec. 1987-88, treas. 1989). Episcopalian. Achievements include rsch. in replacing boiler feedwater regulators, related instrumentation and control systems and blowdown; design of dry fabric dust collectors to remove fly ash from coal-fired boilers' flue gas. Home and Office: C Paul McWilliams PE Cons Engr 1132 Woodbridge Ln Webster NY 14580-8709 Home Phone: 585-872-0505; Office Phone: 585-872-0505. Business E-Mail: paulmcw@frontiernet.net.

MCWILLIAMS, EDWIN JOSEPH, banker; b. Spokane, Washington, Aug. 11, 1919; s. Frank S. and Alice (Conlan) McW.; m. Betty J. Galbreath, Aug. 15, 1944; children: Lawrence, Barbara Anne, Marijoan, Peter Stuart. Student, U. Notre Dame, Ind., 1937-38, Marquette U., Milw., 1938-40; BS in Bus. Adminstrn, Gonzaga U., Spokane, Wash., 1943. With Fidelity Mutual Savings Bank, Spokane, 1940-82, exec. v.p., 1955-58, pres., 1958-82, Fidelity Service Corp., 1983-87. Mem. adv. council Wash. State Dept. Commerce and Econ. Devel., 1977-80; U.S. del. Internat. Savs. Bank Inst., 1975, 76, 79; vice chair, dir. NW Edn. Loan Assn Pres. United Crusade Spokane County, 1966; pres., mem. exec. bd. Inland Empire coun., region 11 exec. com. Boy Scouts Am.; pres. Spokane Unltd.; mem. adv. coun. Sch. Bus., Gonzaga U.; bd. dirs., mem. exec. com. Expo '74 World's Fair, 1973-74; mem. bd. regents Ft. Wright Coll., Spokane, 1960-72; bd. dirs. Sacred Heart Med. Ctr., 1961-70, Fairmont Meml. Assn.; chmn. bd. mem. Spokane Housing Authority, 1972-87; chmn. Spokane C. of C., 1973-75; bd. regents Wash. State U., 1979-92. Lt. USNR, 1943—45. Mem. Nat. Assn. Mut. Savs. Banks (chmn. 1976-77), Mut. Savs. Banks Assn. State of Wash. (pres. 1980), Am. Savs. and Loan Inst. (past gov. dist. XI), Spokane C. of C. (pres. 1974-75, chmn., 1975-77), Clubs: Rotary of Spokane, K.C. Roman Catholic. Home: 2408 E Deerwood Ct Spokane WA 99223

MCWILLIAMS, GRANT, osteopath; s. Kent and Ronda McWilliams; m. Charlene Schambach. D in Osteo. Medicine, Kirksville Coll. Osteo. Medicine, Mo., 2003. Diplomate osteo. medicine AOA, 2003. Resident US Army, Honolulu, 2003—08, physician Ft. Wainwright, Alaska, 2008—. Contbr. articles to profl. jour. (Donald F. Richardson Meml. prize, 2008). Capt. US Army, 2003—08, Ft. Wainwright. Decorated Army Achievement Medal US Army, Goldern Apple award Tripler Army Med. Ctr.; recipient Maj. Gillespie award, Brooke Army Med. Ctr., 2004. Mem.: Am. Soc. Reproductive Medicine, Am. Coll. Ob-Gyn., Am. Osteo. Assn. Protestant. Achievements include research in reproductive endocrinology & infertility, uro-gynecology, & clinical obstetrics. Office: Dept Ob-Gyn 1060 Gaffney Rd #7400 Fort Wainwright AK 99703-7400

MCWILLIAMS, JOHN LAWRENCE, III, lawyer; b. Phila., Dec. 21, 1943; s. John Lawrence Jr. and Elizabeth Dolores (Chevalier) McW.; m. Paula Ann Root, July 19, 1969 (dec.); children: John Lawrence, IV, Robert Root, Anne Elizabeth, David Stanford, Peter Farrell; m. Kathleen Nolan Pradella, Apr. 3, 1993. BS, St. Joseph's U., 1965; JD, Seton Hall U., 1969. Bar: NJ 1969, NY 1975, US Supreme Ct. 1975, Fla. 1977. Trial atty., regional office SEC, NYC, 1969-72; assoc. Mudge Rose Guthrie & Alexander, NYC, 1972-77; mem. Freeman, Richardson, Watson & Kelly, P.A., Jacksonville, Fla., 1977-89, chmn., pres., 1984-89; ptnr. Squire, Sanders & Dempsey, Jacksonville, 1989-98, Livermore, Freeman & McWilliams, P.A., Jacksonville, 1998—. Trustee Mcpl. Svc. Dist. Ponte Vedra Beach, 1981-85, chmn. bd. trustees, 1984-85; treas. Ponte Vedra Cmty. Assn., 1980-82; mem. Leadership Jacksonville, 1981, steering com., 1982; dir. Jacksonville Country Day Sch., 1985-87; pres. Jacksonville Beaches Ponte Vedra Unit Am. Cancer Soc., 1988-90; bd. dirs. Sawgrass Property Owners Assn., Inc., 2000-02. Fellow Am. Coll. Bond Counsel (bd. dir. 2007-); mem. Nat. Assn. Bond Lawyers, The Fla. Bar, Jacksonville C. of C., Jacksonville Cmty. Coun. Inc., Univ. Club, Ponte Vedra Club, Sawgrass Club, River Club. Republican. Roman Catholic. Home: 3040 Timberlake Pt Ponte Vedra Beach FL 32082-3726 Office: Livermore Freeman & McWilliams PA 320 N First St Ste 603 Jacksonville Beach FL 32250 Home Phone: 904-285-2499; Office Phone: 904-399-0500. Personal E-mail: jmcwilliams3@gmail.com. Business E-Mail: jmcwilliams@lfmlaw.net.

MCWILLIAMS, JOHN MICHAEL, lawyer; b. Annapolis, Md., Aug. 17, 1939; s. William J. and Helen (Disharon) McW.; m. Frances Edelen McCabe, May 30, 1970; children: M. Edelen, J. Michael Jr., James McC. BS, Georgetown U., 1964; LL.B., U. Md., 1967; LLD (hon.), U. Balt., 1993. Bar: Md. 1967, U.S. Supreme Ct. 1970, U.S. Ct. Internat. Trade 1991, U.S. Ct. Mil. Appeals 1992; cert. mediator NASD. Law clk. Chief Judge Roszel C. Thomsen, U.S. Dist. Ct. Md., 1967-68; assoc. Piper and Marbury, Balt., 1968-69; asst. atty. gen. Md., 1969-76; gen. counsel Md. Dept. Transp., 1971-76; sr. ptnr. Tydings and Rosenberg, Balt., 1977-97; pres. McWilliams Dispute Resolution, Balt., 1997—. Permanent mem. 4th Jud. Conf.; mem. panel of disting. neutrals CPR Inst. for Dispute

Resolution, 1994—2001; mem. Md. Alt. Dispute Resolution Commn., 1994—2002. Asst. editor Law Rev., U. Md., 1967; mem. nat. bd. advisors Ohio State Jour. Dispute Resolution. Chmn. Md. adv. coun. to Nat. Legal Svcs. Corp., 1975-78; mem. Gov.'s Commn. to Revise Annotated Code of Md., 1973-78; transition dir. Md. Gov.-Elect Harry Hughes, 1978-79; mem. Md. Indsl. Devel. Financing Authority, 1980; mem. Greater Balt. Com., 1979-94; mem. exec. com. Econ. Devel. Coun. Greater Balt., 1979-83; vice chmn. bd. Washington/Balt. Regional Assn., 1980-83; mem. Md. Econ. and Cmty. Devel. Adv. Commn., 1983-87; chmn. bd. Md. Econ. Devel. Corp., 1984-89. Served to 1st lt. U.S. Army, 1958-60. Fellow Am. Bar Found. (bd. dirs. 1986-88, 91-93), Internat. Acad. Mediators (pres. 2006—07), Coll. Comml. Arbitrators (pres. 2004-05), Md. Bar Found. (dir. 1980-82); mem. ABA (pres. 1992-93, mem. ho. of dels. 1976—, chmn. 1986-88, chmn. Md. del. 1976-86, bd. editors jour. 1986-88, 91-93) Md. Bar Assn. (pres. 1981-82), Nat. Conf. Bar Pres. (exec. coun. 1982-85), Bar Assn. Balt. City, Am. Law Inst., Am. Judicature Soc. (dir. 1974-81, exec. com. 1975-77), Am. Acad. Judicature Edn. (dir. 1977), Md. Law Rev. (trustee 1980-83), Md. Inst. Continuing Edn. Lawyers (trustee 1980-83), Inst. Internat. Bus. Law and Practice (corr.), Md. Club, Rule Day Club. Democrat. Roman Catholic. Home: 3 Merryman Ct Baltimore MD 21210-2815 Office: 1106 N Charles St Ste 300 Baltimore MD 21201 Office Phone: 410-244-8124.

MCWILLIAMS, JOHN PROBASCO, JR., English literature educator; b. Cleve., July 22, 1940; s. John Probasco and Ella (Barlow) McW.; m. Mireille Barbaud, July 13, 1985; children: Christopher, Isabel; children by previous marriage: Andrew, Suzannah, Kirsten, Elizabeth. AB, Princeton U., 1962; AM, Harvard U., 1963, PhD, 1968. Asst. prof. U. Calif., Berkeley, 1968-74; assoc. prof. U. Ill., Chgo., 1974-77, assoc. head dept. English, 1975-77; prof. Middlebury Coll., Vt., 1978—, chmn. dept. Am. lit. Middlebury, 1978-90, v.p. acad. affairs, 1995-97; prof. humanities 2004-. Author: Political Justice in a Republic: Fenimore Cooper's America, 1972, (with Bloomfield and Smith) Law and American Literature, 1982, Hawthorne, Melville and the American Character, 1984, The American Epic: Transforming A Gene, 1989, Civil Savagery and Savage Civility, 1994, New England's Crises and Cultural Memory, 2004; contbr. articles to profl. jours; mem. editl. bd. NCL, EAL, 1994—. Woodrow Wilson fellow, 1962; Humanities fellow, 1970-71; NEH fellow, 1982-83, 88-89, 93-94. Fellow Am. Antiquarian Soc.; Phi Beta Kappa. Home: 42 Seminary St Middlebury VT 05753-1219 Office: Middlebury Coll 328 Axinn Ctr Middlebury VT 05753 Home Phone: 802-388-3054; Office Phone: 802-443-5316. Business E-Mail: mcwillia@middlebury.edu.

MCWILLIAMS, KAREN JOAN, writer; b. Alexandria, La., Oct. 12, 1943; d. Steve Peters and Nettie Beatrice Barricklow; step-father: Paul F. McWilliams; m. Charles F. Slezak, June 16, 1973 (div. 1976); m. Julio Espinosa, July 26, 1980 (div. 1988). BA in Elem. Edn., U. No. Colo., 1966; MA in Ednl. Tech./Libr. Sci., San Diego State U., 1976. Tchr. 2d grade Motherlode Union, Diamond Springs, Calif., 1966-67; tchr. 3d grade Redlands (Calif.) Unified Sch. Dist., 1967-69, Dept. of Def. Overseas Schs., various locations, 1969-77; sch. libr. Dept. of Edn., St. Croix, V.I., 1977-83; passage writer Harcourt Brace Edn. Measurement, 1995—97, Pearson Edn. Measurement, 2006—. Author: Pirates, 1989, The Journal of Leroy Jeremiah Jones, 2001, A Fugitive Slave: The Diary of a Slave Girl, Ruby Jo, 2002, The Journal of Darien Dexter Duff Emancipated Slave, 2003 (Royal Palm Young Adult Lit. award, 2003); contbr. articles to Writer's Digest, The Writer, others; children's book reviewer Ind. Pub. mag. Soc. of Children's Book Writers grantee, 1985. Mem. The Authors Guild, Soc. Children's Book Writers and Illustrators (book reviewer). Office Phone: 239-353-0856. Personal E-mail: ksophiedog@aol.com.

MCWILLIAMS, MARGARET ANN, home economist, educator, writer; b. Osage, Iowa, May 26, 1929; d. Alvin Randall and Mildred Irene Edgar; children: Roger, Kathleen. BS, Iowa State U., 1951, MS, 1953; PhD, Oreg. State U., 1968. Registered dietitian. Asst. prof. home econs. Calif. State U., LA, 1961-66, assoc. prof., 1966-68, prof., 1968-92, prof. emeritus, 1992—, chmn. dept., 1968-76; pres. Plycon Press, 1978—. Author: Food Fundamentals, 1966, 8th edit., 2006, 9th edit. 2009, Nutrition for the Growing Years, 1967, 6th edit., 2009, Experimental Foods Laboratory Manual, 1977, 5th edit., 2000, 6th edit., 2005, 7th edit., 2008, Lifelong Nutrition, 2001, (with L. Kotschevar) Understanding Food, 1969, Illustrated Guide to Food Preparation, 1970, 8th edit., 1998, 10th edit., 2009, (with L. Davis) Food for You, 1971, 2d edit., 1976, The Meatless Cookbook, 1973, (with F. Stare) Living Nutrition, 1973, 4th edit., 1984, Nutrition for Good Health, 1974, 2d edit., 1982, (with H. Paine) Modern Food Preservation, 1977, Fundamentals of Meal Management, 1978, 4th edit., 2005, 5th edit., 2008, (with H. Heller) The World of Nutrition, 1984, Foods: Experimental Perspectives, 1989, 4th edit. 2000, 5th edit., 2005, 6th edit., 2008, Food Around the World: A Cultural Perspective, 2003, 2d edit., 2007. Chmn. bd. Beach Cities Symphony, 1991-94. Recipient Alumni Centennial award Iowa State U., 1971, Profl. Achievement award, 1977; Phi Upsilon Omicron Nat. Founders fellow, 1964; Home Economist in Bus. Nat. Found. fellow, 1967; Outstanding Prof. award Calif. State U., 1976. Mem. Am. Dietetic Assn., Inst. Food Technologists, Phi Kappa Phi, Phi Upsilon Omicron, Omicron Nu, Iota Sigma Pi, Sigma Delta Epsilon, Sigma Alpha Iota. Home: PO Box 220 Redondo Beach CA 90277-0220 Personal E-mail: mmcwredondo@aol.com.

MCWILLIAMS, MICHAEL, writer, publisher; b. Detroit, Aug. 28, 1952; s. Henry and Mary (Toarmina) McW. BA, Wayne State U., 1975; MFA, Columbia U., 1978. Free-lance writer Monthly Detroit mag., 1979-82, Village Voice, Rolling Stone, TV Guide, Advt. Age, N.Y. Daily News, L.A. Herald Examiner, NYC, 1982-87; TV critic, 1988—2001; pub. MaryBooks, 2002—. Author: TV Sirens, 1987, (with others) The Premiere Guide to Movies on Video, 1991. Recipient Assn. of Sunday and Feature Editors award, 1st pl. Arts Criticism, 1992. Mem. Phi Beta Kappa. Avocations: television, movies, theater, music.

MCWILLIAMS, MIKE C., lawyer; b. Dallas, Nov. 10, 1948; s. Earl Dewitt and Mary Louise (Campbell) McWilliams; m. Sally Swatzell, Sept. 1, 1973; children: Michael, Matthew. BBA in Fin., U. Tex., 1969, JD, 1973. Bar: Tex. 1973. Assoc. Elliott, Meer, Vetter, Denton & Bates, Dallas, 1973-78; ptnr. Denton & Generis, Dallas, 1978-80, Moore & Peterson, P.C., Dallas, 1980-89, Winstead PC, Dallas, 1989—. Editor: Texas International Law Journal, 1972—73. Mem.: Dallas Bar Assn., Tex. State Bar Assn., Beta Gamma Sigma, Phi Delta Phi. Office: Winstead PC 5400 Renaissance Tower 1201 Elm St Ste 5400 Dallas TX 75270-2199 Office Phone: 214-745-5631. Business E-Mail: mmcwilliams@winstead.com.

MCWILLIAMS, ROBERT HUGH, federal judge; b. Salina, Kans., Apr. 27, 1916; s. Robert Hugh and Laura (Nicholson) McW.; m. Catherine Ann Cooper, Nov. 4, 1942 (dec.); 1 son, Edward Cooper; m. Joan Harcourt, Mar. 8, 1986. AB, U. Denver, 1938, LL.B., 1941. Bar: Colo. bar 1941. Dep. dist. atty. Denver, Co, 1941—42; special agent US Office of Naval Intelligence, 1942—45; sgt. US Army, Office of Strategic Services, 1945—46; dist. atty. Denver, Co., 1946—49; private practice Denver, Co, 1949—52; judge municipal ct., Denver, 1949—52, dist., city, and county, Denver, 1952—61, supreme ct. of Co., 1967—70; instructor U. of Denver, 1954—60; judge US Ct. Appeals (10th cir.), Denver, 1970—84, sr. judge, 1984—. Served with AUS, World War II. Mem. Phi Beta Kappa, Omicron Delta Kappa, Phi Delta Phi, Kappa Sigma. Republican. Episcopalian. Home: 137 Jersey St Denver CO 80220-5918 Office: Byron White US Courthouse 1823 Stout St Rm 216 Denver CO 80257-1823

MCWILLIAMS, ROGER DEAN, physicist, researcher; b. Ames, Iowa, Aug. 18, 1954; s. Donald Arthur and Margaret Ann (Edgar) McW.; m. Carol Lee Carter, Sept. 7, 1985; children: Alice Louise, Corinne Lee. BA, U. Calif., Irvine, 1975; PhD, Princeton U., 1980. Rsch. asst. Princeton (N.J.) U., 1975-80; asst. prof. in physics U. Calif., Irvine, 1980-87, assoc. prof., 1987-91, prof., 1991—, acting dean undergrad. studies, 1994-95, cons., expert witness for physics and law, 1983—, cons., expert witness for physics in sports, 1988—. Mem. IEEE, Optical Soc. America, Am. Phys. Soc., Am. Geophys. Union, Phi Beta Kappa, Sigma Xi. Office: Univ California- Irvine Dept Physics & Astronomy Irvine CA 92697 Home: 3 Dickens Ct Irvine CA 92617 Business E-Mail: mcw@uci.edu.

MCWILLIAMS, TERESSA WYLIE, choreographer; married. MFA, Sam Houston State U., Huntsville, Tex., 1996. Choreographer (concert dance) Whispers of the Spirit (Kans. Arts Commn. award). Mem. OhioDance, Columbus. Mem.: Actors Equity Assn.

MEACHAM, CHARLES HARDING, federal agency administrator; b. Newman, Calif., Sept. 21, 1925; s. Vernon A. and Sara (Paulsen) M.; m. June Lorraine Yunker, June 22, 1946; children— Charles Paulsen, Bruce Herbert. BS, Utah State U., 1950. Biologist Calif. Dept. Fish and Game, 1950-56, Alaska Dept. Fisheries, 1956-59; regional supr. regions II and III Alaska Dept. Fish and Game, 1959-68; dir. internat. fisheries Office Gov. Alaska, 1968-69; commr. U.S. Fish and Wildlife Service, Dept. Interior, 1969-70, dep. asst. sec. for fish and wildlife, pks. and marine resources, commr. Internat. North Pacific Fisheries Commn. and Gt. Lakes Fishery Commn., 1969-70, commr. Internat. Pacific Salmon Fisheries Commn., 1969-70, commr. Great Lakes Fishery Commn., 1969-70, spl. asst. to area dir. Alaska, 1971-74; dir. internat. affairs Office of Gov., Juneau, Alaska, 1975-80; pres. Meacham & Assocs., Anchorage, 1980—. Dep. commr. US North Pacific Fur Seal Commn.; mem. Pacific and North Pacific Fisheries Mgmt. Councils, 1976-81; chmn. nat. park system adv. bd. US Dept. Interior. Bd. dir. Resource Devel. Coun. for Alaska. With USMCR, 1943-46. Mem. Am. Fisheries Soc., Wildlife Soc., Pacific Fisheries Biologists, Internat. Assn. Game, Fish and Conservation Commrs., Ducks Unlimited, Alaska Miners Assn., Am. Legion, USMC Raiders Assn. (pres. 2003—04), Elks. Address: 3389 Harborview Dr Unit 205 Gig Harbor WA 98332

MEACHAM, DAVID ADAM, biologist; b. Malvern, Pa., Aug. 2, 1974; s. Kenneth James and Patricia Ann Klossman; m. Veronica Bachrach, Sept. 17, 1998; children: Aidan David, Liam Emerson. MS in Cell Biology & Biotech., U. Scis. Phila., 2006. Rsch. biologist Merck & Co. Inc, West Point, Pa., 2001—; instr. biology Montgomery County CC, Pottstown, Pa., 2006—. Recipient Lucille Griswold prize, Albright Coll., 2001.

MEACHAM, JON E., editor; b. Chattanooga, 1969; m. Keith Meacham; 2 children. BA in English Lit., summa cum laude, U. of South, Sewanee, Tenn., 1991; LHD (hon.), Yale U. Berkley Div. Sch., 2005, Loyola Coll., Md., 2007. Writer Newsweek mag., NYC, 1995, nat. affairs editor, 1995—98, mng. editor, 1998—2006, editor, 2006—. Contbg. editor The Washington Monthly; writer NY Times Book Review, Washington Post, LA Times Book Review, Washington Post Book World. Author: Franklin and Winston: An Intimate Portrait of an Epic Friendship, 2003 (NY Times bestseller, LA Times Book of Yr., Emery Reves award, Churchill Centre, 2005, William H. Colby Military Writers' Symposium's Book of Yr., 2005), American Gospel: God, the Founding Fathers, and the Making of a Nation, 2006 (NY Times bestseller), American Lion: Andrew Jackson in the White House, 2008 (Publishers Weekly bestseller, Pulitzer prize for biography, 2009); editor: Voices in Our Blood: America's Best on the Civil Rights Movement, 2001. Bd. regents U. of South; leadership coun. Harvard Divinity Sch.; nat. adv. grp. Wash. Nat. Cathedral; active St. Thomas Ch. Fifth Ave., NYC, Trinity Ch. Wall St., NYC. Recipient Hubert H. Humphrey First Amendment Freedoms prize, Anti-Defamation League, 2007. Mem.: Coun. Fgn. Rels. Episcopalian. Office: Newsweek 251 W 57th St New York NY 10019-1894*

MEACHAM, SCOTT, state treasurer; b. Okla. m. Susan Meacham; 4 children. BA in Fin., Univ. Okla., MBA, JD, Univ. Okla. Cert. CFP. Atty.; CEO First Nat. Bank & Trust, Elk City, Okla.; finance dir. State of Okla., treas., 2005—. Office: State Treas Rm 217 2300 N Lincoln Blvd Oklahoma City OK 73105 Office Phone: 405-521-3191. Office Fax: 405-521-4994. Business E-Mail: Okla.Treas@treas.state.ok.us.*

MEACHAM, SUSAN, dietician, educator; d. Thomas and Carol Meacham; children: Aaron Darnton, Kimberly Darnton. PhD, Va. Tech., Blacksburg, 1991. Cert. dietitian Am. Dietetic Assn., 1983. Assoc. prof. UNLV, Las Vegas, Nev., 1998—. Health care com. mem. LWV Las Vegas Valley, 2004—09.

MEACHIN, DAVID JAMES PERCY, investment banker; b. Teignmouth, Devon, Eng., Jan. 1, 1941; arrived in U.S., 1969, naturalized, 1990; s. James Alfred and Ena Annie Meachin; m. Barbara Marshall Maxwell, Sept. 25, 1971; children: Jonathan J.M., Philip D.M. BS in Phys. Sci., U. Natal, South Africa, 1960; BSChemE, U. Cape Town, South Africa, 1963; MS in Petroleum Engring., French Petroleum Inst., Paris, 1965; diploma in Indsl. Mgmt., Cambridge U., Eng., 1966; MBA with distinction, Harvard U., 1971. Project engr. Humphreys and Glasgow Ltd., London, 1966-69; 2nd v.p. investment banking Smith Barney and Co. Inc., NYC and Tokyo, 1971-75; v.p., gen. mgr. internat. corp. fin. Salomon Bros., NYC and London, 1975-81; mng. dir. investment banking divsn. Merrill Lynch Capital Markets, NYC, 1981-91; chmn., CEO Cross Border Enterprises L.L.C.; dir. Ground Round Inc. NASDAQ, 1991—95, Spartek Emerging Opportunities India Fund, 1995—2002, Millennium Chem. Inc., 1996—2004, Lyondell Chem. Co., 2004—07. Mem. adv. bd. Gow & Ptnrs., 2003—, Structured Credit Internat. Corp., 2003—, South African C. of C. Am., 2005—; mem. Corp. Dir. Club, Chief Exec. Officers Club, Nat. Assn. Corp. Dirs. Past chmn. Brit. Am. Ednl. Found.; elder Brick Presbyn. Ch., N.Y.C., 1988—; bd. dirs., vice-chmn. U. Cape Town Fund, N.Y.C., 1985—. Mem.: Kelvin Grove Club (South Africa), Union Club, Harvard Club, United Oxford and Cambridge Club (UK), Misquamicut Club (former bd. govs.). Avocations: sailing, golf, tennis, squash. Home: 351 E 84th St New York NY 10028 Office: 445 Park Ave 9th Fl New York NY 10022 Home Phone: 212-717-5495; Office Phone: 212-682-7400. Business E-Mail: dmeachin@crossborderent.com.

MEACHUM, DANIEL RAY, lawyer; b. Badin, NC, 1955; BA in Polit. Sci. cum laude, NC Ctrl. U., 1977; JD cum laude, Howard U. Sch. Law, Wash. DC, 1981; LLM in Internat. Comparative Law, U. Brussels, 1985. Bar: Pa. Supreme Ct. 1984, Ga. Superior Ct. 2002, US Dist. Ct. (ea. dist.) Pa, US Ct. Appeals (3rd Cir.). Atty. US Atty. Office (so. dist.) NY, Phila.; gen. counsel NY, Atlanta; counsel power brokers Herman J. Russel, Jesse Hill, and Felker Ward, Atlanta; founder Daniel R. Meachum & Assocs. LLC, Atlanta; ptnr., gen. counsel Le Jardin, Atlanta. Recipient Pres. Nat. Citizenship award; Fulbright fellow. Mem.: US Dept. Justice Hon. Program. Achievements include successfully trying 122 out of 126 major jury trials and arbitrations. Office: Daniel R Meachum & Assocs LLC 1995 N Pk Pl Ste 250 Atlanta GA 30339 Office Phone: 770-988-9600. Office Fax: 770-988-9690. Business E-Mail: dmeachum@dmeachumlaw.com.

MEACHUM, PETE (CHARLES PETERSON MEACHUM), legislative staff member; Office mgr., scheduler for Rep. Ginny Brown-Waite, US House of Reps., 2003—04, legis. dir., 2004—05, chief of staff, 2005—. Office: Office of Congresswoman Ginny Brown-Waite 414 Cannon House Office Bldg Washington DC 20515 Office Phone: 202-225-1002. E-mail: pete.meachum@mail.house.gov.*

MEAD, ANDREW M., state supreme court justice; Grad., U. Maine; JD, NY Law Sch. With Paine, Lynch & Weatherbee, Bangor, Maine, 1976—81; chief judge Penobscot Tribal Ct., Maine, 1979—90; ptnr. Mitchell & Stearns, Bangor, 1981—90; judge Maine Dist. Ct., 1990—92, Maine Superior Ct., 1992—2007, chief justice, 1999—2001; assoc. justice Maine Supreme Jud. Ct., 2007—. Jud. liaison Maine Rules of Evidence Adv. Com.; chair Task Force on Electronic Ct. Records; adj. faculty mem. U. Maine. Office: Maine Supreme Jud Ct PO Box 368 Portland ME 04112-0368*

MEAD, CHRISTOPHER, lawyer; b. Richmond, Va., Mar. 20, 1959; BA magna cum laude, Yale Coll., 1981; JD, Yale Law Sch., 1985. Bar: Md. 1985, DC 1988, Va. 1995, admitted to practice: US Ct. Appeals (4th Cir.) 1986, US Ct. Appeals (2nd Cir.) 1986, US Ct. Appeals (7th Cir.) 1986, US Ct. Appeals (11th Cir.) 1986, US Ct. Appeals (DC Cir.) 1986, US Dist. Ct., Dist. Md. 1986, US Dist. Ct. (DC) 1988, US Dist. Ct. (Ea. and Western Dists. Va.) 1995. Law clk. to Hon. Joseph H. Young US Dist. Ct., Dist. Md., 1985—86; assoc. Williams & Connolly, 1986—89; asst. US atty. Dist. Md., 1989—94, spl. asst. US atty., 1994; ptnr. London & Mead, Washington. Author: Champion Joe Lewis, Black Hero in White America, 1985. Named one of 75 Best Lawyers in Washington, Washingtonian Mag., 2002. Fellow: Am. Coll. Trial Lawyers; mem.: Va. State Bar, Md. State Bar Assn., DC Bar. Office: London & Mead 1225 Nineteenth St NW Ste 320 Washington DC 20036 Office Phone: 202-331-3334.

MEAD, DANA GULLING, literature and language professor; b. Knoxville, Tenn., 1961; d. Ronald Dean and Joan Eloise Gulling; m. Andrew David Mead, 1986; children: Deanna Brooke, Savannah Brette. BA, MA, U. Tenn., Knoxville; PhD, Tex. Christian U., Ft. Worth. Assoc. prof. English Elizabethtown Coll., Pa., 1989—, honors program dir., 2005—, pres. faculty assembly, 2008—. Contbr. articles to profl. jours. Mem.: Phi Beta Kappa. Office: Elizabethtown Coll One Alpha Dr Elizabethtown PA 17022 Business E-Mail: meaddg@etown.edu.

MEAD, DANIEL S., telecommunications industry executive; m. Wendy Mead. B in quantitative bus. analysis and fin., Pa. State U., 1975, MBA, 1977. Tooling and equipment plant controller GTE, 1978; founding sr. exec. Verizon Wireless Verizon Comm., 2000, pres. Verizon Wireless midwest region, 2001—05, pres. Verizon Services Corp., 2005—08, pres. Verizon Telecom. Mem. bd. dirs. Vodafone Italia. Recipient Alumni Fellow award, Pa. State Alumni Assn., 2008. Mem.: Behrend Coun. Fellows, Pa. State U. Office: Verizon Comm 140 West St New York NY 10007*

MEAD, JAMES MATTHEW, insurance company executive; b. Erie, Pa., June 10, 1945; s. James Leonard and Olga (Richter) M.; m. Rhoda Ginsburg, Sept. 2, 1967 (div. 1971); m. Elaine Margaret Lytle, Mar. 8, 1975. BS in Econs., Pa. State U., U. Pk., 1967, MA in Econs., 1970. Instr. bus. Pa. State U., Middletown, 1968-71; asst. to ins. commr. Commonwealth of Pa., Harrisburg, 1971-74; asst. to pres. Capital Blue Cross, Harrisburg, 1974-78, sr. v.p., 1978-84, pres., CEO, 1984—2004, vice chmn., 2004—; mng. dir. JM Mead, LLC, 2004—; venture ptnr. Radius Ventures LLC, NYC, 2006—. Bd. dirs. Fed. Res. Bank Phila., 1991-95, chmn., 1994-95; bd. dirs. Internat. Life Scis. Inst., Washington, 2004-; trustee, chmn. Lawyers Fund Client Security, Pa. Supreme Ct., Harrisburg, Pa., 2005-09, Lebanon Valley Coll., Annville, Pa., 2003-09; bd. dirs. Hershey Trust Co., Pa., 2007-, M.S. Hershey Found., Pa., 2007-; bd. mgrs., Milton Hershey Sch., Pa., 2007-, bd. dirs. Utality Group Inc., Chgo., Mgmt. Health Solutions Inc., 2008- Contbr. articles on health care to profl. publs. Mem. bd. advisors Pa. State U., 1985-93; chmn. savs. bond campaign for Ctrl. Pa., U.S. Treasury Dept., Harrisburg, 1986-87; bd. dirs. United Way Capital Region, 1994-98, campaign chair, 1994; bd. dirs. Harrisburg Symphony Assn., 2000-09, chmn. 2005-07; bd. dirs., Found. Enhancing Cmty., 2001-09, trustee, Pa. Lawyers Fund for Client Security, Pa. Supreme Ct. Paul Harris fellow Rotary Internat., 1988, Alumni fellow Pa. State U., 1986. Mem. West Shore Country Club; Camp Hill, Princeton Club. Home: 1752 Conway Heath Camp Hill PA 17011 Home Phone: 717-763-1490; Office Phone: 717-763-1678. Personal E-mail: jim@jmmead.com.

MEAD, KENNETH MINOR, lawyer, former federal agency administrator; b. May 14, 1947; m. Elizabeth Guerry; children: Jennifer, Hillary. Baccalaurette Degree, So. Conn. U., 1970; JD, U. S.C., 1975; John F. Kennedy Sch. Sr. Mgrs. in Govt., Harvard U., 1991. Sr. atty. Office Gen. Counsel U.S. Gen. Acctg. Office, Washington, 1975-82, asst. dir. Office Quality Assurance, 1982-86, assoc., asst. dir. transp., dir. transp. & telecom. issues, 1986-96, dep. asst. comptr. gen. for policy, 1996-97; inspector gen. U.S. Dept. Transp., Washington, 1997—2006; spl. counsel Baker Botts LLP, Washington, 2006—. Mem. Pres. Coun. on Integrity and Efficiency, 1997-05, Comptr. Gen.'s U.S. Domestic Accountability Bd., 2001-05. With USN, 1970—72. Recipient GAO Disting. Svc. award, Meritorious Svc. award. Mem. Am. Numismatic Assn., D.C. Bar Assn., Fed. Bar Assn., Assn. Govt. Accountants Office: Baker Botts LLP The Warner 1299 Pennsylvania Ave NW Washington DC 20004 Office Phone: 202-639-7744. Business E-Mail: ken.mead@bakerbotts.com.

MEAD, LAWRENCE MYERS, JR., retired engineering executive; b. Plainfield, NJ, May 11, 1918; s. Lawrence Myers and Eleanor Whitman (Machado) M.; m. Janet Chase, Feb. 21, 1942; children— Lawrence Myers, Kirtland Chase, Jonathan Taylor, Bradford Machado. BSE, Princeton U., 1940, C.E., 1941; postgrad. mgmt., Harvard Bus. Sch., 1964. With Grumman Corp., Bethpage, NY, 1941-93; v.p. tech. ops. Grumman Aerospace Corp., Bethpage, NY, 1972-75, sr. v.p. dept. ops., 1975-81, sr. v.p. tech. ops., 1981-83; sr. mgmt. cons., 1983-93. Patentee in field. Trustee, police commr., dep. mayor Village of Huntington Bay, N.Y., 1975-80; trustee N.Y.C. Hall of Sci. Fellow Poly. U., 1981. Fellow

AIAA; mem. NAE, L.I. Forum on Tech. (bd. dirs., past chmn. bd.), Soc. Logistic Engrs., Soc. Advancement Materials and Process Engring., Princeton U. Alumni Assn. Democrat. Achievements include designing A6A Intruder Navy All Weather Bomber, Gulfstream III Exec. Jet Transport. Home: 88 Notch Hill Rd Apt 253 North Branford CT 06471-1851

MEAD, LAWRENCE MYERS, III, political science educator; b. Huntington, NY, June 9, 1943; s. Lawrence Myers Jr. and Janet (Chase) M.; m. Robin Elizabeth Brady, May 11, 1996. BA, Amherst Coll., 1966; MA, Harvard U., 1968, PhD, 1973. Mgmt. intern HEW, Washington, 1973-75; rsch. assoc. Urban Inst., Washington, 1975-78; dep. rsch. dir. Rep. Nat. Com., Washington, 1978-79; prof. politics NYU, 1979—. Vis. prof. U. Wis., Madison, spring 1987, Harvard U., Cambridge, Mass., 1993-94, Princeton (N.J.) U., 1994-95; vis. scholar Hoover Instn., Stanford, Calif., 1988; vis. fellow Princeton (N.J.) U., 1995-96, 2001-02. Author: Beyond Entitlement, 1986, The New Politics of Poverty, 1992; author, editor: The New Paternalism, 1997; co-author: From Welfare to Work, 1997, Government Matters, 2004, Welfare Reform and Political Theory, 2005. Adviser on welfare policy Rudolph Giuliani Mayoral Campaigns, N.Y.C., 1993, 97, Reagan Adminstrn., Washington, 1986-87, State of Wis., Madison, 1996—, Human Resources Adminstrn., N.Y.C., 1997—. Fulbright scholar, 1970. Mem. Am. Polit. Sci. Assn. (coun. pub. policy sect. 2000—), Assn. for Pub. Policy Analysis and Mgmt. (conf. com. 1987, 96, 98), Policy Studies Orgn., Am. Soc. for Polit. and Legal Philosophy. Republican. Avocations: sailing, crossword puzzles. Office: NYU Dept Politics 19 W 4th St New York NY 10012 Office Phone: 212-998-8540. Business E-Mail: lmm1@nyu.edu.

MEAD, PHILIP BARTLETT, retired obstetrician, healthcare administrator, educator; b. Poughkeepsie, NY, June 23, 1937; s. Ralph Allen and Altina (Gervin) Mead; m. Ann Elaine Smith, June 27, 1964; children: Ralph Allen II, David Smith. BA, Hamilton Coll., 1959; MD, Cornell U., 1963. Diplomate Nat. Bd. Med. Examiners, Am. Bd. Ob-gyn. Intern in medicine Bellevue Hosp., NYC, 1963-64; resident in ob-gyn. NY Hosp./Cornell Med. Ctr., NYC, 1964-69; asst. prof. U. Vt. Coll. Medicine, Burlington, 1971-76, assoc. prof., 1976-81, prof., 1981—2001, prof. emeritus, 2001—; hosp. epidemiologist Med. Ctr. Hosp. of Vt., Burlington, 1984-93; dir. clin. sys. Vt. Acad. Med. Ctr., Burlington, 1993-95; sr. v.p., med. dir. Fletcher Allen Health Care, Burlington, 1995-97; prof., chmn. ob-gyn. U. Vt. Coll. Medicine, 1997—2001, prof., chmn. emeritus, 2001—; physician leader women's health care svcs. Fletcher Allen Health Care, Burlington, 1997—2001. Lt. comdr. M.C. USN, 1969—71. Fellow: ACOG, Infectious Disease Soc. Am.; mem.: Soc. Hosp. Epidemiologists, Infectious Disease Soc. Ob-Gyn. (pres. 1987—88), Phi Beta Kappa, Alpha Omega Alpha. Home: 203 Pinehurst Dr Shelburne VT 05482-6882 Personal E-mail: pbmeadmd@comcast.net.

MEAD, PHILLIP GUNN, architect, educator; s. David and Martha Mead; m. Kris Mead. BArch, U. Idaho, Moscow, 1984; MArch., U. Tex., Austin, 1991. Registered architect, Calif., 1995. Asst. prof. Tex. Tech. U., Lubbock, 1997—2002; assoc. prof. U. Idaho, 2002—. Adj. prof. New Sch. Architecture, San Diego, 1993—97. Presentation Light, Air & Views: Hist. & Sci. Influences, Smithsonian Inst. Bd. mem. Soc. Light Treatment & Biol. Rhythms, 2005—08. 1st lt. Marines, 1984—88, Camp Lejune. Mem.: AIA (treas. 2001—02). Avocation: travel. Office: Univ Idaho PO Box 442451 Moscow ID 83844-2451 Office Fax: 208-885-9428. Business E-Mail: pmead@uidaho.edu.

MEAD, SUSANAH M., law educator; BA, Smith Coll., 1969; JD, Indiana U. Sch. Law, Indianapolis, 1976. Law clk. for Hon. Paul H. Buchanan Jr, chief judge Ind. Ct. Appeals, 1976—78; lectr. legal writing program to prof. law Ind. U. Sch. Law, Indpls., 1978—, dir. legal writing, 1980—81, assoc. dean academic affairs, 1997—2004, interim dean, 2005. Office: Indian U Sch Law Lawrence W Inlow Hall Rm 313 530 W New York St Indianapolis IN 46202-3225 Office Phone: 317-274-2600. Office Fax: 317-374-3266. E-mail: smead@iupui.edu.*

MEAD, WALTER BRUCE, retired political science professor; b. Cedar Rapids, Iowa, May 25, 1934; s. Otis Bruce Mead and Emma Alvena Schluntz. BA, Carleton Coll., Northfield, MN, 1956; MDiv, Yale Div. Sch., New Haven, 1960; PhD, Duke U., Durham, NC, 1963. Asst. prof. Lake Forest Coll., Govt. Dept., Ill., 1963—67; assoc. prof., prof. Ill. State U., Normal, 1967—95. Editl. bd. mem. Profl. Jours., Europe, 1968—; mem. McLean County Bd., Bloomington, Ill., 1974—78; pres. Michael Polanyi Soc., North America, 2006—. Author: (book) Extremism and Cognition: Styles of Irresponsibility in American Society, The United States Constitution: Personalities, Principles, and Issues; contbr. articles to profl. jours. mem. country budget com., Bloomington, 1974—78; pres. McLean County Mental Health Assn., Ill., 1978—80; mem. City Planning Commn., Normal, Ill., 1983—85, Adv. Com., City Planning, Bloomington, 1992—95; ordained min. Meth. Ch., Wester, NY; dir., internat. study programs Ill. State U., 1988—2002. Recipient award, George Baker Found., Rockefeller Theol. Found., Lilly Found. Earhart Found., 1986—87. Mem.: Michael Polanyi Soc., Am. Acad. Religion, Am. Philos. Assn., Am. Polit. Sci. Assn. Avocations: swimming, skiing. Home: 4 Kenyon Ct Bloomington IL 61701-3320 Personal E-mail: wbmead@ilstu.edu.

MEAD, WILLIAM CHARLES, physicist; b. Hazleton, Pa., Dec. 6, 1946; s. Norman Joseph and Ruth Crawford Mead; m. Carol Edna Jerome, May 24, 1969; 1 child, Bennett R. BS, Syracuse U., Syracuse, NY, 1968; MA, Princeton U., Princeton, NJ, 1970, PhD, 1974. Physicist Lawrence Livermore Nat. Lab., 1973—83; physicist, mgr. Los Alamos Nat. Lab., 1983—94; pres., chief scientist Adaptive Network Solutions Rsch. Inc., 1995—. Cons. Lawrence Livermore Nat. Lab., Livermore, Calif., 1995—99, Whistlesoft, Inc., Los Alamos, N.Mex., 1996—98, Ctr. for Adaptive Sys. Applications, Inc., Los Alamos, N.Mex., 1999, Complexica, Inc., Santa Fe, 1999—2004, Impulse Devices Inc., Grass Valley, Calif., 1999—2003, Los Alamos (N.Mex.) Nat. Lab., 2000—03, Gen. Fusion, Inc., 2003, Environ. Safety Svcs., 2004—06. Contbr. articles to profl. jours. Second lt. USAF, 1973—73. Fellow: Am. Phys. Soc. (fellowship 1987); mem.: Internat. Neural Network Soc. Achievements include being head designer for Cairn 50X Intermediate density target, the first laser-driven target to achieve compression of DT to 10 g/cc and a major milestone of the Inertial Confinement Fusion Program; designed and developed C++ engine for Agent-Based Crisis Simulator; development of the Connectionist Hyperprism Classification network to perform task of automated ion mobility spectrum analysis; Adaptive Teaching and Learning Lab. and an Adaptive Tutor for teaching basic arithmetic facts; research in theoretical and computational effort to explore feasibility of Sonic-Cavitation-Driven Fusion; numerical simulations extending knowledge in areas such as the behavior of fluid instabilities in high-gain ICF pellets and the scaling of laser-driven ablation; testing and extending the understanding of ICF physics, providing ideas, simulations and guidance for laser-plasma coupling experiments. Avocations: classical music, photography. Office: Adaptive Network Solutions Research 10 Bonito Pl Los Alamos NM 87544

MEADER, JOHN DANIEL, judge; b. Ballston Spa, NY, Oct. 22, 1931; s. Jerome Clement and Doris Luella (Conner) M.; m. Joyce Margaret Cowin, Mar. 2, 1963; children: John Daniel Jr., Julia Rae, Keith Alan. BA, Yale U., 1954; JD, Cornell U., 1962. Bar: NY 1963, US Dist. Ct. (no. dist.) NY 1963, US Ct. Appeals (2d cir.) 1966, US Supreme Ct. 1967, US Ct. Mil. Appeals 1973, Ohio 1978, US Dist. Ct. (no. dist.) Ohio 1979, Fla. 1983, US Ct. Appeals (4th cir.) 1992, US Ct. Appeals (fed. cir.) 1993. Sales engr. Albany Internat. Corp., NY, 1954-59; asst. track coach Cornell U., 1959-62; asst. sec., asst. to pres. Albany Internat. Corp., 1962-65; asst. atty. gen. State of NY, Albany, 1965-68; ops. counsel, attesting sec. GE, Schenectady, 1968-77; gen. counsel, asst. sec. Glidden div. SCM Corp., Cleve., 1977-81; chmn. bd., pres. Applied Power Tech. Co., Fernandina Beach, Fla., 1981-84; pres. Applied Energy, Inc., Ballston Spa, 1984-88; judge NY State Workers Compensation Bd., Albany, 1988—. Dir. Saratoga Mut. Fire Ins. Co. Author: Labor Law Manual, 1972, Contract Law Manual, 1974, Patent Law Manual, 1978. Candidate US Ho. of Reps., 29th Dist. NY, 1964, NY Supreme Ct., 1975, 87, 93. Col. JAGC, USAR, 1968-1984, dep. staff judge adv. 3d U.S. Army & Ctrl. Command, 1984, brig. gen. JAGC and Fin. Corps, NY Guard, 1984-2002, state staff judge adv. and state comptr. Nat. AAU High Sch. 1000 Yard Indoor Track Champion, 1949, Nat. AAU Prep. Sch. 440 and 880 Yard Indoor Track Champion, 1950, Nat. AAU Outstanding Performer award, Melrose Games Assn., 1950, Heptagonal Track 880-Yard Champion 1954. Mem. ABA, NY State Bar Assn., Fla. Bar, Amelia Island Plantation Club, Cyprus Temple Club, Yale Club Jacksonville (pres.), Masons. Republican. Presbyterian. Home: 271 Round Lake Rd Ballston Lake NY 12019-1714 Office: NY State Workers Compensation Bd 100 Broadway Albany NY 12241-0001 Office Phone: 518-402-6748. Business E-Mail: john.meader@wcb.state.ny.us.

MEADERS, DONALD W., lawyer; b. Dahlonega, Ga., May 3, 1947; AB, Harvard U., 1969, JD, 1973. Bar: Calif. 1973, States Dist. Ct. (ctrl. dist.) Calif. Ptnr. Manatt Phelps & Phillips LLP. Prog. chmn. 1988 Ann. Meeting Western Pension and Benefits Conf.; mem. steering com. LA chpt. Western Pension and Benefits Conf., 1988-90, sec., 1990-91, pres.-elect, 1991-92, spk. in fields. Contbr. Mem. ABA (mem. employee benefits com., tax sect.), State Bar Calif., LA County Bar Assn. (chmn. employee benefits com., tax sect. 1982-83, mem. exec. com. 1979-82), Calif. Bar Assn., mem. planning com.U. So. Calif. Tax Inst. 2003-2005. Office: Manatt Phelps & Phillips LLP 11355 W Olympic Blvd Los Angeles CA 90064 Office Phone: 310-312-4000, 310-312-4345. Office Fax: 310-312-4224. Business E-Mail: dmeaders@manatt.com.

MEAD-HASKINS, DEBRA, educational consultant, academic administrator, educator; d. John Albert and Norma W. Haskins; m. Lee Mead; children: Julia, Kerry, Donna, Gavin, Jacqueline. BA, SUC Cortland, NY, 1975; MA, SUNY, Stony Brook, 1991; student, Coll. New Rochelle, NY, 1992—94; PhD in Ednl. Psychology, St. John's U., Jamaica, NY, 2009. Cert. social studies educator, grades 7-12, sch. dist. adminstr. Pub. rels. position Taylor Wine Co., Hammondsport, NY, 1973—75; realtor Carriage Home Realty, Smithtown, NY, 1979—81; social studies tchr. Baldwinsville Acad., NY, 1975—79, Sachem Schs., Holbrook, NY, 1983—84, Huntington Unified Sch. Dist., NY, 1981—83, 1984—98, chairperson social studies, 1998—2009, part time ednl. cons., staff developer, 2009—. Exec. bd. tchr. ctr. Huntington Tchr. Ctr., 1999—; exec. bd. mem. Long Island Coun. Social Studies, NY, 2001—03. Women's advocate Chosin Few, LI, 1996—2003. Mentoring Grant for Tchrs., Huntington, NY, 1999—2002, Art and Architecture grant, NEA, 2002—04, Taft scholar, Freedoms Found. Mem.: ASCD, Nat. Coun. Social Studies. Independent. Avocations: painting, writing, reading, travel, dream interpretation. Home: 96 Summit Dr Smithtown NY 11787 Personal E-mail: debhaskins@aol.com.

MEADOR, CHARLES LAWRENCE, management and systems consultant, educator; b. Dallas, Oct. 7, 1946; s. Charles Leon and Dorothy Margaret (Brown), m. Diane E. Collins, May 18, 1985. BSME with honors, U. Tex., 1970; MSME, MS in Mgmt., MIT, 1972. Engring. staff Union Carbide Corp., Houston, 1967-68; instr. Alfred P. Sloan Sch. Mgmt. MIT, Cambridge, 1972-75, asst. dir. Ctr. Info. Systems Rsch., 1976-78, lectr. Sch. Engring., co-dir. Macro-Engring. Rsch. Group, 1978-99. Founder, pres. Decision Support Tech., Inc., 1974-92; co-founder, vice-chmn., dir. Software Productivity Rsch., Inc., 1985-87; pres., dir. The Softbridge Group, 1989-92; founder, CEO, Mgmt. Support Tech. Corp., 1992-99; sr. v.p., chief info. officer CIGNA Property and Casualty, 1995-98; vice-chmn., dir. Condor Tech. Solutions, Inc., 1998-2000; co-founder, chmn., dir. MGI Strategic Solutions, 2001—; commr. Nat. Imagery and Mapping Agy., 2000-01; mem. Def. Sci. Bd. Task Force, 2001. Editor: How Big and Still Beautiful? Macro-Engineering Revisited, 1980, Macro-Engineering: The Rich Potential, 1981, Macro-Engineering and the Future: A Management Perspective, 1982, Macro-Engineering: Global Infrastructure Solutions, 1992, Macro-Engineering: MIT Brunel Lectures on Global Infrastructure, 1997; mem. editorial bd. Computer Comm., 1979-91; contbr. articles to profl. jours. NSF trainee, 1970; MIT Wilfred Lewis fellow, 1971, Draper Lab. fellow, 1974. Mem. Computer Soc. IEEE (vice-chmn. Ea. Hemisphere and Latin Am. Area Com. 1977-83), Am. Soc. for Macro-Engring. (bd. dirs. 1992-96), Cosmos Club, Sigma Xi, Tau Beta Pi, Pi Tau Sigma. Office: MGI Strategic Solutions 85 Speen St Framingham MA 01701

MEADOR, DANIEL JOHN, law educator; b. Selma, Ala., Dec. 7, 1926; s. Daniel John and Mabel (Kirkpatrick) M.; m. Janet Caroline Heilmann, Nov. 19, 1955; children: Janet Barrie, Anna Kirkpatrick, Daniel John. BS, Auburn U., 1949; JD, U. Ala., 1951; LLM, Harvard U., 1954; LLD (hon.), U. S.C., 1998. Bar: Ala. 1951, Va. 1961. Law clk. to Justice Hugo L. Black U.S. Supreme Ct., 1954-55; assoc. firm Lange, Simpson, Robinson & Somerville, Birmingham, Ala., 1955-57; faculty U. Va. Law Sch., Charlottesville, 1957-66, prof. law, 1961-66; prof., dean U. Ala. Law Sch., 1966-70; James Monroe prof. law U. Va., Charlottesville, 1970-94, prof. emeritus, 1994—; asst. atty. gen. US Dept. Justice, 1977-79; dir. grad. program for judges, 1979-95. Fulbright lectr., U.K., 1965-66; vis. prof. U.S. Mil. Acad., 1984; chmn. Southeastern Conf. Assn. Am. Law Schs., 1964-65; chmn. Cts. Task Force Nat. Adv. Commn. on Criminal Justice, 1971-72; dir. appellate justice project Nat. Ctr. for State Cts., 1972-74; mem. Adv. Coun. on Appellate Justice, 1971-75, Coun. on Role of Cts., 1978-84; bd. dirs. State Justice Inst., 1986-92; exec. dir. commn. on structural alternatives Fed. Ct. Appeals, 1998-99. Author: Preludes to Gideon, 1967, Criminal Appeals-English Practices and American Reforms, 1973, Mr. Justice Black and His Books, 1974, Appellate Courts: Staff and Process in the Crisis of Volume, 1974, (with Carrington and Rosenberg) Justice on Appeal, 1976, Impressions of Law in East Germany, 1986, American Courts, 1991, 2nd edit., 2000, Appellate Courts in the United States, 1994, 2nd edit., 2006, His Father's House, 1994, Unforgotten, 1999, Remberton, 2007 (with Baker and Steinman) Appellate Courts: Structures, Functions, Processes, and Personnel, 1994, 2nd edit., 2006; editor: Hardy Cross Dillard: Writings and Speeches, 1995; editor Va. Bar News, 1962-65; contbr. articles to profl. jours. 1st lt. U.S. Army, 1951-53; col. JAGC, USAR ret. Decorated Bronze Star.; IREX fellow German Dem. Republic, 1983 Mem. ABA (chmn. standing com. on fed. jud. improvements 1987-90), Ala. Bar Assn., Va. Bar Assn. (exec. com. 1983-86), Am. Law Inst., Am. Judicature Soc. (bd. dirs. 1975-77, 80-83), Soc. Pub. Tchrs. Law, Am. Soc. Legal History (bd. dirs. 1968-71), Order of Coif, Raven Soc., Phi Delta Phi, Omicron Delta Kappa, Kappa Alpha. Presbyterian. Office: U Va Sch Law 580 Massie Rd Charlottesville VA 22903-1738

MEADOR, JOHN MILWARD, JR., dean, librarian; b. Louisville, Nov. 4, 1946; s. John Milward and Ruth Inez (Miller) M.; m. Judith Ann Hay, Dec. 22, 1969; children: John Milward III, Elise Kathleen. BA, U. Louisville, 1968; MA, U. Tex., 1972, MLS, 1973. Cert. tchr., Ky., Tex. English bibliographer M.D. Anderson Libr., U. Houston, 1973-74, head reference dept. social scis. and humanities, 1974-77, head gen. reference dept., 1977-80; asst. dir. pub. svcs. Marriott Libr., U. Utah, Salt Lake City, 1980-84; dean libr. svcs. S.W. Mo. State U., Springfield, 1984-93; dean librs. U. Miss., Univeristy, 1993—2003; dir. librs. SUNY, Binghamton, 2003—. Bd. dirs. S.W. Mo. Libr. Network, Springfield; cons. Dayco Corp., Springfield, 1984-86; chmn. Mo. Northwestern Online Total Integrated Sys. Users Group, 1988-89. Co-author: The Robinson Jeffers Collection at the University of Houston, 1975; contbr. articles to profl. jours. Sponsor Cmty. Alternative Svc. Program, Springfield and St. Louis, 1985-93; governing bd. Mo. Rsch. and Edn. Network, 1991-93; bd. dirs. Broome Libr. Found., Inc., 2005-07, Broome Leadership Inst. Alumni Assn., 2006—. With U.S. Army, 1969-71, Vietnam. Recipient Nat. Essay award Propeller Club of U.S., 1964; named to Honorable Order of Ky. Colonels, Gov. Ky., 1978; summer scholar English-Speaking Union, Edinburgh, Scotland, 1968; Apple Computer's Higher Edn. Acad. Devel. Donation Program grantee, 1990. Mem. ALA, Am. Assn. for Higher Edn., Assn. Coll. Rsch. Librs., Bibliography Soc. Am., Libr. Adminstrn. and Mgmt. Assn., English-Speaking Union Club, Rotary (chmn. students guests com. Springfield chpt. 1986-89, chmn. scholarships com. 1989-90, bd. dirs. 1990-91, bd. dirs. Oxford chpt. 1995-96), Phi Kappa Phi. Avocations: fishing, book collecting. Office: Binghamton Univ SUNY Bartle Library Binghamton NY 13902-6012 Office Phone: 607-777-2346. Business E-Mail: jmeador@binghamton.edu.

MEADOR, KIMFORD JAY, neurologist, researcher; b. New Orleans, Apr. 28, 1950; s. John D. and Marion (Pierce) M.; m. G. Maggie Pabon; children: Anthony Shane, Mary Catherine, Adrienne Christin, Kellan Jacob. BS in Applied Biology with high honors, Ga. Inst. of Tech., 1972; MD, Med. Coll. of Ga., 1976. Diplomate Nat. Bd. of Med. Examiners, Am. Bd. Neurology and Psychiatry; lic., Ga., S.C. Rsch. asst. Ctr. Disease Control, Atlanta, 1970, 71; intern diversified psychiatry U. Va. Hosp., Charlottesville, 1976-77; lt. comdr. USPHS, 1977-80; residency in neurology Med. Coll. Ga., Augusta, 1980-83; fellow in behavioral neurology U. Fla., Gainesville; asst. prof. neurology Med. Coll. Ga., Augusta, 1984-88, assoc. prof., 1988-93, prof., 1993, Charbonnier prof. neurology; chair neurology Georgetown U., Washington, 2002—04; Melvin Greer prof. neurology U. Fla., Gainesville, 2004—09; prof. neurology, dir. Emory Epilepsy Ctr. Emory U., Atlanta, 2009—. Reviewer: Annals of Neurology, Archives of Neurology, Epilepsia, Exptl. Jour. of Aging, Jour. Clin. Neurophysiology, Neurology, N.Y. State Jour. Medicine, Psychiatry Rsch.; contbr. over 100 articles to Brain, Epilepsia, Neuropsychology, Neuropsychologia, Neurology, Brain and Cognition, Am. Jour. Neuroradiology, Internat. Jour. Neurosci., Archives of Clin. Neuropsychology and others. Scholastic scholar Ga. Inst. Tech. Fellow Am. Acad. Neurology (essay award, 1989); mem. AAAS, AMA, Internat. Neuropsychol. Soc., Am. Neurol. Assn., Am. Epilepsy Soc., The Soc. for Psychophysiol. Rsch., Behavioral Neurology Soc., The N.Y. Acad. of Scis., Ga. Neurol. Assn., Phi Kappa Phi, Beta Beta Beta. Achievements include research in perception, cerebral lateralization, neglect syndrome, memory, Alzheimer's disease, epilepsy, psychopharmacology and psychophysiology. Home: 851 Courtenay Dr NE Atlanta GA 30306 E-mail: Meador@Neuro.mcg.edu.*

MEADOR, ROSS DESHONG, lawyer; b. Mexico City, Aug. 23, 1954; s. Bruce Staffel and Betty Lee M.; m. Michelle Hyunae Chang, Mar. 14, 1997; children: Amy Chang, Leah Chang, Daniel Ross. BA in Comm. and Visual Arts, U. Calif., San Diego, 1980; JD, U. Calif., Berkeley, 1986. Bar: Calif. Co-dir. Overseas Operations Friends of Children of Vietnam, 1974—75; atty. Morrison & Foerster, San Francisco, 1986—89; fgn. legal advisor Kim & Chang, Seoul, 1989—95, Soewito, Suhardiman, Eddymurthy & Kardono, Jakarta, Indonesia, 1996—97; of counsel Morrison & Foerster, 1997—99, Howard, Rice et al, 2000; ptnr. Preston Gates & Ellis, 2001—02, Rogers & Meador, 2003—; internat. legal adv. Vietnam Internat. Law Firm, 2005—. Photographer Escape From Saigon, Gerald Ford Presdl. Mus. Permanent Collection; one man shows include U. Calif. San Diego, 1980; exec. editor Internat. Tax & Bus. Lawyer, 1985-86. Nominee Presdl. Medal of Freedom, 2005. Mem.: Am. C. of C. Vietnam, Calif. Bar Assn. (mem. exec. com. internat. law sect. 2001—04, sec. 2004—05, advisory emeritus 2006—). Avocations: travel, photography. Home: 1270 Campus Dr Berkeley CA 94708-2045

MEADORS, ALLEN COATS, academic administrator, educator; b. Van Buren, Ark., May 17, 1947; s. Hal Barron and Allene Coats (Means) Meadors. AA, Saddleback Coll., 1981; BBA, U. Ctrl. Arki., 1969; MBA, U. No. Colo., 1974; MPA, U. Kans., 1975; MA in Psychology, Webster U., 1979, MA in Health Svcs. Mgmt., 1980; PhD in Adminstrn., So. Ill. U., 1981. Assoc. adminstr. Forbes Hosp., Topeka, 1971-73; asst. dir. health svcs. devel. Blue Cross Blue Shield of Kans., Topeka, 1973-76; asst. dir. Kansas City Health Dept., Mo., 1976-77; program dir., asst. prof. So. Ill. U., Carbondale, 1977—82, Webster U., St. Louis, 1979—82; mem. faculty Calif. State U., Long Beach, 1977-81; assoc. prof., dir. divsn. health adminstrn. U. Tex., Galveston, 1982-84; exec. dir. N.W. Ark. Radiation Therapy Inst., Springdale, 1984-87; mem. grad. faculty Sch. Bus. Adminstrn. U. Ark., Fayetteville, 1984-87; prof., chmn. dept. health adminstrn. U. Okla., Oklahoma City, 1987-90, dean Coll. Pub. Health, 1989—90; dean Coll. Health, Social and Pub. Svcs. Ea. Wash. U., Cheney, 1990—94; chancellor U. NC, Penbroke, 1994—99, Pembroke, 1999—2009; pres. U. Ctrl. Ark., 2009—. Cons. Surgeon Gen. Office and Air Force Sys.; bd. dirs. Lumbar Guartoner Bank, Southeastern Regional Med. Ctr. Contbr. articles to profl. jours. Command bd. dirs. Blair County Hall of Fame, Blair County Hist. Soc., Martin Luther King Hosp., Health Care Svcs. Adv. Bd.; bd. dirs., exec. com. Altoona Symphony Orch.; bd. dirs. Home Health Agy., NC Retirement Fund, Southwestern Regional Med. Ctr. With Med. Svc. Corps USAF, 1969—73. Fellow: Am. Coll. Healthcare Execs.; mem.: Am. Hosp. Assn., C. of C. (v.p.). Office: U Ctrl Ark / Office of Pres Wingo Hall RM 207G 201 Donaghey Ave Conway AR 72035 Office Phone: 501-450-5286. E-mail: ACM@uca.edu.*

MEADORS, C. BRIAN, lawyer; b. Lawrence, Kans., Aug. 18, 1969; s. Carey Wayne Meadors and Norma Meadors Senyard; m. Erika Esterbrook, Feb. 12, 2000; children: August Carey, Tabitha Grace. BS in Engring., U. Mich., Ann Arbor, 1991; JD cum laude, Georgetown U., Washington, 1999. Cert. profl. engr., Va., 1998, Ark., 1998; bar: Va. 1999, DC 2000, Ark. 2001, Mo. 2006, Fla. 2007, Nev. 2007. Atty. Morgan, Lewis & Bockius LLP, Washington, 1999—2002, Pryor, Robertson, Beasley & Smith PLLc, Fort Smith, Ark., 2002—. Elder First

Presbyn. Ch., Fort Smith, 2003—06. Naval nuclear submarine officer USN, 1991—96. Decorated Navy Achievement medal. Avocation: reading. Home: 10712 Hunters Point Rd Fort Smith AR 72903 Office: Pryor Robertson Beasley & Smith PLLC PO Drawer 848 315 N 7th St Fort Smith AR 72902-0848 Office Fax: 479-785-0254. Personal E-mail: brianmeadors@gmail.com. Business E-Mail: cbmeadors@prbsklaw.com.

MEADORS, CONSTANCE YVONNE, engineering educator, researcher; d. Raymond Washington and Carolyn S. Richard-Evans; m. James Edward Meadors, Aug. 17, 1996; children: John Cleveland, Jacob Christian. BS in Physics, Grambling State U., La., 1992; MS in Applied Sci., U. Ark., Little Rock, 1999, PhD in Engring. Scis. Applied Sci., 2008. Chair, dept. electronics ITT Tech. Inst., Little Rock, 2004—06; dean, applied sci. and bus. Ark. Bapt. Coll., Little Rock, 2006—07; asst. prof. mech. engring. Harding U., Searcy, Ark., 2007—. Dir. Nat. Sumer Transp. Inst., Little Rock, 2006—; cons. Inner City Future Net, Little Rock, 2008. Contbr. articles to profl. publs. Adv. bd. Job Corp, Little Rock, 2004—07; tchr. vol. River City Ministries, Little Rock, 2000—05; bd. dirs. City Connections, Little Rock, 2008. STEM Planning grant, NSF, 2002, Ednl. Curriculum Devel. grant, NASA EPSCoR, 2002. Achievements include research in micro-electromechanical systems; NASA hybrid rocket combustion.

MEADORS, MARYNELL, professional basketball coach; B in Health, Phys. Edn. and Recreation, Mid. Tenn. State U., 1965, M in Physiology of Exercise, 1966. Head coach Tenn. Tech. U. Golden Eagles, 1970-86, Fla. State U. Seminoles, 1986-96; head coach, gen. mgr., dir. player and staff pers. Charlotte Sting, 1997-99; dir. scouting Miami Sol, 1999; asst. coach U. Pitts. Panthers, 2003—05, Washington Mystics, 2005—07; head coach, gen. mgr. Atlanta Dream, 2007—. Named Ohio Valley Conf. Coach of Yr., 1978, 83, Metro Conf. Coach of Yr., 1990, Conf. Co-Coach of Yr., 1991; named to Tenn. Tech. Hall of Fame, 1992, Ohio Valley Conf. Hall of Fame, 1992. Office: Atlanta Dream 83 Walton St NW Ste 500 Atlanta GA 30303*

MEADOW, CHARLES, information scientist, writer; b. Paterson, NJ, Dec. 16, 1929; s. Abraham and Florence (Troub) M.; m. Harriet Reiss, Sept. 9, 1956 (div.); children: Debra Lynne, Sandra Lee; m. Mary Louise Shinskey, June 24, 1972; children: Alison Maria, Benjamin Niland. BA, U. Rochester, 1951; MS, Rutgers U., 1954. Employee USN, Rand Corp., GE, IBM, 1954—68; chief sys. devel. divsn. US Nat. Bur. Stds., Gaithersburg, Md., 1968-71; tech. asst. Office of Sci. and Tech. Exec. Office of the Pres., Washington, 1970-71; asst. dir. divsn. mgmt. info. and telecom. sys. US AEC, Washington, 1971-74; prof. Drexel U., Phila., 1974-82; project mgr. Dialog Info. Svcs., Inc., Palo Alto, Calif., 1982-84; prof. U. Toronto, 1984—94, assoc. dean, 1990—94, prof. emeritus, 1994—. Vis. prof. U. Sheffield, 1980-81, U. West Indies, 1990-91, U. NC, 1995; chair Democrats Abroad Victoria, 2007-08. Author or co-author 13 books, including (with Bert R. Boyce, Donald H. Kraft and Carol Barry) Text Information Retrieval Systems, 3d edit., 2007; (with Bert R. Boyce and Donald H. Kraft), Ink Into Bits: A Web of Converging Media, 1998, Making Connections: Communications Through the Ages, 2002, Messages, Meaning and Symbols, 2006, The Number One Dog in Victoria, 2009; editor Jour. Am. Soc. for Info. Sci., 1976-84, Can. Jour. Info. Sci., 1986-87. Lt. USMC, 1951-54. Mem. Am. Soc. Info. Sci. and Tech. (chpt. 1954-59, ann. rsch. award 1995, info. sci. book of yr. award 2000), Can. Assn. Info. Sci. (pres. 1994), NY Acad. Sci. (honorable mention children's sci. book awards 1975), Ret. Academics and Librs. U. Toronto (exec. com. 2000-02, coms. dir. 2001-02), Sigma Xi. Avocation: photography. Home: 1047 Richardson St Victoria BC Canada V8V 3CG E-mail: ct.meadow@shaw.ca.

MEADOW, WILLIAM LEE, medical educator; b. NYC, Oct. 28, 1948; s. Charles and Reine Meadow; m. Susan Goldin, June 20, 1971; children: Alexander Goldin, Nathaniel Goldin, Jacqueline Mollie Goldin. BA, Amherst Coll., 1969; MD, U. Pa., 1974, PhD, 1976. Pediat. Ill., 1981, Soc.Pediat.Rsch. Tex., 1986, Am.Pediat.Soc. Tex., 2001. Prof. pediat. U. Chgo., Chgo., 1981—. Asst. dir. MacLean Ctr. Clin. Med. Ethics, Chgo., 1994—. Office: U Chgo Dept Pediat 5841 South Maryland Ave - MC 6060 Chicago IL 60637 E-mail: wlm1@uchicago.edu.

MEADOWS, DEBORAH RENEE, dean, educator; b. Boise, Idaho, Sept. 7, 1951; d. George Elwood and Clarice Jean Meadows; m. Michael Jon Grinnell, Aug. 19, 1983; children: Daniel Jon Grinnell, Taylor Xavier Grinnell. EdD, Internat. Grad. Sch., St. Louis, 1986. Dean social sci., world lang. bus. & IT Columbia Basin Coll., Pasco, Wash., 1996—, v.p. instrn., 2007—. Bd. chair Tricities Enterprise Assn., Richland, Wash., 1997—2005. Office: Columbia Basin Coll 2600 North 20th Ave Pasco WA 99301 Business E-Mail: dmeadows@columbiabasin.edu.

MEADOWS, GWENDOLYN JOANN, retired behavioral disorders educator; b. Nov. 20, 1944; d. Guss Lee and Bennie Jolene Treadaway; children: Terence Lee Bradley, Melissa Ann Bradley Davis. AA, Norman Coll.; BA, Berry Coll.; M in Behavior Disorders, West Ga. Coll.; ednl. splty. degree in mild learning handicaps, Jacksonville State U., 1988; postgrad. in Adminstrn., U. Ala.; EdD in Human Svcs. and Counseling, U. Sarasota. Cert. tchr. Tchr. Pres. Hillhouse Garden Club, United Daus. of The Confederacy; life mem., bd. dirs. Calhoun Hist. Soc.; life mem. The Deep South Garden Clubs of Ga.; organizer Homebound program for Local Sheriff's Office; mem. Calhoun Red Hats Soc., Calhoun First Bapt. Ch.; bd. dirs. Calhoun Beautification Bd., Garden Club Ga., 2003—04. Named one of Ga. Women of Achievement, 1999. Mem.: Calhoun-Gordon County Ret. Educators Assn., VFW (life), Am. Legion Aux. (pres., 1st v.p., 2d v.p., historian, parliamentarian, chaplain, pres. dept. Ga. 2005—06), Kappa Kappa Iota (1st v.p.). Baptist. Avocations: reading, gardening.

MEADOWS, JUDITH ADAMS, law librarian, educator; b. Spartanburg, SC, June 5, 1945; d. Thomas Taylor and Virginia (Dayton) Adams; m. Bruce R. Meadows; children: Beth Ann Blackwood, Ted Adams Meadows. BA, Am. U., 1967; MLS, U. Md., College Park, 1979. Law libr. Aspen Sys. Corp., Gaithersburg, Md., 1979-81; dir. Fairfax (Va.) Law Libr., 1981-84, State Law Libr., Helena, Mont., 1984—. Vis. prof. U. Wash., Seattle, 1994; adj. prof. U. Great Falls, Mont., 1989-96; presiding ofcl. Gov.'s Conf. on Libr. Info. Svc., Helena, Mont., 1991; cons. Nat. Ctr. for State Cts., 2000—. Author: (book chpts.) From Yellow Pads to Computers, 1991, Law Librarianship, 1994, Encyclopedia of Library and Information Science, 2009; contbr. articles to profl. jours. Bd. dirs. Helena Presents, 1986-92, Holter Mus. Art, 1995-2002, Mont. Supreme Ct. Commn. on Tech., Mont. Equal Justice Task Force, 2001-; bd. dirs. Helena Edn. Found., v.p., 2003, pres. 2005-06; chair Mont. Supreme Ct. Commn. on Self-Represented Litigants, 2004—; mem. Mont. Commn. Continuing Legal Edn., 2006—. Recipient Disting. Svc. award State Bar of Mont., 1991, Pro Bono Pub. award, 2002. Mem. Am. Assn. Law Librs. (treas. 1992-95, v.p. 1996—, pres. 1997-98, past pres. 1998—), N.W. Consortium of Law Librs. (pres.), Mont. Libr. Assn. (sec. 1986-88). Office: State Law Libr Mont PO Box 203004 Helena MT 59620-3004

MEADS, DONALD EDWARD, management services company executive; b. Salem, Mass., Sept. 23, 1920; s. Laurence G. and Gertrude F. Meads; m. Jane Lightner, June 15, 1943; children: Edward G., Robert C., Laurence G., Judith C. Antrim, Suzanne M. O'Neil, Clifford L., Nancy Chapin. AB in Pre-Law, Dartmouth Coll., 1942; MBA in Fin., Harvard U., 1947. V.p., vice chmn. investment com. NY Life Ins Co., NYC, 1947-61; v.p. fin., chmn. investment com. Investors Diversified Svcs. Inc., Mpls., 1961-65; pres., CEO Internat. Basic Economy Corp., NYC, 1965-67, chmn., CEO, 1967-71; exec. v.p., dir., CFO, chmn. investment com. INA Corp., Phila., 1971-74; chmn. bd., CEO CertainTeed Corp., Valley Forge, Pa., 1974-78, dir., 1973-78; chmn. Mateer-Burt Co., Inc., Plymouth Meeting, Pa., 1984-87, Phila. First Group Inc., 1982-90, Carver Assocs., Inc., West Conshohocken, Pa., 1978—. Hon. life trustee Valley Forge Mil. Acad. and Coll., Wayne, Pa.; Capt. USMC, 1942-45. Decorated DFC, Air medals (6). Mem. Harvard Club NYC, Union League (Phila.).

MEADS, MINDY, retail executive; b. 1952; m. Larry Meads; 1 child, Griffin. BS, U. Ill., 1974. With Denver Dry Goods, 1974—78; sr. v.p., v.p., merchandising administr., v.p., store mgr., jeans collection buyer R.H. Macy and Company Inc., 1978—89; operating exec. The Limited, 1989—90; v.p., gen. merchandising mgr. Lands' End Inc., 1991—94; sr. v.p. merchandising & design Lands' End, Inc., 1994—96, exec. v.p. merchandising & design, 1998—2003; sr. v.p., gen. merchandising mgr., merchandising design planning and allocation Gymboree Corp., 1996—98; gen. mgr. apparel Sears Roebuck and Co., 2003—04, exec. v.p., 2003—; pres. Lands' End, Inc., Dodgeville, Wis., 2003—05, CEO, 2004—05; pres. Victoria's Secret Direct, 2005—07; pres., chief merchandising officer Aeropostale, Inc., NYC, 2007—. Office: Aeropostale Inc 112 W 34th St 22nd Fl New York NY 10120

MEADS, WALTER FREDERICK, communications executive, consultant, writer; b. Ft. Wayne, Ind., Mar. 11, 1923; s. Frederick C. and Minnie E. (Stephenson) M.; m. Mary E. Smith, Mar. 21, 1975; children by previous marriage: Kenneth W., Catherine L. BS, Kent State U., 1948; MA, Fairfield U. With Norman Malone & Assos., Akron, Ohio, 1946-48, Griswold-Eshleman Co., Cleve., 1949-53, Fuller, Smith & Ross, Cleve., 1953-55; sr. v.p., head of creative svc., mem. mgmt. com., vice chmn. plans and rev. bds. J. Walter Thompson Co., NYC, 1955-72; pres. Meads & Assocs., 1972—. With USAAF, 1943-45. Recipient numerous nat. and local advt. industry awards. Home: 6761 Trail Ridge Dr Lakeland FL 33813-1844 Personal E-mail: chipmeads@tampabay.it.com. *Creative freedom is probably the core concept at the heart of my life— not only for myself but for others. Life is never static; it either deteriorates or grows. All growth, to me, springs from the creative doers of the world. The rest of humanity goes along for the ride. And creative growth, in any field or endeavor, demands an attitude of freedom to shake off the shackles of habit and find new and better ways of doing things.*

MEAGHER, JAMES PROCTOR, editor; b. Rock Island, Ill., June 2, 1935; s. Edmund Joseph and Pauline Marie (Proctor) M.; m. Marie Therese Lyman, Sept. 12, 1959; children: Kathleen Ann Raffa, Christopher James. BA, U. Notre Dame, 1957. Copy editor Chgo. Tribune Co., 1959-61; staff writer Nat. Observer, Washington, 1961-62, news editor Silver Spring, Md., 1962-65, sr. editor, 1965-76, asst. mng. editor, 1976-77; assoc. editor Barron's Bus. and Fin. Weekly, NYC, 1977-78, news editor, 1978-82, asst. mng. editor, 1982-86, dep. editor, 1986-92, mng. editor, 1992-93, editor, 1993-95; exec. editor Dow Jones Mag. Group, NYC, 1995—2002; ind. edtl. cons., 2002—. Served to 1st lt. US Army, 1957—59. Mem. Soc. Profl. Journalists, Sigma Delta Chi. Roman Catholic. Home: 25 Hedges Ave Chatham NJ 07928-2503 Personal E-mail: meagherj@optonline.net.

MEAL, LARIE, chemistry professor, researcher, consultant; b. Cin., June 15, 1939; d. George Lawrence Meal and Dorothy Louise (Heileman) Fitzpatrick. BS in Chemistry, U. Cin., 1961, PhD, 1966. Rsch. chemist U.S. Indsl. Chems., Cin., 1966-67; instr. chemistry U. Cin., 1968-69, asst. prof., 1969-75, assoc. prof., 1975-90, prof., 1990—, rschr., 1980—. Cons. in field. Contbr. articles to profl. jours. Mem. AAAS, N.Y. Acad. Scis., Am. Chem. Soc., NOW, Planned Parenthood, Iota Sigma Pi. Democrat. Avocation: gardening. Home: 2231 Slane Ave Norwood OH 45212-3615 Office: U Cin 2220 Victory Pky Cincinnati OH 45206-2822 Home Phone: 513-631-5249; Office Phone: 513-556-4364. Business E-Mail: meall@uc.edu.

MEALS, PAMELA F., publishing executive; b. Ill. 1 child, Laura. Student, We. Oreg. State Coll. With advtsg. The Oreg. Statesman and Capital Jour., Salem; advtsg. mgr. The Idaho Statesman, Boise, 1979, pres., publ., 1994-99; publ. Coffeyville (Kans.) Jour., 1979-82, The Palladium-Item, Richmond, Ind., 1982-85, The Olympian, Olympia, Wash., 1985-94, Bellingham Herald, Bellingham, Wash., 1999—. Bd. dirs. Boise Pub. Schs. Edn. Found., Idaho Shakespeare Festival, Albertson Coll. Annual Fund, FUNDSY, William Allen White Found. Mem. Boise Area C. of C. (bd. dirs.), Rotary Club, Idaho Bus. Coun., Pacific N.W. Newspaper Assn. (bd. dirs.), Newspaper Assn. Am. Office: The Bellingham Herald 1155 N State St Ste 1 Bellingham WA 98225-5086

MEALY, DARLENE, city councilwoman; b. Detroit, Mich. Attended, Borough Manhattan Cmty. Coll. Various positions in tech. services div. Dept. of Buses NY Transit Authority, 1989—2006; city councilwoman Dist. 41 NY City Coun., 2006—. Founder & pres. F.A.R.R. Cmty. Assn.; bd. mem. Neighborhood Housing Services; past sec. 81st Pct. Cmty. Coun. Democrat. Office: 1757 Union Street 2nd Floor Brooklyn NY 11213 Office Phone: 718-953-3097. Office Fax: 718-953-3276. Business E-Mail: darlene.mealy@council.nyc.gov.*

MEALY, JOHN BURKE, clinical psychologist; MA in Guidance and Psychology, Assumption Coll., 1966, CAS in Counseling Psychology, 1967; PhD in Clin. Psychology, Duquesne U., 1972. Lic. psychologist, Md; diplomate Profl. Acad. Custody Evaluators, Am. Acad. Forensic Examiners. Clin. psychologist Woodville State Hosp., Carnegie, Pa., 1969-70; dir./psychologist Western State Sch. and Hosp., Canonsburg, Pa., 1970-72; asst. prof. human devel. Calif. State U., Hayward, 1972-73; pvt. practice Md., 1973—; clin. community psychologist Montgomery County Health Dept., Rockville, 1974-78; forensic psychologist Montgomery County Ct., 1978-84. Cons. dist., cir. cts. Montgomery County, 1984-88. Mem.: APA, Am. Orthopsychiat. Assn. Office: JB Mealy and Assocs 15817 Crabbs Branch Way Derwood MD 20855-2635 Office Phone: 301-948-2280. E-mail: drmealy@counselorswithcomparison.com.

MEANS, DWIGHT BARDEEN, JR., financial consultant, educator; b. Pitts., July 21, 1943; s. Dwight B. Sr. and Betty (Feick) M.; div.; children: Melissa Means Morris, Blake Elizabeth. BSEE, Carnegie-Mellon U., Pitts., 1965; MBA, U. Pitts., 1969, PhD, 1984. Various positions Bell Telephone Co. Pa., Pitts., 1965-70; asst. prof., dept. chair CC Allegheny County, Pitts., 1970-78; from asst. to assoc. prof. Saginaw Valley State U., Mich., 1978-86; prof., dept. chair Clarion U. Pa., Pa., 1986-88; asst. prof. U. Memphis, 1988-95; adj. prof. numerous univs., 1996—; cons. Pitts., 1995—. Presenter in field. Reviewer Fin. Practice and Edn., Jour. Econs. and Fin., Jour. Real Estate Rsch., Jour. Applied Bus. Rsch; contbr. articles to profl. jours. Mem. Acad. Fin. Svcs. (program com. 1990-95), Am. Econ. Assn., Midsouth Acad. Econs. and Fin. (dir. 1993-95), Fin. Mgmt. Assn. (program com. 1989), Midwest Fin. Assn. (program com. 1995-96), S.W. Fin. Assn. (program com. 1994-95), So. Fin. Assn. (program com. 1992-95). Avocations: hunting, fishing, camping, reading. Home and Office: 138 Owendale Ave Pittsburgh PA 15227-1951 Office Phone: 412-881-0398. Personal E-mail: meansdb@aol.com.

MEANS, JAMES ANDREW, retired engineer; b. Heavener, Okla., Oct. 11, 1937; s. Edward Andrew and Lorena (Nobles) M.; Therese Louise Zimmermann, Feb. 21, 1959; children: James A. Jr., William R., Charles E., Vicky M. BSEE, U. Ariz., 1962, MSEE, 1966; PhD, U. Calif., Santa Barbara, 1972; MS in Computer Sci., Chapman U., Orange, Calif., 1988. Engr. Pacific Missile Test Ctr., Pt Mugu, Calif., 1962-72, engr. mgr., 1972-79; tech. dir. Space and Missile Test Orgn., Vandenberg AFB, Calif., 1979-89; sr. tech. advisor SRI Internat., Menlo Park, Calif., 1990—2006. Cons. Agri-Craft, Camarillo, Calif., 1968-70, Astro-Geo-Marine, Ventura, Calif., 1972-74; pres. Internat. Found. for Telemetering, 1989-95. Patentee in field. Recipient Allen R. Matthews award, Internat. Test and Evaluation Assn., 1991, Pioneer award, Internat. Found. Telemetering, 2006. Democrat. Baptist. Avocations: waterskiing, fishing, hunting, old cars. Home: 284 St Andrews Way Lompoc CA 93436-1355 Personal E-mail: jim_means@verizon.net.

MEANS, JOHN BARKLEY, director, language educator; b. Cin., Jan. 2, 1939; s. Walker Wilson and Rosetta Barkley (Brower) Means. BA, U. Ill., 1960, MA, 1962, PhD, 1968. U.S. govt. intelligence rsch. analyst on Brazil CIA, Washington, 1962-64; assoc. prof. Spanish and Portugese Temple U., Phila., 1972-82, prof. Portuguese and critical langs., 1982—2003, prof. emeritus, 2003—, co-chmn. dept. Spanish and Portuguese, 1971-75, dir. dept. critical langs., 1975—2003, dir. Inst. for Langs. and Internat. Studies, 1987—2003, chmn. dept. Germanic and Slavic Langs. and lit., 1992-94, chair univ. core programs, 1995-97. Portuguese lang. examiner US Peace Corps, Brazil, 1967—68; cons. on Brazilian-Portuguese and second lang. acquisition and self instrnl. programs for less commonly taught langs., 1968—2003; cons. editor for langs. Norton Pubs., 1979—95; cons. in field. Editor: Essays on Brazilian Literature, 1971; author (with others): Language in Education: Theory and Practice, 1988—; editor: NASILP Manual, 1996; co-dir. CD-ROM Critical Language Series, 1999—; contbr. articles to profl. jours. Trustee Bristol Riverside Theatre, Pa., 1990—2002, 2005—; mng. trustee Means Charitable Trust, 1993—2004. 1st lt. US Army, 1960—62. Grantee, U.S. Dept. Edn., 1979—83, Japan Found., 1980, 1982, 1989—91, ARCO Chem. Found., 1991, 1993; fellow, U. Ill., 1966—68; NDEA fellow, 1962, 1964. Mem.: AAUP, MLA, St. Mary Med. Ctr. (amb. cir.), Linguistic Soc. Am., Joint Nat. Com. for Langs. (bd. dirs.), Nat. Assn. State Univs. and Lang Grant Colls. (commn. on internat. affairs), Nat. Coun. Orgns. Less Commonly Taught Langs. (exec. sec.-treas. 1990—2001), Am. Coun. on Tchg. Fgn. Lang., Nat. Assn. Self-Instrnl. Lang. Programs (exec. dir. 1977—98, editor jour. 1978—94, exec. dir. emeritus 1998—), Nat. Coun. on Langs. and Internat. Studies (bd. dirs.), Sigma Delta Pi, Phi Beta Kappa, Pi Kappa Phi. Home: PO Box 829 Washington Crossing PA 18977-0829 Business E-Mail: means@temple.edu.

MEANS, ROBERT TAYLOR, JR., hematologist, educator, researcher; b. Midland, Tex., July 14, 1957; s. Robert Taylor and Anna Therese (Cassidy) M.; m. Stacey W. McKenzie, May 23, 1992; children: Anna, Robert III, Patrick. BA in Biochemistry, Rice U., Houston, 1979; MD, Vanderbilt U., Nashville, 1983. Diplomate Am. Bd. Internal Medicine; cert. in hematology. Resident Baylor Coll. Medicine, Houston, 1983-86; fellow in hematology Vanderbilt U., Nashville, 1986-88, instr. medicine, 1988-90, asst. prof. medicine, 1990-92; assoc. investigator VA Med. Ctr., 1988-91, asst. chief hematology/oncology Ctr., 1992-98, chief hematology/oncology Charleston, SC, 1998—2004, prof. internal medicine, 2004—, chief med. svc. Lexington, Ky., 2004—06; assoc. prof. med. U. Cin., 1992-98; prof. med., head hematology, assoc. divsn. chief Med. U. SC, 1998-2000, dir. divsn. hematology-oncology, 2000—04; prof. internal medicine U. Ky., 2004—, assoc. rsch. chair internal medicine, 2004—07, interim assoc. dean, 2004—06, sr. assoc. chair, 2007—. Interim dir. Markey Cancer Ctr., 2006—09. Editor (assoc.) Jour. Investigative Medicine; mem. editl. bd. Internat. Jour. Hematology, Am. Jour. Med. Sci., Winthrobe's Clinical Hematology, 12th edit.; contbr. chpts. to books, articles to profl. jours. Recipient Career Devel. award Dept. Veterans Affairs., 1988, Henry Christian award Am. Fedn. Clin. Rsch., 1991, Chief Resident's Faculty of Yr. award, U. Ky., 2006. Fellow Am. Coll. Physicians; mem. Am. Soc. Hematology, Internat. Soc. Exptl. Hematology, Am. Fed. Med. Rsch. (v.p. mtgs., programs, 1998-2002), Southern Soc. Clin. Investigation (councillor, 2005-), Phi Beta Kappa. Achievements include being first to report response of anemia of chronic disease to erythropoietin; first description of erythropoietin receptor in polycythemia. Home: 2204 Abbeywood Rd Lexington KY 40515 Office: J525 Ky Clinic 740 S Limestone St Lexington KY 40536 Home Phone: 859-971-8184; Office Phone: 859-257-5116. Business E-Mail: robert.means@uky.edu.

MEANS, TERRY ROBERT, federal judge; b. Roswell, N.Mex., July 3, 1948; s. Lewis Prude and Doris Emaree (Hightower) M.; m. JoAnn Huffman Harris, June 2, 1973; children: Robert, MaryAnn, Emily. BA, So. Meth. U., 1971, JD, 1974. Bar: Tex. 1974, U.S. Dist. Ct. (no. dist.) Tex. 1976, U.S. Ct. Appeals (5th cir.) 1978, U.S. Dist. Ct. (we. dist., ea. dist.) Tex. 1991. Ptnr. Means & Means, Corsicana, Tex., 1974-88; Presdl. elector, 1980; justice 10th Ct. Appeals, Waco, Tex., 1989-90; judge U.S. Dist. Ct. (no. dist.) Tex., Ft. Worth, 1991—. Chmn. Navarro County Rep. Party, Corsicana, 1976-88; pres. YMCA, Corsicana, 1984, Ft. Worth Youth Soccer Assn., 1996-97. Recipient Disting. Alumni award for jud. svc. So. Meth. U., 2006. Mem. State Bar Tex., Tarrant County Bar Assn. (Silver Gavel award 2006). Baptist. Avocations: coaching soccer, racquetball. Office: 201 US Courthouse 501 W 10th St Fort Worth TX 76102-3637

MEANS, THOMAS CORNELL, lawyer; b. Charleston, SC, Oct. 3, 1947; s. Thomas Lucas and Dean (Cornell) M.; m. Judith Faye Perlmutter, Sept. 10, 1977; children: Benjamin, Samuel. AB, Dartmouth Coll., 1969; postgrad., Princeton Theol. Sem., 1970-71; M of Pub. Adminstrn., U. Colo., 1975; JD, George Washington U., 1978. Bar: D.C. 1978, U.S. dist. Ct. (D.C. dist.), U.S. Ct. Appeals (4th and D.C. cirs.) 1979, U.S. Ct. Appeals (10th cir.) 1983, U.S. Ct. Appeals (6th and 11th cirs.) 1989, U.S. Ct. Appeals (9th cir.) 1992, U.S. Ct. Appeals (8th cir.) 1993, U.S. Ct. Appeals (5th cir.) 1996. Social worker Vinyard Childcare, Ann Arbor, Mich., 1969-70; rsch. analyst, registered lobbyist Colo. Counties, Inc., Denver, 1972-75; assoc. Jones, Day, Reavis and Pogue, Washington, 1978-79; assoc. then ptnr. Crowell & Moring LLP, Washington, 1979—. Mem. state adv. coun. on pub. Pers. Mgmt., Colo. State Govt., Denver, 1974-75; lectr. mining law; chmn. coal com. Energy and Mineral Law Found., 1988-89, chmn. spl. insts., ass sec., 1989-91, sec., 1991-92, v.p., 1992-93, pres., 1993-94, exec. com., 1989-96, trustee, 1989—, mem. bd. editors, 1994—; bd. advisors Nat. Law Ctr., 1993-94, adv. bd. W. Va. Law Review on Nat. Coal Issues, 2001—. Contbr. articles to profl. jours. Recipient Pres.' award, Energy and Mineral Law Found., 2002, Daniel Levy award, Nat. Immigration Project, 2004, John L. McClaugherty award, Energy & Mineral Law Found., 2005; named Best Lawyers in Am., 2006—09. Mem. George Washington Law Alumni Assn. (bd. dirs. 1986-96, exec. com. 1987-96, treas. 1987-88, sec. 1988-90, pres. 1992-94), Order of Coif, Cosmos Club (Washington), Phi Beta Kappa. Home: 6411 Dahlonega Rd Bethesda MD 20816-2101 Office: Crowell & Moring LLP 1001 Pennsylvania Ave NW Fl 10 Washington DC 20004-2595 Home Phone: 301-229-1702; Office Phone: 202-624-2735.

MEARA, ANNE, actress, playwright, writer; b. Bklyn., Sept. 20, 1929; d. Edward Joseph and Mary (Dempsey) M.; m. Gerald Stiller, Sept. 14, 1954; children: Amy, Benjamin. Student, Herbert Berghoff Studio, 1953-54. Apprentice in summer stock, Southold, L.I. and Woodstock, N.Y., 1950-53; off-Broadway appearances include A Month in the Country, 1954, Maedchen in Uniform, 1955 (Show Bus. off-Broadway award), Ulysses in Nightown, 1958, The House of Blue Leaves, 1970, Bosoms and Neglect, 1986, After-Play, 1996; Shakespeare Co., Two Gentlemen of Verona, Ctrl. Park, N.Y.C., 1957, Romeo and Juliet, 1988; Broadway plays: Spookhouse, 1982, Eastern Standard, 1989, Anna Christie, 1993 (Tony nomination Best Supporting Actress); film appearances include The Out-of-Towners, 1968, Lovers and Other Strangers, 1969, The Boys From Brazil, 1978, Fame, 1979, Nasty Habits (with husband Jerry Stiller), 1976, An Open Window, 1990, Mia, 1990, Awakenings, 1991, Reality Bites, 1994, Daytrippers, 1997, The Fish in the Bathtub, 1998, Southie, 1999, The Independent, 2001, Like Mike, 2002, comedy act, 1963—; appearances Happy Medium and Medium Rare, Chgo., 1960-61, Village Gate, Phase Two and Blue Angel, N.Y.C., 1963, The Establishment, London, 1963, QE II, 1990; syndicated TV series Take Five with Stiller and Meara, 1977-78; numerous appearances on TV game and talk shows, also spls. and variety shows; rec. numerous commls. for TV and radio (co-recipient Voice of Imagery award Advt. Bur. N.Y.); star TV series Kate McShane, 1975, Archie Bunker's Place, 1979, Alf, 1986-88; other TV appearances The Sunset Gang, 1990, Avenue Z Afternoon, 1991, Murphy Brown, 1994, Homicide, 1996 (Emmy nomination), Will and Grace, 2002, Sex in the City, 2002-04, The King of Queens, 2003-05, Good Morning Miami, 2003; (TV movie) Jitters, 1997, All My Children, 1994-99, (TV movie) What Makes a Family, 2001; writer, actress TV movie The Other Woman, 1983 (co-recipient Writer's Guild Outstanding Achievement award 1983), Alf, To Make Up to Break Up, The Stiller and Meara pilot; author, actor (play) After-Play, 1996; author (play) Down the Garden Paths, 2000; video host (with Jerry Stiller) So You Want to Be an Actor? Recipient Outer Critic's Cir. Playwriting award for After-Play, 1995, 4th ann. Alan King award in Jewish Humor, 2003, Productive Aging award Jewish Coun. Aging, 2004, Thalia award (w/ Jerry Stiller) Humbert Coll. Toronto; received joint star with husband on the Hollywood Walk of Fame, 2007.

MEARA, JOHN GERARD, plastic surgeon; b. Pitts., Pa., Apr. 15, 1964; BS, U. Notre Dame, Ind., 1986; MD, U. Mich. Med. Sch., Ann Arbor, 1990; DMD, U. Pa., Phila., 1993; MBA, Melbourne Bus. Sch., Australia, 2004. Chief surgery Royal Children's Hosp., Melbourne, 2005—06; plastic surgeon in chief Children's Hosp. Boston, 2006—. Surgeon Partners in Health, Boston, Mass. Fellow: ACS; mem.: Royal Australasian Coll. Surgeons. Office: Children's Hosp Boston 300 Longwood Ave Boston MA 02115 Business E-Mail: john.meara@childrens.harvard.edu.

MEARNS, KENNETH CRAWFORD, retired communications educator; b. Lordsburg, N.Mex., Jan. 7, 1939; s. Walter Crawford and Maizie Patricia Mearns; m. Elva Y. Yanez, Feb. 29, 1996; children: Deborah V. Uroda, Kathryn M. Uroda, Susan E. Uroda, Melissa J. Uroda. BA, Tex. Western Coll., El Paso, 1960; MA in Speech Communication, U. Tex., El Paso, 1987. Cert. educator Tex. State Bd. Educator Cert., 1993. Part time instr. U. Tex., 1982—90, El Paso County CC, 2004—; classroom tchr., pub. sch. campus adminstr. Socorro Ind. Sch. Dist., El Paso, 1986—99, dir. student svcs., 1999—2005; part time instr., facilitator U. Phoenix, Santa Teresa, N.Mex., 2008—. Com. mem. El Paso County Planning Com., 1980—82; dir. MHMR, El Paso, 1981—82. Mem.: Tex. Ret. Tchrs. Assn. Liberal. Roman Catholic. Avocations: travel, walking. Home: 8813 Shaver Dr El Paso TX 79925 Personal E-mail: mearns6@sbcglobal.net.

MEARS, LAINE, engineering educator; m. Kristina Mears, Jan. 1, 1996. BS in Mech. Engring., Va. Tech, Blacksburg, 1993; MS, Ga. Tech, Atlanta, 2004, PhD, 2006. Cert. profl. engr., State Ga., 2006, quality engr., Am. Soc. Quality, 2003. Welding maintenance engr. Va. Power, Louisa, Va., 1990—92; mfg. engr. SKF Bearings, Flowery Branch, Va., 1993—98, mfg. unit mgr., 1998—99; project engr. Hitachi Automotive Products, Monroe, Ga., 1999—2003, asst. engring. mgr., 2003—04; grad. rsch. asst. Ga. Tech, Atlanta, Ga., 2004—06; asst. prof. Clemson U., Clemson, SC, 2006—. Contbr. articles to profl. jours. Grant, NSF, 2007—08, 2008—, Michelin Americas, 2008—, BMW, 2008—. Mem.: ASME, ASQ, SME. Avocation: scuba diving. Office: Clemson Univ ICAR 4 Research Dr Greenville SC 29607 Business E-Mail: mears@clemson.edu.

MEARS, PATRICK EDWARD, lawyer; b. Oct. 3, 1951; s. Edward Patrick and Estelle Veronica (Mislik) M.; m. Geraldine O'Connor, July 18, 1981. BA, U. Mich., 1973, JD, 1976. Bar: NY 1977, Ill. 1996, US Dist Ct. (so. and ea. dists) NY 1977, Mich. 1980, US Dist. Ct. (we. and ea. dists.) Mich. 1980, US Ct. Appeals (6th cir.) 1983, Ill. 1996, US Dist. Ct. (no. dist.) Ill. 1998. Assoc. Milbank, Tweed, Hadley & McCloy, NYC, 1976-79; ptnr. Warner, Norcross & Judd, Grand Rapids, Mich., 1980-91; sr. mem. Dykema Gossett PLLC, Grand Rapids, 1991—2002; equity mem. Dickinson Wright, PLLC, Grand Rapids, 2002—04; equity ptnr. Barnes & Thornburg LLP, 2004—. Adj. prof. Grand Valley State U., Allendale, Mich., 1981-84; dir. Children's Law Ctr., 1994, Grand Rapids Ballet, 1994-99, East Grand Rapids Pub. Sch. Found., 1994-98. Author: Michigan Collection Law, 1981, 2d edit., 1983, Basic Bankruptcy Law, 1986, Bankruptcy Law and Practice in Michigan, 1987, 1995, Revised Article 9 of the UCC in Michigan, 2001; co-author: Strategies for Secured Creditors in workouts and Foreclosures, 2004; contbg. author Collier Bankruptcy Practice Guide; contbr. articles to profl. jours.; editor: Hist. Soc. Jour., US Dist. Ct. (we. dist.)Mich., 2003—. Chmn. legis. com. East Grand Rapids PTA, Mich., 1992—94; bd. dir. Grand Rapids Sister Cities Internat., 2004—06, sec., 2004—06. Fellow: Mich. State Bar Found. (sec. coun. real property sect. 1993—97, chair Uniform Comml. Code com. bus. law sect. 2000—), Am. Coll. Bankruptcy; mem.: ABA (chmn. workouts, bankruptcy and foreclosures 2002—04, vice chair real estate financing group 2004—06, chair real estate financing group 2006—08), Fed. Bar Assn. (chmn. bankruptcy sect. We. Mich. chpt. 1992—94, newsletter editor 1998—2002, pres. 2001—02), Am. Law Inst., Am. Bankruptcy Inst., Mich. State Bar Assn., East Hills Athletic Club. Office: Barnes & Thornburg LLP 171 Monroe Ave NW Ste 1000 Grand Rapids MI 49503-2694 Office Phone: 616-742-3936. Business E-Mail: pmears@btlaw.com.

MEARS, WALTER ROBERT, retired journalist; b. Lynn, Mass., Jan. 11, 1935; s. Edward Lewis and Edythe Emily (Campbell) M.; m. Sally Danton, Dec. 28, 1956 (dec. Dec. 1962); children: Pamela (dec.), Walter Robert Jr. (dec.); m. Joyce Marie Lund, Aug. 4, 1963 (div. 1983); children: Stephanie Joy, Susan Marie; m. Carroll Ann Rambo, Mar. 1, 1986 (div. 1995); m. Frances R. Richarson, July 5, 1997. BA, Middlebury Coll., 1956, LittD (hon.), 1977. Newsman AP, Boston, 1956, corr. Montpelier, Vt., 1956-60, state house corr. Boston, 1960-61, newsman Washington, 1961-69, chief polit. writer, 1969-72, asst. chief Washington bur., 1973-74, spl. corr., 1975, chief, 1977-83, v.p., 1978-2001, exec. editor, 1984-88, v.p., columnist, 1989-2001. Author: (with John Chancellor) The News Business, 1983, The New News Business, 1995, Deadlines Past, 2003. Trustee Middlebury Coll., 1980-84. Recipient ann. award AP Mng. Editors Assn., 1973; Pulitzer prize for Nat. Reporting, 1977. Mem.: Govs. Club, Burning Tree Club, Gridiron Club, Delta Kappa Epsilon, Phi Beta Kappa. E-mail: wmears@nc.rr.com.

MEARSHEIMER, JOHN JOSEPH, political science professor; b. Bklyn., Dec. 14, 1947; s. Thomas J. and Ruth M. (Baumann) Mearsheimer; m. Mary T. Cobb, June 14, 1970; children: Ann, Max, Nicholas. BS, US Mil. Acad., West Point, NY, 1970; MA in Internat. Rels., U. So. Calif., 1974; MA in Govt., Cornell U., NYC, 1978, PhD, 1981. Enlisted US Army, 1965; commd. 2d lt. USAF, 1970, advanced through grades to capt., 1975; resigned, 1975; rsch. fellow Brookings Instn., Washington, 1978—79; postdoctoral fellow Harvard U. Ctr. Internat. Affairs, Cambridge, Mass., 1980-82; asst. prof. dept. polit. sci. U. Chgo., 1982-84, assoc. prof., 1984-87, prof., 1987—, chmn. dept., 1989—92, R. Wendell Harrison disting. svc. prof. polit. sci., 1996—. Whitney H. Shepardson fellow Coun. Fgn. Rels., NYC, 1998—99. Author: Conventional Deterrence, 1983 (Edgar S. Furniss Jr. Book award, 1983), Liddell Hart and the Weight of History, 1988, The Tragedy of Great Power Politics, 2001 (Joseph Lepgold Book prize); co-author (with Stephen M. Walt): The Israel Lobby and U.S. Foreign Policy, 2007 (NY Times bestseller); contbr. articles to profl. jours., chapters to books. Recipient Clark award for Disting. Tchg., 1977, Quantrell award for Excellence in Undergrad. Tchg., U. Chgo., 1985. Fellow: Am. Acad. Arts & Scis.; mem.: Am. Polit. Sci. Assn. Office: U Chgo Dept Polit Sci 5828 S Univ Ave Chicago IL 60637-1515 Office Phone: 773-702-8667. Office Fax: 773-702-1689. Business E-Mail: j-mearsheimer@uchicago.edu.*

MEATH, JAMES V., lawyer; b. Norfolk, Va., May 26, 1948; BA, Old Dominion U., 1971; MUA, Va. Polytechnic Inst. and State U., 1974; JD, U. Richmond, 1979. Bar: Va. 1979, D.C. 1985. Atty. Williams Mullen, Richmond, Va., vice chmn. bd. dirs., regional head Richmond, Charlottesville, chmn. labor and employment sect. Adj. prof. labor law U. Richmond, mem. bd. assocs., 1998—, mem. dean's adv. coun., 1997—. Co-editor: Virginia Employment Law Letter, 1990—2002; contbr. articles to profl. jours. Bd. dirs. Richmond Soc. Prevention of Cruelty to Animals. Named Number One Employment Defendant Atty in Va., Chambers USA; named one of Legal Elite, Va. Bus. Mag.; fellow, Coll. Labor and Employment Lawyers. Mem.: ABA (mem. developing labor law com., mem. alternate dispute com.), Am. Arbitration Assn. (large complex case panel arbitrator 1985—, comml. panel arbitrator, employment panel arbitrator), D.C. Bar Assn., Va. Bar Assn. (chmn. labor rels. and employment sect. 1995—97, mem. exec. com. 2002—, chmn., bd. govs. 2003, pres.-elect 2004, pres. 2005—). Office: Williams Mullen Two James Ctr 1021 E Cary St Richmond VA 23219 also: Williams Mullen PO Box 1320 Richmond VA 23218-1320 Home Phone: 804-783-6507; Office Phone: 804-783-6507. E-mail: jmeath@williamsmullen.com.

MEBANE, JULIE S., lawyer; b. San Antonio, Mar. 13, 1957; d. John Cummins and Mildred (Hill) Mebane; m. Kenneth Jerome Stipanov, Jan. 21, 1984; children: Thomas Kenneth Stipanov, Kristen Hill Stipanov. BA in Polit. Sci., UCLA, 1978, JD, 1981. Bar: Calif. 1981, U.S. Dist. Ct. (so. dist.) Calif. 1981. Assoc. Gray, Cary, Ames & Frye, San Diego, 1981-85, Sheppard, Mullin, Richter & Hampton, San Diego, 1986-90; ptnr. Scalone, Stipanov, Yaffa & Mebane, San Diego, 1990-94, Stipanov & Mebane, San Diego, 1994—2004, Duane Morris LLP, San Diego, 2005—. Panelist Calif. Continuing Edn. Bar, 2000—01, Lorman Edn. Svcs., 2006—07. Bd. dirs. Episcopal Diocese San Diego, 1992—95, Francis Parker Sch., 2003—. Mem.: San Diego Lawyers Club, San Diego County Bar Assn., ABA, Nat. Assn. Women Bus. Owners (bd. dirs. San Diego chpt. 1996—97), UCLA Alumni Assn. (gen. counsel, bd. dirs. 1992—96), Phi Beta Kappa, Kappa Alpha Theta. Avocations: sports, travel. Office: Duane Morris LLP 101 W Broadway Ste 900 San Diego CA 92101-3544 Office Phone: 619-744-2211. Business E-Mail: jmebane@duanemorris.com.

MEBANE, WILLIAM BLACK, controller, financial consultant; b. Vernon, Tex., Dec. 15, 1927; s. David Mitchell and Ida Virginia (Black) M.; m. Joan Hebbard Dumper, Nov. 24, 1956; children— David Alexander, Virginia Ann. BBA, Tex. A&M U., 1952; MBA, Harvard U., 1954. Mem. treas.'s office staff Gen. Motors Corp., NYC, 1954-70; sec.-treas. Alfred P. Sloan Found., NYC, 1971-78; dir. fin. and adminstrn. Am. Diabetes Assn., NYC, 1979-80, dir. planning, 1981; v.p., comptroller NCCJ, Inc., NYC, 1981-86, v.p. for fiscal affairs, 1987-88; fin. cons. Internat. House, NYC, 1989-90; ind. fin. cons., 1990-91; contr. Better Bus. Bur., NYC, 1991-99. Vol. Essex Council Boy Scouts Am., 1967—. Served with USAAF, 1946-49. Recipient Silver Beaver award Boy Scouts Am., 1982 Mem.: Harvard Bus. Sch. (N.Y.C.); Short Hills (N.J.). Republican. Episcopalian. Home: 36 Haddonfield Rd Short Hills NJ 07078-3402 Personal E-mail: bmebane@comcast.net.

MEBANE, WILLIAM DEBERNIERE, newspaper publisher; b. Durham, NC, Jan. 14, 1949; s. John Gilmer and Harriet deBerniere (Elmore) M.; m. Catharine Frampton McGee, May 30, 1970; children— William deBerniere, Harriet Bacot, Jane Bacot, Catharine Frampton, John McGee, Beverly Canby BA, U. N.C., 1971, cert. in exec. program, 1981. V.p. Greenville News-Piedmont, S.C., 1976-82, bus. mgr. S.C., 1976-78, gen. mgr. S.C., 1978-81, co-pub. S.C., 1981-84, pres. S.C., 1982—, pub. S.C., 1984-92, 97-99; v.p. Multimedia Newspaper Co., Greenville, 1984-92, pres., 1989-95; v.p. Multimedia Inc., 1989-95; sr. group pres., newspaper divsn. Gannett Co. Inc., Gannett newspaper operating com., 1995-99; pres. Crescent Pub. LLC, 1999—. Commr. SC Mental Retardation Commn., 1983-89, vice chmn., 1988; past pres. Greenville Symphony Assn.; campaign chmn. United Way Greenville County, 1984, v.p. resource devel., 1985, v.p. mktg. and comms., 1986, 1st v.p., 1987, pres., 1988; treas. Goodwill Industries Upper SC, 1980-81; past pres. Greenville Assn. Retarded Children; mem. First Amendment Congress Bd., 1987-88, NC Soc. Cin., Corp. Coalition Infant Mortality, 1988; bd. dirs. Greenville Hosp. System, 1993-99, chmn. 1999, bd. dirs. Greenville Health Corp., 2008; communicant Christ Episcopal Ch., vestry, 2003-05. Mem. AP (com. 1985—, nominating com. 1991—, chmn. 1992-95), Am. Newspaper Pubs. Assn. (com. 1982—), So. Newspaper Pubs. Assn. (treas. 1990, chmn. com. 1983-84, pres. 1992, chmn. 1993, found. treas. 1996-99), Urban League of Upstate (chair 2006), So. Govs. Assn., SC Press Assn. (treas. 1984-85, v.p. dailies 1986, pres. 1987), Young Pres.'s Orgn., Huguenot Soc., Anglican Compass Rose Soc., Telecom. Commn. Anglican Commmunion, Greenville C. of C. (bd. dirs., v.p. 1981-82, bd. dirs. 1987-88), Poinsett Club, Delta Kappa Epsilon. Avocation: outdoor activities. Home: 119 Crescent Ave Greenville SC 29605-2812 Office: Crescent Pub LLC 109 Laurens Rd Ste 4-C Greenville SC 29607-1860 Office Phone: 864-250-4446. Business E-Mail: bmebane@crescentsc.com.

MECCA, KIMBERLY ANN, psychologist; d. George and JoAnn Weiss; m. William George Mecca, Sept. 25, 1992; children: David, Alanna, Matthew. MA in Psychology, Marywood U., Scranton, Pa., 2002. Psychologist Scranton City Schs., 2002—07, Wake County Pub. Schs., Raleigh, NC, 2007—. Mem.: NASP.

MECCIA, FRANCIS (FRANK) ANTHONY, physician assistant; s. Aniello J. and Marie Celeste Meccia. AA, Kendall Coll., 1976; BS, Columbus Univ., 1998; MS, Trinity So. U., 2000; cert. physician asst., Cook County Hosp., 1989. Cert. advance cardiac life support. Enlisted U.S. Army, 1976, advanced through ranks to staff sgt., 1985, sr. med. aidmen Spangdahlem, Germany, 1976-80, sr. med. advisor Hdqrs. 2d Inf. White House Washington, 1980-83, med. recruiter Ft. Sheridan, Ill., 1983-87, ret., 1987; physician asst. Montefiore Med. Ctr., Bronx, NY, 1989-91; cardiovasc. physician asst. Murphy Otto and Assocs., Evanston, Ill., 1991-98; sr. physician asst. for cardiovasc. svcs. Resurrection Hosp., Chgo., 1998—; staff physician asst. Our Lady of the Resurrection Med. Ctr., Chgo., 2001—; staff physician asst. for cardiovasc. surgery St. Francis Hosp., Evanston, Ill., 2001—. Preceptor U. Health Scis., Chgo. Med. Sch., North Chgo., 1993-94, Cook County Hosp. Physician Asst. Program, Chgo., preceptor 1993—; bd. trustees Alexian Bros. Bonaventure Ho., Chgo., 2005—. Decorated Meritorious Svc. medal USAR, Washington, 1992, Army Commendation medal with oak leaf cluster, 1997; recipient The David award Allied Health Pers., Chgo., 1993. Mem. Am. Assn. Physician Assts. (cert., editor/treas. AAPA caucus GLPA 2003—), Am. Assn. Physician Assts. Surgery, Am. Heart Assn. (cert. advance trauma life support), Assn. Physician Assts. Cardiovasc. Surgery, Ill. Acad. Physician Assts. Avocations: scuba diving, sky diving, skiing. Home: 6219 W Cornelia Ave Chicago IL 60634-4120 Office: Resurrection Hosp 7435 W Talcott Ave Ste 1 Chicago IL 60631-3746 Office Phone: 773-792-7942. E-mail: frank1906@aol.com.

MECCIA, NEIL ROCCO, health facility administrator, physician; b. Evanston, Ill., July 3, 1954; s. Aniello Joseph and Marie Celeste (Ficherelli) Meccia. BA, Northwestern U., 1976; MA, No. Ill. U., 1978; MPA, U. So. Calif., 1980, PhD, 1988; D of Naprapathy, Nat. Coll. Naprapathic Medicine, 2001; D of Naturopathy, Naprapathic Acad. Sci. and Rsch., Chgo., 2004. Diplomate Am. Coll. Healthcare Execs., Am. Acad. Med. Adminstrs., bd. credentialied, diplomate Am. Acad. Med. Adminstrs. Advanced through ranks to lt. col. USAF, 1988—; patient squadron comdr. USAF Med. Ctr., Wright Patterson AFB, Ohio, 1988—90, dep. dir. patient adminstrn., 1988—90, assoc. adminstr. hosp. svcs., 1990—91; command tng. mgr. med. scis. HQ AFMC, Wright Patterson AFB, 1991—95; assoc. to dir. managed care integration Dept. of Def. Health Svc. Region 5, Wright Patterson AFB, 1995—97; assoc. to dep. comdr. 74th Med. Support Squadron, Wright Patterson AFB, 1997—98, assoc. to comdr., 1998—2005; chief resident Noble Family Ctr. for Health, Chgo., 2002—05; assoc. to chief med. edn. and assoc. dean Air Force Inst. Tech., Wright Patterson AFB, 2005—. Cons. adminstr. Great Lakes Podiatric Group, Valparaiso, Ind., 1995—, Family Stress and Pain Clinic, Chgo., 2002—. Contbr. articles to profl. jours. Coord. USMCR Toys for Tots, Chgo., 1997—2004; sci. fair judge Our Lady Immaculate Acad., Oak Park, Ill., 2002—05; charter sponsor Air Force Meml., Washington, 2005—06. Decorated Nat. Def. medal USAF, Air Force Achievement medal, Air Force Commendation medal, Mil. Outstanding Volunteerism Svc. medal USAF; recipient David award for Sci., Italo-Am. Nat. Union, 1990. Fellow: Am. Coll. Healthcare Execs., Am. Acad. Med. Adminstrs. (sec.-treas. 1993—95); mem.: Am. Assn. Physicians & Surgeons, Nutrition for Optimal Health Assn., Assn. Mil. Surgeons US, Chgo. Health Execs. Forum, Healthcare Execs. SW Ohio (charter mem. 1990—91), Mil. Officers Assn. Am. (treas. 2003, cert. of appreciation 2004), Air Force Assn., Am. Legion, Alpha Theta Xi, Phi Theta Kappa, Pi Alpha Alpha, Pi Sigma Alpha, Tau Epsilon Phi. Republican. Roman Catholic. Avocations: aviation, plastic model aircrafts, movies. Home: 6219 W Cornelia Ave Chicago IL 60634-4120 Office: 88th Med Group/SGSX 4881 Sugar Maple Dr Wright Patterson AFB OH 45433-5529 Home Phone: 773-545-1658; Office Phone: 937-257-1976. Office Fax: 937-257-1981. Personal E-mail: majormeccia@hotmail.com.

MECH, TERRENCE FRANCIS, library director; b. Birdorup Park, Wiltshire, Eng., Feb. 24, 1953; s. Emil Paul and Madelyn Mech. BS, U. Wis., Stevens Point, 1975; MS, Ill. State U., 1978; MLS, Clarion U., 1979; EdD, Pa. State U., 1994. Pub. svcs. libr. Tusculum Coll., Greensville, Tenn., 1979-80; libr. dir. Coll. of the Ozarks, Clarksville, Ark., 1980-82, King's Coll., Wilkes-Barre, Pa., 1982—, dir. libr., 1982—, v.p. for info. and instrnl. techs., 1994—2001. Bd. dirs. Northeastern Pa. Bibliographic Ctr., 1982—; mem., officer Coun. Pa. Libr. Networks, 1984-89, chair, 1987-89. Contbr. chpts. to books and articles to profl. jours. Mem. ALA, Pa. Libr. Assn. (bd. dirs. 1986-87, various coms. 1985—). Office: Kings Coll 133 N River St Wilkes Barre PA 18711-0801

MECHAM, GLENN JEFFERSON, lawyer, mayor; b. Logan, Utah, Dec. 11, 1935; s. Everett H. and Lillie (Dunford) M.; m. Mae Parson, June 5, 1957; children: Jeff B., Scott R., Marcia, Suzanne. BS, Utah State U., 1957; JD, U. Utah, 1961; grad., Air Command and Staff Coll., 1984, Air War Coll., 1984. Bar: Utah 1961, Supreme Ct. US, US Ct. Appeals (10th cir.), US Dist. Ct. Utah, US Ct. Claims. Gen. practice law, 1961-65; atty. Duchesne County, Utah, 1962, City of Duchesne, 1962; city judge Roy City, Utah, 1963-66; judge City of Ogden, Utah, 1966-69, mayor, 1992-2000. Lectr. law and govt. Stevens-Henager Coll., Ogden, 1963-75; asst. US atty., 1969-72; ptnr. Mecham & Richards, Ogden, Utah, 1972-82; pres. Penn Mountain Mining Co., South Pacific Internat. Bank, Ltd.; mem. Bur. Justice Stats. Adv. Bd., US Dept. Justice, US Conf. Mayors; chmn. Marina Capital Inc. Chmn. Ogden City Housing Authority; chmn. bd. trustees Utah State U., Space Dynamics Lab; mem. adv. coun. Fed. Home Loan Bank; pres. Utah League Cities and Towns, 1981—82; vice chmn. Wasatch Front Reg. Coun. Col. USAF, 1957; No. Utah liaison U.S. Sen. Robert F. Bennett. Recipient Disting. Svcs. award, Utah State U., Weber State U. Mem ABA, Weber County Bar Assn. (pres. 1966-68), Utah Bar Assn., Am. Judicature Soc., Weber County Bar Legal Svcs. (chmn. bd. trustees 1966-69), Utah Assn. Mcpl. Judges (sec.), Ogden-Weber C. of C. (Order of the Big Hat), Sigma Chi, Phi Alpha Delta. Home: 925 Donner Way 2600 Salt Lake City UT 84108 Home Phone: 801-583-0505; Office Phone: 801-661-8182.

MECHAM, MARK LEONIDAS, music educator, department chairman; s. Leonidas Ralph and Barbara Folsom Mecham; m. Patsy Ann Tomlinson, Aug. 27, 1975; children: Leonidas Carter, Kathryn Ann, Bradley Tomlinson. MusB, U. Utah, Salt Lake City, 1976, MusM, 1978; DMA, U. Ill., Urbana, 1980. Dir. choral activities & asst. prof. music U. Mary, Bismarck, ND, 1980—84, U. Tex., Tyler, 1984—86; dir. choral activities & assoc. prof. music Southern Utah U., Cedar City, 1986—90;

chair & prof. music Lebanon Valley Coll., Annville, Pa., 1990—. Contbr. articles to profl. publs. (Thomas Rhys Vickroy Disting. Tchg. award, 1998). State del. Rep. Conv., Salt Lake City, Utah, 1976—76. Named Outstanding Tchr., U. Mary, 1981. Mem.: AAUP, Pa. Music Educators Assn., Music Educators Nat. Conf., Internat. Fedn. Choral Musicians, Am. Choral Dirs. Assn. (pres. 1989—90). Conservative. Mem. Lds Ch. Avocation: travel. Office: Lebanon Valley Coll 101 N College Ave Annville PA 17003 Business E-Mail: mecham@lvc.edu.

MECHANIC, DAVID, social sciences educator; b. NYC, Feb. 21, 1936; s. Louis and Tillie (Penn) Mechanic; m. Kathleen Mars Wiltshire; children: Robert Edmund, Michael Alexander. BA, CCNY, 1956; MA, Stanford U., 1957, PhD, 1959. Faculty U. Wis., Madison, 1960—79, prof. sociology, 1965—73, John Bascom prof., 1973—79; dir. U. Wis. (Center for Med. Sociology and Health Services Research), 1971—79, chmn. dept. sociology, 1968—70; prof. social work and sociology Rutgers U., New Brunswick, NJ, 1979—, acting dean faculty arts and scis., 1980—81, Univ. prof., dean faculty arts and scis., 1981—84, Univ. prof. and Rene Dubos prof. behavioral scis., 1984—, dir. Inst. for Health, Health Care Policy and Aging Research, 1985—. Panelist on health svcs. rsch. Pres.'s Sci. Adv. Com., 1971—72; coord. panel Pres.'s Commn. Mental Health, 1977—78; mem. Nat. Adv. Coun. Aging, NIH, 1982—86; treatment com. on reduction of cancer mortality Nat. Cancer Inst., 1984; expert adv. panel on mental health WHO, 1984—89; vice-chmn. com. pain, disability and chronic illness behavior Inst. Medicine-NAS, 1985—86, panel on prevention of disability, 1989—90, panel on new data for an aging world, 1999—2000, com. on capitalizing on social sci. and behavioral rsch. to improve the pubs. health, 1999; health adv. bd. GAO, 1987—95; nat. com. on vital and health stats. HHS, 1988—92; commn. on med. edn. Robert Wood Johnson Found., 1990—92, nat. adv. com. scholars in health policy rsch. program, 1993—, nat. dir. investigators awards in health policy rsch. program, 2000—, tech. adv. com. scholars in health policy rsch. program, 2001—02, nat. adv. com. health and soc. scholar's program, 2003—; mem. Com. on Prevention of Mental Disorder, 1992—94; panel on tech., ins. and health care sys. Office of Tech. U.S. Congress, 1992—95; commn. on behavioral and social scis. and edn. NRC, 1992—95; adv. com. Picker/Commonwealth Scholars Program, 1992—99; panel on rethinking disability policy Nat. Acad. Social Ins., 1993—96; vis. scholar Kings Fund Inst., London, 1994—95; professionalism adv. com. Am. Bd. Internal Med. Found., 2002—05; bd. dirs. Acad. Health. Author: Students Under Stress, 1962, 1978, Medical Sociology, 1968, 1978, Mental Health and Social Policy, 1969, 2007, Public Expectations and Health Care, 1972, Politics, Medicine and Social Science, 1974; author: (with Charles E. Lewis and Rashi Fein) A Right to Health, 1976; author: Growth of Bureaucratic Medicine, 1976, Future Problems in Health Care, 1979, From Advocacy to Allocation: The Evolving American Health Care System, 1986, Painful Choices: Research and Essays on Health Care, 1989, Inescapable Decisions: The Imperatives of Health Reform, 1994, The Truth About Health Care: Why Reform is Not Working in America, 2006; author, editor: Symptoms, Illness Behavior and Help-Seeking, 1982; editor: Handbook of Health, Health Care and the Health Professions, 1983, Improving Mental Health Services: What the Social Sciences Can Tell Us, 1987, General Hospital Impatient Psychiatry, 1997, Managed Behavioral Health Care: Current Realities and Future Potential, 1998; co-editor (with Robert Hauser, Archibald Haller and Tess Hauser): Social Structure and Personality, 1982; co-editor: (with Linda Aiken) Applications of Social Science to Clinical Medicine and Social Policy, 1986; co-editor: Paying for Services: Promises and Pitfalls of Capitation, 1989; co-editor: (with Marian Osterweis and Arthur Kleinman) Pain and Disability: Clinical Behavior and Public Policy Perspectives, 1987; co-editor: (with Carl Taube and Ann Hohmann) The Future of Mental Health Services Research, 1989; co-editor: (with Lynn Rogut, David Colby, and James Knickman) Policy Challenges in Modern Health Care, 2005. Recipient Ward medal, CCNY, 1956, Carl Taube award, APHA, 1990, Remc Lapouse award, 2003, Disting. Investigator award, Assn. for Health Svcs. Rsch., 1991, Disting. Contbn. award mental health sect., Soc. for Study of Social Problems, 1991, Emily Mumford medal, Columbia U., 1991, Investigator award in health policy rsch., Robert Wood Johnson Found., 1995—99, Health Svcs. Rsch. prize, Assn. of U. Programs in Health Adminstrn. and the Baxter Allegiance Found., 1997, Senator Frank R. Lautenberg Ann. award, Sch. Pub. Health, U. Medicine and Dentistry NJ, 2003, Benjamin Rush award, Am. Psychiat. Assn., 2004, First Matilda Riley award and lectr., NIH, 2006; fellow Ford Behavioral Sci. fellow, 1956—57, NIMH rsch. fellow, 1965—66, Ctr. for Advanced Study in Behavioral Scis., 1974—75, Guggenheim fellow, 1977—78, Disting. fellow, Assn. Health Svcs. Rsch., 1996. Fellow: AAAS (chmn. sect. social, econ. and polit. scis. 1985), Assn. Health Svcs. Rsch. (disting. 1996); mem.: NAS, Nat. Acad. Sciences, Hogg Found. Mental Health (nat. adv. coun. 1987), Nat. Acad. Social Ins. (founding), Am. Acad. Arts and Scis., Inst. Medicine-NAS (governing coun. 1972—74), Sociol. Rsch. Assn. (pres. 1991—92), Am. Sociol. Assn. (chmn. med. sociol. sect. 1969—70, governing coun. 1977—78, chmn. publs. com. 1989—91, chmn. mental health sect. 1992—93, Disting. Med. Sociologist award 1983, Lifetime Achievement award mental health sect. 1994, Disting. Career award 2001, Disting. Career award for Practice of Sociology 2004), Phi Beta Kappa. Office: Rutgers U Inst Health Policy Aging Rsch 30 College Ave New Brunswick NJ 08901-1283 Home: 5 Overbrook Dr Princeton NJ 08540-3924 Office Phone: 732-932-8415. Business E-Mail: mechanic@rci.rutgers.edu.

MECHEM, CHARLES STANLEY, JR., retired broadcast executive; b. Nelsonville, Ohio, Sept. 12, 1930; s. Charles Stanley and Helen (Hall) Mechem; m. Marilyn Brown, Aug. 31, 1952; children: Melissa, Daniel, Allison. AB, Miami U., Oxford, Ohio, 1952; LLB, Yale U., New Haven, Conn., 1955. Bar: Ohio 1955. Practice in Cin., 1955—67; ptnr. Taft, Stettinius & Hollister, 1965—67; chmn. bd. Taft Broadcasting Co., Cin., 1967—90; commr. LPGA, Daytona Beach, Fla., 1990—95, commr. emeritus, 1995—; chmn. U.S. Shoe, 1993—95; chmn. Cin. Bell, Inc., 1996—98, Convergys Corp., 1998—2000; cons. Arnold Palmer Enterprises, Cin., 1996—. Bd. dirs. Messer Constrn., Inc. Capt. JAGC US Army, 1956—59. Mem.: Cin. C. of C. (pres. 1977), Comml. Club. Office: Taft Stettinius & Hollister LLP 425 Walnut St Ste 1800 Cincinnati OH 45202-4122 Home Phone: 513-759-3011.

MECHER, GREG, legislative staff member; Grad., No. Ky. U., Highland Heights. Intern, Rep. Ken Lucas US House of Reps., Washington, 1999, polit. dir., Rep. Patrick Kennedy, chief of staff to Rep. Steve Driehaus, 2008—. Fundraiser Dem. Nat. Com., 2004; dep. fin. dir. Dem. Congl. Campaign Com., 2006. Democrat. Office: 408 Cannon House Office Bldg Washington DC 20515 Office Phone: 202-225-2216. Office Fax: 202-225-3012.*

MECHREF, YEHIA, biochemist, director; s. Salem H. Mechref and Fayzah Jibloui; m. Reda Z. Rafei, Aug. 23, 1993; children: Farah F., Miriam B. PhD, Okla. State U., Still Water, 1996. Asst. prof. United Arab Emirates U., Al Ain, 1997—2000; dir. Metacyt Biochem. Analysis Ctr. Ind. U., Bloomington, 2005—, asst. dir. Nat. Ctr. Glycomics and Glycoproteomics, 2005—. Contbr. articles to profl. jours. Mem.: ASMS. Achievements include patents for fluid treatment device; device for placement of effluent; high temperature incubation system; glycoprotein cleavage protocol for oligosaccharide analysis; method of preparation of oligosaccharides; glycan markers of hepatocellular carcinoma. Office: Ind Univ 800 E Kirkwood Ave Bloomington IN 47405 Office Fax: 812-855-8300. Business E-Mail: ymechref@indiana.edu.

MECIMORE, CHARLES DOUGLAS, retired accounting educator; b. Belmont, NC, Aug. 20, 1934; s. John Edgar and Hattie (Bolick) M.; m. Barbara Jean Chiddie, June 7, 1959; children: Laura Jean, Charles D. Jr., John Amos. BS, Pfeiffer Coll., 1958; MS, U. N.C., 1962; PhD, U. Ala., 1966. CPA, N.C.; CMA. Asst. prof. U. Ala., Tuscaloosa, 1966-67; assoc. prof. U. Ga., Athens, 1967-71; prof. U. Cin., 1971-79; prof. acctg. Sch. Bus. and Econs., U. N.C., Greensboro, 1980-98; ret., 1998. Head dept. U. N.C. Sch. Bus. and Econs., 1980-89, 96-98. With USAF, 1951—55. Univ. scholar, 1963-66; Haskins and Sells fellow, 1962-64; Beyer bronze medal, 1974. Mem. AICPAs, N.C. Assn. CPAs (Outstanding Educator 1985). Home: 430 Marshall View Ct Winston Salem NC 27101-5285 E-mail: cmecimore@triad.rr.com.

MECKE, WILLIAM MOYN, public information officer; b. Detroit, May 7, 1957; s. Theodore Hart McCalla Jr. and Mary Eleanor (Flaherty) M.; m. Katherine E. Bauer-Mecke. BA, Georgetown U., 1979; MA, Am. U., 1982; postgrad., Oxford U., 1982, U. N.C., 1982-85. Asst. dir. Found. Study Presdl. and Congrl. Terms, Washington, 1979-82; acct. exec. Hill and Knowlton, Inc., Chgo., 1985-86; tchr. The Bolles Sch., Jacksonville, Fla., 1986-88, St. Andrew's Sch., Savannah, 1988-91, Joseph Walker Sch., Marietta, Ga., 1991-92; polit. cons. various Democratic candidates, 1992-95; tech. writer Total Sys. Svcs. Inc., Columbus, Ga., 1995; dir. mktg. Habitat for Humanity Internat., Americus, Ga., 1995-2000, media svcs. mgr., 2000-2001; comm. dir. Ga. Regional Transp. Authority, 2001—. Co-author, editor: Presidential and Congressional Term Limitation: The Issue That Stays Alive, 1981. Asst. dir. Found. Study Presd. and Congl. Terms, Washington, 1979-82. Mem. Pub. Rels. Soc. Am. Office: Ga Regional Transp Authority Ste 900 245 Peachtree Ctr Ave NE Atlanta GA 30303 Office Phone: 404-463-3011. Business E-Mail: wmecke@grta.org.

MECKLENBURG, GARY ALAN, retired hospital administrator; b. June 17, 1946; m. Lynn Kraemer; children: John, Sarah. BA, Northwestern U., 1968; MBA, U. Chgo., 1970. Adminstrv. resident Presbyn.-St. Luke's Hosp., Chgo., 1969-70, adminstrv. asst., 1970-71, asst. supt., 1971-76, assoc. supt., 1976-77, U. Wis. Hosps., Madison, 1977-80; adminstr. Stanford U. Hosp. Clinics, Calif.; pres., CEO St. Joseph's Hosp., Milw., 1980-85; pres. Franciscan Health Care Inc., Milw., 1985; pres., CEO Northwestern Meml. Hosp., Chgo., 1985—2001, Northwestern Meml. HealthCare, Chgo., 2001—06. Preceptor, guest lectr., mem. adv. bd. Kellogg Sch. Mgmt., Chgo., 1986—; pres., CEO, Northwestern Healthcare Network, 1990-92. Recipient Todd Scout award Boy Scouts Am., 1998, Chgo. Bus. Hall of Fame award Jr. Achievement, 2000, GSB Disting. Pub. Svc./Pub. Sector Alumnus award U. Chgo., 2000. Mem. Am. Hosp. Assn. (sect. met. hosps., governing coun. 1984-92, chmn. 1991, 2001, trustee 1996-2002, exec. com. 1997-2002, chmn., 2001, mem. regional policy bd., #5 1984, 87-89, 91-93, 95-99, chmn. 1996-99, 2001, mem. ho. dels. 1984, 87-89, 91—, mem. com. on med. edn. 1976-80), Ill. Hosp. Assn. (bd. dirs. 1988-95, chmn. 1994, mem. adv. panel coun. tchg. hosps. 1997—), U. Chgo. Hosp. Adminstrn. Alumni Assn. (pres. 1985-86), Econ. Club Chgo., Comml. Club Chgo.

MECKSTROTH, WILMA JEAN, piano and organ educator, accompanist; b. Dayton, Ohio, July 5, 1928; d. Edgar B. and Olive M. Andrew; m. Robert C. Meckstroth, Oct. 7, 1950; children: David, John, Carol. MusB, Northwestern U., Evanston, Ill., 1950. Nat. cert. tchr. music Music Tchrs. Nat. Assn. Organist The Luth. Ch. of Our Savior, Dayton, 1957—2003; pvt. piano tchr. Dayton, 1957—; accompanist The Music Appreciation Choral Club, 1957—; chmn. Dayton Organ Acad., 1980—; adjudicator Nat. Guild Piano Tchrs., Am. Coll. Musicians, Austin, 1980—2006. Mem.: Am. Guild Organists (dean 1981—83), Ohio Music Tchrs. Assn. (chmn. west dist. 1994—96, Piano Tchr. of Yr. 1999), Dayton Music Club (pres. 1987—89), Dayton Piano Tchrs. Study Club (pres. 1978—79), Mu Phi Epsilon (pres. 1958—60, 2000—02, Dayton chpt. alumni). Lutheran. Avocations: cooking, tennis. Home: 2142 E Rahn Rd Kettering OH 45440

MECONI, HONEY, musicologist, writer; d. Patrick and Mary Evelyn Meconi; m. Michel Jean-Marie Godts, Mar. 5, 1988; 1 child, Yannick Corentin Godts. BA, Pa. State U., 1974; AM, Harvard U., 1980, PhD, 1986. From asst. to full prof. Rice U., Houston, 1987—2004, dir. Medieval studies, 1998—2004; prof. music U. Rochester, NY, 2004—; prof. musicology Eastman Sch. Music, Rochester, 2004—; dir. Susan B. Anthony Inst., 2007—. Mem. Harvard Grad. Soc. Coun., Cambridge, Mass., 1990—96; mem. adv. bd. Houston Early Music, 2000—02; bd. dir. The Hildegard Project; conf. dir. Constructing Hildegard: Reception and Identity 1098-1998, 1998; music cons. U.S. Cath. Conf., Washington, 1998—99; bd. dirs. Pegasus Early Music. Author: Pierre de la Rue, 2003; editor: Early Musical Borrowing, 2004, (music edit.) Fortuna Desperata, 2001; contbr. articles to profl. jours.; author: Cancionero de Juana la Loca, 2007. Recipient Arts and Architecture Alumna award, Pa. State U., 2006; fellow, Fulbright, Belgium, 1982—84, Villa I Tatti, Florence, Italy, 1986—87, Andrew W. Mellon, U. Pa., 1990—91, Ctr. for the Study of Cultures/Rice U., 2002—03; fellowship, Nat. Endowment Humanities, 2008—. Mem.: Coll. Music Soc., Internat. Musicol. Soc., Am. Musicol. Soc. (pres. S.W. chpt. 1999—2001, bd. dirs. 2005—06, v.p. 2009—, Noah Greenberg award 2006). Avocation: quilting. Office: Univ Rochester 207 Todd Union Rochester NY 14627-0052 Office Phone: 585-275-9399.

MEDAK, PETER, film director; b. Budapest, Hungary; arrived in Eng., 1956; came to U.S., 1979; s. Gyula and Elisabeth (Diamonstein) M.; m. Julia Migenes, July 31, 1989 (div. 2004); children: Christopher, Karen, Joshua, Cornelia, Martina, Jessica. Dir. (films) Negatives, 1968, A Day in the Death of Joe Egg, 1970, The Ruling Class, 1971, Ghost in a Nonnday's Sun, 1973, The Odd Job, 1977, The Changling, 1979, Zorro the Gay Blade, 1980, The Men's Club, 1986, The Krays, 1989, La Voix Humane, 1990, Let Him Have It, 1991, Romeo is Bleeding, 1992, Pontiac Moon, 1994, Hunchback of Notre Dame, 1996, Species 2, 1997, David Copperfield, 1998-99, Feast of All Saints, 2000, (stage) Miss Julie, 1977 (opera) Salome, 1988, La Voix Humane, and others. Mem. Dir.'s Guild of Am., Dir.'s Guild of U.K., Assn. of Cinematographers, Allied Technicians, Dir.'s Guild of Can. Jewish. Office: George Harvey's Office 10100 Santa Monila Blvd Los Angeles CA 90067

MEDALIE, RICHARD JAMES, lawyer; b. Duluth, Minn., July 21, 1929; s. William Louis and Mona (Kolad) M.; m. Susan Diane Abrams, June 5, 1960; children: Samuel David, Daniel Alexander. BA summa cum laude, U. Minn., 1952; cert., U. London, 1953; A.M., Harvard U., 1955, JD cum laude, 1958. Bar: DC 1958, NY 1963. Law clk. to Hon. George T. Washington U.S. Ct. Appeals, Washington, 1958-59; asst. solicitor gen. U.S., 1960-62; assoc. Kaye, Scholer, Fierman, Hays & Handler, NYC, 1962-65; dep. dir. Ford Found. Inst. Criminal Law and Procedure, Georgetown U. Law Ctr., 1965-68; ptnr. Friedman & Medalie and predecessors, Washington, 1968-98; pres. Pegasus Internat., Washington, 1970—; exec. dir. The Appleseed Found., Washington, 1993-94, chmn. bd., 1993—2002, chmn. emeritus, 2003—, pres., 1995-98; pvt. practice Washington, 1998—2006, Hull, Mass., 2006—. Adj. prof. adminstrv. and criminal law Georgetown U. Law Center, 1967—70; mem. D.C. Law Revision Commn., 1975—87; chmn. Criminal Law Task Force, exec. com., 1978—82; mem. panel comml. arbitrators Nat. Arbitration Forum, 2004—; vice chmn. Harvard Law Sch. Fund, 1981—84, chmn. nat. maj. gifts, 1984—86, dep. chmn., 1986—87, chmn., 1987—89; v.p., bd. dirs. Trial Lawyers for Pub. Justice, Washington, 1998—2006. Author: From Escobedo to Miranda: The Anatomy of a Supreme Court Decision, 1966; co-author: Federal Consumer Safety Legislation, 1970; co-author, editor: Commercial Arbitration for the 1990s, 1991; co-author, co-editor American Students Organize: Founding the National Student Association after World War II, 2006; co-editor: Crime: A Community Responds, 1967; staff: Harvard Law Rev., 1956-58; case editor, 1957-58; contbr. articles to legal jours. Bd. dir. alumni assn. Experiment in Internat. Living, Brattleboro, Vt., 1961-64, pres., 1962-63. Fulbright scholar, 1952-53; Ford fellow, 1954-55. Fellow Am. Bar Found., Harvard Law Sch. Assn. D.C. (pres. 1976-77, nat. v.p. 1977-78), Harvard Alumni Assn. (law sch. dir. 1991-95); mem. ABA (program chair 1984, 90, chair legis. subcom. 1986-89, ADR/arbitration com., rep. on adv. com. nat. conf. Emerging ADR Issues in State and Fed. Cts. 1991, vice-chmn. 1991-94, arbitration com. litigation sect., co-chair nat. conf. Critical Issues in Arbitration 1993), Am. Arbitration Assn. (panel comml. arbitrators 1964—), D.C. Unified Bar, Assn. Bar City of N.Y., Am. Law Inst. (life, consultative group, model penal code sentencing), Cosmos Club, Phi Beta Kappa, Phi Alpha Theta. Office: 46 P St Hull MA 02045 Home Phone: 781-925-0138; Office Phone: 202-659-0880. Personal E-mail: rmedalie@att.net.

MEDAVOY, MIKE (MORRIS MIKE MEDAVOY), film company executive, producer; b. Shanghai, Jan. 21, 1941; arrived in U.S., 1957, naturalized, 1962; s. Michael and Dora Medavoy; m. Irena Medavoy; children: Nicholas, Brian. BA, UCLA, 1963; PhD (hon.), Acad. Art san Fransisco, 2009. With Casting dept. Universal Studios, 1963; agt. Bill Robinson Assos., LA, 1963—64; v.p. motion picture dept. GAC/CMA Co., 1965—71, IFA Co., 1971—74; sr. v.p. United Artists Corp., 1974—78; co-founder, exec. v.p. Orion Pictures Co., Burbank, Calif., 1978—82, Orion Pictures Corp. (formerly Orion Pictures Co.), Century City, Calif., 1982—90; chmn. Tri-Star Pictures, Inc., Culver City, Calif., 1990—94; chmn., CEO Phoenix Picture Corp., 1995—. Jury chmn. Tokyo Film Festival 1994; hon. co-chair St. Petersburg (Russia) Film Festival, 1992; adv. bd. Shanghai Film Conf.; co-chmn. Am. Cinematheque, 1997-2004, chmn. emeritus, 2004—. Author: You're Only as Good as Your Next One, 2002. Co-founder Sundance Film Inst.; bd. govs. Sundance Inst., 1980-86; bd. dirs. Calif. Mus. Sci. and Industry, 1984-87, U. Tel-Aviv., UCLA Found.; commr. L.A. Bd. Parks and Recreation, 2001; exec. adv. bd. Calif. Anti-Terrorism Info. Ctr., 2002; bd. advs. Harvard's Kennedy Sch. Gov., co-chair UCLA Burkle Ctr. Internat. Rels., mem. coun. fgn. rels., 2004, bd. dirs. Mus. Sci. & Industry LA, U. Tel Aviv, LA Board Pks. & Recreations., Bd. trustee, UCLA, exec. adv. bd. mem. Calif. Anti-Terrorism Information Ctrs. Recipient Acad. award (mem. of team that green lit), One Flew Over the Cuckoo's Nest, Rocky, Annie Hall, Amadeus, Platoon, Dances with Wolves, Silence of the Lambs, Motion Picture Pioneer award, 1992, Career Achievement award, UCLA Alumni, 1997, Prodrs. award, Cannes Film Festival, 1998, Neil H. Jacoby award, 1999, Fred Zinneman award, Anti-Defamation League, 2001, Film Theater and Prodrs. Guild Am. Vision award, UCLA, 2005, Prodr. of Yr. award, Hollywood Film Festival, 2006, 2007, Lifetime Achievement award, Jerusalem Film Found, 2008; named Chevalier of French Legion Honor, 2009; named to Hollywood Walk of Fame, 2005. Mem. Acad. Motion Picture Arts and Scis. (gov. 1977-81, Hollywood Walk of Fame Star 2005) Business E-Mail: mmedavoy@phoenixpictures.com.

MEDBURY, SCOT DANIEL, botanical garden executive; b. Columbus, Ga., Jan. 28, 1959; s. Paul Randall Medbury and Janet Elaine Stewart; m. Brian K. Lym, Oct. 13, 2003. BA in Internat. Studies, U. Wash., Seattle, 1987, MS in Forest Resources, 1990; studied, U. Calif., Berkeley, 1992—97. Nursery mgr. Nat. Tropical Bot. Garden, Kauai, Hawaii, 1982—83; gardener Crown Estate Commn., Windsor, England, 1985, Pukekura Park, New Plymouth, New Zealand, 1986; edn. assoc. Ctr. for Urban Horticulture, Seattle, 1986—90; curator Honolulu Bot. Gardens, 1990—92; dir. San Francisco Bot. Garden and Conservatory of Flowers, 1999—2005; pres., CEO Bklyn. Botanic Garden, 2005—. Hort. cons. Plant Collections Planning and Mgmt., Berkeley, Calif., 1992—99; bd. dirs. Am. Assn. Botanical Gardens & Arboreta, 2001—04. Author: San Francisco Botanical Garden - A World of Plants, 2005; contbr. articles to profl. jours. Named to Centennial Honor Roll, Am. Assn. Museums, 2006. Mem.: Internat. Dendrology Soc. (coun. mem. 2001—), Garden Club Am. Office: Brooklyn Botanic Garden 1000 Washington Ave Brooklyn NY 11225 Office Phone: 718-623-7269. Business E-Mail: presidentsoffice@bbg.org.

MEDDERS, EMILY ANNA, speech pathology/audiology services professional; d. Emerson C. and Christina Marylene Gillett; children: Gregory, Jeffrey. BS, Phillips U., Enid, Okla., 1980, MS in Speech Pathology, 1982. Cert. clin. competence Am. Speech Lang. Hearing Assn. Speech lang. pathologist Drummond-Lahome Okla. Pub. Sch., 1981—83, Oklahoma City Pub. Sch., 1983—. Mission trip coord. New Covenant Christian Ch., Oklahoma City, 2005—07.

MEDDING, WALTER SHERMAN, retired environmental engineer; b. St. Louis, Mar. 4, 1922; s. Walter Lyman and Elizabeth Steele (Sherman) M.; m. Mary Agnes Patty Johnson, Apr. 22, 1944; children: Jean, Walter, Mauri. BSCE, Va. Poly. Inst., 1947, MS in Sanitary Engring., 1970. Registered profl. engr., Va., N.C., Kans. Various positions U.S. Army, 1942-64; student officer advanced course The Engr. Sch., Ft. Belvoir, Va., 1952—54, head fixed bridges sect., 1954—55; asst. engr. Asmara Eritrea, chief design br. Mediterranean Divsn., Gulf Dist., Tehran, Iran, 1955-57; asst. divsn. engr. 9th Infantry Divsn., Ft. Carson, Colo., 1957-59; resident engr. USACAG, chief constrn. ops. U.S. Army Engring. Command Europe, Frankfurt, Germany, 1959-72; chief contract adminstrn. U.S. Army Engring. Divsn. Europe, Frankfurt, Germany, 1972-75; chief environ. engring. Office, Chief of Engrs., U.S. Army, Washington, 1975-86; sr. engr. Romem Aqua Sys. Co., Woodbridge, Va., 1986-97. Cons. U.S. army Ctr. for Pub. Works, Ft. Belvoir, Va., 1997-98; music tchr. Co-author: (textbook) Non-standard Military Fixed Bridges, 1954, (with E. Farago) Which Musical Instrument Shall I Play?, 1985; editor, pub. Letter to Lyman, 1978; contbr. articles to profl. jours. Mem. ASCE, Am. Waterworks Assn., Water Environ. Fedn., Conf. of Fed. Environ. Engrs. Republican. Episcopalian. Achievements include development of mil. bridge classification procedures for load carrying and rapid field design. Home: 204 Brooke Dr Fredericksburg VA 22408-2004 Personal E-mail: wsmedding@aol.com.

MEDEARIS, MILLER, lawyer; b. Liberty, Mo., Jan. 19, 1921; s. Thomas Whittier and Mara (Miller) Medearis; children: Christy Crochet, Kellee Reed. LLB, Cumberland U., 1948; JD, Stamford U., 1969. Bar: Okla. 1948, Calif. 1957. Claims adjustor Transit Casualty Co., LA, 1950-56, atty., trial counsel, 1956-58; ptnr. Hagenbaugh, Murphy &

Medearis, LA, 1958-69, Medearis and Grimm, LA, 1969—2004; adminstrv. law judge Calif. Employee Ins. Appeals Bd., Sherman Oaks, 2004—. Sec., bd. dirs. Med. Quality Assurance, Sacramento, 1979—84, v.p., 1984—86; commr. LA Bd. Transp., 1986—92; bd. mem. Calif. Unemployment Ins. Appeals Bd., 2000—04; mem. Dem. Bus. Coun., LA, 1980; adminstrv. law judge Calif. Unemployment Ins. Appeals Bd., 2004—; bd. dirs. Pico Rivera Cmty. Hosp., 1975—85. With USN, 1945—46. Mem.: ABA, Okla. Bar Assn., Calif. Trial Lawyers Assn., State Bar Calif., Lawyers Club LA. Democrat. Baptist. Avocations: boating, water-skiing, downhill skiing. Home: 2175 Ridge Dr Los Angeles CA 90049-1153 Home Phone: 310-471-8900; Office Phone: 818-461-3468.

MEDEIROS, ANTONE ARRUDA, retired medical educator; b. New Bedford, Mass., Dec. 29, 1934; s. Sabino Arruda Medeiros and Rosa De Mello Cardosa; m. Beverly Kay Enna, June 25, 1965; children: Chtistina Rose O'Brien, Laurinda Susan Hale, Elena Katherine Van Werkhoven, Evan Sabino, Julia Morgan Berthet, Jamie De Mello, Ann Elizabeth. AB, Brown U., Providence, 1957; MD, Georgetown Med. Sch., Washington, 1961. Diplomate Am. Bd. Internal Medicine, 1970. Epidemic intelligence svc. officer US pub. health svc., Kansas City, 1963—65; asst. prof. medicine peter bent brigham hosp. Harvard Med. Sch., Boston, 1971—76; prof. medicine Brown Med. Sch., Providence, 1984—2006; prof. emeritus Brown U., Providence, 2006. Dir., divsn. infectious diseases Miriam Hosp., Providence, 1976—99. Contbr. chapters to books, articles to profl. jours., scientific papers. Lt. comdr. USPHS, 1963—65, Kansas City. Recipient award, Brown U., 1957. Mem.: Phi Beta Kappa. Democrat. Roman Catholic. Avocations: photography, woodworking, gardening, fishing. Home: 440 Capts Cir Fall River MA 02721 Business E-Mail: antone_medeiros@brown.edu.

MEDEIROS, DENIS MICHAEL, nutrition educator; b. Acushnet, Mass., June 12, 1952; s. Joseph Medeiros and Rita Irene (Brassard) Wilkie; m. Lydia Claire Wiggins, Dec. 28, 1981; 1 child, Kathryn Claire. BS, Cen. Conn. State U., 1974; MS, Ill. State U., 1976; PhD, Clemson U., 1981. Registered dietitian, Ohio. Asst. prof. Miss. State U., Starkville, 1981-84; assoc. prof. nutrition U. Wyo., Laramie, 1984-89, chmn. faculty senate, 1989; prof. human nutrition, assoc. dean for rsch. Ohio State U., Columbus, 1989—. Mem. editorial bd., Biol. Trace Element Rsch., 1984, Nutrition Rsch., 1988; contbr. articles to profl. publs. Grantee, NSF, 1986, NIH, 1988. Mem. Am. Inst. Nutrition, Am. Dietetic Assn., Inst. Food Technologists, Am. Pub. Health Assn., Sigma Xi, Gamma Sigma Delta. Democrat. Roman Catholic. Avocations: rock and roll music, jogging. Office: Ohio State U Dept Human Nutrition & Food Mgmt 265 Campbell Hall 1787 Neil Ave Columbus OH 43210-1295 Home: 8699 Lazelle Commons Dr Lewis Center OH 43035-8841

MEDEL, REBECCA ROSALIE, artist; b. Denver, Mar. 26, 1947; d. Natividad and Josefa (Apodaca) Medel. BFA, Ariz. State U., Tempe, 1970; MFA, UCLA, 1982. Asst. prof. fibers dept. head Tenn. Technol. U., Smithville, 1983-88; lectr. Dept. of Design, UCLA, 1989-91; studio artist, 1991—; prof. Tyler Sch. Art Temple U., 1995—. Lectr. N.C. State U., Raleigh, San Diego State U., SUNY, Purchase, 1992, Penland Sch. Asheville, NC, Textile Study Group, NYC, Calif. Coll. of Arts & Crafts, Oakland, Calif., San Jose State U., Am. Ctr., Kyoto, Japan, City Ctr., Sapporo, Japan, 1986; vis. artist U. ND, 1985. One-woman shows include Thirteen Moons Gallery, Santa Fe, 2003, 05, Brown Grotta Gallery, Wilton, Conn., 1996, Neuberger Mus. of Art, Purchase, NY, 1992-93, Bellas Artes Gallery, NYC, 1991, N.D. Mus. Art, Grand Forks, 1985, Maya Behn Galerie, Zurich, 1984, UCLA, 1982, Thirteen Moons Gallery, Santa Fe, 2003, 05; group shows include Bellas Artes Gallery, Santa Fe, N.Mex., 1992, NC State U. Gallery, 1992, Portland Art Mus., 1995, Madison Art Ctr., Wis., 1995, Santa Monica Art Gallery, 1995, Maya Behn Gallerie, 1991, Mus. Van Bommel-Van Dam, Venlo, Netherlands, 1990, Palo Alto Cultural Ctr., 1990, Barbican Ctr. Concourse Gallery, London, 1998, Montclair State U. Gallery, NJ, 1998, Art Inst. Chgo., 1999, Yokohama Mus. Art, Japan, 1999, Biennial 2000, Del. Art Mus., Wilmington, LA Mus. Art, 2000, Soc. Contemporary Crafts, Pitts., 2001, Westport Arts Ctr., Conn., 2003, many others. Recipient bronze medal Triennial of Tapestry, 1985; visual artist fellow Nat. Endowment for Arts, 1986, 88, fellow for emerging visual artists So. Arts Fedn. NEA, 1985; Pew fellow in the arts, 1999, 2003, fellow Pa. Coun. on Arts, 2001, 03, 07; scholar to Arcosanti, Nat. Endowment for Arts, 1986, 88. Home: 2920 Meyer Ave Glenside PA 19038-1920 Office Phone: 215-782-2728. Business E-Mail: rmedel@temple.edu.

MEDELLIN-AZUARA, JOSUE, environmental scientist; b. Tampico, Tamaulipas, Mex, Dec. 28, 1971; s. Josue Medellin-Rivera and Aurora Azuara-Dominguez; m. Ileana Marcela Sicairos-Lopez; 1 child, Josue Medellin-Sicairos. BS in Mech. and Elec. Engring., Inst. Tech. Monterrey, Mex., 1993, MBA, 1998; MS in Agrl. and Resource Economics, U. Calif., Davis, 2002, PhD in Ecology Water Resources Mgmt., 2006. Cert. quality sys. aditor, Ford, Chrysler, GMC, 1998, environ. mgmt. sys. auditor, Erm Cvs, 1998, in lean mfg., U. Tenn., 1998, Hazardous Waste Handling and Management, Inst. Tech. Monterrey, 1997, cert. in environ. quality, Inst. Tech. Monterrey, 1999. Project engr. Corporativo Copamex SA de CV, San Pedro Garza Garcia, Mexico, 1994—97; environ. coord. Navistar Truck & Engine Corp. Mex., Escobedo, Mexico, 1997—2000; dir. aquatic toxicology outreach program U. Calif., Davis, 2003—05, rschr., 2000—03, 2005—06, 2007—. Cons. Natural Heritage Inst., San Francisco, 2007—08. Mem. Union Concerned Scientists, Davis, 2009. Doctoral fellowship, UCMEXUS, 2000—05, Jastro Shields grant, U. Calif., 2005, Collaborative Grant, UC MEXUS, 2005. Mem.: Air & Waste Mgmt. Assn., Am. Assn. Civil Engrs., Am. Geophys. Union. Office: Univ California Davis Dept Civil and Environ Engring EU III Davis CA 95616 Office Fax: 530-752-7872. Business E-Mail: jmedellin@ucdavis.edu.

MEDER, CORNEL, retired archivist, director; b. Esch/Alzette, Luxembourg, Sept. 23, 1938; s. Nicolas and Susan (Hecker) M.; m. Nicole Wagner, Apr. 10, 1965; children: Charles, Françoise. Grad., State U., Luxembourg, D of Philosophy & Philology. Prof. Lycée de Garçons Esch/Alzette, Esch/Alzette, 1966-69; headmaster Lycée Mathias Adam, Pétange, Luxembourg, 1969-87; dir. Nat. Archives, Luxembourg, 1987—2003. Author 15 books in letters, philology and history; editor Galerie cultur mag., 1982--. Sen. Senate of Luxembourg, 1978-99. Decorated grand officer Order de la Couronne de Chêne (Luxemburg). Mem. Institut Grand-Ducal (pres. linguistics and ethnological sect. 1976-91). Mem. Social Dem. Party. Avocation: lecture. Home: Prinzenberg 69 L-4650 Niederkorn Luxembourg Home Phone: 00352-587045. E-mail: cornel.meder@ci.culture.lu.

MEDEROS, CAROLINA LUISA, public policy consultant; b. Rochester, Minn., July 1, 1947; d. Luis O. and Carolina (del Valle) Mederos. BA, Vanderbilt U., 1969; MA, U. Chgo., 1971. Adminstrv. asst. Lt. Gov. Ill., Chgo., 1972; sr. rsch. assoc. U. Chgo., 1972; project mgr., cons. Urban Dynamics, Inner City Fund and Cmty. Programs Inc., Chgo., 1972-73; legis. asst. to Senate pres. Ill. State Senate, Chgo. and Springfield, 1973-76; program analyst Dept. Transp., Washington, 1976-79, chief, trans. assistance programs div., 1979-81, dir. programs and evaluation, 1981-88, chairwoman, sec.'s safety rev. task force, 1985-88, deputy asst. sec. for safety, policy and internat. affairs, 1988-89; cons. Patton Boggs LLP, Washington, 1990—. Recipient award for Meritorious Achievement, Sec. Transp. 1980, Superior Achievement award U.S. Dept. Transp., 1981, Sec.'s Gold Medal award for Outstanding Achievement, 1986, Presdl. Rank award, 1987. Home: 2723 O St NW Washington DC 20007-3128 Office: Patton Boggs LLP 2550 M St NW Washington DC 20037-1350 Home Phone: 202-337-4107; Office Phone: 202-457-5653. Business E-Mail: cmederos@pattonboggs.com.

MEDHI, DEEPANKAR, computer science educator; b. Guwahati, Assam, India, June 17, 1962; came to U.S., 1983; s. Jyotiprasad and Prity (Chowdhury) M.; m. Karen Thompson, Aug. 15, 1987; children: Neiloy M., Robby S. BSc in Math., Gauhati U., Assam, India, 1981; MS in Math., U. of Delhi, India, 1983; MS in Computer Sci., U. Wis., 1985, PhD in Computer Sci., 1987. Teaching and rsch. asst. U. Wis., Madison, 1983-87; mem. tech. staff AT&T Bell Labs., Holmdel, N.J., 1987-89; rsch. asst. prof. U. Mo., Kansas City, 1989-91, asst. prof. computer sci., 1991-96, assoc. prof., 1996—2000, prof., 2000—. Sr. tech. editor Jour. of Network and Systems Mgmt.; contbr. papers to sci. confs. Mem. IEEE (sr.), Assn. Computing Machinery, Inst. Ops. Rsch. and Mgmt. Sci. (pres. Kansas City chpt. 1991-92). Home: 4009 W 100th Ter Shawnee Mission KS 66207-3740 Office: U Mo Kansas City Sch Computing Engring 5100 Rockhill Rd Kansas City MO 64110-2481

MEDIATE, ROCCO, professional golfer; b. Greensburg, Pa., Dec. 17, 1962; Attended, Fla. Southern U. Profl. golfer, 1985—. Participant World Series of Poker Main Event, 2005; on-course reporter The Golf Channel, 2007. Achievements include being the first player to win a PGA Tour event using a long-handled putter, 1991; PGA Tour wins: Doral-Ryder Open, 1991, KMart Greater Greensboro Open, 1993, Phoenix Open, 1999, Buick Open, 2000, Greater Greensboro Chrysler Classic, 2002. Office: c/o Gaylord Sports Mgmt 13845 N Northsight Blvd Ste 200 Scottsdale AZ 85260

MEDICUS, HEINRICH ADOLF, physicist, researcher; b. Zurich, Switzerland, Dec. 24, 1918; came to U.S., 1950; naturalized, 1995; s. Friedrich Georg and Clara Anna (Frey) M.; m. Hildegard Julie Schmelz, June 15, 1961. Diploma, Swiss Fed. Inst. Tech., Zurich, 1943, DSc, 1949. With Swiss Army, 1938—50; rsch. assoc. Swiss Fed. Inst. Tech., Zurich, 1943-50; visitor Lawrence Berkeley (Calif.) Lab., 1950-51, MIT, Cambridge, Mass., 1951-52, instr., vis. asst. prof., 1952-55; from assoc. prof. to prof. exptl. nuc. physics and history of modern physics Rensselaer Poly. Inst., Troy, NY, 1955-87, prof. emeritus, 1987—. Vis. scientist Atomic Energy Research Establishment Harwell, Eng., 1967-68, Swiss Inst. Nuclear Research, Villigen, 1974-75. Co-author: Fields and Particles, 1973; contbr. articles to profl. jours. Bd. mem. Albany Symphony Orch., NY, 2006—. Fellow Swiss Found., 1950-52 Mem. Am. Phys. Soc., Swiss Phys. Soc., Swiss Am. Hist. Soc., Hudson-Mohawk Swiss Soc. (pres. 1974-06), Delta Tau Delta (pres. house corp. Upsilon chpt. 1984-91, faculty adv. 1991-95), Swiss Alpine Club. Presbyterian. Avocations: wine education, music. Office: Rensselaer Poly Inst Dept Physics Troy NY 12180 Home: 2218 Burdett Ave Apt 109 Troy NY 12180 Home Phone: 518-833-7436. Business E-Mail: medich@rpi.edu.

MEDICUS, HILDEGARD JULIE, retired dentist, orthodontist, educator; b. Frankfurt, Germany, July 25, 1928; came to U.S., 1961, naturalized, 1995; d. Gustav and Elizabeth Berta (Neunhoeffer) Schmelz; m. Heinrich Adolf Medicus, June 15, 1961. DMD, U. Marburg, W. Germany, 1953; orthodontics diploma, U. Düsseldorf, W. Germany, 1957. lic. dentist, N.Y. Postdoctoral fellow dental sch. U. Zürich, Switzerland, 1957; postdoctoral fellow U. Liège, Belgium, 1958, Forsyth Dental Ctr., Boston, 1959, orthodontic rsch. affiliate, 1963—74; sch. dentist Pub. Sch. Sys., Zürich, 1975—76; dental hygiene instr. Hudson Valley C.C., Troy, NY, 1976—77; pvt. practice Troy, NY, 1977—89; ret., 1989. Active Hudson Mohawk Swiss Soc. Mem. AAUW, ADA, European Orthodontic Soc., German Orthodontic Soc. Achievements include study of functional orthodontic appliances and growth and development. Home: 1 The Knoll Troy NY 12180-7284

MEDIN, A. LOUIS, computer company executive; b. Balt., Oct. 2, 1925; s. Nathan and Bessie (Zell) Medin; m. Julia A. Levin, Dec. 24, 1950; children: Douglas, David, Thomas, Linda. BSChemE, Johns Hopkins U., Balt., 1948; PhDChemE, Ohio State U., Columbus, 1951. Registered profl. engr., Md. Chem. engr. AEC, Wilmington, Del., 1951-53; rsch. engr. Ford Motor Co., Dearborn, Mich., 1953-55; chief chem. nuclear reactor tech. ALCO Products, Schenectady, 1955-58; head nuclear rsch. engr. U.S. Steel, Monroeville, Pa., 1958-63; project mgr. missile design AVCO Corp., Wilmington, Mass., 1963-65; mgr. sci. applications IBM, Manassas, Va., 1965-72, mgr. advanced applications, 1975-87; exec. dir. Inst. for Simulation and Tng., Orlando, Fla., 1987-2000. Chmn. sci. and engring. tech. divsn. Nat. Def. Indsl. Assn.; dir. environment and life scis. Dept. Def., 1972—74; lectr. in field. Contbr. articles to profl. and tech. jours. Mem. Monroeville Parks and Recreation Commn., 1960; chmn. Monroeville Mental Health Assn., 1961; mem. Monroeville Zoning and Planning Commn., 1961; chmn. sci. and engring. tech. divsn. Nat. Def. Indsl. Assn., 1999—; dep. precinct chmn. Montgomery County Rep. Com., 1982. With USN, 1944—46, PTO. Recipient award, Am. Chem. Soc., 1957. Fellow: Am. Inst. Chemists; mem.: Am. Metall. Soc., Am. Def. Preparedness Assn. (chmn. sci. and engring. tech. divsn. 1981—, ednl. advisor Def. Jour., Am. Def. award 1984, Gold medal 1990), Am. Inst. Chem. Engrs., Nat. Security Indsl. Assn., Ohio State U. Alumni Assn., Johns Hopkins U. Alumni Assn. Home: 11401 Ridge Mist Ter Potomac MD 20854-7002 Office Phone: 301-762-1290. Personal E-mail: lmedin@comcast.net.

MEDIN, JULIA ADELE, mathematics professor, researcher; b. Dayton, Ohio, Jan. 16, 1929; d. Caroline (Feinberg) Levitt; m. A. Louis Medin, Dec. 24, 1950; children: Douglas, David, Thomas, Linda. BS in Maths. Edn., Ohio State U., Columbus, 1951; MA in Higher Edn., George Washington U., Washington, 1977; PhD in Counseling and Math. Edn., Am. U., Washington, 1985. Cert. tchr. Fla., Md. Rsch. engr. Sun Oil Co., Marcus Hook, Pa., 1951-53; tchr. maths. Montgomery County Pub. Schs., Rockville, Md., 1973-88; asst. prof. maths. U. Ctrl. Fla., Orlando, 1988-90, sr. ednl. technologist Inst. for Simulation and Tng., 1990-99; sr. assoc. Mgmt. and Ednl. Tech. Assocs., 1999—. Adv. steering com. U.S. Dept. Edn. Title II, Washington, 1985-89; sr. math. educator, rschr. Inst. for Simulation and Tng., Orlando, 1988-90; judge, co-chair GII Nar. Awards; co-acad. advisor I/ITSEC Conf.; condr. nationwide rsch. project on effective use of technology in the classroom; spkr. in field Author: Loc. of Cont. and Test Anxiety of Mar. Math. Studies, 1985, Single Sex Public Schools, Who Needs Them and Why, 2005; co-author: Single Sex Public Schools, 2005; contbg. author: Math for 14 & 17 Yr. Olds, 1987; editor: Simulation and Computer-Based Technology for Education; contbr. articles to profl. jours. Dem. committewoman Town of Monroeville, Pa., 1962; religious sch. dir. Beth Tikva Religious Sch., Rockville, 1971; cons. Monroeville Mental Health, 1960 Mem. Nat. Coun. Tchrs. Math., Math. Assn. Am. (task force on minorities in math.), Women in Math. in Edn., Nat. Coalition for Tech. in Edn. and Tng., Phi Delta Kappa, Kappa Delta Pi. Home and Office: 11401 Ridge Mist Ter Potomac MD 20854-7002 Personal E-mail: jmedin@comcast.net.

MEDIN, MYRON JAMES, JR., city manager; b. Ladysmith, Wis., July 8, 1931; s. Myron James and Mildred Clara (Johnson) M.; m. Alice Louise Moholt, May 14, 1955; children: John, Karen, Anne. BA, St. Olaf Coll., 1954; MPA, U. Mich., 1959. Adminstrv. asst. to city mgr. City of Fond du Lac, Wis., 1959-64, city mgr., 1967—83, City of New Ulm, Minn., 1964-67; city adminstr. City of Kansas City, Kans., 1983-85; pres., gen. mgr. Bella Vista Village Property Owners Assn., Ark., 1986-92. Mem. com. human devel. Nat. League of Cities, Washington, 1974-80, com. on govtl. relations, 1971-73; chmn. City Plan Commn., Fond du Lac, Wis., 1967-83 Bd. dirs. United Way, Kansas City, Kans., 1984-85, YMCA, 1984-85, Kansas City C.C. Found., 1984-85; mem. Gov.'s Regionalism Task Force Adv. Com., Madison, Wis., 1968-70; trustee Phillips Pro-Celebrity Golf Tennis Charity Classic, 1991-92; mem. transition task force Bella Vista Incorporation, 2005-06; vol. historic house mus. and gardens. Lt. USAF, 1955-57. Recipient Community Service award Fond du Lac Assn. of Commerce, 1978 Mem. Internat. City Mgmt. Assn., Wis. City Mgmt. Assn. (pres. 1975-76), Wis. League of Municipalities (bd. dirs. 1978-80), Wis. Alliance of Cities (v.p. 1972-73), Am. Soc. Pub. Adminstrn. (bd. dirs. 1984-85, Pub. Adminstr. of Yr. award 1985), Bella Vista-Bentonville C. of C. (bd. dirs. 1987-91), Nat. Trust for Hist. Preservation, Benton County Hist. Soc. Lutheran. Avocations: swimming, reading, tennis, gardening, genealogy. Home: 1 Audley Cir Bella Vista AR 72715-8845

MEDINA, DAVID, state supreme court justice; b. Galveston Island, Tex., 1958; m. Francisca Medina. BS, Southwest Tex. State U., 1980; JD, S. Tex. Coll. of Law, 1989. Joined Cooper Industries Inc., Houston, 1987—89, litigation counsel, 1989; judge 157th State Dist. Ct., Tex., 1990—99; assoc. gen. counsel Cooper Industries Inc., Houston, 2000—04; gen. counsel Gov. Rick Perry, Tex., 2004—05; justice Tex. Supreme Ct., 2005—. Former adjunct prof. S. Tex. Coll. of Law. Former bd. mem. Habitat for Humanity, Houston Metro; bd. mem. Spring Klein Baseball Assn. Mem.: ABA, Mexican Am. Bar Assn., Assn. for Advancement of Mexican Am., Houston Bar Assn. Office: Tex Supreme Ct PO Box 12248 Austin TX 78711 Office Phone: 512-463-1316. Office Fax: 512-463-1365.*

MEDINA, EDUARDO JOSE, language educator; b. Santurce, Pr, Mar. 6, 1956; s. Eduardo Jose Medina and Sylvia Monteserin. BA in Spanish, Towson State U., Md, 1984; BA in French, Towson State U., 1986; MA, Coll. Notre Dame, Balt., 1997. Advanced professional cert. Md., 2008, cert. in teaching Spanish and French grades Towson State U., 1986. Spanish tchr. Towson Cath. HS, 1986—87, Boys Latin Sch. Md, Balt., 1988—94, Carroll County Pub. Sch., Westminster, Md., 1997—98, Anne Arundel County Pub. Sch., Annapolis, Md., 1998—2000, Bishop Mcnamara HS, Forestville, Md., 2002—03; Spanish instr. U. Md, Catonsville, 2003—07, Coll. Notre Dame, Balt., 2004—05, Howard CC, Columbia, Md., 2006—07; Spanish and ESL instr. Prince Georges CC, Largo, Md., 2006—07; mid. sch. French tchr. Montgomery County Pub. Sch., Rockville, Md., 2008—; Spanish and French tchr. Mt. St. Joseph HS, Catonsville, Md., 1995—97; chair fgn. lang. dept Seton Keough HS, Catonsville; Spanish-ESL-success class instr. CC Balt. County, 1998—; Spanish-French-ESL-success class instr. Anne Arundel CC, Arnold, Md., 1999—. Vol. cmty. svc. dir. Boys Latin Sch. Md, 1990—94. Recipient Rev. Marrtin Luther King Jr. award, Boys Latin Sch. Md., 1994. Mem.: Internat. Honor Soc. Edn. Independent. Home: 1720 Glen Keith Blvd Apt F Parkville MD 21234 Office: Montgomery County Pub Sch Rockville MD 20847 Business E-Mail: emedina@ccbcmd.edu.

MEDINA, KATE (KATHRYN BACH MEDINA), associate publisher; b. Plainfield, NJ; d. F. Earl and Elizabeth E. Bach; 1 child. BA, Smith Coll., Northampton, Mass.; MA, NYU. With Doubleday Pub. Co., Inc., NYC, 1965-85; assoc. pub., exec. editl. dir., sr. v.p. Random House Inc., NYC, 1985—, assoc. pub. Random House Publishing Group, 2007—. Assoc. fellow Jonathan Edwards Coll., Yale U., New Haven, 1982—; fellow Bunting Inst., 1994—95; cons., 1995—96, Coun. Fgn. Rels. Editor: books by James Atlas, Peter Benchley, Elizabeth Berg, Amy Bloom, Katherine Boo, Bill Bradley, Tom Brokaw, Anita Brookner, Ethan Canin, Michael Chabon, Robert Coles, Agnes deMille, E.L. Doctorow, Fannie Flagg, Jane Fonda, Max Frankel, Charles Frazier, Henry Louis Gates, Jr., Carol Gilligan, Mary Gordon, David Halberstam, Kathryn Harrison, John Irving, Tracy Kidder, Wynton Marsalis, Bobbie Ann Mason, Jon Meacham, James A. Michener, Sandra Day O'Connor, Jane Pauley, Anna Quindlen, Nancy Reagan, James Reston, William Safire, Maggie Scarf, Gloria Steinem, Christopher Tilghman, Alice Walker, Daniel Yergin. Office: Random House Inc 1745 Broadway New York NY 10019

MEDINA, MARIEMMA, lawyer, educator; b. Bayamón, PR, Sept. 12, 1977; d. Reinaldo Median and Emma Morales; m. Javier Baéz, Sept. 26, 2005. BBA in Human Resources, U. PR, San Juan, 1995—99; JD cum laude, Inter-Am. U., San Juan, 2000—03. Bar: US Ct. Appeals (1st cir.), Mass. 2004, US Fed. Dist. Ct. PR 2006, Supreme Ct. PR 2004. Law clerk Superior Ct. Bayamón, Bayamón, 2002—03; assoc. atty. De La Cruz Skerrett Law Office, PSC, Bayamón, 2004—05, Dr. Juan A. Hernandez Law Offices, PSC, Bayamón, 2005—06; adj. prof. Bayamón Ctrl. U., Bayamón, 2005, San Jacinto Coll. N., Houston, 2006—. Mem.: ABA. Avocation: reading. Business E-Mail: mariemma_medinaesq@yahoo.com.

MEDINA, SANDRA, social worker, educator; b. Tulsa, Oct. 4, 1947; d. James and Erleen (Austin) Meeks; m. Michael Sellman, 1966 (div. 1979); children: Rhainnie, Morgan; m. Ernest Medina, Aug. 21, 1985; 1 child, Brendyn. Cert., Community Coll. of Denver, 1975; BS summa cum laude, Met. State Coll., Denver, 1981; MSW, U. Denver, 1983, postgrad. Lic. clin. social worker, Colo. Dir. Lafayette (Colo.) Presch./Playtime, 1973-75, Bennett (Colo.) Non-Denominational Presch., 1975-76; intern. in clin. social work Brighton (Colo.) Schs., 1981-82; adminstrv. social work intern Jefferson County (Colo.) Schs., 1982-83; med. social worker Las Animas County Health Dept., Trinidad, Colo., 1985-85; psychiat. social worker Colo. State Hosp., Pueblo, 1985-89; clin. social worker PsychCare, Greeley, 1990-92; counselor high sch. U. Northern Colo. Lab. Sch.; pvt. practice Custer, SD, 2007—08. Instr. Trinidad State Jr. Coll., 1984-85; field instr. N.Mex. Highlands U., Las Vegas, 1986-87, U. So. Colo., Pueblo, 1988-89; adj. prof. social work U. Denver, 1996-97; asst. prof. social work, practicum coord. Chadron State Coll., 1997-99. Mem. exec. com. Gov.'s Task Force on Child Abuse, Denver, 1985; bd. dirs. Adams County Rep. Advs. for Children Today, Denver, 1978-79; chairperson membership com. Met. Child Protection Coun., Denver, 1982-83. Mem. NASW. Democrat. Presbyterian. Personal E-mail: bestmedfam@netscape.net.

MEDINA-MORA, MANUEL, bank executive; B in Bus. Adminstrn., Universidad Iberoamericana in Mexico; MBA, Stanford U. Corp. banker Banamex, 1971, CEO, 2001—06, now chmn.; dep. pres. Grupo Financiero Banamex-Accival, 1991, CEO, 1996; chmn., CEO Latin Am. and

Mex. Citigroup Inc., mem. sr. leadership and exec. com. Chmn. bd. dirs. Seguros Banamex, Afore Banamex; bd. dirs. Mexican Stock Exchange; spkr. in field. Bd. dirs. Nat. Arts Mus. Mem.: Mex. Bank Assn. (chmn. 2003). Office: Banamex Isabel la Catolica 44, Colonia 06000 Mexico City Mexico also: Citigroup Inc 399 Park Ave New York NY 10043*

MEDINA-PASCU, ISABEL M., academic administrator; d. Juan Manuel and Margarita Ana Medina. BA student in Orgnl. Leadership, St. Thomas U., Miami Gardens, 2003—. Acquisitions technician IV Barry U., Miami Shores, Fla., 1987—99; acquisitions coord. St. Thomas U., U. Libr., 2000—. Lay min. St. James Cath. Ch., North Miami, Fla., 1996—99. Liberal. Roman Catholic. Avocations: photography, art, travel. Office: St Thomas Univ - Univ Libr 16401 NW 37th Ave Miami Gardens FL 33054 Personal E-mail: milagros55@msn.com. Business E-Mail: imedina@stu.edu.

MEDING, STEPHEN MERCER, research scientist; b. New London, NH, Nov. 11, 1968; s. Stephen Young and Pamela Ann Meding; m. Hillary Laureen Mehl, June 24, 2006; 1 child, Matilda Mehl. BS in Water Resource Mgmt., U. NH, Durham, 1992; MS in Forest Resources, U. Ga., Athens, 1999; PhD in Soils and Biogeochemistry, U. Calif., Davis, 2007. Hydrologist, biol. technician USDA, Durham, 1993—96; sr. rsch. specialist U. Ariz., Tucson, 2007—. Contbr. articles to profl. jours. Mem.: Soil Ecology Soc., Mycol. Soc. America, Soil Sci. Soc. America, Alpha Gamma Rho Frat. (pres. 1991). Avocations: comic book collecting, photography, bicycling, hiking. Personal E-mail: smmeding@gmail.com.

MEDJO ME ZENGUE, MARY, library director; b. Clinton, Iowa, June 9, 1967; d. Edward Lewis WIlliams and Mary Geraldine Williams; m. Christian Medjo Me Zengue; children: Sidonie Damaris, Jean Baptiste. BA, Quincy U., Ill., 1989; MLS, Dominican U., River Forest, Ill., 1991. Reference libr. Niles Pub. Libr. Dist., Ill., 1991—96; asst. head adult svc. Addison Pub. Libr., Ill., 1996—2000, asst. dir. and head adult svc., 2000—04, libr. dir., 2004—. Mem.: ALA, Ill. Libr. Assn. Office: Addison Pub Libr 4 Friendship Plz Addison IL 60101

MEDLIN, JOHN GRIMES, JR., banker, director; b. Benson, NC, Nov. 23, 1933; s. John Grimes and Mabel (Stephenson) M. BS in Bus. Adminstrn., U. N.C., 1956; grad., The Exec. Program, U. Va., 1965. With Wachovia Bank & Trust Co., Winston-Salem, NC, 1959—98, pres., 1974; pres., CEO Wachovia Bank and Wachovia Corp., Winston-Salem, NC, 1977-93; chmn. bd. Wachovia Corp., Winston-Salem, NC, 1987-98, chmn. emeritus, 1998—. Bd.of The Rsch. Triangle Found., Traingle U. Ctr. Advanced Studies; mem. State Jud. Coun. N.C., 2000—; active numerous civic and svc. orgns. With USNR, 1956-59. Mem. Phi Delta Theta. Office: Wachovia Corp 100 N Main St Winston Salem NC 27101 Office Phone: 336-732-5000, 336-732-5938.

MEDLOCK, DONALD LARSON, lawyer; b. Port Chester, NY, Mar. 8, 1927; s. Harold and Emma Adelaide (MacLennan) Medlock; m. Katharine Smedes Nicholson, May 21, 1955; children: Katharine Baird, Margaret MacLennan, William Nicholson. BA with honors, Yale U., 1947, LLB, 1950. Bar: N.Y. 1950, U.S. Dist. Ct. (so. dist.) N.Y. 1951, U.S. Ct. Appeals (2d cir.) 1951, U.S. Dist. Ct. (ea. dist.) N.Y. 1952, U.S. Tax Ct. 1952, U.S. Ct. Custom and Patent Appeals. Assoc. Winthrop, Stimson, Putnam & Roberts, NYC, 1950-56, ptnr., 1957-94, sr. counsel, 1995—. Bd. dirs. Bancard Sys. N.Y. Inc. Editor: Yale Law Jour., 1948—50; former dir. Fin. Times Publs., Economist Newspaper Group. Bd. dirs. Yale Alumni Fund, 1955—, chmn., 1984—86, mem. exec. com., 1980—88, hon., 1988—; bd. dirs. Port Washington Estates Assn., 1958—61; sec., bd. dirs. Port Washington Cmty. Chest, 1959—61; bd. mgrs., mem. exec. com. William Sloane Ho. YMCA Greater N.Y., 1979—84; chmn. Yale Law Sch. Fund, 1974—76; mem. exec. com. Assn. Families U. Denver, 1982—84; mem. ann. fund parents com. Taft Sch., 1979—81; chmn. univ. coun. com. Law Sch. Yale U., 1981—84; mem. Yale U. Council, 1984—86; mem. devel. bd. Yale U., 1984—88, mem. exec. com., 1984—86, Yale Law Sch., 1975—79, hon., 1979—. Recipient citation, Yale Law Sch., 1977, Yale Alumni Fund Chmn.'s award, 1979, 1987, Yale medal, 1994. Mem.: Assn. Bar City of N.Y. (mem. com. profl. ethics 1958—61), Fed. Power Bar Assn., India House, Corbey Ct. Yale Law Sch., Assn. Yale Alumni (rep.-at-large 1979—82, mem. com. undergraduate admissions 1979—82, mem. com. Yale medal 1981, bd. dirs. 1984—86), Mory's Assn., Yale Club N.Y.C., Manhasset Bay Yacht Club, Tuscarora Club (Margaretville, N.Y.) (bd. dirs. 1963—95, sec. 1970—86, v.p. 1984—86), Country Club Landfall, Scroll and Key Soc., Phi Beta Kappa, Phi Delta Phi. Avocations: trout fishing, tennis, reading, crossword puzzles, golf. Home: Landfall 800 Oyster Landing Wilmington NC 28405-5292

MEDLOCK, KENNETH BARRY, economics professor, consultant; b. Lubbock, Tex., Dec. 31, 1970; s. Kenneth Barry and Sandra Turner Medlock; m. Celine Bernadette Verkerk, Jan. 8, 2005; children: Kenneth Cornelis Caleb, Sophia Marie Addison. PhD, Rice U., Houston, 2000. Mgr.,corp. cons. El Paso Corp., Houston, 2000—03; fellow James A Baker III Inst. for Pub. Policy, Rice U., 2003—, Baker Institute; adj. asst. prof. Rice U. Contbr. to scholarly jour. (Award for Outstanding Paper in the Energy Jour., 2001). Mem.: Assn. Comparative Econs. Studies, Am. Econs. Assn., Internat. Assn. Energy Econs. Independent. Avocations: travel, sports, hiking. Office: Rice Univ Econs Dept MS22 6100 Main St Houston TX 77005

MEDNICK, ROBERT, accountant; b. Chgo., Apr. 1, 1940; s. Harry and Nettie (Brenner) Mednick; m. Susan Lee Levinson, Oct. 28, 1962; children: Michael Jon, Julie Eden, Adam Charles. BSBA, Roosevelt U., Chgo., 1962. CPA Ill. Staff asst. Arthur Andersen, Chgo., 1962-63, sr. acct., 1963-66, mgr., 1966-71, ptnr., 1971-98, mng. dir. SEC policies, 1973-76, mng. dir. auditing procedures, 1976-79. Vice chmn. com. on profl. stds. Andersen Worldwide, 1979-82, chmn. com., 1982-98, mng. ptnr. profl. and regulatory matters, 1993-98; mem. faculty Northwestern U. Kellogg Grad. Sch. Mgmt., 1999; mem. panel disting. neutrals in banking, acctg. and fin. svcs. Internat. Inst. for Conflict Prevention and Resolution, 2003—. Contbr. articles to profl. jours. Bd. dirs. Roosevelt U., Chgo., 1977—, vice chmn., 1986-94, sr. vice chmn., 1994—, life trustee, 1999—; bd. dirs. Auditorium Theatre Coun., 1990-96, Lake Shore Drive Synagogue, 1992-07; co-chmn. adv. coun. Chgo. Action for Soviet Jewry, Highland Park, Ill., 1983-87; bd. dirs., mem. exec. com. Am. Judicature Soc., 1990-95, vice chmn., 1993-95; bd. overseers Rand Corp. Inst. Civil Justice, 1994-98; bd. dirs. Nat. Bur. of Econ. Rsch., 1998—, treas., 1999—; acccountability adv. coun. to the Comptr. Gen. of the U.S., 2000—. Sgt. USAFR, 1965-69. Recipient Silver medal Ill. CPA Soc., 1962; named One of Ten Outstanding Young Men in Chgo., Chgo. Jr. C. of C., 1973-74; recipient Rolf A. Weil Disting. Service award, Roosevelt U., Chgo., 1983; Max Block award N.Y. State C.P.A. Soc., 1984; Ann. Literary award Jour. Accountancy, 1986, 88; Andrew D. Bradin award for distinctive contbns. to discipline of accountancy Case Western Res. U., Cleve., 1996; Disting. Alumni award Roosevelt U. Walter E. Heller Coll. Bus. Adminstrn., 1997; Disting. Vis. scholar Hebrew U., Jerusalem, 1999, 2000, Coll. Mgmt., Rishon Litzion, 2003, 05-09, hon. fellow, 2005. Mem. AICPA (bd. dirs. 1986-87, 92-94, 95-98, vice chmn. 1995-96, chmn. 1996-97, numerous coms., Elijah Watt Sells award 1962, Gold Medal for Disting. Svc. 1998), Ill. CPA Soc. (acctg. prins. com. 1973, legal liability com. 1986-89, mgmt. of acctg. practice com. 1991-94, regulation and legis. com. 1998—), Internat. Fedn. Accts. (chmn. compliance adv. panel 2003—). Jewish. Avocations: collecting art, travel. Home Phone: 312-642-4326; Office Phone: 312-642-0571. E-mail: bobmednick@aol.com.

MEDNICK, SHELDON IRA, pharmacist; b. Balt., Apr. 8, 1955; s. Sol Abraham and Doris Asbell Mednick. BSc in Pharmacy, Phila. Coll. Pharmacy, 1979. Registered pharmacist Pa., NJ, Md. Pharmacy intern Cooper U. Hosp., Camden, NJ, 1979—80; staff pharmacist Trenton Psychiat. Hosp., NJ, 1981—86, Phila. Geriatric Ctr., 1986—95, Neighborcare Pharmacy, King of Prussia, Pa., 1997—2001, Girard Med. Ctr., Phila., 2001—. Mem.: Masons (sr. deacon Burlington lodge 1984—85). Jewish. Avocations: reading, music, travel. Home: 2801 Wingate Ct Edgewater Park NJ 08010 Office Phone: 215-787-2460.

MEDOWS, RHONDA M., state agency administrator, public health service officer; married; 3 children. BS, Cornell Univ.; MD, Morehouse Sch. Med., Atlanta. Cert. family medicine. Residency Univ. Hosp., Stony Brook, NY; physician Kaiser Permanente, Atlanta, 1989—93; private practice Mayo Clinic, Jacksonville, Fla., 1993—2000; med. dir. Blue Cross Blue Shield Fla., Jacksonville, 2000—01; sec. Fla. Agy. Health Care Adminstrn., 2001—04; chief med. officer Centers for Medicare & Medicaid Svc. Region IV, Atlanta, 2004—05; commr. Ga. Dept. Cmty. Health, Atlanta, 2005—. Instr. Univ. Fla., Fla. State Univ. Mem.: Am. Acad. Family Physicians, Nat. Med. Assn., Am. Coll. Physician Executives, Fla. Med. Assn., Fla. Acad. Family physicians, Nat. Assn. Managed Care Physicians. Office: Dept Cmty Health 40th Fl 2 Peachtree St NW Atlanta GA 30303*

MEDRANO, PAULINE, city councilwoman, ESL educator; b. Dallas, Nov. 16, 1955; BA, U. Tex., Arlington, 1976. Dist. dir. Texas Dept Agr., Austin, 1988—91; dist. sales supr. GTECH Corp., 1992—95, dist. sales mgr., 1995—2003; ESL instr., adult basic edn. dept. Dallas Ind. Sch. Dist., 2003—; councilwoman, Dist. 2 Dallas City Coun., 2005—, chair transp. & environ. com., Trinity River Corridor Project, mem. housing com., quality of life & govt. svcs. com. Bd. dirs. Friends of Esperanza Hope Medrano Elem. Sch., Dallas; tutor Walnut Hill Elem. Sch., Dallas; translation svcs. to patients Parkland Meml. Hosp., Dallas. Vol. Dallas Summit Youth Volleyball; past bd. dirs. Dallas County Hist. Commn., Maple Ave. Econ. Devel. Corp. Mem.: Mex.-Am. Bus. & Profl. Club (Young Career Woman award 1983). Democrat. Office: Dallas City Hall 1500 Marilla St Rm 5FN Dallas TX 75201 Office Phone: 214-670-4048. Office Fax: 214-670-5117. Business E-Mail: pmedrano@mail.ci.dallas.tx.us.*

MEDVECKY, PATRICIA, retired elementary school educator; b. NYC, Feb. 2, 1936; d. Patrick and Katherine Conneally; m. Thomas E. Medvecky, Aug. 25, 1967; 1 child, Thomas E. II. BA, Hunter Coll., 1961, MS in Edn., 1965. Cert. notary pub. Conn. Tchr. elem. sch. Bd. Edn., NYC, 1961—67, Ridgefield, Conn., 1967—73, ret., 1973; real property abstractor Law Office of T.E. Medvecky, Bethel, Conn., 1973—96. Mem.: Hunter Coll. Alumni Assn., Sheffield Art League. Republican. Roman Catholic. Avocations: history, watercolor painting and etching. Home: PO Box 23 99 Washinee Heights Rd Taconic CT 06079 Personal E-mail: oldpatsy@yahoo.com.

MEDVECKY, ROBERT STEPHEN, lawyer; b. Bridgeport, Conn., Feb. 12, 1931; s. Stephen and Elizabeth (Petro) M.; m. Ellen R. Munt, Nov. 11, 1966; children— Allison L., Beth A., Craig R. AB, Dartmouth, 1952; JD, Harvard, 1955. Bar: Ill. bar 1955, Conn. bar 1958, D.C. bar 1972, Fla. bar 1989. Asso. firm Lord, Bissell & Brook, Chgo., 1955-57; gen. atty. So. New Eng. Telephone Co., New Haven, 1957-71; v.p., gen. counsel, sec. Amtrak, Washington, 1971-75; partner firm Lord, Bissell & Brook, Washington, 1975-78, Reid & Priest, NYC, 1978-87. Clubs: Harvard (N.Y.C.), Fiddlesticks Country (Ft. Meyers, Fla.), Saphire Valley Country (Cashlers, N.C.). Office: 15491 Kilbirnie Dr Fort Myers FL 33912-2424 Home (Summer): 457 Round Hill Rd Sapphire NC 28774 Personal E-mail: bmedvecky@yahoo.com.

MEDVEDOVSKI, EUGENE, ceramics engineer, researcher; b. Moscow, Apr. 22, 1957; arrived in US, 2005; BS, MS, Moscow Mendeleev U. Chem. Engring., Moscow, Russia, 1979; PhD, All-Union Sci. and Project Engring. Inst. Cable Industry, Moscow, Russia, 1987. Registered profl. engr., Nat. Inst. Ceramic Engrs., 2006. From ceramic engr. to head dept. All-Union Rsch. and Mfg. Co. Electroceramics, Moscow, 1979—93; pvt. practice cons. Toronto, Ont., Canada, 1993—94; ceramic engr. Indepor Inc., Medicine Hat, Alta., Canada, 1994—96; sr. devel. engr., sr. ceramist Ceramic Protection Corp., Calgary, Alta., 1996—2005; process engring. mgr. Umicore Indium Products, Providence, 2005—, process devel. mgr., 2005—. Mem. editl. bd. Jour. Advances in Applied Ceramics. Contbr. articles to profl. jours.; editor: (numerous books and chapters to books) Ceramic Armor and Armor Systems. Recipient Pfeil award, 2007. Mem.: Materials Info. Soc., Nat. Inst. Ceramic Engrs., Am. Ceramic Soc. (Corp. Tech. Achievement award 2001). Achievements include research and implementation in the project on armor ceramic tiles technology and body armor plates; development of numerous ceramic materials, processes and products; large size and rotary ITO sputtering targets; development of large size oxide and SiC ceramics for wear, corrosion and thermal shock resistance applications. Office: Umicore Indium Products 50 Sims Ave Providence RI 02909 Business E-Mail: eugene.medvedovski@am.umicore.com.

MEDVIN, NADEEN BETH, psychologist, consultant; b. Miami, Mar. 22, 1960; d. Daniel and Celia Medvin. BA with high honors, Fla. Internat. U., 1981; MS with honors, U. Ga., 1984; PhD with high honors, Fla. Internat. U., 1993. Cert.: Crisis Mgmt. Internat. (corporate crisis intervention) 1997, Fla. Internat. U./Mediation Tng. Group (mediation and conflict resolution) 2003, Fla. Supreme Ct. (mediator) 2006; lic. psychologist Fla., 1996, diplomate Am. Bd. Psychol. Specialties, Am. Coll. Forensic Examiners, 1998, Am. Coll. Disability Analysts, 2000. Staff psychologist, quality assurance comm. chair N. Miami Cmty. Mental Health Ctr., Miami, 1984—88; psychologist, cons. pvt. practice, 1987—; dir. planning & effectivness Miami-Dade C.C., 1994—96; performance cons., quality com. med. ethics com. Bapt. Health Systems South Fla., 1996—2000; applied psychologist City of Miami, 2000—, tng. and devel. coord. employee assistance program adminstr., 2005—. Adj. prof. applied psychology & bus. Fla. Internat. U., 1988—, Barry U., 1988—, healthcare adminstrn. grad prog. leadership devel. strategic planning, 1997—2001; adj. prof. applied psychology & bus. U. Miami, Sch. Medicine Leadership Devel. Sensivity Tng. Patient Relations, 1988—, St. Thomas U., 1988—; mem. adv. bd. human resource mgmt./bus. continuing edn. programs U. Miami, 2002—; lectr. in field; cons. in field. Contbr. articles to profl. jours.; mem. adv. bd.: Chief Learning Officer jour., 2004—. Vol. Switchboard of Miami Crisis Counseling, 1984—86, Red Ribbon Coun./Informed Families, 1986—89; adv. bd. mem. Fla. Internat. U. Inst. Govt., Miami, 2002—03; bus. tech. adv. bd. Dade County Pub. Schs., 2005—; med. edn. tng. South Fla. Aids Network, 1987—88. Fellow: Am. Coll. Forensic Examiners; mem.: APA, Am. Coll. Disability Analysts, Soc. Human Resource Mgmt., Soc. Indsl.-Orgnl. Psychology, Psi Chi, Phi Kappa Phi. Achievements include development of HR metrics, statistical performance models, organizational culture and climate surveys; psychological tests and measures; wellness and health risk assessments, corporate wellness, leadership development and university training programs; leadership, executive assessment and performance coaching. Office: City of Miami 444 SW 2nd Avenue Miami FL 33130 Office Phone: 305-416-2129, 305-815-1129. Personal E-mail: drnadeenmedvin@aol.com.

MEE, ERIN B., theater educator; b. NYC, Oct. 19, 1963; d. Charles and Susie Mee; m. Shanker Satyanath, Jan. 2, 1998; 1 child, Leila Satyanath-Mee. AB, Harvard U., 1985; PhD, NY U., 2004. Asst. prof. Swarthmore Coll., Pa., 2003—. Author: (book) Theatre of Roots: Redirecting the Modern Indian Stage; editor: Drama Contemporary: India; dir.: (play) Aramba Chekkan, Faust, Divided Together, Ottayan, First Love, The Imperialists, The Persians, Antigona Furiosa, Harvest, Big Love. Recipient Fulbright award, 1993, Dean's Dissertation award, NYU, 2000—01, Paulette Goddard award, 2002. Mem.: SSD&C, NY Theatre Workshop, Lincoln Ctr. Theatre Dir.'s Lab. Office: Swarthmore Coll 500 Coll Ave Swarthmore PA 19081

MEE, MAUREEN ADELE See DOZE, MAUREEN

MEECE, DREWRY, retired education educator, minister; b. Russell Springs, Ky., June 26, 1928; s. Drewry and Mauda Wade Meece; m. Shirley Marie Baker, Apr. 25, 1965. AA, Lindsey Wilson Coll., Columbia, Ky., 1948; BA cum laude, Georgetown Coll., Ky., 1950; MA in Edn., U. Ky., Lexington, 1957, EdD, 1965; MDiv, So. Bapt. Theol. Sem., Louisville, Ky., 1970. Cert. tchr. Ky., sch. counselor Ky. Head tchr. Russell County Elem. Schs., Jamestown, Ky., 1953—55; algebra and English tchr. Russell County HS, Jamestown, 1955—58, guidance counselor, 1958—60; adj. in edn. Georgetown Coll., 1963—64; prof. of edn. and chair of divsn. Campbellsville U., Ky., 1965—91; adj. in edn. Ea. Ky. U., Richmond, 1991—95; adj. in sociology St. Catharine Coll., Springfield, Ky., 1995—97, Lindsey Wilson Coll., Columbia, 1997—2000; ret., 2000. Ednl. advisor and tchr. of courses in the mid. east Heritage Travel and Campbellsville U., Louisville, 1972—88; English tchr. China Edn. Assn. for Internat. Exch., Wuxi, China, 1995—99. Editor: Interdisciplinary Readings for Beginning Students in Education. Exec. com., sec.-treas Ky. Assn. Colleges for Tchr. Edn., Frankfort, 1984—85; nursing home ministry Fair Oaks Rest Home, Jamestown, Ky. Recipient Excellence in Tchg. Social Studies award, Ky. Coun. for the Social Studies, 1981, Ten Years of Devoted Svc. award, Ky. Coun. for Internat. Edn., 1991; Haggin fellow, U. Ky., 1961—62, Rsch. grant, Ky. Ed. Assn., 1962—63, Fulbright grant, US Govt., 1982. Mem.: NEA (life), Nat. Coun. for the Social Studies, Ky. Coun. for the Social Studies (pres. 1982—83, v.p. 1981—82), Ky. Edn. Assn., Phi Delta Kappa (life). Baptist. Home: 309 Grant St Campbellsville KY 42718

MEEHAN, JEAN MARIE ROSS, human resources, occupational health and safety management consultant; b. Chgo., Mar. 16, 1954; d. A. Ronald Gonzalez and Barbara Marx Shipley; m. John J. Meehan, 1993; 1 child, Jenna A.; 1 child from previous marriage, Justin L. Ross. DC Diploma in Nursing, St. Mary of Nazareth Hosp., Chgo., 1974; BS in Health Arts with high honors, U. St. Francis, 1988; MPA with honors, Roosevelt U., 2000. Cert. occupl. health nurse specialist COHN-S, cert. pharmacy technician (CPhT); cert. senior professional in human resources SPHR. Staff nurse St. Mary of Nazareth Hosp., Chgo., 1973—75; head nurse ambulatory care Edgebrook Med. Diagnostic Ctr., Chgo., 1975—76; occupl. health nurse Williams Electronics, Inc., Chgo., 1976—84; adminstr. safety and benefits Reliable Power Products, Franklin Park, Ill., 1984—90; dir. corp. human resources MacLean-Fogg Co., Mundelein, Ill., 1990—2005, Navitus Health Solutions LLC, Madison, Wis., 2005—. Pres. Auriel Mgmt. Group, LLC, Island Lake, Ill., 1992—, Claim Masters, LLC, 1998—99; adv. bd. dir. Gt. Lakes Health Care Alliance, 1996—97; spkr. in workshops. Poetry included in Visions of Beauty, 1999 (Editor's Choice award 1999), Tides of Memory, 2000, America at the Millennium—The Best Poems and Poets of the 20th Century, 2000. Guest spkr. local schs. and environ. groups, also I.E.P.A. and U.S. E.P.A. workshops; mem. Ill. Pollution Prevention Adv. Coun., Springfield, Ill., 1993-98; mem. Lake County Employer Coun. Bus./Govt. Partnership, 1996-99; faculty Am. Occupl. Health Conf., 2003-04. Recipient Leadership Civic citation United Way Charities of Lake County, 1993, 94. Mem. AAOHN, Soc. for Human Resources Mgmt., Interventional & Prevention Lake County Employer Coun.(former mem.) Avocations: writing, interior design, reading, arts patronage. Office: Auriel Mgmt Group LLC PO Box 86 Wauconda IL 60084 Home Phone: 847-840-3452; Office Phone: 608-827-7567. Business E-Mail: hrpro@email.com.

MEEHAN, JOHN J., pediatrician, educator; b. Far Rockaway, NY, Dec. 2, 1964; s. James Meehan John and M. Jean Meehan; m. Tammy Denise Fonley, June 17, 1989; children: Taylor Meehan Brianna, Michael Meehan Sean. MD, U. Iowa, 1993. Diplomate in general surgery Am. Bd. Surgery, 1999, in critical care Am. Bd. Surgery, 2000, in pediat. surgery Am. Bd. Surgery, 2004. Asst. prof. U. Iowa Children's Hosp., 2002—07; assoc. prof. Seattle Children's Hosp., 2008—. Dir. Seattle Children's Internat. Robotic Surgery Ctr., 2008—. Contbr. scientific papers to jours. Race dir. Jingle Cross Rock, Iowa City, 2004—. Fellow: ACS; mem.: Am. Assn. Team Cycling Drs., Soc. Am. Gastrointestinal Endoscopic Surgeons, Soc. Laparoendoscopic Surgeons, Internat. Pediat. Endoscopic Group, Minimally Invasive Robotic Assn., Am. Pediat. Surg. Assn. Achievements include first to robotic surgery in infants, neonates and children. Office: Seattle Children's Hosp 4800 Sand Point Way NE Seattle WA 98105 Business E-Mail: john.meehan@seattlechildrens.org.

MEEHAN, JOHN JUSTIN, lawyer; b. NYC, Feb. 14, 1947; m. Daizy Rice; children: John, Jason. Student, Javeriana U., Colombia, 1967; BA cum laude, St. Louis U., 1969, JD, 1975. Bar: Mo. 1976, U.S. Dist. Ct. (we. dist.) Mo. 1976, U.S. Dist. Ct. (ea. dist.) Mo. 1977, U.S. Ct. Appeals (8th cir.) 1978. Tchr. St. Francis Xavier Grad Sch., St. Louis, 1970-72; pvt. practice, St. Louis, 1978—. Tchr. tai chi and qigong St. Louis U., Mo. Bot. Gardens; tchr. tai chi I and II, St. Louis C.C.-Meramec, 1994-98; lectr. in field. Mo. bd. dirs. Chinese Cultural Assn., 1976-80; pres. Chinese Internal Arts Ctr., 1991—; v.p. Lafayette Towne Neighborhood Assn., 1994; bd. dirs. Better Family Life, 1995—, Nigerian Cultural Assn., 1994-2004, Laclede Towne Cmty., 1976-80; active Big Bro. program Pruitt Igoe, 1965-69; mem. John Burroughs Diversity Com., 1998, St. Louis African Chorus, 2000-2004; pro bono legal counsel Eiretrean Assn., Brazilian Assn., Vietnamese Buddhist Assn. Recipient Human Rights award, St. Louis Coalition for Human Rights, 1997, Human Dignity award, YMCA, 2001, Better Family Life Cmty. Svc. award, 2002. Mem. Mo. Bar Assn., Met. Bar Assn. St. Louis, Mound City Bar Assn. (mem.-at-large 1991-92, 98-99, Legal Svc. award 1998), Mo. Asian Bar Assn., NAACP (life). Taoist. Avocations: foreign travel, taiji, qigong. Office: Lafayette Towne Profl Bldg 2734 Lafayette Ave Ste 1 Saint Louis MO 63104-2040 Office Phone: 314-772-9494. Fax: 314-772-3604. E-mail: JJustinMeehan@aol.com.

MEEHAN, MARTIN THOMAS (MARTY MEEHAN), academic administrator, former congressman, lawyer; b. Lowell, Mass., Dec. 30, 1956; s. Martin T. and Alice (Britton) Meehan; m. Ellen T. Murphy; children: Robert Francis, Daniel Martin. BA in Polit. Sci., Edn. cum laude, U. Mass., Lowell, 1978; MPA, Suffolk U., 1981, JD, 1986; student, Harvard U., 1987-88. Adminstrv. asst. to mayor City of Lowell, Mass., 1978-79; press asst. to Rep. James M. Shannon US Congress, Mass., 1979-81; del. Dem. Nat. Conv., 1980, 84, 88; head rsch. analyst Joint Com. on Elec. Laws Mass. State Senate, 1981-84; dir. pub. affairs Commonwealth of Mass., 1985-86, dep. sec. state securities & corporations, 1986-90; 1st asst. dist. atty. Middlesex County, Mass., 1991-92; mem. U.S. Congress from 5th Mass. dist., 1993—2007, mem. armed services. com., judiciary com.; chancellor U. Mass., Lowell, 2007—. Adj. instr. U. Mass., Lowell, 1984-85, U. Harvard, 1987-88 Named Student of Yr. Lowell Exchange Club, 1975. Mem. ABA, Mass. Bar Assn., U. Lowell Alumni Assn., The Newspaper Guild, Internat. Fedn. Journalists. Democrat. Roman Catholic. Office: U Mass Lowell Office of Chancellor One University Ave / Cumnock Hall 2nd Fl Lowell MA 01854 E-mail: Martin_Meehan@uml.edu.

MEEHAN, MICHAEL JOSEPH, lawyer; b. St. Louis, Aug. 28, 1942; s. Joseph Michael and Frances (Taylor) M.; m. Sharon Kay McHenry (div. 1988); m. Patricia Ann Shive, July 8, 1989 (dec. 1999); m. Shelley Fujiko Lee, 2002. BS in Engring., U.S. Coast Guard Acad., 1964; JD with high distinction, U. Ariz., 1971. Bar: Ariz. 1971, US Ct. Appeals (6th, 8th, 9th and 10th cirs.), US Supreme Ct. 1975. Law clk. Assoc. Justice William H. Rehnquist, US Supreme Ct., 1972; assoc. Molloy, Jones & Donahue, P.C., Tucson, 1971-75, shareholder, 1975-93; chmn. exec. com., head trial dept., 1986-93; founder Meehan & Assocs., Tucson, 1993-2001; ptnr. Quarles & Brady/Striech Long, Tucson, 2001—03; pvt. practice Tucson, 2003—; of counsel Munger Chadwick P.L.C., Tucson, 2006—. Mem. fed. appellate rules adv. com. Jud. Conf. US, 1994-99; mem. adv. bd. William H. Reinquist Ctr. Constl. Structures Govt., 2006—. Author chpt. on appellate advocacy: State Bar of Arizona Appellate Practice Handbook. Fellow Am. Acad. Appellate Lawyers (past pres.); mem. Am. Law Inst., Ariz. Bar Assn. (past chair appellate practice sect. 1999-00), Nat. Conf. Appellate Justice (mem. steering com. 2005). Lutheran. Avocation: golf. Office: Munger Chadwick PLC 333 North Wilmot Rd Ste 300 Tucson AZ 85711 Office Phone: 520-721-1900. Business E-Mail: mmeehan@mungerchadwick.com.

MEEHAN, PATRICK LEO, former prosecutor; b. 1955; BA, Bowdoin Coll., 1978; JD, Temple U., 1986. Assoc. Dilworth, Paxon, Kalish and Kauffman; sr. counsel, exec. dir. US Senator Arlen Specter; dist. atty. Delaware County, Pa., 1986—2001; US atty. (ea. dist.) Pa. US Dept. Justice, 2001—08. Mem. corp. fraud task force panel Atty. Gen., 2002—, mem. adv. com., mem. exec. working group.

MEEHAN, SANDRA GOTHAM, communications and creative consultant, writer; b. Tokyo, June 9, 1948; d. Fred C. and Evelyn (Dirr) Gotham; m. James P. Jenkins, June 15, 1970 (div.); m. Dayton T. Carr, Dec. 27, 1986 (div. 1989), m. Michael J. Meehan, II, Jan. 16, 1992. Student, Stanford-in-France, Tours, 1968-69; BA, Stanford U., Calif., 1970, MA, 1971. Acct. exec. Young & Rubicam Inc., NYC, 1972-78, acct. supr., 1978-80; pres. Gotham Prodns., NYC, 1980-82; v.p., mgmt. supr. Ogilvy & Mather, NYC, 1982-85; v.p. Steuben Glass, NYC, 1985-88; sr. v.p. Siegel & Gale, NYC, 1988-92; prin., mng. ptnr. Gotham Meeham Ptnrs., NYC, 1992—. Sr. v.p., dir. corp. comm. Bionutrics, Inc., 1997-98; cons. Congl. coms., FDA, FTC for exec. program Am. Assn. Advt. Agys., Washington, 1978-80; cons. Ctr. Arctic Studies Sorbonne, Paris, in US and Can., 1980-82; seminar dir. NY chpt. Women in Bus., NYC, 1983-84. Author, editor: TV documentary Inuit! The Universal Cry of the Eskimo People, 1981. Trustee, bd. dirs. Rensselaerville Inst., NY; exec. com., bd. dirs. Checkerboard Film Found.; NYC Mayor's rep. to bd. dirs. Bot. Gardens; bd. dirs. Paris Rev. Mag., Agora Found., NYC; pub. Lapham's Quarterly; mem. Century Assn., NYC. Home: 220 E 73rd St New York NY 10021-4319 Office: Gotham Meehan Ptnrs 220 E 73rd St Ste 5G New York NY 10021-4319 Home Phone: 212-734-1249. Office Fax: 212-628-6747. Personal E-mail: gmp7777@aol.com.

MEEHAN, THOMAS, writer; Grad., Hamilton Coll., 1951. Writer (Broadway plays) Annie, 1977 (Drama Desk award, Outstanding Book, Tony award, Best Book of a Musical), I Remember Mama, 1979, Ain't Broadway Grand, 1993 (Tony award, Best Book of a Musical), The Producers, 2001 (Drama Desk award, Outstanding Book of a Musical), Hairspray, 2002 (Drama Desk award, Outstanding Book of a Musical, Tony award, Best Book of a Musical, Laurence Olivier award for London prodn., Best New Musical, 2008), Bombay Dreams, 2004, Young Frankenstein, 2007, Cry-Baby, 2008, (TV films) Annie, the Women in the Life of a Man, 1970 (Emmy award, 1970), Annie: A Royal Adventure!, 1995, Annie, 1999, (films) To Be or Not to Be, 1983, One Magic Christmas, 1985, Spaceballs, 1987, A Child's Garden of Verses, 1992, Hairspray, 2007. Mem.: Dramatists Guild Am. (mem. coun.). Office: Dramatists Guild Am Ste 701 1501 Broadway New York NY 10036

MEEHAN, WILLIAM A., air transportation executive; Pres., COO Continental Micronesia, Inc. Continental Airlines, Inc., Guam, 1998—2002, v.p. Cleve. hub, 2002—03, v.p. Houston hub, 2003—04, sr. v.p. airports svcs. Houston, 2004—. Office: Continental Airlines Inc PO Box 4607 Houston TX 77210 Office Phone: 713-324-5000. Office Fax: 713-324-2637.

MEEHAN, WILLIAM PAUL, pediatrician, educator; b. Medford, Mass., Nov. 27, 1970; BA, Boston Coll., Chestnut Hill, Mass., 1993; MD, Harvard U., Boston, 2002. Physician Children's Hosp. Boston, 2002—, co-founder, concussion and sports clinic, 2008—; instr. pediat. Harvard U., Med. Sch., 2007—. Contbr. articles to profl. jours. Inductee Golden Key Nat. Honor Soc, 1992—93; vol. SJ Vol. Corps., Omak, Wash., 1993—94; neighborhood coord. Menino Adminstrn, Boston, 1994—96. Recipient Cmty. Svc. citation, Mass. State Senate, 1996, Mass. House Representatives, 1996, Boston City Coun., 1996, Boston Fire Dept., 1996, Tchg. award, Harvard Med. Sch., 2005; Enrichment Program Rsch. grant, 1999—2000, grant, Nat. Insts. Health, Ctr. Imegration Medicine and Innovative Tech. Mem.: Am. Coll. Sports Medicine. Avocation: music. Office: Children's Hosp Boston 300 Longwood Ave Boston MA 02115 Office Phone: 617-355-3501. Office Fax: 617-730-0178.

MEEK, BARBARA SUSAN, retired elementary school educator; b. Monaca, Pa., Feb. 8, 1951; d. Michael Frederick and Sarah Ellen (Hall) Fronko; m. Joseph William Meek Jr., Nov. 25, 1977. BS in Edn., Ohio U., Athens, 1973; MA in Edn., Marietta Coll., Ohio, 1999. Cert. elem. tchr., Ohio. 3d grade tchr. Warren Local Schs., Vincent, Ohio. Martha Holden Jennings scholar, 1976-77. Mem. Ohio coun. Tchrs. Math., Ohio Ret. Tchrs. Assn. (life), Wash. County Ret. Tchrs. Assn. Home: 5371 Veto Road Vincent OH 45784-5118

MEEK, ERNEST CARLYSLE, physics professor; b. Merigold, Miss., Sept. 10, 1948; s. Ernest and Sara Bess Meek; children: Joe, Jane. PhD, Miss. State U. Prof. physics Delta State U., Cleve., Miss., 1990—. Editor. Mem.: Miss. Assn. Physicists (bd. mem.). Office: Delta State Univ PO Box 3262 Cleveland MS 38733 Business E-Mail: cmeek@deltastate.edu.

MEEK, FORREST BURNS, retired trading company executive; b. Tustin, Mich., June 11, 1928; s. Robert B. and Electa I. (Gallup) Meek; m. Jean R. Grimes, June 26, 1953; children: Sally, Thomas, Nancy, Charles. AA, Spring Arbor Coll., 1950; AB, Mich. State U., 1953; postgrad., U. Ga., 1965; MA, Ctrl. Mich. U., 1967. Exec. sec., chmn. bd. Edgewood Press, Clare, 1971—; gen. mgr. Blue Water Imports, 1985; dir. Ctr. for Chinese-Am. Scholarly Exchs., Inc., 1989—97; gen. mgr. Blue-Water Internat. Trading Co., Inc., ret., 1998. Vis. prof. Wuhan U., China, 1986—87; dist. office mgr. Fed. Decennial Census, 1990; instr. phys. geology and astronomy Mid Mich. C.C., 2002, instr. astronomy, 2001—03; mem., chmn. Red team East Ctrl. Mich. Planning and Devel. Regional Commn.; bd. sec. ITC Shanghai Maglev, Inc., 2003. Author: Michigan Timber Battleground, 1976, Michigan Heartland, 1979, One Year in China, 1988, Michigan Logging Railroad Era, 1850-1963, 1989, Railways and Tramways, 1990, Lumbering in Eastern Canada, 1991, Pearl Harbor Remembered, 1991, Heroes of The Twentieth Century, 2000. Coord. Clare County Bicentennial Com., 1975-76; Rep. fin. chmn., Clare County, 1966-71, asst. treas. 10th dist. Mich, 1967-69; trustee local sch. bd., 1992-96; chmn. local county jury bd., 1991-98; mem. bd. commrs. Clare County Dist. 4 Commn., 1998-2006. Mem. Am. Entrepreneur Assn., Mich. Sci. Tchrs. Assn., Mich. Hist. Soc., Heartland Mich. Geneal. Soc., White Pine Hist. Soc. (exec. sec.), Steam Locomotive History Soc. Republican. Avocations: astronomy, silviculture. Personal E-mail: forrestburns@gmail.com.

MEEK, JERRY (GERALD FRANCIS MEEK), lawyer, former political organization administrator; b. Fort Worth, Tex., 1971; m. Patrcia Ann Cotham. BA magna cum laude, Duke U., 1992, JD, 1997; MA in Govt., U. Notre Dame, 1995. Congl. page for Rep. Charlie Rose US Congress, 1989; assoc. med. malpractice Law Offices of Wade Byrd, Fayetteville, NC, 1998—99, 2000—08; ptnr. Simpson and Meek, PC, Dallas, 1999—2000, Poyner Spruill LLP, Raleigh & Charlotte, 2008—. Del. Dem. Nat. Conv., 1988. Del. Dem. Nat. Conv., 1988; chmn. Cumberland County Dem. Party, 1997; first vice chair NC Dem. Party, 2003—05, chair, 2005—09. Mem.: Am. Assn. Suicidology. Democrat. Office: Poyner Spruill LLP 301 Fayetteville St Ste 1900 Raleigh NC 27601 also: 301 S College St Ste 2300 Charlotte NC 28202 Office Phone: 910-323-2555, 919-783-6400, 704-342-5250. Office Fax: 910-323-9694, 919-783-1075, 704-342-5264.*

MEEK, KENDRICK B., United States Representative from Florida; b. Miami, Fla., Sept. 6, 1966; m. Leslie Dixon; children: Lauren, Kendrick B. Jr. BS in Criminal Justice, Fla. A&M U., 1989. Devel. rep. Wackenhut Corp., Palm Beach Gardens, Fla.; trooper, capt. Fla. Highway Patrol, 1989—94; mem. Fla. Ho. of Reps., Tallahassee, 1995—98; mem. dist. 36 Fla. State Senate, Tallahassee, 1999—2002; mem. US Congress from 17th Fla. dist., 2003—, mem. armed svcs. com., ways & means com., select com. homeland security. Mem. North Atlantic Treaty Orgn. Parliamentary Assembly, Met. Dade County Urban Revitalization Task Force, Dem. Steering & Policy Com.; chair Congl. Black Caucus Found.; co-chair 30-Something Working Grp.; vice-hair Dem. Congl. Campaign Com.; past-chair Fla. Coalition Reduce Class Size. Founding mem. Men Against Drugs, Defending Against Drugs & Social Disorder (MAD DADS); active Greater Miami Svc. Corps, Cmty. Action Agy., South Fla. Food Recovery. Recipient Outstanding Svc. award, MADD, 1990, Legis. award, 1995, Positive African-Am. Role Models award, Lillie C. Evans Elem. Sch., 1991, Cmty. Svc. award, Fla. Meml. Coll., 1995, Stellar Cmty. Svc. award, South Fla. Assn. Black Journalists, 1996, Legis. Achievement award, Fla. Divsn. Emergency Mgmt., 1996; named a St. Joseph Delaney Hurricane Hero, Metro Dade County Commn., 1995, Quality Floridian, Fla. League of Cities, 1996, Flemming fellow, Ctr. Policy Alternatives, 1996—97; named an 50 Leaders of Tomorrow, Ebony mag., 1995; named one of Most Influential Black Americans, 2006, Power 150, 2008. Mem.: NAACP (life Gwen Sawyer Cherry Meml. award 1997, Adams-Powell Civil Rights award 1996), 100 Black Men South Fla., Biscayne Gardens Homeowners Assn., Fla. Young Dems., Nat. Orgn. Black Law Enforcement Execs., Fla. A&M U. Varsity Club, Omega Psi Phi. Democrat. Office: US Ho Reps 1039 Longworth Ho Office Bldg Washington DC 20515-0917 Office Phone: 202-225-4506. Office Fax: 202-226-0777.*

MEEK, LISA K. S., intervention coordinator, psychotherapist; b. Enid, Okla., Aug. 20, 1962; d. William Frederick and Barbara Ann Seals; m. William Russell Meek, May 18, 1985; children: Ashley Elizabeth, Brandon Alexander. Doctorate in Clin. Psychology, U. of the Rockies, Colorado Springs, 2004—08; Masters of Psychology, Colo. Sch. of Profl. Psychology, Colorado Springs, CO, 2003—04; Masters in Spl. Edn., Tex. Woman's U., Denton, TX, 1995—96; Bachelors in Social Work, U. of Tex. at Austin, Austin, TX, 1980—84. Profl. Tchg. License Colo. Dept. Edn., 2006. Dir. montessori Degroots Acad., Plano, Tex., 1984—86; counselor Cmty. in Schools, Dallas, 1986—87; dir. Colo. Springs Children's Mus., Colo., 1989—91; spl. edn. tchr. Carrollton/ Farmers-Branch, Carrollton, Tex., 1994—97, Acad. Sch. Dist. 20, Colorado Springs, 1997—99; tchr. Classical Acad., Colorado Springs, 1999—2001; pschology intern Falcon Sch. Dist. 49, Falcon, Colo., 2005—07; vol. therapist Franciscan Cmty. Counseling, Colorado Springs, 2004—07; dist. intervention coord. Falcon Sch. Dist., Falcon, Colo., 2008—. Author: (journal of humanistic psychology) Theories of Self: A Post-Modern Perspective (Outstanding Grad. Student, 2008). Mem.: Nat. Assn. of Staff Developers, APA. Achievements include research in Dissertation related to Response to Intervention. Home: 945 Oak Bend Court Colorado Springs CO 80919 Office: Faclon School District 49 11990 Swingline NE Road Falcon CO 80831 E-mail: lmeek@d49.org.

MEEKER, ALAN KEITH, biomedical researcher, educator; b. Newport, RI, Aug. 7, 1960; s. Quentin Stuart Meeker and Vernona Mae McNeil. BS, Fla. Inst. Tech., Melbourne, 1983; MA, Johns Hopkins U., Balt., 1993, PhD, 2001. Asst. prof. pathology & urology Johns Hopkins U. Sch. Medicine, 2005—. Contbr. scientific papers to profl. med. jours. Recipient Larry Ewing Meml. award, Johns Hopkins Sch. Hygiene & Pub. Health, 1996, Paul Ehrlich Rsch. award, Johns Hopkins Sch. Medicine, 1999, Young Investigators Postdoc. Rsch. award., Johns Hopkins Hosp. Dept. Pathology, 2002—03. Mem.: Am. Soc. Investigational Pathology (Merit award. 2004), Am. Assn. Cancer Rsch. (Bristol Meyers Squibb Travel award 1996, AFLAC Scholar-in-Tng. awards 2002), Am. Urol. Assn. Independent. Achievements include discovery of telomere shortening as a prevalent abnormality in human cancer precursors. Avocations: gardening, kayaking, rowing, cooking, guitar, mandolin. Home: 827 Cliffedge Rd Pikesville MD 21208 Office: Johns Hopkins Univ Sch Med 1503 Jefferson St Room B300 Baltimore MD 21231 Personal E-mail: alan.meeker@gmail.com.

MEEKER, CHARLES C., Mayor, Raleigh, North Carolina, lawyer; b. Washington, July 27, 1950; BA, Yale U., 1972; JD, Columbia U., 1975. Bar: NC 1975, DC 1984. Atty. Parker, Poe, Adams & Bernstein, NC, ptnr. NC; mem. Raleigh City Council, NC, 1985—89, NC, 1991—95; mayor City of Raleigh, NC, 2001—. Mem. editorial bd.: Columbia Law Rev., 1974-75. Mem. DC Bar, Mayors Against Illegal Guns Coalition. Named one of Best Lawyers in America in Admin. Law, Woodward/White, 2007—. Democrat. Address: Parker Poe et al PO Box 389 Raleigh NC 27602-0389 Office: Office of Mayor PO Box 590 Raleigh NC 27602: Wachovia Capitol Ctr Ste 1400 150 Fayetteville St Raleigh NC 27601 Office Phone: 919-890-4168. Office Fax: 919-835-4552. Business E-Mail: charlesmeeker@parkerpoe.com, charles.meeker@ci.raleigh.nc.us.*

MEEKER, PAIGE H., science educator; b. Camden, SC, Feb. 3, 1971; d. James Boyce and Martha Welsh Huggins; m. Lee E. Meeker; children: Piper Ashlee, Amber Cherry. PhD, U. SC, Columbia, 2000. Asst. prof. Furman U., Greenville, SC, 2001—04, Presbyn. Coll., Clinton, SC, 2005—. Adj. prof. U. SC, 2005. Grant, Inst. Personal Robots Edn., 2007—08. Mem.: ACM. Baptist. Avocation: reading. Office: Presbyn Coll 503 S Broad St Clinton SC 29325 Business E-Mail: mpmeeker@presby.edu.

MEEKISON, MARYFRAN, writer; b. Napoleon, Ohio, Apr. 9, 1919; d. Frank J. and Elizabeth (Keyes) Shaff; m. David Meekison, June 17, 1939; children: Maureen Meekison Houppert, David Francis, Beth Ann. Student, St. Mary's Coll., Notre Dame, Ind., 1936-39. Hist. writer, photographer, Napoleon, 1963—, St. Augustine Ch., 1983—; citizen com. Napoleon Area HS Award, 2005—. Author: (photographer or many written articles, plus awards at juried shows) Canal Days to Modern Ways Revisited, 1984, History of St. Augustine's 1882-1982, History of St. Augustine Ch., 1983, centennial edit.; (brochure) Canal Days to Modern Ways, 1963; mem. editl. adv. bd. Courier mag., 1989-91; class reporter, Courier Alumnae Mag., 1944-, contbr. articles to mags. Steering com. Napoleon Susquicentennial, 1984; trustee Napoleon Pub. Lib., 1976-01. Recipient Spl. citation Courier Alumnae mag., others, Pres.'s medal, St. Mary's Coll., Notre Dame, Ind., 1991; named Citizen of Yr., Napoleain Area C. of C., 1990; named to St. Mary's Coll. Athletic Hall of Fame Notre Dame, 2001. Mem. Alumnae Assn. St. Mary's Coll. (bd. dirs. 1985-91), Literary Club. Democrat. Roman Catholic. Avocations: tennis, sailing. Home: PO Box 253 Napoleon OH 43545-0253

MEEKS, GREGORY WELDON, United States Representative from New York; b. NYC, Sept. 25, 1953; s. James Weldon and Mary (McNeal) Meeks; m. Simone-Marie Meeks; children: Ebony Renee, Aja J., Nia-Aiyana. BA in Hist., Adelphi U., Garden City, NY, 1975; JD, Howard U. Sch. Law, Washington, 1978. Asst. dist. atty. Queens Dist. Atty.'s Office, 1978-81; asst. spl. narcoties prosecutor Office of Spl. Narcotics Prosecutor, NYC, 1981-83; asst. counsel State Investigations Commn., 1983-84; hearing officer NY Family Ct., 1984-85; judge NY State Workers' Compensation Bd., 1985-87, supervising judge, 1987-93; mem. NY State Assembly, 1993-98, US Congress from 6th NY dist., 1998—, mem. fin. svcs. com., mem. internat. rels. com., mem. fgn. affairs com. Bd. dirs. Rockaway Peninsula Civic Assn., 1983-1991, Peninsula Gen. Hosp., 1989-; chmn. bd. Joseph P. Addabbo Family Health Care Ctr., 1990-92. Recipient NAACP Polit. Leadership award, 1989, Outstanding Vol. Mentor award, NY Mentoring, 1990, Cmty. Leader award Boy Scouts Am., 1992, William Garvin Pub. Svc. award, 2004, Congl. Leadership award, Nat. Urban League, 2006; named one of Most Influential Black Americans Ebony mag., 2006; named to Power 150 Ebony mag., 2008. Mem. ABA, Macon B. Allen Black Bar Assn. (v.p.), Queens County Bar Assn., Far Rockaway NAACP (Polit. Leadership award 1989), Alpha Phi Alpha. Democrat. Baptist. Office: 153-01 Jamaica Ave 2nd Fl Jamaica NY 11432 Office Phone: 202-225-3461, 718-725-6000. Office Fax: 718-725-9868.*

MEEKS, PATRICIA LOWE, literature and language educator, consultant; b. Enid, Okla., Oct. 21, 1928; d. Henry Preston and Veda Gay (Combs) Lowe; m. James Donald Meeks, Feb. 28, 1953 (div. Aug. 1975); children: Mary Gay, Ann Lowe, James Robert David. BA, Phillips U., 1951; MA in English, U. Colo., 1973. Cert. tchr., Colo., Okla. Tchr. English Garber HS, Okla., 1952-53; tchr. English and journalism Hillcrest HS, Dallas, 1955-57; tchg. asst. U. Colo., Boulder, 1965-66; tchr. English Cherry Creek HS, Englewood, Colo., 1966-91; supr. grades K-12 reading and lang. arts Oklahoma City Pub. Schs., 1991-98; English cons., 1998—. Adj. prof. English, Oklahoma City CC, 2002-06, CC Denver, 2006-; cons. Coll. Bd. Rocky Mt. Region, Denver, 1973-91; advanced placement reader, table leader Coll. Bd. and Ednl. Testing Svc., Princeton, N.J., 1970-90, SAT reader, 1989-94, table leader, 1994-98, reader, 1999-04. Grantee Fulbright Found., 1980-81; grantee NEH, 1986; English-Speaking Union, 1987; IDEA fellow. Mem. ACLU, English-Speaking Union (pres. Oklahoma City chpt. 1998-2006), Nature Conservancy, Audubon Soc., US Humane Soc., Defenders of Wildlife, Nat. Resources Defense Coun., Denver Art Mus. Episcopalian. Avocations: art history, bird watching, jazz, reading. Home: 8155 Fairmount Dr 711 Denver CO 80230 Office Phone: 303-269-1616. Personal E-mail: plmeeks@comcast.net.

MEEKS, WILLIAM HERMAN, III, lawyer; b. Ft. Lauderdale, Fla., Dec. 30, 1939; s. Walter Herman Jr. and Elise Walker (McGuire) M.; m. Patricia Ann Rayburn, July 30, 1965; 1 son, William Herman IV; m. 2d, Miriam Andrea Bedsole, Dec. 28, 1971; 1 child, Julie Marie. AB, Princeton U., 1961; LLB, U. Fla., 1964; LLM in Tax, NYU, 1965. Bar: Fla 1964, US Dist. Ct. (so. dist.) Fla. 1965, US Tax Ct. 1966, US Ct. Appeals (11th cir.) 1981, US Supreme Ct. 1985. Ptnr. McCune, Hiaasen, Crum, Ferris & Gardner, Ft. Lauderdale, 1964-89, Fleming, O'Bryan & Fleming, Ft. Lauderdale, 1990-95, Dobbins, Meeks, Raleigh & Dover, Ft. Lauderdale, 1995—. Dir. Attys. Title Svcs., Inc., 1978-79, Attys. Title Svcs. of Broward County, Inc., 1971—, chmn., 1976-77; mem. Attys. Real Estate Coun. Broward County. Mem. ABA, Fla. Bar Assn., Broward County Bar Assn., Attys. Title Ins. Fund, Ft. Lauderdale Hist. Soc., Ft. Lauderdale Mus., Kiwanis, Lauderdale Yacht Club, Tower Club (Ft. Lauderdale), Phi Delta Phi. Democrat. Presbyterian. Office: Dobbins Meeks Raleigh & Dover 3081 E Commercial Blvd Ste 204 Fort Lauderdale FL 33308 Home Phone: 954-567-9151; Office Phone: 954-491-1100. E-mail: whmeeks@ndmrd.com.

MEENAN, ALAN JOHN, clergyman, theology studies educator; b. Belfast, No. Ireland, Feb. 7, 1946; arrived in US, 1970, naturalized, 2001; s. John and Elizabeth (Holland) M.; m. Vicky Lee Woodall, May 6, 1974; children: Kelly Elizabeth, Katie Michelle, Kimberly Brooke. BA, Queen's U., Belfast, 1970; MDiv, Asbury Theol. Sem., Wilmore, Ky., 1972, ThM, 1975; PhD, Edinburgh U., 1981. Ordained to ministry Presbyn. Ch., U.S.A., 1973. Pastor Wilmore Presbyn. Ch., 1972-74; asst. pastor St. Giles' Cathedral, Edinburgh, 1974-77; sr. pastor 3d Presbyn. Ch., Richmond, Va., 1977—84, Canoga Park Presbyn. Ch., Calif., 1984-89, First Presbyn. Ch., Amarillo, Tex., 1989-97, Hollywood Presbyn. Ch., Calif., 1997—2005, Ch. Nations, Glendale, Calif., 2006—; founder, pres. The Word Is Out Internat., LA, 2005. Vis. lectr. Nairobi Grad. Sch. Theology, Kenya, 1983, 89; adj. prof. W. Africa Theol. Sem., Lagos, Nigeria, 2004-, South Asia Inst. Adv. Christian

Studies. 2009-. Contbr. revs. to religious publs., including Asbury Bible Commentary. Tchr. Chogoria High Sch., Meru, Keyna, 1965-66. Yale U. rsch. fellow, 1976—77. Mem. Tyndale Fellowship for Bibl. Rsch., Theta Phi. Avocations: travel, photography, reading, swimming, squash racquets. Office: 11271 Ventura Blvd Ste 509 Studio City CA 91604 Office Phone: 323-969-9090.

MEENGS, WILLIAM LLOYD, cardiologist; b. Zeeland, Mich., Dec. 23, 1942; s. Lloyd Stanley and Gertrude (Wyngerden) M.; m. Helen Delores Van Dyke, June 10, 1964; children: Michelle Rene, William Lloyd, Lisa Ann. AB, Hope Coll., 1964; MD, U. Mich., 1968. Diplomate Am. Bd. Cardiology, Am. Bd. Interventional Cardiology, Am. Bd. Nuc. Cardiology. Intern in internal medicine U. Hosp., Ann Arbor, Mich., 1968-69, resident in internal medicine, 1971-73, fellow in cardiology, 1973-75; practice medicine specializing in cardiology, interventional cardiology and nuc. cardiology Petoskey, Mich., 1975—. Cardiologist Burns Clinic Med. Center, Petoskey, 1975-99, Mich. Heart & Vascular Specialists, 2004-, chmn. dept. cardiology and cardiac surgery, 1978-89; med. dir. No. Mich. Heart Center, 1989-95; pres. Petoskey Cardiology, P.C., 1999-2004; chief sect. cardiology No. Mich. Hosps., 2000-04; cardiologist Little Traverse Hosp., Petoskey, 1975—, dir. coronary care unit, 1986-89; dir. cardiac catheterization lab. No. Mich. Hosps., Petoskey, 1985-87, 92-2004, adult spl. care units, 1986-89; vice chmn. bd. dirs. Burns Clinic Med. Ctr., 1989-92. Contbr. med. articles to profl. jours. Trustee Mich. Heart Assn., 1979-83. Served as surgeon USPHS, 1969-71. Named one of Best Drs. in Am. 2001-02, Best Drs. Inc., 2002, Best Drs. in Am. 2003-04, 2004, Best Drs. in Am., 2005—08. Fellow: Soc. Cardiovasc. Angiography and Interventions, Am. Coll. Cardiology; mem.: Am. Heart Assn. (fellow Coun. on Clin. Cardiology), Alpha Omega Alpha. Home: 1224 Autumn Ln Petoskey MI 49770-9019 Office: Petoskey Cardiology 560 W Mitchell St Ste 400 Petoskey MI 49770-2274 Office Phone: 231-487-2490.

MEENSOOK, CHAROEN, physician, consultant; b. Bangkok, May 20, 1942; s. Song Tiang and Geng Teg (Bae) Ngo; m. Hataya Tantiviwattanapan, Oct. 2, 1976; children: Chayaron, Priya. MD, Siriraj Med. Sch., Bangkok, 1967; diploma of tropical medicine & hygiene, Liverpool U., Eng., 1974. Diplomate Am. Bd. Internal Medicine and Gastroenterology. Med. dir. Thainakarin Hosp., Bangkok, 1993—. Named Excellent Citizen of Thai Soc., 2001, Nat. Exemplary Father, 2007; recipient Excellent Hosp. Adminstr. award Assn. Excellent Adminstrs., Thailand, 1996. Fellow Am. Coll. Gastroenterology, Royal Coll. Physicians Thailand, Am. Coll. Physicians. Avocations: jogging, hiking, stamp collecting/philately, coin collecting/numismatics. Office: Med Dir Office Thai Nakarin Hosp Bangna Bangkok 10260 Thailand Office Phone: 023612727, 023612828. Business E-Mail: medical@thainakarin.co.th.

MEERS, SUZANNE, biology professor; PhD, U. Ga., Athens, 2008. Biology prof. Gainesville State Coll., Watkinsville, Ga., 2007—. Mem.: Am. Soc. Nutrition, Am. Soc. Animal Scis., Gamma Sigma Delta. Office: Gainesville State Coll 1201 Bishop Farms Pky Watkinsville GA 30677 Business E-Mail: smeers@gsc.edu.

MEERSCHAERT, JOSEPH RICHARD, retired physician; b. Detroit, Mar. 4, 1941; s. Hector Achiel and Marie Terese (Campbell) M.; m. Jeanette Marie Ancerewicz, Sept. 14, 1963; children: Eric, Amy, Adam. BA, Wayne State U., 1965, MD, 1967. Diplomate Am. Bd. Phys. Medicine and Rehab., Am. Bd. Pain Medicine. Intern Harper Hosp., Detroit, 1967-68; resident in phys. medicine and rehab. Wayne State U. Rehab. Inst., Detroit, 1968-71; chief divsn. phys. medicine Naval Hosp., Chelsea, Mass., 1971-73; attending physician William Beaumont Hosp., Royal Oak, Mich., 1973—2006, med. dir. rehab. unit, 1979-87; pvt. practice medicine specializing in phys. medicine and rehab. Royal Oak, 1973—2006; pvt. practice specializing in pain medicine, 1990—2006; ret., 2006. Mem. med. adv. bd. Nat. Wheelchair Athletic Assn., 1973—, U.S. team physician VII World Wheelchair Games, Stoke Mandeville, Eng.; clin. instr. Wayne State U., 1973-83, clin. asst. prof. phys. medicine and rehab., 1983—; mem. Mich. Dept. Licensing and Regulation State Bd. Phys. Therapy, 1978-81. Contbr. articles to profl. jours. With M.C. USN, 1971-73. Recipient John Hussey award Mich. Wheelchair Athletic Assn., 1981. Fellow Am. Coll. Pain Medicine; mem. Am. Acad. Phys. Medicine and Rehab. (reviewer, presenter) Am. Congress Rehab. Medicine, Mich. Phys. Medicine and Rehab. Soc., Am. Geriatrics Soc., Am. Assn. Electromyography and Electrodiagnosis, Mich. Rheumatism Soc., Mich. Acad. Phys. Medicine and REhab. (pres. 1986-87, chmn. program com. 1977-78, trustee 1980—, pres. bd. dirs. 1994-97), Oakland County Med. Soc. (bd. dirs. 1991, 97), Alpha Omega Alpha. Roman Catholic.

MEESE, ED (EDWIN MEESE III), law and public policy educator, former United States Attorney General; b. Oakland, Calif., Dec. 2, 1931; s. Edwin and Leone M. Meese; m. Ursula Herrick, 1958; children: Michael James, Dana Lynne. BA, Yale U., 1953; JD, U. Calif., Berkeley, 1958; LLD, Del. Law Sch., Widener U., U. San Diego, Valparaiso U., Calif. Luth. Coll. Dep. dist. atty. Alameda County, Calif., 1959-67; legal affairs sec. to Gov. Ronald Reagan, State of California, Sacramento, 1967-69; exec. asst., chief of staff to Gov. Ronald Reagan, State of Calif., Sacramento, 1969-75; v.p. Rohr Industries, Chula Vista, Calif., 1975-76; pvt. law practice, 1976-80; prof. law U. San Diego, 1977—81, dir. Ctr. for Criminal Justice Policy; counselor to Pres. The White House, Washington, 1981-85; atty. gen. US Dept. Justice, Washington, 1985-88; disting. fellow, Ronald Reagan Chair in Pub. Policy Heritage Found., Washington. Mem. NSC, 1981—88, Iraq Study Group, 2006, Nat. War Powers Commn., 2008; disting. vis. fellow Hoover Instn. Stanford U.; regent emeritus Nat. Coll. Dist. Atty.; bd. dirs. Capital Rsch. Ctr., Landmark Legal Found.; co-chmn. bd. governors The Reagan Ranch Program; co-chmn. Critical Incident Analysis Group. Author: With Reagan: The Inside Story, 1992; co-editor: Making America Safer, 1997; co-author: Leadership, Ethics & Policing. V.p. Lutheran Ch., El Cajon, Calif. Served with US Army. Recipient Life Achievement Award, Nat. Dist. Atty. Assn. Mem.: ABA, Calif. State Bar. Lutheran. Office: Heritage Found 214 Massachusetts Ave NE Washington DC 20002-4958 Office Phone: 202-546-4400.*

MEESE, GEORGE PHILIP ELMAN, literature and rhetoric professor, consultant; b. Cleve., Jan. 17, 1945; s. George Ellsworth and Elma Laura Meese; m. Meese Marie Hoaglund, Dec. 23, 1967; children: Megan Anne Christie, Brenton George. PhD, Chgo., Ill., 1976. Dir., writing excellence program Eckerd Coll., St. Petersburg, Fla., 1986—2008. Fellow NSF & Nat. Endowment Humanities, Wash., 1982—93. Lt. USN, 1968—71, Pearl Harbor. Decorated Navy Commendation medal USN Chief Naval Ops. Democrat. Presbyterian. Office: Eckerd Coll 4200 54th Ave S Saint Petersburg FL 33711 E-mail: meesegp@eckerd.edu.

MEESTER, HOLLY, elementary school educator, music educator, sales executive; b. Grafton, ND, Sept. 1, 1966; d. Gordon and (Alice) Jane Thompson; m. Brent Meester, Sept. 27, 1991; children: Emily, Daniel. BS in Music Edn., N.D. State U., 1989; MA in Music Edn., U. St. Thomas, 2003. Lic. profl. educator N.D., 1989. Asst. dir. Red River Boy Choir, Fargo, ND, 1988—90; tchr. elem. music Fargo Pub. Schs., 1989—; founder, music dir. Lake Agassiz Girls Choir, Fargo, 1990—97. Ind. cons. Mary Kay Cosmetics, Fargo, 1993—; mentor Fargo Pub. Schs., 1999—2002, dir. elem. hand chimes performing group, 1991—, dir. elem. choir, 1989—; adj. prof. Minn. State U., Moorhead, 2004—. Bldg. liaison Fargo Edn. Assn.; bd. mem. Lake Agassiz Girls Choir, Fargo, 1990—98; steering com. mem. North Ctrl. Accreditation - Lewis & Clark Elem., 1992—2005. Mem.: N.D. Music Educators Assn. (state pres. collegiate chpt. 1988—89, Outstanding Collegiate Music Educator 1989), Music Educators Nat. Conf., Orgn. Am. Kodaly Educators, No. Plains Kodaly Chpt. (pres., v.p., past pres., member-at-large 1997—2005), Kappa Delta (life; corr. sec. 1986—87), Sigma Alpha Iota (life). Achievements include Performance at National Organization of American Kodaly Educators while Director of Lake Agassiz Girls Choir. Avocations: reading, piano, scrapbooks, choir. Office: Fargo Pub Schs 415 N 44th St Fargo ND 58102 Office Phone: 701-446-4416.

MEESTER, LEIGHTON (LEIGHTON MARISSA CLAIRE MEESTER), actress; b. Marco Island, Fla., Apr. 9, 1986; Actor(guest appearance): (TV series) Law & Order, 1999, Boston Public, 2001, Family Affair, 2002, Crossing Jordan, 2004, 7th Heaven, 2004, North Shore, 2004, Entourage, 2004, 24, 2005, 8 Simple Rules... for Dating My Teenage Daughter, 2005, Veronica Mars, 2005, Numb3rs, 2006, House M.D., 2006, CSI: Miami, 2007, Shark, 2007,: (films) The Jackalope, 2003, Hangman's Curse, 2003, Flourish, 2006, Inside, 2006, Drive Thru, 2007, The Beautiful Ordinary, 2007, Killer Movie, 2008; (TV series) Tarzan, 2003, Surface, 2005—06, Gossip Girl, 2007— (Choice TV Actress: Drama, Teen Choice Awards, 2009); (TV films) Hollywood Division, 2004, The Haunting of Sorority Row, 2007. Office: c/o Leverage Mgmt 3030 Pennsylvania Ave Santa Monica CA 90404

MEEZAN, ELIAS, pharmacologist, educator; b. NYC, Mar. 5, 1942; s. Morris and Rachel (Epstein) M.; m. Elisabeth Gascard, May 14, 1967; children: David, Nathan, Joshua. BS in Chemistry, CCNY, 1962; PhD in Biochemistry, Duke U., 1966. Asst. prof. physiology and pharmacology Duke U., Durham, NC, 1969-70; asst. prof. pharmacology U. Ariz., Tucson, 1970-75, assoc. prof., 1975-79; prof., chmn. dept. pharmacology U. Ala., Birmingham, 1979-89, prof., dir. Metabolic Diseases Rsch. Lab., 1989-93, prof. dept. pharmacology & toxicology, 1993—. Mem. sci. adv. bd. Aegis Therapeutics, 2004—. Assoc. editor: Life Sci., 1973-79. Helen Hay Whitney postdoctoral fellow, 1966-69; recipient NIH Rsch. Career Devel. award, 1977-79. Mem. Am. Soc. Pharmacology and Exptl. Therapeutics, Am. Soc. Biol. Chemistry, AAUP, AAAS, N.Y. Acad. Sci., Assn. Med. Sch. Pharmacology. Democrat. Jewish. Achievements include isolation of retinal and brain microvasculature; development of method for isolating ultrastructurally and chemically intact basement membranes; co-inventor of method for enhancing nasal absorption of drugs. Home: 1202 Cheval Ln Birmingham AL 35216-2037 Office: U Ala Dept Pharmacology Birmingham AL 35294-0001 Office Phone: 205-934-4577. Business E-Mail: Elias.Meezan@ccc.uab.edu.

MEFFERT, ROLAND MATTHEW, retired periodontist; b. Cross Plains, Wis., June 30, 1932; s. John Michael and Lorraine Catherine (Garfoot) Meffert; m. Marcella Ann Czarnecki, June 12, 1954; children: Jeffrey, Lisa, Sarah, Gregory, Douglas. DDS, Marquette U., 1955; cert. in periodontics, U. Tex., Houston, 1961; cert. in periodontics, Wilford Hall USAF Med. Ctr., 1962. Commd. 1st lt. USAF, 1954, advanced through grades to col., 1970, ret., 1974; prof. dept. periodontics U. Tex. Health Sci. Ctr., San Antonio, 1974—84, 1992—2003, cons. continuing dental edn., 2003—08; assoc. prof. dept. prosthodontics U. Tex. Med. Ctr., San Antonio, 2003—08; prof., chmn. dept. periodontics La. State U. Sch. Dentistry, New Orleans, 1984—92. Editor emeritus Implant Dentistry; editor emeritus: Practical Periodontics and Aesthetic Dentistry; contbr. chapters to books, articles to profl. jours. Recipient Spl. Citation award, Am. Acad. Periodontology, 1993, 1997, Meffert-Mutlu Implant Inst. named in honor, Ankara, Turkey, 1997. Master: Am. Acad. Implant Prosthodontics; fellow: Internat. Colll. Dentists, Am. Coll. Dentists; mem.: Am. Soc. Osseointegration (diplomate, pres. 1992, Oral Implantologist of Yr. 1988), Internat. Congress Oral Implantology (diplomate, pres. 1990, Internat. Edn. award 1992, 1994), Am. Bd. Periodontology (diplomate, dir., chmn. 1990—96).

MEGALLI, MAGUID RAMZI, retired health facility administrator, urologist; b. Cairo, Jan. 26, 1942; arrived in U.S., 1969; s. Ramzi and Lydia Megalli; m. Viviane Wassef, Jan. 28, 1968; children: Michael, Mark. MD, Cairo U., 1965; MBA, Pace U., 1988. Lic. Am. Bd. of Urology. Resident in urology Columbia U., NYC, 1970—74; chief of urology St. Joseph Med. Ctr., Yonkers, NY, 1982—88; chief med. officer Cath. Health Care Sys. Resources, 1999—2002; pres. Benifice Advantage, the Self-Insuring Co. for Archdiocese of N.Y., 2002—; exec. v.p., chief med. officer Our Lady of Mercy Med. Ctr., Bronx, NY, 2003—. Founder, chmn. Servitas IPA, NYC, 1994—99. Contbr. articles to prof. publs. (Valantine Fellowship award, 1974). Lt. col. USAR, 1972—84. Fellow: ACS (life). Home: 35 Island Dr Rye NY 10580 Home Fax: 914-967-3613. Personal E-mail: mmegalli@gmail.com.

MEGDAL, SHARON B., water resource educator, consultant; b. Newark, Apr. 4, 1952; d. William B. and Ann Bernstein; m. Ronald G. Megdal, Aug. 18, 1974; 1 child. AB in Econs., Rutgers U., 1974; MA in Econs., Princeton U., 1977, PhD in Econs., 1981. Asst. prof. econs. U. Ariz., Tucson, 1979-87; pres., owner MegEcon Cons., Tucson, 1987—; assoc. dir. Water Resources Rsch. Ctr., 2002—04, dir., 2004—; prof. agrl. and resource econs. U. Ariz., Tucson, 2002—. Vis. assoc. prof. No. Ariz. U., 1987-88, C.W. Modene Neely Endowed prof., 2008-; spkr., panelist in field. Contbr. articles to profl. jours. Commr. Ariz. Corp. Commn., 1985-87; exec. dir. Santa Cruz Valley Water Dist., 1991-94; chair Ariz. Joint Select Com. State Revenues and Expenditures, 1989; mem. Ariz. State Transp. Bd., 1991-97, vice chair, 1995-96, chair, 1996—; bd. dirs. Tucson Elec. Power Co., Inc., 1989-91, So. Ariz. Water Resources Assn., 1991-95, pres., 1994-95; bd. dirs. United Way, 1989-92; trustee Tucson Med. Ctr., 1990-95, chmn., 1993-95; trustee TMcare Healthpartners of So. Ariz., 1993-99; bd. dirs. Ariz. Hosp. & Healthcare Assn., 1995-99; mem. Tucson Airport Authority, 1990—, Gov.'s Regional Airport Adv. Com., bd. regents Commn. on Status Women, First Leadership Am. Class; participant Econ. Conf. Pres.-elect, Little Rock, 1992; mem. Transp. & Econ. Devel. Com., Transp. Rsch. Bd., Nat. Rsch. Coun.; vol. United Way Greater Tucson, 1982-85, 87-88; co-chmn. Gov.'s Transp. Vision Task Force, 1999-2001; mem. Ariz. Med. Bd., 1999—2007, (vice chmn., 2003); mem. Gov.'s Water Mgmt. Commn., 2000-2001, mem. Ctrl. Ariz. Water Conservation Dist. Bd., 2009-. Richard D. Irwin fellow, Sloan Found., 1976-78; U. Ariz. Rsch. grantee, 1982, 83, Figgle Corp. grantee, 1984. Mem. Am. Econs. Assn. (com. on status women 1983—), Women Execs. in State Govt., Nat. Assn. Regulatory Utility Commrs. (com. on electricity), Phi Beta Kappa, Beta Gamma Sigma. Office: U Ariz Water Resources Rsch Ctr 350 N Campbell Tucson AZ 85719

MEGGERS, BETTY JANE, anthropologist, researcher; b. Washington, Dec. 5, 1921; d. William Frederick and Edith (Raddant) M.; m. Clifford Evans, Sept. 13, 1946. AB, U. Pa., 1943; MA, U. Mich., 1944; PhD, Columbia U., 1952; D (hon.), U. de Guayaquil, Ecuador, 1987, U. Fed. Rio de Janeiro, Brazil, 1994, U. Nat. La Plata, Argentina, 1997, U. Católica de Goiás, Brazil, 1999; D (hon.), U. Fed. do Parana, Brazil, 2006, U. Fed. Rondonia, 2007. Instr. anthropology Am. U., Washington, 1950-51; rsch. assoc. Smithsonian Instn., 1954—, expert, 1981—; founder, pres. Taraxacum Inc., 1977—. Hon. prof. U. de Azuay, Ecuador, 1991. Author: Environmental Limitation on the Development of Culture, 1954, Ecuador, 1966, Amazonia, 1971, 2nd edit., 1996, Prehistoric America, 1972, rev. edit., 2009, Evolucion y Difusion Cultural, 1998, Ecologia y Biogeografia de la Amazonia, 1999, (with Clifford Evans) Archeological Investigations at the Mouth of the Amazon, 1957, Archeological Investigations in British Guiana, 1960, (with Clifford Evans and Emilio Estrada) Early Formative Period of Coastal Ecuador, 1965, (with Clifford Evans) Archeological Investigations on the Rio Napo, Eastern Ecuador, 1968; editor: Prehistoria Sudamericana, 1992. Recipient award for sci. achievement Washington Acad. Sci., 1956; gold medal 37th Internat. Congress of Americanists, 1966; Order Al Merito Govt. Ecuador, 1966; Order Bernardo O'Higgins Govt. Chile, 1985; Sec.'s Gold medal for exceptional service Smithsonian Instn., 1986; Order Andres Bello Govt. Venezuela, 1988; Order Al Mérito por Servicios Distinguidos Govt. Peru, 1989, Order Al Mérito Científico, Casa de la Cultura Ecuatoriana, 2006. Fellow: AAAS, Assn. Tropical Biology (hon.; councilor 1976—78, pres.-elect 1982, pres. 1983); mem.: Ecol. Soc. Am., New Eng. Antiquities Rsch. Assn., Academia Nacional Historia Ecuador (corr.), Am. Anthrop. Assn. (exec. sec. 1959—61), Museo Antropológico de la Cultura Andina (hon.), Soc. Am. Archaeology (exec. bd. 1962—64), Am. Ethnol. Soc., Anthrop. Soc. Wash. (treas. 1955—60, v.p. 1965—66, pres. 1966—68), Phi Beta Kappa, Sigma Xi. Home: 1227 30th St NW Washington DC 20007-3410 Office: Smithsonian Instn Washington DC 20560-0001

MEGHERIAN, YEFKIN, sculptor; b. Troy, NY, Mar. 23, 1924; d. Haroutiun DerBedrosian and Nevart DerVartanian; m. Vartan Megherian, Nov. 30, 1947 (dec. Jan. 1984); children: Gay Zarman, Lori Christine, Narrek Khachig, Talin Yefkin. BA, SUNY, Albany, 1945, MA, 1946; AS in Fine Arts, Queensborough C.C., NYC, 1994. Cert. tchr. secondary schs. NY, tchr. primary grades NY, ancillary cert. tchr. art Bd. Edn., NYC. HS sci. tchr. Warwick Valley Ctrl. Sch., 1946—47; tchr. NYC Bd. Edn., 1967—85; sculptor, 1986—. Ch. sch. supr. St. James Armenian Ch., Evanston, Ill., 1947—55, Armenian Ch. of the Holy Martyrs, Bayside, NY, 1955—72; sec. coun. for religious edn. Diocese Armenian Ch., NYC, 1956—61; cons. for bronze doors St. Vartan Armenian Cath., NYC, 2002—09. Prin. works include Statue of Pope John Paul II, Vatican Mus., Rome, Bust of Vazken I, Catholicos of All Armenians, St. Gregory Illuminator Ch., Westchester, NY, Bust of Archbishop Tiran Nersoyan, Libr. Armenian Seminary, Westchester, Bas-relief, St. Vartan Armenian Cathedral, NYC, St. Peter Armenian Ch., Watervliet, NY, medallions, Med. Mus., Wroclaw, Poland, medallion, Alex Manoogian Mus., St. John Armenian Ch., Southfield, Mich., exhibitions include Franklin Mint, 1994, Pen and Brush Gallery, NYC, 1995—2003, UN Relief Efforts, Lehman Coll., 1995, Canon House Office Bldg. Rotunda, Washington, 1996, Newark Mus., 1996, Nordic Heritage Mus., Seattle, 2004, Nat. Assn. Women Artists, Reading, Pa., 2004—05, Forest Lawn Mus., Calif., 2005, Padded Cell Gallery, Royal Oak, Mich., 2005, Queensborough CC, NYC, 2000, Nat. Assn. Women Artists, Reading, Pa., 2006, FIDEM, ANA Mus., Colorado Springs, 2007, Queensborough CC, NYC, 2009, Medialia Gallery, 2009, Belskie Mus. Art and Sci., Closter, NJ, 2009, pvt. collections, permanent collection of coins and medals, Brit. Mus., London. Mem.: Nat. Assn. Women Artists, Pen and Brush, Inc. (Tallix Foundry award 1996, Merit award 2000, Compleat Sculptor 2003), Fedn. Internat. de la Medaille, Nat. Mus. Women in the Arts, Am. Medallic Sculpture Assn. (bd. dirs. 1997—2000, co-chair medallic sculpture exhbn. 2000), Nat. Sculpture Soc. Avocations: painting, travel, opera, ceramics, reading. Home: 218-37 Grand Central Pkwy Queens Village NY 11427 Office Phone: 718-217-6285. Personal E-mail: yefkin323@aol.com.

MEGHREBLIAN, ROBERT VARTAN, manufacturing executive, physicist; b. Cairo, Sept. 6, 1922; arrived in U.S., 1923, naturalized, 1929; s. Vahan V. and Mary (Kurkjian) M.; m. Mary J. Walton, 1955 (div. 1977); Children: David V., Susan M.; m. Margaret M. Gordon, 1987. B in Engring. (Gotshall-Powell scholar), Rensselaer Poly. Inst., 1943; MS (Guggenheim fellow), Calif. Inst. Tech., 1950, PhD magna cum laude (Guggenheim fellow), 1953. Lectr. Oak Ridge Nat. Lab., 1952-55, assoc. project mgr., 1955-58; chief sect. Physics Jet Propulsion Lab., Calif. Inst. Tech., 1958-60, mgr. space scis. divsn., 1960-68, dep. asst. lab. dir., 1968-71, assoc. prof. applied mechanics, 1960-61; v.p. rsch. and engring. Cabot Corp., Boston, 1971-79, v.p., 1971-87; pres. Distrigas Corp., 1979-85; gen. mgr. Cabot Crystals Bus. Unit, 1985-86, dir. corp. planning and devel., 1986-87. Author: Reactor Analysis, 1960. Vice chair Montecito Planning Commn., Calif., 2003, chair, 2004—06. Lt. (j.g.) USN, 1941—46, PTO, ATO. Fellow: AIAA (assoc.), Am. Nuc. Soc.; mem.: Montecito Assn. (bd. dir. 1992—98, chair archt. rev. com. 1993—95, v.p. 1994, pres. 1995—96, elected hon. dir. 2007, Montecito Citizen of Yr. 2002), Art Found. Santa Barbara (v.p.), Santa Barbara Club (pres. 2009), Tennis Club Santa Barbara, Sigma Xi. Home: 440 Woodley Rd Montecito CA 93108-2006

MEGILL, ALLAN, historian; b. Regina, Sask., Apr. 20, 1947; arrived in US, 1980; s. Ralph Peter and Jean Tudhope (Dickson) M.; div.; children: Jason Robert, Jessica Susan, Jonathan David; m. Rita Felski; 1 child, Maria Megill Felski. BA, U. Sask., 1969; MA, U. Toronto, 1970; PhD, Columbia U., NYC, 1975. From instr. to prof. history U. Iowa, Iowa City, 1974—90; prof. history U. Va., Charlottesville, 1990—. Rsch. fellow in history of ideas Australian Nat. U., Canberra, 1977—79, temp. lectr. modern European studies, 1979; vis. prof. Sch. Advanced Studies in Social Scis., Paris, 1997. Author: Prophets of Extremity, 1985, Karl Marx: The Burden of Reason, 2002, Historical Knowledge, Historical Error: A Contemporary Guide to Practice, 2007, (Russian edn.) Istoricheskaya epistemologia, 2007; editor: Rethinking Objectivity, 1994; co-editor: The Rhetoric of the Human Sciences, 1987; cons. editor Jour. of History of Ideas, 1986—89, mem. editl. bd., 1990—, v.p., 2004—05, pres., 2005—; mem. editl. bd.: U. Press of Va., 1991—94, Rethinking History, 1996—; contbr. articles to profl. jours. Chmn. Page-Barbour and Richard Lectures com. U. Va., 1994-96. Mem.: Internat. Commn. for the History and Theory of Historiography, Internat. Soc. for Intellectual History, Am. Hist. Assn. Office: Univ Va Corcoran Dept History PO Box 400180 Charlottesville VA 22904 Office Phone: 434-924-6414. Business E-Mail: megill@virginia.edu.

MEGNA, STEVE ALLAN, retired secondary school educator; Secondary tchr. Vernon (NJ) H.S., ret., 2006. Recipient Tech. Excellence award Internat. Tech. Edn. Assn. and Tech. Edn. Assn. N.J., 1992, Tech. Program of Yr. award Tech. Edn. Assn. N.J., 1989; named Innovative Tech. Educator, Martinson Family Found., 2002.

MEHAIL, JAMES JOSEPH, aerospace engineer, educator; b. Milw., Apr. 27, 1965; s. James and Mary Jo (Nee Rhomberg) Mehail; m. Despina Stefanidis, Aug. 26, 2006; 1 child, Rachel Marie. BS in Naval Sci., U. Wis. Madison, BSc in Engring. Mechanics, 1987; MSc in Engring. Mgmt. & Fin., Milw. Sch. Engring., 1998. EIT 1992. Project engr. AEGEAN Proprietorship, 1988—; surface warfare officer US Navy, 1987—, engring. officer of watch, 1988—89, engring. auxillaries officer, 1989—98, instr., math. & naval warfare, 1998—; instr., math., physics & computers Milw. Area Tech. Coll., 1991—; instr., math. U. Wis. Milw., 1998—99; product mgr. Rockwell Internat., 1998—2002; asst. program mgr., engring. Astronautics Corp. America, 2006—. Environ. scientist Dept. City Devel., Milw., grad. intern, asst. planner, 1993—95. Contbr. scientific papers. Mem. St. Robert Ch., Shorewood, Wis. Decorated Nat. Def. Ribbon US Navy, Sea Svc. Deployment, Res. Sea Svc. & Expert Pistol; recipient Meritorious Svc. medal, US Navy, Navy Commendation medal, Global War on Terrorism Svc. medal, Navy Achievement medal, Armed Forces Expeditionary medal. Mem.: Res. Officer Assn., Navy Res. Assn. Achievements include patents for engine having external combustion chamber; patents pending in field. Avocations: golf, sailing, computers. Home and Office: 3056 N Barlett Ave Milwaukee WI 53211-3214 Personal E-mail: jmehail@aol.com.

MEHALCHIN, JOHN JOSEPH, entrepreneur, finance company executive; b. Hazleton, Pa., Aug. 8, 1937; s. Charles and Susan (Korba) Mehalchin; 1 child from previous marriage, Martin. BS with honors (1st in class), Temple U., 1964; MBA, U. Calif., Berkeley, 1965; postgrad., U. Chgo., 1964; LHD (hon.), U. Colo., 2002. Supr. costs Winchester-Western, New Haven, 1965-67; mgmt. cons. Booz-Allen & Hamilton, NYC, 1967-68; mgr. planning TWA, NYC, 1968-69; officer Smith Barney, NYC, Paris, 1970-74; CFO Storage Tech., Louisville, 1974-79; sr. v.p. Heizer Corp., 1979—99; pres., founder Highline Fin. Svcs., Inc. and fgn. subs., Boulder, Colo., 1979—98, London, Paris, Frankfurt, Germany; chmn. Highline Capital Corp. and all subs., Boulder, Colo., 1998—. Strategic planning com. Coll. and Grad. Sch. Bus., U. Colo., Denver; bd. advisors U. Colo. Ctr. Entrepreneurship, U. Colo. Bus. Sch., Wolf Ventures. With US Army, 1958—61. Recipient Mack Easton award for Excellence, 1998, Univ. medal, U. Colo., 2002; fellow, U. Calif., Berkeley, 1964, 1965; scholar, U. Chgo., 1964. Mem.: Equipment Leasing Assn., Fin. Execs. Inst., Omicron Delta Epsilon, Beta Gamma Sigma. Home and Office: Highline Fin Svcs Inc 2930 Center Green Ct Ste 200 Boulder CO 80301-5419 Office Phone: 303-443-7267.

MEHALIK, MATTHEW M., industrial engineer, educator; b. Pitts., Pa., Jan. 11, 1970; s. Gilbert G. and Sandra L. Mehalik; m. Deborah L. McGaughey, Apr. 28, 2006. BS in Aerospace Engring. with distinction, U. Va., Charlottesville, 1992, MS in Sys. Engring., 1997; PhD, U. Va., Charlottesville, 2001. Postdoctoral assoc. Sci., Tech., and Soc. U. of Va., Charlottesville, 2001—02; fellow in pub. affairs Coro Ctr. for Civic Leadership, Pitts., 2002—03; postdoctoral rsch. assoc. Learning R&D Ctr. U. of Pitts., Pitts., 2003—05, vis. asst. prof. indsl. engring., 2005—. Cons. Sustainable Pitts., Pitts., 2004—. Author, researcher: Ethical and Environmental Challenges to Engineering, ISO 14001 Concepts and Cases; contbr. articles to profl. jours. (Lous T. Rader award in sys. engring., 2001). Mem. adv. bd. Nat. Found. for Tchg. Entrepreneurship, Pitts., 2003—04; mem. planning com. Nat. Aviary, Pitts., 2006. Recipient Product Realization for Global Opportunities grant, Nat. Collegiate Inventors and Innnovators Alliance, 2005—07, Earth Systems Engring. and Mgmt. Course Devel. grant, AT&T, 2001—03, Bringing Design into Urban High Schools to Teach Sci. grant, NSF, 2005—07, Inventing for a Better Global Environment: A Comparative Analysis of Two Networks grant, 1998—99. Mem.: Assn. for Practical and Profl. Ethics (assoc.), Soc. for the Social Studies of Sci. (assoc.), Am. Soc. for Engring. Edn. (assoc.), Am. Ednl. Rsch. Assn. (assoc.), Inst. for Indsl. Engrs. (assoc.). Office: U Pitts Indsl Engring 1048 Benedum Hall Pittsburgh PA 15261 Office Fax: 412-624-7439. Business E-Mail: mmehalik@pitt.edu.

MEHDI, YUSUF, computer software company executive; m. Stephanie Mehdi; 3 children. BA in Econs., Princeton U.; MBA, U. Wash. Product mgr. Reuters Group PLC; dir. mktg. Microsoft Windows op. sys. Microsoft Corp., Redmond, Wash., dir. mktg. Microsoft Internet Explorer, 1995—99, corp. v.p. MSN personal svcs. and bus., 2002—05, sr. v.p., chief advt. strategist, sr. v.p. strategic partnerships, sr. v.p. online audience bus., 2009—. Office: One Microsoft Way Redmond WA 98052-6399*

MEHL, ALBERT L., pediatrician, poet, composer; s. Clinton Mehl and Alberta Wells; m. Annie Kempe, Aug. 4, 1979; children: Sarah Kempe-Mehl, James Kempe-Mehl. BA, Colo. Coll., Colorado Springs, 1976; MD, U. Colo. Health Scis. Ctr., Denver, 1980. Diplomate Am. Bd. Pediat. Pediatrician Kaiser Permanente, Lafayette, Colo., 1987—. Editl. cons. various publs., Various US states, 1988—; assoc. clin. prof. U. Colo. Health Scis. Ctr., Denver, 2001—. Singer, songwriter: albums Asphalt Cowboy, I'd Rather Be..., writer, performer: albums Cowboy Pottery; contbr. articles to profl. jours. Mem. expert working group effective interventions infants and young children with hearing loss U.S. HHS; gubernatorial appointee Colo. Children's Trust Fund Child Abuse Prevention, Denver, 1992—97, vice chmn., 1995—96; chmn. infant hearing adv. com. Colo. State Dept. Health and Environment, Denver, 1997—. Recipient Peak Performance award, Colo. Acad. Audiology, 1998, Communities Helping Young Children award, Frances Owens, First Lady of Colo., 2005; Boettcher Found. scholar, 1973—77. Fellow: Am. Acad. Pediat. (chmn. nat. task force infant hearing 2005—, appointee U.S. joint com. infant hearing 2005—). Avocations: fly fishing, skiing, golf. Office: Kaiser Permanente Med Offices 280 Exempla Cir Lafayette CO 80026

MEHLENBACHER, DOHN HARLOW, civil engineer, consultant; b. Huntington Park, Calif., Nov. 18, 1931; s. Virgil Claude and Helga (Sigfridson) M.; m. Nancy Moss; children: Dohn Scott, Kimberly Ruth, Mark James, Matthew Lincoln. BSCE, U. Ill., 1953; MS in City and Regional Planning, Ill. Inst. Tech., Chgo., 1961; MBA, U. Chgo., 1972. Registered profl. engr., Ill.; lic. structural engr., Ill. Structural engr., draftsman Swift & Co., Chgo., 1953-54, 56-57, DeLeuw-Cather Co., Chgo., 1957-59; project engr. Quaker Oats Co., Chgo., 1959-61, mgr. constrn., 1964-70, mgr. real property, 1970-71, mgr. engring. and maintenance LA, 1961-64; chief facilities engr. Bell & Howell Co., Chgo., 1972-73; v.p. design Globe Engring. Co., Chgo., 1973-76; project mgr. I.C. Harbour Constrn. Co., Oak Brook, Ill., 1976-78; dir. estimating George A. Fuller Co., Oak Brook, 1978; pres. Food-Tech. Co., Willowbrook, Ill., 1979-80; dir. phys. resources Ill. Inst. Tech., Chgo., 1980-92; cons. Exec. Svc. Corp., Chgo., 1994—; cons. structural engr. Mem. AAA Nat. Roster of Neutrals. With USAF, 1954-56. Fellow ASCE. Home and Office: 436 Leitch Ave La Grange IL 60525-6126 Personal E-mail: dohnh@comcast.net.

MEHLER, GORDON, lawyer, former federal prosecutor; b. Denver, Feb. 27, 1955; s. Irving Martin and Bernice (Steinberg) M.; m. Ariel Zwang; children: Grace, Rachel. BS, U. Colo., 1976; JD, NYU, 1982. Bar: NY 1983, US Dist. Ct. (ea. and so. dists.) NY 1983, US Ct. Appeals (10th cir.) 1984, US Ct. Appeals (2nd cir.) 1986, US Supreme Ct. 2000, US Ct. Appeals (4th cir.) 2009. Assoc. Skadden, Arps, Slate, Meagher & Flom, NYC, 1982-83; law clk. to presiding judge US Ct. Appeals (10th cir.), Denver, 1983-84; fed. prosecutor US Atty.'s Office (ea. dist.), NYC, 1984—99, chief spl. prosecutions (pub. integrity), 1996-98; dep. asst. atty. gen. US Dept. Justice, Washington, 1999-2000; pvt. practice Law Offices of Gordon Mehler, PLLC, NYC, 2000—. Adj. assoc. prof. law Fordham U. Law Sch., NYC, 1988-92; US Dept. Justice resident legal advisor to Romania, Bucharest, 1992. Co-author: (with Gleeson and James) Federal Criminal Practice, 9th edit., 2009; co-editor: New York Criminal Practice, 2d edit., 2005; contbr. articles in field to profl. jours. and newspapers. Bd. dirs. Health Jam, 2004—, Jacob Riis Neighborhood Settlement House, 2007—. Mem. ABA, Fed. Bar Coun., NYC Bar Assn., NY Coun. Def. Lawyers. Office: 747 Third Ave 32nd Floor New York NY 10017-2803 Office Phone: 212-661-2414. Business E-Mail: gmehler@mehlerlaw.com.

MEHLER, PHILIP S., internist; m. Leah Mehler; children: Avi, Ilana, Ben. BA in Biology, U. Colo., Denver, 1979, MD, 1983. Diplomate internal medicine, addiction medicine. Internship and residency U. Colo. Health Sci. Ctr., 1983—87; staff attending physician Denver Health Med. Ctr., Denver, 1987—, chief internal medicine, 1994—2004; assoc. med. dir. Denver Health, 2003—08, chief med. officer, 2008—. V.p. Colo. Prevention Ctr., Denver, 1995—2007; Prof. of Medicine and Glassman endowed prof. Internal Medicine U. Colo. Sch. Medicine, Denver, 2000—. Contbr. articles to profl. jours. Recipient Ciba-Geigy Tchg. award, U. Colo. Sch. Medicine, 1986, Outstanding Faculty award, 1991, Outstanding Tchr. Yr., Denver Health Med. Ctr., 1996, Safety award, NAPH, 1997, Academic Excellence award, Denver Health, 2005, Silver award, U. Colo. Sch. Medicine, Gold award, 2009, Chair award, Patient Safety Nat. Assoc. Pub. Hosp., 2009; named Best Doctors in Am., 5280 Mag., Editl. Bd. Internat. Jour. of Eating Disorders. Fellow: Am. Coll. Physicans; mem.: Phi Beta Kappa, Alpha Omega Alpha. Office: Denver Health Med Ctr 660 Bannock St MC0278 Denver CO 80204

MEHLER, RONALD W., science educator; PhD, U. Tex., Dallas, 2003. Prof. Calif. State U., Northridge, 2005—. Office: Calif State Univ Northridge 18111 Nordhoff St Northridge CA 91326

MEHLINGER, HOWARD DEAN, education educator; b. Hillsboro, Kans., Aug. 22, 1931; s. Alex and Alice Hilda (Skibbe) Mehlinger; m. Carolee Ann Case, Dec. 28, 1952; children: Bradley Case, Barbara Ann, Susan Kay. BA, McPherson Coll., Kans., 1953; MS in Edn, U. Kans., 1959, PhD, 1964. Co-dir. social studies project Pitts. pub. schs., 1963-64; asst. dir. fgn. relations project North Central Assn. Schs. and Colls., Chgo., 1964-65; mem. faculty Ind. U., Bloomington, 1965-97, prof. history and edn., 1974-97, dean Sch. Edn., 1981-90, dir. Ctr. for Excellence in Edn., 1990-99. Social studies adviser Houghton Mifflin Pub. Co.; cons. U.S. Office Edn. Co-author: American Political Behavior, 2d edit., 1977, Count Witte and the Tsarist Government in the 1905 Revolution, 1972, Toward Effective Instruction in the Social Studies, 1974, School Reform in the Information Age, 1995, Technology and Teacher Education: A Guide for Educators and Policymakers, 2002; editl. bd. Education and Society, history tchr.; editor: UNESCO Handbook on the Teaching of Social Studies, 1981; co-editor: Yearbook on the Social Studies, 1981. STAG grantee Dept. State, 1975 Mem. NEA, Nat. Council Social Studies, Phi Beta Kappa, Phi Alpha Theta, Pi Sigma Alpha, Phi Delta Kappa. Home: 3271 N Ramble Rd E Bloomington IN 47408-1094

MEHLMAN, BRUCE P., lobbyist, lawyer, formal federal agency administrator; s. Arthur and Judy Mehlman; married; 3 children. Grad., Princeton U., U. Va. Gen. counsel Nat. Rep. Congl. Com., 1996—99; gen. counsel, policy dir. House Rep. Conf.; telecom. policy counsel Cisco Sys., 1999—2001; asst. sec. for tech. policy US Dept. Commerce, Washington, 2001—04; exec. dir. Computer Systems Policy Project, Washington, 2004—; co-founder, ptnr. Mehlman Vogel Castagnetti, Washington. Exec. dir. Tech. CEO Coun.; mem. Coun. of Fgn. Rels. Named one of 50 Top Lobbyists, Washingtonian mag., 2007. Republican. Office: Mehlman Vogel Castagnetti Ste 1100 1341 G St NW Washington DC 20005 Office Phone: 202-585-0258. Office Fax: 202-393-3031. E-mail: bruce@mvc-dc.com.*

MEHLMAN, EDWIN STEPHEN, endodontist; b. Hartford, Conn., Nov. 30, 1935; s. Sol Abraham and Rose (Slitt) M.; m. Lesley Judith Lunin, June 13, 1959; children: Jeffrey Cole, Brian Scott, Erik Van. BA, Wesleyan U., 1957; DDS, U. Pa., 1961; cert. endodontics, Boston U., 1965. Diplomate Am. Bd. Endodontists. Instr. oral medicine Sch. Dental Medicine Harvard U., Boston, 1965—67; clin. instr. endodontics Sch. Dental Medicine Tufts U., Boston, 1968—70; lectr. endodontics Sch. Dental Medicine, Harvard U., Boston, 1970—72, asst. clin. prof. endodontics, 1972—; staff assoc. Forsyth Dental Ctr., Boston, 1965—; asst. prof. endodontics Boston U. Sch. Dental Medicine, 1995—; pvt. practice Providence, 1965—. Vis. lectr. dental hygiene U. R.I., Kingston, 1965-71, Community Coll. R.I., Lincoln, 1990—; cons. com. on accreditation of Dentists and Dental Aux. Edn. Programs, 1974-78. Contbr. articles to profl. jours. Pres. Temple Habonim, Barrington, R.I., 1968-70, Bur. Jewish Edn. of R.I., 1980-84; area v.p. Jewish Fedn. R.I., 1975-78; mem. R.I. Legis. Commn. to Study Malpractice Crisis, 1985-86; chmn. R.I. Dental Polit. Action Com., 1987-90. Capt. USAF, 1961-63. Recipient Etherington award Six N.E. Dental Assns. for Outstanding Contbns. to Dentistry, Disting. Fellow Internat. Coll. Dentists, 2004, Dist. Alumni award for svc. to dentistry Boston U. Goldman Sch. Dentistry, 2005 Fellow Am. Coll. Dentists (Vol. Yr. 2004), Internat. Coll. Dentists (dep. regent 1994-98), Pierre Fauchard Acad. (Merit award, Leadership award 2006, Rida Kershaw award for outstanding contbn. to cmty. 2006); mem. ADA (coun. on govt. affairs and fed. dental svcs. 1988-92, vice-chmn. 1991-92, 1st v.p. 1994-95, 1st dist. trustee 1999-2003), Am. Assn. Endodontists (dir. 1988-91), R.I. Dental Assn. (pres. 1986-87), N.E. Dental Assns. (Outstanding N.E. Dentist 1995, Disting. Practitioner 2000), NE Dental Soc. (bd. mem. 2009-). Jewish. Avocations: reading, civic activities. Home: 3 Hanley Farm Rd Warren RI 02885-4376 also: 130 Waterman St Providence RI 02906-2010

MEHLMAN, KEN (KENNETH BRIAN MEHLMAN), public relations executive; b. Balt., Aug. 21, 1966; s. Arthur and Judy Mehlman. BA, Franklin & Marshall, 1988; JD, Harvard U., 1991. Bar: DC, Md. Assoc. Akin Gump Strauss Hauer & Feld LLP, 1991—94; legis. dir. to Rep. Lamar Smith US Congress, 1994—96, chief of staff to Rep. Kay Granger, 1996—99; nat. field dir. Bush-Cheney campaign, 1997—2000; dep. asst. to Pres. & dir. pub. affairs The White House, 2001—03; chmn. Bush-Cheney campaign, 2004, Rep. Nat. Com., 2005—07; ptnr. Akin Gump Strauss Hauer & Feld LLP, Washington, 2007—08; mng. dir., head pub. affairs Kohlberg Kravis Roberts & Co., NYC, 2008—. Trustee Harvard U. Inst. Politics; bd. dirs. Nat. Endowment for Democracy. Trustee US Holocaust Meml. Mus., Franklin & Marshall Coll., 2003—, Strong Am. Schools Found. Named Campaign Mgr. of the Yr., Am. Assn. Polit. Consultants, 2005. Mem.: Maryland State Bar Assn., DC Bar Assn., Coun. Fgn. Rels., Phi Kappa Tau. Republican. Jewish. Office: Kohlberg Kravis Roberts & Co 9 W 57th St Ste 4200 New York NY 10019

MEHLMAN, MARK FRANKLIN, lawyer; b. LA, Dec. 18, 1947; s. Jack and Elaine Pearl (Lopater) M.; m. Barbara Ann Novak, Aug. 20, 1972; children: David, Jennifer, Ilyse. BA, U. Ill., 1969; LLB, U. Mich., 1973. Bar: Ill. 1973; U.S. Dist. Ct. (no. dist.) Ill. 1973. Assoc. Sonnenschein, Nath & Rosenthal LLP, Chgo., 1973—80, ptnr., 1980—, mem. policy and planning com., 1989—2006. Trustee Groveland Health Svcs., Highland Park (Ill.) Hosp., 1991-97; trustee, treas., exec. com. Spertus Inst. Jewish Studies, Chgo., 1992-97, vice chmn. bd. trustees, 1996—; vice-chmn. regional bd. Anti-Defamation League, 1987-89, hon. life mem. nat. commn., 1993—. Fellow Am. Bar Found.; mem. ABA (chmn. mortgages and other debt financing subcom. 1991-95, supervisory coun. 1997-2000, sec. RPPT sect. 2004-05), Am. Coll. Real Estate Lawyers (chmn. MDP com. 2000—, chmn. mem. selection com. 2000-01, immediate past pres. 2009-, exec. com. bd. govs. 2000—, sec. 2003-04, treas. 2004-05, v.p. 2005-06, pres.2008-09, chmn. nominating com. 2009) Anglo-Am. Real Property Inst., Legal Club of Chgo., Lake Shore Country Club, Exec. Club of Chgo. Office: Sonnenschein Nath & Rosenthal LLP Ste 7800 233 S Wacker Dr Chicago IL 60606-6491 Office Phone: 312-876-8023. Business E-Mail: mmehlman@sonnenschein.com.

MEHLMAN, MAXWELL JONATHAN, law educator; b. Washington, Nov. 4, 1948; s. Jacob and Betty (Hoffman) M.; m. Cheryl A. Stone, Sept. 15, 1979; children: Aurora, Gabriel. BA, Reed Coll., 1970, Oxford U., England, 1972; JD, Yale U., 1975. Bar: D.C. 1976, Ohio 1988. Assoc. Arnold & Porter, Washington, 1975-84; asst. prof. Case Western Res. U., Cleve., 1984-87, dir. Law-Medicine Ctr., 1986—, assoc. prof., 1987-90, prof. law, 1990-96, Arthur E. Petersilge prof., 1996—, prof. biomed. ethics, 1998—. Spl. counsel N.Y. State Bar, N.Y.C., 1988-94, Nat. Kidney Found., 1991; cons. Am. Assn. Ret. Persons, Washington, 1992. Editor: High Tech Home Care, 1991, (with T. Murray) Encyclopedia of Ethical, Legal and Policy Issues in Biotechnology; author: (with J. Botkin) Access to the Genome: The Challenge to Equality, 1998, (with Andrews and Rothstein) Genetics: Ethics, Law and Policy, 2002, 06, Wondergenes: Genetic Enhancement and the Future of Society, 2003; contbr. articles to profl. jours. Active steering com. AIDS Commn. Greater Cleve., 1986-90. Rhodes scholar, 1970; Rsch. grantee NIH, 1992-94, 97—. Mem. Am. Assn. Law Schs. (chmn. sect. on law, medicine and health care 1990), Phi Beta Kappa. Avocations: skiing, music, kayaking. Office: Case Western Reserve U Sch Law-Law Medicine Ctr Gund Hall 11075 E Blvd Cleveland OH 44106 Office Phone: 216-368-3983. Business E-Mail: mjm10@case.edu.

MEHLTRETTER, KATHLEEN M., prosecutor; b. 1954; BS, Univ. of Dayton; JD, State Univ. of NY at Buffalo. Bar: New York 1979. First asst. US atty. (we. dist.) NY US Dept. Justice, Buffalo, acting US atty. (we. dist.) NY, 2005—06, acting U.S. atty., 2009. Office: US Atty 138 Delaware Ave Buffalo NY 14202 Office Phone: 716-843-5700. Office Fax: 716-551-3052.*

MEHNE, PAUL RANDOLPH, consultant, retired medical educator; b. Wilmington, Del., May 27, 1948; s. Paul Herbert and Doris Ruth (Longfritz) M.; m. Carol Ann (Starner), June 12, 1971; children: Meredith Lynn, and Amy Elizabeth. BS in Environ. Sci., SUNY, Syracuse, 1970; PhD, SUNY, 1976, Syracuse Univ., 1976. Asst. prof. East Carolina U. Allied Health, Greenville, NC, 1975-76; assoc. dir. East Carolina U. Ctr. Edn., Devel., and Evaluation, Greenville, NC, 1976-79; coord. of curriculum East Carolina U. Sch. Medicine, Greenville, NC, 1979—81, asst. dean, 1981-85, assoc. dean, 1985—89, assoc. prof., 1988—89, dir. Ctr. Health Sci., Edn., and Info., 1988—89; assoc. dean U. Pa., Phila., 1989—91; assoc. dean acad. and student affairs, assoc. prof. family medicine Robert Wood Johnson Med. Sch., Piscataway, NJ, 1992—2007; chair U. wide tele medicine video com distance learning com. Univ. Medicine and Dentistry N.J., 1995-2000, chmn. acad. info. tech. adv. com., 1996-98, 2005—06. Chmn. exec. bd. dir. MEDCOMP Super computer Consortium, Athens, Ga., 1986—89; vis. prof. U. N.C., Chapel Hill, 1986, Tulane U., New Orleans, 1988. Contbr. articles to profl. jour. Chmn. Cmty. Appearance Commn., Greenville, NC, 1980—85; ex officio trustee Cooper Univ. Hosp., 2001—07. Grantee NJ Dept. Health and Sr. Svcs., 2003-04; recipient Interactive Video Instrn. Award Digital Equipment Corp., 1985, Med. Edn. Cost Containment award Kate B. Reynolds Health Care Trust, 1985-88, Telemedicine and Med. Informatics Award, 1996-99, US Dept. Commerce NTIA/TIIAP Award for tele-medicine, 1996-98. Mem. IEEE, APHA, Am. Coll. Pers. Assn., Assn. for Med. Edn. and Rsch. on Substance Abuse, Am. Med. Informatics Assn., Am. Edn. Rsch. Assn., Assn. Am. Med. Colls. (chair consortium on student and profl. well being 1993-94, steering com. Clin. Campus Deans 2000—07, chair AAMC Group on Regional Med. Campuses 2005-06, past chmn. 2006—07), Soc. Tchrs. Family Medicine, Alpha Omega Alpha. Office Phone: 610-446-4445. Personal E-mail: pmehne@gmail.com.

MEHO, LOKMAN I., library and information scientist, educator; arrived in US, 1996; s. Ibrahim Y. Meho and Layla S. Hussein. BA in Polit. Sci., Am. U. Beirut, 1991, MA in Polit. Sci., 1996; MS in Libr. Sci., N.C. Ctrl. U., Durham, 1996; PhD in Info. and Libr. Sci., U. N.C., Chapel Hill, 2001. Libr. asst. Am. U. Beirut, 1986—95; freelance bibliographer Lebanon and U.S., 1991—; lectr. Sch. Libr. and Info. Scis. N.C. Ctrl. U., Durham, 1997—98; tchg. fellow Sch. Info. and Libr. Sci. U. N.C., Chapel Hill, 1999—2001; asst. prof. SUNY, Albany, 2001—04, Ind. U., Bloomington, 2004—08, assoc. prof., 2008—, dir., MLS program, 2008—. Author: Libraries and Information in the Arab World, 1999, Kurdish Culture and Society, 2001, Kurdish Question in U.S. Foreign Policy, 2004, Censorship in the Arab World, 2006. Sec. Lebanese Kurdish Charity Assn., Beirut, 1992—95; youth mem. Lebanese Red Cross, Beirut, 1989—95. Mem.: Assn. Libr. and Info. Sci. Edn., Assn. Coll. and Rsch. Librs., ALA, Am. Soc. Info. Sci. and Tech. Avocations: soccer, reading, painting. Office: Ind Univ 1320 E 10th St LI 011 Bloomington IN 47405 Home Phone: 812-320-0437; Office Phone: 812-856-2323. Office Fax: 812-855-6166. Business E-Mail: meho@indiana.edu.

MEHRA, JAGDISH, economics professor; b. Amritsar, Punjab, India, Nov. 12, 1934; came to U.S., 1962; s. Manmohan and Savitri (Devi) M.; m. Sneh L. Mehra, May 19, 1949; children: Reena, Benu. BA, Birla Inst. Tech., Pilani, Rajasthan, 1955, MA, 1957; PhD, SUNY, Buffalo, 1970. Asst. prof. econs. Banasthali U., Rajasthan, 1959-60; rschr. Nat. Coun. Applied Econ. Rsch., New Delhi, 1960-61; asst. prof. Econs. Birla Inst. Tech., Pilani, 1961-62; grad. asst., econs. instr. SUNY, Buffalo, 1962-65; asst. prof. econs. Youngstown (Ohio) U., 1965-71, assoc. prof. econs., 1971-81, prof. econs., 1981—2003, prof. emeritus, 2003—; sr. rsch. fellow Am. Inst. Econ. Rsch., Great Barrington, Mass., 1982-83. Contbr. articles to profl. jours. Avocations: reading, tennis. Office: Youngstown State U Dept Econs 1 University Plz Youngstown OH 44555 Home Phone: 330-792-3363; Office Phone: 330-941-1681.

MEHRA, MANDEEP RAJINDER, cardiologist; b. Delhi, Dec. 3, 1964; came to US, 1989; p. Rajinder Pershad and Neeta (Khanna) M.; m. Gayatri Lall, May 5, 1990; children: Anshul, Lushna, Rishka. MD, Nagpur U., 1988. Intern Mt. Carmel Med. Ctr., Ohio State U., Columbus, 1989-90, resident internal medicine, 1990-92; fellow cardiology Alton Ochsner Med. Found., New Orleans, 1992-95; dir. heart failure Ochsner Med. Instns., New Orleans, 1995—2005, dir. ambulatory svcs. advanced heart failure, 1997—2005, sect. head advanced heart failure, cardiac transplant, 1997—2005; Herbert Berger prof., chief cardiology

U. Md., 2005—. Sci. reviewer Chest, Jour. Heart and Lung Transplantation, IM-Internal Medicine, ACP Jour. Club, Clin. Cardiology, Evidence Based Medicine; contbr. chpts. to books and articles to profl. jours. Mem. ACP, AMA, Am. Coll. Cardiology, Am. Soc. Internal Medicine, Am. Coll. Chest Physicians, So. Med. Assn., Internat. Soc. Heart and Lung Transplantation, Heart Failure Soc. Am., Am. Soc. Transplant Physicians (Young Investigator award 1995). Office: 22 5th Greene St 53B06 Baltimore MD 21201 Home: 4 Padonia Woods Ct Cockeysville MD 21030 Office Phone: 410-328-7716, 410-328-7716. Office Fax: 410-328-4382. E-mail: mmehra@medicine.umaryland.edu.

MEHRA, RAMAN KUMAR, aerospace and defense technology executive, automotion and control engineering researcher; b. Lahore, Punjab, India, Feb. 10, 1943; came to U.S., 1964; s. Madan Mohan and Vidya Vati (Khanna) M.; m. Anjoo Talwar; children: Archana, Mandira, Kunal. BEE, Punjab Engrng. Coll., 1964; MS in Engrng., Harvard U., 1965, PhD, 1968. Assoc. prof. Harvard U., Cambridge, Mass., 1972-76; pres., chief exec. officer Sci. Systems, Co., Inc., Woburn, Mass., 1976—. Author: System Identification, 1976; also tech. papers on model algorithmic control (Best Paper award Internat. Fedn. Automatic Control, 1983). Recipient Eckman award Am. Automatic Control Coun., St. Louis, 1971. Fellow IEEE. Avocations: hiking, golf, tennis. Home: 5 Angier Rd Lexington MA 02420-1608 Office: Sci Systems Co Inc 500 W Cummings Park Woburn MA 01801-6503 Office Phone: 781-933-5355. Personal E-mail: rkmehra@rcn.com. Business E-Mail: rkm@ssci.com.

MEHRBERG, RANDALL ERIC, lawyer, utilities executive; b. Bklyn., Dec. 29, 1955; s. Julius and June (Shapiro) M.; m. Michele Schara, Oct. 20, 1984; children: Dillon, Sam, Eric. BS magna cum laude in Economics, U. Pa., 1977; JD, U. Mich., 1980. Bar: Ill. 1980, US Dist. Ct. (no. dist. Ill.) 1980, US Ct. Appeals (7th cir.) 1981, US Supreme Ct. 1987. Equity ptnr. Jenner & Block, Chgo., 1980—93, 1997—2000; gen. counsel, lakefront dir. Chgo. Pk. Dist., 1993—97; sr. v.p., gen. counsel Exelon Corp., Chgo., 2000—02, exec. v.p., gen. counsel, 2002—06, chief adminstrv. officer, chief legal officer, 2006—08; exec. v.p. planning & strategy PSEG Inc., Newark, 2008—. Asst. sec. Chgo. Pacific Corp., 1984—85; bd. mem. Nuc. Electric Ins. Ltd. V.p. bd. dirs. Gus Giordano Jazzdance Chgo. Recipient Hope for the People award, HOPE Fair Housing, Ill., 1982, commendation for work for the poor, Cath. Charities, 1986, award for def. of civil liberties, ACLU, 1987, Mex. Am. Legal Def. and Edn. Fund Legal Svcs. award, 2001. Mem. ABA, Chgo. Bar Assn. (exec. com. young lawyers sect. 1988-89, David C. Hilliard award), Chgo. Counsel Lawyers, Law Club Chgo. Avocations: tennis, skiing, hockey. Mailing: PSEG PO Box 570 Newark NJ 07101*

MEHRENS, CHRISTOPHER EMILE, musicologist, music librarian; b. Renton, Wash., May 3, 1959; s. George Francis and Gloria Longville Mehrens. MusB in Music History, U. Wash., Seattle, 1982; MA in Music History, U. NC, Chapel Hill, 1987; MLS, Ind. U., Bloomington, 2002—02; PhD in Musicology, U. NC, Chapel Hill, 1998. Music libr. Ind. State U., Terre Haute, 2002—. Cons. Shenyang (China) Conservatory of Music, 2006—. Contbr. biog. dictionary, articles to profl. jours. 1st v.p. Vigo County Hist. Soc., Terre Haute, 2005, mem., 2003. Mem.: ALA, Internat. Music Libr. Assn., Music Libr. Assn. (mem. outreach subcom. 2003—, Walter Gerboth award 2005), Am. Musicol. Soc., Am. Assn. of Museums, Beta Phi Mu. Office: Ind State U Cunningham Memorial Library Terre Haute IN 47809 E-mail: libmehr@isugw.indstate.edu.

MEHRETU, JULIE, artist; b. Addis Ababa, Ethiopia, 1970; Attended, U. Cheik Anta Diop, Dakar, Senegal, 1990—91; BA, Kalamazoo Coll., 1992; MFA with honors, RI Sch. Design, 1997. Greater New York, P.S.1 Contemporary Arts Ctr., NY, 2000, exhibited in group shows, Ctr. Curatorial Studies, Bard College, Annandale-on-Hudson, 2000, Free Style, Studio Mus. Harlem, 2001, The Americans, Barbican Gallery, London, 2001, Busan Biennale, Korea, 2002, 8th Baltic Triennial Vilnius, Lithuania, 2002, Drawing Now: Eight Propositions, Mus. Modern Art, 2002, Painting at the Edge of the World, Walker Art Ctr., 2003, one-woman shows include, Sol Kofler Gallery, Providence, RI, 1995, Ancestral Reflections, Archive Gallery, NY, 1995, Bombastic Righteous Passively Become Apparent Absurdities, Sol Kofler Gallery, Providence, RI, 1996, Recent Work, Barbara Davis Gallery, Houston, 1998, Module, Project Row Houses, Houston, 1999, The Project, NYC, 2001, Art Pace, San Antonio, Tex., 2001, White Cube, London, 2002, Julie Mehretu: Drawing into Painting, Walker Art Ctr. (travelling), 2003, REDCAT, LA, Calif., 2004, Albright-Knox Art Gallery, Buffalo, NY, 2004, Matrix, U. Calif. Berkeley Art Mus., 2004, earlier 1 gebauer, Berlin, Germany, 2004, Drawing, The Project, NYC, 2005, Current, St. Louis Art Mus., 2005, exhibited in group shows at Carnegie Internat., Carnegie Mus. Art, Pitts., Pa., 2004, Sao Paulo Biennial, San Paulo, Brazil, 2004, Whitney Biennal, The Whitney Mus. Am. Art, NYC, 2004, Back to Paint, C&M Arts, NYC, 2004, Firewall, Ausstellungshalle Zeitgenössische Kunst, Munster, Germany, 2004, exhibitions include New Drawings, Kresge Museum Art, East Lansing, 2008, Black City, Louisiana Museum of Modern Art, Humlebaek, Denmark, 2007; contbr. to numerous art articles. Recipient Excellence Award, RI Sch. Design, 1996, Penny McCall Award, 2001, Berlin prize, Am. Acad. in Berlin, 2007, Rhode Island Sch. Design Alumni Council Artistic Achievement award, RI, 2006, Am. Art award, Whitney Museum Art, NY, 2005, Distinguished Alumni achievement awad, Kalamanzoo Coll., Mich., 2005, Artist-in-residency, Walker Art Center, Minneapolis, 2003, Headlands Ctr. Arts, Sausalito, Calif., 2003, Pat Hearn Inaugural award, 2001, CORE Program, Glassell Sch Art, Museum Fine Arts, Houston, 1997—98, Rhode Island Sch. Design Presidential scholar Fall Tuition award, 1995—97; grantee Guna S. Mundeheim fellowship, Am. Acad. in Berlin, 2007, Joan Mitchell Found. grant, 2003, Penny McCall Found. grant, 2002, The Louis Comfort Tiffany Found grant, 2001, Air Program Studio Museum in Harlem, NY, 2001; Core Fellowship, Artist in Residence, Glassell Sch. Art, Mus. Fine Arts, Houston, 1997—99, MacArthur Fellow, John D. and Catherine T. MacArthur Found., 2005. Address: The Project 37 W 57th St 3rd Fl New York NY 10019

MEHRI, CYRUS B., lawyer; b. 1961; BA, Hartwick Coll., 1983; JD, Cornell Law Sch., 1988. Law clk. to Hon. John T. Nixon US Dist. Ct. (middle dist.) Tenn.; founding ptnr. Mehri & Skalet PLLC. Counsel Fritz Pollard Alliance. Co-author: Slipping Back to Business As Usual, Six Months After the Passage of Sarbanes-Oxley, 2003, One Nation, Indivisible: The Use of Diversity Report Cards to Promote Transparency, Accountability, and Workplace Fairness. Recipient Outstanding Youth Alumnus award, Hartwick Coll., Alumni award, Wooster Sch., Distinguished Visitor award, Miami-Dade County Office Mayor & Bd. County Commrs., 2007; named Corp. America's Scariest Opponent, Workforce Mag., 2003; named one of Washington's Ten Most Feared Lawyers, Regardie's Power mag., 2001. Office: Mehri & Skalet PLLC 1250 Connecticut Ave NW Ste 300 Washington DC 20036 Office Phone: 202-822-5100. Office Fax: 202-822-4997. E-mail: cmehri@findjustice.com.*

MEHTA, ASHESH, neurologist; MD in Neuroscience, PhD in Neuroscience, Albert Einstein Coll. Medicine. Resident in neurosurgery Cornell U. NY Presbyterian Hosp.; resident in neuro-oncology Memorial Sloan Kettering Cancer Ctr.; dir. epilepsy surgery Long Island Jewish Med. Ctr. Comprehensive Epilepsy Ctr., 2006—. Mem.: Am. Assn. Stereotactic & Functional Neurosurgery, Congress Neurological Surgeons, Am. Assn. Neurological Surgeons, Soc. for Neuroscience, Am. Epilepsy Soc., Epilepsy Found. Long Island (profl. adv. bd.). Office: 270-05 76th Ave New Hyde Park NY 11040*

MEHTA, EILEEN ROSE, lawyer; b. Colver, Pa., Apr. 1, 1953; d. Richard Glenn and Helen (Wahna) Ball; m. Abdul Rashid Mehta, Aug. 31, 1973. Student, Miami U., 1971-73; BA with distinction, Fla. Internat. U., 1974; JD cum laude, U. Miami, 1977. Bar: Fla. 1977, US Dist. Ct. (so. dist.) Fla. 1977, US Ct. Appeals (11th cir.) 1981. Law clk. to presiding judge US Dist. Ct. (so. dist.) Fla., Miami, 1977-79; asst. atty. County of Dade, Miami, 1979-89; shareholder Fine Jacobson Schwartz Nash Block & England, Miami, Fla., 1989-94; ptnr. Eckert Seamans Cherin & Mellott, Miami, 1994-98, Bilzin Sumberg Baena Price & Axelrod, Miami, 1998—. Lectr. in field. Miami U. scholar, 1971-73. Mem. Fla. Bar Assn., Dade County Bar Assn. Office: Bilzin Sumberg Baena Price & Axelrod 200 S Biscayne Blvd Ste 2500 Miami FL 33131 Office Phone: 305-350-2380. Business E-Mail: emehta@bilzin.com.

MEHTA, JAWAHAR LAL, cardiologist; b. India, Aug. 10, 1946; arrived in US, 1970; s. Mohan L. and Ishwar D. (Valecha) M.; m. Paulette Smedresman, Oct. 20, 1977; children: Asha, Jason. MD, GN Med. Coll. U. Amritsar, 1968; PhD, Uppsala U., Sweden. Diplomate Am. Bd. Internal Medicine, Am. Bd. Cardiovascular Diseases. Intern N.Y. Med. Coll., Valhalla, NY, 1970, resident in pediat., 1971; resident in internal medicine Mt. Sinai-Beth Israel Hosp., NYC, 1971-73; fellow in cardiology SUNY, NY, 1973-75; from asst. prof. to prof. medicine & physiology U. Fla. Coll. Medicine, Gainesville, 1976-2000; dir. molecular cardiology, Stebbins chair in cardiology U. Ark. Med. Sci., Little Rock, 2000—. Rsch. fellow, instr. in medicine U. Minn., Mpls., 1975—76; staff physician VA Med. Ctr., Gainesville, 1976—2000, clin. investigator, 1980—85; dir. cardiology svcs. Ctrl. Ark. Vets. Healthcare Sys., 2000—. Fellow: ACP, Am. Heart Assn., Am. Coll. Cardiology; mem.: Assn. Univ. Cardiologists, Assn. Am. Physicians, Am. Soc. Clin. Investigation. Office: U Ark for Med Scis Slot 532 Little Rock AR 72205-7199

MEHTA, KIRAN H., lawyer; AB magna cum laude, Cornell U., 1978; JD cum laude, Harvard U., 1981. Bar: NC 1983. Law clk. Chief Judge Frank A. Kaufman, US Dist. Ct. (Md. Dist.), 1982—82; ptnr. litigation dept. Kennedy Covington, Charlotte, NC. Contbr. articles to profl. jours., chapters to books. Dean, solid & hazardous waste Charlotte C. of C. Environ. Sch., 1991—94, chmn. hazardous waste/superfund com., 1992—94; dir. Cmty. Sch. Arts, 1997—; mem. supt. council Charlotte-Mecklenburg Sch. Sys., 1999. Mem.: ABA, NC Bar Assn., Mecklenburg County Bar Assn., Phi Beta Kappa. Office: Kennedy Covington Hearst Tower 47th Fl 214 N Tryon St Charlotte NC 28202 Office Phone: 704-331-7437. Office Fax: 704-353-3137. Business E-Mail: kmehta@kennedycovington.com.

MEHTA, LINN CARY, literature educator; b. Chgo., Aug. 8, 1955; d. William Lucius and Katherine L.F. (Cooper) Cary; m. Ved Mehta, Dec. 17, 1983; children: Alexandra Sage, Natasha Cary. BA in English and French, Yale U., 1977; MA in English, Oxford U., 1979; MPhil in Comparative Lit., Columbia U., 1989, PhD in Comparative Lit., 2004. Asst. to pres. Ford Found., NYC, 1980—82, asst. program officer, 1982—85; preceptor Columbia U., NYC, 1990—91; instr. Yale U., New Haven, 1993; instr., adj. asst. prof. English dept. Vassar Coll., Poughkeepsie, NY, 1994—97; lectr. English dept. Barnard Coll., NYC, 2000—; fellow Heyman Ctr. humanities, Columbia U., Spring, 2008. Chair bd. Am. Friends St. Hilda's Coll., Boston, 1995-02; sec. bd. Wrexham Found., New Haven, 1988-94; lit. advisor English adaptation of play "Allende" for Theater for a New City, 2006, Paso Del Norte, 2009. Bd. pres. Ctr. for Traditional Music and Dance, NYC, 1989-94, v.p., 2000—; pres. Lexington 79th Corp., NYC, 1993-97; bd. dirs. Norman Rockwell Mus., Stockbridge, Mass., 1991-96, NY Soc. Libr., 2002—, Goddard Riverside C0mty. Ctr., 2007—; adv. bd. Appalshop, Whitesburg, Ky., 1990-92. Mem. MLA, Am. Comparative Lit. Assn., Thursday Evening Club (pres. 1998-2001), Grolier Club. Avocations: music, poetry, languages. Office: English Dept Barnard Coll Columbia U 3009 Broadway New York NY 10027 Business E-Mail: lmehta@barnard.edu.

MEHTA, MANISH, surgeon; b. New Delhi, Feb. 10, 1967; m. Beulah Mehta; children: Joshuah, Sarah, Hanah. MD, MPH, NY Med. Coll., Valhallah, 1994. Cert. in gen. surgery Am. Bd. Surgery, 2001, in gen. vascular surgery 2003. Dir., endovascular svcs. Vascular Group, PLLC, Albany, NY, 2001—; pres. & CEO Ctr. Vascular Awareness, Albany, 2004—. Assoc. prof. surgery Albany Med. Coll., 2006—. Contbr. articles to profl. jours. Fellow: ACS; mem.: New Eng. Soc. Vascular Surgery, Eastern Vascular Soc., Soc. Clin. Vascular Surgery, Soc. Vascular Surgery. Office: Vascular Group PLLC 43 New Scotland Ave MC157 Albany NY 12208 Office Fax: 518-262-6720.

MEHTA, PRAKASH H., lawyer; b. Boulder, Colo. BS summa cum laude, Georgetown U., Washington, 1991, JD magna cum laude, 1994. Bar: Washington 1994, Md. 1994. Atty. Clifford Chance, Washington; ptnr. Akin Gump Strauss Hauer & Feld LLP, Washington. Mem. adv. bd. Emerging Markets Pvt. Equity Assn. Named one of 50 Most Influential Minority Lawyers in America, Nat. Law Jour., 2008, 10 Rising Stars, Pvt. Equity and M&A Law, Instl. Investor, 2008. Mem.: Indian Am. Bar Assn. Office: Akin Gump Strauss Hauer & Feld LLP 1333 New Hampshire Avenue NW Washington DC 20036 Office Fax: 202-887-4288. E-mail: pmehta@akingump.com.*

MEHTA, RAJENDRA G., research scientist, educator; m. Raksha Mehta, Feb. 23, 1976; children: Sonkulp, Prerak. PhD, U. Nebr., Lincoln, 1974. Sci. advisor IIT Rsch. Inst., Chgo., 1977—92; prof. U. Ill. Med. Sch., 1992—; asst. vice pres., prof. IIT Rsch. Inst., 2004—. Contbr. articles to profl. jours. Mem.: Am. Assn. Cancer Rsch. Home: 11721 Springbrook Ct Orland Park IL 60467 Office: IIT Rsch Inst 10 W 35th St Chicago IL 60616 Personal E-mail: rajuraksha@gmail.com. Business E-Mail: rmehta@iitri.org.

MEHTA, RUBY, pediatric gastroenterologist; b. Bikaner, Rajasthan, India, Jan. 4, 1974; d. Mahendra Singh and Gyanwati Baid Mehta. MD, Jawahar Lal Nehru Med. Coll., 2000, Brookdale U. Hosp. Med. Ctr., 2007, Children's Hosp. Mich., Detroit, 2007. Transitional intern Jawahar Lal Nehru Med. Coll., Ajmer, Rajasthan, India, 1999—2000; rsch. assoc. Advanced Gastro Assocs., Tampa, Fla., 2002—04; resident Brookdale U. Hosp. Med. Ctr., Bklyn., 2004—07; pediat. gastroenterology fellow Children's Hosp. Mich., Detroit, 2007—. Vol. Nat. Pulse Polio, Ajmer, Rajasthan, India, 1995—2000, AAP, Bklyn., 2007. Grantee, Ea. Pediatric Rsch. Soc., 2007. Mem.: AMA, Am. Coll. Gastroenterology, Am. Gastroenterology Assn., N.Am. Soc. Pediat. Gastroenterology, Hepatology and Nutrition, Am. Acad. Pediat. Office: Children's Hospital Mich 3901 Beaubien St Detroit MI 48201

MEHTA, SWATI, electrical engineer, researcher; d. Ashok and Chandrakanta Mehta; m. Sharad Verma, Jan. 9, 2006. BEE, Indian Inst. Tech., Mumbai, India, 1999; MSE ECE, 2001; PhD ECE, Johns Hopkins U., Balt., 2006. Rsch. asst. Johns Hopkins U., 1999—2006; staff engr., sensor design Canesta Inc, Sunnyvale, Calif., 2006—. Intern Intel Corp., Hudson, Mass., 2004. Mem.: IEEE. Office: Canesta Inc 440 N Wolfe Rd Ste 101 Sunnyvale CA 94085

MEHTA, VISHAL M., orthopedist; m. Shefali Oza, May 28, 2000; children: Saachi Vishal, Shiv Vishal, Shaan Vishal. MD, U. Ill. Diplomate Am. Bd. Orthopaedic Surgeon, 2007. Sports medicine surgeon Fox Valley Orthopaedic Inst., Geneva, Ill., 2006—, pres. and founder, 2007—, dir. cartilage restoration, 2006—. Founder Found. Internat. Orthopaedic Devel., Chgo., 2007—09. Mem.: IAOS, AAOS. Achievements include patents for rotator cuff repair device; design of numerous sports medicine devices. Office: 2525 Kaneville Rd Geneva IL 60134

MEHTA, ZARIN, performing company executive; b. Bombay, Oct. 28, 1938; arrived in Can., 1962, naturalized, 1969; s. Mehli and Tehmina Mehta; m. Carmen Lasky, July 1, 1966; children: Rohanna, Rustom. Chartered acct., London, 1957. Acct. Frederic B. Smart & Co., London, 1957—62, Coopers & Lybrand, Mont., Que., Canada, 1962—81; mng. dir. Orchestre Symphonique de Mont., 1981—90; exec. dir., COO Ravinia Festival, 1990—2000; exec. dir. NY Philharm, 2000—, pres., 2004—. Recipient Bravo award, Dominican Repub., 1996, Arts Entrepreneurship award, Columbia Coll., 1997, Dushkin award, Music Inst. Chgo., 1998. Fellow: Inst. Chartered Accts. in Eng. and Wales; mem.: Ordre des Comptables Agrees de Que. Office: NY Philharm Avery Fisher Hall 10 Lincoln Center Plaza New York NY 10023-6990 Business E-Mail: mehtaz@nyphil.org.

MEHURON, WILLIAM OTTO, retired federal official; b. Hammond, Ind., Nov. 20, 1937; s. Arthur and Margaret Irene M.; m. Charlotte Anne Nyheim, Aug. 26, 1982; children: Kimberly Anne, Kristine Lynn, Susan, Geoffrey. BSEE, Purdue U., 1959; MSEE, U. Pa., 1962, PhD, 1966. Tech. dir. naval intelligence Dept. Navy, Washington, 1974-81; dir. rsch. and engrng. Nat. Security Agy., Ft. Meade, Md., 1981-85; v.p., gen. mgr. data systems div. Ampex Corp. subs. Allied-Signal Co., Redwood City, Calif., 1985-86; sr. v.p. product ops. Daisy Systems Corp., Mountain View, Calif., 1986-88; v.p., gen. mgr. Networks and Info. Security div. Security div. Unisys Def. Systems, McLean, Va., 1988-91; pres. Mehuron Assocs. Inc., 1991-95; dir. sys. acquisition office NOAA, USG, Washington, 1995-99; dir. Info. Tech. Lab., Nat. Inst. Stds. and Tech., Gaithersburg, Md., 1999—2002; pres. Mehuron Assocs., Inc., 2002—. Avocations: amateur radio, golf, cooking. Home: 803 S Clay St Hinsdale IL 60521-4541 Office Phone: 630-995-5626. Personal E-mail: wmehuron@comcast.net.

MEI, ANHUA, mechanical engineer, researcher; b. Chongqing, China, Oct. 5, 1955; arrived in US, 2002; s. Dedong Mei and Jiyu Liu; m. Jinghui Wang, May 28, 1984; 1 child, Da. BS, Chongqing U., 1982; MS, Wuhan Tech. U. Surveying and Mapping, China, 1995; D Engrng., Lamar U., Beaumont, Tex., 2006. Asst. prof., lectr. Wuhan Tech. U. Surveying and Mapping, 1982—93, assoc. prof., 1993—98; prof. Wuhan U., 1998—2002; prin. lectr. Harare Poly. U., Zimbabwe, 1999—2002; sr. mech. engr. Perry Equipment Corp., Mineral Wells, Tex., 2006—. Presenter in field. Contbr. articles to profl. jours. Mem.: ASME, Am. Soc. Optical Engrs. Avocations: swimming, ping pong/table tennis. Home: 1676 Holland Lake Dr # 1206 Weatherford TX 76086 Office: Perry Equipment Corp 118 Washington Ave Mineral Wells TX 76086 Personal E-mail: anhuamei2002@yahoo.com.

MEIER, BEVERLY JOYCE LOEFFLER, science educator, consultant; b. Balt., June 28, 1941; d. John Thomas and Frances Lillian Loeffler; m. Thomas Meier, June 8, 1963; children: Thomas Jr., John H. BS, U. Colo., Boulder, 1963, MA, 1969. Sci. tchr. Cherry Creek Sch. Dist., Denever, 1963—65; potter Boulder Potter's Guild, 1970—77; part owner Sturtz Copeland Florist, Boulder, 1970—75; sci. tchr. Boulder Valley Sch. Dist., 1977—. Cons. sci. edn. Nat. Renewal Energy Lab, Golden, Colo., 1989—90, Nat. Oceanic Atmosphere Adminstrn., Boulder, 1993—; cons. Am. Indian Sci. Engr. Soc., Boulder, 1994. Contbr. articles to profl. jour. Adv. bd. Colo. Sci. and Engring. Fair, Ft. Collin., 1990—; dir. sci. fair Boulder Valley Sch. Dist., 1982—. Grantee Boulder Valley Impact grant, 2000, Toyota Tapestry-NSTA, 1998, Boulder Valley Impact on Edn. grant, 2006. Mem.: NSTA, Phi Delta Kappa. Avocations: anthropology, archaeology. Office: Broomfield Heights Mid Sch 1555 Daphne St Boulder CO 80305

MEIER, DIANE EVE, geriatrician, researcher, medical educator; b. Princeton, NJ, Apr. 15, 1952; d. Paul and Louise (Goldstone) Meier; m. Warren Sherman; children: Leo William, Anna Helen. BA, Oberlin Coll., 1973; MD, Northwestern U., 1977. Resident Oreg. Health Scis. U., Portland, fellow; prof. dept. geriatrics and adult devel., medicine Mt. Sinai Sch. Medicine, NYC, 1983—, dir. Hertzberg Palliative Care Inst., 1983—, dir. Ctr. to Advance Palliative Care, Catherine Gaisman prof. medical ethics. Recipient Founders Award, Nat. Hospice and Palliative Care Orgn., 2007, Academic Career Leadership Award, Nat. Inst. Aging, Open Soc. Inst.'s Faculty Scholar's Award of the Project on Death in America, Alexander Richman Commemorative Award for Humanism in Medicine, 50th Anniversary Social Impact Award, AARP, 2008, Physician of Yr. Award, Castle Connelly, 2009, Lifetime Achievement Award, Am. Acad. Hospice and Palliative Medicine, 2009; named a MacArthur Fellow, The John D. and Catherine T. MacArthur Found, 2008. Office: 1440 Madison Ave New York NY 10029 Office Phone: 212-659-8552. E-mail: diane.meier@mssm.edu.*

MEIER, FREDERICK AUGUSTUS, physician, director; b. Boston, May 12, 1948; s. Frederick Augustus and Louise Mary Meier; m. Nancy Lorraine Mason, Sept. 25, 1982; children: Emily Elizabeth Bridget, Frederick Augustus, Robert Mason. AB, Dartmouth Coll., Hanover, NH, 1970; BMS, Dartmouth Med. Sch., Hanover, NH, 1972; MD, McGill U., Montreal, Quebec, Can., CM, 1974. Diplomate in anatomic pathology Am. Bd. Pathology, 1979, in clin. pathology 1981. Staff pathologist Hitchcock Clinic, Hanover, 1980—83; clin. microbiology fellow U. Utah, Salt Lake City, 1983—85; med. dir., clin. microbiology Med. Coll. Va., Richmond, 1985—89, dir. clin. labs., 1989—92; chmn., clin. and anatomic pathology duPont Hosp. Children, Wilmington, Del., 1992—2003; dir. regional labs. Henry Ford Health Sys., Detroit, 2003—. Assoc. prof. pathology and medicine Va. Commonwealth U., Richmond, 1990—92; asso. prof. pathology and pediat. Jefferson Med. Coll., Phila., 1992—2003. Fellow: Am. Soc. Clin. Pathology, Coll. Am. Pathologists. Roman Catholic. Avocations: travel, sailing, tennis. Office: Henry Ford Hosp 2799 W Grand Blvd Detroit MI 48202

MEIER, GAYLE M., library director; b. Jackson, Miss., Sept. 7, 1944; d. Marion Omel Moulton and Dolya Lou Singleton; m. Lawrence W. Meier, Oct. 22, 1971. BA, Emory U., Atlanta, 1966, MLS, 1967, diploma in Librarianship, 1980. Libr. Wash. State U., Pullman, 1867—1968, Atlanta Pub. Libr., 1968—78, Archeol. Survey Cobb-Fulton Counties, Atlanta, 1878—1988; libr. dir. Am. Coll. Applied Arts, Atlanta, Art Inst. Atlanta, 1990—. Office: Art Inst Atlanta 6600 Peachtree Dunwoody Rd Atlanta GA 30328 Office Fax: 770-394-9800. Business E-Mail: gmeier@aii.edu.

MEIER, GEORGE HENRY, vascular surgeon; b. Atlanta, Sept. 11, 1954; m. Margaret Connifey, 4 children. BA, Rice U., 1976; MD, Emory U., 1980. Resident in gen. surgery Mass. Gen. Hosp., Boston, 1980-85, resident in vascular surgery, 1985-86, asst. in surgery, 1986-87; attending surgeon, dir. non-invasive vascular lab. West Haven (Conn.) VA Med. Ctr., 1987—97, Yale-New Haven Hosp., 1987—97; asst. prof. surgery Sch. Medicine Sch. Medicine Yale U., New Haven, 1987-92, assoc. prof., 1992—97, chief vascular surgery, 1993—97, asst. chief surg. svc., 1994—97; assoc. prof. Ea. Va. Med. Sch., 1997—, chief vascular surgery, 2000—, program dir. vascular surgery, 2000—. Welch Found. scholar, 1974-75; NSF grantee, 1975; preceptorship Am. Soc. Anesthesiologists, 1978. Mem. ACS, AMA, AAAS, Assn. Acad. Surgeons, N.Y. Acad. Scis., Internat. Soc. Cardiovascular Surgeons, New Eng. Soc. Vascular Surgeons. Office: Yale U Sch Medicine 333 Cedar St # 137 New Haven CT 06510-3289 Home: 5435 Hobbit Rd Cincinnati OH 45243-3931 Office Phone: 757-622-2649. E-mail: ghm3@aol.com.

MEIER, JOYCE, education educator; children: Amber Cooper, Joseph Cooper. MA in Spl. Edn., Clarke Coll., Dubuque, 2004. Tchr. East Dubuque Elem. Sch., Ill., 1983—2000; instr. edn. Clarke Coll., 2000—. Office: Clarke Coll 1550 Clarke Dr Dubuque IA 52001

MEIER, KATHRYN ELAINE, pharmacologist, educator, academic administrator; b. San Mateo, Calif., Apr. 28, 1953; d. Robert E. and I. Dorothy Hunt; m. G. Patrick Meier, June 16, 1975; children: Adam M., Andrea D. BA in Biology, U. Calif., San Diego, 1975; PhD in Pharmacology, U. Wis., Madison, 1981. Lab. asst., tchg. asst., rsch. fellow U. Calif. San Diego, La Jolla, 1971-75; rsch. asst., fellow U. Wis., Madison, 1975-81; NIH postdoctoral fellow U. Calif. San Diego, La Jolla, 1981-84; assoc., sr. assoc. Howard Hughes Med. Inst., Seattle, 1984-89; rsch. asst. prof. U. Wash., Seattle, 1988-91; asst. prof. Med. U. S.C., Charleston, 1991-96, assoc. prof. pharmacology, 1996—2003; prof. dept. pharm. sci. Wash. State U., Pullman, 2003—, chair dept. pharm. sci., 2003—05, interim asst. dean, 2007, interim-chair nutrition/dietetics, 2007—08, program dir., nutrition & exercise physiology, 2008—. Scientist reviewer Dept. Def., Ft. Detrick, Md., 1996-2005, 2007-09, VA Merit Review, 1999—; Nat. Sci. Fedn. fellowship reviewer, 2004-09. Mem. editl. bd. Jour. Biol. Chemistry, 1993-98, Am. Jour. Physiology, 1996—, Jour. Pharmacology and Exptl. Therapeutics, 1998-2000, Molecular Pharmacology, 2004—; contbr. articles to profl. jours. Recipient Tchg. Excellence award Med. U. SC, 2001; NIH fellow, 1981-84; Rsch. grantee NIH, 1993-96, 2004—, Dept. Def., 1998-2006. Mem. Am. Soc. Biochemistry and Molecular Biology, Am. Soc. Pharmacology and Exptl. Therapeutics, Am. Physiological Soc., Am. Assn. Coll. Pharmacy. Office: Washington State Univ Dept Pharm Scis Wegner Hall PO Box 646534 Pullman WA 99164-6534 Office Phone: 509-335-3573. Business E-Mail: kmeier@wsu.edu.

MEIER, KENNETH JOHN, political scientist; b. Aberdeen, SD, Mar. 3, 1950; s. John and Elizabeth (Malsam) M.; m. Diane Jones Meier, Dec. 31, 1972. BA, U. S.D., 1972; PhD, Syracuse U., 1975. Prof. polit. sci. Rice U., Houston, 1975-78, U. Okla., 1978-85, U. Wis., Madison, 1985-89, Milw., 1989-97; Charles Puryear prof. liberal arts Tex. A&M U., College Station, 1998—2005, Sara Lindsey prof. govt., 2001—04, Charles Gregory chair in liberal arts, 2006—. Fellow com. for hispanic pub. policy issues Inter Univ. Program Social Sci. Rsch. Coun., 1991-92; dir. Ctr. for Presdl. Studies, Policy and Governance, 2001-02. Author: Race, Class and Education, 1989, The Politics of Hispanic Education, 1991, Politics and the Bureaucracy, 1993, The Politics of Sin, 1994, The Case Against School Choice, 1995, Regulation and Consumer Protection, 1995, Applied Statistics for Public Administration, 1997, What Works: A New Approach to Program and Policy Analysis, 2000, The Politics of Fertility Control, 2001, Politics, Policy and Organizations, 2003, Bureaucracy in a Democratic State, 2006, Public Service Performance, Latino Politics, 2007; editor Am. Jour. Polit. Sci., 1994-98; assoc. editor Jour. Pub. Adminstrn. Rsch. and Theory. Recipient Clarence A. Kulp award, 1990, Gustavus Myers award, 1991, 93, Herbert Kaufman award, 1992, 2002, Herbert A. Simon award, 1999, award Acad. Mgmt., 2000, disting. rsch. award, Nat. Assn. Schs. Pub. Affairs and Adminstrn./ASPA, 2003; Big XII Faculty fellow, 2003. Fellow: Nat. Acad. Pub. Adminstrn. (Charles Levine award 2005, William Mosher award 2005), Advanced Inst. Mgmt. (Joseph Wholey award 2004); mem.: APHA, MW Polit. Sci. Assn. (pres.-elect 2004—05, pres. 2005—06), Nat. Pub. Mgmt. Rsch. Assn. (pres. 2003—05), SW Polit. Sci. Assn. (pres.-elect 1998—99, pres. 1999—2000), Am. Polit. Sci. Assn. (Latino Mentor award 2005, John Gaus award 2006). Office: Tex A&M U Dept Polit Sci TAMUS 4384 College Station TX 77843-0001 Office Phone: 979-845-4232. Business E-Mail: kmeier@polisci.tamu.edu.

MEIER, MARK FREDERICK, research scientist, educator, artist, small business owner; b. Iowa City, Dec. 19, 1925; s. Norman C. and Clea (Grimes) M.; m. Barbara McKinley, Sept. 16, 1955; children: Lauren G., Mark S., Gretchen A. BSEE, U. Iowa, 1949, MS in Geology, 1951; PhD in Geology and Applied Mechanics, Calif. Inst. Tech., 1957. Instr. Occidental Coll., LA, 1952-55; chief glaciology project office U.S. Geol. Survey, Tacoma, 1956-85; dir. Inst. Arctic and Alpine Rsch. U. Colo., Boulder, 1985-94; owner MeierArt, 2005—. Vis. prof. Dartmouth Coll., Hanover, N.H., 1964; rsch. prof. U. Wash., Seattle, 1964-86; prof. geol. scis. U. Colo., 1985-96, prof. emeritus, 1997—; pres. Internat. Comn. on Snow and Ice, 1967-71; pres. Internat. Assn. Hydrol. Scis., 1979-83; Mendenhall lectr. U.S. Geol. Survey, 1982, Walter Orr Roberts Disting. lectr. Aspen Global Change Inst., 1992. Contbr. articles to profl. jours. With USN, 1945—46. Recipient 3 medals, Acad. Scis., Moscow, 1970—85, Disting. Svc. award (Gold medal), U.S. Dept. Interior, 1968, Internat. Hydrology prize, Internat. Assn. Hydrol. Scis./World Meteor. Orgn./UNESCO, 1999, Goldthwait Polar medal, Ohio State U., 2002; named Meier Valley (Antarctica) in his honor. Fellow: AAAS (John Wesley Powell Meml. lectr. 1994), Am. Geophys. Union (com. chmn., Robert E. Horton medal 1996); mem.: Arctic Inst. N.Am. (gov. 1987—93), Internat. Glaciol. Soc. (v.p., coun., Seligman Crystal 1985), Geol. Soc. Am. (com. mem.). Office: U Colo Inst Arctic Alpine Rsch 1560 30th St Boulder CO 80309-0450 Home: 4840 Thunderbird Dr 489 Boulder CO 80303 Business E-Mail: mark.meier@colorado.edu.

MEIER, R. PAUL, lawyer; s. Robert Charles and Barbara Joan Meier; m. Kristin Rose Nealey, Sept. 7, 2004; 2 children. BA, Wash. State U., Pullman, Wash., 1994; JD, U. Pa., Phila., 1999. Bar: N.Y. 1999, N.J. 1999, Wash. 2000. Ptnr. Ryan, Swanson & Cleve., PLLC, Seattle, 2000—. Office: Ryan Swanson & Cleveland PLLC 1201 Third Ave Ste 3400 Seattle WA 98033 Business E-Mail: meier@ryanlaw.com.

MEIER, RICHARD ALAN, architect; b. Newark, Oct. 12, 1934; s. Jerome and Carolyn (Kaltenbacher) M.; m. Katherine Gormley, Jan. 21, 1978 (div.); children: Joseph Max, Ana Moss. BArch, Cornell U., Ithaca, NY, 1957; PhD (hon.), U. Naples, Italy, 1991, Parsons Sch. Design, 1998, Wheaton Coll., 1998, Pratt Sch. Fine Arts, 1999, U. Bucharest, 2001, NC State U., 2004, Mercy Coll., 2004. Registered profl. arch., NY, NJ, Conn., Mich., Va., Fla., Ind., Ga., Calif., Ill., Iowa, Tex., Oreg. Arch. Frank Grad & Sons, NJ, 1957, Davis, Brody & Wisniewski, NYC, 1959, Skidmore, Owings & Merrill, 1959—60, Marcel Breuer & Assocs., 1960—63; prin. arch. Richard Meier & Assocs., NYC, 1963—80; arch., prin. Richard Meier & Ptnrs., 1980—. Resident arch. Am. Acad. Rome, 1973-74; vis. critic Pratt Inst., 1960-62, 65, Princeton, 1963, Syracuse U., 1964; William Henry Bishop vis. prof. architecture Yale U., 1975, 77, vis. critic, 1967, 72, 73, 77, Davenport prof., 2008; vis. prof. Harvard U., 1977, UCLA, 1988, Eliot Noyes vis. critic in architecture, 1980-81; Harvey S. Perloff vis. prof. architecture UCLA, 1987, 88, 90, 2000; adj. prof. architecture Cooper Union, NYC, 1963-73; mem. adv. coun. Cornell U. Coll. Art, Architecture and Planning; mem. Jerusalem Com. Exhbns., XV Triennale, Milan, 1973, Mus. Modern Art, NYC, 1975, 81, Princeton U., Biennale, Venice, Italy, 1976, Cooper-Hewitt Mus., NYC, 1976-77, Leo Castelli Gallery, NYC, 1977, 94, Rosa Esman Gallery, NYC, 1978, 80, NJ State Mus., 1978, Modernism Gallery, San Francisco, Wadsworth Atheneum, Hartford, Conn., High Mus. Art, Atlanta Harvard U., Max Protech Gallery, 1980, Syracuse U., Whitney Mus. Art, NYC, 1982, Knoll Internat., Tokyo, Japan, 1988, October Gallery, London, 1990, Royal Palace, Naples, Italy, 1991, Palazzo delle Esposizione, Rome, 1993, Aichi Prefectural Mus. Art, Nagoya, Japan, 1996, LTB Found., London, 2008; prof. Cooper Union, 1963-66, 66-69, 69-73. Prin. works include Westbeth Artists Housing, NYC, Bronx Devel. Ctr., NY, Smith House, Darien, Conn., Douglas House, Harbor Springs, Mich., Shamberg House, Mt. Kisco, NY, Hoffman and Saltzman Houses, East Hampton, NY; houses in Old Westbury, NY, Pound Ridge, NY, Palm Beach, Fla., Pitts.; Twin Parks NE Housing, NYC, Atheneum, New Harmony, Ind., NY, Hartford Sem., Conn., Mus. für Kunsthandwerk, Frankfurt, Germany, Des Moines Art Ctr., High Mus. Art, Atlanta, Bridgeport Ctr., NY, Daimler-Benz Office and Lab. Complex, Ulm, Germany, Weishaupt Forum, Schwendi, Germany, City Hall and Cen. Libr., The Hague, The Netherlands, Corp. Hdqs., Royal Dutch Paper Mills, Hilversum, The Netherlands, Cornell U. Alumni and Admissions Ctr., Ithaca, NY, Canal Hdqs., Paris, Espace Pitot, Montpellier, France, Maybury Office Pk., Edinburgh, Hypolux Bank Bldg., Luxembourg, Mus. Contemporary Art, Barcelona, Spain, Arp Mus., Rolandseck, Germany, Swiss Volksbank, Basel Office Bldg., Singapore, The Getty Ctr., LA, SwissAir Hdqs., Melville, NY, Fed. Courthouse, Islip, NY, Phoenix, Mus. TV & Radio, LA, Gagosian Gallery, LA, Rachofsky House, Dallas, Ch. of Yr. 2000, 173 & 176 Perry St., NYC, 2002 (Royal Inst. Brit. Archs. award 2006), Frieder Burda Collection Mus., Baden-Badem, Germany, 2004 (Royal Inst. Brit. Archs. award 2006), Rome, Ara Pacis, Rome, 2006, 165 Charles St., NYC, 2006, One Grand Army Plz., Bklyn., 2008, Rothschild Tower, Tel Aviv, 2008-, others; author: Richard Meier Architect, vol. 1, 1964-68, vol. 2, 1985-91, vol. 3, 1992-99, vol. 4, 2000-04, On Architecture, 1982, Richard Meier Collages, 1990, The Getty Ctr. Design Process, J. Paul Getty Trust, 1991, Richard Meier Sculpture, 1994; contbr. articles to profl. jours. Decorated officer de l'Ordre des Arts et des Lettres (France), 1984; recipient Arnold Brunner Meml. prize AAAL, 1972, Albert S. Bard Civic award City Club NY, 1973, 1st honor award for excellence in architecture and urban design, 1977, R.S. Reynolds Meml. award, 1977, Archtl. Record award of excellence for design, 1964, 68, 69, 70, 77, Am. Inst. Steel Constrn. award, 1978, 79, design award 1st prize Kunsthandwerk Competition, Frankfurt am Main, Fed. Republic Germany, 1980, Pritzker Prize for Architecture, 1984, Praemium Imperiale, Japan, 1997, Am. Inst. Architects, LA Chpt. Gold Medal, 1998, El Gobierno del Distrito Federal "Huesped Distinguido de la Ciudad de Mexico," 2000, AIA 25-Yr. award for Smith House, 2000, NY Mag. award for Arch., 2003, Frate Sole Internat. award for Sacred Architecture, 2004, Dedalo Minosse Internat. Prize for Commissioning a Bldg. - Quinquennial Hon. award, Associazione Liberi Architetti, 2004, Pratt Legend award, 2004, Sidney L. Strauss award, NY Soc. Archs., 2004, Gold medal for Architecture, Am. Acad. Arts and Letters, 2008, The Pres.'s medal Archtl. League NY, 2009. Fellow AIA (medal of honor NY chpt. 1980, nat. design com. 1972-74, 30 AIA nat. awards 1968-2006, 50 chpt. awards NY 1965-2006, Chgo. Arch. award, 1995, 5 Progressive Architecture awards 1979, 89, 90, 91, 95, Gold medal 1997), Am. Acad. Arts & Sci., 1995; mem. NAD (academician), Internat. Inst. Archs., Royal Inst. Brit. Archs. (Royal Gold medal 1989), Belgian Royal Acad. Art (Lifetime Achievement award Guild Hall 1991, commdr. de l'Ordre des Arts et Lettres, France, 1992). Office: Richard Meier & Ptnrs 475 10th Ave Fl 6 New York NY 10018-1120 Office Phone: 212-967-6060. Office Fax: 212-967-3207. E-mail: mail@richardmeier.com.

MEIER, STEVEN W., orthopedist, surgeon, consultant; b. Elmhurst, Ill., Jan. 11, 1967; s. William P. and Donna L. Meier. MD, Loyola Med. Sch., Chgo., 1993. Diplomate Am. Bd. Orthop. Surgery, 2003. Orthop. surgeon Ctr. Advanced Sports Medicine, Summit, NJ, 2001—06, Adult and Pediatric Orthop. Specialists, Orange and Mission Viejo, Calif., 2006—08, Ctr. Progressive Sports Medicine, 2008—. Contbr. articles to profl. jours. Mem.: Am. Acad. Orthop. Surgeons (assoc.). Office: 1223 Wilshire Blvd #131 Santa Monica CA 90403-5400 Office Phone: 18886152121. Office Fax: 1.714.633.5615. Personal E-mail: oblio54@aol.com.

MEIERAN, EUGENE STUART, materials scientist; b. Cleve., Dec. 23, 1937; s. Elias and Rae (Linetsky) M.; m. Rosalind Berson, Mar. 25, 1962; children: Sharon Elizabeth, Andrew Marc. BS in Metallurgy, MIT, 1961, ScD in Material Sci., 1963; Doctorate (hon.), Purdue U., 2004. Mem. tech. staff Fairchild R&D, Palo Alto, Calif., 1963-73; engring. mgr. Intel Corp., Santa Clara, Calif., 1973-77, sr. mgr. quality assurance, 1977-84, Intel fellow, 1984—, mgr. applications lab., 1989—, Intel sr. fellow, 2003. Dir. rsch. LFM program MIT, 1993—; vis. lectr. Technion, Haifa, Israel, 1970-71, H.H. Wills Physics Lab., Bristol, Eng., 1970-71; mem. adv. bd. Lawrence Berkeley Lab., 1984— Contbr. articles to profl. jours. AEC fellow, 1960; recipient Internat. Reliability awards, 1970, 79, 85, Carnegie medal, 2004; named Disting. Engring. Alumnus Purdue U., 1988, Purdue Band Alumni, 2000, GIA Wall of Fame, 2004. Mem. AIME (chmn. electronic material symposium 1973—), NAE, Electron Microscope Soc. U.S.A., Tau Beta Pi, Phi Lambda Upsilon. Democrat. Jewish. Home: 5421 E Camello Rd Phoenix AZ 85018-1910 Office: Intel Corp 5000 W Chandler Blvd Chandler AZ 85226-3699 Home Phone: 602-840-2870. Personal E-mail: gene.meieran@att.net. Business E-Mail: gene.s.meieran@intel.com.

MEIERHENRY, JUDITH KNITTEL, state supreme court justice; b. Burke, SD, Jan. 20, 1944; m. Mark Vernon Meierhenry, May 14, 1961; children: Todd, Mary. BA in English, U. S.D., 1966, MA, 1968, JD, 1977. Bar: S.D. 1977. H.S. tchr. English Plattsmouth (Nebr.) Pub. Schs., 1966-67; instr. U. SD, 1968-70, Hiram Scott Coll., Scottbluff, Nebr., 1970; tchr. Todd County Pub. Schs., Mission, SD, 1971-74; ptnr. Meierhenry, DeVaney, Krueger & Meierhenry, Vermillion, SD, 1977-79; cabinet sec. SD Dept. Labor, Pierre, 1980-84; sr. mgr., asst. gen. counsel Citibank SD, 1985-88; cabinet sec. edn. and cultural affairs State SD, 1983-84, cir. ct. judge, 1988—2002; justice SD Supreme Ct., 2002—. Mem.: Nat. Assn. Women Judges, SD Bar Assn. Office: SD Supreme Ct 500 E Capital Ave Pierre SD 57501

MEIGEL, DAVID WALTER, retired career officer, musician; b. Chgo., Feb. 27, 1957; s. Thomas Arent and Annie Elizabeth (Thomas) M. Diploma, USAF NCO Leadership Sch., Chanute AFB, Ill., 1981, USAF/CAP SQD Officer Sch., 1987, USAF NCO Acad., Norton AFB, Calif., 1991; BS in Info. Tech. magna cum laude, Nat. U., 2001. Enlisted USAF, 1975; major CAP, Travis AFB, Calif., 1988; ret., 1996; percussionist 724th USAF Band, McChord AFB, Wash., 1976—78, 752d USAF Band, Elmendorf AFB, Alaska, 1978—80, 505th USAF Band, Chanute AFB, Ill., 1980—84, 504th USAF Band, Travis AFB, 1984—96; prin. percussionist, chief of adminstrn. Am.'s Band in Blue, USAF, Travis AFB, 1990—96. Prin. percussionist San Diego (Calif.) Civic Orch., 1973-76, Poway (Calif.) High Sch. Band, 1974-75; percussionist Anchorage (Alaska) Civic Opera, 1979-80, Anchorage (Alaska) Scottish Soc., 1979-80, Fairfield Civic Theatre, Fairfield, Calif., 1984-; comms. officer USAF Civil Air Patrol, Travis AFB, 1986-95; dep. comdr. hdqrs. No. Calif. Group 25, 1995-96. Recipient Gov.'s medal Youkon Internat. Invitational Scottish Games, Whitehorse City Coun., B.C., 1980; decorated USAF Achievement medal 1989, 93, USAF Commendation medal 1996, Comdrs. Commendation medal 1993, 98; named one of Outstanding Young Men Am., 1988, 92, CAP Meritorious Svc. medal, 1989. Mem. AF Musician's Assn, Nat. Assn. Parliamentarians, Calif. State Assn. Parliamentarians. Avocations: amateur radio, golf, bowling, computer ops, target shooting. Home: 8341 Crestshire Cir Orangevale CA 95662-3861

MEIGHER, S. CHRISTOPHER, III, communications and media executive, publisher; b. NYC, Sept. 23, 1946; s. Stephen Christopher and Denise (Connor) Todd; m. Grace Tebbutt, Aug. 8, 1970; children: Elizabeth, Amanda Powers. BA, Dartmouth Coll., 1968; grad. program mgmt. devel., Harvard U., 1974. Dir. circulation Fortune mag., NYC, 1972-74, Sports Illustrated mag., NYC, 1974-76, Time mag., NYC, 1976-79; v.p. circulation Time, Inc., NYC, 1981-83; pres. Time Distbn. Svc., NYC, 1979-81; pub. People mag., NYC, 1983-85, exec. v.p., group pub., 1985-90; pres. Time Inc. Mags. NY, NYC, 1990—92; gen. ptnr., CEO, chmn. Meigher Comm., L.P., NYC, 1993—; CEO Questmedia LLC, 2000—. Bd. dirs. Individual Investor Group, 1998—; bd. vis. Rockefeller Ctr. at Dartmouth Coll., 1997—; delegate U.S. State Dept. USA-USSR, 1988; mem. Bilateral Info. Talks, Moscow. Pub. Saveur mag., Garden Design mag., Quest mag., Smarth Health mag., Friends mag., 1992-2000, Pub Quest Mag., Qmag., Quest Polo Mag., 2000-. Trustee Boys Club NYC, 1979—2008, Internat. House, 1985—92, Am. Ballet Theatre, 1993—, South St. Seaport, 1987—97, St. Paul's Sch., 1997—2002, Episcopal Charities, 2003—; mem. dream team Meml. Sloan Kettering, 1990—, Palm Beach Civic Assn., 2008—; mem. comm. com. St. James Episcopal Ch., 1989—95. Recipient Disting. Service award Brandeis U., 1983 Mem.: Mag. Publs. Assn. (bd. dirs. 1988—92, 1997—2002), Am. Pubs. Assn. (bd. dirs. 1988—92), Everglades Club (Palm Beach), Saratoga Reading Room, Clove Valley Rod and Gun Club, Lake George Club (trustee 1995—2002), NY Yacht Club (trustee 1987—92), Racquet & Tennis Club (NY), Brook Club, Bath & Tennis Club (Palm Beach), River Club. Office Phone: 646-840-3402. E-mail: scmiii@aol.com.

MEIGS, JAMES B., editor-in-chief; Editl. dir. Video Review, 1987—89; sr. editor Entertainment Weekly, 1989—93; editor US Mag., 1993—95; editor-in-chief Premiere Mag., 1996—2000, v.p., 1998—2000; dep. editor features Nat. Geographic Adventure, 2001—03, exec. editor, 2003—04; editor-in-chief Popular Mechanics, 2004—. Freelance writer Rolling Stone, Details, Outside, O: The Oprah Mag., Family Life, Popular Mechanics, others. Contbr. articles to mags. Recipient Nat. Mag award for Personal Svc., Am. Soc. Mag. Editors, 2008. Office: Popular Mechanics Magazine 300 W 57th St Fl 23 New York NY 10019-3741

MEIGS, JOHN FORSYTH, lawyer; b. Boston, Dec. 4, 1941; s. Charles H. Meigs and Florence S. Truitt; m. Carolyn J. Adams, Aug. 11, 2002; children: Amory, Perry, John. BA, Yale U., 1964; LLB, U. Pa., 1969. Bar: Pa. 1969, US Supreme Ct. 1977. Assoc. Saul, Ewing, Remick & Saul (now Saul Ewing, LLP), Phila., 1969-76, ptnr., 1976—. Co-chair estates and trusts Saul Ewing, LLP, 1997—2003, chair personal wealth svcs., 2000—. Contbr. articles to profl. jours. Trustee Independence Seaport Mus., 1978—, Woodmere Art Mus., 1987—. Named one of Top 100 Attys., Worth mag., 2005—08. Mem.: ABA, Phila. Bar Assn., Pa. Bar Assn. Episcopalian. Office: Saul Ewing LLP Centre Sq W 1500 Market St 38th Fl Philadelphia PA 19102-2186 Office Phone: 215-972-7812. Office Fax: 215-972-1870. E-mail: jmeigs@saul.com.

MEIGS, JOSEPH TIMOTHY, lawyer; b. Gainesville, Fla., Sept. 8, 1966; BS in Biology, East Carolina U., Greenville, NC, 1989; JD, U. NC, Chapel Hill, 1993; MS in Biotechnology, Johns Hopkins U., Balt., 2006. Bar: NC 1993, Colo. 1995, DC 2004. Lab technician Burroughs Wellcome Co., Greenville, NC, 1989—90; assoc. atty. Walter Beavers Patent Law Offices, Greensboro, NC, 1993—94; assoc. patent atty. Rhodes, Coats & Bennett LLP, Raleigh, NC, 1994—96; sr. and mng. patent atty. CIBA-Geigy, Novartis and Syngenta Corps., Rsch. Triangle Pk., NC, 1996—2002; sector patent counsel Novartis Corp., Gaithersburg, Md., 2002—03; of counsel Sughrue Mion PLLC, Washington, 2004—05; sr. intellectual property counsel Becton, Dickinson and Co., Rsch. Triangle Pk., NC, 2005—. Mem. biology dept. advancement coun. East Carolina U., Greenville, NC, 2004—; vice-chair, chair edn. com. Am. Intellectual Property Law Assn., Alexandria, 2005—09. Contbr. articles to profl. jours. Recipient Legal Rsch. and Writing award, Am. Soc. Pharmacy Law and Upjohn Co., 1994. Office: BD Technologies 21 Davis Dr Research Triangle Park NC 27709 Office Fax: 919-549-7572. Business E-Mail: timothy_meigs@bd.com.

MEIGS, MONTGOMERY CUNNINGHAM, JR., retired military officer, educator; b. Annapolis, Md., Jan. 11, 1945; s. Montgomery Cunningham and Elizabeth Shoemaker (Griggs) M.; m. Mary Ann Mellenbruch, July 6, 1968; children: William Bradford, Matthew Montgomery. BS, U.S. Mil. Acad., West Point, NY, 1967; MA in History, U. Wis., 1977, PhD in History, 1982. Commd. 2d lt. U.S. Army, 1967, advanced through grades to gen.; internat. affairs fellow Coun. Fgn. Rels., NYC, 1981-82; exec. officer 2d Armored Cavalry Regiment, Nurnberg, Germany, 1982-84; commdr. 1st Squadron, 1st Cavalry, 1st AD, Schwabach, Germany, 1984-86; rsch. fellow Nat. Def. U., Washington, 1986-87; chief strategic applications br. J-5 Joint Staff, Washington, 1987-90; comdr. 2d Bde 1st Armored Divsn., Desert Storm, Erlangen, Germany, 1990-91; chief of staff V U.S. Corps, Frankfurt, Germany, 1993-94; dep. chief of staff Ops. HQ USAREUR & 7th Army, Heidelberg, Germany, 1994; comdg. gen. 3d Infantry Divsn., 1995-96, 1st infantry Divsn., Wurzburg, Germany, 1996-97, COMEAGLE, Bosnia-Herzegovina, 1996-97, Combined Arms Ctr., Ft. Leavenworth, Kans., 1997-98; commdg. gen. U.S. Army, COMSFOR, Bosnia-Herzegovina, 1998-99; comdg. gen. U.S. Army Europe and 7th Army, 1998—2002. Tom Slick vis. prof. LBJ Sch., U. Tex., Austin, 2003—04; Louis A. Bantle chair Maxwell Sch. Syracuse U., 2004—; dir. OSD's

Joint IED Defeat Org., 2005—. Author: Slide Rules and Submarines, 1990; contbr. articles to profl. jours. Decorated Legion of Merit with oak leaf cluster, Bronze Star medal with V device and 2 oak leaf clusters, Purple Heart, officer French Legion of Honor, German Nat. Svc. Order with star, Bavarian Svc. Order, Army Disting. Svc. medal with oak leaf cluster. Avocations: history, hunting.

MEIJER, HANK, retail company executive; b. 1952; BA, U. Michigan, 1973. Asst. advt. dir. Meijer, Grand Rapids, Mich., mktg. dir., vice chmn. bd. dirs., co-chmn. bd. dirs., 1990—, CEO, 2002—05, co-CEO, 2005—07, CEO, 2007—. Office: 2929 Walker Ave NW Grand Rapids MI 49544

MEIJER, PAUL HERMAN ERNST, physicist, educator; b. The Hague, Netherlands, Nov. 14, 1921; came to U.S., 1953, naturalized, 1959; s. Herman Willem and Elisabet (Kossmann) M.; m. Marianne Schwarz, Feb. 17, 1949; children: Onko Frans (dec.), Miriam, Daniel, Mark, Corinne. PhD, U. Leiden, Netherlands, 1951. Research assoc. U. Leiden, 1952-53, Duke U., 1954-55; vis. lectr. Case Inst. Tech., 1953-54; asst. prof. U. Del., 1955-56; asso. prof. Cath. U., Washington, 1956-60, prof. physics, 1960-92, prof. emeritus, 1992—, chmn. dept., 1980-83. Vis. prof. U. Paris, 1964-65, 72, 78, U. Nancy, 1984, 88; part-time appointment Nat. Inst.Stds. and Tech.; short time appointments at Naval Ordnance Lab., Livermore Radiation Lab., Naval Research Lab., Night Vision Lab., Ft. Belvoir. Author:(with P. Papon, J. Leblond) The Physics of Phase Transitions, 2006, (with E. Bauer) Group Theory, 2004; editor: Group Theory and Solid State Physics, 1964. Fulbright grantee, 1953-55, 77-78; Guggenheim grantee, 1964-65; Fulbright sr. fellow, 1978 Fellow Am. Phys. Socs.; mem. European Phys. Soc., Phys. Soc. Netherlands, Fedn. Am. Scientists, Fulbright Alumni Assn., Sigma Xi. Research, publs. statis. mechanics solids and liquids, group theory and other fields. Home: 1438 Geranium St NW Washington DC 20012-1518 Office: Cath U Am Dept Physics Hannan Hall Washington DC 20064 Office Phone: 202-319-5324. Business E-Mail: meijer@cua.edu.

MEIKLE, PHILIP G., engineer, retired government agency executive; b. Glendale, W.Va., Dec. 5, 1937; s. Philip and Caroline Elizabeth (Stephens) M.; m. Linda Kay Price, July 14, 1961 (div. Aug. 1976); children: Philip Kevin, Melissa Kay BS in Mining Engring., W.Va. U., 1961, MS in Mining Engring., 1965; M.Engring. Adminstrn., George Washington U., 1980. Registered profl. engr. Mining engr. Duquesne Light Co., Pitts., 1961-63; research engr. W.Va. U., Morgantown, 1963-66; materials engr. Mobay Chem. Co., New Martinsville, W.Va., 1966-68; asst. dir. Nat. Ash Assn., Washington, 1968-72; staff mining engr. U.S. Bur. Mines, Washington, 1972-82, divsn. chief, 1982-95; ret., 1995. Mem. U.S. Nat. Com. for Tunneling Tech., Nat. Acad. Scis., Washington, 1985-90, chmn., 1988-89; adj. prof. George Washington U., 1985—; pres. Clan Lamont Soc. N.Am., 1998-2002. Contbr. articles to profl. jours., chpts. to books Recipient Superior Svc. award Dept. Interior, 1980, Meritorious Svc. award, 1986, Disting. Svc. award, 1991, Presdl. Rank award, 1991. Mem. Nat. Assn. Ret. Fed. Employees (life), Sr. Execs. Assn. (life), Coun. Former Fed. Execs. (bd. dirs., 2004-06), Sigma Xi, Tau Beta Pi, Sigma Gamma Epsilon, Masons, Shriners. Republican. Baptist. Home: 6819 Brian Michael Ct Springfield VA 22153-1004

MEIKLEJOHN, ALVIN J., JR., state legislator, lawyer, accountant; b. Omaha, June 18, 1923; m. Lorraine J. Meiklejohn; children; Pamela Ann, Shelley Lou, Bruce Ian, Scott Alvin. BS, U. Denver, JD, 1951; LLD (hon.), U. No. Colo., 2000. Mem. Colo. state Senate from 19th Dist., 1976-96, chmn. com. edn.; mem. Edn. Commn. of States, 1981-96; chmn. Colo. Commn. on Ach. in Edn., 1995, mem., 1993-96, Jefferson Sch. Dist. No. R-1 Bd. Edn., 1971-77, pres., 1973-77; commr. Commn. on Uniform State Laws, 1988-96. Dir. Red Rocks C.C. Found.; emeritus dir. Wings Over the Rockies Air and Space Mus. Capt. US Army, 1940—46, maj. USAF, 1947—51. Mem. Arvada C. of C., Masons, Shriners, Transp. Lawyers Assn. (pres. 1972-73). Republican. Home: 7540 Kline Dr Arvada CO 80005-3732 Office: Jones & Keller PC 1625 Broadway Ste 1600 Denver CO 80202-4727 Office Phone: 303-573-1600. E-mail: ajmeiklejohn@joneskeller.com.

MEIKSIN, ZVI H., electrical engineering educator; b. 1926; BSEE, Israel Inst. Tech., Haifa, 1950, Dipl. Ing., 1951; MSEE, Carnegie Mellon U., 1953; PhDEE, U. Pitts., 1959. Registered profl. engr., Pa. Design engr. McGraw Edison, Cannonsburg, Pa., 1953-54; sr. project engr. Westinghouse Electric Corp., Pitts., 1956-59; prof. dept. elec. engring. U. Pitts., 1959-91, prof. emeritus, 1991—; pres. Transtek, Inc., Pitts., 1995—2004; pres., CEO Alertek LLC, Pitts., 2006—. Cons. entr. 33 orgns. in US, Europe, 1959-95; expert witness in field, 1991-95. Author: Thin & Thick Films, 1976, Active Filter Design, 1990; co-author: Electronic Design, 1980, 84, Microprocessor Based Design, 1986; jour. referee profl. publs., 1970—; contbr. articles to profl. jours.; inventor, holder 8 patents in field. Fellow IEEE (award coms.); mem. Eta Kappa Nu, Sigma Xi. E-mail: meiksin@pitt.edu.

MEILAN, CELIA, food products executive; b. Bklyn., Jan. 21, 1920; d. Ventura Lorenzo and Susana (Prego) Meilan. Student, CCNY, 1943—46. Codes and ciphers translator security divsn. U.S. Censorship Office, NYC, 1942—46; sec., treas. Albumina Supply Co., NYC, 1946—55; co-founder, co-owner, sec., treas., fin. officer AnimalFeeds Internat. Corp., Clark, NJ, 1955—86, exec. v.p., 1986—92, pres., 1992—94, chair emeritus, bd. dirs., 1994—, v.p., co-owner, 1998—, dir., v.p., Ctrl. Pacific Trading Corp.; Panama rep.; co-owner AFI Trade Svc. Inc., Clark, NJ, Pacific Oil Panama, 2008; v.p. co-owner Taboquilla Holdings Inc., Panama, Innosi Laria Play Blanca, Panama. Bd. dirs. Pesquera Taboquilla, Panama City, Panama, Inversiones Pesqueras S.A., British Virgin Islands; v.p., bd. dirs. Atlantic Shipers of Tex. Inc., Port Arthur, 1989; bd. dirs. Atlantic Shippers Inc., Morehead City, NC; v.p., dir. AnimalFeeds, Internat., Santiago, Chile. Named One of Top 50 Women Bus. Owners, Working Woman Mag./Nat. Found. Women Bus. Owners, 1994, 1995. Mem.: Nat. Found. Women Bus. Owners, Spanish Benevolent Soc. (bd. dirs. 1955—62). Avocation: Avocations: travel, hand crafts, backgammon, puzzles. Office Fax: 732-827-0188.

MEILMAN, EDWARD, physician; b. Boston, Apr. 6, 1915; s. Harry and Jennie (Sholofsky) M.; m. Rhoeda Berman, Mar. 6, 1946. AB, Harvard U., 1936, MD, 1940. Intern Mt. Sinai Hosp., NYC, 1940-42; resident Beth Israel Hosp., Boston, 1946-48, assoc. in med. and med. research, 1948-53; chmn. dept. medicine L.I. Jewish-Hillside Med. Center, New Hyde Park, NY, 1953-82, chmn. emeritus dept. medicine, 1982—. Prof. medicine SUNY, Stony Brook, 1971— Contbr. articles to profl. jours. Served with USAAF, 1942-46. Fellow N.Y. Acad. Medicine, N.Y. Acad. Scis.; mem. Am. Heart Assn. (fellow council clin. cardiology, council arteriosclerosis), Am. Fedn. Clin. Research, Harvey Soc., Am. Rheumatism Assn., Phi Beta Kappa, Alpha Omega Alpha. Clubs: Harvard (N.Y.C.); Harvard (L.I.). Democrat. Jewish. Office Phone: 516-487-4203. E-mail: emeilman@optonline.net.

MEILTON, SANDRA L., lawyer; b. 1946; BA, Bethany Coll., 1968; attended, U. Pitts.; JD, Dickinson Sch. Law, 1980. Bar: Pa. 1980. Assoc. Hepford, Swartz and Morgan, 1980—87, ptnr., 1987—98; shareholder Tucker Arensberg, P.C., 1998—2006; ptnr. Daley, Zucker, Meilton, Miner & Gingrich, Harrisburg, Pa., 2006—. Bd. dirs. Mechanicsburg Children's Home. Named one of Best Lawyers in Am., 2005—07. Mem.: ABA, Dauphin County Bar Assn., Am. Acad. Matrimonial Lawyers. Office: Daley Zucker Meilton Miner & Gingrich 1029 Scenery Dr Harrisburg PA 17109 Home Phone: 717-697-8810; Office Phone: 717-657-4795. Business E-Mail: smeilton@dzmmglaw.com.

MEIMA, RALPH CHESTER, JR., retired diplomat, real estate company executive; b. Chgo., Mar. 29, 1927; s. Ralph Chester and Grace Georgine (Larson) Meima; m. Elizabeth B. Frazier, 1994; children from previous marriage: Ralph Chester III, Stephen H. BA, U. Ams., Mexico City, 1952; MBA, Am. U., 1964. With Carborundum Co., Perth Amboy, 1952-53, Johns-Manville Corp., NYC, 1953-58, Security Storage Co., Washington, 1958-61, Dept. of Commerce, 1961-68; joined U.S. Fgn. Svc., 1968; consul gen. Marseille, France, 1977-80; on loan export devel. cons. State of Md., 1980-82; pres. Atlantic Eastern Corp., 1982-87, Phoenix Internat. Mktg. Corp., 1987-89; pres., chief exec. officer FTI Inc., Annapolis, Md., 1989-95; pres. DERCO, Inc., Balt., 1995—2002. In govt. rels. iJET Travel Risk Mgmt., Inc. With USN, 1945—46. Office: Hogans Agy 220 High St Chestertown MD 21620 Office Phone: 443-994-6342. Business E-Mail: meimare@yahoo.com.

MEINDL, JAMES DONALD, electrical engineering educator, academic administrator; b. Pitts., Apr. 20, 1933; s. Louis M. and Elizabeth F. (Steinhauser) Meindl; m. Frederica Ziegler, May 21, 1961; children: Peter James, Candace Ann. BS, Carnegie Mellon U., 1955, MS, 1956, PhD, 1958. Engr. Autonetics Co., Downey, Calif., 1957, Westinghouse Co., Pitts., 1958-59; head sect. microelectronics US Army Electronics Command, Ft. Monmouth, NJ, 1959-62, chief br. semiconductors and microelectronics, 1962-65, dir. divsn. integrated electronics, 1965-67; assoc. prof. elec. engring. Stanford U., 1967-70, prof., 1970-84, John M. Fluke prof. elec. engring., 1984-86, assoc. dean rsch., 1984-86, dir. integrated circuits lab., 1969-84; co-founder Telesensory Systems Inc., 1971-84; dir. Electronics Labs. Stanford U., 1972-86, dir. Ctr. Integrated Systems, 1981-86; v.p. acad. affairs, provost Rensselaer Poly. Inst., Troy, NY, 1986-88, prof. sci. and engring., 1986-93, sr. v.p. acad. affairs, provost, 1988-93; Joseph M. Pettit Chair prof. microelectronics Ga. Inst. Tech., Atlanta, 1993—, dir. Microelectronics Rsch. Ctr., 1997—. Cons. to govt., industry. Author: Micropower Circuits, 1969; editor: Brief Lessons in High Technology, 1989; patentee integrated cir. field; contbr. numerous articles to profl. publs. Served to 1st lt. AUS, 1959-61. Recipient Arthur S. Flemming Commn. award Washington Jr. C. of C., 1967; J.J. Ebers award IEEE Electron Devices Soc., 1980, Univ. Rsch. award Semiconductor Industries Assn., 1999. Fellow IEEE (Solid State Circuits Coun. editor jour. 1966-71, Internat. Outstanding Paper ann. awards 1970, 75-78, Beatrice K. Winner award Internat. conf. 1988, solid State Circuits medal 1989, Edn. medal 1990, Third Millenium medal 2000, Medal of Honor 2006), AAAS, Am. Acad. Arts and Scis.; mem. AAUP, NAE, Am. Soc. Engr. Edn. (Benjamin Garver Lamme medal 1991), Electrochemical Soc., Biomedical Engring. Soc. (co-editor Annals of Biomedical Engring. 1976-80), Sigma Xi, Tau Beta Pi, Eta Kappa Nu, Phi Kappa Phi. Office: Ga Inst Tech Microelectronics Rsch Ctr 791 Atlantic Dr Atlanta GA 30332-0001 Home: 1521 Jacksons Ridge Rd Greensboro GA 30642-5210 E-mail: james.meindl@mirc.gatech.edu.

MEINER, SUE ELLEN THOMPSON, nurse, consultant, gerontologist, author, writer; b. Ironton, Mo., Oct. 24, 1943; d. Louis Raymond and Verna Mae Thompson; m. Robert Edward Meiner, Mar. 5, 1971; children: Diane Bubb, Suzanne. AAS, Meramec C.C., 1970; BSN, St. Louis U., 1978, MSN, 1983; EdD, So. Ill. U., Edwardsville, 1991. RN, Nev.; cert. gerontol. nurse practitioner; cert. clin. specialist in gerontol. nursing. Staff RN St. Joseph's Hosp., St. Charles, Mo., 1976-78; nursing supr. Bethesda Gen. Hosp., St. Louis, 1975-76, 71-74; adult med. dir. Family Care Ctr.-Carondelet, St. Louis, 1978-79; program dir., lectr. Webster Coll./Bethesda Hosp., Webster Groves, Mo., 1979-82; diabetes clin. specialist Washington U. Sch. Medicine, St. Louis, 1982; asst. prof. St. Louis C.C., 1983-88, chmn. dept. nursing; vis. nurse assoc. St. Louis, 1970—71; asst. prof. Barnes Hosp. Sch. Nursing, 1988—89; instr. U. Mo., St. Louis, 1989; assoc. prof. St. Charles County C.C., St. Peters, Mo., 1990-92, Deaconess Coll. of Nursing, 1991-93; patient care mgr. Deaconess Hosp., St. Louis, 1993-94; assoc. prof. Jewish Hosp. Coll. of Nursing and Allied Health, 1994-99; gerontol. nurse, rschr. Wash. U. Sch. Med., St. Louis, 1996-2000; asst. prof. nursing U. Nev. Coll. Health Scis., Las Vegas, 2000—05; pvt. practice Nev., 2005—. Nat. dir. edn. Nat. Assn. Practical Nurse Edn. and Svc., Inc., St. Louis, 1984-86; mem. task force St. Louis Met. Hosp. Assn., 1987-88; mem. adv. com. Bd. Edn. Sch. Nursing, St. Louis, 1986-90; grant coord. Kellogg Found. Gerontology and Nursing, 1991-92; project dir. NIH, Nat. Inst. Aging Grant Washington U. Sch. Medicine, St. Louis, 1996-00; mem. editorial bd. Geriatric Nursing Journ., 1999-02; legal nurse cons. Author and editor profl. books; contbr. articles to profl. jours. Chmn. bd. dirs. Creve Coeur Fire Protection Dist. Mo., 1984-89; vice chmn. Bd. Cen. St. Louis County Emergency Dispatch Svc., 1985-87; asst. leader Girl Scouts U.S., St. Louis, 1975; treas. Older Women's League, St. Louis, 1992-93. Recipient Woman of Worth award Gateway chpt. Older Women's League, 1993. Mem.: ANA, Nev N. A. (bd. dir. 2004—05), NCGNP (bd. dir 2004—06), Am. Soc. of Aging, Nat. League for Nursing, Am. Nurses Found., Am. Coll. Nurse Practitioners, Am. Acad. Nurse Practitioners, Job's Daus. (guardian 1979—80), Creve Coeur C. of C., Order Ea. Star (chaplain 1970), Sigma Theta Tau (fin. chmn. 1984, archivist 1985—87, Zeta Kappa chpt. v.p. 2001—03), Kappa Delta Pi, Sigma Phi Omega (Iota chpt. pres. 1990—91). Avocations: travel, reading. Home and Office: 3722 Violet Rose Ct Las Vegas NV 89147-7400 *Personal philosophy: From my earliest memories, I have established goals that were obtainable only through very hard work and perseverance. I always sought support and assistance from significant others as each goal was reached before setting another one. My life has been enriched by family and very dear friends. An important belief and practice has been to return the benefits of my education to my community and to be an advocate for those persons needing assistance. I hold a special place for support of all older adults.*

MEINERT, JOHN RAYMOND, apparel executive, investment banker; b. White Cloud, Mich., Aug. 11, 1927; m. Joyce Macdonell, Nov. 5, 1955; children: Elizabeth Tinsman, Pamela Martin. Student, U. Mich., 1944-45; BS, Northwestern U., 1949. CPA Ill., 1952. With Hart Schaffner & Marx/Hartmarx Corp., Chgo., 1950-90, exec. v.p., 1975-80, vice chmn., 1981-85, sr. vice chmn., 1985-86, chmn., 1987-90, chmn. emeritus, 1990—, also bd. dirs.; prin. investment banking J.H. Chapman Group, LLC, Rosemont, Ill., 1990—, chmn., 1995—. Bd. dirs. County Seat Stores, Inc., N.Y.C., 1998-99, The John Evans Club, BBB, Chgo. C.of C.; trustee Amalgamated Ins. Fund, 1980-90, Rotary Internat. Retirement Fund, 2000-02; dir. Evanston Hosp., 1988-94, Clothing Mfrs. Assn., pres., 1982-87, chmn. 1987-90; instr. acctg. Northwestern U., 1949; faculty Lake Forest Grad. Sch. Mgmt., 1994-95; arbitrator Am. Arbitration Assn., 1993—. Chmn. bus. adv. coun. U. Ill., 1989-90; mem. Fin. Acctg. Stds. Adv. Coun., 1989-92, Chgo. Coun. Fgn. Rels., Sisters City Com.; mem. adv. coun. Northwestern U. Kellogg Grad. Sch. Recipient Alumni Merit award Northwestern U. Kellogg Grad. Sch., 1989; named Humanitarian of Yr., Five Hosp. Found., 1995. Mem. AICPA (v.p. 1985-86, bd. dirs. 1975-78, coun. 1971-93, trustee benevolent fund 1992-95, gold medal 1987), Ill. CPA Soc. (pub. svc. award 1996, pres. 1982-83, bd. dirs. 1966-68, 81-84, hon. award), Chicagoland C. of C. (bd. dirs.), Rotary (pres. Chgo. 1989-90, trustee found. 1991-95, asst. dist. gov. 1997-2000), Univ. Club, Execs. Club, Rolling Green Country Club. Presbyterian (elder). Home: 634 N Ironwood Dr Arlington Heights IL 60004-5818 Office: J H Chapman Group LLC 9700 W Higgins Rd Rosemont IL 60018-4796 Office Phone: 773-693-4800. Business E-Mail: jmeinert@jhchapman.com.

MEINWALD, JERROLD, retired chemistry professor; b. Bklyn., Jan. 16, 1927; s. Herman and Sophie (Baskind) M.; m. Yvonne Chu, June 25, 1955 (div. 1979); children: Constance Chu, Pamela Joan; m. Charlotte Greenspan, Sept. 7, 1980; 1 child, Julia Eve. PhB, U. Chgo., 1947, BS, 1948; MA, Harvard, 1950, PhD, 1952; PhD (hon.), U. Göteborg, 1989. Mem. faculty Cornell U., 1952—80, Goldwin Smith prof. chemistry, 1980—2005, grad. sch. prof., 2006—, mem. sci. directing group Cornell Inst. Rsch. Chem. Ecology, 1992—, emeritus prof., 2006—; rsch. dir. Internat. Centre Insect Physiology and Ecology, Nairobi, 1970-77; A. Mellon Term prof., 1992-95; prof. chemistry U. Calif. at San Diego, 1972-73. Chem. cons. Schering-Plough Rsch. Inst., 1957-99, Procter & Gamble Pharms., 1958-95, Cambridge Neurosci. Rsch., 1988-92, Du Pont, 2006; mem. sci. adv. bd. ENTOMED Inc., 2002-05; vis. prof. Rockefeller U., 1970, Harvard Med. Sch., 1997; Camille and Henry Dreyfus Disting. scholar Mt. Holyoke Coll., 1981, Bryn Mawr Coll., 1983, Dartmouth Coll., 1996; Kolthoff lectr. U. Minn., 1985; Beckman lectr. Calif. Inst. Tech., 1986; Swiss "Troisième Cycle" Lectr., 1986; Russell Marker lectr. Pa. State U., 1987; mem. vis. com. chemistry Brookhaven Nat. Lab., 1969-72, chmn., 1972; mem. med. A chemistry study sect. NIH, 1963-67, chmn., 1965-67; mem. adv. bd. Petroleum Rsch. Found., 1971-73; mem. adv. coun. chemistry dept. Princeton U., 1978-83; mem. adv. bd. Rsch. Corp., 1978-83; mem. adv. bd. chemistry div. NSF, 1979-83; organizing chmn. Sino-Am. Symposium on Chemistry of Natural Products, Shanghai, 1980; mem. adv. bd. A.P. Sloan Found., 1985-91; Frontiers of Rsch. lectr. Coun. Chem. Rsch., 1987; mem. sci. adv. bd. Agridyne Corp., 1989-93; adv. com. chem. ecology Max-Planck Soc., 1994-96, Nat. Inst. Sericulture and Entomol. Scis., Tsukuba, Japan, 1997-01; adv. bd. Xerces Soc., 1995—; adv. com. Biosphere 2, 1999-03; Carlton Coll. Convocation, 1993; Mary Aldridge lectr. Am. U., 1993; K. Pfister lectr. MIT, 1992, Hilldale lectr. U. Wis., 1991, Nat. Undergrad. Rsch. Symposium, Plenary lectr., Mpls., 1992; UNOCAL lectr. Calif. State U., Long Beach, 1992; Max T. Rogers lectr. Mich. State U., 1994; Jean Day lectr. Rutgers U., 1994, Disting. Grad. Sch. lectr. U. Md., 1994. Merck lectr. Lafayette Coll.; plenary lectr. 3d Pan Am. Chem. Congress; Inaugural Paul G. Gassman lectr. Canisius Coll., 1996, Disting. Sci. Lectr. Bard Coll., 1996, hon. visiting sci., Taiwan, 1997, Gassman lectr. U. Minn., 1999, Ptnrs. in Sci. lectr., Rsch Corp., 2000, Iscol award lectr., Cornell U., 2000, Chemistry as a life sci. X Symposium, 2000, IUPAC plenary lectr., Brazil, 2000, W.S. Johnson Symposium, Stanford, 2000, Berzelius Days plenary lectr., Stockholm, 2001, ICSN Symposium on Chemistry of Nat. Products, Gif-sur-Yvette, 2003, Nat. ACS Organic Symposium lectr., 2001, 05, others; mem. internat. sci. com. Programa Brasileiro de Ecologia Molecular/Amazonia, 1997-03; Grandpierre lectr. Columbia U., 1998; sci. adv. bd. Inst. Chemistry and Biochemistry, Czechoslovak Acad. Sci., 1999-05; Gilbert Stork lectr. Columbia U., 2005; mem. Princeton Area Organic Symposium, 2005. Mem. bd. editors Jour. Organic Chemistry, 1962-66, Organic Reactions, 1968-78, Organic Synthesis, 1968-72, Jour. Chem. Ecology, 1974—, Insect Sci., 1979-90, Current Organic Chemistry, 1999—, Chemistry & Biodiversity, 2004—, Procs. Nat. Acad. Sci., 2006—; contbr. articles to profl. jours. Recipient Tyler Environ. Achievement prize U. So. Calif., 1990, Gustavus J. Esselen award for Chemistry in the Pub. Interest, 1991, Heyrovsky medal Acad. Scis. of the Czech Rep., 1996, Pioneer's award Am. Inst. Chemists, 1997; Sloan fellow, 1958-62, Guggenheim fellow, 1960-61,76-77, spl. postdoctoral fellow NIH, 1967-68, fellow Japan Soc. Promotion of Sci., 1983, Ctr. for Advanced Study in Behavioral Sci., 1990-91; Fogarty internat. scholar NIH, 1983-85; Bert L. and Natalie K. Vallee Found., Inc. fellow, 1997. Mem. NAS (exch. scholar 1987), AAAS, Am. Acad. Arts and Scis. (sec. 2005-), Am. Philos. Soc., Am. Chem. Soc. (chmn. organic divsn. 1969, E Guenther award 1985, Disting. Scientist award Kalamazoo sect. 1985, A.C. Cope Scholar award 1989, Roger Adams award in Organic Chemistry 2005, Grand Prize of La Maison de la Chimie, Paris, 2006, R.C. Fuson lectr., U. Nev., 2006, R. Sandin lectr., U. Alberta, 2006, R. Hirschmann lectr., U. Wis., 2006, Novartis lectr., MIT, 2006, John D. Roberts lectr., Caltech, 2007, Clayton Heathcock lectr., U. Calif., Berkeley, 2007), Internat. Soc. Chem. Ecology (pres. 1988, Silver medal 1991), Phi Beta Kappa, Sigma Xi (nat. lectr. 1965, 75, 92-94). Home Phone: 607-257-0035; Office Phone: 607-255-3301. Business E-Mail: circe@cornell.edu.

MEISBURG, RONALD EDWARD, federal agency administrator, lawyer; b. Bowling Green, Ky., July 28, 1947; s. Edward Austin and Jean Lavelle (Knadler) M.; m. Elizabeth Ann Ruark, July 27, 1969 (div. Dec. 1975); m. Roseann Karene Finigan, July 14, 1984 (dec. 1997); m. Mary Helen Ratchford, June 9, 1999. BA, Carson-Newman Coll., 1969; JD, U. Louisville, 1974. Bar: Ky., DC, US Ct. Appeals (2nd, 3rd, 4th, 5th, 6th, 7th, DC, and 9th cirs.). Atty. US Dept. Labor, Washington, 1974-80; assoc. Smith, Heenan and Althen, Washington, 1980-85, ptnr., 1985-97, Heenan Althen & Roles, Washington, 1997—2002; atty., shareholder Ogletree, Deakins, Nash, Smoak & Stewart LLP, Washington, 2002—03; mem. NLRB, Washington, 2004, spl. asst. to assoc. gen. counsel for enforcement, 2005—06, exec. asst. to dep. gen. counsel, 2005—06, gen. counsel, 2006—. Pres., Energy & Mineral Law Found., 1994-95; mem., exec. com. Ea. Mineral Law Found., W.Va. U., Morgantown, 1990—, asst. v.p., 1991-93, v.p., 1993-94, pres., 1994-95; mem., US Coun. Internat. Bus., 1993-98, Employment Lawyers Advisory Coun., 1996-98, Nat. Assn. Mfrs., 1996-98. Contbr. articles to profl. jours. and proceedings; editl. adv. bd. Jour. Natural Resources and Environ. Law, 1987—. Recipient Disting. Achievement award US Sec. of Labor, Washington, 1978. Mem. ABA, Ky. Bar Assn., DC Bar. Roman Catholic. Office: NLRB Office Gen Counsel 1099 14th St NW Rm 10100 Washington DC 20570*

MEISEL, ALAN, law educator; b. Newark, Dec. 24, 1946; s. Stanley and Beatrice (Katz) M.; m. Linda Serody, Mar. 6, 1982; 2 children. BA, Yale U., 1968, JD, 1972. Bar: Conn. 1972, Pa. 1973, U.S. Dist. Ct. Conn. 1972, U.S. Dist. Ct. (we. dist.) Pa. 1973, U.S. Ct. Appeals (3d cir.) 1985. Prof. psychiatry U. Pitts., 1973—, prof. law, 1976—, Dickie, McCamey Chilcote prof. bioethics/law and psychiatry, 1995—, dir. Ctr. for Bioethics and Health Law, 1987—. Asst. dir. for legal studies Pres.'s Commn. for Study of Ethical Problems in Medicine and Biomed. and Behavioral Rsch., Washington, 1982; mem. ethics working group Presdl. Task Force on Healthcare Reform, 1993; mem. adv. coun. NHLBI, 1998—2004. Author: The Right to Die, 1989, 2d edit., 1995, 3d edit. 2004; co-author: Informed Consent: A Study of Decision Making in Psychiatry, 1984, Informed Consent: Legal Theory and Clinical Practice, 1987; contbr.

articles to legal and med. jours. Grantee NIMH, grantee Pres.'s Commn. for Study of Ethical Problems in Medicine and Biomed. and Behavioral Rsch., 1981-82, Founds. Fund for Rsch. in Psychiatry grantee, 1979-82, Legal Svcs. Corp. grantee, 1985-87; fellow Hastings Ctr.; award for The Right to Die Am. Assn. Publs., 1989; Pellegrino medal Contbns. Am. Health Care Ethics Law in Selfless Spirit of Edmund D. Pellegrino, Samford U., 2005. Mem.: Am. Soc. Bioethics and Humanities, Am. Soc. Law, Medicine and Ethics, Am. Health Lawyers Assn. Office: U Pitts Sch Law 3900 Forbes Ave Pittsburgh PA 15260 Business E-Mail: meisel@pitt.edu.

MEISEL, DAN, chemist; b. Tel Aviv, July 4, 1943; s. Arie and Mariasha Miriam (Ribak) M.; m. Osnat Meisel, Dec. 30, 1965; children: Einat, Omer. BSc, Hebrew U., 1967, MSc, 1969, PhD, 1974. Prof. chemistry U. Notre Dame, Ind., 1998—, dir. Radiation Lab. Ind., 1998—2004. Adv. bd.: Jour. Phys. Chem., 1993—2002; editor: Photochem. Energy Conversion, 1989, Semiconductors Nanoclusters, 1997. Mem. AAAS, Am. Chem. Soc., Am. Phys. Soc. Office: U Notre Dame Radiation Lab Notre Dame IN 46556 Office Phone: 574-631-5457. Business E-Mail: dani@nd.edu.

MEISEL, DAVID DERING, retired astronomer; b. Fairmont, W.Va., Mar. 28, 1940; s. Louis D. and Dorothy (Dering) M.; m. Carolyn Mae Conrad; children: Grace Margaret, Catherine Elise. BS in Physics, W.Va. U., 1961; MS in Astronomy, Ohio State U., 1963, PhD in Astronomy, 1967. Asst. prof. U. Va., Charlottesville, 1968-70, SUNY, Geneseo, 1970-76, assoc. prof., 1976-83, prof., 1983—2001, disting. prof., 2001—05; prof. emeritus, 2005—. Assoc. C.E.K. Mees Obs., Bristol, NY, 1973, assoc. dir., 1988—97; sr. assoc. NASA Goddard Space Flight Ctr., Greensbelt, Md., 1977—78. Contbr. articles to profl. jours. NASA grantee U. Va., 1965-67, SUNY, 73-76, NSF grantee, 1976-77, 92—2005. Fellow AAAS, Royal Astron. Soc.; mem. Am. Meteor Soc. (exec. dir. 1972&), Am. Astron. Soc., Internat. Astron. Union, Internat. Info. Acad. (academician). Achievements include study of helium 10830 in early type stars; study of interstellar micrometeors and radio-meteor forward scattering.

MEISEL, JOHN, political scientist; b. Vienna, Oct. 23, 1923; s. Fryda and Ann M. BA, U. Toronto, 1948, MA, 1950; PhD in Polit. Sci., London Sch. Econs., 1959; LLD, Brock U., 1983, U. Guelph, 1985, Carleton U., 1990, U. Toronto, 1993, Queen's U., 1996, U. Regina, 1999, U. Calgary, 2000; DU (hon.), U. Ottawa, 1983; D of Social Scis. (hon.), Laval U., 1988; LittD (hon.), U. Waterloo, 1998. Head dept. polit. studies Queen's U., Kingston, Ont., Canada, 1963-67, Hardy prof. polit. sci., 1963-80, Sir Edward Peacock prof. polit. sci., 1983-93, prof. emeritus. Former chmn. Can. Radio-TV and Telecomms. Commn.; moderator symposia on finding common grounds for polit. issues confronting Yugoslavia, UN, Vienna, 1995. Author: The Canadian General Election of 1957, 1962, Papers on the 1962 Election, 1964, Ethnic Relations in Canadian Voluntary Associations, 1972, Working Papers on Canadian Politics, 1975; editor: Internat. Polit. Sci. Rev., 1979-95, (with Jean Laponce) Debating the Constitution/Débat sur la constitution, 1994. Decorated companion Order of Can.; recipient Killam award Can Coun., 1968-73. Fellow Royal Soc. Can. (pres. 1992-95); mem. Univ. Club (Toronto). Home (Summer): Colimaison Tichborne ON Canada K0H 2V0 Office: Queen's U Kingston ON Canada K7L 3N6 Home (Winter): 70A Johnson St Kingston ON Canada K7L1X7 Business E-Mail: meiselj@queensu.ca.

MEISEL, MARTIN, retired English and comparative literature educator; b. NYC, Mar. 22, 1931; s. Joseph and Sally (Rössler) Mörsel; m. Martha Sarah Winkley, Dec. 22, 1957 (dec. Mar. 2008); children: Maude Frances, Andrew Avram, Joseph Stoddard AB, Queens Coll., 1952; MA, Princeton U., 1957, PhD, 1960; postgrad., U. Rome, 1959. Instr. English Rutgers U., New Brunswick, N.J., 1957-58; instr., asst. prof., assoc. prof. Dartmouth Coll., Hanover, N.H., 1959-65; prof. English U. Wis., Madison, 1965-68; prof. English and comparative lit. Columbia U., NYC, 1968—, Brander Matthews prof. dramatic lit., 1987—, chmn. dept., 1980-83, 99-01, acting v.p. arts and scis., 1986-87, v.p. arts and scis., 1989-93, prof. emeritus, 2004—. Trustee Columbia U. Press, 1990-94. Author: Shaw and the 19th Century Theater, 1963, Realizations: Narrative, Pictorial, and Theatrical Arts in 19th Century England (George Freedley Meml. award Theater Libr. Assn. 1984, Barnard Hewitt award Am. Theatre Assn. 1984), 1983, How Plays Work: Reading and Performance, 2007; mem. editl. bd. Jour. Victorian Studies, PMLA, Jour. Contemporary Lit., Bull. Rsch. in the Humanities, 19th Century Contexts. Served with U.S. Army, 1954-56 Fellow Guggenheim Found., 1963-64, 1987-88, Am. Council of Learned Socs., 1970-71, Inst. for Advanced Studies in the Humanities, Edinburgh, 1977, Huntington Library and Art Gallery, 1978, 80, 83, Nat. Humanities Ctr., 1983-84, Wilson Ctr., Smithsonian Instn., 1987-88. Mem. MLA, Am. Soc. Theatre Rsch., North Am. Victorian Studies Assn., Assn. of Historians of 19 Century Art, Century Assn., Internat. Shaw Soc. Home: 18 Bacon Hill Rd Pleasantville NY 10570-3502 Personal E-mail: mm28@columbia.edu.

MEISEL, STEVEN, advertising photographer; b. NY, 1954; s. Lenny and Sally. Student in Fashion Illustration, Parsons Sch. Design. Illustrator, Halston, Women's Wear Daily; advt. photographer The Gap, Revlon, Valentino, Anne Klein, Calvin Klein, Gianfranco Ferré, Prada, Dolce and Gabbana, Lancome, Barney's, Donna Karan, Versace, Alberta Ferretti, Anna Sui, Max Mara, Clinique; photographer Madonna's Sex, 1992; exhibitions (fashion photos): Fashioning Photography in Fiction since 1990, Mus. Modern Art, NYC, 2004, White Cube 2, London, 2001, Moderna Museet, Stockholm, Nat. Mus.Photography, Film & TV, Bradford, Eng.; free-lance photographer Vogue, Harper's Bazaar. Recipient Spl. award Photography Coun. Fashion Designers Am., 1992, Internat. Fashion Photography award Festival Internat. de la Photo de Mode, 1994. Office: Steven Meisel Studio 64 Wooster St Fl 4 New York NY 10012-4387

MEISEL, ZACHARY FRANKLIN, emergency physician, educator; s. Frederick Lawrence Meisel and Allene Gay Fisch; m. Courtney Anne Schreiber, May 8, 2001; children: Alexander Finn, Dalia Ivy. MD, Johns Hopkins U., Balt., 1999. Cert. Am. Bd. Emergency Medicine, Mich., 2001. Asst. prof. emergency medicine Allegheny Gen. Hosp., Pitts., 2003—05, U. Pa., Phila., 2005—08; clin. scholar Robert Wood Johnson Found. U. Pa., Phila., 2008—. Contbr. articles to profl. jours. Fellow: Am. Coll. Emergency Physicians; mem.: ZaBeCor Pharm. (bd. mem. 2003—08). Avocations: skiing, cooking. Office: Univ Pa 423 Guardian Dr 13th Fl Philadelphia PA 19104 Business E-Mail: zachary.meisel@uphs.upenn.edu.

MEISELBACH, JAMES VINCENT, mechanical engineer, educator; s. Charles John and Maryann Meiselbach; m. Niettchy Neomi Mora, Aug. 4, 1988; children: James Vincent II, Nydia Rose. Degree in Mech. Engring. Tech., Calif. Poly. U., Pomona, 2004. Cert. in fundamental engring., NCEES, Calif. Lic. Bd., 2005. Mfg. engr. Ducommun Aerostructures, Monrovia, Calif., 2004—06; mech. engr. Futek Advanced Sensor Tech., Irvine, Calif., 2006—. Lectr. Calif. Poly. U. Pomona, 2005—. Contbr. scientific papers. Sgt. US Army, 1983—90, Europe. Office: Futek Advanced Sensor Tech 10 Thomas Irvine CA 92618

MEISELES, DANIEL, sports association executive; m. Stephanie Meiseles; 2 children. Grad., St. John's U., NY. Assoc. prodr. NBC, 1988—90, NBA, NYC; sr. v.p. prodn. and programming NBA Entertainment, 2006—07, sr. v.p. prodn., programming and broadcasting, 2007—. Exec. prodr.: NBA Entertainment. Office: NBA Olympic Tower 645 5th Ave Fl 10 New York NY 10022-5986*

MEISELS, GERHARD GEORGE, academic administrator, chemist, educator; b. Vienna, May 11, 1931; came to U.S., 1951, naturalized, 1961; s. Leo and Adele Josefa Maria (Seehofer) M.; m. Sylvia Claire Knopsnider, June 28, 1958; 1 dau., Laura Germaine. Student, U. Vienna, 1949-51, 52-53; MS, U. Notre Dame, Ind., 1952, PhD, 1956. Postdoctoral rsch. assoc. U. Notre Dame, 1955-56; chemist Gulf Oil Corp., Pitts., 1956-59; part-time instr. Carnegie Inst. Tech., Pitts., 1956-58; chemist nuclear divsn. Union Carbide Corp., Tuxedo, NY, 1959-63, asst. group leader, 1964-65; assoc. prof. U. Houston, 1965-70, prof., 1970-75, dept. chmn., 1973-75; prof., chmn. dept. chemistry U. Nebr., Lincoln, 1975-81, dean Coll. Arts and Scis., 1981-88; provost, COO U. South Fla., Tampa, 1988-94; dir. Coalition Sci. Literacy, 1994—, Suncoast Area Ctr. for Ednl. Enhancement (SACEE), 1996-99. Cons. Union Carbide Corp., Gearhart-Owen Industries. Editor (spl. issue) Jour. Radiation Physics and Chemistry, 1980; contbr. writings in field to profl. publs. Sec., pres. Ramsey (N.J.) Jr. C. of C., 1959-64; active rsch. bd. All Children's Hosp.; chmn. Fla. Coalition for Improving Math. and Sci. Edn., 1998—, interim exec. dir. Fulbright fellow, Smith-Mundt fellow, 1951-52; sr. fellow Sci. Rsch. Coun., Eng., 1976. Mem. Am. Chem. Soc. (com. chmn.), Am. Soc. for Mass Spectrometry (charter, com. chmn., v.p. 1984-86, pres. 1986-88, bd. dirs. 1988-90), Fla. Acad. Scis., AAAS, Am. Phys. Soc., Coun. Sci. Soc. Pres. (exec. bd. 1989-92, chmn. elect 1990, chmn. 1991, chmn. com. on sci. priorities), Nat. Alliance State Sci. and Math. Coalitions (bd. dirs. 1999—, v.p., 2007—), Coun. for Chem. Rsch. (bd. dirs. 1982-85), Conformation Judges Assn. Fla. (pres. 1996—), Fla. Higher Edn. Consortium Math. and Sci. (ctrl. steering com. 1995—, chmn. 1998-2000), Houston Kennel Club (bd. dirs. 1968-70), Cornhusker Kennel Club (pres., bd. dirs., del. to Am. Kennel Club 1976-88), St. Petersburg Dog Fanciers Assn. (sec. 1996-98, 2000-04, del. to Am. Kennel Club 1998—), Lakeland-Winter Haven K.C. (pres. 2006-09), Fla. Stem Coun., Sigma Xi. Home: PO Box 1347 Thonotosassa FL 33592-1347 Office: U South Fla 4202 E Fowler Ave/CHE 205 Tampa FL 33620 Office Phone: 813-974-7183. Business E-Mail: meisels@csl.usf.edu.

MEISELS, SAMUEL J., education educator; b. Cleve., Sept. 14, 1945; s. Saul Meisels and Ida Moskowitz; m. Alice Meisels, June 21, 1970; children: Seth, Rebecca Fishman. AB, U. Rochester, NY, 1967; EdM, Harvard U., Boston, 1968, D in Education, 1973. Tchg. fellow edn. Harvard U., Boston, 1968—70; sci. coord. & tchr. Cambridge Montessori Sch., Mass., 1969—70; tchr. Mass. Pub. Schs., Brookline, Mass., 1970—72; lectr. edn. Wheelock Coll., Boston, 1970—72, Simmons Coll., Boston, 1971—73; assoc. prof., dept. child study, Tufts U., Medford, Mass., 1972—80, dir., 1973—78; sr. advisor early childhood devel. Children's Hosp. Med. Ctr., Boston, 1979—80; chmn., spl. edn. program U. Mich., Ann Arbor, Mich., 1980—83, program dir., 1980—83, assoc. prof., 1980—86, assoc. rsch. scientist, 1983—86, prof., sch. edn., 1986—2001, rsch. scientist, ctr. human growth & devel., 1986—2001, prof. edn. emeritus & rsch. scientist emeritus, 2002—, dir.; pres. Erikson Inst., Chgo., 2002—. Lectr. Taiwan Nat. Normal U., Taipei, Taiwan, 1995; mem. Nat. Ctr. Edn. & Economy, Pitts., 1997—98, Nat. Coun. Accreditation Tchr. Edn., Washington, 2008—, Nat. Edn. Goals Panel, Washington, 1990—95, Nat. Assn. State Bds. Edn., Washington, 1991—92, Commn. Behavioral & Social Scis. & Edn., NAS, Washington, 1998—2000, Chgo. Pub. Edn. Fund, Chgo., 2005—, Nat. Reporting Sys., Head Start Bur., Washington, 2002—05, Pew Charitable Trusts, Phila., 2005—07; prin. cons. Merrill-Palmer Inst., Wayne State U., Detroit, 1991—93; advisor Psychol. Corp., Ft. Worth, 1998—2002; co-chair Chgo. Pub. Schs., Chgo., 2002—03. Recipient award, Am. Acad. Pediat., 2005, Outstanding Svc. award, Met. Assn., 2005. Mem.: Zero Three: Nat. Ctr. Infants, Toddlers, & Families (pres. 2001—03), Soc. Rsch. Child Devel., Nat. Soc. Study Edn., Nat. Assn. Edn. Young Children, Coun. Exceptional Children, Am. Edn. Rsch. Assn., Phi Delta Kappa. Office: Erikson Inst 451 N LaSalle St Chicago IL 60654-4510 Office Fax: 312-755-0133.

MEISENHEIMER, FRED E., gas industry company executive; BS, Stephen F. Austin State U.; MBA, Southern Methodist U. Contr. Vartec Telecom Inc.; Audit mgr. Deloitte & Touche LLP, 1970—79; gen. auditor Oryx Energy Corp., 1988—99; asst. contr. Oryx Energy Corp. (formerly Sun Exploration & Prodn. Co.), 1979—99; v.p., contr. Atmos Energy Corp., 2000—09, interim CFO, 2009, sr. v.p., CFO, 2009—. Office: Atmos Energy Corp 1800 Three Lincoln Centre Dallas TX 75240 Office Phone: 972-934-9227. Office Fax: 972-855-3040.*

MEISNER, JOACHIM CARDINAL, cardinal, archbishop; b. Breslau, Germany, Dec. 25, 1933; s. Walter and Hedwig Meisner. Ed., U. Erfurt, Pastoral Sem. at Neuzelle. Ordained priest Diocese of Erfurt-Meiningen, 1962; chaplain St. Agidien, Heiligenstadt, 1963—66, St. Crucis, Erfurt, 1966; rector Diocese of Erfurt, 1966—76; ordained bishop, 1975; aux. bishop Diocese of Erfurt-Meiningen, 1975—80; bishop Diocese of Berlin, 1980—89; pres. Berliner Bischofskonferenz, 1982—89; elevated to cardinal, 1983; cardinal-priest S. Pudenziana, 1983—; archbishop Archdiocese of Cologne, 1989—. Contbr. articles to profl. jours. Roman Catholic. Address: Archdiocese of Cologne Marzellenstrasse 32 50668 Cologne Germany

MEISNER, LORRAINE FAXON, geneticist; d. Morris and Pauline Krimsky Faxon; children: Jeffrey Allen, William Ira, Anne Michelle Meisner - Herrera. PhD, U. Chgo., 1966; FACMG, Am. Coll. Med. Genetics, 1982. Rschr. Cancer Rsch. Inst., Boston, 1962—65; prof. U. Wis., Madison, 1968—2006; chief sci. officer Cell Line Genetics, LLC, Madison, 2006—. Mem.: NY Acad. Scis. Office: Cell Line Genetics LLC 510 Charmany Dr Madison WI 53719-1289 Personal E-mail: lmeisner@clgenetics.com. Business E-Mail: lorraine@slh.wisc.edu.

MEISNER, MARY JO, foundation administrator, former newspaper editor; b. Chgo., Dec. 24, 1951; d. Robert Joseph and Mary Elizabeth (Casey) M.; 1 child, Thomas Joseph Gradel. BS in Journalism, U. Ill., 1974, MS in Journalism, 1976. Copy editor Wilmington (Del.) News Jour., 1975-76, labor and bus. reporter, 1976-79; labor and gen. assignment reporter Phila. Daily News, 1979, city editor, 1979-83, met. editor, 1983-85; PM city editor San Jose (Calif.) Mercury News, 1985-86, met. editor, 1986-87; city editor The Washington Post, 1987-90; mng. editor The Ft. Worth Star-Telegram, 1991-93; editor and v.p. The Milw. Jour., 1993-95; editor, sr. v.p The Milw. Jour. Sentinel, 1995-97; editor, vice chmn. Cmty. Newspaper Co., Needham, Mass., 1997—2001; v.p., comm., pub. affairs Boston Found., 2001—. Mem. AP Mng. Editors (bd. dirs. 1992-95), Am. Soc. Newspaper Editors, Internat. Press Inst. (bd. dirs. 2005-06, Pulitzer prize juror 1994, 97). Mass. Newspaper Pubs. Assn. (bd. dirs.). Office: Boston Foundation 10th Fl 75 Arlington St Boston MA 02116 Office Phone: 617-338-4286. Business E-Mail: mjm@tbf.org.

MEISNER, MAURICE J., history professor; b. Detroit, Nov. 17, 1931; m. Lynn M. Lubkeman, July 11, 1984; 1 child, Matthew Harvey. MA, U. Chgo., PhD, 1962. Rsch. fellow contemporary Chinese studies Harvard U., Cambridge, Mass.; Goldberg prof. history U. Wis., Madison, 1968—. Author: Li Ta-chao and the Origins of Chinese Marxism, Mao's China; Mao's China and After, Mao's China, Third ed, Marxism, Maoism, and Utopianism, The Deng Xiaoping Era, Mao Zedong. Recipient H. Goldberg Chair, U. Wis., 1991—. Avocations: travel, baseball, writing. Home: 1106 Shorewood Blvd Shorewood Hills Madison WI 53705 Office: Univ Wis Madison 435 N Park St Madison WI 53706 Business E-Mail: mmeisner@wisc.edu.

MEISNER, PATRICIA ANN, assistant principal; d. Edward Charles and Eileen Cull Meisner. BS in elem. edn., Ohio U., 1969; M in ednl. adminstrn., U. Hawaii, 1982. Cert. elem. prin. Ohio, elem. tchr. Ohio. Tchr. Northwest Local Sch., Cin., 1969—72, Star of Sea, Honolulu, 1972—83, St. Bartholomew Sch., Cin., 1987—2002; prin. St. Catharine of Siena, Cin., 1983—86; asst. prin. St. Ursula Villa, Cin., 2002—. Trustee N.Am. Ursuline Ednl. Svcs., 2004—. Mem.: Nat. Cath. Edn. Assn., Assn. Supervision and Curriculum Devel. Avocation: travel. Office: St Ursula Villa 3660 Vineyard Pl Cincinnati OH 45226 Office Phone: 513-871-7218 ext. 127. Business E-Mail: p.meisner@stursulavilla.org.

MEISSNER, EDWIN BENJAMIN, JR., retired real estate broker; b. St. Louis, Dec. 27, 1918; s. Edwin B. and Edna (Rice) Meissner; m. Nina Renard, Dec. 17, 1946; children: Edwin Benjamin III, Wallace, Robert; 1 child, Donald. BS, U. Pa., Phila., 1940. Joined St. Louis Car Co., 1934, asst. to pres., v.p., exec. v.p., 1950-56, pres., gen. mgr., 1956-61; pres. St. Louis Car div. Gen. Steel Industries, Inc., 1961-67; sr. v.p., dir. Gen. Steel Industries, Inc., 1968-74; v.p. Bakewell Corp., 1974-85; real estate broker, v.p. Hilliker Corp., St. Louis, 1985-96. Mem. pres.' coun. St. Louis U.; bd. dirs. Washington U. Med. Ctr. Redevel. Corp., Barnard Free Skin and Cancer Hosp.; past bd. dirs. James S. McDonnell USO; overseer St. Louis Symphony Soc.; hon. dir. Humane Soc. Mo.; v.p. Gateway Ctr. Met. St. Louis; past chmn. Ladue Police and Fire Commn., Mo.; mem. Jefferson Nat. Expansion Meml. Commn.; mil. affairs com. Regional Commerce; dir. Ctrl. Inst. for Deaf. Mem. Am. Ordnance Assn. (life), Internat. Assn. Chiefs of Police (assoc.), Mo. Assn. Chiefs of Police, Mo. Athletics Club, Westwood Country Club, Bridlespur Hunt Club, St. Louis Club, Beta Gamma Sigma. Office: Barton Bldg Ste 302 200 S Bemiston Saint Louis MO 63105-1915 Home Phone: 314-993-2959; Office Phone: 314-863-2446.

MEISSNER, LAUREL G., insurance company executive; b. 1959; BS in Acctg. & Sys. Analysis, Taylor U. Held positions KPMG, Cruise Technologies, Initiate Sys.; dir., tech. acctg. Motorola Inc., 2000—01, v.p. fin., 2001—07, asst. contr., 2001—08, corp. v.p. fin., chief acctg. officer, 2008; sr. v.p., global contr. Aon Corp., 2009—, prin. acctg. officer, 2009—. Office: Aon Corp 200 East Randolph St Chicago IL 60601 Office Phone: 312-381-1000.

MEISTER, BERNARD JOHN, retired chemical engineer; b. Maynard, Mass., Feb. 27, 1941; s. Benjamin C. and Gertrude M. Meister; m. Janet M. White, Dec. 31, 1971; children: Mark, Martin, Kay Ellen. BSChemE, Worcester Poly. Inst., 1962; PhD in Chem. Engring., Cornell U., 1966. From engring. rschr. to rsch. scientist Dow Chem. Co., Midland, Mich., 1966—92, rsch. scientist, 1992—2005, ret., 2005. Contbr. articles to profl. jours. Mem.: AIChE (Chem. Engr. of Yr. 1983), Soc. Rheology, Soc. Plastic Engrs., Am. Chem. Soc., Sigma Xi. Methodist. Avocations: fishing, stock market. Home: 2925 Chippewa Ln Midland MI 48640-4181 Personal E-mail: bjjm1@att.net. *Free the mind of things you can't change, and let it focus on things you can accomplish.*

MEISTER, HOWARD SCOTT, marine biologist, educator; b. Tampa, SC, Nov. 27, 1971; s. Howard William Meister and Jackie Denise Preston; m. Sara H. Jones, Oct. 4, 2009. BA in Environ. Studies, Marine Sci., U. NC, Wilmington, 1984. Marine fish biologist SC Dept. Natural Resources, Charleston, 1994—, marine sci. educator, 2006—. Contbr. articles to sci. profl. jours. Mem.: Am. Fisheries Soc., SC Chpt. (Jack Bayless award 2000, 2006), SC Fishery Workers Assn. (pres. 2004—05), SC Marine Educators Assn. (pres. 2009—), Nat. Marine Educators Assn., Assn. Southeastern Biologists. Home: 30 Wyecreek Ave Charleston SC 29412 Office: SC Dept Natural Resources 217 Ft Johnson Rd PO Box 12559 Charleston SC 29422-2559 Office Fax: 843-953-9353. Business E-Mail: meisters@dnr.sc.gov.

MEISTER, JULIA B., lawyer; b. Ft. Thomas, Ky., Nov. 16, 1969; BA, Xavier U., 1991; JD, Notre Dame Law Sch., 1995. Bar: Ohio 1995, Ct. of Appeals Sixth Cir., US Dist. Ct. Southern Dist. Ohio, US Dist. Ct. Southern Dist. Ind. Ptnr. Taft, Stettinius & Hollister LLP, Cin. Mem. Bd. for Cin. Area Sr. Services, Ky. Symphony Orch., Cin., Bd. Cin. Opera Assn. Named a Rising Star, YWCA Acad. Career Women of Achievement; named one of Ohio's Rising Stars, Super Lawyers, 2006; named to Best Lawyers in Am. Mem.: Cin. Bar Assn. (chair, admissions com.). Office: Taft Stettinius & Hollister LLP 425 Walnut St Ste 1800 Cincinnati OH 45202-3957 Office Phone: 513-357-9330.

MEISTER, MARK JAY, museum director, professional society administrator; b. Balt., June 26, 1953; s. Michael Aaron and Yetta (Haransky) M.; m. Carla Steiger, Aug. 7, 1977; children: Rachel, Kaitlin. AB, Washington U., St. Louis, 1974; MA, U. Minn., 1976; cert. mus. mgmt., U. Calif., Berkeley, 1983. Asst. lectr. St. Louis Art Mus., 1974; asst. coord. young people's program Mpls. Inst. Arts, 1975—76, coord. mobile program, 1976, coord. tchrs. resource svcs., 1976—77; dir. Mus. Art and History, Port Huron, Mich., 1978—79, Midwest Mus. Am. Art, Elkhart, Ind., 1979—81; exec. dir. Children's Mus., St. Paul, 1981—86; dir. Mus. Art, Sci. and Industry, Bridgeport, Conn., 1986—89; exec. dir. Archaeol. Inst. of Am., Boston, 1989—99; exec. dir. Archl. Inst. Am. Inst. Archeologique d'Amerique, Boston and Toronto, 1994—99; exec. dir. Dayton Soc. Natural History, 2000—06, pres., CEO, 2006—. Adj. lectr. museology Kenyon Coll., Gambier, Ohio, 1977; adj. lectr. art history Ind. U., South Bend, 1980—81; regional reviewer Inst. Mus. Svcs., Washington, 1985—86, Washington, 1989; treas., vice chmn. Minn. Assn. Mus., St. Paul, 1983—86; ex-officio trustee U.S. com. Internat. Coun. on Monuments and Sites, 1995—99. Bd. dirs. Seaway Arts Coun., St. Clair County, Mich., 1978-79; bd. dirs. Dayton Sister Cities Com., 2000-05, chair, 2003-05; bd. dirs. Dayton Peace Accords Project, 2000-05, vice chair, 2003; bd. dirs. Glen Helen Ecology Inst., 2004—2007, Dayton Coun. on World Affairs, 2005-, pres. 2008-; Greater Dayton Pub. TV, 2006-07, cmty. advisor bd, 2007-; bd. trustees Dayton-Montgomery County Convention & Visitors Bur., 2009-; mem. Mayor's Arts Adv. Com., Elkhart, 1981; mem. exec. com., Conf. Adminstrv. Officers, Am. Coun. Learned Socs., 1994-97; pres. Asian Arts Ctr., Dayton, 2002-05; bd. trustees, Dayton: A Peace Process,

2004-, co-chair, 2007-08, Dayton Literacy Peace Prize Found., 2008-; Prevent Blindness Ohio, Dayton chpt. leadership coun., 2004—, chmn., 2006-. NEH museology fellow, Mpls. Inst. Arts, 1976-77, Kress fellow U. Minn. 1977-78, Bush leadership summer fellow, Bush Found., St. Paul, 1983; named One of Outstanding Young Men Am., 1981. Mem.: Archaeological Conservancy, Assn. Children's Mus., Ohio Mus. Assn. (Profl. of Yr. 2008), Assn. Sci. and Tech. Ctrs., Assn. Zoos and Aquariums, Assn. Sci. Mus. Dirs., Archaeological Inst. Am., Am. Assn. Mus. Office: Dayton Soc Natural History 2600 Deweese Pkwy Dayton OH 45414-5499 Business E-Mail: mmeister@boonshoftmuseum.org.

MEISTER, RYAN EDWARD, marketing executive; b. Washington, July 21, 1973; s. Frederick A. Meister and Susan Danforth; m. Tiffany Meister, June 7, 2008. BA, Colo. State U., Ft. Collins, 1998. Cert.: Colo. POST 1995. V.p. client svcs. GA Wright Mktg., Denver, 2005—. Mem. Denver C. of C., 2005—05. Decorated Meritorious Svc. Commendation CSU Police. Mem.: Gerson Lehman Group. Home: 2915 Woodbriar Dr Highlands Ranch CO 80126 Office: Ga Wright Mktg 10325 E 47th Ave Denver CO 80238 Personal E-mail: denverdiver@gmail.com.

MEIXNER, JOHN B., philosopher, educator; b. Chgo., Dec. 8, 1949; s. Robert H. and Phyllis P. Meixner; children: Monica K. MacMillan, John B. PhD, Johns Hopkins U., Balt., 1975. Asst. prof. Northwestern U., Evanston, Ill., 1975—83; assoc. prof. Ctrl. Mich. U., Mt. Pleasant, Mich., 1983—. Dir. CMU Law Professions Ctr., Mt. Pleasant, 1995—. Contbr. articles to publs. Home: 1007 Glen Ave Mount Pleasant MI 48858 Office: Dept Philosophy Ctrl Mich Univ Mount Pleasant MI 48859 Business E-Mail: john.meixner@cmich.edu.

MEJIA, SISTER CRISTEL, language educator; AA, Trocaire Coll., Buffalo, 1978; BA in Spanish, Calif. State U., Sacramento, 1982; MSEd in Founds. and Tchg., Niagara U., Lewiston, NY, 1987; MA in Spanish Lang. and Lit., PhD in Spanish Lang. and Lit., SUNY, Buffalo, 2008. Spanish tchr. Mt. Mercy Acad., Buffalo, 1987—2000; Spanish instr. SUNY, 2000—08. Sr. lectr. Spanish Niagara U., 2007—08; Spanish instr. Erie CC, Buffalo, 2008—. Named Tchr. of Yr., Diocese Buffalo, 1990. Mem.: MLA.

MEJÍA, JAIME ARMIN, language educator; b. Edinburg, Tex., Feb. 14, 1955; s. Jose Armin and Guadalupe Cortez Mejia. BA, North Tex. State U., Denton, 1978; MA, Pan Am. U., Edinburg, 1985; PhD, Ohio State U., Columbus, 1993. Tchg. assoc., English dept. Ohio State U., 1985—90; assoc. prof., dept. English Tex. State U., San Marcos, 1991—. Recipient Presdl. award, SW Tex. State U., 1996. Mem.: Nat. Assn. Chicana and Chicano Studies, Conf. Coll. Composition and Communication. Office: Tex State Univ San Marcos English Dept Flowers Hall San Marcos TX 78666 Business E-Mail: jm31@txstate.edu.

MEJIA, JORGE MARIA CARDINAL, cardinal, archbishop; b. Buenos Aires, Jan. 31, 1923; Student, Pontifical Biblical Institute, Rome, Seminary of Villa Devoto, Buenos Aires, Argentina; PhD, Theology, Pontifical U. of St. Thomas, Rome, 1948. Ordained priest Archdiocese of Buenos Aires, Argentina, 1945; prof. sacred scripture Catholic U. of Argentina; dir. Catholic Journal Criterio, 1956—77; sec. Dept. Ecumenism CELAM, 1967—77; sec. Pontifical Commn. for Religious Rels. with the Jews, Rome, 1977—86; ordained bishop, 1986; vice-pres. Pontifical Commn. Iustitia et Pax, Rome, 1986—94; archbishop, sec. Congregation of Bishops, Rome, 1994—98; archivist Vatican Secret Archives, Rome, 1998—2003; librarian Vatican Libr., Rome, 1998—2003; elevated to cardinal, 2001; cardinal-deacon S. Girolamo della Carita, 2001—; archivist emeritus Vatican Secret Archives, Rome, 2003—. Roman Catholic. Office: Citta del Baricano 00120 Vatican City Italy

MEJICO, LUIS J., neurologist, educator; s. Sergio O. Mejico and Eugenia H. Sorazu; m. Paula Pons, Oct. 13, 1995; children: Fiona, Vigo. MD, Cath. U. Cordoba, Argentina, 1993, SUNY, Syracuse, 2000. Instr. neurology & ophthalmology Johns Hopkins U. Hosp., Balt., 1999—2000; asst. prof. neurology & ophthalmology SUNY Upstate Med. U., 2000—06, assoc. prof. neurology & ophthalmology, 2006—. Fellow: North Am. Neuro Ophthalmology Soc.; mem.: Am. Headache Soc., Am. Acad. Neurology.

MEKLER, L. ARLEN, lawyer, chemist; b. NYC, May 4, 1943; s. Lev A. and Ethel (Fox) M.; children from previous marriage: Jeffrey Arlen, Rebecca Ann, Ann-Marie Laura, Victoria Arlene, Lamar Adam, Lars Arlen; m. Molly L. Malone, Feb. 3, 1995. BS in Chemistry, Reed Coll.-San Jose State U., 1953; MS in Organic Chemistry, Iowa State U., 1955; PhD, Ohio State U., 1958; JD, Temple U., 1972. Bar: Del. 1972, Pa. 1972, U.S. Supreme Ct. 1976. Sr. rsch. chemist E.I. du Pont de Nemours & Co., Wilmington, Del., 1958-69; ptnr. Mekler and Maurer, Wilmington, 1972—. Chief appellate div. Office Pub. Defender, State of Del., 1973-77; pres. Del. Law Ctr., Wilmington, 1973—; instr. constl. law Wilmington Coll., 1976-80; dir. Bar Rev. Del., 1972—; mem. 3d Circuit Ct. Appeal Jud. Nominating Commn., 1977-81, 3d Circuit Ct. Appeals Jud. Conf. Contbr. monographs to legal publs. Pres. Mental Health Aux. for Gov. Bacon Health Ctr., 1964-66; mem. Citizens Conf. for Modernization of State Legislatures, 1964-68; state chmn., Reform Commn. for Modernization Polit. Party Rules, 1965-68; pres. Del. Citizens for Fair Housing, 1965-69; state commr. Nat. Conf. on Uniform State Laws, 1972—; pres. Democratic Forum Del., 1966-70; mem. Del. Dem. Platform Com., 1966, 68, 72, 76; research dir. Del. Citizens for Humphrey-Muskie, 1968, Citizens for Biden, 1972, 78, 84, Citizens for McDowell, 1986—, Biden for Pres., 1986, 2005; del. Dem. Nat. Conv., 1980, Obama-Biden for pres., 2008, mem. Social Security Medicare Tax Reform Initiative, 2009, 2008; mem. social action com. Unitarian Ch., Wilmington, 1962-68. Recipient Keyman award, 1964, 65; State Govtl. Affairs award, 1964, 65 Mem. ABA, Del. Bar Assn. (com. on rules of criminal procedure 1973-74, supreme ct. com. on revision of criminal law 1973—, supreme ct. com. on rules of evidence 1976—, com. on revised rules of evidence 1976—, com. on revised rules of Del. Supreme Ct. 1974—, family law com. 1979—, continuing legal edn. com. 1981—), Pa. Bar Assn., Am. Chem. Soc., N.Y. Acad. Scis., Chem. Soc. (London), AAAS, Catalyst Club Phila., Wilmington Organic Chemists Club, ACLU (bd. dirs.), Sigma Xi, Phi Alpha Delta Home: Brandywine Hills 714 W Matson Run Pky Wilmington DE 19802-1912 Office Phone: 302-762-8498. Business E-Mail: drlaw@comcast.net.

MELA, CARL FREDERICK, marketing educator; b. Arlington, Mass., Apr. 11, 1961; s. Richard Lawrence and Dorothy Anne M. BSEE, Brown U., 1983; MBA, UCLA, 1987; PhD, Columbia U., 1993. Mktg. support engr. Hewlett-Packard, Lake Stevens, Wash., 1983-85; product line mgr. Proxima Corp., San Diego, 1987-89; asst. prof. dept. mktg. U. Notre Dame, Ind., 1993—. Vice chair Am. Mktg. Assn. Rsch. SIG, Chgo., 1996. Contbr. articles to profl. jours. Am. Mktg. Assn. Doctoral Consortium fellow, 1993. Mem. INFORMS, Am. Mktg. Assn., Assn. for Consumer Rsch., Sigma Xi. Office: Duke U Fuqua Schl of Business Durham NC 27708

MELA, THEOFANIE, physiologist; MD, U. Athens Med. Sch., 1989. Cardiac electrophysiologist Mass. Gen. Hosp., Boston, 2000—, dir., pacemaker & ICD lab, 2003—. Contbr. scientific papers. Office: Mass Gen Hosp 75 Fruit St Boston MA 02114 Office Fax: 617-726-3852. Business E-Mail: tmela@partners.org.

MELAHAJI, JALAL ASSAD, science educator; b. Kamechli, Calif., Syria, July 1, 1956; s. Assad Melahaji Melahaji and Hamdiah Abd Razak Haj Ali Big; m. Judy Mustafa Basha, Oct. 20, 1992; children: Solin Jalal, Simin Jalal, Saman Jalal. BArch, Roger Williams U., Bristol, RI, 1983. Cert. bd. engr., Syria, 1995. Prof. Cuyamaca Coll., El Cajon, Calif., 2001—, San Diego City Coll., 2007—08. Advisor Kamechli corp., Hasaka, Syria, 1995—2000. Recipient Award of Achievment, 1996. Achievements include development of modern community. Home: 1347 Pepper Dr spc 7 El Cajon CA 92021 Office: Cuyamaca Coll 900 Rancho San Diego Pky El Cajon CA 92019 Personal E-mail: melahaji@hotmail.com.

MELAMED, ARTHUR DOUGLAS, lawyer; b. Mpls., Dec. 3, 1945; s. Arthur Charles and Helen Beatrix (Rosenberg) M.: m. Carol Drescher Weisman, May 26, 1983; children: Kathryn Henrie, Elizabeth Allyn. BA, Yale U., 1967; JD, Harvard U., 1970. Bar: DC 1970, US Ct. Internat. Trade 1985, US Ct. Appeals (9th cir.) 1971, US Ct. Appeals (2d cir.) 1975, US Ct. Appeals (DC cir.) 1978, US Ct. Appeals (8th cir.) 1981, US Ct. Appeals (fed. cir.) 1985, U.S. Ct. Appeals (4th cir.) 1989, US Ct. Appeals (10th cir.) 1993, US Supreme Ct. 1981. Law clk. US Ct. Appeals for 9th Circuit, 1970-71; assoc. Wilmer, Cutler, Pickering, Hale & Dorr, Washington, 1971-77, ptnr., 1978-96, 2001—; prin. dep. asst. atty. gen. US Dept. Justice, 1996-2000, acting asst. atty. gen. antitrust divsn., 2000-2001. Vis. prof. Georgetown U. Law Ctr., 1992-93, adj. prof., 1993-94. Editor, Harvard Law Rev.; contbr. articles to profl. jours. Mem. coun. Yale U., 2006-; trustee Nat. Child Rsch. Ctr., 1990-93, Sidwell Friends Sch., 2000-08 Mem. ABA, Am. Law Inst., Yale Club (NYC), Kenwood Country Club. Office: Wilmer Cutler Pickering Hale & Dorr 1875 Pennsylvania Ave NW Washington DC 20006 Office Phone: 202-663-6090. Office Fax: 202-663-6363. Business E-Mail: doug.melamed@wilmerhale.com.

MELAMED, LEO, global consulting firm executive; b. Bialystok, Poland, Mar. 20, 1932; arrived in U.S., 1941, naturalized, 1950; s. Isaac M. and Fayga (Barakin) M.; m. Betty Sattler, Dec. 26, 1953; children: Idelle Sharon, Jordan Norman, David Jeffrey. Student, U. Ill., 1950-52, LittD (hon.), 1999; JD, John Marshall Law Sch., Chgo., 1955. Bar: Ill. 1955. Sr. ptnr. Melamed, Kravitz & Verson, Chgo., 1956-66; chmn., CEO Dellsher Investment Co., 1965—93, Sakura Dellsher, Inc., Chgo., 1993—2000, Melamed & Assoc., Inc., Chgo., 1993—2002; co-chmn. Stevenson, Melamed and Assocs., Chgo., 2002—. Mem. Chgo. Merc. Exch., 1953—, mem. bd. govs., 1967—91, chmn. emeritus, 1991—, chmn. bd., 1969—71, 1975—77, chmn. exec. com., 1985—91, also spl. counsel, apptd. sr. policy advisor, 1997—; chmn. bd. Internat. Monetary Market, 1972—75, spl. counsel, 1976—91; mem. Chgo. Bd. Trade, 1969—; mem. corp. adv. bd. U. Ill., Chgo., 1991—; mayor Chgo. Coun. Manpower and Econ. Advisors, 1972; adv. coun. mem. Grad. Sch. Bus. U. Chgo., 1980—, Leo Melamed endowed chair future markets, 1991; hon. prof. Renmin U., Beijing, 2003; hon. dean Derivatives Sch. Peking U., China, 2007. Author: (sci. fiction novel) The Tenth Planet, 1987, Leo Melamed on the Markets, 1993, Escape to the Futures, 1996; editor: The Merits of Flexible Exchange Rates, 1988. Mem. bd. trustees John Marshall Law Sch., 1991—; coun. mem. US Holocaust Meml. Mus., 1992—, dir. Recipient Human Rights medallion, Am. Jewish Com., 1991, Lifetime Achievement award, Anti-Defamation League, 2001, Medal of Honor, Ellis Island, 2008; named Man Yr., Israel Bonds, 1975; Betty and Leo Melamed Rsch. scholar biomed. rsch., Weizmann Inst. Sci., 1998, Leo Melamed fellow in internat. bus. and trade law, John Marshall Law Sch., 2000. Fellow: Internat. Assn. Fin. Engrs. (sr.); mem.: ABA, Chgo. Bar Assn., Ill. Bar Assn., Am. Judicature Soc., Nat. Futures Assn. (chmn. 1982—89, spl. advisor 1989—), Am. Contract Bridge League (life master), Standard Club, Union League Club, Econs. Club Chgo. Avocations: writing, jogging, bridge. Office: Melamed & Assocs Inc 10 S Wacker Dr Ste 3275 Chicago IL 60606-7442 Office Phone: 312-930-3310. Business E-Mail: lmelamed@melamedassoc.com. E-mail: lm@sdinet.com.

MELAMED, MICHAL L., epidemiologist; d. Abraham Melamed and Hedva Shamir; m. Richard B. Wagreich, Aug. 24, 2003; children: Ethan Wagreich, Aliza Wagreich. MD, Johns Hopkins Sch. Medicine, Balt., 1999; MHS, Johns Hopkins Bloomberg Sch. Pub. Health, Balt., 2005. Diplomate Am. Bd. Internal Medicine, 2003, in nephrology 2005. Asst. prof. medicine and epidemiology and population health Albert Einstein Coll. Medicine, Bronx, NY, 2006—. Achievements include research in vitamin D deficiency. Office: Albert Einstein Coll Medicine 1300 Morris Pk Ave Ullmann 615 Bronx NY 10461

MELANCON, CELINDA REESE, psychologist; b. Ft. Worth, 1969; d. Harold and Betty Reese; m. Michael Melancon, June 11, 2005; 1 child, Margaux. BS, Abilene Christian U., Tex., 1992; MA, U. Richmond, Va., 1996; PhD, La. State U., Baton Rouge, 2000. Asst. prof. Okla. State U., Stillwater, 2001—07, assoc. prof., 2007—. Recipient Coll. Arts and Scis. Jr. Faculty award, Okla. State U., 2007; named Faculty Assoc. of Yr., OSU Residential Life, 2006. Mem.: APA, OSU Psychology Club, Assn. Psychol. Sci., Gerontol. Soc. Am. Achievements include research in relationship between age and memory performance. Office: Okla State Univ 116 North Murray Stillwater OK 74078 Business E-Mail: celinda.reese@okstate.edu.

MELANCON, CHARLES, United States Representative from Louisiana; b. Napoleonville, La., Oct. 3, 1947; s. Joe and Brownie Melancon; m. Alida (Peachy) Clark; children: Charles, Claire. BS, Univ. Southwestern La. Owner Melancon Ins. Agy.; mem. La. Ho. Rep., 1987—93; pres. Am. Sugar Cane League, 1993—2004; mem. US Congress from 3rd La. dist., 2005—. Mem. La. State Dem. Ctrl. Com., 1987—93. Chmn. LSU Agr. Devel. Council; vice chmn. La. Econ. Council. Recipient Outstanding Legislator award, La. Municipal Assn., Disting. Svc. award, La. Restaurant Assn., 1990. Mem.: Ducks Unlimited, UL Lafayette Alumni Assn. Democrat. Roman Catholic. Office: US House Reps 404 Cannon House Office Bldg Washington DC 20515-1803 Office Phone: 202-225-4031. Office Fax: 202-225-3944.*

MELANCON, GLENN, history professor; b. Heidelberg, Germany, Jan. 24, 1966; s. Yves and Anna Mae Melancon; m. Jackie Melancon; children: Christopher, Alexandre. BA in History, U. Southwestern La., 1989, BA in Philosophy, 1989, MA in History, 1991; PhD in History, La. State U., 1994. Instr. history and world religions Acad. Sacred Heart, 1994—95; asst. prof. Southeastern Okla. State U., 1995—2000, assoc. prof., 2000—05, prof., 2005—. Mem. faculty transfer curriculum com.: history Okla. State Regents for Higher Edn., 1995—2005; reviewer social studies curriculum review com. Okla. Commn. Tchr. Preparation, 1998—; com. chair policies and issues Grayson Dem. Party, 2004—05. Cubmaster Cub Scout Pack 9, 1998—2002, com. chair, 2002—05, charter rep., 2005—; mem. adult edn. team St. Mary's Cath. Ch., instr. rite of Christian initiation of adults, 2004—. Mem.: Southwestern Hist. Assn. (pres. 2003—04), Southwestern Social Studies Assn. (sec. 2006—). Democrat. Cath. Office: PO Box 1861 Sherman TX 75091*

MELANI, KENNETH R., insurance company executive; MD, Bowman Gray Sch. of Med., NC, 1979. Pres., CEO West Penn Cares Inc.; pres. Keystone Health Plan West; with Highmark Inc., Pittsburgh, 1989—, exec. v.p. strategic bus. devel. and health services, pres., CEO, 2003—. Mem.: Am. Coll. of Physician Executives, Am. Soc. of Internal Med., Penn. Soc. of Internal Med., Am. Med. Assn., Penn. Med. Soc., Allegheny County Med. Soc. Office: Highmark 120 5th Ave Ste 2015 Pittsburgh PA 15222-3001 Office Phone: 412-544-7000.*

MELANSON, DOROTHY, political organization administrator; b. Boston, Sept. 21, 1953; AS, Westbrook Coll., Maine, 1980. Chairwoman Cumberland County Dem. Com., Maine, 1996—2002; com. woman Maine Dem. Nat., 1996, 2000, 2001—03; presdl. elector Maine, 2000; chairwoman Maine Dem. Party, 2003—; registered nurse Maine Med. Ctr. Democrat.

MELBINGER, MICHAEL S., lawyer; b. Chgo., Sept. 5, 1958; s. Donald G. and Joyce A. (Haynes) M.; m. Karen Mary Melbinger, June 16, 1984; children: Peter Donald, Charlotte Anna, Lucy Grace. BA, U. Notre Dame, 1980; JD, U. Ill., 1983. Bar: Ill., 1983. Assoc. McDermott, Will & Emery, Chgo., 1983-88, ptnr., 1989-93; ptnr., head employee benefits dept. Schiff, Hardin & Waite, Chgo., 1993—97; ptnr., chmn. employee benefits and exec. compensation Winston & Strawn LLP, Chgo., 1997—. Adj. prof. law Northwestern U., U. Ill. Mem. editorial bd. Practical Tax Strategies, Taxation for Lawyers, N.Y.C., 1989—, Employee Benefits Counselor, 1993—, Pension Management, 1995—; author Executive Compensation, 2004, author: Employee Benefit Trust Compliance Manual; contbr. articles to profl. jours. Pro bono Adoptive Families Am., Adoption Advocates. Mem. ABA, Nat. Assn. Stock Plan Profls. Home: 2699 Independence Ave Glenview IL 60025-7730 Office: Winston & Strawn LLP 35 W Wacker Dr Chicago IL 60601-9703 Office Phone: 312-558-7588. Office Fax: 312-558-5700. E-mail: mmelbinger@winston.com.

MELBY, DONNA D., lawyer; b. 1950; BA, U. Calif., Santa Barbara, 1972; attended, Loyola U. Sch. Law, 1977—78, Calif. Western Sch. Law, 1975—77, JD, 1978. Bar: Calif. 1979. Ptnr. Sonnenschein Nath & Rosenthal LLP, LA, 2002—05; ptnr. employment dept. Paul, Hastings, Janofsky & Walker, LA. Mem. Calif. Judicial Selection Adv. Coun., 2004. Recipient Rothchild Pro Bono Award, Sonnenschein Nath & Rosenthall LLP, 2004; named one of The Most Influential & Talented Women Trial Lawyers in Calif., LA Daily Jour. & San Francisco Recorder, 2002—06, 16 leading litigators in the US, Minority Corp. Counsel Assn., 2004, The 100 Most Influential Attorneys in State of Calif., LA Daily Jour. & San Francisco Recorder, 2004, The 50 Most Influential Women Lawyers in Am., Nat. Law Jour., 2007; named to Top 5% So. Calif. Super Lawyers, LA Mag., 2003—06. Fellow: Internat. Soc. Barristers, Am. Coll. Trial Lawyers; mem.: Fed. Bar Assn., Women Lawyers of LA, Calif. Women Lawyers, Assn. Bus. Trial Lawyers, Assn. So. Calif. Def. Counsel, Def. Rsch. Inst. (labor & employment com.), Fedn. Def. and Corp. Counsel, Internat. Assn. Def. Counsel (faculty mem. trial sch.), Am. Bd. Trial Advocates (faculty mem. trial sch. 1993—, mem. bd. dirs. 1994—, mem. found. bd. trustees 2001—, v.p. 2003, pres.-elect 2004, pres. 2005, pres. LA chpt. 2004, Guardian of Constitution award), Chancery Club. Office: Paul Hastings Janofsky & Walker 515 S Flower St 25th Fl Los Angeles CA 90071 Office Phone: 213-683-6098. Office Fax: 213-996-3098. E-mail: donnamelby@paulhastings.com.*

MELBY, EDWARD CARLOS, JR., veterinarian; b. Burlington, Vt., Aug. 10, 1929; s. Edward C. and Dorothy H. (Folsom) M.; m. Jean Day File, Aug. 15, 1953; children: Scott E., Susan J., Jeffrey T., Richard A. Student, U. Pa., 1948—50; DVM, Cornell U., 1954. Diplomate Am. Coll. Lab. Animal Medicine. Practice vet. medicine, Middlebury, Vt., 1954-62; instr. lab. animal medicine Johns Hopkins U. Sch. Medicine, Balt., 1962-64, asst. prof., 1964-66, assoc. prof., 1966-71, prof., dir. div. comparative medicine, 1971-74; prof. medicine, dean Coll. Vet. Medicine, Cornell U., Ithaca, NY, 1974-84; v.p. R & D SmithKline Beecham Animal Health, 1985-90, v.p. sci. and tech. assessment, 1990-91; ind. cons., 1992—. Cons. VA, NRC, NIH. Author: Handbook of Laboratory Animal Science, Vols. I, II, III, 1974-76. Served with USMC, 1946-48. Mem. Am., N.Y. State, Md., Pa. Vet. Med. Assns., Am. Assn. Lab. Animal Sci., Am. Coll. Lab. Animal Medicine, AAAS, Phi Zeta. Home: PO Box 248 Charlotte VT 05445-0248 Office: 736 Lime Kiln Rd Charlotte VT 05445-9141 Home Phone: 802-985-3368; Office Phone: 802-985-3368. Personal E-mail: ecmelby@verizon.net.

MELCHER, ELIZABETH, musician; b. Phoenixville, Pa., Oct. 1, 1965; d. William Diehl Lober and Caroline Merroth Melcher; 1 child, Amy Elizabeth Winger. MusB, Curtis Inst. Music, 1987; MusM, Juilliard Sch., 1990; DMA, Eastman Sch. Music, 1994. Fellow in ch. music Christ and St. Stephen's Episc. Ch., NYC, 1988—89; asst. organist Brick Presbyn. Ch., NYC, 1989—90; organist, choirmaster Ch. of Ascension, Rochester, NY, 1991—94; min. music Ascension Luth. Ch., Balt., 1994—97; dir. music The Luth. Ch. St. Andrew, Silver Spring, 1997—2001; min. music The Ch. Good Shepherd, Burke, Va., 2001—03; organist, choirmaster Grace and Holy Trinity Episc. Ch., Richmond, Va., 2003—. Asst. organist John Wanamaker Grand Ct. Organ, Phila., 1985—87; pvt. tchr. organ and piano, 1999—. Organist: CD recording Pageant, 2001. Recipient 2d prize, Naples Internat. Organ Festival Competition, Fla., 1993, Arthur Poister Nat. Organ Competition, 1995, 1988. Mem.: Am. Guild Organists (recitalist, adjudicator various competitions, 1st prize Nat. Young Artists Competition, Region III 1991, Finalist Nat. Young Artists Competition 1996, 1992). Avocations: tennis, swimming, reading, concerts, travel. Office: Grace and Holy Trinity Episc Church 8 North Laurel St Richmond VA 23220-4797 Office Phone: 804-359-5628 Ext. 18. Office Fax: 804-353-2348. Business E-Mail: emelcherdavis@ghtc.org.

MELCHER, JENNIFER, otolaryngologist, educator; Assoc. prof. otology & laryngology Harvard Med. Sch. Mass. Eye & Ear Infirmary. Mem.: Assn. Rsch. in Otolaryngology, Am. Assn. Advancement Sci., Soc. for Neuroscience. Office: 77 Massachusetts Ave E25-519 Cambridge MA 02139 Office Phone: 617-573-3745. E-mail: jrm@epl.meei.harvard.edu.*

MELCHER, MARTHA ELENA, language educator; b. Taruel, Colombia, Dec. 7, 1955; d. Pacifico and Cornelia Collazos Oliveros; m. Wade Stephen Melcher, Apr. 7, 1998. MS in Philology, Libre U., Bogota, Colombia, 1988. Cert. tchr. Escuela Normal Mixta Neiva, 1980. Spanish tchr. Huila Pub. Sch. Neiva, 1978—81; asst. gen. mgr. Cajanal Bogota, 1984—95; Spanish tchr. children spl. needs Inst. Anzuategui, Bogota, 1997—98; Spanish instr. Mountain State U., Beckley, 2005—07, Coastal Carolina U., Conway, 2007—. Spanish/English interpreter Tazewell County Pub. Sch., Bluefield, Va., 2004—05. Author: (textbook) Secretarial Speed Typing. Home: 1025 Carolina Pines Rd #BB4 Conway SC 29526 Office: PO Box 261954 Conway SC 29528-6054 Personal E-mail: seamountaindev@aol.com. Business E-Mail: mmelcher@coastal.edu.

MELCHER, SARAH J., theology studies educator; b. El Paso, Tex., Feb. 5, 1951; d. Edward Lewis and Jeanne Anderson Melcher. PhD, Emory U., Atlanta, Ga., 2000. Co-dir., ethics-religion & soc. Xavier U., Cin., 2003—06, assoc. prof. hebrew scriptures, 1999—. Co-editor: (book) This Abled Body: Rethinking Disabilities in Biblical Studies; contbr. articles to profl. publs. Mem.: AAUP (treas. Xavier U. 2009), Soc. Bibl. Lit. Office: Xavier Univ 3800 Victory Pky Cincinnati OH 45207-4442 Office Fax: 513-745-3215. Business E-Mail: melcher@xavier.edu.

MELCHERT, JAMES FREDERICK, artist, educator; b. New Bremen, Ohio, Dec. 2, 1930; s. John Charles and Hulda Lydia (Egli) M.; m. Mary Ann Hostetler, June 18, 1954 (dec.); children: Christopher, David, Renee. AB, Princeton U., 1952; MFA, U. Chgo., 1957; MA, U. Calif., Berkeley, 1961. Prof. art U. Calif., Berkeley, 1965-76, 81-84, 88-92, prof. emeritus, 1992—; dir. Am. Acad. in Rome, 1984-88. Dir. Visual Arts Program, Nat. Endowment for Arts, Washington, 1977-81 Exhibited in one man shows at San Francisco Art Inst., 1970, San Francisco Mus. Modern Art, 1975, Holly Solomon Gallery, N.Y.C., 1991; group shows at Biennale de Paris, 1963, Whitney Mus., N.Y.C., 1966, 68, 70, Documenta 5, Kassel, Germany, 1972, World Ceramic Exposition, Korea, 2001; commd. for Artwork (new Biology Bldg.) at MIT, 1993-94, Biomed. Rsch. Bldg. at Case Western Res. U., 1994. Recipient Adaline Kent award San Francisco Art Inst., 1970; Nat. Endowment for Arts artist fellow, 1973; hon. DFA, San Francisco Art Inst., 1984, Md. Inst. Coll. Arts, 1993. Home: 6077 Ocean View Dr Oakland CA 94618-1844 Home Phone: 510-652-2186. E-mail: jfmelchert@gmail.com.

MELCHIOR, IB JORGEN, scriptwriter, author, film director; b. Copenhagen, Sept. 17, 1917; arrived in U.S., 1938; s. Lauritz Lebrecht Hommel and Inger Thora (Nathansen) M.; m. Harriet Hathaway Kale, Mar. 15, 1942 (div. 1960); 1 child, Leif; m. Cleo Baldon, Jan. 18, 1964; stepchild, Dirk Arin. Degree, Stenhus Kostskole, Denmark, 1936; Cand.Phil, U. Copenhagen, 1937. Actor, stage mgr., co-dir. English Players, Paris, 1937—39; stage mgr. Radio City Music Hall, Ctr. Theater, NYC, 1941—42; actor, writer NYC, 1946—49; assoc. dir. CBS-TV, NYC, 1949—53; dir. Perry Como Show, NYC, 1951—54; assoc. prodr. G-L Enterprises, NYC, 1952—53; screenwriter, dir., novelist, 1957—. Author: (novels) Order of Battle, 1973, Sleeper Agent, 1975, The Haigerloch Project, 1977, The Watchdogs of Abaddon, 1979, The Marcus Device, 1980, The Tombstone Cipher, 1983, Eva, 1984, V-3, 1985, Code Name: Grand Guignol, 1987, (biography) Quest, 1990, Order of Battle: Hitler's Werewolves, 1991, (autobiography) Case by Case, 1993; author: (with Cleo Baldon) Steps & Stairways, 1989, Reflections on the Pool, 1997, Lauritz Melchior: The Golden Years of Bayreuth, 2003, A La Carte, 2008; Six Cult Films of the Sixties, 2008; screenwriter Live Fast, Die Young, 1957, The Angry Red Planet, 1959, Reptilicus, 1962, Journey to the 7th Planet, 1962, Ambush Bay, 1965, Robinson Crusoe on Mars, 1964, The Time Travelers, 1964, others; dir. Angry Red Planet, The Time Travelers; translator, narrator (tapes) Hans Christian Andersen Fairy Tales, 1986; creator Space Family Robinson (spl. advisor Lost in Space, 1997-98); subject of biography: (by Robert Skotak) Ib Melchior: Man of Imagination, 2000. Adv. bd. Mayor's Narcotics Info. Clinic, LA, 1972-73; adv. coun. Danish Immigrant Mus., Elk Horn, Iowa, 1985—. With U.S. Army Mil. Intelligence, 1942-46. Decorated Bronze Star, Knight Commander Cross, Militant Order of St. Brigitte of Sweden, 1965; recipient King Christian X Erindringsmedalje, 1948, Medal of Merit Old Guard, 1965, Golden Scroll award Best Writing Acad. Sci. Fiction, 1976, Hamlet award Best Legitimate Play Shakespeare Soc. Am., 1982; named Scandinavian of Yr. Am. Scandanavian Found. L.A., 1995, Mem. Writers Guild Am. West, Dirs. Guild Am., Acad. Sci. Fiction (hon.), Manuscript Soc., Authors Guild Inc., Royal Danish Guard Assn., Danish Luncheon Club (L.A.), Adventures Club (L.A.). Home and Office: 8228 Marmont Ln Hollywood CA 90069-1624 Personal E-mail: ijmelchior@aol.com.

MELCONIAN, LINDA JEAN, state senator, lawyer, educator; b. Springfield, Mass. d. George and Virginia Elaine (Noble) Melconian. BA, Mt. Holyoke Coll.; MA, George Washington U.; JD, George Mason U. Asst. counsel to Spkr. Thomas P. O'Neill, Jr. U.S. Ho. of Reps., Washington; pros. atty. Hampden County Dist. Atty., Springfield, Mass.; state senator Mass. Gen. Ct., Boston, 1983—2004, majority leader emeritus Mass. State Senate. Instr. Mt. Holyoke Coll., Am. Internat. Coll.; vis. asst. prof. Suffolk U., Boston. Ex Officio trustee Ella T. Grasso Found., Conn.; active Dem. State Com., Mass. Home: 465 Dwight Rd Springfield MA 01108 Office Phone: 413-374-3671. Business E-Mail: lindamelconian@comcast.net, lindamelconi@suffolk.edu. E-mail: lmelconi@suffolk.edu.

MELCZEK, DALE JOSEPH, bishop; b. Detroit, Mich., Nov. 9, 1938; AB, St. Mary Coll., Orchard Lake, Mich.; MDiv, St. John Sem., Plymouth, Mich.; MA in Edn., U. Detroit; postgrad., U. Notre Dame. Ordained priest Archdiocese of Detroit, Mich., 1964; assoc. pastor St. Sylvester Ch., Warren, Mich., 1964—70, co-pastor, 1970—72; pastor St. Christine Ch., Detroit, 1972—75; vicar West Detroit Vicariate, 1973—75; asst. vicar for parishes Archdiocese of Detroit, 1975—77, sec. to archbishop and vicar gen., 1977—82, archdiocesan consultor, 1972—83, aux. bishop, titular bishop of Trau, 1982—92; regional bishop Detroit N.W. Region, 1983—92; ordained bishop, 1983; apostolic adminstr. Diocese of Gary, 1992—95, coadjutor Bishop of Gary, 1995—96, bishop, 1996—. Roman Catholic. Office Phone: 219-769-9292.

MELDER, KEITH E., retired curator; b. Seattle, May 13, 1932; s. F. Eugene and Eleanor (Morrill). BA, Williams Coll., Williamstown, Mass., 1954; PhD, Yale U., New Haven, 1964. Asst. curator Nat. Mus. Am. Hist., Smithsonian Inst., Washington, 1962—63, assoc. cur., 1964—85, cur. polit. hist., 1986—94, cur. emeritus, 1995—. Author: City of Magnificent Intentions: A History of Washington, District of Columbia, 1983, Hail to the Candidate: Presidential Campaigns from Banners to Broadcasts, 1992, Beginnings of Sisterhood: The American Woman's Rights Movement, 1800-1850, 1977. Mem. Capitol Hill Cmty. Coun., Washington, 1961—68. Named to Centennial Honor Roll, Am. Assn. Museums, 2006.

MELDER, TREVOR F., physics professor; b. Wilmington, Del. BS, Grove City Coll., Pa.; MS, Ind. U. Pa., Ind. Instr. physics U. La., Monroe, 1992—. Contbr. scientific papers. Vol. Northeastern La. War Vet. Home, Monroe, 2004. Mem.: Multimedia Ednl. Resource Learning and Online Tchg. (assoc. editor 2003), Am. Assn. Physics Tchrs., Omicron Delta Kappa, Sigma Pi Sigma. Home: 300 Warren Dr Apt #304 West Monroe LA 71291 Office: Univ La Monroe 700 University Ave Monroe LA 71209 Business E-Mail: melder@ulm.edu.

MELDMAN, ROBERT EDWARD, lawyer; b. Milw., Aug. 5, 1937; s. Louis Leo and Lillian (Gollusch) M.; m. Sandra Jane Setlick, July 24, 1960; children: Saree Beth, Richard Samuel. BS, U. Wis., 1959; LL.B., Marquette U., Milw., 1962; LL.M. in Taxation, NYU, 1963. Bar: Wis. 1962, Fla. 1987, Colo. 1990, U.S. Ct. Fed. Claims, U.S. Tax Ct. 1963, U.S. Supreme Ct. 1970. Practice tax law, Milw., 1963—; pres. Meldman, Case & Weine, Ltd., Milw., 1975-85; dir. tax div. Mulcahy & Wherry, SC, Milw., 1985-90; shareholder Reinhart, Boerner, Van Deuren, S.C., 1991—2006, of counsel, 2006—. Adj. prof. taxation U. Wis., Milw., 1970—2000, mem. tax adv. coun., 1978—2000, dir. Low Income Taxpayer Clinic, 2005—; adj. prof. Marquette U. Sch. Law, Milw., 2001—02, The U. of Queensland T.C. Beirne Sch. Law, 2002; vice chmn. Internat. Revenue Svc. Taxpayer Adv. Panel, 2003—04; sec. Profl. Inst. Tax Study, Inc., 1978—; bd. dirs. Wis. Bar Found., 1988—94; exec. in residence Deloitte & Touche Ctr. for Multistate Taxation, U. Wis., Milw., 1996—2000. Co-author: Federal Taxation Practice and Procedure, 1983, 1986, 1988, 1992, 1998, 2004, 2007, Practical Tactics for Dealing with the IRS, 1994, A Practical Guide to U.S. Taxation of International Transactions, 1996, 1997, 2004, Federal Taxation Practice and Procedure Study Guide/Quizzes, 1998; editor: Jour. Property Taxation, 1996—2002; mem. editl. bd.: Tax Litigation Alert, 1995—2000; contbr. articles to legal jours. Recipient Adj. Taxation Faculty award UWM Tax Assn., 1987; named Outstanding Tax Profl. 1992 Corp. Reports Wis. Mag. and UWM Tax Assn. Fellow Am. Coll. Tax Coun.; mem. ABA, Fed. Bar Assn. (pres. Milw. chpt. 1966-67), Milw. Bar Assn. (chmn. tax sect. 1970-71), Wis. Bar Assn. (bd. dirs. tax sect. 1964-78, chmn. 1973-74), Internat. Bar Assn., The Law Assn. for Asia and the Pacific (chair tax sect. 2000—, dep. chair bus. law sect.), Friends of Gold Meir Libr. (bd. dirs.), Marquette U. Law Alumni Assn. (bd. dirs. 1972-77), Milw. Athletic Club, Wis. Club (bd. dirs. 2003—), B'nai B'rith (trustee, Ralph Harris Meml. award Century Lodge 1969-70), Phi Delta Phi, Tau Epsilon Rho (chancellor Milw. chpt. 1969-71, supreme nat. chancellor 1975-76, v.p. Wis. chpt., tech. 1992-2000). Jewish (trustee congregation 1972-77).

MELDRUM, DEIRDRE RUTH, electrical engineer, educator; b. Loma Linda, Calif., Mar. 14, 1961; d. Ronald Murray and Barbara Ruth (Howard) M.; m. Peter Jan Wiktor; children: Thaddeus Meldrum Wiktor, Genevieve Meldrum Wiktor. BSCE, U. Wash., 1983; MSEE, Rensselaer Polytech. Inst., 1985; PhDEE, Stanford U., Calif., 1993. Design engr. Wash. State Dept. of Transp., Seattle, 1982-83; mem. tech. staff Jet Propulsion Lab., Pasadena, Calif., 1985-87; NASA fellow, Amelia Earhart fellow Stanford U., Palo Alto, 1989-92; asst. prof. elec. engring. U. Wash., Seattle, 1992-98, assoc. prof. elec. engring., 1998—2001, prof., 2001—06; dean Ira A. Fulton Sch. Engring. Ariz. State U., Tempe, 2007—. Mem. adv. panel ILI Program NSF, Washington, 1993; mem. spl. emphasis panels on genome automation NIH, Bethesda, Md.; dir. CEGS Microscale Life Scis. Ctr. NIH, Bethesda, 2001—, Ctr. Ecogenomics Birdesign Inst. Ariz. State U., Tempe, 2007—. Contbr. articles to profl. jours. Recipient Spl. Emphasis Rsch. Career award NIH, 1993—, Ralph R. Teetor Ednl. award Soc. of Automotive Engrs., 1993, Presdl. Early Career award for Scientists and Engrs., 1996. Fellow AAAS, IEEE; mem. AIAA, Soc. Women Engrs., Sigma Xi Avocations: bicycling, back country skiing, rowing, travel, photography. Business E-Mail: deidre.meldrum@asu.edu.

MELE, ALFRED R., philosophy educator; b. Detroit, May 22, 1951; s. Alfred Emil and Rosemary (Pardo) M.; children: Al, Nick, Angela. BA, Wayne State U., 1973; PhD, U. Mich., 1979. Asst. prof. philosophy Davidson (N.C.) Coll., 1979-85, assoc. prof., 1985-91, prof., 1991-95, Vail prof., 1995-2000; William H. and Lucyle T. Werkmeister prof. Fla. State U., Tallahassee, 2000—. Author: Irrationality, 1987, Springs of Action, 1992, Autonomous Agents, 1995, Self-Deception Unmasked, 2001, Motivation and Agency, 2003, Free Will and Luck, 2006, Effective Initiations, 2009; contbr. articles to profl. jours. Fellow NEH, 1985-86, 92-93, 99-2000, 2007-08, Nat. Humanities Ctr., Rsch. Triangle Park, NC, 1992-93, Australian Nat. U., 1999. Mem. Am. Philos. Assn., Internat. Soc. for Rsch. on Emotion. Avocation: racquetball. Office: Dept Philosophy Fla State Univ Tallahassee FL 32306-1500

MELE, JOANNE THERESA, dentist; b. Chgo., Dec. 5, 1943; d. Andrew and Josephine Jeanette (Calabrese). Diploma, St. Elizabeth's Sch. Nursing, Chgo., 1964; diploma in dental hygiene, Northwestern U., 1977; AS, Triton Coll., 1979; DDS, Loyola U., 1983. RN; registered dental hygienist. Staff nurse medicine/surgery St. Elizabeth's Hosp., Chgo., 1964-66, oper. room nurse, 1966-67; head nurse oper. room Cook County Hosp., Chgo., 1967-76, head nurse ICU, 1976-77; dental hygienist Mele Dental Assocs., Ltd., Oakbrook, Ill., 1977-79, practice dentistry, 1983—. Clin. asst. prof. Loyola U., Chgo., 1988-93. Recipient Northwestern U. Dental Hygiene Clinic award, 1977; Dr. Duxler Humanitarian scholar Loyola U., 1982. Mem. Chgo. Dental Soc., Ill. State Dental Soc., Acad. Gen. Dentistry, Acad. Operative Dentistry, Am. Prosthodontic Soc., Internat. Congress Oral Implantologists, Psi Omega (Kappa chpt.). Roman Catholic. Avocations: reading, music, gardening. Office Phone: 630-573-0420.

MELEIS, AFAF IBRAHIM, dean, nursing educator; b. Alexandria, Egypt, Mar. 19, 1942; d. Abdel Baki Ibrahim and Soad Hussein Hassan; m. Mahmoud Meleis, Aug. 21, 1964; children: Waleed, Sherief. BS magna cum laude, U. Alexandria, 1961; MS, UCLA, 1964, MA, 1966, PhD, 1968; D in Pub. Svc. (hon.), U. Portland, Oreg., 1989; MD (hon.), Linköping U., Sweden, 2007. Instr. U. Alexandria, 1961-62; acting instr. UCLA, 1966-68, asst. prof. nursing, then assoc. prof., 1968-75; assoc. prof., dean Health Inst., Kuwait, 1975-77; prof. nursing U. Calif., San Francisco, 1977—2001, also dir. Study Immigrant Health and Adjustment; Margaret Bond Simon dean of nursing U. Pa. Sch. Nursing, Phila., 2002—, prof. nursing and sociology, dir., WHO Collaborating Ctr. Nursing and Midwifery Leadership. Vis. prof. colls. in Sweden, Brazil, Japan, Saudi Arabia, Kuwait, Egypt; 1st Centennial prof. Columbia U., N.Y.C., 1992-94; cons., speaker in field. Author: Theoretical Nursing: Development & Progress, 1985 (Book of Yr., am. Jour. Nursing, 1985), 2d edit., 1991, 3d edit., 1997; contbr. articles to rsch. and profl. jours. Counsel gen. Internat. Coun. Women's Health Issues; mem. Global Health Coun., Nurses Edn. Fund, Inc., Life Sci. Career Alliance. Recipient Helen Hahm award U. Calif. Sch. Nursing, San Francisco, 1981, Teaching awards U. Calif., San Francisco, 1981, 85, Pres. Hosni Mubarak medal of Excellence, 1990, Chancellor's medal U. Mass., 2000, Global Citizenship award UN Assn. Greater Phila., 2007, Dr. Gloria Twine Chisum award U. Pa., 2007; Kellogg Internat. fellow, 1986-89. Fellow Royal Coll. Nursing, Am. Acad. Nursing, Coll. Physicians Phila.; mem. CARE, Inst. Medicine, Am. Nurses Assn., Coun. Nurse Researchers, Western Soc. Rsch. in Nursing, Pa. Women's Forum, Forum Exec. Women. Avocations: jogging, symphony, reading, politics. Office: Univ Penn Sch Nursing 420 Guardian Dr Rm 465 NEB Philadelphia PA 19104-6096*

MELEKOTE, SWATHANTHRA KUMAR, education educator; s. Swathanthra Kumar Melekote and Gayethri Narayanswamy; m. Gayethri Narayanswamy, Dec. 18, 1964; children: Aswini Kumar, Gautami Kumar. MBBS, Jawaharlal Med. Coll., India, 1989; MD in Pediatrics, Bangalore Med. Coll., India, 1993. Lic. Physician Conn., 2005. Chief resident N.Y. Meth. Hosp., Bklyn., 2003—05; asst. prof. U. Conn., Farmington, 2005—. Mng. dir. Aswini Hosp., Bangalore, India, 1993—98. Prodr.: (movie) Graduation, 2004. Recipient Master, Royal Coll. of Pediatrics, London, 1999—2000, Royal Coll. of Physician Child Health, London, 2000. Achievements include patents pending for New type of laryngoscope. Office: Uconn Health Ctr 273 Farmington Ave Farmington CT 06032 Home: 86 Buff Cap Rd Apt A5 Tolland CT 06084-2639 Office Fax: 860-679-1403. Personal E-mail: swathanthra@yahoo.com.

MELENDEZ, BRIAN, lawyer, political organization administrator; b. Silver Creek, NY, Sept. 26, 1964; s. Gilbert Raymond and Dolores Maried (Valone) M. AB in Govt., Harvard U., 1986, MA in Theological Studies, 1991, JD cum laude, 1991. Bar: Minn., US Ct. Appeals (Fed. Cir.), US Dist. Ct. (Dist. Minn.). Adminstrv. sec. Harvard-Radcliffe Undergrad. Coun., Cambridge, Mass., 1983-84, 85-88; mgr. Copyrite Copy Ctrs., Winter Park, Fla., 1984; rsch. asst. Harvard U., Office of the Sec., Cambridge, 1985, Prog. on Info. Resources Policy, Cambridge, 1986-87; summer assoc. Avrell, Fons, Radey & Hinkle, Tallahassee, 1988, Greenberg, Travrig, Hoffman, Lipoff et al, Miami, Fla., 1989; ptnr. Faegre & Benson LLP, Minneapolis. Counselor Fla. Am. Legion Boys State, Tallahassee, 1982-89; v.p. Ctrl. Minn. Legal Services, 2003-05; bd. trustees Lawyers' Com. Civil Rights Under Law; bd. dirs. Vol. Lawyers Network, Ltd., Fair Vote Minn., 2002-05; mem. adv. com. on gen. rules of practice Supreme Ct. Minn., 2000-04, Minn. Citizens Commn. for Preservation of an Impartial Judiciary; chmn. Mpls. Dem.-Farmer-Labor Party, 1999-2005, Dem.-Farmer-Labor Congl. Dist. 5, 2004-05, Minn. Dem.-Farmer-Labor Party, 2005-; pres. Harvard Divinity Sch. Alumni Assn., 2001-03; mem. Westminster Presbyn. Ch., Mpls. Fellow, Am. Bar Found.; mem. ABA (law student div., chmn. young lawyers divsn. 2000-01, mem. House of Delegates 1997-2004, presdl. appointments com. 2003-04, coun. mem. bus. law sect. 2001-03), Nat. Sr. Classical League (nat. pres. 1985-86), Am. Inst. of Parliamentarians, Hennepin County Bar Assn. (pres. 2001-02), Minn. Bar Assn. (chmn. ct. rules and adminstrn. com., 1998-2001; pres.-elect 2006, pres. 2007), Nat. Assn. Parliamentarian; mem. Minn. Distance Running Assn. Democrat. Office: Faegre & Benson LLP 2200 Wells Fargo Ctr 90 S 7th St Minneapolis MN 55402-3901 also: Minn DFL Party Hdqs 255 E Plato Blvd Saint Paul MN 55107-1623 Office Phone: 612-766-7309, 651-293-1200. Office Fax: 612-766-1600. E-mail: bmelendez@faegre.com.*

MELENDEZ, ROBERT F., ophthalmologist; b. Albuquerque, Dec. 18, 1970; s. Max Carlos and Diane Juliette Melendez; m. Lucille Melendez, May 23, 1992; children: Joshua Jeremiah, Karissa Grace, Jordan Matthew. MD, MS, U. N.Mex., Albuquerque, NM, 2000; MBA, Anderson Sch. Mgmt., U. N.Mex., 2008. Diplomate Am. Bd. Ophthalmology. Sect. chief ophthalmology Presbyn. Hosp., Albuquerque, Lovelace Hosp. Downtown; gen. ophthalmologist Eye Assoc. N.Mex, Ltd., Albuquerque, 2004—, physician dir. clin. devel. program, 2004—09. Cons. CareerPhysician, Grapevine, Tex.; clin. asst. prof. U. N.Mex., Health Sci. Ctr, Albuquerque; spkr. in field. Contbr. articles to profl. jours. (named one of Top Drs. in Albuquerque, The Mag., 2009). Recipient Ray A. Kroc Achievement award, McDonald's Corp., 1989, Pres. of Inter-Hall Presidents' Coun. award, Howard Hughes Med. Inst., 1993, Katali award, U. N.Mex., Sch. Medicine, 1999, Rsch. Honors, 2000, Faculty award for Excellence, 2000; named one of 40 under 40, N.Mex Bus. Weekly, 2007; nominee Congl. award, U.S. Congress, 1989; fellow, Nat. Med. Fellowship, Inc., 1996—97, U. N.Mex., 1996; scholar, Nat. Hispanic Scholarship Fund, 1994—2000, N.Mex Hispanic Med. Assn., 1999. Mem.: Juliette RP Vision Found. (exec. dir., Retinitis Pigments Found. 2008—), N.Mex Acad. Ophthal. (sec.-treas. 2006—08, exec. com. mem., fundraiser dinner com.), Am. Acad. Ophthalmology (assoc.; mem. young ophthalmologist com. 2005—), AMA (assoc.; YPS del., N.Mex. 2008—, Leadership award 2008). R-Consevative. Protestant. Achievements include patents pending for treatment for macular degeneration. Office: Eye Assoc NMex 1740 Grande Blvd Ste B Rio Rancho NM 87124 Office Fax: 505-891-2402. Personal E-mail: rfmelendez@gmail.com.

MELÉNDEZ DE SANTA ANA, THELMA, federal agency administrator; b. June 24, 1958; BA in Sociology, UCLA, 1981; PhD in Edn., U. So. Calif., 1995. Bilingual classroom tchr. Montebello Unified Sch. Dist., Calif., 1982—86, language specialist, v.p., 1986—92; prin. Bandini Elem. Sch., Commerce, 1992—95; dir. instrn. Pasadena Unified Sch. Dist., 1995—97; dir. sch./family initiatives LA Annenberg Met. Project (LAAMP), 1997—99; dept. supt. & chief academic officer Pemona Unified Sch. Dist., 1999—2005, supt., 2006—09; program mgr. Stupski Edn. Found., Mill Valley, 2005—06; asst. sec. for elem. & secondary edn. US Dept. Edn., Washington, 2009—. Contbr. articles to profl. jours. Broad Urban Supts. Acad. fellow, 2006. Office: US Dept Edn Office of Elem and Secondary Edn 400 Maryland Ave, SW Washington DC 20202*

MELENDY, BRENDA, history professor, department chairman; d. Howard Brett and Marian E. Melendy; children: Stefan Schoy, Robin Mario Machuca. AB in Am. Studies, Stanford U., Calif., 1979; MA in History, San Jose State U., Calif., 1984; PhD in History, U. Calif., Santa Cruz, 1998. Prof., chair history dept. Tex. A&M U., Kingsville, 1999—, faculty lectr., 2007, interim asst. dean, Coll. Arts and Scis., 2008—09. Elder 1st Presbyn. Ch., Kingsville, 2007—. Recipient Hall Svc. award, Tex. A&M U., 2008. Mem.: Southern Hist. Assn. (nominating com. mem. 2003—06), World History Assn., German Studies Assn., Am. Hist. Assn. Democrat. Presbyterian. Office: Tex A&M Univ Kingsville 700 University Blvd MSC 166 Kingsville TX 78363

MELENDY, DAVID RUSSELL, newscaster, reporter; b. Corpus Christi, Tex., Oct. 19, 1948; s. Harold Orville and Marguerite Doris (Waller) Melendy; m. Lorna Sandra Katz, Mar. 19, 1972; children: Seth Howard, Andrew Scott. Student, George Washington U., 1966-70; BA magna cum laude, U. Hartford, 1972. News dir. Sta. WINY, Putnam, Conn., 1971-77; news anchor, reporter Sta. WPOP, Hartford, Conn., 1977-80; news dir. Sta. WNVR, Waterbury, Conn., 1980-81; news anchor, reporter St. WDRC, Hartford, Conn., 1980—81; news anchor Sta. WCBS-FM, NYC, 1981; prodr., assignment editor, anchor, reporter AP Broadcast, Washington, 1981—. Instr. journalism Briarwood Coll., Southington, Conn., 1977—81, mem. broadcast adv. com., 1978—81. Prodr., writer, reporter: Star Wars: Strategic Defense Initiative, 1985, Flashback, 1986—2005. Publicity chmn. Woodstock Players Cmty. Theater, Conn., 1972—77, Quinebaug Valley C.C. Found., Danielson, Conn., 1973—75, fundraising chmn., 1976; neighborhood coord. Am. Heart Assn., Washington, 1994, 1999, 2001, 2006, 2007; troop com. mem. Boy Scouts Am., 1998—99, 2005—, pack com. chmn., 2000—01, asst. scoutmaster, 2001—05, advancement chmn., 2003—08, vice chmn. mktg. Horizon dist/nat. Capital Area coun., 2005—. Recipient God and Country award, Episcopal Ch., 1963, Inductee Order of Arrow, Boy Scouts Am., 1963, Eagle Scout award, 1964, Edward R. Murrow award, Radio and TV News Dirs. Assn., 2002. Mem.: Nat. Press Club, Com. Concerned Journalists, News Media Guild/TNG-CWA (v.p.), Radio and

TV News Dirs. Assn., Ho. and Senate Radio-TV Corr. Assn., Elks. Avocations: personal computers, photography, hiking, swimming. Office: AP 1100 13th St NW Ste 700 Washington DC 20005-4076

MELETIADIS, JOSEPH, microbiologist, educator; b. Hannover, Germany, July 13, 1975; s. Emmanuel Meletiadis and Despina Meletiadou. BS, Sch. Biology, Aristotle U., Thessaloniki, Greece, 1998; PhD, Med. Sch., Katholieke U. Nijmegen, Netherlands, 2002. Postdoc. fellow Mycology Rsch. Ctr., Nijmegen, 2002—03; rsch. fellow Pediatric Oncology Br., Nat. Cancer Inst., Bethesda, Md., 2003—07; lectr. Med. Sch., U. Athens, Greece, 2007—. Musician guitarist. Recipient, Hellenic Soc. Med. Micobiology, 2009; Marie Curie Internat. Reintegration grant, European Commn. Mem.: Hellenic Soc. Med. Mycology, European Soc. Clin. Microbiology & Infectious Diseases, Am. Soc. Microbiology. Achievements include research in direct effects of cytokines & corticosteroids on Candida albicans, molecular diagnosis of fungal infections, pharmacogenomics, toxicogenomics & immunogenomics in fungal infections; in vitro susceptibility testing of filamentous fungi & drug interaction of antifungal agents, diagnostic tools & animal models for fungal infections. Office: Attikon Univ Gen Hosp Rimini 1 Haidari Athens Attiki 124 62 Greece Office Fax: 30-210-532-6421. Business E-Mail: jmeletiadis@med.uoa.gr.

MELGREN, ERIC FRANKLIN, federal judge, former prosecutor; b. Minneola, Kans., Dec. 16, 1956; s. Carl James and Louise C. (Loechnor) M.; m. Denise Melgren, June 16, 1979; children: David W., Susan C., Peter J., Abigail J. B, Wichita State U., 1979; JD, Washburn U., Topeka, 1985. Bar: Kans. 1985, US Dist. Ct. Kans. 1985, US Ct. Appeals (10th cir.) 1987, US Tax Ct. 1988, US Supreme Ct. 1995. Law clk. to Hon. Frank G. Theis US Dist. Ct. Kans., Wichita, 1985-87; assoc. Foulston, Siefkin, Powers & Eberhardt, Wichita, 1987-92; ptnr. Foulston & Siefkin, Wichita, 1992—2002; US atty. Dist. Kans. US Dept. Justice, Witchita, 2002—08; judge US Dist. Ct. Kans., Witchita, 2008—. Trustee Leadership Wichita, 1994—. Mem. Christian Legal Soc. (state dir. 1989-94), Wichita State Alumni Assn. (exec. com. 1993—), West Wichita Rotary Club. Republican. Office: US District Court 401 N Market Ste 423 Wichita KS 67202 Office Phone: 316-269-6481, 316-269-6110. Office Fax: 316-269-6111. E-mail: KSD_Melgren_Chambers@ksd.uscourts.gov.*

MELICHER, RONALD WILLIAM, finance educator; b. St. Louis, July 4, 1941; s. William and Lorraine Norma (Mohart) M.; m. Sharon Ann Schlarmann, Aug. 19, 1967; children: Michelle Joy, Thor William, Sean Richard. BSBA, Washington U., St. Louis, 1963, MBA, 1965, DBA, 1968. Asst. prof. fin. U. Colo., Boulder, 1969-71, assoc. prof., 1971-76, prof. fin., 1976—, chmn. fin. divsn., 1978-86, 90, chmn. fin. and econ. divsn., 1993-2000, MBA/MS programs dir., 1990-93, chmn. fin. divsn., 2003—. Assoc. dir. space law bus. and policy ctr. U. Colo., 1986-87; rsch. cons. FPC, Washington, 1975-76, GAO, Washington, 1981, RCG/Hagler, Bailly, Inc., 1985—, Ariz. Corp. Commn., 1986-87, Conn. Dept. Pub. Utility Control, 1989, US SEC, 1992-95; cons. tech. edn. IBM Corp., 1985-91; dir. ann. Exch. Program for Gas Industry, 1975-94; instr. ann. program Nat. Assn. Regulatory Utility Commrs., Mich. State U., 1981-94. Co-author: Real Estate Finance, 1978, 3d edit., 1989, Financial Management, 5th edit., 1982, Finance: Introduction to Markets, Institutions and Management, 1980, 1984, 1988, 1992, Finance: Introduction to Institutions, Investments and Management, 9th edit., 1997, 12th edit., 2006, 13th edit., 2008, Entrepreneurial Finance, 2003, 2d edit., 2006, 3rd edit., 2009; assoc. editor Fin. Mgmt. Jour., 1975—80, The Fin. Rev., 1988—91. Recipient News Ctr. 4 TV Tchg. award, 1987, MBA/MS Assn. Tchg. award, 1988, Boulder Faculty Assembly Tchg. award, 1988, Grad. Bus. Students Tchg. award, 1995, 98; grantee NSF, 1974, NASA, 1986, 87; scholar W.H. Baughn Disting., 1989-2000, U. Colo. Pres.'s Tchg., 1989—. Mem. Fin. Mgmt. Assn. (mem. com. 1974-76, regional dir. 1975-77, v.p. ann. mtg. 1985, v.p. program 1987, pres. 1991-92, exec. com. 1991-93, bd. trustees 1992-99, chmn. 25th Anniversary com. 1994-95, mem. search com. for editor of Fin. Mgmt. Jour., 1995-96, chmn. search com. editor of Fin. Practice and Edn. Jour. 1996, mem. search com. for sec./treas. 1999, 2001), Am. Fin. Assn. Western Fin. Assn. (bd. dirs. 1974-76), Fin. Execs. Inst. (acad. mem. 1975—), Ea. Fin. Assn., Southwestern Fin. Assn., Midwest Fin. Assn. (bd. dirs. 1978-80), Alpha Kappa Psi, Beta Gamma Sigma. Office: U Colo Coll Bus PO Box 419 Boulder CO 80303 Office Phone: 303-492-3182. Business E-Mail: ronald.melicher@colorado.edu.

MELICK, CLIFFORD FRANCIS, sociologist, researcher; b. Albany, NY, Sept. 6, 1947; s. Francis Joseph Melick, Marion Dorothy Campbell; m. Evelyn Louise Mazo, Feb. 24, 2004. BA, Siena Coll., Loudonville, NY, 1971; MA, SUNY, Albany, 1973, PhD, 1979. Rsch. scientist N.Y. State Divsn. for Youth, Albany, 1980—83, dir. revenue and reporting svcs., 1983—86, chief program analysis and rsch., 1986—90; dir. rsch. Greater Balt. Med. Ctr., 1990—2002, dir. clin. info. and rsch., 2002—04; program evaluator Balt. City Pub. Sch. Sys., 2005—. Mem. editol adv. bd. Rsch. in Healthcare Fin. Mgmt., Balt., 2000—; prin. advisor NEMA Rsch., Inc., NYC, 1997—; mem. Greater Balt. Med. Ctr. Instnl. Rev. Bd., Balt., 1990—; bd. dirs. Analytica, Ltd., Albany, NY; adj. Johns Hopkins Sch. Pub. Health, 2005—. Contbr. book Chronic Wound Care, 2nd edit., 1997, Chronic Wound Care, 3d edit., 2001, Current Surgical Therapy, 4th edit., 1992, Current Surgical Therapy, 5th edit., 1995, articles to profl. jours. Mem.: APHA, Soc. of Clin. Rsh. Assoc., Am. Urogynecologic Soc., Acad. Health, Soc. for the Art and Sci. Wound Mgmt., Internat. Soc. for Rschs. in Healthcare Fin. Mgmt., Free State Corvette Club. Avocation: sports cars. Home: 8207 Spring Bottom Way Baltimore MD 21208 Office: Balt City Pub Sch Sys Rsch Evaluation Assessment Account 200 E North Ave Baltimore MD 21202 Office Phone: 410-396-8956. Personal E-mail: cmelick@comcast.net. Business E-Mail: cmelick@bcps.k12.md.us.

MELIKER, JAYMIE R., medical educator; b. Balt., Jan. 31, 1974; married. BA, Oberlin Coll., Ohio, 1996; PhD, U. Mich., Ann Arbor, 2006. Rsch. scientist BioMedware, Ann Arbor, 2006—07; asst. prof. Stony Brook U., NY, 2007—. Mem.: Internat. Soc. Environ. Epidemiology. Office: Stony Brook Univ HSC L3 Rm 071 Stony Brook NY 11794-8338

MELILLO, JERRY M., ecologist; BA, Wesleyan Univ., Middletown, Conn., 1965, MAT, 1968; MFS, Yale Univ., 1972, PhD, 1977. Biology instr. Kakamega Secondary Sch., Kenya, 1966—67, Weston (Conn.) H.S., 1968—73, Foote Sch., 1972—73; tchg. asst. Yale Univ., 1973—75, assoc. rsch., Hubbard Brook Ecosystem Study, 1975—76; dir., ecosystems studies NSF, Washington, 1986—88; assoc. dir., environ., Office of Sci., Tech. Policy Office of Pres., Washington, 1996—97; asst. scientist, Ecosystems Ctr. Marine Biol. Lab, Woods Hole, 1976—82, assoc. scientist, 1982—87, sr. scientist, 1987—, acting dir., 1988—89, co-dir., 1989—. Trustee H. John Heinz III Ctr. Sci., Econ, Environ. Recipient Disting. Alumni award, Wesleyan Univ. Fellow: Am. Acad. Arts & Scis.; mem.: Nat. Assn. Advancement Sci., Am. Geophysical Union, Ecological Soc. Am. (pres.-elect), Cosmos Club. Office: Ecosystems Ctr Marine Biological Lab 7 MBL St Woods Hole MA 02543 Business E-Mail: jmelillo@mbl.edu.

MELILLO, JOSEPH VINCENT, theater producer; b. New Haven, Nov. 15, 1946; s. Vincent and Viola (Fucci) M. BA, Sacred Heart U., 1968; MFA, Cath. U. Am., 1972. Adminstr. City Ctr. Music and Drama, NYC, 1972-75; mktg. dir. The Walnut St. Theatre, Phila., 1975-76; dir. FEDAPT, NYC, 1976-80; gen. mgr. New World Festival of Arts, Miami, Fla., 1982; dir. Next Wave Festival, NYC, 1983-89; artistic dir. N.Y. Internat. Festival, NYC, 1990-91, exec. prodr., 1999—; producing dir. Bklyn. Acad. Music, 1991—, exec. prodr., 1999—. Trustee EnGarde Arts, N.Y.C., 1991-96; v.p., bd. dirs. Assn. Performing Arts Presenters, Washington, 1991-93; cons.-specialist Opera Am. Washington, 1991-93; cons. The Japan Found. "Performing Arts Japan", The Bush Found., St. Paul, Arts Internat., N.Y.C.; adj. prof. Theater Dept. Bklyn. Coll.; co-chair Internat. Presenters Forum; mem. cultural challenge panel N.Y.C. Dept. Cultural Affairs; bd. advisors Etantdonnes, 2000-02; curator Internat. Soc. Performing Arts, 2005. Editor: Market the Arts, 1980. Mem. adv. bd. materials for arts Africa Exch. 651 program com. NJ Performing Arts Ctr., Newark, 1999—; mem. New Haven Festival of the Arts and Ideas; advisor Rolex Mentor and Protege Program, 2002—03, Hermitage Artist Retreat, Sarasota, Fla.; program adv. panel Pew Fellowships in the Arts, 2003, chmn. multidisciplinary panel, 2003, 2007; moderator The Berkshire Conf.; curator panels Internat. Soc. Performing Arts Found., 2005; adv. bd. Rolex Mentor and Protege Program, 2005—. Decorated Order Brit. Empire, chevalier and officer Order of Arts and Letters, Knight Royal Order of the Polar Star, 2007; recipient Documents of Dance award, Dance Library of Israel, 2003, Svc. to Artistic Cmty. award Bang on a Can. Mem.: Century Assn. Democrat. Avocations: reading, travel. Office Phone: 718-636-4107. Business E-Mail: programming@bam.org.

MELIN, ROBERT ARTHUR, lawyer; b. Milw., Sept. 13, 1940; s. Arthur John and Frances Magdalena (Lanser) M.; m. Mary Magdalen Melin, July 8, 1967; children: Arthur Walden, Robert Dismas, Nicholas O'Brien, Madalyn Mary. BA summa cum laude, Marquette U., Milw., 1962, JD, 1967. Bar: Wis. 1966, US Dist. Ct. (ea. dist.) Wis. 1966, US Ct. Appeals (7th cir.) 1966, US Ct. Mil. Appeals 1967, US Supreme Ct. 1975. Law clk. U.S. Dist. Ct. (ea. dist.), Wis., 1966; instr. bus. law U. Ga., Hinesville, 1968; lectr. bus. law U. Md., Asmara, 1970; lectr. law Haile Salassie I. U. Law Faculty, Addis Ababa, Ethiopia, 1971-72; with Walther & Halling, Milw., 1973-74, Schroeder, Gedlen, Riester & Moerke, Milw., 1974-82; ptnr. Schroeder, Gedlen, Riester & Melin, Milw., 1982-84, Schroeder, Riester, Melin & Smith, Milw., 1984—. Author: Evidence in Ethiopia, 1972; contbg. author Ann. Survey African Law, 1974; contbr. numerous articles to legal jours. Rep. Class of 2000, West Point Parent Assn. Wis., 1996—, exec. bd., 1997—; lectr. charitable solicitations and contracts Philanthropy Monthly 9th Ann. Policy Conf., NYC, 1985; chmn. Milw. Young Dems., 1963-64. Capt. JAGC, AUS, 1967-70. Mem.: ABA, Wis. Acad. Trial Lawyers, Wis. Bar Assn., Milw. Bar Assn., Friends Ethiopia, Am. Legion, Delta Theta Phi, Phi Alpha Theta, Pi Gamma Mu. Roman Catholic. Home: 8108 N Whitney Rd Milwaukee WI 53217-2752 Office: 135 W Wells St Milwaukee WI 53203-1807 Office Phone: 414-351-0539.

MELIN, STACY M., literature and language educator; b. Dallas, Oct. 27, 1977; d. Billy Joe Sr. and Suzanne Denise Melin. BA in Lit. cum laude, U. North Tex., Denton, 2003. Cert. tchr. English and lang. arts grades 4-12 State of Tex., 2004. Tchr. lit. grades 7-8 St. Pius X Cath. Sch., Dallas, 2004—. Speech team coach St. Pius X Cath. Sch., Dallas, 2004—. Recipient Work of Heart award, Cath. Diocese of Dallas, 2006. Office: St Pius X Catholic Sch 3030 Gus Thomasson Rd Dallas TX 75228

MELINE, DAVID W., manufacturing executive; b. Owatonna, Minn. BS in Mech. Engring., Iowa State U., Ames; MA in Econs., London Sch. Econs.; MBA, U. Chgo. Product design engr. AT&T Corp.; treasurer's office Gen. Motors, NYC; sr.-level positions GM, Kenya, Brazil, GM Daewoo, Republic of Korea, GM Europe, Switzerland; v.p., CFO GM North America; v.p., corp. contr., chief acctg. officer 3M, St. Paul, 2008—. Office: 3M Corp Hdqs 3M Ctr Saint Paul MN 55144-1000

MELKA, TOMI, language educator, historian; b. Tirana, Albania, Sept. 16, 1965; life ptnr. Mariana G. Hernandez Abreu. MA in Spanish Linguistics, U. Ill., Urbana-Champaign, 2005. Cert. Spanish instr. U. Ill., 2005. Asst. prof. State U. Tirana, Albania, 1988—90; instr. Spanish Parkland Coll., Champaign, Ill., 2005—. Instr. of spanish; tour-leader Gran Canaria Sch. of Languages, Las Palmas de G.C., Spain, 1996—2001. Author: (research article) Cryptologia, 2008; contbr. compilation, correction (Best Promising Youth, 1989); author: (research) Glottotheory: International Journal of Linguistics, Folklore. Scholarship, Ministerio de Cultura, Gobierno de España, 1992. Achievements include research in early forms of writing and other symbolic systems. Office: Parkland Coll Dept Humanities 2400 West Bradley Ave Champaign IL 61821 Business E-Mail: tmelka@parkland.edu.

MELKVIK, JENNIFER KENT, retired mathematics educator; b. Detroit, Mich., Jan. 3, 1953; d. Edgar James and Mary Norton Kent; m. Leslie R Melkvik, July 12, 1980; children: Jennifer M. Thibeault, Sarah J. Millard, Jason E., Chelsie V. BA in edn., Western Mich. U., 1970—74; MS, Ea. Mich. U., 1975—79. Professional Teaching Certification Dept. of Edn./Mich., 1974. Mid. sch. math tchr. East Mid. Sch., Plymouth, Mich., 1974—2006; ret., 2006. Math dept. chmn. East Mid. Sch., Plymouth, Mich., 1987—2005, coach, math counts team, 1995—; founding mem. Girls Excel in Math. and Sci. Com. Plymouth-Canton Schs., Mich., 1992—2006; cooperating tchr. East Mich. U., 1997—2006; Wayne county rep. Mich. Math Leaders Acad., 2002—06. Youth leader Chilson Hills, Am. Bapt. Ch., Brighton, Mich., 1996—2005. Recipient Edythe May Sliffe award, 2004, Math Leadership award for Wayne County Teachers, 2004, Plymouth-Canton Cmty. Schools Extra Miler award, 2003, Detroit Metro Coaching award, Mathcounts, 2003—09. Mem.: Nat. Coun. of Teachers of Math., Mich. Coun. of Teachers of Math., Detroit Area Coun. of Teachers of Math., Math. Assn. of Am. (hon.), Delta Kappa Gamma. Christian. Avocations: exercise, boating, swimming. Home: 10820 Gamewood Dr South Lyon MI 48178 Personal E-mail: jmelkvik@hotmail.com.

MELL, PATRICIA, dean; b. Cleve., Dec. 15, 1953; d. Julian Cooper and Thelma (Webb) M.; m. Michael Steven Ragland. AB with honors, Wellesley Coll., 1975; JD, Case Western Res. U., 1978. Bar: Ohio 1979, Pa. 1988, U.S. Dist. Ct. (so. and no. dists.) Ohio 1979. Asst. atty. gen. State of Ohio, Columbus, 1978-82, sec. of state corps. counsel, 1982-84; vis. asst. prof. Capital U. Law Sch., Columbus, 1984-85, U. Toledo Law Sch., 1985-86; asst. prof. law Widener U. (formerly Delaware Law Sch.), Wilmington, 1986—88; assoc. prof. law Mich. State U. Detroit Coll. of Law, East Lansing, Mich., 1992—2003, prof. law, 1996—2003, assoc. dean for academic affairs, 2000—02; dean John Marshall Law Sch., Chicago, Ill., 2003—. Mediator night prosecutor's program, Columbus, 1984-85. Mem. scholarship screening com. Black Am. Law Student Assn. U. Toledo Law Sch., 1985-86, governing bd. Case Western Res. U. Law Sch., Cleve., 1985-88, Alliance of Black Women, Columbus, 1983-85, Capers for Judge com., Cleve., 1980-86, century club Ohio Dems., 1985-86; chmn. law student com. Young Black Dems., Columbus, 1982-84; coordinator minority affiliations subcom. Citizens for Brown for Gov., Columbus, 1981-82; mem. Nat. Beach MBA, 1986—. Recipient award, 2d Bapt. Ch., Evanston, 2003, Internat. Assn. Corps. Adminstrs., 1983, C.F. Stradford award, 2005; named Chgo. Midwest Honoree, Nat. Coun. Negro Women, 2003, one of Chgo.s 100 Most Influentianl Women, Crain's Chgo. Bus., 2004. Mem. ABA, Nat. Bar Assn., Nat. Conf. Black Lawyers, Am. Arbitration Assn. (comml. arbitrator 1986—), Nat. Black MBA's, 1986-91. Lutheran. Avocations: modern languages, stained glass work, fencing, tennis, piano. Home: 710 Crestview Dr Bolingbrook IL 60440-9059

MELL, RICHARD F., alderman; b. Muskegon, Mich., May 5, 1939; m. Marge Mell; children: Patricia Blagojevich, Deborah, Richard. Student, U. Mich. Owner R.F. Mell Spring & Mfg. Co., Chgo., 1967—; alderman, 33d ward Chgo. City Coun., 1975—; vice mayor City of Chgo., 1979—86. Chmn. committees, rules and ethics com. Chgo. City Coun. Active Logan Sq. Neighborhood Assn., Logan Sq. Lions Club, Northwest Cmty. Org., Fraternal Order Eagles, Polish Am. Alliance; precinct captain 33d Ward Regular Dem Org.; mem., former chmn. Young Democrats Cook County; mem. Cook County Dem. Ctrl. Com. Office: 3649 N Kedzie Ave Chicago IL 60618-4513 also: City Hall 121 N Lasalle St Rm 208 Chicago IL 60602 Office Phone: 773-478-8040, 312-774-6825. Office Fax: 773-478-8006. Business E-Mail: rmell@cityofchicago.org.*

MELLBERG, JAMES RICHARD, retired dental research chemist; b. Manitowoc, Wis., June 3, 1932; s. Millard Filmore Mellberg and Marion Eleanor (Elmer) Zimmerman; m. Gail Maureen Loehning, Sept. 26, 1956; children: Eric, Diane, Laura. BS, Wis. State U., Oshkosh, 1955; MS, Loyola U., Chgo., 1960. Head dental rsch. dept. Kendall Co., Barrington, Ill., 1958-75; assoc. dir. dental rsch. Colgate-Palmolive Co., Piscataway, NJ, 1975-94; ret. Cons. Naval Dental Rsch. Inst., Great Lakes, Ill., 1972-94. Author: Fluoride in Preventive Dentistry, 1983; patentee in field; contbr. over 100 articles in field to sci. publs. Recipient 20 sci. exhibit awards ADA, 1964-87. Mem. Internat. Assn. Dental Rsch. (Disting. Scientist award). Avocations: bicycling, woodworking. Home: 675 Ridge Top Rd Tryon NC 28782 Personal E-mail: mellberg1@windstream.net.

MELLBERG, LEONARD EVERT, physicist; b. Springfield, Mass., Dec. 18, 1935; s. Evert and Dorothy (Baker) M.; m. Pamela Narbeth. BS in Physics, U. Mass., Amherst, 1961; MS in Physics, Trinity Coll., Hartford, Conn., 1968. Rsch. physicist Navy Underwater Sound Lab., New London, Conn., 1961—68, SACLANT Undersea Rsch. Ctr., LaSpezia, Italy, 1968—72, Office of Naval Rsch., London, 1968—72, Naval Underwater Sys. Ctr., Newport, RI, 1972—91; sr. scientist Marine Acoustics Inc., Newport, 1991—94; chief scientist Sci. Applications Internat. Corp., San Diego, 1994—2000, Ocean Physics Assocs., South Dartmouth, Mass., 2000—. Govt. and profl. tech. adv. bds. and coms. Contbr. over 70 articles to profl. jours. Pres. Verdandi Swedish Cultural Found., Providence, 1992-97; bd. dirs. Verdandi Chorus Am. Union Swedish Singers, Providence, 1992—. Recipient Naval Underwater Sys. Ctr. Excellence in Sci. award, 1977, 84, Civilian Navy Meritorious Svc. medal Dept. of Navy, 1991. Fellow Acoustical Soc. Am.; mem. IEEE (life, sr.), AIAA (Svc. award 1977), Am. Geophys. Union, Oceanic Soc. of IEEE. Achievements include research in ocean physics, ocean acoustic propagation, anti-submarine warfare acoustics, Arctic sea-ice ridges and lighter than air vehicles. Home and Office: 109 Wilson St South Dartmouth MA 02748-3021 Home Phone: 508-994-9599. E-mail: lpmellberg@ieee.org.

MELLEN, FRANCIS JOSEPH, JR., lawyer; b. Williamsport, Pa., Dec. 19, 1945; s. Francis Joseph and Mary Emma (Oberst) M.; m. Mary Wilder Davison, Aug. 2, 1975 (div. 1987); m. Beverly Joan Glascock, Sept. 2, 2000; children: Elizabeth, Catherine, Robert, Christine. BA, U. Ky., 1967, MA, 1971; JD, Harvard U., 1973. Bar: NY 1974, Ky. 1975, US Dist. Ct. (so. dist.) NY 1974, US Dist. Ct. (ea. dist.) Ky. 1977, US Dist. Ct. (we. dist.) Ky. 1978, US Ct. Appeals (2d cir.) 1975, US Ct. Appeals (6th cir.) 1982, US Supreme Ct. 2005. Assoc. atty. Rogers & Wells, NYC, 1973-75, Wyatt, Grafton & Sloss, Louisville, 1975-80; ptnr. Wyatt, Tarrant & Combs, Louisville, 1980—. Co-author: Kentucky Mineral Law, 1986, Kentucky Forms and Transactions, 1991; contbr. articles to profl. jours. Spl. study com. Uniform Comml. Code, Ky. Legis. Rsch. Commn., Frankfort, 1984-91; bd. dirs. Leadership Louisville Found., 1995-02, counsel, 1996-98, 2000-02; bd. dirs. Stage One: The Louisville Children's Theatre, 1995-01, v.p., 1997-98, pres., 1998-00; bd. dirs. Louisville-Jefferson County A.W.A.R.E. Coalition, 1994-98; bd. trustees Cherokee Gardens, 2005—. chair, 2007-08, Lt. (j.g.) USNR, 1967-69. Mem. ABA, Am. Arbitration Assn. (panel), Nat. Arbitration Forum (panel), Ky. Bar Assn. (ho. of dels. 1986-92, ethics com. 2004—, arbitration panel 2005—), Louisville Bar Assn. (chmn. com. profl. responsibility 1992-94), Jefferson Club, Filson Club, Am. Mensa, Hon. Order Ky. Cols. Republican. Home: 2944 Lexington Rd Louisville KY 40206-2934 Office: Wyatt Tarrant & Combs LLP 2800 PNC Plz Louisville KY 40202 Home Phone: 502-893-9254; Office Phone: 502-562-7290. E-mail: fmellen@wyattfirm.com.

MELLENCAMP, JOHN (JOHN COUGAR), singer, lyricist; b. Seymour, Ind., Oct. 7, 1951; m. Vicky C. (div.); children: Michelle, Teddy Joe, Justice; m. Elaine Irwin, Sept. 5, 1992; children: Hud, Spec Wildhorse. A. in Broadcasting, Vincennes U., Ind., 1973; Doctorate (hon.), Ind. U., 2000. Albums include Chestnut Street Incident, 1977, Biography, 1978, Johnny Cougar, 1979, Nothing Matters and What If It Did, 1980, Night Dancin, 1980, American Fool, 1982, Uh-huh, 1983, Scarecrow, 1985, The Lonesome Jubilee, 1988, Big Daddy, 1989, Whenever We Wanted, 1991, Human Wheels, 1993, Dance Naked, 1994, Mr. Happy Go Lucky, 1996, The Best That I Could Do...1997, John Mellencamp, 1998, Rough Harvest, 1999, Cuttin' Heads, 2001, Trouble No More, 2003, Words & Music: John Mellencamp's Greatest Hits, 2004, Freedom's Road, 2007, Live, Death, Love & Freedom, 2008; performed one song for Folkways: A Vision Shared (A Tribute to Woody Guthrie and Leadbelly), 1988; film actor, dir., soundtrack performer: Falling From Grace, 1992, Seeing in the Dark, 2000; actor (films) Madison (voice only), 2001, After Image, 2001, Lone Star State of Mind, 2002; TV appearance Bob Dylan: The 30th Anniversary Concert Celebration, 1993, Farm Aid '96, 1996. Co-founder, bd. dirs. Farm Aid, 1985—. Recipient Century award for Creative Achievement, Billboard, 2001, Woody Guthrie award, 2003; named to Rock & Roll Hall of Fame, 2008. Office: John Mellencamp PO Box 6777 Bloomington IN 47407-6777 also: c/o Randy Hoffman Hoffman Entertainment Inc 362 5th Ave Ste 804 New York NY 10001

MELLENDORF, KENNETH ERNEST, physicist, researcher; b. Chicago Heights, Ill., Oct. 7, 1964; s. Kenneth Ray and Donna Rose (Jarchow) M. BA in Physics, U. Chgo., 1986; MS in Physics, U. Ill., 1987, PhD in Physics, 1993. Physics, math. tutor, Dolton, Ill., 1993-96, S. Suburban Coll., South Holland, Ill., 1996; physics prof., tutor Prairie State Coll., Chicago Heights, 1996—2000; physics prof. Ill. Ctrl. Coll., East Peoria, 2000—. Tchg. asst. U. Ill., Champaign, 1986-87, rsch. asst., 1987-93. Mem. Am. Assn. Physics Tchrs., Am. Phys. Soc., Nat. Honor Soc., Sigma Xi. Home: 1900 Highview Rd Apt Gd East Peoria IL 61611 Office Phone: 309-694-5359.

MELLER, JOSE, cardiologist; b. Santiago, Chile, Sept. 29, 1944; MD, Cath. U. Chile, Santiago, 1969. Cert. Internal Medicine, 1973, Cardiovascular Disease, 1975. Intern Elmhurst Gen. Hosp., Queens, NY, 1969—70, resident, 1970—71, Mt. Sinai Hosp., NYC, 1971—74, attending physician, 1974, assoc. attending physician; clin. prof. Mt. Sinai Med. Ctr., NYC. Office: 941 Park Ave New York NY 10028 Office Phone: 212-988-3772. Office Fax: 212-861-4672.

MELLERICK-DRESSLER, DERVLA M., medical association administrator; d. James and Anne Mellerick; m. Gregory Roland Dressler, July 1, 1987; children: Nicole Anne Dressler, Kiera Rose Dressler. BS, U. Ireland, Cork, 1978, MS, 1979; PhD, U. Pa., Phila., 1986. Staff fellow lab., biochem. genetics NHLBI NIH, Bethesda, Md.; asst. rsch. scientist, dept. pediat. U. Mich., Ann Arbor, 1994—99, asst. prof., pathology, 1999—2006; founder Sci. Word Dr. LLC, Ann Arbor, 2007—. Jewelry design. Master: Am. Med. Writers Assn. Business E-Mail: dervla@sciencewordoctor.com.

MELLERT, LUCIE ANNE, writer, photographer; b. Charleston, W.Va., June 6, 1932; d. Wilbur Conant and Grace Martin (Taylor) Frame; m. William Jennings Mellert, March 15, 1957; 1 child, James Floyd Kelly III. Student, Mason Coll. of Music Fine Arts, Charleston, 1937-49, W.Va. U., Morgantown, 1950-51. Pub. rels. exec., asst. treas., office mgr. J. H. Milam, Inc., Dunbar, W.Va., 1959-71; pub. rels. exec., office mgr. Hallcraft, Inc., Dunbar, 1972-74; office mgr. Kanawha Stone Co. Inc., Nitro, W.Va., 1975-78. Vol. photographer Charleston Gazette, 1997—. Beautification commr. City of Dunbar, 1969-72; activity coord., program dir. Dunbar Bicentennial Com., 1971; founder, coordinator Dunbar City wide Beautification and Improvement Com., 1969-72; coord. Kanawha County Elem. Students Anti-Litter Program, Planting the Seed, 1996-03; pres. United Meth. Women of St. Marks; active U. Charleston Builders, W.Va. Humanities Coun., Friends of W. Va. Culture and History, Friends of Clay Ctr.; judge various cmty. events, 1995-04; commr. Kanawha County Pks. and Recreation Commn., 2000—; vol. photographer Charleston Gazette On the Town, 1997-. Recipient West Virginian award, Gov. Cecil Underwood, 2000, Gov. Bob Wise, 2001, West Va. Vol. Spirit award, W. Va. Women's Commn., 2003, commendation for vol. svc., W.Va. Gov. Bob Wise, 2004; named Disting. Mountaineer, W.Va. Gov. Joe Manchin III, 2005. Mem. Nat. Fedn. Press Women, Pioneer Women's (past pres.), Kanawha Valley and Nat. Trust Hist. and Preservation Soc., Women of Moose, W.Va. Soc.Assn. Execs., Mental Health Assn., W. Va. Symphony League, Charleston Area Alliance. Methodist. Avocations: church activities, music, travel, art, photography. Home: 1604 Virginia St E Charleston WV 25311-2114 Home Phone: 304-342-7294; Office Phone: 304-342-7294.

MELLEY, STEVEN MICHAEL, lawyer; b. Rhinebeck, NY, Jan. 3, 1950; s. James Christopher and Virginia (Madonna) M.; children: Aliza, Steven Jonathan, Olivia, Bennett; m. Phoebe Kirwood. BA in Russian Studies with honors, Colgate U., 1972; JD, Tulane U., 1975. Bar: NY 1976, US Dist. Ct. 1976, US Supreme Ct. 1980. Law clk. to hon. Matthew Braniff Criminal Dist. Judge, Orleans Parish, New Orleans; assoc. Woody N. Klose Law Offices, Red Hook, NY, 1975—78; ptnr. Klose & Melley, Rhinebeck, 1978-83; pvt. practice Rhinebeck, 1983—. Atty. Village of Tivoli, NY, 1977-78. Contbg. editor: New York Motor Vehicle Accidents, 1999; assoc. editor Tulane Forum, 1974-75. Named to, NY SuperLawyers, 2007. Mem. ABA, AAJ (sustaining), NY State Bar Assn. (past com. mem. on specialization), Dutchess County Bar Assn. (sustaining), NY State Trial Lawyers Assn., Christian Trail Lawyers Assn., Million Dollar Advocates Forum, Phi Alpha Delta, Kappa Delta Rho. Office: 24 Closs Dr Rhinebeck NY 12572 Office Phone: 845-876-4057. Business E-Mail: melleyinjurylaw@aol.com.

MELLI, MARYGOLD SHIRE, law educator; b. Rhinelander, Wis., Feb. 8, 1926; d. Osborne and May (Bonnie) Shire; m. Joseph Alexander Melli, Apr. 8, 1950; children: Joseph, Sarah Bonnie, Sylvia Anne, James Alexander. BA, U. Wis., 1947, LLB, 1950. Bar: Wis. 1950. Dir. children's code revision Wis. Legis. Coun., Madison, 1950-53; exec. dir. Wis. Jud. Coun., Madison, 1955-59; asst. prof. law U. Wis., Madison, 1959-66, assoc. prof., 1966-67, prof., 1967-84, Voss-Bascom prof., 1985-93, emerita, 1993—. Assoc. dean U. Wis., 1970-72, rsch. affiliate Inst. for Rsch. on Poverty, 1980—; mem. spl. rev. bd. Dept. Health and Social Svcs., State of Wis., Madison, 1973—2002. Author: (pamphlet) The Legal Status of Women in Wisconsin, 1977, (book) Wisconsin Juvenile Court Practice, 1978, rev. edit., 1983, (with others) Child Support & Alimony, 1988, The Case for Transracial Adoption, 1994; co-editor: Child Support: The Next Frontier, 1999; contbr. articles to profl. jours. Bd. dirs. Am. Humane Assn., 1985-95, Frank Lloyd Wright - Wis., 2004-; chair A Fund for Women, Madison, Wis., 2002, 2003; mem. Dane County Ct. Ho. Art Acquisitions com. Named one of five Outstanding Young Women in Wis., Jaycees, 1961, Woman of Distinction, YWCA, Madison, Wis., 2007; grantee NSF, 1983; recipient Belle Case LaFollette award for outstanding svc. to the profession, 1994, Outstanding Contbn. to Advancement of Women in Higher Edn. award, 1991, Lifelong Contbn. to Advancement of Women in the Legal Prof. award, 1994, Sr. Svc. award Rotary, Madison, Wis., Am. Bar Assn. Women Trailblazers. Fellow Am. Acad. Matrimonial Lawyers (exec. editor jour. 1985-90); mem. Am. Law Inst. (cons. project on law of family dissolution), Internat. Soc. Family Law (v.p. 1994-2000, 2002-05), Wis. State Bar Assn. (reporter family law sect., 1976-2005), Nat. Conf. Bar Examiners (chmn. bd. mgrs. 1989, editl. adv. com.). Democrat. Roman Catholic. Avocations: walking, swimming, collecting art. Home: 2904 Waunona Way Madison WI 53713-2238 Office: U Wis Law Sch Madison WI 53706 Home Phone: 608-222-2003; Office Phone: 608-262-1610. Business E-Mail: msmelli@wisc.edu.

MELLINKOFF, SHERMAN MUSSOFF, medical educator; b. McKeesport, Pa., Mar. 23, 1920; s. Albert and Helen Mussoff Mellinkoff; m. June Bernice O'Connell, Nov. 18, 1944; children: Sherrill, Albert. BA, Stanford U., 1941, MD, 1944; LHD (hon.), Wake Forest U., 1984, Hebrew Union Coll., LA, 1988. Diplomate Am. Bd. Internal Medicine, Am. Bd. Gastroenterology, Am. Bd. Nutrition. Intern asst. resident Stanford U. Hosp., San Francisco, 1944—45; asst. resident Johns Hopkins Hosp., Balt., 1947—49, chief resident, 1950—51, instr. in medicine, 1951—53; fellow in gastroenterology Hosp. of U. Pa., Phila., 1949—50; from asst. prof. to prof. medicine UCLA Sch. of Medicine, LA, 1962—86; dean UCLA Sch. Medicine, LA, 1962—86, emeritus prof. of medicine, 1990—; disting. physician of VA Wadsworth VA Medical Ctr., LA, 1990-93. Mem. sci. adv. panel Rsch. to Prevent Blindness, Inc., NYC, 1975—93; mem. program devel. com. Nat. Med. Fellowships, Inc., NYC, 1984—. Editl. bd.: The Pharos, 1986—2009; contbr. articles to profl. jours. Apptd. by Gov. of Calif. to McCone Com., 1965. Capt. US Army, 1945—57. Recipient Abraham Flexner award, Assn. Am. Med. Colls., 1981, J.E. Wallace Sterling Disting. Alumnus award, Stanford U. Sch. of Medicine, 1987. Master: ACP; fellow: Royal Coll. of Physicians; mem.: The Johns Hopkins Soc. of Scholars, Am. Acad. of Arts and Scis., Inst. of Medicine of NAS, Assn. Am. Physicians, Am. Gastroenterol. Assn. Assn. Avocation: reading. Office Phone: 310-825-3473.

MELLINS, CLAUDE ANN, psychologist; BA in Psychology, Brown U., 1982; MS in Clin. Psychology, U. So. Calif., LA, 1987; PhD in Clin. Psychology, U. So. Calif., 1990. Assoc. prof. clin. psychology HIV Ctr.; co-dir. and co-founder Spl. Needs Clinic Children & Families Columbia Presbyn., NYC, 1992—; rsch. scientist dept. psychiatry and sociomed. scis. N.Y. State Psychiat. Inst. and Columbia U., NYC, 1994—. Mem. sci. leadership group exec. com. Pediat. HIV AIDS Cohorts Study; v.p. bd. dirs., Ranapo Children, standing mem., NIH Behavioral & Social Consequenses HIV Study Sect., 2009-. Contbr. chpts. to books and articles to profl. jours. Aaron Diamond Found. fellow. Mem. APA (pediat. psychology subdivsn.).

MELLINS, HARRY ZACHARY, radiologist, educator; b. NYC, May 23, 1921; s. David J. and Ray (Hoffman) M.; m. Judith Alice Weiss, Dec. 26, 1950; children— Elizabeth, William, Thomas. AB, Columbia Coll., 1941; MD, L.I. Coll. Medicine, 1944; MS in Radiology, U. Minn., 1951; AM (hon.), Harvard U., 1970. Intern Jewish Hosp., Bklyn., 1944-45, asst. resident in radiology, 1945-46; resident in radiology U. Minn., Mpls., 1948-50, instr. radiology, 1950-52, asst. prof., 1952-53; clin. asst. prof. radiology Wayne State U., Detroit, 1953-56; dir. radiology Sinai Hosp., Detroit, 1953-56; prof., chmn. dept. radiology SUNY, Coll. Medicine, NYC, 1956-69; chief radiology Kings County Hosp. Center, Bklyn., 1956-69; radiologist-in-chief State Univ. Hosp., Bklyn., 1966-69; prof. radiology Harvard Med. Sch., Boston, 1969—87, prof. radiology emeritus, 1991—; dir. diagnostic radiology Peter Bent Brigham Hosp., 1969-79, Brigham and Women's Hosp., 1980-87, dir. edn. and tng., dept. radiology, 1987-94; co-dir. edn. and tng. dept. radiology, 1994-97; chief of radiology Harvard U. Health Svc., 1988-97; radiologist Brigham and Women's Hosp., 1998-99. Nat. cons. in radiology to surgeon gen. U.S. Air Force, 1968-79; mem. radiation study sect. NIH, 1967-71; mem. subcom. for written exam. in diagnostic radiology Am. Bd. Radiology, 1970-75; mem. radiology tng. com. research tng. grants br. Nat. Inst. Gen. Med. Scis.; mem. diagnostic research adv. group div. cancer biology and diagnosis Nat. Cancer Inst., 1975-79; guest examiner Am. Bd. Radiology. Served to capt. M.C. USAAF, 1946-48. Mem. Bklyn. Radiol. Soc. (pres. 1965-66), N.Y. Roentgen Soc. (pres 1966-67), Assn. Univ. Radiologists (pres. 1969-70, Gold medal 1986), Soc. Uroradiology (pres. 1975-76, Gold medal 2000), Am. Roentgen Ray Soc. (pres. 1977-79, Gold medal 1989), Radiol. Soc. N.Am., New Eng. Roentgen Ray Soc. (pres. 1986-87), Soc. Gastrointestinal Radiology, Alpha Omega Alpha (alumnus).

MELLINS, ROBERT B., pediatrician, educator; b. NYC, Mar. 6, 1928; s. David J. and Ray H. (Hoffman) M.; m. Sue Mendelsohn, Apr. 19, 1959; children: Claude Ann, David Rustin. AB, Columbia U., 1948; MD, Johns Hopkins U., 1952. Intern Johns Hopkins Hosp., 1952—53; mem. epidemic intelligence svc, founder poison control program Ctr. Disease Control, Chgo., 1953—55; resident in pediat. N.Y. Hosp., 1955—56, Presbyn. Hosp., NYC, 1956—57, dir. pediat. ICU, 1970—75; assoc. prof. pediat. Columbia U., NYC, 1970—75, prof. pediat., 1975—, dir. Cystic Fibrosis Ctr., 1976—91, dir. pediat. pulmonary divsn., 1972—97; leloir lectr. USCD, 2008. Christmas Seal prof. Can. Lung Assn., 1979-80; 1st Deans Disting. lectr. in clin. scis. Columbia U. Coll. P&S, 1982; mem. Am. Bd. Pediat., founding mem. sub-bd. on pediat. pulmonology; bd. dirs. A.P. Gold Found. to promote humanism in medicine. Mem. editl. bd. Am. Rev. Respiratory Diseases, 1974-81, assoc. editor, 1984-90; contbr. articles to profl. jours. V.p. Am. Lung Assn., 1987—89; chmn. steering com. multi-ctr. study heart and lung complications of HIV infection in children NIH, 1989—2003; bd. dir. Am. Lung Assn., 1981—83, LA Jonas Found., 1970—78, 1990—, Symphony of UN, 1990—; bd. dirs. Am. Lung Assn. City of N.Y., 2001—05. Recipient Career Devel. award NIH, 1966-71, Career Scientist award Health Rsch. Coun. NYC Health Rsch. Coun., 1975, Stevens Triennial Rsch. award Columbia U., 1980, Health Edn. Rsch. award Nat. Asthma Edn. Program, 1992, Will Ross medal Am. Lung Assn., 1996, 2001, Life & Breath award Am. Lung Assn. NY, Outstanding Alumnus award Babies Hosp., Columbus, 2006. Mem.: Am. Acad. Allergy and Immunology, Soc. Critical Care Medicine, Am. Thoracic Soc. (bd. dir. 1975, 1981—84, nat. pres. 1982—83, v.p., Disting. Achievement award 1996), Am. Acad. Pediat. (Med. Edn. Lay Edn. award 1995, Kendig award 2003), Am. Soc. Pharmacology and Exptl. Therapeutics, Am. Physiol. Soc., Soc. Pediat. Rsch., Am. Pediat. Soc., Fleischner Soc. (pres. 1995—), Gold Humanism Honor Soc., Alpha Omega Alpha. Office: Childrens Hosp NY-Presbyn 3959 Broadway CHC 746 New York NY 10032 Home: 22 W 66th St Apt 5 New York NY 10023-6207 Home Phone: 212-362-3461; Office Phone: 212-305-8430. Business E-Mail: rbm3@columbia.edu.

MELLMAN, MARK STEVE, public opinion researcher; b. Hampton, Va., Sept. 13, 1955; s. Carl B. and Sylvia Shapiro Mellman; m. Mindy Beth Horowitz. AB, Princeton U., 1978; MA, Yale U., 1981. Exec. dir. Com. of Concerned Scientists, NYC, 1976-79; instr. Yale U., New Haven, 1981-85; CEO The Mellman Group, Washington, 1982—. Polit. cons. CBS News; presdl. debate analyst PBS; adj. prof. Grad. Sch. Polit. Mgmt., George Washington U., 1988—. Author: (book chpt.) Political Anti-Semitism, 1995. V.p. Jewish Cmty. Coun., Washington, 1988-89; bd. dirs. United Jewish Appeal Fedn., Washington, 1995-99. Mem. Am. Assn. Polit. Cons. (bd. dirs. 1998—). Democrat. Jewish. Avocation: scuba diving. Office: The Mellman Group 1023 31st St, NW Fifth Fl Washington DC 20007 Office Phone: 202-625-0370. Office Fax: 202-625-0371.*

MELLO, CRAIG C., molecular medicine educator, researcher; b. New Haven, 1960; BS in Biochemistry, Brown U., 1982; tng. in devel. biology, U. Colo., 1982—84; PhD in Biology, Harvard U., 1990. Postdoctoral rsch. fellow Fred Hutchinson Cancer Rsch. Ctr., 1990—94; prof., molecular medicine program U. Mass. Med. Sch., Worcester, Mass., 1994—, Blais U. chair in molecular medicine, 2003—; investigator Howard Hughest Med. Inst., 2000—. Contbr. articles to profl. journals. Recipient Lewis S. Rosenstiel award for Disting. Work in Basic Med. Sci., Massry prize, Wiley Prize in Biomedical Sciences, 2003, Gairdner Found. Internat. award, 2005, Dr. Paul Janssen award for Biomedical Rsch., Johnson & Johnson, 2006, Paul Ehrlich and Ludwig Darmstaedter prize, 2006; co-recipient Nobel Prize in Physiology or Medicine, Nobel Found., 2006; Pew scholar, U. Calif., San Francisco, 1995. Fellow: Am. Acad. Arts and Sciences; mem.: NAS (award in molecular biology 2003). Achievements include discovery of the process now known as RNAi (with Andrew Z. Fire), that double-stranded RNA can quash the activity of specific genes. Office: Univ Mass Med Sch Biotech Two Ste 219 373 Plantation St Worcester MA 01605 also: Howard Hughes Inst Medicine 4000 Jones Bridge Rd Chevy Chase MD 20815-6789 Office Phone: 508-856-1602, 301-215-8500. Office Fax: 508-856-2950. Business E-Mail: craig.mello@umassmed.edu.*

MELLOAN, GEORGE RICHARD, editor; b. Greenwood, Ind., Nov. 10, 1927; s. James and Sara Ollie (Merideth) M.; m. Joan Minner, July 1, 1951; children: James, Melissa, Maryanne. BS, Butler U., 1950. Reporter Logansport (Ind.) Press, 1950, Muncie (Ind.) Press, 1951, Wall Street Jour., Chgo. and Detroit, 1952-59, bur. mgr. Cleve. and Atlanta, 1959-61, page one writer NYC, 1961-66, fgn. correspondent London, 1966-70, editl. writer NYC, 1970—2006, dep. editor, internat., 1973—, op-ed columnist, 1987—2006; ret., 2006. Author: The Great Money Binge, Simont Schuster, 2009; co-author: The Carter Economy, 1978. Sgt. U.S. Army, 1946-47. Recipient Gerald Loeb award G&R Loeb Found., 1981, Daily Gleaner awards Inter-Am. Press Assn., 1983, 87. Mem. Coun. on Fgn. Rels., Dutch Treat Club, Echo Lake Country Club. Avocations: travel, golf, hiking, photography. Office: Wall Street Jour 200 Liberty St New York NY 10281-1003

MELLON, DEFOREST, JR., biology professor, researcher; b. Cleve., Dec. 18, 1934; s. DeForest Mellon and Evelyn Martha Emig; m. Karen Gail Dame, Sept. 30, 1988. PhD, Johns Hopkins U., Balt., 1961. Postdoc. fellow Stanford U., Palo Alto, Calif., 1961—63; asst. prof. U. Va., Charlottesville, 1963—68. Contbr. articles to profl. jour. Treas. Citizens for Albemarle, Charlottesville, 2002—07. Fellow, John Simon Guggenheim Found., 1966—67, Thomas Jefferson Vis. fellow, Downing Coll., Cambridge U., 1978—79. Avocations: scuba diving, flying. Office: Univ Va Dept Biology McCormick Rd Charlottesville VA 22903

MELLON, SEWARD PROSSER, brokerage house executive; b. Chgo., July 28, 1942; s. Richard King and Constance Mary (Prosser) Mellon Burrell; m. Karen Leigh Boyd, Sept. 10, 1966 (div. 1974); children— Catharine Leigh, Constance Elizabeth; m. Sandra Springer Stout, 1975. Grad., Choate Sch., 1960; BA, Susquehanna U., 1965, DH, 1993. With Mellon Nat. Corp., Pitts., 1965-69; with T. Mellon & Sons, Pitts., 1969-71; pres. Richard K. Mellon & Sons, Ligonier, 1971—. Trustee Richard King Mellon Family Found.; trustee, pres. Richard King Mellon Found. Mem. Western Pa. Conservancy (life), LoyalHanna Assn. (pres.), Vintage Club (Palm Springs, Calif.), Duquesne Club (Pitts.), Laurel Valley Golf Club (Ligonier), Rolling Rock Club, Rolling Rock Hunt, Phi Mu Delta. Republican. Home: Huntland Downs Box K Ligonier PA 15658 Office: PO Box Rkm Ligonier PA 15658-0780 Office Phone: 724-238-6671.

MELLON, TAMARA, apparel executive; b. Bershire, Eng., July 7, 1967; d. Tom Yeardye and Ann; m. Matthew Mellon II, 2000 (div. 2005); 1 child, Araminta. Shop asst. Browns; with Phyllis Walters Pub. Rels., Mirabella; accessories editor Brit. Vogue, 1990—96; founder, pres. J. Choo Ltd. (Jimmy Choo), 1996—. Bd. dirs. Revlon, Inc., 2008—; bd. dirs., creative adv. bd. H Company Holdings, LLC. Recipient Brand of Yr. award (for Jimmy Choo) award, Accessories Coun. Excellence awards, 2008. Office: J Choo Ltd Ixworth House 37 Ixworth Pl London SW3 3QH England

MELLOR, CHIP (WILLIAM H. MELLOR), lawyer; Grad., Ohio State U., 1973; JD, U. Denver, 1977. Public interest lawyer Mountain States Legal Found., 1979—83; pres. Pacific Research Institute for Public Policy, 1986—91; pres., gen. counsel, founder Inst. for Justice, 1991—. Office: Institute For Justice 901 N Glebe Rd Ste 900 Arlington VA 22203-1854 E-mail: wmellor@ij.org.

MELLOR, ELI, diversified financial services company executive, writer; b. Bozeman, Mont., Jan. 31, 1945; Student, Sioux Falls Coll., SD, 1963—64, U So. Calif., LA, 1966—69. Cardiovasc. surg. technician LAC, U. So. Calif., LA, 1964—69; founder, CEO Life Sci. Systems, Inc, Burbank, Calif., 1970—75, Better Homes, Upland, Calif., 1978—82; lic. prin, stock broker Bache, Halsey, Stuart, Encino, Calif., 1975—78; exec. recruiter SearchWest, LA, 1983—87; founder, trustee The Time Is Now Inst., Claremont, Calif., 1979—. Author: The Time Is Now, The Time is Still Now, The Time Was or Is Still Now; contbr. articles to profl. publs. Activist The Time Is Now Inst., Claremont, Calif., 1979—2007. Named to Presidents Club, SearchWest, 1983—86. Mem.: Nat. Acad. Polit. Sci. (corr.), LA World Affairs Coun. (corr.). Constitutional. Achievements include patents for Sinbad; Needle-aid; Dia-Kleen; Home Dializer; Shunt-Sim. Office: Time is Now Institute 1500 E Tropicana Ste 100 Las Vegas NV 89119 Office Fax: 702-952-9977. Business E-Mail: spearshakers@bresnan.net.

MELLOR, JOHN WILLIAMS, economist, consultant; b. Paris, Dec. 28, 1928; came to U.S., 1929; s. Desmond W. and Katherine (Beardsley) M.; m. Arlene Patton, June 15, 1950 (div. Sept. 1972); children: Michael, Brian, Mark (dec.); m. Uma Lele, Feb. 17, 1973 (div. Apr. 1992); m. Zarmina Said, Oct. 16, 1997. BS, Cornell U., 1950, MS, 1951, PhD, 1954; Diploma, Oxford U., 1952. Prof. Cornell U., Ithaca, NY, 1953—75; chief economist USAID, Washington, 1975—77; dir. Internat. Food Policy Rsch. Inst., Washington, 1977—91; pres. John W. Mellor Assocs., Inc., Washington, 1991—98; v.p. Abt Assocs., Inc., Washington, 1998—2006; pres. John Mellor Associates, Inc., Washington, 2006—. Mem. bd. on agrl. NAS, 1989-92; mem. Agrl. Credit Commn., Res. Bank India, 1986-88. Author: Economics of Agricultural Development, 1966 (Am. Agrl. Econs. Assn. award 1978), Accelerating Food Production Growth in Sub-Saharan Africa, 1987, Agricultural Price Policy for Developing Countries, 1988 (hon. mention Am. Agrl. Econs. Assn. 1989), Agriculture on the Road to Industrialization, 1992. Mem. Internat. Commn. on Food and Peace, 1988—. Recipient Wihuri Internat. prize Wihuri Found., Helsinki, 1985, Presdl. End Hunger award The White House, 1987, Outstanding Alumni award Cornell U., 1987. Fellow AAAS, Am. Acad. Arts and Scis., Am. Agrl. Econs. Assn. (Best Pub. Rsch. award 1967). Avocations: sailing, skiing. Office: John Mellor Assocs Inc Ste PH18 801 Pennsylvania Ave NW Washington DC 20004-2668 Home Phone: 410-586-1841; Office Phone: 202-347-8802. Business E-Mail: jmellor@jmassocinc.com.

MELLOR, KATHY, English as a second language educator; b. Providence; BS in Elem. Edn., RI Coll., 1970, MEd, 1977; MA in Teaching, with ESL and Cross Cultural studies, Brown U., 1989. Substitute tchr. Cranston, RI Sch. Dept., 1970—74; ESL tchr. Internat. Inst. RI, 1980—85; continuing edn. tchr., english dept. RI Coll., 1985—86; cons. for ESL North Kingstown Sch. Dept., RI, 1985; ESL tchr. Hamilton Elem. Sch., North Kingstown, RI, Davisville Mid. Sch., North Kingstown, RI, 1985—. Nat. and internat. spokesperson for education, 2004—. Named Nat. Tchr. of Yr., Coun. Chief State Sch. Officers, 2004. Achievements include redesigning her school's ESL program, which provides each student with one to three periods per day in classes for English learners. The amount of instruction given depends on their skill level; providing help to students and their families by forming a local parents group called the "Ladybugs" for speakers of other languages. This improved their ability to help their children; has instructed students from virtually every part of the globe (Laos, Korea, Bolivia, Brazil, Puerto Rico, the Philippines and the Dominican Republic); hosts an International Picnic where her students and their families gather to celebrate their achievements during the school year. Office: Davisville Mid Sch 200 School St North Kingstown RI 02852 Office Phone: 401-541-6300.

MELLOR, ROBERT E., building materials company executive, lawyer; b. 1943; BA, Westminster Coll., 1965; JD, So. Meth. U., 1968. Atty. legal dept. Union Oil Co. of Calif., 1968-73; atty. U.S. Leasing Internat. Inc., 1973-75; v.p. dir. Alexander & Bolton Inc., 1975-76; with Di Giorgio Corp., San Francisco, 1976-79, v.p., 1979-80, v.p., gen. counsel, 1980-81, v.p., sec., gen. counsel, 1981-87, sr. v.p., gen. counsel, sec.,

1987, chief adminstrv. officer, exec. v.p., gen. counsel, sec.; counsel Gibson, Dunn & Crutcher, San Francisco, 1990—97; pres., CEO Building Materials Holding Co., San Francisco, 1997—2002, chmn., pres., CEO, 2002—. Bd. dir. Coeur d'Alene Mines Corp., The Ryland Group, Inc., Monroe Muffler Brake, Inc. Office: c/o BMHC 4 Embarcadero Center San Francisco CA 94111

MELLOTT, ANN L., hematologist, oncologist; B, Dartmouth Coll., Hanover, NH; MD, Hahnemann U. Sch. of Medicine, Phila. Cert. Internal Medicine, Oncology, Hematology. With Hematology Oncology Assoc.; residency and fellowship Northwestern U. Sch. of Medicine, oncologist, hematologist & prof.; oncologist, hematologist Hematology Oncology Assoc. of Ill. Office: Hematology Oncology Assoc 676 N Saint Clair St Ste 2140 Chicago IL 60611 Office Phone: 312-664-5400. Office Fax: 312-664-5854. Business E-Mail: ann.mellott@usoncology.com.*

MELLOTT, GREG L., film producer, writer, director; m. Teresa Marie Farrell, Apr. 10. MA, U. Southern Calif., LA. Prof. dir. film program Okla. City CC, 2006—. Dir.(writer): (documentary film on Robert S. Kerr) Dream No Little Dream (Heartland Regional Emmy award, 2007). Dir. campaign videos Allied Arts, Okla. City, 2006—08; dir. fundraising video Okla. Mus. Network, Okla. City, 2007—08; dir. arts, edn. documentary Okla. Pub. Schs. Sys., Okla. City, 2006—07; dir. Okla. Creativity Project, Okla. City, 2007—08. With US Army, 1972—75, Ft. MacArthur, Calif. Grant, Kirkpatrick Found., 2007—08. Mem.: Phi Beta Kappa. Office: Okla City CC 7777 S May Ave Oklahoma City OK 73159 Office Fax: 405-682-7820. Personal E-mail: gregmellott@aol.com. Business E-Mail: gmellott@occc.edu.

MELLOTT, JOHN C., retired publishing executive; Grad., Case Western Reserve U., 1979. CPA. Controller Atlanta Jour.-Constitution, 1987—91, v.p. & gen. mgr., 1992—2000, pub., 2004—09; treas. Cox Enterprises, 1991—92, v.p. bus. devel. & planning, 2000—02; pres. Dent Wizard Internat., 2002—04; ret., 2009.*

MELLOY, MICHAEL J., federal judge; b. Dubuque, IA, 1948; m. Jane Anne Melloy; children: Jennifer, Katherine, Bridget. BA, Loras Coll., 1970; JD, U. Iowa, 1974. With O'Conner & Thomas P.C. (formerly O'Conner, Thomas, Wright, Hammer, Bertsch & Norby, Dubuque, Iowa, 1974-86; judge US Bankruptcy Ct. (no. dist.) Iowa, 1986-92, US Dist. Ct. (no. dist.) Iowa, Cedar Rapids, 1992—2002; chief judge, 1992—99; judge US Ct. Appeals (8th cir.), 2002—. With US Army, 1970-72, USAR, 1972-76. Mem. ABA, Comml. Law League Am., Nat. Conf. Bankruptcy Judges, Eighth Cir. Judicial Coun. (bankruptcy judge rep., bankruptcy com.), Iowa State Bar Assn. (coun. mem. bankruptcy and comml. law sect.), Ill. State Bar Assn., Dubuque County Bar Assn., Linn County Bar Assn., Mason L. Ladd Inn of Ct., Rotary. Address: 625 1st St SE #200 Cedar Rapids IA 52401-2032*

MELMAN, ARNOLD, urologist; b. Bronx, NY, July 23, 1941; m. Lois Ann Melman; children: Lisa, Saul, Rachel. BS, CCNY, 1962; MD, U. Rochester, 1966. Diplomate Am. Bd. Urology. Intern Strong Meml. Hosp., Rochester, 1966-67, resident, 1967-68, urology resident, 1970-74; rsch. fellowship in pathology and anatomy Albert Einstein Coll. of Medicine and Univ. Rochester, 1963; clin. assoc. gerontology rsch. Nat. Inst. Child Health and Human Devel. Ctr., 1968-70; clin. fellowship in nephrology Cedars-Sinai Med. Ctr., LA, 1971-72; instr. in urology UCLA Med. Ctr., 1974; ast. prof. dept. urology Ind. U. Med. Ctr., Indpls., 1974-77, assoc. prof., 1977-79; chief divsn. of urology Indpls. Vets. Hosp., 1974-79; assoc. attending urologist Beth Israel Med. Ctr., NYC, 1979-82, attending urologist, 1982-88, assoc. dir. urology, 1980-86, chief divsn. urology, 1986-88, physician-in-charge Ctr. for Male Sexual Dysfunction, 1981-88; assoc. prof. urology Mount Sinai Sch. Medicine and CUNY, 1979-85, prof. urology, 1985-88; prof., chmn. dept. urology Albert Einstein Coll., Montefiore Med. Ctr., Bronx, N.Y., 1988—. Chmn. subcom. for nomination to rsch. com. Indpls. Vets. Hosp., 1977-78, adv. panel Urologic Devices FDA, 1995—, chmn. subcom. for animal care, 1977-78; mem. com. on scientific activities Beth Israel Med. Ctr., 1979-88, com. on med. edn., 1979-88, pilots project com., 1981-88, subcom. on rsch. space of the com. of scientific activities, 1982-88, ad hoc com. on the revision of the attending staff manual, 1982-88, ad hoc com. on admission priority, 1982-88; mem. acad. coun. Mount Sinai Med. Ctr., 1985-88, mem. search com. chmn. of radiology Montefiore Med. Ctr., Albert Einstein Coll. of Medicine, 1990, mem. search com., chmn. of surgery, neurosurgery, anesthesiology, med. oncology, 1993-95; vis. physician Balt. City Hosp., 1968-79; clin. staff Johnson County Meml. Hosp., Franklin, Ind., 1975-79; staff Wishard Meml. Hosp., Indpls., 1975-79, LaGuardia Hosp., Queens, N.Y., 1979-88, Hosp. for Joint Diseases Orthopedic Inst., N.Y.C., 1979-88, The Workman's Circle, N.Y.C., 1981-88, Union Health Ctr., 1985-88; cons. for penile prostheses Health Ins. Plan of N.Y., 1984—; med. control bd. HIP, 1992; vis. prof. Santa Barbara (Calif.) Clinic, 1984, Tex. A&M Med. Sch., Scott-White Clinic, College Park, Tex., 1985, Queens U., Kingston, Ont., Can., 1985, others. Assoc. editor Sexuality and Disability, 1980-84, editor, 1985-89; editl. reviewer The Jour. of Urology, 1988-90; guest editor Jour. of Marital and Sex Therapy, 1991, The Urologic Clinics of Impotence N.Am., 1995, Seminars in Urologic Oncology, 1996; co-editor Internat. Jour. of Impotence Rsch., 1993—; contbr. articles to profl. jours. including Neurology and Urodynamics, Sexuality and Disability, Urology, Surg. Forum, Jour. Urology, So. Med. Jour., Cytogenetics and Cell Genetics, others. Jonas A. Salk scholarship CCNY, Katherine W. Whipple scholarship U. Rochester, Sol Heuman scholarship. Fellow N.Y. Acad. Medicine; mem. ACS, AAAS, Internat. Soc. Impotence Rsch., Soc. for Study of Impotence, Am. Soc. of Nephrology, Am. Fedn. for Clin. Rsch., Soc. of Univ. Urologists, So. Med. Assn., Am. Urol. Assn. (N.Y. sect.), Internat. Soc. of Nephrology, Urodynamics Soc., Am. Assn. of Clin. Urologists, Internat. Soc. of Urology, Nat. Kidney Found., N.Y. State Urologic Assn., Am. Diabetes Assn., N.Y. County Med. Assn., Internat. Acad. of Sex Rsch., Soc. of Salk Scholars (sec.), Phi Beta Kappa, Sigma Xi (hon.). Home: 23 Agnes Cir Ardsley NY 10502-1706 Office: Dept Urology Montefiore Med Ctr Albert Einstein Coll Med 111 E 210th St Bronx NY 10467-2401

MELMER, RICK, dean, former state official, school system administrator; m. Valerie Melmer; children: Tara, Megan, Sean. BA in Elementary Edn. and Psychology, Dakota Wesleyan U.; MA in Elementary Edn., SD State U.; EdD in Edml. Adminstrn., U. Wyo. Supt. schools Sioux Ctr. Cmty. Sch. Dist., Iowa, 1991—95, Watertown Sch. Dist., 1995—2003; sec. edn. SD Dept. Edn., Pierre, 2003—08; dean Sch. Edn. U. SD, 2008—. Instructed grad. courses U. Sioux Falls, Morningside Coll., Iowa Area Edn. Agy., SD State Univ. Avocations: watching baseball, running, reading. Office: U SD Sch Edn Delzell Edn Ctr 414 E Clark St Vermillion SD 57069 Office Phone: 605-677-5437. Office Fax: 605-677-5438. E-mail: Rick.Melmer@usd.edu.*

MELNGAILIS, JOHN, physicist; b. Riga, Latvia, Feb. 4, 1939; arrived in U.S., 1949; s. John and Jakobine (Zile) M.; m. Susan Toye, Jan. 23, 1967 (div. July 1982); children: Ilze, Sarma; m. Michaele Weissman, Nov. 7, 1982; 1 child, Noah. BS in Physics, Carnegie Mellon Inst., 1960, MS in Physics, 1962, PhD in Physics, 1965. Researcher Westinghouse Rsch., Pitts., 1960-65; postdoctoral fellow Max Planck Inst., Stuttgart, Fed. Republic Germany, 1965, CNRS, Bellevue, France, 1966; mem. staff Lincoln Lab., Lexington, Mass., 1967-79; prin. rsch. scientist MIT, Cambridge, Mass., 1979-90, sr. rsch. scientist Camrbridge, Mass., 1990-93; prof. elec. engring. U. Md., College Park, 1993—. U.S. chmn. workshop on focused ion beam tech. NSF, Osaka, Japan, 1987; co-chair workshops NATO, 1987, 92; chmn. Gordon Conf., 1992. Contbr. chpt. to VLSI Handbook, 1991, also numerous articles to profl. publs. Grantee NSF, DARPA, U.S. Army. Mem. IEEE (sr.), Am. Phys. Soc. Avocation: Tae Kwon Do. Home: 3314 Brooklawn Ter Chevy Chase MD 20815-3901 Office: Univ of Maryland Energy Research Bldg Rm 39 College Park MD 20742-0001

MELNICHENKO, YURI B., physicist; b. Kiev, Ukraine, Dec. 4, 1953; s. Boris and Inna Melnichenko; m. Galina Kalchenko, July 23, 1977; children: Oleg, Yuri Jr. B in Physics, Kiev State U., 1974, MS in Physics, 1976, PhD in Physics, 1984; DSc, Inst. Macromolecular Chemistry, Ukrainian Acad. Sci., 1992. Rsch. assoc. Kiev State U., 1976—84; sr. rsch. assoc. Inst. Macromolecular Chemistry, Kiev, 1984—93; vis. rschr. Max Planck Inst. for Polymer Rsch., Mainz, Germany, 1993—95; sr. rsch. assoc. Ctr. Neutron Scattering Oak Ridge Nat. Lab., Tenn., 1995—. Author more than 110 papers in peer reviewed phys. jours. Fellow, Humboldt Found., 1992, Am. Physics Soc., 2005. Home: 632 Lark Meadow Dr Knoxville TN 37934 Office: Oak Ridge Nat Lab 1 Bethel Valley Rd Oak Ridge TN 37831-6393

MELNICK, JANE FISHER, writer, educator, photographer; b. Boston, Sept. 26, 1939; d. Richard T. and Mary (Holcombe) Fisher; m. Burton A. Melnick, Dec. 1962 (div. 1969); 1 child, Benjamin A.; life ptnr. Eileen Willenborg, 1978—. BA cum laude, Radcliffe Coll., 1962; MA, NYU, 1985, PhD in Am. Studies, 1991. News writer, photographer, freelance editor, 1962—75; editor, writer, photographer In These Times, Chgo., 1976-78; grapnics editor, writer Seven Days, NYC, 1978-81; instr. writing, journalism, Am. lit. and history NYU, 1981-86; instr. writing, Am. lit. Loyola U., Chgo., 1988-91; asst. prof. Elmhurst (Ill.) Coll., 1991-96; writer, coll. prep. tutor Chgo., 1997—2004. Recipient Phi Beta Kappa award for best creative work by an undergrad. Radcliffe Coll., 1959; Mademoiselle mag. fiction contest award, 1962, NEA grantee, 1973, dean's dissertation fellow NYU, 1987. Mem. MLA, Mid-Am. Am. Studies Assn. (exec. bd. 1991-96) Avocations: home renovation, travel. Home: 5000 N Marine Dr Apt 15A Chicago IL 60640-3226

MELNICK, JOHN LATANE, lawyer; b. Alexandria, Va., Apr. 19, 1935; s. Norbert and Myrtle Gray (Waring) M.; m. Marjory Helter, April 28, 1962; children: John, Paul, Kathleen Scott, Laura Thompson. BS in Commerce, U. Va., 1958, JD, 1961. Bar: Va. 1961, U.S. Dist. Ct. (ea.) Va. 1961, U.S. Supreme Ct. 1965. Assoc. Kinney, Smith & Barham, Arlington, Va., 1961-63; asst. commonwealth atty. County of Arlington, 1961-63; ptnr. Ball, McCarthy, Ball & Melnick, Arlington, 1964-67; owner Melnick & Assocs., Arlington, 1967-70; ptnr. Berryman, Sanders & Melnick, Arlington, 1970-77, Melnick & Holmes, Arlington, 1977-91, Melnick & Melnick, Falls Church, Va., 1991—. Bd. dir. Transportaion Inc., Northern, Va., Ctrl. Fidelity Bank, United Savings and Loan; adv. bd. George Mason Bank; past dir. Va. State Bar. Editor Va. Business Rev. Jour., 1958; contbr. articles to profl. jours. Pres. Arlington Symphony, 1986—89, Arlington Sister Cities; mem. House of Delegates Va. Gen. Assembly, 1972—78; bd. dir. Crime Solvers, 2001—03, Wesley Sem. Found., Salvation Army. Recipient Oustanding Contbn. award Humain Socs. Va., 1973, Outstanding Pub. Svc. award Arlington Jaycees. Mem. Arlington Bar Assn. (past pres.), Washington Golf and Country Club. Democrat. Methodist. Avocations: fishing, bicycling. Home: 4710 N Dittmar Rd Arlington VA 22207-4313 Office: Melnick & Melnick 711 Park Ave Falls Church VA 22046-3212 Home Phone: 703-536-8119; Office Phone: 703-276-1000. Personal E-mail: law.jmelnick@verizon.net.

MELNICK, MICHAEL, geneticist, educator; b. NYC, Sept. 24, 1944; s. Lester and Evelyn (Rosenberg) M.; m. Anita Goldberger, June 19, 1966; children: Cliff, Lynn. BA in Biology, NYU, 1966, DDS, 1970; PhD in Genetics, Ind. U., 1978. Instr. oral medicine Ind. U., Indpls., 1973-74, fellow in med. genetics, 1974-77, asst. prof. med. genetics, 1977-78; rsch. assoc. prof. U. So. Calif., LA, 1978-85, assoc. prof., 1985-89, prof. genetics, 1989—. Cons. in human genetics NIH, Bethesda, Md., 1977-88, grant reviewer, 1978—; manuscript referee Am. Jour. Human Genetics, Chgo., 1980—, Am. Jour. Med. Genetics, Helena, Mont., 1980—; MRC vis. prof. McGill U., Montreal, que., 1990. Author, editor 5 books on human genetics; editor-in-chief Jour. Craniofacial Genetics, 1980-2000; contbr. more than 100 articles to profl. jours. Mem. nat. bd. Com. of Concerned Scientists, N.Y.C., 1983—; vice chmn. Youth Towns of Israel, L.A., 1986—. Capt. M.C. U.S. Army, 1970-73. Recipient Ind. U. Disting. Alumnus award, 1984; Warwick James fellow U. London/Guy's Hosp., 1992. Fellow AAAS; mem. Soc. Craniofacial Genetics (pres. 1978-79), Soc. for Developmental Biology, Am. Soc. Human Genetics, Sigma Xi. Achievements include research in delineated major gene causation of cleft lip and palate; delineated insulin-like growth factor, type 2, receptor control of fetal lung, salvary gland and palate development; delineated molecular pathogenesis of viral-induced birth defects; application of probability neural networks and system kinetics to multi-gene analysis; molecular pathology of embryonic CMV infection. Avocations: art, philosophy, chess. Office: Univ So Calif Den 4266 Mc 0641 Los Angeles CA 90089-0641 Business E-Mail: mmelnick@usc.edu.

MELNICK, ROBERT, dean; Dean architecture and applied arts U. Oreg., Eugene; interim exec. dir. Jordan Schnitzer Mus. Art, U. Oreg., Eugene. Office: Architecture Dept Univ Oregon Eugene OR 97403

MELNICK, ROWELL SHEP, political scientist, educator; b. St. Johnsburg, Vt., Apr. 27, 1951; s. Charles Harrington and Barbara (Rowell) M.; m. Katherine M. Hanna, Jan. 22, 1981; children: Hanna E., Hale H. BA in Social Studies, Harvard U., 1973, PhD of Polit. Sci., 1980. Rsch. assoc. Brookings Instn., Washington, 1978-80; asst. prof. Harvard U., Cambridge, Mass., 1981-84; assoc. prof., prof. Brandeis U., Waltham, Mass., 1984-97; Thomas P. O'Neill Jr. prof. Am. Govt. Boston Coll., Chestnut Hill, Mass., 1997—. Vis. prof. Harvard U., 1990, 1996-97, co-chair Program on Constl. Govt., 1986—; associated staff Brookings Instn., Washington, 1981-94. Author: Regulation and the Courts, 1983, Between the Lines, 1994; co-editor: Taking Stock, 1999; contbr. articles to profl. jours. Mem. New Eng. Polit. Sci. Assn. (pres. 2000-01), Phi Beta Kappa. Democrat. Office: Boston Coll Polit Sci Dept 140 Commonwealth Ave Chestnut Hill MA 02467 E-mail: melnicrs@bc.edu.

MELNIK, MIKHAIL, economics professor; MA in Economics, Boston U., Brookline, Mass, 1998; PhD, Ga. State U., Atlanta, 2003. Econ. forecaster Ga. State U., 2001—03, vis. asst. prof. economics, 2005—06, NSU, La., 2004—05; asst. prof. economics Niagara U., NY, 2006—. Office: Niagara Univ PO Box 2201 Niagara University NY 14109 Business E-Mail: mmelnik@niagara.edu.

MELNITCHOUK, SERGUEI, physician; MD, U. Heidelberg Med. Sch., Germany, 2000. Surg. resident BWH, Boston, 2003—07, MGH, Boston, 2007—. Recipient Hans Borst award, European Assn. Cardiothoracic Surgery, 2003. Achievements include research in tissue engineering. Home: 233 Beacon St Apt 5 Boston MA 02116

MELNYK, EUGENE N., professional sports team executive, retired pharmaceutical executive; b. Toronto, May 27, 1959; Founder, pres., CEO Trimel, 1983—91; chmn. bd. dirs. BCI, 1991—94; exec. chmn. Biovail Corp., Mississauga, Ont., Canada, 1994—2007, CEO, 2001—04; owner, gov. & chmn. Ottawa Senators Hockey Club and Scotiabank Place, 2003—. Office: Ottawa Senators Hockey Club Scotiabank Place 1000 Palladium Dr Kanata ON K2V 1A5 Canada

MELODY, MICHAEL EDWARD, publishing company executive; b. Streator, Ill., Dec. 22, 1943; s. Giles Lambert and Rose Mary (Moreschi) M.; m. Carol Ann Weir, June 8, 1968 (div.); 1 dau., Alison Anne; m. Bonnie Kaye Binkert, Mar. 26, 1983. BA, Ala. Coll., 1966. Exec. editor, asst. v.p. Prentice-Hall, Inc., Englewood Cliff, NJ, 1974—79; v.p., editor-in-chief coll. divsn. Macmillan Pub. Co., NYC, 1979-80, sr. v.p., pres. coll. divsn., 1980-87, pres. sch. divsn., 1987—88; v.p. higher edn. group Simon & Schuster, NYC, 1988-90; sr. v.p. Houghton Mifflin Co., Boston, 1990-91, exec. v.p., 1991-95; prin. Michael E. Melody Cons., Boston, 1995-96; v.p., gen. mgr. info. prodn. Inso Corp., Boston, 1996-99; pres, CEO, bd. dirs. Sage Pubs., Inc., Thousand Oaks, Calif., 1999—2005. Chmn. bd. dirs. Appleton & Lange, N.Y.C., 1989-90; bd. dirs. Sage Publs., Ltd., London. Bd. overseers Huntington Theatre Co., Boston, 1993-96; bd. advisors Boston U. Sch. for the Arts, 1997-2000; bd. dirs. Judge Baker Ctr. for Children, Harvard U. Med. Sch., 1997-99, mem. exec. com.; pres. adv. coun. Calif. Luth. U., 2001-05; trustee New West Symphony, 2003-05, So. N.H. U., 2003—06; treas. Santa Fe Symphony Orch., 2006-08, pres., bd. dirs. 2008-. Mem. Assn. Am. Pubs. (vice chmn. coll. divsn. 1981-83, chmn. coll. divsn. 1983-86, exec. com. sch. divsn. 1987-88, exec. com. higher edn. divsn. 1990—), Nat. Assn. Coll. Stores (trustee 1986-87, 94-95). E-mail: michael.melody@gmail.com.

MELONE, JOSEPH JAMES, retired insurance company executive; b. Pittston, Pa., July 27, 1931; s. Dominick William and Beatrice Marie (Pignone) Melone; m. Marie Jane DeGeorge, Jan. 23, 1960; children: Lisa, Carol. BS, U. Pa., 1953, MBA, 1954, PhD in Econs., 1961. CPCU; ChFC. Assoc. prof. ins. U. Pa., 1959-66, mem. pension rsch. coun., 1961-66; rsch. dir. Am. Coll. Life Underwriters, 1966-68; v.p. Prudential Ins. Co., Boston, 1969-76, sr. v.p. Newark, 1976-81, exec. v.p., 1981-84, pres., 1984-90, Equitable Life Assurance Soc. U.S., 1990-94, COO, bd. dirs.; pres. Equitable Cos., Inc., 1992-96, COO, bd. dirs., pres. NYC, 1996-98, CEO; chmn. Equitable Life Assurance Soc. US, NYC, 1994-98. Chmn., CEO Equitable Variable Life Ins. Co.; dir. Federal Home Loan Bank, NY; bd. dirs. BISYS, Inc.; chmn. bd. dirs. Horace-Mann Educators Corp.; chmn. emeritus Equitable Cos. Author: Collectively Bargained Multi-Employer Pension Plans, 1961; co-author: Risk and Insurance, 1963, Pension Planning, 1966. Trustee Newark Mus.; bd. dirs. Greater NY couns. Boy Scouts Am.; chmn. ins. divsn. Caridnal's Commn. Laity NY Archdioceses; bd. overseers Wharton Sch. U. Pa. Mem.: Baltusrol Golf Club, Lost Tree Golf Club, Morris County Country Club, Alpha Tau Omega. Home: Gen Delivery New Vernon NJ 07976-9999 Office: Equitable Cos Inc 1290 Ave of Americas New York NY 10104 Office Phone: 212-314-2060. Personal E-mail: joere@mac.com. Business E-Mail: joseph.melone@axa-financial.com.

MELOY, JUDITH MARIE, retired humanities educator; b. Pitts., Oct. 22, 1951; d. John C. and Miriam Meloy. BA, Denison U., 1973; MST, U. Dayton, 1982; PhD, Ind. U., 1986. Admissions counselor Denison U., Granville, Ohio, 1973—74; tchr. Centerville City Schs., Ohio, 1978—83; program evaluation Conn. State Dept. Edn., Hartford, 1987—89; prof. Vt. State Colls., Castleton, 1989—2006; ret., 2006. Dept. chair, 1994—95; chair tchg. and scholarship com., 2001—03; faculty fellow, 1996—97; adjuct. prof. CSC, 2007—. Author: (book) Writing the Qualitative Dissertation: Understanding by Doing, 1994, Writing the Qualitative Dissertation: Understanding by Doing, 2d edit., 2002; bd. editors Jour. Rsch. Edn., 2004—, Jour. Ethnography and Quantitative Rsch., 2008—. Comty. Svc., Castleton, 1998—; mem. Hayes Found. Bd., 1992—2007. Recipient Outstanding Faculty award, Castleton State Coll. Alumni Assn., 2005. Mem.: Am. Ednl. Rsch. Assn. (chmn. qualitative rsch. spl. interest group 2004—06). Avocations: hiking, writing. Business E-Mail: judy.meloy@castleton.edu.

MELOY, SYBIL PISKUR, retired lawyer; b. Chgo., Dec. 1, 1939; d. Michael M. and Laura (Stevenson) Piskur; children: William S., Bradley M. BS with honors, U. Ill., 1961; JD, Chgo. Kent Coll. Law, 1965. Bar: Ill. 1965, Fla. 1985, DC 1995, US Dist. Ct. (no. dist.) Ill. 1965, US Supreme Ct. 1972, US Ct. Appeals (fed. cir.) 1983, US Dist. Ct. (so. dist.) Fla. 1985, DC 1995. Patent chemist, patent atty., sr. atty., internat. counsel G.D. Searle & Co., Skokie, Ill., 1961-72; regional counsel Abbott Labs., North Chicago, Ill., 1972-78; pvt. practice Arlington Heights, Ill., 1978-79; asst. gen. counsel Alberto Culver Co., Melrose Park, Ill., 1979-83; corp. counsel Key Pharms., Inc., Miami, Fla., 1983-86; assoc. Ruden, Barnett, McCloskey, Smith, Schuster and Russell, Pa., 1987-89, ptnr. Pa., 1990-91, Foley & Lardner, Miami, Washington, 1991—2001. Adj. prof. Univ. of Miami Sch. of Law, 1986-92. Contbr. article on fertility control and abortion laws, book rev. on arbitration to law revs. Recipient Abbott Presdl. award, 1977; Bur. Nat. Affairs prize, 1965; Law Rev. prize for best article. Mem. ABA, Chgo. Bar Assn. (chmn.-elect and vice chmn. internat. and fgn. law com.), Am. Patent Law Assn., Am. Chem. Soc., Licencing Execs. Soc., Phi Beta Kappa, Phi Kappa Phi. Patentee oral contraceptive, 1965. Office: 1676 32d St NW Washington DC 20007-2960 Office Phone: 202-338-5744.

MELROSE, BARRY JAMES, studio analyst, former professional hockey coach and player; b. Kelvington, Sask., Can., July 15, 1956; naturalized, 1998; married; 2 children. Defenseman Winnipeg Jets, 1979—80, Toronto Maple Leafs, 1980—83, Detroit Red Wings, 1983—86; head coach Medicine Hat Tigers, 1987—88, Seattle Thunderbirds, 1988—89, Adirondack Red Wings, 1989—92, gen. mgr., 1990—92; head coach LA Kings, 1992—95, Tampa Bay Lightning, 2008. Studio analyst, hockey commentator ESPN, 1996—2008, 2009—, NHL 2Night, ESPN2, ABC Sports, 2000—02; co-owner Adirondack Frostbite (United Hockey League), 2004—. Contbr. ESPN The Magazine. Achievements include being the coach of Calder Cup Champion Adirondack Red Wings, 1991. Office: ESPN 545 Middle St Bristol CT 06010*

MELROY, PAMELA ANN, astronaut; b. Palo Alto, Calif., Sept. 17, 1961; d. David and Helen M.; m. Douglas W. Hollett. BS in Physics and Astronomy, Wellesley Coll., 1983; MSc in Earth and Planetary Scis., MIT, 1984. Commd. 2nd lt. USAF, 1983, advanced through grades to lt. col.; co-pilot KC-10, aircraft comdr., instr. pilot Barksdale AFB, Bossier City, La.; test pilot C-17 Combined Test Force; shuttle pilot NASA, Houston, pilot STS-92 (Discovery), 2000, pilot STS-112 (Atlantis), 2002, shuttle comdr. STS-120 to Internat. Space Station, 2006, selected as astrounaut, 1994, astronaut, 1995—. Crew mem. STS-92 Discovery Mission, 2000, STS-112 Atlantis Mission; flight comdr. STS-120 Discovery Mission to Internat. Space Station (ISS), 2007. Bd. trustee Wellesley Coll. Decorated Air Force Meritorious Svc. medal with oak leaf cluster, Air medal with oak leaf cluster, Aerial Achievement medal with oak leaf cluster, Expeditionary medal with oak leaf cluster. Mem. Soc. Exptl. Test Pilots, Order of Daedalians, 99s. Achievements include being the second female astronaut to command a US orbiter; With STS-120 mission, first time in the 50 year history of spaceflight that two women (Peggy Whitson-ISS commander) are in charge of two spacecraft at the same time. Avocations: theater, tap and jazz dancing, reading, cooking, flying. Office: Astronaut Office/CB NASA Lyndon B Johnson Space Ctr Houston TX 77058

MELSHEIMER, MEL P(OWELL), venture capitalist; b. LA, July 9, 1939; s. Oscar Merrill M.; m. Sara Sturdevant, Sept. 1, 1962; children: Heidi, Erich, Douglas. AB, Occidental Coll., 1961; MBA, U. So. Calif., 1965. With United Calif. Bank, Los Angeles, 1962-66; sr. fin. analyst Ford Motor Co., Newport Beach, Calif., 1966-67; v.p., chief fin. officer Pepsi Cola Co. Pepsico, Inc., Purchase, NY, 1968-75; exec. v.p., chief operating officer AZL Resources, Inc., 1975-84; chmn. bd., CEO PHX Pacific, Inc., 1984-89; pres., CEO MPM Capital Corp., 1987-89; exec. v.p. Finevest Foods, Inc., Greenwich, Conn., 1989-92; pres., CEO Land-O-Sun Dairies Inc., 1991-92, Atlanta Dairies, Inc., 1991-92; exec. v.p., sec., COO Dairy Holdings, Inc., Johnson City, Tenn., 1992-94; exec. v.p., COO, CFO Sonex Internat. Corp., Brewster, NY, 1994; pres., CEO M.P. Melsheimer & Co., Ridgefield, Conn., 1994-97; pres. NFX, 1995-96; pres., COO, CFO Harris & Harris Group, Inc., NYC, 1997—2004; pres. Linkhorn Capital Advisors, Inc., 2005—; chmn. bd. Patriot Capital Funding Inc., 2006—. Served with U.S. Army, 1961-62. Home: 1418 N Woodhouse Rd Virginia Beach VA 23454 E-mail: melmelsheimer@msn.com.

MELSON, KENNETH E., federal agency administrator, lawyer; b. 1947; BA, Denison U., 1970; JD with honors, George Washington U., 1973. Pvt. law practice, Arlington, Va., 1974—75; asst. commonwealth's atty. Arlington County Commonwealth's Atty.'s Office, Va., 1975—78, chief asst. commonwealth's atty. Va., 1978—80, dep. commonwealth's atty., 1980—83; asst. US atty. (ea. dist.) Va. US Dept. Justice, 1983—86, first asst. US atty. (ea. dist.) Va., 1986—2008, interim US atty. (ea. dist.) Va., 1991, 1993, 2001, dir. Exec. Office US Attorneys (EOUSA) Washington, 2007—09, acting dir. Bur. Alcohol, Tobacco, Firearms & Explosives (ATF), 2009—. Adj. prof. George Washington U. Law Sch.; mem. Am. Soc. Crime Lab. Dirs./Lab. Accreditation Bd. Ethics com. mem., editl. bd. Jour. Forensic Scis. Mem.: Am. Acad. Forensic Scis., Coun. Sci. Soc. Pres. Office: Bureau Alcohol Tobacco Firearms & Explosives (ATF) US Dept Justice 650 Massachusetts Ave Washington DC 20226 E-mail: kmelson@law.gwu.edu.*

MELSON, LISA, psychology educator; b. New Orleans, Nov. 23, 1965; d. Herman and Doris Darby; m. Ted Melson, May 26, 1990; 1 child, Ted. MS in Edn., U. New Orleans, 1992. Cert. in Tchg. La., 1992. Elem. tchr. Orleans Parish Sch. Sys., New Orleans, 1992—2003; early childhood instr. Delgado CC, New Orleans, 2003—, adult edn. instr., 2007—. Grantee, Delgado CC, 2004, 2007. Mem.: Nat. Assn. Edn. Young Children, Greater New Orleans Assn. Edn. Young Children. Home: 4700 Constance St New Orleans LA 70115 Office: Delgado CC 615 City Park Ave New Orleans LA 70119 Business E-Mail: lmelso@dcc.edu.

MELSOP, JAMES WILLIAM, architect; b. Columbus, Ohio, June 2, 1939; s. James Brendan and Juanita Kathryn (Van Scoy) M.; m. Sandra Lee Minnich, Sept. 21, 1957; children: Deborah Lee, Susan Elizabeth, Kathryn Anne. BArch, Ohio State U., 1964; MArch, Harvard U., 1965; MBA, U. Chgo., 1975. Reg. architect, profl. engr. Architect The Austin Co., Chgo., 1967-69, mgr. bus. devel., 1969-74, asst. dist. mgr., 1974-75; pres., mng. dir. Austin Brasil, Sao Paulo, 1975-78; asst. dist. mgr. The Austin Co., Roselle, N.J., 1978-80, dist. mgr. Detroit, 1980-81, v.p., dist. mgr. Cleve., 1986, group v.p., dir., 1986—, exec. v.p. chief oper. officer, 1992, pres., CEO, 1992—, also chmn., bd. dirs.; founder, prin. owner Austin Holdings, Inc., 1997—. Named E&Y Entrepreneur of Yr., 1999. Mem. Am. Inst. Architects., Harvard Club N.Y.C., Presidents' Club, Ohio State U. (Disting. Alumnus award 1989). Home: 3165 Trillium Trail Cleveland OH 44124-5205

MELTON, ARTHUR RICHARD, public health administrator; b. Ysleta, Tex., Apr. 28, 1943; s. Francis Charles and Jean (Graham) M.; m. Frances Bay, Aug. 19, 1965; children: David Bay, Amy Elizabeth. BS, U. Utah, 1969; MPH, U. N.C., 1974, D in Pub. Health, 1976. Dir. labs. S.D. Dept. Health, Pierre, 1976-87; microbiologist Utah Dept. Health, Salt Lake City, 1970-73, dir. divsn. lab. svcs., 1987-92, dep. dir., 1992—. Mem.: Assn. State and Territorial Health Ofcls. (pres. elect 1999—2000, pres. 2000—01), SD Pub. Health Assn. (pres. 1980—81, past. pres. 2001—06), Am. Pub. Health Assn. (governing coun. 1980—83). Mem. Lds Ch. Home: 6835 Heather Way West Jordan UT 84084-2304 Office: PO Box 141000 Salt Lake City UT 84114-1000 Office Phone: 801-538-6111. Personal E-mail: dickmelton@yahoo.com. Business E-Mail: dmelton@utah.gov.

MELTON, CAROL A., communications executive; b. St. Augustine, Fla., 1954; m. Joseph M. Hassett; children: Matthew, Meredith Hassett. BA with honors, Wake Forest U., 1976; MA in Journalism and Comm., U. Fla., 1977; JD with honors, Am. U., 1981. Assoc. in comm. grp. Hogan and Hartson, Washington, 1981-82; asst. gen. counsel Nat. Cable TV Assn., 1983-86, legal adv. to FCC chmn., 1986—87; Washington counsel Warner Comm., 1987-91; v.p. law and pub. policy Time Warner Inc., Washington, 1992-97; exec. v.p. govt. rels., exec. officer Viacom, Inc., Washington, 1997—2005; exec. v.p. global pub. policy, exec. officer Time Warner Inc., 2005—. Trustee The Media Inst., Washington, 1997—2005, Washington Performing Arts Soc., 1997—99, The Potomac Sch., McLean, Va., 1999—2000, Meridian Internat. Ctr., 2001—03, Comm. Econ. Dept., 2007—; mem. Fed. City Coun., 1997—, Coun. on Fgn. Rels., 2006—. Office: Time Warner Inc 800 Connecticut Ave NW Washington DC 20006

MELTON, DAVID REUBEN, lawyer; b. Milw., Apr. 4, 1952; s. Howard and Evelyn M.; m. Nancy Hillary Segal, May 22, 1981; children: Michelle, Hannah. BA, U. Wis., 1974; JD, U. Chgo., 1977. Bar: Ill. 1977, U.S. Dist. Ct. (no. dist.) Ill. 1977, U.S. Ct. Appeals (7th cir.) 1981, U.S. Supreme Ct. 1982, U.S. Fed. Cir. Ct. Appeals, 1991. Assoc. Karon, Morrison & Savikas, Ltd., Chgo., 1977-83; ptnr. Karon, Morrison & Saviskas, Ltd., Chgo., 1983-87, Karon, Savikas & Horn, Ltd., Chgo., 1987-88, Keck, Mahin & Cate, Chgo., 1988-96; counsel Mayer, Brown & Platt, Chgo., 1996-99, ptnr., 2000—07; sr. counsel Foley & Lardner, LLP, Chgo., 2007—. Office: Foley & Lardner LLP 321 N Clark St Ste 2800 Chicago IL 60610 Office Phone: 312-832-4599. Business E-Mail: dmetton@foley.com.

MELTON, DOUGLAS A., molecular and cell biology educator; b. Chgo., Sept. 26, 1953; m. Gail Melton; children: Sam, Emma. BS in Biology, with honors, U. Illinois, Urbana-Champaign, 1975; BA in Hist. and Phil. of Sci., Cambridge U., Eng., 1977, PhD in Molecular Biology, 1980. Asst. prof, dept. bio chem. and molecular biology Harvard U., 1981—84, assoc. prof., 1984—87, J.L. Loeb assoc. prof. nat. sci., 1987, prof. dept. molecular and cellular biology Cambridge, Mass., 1988—; biologist (med.) Mass. Gen. Hosp., Boston; assoc. mem. Children's Hosp., Boston, 1994—; investigator Howard Hughes Med. Inst., 1994—; Thomas Dudley Cabot prof. Natural Sci. Harvard U., Cambridge, Mass., 1999—; co-dir. Harvard Stem Cell Inst., 2004—. Mem. sci. adv. bd. Genetics Policy Inst. Recipient Richard Lounsbery award, NAS, 1995, George Ledlie prize, 2004, Elliot P. Joslin medal; named Policy Leader of Yr., Scientific Am. mag., 2004; named an 50 Who Matter Now, Bus. 2.0, 2007; named one of The World's Most Influential People, TIME mag., 2007, 2009. Mem.: Internat. Soc. for Stem Cell Rsch. (founding mem.), Inst. Medicine. Office: Harvard Univ Dept Molecular & Cellular Bio Sherman Fairchild 7 Divinity Ave Rm 465 Cambridge MA 02138 Office Phone: 617-495-1812. Business E-Mail: dmelton@biohp.harvard.edu.*

MELTON, GARY BENTLEY, psychologist, educator; b. Salisbury, NC, June 4, 1952; s. Harold Sumner Jr. and Marion Adair (Reeves) M.; m. Robin Jo Kimbrough, Aug. 7, 1999; children by previous marriage: Jennifer Lynn, Stephany Beth. BA, U. Va., 1973; MA, Boston U., 1975, PhD, 1978. Asst. prof. psychology Morehead (Ky.) State U., 1978-79, U. Va., Charlottesville, 1979-81; from asst. prof. to full prof. psychology and law U. Nebr., Lincoln, 1981-87, Carl A. Happold prof. psychology and law, 1987-94; prof. neuropsychiatry & behavioral science U. S.C., Columbia, 1994-99, adj. prof. law, pediat. and psychology, 1994-99, dir. Inst. Families in Soc., 1994-99; prof. psychology Clemson U., 1999—. Dir. Inst. Family and Neighborhood Life, Clemson U., 1999—. Author: Child Advocacy: Psychological Issues and Interventions, 1983; coauthor: Community Mental Health Centers and the Courts: An Evaluation of Community-Based Forensic Services, 1985, Psychological Evaluations for the Courts: A Handbook for Mental Health Professionals and Lawyers, 1987, 3d edit., 2007, Pediatric and Adolescent AIDS: Research Findings from the Social Sciences, 1992, Ethical and Legal Issues in AIDS Research, 1995, No Place to Go: Civil Commitment of Minors, 1998; editor numerous books. Mem. U.S. Adv. Bd. on Child Abuse and Neglect, 1989-93, vice-chair, 1991-93. Recipient Frederick Howell Lewis award Psi Chi, 1993, Lynn Stuart Weiss award Am. Psychol. Found., 2000. Fellow: APA (chmn. various coms., cert. recognition for psychology in pub. interest 1981, Disting. Contbn. to Psychology in Pub. Interest award 1985, Nicholas Hobbs award 1992, Harold Hildreth award 1992, Disting. Contbn. to Pub. Svc. award 1999, Disting. Contbn. to Internat. Advancement of Psychology award 2005); mem.: Am. Profl. Soc. on Abuse of Children (Career Achievement in Rsch. award 2005), Prevent Child Abuse Am. (Donna Stone award 1992), Am. Orthopsychiat. Assn. (pres. 2004—05), Am. Psychology-Law Soc. (pres. 1990—91). Unitarian Universalist. Office: Clemson Univ Ctr 225 S Pleasantburg Dr Ste B-11 Greenville SC 29607 Office Phone: 864-656-6271. Personal E-mail: garybmelton@hotmail.com. Business E-Mail: gmelton@clemson.edu.

MELTON, HAROLD D., state supreme court justice; b. Washington; BA, Auburn U.; JD, U. Ga., 1991. Former atty. Ga. Dept. of Law, former section leader, consumer interests div.; former exec. counsel Gov. Perdue; justice Ga. Supreme Ct., 2005—. Former volunteer leader Young Life Ministries. Dir. teen ministry Southwest Christian Fellowship Church; bd. mem. Atlanta Youth Academies. Office: Ga Supreme Ct Ste 300 244 Washington St SW Atlanta GA 30334 Office Phone: 404-656-3470. Office Fax: 404-656-2253.*

MELTON, HOWELL WEBSTER, SR., federal judge; b. Atlanta, Dec. 15, 1923; s. Holmes and Alma (Combee) M.; m. Margaret Catherine Wolfe, Mar. 4, 1950; children— Howell Webster, Carol Anne. JD, U. Fla., 1948. Bar: Fla. 1948. With Upchurch, Melton & Upchurch, St. Augustine, 1948-61; judge 7th Jud. Circuit of Fla., St. Augustine, 1961-77, U.S. Dist. Ct. (mid. dist.) Fla., Jacksonville, 1977-91, sr. judge, 1991—. Past chmn. Fla. Conf. Cir. Judges, 1974; past chmn. coun. bar pres.'s Fla. Bar. Trustee Flagler Coll., St. Augustine. Served with U.S. Army, 1943-46. Recipient Disting. Service award St. Augustine Jaycees, 1953 Mem. ABA, St. Johns County Bar Assn., Jacksonville Bar Assn., Fed. Bar Assn., Fla. Blue Key, Officers Club, Masons, Phi Delta Theta, Phi Delta Phi. Methodist. Office: US Dist Ct 300 N Hogan St Ste 11-300 Jacksonville FL 32202 Office Phone: 904-549-1940.

MELTON, HOWELL WEBSTER, JR., lawyer; b. St. Augustine, Fla., Oct. 26, 1951; BA with high honors, U. Fla., 1973; JD, U. Fla. Coll. Law, 1975. Bar: Fla. 1976, DC 2006, NY 2007, Fla. State Cts., US Dist. Ct. (Middle Dist. Fla.), US Cir. Ct. of Appeals (11th Cir.), US Supreme Ct. With Holland & Knight LLP, NYC, 1975—, mng. ptnr., 2003—08. Bd. dir. Enterprise Fla., Inc., chmn. fin. and compensation com., exec. com.; chmn. Metro Orlando Econ. Develop. Commn., 2000—01; past chmn. Ctrl. Fla. Tech. Partnership. Trustee emeritus U. Fla. Coll. Law; officer, mem. exec. com. bd. trustees Orlando Mus. Art, 1991—97; bd. governors Greater Orlando Region, Nat. Conf. for Community and Justice, 1990—; bd. dir. Ctrl. Fla. Fair, Inc., 1993—; trustee Greater Orlando C. of C.; mem. Orlando Leadership Class, 1990; founder, bd. dir. and sec. Leadership Orlando Alumni Assn.; mem. Orlando Mus. of Art Acquisition Trust, Savant; pres. Fla. Blue Key. Named one of Best Lawyers in Am., 2009. Fellow: Fla. Bar Found., Am. Bar Found.; mem.: NYC Bar, NY County Lawyers Assn., Internat. Bar Assn., DC Bar Assn., Fla. Justice Assn. (commercial litig. sect.), Am. Assn. for Justice, Am. Arbitration Assn. (panel arbitrators), Am. Judicature Soc., Fed. Bar Assn., Orange County Bar Assn., Fla. Bar Assn. (litig. sect.), ABA (litig. sect.), Phi Delta Theta (pres. 1976), Omega Delta Kappa, Phi Delta Phi, Phi Eta Sigma. Office: Holland & Knight LLP 195 Broadway New York NY 10007-3189 Office Phone: 212-513-3544, 212-513-3200, 407-244-5186. Office Fax: 212-513-2339. Business E-Mail: howell.melton@hklaw.com.

MELTON, KATHY A., medical transcription educator; b. Corpus Christi, Tex., Mar. 30, 1952; d. Thomas Rodman Smith and Dorothy Frances Hays; m. Lynn E. White (div.); children: Robert Jason White, Jerrald Martin White; m. Claude E. Melton, Jan. 21, 2005. Student, East Ctrl. State Coll., Ada, Okla., 1970—72, U. Tex., Austin, 1976—77, Houston Lighthouse for Blind, 1977—78. Med. transcriptionist Meth. Hosp., Houston, 1978—80, Cardiovascular Assoc., Athens, Tex., 1997—2002; owner, med. transcriptionist Accutrans, Houston, 1981—85; legal sec. Law Office of David Hamilton, Paris, Tex., 1986—91; receptionist Criss Cole Rehab. Ctr., Austin, 1991—94; relay agt. Relay Tex., Austin, 1994—97; owner, instr. med. transcription medtransclass.com, Enchanted Oaks, Tex., 2003—. Spkr. in field. Pres. Lake Area Coun. Blind, Athens, 1999—2003; vol. Ark. Enterprises for Blind, 1982—83; chairperson Visually Impaired Transcription Alliance, Assn. Healthcare Documentation Integrity; mem. team Walk to Emmaus, 1998—. Mem.: Assn. Healthcare Documentation Integrity, Lions Club (sec. 1987—90, bd. dirs. 1998—2002). Home and Office: 231 Cedarwood Dr Enchanted Oaks TX 75156 Office Phone: 903-451-2720. Business E-Mail: kathy@medtransclass.com.

MELTON, MAURICE K., history professor; b. St. Louis, Apr. 22, 1945; s. Merrel S. and Mildred R. Melton; m. Zoila M. Melton, Dec. 27, 1986; 1 child, Douglas W. BA, SW Mo. State Coll., Springfield, 1967; MA, U. Ga., Athens, 1970; PhD, Emory U., Atlanta, 1978. Assoc. prof. history Stillman Coll., Tuscaloosa, Ala., 2000—03; adj. prof. Am. civil war U. Ala. Coll. Continuing Studies, Tuscaloosa, 2002—; assoc. prof. history Albany State U., Ga., 2003—; adj. prof. grad. course in US mil. history Norwich U., Vt., 2007—. Author monograph. Recipient Faculty Rsch. award, NEH, 2007—08; Rsch. fellowship, Andrew W. Mellon Found., 2000, Gov.'s Tchg. fellowship, State of Ga., 2000, fellowship, Archie K. Davis Found., 2007, grant, Ga. Humanities Coun., 1994, Faculty Rsch. grant, Albany State U., 2001. Mem.: Southern Hist. Assn., Soc. Civil War Historians, Ga. Assn. Historians, Am. Hist. Assn. Office: Albany State Univ 504 College Dr Albany GA 31705 Business E-Mail: maurice.melton@asurams.edu.

MELTON, STEPHEN REID, lawyer; b. Savannah, Ga., Dec. 10, 1949; s. Wallace Reid and Doris Cleone (Bragg) M. BA magna cum laude, Armstrong Coll., Savannah, 1973; JD, U. Ga., Athens, 1976. Bar: Ga. 1976, DC 1979, Tex. 1992, US Supreme Ct. 1980, US Dist. Ct. DC 1980, US Ct. Appeals (DC cir.) 1980, US Ct. Appeals (7th cir.) 1980, US Ct. Appeals (10th cir.) 1981, US Ct. Appeals (5th and 11th cirs.) 1985, US Ct. Appeals (4th cir.) 1986, US Ct. Appeals (6th cir.) 1991. Atty., adviser ICC, Washington, 1976-78; staff lawyer FERC, Washington, 1978-81, dep. gen. counsel, 1981-83, acting gen. counsel, 1983-84; assoc. Beveridge & Diamond, Washington, 1984-85; sr. atty. Tex. Oil & Gas Corp., Dallas, 1985-87; asst. gen. counsel United Gas Pipe Line Co., Houston, 1987-89, asst. v.p., asst. gen. counsel, spl. asst. for regulatory affairs, 1989-90, assoc. gen. counsel, 1990-92; of counsel Akin, Gump, Strauss, Hauer & Feld, 1992—97; v.p. gen. counsel and sec. Columbia Gulf Transmission, 1997—2000; asst. sec. Columbia Gas Transmission Corp., 2000—01; assoc. gen. counsel NiSource Corp. Svcs. Co., 2000—02, dep. gen. counsel, 2002—04, dep. gen. counsel FERC compliance officer, 2004—05, v.p., dep. gen. counsel FERC compliance officer, 2005—. Contbr. articles to profl. jours. Recipient Outstanding Handicapped Employee award, US Dept. Energy, 1983, Disting. Svc. award, US Fed. Energy Regulatory Commn., 1984. Mem. ABA (adminstrv. law sect., utility law sect., bus. law sect.), Energy Bar Assn., Houston Bar Assn., DC Bar Assn. Office: NiSource Corp Svcs Co 5151 San Felipe Ste 2500 Houston TX 77056 Home Phone: 713-932-1358. Office Fax: 713-267-4755. Business E-Mail: smelton@nisource.com.

MELTON, WAYNE CHARLES, real estate executive; b. Oak Ridge, Tenn., Aug. 30, 1954; s. Charles Estel and Una Faye (Hull) M.; m. Maria Tobar-Conde; children: Bonnie Elizabeth, Ingrid Tatiana. AB in European Intellectual History, U. Ga., 1975; MS in Real Estate, Shepperton U., 2001, PhD in Real Estate Fin., 2003. Mgr. Household Internat., Athens, Ga., 1975—76; asst. mgr. Athens and Hickory, NC, Doraville, Ga., 1976—77; pres., CEO Impact Realty-Melton & Assocs. Inc., Athens, 1987—. Cons. Ga. Furniture, Charlotte Realty, NC, 1987—, US Fed. Res. Bank, Atlanta, Ga. Trustee Mu, Inc., Page, Ga. Ho. of Reps., 1968; chmn. Madison County Reps., 1973-74; mem. Congl. Bus. Coun., 2002. Recipient Ronald Reagan award, Rep. Congl. Com., 2004. Mem. AAAR(GR dir., 2004-), NAR, Ga. Cattlemen's Assn., Madison County Cattlemen's Assn., Ga. Assn. Realtors (Fla. & Ga. Charolais growers dir. 2005-, dir. 2006-) Pheonix Club, Pres. Club, Ga. Charlois Assoc., Zeta Beta Tau, Athens Area Assn. Realtors (dir., Good Neighbor award 2005), Riverbend Random Consumer, Ga. (CEO, pres.), Ministerio La Cosecha (dir.), Nat. Ga. Cattlemans Assn., Madison County, Charolais Cattle Assoc. Ga., Fla. Office: Impact Realty Melton & Assoc Inc 855 Sunset Dr Ste 11 Athens GA 30606-7718 Office Phone: 706-549-1799.

MELTON, WILLIAM EVERETT, retired music educator; b. Roanoke, Va., June 28, 1940; s. William Everett and Cordelia Mae Melton; m. Carol Ann Drawdy, Aug. 17, 1963; children: John Morris, Marissa Kaye. BS in Music Edn., Carson-Newman Coll., 1962; MS in Music Edn., U. Tenn., 1970, EdD, 1984. Choral music tchr. Carter H.S., Knoxville, Tenn., 1968—93; instr. Carson-Newman Coll., Jefferson City, Tenn., 1993—2006; ret., 2006. Dir. music ministries Fountain City United Meth. Ch., Knoxville, 1993—2003; min. of music Smithwood Bapt. Ch., Knoxville, 2005—06; dir. traditional worship & music Middlebrook Pike United Meth. Ch., Knoxville, 2008—. Composer, arranger: choral and handbell works. Asst. dir., music dir. Knoxville Nativity Pageant, 1987—95, mem. adv. bd., 1996—2006; vol. Jubilee Project, Sneedville, Tenn., 2004—06; choral clinician, adjudicator East Tenn. Choral Festivals. Recipient Disting. Alumnus award, Carson-Newman Coll., 2001. Mem.: NEA, Tenn. Ret. Tchrs. Assn., Am. Choral Dirs. Assn. (life). Avocations: travel, gardening.

MELTZER, ALLAN H., economist, educator; b. Boston, Feb. 6, 1928; s. George B. and Minerva I. (Simons) M.; m. Marilyn Ginsburg, Aug. 27, 1950; children: Bruce Michael, Eric Charles, Beth Denise. AB, Duke U., 1948; MA, UCLA, 1955, PhD, 1958. Lectr. econs. U. Pa., Phila., 1956-57; faculty Carnegie Mellon U. Grad. Sch. Indsl. Adminstrn., Pitts., 1957-64, prof. econs., 1964—, Maurice Falk prof. econs. and social sci., 1970-80, John M. Olin univ. prof. polit. economy and pub. policy, 1980-91, Univ. prof. polit. economy and pub. policy, 1991-97, Allan H. Meltzer Univ. prof. polit. economy, 1997—. Vis. prof. U. Chgo., 1964-65, Fundacao Getulio Vargas, Rio de Janeiro, 1976-79, City U., London, 1979-2001; vis. fellow Hoover Instn., 1977-78; vis. scholar Am. Enterprise Inst., Washington, 1989—; co-chmn. Shadow Open Market Com., 1974-89, chmn., 1989-2000; cons. US Treasury, joint econ. com. US Congress, 1960; com. on banking and currency US Ho. of Reps., 1963-64; mem. Pres.'s Econ. Policy Adv. Bd., 1988-90; acting mem. Coun. Econ. Advisors, 1988-89; panel econ. advisors Congl. Budget Office, 1995-2009; cons., bd. gov. FRS, FDIC; dir. Cooper Tire & Rubber Co., 1983-98, chmn. audit and compensation com., 1996-98; hon. advisor Inst. Monetary and Econ. Studies Bank of Japan, 1987-2003; bd. dir. Sarah Scaife Found., Commonwealth Found.; dir. Stillhalter Vision AG, Zurich, 1994-2002, Advanced Materials Group, 1994-2001; chmn. Internat. Fin. Instn. adv. com. to US Congress, 1999-2000; advisor Federal Reserve Bank NY, 2005-. Author: Monetary Economics, 1989, Keynes's Monetary Theory: A Different Interpretation, 1988; (with Karl Brunner) Money and the Economy: Issues in Monetary Analysis, 1993; (with Alex Cukierman and Scott Richard) Political Economy, 1991, Report of the International Financial Institution Advisory Commission, 2000, A History of the Federal Reserve, vol. 1, 2003 (Book award Econ. History Assn. 2004-05), vol. 2, 2009; editor: (with Karl Brunner) Carnegie-Rochester Conf. Series, 1976-89; (with Charles Plosser), 1989-97; contbr. articles to profl. jours. Recipient Outstanding Achievement award UCLA, 1983, Money Marketeers, 1997, Educator of Yr. award Pittsburg Hist. Ctr., 2003, Irving Kristol award Am. Enterprise Inst., 2003, David Horowitz prize Israel Bankers Assn., 2004; Social Sci. Rsch. Coun. fellow, 1955-56, Ford Found. fellow, 1962-63; named Man of Yr. in Fin., Pitts., 1995-96. Fellow: Nat. Assn. Bus. Economists (Adam Smith award 2003); mem.: Am. Fin. Assn., Western Econ. Assn. (pres. 1985—86), Internat. Atlantic Econ. Assn. (pres. 1999—2000), Am. Econ. Assn. (v.p. 1990, Disting. fellow 2002), Phila. Soc. (v.p. 1981—83), Cosmos Club. Achievements include research in macroeconomics. Avocations: political economy, monetary history. Office: Carnegie Mellon U Dept Econs Pittsburgh PA 15213 Office Phone: 412-268-2282. Business E-Mail: am05@andrew.cmu.edu.

MELTZER, ARTHUR ADAM, researcher; s. Mayer and Selma Meltzer; m. Adela Valadez-Plascencia. BA, SUNY, Buffalo, 1979; diploma in Human Biology, U. Oxford, 1980; MA, U. Mich., Ann Arbor, 1982; MPH, U. Tex., Houston, 1986, PhD, 1991. Rsch. analyst Ctrs. for Medicare and Medicaid Svcs., Balt., 2000—. Contbr. articles to profl. jours. Mem.: Soc. Epidemiol. Rsch. Achievements include research in population-based health. Avocations: yoga, aerobics. Office: Ctrs Medicare and Medicaid Svcs 7500 Security Blvd Baltimore MD 21224

MELTZER, BRAD, writer; b. Apr. 1, 1970; m. Cori Flam; 2 children. Grad., U. Michigan, Columbia Law Sch. Co-creator (TV series) Jack & Bobby, 2004—05; author: The Tenth Justice, 1998, Dead Even, 1999, The First Counsel, 2001, The Millionaires, 2002, Zero Game, 2004, The Book of Fate, 2006, The Book of Lies, 2008 (No. 1 Publishers Weekly bestseller), (comic books) Justice League of America, Green Arrow, 2003, Identity Crisis, 2005, (short stories) The Best Seat in the House, Final Farewell, An American Lawyer in London, The Craziest Kid in the World. Achievements include participation in a work group along with the CIA, FBI, various psychologists, and Department of Homeland Security intelligence staff to brainstorm new ways that terrorists might attack the US. Home: 20533 Biscayne Blvd Miami FL 33180-1529*

MELTZER, DANIEL J., lawyer, law educator; b. Chgo., Dec. 17, 1951; s. Bernard D. Meltzer; m. Ellen Semonoff. AB in Econs., Harvard U., 1972, JD, 1975. Bar: Ill. 1975, DC 1978, Mass. 1983. Law clk. to Hon. Carl McGowan US Ct. Appeals (DC cir.), 1975-76; law clk. to Justice Potter Stewart US Supreme Ct., 1976-77; spl. asst. to sec. Joseph Califano, Jr. US Dept. Health, Edn. & Welfare, 1977-78; assoc. Williams & Connolly LLP, 1979-81; asst. prof. law Harvard Law Sch., Cambridge, Mass., 1982-87, prof., 1987—2009, Story prof. law, 1998—2009, assoc. dean, 1989-93, vice dean physical planning, 2003—09; prin. dep. counsel The White House, Washington, 2009—. Co-editor: The Judicial Code and the Rules of Procedure in the Fed. Courts, pub. annually, 1988—2000; co-author: Hart & Wechsler's The Federal Courts and the Federal System, 1973, 1988, 1996, 2003. Fellow: Am. Acad. Arts & Sciences. Democrat. Office: The White House 1600 Pennsylvania Ave NW 2nd Fl Washington DC 20502*

MELTZER, DONALD RICHARD, retired treasurer; b. Boston, Sept. 1, 1932; s. Leo N. and Betty (Flesher) M.; m. Mary Douglas Seelye, Dec. 7, 1963; children: Kimberly, Christopher. AB, Dartmouth Coll., 1954, MBA, 1955. Mgr. Peat, Marwick, Mitchell & Co., Boston, 1955-67; asst. controller United Fruit Corp., Boston, 1968-69, controller, 1969-70, v.p., controller, 1970-73; v.p., chief acctg. officer United Brands Co., NYC, 1973-74, v.p. fin. and adminstrn., 1974-76; v.p. fin., treas. Instron Corp., Canton, Mass., 1976-88; v.p. fin. and adminstrn., treas., chief fin. officer Dialogue, Inc., Braintree, Mass., 1988-90. Corp. fin. cons., Sudbury, Mass., 1988-96. Overseer Children's Hosp. Med. Ctr., Boston, 1980-94; fin. com. Town of Sudbury, Mass., 1967; chmn. bd. trustees First Parish Ch., Sudbury, 1970-71, treas., 1991-93; pres. Mass. Parents Assn. for Deaf and Hard of Hearing, Boston, 1976-77, bd. dirs., 1973-86. Mem. AICPA, Mass. Soc. CPAs, Fin. Execs. Inst., Am. Assn. Indsl. Mgmt. (bd. dirs. 1980-85), Walk 'N Mass Volkssport Club (co-pres. 1993-95). Avocations: postal history, stamp collecting/philately. Home: 341 Old Lancaster Rd Sudbury MA 01776-2035

MELTZER, DONNA, medical educator; b. NY; MD, Albany Med. Coll., NY, 1986. Diplomate Am. Bd. Family Medicine, 1989. Clin. asst. prof. Dept. Family Medicine SUNY Stony Brook, assoc. prof., 2003—, residency dir., 2008—. Fellow: AAFP; mem.: AMA, Med. Wilderness Soc., ACSM, STFM. Office: Dept Family Medicine SUNY Stony Brook HSC L4-050 Stony Brook NY 11794-8461

MELTZER, GARY STEPHEN, ancient language educator; BA, Yale Coll., New Haven, 1973; MA, Yale U., New Haven, 1981, MPhil, 1984, PhD, 1987. Vis. asst. prof. classics Union Coll., Schenectady, NY, 1987—88, Cath. U. America, Washington, 1988—90, U. Md., Coll. Pk., 1994—96; asst. prof. classics George Washington U., Washington, 1990—94; assoc. prof. classics Eckerd Coll., St. Petersburg, Fla., 1996—2005; adj. prof. classics, humanities, and English Villanova U., Pa., 2005—08, dir. grad. studies in classics and assoc. prof. classics, 2008—. Vis. scholar Am. Acad., Rome, 2002. Author: Euripides and the Poetics of Nostalgia, 2006; contbr. articles to profl. jour. Office: Humanities Dept Villanova Univ 800 Lancaster Ave Villanova PA 19085-1699 Business E-Mail: gary.meltzer@villanova.edu.

MELTZER, JACK, retired dean; b. Bayonne, NJ, Aug. 21, 1921; s. Louis and Debbie (Gold) M.; m. Rae Libin, June 26, 1944; children: Richard, Marc, Ellen. BA, Wayne State U., 1941; MA, U. Chgo., 1947. Dir. planning Michael Reese Hosp., Chgo., 1953-54; S.E. Chgo. Commn. and U. Chgo., 1954-58; propr. Jack Meltzer Assos. (planners), 1958-63; acting dir. Am. Soc. Planning Ofcls., 1967-68; prof., dir. Center Urban Studies, U. Chgo., 1963-71; prof. div. social scis., prof. Sch. Social Service Adminstrn., 1965-83; prof., dean Sch. Social Scis. U. Tex.-Dallas, 1983-86; pvt. practice cons., 1986—. Cons. to govt. and industry, 1945— Author book revs., articles, books. Village trustee, Park Forest, Ill., 1950-52, mem. plan commn., 1949; Served to capt. USAAF, World War II. Mem. AAUP, Am. Soc. Planning Ofcls. (past treas.), Am. Inst. Planners (past v.p. pvt. practice dept.), Nat. Assn. Housing and Renewal Ofcls., Am. Soc. Pub. Adminstrn. Home: 8100 Connecticut Ave Apt 506 Chevy Chase MD 20815

MELTZER, JAY H., lawyer, consultant; b. Bklyn., Mar. 30, 1944; s. Solomon G. and Ethel L. (Kraft) M.; m. Joan Pike, Aug. 12, 2006; children from previous marriage: Wendy, Elizabeth, Jonathan. AB, Dartmouth Coll., 1964; JD, Harvard U., 1967. Bar: N.Y. 1968, Mass. 1978, U.S. Dist. Ct. Mass. 1979. Law clk. to U.S. dist. judge, 1967-68; assoc. firm Shearman & Sterling, NYC, 1968-72; with Damon Corp., Needham Heights, Mass., 1972-84, gen. counsel, sec., 1973-84, v.p., 1979-84; v.p., corp. counsel The TJX Cos., Inc., Framingham, Mass., 1984-87, v.p., gen. counsel, sec., 1987-89, sr. v.p., gen. counsel, sec., 1989—2005; mng. dir. Kwatcher Legal Consulting, Boston, 2006—08. Dir. coun. Better Bus. Bur., 1990-93. Mem. ABA, Am. Soc. Corp. Secs., Am. Corp. Counsel Assn. (bd. dirs. N.E. chpt. 1991-2000), Retailers Assn. Mass. (bd. dirs., exec. com., sec. 1991-2005), New Eng. Corp. Counsel Assn. (bd. dirs. 1979-2003), Legal Mktg. Assn. Office Phone: 781-259-4360. E-mail: jaymeltzer@comcast.net.

MELTZER, JAY IVAN, medical educator; b. NYC, July 20, 1928; s. Herman and Hannah Meltzer; m. Pamela Privett Meltzer, Aug. 6, 1983. BA, Princeton U., New Jersey, 1949; MD, Columbia U., NYC, 1953. Diplomate Am. Bd. Internal Medicine, 1961. Asst. instr. Columbia Faculty, assoc. clin. prof., asst. clin. prof., 1958—81, clin. prof. medicine, 1981—. Capt. Germany Med. Corps, 1955—57. Mem.: Internat. Soc. Nephrology, Am. Soc. Hypertention, Am. Soc. Nephrology. Avocations: painting, diving, sailing. Home: 25 West 81 St New York NY 10024

MELTZER, MILTON, author; b. Worcester, Mass., May 8, 1915; s. Benjamin and Mary (Richter) M.; m. Hilda Balinky, June 22, 1941; children: Jane, Amy. Student, Columbia, 1932-36. Adj. prof. history U. Mass., Amherst, 1977-80. Author: Mark Twain Himself, 1960; author: (with Walter Harding) A Thoreau Profile, 1962; author: Langston Hughes: A Biography, 1968, Bread and Roses, 1967, Never to Forget: The Jews of the Holocaust, 1976, Dorothea Lange: A Photographer's Life, 1978; author: (with Langston Hughes, C. Eric Lincoln, Jon Michael Spencer) A Pictorial History of African-Americans, 1994; co-editor: Lydia Maria Child: Selected Letters, 1817-1880, 1982, The Black Americans, 1984, Mark Twain: A Writer's Life, 1985, George WAshington and the Birth of Our Nation, 1986, The American Revolutionaries, 1987, Benjamin Franklin: The New American, 1988, Rescue: The Story of How Gentiles Saved Jews in the Holocaust, 1988, Starting From Home: A Writer's Beginnings, 1988, Voices From the Civil War, 1989, Columbus and the World Around Him, 1990, The Bill of Rights: How We Got It and What It Means, 1990, Thomas Jefferson: Revolutionary Aristocrat, 1991, The Amazing Potato, 1992, Slavery: A World History, 1993, Lincoln: In His Own Words, 1993, Andrew Jackson and His America, 1993, Gold, 1993, Cheap Raw Material: How Our Youngest Workers Are Exploited and Abused, 1994, Theodore Roosevelt, 1994, Weapons and Warfare, 1996, Tom Paine, 1996, The Many Lives of Andrew Carnegie, 1997, Ten Queens: Portraits of Women of Power, 1998, Food, 1998, Carl Sandburg, 1999, Witches and Witch Hunts, 1999, Driven from the Land, 2000, They Came in Chains, 2000, Ten Kings, 2001, Ain't Gonna Study War No More, 2002, The Day the Sky Fell, 2002, Great Inventions: The Cotton Gin, 2003, Great Inventions: The Printing Press, 2003, Herman Melville, 2003, Edgar Allan Poe, 2003, Hour of Freedom: American History in Poetry, 2003, Hear That Train Whistle Blow! How the Railroad Changed the World, 2004, Milton Meltzer: Writing Matters, 2005, Emily Dickinson, 2006, Henry David Thoreau, 2007, Not Having Hawthorne, 2007, Tough Tunes: A Novel, 2007, John Steinbeck, 2008, Willa Cather, 2008, Albert Einstein, 2008. Served with USAAF, 1942-46. Recipient Laura Ingalls Wilder award, Am. Libr. Assn., 2001, Regina medal, Cath. Libr. Assn., 2000. Mem. Orgn. Am. Historians, Authors Guild, P.E.N. Address: 263 West End Ave New York NY 10023-2612

MELTZER, PAUL S., geneticist, researcher; BA, Dartmouth Coll., 1967; PhD, Calif. Inst. Tech., 1972; MD, U. Tenn., 1980. Sr. genetics investigator Nat. Human Genome Rsch. Inst., Bethesda, Md.; branch chief Genetics Br., head Molecular Genetics Sect. Ctr. Cancer Rsch., Nat. Cancer Inst., NIH, Bethesda, Md. Office: Nat Cancer Inst Bldg 37, Rm 6138 37 Convent Dr, MSC 4265 Bethesda MD 20892 Office Phone: 301-496-5266. Office Fax: 301-402-3241. E-mail: pmeltzer@mail.nih.gov.*

MELTZER, STEVEN LEE, lawyer; b. Rochester, NY, Sept. 6, 1946; s. Seymour Norman and Ruth (Pekarsky) M.; m. Harriet Vivian Lewis, Aug. 29, 1971; children: Debra, Scott, Jeremy. AB cum laude, Brown U., 1968; MBA with high distinction, Harvard U., 1973, JD, 1973. Bar: Md. 1973, D.C. 1974, Va. 1997. From assoc. to mng. bd. Shaw, Pittman, Potts & Trowbridge, Washington, 1973—2005; ptnr., Corp. & Securities, Health Care, Emerging Growth & Tech. practices, mng. bd. Pillsbury Winthrop Shaw Pittman, McLean, Va., 2005—06. Exec. editor Technology Law Notes, 1986-92. Trustee New Eng. Inst. Tech. 1974-, bd. chmn. 1989-; bd, vis. Coll. Life Sci., U. Md., 2004—; sec., exec. com., legal counsel Tech. Coun. Md.; founder, legal counsel Md. Angels Coun.; bd. visitors, U. Md. Coll. Life Sci., 2004—. Mem. ABA, Internat. Bar Assn., Info. Tech. Assn. Am., Nat. Assn. Corp. Dir., Mid-Atlantic Venture Assn., No. Va. Tech. Council, Biotechnology Industry Org., D.C. Bar Assn., Md. State Bar Assn., Harvard Bus. Sch. Club. Avocations: golf, tennis. Office: Pillsbury Winthrop Shaw Pittman 1650 Tysons Blvd Ste 1400 Mc Lean VA 22102-4859 Office Phone: 703-770-7950. Office Fax: 703-770-7901. Business E-Mail: steven.meltzer@pillsburylaw.com.

MELTZER, YALE LEON, economist, educator; b. NYC, Nov. 3, 1931; s. Benjamin and Ada (Luria) M.; m. Annette Schoenberg, Aug. 7, 1960; children: Benjamin Robert, Philippe David. BA, Columbia U., 1954, postgrad. Sch. Law, 1954—55; MBA, NYU, 1966. Asst. to chief patent atty., prodn. mgr. Beaunit Mills, Inc., Elizabethton, Tenn., 1955—58, prodn. mgr., 1956—58; rsch. chemist N.Y. Med. Coll., NYC, 1958—59, H. Kohnstamm & Co., Inc., NYC, 1959—66, mgr. comml. devel., market rsch., patents and trademarks, 1966—68; sr. security analyst Harris, Upham & Co., Inc., 1968—70; instr. dept. econs. NYU, 1972—79; adj. prof. dept. acctg., fin. and mgmt. Pace U., NYC, 1974—80, adj. assoc. prof., 1980—84; lectr. dept. polit. sci., econs. and philosophy Coll. S.I. CUNY, 1977—82, asst. prof. dept. polit. sci., econs. and philosophy Coll. S.I., 1983—. Lectr. bus., fin., econs., sci. and tech.; presenter papers confs. Author: Soviet Chemical Industry, 1966; Chemical Trade with the Soviet Union and Eastern European Countries, 1967; Chemical Guide to GATT, The Kennedy Round and International Trade, 1968; Phthalocyanine Technology, 1970; Hormonal and Attractant Pesticide Technology, 1971; Urethane Foams: Technology and Applications, 1971; Water-Soluble Polymers: Technology and Applications, 1972; Encyclopedia of Enzyme Technology, 1973; Economics, 1974; Foamed Plastics: Recent Developments, 1976; Water-Soluble Resins and Polymers: Technology and Applications, 1976; Putting Money to Work: An Investment Primer, 1976; (with W.C.F. Hartley) Cash Management: Planning, Forecasting, and Control, 1979; Water-Soluble Polymers: Recent Developments, 1979; Putting Money to Work: An Investment Primer for the '80s, 1981, updated edit., 1984; Water-Soluble Polymers: Developments since 1978, 1981; Expanded Plastics and Related Products: Developments Since 1978, 1983; contbr. articles to profl. publs.; translator Russian, French and German tech. lit. Mem. AAAS, Am. Econ. Assn. Home: 14110 82nd Dr Apt 537 Jamaica NY 11435-1106 Office: Coll Staten Island 2800 Victory Blvd Staten Island NY 10314-6609 Business E-Mail: meltzer@mail.csi.cuny.edu.

MELVILL, MICHAEL W., aircraft company executive, experimental test pilot; b. 1941; arrived in US, 1970; m. Sally Melvill; 1 child. FAA coml. cert., cert. ASEL, AMEL, instrument airplane, Rotorcraft-helicopter and Glider. V.p., gen. mgr., test pilot Scaled Co., Inc., Mojave, Calif., 1985—. Recipient Ivan C. Kincheloe trophy for work on devel. high altitude flight testing of model 281 Proteus, 1999. Mem.: Experimental Aircraft Assn., Aircraft Owners' and Pilots' Assn., Soc. Experimental Test Pilots (assoc. fellow). Achievements include participated in flight testing for Beech Starship prototype (NGBA), Fairchild's Next Generation Trainer for US Air Force (NGT), Ares, Pond Racer; built and flight tested Model 27 Variviggen; built, tested and flew around world in 1997 with Dick Rutan Model 61 Long-EZ; first flight of Model 72 Grizzly prototype, Model 77 Solitaire prototype, Model 81 Catbird prototype, Model 120 Predator prototype, Model 144 UAV prototype, Model 202 Boomerang, Model 226 Raptor; first flight of Model 281 Proteus, Model 316 Spaceshipone; first flight firing of GAU-12/U25mm cannon in Model 151 Ares jet fighter; only person to have flown Voyager Aircraft besides Dick Rutan and Jeana Yeager; holds 4 World and Nat. speed and altitude records in Catbird and Proteus Aircraft; first private manned mission to space, first civilian to fly a spaceship out of the atmosphere, first private pilot to earn astronaut wings, June 21, 2004; Guinness Book of World Records dubbed rocket launch "first ever privately funded manned spaceflight"; manned SpaceShipOne flight on Sept. 29, 2004, which will mark the first of two successful flight that are needed to win the Ansari X Prize. Office: Scaled Composites Inc 1624 Flight Line Mojave CA 93501 Office Phone: 661-824-4541. Office Fax: 661-824-4174.

MELVIN, BILLY ALFRED, clergyman; b. Macon, Ga., Nov. 25, 1929; s. Daniel Henry and Leola Dale (Seidell) Melvin; m. Marcia Darlene Eby, Oct. 26, 1952; children: Deborah Ruth, Daniel Henry II. Student, Free Will Baptist Bible Coll., Nashville, 1947—49; BA, Taylor U., Upland, Ind., 1951, LLD (hon.), 1984; postgrad., Asbury Theol. Sem., Wilmore, Ky., 1951—53; BD, Union Theol. Sem., Richmond, Va., 1956; DD, Azusa Coll., Calif., 1968, Huntington Coll., 1995. Ordained to ministry Free Will Baptist Ch., 1951; pastor First Free Will Baptist Chs., Newport, Tenn., 1951—53, Richmond, Va., 1953—57, Bethany Ch., Norfolk, 1957—59. Exec. sec. Nat. Assn. Free Will Baptists, 1959—67; exec. dir. Nat. assn. Evangelicals, 1967—95. Baptist. E-mail: bam1929@verizon.net.

MELVIN, CAROLE RAMEY, educational consultant; d. Roy Earl and Marjorie Smithson Ramey; m. James Preston Melvin, June 4, 1966; children: LindaJean Melvin Eastland, Robert Wesley. Med, Regent U., 1997. Mid. sch. math tchr. Va. Beach City Pub. Sch., Va., 1965—72, jr. high math tchr., 1989—94, academic, testing coord., 1994—98, libr., computer, testing coord., 1998—2000, sch. improvement specialist, 2000—09; adj. prof. Regent U., Va. Beach, 1997—99, transition specialist, 2009—. Sch. rep. Va. Beach Edn. Assn., 1997—98; facilitator Sch. Planning Coun., Va. Beach, 1999—; mem. Prins. Adv. Com., Va. Beach. Youth leader Va. Beach Christian Ch., 1989—92. Recipient Disting. Student award, Regent U. Mem.: NEA (assoc.), ASCD (assoc.), Va. Edn. Assn. (assoc.), Va. Beach Edn. Assn. (assoc. Outstanding Math Tchr. award 1993, Math. Tchr. award). Office: Renaissance Acad HS 273 NW Witchdack Rd Virginia Beach VA 23456 Business E-Mail: crmelvin@vbschools.com.

MELVIN, CHARLES EDWARD, JR., lawyer; b. Greensboro, NC, July 13, 1929; s. Charles Edward and Mary Ruth (Plunkett) M.; m. Jacklyn McDaniel, Mar. 1, 1958; 1 child, Dana W. BS, U. N.C., 1951, JD with honors, 1956. Bar: N.C. 1956. Of counsel Smith Moore Leatherwood LLP, Greensboro, 1958—. Capt. U.S. Army, 1952-54. Mem. N.C. Bar Assn. (chmn. real property sect. 1981), Am. Coll. Real Estate Lawyers, Greensboro C. of C. (pres. 1978). Office: Smith Moore Leatherwood LLP PO Box 21927 Greensboro NC 27420-1927 Office Phone: 336-378-5204. Business E-Mail: charlie.melvin@smithmoorelaw.com.

MELVIN, DOUG, professional baseball team manager; b. Aug. 8, 1952; Baseball ops. asst. NY Yankees, 1983—84, dir. scouting, 1985; spl. asst., exec. v.p. Balt. Orioles, 1987, dir. player personnel, 1988—89, asst. gen. mgr., dir. player personnel, 1990—94; v.p., gen. mgr. Tex. Rangers, 1996, exec. v.p., gen. mgr., 1997—2001; cons. Boston Red Sox, 2002; sr. v.p., gen. mgr. Milw. Brewers, 2003—. Office: Milw Brewers Miller Pk One Brewers Way Milwaukee WI 53214

MELVIN, JOHN LEWIS, physical and rehabilitation physician, educator, administrator; b. Columbus, Ohio, May 26, 1935; s. John Harper and Ruth Eleanor (Wertenberger) M.; m. Carol Ann Pate, Apr. 10, 1991; children from a previous marriage: Megan Marie, Beth Anne, John Patrick, Mia Michelle. BS, Ohio State U., 1955, MD, 1960, M in Med. Sci., 1966. Rotating Intern Mt. Carmel Hosp., Columbus, 1960—61; resident in phys. medicine U. Hosp. Columbus, 1961, 1963—66; asst. prof. Ohio State U., Columbus, 1966—69, assoc. prof., 1969—73; prof., chmn. dept. Med. Coll. Wis., Milw., 1973—91; prof., dep. chmn. dept Temple U., Phila., 1992—98; v.p. med. affairs Moss Rehab. Hosp., Phila., 1991—2002; dept. chmn. Einstein Medical Ctr., Phila., 1991—2002; Michie prof., dept. chmn. rehab. medicine Thomas Jefferson U., 1998—. Contbr. articles to profl. journals; cons. to numerous U.S. govtl. agys., health care insts.; lectr. in field; research assoc. Ohio State Research Found., Columbus, 1966-68; assoc. coordinator Ohio State Regional Med. Program, Columbus, 1969-71; med. dir. Curative Rehab. Ctr., Milw., 1973-91. Bd. dirs. Vis. Nurses Assn., Milw., 1974-83; mem. com. Mental Health Planning Council, Milw., 1974-75, Wis. Council Devel. Disabilities, Madison, 1979-80; mem. planning and evaluation com. Elizabethtown Hosp. for Children and Youth, Pa., 1977; advisor Nat. Multiple Sclerosis Soc., Milw., 1979-87; mem. Wis. Nicaragua Ptnrs., 1982-91; trustee Easter Seal Research Found., vice chmn., 1985, chmn. 1986-88. Served to capt. M.C. US Army, 1961—63. Recipient cert. of appreciation Goodwill Industries, 1972, spl. recognition award Commn. Accreditation Rehab. Facilities, 1977, Performance award Wood VA Med. Ctr., 1978, Goldschmidt award Nat. Rehab. Hosp., 1990, cert. of appreciation Jour. Rehab. Adminstrn., 1982; Alumni Achievement award Ohio State U., 1985; grantee Rehab. Svcs. Adminstrn., 1979-91, Health Care Financing Adminstrn., 1984-85; Ford Found. fellow, 1951-53. Fellow Am. Acad. Cerebral Palsy and Devel. Medicine, Am. Acad. Phys. Medicine and Rehab. (bd. dirs. 1992-2000, pres. 1999, Zeiter Lectr. award 1987, Krusen award 2000, Disting. Mem. award 2007); mem. Am. Bd. Phys. Medicine and Rehab. (Diplomate, chmn. 1988-93, chmn. residency Rev. Com. 1985-88), Am. Bd. Med. Specialists (exec. com. 1990-92), Med. Soc. Milw. 1973-1991, Milw. Acad. Medicine 1979-1991, Wis. Soc. Phys. Medicine and Rehab. 1973-1991, Am. Assn. Electromyography and Electrodiagnosis (pres. 1979-80, Lifetime Achievement award 2007), Am. Congress Rehab. Medicine (pres. 1987-88, gold medal 1971, 78, Gold Key award 1988, Edward Lowman award 1997), Am. Heart Assn., Am. Hosp. Assn. (sect. rehab. hosp., chmn. 1981), AMA (cert. of appreciation 1976, 82), Am. Paraplegia Soc., Assn. Acad. Physiatrists (pres. 1985-87, Disting. Mem. award 2003), Internat. Fedn. Phys. Medicine and Rehab. (exec. com. 1980-1999, hon. sec. 1980-88, pres. elect 1995-99), Internat. Rehab. Medicine Assn. (bd. dirs. 1992-99), Internat. Soc. Phys. and Rehab. Med. (pres. 1999-2002, Flax Lifetime Achievement award 2005), Rehab. Internat. Med. Comm. 1985-1995, Nat. Assn. Rehab. Facilities (pres. 1981-83, bd. dirs.), Coun. of Med. Splty. Socs. (pres. 1989-90), Found. for Phys. Med. and Rehab. (pres. 2005-07), Alpha Omega Alpha, Delta Chi Fraternity-Internat. Hdqs. (Disting. award, 1997, Delta Chi of Yr., 1999). Office: Thomas Jefferson Univ Dept Rehab Med 25 S 9th St Philadelphia PA 19107-5098 Home Phone: 215-238-9708; Office Phone: 215-955-6574. Office Fax: 215-955-2311. Business E-Mail: John.melvin@jefferson.edu.

MELVIN, LELAND D., astronaut; b. Lynchburg, Va., Feb. 15, 1964; s. Deems and Grace Melvin. BS in Chemistry, U. Richmond, 1986; MS in Materials Sci. Engrng., U. Va., 1991. Rschr. fiber optic sensors group, nondestructive evaluation scis. br. Langley Rsch. Ctr., NASA, Va., 1989—94, head vehicle health monitoring team, 1994—98; astronaut, mission specialist candidate Johnson Space Ctr. NASA, Houston, 1998—. Co-mgr., Educator Astronaut Program NASA; crew mem.

Atlantis STS-122 mission to deliver the European Space Agency's Columbus Lab. to the Internat. Space Station, 2008. Recipient Key to City of Lynchburg, Va.; named Acad. All Am., NCAA Divsn. I; named to U. Richmond Athletic Hall of Fame. Mem.: Soc. for Exptl. Mechanics, Am. Chemical Soc., Nat. Technical Assn. (Hampton Roads chpt. sec. 1993). Achievements include being chosen by the Detroit Lions in the 11th round of the 1986 NFL college draft; participation in Toronto Argonauts and Dallas Cowboys football training camps. Avocations: piano, reading, music, bicycling, tennis, photography, snowboarding. Office: Astronaut Office/CB NASA Johnson Space Ctr Houston TX 77058

MELVIN, PETER JOSEPH, astrophysicist, educator; b. Seattle, Mar. 12, 1944; s. William Leopold and Virginia (Stevens) M.; m. Bernice Stenman, June 6, 1967 (div. July 1974); m. Alice Sue Pfiester, May 25, 1975 (dec. 1994); children: Robert Dennis, Chloe Anne. BA, Western Wash. State Coll., 1965; MS, U. Ill., 1966, PhD, 1970. NASA trainee U. Ill., Urbana, 1966-68, instr. phys. sci., 1970-72, asst. prof., 1972-77; sr. engr. Martin-Marietta Aerospace Co., Denver, 1977-80, staff engr., 1980-83; sr. specialist engr. engring. tech. applications divsn. Boeing Computer Svcs., Seattle, 1983-86; astrophysicist U.S. Naval Rsch. Lab., Washington, 1986-99, ret., 1999; dir. of rsch. B-Gravity, Inc., Waldorf, Md., 1999—. Vis. faculty applied math. divsn. Nat. Bur. Stds. Boulder (Colo.) Labs., 1977. Contbr. articles to sci. jours.; patentee in field. Mem. AIAA, Am. Math. Soc., Soc. Indsl. and Applied Math., Am. Geophys. Uion, Am. Astronautical Soc. Personal E-mail: pjmelvin@comcast.net.

MELVIN, RUSSELL JOHNSTON (JAY MELVIN), magazine publishing consultant; b. New Castle, Pa., Nov. 16, 1925; s. Russell Conwell and Anna Katharine (Johnston) M.; m. Helen Margaret Connery, Aug. 6, 1949; children: Thomas Kirk, Meredith. BA, U. Pa., Phila., 1949. Reporter Phila. Inquirer, 1949; copywriter, then asst. to circulation mgr. Time mag., 1949-53; with Newsweek mag., 1953-86, dir. Pacific edits., 1960-64, mng. dir. internat. edits., 1964-68, mng. editor internat. editorial service, 1969-86; cons. internat. affairs and profl. edn. Mag. Pubs. Am. (formerly Mag. Pubs. Assn.), NYC, 1986—2003. V.p. Newsweek, Inc., 1965-85; founding editor The Journal, Tokyo, 1963; founding dir. Newsweek Feature Service, 1968; mem. UN Communications Adv. Coun. With USNR, 1942—46. Mem. Internat. Advt. Assn. (chmn., CEO 1980-85, exec. dir. Chgos. Corp. 1985-86, bd. dirs. 1988-91, mem. world coun. 1990—), Internat. Fedn. Periodical Press (vice chmn. 1990-94, mgmt. bd.), The Century Assn. Home: 4214 Kendal Way Sleepy Hollow NY 10591

MELVIN, WILLIE VALENTENIA, surgeon, educator; b. Houston, Oct. 9, 1959; s. Willie and Delores Marie Melvin; m. Amy Louise Overall, Jan. 7, 1976; children: Jacob Preston, Sophia Thibodeaux. MD, Meharry Med. Coll., Nashville, 1989. Gen. surgeon Pvt. Practice, Springfield, Tenn., 1995—2000; asst. prof. surg. scis. Vanderbilt U. Med. Ctr., Nashville, 2000—. Roman Catholic. Office: Vanderbilt Univ Med Ctr Nashville TN 37232 Personal E-mail: willie.melvin@gmail.com. Business E-Mail: willie.melvin@vanderbilt.edu.

MELVOLD, ROGER WAYNE, microbiology-immunology educator; b. Henning, Minn., Mar. 21, 1946; s. Sam and Palma (Ronning) M. B.S., Moorhead State U., 1968; Ph.D., U. Kans.-Lawrence, 1973. Assoc. radiation therapy Harvard U., 1972-76, prin. research assoc., 1976-79; asst. prof. medicine and microbiology-immunology Northwestern U., 1979-82, asst. prof. microbiology-immunology, 1982-83; assoc. prof. microbiology-immunology, 1983—92, prof. microbiology-immunology, 1992-97; prof. & chair microbiology-immunology U. ND, 1997-2007; Chester Fritz disting. prof. emeritus microbiology-immunology, 2008; Contbr. articles to profl. jours. Recipient Reverend Elmer & min West Meml. award, Hippocratic Dignity award; NIH grantee, 1979—. Mem. Am. Assn. Immunologists, Transplantation Soc., Sigma Xi. Democrat. Home: 1956 Prairie Rose Ct Grand Forks ND 58201-5896 Office: Univ ND Sch Medicine & Health Scis Dept Microbiology & Immunology 501 N Columbia Rd Grand Forks ND 58202 Home Phone: 707-772-6378. Personal E-mail: rmelvold@gra.midco.net.

MELZACK, RONALD, psychology professor; b. Montreal, Que., Can., July 19, 1929; s. Joseph and Annie (Mandel) M.; m. Lucy Birch, Aug. 7, 1960; children: Lauren, Joel. BSc, McGill U., Montreal, 1950, MSc, 1951, PhD, 1954; DLitt (hon.), U. Waterloo, 1992; DLaws (hon.), Dalhousie U., 2004. Lectr. Univ. Coll., London, 1957-58; assoc. prof. MIT, 1959-63; lectr. psychology McGill U., 1953-54, prof., 1963—, E.P. Taylor prof., 1986. Author: The Day Tuk Became a Hunter, and Other Eskimo Stories, 1967, Raven, Creator of the World, 1970, The Puzzle of Pain, 1973, Why the Man in the Moon is Happy, and Other Eskimo Creation Stories, 1977; author: (with P.D. Wall) The Challenge of Pain, 1982, 2d edit., 1996, 3rd edit., 2008; author: Pain Measurement and Assessment, 1983; author: (with P.D. Wall) Textbook of Pain, 1984, 4th edit., 1999; author: (with D.C. Turk) Handbook of Pain Assessment, 1999, 2d edit., 2001; author: (with P.D. Wall) Handbook of Pain Management, 2003. Decorated Officer, Order of Can., 1995, Order of Quebec, 2000; recipient Molson prize Can. Coun., 1985, Gaston Labat award Am. Soc. Regional Anesthesia, 1989, J.J. Bonica award VI World Congress on Pain, 1990, Prix du Que. Marie-Victorin, 1994, Disting. Contbn. award, Can. Pain Soc., 1995, Rsch. Recognition award, Canadian Anesthesiology Soc., 1997, Janet Travell award Am. Acad. Pain Mgmt., 1997, Killam prize, 2001; named to Can. Med. Hall of Fame, 2009. Fellow APA, AAAS, Royal Soc. Can., Can. Psychol. Assn. (Disting. Contbns. to Psychol. Sci. award 1986, hon. pres. 1988-89, gold medal award 2002); mem. Internat. Assn. Study of Pain (hon., past pres.). Home: 7400 Côte Saint Luc Rd Apt 528 Montreal PQ Canada H4W 3J4 Home Phone: 514-342-3283; Office Phone: 514-398-6084. Business E-Mail: rmelzack@mcgill.ca.

MELZER, PETER, neuroanatomist, educator, research scientist; b. Frankfurt am Main, Hesse, Germany, Dec. 9, 1954; m. Thao Phuong Dang, Mar. 17, 1965; children: Audrey children: Henry. PhD, Johann Wolfgang Goethe U., Frankfurt am Main, 1986. Rsch. fellow NIMH, Bethesda, Md., 1989—92, rsch. assoc., 1992—94; rsch. asst. prof. dept. psychology Vanderbilt U., Nashville, 1996—2006; cons. Brain and Mind Inst., Nashville, 2006—. Fogarty fellow, 1989. Mem.: Soc. Neurosci. Office: Brain and Mind Inst PO Box 0203 Nashville TN 37212 Office Phone: 615-509-6301. Business E-Mail: peter.melzer@brainmindinst.com.

MELZER, RICHARD ANTHONY, historian, educator; b. NYC, Mar. 15, 1949; s. Ben and Gladys Melzer; m. Rena Chavez, Mar. 9, 1984; children: Kam Coveyou, Patrick Richard. PhD, U. N.Mex, 1979. Prof. history U. N. Mex., Valencia, 1979—. Pres. Hist. Soc. N.Mex, 2005—09. Author: (books) Buried Treasures: Famous and Unusual Gravesites in New Mexico History, When We Were Young in the West (Gaspar Perez de Villagra award, 2004), Coming of Age in the Great Depression. Named Tchr. of Yr., U. N.Mex., 1995. Office: U N Mex Valencia 280 La Entrada Los Lunas NM 87031

MEMMOTT, SCOTT A., lawyer; b. Hartford, Conn., July 15, 1965; BS with high honors, USCG Acad., 1987; JD, U. Va., 1996. Bar: Va. 1996, DC. Spl. asst. US atty., Norfolk, Va.; trial atty. civil divsn. US. Dept. Justice, Washington; with Shaw Pittman LLP, Washington; ptnr. Sonnenschein Nath & Rosenthal LLP, Washington, 2004—. Vice-chmn. Nat. Health Care Practice Group, 2007—. Editor-in-chief: Va. Jour. Internat. Law. Founder Sept. 11th Pro Bono Legal Relief Project; mem. standing com. pro bono legal svcs. DC Cir. Jud. Conf.; gen. counsel Pentagon Meml. Fund, Inc. Served to lt. comdr. USCG. Mem.: ABA (mem. health law sect. & litig. sect., white collar crime com.), Healthcare Compliance Assn., Va. Bar Assn., DC Bar Assn. (mem. health law sect.), Am. Health Lawyers Assn. Office: Sonnenschein Nath & Rosenthal LLP Ste 600 E Tower 1301 K St NW Washington DC 20005 Office Phone: 202-408-9169. Office Fax: 202-408-6399. Business E-Mail: smemmott@sonnenschein.com.

MEN, HONGSHENG, biologist, researcher; b. Tongbai, Henan, China, May 18, 1962; s. Jianfeng Men and Shuzhen Li; m. Shunling Tan, May 2, 1989; 1 child, Li. BS, Henan Normal U., Xinxiang, China, 1982—86; MS, Chinese Acad. Scis., Kunming, Yunnan, China, 1986—89; PhD, U. Wis., Madison, 1996—2002. Asst. rschr. Kunming Inst. Zoology, Chinese Acad. Scis., 1986—91, asst. prof., 1992—96; vis. scientist Animal Biotechnology Cambridge Ltd, England, 1991—92; grad. rsch. asst., dept. animal scis. U. Wis., Madison, 1996—2002; rsch. scientist, dept. vet. pathobiology U. Mo., Columbia, 2003—. Rschr. Kunming Inst. Zoology, Chinese Acad. Scis., 1986—96. Contbr. papers to profl. jours. and pubs. Mem.: Soc. Cryobiology, Soc. for Study of Reproduction, Internat. Embryo Transfer Soc. Freedom. Achievements include research in demonstration of cryoinjury to bovine oocytes at DNA level; demonstration of the degeneration mechanism of cryopreserved bovine oocytes to be apotoptic in nature during culture; improvement in the cryosurvival of porcine embryos produced in vitro through chemical delipation; improved monospermic penetration of porcine oocytes employing a modified in vitro fertilization system. Home: 1814 E Broadway 2S Columbia MO 65201 Office: Dept Vet Pathobiology Univ Mo 1600 E Rollins St Columbia MO 65211 Office Phone: 573-882-7343. Office Fax: 573-884-7521. Business E-Mail: menho@missouri.edu.

MENA, DANIEL, lawyer, arbitrator; s. Oswaldo and Martha Mena; m. Maite Pilar Portuondo, Nov. 21, 1997; children: Eric, Sofia. Cert. in Spanish History, U. Salamanca, 1991; BA, Fla. Internat. U., 1992; JD, U. Pa., 1995. Bar: US Dist. Ct. (so. dist.) Fla. 1996, US Dist. Ct. (mid. dist.) Fla. 1997, US Dist. Ct. (no. dist.) Fla. 1998, US Ct. Appeals (11th cir.) 1995, US Supreme Ct. 1999. Assoc. atty. Baker & McKenzie, Miami, Fla., 1993—94; intern civil litig. US Atty.'s Office, Phila., 1994—95; assoc. atty. Gunster, Yoakley & Stewart, Miami, 1995—98; ptnr. Holland & Knight LLP, Miami, 1998—. Mem. civil procedure rules com. Fla. Bar, Tallahassee, 2004—. Contbr. articles to profl. jours. Mem. legal bd. Amigos Together For Kids, Miami, Fla., 2003. Named Selected Up & Comer, South Fla. Legal Guide, 2002; named one of State's Legal Leaders, Fla. Trend's Fla. Legal Elite, 2006. Mem.: ABA (com. internat. law), Dade County Bar Assn. (com. internat. litig.), Chamber South. Independent. Roman Catholic. Avocations: travel, scuba diving, fishing, boating. Office: Holland & Knight LLP 701 Brickell Ave Suite 3000 Miami FL 33131 Office Fax: 305-789-7775. Business E-Mail: daniel.mena@hklaw.com.

MENA, MICHELE M., counselor, therapist; b. Paterson, NJ, Nov. 24, 1953; d. Rev. Miguel Mena and Catalina Alvarez. BA in Psychology, Montclair State U., 1975, MA in Counseling, 1978; MA in Health Edn., NYU, 1985; PhD in Clin. Christian Counseling, Fla. Christian U., 2004. Vocat. rehab. counselor Addiction Rsch. Treatment Corp., NYC, 1984—88; instr. Boricua Coll., NYC, 1988—90; dir. counseling and human svcs. Iron Bd. Edn. Cultural Ctr., Newark, 1992—94; N.G.O. (philanthrope) UN Earth Summit, 1994—; counselor, educator Bridges of America, Fla., 2003—; clin. therapist First Step Adolescent Program, 2007—; evalutor Nat. /State Edn. McGraw Hill Deploit, 2009—. Coll. tutor, peer counselor, English as 2nd lang., reading practitioner, 1972—75. Author: (poetry) Internat. Libr. of Poetry. Guest Presdl. Inaugural-Reagan/Bush, 1984, Nat. Rep. Conv., New Orleans, 1988; mem. Rep. Com. Task Force, Montclair Rep. Com., 1981—91, sec., 1982—84. Recipient grad. assistantship, Dept. Adult Edn., Montclair State U., 1977—78. Mem.: Nat. Assn. Forensic Counselors, Ctrl. Fla. Mental Health Assn., Am. Assn. Christian Counselors, Ctrl. Fla. Soc. for Hist. Preservation, Sanford Hist. Soc., Am. Nat. World War II Mus., Nature Conservancy, Williamsburg Colonial Found., World Wildlife Fund, Audubon Soc., Nat. Geographic Soc., Nat. Wildlife Found., Nat. Trust for Hist. Preservation, Montclair State U. Alumni Assn., White House Historical Soc., Eagle Forum, Montclair Hist. Soc., Orange County Regional History Ctr., Women's Club Upper Montclair, Nat. Garden Club. Republican. Protestant. Avocations: gardening, antiques, poetry, archaeology. Home: 2009 S Magnolia Ave Sanford FL 32771

MENAKER, DANIEL, former publishing executve, television producer; b. NYC, 1941; s. Robert Owen and Mary Grace Menaker; m. Katherine Bouton; 2 children. BA in English, Swarthmore Coll., 1963; MA in English Lit., Johns Hopkins U., 1965. H.S. tchr.; joined as a fact checker The New Yorker, 1969, copy editor, sr. editor; v.p., sr. literary editor Random House, Inc., NYC, 1994—2001; exec. editor Harper Collins, NYC, 2001—03; sr. v.p., editor-in-chief Random House Imprint Random House, Inc., NYC, 2003—04, exec. editor-in-chief, 2004—07. Author: (novels) The Treatment, 1998, (collections of short stories) Friends and Relations, 1976, The Old Left and other stories, 1987.

MENAKER, FRANK H., JR., lawyer; b. Harrisburg, Pa., Aug. 23, 1940; s. Frank H. and Romaine (Sadler) M.; m. Sharon Ann Lynch, Feb. 21, 1981; children: Denise L., Jamie E.; children by previous marriage: David C., Michelle R. BA, Wilkes Coll., 1962; JD, Am. U., 1965. Bar: D.C. 1966, Md. 1975, U.S. Supreme Ct. 1975. Formerly staff counsel Office Gen. Counsel, GAO, Washington; asst. divsn. counsel for aerospace ops. Martin Marietta Corp. Aerospace Divsn., 1970—73, asst. gen. counsel, 1973—77, gen. counsel, 1977—81, Martin Marietta Corp., 1981-95, corp. v.p., 1982—95; v.p., gen. counsel Lockheed Martin Corp., 1995-96, sr. v.p., gen. counsel, 1996—2005; ptnr. DLA Piper Rudnick Gray Cary LLP, Washington, 2006—. Spl. counsel U.S. Commn. on Govt. Procurement, 1971. Mem. ABA (mem. sect. pub. contract law, former chair), Md. Bar Assn., Wash. Met. Corp. Counsel Assn. (bd. dirs. 1988-95). Office: DLA Piper Rudnick Gray Cary 1200 Nineteenth St NW Washington DC 20036 Office Phone: 202-861-6302. Business E-Mail: frank.menaker@dlapiper.com.

MENAKER, MICHAEL, biology professor; b. Vienna, May 19, 1934; came to U.S., 1934; s. William and Esther (Astin) M.; m. Shirley Ann Lasch, June 4, 1955; children: Ellen Margaret, Nicholas. BA in Biology, Swarthmore Coll., 1955; PhD in Biology, Princeton U., 1960; PhD in Math. and Natural Sci. (hon.), U. Groningen, Netherlands, 2009. Asst. instr. Princeton (N.J.) U., 1955-57; postdoctoral fellow Harvard U., Cambridge, Mass., 1960-62; asst. prof. zoology U. Tex.-Austin, 1962-68, assoc. prof., 1968-72, prof., 1972-79; prof. biology U. Oreg., Eugene, 1979-86, dir. interdisciplinary program for neuroscis., 1979-81, dir. Inst. Neurosci., 1981-85; Commonwealth prof. biology U. Va., Charlottesville, 1987—, chmn. dept., 1987-93; dir. Howard Hughes Undergrad. Rsch. Program in Biol. Sci., Charlottesville, 1989-94; core investigator Sci. and Tech. Ctr. in Biol. Timing U. Va., Charlottesville, 1991—. Benjamin Meaker vis. prof. U. Bristol, Eng., 1986. Assoc. editor Behavioral Neurosci., Jour. Biol. Rhythms; contbr. articles to profl. jours. Recipient Lifetime Achievement award Am. Soc. for Photobiology, 2002, Life Achievement in Sci. award Va.'s Outstanding Scientists and Industrialists, 2003, Peter C. Farrell prize Sleep Medicine, 2007, Disting. Scientist award U. Va., 2009; NSF fellow, 1958-59, 60-62; NIH fellow, 1960-62; Guggenheim Found. fellow, 1971-72. Fellow AAAS, Am. Acad. Arts and Scis., Japan Soc. Promotion of Scis. (sr.); mem. Soc. Neuroscis., Am. Physiol. Soc., Soc. Rsch. Biol. Rhythms. Avocations: literature, music, sailing. Office: U Va Dept Biology Gilmer Hall PO Box 400328 Charlottesville VA 22904-4328 Office Phone: 434-982-5767. Business E-Mail: mm7e@virginia.edu.

MENAKER, RONALD HERBERT, retired bank executive; b. NYC, Dec. 17, 1944; s. Harold L. Menaker and Gladys (Bleiberg) Ross; m. Kathleen Sager Thomas, Sept. 11, 1966; children: Meredith E., Kyri D. Student, Queen's Coll., 1965—66. Mng. dir. J.P. Morgan & Co., Inc., NYC, 1966—2000; ret., 2000. Bd. dirs. Reckson Assocs. Realty Corp., 2002—07. Past trustee NYU Med. Ctr. and Health Sys., NYC, 1991, The Am. Kennel Club Mus. of the Dog, St. Louis, 1989—; bd. dirs., chmn. Am. Kennel Club, NYC, 2002; trustee, vice chmn., past chmn. NYU Downtown Hosp., 1991—; bd. overseers U. Pa. Vet. Sch., 2000—. Mem.: Westminster Kennel Club. Avocations: sporting art, judging dogs. Business E-Mail: rhm@akc.org.

MENAMPARAMPIL, THOMAS S.D.B., archbishop; b. Palai, India, Oct. 22, 1936; s. Cheriathu and Annamma Menamparampil. M in English Lit., Calcutta U., 1969, M in History, 1970. Prin. Don Bosco Tech. Sch., Shillong, India, 1975-81; bishop Diocese of Dibrugarh, Assam, India, 1981-92; archbishop Diocese Guwahati, Assam, 1992—. Spl. sec. Asian Synod, Vatican, 1998; founder Religion Leader for Peace, 2004; chmn. Mission Office Asia, Edn. Commission, India, 2006. Author several books; builder of Peace Ctr., Guwahati, 2002. Originator, builder of 50 sch. in Assam; initiator of work for st. children, handicapped and persons terminally sick; builder four hosps. in Assam, 2006; reconciler of ethnic conflicts between Bodo-Adivasi, Kuki-Paite, Dimasa-Hmar, Karbi-Kuki; with joint venture U. Guwahati for Peace, 2006. Recipient Maschio award for Peace and Reconciliation, 1998. Home and Office: Archbishop's House Box 100 Guwahati Assam 781 001 India Home Phone: 094350-15177; Office Phone: 0361-2547664. Fax: 361 2520588. Personal E-mail: menam@sify.com.

MENARCHIK, DOUGLAS EDWARD, federal agency administrator; b. 1945; MA, PhD in Internat. Rels., George Wash. U. With air staff, Middle East/African policy divsn. US Dept. Def.; mil. adv. to v.p. The White House; asst. for terrorism policy US Dept. Def.; dir., def. leadership mgmt. prog. Nat. Def. U., 1997—2000; dir. George Bush Presdl. Libr. & Mus., 2000—04; asst. adminstr. for policy & program coordination US Agy. Internat. Devel. (USAID), 2004—07, asst. adminstr. for Europe & Eurasia, 2007—. Former prof. polit. sci. U.S. Air Force Acad.; former instr. AF Special Ops. Sch.; former prof., dem. def. mgmt. George C. Marshall European Ctr. for Strategic Studies and Def. Econ., Garmisch, Germany. Officer, colonel USAF, 1968—94, vice comdr. 1776 Air Base Wing USAF, Andrews AFB, Md., asst. dir., ops. 443rd Mil. Airlift Wing, Altus AFB, Okla. Office: US Agy Internat Devel (USAID) 1300 Pennsylvania Ave NW Washington DC 20523*

MENARD, JOHN R., JR., home improvement retail executive; b. Eau Claire, Wisc., 1940; s. John Menard Sr. and Rosemary; 6 children. BA/BS, U. of Wis. Madison, 1963. Founder, pres., CEO Menard Inc., Eau Claire, Wis., 1972—; owner, pres. Menard Racing, 1979—. Bd. dirs. Polaris Industries. Named one of Forbes' Richest Americans, 1999—, World's Richest People, Forbes Mag., 2001. Avocation: auto racing. Office: Menard Inc 4777 Menard Dr Eau Claire WI 54703-9625

MENASHE, ALBERT ALAN, lawyer; b. Portland, Oreg., Apr. 24, 1950; s. Solomon A. and Faye F. (Hasson) Menashe; m. Laura L. Richenstein, July 23, 1972 (div. Oct. 1979); 1 child, Shawn Nathan; m. Sandra J. Laniado, June 28, 1980 (div. Jan. 1994); m. Julie D. Howe, Oct. 25, 2003. BS in Polit. Sci., U. Oreg., 1971; JD, Willamette U., 1976. Bar: Oreg. 1977, U.S. Dist. Ct. Oreg. 1977, U.S. Ct. Appeals (9th cir.) 1977, U.S. Supreme Ct. 1980. Assoc. Bullivant, Wright et al, Portland, 1976—79; ptnr. Samuels, Samuels et al, Portland, 1979—80; mng. shareholder Gevurtz, Menashe, Larson & Howe, P.C., Portland, 1982—. Frequent spkr. on family law, 1979—; former pro tem judge County of Clackamas, Oreg. Editor-in-chief: Willamette Law Jour. 1st lt. US Army, 1971—73. Mem.: ABA, Multnomah County Bar Assn. (pres. 1997—98), Oreg. State Bar Assn. (chair family law sect. 1981—82, bd. govs. 2004—07, pres. 2007), Am. Acad. Matrimonial Lawyers (pres. Oreg. chpt. 1996—97), Phi Beta Kappa, Phi Kappa Phi. Office: Gevurtz Menashe Larson & Howe PC 111 SW 5th Ave Ste 900 Portland OR 97204

MENA-WERTH, JOSE, physics professor; s. Jose Mena and Haydee Mena-Werth; m. Jane Werthimer, May 23, 1981; children: Paloma, Rosemary. PhD, U. Wash., Seattle, 1992. Cert. secondary tchr. Calif., 1973. Astronomy grad. student U. Wash., Seattle, 1985—92; prof. physics U. Nebr., Kearney, 1992—. Tchr. St. Ignatius Coll. Prep., San Francisco, 1971—85. Mem.: Am. Astron. Soc. Independent. Office: Univ Nebr 905 W 25th St Kearney NE 68845

MENCER, JETTA, lawyer; b. Coshocton, Ohio, Apr. 7, 1959; d. William J. and Virginia M. (Fry) M. BS, Ohio State U., 1980, JD, 1983. Bar: Ohio, U.S. Dist. Ct. (so. dist.) Ohio. Assoc. Berry, Owens & Manning, Coshocton, 1983-86; asst. pros. atty. Coshocton County, 1983-86, Licking County, Newark, Ohio, 1986-88, asst. atty. gen., 1988-95; pvt. practice Coshocton, 1995-96; prosecuting atty. Coshocton County (Ohio) Prosecutor's Office, 1997-2001; atty. Lee Smith & Assocs., Columbus, Ohio, 2001—03; pvt. practice Columbus, 2003—. Treas. Coshocton County Dem. Cen. & Exec. Coms., 1984-86; chmn., 1986-88; sec., bd. dirs. Heart Ohio Girl Scout Council, Inc., Zanesville, Ohio, 1985-87; fin. chmn., bd. dirs. YMCA, Coshocton, 1985-87. Mem. Ohio State Bar Assn., Coshocton County Bar Assn., Lions Club. Democrat. Methodist. Office: One S Park Pl Newark OH 43055 Office Phone: 740-345-5171. Personal E-mail: jmencer@columbus.rr.com.

MENCER, SUE (CONSTANCE SUZANNE MENCER), former federal agency administrator; b. Nov. 15, 1947; m. John Mencer; children: Jessie, Alex. BA in Spanish, Ohio St. U., 1968; Grad., JFK Sch. Govt., Harvard U., 2003. Tchr. Spanish, 1968—78; spl. agt. FBI, 1978—85, supervisory spl. agt., 1985—90, supr., 1990—98; pvt. cons. Anti-Terrorism Tng., Denver; exec. dir. dept. pub. safety State of Colo., Denver, 2000—03; exec. dir. Office of State & Local Govt. Coordination & Preparedness US Dept. Homeland Security, Washington, 2003—05; sr. policy advisor govt. rels. group Brownstein Hyatt & Farber, PC,

Denver, 2005—. Mem.: Commn. on Jud. Discipline, Soc. Former Spl. Agents. Office: Brownstein Hyatt & Farber PC 410 17th St 22nd Fl Denver CO 80202 E-mail: smencer@bhf-law.com.

MENCH, JOHN WILLIAM, retail executive, electrical engineer; b. NYC, Feb. 27, 1943; s. John William and Edna (Ilgen) M.; m. Rose Irene Miller, Aug. 12, 1962 (dec. Jan. 1997); 1 child, William Ilgen; m. Ann Ward Frentress, Mar. 7, 1998. BSEE, U. S.C., 1969; MBA, Ohio U., 1983; PhD, Calif. Coast U., 1994. Registered profl. engr., Ohio, Ga.; cert. in heating, ventilating and air conditioning; accredited profl. Leadership in Energy and Environ. Design, 2006. Elec. engr. Uniroyal, Shelbyville, Tenn., 1969-74; facility engr. Kroger, Nashville, 1974-77, asst. mgr. facility engring. Atlanta, 1977-79, Kroger mktg. area mgr. facility engring. Columbus, Ohio, 1979-85; divsn. mgr. facility engring., v.p. Safeway Stores, Inc., Oakland, Calif., 1985-86; v.p. constrn., engring. Big V Supermarkets, Inc., Florida, NY, 1986-95; pres. Mench & Assocs. Inc., 1994-98. Assoc. prof. Pa. Coll. Tech., 1996-99; sr. lectr. Southern Poly. State U., 1999—; prof. Am. Contr. Exch., 1999-2003. Author: (tech. manuals) Comments on Commercial Refrigeration, 1998, Comments on Commercial Air Conditioning, 1998, Plan Review, 1995, others, (textbook) Finance for Construction Management 7th edit., 2009. Trustee Meth. Ch., 1987—93; bd. dirs. Goshen Day Care Ctr., 1988—95, Elec. Distbn. Systems, 1993—94; past v.p. Tri State V.W. Assn.; exec. adv. bd. Ohio U. Coll. Bus. Adminstrn., 1992—97, life mem.; v.p. Prime Time Group, 2003—05, pres., 2006. Recipient Outstanding Faculty award, So. Poly. State U., 2007, Engr. of Yr., 2006; named Ga. Engr. of Yr. in Edn., Ga. Profl. Engring. Soc., 2007. Mem. ASHRAE, IEEE (life; sr. mem.), Assn. Energy Engrs. (sr.). Republican. Methodist. Business E-Mail: jmench@spsu.edu.

MENCHER, BRUCE STEPHAN, judge; b. Washington, May 21, 1935; s. Emanuel and Bertha Miriam (Robbin) M.; m. Janet Patricia Whitfield, Nov. 24, 1974; children by previous marriage: Sean Robbin, Marc Nadzo. BA, George Washington U., 1957, JD with honors, 1960. Bar: DC 1960, US Supreme Ct. 1964. Gen. atty. Office Gen. Counsel, Dept. Agr., 1960—61; asst. corp. counsel for D.C., 1961—67; atty.-adviser Office Gen. Counsel, Bur. for Africa, AID, 1967—69; ptnr. Wilkes & Artis, Washington, 1969—75; assoc. judge Superior Ct. D.C., 1975—91, sr. judge, 1991—, presiding judge Family divsn., 1988—90. Professorial lectr. law George Washington U. Nat. Law Ctr., 1982-83; lectr. criminal justice Nat. Cathedral Sch./St. Albans Sch., 1985; faculty advisor Nat. Jud. Coll., 1995. Asst. rsch. editor George Washington Law Rev., 1959-60; contbr. articles to law revs. Mem. gen. alumni gov. bd. George Washington U., 1972-80; bd. dirs. Nat. Child Support Enforcement Assn., 1994-97, The Washington Savoyards Ltd., 1991-96, Trinity Chamber Orch., 2001-. Recipient Alumni Svc. award, 1975, Judge of Yr. award Assn. Plaintiffs Trial Attys., 1983, Samuel Green award for disting. svc. to Washington legal comty. and Phi Delta Phi, 1985, Disting. Alumni Achievement award George Washington U., 1987, also various appreciation and recognition awards local bar assns., DC and fed. govts. for work in area of family law and child support enforcement. Mem. ABA, Bar Assn. D.C., D.C. Bar, George Washington Law Assn. (exec. com. 1972-77), The Barristers (exec. com. 1981), George Washington Am. Inn of Ct. (pres. 1999—2000, Phi Delta Phi (pres. Barrister Inn 1974-75) Office: Superior Ct DC 500 Indiana Ave NW Rm 5520 Washington DC 20001-2131 Office Phone: 202-879-1358. Business E-Mail: mencherbs@dcsc.gov. *While it may sound old-fashioned, I attribute my appointment to the bench, in large part, to hard work, dedication, a love of the law and respect for my fellow man. One should maintain his sense of balance, always try to understand the other person's position and, at all costs, maintain a sense of humor throughout.*

MENCHER, JOAN PHYLLIS, anthropology educator; b. NYC, Jan. 29, 1930; d. Irving W. and Mae (Bodin) M.; m. Franklin C. Southworth, June 21, 1966; children: Devaraj, Leela. BA in Physics and Math. magna cum laude, Smith Coll., 1950; PhD in Anthropology, Columbia U., 1958. cert. trainer in neurolinguistic programming, NLP trainer of trainers. Assoc. prof. Herbert H. Lehman Coll. and City U. Grad. Ctr., 1968-73, prof., 1974—2004; prof. Emeritus Herbert H. Lehman Coll. and City. U. Grad. Ctr., 2004—; chair The Second Chance Found., 2004—. Vis. lectr. Achutha Menon Ctr. of the Sri Chitra Tirunal Inst. of Med. Scis., 1998; presenter NLP workshops, Bangalore, Delhi, 1999, 2003; presenter confs. in field; cons. UNDP, UNIFEM, HIVOS, Women in Devel., Sustainable Agr. India, Women Water, Alternative Agr. Farmers, others. Author: Agriculture and Social Structure in Tamil Nadu: Past Origins, Present Transformations, and Future Prospects, 1978, Social Anthropology of Peasantry, 1983, Where Have All the Men Gone?, 1993, Female Headed/Female Supported Households: A Cross Cultural Comparison, 1993, Mixed Blessings: Women and Religious Fundamentalism, 1996, others; contbr. more than 85 articles to profl. jours. and publs. Grantee in field; Ogden Mills fellow Am. Mus. Natural History, Guggenheim fellow, 1974-75; Fulbright fellow to India, others. Fellow Am. Anthropol. Assn., Soc. Applied Anthroplogy; mem. Assn. Women in Devel., Soc. Internat. Devel., Nat. Assn. Neurolinguistic Programming, Assn. Asian Studies, Indian Sociol. Soc., Indian Anthropol. Assn., Phi Beta Kappa, Sigma Xi. Avocations: snorkeling, swimming. Office Phone: 212-580-5606. Personal E-mail: joan.mencher@gmail.com. Business E-Mail: jmencher@thesecondchance.org.

MENCHER, MELVIN, journalist, educator; b. Bklyn., Jan. 25, 1927; s. Peter and Theresa (Sherman) M.; m. Helen Chamberlain, Aug. 27, 1947; children: Thomas, Marianne, Nicholas. Student, U. N.Mex., 1943-44; BA, U. Colo., 1947; postgrad. (Nieman fellow), Harvard, 1952-53. Reporter UP, 1947-50; state polit. corr. Albuquerque Jour., 1951-54; reporter Fresno (Calif.) Bee, 1954-58; asst. prof. journalism U. Kans., Lawrence, 1958-62; asst. prof. Columbia U., NYC, 1962-65, assoc. prof., 1965-75, prof., 1975-90, assoc. dir. summer program for journalism edn. of minorities, 1971, prof. emeritus, 1990—. Contbg. author: Evaluating the Press, 1973; author: News Reporting and Writing, 1977, Basic Media Writing, 1983; editor: The FNMA Guide to Buying, Financing and Selling Your Home, 1973; contbr. articles to profl. jours. Mem. Soc. Profl. Journalists, Nat. Council Coll. Pubs. Advisers, Kappa Tau Alpha. Home: 450 Riverside Dr New York NY 10027-6801 Home Phone: 212-666-2681. E-mail: mm55@columbia.edu.

MENCHER, STUART ALAN, sales and marketing executive; b. NYC, Apr. 25, 1939; s. Meyer H. and Mildred B. Mencher; m. Judith Leslie Schneider; children: Jane Lizabeth, Tracy Ellen. B in Mgmt. Engring., Rensselaer Poly. Inst., 1960; MBA, NYU, 1965. Sales rep. Sperry Rand Univac, Albany, NY, 1960-62; various sales and mktg. mgmt. positions IBM Corp., White Plains, NY, 1965-78, br. mgr. data processing div. Harrison, NY, 1978-81; dir. market ops. planning, bus. mktg. dept. AT&T, Basking Ridge, NJ, 1981-83; dir. market mgmt., sales and mktg. div. AT&T Info. Systems, Morristown, NJ, 1983, dir. data systems mktg., 1983-84, v.p. mktg., large bus. systems div., 1985-87; sr. v.p. sales and mktg. MCI Communications Corp., Washington, 1987-90; sr. v.p., gen. mgr. U.S. distbn. div. Motorola/Codex Corp., Mansfield, Mass., 1990-91; sr. v.p., gen. mgr. Teleport Communications, NYC, 1992-93, sr. v.p. nat. sales and mktg., 1994-98; v.p. strategic planning AT&T Bus. Svcs., Bridgewater, NJ, 1998-99; mng. ptnr. The Mencher Group LLC, East Hampton, NY, 1999—. Bd. dirs. Broadview Networks, N.Y.C., 2000-05. Pres. Westfield Men's Coll. Scholarship Club, NJ, 1977; coach Westfield Young Soccer Assn., 1976—81; mem. budget rev. com. United Fund, Westfield, NJ, 1983—85; mem. adv. bd. NYC Tech. Coll., 1993; mem. Mayor's Telecomms. Mutual Aid and Restoration Com., NYC, 1992—93; v.p., bd. dirs. Ctr. Children and Families/Safe Space, NYC, 1999—2007; chmn. mktg. adv. com. YMCA Greater N.Y., NYC, 1999—2004. Lt. USCGR, 1962—65. Avocations: golf, travel, theater, arts. Office: PO Box 5134 East Hampton NY 11937-6165

MENCHETTI, DAVID BARRY, lawyer; b. Chgo., Dec. 13, 1959; s. Leo and Diane M.; m. Lorraine C. Dorff, June 2, 1984; children, Cecilia, Quinn. BA, Stanford U., 1981; JD, Loyola U., Chgo., 1984. Bar: Ill. 1984. Staff atty. Ill. State Senate, Sprinfield, 1984-86; ptnr. Cullen, Haskins, Nicholson & Menchetti P.C., Chgo., 1986—. Author: (notebook) Penalties in Workers' Compensation Illinois Trial Lawyers WC Notebook, 1990—. Mem. Ill. State Bar Assn. (chair workers compensation com. 1996-97), Chgo. Bar Assn. (chair workers' compensation com., 1993-94), Workers Compensation Lawyers Assn. (pres. Chgo. 1999, bd. dirs. 1997—), Workplace Injury Litigation Group. Democrat. Roman Catholic. Office: Cullen Haskins Nicholson & Menchetti 35 E Wacker Dr Ste 1760 Chicago IL 60601-2271 Office Phone: 312-332-2545.

MENCHIK, PAUL LEONARD, economist, educator; b. NYC, Sept. 16, 1947; s. Irving and Elinor (Swedlow) M.; m. Bettie Ann Landauer, May 28, 1972; children: Daniel Aron, Jeremy Matthew. BA, SUNY, Binghamton, 1969; AM, U. Pa., 1971, PhD, 1976. Lectr. Rutgers Coll., New Brunswick, NJ, 1974-76; rsch. assoc. Inst. for Rsch. on Poverty, U. Wis., Madison, 1976-79; prof. dept. econs. Mich. State U., East Lansing, Mich., 1979—, chairperson dept. econs., 1992-96, dir. grad. studies, 2005—; sr. economist, econ. policy Office Mgmt. & Budget, Washington, 1990-91. Acad. visitor Stanford (Calif.) U., 1980, London Sch. Econ., 1987-88; vis. assoc. prof. U. Pa., Phila., 1982-83; vis. scholar Congrl. Budget Office, 1997-98; cons., advisor in field. Mem. editl. bd. Jour. Income Distbn., Amsterdam, 1992—; contbr. articles to profl. jour.; Hon. Rsch. Fellow, Univ. Coll., London, 2003. Grantee NSF, Social Security Adminstrn., U.S. Dept. Health and Human Svcs.; recipient Best Article of Yr. award Econ. Inquiry, 1987. Mem. Am. Econ. Assn., Nat. Tax Assn., Nat. Bur. Econ. Rsch. Conf. on Income & Wealth. Avocations: bowling, racquetball, golf, travel, camping. Office: Mich State U 101 Marshall Hall E Circle Dr East Lansing MI 48824 Home Phone: 517-349-5261; Office Phone: 517-355-4553. Business E-Mail: menchik@msu.edu.

MENDE, HOWARD SHIGEHARU, mechanical engineer; b. Hilo, Hawaii, Nov. 19, 1947; s. Tsutomu and Harue (Kubomitsu) M. BS in Mech. Engring., U. Hawaii, 1969; MS in Mech. Engring., U. So. Calif., 1975. Registered profl. engr., Calif. Mem. tech. staff I Rockwell Internat., Anaheim, Calif., 1970-71, LA, 1971-73, mem. tech. staff II, 1973-77, mem. tech. staff IV, 1984-86; devel. engr. AiRsch. Mfg. Co., Torrance, Calif., 1977-83; mech. engr. Def. Contracts Mgmt. East, Santa Ana, Calif., 1987-94, electronics engr., 1994—. Lectr. Pacific States U., LA, 1974-75. Mem. ASME. Democrat. Buddhist. Home: 1946 W 180th Pl Torrance CA 90504-4417 Office: Def Contract Mgmt Agy 2000 E Imperial Hwy El Segundo CA 90245-2463 Personal E-mail: hmende@socal.rr.com. Business E-Mail: howard.mende@dcma.mil.

MENDE, ROBERT GRAHAM, retired engineering association executive; b. Newark, Dec. 4, 1926; s. Herman Ernest and Etta (Hillenbrand) M.; m. Joan B. Tamlyn, Apr. 12, 1958; children: Lisa Anne, Robert Graham Jr. Student, Mass. Inst. Tech., 1944-45; degree, N.Y. State Maritime Acad., 1947; BS, Webb Inst. Naval Architecture, 1951. Project engr. Foster Wheeler Corp., NYC, 1953-56; dist. mgr., naval architect Bird-Johnson Co., NYC, 1956-62; sr. naval architect J.J. Henry Co., Inc., NYC, 1962-69; exec. dir. Soc. Naval Architects and Marine Engrs., 1969-91. Mem. marine engring. coun. Underwriters Labs., Inc., 1969-91; ad hoc vis. com. Engrs. Coun. for Profl. Devel., 1970-72. Bd. dirs. Friends of World Maritime U., 1987-91; trustee Webb Inst. Naval Architecture, 1987-91. Lt. USNR, 1951-53. Fellow Royal Inst. Naval Architects, Soc. Naval Architect and Marine Engrs. (hon. life v.p., chmn. N.Y. sect. 1968-69, Vice Admiral E.S. Jerry Land medal 1991, Robert G. Mende Bldg. hdqrs. bldg. named in his honor); mem. ASME, Am. Soc. Naval Engrs., Am. Soc. Assn. Execs., Coun. Engring. and Sci. Soc. Execs. (bd. dirs. 1988-91), Maritime Coll. Assn., N.E. Coast Inst. Engrs. and Shipbuilders, Webb Alumni Assn. (pres. 1970-72). Personal E-mail: robertgmende@aol.com. *Hard work, perseverance, humility and a dash of deprivation almost always insure success. It also doesn't hurt to be in the right place at the right time.*

MENDEL, JERRY MARC, electrical engineering educator; b. NYC, May 14, 1938; s. Alfred and Eleanor (Deutch) M.; m. Letty Susan Grossman, June 26, 1960; children: Jonathan, Aileen. BMechE cum laude, Poly. U., 1959, MEE, 1960, PhD in Elec. Engring., 1963. Registered profl. engr., Calif. Instr. elec. engring. Poly. Inst. Bklyn., 1960—63; engring. scientist and sect. chief McDonnell-Douglas Astronautics Co., Huntington Beach, Calif., 1963-74; prof. dept. elec. engring. systems U. So. Calif., LA, 1974—, chmn. dept., 1984-91, dir. Signal and Image Processing Inst., 1991-94, assoc. dir. edn. Integrated Media Sys. Ctr., 1996—2004. Pres., founder MENTECH, Culver City, Calif., 1983—; pres. United Signals and Systems, Inc., 1989-2001. Author: Discrete Techniques of Parameter Estimation: The Equation Error Formulation, 1973, Optimal Seismic Deconvolution: An Estimation Based Approach, 1983 (Phi Kappa Phi award 1984), Lessons in Digital Estimation Theory, 1987, Maximum-Likelihood Deconvolution, 1990, Lessons in Estimation Theory for Signal Processing, Communications and Control, 1995; editor: Prelude to Neural Networks: Adaptive and Learning Systems, 1994, Uncertain Rule-Based Fuzzy Logic Systems: Introduction and New Directions, 2001; co-editor: Adaptive Learning and Pattern Recognition Systems, 1970. Fellow IEEE (Centennial medal 1984, Third Millennium medal 2000), IFSA; mem. IEEE Control Systems Soc. (Disting.; pres. 1986), IEEE Computational Intelligence Soc.(AdCom 2004-; Fuzzy Sys. Pioneer award, 2008). Office: U So Calif Dept Elec Engring Sys Eeb 400 Los Angeles CA 90089-2564 Home Phone: 310-837-1993; Office Phone: 213-740-4445. Business E-Mail: mendel@sipi.usc.edu.

MENDEL, JOHN W., automotive executive; With US ops. divsn. Ford Motor Co., 1976, various sales mktg. positions Lincoln Mercury divsn., major markets/dealer advt. mgr., 1990—92, regional ops. mgr. Chgo., 1992, San Francisco, LA, 1993—98, dir. mktg. Ford of Britain, 1999—2002, exec. v.p., COO Mazda N.Am. ops., 2002—04; sr. v.p. automobile ops. Honda/Acura divsn. Am. Honda Motor Co., Inc., 2004—. Bd. dirs. XM Satellite Radio Holdings Inc., 2005—08, Sirius XM Radio, Inc., 2008—. Named a Power Player, Advt. Age, 2008. Office: Am Honda Motor Co 1919 Torrance Blvd Torrance CA 90501 Office Fax: 310-783-3023. Business E-Mail: john_mendel@ahm.honda.com.*

MENDEL, TRACI, composer, educator; b. Lafayette, La., Aug. 26, 1964; d. Raymond Frank Mendel and Norma Nell Noonan. MusD in Music Composition, Fla. State U., Tallahassee, 2002, MusM in Music Composition, 1997; MusB in Theory and Composition, Centenary Coll. La., Shreveport, 1990. Adj. instr. music theory and composition Birmingham-Southern Coll., Ala., 2004—05; adj. instr. music theory and aural skills Appalachian State U., Boone, NC, 2005—. Mem.: Coll. Music Soc., Soc. Composers, Inc., Am. Composers Forum, ASCAP. Office: Appalachian State Univ Hayes Sch ASU Box 32096 Boone NC 28608-2096 Business E-Mail: mendeltr@appstate.edu.

MENDELEJIS, LEONARDO NIERMAN, artist; b. Mexico City, Nov. 1, 1932; s. Chanel and Clara (Mendelejis) N.; m. Esther Ptak, Feb. 16, 1957; children: Monica, Daniel, Claudia. BS in Physics and Math, U. Mexico; degree in bus. adminstrn., U. Mex., 1959, degree in music, degree (hon.), 1960, Concordia U., 1994. One-man shows, Proteo Gallery, 1958, 60, C.D.I. Gallery, 1956, Misrachi Gallery, 1964, Galeria Merkup, 1969, Mus. Modern Art, 1972, all Mexico City, Galeria Sudamericana, N.Y.C., 1958, Hammer Galleries, N.Y.C., 1960, I.F.A. Galleries, Washington, 1952, 62, 65, 68, 71, Edgardo Acosta Gallery, Beverly Hills, Calif., 1961, Art Collectors Gallery, Beverly Hills, 1966, Main St. Gallery, Chgo., 1961, Doll & Richard Gallery, Boston, 1963, Pucker Safrai Gallery, Boston, 1969, El Paso (Tex.) Mus Art, 1964, 71, Wolfard's Gallery, Rochester, N.Y., 1964, Pub. Library Rockville Centre, N.Y., 1964, Little Gallery, Phila., 1964, Neusteters Gallery Fine Arts, Denver, 1965, Judah L. Magnes Meml. Mus., Berkeley, Calif., 1967, Galerie Katia Granoff, Paris, 1969, Little Gallery, Phila., 1970, Aalwin Gallery, London, 1970, Gallery Modern Art, Scottsdale, Ariz., 1971, Mus. Contemporary Arts, Bogota, Colombia, 1973, 74, Galerie Dresdnere, Ont., Can., Casa de la Cultura, Cucuta, Colombia, 1974, also mus., galleries, Haifa, Israel, Rome, Italy, Toronto, Ont., Can., Paris, France, 1962—; exhibited group shows mus., Caracas, Venezuela, 1958, Mexico City, 1958—, Havana, Cuba, 1959, Tokyo, Japan, 1963, Paris, France, 1961, Nagoya, Japan, 1963, Kyoto, Japan, 1963, Osaka, Japan, 1963, Bogota, 1963, Santiago, Chile, 1963, Buenos Aires, Argentina, 1963, Rio de Janeiro, Brazil, 1963, Costa Rica, 1963, Panama, 1963, Oslo, Norway, 1965, Warsaw, Poland, 1965, Madrid, Spain, 1965, Stockholm, Sweden, 1966, Brussels, Belgium, 1966; also exhibitions at the Mus. Contemporary Art, Bogota, Colombia (diploma d'honneur of fine arts in Monaco), 1976, B. Lewin Galleries, Los Angeles, 1977, I.F. A. Galleries, Washington, 1977, Merrill Chase Galleries, Chgo., 1977, Am. Mus., Hayden Planetarium, N.Y.C., 1978, Cumberland Mus. of Sci. Ctr., Nashville, 1978, Fernback Sci. Ctr., Atlanta, 1978, Nahan Galleries, New Orleans, 1980, Broward Galleries, Pompano Beach, Fla., 1980, Mus. Sci. and Industry, Chgo., 1980, Galeria de Arte Misrachi, Mexico City, 1982, Calif. Mus. Sci. and Industry, 1982, Museo de Arte e Historia, Ciudad Juarez, Mexico, 1984, Centro de Artes Visuales e Investigaciones Esteticas, Mexico, 1984, Barbara Gillman Gallery, Miami, 1984, MIT Mus., Boston, 1984, Merrill Chase Galleries, Chgo., 1987, Museo de Arte Costarricense, Art Ctr. Galleries Hawaii Inc., 1988, Maison de L'Amerique Latine de Monaco, Monte Carlo, 1990, Centro Cultural San Angel, Mex.; also exhibited Expo, 1958, also numerous mus., univs., Eastern and Western U.S., Can., 1958—; executed murals, Sch. Commerce University City, Mexico, 1956, Bank San Francisco, 1965, physics bldg., Princeton, 1969; also executed stained glass windows, Mexican synagogues, 1968-69; executed tapestries Concert & Opera House, Salzburg, 1989, Majestic Theatre, San Antonio 1989, Theatre An Der Wein, Austria; prin. sculptures in including at Birmingham (Ala.) Mus. Art, Mexican Nat. U., Yeshiva U., N.Y., Hebrew U. Jerusalem, Sherman Bldg. Mount Scopus, City of Monterrey, Mex., Eleanor Roosevelt Inst., Denver, Wichita (Kans.) Airport; represented in permanent collections, Mus. Modern Art in Mexico, Atlanta Mus., Mus. Modern Art Haifa, Gallery Modern Art, N.Y.C., Phoenix Art Mus., Pan Am. Union, Washington, Detroit Inst. Arts, Bogota Mus. Contemporary Arts, Mus. Contemporary Arts, Madrid, Acad. Fine Arts, Honolulu, Tucson Art Center, Tel-Aviv Mus., Israel Mus., Jerusalem, Kennedy Art Center, Washington, Boston Mus. Fine Arts, U. Va., No. Ill. Univ., Chgo. Art Inst., New Orleans Mus. Art, other mus. and galleries. (Recipient 1st prize Mexican Contemporary Art, Art Inst. Mexico 1964, Palme d'or Beaux Arts, Monaco 1969, gold medal Tomasso Campanella Found. 1972). Patron Acad. St. Martin in the Fields, 1993—. Recipient Gold medal Internat. Parliament for Safety and Peace-U.S.A.-Italy, 1983; named Accademico D'Europe, Centro Studi di Ricerchi L'Accademia D'Europa, Italy; European Banner of Arts Prize, Italy, 1984, Oscar D'Italia, 1984; winner of world-wide competition to do a sculpture for U. Cen. Fla., Orlando, 1986. Life fellow Royal Soc. Arts (London, Eng.). Office: Reforma 16B San Angel 01000 Mexico City 20 Mexico also: Lublin Graphics 95 E Putnam Ave Greenwich CT 06830-5611

MENDELL, JERRY R., hospital administrator; s. Seymour and Dorothy Mendell; m. Joyce N. Mendell, Aug. 14, 1966; children: Felice S. Jenike, Rebecca I. Schmidt, Joshaa T. MD, U. Tex. Southwestern Med. Sch., Dallas, 1966. Cert. in medicine State Ohio, 1972. Rsch. scientist NIH, Bethesda, Md., 1969—72; physician and clinician scientist Ohio State U., Columbus, 1972—2008; dir., ctr. gene therapy Nationwide Children's Hosp., Columbus, 2004—. Contbr. scientific papers (Outstanding Clinician Scientist award, 2004). Comdr. US Pub. Health Svc., 1969—72, Bethesda. U54 grant, NINDS, NIH, 2007—. Fellow: Am. Acad. Neurology. Achievements include research in gene therapy for muscular dystrophy. Office: Nationwide Children's Hosp 700 Childrens Dr Columbus OH 43205

MENDELS, JOSEPH, psychiatrist, educator; b. Cape Town, South Africa, Oct. 29, 1937; came to U.S., 1964; s. Max and Lily (Turecki) M.; m. Ora Kark, Jan. 22, 1960; children: Gilla Avril, Charles Alan, David Ralph. MB, BChir, U. Cape Town, 1960; MD, U. Witwatersrand, Johannesburg, South Africa, 1965. Asst. prof., assoc. prof. psychiatry and pharmacology U. Pa., Phila., 1967-73; prof. U. Pa. and VA Hosp., Phila., 1973-80; med. dir. Fairmount Inst., Phila., 1980-81; hon. prof. psychiatry and human behavior Thomas Jefferson Med. Ctr., 1985—; med. dir. Med. Inst., Phila., 1981-95, Therapeutics PC, Phila., 1981-98. Cons., lectr. in field. Author, editor: Concepts of Depression, 1971, Biological Psychiatry, 1973, Psychobiology of Affective Disorders, 1981; contbr. over 200 articles to med. jours. V.p., mem. bd. govs. Am. Jewish Com. Fellow Internat. Coll. Neuropsychopharmacology, Am. Coll. Neuropsychopharmacology. Personal E-mail: jos737@comcast.net.

MENDELSOHN, DANIEL, writer, humanities professor; b. Long Island, NY, 1960; BA summa cum laude in Jour., U. Va., 1982; PhD Mellon Fell. in Humanities, Princeton U., 1994. Weekly book critic NY Mag., 2000—02; freelance jour., 2002—; lectr., dept. Classics Princeton U., 1994—2002; Charles Ranlett Flint Professor of Humanities Bard Coll., 2002—. Contbr. articles NY Times, New Yorker, NY Review of Books, Esquire Mag., The Nation, The Paris Review (Nat. Book Critics Circle award for Reviewing, 2001); author: (memoirs) The Elusive Embrace: Desire and the Riddle of Identity, 1999 (NY Times Notable Book Yr., 1999), The Lost: A Search for Six of Six Million, 2006 (Nat. Books Critics Circle award for Autobiography, 2006); contbr. chapters to books incl. Best Am. Travel Writing, Republicans Can Be Cured!, Best

Am. Humor Writing. Recipient George Jean Nathan Prize for Drama Criticism; grantee Guggenheim Fell., 2005. Office: c/o Paradigm Agency 360 N Crescent Dr Beverly Hills CA 90210 Office Fax: 310-288-2000.

MENDELSOHN, DAVID EDWARD, lawyer; b. London, July 7, 1964; arrived in US, 1988; LLB, U. Coll. London, 1985; grad., Lancaster Gate Sch. Law, London, 1986; JD, Chgo.-Kent Coll. Law, 1991; Assoc. in Reins. Designation, Ins. Inst. Am., 1995, cert. completion in ins. regulation, 1996. Articled clk. Macfarlanes, London, 1986—88; assoc. DLA Piper and predecessor firms, Chgo., 1988—95, ptnr., 1996—. Mem.: Assn. Fellows and Legal Scholars Ctr. Internat. Legal Studies. Office: DLA Piper US LLP 203 N LaSalle St Chicago IL 60601

MENDELSOHN, JANIS S., pediatrician, educator; b. Fort Smith, Ark., Aug. 02; MD, U. Tenn., 1967. Cert. Pediat., 1973. Intern genetics Children's Meml. Hosp., Chgo., 1968—69, resident, 1969—71, fellowship; pediatrician U. Chgo. Med. Ctr., 1972—; assoc. prof. pediat. U. Chgo. Mem.: Am. Acad. Pediat., Chgo. Pediat. Soc. Office: Ctr Advanced Medicine 5841 S Maryland Ave, MC 1057 Chicago IL 60637 Office Phone: 773-702-6169, 773-834-3862, 773-834-3826. E-mail: jmendels@peds.bsd.uchicago.edu.

MENDELSOHN, LOUIS BENJAMIN, financial analyst; b. Providence, Mar. 26, 1948; s. Alvin Harold and Frances (Leitner) M.; m. Illyce Deborah Greenspan, Aug. 29, 1976; children: Lane Jeffrey, Ean Graham, Forrest Lee. BS, Carnegie Mellon U., 1969; MSW, SUNY, Buffalo, 1973; MBA with hons., Boston U., 1977. Rsch. asst. Mass. Gen. Hosp., Boston, 1969-71; regional health planner Comprehensive Health Planning Coun., Buffalo, 1973-74; adminstv. resident New Eng. Hosp., Boston, 1976; mgmt. specialist Humana Hosp. Bennett, Ft. Lauderdale, Fla., 1977-78; asst. exec. dir. Humana Women's Hosp., Tampa, Fla., 1978-80; pres., CEO Market Techs. Corp., Wesley Chapel, Fla., 1979—, CEO, 2004—, Predictive Techs. Group LLC, Wesley Chapel, 2004—. Author: Trend Forecasting with Techinal Analysis: Unleashing the Hidden Power of Intermarket Analysis to Beat the Market, 2000, Forex Trading Using Intermarket Analysis, 2006, Trend Forecasting with Intermarket Analysis: Predicting Global Markets with Technical Analysis, 2008; contbg. rschr.: The Encyclopedia of Technical Market Indicators, 1988; contbg. author: High Performance Futures Trading, 1990, Virtual Trading, 1995, Artificial Intelligence in the Capital Markets, 1995, Trade Your Way to Financial Freedom, 1999, Trading Chicago Style, 1999, SFO Personal Investor Series: Forex Trading, 2009; contbg. writer Tech. Analysis of Stocks and Commodities Mag.; editor newsletter Neural-Financial News, 1991; developer investment software ProfitTaker, 1979—, VantagePoint, 1988—. USPHS fellow, 1975-77. Mem. Market Technicians Assn., Colleague Internat. Fedn. of Tech. Analysts, Beta Gamma Sigma. Achievements include pioneering strategy backtesting and optimization in technical analysis software for personal computers, 1983; introduction of first commercial strategy testing trading software in financial industry for personal computers and first intermarket analysis software in financial industry for personal computers. Office: Mkt Techs LLC 5807 Old Pasco Rd Wesley Chapel FL 33544-5108 Office Phone: 813-973-0496. E-mail: ww@tradertech.com.

MENDELSOHN, MARTIN, lawyer; b. Bkyln., Sept. 6, 1942; s. Hyman and Gertrude M.; m. Syma Barbara Rossman, Aug. 15, 1964; children: Alice S., James D. BA, Bklyn. Coll., 1963; LLB, George Washington U., DC, 1966. Bar: DC 1967, Ill., 1973, NY, 2003, US Ct. Appeals (DC cir.) 1967, US Supreme Ct. 1970, US Ct. Appeals (3d cir.) 1971, US Ct. Appeals (7th cir.) 1973, Ill. 1973, US Ct. Appeals (9th cir.) 1987, US Tax Ct. 1988, US Ct. Appeals (2d cir.) 1988, US Ct. of Appeals (5th cir.) 2000, US Ct. Appeals (4th cir.) 2002, US Ct. Appeals (8th cir.) 2004. With Gen. Counsel's Office, HEW, Washington, 1966—67; legal svcs. Washington, 1967—70, Pa., 1971—72, Ill., 1973—75; counsel Legal Svcs. Corp., Washington, 1976; adminstrv. asst. US Congress, Washington, 1977; chief spl. litigation US Dept. Justice, Washington, 1977—79, dep. dir. office spl. investigations, 1979—80; counsel House Judiciary Com., 1980; pvt. practice Washington, 1980—88; ptnr. Dilworth, Paxon, Kalish & Kauffman, 1989—91, Verner, Liipfert, Bernhard, McPherson & Hand, 1991—2002, Schnader, Harrison, Segal and Lewis, Washington, 2002—. Author: (with Aaron Freiwald) The Last Nazi, 1994. Decorated officer Order of Merit (Poland), medal of honor Czech Republic; recipient Grand Decoration of High Honor, Austria, 2002, Disting. Achievement in Law award, Bklyn. Coll. Alumni Assn., 2007; named Advocate for Justice, Olender Found., 2007. Mem.: ABA, DC Bar Assn., Cosmos Club. Jewish. Home: 5705 Mckinley St Bethesda MD 20817-3638 Office: 2001 Pennsylvania Ave NW Ste 300 Washington DC 20006 Office Phone: 202-419-4220. Business E-Mail: martinmendelsohn@verizon.net.

MENDELSOHN, ROBERT, educator; b. Mar. 15, 1952; BA, Harvard U., 1973; PhD, Yale U., 1978. Asst. prof. U. Wash., Seattle, 1978-83; assoc. prof. Yale U., New Haven, Conn., 1984-89, prof., 1989-94, Edwin Weyerhauser Davis prof., 1994—. Office: 360 Prospect St New Haven CT 06511-2104

MENDELSON, ALAN CHARLES, lawyer; b. San Francisco, Mar. 27, 1948; s. Samuel Mendelson and Rita Rosalie (Spindel) Brown; children: Jonathan Daniel, David Gary; m. Agnès Marie Barbariol. BA with great distinction, U. Calif., Berkeley, 1969; JD cum laude, Harvard U., 1973. Bar: Calif. 1973. Assoc. Cooley Godward LLP, San Francisco, 1973-80, ptnr. Palo Alto, 1980-2000, mng. ptnr. Palo Alto office, 1990-95, 96-97; sec. acting gen. counsel Amgen Inc., Thousand Oaks, Calif., 1990-91; acting gen. counsel Cadence Design Sys., Inc., San Jose, Calif., 1995-96; sr. ptnr. Latham & Watkins LLP, Menlo Park, Calif., 2000—. Co-chair emerging cos. group Latham & Watkins; mem. bd. advisors Santa Clara Computer and High Tech. Law Jour., 2004—08; bd. adv. UC Berklay Chemistry Dept., 2007—; bd. dirs. Biotech. Industry Orgn., 2004—; mem. US Bd. Dir., Rambam Hosp. Bd. dirs. Bay Bio, pres. Calif. Alumni Assn., 2009—; chmn. Piedmont (Calif.) Civil Svc. Commn., 1978-80; fundraiser Harvard Law Sch. Fund, U. Calif. Berkeley Health Scis. Initiative, Lucille Packard Children's Hosp.; pres., mem. exec. com., bd. dirs. No. Calif. chpt. Nat. Kidney Found., 1986-98; mem. Overseers' Com. to visit Harvard Law Sch., 2005—.bd. trustee U. Calif. Berkley Found., 2008-, With USAR, 1969-75. Recipient Disting. Svc. award Nat. Kidney Found., 1992; named U. Calif. Berkeley Alumni scholar, 1966, Scaife Found. scholar, 1966, One of 100 Most Influential Attys. in U.S. Nat. Law Jour., 1994, 97, 2000, 06. Mem. Bohemian Club, Phi Beta Kappa. Jewish. Home: 76 De Bell Dr Atherton CA 94027-2253 Office: Latham & Watkins LLP 140 Scott Dr Menlo Park CA 94025 Home Phone: 650-853-1343; Office Phone: 650-463-4693. Business E-Mail: alan.mendelson@lw.com.

MENDELSON, ELLIOTT, mathematician, educator; b. NYC, May 24, 1931; s. Joseph and Helen (Bienstock) M.; m. Arlene Zimmerman, Jan. 25, 1959; children: Julia, Hilary, Peter. AB, Columbia U., 1952; MA, Cornell U., 1954, PhD, 1955. Instr. U. Chgo., 1955-56; jr. fellow Soc. Fellows, Harvard U., 1956-58; Ritt instr. Columbia U., 1958-61; mem. faculty Queens Coll., CUNY, 1961—, prof. math., 1965—. Dir., instr. NSF math. program for high sch. students, 1964-71; researcher axiomatic set theory and math. logic, especially ind. various important propositions of axiomatic set theory, axiom of choice, axiom of restriction; participant NSF Time 2000 Project for future secondary sch. math. tchrs., 1998—. Author: Introduction to Mathematical Logic, 1997, Boolean Algebra and Switching Circuits, 1970, Number Systems, 1973, Beginning Calculus, 1997, 3000 Solved Problems in Calculus, 1988, Differential and Integral Calculus, 1997, Quick Calculus, 1999, Introducing Game Theory and Its Applications, 2004; contbr. articles to profl. jours. Mem. Am. Math. Soc., Math. Assn. Am., Assn. for Symbolic Logic, Phi Beta Kappa. Home: 10 Pinewood Rd Roslyn NY 11576-2420 Office: Queens Coll Dept Math Flushing NY 11367 Office Phone: 516-621-0313. Personal E-mail: emenqc@msn.com.

MENDELSON, JOAN RINTEL, lawyer; b. NYC, July 19, 1941; d. Leon and Myra Rintel; m. Neil H. Mendelson, July 30, 1959; children: Debora C., Marie Mendelson Piccarreta. BA with high distinction, with honors in Zoology, Ind. U., 1962, MA, 1963; JD, U. Ariz., 1974. Bar: Ariz. 1975. Co-founder and co-dir. Catonsville Coop. Nursery Sch., Md., 1967—69; assoc. Law Offices of Ann Bowen, Tucson, 1975—76; pvt. practice Tucson, 1977—80; asst. atty. gen. Office of Atty. Gen., Tucson, 1980—2000. Instr. biology U. Md. Balt. County, Catonsville, 1968; spl. magistrate Tucson City Ct., 1984—91; mem. Pima County Child Fatality Rev. Bd., Tucson, 1982—; mem. legal counsel Gov.'s Task Force on Sch. Age Child Care, Phoenix, 1984—86; mem. Pima County Citizen Rev. Bd., Tucson, 2000—; mem. child abuse team Ariz. Health Scis. Ctr., Tucson, 1983—2000; mem. ad hoc com. on child protective svcs. and related child welfare issues Ariz. Legislature, Phoenix, 1994—2000, mem. legal and statutory reform subcom. ad hoc com. on child protective svcs. and related child welfare issues, 1994—2000, chair sys. and policy changes subcom. ad hoc com. on child protective svcs. and related child welfare issues, 1996—2000; mem. model ct. steering com. Pima County Juvenile Ct., Tucson, 1996—2000, mem. model ct. workgroup, 1998—2000; mem. emergency juvenile rules com. Ariz. Supreme Ct., Phoenix, 1998—99, mem. juvenile rules com., 1999—2000, mem. ct. improvement project adv. workgroup, 1998—2003; mem. Pima County Interagency Task Forces on Custodial Interference, Tucson, 1997—2000, Pima County Child Adv. Ctr. Adv. Bd., Tucson, 1997—99; mem. child adv. clinic adv. bd. Coll. Law U. Ariz., Tucson, 1998. Recipient Friend of the Ct. award, Pima County Juvenile Ct., 2006; fellow, Ford Found., 1961, NSF, 1962; NY State Regents scholar, 1958. Mem.: Sigma Xi, Phi Beta Kappa. Personal E-mail: njmend@earthlink.net.

MENDELSON, JOEL STUART, allergist, immunologist; b. Bklyn., Nov. 2, 1956; BS, Bklyn. Coll., 1978; MD, U. Ctrl. East Dominican Rep., 1982. Diplomate Am. Bd. Allergy/Immunology, Am. Bd. Pediatrics, Am. Bd. Pediatric Infectious Diseases. Pres. pedicatrics St. Lukes Roosevelt Med. Ctr./Columbia U., NYC, 1982-85; fellow allergy, immunology and infectious disease U. Med. and Dentistry N.J., Newark, 1985-87; asst. dir. dept. allergy and immunology Childrens Hosp. N.J., Newark, 1987-88; dir. dept. allergy and immunology Beth Israel Med. Ctr., Newark, 1992—; asst. prof. pediat. St. George U. Med. Sch. Cons. in field. Contbr. articles to profl. jours. Fellow Am. Acad. Allergy and Immunology, Am. Coll. Allergy and Immunology, Am. Acad. Pediatrics; mem. Infectious Disease Soc. N.J. Home: 17 Dartmouth Rd Cranford NJ 07016-1651 Office Phone: 908-233-4477. Personal E-mail: jmendelsonmd@msn.com.

MENDELSON, NEIL H., microbial geneticist, educator; b. NYC, Nov. 15, 1937; s. Michael and Rose (Kutner) M.; m. Joan F. Rintel, July 30, 1959; children: Debora C., Marie D. BS, Cornell U., 1959; PhD, Ind. U., 1964. Postdoctoral fellow microbial genetics rsch. unit Med. Rsch. Coun., Hammersmith Hosp., London, 1965-66; asst. prof. U. Md., Catonsville, 1967-69; assoc. prof. U. Ariz., Tucson, 1969-72, prof., 1972—. Vis. prof. Inst. Pasteur, Paris, 1976-77; vis. scientist Cambridge (Eng.) U., 1984, 91. Author: Collected Papers of Neil. H. Mendelson, 2004, Perfect Mistakes, 2005; Contbr. over 80 articles to scholarly and profl. jours. Contrebassist So. Ariz. Symphony Orch., Tucson, 1979—, pres., 1983-86, 90-93. Recipient Rsch. Career Devel. award Nat. Inst. Gen. Med. Sci., 1973-77, J.A. Shannon Dir.'s award Nat. Ctr. for Rsch. Resources NIH, 1992; N.H. Mendelson Collection named in his honor Am. Heritage Ctr., U. Wyo., 1986—. Fellow AAAS, Am. Acad. Microbiology; mem. Cosmos. Jewish. Achievements include discovery of bacterial macrofibers, producer of bacterial thread and related bionites; invention of helix clock theory. Office: U Ariz Molecular & Cellular Biology LSS Bldg Tucson AZ 85721-0106 Business E-Mail: nhm@u.arizona.edu.

MENDELSON, RICHARD DONALD, former communications company executive; b. NYC, Dec. 2, 1933; s. George and Martha (Goodman) M.; m. Marilyn Miller, July 28, 1956; children: Sandra, Kenneth. BS, Wharton Sch. U. Pa., 1955; JD, NYU, 1959. Bar: N.Y., 1960; CPA, N.Y. Asst. atty. gen. N.Y. State Dept. Law, NYC, 1959-70; v.p., treas. Petry TV, NYC, 1971-75; v.p., dir. corp. devel. Katz Communications, Inc., NYC, 1975-77, sr. v.p. ops., 1977-79, sr. v.p., chief fin. officer, 1979-81, exec. v.p., chief operating officer, 1981-82, pres., chief oper. officer, 1982-89; free-lance writer, 1989—. Mem. Employee Stock Ownership Assn. Am. (pres. 1987-88, bd. dirs.), Ballen Isles Country Club (Palm Beach Gardens, Fla.l bd. dirs. 2000-06, pres. 2006). Home and Office: 71 Saint George Pl Palm Beach Gardens FL 33418-4024 Personal E-mail: themeri@aol.com.

MENDELSON, ROBERT ALLEN, polymer scientist, rheologist; b. Cleve., 1930; s. Julius and Theodora Anne M.; m. Lura Lauzon, 1971 (dec. 1999); children: John A. Blackstone, Marie L. Taylor. BS in Indsl. Chemistry, Case Inst. Tech., 1952, PhD in Phys. Chemistry, 1956. From sr. rsch. chemist to sci. fellow rsch. dept. Monsanto Co., Texas City, Tex., 1956-71, sci. fellow Springfield, Mass., 1972-89, sr. sci. fellow, 1989-91; rheology focus area leader Baytown (Tex.) Polymers Ctr. Exxon Chem., 1991-94, rheology prin. investigator, 1995-99; ret., 1999; cons., rheology, IP, 2000—02. Mem. com. for pub. policy Am. Inst. Physics, 1985-89; collaborator Univ. Rsch. Programs, Cornell U., 1989-91. Mem. editl. bd. Journal of Rheology, 1986-99; contbr. chpts. to books and articles to profl. jours.; patentee in field. Mem. AAAS, Soc. Rheology (pres. 1989-91, v.p. 1987-89, sec. 1974-78), Am. Chem. Soc. (Arthur Doolittle award div. organic coatings and plastics 1982). Home: 5001 Woodway Dr Unit 1803 Houston TX 77056-1701

MENDENHALL, BRONCO, college football coach; b. Alpine, Utah; s. Paul Mendenhall; m. Holly Johnston; children: Cutter, Breaker, Raeder. Attended, Snow Coll., Ephraim, Utah, 1984—85; BS in Phys. Edn., Oreg. State U., Corvallis, 1988, MEd in Exercise Physiology, 1990. Grad. asst., defensive line coach Oreg. State U. Beavers, 1989—90, defensive line coach, 1995, defensive coord., secondary coach, 1996, Snow Coll. Badgers, 1991—92; secondary coach No. Ariz. U. Lumberjacks, 1993—94, co-defensive coord., 1994; secondary coach La. Tech. U. Bulldogs, 1997; defensive coord., secondary coach U. N.Mex. Lobos, 1998—2002, asst. head coach, 2002; defensive coord. Brigham Young U. Cougars, 2003—04, head football coach, 2005—. Recipient Leo Gribkoff Meml. award, Oreg. State U., 1987; named Asst. Coach of Yr., BYU Cougar Club, 2003, Region IV Coach of Yr., Am. Football Coaches Assn., 2006; finalist Eddie Robinson Nat. Coach of Yr. award, 2006. Office: Brigam Young Univ Athletics Dept Student Athlete Bldg 220 SAB Provo UT 84602*

MENDENHALL, KATHLEEN F., art educator; d. James M. and Betty A. Flynn; m. Bruce J. Mendenhall, Aug. 3, 1968; 1 child, Amy F. Mendenhall-Mansfield. MA, U. Mo. Kans. City, 1999. Art edn. Paseo HS, Kans., 1968—88, Paseo Acad. Fine & Performing Arts, Kans., 1988—2002, dept. chair, 1993—2001; adj. prof. Avila U., Kans., 1999—, Johnson County CC, Overland Pk., Kans., 2001—. Visual art, Photography and Mixed Media. Recipient Outstanding Secondary Art Tchr. award, Dorothy's Sixty, 1996, Outstanding Art Educator award, Kans. City Art Inst., 2000, Alumni Art Tchr. of Yr. award, Avila U., 2007. Mem.: Soc. Contemporary Photographers. Office: Avila Univ Johnson CC 11901 Wornall Rd Kansas City MO 64145

MENDENHALL, MICHAEL, computer company executive; BS in Bus. Comm., Emerson Coll., Boston, 1984. Nemerous sr. mktg. positions The Walt Disney Co., 1990—2007, including pres. mktg. & synergy, exec. v.p. global mktg. Parks & Resorts, exec. v.p. mktg. & comm.; sr. v.p., chief mktg. officer Hewlett-Packard Co., 2007—. Bd. dirs. USA Swimming Found., San Gabriel Valley coun. Boy Scouts America. Named a Power Player, Advt. Age, 2008; named one of Best Marketers, BtoB Mag., 2008. Mem.: Exec. Mktg. Coun. (sr. adv. bd.), Acad. TV Arts & Scis., CMO Club, CMO Inner Cir., Mktg. 50. Office: Hewlett Packard Co 3000 Hanover St Palo Alto CA 94304-1185 Office Phone: 650-857-1501. Office Fax: 650-857-5518. Business E-Mail: michael.mendenhall@hp.com.*

MENDENHALL, ROBERT W., education technology executive; b. Pasadena, Calif., Nov. 18, 1954; s. Winton L. and Margaret E. (Kerr) Mendenhall; m. Kathleen A. White, 1978; children: Jamie, Robert, Christina, Virginia, Kathleen, Lori, Emily. BS in Univ. Studies, Brigham Young U., Provo, Utah, 1977, PhD in Instrnl. Psychology and Tech., 2003. Gen. mgr. Wicat Inst., Orem, Utah, 1977-80; pres., dir. Wicat Systems Inc., Orem, Utah, 1980—92; exec. v.p., dir. Jostens Learning Corp., San Diego, 1992—94; gen. mgr. IBM K-12 Edn., Atlanta, 1994—96, exec. cons., 1997—98; pres. Western Govs. U., Salt Lake City, 1999—. Mem. bd. bus. and econ. devel. State of Utah, 1997—2001; mem. Commn. Tech. and Adult Learning, 1999—2000; adv. bd. Partnership for 21st Century Skills, 2003—04; mem. Sec. of Edn.'s Commn. on Future of Edn., 2005—06. Missionary and bishop LDS Ch.; bd. dir. Oquirrh Inst., 2002—07; bd. dir. and chair Gina Bachauer Internat. Piano Found., 1980—2000. Office: Western Gov U Ste 700 4001 South 700 East Salt Lake City UT 84107 Office Phone: 801-274-3280. Business E-Mail: rwm@wgu.edu.

MENDES, EVA, actress; b. Houston, Mar. 5, 1974; Spokesperson Revlon Cosmetics. Actor: (films) A Night at the Roxbury, 1998, My Brother the Pig, 1999, Urban Legends: Final Cut, 2000, Exit Wounds, 2001, Training Day, 2001, All About the Benjamins, 2002, 2 Fast 2 Furious, 2003, Once Upon a Time in Mexico, 2003, Out of Time, 2003, Stuck on You, 2003, Hitch, 2005, The Wendell Baker Story, 2005, Trust the Man, 2005, 3 & 3, 2005, Ghost Rider, 2007, Live!, 2007, We Own the Night, 2007, Cleaner, 2007, The Women, 2008, The Spirit, 2008; (TV films) The Disciples, 2000; TV appearances include: ER, 1998; Mortal Kombat: Conquest, 1998; VIP, 1999. Office: c/o Creative Artist Agy 9830 Wilshire Blvd Beverly Hills CA 90212-1825

MÉNDEZ, CARLOS (DON CARLOS MÉNDEZ MARTÍNEZ), political organization administrator, mayor; s. Don Pablo Méndez and Dona Rosita Martinez. Studied at, U. Washington. Mayor, Aguadilla City, PR, 1996—; chmn. Rep. Party of PR, 2007—. Pres. Fedn. of Mayors of PR, 2003—04. Office: Rep Party of PR 1629 Pinero Ave, Ste 203 San Juan PR 00920 Office Phone: 787-793-8084.*

MENDEZ, CELESTINO GALO, mathematics professor, dean; b. Havana, Cuba, Oct. 16, 1944; came to the U.S., 1962; naturalized, 1970. s. Celestino Andres and Georgina (Fernandez) M.; m. Mary Ann Koplau, Aug. 21, 1971; children: Mark Michael, Matthew Maximilian. BA, Benedictine Coll., 1965; MA, U. Colo., 1968, PhD, 1974, MBA, 1979. Asst. prof. maths. scis. Met. State Coll., Denver, 1971-77, assoc. prof., 1977-82, prof., 1982—2002, chmn. dept. math. scis., 1980—83, asst to the v.p. for acad. affairs/provost, 1989—91; vis. assoc. prof. math. U. Mich., Ann Arbor, 2002—03; asst. dir. math program, lectr. dept. applied math. U. Colo., Boulder, 2003—05; dean Coll. Arts and Scis. N.Mex. Highlands U., Las Vegas, N.Mex., 2005—08, prof. math., 2005—08, asst. vice pres., acad. affairs, 2007—08; dean, Coll. Arts & Sci. Northern State U., Aberdeen, SD, 2008—. Assoc. editor Denver Met. Jour. Math. and Computer Sci., 1993—2001; contbr. articles to profl. jours. including Am. Math. Monthly, Procs. Am. Math. Soc., Jour. Personalized Instrn., Denver Met. Jour. Math. and Computer Sci. and newspapers. Mem. advt. rev. bd. Met. Denver, 1973-79; parish outreach rep. S.E. deanery, Denver Cath. Cmty. Svcs., 1976-78; mem. social ministries com. St. Thomas More Cath. Ch., Denver, 1976-78, vice-chmn., 1977-78, mem. parish coun., 1977-78; del. Adams County Rep. Conv., 1972, 74, 94, Colo. 4th Congl. Dist. Conv., 1974, Colo. Rep. Conv., 1982, 88, 90, 92, 96, 98, 2000, 02, 04, Douglas County Rep. Conv., 1980, 82, 84, 88, 90, 92, 94, 96, 98, 2000, 02, 04; alt. del. Colo. Rep. Conv., 1974, 76, 84, 2000, 5th Congl. dist. conv., 1976, mem. rules com., 1978, 80, precinct committeeman Douglas County Rep. Com., 1976-78, 89-92, mem. ctrl. com., 1976-78, 89-92; dist. 29 Rep. party candidate Colo. State Senate, 1990; mem. Colo. Rep. Leadership Program, 1989-90, bd. dirs., 1990-98; Douglas County chmn. Rep. Nat. Hispanic Assembly, 1989—95; bd. dirs. Rocky Mountain Better Bus. Bur., 1975-79, Rowley Downs Homeowners Assn., 1976-78; trustee Hispanic U. Am., 1975-78; councilman Town of Parker, Colo., 1981-84, chmn. budget and fin. com., 1981-84; chmn. joint budget com. Town of Parker-Parker Water and Sanitation Dist. Bds., 1982-84; commr. Douglas County Planning Commn., 1993-97; dir. Mile High Young Scholars Program, 1995-98. Recipient Excellence in Tchg. award U. Colo. Grad. Sch., 1965-67; grantee Benedictine Coll., 1964-65, Math. Assn. Am. SUMMA grantee Carnegie Found. N.Y., 1994; program dir., grantee NSF, 1995-98; nominated candidate for first v.p Math. Assn. Am., 1999, for 2d v.p., 2001. Mem. Math. Assn. Am. (referee rsch. notes sect. Am. Math. Monthly 1981-82, gov. Rocky Mountain sect. 1993-96, investment com. 1996-02, devel. com. 1995-01, task force on reps. 1994-96, sci. policy com. 2000-06, bd. govs. 1993-96, 2002-05, com. mem. 2005-08), Am. Math. Soc., Nat. Coun. Tchrs. Math., Colo. Coun. Tchrs. Math. (bd. dirs. 1994-96), Colo. Internat. Edn. Assn., Assoc. Faculties of State Insts. Higher Edn. in Colo. (v.p. 1971-73). Republican. Roman Catholic. Home: 612 W Paramount Dr Aberdeen SD 57401 Office: Northern State Univ Coll Arts & Sci 1200 S Jay St Aberdeen SD 57401 Office Phone: 605-626-2601. Business E-Mail: tino.mendez@northern.edu.

MENDEZ, JOHN ANTHONY, federal judge; b. Oakland, Calif., 1955; married; 3 children. BA, Stanford U., 1977; JD, Harvard Law Sch., 1980. Bar: Calif. 1980. Assoc. Chickering & Gregory, 1980—81, Orrick, Herrington and Sutcliffe, 1981—84; asst. US atty. (no. dist.)

Calif. US Dept. Justice, 1984—86, 1992—93; assoc., ptnr. Downey, Brand, Seymour and Rohwer, 1986—92; of counsel Brobeck, Phleger and Harrison, 1993—95; shareholder Somach, Simmons and Dunn, 1995—2001; judge Sacramento County Superior Ct., Calif., 2001—07, US Dist. Ct. (ea. dist.) Calif., 2008—. Bd. dirs. Children's Receiving Home. Instr., lector, Eucharistic min. Cath. Ch., Calif. Mem.: Rotary. Office: US Dist Ct 501 I St Ste 4-200 Sacramento CA 95814 Office Phone: 916-930-4000.

MENDEZ, ROSIE, city councilwoman; b. NYC, Feb. 28, 1963; BA, NYU; JD, Rutgers Univ., Newark, 1995. IOLA Legal Services Fellow Bklyn. Legal Services, 1995; chief of staff to City Councilwoman Margarita Lopez; city councilwoman Dist. 2 NY City Coun., 2006—. Chmn. Pub. Housing com. NY City Coun. Democrat. Office: 237 First Ave Suite 504 New York NY 10003 Office Phone: 212-677-1077. Office Fax: 212-677-1990. Business E-Mail: rmendez@council.nyc.gov.*

MENDEZ, RUBEN POLICARPIO, diplomat, educator, economist; b. Manila, Philippines, Jun 28, 1933; came to US, 1948; s. Mauro and Paz Policarpio M.; m. Matilda Currier McEwen, Apr. 8, 1961; children: Katherine McEwen, Tomas Currier. AB cum laude, Harvard U., 1953; MA, Columbia U., 1959; PhD, NYU, 1984. Economist Merrill Lynch, Pierce, Fenner & Smith, NYC, 1959-63; econ. adviser to chmn. Nat. Econ. Coun., Manila, 1964-66; project officer UN Spl. Fund, NYC, 1963-65; various positions UN Devel. Program, NYC, Africa, Asia, 1966-93; chief econ. advisor UN Environ. Program, Nairobi, Kenya, 1977-81; prin. officer, historian UN Devel. Program, NYC, 1993—. Adj. prof., fellow, vis. lectr. NYU, 1991—, Columbia U., 1992, Yale U., 1994—; cons. Oxford U. Press, NY, 1999-2000; panelist academic and mixed intergovtl. confs. US, Europe and L.Am. Author: International Public Finance: A New Perspective on Global Relations, 1992 (and subsequent printings), History of the Riverdale Yacht Club, 2008; contbr. articles to profl. jours., chpts. to books. Yale rep. Acad. Coun. on UN Sys., 1997-98. Grantee Carnegie Corp., NYC, 1995-98, Internat. Devel. Rsch. Ctr., Ottawa, Can., 1994-97. Mem. Am. Econ. Assn., NY Acad. Scis., Soc. Internat. Devel., Harvard Club (NYC), Harvard Faculty Club, Riverdale Yacht Club, United Kenya Club (Nairobi). Avocations: history, philosophy, classical music, sailing, personal computer. Home: 313 W 263d St Riverdale Bronx NY 10471 E-mail: rpmendez@post.harvard.edu.

MENDEZ, VICTOR M., federal agency administrator; b. 1957; BS in Civil Engring., U. Tex., El Paso, 1980; MBA, Ariz. State U., Tempe, 1994. Registered profl. engr. in civil. engring., Ariz. Engr. US Forest Svc., Oreg., Ariz. Dept. Transp. (ADOT), 1985, engring. supr., asst. state engr. Statewide Project Mgmt., dep. state engr. Valley Transp. Group, 1997—99, dep. dir., 1999—2001, dir., 2001—09; adminstr. Fed. Hwy. Adminstrn. US Dept. Transp., Washington, 2009—. Pres. Western Assn. State Hwy. and Transp. Ofcls., 2007, Am. Assn. State Hwy. and Transp. Ofcls., 2007, chair standing com. rsch., chair ops. coun. of standing com. on hwys., chair Transp. Rsch. Bd./Nat. Cooperative Hwy. Rsch. Program oversight group for Long-Term Pavement Performance program. Named Leader of Yr. in Pub. Policy in Transp., Ariz. Capitol Times, 2008. Mem.: Am. Pub. Works Assn. Office: US Dept Transp Fed Hwy Adminstrn (FHA) 1200 New Jersey Ave SE Washington DC 20590 Office Phone: 202-366-4000.*

MENDEZ ASHLA, MARIO, neurologist, educator, internist; b. San Francisco, Oct. 11, 1948; s. Mario Mendez and Carmen Deferby; m. Mary Ashla, Nov. 26, 1982; children: Paul, Mark. MD, U. Tex., Galveston, 1974; PhD, Case We. Res. U., 1991. Diplomate Am. Bd. Internal Medicine, Am. Bd. Neurology. Prof. neurology and psychiatry and biobehavioral scis. UCLA, 1994—. Dir., neurobehavior unit VA Greater L.A., 1994—; dir., Frontotemporal and Focal Dementia Program UCLA, 2001—. Contbr. more than 150 articles to profl. jours. Office: VA Greater Los Angeles Healthcare 11301 Wilshire Blvd Los Angeles CA 90073

MENDILLO, JANE LISA, investment manager; b. 1958; d. Vincent F. Mendillo; m. Ralph Earle, June 14, 1986; children: Elizabeth, Thomas. BA in English, Yale U., 1980, MBA, 1984. Mgr. office of investments Yale U., New Haven, 1980—82; equities analyst Lord, Abbett, Inc., NYC, 1983; mgmt. cons. Bain & Co., Boston, 1984—87; equities analyst domestic stocks Harvard Mgmt. Co. (HMC), 1987—88, prin. private equity group, 1988—89, v.p. private equity, 1989—91, v.p. trusts, 1992—96, v.p. external mgmt., 1997—2002, pres., CEO, 2008—; chief investment officer Wellesley Coll., Wellesley, Mass., 2002—08. Mem. Yale U. Investment Com.; bd. mem. Investment Fund for Founds. Corporator Emerson Hosp. Recipient Industry Leadership award, 100 Women In Hedge Funds, 2007; named one of 100 Most Powerful Women, Forbes mag., 2008, 2009, 50 Women to Watch, The Wall St. Jour., 2008. Mem.: Boston Econ. Club, Boston Com. on Fgn. Rels., Boston Security Analysts Soc., Inc. Office: Harvard Mgmt Co 600 Atlantic Ave Boston MA 02210-2203 Office Phone: 617-523-4400.*

MENDIUS, PATRICIA DODD WINTER, retired editor, educator, writer; b. Davenport, Iowa, July 9, 1924; d. Otho Edward and Helen Rose (Dodd) Winter; m. John Richard Mendius, June 19, 1947; children: Richard, Catherine M. Graber, Louise, Karen M. Chooljian. BA cum laude, UCLA, 1946; MA cum laude, U. N.Mex., 1966. Cert. secondary edn. tchr., Calif., N.Mex. English tchg. asst. UCLA, 1946—47; English tchr. Marlborough Sch. for Girls, LA, 1947—50, Aztec (N.Mex.) HS, 1953—55, Farmington (N.Mex.) HS, 1955—63; chair English dept. Los Alamos (N.Mex.) HS, 1963—86; sr. technical writer, editor Los Alamos Nat. Lab., 1987—2005. Adj. prof. English, U. N.Mex., Los Alamos, 1970-72, Albuquerque, 1982-85; English cons. S.W. Regional Coll. Bd., Austin, Tex., 1975—; writer, editor, cons. advanced placement English test devel. com. Nat. Coll. Bd., 1982-86, reader, 1982-86, project equality cons., 1985-88; book selection cons. Scholastic mag., 1980-82. Author: Preparing for the Advanced Placement English Exams, 1975; editor Los Alamos Arts Coun. bull., 1986-91. Chair Los Alamos Art Pub. Places Bd., 1987-92; chair adv. bd. trustees U. N.Mex., Los Alamos, 1987-93; pres. Los Alamos Concert Assn., 1972-73, 95-98, 2000-04, pres., 2003-04; chair Los Alamos Mesa Pub. Libr. Bd., 1990-94, chair endowment com., 1995-99. Named Living Treasure of Los Alamos, 2005. Mem. Soc. Tech. Communicators, AAUW (pres. 1961-63, state bd. dirs. 1959-63, Los Alamos coordinating coun. 1992-93, pres. 1993-94, 2002-04, sec. 2001-04), DAR, Order Ea. Star, Mortar Bd., Phi Beta Kappa (pres. Los Alamos chpt. 1969-72, 99, v.p. 1996-99, pres. 2000-01, dir. 2002—), Phi Kappa Phi, Delta Kappa Gamma, Gamma Phi Beta. Avocations: swimming, reading, hiking, astronomy, singing. Home: 124 Rover Blvd Los Alamos NM 87544-3634 E-mail: pmendius@cybermesa.com.

MENDLIN, RONALD C., employment specialist, writer; b. San Francisco, Jan. 8, 1936; s. Joseph and Freda Mendlin; m. Lorraine F. Mendlin, Feb. 15, 1964; children: Andrew Scott, Susan Debra. Student, U. San Francisco, San Francisco State U.; degree, San Francisco City Coll., 1958. Vocat edn. tchg. credential Calif. With City and County of San Francisco, 1962-92; employment specialist No. Calif. Svc. League, San Francisco, 1993—; part-time employment specialist San Mateo, Calif. Job developer San Mateo Employment and Tng. Ctr., Advanced Career Tech., Peninsula Placement Agy.; placement counselor Scofield Employment Agy., San Francisco; lectr. in field. Author (with Marc Polonsky): Putting the Bars Behind You, 5 vols., 2000; author: The Double You, Being Job-Ready, Job Search Tools, Networking and Interviewing for Jobs, Keeping Your Job, Up Against The Clock. With N.G. USAR, 1954—63. Recipient numerous accolades, Mayor's Office. Mem.: Fiesta Gardens Home Owners Assn. (v.p.), No. Calif. Svc. League (mock interviewer 1993—). Achievements include credited by California Department of Corrections and California State University's Sacramento Foundation for placing and assisting over 750 ex-felons out of state prisons into jobs; obtaining jobs for residents in work furlough programs and residents who had 3 days or 6 hours to obtain a job or be sent back to prison; saved Municipal Railway from financial embarassment, 1974. Office: No Calif Svc League 40 Boardman Pl San Francisco CA 94103 Office Phone: 415-863-2323.

MENDOLA, JOSEPH ROBERT, philosophy professor, department chairman; b. Rochester, NY, May 2, 1957; s. Joseph R. and Shirley Cook Mendola; m. Therese A. McCarty (div.); 1 child, Lily Yang Griffin. BA, Haverford Coll., Pa., 1979; MA, U. Mich., Ann Arbor, 1981, PhD, 1983. Mellon postdoctoral fellow U. Rochester, 1983—84; vis. asst. prof. NC State U., Raleigh, 1984—85; asst. prof. U. Okla., Norman, 1985—86, U. Nebr., Lincoln, 1986—92, assoc. prof., 1992—98, prof., 1998—, chmn. philosophy dept., 1997—. Author: Human Thought, 1997, Goodness and Justice, 2006, Anti-Externalism, 2008. Mem.: Am. Philos. Assn. (program chmn. 2001), Phi Beta Kappa. Office: U Nebr Dept Philosophy 1010 Oldfather Hall Lincoln NE 68588

MENDONCA, DAVID, engineering educator; PhD, Rensselaer Poly. Inst., Troy, NY, 2001. Assoc. prof. NJ. Inst. Tech., Newark, 2001—. Career award, NSF, 2005—. Mem.: IEEE. Achievements include research in studies of the art of improvisation as practiced in emergency response decision making. Office: New Jersey Inst Tech 323 Martin Luther King Jr Blvd Newark NJ 07102

MENDOZA, GEORGE, poet, author; b. NYC, June 2, 1934; s. George and Elizabeth Mendoza; m. Ruth Sekora, 1967; children: Ashley, Ryan. BA, State Maritime Coll., 1953; postgrad., Columbia U., 1954-56. Author over 100 books for children and adults published worldwide; many included in Boston U.'s George Mendoza Collection, established 1984; children's books on display at the Centre Nat. d'Art et de Culture Georges Pompidou. Works include: And Amedeo Asked, How Does One Become a Man?, (illustrated by Ati Forberg), 1959, The Puma and the Pearl, 1962, The Hawk Is Humming: A Novel, 1964, A Piece of String, Astor-Honor, 1965, Gwot! Horribly Funny Hairticklers (illustrated by Steven Kellog), 1967, The Crack in the Wall and Other Terribly Weird Tales (illustrated by Mercer Mayer), 1968, Flowers and Grasses and Weeds (illustrated by Joseph Low), 1968, The Practical Man (illustrated by Imero Gobbato), 1968, Hunting Sketches (illustrated by Ronald Stein), 1968, A Beastly Alphabet (illustrated by J. Low), 1969, The Digger Wasp (illustrated by Jean Zallinger), 1969, Herman's Hat (illustrated by Frank Bozzo), 1969, The Starfish Trilogy (illustrated by Ati Forberg), 1969, (compiler) The World From My Window: Poems and Drawings (children's writings), 1969, Are You My Friend? (illustrated by F. Bozzo), 1970, The Marcel Marceau Alphabet Book, 1970, The Thumbtown Toad (illustrated by Monika Beisner), 1970, The Inspector, 1970, The Good Luck Spider & other bad luck stories, 1970, The Fearsome Brat (illustrated by F. Bozzo), 1971, Fish in the Sky (illustrated by Milton Glaser), 1971, Moonfish and owl scratchings, 1971, Moonstring, 1971, The Hunter, the Tick and the Gumberoo, 1971, The Marcel Marceau Counting Book, 1971, The Scarecrow Clock (illustrated by Eric Carle), 1971, Big Frog, Little Pond, 1971, The Scribbler, 1971, The Christmas Tree Alphabet Book, 1971, Shadowplay, 1974, Lord, Suffer me to Catch a Fish, 1974, Fishing the Morning Lonely, 1974, (with Carol Burnett) What I Want to Be When I Grow Up, 1975, (with Zero Mostel) The Sesame Street Book of Opposites, 1975, Norman Rockwell's Americana ABC (illustrated by N. Rockwell), 1975, Doug Henning's Magic Book, 1975, Lost Pony, 1976, Norman Rockwell's Boys and Girls at Play, 1976, Secret Places of a Trout Fisherman, 1977, Norman Rockwell's Diary for a Young Girl (illustrated by N. Rockwell), 1978, Magic Tricks, 1978, Mon livre de magic (French edit. of My Book of Magic), Norman Rockwell's Scrapbook for a Young Boy (illustrated by N. Rockwell), 1979, (with Andres Segovia) Segovia, My Book of the Guitar, 1979, Need a House? Call Ms. Mouse! (illustrated by Doris Susan Smith), 1981, Alphabet Sheep (illustrated by K. Reidy), 1982, The Sheepish Book of Opposites, 1982, Silly Sheep and other sheepish rhymes, 1982, Norman Rockwell's Four Seasons, 1982, Norman Rockwell's Happy Holidays, 1983, Henri Mouse (illustrated by Joelle Boucher), 1985, Henri La Souris, 1987, Norman Rockwell's Patriotic Times, 1986, (with Ivan Lendl) Hitting Hot, 1986, (with Sam Snead) Slammin' Sam, 1986, Norman Rockwell's Love and Remembrance, 1986, Top Tennis, 1987, L'Album des Noeuds, 1988, Norman Rockwell's Old Fashioned American Cookbook, 1988, Hairticklers (illustrated by Gahan Wilson), 1989, The Hunter I Might Have Been, reprint 1989, Were You a Wild Duck, Where Would You Go? (illustrated by Jane Osborn-Smith), 1990, Traffic Jam (illustrated by David Stoltz), 1990; also author screenplays for Petals from a Poem Flower, You Show Me Yours and I'll Show You Mine and scripts for Sesame Street; numerous others; over 15 books of poetry including The Hunter I Might Have Been (Lewis Carroll Shelf award 1968), The Mist Men, Goodbye, River, Goodbye; also dozens of articles in The N.Y. Times, Herald Tribune, Stern, Vogue, Harper's Bazaar, Ms., Esquire, Town & Country, Sports Afield, Men's Journal, Philadelphia Inquirer; special travel corr. Toronto Globe & Mail, 1991-94. Cited by Pres. Reagan for Norman Rockwell's Patriotic Times. Avocation: fishing. *I believe we are living in a world where people no longer see each other as individuals. We have become invisible. It is necessary to save our souls. Go out to a field and pick up a fallen leaf. Look at the veins that river the leaf. Follow them until nothing else matters except for the leaf in your hand. Then you will become visible. You will see others and others will see you.*

MENDOZA, JULIE C., lawyer; BA summa cum laude, Tufts U., 1977; JD, U. Chgo., 1981. Bar: DC 1981, US Ct. Internat. Trade, US Ct. Appeals, Fed. Cir. Ptnr., co-chair Internat. Trade Group Kaye Scholer LLP, Washington, DC. Office: Troutman Sanders LLP 401 9th St NW Ste 1000 Washington DC 20004 Office Phone: 202-274-2874. Business E-Mail: julie.mendoza@troutmansanders.com.

MENDOZA, ROBERTO G., JR., banker; b. Cuba, 1945; BA, Yale U., 1967; MBA, Harvard U., 1974. Corp. fin. mgmt. positions with J.P. Morgan & Co., NYC, 1967—90, vice chmn., 1990—2000; mng. dir. Goldman Sachs, NYC, 2000—01; founder & chmn. Integrated Finance Ltd., NYC, 2001—. Bd. dir. Prudential plc, Western Union. Home: Integrated Finance Ltd 245 Park Ave New York NY 10167-0002

MENDOZA, STANLEY ATRAN, pediatric nephrologist, educator; b. Pitts., May 7, 1940; s. Joseph William and Marian Ruth (Atran) M.; m. Carole Ann Klein, June 23, 1963; children: Daniel, Joseph. Student, Harvard U., 1957—59; BA, Johns Hopkins U., 1961, MD, 1964. Diplomate Am. Bd. Pediat. Intern Johns Hopkins Hosp., Balt., 1964-65; jr. asst. resident dept. medicine Children's Hosp. Med. Ctr., Boston, 1965-66; asst. attending physician, dir. renal rsch. labs. Children's Meml. Hosp., Chgo., 1969-71; asst. prof. pediat. U. Calif. Sch. Medicine, San Diego, 1971—73, assoc. prof., 1973—79, prof. pediat. dept. pediat. divsn. pediatric nephrology, 1979—, vice chmn. dept. pediat., 1986—87, chmn. dept. pediat., 1992—2000. Contbr. article in field to profl. publ. Served With USPHS, 1966-69. Fogarty Sr. Internat. fellow, 1978-79; Alan J. Wurtzburger rsch. scholar, 1964; recipient Johns Hopkins Med. Soc. award, 1964, hon. mention Borden Undergrad. rsch. award in medicine, 1964; Eleanor Roosevelt internat. fellow Internat. Union Against Cancer, 1984-85. Mem. Am. Fedn. Clin. Rsch., Am. Pediatric Soc., Am. Physiol. Soc., Am. Soc. Nephrology, Am. Soc. Pediatric Nephrology, Internat. Soc. Nephrology. Office: U Calif San Diego Dept Pediat 9500 Gilman Dr # 0696 La Jolla CA 92093-5004 Home Phone: 858-459-0979. E-mail: samendoza@ucsd.edu.

MENDOZA, WILLIAM A., physics professor; b. NYC; s. Mario Mendoza and Macie Virginia Thrift; married. BSc in Physics, Fla. State U., Tallahassee, MSc, PhD, 1998. Adj. prof. Fla. State U., 1998; vis. prof. Jacksonville U., Fla., 1998—2000, asst. prof., 2000—06; tech. analyst Dept. State, Washington, 2006—07; prof. physics Fla. CC, Jacksonville, 2007—. Mem.: IEEE, Am. Phys. Soc., Nat. Space Soc., Planetary Soc., Sigma Xi. Office: Atom Sci Consulting PO Box 8404 Jacksonville FL 32399 Business E-Mail: atom@sigmaxi.net.

MENEELEY, EDWARD STERLING, artist; b. Wilkes-Barre, Pa., Dec. 18, 1927; s. Edward Sterling and Louina Halter M. Student, Murray Art Sch., Wilkes-Barre, 1947-50, Sch. Visual Arts, NYC, 1952-53. Founder Portable Gallery Press, 1957-67; vis. lectr. Belleville Coll., St. Louis, Art Students League, N.Y.C.; lectr. Lehigh Valley Sch. System, 1987, Rogers College, Istanbul, Turkey, 1991, Lafayette Coll., 1998; pres. ESM Documentations, N.Y.C.; fine arts cons. Arts Initiatives, Inc., N.Y.C.; mem. Penna Artists, 2005. One-man exhbs. include, Donovan Gallery, Phila., 1952, Parma Gallery, N.Y.C., 1962, Teuschr Gallery, N.Y.C., 1966, 68, Inst. Contemporary Arts, London, 1971, Victoria and Albert Mus., London, 1972, U. Sussex, Eng., 1972, Whitechapel Art Gallery, London, 1973, Demos Gallery, Athens, Greece, 1976, Frank Marino Gallery, N.Y.C., 1978, 79, 80, 81, 82, Sordoni Gallery, Wilkes (Pa.) Coll., 1981, Ericson Gallery, N.Y.C., 1980, Portfolio Gallery, Atlanta, 1983, Angela Flowers Gallery, London, 1985, J.T. Gallery, Jim Thorpe, Pa, 1987, 55 Mercer St., N.Y.C., 1987, Anita Shapolsky Gallery, N.Y.C., 1988, Bucknell U. Gallery Art, Lewisburg, 1988, Recent Painting & Sculptute, Coll. Misericordia, Dallas, Pa., 1989, Mixed Media, Craft Alliance Gallery, St. Louis, 1990, Provincetown (Mass.) Art Mus., 1993, De Arte Magick Gallery, Easton, Pa., 1997, New Works, N.Y.C., 1998, 181 Hudson St. N.Y.C., 1998, 70th St. Gallery Collages, 2001, Soho Creative, N.Y.C., 2002, 03, 04, MCI Gallery, 2003, 2004, Anita Shapulsky Art Found., 2005, Joel Finsel Ltd., Wilmington, NC, 2008-, Painting Gallery, Wilming DNC. Served with USNR, 1945-47, 50-52. Nat. Endowment Arts grantee; Pollock-Krasner Found. grantee, 1986, 90, 2002. Mem. Artist Club N.Y.C., Inst. Contemporary Arts London, Josiah White Soc., Weissport, Pa. Office: Anita Shapcsky Found 20 West Broadway Jim Thorpe PA 18229 Personal E-mail: edm7688@yahoo.com.

MENEES, KATHERINE DETERMAN, retired parochial school educator; b. Keyser, W.Va., Mar. 22, 1941; d. Alphonsus William and Bernadette Cosgrove Determan; m. Timothy Ryan Menees, Aug. 24, 1968; children: Timothy Marion, Rebecca Menees Ciccio. EdB in English, Frostburg State U., Md., 1963. Tchr. Surrattsville Jr. HS, Clinton, Md., 1963—69; substitute tchr. Incirlik Am. Sch., Turkey, 1970—71, Bainbridge Island HS, Wash., 1973—74; tchr. St. Valentine Sch., Bethel Park, Pa., 1985—2007; ret., 2007. Forensics team moderator, coach Southwestern Pa. Forensics League, Pitts., 1995—2007; advisor St. Valentine Sch. Newspaper, 1996—2007. Tchr., student advisor St. Mary of Mercy Red Door Program, Pitts., 1987, 1988, 1999, 2005, Food Bank, McKeesport, Pa., 1990; bd. dirs. Children's Ctr. for Theater Arts, Mt. Lebanon, Pa., 1981—90. MAC grantee, McDonalds, Bethel Park, 2004. Mem.: Nat. Cath. Ednl. Assn., Western Pa. Coun. Tchrs. of English, Nat. Coun. Tchrs. of English. Roman Catholic. Avocations: piano, sewing, gardening, reading. Home: 5001 Highland Ave Bethel Park PA 15102 Office: St Valentine Sch 2709 Mesta St Bethel Park PA 15102 Home Phone: 412-833-5378. Personal E-mail: kay@timmenees.com.

MENEFEE, JOHN WILLIAM, III, cinematographer, film producer; b. Washington, Dec. 19, 1944; s. John William Menefee Jr. and Mary Claudia (Tudor) Upchurch. Student, U. Va., 1964-66, Columbia Sch. for Motion Pictures and TV, L.A., 1992. Tour guide Universal Studios, Universal City, Calif., 1970-75, studio transp. driver, 1976; camera asst., trainee Dino d'Laurentis Orgn., Beverly Hills, Calif., 1976, Panavision (formerly Gen. Camera), NYC, 1978; camera person Paramount Pictures, LA, 1980, 20th Century Fox Film Corp., LA, 1987, 96, Sony Pictures Corp., Culver City, Calif., 1992, 97, Paramount Pictures, LA, 2000. Mem. film and TV action com. Bring Hollywood Home, L.A., 1999—; contbr., supporter World Wildlife Fund, Washington, Lambda Legal Def. Fund, N.Y.C., Cato Inst., Washington. Mem. Internat. Cinematographers Guild (cert.), Jamestown Soc. Episcopalian. Avocations: genealogy, vedic astrology, tennis, acting. Home: 1020 San Rafael Ln Pasadena CA 91105-1531 Personal E-mail: mflea3@aol.com.

MENEFEE, LINNEA-NORMA, antique dealer; b. Mpls., Mar. 5, 1924; d. Arthur Wesley and Elsie Ida Buck. Student, U. Minn., Mpls., U. Minn., Duluth, McPhail Sch. Music, Mpls. Chmn. State Vet. Home, Buffalo. Founder Albert Lea (Minn.) Art Ctr., 1959; county chairwoman Goldwater for Pres., Albert Lea. Recipient Conscientious award, 2001; named to Hall of Fame, Washington, 2007. Mem. AAUW, Am. Med. Assn. Alliance, Nat. Fedn. Rep. Women, Nat. Women of the Arts, Nat. Am. Legion Aux., Nat. VFW Aux., Nat. Assn. Family and Cmty. Edn., Order of Ea. Star, Gillette Blue Blades, Kiwanis Internat. (Concientious Kiwanian 2002), Zeta Phi Eta, Omega Upsilon, Zeta Beta Chi. Episcopalian. Avocations: writing, reading, painting, sculpting, travel.

MENEFEE, SAMUEL PYEATT, lawyer, academic; b. Denver, June 8, 1950; s. George Hardiman and Martha Elizabeth (Pyeatt) M.; m. Mary W., April 21, 2000; 1 child: Mary Elizabeth. BA in Anthropology and Scholar of Ho. summa cum laude, Yale U., 1972; diploma in Social Anthropology, Oxford U., Eng., 1973, BLitt, 1975; JD, Harvard U., 1981; LLM in Oceans, U. Va., 1982, SJD, 1993; MPhil in Internat. Rels., U. Cambridge, Eng., 1995. Bar: Ga. 1981, US Ct. Appeals (11th cir.) 1982, Va. 1983, La. 1983, US Ct. Mil. Appeals 1983, US Ct. Internat. Trade 1983, US Ct. Claims 1983, US Ct. Appeals (10th cir.) 1983, US Ct. Appeals (fed., 1st, 3d, 4th, 5th, 6th, 7th, 8th and 9th cirs.) 1984, DC 1985, Nebr. 1985, Fla. 1985, US Supreme Ct. 1985, US Ct. Appeals (DC cir.) 1986, Maine 1986, Pa. 1986. Assoc. Phelps, Dunbar, Marks, Claverie & Sims, New Orleans, 1983-85; of counsel Barham & Churchill PC, New Orleans, 1985-88; sr. assoc. Ctr. for Nat. Security Law U. Va. Sch. Law, 1985—, fellow Ctr. for Oceans Law and Policy, 1982-83, sr. fellow, 1985-89, Maury fellow, 1989—, adv. bd, 1997—, Vis. lectr. U. Cape Town, 1987; vis. asst. prof. U. Mo., Kansas City, 1990; law clk. Hon. Pasco M. Bowman US Ct. Appeals (8th cir.),

1994-95; vis. prof. Regent U., 1996-97, scholar-at-large, 1997—2003, prof., 1998—2003; adv. Am. Maritime Forum/Mariners' Mus., 1997-99; lectr. various nat. and internat. orgns.; mem. ICC Consultative Task Force on Comml. Crime, 1996—. Author: Wives for Sale: An Ethnographic Study of British Popular Divorce, 1981, Contemporary Piracy and International Law, 1995, Trends in Maritime Violence, 1996; co-editor: Materials on Ocean Law, 1982; nat. editor: Assn. Rsch. on Peasant Diaries, 1996-; mem. editl. bd. Internat. Jour. Marine and Costal Law, 1997-2003; contbr. numerous articles to profl. jours. Recipient Katharine Briggs prize Folklore Soc., 1992; Bates traveling fellow Yale U., 1971, Rhodes scholar, 1972; Cosmos fellow Sch. Scottish Studies U. Edinburgh, 1991-92, IMB fellow, ICC Internat. Maritime Bur., 1991—, Piracy Reporting Ctr. fellow, Kuala Lampur, 1993—, Huntington fellow The Mariners Mus., 1997. Fellow Royal Anthrop. Inst., Am. Anthrop. Assn., Royal Asiatic Soc., Royal Soc. Antiquaries Ireland, Soc. Antiquaries Scotland, Royal Geog. Soc., Soc. Antiquaries; mem. ABA (vice-chmn. marine resources com. 1987-90, chmn. law of sea com. subcom. naval warfare, maritime terrorism and piracy 1989—, mem. law of sea com. steering com. 1996—99, mem. working group on terrorism), Southeastern Admiralty Law Inst. (com. mem.), Maritime Law Assn. (proctor, com. mem., chmn. subcom. law of sea 1988-91, vice chmn. com. internat. law of sea 1991—99, chmn. com. internat. law of sea 1999-2003, chair working group piracy 1992—2003, UNESCO study group 1998—), Marine Tech. Soc. (co-chmn./chmn. marine security com. 1991—2004), Selden Soc., Am. Soc. Internat. Law, Internat. Law Assn. (com. mem., rapporteur Am. br. com. EEZ 1988-90, rapporteur Am. br. com. Maritime Neutrality 1992, observer UN conv. on law of sea meeting of states parties 1996, chmn./co-chmn. Am. br. com. on law of sea 1996—2001, rapporteur joint internat. working group on uniformity of law of piracy 1998—2001), Com. Maritime Internat., Am. Soc. Indsl. Security (com. mem.), US Naval Inst., USN League, Folklore Soc., Royal Celtic Soc., Internat. Studies Assn., Royal Scottish Geog. Soc., Royal African Soc., Egypt Exploration Soc., Arctic Inst. N.Am., Internat. Studies Assn., Am. Hist. Soc., Soc. for History of Discoveries, Soc. Nautical Rsch., Internat. Assn. Rsch. on Peasant Diaries, Christian Aid Mission, Nat. Eagle Scout Assn., Raven Soc., Jefferson Soc., Fence Club, Mory's Assn., Elizabethan Club, Yale Polit. Union, Leander Club, Cambridge Union, United Oxford and Cambridge Univ. Club, Yale Club NYC, Paul Morphy Chess Club, Pendennis Club, Round Table Club New Orleans, Phi Beta Kappa, Omicron Delta Kappa. Republican. Avocations: anthropology, archaeology, crew, hiking. Office: PO Box 5291 Charlottesville VA 22905-2591 also: U Va Ctr Nat Sec Law 580 Massie Rd Charlottesville VA 22903-1738 Office Phone: 434-924-7441. Business E-Mail: colp@virginia.edu.

MENENDEZ, BELINDA, broadcast executive; Student, St. Andrews U., Scotland. With internat. TV sales Televisa, 1986—95; mgr. TV sales Cisneros; internat. tv distbn. ops. mgr. Michael Solomon's S.I.E.; exec. v.p. sales Studio Canal (formerly Canal Plus DA); co-pres. NBC Universal Internat. TV Distbn., Universal City, Calif., 2001—04, pres., 2004—. Named one of The 100 Most Influential Hispanics, Hispanic Bus. Mag., The Most Powerful and Influential Latinos, Imagen Found., The 100 Most Powerful Women in Entertainment, Hollywood Reporter; named to Hispanic Women in Entertainment Power 25, Latino Power 50. Office: Universal TV Distbn USA Bldg 1440/3030 100 Universal City Plaza Universal City CA 91608-1002

MENENDEZ, ROBERT (BOB MENENDEZ), United States Senator from New Jersey; b. NYC, Jan. 1, 1954; s. Mario and Evangelina (Lopez) M.; m. Jane Jacobsen, June 5, 1976 (div. 2005); children: Alicia, Robert. BA in Polit. Sci. and Urban Studies, St. Peter's Coll., 1976; JD, Rutgers U., 1979. Bar: NJ 1980. Atty. Diaz and Menendez, Union City, NJ, 1980-92; mayor City of Union City, 1986—92; mem. NJ Gen. Assembly, 1987—91; majority whip NJ State Senate, 1991—92; mem. US Congress from 13th NJ dist., 1993—2006; US Senator from NJ, 2006—; chmn. Democratic Senatorial Campaign Com. (DSCC), 2009—; mem. US Senate Banking Housing & Urban Affairs Com., US Senate Budget Com., US Senate Energy & Nat. Resources Com., US Senate Fin.Com., US Senate Fgn. Rels. Com. Co-chair Hillary Rodham Clinton Presdl. Campaign, 2007—08. CFO Union City Bd. Edn., 1978-82, trustee, 1974-78; mem. Alliance Civic Assn., 1982-92, pres. 1981; mem. Gov.'s Hispanic Adv. Com., Trenton, N.J., 1984—; mem. Gov.'s Ethnic Adv. Com., Washignton, 1985. Recipient Cmty. Svc. award Gran Logia del Norte, 1981, Outstanding Svc. award Hispanic Law Enforcement, 1981, Outstanding Cmty. Svc. Revista Actualidades, 1982, US Conf. Mayors award, 1987, 1988, 1991, Disting. Citizen award U. Medicine and Dentistry N.J., 1994, Man of Yr. award Kiwanis, 1994, Justice of Cyprus award, Cyprus Federation Am., 1995, Am. Hellenic Inst. Public Svc. Achievement award, 1997, Lifetime Achievement award Hispanic Bus. Roundtable, 2000, Excellence in Edn. award, Ana G. Mendez U. System, 2003, Capital award Nat. Coun. of La Raza, 2003, Paraskevaides award, 16th Annual Cyprus Conf., 2005; named Man of the Year, Armenian Nat. Com. NJ, 2007. Mem. ABA, Fed. Bar Assn. NJ Bar Assn., Hispanic Bar Assn., Hudson County Bar Assn., NJ Employment & Training Commn., NJ Mayors Coalition, NJ Hispanic Leadership Opportunities Program (chmn.), Hispanic Elected and Apptd Ofcls. Orgn. (chmn.); Hoboken Elks Club, North Hudson Lawyers Club (chmn.) Democrat. Roman Catholic. Avocations: chess, racquetball. Office: US Senate 317 Hart Senate Office Bldg Washington DC 20510 also: District Office Ste 1100 One Gateway Ctr Newark NJ 07102 Office Phone: 202-224-4744, 973-645-3030. Office Fax: 202-228-2197, 973-645-0502.*

MENÉNDEZ CAMBÓ, PATRICIA, lawyer; b. NYC, June 7, 1966; BBA, U. Miami, 1986; JD, U. Pa., 1989. Bar: Fla. 1991, DC 1993. With Greenberg Traurig, PA, Miami, 1994—2000, shareholder, chair Global Practice Group, 2002—, mem. exec. com.; chief US legal counsel Telefónica S.A., 2000—02. Bd. mem. Coun. of Americas, U. Pa. Sch. Law; adv. bd. mem. Inst. Internat. and Comparative Law; mem. Coun. Fgn. Rels.; spkr. in field. Contbr. articles to profl. jours. Trustee Nat. Alliance for Autism Rsch. Named one of The Top Up and Comers in So. Fla., So. Fla. Legal Guide, 2004, The Top 40 Lawyers Under 40, Nat. Law Jour., 2005, 100 Most Influential Lawyers in America, 2006, 50 Most Influential Women Lawyers in America, 2007, 50 Most Influential Minority Lawyers in America, 2008. Mem.: ABA (mem. Internat. Law Sect.), Internat. Bar Assn. Office: Greenberg Traurig 1221 Brickell Ave Miami FL 33131 Office Phone: 305-579-0766. Office Fax: 305-579-5766. Business E-Mail: pmc@gtlaw.com.*

MENESES (GONZALES), DIANA MARINA, history professor; b. La Paz, Bolivia, June 10, 1980; d. Rolando and Marina Meneses; life ptnr. Casey Iwai. B, U. Incarnate Word, San Antonio, 2002; M, Ariz. State U., Tempe, 2004, PhD in History, 2009. Cert. diplome d'etudes en langue francaise French Govt., in human participants protection Edn. NIH. Tutor/supr. UIW Learning Assistance Ctr., San Antonio, 1998—2002; grad. rsch. asst. ASU Dept. History, 2002—03, grad. tchg. asst. (ta), 2003—06; grad. asst. editor H-AmIndian Listserv, 2004—06; bilingual grant worker ASU Garfield Project, 2005—07; grad. tchg. asst. prof. ASU Dept. History, 2006—08; bilingual scheduler ASU Supporting MAMI Project, Tempe, 2007—08; lead bilingual interviewer ASU Juntos Project, Tempe, 2007—08; grad. fellow,rsch. asst. ASU Inst. Humanities Rsch., Tempe, 2008—; faculty assoc. ASU Dept. History, Tempe, 2008. Bd. mem. ABOR Residency Bd., Tempe, 2005—; student mem. ASU Grad. Coun., Tempe, 2008—; GPSA rep. ASU Dept. History, 2006—08. Del. Global Young People's Convocation, South Africa; mem. staff parish rels. Tempe First United Meth. Ch. Recipient UIW & Nat. Dean's List, 1998—2002, Outstanding Student award, UIW Anthropology, 2001—02, award, UIW Dance, 2002, Dr. Amy Freeman Lee Scholastic Achievement & Svc. Recognition award, UIW Coll. Humanities Arts & Social Sciences, 2002, James E. Tilton Creative Writing award, UIW English, 2002, Best Paper award, Charles Redd Ctr., 2004, Albuquerque Conv. & Visitors Bur. award, SW, Tex. Popular Culture Assn.Am. Culture Assn., 2005, Academic Yr. Lanzate award, SW Airlines & Hispanic Assn. Colleges & Universities, 2007—08, Outstanding Grad. Student award, ASU Grad. Coll., 2007—08, award, Alpha Lambda Delta; Underrepresented Grad. Enrichment Match fellowship, ASU Grad. Coll., Academic Yr. Fgn. Lang. Areas Studies fellowship, U.S. Dept. Edn., 2005—06, Summer Fgn. Lang. Areas Studies fellowship, 2006, Summer Dissertation Rsch. fellowship, ASU Dept. History, 2007, Rsch. grant, ASU Grad. & Profl. Student Assn., 2007—08, Travel grant, Grad. & Profl. Student Assn., 2008. Mem.: Native Am. & Indigenous Studies Assn., Popular Culture Assn., Southwestern Social Sci. Assn., Western History Assn. Avocations: dance, art, languages, travel. Office: 3412 W Ansell Rd Laveen AZ 85339 Business E-Mail: diana.meneses@asu.edu.

MENEZES, IGNATIUS, bishop; b. Mangalore, India, Jan. 3, 1936; s. Jacob and Concepta (D'Mello) M. MA in History, Agra U., India, 1971, MA in Lit., 1973. Tchr. psychology St. Paul's Sem., Lucknow, India, 1964; vice prin. St. Francis Coll., Lucknow, 1965-66, prin., 1977-78; parish priest, prin. St. Joseph's Cathedral and Cathedral Sch., Lucknow, 1966-76; bishop Diocese of Ajmer-Jaipur, Ajmer, India, 1979—. Mem. Cath. Coun. India. Author: I Have Come to Do Thy Will, 1995; contbr. articles to profl. jours. Avocations: reading, studying, badminton, basketball. Home: Bishops House Ajmer 305001 India Office: Diocesan Soc Ajmer-Jaipur Kaiserganj Ajmer 305001 India Home Phone: 0145 2460 337; Office Phone: 0145 2460074. E-mail: bishop@datainfosys.net.

MENG, GUNTER RICHARD, retired surgeon; b. Brühl, Germany, Mar. 31, 1927; US, 1948; s. Richard and Elise Meng; m. Hilde Maria Farrenkopf, Aug. 14, 1954; children: Karin, Peter. BA, Cornell U., 1951, MD, 1955. Internship, surg. residency Syracuse U., NY, 1955—60; gen. surgeon USAF, 1960—82, chief surgery, chief prof. staff; vice comdr. USAF Wright Patterson Med. Ctr.; ret., 1982. Surgery cons. for surgeon gen. USAF, Wash., DC, 1978—82; assoc. clin. prof. surgery Wright-State U. Med. Coll., Dayton, Ohio, 1978—84. Contbr. articles to profl. jours. Mem. All-Am. Soccer Team Cornell U., 1949—50. Col. USAF, 1970—82. Recipient Legion of Merit, USAF, 1982. Fellow: ACS; mem.: Assn. Mil. Surgeons. Republican. Roman Catholic. Home: 12211 Lakewood Ct Fort Myers FL 33908

MENG, TERESA H., electrical engineer, educator; b. Taiwan; BSEE, Nat. Taiwan U., 1983; MS in Elec. Engring. and Computer Sci., U. Calif., Berkeley, 1984, PhD in Elec. Engring. and Computer Sci., 1988. Mem. faculty elec. engring. dept. Stanford U., Calif., 1988—, Reid Weaver Dennis prof. elec. engring. Calif., 2003—; founder, bd. dirs. Atheros Comm., Inc., Calif., 1998—, pres., CEO, 1998—99. Contbr. articles to sci. jours., chapters to books; author: Synchronization Design of Digital Systems, 1990; co-editor: VLSI Signal Processing IX, 1996. Bd. trustees Computer Hist. Mus. Recipient Eli Jury award, U. Calif. Berkeley, 1988, Best Paper award, IEEE Signal Processing Soc., 1989, Presdl. Young Investigator award, NSF, 1989, Young Investigator award, Office of Naval Rsch., 1989, IBM Faculty Devel. award, 1989, Disting. Lectr. award, IEEE Signal Processing Soc., 20/20 Vision award, Chief Info. Officer Mag., 2002, Demo@15 World-Class Innovator award, 2005; named Innovator of Yr., MIT Sloan Sch. eBusiness Awards, 2002; named one of Top 10 Entrepreneurs, Red Herring, 2001. Fellow: IEEE; mem.: NAE. Achievements include patents in field. Office: Dept Elec Engring 209 CIS Bldg 420 Via Palou Mall Stanford CA 94305-4070 Office Phone: 650-725-3636. Office Fax: 650-725-3383. E-mail: meng@ee.stanford.edu.

MENGDEN, JOSEPH MICHAEL, retired investment banker; b. Houston, Sept. 28, 1924; s. Hippolyt Frederick and Amalia (Dittlinger) M.; m. Suzanne Miner, Sept. 30, 1950 (dec. July 1990); children: Anne Elise Mengden Giliberto, Amanda Mary, Michael Joseph, Charles Louis, Melissa Mary Mengden Bunker, Mary Miner Mengden Fitch; m. Dorothy Duggan, July 27, 1991 (dec. Apr. 2006); m. Carolyn Lounsberry, June 22, 2007. Ph.B., U. Notre Dame, 1949. V.p. Nat. Bank of Detroit, 1950-67; exec. v.p. First of Mich. Capital Corp., Detroit, 1967-90, sr. cons., 1990-95. Served to 1st lt. USAAF, World War II. Decorated Air medal with 2 oak leaf clusters. Home: 17111 E Jefferson #11 Grosse Pointe MI 48230-1941 Personal E-mail: men@comcast.net.

MENGE, DAVID MAINA, biomedical researcher; b. Nyamira, Nyanza, Kenya, Jan. 3, 1973; s. Samuel Menge Araka and Joyce Kemunto Menge; m. Catherine Kerubo Misati; children: Albert Lehninger, Louis Pastuer Maringo, Michelle Joyce Kwamboka Maina. BSc with honors, Jomo Kenyatta U. Agric & Tech., Kenya, 1994, PhD, 2004; MSc in Biochemistry, U. Nairobi, Kenya, 1999. Postdoc. fellow U. Calif., Irvine, 2004—06, SUNY, Buffalo, 2004—06; instr., malaria rschr. U. Minn., Mpls., 2006—. Reviewer several jours. Recipient Travel award, MRC, 1998, IUBMB, 2000, 2003, Travel & Trining award, WHO, 2005. Mem.: AAAS, Am. Soc. Tropical Medicine & Hygiene. Achievements include research in mapping genes for disease resistance, genetic epidemiology of malaria and deciphering mechanisms of cerebral malaria pathogenesis. Home: 633D Kingfisher LN Woodbury MN 55125 Office: Univ Minn 2001 6th St SE Minneapolis MN 55455 Office Fax: 612-626-9924. Personal E-mail: davidmenge@gmail.com. Business E-Mail: menge023@umn.edu.

MENGELING, CARL FREDERICK, bishop emeritus; b. Hammond, Ind., Oct. 22, 1930; s. Carl H. and Augusta Huke Mengeling. Attended, St. Meinrad Coll. and Sem., Ind.; Lic. in Sacred Theology, Angelicum U.; STD, Alfonsianum Acad. Ordained priest Diocese of Gary, Ind., 1957; assoc. pastor St. Mark Parish, Gary, 1957—61; tchr. Bishop Noll High Sch., Hammond, St. Joseph Calumet Coll., East Chgo., St. Procopius Sem., Lisle, Ill.; pastor All Saints Parish, Hammond, Ill., 1968—70, Holy Name Parish, Cedar Lake, Ill., 1970—71, Nativity of Our Savior, Portage, Ill., 1971—85, St. Thomas More Parish, Munster, Ill., 1985—95; named monsignor, 1984; founder, chair Inst. Religion, Diocesan of Gary; ordained bishop, 1995; bishop Archdiocese of Lansing, Mich., 1996—2008, bishop emeritus Mich., 2008—. Chair worship com. Diocese of Gary, chair vocations com., mem. Presbyteral coun., mem. ecumenical commn., mem. permanent diaconate formation team. Contbr. Faith Mag. Roman Catholic. Office: 300 W Ottawa St Lansing MI 48933-1530

MENGELING, WILLIAM LLOYD, retired veterinarian, virologist; b. Elgin, Ill., Apr. 1, 1933; s. William Paul and Blanche Joyce (Wormwood) M.; m. Barbara Ann Kethcart, Aug. 23, 1958; children: Michelle, Michael. BS, Kans. State U., 1958, DVM, 1960; MS, Iowa State U., 1966, PhD, 1969. Diplomate M. Coll. Vet. Microbiologists (chmn. 1977-78, bd. dirs. 1975-77). Vet. clinician St. Francis Animal Hosp., Albuquerque, 1960-61; vet. med. officer Nat. Animal Disease Ctr., Ames, Iowa, 1961-69, rsch. leader, 1969—2001, U.S. Sr. Exec. Svc., 1991—; ret., 2001. Cons. numerous state, fed., pvt. U.S. and fgn. agys.; collaborative prof., mem. grad. faculty Iowa State U. Co-editor: Diseases of Swine, 5th, 6th, 7th, 8th editions; contbr. articles to jours., chpts. to books. With U.S. Army, 1953-55. Recipient cert. appreciation USDA, 1978, George Fleming award Brit. Vet. Jour., 1978, Disting. Svc. award USDA, 1984, Gov.'s medal sci. State of Iowa, 1985, Vet. Med. Rsch. award Am. Feed Industry Assn., 1989, Leadership Merit awards USDA, 1989, 90, 91, 93, Alumnus award Kans. State U. Coll. Vet. Medicine and Vet. Med. Alumni Assn., 1999, William P. Switzer award Iowa State U. Coll. Met. Medicine, 2000, Howard Dunne Meml. award, Am. Assn. Swine Vets., 2001; elected to Agrl. Rsch. Svc. Hall of Fame, 2001. Mem. AVMA (Vet. Med. Rsch. award 1989), U.S. Animal Health Assn., Conf. Rsch. Workers in Animal Disease (pres. 1987-88, coun. 1981-86, dedicatee 2005 ann. meeting), Polish Soc. Vet. Sci. (hon.), Kiwanis (pres. 1975-76). Methodist. Avocations: wilderness survival, canoeing, camping, fishing. Home: 4220 Phoenix St Ames IA 50014-3922 Office Phone: 515-292-7060. Personal E-mail: bbmengeling@aol.com.

MENGES, JOHN KENNETH, JR., lawyer; b. Louisville, Sept. 23, 1957; s. John Kenneth and Barbara Jean (Vick) M. BSBA, Boston U., 1979; JD, Harvard U., 1982. Bar: Tex. 1982. Assoc. Akin, Gump, Strauss, Hauer & Feld, Dallas, 1982-89, ptnr., 1989—, now ptnr.-in-charge Dallas office and mem. mgmt. com. Pres. Dallas County Young Dems., 1985-88, Dallas Dem. Forum, 1990-91, bd. dirs., 1986-89; pres. sch. mgmt. Boston U., 1987—, bd. trustees, 1995—; bd. dirs. Friends of Fair Park; bd. trustees Boston U.; Dallas County chair North Tex. Clean Air Coalition. Mem. ABA, Tex. State Bar Assn., Dallas Bus. League (pres. 1989), Dallas Coun. on World Affairs, Dallas Assn. Young Lawyers, Harvard U. Law Sch. Assn. Tex. (bd. dirs. 1984-87, 90-91, pres. 1993), Boston U. Nat. Alumni Coun. (Young Alumni award 1987), Beta Gamma Sigma. Democrat. Methodist. Avocation: basketball. Office: Akin Gump Strauss Hauer & Feld LLP 1700 Pacific Ave Ste 4100 Dallas TX 75201-4675 Office Phone: 214-969-2783. Business E-Mail: kmenges@akingump.com.

MENGES, SUSAN DEBRA FAVREAU, retired protective services official, management consultant; b. Cleve., Dec. 15, 1955; d. Donald Francis and Helen Patricia (Rafferty) F.; m. William J. Menges, Nov. 17, 2001. Student, Cornell U., SUNY. Cert. NY State Police Acad., 1974. Comm. specialist NY State Police, Loudonville, 1974—87, comm. specialist divsn. hdqrs., 1987—98; mgmt. cons., sec.-treas., dir. Don Favreau Assocs., Inc., Clifton Park, NY, 1983—86, v.p., 1986—; comm. specialist divsn. hdqrs. NY State Police, Albany, 1987—98, sys. support specialist divsn. hdqrs., 1998—2005, ret., 2005. Adj. faculty Internat. Assn. Chiefs Police; NYSPIN coord. FBI/Nat. Crime Info. Ctr. cert. program, 1986—; ind. sr. beauty cons. Mary Kay Cosmetics, 2003 Author: Teamwork in the Telecommunication Center, 1986, One More Time: How to be a Mature and Successful Telcommunications Manager, 1987, Law Enforcement Terminal Security, 1991; also NYSPIN cert. manuals. Vol. Suncoast Seabird Sanctuary, Indian Shores, Fla., 2005—06; deacon Ch. of the Isles, Indian Rocks Beach, Fla., 2006—. Recipient Dirs. Commendation NY State Police Acad., 1977, Commendation NY State Police, 1978, Supt.'s Commendation, 1986, Y2K Commendation Gov. George Pataki, 2000 Mem. NAFE, NY State Civil Svc. Assn., Emergency Communicators Profl. Assn. (adv. bd.), Colonie Police Benevolent Assn. (hon.), Am. Soc. Law Enforcement Trainers, Assoc. Pub. Safety Comm. Officers (planning commn. Atlantic chpt. 1991, registration chair ann. N.E. conf. 1991), NY State Troopers Police Benevolent Assn. (hon.), Nat. Bus. Women Am., Internat. Assn. Chiefs Police, Am. Horse Shows Assn., Am. Soc. Law Enforcement Trainers, Capital Dist. Hunter/Jumper Coun Republican. Roman Catholic. Avocations: horseback riding, target shooting, reading, sewing. Office: Hdqrs NY State Police State Office Bldg Campus Bldg # 22 Albany NY 12226 Home: 19701 Gulf Blvd Apt 307 Indian Shores FL 33785-2385 E-mail: susan9g6@aol.com.

MENICHESCHI, EDWARD JOHN, publishing executive; b. June 20, 1959; Graduate, Fasion Inst. of Tech. Edited the retail trade publ. GQ mag, 1982—86, merchandising editor, 1986—90; v.p. mktg. Bidermann Industries, 1990—92; exec. editor Vogue, 1992—94, assoc. publ., 1994—99; pres. IAM.COM, 1999—2001, WWD Media Worldwide, 2001—06; exec. v.p. Fairchild Publications Inc., 2005—06; v.p., publ. Vanity Fair, 2006—. Recipient Outstanding Alumni award, Fashion Inst. Tech., 1988; named to Digital Coast's Top 100 Internet Exec. Office: Vanity Fair 4 Time Square 22nd Fl New York NY 10036

MENICK, FREDERICK J., plastic surgeon; b. July 20, 1945; Grad. in Biology, Fordham Coll., NYC, 1966; MD, Yale Med. Sch., New Haven, Conn., 1970. Cert. Am. Bd. Plastic Surgery, lic. Nat. Bd. Med. Examiners, NY, Ariz. Bd. Med. Examiners, Calif. Bd. Med. Quality Assurance, Ark. State Bd. Intern Stanford Med. Ctr., Palo Alto, Calif., 1970—71, resident, gen. surgery, 1974—75, United Hosp., Port Chester, NY, 1974, U. Ariz. Health Scis. Ctr., Tucson, 1975—79, chief resident, 1977—79; resident, plastic surgery U. Calif., Irvine, 1979—81, chief resident, 1980—81; fellowship, aesthetic plastic surgery of the face Bruce F. Connell, MD, Santa Ana, Calif., 1981; reconstructive plastic surgery, sr. house office, sr. registrar, Mark's Fellow Queen Victoria Hosp., East Grinstead, England, 1981—82; congenital, aesthetic and reconstructive surgery, Millard Fellow D. Ralph Millard, MD, U. Miami, Fla., 1982; chief, divsn. plastic surgery Tucson Vet. Adminstrn. Hosp., 1985—98; clin. assoc. prof. U. Ariz. Hosp., 1982—87; clin. lectr. U. Ariz. Sch. Medicine, 1987—90; clin. assoc. prof., dept. surgery U. Ariz. Coll. Medicine, 1991—, chief, sect. plastic surgery, 1991—95; private practice Guam and Micronesia (Western Pacific), the only plastic surgeon in 800,000 square miles of the Western Pacific, 1981, Tucson, 1983—. Assoc. mem. Ariz. Cancer Ctr., 1991—95; chief, dept. surgery St. Joseph's Hosp., Tucson, 1988—90, Tucson, 1990—92, Tucson, 1994—95; chief, divsn. plastic surgery Tucson Med. Ctr., 1994—96; founding mem. Johnson and Johnson Coun. Advisors of Aesthetic Skin Care, 1998. Contbr. several articles to peer-reviewed jours.; co-author: Aesthetic Restoration of the Nose, 1993; editor: Facial Cosmetic Surgery, Clinics in Plastic Surgery, 1992, Aesthetic Surgery on the Face, Clinics in Plastic Surgery, 1997; guest editor Facial and Nasal Reconstruction, Operative Techniques in Plastic and Reconstructive Surgery, 1998; contbr. chapters to books; editor: Nose Sect., Plastic Surgery Book. Medicine Jour. (www.emedicine.com), 2001; manuscript reviewer Annals of Plastic Surgery, 1991—2002, Plastic & Reconstructive Surgery, 1999—2002. Travels overseas frequently to teach and perform reconstructive charity surgery in Brazil, Philippines, Korea and Vietnam. Lt., submarine med. officer, diving med. officer (hon. discharge) USN, 1973, lt., Sch. Submarine Medicine USN, 1971, New London, Conn., lt., Sch. Deep Sea Diving and Salvage, 1971, Washington, DC. Named to Best Doctors in America: Pacific Region, 1996—97, Best Doctors in America (USA), 1999. Mem.: Tucson Surgical Soc. (v.p. 1994, pres. 1995, 1995), Pima Country Med. Soc. (bd. dirs. 1993—99, mem. media com. 1987—92), Millard Soc., U. Miami Dept. Plastic Surgery, Calif. Soc. Plastic Surgeons, Rhinoplasty Soc. (treas. 2003, v.p. 2004, pres.

2006), Am. Assn. Plastic Surgeons (James Barrett Brown prize in Plastic Surgery 1990, 2003), Am. Soc. for Aesthetic Plastic Surgery, Am. Soc. Plastic and Reconstructive Surgery (internat. programs com., plastic surgery, ednl. found. 1985—98, mem. socioecomomic com. 1986, mem. plastic surgery product assessment commn. 1989, mem. taskforce on long range planning, plastic surgery endl. found. 1990—92, chmn., internat. program com., plastic surgery ednl. found. (PSEF) 1991—94, bd. dirs., reconstructive surgeons vol. program (RSVP), PSEF 1991—98, v.p., bd. dirs. reconstructive surgeons vol. program, PSEF 1992, mem. internat. symposia com. PSEF 1993—94, vis. scholar com. edn. plastic surgery found. 1993—98, pres., chmn. bd. dirs. reconstructive surgeons vol. program, PSEF 1995, membership com. representing zone #5 1995—97, mem. instructional course com., PSEF 1995—99, mem. domestic clin. symposium com., PSEF 1995—99, 1st Pl. Writing award 1995). Office: 1102 N El Dorado Pl Tucson AZ 85715 Office Phone: 520-881-4525. E-mail: drmenick@drmenick.com.

MENICUCCI, AUDREY, artist; b. Santa Rosa, Calif, Sept. 22, 1931; d. Aubrey Joseph and Elaine Zimmerman-Minney Menicucci. Tchr. Sonoma & Marin counties (Calif.). In seascapes; condr. Sebastopol Art Workshop, Pallet Club, Guerneville, Calif.; Artist's Round Table, Santa Rosa, Forestville Art Workshop, one-woman shows include Marin County Civic Ctr., San Rafael, Calif., 1984, exhibited in group shows at San Francisco Civic Ctr. Art Show, 1964, 1984, Falkirk Mansion Cultural, San Rafael, Calif., 1980, Brevard Art Ctr. & Mus., Melbourne, Fla., 1980, Cape Cod Art Assn., Barnstable, Mass., Mus. Arts and Scis., Daytona Beach, Fla., 1982, Atlantic Galleries, Washington, 1985, Sheldon Swope Mus. & Gallery, Terra Haute, Ind., San Luis Obispo Art Ctr., Calif., Ozaukee Art Ctr., Cedarburg, Wis., Represented in permanent collections Brevard Art Ctr. & Mus., Melbourne, Fla., Sausalito Hist. Soc. Recipient Sausalito Art Fest. Spinnaker award, 1973. Mem.: Internat. Soc. Marine Painters. Democrat. Personal E-mail: audreyminney@sbcglobal.net.

MENIER, ROBERT JOSEPH, physiologist; b. Viroflay, France, June 6, 1935; s. Robert Marie Menier and Elisabeth Ocsenas; m. Nicole Jeanine Bodard, (div. 1991); children: Gwennaelle Benedicte, Marie Salome Audrey; m. Arlette Lallemand, 2002. MD, Med. Sch., Paris, 1962, D of Human Biology, 1975; agrégation, Paris, 1975; laureate (hon.), Acad. Med., Paris, 1976. Attaché, asst. physiology Med. Sch., Paris, 1964-68; asst. biology Paris Hosps., Paris, 1968-75; sr. lectr. physiology Med. Sch., Limoges, 1976-90, full prof., 1991—. Chmn. sports medicine Med. Sch., Limoges, 1989—, chmn. physiology, 1994—; deptl. head functional explorations Univ. Hosp., 1994—; dir. Regional Ctr. Sports Medicine, Limoges, 1996—; cons. in rehab. Med. Ctr. Toki Eder, Cambo, 1984—; sci. coun. Univ. Pres., Limoges, 1977-89. Author: Cinématique de la ventilation spontanée chez l'Homme, 1975 (prize Nat. Acad. Medicine 1976); patentee in field. Decorated chevalier Palmes Acad. (France), Legion of Honor (USA), Internat. Order of Merit, Cambridge. Mem. Soc. Limousine de Med. du Sport (pres. 1994-98), Revue European Biomed. Tech. (mem. sci. com. 1989—), Soc. French Sports Medicine, Soc. Physiology, Soc. Electriciens et des Electroniciens. Achievements include research in clinical respiratory physiology (five compartments lung model-kinematics of spontaneous human ventilation) and in physiology of physical activities; follow-up of effects on physical fitness-graded exercise tests-aerobic endurance indicators-physiol. overwork markers-respiratory rehabilitation by retraining & influence of branched-chain amino acids. Avocations: skiing, gardening, travel, reading. Home: 37 Allee de la Garde 87000 Limoges France Office Phone: 33 05 55 05 80 85. Business E-Mail: asp87@wanadoo.fr.

MENIKOFF, JERRY ALAN, health facility administrator, law educator; b. NYC; s. Max and Gloria Menikoff. AB, Harvard Coll., Cambridge, Mass., 1973; JD, Harvard Law Sch., Cambridge, 1977; MPP, Harvard U., Cambridge, 1977; MD, Wash. U., St. Louis, 1986. Assoc. atty. Dewey Ballantine, NYC, 1986—90; fellow ethics and lectr. law U. Chgo., 1991—92; rsch. fellow NY Eye & Ear Infirmary, 1990—91, resident ophthalmology, 1992—95; faculty fellow Program Ethics & Professions, Harvard U., 1995—96; assoc. prof. law, ethics & medicine U. Kans., Mo., 2002—09; dir., office human subjects rsch. NIH, Bethesda, 2007—08; dir., office human rsch. protections US Dept Health and Human Svcs., Rockville, Md. Author: (non-fiction book) What the Doctor Didn't Say: The Hidden Truth about Medical Research, Law and Bioethics (Best of the Best, Assn. Am. U., 2002). Recipient Dirs. award, NIH Clin. Ctr., 2008. Office: Office Human Rsch Protections 1101 Wootton Pkw Ste 200 Rockville MD 20852 Business E-Mail: jmenikof@kumc.edu, jerry.menikoff@hhs.gov.

MENINGALL, EVELYN L., retired educational media specialist; b. Dothan, Ala., July 22, 1935; d. Earl and Luella Koonce; m. A. Richard Meningall, Jan. 17, 1958; children: Dawn, Tracy, Richard. BS in Edn., Wayne State U., 1975; MLS, Rutgers U., 1979. Cert. ednl. media specialist Dept. Edn. State N.J., elem. sch. dept. Dept. Edn. State N.J., profl. librs. cert. Dept. Edn. State N.J. Tchr. Detroit Bd. Edn., 1975—76; libr. East Brunswick (N.J.) Pub. Libr., 1978—80; ednl. media specialist Piscataway (N.J.) Bd. Edn., 1980—98; ret., 1998. Author: A Way of Life: An Anthology of Poems, 2004, Reflections: A Collection of Poems, 2005, (picture book for children) Black is a Way of Life, 2007. Active New Detroit, Inc., Delta Sigma Theta Sorority Ctrl. Jersey; former mem. New Detroit, Inc.; former vol. Holistic Scoring English Test Plainfield HS; recording sec. Scholarship Fund of St. Paul AME Ch. Mem.: ALA (life), Ednl. Media Assn., Nat. Edn. Assn. (life), NJ Edn. Assn. (life), Nat. Sorority Phi Delta Kappa, Inc. (life; basileus 1987—89, exec. advisor 1989—91), Delta Sigma Theta (life). Methodist. Avocations: poetry, reading, fishing. Home: 23 Vauxhall Rd East Brunswick NJ 08816-1719

MENINO, THOMAS M., Mayor, Boston; b. Boston, Dec. 27, 1942; m. Angela Faletra; children: Susan, Thomas Michael, Jr. Grad., Chamberlayne Junior Coll., 1963; degree in Community Planning, U. Mass., 1988; cert. in State and Local Govt. Program, Harvard U. Mem. City Coun., Boston, 1985—, pres., 1993; acting mayor City of Boston, 1993, mayor, 1993—. Sr. rsch. asst. Joint Com. Urban Affairs, 1978-83; pres. U.S. Conf. Mayors, 2002-03. Contbr. articles to historic preservation jours. Regional chmn. Nat. Trust Historic Preservation; bd. dirs. Nat. League Cities, 1985—, mem. various coms. Office: Office of Mayor 1 City Hall Square Ste 500 Boston MA 02201-2013 Office Phone: 617-635-4500. Office Fax: 617-635-2851. Business E-Mail: mayor@cityofboston.gov.*

MENITOFF, PAUL ALAN, psychiatrist; b. Boston, May 4, 1946; s. Ralph and Ethel (Bickoff) M.; m. Susan Mathilde Hirsch, June 8, 1980. BA cum laude, Harvard U., 1969; MD, Cornell U., 1973. Diplomate Am. Bd. Psychiatry and Neurology, Subspecialty Psychosomatic Medicine. Intern in surgery Univ. Hosp., Boston, 1973-74; psychiat. resident Payne Whitney Clinic N.Y. Hosp./Cornell Med. Ctr., NYC, 1974-77; forensic psychiat. fellow U. So. Calif./L.A. County Med. Ctr., 1977-78; forensic psychiat. fellow Med. Sch. U. Md., Balt., 1978-79; staff psychiatrist Clifton T. Perkins Hosp., Jessup, Md., 1978-80; mem. med. staff St. John's Hosp., Lowell, Mass., 1980-93; Saints Meml. Med. Ctr., 1993—; chief divsn. psychiatry, 1996—; mem. med. staff St. Joseph's Hosp., Lowell, 1980-93, Lowell Gen. Hosp., 1980—, chief dept. psychiatry, 1991-93; mem. med. staff New Eng. Rehab. Hosp., Lowell, 1993—; pvt. practice Chelmsford, Mass., 1980—. Clin. inst. psychiatry U. So. Calif. Med. Sch., L.A., 1977-78; clin. asst. prof. psychiatry U. Md. Med. Sch., Balt., 1979-80; clin. asst. prof. psychiatry Tufts U. Sch. Medicine, 2006—. Mem. Am. Psychiat. Assn., Mass. Psychiat. Assn., Acad. Psychosomatic Medicine, Am. Acad. Psychiatry and the Law, Mass. Med. Soc. Democrat. Avocations: movies, theater. Office: Greater Lowell Psychiat Assocs 9 Acton Rd Ste 25 Chelmsford MA 01824-3496 Office Phone: 978-256-6579.

MENIUS, ESPIE FLYNN, JR., electrical engineer; b. New Bern, NC, Mar. 5, 1923; s. Espie Flynn and Sudie Grey (Lyerly) M.; adopted children: James Benfield, Ruben Hughes, James Sechler, Steve Walden. BEE, N.C. State U., 1947; MBA, U. S.C., 1973. Registered profl. engr., N.C., S.C., Tenn., Ga., Fla. With Carolina Power & Light Co., 1947-63, asst. to dist. mgr. Raleigh, Henderson, NC, 1947-50, Sumter, SC, 1947-50, elec. engr. Asheville, Southern Pines and Dunn, NC, 1950-52, dist. engr. Hartsville, SC, 1952-63; sr. elec. engr. Sonoco Products Co., 1963-74, engring. group leader, 1974-89, sr. profl. engr., 1989-91; profl. cons. and elec. engr., 1991—. Instr. Florence-Darlington Tech. Ednl. Ctr. Author: Adoption of Older Children; contbr. articles to profl. jours. Active Hartsville Vol. Fire Dept., 1958-94; Fire dept. and Law Enforcement Chaplain 1985—; Eagle Scout Boy Scouts Am., 1938, scout troop leader New Bern, 1940-41, Raleigh, 1941-47, Henderson, 1948-49, Sumter, 1949-50, Asheville, N.C., 1950, Southern Pines, N.C., 1951-52, Hartsville, 1952-64; bd. mgrs. Nazareth Children's Home, Rockwell, N.C., 1980—; chmn. bd. examiners City of Hartsville, 1980-90; advocate Thornwell Children's Home, Clinton, S.C., 1990-98; bd. dir. Darlington (S.C.) County Youth Home, 1992-98; active Hartsville Leadership Coun., 1993-2000; deacon, elder, trustee, tchr. men's Bible class First Presbyn. Ch., Hartsville. Served with US Army, 1943-46. Recipient Citzenship award S.C. State Firemen's Assn., 1993; named Hartsville Citizen of Yr., Rotary, 1960; named to S.C. Fire Fighters Hall of Fame, 1995. Mem. IEEE, AAAS, VFW, Nat. Assn. Engrs., Am. Legion, Knight of St. Patrick, Scabbard and Blade, Eta Kappa Nu, Pine Burr, Phi Eta Sigma, Theta Tau, Beta Gamma Sigma. Presbyn. Home and Office: 423 W Richardson Cir Hartsville SC 29550-5437 Office Phone: 843-332-8502.

MENJIVAR, CECILIA, social sciences educator; arrived in U.S., 1978; d. Jose and Mercedes Menjivar; m. Victor Agadjanian, Mar. 27, 1992. BA in Psychology and Sociology, U. of So. Calif., LA, 1981, MS in Internat. Ednl. Devel., 1983; MA in Sociology, U. of Calif., Davis, 1986, PhD in Sociology, 1992. Postdoctoral fellow U. of Calif., Berkeley, 1992—94; postdoctoral rschr., cons. RAND Corp., Santa Monica, Calif., 1994—95; disting. prof. sociology Ariz. State U., Tempe, 1996—. Mem., com. on the status of women Ariz. State U., Tempe, Ariz., 2001—02; co-chair Cen. Am. sect. Latin Am. Studies Assn., 2002—; exec. bd. mem. Chgo. Latino Faculty Staff Assoc. Author: Fragmented Ties: Salvadoran Immigrant Networks in America, 2000 (William J. Goode Book award Am. Sociol. Assn. Family Sect., 2001, Hon. Mention Internat. Migration Sect., Outstanding Acad. Title in Social and Behavioral Scis. award, CHOICE award, 02); editor: Through the Eyes of Women: Gender, Social Networks, Family and Structural Change in Latin America and the Caribbean, 2003; co-editor: When States Kill: Latin America, The US, and Technologies of Terror, 2005; mem. editl. bd.: Gender and Identity; contbr. numerous articles to profl. jours. Mem.: Pacific Sociol. Assn. (mem. com. on coms. 2004—06), Latin Am. Studies Assn. (mem. coun. sect. on gender 2004—06), Soc. Study of Social Problems (chmn. minority fellowship selection com. 2001—02), Am. Sociol. Assn. (mem. coun. internat. migration sect. 2003—06, chair Latinola section 2005—06, mem. editl. bd. Am. Sociol. Rev.). Office: Ariz State U Dept Sociology Tempe AZ 85287-4802 Business E-Mail: menjivar@asu.edu.

MENKE, ALLEN CARL, retired manufacturing executive; b. Huntingburg, Ind., Feb. 16, 1922; s. William Ernest and Clara (Moenkhaus) M.; m. Virginia Lee MacDonald, Apr. 14, 1944; children: Janet, William, Sarah. BS in Mech. Engring, Purdue U., 1943, MS, 1948. Instr. Purdue U., 1946-48; with Trane Co., 1948-68, v.p. sales, 1963-64, exec. v.p. sales, mfg. and engring., 1964-68; v.p. Borg-Warner Corp., Chgo., 1969-76; chmn., pres., CEO Artesian Industries, Northbrook, Ill., 1976-88; ret. Bd. dirs. Trane Co., SPS Techs., Hoover Co., Consolidated Papers Corp., York Corp., Am. Air Filter. Pres. Met. Housing Devel. Corp.; founder, pres. Winnetka Interch. Coun.; bd. dirs., past chmn. Presbyn. Home; past chmn. dean's adv. coun. Krannert Sch. Mgmt. Purdue U.; bd. dirs. McCormick Sem., U. Chgo.; trustee Kenilworth Union Ch. Served to 1st lt. AUS, 1944-46. Named Disting. Alumnus, Purdue U., 1965, Outstanding Engr. Grad., 1991, mem. Purdue Hall of Fame, Ind. Basketball Hall of Fame, 1999. Mem. Sigma Chi (Significant Order Constantine awards). Presbyterian (elder). Lodge: Mason. Home: 2 Arbor Ln #208 Evanston IL 60201

MENKE, RICHARD, literature and language professor; s. R. Bruce and Karen Estes Menke; m. Sujata Iyengar; children: Kavya, Kartik. PhD, Stanford U., Calif., 2000. Asst. prof. english U. Ga., Athens, 2000—08, assoc. prof. english, 2008—. Author: (book) Telegraphic Realism: Victorian Fiction and Other Information Systems. Office: Univ GA Dept English Park Hall 254 Athens GA 30602-6205

MENKE, SEAN E., air transportation executive; m. Arminda Menke; 3 children. B in Econs. and Aviation Mgmt., Ohio State U.; MBA, U. Denver. Dir. planning Western Pacific Airlines, Inc.; sr. planner domestic schedule planning United Air Lines, Inc.; dir. mktg. and planning Frontier Airlines, Inc., 1999—2000, v.p. mktg. and planning, 2000—03, sr. v.p. mktg., 2003—04, sr. v.p., chief operating officer, 2004—05, pres., CEO, 2007—; exec. v.p., chief comml. officer Air Can., 2005—07, exec. v.p. comml. strategy, 2007. Bd. mem. Frontier Airlines, Inc., 2007—. Recipient Disting. Alumni award, Ohio State U., 2006. Office: Frontier Airlines Inc 7001 Tower Rd Denver CO 80249 Office Phone: 720-374-4200, 800-265-5505. Office Fax: 720-374-4375.

MENLOVE, FRANCES LEE, psychologist; b. Salt Lake City, June 4, 1936; d. Edwin Fred and Pernecy Greaves Anderson; children: Stephen, Lynelle, Spencer, Lauren. BA, Stanford U., Calif.; PhD, U. Mich., 1963; cert. in Profl. Ethics, Pacific Sch. Religion, 1990, MDiv, 1998. Lic. psychologist N.Mex., 1976, Oreg., 1990. Founder, dir. Coun. Alcholism, Los Alamos, N.Mex., 1973—74; chief psychologist U. Calif., Los Alamos, 1974—86, dir. human resources, 1986—96; ethicist Bioethics Consultation Group, Berkeley, Calif., 1997—2000; asst. min. United Ch. Christ Congl., Lincoln City, Oreg., 2002—. Tchr. ethics U. N.Mex., Los Alamos, 1991—92; trustee Dialogue Jour., Palo Alto, Calif., 1965—72; cons. N.Mex. Dept. Corrections, Albuquerque, 1972—72; dir. Called to Care, Lincoln City, Oreg., 2002—05; psychologist Am. Red Cross, Lincoln City, 2001—; adv. bd. U. N.Mex., Los Alamos, N.Mex., 1993—96. Manuscript editor: Jour. Mormon Thought, 1963—65; author: A Challenge of Honesty, 1966, A Challenge of Honesty-Watershed Articles 35 Years of Dialogue, 2001, Sunstone, 2004; contbr. articles to profl. jours. Recipient Danforth award, Danforth Found., 1954; named Outstanding Young Woman of Yr., New Mex., 1972; fellow, Woodrow Wilson Found., 1959. Mem.: APA (life), Phi Beta Kappa. Avocations: reading, whale watching, travel.

MENN, JULIUS JOEL, retired research scientist, consultant; b. Danzig, Free City (now Poland), Feb. 20, 1929; came to the U.S., 1950, naturalized, 1959; s. David Gregory and Regina (Ajzenstadt) M.; m. Alma R. Zito, Aug. 31, 1952 (div. 1981); children: Leslie, David (dec.), Diana (dec.); m. Dianne R. Sagner, Apr. 17, 1992. BS, U. Calif., Berkeley, 1953, MS, 1954, PhD, 1958. Dir. biochem. and insecticide rsch. Stauffer Chem. Co., Mountain View, Calif., 1957-79; dir. agrichem. rsch. Zoecon Corp., Palo Alto, Calif., 1979-85; nat. program leader crop protection Agrl. Rsch. Svc., USDA, Beltsville, Md., 1985-88; assoc. dep. area dir. Beltsville Agrl. Rsch. Ctr., 1988-94; sr. agrl. policy adviser USDA/FAS, 1999—2006. Internat. cons. crop protection and agr. biotechnology, 1994-; chmn. Gordon Rsch. Conf., 1989; adj. prof. environ. toxicology San Jose State U., Calif., 1979-84; adj. prof. entomology U. Md., College Park, 1986-95; vis. prof. Pa. State U., 1999-2002; mem. U.S./USSR Team on Environ. Pollution, 1974-85; tech. expert UNIDO, UNDCP, 1995—, The World Bank, 1998.; tech. cons. Inst. Post Harvest Tech., MARD, Hanoi, Vietnam, 2003-07. Editor: Insect Juvenile Hormones, 1972, Insect Neuropeptides, 1991, Biopesticides: Use & Delivery, 1999; contbr. articles to 120 sci. jours. Recipient Bussart Meml. award Ea. Br. Entomol. Soc. Am., 1990, Ciba-Geigy Recognition award Ea. Br. Entomol. Soc. Am., 1991, 92. Mem. Am. Chem. Soc. (fellow pesticide chem. divsn. 1973, chmn. 1976, councilor 1981-89, adv. bd. books dept. 1991-94, Agrochem. Divsn. Internat. award for rsch. in pesticide chem. 1979), Internat. Soc. Study Xenobiotics (councilor 1983-86). Achievements include pioneering research in pesticide metabolism, selective insect control agents including juvenile hormones and neuropeptides; patentee in field. Home Phone: 443-745-4091; Office Phone: 301-770-4002. Personal E-mail: menn03@comcast.net.

MENNA, GILBERT G., lawyer; AB magna cum laude, Syracuse U., 1978; JD, Georgetown U., 1982, ML in Taxation, 1983. Bar: Calif. 1982, Mass. 1988. Ptnr., bus. law dept. Goodwin Procter LLP, Boston, mem. mgmt. com. Bd. dir. NYU Real Estate Inst.'s REIT Ctr.; bd. assoc. NAREIT. Frequent lectr., writer in field. Mem.: Phi Beta Kappa. Office: Goodwin & Procter Exchange Pl 53 State St Boston MA 02109-2881 Office Phone: 617-570-1433. Office Fax: 617-523-1231. Business E-Mail: gmenna@goodwinprocter.com.

MENNA, SÁRI, artist, educator; b. San Fracisco, Sept. 29, 1932; m. Ferdinand Carl Menna, Mar. 10, 1949; children: Mark, Diane Menna Clarke. BFA cum laude, Hunter Coll. of CUNY, NYC, 1968, MFA, 1974; post grad., N.Y. U., NYC, 1987—93. Lic. tchr. N.Y. Bd. Edn., 1971. Substitute tchr. Massapequa Pub. Schs., LI, NY, 1968—69; tchr. art N.Y.C. Bd. Edn., 1971—95; ret., 1995. Vol. art tchr. Pres.' Econ. Opportunity Ctr., LI, 1967—68; organizer juried art shows Amity Art League, 1964—67; tchr. cultural workshop Amityville Workshop, LI, 1968. Exhibitions include Salute to Women, Washington, Nairobi, 1991, Women's Art, NYC, 1992, Paintings and Paperworks, CUNY, 1992, Small Works, Kirkland, Wash., 1993, Garden of Delights, Bklyn., 1994, Family Values, NYC, 1994, Hallelujah, 1994, Visions of Reality, Madison, NJ, 1995, A Woman's Pl., NYC, 1995, Points of View, 1995, ADA: Women and Info. Tech., Chgo., 1995—96, The World's Women On Line, Beijing, Tempe, Ariz., online, 1995—96, Fine Arts Mus., LI, NY, 1996, Openings, NYC, 1996, Diversity, 1997, Small Statement Show, Bklyn., 1997, Painterly Forms, NYC, 1997, BWAC 4th Ann. Pier Show, NJ, 1998, Flat Iron Gallery, Peekskill, NY, 1999, Broome St. Gallery, Soho, NYC, 2000, WIA Part II, Canojohri, NY, 2000, Broome St. Gallery, NYC, 2004, Williamsburg Art and Hist. Ctr., Bklyn., 2004, Taller Boriqua Galleries, Julia de Burgos Cultural Ctr., NYC, 2005, Medeung Gallery, Korea, 2005, Art Expo NYC, 2008, LI City Art Orgn. Open Studio, 2008, exhibited in group shows at Pier Show, NYC, 2006, WIA, Venezuelan Ctr., NY, 2007, James Brown House Gallery, NYC, 2008, Represented in permanent collections Nat. Mus. Women in Arts, Washington, Women's Interart Collections, NYC, calendar and cover art, Women Artists, 1983, in pvt. collections, online exhibitions, minipark, NYC, 1974. Pres. Creative Women's Collective, NYC, 1982—85; mem. Women's Caucus Art (N.Y.C. chpt.), 1982—91; mem. Queens Coun. on Art, 2001—. Mem.: Creative Women's Collective, Women in the Arts Found, Inc., Women's Studio Ctr., Artists Equity. Personal E-mail: sarimenna@mac.com.

MENNARD, MIKE, literature and language professor; b. Ft. Worth, July 15, 1967; s. Robert Dallas and Davaleen Louise Mesnard; m. Michelle Mae Velazquez, June 25, 1989; 1 child, Ramsey Robert Francisco Mesnard. MA in English, Sonoma State U., Rohnert Pk., Calif., 2003. Prof., English, communication Union Coll., Linclon, Nebr. Composer (writer and producer): (recording) Pirates Do the Darnedest Things, When Mother Goose Laid an Egg, The Whaler's Inn. Home: 7361 S 30th St Lincoln NE 68516 Office: Union Coll 4800 S 48th St Lincoln NE 68506 Home Phone: 402-420-9794; Office Phone: 402-486-2600 ext. 2321. Business E-Mail: mennard1@mac.com.

MENNICKE, DAVID, music educator, director; BA, St. Olaf Coll., Northfield, Minn., 1983; MusM, U. Ariz., Tucson, 1987, MusD, 1989. Vocal music dir. Benson HS, Minn., 1983—86; choral tchg. asst. U. Ariz., Tucson, 1986—89; sr. choir dir. St. Paul's Episcopal Ch., Tucson, 1986—89, Peace Luth. Ch., Robbinsdale, Minn., 1990—96; dir. choral studies music dept. chair Concordia U., St. Paul, 1989—; dir. adult and youth choirs Bethlehem Luth. Ch., Mpls., 1996—. Melisma editor North Ctrl. Divsn., Am. Choral Directors Assn., St. Paul, 1997—2003. Composer: (choral compositions) Five arrangements published by Morningstar Music; dir.: (choral director) ACDA of Minnesota All-State Children's Choir Director (Outstanding Young Choral Dir. of Yr., 1992, ACDA Minn. Creative Programming award, 1996), Minnesota Music Educators Association All-State Men's Choir Director. Mem.: Music Educators Nat. Conf., Minn. Music Educators Assn., Am. Choral Directors Assn. Office: Concordia Univ St Paul 275 Syndicate St N Saint Paul MN 55104 Business E-Mail: dmennicke@csp.edu.

MENNIN, DOUGLAS STEVEN, psychologist; b. NYC, May 21, 1972; s. Gerald Stanley and Miriam Juliet (Kobrin) M. BA, Oberlin Coll., 1994; MA, Temple U., 1999, postgrad., 1995. Clin. rsch. analyst Mass. Gen. Hosp., Boston, 1994-96; clin. rsch. assoc. Adult Anxiety Clinic Temple U., Phila., 1996-2000; clin. psychology fellow N.Y. Presbyn. Hosp.-Cornell Med. Coll., 2000—. Ad hoc reviewer Cognitive Therapy and Rsch., 1996-99; contbr. articles to profl. jours. Recipient psychology fellow N.Y. Presbyn./Cornell Med. Ctr., 2000—, Congl. medal of merit U.S. Congress, Scarsdale, N.Y., 1990. Mem. APA (student), Assn. Advancement of Behavior Therapy (student), Anxiety Disorders Assn. Am. (student), Sigma Xi. Home: 50 Lexington Ave Apt 16g New York NY 10010-2931

MENNINGER, WILLIAM WALTER, psychiatrist; b. Topeka, Oct. 23, 1931; s. William Claire and Catharine Louisa (Wright) Menninger; m. Constance Arnold Libbey, June 15, 1953 (dec. Apr. 13, 2008);

children: Frederick Prince, John Alexander, Eliza Wright, Marian Stuart, William Libbey, David Henry. AB, Stanford U., 1953; MD, Cornell U., 1957; LittD (hon.), Middlebury Coll., 1982; DSc (hon.), Washburn U., 1982; LHD (hon.), Ottawa U., 1986; LLD (hon.), Heidelberg Coll., 1993, Dominican U., 2007. Diplomate Am. Bd. Psychiatry and Neurology, Am. Bd. Forensic Psychiatry. Intern Harvard Med. Svc., Boston City Hosp., 1957-58; resident in psychiatry Menninger Sch. Psychiatry, 1958-61; chief med. officer, psychiatrist Fed. Reformatory, El Reno, Okla., 1961-63; assoc. psychiatrist Peace Corps, 1963-64; staff psychiatrist Menninger Found., Topeka, 1965—2001, coordinator for devel., 1967-69, dir. law and psychiatry, 1981-85, dir. dept. edn., dean Karl Menninger Sch. Psychiatry and Mental Health Scis., 1984-90, exec. v.p., chief staff, 1984-93, CEO, 1993—2001, pres., 1993—96, 1999—2001, chmn. bd. trustees, 2001—; clin. supr. Topeka State Hosp., 1969-70, sect. dir., 1970-72, asst. supt., clin., dir. residency tng., 1972-81; pres. Menninger Clinic, Topeka, 1991-96; staff Stormont-Vail Hosp., Topeka, 1984-94, assoc., 1994—2002. Adj. prof. Washburn U.; mem. Fed. Prison Facilities Planning Coun., 1970—73; mem. adv. bd. Nat. Inst. Corrections, 1975—88, chmn., 1980—84; cons. U.S. Bur. Prisons; mem. adv. bd. US Bank, Topeka, 1999—. Syndicated columnist: In-Sights, 1975—83; author: (book) Happiness Without Sex and Other Things Too Good to Miss, 1976, Caution: Living May Be Hazardous, 1978, Behavioral Science and the Secret Service, 1981, Chronic Mental Patient II, 1987; editor: Psychiatry Digest, 1971—74, Bull. of Menninger Clinic, 2001—; contbr. articles to profl. jours., chpts. to books. Mem. health and safety com. Boy Scouts Am., 1970—, chmn., 1980—85, mem. nat. exec. bd., 1980—90, mem. nat. adv. coun., 1990—; bd. dirs. Nat. Com. Prevention Child Abuse, 1975—83; mem. nat. adv. health coun. HEW, 1967—71; mem. Nat. Commn. Causes and Prevention Violence, 1968—69; rsch. adv. com. U.S. Secret Svc., 1990—2005; pres. Jayhawk coun. Boy Scouts Am., 1998—2001; mem. Kans. Gov.'s Adv. Commn. Mental Health, Mental Retardation and Cmty. Mental Health Svcs., 1983—90, Kans. Gov.'s Penal Planning Coun., 1970; chmn. Kans. Gov.'s Criminal Justice Coun., 1970; mem. Kans. Gov.'s Commn. on Crime Reduction and Prevention/Koch Commn., 1994—98; ruling elder 1st Presbyn. Ch., Topeka, 1992—95; trustee Kenworthy-Swift Found., 1980—; bd. dirs. Police Found., Washington, 1996—, Koch Crime Inst., 1998—2000; trustee Midwest Rsch. Inst., Kansas City, Mo., 1996—. With USPHS, 1959—64. Fellow: ACP, Am. Coll. Psychiatrists, Am. Psychiat. Assn. (chmn. com. chronically mentally ill 1984—86, chmn. Guttmacher award bd. 1990—96); mem.: AMA, Am. Acad. Psychiatry and Law, Am. Psychoanalytic Assn. (chmn. com. psychoanalysis, cmty. and soc. 1984—93), Inst. Medicine NAS, Group Advancement Psychiatry (chmn. com. mental health svcs. 1974—77, 1991—2002), Stanford Assocs. Office: PO Box 4406 Topeka KS 66604-0406 Office Phone: 785-235-3400. Business E-Mail: wmenninger@menninger.edu.

MENO, JOHN PETER, religious organization administrator; b. Carlinville, Ill., Aug. 22, 1942; s. John Victor and Margaret Mary (Cena) M.; m. Rolanda A. Abyad, Sept. 14, 1968; 1 child, Peter James. MA, Am. U. Beirut, 1969; STM, Union Theol. Sem., 1972. Ordained priest Syrian Orthodox Ch. of Antioch, 1972, elevated to chorepiscopus, 1983. Gen. sec. Archdiocese Syrian Orthodox Ch. US/Can., Lodi, NJ, 1972—95; cathedral dean St. Mark's Syrian Orthodox Cathedral, Teaneck, NJ, 1975—; gen. sec. Archdiocese Syrian Orthodox Ch. Ea. US, Teaneck, 1996—. Co-sec. Standing Conf. of Oriental Orthodox Chs. in America, NYC, 1973—; co-chmn. US Roman Cath.-Oriental Orthodox Cons., 1989—. Editor: Hymns of the Syrian Orthodox Church of Antioch, 1976; contbr. The Oriental Orthodox Chs. in US, 1986, Dictionary of Christianity in America, 1990, Oriental Orthodox-Roman Catholic Interchurch Marriages and Other Pastoral Relationships, 1995, Nelson's New Christian Dictionary, 2001, The Encyclopedia of Christianity, 2003, 2008. Recipient Golden Cross of Archdiocese Syrian Orthodox Ch. US/Can., 1992. Syrian Orthodox. Home: 263 Elm Ave Teaneck NJ 07666-2323 Office: St Mark's Syrian Orthodox Cathedral 260 Elm Ave Teaneck NJ 07666-2318 Personal E-mail: vrjmeno@aol.com.

MENON, JAI M., information technology manager; arrived in U.S., 1977; s. Sreedharan Menon and Radha Sreedharan; m. Sathi Eradi, Aug. 20, 1985; children: Anjali, Vijay V. BS in Tech in Elec. Engring., Indian Inst. Tech., Madras, India, 1977; MS in Computer Sci., Ohio State U., Columbus, Ohio, 1978, PhD in Computer Sci., 1981. From rsch. staff mem. to chief tech. officer IBM, San Jose, Calif., 1982—2003, chief tech. officer, 2003—, dir. storage arch. and strategy, 2003—05, v.p. arch. and strategy, software and strategy, 2005—07, v.p. tech. strategy, 2007—. Session chair CompCon, San Francisco, 1983, 95; mem. program com. conf. Very Large Data Base, 1984, rev. panelist, 1992—96; mem. program com. Internat. Symposium Computer Arch., 1995—95; mem. of steering com. FAST, File and Storage Sys. Tech., 2003—; vice chair IBM Acad. of Tech., San Jose, 2007—; presenter in field. Author: Relational Database Machine Architecture; co-author: Advanced Database Machine Architcture, Disk Array and parallel I/O - Theory and Practice; contbr. over 47 articles to profl. jours. (Best Paper award HICSS-25, 1992); mem. editl. bd.: Jour. Distributed and Parallel Databases, 1993—94; editor, 1994. Chmn. campaign IBM United Way, San Jose, Calif., 2001. Recipient Acad. Tech. award, IBM, 1994, Corp. award, 2000, Disting. Alumnus award, Ohio State U., 2004, Indian Inst. Tech., Madras, 2006; named Master Inventor, IBM, 1995; fellow, 2001; scholar, Govt. India, 1977. Fellow: IEEE (Wallace McDowell award 2002, Reynold B. Johnson award 2006). Achievements include patents in field. Business E-Mail: menonjm@almaden.ibm.com.

MENON, MANI, urological surgeon, educator; b Trichur, Kerala, India, July 9, 1948; came to U.S., 1972, naturalized, 1977; s. Balakrishna and Sumathie Menon; m. Shameem Ara Begum, Oct. 17, 1972; children: Nisha, Roshen. MBBS, Madras U., India, 1971. Diplomate Am. Bd. Urology. Intern Bryn Mawr (Pa.) Hosp., 1973-74; resident Brady Urol. Inst., The Johns Hopkins Hosp., Balt., 1974-80; asst. prof. urology Washington U. Med. Ctr., St. Louis, 1980-83, assoc. prof., 1983; prof. urology, chmn. div. urology and transplant surgery U. Mass. Med. Ctr., Worcester, 1983—; prof. physiology, U. Mass. Med. Ctr., Worcester, 1986—; clin. prof. urology Case Sch. Medicine, U. Toledo, NY U. Contbr. over 300 papers in field robotic surgery, renal transplantation and urolithiasis. Recepient: Dr. B.C.Roy award Pres. of India, 2008. Mem. AAAS, Am. Assn. Genito Urinary Surgeons, Am. Urol. Assn. (Gold Cytoscope award 1990), Am. Fedn. Clin. Rsch., Am. Soc. Transplantation and Vascular Surgery, Rschrs. on Calculus Kinetics, Johns Hopkins Med. and Surg. Assn., Mass. Med. Soc., Mass. Soc. Med. Rsch. Avocations: tennis, puzzles, mystery fiction. Office: Henry Ford Hosp Vattikuti Urology Inst 2799 W Grand Blvd Detroit MI 48202 Office Phone: 313-916-2066. E-mail: mmenon1@hfhs.org.

MENON, RAM KUMAR, neurosurgeon, consultant; b. Allepey, Kerala, India, May 18, 1974; s. Achutha Menon and Kamalamma K. N.; m. Divya Ram Sukumaran, Sept. 15, 2004; 1 child, Dhruv Ram. MBBS, Calicut Med. Coll., Kerala, 1997; MS, Aligarh U., 2002, MCh in Neurosurgery, 2006. Diplomate Ministry Health and Family Welfare, 2003. Sr. registrar King Edward Meml. Hosp., Mumbai, India, 2006; fellow, Barrow Neurological Inst. St. Joseph's Hosp., Phoenix, 2007; fellow Clin. Ctr., U. Hosp., Ljubjana, Slovenia, 2007; cons. neurosurgeon Elite Mission Hosp., Trichur, Kerala, 2007—. Cons. Elite Mission Hosp., Trichur, 2008—. Contbr. articles to rsch. papers. Neurosurgeon Paramekkavu Charitable Hosp., Trichur, 2008—. Recipient Hoechst award, 2001, Nat. award, B. Braun Health Found., 2005; fellow, Hargobind Med. Found., 2007. Mem.: Skull Base Soc. India, Asian Conf. Neurol. Surgeons, Indian Soc. Cerebrovasc. Surgery, Neurol. Soc. India. Office: Univ of Michigan Med Sch Medical Profl Blg Rm D1109 Box 0718 1500 E Medical Center Dr Ann Arbor MI 48109-0718 Office Fax: 0091-487-2424322. Personal E-mail: menon18uk@gmail.com.

MENOTTI-RAYMOND, MARILYN, geneticist, molecular biologist; d. Amel and Mary Menotti; children: James Raymond, Daniel Raymond. BS cum laude, Syracuse U., NY, 1964, MS, 1984, PhD, 1990. Postdoc. fellow Syracuse U., 1990, Nat. Cancer Inst., Frederick, Md., 1990—93, intramural rsch. tng. award fellow, 1993—96, sr. staff fellow, 1996—98, rsch. fellow, 1998—2000, staff scientist, 2000—. Grantee, Nat. Inst. Justice. Mem.: Am. Genetic Assn. Office: Nat Cancer Inst Frederick Bldg 560 Rm 11-38 Frederick MD 21702 Office Fax: 301-846-6327. Business E-Mail: raymond@ncifcrf.gov.

MENSCHEL, ROBERT BENJAMIN, investment banker; b. NYC, July 2, 1929; s. Benjamin and Helen (Goldsmith); m. Joyce Virginia Frank, Dec. 5, 1968; children: David F., Lauren E. BS, Syracuse U., 1951, LLD (hon.), 1991; postgrad., NYU, 1951—53. Mem. N.Y. Stock Exchange, NYC, 1950—51; specialist HW Goldsmith and Co., NYC, 1951—54; with Goldman, Sachs & Co., NYC, 1954—66, gen. ptnr. instl. sales, 1966—78, ltd. ptnr., 1979—2000, sr. dir., 2000—. Author: Markets Mobs & Mayhem, 2002. Trustee Nat. Gallery Art; com. on the arts and the humanities Pres. Clinton; former mem. bd. trustees, investment com. Human Rights Watch; chmn., trustee, exec. and fin. com., mem. investment com., co-chmn. photography com. Mus. Modern Art; trustee Inst. Advanced Study, Princeton, Chess in the Schs., NYC; trustee, exec. com. Syracuse U.; former trustee, mem. exec. com. Montefiore Hosp.; former trustee Guild Hall, East Hampton, NY, past chmn. bd.; pres. bd. trustees, mem. exec. com. Dalton Sch., NYC; past bd. advs. Grad. Sch. Inst. Internat. Bus. Pace U.; exec. bd. NY chpt. Am. Jewish Com., NY; bd. dirs., mem. fin. and exec. com. NY Pub. Libr., NYC; bd. dirs. Parks Coun.; mng. dir. Horace W. Goldsmith Found., Vital Projects Fund; bd. dirs. associated YM-YWHA; v.p. bd. trustees, mem. fin. and exec. com. Temple Emanu-El; trustee NY Presbyn. Hosp. Recipient Recipient George Arents medal, Syracuse U., 1984. Mem.: Coun. Fgn. Rels., City Athletic Club, India Ho. Office: Goldman Sachs & Co 85 Broad St New York NY 10004-2456 Home: 980 5th Ave New York NY 10075 also: Further Lane Amagansett NY 11930 Office Phone: 212-902-6913. Business E-Mail: robert.menschel@gs.com.

MENSCHER, BARNET GARY, steel company executive; b. Laurelton, NY, Sept. 5, 1940; s. Samuel and Louise (Zaimont) M.; m. Diane Elaine Gachman, June 12, 1966; children: Melissa Denise, Corey Lane, Scott Jay. Student, Centenary Coll., 1958-59; BBA, U. Tex., 1963. Vice pres. mktg. Ella Gant Mfg., Shreveport, La., 1964-66; warehouse mgr., dir. material control Gachman Steel Co., Fort Worth, 1966-68, gen. mgr. Houston, 1968-70; v.p. sales Gachman Metal Co., Houston, 1971-76; pres. Menko Steel Service, Inc., Houston, 1979—; CEO NEXTLEVEL, Houston, 1998—. Investment cons. D & L Enterprises, 1966—. Mem. solicitation com. United Fund, 1969-76; mem. Nat. Alliance of Businessmen Jobs Program, 1969—. Served with AUS, 1963-65. Mem. Tex. Assn. Steel Importers, Purchasing Agts. Assn. Houston, Credit Assn. Houston, Am. Mgmt. Assn., Assn. Steel Distbrs., Nat. Assn. Elevator Contractors, Phi Sigma Delta, Alpha Phi Omega. Home: Apt 1002 3388 Sage Rd Houston TX 77056 Home Phone: 713-464-8700. Personal E-mail: bdmenscher@gmail.com.

MENSE, ALLAN TATE, research and development engineering executive; b. Kansas City, Mo., Nov. 29, 1945; s. Martin Conrad Mense and Nancy (Tate) Johnson; children from previous marriage: Melanie Georgia Thomas, Eileen Mense Hartzell. BS, U. Ariz., 1968, MS, 1970; PhD, U. Wis., 1977; MS in Indsl. Engring., Ariz. State U., 1999. Registered profl. indsl. engr., ASQ cert. reliability engring. Scientist Oak Ridge (Tenn.) Nat. Lab, 1976-79; sr. staff sci. and tech. comm. U.S. Ho. Reps., Washington, 1979-81; sr. scientist McDonnell Douglas Astro. Co., St. Louis, 1981-85; from dep. chief scientist to chief scientist Dept. Def. Strategic Def. Initiative Orgn., Washington, 1985-88; v.p. rsch. Fla. Inst. Tech., Melbourne, 1988-92; pres. Advanced Tech. Mgmt., Inc., Tempe, Ariz., 1992-97; lead sys. engr. Motorola Space Sys. Tech. Group, Chandler, Ariz., 1998—2001; chief engr., prin. engring. fellow Raytheon Missile Sys., 2002—. Vis. scholar Sloan Sch., MIT, 1995-96; mem. U.S. Army Sci. Bd., 2005—. Contbr. over 60 articles to profl. jours. Ariz. State U. scholar, 1996-97. Mem. AIAA (sr. mem.), IEEE (chmn. energy com. 1985—, sr. mem.), Nat. Def. Industries Assn., Am. Phys. Soc., Am. Nuclear Soc., Inst. Indsl. Engrs., Fla. Com. Nat. Space Club (charter), Sigma Xi, Theta Tau, Pi Mu Alpha. Episcopalian. Office: 1151 E Hermans Rd B840/MS8 Tucson AZ 85706 Home: 116 E Camino Limon Verde Sahuarita AZ 85629 Office Phone: 520-794-4720. Business E-Mail: allan_t_mense@raytheon.com.

MENSES, JAN, artist, draftsman, muralist; b. Rotterdam, Netherlands, Apr. 28, 1933; emigrated to Can., 1960, naturalized, 1965; s. Jan and Elisabeth Wilhelmina (Schwarz) M.; m. Rachel Régine Kadoch, Dec. 7, 1958; children: Salomon, Hnina Sarah, Nechamah Elisabeth Halo. Student, Acad. Fine Arts, Rotterdam, Officers Acad. Royal Dutch Air Force, 1953-55. Cert. Royal Can. Academician, Academician of Nations, Academician of Europe, Academician of Italy. Lectr. in fine arts Concordia U., Montreal, 1973-76, others. One-man shows include Montreal Mus. Fine Arts, 1961, 65, 76, Isaacs Gallery, Toronto, Ont., Can., 1964, Delta Gallery, Rotterdam, 1965, Galerie Godard Lefort, Montreal, 1966, Gallery Moos, Toronto, 1967, Rotterdam Art Found., 1974, Galerie Mira Godard, Toronto, 1977, Montreal, 1978, Seasons Galleries, The Hague, 1980, U. B.C. Fine Arts Gallery, Vancouver, 1981, Galerie Don Stewart, Montreal, 1981, Mead Art Mus., Amherst, Mass., 1983, Agnes Etherington Art Mus., 1984, Blom and Dorn Gallery, N.Y.C., 1985, 86-93, Marywood Coll. Mus., Scranton, Pa., 1985, Saraya-Wolfson Ctr., Safed, Israel, 1987, Mayanot Gallery, Jerusalem, 1987-88, Esperanza Gallery, Montreal, 1988, 89, Gallery Hamaayan Haradum, Safed, Israel, 1989—, Blom and Dorn Gallery, Hartford, Conn., 1995, Nora Gallery, Jerusalem, 1995, 96, 97, Artist's Colony, Safed, Israel; over 300 group shows include Montreal World Exhbn., 1967, Salon Internat. Art, Basel, Switzerland, 1972, 74, Can. Nat. Exhbn., 1972, Centennial Exhbn., Royal Can. Acad., Toronto, 1980, Que. Biennale I, II, III, Montreal, 1977, 79, 81, Foire Internat. D'Art Contemporain Paris and Internat. Fair Koln Germany, 1986, Migdal Ha-Emek, Israel, 1988, Group of 8 Israel, Toronto, 1990, Royal Can. Acad. Show, Toronto, 1991, Bezalel Acad., Jerusalem, 2004; represented in permanent exhbn. Gallery Hamaayan Haradum, Safed, Profl. Artists' Assn., Artists Colony, Safed, Menses Mus. Contemporary Art, Safed, Israel; represented in permanent collections Pushkin Mus., Moscow, former Soviet Union, U. Coll. Cape Breton Art Gallery, Sydney, NS, Can. Museo Ciani di Villa Caccia, Lugano, Switzerland, The Art Gallery of Hamilton, Ont.,Can., David Giles Carter Collection, New Haven, Gallery of N.S.-Halifax, Can, Jewish Pub. Libr. Collection, Montreal, Cadillac Fairview Collection, Toronto, Mus. Modern Art, NYC, Phila. Mus. Art, Solomon R. Guggenheim Mus., NYC, Yivo Inst., NYC, Bklyn. Mus., Art Inst. Chgo., Cleve. Mus. Art, Detroit Inst. Arts, Yale U., U. Montreal, Queens U., Kingston, Mead Art Mus., Amherst Coll., Jonathan Edwards Coll., New Haven, Victoria and Albert Mus., London, Vatican Mus., Rome, Quebec Art Bank, Concordia U., Montreal, Haifa Mus. Modern Art, Hebrew U., Jerusalem, Govt. of Que., Yad Vashem Holocaust Meml., Jerusalem, Mus. Boymans-van Beuningen, Rotterdam, Stedelijk Mus., Amsterdam, Rijksmuseum, Amsterdam, Nat. Gallery Can., Ottawa, Gallery Stratford, Montreal Mus. Fine Arts, Musée d'Art Contemporain, Montreal, Que. Provincial Mus., Que. Art Bank, Art Bank of the Can. Coun., Ottawa, Ariz. State Mus., Tucson, Hebrew U., Jerusalem, City of Safed-Israel, Holocaust Mus., Majdanek, Poland, Holocaust Meml. Ctr., Toronto, Lavalin Mus. Coll, Montreal, Oshawa Mus., Ont., Dept. External Affairs Govt. Can., Ottawa, Can. Jewish Congress Mus., Montreal, Israel Mus., Jerusalem, Holocaust Mus., Majdanek, Poland, McGill U., Montreal, Olympia and York Collection, Toronto, CBC Collection, Montreal, Kingston (Ont.) U. Mus. Collection, NY Pub. Libr., Worcester (Mass.) Art Mus., Currier Gallery Art, Manchester, NH, Gallery of U. NH, Durham, Mus. Art. RI Sch. Design, Providence, Olympia & York Collection, Toronto, Collection Rishon Le'Zion, Jerusalem, Rose Art Mus., Brandeis U., Waltham, Mass., C.I.L. Collection Montreal, McGill U. Coll., Montreal, Can. Jewish Congress Mus., Montreal, Young Israel of Montreal (Coll.), Can., Confedn. Art Ctr., Charlottetown-Prince Edward Island, Can., Thomas More Inst., Montreal, Menses Mus. Contemporary Art, Safed, Israel, Pushkin Mus., Moscow, The Bronfman Collection Can. Art Montreal Mus. Fine Arts, CEMP Collection Montreal, Mt. Allison U., Sackville, NS, Ont. Heritage Found., Toronto, Denbo Collection, L.A., Oziel Collection, Israel, Edelstein Collection, Montreal, many others; paintings include Klippoth Series, 1963-78, Kaddish Series, 1964-80, Hechaloth Series, 1973—, Tikkun Series, 1978—, Doomed Children Series, Kings Series, Victor's Series, Metamorphasis Series, ShevirotHakelim Series, Diabolica Series, Lepers Series, Angels Series, Hiroshima Cycle; mural for Montreal Holocaust Meml. Ctr., My Three Sisters from Hiroshimah, Japan, Loto Quebec Coll., Can. Mem. pres.'s coun. U. N.H. Served with Royal Dutch Air Force Res., 1953-55. Recipient 5 1st prizes Nat. Art Exhbn., Quebec, Que., 1960-65; Grand prize Concours Artistiques de la Province de Que., 1965; prize X and XI Winnipeg (Man., Can.) Shows, 1966, 68; prize IX Internat. Exhbn. Drawings and Prints, Lugano, 1966; prize Ofcl. Centennial Art Competition, Toronto; 1st prize Hadassah, 1969, 71, 82; Recipient Imago award U. Montreal, 1971; award Reeves of Can., 1969; Tigert award Ont. Soc. Arts, 1970; Loomis and Toles award, 1972; J. I. Segal award J. I. Segal Fund Jewish Culture, 1975; Gold medal Accademia Italia Delle Arte, Italy, 1980; Gold medal Internat. Parliament U.S.A., 1982; Gran Premio delle Nazioni, Italy, 1983, European Banner of Arts with Gold medal, 1984, Oscar d' Italia, 1985, 1st prize III Que. Biennale, 1981, OSA award of merit, Toronto, 1981, 82; World Culture prize Italy, 1984; Golden Flame of World Parliament (U.S.A.) award, 1986; Ish Shalom award Jerusalem, 1993; numerous others; Can. Council sr. arts fellow, 1969-70, 71-72, 81-82; grantee, 1966-67, 67-68; travel grantee, 1968, 73 Mem. Royal Can. Acad. Arts, Acad. Italia Arte e del Lavoro, Acad. Nazioni, Maestro Accademico-Accademia Bedriacense (Italy), Jewish Am. Acad. Arts and Scis., Israeli Art Assn. (Telaviv), Israel Assn. Profl. Artists Safed, Acad. Europa, Academician Italy, Israel Assn. Visual Art (Jerusalem). Jewish. Address: PO Box 43150 HAR NOF Jerusalem 91400 Israel Home Phone: 026518014. Personal E-mail: tikkun@janmenses.com. *My works have dealt with death, the eclipse of faith, exile, the Galut. They are shaped by my childhood experiences, real and imagined, in Nazi-occupied Europe; influenced by and rooted in my principles and standards of conduct as an Orthodox Jew in the post-holocaust/pre-Messianic era. They are an attempt to translate these experiences into visual contemporary terms (imagery conflicts and reconciliations of conflicts) in order to ascend from the personal/specific to the universal/general. They are a lament, an elegy, a denial and confirmation, an expression of the attitude of the soul in its debasement and dignity towards its Creator; a striving towards serenity in anticipation of the Redemption: a form of prayer.*

MENTEL, MICHAEL C., city council president, lawyer; b. Columbus, Ohio, Nov. 27, 1961; s. James Michael and Victoria K. (Haslett) Mentel; m. Marisa Ann Rotolo, Oct. 7, 1989; children: Angela, Connor. BA in Polit. Sci. and Hist., Capital U., Bexley, Ohio, 1984; JD, Capital U. Law Sch., 1987. Bar: Ohio 1988, US Supreme Ct. 1992, US Ct. Appeals (6th cir.), Ohio 1994, US Dist. Cts. (so. and no. dists.), Ohio 1995. Intern US senator John Glenn/Washington Workshops, Washington, 1980; account clk. Ohio Atty. Gen., Columbus, 1981-82; intern Columbus City Atty., 1983-84; legal intern Franklin County Pub. Defender, Columbus, 1987-88, staff atty., 1988-89; atty. Ohio EPA, Columbus, 1990-93, supr. atty., 1993-94; atty. Crabbe, Brown, Jones, Potts & Schmidt, 1994-99, Blaugrund Herbert & Martin, 1999; pvt. practice atty., 1999—; councilman Columbus City Coun., 1999—, pres., 2007—; chair Fin. Com. Mem. Franklin County Criminal Justice Planning Bd. Vol. Operation Feed Columbus, Charity Newsies. Mem.: ABA, Columbus Bar Assn., Ohio State Bar Assn., Shamrock Club, Agonis Club, Ancient Order of Hibernians. Democrat. Roman Catholic. Avocations: golf, Irish culture. Office: Columbus City Council 90 W Broad St Rm 231 Columbus OH 43215-9015

MENTER, M(ARTIN) ALAN, dermatologist; b. Doncaster, Eng., Oct. 30, 1941; came to U.S., 1975; s. Harry Menter and Esme (Green) Behr; m. Pamela Mary Williams, Dec. 4, 1966; children: Keith, Colin, Kerith. MB, BChir, U. Witwatersrand, 1966; MMed in Dermatology, U. Pretoria, 1971. Diplomate Am. Bd. Dermatology. Intern Johannesburg Gen. Hosp., South Africa, 1967, sr. intern, 1968; resident in dermatology U. Pretoria and Pretoria Gen. Hosp., 1968-71; sr. resident in dermatology Guy's Hosp., London, 1972; sr. resident, tutor in dermatology St. John's Hosp. for Disease of Skin, London, 1972-73; cons. dermatologist Pretoria Gen. Hosp., 1973-75; dermatologist Baylor U. Med. Ctr., Dallas, 1975—, chmn. divsn. dermatology, 1992—; dir. Baylor Psoriasis Rsch. Ctr., 2007—; med. dir. Nat. Psoriasis Found. Tissue Bank, Dallas, 1993—99; clin. prof. dermatology U. Tex. Southwestern Med. Sch., 1996—. Fellow dept. dermatology U. Tex. Southwestern Med. Sch., Dallas, 1977-79, assoc. clin. prof. dermatology, 1977-95; med. dir. Psoriasis Ctr., Baylor U. Med. Ctr., Dallas, 1979—; clin. assoc. prof. dept. periodontics Baylor Coll. Dentistry, Dallas, 1985—; presenter in field. Mem. editl. bd. Jour. Am. Acad. Dermatology, 1993—2003; contbr. numerous articles to profl. jours., chpts. to books. Tex. state chmn. Dermatology Found.; rsch. chmn. Nat. Psoriasis Found., med. adv. bd. exec. com.; coach Rugby football team U. Pretoria, 1974; represented S. Africa Nat. Rugby football team, 1968; coach, commr. Boys Under 12 Classic League Soccer, Dallas, 1978-82; active various local civic organizations and coms. Recipient Clin. Rsch. award Imperial Chem. Industries, 1972-73. Mem. AMA, Acad. Dermatology (mem. com. on psoriasis 1988-93, chmn. 1990-93, mem. com. on stds. care for psoriasis 1988-92, 2007, chmn. 1989-92, 2007, dir. Psoriasis Symposium 1990-93, bd. dirs. 1995-97), Am. Acad. Dermatol. Surgery, Brit. Assn. Dermatology, Dallas County Med. Soc. (mem. med. student rels. com. 1989-94), Dallas Dermatol. Soc. (sec.-treas. 1979, pres. 1980, rep. to adv. coun. Am. Acad. Dermatology 1987-89), Dermatol. Therapy Assn. (pres. 1985), Tex. Dermatol. Soc. (program coord. 1987-93, pres. 1995-96), Tex. Med. Assn. (mem. subcom. on joint sponsorship 1992-95), Internat. Psoriasis Coun. (pres. 2005—). Home: 5230 Royal Ln

Dallas TX 75229-5525 Office: Baylor Rsch Inst Baylor Medical Pavilion 3900 Junius St #125 Dallas TX 75246-1613 Office Phone: 972-386-7546. Personal E-mail: alanmenter@gmail.com.

MENTHENA, ANURADHA, research scientist; arrived in US, 2000; d. Bangar Raju and Ammaji Mantena. Student, St. Ann's Coll., Hyderabad, India, 1988—89; MBBS, U. Health Sci., Hyderabad, 1996. House officer Shanti Nursing Home, Hyderabad, 1997—2000; rsch. assoc. Live Rsch. Ctr. Albert Einstein Coll. Medicine, Bronx, NY, 2001—05; rsch. assoc. dept. devel. and molecular biology Albert Einstein Coll. Medicine, Bronx, 2005—08, rsch. assoc. dept. pathology, 2008—. Contbr. articles to profl. jours. Avocations: opera, music, travel, cooking, reading. Office: Albert Einstein Coll Medicine Dept Pathology 1300 Morris Park Ave Ullmann 423 Bronx NY 10461 E-mail: anu_48089@yahoo.com.

MENTON, TANYA LIA, lawyer, educator; b. Chgo., Sept. 13, 1964; d. Joseph Bernard and Rosalind Marie (Macey) M. BA magna cum laude, Northwestern U., 1986, JD, 1989. Bar: Calif. 1989, N.Y. 1993. Counsel Townley and Updike, NYC, 1991—96; v.p. litigation and employment practices ABC, Inc., LA, 1995—. Adj. prof. Mercy Coll., Dobbs Ferry, N.Y., 1993-2000; lectr. on sexual harassment, discrimination and mgmt. tng. various orgns. Editor: (legal publ.) California Employment Law Letter, 1989-91. Nat. Harry S. Truman scholar, 1982-86. Mem. ABA, Calif. Bar Assn. (labor and employment sect.), N.Y. State Bar Assn. (labor and employment sect.). Democrat. Avocation: horseback riding. Home: # 17P 301 E 79th St Apt 17P New York NY 10021-0940 Office: ABC Inc 77 W 66th St New York NY 10023-6201 Office Phone: 212-456-6178.

MENTZ, HENRY A., III, plastic surgeon; b. New Orleans, Apr. 9, 1958; s. Henry A. Jr. and Ann (Lamantia) M.; m. Paula Comiskey, May 20, 1989; children: Henry A. IV, James August. BS, La. State U., 1980, MD, 1984. Diplomate Am. Bd. Facial Plastic and Reconstructive Surgery, Am. Bd. Otolaryngology, Am. Bd. Plastic Surgery. Intern otolaryngology Tulane U., New Orleans, 1984-89; resident plastic surgery St. Joseph's Hosp., Houston, 1989-91; founder, ptnr. Aesthetic Ctr. for Plastic Surgeons, Houston, 1991—. Clin. assoc. prof. Baylor U., Houston, 1992—, St. Joseph U., Houston, 1992—; chief surgery Sharpstown Gen. Hosp., Houston, 1994—, chief plastic surgery, 1994—; pres., Houston Soc. of Plastic Surgeons, 2000-01. Fellow ACS, Internat. Coll. Surgeons, Am. Acad. Otolaryngology; mem. Am. Soc. Plastic and Reconstructive Surgeons, Am. Soc. Plastic Surgeons, Am. Soc. Aesthetic Plastic Surgeons, Internat. Soc Aesthetic Plastic Surgeons, Am. Acad. Otolaryngology Head and Neck Surg, AMA, Tex. Medical Assn., Houston Soc. Plastic Surgeons, Harris County Medical Soc. Republican. Episcopalian. Office: Aesthetic Ctr for Plastic Surgery Ste 300 Kimberly Profl Bldg 12727 Kimberley Houston TX 77024

MENTZER, ROSLYN, academic administrator; b. NYC, Oct. 26, 1935; d. Morris and Etta B. (Greenberg) Moskowitz; m. Alan D. Mentzer, June 21, 1953; children: Michelle, Stuart. BA, Queens Coll., 1965; MA, UCLA, 1968. Instr. L.A. Community Coll. Dist., 1968-69; v.p. United Coll. of Bus., LA, 1969—. Pres. CAPPS, Calif., 1984-87. Mem. LWV (v.p. Beverly Hills, Calif. chpt. 1969), Phi Beta Kappa. Avocations: tennis, bridge, writing. Office: United Coll of Bus 445 S Figueroa St Bldg 2400 Los Angeles CA 90071-1602 Home: 78240 Gray Hawk Dr Palm Desert CA 92211-2335

MENUGE, ANGUS JL, philosopher, educator; s. Hagen and Penelope Menuge; m. Vicki Hubert, June 18, 1988; children: Aidan, Corin. PhD, U. Wis., Madison, 1989. Diploma in christian apologetics Internat. Acad. Apologetics, Strasbourg France, 2003. Assoc. prof. philosophy Concordia U. Wis., Mequon, 1997—2004, prof. philosophy, 2004—. Co-dir. Cranach Inst., Ft. Wayne, Ind., 2004—. Author: (books) Agents Under Fire: Materialism and the Rationality of Science, 2004 (Discovery Inst. fellowship, 2002); editor: C.S. Lewis: Lightbearer in the Shadowlands, 1997, Christ and Culture in Dialogue, 1999, Reading God's World, 2004. Expert witness on sci. edn. stads. State of Kans. Sch. Bd., Topeka, 2005. Named one of Outstanding Academics, Internat. Biographic Ctr., Cambridge, 2004, Outstanding Intellectuals, Internat. Biog. Ctr., Cambridge, 2005. Office: Concordia Univ Wis 12800 N Lake Shore Dr Mequon WI 53097

MENUTIS, RUTH ANN, small business owner; b. Lafayette, La., Aug. 7, 1939; d. Minus and Annie (Duhon) Pellerin; ed. S.W. La. Inst., Patricia Stevens Sch. Modeling; m. Jimmie Menutis, Feb. 15, 1960; children: Jamie, Marika, Dimitri. Comml. announcer, traffic mgr. KLFY-TV, 1957-58; hostess Trans Tex./Tex. Internat. Airlines, also model Dallas Apparel Mart, 1958-68; owner, mgr. Playgril Shop of Am. and Ruth Ann Fashion, New Orleans, 1960-80; owner Natural Energy Unltd., Inc. (doing bus. as Grove), 1980-2004; owner Menutis Investments, New Orleans/Lafayette, La.; pres. Branded Works Inc.; acting pres. French Market Corp.; real estate developer; clothing designer Miss Jane of Miami & More by Ruth Ann. Bd. dirs. Better Bus. Bur., Contemporary Arts Ctr.; chmn. La. del. to White House Small Bus. Conf., 1980; vice chmn. midwest U.S.A. Small Bus. Nat. Unity Council; chmn. New Orleans Mayor's, French Quar. Task Force. Mem. Vieux Carre Action Assn. (v.p.), Bourbon Mchts. Assn. (pres.), Daus. of Penelope. Greek Orthodox. Office: 110 Travis St # 100 Lafayette LA 70503-2453 Home: 110 Travis St Lafayette LA 70503-2452 Business E-Mail: rmenutis@brandedworksinc.com.

MENZ, ROBERT L., psychotherapist, minister; b. Cape Girardeau, Mo., June 29, 1949; s. Robert A. and Vivian Marie Menz; m. Ruth A. Hageman, Jan. 7, 1994; children: Gwendolyn J. Menz Ogle, Shawn E. BS in Edn. and Sci., SE Mo. U., Cape Girardeau, 1975; MDiv, Midwestern Bapt. Sem., Kansas City, Mo., 1979; DMin in Counseling, So. Bapt. Sem., Louisville, 1987. Ordained Am. Bapt. Ch., 1974. Resident chaplain Bapt. Meml. Hosp., Kansas City, 1980—81; chaplain Meml. Med. Ctr., Springfield, Ill., 1981—87; dir. pastoral care Bapt. Home DC, Washington, 1987—91; employee counselor Emerson Climate Techs., Sidney, Ohio, 1991—. Adj. asst. prof. So. Ill. U., Springfield, 1982—87; adj. faculty Edison State Coll., Piqua, Ohio, 1993—. Author: A Memoir of a Pastoral Counseling, 1997, A Pastoral Counselor's Model of Wellness in the Workplace, 2003; editor: Social Change: Vision 2020, 2009. Counsel mem., past pres. Shelby County Cmty. Svcs., Sidney, 1991—; counsel mem. Wilson Home Health Hospice, Sidney, 1998—; bd. dirs., past chmn. Shelby County Counseling Ctr., Sidney, 2002—. With US Army, 1970—71, Vietnam. Decorated Commendation medal US Army. Fellow: Am. Assn. Pastoral Counselors; mem.: Employee Assistance Profl. Assn. (bd. cert.), Am. Psychotherapy Assn. (diplomate 2002—), Nat. Employee Assistance. Avocations: flying, running, mountain climbing, hiking, writing. Home: 1290 Dritwood Trail Sidney OH 45365 Office: Emerson Climate Techs 1650 W Campbell Rd Sidney OH 45365 Office Phone: 937-498-3609.

MENZA, CLAUDIA MARCELLA, literary agent; b. NYC, June 11, 1947; d. John Gaetano and Antonina (di Lorenzo) M.; m. James R. Forker, May 29, 1971 (div. 1980); m. Charles Anthony Frye, Dec. 16, 1989 (dec. Oct. 1994). BA, Oberlin Coll., 1969. Asst. editor Evergreen Rev., NYC, 1969-73; gen. editor, prodn. mgr. Grove Press, Inc., NYC, 1973-83; sr. editor Art Dir. News, NYC, 1983-85; ptnr. Menza-Barron Agy., NYC, 1983—. Cons. Riverrun Press, N.Y.C., 1983-96; guest lectr. Tex. A&M U., Prairie View, Tex., 1986, NYU, N.Y.C., 1986-87; cons., panelist Nat. Civil Rights Mus. Conf. The Power of the Word, Memphis, 1995; panelist NYU, 1998, The New Sch., N.Y.C., 2000, The Lost State Writers Conf., Greeneville, Tenn., 2000, Harlem Book Fair, 2001; panelist African Am. Lit. Conf., Raleigh, NC, 2003. Author: Cage of Wild Cries, 1990, The Lunatics Ball, 1994, (play), 2006; contbg. author: The Dream Book: An Anthology of Writing by Italian-American Women, 1985 (Am. Book award, 1985); actor: Damned Pub. Riverside Studios, 1999. Working mem. Congress of Racial Equality, Hempstead, N.Y., 1961, Student Nonviolent Coord. Com., Oberlin, Ohio, 1965, Students for Dem. Soc., Oberlin, 1965, The West Village Com., N.Y.C., 1980. Mem. PEN (trustee, chair prison writing com.), Internat. Platform Assn., Acad. Am. Poets, Italian-Am. Writers Assn., Assn. Authors Reps. Avocations: reading, music, theater. Office: Menza-Barron Agy 511 Ave Americas # 51 New York NY 10011 Business E-Mail: claudia@menzabarron.com.

MENZA, MATTHEW A., psychiatrist; b. Sept. 11, 1950; BA, U. Va., 1973; MD, Temple U., 1980; postgrad., Harvard U., 1985. Intern NYU Med. Sch. Bellvue Hosp., NYC, 1980—81, resident, 1981—84; chief divsn. clin. psychopharmacology Robert Wood Johnson Med. Sch., Piscataway, NJ, 1996—, interim chmn. dept. psychiatry, 2003—. Contbr. articles to profl. jours. Bd. govs. Univ. Med. Group, New Brunswick, N.J., 1999—. Office: Robert Wood Johnson Med Sch Dept Psychiatry 675 Hoes Ln Piscataway NJ 08854-5627 Home Phone: 732-868-0840. Business E-Mail: menza@umdnj.edu.

MENZEL, IDINA, actress, singer; b. Syosset, May 30, 1971; d. Stuart and Helene Mentzel; m. Taye Diggs, Jan. 11, 2003. BFA in Drama, NYU. Actor: (Broadway plays) RENT, 1995—97 (Tony award nominee), Aida, 2001, Funny Girl, 2002, Wicked, 2003—05 (Tony award best actress in a musical, 2004); (plays) The Wild Party, 1999, Summer of '42, 2000, Hair, 2001, The Vagina Monologues, 2002, See What I Wanna See, 2005; singer: (albums) Still I Can't Be Still, 1998, Here, 2004, I Stand, 2008; actor: (films) Kissing Jessica Stein, 2001, Just a Kiss, 2002, The Tollbooth, 2004, Rent, 2005, Ask the Dust, 2006, Enchanted, 2007; singer: (film soundtracks) The Other Sister, 1998, Rent, 2005, Beowulf, 2007. Office: 156 W 56th St Ste 1803 New York NY 10019

MENZEL, JIŘI, film and theater director, actor; b. Prague, Czechoslovakia, Feb. 23, 1938; s. Josef and Bozena Menzel. Student specialization in film directing, Film Acad. Performing Arts, Prague, 1957-61. Film dir., actor, 1962—; head, dept. film directing Film Acad. Performing Arts, Prague, Czech Republic, 1990-92; prodr. Studio 89, 1991-98; artistic dir. Theater Vinohrady, Prague, Czech Republic, 2000—03. Working in theaters Prague, Zagreb, Sofia, Budapest. Dir.: (films) Pearls of the Deep, 1965, Crime at a Girl's School, 1965, Closely Watched Trains, 1966 (Best Fgn. Lang. Film Acad. award), Capricious Summer, 1968, Crime in a Night Club, 1968, Larks on a String, 1969, Who Looks for Gold?, 1974, Seclusion Near a Forest, 1976, Those Wonderful Men with a Crank, 1978, Short Cut, 1980, The Snowdrop Festival, My Sweet Little Village, 1986, The End of Old Times, 1989, The Beggar's Opera, 1991, The Life and Extraordinary Adventures of Private Ivan Chonkin, 1994, short film, "One Moment" part of the project "The Cello", I Served The King Of England, 2006. Home Phone: ++420-233325208; Office Phone: ++420-602237211. Personal E-mail: radova.mila@quick.cz.

MENZEL, PAUL THEODORE, philosophy educator; b. Elmhurst, Ill., Sept. 18, 1942; s. Theophil William and Annemarie Eva (Mueller) M.; m. Susan L. Johnson Blank, May 5, 1984(dec. Sept 28, 2007); children— Tam, Heidi, David, Matthew. B.A., Coll. Wooster, 1964; B.D., Yale U., 1967; Ph.D., Vanderbilt U., 1971. From asst. prof. to prof. philosophy Pacific Luth. U., Tacoma, Wash., 1971—. Author: Strong Medicine: The Ethical Rationary of Health Care, 1990; Danforth Found. fellow, 1964-70, NEH fellow, 1975, 77, 82. Mem. Am. Philos. Assn., Hastings Ctr., Phi Beta Kappa. Home: 537 Race Rd Coupeville WA 98239-4006 Business E-Mail: menzelpt@plu.edu.

MENZER, JOHN BRUCE, retail executive; b. Chgo., Mar. 27, 1951; s. John and Lorraine (Glugla) M. m. Kathleen A. Leahy, Oct. 23, 1976; 1 child, Christine. BBA in Pub. Acctg., Loyola U., 1972, MBA in Fin., 1980. CPA, Ill. Supr. acctg. systems Am. Internat., Mount Prospect, Ill., 1973-75; supr. audit Pannell, Kerr, Forster & Co., Chgo., 1975-77; sr. v.p. Bally Mfg. Corp., 1977-85, Ben Franklin Retail Stores, Carol Stream, Ill., 1985—88, exec. v.p., 1988—91, COO, CFO, 1991—93, pres., 1993—95; exec. v.p., CFO Wal-Mart Stores, Inc., 1995—99; pres., CEO Wal-Mart Internat., 1999—2005; vice chmn. U.S. Wal-Mart Stores, Inc., 2005—08; CEO Michaels Stores Inc., Irving, Tex., 2009—. Bd. dirs. Wal-Mart de Mex., Seiyu Ltd., Japan, Emerson Electric, U.S.-China Bus. Coun., Guangdong Province Gov.'s Econ. Advisors in China. Bd. dirs. Jr. Achievement, Chgo., 1973-75. Mem. Fin. Execs. Inst., Ill. State Soc. CPAs, Nat. Retail Mchts. Assn., Am. Inst. CPAs, Internat. Franchise Assn. (chmn. fin. and tax com., conf. coordinator). Avocations: golf, tennis. Mailing: Michaels Stores Inc PO Box 619566 Dallas TX 75261-9566*

MENZER, ROBERT EVERETT, retired toxicologist, educator; b. Washington, Dec. 21, 1938; s. Russell Ernest and Ora Taylor (Oates) M.; m. Sara Lee Gribbon, Dec. 29, 1962; children: R. Eric, Paul D., Joan Coleraine. BS in Chemistry, U. Pa., 1960; MS, U. Md., 1962; PhD, U. Wis., 1964. Instr. U. Wis., Madison, 1964; mem. faculty U. Md., 1964-89, asst. prof. entomology, 1964-69, assoc. prof., 1969-73, prof., 1973-89, assoc. dean grad. studies and research, 1974-77, acting dean, 1977-80, chmn. grad. program marine-estuarine-environ. scis., 1978-89, dir. Water Resources Research Ctr., 1981-89; dir. environ. rsch. lab. EPA, Gulf Breeze, Fla., 1989-95, sr. sci. advisor Nat. Ctr. for Environ. Rsch. Washington, 1995—2001; ret., 2001. Prof. emeritus U. Md., 1990—; chmn. hazardous substances data bank rev. panel Nat. Library Medicine, 1973-97, mem. 2008-; cons. in field, 2001-. Contbr. articles to profl. jours. Recipient U. Md. Alumni award, 1974 Fellow Washington Acad. Scis.; mem. AAAS, Am. Chem. Soc., Soc. Toxicology, Estuarine Rsch. Fedn., Sigma Xi, Phi Kappa Phi. Clubs: Cosmos (Washington). Republican. Episcopalian. Home: 90 Highpoint Dr Gulf Breeze FL 32561-4014 Home Phone: 850-934-7765. Personal E-mail: robertmenzer@bellsouth.net.

MENZIES, HENRY HARDINGE, architect; b. Hickory, NC, Apr. 20, 1928; s. Henry Hardinge and Hallie (Lloyd) M. AB in Lit., U. N.C., 1948; postgrad., U. So. Calif., 1948-49; BArch, N.C. State U., 1958. Founder, ptnr. The Architects Group, Boston, 1962-63; individual practice architecture Boston, 1964-78; ptnr. Menzies and LeMieux, NYC, 1978-82; pvt. practice architecture New Rochelle, N.Y., 1983—. Lectr. in field. Works include coll. and seminary, Natick, Mass., 1964, Heights Sch., Washington, 1965, St. Marie's Ch., Lowell, Mass., 1966, Central Cath. H.S., Lawrence, Mass., 1971, Walker Sch., Needham, Mass., 1972, Baird Residence, Sherborn, Mass., 1972, Layton Cultural Ctr., Brookfield, Wis., 1974, Shellbourne Conf. Ctr., Valparaiso, Ind., 1974, Wespine Study Ctr., Pembroke, Mass, 1982, alterations to residences in Greenwich, Conn., 1984, Garwood Bldg. at Arnold Hall, 1986, Midtown Ctr., Chgo., 1986, Student Ctr., Houston, 1986, Windmoor Ctr., South Bend, Ind., 1986, alterations to student residences in Milw. and Providence, 1989-91, renovation of interior St. Aloysius Ch., New Canaan, Conn., 1993-96, chapel at Warwick House, Pitts., 1993, chapel at Westfield Residence, L.A., 1994, chapel at Allview Ctr., Columbia, Md., 1994, chapel at St. John Fisher Residence, Stamford, Conn., 1994, master plan, crypt chapel St. Mary of the Angels Ch., Chgo., 1996—, Shrine at Conf. Ctr., Schulenberg, Tex., chapel Lincoln Green student residence, Urbana, Ill., 1997—, new facade of St. Aloysius Ch., New Canaan, 1997—, Willows Acad., Chgo., 1997—, Cath. Info. Ctr. Washington, 1999-2000, St. Michael's Ch., Gastonia, N.C., 2000—, Cathedral St. Augustine, Bridgeport, Conn., 2003, Paducah, Ky., 2003, H.S. Charlotte, 2003, St. Ann's Ch., Bridgeport, 2006, Heights Sch. Chapel, 2006, New Chapels, ShellBourne Conf. Ctr., 2009, Chapel at St. Paul's Cath. Ctr. U. Wisc., Chapel In IESE Bldg., NY, 2009; contbr. articles to profl. jours. Served to 1st lt. USNR, 1951-55. Mem. AIA (N.Y. chpt. 1978-84, Westchester/Mid-Hudson chpt. 1985—). Roman Catholic. Office: 99 Overlook Cir New Rochelle NY 10804-4501 Office Phone: 914-637-9597. E-mail: hmenzies@gmail.com.

MENZIES, IAN STUART, newspaper editor; b. Glasgow, Scotland, Mar. 11, 1920; came to U.S., 1944, naturalized, 1948; s. John S. and Gertrude (Mephius) M.; m. Barbara Edith Newton, June 16, 1945; children: Marla Ann, Gillian Jean, Alexa Stuart, Deborah Newton. Student, Royal Tech. Coll., 1937-39; LHD, Salem State Coll., Mass., 1978. Reporter Boston Globe, 1948-57, sci. editor, 1957-63, fin. editor, 1963-65, mng. editor, 1965-70, assoc. editor, 1970-85; sr. fellow John McCormack Inst. Pub. Affairs, U. Mass., Boston, 1985—95, sr. fellow emeritus, 1995—. Vis. assoc. Joint Ctr. for Urban Studies, Mass. Inst. Tech.-Harvard, 1970-71. Mem. Hingham Sch. Com., Mass., 1962-68. Served to lt. Royal Naval Vol. Res., 1939-46. Decorated D.S.C.; recipient Pub. Service award Nat. Edn. Writers, 1961, Pub. Service award AAAS, 1963, Heywood Broun award, 1961, Sevellon Brown award, 1959, Rudolph Elie award, 1959, A.P. Big City award, 1958, U.P.I. award, 1959; Nieman fellow Harvard U., Cambridge, Mass., 1961-62. Mem. Brit. Officers Club New Eng. Home and Office: Apt 527 303 Linden Ponds Way Hingham MA 02043-4705 Home Phone: 781-749-2188.

MENZIN, ANDREW, gynecologist; b. Hempstead, Ny, Dec. 31, 1963; m. Lauren Menzin. MD, Ny U. Sch. Medicine. Diplomate Am. Bd. ob-gyn. Physician North Shore U. Hosp., Manhasset, NY, 1995—2008. Achievements include patents for medical instruments. Office: N Shore Univ Hosp 300 Community Dr Manhasset NY 11030 Office Fax: 516-562-2805.

MEPHAM, DEREK JOHN AMOORE, business investor; b. Inverell, N.S.W., Australia, Mar. 26, 1954; s. Norman Francis Amoore and Marie Agnes (Cannons) M. m. Rong Wei Mepham. B Econs., New Eng. U., Armidale, Australia, 1978; MBA, Queensland Ctrl. U., Australia, 1998. Trainee acct. Wayland & Wayland, Sydney, NSW, Australia, 1977; trainee Hyland Downs, Armidale, NSW, Australia, 1978-80, owner, exec. Clermont, Queensland, Australia, 1980—. Mem. Liberal Party. Avocations: golf, tennis, swimming, exercise, football. Home and Office: PO Box 344 Hyland Downs Queensland Clermont 4721 Australia Office Phone: 61-07-4983-5184. Home Fax: 61-07-7983-5479. E-mail: mephamderek@bigpond.com.

MÉRAS, PHYLLIS LESLIE, journalist; b. Bklyn., May 10, 1931; d. Edmond Albert and Leslie Trousdale (Ross) M.; BA, Wellesley Coll., Mass., 1955; MS in Journalism, Columbia U., NYC, 1954; Swiss Govt. Exchange fellow, Inst. Higher Internat. Studies, Geneva, 1957; m. Thomas H. Cocroft, Nov. 3, 1968. Reporter, copy editor Providence Jour., 1954-57, 59-61; feature writer Ladies Home Jour. mag., 1957-58; editor Weekly Tribune, Geneva, Switzerland, 1961-62; copyeditor, travel sect. NY Times, 1962-68; mng. editor Vineyard Gazette, Edgartown, Mass., 1970-74, contbg. editor, 1974—; assoc. editor Rhode Islander, Providence, 1970-76; travel editor Providence Jour., 1976-95; editor Wellesley Alumnae mag., 1979-96; assoc. in journalism U. RI, 1974-75; adj. instr. Columbia U. Sch. Journalism, 1975-76. Author: First Spring: A Martha's Vineyard Journal, 1972, A Yankee Way With Wood, 1975, Miniatures: How to Make Them, Use Them, Sell Them, 1976, Vacation Crafts, 1978, The Mermaids of Chenonceaux and 828 Other Tales: An Anecdotal Guide to Europe, 1982, Exploring Rhode Island, 1984, Castles, Keeps and Leprechauns: Tales, Myths and Legends of Historic Sites in Great Britain and Ireland, 1988, Eastern Europe: A Traveler's Companion, 1991; co-author: Christmas Angels, 1979, Carry-out Cuisine, 1982, New Carry Out Cuisine, 1986, Country Editor: Henry Beetle Hough and the Vineyard Gazette, 2006, The Historic Shops and Restaurants of Boston, 2007, Martha's Vineyard: Quiet Pleasures, 2008, Rhode Island Explorer's Guide, 2008. Pulitzer fellow in critical writing, 1967. Mem. Soc. Am. Travel Writers. Home: Music St PO Box 215 West Tisbury MA 02575-0215 Office Phone: 508-693-1439. E-mail: pmcocroft@aol.com.

MERAYYAN, SAAD M., engineering educator; m. Amani J. Younis, July 20, 1997; children: Zayd S., Noor S. BS, Jordan U., 1992; MS, U. Mo., Columbia, 1996; PhD, Wayne State U., Detroit, 2001. Asst. prof. Calif. Poly. State U., San Luis Obispo, 2004—06, Calif. State U., Sacramento, 2006—. Engr. Tetra Tech, Ann Arbor, Mich., 2001—04. Mem.: ASCE. Office: Calif State Univ 6000 J St Sacramento CA 95819-6029 Office Fax: 916-278-7957; Home Fax: 916-278-7957. Business E-Mail: merayyan@csus.edu.

MERCADAL, LUCILE, nephrologist; b. Paris, Feb. 1, 1968; d. Georges Mercadal and Danielle Yvars; children: Maxime Lebourg, Juliette Lebourg, Marie Lebourg. PhD, Paris 11 U., MD in Nephrology, 1998. Physician, nephrology dept. Pitié Salpétrière Hosp., Paris, 1998—. Contbr. articles to profl. publs. Office: Pitié Salpétrière Hosp 83 Bd De Hosp Paris 75013 France Office Phone: 33142177211. Business E-Mail: lucile.mercadal@psl.aphp.fr, lucile.mercadal@psl.ap-hop-paris.fr.

MERCADO, MOSES C., lobbyist; b. Tex. B, U. Tex., Austin, 1986; JD, So. Tex. Coll. Law, Houston, 1991. Bar: Tex. Officer Travis County Sheriff's Dept., Tex., 1986—88; asst. atty. gen. State of Tex., 1992; chief of staff US Congressman Gene Green, 1993—97; dep. chief of staff, sr. policy advisor US Congressman Dick Gephardt, 1997—2002; v.p. fed. affairs Am. Ins. Assn., 2003—04; state dir., N.Mex. Senator John Kerry's Presdl. Campaign, 2004; dep. exec. dir. inter-govtl. affairs Dem. Nat. Com., 2005—07; sr. v.p. Ogilvy Govt. Rels., Washington, 2007, mng. dir., 2007—. At-large mem. Dem. Nat. Com.; bd. mem. Congl. Hispanic Caucus Inst., 2008—. Super del. Dem. Nat. Convention, 2008. Mem.: ABA. Office: Ogilvy Govt Rels 1111 19th St NW Ste 1100 Washington DC 20036 Office Phone: 202-729-4200. Office Fax: 202-530-9777.*

MERCANDO, ANTHONY DOMINIC, cardiologist; b. Yonkers, NY, Oct. 6, 1954; s. Dominic and Ida Mercando; m. Lee-Ann Davis, May 3, 1980; children: Michelle, Christina, Andrew, Anne Marie. BSEE,

Manhattan Coll., Bronx, 1976; MD, Harvard U., 1980. Lic. physician, N.Y. Med. intern Montefiore Med. Ctr., Bronx, 1980-81, med. resident, 1981-83, cardiology fellow, 1984-86, attending arrhythmia svc., 1986-88; ptnr. Westchester Cardiology Assocs., Scarsdale, NY, 1988—. Founder, pres. Amadeus Multimedia Technologies, Ltd., Irvington, N.Y., 1995—; dir. ACLS Montefiore Hosp., 1991—. Contbr. articles to profl. jours., chpts. to books; computer editor Jour. Pacing and Clin. Electrophysiology, 1993—. Bd. dirs. Home Nursing Assn. Westchester, Tuckahoe, 1994—; tech. com. Irvington Sch. Bd., 1995—. R. Rosen fellow in pacing and electrophysiology N. Am. Soc. Pacing and Electrophysiology, 1986, Sable Meml. Heart fellow United Order Odd Fellows, 1985. Fellow Am. Coll. Cardiology; mem. N.Am. Soc. Pacing and Electrophysiology. Roman Catholic. Avocations: biking, skiing. Office: Westchester Cardiology 688 White Plains Rd # 201 Scarsdale NY 10583-5059 Office Phone: 914-722-6300. Business E-Mail: adm@webaxis.com.

MERCAY, JESSIE JARDINE, academic administrator, educator; b. Poughkeepsie, NY., Dec. 5, 1945; d. Lorance Edwin and Jessie Patty Mercay. BA, Colo. State U., Ft. Collins, 1973; MA, Appalachian State U., Boone, NC, 1977; PhD, U. Iowa, 1985, Internat. Inst. Mayonic Sci. & Tech., Chennai, India, 2006. Cert. in Mayonic sci. & tech. & traditional Indian architecture, Vaastu Vedic Rsch. Found., 1985. Chancellor Am. U. Mayonic Sci. & Tech., Alamos, Sonora, Mexico, 2006—09, prof., 2006—09. Archtl. cons. vaastu shastra, 2005—09. Author: (books) Fabric of The Universe; contbr. articles. Tchr. Soc. Internat. Vaastu Architecture, Internat. Capt. US Army, 1964—71, Worldwide. Achievements include research in compilation of knowledge in vaastu architecture, traditonal Indian art & architecture.

MERCER, DEBBIE K., dean; PhD, Kans. State U., Manhattan. Dean, coll. edn. and tech. Ft. Hays State U., Kans., 2005—. Mem.: Internat. Reading Assn. (state kra pres.), Rotary Internat. Club, Kappa Delta Pi (counselor), Phi Delta Kappa (past pres.). Office: Fort Hays State Univ 600 Park St Hays KS 67601 Office Fax: 785-628-4447. Business E-Mail: dmercer@fhsu.edu.

MERCER, DOROTHY MAY, real estate company executive; b. Spring Arbor, Mich., June 12, 1932; d. Leon Luther and Esther Elizabeth (Dodes) Douglas; m. David Neal Mercer, Mar. 17, 1951; children: Shelley Lynn, Ann Elizabeth. AA, Grand Rapids Jr. Coll., Mich., 1975; MusB summa cum laude, Western Mich. U., Kalamazoo, 1981; postgrad., Perkins Sch. Theology, Highland Park, Tex., 1987. Cert. dir. mus. and healing and wholeness ministries United Meth. Ch. Dir. music Grandville United Meth. Ch., Grandville, Mich., 1979—80, Burton Hts. United Meth. Ch., Grand Rapids, Mich., 1980—81, Faith United Meth. Ch., Grand Rapids, 1981—88, Northland United Meth. Ch., Stanwood, 1994—2004; pvt. tchr. piano, voice and guitar Grand Rapids and Stanwood, 1970—2005; pres. Mercer Pubs., Inc., Stanwood, 1986—, Swains Lake Farms, Inc., Concord, Mich., 1992—. Deacon United Meth. Ch., 1997—2003; cons. in healing and wholeness ministries; condr. seminars and workshops in field; dir. MerriMen Chorus, Canadian Lakes, Mich., 1995—. Author: (autibiography) Stories I Haven't Told, 2009; composer: numerous piano, guitar and choral works; author: numerous books on healing and wholeness, Stories I Havent Told Memoirs of a Depression Baby. Fundraiser Habitat for Humanity, Mecosta County, Mich., 1993—; leader Girls Scouts US, Grand Rapids, 1962—70; fundraiser WWII Meml., Washington, 2000—05; pres. Swains Lake Farms Property Owners Assn., Concord, 2003—05; vol. in mission Zimbabwe, South Africa; chmn. bd. diaconal ministry West Mich. Conf., United Meth. Ch., 1994. Republican. Methodist.

MERCER, EDWIN WAYNE, lawyer; b. Kingsport, Tenn., July 19, 1940; s. Ernest LaFayette and Geneva (Frye) M. BBA, Tex. Tech U., 1963; JD, S. Tex. Coll. Law, 1971. Bar: Tex. 1971, U.S. Dist. Ct. (no. dist.) Tex 1975, U.S. Supreme Ct. 1976, U.S. Ct. Appeals (5th Cir.) 1979. Pvt. practice, Houston, 1971-73; gen. counsel, corp. sec. Alcon Labs., Inc., Ft. Worth, 1973-81; ptnr. Gandy Michener Swindle Whitaker Pratt & Mercer, Ft. Worth, 1981-84; v.p., gen. counsel, corp. sec. Pengo Industries, Inc., Ft. Worth, 1984-90, also bd. dirs.; pvt. law practice, 1990—. Bd. dirs. Soc. for Prevention Blindness, 1979—. Mem. ABA, State Bar Tex., Ft. Worth-Tarrant County Bar Assn., South Tex. Coll. Law Alumni Assn., Tex. Tech U. Ex-Assn., Ft. Worth Club, Delta Theta Phi, Phi Delta Theta. Methodist. Office Phone: 817-731-1959.

MERCER, EVELYN LOIS, retired counseling administrator; b. Ellensboro, NC, Apr. 25, 1934; d. Milton Bernadine Robinson Sr. and Lois Lenora Robinson; m. Theodore Roosevelt Mercer Sr. (div. June 1978); children: Theodore Roosevelt Jr., Brian Vincent, David Lemuel. BS in Math., Livingstone Coll., 1957; MEd in Guidance and Counseling, U. Cin., 1972; student, U. Akron, Ohio, 1973, student, 1974, Miami U., 1973—75. Cert. math tchr. Ohio, 1963, guidance counselor Ohio, 1972, lic. profl. counselor Ohio Counselor & Social Worker Bd., 1984. Math tchr. Jackson County Pub. Schs., Gumberry, NC, 1957—60, Cin. Pub. Schs., Cin., 1963—72, guidance counselor, 1972—73, Winton Woods City Sch. Dist., Cin., 1973—94, ret., 1994. Mem. adv. com. conselor edn. U. Cin., Cin., 1975—76; admissions adv. bd. Cin. Tech. Coll., Cin., 1975—81, The Ohio State U., Columbus, Ohio, 1982—85; nursing sch. adv. bd. Deaconess Hosp. Sch. Nursing, Cin., 1983—88; dir. Sch. Counseling Cons. Svc., Cin., 1994—, Charlotte, NC, 1994—. Mem. housing commn. City of Forest Park, Cin.; Dem. precinct exec. Hamilton County Bd. Elections, Cin., 1974—96. Named Outstanding Counselor of Yr., Inroads of Cin., 1984. Mem.: NEA, AAUW (pres. Charlotte br. 2001—03), Am. Assn. U. Women of NC (immediate past state v.p. membership), Am. Assn Coll. Admissions Counselors, Ohio Assn. Coll. Admissions Counselors, Ohio Sch. Counselors Assn., Ohio Edn. Assn., Livingstone Coll. Alumni Assn., U. Cin. Alumni Assn., Nat. Assn. Advancement for Colored People, Les Birdies Golf Club Charlotte (founder 1999, pres. 1999—2001), Order of Eastern Star, Zeta Phi Beta. Democrat. Methodist. Avocations: golf, travel, bridge, volunteering, gardening. Home and Office: 4101 Rye Mill Ct Charlotte NC 28277

MERCER, JAMES LEE, management consultant; b. Sayre, Okla., Nov. 7, 1936; s. Fred Elmo and Ora Lee (Davidson) M.; m. Karolyn Lois Prince, Nov. 16, 1962; children: Tara Lee, James Lee. BS, U. Nev., Reno, 1964, MBA, 1966; postgrad. exec. devel. program, Cornell U., Ithaca, NY, 1979. Cert. in mcpl. adminstrn. U. NC, 1971, lifetime Jr. coll. tchng. credential Calif., cert. mgmt. cons. Methods and results supr. Pacific Tel. & Tel., Sacramento, 1965-66; prodn. control supr. Gen. Dynamics, Pomona, Calif., 1966-67; nuclear submarine project mgr. Litton Industries, Pascagoula, Miss., 1967-70; asst. city mgr. City of Raleigh, NC, 1970-73; nat. program dir. Pub. Tech., Inc., Washington, 1973-76; gen. mgr. Battelle So. Ops., Atlanta, 1976-79; v.p. Korn/Ferry Internat., Atlanta, 1979-81; pres. James Mercer & Assocs. Inc.; mgmt. cons. Atlanta, 1981-86; chief Indsl. Ext. Divsn. Ga. Inst. of Tech., Atlanta, 1981-83, dir. Ga. Productivity Ctr.; dir. govtl. cons. svc. Coopers & Lybrand, 1983-84; regional v.p. Wolfe & Assocs., Inc., 1984-86; pres., CEO, chmn. Mercer, Slavin & Nevins, Inc., 1986-90, The Mercer Group, Inc., 1990—. Ad hoc prof. NC State U., 1972-73; bd. dirs. Taratec Corp., lectr., spkr. in field. Author: Public Management Systems, 1978, Public Technology, 1981, Managing Urban Government Services, 1981, Strategic Planning for Public Managers, 1990, Public Management in Lean Years, 1992; contbr. numerous articles to profl. jours. Chmn. Raleigh Mayor's Civic Ctr. Authority Study Commn., 1971; founding bd. dirs. Mordecai Sq. Hist. Soc., Nat. Civic League; founding mem. Calif. Poly. State U., adv. coun. Coll. Bus. Adminstrn., San Luis Obispo, 1980-95, bd. mem. emeritus, 1995—; founding mem., bd. trustees U. Nev. Found., Reno, 1985-91, trustee emeritus, 1991—; founding mem. U. SC and Coll. Charleston, M Pub. Adminstrn. adv. bd., 1987-97. Mem.: NC League of Municipalities (George C. Franklin award 1971), Instit. Mgmt. Cons. (Atlanta Chpt. (v.p. membership 1991—97, bd. dirs. 1991—97), Contract Svcs. Assn. Am. (bd. dirs. Wash. DC 1990—2006), Ga. Indsl. Devel. Assn., Tech. Transfer Soc. (dir. 1978—87, treas. 1985—86), Internat. Pers. Mgmt. Assn., Govtl. Fin. Officers Assn., Inst. Indsl. Engrs. (chpt. pres. 1969—70, past pres.'s award 1970), Am. Soc. Pub. Adminstrn., Internat. City-County Mgmt. Assn., Raleigh Forward Leadership Orgn., U. Nev. Alumni Assn. (exec. com. 1969—79, Oustanding Alumnus), Shriners, Rotary, Atlanta C. of C., Masons, Beta Gamma Sigma. Home: 28 Sierra del Sol Santa Fe NM 87508-2136 Office: 551 W Cordova Rd Ste 726 Santa Fe NM 87505-1825 Office Phone: 505-466-9500. Personal E-mail: mercer@mindspring.com.

MERCER, JENNIFER LYNN, research scientist; b. Deadwood, SD, Oct. 20, 1974; d. Gordon G. and Sharon M. Mercer. BS, Black Hills State U., Spearfish, SD, 1997; PhD, Dartmouth Coll., Hanover, NH, 2002. Rsch. asst. Dartmouth Coll., 1997—2002, postdoc. rsch. assoc., 2002—03, U. Wyo., Laramie, 2003—05, assoc. rsch. scientist, 2005—. Co-prin. investigator NSF Office Polar Programs, 2006—; ind. cons. Arbonne Internat., 2007—. Contbr. articles to profl. jours. Mem. Albany County Democrats, Laramie, 2006—. Recipient Young Alumni Achievement award, Black Hills State U., 2003, Gary Malone award, Dartmouth Coll., 2003; named a Daschle Scholar, Internat. Honor Del., Acad. Achievement, 2004; vis. scholar student fellow, Woods Hole Oceanog. Instn., 1997. Mem.: Am. Geophys. Union, Sigma Xi. Democrat. Achievements include profiled by Ann Curry and NBC's Today Show in November 2007; climbed Mt. Kilimanjaro and Mt. Fuji. Avocations: snowboarding, travel (visited all 7 continents), backpacking, skiing. Office: Univ Wyo Dept Atmospheric Sci Laramie WY 82071

MERCER, JOHN T.W., lawyer; b. Mpls., 1949; AB, Univ. Mich., 1973, JD, 1977. Bar: Ga. 1977. Assoc. Troutman Sanders LLP, Atlanta, 1978—84, ptnr., corp. and securities, 1985—, and practice group leader, project develop. and fin. Named Ga. Super Lawyer in Securities and Corp. Fin., Atlanta Mag., 2007; named one of Am. Leading Lawyers for Energy and Natural Resources, Chambers USA, 2005, 2006. Mem.: ABA, State Bar Ga. Office: Troutman Sanders LLP 600 Peachtree St NE Ste 5200 Atlanta GA 30308-2216 Office Phone: 404-885-3182. Office Fax: 404-962-6632. Business E-Mail: john.mercer@troutmansanders.com.

MERCER, RICHARD JAMES, lawyer; b. New London, Conn., Oct. 2, 1950; s. James Wilson and Marianne (Wieczorek) Mercer; m. Ann Holly Gutting, Oct. 9, 1970 (div. 1977); 1 child, James; m. Harriet Allston Jopson, June 1, 1982. BBA, Old Dominion U., 1972; JD, Coll. William and Mary, 1975; LLM in Taxation, Boston U., 1977, LLM in Banking, 1986. Assoc. Epstein & Epstein, Norfolk, Va., 1975, Bernard A. Kaplan, Boston, 1975—76; sole practice, 1976—80; ptnr. Shagory & Shagory, Boston, 1978—79, Alpert, Thurman & Mercer, Boston, 1980—86; assoc. counsel First Nat. Bank Boston, 1983—85, asst. v.p., assoc. counsel, 1985—86, sr. counsel, 1986—90; ptnr. Parker, Coulter, Daley & White, Boston, 1990—91; pvt. practice Dover, Mass., 1991—. Mem.: Va. Bar Assn., Mass. Bar Assn. Republican. Anglican. Office Phone: 508-785-1831.

MERCER, WILLIAM W., prosecutor; b. Jan. 7, 1964; BA in Polit. Sci., U. Mont., 1986; MPA, Harvard U., 1988; JD, George Mason U., 1993. Counselor to asst. atty. gen., sr. policy analyst Office of Policy Devel. US Dept. Justice, 1989—94, prin. assoc. dep. atty. gen. Washington, 2005—06, acting assoc. atty. gen., 2006—07, asst. US atty. Dist. Mont. Billings, Mont., 1994—2001, US atty., 2001—. Mem. president's adv. coun. U. Mont.; mem. bd. visitors U. Mont. Sch. Law; mem. atty. gen.'s adv. com. Office: US Attys Office PO Box 1478 Billings MT 59103 E-mail: askdoj@usdoj.gov.*

MERCHANT, JUANITA LYNNE, gastroenterologist, educator; MD, PhD, Yale U., 1984. Cert. Internal Medicine, 1987, Gastroenterology, 1993. Resident Mass. Gen. Hosp., 1987, fellow in gastroenterology, 1990, UCLA, 1991; faculty U. Mich., Ann Arbor, 1991—, prof. internal medicine, prof. molecular and integrative physiology, mem. Cancer Ctr.; investigator Howard Hughes Med. Inst., 1994—2002. Mem.: Inst. Medicine, Am. Soc. Clin. Investigation (Robert and Sally Funderburg award), Am. Soc. Biochemistry and Molecular Biology, Am. Assn. Cancer Rsch., Ctrl. Soc. Clin. Rsch., Midwest Gut Club, Am. Fedn. Clin. Rsch., Am. Gastroenterological Assn. (Outstanding AGA Women in Sci. 2008), Am. Soc. Microbiology, Gastroenterology Rsch. Group, Alpha Omega Alpha. Office: Med Sci Rsch Bldg I Rm 3510 1150 W Med Ctr Dr Ann Arbor MI 48109-0682 Office Phone: 734-647-2944. Office Fax: 734-936-1400. E-mail: merchanj@umich.edu.*

MERCHANT, P. GLENN, JR., military officer, physician; b. Quonset Point, RI, Jan. 6, 1953; s. Paul Glenn and Mary Jean Merchant; m. Debra Colleene Brown, Nov. 25, 1951; children: Nicholas Ryan, Kaitlin Elizabeth, Joshua Daniel. BS in Biology, The Citadel, 1980—83; MD, Med. U. of SC., 1983—87; BA in Polit. Sci., The Citadel, 1971—75; Masters in Pub. Health and Tropical Medicine, Tulane U. Sch. of Pub. Health & Tropical Medicine, 1991—92. Diplomate Am. Bd. of Preventive Medicine, 1994. Marine aviator VMA-542, Cherry Point, NC, 1975—80; commd. 2d lt. USMC, 1975, advanced through grades to capt., 1980; intern in family medicine Naval Hosp., Charleston, SC, 1987—88; flight surgeon 2d MAW, 1988—91; resident in aerospace medicine Naval Aerospace Med. Inst., Charleston, SC, 1992—94; sr. med. officer USS John C. Stennis (CVN 74), Norfolk, 1994—97; prof. Uniformed Svcs. U., Bethesda, 1997—2005; mem. Med. Exam. Review Bd. Dept. of Def., USAF Acad., Colo., 2005—07, dir. Med. Exam Review Bd., 2007—. Chair Am. Bd. Preventive Medicine, Chgo., 2003—07. Recipient Delta Omega Scholastic Honor Soc., Tulane U. Sch. of Pub. Health, 1992, Phi Kappa Phi Honor Soc., The Citadel, 1983. Fellow: Am. Coll. of Preventive Medicine, Aerospace Med. Assn. (v.p. 2001—03); mem.: Am. Bd. Preventive Medicine (chair). Methodist. Office: Dept of Def Med Exam Review Bd 8034 Edgerton Dr Ste 132 U S A F Academy CO 80840-2200 Business E-Mail: glenn.merchant@dodmerb.tma.osd.mil.

MERCHANT, RAHUL, former mortgage company executive; BSEE, Bombay U., India; MSc in Computer Sci., Memphis State U.; MBA, Temple U., Phila. Control systems programmer Leeds & Northrop Co.; 1st v.p. Lehman Brothers, Inc.; sr. v.p. Sanwa Fin. Products; exec. v.p. Dresdner, Kleinwort and Benson; head, global bus. tech. Merrill Lynch & Co.; exec. v.p., chief info. officer Fannie Mae, Washington, 2006—08. Bd. dirs. GCI, Inc. Bd. advisors Am. India Found.

MERCHANT, ROLAND SAMUEL, SR., retired health facility administrator, educator; b. NYC, Apr. 18, 1929; s. Samuel and Eleta (McLymont) M.; m. Audrey Bartley, June 6, 1970; children: Orelia Eleta, Roland Samuel, Huey Bartley. BA, NYU, 1957, MA, 1960; MS, Columbia U., 1963, MSHA, 1974. Asst. statistician NYC Dept. Health, 1957-60, statistician, 1960-63, NY Tb and Health Assn., NYC, 1963-65; biostatistician, adminstrv. coord. Inst. Surg. Studies, Montefiore Hosp., Bronx, NY, 1965-72; resident in adminstrn. Roosevelt Hosp., NYC, 1973-74; dir. health and hosp. mgmt. Dept. Health, City of NY, 1974-76; from asst. adminstr. to adminstr. West Adams Cmty. Hosp., LA, 1976; spl. asst. to assoc. v.p. for med. affairs Stanford U. Hosp., Calif., 1977-82, dir. office mgmt. and strategic planning Calif., 1982-85, dir. mgmt. planning Calif., 1986-90; v.p. strategic planning Cedars-Sinai Med. Ctr., LA, 1990-94; cons. Roland Merchant & Assocs., LA, 1994—. Clin. assoc. prof. dept. family, cmty. and preventive medicine Stanford U., 1986—88; dept. health rsch. and policy Stanford U. Med. Sch., 1988—90. Author: Passion-Sustained Commitment to Excellence: Family-Oriented Parenting and Training, 2004. With US Army, 1951—53. Fellow, USPHS. Fellow: APHA, Am. Coll. Healthcare Execs. (life); mem.: NY Acad. Scis. Home: 4445 Arcola Ave Toluca Lake CA 91602

MERCHANT, SUZY, women's college basketball coach; b. Dearborn, Mich., July 26, 1969; married; 1 child, Tyler. BA, Ctrl. Mich. U., 1991; MA in Edn., Saginaw Valley St. Asst. coach Oakland U., 1992—95; head coach Saginaw Valley State U., 1995—98, Ea. Mich. U., 1998—2007, interim assoc. athletics dir., sr. women's adminstr., 2005—06; head coach Mich. State U., 2007—. Named Coach of Yr., Basketball Coaches Assn. Mich., 2004. Office: Mich State Univ Womens Basketball Berkowitz Complex Ste 110 East Lansing MI 48824 Office Phone: 517-353-8613. E-mail: msuwbbhoops@ath.msu.edu.*

MERCIER, EILEEN ANN, pension fund chairman; b. Toronto, Ont., Can., July 7, 1947; d. Thomas Sidley and Frances Katherine (Boone) Falconer; m. Ernest Cochrane Mercier, Feb. 8, 1980 (dec.); children: Jenny, Sheelagh, Peter, Michael, Stuart; m. Charles H. Hantho Mercier, Jan. 19, 2008. BA with honors, Waterloo Luth. U., 1968; MA, U. Alta., Can., 1969; fellow, Instn. Can. Bankers, 1975; MBA, York U., 1977. Mgr. corp. fin. Toronto-Dominion Bank, 1972-78, portfolio mgr. TD capital; dir., U.S. comm. ops. Canwest Capital Corp., Toronto, 1978-81; mgr. fin. strategy & planning Gulf Can. Ltd., Toronto, 1981-86, mgr. corp. fin.; v.p. The Pagurian Corp., Toronto, 1986-87; v.p., treas. Abitibi-Price, Inc., Toronto, 1987-88, v.p. corp. devel., 1989-90, sr. v.p., CFO, 1990-95. Bd. dirs. TeeKay Corp., The CGI Group Inc., ING Bank Can., Intact Fin. Corp.; chmn. Ont. Tchrs. Pension Plan. Past chmn., mem. bd. govs. Wilfrid Laurier U., Waterloo, Ont., York U. Recipient Outstanding Bus. Leader award Wilfrid Laurier U., 1991, Award for Outstanding Contbn. Schulich Sch. of Bus. York U., 1997, fellow Inst. Corporate Dirs., 2009. Office: 1 Post Rd Apt 407 Toronto ON Canada M3B 3R4

MERCKER, MARY ALICE, aviation school administrator; b. Kansas City, Mo., June 29, 1932; d. Kenneth Foster Rhees and Catherine Mary Henel; m. Reid Martin, Nov. 23, 1950 (div. Nov. 1969); children: Reid J., Kenneth C., Mark T., Mary M., Theodore H., Sylvia R., Ben X., Teresa I. Student, Phoenix Coll., 1949-50; AA, Pima Coll., 1990-93; student, U. Ariz., 1994. Fed. aviation adminstr.; comml. pilot; cert. flight instr. Instr. Ariz. Sch. Aviation, Tucson, 1979, Tucson Cmdr., 1980, AVRA Flt. Ctr., Marana, Ariz., 1976-78; pres., founder Alpha Air, Inc., Tucson, 1980—; sec., treas. Manasco Inc., Tucson, 1987—. Aviation cons., Tucson, 1987—; adj. prof aviation Pima C.C., Tucson, 1988-94, curriculum cons., 1988-93. Author: Northumberland Dreaming, 1998, numerous poems. Recipient 2nd Place Sparrowgrass Poetry Forum, 1996, 1st Place Sparrowgrass Chapbook award, 2001. Mem. Ariz. Pilots Assn., Aircraft Owners and Pilots Assn., 99's (life). Home: 6220 W Belmont Rd Tucson AZ 85743-9212 Office: Alpha Air Inc HC 2 Box 282 Tucson AZ 85735-9709 Home Phone: 520-744-1696. Personal E-mail: alphair@msn.com.

MERCURIO, MARK R., pediatrician, educator; AB in Biochemical Scis., Princeton U., NJ; MA in Philosophy, Brown U., Providence; MD, Columbia U., NYC. Cert. neonatology and pediatrics Am. Bd. Pediat. Attending neonatologist Yale New Haven Children's Hosp., 1988—; dir., yale pediatric ethics program Yale U., New Haven, 2007—. Office: Yale Univ Sch Medicine PO Box 208064 333 Cedar St New Haven CT 06520 Business E-Mail: mark.mercurio@yale.edu.

MERCURIO, RENARD MICHAEL, real estate company executive; b. NYC, June 22, 1947; s. Pasquale J. and Ann F. Mercurio; m. Abbie Gonzalez, June 29, 1968; children— Kristin, Allison. BA, Queens Coll., NYC, 1968; MBA, U. Rochester, 1969. CPA, N.Y.; lic. real estate broker, Calif. Sr. accountant Peat, Marwick & Mitchell, NYC, 1969-73; mgr. Gulf & Western Industries, Inc., NYC, 1973-78; v.p., treas. Famous Players Ltd., Toronto, Ont., Canada, 1978-81; exec. v.p. Famous Players Realty Ltd., Toronto, 1981-84; pres. Design Twenty-Seven Ltd., Toronto, 1984—; v.p. Renric Holdings, Ltd., 1987—; CFO Schickedanz Real Estate, Palm Beach Gardens, Fla., 1999—2003. Mem. AICPA, NY State Soc. CPAs. Personal E-mail: amercu6@aol.com.

MERDINGER, CHARLES JOHN, civil engineer, educator, military officer, academic administrator; b. Chgo., Apr. 20, 1918; s. Walter F. and Catherine (Phelan) M.; m. Mary McKelleget, Oct. 21, 1944; children: Anne, Joan, Susan, Jane. Student, Marquette U., 1935-37; BS, U.S. Naval Acad., 1941; BCE, Rensselaer Poly. Inst., 1945, MCE, 1946; DPhil (Rhodes scholar), Brasenose Coll., Oxford U., Eng., 1949; LHD (hon.), Sierra Nev. Coll., 1987; DLitt (hon.), U. Nev., Reno, 1994. Registered profl. engr., Wis. Commd. ensign USN, 1941, advanced through grades to capt. Civil Engr. Corps, 1959; served aboard USS Nevada, USS Alabama Atlantic and Pacific, 1941-44; design, constrn. pub. works Panama, 1946—47, Washington, Bremerton, Adak, Miramar, 1949—56; comdg. officer, dir. U.S. Naval Civil Engring. Lab., Port Hueneme, Calif., 1956-59; pub. works officer U.S. Fleet activities, Yokosuka, Japan, 1959-62; head English, history and govt. dept. U.S. Naval Acad., Annapolis, Md., 1962-65; asst. comdr. ops. & maintenance Naval Facilities Engring. Command, Navy Dept., 1965-67; pub. works officer Seabees (NSA), DaNang, Vietnam, 1967-68; comdg. officer Western div. Naval Facilities Engring. Command, San Bruno, Calif., 1968-70; pres. Washington Coll., Chestertown, Md., 1970-73; v.p. Aspen Inst. Humanistic Studies, Colo., 1973-74; dep. dir. Scripps Instn. Oceanography, La Jolla, Calif., 1974-80; dir. Avco, 1978—. Author: Civil Engineering Through the Ages, 1963; contbr.: articles to Ency. Britannica; others. Mem. Md., Calif., Oreg. and Nev. Selection Coms. for Rhodes Scholars, sec. Nev. Com., 1982-89; exec. vol. Boy Scouts Am.; sec., mem. exec. com. Md. Ind. Coll. and Univ. Assn., 1971-72; mem. So. Regional Edn. Bd, 1971-73, Nat. Com. History and Heritage of Am. Civil Engring., 1965-72; Alumni trustee U.S. Naval Acad., 1971-74; mem. coun. Rensselaer Poly. Inst., 1972—; trustee Found. for Ocean Rsch., 1976-80, Desert Rsch. Inst. Found., Nev., 1983-92, U. Nev. Reno Found., 1986-93; chmn. bd. trustees Sierra Nev. Coll., 1980-87, chmn. bd. emeritus, 1987; commr. N.W. Assn. Commn. on Colls., 1988-93. Pfc Wis. Nat. Guard, 1935—37. Decorated Legion of

Merit with combat V; named All-Am. in lacrosse, 1945, Papal Knight Grand Cross Equestrian Order of Holy Sepulchre of Jerusalem, 1992; inducted into Rensselaer Athletic Hall of Fame, 1983; recipient Disting. Eagle Scout award, 1984. Fellow ASCE (Nat. History and Heritage award 1972), Explorers Club, Soc. Am. Mil. Engrs. (Toulmin medal 1952, 57, 61); mem. NSPE, Am. Soc. Engring. Edn., Brasenose Soc., Pearl Harbor Survivors Assn., Nat. Eagle Scout Assn. (regent), Phalanx, Sigma Xi, Tau Beta Pi, Chi Epsilon. Clubs: Vincent's, Oxford. Roman Catholic. Home: The Forum 305 D 23500 Cristo Roy Dr Cupertino CA 95014 Business E-Mail: charles.merdinger@forumrsa.com.

MEREDITH, ANDREA L., medical educator; b. Washington, Dc, Oct. 1, 1973; d. George R. and Carol A. Meredith. BS, Univ. Md. Balt., 1994; PhD, Univ. Tex. Southwestern Med. Sch., Dallas, 2000. Student rsch. asst. Gerontology Rsch. Ctr. (NIA, NIH), Balt., 1992—94; postdoc. fellowship Stanford U., Palo Alto, Calif., 2000—06; asst. prof. U Md. Sch. Medicine, Md., 2006—. Vol. Nat. Alliance Mentally Ill, Arlington, Va., 2008—; pres. Grad. Student Orgn. (UTSW), Dallas, 1997—98. Recipient Inducted award, Kappa Theta Episilon, 1993, Performance Award, Gerontology Rsch. Ctr., 1993, Oral Presentation, SW Regional Conf., 1998, Ida Green award, Cecil & Ida Green Found., 1999, Travel award, Beckman Ctr. Molecular Genetic Medicine, 2005, Md. Outstanding Young Scientist award, Md. Sci. Ctr., 2008—, Allen C. Davies Medal, 2008—; fellow Cell & Molecular Biology Tng. grant, NIH, 1998; Scientist Devel. award, Am. Heart Assn., 2008—. Mem.: Am. Heart Assn., Soc. Rsch. Biol. Rhythms, Am. Physiol. Soc., Soc. Neuroscience. Achievements include invention of Slo1 conditional knockout mice, licensed through Standford university.

MEREDITH, DALE DEAN, civil engineering educator; b. Centralia, Ill., Mar. 24, 1940; s. Leslie Edward Meredith and Beulah Marie (McClelland) Nattier; m. Linda Jean Hutson, July 3, 1965; children: Sarah Elizabeth, Laura Jane. AA, Centralia Twp. Jr. Coll., 1961; BS, U. Ill., 1963, MS, 1964, PhD, 1968. Registered profl. engr., N.Y., Ill. Asst. prof. U. Ill., Urbana, 1968-73; assoc. prof. civil engring. SUNY, Buffalo, 1973-79, prof., 1979-2000, chmn. dept. civil engring., 1987-96, prof. emeritus, 2000—; pastor U. Baptist Ch., Getzville, NY, 1996—. Co-author: Design and Planning Engineering Systems, 1973, 2d edit., 1985; also over 50 articles. Vice pres. Baptist Conv. N.Y., Syracuse, 1982-84, 94-95, chmn. exec. bd., 1987. Grantee U.S. Office Water Research and Tech., 1966-73, 75-78, U.S. Dept. Interior, 1968-79, U.S. Dept. Commerce, 1976-79, various pvt. cos., 1979—, N.Y. State Agys., 1980-2000. Fellow ASCE (chmn. exec. com. Water Resources Planning and Mgmt. div., 1988, editor jour. Water Resources Planning and Mgmt. 1982-84); mem. Am. Geophys. Union, Am. Soc. Engring. Edn., Am. Water Resources Assn. (editor Water Resources Bull. 1990-91). Office: SUNY Dept Civil Engring Buffalo NY 14260-4300 E-mail: ciedale@eng.buffalo.edu.

MEREDITH, JOANNE CUSICK, retired special education educator; b. Pitts., Dec. 2, 1952; d. Joseph Francis and Anne Amelia (Fiorillo) Cusick; m. Richard Burdette Meredith, Nov. 25, 2001. BS in speech and hearing, Ind. U. of Pa., 1974, MS in Speech Pathology, 1979. Cert. spl. edn. supr. Slippery Rock U. Pa., 1987, sch. psychologist Duquesne U., Pa., 1992, speech correction profl. level II Ind. U. Pa., supr. spl. edn. profl. level II Slippery Rock U. of Pa., 1987, sch. psychologist level I. Speech/lang. therapist Seneca Valley Sch. Dist., Harmony, Pa., 1974—96; part-time speech pathologist Rehab. Specialists, Pitts., 1980—81; sch. psychologist intern Seneca Valley Sch. Dist., Harmony, Pa., 1991—92, dir. spl. edn., 1996—2008; ret. Pres. Seneca Valley Edn. Assn., Harmony, Pa., 1986—90, chief negotiator, 1989—95, v.p., 1990—92. Recipient Gift of Time award, Am. Family Inst., ACE award, Am. Speech/Lang./Hearing Assn., Appreciation award, Pa. State Assn. for Health, PE, Recreation and Dance, 1995. Mem.: Butler County ARC (bd. dirs.), Pa. Speech/Lang. Assn., Am. Speech, Lang. and Hearing Assn., Phi Delta Kappa. Democrat. Avocation: motorcycling. Home: 345 Beacon Rd Renfrew PA 16053 Home Phone: 724-586-7635. Personal E-mail: meredithjoanne@ymail.com.

MEREDITH, LISA ANN MARIE, literacy coach, consultant; d. Robert Lee and Carol Ann Meredith; life ptnr. Thomas J. Unrath; children: Brittany, Bethanne. BA, Alvernia Coll., Reading, Pa., 1990—91; MA in Am. History, Chevnev U., Pa., 2006. Cert. elem. sch. tchr. Commonwealth of Pa., 1991, mid. sch. tchr. Commonwealth of Pa., 2005. Tchr. Reading Sch. Dist., Pa., 1991—2003, Sch. Dist. Phila., 2001—; edn. coord. Nat. Constn. Ctr., Phila., 2003—04. Asst. coord. Ctr. for Civic Edn., Phila., 2003—04; cons. Pa. Gov.'s Inst. for Social Studies Educators, Harrisburg, 2004—; bd. mem. Buck's County Commr.'s Adv. Coun. for Women, 2005—07, steering com., 2005—07. Mem. Champions for Caring, Phila., 2003—04; activist, rep. Reading Edn. Assn., Pa., 1998—2000; activist Phila. (Pa.) Citizens Children and Youth, 2002—03, Phila. Fedn. Tchrs., 2004—05. Grantee, Eisenhower Grants, 1995—96, Tchg. Am. History, 2002—03. Mem.: NEA, ASCD, Pa. State Edn. Assn., Nat. Coun. Social Studies Tchrs. (assoc.), Reading Edn. Assn. (assoc.). Democrat. Lutheran. Avocations: history, travel, golf, reading, cooking. Business E-Mail: lameredith@phila.k12.pa.us, mereditl@readingsd.org.

MEREDITH, THOMAS BRIAN, healthcare consultant; b. Grand Rapids, Mich., Dec. 31, 1957; s. George William and Lucille Francis (Calandrino) M.; m. Colleen Masterson, Oct. 10, 1987; children: Mark Thomas, Brian Christopher. BS in Bus. Adminstrn. Acctg., Ohio State U., 1980. CPA. Acct. Shaker Med. Ctr., Cleve., 1980—83; asst. acctg./budget mgr. Luth. Med. Ctr., Cleve., 1983—85; sr. mgr. KPMG Peat Marwick, Cleve., 1985—95; prin. Advantage Consulting, Inc., Independence, Ohio, 1995—2008; pres. Spectrum Consulting LLC, Cleve., 2008—. Mem. AICPAs, Healthcare Fin. Mgmt. Assn. (Follmer Bronze Merit award 1995, advanced mem., Reeves Silver award 1999), Healthcare Fin. Mgmt. Assn. Northeast Ohio (bd. dirs. 1996-98). Avocations: reading, music, golf.

MEREDITH, THOMAS J., investment company executive; b. 1950; m. Lynn Maureen Mullen; 4 children. BA in Polit. Sci., St. Francis Coll., Loretto, Pa., 1972; JD, Duquesne U. Law, 1975; LLM in Taxation, Georgetown U., 1977; PhD (hon.), St. Francis, Duquesne U. Bus. Sch. Bar: Calif., DC, Pa. Dir. tax rsch. and planning Castle & Cooke, Inc.; sr. tax cons. Arthur Young & Co.; co-founder, gen. mgr. Amdahl Capital Corp., 1979—89; v.p., treas. Sun Microsystems, Inc., 1989—92; sr. v.p., CFO Dell Computer Corp., Round Rock, Tex., 1992—2000, sr. v.p., bus. devel & strategy, 2000—01; mng. dir. Dell Ventures, 2000—01; co-founder, gen. ptnr. Meritage Capital, L.P., 1998—; CEO MFI Capital, LLC; acting CFO Motorola, Inc., Schaumburg, Ill., 2007—08. Bd. dir. Freemarkets, Inc., Divine, Inc., VoxPath Networks, Tipping Point, 2001—, Motive, Inc., 2003—, Motorola, Inc., 2005—; adj. prof., McCombs Sch. Business Univ. Texas; adv. bd. Wharton Sch., U. Pa., U. Tex., adj. prof., McCombs Sch. Bus. Chair, pres. Meredith Private Found., 1998—; founding investor & chair Austin Idea Network. Mem.: Fin. Execs. Inst. Office: MFI Capital LLC 248 Addie Roy Rd Austin TX 78746*

MEREDITH, WENDI SUE, music educator; d. Dennis Wayne and L Imogene Meredith. BS in Elem. Edn., Bapt. Bible Coll., 1992, BA in Ch. Music, 1997; MusM, SW Mo. State U., 2001. Level 1 Orff Schulwerk Certification Am. Orff Schulwerk Assn., 1999, Improving Strategies in Tchg.AQA GCSE Music Specification Keynote Ednl., 2004, Form Tutors: Role, Skills and Responsibilities Lighthouse Profl. Devel., 2004. English, music tchr. Quint City Bapt. Sch., Davenport, Iowa, 1992—95; prof. voice Bapt. Bible Coll., Springfield, Mo., 1997—2004; tchr. music Egerton Rothesay Sch., Berkhamsted, Hertfordshire, England, 2004—06, peripatatic singing tchr., 2005—, head music, 2006—, coord. musical events, 2006—. Traveling recruiter Bapt. Bible Coll., Springfield, Mo., 1990—92, 1995—2001, coord. traveling recruitment teams, 1999—2001, co-writer, co-producer of drama, 1998—99; soprano Cmty. Choir SW Mo. State U., Springfield, 1998—2003; coord. program for woman's conf. Cherry St. Bapt. Ch., Springfield, 2000—04, dir. woman's conf., 2003—04; children's and musical dir. Bible Bapt. Ch., Wendover, Buckinghamshire, England, 2003—, worship leader, 2004—, vocal instr., Resonant Praise, 2007; mem. chorus Springfield Regional Opera/Messiah Project, 2003—03; soprano Cmty. Choir Bapt. Bible Coll., Springfield, 2003—04; spkr. in field; coord., group leader ERS2USA Music Trip, 2009. Composer: (song) For Such a Time as This. Choir dir. Voices of St. Francis concert Egerton Rothesay Sch., 2006; singing team leader for youth camp and youth events Bapt. Bible Fellowship Internat., Springfield, Mo., 1995—2002; children's choir tchr. Cherry St. Bapt. Ch., Springfield, Mo., 1995—2004; christian sch. tchr. Quint City Bapt. Ch., Davenport, Iowa, 1992—95; music coord. youth event, Berkhamsted, 2006—07; music coord., leader LIFE Camp, Tonbridge, Kent, England, 2006—07. Civilian day camp worker US Army, 1990—93, Rock Island Illinois. Mem.: Nat. Trust, Nat. Union Tchrs., Gospel Music Assn., Am. Orff Schulwerk Assn.

MEREL, GAIL, lawyer; m. Christopher E.H. Dack. BS, Cornell U., Ithaca, NY, 1969; PhD, Harvard U., Cambridge, Mass., 1974, JD, 1977. Tchg. asst. Cornell U., 1968—69, Harvard U., 1972; asst. prof. Case We. Res. U., Cleve., 1974; assoc. atty. Cleary Gottlieb Steen & Hamilton LLP, NY, 1977—82; assoc. Schulte Roth Zabel, LLP, NY, 1982—85, ptnr., 1985—87, Mayor, Day, Caldwell & Keeton, LLP, Houston, 1987—2001, Andrews Kurth, LLP, Houston, 2001—. Mem. com. Glassell Sch. Art, Houston, 1998—2009. Fellow, NSF, 1969—71. Mem.: ABA (mem. legal opinions com. bus. law sect.), DirectWomen (steering com. mem. 2009), Working Group Legal Opinions (editor in chief 2006—, steering com. mem. 2007—), Houston Comml. Fin. Lawyers Forum, Tex. Bus. Law Found. (dir. 1995—), State Bar Tex. (chmn. bus. law sect. 2004—05, past chmn., mem. legal opinions com.). Office: Andrews Kurth LLP 600 Travis St Ste 4200 Houston TX 77002

MERENDINO, K. ALVIN, surgeon, educator; b. Clarksburg, W.Va., Dec. 3, 1914; s. Biagio and Cira (Bivona) M.; m. Shirley Emma Jane Hill, July 6, 1943; children: Cira Anne Watts, Nancy Jane Napuunoa, Susan Hill Mitchell, Nina, Maria King Merendino-Stillwell. BA summa cum laude, Ohio U., Athens, 1936, LLD (hon.), 1967; MD, Yale U., New Haven, Conn., 1940; PhD, U. Minn., Mpls., 1946. Diplomate Am. Bd. Surgery, Am. Bd. Thoracic Surgery. Intern Cin. Gen. Hosp., 1940-41; resident U. Minn. Hosp., Mpls., 1941-45; rsch. asst. Dr. Owen H. Wangensteen, 1942-43; trainee Nat. Cancer Inst., 1943-45; dir. program in postgrad. med. edn. in surgery Ancker Hosp., St. Paul, 1946-48; instr. dept. surgery U. Minn., Mpls., 1944-45, asst. prof. dept. surgery, 1945-48; assoc. prof. dept. surgery U. Wash., Seattle, 1949-55, dir. exptl. surgery labs., dept. surgery, 1950-72, prof. dept. surgery, 1955-81, prof. emeritus, 1981—, prof. and adminstrv. officer dept. surgery, 1957-64, prof., chmn., 1964-72; chmn. dept. surgery King Faisal Specialist and Rsch. Ctgr., Riyadh, Saudi Arabia, 1975—76, dir. med. affairs, 1976-79, chmn. dept. energy, dir. Cancer Therapy Inst., spl. cons. to Coun., supr. for exec. mgmt., assoc. dir. med. affairs Riyadh, Saudi Arabia, 1981-82; dir. ops. King Faisal Med. City, Riyadh, 1981-85. Mem. adv. com. for med. rsch., Boeing Airplane Co., 1959-67, chmn., 19621 cons. Children's Orthopedic Hosp., Seattle, 1972-82; mem. adv. com. on heart disease and surgery for crippled children's svc., Wash. State Dept. Health and Div. Vocational Rehab., 1961; mem. surgery study sect. NIH, 1958-62, subcom. on prosthetic valves for cardiac surgery, chm. 1st Nat. Conf., 1960, mem. adv. com. 2d Nat. Conf. on Prosthetic Heart Valves, 1969, Surgery A study sect. chmn., 1970-72, Nat. Heart and Lung Inst. Tng. Com., 1965-69; cons. VA, Seattle, 1949-59, 65-81; mem. adv. com. on hosps. and clinics, USPHS, 1963-66; mem. surgery test com. Nat. Bd. Med. Examiners, 1963-67; mem. surgery resident rev. com., Conf. Com. on Grad. Edn. in Surgery, 1963-73, vice-chmn., 1972-73; chmn. 2d Saudi Arabian Med. Conf., Riyadh, 1978; mem. com. on postgrad. med. edn., Kingdom of Saudi Arabia Ministry of Health, 1978-79; vis. prof. established open heart surgery program Malaysia U. Hosp., Kuala Lumpur, 1971, edn. and tng. jr. faculty (surg. residents) faculty medicine U. Saigon and Mil. M.C. (army surgeons) Binh Dan Hosp. Saigon, Vietnam. Editor in chief: Prosthetic Valves for Cardiac Surgery, 1961; assoc. editor: Prosthetic Heart Valves, 1969; mem. editorial bd. Am. Jour. Surgery, 1958-83, Jour. Surg. Rsch., 1961-69, Pacific Medicine and Surgery, 1964-68, King Faisal Hosp. Medicine Jour. (renamed Annals of Saudi Medicine), 1981-85; contbr. articles to profl. jours., chpts. to books; producer movies on surgery. Recipient cert. of merit Ohio U. Alumni Assn., 1957, Outstanding W.Va. Italian-Am. award W.Va. Italian Heritage Festival Inc., Clarksburg, W.Va., 1984, Spirit of Freedom award A. James Mancin, Sec. State W.Va., 1984, Disting. W. Virginian award Gov. John D. Rockefeller IV., State of W.Va., 1984, John Baird Thomas Meml. award Ohio U.; named Surgery Alumnus of Yr., U. Minn., 1981, Disting. Citizen Wash. State, Lt. Gov. John Cherberg, 1981, K. Alvin Merendino Day Seattle, Mayor Charles Royer, 1981; NIH grantee, 1951-76; Verdi scholar Yale U., Dr. K. Alvin and Shirley Merendino Professorship, 2008 Fellow ACS (numerous coms., bds.), Soc. of Univ. Surgeons (councilman at large 3 yrs.), Internat. Soc. Surgery; mem. Am. Surg. Assn. (adv. mem. com. 1959-64, v.p. 1972-73), Am. Assn. for Thoracic Surgery, Halsted Soc., Henry N. Harkins Surg. Soc., N. Pacific Coast Surg. Assn., Seattle Surg. Soc. (honored special tribute annual meeting 1997), So. Surg. Soc. (Arthur H. Shipley award 1972), Am. Bd. Surgery 1958-64 (vice chmn. 1962-63, chmn. 1963-64, emeritus 1964—); University Club, Seattle Golf Club, Phi Beta Kappa, Sigma Xi, Beta Theta Pi (sec., pres.), Phi Beta Pi (hon.). Republican. Episcopalian. Avocations: golf, fly fishing, bird hunting, gardening. Home: The Highlands Shoreline WA 98177 Personal E-mail: k.merendinomd@comcast.net.

MERGENTHALER, FRANK, corporate financial executive; BS, Providence Coll. CPA. Acctg. positions Price Waterhouse, 1983—96; asst., treas., corp. contr. to sr. v.p. fin. Seagram, 1996—2001; sr. v.p., dep. CFO Vivendi Universal, 2001—02; exec. v.p., CFO Columbia House Co., 2002—05, Interpublic Group of Companies, NYC, 2005—. Mem.: AICPA, Fin. Executives Inst., NY State Soc CPAs. Office: Interpublic Group 1114 Ave of the Americas New York NY 10036

MERGLER, H. KENT, investment counselor; b. Cin., July 1, 1940; s. Wilton Henry and Mildred Amelia (Pulliam) M.; m. Judith Anne Metzger, Aug. 17, 1963; children: Stephen Kent, Timothy Alan, Kristin Lee. BBA with honors, U. Cin., 1963, MBA, 1964. CFA, C.I.C. Portfolio mgr. Scudder, Stevens & Clark, Cin., 1964-68, exec. v.p. Chgo., 1970-73; v.p. Gibralter Rsch. & Mgmt., Ft. Lauderdale, Fla., 1968-70; ptnr. Stein Roe & Farnham, Ft. Lauderdale, 1973-84; ptnr., pres., dir., prin., mem. exec. com. Stein Roe & Farnham, Inc., Chgo., 1984-91; pres. Stein Roe Investment Trust, 1988—91; mng. ptnr., chief investment officer Loomis, Sayles & Co., L.P., Palm Beach Gardens, Fla., 1992-2000; pres. Northstar Capital Mgmt., Inc., 2002—04, chmn., 2005—. Arbitrator Nat. Assn. Security Dealers, Inc., 1976-82. Chmn. adminstrv. bd. Christ United Meth. Ch., Ft. Lauderdale, 1981—83; mem. fin. com. Kenilworth Union Ch., 1989—92; elder, chmn. fin. com. First Presbyn. Ch., Stuart, 2001—04, 2006—09; chmn. Presbytery of Tropical Fla.-Coral Gables Fund, 2006—; chmn. investment com. Cmty. Found. Broward, 1992—2001, bd. dirs., chmn. investment com., 1994—2001; mem. Martin County Econ. Coun., 1992—2000; bd. dirs. Pine Crest Prep. Sch., 1982—84, bd. advisors, 1984—87; corp. adv. bd. U. Cin. Coll. Bus. Adminstrn., 1991—94; bd. dirs. Hibiscus House Children's Found., 1993—99, 2001—07, chmn. investment, endowment com., 1994—99, 2001—. Mem. Fin. Analysts Soc. So. Fla. (bd. dirs. 1974-78, pres. 1975), Bond Club Ft. Lauderdale (bd. dirs. 1978-82), Yorktown University (bd. trustees, 2006-), Cullasaja Club (Highlands, N.C.), Mariner Sands Golf Club, Beta Gamma Sigma, Beta Theta Pi (found. bd. dirs. 2008-). Republican. Presbyterian. Home: 6306 SE Oakmont Pl Stuart FL 34997 Office: 3801 PGA Blvd Ste 904 Palm Beach Gardens FL 33410 Office Phone: 561-775-5880.

MERIDEN, TERRY, physician; b. Damascus, Syria, Oct. 12, 1946; arrived in U.S., 1975; s. Izzat and Omayma (Aidi) Meriden; m. Lena Kahal, Nov. 17, 1975; children: Zina, Lana. BS, Sch. Sci., Damascus, 1968; MD, Sch. Medicine, Damascus, 1972, doctorate cum laude, 1973. Diplomate Am. Bd. Internal Medicine. Resident in infectious diseases Rush Green Hosp., Romford, Eng., 1973; house officer in internal medicine and cardiology Ashford Group Univ. Hosps., England, 1973-74; sr. house officer in internal medicine and neurology Grimsby Group Univ. Hosps., England, 1974; registrar in internal medicine and rheumatology St. Annes Hosp., London, 1974-75; jr. resident in internal medicine Shadyside Hosp., Pitts., 1975-76, sr. resident in internal medicine, 1976-77; fellow in endocrinology and metabolism Shadyside Hosp. and Grad. Inst., Pitts., 1976-77; clin. asst. prof. U. Ill., Peoria, 1979; pres. Am. Diabetes Assn., Peoria, 1982-84; dir. Proctor Diabetes Unit, Peoria, 1984—, 1984—. Adviser Gov. of Ill. on diabetes. Mem. editl. bd. Diabetes Forecast mag., Clin. Diabetes, 1990; contbr. articles to profl. jours. Fellow: ACP, Am. Coll. Endocrinology; mem.: ADA (chmn. profl. edn. and rsch. 1980—, mem. editl. bd., mem. Spanish lit. bd., nat. bd. dirs. 1986—, vice chmn. nat. com. on diabetes edn. and affiliate svcs. 1986—, Outstanding Svc. award 1984, Outstanding Diabetes Educator award 1986), AMA (Recognition award 1985), Am. Coll. Endocrinology, Am. Assn. Clin. Endocrinology (founding), Am. Cancer Soc. (Life Line award 1983), Obesity Found. (Century award 1984, Recognition award 1985). Home: 115 E Coventry Ln Peoria IL 61614-2103 Office: 900 Main St Ste 300 Peoria IL 61602-1049 Office Phone: 309-673-1717. Personal E-mail: tmeriden@aol.com.

MERINI, RAFIKA, humanities and foreign languages educator, writer; b. Morocco; arrived in U.S., 1972; d. Mohamed M. and Fatima Merini. BA in English cum laude, U. Utah, 1978, MA in Romance Langs. and Lits., 1981; postgrad., U. Wash., 1980-82; cert. in translation, SUNY, Binghamton, 1988, PhD in Comparative Lit., 1992. Tchg. asst. U. Utah, Salt Lake City, 1978-80, U. Wash., Seattle, 1980-82; adminstrv. asst., tchr. French, interpreter, translator Internat. Lang. Sch., Seattle, 1982—83; lectr. Pacific Luth. U., Tacoma, 1983; instr. French and Spanish Ft. Steilacoom C.C. (now Pierce C.C.), 1983—85; tchg. asst. dept. romance langs. SUNY, Binghamton, 1985-87, tchg. asst. women's studies dept., 1988, tchg. asst. comparative lit. dept., 1986-88; vis. instr. humanities and French Union Coll., Schenectady, NY, 1988—89; vis. instr. dept. fgn. langs. and lits. Skidmore Coll., Saratoga Springs, NY, 1989-90; asst. prof. dept. modern and classical langs. State U. Coll., Buffalo, 1990—96, assoc. prof. dept. modern and classical langs., 1996—. Coord. Buffalo State Coll. women's studies interdisciplinary unit State U. Coll., Buffalo, 1993-99, adviser French Club, 1990-93, 2007-; v.p., acting pres. Faculty Student Assn., 2006-08, pres., 2008-; sponsor, founder, dir. Trois-Pistoles French Immersion Program, U. Western Ont.-Buffalo State Coll.1994, 95, 2005-; presenter, spkr., organizer numerous inter-disciplinary confs. Author: Two Major Francophone Women Writers, Assia Djébar and Leïla Sebbar: A Thematic Study of Their Works, 1999, 2d printing, paperback edit., 2001; mem. editl. bd. Jour. Middle Eastern and North African Intellectual and Cultural Studies, 2002-07; contbr. articles to profl. jours Grantee Nat. Defense Student award U. Utah, 1974; also numerous other grants and awards. Mem. MLA, Pi Delta Phi. Achievements include being interviewed on WBNY (BSC), Radio-Canada, FranceInter twice, Radio-France (Allo la Planete), Radiodiffusion Television Marocaine & by the FranceInter. Office: State Univ Coll-Buffalo Modern & Classical Langs 1300 Elmwood Ave Buffalo NY 14222-1095 Home: PO Box 1063 Buffalo NY 14213-1063

MERINO, ADRIANA GRACIELA, language educator; d. Oscar Merino and Ma. Virginia Tantucci; m. Gerardo Massaccesi; children: Guillermo Massaccesi, Guido Massaccesi. BA in English Tchg. and Lit., Inst. Nat. Lenguas Vivas Juan Ramon Fernandez, Buenos Aires, 1984; MA in Linguistics, U. Comahue, Gen. Roca, Rio Negro, Argentina, 1998; PhD in Applied Linguistics summa cum laude, UNED, Madrid, 2008. Assoc. prof. U. Nat. Comahue, Gen. Roca, 1986—2001, ext. sec., Escuela Superior Idiomas, 1995—2001, cons., in-svc. trainer, Inst. Nuevo Siglo, 1998—99, ESI program developer, assessment and syllabus designer, 2007—08, profl. devel. trainer; vis. internat. faculty VIF Program, Asheville, NC, 2001—03; Spanish instr. Holy Family U., Phila., 2004—. Contbg. editor Piensa en Espanol, Instrnl. Mag., La Jolla, Calif., 2003—04; external cons. Escuela Superior Idiomas, Gen. Roca, 2007—08. Contbr. scientific papers to numerous profl. jours.

MERINO, DENNIS ILIGAN, mathematics educator, researcher; b. La Carlotta, The Philippines, May 17, 1966; came to U.S., 1988; s. Menandro Villas and Zenaida (Iligan) M. BS in Math., U. Philippines, Manila, 1986; MS in Engring., Johns Hopkins U., 1990, PhD, 1992. Instr. U. Philippines, 1986-88; teaching asst. Johns Hopkins U., Balt., 1989-92, rsch. asst., 1991; asst. prof. math. Southeastern La. U., Hammond, 1992—. Mathematician NIH, Bethesda, Md., summer 1990. Abel Wolmann fellow Johns Hopkins U., 1988. Mem. Math. Assn. Am. Roman Catholic. Avocations: playing tennis, chess, singing. Home: 2200 N Morrison Blvd Apt 64 Hammond LA 70401-1233 Office: Dept Math Southeastern Ln # U Hammond LA 70402-0001

MERINO, ENRIQUE, retired geochemistry professor; b. Madrid, Jan. 21, 1942; s. Félix Merino and Maria-Luisa Muedra; m. Consuelo López-Morillas, June 11, 1971; children: Diego, Miguel. PhD, U. Calif., Berkeley, 1973. Cert. ingeniero minas, Sch. Mining Engring., Madrid, 1965. Vis. asst. prof. U. Western Ont., London, Canada, 1973—74; postdoc. fellow Case Western Res. U., Cleve., 1975—76; prof. geology dept. Ind. U., Bloomington, 1976—2006, prof. emeritus; vis. prof. U. Aix-Marseille III, France, 1991; fellow Gesthermal Inst., U. Auckland, New Zealand, Acad. Scis., Oslo, 2001. Fellow, Fulbright Found., Del Amo Found., 1967—71. Mem.: Geochem. Soc. Achievements include research in chemical-geodynamic and self-patterning phenomena. Avocations: travel, soccer, music. Home: 1320 E First St Bloomington IN 47401 Office: Ind Univ Dept Geol Scis 1005 E Tenth St Bloomington IN 47405 Office Fax: 812-855-7899. Business E-Mail: merino@indiana.edu.

MERIWETHER, HEATH J., newspaper consultant, retired publisher, educator; b. Columbia, Mo., Jan. 20, 1944; s. Nelson Heath and Mary Agnes (Immele) Meriwether; m. Patricia Hughes, May 4, 1979; children: Graham, Elizabeth. BA in History, BJ, U. Mo., 1966; MAT, Harvard U., 1967; Advanced Exec. Program, Northwestern U. Journalism fellow Stanford U.; reporter Miami (Fla.) Herald, 1970—72, editor Broward and Palm Beach burs., 1972—77, exec. city editor, 1977—79, asst. mgr. editor news, 1979—80, mng. editor, 1981—83, exec. editor, 1983—87, Detroit Free Press, 1987—95, pub., 1996—2004; newspaper cons., 2004—. Adj. prof. grad. sch. journalism City U. NY, 2006—. Chair Rails to Trails Conservancy, 2005—07. Lt. USNR, 1967—70. Office Phone: 646-758-7824. Personal E-mail: hjm4491@yahoo.com.

MERK, FREDERICK BANNISTER, biomedical educator, researcher; b. Cambridge, Mass., Feb. 21, 1936; s. Frederick and Lois Alberta (Bannister) M.; m. Linda Jean Poole, Oct. 22, 1966 (dec. Dec. 1994); children: John F., R. Daniel; m. Laura Ann Bradford, July 11, 1998; 1 stepchild, Letty A. Bradford. AB, Harvard Coll., 1958; PhD, Boston U., 1971. Asst. prof. pathology Boston U. Sch. Medicine, 1972-73; assoc. prof. dept. pathology Tufts U. Sch. Medicine, Boston, 1973—2002, assoc. prof. dept. anatomy, 1973—2002, emeritus prof. pathology and anatomy, 2002—, part time tchr. anatomy, 2002—, dir. electron microscopy facility, 1975-85. Cons. electron microscopy Mass. Gen. Hosp., Boston, 1964-85; cons. toxicol. testing Transgenic Scis., Worcester, Mass., 1988-91, U.S. Army, 1998-2001. Contbr. more than 60 articles to profl. jours. Trustee Broadway United Meth. Ch., Lynn, Mass., chmn. 1994-2000; lay rep. Grace United Meth. Ch. to ann. New Eng. Conf., 2000—; trustee Frederick and Paula Anna Markus Found., Audubon Soc., Moultonboro, NH, 2005—. Recipient Disting. Career in Tchr. award, 2002; grantee, NIH, 1994—98. Mem. Am. Soc. Cell Biology, Fedn. Am. Soc. Exptl. Biology, Am. Assn. Anatomists, Microscopy Soc. Am., Boston Cancer Rsch. Assn., Sigma Xi. Achievements include research on biology of cells in target organs responding to hormones with emphasis on benign prostatic hypertrophy (enlargement) and prostate cancer. Avocations: gardening, photography, swimming, scuba diving. Home: 28 Warwick Rd Melrose MA 02176 Office: Tufts Univ Sch Medicine Dept Anatomy 136 Harrison Ave Boston MA 02111-1800 Personal E-mail: fmerk@hotmail.com.

MERK, P. EVELYN, retired librarian; b. Macon, Ga., Dec. 8, 1943; d. Charlie B. and Gladys (Perry) M. BA, Mercer U., 1966; MEd, U. Ga., 1973; MLS, Emory U., 1987. Tchr. East Laurens HS, Dublin, Ga., 1966-68, Westside Sch., McDonough, Ga., 1968-70, Brantley County HS, Nahunta, Ga., 1970-72; sch. media specialist Mary Persons Sch., Forsyth, Ga., 1973-75; tech. services libr. Houston County Pub. Libr., Warner Robins, Ga., 1975-76, reference libr., 1976-77, libr., 1977—96, asst. dir., 1996—2002, libr. cons., trainer, 2002—06; ret., 2007. Bd. dirs. Warner Robins Day Care Ctr. Inc., chmn. 1984-85, 91. Mem. ALA, AAUW, Bus. and Profl. Women, Southeastern Library Assn., Ga. Library Assn., Warner Robins Pioneers. Avocations: reading, candle making, travel. Home: 293 Peachtree Cir Warner Robins GA 31088-4448 Personal E-mail: evelynmerk@aol.com.

MERKEL, ANNE D., science educator; b. Wilmington, Del., Nov. 4, 1942; d. George and Eileen Davis; m. James A. Merkel, June 3, 1970. BS, U. Del., Newark, 1964; MEd in Chemistry, U. Del., 1971. Registered med. technologist ASCP, Chgo., 2008. Dir. med. assisting program Beal Coll., Bangor, Maine, 1979—81; instr. Eastern Maine CC, Bangor, 1981—. Grader for coll. bd. essays in ap biology Ednl. Testing Svcs., Newark, 2002—04; program dir. med. lab. tech. Eastern Maine CC, 1996—2001; supr. microbiology dept. Maine Coast Meml. Hosp., Ellsworth, 1977—79; rsch. assoc. virology DuPont Co., Newark, 1965—69. Mem.: NEA, Am. Soc. Clin. Pathology, Maine Tchrs. Assn. Independent. Roman Catholic. Achievements include curriculum development for programs at Jackson Laboratory, Beal College and East Maine Community College; serving on accrediting teams for New England Association of Schools and Colleges. Avocations: bicycling, swimming, travel. Home: 298 Ohio St Bangor ME 04401 Office: Eastern Maine Cmty Coll 354 Hogan Rd Bangor ME 04401 Business E-Mail: amerkel@emcc.edu.

MERKEL, PATRICIA MAE, retired school system administrator; b. Spokane, Wash., June 18, 1935; d. Hugo Oscar and Mary Jane (Blackwelder) Koenig; m. Gordon Henry, Nov. 10, 1956 (div. 1973); children: Katherine Marie Merkel Fisk, Karol Ann Merkel Korte, John Henry. BA cum laude, Ea. Washington U., 1989. Cert. ednl. office employee. Acctg. clk. Pacific N.W. Bell, Spokane, 1954-56; book-keeper Edwall (Wash.) Sch. Dist., 1969-75, Reardan (Wash.)-Edwall Sch. Dist., 1975-78, bus. mgr., 1978-82; asst. to supr. fin. Dayton (Wash.) Sch. Dist., 1982-99. Mem. Town of Reardan Planning Commn., 1977-82, sec., 1978-82; treas. Citizens for Edn. Com., Dayton, 1983-91, Columbia County Courthouse Restoration Project, Dayton, 1988-99; fin. adv. com. Dayton Gen. Hosp., 1986-90, Dayton City Coun., 1986-87; vocat. bus. adv. com. Dayton HS, 1990-96. Recipient Mary Shields Wilson Medallion award; George F. Hixson fellow, 2005. Mem. AAUW, Wash. Assn. Ednl. Office Profls. (treas. 1984-86, pres.-elect 1986-87, pres. 1987-88, Ednl. Office Profl. of Yr. award 1990), Nat. Assn. Ednl. Office Profls. (Ednl. Office Profl. of Yr. award 1990), Assn. Assn. Sch. Bus. Ofcls. (chmn. com. 1978-81), S.C. Assn. Ednl. Office Profls. (pres. 1991-92), Blue Mountain Assn. Ednl. Office Profls., Assn. Sch. Bus. Ofcls. Internat. (com. 1984-86, scholar 1987), Order of Eagles, Kiwanis (sec. 1991-99, pres.-elect Tri Cities 2002-03, pres. 2003-04, Kiwaniain of Yr. 1993, 99, George F. Hixson award 2006). Democrat. Methodist. Avocations: reading, quilting, needle work, doll and bear making. Home: 3324 W 19th Ave Trlr 102 Kennewick WA 99338-2292 Personal E-mail: patmmerkel@aol.com.

MERKEL, PAUL BARRETT, chemist, consultant; b. Rochester, NY, May 14, 1945; s. Paul A. and Jeanette B. M. BS, St. John Fisher Coll., 1967; PhD, U. Notre Dame, 1970. Postdoctoral rsch. Univ. Calif., Riverside, 1970-71; rsch. chemist Eastman Kodak Co., Rochester, NY, 1971—2001; jr. scientist, dept. chemistry U. Rochester, 2002—. Patentee in field; contbr. articles to profl. jours. Mem. Am. Chem. Soc., Sigma Xi. Home: 7749 Dryer Rd Victor NY 14564-9191 Home Phone: 585-742-2933.

MERKEL-MORAN, CHRISTA ILSE, investor, linguist, educator; b. Leipzig, Saxony, Germany, Jan. 5, 1946; arrived in US, 1968; d. Erich Harry and Ilse Dora (Waehnert) Merkel; m. William Joseph Moran, May 5, 1967 (dec. Mar. 4, 1979); children: Leslie Paige, Linda Christa. BA, U. Tuebingen, 1968; postgrad., U. Alaska, 1968—69. German linguistics. Clk. Anchorage Westward Hotel, 1969—71; sales mgr. Windsor Park Hotel, Washington, 1971—75; linguist, instr. Def. Lang. Inst., Dept. Def., Washington, 1975—79; investor in real estate, sports cars Atlanta, 1979—. Real estate agt., Northside Realty Co., Atlanta, 1992—. Author: Die Millie Miglia, 1969; Der Nuerburgring, 1975; German Culture, 1977. Chairperson for a United Germany Com., Washington, Atlanta, Leipzig chpt.; fundraiser UNICEF. Named Sportswriter of Yr., ADAC of Germany, 1977. Democrat. Home: PO Box 34165 Pensacola FL 32507-4165 Office: Buckhead Brokers 5395 Roswell Rd NE Atlanta GA 30342-1976 Home Phone: 850-261-0700; Office Phone: 850-492-0025. Personal E-mail: christamoran@bellsouth.net.

MERKEN, MELVIN, chemistry professor; b. Peabody, Mass., Jan. 19, 1927; s. Harry and Annie (Ossoff) M.; m. Dec. 23, 1956; children: Stephen Robert, Naomi Cheryl, Aaron Jeffrey. BS, Tufts U., 1950, AM, 1951; EdD, Boston U., 1967. Tchr. sci. Old Lyme H.S., Conn., 1951—57, Norwalk H.S., Conn., 1957—58; prof. chemistry Worcester State Coll., Mass., 1958—. Author: Physical Science with Modern Applications, 1st edit., 1976, 2d edit., 1980, 3d edit., 1985, 4th edit., 1989, 5th edit., 1993; co-author: (lab. manual) Exptl. Coll. Phys. Sci., 1964, 67. With U.S. Army, 1944-46, PTO. Westinghouse fellow, 1952, NSF fellow, 1959-63. Fellow AAAS, Am. Inst. Chemists; mem. AAUP, Am. Chem. Soc., Am. Assn. Physics Tchrs., Phi Delta Kappa. Home: 1 St Paul Dr Worcester MA 01602-1519 Office: Worcester State Coll 486 Chandler St Worcester MA 01602-2832 Office Phone: 508-929-8621. Business E-Mail: mmerken@worcester.edu.

MERKER, STEVEN JOSEPH, lawyer; b. Cleve., Feb. 21, 1947; s. Steven Joseph and Laverne (Zamenik) Merker; m. Janet L. Whyatt; children: Steven, Rena, Ashley, Matthew. BS, Case Inst. Tech., 1968; MS, U. Fla., 1973; JD, George Washington U., 1976. Bar: Ohio 1976, US Dist. Ct. (no. dist.) Ohio 1976, US Dist. Ct. Colo. 1979, US Ct. Appeals (10th cir.) 1979, US Supreme Ct. 1989, US Patent & Trademark Office. Assoc. Jones, Day, Reavis & Pogue, Cleve., 1976-78, Davis, Graham & Stubbs, Denver, 1978-82, ptnr., 1983-96, chmn. labor and employment group, 1989-96; chmn. litig., labor and employment groups Merrick, Calvin & Merker, LLP, 1996-97; ptnr. Dorsey & Whitney LLP, Denver, 1997—, mng. ptnr. Denver office, 2000—. Mem. Tenth Cir. Adv. Com., 1997—2000. Bd. dirs. Very Spl. Arts, Colo., 1994—, Am. Liver Found., 2002—; legal counsel Coloradans for Lamm-Dick campaign, Denver, 1982, Nancy Dick for US Senate Com., Denver, 1984, Cantrell for Dist. Atty., Jefferson County, Colo., 1984. Capt. USAF, 1969—72. Mem.: ABA, Am. Intellectual Property Law Assn., Intellectual Property Owners Assn., Denver Bar Assn., Colo. Bar Assn. Office: Dorsey & Whitney LLP 370 17th St Ste 4700 Denver CO 80202-5644 Office Phone: 303-628-1514. Business E-Mail: merker.steve@dorsey.com.

MERKERSON, S. EPATHA, actress; b. Saginaw, Mich., Nov. 28, 1952; m. Toussaint L. Jones, Mar. 1994 (div. Feb. 14, 2006). BFA, Wayne State U. Broadway and Off-Broadway productions include The Piano Lesson, I'm Not Stupid (Obie award 1992), The Old Settler, Birdie Blue, 2005 (OBIE award Village Voice 2006), Come Back, Little Sheba, 2008; appeared in films including Terminator II, Jacob's Ladder, Navy Seals, Loose Cannons, Random Hearts, 1999, The Rising Place, 2001, Radio, 2003, Jersey Girl, 2004, Black Snake Moan, 2006; television guest appearances include The Cosby Show, Equal Justice, Elysian Fields, Moe's World; television series roles include Pee Wee's Playhouse, Mann & Machine, Here & Now, Law & Order (Outstanding Supporting Actress in a Drama Series, NAACP Image award, 2006), A Place for Annie, 1994, A Mother's Prayer, 1995, Breaking Through, 1996, An Unexpected Life, 1998, Exiled, 1998, Lackawanna Blues, 2005 (Emmy award for outstanding lead actress in a miniseries or a movie, 2005, best performance by an actress in a mini-series or motion picture made for television, Hollywood Fgn. Press Assn. (Golden Globe award), 2006, outstanding performance by an female actor in a TV movie or miniseries, Screen Actors Guild award, 2006, Outstanding Actress in a TV Movie, Mini-Series, or Dramatic Spl., NAACP Image awards, 2006). Nominated for Tony award, 1990, Drama Desk award, 1990, Helen Hayes award, 1990, L.A. Theater Critics award, 1990. Office: Law & Order c/o Universal Television 100 Universal City Plz Universal City CA 91608-1002

MERKIN, ALBERT CHARLES, pediatrician, allergist; b. Chgo., Sept. 4, 1924; s. Harry A. and Goldie (Lamasky) M.; m. Eunice Aprill, Aug. 22, 1948; children: Audrey, Ellen, Joseph. Student, U. Ill., 1942-44; MD, U. Ill., Chgo., 1949. Diplomate Am. Bd. Allergy and Immunology, Am. Bd. Pediat. Intern, resident Cook County Hosp., Chgo.; resident Children's Meml. Hosp., Chgo.; with Valley Pediatric and Allergy Clinic, Las Vegas, Nev. Capt. USAF, 1950-53. Fellow Am. Acad. Pediatrics (state chmn. Nev. 1961-64, sect. allergy and immunology), Am. Coll. Allergy; mem. Am. Acad. Allergy, Allergy Subsplty. Group of Acad. Pediatrics (cert. pediatric allergist). Avocations: reading, travel. Office Phone: 702-341-8695.

MERKIN, WILLIAM LESLIE, retired lawyer; b. NYC, Apr. 30, 1929; s. Jules Leo Merkin and Rae (Levine) Lesser; children: Monica Jo, Lance Jeffrey, Tiffany Dawn. BA, U. Tex., Austin, 1950; JD, St. Mary's U., San Antonio, 1953. Bar: Tex. 1953, U.S. Ct. Mil. Appeals 1954, U.S. Dist. Ct. (we. dist.) Tex. 1957, U.S. Ct. Appeals (5th cir.) 1969, U.S. Supreme Ct. 1970. Pvt. practice, El Paso, Tex., 1956-71; sr. ptnr. Merkin & Gibson, El Paso, Tex., 1972-78, Merkin, Hines & Pasqualone, El Paso, Tex., 1978-90; ret. Lectr. U. Tex.-El Paso, 1978—; cons. in field. Served to capt. JAGC US Army, 1953—56. Mem. Tex. State Bar Assn., Soc. Profls. in Dispute Resolution, Am. Trial Lawyers Assn., Tex. Trial Lawyers Assn., Common Cause, Internat. Wine and Food Soc. (pres. 1979-80), Am. Arbitration Assn. (part-time arbitrator), Nat. Assn. Securities Dealers (part-time arbitrator), Del Norte Club (El Paso), B'nai B'rith (pres. 1961-62), Phi Delta Phi. Home and Office: 1442 Seacoast Dr Imperial Beach CA 91932-3183 Office Phone: 619-423-1718.

MERKLE, ALAN RAY, lawyer; b. Boise, Idaho, Oct. 14, 1947; s. John William and Arlene June (Hawkins) M.; m. Diane M. Martin, June 15, 1973 (div. 1978); m. Linda Jo Todd, Mar. 15, 1980; children: Amanda, Lindsay. AS, Boise State U., 1967; BSME, U. Idaho, 1970, MBA, 1971; JD, Lewis & Clark Coll., 1982. Bar: Oreg. 1983, Wash. 1983, U.S. Dist. Ct. (Oreg.) 1983, U.S. Dist. Ct. (we. dist.) Wash. 1984; registered profl. engr. Wash., Oreg., Idaho. Field engr. GE, NY, Oreg., Wash., other location, 1971-74, svc. specialist Seattle, 1974-77, svc. mgr. steam turbines Portland, Oreg., 1977-80, mgr. hydro ops., 1980-82; assoc. Stoel, Rives LLP, Seattle, 1982-86, ptnr., 1987—, chair firm, 2009—. Author: Construction Law, Licensing and Registration, 1988, Damages, Liability of Architects and Engineers, 1989, 93, Public Contracting in Washington, 1992, 93, 94, Washington Lien Law, 1992, Defending Claims Against the Owner, 1994, 96, 99, 2000, Construction Law, 1996, 97, Advanced Construction Law in Washington, 1997-2002, Sick Building Syndrome, 2001. Apptd. Mercer Is. City Coun., 1996, elected 4 yr. term, 1997, dep. mayor, 1999, mayor, 2000-05. Recipient Cornelius Honor award, 1982; named Super Lawyer, Washington Law and Politics Mag., 2005—09; named one of Seattles Best 100 Lawyer, Seattle Mag., 2005. Mem. AIA (bd. dirs., hon. 2006), ABA, Oreg. State Bar Assn., Wash. State Bar Assn., Fed. Energy Bar Assn. (past chair pub. procurement, pvt. law sect., associated gen. contractors, legal affairs com.), French Am. C. of C. (pres., 2009-). Democrat. Avocations: skiing, sailing, fishing. Office: Stoel Rives LLP 3600 One Union Sq 600 University St Seattle WA 98101-1176 Office Phone: 206-386-7636. E-mail: armerkle@stoel.com.

MERKLE, SARAH LYNN, research scientist; b. Chambersburg, Pa., Aug. 5, 1971; d. Dale Gordon and Mary Lynn Merkle; m. Brian Talmadge Murphey, Aug. 24, 2002; children: Samuel Alexander Murphey, Zachary Dale Murphey. BA, Macalester Coll., St. Paul, MN, 1993; MPH, U. NC, Chapel Hill, 2000. Esl. tchr. Montgomery County Pub. Sch., Silver Spring, Md., 1993—95; sch./cmty. coord. San Francisco Sch. Vols., 1995—98; health scientist Ctrs. Disease Control and Prevention, Atlanta, 2000—. Contbr. to numerous profl. jours. (CDC/DASH Rsch. Application Br. Employee of Yr., 2006). Recipient Honor award, CDC, 2005. Office: Ctrs Disease Control and Prevention 4770 Buford Hwy NE Atlanta GA 30341

MERKLEY, JEFFERY A., United States Senator from Oregon; b. Eugene, Oreg., Oct. 24, 1956; m. Mary Sorteberg; 2 children. BA, Stanford U., 1979; MA, Princeton U., 1982. Presdl. intern, 1982—85; analyst Congrl. Budget Office, 1985—89; mng. ptnr. Computer Medics, 1989—91; exec. dir. Portland Habitat for Humanity, 1991—94; dir. Housing Devel., Human Solutions, 1995—96; exec. dir. World Affairs Coun. Oreg., 1996—2003; mem. Oreg. Ho. of Reps., 1998—2009, spkr., 2007—09; US Senator from Oreg., 2009—. Democrat. Protestant. Office: PO Box 33167 Portland OR 97292-3167 also: B40B Dirksen Senate Office Bldg Washington DC 20510 Office Phone: 202-224-3753.*

MERLE, PATRICK F., communications educator; b. Auxerre, France, Sept. 13, 1975; s. Max Merle and Edith Marquet. Postgrad. Communication, Inst. Francais De Presse, France, 1998. Reporter to editor Eurosport Internat., Paris, 2000—02; asst. prof. communication Ancilla Domini Coll., Donaldson, Ind., 2003—08. Journalist IAAF, Monaco, 2002—08. Mem.: Soc. Profl. Journalists. Home: 115 1/2 N Mich St Plymouth IN 46563

MERLINO, ANTHONY FRANK, orthopedist; b. Providence, Jan. 21, 1930; s. Anthony Frank and C. Mildred (Campagna) Merlino; m. Dolores Mary Aucello, Nov. 22, 1956; children: Christa Marianne, Paula Nicole. BS, Providence Coll., 1951; MS, U. Conn., 1952; MD, Jefferson Med. Coll., 1956. Diplomate Am. Bd. Ortho. Surgery. Intern St. Joseph Hosp., Providence, 1956—57; resident orthop. surgery VA Hosp., Phila., 1959—63; orthop. surgeon Phila., 1963—68, Providence, 1968—. Attending orthop. surgeon, pres. med. staff St. Joseph Hosp., Providence, 1974—75, trustee, 1973—76, med. staff, trustee joint conf. com., 1982; attending orthop. surgeon Our Lady of Fatima Hosp., North Providence, RI; vis. orthop. surgeon R.I. State Hosp., Howard, 1968—75; asst. orthop. surgeon Hahnemann Med. Coll., Phila., 1965—69; pediat. orthop. surg. cons. Crippled Children's Program of R.I., 1968—86; cons. orthop. surgeon Roger Williams Gen. Hosp., Providence, 1969—89; v.p. R.I. Orthop. Group, Inc., Providence, 1969—83, pres., 1983—; team physician hockey and basketball teams Providence Coll., 1968—87; mem. R.I. Gov.'s Med. Malpractice Commn., 1975—77, R.I. Bd. Examiners in Chiropractic, 1977—80; mem. study commn. R.I. Med. Rev. Bd., 1977—85; mem. corp. Blue Cross/Blue Shield R.I., 1976—87; physician, adv. R.I. Assn. Med. Assts., 1979—84; mem. R.I. Worker's Compensation Adv. Panel, 1978—88; mem. adv. bd. Cath. Social Svcs., 1981—84; police surgeon Am. Law Enforcement Officers' Assn., 1980; cons. orthop. surgery Am. Assn. Medicolegal Cons., 1980—90. Contbr. articles to profl. jours. Pres. Hindle Bldg. Assocs., 1983—; mem. med. splty. adv. bd. Med. Malpractice Prevention, 1985—90. Capt. med. corp. USAF, 1957—59. Recipient Dr. William McDonnell award, Providence Coll. Alumni Assn., 1981. Fellow: ACS (pres. R.I. chpt. 1982—84), Latin Am. Soc. Orthop. and Traumatology, Internat. Coll. Surgeons, Am. Acad. Orthop. Surgeons; mem.: AMA, Providence Med. Soc., Jefferson Orthop. Soc., R.I. Med. Soc. (commr. profl. rels. 1976, ho. of dels. 1976—82, commr. internal affairs 1982), R.I. Orthop. Soc. (sec.-treas. 1978—80, v.p. 1980—82, pres. 1982—84), Ea. Orthop. Soc., New Eng. Orthop. Assn., Am. Soc. Law and Medicine, Internat. Soc. Rsch. in Orthop. and Trauma, Internat. Soc. Orthop. and Traumatology, Am. Med. Photography Assn., Am. Orthop. Soc. for Sports Medicine, Am. Coll. Sports Medicine, Am. Acad. Compensation Medicine, Am. Profl. Practice Assn., Pan-Pacific Surg. Assn., Am. Fracture Assn., Am. Coll. Legal Medicine, Orthop. Rsch. and Edn. Found. (life), Thomistic Inst. Drs. Guild, R.I. Hist. Soc., 100 of R.I. Club, Mal Brown Club, Boston Orthop. Club. Roman Catholic. Home: 2 Countryside Dr North Providence RI 02904-3419 Office: 655 Broad St Providence RI 02907-1444

MERLINO, GLENN T., medical researcher; BA, Adelphi U., LI, 1975; PhD, U. Mich., Ann Arbor, 1980. Lab. technician NY State Inst. Basic Rsch. in Mental Retardation, 1974—75; grad. fellow Cellular and Molecular Biology Dept. U. Mich., 1975—80; postdoctoral fellow Nat. Cancer Inst., NIH, 1980—82, staff fellow Lab. Molecular Biology, 1982—92, sr. investigator, chief Lab. Cell Regulation and Carcinogenesis, Ctr. Cancer Rsch., head Molecular Genetics Group, now chief Lab. Cancer Biology and Genetics, head Cancer Modeling Section. Past adj. asst. prof. Dept. Biochemistry George Washington U.; past adj. assoc. prof. Dept. Pathology Georgetown U. Mem.: AAAS, Am. Soc. Investigative Pathology, Am. Assn. Cancer Rsch. Office: Nat Cancer Inst Ctr Cancer Rsch 37 Convent Dr Bldg 37 Rm 5002 Bethesda MD 20892-4264 Office Phone: 301-496-4270. Office Fax: 301-480-7618. E-mail: gmerlino@helix.nih.gov.*

MERLINO, JOSEPH P., psychiatrist, director; b. Jersey City, Feb. 12, 1952; s. John A. Merlino and Eleanor Crescetelli; m. Ronald W. Goralewicz, Mar. 3, 2008. MD, NY Med. Coll., NYC, 1978; MPA, Baruch Coll., NYC, 1992. Diplomate in psychiatry Am. Bd. Psychiatry & Neurology, 1983, cert. in psychoanalysis NY Med. Coll., 1986, in ethics & med. humanities Coll. Physicians & Surgeons, Columbia U., 1997. Assoc. dir. psychiatry Lenox Hill Hosp., NYC, 1985—99; dir. ambulatory & cmty. psychiatry Bellevue Hosp. Ctr., NYC, 2001—03; dir. psychiatry Queens Hosp. Ctr., Jamaica, NY, 2003—. Cons. Forensic Panel, NYC, 2002—08. Editor: (book) American Psychiatry & Homosexuality, Freud at 150. Chairperson bd. Opportunity Charter Sch., NYC, 2006—08. Recipient Wholeness Life award, Healthcare Chaplaincy, 1998, Behavioral Health award, Queens Hosp. Ctr., 2008. Fellow: Am. Psychiat. Assn., Am. Acad. Psychoanalysis & Dynamaic Psychiatry (pres. 2004—06); mem.: Group Advancement Psychiatry, Am. Coll. Psychiatrists. Office: Queens Hosp Ctr 82-68 164th St Jamaica NY 11432 Office Fax: 718-883-6135. Business E-Mail: merlinjo@nychhc.org.

MERLO, LARRY J., retail executive; Sr. v.p. stores CVS Pharmacy, Inc., Woonsocket, RI, 1994—98, exec. v.p. stores, 1998—2000, CVS Corp., Woonsocket, 2000—07; exec. v.p., pres. CVS Pharmacy Retail CVS Caremark Corp., Woonsocket, RI, 2007—. Office: CVS Caremark Corp Corp Hdqrs 1 CVS Dr Woonsocket RI 02895*

MERMELSTEIN, JULES JOSHUA, lawyer, educator, commissioner; b. Phila., Apr. 25, 1955; s. Harry and Ellen Jane (Greenberg) M.; m. Ruth Susan Applebaum, Aug. 18, 1974; children: Hannah Leona, Benjamin Isaac. BA, Temple U., Phila., 1977; JD, Am. U., Washington, DC, 1979; MEd, Beaver Coll., Glenside, Pa., 1994. Bar: Pa. 1980, US Dist. Ct. (ea. dist.) Pa. 1980, US Ct. Appeals (3d cir.) 1982, US Supreme Ct. 1983. Ptnr. Mermelstein & Light, Norristown and Hatboro, Pa., 1980-83; v.p., gen. counsel Am. Ins. Cons., Feasterville, Pa., 1983; staff atty. Hyatt Legal Svcs., Phila., 1983-84, mng. atty., 1984-85; pvt. practice Phila./Montgomery County, 1985-93; tchr., social studies coord. The Bridge, 1997-99; atty. Levin & Assocs., Wyncote, Pa., 1998—2001, mng. atty., 2002—03; title agt. Forward Abstract, LLC, Glenside, Pa., 2002—05; social studies tchr. Sch. Dist. Phila., 2005—07, Upper Dublin Sch. Dist., 2007—. Prof. law St. Matthew Sch. Law, Phila., 1985—87; adj. prof. criminal justice Glassboro State U., NJ, 1988; faculty polit. sci. dept. Temple U., 1989; ednl. cons. Interim Ho., 1998—2000. Editor: The Montco Democrat, 1990-92. Vol. atty. ACLU, Phila., 1980-93; chmn. Tikkun Olam (Repair the World) Com., 1989-92, 98-2000; area rep. Montgomery County Dem. Exec. Com., 1982-85, 88-94; treas., 1994-98, candidate coord., 1982, nominee for dist. atty., 1983, committeeman, 1973-77, 82-85, 88-92, campaign mgr. Talbot for state legis., 1988; Upper Dublin chmn. Dukakis-Bentsen, 1988, chair Upper Dublin Dem. Com., 1990-91, commr. Upper Dublin Twp., 1992—, v.p., 2006-08, pres., 2008-; Dem. candidate Pa. State Legis., 2000; bd. dirs. Reconstructionist Congregation Or Hadash, Ft. Washington, Pa., 1988-92, 96-2000, 2001-2003, 2006-08, confirmation tchr., 1994-. Jewish. Home: 18 Northview Dr Glenside PA 19038-1318 Personal E-mail: Jules.Mermelstein@gmail.com.

MERMOUD, J. FRANK, United States Special Representative, Commercial and Business Affairs; BS, Georgetown U. Sch. Fgn. Svc., Washington. Dir. fed. bus. procurement and export devel. US Fgn. Comml. Svc.; assoc. dir., EXPORT NOW presdl. initiative US Dept. Commerce; Congl. liaison officer US Info. Agency; dir. legis. affairs US Dept. State, spl. rep. comml. and bus. affairs, 2002—; exec. v.p. internat. and corp. affairs, mem. bd. dirs. Aegis Comm.; co-founder, exec. v.p., pres. internat. SageMetrics Corp., 1999—2002. Conf. coord. Pvt. Sector Reconstrn. for Iraq, Madrid, 2003; lead positions for various internat. presdl. initiatives. Mem. tech. nat. steering com. Bush-Cheney Presdl. Campaign, 2000, mem. nat. fin. com., 2000. Office: US Dept State 2201 C St NW Washington DC 20520*

MEROLLA, MICHELE EDWARD, chiropractor, broadcaster; b. Providence, Feb. 20, 1940; s. Joseph and Viola (Horne) M.; m. Ednamarie G.; children: Michele Edward II, Matthew Joseph, Samantha Joan, Alexandra Marie. BS, Bryant Coll., 1961; DC, Chiropractic Inst. N.Y., 1965; LHD, Logan Chiropractic Coll., St. Louis, 1973. Owner chiropractic clinics chiropractic clinics, New Bedford, Taunton, Somerset, Seekonk, Attleboro, others, Mass., 1965—. Daily Network radio talk show hoset Holistic Hotline; owner radio sta. WJYT-AM, Attleboro, Mass. Editor: New Eng. Jour. Chiropractic. Mem. New Bedford City Coun., 1969-73, Airport Commn., 1972-75, Sch. Com., 1978-86, Recreation Commn., 1983-89, Fairhaven (Mass.) Sch. Com., 2000—; pres. New Bedford Aid Ctr., 1977; bd. dir. Your Theatre Inc. Recipient Svc. award New Eng. Chiropractic Coun., 1973. Mem. Am. Chiropractic Assn., Nat. Assn. Broadcasters, Mass. Assn. Broadcasters, Southeastern Mass. Chiropractic Soc. (bd. dir.), Mass. Chiropractic Soc., NY Acad. Sci., Fla. Chiropractic Soc., New Bedford Preservation Soc. (bd. dir.). Office: 73 Alden Rd Fairhaven MA 02719 Home: PO Box 806 Sandwich MA 02563 Office Phone: 508-888-7122. Personal E-mail: DRMEROLLA@AOL.COM.

MERON, DANIEL, lawyer; s. Theodor and Roxandra Meron, Monique Meron (Stepmother); m. Jennifer Rachel Hersch, June 28, 1992; 4 children. AB in Govt., magna cum laude, Harvard Coll., 1986; JD magna cum laude, Harvard Law Sch., 1992; PhD in Social Thought, U. Chgo. Bar: DC 1996. Law clk. Hon. Anthony M. Kennedy, US Supreme Ct., Hon. Laurence H. Silberman, US Ct. Appeals (DC cir.); appellate/regulatory litigation ptnr. Sidley Austin LLP, Washington; prin. dep. asst. atty. gen. civil divsn. US Dept. Justuce, 2003—06; gen. counsel US Dept. Health & Human Svcs., 2006—08; ptnr., global co-chair healthcare/life scis. practice grp. Latham & Watkins LLP, 2008—. Sr. policy adv. healthcare transparency initiative US Dept. Health & Human Svcs. Office: Latham & Watkins LLP 555 Eleventh St NW Ste 1000 Washington DC 20004 Office Phone: 202-637-2218. Office Fax: 202-637-2201. Business E-Mail: daniel.meron@lw.com.*

MERON, THEODOR, judge, educator, researcher; b. Kalisz, Poland, Apr. 28, 1930; came to U.S., 1978, naturalized, 1984; s. Yhiel and Bluma (Lipschitz) Znamirowski; m. Monique Jonquet, Mar. 13, 1981; children: Daniel, Amos. M.J., Hebrew U., 1954; LL.M., Harvard U., 1955, S.JD, 1957; diploma in Pub. Internat. Law, Cambridge U., Eng., 1957. Bar: Israel 1971, N.Y. 1984. Legal adv. Fgn. Ministry of Israel, 1967-71, Israeli amb. to Can. Ottawa, 1971-75; permanent rep. UN, Geneva, 1977; prof. law NYU Law Sch., NYC, 1977—94, Charles L. Denison prof., 1994—2005, Charles L. Denison prof. emeritus, jud. fellow, 2006—. Carnegie lectr. Hague Acad. Internat. Law, 1980; Sir Hersch Lauterpacht Meml. lectr.; vis. fellow All Souls Coll., Oxford U., England, Max-Planck Inst., Heidelberg, Germany; vis. prof. Grad. Inst. Internat. Studies, Geneva, prof. law, 1991—95; pub. mem. US Del. Conf. on Human Dimension Conf. on Security and Coop. in Europe, Copenhagen, 1998; mem. U.S. del. Rome Diplomatic Conf. on the Establishment of an Internat. Criminal Ct.; vis. prof. law Harvard U., Berkeley Law Sch.; counselor on internat. law US Dept. State, 2000—01; judge appeals chamber Internat. Criminal Tribunal for former Yugoslavia, 2001—, Internat. Criminal Tribunal for Rwanda, 2001—, pres., 2003—05. Author: Investment Insurance in International Law, 1976, The United Nations Secretariat, 1977, Human Rights Law-Making in the United Nations, 1986, Human Rights in Internal Strife: Their International Protection, 1987, Human Rights and Humanitarian Norms as Customary Law, 1989, Henry's Wars and Shakespeare's Laws, 1993, Bloody Constraint: War and Chivalry in Shakespeare, 1998, International Law in the Age of Human Rights, 2004, The Humanization of International Law, 2006; editor: Human Rights in International Law, 1984; editor in chief: Am. Jour. Internat. Law, 1983-88; contbr. articles to profl. jours. Rockefeller Found. fellow, 1975-76; Humanitarian Trust student Cambridge U., 1956-57;recipient Rule of Law award, Internat. Bar Assn., 2005, Homer Haskins prize Am. Coun. Learned Socs., 2008. Fellow: Am. Acad. Arts and Socs.; mem. AAAS, Am. Soc. Internat. Law (Cert. Merit 1987, Hudson medal 2006), French Legion of Honor (officer 2007); Inst. Internat. Law, Internat. Law Assn., Coun. on Fgn. Rels., Inst. Internat. Humanitarian Law, French Inst. Internat. Law. Office: NYU Law Sch 40 Washington Sq S New York NY 10012-1099 also: Churchillplein 2501 EW The Hague Netherlands Business E-Mail: meront@un.org.

MEROPOL, NEAL J., oncologist, researcher; AB, Princeton U., 1981; MD, Vanderbilt U., 1985. Cert. Am. Bd. Internal Medicine, Internal Medicine, Med. Oncology. Intern, resident in internal medicine Case Western Res. U., Cleve., 1985—88; fellow in med. oncology and hematology U. Pa., Phila., 1988—92; asst. prof. medicine Roswell Park Cancer Inst., 1992—98; dir. Gastrointestinal Cancer Program Fox Chase Cancer Ctr., Phila., 1998—, dir., Gastrointestinal Tumor Risk Assessment Program. Prof. medicine Temple U. Sch. Medicine, 2006—. Contbr. articles to profl. publications. Named one of Top Doctors, Phila. mag., 2008. Mem.: Am. Assn. for Cancer Rsch., Am. Soc. Clin. Oncology. Office: Fox Chase Cancer Ctr 333 Cottman Ave Philadelphia PA 19111-2497*

MEROW, JAMES F., federal judge; AB, George Washington U., 1953, JD, 1956. Bar: Va., 1956, DC, 1958. Trial atty., br. dir., civil divsn. US Dept. Justice, Washington, 1959-78; trial judge US Ct. Claims, Washington, 1978-82; judge US Ct. Fed. Claims, Washington, 1982—. With JAGC, US Army, 1956-59. Mem. ABA, Fed. Bar Assn., Va. State Bar, DC Bar. Office: US Ct Fed Claims 717 Madison Pl NW Washington DC 20005*

MEROW, JOHN, lawyer; b. Little Valley, NY, Dec. 20, 1929; s. Luin George and Mildred Elizabeth Merow; m. Mary Alyce Smith, June 19, 1957; 1 child, Alison. Student, UCLA, 1947—48; BS in Engring., U. Mich., 1952; JD, Harvard U., 1958. Bar: N.Y. 1958, U.S. Supreme Ct. 1971. Assoc. Sullivan & Cromwell, NYC, 1958-64, ptnr., 1965-96, vice chmn., 1986-87, chmn., sr. ptnr., 1987-94, sr. counsel, 1997—; sr. mng. dir. Brock Capital Group, LLC, 2007—. Bd. dirs. Seligman Group Investment Cos., 1969-2005, Kaiser Aluminum and Chem. Corp., 1971-1987, Commonwealth Industries, 1995-2005, Aleris Internat. Inc., 2005-06; trustee, vice chmn. N.Y. Presbyn. Healthcare Sys., Inc.; trustee N.Y. Presbyn. Hosp.; trustee, sec. Friends of the Archbishop of Canterbury's Anglican Communion Fund. Chmn. bd. dirs. Am.-Australian Assn., 1986—99; bd. dirs. Mcpl. Art Soc. N.Y.; mem. exec. com., sec. US Coun. Internat. Bus.; bd. dirs., sec. Met. Opera Club, 1986—94; dir., treas. Foreign Policy Assn., 1990—2003; trustee Anglican Investment Agy. Trust, Archbishop of Canterbury's Anglican Communion Fund. Lt. USN, 1952—55. Named hon. officer Order of Australia. Mem. Am. Law Inst. (advisor corp. governance project 1978-92), Coun. on Fgn. Rels., Soc. Mayflower Desc., Links Club, Pilgrims, Piping Rock Club, Down Town Assn., Union Club, Griffis Faculty Club, River Club. Home: 435 E 52d St New York NY 10022 also: 51 Fruitledge Rd Glen Head NY 11545-3316 Office: Sullivan & Cromwell LLP 125 Broad St New York NY 10004-2498 Office Phone: 212-558-3616. E-mail: merowj@sullcrom.com.

MERRELL, JAMES LEE, writer, minister; b. Indpls., Oct. 24, 1930; s. Mark W. and Pauline F. (Tucker) M.; m. Barbara Jean Burch, Dec. 23, 1951; children: Deborah Lea Merrell Griffin, Cynthia Lynn Archer, Stuart Allen. AB, Ind. U., 1952; MDiv, Christian Theol. Sem., 1956; LittD, Culver-Stockton Coll., 1972. Ordained to ministry Christian Ch., 1955; asso. editor World Call, Indpls., 1956-66, editor, 1971-73; pastor Crestview Christian Ch., Indpls., 1966-71; editor The Disciple, St. Louis, 1974-89; sr. v.p. Christian Bd. Publ., 1976-89; sr. minister Affton Christian Ch., St. Louis, 1989-94; interim chaplain Culver-Stockton Coll., Canton, Mo., 1995; interim sr. pastor Friedens United Ch. of Christ, Warrenton, Mo., 1995-98, St. Johns United Ch. of Christ, Mehlville, Mo., 1998—2002, Hamilton Christian Ch., Creve Coeur, 2002—03, Redeemer Evang. Ch., St. Louis, 2003—05, Trinity United Ch. Christ, 2005—. Bd. dirs. Horizons mag., 1995-98. Author: They Live Their Faith, 1965, The Power of One, 1976, Discover the Word in Print, 1979, Finding Faith in the Headlines, 1985, We Claim Our Heritage, 1992, Seeing Life: Finding God, 2006. Chmn. bd. Kennedy Meml. Christian Home, Martinsville, Ind., 1971-73; trustee Christian Theol. Sem., 1978-81. Recipient Faith and Freedom award Religious Heritage of Am., 1983; lifetime achievement award Mo. State Sen., 2000. Mem. Associated Ch. Press (award 1973, 79, 80, 81, 82, dir. 1974-75, 78-81, 1st v.p. 1983-85), Christian Theol. Sem. Alumni Assn. (pres. 1966-68), Religious Pub. Rels. Coun. (awards 1979, 80, 84, 87, 90, pres. St. Louis chpt. 1985-86), Sigma Delta Chi (award 1952), Theta Phi. Home: 112 E Bodley # 204 Saint Louis MO 63122 Personal E-mail: JLeeMer@aol.com. *As a religious communicator and as a pastor, I have always believed in applying the same standards in the sacred realm as in the secular. I have tried to pursue the truth, to keep my constituency informed, to celebrate the noble in life, to fight against those who would lie, distort and hide God's truth in the name of some supposed good.*

MERRELL, JESSE HOWARD, writer; b. Shelby, Ala., Dec. 9, 1938; s. James Walton and Emma Thelma (Davis) M.; m. Betsy Lee Davis, Jan. 11, 1964 (div. 1979); children: Sandra, Mark, Brad, Carolyn, Gwen. Grad., Shelby High Sch., Columbiana, Ala., 1957. Pitcher Cin. Redlegs, 1958-62; reporter, news dir. WHAP Radio, Hopewell, Va., 1963; writer/editor Hopewell News, 1963-65; state editor Daily Progress, Charlottesville, Va., 1965-68; assoc. editor Transport Topics, Washington, 1968-75; spl. asst. to pres. Am. Trucking Assn., Washington, 1975-76; editor Transport Topics, Washington, 1976-77; pres. Merrell Ent., Washington, 1977—. Pub. rels. com. Am. Movers Conf., Washington, 1969-72; instr. Dale Carnegie courses, Washington, 1974-81, 1st pres., 1980-81; cons. Mid. Atlantic Conf., Riverdale, Md., 1981-82, Contract Carrier Conf., 1977-82; speechwriter ICC, Washington, 1982. Author: (novel) A Christmas Gift, 1979; syndicated columnist Religion and the Times, Washington Welter, (genealogy) The Merrells of Alabama, 1995, My Name is America! I Was Born at Jamestown!, 2002. Mem. Nat. Trust for Hist. Preservation, Assn. Preservation Va. Antiquities. With U.S. Army, 1960-62. Recipient George Washington Honor award Freedoms Found., 2002, Liberty award Congress of Freedom, Jackson, Miss., 1970, 71, Honor Cert., Freedoms Found., 1972, 1st place editorial writing Va. Press Assn., 1965, 1st place news writing, 1966. Mem. Nat. Press Club, Assn. Preservation Va. Antiquities, Gen. Washington's Coun. of the 1607 Soc. (charter mem.), Regent's Circle of Mt. Vernon, Jamestown 2007 Spkrs. Bur., Jamestown-Yorktown Found., Colonial Williamsburg Raleigh Tavern Soc. Avocation: photography. Office: Merrell Ent 2610 Garfield St NW Washington DC 20008-4104 Office Phone: 202-288-3334. Personal E-mail: jessemerrell@comcast.net.

MERRELL, KEITH P., elementary school educator; s. Sandra Gardner and Purless Merrell; m. Bernadette Merrell, Mar. 28, 1998; children: Trenetta Merrell-Scott, Jasimine Brightman, Keith Jr., James Brightman III, Khristian. BS, Fla. State U., Tallahassee, 1978; MA, Webster U., Merritt Island, Fla., 1996. Cert. in bus. edn. Fla. Dept. Edn., 1998, in computer sci. edn. Fla. Dept. Edn., 1998. Maj. US Army, Fort Bragg, NC, 1978—96. Mem. NAACP, Cocoa, Fla., Afghanistan, 1996—2008, Youthful Souls, Atlanta, 2004—08, Youth Build, Orlando, Fla., 2006—08; pres. Nat. Tech. Assn., Titusville, Fla., 1996—2008. Decorated Meritorious Svc. medal US Army; named Tchr. of Yr., Southwest Mid. Sch., 2002; grant, Best Buy, 2006. Mem.: Alpha Phi Alpha (v.p. 2006—08). Office: Southwest Mid Sch 451 Eldron Blvd Palm Bay FL 32909 Personal E-mail: golden0622@yahoo.com. Business E-Mail: merrellk@brevard.k12.fl.us.

MERRELL, RONALD CLIFTON, surgeon, educator; b. Birmingham, Ala., June 18, 1946; s. Greene Lawrence and Florence (Jones) M.; m. Marsha Karen Cox, Dec. 24, 1966; children: Alexandria, Alison, R. Clifton. BS in Chemistry, U. Ala., 1967, MD, 1970. Diplomate Am. Bd. Surgery. Resident and fellow in surgery Wash. U., St. Louis, 1970-77; asst. prof. surgery Stanford U., Calif., 1979-84; assoc. prof. surgery U. Tex. Med. Sch., Houston, 1984-88, prof. surgery, 1988—93, M.D. Anderson Cancer Ctr., Houston, 1988—93; assoc. dean clin. affairs U. Tex. Med. Sch., Houston, 1988-92, vice dean, 1992-93; Lampman prof. surgery, chmn. dept. surgery Yale U., 1993—99; Stuart McGuire prof. surgery, chmn. dept. surgery Va. Commonwealth U., Richmond, 1999—2003, prof. surgery, 2003—; dir. Med. Informatics Tech. Applications Consortium, 1997—2008. Editor-in-chief Telemedicine and e-Health. Contbr. chapters to books, articles to profl. jours. Maj. US Army, 1977—79. Recipient Basil O'Connor award March of Dimes, 1979, Rsch. Career Devel. award NIH, 1979-84, Henry J. Kaiser award Stanford U., 1982, 83, John P. McGovern Outstanding Tchr. award U. Tex. Med. Sch., 1988, Dean's Teaching Excellence award, 1983-89, Pub. Svc. medal NASA, 1998, 2005, 06, Disting. medal as Friend of Democritus, U. Thrace, Greece, 1998; grantee NASA, Dept. Def., Internat. Coop. medal, Russian Space Agy., 2005. Fellow: ACS, Soc. Univ. Surgeons; mem.: Am. Surg. Assn., Am. Assn. Endocrine Surgery, Alpha Omega Alpha. Democrat. Episcopalian. Achievements include research in telemedicine and in the transplantation of islets of Langerhans. Office: Va Commonwealth U PO Box 980480 1200 E Marshall St Richmond VA 23298-0519 Office Phone: 804-827-1031. Office Fax: 804-827-1029. Business E-Mail: rmerrell@mcvh-vcu.edu.

MERRELL, WOODSON C., integrative medicine specialist; Asst. clinical prof. medicine Columbia U. Coll. Physicians & Surgeons; attending physician St. Luke's-Roosevelt Hosp., Beth Israel Med. Ctr.; past chmn. NY State Bd. Acupuncture; bd. mem. NY State Office Profl. Med. Conduct, 1995—; chmn. dept. intregative medicine Beth Isreal Info. Ctr. Author: The Source, 2008. Office: 44E 67st New York NY 10065 Office Phone: 212-535-1012.

MERRIAM, DIANE LOUISE, ESL educator; b. Balt., Aug. 5, 1945; d. Robert Frederick and Margaret Amelia Merriam. BA, Towson U., Md., 1966; MA, Columbia U., NYC, 1970, U. Md., 1998. Advanced profl. cert. Md. State Bd. Edn. Elem. classroom tchr. Balt. County Pub. Schs., Towson, 1966—80; ESL tutor Fgn. Immigrants Referral Network, Columbia, Md., 1993—94; home and hosp. tchr. Howard County Pub. Schs., Ellicott City, Md., 1994—95; adult edn. instr. ESL Montgomery County Alternative Edn. Progs., Md.; grad. asst. U. Md., Balt., 1996—98; adj. ESL tchr. Balt. City CC, 2001—02; sr. tchr. George Meany Nat. Labor Coll., Silver Spring, Md., 2002—03; assoc. prof. ESL Prince George's CC, Largo, Md., 2004—06; ESL tchr. Prince George's County Pub. Schs., Beltsville, 2006—; dept. chair Martin Luther King Jr. Mid. Sch., 2008—. Rschr. KIA, Sake Excursions; specialist in humanities/internat. svc. Kanagawa Internat. Assn., Yokohama, 1998—2000; lectr. in field. Women's com. mem. Kanagawa-Md. Sister States Com., Annapolis, 2005—06. Work-Study grantee, Kanagawa Internat. Assn., 1998—2000. Mem.: NEA, TESOL, Md. State Tchrs. Assn., Wash. Area TESOL, Md. TESOL, Wash. Internat. Piano Arts Coun., Phi Kappa Phi. Democrat. Methodist. Avocations: travel, classical piano, language study. Home: 8983 Footed Ridge Columbia MD 21045 Office: Prince George's County Pub Schs 4545 Amendale Rd Beltsville MD 20705 Office Phone: 301-572-0650. Personal E-mail: dmerri1@comcast.net. Business E-Mail: diane.merriam@pgcps.org.

MERRIAM, ROBERT W., engineering executive, educator; b. Providence, July 18, 1923; s. Paul Adams and Marian Lewis M.; m. Nancy Ann Allen, Dec. 21, 1954; children: Susan Allen Jones, Paul Adams, II. BS in Engring. Sci. and Applied Physics, Harvard Coll., 1949; MS in Engring. Sci. and Applied Physics, Harvard Engring. Sch., 1950. Reg. profl. engr., R.I. Instr. elec. engring. Swarthmore (Pa.) Coll., 1950-52; engr. Metals & Controls Corp., Attleboro, Mass., 1953-55; pres. Merriam Instruments, East Greenwich, R.I., 1955-99. Assoc. prof. U. R.I., Kingston, 1969-79. Editor: History of Wireless Communication in the U.S., 1989; patentee in field; contbr. articles to popular publications. Pres., dir. N.E. Wireless and Steam Mus., East Greenwich, 1964—; chmn. Planning Bd., East Greenwich, 1970s; hon. trustee Heritage Trust of R.I. With U.S. Army Signal Corp., 1942-46, ETO. Recipient Antoinette Downing award State of R.I., 1998; named Engr. of Yr., Nat. Assn. Power Engrs., 1998, award Soc. Indsl. Archeology Gen. Tools, 2001, Preserve R.I. Merit award, 2005. Fellow Radio Club Am. (Batcher award 1979); mem. IEEE (life), Am. Radio Relay League (life), Nat. Marine Electronic Assn. (hon., dir. 1957), Nat. Assn. Power Engrs. (hon.), Vet. Wireless Assn. (Marconi Gold medal 1995), 20:00 Club (Meritorious Amateur Seamanship award 1955), Rhode Soc. Profl. Engrs. (Engr. of Yr. 1999), Hope Club, Harvard Club (Boston).

MERRICK, FRED HAROLD, retired marine engineer; s. Fred C. Merrick and Irene Louise Carpenter; m. Cheryl Ann Cain, Apr. 2, 1977. BS, UCLA, 1963; MDiv, Ch. Div. Sch. Pacific, Berkeley, Calif., 1973—76; Cert. Advanced Profl. Study, Pacific Sch. Religion, Berkeley, 1976—78; Cert. Supervision & Mgmt., San Francisco City Coll., 1994—95. Engr. Nat. Aeronautics & Space Adminstrn., Edwards, Calif., 1962; commd. officer USN, 1963—72, 1st commanding officer deep submergence rescue vehicle 2, 1969—72; sr. marine engr. Planning Rsch. Corp., Marine Sys., San Francisco, 1977—79; project mgr., sr. marine engr. Morris Guralnick Assocs., San Francisco, 1979—90; supervising engr. Earl & Wright Cons. Engrs., San Francisco, 1990—91; asst. program mgr. John J. McMullen Assocs., Inc., San Francisco, 1993—2000, Cammisa & Wipf Cons. Engrs., San Francisco, 1991—93, computer sys. mgr., 1993—2005; ret., 2005. Expert witness in marine engring., San Francisco, 1980—. Singer public performances, solos, duets & quartets. Assoc. pastor Christ Ch. Luth., San Francisco, 1981—85; sec. Luth. Campus Ministry, San Francisco, 1982—95; pastor Bayview Luth. Ch., San Francisco, 1986—98; chaplain Vets. Adminstrn. Med. Ctr., San Francisco, 2000—05; publicity dir. Calif. Geneal. Soc., San Francisco, 1985—90; pres., program dir. Landberg Ctr. Health & Ministry, San Francisco, 1985—2006. Lt. USN, 1963—72. Mem.: VFW (life). Reform. Luth. Avocations: singing, genealogy, travel. Home: 1623 12th Ave San Francisco CA 94122 Personal E-mail: fmerrick@pacbell.net.

MERRICK, JOAV, pediatrician, government agency administrator, researcher; b. Copenhagen, Sept. 26, 1950; s. Abraham and Yona (Michaelson) Merrick; m. Geula Gadassi; children: Michael Talia, Efrat Miriam, Etai Jaakov, Alona Yona, Amir David, Maya Rachel. MD, MMedSci, U. Copenhagen, 1977, DMSc, 1989. Rotating intern internal medicine and surgery unit Hosp. Rigshospitalet, Copenhagen, 1977—78, resident ambulatory, cmty. and social pediats., 1979—81, sr. resident in pediat., 1983—84, attending physician, dir. sect. ambulatory, cmty. and social pediats., dept. pediat., sr. lectr. cmty. pediat., 1984—86, clin. prof. child health and cmty. pediat., 1986—89, from rsch. pediatrician to dir. Prospective Pediat. Rsch. Unit, 1980—87; intern in internal medicine Vestre Hosp., Copenhagen, 1978—79; resident in gen. pediat. Roskilde County Hosp., Denmark, 1981—82; resident Hosp. for Sick Children, Fuglebakken, Denmark; cons. cmty. pediatrician, dir. child protection team Copenhagen County Dept. Social Svc., 1984—89; attending physician pediat., dir. ambulatory pediat. dept. pediat. Holbaek (Denmark) Ctrl. Hosp., 1986—89; attending physician pediat. Chaim Sheba Med. Ctr., Tel-Hashomer, Israel, 1989—91; dir. Children's House and Nat. Ctr. Prevention Child Abuse and Neglect, Copenhagen,

1987—89; med. dir. divsn. mental retardation Min. Social Affairs, State of Israel, Jerusalem, 1991—; dir. Nat. Inst. Child Health and Human Devel., Jerusalem, 1999—; prof. pediat. U. Ky. Children's Hosp., Lexington, 2007—. Clin. and vis. prof. child health and human devel. U. Copenhagen, U. Chgo., U. Colo., U. Gottenburg, U. Ben Gurion, U. Tel Aviv, 1984—. Author: Children and the Emergency Room, 1980, Child Abuse and Neglect, 1984, The Baby and Child Medical Handbook, 1988, Principles of Holistic Medicine, 2005, 2006; editor: Incest and Child Sexual Abuse, 1983, Child Health and Development. The Scandinavian Textbook on Social and Community Pediatrics, 1984, Children in Alcohol-and-Drug-Abusing Families, 1985, A Scandinavian Textbook on Child Abuse and Neglect, 1985, Suicidal Behavior in Adolescence, 2005, Adolescence and Alcohol, 2006, Alcohol and Suicide, 2007; mem. editl. bd. Jour. Religion Disability and Health, 1999—, editor-in-chief Internat. Jour. Adolescent Med. Health, 2000—, Scientific World Jour., 2003—, Internat. Jour. Disability and Human Devel., 2005—; editor-in-chief: TSW-Holistic Health and Medicine, 2006—, Internat. Jour. Child Health Human Devel., 2008—, Internat. Jour. child Adolescent Health, 2008—, Jour. Pain Mgmt., 2008—. Capt. reserves Israel Def. Forces, 1991—2003. Recipient Peter Sabroe Child award, Danish Child Welfare Found., 1985, Internat. LEGO prize, LEGO Internat, 1987. Mem.: Lego International, Intellectual and Devel. Disabilities, Assn. for Child Psychology and Psychiatry, Internat. Assn. Sci. Study Intellectual Disabilities, Am. Assn. on Mental Retardation, Am. Profl. Soc. and the Abuse of Children, Internat. Soc. for Prevention Child Abuse and Neglect (exec. coun. 1984—86, editl. bd. and rev. internat. jour. 1986—), Israeli Pediat. Soc. Office: Ministry Social Affairs Divsn Mental Retardation PO Box 1260 IL-91012 Jerusalem Israel Office Fax: 972-2-6703657; Home Fax: 972-8-9201917.

MERRIFIELD, DUDLEY BRUCE, finance educator, federal official; b. Chgo., June 13, 1921; s. Fred and Anna (Marshall) M.; m. Paula Sorensen, June 8, 1949; children: Bruce, Robert, Marshall. AB in Chemistry, Princeton U., 1942; MS in Chemistry, U. Chgo., 1948, PhD in Chemistry, 1950. Disting. vis. prof. Georgetown U. Bus. Sch., Washington. Sr. rsch. chemist Monsanto, St. Louis, 1950-56; mgr. polymer rsch. Tex.-U.S. Chem. Co., Parsippany, NJ, 1956-63; dir. R & D Petrolite Corp., St. Louis, 1963-68; v.p. tech. and ventures Occidental Petroleum Co., Houston, 1968-77; v.p. tech. and venture mgmt. Continental Group, Stamford, Conn., 1977-82; asst. sec. for productivity, tech. and innovation Dept. Commerce, Washington, 1982-89; undersec. econ. affairs, 1986-87; Walter Bladstrom prof., emeritus Wharton Bus. Sch., U Pa., Phila., 1989-94; pres., CEO Pinnacle Rsch. Inst. Devel. Co., 1991—; ptnr. Innovation Alliance, 2007—. Adv. bd. Binat R & D Found., U.S., Israel, France, India, 1979—; disting. vis. prof. mgmt., Georgetown U., Washington. Contbr. articles to profl. jours.; patentee in field. Exec. coun. Episcopal Ch., 1973-79; chmn. Princeton Alumni Coun., 1968-72. With USMC, 1943-46. Fellow AAAS, Inst. for Chemists; mem. Am. Chem. Soc., Indsl. Rsch. Inst. (dir., pres.-elect 1977-82 M. Holland award), Am. Mgmt. Assn. Hall of Fame (trustee, chmn. rsch. coun.), Dirs. Rsch., Sigma Xi Republican. Episcopalian. Office: Pridco Mgmt Corp Ste 604 1316 New Hampshire NW Washington DC 20036 Office Phone: 202-887-0877. Personal E-mail: pridco@verizon.net.

MERRIFIELD, JEFFREY S., engineering company executive, former commissioner; b. Antrim, NH, 1963; m. Diana M. Merrifield; 3 children. BA magna cum laude, Tufts U., 1985; JD, Georgetown U.Law Ctr., 1992. Bar: NH, DC. Legis. asst. to Senator Gordon Humphrey US Senate, Washington, 1987—90, legis. asst. to Senator Robert Smith, 1990—92; assoc. McKenna & Cuneo LLP, Washington, 1992—95; majority coun. & staff dir. Senate Subcommittee on Superfund, Waste Control and Risk Assessment, Washington, 1995—98; commr. US Nuclear Regulatory Commn., Rockville, 1998—2007; sr. v.p. Power Group The Shaw Group Inc., Charlotte, NC, 2007—; dir. Am. Ecology, 2007—. Mem.: DC Bar Assn., NH State Bar Assn. Achievements include appointed by president Clinton and reappointed by president Bush for two terms as an NRC Commission. Office: The Shaw Group Inc 128 S Tryon St Charlotte NC 28202 Office Phone: 301-415-1855, 701-378-5227.

MERRIFIELD, LANE, Internet company executive; b. Lethridge, Alta., Canada, 1978; With Disneyland, Burbank, Calif., 1995; sales rep. New Horizon Prodns., Kelowna, BC, 2003—05; co-founder, CEO Club Penguin, 2005—07, gen. mgr., 2007—; exec. v.p. Walt Disney Internet Grp., Burbank, Calif., 2007—. Office: Club Penguin 410-1620 Dickson Ave Kelowna BC V1Y-9Y2 Canada

MERRIGAN, JOHN A., lobbyist, lawyer; AB, Georgetown U., 1970; JD cum laude, Loyola U., 1973. Bar: DC 1973. Atty. Verner Liipfert, co-founder fed. affairs practice; ptnr. DLA Piper, Washington, 2002—. Chmn. Dem. Bus. Coun. Dem. Nat. Party, 1996—2000, Middle Atlantic fin. chmn. for Kerry for Pres. Campaign, 2002—04; bd. advisors George Washington Grad. Sch. of Polit. Mgmt.; mem. Nat. Coun. Polit. Mgmt., George Washington U.; bd. dirs. New Dem. Network; spkr. in field. Bd. mem. Children Uniting Nations. Named one of 50 Top Lobbyists, Washingtonian mag., 2007. Mem.: ABA. Office: DLA Piper 500 Eighth St, NW Washington DC 20004 Office Fax: 202-799-4310, 202-799-5310. E-mail: john.merrigan@dlapiper.com.*

MERRIGAN, KATHLEEN ANN, federal agency administrator; b. 1959; BA in Polit. Sci. & English, Williams Coll., 1982; MA in Pub. Affairs, Lyndon Johnson Sch. Pub. Affairs, U. Tex., 1987; Ph.D in Environmental Planning & Policy, MIT, 2000. Mgr. John Olver for State Senate Campaign, 1982; rsch. analyst Mass. Joint Com. on Taxation, 1983; chief of staff to Senator John Olver Mass. State Senate, 1983—85; spl. asst. regulatory divsn. Tex. Dept. Agrl., 1986—87; staff mem. US Senate Agrl., Nutrition, & Forestry Com., 1987—92; sr. analyst Henry A. Wallace Inst. for Alternative Agrl., 1994—99; adminstr. Agrl. Mktg. Services USDA, 1999—2001; asst. prof. Friedman Sch. Nutrition Sci., Tufts U., Boston, 2001—09, dir. Agrl. Food & Environment Program, 2001—09; dep. sec. USDA, Washington, 2009—. Expert cons. Food Agrl. Orgn. UN, 1998, 2008; rsch. asst. MIT, 1992—93, 1993—94, instr., 1993; mem. USDA Nat. Organic Standards Bd., 1995—99, U.S. EPA Food Safety Advisory Com., 1996—98, USDA Facilities Reform Commn., 1997—99. Bd. dirs. Organic Farming Rsch. Found., 1992—95, The Organic Ctr., 2004—; mem. steering com. Nat. Campaign for Sustainable Agrl. Steering Com., 1994—99, Kellogg Found. for Integrated Food & Farming Systems Network, 1996—98; mem. standards com. Human Farm Animal Care, 2003—07. Recipient Organic Leadership award, Organic Trade Assn., 2000, Plow Honor award, USDA, 2001. Mem.: Am. Acad. for the Advancement of Sci. (AAAS). Democrat. Office: USDA 12th & Jefferson Dr SW Rm 202-B Washington DC 20250*

MERRILL, ANDREA O., music educator; BS in Music Edn., Coll. St. Rose, Albany, NY, 1970; MusM in Piano Pedagogy, Cath. U., Washington, 1971; student, Am. Inst. Mus. Studies, Graz, Austria. Cert. K-12 music tchr. NY. Tchr. Mechanicville Pub. Schs., NY, Doane Stuart Sch., Albany, NY, 1975—85, Acad. Holy Names, Albany, 1976—. Mus. dir. Schenectady Light Opera Co., NY, 1985—; accompanist concert choir Rensselaer Poly. Inst., Troy, NY, 1995—. Mem.: Theatre Assn. NY State (music dir. award 2007, 2009), Suzuki Assn. Ams., Music Tchrs. Nat. Assn., Music Educators Nat. Conf. Office: Acad of Holy Names 1075 New Scotland Rd Albany NY 12208 Personal E-mail: andmerrill@aol.com.

MERRILL, ANDREA TAI, musician, educator; b. Allentown, Pa., Dec. 23, 1973; d. John Sefton Flick and Linda Kay Gardner; m. Paul Robert Merrill, May 23, 1998; 1 child, Jacob Nicholas. MusB, Ithaca Coll., NY, 1995; MusM, Ariz. State U., Tempe, 1997; PhD in Musical Arts, U. Rochester, NY, 2005. Asst. prof. Ithaca Coll., 2005—. Office: Ithaca Coll 953 Danby Rd Ithaca NY 14850

MERRILL, CHARLES EUGENE, lawyer; b. San Antonio, Aug. 26, 1952; s. Charles Perry and Florence Elizabeth Merrill; m. Carol Ann Rutter, Apr. 28, 1984; children: Elizabeth C., Charles C. AB, Stanford U., 1974; JD, U. Calif., Berkeley, 1977. Bar: Mo. 1977, Calif. 1983, Ill. 1993. Mem. Husch & Eppenberger, LLC, St. Louis, 1977—2007; ptnr. Husch Blackwell Sanders, LLP, 2008—. Mem. ABA, Bar Assn. of Met. St. Louis. Office: Husch Blackwell Sanders LLP 190 Carondelet Plz Ste 600 Saint Louis MO 63105-3441 Business E-Mail: charles.merrill@huschblackwell.com.

MERRILL, CHARLES J., language educator; b. Winfield, Kans., Sept. 21, 1950; s. John C. and Dorothy J. Merrill; children: Susanna Mary, John Thomas. BA, Dartmouth Coll., Hanover, NH, 1972; PhD, Duke U., Durham, NC, 1978. Asst. prof. Hood Coll., Frederick, Md., 1978—81; assoc. prof. Mt. St. Mary's U., Emmitsburg, Md., 1981—. Author: (history book) Colom of Catalonia. Scholar, Fulbright Commn., 1976—77. Mem.: Cercle d'Estudis Colombins. Roman Catholic. Office: Mt St Mary's Univ 6300 Old Emmitsburg Rd Emmitsburg MD 21727 Business E-Mail: merrill@msmary.edu.

MERRILL, CHRISTOPHER LYALL, writer; b. Northampton, Mass., Feb. 24, 1957; s. Charles Francis Merrill and Suzanne Sigmund France; m. Lisa Ellen Gowdy, June 4, 1983; children: Hannah Frances, Abigail Rose. BA, Middlebury Coll., 1979; MA, U. Wash., 1982. Dir. Santa Fe Writers Conf., 1987-90, Santa Fe Literary Ctr., 1988-92; William H. Jenks chair Contemporary Letters Coll. of the Holy Cross, Worcester, Mass., 1995-2000; dir. internat. writing program U. Iowa, Iowa City, 2000—. Author: The Old Bridge: The Third Balkan War and The Age of the Refugee, 1995, Watch Fire, 1994, The Grass of Another Country: A Journey Through The World of Soccer, 1993, From the Faraway Nearby: Georgia O'Keefe As Icon, 1992, Only the Nails Remain: Scenes from the Balkan Wars, 1999, Brilliant Water, 2001, Things of the Hidden God, 2005; poetry editor Orion Mag., 1993-2003; contbg. editor Paris Rev., 1991-95; gen. editor-poetry series Gibbs Smith Pub., Layton, Utah, 1987-2001. Recipient Ingram Merrill Found. award, 1991, Pushcart Prize in Poetry, 1990, Arts and Letters chevalier French Govt., 2006. Mem. Acad. Am. Poets (Peter Lavan Younger Poets award 1993, Bosnian Stecak award 2001, Kostas Kyriazis Internat. Lit. award 2005). Episcopalian. Avocations: gardening, hiking, reading. Office: U Iowa Internat Writing Program Shambaugh House Iowa City IA 52242-2020 Office Phone: 319-335-2609. Business E-Mail: christopher-merrill@uiowa.edu.

MERRILL, DANIEL A., program manager; b. NJ; m. Shelly Merrill, 1989; children: Nick, Stephanie. Project mgmt. profl., Project Mgmt. Inst., 2007; info. tech. infrastructure libr. found. cert. Exin/Loyalist, 2007, cert. info. sys. security profl. Internat. Info. Sys. Security Cert. Consortium, 2009. Data ctr. shift supr. Volt Info. Scis., 1984—85; image analyst DBA Sys., 1985—87; data ctr. supr. sys. divsn. TRW, 1987—89; info. tech. ops. mgr. advanced client/server devel. group Wollongong/Attachmate, 1989—99; mgr. internat. CPE cert. global product engring. UUNET Tech., 1999—2001; tech. project mgr. IP VPN product devel., comm. svcs. engring. Worldcom, Inc., 2001—02; info. tech. mgr. RDR, Inc., 2003—04; program mgr. Metters Industries, Inc., 2004—06, ManTech Internat., 2006—. Mgr. Internet Protocol Devel. Teams., Software Devel. Teams, Sys. Devel. Teams, Network Security Product Devel. Teams, Application Svc. Provider Orgn. Pres. Home Owner's Assn., Clearbook, 2002—05. With USN, 1980—84. Recipient Disting. Svc. award, RDR, Inc., 2003; named Employee of Yr., Wollongong/Attachmate, 1994. Mem.: Gerson Lehman Group, Nat. Contract Mgmt. Assn., Project Mgmt. Inst., Internat. Info. Systems Security Cert. Consortium, Armed Forces Comm. and Engring. Assn., Internet Engring. Task Force, Am. Mgmt. Assn., Wash. Network Group, US Tennis Assn., Appalachian Mountain Club, Am. Legion. Avocation: travel. Home: 2015 Chapel Ct Frederick MD 21702-2624

MERRILL, DAVID, entrepreneur, researcher; BS in Symbolic Sys., Stanford U., Calif., 2000, MS in Computer Sci., 2002; Attending, MIT Media Lab., Cambridge, Mass., 2002—. Lectr. Stanford U., 2002; rschr. MIT Media Lab, 2002—09. Freelance cons. Pvt. Practice, Somerville, Mass., 2000—09. Mem.: IEEE, ACM Sigchi, ACM Siggraph. Liberal. Avocations: photography, surfing. Office: MIT Media Lab 20 Ames St E15-313 Cambridge MA 02139

MERRILL, DEANE WHITNEY, JR., education educator, consultant; b. Orange, NJ, May 9, 1938; s. Deane Whitney Merrill Sr. and Harriet Mary (Ray); m. Colette Marie Yvonne Bruvry, June 20, 1964 (div. 1971); m. Jane Elizabeth Brockmeyer, Dec. 6, 1975 (div. 1985); m. Anna Christine Morben, July 2, 1995. AB, Williams Coll., 1960; MA in Physics, U. Calif., Berkeley, 1962, PhD in Physics, 1967, DPH, 1998. Scientist Lawrence Berkeley Lab., Calif., 1960—98; tchr. Mohawk Trl. Regional HS, Buckland, Mass., 2001—06, Asheville-Buncombe Tech. CC, NC, 2006—, South Coll., Asheville, 2007—. Cons. in field. Author: numerous publs. in physics, demography, pub. health, biostats. and epidemiology. Achievements include development of density equalizing map projections (cartograms). Home: 96 Beverly Rd Asheville NC 28805 Personal E-mail: dwmerrill@charter.net.

MERRILL, DONNA, special education educator; b. Raymond, Nebr., Oct. 30, 1933; d. Donald Frank and Edith Marie (Brightenburg) Spellman; m. Robert Henry Merrill, May 29, 1952; children: Nancy, Catherine, Robert, Barbara. BA, Park Coll., Parkville, Mo., 1955; MA, U. Mo., Kansas City, 1975, PhD, 1983. Editor publs. Park Coll., Parkville, Mo., 1953-57; tchr. Smithville Sch. Dist., Mo., 1965-85, Shawnee Mission Sch. Dist., Mo., 1985—2001, St. Agnes Sch., Mission, Kans., 2000—07. Adj. faculty U. Mo., Kansas City, 1985-1995; co-dir. Signet Summer Camp, Kansas City, 1985-88. Mem. Gifted Assn. Mo., Kans. Gifted-Talented Assn., Alpha Delta, Phi Kappa Phi, Pi Lambda Theta, Phi Delta Kappa. Avocation: travel. Home: 19626 SE Dykes Rd Holt MO 64048-8782 Home Phone: 816-320-2408. Personal E-mail: dmerrill915141@embarqmail.com.

MERRILL, EDWARD WILSON, chemical engineering professor; b. New Bedford, Mass., Aug. 31, 1923; s. Edward Clifton and Gertrude (Wilson) M.; m. Genevieve de Bidart, Aug. 19, 1948; children: Anne de Bidart, Francis de Bidart. AB, Harvard U., 1945; DSc, MIT, 1947. Research engr. Dewey & Almy div. W.R. Grace & Co., 1947-50; mem. faculty MIT, 1950-98, prof. chem. engring., 1964-98, Carbon P. Dubbs prof., 1973-96, emeritus, 1998—. Cons. in field. Contbr. articles to profl. jours. Pres. bd. trustees Buckingham Sch., Cambridge, 1969-74; trustee Browne and Nichols Sch., Cambridge, 1972-74, hon. trustee, 1974—. Fellow Am. Inst. for Med. and Biol. Engring., Am. Acad. Arts and Scis.; mem. AIChE (Alpha Chi Sigma award 1984, Charles M.A. Stine award 1993, Founders award 2000), Am. Chem. Soc., Soc. for Biomaterials (Clemson U. Award 1990, Founders award 2003). Achievements include patents for chemical and rheological instruments; research in polymers, rheology, medical engineering. Home: 90 Somerset St Belmont MA 02478-2010 Home Phone: 617-484-1578; Office Phone: 617-253-4593. Office Fax: 617-489-2165. Business E-Mail: emerrill@mit.edu.

MERRILL, GEORGE VANDERNETH, lawyer, investment executive; b. NYC, July 2, 1947; s. James Edward and Claire (Leness) M.; m. Janice Anne Humes, May 11, 1985; children: Claire Georgina, Anne Stewart. Student, Phillips Exeter Acad., 1960—64; AB magna cum laude, Harvard U., 1968, JD, 1972; MBA, Columbia U., 1973. Bar: NY 1973, US Dist. Ct. (so. and ea. dists.) NY 1974, US Ct. Appeals (2d cir.) 1974. Assoc. Cleary, Gottlieb, Steen & Hamilton, NYC, 1974-77, Hawkins, Delafield & Wood, NYC, 1977-79; v.p. Irving Trust Co., NYC, 1980-82, Listowel, Inc., NYC, 1982-84, bd. dirs., exec. v.p., 1984-93; v.p. instl. portfolio mgmt. Shawmut Investment Advisors, 1993-95; also co-mgr. Shawmut Growth & Income Equity Mut. Fund; v.p. instl. portfolio mgmt. Fleet Investment Advisors, 1995-96, also co-mgr. Galaxy Growth & Income Equity Mut. Fund.; v.p. trust and instl. portfolio mgmt., mem. Fla. equity com. No. Trust Corp., Chgo., 1996-2000; v.p., sr. personal investment officer, sector head Bank of NY Mellon, NYC, 2000—, mem. investment policy com., 2004—. Pres. Northfield Charitable Corp., NYC, 1986-93; v.p., sec. Brougham Prodn. Co., NYC, 1986-89, sr. v.p., sec., 1990-93; v.p., sec. Marinetics Inc., NYC, 1988-90, sr. v.p., sec., 1991-93; v.p. Sci. Design and Engring. Co., Inc., NYC, 1987-88, exec. v.p., 1989-93 Bd. dirs. Pres. Arell Found., NYC, 1985—93. Recipient Detur award, Harvard U., 1968; John Harvard scholar. Mem. ABA, Am. Mgmt. Assn., Nat. Cum Laude Soc., Series 65 Cert., The Brook, Union Club (NYC), Down Town Assn., Racquet and Tennis Club, Somerset Club (Boston), Signet Soc. (Cambridge), Pilgrims of US. Home: 2 Pierce Rd Riverside CT 06878 Office: BNY Mellon Wealth Mgmt 200 Pk Ave 54th Fl New York NY 10166 Business E-Mail: george.merrill@bnymellon.com.

MERRILL, HARVIE MARTIN, retired manufacturing executive; b. Detroit, Apr. 26, 1921; s. Harvie and Helen (Nelson) M.; m. Mardelle Merrill; children— Susan, Linda. BS in Chem. Engring, Purdue U., 1942, Bd Che magma cum laude. Devel. engr. Sinclair Refining Co., 1946-47; research and gen. mgr. 3M Co., St. Paul, 1947-65; v.p. fabricated products Plastics div. Stauffer Chem. Co., NYC, 1965-69; with Hexcel Corp., San Francisco, 1969-86, pres., chief exec. officer, 1969-86, chmn. bd., 1976-88. With USAF, 1942-46. Mem.: Interlachen Country Club. Home: 664 Osceola Ave Winter Park FL 32789 Home Fax: 407-628-3130.

MERRILL, JEAN FAIRBANKS, writer; b. Rochester, NY, Jan. 27, 1923; d. Earl Dwight and Elsie (Fairbanks) M. BA, Allegheny Coll., 1944; MA, Wellesley Coll., 1945. Feature editor Scholastic Mags., 1947-50; editor Lit. Cavalcade, 1956-57; publs. div. Bank St. Coll. Edn., 1964-65. Children's books include Henry, the Hand-Painted Mouse, 1951, The Woover, 1952, Boxes, 1953, The Tree House of Jimmy Domino, 1955, The Travels of Marco, 1956, A Song for Gar, 1957, The Very Nice Things, 1959, Blue's Broken Heart, 1960, Shan's Lucky Knife (Jr. Lit. Guild selection), Emily Emerson's Moon, 1960 (Jr. Lit. Guild selection), The Superlative Horse (Jr. Lit. Guild selection), 1961 (Lewis Carroll Shelf award 1963), Tell About the Cowbarn, Daddy, 1963, The Pushcart War (Lewis Carroll Shelf award), 1964 (Boys Club Am. Jr. Book award), High, Wide & Handsome, 1964 (Jr. Lit. Guild selection), The Elephant Who Liked to Smash Small Cars, 1967, Red Riding, 1968, The Black Sheep, 1969, Here I Come-Ready or Not!, 1970, Mary, Come Running, 1970, How Many Kids are Hiding on My Block?, 1970, Please, Don't Eat My Cabin, 1971, The Toothpaste Millionaire (Dorothy Canfield Fisher Meml. award 1975-76), 1972 (Sequoyah award 1977), The Second Greatest Clown in the World, 1972, The Jackpot, 1972, The Bumper Sticker Book, 1973, Maria's House, 1974, The Girl Who Loved Caterpillars, 1992; poetry books edited include A Few Flies and I, 1969; libretto for chamber opera Mary Come Running, 1983. Fulbright fellow, India, 1952—53. Mem. Authors League, Vt. Arts. Coun., Vt. Inst. Natural Sci., Vt. Nat. Resources Coun., Fulbright Assn., Women's Internat. League Peace and Justice, Sierra Club, Audobon Soc., Women's Internat. League Peace and Justice, Phi Beta Kappa. Home Phone: 802-728-9549; Office Phone: 802-728-9549. *My interest in writing children's books may have derived from the impact certain books had on me as a child, and a wish to recreate the quality of that experience. As to my general motivation as a writer, I would say that it is to celebrate those aspects of the human experience that affirm the creative and life-reverencing instinct in man. I always hope that my stories may be essentially liberating, opening the reader to emotional, as well as intellectual experience, and that they may be entertaining, encouraging the capacity for joy by evoking the free play of a reader's curiosity, humor and inventiveness.*

MERRILL, JONATHAN ALDEN, retired newsletter editor; b. Washington, May 25, 1945; s. Deane Whitney and Harriet Mary (Ray) M. BME, Westminster Choir Coll., 1969. Music tchr. various pub. schs., N.J., Vt., 1969-78; clerical adminstr., fin. mgr. AT&T, Morristown, NJ, 1982—2009. Tax preparer Hour Block, 2007—. Editor (newsletter) Annie People, 1983-98. Troop leader Girl Scouts Am., Somerville, N.J., 1983-84. With U.S. Army, 1978-82. Democrat. Episcopalian. Avocation: collecting and researching Little Orphan Annie lore and memorabilia. Home: 285 Haw Creek Mews Dr Asheville NC 28805 Home Phone: 828-505-1043.

MERRILL, JOSEPH MELTON, medical educator; b. Andalusia, Ala., Dec. 8, 1923; s. Walter C. and Mary T. (McLaney) M.; m. Gudrun Wallgren, Sept. 15, 1960; children: Maria, Caroline. MD, Harvard Med. Sch., 1948. Diplomate Am. Bd. Internal Medicine. With VA Med. Ctr., Nashville, 1960-64; chief Gen. Clin. Rsch. Ctrs. NIH, Bethesda, 1964-67; dean sci. affairs Baylor Coll. Medicine, Houston, 1967-77, prof., 1967—. Capt. USAF, 1951-53.

MERRILL, RICHARD JAMES, retired educational director; b. Milw., Apr. 15, 1931; s. Henry Baldwin and Doris (Lucas) M.; m. Kathleen Emden Keely, June 14, 1953 (dec. Jan. 1974); children: Wendy Ann, Vicki Louise, Robin Kay, Christina Suzanne; m. Terry Bradley Alt, Aug. 10, 1974 (div. 1976); m. Shannon Ann Lynch, June 19, 1977. BS, U. Mich., 1953; MA, Columbia U., 1957, EdD, 1960. Tchr. sci. Ramona H.S., Riverside, Calif., 1958-62; secondary sci. coord. Riverside City Schs., 1960-62; exec. dir. chem. edn. material study Harvey Mudd Coll. and U. Calif. at Berkeley, 1962-65; curriculum specialist Mt. Diablo Unified Sch. Dist., Concord, Calif., 1965-91, dir. curriculum, 1980-81; assoc. dir. Inst. for Chem. Edn. and Project Phys. Sci., U. Calif., Berkeley, 1990—94; ret. Bd. dirs. San Francisco Bay Area Sci. Fair; mem. sci. adv. com. Calif. Assessment Program, 1983-89, also mem. assessment adv. com. to state supt., pub. instrn., 1984-86; dir. N. Calif.

W. Nev. Jr. Sci. and Humanities Symposium, 1993-2004; lectr. Calif. State U., Hayward, 1996-99. Author: (with David W. Ridgway) The CHEM Study Story, 1969; co-author: National Science Teachers Association Guidelines for Self-Assessment of Secondary Science Programs, 1975, Science Framework for California Public Schools, 1978, 84; co-author, editor: The Physical Science of Living in California, 1993. Bd. dirs. Ctr. for New Ams., Concord, 1984-91. Served from ensign to lt. (j.g.) USN, 1953-56. Named to Hall Of Fame, Washington Pk. HS, 2008. Mem. NSTA (past pres., past mem. exec. com.), Nat. Sci. Suprs. Assn., Elem. Sch. Sci. Assn. (coun. 1975-82, pres. 1983), Calif. Sci. Tchrs. Assn. (Disting. Svc. award 1990), Assn. Calif. Sch. Adminstrs., Acacia, Phi Delta Kappa. Home: 1862 2d Ave Walnut Creek CA 94597-2553 E-mail: randsmerrill@sbcglobal.net.

MERRILL, STEPHEN, lawyer, consultant, Former Governor, New Hampshire; b. June 21, 1946; m. Helen Walker. BA magna cum laude, U. NH, 1969; JD, Georgetown U., 1972. Former personal counsel to Sec. Air Force, Pentagon; atty. gen. State of NH, Concord, 1985—89, gov., 1993—97; of counsel Choate, Hall and Stewart, Boston, 1997—99; pres. Bingham Consulting Group, Boston, 1999—; ptnr. Bingham McCutchen LLP, Boston, 1999, of counsel. Mem. NH task force on Child Abuse and Neglect, former pres., legal counsel. Served to capt. USAF. Recipient AG Profl. award, Nat. award for Human Svc., Disting. Citizen of Yr. award, Daniel Webster Coun.; Georgetown Law Fellow, Ford Found. Scholar, Univ. NH. Fellow: ABA (life); mem.: Manchester Bar Assn., Pa. Bar Assn., DC Bar Assn., NH Bar Assn., Nat. Attys. Gen. Emeritus (co-chmn.), Nat. Gov.'s Assn. Emeritus, Ea. Assn. Attys. Gen. (chmn.), Phi Beta Kappa (Ford Found. scholar). Republican. Episcopalian. Office: Bingham McCutchen 150 Federal St Boston MA 02110-1726 Office Phone: 617-951-8828. Office Fax: 617-951-8736. Business E-Mail: stephen.merrill@bingham.com.

MERRILL, SUSAN L., financial regulatory service executive, lawyer; b. 1957; Grad. cum laude, U. Md., 1979; JD summa cum laude, Bklyn. Law Sch., 1986. Law clk. to Hon. Francis L. Van Dusen US Ct. Appeals (3rd cir.), 1986—87; assoc. Davis Polk & Wardwell, 1987—2004, ptnr., 1994—2004; exec. v.p. enforcement NYSE Group, Inc. (formerly NY Stock Exch.), 2004—07, Fin. Industry Regulatory Authority, Inc. (FINRA), Washington, 2007—. Office: Financial Industry Regulatory Authority Inc 1735 K St NW Washington DC 20006 Office Phone: 212-656-3000.*

MERRILL, WALTER HILSON, surgeon; b. Montgomery, Ala., Oct. 27, 1947; s. Mary Jim Pianowski; m. Morgan Van Zandt, June 10, 1972; children: Virginia Kelly, Elizabeth Gibson, Mary Knox, Walter Joseph Hilson. BA, U. South Sewanee, Tenn., 1970; MD, Johns Hopkins U. Sch. Medicine, Balt., 1974. Diplomate Am. Bd. Thoracic Surgery, 1983. Dept. cardiothoracic surgery Vanderbilt U., Nashville, 1983—2002; chief, sect. cardiothoracic surgery U. Cin. Office: Univ Cin 231 Albert Sabin Way ML 0558 Cincinnati OH 45267-0558

MERRILL, WENDY JANE, realtor; b. Waterbury, Conn., Dec. 4, 1961; d. David Kenneth and Jane Joy (Nevius) Merrill; m. Aidan T. Harrison (div. Nov. 1998); children: Christopher Harrison, Charlotte Harrison, Ryan Harrison; m. Michael G. Kelly, Oct. 2, 1999 (dissolved Nov. 2004). BA in Journalism, George Washington U., 1981; MBA in mgmt., Cornell U., 1992. Intern edn. HEW, Washington, 1978, writer, 1979; rsch. asst. dept. health svcs. adminstrn. George Washington U., Washington, 1979—81; sec. Nat. Assn. Beverage Importers, Washington, 1981; account exec. Staff Design, Washington, 1982; adminstrv. aide Internat. Food Policy Rsch. Inst., Washington, 1983—86; program assoc. Acad. for Ednl. Devel., Washington, 1986—87; pvt. practice cons. Washington, 1987—88; adminstrv. mgr. food and nutrition policy program Cornell U., Ithaca, NY, 1988—92; cons. mgmt. of med. practices Med. Bus. Mgmt., Ithaca, 1994—95; realtor Century 21 Alpha, 1995—97; compensation mgr. Santa Clara U., Calif., 1996—98; sr. compensation analyst Stanford U., Calif., 1998—99; human resources cons. Siemens Info. and Comm. Networks, 2000; compensation and benefits mgr. Kana Comms., 2000—01; U.S. compensation mgr. KLA-Tencor, 2001—02; pres. Total Solutions Ins. Agy., Inc., Calif., 2003—, Total Solutions Comml. Ventures, Inc., 2003—, Ruby Enterprises LLC, 2007—; realtor presdl., 2009—. Cons., editor George Washington U., 1986; cons., rapporteur Internat. Food Policy Restaurant Inst., Washington and Copenhagen, Denmark, 1987; cons., adminstr. Hansell & Post, Washington, 1987-88, Cornell U., Washington and Ithaca, 1988; pvt. practice cons., 2001—. Sponsor Worldvision, Tanzania, 1988-91. George Washington U. scholar, 1979-81. Mem. Zonta Club (charter pres. Silicon Valley chpt. 2006—), Sigma Delta Xi (scholar 1980). Democrat. Avocations: piano, hiking, swimming. Home: 9000 Las Vegas Blvd S #1102 Las Vegas NV 89123 Business E-Mail: wendy@totalsolutionscv.com.

MERRILL, WILLIAM DEAN, retired architect, medical facility planning consultant; b. Portland, Oreg., June 1, 1915; s. Charles O. and Grace (Ruhl) Merrill; m. Bernice E. Wickham, Apr. 19, 1943 (dec. Sept. 1996); 1 child, Sue Ann Merrill Boardman; m. Irene Moe Merrill, July 30, 2001. Student in Fine Arts and Forestry, Oreg. State U., Corvallis, 1936—38; student in Architecture, U. Oreg., Eugene, 1939—42. Registered architect, Oreg., Calif. NCARB prin., Portland, 1956—64; architect, ptnr. Bissell & Merrill, Architects, Stockton, Calif., 1964—68; architect design and constrn. Kaiser Engrs. Kaiser Found. Hosps., 1968—81; pvt. practice Bay Area, 1981—91; hosp. and sch. constrn. insp. Office State Health Planning & Devel., Calif., 1984—93; ret., 1996. Served as lt. (j.g.) USNR, 1942—44, PTO. Mem.: AIA (emeritus mem.). Republican. Home: 25411 E Cedar Glen Loop Welches OR 97067

MERRIMAN, SHAWNE DEANDRE, professional football player; b. Washington, May 25, 1984; Student in Criminology and Criminal Justice, U. Md., College Park, 2002—04. Linebacker San Diego Chargers, 2005—. Named NFL Defensive Rookie of Yr., AP, 2005, First Team All-Pro, NFL, 2006; named to Am. Football Conf. Pro Bowl Team, 2005—07. Achievements include leading the NFL in: sacks (17), 2006. Office: San Diego Chargers PO Box 609609 San Diego CA 92160-9609*

MERRIN, SEYMOUR, computer company executive; b. Bklyn., Aug. 13, 1931; s. Joseph and Esther Bella (Manelis) M.; m. Elaine Cohen, Sept. 4, 1960 (dec. May 1962); m. Elizabeth Jenifer Slack, Oct. 12, 1963 (dec. Mar. 1995); children: Charles Seymour, Mariamne Jenifer Weights; m. Helene Claire Singer, Sept. 1, 2001 BS, Tufts Coll., 1952; MS, U. Ariz., 1954; PhD, Pa. State U., 1962. Geologist Magma Copper Co., Superior, Ariz., 1954, U.S. Geol. Survey, 1956-58; chemist IBM, Poughkeepsie, NY, 1962-64; mgr. package devel., mgr. reliability and failure analysis Sperry Semiconductor divsn. Sperry Rand, Norwalk, Conn., 1965-68; cons. materials tech. Fairfield, Conn., 1967-69; v.p., dir. Innotech Corp., Norwalk, 1969-74; divsn. mgr. Emdex divsn. Exxon Enterprises, Milford, Conn., 1974-78; chmn., dir. Computerworks, Westport, Conn., 1978-85; v.p., dir. personal computing svc. Gartner Group, Inc., Stamford, Conn., 1984-87; pres. Merrin Resources, Southport, Conn., 1987-89, Merrin Info. Svcs., Inc., Santa Fe, 1987—. Bd. dirs. Micrografx Corp., Allen, Tex.; adv. panel Apple Computer Co., Cupertino, Calif., 1982-83; adv. bd. Compaq Computer Corp., Houston, 1984-85, Computer and Software News, NYC, 1984-89; program adv. bd. Comdex, Boston, 1985—; lectr. in field. Contbr. numerous articles to profl. publs.; patentee in field. Bd. dirs. Futures for Children, Albuquerque, 2004—, Santa Fe Internat. Folk Market, Couse Found., Taos, N.Mex. With US Army, 1954—56. Fellow Geol. Soc. Am., Am. Inst. Chemists; Computing Tech. Industry Assn. (founder, pres. 1981-83, bd. dirs. 1981-84). Home and Office: 840 Camino de las Trampas Santa Fe NM 87501 Personal E-mail: smerrin@aol.com.

MERRISS, PHILIP RAMSAY, JR., banker; b. NYC, June 7, 1948; s. Philip Ramsay and Elisabeth (Paine) M.; m. Janet Henry Hylan, Oct. 27, 1973. AB in Econs. magna cum laude, Lafayette Coll., 1970; MBA with high distinction, Dartmouth Coll., 1972. Assoc. corp. fin. dept. A.G. Becker and Co. Inc., NYC, 1972-73; fin. analyst corp. banking dept. Chase Manhattan Bank, 1973, asst. treas. N.Y.C. dist., 1974-75, 2d v.p. mining and metals div., 1976-78, 2d v.p. petroleum div., 1979-86, client exec., v.p. pub. utilities component, 1987-89, credit supv. officer, div. exec., v.p. U.S. pvt. banking, 1989-94; credit exec. J.P. Morgan Pvt. Bank, NYC, 1994-97, mng. dir. and credit exec., 1997—. Capt. US Army, 1978. Tuck scholar Dartmouth Coll., 1972. Mem. Am. Econ. Assn., Aircraft Owners and Pilots Assn., Weston Gun Club, Yale Club, Fairfield County Hunt Club, Phi Beta Kappa. Republican. Episcopalian. Home: 11 Katydid Ln Weston CT 06883-1808 Office: JP Morgan Chase & Co 345 Park Ave New York NY 10154-1002

MERRITT, BETTY L., medical/surgical and mental health nurse; b. Greenville, SC, Apr. 16, 1939; d. Milton and Lola (Wofford) Alexander; m. Otis Merritt Jr., Mar. 8, 1957; children: Belinda Lorezia, Otis III, Milton Otto, Glenda Frencestia, Lucinda Yvette. ADN, Community Coll. Balt., 1976; AA, Balt. City Hosp. Sch. Nursing, 1973. LPN; cert. psychiat./mental health nurse, ANA; cert. legal nurse cons. The Legal Nurse Cons. Inst. Student advisor Community Coll. Balt.; nurse coord. partial hospitalization svcs. Provident Hosp., Balt.; charge nurse Balt. City Hosp.; clin. nurse supr. Crownsville (Md.) State Hosp.; psychiat. and med.-surg. nurse Liberty Med. Ctr., Balt., alternate nurse mgr. dept. psychiatry; acting nurse, divsn. chief Crownsville (Md.) State Hosp. Cons. psychiat. and mental health nursing Blue Cross/Blue Shield Md. Home: 3212 Burleith Ave Baltimore MD 21215-7908 Business E-Mail: bettylnc1@aol.com.

MERRITT, BRUCE GORDON, lawyer; b. Iowa City, Oct. 4, 1946; s. William Olney and Gretchen Louise (Kuever) M.; m. Valerie Sue Jorgensen, Dec. 28, 1969; children: Benjamin Carlyle, Alicia Marie. AB magna cum laude, Occidental Coll., 1968; JD magna cum laude, Harvard U., 1972. Bar: Calif. 1973, NY 1996. Assoc. Markbys, London, 1972—73, Nossaman, Krueger & Marsh, LA, 1973—79, ptnr., 1979—81; asst. US Atty., LA, 1981—85; ptnr. Debevoise & Plimpton, LA, 1989—95, NYC, 1996—2001. Adj. prof. law Loyola Law Sch., LA, 2003—08. Vestryman St. Mark's Episcopal Ch., Glendale, Calif., 2006—09; bd. dir. Inner Law Ctr., LA, 1991—96. Fellow Am. Coll. Trial Lawyers; mem. Calif. State Bar Assn. (exec. com. litig. sect. 1992-95), Phi Beta Kappa. Episcopalian. Office Phone: 818-521-1812. Personal E-mail: brucegmerritt@sbcglobal.net.

MERRITT, GILBERT STROUD, federal judge; b. Nashville, Tenn., Jan. 17, 1936; s. Gilbert Stroud and Angie Fields (Cantrell) M.; m. Louise Clark Fort, July 10, 1964 (dec.); children: Stroud, Louise Clark, Eli. BA, Yale U., 1957; LLB, Vanderbilt U., 1960; LLM, Harvard U., 1962. Bar: Tenn. 1960. Asst. dean Vanderbilt U. Law Sch., 1960-61, lectr., 1963-69, 71-75, assoc. prof. law, 1969-70; assoc. Boult Hunt Cummings & Conners, Nashville, 1962-63, adj. prof., 2003—; asst. metro. atty. City of Nashville, 1963-66; US Dist. atty. for (mid. dist.) Tenn., 1966-69; ptnr. Gullett, Steele, Sanford, Robinson & Merritt, Nashville, 1970-77; judge US Ct. Appeals (6th cir.), Nashville, 1977-2001, chief judge, 1989—96, sr. judge., 2001—; chmn. exec. com. US Judicial Conf., 1993—96; chmn. internat judicial rel. com. US Judiciary, 1993—95. Exec. sec. Tenn. Code Commn., 1977. Mng. editor: Vanderbilt Law Rev, 1959-60; contbr. articles to law jours. Del. Tenn. Constl. Conv., 1965; chmn. bd. trustees Vanderbilt Inst. Pub. Policy Studies. Mem. ABA, Fed. Bar Assn., Tenn. Bar Assn., Nashville Bar Assn., Vanderbilt Law Alumni Assn. (pres. 1979-80), Am. Law Inst., Order of Coif. Episcopalian. Office: US Ct Appeals Customs House 701 Broadway Ste 303 Nashville TN 37203-3967*

MERRITT, JEAN, consulting firm executive, psychotherapist; b. NYC, Oct. 29, 1952; d. Harry and Ruth (Happel) Packman; m. Richard L. Kashinsky, Aug. 2, 1976 (div.); m. Richard L. Merritt, May 5, 1985 (div. June 2002); children: Courtney Morgan, Melissa Morgan Grad. high sch., Bayside, NY. From contr. to v.p., sec., treas. Kaswol Corp., Richmond Hill, NY, 1973—85; corp. exec. Federated Cons. Svc., Inc., Bayside, NY, CFO Jupiter, Fla., 1985—2002, psychotherapist, 2004—, dir. mktg., 2005—, holistic life coach, 2007—. Coach Queens Spl. Olympics, 1985. Mem. Nat. Trust for Hist. Preservation, Nat. Fedn. Wildlife, Ctr. for Environ. Edn., Defenders of Wildlife, Nat. Resource Def. Coun., Humane Soc. of U.S., Sierra Club, Amnesty Internat. Avocations: flying, art collecting, painting, interior design, gourmet cooking. Home: 4856 Katherine Ave Sherman Oaks CA 91423 Office Phone: 917-319-0184. E-mail: jeanie22m@aol.com.

MERRITT, LIBBIE, safety engineer; d. Robert and Janet Lingenfelter; m. Lynn Lingenfelter, July 5, 1980; children: Deanna Hart, Joni Lewis, Christy Ray. Cert. notary Wash., 2008. Adminstrn. asst. mgr KBR, Houston, 1987—97; safety adminstr. Jacobs, Houston, 2004—05, contracts adminstr., 2005—07, office mgr., 2007—. Youth leader Foursquare, Mount Vernon, Wash., Ch., Slidell, La.

MERRITT, NANCY-JO, lawyer; b. Phoenix, Sept. 24, 1942; d. Robert Nelson Meeker and Violet Adele Gibson; children: Sidney Kathryn, Kurt, Douglas. BA, Ariz. State U., 1964, MA, 1974, JD, 1978. Bar: Ariz. 1978, U.S. Dist. Ct. Ariz. 1978, U.S. Ct. Appeals (9th cir.) 1984. Shareholder Fennemore Craig, P.C., Phoenix. Author: Understanding Immigration Law, 1993; sr. editor: Immigration and National Law Handbook, 1993—; contbr. articles to profl. jours. Chair bd. dirs. TERROS, 1995-97. Fellow Ariz. Bar Found.; mem., Ariz. Lost Boys Ctr. (pres., bd. dirs.), ABA, Am. Immigration Lawyers Assn. (chairperson Ariz. chpt. 1985-87, several coms., Pro Bono award), Ariz. Bar Assn. (immigration sect.), Nucleus Club. Democrat. Avocations: modern literature, south american literature, hiking, gardening. Office Phone: 602-916-5411, 702-692-8003. Business E-Mail: njmerritt@fclaw.com.

MERRITT, PHYLLIS JUNE, music educator, director; b. Elizabethton, Tenn., Mar. 28, 1939; d. Earl H. and Willie Greene Merritt. BS in Music Edn., East Tenn. State U., 1960; MusM in Edn., Fla. State U., 1972. Tchr. music Kingsley Elem. Sch., Kingsport, Tenn., 1960—61, Weis Elem. Sch., Pensacola, Fla., 1961—62; dir. choral music Brownsville Jr. H.S., Pensacola, 1962—65, Escambia H.S., Pensacola, 1965—76, Meigs Jr. H.S., Shalimar, Fla., 1976—80, Niceville H.S., Fla., 1980—90; dir. music Trinity United Meth. Ch., Fort Walton Beach, Fla., 1991—98, ret., 1998; founder Phyllis Merritt Singers, Pensacola, 2003—, artistic music dir., 2003—. Singer, conductor Inst. European Studies Concert Tour, 1970, Internat. Assn. Cultural European Concert Tour, 1973, Young Americans Nat. Choral Festival, 1985, Big Apple Choral Festival, 1986. Recipient Disting. Alumni in Arts award, East Tenn. State U., 1990; named Tchr. of Yr., Escambia County, Fla., 1971, Okaloosa County, Fla., 1986. Mem.: Fla. Vocal Assn. (chmn. dist. 1967—69, pres. 1970—73), Am. Choral Dirs. Assn. (state pres. 1975—77, pres. divsn. 1979—81, bd. dirs., dir. various convs., musician various concerts, Wayne Hugoboom Disting. Svc. award 1989, So. Divsn. Excellence in Choral Art award 2000). Avocation: travel. Home: 431 Gregory Ave Valparaiso FL 32580 Personal E-mail: phe@valp.net.

MERRITT, SUSAN MARY, computer science educator, dean; b. New London, Conn., July 28, 1946; d. Nelson Alfred and Mary (Cory) M. BA summa cum laude, Cath. U. Am., 1968; MS, NYU, 1969, PhD, 1982; Cert., Inst. for Edn. Mgmt., Harvard U., 1985. Joined Sisters of Divine Compassion, 1975; permanent cert. tchr., N.Y. Systems programmer Digital Equipment Corp., Maynard, Mass., 1969-70; tchr. Good Counsel Acad. High Sch., White Plains, N.Y., 1970-75; adj. instr. computer sci. Pace U., 1972-78, asst. prof. White Plains, 1978-82, assoc. prof., 1982-85, prof., 1985—, chmn. dept., 1981-83, dean Sch. Computer Sci., 1983—2008. Spkr. in field, mem. gen. coun. Sisters Divine Compassion, 1988-92. Contbr. articles to profl. jours. Recipient Carol S. Russett Award for Disting. Svcs., ACE Nat. Women's Leadership Network, Recipient Cert. of Appreciation, IEEE, 1990, endowment, Ivan G. Seidenberg Sh. Computer Sci. and Info. Sys., 2005. Mem. Assn. for Computing Machinery (edn. bd. 1988—), Phi Beta Kappa, Sigma Xi(pres., 2008-) Roman Catholic.

MERRITT, THOMAS BUTLER, lawyer; b. Toledo, Apr. 3, 1939; s. George Robert and Bernice (Gerwin) M.; m. Mary Jane Bothfeld, July 23, 1966; children— Thomas Butler, Haidee Soule, Theodore Bothfeld AB magna cum laude, Harvard U., 1961, LLB cum laude, 1966. Bar: Mass. 1966, NH 1994, Vt. 2006, Maine 2007, US Ct. Appeals (1st cir.) 1999, US Supreme Ct. 1974. With N.Y. State Dept. Civil Svc., Albany, 1961—63; intern Office of Legal Advisr U.S. Dept. State, Washington, 1965; law clk. to assoc. justice Arthur E. Whittemore Supreme Jud. Ct. Mass., Boston, 1966-67; assoc. Nutter, McClennen & Fish, Boston, 1967-69, Palmer & Dodge, Boston, 1969-73; asst. counsel to Gov. Mass., 1973; reporter of decisions Supreme Jud. Ct. Mass., Boston, 1974-94; pvt. practice NH, 1994—. Contbr. articles to profl. jours. Mem. Conservation Commn. Town of Sherborn, Mass., 1969-74, chmn., 1972-74; planning bd. Town of Hollis, NH, 1995-98; mem. NH Bd. Natural Scientists, 2005—. 1st lt. US Army, 1962—63, capt. USAR, 1963—69. Mem.: Assn. Reporters Jud. Decisions (pres. 1983—84), NH Bar Assn. (sec. sec. mil. law), Mass. Bar Assn., Am. Law Inst. (life), Harvard Faculty Club (Cambridge), Harvard Club Boston. Episcopalian. Office: PO Box 324 Littleton NH 03561-0324 Home Phone: 603-444-5354.

MERRIWEATHER, FREDA E., education educator; d. Oscar and Eura Merriweather; m. William M. Norvell, III, Apr. 30, 1961 (div.); children: Stacy LePrix Norvell, Tracy Norvell Dukes. BS, So. Ill. U., 1964; MS, U. Wis., Milwaukee, 1971; EdD, U. Louisville, 1992. Cert. tchr. So. Ill. U., 1964, Principal U. Wis., 1972, Superintendent State of Ky., 1991. Tchr. Siefert Elem. Sch., Milw., 1964—73; prin. Md. Ave. Sch., Milw., 1974—76, James Whit Comb Riley, Milw., 1977—80, Price Elem. Sch. - JCPS, Louisville, 1984—87; vice-prin. William McKinley Intermediate Sch., Milw., 1976—80; edn. cons. Ingham Internat. Sch. Dist., Holt, Mich., 1982—84; dir. Jefferson County Pub. Sch., Louisville, 1987—91, exec. dir., 1991—93, asst. supt., 1993—2002, 1993—2002; practitioner in residence U. Louisville, Louisville, 2002—. Mem. Gov.'s Literacy Task Force, Frankfort, Ky.; alumni bd. U. Louisville, 1993—95; alumni Supt. Prepared-McKenzie Group, Washington, 1995. Mem. Jr. Achieve., Louisville, Urban League, Louisville. Recipient Adminstrv. Leadership award, Collaborative for Tchg. and Learning, 2001, award, Sarah Scott Leadership, 1978, Valedictorian, H.S. Class, Alumni Fellow, Coll. of Edn., U. Louisville, 1999, Bingham Fellows, 1993, Grad. Sch. Dean's Citation, 1991, Ky. Edn. Leadership Inst., 1990, Outstanding Prin., Nat. Schools of Excellence, 1987; grantee, Leadership Louisville, 1992, Bd. of Alderman, 1992; Doctoral Program scholarship, Scottish Rites Found. Mem.: NAACP, Greater Louisville Alliance of Black Sch. Educators, Nat. Alliance of Black Sch. Educators, Urban League (dir.), Louisville Chpt. of Moles (parliamentation), Delta Sigma Theta Sorority. Avocations: dancing, card games, reading. Personal E-mail: femerr01@aol.com.

MERSEL, MARJORIE KATHRYN PEDERSEN, lawyer; b. Manila, Utah, June 17, 1923; d. Leo Henry and Kathryn Anna (Reed) Pedersen; m. Jules Mersel, Apr. 12, 1950; 1 child, Jonathan. AB, U. Calif., 1948; LLB, U. San Francisco, 1948. Bar: DC 1952, Calif. 1955. Pvt. practice, Beverly Hills, Calif., 1961—71, LA, 1997—; staff counsel Dept. Real Estate State of Calif., LA, 1971—97. Pub. counsel, 2000—02. Mem.: ABA, Current Affairs Forum, World Affairs Coun., So. Calif. Women Lawyers Assn. (treas. 1962—63), Trial Lawyers Assn., LA County Bar Assn., Beverly Hills Bar Assn., Beverly Hills C. of C., LA-Guanghou Sister City Assn., Sierra Club, LA Athletic Club. Home and Office: 13007 Hartsook St Sherman Oaks CA 91423-1616

MERSEREAU, JOHN, JR., literature and language professor; b. San Jose, Calif., Apr. 16, 1925; s. John Joshua and Winona Beth (Roberts) M.; m. Nanine Landell, July 11, 1953; children: Daryl Landell, John Coates. AB, U. Calif., 1945, MA, 1950, PhD, 1957. Teaching fellow, Slavic dept. U. Calif., Berkeley, 1950-52, research asst., 1953-54; instr. Slavic dept. U. Mich., Ann Arbor, 1956-59, asst. prof., 1959-61, assoc. prof., 1961-63, prof., 1963—, chmn. dept., 1961-71, 85-89, prof. emeritus, 1990—, dir. Residential Coll., 1977-85. Mem. Joint Com. Eastern Europe of Am. Council Learned Socs./Social Sci. Research Council, 1971-74, chmn., 1973-74. Author: Mikhail Lermontov, 1962, Baron Delvig's Literary Almanac: Northern Flowers, 1967, Translating Russian, 1968, Russian Romantic Fiction, 1983, Orest Somov, 1989, How to Grill a Gourmet, 2000, Overdue at Immokalee, A Tale of Preemptive Assassination, 2003, The Russian Novel of Psychological Realism, 2005; assoc. editor Mich. Slavic Publs., 1962—; contbr. articles to profl. jours. Served to lt. (j.g.) USNR, 1943-46, PTO. Calmerton Slavic scholar U. Calif., Berkeley, 1954-55; Ford Found. fellow, London and Paris, 1955-56, Guggenheim fellow, 1972-73; recipient Disting. Service award U. Mich., Ann Arbor, 1961. Mem. Am. Assn. Advancement Slavic Studies, U. Mich. Research Club. Clubs: Waterloo Hunt (Grass Lake, Mich., sec. 1970-80); Commanderie de Bordeaux (Detroit). Avocations: flying, gourmet cuisine, raising horses. Office: U of Mich Slavic Dept Ann Arbor MI 48109 Business E-Mail: mersera@aol.com.

MERSFELDER, TRACEY, pharmacist, educator; PharmD, U. Cin., 1997. Cert. Bd. Pharm. Spltys., 1999. Contbr. articles to profl. jours. Faculty Mentor scholar, Am. Assn. Coll. Pharmacy, 2005. Mem.: Am. Coll. Clin. Pharmacy.

MERSINI - HOUGHTON, LAURA, physicist, educator; d. Nexhat and Stela Mersini; m. Jeffrey Houghton, Feb. 2, 2003. MSc in Physics, U. Md., 1997; PhD, U. Wis., Milw., 2000. Cert. theoretical physics U. Wis., Milw. Physics Dept., 2000. Rsch. fellow Scuola Normale Superiore, Pisa, Italy, 2000—02; postdoctoral fellow Syracuse U., Physics Dept., NY, 2002—03; vis. prof. Perimeter Inst. Theoretical Physics, Waterloo, Ontario, Canada, 2003—04; asst. prof. physics U. NC, Chapel Hill, 2004—. Contbr. articles to profl. jours. Fellow, Fulbright Found., 1994. Achievements include research in addressing fundamental problems of cosmology and modern physics by means of a new field and direction, string cosmology. Connecting and testing models and the new field to astrophysical observables. Office: U NC Dept Physics and Astronomy Phillips Hall UNC-Chapel Hill Chapel Hill NC 27599 Office Fax: 919-962-0480. Business E-Mail: mersini@physics.unc.edu.

MERSKI, RICHARD P., insurance company executive; B in Polit. Sci. and Economics, Georgetown U.; M in Polit. Sci., Columbia U.; JD, U. Va. Bar: DC, Commonwealth of Va., DC Ct. Appeals, US Ct. Appeals, DC Cir., US Dist. Ct., DC, US Ct. Internat. Trade. Atty. Collier, Shannon, Rill & Scott; legis. dir., counsel Congressman Richard T. Schulze; joined Am. Internat. Group, Inc. (AIG), 1985, v.p. corp. affairs, counsel; sr. v.p., head fed. affairs Zurich Fin. Svcs. Group, Washington, 2009—. Mem. World Affairs Coun., Washington, vice chmn. bd. dirs. Office: Zurich Fin Svcs Group 1201 F St Nw Ste 250 Washington DC 20004*

MERSON, MICHAEL HOWARD, public health physician, epidemiologist, educator; b. NYC, June 7, 1945; s. Leo and Paula Enid (Katz) M.; 1 child: Jonathan. BA, Amherst Coll., 1966; MD, SUNY, Bklyn., 1970. Commd. officer USPHS, 1972, advanced through grades to capt.; chief enteric disease br. Ctrs. for Disease Control, Atlanta, 1974-75; chief epidemiologist Cholera Rsch. Lab., Dacca, Bangladesh, 1977-78; dir. diarrheal diseases control program WHO, Geneva, 1978-90, dir. global program on AIDS, 1990-95; prof., dean pub. health Sch. Medicine Yale U., New Haven, 1995—2004, Anna M.R. Lauder prof. pub. health; prof., dir. Duke U. Global Health Inst., 2006—. Trustee, bd. dirs. Internat. Ctr. for Diarrheal Diseases, Dacca, 1985-90. Recipient Arthur Fleming award U.S. Jaycees, 1975. Mem. Royal Soc. Tropical Medicine and Hygiene, Internat. Epidemiol. Assn., Am. Soc. for Epidemiology, Soc. Scholars. Office: Duke U Box 90519 Global Health Inst Durham NC 27708 Office Phone: 919-681-7760. E-mail: michael.merson@duke.edu.

MERSON, SUSAN ILENE, actor, writer, producer; d. Louis Merson and Shirley Rebecca Lubin; m. Tony Shultz (dec.); 1 child, Sofia Angelique Shultz. MFA, Goddard Coll., Plainfield, Vt., 2003. Actor: (Broadway plays) Vanities and Many New Plays (named Best Actress, 1991); author: (novel) Dreaming in Daylight; playwright (numerous plays) Bounty of Lace; author: (nonfiction book) Your Name Here: An Actor/Writers Guide to Solo Performance. Ny bd. Ensemble Studio Theatre, NYC, 2006—08. Recipient ATHE Religion and Theatre award, 2008. Mem.: Dramatists Guild, Actors Equity Assn., AFTRA, SAG. Avocations: yoga, crafts.

MERSZEI, GEOFFREY E., corporate financial executive; BA, Albion Coll. With Dow Chem. Co., Midland, Mich., 1977—2001, treas. Germany Frankfurt, 1983—85, treas. Ea. Europe, 1985—86, fgn. exch. mgr. Midland, Mich., 1986—88, dir. fin. Asia Pacific Hong Kong, 1988—91, dir. fin. Europe Horgen, Switzerland, 1991—96, v.p., treas. Midland, Mich., 1996—2001; exec. v.p., CFO Alcan, Inc., 2001—05, Dow Chem. Co., Midland, Mich., 2005—, bd. dirs., mem. Office of the Chief Exec., 2005—. Bd. dir. Dow Corning Corpn.; mem. Conf. Bd. Com. Coun. Fin. Execs.; mem. corp. exec. bd. working coun. for CFOs. Office: Dow Chem Co 2030 Dow Ctr Midland MI 48674*

MERTA DE VELEHRAD, JAN, safety engineer, psychologist; b. Stare Mesto, Czech Republic, Apr. 24, 1944; arrived in Can., 1968; s. Jan and Marie (Sebkova) M.; m. Margaret; 1 child, Iveta. Diploma, Ucnovská Skola Technická, Slusovice, 1962, Coll. Social Law, Prague, 1968; BS, McGill U., Montreal, Can., 1971; PhD in Psychology, U. Aberdeen, Scotland, 1978. Pres. pub. Jan's Pub. Co., Montreal, 1972-74; deep sea diver, diving supr. North Sea, Mid. East, Africa, 1974-78; dir. R & D Wharton-Williams Ltd., Aberdeen, 1978-79, Oceaneering, Inc., Houston, 1979-81; chief insp. diving Govt. of Can., 1981—2005, insp. officer, health and safety officer. Co-author: Exploring The Human Aura, 1976, Canadian Oil and Gas Diving Regulations, 1989, 99. Chmn. com. for survival suits Can. Gen. Stds. Bd., 1983-96; br. chmn. Czech Assn. of Can., 1986-91; hon. appt. bd. Seneca Coll. Ont., 1983; chmn. com. for diving competency Can. Stds. Assn., 1994-2000; chmn. Z-275 tech. com. Can. Stds. Assn., 2000—. Recipient Spl. Industry award Can. Assn. Diving Contrators, 1985, award for svc. to sub-sea industry, 1988, Internat. Cultural Diploma of Honour, 1989, Commemorative Medal of Honour, 1988, Silver Shield of Valor, 1992, Alta. Centennial medal, 2005; named Pursuivant, Spanish Coll. Arms, 1990, to Internat. Leadership Hall of Fame, 1988, Internat. Hall of Leaders, 1988; named Man of Yr., U.K., 1990, World Intellectual, 1993, One in a Million, U.K., 1992, hon. citizen Town of Modra, Czech Republic, 2001. Fellow Inst. Diagnostic Engrs., Inst. Petroleum; mem. Soc. Fire Protection Engrs., Am. Soc. Safety Engrs., Brit. Psychol. Soc., Internat. Soc. Hyperbaric Medicine (v.p. 1990-96), Undersea Med. Soc., Soc. Petroleum Engrs., Submarine Pilot Assn., Soc. Naval Archs. and Marine Engrs., Am. Soc. Safety Engrs. Achievements include two British patents, 4 patents pending. Address: Tkida Spojencu 29 Olomouc 77200 Czech Republic

MERTE, HERMAN, JR., mechanical engineering educator; b. Detroit, Apr. 3, 1929; s. Herman and Anna Marie (Mitterer) M.; m. Bernice Marie Brant, Sept. 17, 1952; children: Kenneth Edward, James Dennis, Lawrence Carleton, Richard Brant, Robert Paul. BS in Marine Engring, U. Mich., Ann Arbor, 1950, BS in Mech. Engring, 1951, MS, 1956, PhD, 1960. Faculty U. Mich., 1959—67, prof. mech. engring. Ann Arbor, 1967—2000, prof. emeritus, 2000—. Vis. prof. Tech. U. Munich, Germany, 1974-75 Served to lt. (j.g.) USNR, 1952-55. NSF sr. postdoctoral fellow, 1967-68 Mem. ASME, AIAA, Am. Soc. Engring. Edn., Am. Assn. U. Profs., Sigma Xi. Home: 3480 Cottontail Ln Ann Arbor MI 48103-1706 Office: U Mich Heat Transfer Lab 2260 G G Brown Lab Ann Arbor MI 48109-2125 Home Phone: 734-662-6253; Office Phone: 734-647-9475. Business E-Mail: merte@umich.edu.

MERTENS, JOAN R., museum curator, art historian; b. NYC, Oct. 10, 1946; d. Otto R. and Helen H. M. BA, Radcliffe Coll., 1967; PhD, Harvard U., 1972. Curatorial asst. Met. Mus. Art, NYC, 1972-73, asst. curator, 1973-76, assoc. curator, 1976-81, curator Greek and Roman dept., 1981—, curator, adminstr., 1983-90, mem. editorial bd. Mus. Jour., 1976—. Lectr. NYU, Inst. Fine Arts, 1992—. Author: Attic White-Ground*Its Development, 1977, Greek Bronzes in the Metropolitan Museum of Art, 1985; author: (with others) Ancient Art from Cyprus: The Cesnola Collection in the Metropolitan Museum of Art., 2000, The Cesnola Collection: Terracottas, 2004, The Art of the Classical World in the Metropolitan Museum of Art, 2007. Mem. Archaeol. Inst. Am., German Archael. Inst. (corr. mem.) Home: 124 E 84th St New York NY 10028-0915 Office: Met Mus Art Fifth Ave at 82nd St New York NY 10028

MERTENS, THOMAS ROBERT, biology professor; b. Fort Wayne, Ind., May 22, 1930; s. Herbert F. and Hulda (Burg) M.; m. Beatrice Janet Abair, Apr. 1, 1953; children: Julia Ann, David Gerhard BS, Ball State U., 1952; MS, Purdue U., 1954, PhD, 1956. Research assoc. dept. genetics U. Wis.-Madison, 1956-57; asst. prof. biology Ball State U., Muncie, Ind., 1957-62, assoc. prof., 1962-66, prof., 1966-93, dir. doctoral programs in biology, 1974-93, George and Frances Ball disting. prof. biology edn., 1988-93, prof. emeritus, 1993—. Author: (with A. M. Winchester) Human Genetics, 1983 (with R.L. Hammersmith) Genetics Laboratory Investigations, 13th edit., 2006 (co-recipient William Holmes McGuffey Longevity award Text and Acad. Authors Assn. 1998); contbr. numerous articles to profl. jours. Co-recipient Gustav Ohaus award for innovative coll. sci. tchg. NSTA, 1986, recipient Disting. Svc. to Sci. Edn. citation, 1987; fellow NSF, 1963-64, Ind. Acad. Scis., 1969. Fellow AAAS; mem. Nat. Assn. Biology Tchrs. (pres. 1985, hon. mem. 1988), Am. Genetic Assn., Genetics Soc. Am. Episcopalian. Home: 4501 N Wheeling 9B-4 Muncie IN 47304-1277 Office: Ball State U Dept Biology Muncie IN 47306-0001 Office Phone: 765-285-8820. Personal E-mail: t.mertens@att.net.

MERTINS, DETLEF, architect, educator; BArch, U. Toronto, 1980; PhD in Architecture, Princeton U., 1996. Instr. U. Toronto, 1991—2003, Can. Rsch. chair in architecture, 2001—03; prof., chair dept. architecture U. Pa. Sch. Design, 2003—. Vis. prof. Columbia U., Harvard U., Princeton U., Rice U. Author: The Presence of Mies, 1994, The Victory of Building a Style, 2000, others. Recipient Konrad Adenauer Rsch. prize, Alexander von Humboldt Found. and Royal Can. Soc., 2003; vis. scholar fellow, Can. Ctr. for Architecture, 1998. Office: Univ Pa 207 Meyerson Hall Philadelphia PA 19104-6311

MERTINS, JAMES WALTER, entomologist; b. Milw., Feb. 18, 1943; s. Walter Edwin and Harriet Ellen (Sockett) M.; m. Marilee Eloise Joeckel, Dec. 8, 1979. BS in Zoology, U. Wis., Milw., 1965; MS in Entomology, U. Wis., 1967, PhD in Entomology, 1971. Project assoc. dept. entomology U. Wis., Madison, 1971-75, rsch. assoc. dept. entomology, 1975-77; asst. prof. dept. entomology Iowa State U., Ames, 1977-84; entomol. cons. Ames, 1984-89; entomologist Nat. Vet. Svcs. Labs. USDA Animal and Plant Health Inspection Svc., Ames, 1989—. Co-author: (textbook) Biological Insect Pest Suppression, 1977, Russian edit., 1980, Chinese edit., 1988; contbr. articles to profl. jours. NSF Grad. fellow, 1970. Mem. Entomol. Soc. Am. (Insect Photography award 1984, 86, 2003), Entomol. Soc. Can., Mich. Entomol. Soc., Wis. Entomol. Soc. (pres., sec., treas., bd. dirs.), Cyclone Corvettes, Inc. (co-founder, pres. 1978, 79, sec., treas., bd. dirs., Mem. of Yr. 1982), Am. Mensa. Avocations: insect photography, Corvette automobile activities, gardening, movies, insect collecting. Office: USDA Animal and Plant Health Inspection Svc PO Box 844 Ames IA 50010-0844 Business E-Mail: James.W.Mertins@aphis.usda.gov.

MERTON, ROBERT C., economist, educator; b. NYC, July 31, 1944; s. Robert K. and Suzanne (Carhart) M., 3 c. BS in Engring. Math., Columbia U., 1966; MS in Applied Math., Calif. Inst. Tech., 1967; PhD in Econs., MIT, 1970; MA (hon.), Harvard U., 1989; LLD (hon.), U. Chgo., 1991; Prof. honoris causa degree, HEC Sch. Mgmt., Paris, 1995; D Econ. Sci. (hon.), U. Lausanne, Switzerland, 1996; Dr honoris causa, U. Paris Dauphine, 1997, Universidad Nacional Mayor de San Marcos, Lima, Peru, 2004; D of Mgmt. Sci. (hon.), Nat. Sun Yat-sen U., Kaoshiung, Taiwan, 1998; DS (hon.), Athens U. Econs. and Bus., 2003; DPhil (hon.), U. Nacional Federico Villarreal, Lima, Peru, 2004. Instr. econs. MIT, Cambridge, 1969-70; asst. prof. fin. Alfred P. Sloan Sch. Mgmt., 1970-73, assoc. prof., 1973-74, prof., 1974-80, J.C. Penney prof. mgmt., 1980-88; vis. prof. fin. Harvard U., Boston, 1987-88, George Fisher Baker prof. bus. adminstrn., 1988-98, John and Natty McArthur University prof., 1998—. Rsch. assoc. Nat. Bur. Econ. Rsch., 1979—; mem. internat. bd. sci. advisors Tinbergen Inst.; co-founder Long-Term Capital Mgmt., L.P., Greenwich, Conn., 1993—99; mem. governing bd. AlphaSimplex Group, 2001—; acad. adv. bd. Real Option Group, 1999—; bd. dirs. Vical Inc., MF Risk, Inc., Dimensional Funds, Cmty. First Fin. Group, Peninsula Banking Group; co-founder, chief sci. officer, mem. bd. dirs. Integrated Fin. Ltd., 2002—; mem. competitive markets adv. coun. Chgo. Merc. Exch., 2004—. Author: Continuous-Time Finance, 1990, rev. edit., 1992; co-author: Casebook in Financial Engineering: Applied Studies of Financial Innovation, 1995, The Global Financial System: A Functional Perspective, 1995, Finance, 2000, Transparency, Risk Management and International Financial Fragility, 2003; editor: The Collected Scientific Papers of Paul A. Samuelson, vol. III, 1972; mem. editl. bd. Internat. Econ. Rev., 1972-77, Jour. Fin., 1973-77, Jour. Money, Credit and Banking, 1974-79, Jour. Fin. Econs., 1974-83, Jour. Banking and Fin., 1977-79, 92-2003, Fin. India, 1988—, Geneva Papers on Risk and Ins., 1989-96, Jour. Fixed Income, 1991—, Fin. Rev., 1992-97, Jour. Fin. Edn., 1995—, European Fin. Rev. (now Rev. Fin.), 1997-2004; mem. adv. bd. The New Palgrave Dictionary of Money and Finance, Math. Fin., Rev. Derivatives Rsch., Nihon Finance Gakkai, The Brookings-Wharton Papers on Financial Policy, Internat. Jour. Theoretical and Applied Finance, Jour. Investment Mgmt., North Holland Series of Handbooks in Finance, Jour. Banking and Fin., 2003—, Annals of Fin., 2004—, Jour. Fin. Lit., 2004—; mem. adv. coun. Fin. Analyst Jour., 2003—; contbr. articles to profl. jours. Mem. hon. bd. Internat. Raoul Wallenberg Found., 2003—, Angelo Roncalli Internat. Com., 2003—. Recipient Leo Melamed prize U. Chgo. Sch. Bus., 1983, Roger Murray prize Inst. for Quantitative Rsch. in Fin., 1985, 86, Disting. Scholar award Ea. Fin. Assn., 1989, Internat. INA-Nat. Acad. Lincei prize Nat. Acad. Lincei, Rome, 1993, FORCE award for fin. innovation Fuqua Sch. Bus., Duke U., 1993, Fin. Engr. of Yr. award Internat. Assn. Fin. Engrs., 1993, Alfred Nobel Meml. Prize in Econ. Scis., 1997, Heroes Among Us award Boston Celtics, 1997, Michael Pupin medal Columbia U., 1998, Disting. Alumni award Calif. Inst. of Tech., 1999, MFD Lifetime Achievement award Boston U., 1999, Lifetime Achievement award Risk Mag., 2003, Nicholas Molodovsky award Assn. Investment Mgmt. Rsch., 2003, Graham and Dodd award Fin. Analysts Jour., 2003; inducted Derivatives Hall of Fame, 1998, named Risk Hall of Fame, Risk Mag., 2002. Fellow Internat. Assn. Fin. Engrs. (sr.), Econometric Soc., Am. Acad. Arts and Scis., Inst. Quantitative Rsch., Fin. Mgmt. Assn., Am. Fin. Assn. (dir. 1982-84, pres. 1986, fellow 2000—); mem. NAS, Bachelier Fin. Soc., Soc. for Fin. Studies (v.p. 1993), Hon. Order Ky. Cols., Tau Beta Pi, Sigma Xi. Office: Harvard U Grad Sch Bus Adminstrn Baker Libr 353 Soldiers Field Rd Boston MA 02163 Home Phone: 617-374-9511. Business E-Mail: rmerton@hbs.edu.*

MERTZ, FRANCIS JAMES, university president; b. Newark, Sept. 24, 1937; s. Frank E. and Marian E. (Brady) M.; m. Gail Williams, Apr. 11, 1964; children: Lynn, Christopher, Suzanne, David, Amy, Jonathan. BA, St. Peter's Coll., 1958; JD, NYU, 1961; LLD (hon.), Felician Coll., 1984, Stevens Inst. Tech., Hoboken, NJ, 1988, Fairleigh Dickinson U., 1999, Kunghnam Univ., 1999, Coll. St. Elizabeth, 2002. Bar: N.J. 1967. Exec. v.p. St. Peter's Coll., Jersey City, 1972-78; v.p., CFO N.Y. Med. Coll., Valhalla, 1978-79; dir. adminstrn. Sage Gray Todd and Sims, NYC, 1979-81; pres. Ind. Coll. Fund N.J., Summit, 1981-90, Assn. Ind. Colls. and Univs. N.J., Summit, 1982-90, Fairleigh Dickinson U., Teaneck, NJ, 1990-99, pres. emeritus. Bd. dirs., chmn. St. Joseph's Home for the Blind, 1998—2008; mem. bd. trustees Coll. St. elizabeth, 2007-; mem. bd. regents Seton Hall U., 2002-04; chair N.J. Commn. on Higher Edn., 2004-06, N.J. Higher Edn. Student Assistance Authority, 2004-06, N.J. Ednl. Facilities Authority, 2004-06. Home: 54 Woodcrest Dr Morristown NJ 07960-4541 Home Phone: 973-984-6455; Office Phone: 973-267-1506. Business E-Mail: mertz@fdu.edu.

MERTZ, JANET ELAINE, molecular biology researcher, educator, consultant; b. NYC, Aug. 9, 1949; d. Harry and Pauline (Schwartz) M.; m. Jonathan Michael Kane, Mar. 16, 1980; children: Daniel Morris Mertz Kane, Jeremy Solomon Mertz Kane. BS in Life Scis. and Elec. Engring., MIT, 1970; PhD in Biochemistry, Stanford U., Calif., 1975. Teaching asst. dept. biochemistry Stanford U., 1970-73; postdoctoral fellow Med. Rsch. Coun. Lab. Molecular Biology, Cambridge, Eng., 1975-76; asst. prof. oncology McArdle Lab. for Cancer Rsch. U. Wis., Madison, 1976-83, assoc. prof. oncology, 1983-92; prof. oncology McArdle Lab. for Cancer Rsch. U. Wis., Madison, 1992—. Ad hoc mem. study sects. NIH, Bethesda, Md., 1981—; panel mem. NSF, 1993-97; cons. Agrigenetics Corp., Madison, Wis., 1983-84. Mem. editorial bd. Molecular and Cellular Biology Jour., 1985-90, Virology Jour., 1988—, Jour. Virology, 1999—; contbr. numerous articles to profl. jours. Recipient Kallman award Stanford U., 1973; Jane Coffin Childs Meml. Fund fellow, 1975-76; numerous rsch. grants. Mem. AAAS, Am. Assn. for Cancer Rsch., Am. Soc. for Biochemistry and Molecular Biology, Am. Soc. for Microbiology, Am. Soc. for Virology, Assn. for Women in Sci. Office: U Wis McArdle Lab 1400 University Ave Madison WI 53706-1599 E-mail: mertz@oncology.wisc.edu.

MERTZ, PAUL ERIC, retired history professor, writer; b. Bartlesville, Okla., Feb. 27, 1943; s. Floyd E. and Mary O. Mertz; m. Lyndall Ruth Kauffman, Jan. 28, 1966; children: Mary Kathryn Mertz Carney, Paul Eric Jr. BA, Phillips U., Enid, Okla., 1965; MA, U. Okla., Norman, 1967, PhD, 1971. Instr. history U. Wis., Stevens Point, 1969—72, asst. prof., 1972—77, assoc. prof., 1977—82, prof. history, 1982—2006; prof. emeritus, 2006—. Chair dept. history U. Wis., Steven Point, 1992—98. Author: New Deal Policy and Southern Rural Poverty, 1978. Chair Dem. Party, Portage County, Wis., 1999; elder Frame Meml. Presbyn. Ch., 1972—. Woodrow Wilson Nat. fellow, 1965—66. Mem.: Wis. State Hist. Soc., So. Hist. Assn., Orgn. Am. Historians. Democrat. Presbyterian. Avocation: leading bicycle tours in Europe. Office: Dept History U Wis Stevens Point WI 54481

MERWADE, VENKATESH M., hydrologist; PhD, U. of Tex. at Austin, 2004. Project engr. Montgomery Watson Harza, Mumbai, India, 1997—99; post-doctoral fellow Ctr. for Rsch. in Water Resources, Austin, Tex., 2004—. E-mail: vmmerwade@mail.utexas.edu.

MERWIN, DAVIS UNDERWOOD, newspaper executive; b. Chgo., June 22, 1928; s. Davis and Josephine (Underwood) M.; m. Nancy Snowden Smith Tailer, Nov. 14, 1958 (dec. Feb. 1995); children: Davis Fell, Laura Howell; m. Sharon Adkins Todd, May 12, 1998. AB, Harvard U., 1950; LLD (hon.), Ill. Wesleyan U., 1991. Pres. Evergreen Comm., Inc., Bloomington, Ill., 1969-80; pub. Daily Pantagraph, 1968-80; pres. Wood Canyon Corp., Tucson, 1989-93; vice-chmn. Bloomington Broadcasting Corp., 1993-99. Dir. State Farm Growth, Balanced Mcpl. Bond and Interim Funds, State Farm Variable Products Funds. Trustee emeritus Ill. Wesleyan U.; trustee Ill. Nature Conservancy. Recipient Disting. Svc. award U.S. Jaycees, 1959 Mem. Am. Newspaper Pubs. Assn., Inland Daily Press Assn. (pres. 1977, chmn. bd. dirs. 1978), Harvard Club (Chgo.), Phoenix-SK Club, Hasty Pudding Club, Bloomington Country Club, Ristigouche Salmon Club. Republican. Unitarian Universalist. Office: 2422 E Washington St Bloomington IL 61704-4478 Mailing: PO Box 1665 Bloomington IL 61702-1665 E-mail: DUMerwin@aol.com.

MERWIN, JOHN DAVID, lawyer, former Governor of the Virgin Islands; b. Frederiksted, St. Croix, VI, Sept. 26, 1921; s. Miles and Marguerite Louise (Fleming) M.; m. Marjorie Davis Spaulding, Feb. 18, 1993. Student, U. Lausanne, Switzerland, 1938-39, U. P.R., 1939-40; BSc, Yale U., 1943; JD, George Washington U., 1948. Bar: Conn., VI 1949, US Supreme Ct. Practice law, St. Croix, VI, 1949-50, 1953-57, 67-85; gen. counsel, v.p. Rob't L. Merwin & Co., Inc., 1953-57; senator-at-large VI Legislature, 1955-57; govt. sec. for VI, 1957-58; gov. VI, 1958-61; rep. Chase Manhattan Bank, Nassau, Bahamas, 1961-65; exec. v.p. Equity Pub. Corp. Orford, NH, 1965-67; ret. Chmn. VI Port Authority, 1972-75; Rep. candidate for Pres. NH Primary Election, 1992; pres. The Nason Found., Cleve., 1981-2002. Capt. F.A. AUS, 1942-46, 50-53. Decorated Bronze Star; Croix de Guerre with silver star. Mem. Tennis Club St. Croix (VI), Yale Club (NYC), Cosmos Club (Washington), Country Club of Hudson, Phi Delta Phi. Episcopalian. Home and Office: PO Box 1029 Hudson OH 44236 E-mail: jdmerwin@hotmail.com.

MERWIN, WILLIAM STANLEY, poet; b. NYC, Sept. 30, 1927; AB, Princeton U., NJ, 1948. Translator, London, 1951-54; playwright-in-residence Poet's Theatre, Cambridge, Mass., 1956—57; poetry editor The Nation, 1962. Author: (poetry collections) A Mask for Janus, 1952 (Yale Younger Poets prize, 1952), The Dancing Bears, 1954, Green with Beasts, 1956, The Drunk in the Furnace, 1960, The Moving Target, 1963 (Nat. Book award for poetry, 1963), The Lice, 1967, The Carrier of Ladders, 1970 (Pulitzer prize for poetry, 1971), Writings to an Unfinished Accompaniment, 1973, The First Four Books of Poems, 1975, The Compass Flower, 1977, Finding the Islands, 1982, Opening the Hand, 1983, Selected Poems, 1988, The Second Four Books of Poems, 1993, Travels, 1993, The Vixen, 1996, Flower & Hand, 1997, The Folding Cliffs: A Narrative, 1998, The River Sound, 1999, The Pupil, 2001, Lament for the Makers, 2002, Migration: New & Selected Poems, 2005 (Nat. Book award for poetry, 2006), Present Company, 2005, The Shadow of Sirius, 2008 (Pulitzer prize for poetry, 2009), (prose) The Miner's Pale Children, 1970, Houses and Travellers, 1977, Unframed Originals: Recollections, 1982, Regions of Memory, 1987, The Lost Uplands: Stories of Southwest France, 1992, The Mays of Ventadorn, 2002, The Ends of the Earth, 2004, The Book of Fables, 2007, (memoir) Summer Doorways, 2005; translator (Spanish, French, Italian, Latin poetry): The Poem of the Cid, 1959, The Satires of Persius, 1960, Spanish Ballads, 1961, Lazarillo de Tormes, 1962, The Song of Roland, 1963, Selected Translations, 1948 - 1968, 1968 (PEN/Book-of-the-Month Club Translation prize, 1969), Twenty Love Poems and a Song of Despair, Poems by Pablo Neruda, 1969, Products of the Perfected Civilization, Selected Writings of Chamfort, 1969, Voices, Poems of Antonio Porchia, 1969, Transparence of the World, Poems by Jean Follain, 1969, Asian Figures, 1973, Osip Mandelstam: Selected Poems, 1974, Euripedes' Iphigeneia at Aulis, 1978, Selected Translations, 1968-1978, 1979, Four French Plays, 1985, From the Spanish Morning, 1985, Vertical Poetry, Poems by Roberto Juarroz, 1988, Sun at Midnight, Poems by Muso Soseki, 1989, Pieces of Shadow: Selected Poems of

Jaime Sabines, 1996, East Window: The Asian Translations, 1998, Purgatorio from The Divine Comedy of Dante, 2000, Sir Gawain and the Green Knight, 2005. Recipient Bess Hokin prize, 1962, Harriet Monroe Meml. prize, 1967, Shelley Meml. award, 1974, Bollingen prize for poetry, 1979, Tanning prize, Acad. Am. Poets, 1994, Lannan Lit. award for lifetime achievement, 2004; grantee Nat. Inst. Arts & Letters, 1957, Britain Bursary, 1957, Rabinowitz Found., 1961, Ford Found., 1964—65; fellow Rockefeller Found., 1956, John Simon Guggenheim Meml. Found., 1973, 1983. Address: PO Box 809 Haiku HI 96708-0809 Mailing: care Copper Canyon Press Bldg 313 Ft Worden State Pk PO Box 271 Port Townsend WA 98368*

MERZ, JAMES LOGAN, electrical and materials engineering educator, researcher; b. Jersey City, Apr. 14, 1936; s. Albert Joseph and Anne Elizabeth (Farrell) M.; m. Rose-Marie Weibel, June 30, 1962; children: Kathleen, James, Michael, Kimarie. BS in Physics, U. Notre Dame, 1959; postgrad., U. Göttingen, Fed. Republic Germany, 1959-60; MA, Harvard U., 1961, PhD in Applied Physics, 1967; PhD (hon.), Linköping U., Sweden, 1993. Mem. tech. staff Bell Labs., Murray Hill, NJ, 1966-78; prof. elec. engring. U. Calif., Santa Barbara, 1978-94, prof. materials, 1986-94, chmn. dept. elec. and computer engring., 1982-84, assoc. dean for rsch. devel. Coll. Engring., 1984-86, acting assoc. vice chancellor, 1988, dir. semiconductor rsch. corp. core program on GaAs digital ICs, 1984-89, dir. Compound Semiconductor Rsch. Labs., 1986-92, dir. NSF Ctr. for Quantized Electronic Structures, 1989-94; Freimann prof. elec. engring. U. Notre Dame (Ind.), 1994—2009, v.p. for grad. studies and rsch., dean Grad. Sch., 1996-2001, interim dean engring., 2006—08, prof. emeritus, 2009—, UC Santa Barbara, 1994—. Mem. exec. com. Calif. Microelectronics Innovation and Computer Rsch. Opportunities Program, 1986-92; mem. NRC com. on Japan, NAS/NAE, 1988-90; mem. internat. adv. com. Internat. Symposium on Physics of Semiconductors and Applications, Seoul, Republic of Korea, 1990, Conf. on Superlattices and Microstructures, Xi'an, China, 1992, mem. bd. dirs. Tyndall nat. Inst. Ireland; participant, mem. coms. other profl. confs. and meetings. Contbr. over 450 articles to profl. jours.; patentee in field. Fulbright fellow, Danforth Found. fellow, Woodrow Wilson Found. fellow; Alexander von Humboldt rsch. awardee, 2002. Fellow IEEE, AAAS, Am. Phys. Soc., Materials Rsch. Soc.(IEEE Millenium medal, 2000); mem. IEEE Lasers and Electro-Optics Soc. (program com. annual mtg. 1980), IEEE Electron Device Soc. (sec. 1994, 95, 2008-), Am. Vacuum Soc. (exec. com. electronic materials and processing divsn. 1988-89), Materials Rsch. Soc. (editl. bd. jour. 1984-87), Soc. for Values in Higher Edn., Inst. Electronics, Info. and Comm. Engrs. (overseas adv. com.), Sigma Xi, Eta Kappa Nu. Achievements include research in field of optoelectronic materials and devices: semiconductors and ionic materials; optical and electrical properties of implanted ions, rapid annealing; semiconductor lasers, detectors, solar cells, other optoelectronic devices; low-dimensional quantum structures, nanostructures. Home: 1530 Marigold Way South Bend IN 46617-1016 Office: U Notre Dame Dept Elec Engring 203B Cushing Hall Notre Dame IN 46556-5637 Business E-Mail: jmerz@nd.edu.

MERZ, KENNETH M., JR., chemistry professor; b. Niagara Falls, NY, Jan. 24, 1959; s. Kenneth M. and Dorothea L. Merz; m. Deborah S. Johnston, Feb. 26, 1958; children: Charles K., Margaux R. BS, Wash. Coll., Chestertown, Md., 1981; PhD, U. Tex. Austin, 1985. Prof. chemistry Pa. State U., University Park, 1989—2005, U. Fla., Gainesville, 2005—08. Sr. dir. Pharamcopeia, Inc., Princeton, NJ, 1998—2001. Contbr. scientific papers to profl. publs. Grantee, NIH, 1989—2008, NSF, 1989—2008, ONR, 1989—95, DOE, 1997—98. Fellow: AAAS. Independent. Avocations: travel, reading, bicycling. Office: Univ Florida Dept Chemistry Gainesville FL 32611 Business E-Mail: merz@qtp.ufl.edu.

MERZBACHER, EUGEN, retired physics professor; b. Berlin, Apr. 9, 1921; came to U.S., 1947, naturalized, 1953; s. Siegfried and Lilli (Wilmersdoerffer) M.; m. Ann Townsend Reid, July 11, 1952; children: Celia, Charles, Matthew, Mary (dec.). Licentiate, U. Istanbul, 1943; AM, Harvard U., 1948, PhD, 1950; DSc (hon.), U. N.C., Chapel Hill, 1993. HS tchr., Ankara, Turkey, 1943—47; mem. Inst. Advanced Study, Princeton, NJ, 1950—51; vis. asst. prof. Duke U., Durham, NC, 1951—52; from mem. faculty to Kenan prof. physics U. N.C., Chapel Hill, 1952—91, Kenan prof. emeritus, 1991—; ret., 1991. Vis. prof. U. Wash., 1967-68, U. Edinburgh, Scotland, 1986; Arnold Bernhard vis. prof. physics Williams Coll., 1993; chair Internat. Conf. on Physics of Electronic and Atomic Collisions, 1987-89; sr. advisor APS, 1998-99. Author: Quantum Mechanics, 3d edit., 1998; also articles. NSF Sci. Faculty fellow U. Copenhagen, Denmark, 1959-60; recipient Thomas Jefferson award U. N.C., 1972; Humboldt sr. scientist award U. Frankfurt, Germany, 1976-77. Fellow AAAS, Am. Phys. Soc. (pres. 1990); mem. Am. Assn. Physics Tchrs. (Oersted medal 1992), Sigma Xi. Achievements include research on applications of quantum mechanics to study atoms and nuclei. Home: 750 Weaver Dairy Rd #119 Chapel Hill NC 27514-1439 Home Phone: 919-918-3675. Personal E-mail: merzie@mindspring.com.

MERZENICH, MICHAEL, neuroscientist, educator; m. Diane Merzenich. B in Gen. Sci., U. Portland; PhD, John Hopkins U.; tng., U. Wis. Founder Neuroscience Solutions Corp., 2003; founding CEO, dir. Scientific Learning, Oakland, Calif., 1996—; co-founder, chief scientific officer Posit Science Corp., San Francisco, 2003—; Francis A. Sooy chair of Otolaryngology, Keck Ctr. for Integrative Neurosciences U. Calif. San Francisco, 1998—2007, prof. emeritus otolaryngology, founding mem. Keck Ctr. Integrative Neuroscience. Contbr. several articles to peer-reviewed jours., including Science and Nature, chapters to books, articles to NY Times, Wall Street Jour., Time and Newsweek; editor: Cochlear Implants; guest appearances Sixty Minutes II, CBS Evening News, Good Morning America. Recipient IPSEN prize, Zülch prize, Max-Planck Inst., Thomas Alva Edison Patent award, Purkinje medal. Mem.: Inst. Medicine, NAS. Achievements include patents in field; In the late 1980's, was part of the team that developed the first models of a commercial coclear implant; developed software to help children with dyslexia and other disorders learn how to read; leading pioneer in brain plasticity. Office: Posit Science Corp 225 Bush St 7th Fl San Francisco CA 94104 also: Scientific Learning 300 Frank H Ogawa Plz Ste 600 Birds Landing CA 94512-2040 also: U Calif San Francisco Dept Otolaryngology Box 0732 513 Parnassus HSE-828 San Francisco CA 94143-0732 Office Phone: 800-514-3961, 888-665-9707, 415-476-0490. Office Fax: 415-986-2829, 510-444-3580. Business E-Mail: merz@phy.uscf.edu.*

MESCHAN, LYNN, psychology professor; d. Harrison and Dorothy Rowe; m. Bill Meschan; 1 child, Sharana. MA in Humanistic Psychology, Sonoma State U., Rohnert Pk., Calif., 1975. Cert. counseling U. Calif., Santa Barbara, 1990; tchg. & counseling credential CA State Bd. Edn., 1975. Psychology instr. Ventura Coll., Calif., 1975—; co-dir. Ctr. Holistic Living, 1980—90; prof., psychology Moorpark Coll., 1990—, mentor, 2005—. Photographer (nature photography) Photography Show Return to Your Center. Vol. Ventura County Master Chorale & Ventura Music Festival, 1985—. Avocation: travel.

MESELSON, MATTHEW STANLEY, biochemist, educator; b. Denver, May 24, 1930; s. Hymen Avram and Ann (Swedlow) M.; m. Jeanne Guillemin, 1986; children: Zoe, Amy Valor. Ph.B., U. Chgo., 1951, D.Sc. (hon.), 1975; PhD, Calif. Inst. Tech., 1957; Sc.D. (hon.), Oakland Coll., 1964, Columbia, 1971, Yale U., 1987, Princeton U., 1988. Asst. prof. chemistry Calif. Inst. Tech., 1958—59, sr. rsch. fellow chem. biology, 1959—60; assoc. prof. molecular biology Harvard U., 1964—76, Thomas Dudley Cabot prof. natural scis., 1976—. Cons. U.S. Arms Control and Disarmament Agency, 1963; adj. scientist Josephine Bay Paul Ctr. Comparative Molecular Biology and Evolution Marine Biol. Lab., Woods Hole, Mass., 2000—. Recipient Eli Lilly award microbiology and immunology, 1964, Alumni medal U. Chgo., 1971; Lehman award 1975, Presidential award 1983, N.Y. Acad. Scis., 1975; Alumni Disting. Svc. award Calif. Inst. Tech., 1975; Leo Szilard award Am. Phys. Soc., 1978; MacArthur fellow, 1984-89, Lasker-Koshland Spl. Achievement award in Med. Sci., Lasker Found., 2004, Mendal medal Genetics Soc., 2008. Fellow AAAS (Sci. Freedom and Responsibility award, 1990); mem. NAS (Molecular Biology prize 1963), Inst. Medicine, Am. Acad. Arts and Scis., Fedn. Am. Scientists (chmn. 1986-88, Pub. Svc. award 1972), Coun. Fgn. Rels., Accademia Santa Chiara, Am. Philos. Soc., Royal Society (London), Académie des Sciences (Paris), Genetics Soc. Am. (Thomas Hunt Morgan medal 1995). Office: Harvard U Fairchild Biochem Bldg 7 Divinity Ave Cambridge MA 02138-2019

MESEREAU, THOMAS ARTHUR, JR., lawyer; b. West Point, NY, 1951; m. Heidi Gold (div.). BA cum laude, Harvard U., 1973; MSc, London Sch. Econ., 1975; JD, U. Calif., 1979. Bar: Calif. 1979. Assoc. Hunton & Williams, Washington, 1979—81; dep. dist. atty. Orange County, Calif., 1981—82; exec. Getty Synthetic Fuels Inc., 1982—85; ptnr. Collins, Mesereau, Reddock & Yu, LLP (now Mesereau and Yu, LLP), LA, 1985—. Lectr. in field. Founder Mesereau-Ephriam-Villaraigosa Free Legal Clinic First African Meth. Episcopal Ch.; vol. Save Our Sons, Families to Amend Calif. Three Strikes, N-Action Family Network. Recipient Pro Bono award, State Bar Calif., Commendation, LA Bd. Supr., Sarah Allen Trailblazer award, Cert. Appreciation, LA County Supr., Compton award, Calif. Sch. Bd., Humanitarian award, Nat. Assn. Blacks in Criminal Justice; named Criminal Def. Lawyer Yr., Century City Bar Assn.; named one of The 10 Most Fascinating People of 2005, Barbara Walters Special. Mem.: Italian Am. Lawyers Assn. (former mem. bd. gov.), Calif. Atty. Criminal Justice. Achievements include leading def. atty. in Michael Jackson child molestation trial, 2005. Office: Mesereau & Yu LLP 10390 Santa Monica Blvd Ste 220 Los Angeles CA 90025 Office Phone: 213-384-0982, 310-789-1177. Office Fax: 213-380-4820, 310-861-1007. Business E-Mail: mesereau@mesereauyu.com.*

MESERVE, RICHARD ANDREW, lawyer, administrator; b. Medford, Mass., Nov. 20, 1944; s. Robert William and Gladys Meserve; m. Martha Anne Richards, Sept. 20, 1966; children: Amy, Lauren. BA, Tufts U., 1966; JD, Harvard U., 1975; PhD in Applied Physics, Stanford U., 1976. Bar: Mass. 1975, DC 1980, U.S. Supreme Ct. 1982. Law clk. Mass. Supreme Jud. Ct., Boston, 1975-76; law clk. to presiding justice U.S. Supreme Ct., Washington, 1976-77; legal counsel Pres. Sci. Adviser, Washington, 1977-81; ptnr. Covington & Burling, Washington, 1981-99, sr. of counsel, 2004—; bd. dirs. Carnegie Instn. Washington, 1992—2003, pres., 2003—; chmn. U.S. Nuc. Regulatory Commn., Washington, 1999—2003. Chmn. com. assess safety and tech. issues Dept. Energy reactors NAS, 1987—88, chmn. com. fuel economy automobiles and light trucks, 1991—92, chmn. com. declassification info. Dept. Energy's environ. programs, 1994—95; chmn. nuc. and radiation studies bd. NAS-NAE, 2004—; co-chmn. AAAS-ABA Nat. Conf. Lawyers and Scientists, 1988—94; mem. bd. overseers arts and scis. Tufts U., 1994—2002; mem. adv. bd. Sec. Energy, 1996—99; bd. dirs. Univs. Rsch. Assn., Inc., 2004—, PG&E Corp., 2006—, Luminant Holding Co., 2008—; chmn. internat. nuc. safety group IAEA, 2003—; mem. Nat. Commn. on Energy Policy, 2006—; bd. overseers Harvard U., 2007—. Recipient Gold medal, Sec. of Energy, 1999. Fellow: AAAS (bd. dirs. 2000—06, Abelson prize 2009), Am. Acad. Arts and Scis. (coun. and exec. com. 2005—), Am. Phys. Soc.; mem.: NAE, Am. Philos. Soc., Sigma Xi, Phi Beta Kappa. Democrat. Home: 708 Berry St Falls Church VA 22042-2402 Home Phone: 703-533-0775; Office Phone: 202-387-6404. Business E-Mail: rmeserve@ciw.edu.

MESERVE, WILLIAM GEORGE, lawyer; b. Medford, Mass., June 14, 1940; s. Robert William and Gladys Evangeline (Swenson) M.; m. Susan Mary Rycroft, Oct. 21, 1967; children: Daniel Scott, Susan Elizabeth, Jonathan Robert. BA, Tufts U., Medford, Mass., 1962; LLB, Harvard U., Cambridge, Mass., 1965; MSc, London Sch. Econs., 1966. Bar: Mass. 1966, US Dist. Ct. Mass. 1970, US Ct. Appeals (1st cir.) 1973. Legal asst. to commr. FTC, Washington, 1966-67; staff counsel com. commerce US Senate, Washington, 1967-69; assoc. Ropes & Gray, Boston, 1970-76, ptnr., 1976—2002, sr. counsel, 2002—06, of counsel, 2007—. Geology field asst. McMurdo Sound, Antarctica, 1959-60, Inglefield Land, Greenland, summer 1965. Trustee Tufts U., Medford, 1979—97, AFS Intercultural Programs Inc., NYC, 1979—92, 1993—96, 2006—, Boston Fulbright Com., Inc., 1999—, New Eng. Med. Ctr., Inc., Boston, 1988—97, Lifespan of Mass., Inc., 1997—2002; bd. visitors Fletcher Sch. Law and Diplomacy Tufts U., Medford, 1971—2008; bd. dirs. United South End Settlements, Boston, 1979—, Earthwatch Inst., Maynard, 1996—2007, AFS-USA, NYC, 1999—2006, Conservation Edn. and Rsch. Trust, Oxford, England, 2004—07; bd. govs. New Eng. Med. Ctr. Hosps., Boston, 1982—94, 1995—97, 2004—. Fellow Am. Coll. Trial Lawyers; mem. ABA, Boston Bar Assn., Phi Beta Kappa. Clubs: Appalachian Mountain (Boston) (rec. sec. 1977-78). Democrat. Office: Ropes & Gray 1 International Pl Fl 41 Boston MA 02110-2624 Business E-Mail: william.meserve@ropesgray.com.

MESEV, VICTOR, geographer, educator; s. Alexsandar Mesev and Mirjana Cekova; 1 child, Emily Victoria. BA, U. Leicester, Eng., 1989; MA, Ohio State U., Columbus, 1991; PhD, U. Bristol, Eng., 1995. Lectr. geography Ulster U., Coleraine, Northern Ireland, 1999—2004; prof. geography Fla. State U., Tallahassee, 2004—, chair geography, 2006—. Editor: (book) Remotely Sensed Cities, Integration of GIS and Remote Sensing. Rsch. grant, Brit. Leverhulme Trust, 1995, European Union, 2000. Office: Fla State Univ 113 Collegiate Loop Tallahassee FL 32306 Office Fax: 850-644-5913. Business E-Mail: vmesev@fsu.edu.

MESGARANI, NIMA, electrical engineer, researcher; arrived in U.S., 2002; BSc in Elec. Engring., Sharif U. Tech., Iran, 1999; MSc, U. Md., 2004. Rsch. asst. U. Md., College Park, Md., 2002—. Officer Iranian Grad. Students' Found., College Park, Md., 2004—05. Recipient Outstanding Sys. Engring. award, Inst. for Sys. Rsch., U. Md. Mem.: IEEE, U. Md. ECE Grad. Studies Assn. (v.p. acad. affairs 2005—06). Achievements include patents pending for. Office: University of Maryland 1103 AVWilliams Building College Park MD 20742 Business E-Mail: mnima@glue.umd.edu.

MESHACK, GENEVA TUCKER, retired elementary school educator; b. Marion, Ala., Aug. 31, 1939; d. Lovelace and Louise (Kynard) Tucker; m. Hugh von Meshack, Aug., 1962 (div. 1978). BS, MS, Prairie View A&M. Tchr. Temple ISD, Temple, Tex., 1965—2004; ret., 2004. Mem. PTO, Temple; music dept. Mt. Zion Bapt. Ch., Temple, Tex., pres. women ministry. Mem. NEA, Tex. State Tchr. Assn., Nat. Sci. Assn., Ebony Culture Soc., Prairie View A&M U. Alumni, Zeta Phi Beta. Democrat. Home: 1016 E Adams Ave Temple TX 76501-4621

MESHBESHER, RONALD I., lawyer; b. Mpls., May 18, 1933; s. Nathan J. and Esther J. (Balman) M.; m. Sandra F. Siegel, June 17, 1956 (div. 1978); children: Betsy F., Wendy S., Stacy J.; m. Kimberly L. Garnaas, May 23, 1988; 1 child, Jolie M. BS in Law, U. Minn., 1955, JD, 1957. Bar: Minn. 1957, U.S. Supreme Ct. 1966. Prosecuting atty. Hennepin County, Mpls., 1958-61; pres. Meshbesher and Spence Ltd., Mpls., 1961—. Lectr. numerous legal and profl. orgns.; mem. adv. com. on rules of criminal procedure Minn. Supreme Ct., 1971-91; cons. on recodification of criminal procedure code Czech Republic Ministry of Justice, 1994. Author: Trial Handbook for Minnesota Lawyers, 1992; mem. bd. editors Criminal Law Advocacy Reporter; mem. adv. bd. Bur. Nat. Affairs Criminal Practice Manual; contbr. numerous articles to profl. jours. Mem.: ABA, ATLA (bd. govs. 1968—71),Calif. Attys. for Criminal Justice, Trial Lawyers for Pub. Justice, Minn. Assn. Criminal Def. Lawyers (pres. 1991—92, Disting. Svc. award 2001), Minn. Trial Lawyers Assn.(pres 1973—74, (Lifetime Achievement award 2001), Nat. Assn. Criminal Def. Lawyers (pres. 1984—85), Am. Acad. Forensic Scis., Am. Bd. Criminal Lawyers (v.p. 1983, bd.gov.) Am. Bd. Trial Advs., Am. Coll. Trial Lawyers (Lifetime Achievement sward, Minn. chpt., 2006), Internat. Acad. Trial Lawyers, Minn. Bar Assn. Avocations: bicycling, photography, travel, flying, theater. Office: Meshbesher & Spence 1616 Park Ave Minneapolis MN 55404-1695 Office Phone: 612-339-9121. E-mail: rmeshbesher@meshbesher.com.

MESHEJIAN, WAYNE KIT, retired physics professor; b. Md. s. John and Dolly Meshejian; m. Brenda Josephine Mani; 1 child, Anna. BS in Physics and Math., Samford U., Birmingham, Ala., 1967; MS in Physics, Va. Poly. Inst., Blacksburg, 1968. Asst. prof., physics Longwood U., Farmville, Va., 1968—2008. Recipient Faculty Recognition award, Longwood U., 2007. Business E-Mail: meshejianwk@longwood.edu.

MESHEL, HARRY, former state senator, political party official; b. Youngstown, Ohio, June 13, 1924; s. Angelo and Rubeni (Markakis) Michelakis; children: Barry, Melanie. BSBA, Youngstown Coll., 1949; MS, Columbia U., 1950; LLD (hon.), Ohio U., Youngstown State U., Ohio Coll. Podiatric Medicine; LHD (hon.), Youngstown State U. Exec. asst. to mayor City of Youngstown, Ohio, 1964-68, urban renewal dir. Ohio, 1969; mem. 33d district Ohio Senate, Columbus, 1971-93, Dem. minority leader, 1981-82, 85-90, pres. and majority leader, 1983-84, com. mem. econ. develop., sci. & tech., state & local govt., ways & means, commerce & labor, controlling bd., state employment compensation bd., fin. chmn., 1974-81, rules chmn., 1983-84, com. mem. rules, reference & oversight, 1985-90; state chair Ohio Dem. Party, 1993-95. Real estate broker; adj. prof. polit. sci. Ohio U.; faculty mem. (limited svc.), bd. trustees Youngstown State U.; div. mgr. investment firm; Ohio Senate special com. mem. Task Force on Drug Strategies, Ohio Acad. Sci. Centennial Celebration Commn., Motor Vehicle Inspection & Maintenance Program, Legis. Oversight Com., Ohio Boxing Commn., Correctional Inst. Inspection Com., Ohio Small Bus. & Entrepreneurship Coun., Gov.'s Adv. Coun. Travel & Tourism, Legis. Svc. Commn., Capital Sq. Rev. & Adv. Bd., others. Past pres., past lt. gov. Am. Hellenic Ednl. Prog. Assn. (AHEPA); precinct committeeman Mahoning County Dem. Party, ward captain, mem. exec. com.; campaign mgr. local candidates, county campaign mgr. presdl. candidates; del. Dem. Mid-Term Conv., 1981; founder Great Lakes/N.E. Legis. Coalition; chmn., founder Nat. Dem. State Legis. Leaders Assn.; dir. State Legis. Leaders Found.; state/fed. assembly, mem. communications com. Nat. Conf. State Legis., legis. mgmt. com., govt. opers. com.; chair fiscal affairs com. Midwest Conf. Coun. State Govts., task force on econs. & fiscal affairs; del., exec. com. Dem. Nat. Com.; mem. Dem. Leadership Coun., State Dem. Exec. Com.; exec. com. Assn. State Dem. Chairs; bd. trustees Nat. Hall of Fame for Persons with Disabilities, Youngstown State U.; mem. St. Nicholas Greek Orthodox Ch.; mem. Mill Creek Metro Park Bd. Commrs. With USN, 1943-46. Decorated two Bronze Battle Stars; recipient Dist. Svc. award Office of Pres., Top Legislator award Ohio Union Patrolmen Assn., Dist. Citizen award Med. Coll. Ohio, City of Hope Leadership award, 1993, Legis. Leadership award Ohio Coalition for Edn. of Handicapped Children, Phillips Medal of Pub. Svc., Ohio U., John E. Fogarty award Gov.'s Com. of Employment of Handicapped, Gov.'s award, 1992, U. Cin. Award for Excellence, Lamp of Learning award Ohio Edn. Assn., Black Cultural Soc. award East Liverpool, Mahoning Valley Man of Yr. award, Mahoning Valley Econ. Devel. Corp., Office Holder of Yr. award Truman-Johnson Dem. Women, Best Interest of Children award Fathers of Equal Rights, Founders Day award Circle of Friends Found., Helping Hand award Easter Seal Soc., Honorary Riverboat Captain award Mahoning County Dem. Party, Community Svc. and Special Svcs. awards Eastern Orthodox Men's Soc., Periclean award AHEPA, Academy of Achievement award Nat. AHEPA Ednl. Found., Nat. Svc. Dem. award AHEPA, 1994, Disting. Citizen award Youngstown State U. Alumni Assn., numerous appreciation and recognition awards; recipient Outstanding Legislator awards Ohio Acad. Trial Lawyers, Ohio Assn. Pub. Sch. Employees, Ohio Rehab. Assn., League Ohio Sportsmen; recipient Dist. Svc. awards Youngstown State U., Ohio Edn. Assn., Ohio Union Patrolmen Assn., Ohio Disabled Vets., AFL-CIO Ohio Barbers Union, AFL-CIO Nat. Assn. of Theatre Owners of Ohio, Edward DeBartolo Meml. award; named Guardian of the Menorah, Youngstown B'nai B'rith, Outstanding Dem., Fairfield Dem. Club, 1993; named to Ohio Vets. Hall of Fame. Mem. (life) NAACP, ACLU, AMVETS (Legislator of Yr. 1993), VFW, Am. Legion, Cath. War Vets (Dist. Legislator award), Vet. Boxers Assn. Mercer County, Pa., Trumbull County Boxers' Legends of Leather (Man of Yr. award Hall of Fame), William Holmes McGuffey Hist. Soc., Buckeye Elks Lodge (hon.); mem. Kiwanis Internat., Urban League, Alliance C. of C., Southern Community Jaycees (hon.), Soc. for Preservation of Greek Heritage, Greek Am. Progressive Assn., Pan Cretan Assn., Arms Hist. Mus. Soc., Eagles, Moose, The Stambaugh Pillars.

MESHER, BARRY NEAL, lawyer; b. Portland, Oreg., Oct. 26, 1951; s. Louis N. Mesher and Mildred (Schwartz) Friendly; m. Deborah Anne Barrett, May 4, 1980. BS, U. Puget Sound, 1973; MA, Claremont U., 1974, JD, 1977. Bar: Washington 1977, U.S. Dist. Ct. (we. dist.) Washington 1977, U.S. Ct. Appeals (4th cir.) 1977, U.S. Tax Ct. 1985, U.S. Supreme Ct. 1985. Assoc. Dolack, Hansler, Tacoma, 1977-80, Billett Comfort & Rosenow, Tacoma, 1980-87; ptnr. Comfort & Mesher, Tacoma, 1987; assoc. Lane Powell Moss & Miller, Bellevue, Wash., 1987—. Cons. Lakeside Country Club, 1982—. Mem. com. bldg. fund YMCA, 1986. Mem. Washington State Bar Assn., Fed. Bar Assn., Seattle-King County Bar Assn., Washington Def. Trial Lawyers Assn., Def. Rsch. & Trial Lawyers Assn., Tacoma Country & Golf Club,

Washington Athletic Club, Tyee Club. Home: 9 Lakeside Country Clb SW Tacoma WA 98498-5250 Office: Lane Powell Spears Lubersky 1420 5th Ave Ste 4100 Seattle WA 98101-2338

MESHII, MASAHIRO, materials science educator; b. Amagasaki, Japan, Oct. 6, 1931; arrived in US, 1956; s. Masataro and Kazuyo M.; m. Eiko Kumagai, May 21, 1959; children: Alisa, Erica. BS, Osaka U., Japan, 1954, MS, 1956; PhD, Northwestern U., 1959. Lectr., rsch. assoc. dept. materials sci. and engring. Northwestern U., Evanston, Ill., 1959-60, asst. prof., assoc. prof., then prof., 1960-88, chmn. dept. materials sci. and engring., 1978-82, John Evans prof., 1988—2003, John Evans prof. emeritus, 2003—. Vis. scientist Nat. Rsch. Inst. Metals, Tokyo, 1970-71; NSF faculty rsch. participant Argonne (Ill.) Nat. Lab., 1975; guest prof. Osaka U., 1985; Acta/Scripta Metallurgica lectr., 1993-95. Co-editor: Lattice Defects in Quenched Metals, 1965, Martensitic Transformation, 1978, Science of Advanced Materials, 1990; editor: Fatigue and Microstructures, 1979, Mechanical Properties of BCC Metals, 1982; contbr. over 245 articles to tech. publs. and internat. jours. Recipient Founders award Midwest Soc. Electron Microscopists, 1987, Albert Easton White Disting. Tchr. award, 2008; named Best Tchr. of Yr., Engring. Students of Northwestern U., 1978; Fulbright grantee, 1956; Japan fellow, 1957. Fellow ASM (Henry Marion Howe medal 1968, Best Acad. Paper award 1994), Japan Soc. Promotion of Sci.; mem. AIME (Meritorious award for Best Paper Iron and Steel Soc. 1993), Metall. Soc., Japan Inst. Metals (hon., Achievement award 1972), Toastmasters Internat. (Disting. Toast Master, 1987, 2007). Office: 22879 NE 127th Way Redmond WA 98053-5657 Office Phone: 425-836-2334. Personal E-mail: mmeshii@hotmail.com.

MESHKATY, SHAHRA, academic administrator; d. Hossein-Ali Salar Meshkaty and Mahrokh Bolgari; m. Dean Ehya, Oct. 28, 1980; 1 child, Shahrzad Sherry Ehya. Degree in Psychology, San Diego State U., 1979; degree in Public Adminstrn., San Diego, 1981, MA in Instructional Tech., 2004. Cert. State Calif., 1985. Adminstr. U. San Diego, 1996—2005, adj. faculty, 1999—2005, sr. dir. academic computing, 1996—. Mem.: Educause.

MESHKI, HAMED, lawyer; b. Tehran, Iran, Dec. 28, 1978; s. Cyrus Meshki and Aida S. McNamara. BA, UCLA, 2000; postgrad., Georgetown U., Washington, 2000—01; JD with hons., U. Chgo., 2003. Bar: Calif. 2003. Assoc. Skadden, Arps, Slate, Meagher & Flom LLP, LA, 2003—05, Kirkland & Ellis LLP, LA, 2005—. Presenter in field; founder, chmn. com. Chgo. Transfer Com., 2002—03; mem. Chgo. Investment Law Group, 2002—03; course instr. Law Sch. Admissions Test, 1999—2000; asst. mgr., sales rep. Bernini, Inc., 1997—2000. Contbr. articles to mags. Pro bono atty. Pub. Counsel, LA, 2003; vol. Habitat for Humanity, LA, 2005; pro bono atty. Small Wonders Found., LA, 2004—05, Hope Renews, Inc., LA, 2004—05, Alliance Children's Rights, LA, 2006. John M. Olin scholar in law and econ., U. Chgo. Law Sch., 2001—02. Mem.: Calif. Young Lawyers Assn., LA County Bar Assn., Calif. State Bar Assn., Order of Coif. Avocations: literature, wine, travel. Office: Kirkland & Ellis LLP 777 S Figueroa St Los Angeles CA 90017

MESHLOVITZ, MARY E., educational consultant, special education educator; b. Buffalo, Apr. 6, 1967; d. John and Kathleen C. Kroll; m. Kenneth Peter Meshlovitz, Mar. 15, 1997; 1 child, Kenneth John. BS in Elem. and Spl. Edn., SUC Geneseo, 1989; MS in Reading Edn., SUNY, Buffalo, 1999. Cert. reading, elem. edn., spl. edn. Spl. edn. tchr. Monroe Boces II, Spencerport, NY, 1989—90, Gateway-Longview Sch., Williamsville, 1990—98; spl. edn. resource tchr. Buffalo Pub. Sch., 1998—99, reading tchr., 1999—2003, reading first coach, 2003—07, staff developer K-6, 2007—. Mem.: Coun. for Exemption Children, Internat. Reading Assn. Democrat. Roman Catholic. Avocations: reading, travel, cross stitch. Home: 302 Hartford Rd Buffalo NY 14226 Office: #70 Buffum St Buffalo NY 14207 Personal E-mail: new1211997@netzero.net.

MESKILL, VICTOR P., academic administrator, educator; b. Albertson, NY, May 9, 1935; s. James Joseph and Ida May (Pfalzer) M.; m. Gail King Heidinger, 1986; children by previous marriage— Susan Ann, Janet Louise, Gary James, Glenn Thomas, Kenneth John, Matthew Adam. BA, Hofstra U., 1961, MA, 1962; PhD, St. John's U., 1967; student, Ohio State U., Harvard U., NYU; DSc (hon.), Samara State Aerospace U., Russia, 1993; LHD (hon.), St. John's U., 1995; DCL (hon.), Moscow Internat. U., Russia, 1996; D (hon.), Coll. Puschino State U., Moscow, 1996; PhD of Pedagogy (hon.), Dowling Coll., 1997; D of Econs. (hon.), U. Istanbul, Turkey, 1997; D of Sci., Yanshan U., Peoples' Republic of China, 1998. Lab. asst., instr. biology Hofstra U., 1960-62; N.Y. State teaching fellow St. John's U., 1962-63; instr. biology Nassau C.C., NY, 1963-64; tchr. sci. Ctrl. HS Dist. 2, Floral Park, NY, 1963-64; lectr. biology C.W. Post Coll., Greenvale, NY, 1963-64, instr. biology, 1964-67, asst. prof., 1967-68, assoc. prof., 1968-74, assoc. dir. Inst. for Student Problems, supr. student tchrs., 1967-68, asst. dean Coll., dean summer sch., coordinator Admissions Office, coordinator adult and continuing edn. programs, 1968-69; dean adminstrn. C.W. Post Ctr. LI U., 1969-70, v.p. adminstrn., 1970-77, prof. biology, 1975-77; pres. Dowling Coll., Oakdale, LI, 1977-2000, pres. emeritus, 2000—. Cons. in edn. and biology; chem. technician, detective Tech. Rsch. Bur., Nassau County Police Dept., 1958-63, mem. sci. adv. com., 1970; mem. adv. coun. Aerospace Edn. Coun. Inc., 1968; trustee, mem. state legis. com. Commn. Ind. Colls. and Univs.; mem. evaluation teams Mid. States Assn., 1971—; mem. higher edn. adv. com. NY State Senate; mem. Nassau-Suffolk Comprehensive Health Planning Coun.; chmn. Internat. and Mediterranean Studies Group Conf. Contbr. articles to profl. jours. Founding mem., vice-chmn. bd. trustees Nassau Higher Edn. Consortium; bd. dirs. Suffolk County coun. Boy Scouts Am.; mem. NY State Energy Rsch. and Devel. Authority, Town of Islip Devel. Commn.; chmn. bd. trustees LI Regional Adv. Coun. Higher Edn.; chmn. L.I. Mid Suffolk Bus. Action; bd. dirs. Southside Hosp., NY; v.p. LI Forum for Tech.; former commr. Suffolk County Vanderbilt Mus.; mem. Bus. Coun. NY; hon. mem. U. Pau and Pays de l'Adour, Pau, France, 1994; hon. prof. Minjiang U., Fuzhou, Peoples Republic of China, 1994; active mem. Universal Life Keeping Problems Acad., Dept. Justice Russian Fedn., Moscow. Decorated commendatore dell'Ordine al Merito (Italy); NSF rsch. grantee, 1967-69; Named Tchr. of Yr., Aesculapius Med. Arts Soc., C.W. Post Coll. of LI U., 1967; Disting. Faculty Mem. of Year, C.W. Post Ctr. LI U., 1977, Educator of Yr. WLIW Channel 21, 1996, Officier dans l'ordre des Palmes Académiques, 2001; recipient George M. Estabrook award Hofstra U., 1978, Higher Edn. Leadership award Corning Glass Works, 1987, Disting. Leadership award LI, 1989, Diploma Merito, Garibaldi Inst., Rome, Diploma of Honor, Rsch. Ctr. for Islamic History, Art and Culture, Istanbul, Turkey, Advancement Commerce and Industry Disting. Svc. award in edn., 1997. Mem. AAAS, Coun. Advancement and Support of Edn., Am. Assn. Collegiate Registrars and Admissions Officers, Am. Assn. Higher Edn., Am. Inst. Biol. Scis., Am. Soc. Zoologists, Am. Assn. U. Adminstrs., Commn. on Ind. Colls. and Univs. (trustee), Nat. Assn. Biology Tchrs., Nat. Sci. Tchrs. Assn., Soc. Protozoologists, NY Acad. Scis., Camilo Josè Cela Found. (hon.), Met. Assn. Coll. and Univ. Biologists (founder, mem. steering com.), Bus. Coun. NY, Oakdale C. of C. (founding mem., dir.), Russian Soc. Plant Physiologists (corr.), Universal Life Keeping Problems Acad. Moscow, Tsiolkovski Space Acad. Moscow (fgn.), Univ. Club (NYC), Wings Club (NYC), Nat. Arts Club (NYC), LI Coun. Fgn. Rels., LI Assn. Commerce and Industry (v.p. edn., dir.), Alpha Chi, Kappa Delta Pi, Phi Delta Kappa, Sigma Xi, Beta Beta Beta, Alpha Eta Rho, Delta Mu Delta, Kappa Delta Rho. E-mail: vpmphd@aol.com.

MESNEY, KATHRYN, theater educator; b. NYC, Feb. 6, 1948; d. Peter and Dorothy Mesney; m. Louis Hetler, Dec. 30, 1979. MA, SUNY, Binghamton, 1974. Cert. in advanced studies somatic experiencing Found. Human Enrichment, Boulder, Colo., 2007. Instr., bfa theatre program Ithaca Coll., NY, 1974—76; instr., voice and speech KiiS Broadcasting Workshop, LA, 1977; prof. Cornish Coll. Arts, Seattle, 1978—. Actor: (film) The Dark Horse, (numerous theatrical prodn.), (film and television prodn.). Mem.: Am. Fedn. TV and Radio Artists (actor 1981—2001), Actors Equity Assn. (actor 1981—), SAG (actor 1984—). Home Fax: 206-567-5415. Personal E-mail: kmesney@aol.com. Business E-Mail: kmesney@cornish.edu.

MESSA, CHARLES ANGELO, III, plastic surgeon; b. Phila., Feb. 8, 1963; s. Charles Angelo Jr. and Roberta Elizabeth (Price) M.; m. Linda Mary Schultz, Aug. 13, 1988; children: Charles Angelo IV, William Joseph. BA magna cum laude, LaSalle U., 1985; MD, Pa. State U., 1989. Diplomate Am. Bd. Surgery. Intern U. Mass. Sch. Medicine, 1989-90; resident in surgery U. Mass. Sch. Medicine Ctr., Worcester, 1990-94; resident in plastic and reconstructive surgery U. Pa. Med. Ctr., Phila., 1994-96; surgeon Cosmetic Surgery Ctr., Weston, Fla. Presenter in field. Contbr. articles to profl. jours. Fellow ACS (assoc.), Am. Soc. Laser Med. and Surg.; mem. AMA, Pa. Med. Soc., Fla. Med. Assn., Mass. Med. Soc. Republican. Roman Catholic. E-mail: drmessa@westoncosmeticsurgery.com.

MESSAM, LEROY ANTHONY, accountant; b. Kingston, Jamaica, West Indies, July 24, 1923; came to U.S., 1951; s. David A. and Irene Beatrice (Patterson) M.; m. Ruby Patricia Jackson, July 25, 1964; children: LeRoy Jr., Andrea, Conrad, Mahalia. BA in Bus. Adminstr., Bryant & Stratton, Boston, 1958; MEd, Cambridge Coll., 1983; DD, Free Anglican Ch. in Am., 1979; DBA, Southland (Lassell) U., Pasadena, Calif., 1986; grad., Harvard U., 1980. CPA; accredited Accreditation Coun. for accountancy. Prin. Leroy A. Messam, Pub. Acct., Boston, 1962—; bishop St. John's Episcopal Ch., Mattapan, Mass., 1986—. Author: Resource Handbook for Black & Minority Entrepreneurs, 1983; co-author Pub. Adminstrn. of Our Nat. Economy, 1983. Treas. NAACP, Boston, 1962; coord. Boy Scouts Am., Boston, 1984—; del. White House Conf. on Small Bus., Washington, 1986; bd. dirs. Mass. Dept. Social Svcs., Boston, 1987; chmn. Jamaican Hurricane Relief, 1988—. Recipient Community Svcs. award Boston Soc. Vulcans Inc., Black Profl. Fire Fighters, 1989, Medal of Freedom US Congress, 2004, Peace Through Strength medal USS Ronald Reagan. Fellow Reg. Pub. Accts. of Jamaica (v.p. 1975-76); mem. Nat. Soc. Pub. Accts., Mass. Assn. Pub. Accts., Jamaican Culture Soc. (pres. 1962-73), The Friends of BOAF (sec. 1989—). Republican. Episcopalian. Office: 96 Greenfield Rd Mattapan MA 02126-3203 Office Phone: 16172989432.

MESSBARGER, REBECCA MARIE, literature and language professor; d. Paul Robert and Patricia Anne Messbarger; m. Salvatore Joseph Fiorello, Aug. 22, 1987; children: Julian Graham Fiorello, Maxwell Olivieri Fiorello, Audrey Li Ai Fiorello. BA, Loyola U., Chgo., 1983; MA, U. Wis., 1986; PhD, U. Chgo., 1994. Assoc. prof. Italian Wash. U., St. Louis, 1995—. Author: The Century of Women: Representations of Women in Eighteenth-Century Italian Public Discourse, 2002, The Contest for Knowledge: Debates Over Women's Learning in Eighteenth-Century Italy, 2005. Fellow, Nat. Endowment Humanities, 2000, Am. Philos. Soc., 1999, Fulbright Orgn., 1991; New Directions fellowship, Mellon Found., 2005. Mem.: Midwest MLA (exec. bd. 1996—99), Am. Soc. Italian Studies, MLA, Am. Soc. Eighteenth-Century Studies (nominating com. 2007). Office: Wash Univ Box 1077 One Brookings Dr Saint Louis MO 63130 Office Fax: 314-726-3494.

MESSENGER, BARBARA BEALL, artist; d. John Murray and Anne Bryant (Dorsey) Beall; m. Donald White Messenger, Aug. 16, 1960; children: Colleen Beall Messenger-Baldwin, Melanie Dorsey Messenger Davis. BS, Western Md. Coll., 1960; postgrad., Md. Inst. Art, 1978, Howard C.C., Columbia, Md., 1979—80. Art educator, dept. chair Md. Pub. Sch. Sys., New Carrollton, 1960—66; art dir. Bellassai Gallery, Ellicott City, Md., 1980—84; proprietor Art and Frame Shop Ellicott Mills Gallery, Ellicott City, 1984—2000. Set, costume and program designer Calverton Players, Beltsville, Md., 1970—73; art critic, writer Laurel Newsleader, Md., 1974—80; substitute tchr. Howard County Sch. Sys., Ellicott City, 1984, Ellicott City, 85; publicity chmn. Laurel Art Guild. Exhibited in group shows at Laurel Art Guild, 1979, Bellassai Gallery, 1980—84, Villa Julia, Stevenson, Md., 1983, exhibited in group shows, Camden, Maine, 1988, exhibitions include Ellicott Mills Gallery, Md., Represented in permanent collections, Honduras, Turkey, Italy, German, U.S.A., and many islands. Active PTA, Howard County; membership chmn., v.p. Howard County Rep. Women; events coord. Howard County Rep. Party. Recipient Best of Balt. Original Art Gallery, Balt. Mag., 1980. Mem.: Md. State Arts Coun. (bd. mem. 2003—), Nat. Mus. Women in the Arts (charter). Avocations: painting, crafts, reading, writing, photography. Home and Office: 616 Traveller Ct Lothian MD 20711

MESSENGER, GEORGE CLEMENT, engineering executive, consultant; b. Bellows Falls, Vt., July 20, 1930; s. Clement George and Ethel Mildred (Farrar) M.; m. Priscilla Betty Norris, June 19, 1954; children: Michael Todd, Steven Barry, Bonnie Lynn. BS in Physics, Worcester Poly U., 1951, PhD (hon.) in Engring., 2008; MSEE, U. Pa., 1957; PhD in Engring., Calif. Coast U., 1986; Deng (hon.), Woncester Poly. U., 2009. Rsch. scientist Philco Corp., Phila., 1951-59; engring. mgr. Hughes Semicondr., Newport Beach, Calif., 1959-61; divsn. mgr. Transitron Corp., Wakefield, Mass., 1961-63; staff scientist Northrop Corp., Hawthorne, Calif., 1963-68; cons. engr. Las Vegas, Nev., 1968—. Lectr. UCLA, 1969-75; v.p., dir. Am. Inst. Fin., Grafton, Mass., 1970-78; gen. ptnr. Dargon Fund, Anaheim, Calif., 1983—; v.p., tech. dir. Messenger and Assoc., 1987—, registered investment adviser, 1989—. Co-author: The Effects of Radiation on Electronic Systems, 1986, Single Event Phenomena, 1997; contbg. author: Fundamentals of Nuclear Hardening, 1972, Nonvolatile Semiconductor Memory Technology, 1998; contbr. articles to profl. jours.; patentee microwave diode, hardened semicondrs. Recipient Naval Rsch. Lab. Alan Berman award, 1982, Best Paper award HEART Conf., 1983, Spl. Merit award, 1983, Pete Haas award, 1992, Goddard award for outstanding profl. achievement Worcester Poly. Inst., 1996, Archimedes award for contbns. to semicondr., solid state and nuc. physics rsch., 2006. Fellow IEEE (Merit award 1986); mem. Rsch. Soc. Am., Am. Phys. Soc. Congregationalist. Home and Office: 3111 Bel Air Dr Apt 7F Las Vegas NV 89109-1510

MESSER, DONALD EDWARD, author, theology educator, administrator; b. Kimball, SD, Mar. 5, 1941; s. George Marcus and Grace E. (Foltz) M.; m. Bonnie Jeanne Nagel, Aug. 30, 1964; children: Christine Marie, Kent Donald. BA cum laude, Dakota Wesleyan U., 1963, LHD (hon.), 1977; MDiv magna cum laude, Boston U., 1966, PhD, 1969. Asst. to commr. Mass. Commn. Against Discrimination, Boston, 1968-69; asst. prof. Augustana Coll., Sioux Falls, SD, 1969-71; assoc. pastor 1st United Meth. Ch., Sioux Falls, 1969-71; pres. Dakota Wesleyan U., Mitchell, SD, 1971-81, Iliff Sch. Theology, Denver, 1981-2000, pres. emeritus and prof. practical theology emeritus, 2000—; exec. dir. Ctr. for the Ch. and Global AIDS, 2007—. Author: Christian Ethics and Political Action, 1984, Contemporary Images of Christian Ministry, 1989, Send Me? The Intineracy in Crisis, 1991, The Conspiracy of Goodness, 1992, Caught in the Crossfire: Helping Christians Debate Homosexuality, 1994, Calling Church and Seminary Into the 21st Century, 1995, Unity, Liberty, and Charity: Building Bridges Under Icy Waters, 1996, How Shall We Die? Helping Christians Debate Assisted Suicide, 1997, The Befuddled Stork: Helping Persons of Faith Debate Beginning of life Issues, 2000, Breaking the Conspiracy of Silence: Christian Churches and the Global AIDS Crisis, 2004; co-author: (with George McGovern, Bob Dole) Ending Hunger Now, 2005; co-editor: Connected Spirits: Friends and Spiritual Journeys, 2007, Cherishing Life and Love, 2009, 52 Ways to Create an AIDS-FREE World, 2009, Names, Not Just Numbers: Facing Global AIDS and World Hunger, 2009; contbr. articles to Face to Face, The Christian Century, The Christian Ministry. Active Edn. Commn. of U.S., 1973-79; co-chmn. Citizens Commn. Corrections, 1975-76; vice chmn. SD Commn. on Humanities, 1979-81. Dempster fellow, 1967-68; Rockefeller fellow, 1968-69; named to SD Hall of Fame, 2008, Alumnus of Yr. Dakota Wesleyan U., 2008; recipient Lifetime Achievement award MGR Med. U., India, 2005. Mem. Soc. Christian Ethics, Am. Acad. Religion, Assn. United Meth. Theol. Schs. (v.p. 1986-91, pres. 1991-92). Democrat.

MESSER, JAY JAMES, environmental scientist; b. Joplin, Mo., Jan. 31, 1946; s. Nelson Anders and Virginia Lee (Fields) M.; m. Janice Marie Felgenhauer, Jna. 1, 1978; children: John Nelson, Elizabeth Ann. BS, Jacksonville U., 1969; MS, U. Fla., 1975, PhD, 1978. Sci. tchr. Bishop Kenney H.S., Jacksonville, Fla., 1969-71; textbook salesman Allyn & Bacon, Tampa, 1971-72; sci. tchr. The Bolles Sch., Jacksonville, 1972-73; vis. asst. prof. U. Fla., Gainesville, 1978-79; rsch. asst. prof. Utah State U., Logan, 1980-82, rsch. assoc. prof., 1983-88; program dir. U.S. EPA, Research Triangle Park, N.C., 1988-91, dep. dir., atmospheric rsch. and exposure assessment lab., 1992-95, sr. scientist, 1995—; vis. prof. N.C. Ctrl. U., Durham, 1996—. Sci. advisor Senator Daniel Ptrick Moynihan, Washington, 1991; mem. adv. bd. Nat. Ctr. for Transp. and the Environ., Raleigh, N.C., 1993—2005; active EPA Risk Assessment Forum, 1995-98; dir. environ. scis. divsn. EPA Nat. Exposure Rsch. Lab., 1997-98, assoc. dir. ecology EPA Nat. EXposure Res. LAS, 1999-2001, Off EYA Wbpelida Gen, 2001-02, sci. advisor, EPA Nat. Ctr. Environ. Assasement, 2002- Contbr. articles to profl. jours., chpts. to books. Mem. Sigma Xi, Tau Beta Pi, Phi Kappa Phi. Achievements include development of EPA's national stream survey and environmental monitoring and assessment program;EPAs report on the environment. Home: 1215 Clearwater Farm Trl Chapel Hill NC 27517-7740 Business E-Mail: zekemessor@earthlink.net.

MESSER, THOMAS MARIA, museum director; b. Bratislava, Czechoslovakia, Feb. 9, 1920; came to U.S., 1939, naturalized, 1944; s. Richard and Agatha (Albrecht) M.; m. Remedios García Villa, Jan. 10, 1948. Exch. student, Inst. Internat. Edn., 1939; student, Thiel Coll., Greenville, Pa., 1939-41; BA, Boston U., 1942; degree, U. Sorbonne, Paris, 1947; MA, Harvard U., 1951; DFA (hon.), U. Mass., 1962, U. of Arts, Phila., 1988. Dir. Roswell (N.Mex.) Mus., 1949—52, Am. Fedn. Arts, NYC, 1952—56, Inst. Contemporary Ary, Boston, 1957—61, Solomon R. Guggenheim Mus., NYC, 1961—88, Peggy Guggenheim Collection, Venice, Italy, 1980—88, Solomon R. Guggenheim Found., NYC, trustee, 1980—90, dir. emeritus, 1990—; chief curator Schirn Kunsthalle, Frankfurt, 1994—99. Adj. prof. Harvard U., 1960, Barnard Coll., 1966, 71; prof.ü Hochschule für Angewandte Kunst, Vienna, 1984; pres. Assn. Art Mus. Dirs., 1974—75; pres. Icom's internat. com. Modern Art Mus., 1976—80, hon. mem., 2000—; pres. The MacDowell Colony Inc., 1977—78; founding mem. Am. Arts Alliance, Washington, 1978—81; mem. adv. bd. Palazzo Grassi, Venice, 1986—97; sr. advisor visual arts Caixa Found, 1991—96; mem. adv. com. Nat. Gallery, Czech Republic, 1994—99; hon. prof. Johann Wolfgang Goeth U., Frankfurt, 1997—. Author: Edvard Munch, 1973, Vasily Kandinsky, 1997; contbr. to mus. catalogues, art jours. Trustee The Isamu Noguchi Found., NYC, 1988—2006, Tokyo, 1988—, Inst. Internat. Edn., 1990—98, Fontana Found., Milan, 1996—2003; sr. cultural advisor, trustee Am.'s Soc., 1988—2006; hon. mem. Inst. Internat. Edn., 1998—. Decorated chevalier Legion d'Honneur, France, 1980, Officier Legion d'Honneur, France, 1989; recipient Goethe medal Fed. Republic Germany; spl. fellow for study in Brussels Belgian-Am. Ednl. Found., 1953; sr. fellow Ctr. Advanced Studies, Wesleyan U., 1966. Mem.: Assn. Art Mus. Dirs. (hon.; pres. 1974—75), Century Assn. (N.Y.C.). Home: 35 Sutton Pl New York NY 10022-2464 Office Phone: 212-486-1393. E-mail: tmmesser@aol.com.

MESSERLE, JUDITH ROSE, retired medical librarian, public relations executive; b. Litchfield, Ill., Jan. 16, 1943; d. Richard Douglas and Nelrose B. Wilcox; m. Darrell Wayne Messerle, Apr. 26, 1968; children: Kurt Norman, Katherine Lynn. BA in Zoology, So. Ill. U., 1966; MLS, U. Ill., 1967. Cert. med. libr. Libr. St. Joseph's Sch. Nursing, Alton, Ill., 1967-71, dir. med. info. ctr., 1971-76, dir. info. svcs., 1976-79; dir. ednl. resources and cmty. rels. St. Joseph's Hosp., 1979-84; dir. Med. Ctr. Libr. St. Louis U., 1985-88; libr. Francis A. Countway Libr. Harvard Med. Sch. and Boston Med. Libr., 1989—2004; ret. Instr. Lewis and Clark Coll., 1975, Med. Libr. Assn.; cons. in field. Bd. dirs. Family Svcs. and Vis. Nurses Assn., Alton, 1976-79. Fellow AAAS, Med. Libr. Assn. (search com. for exec. dir. 1979, dir. 1981-84, pres. 1986-87, legis. task force 1986-90, task force for knowledge and skills 1988-92, nominating com. 1996); mem. OCLC (spl. libr. adv. com. 1994-98), AMA (com. on allied health edn. and accreditation 1991-94), Assn. Acad. Health Sci. Libr. Dirs. (editl. bd. for ann. stats. 1989-94, Region 8 adv. bd. 1992-93, joint legis. task force 1992-96, pres. 1993, charting the future task force 2001-03, scholarly communication task force 2003-05), Am. Med. Informatics Assn. (planning com. 1990, publs. com. 1994-96, ann. mtg. com. 1996-98), Ill. State Libr. Adv. Com., Midwest Health Sci. Libr. Network (divsn. health sci. coun.), St. Louis Med. Librs., Hosp. Pub. Rels. Soc. St. Louis, Nat. Libr. Medicine (biomed. libr. rev. com. 1988-92).

MESSERSCHMIDT, WILLIAM HARCLERODE, retired noncommissioned officer, musician; b. Lebanon, Pa., Apr. 30, 1947; s. Harry Edgar and Sylva (Harclerode) M.; m. Janice Andersen, Dec. 28, 1971; children: William F., Ann K., Dorothy R., Edward D. MusB with distinction, Eastman Sch. Music, 1969; postgrad., Cath. U. Am., 1983, Va. Theol. Sem., 1992-96. Enlisted man U.S. Army, 1969, advanced through grades to sgt. maj., 1994; percussionist U.S. Army Field Band, Ft. George G. Meade, Md., 1969-74, U.S. Army Band (Pershing's Own), Ft. Myer, Va., 1974-85, asst. sect. leader, 1985-89, leader percussion sect., 1989-94, leader percussion group, 1994—2002; ret., 2002. Pvt. tchr. percussion, Springfield and Woodbridge, Va., 1975—; adj. instr. percussion No. Va. C.C., Woodbridge, 1983—, adj. percussion instr., Va. Commonwealth U. Richmond, 2008-; percussionist Prince William

Symphony Orch., Lake Ridge, Va., 1989-93, The Fifes and Drums of Prince William, III, Murrells Inlet, SC, 2003—, March Militaire, Capital Band, Annandale, Va., 2003-; timpanist, percussionist orchs. with Nt. Christian Choir, Gaithersburg, Md., 1990—, Old Bridge Chamber Orch., Woodbridge, Va., 1999-, ad hoc Lynchburg Symphony Orchestra, Va., 2003-07, Roanoke Symphony Orchestra, Va., 2007-, Annapolis Symphony Orchestra Md., 2008 Choir dir. Grace Ref. Presbyn. Ch., Woodbridge, 1985-93, Salvation Army Leadership Coun. Mem. Nat. Audubon Soc., Am. Soc. Prevention Cruelty to Animals, Humane Soc. US, Am. Fedn. Musicians, Vic Firth Edn. Team, Am. Legion, SAR, Kappa Delta Pi, Percussive Arts Soc., Nat. Assn. Coll. Wind and Percussion Instrs., Coll. Music Soc., Music Educators Nat. Conf., Coll. Music Soc. Avocations: reading, philosophy, tennis, languages. Home: 5400 Staples Ln Woodbridge VA 22193-3562 Office Phone: 703-590-9834. Personal E-mail: messperc@aol.com.

MESSERSMITH, PHILLIP B., biomedical engineer, educator; BS in Life Sciences, U. Ill., Urbana, 1985, PhD in Materials Sci., 1992; MS in Bioengineering, Clemson U., 1987. Asst. prof. restorative dentistry & bioengineering U. Ill. Chgo., 1994—97; asst. prof. divsn. biological materials Northwestern U., 1997—98, asst. prof. dept. physical medicine & rehabilitation, 1998—99, asst. prof. dept. biomedical engring., 2000—03, assoc. prof. dept. biomedical engring, materials sci. & engring., 2003—05, prof. dept. biomedical engring, materials sci. & engring., 2006—. Chief scientific adv. Nerites Corp., 2004; editorial bd. Nanomedicine, 2005, Biointerphases, 2006. Recipient First award, Nat. Inst. Health, 1997. Mem.: Inst. for BioNanotechnology in Advanced Medicine, Implant Dentistry Rsch. & Edn. Found. (scientific adv. bd.). Office: Northwestern University Biomedical Engineering Dept 2145 Sheridan Rd Evanston IL 60208 Office Phone: 847-467-5273. Office Fax: 847-491-4928. E-mail: philm@northwestern.edu.*

MESSIAH, SARAH ELIZABETH, medical researcher; b. Ann Arbor, Mich., May 11, 1967; d. Edith Kimm and Charles Emil Sova; children: Jonah Eric, Jasmine Summer, Jayden Stephen. BA, Skidmore Coll., Saratoga Springs, NY, 1989; MPH, Fla. Internat. U., Miami, 1997; PhD, U. Miami Miller Sch. Medicine, Fla., 2005. Rsch. asst. prof. pediat., divsn. pediatric clin. rsch. U. Miami Miller Sch. Medicine, 2005—. Contbr. scientific papers to profl. jours. Pres. neighborhood assn. Ives Estates Cmty. Assn., North Miami Beach, Fla., 1999—2008; chair, health and wellness com. Ada Merritt K-8 Ctr., Miami, 2006—08. Recipient New Rsch. award, Thrasher Rsch. Fund, 2006—07. Mem.: Soc. Perinatal and Pediatric Rsch. Office: Univ Miami Miller Sch Med Batchelor Children's Rsch Inst Miami FL 33130 Office Fax: 305-243-8475. Business E-Mail: smessiah@med.miami.edu.

MESSICK, ANDREW, marketing executive; BA in Econs. and Psych., U. Calif., Davis; MBA, Yale Sch. Mgmt. With McKinsey & Co., Chgo. and Amsterdam; various bus. devel., mktg. and gen. mgmt. positions Sara Lee Corp.; sr. v.p. internat. NBA; exec. v.p. mktg. and internat. AEG, 2007—. Office: AEG 1100 S Flower St Los Angeles CA 90015 Office Phone: 213-763-7700.*

MESSICK, FREDERIC MORTON, librarian; b. South Bend, Ind., Apr. 20, 1935; s. Francis Morton Messick and Mary Elizabeth Muessel; m. Carol Louise Reitzel, May 15, 1993; m. Claire Laverne Bowen, Dec. 18, 1965 (div. July 15, 1990); children: Elizabeth Ann Webber, David Morton. AB, Ind. U., 1959, AMT, 1963; MLS, U.Mich., 1965. Social sci. tchr. Elkhart Pub. Schools, Ind., 1963—64; ref. libr. Am. U., Washington, 1965—67; libr., bibliographer Ctrl. Mich. U., Mount Pleasant, Mich., 1967—97, ret., 1997, prof. emeritus, 1997—. Author: (reference book) Primary Sources in European Diplomacy, 1914-1945: A Bibliography of Published Memoirs and Diaries; contbr. articles to profl. jour. Bd. dirs. Mt. Pleasant Area Internat. Rels. Com., Mich., 1994—2001. Mem.: Am. Hist. Assn., Beta Phi Mu. Unitarian. Avocations: sailing, swimming. Home: 1333 Crestwood Dr Mount Pleasant MI 48858 Personal E-mail: f.messick@cmich.edu.

MESSIER, JEAN-MARIE, corporate financial executive; b. Grenoble, France, Dec. 13, 1956; married Antoinettte Fleisch, 1983; 5 children. Grad., Ecole Polytech., 1979, Ecole Nat. Adminstrn., 1982. Inspector French Min. Economy & Fin., 1982-86; head cabinet Camille Cabana, min. in charge, min. economy, 1986-88; gen. ptnr. Bank Lazard Freres, 1989—94; chmn. exec. com., CEO Compagnie Gen. Des Eaux, 1994; chmn., CEO Vivendi, Paris, 1994—2002; founder, CEO Messier Partners, NYC, 2003—. Office: Messier Partners LLC One Rockefeller Plz New York NY 10020 Office Phone: 212-332-6050.

MESSIER, LUC J., oil industry executive; BS in Civil Engring., U. Sherbrooke; studied at, McGill U., INSEAD. Engring., project mgmt. and mng. dir. Bouygues Construction and Pomerlau; COO Technip USA, 2003, pres., CEO Technip Offshore Inc., pres., CEO, 2005—07; sr. v.p. project devel. ConocoPhillips, Houston, 2007. Spkr. in field. Bd. trustees AWTY Internat. Sch. Office: ConocoPhillips PO Box 2197 Houston TX 77252-2197*

MESSIER, MARK DOUGLAS, professional sports team executive, retired professional hockey player; b. Edmonton, Alta., Can., Jan. 18, 1961; children: Lyon, Douglas Paul, Jacqueline Jean. Center Indpls. Racers, 1978, Cin. Stingers, 1979, Edmonton Oilers, 1979—91, capt., 1988—91; center, capt. NY Rangers, 1991—97, 2000—05, Vancouver Canucks, 1997—2000; hockey analyst NHL on Versus; spl. asst. to pres. NY Rangers, 2009—. Recipient Conn Smythe Trophy, 1984, Lester B. Pearson Award, 1989—90, 1991—92, Hart Meml. Trophy, 1990, 1992; named NHL Player of Yr., Sporting News, 1990, 1992; named to Sporting News All-Star Team, 1981—82, 1982—83, 1989—90, 1991—92, NHL All-Star Game, 1982—84, 1986, 1988—92, 1994, 1996—98, 2000, 2004. Achievements include being a member of Stanley Cup Champion Edmonton Oilers, 1984, 1985, 1987, 1988, 1990, New York Rangers, 1994; having his number, 11, retired by New York Rangers, 2006, Edmonton Oilers, 2007; being inducted into the Hockey Hall of Fame, 2007. Office: c/o NY Rangers 2 Pennsylvania Plaza New York NY 10121*

MESSIER, PIERRE, lawyer, manufacturing executive; b. Montreal, Que., Can., Mar. 3, 1945; s. Lionel and Anita (Caron) M.; m. Ginette Piche, July 11, 1970; 1 child, Mathieu. BA, Coll. St. Viateur, Outremont, Que., 1964; Lic. in Law, U. Montreal, 1968; diploma in adminstrv. scis., Ecole Hautes Etudes Commerciales, Montreal, 1973. Bar: Que. 1969. Assoc. Lemay & Messier, Montreal, 1969-75; v.p., sec. gen. counsel Can. Cement Lafarge, Ltd., Montreal, 1975-84; v.p., sec. Lafarge Corp., 1983-84; v.p. bus. devel., legal affairs Norsk Hydro Can. Inc., Montreal, 1989-98; lawyer Leduc LeBlanc, Montreal, 1998-2000; pvt. practice, cons., 2000—02, 2003—; sr. legal counsel Bombardier, Inc., Montreal, 2002—03. V.p. Que. Bar Svc. Corp., 1995-2006, chmn. Que. Bar Investment Fund Super. Com., 1995—. Pres. Centre Pedagogique Lucien-Guilbault Inc., 1999—; v.p. Coll. Jean de Brebeuf, 1991-97; pres. Greenfield Park Bd. Revision, 1973-74; bd. dirs. Societe Progres Rive Sud, Longueuil, Que., 1974-75, Que. Bar Profl. Liability Ins. Fund, 2006—. Mem. Can. Bar Assn. (pres. young lawyers sect. 1976, nat. exec. 1977-78), Montreal Jr. Bar (treas. 1972), Que. Mfrs. and Exporters Alliance (bd. dirs. 1996-98), St. Denis Club (Montreal), Que. Secs. and Gen. Counsel Assn. (sec. 1998). Office Phone: 514-344-5001 ext 6005. Business E-Mail: pierre.messier@defense.bombardier.com.

MESSIN, MARLENE ANN, plastics company executive; b. St. Paul, Oct. 6, 1935; d. Edgar Leander and Luella Johanna (Rahn) Johnson; m. Eugene Carlson (div. 1972); children: Rick, Debora, Ronald, Lori; m. Willard Smith (dec. 1975); m. Frank Messin, Sept. 24, 1982; 5 stepchildren. Bookkeeper Jeans Implement Co., Forest Lake, Minn., 1952-53, 1953—57, Great Plains Supply, St. Paul, 1960-62, Plastic Products Co., Inc., Lindstrom, Minn., 1962-75, pres., 1975—; co-owner, treas. Gustaf's Fine Gifts, Lindstrom, 1985—. Bookkeeper Trinity Luth. Ch., Lindstrom, 1976—81. Recipient award, Diversity 2000/Woman-Owned Bus. in Minn. Mem. Soc. Plastic Engrs., Swedish Inst., Soc. Plastic Industry, Minn. State Hist. Soc., Chgo. County Hist. Soc. Home: 28968 Olinda Trl Lindstrom MN 55045-9429 Office: 30355 Akerson St Lindstrom MN 55045-9456

MESSINA, CHARLES, artist; b. Wilmington, Del., Jan. 6, 1950; s. Joseph and Mae C. Messina; m. Patricia Simmons (div.); 1 child, Charlene. Oil painter, wood carver, sculptor. Represented in permanent collections Rattenni Children Edn. Fund, Wilmington, Am. Diabetes Assn., Leukemia and Lymphoma, Del. Recipient Salute for Participation, Soc. da Vinci, 2004, cert. appreciation, City of Wilmington, 2004. Mem.: Order Sons Italy Am., St. Anthony's Club. Avocations: art, crafts. Home: 1902 W 6th St Wilmington DE 19805

MESSINA, JIM (JAMES A. MESSINA), federal official; b. Denver, 1969; s. Jan and Rick Heller (Stepfather). BA in Polit. Sci., U. Mont., 1993. Chief of staff to Senator Mike Halligan Mont. State Senate, Mont., 1995; chief of staff to Senator Max Baucus US Senate, Washington, 1995—2001, 2005—08, campaign mgr. to Senator Max Baucus, 1996, 2002; chief of staff to Rep. Carolyn McCarthy US Congress, 1999—2001; chief of staff to Senator Byron Dorgan US Senate, 2003—05; dir. pers. Barack Obama Presdl. Transition Team, 2008; dep. chief of staff to Pres. The White House, Washington, 2009—. Democrat. Office: The White House Office Dep Chief Staff 1600 Pennsylvania Ave NW Washington DC 20500*

MESSING, DEBRA, actress; b. Bklyn., Aug. 15, 1968; m. Daniel Zelman, Sept. 3, 2000; 1 child, Roman Walker. Grad., Brandeis U.; M in Drama, NYU. Actor: (films) Walk in the Clouds, 1995, McHale's Navy, 1997, Prey, 1997, Celebrity, 1998, Mothman Prophecies, 2002, Hollywood Ending, 2002, Along Came Polly, 2004, (voice) Garfield, 2004, The Wedding Date, 2005, (voice) Open Season, 2006, Purple Violets, 2007, Lucky You, 2007, The Women, 2008, Nothing Like the Holidays, 2008; (TV series) Ned and Stacey, 1995, Prey, 1998, Will & Grace, 1998—2006 (Emmy award best actress in a comedy, 2003); (TV miniseries) The Starter Wife, 2007—; TV appearances include: NYPD Blue, 1994, 1995; Partners, 1995; Seinfeld, 1996, 1997; (voice) King of the Hill, 2002. Office: c/o Gersh Agy 232 N Canon Dr Beverly Hills CA 90210

MESSINGER, DONALD HATHAWAY, lawyer; b. Lyons, NY, July 1, 1943; s. Donald H. and Thelma (Hubbard) M.; m. Sara L. Stock, June 3, 1967; children: Michael David, Robert Stephen, Daniel Mark. BA, Colgate U., 1965; JD, Duke U., 1968. Bar: Ohio 1968. Assoc. Thompson Hine LLP, Cleve., 1968-76, ptnr., 1976—, vice chair corp. practice group, 1989-92, ptnr.-in-charge Cleve. office, 1991-96, mem. exec. com., 1996-2000. Sec., bd. dirs. Am. Steel and Wire Corp., 1986-93; sec., bd.dirs. Lee Wilson Engineering C., Inc., 1989-94; bd. dirs. Cedar Fair Mgmt. Co., 1993-2002. Trustee Cmty. Info.-Vol. Action Ctr., 1981-88, pres. 1981-84; trustee Free Med. Clinic Greater Cleve., 1970—, sec., 1970-82, v.p. 1982-86, 96-2002, pres. 2002-04; trustee Cleve. Hearing and Speech Ctr. 1980—, v.p. 1984-86, 92-93, pres., 1986-88, 98-2000; dir. Colgate U. Alumni Corp., 1979-83; trustee U. for Young Ams., 1982-95, sec.,1982- 1982-86, pres., 1986-88, chmn. 1991-95; mem. exec. bd. Boy Scouts Am., 1983-88; Leadership Cleve., 1984—, class v.p. 2007-; trustee, sec. Bus. Vols. Unltd., 1992—; sec. Buckeye Area Devel. Corp., 1970-90; mem. adv. bd. Greater Cleve. New Stadium; dir., Cleve. Pops Orch., 2006-. Recipient Cmty. Svc. award Fedn. for Community Planning, 1981-82, Daniel D. Dauby award Cleve. Hearing & Speech Ctr. 2007.; named one of Outstanding Young Citizens of Greater Cleve., 1971-75, BTI Client Svc. All Star 2006. Mem. ABA, Ohio Bar Assn., Cleve. Met. Bar Assn. (trustee 1975-79, chmn. securities law inst. 1983), Nat. Assn. Bond Lawyers Home: 21550 Shelburne Rd Shaker Heights OH 44122 Office: 3900 Key Ctr 127 Public Sq Cleveland OH 44114 Business E-Mail: don.messinger@thompsonhine.com.

MESSITTE, PETER JO, federal judge; b. Washington, July 17, 1941; s. Jesse B. and Edith (Wechsler) M.; m. Susan P. Messitte, Sept. 5, 1965; children: Zachariah, Abigail. BA cum laude, Amherst Coll., Mass., 1963; JD, U. Chgo., 1966. Bar: Md. 1969, DC 1969, US Ct. Appeals (4th cir.) 1977, US Supreme Ct. 1973, US Ct. Appeals (DC cir.) 1982, US Ct. Appeals (5th cir.) 1983. Assoc. Zuckert, Scoutt & Rasenberger, Washington, 1968-71; solo practice Chevy Chase, Md., 1971-75; mem. Messitte & Rosenberg, P.A., Chevy Chase, 1975-81; prin. Peter J. Messitte, P.A., Chevy Chase, 1981-85; assoc. judge Cir. Ct. for Montgomery County Rockville, Md., 1985-93; judge U.S. Dist. Ct. Md., Greenbelt, 1993—; mem. adv. bd., World Justice Project U. Fla. Levin Coll. Law, 2009—. Mem. Internat. Jud. Rels. Com. Jud. Conf. US, 1997-2003. Bd. dirs. Cmty. Psychiat. Clinic, Montgomery County, Md., 1974-85, v.p. 1980-85; Peace Corps vol., Sao Paulo, Brazil, 1966-68; Md. del. Dem. Nat. Conv., NYC, 1980. Recipient tchg. citations Fed. Deposit Ins. Corp. Bank Exam. Sch., 1975, 79, Am. Inst. Banking, 1978, Elizabeth Scull award for Outstanding Svc. to Montgomery County, Md., 1993, Spl. citation Divorce Roundtable Montgomery County, 1993, Gran Cruz da Ordem São José Operário-Brazilian Labor Tribunal, Mato Grosso, 2001, Medalha de Mérito Académico, Academia Paulista de Magistrados, 2002, 09, Contbr. Mental Health Cmty. Psychiat. Clinic, 1986, Leadership in Law award, Md. Daily Record, 2002, Medal of Commendation Sao Paulo Acad. Judges, 2009, Diploma Honor and Merit, Assn. São Paulo Magistrates, 2007, 09; named an honorary citizen Riberão Preto, Brazil, 2007, 09, Uberlândia, Brazil, 2007, City of Sao Paulo, 2008, Jon Mills award U. Fla. Levin Coll. Law, 2009. Fellow: Md. Bar Found. (H. Vernon Eney award for contbn. to adminstrn. of justice 2001); mem.: ABA, Jud. Inst. Md. (bd. dirs. 1989—93), Charles Fahy Inn of Ct. (master 1987—88), Fed. Judges Assn. (4th jud. cir.), Am. Law Inst., Instituto Paulista de Advogados (hon.), Montgomery County Bar Assn. (Century of Svc. award 1999), Md. Bar Assn., DC Bar Assn., Fed. Bar Assn., Montgomery County Inn of Ct. (pres. 1988—90). Jewish. Office: US Courthouse 6500 Cherrywood Ln Greenbelt MD 20770-1249

MESSMER, DONALD JOSEPH, business management educator, marketing consultant; b. St. Louis, July 30, 1936; s. Edgar Louis and Lucille Louise (Straub) Messmer; m. Charlotte Jean Fox; 1 child, Angeline Charlotte. BSBA with honors, Washington U., St. Louis, 1969, PhD, 1974. Asst. mgr. M.A. Bell Co., St. Louis, 1956-61; dist. sales exec. U. S. Gypsum Co., St. Louis, 1962-65; br. sales exec. Victor Comptometer Corp., St. Louis, 1965-68; pres. The Wessex Group, Ltd., Williamsburg, 1979—; asst. prof. Coll. William and Mary, Williamsburg, Va., 1973-76, assoc. prof., 1976-81, prof., 1981—2006, J.S. Mack prof., 1982—2006, J.S. Mack prof. emeritus, 2006—. Bd. dirs. Williamsburg Winery, Ltd., 2005—07, chmn. bd. dirs., 2005—07; co-founder, mem. adv. com. Coll. William and Mary Exec. Ptnrs. Editor (assoc ed): Decision Scis Jour, 1985—88; contbr. articles to profl jours. Bd. dirs., treas. Cmty. Action Agy., Williamsburg, 1984—91, United Way Greater Williamsburg, 1985—91, pres., 1989; founder Cmty. Svcs. Coalition, pres., chmn., 1992—98, bd. dirs., 2008—; owner Hist. Triangle Cmty. Svcs. Bldg. Recipient Pres.'s cmty. svc. award, Coll. William and Mary, 1999. Mem.: Greater Williamsburg Chamber and Tourism Alliance's (chmn. ednl. liaison com. 2008—), Southeastern Decision Scis Inst (pres 1985—86), Am Mkt Asn (Dissertation award 1974), Decision Scis Inst (mkt coord 1985—86), Rotary (bd. dirs. 1990—92, program chair 2003, bd. dirs. 2003—07, pres. 2004), Beta Gamma Sigma, Alpha Mu Alpha. Republican. Avocations: fishing, golf. Office Phone: 757-253-5606. Personal E-mail: don.messmer@cox.net. Business E-Mail: don.messmer@wessexgroup.com.

MESSMER, HAROLD MAXIMILIAN, JR., (MAX MESSMER), consulting company executive; b. Jackson, Miss., Feb. 20, 1946; s. Harold Maximilian and Margaret (Dee) M.; m. Marcia Elizabeth Nesmith, Apr. 5, 1973; children: Michael Christopher, Matthew Gordon. AB summa cum laude, Loyola U., 1967; JD cum laude, NYU, 1970. Ptnr. corp. law and securities O'Melveny & Myers, Los Angeles, 1970-81; sr. v.p., gen. counsel Pacific Holding Corp., Los Angeles, 1981-82, pres., chief operating officer, 1982-85; pres., dir., chief operating officer Cannon Mills Co. (subs.), Kannapolis, N.C., 1982-85; chmn., dir. Castle & Cook Inc., San Francisco, 1985; chmn., pres., chief exec. officer Robert Half Internat. Inc., Menlo Park, 1985—2004, chmn., CEO, 2004—. Adj. prof. Claremont Grad. Sch. Bus.(exec. mgmt. program), 1979-82; bd. dirs. Health Care Property Investors, Los Angeles, BF Enterprises Inc., N.C. Nat. Bank, Charlotte. Trustee Davidson (N.C.) Coll., 1984—; appointee Pres. Reagan's Adv. Com. on Trade Negotiations, 1985-87. Served with USAR, 1971-75. Mem. ABA, Los Angeles County Bar Assn., Calif. Bar Assn. Served with USAR, 1971-75. Office: Robert Half Internat Inc 2884 Sand Hill Rd Ste 200 Menlo Park CA 94025-7059

MESSNER, ROBERT THOMAS, lawyer, bank executive; b. McKeesport, Pa., Mar. 27, 1938; s. Thomas M. and Cecilia Mary (McElhinny) M.; m. Anne Margaret Lux, Dec. 3, 1966; children: Megan Anne, Michael Thomas. AB, Dartmouth Coll., 1960; LL.B., U. Pa., 1963. Bar: Pa. 1965. With firm Rose, Schmidt & Dixon, Pitts., 1965-68; with G.C. Murphy Co., McKeesport, 1968-86, corp. sec., 1974—, gen. counsel, 1975-86, v.p., 1976-86; v.p., gen. counsel, corp. sec. Dollar Bank, Pitts., 1986—2006. Dir. G.C. Murphy Found. Author: Reflections from Braddock's Field, 2005. Mem. Point State Park planning com. City of Pitts.; Rep. candidate Pa. Legis., 1966; mem. Mayor's Com. on Fort Duquesne, Pitts.; bd. dirs. McKeesport YMCA, Downtown Pitts. YMCA, Braddock's Field Hist. Soc., 1994—, Mon-Yough Heritage Found., 2003—; mem. adv. bd. Pa. Human Rels. Commn., 1968—69. 1st lt. US Army, 1963—65. Decorated Commendation medal. Mem. ABA, Pa. Bar Assn. (chmn. corp. law dept. com.), Allegheny County Bar Assn. (coun. on corp., banking and bus. law), Am. Soc. Corp. Secs. (pres. Pitts. regional group, dir.), Am. Mgmt. Assn., Pa. Assn. Savs. Instns. (chmn. legal com. 1989—), Am. Corp. Counsel Assn., Braddock's Battlefield Assn. (bd. dirs. 2004—), Theta Delta Chi. Clubs: Dartmouth Western Pa., Rivers. Personal E-mail: r.messner@comcast.net.

MESSNER, ZBIGNIEW, former Prime Minister of Poland, politician, economist; b. Stryj, Poland, Mar. 13, 1929; married; 2 children. Grad., Higher Sch. of Econs., Katowice, 1951; M. Econs., Higher Sch. Econs., Cracow, 1952, Dr. Econs., 1961, Dr. Habilitatis, 1969. Extraordinary prof. of econs. 1972, ordinary prof. econs. 1977. Author: numerous publs. in field. Decorated Comdrs. Cross of Polonia Restituta, First Class Banner of Labour; recipient Prizes of Ministry of Sci., Higher Edn. and Tech., Nat. Edn. Commn. medal, 1973, award Meritorious Tchr. of People's Poland, 1974; named Hon. Miner of Polish People's Republic, 1983. Mem.: Polish Acct. Standards Com. (chmn. 2002—), Acctg. Inst. Econs. U. (head), Polish Exam. Com. for Candidates for Cert. Auditors, Polish Acctg. Assn. (chmn. sci. coun.), Accts. Assn. in Poland (chmn. sci. coun. 1992—2003, pres. 2003—), Polish Econ. Soc. (v.p. main bd. 1971—81). Office: Ul Bogucicka 3 40-226 Katowice Poland Home Phone: 48-022-756-38-65; Office Phone: 48-32-257-7276.

MESTAYER, MARY FRANCES, science educator; b. Raceland, La., Sept. 2, 1952; d. Thomas Francis and Del Monte Mary Arabie Mestayer. BA in Edn., U. Southwestern La., Lafayette, 1974; student, Lea Castle Equestrian Riding Sch., Worcester, Eng., 1977, Moyfield Equestrian Riding Sch., 1978; cert, in advanced Bible Study, Layman's Sch. Training Christian Cmty. Ch., Pietersburg, South Africa, 1997—99. Cert. Rhema Bible Training Ctr., Johannesburg, South Africa, 1992; tchr. type B State of La., 1977, tchr. South African Tchr.'s Coun., 1986, South African Coun. Educators, 2000, highly qualified sci. and elem. edn. State of La. Tchr. Raceland (La.) Lower Elem. Sch., 1974—86; sci. tchr. Sunward Park H.S., South Africa, 1986—90; staff Rhema Missions Ctr. Rhema Ministries South Africa, Lanseria, 1991—92; sci. tchr. Southside Elem., Bastrop, La., 1993; sci. tchr., coord. and facilitator Pepps Polokwane Prep. Sch. and Coll., Pietersburg, South Africa, 1994—2001; sci. tchr. Larose- Cut Off Mid. Sch., Cut Off, La., 2001—. Sci. fair coord. Pepps Polokwane Prep. Sch. and Coll., Pietersburg, South Africa, 1994—2000; sci. facilitator Sci. Math. Found., 1996, Power Matric, South Africa, 1996, Africa Growth Network, 1996; sch. dir. after care Pepps Polokwane Prep. Sch. and Coll., 1999; sci. fair coord. Larose- Cut Off Mid. Sch., Cut Off, La., 2002—07; sci. fair team mem. Lafourche Parish Schs., Thibodaux, La., 2002—07; fellow Ag in the Classroom, La., 2002—09; mem. Nat. Energy Ednl. Devel. Project, 2004—, Jason Project, 2006—07, Immersion, 2007—08, La. Environ. Edn., 2008—, LSU Coastal Erosion, 2008—. Recipient Mestayer Sci. Trophy, Pepps Polokwane Prep. Sch. and Coll., 2000. Mem.: La. Fedn. Tchrs. Republican. Avocations: missions, horseback riding, gardening, reading, travel. Office: Larose Cut Off Mid Sch 13356 W Main St Cut Off LA 70345-2500 Office Phone: 985-693-3273. Business E-Mail: mmestayer@lafourche.k12.la.us.

MESTECHKIN, MIKHAIL MARKOVICH, retired mathematics physicist; b. Kiev, USSR, June 2, 1932; s. Mark Mikhailovich and Bella Grigorjevna (Greben') M.; m. Liya Semenovna Gutyrya, Apr. 23, 1955; 1 child, Tanya. MS, Odessa State U., 1955; PhD in Math./Physics, Leningrad State U., 1961, ScD in Math./Physics, 1970. Tchr. high and mid. sch. Railway Sta., Yasinovataja, Ukraine, 1955-57; asst. prof. Mordovian State U., Saransk, 1960-65; head theoretical chemistry dept., prof. Inst. Phys. Organic and Coal Chemistry, Donetsk, Ukraine, 1965-96; ret. Author: Density Matrix Method in Theory of Molecules, 1977, Spin-Extended Hartree-Fock Method, 1983 (Bronze medal of Soviet Ind. Exhbn., 1990), Hartree-Fock Instability Theory and Molecular Stability, 1986; contbg. author: Density Matrices and Density Functionals, 1987, Fullerene Science and Technology, 1997; contbr.

articles to profl. jours. including Jour. Phys., Chemistry Ref. Data, Proc. Internat. Soc. Opt. Engring., others. Mem.: World Assn. Theoretical Organic Chemists (diploma Soviet Union br.). Home: Unit 33 12773 Seabreeze Farms Dr San Diego CA 92130-3752 Home Phone: 858-847-9029. Personal E-mail: mestechkinmm@gmail.com.

MESTEL, MARK DAVID, lawyer; b. May 15, 1951; s. Oscar L. and Katherine (Waldner) M.; m. Linda Antonik, Jan. 6, 1984; children: Brenton V., Spenser Andrew. BA, Northwestern U., 1973; JD, U. Mich., 1976. Bar: Mich. 1976, DC 1977, Wash. 1978, US Dist. Ct. (we. dist.) Wash. 1979, US Ct. Appeals (9th cir.) 1984, US Dist. Ct. (ea. dist.) Wash. 1986, US Supreme Ct. 1991; cert. criminal trial specialist Nat. Bd. Trial Advocacy, 1982, 86, 91. Atty. EPA, Washington, 1976-77; pvt. practice Washington, 1977-78, Everett, Wash., 1981-84; staff atty. Snohomish County Pub. Defender, Everett, 1978-80, dir., atty., 1980-81; ptnr. Mestel & Muenster, Everett, 1984-94; pvt. practice, 1994—. Mem. Nat. Assn. Criminal Def. Lawyers, Wash. Assn. Criminal Def. Lawyers. Office: Mark D Mestel Inc PS 3221 Oakes Ave Everett WA 98201-4407 Office Phone: 425-339-2383. Personal E-mail: mdmestel@verizon.net.

MESTEL, SHERRY Y., social worker, school psychologist, art therapist; b. Bklyn., Dec. 7, 1952; d. Robert and Miriam Mestel; children: Jessica, Iris. MSc in Bilingual Edn., CCNY, 1976; MSW, SUNY, Stonybrook, 1979; MSC in Sch. Psychology, LI U., 1992; PhD, Nat. Inst. Expressive Therapy, 1995; cert. in traumatic brain injury and children, Mt. Sinai Hosp. and Hunter Coll., 1999. Lic. social worker; cert. bilingual Spanish/English elem. tchr. NY, sch. psychologist NY. Puppeteer NYC Dept. Pks., 1972—74; elem. sch. tchr. NYC Bd. Edn., 1974—75, sch. social worker, 1987—92; psychiat. social worker Rockland Children's Psychiat. Ctr., Orangeburg, NY, 1979—81; psychotherapist NY Psychotherapy & Counseling Ctr., Bklyn., 1981—87; sch. psychologist NYC Dept. Edn., Bklyn., 1992—; social worker For the Children, Para los Ninos, PLLC, Bklyn., 2000—. Spkr. NY State Early Childhood Conf., Bklyn., 1999—, YAI, NYC, 1999—; owner Earth Rites Press, Bklyn. Editor: Herbal Remedies, 1978, Women's Rituals, 1979; exhibitions include A.I.R. Gallery, NYC, B.W.A.I.C., Bklyn. Recipient Elem. Sch. Book award, Queens Coll., Flushing, NY, 1974. Mem.: NASP, NASW, Am. Art Therapy Assn. (cert.), Nat. Expressive Therapy Assn., Assn. Humanistic Psychology, Nuyagi Keetowah Soc., Bklyn. Women's Chorus, Bklyn. Working Artist Coalition, Backyard Garden.

MESTICE, ANTHONY FRANCIS, Bishop Emeritus; b. NYC, Dec. 6, 1923; Grad., St. Joseph Sem., NYC. Ordained priest Archdiocese of NY, 1949, aux. bishop, 1973—2001, aux. bishop emeritus, 2001—; ordained bishop, 1973; bishop Parish of Resurrection, Rye, NY. Roman Catholic. Office: Archdiocese of NY 1011 1st Ave New York NY 10022-4106

MESTRES, RICARDO A., III, film company executive; b. NYC, Jan. 23, 1958; s. Ricardo Angelo Jr. and Ann M.; m. Tracy Stewart (div.); children: Alexander Carson, Carrie Ann (dec.). AB, Harvard U., 1980; postgrad., U. So. Calif., 2007—. Creative exec. Paramount Pictures, LA, 1981-82, exec. dir. prodn., 1982-84, v.p. prodn., 1984-85, Walt Disney Pictures, Burbank, Calif., 1985-86, sr. v.p. prodn., 1986-88; pres. prodn. Touchstone Pictures, Burbank, Calif., 1988-89; pres. Hollywood Pictures, Burbank, Calif., 1989-94; co-founder Great Oaks Entertainment, Burbank, Calif., 1995-97; prin. Ricardo Mestres Prodns., Disney Studios, Burbank, Calif., 1997. Prodr: Jack, 101 Dalmations, Flubber, Home Alone 3, The Visitors, The Hunted. Mem. Acad. Motion Picture Arts and Scis. Personal E-mail: mestres@usc.edu. Business E-Mail: ricardo@rmp.com.

MESZAROS, MILAN, astrophysicist; b. Devavanya, Hungary, Oct. 3, 1954; s. Istvan and Istvanne (Vozary Klara) M.; children: Balazs, Veronika. Cert. physicist, Roland Eotvos U., 1980, cert. philosopher, 1984. Rsch. scientist dept. logic Roland Eotvos U., Budapest, 1980-86; rsch. scientist inst. physics Tech. U. Budapest, 1986-94; rsch. head, sci. advisor Rsch. Inst. and Innovation Co. for Telecom., Budapest, 1994-97; chief counsellor Data Processing Office, Hungarian Ministry Interior, Budapest, 1997-99; chief counsellor Hungarian Ministry of EPA, Budapest, 1999-2000, dir., 2000—. Chmn. curatorium 137 Found. for Theoretical Phys. Rsch., Budapest, 1995—; pres. Alpha Group Labs. Soc., Inc., 2004-; head dept. physics Real Green Soc., Hungary, 1992—. Editor: The Enigmatic Photon, Vol. 5: Photon and Poincare Group, 1999; contbr. articles to profl. jours. and books. Buddhist priest, 1989. Named Man of the Yr. Am. Biol. Inst., 1997, Key award, 1997, World Lifetime achievement award, 1997, Man of the Yr., 1998, 2000, 2008, Millennium Medal of Honor, 1998, Internat. Man of the Yr. award Internat. Biol. Ctr., 1997-98, Gold Star award, 1997, 20th Century award for achievement, 1998. Mem. London Diplomatic Acad. (founder mem. of diplomatic coun., 2000), Nat. Geographic Soc., N.Y. Acad. Scis., IEEE Nuclear and Plasma Scis. Soc., Planetary Soc., Internat. Union Radio Sci. Achievements include patents for capacitance eletromotor. Home: 11 Rutafa St H-1165 Budapest Hungary Office: Alpha Group Labs Inc 11 Rutafa St Bldg H H-1165 Budapest Hungary Office Phone: +36 (1) 4034589. Business E-Mail: society@neumann-alpha.hu.

MESZNIK, JOEL R., investment banker; b. Oct. 3, 1945; m. Lynne Gladstein, Mar. 25, 1979; children: Daniel, Jared, Kara. BS, CCNY, 1967; MBA, Columbia U., 1970. Engr. Ebasco Svcs., NYC, 1967-70; banker Citibank, NYC, 1970-71, Newhouse Capital, NYC, 1971-72, Matthews & Wright, NYC, 1972-76; mng. dir. Drexel Burnham Lambert, NYC, 1976-89; pres. Mesco Ltd., 1990—. Bd. dirs. Pharma/wHealth. Office: 470 Main St Ste 315 Ridgefield CT 06877-4516

METALLO, CLAUDINE, language educator; b. NJ; Adj. prof. Italian Seton Hall U., South Orange, NJ, 1999—; instr. Italian Montclair State U., 2001—, Rutgers U., New Brunswick, 2004—, instr. collegiate, 2004—.

METALLO, FRANCES ROSEBELL, mathematics professor; b. Jersey City; d. Vincenzo James and Lucille (Frank) M. BA in Math., Jersey City State Coll., 1985, MA in Math. Edn., 1987. Math. tchr. Emerson HS, Union City, NJ, 1990-92; math tchr. gifted/talented program Jefferson Annex Woodrow Wilson Sch. Dist. Union City, 1992-95; math tchr. Woodrow Wilson Sch., Dist. Union City, 1995—. Adj. tchr. math. Hudson County CC, 1987—, Jersey City State Coll., 1986—, tutor, 1983-86; reviewer for Nat. Coun. Tchrs. Math mag., A Plus for Kids Tchr. Network, 1994, grantee 1993, 96 Contbr. articles to profl. publs.; author, History of the Abacus and Study of Soroban, 1987, The Abacus: It's History and Application Module 17, 1990, A Concise Dictionary of Math and Symbols, 1992, Smile, Basic Algebra is Fun, 1999. Recipient St. Jude's Children's Rsch. Hosp. award, 1995, 1996; named Most Admired Woman of Decade; nominee Pres. award for sci. and math tchg., 1996, EWT Com. of NJ, 1996. Mem. Nat. Coun. Tchrs. Math., Assn. Math. Tchrs. of NJ, Alumni Assn. Jersey City State Coll., Math. Assn. Am., Am. Soc. Prevention of Cruelty to Animals, Assn. of Women in Math., Am. Math. Soc., Dozenal Soc., Kappa Delta Pi (mem. Wall of Tolerance, 2005, 06), Phi Delta Kappa. Avocations: crochet, embroidery, piano. Home: 201 Hancock Ave Jersey City NJ 07307-1916

METCALF, CHARLES DAVID, museum director, retired military officer; b. Anamosa, Iowa, June 18, 1933; m. Patricia (Sedlacek) M.; children: Christin, Karen. BA, Coe Coll., 1955; MBA, Mich. State U., 1964. Commd. 2d lt. USAF, 1955; advanced through grades to maj. gen., 1986; various fin. mgmt. duties USAF; asst. dir. Defense Security Assistance Agy.; commdr. Air Force Acctg. and Fin. Ctr.; ret., 1991; dir. USAF Mus., Wright-Patterson AFB, Ohio, 1996—. Decorated D.S.M. with one oak leaf cluster, Def. Superior Svc. medal, Legion of Merit. Office: USAF Mus 1100 Spaatz St Wright Patterson AFB OH 45433-7102

METCALF, JAMES S., manufacturing executive; b. 1959; married; 3 children. BS, Ohio St. Univ., 1980; MBA, Pepperdine Univ., Calif., 1983. Former sr. v.p., L&W Supply Distribution Subs., USG Corp.; with USG Corp., 1981—, dir., retail strategy, 2004, exec. v.p., pres. building sys. divsn., 2005—06, pres., COO, 2006—. Bd. dirs. Molex Inc., 2008—. Office: USG Corp 550 W Adams St Chicago IL 60661 Office Phone: 312-436-4000. Office Fax: 312-672-4093.

METCALF, JOHN STEVENSON, surgical pathologist, dermatologist; s. Isaac Stevens Halstead and Margaret Schnabel Metcalf; m. Murilyn Sadler Metcalf; 1 child, Christian Halstead. MD, Med. U. SC, Charleston, 1974. Diplomate in dermatopathology Am. Bd. Pathology and Dermatology, 1983, in anatomic pathology Am. Bd. Pathology, 1977, Am. Bd. Pathology, 2008. Asst. prof. pathology Med. U. SC, 1978—86, assoc. prof. pathology and dermatology, 1986—95, prof. pathology and dermatology, 1995—. Fellow: Coll. Am. Pathologists. Independent. Avocations: photography, motorcycling, scuba diving. Office: MUSC Dept Pathology and Lab Med 165 Ashley Ave Charleston SC 29425 Business E-Mail: metcalfj@musc.edu.

METCALF, KAREN, retired foundation executive; b. Reading, Mass., Dec. 12, 1936; d. Albion Edmund and Natalie Viola (Ives) M. AB, Vassar Coll., 1958; MBA, Harvard U., 1968. CFA. Sec. Radio Liberty Com., NYC, 1958-60; rsch. asst. Air Inc., Cambridge, Mass., 1960-64; sys. analyst Keydata Corp., Watertown, Mass., 1964-66; customer edn. cons. Interactive Data Corp., NYC, 1968; portfolio mgr. Scudder, Stevens & Clark, NYC, 1969-81; v.p. fin. and adminstrn. N.Y. Cmty. Trust, NYC, 1981—2002. Episcopalian. Avocations: travel, opera.

METCALF, LAURIE (LAUREN OPHELIA METCALFE), actress; b. Edwardsville, Ill., June 15, 1955; m. Jeff Perry (div.); 1 child, Zoe; m. Matt Roth; 2 children Will Theron, Mae BA in Theatre, Ill. State U., 1976. Founding ensemble mem. Steppenwolf Theatre, Chgo. Off-Broadway appearances: Balm in Gilead (debut, Theatre World award), 1984; stage appearances: Who's Afraid of Virginia Woolf?, 1982, Coyote Ugly, 1985, Bodies Rest, and Motion, 1986, Educating Rita, 1987 (Joseph Jefferson award best performance by principal actress in a play), Little Egypt, 1987, Killers, 1988, All My Sons, 2006 (LA Ovation award lead actress in a play 2006); Broadway plays: My Thing of Love, 1995, November, 2008; films: Desperately Seeking Susan, 1985, Making Mr. Right, 1987, Stars and Bars, 1988, The Appointments of Dennis Jennings, 1988, Candy Mountain, 1988, Miles from Home, 1988, Uncle Buck, 1989, Internal Affairs, 1989, Pacific Heights, 1990, Frankie and Johnny, 1991, JFK, 1991, Mistress, 1992, A Dangerous Woman, 1993, Blink, 1994, The Secret Life of Houses, 1994, Leaving Las Vegas, 1995, Dear God, 1996, (voice) Toy Story, 1995, Hellcab, 1997, U-Turn, 1997, Scream 2, 1997, Bulworth, 1998, (voice) Toy Story 2, 1999, Treasure Planet, 2002, Steel City, 2006, Beer League, 2006, (voice) Meet the Robinsons, 2007, Georgia Rule, 2007, Stop-Loss, 2008; TV films: Execution of Raymond Graham, 1985, Always Outnumbered, 1998, The Long Island Incident, 1998, Ballon Farm, 1999, Two Families, 2002, Phil at the Gate, 2003; TV series: Saturday Night Live, 1981, Roseanne, 1988-97 (Emmy award, Outstanding Supporting Actress in a Comedy Series, 1993, 94), The Norm Show, 1999, (voice) God, The Devil and Bob, 2000; TV appearances: The Equalizer, 1986, The Dharma & Greg, 1997, King of the Hill, 1997, 3rd Rock from the Sun, 1998, The Norm Show, 2001, Malcolm in the Middle, 2004, Frasier, 2004, Without a Trace, 2005, Monk, 2006, Grey's Anatomy, 2006, Desperate Housewives, 2006.

METCALF, WILLIAM EDWARDS, museum curator, educator; b. East Grand Rapids, Mich., Dec. 16, 1947; s. George Ellington and Ruthanne (Schnitzler) M.; m. Margaret Mary Finn, May 21, 1972 (annulled 1984); 1 son, Daniel F.; m. Jane Salinger, Oct. 26, 1991; 1 child, Lydia Qiao Salinger. BA, U. Mich., 1969, MA, 1970, PhD in Classical Studies (Horace H. Rackham prize fellow), 1973. Asst. curator Roman and Byzantine coins Am. Numismatic Soc., NYC, 1973-75, assoc. curator, 1975-78, curator, dep. chief curator, 1978-79, chief curator, 1979-2000, hon. curator, 2000—; prof. classics Yale U., 2002—, curator coins and medals Art Gallery, 2002—. Adj. prof. art history and archaeology Columbia U., 1978—97, adj. prof. classics, 1998; adj. prof. history, 1993; adj. prof. classics NYU, 1996, 2000-01, Princeton U., 1999, Bryn Mawr Coll., 2000; vis. prof. classics NYU, 2001-02. Author: The Cistophori of Hadrian, 1980, The Silver Coinage of Cappadocia, Vespasian-Commodus, 1996; editor: Studies in Early Byzantine Gold Coinage, 1988, America's Gold Coinage, 1990, Mnemata: Papers in Memory of Nancy M. Waggoner, 1991; adv. com. Lexicon Iconographicum Mythologiae Classicae, 1979—; adv. bd. Am. Jour. Archaeology, 1980-97; editor book revs. Am. Jour. Numismatics, 1989-2000; mem. editl. bd. Revue Suisse de Numismatique, 2002—contbr. articles on Roman and Byzantine coinage to profl. jours. NEA fellow for mus. profls., 1978; mem. Inst. for Advanced Study, 1988-89 Fellow Am. Numismatic Soc. (life), Soc. Antiquaries London; mem. Royal Numismatic Soc., Am. Philol. Assn. (subcom. on classical bibliography 1979-89), Archaeol. Inst. Am. (exec. com. NY 1976-80, chmn. numismatics com. 2000--), Columbia U. Seminar on Classical Civilization, Internat. Numismatic Commn. (1st v.p. 1997-2003). E-mail: william.metcalf@yale.edu.

METCALFE, ELIZABETH BROKAW, art educator; b. St. Louis, Feb. 14, 1941; d. Augustus Van Liew and Elizabeth Cabell Gray Brokaw; m. James Walter Metcalfe, June 7, 1969; children: James Kenneth Brokaw, Elizabeth Cabell. BA, Washington U., St. Louis, 1962, MA, 1965. Instr. Pierce Coll., Athens, Greece, 1966; instr. art history Maryville U., St. Louis, 1968—72, 1981—. Lectr. and book reviewer. Mem. St. Louis Art Mus., 1970—, Chgo. Art Inst., 1970—. Mem.: Archeol. Inst. Am., Nat. Soc. Colonial Dames Am. Republican. Episcopalian. Avocations: reading, walking, running, travel, hiking. Home: 65 Berry Rd Pk Saint Louis MO 63122 Office: Maryville Univ 13550 Conway Rd Saint Louis MO 63141 Personal E-mail: stlouis65@juno.com.

METCALFE, LAUREN OPHELIA See METCALF, LAURIE

METCALFE, ROBERT DAVIS, III, lawyer; b. Bridgeport, Conn., July 2, 1956; s. Robert Davis Jr. and Barbara Ann (Peaslee) M. BA summa cum laude, U. Conn., 1978, JD, 1981; MA, Trinity Coll., 1982, Am. Mil. U., 1997. Bar: Conn. 1981, U.S. Supreme Ct. 1986, D.C. 1990, Md. 1991. Judge adv. USN, Norfolk, Va., 1982-85; spl. asst. U.S. atty. U.S. Dept. Justice, Norfolk, 1985, trial atty. Washington, 1985—. Instr. ARC, Hartford, Conn., 1976-80; legis. asst. Conn. Gen. Assembly, Hartford, 1977. Served to lt. USN, 1982-85. Mem. Fed. Bar Assn., Conn. Bar Assn., Judge Adv. Assn., Mensa, Phi Beta Kappa. Republican. Roman Catholic. Avocations: martial arts, reading, sailing, trap and skeet shooting, stamp collecting/philately.

METCALFE, ROBERT M., venture capitalist, former science engineer, publishing executive, writer; b. Bklyn., Apr. 7, 1946; BS in Electrical Engring. and Computer Sci., B in Mgmt., MIT, 1969; MS in Applied Math., Harvard U., 1970, PhD in Computer Sci., 1973; doctorate (hon.). With computer sci. lab. Xerox Palo Alto Rsch. Ctr., 1973-79; founder 3Com Corp., Santa Clara, Calif., 1979-90; v.p. tech. Internat. Data Group, Boston, 1990—92; CEO, pub. Info World Pub. Co., San Mateo, Calif., 1992—95, columnist, exec. corr., 1995—2000; venture capitalist, gen. ptnr. Polaris Venture Partners, Waltham, Mass., 2001—. Vis. fellow U. Cambridge, 1991—92; bd. dir. Avistar, EarthLink, Ember, IDC, IDG, Jeknscitt, MediaLabEurope, MIT, Nanosys, Narad, MIT Tech. Review Mag., Mintera Corp.; chmn. Paratek; bd. dir. SiCortex; founder (conferences) Pop!Tech, 1997, dir. conferences; produced conferences for Agenda, Vortex. Author: (books) Packet Communication, Internet Collapses and Other InfoWorld Punditry, Beyond Calculation: The Next Fifty Years of Computing. Bd. trustees MIT; bd. dir. St. Mark's Sch. Recipient Grace Murray Hepper award, Assn. for Computing Machinery, 1980, Alexander Graham Bell medal, IEEE 1988, Pub. Understanding of Sci. award, 1995, Medal of Honor IEEE 1996, Nat. Medal Tech., 2005; Marconi Internat. Fellowship 2003; inducted into Bay Shore HS Hall of Fame, 2003, Nat. Inventors Hall of Fame, 2007. Mem. Am. Acad. Arts and Sciences, NAE, Internat. Engring. Consortium Achievements include helping build the early Internet; invention of Ethernet for which he holds four patents. Office: Polaris Venture Partners Ste 3350 1000 Winter St Waltham MA 02451

METCALFE, WALTER LEE, JR., lawyer; b. St. Louis, Dec. 19, 1938; s. Walter Lee and Carol Metcalfe; m. Cynthia Williamson, Aug. 26, 1965; children: Carol, Edward. AB, Washington U., St. Louis, 1960; JD, U. Va., 1964. Bar: Mo. 1964. Ptnr. Armstrong, Teasdale, Kramer & Vaughan, St. Louis, 1964—81; sr. ptnr. Bryan Cave LLP, St. Louis, 1982—, former chmn.; chmn. Fed. Res. Bd., St. Louis. Bd. dirs. BJC Health Care, St. Louis. Bd. dirs. Washington U., St. Louis, Danforth Found., Pulitzer Found. Arts, St. Louis Children's Hosp. Named one of 100 Most Influential Lawyers, Nat. Law Jour., 2006. Mem.: ABA, St. Louis Bar Assn., Mo. Bar Assn., Noonday Club, Bogey Club. Episcopalian. Office: Bryan Cave 211 N Broadway 1 Metropolitan Sq Ste 3600 Saint Louis MO 63102-2750 Home: 150 Carondelet Plz Apt 1702 Saint Louis MO 63105-3453 Office Phone: 314-259-2000.

METRIONE, LARA, biomedical researcher; b. Washington, Dc, Dec. 2, 1982; d. Michael and Patricia Metrione. BS, U. Md., 2003; MS, Southern Ill. U., Carbondale, 2005; attending, Dept. Evolution, Ecology and Organismal Biology.,Ohio State U., 2009. Rsch. intern White Oak Conservation Ctr., Yulee, Fla., 2006—07; grad. tchg. assoc. Ohio State U., Columbus, 2008—. Instr. US Pony Club, Olney, Md., 1999—2007; rating examiner Redland Hunt Pony Club, Olney. Recipient Frank Bierman award, US Pony Club, 1999. Mem.: Internat. Rhino Keepers Assn., US Equestrian Fedn., US Eventing Assn. Roman Catholic. Avocation: horseback riding. Office: Ohio State Univ 318 W 12th Ave Columbus OH 43210

METROS, MARY TERESA, librarian; b. Denver, Nov. 10, 1951; d. James and Wilma Frances (Hanson) Metros. BA in English, Colo. Women's Coll., 1973; MA in Librarianship, U. Denver, 1974. Adult svcs. libr. Englewood Pub. Libr., Colo., 1975—81, mgr. adult svcs., 1983—84; sys. cons. Dataphase Sys., Kansas City, Mo., 1981—82; circulation libr. Westminster Pub. Libr., Colo., 1983; supr. pub. svcs. Tempe Pub. Libr., Ariz., 1984—90, libr. dir., 1990—. Mem.: ALA, Ariz. Libr. Assn., Pub. Libr. Assn. Democrat. Office: Tempe Pub Libr 3500 S Rural Rd Tempe AZ 85282-5405 Home Phone: 480-777-8530; Office Phone: 480-350-5551. Business E-Mail: teri_metros@tempe.gov.

METTEE, HOWARD DAWSON, chemistry professor, consultant; s. Milton Howard Mettee and Marjorie Muther; children: Michael Stewart, Nancy, Travis Dawson. BA in Chemistry, Middlebury Coll., Vt., 1961; PhD in Physical Chemistry, U. Calgary, Canada, 1964. Postdoctoral fellow NRC, Ottawa, Ontario, Canada, 1964—66; posdoctoral fellow U. Tex., Austin, 1966—68; asst. prof. chemistry Youngstown State U., Ohio, 1968—72, assoc. prof. chemistry, 1972—82; sr. scientist U. Calif., Berkeley, 1979—80; prof. chemistry Youngstown State U., 1982—; vis. prof. Forest Tech. Acad., St. Petersburg, Russia, 1997—98; rsch. scientist Forestry Acad., St. Petersburg, 2006—07. Pres. M & M Cons., Youngstown, 1983—. Editor: (reference book) Directory of Russian Scientists and Engineers. Founding bd. mem. Youngstown State U. Tech. Devel. Corp., 1989—97. Recipient Edward Piszek award, Rotary Found., 1992; Fulbright scholarship, Coun. Internat. Exch. Scholars, 1997—98. Mem.: Am. Chem. Soc., Boardman Rotary (pres. 2004—05). Achievements include research in IR spectroscopy, photochemistry and photoelectrochemical water splitting and biomass conversion. Avocations: skiing, tennis, guitar. Office: Youngstown State Univ One University Plz Youngstown OH 44555 Office Phone: 330-941-3669. Office Fax: 330-941-1579; Home Fax: 330-941-1579. Business E-Mail: hdmettee@ysu.edu.

METTEE-MCCUTCHON, ILA, municipal official, retired military officer; b. Mobile, Ala., May 1, 1945; d. John Martin and Anna Ruth (Cleveland) Mettee; m. John Robert McCutchon, Oct. 13, 1974; 1 child, Erin Tempest. BS, Auburn U., Ala., 1967, MS, 1969; grad., various army schs. Rsch. psychologist VA Hosp., Tuskegee, Ala., 1967-69; clin. psychologist U. Ala. Med. Ctr., Birmingham, 1969-71; commd. 1st lt. U.S. Army, 1971, advanced through grades to col., 1992. Officer in charge Alcohol and Drug Abuse Rehab. Ctr., Presidio, San Francisco, 1971-73; strategic intelligence officer 8th Psychol. Bn., 1973-75; tactical intelligence officer, ops. officer, co. comdr. 525th MI Brigade (Airborne), Ft. Bragg, N.C., 1976-79; project officer Command, Control, Comms. and Intelligence Directorate, Combined Arms Combat Devel. Activity, Ft. Leavenworth, Kans., 1979-82; student Command and Gen. Staff Coll., 1982-83; ops. officer Army Spl. Security Group, Washington, 1983-86; Def. Lang. Inst. Presidio of Monterey, 1986-87; chief U.S. So. command Joint Intelligence Ctr., Republic of Panama, 1987-89; comdr. 741st M.I. Bn., Ft. Meade, Md., 1989-91; U.S. Army War Coll., 1991-92; strategic intelligence officer Internat. Mil. Staff NATO, Brussels, 1992-94; comdr. Presidio of Monterey and Ft. Ord, Calif., 1994-96, chief base realignment and closure/environ. mgmt., 1996-97, ret. with honors, 1997. Elected to Marina City Coun., 1998, Rep. ctrl. com. Monterey County, 2000, Mayor City of Marina, 2002—, reelected, 2004, 2006; apptd. Monterey County supr. by gov. of Calif., 2008; chair bd. dirs. Ft Ord Reuse Auth., 2004-2006 Decorated Army Commendation medal (3), Meritorious Svc. medal (4), Def. Meritorious Svc. medal, Army Achievement award (2), Legion of Merit (2), Def. Superior Svc. medal; named Woman of Yr. Marina, 2001, Philanthropist of Yr., 2001, Citizen of Yr., 2005; fellow, Calif. State U. Monterey Bay, 2003. Mem. NAFE, Nat. Assn. Univ. Women, VFW, Assn. U.S. Army, Alumni Assn. U.S. Army War Coll., Am. Legion (post 694), Ft. Ord Alumni Assn. (adv. bd.), Girl Scouts of Monterey Bay (bd. dirs.), Cmty. Human Svcs. (bd. dirs.), Rotary Internat. (local chpt.), Monterey Rep. Women, Marina C. of C. Home: 3181 DeForest Rd Marina CA 93933 Office: Monterey County Supr 4th Dist Alisal Ave Salinas CA 93905 Home Phone: 831-884-9042; Office Phone: 831-883-2570. Personal E-mail: ilamm4@aol.com.

METTERS, RICHARD, finance educator; b. Kans. City, Kans., Jan. 30, 1957; PhD, U. NC, Chapel Hill, 1993. Prof. Emory U., Atlanta, Ga., 1993—2008. Author: (book) Successful Service Operations Management; contbr. articles to academic bus. jours. Office: Emory Univ 1300 Clifton Rd Atlanta GA 30322 Business E-Mail: richard_metters@bus.emory.edu.

METWALLI, APRIL BEEMAN, legislative staff member; BA in Polit. Sci. and Comm., Elizabethtown Coll., 1997; JD, Wake Forest U., 2000. Press. sec. Bob Casey for Congress, 1998; pub. affairs specialist Nat. Ctr. for Family Literacy, 2000; regional dir. Okla./Ark. Alzheimer's Assn., 2001—05; sr. adviser Christopher Carney for Congress; chief of staff for Rep. Christopher Carney, US House of Reps., Washington, 2007—. Office: Office of Congressman Christopher Carney 416 Cannon House Office Bldg Washington DC 20515 Office Phone: 202-225-3731. Office Fax: 202-225-9594. E-mail: april.metwalli@mail.house.gov.*

METZ, ADAM S., real estate company executive; BA, Cornell U.; MMgmt, Northwestern U. Corp. lending officer 1st Nat. Bank Chgo., 1983-87; v.p. Capital Markets Group, JMB Realty, 1987-93; treas., CFO, exec. v.p, dir. acquisitions Urban Shopping Ctrs., Inc., 1993-2000, pres., 2000—01; co-founding ptnr. Polaris Capital LLC, Northbrook, Ill., 2003—; CEO Gen. Growth Properties, Inc., 2008—. Trustee Amli Residential Properties, 2003—, Ctr. for Urban Land Econs. Rsch., U. Wis., 1997—. Mem. Internat. Coun. Shopping Ctrs. Office: Polaris Capital LLC 1033 Skokie Blvd Ste 660 Northbrook IL 60062 Home Phone: 847-835-4171; Office Phone: 847-480-9180. E-mail: metza@comcast.net.*

METZ, CHARLES EDGAR, radiology educator; b. Bayshore, NY, Sept. 11, 1942; s. Clinton Edgar and Grace Muriel (Schienke) M.; m. Maryanne Theresa Bahr, July, 1967 (div. 1988); children: Rebecca, Molly. BA, Bowdoin Coll., 1964; MS, U. Pa., 1966, PhD, 1969. Instr. radiology U. Chgo., 1969-71, asst. prof., 1971-75, assoc. prof., 1976-80, dir. grad. programs in med. physics, 1979-85, prof., 1980—, prof. structural biology, 1984-86, prof. med. physics, 2003—. Mem. diagnostic rsch. adv. group Nat. Cancer Inst., 1980-81; mem. sci. com. Nat. Coun. on Radiation Protection and Measurements, 1982-85, 2001-, Internat. Commn. on Radiation Units and Measurements, 1988-96, chmn. sci. com., 1992-99; cons. and lectr. in field. Assoc. editor: Radiology Jour., 1986—91, Med. Physics Jour., 1992—95, mem. editl. bd.: Med. Decision Making Jour., 1980—84; contbr. over 250 articles to sci. jours. and chpts. to books. Recipient L.H. Gray medal, Internat. Commn. on Radiation Units and Measurements, 2005. Fellow Am. Assn. Physicists in Medicine; mem. Radiol. Soc. N.Am., Am. Assn. Physicists in Medicine, Soc. Med. Decision Making, Assn. Univ. Radiologists, Phi Beta Kappa, Sigma Xi. Achievements include development of software for ROC analysis used in more than 10,000 labs worldwide. Office: U Chgo Dept Radiology MC2026 5841 S Maryland Ave Chicago IL 60637-1463

METZ, CRAIG HUSEMAN, lawyer; b. Columbia, SC, Aug. 26, 1955; s. Leonard Huseman and Annette (Worthington) M.; m. Karen Angela McCleary, Aug. 11, 1984; 1 child, Preston Worthington. BA, U. Tenn., 1977; JD, U. Memphis, 1986; cert., U.S. Ho. of Reps. Rep. Leadership Parliamentary Law Sch., 1987. Bar: S.C., D.C., U.S. Ct. Fed. Claims, U.S. Supreme Ct., U.S. Ct. Appeals (4th cir.). Canvass coord., liaison Campaign to Re-elect Congressman Floyd Spence, 1978; del., chmn. Shelby County Del. to 1983 Tenn. Young Rep. Fedn. Conv.; vice chmn. Shelby County Young Reps., 1983-84, chmn., 1984-85; Shelby County adminstr., asst. to Tenn. state exec. dir. Reagan-Bush Campaign, 1984; field rep. Campaign to Re-elect Congressman Floyd Spence, 1986; spl. asst. to Congressman Floyd Spence, 1986-88; counsel com. on labor and human resources U.S. Senate, 1988-90; commr.'s counsel U.S. Occupl. Safety and Health Rev. Commn., Washington, 1990-91; spl. asst. to asst. sec. for legis. and congl. affairs, dep. asst. sec. for congl. liaison US Dept. Edn., 1991—93; asst. dir. Divsn. Congl. Affairs AMA, Washington, 1993; chief of staff Congressman Floyd Spence, Washington, 1993—2001; adminstr. Office of the Second Congl. Dist. of S.C., U.S. Ho. of Reps., Washington, 2001; govt. rels. EMC Corp., Arlington, Va., 2001—07; atty. Venable LLP, Washington, 2007—. Judge nat. writing competition U.S. Constn. Bicentennial, SC, 1987—88; mem. U.S. adv. bd. Churchill Archives Ctr., Churchill Coll., U. Cambridge; mem. bd. trustees Dwight D. Eisenhower Soc.; adv. bd. South Carolina Political Collections; advisor catesby Commemorative Trust; mem. Ch. of the Ascension and Saint Agnes, Washington, Friends of the Ch. of the Resurrection, NYC, Guild of All Souls. Recipient award of merit Rep. Party of Shelby County, 1985, Outstanding Leadership award Shelby County Young Reps., 1985, Meritorious Svc. medal Mil. Dept. S.C., Legis. award Res. Officers Assn. U.S., Order of the Palmetto, Palmetto Patriot award, Pres.'s award of N.G. Assn. S.C.; Hon. Washington fellow U. S.C. Washington Fellows Program. Mem.: SAR, La Soc. Française Bienfaisance Charleston, SC, Nat. Soc. Am. Royal Descent, Soc. Colonial Wars, Rep. Nat. Lawyers Assn. (state chmn. S.C. chpt. 1987—90), Millitary Order Crusades, Baronial Order Magna Charta, The Welsh Socs. Phila., Order of Merovingian Dynasty, Royal Oak Found., Ky. Col., Nat. Cathedral Assn., U. Tenn. Nat. Alumni Assn., Soc. of Friends of St George's and Descs. of Knights of the Garter, Order St. John, St. George's Soc. Balt., NY, Supreme Ct. Hist. Soc., St. David's Soc., NY, Charleston, SC, Sons of Am. Colonists, St. Andrew's Soc. Washington, Royal Soc. St. George, Mil. Soc. War of 1812, Vet Corps Arty., Gen. Soc. War of 1812, Mil. Order Loyal Legion of U.S., Mil. Order Stars and Bars, Sons and Daus. Colonial and Antebellum Bench and Bar 1565-1861, Freedoms Found. Valley Forge, Va. Hist. Soc., Assn. for Preservation Va. Antiquities, Land Trust of Va., Preservation Alliance of Va., Va. Geneal. Soc., U. South Caroliniana Soc., Palmetto Trust for Historic Preservation, Palmetto Conservation Found., Lowcountry Heritage Soc., Orangeburg County Hist. Soc., Savannah River Valley Geneal. Soc., The Oyster Bay Hist. Soc., Hist. Soc. of Washington County, Va., Randolph County Geneal. Soc., Nat. Trust for Hist. Preservation (assoc. Capital region), Soc. King Charles the Martyr, Clan Lockhart, Am. Clan Lockhart Soc., English Spkg. Union, The Churchill Ctr., Geman Soc. Md., Propeller Club Washington, Nat. Mus. U.S. Army (founding sponsor), Order of Crown Charlemagne in Am., St. Nicholas Soc., NY, Friends of Stratford Hall, NY Caledonian Club, Touchdown Club, Phi Alpha Delta (v.p. McKeller chpt., Outstanding Svc. award 1983), Sigma Alpha Epsilon. Republican. Episcopalian. Office: 575 7th St NW Washington DC 20004 Home: 3718 Cumberland St NW Washington DC 20016-1816

METZ, ERIC D., professional sports agent; b. Monroeville, Pa., Mar. 1961; married; 3 children. Grad., Pa. State U., 1983. Sports agent Lock, Metz & Malinovic, LLC, Tempe, Ariz. Office: Lock Metz Malinovic Llc PO Box 28245 Tempe AZ 85285-8245 Office Phone: 480-921-9770.

METZ, MARY SEAWELL, retired foundation and academic administrator; b. Rockhill, SC, May 7, 1937; d. Columbus Jackson and Mary (Dunlap) Seawell; m. F. Eugene Metz, Dec. 21, 1957; 1 dau., Mary Eugena. BA summa cum laude in French and English, Furman U., 1958; postgrad., Institut Phonetique, Paris, 1962-63, Sorbonne, 1962-63; PhD magna cum laude in French, La. State U., 1966; HHD (hon.), Furman U., 1984; LLD (hon.), Chapman Coll., 1985; DLT (hon.), Converse Coll., 1988. Instr. French La. State U., 1965-66, asst. prof., 1966-67, 1968-72, assoc. prof., 1972-76, dir. elem. and intermediate French programs, 1966-74, spl. asst. to chancellor, 1974-75, asst. to chancellor, 1975-76; prof. French Hood Coll., Frederick, Md., 1976-81, provost, dean acad. affairs, 1976-81; pres. Mills Coll., Oakland, Calif., 1981-90; dean of extension U. Calif., Berkeley, 1991-98; pres. S.H. Cowell Found., San Fransisco, 1999—. Vis. asst. prof. U. Calif.-Berkeley, 1967-68; mem. commn. on leadership devel. Am. Coun. on Edn., 1981-90, adv. coun. Stanford Rsch. Inst., 1985-90, adv. coun. Grad. Sch. Bus., Stanford U.; bd. dirs. PG&E, AT&T, Inc., Union Bank, Longs Drug Stores. Author: Reflets du monde francais, 1971, 78, Cahier d'exercices: Reflets du monde francais, 1972, 78, (with Helstrom) Le Francais a decouvrir, 1972, 78, Le Francais a vivre, 1972, 78, Cahier d'exercices: Le Francais a vivre, 1972, 78; standardized tests; mem. editorial bd. Liberal Edn., 1982—. Trustee Am. Conservatory Theater. NDEA fellow, 1960-62, 1963-64; Fulbright fellow, 1962-63; Am. Council Edn. fellow, 1974-75 Mem. Western Coll. Assn. (v.p. 1982-84, pres. 1984-86), Assn. Ind. Calif. Colls. and Univs. (exec. com. 1982-90), Nat. Assn. Ind. Colls. and Univs. (govt. rels. adv. coun. 1982-85), So. Conf. Lang. Teaching (chmn. 1976-77), World Affairs Coun. No. Calif. (bd. dirs. 1984-93), Bus.-Higher Edn. Forum, Women's Forum West, Women's Coll. Coalition (exec. com. 1984-88), Phi Kappa Phi, Phi Beta Kappa. Address: PO Box 686 Stinson Beach CA 94970-0686

METZ, RICARDO BAER, chemistry professor; b. Santiago, Chile, May 22, 1965; s. Manuel and Margarita Metz; m. Jacqueline Scott, July 20, 1996; children: Ethan Brian, Aidan David. BA in Chemistry, Johns Hopkins U., Balt., 1986; PhD in Chemistry, U. Calif., Berkeley, 1991. Postdoc. fellow dept. chemistry U. Wis., Madison, 1991—95; asst. prof. Dept. Chemistry, U. Mass., Amherst, 1995—2001, assoc. prof., 2001—. Contbr. articles to profl. jours. Recipient New Faculty award, Camille & Henry Dreyfus Found., 1995, NSF Career award, 1998; grant, Am. Chem. Soc., Petroleum Rsch. Fund, 2001—03, NSF, 2003—. Mem.: Am. Soc. Mass Spectrometry, Am. Chem. Soc. Office: Dept Chemistry Lederle GRC Univ Mass Amherst MA 01003

METZ, ROBERT C., media company executive; b. Feb. 13, 1953; married; 2 children. Grad., U. Mich. With PRIMEDIA Inc. (formally PRIMEDIA Consumer Guides, HPC Publs.), 1975—, various positions including publisher, COF, COO, pres., chmn. bd., v.p., 2000—; pres., CEO PRIMEDIA Inc.; CEO Consumer Source Inc. Bd. dirs. Guia Qual. Bd. dirs. Big Brothers program; coach various children's sports teams. Office: PRIMEDIA Consumer Source Inc 3585 Engineering Dr Ste 100 Norcross GA 30092 Office Phone: 678-421-3000.

METZ, ROXIE ANNE, art educator; b. New Rochelle, NY, July 2, 1955; d. Calvin Leon and Dorothy Mary (Belton) Metz. BFA, Coll. New Rochelle, 1978, MA in Art/Psychology, 1984. Asst. residence supr. Westchester Assn. for Retarded Citizens, White Plains, NY, 1978-79; art tchr. New Rochelle City Sch. Dist., 1979—. Vol. New Rochelle Hosp. Med. Ctr., 1977—; active New Rochelle Community Action Agy., 1973-74; art tchr. Hawthorne Cedar Knolls Union Free Sch. Dist., NY. Mem. NY State United Tchrs., Am. Fedn. Tchrs. Democrat. Christian. Address: 80 Guion Pl Apt 8T New Rochelle NY 10801-3837 Office Phone: 914-576-4300. Personal E-mail: preciousmetz@optonline.net.

METZ, T(HEODORE) JOHN, librarian, educator; b. Erie, Pa., Nov. 5, 1932; s. Theodore John and Dorothy Pearl (Schutte) M.; m. Dorothy Page Neff, June 11, 1955; 1 child, Margaret Elizabeth MusB, Heidelberg Coll., 1954; MA in Music, Miami U., Oxford, Ohio, 1955; MLS, U. Mich., 1959. Libr. II U. Wis., Madison, 1959-61; asst. libr. Lawrence U., Appleton, Wis., 1961-67; dir. librs. U. Wis.-Green Bay, 1967-75; exec. dir. Midwest Region Library Network, Evanston, Ill., 1975-79; coll. libr., assoc. prof. Carleton Coll., Northfield, Minn., 1979-97, coll. libr. emeritus, 1998—. Speaker, participant, coord. numerous confs. and insts., 1969—; chmn. several state libr. groups, 1971-76; mem. several nat. libr. adv. coms., 1974-80; bldg. cons. Carleton Coll., others, 1978—; mem. Citizen Amb. Rsch. Librs. del. to Ea. Europe, 1992. Author: MIDLNET Symposium Report, 1976 Chmn. Green Bay Symphony, 1971-76; mem. various bds. coms., relating to mus. activities; performer Green Bay and other orchs., 1955— Library Service scholar U. Mich., 1957; Library Service fellow U. Mich., 1958 Mem. ALA, Assn. Coll. Rsch. Librs., Internat. Fedn. Libr. Assns. Avocations: music, hunting, fishing, gardening. E-mail: tmetz@carleton.edu.

METZ, THOMAS FREDERIC, career military officer; b. Elkin, NC, Sept. 21, 1948; m. Pamela Redmond; children: Elizabeth, Cade, Patrick. BS, U.S. Mil. Acad., 1971; M in Mech. Engring., N.C. State U., 1980; grad., Command and Gen. Staff Coll., Army War Coll. Registered profl. engr., Va. Enlisted U.S. Army, 1966, commd. 2nd lt. inf., 1971, advanced through grades to lt. gen., 2002, various positions, 1972-76, aide-de-camp for Comdr., Readiness Region VI Ft. Knox, Ky., 1976, comdr. C Co., 4th Bn., 54th Inf., 194th Armor Brigade, 1977-78; asst. prof. mech. engring. dept. U.S. Mil. Acad., West Point, N.Y., 1981-84; S-3/XO 3d Bn., 7th Inf., S-3 197th Separate Inf. Brigade Ft. Benning, Ga.; divsn. chief Inf. Sch. Combat Devel. Directorate, 1984-87; comdr. 4th Bn., 15th Inf., 194th Armor Brigade Ft. Knox, 1987-89; G-3, 2d Inf. Divsn. Republic of Korea, 1990-92; comdr. 2d Brigade, 1st Inf. Divsn., 1992-94; chief of staff Ft. Riley, 1994-95; dir. exptl. force coordination cell, 4th Inf. Divsn. U.S. Army, Fort Hood, 1995-97; asst. divsn. comdr. for support 4th Inf. Divsn., 1997-98; dep. dir. Joint Warfighting Capability Assessment, J-8 The Joint Staff, Washington, 1998-2000, vice dir., force structure, resources, & assessment (J-8), 2000—01; comdr., 24th Infantry Divsn. (Mechanized) US Army, Fort Riley, Kans., 2001—03; chief of staff US Centl. Command, Operation Enduring Freedom, 2002—03; comdr., III US Corps US Army, Fort Hood, Tex., 2003—06; comdr. Multi-Nat. Corps. Iraq, Baghdad, 2004—05; dep. commdg. gen., chief of staff US Army Training & Doctrine Command (TRADOC), Ft. Monroe, Va., 2006—07; dir. Joint IED Defeat Orgn. (JIEDDO), Washington, 2007—. Decorated Legion of Merit with two oak leaf clusters, Bronze Star medal, Meritorious Svc. medal with three oak leaf clusters, Army Commendation medal with two oak leaf clusters, Good Conduct medal. Office: JIEDDO 5000 Army Pentagon Washington DC 20310-5000 Office Phone: 703-601-3837. E-mail: thomas.metz@jieddo.dod.mil.*

METZEL, ALAN BARRY, manufacturing engineer; b. Hagerstown, Md., Sept. 25, 1944; s. Richard Cavanaugh (Stepfather) and Honora Irene McCoppin; m. Sheila Eileen Shobe, July 28, 1967; children: Michael Alan, Amanda Eileen. AS in Engring. Tech., Hagerstown Jr. Coll., 1965; BS in Mech. Engring., Univ. Tenn., Knoxville, 1969. Tooling supr. Ea. Products Corp., Hagerstown, Md., 1969—73; mfg. engr. Mack Trucks Powertrain Divsn., Hagerstown, Md., 1973—91; mfg. liaison United Def., York, Pa., 1998—99; quality engr. Northrop Grumman Electronic Sector, Linthicum, Md., 2000—. Past pres., past v.p., past exec. comm. mem. Hagerstown Jr. Coll. Alumni Assn., 1970. Mem.: Coordinate Measurement Sys. Com., Am. Soc. Quality, Soc. Mfg. Engrs. Home: 12637 Bradbury Ave Smithsburg MD 21783-1417 Office: Northrop-Grumman 7323 Aviation Blvd Linthicum MD 21090 Personal E-mail: almetzel@aol.com.

METZGER, DENNIS W., medical educator, immunologist, researcher; b. Suffern, NY, Sept. 14, 1951; s. Gertrude Metzger; m. Colleen Walsh, Feb. 14, 1991; children: Jacqueline, Christina, Caroline, Natalie, Gregory. BS in Biology, U. Ill., Champaign, 1973; MS in Microbiolog and Immunology, U. Ill., Chgo., 1976, PhD, 1978. Postdoctoral fellow dept. microbiology UCLA, 1978—80; rsch. assoc. dept. immunology St. Jude Children's Rsch. Hosp., Memphis, 1980—82, asst. mem. dept. immunology, 1982—86, assoc. mem., 1986—90; assoc. prof. microbiology and immunology Med. Coll. Ohio, Toledo, 1990—96, prof. microbiology and immunology, 1996—99, dir. molecular basis of disease grad. program, 1996—99; Theobald Smith Alumni chair, dir. ctr. for immunology and microbial disease Albany Med. Coll., 1999—. Adj. prof. dept. biomed. engring. Rensselear Poly. Inst., Troy, 2000—; affiliated scientist NY State Dept Health, Wadsworth Ctr., Albany, 2005—. Contbr. scientific papers to profl. jours. Grantee, NIH, 1980—. Mem.: Am. Assn. Immunology. Achievements include patents in field. Home: 504 Windsor Ct Niskayuna NY 12309 Office: Albany Med Coll MC-151 43 New Scotland Ave Albany NY 12208-3478 Office Fax: 518-262-6053. Business E-Mail: metzged@mail.amc.edu.

METZGER, ERNEST HUGH, aerospace engineer, research scientist; b. Nurnberg, Germany, Oct. 22, 1923; came to U.S., 1939, naturalized, 1943; s. Paul Arthur and Charlotte Babette (Kann) M.; m. Sarah Temple Grinnell, Nov. 19, 1956; children: Lisa Metzger Dunning, Charlotte Bennett (dec.), George Grinnell. BS, CCNY, 1949; MS, Harvard U., 1950. Automatic control engr. Bell Aerospace Co. div. Textron, Buffalo, 1950-54, tech. dir. inertial nav. systems, 1954-60, chief engr., inertial instruments, 1960-70, chief engr., gravity gradiometer systems, 1970-83, dir. gravity sensor systems, 1983-86, exec. dir. engring., 1986-89, cons., 1989-95, Bell Geospace Inc., Buffalo, 1995—. Mem. panel future navigation systems Nat. Acad. Sci., com. on geodesy NRC, 1988-89, accelerator criteria com. NASA, tech. com. navigation guidance and control, AIAA, 1989—; vis. lectr. dept. aernautics and astronautics Stanford U., 1990 Contbr. articles to profl. jours.; patentee in field Served with AUS, 1943-46 Recipient Aerospace Pioneer award Niagara Frontier sect. AIAA, 1977; named to Niagara Frontier Aviation Hall of Fame, 1992. Mem. IEEE, Inst. Navigation (Thurlow award for outstanding contbn. to sci. navigation 1983), AAAS, Air Force Assn., N.Y. Acad. Scis., Explorers Club, Sigma Xi, Tau Beta Pi, Eta Kappa Nu Clubs: Harvard, Buffalo Ski. Home: 663 Downing Ln Williamsville NY 14221 E-mail: semetz@roadrunner.net.

METZGER, ROBERT MELVILLE, chemistry educator; b. Yokohama, Kanagawa, Japan, May 7, 1940; s. Ferdinand Joseph and Gabriella I. (Szigeti) M.; m. Christina D. Csoeke-Poeckh, Sept. 12, 1970; children: Gian-Lorenzo R., Alissa D., Carin E. BS, UCLA, 1962; PhD, Calif. State Poly. U., 1968. Asst. prof. chemistry U. Miss., University, 1971-76, assoc. prof., 1976-83, prof., 1983-84, Coulter prof., 1984-86; prof. U. Ala., Tuscaloosa, 1986—. Gast prof. U. Heidelberg, Fed. Republic Germany, 1979-80; maitre de conf. U. Bordeaux, France, 1980; guest researcher Ministry of Sci. and Technology, Tsukuba, Japan, 1983; professore a contratto U. di Parma, Italy, 1991. Editor (books) Crystal Cohesion and Conformational Energies, 1981, Higher Temperature Superconductivity, 1988, Lower-Dimensional Systems and Molecular Electronics, 1988. Grantee NSF, Office of Naval Rsch., NATO, Naval Air Systems Command, Japan Victor Co. Mem. Am. Chem. Soc. Avocation: stamp collecting/philately. Home: 4950 Northwood Lake Dr E Northport AL 35473-2007 Office: U Ala Dept Chemistry Tuscaloosa AL 35487-0001

METZGER, ROBERT STREICHER, lawyer; b. St. Louis, Sept. 27, 1950; s. Robert Stanley and Jean Harriet (Streicher) M.; children: Michael, Kristen, Marisa. BA, Middlebury Coll., 1974; JD, Georgetown U., 1977. Bar: Calif. 1978, D.C. 1978. Legis. aide US Rep. Robert F. Drinan, Washington, 1972-73; legis. asst. US Rep. Michael J. Harrington, Washington, 1973-75; rsch. fellow Ctr. for Internat. Affairs Harvard U. Grad. Sch. Arts and Sci., Cambridge, Mass., 1977, Harvard U., Kennedy Sch. Govt., Cambridge, Mass., 1978; assoc. Latham & Watkins, LA, 1978-84, ptnr., 1984-90, Kirkland & Ellis, LA, 1990-93, Troop, Meisinger, Steuber & Pasich and predecessor, LA, 1993-97, Gibson, Dunn & Crutcher LLP, LA, 1997—2007; ptnr. corp. and securities Pillsbury Winthrop Shaw Pittman LLP, LA, 2007—. Chmn. Aerospace and Govt. Practice Group, 1997—2006, Telecom. Practice Group, 2000-06; cons. Congl. Rsch. Svc., Washington, 1977-78. Contbr. articles to profl. jours. Trustee Sierra Canyon HS Found., 2007, 2009; mem. dean's alumni leadership coun. Kennedy Sch. Govt. Harvard U., 2005—09. Mem. ABA (litig. pub. contracts sect.), Fed. Comm. Bar Assn., Internat. Inst. for Strategic Studies, Jonathan Club. Office: Pillsbury Winthrop Shaw Pittman LLP 725 S Figueroa St Ste 2806 Los Angeles CA 90017-5406 Office Phone: 213-488-7437, 310-729-9392. Business E-Mail: robert.metzger@pillsburylaw.com.

METZGER, SIDNEY, retired communications engineer; b. NY, Feb. 1, 1917; m. Miriam Lipstein; children: David, Sally, Philip. BSEE, N.Y. Univ., 1937; MEE, Polytech. Inst. Bklyn., 1950. Engr. U.S. Signal Corps. Lab., NJ, 1939—45; head radio relay divsn. Fed. Telecommunications Labs. Internat. Tel. & Tel. Corp., 1945—54; mgr. communications engring. Astro Elect. Prod. Divsn. RCA, 1954—63; mgr. engring. divsn. Communications Satellite Corp., 1963-67, asst. v.p. and chief engr., 1968-72, asst. v.p. and chief scientist, 1972-80, v.p. and chief scientist, 1980-82; cons. engr., 1982—93; ret., 1993. Recipient Aerospace award Aerospace & Elec. Systems Soc., 1975, Internat. Communication award IEEE, 1976, Koji Kobayashi Computers & Communication award, 1985, Aerospace Communication award Am. Inst. Aeronaut. & Astronaut., 1984. Fellow IEEE, AIAA; mem. Nat. Acad. Engring, Sigma Xi. Address: 700 John Ringling Blvd Apt N-206 Sarasota FL 34236-1500 Personal E-mail: mimsid7@comcast.net.

METZGER, VERNON ARTHUR, management educator, consultant; b. Baldwin Park, Calif., Aug. 13, 1918; s. Vernon and Nellie C. (Ross) Metzger; m. Beth Alrene Metzger, Feb. 19, 1955; children: Susan,

Linda, David. BS, U. Calif., Berkeley, 1947, MBA, 1948. Estimating engr. C.F. Braun & Co., 1949; prof. mgmt. Calif. State U., Long Beach, 1949—89, prof. emeritus, 1989—, founder Sch. of Bus. Mgmt. cons. Mem. Fire Commn., Fountain Valley, Calif., 1959—60; mem. mgmt. task force to promote modern mgmt. in Yugoslavia, U.S. State Dept., 1977; mem. State of Calif. Fair Polit. Practices Commn., Orange County Transit Com.; pres. Orange County Dem. League, 1967—68. With USNR, 1942—45. Recipient Outstanding Citizen award, Orange County. Fellow: Soc. Advancement Mgmt. (life; dir.); mem.: Orange County Indsl. Rels. Rsch. Assn. (v.p.), Acad. Mgmt., Tau Kappa Upsilon, Alpha Kappa Psi, Beta gamma Sigma. Home: 1938 Balearic Dr Costa Mesa CA 92626-3513 Office: 1250 N Bellflower Blvd Long Beach CA 90840-0006 Office Phone: 714-557-6415.

METZLER, JAMES ROBERT, musician; b. Worcester, Mass., June 20, 1947; adopted s. Robert Adolph Metzler and Olga Slonin; m. Diane Pearl Fought, Aug. 27, 1988; children: Yurii Wynn Fought, Jeffrey David. MusB, Westminster Choir Coll., 1969; MusM, Hartt Coll. Music, U. Hartford, 1975; diploma, Cambridge Soc. Musicians; diploma (hon.), Nat. Coll. Music & Arts; diploma in Choir Tng., Am. Guild Organists, 1977; D in Organ and Musicology, U. Mich., Ann Arbor, 1987. Organist and choirmaster St. James' Episcopal Ch., New London, Conn., 1969—71, First Presbyn. Ch., Hartford, Conn., 1971—72, Trinity Episcopal Ch., Toledo, 1972—96; adj. prof. organ U. Toledo, 1984—89; organist and dir. music Trinity Episcopal Cathedral, Little Rock, 1996—2006, Pk. Congl. Ch., Grand Rapids, 2006—. Recipient S. Lewis Elmer (First Prize on Guild Exams), Am. Guild of Organists, 1977. Mem.: Royal Sch. Ch. Music, Assn. Anglican Musicians, Am. Guild Organists, Am. Guild of English Handbell Ringers. Episcopalian. Achievements include organ recitals at Notre-Dame Cathedral, Westminster Abbey, St. Paul's Cathedral, Norwich Cathedral, King's College Chapel, Westminster Cathedral, and Washington National Cathedral; director of the Canterbury Singers USA for more than 90 choral services at major British cathedrals and Westminster Abbey. Office: Pk Congl Ch 10 E Park Pl NE Grand Rapids MI 49503 Office Fax: 616-459-0918. Business E-Mail: jmetzler@parkchurchgr.org.

METZMEIER, KURT X., legal association administrator; s. Frank X. Metzmeier. JD, U. Louisville, Ky., 1995, MA in History, 1989; MSLIS, U. Ky., Lexington, 1998. Libr., IT mgr. U. Ky., 1995—2000; assoc. dir. U. Lousville Law Libr., 2000—. Contbr. articles to profl. jours. Fellow: Louisville Bar Found.; mem.: Ky. Hist. Soc., Ky. Bar Assn., Ohio Regional Assn. Law Librs. (bd. mem. 2001—03), Am. Assn. Law Librs. (chair, legal history and rare books SIS 2002—03), Beta Phi Mu, Phi Alpha Theta, Louis Dembitz Brandeis. Office: Law Libr University Louisville Louisville KY 40292 Business E-Mail: kurt.metzmeier@louisville.edu.

METZNER, DAVID MARK, plastic and reconstructive surgeon; b. Cleve., Jan. 16, 1939; children: Damon Hires, Rowan Aliya von Zanthier. AB, U. Mich., 1960; MD, Case Western Res. U., 1964. Diplomate Am. Bd. Otolaryngology, Am. Bd. Plastic Surgery, Nat. Bd. Med. Examiners; lic. MD, Ohio, Calif., Mass., La. Internship Mt. Sinai Hosp., Cleve., 1964-65, residency in gen. surgery, 1965-66; residency in otolaryngology Harvard Med. Sch., Boston, 1966-69; chief of otolaryngology The Cambridge (Mass.) Hosp., 1971-74; residency in plastic and reconstructive surgery La. State U., New Orleans, 1975-76; active staff Lakeside Hosp., Metairie, La., 1977—2007, Highland Pk. Hosp., Covington, La., 1997—2007, Prytania Surgery Ctr., New Orleans, 1986—2007; pvt. plastic surgery New Orleans & Covington, 1977—2007; plastic surgeon Vermont Ctr. Plastic Surgery Dermatology. Active, courtest staff So. Bapt. Hosp., New Orleans, 1977—; courtesy staff St. Tammany Parish Hosp., Covington, 1977—; clin. instr. Harvard Med. Sch., 1971-75; vis. prof. Nassau County, N.Y. Med. Ctr., 1988, Med. Coll. Wis., 1992; vis. lectr. U. Calif. San Diego, 1991; clin. asst. prof. La. State U., 1994-2007; lectr. in field. Recipient AMA Physician's Recognition award, 1981, 84, 87, 90, Appreciation award North Am. Med./Dental Assn.; named one of Top Plastic Surgeons, New Orleans Mag. Mem. Am. Soc. Plastic and Reconstructive Surgeons, Inc., The Am. Soc. for Aesthetic Plastic Surgery (Walter Scott Brown award, 1989), Southeastern Soc. Plastic and Reconstructive Surgeons, Inc., Am. Acad. Facial Plastic and Reconstructive Surgery, Inc., Am. Acad. Otolaryngology-Head and Neck Surgery, Inc., La. Soc. Plastic and Reconstructive Surgeons (pres.), The Double Boarded Soc. (pres.), Southeastern Soc. Plastic and Reconstructive Surgeons, La. Soc. Plastic and Reconstructive Surgeons, La. State Med. Soc., Orleans Parish Med. Soc., Harvard Club La. (pres.). Avocations: art, sculpting, jewelry. Office: 106 Park Pl Ste 115 Covington LA 70433 also: 69 Union St PO Box 147 Manchester VT 05254 Office Phone: 802-362-5655.

METZNER, RICHARD JOEL, psychiatrist, psychopharmacologist, educator; b. LA, Feb. 15, 1942; s. Robert Gerson and Esther Rebecca (Groper) M.; children: Jeffrey Anthony, David Jonathan; m. Leila Kirkley, June 26, 1993. BA, Stanford U., 1963; MD, Johns Hopkins U., 1967. Diplomate Am. Bd. Psychiatry and Neurology. Intern Roosevelt Hosp., NYC, 1967-68; resident in psychiatry Stanford U. Med. Ctr., 1968-71; staff psychiatrist divsn. manpower and tng. NIMH-St. Elizabeths Hosp., Washington, 1971-73; chief audiovisual edn. sys. VA Med. Ctr. Brentwood, LA, 1973-79; from asst. prof. psychiatry to assoc. clin. prof. UCLA Neuropsychiat. Inst., 1980-96, clin. prof., 1996—. Lectr. Sch. Social Welfare, 1975-84; pvt. practice medicine specializing in psychiatry, Bethesda, Md., 1972-73, L.A., 1973—, Sedona, Ariz., 1997—; dir. Western Inst. Psychiatry, L.A., 1977—; pres. Psychiat. Resource Network, Inc., 1984-90, chair, Clin. Neuropharmacology, UCLA, 2007. Contbr. articles to profl. jours.; prodr., writer numerous films and videotapes. With USPHS, 1968-71. Recipient 6 awards for film and videotape prodns., 1976-80, Career Achievement award, Psychiat. Clin. Faculty Assn., UCLA 2006 Fellow: Am. Psychiat. Assn. (life Disting.); mem.: UCLA Psychiat. Clin. Faculty Assn. (pres. 2001—02), Mental Health Careerists Assn. (chmn. 1972—73), So. Calif. Psychiat. Soc., Phi Beta Kappa. Democrat. Jewish. Office: 25 Cindercone Cir Sedona AZ 86336 Office Phone: 928-204-5850. E-mail: rmetzner@ucla.edu, rmetzner@earthlink.net.

MEUCCI, OLIMPIA, medical educator; b. Napoli, Italy, Aug. 22, 1963; d. Dante Meucci and Rosaria Rago; m. Alessandro Fatatis; 1 child, Andrea Fatatis. MD, PhD, U. Naples, 1994. Rsch. asst. prof. U. Chgo., 1994—2000; prof. Drexel U. Coll. Medicine, Phila., 2000—. Fund raiser Am. Cancer Soc. Recipient Excellence Rsch. award, Drexel U., 2002—04, Travel award, Italian Assn. Neurology Rsch.; AIDS rsch. fellowship, Italian Ministry Health, 1994—96. Mem.: AAAS, Italian Soc. Neurochemistry, Soc. NeuroImmunepharmacology, Soc. Neurovirology, Soc. Neuroscience. Achievements include discovery of role of chemokines in neuronal signaling and signalling, cell cycle proteins in HIV neuropathology; research in cellular and molecular mechanisms of HIV neuropathology. Office: Drexel Univ Coll Medicine 245 N 15th st Philadelphia PA 19102 Office Fax: 215-762-2299. Business E-Mail: omeucci@drexelmed.edu.

MEURER, WILLIAM JOSEPH, emergency physician, educator; s. Gregory John and Gail Patricia Meurer; m. Elizabeth Ann Beiler, June 23, 2001; children: William Jr. (Liam) Joseph, Andrew (Drew) Thomas. BA, Ohio State U., Columbus, 1999; MD, U. Cin., Ohio, 2003; MS, U. Mich. Sch. Pub. Health, Ann Arbor, 2009. Diplomate Am. Bd. Emergency Medicine, 2008. Resident MetroHealth Med. Ctr. emergency medicine, Cleve., 2003—06, chief resident, 2005—06; clin. lectr. U. Mich. Health Sys., Ann Arbor, 2006—. Rsch. fellowship, Emergency Medicine Found., 2008. Mem.: AMA, Am. Acad. Emergency Medicine, Am. Heart Assn., Soc. Academic Emergency Medicine, Am. Coll. Emergency Physicians, Ohio State Alumni Assn.

MEUS, JONATHAN A., engineering educator; Adj. asst. prof. Marquette U., Milw., 1992—. Mem.: ASCE. Office: Marquette Univ Coll Engring PO Box 1881 Milwaukee WI 53201-1881 Business E-Mail: jonathan.meus@mu.edu.

MEUSER, FREDRICK WILLIAM, retired church administrator, historian; b. Payne, Ohio, Sept. 14, 1923; s. Henry William and Alvina Maria (Bouyack) Meuser; m. Jeanne Bond Griffiths, July 29, 1951; children: Jill Martha, Douglas Griffiths. AB, Capital U., 1945, BD, 1948, DD (hon.), 1989; STM, Yale U., 1949, MA, 1953, PhD, 1956; DD (hon.), Tex. Luth. Coll., 1980, Capital U., 1989; LHD (hon.), Augustana Coll., 1985. Ordained to ministry Am. Lutheran Ch., 1948; asst. pastor 1st Luth. Ch., Galveston, Tex., 1948, Christ Luth. Ch., North Miami, Fla., 1949—51; luth. campus minister Yale U., 1951—53; prof. ch. history Luth. Theol. Sem., Columbus, Ohio, 1953—78, dean grad. studies, 1963—69, pres., 1971—78; exec. sec. div. theol. studies Luth. Council in U.S.A., 1969—71; pres. Trinity Luth. Sem., Columbus, 1978—88; del. World Council Chs., 1968, Luth. World Fedn., 1970; v.p. Am. Luth. Ch., 1974—80; mem. Commn. for a New Luth. Ch., 1982—86; asst. pastor St. Paul Luth. Ch., Westerville, Ohio, 1995—97. Author: The Formation of the American Lutheran Church, 1958, Luther the Preacher, 1983; author: (with others) Church in Fellowship, 1963, Lutherans in North America, 1975; translator: (with others) What Did Luther Understand by Religion, 1977, The Reconstruction of Morality, 1979; editor and author: (with others) Interpreting Luther's Legacy, 1967; contbr. articles to profl. publs. Recipient Disting. Churchman's award Tex. Luth. Coll., 1972, Joseph Sittler award Trinity Luth. Sem., 1990; named Outstanding Alumnus Capital U., 1977; Am. Assn. Theol. Schs. fellow, 1961-62 Home: 2055 S Floral Ave Lot 240 Bartow FL 33830-7157 Personal E-mail: fredmeuser@aol.com.

MEVERS, FRANK CLEMENT, state agency administrator, archivist; b. New Orleans, Oct. 10, 1942; s. Lloyd F. and Mary Ashley (Collins) M.; m. Kathryn Ann Hayes, Dec. 23, 1967; children: John F., Lauren K. BA in History, La. State U., 1965; PhD in Am. History, U. NC, 1972; MA, La. State U., 1967. Editor Papers of James Madison, Charlottesville, Va., 1972-74, Papers of Josiah Bartlett, Concord, NH, 1974-77, Papers of William Plumer, Concord, 1977-79; state archivist State of NH, Concord, 1979—. Editor, author: New Hampshire: State That Made US a Nation, 1989. Mem. Pub. Libr. Bd. Trustees, Concord, 1979-99. With US Army, 1967-69, Korea. Episcopalian. Avocation: stamp collecting/philately. Home: 29 Bradley St Concord NH 03301-6432 Office: NH State Archives 71 S Fruit St Concord NH 03301-2410 Office Phone: 603-271-2236. Personal E-mail: eatright@comcast.net. Business E-Mail: fmevers@sos.state.nh.us.

MEW, CALVIN MARSHALL, advertising executive; b. Oakland, Calif., Oct. 27, 1947; s. Thomas Bing and May (Jan) m. Mary Farnham Crawford, Oct. 20, 2001. BA, Yale U., 1969; MDiv, Union Theol Sem., 1973; postgrad., Columbia U., 1973-79, Harvard U., 1984. Tutor Union Theol. Sem., 1973-77; adj. lectr. Hunter Coll., 1977-79; market analyst Kenyon & Eckhart Advt., Inc., NYC, 1979-82, v.p. market plans, 1982-83, rev. v.p. strategic plan, 1983-85, v.p. strategic mktg. svcs., 1985-88, sr.v.p. strategic and forward planning, 1988-90; sr. v.p., mng. dir. Bozell, Inc., 1990-93, exec. v.p., mng. dir., 1993—. Gen. mgr. Bozell Austria, 1994; exec. v.p., regional dir. L.Am. Bozell Worldwide, Inc., 1996; dir. Capritauro Investments, Ltd., 2002; adv. bd. Columbia U. Librs., 2006—. Contbr. articles to profl. jours. Bd. dirs. Union Theol. Sem., 1984—, vice chmn., 1992—; mem. advisory bd. Columbia U. Libr., 2006-, trustee Mus. Biblical Art, 2007, James Lenox House Assn., 2008. Recipient Cogswell award Yale U., 1969; Columbia U. fellow, Rockefeller Bros. Fund fellow. Mem. Am. Acad. Religion, Soc. Bibl. Lit., Harvard Bus. Sch. Club (mem. adv. bd. N.Y. chpt. 2004). Presbyterian. Home: 895 W End Ave New York NY 10025-3500 Office: Bozell Jacobs Kenyon Eckhart 13801 Fnb Pkwy Omaha NE 68154-5230 Business E-Mail: calvinmew@post.harvard.edu.

MEW, THOMAS JOSEPH, III, (TOMMY), artist, educator; b. Miami, Fla., Aug. 15, 1942; s. Thomas Joseph and Maude Edith (Perry) M.; m. Mary Ann Kelley, June 17, 1966; 1 son, Thomas Joseph IV. BS, Fla. State U., 1962, MA, 1964; PhD, NYU, 1966. Grad. instr. Fla. State U., 1963; asst. prof. art Troy State U., 1966-68, Jacksonville U., 1968-70; prof., chmn. dept. art Berry Coll., 1970—, Dana prof. art. Juror art shows: vis. artist; lectr. in field, cons. art; dir. Fluxus West/Southeast; dir. Moon Gallery. Exhibited in one-man shows Parkway Gallery, Miami, 1962-63, 319 Gallery, NYC, 1968, Meridian (Miss.) Mus., 1976, C.D.O. Gallery, Parma, Italy, 1978, Calif. State U., Sacramento, 1979, Miss. Mus. Art, Jackson, 1979, Art Inst. for Permian Basin, ITex, Arte Studio, Bergamo, Italy, Queen Street Gallery, Belfast, No. Ireland; group shows include High Mus., Atlanta, 1971, 72, 74, New Reform Gallery, Aalst, Belgium, 1975, U. Guelph, Ont., Can., 1975, Neuberger Mus., Purchase, NY, 1978, Arte Fiera, Bologna, Italy, 1979; represented in permanent collections, Kansas City Art Inst., Mildura Art Centre, Australia, Wichita Art Mus., Jacksonville (Fla.) Art Mus., Macon Mus. Art, AT&T, Harn Mus., U. Iowa; host: Cable TV show Art: The Mew View, 1978—; Filmmaker, 1966-69; contbr. articles to profl. jours. Bd. dirs. Rome Arts Coun., 1984—, Interface. Recipient Gellhorn award NYU, 1966; Cowperthwaite grantee, 1972; Lilly Found. grantee, 1975; Gulf Life grantee, 1977. Mem. Southeastern Coll. Art Conf., Coll. Art Assn. Am., Am. Fedn. Arts, Nat. Art Edn. Assn., Am. Assn. Art Dealers, Omicron Delta Kappa, Phi Kappa Phi. Home: 28 Virginia Cir Rome GA 30161 Office: Berry Coll Art Dept PO Box 580 Mount Berry GA 30149 Home Phone: 706-292-9234; Office Phone: 706-236-2219. Business E-Mail: tmew@berry.edu. *I've always moved in the direction of my dreams... always tried to make the great dream a reality.*

MEWSHAW, RICHARD ERIC, chemist; b. Balt., Oct. 20, 1955; s. Thomas James and Laura Jean Mewshaw; 1 child, Rachelle Stephanie. PhD, U. Pa., Phila., 1985. Chemist Smith Kline & French, King of Prussia, Pa., 1988—90, Nova Pharms., Balt., 1990—93, Wyeth, Radnor, Pa., 1985—87, Princeton, NJ, 1993—99, Collegeville, Pa., 1999—. Contbr. articles to profl. sci. jours. Mem.: Am. Chem. Soc. Achievements include being the inventor or coinventor on 50 US patents. Avocations: travel, golf, dance, languages.

MEYBURG, ARNIM HANS, transportation engineer, educator, consultant; b. Bremerhaven, W. Ger., Aug. 25, 1939; came to U.S., 1965; s. Friedel and Auguste (Kleeberg) M.; 1 child, Jennifer Susan. Student, U. Hamburg, 1960-62, Free U. Berlin, 1962-65; MS (Fulbright travel grantee), Northwestern U., 1968, PhD, 1971. Research assoc. Transp. Center, Northwestern U., 1968-69; asst. prof. transp. engring. Cornell U., 1969-75, assoc. prof., 1975-78, prof., 1978—, prof. emeritus, 2008—, acting chmn. dept., 1977-78, chmn. dept., 1980-85, dir. Sch. Civil and Environ. Engring., 1988-98, chmn. bd. Univ. Transp. Rsch. Ctr., 1992-95; dir. Transp. Infrastructure Rsch. Consortium, 1995—. Vis. mem. faculties U. Calif., Irvine, Tech. U. Munich, Germany, (Fulbright lectr.) U. Sao Paulo, Brazil, 1984, Tech. U. Brunswick, W. Ger., 1985-86; Humboldt Found. research fellow, 1978-79; prin. investigator projects Dept. Transp., NSF, Nat. Coop. Hwy. Research Program, N.Y. State Dept. Transp., U.S. Dept. Transp. Author: (with others) Urban Transportation Modeling and Planning, 1975, Transportation Systems Evaluation, 1976, Survey Sampling and Multivariate Analysis for Social Scientists and Engineers, 1979, Survey Methods for Transport Planning, 1995; co-editor: (with others) Behavioral Travel-Demand Models, 1976, New Horizons in Travel-Behavior Research, 1981, Selected Readings in Transport Survey Methodology, 1992; contbr. articles to profl. jours., chpts. to books. NSF Research Initiation grantee, 1973; recipient Humboldt U.S. Sr. Scientist award, 1984, Fulbright sr. lectr. award, 1984. Mem. ASCE, AAUP, Transp. Rsch. Bd., Transp. Rsch. Forum, Sigma Xi, Chi Epsilon. Office: Cornell U 220 Hollister Hall Ithaca NY 14853-3501 Office Phone: 607-255-7519. E-mail: ahm2@cornell.edu.

MEYER, ALBERT JAMES, educational researcher; b. Cleve., Sept. 24, 1929; s. Jacob Conrad and Esther Agnes (Steiner) M.; m. Mary Ellen Yoder, Aug. 21, 1954; children: Richard, Anne, Kathryn, Barbara, Elaine. BA, Goshen Coll., 1950; MA, Princeton U., 1952, PhD, 1954. Asst. in teaching and rsch. Princeton (N.J.) U., 1950-53; fellow U. Basel, Switzerland, 1953-54, rsch. assoc., 1956-57; dir. for France, rep. European peace sect. Mennonite Ctrl. Com., 1954-57; asst. prof. physics Goshen (Ind.) Coll., 1958-61, prof., rsch. prof., 1967-89, adj. rsch. prof., 1989—; acad. dean, prof. Bethel Coll., North Newton, Kans., 1961-66, Menno Simons lectr., 1993; exec. sec., pres. Mennonite Bd. Edn., Elkhart, Ind., 1967-95; vis. fellow Princeton (N.J.) U., 1995-96. Exec. for secretariat Puidoux Theol. Confs., 1955-57; former mem. staff Mennonite Student Svcs. Com.; former coord. com. on liberal arts edn. North Ctrl. Assn. Colls. and Secondary Schs.; vis. rsch. scientist U. Paris, 1974-75; vis. rschr. New Coll. Berkeley, 1986-87; presenter in field; former cons. Conrad Grebel Coll., U. Waterloo, Ont., Can.; mem. peace and social concerns com. Mennonite Ch., 1959-71; former mem. Continuation Com. of Hist. Peace Chs.; mem. interch. rels. staff Mennonite Ch. U.S.A., 1997—; mem secretariat Nat. Assn. Ind. Colls. and Univs. Contbr. articles to profl. jours. Princeton U. exch. fellow and Charles Foster Kent fellow Nat. Coun. for Religion in Higher Edn., 1953-54. Mem.: Soc. for Values in Higher Edn., Nat. Assn. Ind. Colls. and Univs. (secretariat), Am. Assn. Physics Tchrs., Denominational Execs. for Ch.-Related Higher Edn. (chmn. 1984—86). Avocations: hiking, camping. Home: 708 Emerson St Goshen IN 46526-3904

MEYER, ALICE VIRGINIA, state official; b. NYC, Mar. 15, 1921; d. Martin G. and Marguerite Helene (Houzē) Kliemand; m. Theodore Harry Meyer, June 28, 1947; children: Robert Charles, John Edward. BA, Barnard Coll., 1941; MA, Columbia U., 1942; D of Humanitarian Svcs. (hon.), Briarwood Coll., 2006. Tchr. pub. schs., Elmont, N.Y., 1942-43; tchr. Fairlawn (N.J.) High Sch., 1943-47; office mgr., sales rep. NYC, 1948-55; substitute tchr. Pub. Schs., Easton, Conn., 1965-72; state rep., asst. minority leader Conn. State Legislature, Hartford, 1976-93. Mem. Ct. Bd. of Govs. Higher Edn., 1993-05, vice-chair, chair. bd. govs. higher edn.; bd. dirs. 3030 Fairfield Health Ctr., 1994-06. Mem. Edn. Commn. of the States, 1985—87; life trustee Discovery Mus., 1980—; trustee United Way Regional Youth Substance Abuse Project, Bridgeport, 1983—93; mem. strategic planning com. Town of Easton, 1993—96; vice chmn. ct. adv. coun. on intergovtl. rels., 1988—; mem. Conn. Commn. on Quality Edn., 1992—93; supporter Conn. Small Towns, 1988; mem. Conn. Humanities Coun., 1974—76, Conn. Film Commn., 1985—88; co-chair Com. on State Plan of Conservation and Devel., 1985—87; mem. Lt. Gov.'s Commn. on Mandate Reduction, 1995; sec. Easton Free Sch. Scholarship Fund, 1980—; pres. Barnard Class of 1941, 1996—; justice of the peace, 2001—; ct. adv. coun. career and vocat. edn., 1980—88; mem. Easton Rep. Town Com., 1965—, vice chmn., 1970—78; bd. dirs. Bridgeport Ch. Women United, 1950—58, pres., 1955—57; chair Small Bus. Adv. Commn., 1984—88; Fairfield County Lit. Coalition Bridgeport, 1988—94; bd. dirs. 3030 Park, 1993—2006. Named Legislator of Yr. Conn. Libr. Assn., 1985; Guardian Small Bus. grantee Nat. Fedn. Ind. Bus., 1987; honoree Fairfield YWCA Salute to Women, 1988, Conn. Assn. Small Towns, 1990; named grant to AAUW Fellowship Fund, Bridgeport Br., 1970, Conn. State AAUW, 1974; recipient Conn. Friends of Libr. Hon. award, 1984, Disting. Svc. award Conn. State Coun. on Voc/Tech. Edn., 1986, Sacred Heart U. Ctr. for Policy Issues award, 1988, citation Conn. Bd. for Acad. Affairs, 1992, citation Charter Oak Coll., 1993, Spl. Day Recognition, Town of Weston, 1993, Cert. of Recognition, Town of Westport, 1993, Citation for Fostering Open Access to Higher Edn., AAUW, 1994, Disting. Rep. award Easton Rep. Town Com., 2000, Pub. Svc. award Conn. Sec. of State, 2003, others; named in her honor Alice V. Meyer Day, Gov. M. Jodi Rell, Conn., 2005; scholarship named in her honor, 2006. Mem.: LWV, AAUW (local pres. 1976, bd. dirs. 1982), Nat. Order Women Legislators (regional dir. 1987—91, past pres. Conn. chpt.), Conn. Assn. Sch. Adminstrs. (hon.), Bus. and Profl. Women. Congregationalist. Avocations: swimming, sailing, bridge. Home: 18 Lantern Hill Rd Easton CT 06612-2218

MEYER, AUGUST CHRISTOPHER, JR., broadcast executive, lawyer; b. Champaign, Ill., Aug. 14, 1937; s. August C. and Clara (Rocke) M.; m. Karen Haugh Hassett, Dec. 28, 1960; children: August Christopher F., Elisabeth Hassett. BA cum laude, Harvard U., Cambridge, Mass., 1959, LLB, 1962. Bar: Ill. 1962. Founding ptr. Meyer-Capel, Champaign, Ill., 1962-77, of counsel, 1977—2003; owner, dir., officer Midwest TV, Inc., Sta. KFMB-TV-AM-FM, San Diego, Sta. WCIA-TV, Champaign, Ill., Sta. WMBD-TV-AM, WMXP, Peoria, Ill., 1968—, pres., 1976—2007, chmn. bd. of dirs., 2007—. Bd. dirs. Bank Ill., Main St. Trust Inc., First Busey Corp., (bank holding co.); spl. asst. atty. gen. State of Ill., 1968-76. Chmn. bd. trustees Carle Found. Hosp., Urbana, Ill. Mem. Ill. Bar Assn., Champaign County Bar Assn. Clubs: Champaign Country. Office: Midwest TV Inc PO Box 197 100 W University Ave # 401 Champaign IL 61824-0197 also: Sta KFMB PO Box 85888 7677 Engineer Rd San Diego CA 92111-1515

MEYER, BARRY MICHAEL, motion picture executive; b. NYC, Nov. 28, 1943; s. Perry and Lillian Helen (Katz) M.; m. Barbara Patricia, June 12, 1966; children: Matthew, Elizabeth. BA, U. Rochester, 1964; JD, Case Western Res. U., 1967. Bar: NY, Ohio. Legal counsel ABC, NYC, 1968-70, dir. bus. affairs LA, 1970-71, Warner Bros. TV, LA, 1971—72, v.p. bus. affairs, 1972—78, exec. v.p., 1978—84, Warner Bros. Entertainment, Inc., LA, 1984—94, exec. v.p., COO, 1994—99, chmn., CEO, 1999—. Mem. bd. councilors USC Sch. Cinema-TV; bd. dirs. Motion Picture Assn. Am., Mus. Radio and TV, Am. Film Inst. Contbr. articles to profl. jours. Bd. dirs. Human Rights Watch, San Fernando Valley Child Guidance Clinic, Calif.; bd. trustees U. Rochester. Named one of 50 Most Powerful People in Hollywood, Premiere mag., 2004—06. Mem. Hollywood Radio and TV Soc., Nat. Acad. TV

Arts and Scis. (former gov.), Am. Mgmt. Assn., Acad. Motion Pictures Arts & Scis. Office: Warner Bros Entertainment Inc 4000 Warner Blvd Burbank CA 91522-0002 Office Phone: 818-954-1464.*

MEYER, BRUCE D., lawyer; b. Aug. 31, 1945; BA, U. Ill., 1967, JD with high honors, 1970. Bar: Calif. 1971. Assoc. Gibson Dunn & Crutcher, LA, 1970—73, ptnr., 1979—81, Riyadh, Saudi Arabia, 1981—83, ptnr. corp. transactions and securities LA, 1983—; v.p., asst. gen. counsel Whittaker Corp., LA, 1973—79. Mem. exec. com. Gibson Dunn & Crutcher. Mem.: ABA (chmn. Middle East law com., internat. law section 1984—85), LA County Bar Assn., Order of Coif. Office: Gibson Dunn & Crutcher LLP 333 Grand Ave Los Angeles CA 90071-3197 Office Phone: 213-229-7979. Office Fax: 213-229-6979. Business E-Mail: bmeyer@gibsondunn.com.

MEYER, CHARLOTTE LOIS, medical geriatric social worker, consultant; b. Chelsea, Mass., June 15, 1932; d. James and Anne (Berson) Sampson; m. Irving Meyer; children: Fredric B., Marc H., James S. BS, Simmons Coll., 1952, MS in Social Work, 1954; cert in Psychotherapy, Smith Coll., 1996. Bd. cert. in clin. social work. Pvt. practice med./geriat. social work. Mem.: Acad. Cert. Social Workers.

MEYER, CHRISTOPHER HAWKINS, lawyer; b. Springfield, Mo., Sept. 29, 1952; s. Richard DeWitt and Nancy (Hawkins) M.; m. Karen Anne Adams, Aug. 8, 1987; 1 child, C. Andrew Meyer. BA in Econs. magna cum laude, U. Mich., 1977, JD cum laude, 1981. Bar: DC 1981, US Ct. Appeals (DC cir.) 1982, US Ct. Appeals (9th cir.) 1983, Colo. 1985, US Ct. Appeals (10th cir.) 1985, Idaho, US Ct. Appeals (8th cir.). Counsel water resources program Nat. Wildlife Fedn., Washington, 1981-84; assoc. prof. U. Colo. Law Sch., Colo., 1984-91; ptnr. Givens Pursley, Boise, 1991—. Counsel Rocky Mountain Natural Resources Clinic, Boulder, Colo., 1984—91. Contbr. articles to profl. publs. Mem. steering com. Idaho Environ. Forum. Named one of Best Lawyers in Am., Chambers USA, Super Lawyers of Intermountain West. Mem. Phi Beta Kappa. Home: 3443 S Millspur Way Boise ID 83716-8648 Office: Givens Pursley LLP 601 W Bannock St Boise ID 83702-7720 Home Phone: 208-336-2485; Office Phone: 208-388-1236. Business E-Mail: chrismeyer@givenspursley.com.

MEYER, SIR CHRISTOPHER J.R., former ambassador; b. Beaconsfield, Eng., Feb. 22, 1944; m. Catherine Laylle; 2 sons, 2 stepsons. Student, Lancing Coll., Eng., Peterhouse, Cambridge, Eng., Paul Nitze Sch., Bologna, Italy; MA in History, Cambridge U., 1965. Joined Diplomatic Svc., London, 1966-68, with Moscow, 1968-70, Madrid, 1970-73; head Soviet sect. East European and Soviet dept. Fgn. and Commonwealth Office, London, 1973-76; speech-writer to fgn. sec. policy planning staff Diplomatic Svc., London, 1976-78; mem. UK rep. to European Comtys., Brussels, 1978-82; polit. counselor British Embassy, Moscow, 1982-84; fgn. office spokesman, press sec. to fgn. sec. Fgn. and Commonwealth Office, London, 1984-88, min. Washington, 1989-92; min., dep. head mission British Embassy, 1992—93, govt. spokesman, press sec. to prime min. London, 1994—96, Brit. amb. to Fed. Rep. Germany, 1997; UK amb. to U.S. Washington, 1997—2003; chmn. U.K. Press Complaints Commn., 2003—09. Vis. fellow Harvard U. Ctr. for Internat. Affairs, 1988-89; hon. fellow Peterhouse, Cambridge U., 2001—; non-exec. dir. GKN Plc., Arbuthnot Banking Group; gov. English Speaking Union. Named Knight Comdr. of the Order of St. Michael and St. George, 1998. Mem.: Fleishman-Hillard (internat. adv. bd.). Avocations: tennis, watching soccer, listening to jazz music. Home: 48 Rawlings St London SW3 2LS England Office: Arbuthnot Banking Group 20 Ropemaker St London EC2Y 9AR England Office Phone: 44 2070 122420.

MEYER, DANNY, restaurateur; b. St. Louis; m. Audrey Meyer; children: Hallie, Charles, Gretchen, Peyton. Degree in Polit. Sci., Trinity Coll. Cook County field dir. John Anderson's presdl. campaign, Chgo.; asst. mgr. Pesca, NYC, 1984; pres. Union Square Hospitality Group, 1998—. Co-author: Union Square Cafe Cookbook, 1994 (Julia Child award Internat. Assn. Culinary Profls.), Second Helpings from Union Square Cafe, 2001; author: Setting the Table, 2006. Co-chair Union Square Partnership; mem. bd. dirs. Share Out Strength, City Strength; mem. exec. com. NYC & Co., Madison Square Park Conservancy. Recipient Outstanding Restaurant award (Gramercy Tavern), James Beard Found., 2008; named one of 25 Leaders Reshaping NY, Crain's NY mag., 2008. Office: Union Square Hospitality Group 24 Union Square E New York NY 10003 Office Phone: 212-228-3585.

MEYER, DAVID ALAN, lawyer; b. St. Louis, Feb. 23, 1968; s. Robert L. and Jeanette Z. Meyer. BA, Williams Coll., Williamstown, Mass., 1990; JD, Boston U., 1994, MA, 1995. Bar: Ill. 1994, Mo. 1995. Asst. atty. gen. Office of Atty. Gen. Mo., Jefferson City, 1997—2001; sr. counsel Mo. Pub. Svc. Commn., Jefferson City, 2001—07; asst. city counselor & counsel St. Louis Devel. Corp., 2007—. Office: 1015 Locust Ste 1200 Saint Louis MO 63101

MEYER, DAVID GILBERT, engineering educator; b. Cleve., Mar. 23, 1944; s. Casper Joseph Meyer and Evelyn Weber; m. Kathleen Grewe, Sept. 14, 1968; children: Jennifer Lynn, Jeffery Paul, David Michael. BS in Indsl. Tech., Ohio State U., Columbus, 1969, PhD, 2008; MBA, Jones Internat., Denver, 2003. Registered profl. engr., Ohio Profl. Engrs., 1980; lic. pilot Soc. Mfg. Engrs. Engring. ops., plant mgmt., Dayton, 1969—2000; coll. prof. Sinclair CC, Dayton, 2000—. Contbr. scientific papers. Trustee and advisor PolymerOhio, Columbus, 2000—04, cons. mfg., 2000—08. With USAF, 1962—65, Wethersfield, Eng. Recipient ASC Outstanding Scientists & Engrs. award, Affiliates Socs. Coun. Dayton, 2005. Mem.: Dayton Soc. Profl. Engrs. Independent. Achievements include patents for punch trainer tooling. Avocation: flying. Home: 1375 Black Oak Dr Dayton OH 45459 Office: Sinclair CC 444 W Third St Dayton OH 45402-1460 Office Fax: 937-512-4530. Business E-Mail: meyer@osu.edu.

MEYER, DEBORAH WAHL, automotive executive; b. Detroit, 1962; married; 1 child. BA in Econs., Wellesley Coll., Mass., 1986; MBA, U. Pa. Wharton Sch. Bus.; MS, U. Pa. Joseph H. Lauder Inst. Mgmt. Internat. Studies, 2005. With Chase Manhattan Bank, NY; product mgr. W.L. Gore & Assocs., Paris; various positions Ford Motor Co., including mktg. comm. mgr. Lincoln Mercury divsn., group mgr. brand strategy/comm. Mazda N.Am. ops., brand mgr. Ford do Brasil; corp. mktg. mgr. Toyota Motor Sales USA Inc., 2001—05, v.p. mktg. Lexus divsn., 2005—07; v.p., chief mktg. officer Chrysler LLC, Auburn Hills, Mich., 2007—. Bd. dirs. Assn. Nat. Advertisers. Trustee Long Beach Mus. Art, 2005—. Named a Woman to Watch, Fortune mag., 2007, Power Player, Advt. Age mag., 2008; named one of 100 Leading Women in N.Am. Automotive Industry, Automotive News, 2005; named to Hall of Advt. Achievement, Am. Advt. Fedn. Office: Chrysler LLC 1000 Chrysler Dr Auburn Hills MI 48326 Office Phone: 248-576-5741. Business E-Mail: deborahmeyer@chryslerllc.com.*

MEYER, DENNIS IRWIN, lawyer; b. Dayton, Ohio, Oct. 20, 1935; s. Luther Edward and Mary (McGee) Meyer; m. Rita Murray, June 23, 1962; children: Matthew, Michael, Rita Catherine, Peter, Denise, Abigail. BS, U. Dayton, 1957; LLB, Georgetown U., 1960, LLM, 1962. Bar: Ohio 1960, DC 1962. Atty.-advisor US Tax Ct., Washington, 1960—62; sr. counsel Baker & McKenzie, Washington, 2002—. Bd. dirs. United Fin. Banking Cos., Vienna. Mem.: ABA, Internat. Fiscal Assn., Robert Trent Jones Golf Club, Avenel Golf Club, Belle Haven Country Club, Met. Club. Roman Catholic. Office: Baker & McKenzie 815 Connecticut Ave NW Washington DC 20006-4004 Home Phone: 703-768-3482; Office Phone: 202-452-7008. Business E-Mail: dennis.i.meyer@bakernet.com.

MEYER, DIANNE A., lawyer; b. Phila., Apr. 9, 1953; JD, U. Pa., 1986. CPA 1978; bar: Pa., Supreme Ct. Pa. CPA Audit and Mgmt. Adv. Svcs., 1978—81; asst. mgr. fin. svcs. Reliance Ins. Co., 1981—83; assoc. Blank, Rome, Comisky & McCauley, Phila., 1986—88, Saul, Ewing, Remick & Saul, Phila., 1988—89, Duane Morris LLP, 1989—95, ptnr., 1995—. Bd. mem. Woodmere Art Mus., Chestnut Hill, Pa. Named to America's Leading Bus. Lawyers, Chambers USA, 2006—09. Mem.: Phila. Bar Assn., Pa. Inst. CPA, Pa. Assn. Bond Lawyers (pres. 2002—03), Nat. Assn. Bond Lawyera. Office: Duane Morris LLP 30 South 17th St Philadelphia PA 19103 Office Phone: 215-979-1222. Office Fax: 215-689-3603. Business E-Mail: DAMeyer@duanemorris.com.*

MEYER, DIRK (DERRICK R. MEYER), information technology executive; b. La Grange, Ill., 1961; BS in Computer Engring., U. Ill.; MBA, Boston U. With microprocessor design group Intel Corp.; with Digital Equipment Corp., 1985—95; joined Advanced Micro Devices, Inc., Sunnyvale, Calif., 1995—, dir. engring. Austin, Tex., 1996—99, v.p. engring., computation products group Sunnyvale, Calif., 1999—2001, group v.p., computation products group, 2001—02, sr. v.p., computation products group, exec. officer, 2002—04, exec. v.p., computation products group, 2004—05, pres., COO, microprocessor solutions sector, 2005—06, pres., COO, 2006—08, pres., CEO, 2008—. Bd. dirs. Advanced Micro Devices, Inc., 2007—. Recipient Maurice Wilkes award, Assn. Computing Machinery, 2003. Office: Advanced Micro Devices Inc 1 AMD Pl Sunnyvale CA 94088

MEYER, DOROTHY JEAN, nursing consultant, director; d. Frederick G. and Dorothy Marie Meyer. BS in Nursing, Ariz. State U., Tempe, 1974; MPH, Johns Hopkins Sch. Pub. Health, Balt., 1979; Diploma in Nursing, Luth. Hosp. Sch. of Nursing, St. Louis, 1966. Cert. nurse midwife, Am. Coll. Nurse Midwives, 1979. Staff nurse gen. surgery St. Louis Children's Hosp., 1969—70; hosp. staff nurse pediat. PHS Indian Hosp., Tuba City, Ariz., 1970—72, pub. health nurse & home care coord., 1974—77, staff nurse midwife, 1979—83, Fort Yates, ND, 1983—85; capt. US Pub. Health Svc., 1979—2002; pub. health adminstrv. residency Nat. Health Svc. Corps, Boston, 1985—86; maternal child health cons. Phoenix Area Indian Health Svc., 1986—2002; vol. med. cons. Cameroon Bapt. Conv. Health Bd., Bamanda, Cameroon, 1998—. Dir. Flagstaff Internat. Health & Edn. Fund, Ariz., 2005—. Contbr. articles to profl. jours. Vol. peace corps, Sabah, Malaysia; vol. dir. Flagstaff Internat. Health & Edn. Fund, 2005—08. Decorated Outstanding Svc. Medal USPHS, Commendation Medal; recipient Cert. Appreciation, Ariz. Dept. Health Svcs., 1988, US Dept. Justice, 1990, Native Am. Child Advocacy award, Am. Acad. Pediat., 1999, Govs. Recognition award, Ariz. Gov., 1996, Mabel May Wagner award, USPHS, 1998, Chief Nurse Officer award, 1996, Asst. Sec. Health's award, 1985, Champions Children, Ariz. Republic Newspaper, 1999; named to Woman of the Yr., Fed. Woman's Program, 1991, PHS Nurse Adminstr. of the Yr., Indian Health Svc., 1990. Mem.: Am. Coll. Obstetricians & Gynecologists, Am. Coll. Nurse Midwifery. Personal E-mail: dotjmeyer@aol.com.

MEYER, DOROTHY VIRGINIA, retired education educator; b. Boston, Apr. 15, 1930; d. Arnold S. and Hilda M. (Cann) M. BA, Houghton Coll., NY, 1952; MEd, Boston U., 1959, EdD, 1976. Tchr. Wellesley Pub. Schs., Mass., 1954-69; dir. edn. Cambridge Model Cities, Mass., 1969-71, dir. program ops., 1971-73; asst. prof. Newton Coll., Mass., 1973-75, Grad. Sch. Edn. U. Mass.-Lowell, Mass., 1975-79, assoc. prof. and coord. Ctr. Adminstrn., Planning and Policy, 1979—99, chmn. faculty Edn., 1983, 84-88, prof. emerita, 2000. Bd. dirs. Mass. Coun. Pub. Schs., 1963-66, Mass. Coun. Tchr. Edn., 1964-66; mem. adv. com. U.S. Office Edn. Nat. Tchr. Corps, 1970-72, panel cons.'s Ednl. Personnel Devel. Div., 1967-69, Mass. Bi-Lingual Adv. Bd., 1971-75. Contbr. articles to ednl. jours. Bd. dirs. Bishop Guetrin High Sch., Nashua, N.H., 1987-93, Commn. on Ministry to Higher Edn. Mass. Episc. Diocese, 1983-90. Mem. NEA (commr. nat. commn. tchr. edn. and profl. standards 1966-70, chmn. 1968-69, bd. dirs. Ctr. for Study Instrn. 1967-71, co-editor publ., 1980), Mass. Soc. Profs., Mass. Tchrs. Assn. (bd. dirs. 1957-67, exec. com. 1963-67, v.p. 1962-65, pres. 1965-66), Nat. Assn. State Edn. Assns. (exec. com. 1965-67, v.p. 1967-68), Internat. Soc. Ednl. Planning, Nat. Coun. Accreditation Tchr. Edn. (mem. coordinating bd. 1968-70, mem. evaluation bd. 1971-74) Home: 43 Linnaean St Cambridge MA 02138-1544 Business E-Mail: Dorothy_Meyer@uml.edu.

MEYER, EDMOND GERALD, retired chemistry professor, energy scientist, academic administrator; b. Albuquerque, Nov. 2, 1919; s. Leopold and Beatrice (Ilfeld) M.; m. Betty F. Knobloch, July 4, 1941 (dec.); children: Lee Gordon, Terry Gene, David Gary. BS in Chemistry, Carnegie Mellon U., 1940, MS, 1942; PhD, U. N.Mex., 1950. Chemist Harbison Walker Refractories Co., 1940-41; instr. Carnegie Mellon U., 1941-42; asst. phys. chemist Bur. Mines, 1942-44; chemist research div. N.Mex. Inst. Mining and Tech., 1946-48; head dept. sci. U. Albuquerque, 1950-52; head dept. chemistry N.Mex. Highlands U., 1952-59; dir. Inst. Sci. Rsch., dean Grad. Sch. U. Wyo., 1957—63, dean Coll. Arts and Sci., 1963-75, v.p. rsch., 1974-80, prof. energy and natural resources, 1981-89, prof. and dean emeritus, 1989—; pres., CEO Advanced Clean Coal Techs. LLC, 1999—. Exec. cons. Diamond Shamrock Corp., 1980; sci. adviser Gov. of Wyo., 1964-90; pres. Coal Tech. Corp., 1981—; cons. Los Alamos Nat. Lab., NFS, HHS, GAO, TVA, Wyo. Bancorp; contractor investigator Rsch. Corp., Dept. Interior, AEC, NIH, NSF, Dept. Energy, Dept. Edn.; Fulbright exch. prof. U. Concepcion, Chile, 1959. Co-author: Chemistry-Survey of Principles, 1963, Legal Rights of Chemists and Engineers, 1977, Industrial Research & Development Management, 1982; contbr. articles to profl. jours.; patentee in field. Mem. Laramie Regional Airport Bd., 1989-93, treas., 1994-97, chair; active Laramie City Coun., 1997-2001, vice mayor, 1998-2001. Lt. comdr. USNR, 1944-46, ret. Recipient Disting. Svc. award Jaycees, Disting. Faculty award 2009; rsch. fellow U. N.Mex., 1948-50. Fellow: AAAS, Am. Inst. Chemists (hon.; pres. 1992—93, chmn. 1994—95); mem.: AIChE (sr.), Coun. Coll. Arts and Scis. (pres. 1971, sec.-treas. 1972—75, dir. Washington office 1973), Biophys. Soc., Am. Chem. Soc. (councilor 1962—90, chmn. Wyo. sect. 1997, 2002, chmn. Rocky Mountain region 1972—88, 2000, 2009, nat. vol. svc. award 2006), Assn. Western Univs. (chmn. 1972—74), Laramie C. of C. (pres. 1984), Sigma Xi. Home: 1058 Colina Dr Laramie WY 82072-5015 Office: U Wyo Coll Arts Scis Laramie WY 82073-0966 Office Phone: 307-766-5445. Business E-Mail: egmeyer@uwyo.edu.

MEYER, ELLEN L., academic administrator; BA and MS Geo Wash U. V.p. mktg. dean continuing studies, dir. extension program and summer sch. Mpls. Coll. Art and Design; dir. continuing edn. and spl. programs RI Sch. Design; pres. Atlanta Coll. Art, 1992—2007, Watkins College of Art, Design & Film, Nashville, 2008—. Mem.: Nat. Black Arts Festival (bd. dirs.), Metro Atlanta Arts Fund (adv. bd. mem.). Office: Watkins College of Art, Design & Film 2298 Rosa L Parks Blvd Nashville TN 37228*

MEYER, ERNST A., oil industry executive, consultant; s. Trygve Arild and Marina Meyer; m. Randi Sundt Meyer; children: Henrik Sundt, Sundt Meyer Frida. MS (hon.), U. Trondheim, 1995. Prin. cons. Det Norske Veritas, Oslo, 2001—03, dir. DNV energy, 2006—, head DNV consulting upstream Houston, 2003—06. Lt. Norwegian Army, 1989—90, Northern Norway. Home: 2200 Eldridge Pky 4103 Houston TX 77077 Office: Det Norske Veritas Inc 16340 Park Ten Pl 100 Houston TX 77084

MEYER, FERDINAND CHARLES, JR., lawyer; b. San Antonio, Sept. 30, 1939; Student, Tulane U.; BBA, U. Tex., 1961, LLB, 1964. Bar: Tex. 1966, U.S. Dist. Ct. (we. dist.) Tex. 1969, U.S. Ct. Appeals (5th cir.) 1971, U.S. Supreme Ct. 1975, U.S. Ct. Appeals (11th cir.) 1979, D.C. 1986. V.p., gen. counsel CSW Svcs.; ptnr. Matthews & Branscomb, San Antonio; v.p. asst. gen. counsel CSW Corp., 1986-88; v.p., gen. counsel Ctrl. & S.W. Corp., 1988-90, sr. v.p., gen. counsel, 1990-98, gen. counsel, 1990-2000, exec. v.p., gen. counsel, 1998-2000. Instr. trial advocacy St. Mary's Sch. Law, 1980-86. Capt. USAR. Fellow Am. Coll. Trial Lawyers, Tex. Bar Found.; mem. ABA, Am. Bd. Trial Advs. (adv.), State Bar Tex., Dallas Bar Assn., San Antonio Bar Assn., Internat. Assn. Def. Counsel, Phi Alpha Delta. Office: PO Box 7616 Dallas TX 75209-7616

MEYER, G. CHRISTOPHER, lawyer; b. Fremont, Nebr., Mar. 27, 1948; s. Gerald William and Mildred Ruth (Clauson) M.; children: Kate, Stacy, Jon, Robert. Student, Grinnell Coll., Iowa, 1966—69; BA, U. Kans., 1970; JD, U. Pa. Law Sch., 1973. Bar: Ohio 1973, US Dist. Ct. (no. dist.) Ohio 1975, US Ct. Appeals (6th cir.) 1982. Assoc. Squire, Sanders & Dempsey, L.L.P., Cleve., 1973-82, ptnr., 1982—. Bd. mem. Cleve. Rape Crisis Ctr., past chmn. Named one of Best Lawyers in Am., Ohio Super Lawyers. Mem. ABA, Metro Cleve. Bar Assn.(bd. mem.), Fellow Am. Coll. Bankruptcy. Office: Squire Sanders & Dempsey LLP 4900 Key Tower 127 Public Sq Cleveland OH 44114-1304 Home: 5455 N Marginal Rd Cleveland OH 44114-3951 Office Phone: 216-479-8692. Business E-Mail: cmeyer@ssd.com.

MEYER, GEORGE HERBERT, lawyer; b. Detroit, Feb. 19, 1928; s. Herbert M. and Agnes F. (Eaton) Meyer; m. Carol Ann Jones, 1958 (div. 1981); children: Karen Ann, George Herbert Jr.; m. Katherine Palmer White, Nov. 12, 1988. BA, U. Mich., 1949; JD, Harvard U., 1952; cert., Oxford U., Eng., 1955; LLM in Taxation and Labor Law, Wayne U., 1962. Bar: DC 1952, Mich. 1953. Assoc. firm Fischer, Franklin & Ford, Detroit, 1956-63, mem. firm, 1963-74; established firm George H. Meyer, 1974-78; sr. mem. firm Meyer and Kirk, 1978-85; sr. mem. Meyer, Kirk, Snyder & Safford PLLC, Bloomfield Hills and Detroit, Mich., 1985-99; mng. mem. Meyer, Kirk, Snyder & Lynch PLLC, Bloomfield Hills and Detroit, Mich., 2000—07, Meyer & Kirk PLLC, 2007—. Curator Step Lively exhibit Mus. Am. Folk Art, NYC, 1992; lectr. Am. Folk Art. Author: Equalization in Michigan and Its Effect on Local Assessments, 1963, Folk Artists Biographical Index, 1986, American Folk Art Canes: Personal Sculpture, 1992. Chmn. Birmingham Bd. Housing Appeals, Mich., 1964—68; vice chmn. Birmingham Bd. Zoning Appeals, 1968—69; mem. Birmingham Planning Bd., 1968—70; trustee Bloomfield Village, Mich., 1976—80, pres., 1979—80; trustee Am. Mus. Folk Art, NYC, 1987—2004; mem. exec. bd. Detroit area coun. Boy Scouts Am., 1976—, counsel, 1986—95; trustee Detroit Sci. Ctr., 1985—99, Assocs. Am. Wing, 2009—, Detroit Inst. Arts, 2005—, pres., 2009—; trustee Mich. Hist. Found., 2007—, pres., 2009—. 1st lt. JAG USAF, 1952—55, maj. USAFR. Recipient Silver Beaver award, Detroit area coun. Boy Scouts Am., 1989. Mem.: ABA, Cranbrook Writers Guild (pres. 2002—04), State Bar Mich., Oakland County Bar Assn., Detroit Bar Assn., Am. Folk Art Soc. (pres. 2000—04), Detroit Sci. Mus. Soc. (pres. 1961—74, chmn. 1974—76), Harvard Law Sch. Assn. Mich. (dir. 1959—78, pres. 1970—78), Detroit Athletic Club, Harvard Club NYC, Prismatic Club (pres. 2002—03), Scarab Club, Birmingham Athletic Club, Rotary, Freemasons, Phi Beta Kappa, Pi Sigma Alpha, Alpha Phi Omega. Republican. Unitarian. Office: Meyer & Kirk PLLC 100 W Long Lake Rd Ste 100 Bloomfield Hills MI 48304-2773 Office Phone: 248-647-5111. Business E-Mail: gmeyer@meyerkirk.com.

MEYER, HELEN M., state supreme court justice; BSW, U. Minn.; JD, William Mitchell Coll. Law. Ptnr. Pritzker & Meyer, 1987—96, Meyer and Assocs., 1996—2002; assoc. justice Minn. Supreme Ct., St. Paul, 2002—. Office: Minn Jud Ctr 25 Rev Dr Martin Luther King Jr Blvd Saint Paul MN 55155*

MEYER, HENRY LEWIS, III, bank executive; b. Cleve., Dec. 25, 1949; s. Henry Lewis and Anne (Taylor) M.; m. Jane Kreamer, July 15, 1978; children: Patrick Harrison, Andrew Taylor, Christopher Bicknell. BA, Colgate U., 1972; MBA, Harvard U., Boston, 1978. Asst. v.p. Soc. Nat. Bank, Cleve., 1972-76, v.p., 1978-81, sr. v.p., 1981-83; exec. v.p. Soc. Bank, Dayton, Ohio, 1983-85, pres., chief operating officer, 1985-87; sr. exec. v.p. Soc. Nat. Bank, Cleve., 1987-89, vice chmn. bd., 1989-90, pres., COO, 1990-93, pres., CEO, 1993-94, chmn. bd., CEO, 1994-95; exec. v.p. Soc. Corp., 1987-91, vice chmn. bd., 1991-94; exec. v.p. KeyCorp, 1994-95, sr. exec. v.p., COO, 1995-96, vice chmn. bd., COO, 1996-97, pres., COO, 1997—2001, chmn., CEO, 2001. Bd. dirs. Continental Airlines, Inc., Fed. Res. Bank Cleve. Trustee Cleve. Mus. Nat. History, Ideastream (WVIZ/PBS and WCPN); with Law Enforcement Found., Northeast Ohio Coun. Higher Edn., United Way Greater Cleve., Univ. Sch.; bd. dirs. U. Hosps. Health Sys., Inc. Mem.: Club at Key Ctr., Chagrin Valley Hunt Club, Pepper Pike Club, The Union Club, Kirtland Country Club. Republican. Episcopalian.

MEYER, HERMANN BELTON PERRIN, retired neonatologist, health facility administrator, bioethicist; b. Stockton, Calif., Apr. 5, 1935; s. Hermann Perrin and Margaret Anna (Kammerer) Meyer; m. Marion Annette Pinkerton, July 2, 1961; children: Paul Belton, Christopher Charles. AA, Sacramento Jr. Coll., Calif., 1955; BA, U. Calif., Berkeley, 1957; MD, U. Calif., San Francisco, 1960; MS, Ariz. State U., Tempe, 1999, PhD, 2006. Diplomate Am. Bd. Pediat., 1969, perinatal medicine Am. Bd. Pediat., 1975. Rotating internship Highland-Alameda County Hosp., Oakland, Calif., 1960—61; sr. pediat. intern U. Calif. Med. Ctr., San Francisco, 1963—64, pediat. residency, 1964—65; fellowship, NIH Newborn Respiratory Physiology Ctr. for Premature Infants, Stanford U., Palo Alto, Calif., 1965—67; med. dir. newborn transport and intensive care Ariz. State Health Dept., Phoenix, 1967—91; med. dir. nurseries Good Samaritan and Phoenix Children's Hosps., Phoenix, 1967—86, 1990—91; med. dir. Ariz. Health Care Cost Containment Sys., Phoenix, 1992—97, ret., 1997. Trustee Ariz. Perinatal Trust, Phoenix, 1980—, trustee emeritus, 2008—; chmn. bioethics com. Good Samaritan Hosp., 1983—89; mem. cmty. bd. St. Joseph's Hosp. and Med. Ctr., Phoenix, 2002—08; sec., adv. com. Cath. Social Svcs., Phoenix, 2003—06; chmn. bioethics com. Phoenix Children's Hosp.; cons. in field. Contbr. articles to profl. jours. Chmn. premature adv. com. Ariz. Health Dept., 1970—73; chmn. bioethics workgroup Kino Inst. Cath. Diocese, Phoenix, 1980—83. Lt. med. corps. USN, 1961—63, med. officer USN, 1961—62, USS Lenawee, asst. med. officer, med. dept. US Naval Air Reserve Training Sta., 1962—63, Los Alamitos, Calif. Recipient various Lifetime Achievement awards, Dr. William Beaumont Outstanding Contbn. by Physician Under 50 award, AMA, 1978. Mem.: SAR (Ariz. and nat. soc. 2006—), Ariz. Med. Assn. (bd. dirs. 1967—, chmn. govt. svcs. 1983—90, chmn. bioethics 1990—96, A.H. Robins Physician Cmty. Svc. award 1978), Maricopa Med. Soc., Knights Malta (mem. Malta ctr. bd. 1991—98, named Knight Magistral Grace 1991). Democrat. Roman Catholic. Avocations: painting, ceramics, philosophy, reading. Home: 901 West Monte Vista Rd Phoenix AZ 85007 Office Phone: 602-663-1907. Personal E-mail: belhpmar@f.com.

MEYER, HORST, physics professor; b. Berlin, Mar. 1, 1926; arrived in US, 1957; BS, U. Geneva, 1949; PhD in physics, U. Zurich, 1953. Fellow Swiss Assn. Rsch. Physics and Math. Studies, Oxford, Eng., 1953-55; Nuffield fellow Clarendon Lab. U. Oxford, 1955-57; lectr., rsch. assoc. dept. engring. and applied physics Harvard U., Cambridge, Mass., 1957-59; from asst. prof. to prof. Duke U., Durham, NC, 1959-84, Fritz London prof. physics, 1984—2004, Fritz London prof. physics emeritus, 2004—. Vis. prof. Technische Hochschule, Federal Republic of Germany, 1965, Tokyo U., 1980, 81, 83; traveling fellow Japanese Soc. for Promotion Sci., 1971, vis. scientist, 1979; guest scientist Inst. Laue-Langevin, France, 1974, 75; Yamada Found. fellow, Japan, 1986; guest scientist USSR Acad. Sci., 1988; guest prof. Toyota Inst. Tech., Nagoya, Japan, Oct. 1998; chmn. Gordon Conf. on Solid H2, 1990; western chmn. conf. quantum crystals, Almaty, Kazakhstan, 1995. Editor Jour. Low Temperature Physics, 1992—, mem. editorial bd., 1988-92; contbr. articles to profl. jours. Alfred P. Sloan fellow, 1961-65. Fellow Am. Phys. Soc. (Jesse Beams prize, 1982, Fritz London prize 1993). Achievements include exptl. rsch. on the properties of liquid and solid helium, critical phenomena in fluids, solid hydrogen and deuterium, magnetic insulators, phase transitions, convection in supercritical helium. Office: Duke U Dept Physics PO Box 90305 Durham NC 27708-0305 Office Phone: 919-660-2520, 919-660-2522. Business E-Mail: hm@phy.duke.edu.

MEYER, IRWIN STEPHAN, lawyer, accountant; b. Monticello, NY, Nov. 14, 1941; s. Ralph and Janice (Cohen) M.; children: Kimberly B., Joshua A. BS, Rider Coll., 1963; JD, Cornell U., 1966. CPA NJ; bar: NY 1966. Tax mgr. Lybrand Ross Bros. & Montgomery, NYC, 1966—71; mem. Ehrenkranz, Ehrenkranz & Schultz, NYC, 1971—74; prin. Irwin S. Meyer, 1974—77, 1982—97; mem. Levine, Honig, Eisenberg & Meyer, 1977—78, Eisenberg, Honig & Meyer, 1978—81, Eisenberg, Honig, Meyer & Fogler, 1981—82, Janow & Meyer, LLC., 1997—2004; prin. Irwin S. Meyer, LLC, Pearl River, NY, 2004—. With US Army, 1966—71. Mem.: ABA, NY Bar Assn., Am. Assn. Atty.-CPA, NY Assn. Atty.-CPAs, NJ Soc. CPAs. Office: 1 Blue Hill Plz Ste 1006 Pearl River NY 10965-3100 Business E-Mail: info@nytaxplanner.com.

MEYER, J. EDWARD, state legislator; b. NYC, Apr. 15, 1935; s. J. Edward Jr. and Carolyn (Starring) M.; m. Patricia Ann Reese, Mar. 3, 1979; children: Daniel, Elizabeth, Jeffrey, Tory, Timothy, Andrew. BA, Yale Coll., 1957, LLB, 1961; LHD, Marymount Coll., 1983. Bar: NY 1963. Assoc. atty. Davis Polk & Wardwell, NYC, 1961-64; asst. US atty. US Dept. of Justice, NYC, 1964-67; ptnr. Spengler Carlson, NYC, 1968-85, Meyer & Wild, NYC, 1987—2004; mem. Dist. 12 Conn. State Senate, 2005—. State assemblyman NY State Assembly, Albany, 1971-75; regent NY State Bd. of Regents, Albany, 1977—2000; del. for Bill Bradley Dem. Nat. Convention, 2000. Scholarship Cambridge U., 1957-58. Mem. Bar of US Supreme Ct., South 40 Corp. (dir. 1963—). Democrat. Presbyterian. Avocations: tennis, golf. Office: Legis Office Bldg Rm 3200 Hartford CT 06106 Office Phone: 860-240-8600. Office Fax: 860-240-0208. Business E-Mail: meyer@senatedems.ct.gov.

MEYER, JACK ALLEN, historian, consultant; b. Sugar Camp, Wis., Nov. 13, 1934; s. John Charles Meyer and Loretta Bertha Basch; m. Martha Elise Robinson, Dec. 18, 1970. BA summa cum laude, U. Md., 1973; MA, U. SC, 1979, PhD, 1984. Enlisted USAF, 1953, advanced through grades to chief master sgt., 1975, ret., 1976; lectr. U. SC, Columbia, 1983—85, vis. asst. prof., 1985—87, sr. lectr., 1987—93, 2008; self-employed Tower Armory, Winnsboro, SC, 1993—; commd. SC State Guard, 1993, col., 2001—. Cons. SC State Mus., Columbia, 1979—; presenter in field. Author: South Carolina in the Mexican War, 1996, (monograph) William Glaze & the Palmetto Armory, 1982, 1994; editor: Annotated Bibliography-Napoleonic Era, 1987; author: The South Carolina State Guard, A Brief History, 2007; contbr. articles to profl. jours. Chmn. Fairfield County Airport Commn., 1976—79, 2008—, mem., 2006—; bd. mem. Columbia Choral Soc., 1988—90, treas., 1991—92; chmn. Fairfield County Hist. Commn., 1987—89, mem., 1990—94; spl. advisor Laotian Airborne Assn.; trustee Greenbrier United Meth. Ch., 1980—87, 1998—2000, 2002—07, chmn., 2005—06. Decorated Bronze Star, Meritorious Svc. medal, Air Force Commendation medal,; recipient Disting. Faculty award, ROTC, 1992, President's Vol. Svc. award, 2007, Order of the Palmetto, Governor of South Carolina, 2009. Fellow: Internat. Napoleonic Soc.; mem.: SAR, VFW, Royal Soc. St. George, Sumter Guards, SC Soc. SAR (pres. 2001—06), State Guard Assn. US, Internat. Chivalric Inst., Am. Inst. for Conservation and Preservation of Historic and Artistic Works, Orders and Medals Rsch. Soc., Orders and Medals Soc. Am. (Lit. medal 1991), Am. Numismatic Assn., Arms and Armour Soc., SC Arms Collectors Assn., Univ. South Caroliniana Soc., SC State Mus. Found. (founding mem., treas. 1981—83, dir. 1983—88), Fairfield County Hist. Soc. (dir. 1978, pres. 1979—80, dir. 1984—87), Co. Mil. Historians, SC Hist. Soc., Soc. for Army Hist. Rsch., US Parachute Assn., Am. Legion, Soc. for Mil. History, Alpha Sigma Lambda, Phi Kappa Phi, Phi Alpha Theta. Methodist. Avocations: private pilot, skydiving, collecting antiques. Home: Aeolia 1029 Greenbrier/Mossydale Rd Winnsboro SC 29180 Personal E-mail: drjameyer@mindspring.com.

MEYER, JOHN FREDERICK, engineering educator; b. Grand Rapids, Mich., July 26, 1934; s. Frederick Albert and Harriet (Stibbs) M.; m. Nancy Shaw Briggs, July 4, 1959; children: John, Patricia, James. BS, U. Mich., 1957; MS, Stanford U., 1958; PhD, U. Mich., 1967. Data systems engr. Douglas Aircraft Corp., Santa Monica, Calif., 1957; research engr. Caltech, Jet Propulsion Lab., Pasadena, Calif., 1958-67; asst. prof. U. Mich., Ann Arbor, 1968-71, assoc. prof., 1971-76, prof. elec. engring. and computer sci., 1976—2002, dir. Computing Research Lab., 1984-89, prof. emeritus elec. engring. and computer sci., 2002—. Cons. Calif. Inst. Tech. Jet Propulsion Lab., 1979—91, Indsl. Tech. Inst., Ann Arbor, 1985-92, CIMSA, Paris, 1992, Bendix Advanced Tech. Ctr., Columbia, Md., 1977-85, Thomson CSF, Paris, 1975, Italtel, Milan, 1990—99, Applied Scis. Corp., Reading, Mass., 1993, U. Ill., 2002-05. Precinct chmn. 3d ward Democratic Party, Ann Arbor, 1971-74. Recipient Disting. Service Award U. Mich., 1964, Silver Core award IFIP, 1995, Golden Core award 1996; IBM fellow, 1957 Fellow IEEE; mem. AAAS, IEEE Computer Soc. (Cert. of Appreciation 1981, 95, Meritorious Svc. award 1985). Achievements include patents for time division multiplexer; admission control of mixed variable bitrate sources in broadband networks. Home: 1946 Ridge Ave Ann Arbor MI 48104-6306 Office: U Mich 3636 CSE Bldg Ann Arbor MI 48109-2121 Business E-Mail: jfm@umich.edu.

MEYER, JOHN ROBERT, economist, educator; b. Pasco, Wash., Dec. 6, 1927; s. Philip Conrad and Cora (Kempter) M.; m. Lee Stowell, Dec. 17, 1949 (dec.); children: Leslie Karen, Ann Elizabeth, Robert Conrad. Student, Pacific U., 1945-46; BA, U. Wash., 1950; PhD (David A. Wells prize), Harvard U., 1955. Jr. fellow Harvard U., 1953-55, asst. prof., 1955-58, assoc. prof., 1958-59, prof. econs., 1959-68, 1907 Found., prof. transp. and logistics, 1973-83; prof. Yale U., 1968-73; Harpel prof. capital formation and econ. growth Harvard U., 1983-96, prof. emeritus, 1997—. Vice chmn. Union Pacific Corp., 1982-83, dir., 1978-99; trustee Pacific U. Author (with Edwin Kuh): The Investment Decision-An Empirical Inquiry, 1957; author: (with others) Competition in the Transportation Industry, 1959, The Urban Transportation Problem, 1965, Techniques of Transport Planning, 1970, Economics of Competition in the Telecommunications Industry, 1980, Autos, Transit and Cities, 1981, Deregulation and the Future of Intercity Passenger Travel, 1987, Going Private: The International Experience with 'Transport Privatization, 1993, Moving to Market: Restructuring Transport in the Former Soviet Union, 1996, Chile: Political Economy of Urban Development, 2002, other books; contbr. articles. Mem. Presdl. Task Forces on Transp., 1964, 80, Presdl. Commn. on Population Growth and Am. Future, 1970-72; pres. Nat. Bur. Econ. Research, 1967-77. Served with USNR, 1946-48. Recipient Roy W. Crum award, transp. rsch. bd. Nat. Acad. Scis. and Nat. Acad. Engring., 2002; Guggenheim fellow, 1958. Fellow: Econometric Soc., Am. Acad. Arts and Scis.; mem.: Econ. History Assn., Coun. Fgn. Rels., Am. Econ. Assn. (mem. exec. com. 1971—73). Home: 572 Kinzie Island Ct Sanibel FL 33957-5021 Office: Harvard U Jt Ctr Housing Studies 1033 Massachussetts Ave 5th Fl Cambridge MA 02138-5801 Personal E-mail: jrobtmeyer@aol.com.

MEYER, JON KEITH, psychiatrist, psychoanalyst, educator; b. Springfield, Ill., May 6, 1938; m. Eleanor Fumie Yamashita, June 6, 1964; children: David Christopher, Laura Tamiko. AB summa cum laude, Dartmouth Coll., 1960; MD, Johns Hopkins U., 1964; grad., Washington Psychoanalytic Inst, 1980. Intern internal medicine Johns Hopkins Hosp., Balt., 1964-65, resident in psychiatry, 1965-67, 69, St. Elizabeth's Hosp., Washington, 1968; spl. asst. to dir. NIMH, Bethesda, Md., 1969-71; asst. prof. psychiatry Johns Hopkins Med. Sch., Balt., 1971-76, assoc. prof., 1976-83; prof. psychiatry Med. Coll. Wis., Milw., 1983—2003, prof. psychoanalysis, 1996—2003, prof. family medicine, 1990—2003, prof. psychiatry and psychoanalysis emeritus, 2003—; tng. and supervising analyst Chgo. Inst. for Psychoanalysis, 1987—2002; vice chmn. Dept. of Psychiatry, 1993—2003; chief psychiatry Froedtert Meml. Luth. Hosp., Milw., 1994-97; tng. and supervising analyst Wis. Psychoanaltic Inst., Milw., 2001—07, Washington Psychoanalytic Inst., 2004—; tchg. analyst Balt.-Washington Psychoanalytic Inst., 2004—; clin. prof. psychiatry Georgetown U. Sch. Medicine, 2006—. Clin. prof. psychiatry U. Maryland Sch. of Medicine, 2006-, med. dir. Wis. Psychoanalytic Found., Milw., 1987-91, sec. bd. dir., 1988-91; part time assoc. prof. psychiatry Johns Hopkins Med. Sch., 2003-. Author books; editl. bd. Jour. Am. Psychoanalytic Assn., 1991-94; nat. editor: The American Psychoanalyst, 1997-2001; mem. steering com. Psychodynamic Diagnostic Manual; contbr. chpts. to books, numerous articles to profl. jours. Comdr. USPHS, 1967—71. Recipient Dennison Rsch. prize, Johns Hopkins Med. Sch., 1964; Sr. fellow, Dartmouth Coll., 1959—60, Daniel Webster Nat. scholar, 1956—60, Rufus Choate scholar, 1960, Erik Erikson scholar, Austen Riggs Ctr., Stockbridge, Mass., 1991—92, Ctr. Advanced Psychoanalytic Studies, Princeton, NJ, 1998—. Fellow: Am. Coll. Psychoanalysts, Am. Psychiat. Assn. (disting. life fellow); mem.: Task Force Psychoanalysis & Arts, Washington Ctr. Psychoanalysis (bd. dirs. 2007—), Wash. Psychoanalytic Soc., Balt.-Wash. Psychoanalytic Soc., Can. Psychoanalytic Soc. (hon.), William Alanson White Psychoanalytic Soc. (hon.), Wis. Psychoanalytic Soc. (pres. 1989—91), Assn. Child Psychoanalysis (candidate councilor 2001—03), Am. Psychoanalytic Assn. (exec. councilor 1993—97, chmn. com. on exec. coun. structure and function 1995—98, sec. 1997—2001, chmn. com. on cmty. clinics 1997—2002, exec. com. 1997—2002, adminstrv. bd. Jour. Am. Psychoanalytic Assn. 1997—2002, com. on insts. 1998—2002, com. on bylaws 2001—02, pres.-elect 2002—04, adminstrv. bd. Jour. Am. Psychoanalytic Assn. 2002—06, exec. com. 2002—06, pres. 2004—06, chmn. exec. com. 2004—06, presiding officer exec. coun. 2004—06, chmn. steering com. 2004—06, exploratory subcom. nominating com. 2006—08, exec. councilor 2006—, chair task force on access to care 2007—08, Edith Sabshin Tchg. award 1999), Internat. Psychoanalytical Assn. (com. on constn. and by-laws 1997—2001, com. on procedural codes 1997—2001, task force on structure and mission 1997—2001, ho. dels. 1998—2001, chair ho. of dels. 1999—2000). Avocations: photography, hiking, kayaking. Office: 2210 Dalewood Rd Lutherville Timonium MD 21093

MEYER, JOSEPH B., state treasurer; b. Casper, Wyo., 1941; m. Mary Meyer; 2 children. Student, Colo. Sch. Mines; BA, U. Wyo., 1964, JD, 1967; postgrad., Northwestern U., 1968. Dep. county atty. Fremont County, Wyo., 1967-69; assoc. Smith and Meyer, 1968-71; asst. dir. legis. svc. office State of Wyo., Cheyenne, 1971-87, atty. gen., 1987-95, sec. state, 1999—2006, state treas., 2007—; spl. asst. to pres. govt. rels. U. Wyo., Laramie, 1995-98. Condr. numerous govt. studies on state codes including Wyo. probate, criminal, state adminstrn., banking, domestic rels.; negotiator with Office of Surface Mining for Wyo. state preemption; lectr. Rocky Mountain Mineral Law Found., 1977; instr. Wyo. Coll. Law, fall, 1986; chmn. Conf. Western Atty. Gen., 1992—93; mem. Bush-Cheney Transition Team, 2000—01. Chmn. Cheyenne Bd. of Health, 1999—; bd. dirs. Longs Peak coun. Boy Scouts Am., Wyoming Cmty. Devel. Authority. Named BSA Citizen Yr., Longs Peak Coun., 2007, UPRR Honoree, RNC Nat. Convention, 2008. Mem.: Nat. Assn. Atty. Gen. (exec. com. 1991—93). Republican. Congregationalist. Avocations: golf, tennis, gardening, wood carving, rock hunting. Office: Treasurer's Office 200 W 24th St Cheyenne WY 82002 Office Phone: 307-777-7408. Office Fax: 307-777-5411. Business E-Mail: treasurer@state.wy.us.*

MEYER, JOYCE, television minister, author; b. St. Louis, Mo., June 4, 1943; m. Dave Meyer; 4 children. PhD in Theology, Life Christian U., Tampa, Fla.; PhD in Divinity (hon.), Oral Roberts U., Tulsa, Okla.; PhD in Sacred Theology (hon.), Grand Canyon U., Phoenix. Mem. Life Christian Ch., assoc. pastor, 1980—86; founder Joyce Meyer Ministries, 1986—; TV minister Enjoying Everyday Life, 1993—. Author: Battlefield of the Mind: Winning the Battle in Your Mind, 1993, Me and My Big Mouth: Your Answer is Right Under Your Nose, 2002, How to Hear from God: Learn to Know His Voice and Make Right Decisions, 2003, The Secret Power of Speaking God's Word, 2004, In Pursuit of Peace: 21 Ways to Conquer Anxiety, Fear, and Discontentment, 2004, Straight Talk: Overcoming Emotional Battles with the Power of God's Word, 2005, Approval Addiction: Overcoming Your Need to Please Everyone, 2005, Look Great Feel Great: Joyce Shares Twelve Practical Keys That Will Help You Look and Feel Great, 2006. Founder St. Louis Dream Ctr. Named one of 25 Most Influential Evangelicals, Time Mag., 2005. Evangelical. Office: Joyce Meyer Ministries PO Box 655 Fenton MO 63026 Office Phone: 800-727-9673. E-mail: mediacontact@joycemeyer.org.

MEYER, KARL ERNEST, retired journalist; b. Madison, Wis., May 22, 1928; s. Ernest Louis and Dorothy (Narefsky) M.; m. Sarah Nielsen Peck, Aug. 12, 1959 (div. 1972); children: Ernest, Heather, Jonathan; m. Shareen Blair Brysac, Jan. 6, 1989. BA, U. Wis., 1951; MPA, Princeton U., NJ, 1953, PhD, 1956. Reporter N.Y. Times, NYC, 1952, mem. editl. bd., 1979-98; editl. writer Washington Post, 1956-65, chief London Bur., 1965-70, N.Y.C. corr., 1970-71; Washington corr. New Statesman, 1961-65; sr. editor, TV critic Saturday Rev., NYC, 1975-79; corr. in residence Fletcher Sch. Law and Diplomacy, Tufts U., 1979; editor World Policy Jour., NYC, 2000—08; editor emreitus, 2000—. Vis. journalist fellow Duke U., Durham, NC, 1988; vis. prof. Yale U., New Haven, 1983, New Haven, 90; McGraw prof. in writing Princeton U., 1993—94; vis. prof. Bard Coll., NY, 2002. Author: The New America, 1961, (with Tad Szulc) The Cuban Invasion, 1962, Fulbright of Arkansas, 1963, The Pleasures of Archaeology, 1971, The Plundered Past, 1973, Teotihuacán, 1975, The Art Museum: Power, Money, Ethics, 1979, Pundits, Poets and Wits: An Omnibus of American Newspaper Columns, 1990, (with Shareen Brysac) Tournament of Shadows: The Great Game and Race for Empire in Central Asia, 1999, The Dust of Empire, 2003, Kingmakers: The Invention of the Modern Middle East, 2009. Recipient citation for excellence Overseas Press Club (with Shaveen Brysac) Kingmakers: Invention Modern Mid. East, 2008, Bronze medal for editl. writing Sigma Delta; George Foster Peabody Broadcasting award 1983, Disting. Achievement award Sch. Journalism, U. Wis., 1985; Davenport Coll. of Yale U. fellow; Wisenschaftskolleg Inst. Adv. Studies (Berlin) fellow, 1994-95, Reuter fellow Oxford (Eng.) U., 1996-97. Mem. PEN Club Internat., Coun. on Fgn. Rels., Century Assn., Authors League Am Home: 50 W 96th St New York NY 10025-6526 Home Phone: 212-663-0162. Personal E-mail: karlmeyer@optonline.net. Business E-Mail: meyerk@newschool.edu.

MEYER, KARL WILLIAM, retired university president; b. Ft. Wayne, Ind., May 8, 1925; s. K.W. and L. (Hofacker) M.; m. Margery R. Hamman, Apr. 15, 1950; children— Mary, William, Frederick, Ann, Jean. AB, Valpariaso U., 1948; M.F.S., U. Md., 1949; PhD, U. Wis., 1953; postgrad., U. Basel, Switzerland, 1948-49; postdoctoral fellow, U. Mich., 1958-59. Faculty Valparaiso U., 1952-53, Augustana Coll., 1953-55, Wis. State U., 1955-58; dean instrn., dir. grad. studies Wayne State Coll., 1959-63; asst. dir. bd. regents Wis. State Colls., Madison, 1963-64; pres. U. Wis.-Superior, 1964-87. Author: Karl Liebknecht: Man Without a Country, 1957; Contbr. articles to profl. jours. Served with USAAF, 1943-46, ETO. Home: W7861 Homestead Ct Holmen WI 54636-9440 E-mail: meyk25@aol.com.

MEYER, LAWRENCE GEORGE, lawyer; b. East Grand Rapids, Mich., Oct. 2, 1940; s. George and Evangeline (Boerma) M.; children from previous marriage: David Lawrence, Jenifer Lynne; m. Linda Elizabeth Buck, May 31, 1980; children: Elizabeth Tilden, Travis Henley. BA with honors, Mich. State U., 1961; JD with distinction, U. Mich., 1964. Bar: Wis., 1965, Ill. 1965, US Supreme Ct. 1968, DC 1972. Assoc. Whyte, Hirschboeck, Minahan, Hardin & Harland, Milw., 1964-66; atty. antitrust div. U.S. Dept. Justice, Washington, 1966-68; legal counsel U.S. Senator Robert P. Griffin, Mich., 1968-70; dir. policy planning FTC, 1970-72; ptnr. Patton, Boggs & Blow, Washington, 1972-85, Arent, Fox, Kintner, Plotkin & Kahn, Washington, 1985-96, Gadsby & Hannah, 1996-2001; pvt. practice Washington, 2001—. Contbr. articles to profl. jours.; asst. editor. U. Mich. Law Rev., 1960-61. Bd. dirs. Hockey Hall of Fame, Toronto, 1993-99, Woodrow Wilson House, 1997-2007. Recipient Disting. Svc. award FTC, 1972. Mem.: ABA, Ill. Bar Assn., Wis. Bar Assn., DC Bar Assn., Congl. Country Club. Home: 9602 Beman Woods Way Potomac MD 20854-1610 Office Phone: 202-262-1964. Business E-Mail: larry@lawlgm.com.

MEYER, MARA ELLICE, special education educator, consultant, academic administrator; b. Chgo., Oct. 28, 1952; d. David and Harriett (Lazar) Einhorn; m. Leonard X. Meyer, July 20, 1986; children: Hayley Rebecca, David Joseph. BS in Speech and Hearing Sci., U. Ill., 1974, MS in Speech and Lang. Pathology, 1975, postgrad., 1990—95; EdD in Ednl. Policy and Leadership, Nat. Louis U., Chgo., 2009. Cert. speech and lang. pathologist, spl. edn. tchr., reading tchr, gen. edn. tchr. reading, lang. arts. Speech and lang. pathologist Macon-Piatt Spl. Edn. Dist., Decatur, Ill., 1975-76, Cmty. Consolidated Sch. Dist. # 59, Arlington Heights, Ill., reading specialist, learning disabilities coord., 1976—87; speech and lang. pathologist Adlai Stevenson HS, Lincolnshire, Ill., 2006—07, Lincolnshire-Prairie View Sch. Dist., 2007—09. Adj. prof. Nat. Louis U., 1985—87, 2003—; test cons. Psychol. Corp., San Antonio, 1987—89, ednl. cons., 1987—89, Am. Guidance Svc., Circle Pines, Minn., 1989—94; project dir. Riverside Pub. Co., Chgo., 1993—94; pvt. practice ednl. cons., Deerfield, Ill., 1994—; cons. Spl. Edn. Dist., Lake County, 1995—, Lake Zurich Pub. Schs., 1996—98, Waukegan Pub. Schs., Ill., 1997; asst. prin., inclusion coord. Mundelein Sch. Dist., Ill., 1999—2001; spl. edn. adminstr. Wilmette Schs., 2001—03; spl. cons. Avoca Sch. Dist. 37, Wilmette, Ill., 2003—05; prin. ednl. cons. Ill. State Bd. Edn., 2004—06. Mem. adv. coun. to Headstart, Dept. Human Svs., Chgo., 1990-99; pres. Park West Condo Assn., Lake County, 1983-88; area coord. Dem. Party, Lake County, Ill., 1978—. Mem. NEA, ASCD, Nat. Assn. Elem. Prins., Nat. Family Partnership Network, Am. Speech-Lang. and Hearing Assn., Ill. Speech-Lang. and Hearing Assn., Ill. Prins. Assn., Internat. Reading Assn., Coun. on Exceptional Children. Avocations: swimming official, leisure reading, technical reading. Home: 1540 Central Ave Deerfield IL 60015-3963 Office Phone: 847-431-0767. Personal E-mail: maraemeyer@comcast.net.

MEYER, MARK ALAN, lawyer; b. NYC, Dec. 19, 1946; s. Paul and Tilly M. BA, Fairleigh Dickinson U., 1968; JD, St. Johns U., 1971; LLM, Harvard U., 1972; LLD (hon.), St. Johns U., 2007. Bar: NY 1972, US Dist. Ct. (so. and ea. dists.) NY 1973, US Ct. Appeals (2d cir.) 1973, US Supreme Ct. 1977. Instr. law Boston U., 1971-72; asst. dist. atty. NY County Dist. Atty., 1972-74; assoc. Golenbock & Barell, 1975-77, Solinger & Gordon, 1977-82; ptnr. Goldschmidt, Oshatz, Powsner & Saft, NYC, 1982-85, Spitzer & Feldman PC, 1985-87, Hall, Dickler, Lawler, Kent & Friedman, NYC, 1987-94, Herzfeld & Rubin PC, NYC, 1995—. Adj. prof. law St. John's U., 2006—. Chmn. Am-Romanian Cultural Found., 1995—. Decorated Comdr. Romanian Nat. Order of merit, Moldovan Order of Civic merit; recipient Harvard Law Sch. Traphagen Disting. Alumnus award, 2004, Pinnacle award, Fairleigh Dickinson U., 2004, Civic Merit medal, Pres. Republic Moldova, 2006. Fellow Am. Bar Found.; mem. Assn. Bar City NY (chmn. com. on European affairs, 2004-07, chmn. Fgn. and Comparative Law Com.

2008-), Romanian-Am. C. of C. (chmn. 1990—), Internat. Panel of Arbitrators, Am. Arbitration Assn., Romanian Ct. Internat. Arbitration (panel of arbitrators 2006-). Avocations: art, boating. Home: 35 Overlook Rd Dobbs Ferry NY 10522-3209 also: Herzfeld & Rubin PC 26 Broadway New York NY 10004-1703 Office Phone: 212-471-8453. Business E-Mail: mmeyer@herzfeld-rubin.com.

MEYER, MAX EARL, lawyer; b. Hampton, Va., Oct. 31, 1918; s. Earl Luther and Winifred Katherine (Spacht) M.; m. Betty Maxwell Dodds, Sept. 22, 1945; children: Scott Maxwell, Ann Culliford. AB, U. Nebr., 1940, JD, 1942. Bar: Nebr. 1942, Ill. 1946. Assoc. firm Lord, Bissell & Brook, Chgo., 1945-53, ptnr., 1953-85; chmn. Chgo. Fed. Tax Forum, 1965, U. Chgo. Ann. Fed. Tax Conf., 1972; mem. Adv. Group to Commr. of IRS, 1967; assoc. firm Lolke Lord Bissell & Lidell LLP. Lectr. in field. Bd. dirs. Music Acad. of the West, chmn., 1993—94. Mem.: ABA (coun. tax sect. 1969—72), Am. Coll. Tax Counsel, Chgo. Bar Assn. (chmn. taxation com. 1959—61), Nebr. Bar Assn., Ill. Bar Assn. (coun. tax sect. 1973—76), Birnam Wood Golf Club, Valley Club of Montecito, Law Club (Chgo.), Legal Club, Masons. Republican. Presbyterian.

MEYER, MICHAEL EDWIN, lawyer; b. Chgo., Oct. 23, 1942; s. Leon S. and Janet (Gorden) M.; m. Catherine Dieffenbach, Nov. 21, 1982; children: Linda, Mollie, Patrick, Kellie. BS, U. Wis., 1964; JD, U. Chgo., 1967. Bar: Calif. 1968, U.S. Supreme Ct. 1973. Assoc. Lillick & McHose, LA, 1967-73, ptnr., 1974-90, mng. ptnr., 1986-87; ptnr. Pillsbury Madison Sutro, 1990—, mem. mgmt. com., 1990-92; mng. ptnr. Pillsbury Winthrop, LA, 1999—2003, Piper Rudnick LLP (now DLA Piper Rudnick Gray Cary), 2004—. Judge pro tem Beverly Hills Mcpl. Ct., Calif., 1976-79, Los Angeles Mcpl. Ct., 1980-86; lectr. in field. Bd. dirs. Bldg. Owners and Mgrs. Assn. Greater L.A., L.A. coun. Boy Scouts Am., L.A. Sports and Entertainment Commn., L.A. Econ. Devel. Corp.; pub. counsel United Way Greater L.A., Los Angeles County Bar Found., trustee, 1997—, Reviving Baseball in Inner Cities; mem. L.A. County Sheriff Youth Found., Jackie Robinson Found. Recipient Good Scout award L.A. Coun. Boy Scouts Am., 1992, Man of Yr. award United Way, 1996, Real Estate Profl. of Yr. award NACORE, 2002, Reviving Baseball in Inner-Cities CB award Major League Baseball, 2005, Spirit L.A. award L.A. Hdqs. Assn., 2005, Outstanding Cmty. Svc. award Weingart Ctr., 2006; named to Top Ten So. Calif. Super Lawyers LA Mag., 2006, Top Five Calif. Real Estate Lawyers Chambers USA, 2005. Mem. ABA, Am. Arbitration Assn. (arbitrator), Calif. Bar Assn., Los Angeles County Bar Assn. (trustee 1997—), L.A. Bar Assn., Am. Coll. of Real Estate Lawyers, U. Chgo. Alumni Assn. So. Calif. (pres. 1980-82), Calif. Club, U. L.A. Club (dir. 1979-85, pres. 1984-85), L.A. Country Club. Jewish. Office: DLA Piper Rudnick Gray Cary Ste 2300 550 S Hope St Los Angeles CA 90071 Home Phone: 310-546-5500, 213-505-2113; Office Phone: 213-330-7777. Office Fax: 213-330-7577. Business E-Mail: michael.meyer@dlapiper.com.

MEYER, MILTON EDWARD, JR., retired lawyer, artist; b. St. Louis, Nov. 26, 1922; s. Milton Edward and Jessie Marie (Hurley) M.; m. Mary C. Kramer, Nov. 5, 1949 (dec. Dec. 1999); children: Milton E. III, Melanie M. Meyer Francis, Daniel K., Gregory N.; m. Mildred R. Emrick, Nov. 18, 2003. BS in Bus. Adminstrn, Washington U., 1943; LL.B., St. Louis, U., 1950; LL.M., N.Y. U., 1953. Bar: Mo. 1950, Colo. 1956. Trust adminstr. Mississippi Valley Trust Co., St. Louis, 1946-50; asso. firm Burnett, Stern & Liberman, St. Louis, 1953-56; founding partner firm Hindry & Meyer, Denver, 1956-79, chmn. bd., 1970-79; spl. counsel Schmidt, Elrod & Wills, and predecessors, 1979-83, pres., 1980-82; sec. C.A. Norgren Co., Littleton, Colo., 1960-78, dir., 1971-78; ret., 1978. Contbr. articles to profl. jours. Chmn. Denver Rotary's Artists of Am. Exhbn., 1990—92; bd. dirs. Nat. Club Assn., 1971—91, pres., 1976—78; bd. dirs. Denver Cmty. Concert Assn., 1960—64, Sewall Rehab. Ctr., Denver, 1965—68, Carl A. Norgren Found., 1960—70; Denver Leadership Found., 1983—93, Found. Colo. Women's Coll., 1982—86, chmn., bd. dirs., 1984—86; bd. dirs. Conf. Pvt. Orgns., 1982—89, chmn., bd. dirs., 1984—88. Officer, U.S. Airborne Infantry US Army, 1943—46, World War II, officer, U.S. Airborne Infantry US Army, 1950—52, Korean War. Recipient Wisdom Soc. award of honor. Mem.: ABA, Colo. Bar Assn., Denver Bar Assn., Greater Denver Tax Counsels Assn. (founder, chmn. 1957), Denver Estate Planning Coun. (founder, pres. 1958), Am. Coll. Probate Counsel, Knickerbocker Artists, Pastel Soc. Am., Pastel Soc. West Coast (disting. pastellist award), Internat. Assn. Pastel Socs (founder, dir. 1994—2003), Salmagundi Club, Pinehurst Country Club (pres. 1979—80, dir. 1960—97), Hundred Club Denver, Denver Execs. Club, Cherry Hills Country Club, Rotary (bd. dirs. 1991—93), Phi Eta Sigma, Beta Gamma Sigma, Omicron Delta Kappa, Beta Theta Pi. Republican. Roman Catholic. Home: 7123 W Belmont Dr Littleton CO 80123 E-mail: miltonmeyer@comcast.net.

MEYER, NICK, film company executive; BA in Romance Languages and Literatures, Wesleyan U., Middletown, Conn.; MA in French, Middlebury Coll., Vt. With advt. & publicity dept. Sony Pictures Classics; dir. worldwide sales and acquisitions, Columbia Tri-Star Motion Picture Group Sony Pictures Entertainment; co-prexy Lionsgate Internat., 2001—03, pres.; co-prexy Paramount Vantage, 2006—08, pres., 2008—. Mem. bd. dirs. Ind. Film and TV Alliance. Office: Paramount Vantage Chevalier Bldg 2nd Fl 555 Melrose Ave Los Angeles CA 90038

MEYER, PAUL, information technology executive; Studied Politics, Philosophy and Econs., Oxford U.; grad., Pomona Coll.; JD, Yale U. Rschr. & speechwriter for Pres. Clinton The White House, 1993—95; CEO Endeavor Initiative; with Internat. Rescue Com.; sr. fellow Markle Found.; founder, chmn. IPKO, Kosovo, 1999; co-founder, pres. & CEO Voxiva, Washington, DC, 2001—. Recipient Tech. in Service of Humanity Award, MIT Tech. Review; named one of the world's 100 Top Young Innovators, 100 Global Leaders for Tomorrow, World Econ. Forum. Fellow: Foreign Policy Assn. Office: Voxiva Inc 1990 K St NW Ste 401 Washington DC 20006-1180

MEYER, PAULETTE ANN, history professor; b. Newport, Oreg., Feb. 20, 1945; d. Paul Merrill and Shirley (Cooper) Billbe; m. Richard John Meyer, Jan. 9, 1965; children: Erika Meyer, Rodrick Meyer. AB in History, Stanford U., Calif., 1966, AM in Edn., 1967; PhD, U. Minn., 1997. Cert. secondary tchr., Calif. Instr. world history U. Minn., Mpls., 1992; instr. European intellectual history S.W. State U., Marshall, Minn., 1994; lectr. history of biology, world history Humboldt State U., Arcata, Calif., 1995—2001. Presenter in field. Author: They Met in Zürich-German and Russian Women Physicians, 1997, From 'Uncertifiable' Medical Practice to the Berlin Clinic of Women Doctors: The Medical Career of Franziska Tiburtius, 1999, Maternal Feminism and Physiatrie: Dr. Anna Fischer-Dückelmann (M.D. Zürich, 1896) Critiques German Academic Medicine, 2002, Dr. Maríe Zakrzewska (1829-1902) and the Reform of Medical Institutions, 2004, Gender and Medical Relief Across Borders, 2005, German Women Pioneers in Medical Specialties, 2006, German Experiments in Feminine Respectability, 2008. Action chair LWV, Humboldt; bd. suprs. Recreational Trails Com., Humboldt. Fellowship U. Minn., 1989; Nat. Merit scholar. Mem. Western Assn. Women Historians, Columbia History of Sci. Group, Social Sci. History Assn. United Methodist. Avocation: training Arabian horses. Home: 1615 SE 58th Ave Portland OR 97215-3414

MEYER, PHILIP EDWARD, journalism educator; b. Deshler, Nebr., Oct. 27, 1930; s. Elmer Edward and Hilda Grace (Morrison) M.; m. Sue Quail, Aug. 5, 1956; children: Caroline, Katherine, Melissa, Sarah. BS, Kans. State U., 1952; MA, U. N.C., 1963. Asst. state editor Topeka (Kans.) Daily Capital, 1954-56; reporter Miami (Fla.) Herald, 1958-62; Washington corr. Akron Beacon Jour., 1962-66; nat. corr. Knight-Ridder, Inc., Washington, 1967-78, dir. news research Miami, 1978-81; William Rand Kenan Jr. prof. journalism U. N.C., Chapel Hill, 1981-93; Knight prof., 1993—2008; prof. emeritus, 2008—. Author: Precision Journalism, 1973 (Sigma Delta Chi Disting. Service award 1974), The Newspaper Survival Book, 1985, Ethical Journalism, 1987, The New Precision Journalism, 1991, The Vanishing Newspaper, 2004; co-author: To Keep the Republic, 1975; co-editor: Evaluating Public Journalism, 1998; editor: Letters From The Editor, 2007. Project dir. Russell Sage Found., N.Y.C., 1969-70. Served with USNR, 1952-54. Recipient Disting. Contbns. to Journalism award Nat. Press Found., 1994, Disting. Contbns. to Media and Media Studies award Freedom Forum Media Studies Ctr., 1995, award of merit Newspaper Assn. Am. Rsch. Fedn., 1996; Nieman fellow Harvard U., 1966-67, fellow Freedom Forum Ctr. for Media Studies, 1985. Fellow Soc. Prof. Journalists, mem. Am. Assn. for Pub. Opinion Rsch. (pres. 1989-90, award exceptionally disting. achievement 2000), World Assn. for Pub. Opinion Rsch. (pres. 1994-95), Assn. for Edn. in Journalism and Mass Comm. (mem. USA Today bd. contbrs. 1998—), Nat. Press Club (Washington), NC Journalists (Hall of Fame). Democrat. Episcopalian. Avocation: photography. Office Phone: 919-962-4085. Business E-Mail: philip_meyer@unc.edu.

MEYER, PHILIP GILBERT, lawyer; b. Louisville, June 26, 1945; s. Henry Gilbert and Adele (Gutermuth) M.; m. Jackie Darlene Watson, Jan. 30, 1971 (div. Apr. 1976); m. Sylvia Saunders, Oct. 9, 1976. BBA, U. Mich., Ann Arbor, 1967; JD, U. Tex., Austin, 1970. Bar: Tex. 1970, Mich. 1971, U.S. Tax Ct. 1972, U.S. Dist. Ct. (ea. dist.) Mich. 1971, U.S. Ct. Appeals (6th cir.), 1972, U.S. Dist. Ct. (no. dist.) Ohio 1976, U.S. Dist. Ct. (we. dist.) Mich. 1993, U.S. Dist. Ct. (no. dist.) Ill. 1998. Law clk. Wayne County Cir. Ct., Detroit, 1970-72; atty. Leonard C. Jaques, Detroit, 1972; assoc. Christy & Robbins, Dearborn, Mich., 1972-73; ptnr. Foster, Meadows & Ballard, Detroit, 1973-79; of counsel Christy, Rogers & Gantz, Dearborn, 1979-81, Rogers & Gantz, Dearborn, 1981-86; prin. Philip G. Meyer and Assocs., Farmington Hills, 1986—. Adj. prof. U. Detroit Sch. Law, 1979. Mem. ABA (com. vice chmn. rules and procedure 1982-88), Maritime Law Assn. U.S., Mich. Bar Assn. (vice chmn. admiralty sect. 1978), Tex. Bar Assn., Detroit Bar Assn. (vice chmn. admiralty com. 1991-93, chmn. admiralty sect. 1993-95), Propeller-Port of Detroit Club (pres. 1984-85). Independent. Home: 5905 Independence Ln West Bloomfield MI 48322-1854 Office: Ste 113 30300 Northwestern Hwy Farmington Hills MI 48334-3212 Home Phone: 248-626-4677; Office Phone: 248-737-0700. Business E-Mail: pgm@meylaw.com.

MEYER, PIOTR JAN, electronics engineer; b. Szczecin, Poland, May 31, 1969; arrived in US, 2000; s. Zygmunt and Maria Meyer. MS in Electronics Engring., Tech. U. Szczecin, 1992. Devel. engr., mechatronic sys. Philips Applied Technologies, Eindhoven, Netherlands, 1994—2000, sr. specialist mechatronic sys. Lynnfield, Mass., 2000—08, cons. ind. robotics & position metrology, 2008—. Guest lectr. series MIT, Cambridge, Mass., 2006. Contbr. scientific papers. Mem.: Boston Com. on Foreign Rels., Math. Assn. Am., German Scholars Boston (bd. dirs. 2003—06), IEEE Robotics and Automation Soc. (chmn. chpt. 2006—). Achievements include patents for fast and accurate motion of industrial robots; research in mathematical modelling, analysis, simulation and optimization of industrial robot motion for nanometer-level accuracy in semiconductor manufacturing; development of mathematical modelling, analysis, simulation and optimization of commercial LED-based light sources. Avocations: history, philosophy, fine arts, classical music, mountain climbing. Business E-Mail: p.j.meyer@ieee.org.

MEYER, PRISCILLA ANN, literature and language professor; b. Aug. 26, 1942; d. Herbert Edward and Marjorie Rose (Wolff) M.; m. William L. Trousdale, Sept. 15, 1974; 1 dau., Rachel V. BA, U. Calif., Berkeley, 1964; MA, Princeton U., 1966; PhD, 1971. Lectr. in Russian lang. and lit. Wesleyan U., Middletown, Conn., 1968-71, asst. prof., 1971-75, assoc. prof., 1975-88, prof., 1988—. Vis. asst. prof. Yale U., 1973, adv. coun. dept. Slavic lang. and lit. Princeton U., 1998-2002. Author: Find What the Sailor Has Hidden: Vladimir Nabokov's Pale Fire, 1988, Russian Translation, 2007, How the Russians Read the French: Lermontov, Dostoevsky, Tolstoy, 2008; editor: Notes and Brief Commentaries, The Nabokovian, 2001-, Life in Windy Weather (by Andrei Bitov), 1986; co-editor: Dostoevsky and Gogol, 1979, Essays on Gogol: Logos and the Russian Word, 1992, Nabokov's World, 2001, Yuz! Essays on the Occasion of the 75th Birthday of Yuz Aleshkovsky, 2005; translator stories; mem. editl. bd. Slavic and East European Jour., 1999—; contbr. articles to profl. jours. Scholar Internat. Rsch. and Exch. Bd., 1973; grantee Ford Found., 1964-68, 70; hon. vis. fellow Sch. Slavonic and East European Studies London U., 1997, 2001. Mem. Am. Coun. Tchrs. Russian (dir. 1983-86), Am. Assn. Tchrs. Slavic and East European Studies, Internat. Vladimir Nabokov Soc. (v.p. 1983-85, 2002-04, pres. 1985-87, 2004-06), Tolstoi Soc., Dostoevsky Soc., Conn. Acad. Arts and Scis. Office: Russian Dept Wesleyan U Middletown CT 06459-0001 Office Phone: 860-685-3127. E-mail: pmeyer@wesleyan.edu.

MEYER, PUCCI, editor; b. NYC, Sept. 1, 1944; d. Charles Albert and Lollo (Offer) M.; m. Michael V. McGill, Oct. 28, 2001. BA, U. Wis., 1966. Asst. editor Look mag., NYC, 1970-71, editorial asst. Paris, 1967-69; reporter Newsday, Garden City, L.I., NY, 1971-73; style editor N.Y. Daily News Sunday Mag., NYC, 1974-76, assoc. editor, 1977-82, editor, 1983-86; sr. editor Prodigy, White Plains, NY, 1987; spl. projects editor N.Y. Post, NYC, 1988-89, style editor, 1990-92, food editor, 1992-93, assoc. features editor, 1993—94, travel editor, 1994—2004. Contbr. articles to various nat. mags. Recipient Pulitzer prize as mem. Newsday investigative team that wrote articles and book The Heroin Trail, 1973.

MEYER, RICHARD CHARLES, microbiologist, educator; b. Cleve., May 2, 1930; s. Frederick Albert and Tekla Charlotte (Schrade) M.; m. Carolyn Yvonne Patton, Apr. 6, 1963; children: Frederick Gustav, Carl Anselm. B.Sc., Baldwin-Wallace Coll., 1952; M.Sc., Ohio State U., 1957, PhD, 1961. Teaching and research asst. Ohio State U., 1956-61, research assoc., 1961-62; microbiologist Nat. Cancer Inst., NIH, Bethesda, Md., 1962-64; asst. prof. vet. pathology and hygiene and microbiology U. Ill., Urbana-Champaign, 1965-68, assoc. prof., 1968-73, prof., 1973-89, prof. emeritus, 1989—. Served with C.E. U.S. Army, 1952-54. Mem. Am. Acad. Microbiology, AAAS, Am. Inst. Biol. Sci., Am. Soc. Microbiology, Sigma Xi, Gamma Sigma Delta, Phi Zeta. Republican. Lutheran. Home: 1504 S Buckthorn Ln Mahomet IL 61853-3632 Office: Dept Vet Pathobiology U Ill at Urbana-Champaign Urbana IL 61801

MEYER, RICHARD W., retired university librarian; b. St. Louis, Jan. 22, 1943; s. Norman K. Meyer and Melba R. Reisel; m. Clare A. Siesennop, Apr. 12, 1944; children: Sharyn C. Moore, Karyn A. BS in Chemistry, U. Mo., 1967; BA in Libr. Sci., U. Mo., Columbia, 1967; MS in Libr. Sci., U. Ill., Champaign, 1970; MA in Econs., Clemson U., SC, 1986. Asst. libr. E.I. duPont de Nemours, Aiken, SC, 1967—69; asst. dir. libr. U. Tex. at Dallas, Richardson, 1970—76; dir. libr. tech services Ind. State U., Terre Haute, Ind., 1976—79; assoc. dir. libraries Clemson U., 1979—91; dir. libr. Trinity U., San Antonio, 1991—2000; dean, dir. libraries Ga. Inst. Tech., Atlanta, 2000—08. Cons. Harris Corp., Melbourne, Fla., 1985—86, Chemists Club, NYC, 1991—92, Mackenzie U., Sao Paulo, Brazil, 1998—99, Mercer U., 2001, Westminster Coll., 2003, Winona St. U., 2004. Contbr. articles to profl. jours. Field svc. rev. team mem. United Way of San Antonio, 1998—2000; Solinet Bd., 2004—07. Recipient G.K. Saur Best Article award, Coll. and Rsch. Libraries, 1999; grantee, Andrew W. Mellon Found., 1995—2000; Blackwell scholarship, Coll. and Rsch. Libraries, 2002. Mem.: So. Assn. Colls. and Schs. (mem. reaffirmation rev. teams 1999—2002), ALA. Conservative. Personal E-mail: rwmeyer@charter.net.

MEYER, ROBERT ALAN, management consultant; b. NYC, Mar. 20, 1946; s. Leonard and Mildred M.; m. Gail Rein, Oct. 29, 1967; children: Jonathan, Caroline. BA in Econs., Am. Internat. Coll., Springfield, Mass., 1967; MBA, NYU, 1973. 2nd v.p., mgr. mcpl. bond research Smith Barney Harris Upham and Co., Inc., NYC, 1973-76; 1st v.p., dir. mcpl. bond research E.F. Hutton and Co. Inc., NYC, 1976-82; v.p., mgr. mcpl. bond research Merrill Lynch Pierce Fenner and Smith Inc., NYC, 1982-84; pres. Bond Investors Guaranty Ins. Co., NYC, 1984-90; pres., chief exec. officer Greig Fester Fin. Guaranty Brokers, Inc., NYC, 1991-94; prin. Meyer Cons. Group Inc., Holmdel, N.J., 1994-98; chmn., pres., CEO RAM Reinsurance Co. Ltd., Hamilton, Bermuda, 1998-2001; prin. Meyer Cons. Group Inc., Holmdel, NJ, 2001—08; fin. advisor Morgan Stanley, NJ, 2008—. Mem. India House. Office: Morgan Stanley 1 Linden Pl Red Bank NJ 07701 Office Phone: 732-335-9536. Personal E-mail: mcgramgm@msn.com.

MEYER, ROBERT ALLEN, finance educator; b. Wisconsin Rapids, Wis., May 31, 1943; s. Charles Harold and Viola Bertha (Stoeckmann) M.; 1 child, Timothy Charles. BA, Valparaiso U., Ind., 1966; MA, Mich. State U., 1967, PhD, 1972, postgrad., 1981. Asst. prof. Muskingum Area Tech. Coll., Zanesville, Ohio, 1972-74; adj. prof. U. Fla., Gainesville, 1974-80; dean acad. affairs Santa Fe Community Coll., Gainesville, 1974-80; asst. prof. Purdue U., W. Lafayette, Ind., 1982-84, Ga. State U., Atlanta, 1985-89; assoc. prof., program coord. U. N. Tex., Denton, 1989-91; Fulbright profl. scholar, Bangkok, 1991-92; coord. travel, tourism, hotel, restaurant mgmt. program U. Hawaii Manoa Campus, Honolulu, 1992-97; dir. distance edn., dir. travel, hotel and restaurant mgmt. SPC, St. Petersburg, Fla., 1997—; 21573325. Investor, asst. mgr. LaSiene Restaurant, Ann Arbor, Mich., 1970-72; investor, cons. Cafe Brittany St. Thomas, U.S. V.I., 1974-80, owner, operator, Houston, 1980; pres. RTM Cons., Honolulu, Hawaii, 1989—; educator World Tourism Orgn., 1993—; mem. vis. ind. coun. C. of C., 1993—; club mgr. Assn. Am., 1994—; dir. edn. Am. Assoc. Real Estate License Law Officials. Contbr. articles to profl. jours. Founding mem. Fla. Distance Learning Consortium, 1998—; bd. dirs., founder Fla. Virtual Campus, 1998—, dir. hospitality program, 1998—. Recipient White House Commendation for Partnerships with Industry and Higher Edn.,1984, George Washington Medal of Honor for innovations in higher edn., Freedoms Found., 1985, 86, Achievement award in hospitality edn. Coun. of Hotel, Restaurant & Instl. Edn., 1987. Mem. Assn. Real Estate Lic. Law Ofcls. (distance edn. coun. bd. mem. 1999—), Tarrant County Hotel and Motel Assn., Dallas Hotel Assn., Am. Soc. Tng. and Devel., Travel Ind. Assn. Tex., Hotel Sales & Mktg. Assn. (bd. dirs. 1985-89), Coun. of Hotel, Restaurant and Instl. Edn. (grad. com. 1989-90). Office: St Petersburg Coll PO Box 13489 Saint Petersburg FL 33733-3489 Home: 15184 Ganster Dr Brooksville FL 34613 Office Phone: 727-394-6165. Business E-Mail: rmeyer.robert@spcoiiege.edu. E-mail: meyer1@tampabay.rr.com.

MEYER, ROBERT R., retired science educator; Prof. Computer Sci. Dept., U. Wis., Madison, 1973—2008, prof. emeritus, 2008—. Rsch. grant, NSF, 1974—2006.

MEYER, RON, film company executive; b. 1944; m. Kelly Chapman; children, Jennifer, Sarah, Carson, Eli. With Paul Kohner Agency, 1964-1970; agent William Morris Agency, Beverly Hills, CA, 1970-1975; co-founder, pres. Creative Artists Agency, Inc., Beverly Hills, CA, 1975-95; pres., COO Universal Studios Inc., Universal City, 1995—. Served with USMC. Recipient Milestone award, Producers Guild Am., 2007; named one of 50 Most Powerful People in Hollywood, Premiere mag., 2004—06. Office: Universal Studios Inc 100 Universal City Plz Universal City CA 91608 Office Phone: 818-777-1000.*

MEYER, RUTH A., mathematics professor; d. Donald A. Janssen and Adela Marie Brase; m. Bruce E. Meyer, Jan. 7, 1984; children: Ben Martin, Mark Edward. BA in Edn., Wichita State U., 1981, MS in Math., 1984, PhD in Applied Math., 1993. Math. instr. Wichita State U., 1984—90, Butler CC, El Dorado, Kans., 1995—; vis. asst. prof. Tabor Coll., Hillsboro, Kans., 1993—94; asst. prof. math. Northwest Mo. State U., Maryville, 1994—95. Contbr. articles to profl. joursa. Mem.: Math. Assn. America. Office: Butler CC 901 S Haverhill Rd El Dorado KS 67042 Business E-Mail: rmeyer@butlercc.edu.

MEYER, STEPHENIE, writer; b. Hartford, Conn., Dec. 24, 1973; m. Christiaan Meyer, 1994; children: Gabe, Seth, Eli. BA in English, Brigham Young U., Provo, Utah. Author (Twilight Saga Series): Twilight, 2005 (Top Ten Best Book for Young Adults, ALA, Publishers Weekly Best Book of Yr.), New Moon, 2006, Eclipse, 2007, Breaking Dawn, 2008; author: The Host, 2008 (Publishers Weekly Bestseller); co-author: Prom Nights from Hell, 2007. Named one of The 100 Most Influential People in the World, TIME mag., 2008, 10 People Who Mattered, Newsweek, 2008. Office: c/o Hachette Book Group USA Little, Brown Young Readers 237 Park Ave New York NY 10017

MEYER, SUSAN MOON, speech pathologist, educator; b. Hazleton, Pa., Mar. 8, 1949; d. Robert A. and Jane W. (Walters) Moon; m. John C. Meyer Jr., Feb. 16, 1989; children: Chris, Scott. BS, Pa. State U., 1971, MS, 1972; PhD, Temple U., 1983. Cert. tchr., Pa. Speech-lang. pathologist, instr. Elmira (N.Y.) Coll., 1973-74; speech-lang. pathologist Arnot-Ogden Hosp., Elmira, 1973-74; supr. Sacred Heart Hosp. Speech and Hearing Ctr., Allentown, Pa., 1974-75; speech-lang. pathology instr. Kutztown (Pa.) U., 1975-78, asst. prof., 1978-82, assoc. prof., 1982-85, prof., 1985—. Owner Speech and Lang. Svcs., Allentown, 1975-87; cons. Vis. Nurses Assn., Allentown, 1975-85, Home Care, Allentown, 1975-85. Author: Survival Guide for the Speech-Language Clinician, 1998, 2004. Mem. Am. Speech-Lang.-Hearing Assn. (cert., councilor 1986-89, numerous Continuing Edn. awards), Pa. Speech-Lang.-Hearing Assn. (cert., v.p. profl. preparation 1985-89, Appreciation award 1987-89, 2001), Northea. Speech and Hearing Assn. Pa. (pres. 1984-86, Outstanding Dedication award 1985, Honors of the Assn. award 1999), Coun. Suprs. Speech-Lang. Pathology and Audiology. Avocations: cross country skiing, reading, water gardening. Office: Kutztown U Dept Speech-Lang Kutztown PA 19530 Office Phone: 610-683-4297. Business E-Mail: smeyer@kutztown.edu.

MEYER, THEO E., cardiologist; b. Pretoria, South Africa, Feb. 22, 1953; s. Mauritius and Nini Meyer; m. Susanna E. Le Roux; children: Joseph, Teresa. MD, U. Pretoria, South Africa, 1976; PhD, Oxford U., Eng., 1976. Diplomate in cardiovasc. diseases Am. Bd. Internal Medicine, 1997. Cardiologist U. Mass. Meml., Worcester, 1987—. Achievements include research in cardiovascular medicine. Office Fax: 508-856-4571. Business E-Mail: meyert@ummhc.org.

MEYER, URBAN, college football coach; b. Ashtabula, Ohio, July 10, 1964; m. Shelly Mather, 1986; children: Nicole, Gigi, Nate. Grad., U. Cin., 1986. Tight ends coach Ohio State U. Buckeyes, 1986, receivers coach, 1987; linebackers coach Ill. State U. Redbirds, 1988, quarterbacks/wide receivers coach, 1989; wide receivers coach Colo. State U. Rams, 1990—95, U. Notre Dame Fighting Irish, 1996—2000; head coach Bowling Green U. Falcons, 2001—02, U. Utah Utes, 2003—04, U. Fla. Gators, Gainesville, 2005—. Recipient Nat. Coach of Yr., Pro Football Weekly, 2004, George Munger award for Collegiate Coach of Yr., Maxwell Club, 2004, Woody Hayes Trophy award, Columbus Touchdown Club, 2004, Victor award, 2004; named Mid. Am. Conf. Coach of Yr., 2001, Nat. Coach of Yr., The Sporting News, 2003, Mountain West Conf. Coach of Yr., 2003, 2004, Nat. Coach of Yr., Home Depot, 2004, Eddie Robinson Coach of Yr., Football Writers Assn. Am., 2004. Achievements include coaching the University of Florida Gators to the BCS National Championship, 2006, 2008. Office: U Fla Gators Ben Hill Griffin Stadium Univ Ave & North South Dr Gainesville FL 32611*

MEYER, WILLIAM H., pediatrician, educator; b. Williamsport, Pa., Algeria, Nov. 30, 1951; s. Henry W. and Ruth G. Meyer; m. Irma DeVaul, Apr. 8, 1978; children: Eric J., Meghan N., Rachel D. BS, Penn State U., Univ. Pk., 1972; MD, Jefferson Med. Coll., Pa., 1974. Diplomate pediatric hematology-oncology Am. Bd. Pediat., 1980. Asst. prof. U. Va. Med. Sch., Charlottesville, 1980—83; asst. mem. - full mem. St. Jude Children's Rsch. Hosp., Memphis, 1983—97; CMRI Ben Johnson endowed prof. pediat. U. Okla. Health Sci. Ctr., Okla. City, 1997—. Office: Univ Okla Health Sci Ctr 940 NE 13th St Rm 3308 Oklahoma City OK 73104 Business E-Mail: william-meyer@ouhsc.edu.

MEYER-BAESE, UWE, engineering educator; m. Anke Meyer-Baese. Deng., Darmstadt U. Tech., Germany, 1995. Prof. FSU, Tallahassee, 2001—. With Moerser German Army, 1984—85. Recipient Habilitation award, TU Darmstadt, 2003. Mem.: IEEE. Achievements include patents in field. Office: FL State Univ 2525 Pottsdamer St Tallahassee FL 32301

MEYER-BAHLBURG, HEINO F.L., psychology professor; b. Hamburg, Germany, Feb. 26, 1940; came to U.S., 1969; s. Wilhelm and Marie Luise Meyer-B. Vordiplom in Psychology, U. Hamburg, 1963, Diplom Psychology, 1966; D in Natural Scis., U. Düsseldorf, Germany, 1970. Sci. asst. U. Düsseldorf, 1970; rsch. asst., then rsch. assoc. prof. psychiatry and pediat. SUNY Med. Sch., Buffalo, 1970-77; rsch. scientist N.Y. State Psychiat. Inst., NYC, 1977—; from assoc. clin. prof. med. psychology to prof. clin. psychology in psychiatry Columbia U. Coll. Physicians and Surgeons, 1978—; pediat. behavioral endocrinologist Presbyn. Hosp., NYC, 1978-90, prof. psychologist in psychiat. svc., 1990—. Contbr. numerous articles to profl. publs. Recipient Disting. Sci. Achievement award Soc. for Sci. Study of Sex, 1993; grantee NIMH, NICHD. Mem. AAAS, APA, Soc. Pediat. Psychology, Internat. Acad. Sex Rsch., Soc. Sci. Study Sex, Soc. Rsch. Child Devel., Soc. Sexual Therapy and Rsch., Lawson Wilkins Pediat. Endocrine Soc., World Profl. Assn. for Transgender Health. Office: Columbia U Dept Psychiatry 1051 Riverside Dr Unit 15 New York NY 10032-2695 Office Phone: 212-543-5299. Business E-Mail: meyerb@childpsych.columbia.edu.

MEYER-BROSDAHL, DEBORAH J.C., educator, researcher; d. Marvin V. and Lois D. Colton; m. Alan D. Brosdahl, Dec. 3, 2005; children: Nicole Meyer, W. Colton Meyer, Morgan M. Brosdahl. BS, Iowa State U., Ames, 1979; PhD, 1995; MS, U. Mo., Columbia, 1990. Buyer mgr. Fashion Ctr. Bridal & Formal, Phoenix, 1979—84; dept. head faculty Maricopa Comm. Coll. Skill Ctr., Phoenix, 1984—86; owner RSVP, Glasgow, Mo., 1987—2000; asst. prof. apparel merchandising Wash. State U.; Apparel, Merchandising, & Int. Design, Pullman, Wash., 1995—98; assoc. prof. apparel mktg.; dir. grad. studies KSU-Apparel, Textiles & Interior Design, Manhattan, Kans., 1998—2009; assoc. prof. & dir. grad. studies Dept. Retailing, U. SC. Contbr. articles to profl. jours. Recipient Textile & Apparel Mgmt. Outstanding Tchg. Asst. award, U. Mo.-Columbia, 1989—90, Superior Grad. Student Achievement award, 1988—90, All Star award, Apparel Mag., 2006—08, Dean Barbara S. Stowe Endowed Faculty Devel. Fund award, Coll. Human Ecology, 2005—06, 2008—09, Alford-Myers Outstanding Tchg. award, 1999—2000, award, Kans. State Faculty Exch., 2004—05, 2008—09, ITAA Faculty Travel award, Am. Internat. U. & Internat. Textile and Apparel Assoc., 2005, Faculty award, Eden Travel & Internat. Textile and Apparel Assn., 2004, Outstanding KSU Faculty, Pi Beta Phi, 2004; grantee Educating Future Leaders, USDA Challenge Grant Program, 2003; grant, USDA, K-State Agrl. Expt. Sta., 2006—, USDA Challenge Grant Program, 1997—2000, Internat. Coun. Shopping Ctrs., 2000—01, Internat. Textile & Apparel Assoc., 1997—98, Wakonse fellow, Kans. State U., 2003, Grad. Fellowship award, Internat. Textile & Apparel Assn., 1994. Mem.: Am. Family and Consumer Sciences Assn., Am. Collegiate Retail Assn., Internat. Colour Congress, Internat. Textile & Apparel Assn. (sec. 2006—08), Kappa Omicron Nu. Office: Univ SC Dept Retailing Carolina Coliseum Columbia SC 29201 Office Fax: 785-532-3796. Business E-Mail: brosdahl@ksu.edu.

MEYERHARDT, JEFFREY ABRAHAM, internist, oncologist; b. Englewood, NJ, Oct. 26, 1969; MD, Yale U. Sch. Med., 1997. Resident, internal medicine Beth Israel Deaconess Med. Ctr., Boston, 1997; fellow, med. oncology Dana-Farber Cancer Ctr. Inst., Boston, hosp. appointment, Gastrointestinal Cancer Ctr., dept. med. oncology, 2002—; asst. prof. medicine Harvard Med. Sch., Boston, 2004—. Contbr. articles to profl. jours. Office: Dana-Farber Cancer Inst Mailstop DL 1220 44 Binney St Boston MA 02115 Office Phone: 617-632-6855. Office Fax: 617-632-5370.

MEYERHOFF, ANDREA NIKKI, former federal agency administrator, biodefense executive, medical educator; b. Boston, July 31, 1959; d. Joseph and Ruth Meyerhoff; m. Jacob Gregg Thiessen, Apr. 27, 1991. BA in History, Wellesley Coll., Mass., 1981; MD, Albert Einstein Coll. Medicine, Bronx, NY, 1985; MSc in Clin. Tropical Medicine, London Sch. Hygiene and Tropical Medicine, 1990. Diplomate infectious diseases Am. Bd. Internal Medicine, 1996, Am. Bd. Internal Medicine, 1988, tropical medicine and hygeine RCP, LOndon, 1990. Resident internal medicine Boston City Hosp., 1985—88; internist Neighborhood Health Ctrs., Boston, 1988—91; rsch. asst. NIH Parasitic Diseases Lab., Bethesda, Md., 1992; fellow, infectious disease Brown U., Providence, 1993—95; infectious disease physician Frederick Meml. Hosp., Md., 1995—96; med. officer US FDA, Rockville, Md., 1996—2001, dir. counterterrorism, 2001—03; assoc. prof. clin. medicine Georgetown U., Washington, 1997—; dir., med. wmd def. US Dept. Def., Office of Sec., Arlington, Va., 2003—04; CEO GexGroup, Inc, Washington, 2005—. Instr. Peace Corps Med. Officers, Washington, 2002—04; mem. White House Interagency Working Group Med. Countermeasures for Biodefense, 2003—04; adj. assoc. prof. Johns Hopkins Sch. Medicine, Balt., 2006—. Contbr. articles to profl. pubs., chapters to books. Recipient Commr. Spl. Citation, US FDA, 2002; Fulbright scholarship, UK, 1989—90. Mem.: ACP, Humane Soc. US (special friend), Royal Soc. Tropical Medicine and Hygiene, Am. Soc. Tropical Medicine and Hygiene, Infectious Diseases Soc. Am., Fulbright Assn. (life), Phi Beta Kappa. Office: GexGroup Inc 5185 MacArthur Blvd NW 610 Washington DC 20016 Business E-Mail: ameyerhoff.gex@verizon.net.

MEYERHOFF, ERICH, librarian, director; b. Braunschweig, Germany, Nov. 24, 1919; came to US, 1935; s. Karl and Irma Meyerhoff; m. Inge Zuber; children: Tina, C. Michael BS, CCNY, 1943; MS, NY Sch. Social Work, 1949; MSLS, Columbia U., 1951, cert. advanced librarianship, 1974. Social worker various orgns., to 1951; reference librarian Columbia U. Med. Library, NYC, 1951-57; librarian, asst. prof. Downstate Med. Ctr., SUNY, Bklyn., 1957-61; dir. Med. Library Ctr. NY, 1961-67; librarian Health Scis. Library, SUNY-Buffalo, 1967-70, Cornell U. Med. Coll., NYC, 1970-86, asst. dean, 1977-86; chief library svc. VA Med. Ctr., NYC, 1986-88; archives librarian NYU Med. Ctr., 1980-91; asst. curator Ehrman Med. Libr.-Archives, NYU Sch. Medicine, 1991—. Adj. instr. biomed. comms. Columbia U., 1976-81; cons. U. Mich., Ann Arbor, 1968, NY Met. Reference Rsch. Libr. Agy., 1968-69, Coll. Physicians Phila., 1969-70. Fellow AAAS, Med. Library Assn. (cert., bd. dirs. 1972-76, chmn. various coms. 1968-72, 78-81, Inst. for Sci. Info. award 1981-82, Janet Doe lectr. 1977, Marcia C. Noyes award 1997), NY Acad. Medicine; mem. AAUP, Spl. Libraries Assn., Archons Colophon, Am. Assn. History Medicine, Am. Printing History Assn., Met. NY Archivists Roundtable. Avocation: travel. Home: 90 La Salle St New York NY 10027-4719 Office: NYU Med Ctr Archives 550 1st Ave New York NY 10016-6402 Office Phone: 212-263-8280. Business E-Mail: meyere01@library.med.nyu.edu.

MEYERHOFF, JAMES LESTER, medical researcher; b. Phila., Dec. 12, 1937; s. Lester Bacharach and Natalie Hatch (Rosenberg) M. BA, U. Pa., 1962, MD, 1966. Diplomate Nat. Bd. Med. Examiners, Am. Bd. Psychiatry and Neurology; lic. physician, Md. Intern Misericordia Hosp., Phila., 1966-67; resident U. Chgo. Hosp., 1967-70; postdoctoral fellow Johns Hopkins U., 1970-71; rsch. assoc. Walter Reed Army Inst. Rsch. and Med. Ctr., Washington, 1971-72, head neurochemsitry sect., 1972-74, chief dept. neuroendorcinology, 1974-76, chief neuroendocrinology and neurochemistry bd., 1976—. Clin. assoc. prof. psychiatry Georgetown U., 1977., adj. prof. physiology, 2007-; rsch. prof. psychiatry Uniformed Svcs. U. Health Scis., 1978-96, rsch. prof. neurology, 1996-2003, rsch. prof. med. psychology 2003-. Contbr. numerous articles to profl. jours.; mem. editl. bd. Psychosomatic Medicine. Maj. M.C., U.S. Army, 1969-72. Fellow APA, Acad. Behavioral Medicine; mem. Am. Psychosomatic Soc., Soc. for Neurosci. Achievements include patents in field. Personal E-mail: james.meyerhoff@rcn.com.

MEYERINK, VICTORIA PAIGE, film producer, actress; b. Santa Barbara, Calif., Dec. 27, 1960; d. William Joseph Meyerink and Jeanne Baird; m. Lawrence David Foldes, Apr. 24, 1983. Student, U. So. Calif., 1978-80. Actress, 1962—; v.p. Star Cinema Prodn. Group, Inc., 1981-85; pres. Star Entertainment Group, Inc., LA, 1985—. Mem. faculty Internat. Film & TV Workshops, 1991—; lectr. colls. & film festivals, co-editor Indeependence Filom Festival, Colo., 2007-. Prodr. (motion pictures) The Great Skycopter Rescue, 1982, Young Warriors, 1984, Night Force, 1987, Prima Donnas, 1996, Finding Home, 2004; actress (TV series) The Danny Kaye Show, Green Acres, My Three Sons, Family Affair, The FBI, Adam 12, (motion pictures) Speedway, Night of The Grizzly, Seconds, Brainstorm, The Littlest Hobo, (TV spl.) It Isn't Easy Being a Teenage Millionairess, numerous comms. Recipient Mayoral Proclamation for Outstanding Achievement award City of LA, 1984, Recognition Cert. for 25 Yrs. Outstanding Contbns. to the Entertainment Industry City of LA, 1985, Outstanding Achievement award Acad. Family Films & TV, Former Child Star Lifetime Achievement award, 2006. Mem. Acad. Motion Picture Arts & Scis. (exec. com. Student Acad. Awards 1996—), L.A. Film Tchrs. Assn. Avocations: languages, travel, music, scuba diving, gourmet cooking.

MEYEROWITZ, ELLIOT MARTIN, biology professor; b. Washington, May 22, 1951; s. Irving and Freda (Goldberg) Meyerowitz; m. Joan Agnes Kobori, June 17, 1984; 2 children. AB, Columbia U., 1973; MPhil, Yale U., 1975, PhD, 1977; D (hon.), École Normale Supérieure, Lyon, France, 2007. Rsch. fellow Stanford U., Calif., 1977-79; asst. prof. biology Calif. Inst. Tech., Pasadena, 1980-85, assoc. prof., 1985-89, prof., 1989—, George W. Beadle prof. biology, 2002—, chair, divsn. biology, 2000—. Mem. editl. bd. Trends in Genetics, Current Biology, Devel, Genome Biology, Philos. Transactions Royal Soc. B, 2006; mem. editl. bd.: Current Opinion in Plant Biology, Jour. of Biology; contbr. articles to profl. jours. Recipient LVMH Sci. pour l'Art Sci. prize, 1996, Internat. prize for biology, Japan, 1997, Mendel medal, UK, 1997, Wilbur Cross medal, Yale U., 2001, Ross Harrison prize, Internat. Soc. Devel. Biologist, 2005, Balzan prize, 2006; Jane Coffin Childs Meml. Fund fellow, 1977—79, Sloan Found. fellow, 1980—82. Fellow: AAAS; mem.: NAS (councilor 2006—09, Lounsbery award 1999), Royal Soc., Soc. Devel. Biology (pres. 2005—06), Academie des Scis. (fgn. mem. France), Internat. Soc. for Plant Molecular Biology (pres. 1995—97), Genetics Soc. Am. (pres. 1999, medal 1996), Bot. Soc. Am. (Pelton award 1994, Centennial award 2006), Am. Soc. Plant Biologists (Gibbs medal 1995), Am. Acad. Arts and Scis., Am. Philos. Soc. Office: Calif Inst Tech Divsn Biology 156 29 Pasadena CA 91125-0001 Home Phone: 626-844-4555; Office Phone: 626-395-6889. Business E-Mail: meyerow@caltech.edu.

MEYERS, ALAN HOGE, lawyer; b. Brookfield, Mo., Nov. 2, 1949; s. Francis E. and Dorothy K. (Hoge) Meyers; m. Nancy Blaker Mitchell, July 31, 1976; children: Meredith Blaker, Courtney Alyson Lyon, Mitchell Cutler. BA with honors, U. Tex., 1973, JD, 1976. Bar: Tex. 1977, U.S. Tax Ct. 1978. Assoc. J.C. Blazier, Austin, 1976—78; from assoc. to ptnr. Cotton, Bledsoe, Tighe & Dawson, Midland, Tex., 1978—96; ptnr. Morgan, Leeton & Meyers, P.C., Midland, 1996—2004; pvt. practice Midland, 2004—. Participant Leadership Midland, 1981—82; elder 1st Presbyn. Ch., Midland; trustee Cmty. Bible Study, Colorado Springs, Colo. Served to 1st lt. U.S. Army N.G., 1971—78. Mem.: Midland County Bar Assn. (pres. 2004—05), Tex. State Bar Assn. Home: 1704 Normandy Ln Midland TX 79705-1701 Office: Law Offices of Alan H Meyers PC 505 N Big Spring Ste 104 Midland TX 79701 Office Phone: 432-682-5800, 432-312-1361. Personal E-mail: meyers11@sbcglobal.net.

MEYERS, AMY, museum director; m. Jack Meyers; 1 child, Rachel. BA, U. Chgo.; PhD in Am. Studies, Yale U. Rschr. Dumbarton Oaks; rschr. Ctr. for Advanced Study in Visual Arts, Nat. Gallery; curator Am. Art, Henry E. Huntington Libr., Art Collections and Bot. Gardens, San Marino, Calif.; dir. Yale Ctr. for Brit. Art; adj. prof. art hist. Yale U. Adj. faculty Calif. Inst. Tech.; vice chair, Huntington rep. Assn. Rsch. Insts. in History of Art, 1995—2000. Editor (with Margaret Pritchard): Empire's Nature: Mark Catesby's New World Vision; editor: (with Alan Trachtenberg) Classic Essays on Photography. Office: Yale Ctr for Brit Art PO Box 208280 1080 Chapel St New Haven CT 06520-8280

MEYERS, CHRISTINE LAINE, marketing and media executive, consultant; b. Detroit, Mar. 7, 1946; d. Ernest Robert and Eva Elizabeth (Laine) M.; 1 child, Kathryn Laine; m. Oliver S. Moore III, May 12, 1990. BA, U. Mich., 1968. Editor indsl. rels. diesel divsn. Gen. Motors Corp., Detroit, 1968; nat. advt. mgr. J.L. Hudson Co., Detroit, 1969-76, mgr. internal sales promotion, 1972-73, dir. pub., 1973-76; nat. advt. mgr. Pontiac Motor divsn., Mich., 1976-78; pres., owner Laine Meyers Mktg. Cos., Inc., Troy, Mich., 1978—; founder, owner CORP! Mag., 1998—. Dir. Internat. Inst. Met. Detroit, Inc. Contbr. articles to profl. publs. Bus. adv. coun. Ctrl. Mich. U., 1977-79; pub. adv. com. on jud. candidates Oakland County Bar Assn.; adv. bd. Birmingham Cmty. Hosp., Bank of Am., 1999-2001; bd. dirs. YMCA, Mich., 1992-98, Haven, 1997—, Automation Alley, Oakland County, 1999—. Named Mich. Ad Woman of Yr., 1976, one of Top 10 Working Women, Glamour mag., 1978, one of 100 Best and Brightest Advt. Age, 1987, one of Mich.'s top 25 female bus. owners Nat. Assn. Women Bus. Owners, One of Top 10 Women Owned Bus., Mich., 1994; recipient Vanguard award Women in Comm., 1986, Lifetime Achievement award Northwood U., 2002. Mem. Internat. Assn. Bus. Communicators, Adcraft Club, Women's Advt. Club (1st v.p. 1975), Women's Econ. Club (pres. 1976-77), Internat. Women's Forum Mich. (founding pres. 1986-97), Internat. Inst. Detroit (bd. dirs. 1986-89), Detroit C. of C., Troy C. of C., Mortar Bd., Quill and Scroll, Pub. Rels. Com. Women for United Found., Founders Soc. Detroit Inst. Arts, Fashion Group, Pub. Rels. Soc. Am., First Soc. Detroit (exec. com. 1970-71), Kappa Tau Alpha. Home: 604 Courtside Dr Naples FL 34105-7133 Office Phone: 248-458-2677 ext.301. Business E-Mail: cmyers@corpmagazine.com.

MEYERS, CHRISTOPHER, humanities educator, consultant; s. Diana Meyers and Ehrhard Bahr (Stepfather); m. Donna Elsdon, Apr. 6, 1997; 1 child, Natasha Leigh Meyers-Cherry stepchildren: Renee Elsdon, Jonathon Elsdon. BA, U. Calif., Santa Cruz, 1980; cert. in clin. ethics, U. Tenn., 1984, D, 1986. Prof. philosophy Calif. State U., Bakersfield, 1986—, exec. dir. Kegley Inst. Ethics, 1987—; clin. ethicist Kern Med. Ctr., Bakersfield, 1997—. Ethics cons., instr. Mercy Healthcare, Bakersfield, 1991—, San Joaquin Cmty. Hosp., Bakersfield, 1995—. Author: (book) A Practical Guide to Clinical Ethics Consulting: Ethics, Power & Expertise, 2007; contbr. articles to profl. jours. Ethics cons., instr. Multiple Bus. and Philanthropic Groups, Bakersfield, 1987—2006. Mem.: Am. Soc. Bioethics and Humanities, Assn. Practical and Profl. Ethics, Am. Philos. Assn. Avocations: fly fishing, hiking, bicycling. Office: Calif State U Bakersfield 9001 Stockdale Hwy Bakersfield CA 93311 Business E-Mail: cmeyers@csub.edu.

MEYERS, DALE (MRS. MARIO COOPER), artist; b. Chgo. d. Walter Herman and Gertude Wetterer; m. Mario Cooper, Oct. 11, 1964; children: Dale, Steven R. Student, Glendale Coll., Corcoran Gallery Sch. Art, Washington, 1962-63, Art Student's League, NYC, 1964-78. Instr. Art Students League, 1979—; ofcl. artist NASA, USCG.; lectr. Parson's Sch. Design, Nat. Acad. Sch. Author The Sketchbook, 1983; contbr.: Watercolor Bold and Free, Am. Artist mag, Diversion mag.; solo exhbns. include, West Wing Gallery, Ringwood (N.J.) State Park, 1970, Manor Club, Pelham Manor, N.Y., 1970, Apollo Art Gallery, Oklahoma City, 1972, Quadrangle Gallery, Dallas, 1972, Galveston Ctr. for Arts, 1974, Fla. Gulf Coast Art Ctr., 1977, 86, Okura Hotel, Tokyo, Japan, 1977, Owensboro Mus. Art, 1983, Salmagundi Club, 1986, 88, Stehle-Reed Gallery, Midland, Tex., 1987, others; artist-in-residence, Galveston Arts Ctr., 1974, Owensboro Mus. Art, 1983, Asilomar, Calif., 1983, 84; group exhbns. include Two Hundred Years of Watercolor Painting in Am, Met. Mus. Art, 1966, Eyewitness to Space, Nat. Gallery Art, Washington, 1969, Smithsonian Instn., 1961-63, Corcoran Gallery, 1963, Museo de la Acuarela, Mexico City, 1968, 89, London (Ont., Can.) Mus. Art, 1971-72, Art Gallery Hamilton, Ont., Can., 1971-72, Ont. Inst. Edn., 1971-72, Butler Inst. Art, 1962—, Frye Mus., 1962—; represented in permanent collections, Calif. Palace of Legion of Honor, San Francisco, Nat. Acad. N.Y.C., Avon Fine Arts Collection, NASA, EPA, Museo de la Acuarela, Schumacher Gallery, Columbus, Ohio, Slater Mus., Conn., Portland (Maine) Mus., U. Utah Fine Arts Collection, Frye Mus., Seattle, Owensboro Mus. Art, Coll. Misericordia, Dallas, Pa, Canton Art Inst., Ohio, Arnot Mus., Elmira, N.Y.; internat. watercolor exhbn. Can., U.S., Gt. Britain, 1991-94, Chung Cheng Gallery, Taipei, 1994. Recipient Henry W. Ranger award Nat. Acad. Design, 1968, Samuel F.B. Morse medal, 1973, Anna Hyatt Huntington Bronze medal, 1971, Knickerbocker Artists Gold medal, 1981, 88, Allied Artists Am. award, 1969, Gold medal honor Nat. Arts Club, 1972, Anna Hyatt Huntington Gold medal, 1974, Adolf and Cara Obrig award Nat. Acad., 1974, 81, Walter Biggs award, 1976, Allied Arts Gold medal, 1978, Audubon ARtists Silver medal, 1984. Fellow Royal Soc. Arts (Grumbocher Gold medals 1988, 90); mem. Am. Watercolor Soc. (pres. 1993-03, pres. emeritus 2003-, editor jours. 1962-79, Bronze medal honor award 1968, awards 1970, 72, 78, 79, 81, 82, 83, 85, 87, 89, 93, 98, High Winds medal 2001, 05, Dolphin medal 2000), Nat. Acad. (academician), Allied Artists Am. (pres. 1975-78), Art Students League N.Y., La. Watercolor Soc. (hon.), Ky. Watercolor Soc., Ohio Watercolor Soc. (hon.), Watercolor Soc. Mex., Fla. Watercolor Soc. (hon.), Audubon Artists, Salimagundi Club (medal of honor 1994). Office: Art Students League 215 W 57th St New York NY 10019

MEYERS, DAVID GEORGE, internist, cardiologist, educator; b. Muscatine, Iowa, Oct. 5, 1950; BS, Loras Coll., 1972; MD, U. Iowa, 1976; MPH, Med. Coll. Wis., 1998. Cert. in cardiology Am. Bd. Internal Medicine, Am. Bd. Preventive Medicine, Am. Bd. Clin. Lipidology. Intern Creighton U., 1976-77, resident medicine, 1977-79; fellow cardiology Med. Coll. Va., 1979-81; from asst. prof. internal medicine to assoc. prof. Neb. U. Med. Ctr., Omaha, 1981-93; mem. faculty U. Kans. Med. Ctr., Kansas City, 1994, prof. internal medicine and preventive medicine, 1994—, dir. of preventive Cardiology, 1994—. Recipient Chancellor's Outstanding Classroom Tchg. award, U. Kans., 1997. Fellow ACP, Am. Coll. Cardiology, Am. Coll. Chest Physicians, Am. Heart Assn., Am. Coll. Preventive Medicine, Nat. Lipid Assn.; mem. Am. Coll. Epidemiology, Am. Soc. Preventive Cardiology, Soc. Civil War Surgeons, Internat. Wine and Food Soc., Am. Inst. for Wine and Food. Office: U Kans Med Ctr 3901 Rainbow Blvd Kansas City KS 66160-0001 Office Phone: 913-588-6015. Business E-Mail: dmeyers@kumc.edu.

MEYERS, ERIC MARK, religion educator; b. Norwich, Conn., June 5, 1940; s. Karl D. and Shirlee M. (Meyer) M.; m. Carol Lyons, June 25, 1964; children: Julie Kaete, Dina Elisa. AB, Dartmouth Coll., 1962; MA, Brandeis U., 1964; PhD, Harvard U., 1969. Lerner prof. religion, archeol., bibl. study, ancient hist. Duke U., Durham, NC, 1969—, dir. grad. program in religion, 1979—86, 2001—06; dir. Annenberg Inst., Phila., 1991-92, Ctr. Jewish Studies, 1972—90, 2000—. Pres. Am. Schs.

Oriental Rsch., Boston, 1990—96, 2006—07; commentator on biblical archaeology; dir. 8 digs Israel, Italy, 1970—2000; co-dir. NEH seminar Duke U., 2004; dir. Jewish St. Program, 1972—90, 2002—. Author: 10 books; co-author: The Cambridge Companiion to the Bible, 1997, 2008; editor (in chief): The Oxford Encyclopedia of Archaeology in the Near East, 5 vols., 1997; contbr. articles more than 400 to profl. jours.; frequent guest (TV series) A&E channel, Discovery channel; frequent guest: History Channel. Jewish. Avocations: singing (baritone), golf, the arts, travel. Home: 3202 Waterbury Dr Durham NC 27707-2416 Office: Duke U 118 Gray Bldg PO Box 90964 Bldg Durham NC 27708-0964 Office Phone: 919-660-3517. Business E-Mail: emc@duke.edu.

MEYERS, GERALD CARL, finance educator, retired automotive executive; b. Buffalo, Dec. 5, 1928; s. Meyer and Berenice (Meyers) M.; m. Barbara Jacob, Nov. 2, 1958. BS, Carnegie Inst. Tech., 1950, MS with distinction, 1954. With Ford Motor Co., Detroit, 1950-51, Chrysler Corp., Detroit and Geneva, 1954-62, Am. Motors Corp. (AMC), Detroit, 1962-84, v.p., 1967-72, group v.p. product, 1972-75, exec. v.p., 1975-77, pres., 1977-84, COO, 1977, chmn., CEO, 1977-82; Ford Disting. prof. Grad. Sch. Indsl. Adminstrn. Carnegie Mellon U., Pitts., 1985-96; prof. U. Mich. Bus. Sch., Ann Arbor, 1995—. Pres. Gerald C. Meyers Assocs., Inc., West Bloomfield, Mich.; adj. prof. Sch. Bus. U. Mich., Ann Arbor. Author: When It Hits the Fan, Managing the Nine Crises of Business; co-author: Dealers, Healers, Brutes and Saliors; bus. commentator Nat. Pub. Radio, Fox News Cable TV, CNBC TN Network; contbr. articles to N.Y. Times, Wall St. Jour., L.A. Times. 1st lt. USAF, 1951-53. Decorated Legion of Honor (France). Mem. Econ. Club Detroit, Tau Beta Pi, Phi Kappa Phi, Omicron Delta Kappa. Address: U Mich Bus Sch D 3246 701 Tappan Ave Ann Arbor MI 48109-1217 Office: 5600 W Maple Rd Ste B216 West Bloomfield MI 48322-3787*

MEYERS, KAREN DIANE, lawyer, educator; b. Cin., July 8, 1950; d. Willard Paul and Camille Jeannette (Schutte) M.; m. William J. Jones, Mar. 27, 1978. BA summa cum laude, Thomas More Coll., 1971; MBA, MEd, Xavier U., 1978; JD, Chase Coll. Law, U. Ky., Covington, 1978. Bar: Ohio 1978, Ky. 1978; CLU; CPCU; cert. structured settlement cons. Clk. to mgr. Baldwin Co., Cin., 1970-78; adj. prof. bus. Thomas More Coll., Crestview Hill, Ky., 1978—, CSSC-U. Notre Dame, 1994, CSSC, 1994; asst. sec., asst. v.p., sr. counsel The Ohio Life Ins. Co., Hamilton, 1978-91; prin. KD Meyers & Assocs., 1991—; v.p. Benefit Designs, Inc., 1991-96, Little, Meyers & Assocs., Ltd., Cin., 1996—; adj. lectr. Miami U., 1998—. Adj. lectr. U. Notre Dame, South Bend, Ind., 2005—07. Bd. dirs. ARC, Hamilton, 1978-83, vol. Christ Hospital Family Advisory Council, 2008-, 1978—; bd. dirs. YWCA, Hamilton, 1985-91. Gardner Found. fellow, 1968-71; recipient Ind. Progress award Bus. & Profl. Women, 1990. Fellow Life Mgmt. Inst. Atlanta; mem. ABA, Soc. Chartered Property Casualty Underwriters (instr. 1987—), Cin. Bar Assn., Butler County Bar Assn., Ohio Bar Assn., Ky. Bar Assn. Roman Catholic. Avocations: aerobics, jogging, crafts. Home: 903 Hickory Hill Ln Cincinnati OH 45241-1363 Office Phone: 513-871-8900.

MEYERS, KENNETH RAYMOND, telecommunications industry executive; b. Chgo., Jan. 16, 1954; s. Raymond F. and Rita L. (Dunlevy) M.; m. Chere L. Lazzare, Mar. 10, 1984; children: Kristin, Kathryn. BBA, Loyola U., Chgo., 1977; M in Mgmt., Northwestern U., 1994. CPA. Various fin. positions including divsn. contr. and audit mgr. The Marmon Group, Chgo., 1977-84; contr. to treas. to v.p. fin. Imi-Tech Corp., Elk Grove, Ill., 1984-87; various sr. mgmt. fin. positions US Cellular Corp., Chgo., 1987—99, exec. v.p., CFO, 1999—2007, Tel. and Data Systems, 2007—. Bd. dirs. US Cellular Corp., Tel. and Data Systems. Mem. alumni adv. bd. Northwestern U. J.L. Kellogg Sch. Mgmt. Mem. AICPA, Fin. Exec. Inst., Cellular Tel. Industry Assn. (fin. com.). Roman Catholic. Avocations: boating, golf. Office: Tel and Data Systems 30 N LaSalle St Ste 4000 Chicago IL 60602 Office Phone: 312-630-1900. Office Fax: 312-630-1908.

MEYERS, KENT, literature and language professor, writer; b. Redwood Falls, Minn., Aug. 1, 1955; s. Wayne M. and Marguerite E. Meyers; m. Zindie Z. Ziemke, Oct. 1, 1977; children: Derek, Lauren, Jordan. MA, Wash. State U., Pullman, 1980. Writer-in-residence, assoc. prof. Black Hills State U., Spearfish, SD, 1980—. Author: (novels) Twisted Tree, The Work of Wolves, The River Warren (Barnes and Nobel New Voices award, 1998), (books) Light in the Crossing, (memoir) The Witness of Combines (Friends of Am. Authors award, 1998). Bd. mem. Cath. Social Svcs. Rapid City, Rapid City, SD, 2005—08. Recipient Minn. Book award, 2004; fellowship, Nat. Endowment Arts, 1992. Mem.: Western Lit. Assn. Avocations: tennis, cross country skiing. Office: Black Hills State Univ 1200 University Spearfish SD 57799 Business E-Mail: kentmeyers@bhsu.edu.

MEYERS, KEVIN OMAR, oil industry executive; b. 1953; BS in Chemistry and Math., Capital U., Columbus, Ohio, 1975; PhD in Chem. Engring., MIT. Joined exploration and prodn. tech. ARCO, Plano, Tex., 1980, various positions in exploration and prodn. ops. Tex., Alaska, 1980—96, sr. v.p., Prudhoe Bay bus. unit, 1996—98, pres., ARCO Alaska, Inc., 1998, CEO, ARCO Alaska, Inc., 1998—2000; sr. v.p. Atlantic Richfield Co., 1998—2000; sr. v.p. Alaska prodn. and ops. and pres., CEO Phillips Alaska, Inc., 2000—01; exec. v.p. Alaska prodn. ops. Phillips Petroleum Co., 2001—02; pres., Alaska ConocoPhillips, 2002—04, pres., Russia & Caspian region Moscow, 2004—06, pres. exploration & prodn. Can. Calgary, 2006—09, sr. v.p. exploration & prodn. Americas Houston, 2009—. Bd. regents U. Alaska; bd. dirs. Alaska Oil and Gas Assn., Anchorage Symphony Orch., Nature Conservancy Alaska, Anchorage Mus. Found., Kenai River Sportfishing Assn., USAF Civilian Adv. Bd., Alaska Command. Named one of Top 25 Most Powerful Alaskans, Alaskan Jour. of Commerce, 2002. Office: ConocoPhillips PO Box 2197 Houston TX 77252*

MEYERS, MARLENE O., retired hospital administrator; m. Eugene Meyers; children: Lori, Lisa, Dean. BSN, U. Sask., 1962; postgrad., U. Oslo, Norway, 1973; MSc, U. Calgary, Alta., Can., 1976; continuing edn., Harvard U., 1980, Banff Sch. Mgmt., 1985, U. Western Ont., Can., 1993; EMT-B, Scottsdale C.C., 2000. RN, Ariz. Various nursing positions, Alta. and B.C., Can., 1962-69; instr., chair Mount Royal Coll. Allied Health, Calgary, 1969-82; asst. exec. dir. Rockyview Hosp., Calgary, 1982-85; v.p. patient svcs. Calgary Gen. Hosp., 1985-91, pres., CEO, 1991-95, Meyers and Assocs. Health Care Mgmt. Cons., Calgary, 1995—98; clin. nurse Scottsdale Behavioral Health Ctr., 1999—2006. Surveyor Can. Coun. on Health Facilities Accreditation, 1986-97; mem. adv. com. for South Caucasus Health info. project, Can. Adv. Com. Named Calgary Woman of Yr. in field of Health, 1982; recipient Heritage of Svc. award, 1996. Mem. Alta. Assn. RNs (hon.), Can. Coll. Health Svcs. Orgn., Can. Exec. Svcs. Orgn., Can. Soc. for Internat. Health (bd. dirs. 1997-2001, South Caucasus adv. com. 2001—), Rotary Internat. PEO also: 10464 E Cannon Dr Scottsdale AZ 85258-4929

MEYERS, MARSHA LYNN, retired social worker; b. Springfield, Ohio, Dec. 3, 1948; d. Dennis Wathan and Juanita E. (Ratliff) Easterling; m. Wade Trent Meyers, Oct. 5, 1974; children: Lindsay Dionne, Whitney Jane. BA in Sociology, Olivet Nazarene U., Bourbonnais, Ill., 1972. Lic. social worker, Ohio. Formerly social work coord. Mercy Meml. Hosp. and Home Health Care, Urbana, Ohio. Former bd. dirs. Champaign County chpt. Am. Cancer Soc.; mem. adv. bd. Mercy Meml. Hosp. Home Health Care Hospice. Named Social Worker of the Yr. for excellence in small depts. Ohio Soc. Hosp. Social Workers, 1995, Social Worker of Yr., Cedarville U. chpt. Phi Alpha Theta, 2000. Mem. Soc. of Hosp. Social Work Dirs., Nat. Assn. Christian Social Workers (past v.p.). Home: 223 College St Urbana OH 43078-2405

MEYERS, MARY ANN, foundation administrator, consultant, writer; b. Sodus, NY, Sept. 30, 1937; d. Harold Galpin and Clarice Mildred (Daniel) Dye; m. John Matthew Meyers D., Aug. 22, 1959; children: Andrew Christopher, Anne Kathryn. BA magna cum laude, Syracuse U., 1959; MA, U. Pa., 1965, PhD, 1976. Editorial asst. Ladies' Home Jour., Phila., 1959-62; editor, asst. dir. news bur. U. Pa., Phila., 1962-65, asst. to pres., 1973-75, univ. sec., lectr. Am. civilization, 1980-90; contbg. writer The Pennsylvania Gazette, Phila., 1965—97; dir. coll. rels., editor Haverford Horizons, lectr. in religion Haverford (Pa.) Coll., 1977-80; pres. The Annenberg Found., St. Davids, Pa., 1990-92; v.p. for external affairs Moore Coll. Art and Design, Phila., 1995-97; sr. fellow The John Templeton Found., Radnor, Pa., 1997—. Vis. com. dept. biology U. Pa., 1996—2002; mem. bd. advisors The Peter Gruber Found., St. Thomas, U.S. V.I., 2001—. Author: A New World Jerusalem, 1983, Art, Education and African American Culture: Albert Barnes and the Science of Philanthropy, 2004, 06; contbg. author: Death in America, 1975, Gladly Learn, Gladly Teach, 1978, Coping with Serious Illness, 1980, Religion in American Life, 1987; contbr. articles to profl. jours. Judge recognition program Coun. for Advancement and Support Edn., Washington, 1977—78, chair creative editing and writing workshop, 1978; mem. Picker Found. Program on Human Qualities in Medicine, NYC and Phila., 1980—83; del. Phila.-Leningrad Sister Cities Project, 1986; trustee U. Pa. Press., 1985—2003; vice chmn. U. Pa. 250th Anniversary Commn., 1987—90; mem. steering com. of bd. trustees U. Pa., Annenberg Sch. for Comm., 1990—92; mem. adv. bd. U. Pa., Annenberg Ctr. for the Performing Arts, 1990—98; mem. bd. overseers U. Pa., Sch. Arts and Scis., 1990—97; mem. steering com. of bd. trustees Annenberg Ctr. for Comm., U. So. Calif., LA, 1990—92, The Annenberg Washington Program in Comm. Policy Studies of Northwestern U., Washington, 1990—92; dir., sec. Am. Acad. Polit. and Social Sci., 1992—, World Affairs Coun. Phila., 1990—95; dir. Diagnostic and Rehab. Ctr., Phila., 1993—2002. Recipient Excellence award Women in Communications, Inc., 1973-74, award for pub. affairs reporting Newsweek/Coun. for Advancement and Support Edn., 1977, Silver medal Coun. for Advancement and Support Edn., 1986. Mem. Am. Acad. Polit. and Social Sci. (sec. and dir. 1992-), Cosmopolitan Club, Sunday Breakfast Club, Phi Beta Kappa (mem. steering com. Delaware Valley chpt. 1995-97). Roman Catholic. Home: 414 Old Lancaster Rd Apt 203 Haverford PA 19041-1571

MEYERS, MORTON ALLEN, radiologist, educator; b. Troy, NY, Oct. 1, 1933; s. David and Jeanne Sarah (Dunn) M.; m. Beatrice Applebaum, June 1, 1963; children— Richard, Amy. MD, SUNY, Upstate Med. Coll., 1959. Diplomate Am. Bd. Radiology, 1965. Intern Bellevue Hosp., NYC, 1959-60; resident in radiology Columbia-Presbyn. Med. Ctr., NYC, 1960-63; fellow Am. Cancer Soc., 1961-63; prof. dept. radiology Cornell U. Med. Ctr., NYC, 1973-78; radiologist in chief Stony Brook U. Hosp., 1978—91; prof., chmn. dept. radiology SUNY Sch. Medicine, Stony Brook, 1978-91, prof. dept. radiology, 1991-98, disting. univ. prof., 1998—. Cons. Northport VA Hosp.; vis. investigator St. Mark's Hosp., London, 1976; spkr. in field. Author: Diseases of the Adrenal Glands: Radiologic Diagnosis, 1963, Dynamic Radiology of the Abdomen: Normal and Pathologic Anatomy, 1976, 5th edit., 2000, tranl. in Spanish, 1980, Japanese, 1985, 1991, Italian, 1992, Portuguese, 1999, Iatrogenic Gastrointestinal Complications, 1981; series editor: Computed Tomography of the Gastrointestinal Tract: Including the Peritoneal Cavity and Mesentery, 1986, Neoplasms of the Digestive Tract: Imaging, Staging, and Management, 1998, Happy Accidents: Serendipity in Modern Medical Breakthroughs, 2007, founding editor-in-chief: Abdominal Imaging, 1976—, mem. editl. bd.: Iatrogenics; mem. editl. bd. Surg. and Radiol. Anatomy; contbr. chapters to books, articles to profl. jours. Served to capt. M.C. U.S. Army, 1963-65. Recipient Gold medal, U. Leeds, 1980, Radiol. Soc. Republic of China, 1986, Asian-Oceanian Congress Radiology, 1987, European Congress of Radiology, 1995, Indian Radiol. and Imaging Assn., 1999. Fellow: European Soc. Gastrointestinal and Abdominal Radiology, Am. Coll. Gastroenterology, Am. Coll. Radiology; mem.: European Soc. Urogenital Radiology, NY Acad. Gastroenterology, NY Roentgen Ray Soc., Assn. Univ. Radiologists, Israel Radiol. Soc. (hon.), Italian Radiol. Soc. (hon. Medal of honor 1983), Royal Belgian Soc. Gastroenterology (hon.), Spanish Radiol. Soc. (hon.), European Assn. Radiology (hon.), Soc. Gastrointestinal Radiologists (Cannon medal 1993, Hartman medal 1995), Soc. Uroradiology, Am. Gastroenterol. Assn., Am. Roentgen Ray Soc. (Gold medal 1975, 1980), Radiol. Soc. N.Am. (ann. orator 1986), Alpha Omega Alpha. Home: 14 Wainscott Ln East Setauket NY 11733-3816 Office: SUNY Health Scis Ctr Sch Medicine Dept Radiology Stony Brook NY 11794-8460 Office Phone: 631-751-3685. Business E-Mail: jimenez1234@optonline.net.

MEYERS, NICHOLAUS, music educator; s. Walden Augustus and Cheryl Renee Meyers. MusB, Augusta State U., 1997—2002; MusM, U. of Tenn., 2002—04. Grad. libr. asst. U. Tenn., Knoxville, 2003—04; instr. music Augusta State U., 2004—, Augusta Tech. Inst., 2007—. Percussion instr. Lakeside HS, Evans, Ga., 2001—; instr. Troy U., 2008—; percussionist Augusta Opera, 2002—; timpanist Augusta Choral Soc., 2004—; percussionist Oakridge Symphony, Tenn., 2004. Composer: (composition) A Glimpse Ahead, Reflections, Three Shorts, Altered Stages, Contrasting Opinions, Two Holy Songs, Two Songs of Love, Concerto for Marimba, The Picture in My Mind, The New Found Feeling. Maxwell Meml. Music scholarship, Augusta State U., 1998—2002, Mauldin Music scholarship, 1999—2002. Mem.: ASCAP, Percussive Arts Soc., Soc. of Composers, Coll. Music Soc. Achievements include research in Guide to Timpani Concertos. Home: 495 Creekwalk Cir Augusta GA 30907 Personal E-mail: nmeyers@aug.edu.

MEYERS, PAMELA SUE, lawyer; b. Lakewood, NJ, June 13, 1951; d. Morris Leon and Isabel (Leibowitz) M.; m. Gerald Stephen Greenberg, Aug. 24, 1975; children: David Stuart Greenberg, Allison Brooke Greenberg. AB with distinction, Cornell U., 1973; JD cum laude, Harvard U., 1976. Bar: NY 1977, Ohio 1990. Assoc. Stroock & Stroock & Lavan, NYC, 1976-80; staff v.p., asst. gen. counsel Am. Premier Underwriters, Inc., Cin., 1980-96; legal counsel Citizens Fed. Bank, Dayton, Ohio, 1997-98; gen. counsel, sec. Mosler Inc., Hamilton, Ohio, 1998—2001. Bd. dirs. Hamilton County Alcohol and Drug Addiction Svc. Bd., 1996-2000, Adath Israel Congregation, 1999-2005; dir. Gorman Heritage Farm Found., 2006-2007; trustee Carpenters Creek Civic Assn., 2004-06; mem. Village Evendale Recreation Commn., 2006-; docent Cincinnati Art Mus., 2008- Mem. Cin. Bar Assn., Harvard Club of Cin. (pres. 1998-99, bd. dirs. 1993-2000, 2009-), Phi Beta Kappa. Jewish. Avocations: piano, reading, tennis. Home: 3633 Carpenters Creek Dr Cincinnati OH 45241-3824 Personal E-mail: psmeyers@fuse.net.

MEYERS, PHILIP ALAN, geochemistry educator, researcher; b. Hackensack, NJ, Mar. 3, 1941; s. Harold Grove and Gertrude Myra (Smith) M.; m. Judith Arlene Brown, May 15, 1965; children: Shelley, Suzanne, Christopher. BS, Carnegie-Mellon U., 1964; PhD, U. R.I., 1972. Rsch. chemist Inmont Corp., Clifton, N.J., 1967-68; prof. U. Mich., Ann Arbor, 1972—. Cons. Marathon Oil Co., BP Oil Co., Chevron Oil Co., Cities Svc. Oil. Co., 1980; dir. Ct. Lakes and Marine Waters Ctr., U. Mich., 1982-83; vis. prof. Eidgenossische Technische Hochschule, Zurich, Switzerland, 2003, Hokkaido U., Sapporo, Japan, 2008 Contbr. articles to profl. jours. Lt. (j.g.) USNR, 1964-67. NOAA summer fellow, 1981, vis. fellow Hanse-Wissenschaftskolleg, 2000, 2002; recipient Disting. Svc. award U. Mich. Class of 1938, Engring., 1976, vis. scientist award Ind. U., 1979-80; named Disting. Lectr. Sigma Xi, 2007-09. Fellow AAAS, Geol. Soc. Am., Am. Geophys Union, Geochem. Soc.; mem. Am. Assn. Limnology and Oceanography, European Assn. Organic Geochemists, Huron Valley Tennis Club. Avocations: tennis, travel, photography, running. Office: U Mich 3514 C C Little Bldg Ann Arbor MI 48109-1005 Home Phone: 734-769-2740; Office Phone: 734-764-0597. Business E-Mail: pameyers@umich.edu.

MEYERS, REBECKA LOUISE, pediatric general surgeon; b. Salt Lake City, May 11, 1958; MD, Oreg. Health Scis. U. Sch. Medicine, 1985. Cert. Gen. Surgery, Pediatric Gen. Surgery. Intern, gen. surgery U. Calif. Med. Ctr., San Francisco, 1985—88, fellow, cardiovascular diseases, 1988—90, resident, gen. surgery, 1990—92; fellow St. Christopher's Hosp. for Children in Pediatric Surgery, Phila., 1992—94; pediatric surgeon Primary Children's Med. Ctr., Salt Lake City, 1994—; chief, divsn. pediatric surgery Univ. Utah Hosp. (now called U. Utah Health Scis. Ctr.), Salt Lake City, 2001—; asst. prof. U. Utah, Salt Lake City, 1994—99, assoc. prof., 1999—2007, prof., 2007—. Mem.: UMA, Pacific Assn. of Pediatric Surgeons, Internat. Pediatric Endosurgery Grp., Assn. Women Surgeons, Am. Pediatric Surgical Assn., Am. Coll. Surgeons, Am. Acad. Pediat. Office: U Utah Health Services Ctr 50 N Medical Dr Salt Lake City UT 84132 also: Primary Childrens Med Ctr 100 N Mario Capecchi Dr Ste 2600 Salt Lake City UT 84113 Office Phone: 801-662-2950.

MEYERS, ROBERT ALLEN, chemist, publisher; b. LA, May 15, 1936; s. Jack B. Meyers and Pearl (Cassell) Thorpe; m. Roberta Lee Hart, June 24, 1961 (div. 1976); children: Tamara, Robert Jr.; m. Ilene Braun, Feb. 27, 1977; children: Jenifer, Jacalyn. BA, San Diego State U., 1959; PhD, UCLA, 1963. Postdoctoral fellow, mem. faculty Calif. Inst. Tech., Pasadena, 1963-64; rsch. scientist Bell & Howell Rsch. Ctr., Sierra Madre, Calif., 1965; project mgr. TRW Def. & Space, Redondo Beach, Calif., 1966-81; bus. area mgr. TRW Energy Group, Redondo Beach, 1981-86; mgr. process devel. TRW Def. & Space, Redondo Beach, 1986-88, mgr. new projects devel., 1988-95; pres. Ramtech Ltd., Mill Valley, Calif., 1995—. Del. U.S.-USSR Working Group, Washington and Moscow, 1973-80; chmn. adv. bd. Guide to Nuclear Power Tech., NYC, 1982-84; adv. coun. chemistry dept. UCLA, 1991—. Author: Coal Desulfurization, 1977; editor: Handbook of Petroleum Refining Processes, 1986, 3d edit., 2003, Handbook of Synfuels Technology, 1984, Handbook of Energy Technology and Economics, 1983, Handbook of Chemicals Production Processes, 1986, 2d edit., 2004, others; editor-in-chief Ency. Phys. Sci. and Tech., 1987, 1992, 2001, Ency. of Modern Physics, 1990, Ency. Lasers and Optics, 1991, Ency. Telecomm., 1989, Molecular Biology and Biotech., 1995, Ency. Molecular Biology and Molecular Medicine, 1995, Ency. Environ. Analysis and Remediation, 1998, Ency. Environ. Pollution and Control, 1999, Ency. of Analytical Chemistry, 2000, Ency. Molecular Cell Biology and Molecular Medicine, 2004, 2005, Handbook of Petrochems. Prodn. Processes, 2004; author: Encyclopedia of Complexity & Sys. Sci., 2009. Mem.: Am. Phys. Soc., Am. Soc. Cell Biology, Am. Inst. Chem. Engrs., Am. Chem. Soc. Avocations: swimming, bicycling, tennis, golf. Personal E-mail: robert.meyers@ramtechlimited.org.

MEYERS, RONALD J., literature and language professor; b. NYC, Mar. 1, 1936; s. Percy and Gitelle S. Meyers; m. Rina Buchshriber, Aug. 30, 1959; children: Adam Elan, Orna Jacqueline Kliger. PhD, NYU, 1963. English prof. East Stroudsburg U., Pa., 1966—. Recipient Sophomore award, Bklyn. Coll., 1954. Liberal. Jewish. Avocations: languages, travel, golf. Home: 69 East McClellan Ave Livingston NJ 07039 Office: East Stroudsburg Univ 200 Prospect St East Stroudsburg PA 18301 Personal E-mail: ronaldjmeyers@comcast.net. Business E-Mail: ronald.meyers@po-box.esu.edu.

MEYERS, TEDSON JAY, lawyer; b. Bayonne, NJ, May 6, 1928; s. Irving and Norma Miriam (Anson) M.; m. Patricia Elizabeth Sullivan, Apr. 10, 1965 (div. Apr. 1978); children: Mary, John, Katherine; m. Lynn Scholz, Aug. 6, 1978 (div. Oct. 1992); m. Arden Schell, Dec. 27, 2000. Student, Ohio State U.; BA, NYU, 1949, MA, 1950; JD, Harvard U., 1953. Bar: DC 1953, NY 1957, US Supreme Ct. 1971. Asst. counsel Office Gen. Counsel, Dept. Navy, Washington, 1955-56; assoc. Liebman, Eulau & Robinson, NYC, 1956-58; staff counsel for govt. regulations ABC, NYC, 1958-61; adminstrv. asst. to chmn. FCC, Washington, 1961-62; asst. to dir., dir. overseas ednl. TV projects Peace Corps, Washington, 1962-68; pvt. practice Washington, 1968-70; ptnr. Sullivan Beauregard Meyers & Clarkson, Washington, 1970-74, Peabody Lambert & Meyers, Washington, 1974—84, Reid & Priest, Washington, 1984-96, Coudert Brothers, Washington, 1996—2003. Adj. prof. comm. San Diego State U., 1993—; founding pres. Harvard Legis. Rsch. Bur., 1952—53; mem. White House Task Force on Ednl. TV Overseas, 1966—68; trustee Global Legal Info. Network Found., 2001—; mem. adv. panel internat. telecomm. law US State Dept., 1987—; bd. govs. Internat. Coun. Computer Comm., 1986—, pres., 2000—02; bd. dirs. Cyber Century Forum. Contbr. conf. papers and articles to profl. publs. Mem. City Coun. Washington, 1972-75; bd. govs. Met. Washington Coun. Govts., 1973-75; chmn. Bicycle Fedn. of Am., 1977-2008, bd. dirs. 2009-, U.S. Coun. for World Comm. Yr. 83, 1982-84; dir. The Arthur C. Clarke Found. of the US Inc., 1987—, chmn., 2003—; bd. dirs. Friends of Law Libr. Congress, 2001-. Lt. USMC, 1953-55, Korea. Recipient Sec. of Army Pub. Svc. medal; rsch. fellow Carnegie Found., 1949. Fellow: Am. Bar Found.; mem.: ABA (sect. sci. and tech. 1982—85, coun. mem. sect. sci. and tech. 1983—87, chmn. standing com. law libr. congress 2000, co-founder and chmn. internat. telecomm. com.), Internat. Telecomm. Acad. Russia (hon. academician 2002—), Cosmos Club Found. (trustee, chmn. 1985—88, 1990—), Cosmos Club (pres. 1988—90), Alpha Epsilon Pi. Avocations: bicycling, motorcycling, computers, sculling, music. E-mail: tmeyers@tedson.com.

MEYERS, WAYNE MARVIN, microbiologist, physician; b. Huntingdon County, Pa., Aug. 28, 1924; s. John William and Carrie Venca (Weaver) Meyers; m. Esther Louise Kleinschmidt, Aug. 26, 1953; children: Amy, George, Daniel, Sara. BS in Chemistry, Juniata Coll., Huntingdon, Pa., 1947, DSc (hon.), 1986; diploma, Moody Bible Inst., Chgo., 1950; MS in Med. Microbiology, U. Wis., 1953, PhD in Med. Microbiology, 1955; MD, Baylor Coll. Medicine, 1959. Instr. Baylor Coll. Medicine, 1955-59; intern Conemaugh Valley Meml. Hosp., Johnstown, Pa., 1959-60; staff physician Berrien Gen. Hosp., Berrien Center, Mich., 1960-61; missionary physician Am. Leprosy Missions,

Congo/Zaire, Burundi, 1961-73; prof. pathology Sch. Medicine U. Hawaii, Honolulu, 1973-75; chief microbiology divsn. Armed Forces Inst. Pathology, Washington, 1975-89, chief mycobacteriology, 1989—2005, registrar leprosy registry, 1975—2005, asst. to registrar leprosy registry, 2005—, vis. scientist, 2005—; mem. leprosy panel US-Japan Coop. Med. Sci. Program, 1976-83; mem. sci. adv. bd. Leonard Wood Meml., 1981-85, sci. cons. dir., 1985-87, sci. dir., 1987-90, cons., 1990—2004; rsch. affiliate Tulane U., 1981—2005. Bd. dirs. Gorgas Meml. Inst. Tropical and Preventive Medicine, Inc., Leonard Wood Meml. Bd. dirs. Jour. Leprosy, 1978—93; contbr. chapters to books, articles to profl. jours. Adv. bd. Damien-Dutton Soc. Leprosy Aid, Inc., 1983—96, corp. bd. dirs., 1996—; adv. bd. Am. Leprosy Missions, Inc., 1979—88, chmn. bd. dirs., 1985—88, program cons. to bd. dirs., 1988—2003, mem. bd. references, 1988—; mem. Hansen's Disease rsch. adv. com. Gillis W. Long Hansen's Disease Ctr., Carville, La., 1985—92, chmn., 1985—92; mem. Buruli Ulcer task force WHO, 1998—2004. With US Army, 1944—46. Allergy Found. Am. fellow, 1957, 1958, WHO Rsch. grantee, 1978—87. Mem.: Internat. Soc. Travel Medicine, Binford-Dammin Soc. Infectious Disease Pathologists (sec.-treas. 1988—91, pres. 1995—96), Am. Soc. Microbiology, Am. Soc. Tropical Medicine and Hygiene, Internat. Soc. Tropical Dermatology, Internat. Acad. Pathology, Internat. Leprosy Assn. (councillor 1978—88, pres. 1988—93), Sigma Xi. Achievements include research in human and experimental leprosy, and other mycobacterial diseases. Office: Armed Forces Inst Pathology Washington DC 20306-6000 Office Phone: 202-782-1873. Personal E-mail: wmekmeyers@comcast.net.

MEYERSON, ADAM, foundation administrator; b. Phila., Aug. 2, 1953; s. Martin and Margy Ellin (Lazarus) M.; m. Nina Hope Shea, Sept. 13, 1986; children: Thomas Abraham, William Ulysses, Henry Elijah. BA, Summa Cum Laude, Yale U., 1974; student, Harvard U., 1977-79. Mng. editor The Am. Spectator, Bloomington, Ind., 1974-77; editorial writer Wall St. Jour., NYC, 1979-83; editor Policy Rev. The Heritage Found., Washington, 1983-98, v.p. ednl. affairs, 1993—2001; pres. Philanthropy Roundtable, Washington, 2001—. Co-editor: The Wall Street Journal on Management, 1985. Home: 3714 Ingomar St NW Washington DC 20015-1820 Office: Philanthropy Roundtable 1150 17th St NW # 503 Washington DC 20036 Office Phone: 202-822-8333. E-mail: ameyerson@philanthropyroundtable.org.

MEYERSON, IVAN D., lawyer, former corporate financial executive; AB, U. Calif., Berkeley, 1966; JD, Stanford U., 1969. Bar: Calif. 1970. Assoc. Herzstein & Maier, San Francisco, 1970-75, ptnr., 1976-78; atty. SEC, 1975-76; assoc. gen. counsel McKesson Corp., San Francisco, 1984-87, v.p., gen. counsel, 1987-98; exec. v.p., gen. counsel McKesson - HBOC Inc., San Francisco, 1998—2006.

MEYERSON, MORTON HERBERT, investor, real estate company executive; b. Ft. Worth, June 3, 1938; s. Maurice Brudus and Bernice Estell (Gressman) M.; m. Marlene Nathan, Apr. 26, 1964; children: David Nathan (dec.), Marti Ann, Leslie. BA in Philosophy and Econs., U. Tex., 1960. Computer software trainee Bell Helicopter; v.p. Electronic Data Systems Corp., Dallas, 1966-71, pres., 1979-86, vice chmn., 1986; pres. E.D.S. Fed. Corp. subs. Electronic Data Systems Corp., Dallas, 1975-79; pres., bd. dirs. duPont Glore Forgan Inc., NYC, 1971-75; pres. Nat. Heritage Ins. Co. (subs. E.D.S.), NYC, 1976-86; now chmn., CEO 2M Companies Inc.; also chmn. Morton H. Meyerson Family Tzedakah Fund; and chmn. E2M Partners real estate fund. Bd. govs. Dallas Symphony Orchestra, chmn. concert hall com., 1980-86, bd. dir. Nat. Park Found. Served with US Army, 1961-63, USAR, 1963-69. Fellow Am. Acad. Arts & Scis. Jewish. Office: 2M Cos 3401 Armstrong Ave Dallas TX 75205-3949 Office Phone: 214-443-1900. Office Fax: 214-443-1980.

MEYERSON, SEYMOUR, retired chemist; b. Chgo., Dec. 4, 1916; s. Joseph and Rena (Margulies) M.; m. Lotte Strauss, May 22, 1943; children: Sheella, Elana. SB, U. Chgo., 1938, postgrad., 1938-39, 47-48, George Williams Coll., 1939-40; DSc (hon.), Valparaiso U., 1995. Inspector powder & explosives Kankakee Ordnance Works, Joliet, Ill., 1942; chemist Deavitt Labs., Chgo., 1941-42; from chemist to rsch. cons. Amoco Corp., Whiting, Ind., 1946—84, Naperville, Ill., 1946—84. Mem. indsl. adv. coun. chemistry dept. U. Okla., Norman, 1967-69; Frontiers in Chemistry lectr. Wayne State U., 1965; invited spkr. James L. Waters Symposium, Pitts. Conf., Chgo., 1995. Charter mem. editl. adv. bd. Organic Mass Spectrometry, 1968-87, Mass Spectromony Revs., 1980-87; author, co-author 190 sci. publs. 2d. lt. AUS, 1943—46, ETO. Mem. Am. Chem. Soc. (Frank H. Field and Joe L. Franklin award for outstanding achievement in mass spectrometry 1993), Am. Soc. for Mass Spectrometry., Phi Beta Kappa. Secular Humanist. Achievements include research in chemistry of gas-phase organic ions; patents in field. Home: 43 Vermont Ct Unit A1 Asheville NC 28806-3058 Personal E-mail: meyerson43@hotmail.com.

MEYLER, WILLIAM ANTHONY, financial analyst; b. Newark, Oct. 29, 1944; s. Raymond Francis and Margaret (Loveless) Meyler; m. Dana Irene Brennan, May 3, 1975; children: Daniel, Diana. BS, St. Joseph's Coll., 1966; MBA, Fairleigh Dickinson U., 1974. CPA NJ. Sr. acct. Ernst & Young, Trenton, NJ, 1970; dir. acctg. Baker Industries, Inc., Parsippany, NJ, 1971—72; mgr. corp. acctg. Witco Chem. Corp., NYC, 1973—75, asst. to contr., 1976—79, asst. contr. world-wide ops., 1977—82, asst. contr. mgmt. info. sys., 1982—84; ptnr. Letters, Meyler & Co. CPA, 1984—91, Meyler & Co. LLC, 1982—. Cons., exec. v.p. Investment Techs., Inc., Edison, NJ, 1985—91, bd. dirs.; exec. v.p., CFO Gateways to Space, Inc., 1994—96, bd. dirs.; adj. prof. Monmouth Coll., 1983—85. Fellow: NJ Soc. CPA; mem.: AICPA, Am. Acctg. Assn., Middletown C. of C., Rotary. Home: 30 Southview Ter S Middletown NJ 07748-2415 Office: One Arin Park 1715 Highway 35 Middletown NJ 07748-1867

MEYROWITZ, CAROL M., retail executive; b. 1954; With TJX Cos., Inc., Framingham, Mass., 1983; exec. v.p. merchandising Chadwick's of Boston (divsn. previously held by TJX), 1996—99; sr. v.p. merchandising The Marmaxx Group, 1999—2000, exec. v.p. merchandising Framingham, Mass., 2000—01, pres., 2001—05; exec. v.p. TJX Cos., Inc., Framingham, Mass., 2001—04, sr. exec. v.p., 2004—05, adv. cons., 2005, pres., 2005—, CEO, 2007—. Bd. dirs. Yankee Candle, 2004—, TJX Cos., Inc., 2006—, Staples Inc., 2007—. Named one of 50 Most Powerful Women in Bus., Fortune mag., 2006—08, 100 Most Powerful Women, Forbes mag., 2008, 2009. Office: TJX Companies 770 Cochituate Rd Framingham MA 01701*

MEYSENBURG, MARY ANN, principal; b. LA, Sept. 16, 1939; d. Clarence Henry and Mildred Ethel (McGee) Augustine; m. John Harold Meysenburg, June 17, 1967; children: Peter Augustine, Amy Bernadette. BA magna cum laude, U. So. Calif., 1960; MA Pvt. Sch. Adminstrn. magna cum laude, U. San Francisco, 1995. Cert. elem. tchr., Calif. Auditor, escrow officer Union Bank, LA, 1962-64; v.p., escrow mgr. Bank of Downey, Calif., 1964-66; cons., tchr. Santa Ana (Calif.) Coll. Bus., 1964-66; elem. tchr. St. Bruno's Sch., Whittier, Calif., 1966-70, Pasadena (Calif.) Unified Sch. Dist., 1971-84, Holy Angels Sch., Arcadia, Calif., 1985-89; vice prin., computer coord. Our Mother of Good Counsel, LA, 1989-93; prin. St. Stephen Martyr, Monterey Park, Calif., 1993-2000, Holy Trinity Sch., LA, 2000—05. Mem. Writing to Read Bd., Holy Trinity Sch., 2000—05; trainer Riordan Found., 1998—2001; master catechist religious edn. L.A. Archdiocese, 1988—; supr. BTSA Induction Program L.A. County Office of Edn., 2005—, cons. BTSA, intern tchrs., 2005—. Author: History of the Arms Control and Disarmament Organization, 1976; organizer, editor newsletter Cath. Com. for Girl Scouts and Campfire. Counselor Boy Scouts Am., 1985—; eucharistic min. Our Mother of Good Counsel, 1985—95, Holy Angels Ch., Arcadia; sec. of senatus Legion of Mary, 1980—85; mem. Cath. com.Girls Scouts U.S.A. and Campfire; vice chmn. acad. affairs L.A. Archdiocese, 1985—90, deanery chairperson Dept. of Edn.; bd. dirs. Alumni Assn. Immaculate Heart H.S., 1999—. Recipient Pius X medal L.A. Archdiocese, 1979, St. Elizabeth Ann Seton award Cath. Com. for Girl Scouts, 1988, St. Anne medal Cath. Com. for Girl Scouts, 1989, Bronze Pelican award Cath. Com. for Boy Scouts, 1989; grantee Milken Family Found., 1989, 92. Mem.: Western Assn. Schs. and Colls. (team chairperson), Phi Kappa Phi, Phi Delta Kappa (historian 1991—92, founds. rep. 1992—93, treas. 1993—94, 1st v.p. 1994—95, pres. 1995—96, advisor 2001—02, Svc. award 1999), Phi Beta Kappa, Chi Lambda Theta, Phi Lambda Theta. Avocations: tennis, walking, swimming, reading. Home: 6725 Brentmead Ave Arcadia CA 91007-7708 Office: LA County Office Edn 9300 Imperial Hwy Downey CA 90242-2813

MEZA, JUAN C., mathematician, computer scientist; s. Camilo and Carmen Meza. BEE, Rice U., Houston, 1978, MEE, 1979, PhD in Computational Math., 1986. Disting. mem. tech. staff Sandia Nat. Lab., Livermore, Calif., 1987—2002; dept. head Lawrence Berkeley Nat. Lab., Calif., 2002—. Recipient Blackwell-Tapia award, 2008; named Disting. Scientist, SACNAS, 2008. Mem.: AAAS, SIAM (bd. mem. 2006—08), SACNAS. Office: Lawrence Berkeley Nat Lab 1 Cyclotron Rd Berkeley CA 94720 Business E-Mail: jcmeza@lbl.gov.

MEZA, LUIS ALBERTO, internist, researcher; s. Luis Alberto and Susana Cartes Meza; m. Teresa I. Ibarra, Sept. 3, 1966; children: Luis A. Jr., Monica Meza Hernandez, Leticia Ann Canizaro, Lisa Cristina Harrell. MD, U. Nat. Asuncion, Paraguay, 1966. Diplomate Am. Bd. Internal Medicine, Am. Bd. Oncology, Am. Bd. Hematology. Intern Mercy Hosp., Des Moines, 1970—71; resident in internal medicine La. State U., New Orleans, 1971—74; fellow Ochsner Found. Hosp., New Orleans, 1974—76; assoc. prof. medicine La. State U., Lafayette, 1976—; physician SW Oncology, Lafayette, 1979—. Chief med. staff Southpark Hosp., Youngsville, La., 2005—06. Capt. Paraguay Nat. Army, 1964—69. Fellow: ACP, Internat. Soc. Hematology; mem.: Am. Soc. Hematology, So. Assn. for Oncology, La. State Med. Soc., So. Med. Assn., Am. Soc. of Clin. Oncology, Lafayette Parish Med. Soc. Roman Catholic. Achievements include research in growth factor support in treating side effects related to chemotherapy. Avocations: travel, golf, photography. Office: Southwest Oncology 443 Heymann Blvd Ste A Lafayette LA 70503 Office Fax: 337-235-4272. Personal E-mail: lamezamd@aol.com.

MEZENCEV, ROMAN, arms control expert, consultant, translator; b. Kosice, Slovakia, Jan. 20, 1970; s. Vladimir Mezencev and Luboslava Mezencevova; m. Andrea Zatrochova, Sept. 19, 1992; children: Romana Mezencevova, Denis. BS, Pavol Jozef Safarik U., Kosice, MS, 1993, RNDr. in Chemistry, 1999, PhD in Pharmacology, 2007; MS in Biology, Ga. Inst. Tech., Sch. Biology, Atlanta, 2007. Forensic scientist, Inst. Forensic Medicine Pavol Jozef Safarik U., 1993—96, rsch. project cons., faculty sci., 2006—; prin. sci. officer Ministry Economy, Bratislava, Slovakia, 1997—99; clin. rsch. monitor Pharmacia & Upjohn, Bratislava, 1998—2002; insp. roster pers. UNMOVIC, NYC, 2000—07, insp. & biol. team leader & arms control expert, 2002—06; postdoc. rschr. Ga. Inst. Tech., Sch. Biology, 2008—09, rsch. scientist, 2009—. Translator: (non-fiction novel) Bob Drogin: Curveball; contbr. scientific papers to profl. jours., chapters to books. Mem.: AAAS, Am. Chem. Soc., Am. Assn. Cancer Rsch. Achievements include patents pending for the use of brassinin and its derivatives for the treatment of chagas disease & cholera; metabolomics-based identification of anticancer compounds. Office: Ga Inst Tech 310 Ferst Dr Atlanta GA 30332 Personal E-mail: romanmez@gmail.com. Business E-Mail: roman.mezencev@biology.gatech.edu.

MEZENTSEV, ALEXANDRE VICTOR, aerospace scientist, researcher; b. Moscow, July 2, 1966; arrived in US, 1998, permanent resident, 2004; s. Victor Mezentsev and Inna Mezentseva. MSc in Biology with honors, Moscow State U., 1991; PhD, AN Bakh Inst. Biochemistry, Moscow, 1996. Rsch. student AN Bakh Inst. Biochemistry, Russian Acad. Scis., Moscow, 1991—93, jr. rsch. scientist, 1993—95, rsch. scientist, 1995—97; postdoctoral fellow Dept. Pediat. Svc. Genetic Medicine L'Hopital Ste, Justine Ctr. Rsch., Montreal, Quebec, Canada, 1996—98; postdoctoral fellow U. of Tex. Health Ctr., San Antonio, 1998—2000; rsch. assoc. NY Med. Coll., Valhalla, 2000—05; post doctoral rschr. Columbia U., NYC, 2005—06, rsch. assoc. scientist, 2006—. Invited scientist NASA Space Radiation Summer Sch., 2007. Recipient Acknowledgement award, Russian Acad. Sci., Inst. Biochemistry, 1995, Rsch. to Prevent Blindness, Inc., 2003. Mem.: Soc. for Investigative Dermatology, Assn. for Rsch. and Vision in Ophthalmology, NY Acad. Scis., Internat. Soc. Imaging in the Eye. Orthodox. Achievements include research in lysosomal storage diseases and sialidase deficiency in galactosialidosis; ocular surface inflammation, discovery of proinflammatory eicosanoid signaling mechanism in the cornea; role of Arnt signaling in epidermal keratinocytes and regulation of gene expression. Avocations: Bingo, cooking. Office: Columbia U VC 110215 630 West 168th St New York NY 10032 Home: 124 Overlook Ave Peekskill NY 10566-3008 Office Phone: 212-305-3911. Office Fax: 212-305-3229. Personal E-mail: mesentsev@yahoo.com.

MEZEY, ESTEBAN, internist, gastroenterologist, educator; b. Vienna, Oct. 12, 1936; came to U.S., 1953; s. Kalman Coloman and Elisabeth (Jaberg) M.; m. Anne Elizabeth Lindeman, June 3, 1962; children: Lillian, Paul Stephen, Marina. BA in Zoology, Yale U., 1958; MD, Harvard U., 1962. Diplomate Am. Bd. Internal Medicine, Am. Bd. Gastroenterology. Intern Pa. Hosp., Phila., 1962-63; resident St. Luke's Hosp. Ctr., NYC, 1963-65, fellow in gastroenterology, 1965-66, NIH postgrad. rsch. fellow, 1966-67, rsch. assoc., 1966-67; Norman Jolliffe fellow in clin. nutrition Columbia U., NYC, 1966-67; from instr. to prof. medicine Sch. Medicine, Johns Hopkins U., Balt., 1968-82, prof., 1982—; mem. staff divsn. gastroenterology Johns Hopkins Hosp., Balt., 1968—, chief hepatology, 1988—, chief clinical gastroenterology, 2002—05. Chief hepatology Francis Scott Key Med. Ctr., Balt., 1968-84, med. dir. alcoholism svcs., 1972-84; med. dir. alcoholism treatment program, phase I, Johns Hopkins Hosp., 1985-87; dir. Johns Hopkins Alcohol Rsch. Ctr., 1985-88; cons. liver diseases VA Hosp., Ft. Howard, Md., 1968-96; med. rsch. svc. merit rev. bd. gastroenterology VA, 1983-87; mem. adv. bd. Liver Ctr., Yale U., New Haven, 1985-93; mem. coms. and subcoms. profl. and ednl. instns. Mem. editl. bd. Alcohol, 1983-87, 93—, Hepatology, 1986—, assoc. editor, 1992-96; mem. editl. bd. Alcoholism: Clin. and Exptl. Rsch., 1988-93, Pharmacology adn Therapeutics; field editor Jour. Alcohol Studies, 1989-92; mem. editl. adv. bd. Biochem. Pharmacology, 1984-96; mem. staff contbrs. Selected Summaries in Gastroenterology, 1974-85; contbr. articles (with others) to profl. jours. Bd. dirs. Balt. Area Coun. on Alcoholism, v.p., 1972-76, pres., 1976-77; bd. dirs. Am. Coun. on Alcoholism, 1980-89; mem. med. adv. bd. Alcoholic Beverage Med. Rsch. Found., 1987-93, chmn., 1992-93; mem. alcoholism adv. coun. to mayor City of Balt., 1987-88; mem. alcoholism rsch. rev. com. biomed. br. Nat. Inst. Alcohol Abuse and Alcoholism, 1979-83, mem. nat. adv. coun., 1985-88, mem. extramural sci. adv. bd., 1990-93, mem. bd. sci. counselors, 1994-98, chmn. 1996—. Fellow ACP; mem. Assn. Am. Physicians, Am. Soc. Clin. Investigation, Am. Assn. for Study of Liver Diseases (pres. 1993, councilor 1989-97, chmn. publs. com. 1986-88), Am. Gastroent. Assn., Internat. Assn. for Study of Liver, Internat. Soc. for Biomed. Rsch. on Alcoholism, Pan Am. Med. Assn. (past counselor alcoholism sect.), Rsch. Soc. on Alcoholism (program com.), Colombian Soc. Gastroenterology (corr.), Argentinian Soc. Pathology, Ibero-Am. Assn. for Study of Problems of Alcoholism, Ea. Gut Club, Am. Liver Found. (bd. dirs. 1995—). Republican. Roman Catholic. Avocations: sailing, swimming. Office: Johns Hopkins U Sch Medicine 720 Rutland Ave Baltimore MD 21205-2109 Office Phone: 410-614-0144.

MEZEY, ROBERT, poet; b. Phila., Feb. 28, 1935; s. Ralph and Clara M.; m. Olivia Simpson (div.); children: Naomi, Judah, Eve. Student, Kenyon Coll., 1951-53; BA, U. Iowa, 1959; postgrad., Stanford U., 1960-61; degree (hon.), Kenyon Coll., 2008. Lectr. Western Res. U., Cleve., 1963-64, Franklin & Marshall Coll., Lancaster, Pa., 1965-66; asst. prof. Fresno (Calif.) State U., 1967-68, U. Utah, Salt Lake City, 1973-76; prof., poet-in-residence Pomona Coll., Claremont, Calif., 1976-99; ret., 1999. Author: (poems) The Lovemaker, 1960 (Lamont award), White Blossoms, 1965, The Door Standing Open, 1970, Selected Translations, 1981, Evening Wind, 1987 (Bassine citation, PEN prize 1989), Collected Poems 1952-1999, 2000 (Poets prize 2002); editor Naked Poetry, 1968, Poems from the Hebrew, 1973, Collected Poems of Henri Coulette, 1990, Selected Poems of Thomas Hardy, 1998, The Poetry of E.A. Robinson, 1999, Poems of the American West, 2002, A Word Like Fire: Selected Poems of Dick Barnes, 2005; translator: Tungsten (César Vallejo), 1988. With US Army, 1953—55. Fellow Ingram Merrill, 1973, 89, Guggenheim Found., 1977, Stanford U., 1960, NEA, 1987; recipient Poetry prize Am. Acad. Arts and Letters, 1982. Avocations: tennis, chess. Home: 960 E Bonita Ave # 28 Pomona CA 91767 Personal E-mail: mezteadancer@gmail.com.

MEZGER, JEFFREY T., construction executive; b. Chgo., 1955; BA in Econs., DePauw U., Greencastle, Ind., 1977. Pres. ctrl. Calif. divsn. US Home, Calif., 1983—93; pres. Antelope Valley divsn. KB Home Corp., LA, 1993—95, pres. KB Home Ariz., sr. v.p., regional mgr. SW divsn., 1995—99, exec. v.p., COO, 1999—2006, pres., CEO, 2006—. Mem. exec. bd. USC Lusk Ctr. for Real Estate; mem. policy adv. bd. Harvard Joint Ctr. for Housing Studies. Mem.: Nat. Assn. Home Builders (mem. high prodn. builders coun.). Office: KB Home Corp 10990 Wilshire Blvd 7th Fl Los Angeles CA 90024

MEZHIR, JAMES A., law educator; s. Viola Virginia Torcasio; m. Tricia Ann Mezhir, Dec. 19, 1984; children: James John, John Joseph, Ryan Michael, Daniel Michael, Brittany Grace. BS, SUNY, Buffalo, 1970, MS, 1980, Niagara U., Lewiston, NY, 1974. Coll. prof. NCCC, Sanborn, NY, 1974—; cons. JA Mezhir Consulting Enterprise, Lewiston, NY, 1980—. Command sgt. maj. US Army Res., Buffalo, 1966—97. V.p. Lewiston Porter Sch. Bd., NY, 2005—08. Recipient Pres. award, Niagara County CC, 1987, NYS Chancellors award, SUNY, 1988, Nat. Tchg. Excellence award, U. Tex. Study, 1989. Mem.: Am. Soc. Indsl. Security. Conservative. Roman Catholic. Avocations: walking, jogging, reading, bicycling, weightlifting. Home: 588 Briarwood Ln Lewiston NY 14092 Office: Niagara County CC 3111 Saunders Settlement Rd Sanborn NY 14132 Office Fax: 716-614-6763; Home Fax: 716-614-6700. Personal E-mail: jmezhirconsulting@yahoo.com.

MEZO, RICHARD EUGENE, literature and language professor, writer; b. Carterville, Ill., Aug. 17, 1938; s. William Leonard Mezo and Madeline Helen Wilkerson; m. Sun Hee Choe Mezo; children: Harmony Suzanne, Julia Ann. AA, San Diego City Coll., 1969; MA, Calif. State U., 1972; PhD, U. ND, 1978. Cert. Teacher 6-12 Western Wash. U., 1988. English instr. Several Overseas U. (Saudi Arabia, Taiwan, Korea), 1979—85, Pierce Coll., Tacoma, 1985—86, Olympic Coll., Bremerton, Wash., 1986—87; asst. prof. Maville State U., ND, 1988—89; assoc. prof. U. Guam, 1989—99; lectr. U. Md., Asian Divsn., 1992—2001; tchr. Dept. Def. Edn. Activity, Arlington, Va., 2001—07; instr. Germanna Comm. Coll., Va., 2007—. Reader ETS Coll. Bd., Daytona, Fla., 1997—; chmn., divsn. English and applied linguistics U. Guam, 1990—92. Author: (reference book) Am. Nat. Bio., 1999, World Edn. E.ncy, 2001. Mem.: MLA (field bibliographer 2002—), Assn. Lit. Scholars and Critics, Acad. Am. Poets. Democrat. Protestant. Avocation: reading. Home: 27 Wallace LN Stafford VA 22554-8836 Personal E-mail: remezo@yahoo.com.

MEZZULLO, LOUIS ALBERT, lawyer; b. Balt., Sept. 20, 1944; m. Judith Scales, Jan. 2, 1970. BA, U. Md., 1967, MA, 1976; JD, T.C. Williams Law Sch., 1976. Bar: Va. 1976, Calif. 2006. Sales rep. Humble Oil (name now Exxon), Richmond, Va., 1970-72; acctg. Marcoin, Inc., Richmond, 1972-73; pvt. practice bookkeeping, tax preparation, Richmond, 1973-76; assoc. McGuire, Woods, Battle and Boothe, Richmond, 1976-79; dir. Mezzullo & McCandlish, Richmond, 1979-2000; mem. Mezzullo & Guare, PLC, Richmond, 2000—03, McGuire Woods, 2004—06, Luce, Forward, Hamilton & Scripps, Carlsbad, Calif., 2006—. Contbr. articles to profl. jours. Former pres. Southampton Citizens Assn., Richmond, 1986; former bd. dirs. Richmond Symphony; bd. dirs. Va. Mus. Fine Arts Found., San Diego Opera. Served with USAR, 1969—75. Mem.: ABA (tax sect., vice chair publs.), Am. Coll. Employee Benefits Counsel, Trust Adminstrs. Coun., Estate Planning Coun. Richmond, Va. Law Found., Am. Bar Found., Va. Bar Assn., Am. Coll. Employee Benefit Counsel, Va. State Bar (tax sect.), Am. Coll. Tax Counsel (chair), Am. Coll. Trust and Estate Counsel (treas.), Internat. Acad. Estate and Trust Law, Willow Oaks Country Club. Home: 7326 Grebe Dr Carlsbad CA 92011 Office Phone: 858-381-8014. Business E-Mail: lmezzullo@luce.com.

M.I.A., See ARULPRAGASAM, MATHANGI

MIAH, ABDUL JALIL, library director; m. Sakina Khanum; 1 child, Azhar Jalil. EdD, Va. Poly. and State U., Blacksburg, 1989. Dir. libraries and info. svc. J. Sargeant Reynolds CC, Richmond, Va., 1965—, dir. lib. Pres., chmn. Islamic Ctr. Va., Richmond, 1978—2005. Office: J Sargeant Renoldsedu E Parham Rd PO Box 85622 Richmond VA 23285 Office Phone: 804-523-5323. Home Fax: 804-786-5623. Business E-Mail: amiah@renolds.edu.

MIALON, SUE, economics professor; d. Joon Sung Hwang and Sun Ye Park; m. Hugo Mialon, Dec. 22, 2002. PhD, U. Tex., Austin, 2002. Asst. prof. U. ND, Grand Forks, 2006—08, Emory U., Atlanta, 2008—. Contbr. articles to profl. jours. Recipient Meritorious Rsch. award, 2006—07. Mem.: Am. Econ. Assn. Office: Emory Univ Dept Economics 1602 Fishburne Dr Atlanta GA 30322 Office Phone: 404-712-8169. Office Fax: 404-727-4639. Business E-Mail: smialon@emory.edu.

MIAN, SHABBIR M., physicist, educator; s. Abdul Jalil and Hasina Mian; m. Mahmuda Khatun, Aug. 20, 2003. PhD, Okla. State U., Stillwater, 1996. Vis. asst. prof. Gettysburg Coll., Pa., 1996—98; postdoc. rsch. fellow Applied Optics Ctr. Del., Dover, 1998—99; assoc. prof. McDaniel Coll., Westminster, Md., 1999—. Chmn. bd. Islamic Soc. Carroll County, Westminster, Md., 2007—. Edn. grant, NSF, 2002—05, Rsch. grant, Petroleum Rsch. Fund, 2003—05. Achievements include patent for method and apparatus for measuring thin films. Office: McDaniel Coll Dept Physics 2 College Hill Westminster MD 21157 Office Fax: 410-386-2483. Business E-Mail: smian@mcdaniel.edu.

MIAN, SHAHZAD, ophthalmologist; married. MD, Emory U., Atlanta, 1996. Diplomate Am. Bd. Ophthalmology, 2001. Asst. prof. U. Mich., Ann Arbor, 2004—. Office: Univ Mich WK Kellogg Eye 1000 Wall St Ann Arbor MI 48105

MIANO, LOUIS STEPHEN, arts advisor; b. NYC, July 28, 1934; s. Louis Clyde and Zefira (Palombo) M. BA, Dartmouth Coll., 1955; MA, Columbia U., 1958. Writer Look Mag., NYC, 1960-61; editor Show Mag., NYC and L.A., 1961-63; assoc. producer ABC-TV, NYC and L.A., 1963-66; vice-chmn., dir. creative services AC&R Advt., NYC, 1966-90. Sec. EEE Theatrical Ventures, N.Y.C., 1974—; bd. trustees Met. Opera Guild; v.p.; cons. in field. Co-producer plays: Design for Living, Corpse, The Seagull, Legends, Inner Voices, 1974-86 Trustee Marymount Manhattan Coll., N.Y.C., 1980-2002; cons. Home Box Office, 1991-92; bd. dirs. Nat. Bd. of Rev. of Motion Pictures, 1995—, Gotham Chamber Opera, 2000—, Met. Opera Guild, 2005—, vice pres. Circle-in-the Square, sec.; gen. dirs. coun. N.Y.C. Opera, 1998—. Mem. Century Assn. Home and Office: 430 E 57th St New York NY 10022-3061 Office Phone: 212-753-2860.

MIAO, WUJIAN, chemistry professor; b. Rudong, Jiangsu, China, Dec. 26, 1962; s. Siyou Miao and Bafeng Yang; m. Zhilan Ge, Nov. 25, 1986; children: Jingfan, Kevin Liu. BS, Nantong U., Nantong, China, 1979—82; MSc Courses Diploma, Jinan U., Guangzhou, China, 1985—86; MSc, Zhongshan U., Guangzhou, China, 1988—91; PhD, Monash U., Melbourne, Australia, 1996—99. U. tchr. qualification credential Edn. Commn., Jiangsu Province, China, 1996. Chemistry technician, dir. chemistry dept. labs, lectr., vice-head, dept. chemistry Nantong U., 1982—95; vis. scholar Monash U., Melbourne, Australia, 1995—96; rsch. scientist Commonwealth Sci. and Industrian Orgn., Melbourne, 2000; post-doctoral fellow U. Tex., Austin, 2001—04; asst. prof. U. So. Miss., Hattiesburg, 2004—. Adv. Overseas Exch. Assn. of Nantong City, Jingsu, China, 1998—2002; sec. gen. Chinese Student Club, Monash U., 1996—98. Recipient Top Postgrad. award, Zhongshan U., 1991, Dean's Rsch. Initiative Program award, U. So. Miss., 2004, Keith Lucas & Ella Ginn Lucas Endowment Faculty Excellence award, 2008; named Top Young Tchr. in Gen. Univs. and Colls., Edn. Commn, Jiangsu Province, China, 1994; Guanghua Edn. scholar, Zhongshan U., 1990, Yao Wannian scholar, 1990, Study Abroad scholar, State Edn. Commn., China, 1995, Grad. scholar, Monash U., 1996—99, Study Abroad scholar, State Edn. Commn., China, 1997, Internat. Planning Visit grantee, NSF, 2006. Fellow: China's Tchrs. Coll. Assn. Analytical Chemistry, Universities & Colleges Laboratorial Mgmt. Soc., Jiangsu Province; mem.: Miss. Acad. Scis., Soc. Electroanalytical Chemistry, Electrochem. Soc., Am. Chem. Soc. Achievements include patents for methods and compositions for the detection of biological molecules using a two particle complex. Office: Univ So Miss 118 College Dr Box 5043 Hattiesburg MS 39406 Office Fax: 601-266-6075. Business E-Mail: wujian.miao@usm.edu.

MIAOULIS, IOANNIS NIKOLAOS, museum director, mechanical engineer, educator; b. Athens, Greece, July 24, 1961; came to U.S., 1980; s. Nikolaos Ioannis and Titika Photini (Kokkinopoulou) M.; m. Beth Karen, Sept. 23, 1984; children: Marina, Katrina. BSME, Tufts U., 1983, MA in Econs., 1986, PhD in Mech. Engring., 1987; MME, MIT, 1984. Asst. prof. mech. engring. Tufts U., Medford, Mass., 1987-93, assoc. prof., 1993-97, assoc. dean engring., 1993-94, dean, Sch. Engring., 1994—2002, prof., 1997—2002, interim dean, Sch. Arts and Scis., 2001, assoc. provost, Sch. Arts and Scis., 2001—02; pres., dir. Mus. Sci., Boston, 2003—. Spkr. in field. Contbr. over 100 articles to profl. jours. Elected mem. Mass. Tech./Engring. Edn. Adv. Bd., 1999—, chair 2000—; elected mem. Mass. Math. & Sci. Edn. Bd., 1995-99, Tufts Alumni Coun., Medford, 1994-2002; elected coun. mem. Pompositticut Sch., Stow, Mass., 1993-98; trustee Tufts U. Recipient Presdl. Young Investigator award NSF, 1991, Inventor's Assn. award, New. Eng., 1990, William P. Desmond award Citizen's Edn. Resource Ctr., Mass., 1996, Cmty. & Leadership award Toastmasters Internat., Mass., 1995, Jaycees Outstanding Young Leader award, 1999, Outstanding Svc. Alumni award Tuffi Univ., 2003, Sophia award Hellenic Inst., 2004. Mem. ASME, AAAS, Am. Soc. Engring. Edn., ASTK, Materials Rsch. Soc. Achievements include 2 U.S. patents; research in area of heat transfer in materials processing, microscale heat transfer, comparative biomechanics. Office: Mus Sci Science Pk Boston MA 02114 Office Phone: 617-723-2500.

MICA, JOHN L., United States Representative from Florida; b. Binghamton, NY, Jan. 27, 1943; s. John and Adeline (Resciniti) Mica; m. Patricia Szymanek, 1972; children: D'anne, Clark. AA, Miami-Dade C.C., 1965; BA, U. Fla., 1967. Pres. MK Devel. Inc., 1976—92; mem. Fla. Ho. of Reps., 1976—80, mem. appropriations com., mem. ethics com., mem. elections com., mem. cmty. affairs com.; chief of staff US senator Paula Hawkins, Washington, 1981—85; mng. gen. ptnr MD Cellular Comm., 1987—92; mem. US Congress from 7th Fla. Dist., Washington, 1993—, mem. transp. & infrastructure com., govt. reform & oversight com., chair civil svc. subcom., 1995—99, chair subcom. aviation, 2001—06, chmn. subcom. on aviation, 2001—06, ranking rep. transp. infrastructure com., 2007—. Exec. dir. Local Govt. Study Commn. Palm Beach/Orange County, 1970—72; spkrs. rep. US Capitol Preservation Commn.; mem. Ho. Adminstrn. Com., Ho. Oversight Com., Govt. Reform Com.; co-chair Speaker's Task Force Drug-Free America, 1998—, US Capitol Preservation Commn., 1998—. Mem. bd. vis. US Coast Guard; bd. trustees Kennedy Ctr. Recipient Outstanding Svc. award, Fla. Conservative Union, Fla. Cancer Soc. Mem.: Fla. Jaycees (Good Govt. award 1973), Winter Park Jaycees (Good Govt. award 1972), Tiger Bay Club, Kiwanis, Delta Chi. Republican. Episcopalian. Office: US House Reps 2313 Rayburn House Office Bldg Washington DC 20515-0907 Office Phone: 202-225-4035.*

MICALE, FRANK JUDE, lawyer; b. Pitts., Jan. 10, 1949; s. Frank Jacob and Catherine Anna (Wagner) M.; m. Jane Sincler Czak. BA, Duquesne U., 1971, JD, 1977. Bar: Pa. 1977, US Dist. Ct. (we. dist.) Pa. 1977, US Ct. Appeals (3rd cir.) 1978. US Supreme Ct. 1986; cert. Nat. Bd. Trial Advocacy. Law clk. to judge US Ct. Appeals (3rd cir.), 1977-78, US Dist. Ct. (we. dist.) Pa., 1978-79; assoc. Egler & Reinstadtler, Pitts., 1979-80; dep. atty. gen., sr. dep. atty. gen. in charge torts litigation sect. western region Office of Atty. Gen. Commonwealth of Pa., 1980-92; pvt. practice, 1992—. Mem. ABA, Am. Arbitration Assn., Pa. Bar Assn., Allegheny County Bar Assn., Acad. Trial Lawyers Allegheny County. Home: 5521 Claybourne St Pittsburgh PA 15232-1634 Office: 1042 Summitt St Mc Keesport PA 15132 Personal E-mail: frankmac@msn.com.

MICCIANCIO, DANIELE, computer scientist; b. Palermo, Sicily, Italy, Nov. 23, 1971; s. Stefano Micciancio and Maria Stella Giammarinaro. Diploma, Scuola Normale Superiore, Pisa, Italy, 1994; degree, U. of Pisa, 1994; MS, PhD, MIT, 1998. Postdoctocal assoc. MIT Lab. for Computer Sci., Cambridge, Mass., 1998—99; asst. prof. Dept. Computer Sci. and Engring. U. of Calif., San Diego, 1999—2005, assoc. prof. La Jolla, Calif., 2005—. Author: Complexity of Lattice Problems: a Cryptographic Perspective, 2002. Recipient Machtey award, 1998, Sprowls award, 1999; grantee, NSF, 2001, 2003, 2004, Sloan Found., 2003; fellow, Hellman Found., 2001. Mem.: Assn. Computing Machinery, Internat. Assn. for Cryptologic Rsch., IEEE Computer Soc. Office: University of California San Diego 9500 Gilman Dr Mail Code 0404 La Jolla CA 92093

MICCICHE, DANIEL JOHN, lawyer; BA, SUNY, Stony Brook, 1978; JD, U. Chgo., 1981. Profl. corp. ptnr. Akin Gump Strauss Hauer and Feld LLP, Dallas, 1988—. Mem. comptroller's tax adv. group Tex. Comptroller Pub. Accounts. Mem. sch. fin. task force Greater Dallas Chamber; bd. dirs. Tex. C-BAR (Cmty. Bldg. through Atty. Resources), Am. Found. Blind S.W. Region. Mem. ABA, State Bar Tex.(chair state taxation com., 2002-04, chair corp. taxation com., 1998-99), Dallas Bar Assn. (chair tax section, 2001), State Bar N.Y. Office: Akin Gump Strauss Hauer & Feld LLP 1700 Pacific Ave Ste 4100 Dallas TX 75201-4675

MICCO, VINCENT, banker; b. Hackensack, NJ, July 19, 1971; m. Jennifer Micco; 4 children. Grad. in counter-intelligence, US Army Intelligence Acad., Ft. Huachuca, 1997. Cert. in NJ real estate Am. Bus. Sch., 1999, in GE mortgage ins. Loan Officer U., in principles mortgage fin. & FHA/VA loans Capstone Inst. Mortgage Fin. Counter-intelligence agent, B Co., 325th Mil. Intelligence Bn. US Army, 1996—2004; mortgage banker Kearny Federal Savings Bank, 1998—. Mem. govtl. affairs com. NJ Commerce and Industry Assn. Dir. Rutherford C. of C., 2005—06; com. mem. Young Profls. Network-Meadowlands C. of C., 2006; chmn. March of Dimes WalkAmerica, 2007; exec. dir. Bergen County Rep. Org., 1997—98; chmn. Bergen County Young Reps., NJ, 2002, 2004; polit. dir. DiGaetano for Gov., 2004—05; electoral appointee Presdl. Electoral Coll., NJ, 2004. Sgt. US Army, Irag. Decorated Army Commendation Medal, Global War on Terrorism Expeditionary Medal; recipient Leadership award, Meadowlands Regional C. of C., 2007. Mem.: UNICO, Elks. Republican. Office: Kearny Fed Savings Bank 250 Valley Blvd Wood Ridge NJ 07075 Office Phone: 201-939-3400 ext. 116.

MICELI, WILLIAM CYRIL, SR., director; b. Chgo., Jan. 9, 1949; s. Cyril Francis and Mary Elizabeth Miceli; m. Phyllis M. Michaud, Aug. 22, 1976 (div. May 1998); 1 child, William Cyril Jr.; m. Candi F. Metz Miceli, July 18, 2001. BS in Edn., No. Ill. U., 1970; MA in History, Northeastern Ill. U., 1974. Tchr. Jones H.S. Chgo. Pub. Schs., 1971—78, asst. prin., scheduler Jones H.S., 1978—98, scheduler Jones H.S., 1998—2003, programmer, troubleshooter dept. H.S. programs, 2003—04, dir. citywide student scheduling svcs. Office of H.S. Programs, 2004—. Acting prin. Jones H.S. Chgo. Pub. Schs., 1988. Founder Mayfair Youth Orgn., 1967—, Thai Found., 1977—; bd. dirs. Old Timers Baseball Assn.; co-chair econ. devel. subcom. City of Chgo., 2006—; committeman 39th Wd. Chgo. Rep., 2008. Republican. Roman Catholic. Avocations: coin collecting/numismatics, coaching, political activities. Home: 5157 N Lowell Chicago IL 60630 Office: Chgo Pub Schs Dept HS Programs 125 S Clark 12th Fl Chicago IL 60603 Office Phone: 773-553-2073. Personal E-mail: wcmiceli@aol.com.

MICHA, DAVID ALLAN, chemistry and physics professor; came to U.S., 1966, naturalized, 1974; s. Simon David and Catalina (Cohen) M.; m. Rebecca Stefan, 1991; children: Michael F., Anna K. MS, U. Cuyo, Bariloche, Argentina, 1962; DSc, U. Uppsala, Sweden, 1966. Rsch. assoc. Theoretical Chemistry Inst. U. Wis., Madison, 1966-67; asst. rsch. physicist Inst. Pure and Applied Sci. U. Calif., La Jolla, 1967-69; assoc. prof. chemistry and physics U. Fla., Gainesville, 1969-74, prof., 1974—, dir. Ctr. Chem. Physics, 1982-91, head phys. chem. divsn., 1999—2004. Vis. prof. U. Gothenburg, Sweden, 1970, Harvard U., 1972, 90, 98, 2000, 01, Max-Planck Inst., Göttingen, Germany, 1976, 96, Imperial Coll., London, 1977, U. Calif., Santa Barbara, 1982, U. Colo. and Weizmann Inst., Israel, 1983, U. Buenos Aires, 1988, 95, Supercomputer Inst., Fla. State U., 1991, Ecole Normale Superieure, Paris 2004, 05, 07, Inst. Math. Applications, U. Minn., 2009; mem. adv. panel div. advanced sci. computing NSF, 1990-92, Max-Planck Inst. Astrophysik, Munich, Germany, 1996, 97. Mem. editl. bd. Internat. Jour. Quantum Chemistry, 1979-88, Few-Body Systems, 1985—; editor Finite Systems and Multiparticle Dynamics, 1990-2005, 2 symposium procs., 5 workshop books; contbr. several book chpts., numerous articles to sci. jours. Recipient U.S. Sr. Scientist award A. Von Humboldt Found., 1976, Sr. Faculty Rsch. award Sigma Xi, 1985; Alfred P. Sloan Found. fellow, 1971-74; Nat. Bur. Standards JILA fellow, 1983, Mentors award, Dreyfus Found., 2009. Fellow Am. Phys. Soc. (vice chmn. topical group on few body sys. and multi-particle dynamics 1986-88, chmn. 1988-89); mem. Am. Chem. Soc. Office: U Fla 2318 New Physics Bldg Gainesville FL 32611-8435

MICHAEL, ALAN C., dean, law educator; AB, Harvard Coll., Cambridge, Mass., 1983; JD, Columbia U. Sch. Law, NYC, 1986. Bar: NY 1st Dept. 1995. Chief asst. to trademark atty. IBM Corp., Valhalla, NY, 1982; legal intern NY County Dist. Atty. Office, 1984, asst. dist. atty., 1991—95; summer assoc. Debevoise & Plimpton, NYC, 1985, Paul, Weiss, Rifkind, Wharton & Garrison, NYC, 1986; law clk. to Hon. Wilfred Feinberg US Ct. Appeals (2d cir.), 1986—87; law clk. to Hon. Harry A. Blackman US Supreme Ct., 1987—88; of counsel, Maj. League Baseball Players Assn. McGuire & Tiernan, NYC, 1989—91; faculty mem. Ohio State U. Moritz Coll. Law, Columbus, 1995—, assoc. prof. law, 1999—2002, assoc. dean, faculty, 2001—03, prof. law, 2002—, Cooperman designated prof. law, 2002—08, interim dean, 2008, dean, 2008—. Vis. prof. law U. Mich. Law Sch., 2003; print and broadcast media commentator on criminal law and sports law; lectr., presenter, moderator and panelist in field. Co-author (with J. Dressler): Understanding Criminal Procedure: Investigation (4th ed.), 2006, Understanding Criminal Procedure: Adjudication (4th ed.), 2006; contbr. articles to profl. jours., chapters to books. Bd. trustees Bexley Pub. Libr., 2009—. Mem.: ABA, Assn. Am. Law Schools (mem. criminal justice and law & sports sects.). Office: Michael E Moritz Coll Law Ohio State Univ 55 W 12th Ave Columbus OH 43209 Office Phone: 614-292-0574. Office Fax: 614-292-1383. Business E-Mail: michaels.23@osu.edu.*

MICHAEL, ALFRED FREDERICK, JR., physician, medical educator; b. Phila. s. Alfred Frederick and Emma Maude (Peters) M.; m. Jeanne Jones; children: Mary, Susan, Carol. MD, Temple U., 1953. Diplomate Am. Bd. Pediatrics (founding mem. sub-bd. pediatric nephrology, pres. 1977-79). Pediat. diagnostic lab. immunology and pediatric nephrology intern Phila. Gen. Hosp., 1953-54; resident St. Christopher's Hosp., Phila., 1954, Children's Hosp. and U. Cin. Coll. Medicine, 1957-60; postdoctoral fellow dept. pediatrics and biochemistry Med. Sch., U. Minn., Mpls., 1960-63, assoc. prof., 1965-68, prof. pediatrics, lab. medicine and pathology, 1968-88, co-dir. pediatric nephrology, 1968—86, Regents' prof., 1986—, head dept. pediatrics, 1986-97, dean, 1996—2002. Established investigator Am. Heart Assn., 1963-68. Past mem. editl. bd. Internat. Yr. Book of Nephrology, Am. Jour. Nephrology, Kidney Internat., Clin. Nephrology, Am. Jour. Pathology; contbr. articles to profl. jours. Physician founder Vikings Children's Fund, Univ. Pediat. Found.; bd. dirs. St. Mary's Health Clinics, Minn. Vikings Children's Fund. Served with USAF, 1955—57. Recipient Alumni Achievement award Temple U. Sch. Medicine, 1988, John Peters award, 1992, Diehl award, 2003; NIH fellow, 1960-63, Guggenheim fellow, 1966-67, NIH Merit awardee, 1992-2002, Bolles Rogers award, Shotwell award. Fellow AAAS; mem. Am. Soc. Clin. Investigation, Assn. Am. Physicians, Am. Pediat. Soc., Soc. for Pediat. Rsch., Am. Assn. Investigative Pathology, Am. Soc. Cell Biology, Am. Soc. Nephrology (coun., pres.-elect 1992—, pres. 1993, John Peters award), Internat. Soc. Nephrology, Soc. for Exptl. Biology and Medicine, Minn. Med. Assn. Home: 1986 Lower Saint Dennis Rd Saint Paul MN 55116-2820 Office Phone: 612-626-4900. Business E-Mail: micha003@umn.edu.

MICHAEL, ANDREW JAY, geophysicist; s. Paul Andrew and Norma Michael; m. Stephanie Louise Ross. BS, MIT, Cambridge, Mass., 1981; MS, Stanford U., Calif., 1983, PhD, 1985. Postdoctoral scholar and tchr. dept. geophysics Stanford U., 1985—86; postdoctoral scholar br. seismology US Geol. Survey, Menlo Park, Calif., 1986—88, geophysicist Earthquake Hazards Team, 1988—. Editor: (jour.) Bulletin Seismol. Soc. Am., 2004—; composer: (music) Earthquake Quartet #1; lectr., musician (performance) The Music of Earthquakes. Mem., pres. Coastside Cmty. Orch., Half Moon Bay, Calif., 1995—2003; founding dir. Coastside Jewish Cmty., Half Moon Bay; bd. mem. Patients Against Lymphoma, Rieglesville, Pa., 2005—. Mem.: Seismol. Soc. Am., Am. Geophys. Union (life). Achievements include research in Stress and Structure Around Active Faults, Earthquake Prediction, Hazards Assessment, Rapid Dissemination of Earthquake Information. Avocations: jazz, classical music, squash, canoe camping, winemaking. Office: USGS - Ms 977 345 Middlefield Rd Menlo Park CA 94025 Business E-Mail: michael@usgs.gov.

MICHAEL, DIETRICH, biology professor; b. Huntsville, Ala., Nov. 7, 1963; s. Regis and Sarah Dietrich; m. Laura Lovett, Aug. 6, 1989; children: Lydia Lovett-Dietrich, Arlena Lovett-Dietrich. BA, Va. Tech, Blacksburg, 1985; PhD, U. Calif. San Diego, 1991. Assoc. prof. U. Calif. Davis, 1990—98; prof. Dartmouth Coll., Hanover, NH, 1998—. Author: Rebels, Mavericks, and Heretics in Biology. Mem.: Internat. Soc. History, Philosophy, & Social Study Biology (pres. 2003—05). Home: 35 McClure St Amherst MA 01002

MICHAEL, ERNEST ARTHUR, mathematics professor; b. Zurich, Switzerland, Aug. 26, 1925; came to U.S., 1939; s. Jakob and Erna (Sondheimer) M.; m. Colette Verger Davis, 1956 (div. 1966); children: Alan, David, Gerard; m. Erika Goodman Joseph, Dec. 4, 1966; children: Hillary, Joshua. BA, Cornell U., 1947; MA, Harvard U., 1948; PhD, U. Chgo., 1951. Mem. faculty dept. math. U. Wash., Seattle, 1953—, asst. prof., 1953-56, assoc. prof., 1956-60, prof., 1960-93, prof. emeritus, 1993—. Mem. Inst. for Advanced Study, Princeton, 1951-52, 56-57, 60-61, 68, Math. Research Inst., E.T.H., Zürich, 1973-74; vis. prof. U. Stuttgart, Ger., 1978-79, U. Munich, Fed. Republic Germany, 1987, 88, 92-93. Editor: Procs. Am. Math. Soc., 1968-71, Topology and Its Applications, 1972-94, Set-Valued Analysis, 1993—; contbr. articles to profl. jours. With USNR, 1944—46. Grantee, AEC, Office Nav. Rsch., NSF, Guggenheim Found., Humboldt Found. Mem. Am. Math. Soc., Math. Assn. Am., ACLU, Amnesty Internat. Jewish. Home: 22200 Chinook Rd Woodway WA 98020-7200 Office: U Washington Dept Math Box 354350 Seattle WA 98195-4350 Home Phone: 425-640-3200. Personal E-mail: ernie@eemichael.net.

MICHAEL, GEORGE T., real estate manager, developer; s. Lorriane Cooper; m. Terrelyn Michael, Sept. 9, 1989. AA, Bronx C.C., 1978; diploma, NYU Grad. Sch. of Bus., 1980. Mgr., owner various real estate properties, NYC, 1980—. Author: (sch. newspaper) The Communicator, 1975. V.p. Adults & Youth for a Better Baisley Inc., Jamaica, 1984. Avocations: book collecting, stamp collecting/philately, track. Office Phone: 718-468-4481. Office Fax: 718-468-1512. E-mail: gtmdred@aol.com.

MICHAEL, HANNIGAN OWEN, biology educator; b. Houlton, Maine, May 5, 1965; s. Thomas Owen and Linda Anne Hannigan; m. Denise Martine Pelletier, Aug. 12, 1989; children: Gabriel Jacques-Thomas Hannigan, Seth Ryan Hannigan, Heather Rose Hannigan. PhD, U. Conn., Farmington, 1998. Cert. tchr. Maine, 2007. Postdoc. fellow U. Conn., 1998—2001, U. Conn. Health Ctr., 2001—03; tchr. dept. life sci. Houlton HS, 2003—. Youth leader Boy Scouts Am., Houlton, 1996—2007; mem. Elks, Houlton, 2008—. Recipient Sister Mary Bouchard Excellence Tchg. award, St. Joseph's Coll., 1988, Excellence award, ETS, Princeton, NJ, 2007—08. Mem.: ISTE. Home: 72 Pleasant St Houlton ME 04730 Office: Houlton HS 7 Bird St Houlton ME 04730 Personal E-mail: michaelhanniga@snet.net. Business E-Mail: mihannigan@msln.net.

MICHAEL, JERROLD MARK, public health service officer, educator, retired dean; b. Richmond, Va., Aug. 3, 1927; s. Joseph Leon and Esther Leah M.; m. Lynn Y. Simon, Mar. 17, 1951; children: Scott J., Nelson L BCE, George Washington U., 1949; MSE, Johns Hopkins U., 1950; MPH, U. Calif., Berkeley, 1957; DrPH (hon.), Mahidol U., 1983; ScD (hon.), Tulane U., 1984. Commd. ensign USPHS, 1950, advanced through grades to rear adm., asst. surgeon gen., 1966; ret., 1970; dean Sch. Pub. Health, U. Hawaii, Honolulu, 1971-92, prof. pub. health, 1971-95; emeritus prof. pub. health U. Hawaii, Honolulu, 1995—; adj. prof. global health George Washington U., 1997—. Bd. dirs. Nat. Health Coun., 1967-78, Nat. Ctr. for Health Edn., 1977-90; mem. nat. adv. coun. on health professions edn., 1978-81; chmn. bd. dirs. Kuakini Med. Ctr., Honolulu; sec., treas. Asia-Pacific Acad. Consortium Pub. Health; vis. prof. U. Adelaide, 1993, George Washington, 1994; hon. prof. Beijing Med. U., 1994; adj. prof. internat. pub. health Goerge Washington U., 1997- Contbr. articles to profl. jours.; assoc. editor Jour. Environ. Health, 1958-80, Asia-Pacific Jour. of Pub. Health, 1986-95 Pres. Commd. Officers Found., 2000—. Served with USNR, 1944-47 Decorated Meritorious Svc. medal, comdr. Royal Order of Elephant (Thailand); recipient Walter Mangold award, 1961, J.S. Billings award for mil. medicine, 1964, Gold medal Hebrew U., Jerusalem, 1982, San Karcil Gold medal, Malaysia, 1989, Disting. Svc. award Pacific Island Health Officers Assn., 1992, USPHS awards, Commd. Officers Assn. Brutsche award, 1999, Founders award Asia-Pacific Acad. Consortium Pub.

Health, 2003, U.S. Surgeon Gen.'s medallion, 2005, Michael Ednl. Fellowship, PHS Found., 2007, Adm. Michael PHS Engr. award, 2008,Theta Tau Laureate Alumni Hall Of Fame, others Fellow Am. Public Health Assn.; mem. Am. Acad. Health Adminstrn., Am. Soc. Cert. Sanitarians, Nat. Environ. Health Assn., Am. Acad. Environ. Engrs. Clubs: Masons

MICHAEL, M. BLANE, federal judge; b. Charleston, SC, Feb. 17, 1943; AB, W.Va. U., 1965; JD, NYU, 1968. Bar: NY 1968, US Dist. Ct. (so. and ea. dists.) NY 1968, W.Va. 1973, US Ct. Appeals (4th cir.) 1974, US Dist. Ct. (so. dist.) W.Va. 1981. Counsel to Gov. W.Va. John D. Rockefeller IV, 1977—80; atty. Jackson & Kelly, Charleston, W.Va., 1981—93; fed. judge US Ct. Appeals (4th cir.), Charleston, W.Va., 1993—. Mem.: ABA, Kanawha County Bar Assn., W.Va. Bar Assn., Phi Beta Kappa. Office: US Circuit Judge Robert C Byrd US Courthouse 300 Virginia St E Rm 7404 Charleston WV 25301-2504 Office Phone: 304-347-3516.*

MICHAEL, MARK ALBER, cardiologist, researcher; Degree in Medicine, Tanta U. Sch. Medicine, Egypt. Internal medicine house staff Ind. U. Sch. Medicine, Indpls., 2005—08; fellow cardiovasc. medicine Krannert Inst. Cardiology, Indpls., 2008—; rsch. scientist Amyloidosis Rsch. Group, Indpls. Contbr. articles to numerous profl. jours. Recipient First Pl. winner, Dept. Medicine, Ind. U., 2006, 2007, Fourth Pl. winner, ACP, 2006; Cardiology fellowship, Krannert Inst. Cardiology, Indpls., 2008. Mem.: ACP, Am. Bd. Internal Medicine, Heart Rhythm Soc., Am. Coll. Cardiology, Am. Heart Assn. Achievements include first to fragmented wide QRS on a 12-Lead ECG: a sign of myocardial scar and poor prognosis; fragmented QRS complexes on a 12-Lead ECG predict arrhythmic events in patients with an ICD; segmental wall motion abnormalities in nonischemic cardiomyopathy patients with implantable cardioverter-defibrillators predicts appropriate device therapy; fragmented QRS predicts cardiac events and mortality in patients with narrow QRS on 12-lead electrocardiogram; fragmented QRS (fQRS) on 12-lead EKG is a predictor of arrhythmic events and mortality in patients with dilated cardiomyopathy.

MICHAEL, NOREEN, academic administrator; PhD in Ednl. Psychology, U. Ill. Commr. of edn. Virgin Islands Dept. Edn., Charlotte, Amalie, Virgin Islands, 2002—07; chief of staff, Office of President U VI, St. Thomas, 2007—. Office: 2 John Brewer's Bay St Thomas VI 00802-9990 Office Phone: 340-774-0100, 340-693-1003. Office Fax: 340-779-7153. Business E-Mail: nmichael@uvi.edu.

MICHAEL, SIMON R., physician scientist, educator; MD, NY U., 1969. Diplomate Am. Bd. Internal Medicine, 1975, Am. Bd. Allergy & Immunology, 1977, Am. Bd. Med. Lab. Immunology, 1985. Clin. prof. emeritus Wayne State U. Sch. Medicine, Detroit, 2006—; pres., sec. IgA, Inc., Ann Arbor, Mich., 2007—. Exec. com. Mich. Allergy & Asthma Soc., East Lansing, 1994—; mem., bioethics com. Mich. State Med. Soc., 2000—. Fellow: ACP, Am. Acad. Allergy, Asthma & Immunology, Am. Coll. Allergy, Asthma & Immunology, Royal Coll. Physicians & Surgeons Can.

MICHAELIDES, CONSTANTINE EVANGELOS, architect, educator; b. Athens, Greece, Jan. 26, 1930; came to U.S., 1955, naturalized, 1964; s. Evangelos George and Kalliopi Constantine (Kefallonitis) M.; m. Maria S. Canellakis, Sept. 3, 1955; children: Evangelos Constantine, Dimitri Canellakis. Diploma in Architecture, Nat. Tech. U., Athens, 1952; M.Arch., Harvard U., 1957. Practice architecture, Athens, 1954-55, St. Louis, 1963—; asso. architect Carl Koch, Jose Luis Sert, Hideo Sasaki, Cambridge, Mass., 1957-59, Doxiadis Assos., Athens and Washington, 1959-60, Hellmuth, Obata & Kassabaum, St. Louis, 1962; instr. Grad. Sch. Design Harvard U., 1957-59, Athens Inst. Tech., 1959-60; asst. prof. architecture Washington U., St. Louis, 1960-64, assoc. prof., 1964-69, prof., 1969-94, assoc. dean Sch. Architecture, 1969-73; dean Washington U., Sch. Architecture, 1973-93, dean emeritus, 1993—; Ruth and Norman Moore vis. prof. Washington U., St. Louis, 1995. Vis. prof. (Sch. Architecture), Ahmedabad, India, 1970; counselor Landmarks Assn. St. Louis., 1975-79 Author: Hydra: A Greek Island Town: Its Growth and Form, 1967, The Aegean Crucible: Tracing Vernacular Architecture in Post-Byzantine Centuries, 2003; contbr. articles to profl. jours. Mem. Mcpl. Commn. on Arts, Letters, University City, Mo., 1975-81. With Greek Army Res., 1952-54. Fellow AIA (Rsch. award 1963-64, Presdl. Citation 1992); mem. Tech. Chamber of Greece, Soc. Archtl. Historians, Modern Greek Studies Assn., Hellenic Soc. St. Louis (pres. 1991, 95, 96). Home and Office: 735 Radcliffe Ave Saint Louis MO 63130-3139 Business E-Mail: info@delospress.com.

MICHAELIDES, DOROS NIKITA, internist, medical educator; b. Nicosia, Cyprus, Jan. 7, 1936; came to U.S., 1969; s. Nikita P. and Elpinike (Taliadorou) M.; m. Eutychia J. Loizides, Feb. 27, 1965; children: Nike-Elsie, Joanna-Doris. MD magna cum laude (Royal Greek Govt., Scholar) U. Athens, 1962; DTM and H (Greek State Scholarship, Found. Scholar) U. Liverpool, Eng., 1967; MSc in Clin. Biochemistry (Greek State, Scholarship Found. Scholar), U. Newcastle-upon-Tyne (Eng.), 1969. Diplomate Am. Bd. Family Practice, Am. Bd. Allergy and Immunology; qualified Am. Bd. Internal Medicine; cert. in infectious diseases and immunochemistry, Eng. Clk., intern U. Uppsala, Sweden, 1962; resident Nicosia Gen. Hosp., 1963—66; fellow U. Liverpool Hosps., 1967; fellow internal and clin. medicine Royal Infirmary U. Edinburgh, 1967—68; rsch. fellow Royal Victoria Infirmary U. Newcastle-upon-Tyne, 1968—69; resident internal medicine Bapt. Meml. Hosp., Memphis, 1969—72; fellow in chest diseases We. Okla. Chest Disease Hosp., 1970—71; chief clin. immunology/respiratory care ctr. Erie, Pa.; chief respiratory care ctr. VA Med. Ctr., Erie, 1972—84, acting chief dept. medicine, 1980—81; asst. clin. prof. medicine Hahnemann U. Sch. Medicine, Phila., 1977—, Gannon U., Erie, 1977—. Mem. staff internal medicine Hamot Med. Ctr., immunology and chest diseases Metro Health Ctr., Erie; preceptor medicine St. Vincent's Health Ctr.; affiliate staff Cleveland Clinic Found.; vol. physician Greek Nat. Guard, Cyprus, 1964. Author: The Occurrence of Proteolytic Inhibitors in Heart and Skeletal Muscle, 1969; Blood Gases, Acid-Base and Electrolytes Disturbances, 1980; Immediate Hypersensitivity: The Immunochemistry and Therapeutics of Reversible Airway Obstruction, 1980; The Equivalent Potency of Corticosteroid Preparations used in Reversible Airway Obstruction, 1981; contbr. articles to med. jours. Recipient citation for outstanding svcs. to vets. DAV, 1975, citation Adminstr. U.S. Vets. Affairs, 1978. Fellow ACP (life), Am. Assn. Cert. Allergists, Am. Coll. Allergy and Immunology (com. autoimmune diseases), Am. Assn. Clin. Immunology and Allergy (pulmonary com.), Am. Coll. Chest Physicians (life; critical care com.), Royal Soc. Medicine, Am. Coll. Angiology, N.Y. Acad. Scis., Am. Coll. Clin. Pharmacology, Am. Assn. Cert. Allergists. Greek Orthodox. Home: 4107 State St Erie PA 16508-3129 Office: Doros N Michaelides MD 4107 State St Erie PA 16508-3129 Personal E-mail: dorosmichaelides@yahoo.com. Business E-Mail: dnm777@pol.net.

MICHAELIS, KENNETH A., biology professor; b. Phila., Mar. 21, 1948; s. Kenneth F. and Ella M. Michaelis. BA, Columbia Union Coll., Takoma Park, Md., 1970; MA, Walla Walla Coll., College Place, Wash., 1972. Full prof. San Bernardino CC Dist.,Calif., 1972—. Treas. SBVC Faculty Assn., San Bernardino, Calif., 1983—2008, Highland SDA Ch., Calif., 1985—89, Calimesa SDA Ch., Calif., 1992—96. Independent. Office: San Bernardino Valley Coll 701 South Mt Vernon Ave San Bernardino CA 92410 Business E-Mail: kmichael@sbccd.cc.ca.us.

MICHAELIS, MICHAEL, management and technical consultant; b. Berlin, June 8, 1919; s. George and Martha (Bluth) M.; m. Diana Ordway Tead, Sept. 11, 1954; children: Ordway Peter, David Tead; m. Cintra McIlwain Williams, Mar. 19, 1966 (div. Nov. 1975); m. Caroline Crutcher Bishop, Mar. 17, 1984. BSc in Engring., U. London, 1941. Rsch. asst., group leader Rsch. Labs. Gen. Electric Co., Ltd., U.K., 1935-45, staff physicist and cons., 1945-49; dir. physics divsn. Radiochem. Centre, U.K. Atomic Energy Authority, 1949-51; cons. Arthur D. Little, Inc., Cambridge, Mass., 1951-52, staff cons., 1952-61, sr. asso., 1957-61, head nuclear mgmt. cons. services, 1956-61, internat. bus. devel. services, 1959-61, policy adviser to several large corps, 1954-61, mgr. Washington ops., 1963-72, sr. cons., 1972-81; pres., CEO Partners In Enterprise, Inc., 1981—2000. Cons. to Pres.'s Spl. Asst. Sci. and Tech., The White House, 1961-63; exec. sec. The White House Panel on Civilian Tech., 1961-63; exec. dir. rsch. mgmt. adv. panel, com. on sci. and tech. U.S. Ho. of Reps., 1963-67; dep. coord. then Pres.-elect Carter's Task Force on Sci. and Tech. Policy, 1976; mem. tech. adv. bd. to U.S. Sec. Commerce, 1978-81; mem. citizens adv. coun. Congl. Caucus for Sci. and Tech., 1983-86; mem. nat. com. Am. Goals and Resources, Nat. Planning Assn., 1964-67, mem. adv. com. sci., tech. and economy, 1966-68; vice chmn. com. internat. affairs Atomic Indsl. Forum, 1958-60; assoc. with Anglo-Am. Radar Rsch. Project, World War II. Editor, project dir.: Federal Funding of Civilian Research and Development, 1976; Contbr. articles to profl. jours. Fellow AAAS (chmn. engring. sect. 1980-82, exec. dir. sr. scientists and engrs. program 1989-90); mem. IEEE (sr.), Sci. Film Assn. (founder 1943, sec. 1943-48, v.p. 1948-51), Am. Nuclear Soc., Boston Com. Fgn. Rels., Royal Inst. Physics and Phys. Soc., Soc. Internat. Devel., Royal Instn. Elec. Engrs., Assn. Hosp. Physicists, Nat. Planning Assn., World Future Soc. (dir.), U.S. C. of C. (chmn. com. on govt.-industry rels. in sci. and tech. 1963-64), Interdisciplinary Comm. Assocs. Inc. (dir. 1969-79), Am. Econ. Assn., Am. Soc. Cybernetics, Am. Soc. for Pub. Adminstrn., Atlantic Coun. U.S., Cosmos Club (Washington, sec. 1994-97, v.p. 1997-98, pres. 1998-99), Harvard Faculty Club. Home and Office: 6812 Meadow Ln Chevy Chase MD 20815-5018 Home Phone: 301-657-8847; Office Phone: 301-986-1950. Personal E-mail: zmichael@verizon.net. *The Constitution of the U.S. diffuses power so as to better secure liberty. But it also intends that practice will integrate the dispersed powers into a workable government. It confers upon its branches autonomy but also reciprocity, separateness but also interdependence. It is incumbent on each of us to help make this system work, and to make it responsive to the human needs of our country and the world.*

MICHAELIS, PAUL CHARLES, engineering physicist executive; b. Bronx, June 18, 1935; s. Paul Fredrick and Rose (Landsbury) M.; m. Geraldine A. DeCuollo, June 29, 1958; 1 son, Paul Charles. BS in Elec. Engring, Newark Coll. Engring., 1964, MS in Physics, 1967. Cert. account mgr. With AT&T Bell Labs., Murray Hill and Whippany, NJ, 1953-96; assoc. mem. tech. staff Bell Telephone Labs., 1963-67, mem. tech. staff, 1967-82, tech. mgr., 1982-96, ret., 1996; founder P.C. Michaelis Tech. Cons. Inc., Watchung, NJ, 1996—. Guest lectr. USSR Acad. Scis., 1972 Contbr. articles to profl. jours.; patentee in optics, magnetics, mechanics and electronics. Mem. IEEE (life; Morris N. Liebmann award 1975), AAAS, Am. Phys. Soc., U.S. Naval Inst., Am. Soc. Naval Engrs., Lions (past pres. Watchung club, Melvin Jones fellow), Raritan Yacht Club (sec.). Avocation: sailing. Home: 103 High Tor Dr Watchung NJ 07069-5424 also: 151 Amherst Dr Bayville NJ 08721 Office: P C Michaelis Tech Cons Inc 103 High Tor Dr Watchung NJ 07069-5424 E-mail: pmichaelis@optonline.net.

MICHAELS, AL (ALAN RICHARD MICHAELS), sportscaster; b. Bklyn., Nov. 12, 1944; s. Jay Leonard and Lila Ruth (Ross) Michaels; m. Linda Anne Stamaton, Aug. 27, 1966; children: Steven, Jennifer. BA, Ariz. State U., 1966. TV/radio play-by-play announcer Cin. Reds, 1971—73, San Francisco Giants, 1974—76; sports commentator ABC TV Network, NYC, 1976—2006, lead announcer, Monday Night Football, 1986—2006, lead announcer, NBA, 2003—06, NBC Sunday Night Football, 2006—. Recipient Nat. Sportscaster of Yr. award, Nat. Sportscasters and Sportswriters Assn., 1980, 1983, 1986, Emmy award, 1987, Emmy award, Outstanding Sports Personality - Play-by-Play, 2007; named one of Top 50 Sportscasters, Am. Sportscasters Assn., 2009. Avocations: reading, tennis. Office: c/o NBC Sports 30 Rockefeller Plaza New York NY 10112*

MICHAELS, CLAIRE FARLEY, psychology educator; b. New London, Conn., Sept. 13, 1948; d. Walter Dixson and Anna Emerancia (DeNeve) Farley; m. Robert James Michaels, Nov. 29, 1969 (div. Dec. 1981). BA, U. Conn., 1969, MA, 1972, PhD, 1974. Prof. psychology Lake Forest (Ill.) Coll., 1973-91; with Vrike U. Amsterdam, The Netherlands, 1991—. Co-author: Direct Perception, 1981; cons. editor Jour. of Experimental Psycholo gy, 1989–; contbr. articles to profl. jours. Recipient Outstanding Teaching award Inland Steel-Ryerson Found., 1979. Mem. AAAS, Internat. Soc. Ecol. Psychology (bd. dirs. 1985-87, 1990-92), Psychonomic Soc., Sigma Xi. Democrat. Avocations: skiing, fishing. Office: Univ of Connecticut 406 Babbidge Rd Storrs Mansfield CT 06269 Home: 136 Beech Mountain Mansfield Center CT 06250 Business E-Mail: claire.michaels@uconn.edu.

MICHAELS, JAMES EDWARD, bishop emeritus; b. Chgo., Ill., May 30, 1926; Ordained priest Missionary Soc. of St. Columban, Dublin, 1951; ordained bishop, 1966; aux. bishop Archdiocese of Kwangju, Republic of Korea, 1966—73, Diocese of Wheeling-Charleston, W.Va., 1973—87, aux. bishop emeritus, 1987—. Roman Catholic. Office: Diocese of Wheeling-Charleston 1300 Byron St Wheeling WV 26003-0230

MICHAELS, JENNIFER TONKS, foreign language educator; b. Sedgley, England, May 19, 1945; d. Frank Gordon and Dorothy (Compston) Tonks; m. Eric Michaels, 1973; children: Joseph, David, Ellen. MA, U. Edinburgh, 1967, McGill U., 1971, PhD, 1974. Teaching asst. German dept. Wesleyan U., 1967-68; instr. German dept. Bucknell (Pa.) U., 1968-69; teaching asst. German dept. McGill U., Canada, 1969-72; prodn. asst. Pub. TV News and Polit. program, Schenectady, NY, 1974-75; from asst. prof. to assoc. prof. Grinnell (Iowa) Coll., 1975-87, prof., 1987—. Vis. cons. German dept. Hamilton Coll., 1981; cons. Modern Lang. dept. Colby Coll.; panelist NEH, 1985; spkr. in field. Author: D.H. Lawrence, The Polarity of North and South, 1976, Anarchy and Eros: Otto Gross' Impact on German Expressionist Writers, 1983, Franz Jung: Expressionist, Dadaist, Revolutionary and Outsider, 1989, Franz Werfel and the Critics, 1994; contbr. numerous articles, revs. to profl. jours. Mem. MLA, Rocky Mt. MLA (v.p. 2005), Am. Assn. Tchrs. of German, Soc. Exile Studies, German Studies Assn. (sec. treas. 1991-92, v.p. 1992-94, pres. 1995-96, numerous coms.). Democrat. Avocations: music, travel, reading. Office: Grinnell Coll German Dept PO Box 805 Grinnell IA 50112-0805 Business E-Mail: michaels@grinnell.edu.

MICHAELS, LORNE, television producer; b. Toronto, Ont., Can., Nov. 17, 1944; m. Rosie Schuster, 1973 (div. 1980); m. Susan Forristal, 1984 (div. 1987); m. Alice Barry, 1991; 3 children. Grad., U. Toronto, 1966; doctorate (hon.), Ryerson U. Former prodr. CBC, Toronto; writer Rowan and Martin's Laugh-In, NBC, also other TV series, LA, 1968-75; chmn. bd., founder Broadway Video, NYC. Writer, prodr. (TV series) The Hart & Lorne Terrific Hour, 1970, writer, exec. prodr. Saturday Night Live, 1975—80 (Best Comedy/Variety - Series, Writers Guild America, 2009), 1985—; prodr.: (TV series) The New Show, 1984; exec. prodr.: Sunday Night, 1988, The Kids in the Hall, 1989—94, Late Night with Conan O'Brien, 1993—, The Vacant Lot, 1994; writer, prodr. (TV special) Lily Tomlin, 1975, The Paul Simon Special, 1977, Steve Martin's Best Show Ever, 1981; exec. prodr.: (TV special) Late Night with Conan O'Brian: 10 Anniversary Special, 2003, Night of Too Many Stars, 2003, Saturday Night Live: 25th Anniversary; co-exec. prodr. (TV special) Rolling Stone Presents Twenty Years of Rock & Roll, 1987; prodr.: (TV films) Things We Did Last Summer, 1977; exec. prodr.: The Rutles: All You Need Is Cash, 1978, Mr. Mike's Mondo Video, 1979, Simon and Garfunkel: The Concert in Central Park, 1982, The Rutles 2: Can't Buy Me Lunch, 2002; (TV series) 30 Rock, 2006— (Primetime Emmy for Outstanding Comedy Series, Acad. TV Arts and Scis., 2007, 2008, Danny Thomas Prodr. of Yr. Award in Episodic TV - Comedy, Prodrs. Guild America, 2009); co-writer (TV films) Gilda Live, 1980, writer, prodr. (films) Three Amigos, 1986; prodr.: (films) Coneheads, 1983, Nothing Lasts Forever, 1984, Wayne's World, 1992, Coneheads, 1993, Wayne's World II, 1993, Tommy Boy, 1995, Stuart Saves His Family, 1995, Black Sheep, 1996, Kids in the Hall: Brain Candy, 1996, A Night at the Roxbury, 1998, Superstar, 1999, The Ladies Man, 2000, Enigma, 2001, Mean Girls, 2004, Hot Rod, 2007, Baby Mama, 2008. Recipient George Foster Peabody award for Saturday Night Live, 1990, Mark Twain Prize, John F. Kennedy Ctr. Performing Arts, 2004, Herb Sargent award for Comedy Excellence, Writers Guild of America, 2007, 11 Emmy awards, star on Hollywood Walk of Fame, Webby Film & Video Lifetime Achievement, Internat. Acad. Digital Arts and Scis., 2008; named Broadcaster of Yr., Internat. Radio and TV Soc., 1992; named one of The 100 Most Influential People in the World, TIME mag., 2008; named to TV Acad. Hall of Fame, 1999, Order of Canada, 2002. Office: Broadway Video 1619 Broadway Fl 9 New York NY 10019-7463

MICHAELS, PATRICK JOSEPH, climatologist; b. Berwyn, Ill., Feb. 15, 1950; s. Joseph Matthew and Cecelia Bernadette (Stonich) M.; m. Erika Nellie Kancler, Sept. 24, 1983; 1 child, Erika. AB, U. Chgo., 1971, SM, 1975; PhD, U. Wis.-Madison, 1979. Asst. prof. U. Va., Charlottesville, 1979-86, Va. state climatologist Dept. Envion. Scis., 1980, assoc. prof., 1986, now prof. environ. sci.; sr. fellow environ. studies Cato Inst., Washington. Vis. scientist Marshall Inst., Washington. Author: Sound and Fury: The Science and Politics of Global Warming, 1992, The Satanic Gases, 2000, Meltdown: The Predictable Distortion of Global Warming by Scientists, Politicians, and the Media, 2004, Shattered Consensus: The True State of Global Warming, 2005; contbr. articles to profl. jours. Grantee in field. Mem. Am. Assn. State Climatology (pres. 1987-88), Am. Meteorol. Soc. (program chmn. com. on applied climatology 1988-89). Avocations: gardening, competitive softball. Home: RR 1 Box 234 Waynesboro VA 22980-9737 Office: Cato Inst 1000 Massachusetts Ave, NW Washington DC 20001-5403 also: Va State Climatology Office Clark Hall, I051 PO Box 400123 Charlottesville VA 22903 Office Phone: 434-924-0549, 202-789-5200. Office Fax: 434-982-2137, 202-789-5226. E-mail: pjm8x@p.mail.virginia.edu, pmichaels@cato.org.

MICHAELS, PAUL S., food products executive; Pres. Masterfoods USA; Americas regional pres. Mars, Inc., global pres. Office: Mars Inc 6885 Elm St Mc Lean VA 22101 Office Phone: 703-821-4900.

MICHAELS, RANDY (BENJAMIN HOMEL), multimedia company executive; b. 1952; BA, SUNY, 1983. Engr. coll. station SUNY; radio, TV ops., v.p. programming Taft Broadcasting, Buffalo, Cin., 1973—83; co-founder Seven Hills Comm. (merged with Jacor Comm.), 1983—96; exec. v.p. programming, co-chief oper. officer Jacor Comm., 1986—93, pres., COO, 1993—96; CEO Jacor Comm. (acquired by Clear Channel Comm.), 1996—99; divsn. pres., chmn., CEO Clear Channel Comm., 1999—2002; founder RadioActive LLC, Product 1st; acquisition ops. Oak Hill Capital ptnrs., 2005—07; CEO Local TV, LLC, 2007; exec. v.p., CEO interactive, broadcasting ops. Tribune Co., Chgo., 2007—08, COO, 2008—. Mem.: Nat. Assn. Broadcasters TV Bd. Office: Tribune Co 435 N Mich Ave Chicago IL 60611 Office Phone: 312-222-9100. Business E-Mail: corp.info@tribune.com.

MICHAELS, RICHARD EDWARD, lawyer; b. Chgo., June 10, 1952; s. Benjamin and Lillian (Borawski) Mikolajczewski; m. Karen Lynn Belau Michaels, May 17, 1980; children: Jonathan R., Timothy R., Matthew R. BS in Commerce summa cum laude, DePaul U., 1973; JD, Northwestern U., 1977. Bar: Ill. 1977, U.S. Dist. Ct. (no. dist.) Ill. 1977, U.S. Ct. Appeals (7th cir.) 1977; CPA, Ill. Acct. Touche Ross & Co., Chgo., 1973-74; assoc. Schuyler, Roche & Zwirner and predecessor firm Hubachek & Kelly Ltd., Chgo., 1977-83; ptnr. Schuyler, Roche & Zwirner, Chgo., 1983—2008, pres., 1994—2007, chmn., 2007—08; ptnr. Baker & Daniels LLP, Chgo., 2008—, mng. ptnr., 2009—. Mem. bd. dir. First Person Bank; mem. adv. bd. Thrivent Fin., 2002—08. Mem. Northwestern U. Law Rev., 1976-77. Mem. adv. bd. Greater Chgo. agy. Luth. Brotherhood, 1999—2002; chmn. Hawkswimming Maine South H.S., 2001—02; vice chmn. congregation St. Andrew's Luth. Ch., Park Ridge, Ill., 1990—92, 2009—, chmn. congregation Park Ridge, Ill., 1992—94. Mem. ABA, Internat. Bar Assn., Ill. Bar Assn., Chgo. Bar Assn., DePaul U. Alumni Assn., DePaul U. Boosters, Chgo. Athletic Assn., Northwestern Club, Union League Club, Beta Gamma Sigma, Pi Gamma Mu, Beta Alpha Psi. Lutheran. Avocations: photography, golf. Home: 808 Elm St Park Ridge IL 60068-3312 Office: Baker & Daniels LLP 311 S Wacker Dr Ste 4400 Chicago IL 60606 Office Phone: 312-212-6549. Business E-Mail: rick.michaels@bakerd.com.

MICHAELS, WILLARD A. BILL (BILL MICHAELS), retired broadcasting executive; b. Omaha, May 13, 1917; s. Gus M. and Bessie (Kerstine) M.; m. Helen Louise Mintel, Nov. 20, 1938 (dec. Sept. 2000); children: Marcella, Lawrence Richard, Betty Michaels Westbrook BA, Trinity U., 1940. Asst. sports editor San Antonio Express, 1937-40; sports announcer, sales mgr., gen. mgr. KABC, San Antonio, 1940-53; gen. mgr. KGBS-TV, 1954; v.p. WJBK-TV, Detroit, 1955-61; dir. Storer Broadcasting Co., Miami Beach, Fla., 1960-85, TV v.p., 1961-66, exec. v.p., 1966-67, pres., 1967-74, chmn., 1974-82, ret., 1982. Chmn. New Boston Garden Corp. (Boston Bruins), 1972-75; dir., mem. exec. com. Northeast Airlines, 1965-72, pres., 1970-72; dir. Delta Airlines, 1972-90, adv. dir., 1990-2009. Trustee Storer Found, 1960-2009. Home: 154 Manchester Way Shavano Pk San Antonio TX 78249 Personal E-mail: bmich76299@aol.com.

MICHAELSON, ARTHUR M., lawyer; b. NYC, May 16, 1927; s. Samuel H. and Augusta L. M.; m. Arline L. Kahn, June 30, 1957; children: Barbara L., Sarah E., David N. AB, Columbia U., 1947; LLB, Yale U., 1950. Bar: NY 1950, US Supreme Ct 1964. Partner Wachtel & Michaelson, NYC, 1957-66; v.p. McCrory Corp., NYC, 1966-68, Glen Alden Corp., NYC, 1968-73; partner Miller, Singer, Michaelson & Raives, NYC, 1973-84; counsel Hofheimer Gartlir & Gross, 1984—. Author: (with J. Blattmachr) Income Taxation of Estates and Trusts, 1980, 85, 89, 95, 96, 98. Bd. dirs., mem. exec. com. Amnesty Internat. of USA, Inc., 1972-81, vice chmn., 1975-76. Served with USN, 1945-46. Fellow Am. Bar Found.; mem. ABA, Assn. Bar City NY Office: 530 5th Ave New York NY 10036-5101

MICHAELSON, MARTIN, lawyer; b. Boston, Apr. 12, 1943; s. Eliot D. and Charlotte (Selib) M.; m. Anne Taylor, Aug. 30, 1987; children: Andrew M., Daniel M.; stepchildren: Rachel T., Hannah T. BA, U. Chgo., 1965; JD, Boston Coll., 1968. Bar: NY 1968, DC 1973, US Supreme Ct. 1973, Mass. 1983, US Dist. Ct. NY 1969, DC 1973, US Ct. Appeals (1st, 2d, 3d, 4th, 6th and 9th cirs.). Atty. Cravath, Swaine & Moore, NYC, 1968-71; legis. asst. Congressman Robert F. Drinan, Washington, 1971-73; atty. Hogan & Hartson, Washington, 1973-76, ptnr., 1976-83, 89—. Dep. gen. counsel Harvard U., Cambridge, Mass., 1983-88, univ. counsel, 1989, lectr. Harvard Grad. Sch. of Education, 1999. Consulting editor Trusteeship mag. Fellow: Nat. Assn. Coll. and Univ. Attys. Office: Hogan & Hartson Columbia Square 555 13th St NW Ste 800E Washington DC 20004-1161 Office Phone: 202-637-5748. Business E-Mail: mmichaelson@hhlaw.com.

MICHAELSON, PETER LEE, lawyer; b. NYC, Aug. 29, 1952; BS in Elec. Engring. and Econs., Carnegie-Mellon U., 1974, MSEE, 1975; JD, Duquesne U., 1979; LLM in Trade Regulation, NYU, 1985; postgrad., Harvard U., 1993, 96, 97. Bar: Pa. 1979, NJ 1980, (US Patent and Trademark Office) 1980, (US Dist. Ct. NJ) 1980, (US Ct. Claims) 1980, (US Ct. Mil. Appeals) 1980, (US Tax Ct.) 1980, (US Ct. Appeals (3rd cir.)) 1981, (US Ct. Appeals (fed. cir.)) 1983, NY 1986, (US Supreme Ct.) 1986, Alaska 2000, cert.: Ctr. Effective Dispute Resolution (mediator), lic.: Chartered Inst. Arbitrators, Eng. (arbitrator). Electronics project engr. Control Systems Research, Inc., Pitts., 1975-76; electronics devel. engr. Aluminum Co. Am., Alcoa Tech. Ctr., Prodn. Equip. Lab., Pitts., 1976-77, Rockwell Internat. Corp., Pitts., 1977-79; corp. patent atty., mem. patent and legal staff Bell Telephone Labs., Holmdel, NJ, 1979-82; atty. Pennie & Edmonds, NYC, 1982-84; prin. Michaelson & Assocs., Counsellors at Law, Red Bank, NJ, 1984—. Mem. disting. panel neutrals tech., e-discovery, ICANN domain names and Y2K panels CPR Inst. Dispute Resolution, NYC; accredited mediator Ctr. Effective Dispute Resolution, London; approved mediator/arbitrator in intellectual property and ICANN domain name and keyword disputes World Intellectual Property Orgn., Geneva; arbitrator ICANN domain name disputes, mem. adv. com. IP panel, bd. dir., mem. transfer dispute resolution policy panel Nat. Arbitration Forum, Mpls.; arbitrator, mediator US Dist. Ct. (ea. dist.) NY; arbitrator London Ct. Internat. Arbitration, N.Am. Coun., Internat. C. of C., Paris, Internat. Ct. Arbitration, US Coun. Internat. Bus., NYC, Fin. Industry Regulatory Authority, NY Stock Exch., NYC; mediator NJ Superior Ct.; master Justice Marie Garibaldi Am. Inn of Ct. for Alternative Dispute Resolution; mem. CPR arbitration com. Ctr. Dispute Resolution, mem. patent commn., mem. e-discovery com.; chartered arbitrator Chartered Inst. Arbitrators, London; arbitrator Comml. and Tech. Panels, Am. Arbitration Assn., Internat. Ctr. Dispute Resolution, NYC, Australian Ctr. Internat. Comml. Arbitration, Sydney, Asian Domain Name Dispute Resolution Ctr., Hong Kong Internat. Arbitration Ctr.; fellow Australian Ctr. Internat. Comml. Arbitration; presenter in field US and abroad. Contbr. articles to profl. jours. Mem. Sch. Budget Adv. Com., Rumson, NJ, 1981—85, Zoning Bd. Adjustment, Rumson, 1988—93. Named AV rated attorney. Fellow: Coll. Comml. Arbitrators, Australian Ctr. Internat. Comml. Arbitration (arbitrator), Chartered Inst. Arbitrators; mem.: AIPPI, NY State Bar Assn., Internat. Bar Assn., Am. Arbitration Assn. (nat. patent adv. coun.), Assn. Fed. Bar N.J., Fed. Bar Assn., N.J. Intellectual Property Law Assn., Am. Intellectual Property Law Assn. Home: 15 Holly Tree Ln Rumson NJ 07760-1950 Office: Michaelson Associates 1161 Broad St Ste 118 Shrewsbury NJ 07702 Office Phone: 732-542-7800. Office Fax: 732-542-7858. Business E-Mail: pete@mandw.com.

MICHAILOFF, IAN ROBERT, real estate broker, land use planner; b. Santa Clara, Calif., Sept. 13, 1973; s. Michael Gregory and Victoria Jean Michailoff; m. Robyn Michelle Clark, Mar. 10, 2001; children: Raiden Anthony, Jennika Simone. Diploma in bus. mgmt. info. sys. and acctg., Calif. State U., Sacramento, 1998; Microsoft Cert. Sys. Engr., HEALD, Calif., 1999. Cert. Real Estate Broker Calif., 2004. Broker, founder HouseLynk Realty & Loan, Stockton, Calif., 2003—, RentLynk Property Mgmt., Stockton, Calif., 2003—. Land developer DYB, LLC, Stockton, Calif., 2004—. Sgt. US Army, 1991—95. Decorated Airborne Jump Wings U.S. Army, Ranger Tab, Can. Jump Wings, Jordanian Jump Wings. Mem.: Santa Clara Assn. Realtors (licentiate), Lodi Assn. Realtors (licentiate), Calif. Assn. Realtors (licentiate), Nat. Assn. Realtors (licentiate), Stockton C. of C. (assoc.), Stockton Golf & Country Club (licentiate), Gracie Jiu Jitsu (assoc.), Sigma Phi Epsilon Frat. (assoc.; social chmn. 1997—98). Conservative. Roman Catholic. Avocations: golf, Ju Jitsu, kickboxing, renovating properties. Office: House-Lynk Realty & Loan 1904 Country Club Blvd Stockton CA 95204 Home: 1466 Middlefield Ave Stockton CA 95204-4925 Business E-Mail: robm@houselynk.com.

MICHALAK, JANET CAROL, childhood education educator, coordinator; b. Buffalo, Mar. 22, 1949; d. Theodore and Thelma Ruth (Roesch) Vukovic; m. Gerald Paul Michalak, June 19, 1971; children: Nathan, Justin. BS in Edn., SUNY Coll. at Buffalo, Buffalo, 1970; MS in Edn., SUNY, Buffalo, 1971, EdD, 1981. Cert. tchr. nursery, kindergarten, grades 1-6, reading tchr., English tchr. grades 7-12, N.Y. Reading tchr. Tonawanda (N.Y.) Sch. System, 1971-80; instr. Niagara County C.C., Sanborn, N.Y., 1980-82, asst. prof., 1982-85, assoc. prof., 1985-91, prof., 1991—2004, prof. emeritus, 2004, coord., prof. childhood edn. Adj. lectr. SUNY, Buffalo, 1990—91. Recipient Pres.'s award for Excellence in Teaching, Niagara County C.C., 1990, Nat. Inst. for Staff & Orgnl. Devel. Excellence award, 1991, SUNY Chancellor's award for Excellence in Teaching, 1991. Mem. Coll. Reading Assn., Internat. Reading Assn., N.Y. Coll. Learning Skills Assn., Niagara Frontier Reading Coun. (bd. dirs. 1986-88, 97—). Republican. Avocation: reading. Office: Niagara County CC 3111 Saunders Settlement Rd Sanborn NY 14132-9487 Home: 90 Lord Byron Ln Buffalo NY 14221-1997

MICHALAK, JO-ANN, library director; Grad., Syracuse U., U. Ill., Columbia U. Libr. U. Ill., Ind. U., Columbia U., U. Pitts.; now dir. Tisch Libr. Tufts. U., Medford, Mass. Pres. Boston Libr. Consortium, 2006—; mem. adv. bd. for univ. librs. Carnegie Mellon U., 2006—; bd. dirs. NELINET. Mem.: Soc. For Scholarly Pub. Office: Tisch Libr Tufts U 35 Professors Row Medford MA 02155 Office Phone: 617-627-3345. Office Fax: 617-627-3002. E-mail: jo-ann.michalak@tufts.edu.

MICHALAK, MICHAEL WALTER, United States Ambassador to Vietnam; b. Detroit; married; 3 children. BS in Physics, Oakland U., Rochester, Mich., 1968; MS in Physics, Cath. U., Washington; MPA, Harvard U., Cambridge, Mass. Various positions in Tokyo, Sydney, Islamabad, Pakistan and Beijing US Dept. State, various positions in Bur. East Asian and Pacific Affairs, Office for Japan and the Office of Chinese and Mongolian Affairs Washington, US sr. ofcl. to Asia-Pacific Econ. Cooperation, Bur. East Asia Pacific Affairs, 2005—07, US amb. to Vietnam Hanoi, 2007—. Recipient Disting. Alumni Svc. award, Oakland U., 1968. Office: DOS Amb 4550 Hanoi Pl Washington DC 20521-4550*

MICHALAK, SARAH C., university librarian; BA in English, Univ. Calif. Riverside, 1969; MLS, UCLA, 1970. Previous head Bio-Agrl. Dept. Univ. Calif. Riverside; previous libr. Univ. Wash., Seattle; dir. J. Willard Marriot Libr. Univ. UT, Salt Lake City, 1995—2004; univ. libr. and assoc. provost for univ. libraries U. NC, Chapel Hill, 2004—. Mem.: Scholarly Pub. and Academic Resources Coalition (steering com.), Libr. Adminstrn. and Mgmt. Assn., Assn. Rsch. Libr. Office: Univ NC Walter Clinton Jackson Library PO Box 26170 Greensboro NC 27402 Office Phone: 919-962-1301. E-mail: smichala@email.unc.edu.

MICHALIK, JOHN JAMES, legal association administrator; b. Bemidji, Minn., Aug. 1, 1945; m. Diane Marie Olson, Dec. 21, 1968; children: Matthew John, Nicole, Shane. BA, U. Minn., 1967, JD, 1970. Legal editor Lawyers Coop. Pub. Co., Rochester, NY, 1970—75; dir. continuing legal edn. Wash. State Bar Assn., Seattle, 1975—81, exec. dir., 1981—91; asst. dean devel. and cmty. rels. Sch. Law U. Wash., 1991—95; dir., CEO Assn. Legal Adminstrs., Lincolnshire, Ill., 1995—. Fellow: Coll. Law Practice Mgmt.; mem.: Nat. Trust Hist. Preservation, Am. Mgmt. Assn., Am. Soc. Assn. Execs. Lutheran. Office: Assn Legal Adminstrs 75 Tri-State Internat Ctr # 222 Lincolnshire IL 60069-4435 Home Phone: 847-821-9533; Office Phone: 847-267-1360. Business E-Mail: jmichalik@alanet.org.

MICHALSKI, PAUL PETER, lawyer; b. Amsterdam, NY, Aug. 11, 1961; s. Steven Robert (stepfather) and Marilyn Lee (Januszewski) Cevera; m. Elizabeth L. Butterworth, 1994; children: James, Anne. AB, Harvard U., 1983, JD, 1986. Bar: Mass. 1986, N.Y. 1987. Assoc. Cravath, Swaine & Moore LLP, NYC, 1986-94, ptnr., corp., 1994—2009. Adv. bd. Capital Markets Law Jour. Chmn. Benjamin Franklin Ho. Found., NYC., James Beard Found. fellow. Mem. ABA, Internat. Bar Assn., N.Y. State Bar Assn., City of N.Y. Bar Assn., The Blue Hill Troupe Ltd., Mosimann's Club, Harvard Club, New Canaan Soc. (dir., v.p.Roton Point Assn., Royal Soc. for Encouragement of Arts (Mfg. and Commerce fellow), NY Law Inst. (exec. com.), ABA Internat. Security & Capital Mkt. Cmty (vice chair). Republican. Office: 371 Middlesex Rd Darien CT 06820 Office Fax: 203-662-9551.

MICHALSKI, THOMAS JOSEPH, writer, political activist, retired city planner, developer; b. Waukesha, Wis., Jan. 28, 1933; s. Thomas and Anna (Benca) M. B.Arch., U. Mich., 1956, M.City Planning, 1959; postgrad., Magdalene Coll., U. Cambridge, Eng., 1988—89. Urban renewal planner City of Milw., 1956-57; land planner, urban designer Baltimore County, Md., 1959-60; planning cons. City of N.Y., 1961-77; project mgr. Yanbu Indsl. City for Royal Commn., Saudi Arabia, 1980-83; cons. UN Ctr. for Human Settlements, Habitat Nairobi, Kenya, 1984—2005; bd. Community Housing Initiative Trust, 1993-98; faculty U. Mich., 1994; bd. dirs., cons. EMTEL, Inc., 2000—02; ret., 2005. Mem. faculty NYU, 1965-66, CUNY, 1970-71, Rollins Coll., 1992-96; town planning cons. new town in Iran, 1977; mem. Community Bd. 8, N.Y.C., 1972-76, chmn. landmarks com.; cons. Islamic Devel. Bank, 1989-95, Fla. Solar Energy Ctr. Affordable Living Conf., 1991. Author: In Search of Purpose: Essays on Planning the Human Environment, 1961, Human Values and the Emerging City, 1967 Founding mem. Friends of Cen. Park; 1000 Friends of Fla., 1987-98; pres. Brevard 21 Inc., 1988-2000; bd. govs. Coll. Architecture and Urban Planning, U. Mich., 1984-88; bd. ACLU, 1993—. Wis. Architects Found. scholar, 1953-56; Vincent Astor Found. grantee, 1971, World Wildlife Fund Successful Communities grantee, 1991. Fellow Am. Hort. Soc.; mem. Am. Planning Assn. (charter), Am. Inst. Cert. Planners, Royal Town Planning Inst., Town and Country Planning Assn., Internat. Fedn. Housing and Planning, Nat. Trust for Historic Preservation, Wis. Soc. Archtl. Historians, Mich. Urban Planning Alumni Soc. (bd. dirs. 1984-88), Audubon Soc. Fla. (chmn. conservation com. 1987-91), Assn. for Asian Studies, Worldwatch Inst., English-Speaking Union (London), Brevard County (Fla.) Democratic exec. com., So. Poverty Law Ctr., U. Mich. Club (N.Y.C.), Sierra Club, Delta Chi (Morrey Outstanding Alumnus award 1984), Cambridge in Am. and Magdalene in Am. Democrat. Roman Catholic. Home: 1925 Greenway Dr Apt 11 Melbourne FL 32901-4446 E-mail: tjmichalski1@aol.com. *The educated person prepares mightily to do something constructive about that which is displeasing, to sustain that which is good, and to discriminate the one from the other.*

MICHALSON, GORDON E., JR., academic administrator; BA magna cum laude, Yale U., 1970; RelM in Philosophy of Religion/Theology, Claremont Sch. Theology, 1972; PhD in Philosophy of Religion, Princeton U., 1976. Tchg. asst. Princeton U., 1974—75; from instr. to asst. prof. Dept. Religion Davidson Coll., 1975—79; from asst. prof. to prof. Oberlin Coll., 1977—92, dept. chair, 1989—92; dean, warden New Coll., U. So. Fla., 1992—97, prof. humanities, 1992—; acting pres. New Coll. of Fla., Sarasota, 2001, pres., 2001—. Bd. trustees Leroy Collins Inst. Pub. Policy, 2004. Author: Kant and the Problem of God, 1999; contbr. articles to profl. jours. Mem.: Am. Theol. Soc. Office: New Coll of Fla 5800 Bay Shore Rd Sarasota FL 34243-2109 Office Phone: 941-487-4100.

MICHAUD, GEORGES JOSEPH, physics professor; b. Quebec, Can., Apr. 30, 1940; s. Marie-Louis and Isabelle (St. Laurent) M.; m. Denise Lemieux, June 25, 1966. BA, U. Laval, Que., 1961, BSc, 1965; PhD, Calif. Tech. Inst., Pasadena, 1970. Prof. U. Montreal, Canada, 1969—2005, prof. emeritus, 2005—; dir. Ctr. Rsch. en Calcul Appliqué, 1992-96, assoc. dean of grad. studies, 1997-2000. Recipient Steacie prize NRC, 1980, Medaille Janssen, Acad. Scis., Paris, 1982, Prix Vincent, ACFAS, 1979; Killam fellow Conseil des Arts, 1987-89. Mem.: Royal Soc. Can., Internat. Astron. Union, Can. Astron. Soc. (Beals award 2006), Am. Astron. Soc. Office Phone: 514-343-6672. Business E-Mail: michaudg@astro.umontreal.ca.

MICHAUD, MICHAEL HERMAN, United States Representative from Maine; b. Millinocket, Maine, Jan. 18, 1955; s. James Leroy and Jean (Morrow) M. Grad., Schenck H.S., 1973; student, U. Maine, 1979. Papermaker Gt. No. Paper Co., 1973-80, mem. staff finishing dept., 1981—; mem. dist. 134 Maine Ho. Reps., Augusta, 1980—94, mem. regional conf. task force on environment, chmn. energy and natural resources com., spkr. pro tem, chmn. appropriations and fin. affairs com., mem. legis. svc. com.; mem. Dist. 3 Maine Senate, Augusta, 1994—2002, pres. pro tem.; mem. US Congress from 2nd Maine dist., 2003—. Mem. com. Eastmill Fed. Credit Union, 1979—; area coord. Merril for Gov. campaign, 1978; v.p. Maine Young Dems., 1978-80, del. state conv., 1980, 82, 84, del. nat. conv., 1979. Mem. Nat. Conf. State Legislators, Katahdin Friend of Retarded Children Assn., East Br. Snow Rovers, KC. Democrat. Office: US Ho Reps 437 Cannon Ho Office Bldg Washington DC 20515-1902 also: Great Northern Paper Co Bowater Main St East Millinocket ME 04430 Home: 3 Birch St East Millinocket ME 04430-1001*

MICHAUD-DANIEL, DIDIER, manufacturing executive; Grad. in Bus. Mgmt., Ecole Superieure de Commerce; mgmt. grad., INSEAD. Positions in svc. sales and sales, br., and field support mgmt. Otis France, 1981—91, field ops. dir., 1991—92, Paris field and sales ops. dir., 1992—98, dep. gen. mgr. ops., 1998—2001; mng. dir. Otis UK and Ireland, 2001—04; pres. UK and Ctrl. Europe area Otis Elevator Co., 2004—08, pres., 2008—. Mem. bd. trustees Kingswood-Oxford Sch., West Hartford, Conn. Office: Otis Elevator Co 10 Farm Springs Rd Farmington CT 06032 Office Phone: 860-676-5992.

MICHAUDON, ANDRÉ FRANCISQUE, physicist; b. Cavaillon, Vaucluse, France, May 14, 1929; s. Maurice Louis and Jeanne Francoise (Chatal) Michaudon; children: Claire Hello, Helene Caron. Engring. degree, Ecole Supérieure Ingenieurs Arts et Métiers, Paris, 1951, Ecole Supérieure Electricite, 1953; DS, Sorbonne, 1964. Rsch. engr. Le Materiel Teléphonique, Boulogne, France, 1954-56; group leader Commissariat à Energie Atomique, Cen Saclay, France, 1956-64, 65-72, div. head Bruyeres le Chalel, France, 1972-79, dept. dept. head Limeil, France, 1979-83; theorist MIT, Cambridge, 1964-65; French co-dir. Inst. Laue Langevin, Grenoble, France, 1983-89; prof. Inst. Nat. des Scis. et Techniques Nucléaires, Saclay, Orsay, France, 1969-84; sr. sci. adv. Los Alamos (N.Mex.) Nat. Lab., 1989. Mem. exec. coun. European Sci. Found., Strasbourg, France, 1987—90; mem. adv. coun. Census Bur. for Nuc. Measurements, European Union, Geel, Belgium, 1990—95; cons. Orgn. for Econ. Cooperation and Devel., Paris, 1989—92. Contbr. articles to profl. jours.; author (author, editor): (book) Nuclear Fission, 1981; editor (co-gen. editor): Neutron Sources, 1983, Neutron Radiative Capture, 1984, Probability & Statistics, 1991. Lt. French Navy, 1953-54. Recipient written congratulations, Minister of the Navy, France, 1954, award, Acad. des Scis., Paris, 1980; named knight, Order of Merit, Paris, 1984. Fellow: Am. Nuclear Soc., Am. Phys. Soc.; mem.: N.Y. Acad. Scis., Francaise de Physique, Cosmos Club. Avocations: music, tennis, skiing, golf, hiking. Home: 333 Otero St Unit 6 Santa Fe NM 87501-6212 Office: Los Alamos Nat Lab Lansce Ns Ms H 855 Los Alamos NM 87545-0001 Home Phone: 505-820-0944; Office Phone: 505-665-2883. Personal E-mail: amichaudon@aol.com. Business E-Mail: michaudon@lanl.gov.

MICHEL, ALIX JAMES, President of Seychelles; b. Seychelles, Aug. 16, 1944; Student, tchr. tng. coll., Victoria, Seychelles, 1960-61. Tchr. primary and secondary schs., Anse Boileau, 1960-61; with Cable & Wireless Ltd., 1961-71, Hotel des Seychelles, 1971-74; min. adminstrn. and info., 1977-79; editor ofcl. party newspaper The People, 1971—; min. edn. and info. Govt. Seychelles, 1979-89, min. finance and comm., min. def., now min. fin., comm., def. and environment); v.p., 1996—; Pres. Republic of Seychelles, 2004—06, 2006—; Minister of Defense, Minister of Legal Affairs, Minister of Police, Minister for Internal Affairs, Minister for Risk and Disaster Mgmt., 2006—. Mem. exec. com. Seychelles People's United Party, 1974; dep. sec.-gen. Seychelles People's Progressive Front, 1984-94, sec.-gen., 1994—. Recipient Outstanding Civilian Svc. medal U.S. Army, 1995. Office: State House PO Box 55 Victoria Mahe Seychelles

MICHEL, BOB (ROBERT HENRY MICHEL), lobbyist, former United States Representative from Illinois; b. Peoria, Ill., Mar. 2, 1923; m. Corinne Woodruff, Dec. 26, 1948 (dec. Mar. 26, 2008); children: Scott, Bruce, Laurie, Robin. BS, Bradley U., Peoria, 1948. Adminstrv. asst. to Rep. Harold Velde US Congress, 1948—56; mem. US Congress from 18th Ill. dist., 1957—95, minority whip, 1975—81, minority leader, 1981—95; chmn. Nat. Republican Congressional Com., 1973—74; sr. adv. Hogan & Hartson LLP, Washington, 1995—. Bd. dirs. Dirksen Congl. Ctr., Pekin, Ill., BNFL, Inc. Bd. trustees Bradley U.; del. Rep. Nat. Convention, 1960—2000, permanent chmn., 1984, 1988, 1992. With 39th inf. rgt. US Army, 1943—46, England, France, Belgium, Germany. Decorated Purple Heart, Bronze Star (2); recipient Presdl. Citizens Medal, 1989, Presdl. Medal of Freedom, The White House, 1994, Congl. Disting. Svc. Medal, US Ho. of Reps., 2003, Campaign for Med. Rsch. award, NIH, Edwin C. Whitehead award for med. rsch. advocacy, Research!America, Nat. Security Leadership award, Reserve Officers Assn./Am. Security Coun., Jefferson award, Am. Inst. Pub. Svc., Spirit of Enterprise award, US C. of C., Bryce Harlow Found. award, Lincoln Acad. Ill. Laureate award, Alumnus award, Bradley U., 1961. Mem.: Capitol Hill Club (bd. dirs.). Republican. Office: Hogan & Hartson LLP 555 13th St NW Washington DC 20004 Office Phone: 202-637-5804. Office Fax: 202-637-5910. Business E-Mail: rhmichel@hhlaw.com.*

MICHEL, DONALD CHARLES, editor; b. Ventura, Calif., Nov. 17, 1935; s. Charles J. and Esther Caroline (Heilert) M.; m. Loretta Perron, May 4, 1963; children: Edwin, Robert, Christopher. BA, UCLA, 1958, MS, 1959. Editor San Fernando (Calif.) Sun, 1958-60; successively reporter, weekend editor, mng. editor Valley Times Today, North Hollywood, Calif., 1960-63; feature editor Houston Chronicle, 1963-68; asst. mng. editor features Chgo. Daily News, 1968-77; exec. v.p., editor Chgo. Tribune-N.Y. News Syndicate, 1977-84; v.p. adminstrn. and editl. devel. L.A. Times Syndicate, 1984-93, dir. book devel., 1993-97; cons. LA. Times Syndicate, 1998-99; ret. Photo exhbn., Sedona, 2001; founder DLM Images, 2003. Home: 3000 Adornos Way Burbank CA 91504-1609 Personal E-mail: donmichel@charter.net.

MICHEL, GEORGE FREDERICK, psychology professor, researcher; s. George Frederick and Viola Michel; m. Theresa Lillian Williams, Aug. 26, 2001; 1 child, Jennifer Lynn; m. Celia Lanell Moore, Apr. 8, 1967 (div. Mar. 20, 1995). PhD, Rutgers U., Newark, 1972. Asst. prof. psychology Boston U., 1972—77; vis. asst. prof. psychology U. Mass., Boston, 1977—78; NICHHD postdoc. fellow Children's Hosp. Med. Ctr., Boston, 1978—80, preceptor, 1980—88; officer Harvard U., Cambridge, Mass., 1981—93; prof. psychology DePaul U., Chgo., 1988—2004; head psychology U. NC Greensboro, 2004—. NICHHD Rsch. grant, NIH, 1987—91, Rsch. grant, NSF, 2007—. Fellow: APA; mem.: Internat. Soc. Devel. Psychobiology (pres. 2005—06). Independent. Avocations: dance, travel, reading, movies.

MICHEL, JESSE STEVEN, psychology professor; b. Cresco, Iowa, Jan. 2, 1977; s. George and Deanna Michel; m. Kristina Jung, Jan. 26, 2007; 1 child, Fritz. BA, U. Minn., Twin Cities, 2001; PhD, Wayne State U., Detroit, 2007; postdoc, Mich. State U., East Lansing, 2007—08. Vis. asst. prof. Mich. State U., 2007—08; asst. prof. Fla. Internat. U., Miami, 2008—. Consulting editor Jour. Psychology, 2009—. Contbr. chapters to books, articles to profl jours. on psychology. Mem.: APA, Assn. Psychol. Sci., Acad. Mgmt. Office: Fla Internat Univ 11200 SW 8th St DM 256 Miami FL 33199

MICHEL, MARY ANN KEDZUF, retired nursing educator; b. Evergreen Park, Ill., June 1, 1939; d. John Roman and Mary Kedzuf; m. Jean Paul Michel, 1974. Diploma in nursing, Little Company of Mary Hosp., Evergreen Park, 1960; BSN, Loyola U., Chgo., 1964; MS, No. Ill. U., 1968, EdD, 1971. Staff nurse Little Co. of Mary Hosp., 1960-64; instr. Little Co. of Mary Hosp. Sch. Nursing, 1964-67, No. Ill. U., DeKalb, 1968-69, asst. prof., 1969-71; chmn. dept. nursing U. Nev., Las Vegas, 1971-73, prof. nursing, 1975—2008, dean Coll. Health Scis., 1973-90, prof. emeritus coll. health scis., 2006—08; pres. PERC, Inc.; mgmt. cons., 1993—95; eneritas dean Coll. Health Professions. Mgmt. cons. Nev. Donor Network, 1993; mem. So. Nev. Health Manpower Task Force, 1975; mem. manpower com. Plan Devel. Commn., Clark County Health Sys. Agy., 1977-79, mem. governing body, 1981-86; mem. Nev. Health Coordinating Coun., Western Inst. Nursing, 1971-85; mem. coordinating com. assembly instnl. adminstrs. dept. allied health edn. and accreditation AMA, 1985-88; mem. bd. advisors So. Nev. Vocat. Tech. Ctr., 1976-80; sec.-treas. Nev. Donor Network, 1988-89, chmn. bd., 1988-90. Contbr. articles to profl. jours. Trustee Desert Spring Hosp., Las Vegas, 1976-85; bd. dirs. Nathan Adelson Hospice, 1982-88, Bridge Counseling Assocs., 1982, Everywoman's Ctr., 1984-86; chair Nev. Commn. on Nursing Edn., 1972-73, Nursing Articulation Com., 1972-73, Yr. of Nurse Com., 1978; moderator Invitational Conf. Continuing Edn., Am. Soc. Allied Health Professions, 1978; mgmt. cons. Nev. Donor Network, 1994-95, Donor Organ Recovery Svc., Transplant Recipient Internat. Orgn., SW Eye Bank, SW Tissue Bank. Named Outstanding Alumnus, Loyola U., 1983; NIMH fellow, 1967-68. Fellow Am. Soc. Allied Health Professions, 1991, (chair nat. resolutions com. 1981-84, treas. 1988-90, sec's. award com. 1982-83, 92-93, nat. by-laws com. 1985, conv. chair 1987); mem. AAUP, Am. Nurses Assn., Nev. Nurses Assn. (dir. 1975-77, treas. 1977-79, conv. chair 1978), So. Nev. Area Health Edn. Coun., Western Health Deans (co-organizer 1985, chair, 1988-90), Nat. League Nursing, Nev. Heart Assn., So. Nev. Mem. Hosps. (nursing recruitment com. 1981-83, mem. nursing practice com. 1983-85), Las Vegas C. of C. (named Woman of Yr. Edn.) 1988, Slovak Catholic Sokols, Phi Kappa Phi (chpt. sec. 1981-83, pres.-elect 1983, pres. 1984, v.p. Western region 1989-95, editl. bd. jour. Nat. Forum 1989-93), Alpha Beta Gamma (hon.), Sigma Theta Tau, Zeta Kappa. Personal E-mail: m.a.michel@worldnet.att.net.

MICHEL, PAUL REDMOND, federal judge; b. Phila., Feb. 3, 1941; s. Lincoln M. and Dorothy (Kelley) Michel; m. Brooke England, 2004; children: Sarah Elizabeth, Margaret Kelley. BA, Williams Coll., 1963; JD, U. Va., 1966. Bar: Pa. 1967, US Supreme Ct. 1970. Asst. dist. atty. Dist. Atty.'s Office, Phila., 1967—71, dep. dist. atty. investigations, 1972—74; asst. spl. prosecutor Watergate investigation US Dept. Justice, Washington, 1974—75, dep. chief pub. integrity sect., Criminal div. and prosecutor "Koreagate" investigation, 1976—78, assoc. dep. atty. gen., 1978—81; asst. counsel intelligence com. US Senate, 1975—76, counsel and adminstrv. asst. to Sen. Arlen Specter, 1981—88; judge US Ct. Appeals (Fed. cir.), Washington, 1988—2004, chief judge, 2004—. Instr. appellate practice and procedure George Washington U. Nat. Law Ctr., 1991—2002. 2d lt. USAR, 1966—72. Office: US Ct Appeals Fed Cir 717 Madison Pl NW Washington DC 20439 Office Phone: 202-633-6297. E-mail: michelp@cafc.uscourts.gov.*

MICHEL, VERLYN LYLE, mayor, consultant; b. Nampa, Idaho, Sept. 25, 1938; s. Wolford and Ruth Alleta (Kimes) Michel; m. Betty Vernette, Nov. 1, 1974; children: Verlyn Lyle II, Eric Ryan. Student, Foothill Coll., Los Altos Hills, Calif., 1969—70, De Anza Coll., Cupertino, Calif., 1969—70, Lassen County Coll., Susanville, Calif., 1971. Com. mem. USAF/State of Idaho, Mountain Home AFB, 1963—67; cons. State Senator Hansen, Mountain Home AFB, 1964—66, Amb. Perez from Peru, Hemet, Calif., 1990; mayor Town of Quartzsite, Ariz., 2000—; com. leader Ariz. Western Coll., Yuma, 2004. Past pres. Western Ariz. Coun. Govts.; mem. exec. com. Western Ariz. Econ. Devel. Dist., Ariz. League Cities and Towns, Pandemia Flu H5N1; mem. com. APS Focused Future; mem. adv. com. Ariz. Western Coll. Staff sgt. USAF, 1963—67. Recipient cert. appreciation, DAV, Good Conduct medal, US Army, Nat. Def. Svc. medal, Armed Forces Res. medal, Presdl. Unit citation, Outstanding Unit award, USAF, Good Conduct medal, Longevity Svc. award ribbon, Tng. Ribbon, Cold War medal. Mem.: Toastmasters, Disabled Vets. Assn., Quartzsite Vets. Assn., Quartzsite Basin Model RR (pres. 2004). Republican. Baptist. Avocations: amateur radio, model railroads, woodworking. Home: PO Box 1353 Quartzsite AZ 85346 Office: Town of Quartzsite PO Box 2812 Quartzsite AZ 85346 Office Phone: 928-927-4333. Fax: 928-927-4400. Business E-Mail: mayormike@ci.quartzsite.az.us.

MICHELASSI, FABRIZIO, surgeon; b. Pisa, Italy, Nov. 5, 1950; MD summa cum laude, U. Pisa, Italy, 1975. Diplomate Am. Bd. Surgery; lic. NY, Ill. Intern NYU Med. Ctr., 1977-81, resident gen. surgery, 1983-84, instr. surgery, 1983—84, tchg. asst. surgery, 1977—81; rsch. fellow Mass. Gen. Hosp., Harvard U., Boston, 1981-83; asst. prof. surgery U. Chgo., 1984-90, attending surgeon, 1984—2004, mem. cancer rsch. ctr., 1985—91, assoc. prof. surgery, 1990-95, consulting surgeon, Louis A. Weiss meml. hosp., 1990—2004, prof. surgery, 1995—2004, dir., ctr. excellence minimally invasive surgery, 1999—2004, chief gen. surgery, 1994—2004, vice chmn. dept. surgery, 2000—04; Lewis Atterbury Stimson prof. surgery Weill Cornell Med. Coll., NY, 2004—, chmn. dept. surgery, 2004—, bd. overseers, faculty rep., 2007—, trustee, alumni coun., 2008—. Surgeon-in-chief NY Presbyn. Hosp., 2004-, chmn. operating rm. com., 2004-; lectr. in field. Contbr. articles to profl. jours., chapter to books; participant in films. Recipient Andrew W. Mellon Found. award, 1985, 86, Am. Cancer Soc. Devel. award, 1987-90, Silver medal U. Bologna, 1988, Disting. Leadership award, Crohn & Colitis Found. America, 1996, Best Poster Presentation award U. Chgo., 1995; honoree Crohn's and Colitis Found. Am., 1996; named one of Best Drs. in America, 2007, Top Drs., Chgo. Mag. Surgery, 1997, 98, 99, Castle Connolly Med. Ltd., 2007, NY Super Drs. NY Times Mag., 2008-09. Fellow ACS (mem. com. on med. motion pictures 1992-99, mem. exec. com. on med. motion pictures 1993-96, councilor Met. Chgo. chpt. 1991-94); mem. Acad. Surg. Rsch., Am. Assn. Cancer Rsch., Am. Bd. Surgery (dir. & rep. CSA 20069-), Am. Coll. Surgeons (mem. ocology group colozected exec. com. 1998—, mem. com. med. motion pictures, 1992-2002, mem. exec. com., 1993-96, adv. coun. gen. surgery 2003-), Am. Gastroenterologic Assn., Am. Pancreatic Assn., Am. Radium Soc., Soc. Surg. Oncology (various coms.), Soc. Univ. Surgeons (mem. com. on publs. 1991-94), Spencer Surg. Soc. (sec. 1990-91, pres. 1991-92), U. Chgo. Surg. Soc., Western Surg. Assn. (mem. program com. 1993-95, chmn. program com. 1995-96, chmn. com. on local arrangements for 1995 meeting, recorder 1997—), Am. Soc. Clin. Oncology, Am. Soc. Colon and Rectal Surgeons, Am. Soc. Liver and Pancreas Surgery, Am. Surg. Assn. (ASA rep. to ACS adv. coun. gen. surgery 2003-06), Assn. Acad. Surgery, Ctrl. Surg. Assn. (mem. membership com. 1993-96, 2000-03, mem. local arrangement com. 1994, mem. nominating com. 1997, sec. 2000—), Ill. Surg. Soc. (co-chmn. com. on local arrangements for the spring 1992 meeting, sec. 1993-96, treas. 1993-96, v.p. elect, 1989-99, v.p., 1999—, pres. elect 2000—), Chgo. Surg. Soc. (mem. program com. 1995, chmn. program com. 1996-99,ex-officio mem. 2005-06, treas. 2006-07), Collegium Internat. Chirurgiae Digestivae (mem. program com. 15th World Congress), Crohn's and Colitis Found. Am., European Soc. for Surg. Rsch., internat. Assn. Pancreatology, Internat. Gastro-Surg. Club (mem. adv. bd. 1990—, mem. clin. trials com. 1990—, mem. coun. of the exec. com. 1991—, internat. sci. com. 4th internat. meeting 1993), World Assn. Hepato-Pancreatico-Biliary Surgery, Internat. Hepato-Pancreatico-Biliary Assn., Pancreas Club (mem. planning session com. 1994, adv. coun. mem. 1995—), Soc. for Clin. Trials, Soc. for Surgery of the Alimentary Tract, Sigma Xi. Achievements include development of insight in the surgical treatment of pancreatic and colorectal cancers, ulcerative colitis and Crohn's disease; new techniques that ensure better outcomes and improved quality of life for patients with rectal cancer and ulcerative colitis. Office: Weill Cornell Med Coll Dept Surgery 525 East 68th St Rm F739 PO Box 129 New York NY 10065 Office Phone: 212-746-5144, 212-746-6006. Office Fax: 212-746-8753. Business E-Mail: fam2006@med.cornell.edu.

MICHELBERGER, PAL, mechanical engineer, educator; b. Vecses, Hungary, Feb. 4, 1930; s. Pal and Maria (Komaromy) M.; m. Ilona Torma, Sept. 21, 1957; children: Agnes, Pal. MSc in Mech. Engring., Tech. U., Budapest, Hungary, 1952, PhD, 1960; DSc, Hungarian Acad. Scis., Budapest, 1970. Asst. Tech. U., 1952-56, prof., 1968—, dean, 1985-90, pres., 1990-94; design engr., chief designer Ikarus Bus Factory, Budapest, 1956-63; dept. leader, tech. dir. Trust Automobile Industry, Budapest, 1963-68. Chmn. bd. Hungarocamion Ltd., Budapest, 1992-94; chair supervisory com. Bakonymüvek Ltd., Veszprem, 1992-95; bd. dirs. Ikarus Bus Factory Ltd. Mem. editl. bd. Vehicle System Dynamics, 1984—. Capt. Hungarian Air Force, 1950—56. Recipient Pattantyus prize Hungarian Soc. Mech. Engring., 1973, Eotvos L prize Min. Industry, 1994, Szechenyi prize Pres. Hungarian Republic, 1995, Mem. Internat. Fedn. Automotive Engrs. Soc., Hungarian Soc. Mech. Engring., Verein Deutsch Eng., Hungarian Acad. Scis. (v.p. 1993—). Roman Catholic. Office: Tech U Budapest Muegyetem RKP3 H1111 Budapest Hungary Home Phone: 36 23 422 668. Business E-Mail: jvkt@kme.bme.hu.

MICHELE, CHRISETTE (CHRISETTE MICHELE PAYNE), singer; b. Central Islip, NY, Dec. 2, 1982; Attended, Five Towns Coll., Dix Hills, NY. Signed to Island Def Jam Music Group, 2007. Singer: (albums) I Am, 2007, (songs) (with will.i.am) Be OK, 2007 (Grammy award for Best Urban/Alternative Performance, 2009). Office: Trea Day Mgmt and Publicity 11325 Vedrines Dr Ste A-1 Alpharetta GA 30022*

MICHELINI, SYLVIA HAMILTON, auditor; b. Decatur, Ala., May 16, 1946; d. George Borum and Dorothy Rose (Swatzell) Hamilton; m. H. Stewart Michelini, June 4, 1964; children: Stewart Anthony, Cynthia Leigh. BSBA summa cum laude, U. Ala., Huntsville, 1987. CPA, Ala.; cert. govt. fin. mgr., fraud examiner. Acct. Ray McCay, CPA, Huntsville, 1987-88; auditor Def. Contract Audit Agy., Huntsville, 1989-92; auditor-office of inspector general George C. Marshall Space Flight, Center, Ala., 1992-97; contr. Hamilton Hotels, Inc., 1997-2001; ret.; pres. HiCotton, 2009—. Exec. bd. Decatur City PTA, 1976-78; pres., v.p. Elem. Sch. PTA, Decatur, 1977-79; leader Girl Scouts U.S. and Cub Scouts, Decatur, 1972-77; active local ARC, 1973-77; pres., chmn. bd. High Cotton Co. Mem.: AAUW (chpt. treas. 1988—90), AICPA, Inst. Mgmt. Accts. (v.p. comm., dir. program book 1991—94, Dixie coun. dir. newsletters 1992—93, dir. ednl. programs 1992—93, 1993—94, nat. com. ethics 1990—97, nat. fin. com. 1997—98, nat. bd. dirs. 1994—97), Inst. Internal Auditors (dir. awards and recognition 1996—97, sec. 1999—2001, 2003—04), Ala. Soc. CPAs (profl. ethics com. 1993—94, govtl. acctg. and auditing com. 1994—95), Assn. Govt. Accts. (sec. 1992—93, chmn. pub. rels. 1993—94), Am. Soc. Women Accts. (chpt. treas. 1989—90, dir. chpt. devel. 1989—90), Nat. Notary Assn., Nat. Assn. Accts. (dir. cmty. svc. 1987—88, v.p. adminstrn. and fin. 1988—89, pres. 1989—90, nat. com. on ethics 1990—91), Phi Kappa Phi. Baptist. Avocations: reading, walking, sewing, research, music. Home and Office: 2801 Sylvia Dr SE Decatur AL 35603-5643 E-mail: nimi@hiway.net.

MICHELIS, MICHAEL FRANK, nephrologist; b. Bklyn., Dec. 11, 1938; s. Michael and Gisella (Gammer) M.; m. Mary Ann Wolak, July 28, 1973; children: Elizabeth Ann, Katherine Clare. BA, Columbia U., 1959; MD, George Washington U., 1963. Intern, resident Lenox Hill Hosp., NYC, 1963-65; resident Hosp. Med. Coll. Pa., Phila., 1965-67; fellow in renal disease, dept. medicine U. Pitts. Sch. Medicine, 1969-70, asst. prof. medicine, 1971-75; chief renal diagnostic unit VA Hosp., Pitts., 1971-75; asst. prof. clin. medicine NYU Med. Sch., 1975-93; assoc. prof. clin. medicine N.Y. Med. Coll., 1980-87, prof., 1987-92; assoc. prof. clin. medicine Cornell U. Med. Coll., 1992-93; prof. clin. medicine NYU Med. Coll., 1993—; dir. nephrology sect. Lenox Hill Hosp., NYC, 1975—. Spl. lectr. Georgetown U. Med. Sch., 1973-85; invited spkr., Various Med. Schs. & Socs., 2004-; lectr. Western Pa. Continuing Edn. for Physicians, 1972-75, vis. prof., 1976; mem. merit rev. bd. VA, 1973-76; cons. clin. fellowship rev. com. NIH, 1981-85; mem. exec. com. End Stage Renal Disease Network, N.Y.C., 1981-85; mem. med. adv. bd. Nat. Kidney Found. of N.Y./N.J., 1987-2001; vice-chair med. adv. bd., trustee Kidney and Urology Found. Am., 2001—, v.p., 2005—. Mem. editl. bd. Clin. Nephrology, 1979-89, Geriat. Nephrology, 1986, Jour. Geriatric Nephrology and Urology, 1989—, Am. editor, 1989-98; contbr. articles to profl. jours. Served to maj. M.C., AUS, 1967-69. Decorated Army Commendation medal; Health, Rsch. and Svcs. Found. grantee, 1970, 72, 74. Mem. AMA (invited lectr. 1973-75), ACP, Am. Fedn. Clin. Rsch., Am. Soc. Nephrology, Internat. Soc. Nephrology, Internat. Soc. for Geriatric Nephrology and Urology (pres. 1999-2003), Ctrl. Soc. Clin. Rsch. Greek Orthodox. Home: 16 Woodland Park Dr Tenafly NJ 07670-3027 Office: Lenox Hill Hosp 100 E 77th St New York NY 10075-1850 Home Phone: 201-871-3769; Office Phone: 212-988-3506. E-mail: mfmich@ix.netcom.com.

MICHEL-KERJAN, ERWANN O., finance educator; b. Paris; PhD, Polytechique, Paris, 2002. Mng. dir. Ctr. for Catastrophic Risk Mgmt., Wharton Sch., Phila., 2002—. Advisor to pres. OECD. Mem.: World Econ. Forum's Young Global Leader. Office: The Wharton School 3730 Walnut St Philadelphia PA 19104 Business E-Mail: erwannmk@wharton.upenn.edu.

MICHELLE, MILLAY KATHLEEN, sculptor; b. Dayton, Ohio, Dec. 18, 1961; d. Albert Kenneth and Joan Millay; life ptnr. Joey Orosco. AA, Ringling Sch. Art & Design, Sarasota, Fla., 1983. Pvt. practice, Sherman Oaks, Calif., 1991—. Personal E-mail: michellemillay@sbcglobal.net.

MICHELS, DALE E., physician; b. Wayne, Nebr., Mar. 24, 1948; s. R.B. and Florence A. (Peterson) M.; m. Roylene C. Gustafson, Jan. 25, 1969; children: Gretchen, Sheila, Joel. BA in Medicine, U. Nebr., Omaha, 1969, MD, 1973. Diplomate Am. Bd. Family Practice. Practicing family physician Lincoln (Nebr.) Family Med. Group, 1974—. Med. cons. Comm. Blood Bank of LCMS, Lincoln, 1992-2007; v.p. Wellmark Health Plan of Nebr., Lincoln, 1996-2000; vice-chair bd. trustees Back to the Bible, Lincoln, 1986-2004 chair bd. trustees, 2004—; sec.-treas. Family Care, PC, Lincoln, 1986-97; med. dir. Nebr. Found. for Med. Care, 2001-07; pres. EMS, Inc., 2002-07l med. dir. QualisHealth NE, 2007-. Pres. Lancaster County Med. Soc., Lincoln, 1991-92, Nebr. Acad. of Family Physicians, Omaha, 1987, Nebr. Heart Assn., 1983, Lincoln Christian Sch. Bd., Lincoln, 1990-97. Recipient J.J. Hanigan award Lincoln Lancaster Comm. Health Dept., 1994, Pub. Health Leadership awrd, 2000; named Family Physician of Yr., Nebr. Acad. Family Physicians, 1999. Mem. Am. Med. Dirs. Assn. (pres. N.E.), Nebr. Med. Dirs. Assn. (pres. 2006-07), Lancaster County Med. Soc., Nebr. Acad. Family Physicians (Family Physician of Yr. 1999), Christian Med. Dental Soc., Am. Acad. Family Physicians, Nebr. Med. Assn. (pres. 1999-2000). Republican. Avocations: flying, photography, gardening. Office: Lincoln Family Med Group PC 7441 O St Ste 400 Lincoln NE 68510-2466 Home Phone: 402-488-8760; Office Phone: 402-488-7400. E-mail: dale.michels@gmail.com.

MICHELS, DIRK, lawyer; b. Wupperful, Germany, Mar. 10, 1962; s. Wolfgang and Ingrid Michels; m. Claudia I. Olson, Aug. 2, 1995. BWL Vordiplom, U. Hamburg, Germany, 1986, JD Erstes Staatsexamen, 1988; LLM, U. San Diego, 1996. Bar: Hamburg 1992, Calif. 1996. Law clk. Hamburg Ct. Appeals, 1989-92; assoc. Huth Dietrich Hahn, Hamburg, 1992-95, Hillyer & Irwin, San Diego, 1996-2000; assoc. to ptnr. K & L Gates LLP, San Francisco, 2000—. Contbr. articles tp profl. jours. Mem. ABA (internat. sect.), Council of Bars & Law Soc. of European Cmty., German-Am. Bus. Assn. (bd. dir.), German-Am. Lawyers Assn., German-Am. Cultural Soc., Am. Coun. on Germany. Office: K&L Gates LLP 630 Hansen Way Palo Alto CA 94304 Office Phone: 650-798-6709. Business E-Mail: dirk.michels@klgates.com.

MICHELS, H. HARVEY, physicist; b. Phila., Dec. 9, 1932; s. Nicholas A. and Martha A. (Tweeddale) M.; m. Joan A. Grigger, Sept. 20, 1958 (div. Aug. 1974); children: William H., Jonathan T.; m. Nancy A. Gubbins, Oct. 24, 1975. BS, Drexel Inst. Tech., 1955; MS, U. Del., 1957, PhD, 1960. Chemist G & W.H. Corson Co., Plymouth Meeting, Pa., 1951-54, Gulf Oil, Phila., 1955; chem. physicist United Techs. Rsch. Ctr., East Hartford, Conn., 1959—; chemistry educator U. Hartford, West Hartford, Conn., 1975—; educator Rensselaer Polytechnic Inst./Hartford Grad. Ctr., Hartford, 1960-73. Fellow Joint Inst. Lab. Astrophysics, Boulder, Colo., 1970-73; vis. scholar U. Calif., Santa Barbara, 1971. Author: (books) Excited State in Chemical Physics, 1980, Methods in Computational Physics, Vol. 10, 1971, Adv. in Chemical Physics, Vol. 13, 1967; contbg. author: DNA Handbook, 1979; contbr. articles to profl. jours. Scoutmaster Boy Scouts Am., West Hartford, 1974-79. Fellow Am. Phys. Soc.; mem. Am. Chem. Soc. (councilor 1980), Conn. Acad. Sci. and Engring., Sigma Xi. Office: United Tech Rsch Ctr 400 Main St East Hartford CT 06118-1873

MICHELS, ROBERT, psychiatrist, educator; b. Chgo., Jan. 21, 1936; s. Samuel and Ann (Cooper) M.; m. Verena Sterba, Dec. 23, 1962; children: Katherine, James. BA, U. Chgo., 1953; MD, Northwestern U., 1958. Intern Mt. Sinai Hosp., NYC, 1958-59; resident in psychiatry Columbia Presbyn.-N.Y. State Psychiat. Inst., NYC, 1959-62; mem. faculty Coll. Physicians and Surgeons, Columbia U., NYC, 1964-74, assoc. prof., 1971-74; psychiatrist student health service Columbia U., 1966-74; supervising and tng. analyst Columbia U. Center for Psychoanalytic Tng. and Research, 1972—; attending psychiatrist Vanderbilt Clinic, Presbyn. Hosp., NYC, 1964-74; Barklie McKee Henry prof. psychiatry Cornell U. Med. Coll., NYC, 1974-93, chmn. dept. psychiatry, 1974-91, Stephen and Suzanne Weiss dean, 1991-96; provost for med. affairs Cornell U., 1991-96, Walsh McDermott U. prof. of medicine, 1996—, univ. prof. psychiatry, 1996—; psychiatrist-in-chief N.Y. Hosp., 1974-91, attending psychiatist, 1991—. Attending psychiatrist St. Luke's Hosp. Ctr., NYC, 1966—. Co-author: The Psychiatric Interview in Clinical Practice, 1971, 2d edit., 2006; contbr. articles to profl. jours. Served with USPHS, 1962-64. Mem. Am. Psychiat. Assn., Am. Coll. Psychiatrists, NY Psychiat. Soc., Royal Medico-Psychol. Assn., Psychiat. Rsch. Soc., Assn. Rsch. in Nervous and Mental Diseases, Assn. Acad. Psychiatry, Am. Psychoanalytic Assn., Internat. Psychoanalytic Assn., Ctr. Advanced Psychoanalytic Studies, NY Acad. Scis., Alpha Omega Alpha. Office: Cornell U Med Coll 418 E 71st St New York NY 10021-4894 Office Phone: 212-746-6001. E-mail: rmichels@med.cornell.edu.

MICHELSEN, CHRISTOPHER BRUCE HERMANN, surgeon; b. Boston, Aug. 18, 1940; s. Jost Joseph and Ingeborg Elizabeth (Dilthey) M.; m. Kethleen Mary; children: Heidi Elizabeth, Matthew Christopher, Joshua Jost. BA, Bowdoin Coll., 1961; MD, Columbia U., 1969. Diplomate Am. Bd. Orthop. Surgery, Am. Bd. Forensic Medicine. Intern Columbia Presbyn. Med. Ctr., NYC, 1969—70, resident, 1970—71; orthop. resident N.Y. Orthop. Hosp., NYC, 1971—73, jr. Anne C. Kane fellow, 1973—74, sr. Anne C. Kane fellow and hip fellow, 1974—75, traveling fellow, 1975—76; intenrat. A-O fellow, postgrad. fellow in biomechanics Case Western Res. U., NYC, 1975—76, instr. biomed. engring., 1975—76; prof. clin. orthop. surgery, orthop. surgeon Columbia Coll. Physicians and Surgeons, 1976, vice chmn. dept. orthop. surgery, 2002—; chief orthop. svc. Allen Pavillion, Columbia Presbyn. Med. Ctr., 1993—, chief orthop. spine surgery svc., 1998—. Col. USAR, ret. Fellow ACS, Am. Assn. for Surgery of Trauma, Am. Orthop. Assn., N.Am. Spine Soc., Am. Acad. Orthop. Surgeons, Internat. Coll. Surgeons, N.Y. Acad. Medicine; mem. AMA, Am. Coll. Physicians Execs., Orthop. Rsch. Soc., Am. Soc. Bone and Mineral Rsch., Royal Soc. Medicine (affiliate). Office: 5141 Broadway New York NY 10034-1159 Home: 10 Rossa Ln Ossining NY 10562-2568

MICHELSON, GERTRUDE GERALDINE, retired retail executive; b. Jamestown, NY, June 3, 1925; d. Thomas and Celia Rosen; m. Horace Michelson, Mar. 28, 1947 (dec. Apr. 2002); children: Martha Ann (dec.), Barbara Jane. BA, Pa. State U., 1945; LLB, Columbia U., 1947; LLD with honors, Adelphi U., 1981; DHL with honors, New Rochelle Coll., 1983; LLD with honors, Marymount Manhattan Coll., 1988; PhD in Policy Analysis, Rand Grad. Sch., 2002. Mgmt. trainee Macy's NY, 1947-48, various mgmt. positions, v.p. employee personnel, 1963-70, sr. v.p. labor consumer rels., 1970—72; sr. v.p. pers. labor consumer rels. Macy & Co., Inc., 1972-79, sr. v.p. external affairs, 1979-80, R.H. Macy & Co., Inc., 1980-92, sr. advisor, 1992-94; ret., 1995. Chmn. Helena Rubinstein Found.; chmn. emeritus bd. trustees Columbia U.; life trustee Spelman Coll.; past pres. bd. overseers Tchrs. Ins. Annuity Assn. Am. Coll. Retirement Equities Fund. Recipient Disting. Svc. medal Pa. State U., 1969. Mem. NYC Ptnrship. (vice chmn.), Women's Forum, Econ. Club NY Home: 70 E 10th St New York NY 10003-5102 Office: Macy's Dept Stores Inc 151 W 34th St New York NY 10001-2101

MICHELSON, LILLIAN, librarian, researcher; b. NYC, June 21, 1928; d. Louis and Dora (Keller) Farber; m. Harold Michelson, Dec. 14, 1947; children: Alan Bruce, Eric Neil, Dennis Paul. Vol. Goldwyn Libr., Hollywood, Calif., 1961-69; owner Former Goldwyn Rsch. Libr., Hollywood, 1969—; ind. location scout, 1973—. Mem. Motion Picture Libr. Found., 2002—, Friends L.A. Pub. Libr. Mem.: Acad. Motion Picture Arts and Scis. Office: c/o Dreamworks SKG Rsch Libr 1000 Flower St Glendale CA 91201-3007 Home Phone: 323-654-7177. E-mail: lmichelson@dreamworks.com.

MICHELSON, SARAH, choreographer; b. Manchester, England, 1964; BA, London U., 1984; performance diploma, Laban Contemporary Dance, London, 1985; MFA, Mills Coll., Oakland, Calif, 1991. Yoga instr. The Shala, NYC; assoc. curator performance, mem. adv. bd. The Kitchen, NYC. Choreographer Group Experience, Performance Space 122, NYC, 2001, Grivdon at the Grivdon Lawn, Jacob's Pillow Dance Festival, 2002, Grivdon at the Grivdon Concrete, The Kitchen, NYC, 2002, The Experts, White Oak Dance Project, 2002, Shadowmann, The Kitchen & Performance Space 122, traveling, 2003, Love is Everything, Lyon Opera Ballet, 2005, Daylight, Performance Space 122, 2005, Daylight (for Minneapolis), Walker Art Ctr., 2005, DOGS, New Wave Festival, Bklyn. Acad. Music, 2006. Recipient NY Dance & Performance "Bessie" award, 2002, 2003, 2008, MAP Fund award, 2004, 2007, Alpert award in Dance, 2006; grantee Creative Capital, 2006, Found. Contemporary Arts, 2008; fellow John Simon Guggenheim Meml. Found., 2009. Office: The Kitchen 512 W 19th St New York NY 10011 also: The Shala 2nd Fl 815 Broadway New York NY 10003*

MICHENER, CHARLES DUNCAN, entomologist, researcher, educator; b. Pasadena, Calif., Sept. 22, 1918; s. Harold and Josephine (Rigden) Michener; m. Mary Hastings, Jan. 1, 1941; children: David, Daniel, Barbara, Walter. BS, U. Calif., Berkeley, 1939, PhD, 1941. Tech. asst. U. Calif., Berkeley, 1939-42; asst. curator Am. Mus. Natural History, NYC, 1942-46, assoc. curator, 1946-48, rsch. assoc., 1949—; assoc. prof. U. Kans., 1948-49, prof., 1949-89, prof. emeritus, 1989—, chmn. dept. entomology, 1949-61, 72-75, Watkins Disting. prof. entomology, 1959-89, acting chmn. dept. systematics, ecology, 1968-69, Watkins Disting. prof. systematics and ecology, 1969-89; dir. Snow Entomol. Museum, 1974-83, state entomologist, 1949-61. Vis. rsch. prof. U. Paraná, Curitiba, Brazil, 1955—56. Author: The Social Behavior of the Bees, 1974, The Bees of the World, 2000, 2d edit., 2007; author: (with Mary H. Michener) American Social Insects, 1951; author: (with S. F. Sakagami) (book) Nest Architecture of the Sweat Bees, 1962; author: (with M. D. Breed and H. E. Evans) The Biology of Social Insects, 1982; author: (with D. Fletcher) Kin Recognition in Animals, 1987; author: (with R. McGinley and B. Danforth) The Bee Genera of North and Central America, 1994; contbr. articles to profl. jours.; Am. editor: Insectes Sociaux, 1954—55, 1962—90; editor: (jour.) Evolution, 1962—64; assoc. editor: Ann. Rev. Ecology and Systematics, 1970—90. Served to capt. San Corps AUS, 1943—46. Recipient Disting. Rsch. medal, Internat. Soc. Hymenopterists, 2002; fellow Guggenheim, U. Paraná, 1955—56, Africa, 1966—67, Fulbright, U. Queensland, 1958—59; scholar Rsch., U. Costa Rica, 1963. Fellow: AAAS, Royal Entomol. Soc. London, Am. Acad. Arts and Sci., Am. Entomol. Soc., Entomol. Soc. Am. (C. V. Riley award 1999); mem.: NAS, Kans. Entomol. Soc. (pres. 1950), Linnean Soc. London (corr.), Russian Entomol. Soc. (hon.), Soc. Systematic Zoologists (hon.; pres. 1969), Netherlands Entomological Soc. (hon.), Brazilian Acad. Sci. (corr.), Internat. Union Study Social Insects (pres. 1977—82), Am. Soc. Naturalists (pres. 1978), Soc. Study Evolution (pres. 1967). Home: 1706 W 2nd St Lawrence KS 66044-1016 Home Phone: 785-843-4598; Office Phone: 785-864-4610. Business E-Mail: michener@ku.edu.

MICHENER, JAMES LLOYD, medical educator; b. Dec. 19, 1952; m. Gwendolyn Curtis Murphy; children: Rebecca Liane, Joshua Kieran. BA, Oberlin Coll., Ohio, 1974; MD, Harvard Med. Sch., 1978. Diplomate Am. Bd. Family Practice. Resident in family medicine Duke U. Med. Ctr., Durham, NC, 1978-81, Kellogg fellow, 1981-82, prof. dept. cmty. and family medicine, 1994—, chmn. dept. cmty. and family medicine, 1994—; dir. Duke Ctr. Cmty. Rsch., 2006—. V.p. Durham Health Care, Inc., 1985-86; project reviewer Ctrs. Disease Control and Prevention, 2002-; vis. prof. work group pub. health and med. edn. Ctrs. Disease Control, Atlanta, 2005. Co-author: Nutrition in Practice, 1990, 2d edit., 1992; contbr. numerous articles to med. pubs. including Academic Medicine, The Jour. of Family Practice, Medical Care, others; mem. editl. bd. Rx Nutrition, 1989-91; presenter in field. Bd. dirs. N.C. Med. Soc. Found., 1995—2004; STFM rep. resource com. on nutrition edn. Am. Acad. Family Practice Found., 1987-91. Grantee The Fullerton Found., Inc., The Josiah Macy, Jr. Found., U.S. Dept. Health and Human Svcs., Kate B. Reynolds Charitable Trust, N.C. Health and Wellness Trust. Mem. AMA, NIH (co chair com. engagement com., NCRR, 2007-, Fogarty/Ellison fellowship selection com. 2005-), Assn. Am. Med. Colls. (exec. com. 2005-06, exec. coun. 2001-07, bd. dirs. 2008-), Assn. Tchrs. Preventive Medicine (chmn. coun. acad. units 2002-, pres. 2008-), Am. Acad. Family Physicians Found., N.C. Acad. Family Physicians, Assn. Dept. Family Medicine (bd. dir. 1997—, sec. 1998—2005), Coun. Acad. Socs. (adminstrn. bd. 2000-07, chair 2005-06), World Orgn. Nat. Colls., Acads. and Academic Assn. Gen. Practitioners and Family Physicians, Am. Austrian Founds. Internat. Health Forum (mem. steering com.), Nat. Patient Safety Found. (bd. govs. 2009). Home: 4011 Duck Pond Trail Chapel Hill NC 27514-9758 Office: Duke U Med Ctr PO Box 2914 Durham NC 27710-0001 Business E-Mail: miche001@mc.duke.edu.

MICHENER, JOHN RUSSELL, electrical engineer; b. Oakland, Calif., Oct. 6, 1951; s. John Harrold and Ann (Crabtree) M.; m. Ann Gardner, Dec. 30, 1974 (div. 1995); children: Robin Ann, Kristen Lee; m. Vera Grabovetska, June 18, 1996; children: Sophia Maria, John Yaroslav. MS, U. Rochester, 1979, PhD, 1984. Rsch. physicist Kodak, Rochester, NY, 1974—79; prin. investigator Siemens Rsch., Princeton, NJ, 1982—89; v.p., chief scientist Wave Systems Corp., Princeton, 1989—96; security architect Novell Inc., 1996—99; security architect and chief tech. officer Enterprises Solutions, Inc., 1999—2002; chief scientist, v.p. for bus. devel. BBX Technologies, NYC, 2002—03; security arch. Microsoft Co., 2003—. Arms analyst Princeton Arms Study Program and Am. Inst. Physics, 1983—. Contbr. articles to profl. jours. Mem. IEEE, Am. Phys. Soc., Assn. for Computing Machinery, Soc. Indsl. and Applied Math. Achievements include 8 patents in field. Home: 2019 264 Pl SE Sammamish WA 98075 Office: Microsoft Corp One Redmond Way Redmond WA 98052-6399

MICHENFELDER, ALBERT A., lawyer; b. St. Louis, July 21, 1926; s. Albert A. and Ruth Josephine (Donahue) M.; m. Lois Barbara Sullivan, Sept. 03, 1949 (div. May 2, 1967); children: Michael J., Ann C. Michenfelder Yancey, Elizabeth D. Michenfelder Brown; m. Ramona Jo Dysart, July 12, 1968 (dec. Jan. 2, 1998); 1 child, Julie D. Michenfelder Wolfe. B of Naval Sci., Marquette U., 1946; LLB, St. Louis U., 1950. Bar: Mo. 1950, U.S. Dist. Ct. (ea. dist.) Mo. 1950, U.S. Supreme Ct. 1975. Assoc. Flynn & Challis, St. Louis, 1950-54; pvt. practice St. Louis, 1954-55; of counsel Husch & Eppenberger LLC, St. Louis. Mem. 21st Cir. Jud. Commn., St. Louis, 1981-87. Contbr. articles to profl. jours. City atty. City of Webster Groves, Mo., 1966-79; mem. John Marshall Club, St. Louis. Lt. (j.g.) USNR, 1944-47. Mem. Mo. Bar Assn., Bar. Assn. Met. St. Louis, St. Louis County Bar Assn. (pres. 1966), Westborough Country Club. Republican. Avocations: golf, tennis. Office: Husch & Eppenberger LLC 190 Carondelet Plz Ste 600 Saint Louis MO 63105-3441 Home Phone: 314-991-2846; Office Phone: 314-480-1730. Business E-Mail: al.michenfelder@husch.com.

MICHEV, DIMITAR PEROV, mathematics professor; s. Pero Mishev and Dimitra Misheva; m. Tatiana A. Micheva; children: Ilia D. Mishev, Antoan D., Elizabeth D. Micheva. MS in Math., Sofia U., Bulgaria, 1977, PhD, 1989. Assoc. prof. dept. math. Tech. U., Sofia, 1985—93, head dept. math., 1993—98; lectr. Southern Ill. U., Carbondale, 1999—2001; assoc. prof. dept. math. Prairie View A & M U., Tex., 2001—. Co-author (with D.D.Bainov): (book) Oscillation theory for neutral differential equations with delay, Adam Hilger, Bristol, Philadelphia, New York, Oscillation theory of operator-differential equations, World Scientific, Singapore, New Jersey, London, Hong Kong; coauthor: (with A. M.Haghighi) Queueing Models in Industry and Business. Named Outstanding Rschr. of Yr., Dept. Math., Prairie View A & M U., 2002, Outstanding Tchr. of Yr., Coll. Art & Scis., Prairie View A & M U., 2007. Mem.: Internat. Soc. Difference Equation, Union Mathematicians Bulgaria, Union Scientists Bulgaria, Am. Math. Soc. Office: Prairie View A & M Univ Dept Math Prairie View TX 77446-2967 Business E-Mail: dimichev@pvamu.edu.

MICHNICH, MARIE E., health policy analyst, consultant, educator; BS in Nursing, U. Conn.; M in Health Svs. Adminstrn., UCLA, DrPH in Health Svs. Rsch. Legis. asst., health policy Medicare, Medicaid, maternal and child health; legis. asst. U.S. Senate Majority Leader Robert Dole; asst. prof. health services U. Washington; sr. exec. v.p. Health Policy and Clin. Practice and Sci. Services Divisions, Am. Coll. Cardiology; dir., Health Policy Ednl. Programs and Fellowships Bd. Inst. of Medicine-Nat. Academies, 2002—; exec. dir. President's Commn. on Care America's Returning Wounded Warriors, 2007. Cons. & spkr. in field; mem. several nat. health policy groups; bd. mem. then chair Health Care Quality Alliance, 1994—2001. Recipient Disting. Alumni Leadership award, U. Conn., Outstanding Achievement award, Sec. Def.; Robert Wood Johnson Health Policy fellow. Mem.: Am. Pharm. Assn. Found. (1st pub. mem. bd. dirs. 2002—), Robert Wood Johnson Health Policy Fellows Program (mem. adv. bd., dir.), Health Care Quality Alliance (former chmn.). Office: Institute of Medicine 500 5th St NW Washington DC 20001 Office Phone: 202-334-1296. Business E-Mail: mmichnich@nas.edu.*

MICHOPOULOS, ARISTOTLE V., humanities educator, researcher; b. Kotylion, Arcadia, Peloponnesos, Greece, Apr. 22, 1944; s. Vassilios A. Michopoulos and Anastasia D. Papazafeiropoulos; m. Despina Dimitropoulos (div. Jan. 30, 1996). BA, U. Athens, 1967; MA, CUNY, 1976; PhD, Fla. State U., Tallahassee, 1980. Translator Greek Orthodox Archdiocese of N.Am. and S. Am., NYC, 1970—71; translator and adminstr. Hellenic Indsl. Devel. Corp., NYC, 1972—74; h.s. tchr. Bd. of Edn. of NYC, 1975—76; adj. instr. Fla. State U., Tallahassee, 1977—78, asst. project dir. and curriculum writer, 1978—80; asst. prof. U. Fla., Gainesville, 1980—87; prof., dir. Greek studies Hellenic Coll., Brookline, Mass., 1987—2008. Dean Hellenic Coll., Brookline, Mass., 1995—2002, Greek studies dept. dir., 1987—; translator, cons. Various Organizations, Many, 1980—. Rep. to U.S. Dept. Edn., Greek Orthodox Archdiocese, N.Y.C., 1992—98; del., com. mem. Coun. on Hellenes Abroad, Chgo., 1995—2002; nat. coord. Paideia project, Greece, 1999—2008. Recipient Socratic award, U. Fla., 1999, Capitol award, US Congress, 2008; fellow, US Dept. HEW, 1976—79; Fulbright awardee, 1977. Mem.: Kotylion Syllogos (cons. 1980—2005, Merit Award 2000), Am. Hellenic Edn. Assn. (AHEPA), Modern Greek Studies Assn. Avocations: tennis, swimming, backgammon, travel. Office: Hellenic Coll 50 Goddard Ave Brookline MA 02445 Office Phone: 617-850-1271.

MICHOPOULOS, JOHN GEORGE, research civil engineer; b. Athens, Greece, Sept. 26, 1956; came to U.S., 1982; s. George and Vasiliki (Nikolakopoulos) M.; m. Athina Tsikoula, June 6, 1982; 1 child, Vasiliki. B.Sc. in Elec. Engring., N.Y. Inst. Tech., 1978; M.Sc. in Civil Engring., Nat. Tech. U., Athens, 1979, Ph.D. in Applied Mechanics, 1982. Research assoc., teaching asst. Nat. Tech. U. Athens, 1979-82; research asst. Packard lab. Inst. Fracture/Solid Mechanics, Lehigh, U., Bethlehem, Pa., 1982-83, research engr., 1983—; cons. Comptek Corp., Pa., 1984-85. Contbr. articles. to profl. publs., 1980—. Greek Nat. Found. Scholarships hon. scholar, 1975; A.S. Onassis Pub. Benefit Found. hon. fellow, 1982-84. Mem. Am. Acad. Mechanics, N.Y. Acad. Scis., ASME, AAAS, Optical Soc. Am., Sigma Xi. Avocations: writing and reading poetry; painting; music. Office: Lehigh U Inst Fracture/Solid Mechanics Packard Lab 19 Bethlehem PA 18015

MICIC, MIODRAG, chemist, researcher; b. Belgrade, Serbia-Monteneg, Sept. 19, 1973; s. Zivorad and Nadezda Micic. B in Mech. and Navel Arch. Engring., Poly. Acad., Belgrade, 1991; BS in Physics and Fundamentals of Engring., U. Belgrade, Serbia, 1996, MS in Phys. Chem., 1998, DS in Phys. Chem., 2001; PhD in Chemistry, MS in Chemistry, U. Miami, Coral Gables, 2002; M in Tech. Mgmt., Wash. State U., Pullman, 2003. Pres., CEO Mimitech D.O.O., Belgrade, Serbia and Montenegro, 1991—98; rsch. assoc. U. Belgrade, Faculty Phys. Chemistry, 1996—98; tchg. and rsch. asst. U. Miami, Chemistry Dept., Coral Gables, 1998—2002; sr. applications scientist Veeco Instruments, Inc., Santa Barbara, Calif., 2003—04; v.p., r & d MP Biomedicals LLC, Irvine, Calif., 2004—. Grants reviewer Inst. for Publich Health and Water Rsch., Napperville, Ill., 2005—, Ministry Sci. and Environ. Protection, Belgrade, 2004—, Vojvodina Region, Provincial Secretariat Sci. and Tech. Devel., Novi Sad, 2004—; symposia chmn. 40th Regional Meeting Western Region Am. Chem. Soc., Annaheim, Calif., 2006—. Fellow, Battelle Meml. Inst., Pacific NW Nat. Lab., Richland, 2002—03. Mem.: Am. Chem. Soc., Exptl. Aircraft Assn., Aircraft Owners and Pilots Assn., Masons (Master Mason 2001, plural membership 2004, 2002), Scottish Rite (32nd degree), Sigma Xi, Alpha Epsilon Lambda (hon.). Achievements include discovery of methods for AFM imaging of microorganisms; research in single molecular electron transfer; development of an aurora-3/SPEC near field scanning optical microscopy system. Home: 3 Hutton Centre Dr Ste 100 Santa Ana CA 92707-8757 Office Fax: 959-859-5095; Home Fax: 949-387-0841. Personal E-mail: drmicic@aol.com. E-mail: mmicic@mpbio.com.

MICK, DAVID GLEN, finance educator; b. Hammond, Ind., Dec. 5, 1951; married. PhD, Ind. U., Bloomington, 1987. Prof. mktg. U. Va., Charlottesville, 2000—. Editor Jour. Consumer Rsch., Chgo., 1999—2003; pres. Assn. Consumer Rsch., Duluth, Minn., 2005—06. Religious edn. tchr. Thomas Jefferson Meml. Ch., Charlottesville, 2004—08. Recipient Maynard award. Fellow: Soc. Consumer Psychology. Office: Univ Va Rouss & Robertson Halls Charlottesville VA 22904 Business E-Mail: dmick@virginia.edu.

MICK, DIANE JOAN, nurse; b. Pottsville, Pa., June 21, 1955; d. Stanley Philip and Helen Josephine (Padrezas) M. BA, West Chester U., Pa., 1977; AS in Nursing, Gwynedd-Mercy Coll., 1983, MS in Nursing, 1991. Critical Care RN, Pa. Instr. music Braun Sch. Music, Pottsville, 1978-79; nurse Sacred Heart Hosp., Norristown, Pa., 1983; critical care nurse Grand View Hosp., Sellersville, Pa., 1983-84, Montgomery Hosp., Norristown, Pa., 1984-91; instr. nursing Geisinger Med. Ctr. Sch. Nursing, Danville, Pa., 1991—. Guest lectr. Wilkes U., Wilkes Barre, Pa. Contbr. articles to profl. publs. Mem. AACCN, Nat. League Nursing, West Chester Univ. Alumni Assn., Gwynedd-Mercy Coll. Alumni Assn. (diplomat), Sigma Theta Tau, Gamma Theta Upsilon. Democrat. Roman Catholic. Avocations: travel, performing music, community theater.

MICKEL, EMANUEL JOHN, foreign language educator; b. Lemont, Ill., Oct. 11, 1937; s. Emanuel John and Mildred (Newton) M.; m. Kathleen Russell, May 31, 1959; children: Jennifer, Chiara, Heather. BA, La. State U., 1959; MA, U. N.C., 1961, PhD, 1965. Asst. prof. U. Nebr., Lincoln, 1965-67, assoc. prof., 1967-68, Ind. U., Bloomington, 1968-73, prof., 1973—, dir. Medieval Studies Inst., 1976-91, chmn. French and Italian, 1984-95, 2009—. Cons. NEH; French advisor Soc. Rencesvals, 1995-98; adv. bd. mem. Nineteenth Century French Studies, 1995-, Mediaevalia, 2007, vis. scholar Pembroke Coll., U. Cambridge, 2006. Author: Marie de France, 1974, Eugene Fromentin, 1982, Ganelon Treason and the Chanson de Roland, 1989, Jules Vernes Complete Twenty Thousand Leagues Under the Sea, 1992, Enfances Godefroi and Retour de Cornumarant, 1999. Capt. U.S. Army, 1963-65. Grantee NEH, Washington, 1978-84; Lilly Open fellow Lilly Found., Indpls., 1981-82; Chevalier dans l'Ordre des Palmes Academiques, 1997. Avocations: music, theater, sports, travel, ancient literature. Office: French & Italian Dept Indiana Univ 642 Ballantine Hall Bloomington IN 47401-5020 Home Phone: 812-336-3992.

MICKELSON, PAUL A., biology professor, consultant; b. Evanston, Ill., Mar. 1, 1963; s. Judy Mickelson; m. Lora Johnson, Nov. 24, 2000; children: Stephanie, Linsy, Alexis Cartwright. MS, U. Minn., Mpls., 1988. Faculty Fond du Lac CC, Cloquet, Minn., 1995—2000, Ctrl. Lakes Coll., Brainerd, Minn., 2000—. Ednl. cons. Ednl. Policy Improvement Ctr., Wash., 2005—. Home: 504 Johnson Ave Cloquet MN 55720 Office: Ctrl Lks Coll 501 W College Dr Brainerd MN 56401

MICKELSON, PHIL (PHILIP ALFRED MICKELSON JR.), professional golfer; b. San Diego, June 16, 1970; s. Philip and Mary Mickelson; m. Amy McBride, Nov. 19, 1996; children: Amanda Brynn, Sophia Isabel, Evan. BS in Psych., Ariz. State U., 1992. Profl. golfer PGA, 1992—. Mem. US team Presidents Cup, 1994, 96, 98, 2000, 03, Ryder Cup, 1995, 97, 99, 2002, 04, 06, 08. Co-author (with Donald T. Phillips): One Magical Sunday (But Winning Isn't Everything), 2005; appeared in (TV series) Entourage, 2008. Founder The Phil and Amy Mickelson Charitable Fund. Recipient Fred Haskins award, 1990, 91, 92, Jack Nicklaus award, 1990, 91, 92; won NCAA Championships, 1989, 90, 92; 1st team All-Am. with Sun Devils; Espy Award for Best Male Golfer, Best Championship Performance, ESPN, 2004; named one of The 100 Most Powerful Celebrities, Forbes.com, 2008. Achievements include 1st left-hander to win US Amateur, 1990; 1st player in PGA history to win same tournament as amateur and profesional (No. Telecom Open); winner Major Championships: The Masters, 2004, 06; PGA Championship, 2005; 36 career PGA Tour Victories; member of the Ryder Cup winning US team, 2008; winner World Golf Championships: CA Championship, 2009. Avocation: flying. Office: c/o PGA Box 109601 100 Avenue Of Champions Palm Beach Gardens FL 33418*

MICKENBERG, JULIA LYNN, American studies professor; b. Bethesda, Md., May 28, 1968; d. Ira Douglass and Yvette Alter Mickenberg; m. Daniel Jay Birkholz, Sept. 6, 1998; children: Lena Janet Mickenberg Birkholz, Edie Brigid Mickenberg Birkholz. AB, Brown U., Providence, 1990; PhD, U. Minn., Mpls., 2000. Asst. prof. Am. Studies U. Tex., Austin, 2001—07, dir. grad. studies, assoc. prof. Am. Studies, 2007—. Contbr. articles to profl. jours. Recipient Children's Lit. Book prize, Grace Abbott Book prize, Hamilton Book award, Pacific Coast Br. award. Office: Univ Tex Austin 1 Univ Sta B7100 Austin TX 78712 Office Fax: 512-471-3540. Business E-Mail: mickenberg@mail.utexas.edu.

MICKENS, RONALD ELBERT, mathematician, physics professor; b. Petersburg, Va., Feb. 7, 1943; s. Joseph Persival and Daisy (Brown) M.; m. Maria Kelker, Aug. 13, 1977; children James Williamson, Leah Maria. BA, Fisk U., 1964; PhD, Vanderbilt U., 1968. NSF postdoctoral fellow MIT, Cambridge, 1968-70, vis. prof., 1973-74; prof. physics Fisk U., Nashville, Tenn., 1970-81, Clark Atlanta U., 1982—, Callaway prof., 1986. Vis. prof. Morehouse Coll., Atlanta, 1979-80, Joint Inst. for Lab. Astrophysics, Boulder, Colo., 1981-82; cons. adv. bd. NSF, Nat. Urban Coalition, Nat. Rsch. Coun., Am. Inst. Physics and a variety of univs. and nat. labs. Author: Nonlinear Oscillations, 1981, Difference Equations, 1987, Difference Equations: Theory and Applications, 1990, Nonstandard Finite Difference Models of Differential Equations, 1994, Oscillations in Planar Dynamical Systems, 1996; editor: Mathematics and Science, 1990, Applications of Nonstandard Finite Difference Schemes, 2000, Edward Bouchet: The First African American Doctorate, 2002, Mathematical Methods for the Natural and Engineering Sciences, 2004; editor: Advances in the Applications of Nonstandard Finite Difference Schemes, 2005; co-editor: Mathematical Studies on Human Disease Dynamics, 2006; contbr. numerous rev. articles, abstracts and gen. articles to publs. Fellow Woodrow Wilson Found., Danforth Found., UNCF, Joint Inst. for Lab. Astrophysics; grantee ARO, NSF, DOE, NASA, NIH, 1968—. Fellow Am. Phys. Soc. (con., adv. bd.); mem. AAAS, European Phys. Soc., Soc. Indsl. and Applied Math., Am. Math. Soc. Achievements include construction of new finite-difference schemes for numerical solution of differential equations; new perturbation techniques for nonlinear difference and differential equations; construction of global methods for nonlinear oscillatory systems; investigation of properties of rate constants for third-order chemical react; mathematical modeling in the biosciences; history of African American scientists. Office: Clark Atlanta U Physics Dept Atlanta GA 30314 Home Phone: 404-696-0739; Office Phone: 404-880-6923. Business E-Mail: rohrs@math.gatech.edu.

MICKES, LAURA, psychology professor; MS, U. Calif. San Diego, La Jolla, attending, 2009. Co-creator Bumpy Brains, La Jolla, Calif., 2008—. Summer Grad. Tchg. fellowship, U. Calif. San Diego, 2007. Mem.: Assn. Psychol. Sci. Personal E-mail: lmickes@ucsd.edu.

MICKIEWICZ, ELLEN PROPPER, political and social science educator; b. Hartford, Conn. d. George K. and Rebecca (Adler) Propper; m. Denis Mickiewicz; 1 son, Cyril. BA, Wellesley Coll.; MA, Yale U., PhD, 1965. Lectr. dept. polit. sci. Yale U., 1965-67; asst. prof. dept. polit. sci. Mich. State U., East Lansing, 1967-69, assoc. prof., 1969-73, prof., 1973-80; prof. dept. polit. sci. Emory U., Atlanta, 1980-88, dean Grad. Sch. Arts and Scis., 1980-85, Alben W. Barkley prof. polit. sci., 1988-93; James R. Shepley prof. pub. policy, prof. polit. sci. Duke U., Durham, N.C., 1994—, dir. DeWitt Wallace Ctr. for Comm. and Journalism Terry Sanford Inst. Pub. Policy, 1994—. Vis. prof. Kathryn W. Davis Chair Wellesley Coll., 1978; vis. com. dept. Slavic lang. and lit. Harvard U., 1978-85, vice chmn. vis. com. Russian Rsch. Ctr., Harvard U., 1986-92; mem. subcom. on comms. and society Am. Coun. Learned Socs./Soviet Acad. Scis., 1986-90; mem. com. on internat. security studies, Am. Acad. Arts and Scis., 1988-90; fellow The Carter Ctr., 1985—, dir. Commn. on Radio and TV Policy; mem. area adv. com. for Ea. Europe and USSR, Coun. for Internat. Exch. Of Scholars, 1987-90; mem. acad. adv. coun. The Kennan Inst. for Advanced Russian Studies, 1989-93; mem. bd. overseers Internat. Press Ctr., Moscow, 1995; dir., commr.

Commn. Radio and TV Policy, 1990. Author: Soviet Political Schools, 1967, Media and the Russian Public, 1981, Split Signals: Television and Politics in the Soviet Union, 1988 (Electronic Book of Yr. award Nat. Assn. Broadcasters and Broadcast Edn. Assn. 1988); co-author: Television and Elections, 1992, Television/Radio News and Minorities, 1994, Changing Channels: Television and the Struggle for Power in Russia, 1997, revised and expanded edit., 1999; editor: Soviet Union Jour., 1980-90; co-editor: International Security and Arms Control, 1986, The Soviet Calculus of Nuclear War, 1986; editor, contbr.: Handbook of Soviet Social Science Data, 1973; mem. editl. bd. Jour. Politics, 1985-88, Harvard Internat. Jour. Press/Politics, 1995—, Polit. Comms., 1996—, Polit. Comm., 1995—. Founder, 1st chmn. bd. dirs. Opera Guild of Greater Lansing, Inc., 1972-74. Recipient Outstanding Svc. to Promote Dem. Media in Russia award Journalists Union of Russia, 1994; Ford Found. Fgn. Area Tng. fellow, 1962-65, Guggenheim fellow, 1973-74; Sigma Xi grantee, 1972-74, John and Mary R. Markle Found. grantee, 1984-88, 94-96, 95—, Ford Found. grantee, 1985, 88-91, 92—, Rockefeller Found. grantee, 1985-87, W. Alton Jones Found. grantee, 1987-88, Eurasia Found. grantee, 1993-94, Carnegie Corp. of N.Y. grantee, 1996—. Mem. Am. Assn. for Advancement Slavic Studies (bd. dirs. 1978-81, mem. awards com., mem. endowment com. 1984-86, pres. 1987-88), Am. Polit. Sci. Assn.,Internat. Studies Assn. (v.p. N.Am. 1983-84), Dante Soc. Am., So. Conf. Slavic Studies (exec. com. 1983-84), Counc. Fgn. Rels. Office: Duke U Sanford Inst Pub Policy PO Box 90241 Durham NC 27708-0241

MICK III, LEONARD SILAS, language educator; b. Aug. 2, 1980; s. Leonard and Deborah Mick. BA, Va. Commonwealth U., Richmond. Cert. German K-12 tchr. Va., 2006. German tchr. Richmond Pub. Sch., 2005—, Va. Commonwealth U., 2007—, Governor's German Acad., Richmond, 2008—. Author: (book) Deutsche Minderheiten in anderen Laendern. With USN. Recipient Claes Nobel Educator Distinction award, Nat. Soc. HS Scholars, 2007. Mem.: AVER, Fgn. Lang. Assn. Va., Am. Coun. Tchg. Fgn. Lang., Am. Assn. Tchrs. German, Am. Legion Post 448. Green Party. Achievements include research in German speaking minorities in Africa, South America and Oceania; German langauge instruction in the urban American high school.

MICKLE, MARLIN HOMER, electrical engineer, educator; b. Windber, Pa., July 5, 1936; s. Howard T. and Ruth Elma (Corle) Mickle. BS, U. Pitts., 1961, MS, 1963, PhD, 1967. Jr. engr. IBM, 1962; engr. Westinghouse Co., 1964; mem. faculty U. Pitts., 1962—, assoc. prof. elec. engring., 1968-75, prof., 1975—, dir. computer engring. program, 1982-84, Nickolas A. DeCecco prof., 2001—. Program dir. sys. theory & applications NSF, 1974—75; pres. Mickle Computer Techs., Inc., Pitts., 1979—85; v.p., bd. dirs. Power Resources, Inc., Pitts., 1980—84; dir. Univ. R & D Assocs., Inc., 1985—2004; exec. dir. Swanson Ctr. Product Innovation, 2004—06; dir. Radio Frequency Identification Ctr. Excellence, 2005—; cons. in field. Author (with T. W. Sze): Optimization in Systems Engineering, 1972; mem. editl. bd. Jour. Interdisciplinary Modeling and Stimulation, 1978—80; editor-in-chief: Internat. Jour. Paralle and Distributed Systems and Networks, 1997—2002; editor: Internat. Jour. Radio Frequency Tech. Applications, 2004—; contbr. articles to profl. jours. Bd. dirs. Asbury Heights, Pitts., 1982—, Wesley Hills Mt. Lebanon, Pitts., 1985—86; chmn. bd. dirs. Emory Sr. Housing, Pitts., 2000—; dist. lay leader Pitts. Dist. United Meth. Ch., 1971—73; elder Shadyside Presbyn. Ch., 2004—. Radar tech. Airborne USAF, 1954—58. Recipient sys. rsch. and cybernetics award, Internat. Inst. Advanced Studies in Sys. Rsch. and Cybernetics, 1988, excellence in corp. innovation award, Carnegie Sci. Ctr., 2005, Pitt Innovator award, U. Pitts., 2005, 2006, 2007, 2008, Disting. Alumni award, ECE Dept., Pitts., 2008. Fellow: IEEE (life); mem.: Cathedral Learning Soc. Republican. Home: 4601 5th Ave Apt 723 Pittsburgh PA 15213-3657 Office: U Pitts Dept Elec and Computer Engring Pittsburgh PA 15261-0001 Office Phone: 412-600-3606. Business E-Mail: mickle@pitt.edu.

MICKLETHWAIT, JOHN, editor-in-chief; m. Fevronia Micklethwait. Formerly with Chase Manhattan Bank; joined The Economist, London, 1987, LA bur. chief, media corr., 1990—93, bus. sect. editor NYC, 1993—97, NY bur. chief, 1997—99, US editor, 1999—2006, editor-in-chief London, 2006—. Co-author (with Adrian Wooldridge): The Witch Doctors: Making Sense of the Management Gurus, 1996, A Future Perfect: The Challenge and Hidden Promise of Globalization, 2000, The Company: A Short History of a Revolutionary Idea, 2003, The Right Nation: Conservative Power in America, 2004, God is Back, 2009. Named Young Financial Journalist of the Yr., Harold Wincott Found., 1990. Office: The Economist 25 St James St London SW1A 1HG England Office Phone: (44) 207 830 7000.*

MICKO, ALEXANDER S., corporate financial executive, educator, treasurer; b. Munich, May 8, 1947; came to U.S., 1952, naturalized, 1957; s. Zygmunt and Maria (Huber) M.; m. Sharon E. Judge, June 7, 1969; 1 child, Brian A. BS, LaSalle U., 1969. CPA, NJ, Pa. Audit mgr. Price Waterhouse Coopers, Phila., 1970—77; asst. chief fin. investigations div. of Casino Gaming Enforcement, State of NJ, Trenton, NJ, 1977—79; v.p. fin. TeleScis., Inc., Mt. Laurel, NJ, 1979—87, Nat. Environ. Testing, Inc., Thorofare, NJ, 1988—92; controller AAA Mid-Altantic, Inc., Phila., 1992—2006; pres. Alexander & Assocs., CPA, LLC, 2006—; dir. Nat. Championships Phila., 2007—. Cons. United Computer Svcs., Berlin, 1982; lectr. in field. Bd. dirs. Forest Hills Civic Assn., Williamstown, NJ, 1976. With USMC, 1969-75. Recipient Michael A. DeAngelis Outstanding Profl. Achievement award, LaSalle U., Phila., 1985. Mem. AICPA, NJ Soc. CPAs, Pa. Inst. CPAs, Fin. Execs. Inst., Nat. Assn. Accts. Roman Catholic. Avocations: skiing, golf. Home: 5 Huntington Cir Medford NJ 08055-3315 Office Phone: 856-273-1040.

MICZEK, KLAUS ALEXANDER, psychology professor; came to U.S., 1967; s. Erich and Irene (Wirthl) M.; m. Christiane Baerwaldt, Aug. 8, 1970; 1 child, Nikolai A. Tchrs. cert., Paedagogische Hochschule, Berlin, 1966; PhD, U. Chgo., 1972. Asst. prof. Carnegie-Mellon U., Pitts., 1972-74, assoc. prof., 1974-79, Tufts U., Medford, Mass., 1979-83, prof., 1983-93, Moses Hunt prof. psychiatry, psychology, pharmacology and neuroscience, 1993—. Cons. Solvay-Pharma v.b., Weesp, The Netherlands, 1984-99, NIH, Rockville, Md., 1984—, Forest Labs., N.Y.C., 2003-; Boehringer Ingelheim, Germany, 2003-; Boerhaave prof. U. Leiden, The Netherlands, 1987; mem. panel on violence, NAS, 1989-92. Editor: Ethopharmacology, 1983, Ethopharmacological Aggression Research, 1984; field editor, coord. editor Behavioral Pharmacology, Jour. Psychopharmacology; contbr. articles on psychopharmacology, 1973—. Rsch. grantee Nat. Inst. Drug Abuse, 1973—, Nat. Inst. Alcoholism and Alcohol Abuse, 1981—; recipient Solvay-Duphar award APA, 1993, Bundesverdienstkreuz Cross of Merit, Fed. Republic of Germany, 1996, Gold medal Charles U., Prague, 2004; named disting. scholar Tufts U., 2006, recipeint disting. achievement award European Behavioural Pharmacy Soc., 2007. Fellow AAAS, APA (program chmn. 1981, pres. div. psychopharmacology 1990-91, master lectr. 1999), Behavioral Pharmacol. Soc. (pres. 1992-94), Internat. Soc. for Rsch. on Aggression (councilor 1987); mem. Soc. Neurosci., N.Y. Acad. Scis., Internat. Primatol. Soc. Office: Tufts U Dept Psychology 530 Boston Ave Medford MA 02155-5532 Business E-Mail: klaus.miczek@tufts.edu.

MIDCALF, RANDALL, language educator, director; b. Saginaw, Mich., Feb. 10, 1959; MA in English, Oakland U., Rochester, Mich., 1989. Assoc. prof. English Maranatha Bapt. Bible Coll., Watertown, Wis., coord. English program, 1997—. Contbg. editor (mag.) In Focus. Instr. Sunday sch. Calvary Bapt. Ch., Watertown, 1994—. Mem.: NCTE. Office: Maranatha Bapt Bible Coll 745 W Main St Watertown WI 53094 E-mail: rmidcalf@mbbc.edu.

MIDDAUGH, ROBERT BURTON, artist; b. Chgo., May 12, 1935; s. John Burton and Mae Knight (Crooks) M. Student, U. Chgo., 1960-64; BFA, Art Inst. Chgo., 1964. Curator art collection 1st Nat. Bank Chgo., 1971-83. Designed, executed ednl. display, Prehistoric Project at Oriental Inst. of U. Chgo., 1968; one-man shows include, Kovler Gallery, Chgo., 1965, 67, 69, Martin Schweig Gallery, St. Louis, 1970, 72, 79, 83, U. Wis., 1976, 81, 82, Fairweather Hardin Gallery, Chgo., 1977, 80, 83, 85, Rockford Art Mus., 1987, Zaks Gallery, Chgo., 1992, 93, 97, Printworks Gallery, Chgo., 2006; group shows, including, Art Inst. Chgo., 1964, 66, 78, 79, Evanston (Ill.) Art Ctr., 1966, Joslyn Art Mus., Omaha, 1968, U. Notre Dame, 1969, Va. Mus. Fine Arts, Richmond, 1966; represented in permanent collections, Art Inst. Chgo., Boston Mus. Fine Arts, Fine Art Mus. of South, Mobile, Ala., Los Angeles County Mus., Phoenix Art Mus., Worcester (Mass.) Art Mus., Ill. State Mus., Springfield. Served with U.S. Army, 1958-60. Archivist, Chgo. Park Dist., 1998-2005. Mem. Arts Club Chgo.

MIDDELHOEK, ANDRÉ J., retired international organization administrator, auditor; b. The Netherlands, 1931; m. Geertruida Johanna Van den Broek; 2 children. Degree, U. Amsterdam, 1957. Various posts Netherlands Cen. Planning Bur., The Hague, 1958-66; lectr. Internat. Inst. for Social Studies, 1960-69; dep. dir. Netherlands Cen. Planning Bur., 1966-69; dir. gen. budget Ministry of Finance, 1969-77; mem. ct. of auditors The European Cmty., 1977-95, pres. ct. of auditors, 1993-95; ret., 1996. Mem. bd. dirs. Koninklijke Ned. Hoogovens N.V., Hoogovens Ijmuiden B.V., 1970-77; mem. Nat. Phys. Planning Com., 1966-77; mem., v.p. econ. policy com. European Cmty., 1969-77, mem., vice chmn. staff establishment com., 1969-77, chmn. com. for devel. of policy analysis, 1970-77, mem. extraordinary sci. coun. for govt. policy, 1972-77. Contbr. articles to profl. jours. Decorated comdr. Orde van Nederlandse Leeuw, knight Orde Van de Nederlandse Leeuw; Grand Croix Ordre Grand-Ducal de la Couronne de Chêne (Luxemburg). Personal E-mail: andre.middelhoek@skynet.be.

MIDDELKAMP, JOHN NEAL, pediatrician, educator; b. Kansas City, Mo., Sept. 29, 1925; s. George H. and Clara M. (Ordelheide) M.; m. Roberta Gill, Oct. 3, 1949 (div. 1970); children— Sharon Ann, Steven Neal, Susan Jean, Scott Alan; m. Lois Harper, Mar. 1, 1974 BS, U. Mo., 1946; MD, Washington U., St. Louis, 1948. Diplomate Am. Bd. Pediatrics. Intern D.C. Gen. Hosp., Washington, 1948-49; resident St. Louis Children's Hosp., 1949-50, 52-53; instr. pediatrics Washington U., 1953-57, asst. prof. pediatrics, 1957-64, assoc. prof., 1964-70, prof., 1970-98, prof. emeritus, 1998—; dir. ambulatory pediatrics St. Louis Children's Hosp., 1974-91. Author: Camp Health Manual, 1984; contbr. articles, chpts. to profl. publs. Served to comdr. M.C., USNR, 1943-66. NIH postdoctoral fellow, 1961-62 Mem. Am. Acad. Pediatrics, Am. Soc. Microbiology, Infectious Diseases Soc. Am., Am. Pediatric Soc., Ambulatory Pediatric Assn., Sigma Xi, Alpha Omega Alpha Home: 8845 Paragon Cir Saint Louis MO 63123-1114 Office: Office Assoc Dean for Grad Med Edn Washington Univ Sch Medicine 660 S Euclid Box 8033 Saint Louis MO 63110 Office Phone: 314-747-4479.

MIDDENDORF, J. WILLIAM, II, investment banker; b. Balt., Sept. 22, 1924; m. Isabelle Paine, Mar. 7, 1953; children: Frances, Amy, John W. IV, Ralph Henry. B in Naval Sci., Holy Cross Coll., 1945; AB, Harvard U., 1947; MBA, NYU, 1954; LLD (hon.), Troy State U.; LittD (hon.), Sch. of Ozarks, Am. Christian Coll.; D. Social Scis. (hon.), Netherlands-Am. Inst. Commd. ensign USN, 1945, advanced through grades to lt. (j.g.), ret., 1946; with credit dept. Chase Manhattan Bank, 1947-52; ptnr. Wood Struthers and Co., 1958-61; sr. ptnr. Middendorf, Colgate and Co., 1962-69; ambassador to The Netherlands, 1969-73; sec. USN, 1974-77; pres., CEO Fin. Gen. Bankshares, Inc., 1977-81; ambassador to Orgn. Am. States, 1981-85, European Communities, 1985-87; chmn. Middendorf & Assocs., Inc., 1989—. Chmn. presdl. task force Project Econ. and Social Justice, 1986-90; mem. U.S. Del. to supervise elections in Suriname, 1988; treas. Internat. Rep. Inst. Composer 8 symphonies, 100 marches, (opera) King Richard, nat. independence march for Belize, other compositions for Latin Am. countries; guest condr. Boston Pops, St. Louis Symphony, Ind. U., others; contbr. articles to profl. jours. Mem. U.S. Olympic com., 1979-89, U.S. Olympic Selection com. for field hockey; judge field hockey Olympics, Rome, 1960; former mem. vis. com. dept. Am. paintings Met. Mus. Art, N.Y.C., vis. com. dept. Am. Art, Mus. Fine Arts, Boston; hon. v.p. Naval Hist. Found.; treas. Goldwater for Pres. com., 1962-64, Presdl. Transition com. 1968, Rep. Nat. Com., 1964-69; alt. del. for Gov. Reagan, 1980; del. State of Conn., 1964, 68, State of Va., 1996; co-chmn. Virginians for Reagan, 1980, fin. com. Va. GOP, 1980-81; coord. internat. econ. and naval adv. com. Reagan for Pres. campaign, 1980; chmn. Congl. Boosters com., 1978-81; chmn. CIA Transition Team, 1980-81; chmn. fin. com. Pres. Reagan's 1981 Inaugural com.; trustee Naval War Coll. Found., Heritage Found., Washington; past trustee Hoover Instn. for War Revolution and Peace, Corcoran Gallery, N.Y. Hist. Soc., Balt. Mus. Art, Greenwich Hist. Soc., Boston Symphony, Middlesex Sch., Concord, Mass., Nat. Symphony Orch., Mass. Gen. Hosp., Boys Club N.Y.; bd. electors Ins. Hall of Fame; bd. dirs. Georgetown U., John Philip Sousa Meml. Found., Newport Art Mus. and Mariners' Mus., Norfolk, Va.; chmn. bd. dirs. council statesmen Ludwig von Mises Inst.; chmn. Com. for Monetary Rsch. and Edn. Inc., Netherlands-Am. Amity Trust, Def. Forum Found., Navy League Awards com., 1977—; former mem. com. Dept. State Fine Arts Com.; founding chmn. U.S. Navy Meml. Found.; past chmn. Netherlands-Am. Inst., Wolf Trap Farm Park, John Carter Brown Library Assocs., Providence, Asian Composers Expo., European Council of Boy Scouts. Decorated Grand Master Order of Orange Nassau (Netherlands), Order of Arab (Republic Egypt), Grand Master of Order of Naval Merit (Republic Brazil); recipient Superior Honor award Dept. State, 1974, Disting. Pub. Svc. award Dept. Def., 1975, 76, Navy Disting. Pub. Svc. award, 1976, Naval Disting. Svc. medal Republic Brazil, 1976, Ludwig von Mises Free Market award, 1985, Inter-Am. Music Coun. award, 1985, Edwin Franko Goldman award Am. Bandmasters Assn., 1987, Assn. Harvard Clubs Am. award, Disting. Svc. medal Purdue Univ. Bands, Netherlands Soc. Phila. Gold medal, Good Citizenship medal Nat. Soc. SAR, Medal of Honor, Midwest Nat. Band Assn., Invest in Am. Am. Eagle award, 1988, Eugene J. Keogh Disting. Pub. Svc. award NYU, 1989, Nat. Commendation award Pres.' Coun. Phys. Fitness and Sports, 1989, Leadership award Am. Friends of Turkey, 1989, Adm. Arleigh Burke Leadership award, 1998, Arleigh Burke award 1998, Gold medal Holland Soc., Spl. Recognition award Surface Navy Assn., 2007; named Alumnus of Yr. NYU, 1978; Nat. Masters Sculling champion, 1979. Mem. Am. Antiquarian Soc., Harvard Alumni Assn. (permanent class com. 1947), Soc. Cin. (hon.), ASCAP, Walpole Soc., Co. Mil. Historians, Mil. Order Loyal Legion, SAR, Soc. of SAR, Field Hockey Assn. Am. (past pres., player/mgr. nat. team 1963), U.S. Naval Inst., Navy League. Clubs: Angler's, Downtown Assn., Union (N.Y.C.); Army-Navy, Capitol Hill, Met., Potomac Boat (Washington); Sakonnet Golf (Little Compton, R.I.); Somerset (Boston). Mailing: PO Box 1037 Little Compton RI 02837

MIDDLEBROOKS, DELORIS JEANETTE, retired nursing educator; b. Cedar Rapids, Iowa, Apr. 9, 1931; d. Harland R. and Rosa V. (Anderson) Hickey; m. Johnnie L. Middlebrooks, Apr. 25, 1962 (dec.); children: James, Kathleen. Diploma, Evang. Hosp. Sch. Nursing, 1956; BSN, State U. Iowa, 1958; MS in Nursing, U. Calif., San Francisco, 1960; EdD, U. Nev., Las Vegas, 1985. Instr., coord. Nev. State Hosp. Sch. Practical Nursing, Sparks, 1963-66; staff nurse St. Mary's Hosp., Reno, 1968; instr., coord. Reno VA Sch. Practical Nursing, 1968-72; instr., coord. health occupations Wooster High Sch., 1972-73; nursing faculty Truckee Meadows C.C., 1973-94, ret., 1994; intermittent staff nurse VA Hosp., 1984-86; instr., review course Stanley Kaplan Ednl. Ctr., 1987-89; clin. nursing faculty Western Nev. C.C., Carson City, 1987, Northern Nev. C.C., Elko, 1979-93; guest assoc. prof. nursing Lewis-Clark State Coll., Lewiston, Idaho, 1989. Cons. Irish Bd. Nursing, Dublin, Ireland, 1985. Nominated Nev. Voc. Tchr. of Yr., 1975, 79, 88, 89; Recipient March of Dimes Community Leadership award, 1990. Mem.: ANA, Am. Assn. for the History of Nursing, Nev. Nurses Assn., Phi Kappa Phi, Sigma Theta Tau. Home: 1385 Ebbetts Dr Reno NV 89503-1918

MIDDLEBROOKS, EDDIE JOE, environmental engineer; b. Crawford County, Ga., Oct. 16, 1932; s. Robert Harold and Jewell LaVerne (Dixon) M.; m. Charlotte Linda Hardy, Dec. 6, 1958; 1 child, Linda Tracey. BCE, U. Fla., 1956, MS, 1960; PhD, Miss. State U., 1966. Registered profl. engr., Ariz., Miss., Utah, Wash., Colo.; registered land surveyor, Fla. Asst. san. engr. USPHS, Cin., 1956-58; field engr. T.T. Jones Constrn. Co., Atlanta, 1958-59; grad. teaching asst. U. Fla., 1959-60; research asst. U. Ariz., 1960-61; asst. prof., then assoc. prof. Miss. State U., 1962-67; research engr., asst. dir. San. Engring. Research Lab., U. Calif.-Berkeley, 1968-70; prof. Utah State U., Logan, 1970-82, dean Coll. Engring., 1974-82; Newman chair natural resources engring. Clemson U., 1982-83; provost, v.p. acad. affairs Tenn. Tech. U., 1983-88, U. Tulsa, 1988-90, prof. chem. engring., 1988-92, Trustees prof. chem. engring., 1990-92, acting pres., 1990; prof. civil engring. U. Nevada, Reno, 1992-97. Mem. nat. drinking water adv. council EPA, 1981-83; cons. EPA, UN Indsl. Devel. Orgn., Calif. Water Resources Control Bd., City and County of San Francisco, State of Colo., South Fla. Water Mgmt. Dist. (Everglades), also numerous indsl. and engring. firms. Author: Modeling the Eutrophication Process, 1974, Statistical Calculations-How to Solve Statistical Problems, 1976, Biostimulation and Nutrient Assessment, 1976, Water Supply Engineering Design, 1977, Lagoon Information Source Book, 1978, Industrial Pollution Control, Vol. 1: Agro-Industries, 1979, Wastewater Collection and Treatment: Principles and Practices, 1979, Water Reuse, 1982, Wastewater Stabiliation Lagoon Design, Performance and Upgrading, 1982, Reverse Osmosis Treatment of Drinking Water, 1986, Pollution Control in the Petrochemicals Industry, 1987, Natural Systems for Waste Management and Treatment, 1988, 2d edit., 1995, Japanese transl., Natural Wastewater Treatment Systems, 2006; contbr. tech. articles to profl. jours. Fellow ASCE; mem. Water Environment Fedn. (dir. 1979-81, 91-92), Eddy medal 1969), Assn. Environ. Engring. Profs. (pres. 1974), Utah Water Pollution Control Assn. (pres. 1976), Internat. Assn. on Water Quality, Am. Soc. Engring. Edn., Am. Acad. Environ. Engrs. (diplomate, trustee 1992-95, v.p. 1995, pres. 1997-98), Sigma Xi, Omicron Delta Kappa, Phi Kappa Phi (Disting. mem.), Tau Beta Pi, Sigma Tau. Home and Office: 2128 Imperial Ln Superior CO 80027 Office Phone: 303-664-5292. Personal E-mail: Joemiddle@aol.com.

MIDDLEDITCH, LEIGH BENJAMIN, JR., lawyer, educator; b. Detroit, Sept. 30, 1929; s. Leigh Benjamin and Hope Tiffin (Noble) M.; m. Betty Lou Givens, June 27, 1953; children: Leigh III, Katherine Middleditch McDonald, Andrew B. BA, U. Va., 1951, LLB, 1957. Bar: Va. 1957. Assoc. James H. Michael, Jr., Charlottesville, Va., 1957-59; ptnr. Battle, Neal, Harris, Minor & Williams, Charlottesville, 1959-68; legal adviser U. Va., Charlottesville, 1968-72; ptnr. McGuire, Woods, Battle & Boothe (now McGuire Woods LLP), Charlottesville, 1972-99, of counsel, 2000—; v.p. McGuire Woods Cons. LLC, Charlottesville, 2001—. Lectr. Grad. Bus. Sch., U. Va., Charlottesville, 1958-90, lectr. Law Sch., 1970-90. Co-author: Virginia Civil Procedure, 1978, 2d edition, 1992; contbr. articles to profl. jours. Chmn. U. Va. Health Svcs. Found., 1988-97; bd. mgrs. U. Va. Alumni, 1994-2001, pres., 2000-01; bd. dirs., chmn. Va. Health Care Found., 1997-98; trustee Claude Moore Found., 1991—; bd. visitors U. Va., 1990-94; trustee Thomas Jefferson Meml. Found., Monticello, 1994-2002; chair U. Va. Miller Found. for Study of Presidency, 2000—. Fellow Am. Bar Found., Va. Bar Found.; mem. ABA (bd. govs. 1999-2002), Va. State Bar (coun., chmn. bd. govs. various sects.), Charlottesville-Albemarle Bar Assn. (pres. 1979-80), U. Va. Law Sch. Alumni Assn. (pres. 1979-81), U.S. C. of C. (bd. dirs. 1998—2004), Va. C. of C. (pres. 1988-90), Omicron Delta Kappa. Episcopalian. Office: McGuire Woods LLP PO Box 1288 Charlottesville VA 22902-1288 Office Phone: 434-977-2543. E-mail: lmiddleditch@mcguirewoods.com.

MIDDLEKAUFF, ROBERT LAWRENCE, historian, educator, academic administrator; b. Yakima, Wash., July 5, 1929; s. Harold and Katherine Ruth (Horne) M.; m. Beverly Jo Martin, July 11, 1952; children: Samuel John, Holly Ruth. BA, U. Wash., 1952; PhD, Yale U., 1961. Instr. history Yale U., New Haven, 1959-62; asst. prof. history U. Calif., Berkeley, 1962-66, assoc. prof., 1966-70, prof., 1970-80, Margaret Byrne prof. history, 1980-83, prof. history, 1988-92, emeritus prof., 2000—, Preston Hotchkis prof., 1992—; dir. Huntington Libr., Art Gallery and Bot. Gardens, San Marino, Calif., 1983-88; Harmsworth prof. history Oxford (Eng.) U., 1996-97. Mem. coun. Inst. Early Am. History and Culture, Williamsburg, Va., 1974-76, 85-88, chair exec. bd., 1992-96. Author: Ancients and Axioms, 1963, The Mathers, 1971, The Glorious Cause: The American Revolution, 1763-1789, 1982, 2nd edit., rev., 2005, Benjamin Franklin and His Enemies, 1996. Served to 1st lt. USMC, 1952-54, Korea. Recipient Bancroft prize, 1972, Commonwealth Club Gold medal, 1983; fellow Am. Coun. Learned Socs., 1965, NEH, 1973, Huntington Libr., 1977. Fellow Am. Acad. Arts and Scis.; mem. Am. Hist. Assn., Orgn. Am. Historians, Am. Philos. Soc., Soc. Am. Historians, Am. Antiquarian Soc., Assocs. Early Am. History and Culture (chmn. exec. com.), Colonial Soc. Mass. (corr.), Mass. Hist. Soc. Home: 5868 Ocean View Dr Oakland CA 94618-1535 Office: Univ Calif Dept History Berkeley CA 94720-2550 Office Phone: 510-642-1971.

MIDDLEMAN, RAOUL FINK, artist; b. Balt., Apr. 3, 1935; s. Paul B. and Elizabeth (Fink) M.; m. Pat Bird (div.); m. Ruth Katherine Channing, Dec. 2, 1971; children: Raphael Bachrach, Benjamin Jacob, Nathaniel John. BA, Johns Hopkins U., 1955; postgrad., Penn. Acad. Fine Arts, 1957—61, Bklyn. Mus., 1961. Faculty Md. Inst. Coll. of Art,

Balt., 1961-85. Vis. critic Vt. Studio Sch. Summer Program,1 985; resident dir. Summer Landscape Painting Program, Md. Inst. Coll. of Art, 1981-83; vis. artist Artists for Environment Found., Walpack Ctr., 1977-81; artist-in-residence Hoffberger Sch. of Painting, 1973-74; lectr. for Figurative Alliance, Studio Sch., N.Y.C., Nat. Gallery in Edinborough, Yale Norfolk, 1980, Md. Inst. Coll. of Art, 1985. One-man shows include Swanston Fine Arts, 1988, Allan Stone Gallery, 1985, 1981,1975, 1972, 1969, 1968, Grimaldis Gallery, 1984, 1981, 1979, 1978, 1999, 2003, William Capro Gallery, 1983, The Water Gap Art Gallery, 1982, The Md. Inst., Coll. of Art, 1974, Krasner Gallery, 1966, Ice Gallery, NYC, 1996, 1997, 1998, Univ. Md., 1999, Troika Gallery, Easton, Md., 1999, MB Modern Gallery, NYC, 2000, Rodger LaPelle Galleries, Phila., 2001, Bavarian Paintings, Murnau, Germany, 2001, Md. Art Place, Balt., 2002; exhibited in groups shows at Nat. Acad. Design, 1990, Md. Inst., 1989-90, Gaumann Cicchino Gallery, 1989, Ingber Gallery, 1989, Bendann Gallery, 1989, Swanston Fine Arts, 1988, Haus der Kunst, 1986, Kornbluth Gallery, 1985, Steven Scott Gallery, and others; respresented in permanent collections at ABC Network, Balt. Mus. Art, Corcoran Gallery, Frye Mus. Art, Johns Hopkins Hosp. NAD, Met. Mus. Art, NY Public Libr., Syracuse Univ., Towson Univ., Univ. Md. Recipient Robert and Rochelle Phillipp prize Nat. Acad. Design, 1990. Mem. Nat. Acad. Design (pres. 1998-2001). Avocation: violin. E-mail: rmiddleman@earthlink.net.

MIDDLESWORTH, WILLIAM, pediatric surgeon; b. Atlantic City, May 30, 1961; BA, Dartmouth Coll., Hanover, NH, 1983; MD, U. Medicine and Dentistry NJ Robert Wood Johnson Med. Sch., Camden, 1989. Cert. Am. Bd. Surgery, 2007, in pediatric surgery Am. Bd. Surgery, 2007. Rsch. fellowship Children's Hosp., Harvard Med. Sch., Boston, 1983—85, The John Radcliffe Hosp., Oxford U., England, 1985, U. Pa., Phila., 1986; internship in gen. surgery U. Md. Med. Sys., Balt., 1989—91, residency in gen. surgery, 1992—95; rsch. fellowship Royal Children's Hosp., U. Melbourne, Australia, 1991—92; pediatric surgery resident Morgan Stanley Children's Hosp. NY Presbyn., NYC, 1995—97, attending surgeon, 1997—, dir., regional pediatric trauma program, 2005—; asst. prof. surgery & pediatric surgery Columbia U. Coll. Physicians & Surgeons, NYC, 1997—; chief, divsn. pediatric surgery Bronx-Lebanon Hosp. Ctr., Bronx, NY, 1997—, St. Barnabas Hosp., Bronx, 1999—. Chair, quality assurance com., dept. surgery NY Presbyn. Hosp. Columbia U. Med. Ctr., quality and patient safety com.; quality assurance com. Morgan Stanley Children's Hosp. NY Presbyn., operating rm. com.; faculty coun. Columbia U. Coll. Physicians & Surgeons, Faculty Medicine. Contbr. articles to profl. jours. Mem.: ACS, Assn. Academic Surgery, Children's Oncology Group, Am. Pediatric Surg. Assn., Internat. Pediatric Endosurgery Group, Am. Acad. Pediat. Surg. Sect. Office: Morgan Stanley Children's Hosp NY-Presbyn Babies & Children's Hosp N Rm 3959 Broadway New York NY 10032 Office Phone: 212-305-5804. Office Fax: 212-305-5971.

MIDDLETON, ANTHONY WAYNE, JR., urologist, educator; b. May 6, 1939; s. Anthony Wayne and Dolores Caravena (Lowry) M.; m. Carol Samuelson, Oct. 23, 1970; children: Anthony Wayne, Suzanne, Kathryn, Jane, Michelle. BS, U. Utah, 1963; MD, Cornell U., 1966. Intern U. Utah Hosps., Salt Lake City, 1966-67; resident in urology Mass. Gen. Hosp., Boston, 1970-74; practice urology Middleton Urol. Assocs., Salt Lake City, 1974—2005; physician cons. LDS Ch., 2008—. Mem. staff LDS Hosp., chmn. divsn. urology, 1995—2004, Salt Lake Regional Med. Ctr., 1977—79, 1984—86; assoc. clin. prof. surgery U. Utah Med. Coll., 1977—2005, staff mem., divsn. urology, 2009—; vice-chmn. bd. govs. Utah Med. Self-Ins. Assn., 1980—81, 1996—2005, chmn., 1985—87; chmn. med. adv. bd. Uroquest Co., 1996—99; med. dir. Uromed, prostate microwave co., 1999—2000, Utah divsn. Rocky Mountain Prostate, 2001—04, Utah-Idaho Lithotripsy, 2001—03; staff Mission Med., LDS Ch., 2008—. Editor: AACU-FAX, 1992-2005; assoc. editor Millenial Star Brit. LDS mag., 1960-61; contbr. articles to profl. jours. Mem. U. Utah Coll. Medicine Dean's Search Com., 1983—84; bd. dirs. Utah Symphony, 1985—2002, Primary Children's Found., 1989—96; mem. Utah Crime Reparations Bd., 2000—05, chmn., 2002—05; staff pres. Primary Children's Med. Ctr., 1982; vice chmn. Utah Med. Polit. Action Com., 1978—81, chmn., 1981—83, Utah Physicians for Reagan, 1983—84; del. Utah State Rep. Conv., 2000—01; bishop, later stake presidency Ch. Jesus Christ Latter-day Saints; mission pres. Canada Vancouver Mission, 2005—08; bd. dirs. Utah chpt. Am. Cancer Soc., 1978—86, Utah Symphony and Opera, 2002—05, Timpanogos Club, 1978—, 2d asst. to pres., 2002—03, 1st asst. to pres., 2003—04, pres., 2004—05. Capt. USAF, 1968—70. Mem.: AMA (del. to Ho. of Dels. 1998—2005, chmn. ref. com. I 2001, mem. governing coun. SSS 2002—05, alt. del. to Ho. of Dels., 1987-88, 89-92, 94, 96-98), ACS, Am. Assn. Clin. Urologists (bd. dirs. 1989—90, nat. pres.-elect 1990—91, pres. 1991—92, nat. bd. chmn. urologic polit. action com. UROPAC 1992—98, Disting. Svc. award 2000), Salt Lake Surg. Soc. (treas. 1977—78), Utah Urol. Assn. (treas. 1977—78, pres. 1978—79), Salt Lake County Med. Assn. (sec. 1965—67, pres. liaison com. 1980—81, pres.-elect 1981—83, pres. 1984), Am. Urologic Assn. (socioecons. com. 1987—90, chmn. western sect. socioecons. com. 1989—90, chmn. western sect. health policy com. 1990—2002, pres.-elect western sect. 1999—2000, pres. 2000—01, Outstanding Svc. award 2005), Utah Med. Assn. (pres. 1987—88, bd. dirs. 1998—2005, Disting. Svc. award 1993), Beta Theta Pi (chpt. pres. Gamma Beta 1962), Alpha Omega Alpha, Phi Beta Kappa. Republican. Home: 2798 Chancellor Pl Salt Lake City UT 84108-2835 Office: 1060 East 1st South Salt Lake City UT 84102-1520 Office Phone: 801-531-9453, 801-707-5482. Personal E-mail: awmiddleton@msn.com.

MIDDLETON, CHRISTOPHER, Germanic languages and literature educator; b. Truro, Cornwall, Eng., June 10, 1926; arrived in US, 1966; s. Hubert Stanley and Dorothy May (Miller) M. BA, U. Oxford, Eng., 1951, DPhil, 1954. Lectr. King's Coll., London, 1955-65; prof. Germanic langs. and lit. U. Tex., Austin, 1966-98. Author: Selected Writings, 1989, Andalusian Poems, 1993, The Balcony Tree, 1992, Intimate Chronicles, 1996, Twenty Tropes for Doctor Dark, 2000, The Word Pavilion and Selected Poems, 2001, Of the Mortal Fire, 2003, Jackdaw Jiving: Essays on Poetry and Translation, 1998, In the Mirror of the Eighth King, 1999, Faint Harps and Silver Voices-Selected Translations, 2000, Crypto-Topographia: Stories of Secret Places, 2002, Palavers and A Nocturnal Journal, 2004, The Anti-Basilisk, 2005, The Tenor on Horseback, 2007, Collected Poems, 2008. Recipient trans. prize Schlegel-Tieck/Govt. Fed. Republic Germany, 1985, Anglo-Swiss Cultural Rels. prize Max Geilinger Stiftung, Zurich, Switzerland, 1987; Guggenheim Found. poetry fellow, 1974-75, NEH poetry fellow, 1980. Mem. Akademie der Künste Berlin. Office: U Tex Dept Of Germanic Langs Austin TX 78712

MIDDLETON, HERMAN DAVID, SR., retired theater educator; b. Sanford, Fla., Mar. 24, 1925; s. Arthur Herman and Ruby Elmerry (Hart) Middleton; m. Amelia Mary Eggart, Dec. 1, 1945; children: Herman David, Kathleen Hart. BS, Columbia U., 1948, MA, 1949; PhD, U. Fla., 1964; postgrad., N.Y. U., 1950, Northwestern U., 1951. Instr., dir. drama and speech Maryville (Tenn.) Coll., 1949-50; instr., designer, tech. dir. theatre U. Del., 1951-55; asst. prof., head dept. drama U. N.C., Greensboro, 1956-59, assoc. prof., head dept. drama and speech, 1959-65, prof., head dept., 1965-74, prof., 1974-79, Excellence Fund prof. dept. communication and theatre, 1979-90, prof. emeritus, 1990. Stage mgr. Unto thee Hills Cherokee Hist. Assn., 1953—56; designer Chucky Jack Gt. Smokey Mountains Hist. Soc., Gatlinburg, Tenn., 1956, designer, dir., 57; comm. cons. NC Nat. Bank, 1968, Jefferson Std. Life Ins. Co., Greensboro, NC, 1969, Gilbarco, Inc., Greensboro, 1969—70, Greensboro, 1973. Drama critic, columnist: Sunday Star, 1952, theater editor: Players Mag., 1959—61, theater columnist: Sunday edits. Greensboro Daily News, 1959—62; contbr. articles to profl. jours. Mem. NC Arts Coun. Commn., 1964—66, Guilford County Bi-Centennial Celebration Commn., 1969—70; pres. Shanks Village Players, Orangeburg, NYC, 1947—48, Univ. Drama Group, Newark, Del., 1954—55; bd. dirs. Broadway Theatre League Greensboro, 1958—60, Greensboro Cmty. Arts Coun., 1964—67, 1969—72, Greensboro Cmty. Theatre, 1983—86, Carolina Theatre commn., 1990—93; organizer-cons. Market Players, W. Market St. United Meth. Ch., 1979—82. With USN, 1943—46. Recipient O. Henry award, Greensboro C. of C., 1966, Gold medallion, Amoco Oil Co., 1973, Suzanne M. Davis award, Southeastern Theatre Conf., 1975, Marian A. smith Disting. Career award, NC Theatre Conf., 1990. Mem.: Assn. Theater Higher Edn., NC Theater Conf. (co-organizer 1971, bd. dirs. 1984—92, pres. 1987—88), NC Drama and Speech Assn. (pres. 1966—67), Carolina Dramatic Assn. (bd. dirs. 1958—59), Southeastern Theatre Conf. (bd. dirs. 1963—68, 1987—92, pres. 1965, pres. pro tem 1966), Nat. Collegiate Players, Speech Communication Assn. Am., Assn. Theatre Higher Edn. (founding mem. 1986—87), Am. Coll. Theatre Festival (regional festival dir. 1973, 1980, regional dir., mem. nat. com. 1978—80), Am. Theatre Assn. (chmn. bd. nominations 1971—72), Am. Nat. Theatre and Acad. (organizer, exec. v.p. Piedmont chpt. 1957—60), Alpha Psi Omega, Theta Alpha Phi, Phi Kappa Phi, Phi Delta Kappa. Democrat. Methodist. Home: 203 Village Ln Unit A Greensboro NC 27409-2517 Personal E-mail: hmiddleton@triad.rr.com.

MIDDLETON, JACK BAER, lawyer; b. Phila., Jan. 13, 1929; s. Harry C. and Mildred Cornell (Baer) M.; m. Ann (Dodge), Aug. 22, 1953; children: Susan D., Jack B. Jr., Peter C. BA, Lafayette Coll., 1950; JD (hon.), Boston U., 1956. Bar: NH 1956, US Dist. Ct. Vt. 1988, US Ct. Appeals (1st cir.) 1957, US Supreme Ct. 1972. Assoc. McLane, Graf, Raulerson, and Middleton, Manchester, NH, 1956—62; ptnr., dir. McLane, Graf, Raulerson, and Middleton, Manchester, NH, 1962—. Spl. justice Merrimack, NH Dist. Ct., 1964-87; commr. Uniform State Laws, 1971-74. Author: (with others) Summary of New Hampshire Law, 1964, Compendium of New Hampshire Law, 1969, Trial of a Wrongful Death Action in New Hampshire, 1977; editor Boston U. Law Rev., 1954-56; contbr. articles to profl. jours. Active Mt. Washington Commn., 1969—, Bedford, NH Sch. Bd., 1960-66; adv. bd. Merrimack Valley Coll.; trustee, v.p. Mt. Washington Obs., 1957—; chmn. bd. trustees White Mountain Sch., 1976-79; campaign chmn. United Way Greater Manchester, 1987, bd. dirs., 1986-92, chmn., 1990-91; bd. dirs. NH Pub. Radio, 1988-91; bd. gov. NH Pub. TV, 1994-2003, chmn., 1997-99; trustee New Eng. Law Inst., 1977-80, Franklin Pierce Law Ctr., 2003—. Sgt. USMCR, 1950-52. Fellow Am. Coll. Trial Lawyers (chmn. NH sect. 1988-90), Am. Bar Found. (life); mem. ABA (ho. dels. 1984-2005, bd. gov. 1996-2002, sec. elect 1998-99, sec. 1999-2002), New Eng. Bar Assn. (bd. dir. 1977-88, pres. 1982-83), NH Bar Assn. (pres. 1979-80), NH Bar Found. (bd. dir. 1979-92, chair 1983-90), Nat. Ctr. State Ct. (dir. 1999-2005), Nat. Conf. Bar Found. (trustee 1985-92, pres. 1989-90), Nat. Conf. Bar Pres. (exec. coun. 1987-95, pres. 1993-94), NH Bus. and Industry Assn. (bd. dir. 1988-2005, sec. 1990-2005), Manchester C. of C. (bd. dir. 1967-89, chmn. 1984-85), New Eng. Coun. (bd. dirs. 1991-2004), New Eng. Legal Found. (bd. dirs. 2001-04). Office: McLane Graf Raulerson and Middleton 900 Elm St Ste 1001 Manchester NH 03101-2029 Home Phone: 603-539-6305; Office Phone: 603-628-1446, 603-625-6464. Business E-Mail: jack.middleton@mclane.com.

MIDDLETON, NORMAN GRAHAM, social worker, psychotherapist; b. Jacksonville, Fla., Jan. 21, 1935; s. Norman Graham and Betty (Quina) M.; m. Judy Stephens, Aug. 1, 1968; stepchildren: Monty Stokes, Toni Stokes. BA, U. Miami, Fla., 1960; MSW, Fla. State U., 1962. Casework counselor Family Svc., Miami, 1962-64; psychiat. social worker assoc. firm Drs. Watson, Steele, Wiener, Sarasota, Fla., 1964-66; psychotherapist Sarasota, 1966—. Instr. Manatee Jr. Coll., Bradenton, Fla., 1973-76. Author: The Caverns of My Mind, 1985, Imaginative Healing, 1993, Spirited Imagination, 2002. Pres. Coun. on Epilepsy, Sarasota, 1969-70. Served with USAF, 1954-58. Fellow Fla. Soc. Clin. Social Work (pres. 1978-80); mem. Am. Group Psychotherapy Assn., Am. Assn. Sex Educators and Counselors (cert. sex educator). Democrat. Episcopalian. Home: 16626 Winburn Dr Sarasota FL 34240-9221 Office: 1257 S Tamiami Trail Sarasota FL 34239-2219 Office Phone: 941-366-3334. Personal E-mail: imageside@aol.com.

MIDDLETON, VICTORIA J., legislative staff member; b. Leesburg, Va. Degree, Mary Washington Coll., Fredericksburg, Va., 1978; BA in Polit. Sci. cum laude, Hollins Coll., Va., 1981. Legis. asst. for Rep. Duncan Hunter US House of Reps., Washington, 1982—84, chief of staff, 1985—. Mem.: Omicron Delta Kappa, Hollins Columns. Avocations: hockey, needlecrafts, reading, horseback riding. Office: Office of Congressman Duncan Hunter 1429 Longworth House Office Bldg Washington DC 20515 Office Phone: 202-225-5672. Business E-Mail: victoria.middleton@mail.house.gov.*

MIDDLETON-KAPLAN, RICHARD EDWARD, literature and language professor; b. LA, Sept. 10, 1961; s. Harold and Eva Evelyn Kaplan; m. Marcia Ann Middleton-Kaplan, Mar. 20, 2004. PhD, U. Calif., LA, 1993. Sr. staff editor Coffey Comm. Inc., Walla Walla, Wash., 1993—2002; assoc. prof. dept. English Harper Coll., Palatine, Ill., 2002—. Contbr. articles to profl. pubs. Lay leader Congregation Beth Israel, Walla Walla, 1993—2002; bd. dirs. Elgin Youth Symphony Orch., Ill., 2003—08, Walla Walla Symphony Orch., 1997—2002. Fellowship, Harper Coll. Ctr. Multicultural Learning, 2004. Mem.: MLA, N.Am. Levinas Soc., Nineteenth-Century Studies Assn., Melville Soc., MELUS, Am. Fedn. Tchrs., Am. Culture Assn. Liberal. Jewish. Office: Harper Coll 1200 W Algonquin Rd Palatine IL 60067 Office Fax: 847-924-6039. Business E-Mail: rkaplan@harpercollege.edu.

MIDDLEWOOD, MARTIN EUGENE, writer, consultant; b. Galesburg, Ill., Mar. 21, 1947; s. Martin and Bernetta Maxine (Henderson) M.; m. Mona Marie Jarmer, Sept. 10, 1971; children: Erin, Martha, Emily, Margaret. BA, Ea. Wash. U., 1973, MA, 1980. Writer tech. manuals Tektronix, Inc., Beaverton, Oreg., 1976-77, tech. writer, 1977-79, sr. tech. writer, 1979-82, supr. pub. rels., 1982-84, mgr. pub. rels., 1984-85, mgr. mktg. communications Vancouver, Wash., 1985-86; dir. info. strategy and svcs. Waggener Edstrom, Portland, Oreg., 1986-98; pub. Cognizer Report, Portland, Oreg., 1990-94. Chmn. adv. bd. sci. and tech. writing, Clark Coll., Vancouver, 1984-2004; owner communications cons. firm, Vancouver, 1978-98; pres., owner Frontline Strategies, Inc., 1998—. Author: (ednl. brochure series) Oscilloscope Measurements, 1979 (award of excellence Willamette Valley chpt., Network Svcing., won Awd. of Distinction, 1980, Soc. Tech. Communication, 1980); assoc. pub. Builder News, 2004-2005; contbr. articles to profl. jours. Served with USMC, 1967-70. Recipient cert. recognition Clark Coll., Vancouver, 1984, 86, 89, 92-99, award of excellence Pacific N.W. chpt. Internat. Assn. Bus. Communicators, 1985. Mem. Soc. Tech. Communication (pres. Willamette Valley chpt. 1983-85, award of recognition 1986, chpt. pub. achievement award 1985, awards of distinction, 1980, 81). Avocations: photography, martial arts. Home and Office: 10816 NW Oxbow Ridge Dr Vancouver WA 98685

MIDELFORT, HANS CHRISTIAN ERIK, retired history professor; b. Eau Claire, Wis., Apr. 17, 1942; s. Peter Albert and Gerd (Gjems) M.; m. Corelyn Forsyth Senn, June 16, 1965 (div. Dec. 1981); children: Katarina, Kristian; m. Cassandra Clemons Hughes, May 25, 1985 (div. April 1996); 1 child, Lucy; m. Anne L. McKeithen, June 22, 1996. BA, Yale U., 1964, MPhil, 1967, PhD, 1970. Instr. Stanford U., Calif., 1968-70; asst. prof. U. Va., Charlottesville, 1970-72, assoc. prof., 1972-87, prof., 1987—2009, Charles Julian Bishko prof. history, 1996—2009. Vis. prof. Harvard U., Cambridge, Mass., 1985, U. Stuttgart, Germany, 1988, U. Bern, Switzerland, 1988, Wolfson Coll., Oxford U., 2002, Yale U., 2003; prin. Brown Coll., U. Va., 1996-2001; Dwight Terry lectr. Yale U., 2003; vis. fellow All Souls Coll., Oxford U., 2005. Author: Witch Hunting in Southwestern Germany, 1972 (Gustave Arlt prize 1972), Mad Princes of Renaissance Germany, 1994 (Roland H. Bainton prize 16th Century Studies Conf. 1995), A History of Madness in 16th Century Germany, 1999 (Ralph Waldo Emerson prize, Phi Beta Kappa, 1999, Roland H. Bainton prize 16th Century Studies Conf. 2000), Exorcism and Enlightenment, 2005, Ideas and Cultural Margins in Early Modern Germany, 2009; editor: Johann Weyer, On Witchcraft, 1998; co-editor: Europe, 1450-1789. Encyclopedia of the Early Modern World, 2003; translator: Imperial Cities and the Reformation (Bernd Moeller), 1972, Revolution of 1525 (Peter Bickle), 1981, Shaman of Oberstdorf (Wolfgang Behringer), 1998, Witchcraft and the Papacy (Rainer Decker), 2008. Mem. Soc. Reformation Rsch. (pres. 1992-93). Business E-Mail: hem7e@virginia.edu.

MIDKIFF, DINAH LEE, retired elementary and middle school educator; b. Ashland, Ky., Dec. 23, 1954; d. Marie Ramey Midkiff. AA, Ashland Cmty. Coll., 1974; BA, Morehead State U., 1976, MA, 1978, cert. in adminstrn. and supervision, 1980. Tchr. Boyd County Bd. Edn., Ashland, 1976—85, Boone County Bd. Edn., Hebron, Ky., 1989—90, Franklin County Bd. Edn., Frankfort, Ky., 1990—2003, Jessamine County Bd. Edn., Nicholasville, Ky., 2003—04; ret., 2004—. Cons. Ky. Dept. Edn., Frankfort, Ky., 1986—89. Co-author: Jazz Up Reading: A Conference Overview, Informal Selection Process for Grade One Placement. Recipient Drug Abuse Resistance Edn. award, 2002; named Ky. Col., 2001. Mem.: NOW, AAUW, Am. Assn. Ret. Persons, Ky. Ret. Tchr. Assn. Democrat. Avocations: travel, reading, gardening. Home: 1338 Shun Pike Nicholasville KY 40356

MIDLARSKY, ELIZABETH RUTH, psychologist, researcher, educator; b. NYC; d. Abraham Allan and Frances Lucille (Wiener) Steckel; m. Manus Issachar Midlarsky, June 25, 1961; children: Susan Rachel, Miriam Joyce, Michael George. BA, CUNY, 1961; MA, Northwestern U., 1966, PhD, 1968. Lic. psychologist, N.J., Mich., Colo. Asst. prof. U. Denver, 1968-73; dir. rsch. and evaluation Malcolm X Mental Health Ctr. (now Park East), Denver, 1973-75; assoc. prof., dir. psychol. tng. program Met. State Coll., Denver, 1975-77; assoc. prof. psychology U. Detroit, 1977—83, prof. psychology, 1983-90, chair dept. psychology, 1978-81, dir. Ctr. Study Devel. and Aging, 1982—90; prof. clin. psychology Tchrs. Coll. Columbia U., NYC, 1990—, dir. Ctr. for Lifespan and Aging Studies, 1992—, founding coord. MA program, 1998—, co-chair dept. counseling and clin. psychology, 2006—09; rsch. scholar Phila. Geriatric Ctr., 1997—2000. Mem. initial rev. group NIMH, Bethesda, Md., 1976-82; mem. ad hoc rev. groups NHLBI, Bethesda, 1985-95; mem. study sect. NIH, Bethesda, 1986-91; mem. nat. reviewers reserve, 1991-94, rev. groups, Congressionally Directed Med. Rsch. Program, 2007 Author: Altruism in Late Life, 1994; co-editor Humboldt Jour. Social Rels., 1985-86, Violence in Schools, 2005; editor Acad. Psychol. Bull., 1982-86, mem. editl bd. Jour. Traumatic Stress, 2000-2008, Jour. Religion Health, 2007-, Psychology Religion and Spirituality, 2008-; contbr. chpts. to books and articles to profl. jours. Mem. exec. coun. Mich. Psychol. Assn. Grantee Nat. Inst. Aging, 1982-85, 87-90, AARP, 1982-83, 88-89, 92-95; postdoctoral rsch. fellow AAUW, 1974-75. Fellow APA (divsn. 12, 20, publs. com. 1990-92, election com. 2005—, student award com. 1990), Assn. Psychol. Sci., Am. Orthopsychiat. Assn., Gerontol. Soc. Am. (exec. com. on program com. 1983-84); mem. Soc. Psychol. Study Social Issues, Internat. Assn. Genocide Scholars, Dept. Defense (CDMRP) Panel. Jewish. Avocations: writing poetry, needlepoint, piano, reading. Home: 3 Falcon Rd East Brunswick NJ 08816-2716 Office Phone: 212-678-3124. Business E-Mail: em142@columbia.edu.

MIDLER, BETTE, singer, entertainer, actress; b. Honolulu, Dec. 1, 1945; m. Martin von Haselberg, 1984; 1 child, Sophie. Student, U. Hawaii. Debut as actress (films), Hawaii, 1965, mem. cast Fiddler on the Roof, N.Y.C, 1966—69, Salvation, 1970, Tommy, Seattle Opera Co., 1971, nightclub concert performer on tour U.S., from 1972; appearance Palace Theatre, N.Y.C., 1973, Radio City Music Hall, 1993, TV appearances include The Tonight Show, Bette Midler: Old Red Hair is Back, 1978, Gypsy, 1993 (Golden Globe award best actress in a mini-series or movie made for television, 1994, Emmy nomination, Lead Actress - Special, 1994), Seinfeld, 1996, Diva Las Vegas, 1997, Murphy Brown, 1998, appeared Clams on The Half-Shell Revue, N.Y.C., 1975, recs. include The Divine Miss M, 1972, Bette Midler, 1973, Broken Blossom, 1977, Live at Last, 1977, The Rose, Thighs and Whispers, 1979, Songs for the New Depression, 1979, Divine Madness, 1980, No Frills, 1984, Mud Will Be Flung Tonight, 1985, Beaches (soundtrack), 1989, Some People's Lives, 1990, Bette of Roses, 1995, Bathhouse Betty, 1998, Bette, 2000, Bette Midler Sings The Rosemary Clooney Songbook, 2003; actor: (films) Hawaii, 1966, The Rose, 1979 (Academy award nomination best actress, 1979), Divine Madness, 1980, Jinxed, 1982, Down and Out in Beverly Hills, 1986, Ruthless People, 1986, Outrageous Fortune, 1987, Oliver and Company (voice), 1988, Big Business, 1988, Beaches, 1988, Stella, 1990, Scenes From a Mall, 1991, For the Boys, 1991 (Academy award nomination best actress, 1991), Hocus Pocus, 1993, Get Shorty, 1995, The First Wives Club, 1996, That Old Feeling, 1997, Get Bruce, 1999, Isn't She Great, 1999, Drowning Mona, 2000, Isn't She Great, 2000, The Stepford Wives, 2004, The She Found Me, 2007, The Women, 2008; appeared in cable TV (HBO) prodn. Bette Midler's Mondo Beyondo, 1988; author: A View From A Broad, 1980, The Saga of Baby Divine, 1983; exec. prodr., composer (TV show) Bette, 2000, exec. prodr. Some of My Best Friends, 2001, (films) Divine Secret of the Ya-Ya Sisterhood, 2002. Recipient After Dark Ruby award, 1973, Grammy awards, 1973, 1990, spl. Tony award, 1973, Emmy award for NBC Spl., Ol' Red Hair is Back, 1978, 2 Golden Globe awards for The Rose, 1979, Golden Globe award for The Boys, 1991, Emmy award The Tonight Show appearance, 1992. Office: c/o Miss M Prodns 1222 16th Ave S 3rd Fl Nashville TN 37212

MIDLER, LAURENCE H. (LARRY), lawyer, real estate company executive; BA with hon., U. Va., 1987; JD, NYU, 1990. Bar: NY State 1990. Former assoc. atty. Latham & Watkins Law Offices, NYC; former v.p., gen. counsel Serviscope Corp.; former head facilities corp. svcs.

dept., gen. counsel Micro Warehouse, Inc.; exec. v.p., gen. counsel CB Richard Ellis Group, 2006—. Office: CB Richard Ellis Ste 2700 355 S Grand Ave Los Angeles CA 90071*

MIEARS-CUTSINGER, MARY ELLEN, artist, gallery owner; b. Ratliff, Okla., Jan. 23, 1931; d. Elmer Cecil and Ruth Collins Miears; m. Leroy Gene Meyers (dec.); children: Kathryn, Melissa, Mary Teresa, Marsha, Donna; m. Charles Wesley Cutsinger, Oct. 10, 1979. Student, Mt. San Antonio Coll., Walnut, Calif., 1975—76. Freelance comml. and portrait artist, 1949—76; staff artist Pomona (Calif.) Progress Bull., 1976—77; studio artist Miears Fine Art, Ridgecrest, Calif., 1979—; art tchr. Studio Eight, Ridgecrest, 1989—96; studio artist Miears Fine Art and Studio Eight Gallery, Ridgecrest, 1979—. Mem. gallery com. Maturango Mus., Ridgecrest, 1990. Recipient Top 100 Paintings award, Premier Arts for the Parks Nat., 1987, Wingspread Guide to N.Mex. award, Ann. Nat. Exhbn., 2000, 2d pl. award, Sierra Pastel Soc. Internat., 2004. Mem.: Allied Artists, Pastel Soc. West Coast (signature mem.), Catharine Lorillard Wolfe Art club (signature mem.). Home: 1125 W Benson Ridgecrest CA 93555 Office: 995 N Norma St Ste # Ridgecrest CA 93555 Office Phone: 760-446-7977. E-mail: mary@kuanyin-images.com.

MIEKKA, JEANETTE ANN, retired science educator; b. Kenmore, NY, Aug. 25, 1931; d. Harry Whittier and Beulah Laura Lambe; m. Richard George Miekka, June 22, 1958; children: James Richard, Frederick Noah, Cynthia Marie Bordas-Miekka. BSc, Boston U., 1949—53, MEd, 1954—57. Teacher of All Sciences Mass., 1954. Tchr. of chemistry, physics, biology, gen. sci. Meridith H.S., Meridity, NH, 1953—54; sci. tchr. and dept. chmn. Hicksville Jr. H.S., 1954—56; biology and physiology tchr. Newton H.S., Mass., 1956—60; instr. of comparative physiology Allied Health Jr. Coll., Holliston, Mass., 1978—79; ret., 1979. Sophomore class advisor Meridith H.S., NH, 1953—54; supr. of student teachers Newton H.S., Mass., 1957—60, advisor, future teachers of am., 1956—60. Contbr. articles to profl. jours. Pres. Am. Field Svc., Natick, Mass., 1964—65; dir. F.I.S.H., Natick, Mass., 1964—65; chmn., publicity Sudbury Women's Club, Mass., 1971—74; mem. Sun Coast Opera Guild; cons. St. Francis Sch., Loiseau, Haiti, 2002—05; assoc. St. Margaret's Convent, Boston; lay eucharistic min. St. Matthews Ch., St. Petersburg, Fla., 2004—05, vestry mem. Episcopal. Avocations: travel, bridge, book club, cooking, writing.

MIEL, JAN, humanities educator; b. Wayne, Pa., Oct. 10, 1930; s. Charles Jan and Mary (Long) M.; m. Elizabeth MacKiernan, Sept. 10, 1960; children: Persephone, Justin. AB, Harvard U., 1952; MA, Princeton U., 1960, PhD, 1965. Instr. Goucher Coll., Towson, Md., 1960-62; asst. prof. MIT, Cambridge, Mass., 1962-64, Wesleyan U., Middletown, Conn., 1964-70, assoc. prof., 1970-78, prof., 1978-99. Author: Pascal and Theology, 1970, Pascal and Theology (Japanese transl), 2000; contbr. articles to profl. jours. Mem. exec. coun. Diocese of Conn., Hartford, 1999-2002. Cpl. U.S. Army, 1953-55. Fellow Johns Hopkins U., 1968, NEH, 1976, Guggenheim Found., 1977. Mem. MLA, N.Am. Soc. for 17th Century French Lit. Anglican. Home: 29 Gordon Pl Middletown CT 06457 Office: Wesleyan U Coll Letters Middletown CT 06459

MIELE, ANGELO, engineering educator, researcher, consultant, author; b. Formia, Italy, Aug. 21, 1922; arrived in U.S., 1952, naturalized, 1985; s. Salvatore and Elena (Marino) Miele. DCivil Engring., U. Rome, Italy, 1944, DAero. Engring., 1946; DSc (hon.), Inst. Tech., Technion, Israel, 1992. Asst. prof. Poly. Inst. Bklyn., 1952- 55; prof. Purdue U., 1955-59; dir. astrodynamics Boeing Sci. Rsch. Labs., 1959-64; prof. aerospace scis., math. scis. Rice U., Houston, 1964-88, Foyt Family prof. engring., 1988-93, Foyt prof. emeritus engring., aerospace scis., math. scis., 1993—, rsch. prof., 2001—. Cons. Douglas Aircraft Co., 1956—58, U.S. Aviation Underwriters, 1987, Boeing Comml. Airplane Co., 1989, European Space Tech. Engring. Ctr., 2002; cons. Allison divsn. GM Corp., 1956—58; Breakwell Meml. lectureship Internat. Astron. Fedn., 1994; Gaspare Santangelo Meml. lectureship Italian Assn. of Aeronautics and Astronautics, 2001. Author: Flight Mechanics, 1962; editor: Theory of Optimum Aerodynamic Shapes, 1965, Applied Mathematics in Aerospace Science and Engineering, 1994, Advanced Design Problems in Aerospace Engineering, 2003; editor-in chief Jour. Optimization Theory and Applications, 1966—, assoc. editor Jour. Astronautical Scis., 1964—93, Applied Math. and Computation, 1975—, series editor Math. Concepts and Methods in Sci. and Engring., 1975—. Optimal Control Applications and Methods, 1979—, mem. editl. bd. RAIRO-Ops. Rsch., 1990—, mem. adv. bd. AIAA Edn. Series, 1991—98; contbr. articles to profl. jours. Pres. Italy in Am. Assn., 1966—68. Decorated knight comdr. Order Merit Italy; recipient Levy medal, Franklin Inst. of Phila., 1974, Brouwer award, AAS, 1980, Schuck award, Am. Automatic Control Coun., 1988, Latina prize, 2002, Flight Mechanics award, AIAA, 1982, Pendray Aerospace Lit. award, 1982. Fellow: Am. Astronautical Soc., AIAA (hon. Pendray Aerospace Lit. award 1982, Mechs. and Control of Flight award 1982), Franklin Inst.; mem.: Tex. Acad. Engring., Scis. and Medicine, Nat. Acad. Engring. of Argentina (corr.), Internat. Acad. Astronautics, Acad. Scis. Turin (corr.), Russian Acad. Scis. (fgn.), NAE. Achievements include research in aerospace engring., windshear problems, hypervelocity flight, interplanetary flight, math. programming, optimal control theory and computing methods. Home: 3106 Kettering Dr Houston TX 77027-5504 Office: Rice Univ MS-322 Aero-Astronautics Group 6100 Main St Houston TX 77005-1827 Office Phone: 713-348-4907. Business E-Mail: miele@rice.edu.

MIELE, JOEL ARTHUR, SR., civil engineer; b. Jersey City, May 28, 1934; s. Jene Gerald Sr., and Eleanor Natalie (Bergida) M.; m. Faith Roseann Trombetta, July 21, 1952 (div. 1954); m. 2d Josephine Ann Cottone, Feb. 14, 1959; children: Joel Arthur, Jr., Vita Marie, Janet Ann. BCE, Poly. Inst. Bklyn., 1955. Lic. profl. engr. NY, NJ, Fla.; profl. planner NJ; chartered engr., UK. Civil engr. Yudell & Miele, Queens, NY, 1955-57; chief engr. Jene G. Miele Assocs., 1960—68; prin. and CEO Miele Assocs., 1968—94; commr. NYC Planning Commn., 1990—94; commr. dept. bldgs. City of NY, 1994—96; commr. Dept. Environ. Protection, 1996—2002, NYC Bd. Stds. and Appeals, 2002—05; pvt. practice cons. engr., 2005—. Mem. NY State Bd. for Engring. and Land Surveying, 1997—, chmn. 2005-07. Patentee masonry wall constrn. Mem. Cmty. Bd. 10, Queens, 1971-90, chmn., 1978-90; mem. bd. visitors Creedmoor State Hosp., 1978—, pres., 1979—; trustee Queens Borough Pub. Libr., 1979—, pres., 1995-96; bd. dirs. Peninsula Hosp. Ctr., 1984—, chair, 1990—; bd. mem. Peninsula Gen. Nursing Home, 1985—, chair, 1990—; bd. dirs. Queens County Overall Econ. Devel. Corp., 1989-94, pres., 1991-94; trustee, bd. chair Queens Pub. Comm. Corp., 1983—; exec. v.p. Queens County and mem. Nat. Coun. Boy Scouts Am., 1991—; bd. mem. Am. Parkinson Disease Assn., 1985—, mem. exec. com., 1987—, v.p., 1996—2008; pres. 2009-; pres. Internat. Parkinsons Fond, Netherlands, 1997—, bd. chair, 2009-; dir. Queens Libr. Found., 1997—; dir. Assn. Met Water Agys., 1997-02, Assn. Met. Sewerage Agys., 1997-02; mem. Nat. Coun. Examiners Engring. & Surveying, 1997—; founder, co-pres., Internat. Parkinsons Fond GmbH, Germany, 2006-. Lt. (j.g.) USN, 1957-60; capt. USNR, 1960-88, ret., 1988; RADM LH NY Naval Militia, 1998. Named Italian-Am. of Yr. Ferrini Welfare League, Queens, 1980, Hon. Mem. of Queens Chpt. AIA, 1994, Hon. Profl. Affiliated Mem. NY Soc. Archs., 1994; recipient Outstanding Cmty. Leader award Boy Scouts Am., 1987, Pride of Queens award, 1990, Pub. Servant Extraordinaire award United Cerebral Palsy of Queens, 1994, Good Scout award Greater NY Coun. Boy Scouts Am., 1994, Nat. Silver Beaver Court of Honor award, Boy Scouts of America, 1997, United Hosp. Funds Disting. Trustee award for Extraordinary Svc., 1997, NYSSPE Outstanding PE Mgr. of Yr. award, 1997, Disting. Alumni award, Poly. U., 1998, Humanitarian of Yr. award Guide Dog Found., 2000, Spl. Recognition for Pub. Svc. award NY Bldg. Congress, 2002, Golden Eagle award Boy Scouts Am., 2002. Fellow ASCE (life), NSPE (trustee polit. action com. 1990-96); mem.NY State Soc. Profl. Engrs. (v.p. 1984-86, pres. 1988-89, nat. dir. 1987-90, Engr. of Yr. 1983), NY State Assn. of Professions (founding). Democrat. Congregationalist. Office Phone: 718-848-8013. Personal E-mail: jmiele2@nyc.rr.com.

MIELE, LUCIO, physician, medical researcher, pharmacologist; b. Naples, Italy, Mar. 13, 1957; s. Armando and Agata Liana (Vassallo-Paleologo) Miele; m. Carolyn Margaret Duncan, Oct. 16, 2005; stepchildren: Charles Joseph Duncan, Margaret Ann Duncan, Caroline Elizabeth Duncan. MD, U. Naples, Italy, 1981—81, PhD, 1987. Vis. fellow NIH, Bethesda, Md., 1986—89, vis. assoc., 1989—93; tenure-track prin. investigator Ctr. for Biologics Evaluation and Rsch., FDA, Bethesda, 1994—96, acting chief lab. cell biology, 1996—98; asst. prof. pathology Loyola U. Med. Ctr., Maywood, Ill., 1998—2001; assoc. prof. pharmacology U. Ill., Chgo., 2001—05; prof. pathology, pharmacolgy and exptl. therapeutics Loyola U. Med. Ctr., Maywood, Ill., 2005—. Vis. prof. Temple U., Phila., 2005—06; dir. breast cancer pre-clinical rsch. program Cardinal Bernardin Cancer Ctr., Loyola U. Chgo., Maywood, Ill., 2005—; organizer EMBO Conf. on Notch Signaling, 2005; spkr., cons. in field. Editor: Jour. Expt. Clin. Oncology, 2004—06; mem. editl. bd.: Jour. Cell Biochem., 2003—06, Women's Oncology Reviews, 2002—06; contbr. articles to profl. jours. Drug discovery and molecular pharmacology study sect. Nat. Cancer Inst./NIH, Bethesda, 2002—06; breast cancer rsch. study sections Dept. of Def., Washington, 2002—06; dept. pub. health penny severns women's oncology rsch. awards study sect. State of Ill., Springfield. Recipient Outstanding Young Scientist award, Italian Acad. Medicine and Surgery, 1983, FDA award, 1997, Excellence in Women's Oncology Rsch. award, Ill. Dept. Pub. Health, 2000—01; grantee, NCI, 1999—2004, Ill. Dept. Pub. Health, 1999—2002, 2006—, Nat. Inst. Child Health and Human Devel., 2002—06; Idea grant, DOD, 2004—, Program Project grant, NCI/NIH, 2006—. Mem.: Am. Assn. for Cancer Rsch. Democrat-Npl. Roman Catholic. Achievements include development of recombinant human CC10/Uteroglobin; research in role of notch signaling in various cancers, notch inhibition has anti-neoplastic activity in vivo. Avocations: horsemanship, scuba diving, photography, poetry, philosophy. Office: Loyola Univ Med Ctr 2160 S First Ave Maywood IL 60153 Office Fax: 708-327-2245. Business E-Mail: lmiele@lumc.edu.

MIELKE, CLARENCE HAROLD, JR., hematologist; b. Spokane, Wash., June 18, 1936; s. Clarence Harold and Marie Katherine (Gillespie) M.; m. Marcia Rae, July 5, 1964; children: Elisa, John, Kristina. BS, Wash. State U., 1959; MD, U. Louisville, 1963. Intern San Francisco Gen. Hosp., 1963-64; resident in medicine Portland VA Hosp., 1964-65, San Francisco Gen. Hosp., 1965-67; fellow in hematology U. So. Calif., 1967-68; tchg. fellow, asst. physician, instr. Tufts-New Eng. Med. Ctr. Hosps., Boston, 1968-71; sr. scientist Med. Rsch. Inst., San Francisco, 1971-90; chief hematology Presbyn. Hosp., San Francisco, 1971-82; asst. prof. clin. medicine U. Calif. Sch. Medicine, San Francisco, 1971-80, assoc. clin. prof., 1979-90, bd. dirs. Inst. Cancer Rsch., 1992—; with Regent Gonzaga U., 2009. Trustee, bd. dirs. Med. Rsch. Inst. San Francisco, Sacred Heart Hosp. Found., 1997-2000, Rockwood Clinic Found., 1994—; dir. emeritus Inst. Cancer Rsch.; trustee emeritus, bd. dirs. Med. Rsch. Inst., 1988—; dir. Health Rsch. and Edn. Ctr., Wash. State U., 1989-2005, prof. pharmacology, 1989—, prof. vet. medicine, 1989—, assoc. dean rsch., 1992-2004; dir. Spokane (Wash.) Heart Study, 1994-2006. Editor emeritus Jour. Clin. Aphesis, 1981; contbr. chpts. to books, articles to med. jours. Named Nat. Disting. Eagle Scout, 1998; NIH grantee, 1973-88. Fellow ACP, Am. Heart Assn.; mem. AAAS, AMA, Am. Heart Assn., Internat. Acad. Clin. and Applied Thrombosis and Hemostasis, Internat. Soc. Hematology, Am. Coll. Angiology; mem. Am. Soc. Internat. Medicine, Internat. Soc. Thrombosis and Hemostasis, N.Y. Acad. Scis., Spokane Med. Soc., Internat. Soc. Angiology. Office: 25415 E Misson Ave Liberty Lake WA 99019 Office Phone: 509-358-7630. Business E-Mail: mielkeh@wsu.edu, harry@arborcrest.com.

MIELKE, PAUL WILLIAM, JR., statistician, consultant; b. St. Paul, Feb. 18, 1931; s. Paul William and Elsa (Yungbauer) M.; m. Roberta Roehl Robison, June 25, 1960; children: William, Emily Spear, Lynn Basila. BA, U. Minn., 1953, PhD, 1963; MA, U. Ariz., 1958. Tchg. asst. U. Ariz., Tucson, 1957—58, U. Minn., Mpls., 1958—60, statis. cons., 1960—62, lectr., 1962—63; from asst. to assoc. prof. dept. stats. Colo. State U., Fort Collins, 1963—72, prof. dept. stats., 1972—. Co-author: Permutation Methods: a Distance Function Approach; contbr. articles Am. Jour. Pub. Health, Jour. of Statis. Planning and Inference, Ednl. and Psychol. Measurement, Biometrika, Earth-Sci. Revs., Weather and Forecasting, Jour. Behavioral and Ednl. Stats. Capt. USAF, 1953-57. Fellow Am. Statis. Assn.; mem. Am. Meteorol. Soc. (Banner I. Miller award 1973, 94), Biometric Soc. Achievements include rsch. in common statistical methods (t test and analysis of variance) based on counter intuitive geometric foundations and provided alternative statistical methods which are based on appropriate foundations. Home: 736 Cherokee Dr Fort Collins CO 80525-1517 Office: Colo State U Dept Stats Fort Collins CO 80523-1877 Home Phone: 970-484-3374; Office Phone: 970-491-6465. Business E-Mail: paul.mielke@colostate.edu.

MIELKE, THOMAS J., lawyer, health products executive; BA, Gustavus Adolphus Coll., 1980; JD, Univ. Minn., 1983. Patent atty. Spensley, Horn, Jubas & Lubitz, LA, Dow Chem. Co., Midland, Mich.; v.p., chief patent counsel, and chief counsel for No. Am. consumer bus. Kimberly-Clark Corp., Dallas, 1998—2007, sr. v.p. law & govt. affairs, chief compliance officer, 2007—. Mailing: Kimberly-Clark PO Box 19100 Dallas TX 75261-9100*

MIERS, HARRIET ELLAN, lawyer, former federal official; b. Dallas, Aug. 10, 1945; BS in Mathematics, So. Meth. U., 1967, JD, 1970; LLD (hon.), Pepperdine U. Sch. of Law. Bar: Tex. 1970. Law clk. to Hon. Joe E. Estes US Dist. Ct. (no. dist.) Tex., 1970—72; assoc. Locke Purnell Rain Harrell (formerly Locke, Purnell, Boren, Laney & Neely PC), Dallas, 1972—78, ptnr, 1978—99, pres., 1996—99; mng. ptnr. Locke Liddell & Sapp LLP, Dallas, 1999—2001; asst. to Pres. & staff sec The White House, Washington, 2001—03, asst. to Pres. & dep. chief of staff for policy, 2003—05, gen. counsel to Pres., 2005—07; nominee for assoc. justice US Supreme Ct., 2005, withdrew nomination, 2005; ptnr. Locke Liddell & Sapp LLP, Dallas, 2007—. Chairwoman, Tex. Lottery Commn., 1995-2000 Comments editor Southwestern Law Jour., 1969-70. Mem.-at-large Dallas City Coun., 1989-91 Named Outstanding Young Lawyer of Dallas, Dallas Assn. of Young Lawyers, 1978; named 1 of Top 100 Most Powerful Attys., Top 50 Most Influential Women Lawyers, Top 100 Most Influential Lawyers in America, Nat. Law Jour., 1997, 1998, 2000; Nat. award for Leadership and Commitment, Girls Clubs, 1987; Am. Jewish Comm. Human Relations award, 1992; DBA's Justinian award for Community Svc., 1992; Sarah T. Hughes award, Women in Law Section State Bar of Tex., 1993; Louise B. Raggio award, Dallas Women Lawyers Assn., 1996; Hon. Merrill Hartman award, Legal Svcs. of No. Tex., 1996; Jurisprudence award, Anti-Defamation League, 1996; Woman of Excellence award, Woman's Enterprise Mag., 1997; Woman of the Year, Today's Dallas Woman, 1997; SMU Robert G. Storey award for Distinguished Achievement, 2005; Spirit of Thanks-Giving award, 2006; DOJ Edmund J. Randolph award, 2007; Agy. Seal award CIA, 2007, YWCA Centennial award, 2008. Fellow Am. Bar Found., Tex. Bar Found. (life); mem. ABA (jour. bd. editors, ho. dels., chair credentials and admissions com., election law com., bus. and cmty. activities), Dallas Bar Found., Dallas Bar Assn. (chmn. bd. dirs. 1981, pres., 1985-90), State Bar Tex. (pres. 1992-93, dir. 1986-89), Attys. Liability Assurance Soc. (former bd. dirs.). Office: Locke Lord Bissell & Liddell LLP 2200 Ross Ave Ste 2200 Dallas TX 75201-6776 also: 100 Congress Ave Ste 300 Austin TX 78701 Office Phone: 214-740-8450, 512-305-4888, 202-220-6925. Office Fax: 214-740-8800, 512-305-4800. E-mail: hmiers@lockelord.com.

MIGAJ, DAVID, language educator; b. Madrid; BA, Northern Ill. U., DeKalb, 1997, MA, 1998. Instr. Northern Ill. U., 1998—2000; asst. prof. Wilbur Wright Coll., Chgo., 2000—. Personal E-mail: dmigaj@yahoo.com.

MIGAKI, JAMES M., education educator; b. Spokane, Wash., Sept. 27, 1931; s. Kametaro and Ichiye (Hashimoto) M.; m. Ruth M.K. Tsai, Aug. 19, 1967 (div. July 1974); children: Grace, Paul. BA, Wash. State Coll., 1954; EdD, Wash. State U., 1978. Cert. elem. and secondary edn. tchr. and prin., Wash. Rsch. mechanic dept. math. Washington State Coll., Pullman, 1950-51; substitute tchr. physics Spokane Sch. Dist. 81, 1953, elem. sch. tchr., 1954-59, acting prin., tchr., 1959, secondary sci. and math. tchr., 1959-65; teaching asst. Wash. State U., 1966-67, from instr. to assoc. prof. elem. and secondary edn., 1967—69, dir. Peace Corp/Master of Edn. Program, 1968—69, dir. first tenured faculty mem. in Asian-Am. Studies program, 1975—77; dir. Masters'-Peace Corp Program Coll. Edn. and Internat. Devel. Office, Wash. State U., 1990—; prof. emeritus of sci. edn. Wash. State U., 1993; pres. Sci. Edn. Cons. Svcs. Internat., 1994—. Dir. Saturday Sci. Project, Spokane Tech. and Profl. Coun., 1963-65; vis. faculty sci. and math. Wash. State U., 1965; dir., assoc. dir., acting dir. numerous projects NSF, 1965-92; cons. to numerous sch. dists. Inventor math. model for higher plane curves in rotation, 1950; contbr. numerous articles to profl. jours. Del. Gov.'s Conf. on Health Care, Seattle, 1967; bd. mem. Palouse Asian-Am. Assn., 1967-74, charter mem., pres. 1997-99; bd. mem. Wesley Found., 1998-2004; recorder Gov.'s Conf. on Edn., Seattle and Olympia, Wash., 1967-68; cons., mem. evaluation panel NSF, Washington, 1974; del. nat. fgn. policy conf. US Dept. State, 1980. Named Patron of Youth, YMCA, 1978; recipient numerous awards and scholarships. Mem. NEA (life, state rep.), Wash. Sci. Tchrs. Assn. (charter; pres., other offices), YMCA (pres. 1966-81, bd. trustees 1966-81, bd. pres. 1980-81), Nat. Sci. Tchrs. Assn. (life; various coms.), Palouse Asian Am. Assn. (founding mem., bd. mem., pres., 1992-98), Phi Delta Kappa (life; pres. 1969-83, svc. award 1981), Kappa Delta Pi, PAAA Investment Club (charter mem., sec. 1981-90, pres. 1991-92), Clarkston Golf and Country Club. Avocations: automobiles, fishing, bowling, trapshooting, sports. Home: 914 Coulter Ln Clarkston WA 99403-1116

MIGALA, LUCYNA J., journalist, broadcast executive, artistic director; b. Krakow, Poland, May 22, 1944; came to U.S., 1947, naturalized, 1955; d. Joseph and Estelle (Suwala) M.; m. Frank A. Cizon, Oct. 9, 1998. Student, Loyola U., Chgo., 1962-63, Chgo. Conservatory of Music, 1963-70; BS in Journalism, Northwestern U., 1966. Radio announcer, prodr. Sta. WOPA, Oak Park, Ill., 1963—66; writer, reporter, prodr. NBC News, Chgo., 1966—69, 1969—71; prodr. NBC local news, Washington, 1969; prodr., coord. NBC network news, Cleve., 1971—78, field prodr. Chgo., 1978—79; v.p. Migala Comm. Corp., 1979—. Program and news dir., on-air personality Sta. WCEV, Cicero, Ill, 1979—; lectr. City Colls., Chgo., 1981, Morton Coll., 1988. Columnist Free Press, Chgo., 1984-87. Founder, artistic dir., gen. mgr. Lira Ensemble (formerly The Lira Singers), Chgo., 1965—, Artist-in-residence, Loyola U., Chgo.; mem., chmn. various cultural coms. Polish Am. Congress, 1970-80; bd. dir. Nationalities Svcs. Ctr., Cleve., 1973-78; bd. dir., v.p. Cicero-Berwyn Fine Arts Coun., Cicero, Ill., 1980-87; v.p. Chgo. chpt. Kosciuszko Found., 1983-86; bd. dir. Polish Women's Alliance Am., 1983-87, Ill. Humanities Coun., 1983-89, mem. exec. com., 1986-87; founder, gen. chmn. Midwest Chopin Piano Competition (later Chgo. Chopin Competition), 1984-86; founding mem. ethnic and folk arts panel Ill. Arts Coun., 1984-87, 92-94; mem. City Arts I and II panels Chgo. Office Fine Arts, 1986-89, 94; bd. dir. Ill. Arts Alliance, 1989-92, Polish-Am. Leadership Initiative, Chgo., 2001-05; mem. Polonia Census 2000 Com.; bd. dir.trustee Lincoln Acad. Ill., 2005—; mem. bd. Berwyn Cicero Coun. on Aging, 2007-. Fellow Washington Journalism Ctr., 1969; decorated Cavalier's Cross of Merit Govt. Poland; recipient AP Broadcasters award, 1973, Emmy award NATAS, 1974, Cultural Achievement award Am. Coun. Polish Culture, 1990, award of merit Advocates Soc. Polish Am. Attys., 1991, Human Rels. Media award City of Chgo., 1992, Outstanding Achievement award Minister Fgn. Affairs Rep. of Poland, 1994, Civic Achievement award Polish Am. Hist. Assn., 2000, Nat. Creative Arts award Polish Am. Hist. Soc., 2003, Beautiful Spirit award Keep Chgo. Beautiful, Inc., 2005, SOR Juana award Nat. Mus. Mexican Art, Chgo., 2007. Mem. Soc. Profl. Journalists,Solutions Care Cicero,Ill.(bd. dir.). Office: Sta WCEV 5356 W Belmont Ave Chicago IL 60641-4103 also: The Lira Ensemble 6525 N Sheridan Rd # CH-LL Chicago IL 60626-5344 Personal E-mail: lmigala@wcev1450.com. Business E-Mail: lmigala@liraensemble.com.

MIGDOL, MARVIN JACOB, public relations and marketing executive, consultant; b. Rochester, NY, Jan. 11, 1937; s. Frank and Dorothy (Krieger) M.; m. Frances Scheiner, June 13, 1959 (div. June 1970); children: Helene Ellen, Steven Gary, Larry Jay; m. Grace Miron, Dec. 26 1970 (div. Aug. 1986); children: Michael Alan, Susan Renee, Honi Faith; m. Roni Habel, June 30, 1991 (div. Dec. 1992); m. Fay Herschberg, Dec. 27, 2003. BA in Sociology, U. Buffalo, 1959; postgrad., U. Miami, 1959-60; MS in Communications, Boston U., 1961. Dir. pub. rels. United Fund, Reading, Pa., 1961-63, Rensselaer Poly. Inst., Troy, NY, 1963-64, Touro Infirmary, New Orleans, 1964, Hamot Hosp., Erie, Pa., 1964-65, United Jewish Fedn., Buffalo, 1965-68; pres. Marvin J. Migdol Inc., Dallas, 1968—. Instr. Boston U., 1962—, Pa. State U., 1962—, U. Tex., 1962—, Collin County C.C., Plano, 1990-91. Author: Public Relations Handbook, 1963, Comics as a Public Relations Tool in Communications, 1971, The Migdol Manual, 1972, Success in the 1990's, 1987, Greater Virility: Overcoming Impotence, 1993; contbr. numerous articles to profl. jours. Reporter Rep. Nat. Conv., Dallas, 1964; asst. dist. commr. Boy Scouts Am., Dallas, 1980-85; exec. bd. dirs. EPCOT Resorts, Lake Buena Vista, Fla., 1992—; v.p. Am. Jewish Congress, S.W. Region, 2001-05; v.p. Am. Friends of Magen David

Adoin, 2004-07; commencement U. Phoenix, Dallas, 2005. Recipient Pub. Rels. award Coun. Jewish Welfare Funds & Fedn., N.Y.C., 1967, Nat. Bus. League, West Palm Beach, Fla., 1968, Merit award Big Brothers & Sisters, Dallas, Tex., 1987, Major League Volleyball award San Jose, Calif., 1987.; named Entrepreneur of the Yr. Venture Mag., Dallas, Tex., 1987 Mem. U.S. Profl. Mktg. Assn. (pres. 1990—), Am. Assn. Indsl. Editors (bd. dirs. 1967-70), Am. Coll. Pub. Rels. Assn. (bd. dirs. 1964-66), Inst. for Info. and Comm. (bd. dirs. 1971—), Dallas Belles (dir. mktg. and pub. rels. 1987—), Jewish Nat. Fund (area dir.), Dallas Bridge Assn. (chmn. publicity, Tex. Star award, 2009), Dallas C. of C. (mem. econ. and internat. coun.), U. Buffalo Alumni Assn. We. Pa. and Tex. (Cert. Recognition Outstanding Dedicated Svc., 2007), 1964-65, Temple Shalom (vice chmn. bldg. fund 1971-72, mem. Brotherhood bd. 1985-86), Jewish Cmty. Ctr., Am. Contract Bridge League (chmn. pub. rels. 1983—, award Memphis chpt. 1983-87), Alpha Epsilon Pi (gov., 1970-79), Phi Delta Phi, (v.p. 1959-60, treas. 1960—). Jewish. Avocations: writer, lecturer, baseball and softball umpire, Boy Scout leader. Home: 18715 Gibbons Dr Dallas TX 75287-4045 Office Phone: 972-978-5487. Personal E-mail: fmmigdol@gmail.com.

MIGEON, CLAUDE JEAN, pediatrics educator; b. Lievin, Pas-De-Calais, France, Dec. 22, 1923; came to U.S., 1950, naturalized, 1967; s. André and Pauline (Descamps) M.; m. Barbara Lou Ruben, Apr. 2, 1960; children: Jacques, Jean-Paul, Nicole. MD, Sch. Medicine, U. Paris, 1950. Fellow dept. pediatrics Sch. Medicine, Johns Hopkins U., 1950-52, asst. prof., 1954-60, asso. prof., 1960-71, prof. pediatrics, 1971—; instr. biochemistry U. Utah, 1952-54; pediatrician Johns Hopkins Hosp., 1954—. Mem. diabetes metabolism tng. grants com. NIH, 1963-67, gen. clin. rsch. ctrs. com., 1968-71, mem. endocrinology study sect., 1974-78; cons. Med. Rsch. Coun. Can., 1969-85, mem. Nat. Ctr. for Rsch. Resources data and safety monitoring bd. NIH, 2006-, others; vis. prof. Maadi Armed Forces Hosp., Cairo, 1985, Guy's Hosp., London, 1986. Co-editor: (textbook) The Diagnosis and Treatment of Endocrine Disorders in Childhood and Adolescence, 4th edit., 1994; mem. editl. bd.: Johns Hopkins Med. Jour., 1970-72, Jour. Clin. Endocrinology and Metabolism, 1971-77, Hormone Rsch., 1979—; contbr. articles to profl. jours. Fulbright fellow, 1950; Am. Field Svc. fellow, 1950-51; Andre and Bella Meyer fellow, 1951-52; recipient rsch. career award NIH, 1964-85. Fellow AAAS; mem. Endocrine Soc. (coun. 1971-74, chmn. pub. affairs com. 1974-91, Ayerst award, Williams award), Soc. Pediatric Rsch. (emeritus), Am. Pediatric Soc., Lawson Wilkins Pediatric Endocrine Soc. (founding pres. 1972, Van Wyk prize, 2009), Am. Soc. Clin. Investigation (emeritus), Am. Physiol. Soc., Japanese Pediatric Endocrine Soc. (hon.), Found. Am. Meml. Hosp. (bd. dirs. 1985—, v.p. 2001-), Soc. Francaise d'Endocrinologie (fgn. corr. mem.). Home: 502 Somerset Rd Baltimore MD 21210-2720 Office: Johns Hopkins Hosp Harriet Ln Children Ctr 200 N Wolfe St Baltimore MD 21287-2520 Office Phone: 410-502-8326. Business E-Mail: cmigeon@jhmi.edu.

MIGHELL, ALAN DONALD, physical chemist; b. Amherst, Mass., Jan. 1, 1935; s. Ronald Lester and Anna Marie Mighell; m. Anna D. DeKonschin, June 24, 1962; children: Mark Alan, Gregory Ronald. BS, George Washington U., Washington, 1957, MS, 1959; PhD, Princeton U., NJ, 1963. Postdoc. rschr. Princeton U., NJ, 1963—64; rsch. phys. chemist Nat. Inst. Stds. and Tech., Gaithersburg, Md., 1964—. Contbr. articles to profl. jours. Recipient Silver Medal award, Nat. Inst. Stds. and Tech., US Dept. Commerce, 1975. Mem.: Internat. Ctr. Diffraction Data, Microscopy Soc. America, Am. Crystallographic Assn., Phi Beta Kappa. Achievements include development of pioneering vector techniques for extracting crystal structures from 3-dimensional Patterson Fourier maps; a prototype computer control system for coordinating x-ray diffraction structure solution programs; patents for apparatus and methods for identifying and comparing lattice structures and determining lattice structure symmetries. Home: 510 Lynch St Rockville MD 20850 Office: Nat Inst Stds & Tech 100 Bureau Dr Gaithersburg MD 20899-8520 Personal E-mail: alan_mighell@msn.com. Business E-Mail: alan.mighell@nist.gov.

MIGHELL, KENNETH JOHN, lawyer; b. Schenectady, NY, Mar. 17, 1931; s. Richard Henry and Ruth Aline (Simon) M.; m. Julia Anne Carstarphen, Aug. 24, 1961; children: Thomas Lowry, Elizabeth Anne. BBA, U. Tex., 1952, JD, 1957. Bar: Tex. 1957. Assoc. Scurry, Scurry, Pace & Wood, Dallas, 1957-61; asst. U.S. Atty. Justice Dept., Dallas, 1961-77; 1st asst. No. Dist. Tex., 1972-77; U.S. Atty. No. Dist., Tex., 1977-81; ptnr. Cowles & Thompson, Dallas, 1981-96, of counsel, 1996—. Chmn. bd. mgmt. Downtown Dallas YMCA, 1974-76; pres. Dallas Area Am. Lung Assn., 1985-87; bd. dirs. YMCA Met. Dallas, 1987—; chmn. adv. bd. Southwestern Law Enforcement Inst., 1994-98; mem. SW Legal Found., CLE adv. com. 1999-2003. With USN, 1952-54; capt. USNR, 1954-78. Mem.: FBA, Nat. Assn. Former U.S. Attys. (pres. 1995), State Bar Tex. (bd. dirs. 1994—95), Dallas Bar Found. (trustee 1994—2001, vice chmn. 1999—2000, chmn. 2001—02), Dallas Bar Assn. (bd. dirs. 1984—89, chmn. 1989, v.p. 1990—91, pres. 1993). Democrat. Methodist. Office: Cowles & Thompson 901 Main St Ste 3900 Dallas TX 75202-3793 E-mail: kmighell@cowlesthompson.com.

MIGIRO, ASHA-ROSE, international organization official; b. Songea, Tanzania, July 9, 1956; m. Cleophas Migiro; 2 children. LLM, U. Dar es Salaam, Tanzania, 1984; LLD, U. Konstanz, Germany, 1992. Mem. faculty of law to sr. lectr. U. Dar es Salaam, head dept. constl. and adminstrv. law, 1992—94, head dept. civil and criminal law, 1994—97; min. cmty. devel., gender and children United Republic of Tanzania, min. fgn. affairs and internat. cooperation, 2006—07; dep. sec.-gen. UN, NYC, 2007—. Mem. Tanzania Law Reform Commn., 1997, UN Com. on Elimination of Discrimination against Women, 2000; pres. UN Security Coun.; chair So. African Devel. Cmty. Ministerial Com. Organ on Politics, Def. and Security Cooperation; chair Coun. of Mins.' meetings Internat. Conf. of Gt. Lakes Region. Contbr. articles to profl. jours. Office: UN First Ave at 46th St New York NY 10017

MIGLIARO, MARCO WILLIAM, electrical engineer; b. NYC, Mar. 29, 1948; s. Marco Salvatore and Anna (Dalton) M.; children: Kristen Marie, Meredith Anne, Marie Angela, Marco Thomas; m. Jasoda Badlu, Nov. 19, 1988. BEE, Pratt Inst., 1969; postgrad., N.J. Inst. Tech., 1970-72. Registered profl. engr., N.Y., N.J., Pa., Mass., Fla. Engr. Am. Electric Power, NYC, 1969-78; staff engr. Gibbs & Hill, Inc., NYC, 1978-81; sr. cons. engr. Ebasco Svcs., Inc., NYC, 1981-88; tech. mgr. ABB Impell Corp., Melville, NY, 1988-90; sr. staff specialist for nuc. engring. Fla. Power & Light, Juno Beach, 1990-96, chief elec./I&C engr., 1996—2003; pres. ESA Cons. Engrs., PA, Jupiter, Fla., 2003—; pres., CEO IEEE Industry Stds. and Tech. Orgn., 2003—. Developer seminar on stationary batteries, 1987. Contbg. author: Handbook of Power Calculations, 1984, 99, Standard Handbook for Electrical Engineers, 1999, 2006; also articles. Recipient Meritorious Svc. award Am. Nat. Standards Inst., 1994. Fellow IEEE (pres. 2001—, stds. assn. bd. govs. 1998—, bd. dirs. 1990-92, 2001, fin. com. 1990-92, dir. stds. 1990-91, mem. exec. com. 1992, v.p. stds. activities, 1992, 2001, Stds. medal 1986, Stds. Bd. Disting. Svc. award 1993, Charles Proteus Steinmetz award 1996, Third Millennium medal 2000); mem. IEEE Power Engring. Soc. (Disting. Svc. award 1988, 92), Industry Standards and Tech. Orgn. (bd. dirs. 2000—, chmn. 2000-03). Avocations: fishing, travel, music. Home: PO Box 9253 Jupiter FL 33468-9253 Office: ESA Cons Engrs PA PO Box 9251 Jupiter FL 33468-9251 Home Phone: 561-624-4743; Office Phone: 561-691-1946. Business E-Mail: marco@esaconsulting.com.

MIGLIAZZO, ARLIN C., history professor; b. South Gate, Calif., Sept. 20, 1951; BA, Biola U., La Mirada, Calif., 1974; MA, No. Ariz. U., Flagstaff, 1975; PhD, Washington State U., Pullman, 1982. Asst. prof. history and polit. sci. Judson Bapt. Coll., The Dalles, Oreg.; asst. to full prof. history Whitworth U., 1983—. Editor: (book) Lands of True and Certain Bounty, 2002, Teaching As An Act of Faith, 2002; author: To Make This Land Our Own, 2007. Scholar, Fulbright Found., 1990; Rsch. Fellowship, Weyerhaeuser Ctr. for Faith and Learning, 1999. Mem.: Conf. in Faith and History, Ea. Wash. State Hist. Soc., SC Hist. Soc., So. Hist. Assn., Spokane City-County Hist. Landmarks Commn., Phi Alpha Theta. Office: Whitworth U Dept History 300 W Hawthorne Rd Spokane WA 99251 Home Phone: 509-467-6198; Office Phone: 509-777-4367.

MIGLIORE, MARCUS CHARLES, lawyer; b. Rochester, NY, Apr. 12, 1961; s. Charles T. and Virginia (DeCesare) M. BA, U. Rochester, 1983; JD, George Washington U., 1986. Bar: N.Y. 1987, D.C. 1987. Law clk. to chief judge D.C. Ct. Appeals, Washington, 1986-87; assoc. Dickstein, Shapiro & Morin, Washington, 1987—91; appellate counsel Fed. Election Commn., 1991—93; atty. to mng. atty., legal dept. Air Line Pilots Assn., AFL-CIO, Washington, 1993—. Mem. ABA, N.Y. State Bar Assn., D.C. Bar Assn., Order of Coif, Phi Beta Kappa. Office: ALPA 1625 Massachusetts Ave NW Washington DC 20036-2212 Business E-Mail: marcus.migliore@alpa.org.

MIGNONE, MARIO B., language educator; came to U.S., 1960; m. Lois Mignone, June 29, 1968; children: Pamela Anne, Cristina Maria, Elizabeth Maria. BA, CCNY, 1967; MA, Rutgers U., 1969, PhD, 1972. Disting. prof. Italian lang. SUNY, Stony Brook, 1970—, dir. undergrad. studies, 1976-83, dir. grad. studies, 1983-87; founder, exec. dir. Ctr. for Italian Studies, chmn. French and Italian dept., Stony Brook, 1988—98. Author: The Theater of Eduardo De Filippo, 1974, Abnormality and Anguish in the Narrative of Dino Buzzati, 1981, Eduardo De Filippo, 1984, Pirandello in America, 1988, Columbus: Meeting of Cultures, 1993, Italy Today: A Country in Transition, 1995, Italy Today: At the Crossroads of the New Millennium, 1998, Italy Today: Facing the Challenges of the New Millenium, 2008; assoc. mng. editor Forum Italicum, 1986-94, editor, 1994—; contbr. articles to profl. jours. Mem. coll. coun. SUNY, Old Westbury. Mem. Am. Assn. Tchrs. Italian (pres. 1982-84), Assn. Italian Am. Educators (pres. 1997—), Am. Italian Hist. Assn. (nat. exec. com.). Office: SUNY Dept European Langs Lits Stony Brook NY 11794-3359 Office Phone: 631-632-7444. Business E-Mail: mmignone@notes.cc.sunysb.edu.

MIGNOT, EMMANUEL, medical researcher; Student, Ecole Normale Supérieure, Paris; MD, René Descartes Sch. Medicine, Paris V Univ., 1984; PhD, Paris VI Univ., Pierre and Marie Curie U., 1984. Cert. Sleep Disorders Am. Bd. Sleep Medicine. Resident Necker Enfants Malades Hosp., Paris, 1985, intern, 1984; dir. Stanford Ctr. for Narcolepsy Stanford U. Sch. Med., 1993—, acting asst. prof. psychiatry & behavioral sciences, 1993—2001, prof. psychiatry & behavioral sciences, 2001—, assoc. prof. medicine; founder Hypnion Inc., 2000—; investigator Howard Hughes Med. Inst., 2002—. Bd. dirs. Nat. Sleep Found., chair Narcolepsy Coun.; chair, Nat. Ctr. on Sleep Disorders Rsch. Adv. Bd. NIH. Mem. editl. bd. Sleep, Sleep Medicine, Sleep Research Online; contbr. articles to profl. jours. Recipient Health Rsch. award, Nat. Sleep Found., Rsch. award, NIH, Profl. Svc. award, Narcolepsy Network, Drs. C. & F. Demuth 11th award for Young Ingestigators in the Neurosciences, WC Dement Academic Achievement award, McKnight Found. Achievement award, W. Alden Spencer award, Jacobaeus Prize. Mem.: Inst. Medicine. Achievements include discovery of cause of narcolepsy. Office: Stanford Hosp Sleep Disorders Clinic #3301 MC 5730 401 Quarry Rd Stanford CA 94305-5730 also: Ctr for Narcolepsy Stanford U Sch Med Dept Psychiatry and Behavioral Scis 701 B Welch Rd Rm 143 MC 5742 Palo Alto CA 94304-5742

MIGRO, ASHA-ROSE, international organization official; b. Songea, Ruvuma Region, Tanzania, July 9, 1956; LLB, LLM, U. Dar-es-Salaam; PhD, U. Konstanz. Sr. lectr. faculty of law U. Dar-es-Salaam; min. cmty. devel., gender & children Govt. of Tanzania, 2000—06, min. fgn. affairs & internat. cooperation, 2006—07; dep. sec.-gen. UN, NYC, 2007—. Office: UN UN Plz 46th St at First Ave New York NY 10017

MIGUDA, EDITH ATIENO, history professor; d. Ondiek Chillo Miguda and Rosbella Ofweny Ondiek; children: Vivienne Audrey Ndun'gu, Marvin Atuko, Arnold Winga. EdB, Kenyatta U., Kenya; MA in History, U. Nairobi, Kenya, 1988; PhD, U. Adelaide, 2005. Tchr. Alliance Girl's HS, Nairobi, 1987—88; lectr. U. Nairobi, 1988—99; hs tchr. Trinity Coll., Gawler, South Australia, 2000—02; sr. cons. Aus. training Flinders U., Adelaide, 2002—04, sr. trainer, 2002—04; project officer Dept. Edn., Adelaide, 2005—06; postdoc. fellow, ctr. women's intercultural leadership St. Mary's Coll., South Bend, Ind., 2006—07, asst. prof. history, 2007—. Rschr. women and politics Adelaide U. Ctr. Women's Intercultural Leadership, 2000. Recipient award, African Studies Assn. Australasian and Pacific, 2004. Mem.: Internat. Knowledge Network Women and Politics (expert 2006). Avocations: travel, reading. Business E-Mail: emiguda@saintmarys.edu.

MIGUE, JEAN LUC, economics professor; b. Montreal, Que., Can., Apr. 13, 1933; s. Joseph Alfred and Marie Laurence (Venne) M.; m. Renee Caron, Sept. 13, 1958; children: Paule, Pascal, Nicolas. BA in Econs, U. Montreal, 1953, MA, 1956; PhD in Econs, Am. U., 1968. Researcher Bank of Can., 1957-58; prof. Laval U., 1962-70; prof. econs. Nat. Sch. Public Adminstrn., Quebec, 1970-99. Mem. staff Econ. Coun. Can., 1973-74 Author: The Price of Health, 1974, Le Prix du Transport, 1978, Nationalistic Policies of Canada, 1979, L'Economiste et La chose Publique, 1979, The Public Monopoly of Education, 1989, Federalism and Free Trade, 1993, Etatisme et Declin du quebec, 1999, Le Monopole de La Santé, 2001, Statism and Health in France, 2005, On N'a Pas Les Gouvernements Qu'on Merite, 2007. Fellow Massey Found., 1956, sr. fellow, The Fraser Inst. Fellow Royal Soc. Can.; mem, Mont Pelerin Soc. Roman Catholic. Office Phone: 418-651-1968. E-mail: jlmigue@videotron.ca.

MIGUEL, CAIO F., psychology professor; b. Sao Carlos, Brazil, Sept. 3, 1975; s. Joao Paulo and Cristina A. Miguel; m. Danielle L. LaFrance. BA in Psychology, Pontificia U. Catolica de Sao Paulo, Brazil, 1997; PhD in Applied Behavior Analysis, Western Mich. U., Kalamazoo, 2004. Cert. Behavior Analysis Certification Bd., 2004. Case mgr. Western Mich. U. Ctr. for Autism, 2000—01; clin. cons. St. Amant Ctr., Winnipeg, Canada, 2003—04; prog. specialist New Eng. Ctr. for Children, Southborough, Mass., 2004—06; clin. asst. prof. Northeastern U., Boston, 2004—06; asst. prof. Calif. State U., Sacramento, 2006—. Vis. prof. Pontificia U. Catolica de Sao Paulo, 2004; adj. prof. U. de Sao Paulo, 2004—; guest faculty Ohio State U., 2006; adj. prof. Chgo. Sch. Profl. Psychology, 2008—. Guest reviewer: Jour. Applied Behavior Analysis, 2003—, mem. editl. bd.: Internat. Jour. Behavioral Consultation and Therapy, 2004—, Brazilian Jour. Behavioral Analysis, 2008—, assoc. editor: Jour. Speech and Lang. Pathology-Applied Behavior Analysis, 2005—; editor: Analysis of Verbal Behavior, 2008—; contbr. articles to profl. jours., chapters to books. Mem. governing bd. Behavior Analyst Online, Pa., 2007—. Recipient Creative Scholar award, Western Mich. U., 2002, Verbal Behavior Student Rsch. award, 2002, Grad. Tchr. award, 2003, Exptl. Analysis Human Behavior Student Rsch. award, 2005, Rsch. Creative Activity award, Calif. State U., Sacramento, 2006; Sidney and Janet Bijou fellowship, Soc. the Advancement Behavior Analysis, 2003, Travel Grant, Western Mich. U., 2001, 2003, Rsch. Grant, 2004, Travel Grant, Calif. State U., Sacramento, 2006, 2007, 2008. Mem.: Orgnl. Behavior Mgmt. Network, Calif. Assn. Behavior Analysis (bd. dirs. 2007—), Assn. Behavior Analysis Internat. (Presenter's grant 2002, 2003), Verbal Behavior Spl. Interest Group (co-editor, verbal behavior newsletter 2007—), Phi Kappa Phi. Achievements include research in the acquisition of language and language-mediated behaviors; specific environmental arrangements that would give rise to novel behavior in children diagnosed with autism. Office: Calif State U Sacramento Dept Psych 6000 J St Sacramento CA 95819

MIGUEL, LUIS, musician; b. San Juan, Apr. 19, 1970; m. Aracely Arámbula, 2006; 1 child, Miguel. Albums include Directo Al Corazon, 1982, Un Sol, 1982, Decidete, 1983, Fiebre de Amor, 1985, Soy Como Quiero Ser, 1987, Busca Una Mujer, 1988, 20 Anos, 1990, Romance, 1991, Del Corazon del Hombre, 1992, El Idolo De Mexico 1992, Los Idolos De Mexico, 1993, Aries, 1993 (Grammy award, Best Latin Pop Perfomance), Segundo Romance, 1994 (Grammy award, Best Latin Pop Performance), Musipistas, 1995, El Concierto, 1995, Nada Es Igual, 1996, Romances, 1997 (Grammy award, Best Latin Pop Performance), Amarte Es Un Placer, 1999 (Album of the Yr. award Latin Grammy Awards, Best Pop Album award Latin Grammy Awards), Vivo, 2000, 21 Black Jack, 2000, Vallenato, 2001, Mis Romances, 2001, Amandote a la Italiana, 2002, 33, 2003, Palabra de Honor, 2004, Mexico en la Piel, 2005 (Grammy award, Best Mexican-Am. Album), Perfil, 2006, Navidades, 2006; songs include Me Gustas Tal Como Eres, 1984 (Grammy award, Best Mexican-Am. Music Performance). Recipient 5 Grammy awards, star, Hollywood Walk of Fame, 1996.

MIHAESCU, MIHAI, engineering educator, researcher; BSc in Automotive Engring., Tech. U. Cluj-Napoca, Romania, 1999, Postgrad. student in Mech. Engring., 2000; PhD, Lund U., Sweden, 2005. Tchg. asst. Tech. U. Cluj-Napoca, 2000—01; rsch. asst. prof. U. Cin., 2009, postdoc. rsch. assoc., 2009. Reviewer AIAA Jour., Jour. Applied Acoustics. Contbr. scientific papers. Recipient First Pl. Poster award, COSM/ASPO, 2007; fellowship, EUA4X, von Karman Inst. Fluid Dynamics, Rhode-Saint-Genese, Belgium, 2006, URC Interdisciplinary grant, U. Cin., 2008. Mem.: AIAA. Office: Univ Cin 745 Baldwin Hall ML0070 Cincinnati OH 45221

MIHAI, FLORIN MARIUS, language educator; b. Iasi, Romania, Feb. 19, 1969; s. Mihai and Olga Mihai; m. Cristina Moisii, Nov. 2, 1997. BA, Al. I. Cuza U., Iasi, Romania, 1992; MS, Fla. State U., Tallahassee, 1997, PhD, 2003. Vis. asst. Fla. State U., Tallahassee, 2003—06; asst. prof. English as 2d lang. U. Ctrl. Fla., Cocoa, 2006—. Mem.: TESOL, Am. Ednl. Rsch. Assn., Internat. Assn. Applied Linguistics, Am. Assn. Applied Linguistics, Pi Lambda Theta. Office: University of Central Florida 1519 Clearlake Rd Cocoa FL 32922 Business E-Mail: fmihai@mail.ucf.edu.

MIHAILA, BOGDAN, physicist; b. Bucharest, Romania, July 26, 1964; arrived in US, 1992, naturalized, 2007; s. Dumitru and Georgeta Mihaila; m. Ioana C. Chiribelea, June 4, 1988; children: Iulia, Cornelia. Diploma in Physics and Engring., U. Bucharest, Romania, 1989; PhD in Theoretical Physics, U. NH, Durham, 1998. Tech. staff mem. Nat. Inst. Meteorology and Hydrology, Bucharest, Romania, 1989—90, Inst. Environ. Rsch. and Engring., Bucharest, 1990—92; grad. rsch. assoc. U. NH, Durham, 1992—98; post doctoral fellow Oak Ridge Nat. Lab., Tenn., 1998—99, Argonne Nat. Lab., Ill., 2000—02, Los Alamos Nat. Lab., N.Mex., 2003—06, tech. staff mem., 2006—. Vis. prof. physics Coastal Carolina U., Conway, SC, 1999—2000; sr. fellow Inst. Complex Adaptive Matter, Los Alamos, N.Mex., 2005—06. Contbr. articles to profl. and peer-reviewed jours., scientific papers. Mem.: Am. Phys. Soc., Sierra Club. Achievements include research in many-body theory with applications to cold atoms, condensed matter, nuclear and high-energyphysics; high-performance computing and algorithm development. Avocations: hiking, travel, photography, reading. Home: 1124 Grand Canyon Brea CA 92821 Office: Los Alamos Nat Lab MS G755 Los Alamos NM 87545 Office Fax: 505-665-9224. Personal E-mail: bogdan.mihaila@gmail.com. Business E-Mail: bmihaila@lanl.gov.

MIHAL, SANDRA POWELL, research scientist; b. Balt., Dec. 15, 1941; d. Sanford William and Mary Louise (Barry) Powell; m. James George Anderson, June 15, 1963; children: Robin Marie, James Brian, Melissa Lee, Derek Clair; m. Charles Turner Barber, Apr. 18, 1978; stepchildren: Gretchen Jayco, Katrina Hope; m. Ladislaw Paul Mihal, May 25, 1991; stepchildren: Alexander Paul, Suzie May, Natasha Elizabeth, Rudy Darius. BA, Mt. St. Agnes Coll., 1963; MA, N.Mex. State U., 1970, Purdue U., 1975; EdD, Vanderbilt U., 1990. Cert. tchr., Md. Tchr. Ridgely-Dulaney Jr. H.S., Towson, Md., 1964; grad. asst. N.Mex. State U., Las Cruces, 1967—69; acad. advisor, instr. polit. sci. Purdue U., West Lafayette, Ind., 1974—78; prof., acad. sys. analyst U. So. Ind., Evansville, 1978—82; assoc. prof., chair dept. computer info. sys. Henderson (Ky.) C.C., 1982—88; prof. computer tech., divsn. chair Anne Arundel C.C., Arnold, Md., 1988—91; sys. analyst immigration and naturalization svc. Dept. of Justice, Washington, 1991—92, sr. rsch. sys. analyst immigration and naturalization svc. Glynco, Ga., 1995—; dep. program mgr. distributed learning Fed. Law Enforcement Training Ctr., Homeland Security, Glynco, Ga., 2002—. Bd. dirs. Ind. Polit. Sci. Assn., Muncie, 1984-88, Internat. Studies Assn.-Midwest, Chgo., 86-88; pres. Ky. Acad. Computer Users' Group, Lexington, 1985-86; telecom. adv. bd. C.C. Sys., Annapolis, Md., 1990-91; computer sys. network analyst CLARC Svcs., Pt. Charlotte, Fla., 92-95; adj. prof. history and polit. sci. Edison C.C., Punta Gorda, Fla., 1993-95; spkr. in fied Author: Learning By Doing BASIC, 1983, Computers Learning By Doing, 1984; contbr. articles to profl. jours Block coord. several neighborhood assns.; computer adv. bd. Henderson County Sch., 1982-88; chmn. Newburgh (Ind.) Youth Orgn., 78-86; judge Sci. Fair, Annapolis, 1988-90; nomination bd. Ky. Higher Edn. Assn., 1989-91; mem. Charlotte Chorale, Port Charlotte, 1992-94, Peace River Power Squadron, Port Charlotte, 1994-96. Coast Guard Aux., 1995-97. Fellow, Sloan Found., 1973—75, U. Ky., 1984, Ky. Col., 2003; scholar, Md. State Tchr. Bd. Edn., 1960—63. Mem, Soc. Applied Learning Tech., Assn. Computing Machinery (v.p. 85—), Am. Legion, Pi Gamma Mu. Democrat. Mem. Ch. Of Christ. Avocations: sailing, singing, swimming, cooking, music. Home: 112 Oak Ridge Rd Brunswick GA 31523-9741 Home Phone: 912-261-9623; Office Phone: 912-265-3474. Business E-Mail: sandy.mihal@dhs.gov, sandramihal@bellsouth.net.

MIHALAS, DIMITRI MANUEL, astrophysicist, educator; b. LA, Mar. 20, 1939; s. Emmanuel Demetrious and Jean (Christo) M.; children: Michael Demetrious, Alexandra Genevieve. BA with highest honors, UCLA, 1959; MS, Calif. Inst. Tech., 1960, PhD, 1963. Asst. prof. astrophys. scis. Princeton U., 1964-67; asst. prof. physics U. Colo., 1967-68; asso. prof. astronomy and astrophysics U. Chgo., 1968-70, prof., 1970-71; adj. prof. astrogeophysics, also physics and astrophysics U. Colo., 1972-80; sr. scientist High Altitude Obs., Nat. Center Atmospheric Research, Boulder, Colo., 1971-79, 82-85; astronomer Sacramento Peak Obs., Sunspot, N.Mex., 1979-82; mem. staff Los Alamos (N.Mex.) Nat. Lab., 1998—2004, fellow, 2004—; G.C. McVittie prof. astronomy U. Ill., 1985-98, g. c. prof. astronomy emeritus, 1998—. Cons. Los Alamos Nat. Lab, 1981-98; vis. prof. dept. astrophysics Oxford (Eng.) U., 1977-78; sr. vis. fellow dept. physics and astronomy Univ. Coll., London, 1978; mem. astronomy adv. panel NSF, 1972-75 Author: Galactic Astronomy, 1969, 2d edit, 1981, Stellar Atmospheres, 1970, 2d edit., 1978, Theorie des Atmospheres Stellaires, 1971, Foundations of Radiation Hydrodynamics, 1984; assoc. editor Astrophys. Jour, 1970-79, Jour. Computational Physics, 1981-87, Jour. Quantitative Spectroscopy, 1984-94; mem. editorial bd. Solar Physics, 1981-89. NSF fellow, 1959-62; Van Maanen fellow, 1962-63; Eugene Higgins vis. fellow, 1963-64; Alfred P. Sloan Found. Research fellow, 1969-71; Alexander von Humboldt Stiftung sr. U.S. scientist awardee, 1984. Mem. U.S. Nat. Acad. Sci., Internat. Astron. Union (pres. commn. 36 1976-79), Am. Astron. Soc. (pub. bd. 1995-99, mem. coun. 2000—03, Helen B. Warner prize 1974), Astron. Soc. Pacific (dir. 1975-77) Home: 15 Withers Peak Santa Fe NM 87508 Office: Los Alamos Nat Lab x-2 MS-T087 Los Alamos NM 87545 Office Phone: 505-665-4529. Business E-Mail: dmihalas@lanl.gov.

MIHALEF, VIOREL, research scientist; b. Galati, Romania, Jan. 19, 1972; s. Virgil Valeriu and Leonila Mihalef. PhD, Rutgers U., New Brunswick, 2007. Rsch. assoc. Rutgers U., Piscataway, NJ, 2008—. Achievements include invention of marker level set method. Home: 219 Sunnyview Oval Keasbey NJ 08832 Office: Rutgers Univ DCIS 110 Frelinghuysen Rd Piscataway NJ 08854 Business E-Mail: mihalef@cs.rutgers.edu.

MIHALOPOULOS, CATHERINE ELIZABETH, art educator; m. Frank G. Mihalopoulos; children: George, Aphrodite. PhD, U. Southern Calif., LA, 2001. Asst. prof. art history Calif. State U. Channel Islands, Camarillo, 2007—; vis. asst. prof. art history Ucsanta Barbara, Santa Barbara, Calif. Adj. prof. classics Loyola Marymount U., LA, 2001—06. Contbr. chapters to books. Vol. SOS, World Villages Children, Calif. Mem.: Assn. Specialized and Cooperative Libr. Agys. (sr. rsch. scholar 2004—08). Greek Orthodox. Office: Calif State Univ Channel Islands One University Dr Camarillo CA 93012 Business E-Mail: catie.mihalopoulos@csuci.edu.

MIHALY, EUGENE BRAMER, management consultant; b. The Hague, The Netherlands, Nov. 11, 1934; arrived in US, 1940; s. Eddy and Cecile (Bramer) Kahn; stepson of Eugene Mihaly; m. Stacey Beth Pulner, Apr. 21, 1996; children: Lisa Klee, Jessica; stepchildren: Stephanie Pulner, Andrew Pulner. AB magna cum laude, Harvard U., 1956; PhD, London Sch. Econs. and Polit. Sci., 1964. Aviation/space editor Hartford (Conn.) Courant, 1960-61; internat. economist AID, Washington, 1964-65; dep. dir. Peace Corps, Tanzania, 1966, dir., 1967-68, dep. dir. East Asia/Pacific bur. Washington, 1969, dir. office program devel., evaluation and rsch., 1969-70; assoc. dir. Inst. Internat. Studies, U. Calif., Berkeley, 1970-72; pres. Mihaly Internat. Corp., 1972—2006, chmn., 2006—; chmn. bd. Mihaly Internat. Can., Ltd., 1992—; sr. lectr. Haas Sch. Bus. U. Calif., Berkeley, 1991-95. Adj. prof. Amos Tuck Sch. Dartmouth Coll., 1997-2002; chmn. adv. bd. Northwood Fund Mgmt. Inc. Author: Foreign Aid and Politics in Nepal: A Case Study, 1965; contbr. articles to profl. jours., chpts. to books. Chmn. Global R.I.; dir. Common Cause R.I.; trustee CC of R.I. Found.; chmn. emeritus and dir., RI Pub. Radio; trustee Inst. Study and Practice Nonviolence. Mem. Coun. on Fgn. Rels. (chmn.), Exec. Svc. Corps (cons, team leader) Appalachian Mountain Club (Narragansett chpt.). Home: 4 Half Mile Rd Barrington RI 02806 Office Phone: 401-247-1418.

MIHALY, LASZLO, physics professor; PhD, Eotvos U., Budapest, 1977; PhD in Phys. Sci., Hungarian U., Budapest, 1993. Rschr. various positions Ctrl. Rsch. Inst. Physics, Budapest, 1975—89; visitor Inst. Laue-Langevin, Grenoble, 1975—76, Tech. U., Budapest, 2005—06, U. Paris, Orsay, 1980—82; visitor, dept. physics U. Calif., LA, 1983—86; prof. physics Stony Brook U., NY, 1989—, grad. program dir., dept. physics and astronomy, 2003—. Author: (book) Solid State Physics: Problems and Solutions. Recipient Chancellor's award, SUNY, 2003, Dean's award, Stony Brook U., 2008; Szent-Gyorgyi fellowship, Hungarian Acad. Sci., Ministry Edn., 2005, fellow, Am. Phys. Soc., 2006.

MIHAN, RICHARD, retired dermatologist; b. Dec. 20, 1925; s. Arnold and Virginia Catherine (O'Reilly) M. MD, St. Louis U., 1949. Diplomate Am. Bd. Dermatology. Intern L.A. County Gen. Hosp., 1949-51, resident in dermatology, 1954-57; pvt. practice in dermatology LA, 1957-95; prof. emeritus U. So. Calif., 1989—. Lt. Comdr. USNR, 1951-53. Fellow ACP; mem. AMA, Pacific Dermatol. Assn. (exec. bd. 1971-74), Am. Acad. Dermatol., Calif. Med. Assn. (chmn. dermatol. sect. 1973-74), L.A. Met. Dermatology Soc. (pres. 1975-76), L.A. Acad. Medicine (pres. 1988-89), Order of St. John of Jerusalem, of Rhodes, and of Malta, Order of St. Lazarus (comdr.), Calif. Club. Roman Cath. Home: 3278 Wilshire Blvd Apt 503 Los Angeles CA 90010-1431

MIHM, MARTIN CHARLES, JR., pathologist, educator; s. Martin Charles and Cecilia Matilda (Hepp) M. AB, Duquesne U., 1955; MD, U. Pitts., 1961; MA (hon.), Harvard U., Cambridge, Mass., 1990. Diplomate Am. Bd. Dermatology, Am. Bd. Pathology. Intern Mt. Sinai Hosp., NYC, 1961-62, resident in medicine, 1963-64; resident in dermatology Mass. Gen. Hosp., Boston, 1964-67, resident in Pathology, 1968-72, chief dermatopathology, 1973-94; asst. prof. pathology Harvard U. Med. Sch., Boston, 1972-75, assoc. prof., 1975-79, chief dermatopathology, 1982-93; prof. pathology Mass. Gen. Hosp.-Harvard U., Boston, 1980-93; prof., chief dermatopathology, dermatology Albany (N.Y.) Med. Coll., 1993—. Pathologist Malignant Melanoma Coop. Group, 1972—77; chmn. pathology com. Intergroup Melanoma Study, 1983—88; chief sr. adminstr. Wellman Labs., Mass. Gen. Hosp., 1985—93; cons. WHO, 1985—; adj. prof. pathology Vanderbilt U., 1989—; chmn. pathology standing com., 1991—; clin. prof. pathology Harvard Med. Sch., 1996—; sr. dermatopathologist and pathologist Mass. Gen. Hosp., 1996—; adj. prof. Thomas Jefferson Med. Sch., 2000—; prof. otolaryngology U. of Ark. Sch. of Med. Scis., 2002—. Author: Primer of Dermatopathology, 1984, 2d edit., 1992, Problematic Pigmented Lesions, 1990; co-author: Melanoma and Nevi, 1997, The Melanocytic Proliterations, 2001; editor: Lymphoproliferative Disorders of the Skin, 1986, Pathbiology and Recognition Malignant Melanoma, 1988, Dermatologia Practica, 2005; contbr. articles to med. jours.; overseer Boston Symphonic Orch., 2001—. Bd. overseers Boston (Mass.) Symphony Orch., 2001—. Served to comdr. USPHS, 1967-69. Recipient Gold Humanism award, Harvard Med. Sch., 2004. Fellow: ACP, Am. Soc. Dermatopathology, Am. Acad. Dermatology; mem.: AMA (Harvard Med. Sch. rep. to med. sch. sect. 1991), Annenberg Cir. of Dermatologic Found., Italian Assn. Ambulatory Dermatologists (hon.), Soc. of Dermatology, Mexico (hon.), Italian Soc. of Anatomic Pathology (hon.), Austrian Dermatology Soc. (hon.), Harvard Dermatology House Officer's Assn. (pres. 1982), Fort Orange Club, Albany, Harvard Club (Boston, N.Y.C.), Pi Gamma Mu, Alpha Omega Alpha. Independent. Roman Catholic. Home: 27 Chilton St Brookline MA 02446 Office: Mass Gen Hosp Warren Bldg 827 55 Fruit St Boston MA 02114 Office Phone: 617-724-1350. Business E-Mail: mmihm@partners.org.

MIHRAM, GEORGE ARTHUR, mathematician; b. Norman, Okla., Sept. 21, 1939; s. Russell George and Ella Lee (Stanaland) M.; m. Danielle Redibaum, Dec. 22, 1965. BS summa cum laude, U. Okla., 1960; postgrad., Wash. State U., Pullman, 1960—61; MS, Okla. State U., 1962, PhD, 1965. Operational rschr. Ops. Rsch., Inc., Silver Spring, Md., 1965-66; systems analyst Joint Chiefs of Staff, Washington, 1966-68; asst. prof. U. Pa., Phila., 1968-74; mem. faculty U. So. Calif., University Park, 1978-79. Cons. IBM Corp., East Fishkill, NY, 1973, Acad. Natural Scis., Phila., 1970-71, Office Asst. Sec. Def., 1969, Hdqrs. USAF, 1968-69. Author: Simulation: Statistical Foundations and Methodology, 1972, An Epistle to Dr. Benjamin Franklin, 1975, A Critique of World Models, 1975; co-author: Human Knowledge: Role of Models, Metaphors, and Analogy, 1974, Religion: Man's Earliest Science, 1978, Credibility: Every Computer Programme is a Simulation Model, 1985, Tele-cybernetics: Implications for the International Marketplace, 1988, Tele-cybernetics: Inferences from Living Systems to Both Science and Political Science, 1994, The Enhanced Electronic Postmark, 1997, Resolving Two Congressional Duties, 2000, The Scientific Method, 2003, An Open Letter to Diplomats Concerned About America's Middle Eastern Policy, 2006, The Philosophy of Science as a Biological Process, 2008, An Unsuspected Attribute of Darwinism, 2009; assoc. editor: Simulation, 1973-75, Internat. Jour. Gen. Systems, 1973—, Modeling and Simulation, 1974-92; contbr. Oxford English Dictionary, 2d edit. Mem. peer rev. panels NSF, Washington, 1974, 82. Capt. U.S. Army, 1966-68. Decorated Joint Svcs. Commendation medal; recipient award Conf. Simulation of Large Systems, Bielefeld, Germany, 1980, award Conf. Systems Rsch. Cybernetics, Baden-Baden, Germany, 2003; Fulbright scholar U. Sydney, Australia, 1964-65; NSF rsch. initiation grantee, 1970-72, internat. travel grantee, 1975, NATO grantee, 1977. Mem. AAAS (fellow nominee 1974, profl. socs. ethics group 1987-95, program liaison to Am. Math. Soc. com. 1992-94), Am. Philos. Assn., Soc. Study Social Problems, Internat. Soc. Sys. Sci., Soc. Computer Simulation (chmn. tech. com. on verification and validation 1974-75), Soc. Lit. and Sci., Internat. Assc. Statis. Computing, Internat. Assn. Cybernetics, Math. Assn. Am., Am. Math. Soc., Am. Statis. Assn., Biometric Soc., Can. Math. Soc., Assn. Computing Machinery, Interface (of Computer Sci. and Stats.) Found., Ops. Rsch. Soc. Am. (ethics and profl. practice com. 1983-95), Statis. Soc. Canada, Sigma Xi, Phi Beta Kappa, Pi Mu Epsilon, Phi Eta Sigma Avocation: mankind's search for truth mimes nature's biochemical process ensuring survival.

MIKA, JOSEPH JOHN, library and information scientist, educator; b. McKees Rocks, Pa., Mar. 1, 1948; s. George Joseph and Sophia Ann (Stec) Mika; m. Marianne Hartzell; 4 children. BA in English, U. Pitts., 1969, MLS, 1971, PhD in Libr. Sci., 1980. Asst. libr., instr. Ohio State U., Mansfield, 1971-73; asst. libr., asst. prof. Johnson State Coll., Vt., 1973-75; grad. asst., tchg. fellow Sch. Libr. and Info. Sci., U. Pitts., 1975-77; asst. dean, assoc. prof. libr. svc. U. So. Miss., Hattiesburg, 1977-86; dir. libr. and info. sci. program Wayne State U., 1986—95, 2002—07, prof., 1986—. Co-owner Hartzell-Mika Consulting; cons. to librs. Editor: Jour. Edn. Libr. and Info. Sci., 1995—2005. Retired col. USAR. Decorated DSM. Mem.: ALA (councilor 1983—86, chmn. constn. and bylaws com. 1985—86, councilor 1998—2001), Mich. Ctr. for Book (chair 1994—2001), Soc. Miss. Archivists (treas., exec. bd. 1981—83), Assn. Coll. and Rsch. Librs. (chmn., chmn. budget com. 1982—83), Leadership Acad., Mich. Libr. Assn., Miss. Libr. Assn. (pres.-elect 1985, chair libr. edn. com. 1989), Assn. Libr. and Info. Sci. and Edn. (chmn. nominating com. 1982, chmn. membership com. 1982—83, exec. bd. 1986), Kiwanis (Hattiesburg), Phi Delta Kappa, Beta Phi Mu (pres-elect 1987—89, pres. 1989—91). Home: 222 Abbott Woods Dr East Lansing MI 48823-1995 Office: Wayne State U Libr and Info Sci Program 106 Kresge Library Detroit MI 48202 Office Phone: 313-577-6196. Business E-Mail: aa2500@wayne.edu.

MIKABERIDZE, ALEXANDER, history professor, researcher; b. Aktiubinsk, Kazakhstan, Jan. 27, 1978; s. Levan and Marina Mikaberidze; m. Anna Kankia. JD in Internat. Law, Tbilisi State U., Rep. Ga., 1999; MA in History, Fla. State U., Tallahassee, 2001, PhD, 2003. Internat. law expert Ministry Fgn. Affairs Ga., Tbilisi, 1996—2000; lectr. Inst. Law and Psychology, Tbilisi, 1999—2000; vis. lectr. US Naval War Coll., Newport, 2004—07; asst. prof. history Miss. State U., Starkville, 2004—05, La. State U., Shreveport, La., 2007—. Editor, manuscript reviewer ABC-CLIO, Santa Barbara, Calif., 2005. Editor: (editorial) Dictionary of Georgian National Biography; contbr. articles to profl. publs.; author: The Russian Officer Corps in the Revolutionary and Napoleonic Wars, 179201815, 2005, The Czar's General: The Memoirs of a Russian General in the Napoleonic Wars, 2005, The Battle of Borodino: Napoleon versus Kutuzov, 2007, Historical Dictionary of Georgia, 2007, Great Escape: The Battle of the Berezina, 2009. Recipient Lit. award, Internat. Napoleonic Soc., 2005. Mem.: Consortium Revolutionary Era (bd. dirs. 2007), Soc. Mil. History, Napoleonic Soc. Ga. (pres. 1999—2007). Office: LA State Univ One University Place Shreveport LA 71115 also: 9431 Shartel Dr Shreveport LA 71118 Business E-Mail: alexander.mikaberidze@lsus.edu.

MIKAELIAN, TSOLINE, aerospace engineer; b. Beirut, Feb. 15, 1980; d. Hratch Kaspar Mikaelian and Alice Karapet Koucherian; m. Jonathan William Babb. BSc in Space and Comm. Scis., York U., Toronto, Ont., Can., 2002; MS in Aeronautics and Astronautics, MIT, Cambridge, Mass., 2005; PhD in Aerospace Sys. Engring., MIT, Cambridge, 2009. Tchg. asst., rschr. Atomic Physics Lab., York U., 2000—02; rschr. Spectral Applied Rsch., Inc., Concord, Ont., 2002, MIT Computer Sci. and Artificial Intelligence Lab., Cambridge, 2003—07, MIT Sys. Engring. Advancement Rsch. Initiative, 2007—. Rsch. cons. Toyota Tech. Ctr., Inc., Cambridge, 2004—06. Contbr. articles to profl. jours. Gen. advisor Armenian Generic Benevolent Union, Young Profls. Group, Boston, 2005. Recipient Herschel prize dept. physics and astronomy, York U., 2000, Ruth Hill Meml. award, 2001, Gold medal of the Faculty of Pure and Applied Sci., 2002, Normal Bethune Coll. Master's prize for academic excellence, 2002, Academic medal, Gov. Gen. of Can., 2002; scholar, Calouste Gulbenkian Found., Portugal, 1999, 2000, 2001; Presdl. fellow, MIT, 2003, Amelia Earhart fellow, Zonta Internat. Found., 2004—05. Mem.: Can. Assn. Physicists, Assn. for Advancement Artificial Intelligence, MIT Enterprise Forum. Armenian Orthodox. Avocations: painting, photography, travel. Business E-Mail: tsoline@alum.mit.edu.

MIKALS-ADACHI, EILEEN B., translator, educator; d. John J. and Eleanor F. Mikals; m. Misao Mikals-Adachi, July 20, 1975; children: Jo F., Ken J. PhD, Ochanomizu U., Tokyo, 1992. Instr. Manhattanville Coll., Purchase, NY, 1981—84; asst. prof. Kunitachi Music Coll., Tokyo, 1986—90, Bucknell U., Lewisburg, Eckerd Coll., St. Petersburg; assoc. prof. U. Notre Dame, Ochanomizu U., Tokyo. Translator: (history) The Roots of Contemporary Japan; contbr. articles to profl. publs. Mombusho grant, Japanese Govt., 1984—92, Japanese Tchg. Materials grant, Japan Found., 2007. Mem.: Nat. Coun. Japanese Lang. Tchrs., Assn. Fla. Tchrs. Japan, Assn. Tchrs. Japanese, Assn. Japanese Lit. Studies, Assn. Asian Studies (NEAC Rsch. Travel grant 1995, 2007). Office: Eckerd Coll 4200 54th Ave S Saint Petersburg FL 33711 Office Fax: 727-864-7995. Business E-Mail: mikalseb@eckerd.edu.

MIKALSON, BARBARA G., economics professor; b. Longview, Wash., Oct. 21, 1952; 1 child, Kerstin Mikalbrown. JD, UCLA Law Sch., 1991. Lectr. Princeton U., NJ, 1989—92, UC Irvine, Calif., 1984—88; assoc. Crowell & Moring, Newport Beach, 1992—93; assoc. atty. Buchalter Nemer, San Francisco, 1994—95; chef Sisters, Mamma Giovanna's, Idyllwild, 1995—97; co-founder & prin. Idyllwild Charter HS, 1998—2000; prof. Rio Hondo Coll., Whittier, 2001—. Home: 2825 Mariquita St Long Beach CA 90803 Office: Rio Hondo Coll 3600 Workman Mill Rd Whittier CA 90601 Business E-Mail: bmikalson@riohondo.edu.

MIKALSON, JON DENNIS, classics educator; b. Milw., Aug. 1, 1943; s. John Martin and Evelyn Kathryn (Heuser) M.; m. Mary Helen Villemonte, Aug. 28, 1966; children: Melissa, Jacquelyn. BA, U. Wis., 1965; postgrad., Am. Sch. Classical Studies, Athens, Greece, 1968-69; PhD, Harvard U., 1970. Asst. prof. classics U. Va., Charlottesville, 1970-75, assoc. prof., 1975-84, prof., 1984—, William R. Kenan Jr. prof. classics, 1999—, chmn. dept. classics, 1978-90, Dir. Echols Scholar Program, 1997-2000; vis. scholar Corpus Christi Coll., Cambridge, Eng., 1977-78; mem. Inst. for Advanced Study, Princeton, N.J., 1984-85; Whitehead prof. Am. Sch. Classical Studies, 1995-96. Author: The Sacred and Civil Calendar of the Athenian Year, 1975, Athenian Popular Religion, 1983, Honor Thy Gods: Popular Religion in Greek Tragedy, 1991, Religion in Hellenistic Athens, 1998, Herodotus and Religion in the Persian Wars, 2003, Ancient Greek Religion, 2004; contbr. articles to profl. and scholarly jours. James Rignall Wheeler fellow Am. Sch. Classical Studies, 1968-69, NEH fellow, 1977-78, Herodotus fellow Inst. for Advanced Study, 1984-85. Mem. Am. Philol. Assn., Am. Sch. Classical Studies, Archeol. Inst. of Am., Classical Assn. of Middle West and South (pres. so. sect. 1988-90), Classical Assn. of Va., Phi Beta Kappa, Phi Eta Sigma, Phi Kappa Phi, Omicron Delta Kappa. Clubs: Lions. Home: PO Box 664 Crozet VA 22932-0664 Office: U Va Dept Classics PO Box 400788 B002 Cocke Hall Charlottesville VA 22904-4788 Home Phone: 434-823-2163; Office Phone: 434-823-2163, 434-924-3008. Business E-Mail: jdm9x@virginia.edu.

MIKAN, G. MIKE, healthcare services company executive, corporate financial executive; Mgmt. positions, corp. devel. group UnitedHealth Group, Minnetonka, Minn., 1998, CFO specialized care svcs., 2001—04, sr. v.p. fin., 2006, exec. v.p., CFO, 2006—; pres. UnitedHealth Networks, Minnetonka, Minn., 2004—06. Bd. dirs. Best Buy Co., Inc., 2008—. Bd. dirs. Make-a-Wish Found. Minn., 2004—, Children's Theatre Co., Best Buy Co. Office: UnitedHealth Group PO Box 1459 Minneapolis MN 55440-1459*

MIKELLS, KATHRYN ANN, air transportation executive; b. 1965; BS in Fin., U. Ill., Urbana-Champaign; MBA, U. Chgo. With Household Internat., Can. Imperial Bank; with corp. fin. grp. GE Capital Solutions; fin. analyst United Air Lines, Inc., 1994, dir. fin. analysis, mgr. oper. budgets/treasury, v.p. and treas., 1994—2007, v.p. corp. real estate, 2003—05, v.p., treas., 2005—06, v.p. financial planning & analysis, 2006—07, v.p. investor rels., 2007—08, sr. v.p., CFO, 2008—09, exec. v.p., CFO, 2009—; sr. v.p., CFO UAL Corp., 2008—09, exec. v.p., CFO, 2009—. Office: UAL Corp World Hdqs PO Box 66100 Chicago IL 60666 Office Phone: 312-997-8610. Office Fax: 312-997-8610.*

MIKELS, JO, science educator; b. Findlay, Ohio, Oct. 24, 1952; d. A. Robert and Mary Welsh Kostyo; m. John Kenneth Mikels, Aug. 28, 1952; children: Shana, Erin. BA, U. Tex. at Pan Am., Edinburg, 1974. Cert. tchr. Tex., 1974, early adolescence, sci. tchr. Nat. Bd. for Profl. Tchg. Stds., 2003. Tchr. Austin Ind. Sch. Dist., Tex., 1982—. Tchr., cons. Tex. Mining and Reclaimation Assn., Austin, 2001—. Recipient Tchr. of Yr. award, Mendez Mid. Sch., 1998, Mid. Sch. Tchr. of Yr. award, Tex. Mining and Reclaimation Assn., 2002. Mem.: Edn. Austin, Phi Delta Kappa, Delta Kappa Gamma (Alpha State Lambda Iota chpt. pres. 2006—). Avocation: reading. Home: 7205 Towering Oaks Dr Austin TX 78745 Office: Clint Small Jr Mid Sch 4801 Monterey Oaks Blvd Austin TX 78749 Office Fax: 512-841-6703. Personal E-mail: koszmik@gmail.com. E-mail: jmikels@austinisd.org.

MIKELS, RICHARD ELIOT, lawyer; b. Cambridge, Mass., July 14, 1947; s. Albert Louis and Charlotte Betty (Shapiro) M.; m. Deborah Gwen Katz, Aug. 29, 1970; children: Allison Brooke, Robert Jarrett. BS in Bus. Adminstrn., Boston U., 1969, JD cum laude, 1972. Bar: Mass. 1972, US Dist. Ct. Mass. 1974, US Ct. Appeals (1st Cir.) 1978. Legal examiner ICC, Washington, 1972-74; ptnr. Riemer & Braunstein, Boston, 1974-80; ptnr., chmn. Comml. Law Sect. Peabody & Brown, Boston, 1980-88; mem., chmn. Comml. Law Sect. Mintz, Levin, Cohn, Ferris, Glovsky and Popeo, PC, Boston, 1988—, ptnr. Contbr. articles to profl. jour.; editor: Boston U. Law Rev., 1971—72. Tng. adv. com. Jewish Vocat. Svc., Boston, 1991, 1995, 1996, bd. dir., 1995—99, vice chair microenterprise adv. com., 1997; vice chair lawyers com. Combined Jewish Philanthropies, 1994, 1995; co-chair Boston U. Law Sch. Law Fund. Fellow Am. Coll. Bankruptcy (1st cir. regent 2005-09, bd. dir., 2009); mem. ABA, Am. Bankruptcy Inst. (bd. dirs. 2000-06), Assn. Comml. Fin. Attys., Comml. Law League Am., Mass. Bar Assn., Boston Bar Assn., Boston U. Law Alumni Assn. (mem. exec. com., pres. exec. com. 2000-01). Office: Mintz Levin Cohn Ferris Glovsky & Popeo PC 1 Financial Ctr Fl 39 Boston MA 02111-2657 Office Phone: 617-348-1691. Office Fax: 617-542-2241. Business E-Mail: rmikels@mintz.com.

MIKESELL, ELIZABETH BREMOND, foundation administrator; b. Tucson, Ariz., Dec. 11, 1946; d. Howard Swart Bremond and Mary Miner Carson; m. Robert Eugene Mikesell, Jan. 23, 1984; children: Victor Eugene, Frances Elizabeth 1 stepchild, Amber Sinclair. BFA, U. Ariz., Tucson, 1969. Cert. exec. chef Am. Culinary Fedn., Fla., 1992. Exec. chef Country Club Green Valley, Ariz., 1987—2001; chef instr. Pima CC Desert Vista Campus, Tucson, 2002—08. Pres. ACF Chefs Assn. Southern Ariz., Tucson, 1998—2001, chmn. bd. dirs., 2001—05, v.p., 2005—; mem. rels. chair Am. Acad. Chefs, St. Augustine, 2003—07; chair ACF Chef Child Found., St. Augustine, 2005—. Dancer (ballets) The Nutcracker. Chair ACF Chef Child Found., 2005—08. Recipient The Good Taste award, Am. Acad. Chefs, 2006; named Chef of Yr., ACF Chefs Assn. So. Ariz., 1994, 2007, Vocat. Instr. of Yr., Pima C.C., 2003—04. Home: 1515 W Calle Guadaljara Tucson AZ 85713 Office: Pima CC 5901 S Calle Santa Cruz Tucson AZ 85709 Office Fax: 520-206-5196. Business E-Mail: elizabeth.mikesell@pima.edu.

MIKESKA, NOEL RHEA, entrepreneur, health advocate; b. Garland, Tex., Nov. 28, 1975; s. Gary and Kimberlee Mikeska; m. Erinn Teresa Blake, Sept. 22, 2001. BA, Abilene Christian U., Tex., 2000. Cert. Nat. Assn. Health and Fitness Am.,Tex., 2000. CEO Your Body Fitness Inc, Dallas, 1997—, America's Fitness Corp., 2001—, Abb-Solute Fitness, Dallas, 2003—; exec. dir. Noel Mikeska Enterprises Inc., Irving, 2004—. Founder America's Fitness Inst., 2006; pres. Fitnex Comml.; health expert ABC-TV; talk show host local Dallas TV. Contbr. articles to periodicals. Mem.: CEO Club, Sigma Nu. Achievements include being featured in the Dallas Morning News.

MIKHAEL, JOSEPH, hematologist; MD, U. Ottawa, Can., 1997; MEd, U. Toronto-OISE, Ont., Can., 2003. Cert. in internal medicine Royal Coll. Physicians and Surgeons Can., 2001, in hematology 2002. Staff hematologist Princess Margaret Hosp., Toronto, 2004—08; cons. hematologist Mayo Clinic Ariz., Scottsdale, 2008—. Office: Mayo Clinic 13400 E Shea Blvd Scottsdale AZ 85259 Office Fax: 480-301-4675. Business E-Mail: mikhael.joseph@mayo.edu.

MIKHAILOV, STEPAN FEDOROVICH, physicist, researcher; b. Norilsk, Krasnoyarsk region, Russia, Nov. 29, 1960; arrived in US, 2000; s. Feodor K. and Valentina M. Mikhailov; m. Natalia A. Makhanova, June 8, 2000; 1 child, Andrei M. Makhanov. MS, Novosibirsk State Tech. U., Russia, 1982. Rsch. scientist Budker Inst. Nuc. Physics, Novosibirsk, 1982—2000; sr. rsch. scientist FEL Lab. Duke U., Durham, NC, 2000—. Office: Duke U DFEL Lab PO Box 90319 LaSalle St Extension Durham NC 27708-0319 Home: Apt K 103 Misty Woods Cir Chapel Hill NC 27514 Office Fax: 919-660-2671. Business E-Mail: smikhail@fel.duke.edu.

MIKHELASHVILI, TIM, pharmaceutical executive; s. Nodari Mikhelashvili. BS, Tulane U., New Orleans, 2000; PharmD, Xavier Coll. Pharmacy, New Orleans, 2004. Lic. pharmacist Bd. Pharmacy, NJ, 2004. Sci. publs. and med. edn. postdoc. fellow Sanofi-Aventis Pharms., Bridgewater, NJ, 2004—05, Ernest Mario Sch. Pharmacy, Rutgers U., Piscataway, NJ, prof., adj. faculty, 2004—05; regional sci. mgr. AstraZeneca Pharms., Bklyn., 2005—. Contbr. scientific papers. Pharm. industry com. chmn. NY Soc. Health-Sys. Pharmacists, Royal Counties chpt., Bklyn., 2008. Mem.: Am. Soc. Health Sys. Pharmacists, Assn. Health Sys. Pharmacists, Am. Heart Assn. Avocation: soccer. Home Fax: 718-996-1528. Personal E-mail: tim.mikhelashvili@astrazeneca.com.

MIKHELSON, SERGEI, mathematician, educator; b. Saint Petersburg, Russia, May 17, 1970; s. Stanislav and Eleonora (Guretskaya) Mikhelson. BA, Russian State Pedagogical U., St. Petersburg, Russia, 1993; MA, Russian State Pedagogical U., 1993, Columbia U., NYC, 1994. Math. and logic tchr. Gymnasia 56, St. Petersburg, Russia, 1991—97; program dir., dept. head Ctr. of Alternative Edn., St. Petersburg, 1994—98; vice-prin. Gymnasia 56, St. Petersburg, 1995; math. adj. instr. NYU, NYC, 1999—2005, Borough of Manhattan C.C., NYC, 1998—2001; math. tchr. Bklyn Friends Sch., 2002—08, Little Red Sch. House & Elizabeth HS, 2008—. Internat. debate trainer Internat. Debate Edn. Assn., NYC, 1998—2002. Co-author (publication) Mathematics Education in Russia. Mem.: Nat. Coun. of Tchrs. of Math. Office Phone: 212-477-5316. Business E-Mail: ssm21@columbia.edu.

MIKIEWICZ, ANNA DANIELLA, marketing and international business export manager; b. Chgo., Dec. 22, 1960; d. Zdislaw and Lucy (Magnusewska) M. BS in Mktg., Elmhurst Coll., 1982; postgrad., Triton Coll. Asst. to midwestern regional mgr. Melster Pub. Co., Chgo., 1983; sales rep. First Impressions, Elk Grove, Ill., 1984; asst. to Midwestern dist. mgr. Airco Ind. Gases, Broadview, Carol Stream, Ill., 1985; customer svc. & ops. Yamazen USA, Inc., Schaumburg, Ill., 1985-88; nat. sales & mktg. coord. Kitamura Machinery U.S.A. Inc., 1988-95; mktg. mgr. Beth Lee Boutique, 1995-97; internat. bus. export control mgr. MHI Machine Tool USA, Inc. subs. Mistubishi Heavy Industries, 1997-99; internat. bus. asst. to exec. v.p. sales America Excel, Inc., Elk Grove Village, Ill., 1999—; internat. account mgr. Brazil Market JST Sales Am., Inc., Waukegan, Ill., 2000—04; NAFTA program mgr. global worldwide market Anixter, Inc., 2005—; NAER cons. NAFTA & Export Rescue, 2007—; internat. bus.-export compliance cons. Projects Longterm-Shortterm. Named Chgo. Polish Queen Polish Am. Culture Club, 1983-84. Mem.: NAFE. Republican. Roman Catholic.

MIKITKA, GERALD PETER, brokerage house executive, consultant; BSBA in Fin., Roosevelt U., 1966, postgrad., 1967. Diplomate: registered investment advisor. Sr. investment exec. Shearson Hammill & Co., Chgo., 1967-73; chmn., pres. Capital Directions, Inc., Chgo., 1973—. Pres. CDI Fin. Advisors, Chgo., 1974—, CDI Properties, Chgo., 1974—, CDI Communications, Inc., Chgo., 1978—, A.B. Properties Inc., Chgo., 1986—, Am. Eagle Realty Inc., Chgo., 1988—, Grand Caribbean Properties Inc., Chgo., 1988, Cain Estates Inc., Chgo., 1988—, Caribbean Sea Properties Inc., Chgo., 1989—. Served with U.S. Army, 1967-69. Mem. Nat. Assn. Securities Dealers, Securities Investment Protection Assn., Broadcast Fin. Mgmt. Assn., Nat. Radio Broadcast Assn., Internat. Assn. Fin. Planning. Lodges: Rotary.

MIKLOS, ATHENA PAULINE, business educator, property management company executive; b. Athens, Ohio, May 13, 1950; d. Mike J. and Rallia (Psaltakis) Chakiris; m. Robert R. Miklos, June 18, 1983. B. in Gen. Studies, Ohio U., 1972. Display coordinator Lerner Shops, Pitts., 1972-75, tng. supr., 1976-78; mgr. Ups and Downs, Pitts., 1975-76; city planner City of Athens, 1980-82; mem. faculty Hocking Tech. Coll., Nelsonville, Ohio, 1982—; property mgr. Phil Chakiris, Athens, 1982—, Cathy Antonopoulos, Athens, 1982-83; bus. adviser Beaver Industries, Nelsonville, 1983—; instr. Hocking Correctional Facility, Nelsonville, 1984—; guest lectr. Methodist Ch., The Plains, Ohio, 1985. Trustee, Athens County Tourism Bur., 1982—. Grantee Ohio Hist. Soc., 1981. Mem. Ohio Mktg. Mgmt. Educators, Beta Sigma Phi. Greek Orthodox. Avocations: photography; interior design; reading; antiques; auctions. Office: College of Southern Maryland 8730 Mitchell Rd, PO Box 910 La Plata MD 20646 Business E-Mail: athenam@csmd.edu.

MIKOLAVICH, DANIEL KEITH, literature and language professor, consultant; b. San Francisco, Feb. 2, 1964; s. Daniel Carl Mikolavich and Barbara Faith Davison; m. Ema Fischer, June 30, 2007. BA in English Lit., San Francisco State U., 1987, MA in English, 1990. Tchr., cons. U. Calif., Berkeley's Bay Area Writing Project, 1992—. Democrat. Avocations: farming, architecture, beekeeping, reading. Office: Diablo Valley Coll 321 Golf Club Rd Pleasant Hill CA 94523

MIKULICH GILBERTSON, SUSAN KAY, science educator; b. Portland, Colo., Sept. 11, 1966; d. Edna Mae Paul; m. Richard Arn Gilbertson, July 2, 2003; 1 child, Daniel Gilbertson. PhD, U. Colo., Denver, 2000. Assoc. prof., biostats. U. Colo., Denver, 1990—. Musician live performances & recs. Recipient Strother Walker award, U. Colo., 2001, Early Investigator award, Coll. Problems Drug Dependence, 2001; Doctoral fellowship, U. Colo. Health Scis. Ctr. Grad. Sch., 1997. Mem.: Am. Statis. Assn. (Maurice Davies award, Colo. Wyo. Chpt. 1996). Home: 94 S Joyce St Golden CO 80401 Office: Univ Colo Denver 12469 E 17th Pl Bldg 400 Rm 211 Aurora CO 80045 Business E-Mail: susan.mikulich@ucdenver.edu.

MIKULICS, MICHAEL P., literature and language educator; s. Michael Charles and Marilyn Stella Mikulics. BA in English, Calif. State U., Fullerton, 1979; MEd, US Internat. U., 1985, EdD, 1998. English tchr. Canyon Springs HS, Moreno Valley, Calif., 1995—. GATE facilitator adj. prof. edn. Chapman U., Azusa-Pacific U., Concordia U., U. Calif., Riverside.

MIKULSKI, BARBARA ANN, United States Senator from Maryland; b. Balt., July 20, 1936; d. William and Christine (Kutz) M. BA in Sociology, Mt. St. Agnes Coll., 1958; MSW, U. Md., 1965; LLD (hon.), Goucher Coll., 1973, Hood Coll., 1978, Bowie State U., 1989, Morgan State U., 1990, U. Mass., 1991; DHL (hon.), Pratt Inst., 1974. Tchr. Vista Tng. Ctr. Mount St. Mary's Sem., Balt.; social worker Balt. Dept. Social Services, 1961-63, 66-70; mem. Balt. City Council, 1971-76, 95th-99th Congresses from 3d Md. Dist., 1977-87; US Senator from Md., 1987—; sec. Dem. Conf. 104th-106th Congress. Adj. prof. Loyola Coll., 1972-76; mem. U.S. Senate labor and human resources com., 1987—, ranking mem. subcom. on aging, 1993—; mem. appropriations com., 1987, ranking mem. subcom. on vets., housing, and ind. agys., 1987—. Bd. visitors U.S. Naval Acad.; bd. adv. Space Awareness Alliance. Recipient Nat. Citizen of Yr. award Buffalo Am.-Polit. Eagle, 1973, Woman of Yr. Bus. & Profl. Women's Club Assn., 1973, Outstanding Alumnus U. Md. Sch. Social Work, 1973, Govt. Social Responsibility award, 1991, Disting. Svc. award Ctrl. and East European Coalition, 1996, Louis D. Brandeis award Baltimore, Md. Zionist Dist., 1996, Public Svc. award Am. Inst. Aeronautics and Astronautics, 1998, Order of Merit Commanders Cross with Star Govt. Poland, 2001, Good Housekeeping/Wyeth award women's health, 2002, Connie Mack Lifetime Avhievement award Susan G. Komen Breast Cancer Found., 2003, Elmer P. Martin Public Svc. award Great Blacks in Wax Mus., 2003, Public Svc. award Emergency Nurses Assn., 2004, Nat. Leadership award Big Brothers and Big Sisters of Ctrl. Md., 2005. Mem. LWV. Democrat. Roman Catholic. Office: US Senate 503 Hart Sen Office Bldg Washington DC 20510-0001 also: Brown's Wharf Ste 400 1629 Thames St Baltimore MD 21231 Office Phone: 202-224-4654, 410-962-4510. Office Fax: 202-224-8858, 410-962-4760.*

MIKUMO, AKIKO, lawyer; BA, U. Calif., Berkeley, 1978; JD, NYU, 1982. Assoc. Weil, Gotshal & Manges LLP, NYC, 1982—90, ptnr., 1990—, head U.S. practice London, 1998—2002. Mem.: ABA (mem. com. on corp. law 1993—), Assn. of the Bar of the City of N.Y. (com. Asian affairs). Office: Weil Gotshal & Manges LLP 767 Fifth Ave New York NY 10153 Office Phone: 212-310-8000.

MIKUS, ELEANORE ANN, artist; b. Detroit, July 25, 1927; d. Joseph and Bertha (Englot) M.; m. Richard Burns, July 6, 1949 (div. 1963); children: Richard, Hillary, Gabrielle. Student, Mich. State U., 1946-49, U. Mex., summer 1948; B.F.A., U. Denver, 1957, MA, 1967; postgrad., Art Students League, 1958, NYU, 1959-60. Asst. prof. Cornell U., Ithaca, NY, 1979-80, assoc. prof., 1980-92, prof. art, 1992-94, prof. emerita, 1994—. Asst. prof. art Monmouth Coll., West Long Branch, N.J., 1966-70, prof. Cornell, Rome, 1989; vis. lectr. painting Cooper Union, N.Y.C., 1970-72, Central Sch. Art and Design, London, 1973-77, Kensington Inst., London, 1974-77, Harrow (Eng.) Coll. Tech. and Art, 1975-76. One-woman shows include Pace Gallery, NYC, 1963-65, O.K. Harris Gallery, NYC., 1971-74, Baskett Gallery, Cin., 1982, 84-85, Claudia Carr Gallery, 1998—, Mitchell Algus Gallery, NYC, 1998, 2003-04, The Drawing Ctr., NYC, 2006-07, Marlborough Gallery, NYC, 2008, Artnot Art Mus. Elmira, NY, 2009; represented in permanent collections including Met. Mus. Art, NYC, Mus. Modern Art, NYC, Whitney Mus., NYC, LA County Mus., Cin. Mus., Birmingham Mus. Art, Ala., Norton Simon Mus., Pasadena, Bklyn. Mus., Honolulu Acad. Arts, Indpls. Mus. Art, Nat. Gallery Art, Washington, Victoria and Albert Mus., London, Libr. of Congress, Washington, Tucson Mus. of Art, Blanton Mus. U. Tex., U. Ariz. Mus. Art, Tucson, Univ. Ariz., Tucson, De Cordova Mus., Lincoln, Mass.; subject of book Eleanore Mikus, Shadows of the Real (by Robert Hobbs and Judith Bernstock), 1991. Fellow, Guggenheim, 1966—67, Tamarind, 1968, McDowell, 1969, Yaddo drawing and painting, 2004. Home: PO Box 4775 Ithaca NY 14852-4775 Office: Cornell U Dept Art Tjaden Hall Ithaca NY 14853 also: 270 Luce Rd Groton NY 13073-9747 Office Phone: 607-533-7766. Personal E-mail: mikusart44@hotmail.com.

MIKVA, ABNER JOSEPH, lawyer, retired judge; b. Milw., Jan. 21, 1926; s. Henry Abraham and Ida (Fishman) M.; m. Zoe Wise, Sept. 19, 1948; children: Mary, Laurie, Rachel. JD cum laude, U. Chgo., 1951; DL (hon.), U. Ill., 1980, Am. U., 1991, Northwestern U., 1991, Tulane U., 1993, Ill. Inst. Tech., 1997, Santa Clara U., 2000, Wm. Mitchell Coll. Law, 2001; DHL (hon.), Hebrew U., 1989, U. Wis., 1995, De Paul U. Law Sch., 2002, So. Ill. U., 2006. Bar: Ill. 1951, D.C. 1978. Law clk. to Hon. Sherman Minton U.S. Supreme Ct., 1951; ptnr. Devoe, Shadur, Mikva & Plotkin, Chgo., 1952-68, D'Ancona, Pflaum, Wyatt & Riskind, 1973-74; lectr. Northwestern U. Law Sch., Chgo., 1973-75, U. Pa. Law Sch., 1983-85, Georgetown Law Sch., 1986-88, Duke U. Law Sch., Durham, NC, 1990-91, U. Chgo. Law Sch., 1992-93; mem. Ill. Gen. Assembly from 23d Dist., 1956-66, US Congress from 2d Dist. Ill., 1969—73, US Congress from 10th Ill. Dist., 1975—79, mem. ways and means com., judiciary com.; chmn. Dem. Study Group, 1979; judge U.S. Ct. Appeals (D.C. cir.), 1979-94; chief judge U.S. Ct. Appeals (D.C. cir), 1991-94; counsel to the Pres. The White House, Washington, 1994-96; arbitrator JAMS, Inc., 1997—. Vis. prof., Walter Schaefer chair in pub. policy U. Chgo., 1996-98; vis. prof. U. Ill. Coll. Law, 1998-2000, U. Chgo., 2000—. Author: The American Congress: The First Branch, 1983, The Legislative Process, 1995, An Introduction to Statutory Interpretation, 1997. With USAAF, WWII. Sr. fellow Inst. Govt. & Pub. Affairs U. Ill., 1998-2000; recipient Page One award Chgo. Newspaper Guild, 1964, Best Legislator award Ind. Voters Ill., 1956-66, Alumni medal U. Chgo., 1996, Paul Douglas Ethics in Govt. award, 1998, Thurgood Marshall award, ABA, 2005; named one of Ten Outstanding Young Men in Chgo., Jr. Assn. Commerce and Industry, 1961. Fellow Am. Acad. Arts and Scis.; mem. ABA, Chgo. Bar Assn. (bd. mgrs. 1962-64), D.C. Bar Assn., Am. Law Inst., U.S. Assn. Former Mems. Congress, Order of Coif, Phi Beta Kappa. Home: Ph 6 5020 S Lake Shore Dr Chicago IL 60615-3253 Home Phone: 773-241-5048; Office Phone: 773-834-5852. Personal E-mail: zmikva@aol.com. Business E-Mail: amikva@law.uchicago.edu.

MIKVA, LAURIE I., lawyer; b. 1955; d. Abner and Zoe. JD, NYU, 1983. Clk. Judge Luther M. Swygert, 1983—84; asst. pub. defender Md. Pub. Defenders Office Appellate Divsn., Urbana, Ill., 1988—91; atty. Land of Lincoln Legal Assistance Found., 1993—2008; staff atty. Ill. Dept. Employment Security Office Legal Counsel; bd. dirs. Legal Svcs. Corp., 2009—. Instr. legal writing U. Ill. Coll. Law, founder Domestic Violence Clinic; fellow Women's Law & Pub. Policy Program Georgetown U. Law Sch. Office: 3333 K St NW 3rd Fl Washington DC 20007-3522 Office Phone: 202-295-1500. Office Fax: 202-337-6797. E-mail: info@lsc.gov.*

MILAM, JOHN DANIEL, pathologist, educator; b. Kilgore, Tex., May 22, 1933; s. Ott G. and Effie (White) Milam; m. Carol Jones, Aug. 1, 1959; children: Kay, Beth, John Daniel, Julie. BS, La. State U., 1955, MS, 1957, MD, 1960. Attending pathologist St. Luke's Episcopal Hosp., Houston, 1967—89, chief of staff, 1981—83; emeritus Tex. Children's Hosp., Houston, 2000—; adj. prof. lab. medicine M.D. Anderson Cancer Ctr., U. Tex., Houston, 1990—2001; prof. pathology and lab. medicine U. Tex. Med. Sch., Houston, 1989—2001, prof. emeritus, 2001—; active med. staff Hermann Hosp., Houston, 1988—, med. dir. lab. svcs., 1990—95; chief pathology Lyndon B. Johnson Gen. Hosp., Houston, 1995—2001. Trustee Am. Bd. Pathology, 1985—96, pres., 1995, life trustee, 1996—; cons. in field. Contbr. articles and abstracts to profl. jours., chapters to books. Bd. dirs. Greater Houston area chpt. ARC, 1978—. Recipient Disting. Physician award, Hermann Hosp., 1996. Mem.: Coll. Am. Pathologist (bd. govs., vice spkr. house of dels. 2005—), Houston Soc. Clin. Pathologists (pres. 1975, Harlan J. Spjut award 2003), Am. Soc. Clin. Pathologists (Commn. on Continuing Edn. Disting. Svc. award 1993, Israel Davidsohn Disting. Svc. award 2001), Tex. Soc. Pathologists (pres. 1978, George T. Caldwell award 1981), Am. Assn. Blood Banks (pres. 1984, Disting. Svc. award 1988). Republican. Baptist. Home: 11927 Arbordale Ln Houston TX 77024-5001 Office: U Tex Houston Med Sch Rm 2-022 Dept Pathology 6431 Fannin St Houston TX 77030-1501 Office Phone: 713-500-5336. Business E-Mail: john.d.milam@uth.tmc.edu.

MILAM, LYNNE MORGAN, special education educator; b. Harlan, Ky., Oct. 19, 1943; d. James T. and Dorothy O. Morgan; m. Jon Milam, June 20, 1970; 1 child, Morgan M. Cressman. BA with distinction in Edn., U. Ky., Lexington, 1967; MA in Spl. Edn., West Ga. Coll., Carrollton, 1990. Cert. tchr. speech grades 7-12 Ky., 1967, Ga., 1989, tchr. learning disabilities grades K-12 Ga., 1991. Tchr. English/speech Loyall Jr. H.S., Ky., 1966—73; tchr. speech/drama James A. Cawood H.S., Harlan, 1969—73; tchr. learning disabilities The Bedford Sch., Fairburn, Ga., 1985—. Recipient Outstanding Young Ky. Speech Tchr., Ky. Assn. Comm. Arts, Lexington, 1969, Outstanding Harlan County Educator, Harlan County Jaycees, 1970; named one of Outstanding Young Women in Am, 1967, 1970. Mem.: Orton Dyslexia Assn., Ga. Coun. Tchrs. of English, Phi Kappa Phi. Republican. Christian. Avocations: reading, writing, singing. Office: The Bedford Sch 5665 Milam Rd Fairburn GA 30213 Business E-Mail: lmilam@thebedfordschool.org.

MILAM, WILLIAM BRYANT, senior policy scholar, former ambassador; b. Bisbee, Ariz., July 24, 1936; s. Burl Vivian and Alice Vera (Pierce) M.; m. Faith A. Handley; step-children: Erika, Fred. AB, Stanford U., 1959; MA, U. Mich., 1970; postgrad., Am. U., 1973. Polit. officer Dept. State, Washington, 1967-69; fin. economist Dept. State and Am. Embassy, Washington and London, 1970-75; energy economist Dept. State, Washington, 1975-77, dep. office dir., 1977-80, office dir., 1980-83, dep. chief of mission Yaounde, Cameroon, 1983-85, dep. asst. sec. Washington, 1985-90, U.S. amb. to Bangladesh, 1990-93, spl. negotiator oceans environ. sci. Washington, 1993-95, chief of mission Monrovia, Liberia, 1995-98, US amb. to Pakistan Islamabad, 1998-2001, interim chief of mission Tripoli, Libya, 2007—08; sr. policy scholar Woodrow Wilson Internat. Ctr. for Scholars, 2002—. Author: (bi-weekly op-ed column) Pakistan Daily Times. Calif. State scholar, 1956-59; recipient James Clement Dunn award Dept. of State, 1981, Superior Honor award, 1983, Pres.'s Meritorious Svc. award U.S. Govt., 1990, Pres. Outstanding Svc. award, 1991. Avocations: reading, golf, writing. Office: One Woodrow Wilson Plz 1300 Pennsylvania Ave NW Washington DC 20004 Business E-Mail: william.milam@wilsoncenter.org.*

MILAN, STOJANOVIC P., medical educator, director; s. Petar and Tatjana Stojanovic; m. Maja Nikolic; children: Stefan Stojanovic, Petar Stojanovic. MD, U. Belgrade, 1985. Founder and dir., interventional pain program Mass. Gen. Hosp., Harvard Med. Sch., Boston, 1997—2008; dir., outpatient clinic MGH Pain Ctr., Mass. Gen. Hosp., Harvard Med. Sch., Boston, 1997—99; co-medical dir. Cape Cod Hosp. Pain Ctr., Hyannis, Mass., 2002—08; co-founder Spine and Pain Inst. New Eng., Dedham, Mass.; asst. prof. Harvard Med. Sch., Boston, 2003—; dir. at large Am. Soc. Interventional Pain Physicians, Paducah, Ky., 2007—. E-mail: mpstmd@yahoo.com.

MILANA-PANOPOULOS, MARIA, artist, model; b. Oceanside, NY, Nov. 13, 1965; d. Thomas F. and Angelina M. Milana; m. S. Michael Panopoulos, May 1988; children, Thomas, Nicholas Student, Kingsborough CC, Manhattan Beach, NY, 1983—84, Nassau CC, Garden City, NY, 1984—85. Cert. herbologist Herbal Healer Acad. Freelance model, NY, 1981—, Fla.; owner Artistic Creations, 2006—, Custom Faux You!, 2006—, Mia Milana Collections, 2006—. Mem. adv. bd. Trinity Oaks Homeowners Assn., New Port Richey, Fla., 1992-93. Mem. Tarpon Springs Art Assn. (bd. dirs. 1998—), Herbal Healer Acad. Republican. Roman Catholic. Achievements include patent for knee brace. Mailing: PO Box 1234 Elfers FL 34680 Business E-Mail: cre8tive@tampabay.rr.com.

MILANDER, HENRY MARTIN, educational consultant; b. Northampton, Pa., Apr. 17, 1939; s. Martin Edward and Margaret Catherine (Makovetz) M.; children: Martin Henry, Beth Ann. BS summa cum laude, Lock Haven U., Pa., 1961; MA, Bowling Green State U., Ohio, 1962; EdS (Future Faculty fellow 1964), U. No. Iowa, 1965; EdD, Ill. State U., Normal, 1967. Instr. Wartburg Coll., Waverly, Iowa, 1962-64; asst. prof. Ill. State U., 1966-67; dean instrn. Belleville (Ill.) Area Coll., 1967-69; v.p. acad. affairs Lorain County Community Coll., Elyria, Ohio, 1969-72; pres. Olympic Coll., Bremerton, Wash., 1972-87, Northeastern Jr. Coll., Sterling, Colo., 1988-95; edn1. cons., 1995—. Pres. Bremers, Inc., 1986-87. Contbr. articles to profl. jours. Pres. Kitsap County Comprehensive Health Planning Council, 1975-76; pres. Logan County Colo. United Way, 1992-93. Recipient Faculty Growth award Wartburg Coll., 1963, Cmty. Svc. award, 1975, Chief Thunderbird award, 1985. Mem. Am. Assn. C.C., Am. Assn. Sch. Adminstrs., N.W. Assn. Cmty. and Jr. Colls., Wash. Assn. C.C. (pres. 1984-85), Wash. C.C. Computing Consortium (chmn. bd. dirs. 1985-87), Puget Sound Naval Bases Assn. (pres. 1982-86), Wash. Assn. C.C. Pres. (pres. 1984-85), Bremerton Area C. of C. (pres. 1977-78), Colo. Assn. C.C. Pres. (pres. 1993-94), Rotary (pres. Sterling Club 1992-93), Kappa Delta Pi, Phi Delta Kappa. Lutheran. Home: 709 E Pointes Dr West Shelton WA 98584-6305

MILANI, ABBAS SADEGHZADEH, professor; PhD in Engring., McGill U., Montreal, Can., 2005. Postdoc. fellow, NSERC MIT, Cambridge, 2005—07; asst. prof. U. BC, Kelowna, Canada, 2007—. Vis. rsch. assoc. Indsl. Materials Inst. Nat. Rsch. Coun., Boucherville, QC, Canada, 2001—02. Postdoc. fellow, Natural Scis. and Engring. Rsch. Coun., Can., 2005—07. Achievements include research in a multi-objective inverse method for obtaining constitutive material parameters of textile composites using two hyperelastic models. Office: Univ BC 3333 Univ Way Kelowna BC V1V 1V7 Canada Office Fax: 250-807-9850. Business E-Mail: abbas.milani@ubc.ca.

MILANICH, JERALD THOMAS, archaeologist, writer, curator; b. Painesville, Ohio, Oct. 13, 1945; s. John Joseph and Jean Marie (Bales) M.; m. Maxine L. Margolis, Dec. 20, 1970; 1 child, Nara Bales. BA, U. Fla., 1967, MA, 1968, PhD, 1971. Fellow Smithsonian Inst., Washington, 1971-72; asst. prof. anthropology U. Fla., Gainesville, 1972-75; asst. curator Fla. Mus. Natural History, 1975-77, assoc. curator, 1977-81, chmn. dept. anthropology, 1981-83, 91-94, curator, 1981—. Author: (with Samuel Proctor) Tacachale -- Essays on the Indians of Florida and Southeastern Georgia During the Historic Period, 1978; (with Charles Fairbanks) Florida Archaeology, 1980; McKeithen Weeden Island, 1984; Early Prehistoric Southeast, 1985; (with Susan Milbrath) First Encounters, Spanish Explorations in the Caribbean and the United States, 1492-1570, 1989; The Hernando de Soto Expedition, 1990; Earliest Hispanic-Native America Interactions in the Greater American Southwest, 1991; (with Charles Hudson) Hernando de Soto and the Indians of Florida, 1993, Archaeology of Precolumbian Florida, 1994, Florida Indians and the Invasion of Europe, 1995, The Timucua, 1996, Archaeology of Northern Florida, 1997, Florida Indians From Ancient Times to the Present, 1998, Laboring in the Fields of the Lord: Spanish Missions and Southeastern Indians, 1999, 2006, Famous Florida Sites: Mount Royal and Crystal River, 1999, (with Theodore Morris) Florida's Lost Tribes: Through the Eyes of an Artist, 2004, Frolicking Bears Wet Vultures and Other Oddities: A New York City Journalist in Nineteenth Century Florida, 2005, A Remarkable Commodity: Dispatches From a New York City Journalist's 1873 Railroad Trips Across The American West, 2008; mem. editl. bd.: Archaeology Mag., 1992-2002, contbg. editor, 2002—. Trustee Archeol. Inst. Am., 2004—. Recipient Ripley P. Bullen award, 1980, Rembert Patrick Book award, 1994-95, James Mooney Book award, 1995, medal Fla. Acad. Sci., 2004, Lifetime Achievement award Fla. Archeol. Coun., 2005; grantee NSF, 1970-71, 73-75, 77-82, 2003, Wentworth Found., 1976-77, 81-84, 91, NEH, 1985, 87-89, Fla. Divsn. Hist. Resources, 1981, 83-89, 91, 96-97, 00-02, 03-04. Mem. Soc. Am. Archaeology (exec. bd. 1990-93), Soc. Profl. Archeologists (cert., pres. 1981-82), So. Anthrop. Soc., S.E. Archeol. Conf. (pres. 1986-88). Office: Fla Mus Natural History Gainesville FL 32611-7800

MILANO, ALYSSA, actress; b. NYC, Dec. 19, 1972; d. Thomas M. and Lin Milano.; m. Cinjun August Tate, Jan. 1, 1999 (div. Nov. 20, 1999); m. David Bugliari, Aug. 15, 2009. Student, Bel Air Prep. Sch., LA. Actress: (TV series) Who's the Boss?, 1984-92, Melrose Place, 1997-98, Charmed, 1998-2006; (TV movies) The Canterville Ghost, 1986, Dance'Til Dawn, 1988, Conflict of Interest, 1992, Candles in the Dark, 1993, Casualties of Love: The Long Island Lolita Story, 1993, Confessions of a Sorority Girl, 1994, The Surrogate, 1995, To Brave Alaska, 1996, Goldrush: A Real Life Alaskan Adventure, 1998, Diamond Hunters, 2001, (voice only) Jimmy Neutron: Win, Lose and Kaboom, 2004, Reinventing the Wheelers, 2007, Wisegal, 2008; (films) Old Enough, 1982, Commando, 1985, Speed Zone, 1989, Where the Day Takes You, 1992, Little Sister, 1992, Double Dragon, 1993, Embrace of the Vampire, 1995, At Home with the Webbers, 1993, The Surrogate, 1995, Public Enemy # 1, 1995, Fear, 1996, Glory Daze, 1996, Jimmy Zip, 1996, Below Utopia, 1997, Hugo Pool, 1997, Buying the Cow, 2002, Kiss the Bride, 2002, Dickie Roberts: Former Child Star, 2003, (voice only) Dinotopia: Quest for the Ruby Sunstone, 2005, The Blue Hour, 2007, Pathology, 2008; actress, exec. prodr.: Below Utopia, 1997; actress: (TV appearances) The Outer Limits, 1995, Spin City, 1997, 2001, Fantasy Island, 1998, My Name Is Earl, 2008; (stage appearances) Annie, 1981, All Night Long, Second Stage Theatre Co., N.Y.C., 1984, Jane Eyre, Theatre Opera Music Inst., N.Y.C. Recipient Best Supporting Actress award Youth Films Awards; Silver prize Tokyo Music Festival, 1989. Mem. SAG, AFTRA, Actors' Equity Assn. Office: c/o Creative Artists Agy 2000 Avenue of the Stars Los Angeles CA 90067*

MILANOVICH, NORMA JOANNE, training services executive; b. Littlefork, Minn., June 4, 1945; d. Lyle Albert and Loretta (Leona) Drake; m. Rudolph William Milanovich, Mar. 18, 1943 (dec.); 1 child, Rudolph William Jr. BS in Home Econs., U. Wis., Stout, 1968; MA in Curriculum and Instrn., U. Houston, 1973, EdD in Curriculum and Program Devel., 1982. Instr. human svcs. dept. U. Houston, 1971-75; dir. videos project U. N.Mex., Albuquerque, 1976-78, dir. vocat. edn. equity ctr., 1978-88, asst. prof. occupational edn., 1982-88, coord. occupational vocat. edn. programs, 1983-88, dir. consortium rsch. and devel. in occupational edn., 1984-88; pres. Alpha Connection Tng. Corp., Albuquerque, 1988—; exec. dir. Trinity Found., 1991—; pres. Athena Leadership Ctr., 1994—. Adj. instr. Cen. Tng. Acad., Dept. Energy, Wackenhut; faculty U. Phoenix; adj. faculty So. Ill. U., Lesley Coll., Boston; lectr. in field Author: Model Equitable Behavior in the Classroom, 1983, Handbook for Vocational-Technical Certification in New Mexico, 1985, A Vision for Kansas: Systems of Measures and Standards of Performance, 1992, Workplace Skills: The Employability Factor, 1993; editor: Choosing What's Best for You, 1982, A Handbook for Handling Conflict in the Classroom, 1983, Starting Out...A Job Finding Handbook for Teen Parents, Going to Work...Job Rights for Teens; author: JTPA Strategic Marketing Plan, 1990, We, The Arcturians, 1990, Sacred Journey to Atlantis, 1991, The Light Shall Set You Free, 1996; editor: Majestic Raise newsletter, 1996—, Celestial Voices newsletter, 1991—; conf. presenter in field; dir. (film and book) Building Feng Shui Dream Homes, 2009. Del. Youth for Understanding Internat. Program, 1985—90; adv. bd. Southwestern Indian Poly. Inst., 1984—88; com. mem. Region VI Consumer Exch. Com., 1982—84; coord. various countries Worldwide Conf. for Peace on Earth, 1999—2009; coord. Customized Leadership Programs, 2003—09; bd. dirs. Albuquerque Single Parent Occupational Scholarship Program, 1984—86. Grantee N.Mex. Dept. Edn., 1976-86, HEW, 1979-81, 83-87. Mem. ASTD, Am. Vocat. Assn., Vocat. Edn. Equity Coun., Nat. Coalition for Sex Equity Edn., Am. Home Econs. Assn., Inst. Noetic Scis., N.Mex. Home Econs. Assn., N.Mex. Vocat. Edn. Assn., N.Mex. Adv. Coun. on Vocat. Edn., Greater Albuquerque C. of C., NAFE, Feng Shui Conf. and Modules for Success, Phi Delta Kappa, Phi Upsilon Omicron, Phi Theta Kappa. Democrat. Roman Catholic. Avocation: fung shui. Office: Athena Leadership Ctr Scottsdale AZ 85259 Office Phone: 480-767-5346. Business E-Mail: info@athenalctr.com.

MILBOURNE, WALTER ROBERTSON, lawyer; b. Phila., Aug. 27, 1933; s. Charles Gordon and Florie Henderson (Robertson) M.; m. Georgena Sue Dyer, June 19, 1965; children: Gregory Broughton, Karen Elizabeth, Walter Robertson, Margaret Henderson AB, Princeton U., 1955; LL.B., Harvard U., 1958. Bar: Pa. 1959. Assoc. firm Pepper, Hamilton & Sheetz, Phila., 1959-65, Obermayer, Rebmann, Maxwell & Hippel, Phila., 1965-67, ptnr., 1968-84, Saul, Ewing, Remick & Saul, 1984-2000, of counsel, 2001—. Bd. dir. Phila. Reins. Corp.; co-chmn. Nat. Conf. Lawyers and Collection Agys., 1979-90; chmn. bus. litigation com. Def. Rsch. Inst., 1986-89, mem. law instsn. com., 1989-95; mem. panel of disting. neutrals CPA Inst. Dispute Resolution, 2000- Chmn. mental health budget sect. Phila. United Fund, 1967—70; pres. Found. Internat. Assn. Def. Counsel, 1997—2001. Fellow: Am. Coll. Trial Lawyers (mem. internat. com. 1992—96); mem.: ABA, Phila. Bar Assn., Pa. Bar Assn., Phila. Lawn Tennis Assn. (pres. 1969—70), Merion Cricket Club. Republican. Home: 689 Fernfield Cir Wayne PA 19087-2002 Office: Saul Ewing LLP 3800 Centre Sq W Philadelphia PA 19102 Office Phone: 215-972-1975. Personal E-mail: waltermilb@aol.com.

MILBURN, RICHARD HENRY, physics professor; b. Newark, June 3, 1928; s. Richard Percy and Lucy Elizabeth (Karr) M.; m. Nancy Jeannette Stafford, Aug. 25, 1951; children— Sarah Stafford, Anne Douglas. AB, Harvard U., 1948, A.M., 1951, PhD, 1954. Instr. Harvard U., Cambridge, Mass., 1954, 56-57, asst. prof., 1957—61; assoc. prof. physics Tufts U., Medford, Mass., 1961-65, prof., 1965-98, John Wade prof., 1990-98, rsch. prof., 1998—2003, prof. emeritus, 2003. Fulbright lectr., India, 1984 Trustee Cambridge Friends Sch., 1989-95. With U.S. Army, 1954-56. Sheldon travelling fellow, 1948-49; NSF fellow, 1952-53; Guggenheim fellow, 1960 Fellow Am. Phys. Soc. (past chmn. New Eng. sect.); mem. Am. Assn. Physics Tchrs., AAAS. Achievements include research on high energy and elementary particles physics. Home: 299 Cambridge St Unit 323 Winchester MA 01890-2390 Business E-Mail: rmilburn@tufts.edu.

MILBURY, MIKE (MICHAEL JAMES MILBURY), sports analyst, former professional sports team executive; b. Brighton, Mass., June 17, 1952; m. Ginger Milbury; children: Owen, Luke, Jake, Jake Patrick, Caitlin, Alison. Grad., Colgate U. Defenceman Boston Bruins, 1976—87, asst. coach, 1985—86, head coach, asst. gen. mgr., 1989-91, asst. gen. mgr., 1991—95; head coach Maine Mariners (Am. Hockey League), 1987—89, NY Islanders, 1995—97, 1998, gen. mgr., 1996—98, 1999—2006, sr. v.p. sports properties, 2006—07. In-studio analyst ESPN, 1994—95; gen. mgr. US Nat. Hockey Team, 1995—96, 1996—97; sr. v.p. mktg. Bridgeport Sound Tigers, NY Dragons, 2006—07; studio analyst TSN, 2007—08, NBC Sports, 2007—08, Hockey Night in Can., CBC, 2008—. Named Coach of Yr., Sporting News, 1990, The Hockey News and The Sporting News, 1990. Office: CBC 250 Front St W PO Box 500, Station A Toronto ON M5W 1E6 Canada

MILCH, DAVID, screenwriter, producer; b. Buffalo, Mar. 23, 1945; s. Elmer and Molly (Pies) M.; m. Rita Stern, Oct. 30, 1982; children: Elizabeth, Benjamin, Olivia. BA in English summa cum laude, Yale U., 1966; MFA with distinction, Iowa U., 1970. Co-founder Redboard Productions, 2001—. Vis. lectr. Yale U., New Haven, 1971-82. Writer: TV series Hill Street Blues, 1982—84 (Emmy award for Best Writing in a Drama series, Writer Guild award, Humanitas prize, 1982), Bay City Blues, 1983, Murder One, 1995, Total Security, 1997; prodr.: (TV series) Hill Street Blues, 1984—85; exec. prodr.: (TV series) Hill Street Blues, 1985, 1986—87, Beverly Hills Buntz, 1987—88, Brooklyn South, 1997; writer, exec. prodr.: TV series The Big Apple, 2001, NYPB Blue, 1993—2005 (Emmy award for Best Writing in a Drama series, 1997, 1998, Humanitas prize, Edgar award for Screenwriting), Capital News, 1990, Deadwood, 2004—06, John from Cincinnati, 2007—; actor: (TV appearances) L.A. Law, 1987—94; editor: (textbook) History of American Literature, 1974. Recipient Tinker prize for Highest Achievement in English, Yale U. Mem. Writers Guild Am. (Writers Guild award 1983, 84), Phi Beta Kappa (Tinker prize). Office: c/o HBO 1 Time Warner Ctr New York NY 10019

MILCH, PETER STEPHEN, retired finance educator; b. Bklyn., Dec. 16, 1939; s. Harold Carlton and Harriet Milch; m. Shiela Susan Woda, Dec. 21, 1963; m. Linda Beth Leavell, July 7, 1990; children: Jennifer Ann, Helaine Cynthia. BS in Bus., Miami U., Oxford, Ohio, 1960; MBA, NYU, 1963. Spl. edn. tchr. Houston Ind. Sch. Dist., 1992—2004, Chairperson faculty adv. com., 2000—03; economics instr. Houston CC, 1992—. Wiith US Army, 1962—68. Recipient Tchr. of Yr., TH. Roges Sch., 2000. Business E-Mail: pmilch@sbcglobal.net.

MILCH, RANDAL S., telecommunications industry executive, lawyer; b. 1958; BA, Yale U.; JD, NYU. Ptnr. Donovan Leisure Newton & Irvine, Washington; v.p., gen. counsel, sec. Bell Atlantic-Maryland, Inc., 1994; assoc. gen. counsel Bell Atlantic (merged with GTE to become Verizon Comm. Inc., 2000); sr. v.p., dep. gen. counsel Verizon Communications Inc., sr. v.p. legal/external affairs Verizon Bus., exec. v.p., gen. counsel, 2008—. Office: Verizon Communications Inc Hdqs 140 West St New York NY 10007

MILCHAN, ARNON, film producer; b. Britis Palestine (now Israel), Dec. 6, 1944; 4 children. Student, London Sch. of Economics, U. Geneva Interpreters Sch. Founder, co-owner New Regency Productions, 1991—. Prodr. (plays) Tomb, It's So Nice To Be Civilized, Amadeus (Paris prodn.), (TV) MASADA, 1981, (TV series) The Client, 1995, (films) Black Joy, 1977, The Medusa Touch, 1978, Dizengoff 99, 1979, The King of Comedy, 1983, Once Upon a Time in America (also actor), 1984, Brazil, 1985, Stripper, 1986, Legend, 1986, Man on Fire, 1987, The Adventures of Baron Munchausen, 1989, Who's Harry Crumb, 1989, The War of the Roses, 1989, Big Man on Campus, 1990, Pretty Woman, 1990, Q&A, 1990, Guilty by Suspicion, 1991, JFK, 1991, Switch, 1991, The Mambo Kings, 1992, Memoirs of an Invisible Man, 1992, The Power of One, 1992, Under Siege, 1992, Sommersby, 1993, Falling Down, 1993, Made in America, 1993, Free Willy, 1993 (exec. prodr.), The Nutcracker, 1993, That Night, 1993, Heaven and Earth, 1993, The New Age, 1993, Striking Distance, 1993, Six Degrees of Separation, 1993, Second Best, 1994, Boys on the Side, 1994, Natural Born Killers, 1994, The Client, 1994, Cobb, 1994, Bogus, 1995, Under Siege 2: Dark Territory, 1995, Free Willy 2: The Adventure Home, 1995, Empire Records, 1995, Copycat, 1995, Heat, 1995, The Sunchaser, 1996, Carpool, 1996, Bogus, 1996, A Time to Kill, 1996, The Mirror Has Two Faces, 1996, Tin Cup, 1996, L.A. Confidential, 1997, Murder at 1600, 1997, Free Willy 3: The Rescue, 1997, The Devil's Advocate, 1997, Breaking Up, 1997, The Man Who Knew Too Little, 1997, Dangerous Beauty, 1998, City of Angels, 1998, The Negotiator, 1998, A Midsummer Night's Dream, 1999, Simply Irresistable, 1999, Goodbye Lover, 1999, Fight Club (exec. prodr.), 1999, Entrapment, 1999, The Hunt for the Unicorn Killer, 1999, Big Momma's House, 2000, Tigerland, 2000, Joe Somebody (exec. prodr.), 2001, Don't Say A Word, 2001, Black Knight, 2001, Freddy Got Fingered (exec. prodr.), 2001, Joy Ride (exec. prodr.), 2001, High Crimes, 2002, Life or Something Like It, 2002, Unfaithful (exec. prodr.), 2002, Daredevil, 2003, Runaway Jury, 2003, Down with Love (exec. prodr.), 2003, The Girl Next Door (exec. prodr.), 2004, Man on Fire, 2004, First Daughter (exec. prodr.), 2004, Elektra, 2005, Mr. and Mrs. Smith, 2005, Bee Season (exec. prodr.), 2005, Stay, 2005, Date Movie, 2006, The Sentinel, 2006, Just My Luck, 2006, My Super Ex-Girlfriend, 2006, The Fountain, 2006; (TV); exec. prodr.: Squach, 2000, Noriega: God's Favorite, 2000 (TV), Up at the Villa, 2000 Named one of World's Richest People, Forbes mag., 2004—. Office: New Regency Enterprises 10201 W Pico Blvd Bldg 12 Los Angeles CA 90064-2606

MILDENHALL, JONATHAN, beverage company executive; b. 1967; Student, Manchester Poly.; grad. in Advanced Mgmt. Prog., Harvard Bus. Sch., 2005. Grad. trainee McCann-Erickson, 1990—93; with Bartle Bogle Hegarty, 1993—96; account dir. Smirnoff worldwide Lowe Howard-Spink, 1996—97, bd. dirs., 1997; head account mgmt. HHCL & Ptnrs., 2000—02; joint mng. dir. TBWAflONDON, 2002—03, mng. dir., 2003—05; strategy dir. Mother Coca-Cola Co., London, 2005—06, v.p. global mktg. strategy and creative comm. Atlanta, 2007—. Co-chair ethnic diversity com. IPA, coun. steering mem. Fellow: British Am. Project. Office: Coca-Cola Co PO Box 1734 Atlanta GA 30301

MILDVAN, DONNA, infectious diseases physician; b. Phila., June 20, 1942; d. Carl David and Gertrude M.; m. Rolf Dirk Hamann; 1 child, Gabriella Kay. AB magna cum laude, Bryn Mawr Coll., 1963; MD, Johns Hopkins U., 1967. Diplomate Am. Bd. Internal Medicine and Infectious Diseases. Intern, resident Mt. Sinai Hosp., NYC, 1967-70, fellow, infectious diseases, 1970-72; asst., assoc. prof. clin. medicine Mt. Sinai Sch. Medicine, NYC, 1972-87; prof. clinical medicine Dept. Medicine, Mt. Sinai Sch. Medicine, NYC, 1987-88, prof. medicine, 1988-94; physician-in-charge infectious diseases Beth Israel Med. Ctr., NYC, 1972-79, chief, div. infectious diseases, 1980—; prof. medicine Albert Einstein Coll. of Medicine, NYC, 1994—. Mem. AIDS charter rev. com., NIH/Nat. Inst. Allergy and Infectious Diseases, Bethesda, 1987—; cons. FDA, Rockville, 1987—, Ctrs. for Disease Control, Atlanta, 1985-86; among first to describe AIDS, "Pre-AIDS", AIDS Dementia, 1982, among first to study AZT, 1986; Keynote speaker, II Internat. Conf. on AIDS, Paris, 1986 and other achievements in field; Sophie Jones Meml. lectr. in infectious diseases U. Mich. Hosps., 1984. Contbr. numerous articles to profl. jours; co-editor two books, many book chpts. and abstracts on infectious diseases and AIDS; editor: Atlas of AIDS, edits. 1-4. Grantee N.Y. State AIDS Inst., 1986-87; Henry Strong Denison scholar Johns Hopkins U. Sch. Medicine, 1967; recipient Woman of Achievement award AAUW, 1987, Hero in Medicine award Internat. Assn. Physicians in AIDS Care, 2000; contract for antiviral therapy in AIDS, Nat. Cancer Inst./Nat. Inst. Allergy and Infectious Diseases, 1985-86, subcontract Nat. Inst. Allergy and Infectious Diseases, ACTU, 1987-99, prin. investigator, 2000-09. Fellow Infectious Diseases Soc. Am.; mem. Am. Soc. Microbiology, AAAS, Harvey Soc., Internat. AIDS Soc. Democrat. Jewish. Avocation: old movies. Office: Beth Israel Med Ctr 1st Ave New York NY 10003-7903

MILECOFSKY, MARC See ECKO, MARC

MILES, AMY E., theatre company executive; With Pricewaterhouse-Coopers, LLC, 1989—98; sr. mgr. Deloitte & Touche, 1998—99; sr. v.p. fin. Regal Cinemas, Inc., 1999—2000, exec. v.p., treas., CFO, 2000—02, Regal Entertainment Group, 2002—09, CEO, 2009—. Office: Regal Entertainment Group 7132 Regal Ln Knoxville TN 37918*

MILES, BRIAN JOHN, urologist; b. Belfast, No. Ireland, Nov. 8, 1946; s. William Livingston and Kathleen (Jamison) M.; m. Renee' Gig DeBlaise, Sept. 15, 1990. BS, Mich. State U., 1967; MS in Engring., U. Mich., 1968, MD, 1974. Diplomate Am. Bd. Urology. Surg. intern Georgetown U., Washington, 1974-75; resident in urology Walter Reed Army Med. Ctr., Washington, 1978-82; instr. dept. urology Army Med. Ctr., Tacoma, 1982-84; instr. dept. surgery U. Wash., Seattle, 1982-84; staff physician dept surgery Henry Ford Hosp., Detroit, 1984-91; assoc. prof. U. Mich., Ann Arbor, 1984-93; dir. resident edn. Henry Ford Hosp., Detroit, 1987-93, dir. urologic oncology, 1988—91; assoc. prof. Scott Dept. Urology, Houston, 1993-2000, prof., 2000—08, disting. Cullen chair in Urology, 2003—08; chief of urology VA Med. Ctr., Houston, 1993-98, St. Luke's Episcopal Hosp., Houston, 1993—; med. dir. Tex. Cancer Inst., 1999—2008; assoc. dir. for clin. affairs Baylor Comprehensive Cancer Ctr., Houston, 2006—08; clin. prof. urology, 2008—. Assoc. editor: Comprehensive Textbook of Genitourinary Oncology, 1995. Lt. col M.C., U.S. Army, 1975-84. Mem. ACS, Am. Urologic Assn. (Prostate Cancer Outcomes Analysis Grant 1995, 96), Soc. Urologic Oncology, Soc. Univ. Urologists, Internat. Soc. Urology. Avocations: history, sports, reading. Home: 3781 Farbar St Houston TX 77005-3713 Office: 6560 Fannin St Ste 2110 Houston TX 77030-2769 Office Phone: 713-441-8110. Business E-Mail: bmiles@drbrianmiles.com.

MILES, CHRISTINE MARIE, museum director; b. Madison, Ind., Mar. 2, 1951; d. Leland Weber and Mary Virginia (Geyer) M.; m. John J. Kelliher, 1990. BA, Boston U., 1973; MA in Mus. and Am. Studies, George Washington U., 1982; postgrad., Mus. Mgmt. Inst., 1985. Curatorial asst. Mus. City of NY, 1973-75; art gallery dir. South St. Seaport Mus., NYC, 1975-77; rschr. The Octagon, AIA Found., Washington, 1978-80; dir. Fraunces Tavern Mus., Washington, 1980-86, Albany Inst. History and Art, NY, 1986—. Bd. dirs. SUNY-Albany Found. Author, writer/coordinator, compiler of catalogs in field. Mem. Arts Commn. City of Albany; pres. Gallery Assn. N.Y. State, 1991-93, Mus. Assn. N.Y. State. Mem. Am. Assn. Mus. Office: Albany Inst History and Art 125 Washington Ave Albany NY 12210-2296 Office Phone: 518-463-4478. Office Fax: 518-463-5506. Business E-Mail: milesc@albanyinstitute.org.

MILES, DAVID LOREN, museum director; b. Charlevoix, Mich., Feb. 14, 1940; s. Robert Clarence and Esther Miles. BA, MA, U. Mich., 1963. Asst. cashier U. Mich., Ann Arbor, 1966—68, dir. statistical svcs., 1968—70; night mgr. Lodge Motel, Charlevoix, 1972—2000; co-dir. Charlevoix Hist. Soc. Harsha House Mus., 2000—. Writer, prodr., rschr. (town heritage book) Bob Miles' Charlevoix II, 2002. Mem. C. of C. Home: 109 Park Ave Charlevoix MI 49720 Office: Charlevoix Hist Soc PO Box 525 Charlevoix MI 49720 Office Phone: 231-547-0373. Personal E-mail: miles.david@att.net. Business E-Mail: chxhistory@sbcglobal.net.

MILES, DAVID MICHAEL, lawyer; b. Jackson, Mich., Aug. 5, 1954; s. Richard George and Joann Marie (Stefanoff) M.; m. Noelle Suzanne McHugh, Sept. 6, 1986; children: Amy Elizabeth, Margaret Noelle, Lane McHugh. Student, U. Mich., 1972-74; BA cum laude, Clark U., 1976; JD magna cum laude, George Washington U., 1979. Bar: DC 1979, US Ct. Appeals (4th cir.) 1980, US Dist. Ct. Md. 1980, US Dist. Ct. DC 1983, US Supreme Ct. 1983, U.S. Ct. Appeals (DC cir.) 1981, US Ct. Appeals (9th cir.) 1984, US Ct. Appeals (2d cir.) 1986. Law clk. to Chief Judge Edward Northrop, US Dist. Ct. Md., 1979-80; law clk. to Cir. Judge George MacKinnon US Ct. Appeals, Washington, 1980-81; assoc. Fried, Frank, Harris, Shriver & Jacoboson, Washington, 1981-86, ptnr., 1986-92, Sidley Austin LLP, Washington, 1992—. Co-author: The Law of Financial Services, 1988; contbr. articles to profl. jours. Home: 5229 Westpath Way Bethesda MD 20816 Office: Sidley Austin LLP 1501 K St NW Washington DC 20005 Home Phone: 301-229-9240; Office Phone: 202-736-8556. Personal E-mail: DavidM9876@aol.com. Business E-Mail: dmiles@sidley.com.

MILES, ELIZABETH JANE, social worker; b. Upper Fairmount, Md., Mar. 13, 1927; d. Harry Budd Miles and Elizabeth Thomas. AA, St. Mary's Coll., St. Mary's City, Md., 1947; BA, Scarritt Coll., 1949; MSW, Vanderbilt U., 1951. Dir. Christian edn. Meth. Ch., Gaithersberg, Md., 1952—53; mgr., owner Edn. Assn., Pitts., 1954—60, Frontier Press, Balt., 1960—70; social worker, bd. dirs. Home-Coming Mental Health, Bel Air, Md., 1970—90; resident supr. VA Home Programs, Perry Point, Md., 1990; pvt. cons. in field. Mem. bd. Commn. on Aging, Somerset County, Md., 1990—; deaconess Meth. Ch..., Balt., 1951—52;

bd. dirs. Country Retreat-Christian Retreat, Bradenton, Fla., 1991—. Scholar, Md. State Senator, 1945, Meth. Missionary Bd. Mem.: Nat. Hist. Trust Assn., Bus. and Profl. Club. Republican. Methodist. Avocations: horses, antiques, restoring family home. Home (Summer): PO Box 144 Manokin MD 21836

MILES, FRANK CHARLES, retired newspaper executive; b. Detroit, Jan. 1, 1926; s. Nelson and Ethel Jane (Mennill) M.; m. Catharine Estelle Coleman, Sept. 4, 1948 (dec. Aug. 2000); children: Barbara Ann, Diana Estelle; m. Joan Ashkin, Feb. 1, 2003 (div. Dec. 15, 2006). Student, Westervelt Bus. Coll., 1947-48. With Thomson Newspapers Ltd., Cambridge, Ont., Canada, 1950-52, 54-55; bus. mgr. Sarnia (Ont.) Obs., 1952-54; gen. mgr. Pembroke (Ont.) Obs., 1956-58, Moose Jaw (Sask.) Times-Herald, Canada, 1958-62; pub. Austin (Minn.) Daily Herald, 1962-66; sr. v.p., gen. mgr. Thomson Newspapers Inc., Des Plaines, Ill., 1966-89, exec. v.p. acquisitions, 1990-91, ret., 1991, also bd. dirs. Vol. assignments Internat. Media Fund, Baltics, Albania, 1992-93; Knight fellowship Moscow, 1994, Ctrl. for Ind. Journalism, Bucharest, Romania, 1995, Kocise Slovakia, 1996, Internat. Rsch. & Exch. Corp., Zagreb, Croatia, Belarus, 1997, Brest, Minsk, Belarus, 1997-98. Sigma Delta Chi. Independent Home Phone: 512-296-2219. Personal E-mail: fmiles001@austin.rr.com.

MILES, JOANNA, actress, playwright, director; b. Nice, France, Mar. 6, 1940; came to U.S., 1941, naturalized, 1941; d. Johannes Schiefer and Jeanne Miles; m. William Burns, May 23, 1970 (div. 1977); m. Michael Brandman, Apr. 29, 1978; 1 child, Miles. Grad. H.S., Putney, Vt., 1958. Mem. Actors Studio, Playwrites and Dirs. Workshop, NYC, 1966; co-founder, mem. LA Classic Theatre, 1986. Founder, artistic dir. Playwrights Group/LAWW, 1991-98. Starred in: (motion pictures) The Way We Live Now, 1969, Bug, 1975, The Ultimate Warrior, 1975, Golden Girl, 1978, Cross Creek, 1983, As Is, 1986, Blackout, 1988, Rosencrants and Guildenstern are Dead, 1991, The Rhinghart Theory, 1994, Judge Dredd, 1994, Alone, 1996, Sex & Breakfast, 2006; numerous television films including In What America, 1965, My Mothers House, 1963, Glass Managerie, 1974, Born Innocent, 1974, Aloha Means Goodbye, 1974, The Trial of Chaplain Jensen, 1975, Harvest Home, 1977, Fire in the Sky, 1978, Sophisticated Gents, 1979, Promise of Love, 1982, Sound of Murder, 1983, All My Sons, 1987, The Right to Die, 1987, The Habitation of Dragons, 1991, Heart of Justice, 1991, Water Engine, 1991, Cooperstown, 1992, Legionnaires, 1992, Life Lessons, 1992, Willing to Kill, 1992, The American Clock, 1993, Dark Reflections, 1993, Outcry, 1994, Everything to Gain, 1995, Small Vices, 1998, Crossfire Trail, 1999, Thin Aire, 1999, Monty Walsh, 2002, Jane Doe: Shaken & Stirred, 2006, Grave Misconduct, 2007, Thin Ice, 2008; episodes in numerous TV series including: Barney Miller, Dallas, St. Elsewhere, The Hulk, Trapper John, Kaz, Cagney and Lacey, Studio 5B, 1989, Star Trek: The Next Generation, 1990, 91, Life Stories, 1991, HBO Life Stories, 1993, Total Security, 1997, Nothing Sacred, 1998, Chicago Hope, 1998-99, ER, 2000, 01, Family Law, 2000, Judging Amy, 2003; stage plays include Once in a Life Time, 1963, Cave Dwellers, 1964, Drums in the Night, 1968, Dracula, 1968, Home Free, 1964, One Night Stands of a Noisy Passenger, 1972, Dylan, 1973, Dancing for the Kaiser, 1976, Debutante Ball, 1985, Kramer, 1977, One Flew Over the Cuckoo's Nest, 1989, Growing Gracefully, 1990, Cut Flowers, 1994; performed in radio shows Sta. KCRW Once in a Lifetime, 1987, Babbit, 1987, Sta. KPFK, Grapes of Wrath, 1989, The White Plague, Sta. KCRW, 1991, Chekhov Short Stories, Sta. KCRW, 1992; playwright, v.p. Brandman Productions; author: (plays) Ethanasia, A Woman in Reconstruction, Hostages, Feathers, On the Shelf, (films) An Offereing of Oranges, Breaking the Rules. Pres. Children Giving to Children. Recipient 2 Emmy awards, 1974, Women in Radio and TV award, 1974, Actors Studio Achievement award, 1980, Dramalogue award, 1996, Vision award 2003; nominated Golden Globe, 1974. Mem. Acad. Motion Picture Arts and Scis. Office: Brandman Prodns 2062 Vine St Apt 5 Hollywood CA 90068-3928 Office Phone: 323-463-3224. Personal E-mail: jmilesb@aol.com.

MILES, JOHN BENJAMIN, lawyer; b. Greensboro, NC, Oct. 19, 1930; s. John Richard and Lois (Wilson) Miles; m. Daphne Rees, June 25, 1960; children: Lois Rose, John Benjamin Jr. BA, Guilford Coll., 1952; LLB, Wake Forest U., 1955. Bar: NC 1955, US Dist. Ct. (mid. dist.) NC 1959. Pvt. practice law, Greensboro, 1958—61, 1969—2008; mcpl. judge City of Greensboro, 1961—68. With US Army, 1955—58. Mem.: NC Bar, Phi Delta Phi. Republican. Presbyterian. Home: 5045 Harvest Rd Mc Leansville NC 27301-9702

MILES, LAVEDA ANN, advertising executive; b. Greenville, SC, Nov. 21, 1945; d. Grady Lewis and Edna Sylvia (Mahaffey) Bruce; m. Charles Thomas Miles, Nov. 10, 1974; 1 child, Joshua Bruce. A in Bus. Adminstrn., North Greenville Jr. Coll. Traffic mgr. WFBV-TV, Greenville, 1968-74; pub. svc. dir., traffic mgr. WTCG-TV, Atlanta, 1974-75; traffic mgr. Henderson Advt. Co., Greenville, 1975-77, broadcast coord., 1977-79, dir. broadcast bus., 1979-82, v.p., dir. broadcast bus., 1982-89, bus. mgr. creative dept., 1989-91, dir. creative svcs., 1991-93, sr. v.p., 1994-96, v.p., dir. creative svcs., 2000—06; creative svcs. mgr. The Bounce Agy., 2006—; owner Altamont Mktg., 1996-99. Mem. Leadership S.C., 1994-95; bd. dirs. Boys Home of the South, 2003—. Named one of 100 Best and Brightest Women, Ad Age and Advt. Women of N.Y., 1988. Mem. Advt. Fedn. Greenville (sec. 1979-81), Greenville Ad Club (sec. 1999-2000, pres. 2000—02, Silver medal award 2003). Republican. Baptist. Office Phone: 864-271-8340. E-mail: laveda.miles@thebounceagency.com.

MILES, LELAND WEBER, retired academic administrator; b. Balt., Jan. 18, 1924; s. Leland Weber and Marie (Fitzpatrick) M.; m. Mary Virginia Geyer, July 9, 1947; children: Christine Marie, Gregory Lynn. AB cum laude, Juniata Coll., 1946; MA, U. N.C., 1947, PhD, 1949; postgrad., Duke U., 1949; DLitt (hon.), Juniata Coll., 1969; LHD (hon.), Rosary Hill Coll., 1970; LLD (hon.), Far East U., 1979; DHC (hon.), U. Guadalajara, Mex., 1984; Order of Merit, Alfred U., 1986. Assoc. prof. English Hanover Coll., 1949-50, prof., chmn. English dept., 1950-60; assoc. prof., asst. to head English dept. U. Cin., 1960-63, prof., 1963-64, founder humanities reading program for engrs., 1961; dean Coll. Arts and Scis., U. Bridgeport, Conn., 1964-67; pres. U. Bridgeport, 1974-87; founder U. Bridgeport Sch. Law, 1977; pres. emeritus U. Bridgeport, 1987—; pres. Alfred U., 1967-74. Bd. dirs. United Illuminating, 1978-94, chmn. audit com., 1992-94, Grolier, 1984-88, Wright Managed Investment Funds, 1988-04, Internat. Peace Acad., 1982-90; Danforth scholar Union Theol. Sem., 1956; Lilly fellow Sch. Letters Ind. U., 1959; Am. Council Learned Socs. fellow Harvard, 1963-64; Sr. Fulbright Research scholar Kings Coll. U. London, 1964, vis. scholar, 1972; seminar leader, deans and presidents insts. Am. Council on Edn., 1973-79; chmn. bd. Acad. Collective Bargaining Info. Service, Washington, 1977-79; producer, moderator Casing the Classics CBS Sta. WHAS-TV, Louisville, 1958-61; moderator Aspen (Colo.) Inst. for Humanistic Studies, 1969-70; lectr. Keedick Lecture Bur., N.Y.C., 1956-83; vis. prof. New Coll., Sarasota, Fla., 1989. Author: John Colet and the Platonic Tradition, 1961; editor: St. Thomas More's Dialogue of Comfort Against Tribulation, 1965, Where Do You Stand On Linquistics?, 1964, revised, 1968; sr. editor: (with Stephen Graubard and later Stephen B. Baxter) Studies in British History and Culture, 1965-79, Provoking Thought: What Colleges Should Do For Students, 2001; contbg. editor Nat. Forum, 1983-91; contbr. articles to learned jours., chpts. in books. Trustee Western NY Nuc. Rsch. Ctr., 1967-73; chmn. bd. Coll. Ctr. Finger Lakes, 1968-71; vice-chmn. bd. Empire State Found., 1969-71, chmn., 1971-73; mem. New Eng. Bd. Higher Edn., 1985-87, Ambs. Roundtable World Affairs Forum, 1986-92, Fuld Found./Nat. League Nursing Adv. Coun. on Accreditation, 1986-88; chmn. Ettinger scholarship com. Ednl. Found. Am., 1987-93; bd. dirs. Conn. Grand Opera, 1978-89, Bridgeport Bus. Coun., 1982-88; bd. dirs. Save the Children, 1988-95, chmn. adv. coun., 1990-95; adviser Asolo Theater-Fla. State U. Conservatory Actors Tng., 2004-. 1st lt. USAAF, 1944-45; capt. USAFR. Decorated DFC with oak leaf cluster, Crown Decoration of Honor 3rd Order Iran, 1978; chevalier l'Ordre des Palmes Académique (France), 1984; recipient Rosa and Samuel Sachs prize Cin. Inst. Fine Arts, 1961, Cultural medal Republic of China, 1983, Disting. Svc. award Greater Bridgeport Bar Assn., 1986, Outstanding Civilian Svc. medal Dept. Army, 1988; Miles scholars Alfred U., 1995—. Fellow Royal Soc. Arts, Manufactures and Commerce (life); mem. Renaissance Soc. Am., English Speaking Union (bd. dirs. Greenwich, Conn. chpt. 1998-04), UN Assn. (bd. dirs. Sarasota Manatee chpt., coord. young profl. for internat. coop. 2005-08), Internat. Assn. Univ. Pres. (pres. 1981-84, pres. emeritus 1984—, chief UN mission 1988-97, World Peace award 1987, chmn. UN commn. on arms control edn. 1991-96, mem. coun. sr. advisers 1992—), Knights of Malta (order of the Orthodox Knights Hospitaller of St. John of Jerusalem, Russian Orthodox br.), Mil. Officers Assn. Sarasota, West Coast Symphony Assn., Sarasota Opera Guild, Univ. Club (NYC), Phi Delta Kappa. Episcopalian. Home (Summer): 87 Field Point Dr Fairfield CT 06824-6329 Home (Winter): 2110 Ben Franklin Dr Sarasota FL 34236 Office Phone: 941-525-3095. Personal E-mail: lelandwmiles@yahoo.com.

MILES, LES (LESLIE EDWIN MILES), college football coach; b. Elyria, Ohio, Nov. 10, 1953; m. Kathy Miles; children: Kathryn, Leslie Matthew, Benjamin, Macy Grace. BS in Econs., U. Mich., Ann Arbor, 1976. Grad. asst. U. Mich., 1980—81, asst. coach, 1987—94, U. Colo., 1982—86; offensive coord. Okla. State U., Stillwater, 1995—97, head coach, 2001—04, La. State U., Baton Rouge, 2005—; tight ends coach Dallas Cowboys, 1998—2000. Active Spl. Olympics; event host Children's Miracle Network; active celebrity waiter event Baton Rouge Children's Advocacy Ctr.; active Mary Bird Perkins Cancer Ann. Fundraiser. Named Big 12 Conf. Coach of Yr., 2002. Achievements include coaching La. State U. to the 2007 BCS Nat. Championship. Office: LSU Athletic Dept Football PO Box 25095 Baton Rouge LA 70894 Office Phone: 225-578-1151. Business E-Mail: lem042@lsu.edu.

MILES, MARY ELLEN, retired human resources specialist; d. Monroe and Leona (Simmons) Jackson; m. Monte Sanford, Sept. 21, 1956 (div.); children: Dean Sanford, Marisa Sanford(dec.), Mark Sanford. Degree in secretarial sci., Orlando Jr. Coll., Fla., 1962. Cert. OSHA inspector, EEO investigator. Exec. sec. Dept of Def./AAFES, Montgomery, Ala., 1974, employee devel. specialist Wright Patterson AFB, Ohio, 1974—77, tech. publs. writer/editor Munich, 1977—79, pers. asst Ft. Rucker, Ala., 1979—82, pers. asst, employee devel. specialist Langley AFB, Va., 1982—85, human resources mgr. Ft. Eustis, Va., 1985—87, Ft. Knox, Ky., 1987—91, Ft. Carson, Colo., 1990—93, Ft. Hood, Tex., 1993—95, Hickam AFB, Hawaii, 1995—98, sr. human resources policy specialist/policy devel. Dallas, 1998—2002. HR subject matter expert, cons., Decatur, Ala., 2002. Author: (cookbook) From the Heart. Newsletter writer, editor Newport News Literacy Coun., Va., 1985—86, Clean Cmty. Commn., Newport News, 1985—86; mem. Mayor's Coun. Handicapped Employment, Newport News, 1985—87; vol. Duncanville Pub. Libr., Tex., 2002, Carnegie Visual Arts Ctr., Decatur, 2003; mem. Ala. Citizens for Constn. Reform, Huntsville, 2003—06, Acad. for Lifetime Learning, U. Ala., Huntsville, 2003—05, Leadership Coun., So. Poverty Law Ctr., Montgomery, Ala., 2003, Morgan County Diversity Coun., 2004, Princess Theater, Decatur, 2006; vol. Decatur City Schs., 2004—06, Cmty. Free Clinic, Decatur, 2005, Habitat for Humanity, Decatur, 2006, Morgan County Pub. Libr., Decatur, 2006; docent Carnegie Visual Arts Ctr., 2003. Recipient Commander's Coin, Cold War Recognition Cert. for Fed. Govt. Svc. Mem.: Am. Bus. Women's Assn. Republican. Avocations: reading, writing, art, antiques, collectibles, cooking. Home: 2433 CAMMERON ST SW Decatur AL 35603-2952

MILES, MICHAEL A., JR., retail executive; BA, Yale U., New Haven, 1983; MBA, Harvard U., 1987. Sr. v.p. concept devel. & franchise Pizza Hut Yum! Brands, Inc., 1996—99, COO Pizza Hut, 2000—03; COO Staples, Inc., Framingham, Mass., 2003—, pres., 2006—. Bd. dir. Western Union. Office: Staples Inc 500 Staples Dr Framingham MA 01702

MILES, REBECCA, urban planner, educator; d. Frank Vernon and Patricia Beatty Miles; m. Ward M. Broderson, July 6, 2002; m. Peter L. Doan, Aug. 8, 1981 (div. Oct. 4, 2000); children: Jessamyn Jessup Doan, Daniel Miles Doan. BS, Harvard U., Cambridge, Mass., 1977; MS in Urban Studies, Cornell U., Ithaca, NY, 1983, PhD, 1988. Asst. prof. Fla. State U., Tallahassee, 1993—99, assoc. prof., 1999—. Cmty. devel. advisor Nr. East Found. Amman Municipality, Jordan, 1984—86. Adv. bd. mem. Am. Friends Svc. Com., Phila., 1994—2001; vol. cons. Fla. Assn. Voluntary Agys. Caribbean Action, Tallahassee, 1994—99. Recipient Outstanding Vol. Achievement, Fla. Assn. Voluntary Agys. Caribbean Action, 2000; Rsch. grant, Ctrs. Disease Control, 2001—02, Fulbright, 1996, Harry Frank Guggenheim Found., 1992, 1994. Mem.: Assn. Collegiate Schs. Planning (pres. faculty women's interest group 2008). Achievements include research in urban planning & health. Office: Fla State Univ 113 Collegiate Loop PO Box 3062280 Tallahassee FL 32306-2280

MILES, RUBY WILLIAMS, secondary school educator; b. Petersburg, Va., Jan. 19, 1929; d. Richard Allen and Elizabeth (Penny) Williams; m. John Oscar Miles, Jan. 7, 1950 (div. 1966); children: Karen Jonnia Miles George, Steven Ricardo. BA, Va. State Coll., Petersburg, 1971, MA, 1977. Cert. high sch. tchr., Va. Tchr. English Dinwiddie (Va.) Sch., 1971-78, Clarksville (Tenn.) Sch., 1978-80, Petersburg Pub. Schs., 1982—, head English dept., 1991-96, ret., 1996; instr. St. Paul's Coll., Lawrenceville, Va., 1981-82; asst. prof. St. Leo Coll., Ft. Lee, Va., 1988; instr. english/speech Bethany Baptist Church, Petersburg, VA, 1998—. Tchr., counselor Upward Bound project Va. State U., summer, 1974; tchr. Hopewell Pub. Schs., Va. summer 1983—; instr. John Tyler C.C., Fort Lee, Va., 1992—; adj. prof. Richard Bland Coll., Coll. William and Mary, 2001-02. Songwriter: A Day in September; author: Deal With the Downs, 2003. Bd. dirs. Playmaker Fellows Ltd., Petersburg, 1983; co-dir. Exclusively Youth Models, 1984-85. Recipient Leadership award Va. Edn. Assn., 1985. Mem. Petersburg Edn. Assn. (past pres.), Am. Bus. Women's Assn., Nat. Orgn. for Women, Nat. Assn. Female Execs., NEA, Nat. Coun. Tchrs. English, Jr. Civic League, Delta Sigma Theta, CHUMS Inc. Avocations: writing, travel. Home: 2733 Rollingwood Rd Petersburg VA 23805-2317 Personal E-mail: rlmiles44@verizon.net.

MILES, SHIRLEY, school system administrator; b. Panama; B in Bus. Adminstrn., U. Colo., 1984, M in Pub. Adminstrn., 1990; PhD in Curriculum and Instruction, U. Denver, 2001. Tchr. history, econs. and law Air Acad. Sch. Dist., Colorado Springs, Colo., human resources dir.; asst. prin. than HS prin. Denver; supt. Tempe Union HS Dist., Tempe, Ariz.; assoc. dir. edn., prin. dep. dir. Dept. Def. Edn. Activity (DoDEA), Arlington, Va., dir., 2008—. Adj. prof. U. Colo., Colorado Springs. Mem.: Am. Assn. Sch. Adminstrs., Assn. Supervision and Curriculum Devel., Colo. Sch. Adminstrs. Assn. Office: Dept Def Edn Activity Office of Dir 4040 N Fairfax Dr Arlington VA 22203 Office Phone: 703-588-3200.*

MILES, THOMAS CASWELL, mechanical engineer; b. Atlanta, Mar. 21, 1952; s. Franklin Caswell and Eugenia Frances (Newsom) M.; m. Linda Susan Duggleby, Aug. 10, 1980. BMET, So. Poly. State U., 1977; postgrad., Troy State U., 1978-80. Assoc. engr. aircraft design Lockheed Martin Aero. Co., Marietta, Ga., 1980-82, engr., aircraft design, 1982-85, sr. engr., aircraft design, 1985-89, group engr., 1989-90, specialist engr., 1990-98, sr. specialist engr., 1998-2001, staff engr., 2001—. Mem. SAE-A-6 Mil. Aircraft & Helicopter Panel, 1987-91, SAE-A-10 Aircraft Oxygen Equipment Com., 1996—. Mem. AIAA, (assoc. fellow), ASME, ASTM, Nat. Mgmt. Assn. (bd. dirs. 1996-2000), Soc. Automotive Engrs. (SAE co. rep., SAE Atlanta sect. vice chmn. aircraft), Oxygen Standardization Coord. Group, Assn. Fraternity Advisors (affiliate), Wick's Lake Homeowners Assn. (pres. 1995, v.p. 1996, 97), Tau Kappa Epsilon (Providence advisor 1999-2002, dist. pres. 1987-88, dist. v.p. 1984-99, chpt. advisor 1980-87, key leader 1985, 90, So. Order of Honor 1989, Edn. Found. medal of excellence 2002). Avocations: sailing, screen printing, bicycling. Home: 1926 Wicks Ridge Ln Marietta GA 30062-6777 Personal E-mail: tekezeke@aol.com.

MILES, VERYL VICTORIA, dean, law educator; Grad., Wells Coll.; JD, Cath. U. of America. Law faculty mem. George Mason U. Sch. Law; prof. law Columbus Sch. Law, Cath. U. of America, Washington, 1987—, assoc. dean academic affairs, 1997—99, dean, 2005—. Tchr. summer sch. program Washington U. Sch. Law, St. Louis; adj. prof. Am. U. Law, Washington. Contbr. articles to law jours. Mem.: ABA (mem. Accreditation Com. 2008—), Assn. Am. Law Schs. (dep. dir. 2001—03). Office: Cath U of America Columbus Sch Law 3600 John McCormack Rd, NE Washington DC 20064 Office Phone: 202-319-5140. E-mail: miles@law.edu.*

MILES, WILLIAM TRICE, state legislator; b. Fulton, Miss., Jan. 6, 1938; s. Ira Matison and Ellen Ozema (Webb) M.; m. Patricia Ann Reed, May 16, 1957; William T. Jr., Pattie Miles Cox. BA, U. Miss., 1959. Journalist Itawamba Times, Fulton, Miss., 1954-56; pub. rels. exec. Miss. State U., Starkville, Miss., 1958-59; journalist Tupelo (Miss.) Jour., 1959-63; journalism instr. Itawamba C.C., Fulton, 1959-69; CEO Bill Miles Assocs., Inc., Tupelo, 1963-95; editor, publisher, owner The Amory (Miss.) Advertiser, 1972-80, The Nettleton (Miss.) News, 1975-80; rep. 21st dist. Miss Ho. of Reps., Jackson, Miss., 1996—. Author: (manual) How to Gain and Maintain Public Confidence for Police Organizations, 1968 Mem. Itawamba County Devel. Coun., Fulton, Miss., 1985—. Mem. Sigma Delta Chi. Democrat. Mem. Ch. of Christ. Avocation: golf. Home: PO Box 246 Fulton MS 38843-0246

MILEY, BRYAN S., language educator, real estate broker; s. Harold and Sally Miley; m. Shirley Bush, Oct. 12, 1991; children: Madelyn, Allyson, Sarah, Evelyn, Emily. MBA, Thunderbird, Am. Grad. Sch. Internat. Mgmt., Glendale, Ariz., 1991. Dir. internat. ops. MONY Life Ins. Co. Americas, Quito, Ecuador, 1994—98; prof. langs. GCC, Glendale, 1998—. Real estate broker 50 States Realty, Surprise, Ariz., 1998—. Sgt. USAF, 1983—87. Recipient John Levitow Leadership award, Hill AFB NCO Prep Acad., 1987. Conservative. Avocation: motorcycling. Personal E-mail: bryanmiley@juno.com.

MILEY, GEORGE H., nuclear and electrical engineering educator, plasma engineer, energy conversion scientist; b. Shreveport, La., Aug. 6, 1933; s. George Hunter and Norma Angeline (Dowling) M.; m. Elizabeth Burroughs, Nov. 22, 1958; children: Susan Miley Hibbs, Hunter Robert. BS in Chem. Engring., Carnegie-Mellon U., 1955; MS, U. Mich., 1956, PhD in Chem.-Nuclear Engring., 1959. Nuclear engr. Knolls Atomic Power Lab., Gen. Electric Co., Schenectady, 1959-61; mem. faculty U. Ill., Urbana, 1961—, prof., 1967—, chmn. nuclear engring. program, 1975-86, dir. Fusion Studies Lab., 1976—, fellow Ctr. for Advanced Study, 1985-86; dir. rsch. Rockford Tech. Assocs. Inc., 1990-94; pres., dir. rsch. NPL Assocs. Inc., 1994—; chief scientist Lattice Energy, LLC, 2001—03. Vis. prof. U. Colo., 1967, Cornell U., 1969-70, U. New South Wales, 1986, Imperial Coll. of London, 1987; mem. Ill. Radiation Protection Bd., 1988—; mem. Air Force Studies Bd., 1990-94; chmn. tech. adv. com. Ill. Low Level Radioactive Waste Site, 1990-96; chmn. com. on indsl. uses of radiation Ill. Dept. Nuclear Safety, 1989-2000. Author: Direct Conversion of Nuclear Radiation Energy, 1971, Fusion Energy Conversion, 1976; editor Jour. Fusion Tech., 1980-2001; U.S. assoc. editor Laser and Particle Beams, 1982-86, mng. editor, 1987-91, editor-in-chief, 1991-2002; U.S. editor Jour. Plasma Physics, 1995-2003. Served with C.E. AUS, 1960. Recipient Western Electric Tchg.-Rsch. award, 1977, Halliburton Engring. Edn. Leadership award, 1990, Edward Teller medal, 1995, Scientist of Yr. award Inst. New Energy, 1996, Cert. Recognition award NASA, 2003; NATO sr. sci. fellow, 1975-76, Guggenheim fellow, 1985-86, Japanese Soc. Promotion of Sci. fellow, 1994, CMNS Preparata medal, 2006, Integrity in Rsch. award, 2006. Fellow IEEE (Fusion Engring. and Sci. award, 2004), Am. Nuclear Soc. (dir. 1980-83, Disting. Svc. award 1980, Outstanding Achievement award Fusion Energy divsn. 1992, Radiation Sci. and Tech. award 2004), Am. Phys. Soc., AIAA (assoc.); mem. Am. Soc. Engring. Edn. (chmn. energy conversion com. 1967-70, pres. U. Ill. chpt. 1973-74, chmn. nuclear divsn. 1975-76, Outstanding Tchr. award 1973), Sigma Xi, Tau Beta Pi. Presbyterian. Achievements include research in fusion, energy conversion, reactor kinetics, and fuel cells. Avocations: tennis, hiking. Office: 216 Talbot Lab 104 S Wright St Urbana IL 61801-2901 Home Phone: 217-356-5402; Office Phone: 217-333-3772. E-mail: georgehm@aol.com. *My professional goal has been to insure that future generations have a plentiful supply of economical, readily available energy such as offered by fusion and renewable energy sources. Not only should this insure a continued improvement in the standard of living for persons in all nations, but it should help maintain peace which is threatened by the struggle to obtain and control limited natural sources of energy.*

MILEY, JENNA YVONNE, education educator, consultant; b. S. Charleston, W.Va., Nov. 23, 1951; d. Edgar M. and Retha M. (Barnes) Gillespie; m. Stanley Leon Miley, Apr. 19, 1985; 1 child, James E. Caruthers. AS, Mohegan C.C., Norwich, Conn., 1990; BS, So. Ill. U., 1991; MA, Webster U., St. Louis, 1994; postgrad., Capella U., PhD, 2008. Instr. Owensboro C.C., Ky., 1995—96; summer intern GRADD, Owensboro, Ky., 1996; instr. Jefferson C.C., Louisville, 1997, Carolina C.C., Sanford, NC, 1998—99, Al Ain Women's Coll., United Arab Emirates, 1999—2002; asst. prof. Bainbridge (Ga.) Coll., 2002—. Dir. mini-grant Svc. Learning. Author: (newsletter) College Success. Mem. steering com. Leadership Decatur County, 2004—05. Decorated Outstanding Unit Ribbon USAF; Gov.'s Tchg. fellow, 2005—06. Mem.: AAUW (pres. Bainbridge chpt. 2005—06), AAUP, Lions. Republican. Pentecostal. Avocation: travel, reading. Office: Bainbridge Coll 2500 E Shotwell St Bainbridge GA 39819 Personal E-mail: jmiley@bainbridge.edu.

MILFORD, FREDERICK JOHN, retired research and development company executive; b. Cleve., July 1, 1926; s. Frederick Charles and Florence M.; m. Jean Irene Olson, Sept. 8, 1951; 1 child, Cheryl Lynn. BS in Physics, Case Inst. Tech., 1949; PhD in Physics, M.I.T., 1952. Instr. Case Inst. Tech., Cleve., 1952-56, asst. prof., 1956-59; div. cons. Battelle Columbus Labs., 1959-62, div. chief, 1962-64, sr. fellow, 1964-66, dir. research in phys. scis., 1966-73, scientist, 1973, dept. mgr., 1973-76, assoc. dir., 1976-85, chief scientist, 1985-87, v.p. spl. programs, 1987-89, ret., 1989. Vis. prof. physics U. Wash., 1969 Author: (with J.R. Reitz) Foundations of Electromagnetic Theory, 1960, 4th edit., 1993. Emeritus mem. adv. bd. Central Ohio Salvation Army. Served with USNR, 1945-46. George Eastman fellow, 1951-52; Focke scholar, 1948-49 Fellow Am. Phys. Soc.; mem. Masons, Kit Kat Club, Ctrl. Ohio Lions Eye Bank (oper. bd. 1993—). Home: 1411 London Dr Columbus OH 43221-1543

MILFORD, MURRAY HUDSON, retired soil science educator; b. Honey Grove, Tex., Sept. 29, 1934; s. Murray Lane and Vivian Ione (Hudson) M.; m. Marsha Ann Rasmussen, July 21, 1961; children: Rebecca Ione, Murray Daniel. BS in Agronomy, Tex. A&M, 1955, MS in Agronomy, 1959; PhD in Soil Science, U. Wis., 1962. Cert. profl. soil scientist. Rsch. assoc. Cornell U., Ithaca, NY, 1962-63, asst. prof., 1963-68, assoc. prof., 1968, Tex. A&M U., College Station, 1968-74, prof., 1974-2001; ret., 2001. Author: (lab. manual) Soils and Soil Science-Lab. Exercises, 1970. 1st lt. USAR, 1955-57. Recipient so. region award for excellence in coll. and univ. tchg. in food and agrl. scis. Nat. Assn. State Univs. and Land Grant Colls., Higher Edn. Program, USDA, 1995. Fellow AAAS, Am. Soc. Agronomy (pres. Tex. chpt. 1982-83, Resident Edn. award 1978), Soil Sci. Soc. Am. (Edn. award 1988). Democrat. Presbyterian. Home: 3606 Tanglewood Dr Bryan TX 77802-3320

MILGRAM, ANNE M., state attorney general; b. Dec. 1, 1970; BA in English & Polit. Sci., Rutgers Coll., 1992; MPhil in Social & Polit. Theory, U. Cambridge, Eng., 1993; JD, NYU, 1996. Law clk. to Hon. Anne E. Thompson US Dist. Ct. NJ, Trenton, 1996—97; asst. dist. atty. NYC, 1997—2001; prosecutor criminal sect. US Dept. Justice, 2001, lead fed. prosecutor; counsel to Gov. Jon Corzine State of NJ, Trenton, 2005, acting atty. gen., 2006, first asst. atty. gen., 2006—07, atty. gen., 2007—. Recipient Spl. Commendation for Outstanding Svc., US Dept. Justice, 2004, Director's award, 2006. Democrat. Office: Office Atty Gen Richard J Hughes Justice Complex 25 Market St 8th Fl West Wing Trenton NJ 08625-0080 Office Phone: 609-292-8740.*

MILGRAM, JEROME H., retired marine and ocean engineer, educator; b. Phila., Sept. 23, 1938; s. Samuel J. and Fannie M. BSEE, MIT, 1961, BS in Naval Architecture and Marine Engring., 1961, MS, 1962, PhD in Hydrodynamics, 1965. Registered profl. engr., Mass. With Scripps Inst. Oceanography, San Diego, summer 1961; project engr. Block Assocs., Cambridge, Mass., 1961-67; asst. prof. MIT, Cambridge, 1967-70, assoc. prof., 1970-77, prof. ocean engring., 1977-89, William I. Koch prof. marine tech., 1989—2007, prof. mech. engring., 2005—, emeritus prof. marine tech., 2007—. Rsch. assoc. in biophysics Harvard U. Med. Sch., 1974-76; vis. prof. in naval architecture and marine engring. U. Mich., 1988-89; design dir. Am. 3 Found., 1991-95; guest investigator Woods Hole Oceanog. Instn., 1996—; vis. prof. Johns Hopkins U., 1996-97; investigator and expert witness for marine casualties. Contbr. articles to profl. jours.; patentee in field. Recipient Am. Bur. Shipping award, 1961, Alan Berman Outstanding Rsch. Publ. award U.S. Naval Rsch. Lab., 1990, AT&T Design Innovation award, 1992. Fellow Soc. Naval Archs. and Marine Engrs. (life); mem. NAE (life), Nat. Rsch. Coun. (marine bd. 1998-2001). Home: 20 Blossom Hill Rd Winchester MA 01890-3455 Office: MIT 77 Massachusetts Ave Rm 5-318 Cambridge MA 02139-4307 Business E-Mail: jmilgram@mit.edu.

MILGRAM, R. JAMES, mathematics professor; s. Arthur Norton and Miriam Bernice Milgram; m. Judith Ann Krekelberg, Mar. 20, 1964; children: Arthur Jules, Jean Rose Kornmuller. BSc, U. Chgo., 1960, MSc, 1961; PhD, U. Minn., 1964. Instr. Princeton U., NJ, 1964—66, vis. full prof., 1969—70; asst. prof. U. Ill., Chgo., 1966—67, prof., 1968—69; prof. math. Stanford U., Calif., 1969—. Vis. prof. Aarhus U., Denmark, 1976—77; ordway vis. prof. U. Minn., 1986—86; gauss prof. U. Goettingen, Germany, 1987—88; regents prof. U. N.Mex, Albuquerque, 1993—95; vis. prof. U. Montreal, Canada, 1995—96; disting. vis. prof. Chinese Acad. Sci., Beijing, 2000; mem, math. adv. panel Achieve, Washington, 2000—; disting. vis. prof. U. Lille, France, 2001; mem. nat. bd. Inst. Edn. Sci., US Dept. Edn., Washington, 2004—07; mem., math adv. bd. W. H. Sadlier Inc., NYC, 2004—; mem. adv. coun. NASA, Washington, 2005—; bd. advisors Reasoning Mind, Houston, 2006—. Rsch. grant, NSF, 1970—2006, Cargo grant, 2002—07, Spl. grant, 2005, FIE grant, Sec. Edn. Rod Paige, 2002—05. Office: Stanford Univ Dept Math Stanford CA 94305 Business E-Mail: milgram@math.stanford.edu.

MILGRAUM, SANDY, surgeon, educator; s. Aria Lee and Sacia Chia Milgraum. MD, U. Western Australia, Perth, 1978. Cert. NJ., 1986. Pvt. practice, East Brunswick, NJ, 1986—2008; assoc. prof. Robert Wood Johnson Med. Sch., Piscataway, NJ, 1986—2008, tchr., 1986—2008. Office: Sandy Milgraum MD 81 Brunswick Woods Dr East Brunswick NJ 08816

MILGRIM, ROGER MICHAEL, lawyer; b. NYC, Mar. 22, 1937; s. Israel and Iola (Lash) Milgrim; 1 child, Justin. BA, U. Pa., 1958; LLB, NYU, 1961, LLM, 1962. Bar: NY, US Supreme Ct. Assoc. Baker & McKenzie, Paris, 1963-65, Nixon Mudge et al, NYC, 1965-68; mem. Milgrim Thomajan & Lee P.C., NYC, 1968-92; ptnr., chmn. intellectual property group Paul, Hastings, Janofsky & Walker LLP, NYC, 1992—2005, chmn. litig. dept., 1999—2000. Adj. prof. sch. law NYU, NYC, 1974—95. Author: Milgrim on Trade Secrets, 1967, supplement, 2009, Milgrim on Licensing, 1990, supplement, 2009. Trustee Coll. Wooster, 1994-97, Bklyn. Hosp., 1982-91; bd. dirs. Fulbright Assn., 1998—2004, chmn. Fulbright Prize com., 1999-2001; bd. dirs. Technip, 1998—2009 Mem. Knickerbocker Club. Republican. Home: 431 Paxinosa Rd E Easton PA 18040-1337 Home Phone: 610-438-4418. Business E-Mail: rogermilgrim@gmail.com.

MILGROM, PAUL ROBERT, economics educator; b. Detroit, Apr. 20, 1948; s. Abraham Isaac and Anne M. (Finkelstein); m. Eva Meyersson Milgrom, Sept. 17, 2000; m. Jan Thurston, Dec. 10, 1977; children: Joshua, Elana. AB in Math. with high honors, U. Mich., 1970; MS in Stats., Stanford U., 1978, PhD in Bus., 1979; MA (hon.), Yale U., 1983. Actuarial trainee Met. Life Ins. Co., 1970-71; conulting actuary Nelson and Warren, Inc., 1972-75; asst. prof. dept. managerial econs. and decision scis. Kellogg Grad. Sch. Mgmt. Northwestern U., 1979-81, assoc. prof., 1981-82, prof., 1982-83; prof. econs. and mgmt. Yale U., 1983-85, Williams Bros. prof. mgmt. studies, prof. econs., 1985-87; prof. econs. Stanford U., 1987—, Shirley R. and Leonard W. Ely, Jr. prof. humanities and scis., 1993—. Vis. rsch. assoc. econs. Stanford U., 1981; vis. prof. Yale U., 1982-83; Ford vis. prof. econs. U. Calif. Berkeley, 1986-87; IBM rsch. chair Northwestern U., 1981; Williams Bros. chair mgmt. studies Yale U., 1985; Olin disting. lectr. Princeton U., 1988; dir. Stanford Inst. for Theoretical Econs., 1989-1991; past cons. So. New Eng. Telephone Co., Rand Corp., Arctic Slope Regional Corp., Ga. Pacific, Exxon, Pacific Telesis, Bell Atlantic, Google, Yahoo, Microsoft Network, Govt. of Mex., others; lectr. in field. Author: (with John Roberts) Economics, Organization and Management, 1992, (with John Roberts), Instructor's Manual for Economics, Organization and Management, 1992; assoc. editor Jour. Econ. Theory, 1983-87, Rand Jour. Econs., 1985-89, Econometrica, 1987-90, Jour. Fin. Intermediation, 1989-92, Games and Econ. Behavior, 1990-92; co-editor Am. Econ. Review, 1990-93; contbr. over 50 articles to profl. jours. Recipient Leonard J. Savage Meml. Thesis award, 1980, Rsch. grant NSF, 1980, 82, 85, 88-91, 89, 91, 07, Rsch. award Actuarial Edn. and Rsch. Fund, 1983, John Simon Guggenheim fellowship, 1986, Best Paper of Yr. award, 1987, Rsch. grant Ctr. Econ. Policy, 1988, 90, Erwin Plein Nemmers Prize in Econs., Am. Math. Soc., 2008. Fellow Am. Acad. Arts and Scis., Econometric Soc. (plenary lectr. 5th World Congress 1985, mem. exec. com. 2005), Morse Coll., Inst. Advanced Studies Hebrew U. Jerusalem, Ctr. Advanced Study in Behavioral Scis., Soc. Actuaries (Triennial Paper prize 1976); mem. NAS, Am. Econ. Assn., Western Econ. Assn. Internat. (pres. 2007). Office: Stanford Univ Dept Econs Stanford CA 94305 E-mail: milgrom@stanford.edu.

MILHORAT, THOMAS HERRICK, neurosurgeon; b. NYC, Apr. 5, 1936; s. Ade Thomas and Edith Caulkins (Herrick) M.; m. Edith Mostile, 1961; children: John Thomas, Robert Herrick. BA, Cornell U., 1957, MD, 1961. Intern, asst. resident in gen. surgery N.Y. Hosp.-Cornell Med. Ctr., 1961—63, asst. resident, chief resident in neurosurgery, 1965—68, asst. neurosurgeon NIH, 1968—71; clin. assoc., dept. surg. neurology Nat. Inst. Neurol. Diseases and Blindness, Bethesda, 1963—65; assoc. prof. neurol. surgery, assoc. prof. child health and devel. George Washington U. Sch. Medicine, Washington, 1971—74, prof. neurol. surgery, prof. child health and devel., 1974—81; chmn. dept. neurosurgery Children's Hosp. Nat. Med. Ctr., Washington, 1971—81; prof. neurol. surgery, dept. chmn. SUNY Health Sci. Ctr., Bklyn., 1982—2001; chmn. dept. neurosurgery North Shore/L.I. Jewish Health System, 2002—; founder, dir. Chiari Inst. North Shore Univ. Hosp., 2002—; dir. Harvey Cushing Insts. Neurosci., Northshore-LI Jewish Health System, 2006—; prof. neurol. surgery NYU Sch. Medicine, 2002—07. Neurosurgeon-in-chief Kings County Hosp. Ctr., 1982—2001; regional chmn. neurol. surgery LI Coll. Hosp., 1986—2001; program dir. Neurosurgery Rsch. Tng. Program, 1982—2001; mem. Nat. Coun. Scientists NIH, 1969—82; dir. Harvey Cushing Inst. Neurosci. North Shore LI Jewish Health Sys., NY, 2006—. Author: Hydrocephalus and Cerebrospinal Fluid, 1972, Pediatric Neurosurgery, 1978, Cerebrospinal Fluid and the Brain Edemas, 1987; (with M.K. Hammock) Cranial Computed Tomography in Infancy and Childhood, 1981; mem. editl. bd. Neurosurgery, 1997—, Neurosug Focus: Syringomyelia, 2000—; contbr. more than 325 articles to profl. jours. Lt. comdr. USPHS, 1963—65. Recipient 1st prize in pathology, Cornell U. Med. Sch. Dept. Ob-Gyn., 1960, Charles L. Horn prize Cornell Med. Sch., 1961, Best Paper award ann. combined meeting NY Acad. Medicine/NY Neurosurg. Soc., 1965, Pudenz award for Excellence in CSF Physiology, 1994, E. Jefferson Browder award for excellence in Neurosurgery, 1996, Arthur A. Kaplan award for excellence in neurosurgery, 1999, White House Recognition award,2008. Mem. AAAS, Internat. Soc. Pediat. Neurosurgery, Am. Assn. Neurol. Surgery, Am. Syringomyelia Alliance Project (chmn. med. adv. bd. 1996-2007, bd. dirs. 1996-2007), Am. Acad. Pediat. (surg. sect.), Soc. Pediat. Rsch., NY Acad. Medicine, NY Soc. Neurosurgery (pres. 1988-90), Bklyn. Neurologic Soc. (pres. 1988-95), Soc. Neurosci., Internat. Soc. Neurosci., Soc. Neurol. Surgeons, Sigma Xi. Avocations: golf, billiards, gardening. Office: North Shore Univ Hosp Dept Neurosurgery Manhasset NY 11030 Office Phone: 516-562-3020. Business E-Mail: milhorat@nshs.edu.

MILHOUS, ELIZABETH, social studies educator; b. Fort Polk, La., Aug. 28, 1974; d. W. K. and V. G. Milhous. BA, Clemson U., SC, 1997, MEd, 1999. Cert. in tchg. Ga., 2002. Social studies tchr. Langston Charter Mid. Sch., Greenville, SC, 2005—. Mem. sch. bd. Langston Charter Mid. Sch., 2005—, after sch. prog. dir., 2005—; dir. outreach Clemson Alumni Assn., SC. Elected chair Clemson U. Women's Alumni Coun., 2000—06; bd. mem. Greenville Clemson Club, 2004—06. Named Young Alumnus of Merit, Clemson U., 2003. Mem.: NEA, SC Edn. Assn., SC Coun. Social Studies, Nat. Coun. Social Studies (archives com. mem. 2006—), Kappa Delta Pi. Office: Clemson Alumni Assn 109 Daniel Dr Clemson SC 29631 also: Langston Charter Middle School 212 Roper Mountain Road Ext Greenville SC 29615-4825 Personal E-mail: milhous@alumni.clemson.edu. Business E-Mail: emilhous@langstonchartermiddleschool.com.

MILIAN, AYDA R., secondary school educator; d. Rafael R. Milian and Aida A. Suarez. MA, U.North Tex., Denton, 1976. Cert. tchr. State Tex., 1978. Sr. mgr. internat. mktg. Nortel Networks, Richardson, Tex., 1983—99, new product intro. L.Am. Sunrise, Fla., 1992—99. Active tchr. Cath. Ch. Broward County, Hialeah, Fla., 1996—99. Study fellowship, Richardson Found., 2008. Mem.: AATSP (pres. 2008). Office: Little Elm HS 1900 Walker Ln Little Elm TX 75068

MILIC-EMILI, JOSEPH, physiologist, educator; b. Sezana, Slovenia, May 27, 1931; arrived in Can., 1963; s. Joseph Milic-Emili and Giovanna Milic-Emili Perhavec; m. Ann Harding, Nov. 2, 1957; children: Claire, Anne-Marie, Alice, Andrew. MD, U. Milan, 1955; Dr. honoris causa, U. Louvain, Belgium, 1987, Kunming Med. Coll., China, 1987, U. Montpellier, France, 1994, U. Ferrara, Italy, 1996, U. Athens, Greece, 1998, U. Ljubljana, Slovenia. Asst. prof. physiology and exptl. medicine McGill U., Montreal, Que., Canada, 1963-65, assoc. prof., 1965-69, prof., 1970-97, prof. emeritus, 1998—, dir. Meakins-Christie Labs., 1979-94. Vis. prof. Lab. de Physiologie Faculte de Medecine Saint-Antoine, Paris, Svc. de Pneumologie Hosp. Beaujon, Paris, 1978-79, 94-95, chmn. dept. physiology, 1973-78; vis. cons. medicine Royal Postgrad. Med. Sch., London, 1969-70; vis. cons. Aeronautics Imperial Coll. Tech., London, 1969-70; asst. prof. physiology U. Liege, Belgium, 1958-60; asst. prof. U. Milan, 1956-58. Mem. editl. bd. Jour. Applied Physiology, 1970-76, Rev. Française des Maladies Respiratories, 1979-96, Rivista de Biologia, 1979-86, Am. Rev. Respiratory Disease, 1982-89, Reanimation, Soins Intensifs, Medicine d'Urgence, 1984-95. Mem. applied physiology and bioengring. study sect. NIH, 1975-78. Decorated Order of Can.; recipient Gold medal C. Forlanini U. Pavia, Italy, 1982, Am. Coll. Chest Physicians medal, 1984, 98, Harry Wunderly medal Thoracic Soc. Australia, 1988, medal Italian Sch. Mil. Medicine, 1990, medal Med. Sch. Brest, 1997, medal Med. Sch. Ferrara, 1997, medal Med. Sch. Bologna, 2006, Trudeau medal Am. Thoracic Soc., 2006; author of one of 100-most cited articles in clin. rsch. of 1960s; named one of 1,000 most-cited contemporary scientists, 1965-78, 1998 Presdl. award European Respiratory Soc., 1998 Disting. Lectr. in Physiology Am. Coll. Chest Physicians. Fellow Royal Soc. Can., Slovenian Acad. Sci. (fgn. corr.), Soc. Med. Clin. Bononiensis Sci.; mem. Am. Physiol. Soc., Can. Physiol. Soc., Can. Thoracic Soc., Med. Rsch. Coun. (mem. grants com. 1980), Soc. Pneumologie Belge (hon.), Brazilian Physiol. Soc. (hon.), Hellenic Thoracic Soc. (hon.), Polish Pneumological Soc. (hon.), Chilean Resp. Soc. (hon.). Home: 4394 Circle Rd Montreal PQ Canada H3W 1Y5 Office: McGill U Meakins-Christie Labs 3626 St Urbain St Montreal PQ Canada H2X 2P2 Office Phone: 514-398-3864 ext. 80144. Business E-Mail: joseph.milic-emili@mcgill.ca.

MILICIC, DARKO, professional basketball player; b. Novi Sad, Serbia and Montenegro, June 20, 1985; Profl. basketball player Yugoslavia, 2001—02, Hemofarm Vrsac, 2002—03; forward-ctr. Detroit Pistons, 2003—05, Orlando Magic, Fla., 2005—07, Memphis Grizzlies, 2007—09, KY Knicks, 2009—. Mem. Yugoslavian Team European Cadet Championships, 2001. Office: NY Knicks Madison Sq Garden 4 Pennsylvania Plz New York NY 10001*

MILIOTIS, DEMITRIOS, physics professor; b. Korinth, Greece, Jan. 1, 1930; s. Menelaos and Angellika Miliotis; m. Louly Grifsa, June 10, 1960; 1 child, Menelaos. Diploma in Physics, Nat. U., Athens, Greece, 1957, PhD in Physics, 1964. Rsch. asst. Nat. Found. Rsch., Athens, 1958-65, rsch. assoc., 1969-71; rsch. asst. physics dept. U. Ill., Urbana, 1965-66, rsch. assoc., 1966-68; asst. prof. physics dept. U. Athens, 1971-72; assoc. prof. U. Ioannina, Greece, 1972-75, prof., chmn. applied physics, 1975-77, head physics and math. depts., 1978-80, prof. dept. physics, 1981-85, prof. emeritus, 1985—. Invited prof. U. Crete, Heraklion, Greece, 1977-78; vis. prof. physics dept. U. Ill., 1980-81. Author books on circuit analysis and semiconductor physics; contbr. articles to profl. jours. Lt. Greek Army, 1954-56. Home: 27A Kifissias Ave 11523 Athens Greece

MILKE, LINDA JEAN, elementary school educator; b. Muskegon, Mich., Sept. 30; d. John Carl and Helen Maxine Milke. BA, Western Mich. U., Kalamazoo, 1973; MEd in Curriculum and Instrn., Ariz. State U., Tempe, 2002. With Smitty's of Ariz., 1973—90; tchr. Tempe Elem. Dist., 1992—98; tchr. in sch. intervention Gililland Mid. Sch., Tempe, 1998—2003, tchr. 6th grade social studies, 2003—. Co-chair pride com. Gililland Mid. Sch., 2000—06, co-chair leadership team, 2003—04, mem. site coun., 2004—, mem. ASIP acad. coun., 2006—07. Mem. Project Upward Bound Western Mich. U., 1967—69. Mem.: NEA (assoc.), Nat. Assn. Bilingual Educators (assoc.), Phi Kappa Phi. Avocations: antiques, home decorating, reading. Home: 7026 E Kiva Ave Mesa AZ 85209 Office: Gililland Middle Sch 1025 S Beck Ave Tempe AZ 85281 Personal E-mail: lindamilke@msn.com. Business E-Mail: lindamilke@tempeschools.org.

MILKEN, MICHAEL R., think-tank executive, philanthropist; b. Calif., July 4, 1946; m. Lori Milken, Aug. 11, 1968; 3 children. Grad. summa cum laude, U. Calif., Berkeley; MBA, U. Pa. Securities trader Drexel Burnham Lambert, until 1990; chmn. The Milken Inst., 1991—; founder Prostate Cancer Found. (formerly CaPCure), 1993—; chair Knowledge Universe, 1996—; chmn. FasterCures/Ctr. for Accelerating Med. Solutions, 2003—. Author: Taste for Living Series cookbooks. Chair Assn. Cure of Cancer of the Prostate; co-founder Milken Family Found., 1982. Named one of 400 Richest Ams., Forbes mag., 2006. Office: Milken Inst 1250 Fourth St Ste 200 Santa Monica CA 90401

MILL, THEODORE, chemist, researcher; b. Apr. 17, 1931; BS, Wayne State U., 1953; PhD, U. Wash., 1956. Fellow Hickrill Rsch. Found., Katonah, NY, 1956-57; chemist DuPont Expt. Sta., DuPont Co., Wilmington, Del., 1957-60, Stanford Rsch. Inst., Menlo Park, Calif., 1960-64, dir. phys. organic chemistry dept., 1964-85, sr. scientist, 1985—. Fellow Stanford Rsch. Inst., 1996; cons. in field. Contbr. articles to profl. jours. Patentee in field. Grantee NSF, 1975-80, NIH, 1976-82, EPA, 1976-99, Dept. Energy, 2002-04. Mem. ACS (chmn. local sect. 1976), AAAS, Am. Geophys. Union, Sierra Club, Audubon Soc. Office: SRI 333 Ravenswood Ave PS 239 Menlo Park CA 94025-3493 Home Phone: 650-328-1069; Office Phone: 650-859-3605. Personal E-mail: ted.mill@srl.com.

MILLAN, CESAR, television personality; b. Culiacán, Mex., May 12, 1969; s. Felipe Millan Guillen and Maria Teresa Favela de Millan; m. Ilusion Wilson Millan; children: Andre, Calvin. Owner, founder, dog trainer Dog Psychology Ctr., LA; CEO Cesar Millan, Inc.; co-founder Cesar and Ilusion Millan Found., Burbank, Calif., 2007—. Host (TV series) Dog Whisperer with Cesar Millan, 2004—; co-author: (books) Be the Pack Leader: Use Cesar's Way to Transform Your Dog...and Your Life, 2007, Cesar's Way: The Natural, Everyday Guide to Understanding and Correcting Common Dog Problems, 2007; creator: (instructional DVDs) People Training for Dogs; Becoming a Pack Leader; Your New Dog: First Day and Beyond; cinematographer:. Active K-9 Connection, Pups on Parole, Pets911; founder Cesar and Ilusion Millan Found. Recipient Genesis award, Nat. Humane Soc., 2005, Michael Landon award, 2007. Mem.: Internat. Assn. Canine Profls. (hon.). Office: Cesar Ilusion Millan Foundation PO Box 2039 Burbank CA 91507-2039

MILLANE, LYNN, retired municipal official; b. Buffalo, Oct. 14, 1928; d. Robert P. and Justine A. Schermerhorn; m. J. Vaughan Millane Jr., Aug. 16, 1952; children: Maureen, Michele, John, Mark, Kathleen. EdB, U. Buffalo, 1949, EdM in Health Edn., 1951. Coun. mem. Amherst Town Bd., NY, 1982—96, dep. town supr., 1990-96, supr., 1996. Founder, liaison 1st adult day svcs. adv. bd. Town of Amherst, 1988, liaison to ad hoc cable TV com., 1992—96, liaison to Amherst C. of C., 1993—96, 1st records mgmt. adv. bd., liaison ethics bd., 1994—96; legis. liaison SUNY Family Violence Clin. Sch. Law, Buffalo, 1997—98; pres. E.J. Meyer Hosp. Jr. Bd., 1962—64; commr. (apptd. by Gov. George Pataki) NY State Ethics Commn., 1999—2004, 2004—07; adv. bd. NY State Office Aging, 1996—2005, chair adv. bd., 1997—2005; spkr. in field. Pres. Aux. to Erie County Bar Assn., 1966-68, Womens Com. Buffalo Philharm. Orch., 1976-78, v.p. adminstrn., 1975-76, v.p. pub. affairs, 1974-75, chair. adv. bd., 1979-82; v.p. Buffalo Philharm. Orch. Soc., Inc., 1976-78, coun. mem., trustee, 1979-87, bd. overseers, 1987-92; dir. 8th jud. dist. NY State Assn. Large Towns, 1989-91; bd. dirs. oper. bd. Millard Fillmore Suburban Hosp., 1992-98; 1st v.p. Fams for 17, 1980-82, Friends of Baird Hall SUNY, Buffalo, 1980-82; exec. bd. Womens Exec. Coun. Erie County Rep. Com., 1969-71, Longview Protestant Home for Children, 1979-85, 2d v.p., 1982-85; bd. dirs. Amherst br. ARC, 1982-91, by-laws com., 1981, 84, chair sr. concerns com., 1982-91, liaison code of ethics com., 1987-89; nat. music com. Womens Assn. for Symphony Orchs. in Am. and Can., 1977-79; coun. mem. Am. Symphony Orch. League; sec. Amherst Sr. Citizens Adv. Bd., 1980-81, liaison from Amherst Town Bd., 1982-96; liaison to the Alternate Fuel and Clean Cities Com., 1994-96; dir.-at-large cmty. adv. coun. SUNY, Buffalo, 1981-91; co-assoc. chair maj. gift divsn. capital campaign Daemen Coll., 1983-84, trustee, 1998-; chair mem. com. Daemen Coll Trustees, 2003—; co-chair Women United Against Drugs Campaign, 1970-72; founding mem.

Lunch and Issues, Amherst, 1981—; edn. com., bd. dirs. Network in Aging of Western NY, Inc., 1982-89, housing com., 1987-89; bd. dirs. Amherst Elderly Transp. Corp., 1982-99; committeeman dist. Town of Amherst Rep. Com.; treas. Town and Country Rep. Club, 1980-81; nominating com. Fedn. Rep. Womens Clubs Erie County, 1980; del. NY State Govs. Conf. on Aging, 1995, White House Conf. on Aging, 1995, named mem. aging svcs.; mem. Erie County Indsl. Devel. Agy. Erie County Regional Devel. Corp., 1996-97; mem. adv. bd. Amherst Symphony Orch., 2003-; vol. life project Greater Buffalo chpt. ARC, 2002-05, mem. svc. to older adults com., 2002-05. Recipient Good Neighbor award, Courier Express, 1978, Merit award, Buffalo Philharm. Orch., 1978, Edn. Rep. Womens Clubs Erie County award, 1982, Disting. Svc. award, Town of Amherst Sr. Ctr., 1985, Amherst Adult Day Care and Vis. Nurses Assn., 1994, Susan B. Anthony award, Interclub Coun. Western NY, 1991, Cmty. Svc. award, Amherst Rep. Com., 1991, D.A.R.E. award, Town of Amherst Police Dept., 1994, Amherst South Rotary Club, 1997, Outstanding Cmty. Svc. award, Amherst Sr. Citizen Found., 1997, Lynn Millane Cmty. Svc. award named in her honor, Rep. honoree, award for svc., Town of Amherst Youth Bd., 1996, award for care and assistance to sr. citizens of N.Y. State, Batavia Nursing Home, 2000, Woman of Distinction award, NY State Senate, 2003; named Homemaker of Yr., Family Circle mag., 1969, Woman of Substance, 20th Century Rep. Women, 1983, Woman of Yr., Buffalo Philharm. Orch. Soc., Inc., 1982, Outstanding Woman in Cmty. Svc., SUNY, Buffalo, 1985; hon. Paul Harris fellow. Mem. Amherst C. of C. (VIP dinner com. 1984), LWV, SUNY Buffalo Alumni Assn. (life, presdl. advisor 1977-79), Amherst Symphony Orch. Assn. (bd. dirs. 1981-87, roster chair. 1982-84, nominating chair 1985-86, vice-chair 50th ann. com. 1994-96, trustee 2003-09), Niagara Connect, Amherst Rep. Womens Club (bd. dirs. 1963-65, 99), Zonta (pres. Amherst chpt. 1986-88, Zontian of Yr. 1992); Pi Lambda Theta (hon.), Twentieth Century Club (pres. 2009-).

MILLAR, GORDON HALSTEAD, mechanical engineer, agricultural products executive; b. Newark, Nov. 28, 1923; s. George Halstead and Dill E. (McMullen) M.; m. Virginia M. Jedryczka, Aug. 24, 1957; children: George B., Kathryn M., Juliet S., John G., James H. B.M.E., U. Detroit, 1949, D.Sc. (hon.), 1977; PhD, U. Wis., 1952; L.H.D., West Coast U., 1984; D.Sc. (hon.), Western Mich. U., 1986. Registered profl. engr., Fla., Ill., Iowa, Mich., Minn., Ohio. Supr. new powerplants Ford Motor Co., 1952-57; engring. mgr. Meriam Instrument Co., Cleve., 1957-59; dir. new products McCulloch Corp., Los Angeles, 1959-63; with Deere & Co., 1963-84, v.p. engring. Moline, Ill., 1972-84; exec. assoc. Southwest Research Inst., 1987. Mem. Fed. Adv. Com. Indsl. Innovation, 1979; chmn. West Ctrl. Ill. Ednl. Telecom. Corp.; pres. Accreditation Bd. for Engring. and Tech., 1983-85; pres., fellow Accreditation Bd. for Engring. and Tech. Editor: The Sheerline, Antique and Classic Boat Soc. (Sunnyland chpt.), 1995-; contbr. articles to profl. jours.; patentee in field. Chmn. Quad Cities chpt. United Way, 1976-77; bd. dirs.; adv. council Bradley U. Coll. Engring. and Tech.; mem. exec. com. Illowa council Boy Scouts Am., 1977-79. Served with U.S. Army, World War II. Decorated Purple Heart, Combat Inf. Men's Badge, Bronze Star; recipient Alumnus of Year award U. Detroit, 1976, Comdrs. medal for pub. svc. Dept. Army, 1989 Fellow ASME (hon. life mem.), Soc. Automotive Engrs. (pres. 1984, bd. dirs. 1984-86, mem. nat. nominating com.); mem. NAE, NSPE, Engrs. Joint Coun., Indsl. Rsch. Inst., Engring. Soc. Detroit, Am. Soc. Agrl. Engrs., Ill. Soc. Profl. Engrs., Moline C. of C., Aviation Coun, Boat Modelers Club, North Fl. O.R.C.A.S. Ship Modelers Club, North Am. Steam Modelers Assn. Home: 1840 Wiley Post Trl Port Orange FL 32128-6756 Home Phone: 386-788-0213.

MILLAR, JOHN DONALD, physician, occupational & environmental health services consultant, musician; b. Newport News, Va., Feb. 27, 1934; s. John and Dorothea Virginia (Smith) M.; m. Joan M. Phillips, Aug. 17, 1957; children: John Stuart, Alison Gordon, Virginia Taylor. BS, U. Richmond, 1956; MD, Med. Coll. Va., 1959; DTPH, London Sch. Hygiene and Tropical Medicine, 1966; D of Pub. Svc. (hon.), Greenville Coll., Ill., 1994. Cert. specialist in Gen. Preventive Medicine 1969. Intern U. Utah Affiliated Hosps., Salt Lake City, 1959-60, asst. resident in medicine, 1960-61; chief Epidemic Intelligence Svc., Ctr. for Disease Control, USPHS, HEW, Atlanta, 1961-63, dep. chief surveillance sect. epidemiology br., 1962-63, chief smallpox unit, 1963-65, dir. smallpox eradication program, 1966-70, dir. Bur. State Svcs., 1970-78, asst. dir. Ctr. for Disease Control for Pub. Health Practice, 1979-80; dir. Nat. Ctr. Environ. Health, Atlanta, 1980-81, Nat. Inst. for Occupation Safety and Health, Atlanta, 1981-93, chmn. exec. com. Nat. Toxicology Program, 1989-93; pres. Don Millar & Assocs., Inc., Atlanta, 1993—. Adj. prof. occupl. and environ. health Sch. Pub. Health Emory U., Atlanta, 1988-98; cons. on smallpox, smallpox eradication, immunization programs and occupl. and environ. health WHO; mem. WHO expert adv. panel on occupl. health; bd. dirs. Farm Safety 4 Just Kids, 1993-98; tech. adv. bd. Ctr. Protect Workers' Rights, 1993; disting. fellow, vice chmn. Pub. Health Policy Adv. Bd., Inc., Washington, 1998-2007; mem. bd. dirs. Coll. Pub. Health, U. Ga., 2007-08, mem. Dean's Practice Com., 2008-; mem. string bass sect. DeKalb Symphony Orch., 1982-06, Gainesville (Ga.) Symphony Orch., 2000-04, N.E. Ga. Mountain Chamber Orch., 2001-05, Truett-Macconnell Coll. Wind Symphony, 2002—, Toccoa Falls Coll. Orch., 2005—, Toccoa Symphony Orch., 2005—. Mem. editl. bd. Am. Jour. Indsl. Medicine, 1985-05, Am. Jour. Occupl. Psychology, 1993-00, Am. Jour. Preventive Medicine, 1993-00; contbr. articles to profl. jours. Recipient Surgeon Gen's. Commendation medal, 1965, Okeke prize London Sch. Hygiene and Tropical Medicine, 1966, Presdl. award for mgmt. improvement, 1972, W.C. Gorgas medal Assn. Mil. Surgeons U.S., 1987, Lucas lectr. Faculty Occupational Medicine Royal Coll. Physicians, London, 1987, Outstanding Med. Alumnus award Med. Coll. Va., 1988; also recipient Equal Employment Opportunity award, 1975, Medal of Excellence, 1977, Joseph W. Mountin lectr. award, 1986, Alexander D. Langmuir MD Meml. lectr. award, 2001, all from Ctrs. for Disease Control, Disting. Svc. medal USPHS, 1983, 88, Exemplary Svc. medal Surgeon Gen. U.S., 1988, Giants in Occupational Medicine lectr. U. Utah, 1989, William S. Knudsen award Am. Coll. Occupational Medicine, 1991, presdl. citation APA, 1991, William Steiger Meml. award Am. Conf. Govtl. Indsl. Hygienists, 1993, Health Watch award for outstanding contbns. toward improving health of minority populations, 1992, Award of Merit Minerva Edn. Inst., 1993, Alumni Disting. Svc. award U. Richmond, 1993, Jeff Lee Mem. Lectr. Am. Indusl. Hygiene Assoc. San Diego, Calif., 2002; named to Order Bifurcated Needle, World Health Orgn., 1978, Faculty Occupational Medicine, Royal Coll. Physicians, London, 1990; elected Safety and Health Hall of Fame Internat., Nat. Safety Coun., 1997. Mem. Am. Indsl. Hygiene Assn. (hon.), Am. Coll. Occupl. and Environ. Medicine, Am. Epidemiol. Soc., Collegium Ramazzini, Am. Assn. Pub. Health Physicians., Assn. Mil. Surgeons U.S., Pub. Health Svc. Commissioned Officers Assn., Alpha Omega Alpha.

MILLAR, RICHARD WILLIAM, JR., lawyer; b. LA, May 11, 1938; LLB, U. San Francisco, 1966; JD (hon.), Western State U., Coll. Law, 2008. Bar: Calif. 1967, US Dist. Ct. (cen. dist.) Calif. 1967, US Dist. Ct. (no. dist.) Calif. 1969, US Dist. Ct. (so. dist.) Calif. 1973, US Supreme Ct. Assoc. Iverson & Hogoboom, Los Angeles, 1967-72; ptnr. Eilers, Stewart, Pangman & Millar, Newport Beach, Calif., 1973-75, Millar & Heckman, Newport Beach, 1975-77, Millar, Hodges & Bemis, Newport Beach, 1979—. Trustee Western State U. Coll. Law, 2004—. Fellow: Am. Bar Found. (life); mem.: ABA (litigation sect. trial practice com., ho. of dels. 1990—), Orange County Bar Assn. (chmn. bus. litig. sect. 1981, chmn. judiciary com. 1988—90, sec. 1999, treas., dir. charitable fund 2000, pres.-elect 2001, pres. 2002, treas., dir. charitable fund 2003), Calif. Bar Assn. (lectr. CLE), Pacific Club, Bohemian Club (San Francisco). Home: 71 Hillsdale Newport Beach CA 92660 Office: Millar Hodges & Bemis One Newport Pl Ste # 900 Newport Beach CA 92660 Office Phone: 949-752-7722. Personal E-mail: millar@mhblaw.net.

MILLARD, CHARLES WARREN, III, retired museum director, writer; b. Elizabeth, NJ, Dec. 20, 1932; s. Charles Warren and Constance Emily (Keppler) M. AB magna cum laude, Princeton U., 1954; MA, Harvard U., 1963, PhD, 1971. Asst. to dir. Fogg Art Mus. Harvard U., Cambridge, Mass., 1963-64; asst. to dir. Dumbarton Oaks, Washington, 1965-66; dir. Washington Gallery Modern Art, 1966-67; teaching fellow Harvard U., 1968-69; curator 19th Century European art L.A. County Mus. Art, 1971-74; chief curator Hirshhorn Mus. and Sculpture Garden Smithsonian Instn., Washington, 1974-86; adj. prof. Johns Hopkins U., Balt., 1983-86; dir. Ackland Art Mus. U. N.C., Chapel Hill, 1986-93, adj. prof., 1986-93; chmn. vis. com. to fine arts dept. Boston U., 1977-80. Chmn. nat. adv. bd. Ackland Art Mus., 2000-04. Author: The Sculpture of Edgar Degas, 1977, La Vie d'Auguste Preault, Auguste Preault Sculpteur Romantique, 1809-1879, 1997; art editor Hudson Rev., 1972-87; contbr. articles to profl. jours. With USN, 1956-59.

MILLARD, NEAL STEVEN, lawyer, educator; b. Dallas, June 6, 1947; s. Bernard and Adele (Marks) Millard; m. Janet Keast, Mar. 12, 1994; 1 child, Kendall Layne. BA cum laude, UCLA, 1969; JD, U. Chgo., 1972. Bar: Calif. 1972, US Dist. Ct. (ctrl. dist.) Calif. 1973, US Tax Ct. 1973, US Ct. Appeals (9th cir.) 1987, NY 1990. Assoc. Willis, Butler & Schiefly, LA, 1972-75; ptnr. Morrison & Foerster, LA, 1975-84, Jones, Day, Reavis & Pogue, LA, 1984-93, White & Case, LA, 1993—. Instr. Calif. State Coll., San Bernardino, 1975—76; lectr. Practising Law Inst., NYC, 1983—90, Calif. Edn. Bar, 1987—90; adj. prof. U. So. Calif. Law Ctr., LA, 1994—. Mem. citizens adv. com. LA Olympics, 1982—84; trustee Altadena Libr. Dist., Calif., 1985—86; bd. dirs. Woodcraft Rangers, LA, 1982—90, pres., 1986—88; bd. dirs. LA County Bar Found., 1990—2000; pres. Los Angeles County Bar Found., 1997—98; mem. Energy Commn. county/cities of LA, 1995—99; mem. jud. procedures commn. LA County, 1999—, chair, 2000—02; mem. Pub. Safety Commn. LaCanada-Flintridge, 2006—, chair, 2008—09; bd. dirs. Inner City Law Ctr., 1996—99; bd. dirs., sec. LaCanada-Flintridge Ednl. Found., 2002—06; bd. dirs. Alliance Coll.-Ready Pub. Schs., 2004—. Mem.: Am. Law Inst., Pub. Counsel (bd. dirs. 1984—87, 1990—93), LA County Bar Assn. (trustee 1985—87), NY State Bar Assn., Calif. Bar Assn., U. So. Calif. Inst. Corp. Counsel (mem. adv. bd. 1998—2006), U. Chgo. Law Alumni Assn. (pres. 1998—2001), Flintridge Riding Club, Calif. Club, Chancery Club, Beach Club, Phi Beta Kappa, Phi Delta Phi, Pi Gamma Mu. Office: White & Case 633 W 5th St Ste 1900 Los Angeles CA 90071-2087 Office Phone: 213-620-7773. Business E-Mail: nmillard@whitecase.com.

MILLARD, WENDA HARRIS, multi-media company executive; b. Alexandria, Va., July 9, 1954; d. Roger and Joan Marie (Kelliher) Harris; m. William John Millard, Oct. 8, 1983. BA in English, Trinity Coll., Hartford, Conn., 1976; MBA, Harvard U., 1983. Sales promotion mgr. Am. Home mag., 1976-77, Ladies' Home Jour., 1977-79; sales devel. mgr. NY mag., 1979-81; gen. mgr. Working Woman Ventures, 1983-85; exec. v.p., group pub. Adweek, Mediaweek and Brandweek mags., NYC, 1985-89; gen. mgr., ptnr. The Peer Group, Westport, Conn., 1989; sr. v.p., pub. Family Circle mag.; pres., group pub. SRDS; founding mem., exec. v.p. DoubleClick, 1996—2000; chief internet officer Ziff Davis Media; pres. Ziff Davis Internet, 2000—01; chief sales officer Yahoo! Inc., 2001—07; pres. media Martha Stewart Living Omnimedia, Inc., NYC, 2007—08, co-CEO, 2008—09; pres. Media Link, LLC, NYC, 2009—; interim pres. sales/mktg. MySpace, 2009—. Exec. prodr. Working Woman radio report, Nat. Commn. on Working Women, 1984; bd. dirs. Martha Stewart Living Omnimedia, 2004—07, Millennial Media, Inc., 2009—. Editor: Fashion Capital News, 1980; contbr. articles to profl. jours. Bd. trustees Trinity Coll., 1980—; bd. mem. James Beard Found. Recipient Women at Work Broadcast Award, IABC Award for Innovation, Univ. Settlement House, Gary McQuaid Award for Excellence in Bus. Leadership, Matrix award for "Women Who Changed the World", 2005, "Advt. Person of the Yr." Silver Medal award, The Am. Advt. Fedn., 2006, John A. Reisenbach award for Disting. Citizenship, 2007; named Digital Media Master, Advertising Age, 1999; named one of 100 Young Women of Promise, Good Housekeeping mag., 1985. Mem.: Advt. Club NY (Andy award 1988, 1999), Women's Equity Action League, Women in Comms., Advt. Women NY, Harvard Club. Republican. Office: Media Link LLC 845 Third Ave 6th Fl New York NY 10022 Office Phone: 646-290-5122. Office Fax: 646-290-5116.*

MILLBERG, JOHN C., lawyer; b. New London, Conn., Jan. 4, 1956; s. Melvin Roy and Dorothy (Van Zandt) M.; m. Lori Bruce, Oct. 18, 1981; children: Kathryn Faye, Rebecca Ann, Melvin Roy III. BA, Bowling Green State U., 1977; JD, Wake Forest U., 1980. Bar: Tex. 1980, NC 1986, SC 2000, US Dist. Ct. (so. dist.) Tex. 1981, US Ct. Appeals (5th and 11th cirs.) 1981, US Dist. Ct. (ea., mid. and we. dists.) NC 1986, US Ct. Appeals (4th cir.) 1986, US Dist. Ct. SC 2002. Assoc. Crain Caton James & Womble, Houston, 1981—85; assoc., dir. Maupin, Taylor, Ellis & Adams, Raleigh, NC, 1985—94; mng. ptnr. Millberg, Gordon & Stewart, PLLC, Raleigh, NC, 1994—. Mem. bar candidate com. NC Bd. Law Examiners, 1988-90. Scholar Wake Forest U. Sch. Law, 1977-80. Mem. NC Assn. Def. Attys. (exec. com., v.p. southeastern region), Nat. Assn. R.R. Trial Counsel. Office: Millberg Gordon & Stewart PLLC S 104 1101 Haynes St Raleigh NC 27604-1455

MILLEA, THOMAS FRANCIS, photographer; b. Bridgeport, Conn., Sept. 30, 1944; s. Thomas Francis and Mildred Claire Millea. BA in History, Western Conn. State U., Danbury, 1966. Artist in residence Yosemite Valley Nat. Pk., 1988—99. Photographer (permanent collections), The Getty Mus., The Smithsonian, San Francisco Moma, Boston Mus. Fine Arts, in over 40 museums worldwide. Named Alumnus of Yr., Western Conn. State U., 2006; Rutenburg grant, 1984. Achievements include re-introduction and refinement of platinum printing for photography. Avocations: travel, philosophy. Business E-Mail: tmillea@aol.com.

MILLER, A. TROY, city councilman, information technology executive; BS in Health Svcs. Adminstrn., U. Cin.; MBA, Ohio Dominican U. Mgr. corp. devel. Ctrl. Benefits Mutual Ins. Co., Westerville, Ohio; acct. exec. ACNielsen; market rsch. analyst Abbott Labs.; med. staff. devel. planning mgr. OhioHealth, Columbus; owner, pres. ATM Ctrl. Devel., LLC, Columbus, 2007—; councilman Columbus City Coun., 2009—, chair adminstrn. com. Bd. dirs. St. Vincent Family Ctr.'s. Recipient Edgar Ingram, Jr. Innovation award, Ohio Dominican U., 2006. Mem.: Am. Hosp. Assn. Soc. Healthcare Strategy & Market Devel., Healthcare Info. Mgmt. Sys. Soc., Am. Coll. Health Care Execs. Office: Colombus City Coun 90 West Broad St 2nd Fl Columbus OH 43215 also: ATM Ctrl Devel LLC 4100 Regent St Ste U Columbus OH 43219 Office Phone: 614-414-0410. Office Fax: 614-414-0848. Business E-Mail: troy@atmcentraldev.com.

MILLER, AARON DAVID, political scientist, writer; b. Cleve., Mar. 25, 1949; s. Samuel H. and Ruth Ratner Miller; m. Lindsay Miller; children: Jennifer, Daniel. BA, U. Mich., 1971, PhD in Am. Diplomatic and Middle East History, 1977. With US Dept. State, Washington, 1978—2003, historian Bur. Public Affairs, 1978, analyst Lebanon and the Palestinians Bur. of Intelligence and Rsch. (INR), 1980, temporary tour US Embassy Amman, Jordan, advisor to sec. of state Washington, 1985—93, dep. spl. Middle East coord. Arab-Israeli negotiations, 1993, sr. mem. policy planning staff Bur. Intelligence and Rsch., sr. mem. Office of the Historian, sr. advisor Arab-Israeli negotiations Bur. Near Eastern Affairs; pres. Seeds of Peace, 2003—06; pub. policy fellow Woodrow Wilson Internat. Ctr. for Scholars, 2006—. Fellow Coun. on Fgn. Rels., 1982—83; resident scholar Georgetown Ctr. for Strategic and Internat. Studies, 1982—83; mem. US Holocaust Meml. Coun., 1998—2000; spkr. in field. Author: PLO: Politics of Survival, 1983, The Arab States and the Palestine Question: Between Ideology and Self-Interest, 1986, Search for Security: Saudi Arabian Oil and American Foreign Policy, 1939-1949, 1991, The Much Too Promised Land: America's Elusive Search for Arab-Israeli Peace, 2008. Recipient Disting., Meritorious and Superior Honor Awards, US Dept. State, Ellis Island Medal of Honor, 2005. Office: Woodrow Wilson Internat Ctr for Scholars One Woodrow Wilson Plaza 1300 Pennsylvania Ave, NW Washington DC 20004-3027 Office Phone: 202-691-4040. E-mail: Aaron.Miller@wilsoncenter.org.*

MILLER, ALAN, computer company executive, management consultant; b. Bklyn., Apr. 20, 1954; s. Michael and Lillian Charlotte (Garment) M.; m. Zelda Sara Bochlin; Nov. 16, 1974; children: Michael Glenn, Dara Jennifer. BS in Computer Sci., magna cum laude, SUNY, 1975; MBA in Mgmt., with honors, Adelphi U., 1982. Tech. svcs. mgr. Guardian Life Ins. Co., NYC, 1977-81; project mgr. Mfrs. Hanover Trust Co., NYC, 1981-83; asst. v.p. Bankers Trust Co., NYC, 1983-86; v.p., MIS dir. Bank Am. Trust Co. NY, NYC, 1986-87; assoc. John Diebold and Assocs., NYC, 1987-89; mgr. banking practice AGS Info. Svcs., NYC, 1989-90; v.p. mktg. and bus. devel., product mgr. global trade fin. BIS Banking Systems, NYC, 1990-93; sr. cons. Computer Scis. Corp., 1994-95; solution exec. global fin. industries IBM Software Group, Somers, NY, 1995—98; client exec. Goldman Sachs Group IBM Corp., NYC, 1998—2001; client exec. NY Life, 2002—05; client unit exec. Wall St., 2006—. Chmn. Sch. Dist. Adv. Com., Plainview, NY, 1981-83; exec. producer Oklahoma prodn. Patio Players, Plainview, 1990-91; bd. dirs. men's club Plainview Jewish Ctr., 1986-95. Mem. Delta Mu Delta. Jewish. Avocations: softball, theater, games shows, volleyball. Home: 21 Beaumont Dr Plainview NY 11803-2507 Office: IBM 33 Maiden Ln New York NY 10038-4598 Home Phone: 516-935-5965; Office Phone: 917-472-3443. Business E-Mail: alan.miller@us.ibm.com.

MILLER, ALAN B., hospital management executive; b. NYC, Aug. 17, 1937; s. Daniel and Mary (Blumenthal) M.; m. Jill K. Stein, Oct. 5, 1968; children: Marc Daniel, Marni Elizabeth, Abby Danielle. BA, Coll. William and Mary, 1958; MBA, U. Pa., 1960; PhD (hon.), U. SC. V.p. Young & Rubicam, Inc., NYC, 1964-69; sr. v.p. Am. Medicorp., Inc., LA, 1970, pres., chief exec. officer Phila., 1973-77, chmn. bd., 1977, Hosp. Underwriting Group, 1977-78; founder, chmn., pres., CEO Universal Health Services, King of Prussia, Pa., 1978—; chmn., founder UHT-Real Estate Trust, King of Prussia, Pa., 1986—. Formerly health care adviser Fed. Mediation and Conciliation Svc.; chmn., pres. Universal Health Svcs. Real Estate Investment Trust, N.Y. Stock Exch., 1986—, former dir., Broadlane, Penn Mut. Life Ins., bd. dirs. CDI Corp., N.Y. Stock Exch.; mem. exec. bd. Wharton Sch., U. Pa., 1996-2004, mem. bd. overseers, 2005-. Former chmn. Opera Co. of Phila.; dir. Regional Performing Arts Ctr. Capt. 77th Inf. Divsn. US Army. Recipient Ellis Island Medal of Honor, 1998, William and Mary medallion, George Washington U. Pres.'s medal. Home: 57 Crosby Brown Rd Gladwyne PA 19035-1512 Office: Universal Health Svcs Inc PO Box 61558 367 S Gulph Rd King Of Prussia PA 19406 Office Phone: 610-768-3300.

MILLER, ALAN J., retired financial company executive; b. Bklyn., July 11, 1936; s. Louis and Claire (Maltz) M.; m. Susan Ruth Morris, Oct. 29, 1961; children— Laurie Ann, Adam Louis. BA, Cornell U., 1957. Chartered fin. analyst. Pres. Analysis-in-Depth Inc., NYC, 1965-67; mng. editor Value Line Investment Survey, NYC, 1967-68; rsch. dir. Emanuel Deetjen & Co., NYC, 1968-69; exec. v.p., dir. Intersci. Capital Mgmt. Corp., NYC, 1969-71; pres., dir. ICM Equity Fund Inc., NYC, 1970-71, ICM Fin. Fund Inc., NYC, 1970-71; v.p., assoc. rsch. dir. Bache & Co., Inc., NYC, 1972, G.H. Walker & Co., Inc., NYC, 1972-73; 1st v.p., assoc. rsch. dir. Blyth Eastman Dillon & Co. Inc., NYC, 1974-76; dir. rsch. E.F. Hutton & Co., Inc., NYC, 1976-81, sr. v.p., 1976-80, exec. v.p., 1981-88; dir. Hutton Investment Mgmt., 1976-88; mng. dir. SLH Asset Mgmt. Shearson Lehman Hutton, Inc, NYC, 1988-90; sr. v.p. Martin E. Segal Co., NYC, 1990-92. Adj. assoc. prof. Columbia U. Grad. Sch. Bus., 1978-79; mem. faculty NY Inst. Fin., 1977-98; adj. prof. Adelphi U. Coll., 1993-98; rare book dealer, 1998-2006. Author: Socially Responsible Investing: How to Invest with Your Conscience, 1991, Standard and Poor's 401(k) Planning Guide, 1995. Home Phone: 212-300-4488. Personal E-mail: amiller202@aol.com.

MILLER, ALAN M., writer, educator, television host; b. NYC, July 24, 1934; s. Philip and Sylvia (Lubash) M.; children: Neil, Peter, Stephanie Cook, Douglas; m. Sharon A. Tanenbaum, Aug. 29, 1996; step-children: Holly Harouche, Becky Theodoratos. AB, Syracuse U., 1955, LLB, 1958, JD, 1968. Asst. counsel 3 joint legis. coms. NY State Legislature, 1968-70; counsel to minority Nassau County Bd. Suprs., 1974-75; prin. atty. editor Thomson/West, Eagan, Minn., 1985—2004. Faculty cinema divsn. Mpls. Coll., 1999—, Hofstra U., 1990-97, Discovery Ctr., 1990-94, NY Inst. Tech., Old Westbury, 1987-89; humanities faculty, Inver Hills CC, 2004—; bd. mem. Inver Hills Found., 2005—. Columnist South Shore Record, Woodmere, NY, Another Viewpoint, 1985-99 (awards NY Press Assn. 1988, 89, 94, Best column award 1992), Single-Minded, 1991-92, NY Bowler, 1991-93 (Bowling Mag. awards 1990-93, Best column award 1992), Nostalgia Mag., 1990-91; writer-editor USCAdvantage, 1995-99 (Immy awards 1996, 97); editor: Beyond the Bar, Thomson West Group, 2000-02, 05; contbr. articles to publs., including NY Times, Newsday, Newsday Mag., Mpls. Star-Tribune, St. Paul Pioneer Press, Humanistic Judaism; host and prodr. cable TV Access to Democracy, 1999—, TwinsTalk, 2003-; guest host Air Am. Radio, Minn., 2005—. Assembly dist. leader NY State Dem. Com., 1965-76; Commr. Village of Woodsburgh, NY, 1980, telecomm. com. City of Eagan, Minn., 1999-2005, chmn., 2002, vice-chmn., 2003; citizens adv. com. Minn. Twins, 2000-02; vice-chmn. Minn. Assn. Cable TV Adminstrs., 2002-03; presenter, Holocaust and Genocide Seminar, Met. State U., 2006, coord. Human Right & Social Justice Seminar,

2009. Recipient multiple awards for coverage of Persian Gulf War from Israel, 1991, Citizens Impact award Burnsville/Eagan Telecomm., 2003-04, Millenium Club award, 2004, Century Club award, 2005. Mem. Screenwriters Workshop, Ind. Film Pub., Assn. Holocaust Orgns., Burnsville Breakfast Rotary. Jewish. Home: 4316 Aries Ct Eagan MN 55123 Office: 1501 Hennepin Ave T-3068 Minneapolis MN 55403 Personal E-mail: alanmillermn@comcast.net.

MILLER, ALBERT, physician, researcher; b. NYC, July 28, 1936; m. Elaine Grant, June 6, 1959; children: Dina, Jeffrey, Neil, Michele. BA, U. Wis., 1955, MD, 1959. Diplomate Am. Bd. Internal Medicine, Am. Bd. Pulmonary Medicine; cert. expert pneumoconiosis Am. Bd. Radiology, Nat. Inst. Occupational Safety and Health. From assoc. clin. prof. to clin. prof. medicine Mt. Sinai Med. Sch., NYC, 1981—94, from assoc. clin. prof. to clin. prof. cmty. medicine, 1981—94; dir. pulmonary divsn. St. Vincent Cath. Med. Ctr. Bklyn. and Queens, 1994—2009; prof. clin. medicine N.Y. Med. Coll., 2003—. Editor, chief author: Pulmonary Function Tests in Clinical and Occupational Lung Disease, 1986, Pulmonary Function Tests: A Guide for the Student and House Officer, 1987; contbr. over 110 articles to profl. jours. Comdr. USPHS, 1962-64. Fellow ACP, Am. Coll. Chest Physicians; mem. Am. Thoracic Soc., Am. Pub. Health Assn., Phi Beta Kappa, Alpha Omega Alpha. Office: 42-23 Francis Lewis Blvd Bayside NY 11361 Office Phone: 718-670-4192.

MILLER, ALBERT J., cardiologist, internist; b. Chgo., 1922; MD, Northwestern U., 1946. Diplomate Am. Bd. Internal Medicine, Am. Bd. Cardiovascular Diseases. Intern Michael Reese Hosp., Chgo., 1945-46, resident in medicine, 1950, fellow in cardiology rsch. Cardiovascular Inst., 1948-50; resident in medicine VA Hosp., Hines, Ill., 1950-51; attending physician Northwestern Meml. Hosp., Chgo.; prof. clin. medicine, cardiology Northwestern U. Med. Sch. Author: The Lymphatics of the Heart, 1982, Diagnosis of Chest Pain, 1988, Chest Pain, When and When Not to Worry, 2005; has done basic rsch. on lymphatics of the heart. Fellow ACP, Am. Coll. Cardiology, Am. Fedn. for Clin. Rsch., Ctrl. Soc. for Clin. Rsch. Office: Clin Cardiol Group Ltd 333 Lakeside Pl Highland Park IL 60035 Personal E-mail: ajmiller22@sbcglobal.net.

MILLER, ALBERT JAY, retired library director; b. Beaver Falls, Pa., Dec. 7, 1927; s. Joseph Jefferson and Alberta Fae (Shaffer) Miller. BS, Geneva Coll., 1952; MLS, Rutgers U., 1958; postgrad., U. Chgo., 1960-61, U. Pitts., 1963-68, U. Mich., 1969. Libr. West Allegheny Jr. H.S., Imperial, Pa., 1959-60, Butler (Pa.) Area Sr. H.S., 1962-67, Pa. State U., New Kensington, 1969-89, tchr.-libr. continuing edn. dept., 1970-89, ret. libr. and info. svcs. dir. emeritus, 1989, prof. emeritus, mem. alumni. assn., 2009—. Author: A Selective Bibliography of Existentialism in Education and Related Topics, 1969, Confrontation, Conflict and Dissent, 1972, Death: A Bibliographical Guide, 1977; book and media rev. editor: Learning Today, 1978—; mem. editl. bd. Learning Today, 1979—. Tchr., judge Nat. Baton Twirling Assn., 1998; instr. water safety ARC, New Kensington, 1969—, Citizens Gen. Hosp., 1971—72; active Boy Scouts Am., 1970—; bd. dirs. Westmoreland County, Butler County mental health issues; mem. Allegheny-Kiski Human Rels. Coun., 1976—77; bd. dirs. Allegheny-Kiski Sr. Citizens Ctr., 1976—77, fund raising chmn., 1989—90, 2d v.p., 1997—98, pres., 1998—; mem., pub. rels. dir. Twirling Unlimited, Akron, Ohio; baton twirler Kensington Firemens Band; entrepreneur Al's Terrific Twirling Tricks-Catch It; book reader People's Libr., New Kensington; Sunday sch. tchr. Manchester Reformed Presbyn. Ch., 1970—, elder, clk. session, 1984—, Sabbath sch. supt., 1990; elder emeritus Eastvale Reformed Presbyn. Ch., mem. Christian edn. com., tchr. adult Sabbath sch., 2003; bd. corporators Geneva Coll., Beaver Falls, Pa., 1987—, vol. adv., 2008—. Named Twirling champion, N.Y. State Hall of Fame, 1999. Mem.: ALA, NEA (life), U.S. Twirling Assn., Pa. Libr. Assn., Pa. Edn. Assn. (life). Democrat. Home: 160 Crosswynds Dr Beaver Falls PA 15010-1182 Office Phone: 724-891-2369. Personal E-mail: millercrosswynds@comcast.net.

MILLER, ALISA DOROTHY NORTON, artist; b. Wellsville, NY, Nov. 18, 1920; d. Oak Duke and Gladys Virginia (Dexter) Norton; m. Robert E. Miller, Oct. 12, 1974; children from previous marriage: Richard, Linda, Michael. Student, Rochester Inst. Tech., 1968—69, San Jose State U., 1981; AA in Fine Arts, West Valley Coll., Saratoga, Calif., 1983. With Airline stewardess Colonial Airlines, NYC, 1944—45; art supr. Eastman Kodak Co., Rochester, 1962—70; exec. sec. 3M Corp., Rochester, 1970—72; med. sec., asst. Los Gatos, 1972—76; portrait artist Art Studio, Los Gatos, 1976—90. One-man shows include Norton Gallery, Rochester, 1972, exhibited in group shows at Glossinger Cultural Mus., Xenia, Ohio, 1964, Rosicrucian Mus., San Jose, Calif., 1981, Triton Mus., Santa Clara, Calif., 1982, Represented in permanent collections Glossinger Cultural Mus., numerous pvt. collections. Home and Office: 2561 Sadies Drive Hollister CA 95023-8320

MILLER, ALLAN JOHN, retired lawyer, oil industry executive; b. Beachwood, Ohio, Oct. 17, 1921; s. Carl Frederick and Rhoda (Warren) M.; m. Marjorie Hewitt Pirtle, Aug. 10, 1946; children: James W., Patricia Anne Costas. BBA, Fenn Coll., 1946; LLB, Western Res. U., 1948; D (hon.), Dyke Coll., Cleve., 1986. Bar: Ohio 1948. With Standard Oil Co., Ohio, 1948-77, treas., 1967-77; mem. firm Kiefer, Knecht, Rees, Meyer & Miller, Cleve., 1977-81. Dir. United Screw & Bolt Corp., 1977—97. Pres. South Euclid-Lyndhurst Recreation Com., Ohio, 1953-56; division chair unit plan divsn., United Way Cleve., 1966-69; Chmn. bd. dirs. Luth. Med. Ctr., Cleve., 1967-82; pres. Luth. Med. Ctr. Med. Staff Found., 1979-85; bd. dirs. Christian Residencies Found., 1972-77, St. Luke's Hosp. Assn., 1973-84; chmn. bd. trustees Dyke Coll., Cleve., 1971-86; vol. tax aide AARP, 2005-. Sgt. Corp. Engrs. US Army, 1943—46, Asiatic Pacific. Named Man of Yr., Cleve. State U. Alumni, 1982, Lutheran Med. Ctr., Cleve., 1984. Mem. Capri Isles Golf Club (Venice, Fla.). Presbyterian. Avocations: golf, bridge, music. Home: Apt 531 900 Tamiami Trl S Venice FL 34285-3627

MILLER, ALLEN RICHARD, retired mathematician; b. Bklyn., 1942; BS, Bklyn. Coll., 1965; MA, U. Md., 1971. Mathematician U.S. Naval Rsch. Lab., Washington, 1968-93; prof. George Washington U., Washington, 1992-95. Reviewer: Math. Revs. With U.S. Army, 1965-67.

MILLER, ALLEN TERRY, JR., lawyer; b. Alexandria, Va., Sept. 19, 1954; s. Allen Terry and Eleanor Jane (Thompson) M.; m. Maureen Ann Callaghan, June 22, 1985; children: Brendan Allen, Patrick Joseph, Brigit Eleanor. BA, U. Va., 1977; JD, Seattle U., 1982. Bar: Wash. 1982, US Dist. Ct. (we. dist.) Wash. 1982, US Ct. Appeals (9th cir.) 1985, US Dist. Ct. (ea. dist.) Wash. 1986, US Dist. Ct. (no. dist.) NY 1990, US Dist. Ct. (we. dist.) Mich. 1990, US Supreme Ct. 1990, US Ct. Appeals (2d and 6th cirs.) 1991. Legis. asst. Congressman Paul N. McCloskey Jr., Washington, 1978-79; asst. atty. gen. State of Washington, Olympia, Wash., 1982-92; prin. Connolly, Tacon & Meserve, 1992—2004; chief dep. prosecuting atty. environ. and land use Thurston County Crthse., 2004—06; atty. pvt. practice, Olympia, 2006—. Adj. prof. environ. law Seattle U., 1991—2001. Commr. Olympia Planning Commn., 1987-92, vice-chair, 1991, chair, 1992; sec. North Capitol Campus Heritage Pk. Devel. Assn., 1989-90, pres., 1991—; pres. Olympia Chorale and Light Opera Co., 1984-85; mem. St. Michael's Sch. Bd., 1993-96, chair, 1994-96, mem. Olympia Sch. Bd., 2008-; bd. dirs. South Sound YMCA, 1996—, Olympia Symphony, 1999-2001, Olympia Sch. Dist. Found., 1998-2002; pres. bd. dirs. United Way Thurston County, 1998-2003, pres. 2000-02, campaign chair, 2002-05; pres. Olympia Kato Sister City Assn., 2001-02, 2007-, bd. dirs. Olmpia Sch. Dist., 2008-. Recipient Merit award Am. Planning Assn., 1989, 92, Citizen of Yr. award Thurston County, 1998. Mem. ABA, Wash. Bar Assn. (mem. environ. law sect. 1984—, ct. rules com. 1985-89, jud. recommendation com. 1991-94, legis. com. 1994-97, ct. improvement com. 1997-2000, character and fitness com. 2002-06, vice chmn. 2004-06, fee arbitration panel, 2005—09), Thurston County Bar Assn.(pres., 2009-), Leadership Thurston County, Olympia-Thurston C. of C. (trustee 1996-00, pres. 1998), Rotary (Olympia, bd. dirs. 2002-08, pres. 2006-07). Roman Catholic. Avocations: mountain climbing, kayaking, tennis, piano. Office: 1801 W Bay Dr SW Ste 205 Olympia WA 98502 Home: PO Box 6059 Olympia WA 98507-6059 Office Phone: 360-754-9156. Business E-Mail: allen@atmlawoffice.com.

MILLER, ALWIN VERMAR, educational association administrator, consultant; b. Dardanelle, Ark., Oct. 12, 1922; s. William Marshall and Ollie Vernice (Green) M.; m. Patricia Jane Knox, Dec. 31, 1945; children: Carol, Alwin, William, Nitiya, Thomas. AA, Ark. Poly. Inst., 1939; BS, UCLA, 1947, BA with honors, 1947, MEd, 1948, EdD, 1956; cert., Internat. Inst. Ednl. Planning, (UNESCO), 1967—68. Instr. Chico (Calif.) State Coll., 1948-49; assoc. prof. So. Oreg. Coll., Ashland, 1949-57; edn. advisor AID, Washington, 1957-75; pvt. practice Upper Marlboro, Md., 1975—. Cons. in field. Lt. col. USAF, 1942-46. Mem. ASTD, Soc. Internat. Devel., Internat. Soc. Ednl. Planning, Res. Officers Assn. (v.p. DC dept. 1986-87, treas. 1991-97, pres.-elect 1997-98, pres. 1998-99), Reilly Meml. Scholarship com. 1999-2002, retirement com. 2002—), Am. Legion (post comdr. 1995-96, 99-2000, 2007-, dept. vice comdr. 1996-97, dept. comdr. 1997-98, vice chmn. nat. security 1999-2004), Mil. Order World Wars (chpt. pres. 1999-2002, nat. security com. 2002—, nat. legis. com. 2002—, sr. vice comdr. Dept. of Md., 2003-04, comdr. dept. Md. 2004—06), Nat. Sojourners (v.p. 2006-07, pres. 2007—), Mil. Order of Temple of Jerusalem, Forty and Eight (grand conducteur 2000-01), Lions, Masons (trustee Mt. Hermon lodge no. 179, 2005-06, treas. 2005—), Shriners, K.T., Phi Delta Kappa. Democrat. Office: 9544 Franklin Ave Lanham MD 20706-4010 Office Phone: 301-577-7277. Personal E-mail: avmiller46@verizon.net.

MILLER, ANDRE LLOYD, professional basketball player; b. Mar. 19, 1976; s. Andrea Robinson. BS in Sociology, U. Utah, Salt Lake City, 1998, grad. student, 1998—99. Guard Cleve. Cavaliers, 1999—2002, LA Clippers, 2002—03, Denver Nuggets, 2003—07, Phila. 76ers, 2007—09, Portland Trailblazers, 2009—. Recipient Gold medal, Goodwill Games, 1998; named to NBA All-Rookie Team, 1999—2000. Office: Portland Trailblazers 1 N Center Court St Portland OR 97227*

MILLER, ANDREA LYNN, communications educator; b. Lincoln, Nebr., Oct. 7, 1967; d. Benjamin Junior Warrenburg and Doris Ann Miller; m. Douglas Glenn Miller, Nov. 7, 1992; children: Lindsay Grace, Zachary Glenn. BA, Tex. A&M U., Coll. Sta., 1990; MS, Tex. Christian U., Ft. Worth, 2000; PhD, U. Mo., Columbia, 2003. Assoc. prodr. KBTX-TV, Bryan, Tex., 1990—92, reporter Coll. Sta., 1990—92; prodr. KVII-TV, Amarillo, Tex., 1992—93, anchor, 1992—93; field prodr. WFAA-TV - Prime Time Tex., Dallas, 1993—94, rschr., 1993—94; prodr. KTVT-TV, Ft. Worth, 1994—2000; advisor Tiger TV La. State U., 2003—07, asst. prof., manship sch. mass communication, 2003—, media cons., 2004—05. Contbr. articles to profl. jours. Mem. Dutchtown Primary Sch. Ptnrs. Edn., Geismar, La., 2003, First United Meth. Ch., Gonzales, La., 2008. Recipient 2nd prize, Assn. Edn. Journalism & Mass Comm., 2003; grantee grant, La. State U., 2005—06; Survey Rsch. grant, 2004, Doris Westmoreland Darden Professorship grant, 2004—05, Bart R. Swanson Meml. Professorship grant, 2006—07, 2007—08, Belo Corp. Professorship grant, 2008—. Mem.: Assn. Edn. Journalism & Mass Communication, Kappa Tau Alpha (life). Methodist. Avocations: travel, reading. Office: La State Univ Manship Sch Mass Communication 211 Journalism Bldg Baton Rouge LA 70803 Office Fax: 225-578-2125. Business E-Mail: almiller@lsu.edu.

MILLER, ANDREA R., application developer, educator; b. Chgo., 1954; BA in Early Childhood Edn., Northwestern U., Evanston, Ill. Teaching asst. St. James Elem. Sch.; various positions in ins., banking and tech. sales fields; founder The Learning Club, San Francisco; with Social Security Adminstrn.; lectr. computer applications Howard CC Ctr. Workforce Devel., Johns Hopkins Sch. Continuing Studies Lifelong Learning Divsn.; founder, pres. Data Acqsys, Inc.; WebEOC trainer Va., Washington, Md. Instructional designer WebLearningIT, 2003. Statewide coord. Va. Congressman Dennis Kucinich's Presdl. Campaign, regional coord., MoveOn.org; mem. Chesterfield County Dem. Com., Va. Anti-War Network. Mem.: Progressive Dems. America. Democrat. Office: Data Acqsys Inc 10608 Abigail Dr Columbia MD 21044 Office Phone: 410-740-0157. Office Fax: 443-583-0070. Business E-Mail: amiller@weblearningit.com.

MILLER, ANDREW PICKENS, lawyer; b. Fairfax, Va., Dec. 21, 1932; s. Francis Pickens and Helen (Hill) M.; m. Penelope Farthing, Nov. 18, 1990; children: Julia Lane, Andrew Pickens, Elise Givhan, Winfield Scott, Lucia Holcombe. AB magna cum laude, Princeton U., 1954; postgrad., New Coll., Oxford U., Eng., 1954-55; LLB, U. Va., 1960. Bar: Va. 1960, U.S. Supreme Ct. 1967, D.C. 1979. Asso. Penn, Stuart & Stuart, 1960-62; ptnr. Penn, Stuart & Miller, Abingdon, Va., 1963-69; atty. gen. State of Va., 1970-77; ptnr. Mays, Valentine, Davenport & Moore, Richmond, Va., 1977-78, Dickstein, Shapiro, Morin & Oshinsky, LLP, Washington, 1979—2002, Powell Goldstein LLP, Washington, 2002—08, Hunton Williams LLP, 2009—. Pres., Young Democratic Clubs Va., 1966-67; chmn. Washington County Dem. Com., 1967-69; Dem. nominee for U.S. Senate from Va., 1978; bd. dirs. Barter Found., 1962-69; trustee King Coll., 1966-74; mem. adv. bd. Ams. for Effective Law Enforcement, 1973-77, Ctr. for Oceans Law and Policy, 1975-79; vice-chmn. Va. Bd. Corrections, 1983-86. Served to 1st lt. AUS, 1955-57. Fellow Am. Bar Found., ABA (ho. dels. 1971-76, action commn. to reduce ct. costs and delay 1979-84, commn. on pub. understanding about the law 1992-95); mem. So. Conf. Attys. Gen. (vice chmn. 1972-73, chmn. 1973-74), Nat. Assn. Attys. Gen. (exec. com. 1973-74, chmn. antitrust com. 1971-76, Wyman Meml. award 1976), Va. Bar Assn. (chmn. young lawyers sect. 1967-68, exec. com. 1985-88), Am. Judicature Soc. (bd. dirs. 1973-76, exec. com. 1974-76), Soc. of Cin. (Va. standing com. 1986-89, 93-96, asst. sec. gen., 1992-95, sec. gen. 1995-98), Nat. Maritime Heritage Found. (bd. dirs. 2005-, v.p. 2008-), The John Marshall Found. (pres. 1987-89), Phi Beta Kappa, Omicron Delta Kappa. Presbyterian. Home: 1503 35th St NW Washington DC 20007-2729 Office: Hunton Williams LLP 1900 K St NW Washington DC 20006-1109 Office Phone: 202-419-2126. Business E-Mail: amiller@hunton.com.

MILLER, ANTHONY BERNARD, physician, researcher; b. Woodford, Eng., Apr. 17, 1931; married, 1952; 5 children. BA, U. Cambridge, 1952, MB, BChir, 1955; MA, 2004, MD, 2006. House officer Oldchurch Hosp., Romford, Eng., 1955-57; med. registrar Luton and Dunstable Hosp., Eng., 1959-62; mem. sci. staff Med. Research Council Tb and Chest Disease Unit, London, 1962-71; assoc. prof. preventive medicine and biostats. U. Toronto, 1972-76, prof., 1976-96, chmn. dept., 1992-96, dir. grad. program in epidemiology, 1986-91; dir. epidemiology unit Nat. Cancer Inst. Can., Toronto, 1971-86; dir. Nat. Breast Screening Study, 1980—, WHO Collaborating Ctr. on Evaluation of Screening for Cancer, 1991-2000; prof. emeritus pub. health scis., 1997—; head divsn. of clin. Epidemiology German Cancer Rsch. Ctr., Heidelberg, 1999—2003; assoc. dir. rsch. Dalla Lana Sch. Pub. Health, 2009—. Nat. Health scientist, 1988-93; mem. working cadre Bladder Cancer Project, U.S., 1973-75; mem. epidemology com. Breast Cancer Task Force, U.S., 1973-77, chmn., 1975-77; mem. Fed. Task Force Cervical Cytol. Screening, Can., 1974-76, 80-81, Union Internat. Contre le Cancer com., controlled therapeutic trials, 1978-82, Multidisciplinary project breast cancer, 1978-82, chmn. project on screening, 1982-93; mem. sci. council Internat. Agy. Research Cancer, Lyon, 1981-85, chmn., 1985; mem. com. on diet, nutrition and cancer NRC of U.S., 1980-83, mem. oversight com. radioepidemiologic tables, 1983-84, com. on diet and health, 1986-89, com. on dietary guidelines implementation, 1988-91, chmn. com. on environmental epidemiology, 1990-94; chmn. Ont. Task Force on Primary Prevention of Cancer, 1994-95; mem. Coun. Can. Strategy Cancer Control, 2000-06; mem. adv. coun. Can. Partnership Against Cancer, 2007—. Served with RAF, 1957-59. Mem. Can. Oncology Soc. (sec.-treas. 1975-79, pres. 1980-81), Soc. Epidemiology Research, Internat. Epidemiology Assn., Am. Soc. Preventive Oncology (pres. 1983-85), Am. Coll. Epidemiology (bd. dirs. 1987-89). Office Phone: 416-946-0911. Personal E-mail: ab.miller@sympatico.ca. Business E-Mail: ab.miller@utoronto.ca.

MILLER, ANTHONY WILDER (TONY MILLER), federal agency administrator; m. Carole Miller; 1 child. BS in Indsl. Engring., Purdue U., West Lafayette, Ind., 1989; MBA, Stanford U., Calif., 1992. Western regional mktg. mgr. Delco Electronics; ptnr. McKinsey & Co.; exec. v.p. ops. LRN Corp., 2003—06; oper. ptnr. Silver Lake, 2007—09; dep. sec. US Dept. Edn., Washington, 2009—. Cons. LA Unified Sch. Dist., 1997—2000, Santa Monica-Malibu Unified Sch. Dist., 2001; ex officio mem. budget and fin. com. Bd. Edn. of City of LA, 2002, 03. Office: US Dept Edn 400 Maryland Ave SW Washington DC 20202*

MILLER, ARJAY, retired university dean; b. Shelby, Nebr., Mar. 4, 1916; s. Rawley John and Mary Gertrude (Schade) M.; m. Frances Marion Fearing, Aug. 18, 1940; children: Kenneth Fearing, Ann Elizabeth (Mrs. James Olstad). BS with highest honors, UCLA, 1937; postgrad., U. Calif., Berkeley, 1938-40; LLD (hon.), Washington U., St. Louis, 1964; LLD, Whitman Coll., Walla Walla, Wash., 1965, U. Nebr., 1965, Ripon Coll., Wis., 1980. Teaching asst. U. Calif. at Berkeley, 1938-40; research technician Calif. State Planning Bd., 1941; economist Fed. Res. Bank San Francisco, 1941-43; asst. treas. Ford Motor Co., 1946-53, controller, 1953-57, v.p., controller, 1957-61, v.p. finance, 1961-62, v.p. of staff group, 1962-63, pres., 1963-68, vice chmn., 1968-69; dean Grad. Sch. Bus., Stanford U., 1969-79, emeritus, 1979—. Former chmn. Automobile Mfrs. Assn., Econ. Devel. Corp. Greater Detroit; councillor The Conf. Bd.; past chmn., life trustee Urban Inst.; mem. Public Adv. Commn. on US Trade Policy, 1968-69, Trilateral Commn., 1977-83; Pres.'s Nat. Commn. on Productivity, 1970-74. Trustee Internat. Exec. Svc. Coirps.; hon. trustee The Brookings Instn.; dir. emeritus S.R.I. Internat.; former chmn. Pub. Policy Inst. Calif.; former pres. Detroit Press Club Found.; former chmn. Bay Area Coun. Capt. USAAF, 1943—46. Recipient Alumnus of Year Achievement award UCLA, 1964, Disting. Nebraskan award, 1968, Nat. Industry Leader award B'nai B'rith, 1968; named to Automotive Hall of Fame, 2006. Fellow Am. Acad. Arts and Scis. Clubs: Pacific Union, Bohemian. Presbyterian. Home Phone: 650-851-1217.

MILLER, ARNOLD, electronics executive; b. NYC, May 8, 1928; s. Sam and Mina (Krutalow) M.; m. Beverly Shayne, Feb. 5, 1950; children: Debra Lynn, Marla Jo, Linda Sue BS in Chemistry, UCLA, 1948, PhD in Phys. Chemistry, 1951; DHL (hon.), So. Calif. Coll. Optometry, 2007. Registered profl. engr., Calif. Rsch. phys. chemist Wrigley Rsch. Co., Chgo., 1951; supr. phys. chemistry Armour Rsch. Found., Chgo., 1951-54, mgr. chemistry and metals, 1954-56; chief materials sci. dept. Borg-Warner Rsch. Ctr., Des Plaines, Ill., 1956-59; dir. rsch. Rockwell Corp., Anaheim, Calif., 1959-66, dir. microelec. ops., 1967-68; group exec. materials ops. Whittaker Corp., LA, 1968-70; pres. Theta Sensors, Orange, Calif., 1970-72; mgr. xeroradiography Xerox Corp., Pasadena, Calif., 1972-75, corp. dir. rsch. and adv. devel. Stamford, Conn., 1975-78, El Segundo, Calif., 1978-81, v.p. electronics div., 1981-84, pres. electronics div., 1984-87, corp. officer Stamford, 1984-87; pres. Tech. Strategy Group, Fullerton, Calif., 1987—; prodr. Remembrance Films, 2004—. Bd. dirs. Spectro Diode Labs, San Jose, Calif., Semicondr. Rsch. Corp., Colorep Inc., Carlsbad, Calif.; bd. dirs., chair audit com. Merisel Computer Products, El Segundo, Calif., lead dir., 1989—; mem. vis. com. on materials sci. U. So. Calif., L.A., 1966-68; mem. State of Calif. Micro Bd., 1984-2000. Editorial adv. bd. Advances in Solid State Chemistry; co-editor Electronics Industry Development, Trends in IT, Trends In IT; contbr. numerous articles to profl. jours. and monographs; patentee in field. Mem. civilian adv. group Dept. Commerce, 1959-60; mem. 5th decade com., also adv. com. on engring. and mgmt. program UCLA, 1984-; mem. com. on scholarly commn. with People's Republic of China, Tech. Transfer Task Force, Nat. Acad. Sci., Washington, 1985; bd. dirs. Orange County Pacific Symphony, Fullerton, Calif., 1982-; mem. univ.'s adv. bd. Calif. State U.-Fullerton, 1986-2006, chair, 1991-2006; v.p., bd. dirs. Heritage Pointe Home for the Aging, 1987-97; chmn. Indsl. Assocs. sch. engring. and computer sci. Calif. State U., 1987-97, trustee continuing learning ctr., 1993-, cmmencement spkr., 2009; mem. Overseas Devel. Coun., 1988-; mem. Nat. Com. U.S.-China Rels., 1990-; trustee So. Calif. Coll. of Optometry, 1996-, sec.-treas. 1997-2003; bd. mem. Cmty. Found., 1995-, v.p., 1997-. Recipient Sci. Merit award Navy Bur. Ordnance/Armour Rsch. Found., 1952, IR-100 award, 1964, 69, U. medal Inst. Gerontology Calif. State U., Fullerton, 2002; named Hon. Alumnus Calif. State U., Fullerton, 1996, Hon. Dr. Humane Letters So. Calif. Coll. Optometry, 2007. Fellow AAAS; mem. IEEE, Am. Chem. Soc., So. Calif. Coalition Edn. Mfg. Engring. (bd. dirs. 1994-98, ind. living partnership, 2009-), Independent Living Partnership (bd. dirs. 2009-), Elec. Industry Assn. (past chmn. microelectronics), Phi Beta Kappa, Sigma Xi, Phi Lamda Upsilon Home: 505 Westchester Pl Fullerton CA 92835-2706 Office: Tech Strategy Group PO Box 5769 Fullerton CA 92838-0769 Home Phone: 714-738-0368; Office Phone: 714-447-8887. Business E-Mail: amiller@fullerton.edu.

MILLER, ARTHUR JOSEPH, neurophysiology and craniofacial biology researcher; b. San Francisco, Jan. 18, 1943; s. Arthur Joseph and Theresa (Walczak) M.; m. Marilyn Loushin, Aug. 21, 1965; children: Garreth, Ashleigh, Heath. BA, San Jose State U., 1965; postgrad., Brain Research Inst., 1966-70; PhD, UCLA, 1970. Asst. prof. U. Ill., Chgo., 1970-75; asst. prof. growth devel., physiology U. Calif., San Francisco, 1975-78, assoc. prof., 1978-84, prof., 1984—. Author: Craniomandibular Muscles: Their Role in Form and Function; mem. editorial bd. Dysphagia; reviewer for Brain Rsch., Exptl. Neurology, Archives Oral

Biology, Am. Jour. Orthodontics, others; ad hoc reviewer NIH, Can. Med. Rsch. Coun., NSF; contbr. articles to profl. jours. Mem. Neurosci. Soc., Internat. Assn. for Dental Research, Internat. Brain Research Assn., Dysphagia Rsch. Soc., Omicron Rho Upsilon. Democrat. Roman Catholic. Home: 160 Leslie Dr San Carlos CA 94070-3461 Office: U Calif Dept Orofacial Scis San Francisco CA 94143-0438

MILLER, ARTHUR MADDEN, lawyer, investment banker, brokerage house executive; b. Greenville, SC, Apr. 10, 1953; s. Charles Frederick and Kathryn Irene (Madden) M.; m. Roberta Beck Connolly, Apr. 17, 1993; children: Isabella McIntyre Madden, Roberta Beck Connolly. AB in History, Princeton U., 1973; MA in History, U. NC, 1976; JD with distinction, Duke U., 1978; LLM in Taxation, NYU, 1982. Bar: NY 1979, US Dist. Ct. (so. dist.) NY 1979. Assoc. Mudge Rose Guthrie Alexander & Ferdon, NYC, 1978—85; v.p. pub. fin. Goldman, Sachs & Co., NYC, 1985—. Trustee Convent of the Sacred Heart, NY, 2003—08, St. Andrew's Sch., Del., 2003—, Cathedral Sch. St. John Divine, NYC, 2008—; adv. bd. Mary Baldwin Coll., Staunton, Va., 1982—86; trustee Princeton U. Rowing Assn., NJ, 1980—, pres., 1986—95; trustee Rebecca Kelly Dance Co., NYC, 1984—86; steward Power Ten, 1992—95. Mem. ABA (tax sect. com. on tax exempt financing 1985—), Nat. Assn. Bond Lawyers (lectr. 1985—), Securities Industry & Fin. Market Assn. (cons. 1985—), Practising Law Inst. (lectr. 1980, editor/author course materials 1980—), Bond Attys. Workshop (editor/author course material 1983—, lectr. 1983—), Princeton Club. Office: Goldman Sachs & Co 85 Broad St New York NY 10004-2456

MILLER, AUDREY THORNTON, retired vice principal; b. Glassboro, NJ, June 22, 1937; d. Aubrey and Rebecca Thornton; m. Kenneth C. Miller, Sr., Nov. 20, 1967; children: Yvette A. Rudd, Kenneth C. Jr. BS, Cheyney U., 1963; MEd, Rutgers U., 1974; EdD, Nova Southeastern U., 1998. Cert. prin., supr. NJ. Tchr. Camden Bd. Edn., NJ, 1963-74, asst. to prin., 1974-97, vice prin. H.C. Sharp Sch., 1997-2000; ret., 2000. Author Using the Writing Process to Enchance Elementary Students Writing Proficiency and Teachers' Instructional Strategies, 1998; advisor Theta Chi City Wide chpt. Rowan U., 1980-85, Sharp Sch. Safety Patrol, Camden, 1991-95, Network III Drug Program, Camden, 1993-96; adv. bd. Carter's Psychol. Svc., Camden County, 1995—. V.p. Garden City Alumnae of Delta Sigma Theta Sorority, Inc., Sicklerville, NJ, 1989-91; chair Career Women's Ministry, St. Matthews Bapt. Ch. Williamstown, NJ, 1993-96, chief ednl. svcs. comty. devel. ctr. programs SMCDC, 2003-07, dir. tutoring svcs., 2007-; mem. Camden County LWV. Recipient Set a Good Example award Gov. Christie Whitman, Trenton, 1994, Disting. Achievement award, Camden Bd. Edn., 1994, 96, Proclamation, Bd. Chosen Freeholders, Camden County, 2000, Cheyney U. Alumni Outstanding Service Award, 2003. Mem. NAACP, AFL-CIO, Cheyney U. Alumni Assn. (life, area rep. S. Jersey chpt., 2000-), Nova Southeastern U. Alumni Assn., Rutgers U. Alumni, Black Women's Edn. Alliance (Educator's award 1992), Camden City Fedn. Sch. Adminstrs., NJ State Fedn. Colored Women's Club (Outstanding Svc. in Edn. award 2000, Kappa Educators award 2007, Ednl. Appreciation award 2007), Delta Sigma Theta (life, mem. ea. region leadership team 2005), Kappa Delta Pi. Democrat. Avocations: interior decorating, travel, tennis. Home: 4 Pierson Pl Sicklerville NJ 08081-2006 Personal E-mail: milerau@aol.com.

MILLER, BARBARA KENTON, retired librarian; b. NYC, Sept. 21, 1934; d. Robert Alfred and Kathleen Hope (Levy) Kenton; m. John Arnold Miller, June 15, 1955; children: Valerie Ann Miller, Jennifer Karen Kraft. BA distinction, Finch Coll., 1960; MLS, C.W. Post, 1976. Cert. libr., N.Y. Libr., cons. archivist Coun. Fgn. Rels., NYC, 1977—2000; ret., 2000. Cons. archivist Coun. on Fgn. Rels. Mem. Spl. Librs. Assn., Beta Phi Mu. Avocations: dogs, golf. Office: Coun Fgn Rels 58 E 68 St New York NY 10021-5953 Personal E-mail: bkmiller55@aol.com.

MILLER, BARRY RIXMANN, lawyer; b. Tempe, Ariz., Feb. 8, 1945; s. Ray E. and Dorothy (Rixmann) Miller; m. Patricia A. Cunningham, Aug. 10, 1968; children: Christy, Brandy Ann. BS with honors, U. Ill., 1967, JD with honors, 1970. Bar: Ill. 1970, Tex. 1972, US Tax Ct. 1972. Mem. firm Andrews & Kurth, Houston, 1972—79, ptnr., 1979, mgmt. com., 1990—92; ptnr., co-head tax law sect. Vinson & Elkins, LLP, 2003—05; treas. Askew PTO, 1980. Contbr. articles to profl. jours. Served to 1st lt. US Army, 1970—72. Decorated Army Commendation medal US Army; recipient Bronze Tablet, U. Ill., 1967; James scholar, 1963. Mem.: ABA (sect. on taxation), Tex. Bar Assn., Phi Alpha Mu, Beta Alpha Psi, Order of Coif, Sigma Chi. Republican. Office: Vinson & Elkins LLP First City Tower 1001 Fannin St, Ste 2300 Houston TX 77002 Office Phone: 713-758-4438. Business E-Mail: brmiller@velaw.com.

MILLER, BEVERLY A(NN), reference librarian, professor; b. Tulsa, Dec. 22, 1941; d. Buford Maxwell and Wilda (Durfee) M. BA, Thiel Coll., Greenville, Pa., 1964; MA in Libr. Sci., U. Denver, 1965; MA in History, Boise U., Idaho, 2003. Periodicals libr. Minot (N.D.) State Coll., 1966-67; asst. libr. Rocky Mountain Coll., Billings, Mont., 1967-68; circulation libr. Boise (Idaho) State Coll., 1968-71; reference and interlibr. libr. Boise (Idaho) State U., 1971—, bd. dirs., faculty advisor Women's Ctr., 1992-93. Bd. dirs. Higher Edn. Resource Svcs./West, Boise, 1991—. Book reviewer Libr. Jour., 1975-95; author, adv. bd. mem. Sage Woman Mag., 1980's; contbg. editor: Idaho Women in History, 1990. Mem. AAUP (bd. dirs. Boise State U. chpt. 1994-2003, treas.), NOW (bd. dirs. Boise 1978-79, Idaho 1979-80), Am. Fedn. Tchrs. (v.p. 1979-81 Boise State U.), Pacific N.W. Libr. Assn., Pacific N.W. Women's Studies Assn., Idaho Libr. Assn., Idaho Womens Network (bd. dirs. 1987-92), Snake River Alliance (bd. dirs. 1986). Avocations: women's history, dog sports. Home Phone: 208-343-5329.

MILLER, BEVERLY WHITE, former college president, educational consultant; b. Willoughby, Ohio, 1923; d. Joseph Martin and Marguerite Sarah (Storer) White; m. Lynn Martin Miller, Oct. 11, 1945 (dec. 1986); children: Michaela Ann, Craig Martin, Todd Daniel, Cass Timothy, Simone Agnes. AB, Western Res. U., 1945; MA, Mich. State U., 1957; PhD, U. Toledo, 1967; LHD (hon.), Coll. St. Benedict, St. Joseph, Minn., 1979; LLD (hon.), U. Toledo, 1988. Chem. and biol. researcher, 1945-57; tchr. schs. in Mich., also Mercy Sch. Nursing, St. Lawrence Hosp., Lansing, Mich., 1957-58; mem. chemistry and biology faculty Mary Manse Coll., Toledo, 1958-71, dean grad. div., 1968-71, exec. v.p., 1968-71; acad. dean Salve Regina Coll., Newport, RI, 1971-74; pres. Coll. St. Benedict, St. Joseph, Minn., 1974-79, Western New Eng. Coll., Springfield, Mass., 1980-96, pres. emerita, 1996—. Higher edn. cons., 1996—; cons. U.S. Office Edn., 1980; mem. Springfield Pvt. Industry Coun./Regional Employment Bd., exec. com., 1982-94; mem. Minn. Pvt. Coll. Coun., 1974-79, sec., 1974-75, vice chmn., 1975-76, chmn., 1976-77; cons. in field. Author papers and books in field. Corporator Mercy Hosp., Springfield, Mass. Recipient President's citation St. John's U., Minn., 1979; also various service awards; named disting. alumna of yr. U. Toledo, 1998. Mem. AAAS, Am. Assn. Higher Edn., Assn. Cath. Colls. and Univs. (exec. bd.), Internat. Assn. Sci. Edn., Nat. Assn. Ind. Colls. and Univs. (govt. rels. adv. com., bd. dirs. 1990-93, exec. com. 1991-93, treas. 1992-93), Nat. Assn. Biology Tchrs., Assn. Ind. Colls. and Univs. of Mass. (exec. com. 1981-96, vice chmn. 1985-86, chmn. 1986-87), Nat. Assn. Rsch. Sci. Tchg., Springfield C. of C. (bd. dirs.), Am. Assn. Univ. Adminstrs. (bd. dirs. 1989-92), Delta Kappa Gamma, Sigma Delta Epsilon. Office: 6713 County Road M Delta OH 43515-9778

MILLER, BILL, III, (WILLIAM HERBERT MILLER), hedge fund manager; b. Fla., 1950; m. Leslie Miller, 1974. BA in European Hist. & Econs., Washington & Lee U., Lexington, Va., 1972; student, Johns Hopkins U., Balt. Cert. CFA 1986. Treas. J.E. Baker Co., York, Pa., 1977—81; dir. rsch. Legg Mason, Inc., Balt., 1981—85, co-mgr. value trust mutual fund, 1982—90, portfolio mgr. Legg Mason Value Trust (LMVTX), 1990—, chmn., chief investment officer Legg Mason Capital Mgmt., Inc. Vice chmn. bd. trustees Santa Fe Inst., 2001—05, chmn., 2005—. Officer Mil. Intelligence Corps US Army, 1972—75, Europe. Named Greatest Money Mgr. of the 90's, Money mag., Domestic Equity Mgr. of Yr., Morningstar, Inc., 1998, Fund Mgr. of Decade, Morningstar.com, 1999; named one of 30 Most Influential People in Investing, SmartMoney, Best Fund Managers 2006, BusinessWeek.com; named to All-Century Investment Team, Barron's Fin. News, 1999. Office: Legg Mason Capital Management Inc 100 Light St Baltimore MD 21202-1099*

MILLER, BODE (SAMUEL BODE MILLER), professional skier; b. Easton, NH, Oct. 12, 1977; s. Woody and Jo (Kenney) Miller. Attended, Carrabassett Valley Acad. Mem. US Ski Team, 1996—2007; founder Team Am., 2007—; co-founder The Turtle Ridge Found., 2005—; co-founder, CEO SkiSpace.com, 2007—. Co-author (with Jack McEnany): Bode: Go Fast, Be Good, Have Fun, 2005. Recipient Giant Slalom Title, World Cup, 2004, Super G Title, 2005, 2006, Six US Nat. Championship Medals, Silver medal, giant slalom, XIX Olympic Games, Salt Lake City, 2002, Silver medal, combined, 2002, Silver Medal, Two Gold Medals, World Championships, 2003, Two Gold Medals, 2005, Super G Title, US Alpine Championships, 2007; named Combined Champion, World Cup, 2003, 2008, Overall Champion, 2005, 2008. Achievements include first US skier in 22 yrs. to win World Cup overall championship, 2005, the most successful US skier with 28 World Cup victories. Office: The Turtle Ridge Found 392 Streeter Pond Rd Sugar Hill NH 03586 E-mail: bode@bodemillerusa.com.

MILLER, BONNIE SEWELL, marketing professional, writer; b. Junction City, Ky., July 24, 1932; d. William Andrew and Lillian Irene (McCowan) Sewell; m. William Gustave Tournade Jr., Nov. 5, 1950 (div. 1974); children: Bonnie Sue Tournade Zaner, William Gustave III, Sharon Irene Tournade Leach; m. Bruce George Miller, Nov. 15, 1981. BA, U. South Fla., 1968, MA, 1973. Cert. tchr., Fla. Chair dept. English Tampa Cath. H.S., Fla., 1972—78; tchr. Clearwater H.S., Fla., 1978—80; mgr. prodn. svcs. Paradyne Corp., Largo, Fla., 1980—83; freelance writer, cons. Tampa, 1983—84; mgr. product documentation PPS, Inc., Largo, 1984—86, mgr. mktg. comm., 1986—87; writer Nixdorf Computer Corp., Tampa, 1988—89; mktg. dir. Suncoast Schs. Fed. Credit Union, Tampa, 1989—98; co-owner, v.p., writer, cons. Need-A-Writer, Inc., Tampa, 1998—; instr. profl. and tech. writing and comm. for engrs. U. South Fla., 2004—. Instr. English, Hillsborough C.C., Tampa, Fla., 1975—87; cons. bus. writing Coronet Instrnl. Media Writing Project, 1976, Nat. Mgmt. Assn., 1981—87; adj. instr. profl. writing U. South Fla., 1993; adj. instr. tech. writing U. Tampa, 2002—, English instr., 2002—; adj. instr. profl. and tech. writing U. South Fla., 2004—. Author: Youth Financial Literacy, 1999, Effective Business Writing for Credit Unions, 2000, Meeting for a Lifetime, 2007; contbr. articles to profl. jours. Bd. dir. SERVE, Tampa, Credit Union Mktg. Assn. Coun., Sing Parent Displaced Homemakers Group; legis. chair Tampa PTA, 1965; judge speech contest Am. Legion, Tampa, 1976; vol. North Tampa Vol. Libr., 1988. NEH fellow, 1975. Mem. NAFE, Soc. Tech. Communicators, Am. Assn. Bus. Women, U. South Fla. Alumni Assn., Kappa Delta Pi. Democrat. Methodist. Avocations: writing, sewing, gardening, travel, decorating. Home and Office: 516 2d Ave SE Lutz FL 33549 Business E-Mail: bmiller115@tampabay.rr.com.

MILLER, BRAD (RALPH BRADLEY MILLER), United States Representative from North Carolina; b. Fayetteville, NC, May 19, 1953; s. Nathan David and Margaret Virginia (Hale) Miller; m. Esther Susan Hall, Dec. 19, 1981. BS in Polit. Sci., U. NC, Chapel Hill, 1975; MSc in Polit. Sci., London Sch. Econs., 1978; JD, Columbia U., 1979. Bar: NC 1979, US Dist. Ct. (ea. dist.) NC 1980, US Ct. Appeals (4th cir. 1980), US Dist. Ct. (mid. dist.) NC 1983. Law clk. to Hon. J. Dickson Phillips, Jr. US 4th Cir. Ct. Appeals, 1979-80; assoc. Allen, Steed & Allen, Raleigh, NC, 1980-82, Barringer, Allen & Pinnix, Raleigh, NC, 1982-84, LeBoeuf, Lamb, Leiby & MacRae, Raleigh, NC, 1985-88; prin. Nichols, Miller & Sigmon, Raleigh, NC, 1988-90; pvt. practice Raleigh, NC, 1991—; mem. NC State Ho. Reps., 1992—96, NC State Senate, 1997—2002, chmn. sen. jud. II com.; mem. US Congress from 13th NC dist., 2003—. Mem. fin. svcs. com. US Congress, mem. fgn. affairs com., mem. sci. and tech. com., mem. internat. rels. com., chmn. subcommittee on investigations and oversight. Chmn. Wake County Dem. Com., 1985-87; mem. state exec. com. NC Dem. Com., 1985-89, 91-97; mem. NC Environ. Rev. Commn., 1994-95, mem. sentencing and policy adv. com. Mem. ATLA, NC Bar Assn., Wake County Bar Assn., NC Acad. Trial Lawyers, Am. Judicature Soc. Democrat. Episcopalian. Office: US House Reps 1722 Longworth House Office Bldg Washington DC 20515 Office Phone: 202-225-3032. Office Fax: 202-225-0181.*

MILLER, BRAD (BRADLEY ALLEN MILLER), professional basketball player; b. Ft. Wayne, Ind., Apr. 12, 1976; s. Rosie Miller. BS in Restaurant/Hotel, Instn. and Tourism Mgmt., Purdue U., Ind., 1998. Ctr. Bini Viaggi Livorno, Italy, 1998, Charlotte Hornets, 1998—2000, Chgo. Bulls, 2000—01, 2009—, Ind. Pacers, 2001—03, Sacramento Kings, 2003—09. Mem. US Men's World Basketball Team, 1998, 2006. Active Big Brothers and Big Sisters. Recipient Bronze medal, FIBA World Championships, 1998, 2006; named to Ea. Conf. All-Star Team, NBA, 2003, We. Conf. All-Star Team, 2004. Office: Chgo Bulls United Ctr 1901 W Madison St Chicago IL 60612*

MILLER, BRENDA, Johrei practitioner; b. Gary, Ind., Dec. 31, 1957; d. Earl Miller and Essie Birdsong Hill; m. Petion Michael Nemorin, Feb. 14, 1987 (div. Mar. 1989); 1 child, Chris. BA, Howard U., 1979; JD, U. West L.A., 1995. Domestic violence cert. adv. Haven Hills Shelter, 1999. 60 Minutes archives asst. CBS Broadcast Ctr., NYC, 1978; mdse. supr. Universal Studio Tour, Universal City, Calif., 1981—83; employment liaison specialist Mayor's Office for the Disabled, LA, 1984—86; ind. sales contractor various orgns., LA, 1988—98; nutrition team mem. Whole Foods Market, Woodland Hills, Calif., 1999—2001; in-house security LA Family Housing Shelter, North Hollywood, 2002—04; Home Mag. staff writer Womens Care Cottage Shelter, North Hollywood, Calif., 2002—04; sr. investment analyst 1031 Commercial Exchange, Beverly Hills, Calif., 2003—05; Johrei practitioner Inunome Assn. Calif. Ctr., 2006—. Resident adv. com. mem. Haven Hills Shelter, Canoga Park, Calif.; mentor for youth prison Calif. Youth Authority, Camarillo; adv. for women's prison Calif. Instn. for Women, Corona. Author poetry. Pro-bono legal work San Fernando Valley Legal Aide, Pacoima, Calif., 1994; pub. rels. co-chair Lawyers for Human Rights, LA, 1995; domestic abuse response team Haven Hills Shelter/L.A. Police Dept., Van Nuys, Calif., 1999; Infinite Way meditation tape group leader, 1998—. Recipient Wiley M. Manuel for Pro Bono Legal Svc., State Bar Calif., 1994—95, Battered Women's Svc. award, Convicted Women Against Abuse, Calif. State Prison, 2000, Courageous Achievers award, Billy Blanks Found., 2001. Mem.: Divine Light Program, Alpha Kappa Alpha (Sigma Lamda Omega chpt. San Fernando Valley). Democrat. Office Phone: 310-836-3691.

MILLER, BRETT, communications educator, consultant; b. Valparaiso, Ind., Sept. 12, 1964; s. George and Dona Miller; m. Betsy Wammack; children: Cassidy, Carsen. PhD, U. Mo., Columbia, 1999. Tchr.-debate coach Parkview HS, Springfield, Mo., 1989—98; prof. comm. SW Bapt. U., Bolivar, Mo., 1998—. Author: (book) Divine Apology: The Discourse of Religious Image Restoration. Team leader Obama's Campaign Change, Springfield, 2008. Independent. Avocations: singing, writing. Office: SW Bapt Univ 1600 Univ Ave Bolivar MO 65613 Business E-Mail: bmiller@sbuniv.edu.

MILLER, BRIAN A., lawyer, electric power industry executive; BA, Boston Coll.; JD, Univ. Conn. Counsel Chadbourne & Parke LLP; v.p., dep. gen counsel, corp. sec. AES Corp., 2001—05, gen. counsel & corp. sec., 2005—. Office: AES Corporation 11th Fl 4300 Wilson Blvd Arlington VA 22203*

MILLER, BRIAN DANIEL, music educator, organist; b. Charlotte, NC, Nov. 3, 1971; s. Vincent LaFollette and Jettie Rea Miller. BA in History, U. NC, 1994, B in Music Edn., 1995. Band tchr. Louisburg HS, NC, 1995—. Mem. NC Music Educators Conf., 1995—; fine arts dept. chair Louisburg HS, 1996—, mem. sch. planning team; mem. supt. dropout adv. team Franklin County Schs., 2004—05. Composer: The Louisburg March, 2001. Pianist Lions Club, Louisburg, NC, 2000—. Recipient Never Stop Learning Educator award, WTVD-11; named Young Educator of Yr., Louisburg Jaycees, 2000, Tchr. of Yr., Franklin County Schs., 2000, Artist of Yr., Franklin County Arts Coun., 2001, Tchr. of Yr., Wal-Mart, 2002, 2003, 2004. Mem.: Am. Theatre Organ Soc., Am. Guild Organists, Ctrl. Dist. Bandmasters Assn., James A. Johnson Masonic Lodge, Phi Mu Alpha Sinfonia, Phi Eta Sigma, Phi Beta Kappa. Republican. So. Baptist. Avocations: reading, collecting books and music, antique lamp repair, restoring typewriters and reed organs. Home: 102 Person St Louisburg NC 27549 Office Phone: 919-496-4722 ext. 225. Personal E-mail: bdmiller1935@aol.com.

MILLER, BRIAN DAVID, federal agency administrator; JD, U. Tex. Sr. counsel to dep. atty. gen. and spl. counsel on health care fraud US Dept. Justice, asst. US atty., with Eastern Dist. Va., 2002—05; inspector gen. US Gen. Svcs. Adminstrn., 2005—. Mem. President's Coun. on Integrity and Efficiency; mem. Hurricane Katrina task force US Dept. Justice, vice chair National Procurement Fraud task force, 2006. Featured in (articles) Those Who Dared: 30 Officials who Stood Up for Our Country, 2008. Recipient Dir.'s award, Exec. Office for US Attys., Disting. Svc. award, US Atty. Gen., 2008; named one of The most influential person in business ethics, Ethisphere mag., 2007. Office: US Gen Svcs Adminstrn 1800 F St NW Rm 5340 Washington DC 20405 Office Phone: 202-501-0450. Business E-Mail: brian.miller@gsa.gov.

MILLER, BRIAN STACY, federal judge; b. Pine Bluff, Ark., 1967; AA, Phillips CC of U. Ark., 1990; BS, U. Ctrl. Ark., 1992; JD, Vanderbilt Law Sch., 1995. Bar: Tenn. 1995, Ark. 1996. Assoc. atty. Martin, Tate, Morrow, & Marston PC, 1995—2006; city atty. City of Helena, Ark., 1999—2005; dep. prosecuting atty. Phillips County, Ark., 2000—06; judge Ark. Ct. Appeals, 2007, US Dist. Ct. (ea. dist.) Ark, 2008—. Served with USNR, 1984, 1989-92, served with USN, 1985—89. Mem.: ABA, Memphis Bar Assn. (pub. coun. 1997), Phillips County Bar Assn., Tenn. Bar Assn., Ark. Bar Assn., Nat. Bar Assn. Office: US Dist Ct 500 W Capitol Ave Little Rock AR 72201 Office Phone: 501-604-5351.

MILLER, BRUCE ABRAHAM, lawyer; b. Bklyn., Oct. 11, 1927; s. Charles X. and Lydia Keyes (Barnett) M.; m. Edna Powell, Feb. 27, 1960; children: E. Powell, Ann L., Elizabeth D. JD, Wayne St. U., 1954. Bar: Mich. 1956. Former gen. coun. Metro-Detroit AFL-CIO; sp. counsel United Steelworkers Am., AFL-CIO-CLC, Am. Fed. Tchrs., AFL-CIO; atty. Miller Cohen, Detroit. Former officer-at-large Mich. Dem. Com.; treas. 13th Congl. Dist. Dem. Com.; chmn. Wayne County Dem. Com. With U.S. Army, 1946-48. Office: 600 W Lafayette Blvd 4th Fl Detroit MI 48226-3195 Home Phone: 248-540-8677; Office Phone: 313-964-4454. Business E-Mail: brucemiller@millercohen.com.

MILLER, BRUCE LAWRENCE, neurologist, educator; b. Indpls., Aug. 24, 1949; s. Milton Howard and Harriet Bernice Miller; m. Deborah Scofield Heintz, May 7, 1977; children: Hannah Amanda, Elliott Clemens. BS, Butler U., Indpls., 1974; MD, U. B.C., 1978. Diplomate Am. Bd. Neurology 1985. Resident, internal medicine Vancouver Gen. Hosp., 1980; fellow, neurology U. Western Ont., 1981; asst. to prof. UCLA, LA, 1985—98; prof. neurology & psychiatry, A.W. and Mary Margarfet Clausen disting. chair U. Calif., San Francisco, 1998—. Med. dir. John Douglas French Found. for Alzheimer's Disease Rsch., LA, 1984—; dir. Memory and Aging Ctr., U. Calif., San Francisco. Author: (textbook) The Human Frontal Lobes, editions 1 and 2; contbr. several articles to profl. jours. Jewish. Office: UCSF Memory and Aging Center 350 Parnassus Avenue Ste 905 San Francisco CA 94143-1207 Office Fax: 415-476-4800. E-mail: bmiller@memory.ucsf.edu.*

MILLER, BUFFY, dancer; b. Atlanta; Studies with, Patricia Bromley; student, New Ballet Sch. Mem. Feld Ballet Tech. Soc., 1986—97; with Ballet Tech., 1997—. Home: 854 Carpenter LN Philadelphia PA 19119-3408

MILLER, C. ARDEN, physician, educator; b. Shelby, Ohio, Sept. 19, 1924; s. Harley H. and Mary (Thuma) Miller; m. Helen Meihack, June 26, 1948; children: John Lewis, Thomas Meihack, Helen Lewis, Benjamin Lewis. Student, Oberlin Coll., Ohio, 1942—44; MD cum laude, Yale U., New Haven, Conn., 1948. Intern, then asst. resident pediatrics Grace-New Haven Community Hosp., 1948—51; faculty U. Kans. Med. Center, 1951—66, dir. childrens rehab. unit, 1957—60, dean Med. Sch., dir., 1960—66; prof. pediatrics and maternal and child health U. N.C., Chapel Hill, 1966—98, emeritus, 1998—, vice chancellor health scis., 1966—71, chmn. dept. maternal and child health, 1977—87. Chmn. exec. com. Citizens Bd. Inquiry into Health Svcs. for Am., 1968—71. Mem. editl. bd.: Jour. Med. Edn., 1960—66; contbr. articles to profl. jours. Trustee Appalachian Regional Hosps., 1974—84, Planned Parenthood Fedn.; chmn. Alan Guttmacher Inst., 1978—84, 1986—. Recipient Robert H. Felix Disting. Svc. award, St. Louis U., 1977, Martha Mae Eliot award in pub. health, 1984, O. Max Gardner award, U. N.C., 1987; scholar Am. Markle scholar in med. scis., 1955—60. Fellow: Royal Soc. Health (hon.), Clare Hall Cambridge (Eng.) U. (life); mem.: APHA (chmn. action bd. 1972—75, pres.

1974—75, Sedgewick Meml. medal 1986), Inst. of Medicine NAS, Assn. Am. Med. Colls. (v.p. 1965—66), Soc. Pediat. Rsch., Delta Omega, Alpha Omega Alpha, Sigma Xi. Home: 350 Carolina Meadows Villa Chapel Hill NC 27517-7549

MILLER, CANDICE S., United States Representative from Michigan; b. Clair Shores, Mich., May 7, 1954; m. Donald G. Miller; 1 child, Wendy Nicole. Student, Macomb County C.C., 1973—74, Northwood U., 1974. Sec., treas. D.B. Snider, Inc., 1972-79; trustee Harrison Twp., 1979-80, supr., 1980-92; treas. Macomb County, 1992-95; sec. of state State of Mich., Lansing, 1995—2003; mem. US Congress from 10th Mich. dist., 2003—. Mem. Lake St. Clair Blue Ribbon Commn. Chair John Engler for Gov. campaign, Macomb County; del. Rep. Nat. Conv., 1996; co-chair Rep. Platform Com., 1996, Dole/Kemp Presdl. Campaign, Mich., 1996, Bush/Cheney Presdl. Campaign, Mich., 2000; mem. Carehouse-Macomb County Child Adv. Ctr., Selfridge Air Nat. Guard Base Cmty. Coun., Detroit Econ. Club; mem. adminstrv. bd. Mich. State, mem. safety commn. Recipient Macomb Citizen of Yr. award, March of Dimes, 1997, Woman of Distinction award, Macomb County Girl Scouts, Adjutant General's Patriot award, Mich. Nat. Guard, 2002, GH award women in govt., Good Housekeeping mag., 2003, Econ. Excellence award, Macomb C. of C.; Paul Harris Internat. fellow. Mem.: Nat. Assn. Secretaries of State, Boat Town Assn. Republican. Presbyterian. Avocations: boating, yacht racing. Office: US Congress 228 Cannon HOB Washington DC 20515 also: District Office 48653 Van Dyke Ave Shelby Township MI 48317-2560 Office Phone: 202-225-2106, 586-997-5010. Office Fax: 202-226-1169, 586-997-5013.*

MILLER, CAROL A., pediatrician, educator; b. Kansas City, Kans., Oct. 28, 1948; MD, Stanford U., 1975. Intern pediat. Mt. Zion Hosp. and Med. Ctr., San Francisco, 1975—76, resident, 1976—77, fellowship neonatology, 1977—79; attending physician U. Calif. Med. Ctr., San Francisco, dir. Well-Baby Nursery; faculty mem. U. Calif. San Francisco Sch. Medicine, 1989—, clin. prof. pediat. Adv. coll. mentor Sinkler Miller Med. Assn., exec. bd. mem.; com. mem. Shaken Baby Syndrome Prevention; physician edn. com. San Francisco Immunization Coalition. Named one of Top Docs-the Top 425 Doctors in the Bay Area, San Francisco Mag., 2001, 2002; named to Acad. Med. Educators, U. Calif. San Francisco Sch. Medicine, 2002. Office: UCSF Sch Medicine AC - 01, Box 0374 400 Parnassus Ave San Francisco CA 94143 Office Phone: 415-353-2000. Office Fax: 415-353-2822. E-mail: millerc@peds.ucsf.edu.

MILLER, CAROLE ANN LYONS, writer, editor, publisher, marketing executive; b. Newton, Mass. d. Markham Harold and Ursula Patricia (Foley) Lyons; m. David Thomas Miller, July 4, 1978. BA, Boston U., 1964. Cert. in Bus. Hickox Sch., Boston, 1964, advt./mktg. profl. UCLA, 1973, retail mgmt. profl. Ind. U., 1976. Editor Triangle Topics, Pacific Telephone, LA; programmer LA Ctrl. Area Spkrs. Bur., 1964-66; mng. editor, mktg. dir. Teen mag., LA, NYC, 1966-76; advt. dir. L.S. Ayres & Co., Indpls., 1976-78; v.p. mktg. The Denver, 1978-79; founder, editor, pub. Clockwise mag., Ventura, Calif., 1979-85; mktg. mgr., mgr. pub. rels. and spl. events Robinson's Dept. Store, LA, 1985-87; exec. v.p., dir. mktg. Harrison Svcs., LA, San Francisco, 1987-93; pres. divsn. Miller & Miller MillerMania, Video Image and Mktg., Camino, Calif., 1993—. Instr. retail advt. Ind. U., 1977-78. Author: AICI Publicity Handbook, 2005; editor: Style Source: The Power of the Seven Universal Styles for Women and Men, 2008. Recipient Pres.'s award Advt. Women of NY, 1974, Seklemian award, 1977, Pub. Svc. Addy award, 1978, Disting. Svc. award Bay Area chpt. Assn. Image Cons., Internat., 2003. Mem. Image Cons., Internat. (1st Ever Oustanding Svc. award Bay Area chpt. 2004), Advt. Women NY, Retail Advt. and Mktg. Assn., Fashion Group Internat., Bay Area Integrated Mktg., San Francisco Fashion Group, UCLA Alumni Assn. (life), Media Coms. (life), Assn. Image Cons. Internat. Home Phone: 530-644-3104; Office Phone: 530-644-4919. E-mail: caroleann@millermania.com.

MILLER, CAROLYN LYONS, microbiologist, military officer; b. Birmingham, Ala., June 28, 1955; d. John Henry and Annie Lois Lyons; m. Brian Lenny Miller, July 28, 1984; 1 child, Brian Lenny Miller, Jr. BS, U. Ala., 1977; MS, Ala. A&M U., 1979; PhD, Rutgers U., 1984; degree, Air U., 2000. Lic. medical technologist Am. Soc. Clin. Pathologists, 1984, cert. clin. lab. scientist Nat. Certification Agy, Lenexa, KS, 1984. Student asst. Dept. Biology and Microbiology U. Ala., Birmingham, Ala., 1973—77; rsch. asst. Dept of Biology and Food Sci. and Tech. Ala. A&M U., Normal, Ala., 1977—79; rsch. asst. Dept Pedodontics Sch. of Dentistry U. Ala., 1980; tchg. asst. biology and microbiology Cook Coll. Rutgers U., New Brunswick, NJ, 1980—83, asst. area coord. student life Douglass Coll., 1983—84; med. tech. intern Wilford Hall Med. Ctr., Lackland Air Force Base, Tex., 1985—86; chief quality control/epidemiology divsn. Air Force Sch. Aerospace Medicine, Brooks Air Force Base, Tex., 1986—89; comdr. 421st med. svc. squadron Wilford Hall Med. Ctr., Lackland Air Force Base, 1997—98; assoc. prof. Dept. Biology USAF Acad., Colorado Springs, Colo., 1989—93, exec. officer to the dean of the faculty, 1993—95; exec. officer to the comdr. Human Sys. Ctr., Brooks Air Force Base, Tex., 1995—97; ops. staff officer/dir., quality assurance & regulatory affairs 59th Med. Diagnostics and Therapeutics Group, Lackland Air Force Base, Tex., 1998—99; v.p. recruitment & diversity affairs Uniformed Svcs. U. Health Scis., Bethesda, Md., 1999—2002; pathology flight comdr. 375th Med. Group, Scott AFB, Ill., 2002—05; dep. med. support squadron comdr. 375th Med. Support Squadron, Scott Air Force Base, Ill., 2002—05; biomed. sci. corps exec. 375th Airlift Wing, Scott AFB, Ill., 2002—05; dir. chem., biol., nuc. and clin. surveilance Air Force Inst. for Operational Health, Brooks City AFB, Tex., 2005—. Faculty advisor for vol. cmty. med. clinic Med. Sch. Uniformed Svcs. U., Bethesda, 1999—2002; coach odyssey of the mind White Oaks Elem. Sch., Burke, Va., 2000—02; vol. instr. Incarnate Word Coll., San Antonio, 1995—97; chmn. parent adv. com. Child Devel. Ctr., Colorado Springs, Colo., 1991—95; mem., leadership coun. for cmty. svc. Alamo Fed. Exec. Bd., San Antonio, 1995—99; cons. in field. Contbr. articles to profl. jours. Cmty. mem. Alamo Fed. Exec. Bd., San Antonio, Tex., 1995—99; ch. med. vol. Emmanuel Ch., San Antonio, Tex., 1985—89; advisor to the bd. Uniformed Svcs Med. Sch., Bethesda, Md., 1999—2002; mil. deployment Mil., Overseas, Non-U.S., Classified, 2003—03. Col. USAF, 1985, Scott and various other Air Force Bases, over 20 years of service. Decorated Expeditionary Svc. Ribbon with Gold Border USAF, Air Force Outstanding Unit Award with Valor US; fellow, 81Rutgers U., 1984; Pell grant, U. of Ala., 1974—77. Master: Biomedical Scis. Corps (licentiate; licensure 1985, Chief Mastery badge 1995); mem.: Soc. Armed Forces Mil. Lab. Scientists (sr. mem. 1986, Best Rsch. Poster Presentation 1999), Am. Soc. Microbiologists (corr.; mem. 1978, Grad. Student award 1983), Assn.Mil. Surgeons of U.S. (corr.; mem. 1996), Am. Soc. Clin. Pathologists (assoc.; assoc. mem. 1990), Officers Club (assoc.; mem. 1986), Beta Beta Beta (hon.; honor mem. 1979), Zeta Phi Beta (corr.; pres. 1975—77, Cmty. Charity Supporter 1976). Achievements include research in converting urine to potable water to prevent discharge in space; development of medical laboratory in deployed location; first to tri-service military and federal medical school recruitment to help meet nation's need for physicians, women and minorities. Avocations: reading, horseback riding, running, walking, interior decorating. Home: 23003 Whisper Canyon San Antonio TX 78258-3211 Office: 2350 Gillingham Dr Brooks City-Base TX 78235 Personal E-mail: bbcmiller@earthlink.net. Business E-Mail: carolyn.miller@brooks.af.mil.

MILLER, CATHERINE H., nursing administrator, property manager; d. Lawrence James Gleason, Jr. and Arlene Joan Woolsey; m. Thomas Dewayne Keyser (div.); children: Kenneth James Keyser, Kerry Lee Keyser, Gary Wayne Keyser; m. James H. Miller, Dec. 14, 1996. Certificate acctg., Brown's Bus. Sch., Hempstead, NY, 1966; certificate cmty. health agt., certificate nursing asst., Dabney S. Lancaster CC, Clifton Forge, Va., 1977, AAS, 1981. RN Va., 1981. Sec., bookkeeper Aluminum Specialties Home Improvement, Levittown, NY, 1960—76; cert. nursing asst. Liberty House Nursing Home, Clifton Forge, 1977—79, RN charge nurse, 1981—83, 1985—97, RN supr., 1997—2005; staff devel. dir. Alleghany Rehab./Health Care, Clifton Forge, 2006; RN supr. Beverly Health Care, Alleghany Rehab./Health Care, Clifton Forge, 2006—. Nurse, adult CPR instr. Am. Red Cross, Covington, Va., 1997—. Worthy matron Order of Ea. Star Martha chpt. 21, Covington, 1985. Named to Wall of Tolerance, Nat. Campaign for Tolerance, founding chair Rosa Parks, 2005. Avocation: painting. Office: Alleghany Highlands Cmty Svcs Adult Day Ctr 550 Pine St Clifton Forge VA 24422

MILLER, CHARLES E. (CHUCK MILLER), judge; b. Washington, Sept. 26, 1944; s. Charles Edward Miller and Mary (Cox) M.; divorced; 1 child, Samantha Mcgill Cox. BA, So. Meth. U., 1971, JD, 1972. Bar: Tex. 1972. Assoc. Roseborough & Curlee, Dallas, 1972-77; judge County Criminal Ct. #7, Dallas, 1977-82, Ct. Criminal Appeals, Austin, Tex., 1983-94; state judge at large State of Tex., 1995—. Adj. prof. criminal law So. Meth. U. Law Sch., Dallas, 1980—82; arbitrator comml., employment and labor panels Am. Arbitration Assn., 1995—; labor abitrator Fed. Mediation and Conciliation Svc., 2002—, arbitrator, labor roster, 2003—; arbitrator comml. and employment Nat. Arbitration Forum, 2004. Author and lectr. in field. Mem. nat. adv. coun. Nat. victim Ctr., NYC and Washington; mem. nat. steeringcom. Victims Constitutional Amendment Network; mem. adv. bd. victims Organized to Ensure Rights and Safety; mem. victim assistancecom. Tex. Young Lawyers Assn.; parliamentarian state exec. bd. People Against Violent Crime. With US Army, 1966-70. Named Disting. Mil. Grad., Officer Candidate Sch., Ft. Sill, Okla., 1968, Best Dallas Misdemeanor Ct. Judge, Dallas Bar Assn., 1982, Best Dallas Criminal Ct. Judge, Dallas County Criminal Bar Assn., 1982; decorated Army Commendational medal, 1970; recipient Sunny von Bulow Nat. Victim Advocacy Ctr. Appreciation cert., 1987, US Dept. Justice Victims of Crime Appreciation cert., 1992, Victims Organized to Ensure Rights and Safety Advocate for Justice award, 1993, People Against Violent Crime Appreciation cert., 1993. Mem. SAR, State Bar Tex. (chmn. criminal law sect. 1981-82, course dir. advanced criminal law course 1990, chmn. crime victim com. 1992-94, crime victim & witness, 1994, cert. specialist in criminal law), Coll. State Bar Tex., Tex. Bar Found. Republican. Home and Office: 300 Woods Loop Ste 100 Driftwood TX 78619 Home Phone: 512-829-4725; Office Phone: 512-496-6666. Personal E-mail: judgechuckmiller@att.net.

MILLER, CHARLES E., gynecologist; b. Iron Mountain, Mich., Aug. 18, 1953; s. Alfred and Muriel Miller; m. Laura Miller; children: Benjamin, Abagayle, Alec. BS in Medicine, Northwestern U., Chgo., 1975, MD, 1977. Diplomate Am. Bd. Ob-gyn., 1984. Dir. reproductive endocrinology and infertility Luth. Gen. Hosp., Park Ridge, Ill., 1983—85, dir. Ctr. for Advanced Reproduction for In-vitro Fertilization and Gamete Intrafallopian Transfer, 1989—95, dir. minimally invasive gynecol. surgery, 2005—; med. dir., med. dir. divsn. endoscopic surgery Ctr. for Human Reproduction, Schaumburg, Ill., 1995—99; dir. Ctr. for Minimally Invasive Gynecologic Surgery Glenbrook Hosp., Ill., 1997—2001; pvt. practice Arlington Heights, Ill., 1999—2001, Charles E. Miller, MD & Assocs., Arlington Heights and Naperville, Ill., 2001—. Cons. Ethicon Endo-Surgery, Cin., 2004—, Ethicon Women's Health and Urology, Somerville, NJ, 2004—, Galil Med., Ltd., Yokneam, Israel, 2006—, Serono, Rockland, Mass.; cons., mem. spkrs. bur. Smith & Nephew, Andover, Mass., 2005—; mem. spkrs. bur. Boston Sci., Natick, Mass., 2005—; clin. assoc. prof. dept. ob-gyn. U. Ill., Chgo., clin. assoc. dept. ob-gyn. Mem. adv. bd.: Jour. Minimally Invasive Gynecology, mem. editl. bd.: OB/GYN News; contbr. chapters to books, articles to profl. jours. Fellow: ACOG (cert. accreditation coun. for gynecologic endoscopy); mem.: Chgo. Assn. Gynecologic Endoscopists, Chgo. Assn. Reproductive Endocrinology, Soc. Reproductive Surgeons, Endometriosis Assn. (clin. adv. bd., bd. dirs. 2006), Am. Assn. Gynecologic Laparoscopists (pres. elect, sec. - treas. 2006), RESOLVE - The Nat. Fertility Assn. (clin. adv. bd. mem., Lifetime Achievement award 2005), Am. Soc. Reproductive Medicine (bd. mem.). Office: Charles E Miller MD & Associates 120 Osler Dr Naperville IL 60540 Office Fax: 630-428-0083. Business E-Mail: lmaki@charlesemillermd.org.

MILLER, CHARLES HAMPTON, lawyer; b. Southampton, NY, Jan. 25, 1928; s. Abraham E. and Ethel (Simon) M.; m. Mary Fried, Aug. 26, 1956; children: Cathy Lynn Castaneda, Steven Scott, Jennifer Lee Miller-Grady. BA, Syracuse U., 1949; LLB, Columbia U., 1952. Bar: NY 1952, Republic of Korea 1954, US Ct. Appeals (2d cir.) 1958, US Supreme Ct. 1969, US Ct. Appeals (3d cir.) 1972, US Ct. Appeals (7th cir.) 1973, US Ct. Appeals (9th cir.) 1995; cert. mediator (so. and ea. dists.) NY, mediator Supreme Ct. NY County; arbitrator Ea. dist. NY. Asst. counsel Waterfront Commn., NY Harbor, 1954-56; asst. atty. US Atty. So. Dist. NY, 1956-58; assoc. Cole & Deitz, NYC, 1958-61, Marshall Bratter Greene Allison & Tucker, NYC, 1961-64, ptnr., 1964-82, Hess Segall Guterman Pelz Steiner & Barovick, NYC, 1982-86, Loeb & Loeb LLP, NYC, 1986-2000, counsel, 2000—. Mem. faculty Continuing Legal Edn., Columbia U. Law Sch., 1976-82. With US Army, 1952-54. Fellow: Am. Bar Found.; mem.: ABA, Assn. of Bar of City of NY. Home: 171 Ralph Ave White Plains NY 10606-3813 Office: Loeb & Loeb LLP 345 Park Ave Fl 18 New York NY 10154-1895 Office Phone: 212-407-4910. Personal E-mail: marbuzz@msn.com. Business E-Mail: cmiller@loeb.com.

MILLER, CHARLES RICKIE, systems analyst, engineering executive; b. New Albany, Ind., Oct. 4, 1946; s. Marshall Christian and Thelma Virginia (Martin) M.; m. Janel Howell, Nov. 24, 1968; children: Kimberly, Brian, Audrey, Rachel. BA in Physics, DePauw U., 1969; postgrad., Rice U., 1969-70, U. Houston, 1972-76. Tech. editor ITT/Fed. Electric Corp., Houston, 1970-71, LTV/Svc. Tech. Corp., Houston, 1971; sys. safety engr. Boeing Aerospace Corp., Houston, 1971-76; thermal analyst space sys. divsn. Rockwell Internat. Corp., Houston, 1976-89; mgr. thermal and fluid sys. for space shuttle payloads Space Shuttle Program Office, NASA/L.B. Johnson Space Ctr., Houston, 1989—. Mem. editl. team Apollo 14, 15 preliminary sci. reports, 1971-72; mem. sys. integration negotiating team for Space Shuttle to Mir Space Sta. rendezvous and docking missions, 1993-98, chmn. negotiating team for Space Shuttle to Mir Space Sta. water preparation and transfer, 1994-98, space shuttle program co-chmn. for shuttle/internat. space sta. program joint tech. working groups for thermal control, environ. control and life support sys., 1996—. Bd. dirs. Space City Aquatic Team, Houston, 1990-91. Rector scholar DePauw U., 1964-68; Rice fellow Rice U., 1969-70. Mem. AIAA, ASME, Nat. Space Soc., Air Force Assn., Am. Inst. Physics, Planetary Soc., Sigma Pi Sigma. Avocations: children's sports, jogging, science fiction, military history. Home: 806 Walbrook Dr Houston TX 77062-4030 Office: NASA Mail Code MO2 LB Johnson Space Ctr Houston TX 77058 Office Phone: 281-483-1229. Business E-Mail: c.r.miller@nasa.gov.

MILLER, CHARLES T., prosecutor; b. Winslow, Wash., June 27, 1948; s. Charles Wilbur and Pharoeba H. (Good) M.; m. Rebecca Louise Campbell, Aug. 17, 1974; children: Angela Dawn, Emily Grace, Kathryn Louise. BS in Criminal Justice, W.Va. State Coll., 1973; JD, W.Va. U., 1977. Bar: W.Va. 1977, U.S. Ct. Appeals (4th cir.) 1977. Asst. prosecuting atty., Kanawha County, W.Va., 1977-82; assoc. and ptnr. E. F. Thaxton Attys., Charleston, 1982-84; 1st asst. US atty. (so. dist.) W.Va. US Dept. Justice, Charleston, 1984—, interim US atty., 1991—92, 1993, 2001, interim US atty. (so. dist.) W.Va., 2006—. With USN, 1966-69, Vietnam; maj. W.Va. Army Nat. Guard; lt. col. W.Va. Air Nat. Guard. Decorated Navy Achievement medal, Rep. of Vietnam Svc. medal, Rep. of Vietnam Campaign ribbon, Rep. of Vietnam Cross of Gallantry, Combat Action ribbon, Presdl. Unit citation. Presbyterian. Avocation: carpentry. Office: US Atty's Office PO Box 1713 Charleston WV 25326

MILLER, CHARLES WALLACE, historian, retired environmental geologist, educator; b. Phoenix, July 7, 1946; s. Charles W. and Emabel O. Miller; m. Connie Raschke, June 3, 1972; 1 child, Geoffrey Wallace. BA, U. Md., 1969; MA, U. Tex., Austin, 1970; BS, SUNY, Albany, 1978; PhD, Union Inst., Cin., Ohio, 1990. Tchr. pub. schs., San Antonio, 1971-76; instr. San Antonio Coll., 1972-78, St. Mary's Univ., San Antonio, 1976-78, Cochise Coll., Sierra Vista, Az., 1989-90, Pima C.C., Tucson, 1998—, Yorktown U., 2003—; environ. geologist U.S. Geol. Survey, Metairie, La., 1978-80; field geologist U.S. Bur. Land Mgmt., Moab, Utah, 1980-84; historian U.S. Bur. Reclamation, Salt Lake City, 1990-94; environ. scientist USAF, Tucson, 1994—2009. Mineral cons., Tucson, 1984-89. Author: Stake Your Claim! The Tale of America's Enduring Mining Law, 1991, The Spirit of the Pioneers Still Rules, 1997, The Automobile Gold Rushes, 1998. Vol. East Tucson Bapt. Ch.; asst. scoutmaster Boy Scouts Am.; group coord. Combined Fed. Campaign. Recipient Outstanding Alumni award, SUNY Albany (now Excelsior Coll.), 2005. Mem. SAR, Nat. Eagle Scout Assn., Mining History Assn., James Madison Brigade for Preservation of the U.S. Constn., Mensa, Hist. Soc., Golden Key, Phi Alpha Theta, Pi Sigma Alpha. Achievements include climbing two tallest peaks in the lower 48 and 13 others over 14,000 feet; rim-to-rim trek across Grand Canyon. Avocations: backpacking, scuba diving, photography, lifeguarding, hunting. Home: 1207 Nicole Ln Fredericksburg TX 78624

MILLER, CHRIS J., legislative staff member; Constituent services rep., Senator Gordon Smith US Senate, Washington, 2001, legis. correspondent, Senator Tim Hutchinson, 2001—02, rsch. asst., health, edn., labor and pensions com., 2002; legis. asst., Rep. Jennifer Dunn US House of Reps., 2003—04, sr. legis. asst., Rep. Gary Miller, 2004—05, legis. dir., Rep. David Reichert, 2005—08, chief of staff to Rep. David Reichert, 2008—. Republican. Office: 1730 Longworth House Office Bldg Washington DC 20515 Office Phone: 202-225-7761. Office Fax: 202-225-4282.*

MILLER, CHRISTINE MARIE, sales, marketing and public relations executive; b. Williamsport, Pa., Dec. 7, 1950; d. Frederick James and Mary (Wurster) M.; m. Robert M. Ancell, Mar. 30, 1985. BA, U. Kans., Lawrence, 1972; MA, Northwestern U., Evanston, Ill., 1978, PhD, 1982. Pub. rels. asst. Bedford County Commr., Pa., 1972—73; tchg. asst. Northwestern U., Evanston, Ill., 1977—80; asst. prof. U. Ala., Tuscaloosa, 1980—82, Loyola U., New Orleans, 1982—85; vis. prof. Ind. U. Sch. Journalism, Bloomington, 1985—86; dir. mktg. Nat. Inst. Fitness & Sport, Indpls., 1986—88; mgmt. assoc. cmty. and media rels. Subaru-Isuzu Automotive, Inc., Lafayette, Ind., 1988—91; dir. pub. rels. Giddings & Lewis, Fond Du Lac, Wis., 1991—93; v.p. comm. and enrollment mgmt. Milton Hershey Sch., Pa., 1993—94, dir. adminstrn., 1994—95; account mgr. Verizon Bus., Vienna, Va., 1995—2007, Terremark Fed., 2007—08; strategic comm. analyst Navy Warfare Devel. Command, 2008—. Program dir. Nat. Entrepreneurship Acad., Bloomington, 1986—88. Co-author: The Biographical Dictionary of World War II General and Flag Officers, 1996; contbr. articles to profl. jours. Bd. dirs. Indpls. Entrepreneurship Acad., 1988-91, Area IV Agy., Greater Lafayette Mus. Art, 1989-91. With USN, 1973-77, capt. USNR, 1977—. Mem. Armed Forces Comm. Electronics Assn., Pub. Rels. Soc. Am., Naval Order of the U.S. (nat. pub. affairs com.), U.S. Naval Pub. Affairs Alumnae Assn. (bd. dirs.), Naval Res. Assn., Res. Officers Assn. Presbyterian. Avocations: cooking, swimming, reading, travel, bicycling. Office: STRAT EGIC Comm Analyst Navy Warface Devel Command 1474 Gilbert St Norfolk VA 23511-2723 Home: 1515 Runnymede Rd Norfolk VA 23505 Home Phone: 703-444-8174; Office Phone: 757-444-8174. Business E-Mail: christine.miller@gdit.com.

MILLER, CHRISTINE ODELL COOK, federal judge; m. Dennis F. Miller; 2 children. BA in Polit. Sci., Stanford U., 1966; JD, U. Utah, 1969. Bar: DC, Calif. Law clk. to Honorable David T. Lewis US Ct. Appeals (10th circuit), Salt Lake City; trial atty. US Dept. Justice, US Ct. Claims; team leader atty. FTC; atty. Hogan & Hartson, Washington; spl. counsel Pension Benefit Guaranty Corporation; dep. gen. counsel US Rlwy. Assn.; ptnr. Shack & Kimball, Washington; judge US Ct. Fed. Claims, Washington, 1983—. Comment editor Utah law Review Scholar U. Utah Coll. Law. Mem. DC Bar Assn., Calif. State Bar, Order of Coif, Cosmos Club. Avocation: gemology. Office: US Ct Fed Claims 717 Madison Pl NW Ste 716 Washington DC 20005-1011*

MILLER, CHRISTOPHER JOHN, statistician; m. Christina Lynn Miller. BS, Loyola Coll. Md., Balt., 1990; MS, NC State U., Raleigh, 1992. Statistician Abbott Labs.; sr. dir., biostatistics AstraZeneca, Wilmington, Del., 2006—. Office: AstraZeneca 1800 Concord Pike PO Box 15437 Wilmington DE 19850 Business E-Mail: chris.miller@astrazeneca.com.

MILLER, CLAIRE ELLEN, editor, educator, writer; b. Milw., July 17, 1936; d. Emil George Benjamin and Phyllis Dorothy (Rahn) Holtzen; m. Gerald Ray Miller, June 21, 1958; children: Karin, Russell. BS in Edn., Concordia U., 1961. Tchr. Grace Episcopal Day Sch., Silver Spring, Md., 1971-77, The Norwood Sch., Bethesda, Md., 1977-79; writer Media Materials, Balt., 1980; project editor Ednl. Challenges, Alexandria, Va., 1981; asst. mng. editor Ranger Rick Mag., Nat. Wildlife Fedn., Vienna, Va., 1981-87, mng. editor, 1988-2001, contbg. editor, 2002—; propr. Claire Miller, Writing and Editing, Rockville, Md., 2001—. Author numerous activity books for presch. thru mid. sch., 1979-80; project editor 6 vocabulary books, 1981; author numerous children's mag. and newspaper stories and books, 1981—. Mem. Md. Ornithol. Soc. Democrat. Lutheran. Avocation: birding. Home and Office: 17501 Kirk Ln Rockville MD 20853-1033 Personal E-mail: clairemiller2@verizon.net.

MILLER, CLAUDE HAROLD, communications educator; s. Mary Amie Miller-Pikul; m. Katharine Weld Leggett, May 30, 1997; 1 child, Madeline Blake. PhD, U. Ariz., Tucson, 2000. Asst. prof. Wake Forest U., Winston-Salem, NC, 2001—02; assoc. prof. U. Okla., Norman, 2002—, spkr., svc. program, 2003. Contbr. chapters to books, articles to profl. jours. Spkr. Mornings with Prof. Program, Sr. Adult Svcs., OU Outreach, Norman, Okla., 2003. Mem.: Nat. Communication Assn. (rsch. com. chair 2007, Top Paper award 2004). Libertarian. Achievements include research in identifying principal factors predicting emerging adult health risk behavior. Avocations: photography, painting. Office: Univ Okla 610 Elm Ave Norman OK 73019

MILLER, CLIFFORD ALBERT, merchant banker; b. Salt Lake City, Aug. 6, 1928; s. Clifford Elmer and LaVeryl (Jensen) M.; m. Judith Auten, Sept. 20, 1976; 1 child, Courtney; children by previous marriage, Clifford, Christin, Stephanie. Student, U. Utah, 1945-50, UCLA, 1956. Pres. Braun & Co., LA, 1955-82, chmn., 1982-87; exec. v.p. Gt. Western Fin. Corp., Beverly Hills, Calif., 1987-91; chmn. Clifford Group, Inc., bus. cons., 1992—; mng. dir. Shamrock Holdings, Inc., 1992—, Shamrock Capital Advisors, L.P., 1992—. Bd. dirs. Frontier Bank, Park City, Utah, Triad Broadcasting Co., Inc., Monterey, Calif., 2005—, Western Cmty. Bancshares, Park City, Utah; cons. to White House, 1969—74. Trustee Harvey Mudd Coll., Claremont, Calif., 1974—, chmn. bd. trustees, 1991-98; chmn. bd. dirs. L.A. Master Chorale, 1989-93, chmn. emeritus, 1993; mem. chmn.'s coun. Music Ctr. Unified Fund Campaign; bd. trustees Keck Grad. Inst. Applied Life Scis., Claremont, 1997—. Mem. Calif. Club, Wilshire Country Club, Park Meadows Country Club, Pi Kappa Alpha. Office: Shamrock Holdings Inc 4444 W Lakeside Dr Burbank CA 91510-7774 Office Phone: 818-973-4297.

MILLER, CORBIN RUSSELL, investment company executive; b. Huntington, W.Va., Apr. 6, 1948; s. Corbin Russell and Ernestine (Thorne) M.; m. Kathryn Ann Anderson, Sept. 16, 1978. AB cum laude, Princeton U., NJ, 1971. Trainee Morgan Guaranty Trust Co., NYC, 1972-74, asst. treas., 1974-77; assoc. Wm. Sword & Co. Inc., Princeton, 1977-79; v.p. J. Henry Schroder Corp., NYC, 1979-83, J. Henry Schroder Bank & Trust, NYC, 1983-87; sr. v.p. IBJ Schroder Bank & Trust Co., NYC, 1987-90; chmn. Koala Techs. Corp., Pleasanton, Calif., 1990-91; mng. dir. Regent Ptnr. Inc., NYC and Denver, 1991-92; exec. v.p. S.N. Phelps & Co., Greenwich, Conn., 1992-95; exec. v.p., CFO, dir. Carey Internat., Inc., Washington, 1995-96; pres. Lombard North Am. Inc., San Francisco, 1997-99; sr. ptnr. Continuum Ventures LLC, NYC, 2000—. Bd. dirs. Met. Opera Guild, N.Y.C., 1994-2008. Mem. Am. Soc. Order St. John of Jerusalem (chancellor 1999-2002), Met. Opera Club (pres. 1992-94), Knickerbocker Club, Rockaway Hunting Club, Racquet and Tennis Club, The Brook. Republican. Episcopalian. Avocation: golf. Home: 1165 5th Ave New York NY 10029-6931 Office: Continuum Ventures LLC 300 Park Ave Fl 17 New York NY 10022-7402 E-mail: cm@corbinmiller.us.

MILLER, CORY D., science educator; b. East Stroudsburg, Pa., Sept. 26, 1966; s. Donald F. Miller and Susan M. Piazza, Sylvia Miller (Stepmother), David J. Piazza (Stepfather); m. Patricia G. Rowe; 1 child, Vernon C. Rowe. BA Music Merchandising, U. Pa., Mansfield, 1988; MS in Advanced Classroom Instrn., Capella U., Mpls., 2008; PhD, Capella U., 2008. Sci. educator Horizons Acad., Bradenton, Fla., 2002—. Office: Horizons Acad 2710 27th St E Bradenton FL 34208 Business E-Mail: millerc@manateeschools.net.

MILLER, CRYSTAL ANN, respiratory therapist; b. San Diego, Apr. 18, 1979; d. Thomas Howard and Sharon Ann Miller; life ptnr. Robert Marshall Miller; children: Thomas James children: Jade Leinani. AA in Arts & Scis., Olympic Cmty. Coll., Bremerton, Wash., 1997; BA in Human Svcsi., Hawaii Pacific U., Kaneohe, 2000; AA in Sci. Respiratory, Tidewater Cmty. Coll., Va. Beach, 2001; MBA in Healthcare Mgmt., U. Phoenix, 2005. Cert. respiratory therapist Nat. Bd. Respiratory Care, 2001, registered Nat. Bd. Respiratory Care, 2005. Respiratory therapist Med. Staffing Network, Seattle, 2004—08; respiratory theapist Overlake Hosp., Bellevue, Wash., 2004—08; clin. specialist, project mgr. Masimo, 2008—. Respiratory agent on assignment, Seattle, 2005—. High priestess Druid, Lakebay, Wash., 1994—. Specialist US Army, 2001—02, Ft. Leonardwood, Mich. Recipient Employee Recognition award, Overlake Hosp., 2004—06. Mem.: Mensa (life). Achievements include research in medical instruction and education. Home: 221 195th Ave KP S Lakebay WA 98349 Office: 40 Parker Irvine CA 92618 Personal E-mail: sweetc11@yahoo.com. Business E-Mail: cmiller@masimo.com.

MILLER, CYNTHIA S., healthcare insurance company executive; BS, Ohio State U.; MA in Math., Ind. U. Actuarial student Am. United Life Ins. Co.; asst. actuary Indpls. Life Ins. Co.; assoc. actuary Anthem, Inc., 1986, mgmt. positions, 1986—95, v.p., chief actuary, 1996—2004; v.p., corp. actuary WellPoint, Inc. (formerly Anthem, Inc.), 2004—05, sr. v.p., chief actuary, chief of staff to CEO, 2006, exec. v.p., chief actuary, integration mgmt. officer, 2007—. Mem. bd. dirs. BCS Fin. Corp., Jr. Achievement Ctrl. Ind., Inc. Fellow: Soc. Actuaries (mem. bd. dirs., chair health sect. coun.); mem.: Am. Acad. Actuaries, Indpls. Actuarial Club (pres.). Office: WellPoint Inc 120 Monument Cir Indianapolis IN 46204*

MILLER, D. CRAIG, cardiovascular surgeon; b. Dec. 3, 1946; Student in Chemistry and Math., Dartmouth Coll., 1965-68; BS in Basic Med. Scis., Stanford U. Sch. Medicine, 1969, MD, 1972. Lic. Calif., cert. Am. Bd. Surgery, Am. Bd. Thoracic Surgery, Am. Bd. Surgery (spl. qualifications gen. vascular surgery). Resident, gen. surgery Stanford U. Med. Ctr. and Affiliated Hosps., Calif., 1972—75; chief resident, peripheral vascular surgery Stanford U. Med. Ctr., Calif., 1975—76, chief resident, cardiovasc. surgery Calif., 1976—77, chief resident, thoracic surgery Calif., 1977, program dir., vascular surgery residency Calif., 1985—93; chief, cardiac surgery sect. VA Med. Ctr., Palo Alto, Calif., 1978—86, staff surgeon, cardiac surgery sect., 1978—96; clin. asst. prof., cardiovasc. surgery Stanford U. Sch. Medicine, Calif., 1978, assoc. prof., cardiovasc. surgery Calif., 1983—89, prof., cardiovasc. surgery Calif., 1989—; Thelma and Henry Doelger Prof., Cardiovasc. Surgery Stanford U., 1998—. Invited lectr. in field. Guest editor, circulation supplement Cardiovasc. Surgery, 1990—92, mem. editl. bd. Jour. Thoracic and Cardiovasc. Surgery, 1984—91, assoc. editor (acquired heart disease), 1998—2007, mem. editl. bd. Jour. Cardiac Surgery, 1985—95, Cardiac Chronicle, 1985—93, Jour. Surgical Rsch., 1990—94, Circulation, 1991—93, Jour. Heart Valve Disease, 1992—, Heart and Vessels, 1998—, ad hoc referee for several peer-reviewed publications; contbr. several articles to peer-reviewed jours. Lt. med. corps. USNR, 1970—82. Recipient Stanford U. Med. Sch. Disting. Alumni award, 1997, Wilfred Bigelow award, Canadian Cardiovasc. Soc., 2000, Antoine Marfan award, Nat. Marfan Found., 2001. Mem.: Santa Clara County Med. Soc. (mem. ethics com. 1980—82, Outstanding Achievement in Medicine award 2004), AMA, Calif. Med. Assn., San Francisco Surgical Soc., Am. Fedn. for Clin. Rsch., Pan-Pacific Surgical Assn., Sociedad de Cardiocirujanos (Spain) (pres. 1987—88), Soc. Thoracic Surgical Edn., Soc. for Clin. Vascular Surgery, Bay Area Soc. Thoracic Surgeons, Northern Calif. Vascular Soc., Am. Coll. Chest Physicians, Am. Coll. Cardiology (scientific abstract review com. 1986, 1990, peripheral vascular disease com. 1994—98), ACS (cardiovasc. surgery com. 1986—88, exec. com. 1987—88), Soc. Heart Valve Disease, Am. Heart Assn. (bd. dirs., Santa Clara County Chpt. 1980—82, mem. rsch. com., Santa Clara County Chpt. 1981—83, optimal resources for vascular surgery com. 1985—89, program com., cardiovasc. surgery coun. 1988—92, chmn. 1989—92, vice-chmn., cardiothoracic-vascular surgery coun. 1993—95, chmn., cardiothoracic and vascular surgery coun. 1995—97, chmn., cardiothoracic-vascular surgery coun. 1995—97, Disting. Scientist 2003), Western Vascular Soc. (co-chmn., com. scientific sessions 1992—93), Soc. for Thoracic Surgeons, Western Thoracic Surgical Assn. (prog. com. 1983—88, sec. 1989—93, v.p. 1993—94, pres. 1994—95), Soc. for Vascular Surgery (chmn. 1986—88), Soc. Univ. Surgeons, Am. Assn. for Thoracic Surgery (coun. 2003—07, pres. 2007—08), Am. Surgical Assn., Soc. Clin. Surgery, Cardiac Soc. Australia and New Zealand (corr.) (hon.), Sociedad Chilena de Cardiologia y Cirugia Cardiovasc. (Chile) (hon.), Sociedad Colombiana de Cirugia (Columbia) (hon.), Sociedad Espanola de Cirugia Cardiovasc. (Spain) (hon.), European Assn. for Cardio-Thoracic Surgery (hon.), Cardiac Surgery Biology Club. Office: Dept Cardiothoracic Surgery Falk Cardiovasc Rsch Ctr Stanford U Sch Medicine 300 Pasteur Dr Stanford CA 94305-5407 Office Phone: 650-723-5771, 650-725-3826. Office Fax: 650-725-3846. Business E-Mail: dcm@stanford.edu.

MILLER, DALE EUGENE, philosopher, educator; b. Wichita, Kans. m. Cindy Sue Miller. MA in Economics, U. Pitts., 1999, PhD in Philosophy, 1999. Assoc. prof. philosophy and religious studies Old Dominion U., Norfolk, Va., 2005—.

MILLER, DAN, information technology executive; m. Sheryl Miller; 2 children. BSBA, U. Colo., Boulder. Various product mktg., sales and mgmt. positions NBI, Inc., Colo.; dir. Reseller Channel Orgn. Sun Microsystems, Inc., dir. Telco Sales for US Western Market, various leadership positions in Global Sales Orgn. including v.p. US Telecom. Market Area, v.p. Global Svc. Provide Strategy Group, pres. Global Electric Motors Japan, sr. v.p. global systems practice. Office: Sun Microsystems Inc 4150 Network Cir Santa Clara CA 95054 Office Phone: 650-960-1300.

MILLER, DARREN JOHN, social worker; b. Salem, Ohio, May 27, 1973; s. Rachel Culp and Herman Jay Miller; m. Elizabeth Martha Tesner, Nov. 20, 1999; children: Trinity Elisabeth, Christian Vincent. Degree in Social Work, Youngstown State U., Ohio, 1996. Lic. Counselor and Social Worker Bd., Marriage and Family Therapist Bd., 1996. Officer Columbiana County Juvenile Ct., Lisbon, Ohio, 1996—2000; safe and drug free coord. East Palestine City Schs., Ohio, 2000—. Social svc. cons. Sunrise Homes, Lisbon, 1994—99. Recipient Asset Bldg. award, Ohio Dept. Edn., 2003. Mem.: Nat. Social Workers. Avocations: soccer, mountain climbing, travel, reading. Home: 60 South Pleasant Dr East Palestine OH 44413 Office: East Palestine City Schs 360 West Grant St East Palestine OH 44413 Office Fax: 330-426-5105. E-mail: epal_djm@access-k12.org.

MILLER, DAVID BRUCE, investment company executive; b. Dallas, Feb. 17, 1950; s. Van Roy and Fay Ann (Luther) M.; m. Mary Lee Filgo, May 27, 1972; children: Kyle, Meredith. BBA, So. Meth. U., 1972, MBA, 1973. V.p. Republic Bank Dallas, 1973-78; v.p., mgr. Republic Energy Fin. Corp. subs. Republic Bank, Denver, 1978-81; chmn., chief exec. officer MAZE Exploration Inc., Englewood, Colo., 1981-86; pres. PMC Acquisition Co., Dallas, 1988—96; ptnr. EnCap Investments LP, Dallas, 1994—. Bd. dirs. Practical Parent Edn. Mem. adminstrv. bd. and exec. com. St. Andrew United Meth. Ch., 1987—. Mem. Ind. Petroleum Assn. Am., Ind. Petroleum Assn. Mountain States (bd. dirs. 1984—), Tex. Ind. Producers and Royalty Owners Assn., So. Meth. U. Alumni Assn. (bd. dirs. 1974-84, pres. Denver chpt. 1979-84)., So. Meth. U. Letterman's Assn. (bd. dirs. 1977-78). Clubs: Metro Denver Executives, Denver Assocs. (pres. 1985-86); So. Meth. U. Mustang (Dallas) (bd. dirs. 1976-78); Leadership Plano, Gleneagles Country. Republican. Methodist. Avocations: tennis, skiing, hunting. Office: EnCap Investments LP 3811 Turtle Creek Blvd Dallas TX 75219*

MILLER, DAVID L., lawyer; b. Bklyn., Nov. 4, 1954; BA with distinction, George Washington U., 1976; JD magna cum laude, U. Mich., 1979. Bar: DC 1979, Va. 1986. Ptnr. Real Estate practice, former mem. bd. dir., former chmn. Legal Opinion com. Pillsbury Winthrop Shaw Pittman, McLean, Va. Former bd. mem. Appleseed Found.; bd. mem. Langley Sch., McLean, Va. Mem.: ABA (former chmn. com. on legal opinions in real estate transactions), Am. Coll. Real Estate Lawyers (former chmn. com. on legal opinions), Urban Land Inst., Nat. Assn. Industrial & Office Properties, Va. State Bar Assn., DC Bar Assn. (former vice chmn. steering com. sec.), Phi Beta Kappa, Order of the Coif. Office: Pillsbury Winthrop Shaw Pittman 1650 Tysons Blvd Mc Lean VA 22102-4859 Office Phone: 703-770-7925. Office Fax: 702-770-7901. Business E-Mail: david.miller@pillsburylaw.com.

MILLER, DAVID R., academic administrator; BS, U. Calif., Berkeley; PhD, Princeton U. Acting dean engring. U. Calif. San Diego, La Jolla, assoc. dean engring., assoc. vice chancellor, acting sr. vice chancellor, assoc. vice chancellor. Office: UCSD Office Sr Vice Chancellor Acad Affairs 9500 Gilman Dr Dept 0001 La Jolla CA 92093-0001 Business E-Mail: milleravc@ucsd.edu.

MILLER, DAVID SAMEUL, physiologist; b. Bklyn., July 24, 1945; m. Mimi Salisbury, Apr. 15, 1978; 1 child, Alexander. BS, Bklyn. Coll., 1966; PhD, U. Maine, 1973. Rsch. assoc. Mt. Desert Inst. Biol. Lab., Salisbury Cove, Maine, 1973-78; rsch. scientist Mountain Desert Inst. Biol. Lab., Salisbury Cove, Maine, 1978-81; asst. mem. Mich. Cancer Found., Detroit, 1981-85; expert rsch. physiologist NIH/NIEHS, Research Triangle Park, N.C., 1985-90; rsch. physiologist NIH/NIGHS, Research Triangle Park, N.C., 1990—. Adj. scientist Mich. Cancer Found., Detroit, 1985—. Author: (chpt.) Proximal Tubular Transport of Organic Antons and Rations, 1991. Mem. Am. Physiol. Soc. Achievements include research on role for intracellular receptors in action of insulin; mechanisms of organic anion and cation transport in intact renal tissue; effects of ingested crude oil on seabirds; mechanism of organochlorine induced eggshell thinning. Office: NIH/NIEHS PO Box 12233 Durham NC 27709-2233

MILLER, DAVID WILLIAM, historian, educator; b. Coudersport, Pa., July 9, 1940; s. Arthur Charles and Kathryn Marie (Long) M.; m. Margaret Vick Richardson, Aug. 22, 1964; 1 child, Roberta Neal. BA, Rice U., 1962; MA, U. Wis., 1963; PhD, U. Chgo., 1968. Instr. history Carnegie Mellon U., Pitts., 1967-68, asst. prof., 1968-73, assoc. prof., 1973-80, prof., 1980—. Adj. prof. religious studies U. Pitts., 1998—. Author: Church, State and Nation in Ireland, 1898-1921, 1973, Queen's Rebels: Ulster Loyalism in Historical Perspective, 1978; editor: Peep o'Day Boys and Defenders: Selected Documents on the Disturbances in County Armagh, 1784-1796, 1990; co-editor: Piety and Power in Ireland, 1760-1960, 2000; assoc. editor: Oxford Dictionary of National Biography, 2004, Encyclopedia of Irish History and Culture, 2004; prin. developer: (interactive atlas) Great American History Machine, 1994. Sr. research fellow Inst. Irish Studies Queen's U., Belfast, Northern Ireland, 1975-76. Democrat. Presbyterian. Avocations: walking, singing. Office: Carnegie Mellon Univ Dept of History Schenley Park Pittsburgh PA 15213 Home Phone: 412-362-3953; Office Phone: 412-268-2953. Business E-Mail: dwmiller@cmu.edu.

MILLER, DEBRA LYNN, political scientist; b. Chgo., Dec. 8, 1952; d. Arnold and Beverly S. Miller; children: Abigail Suzanne Davidow, Molly Hannah Davidow stepchildren: Elizabeth Brooks Davidow, Judith Loraine Davidow. AB, U. Calif., Berkeley, 1974; PhD, Harvard U., Cambridge, Mass., 1979. Intern Office of Senator Birch Bayh, Washington, 1973, Office of Congressman John M. Murphy, 1973, U.S. Dept. State, 1974; asst. prof. Barnard Coll. and Columbia U., NYC, 1979—87; internat. economist Office of Indsl. Trade U.S. Dept. Commerce, Washington, 1988—90; sr. fellow and project dir. Ctr. Strategic and Internat. Studies, 1990—93, program dir., 1993—94, polit. scientist, 2006—. Cons. Ednl. Testing Svc., Princeton, NJ, 1984, 85; v.p. Tech. Strategy Group, 1987—88; dir. Strengthening of Am. Commn., Washington, 1990—94; adj. faculty George Mason U., Fairfax, Va., 1990—97; faculty Salzburg Seminar on a changing Europe, 1990; spkr. internat. politics Intellectual Property Rights Internat. Trade. Author: Principles for Health Care Reform: The Second Report of the CSIS Strengthening of America Commission, 1994; editor: A Commerce Department Analysis of European Community Directives vols. 1-3, 1989—90; contbr. chapters to books, articles to profl. jours. John Compton Predoctoral fellow, Princeton U., 1977—78, Dorothy Danforth Compton fellow, Inst. Study of World Politics, 1977—78, Mellon grant non-tenured faculty, Barnard Coll., 1980. Mem.: Coun. Fgn. Rels. Home: 1328 Maryland Ave NE # 2 Washington DC 20002-4402

MILLER, DECATUR HOWARD, lawyer; b. Balt., June 29, 1932; s. Lawrence Vernon and Katherine Louise (Baum) M.; m. Sally Burnam Smith, Nov. 23, 1963; 1 dau., Clemence Mary Katherine. BA, Yale U., 1954; LL.B., Harvard U., 1959. Bar: Md. 1959. Assoc. Piper & Marbury, Balt., 1959-62, 1963-66, ptnr., 1967-94, ptnr. emeritus, 1995—, mng. ptnr., 1974-87, chmn., 1987-94; Md. Securities commr., 1962-63. Bd. dirs. PNC Funds. Trustee Enoch Pratt Free Libr., 1975—2005, v.p., 1977—85, pres., 1985—89; trustee Calvert Sch., Balt., 1976—89, pres., 1982—87; trustee Walters Art Gallery, Balt., 1987—91; bd. sponsors Sellinger Sch. Bus. and Mgmt. Loyola Coll., 1990—98; active Mayor's Bus. Adv. Coun., 1993—99; bd. vis. U. Md. Balt. County, 1994—2000; bus. sch. adv. coun. Morgan State U., 1994—96; chmn. Equal Justice Coun., 1999—2003; bd. dirs. Balt. Symphony Orch., 1970—, v.p., 1978—86, 1988—90, pres., 1990—92, life dir., 2002—; bd. dirs. United Way Ctrl. Md., 1988—91, The Leadership, 1990—93, Empower Balt. Mgmt. Corp., 1995—, Coll. Bound Found., 1990—2001, chmn., 1994—96; bd.dirs. Greater Balt. Com., 1988—96, chmn., 1992—94; bd. dirs. U. Md. Found., 2000—03. With US Army, 1954—56. Mem. Md. Bar Assn., Am. Law Inst., Am. Bar Found., Md. Bar Found., Century Assn., Elkridge Club, Ctr. Club, Elizabethan Club, Lawyers Round Table. Home: 3704 N Charles St Apt 1305 Baltimore MD 21218 Personal E-mail: dhm26@mindspring.com.

MILLER, DENNIS, comedian; b. Pitts., Nov. 3, 1953; m. Ali Espley, April 10, 1988; 2 children, Holden, Marlon. BA, Point Park Coll. Stand-up comic, cast mem. Saturday Night Live, 1985-91; prodr., writer, host Dennis Miller Show, 1992; exec. prodr., writer, host Dennis Miller Live, 1994—2002; announcer Monday Night Football, 2000—02; exec. prodr., host Dennis Miller, 2004—05; contbr., Hannity & Colmes Fox News, 2006—. HBO spls. include: Mr. Miller Goes to Washington (also exec. prodr.), 1988, host 13th Annual Young Comedians Show (also prodr., writer), 1989, Black & White, 1990, They Shoot HBO Specials, Don't They? (also exec. prodr.), 1993, Dennis Miller: Citizen Arcane (also exec. prodr.), 1996, Dennis Miller: The Millenium Special-1,000 Years, 100 Laughs, 10 Really Good Ones (also exec. prodr., writer), 1999, Raw Feed (also writer), 2003; host Freedomfest: Nelson Mandela's 70th Birthday Celebration, The America's Choice Awards, 1990, 43d Annual Primetime Emmy Awards Presentation, 1991; albums include The Off-White Album, 1989; actor (films) Disclosure, 1994, The Net, 1995, Tales From the Crypt Presents: Bordello of Blood, 1996, Murder at 1600 Pennsylvania Avenue, 1997, Joe Dirt, 2001; TV appearances include Sam Kinison: NewsRadio, 1995, Why Did We Laugh?, 1998, Saturday Night Live: The Best of Phil Hartman, 1998, The Best of Chris Farley, 1998, Bad Boys of Saturday Night Live, 1998; (video) The Best of Mike Myers, 1998, 25th Anniversary, 1999, SportsCenter, 2000, Primetime Glick, 2001, Boston Public, 2003, The View, 2004; author: The Rants, 1996, Ranting Again, 1998, I Rant Therefore I Am, 2000, The Rant Zone: An All-Out Blitz Against Bush League Politics, Twisted Child Stars, Soul-Sucking Jobs and People Who Eat Their Jobs, 2001. Recipient Best Writing Emmy award for a Variety/Music Program for Dennis Miller Live, 1994, 1995, 1996, 1998. Office: Fox New Network LLC 1211 Ave Americas New York NY 10036*

MILLER, DENNIS DIXON, economics professor; b. Chillicothe, Ohio, May 1, 1950; s. Kermit Baker and Martha (Ralston) M. BA, Heidelberg Coll., Tiffin, Ohio, 1972; MA, U. Colo., 1979, PhD, 1985; D (hon.), Ternopil Acad. Nat. Economy, Ukraine, 2000. Instr. in econs. Am. U., Cairo, 1982-84; internat. economist USDA, Washington, 1985-86; prof. Baldwin-Wallace Coll., Berea, Ohio, 1987—, chmn. dept. econs., 2007—, social sci. divsn. chair, 2008—. Rsch. assoc. Internat. Ctr. Energy and Econ. Devel., Boulder, 1979—82, Inst. Behavorial Sci., Boulder, 1979—82, Boulder, 1984—85; vis. scholar Hoover Instn., Stanford U., Palo Alto, 1986; acad. advisor Heartland Inst., Chgo., 1988—95, Buckeye Ctr; book reviewer Choice mag., 1984—; manuscript reviewer Dryden Press, 1994—96; pub. policy advisor Heritage Found.'s Listing, Washington, 1991—; econ. cons. gen., 1991—; vis. prof. Mithibai Coll., U. Bombay, 1991; coord. agy. Air Quality Pub. Adv. Task Force, 1993; v.p. Adam Ferguson Inst., 1996—97; vis. prof. The U. of the Autonomous Regions of the Caribbean Coast of Nicaragua, Bluefields, 1996, The Ternopil Acad. of Nat. Economy Ukraine, 1997; Fulbright sr. specialist Discipline Peer Rev. Com., 2001. Fellow, Found. Def. of Democracies, 2003—; Earhart Found. fellow, 1977—78, Fulbright scholar, 1999—2000, Ukraine, 2004—05. Mem. Am. Econs. Assn., Cleve. Coun. on World Afairs, Assn. Pvt. Enterprise Edn., Ohio Assn. Economists and Polit. Scientists (v.p. 2000-01, pres. 2001-02), NE Ohio Fulbright Assn. (treas. 2006—), Intertel, Middle East Inst., Sierra Club, Nature Conservancy, Mensa, Eagle Scout. Avocations: running, tennis, reading, travel. Office: Baldwin Wallace Coll Dept Of Econs Berea OH 44017 Office Phone: 440-826-2002. Business E-Mail: dmiller@bw.edu.

MILLER, DENNIS EDWARD, health medical executive; b. Detroit, Dec. 21, 1951; m. Deborah Ann Keith, Feb. 12, 1977. BS, Austin Peay State U., 1973; MBA, U. South Fla., 1981. CPA. Chief exec. officer Hosp. Corp. of Am., Bennettsville, SC, 1976-84; div. v.p. Westworld Community Healthcare, Waco, Tex., 1984-86; group v.p. Nat. Healthcare, Inc., Dothan, Ala., 1986-87; COO Healthcare Connections, Brentwood, Tenn., 1988; cons. VHA Physician Svcs., Inc., Dallas, 1988-90; asst. adminstr., CFO Clarksville (Tenn.) Meml. Hosp., 1990; Franklin,

Tenn., 1990; sr. v.p., COO Eastside Ventures, Inc., Birmingham, Ala., 1990-93; sr. v.p. Ea. Health System, Inc., Birmingham, 1993—2002; CEO Williamson Med. Ctr., Franklin, 2002—. Chmn. Minority Leadership Task Force, Ea. Health System, Inc., 1994-95. Sec. Ala. Health Svcs. Bd.; mem. Literacy Coun. Ala., Ala. Hosp. Assn. State Legis. Com., future directions com.; chmn. Birmingham Regional Healthcare Exec. Forum; chmn. friends of scouting campaign Boy Scouts Am., 1996; mem. Franklin Land Use Steering Com. subcom., Leadership Franklin, 2002, Franklin Tomorrow, Williamson 25, 2004, 05, Franklin Bus. Leadership Coun., 2006, Hosp. Alliance Tenn., 2006, Tenn. Hosp. Ass., 2006; chmn. Healthcare Exec. Forum Mid. Tenn., 2006; mem. coun. Boy Scouts Mid. Tenn., 2006; mem. archives and mus. com. Williamson County, 2006; adv. com. mem. Tenn. Pub. Health Emergency, 2006-08. Fellow Am. Coll. Healthcare Execs. (chmn diplomate credentials com., pres. mid. Tenn. chpt. 2006, Ala. Regent's award for exec. excellence 1995), Hosp. Fin. Mgmt. Assn. (Follmer Bronze Merit award for outstanding svc.); mem. AICPA, Tenn. Soc. CPAs, Ala. Soc. CPAs (chmn. state legis. com.), Ala. Hosp. Assn. (future directions com.), Birmingham C. of C. (chmn. memberhsip com.), Birmingham East Rotary Club (pres., chmn. membership com.), Leadership Franklin Class 2003, Franklin Noon Rotary Club, Mensa, Shriners, Masons, Birmingham Touchdown Club, Sigma Chi. Avocations: hunting, fishing, gardening, antiques. Office: Williamson Med Ctr 2021 Carothers Rd Franklin TN 37067 Home Phone: 615-599-0325; Office Phone: 615-435-5151.

MILLER, DIANE WILMARTH, retired human resources director; b. Clarinda, Iowa, Mar. 12, 1940; d. Donald and Floy Pauline (Madden) W.; m. Robert Nolen Miller, Aug. 21, 1965; children: Robert Wilmarth, Anne Elizabeth. AA, Colo. Women's Coll., 1960; BBA, U. Iowa, Iowa City, 1962; MA, U. No. Colo., Greeley, 1994. Cert. tchr., Colo.; vocat. credential, Colo.; cert. sr. profl. in human resources; lic. Colo. Ins. Prodr. Sec.-counselor U. SC Rep., Myrtle Beach AFB, 1968-69; instr. Coastal Carolina Campus U. SC, Conway, 1967-69; tchr. bus. Poudre Sch. Dist. R-1, Ft. Collins, Colo., 1970-71; travel cons. United Bank Travel Svc., Greeley, Colo., 1972-74; dir. human resources Aims C.C., Greeley, 1984—2001, ret., 2001. Instr. Aims CC, 1972—89; bd. dirs. U. No. Colo. Found., Greeley, 2003—, chair, 2007—08. Bd. trustees 1st Congl. Ch., Greeley, 2005—. Mem.: Philanthropic Ednl. Orgn. (pres. 1988—89), Women's Investment Network (pres. 2007—08), Women's Panhellenic Assn. (pres. 1983—84), Questers (pres. 2002—04), WTK Club (pres. 2006—07), Scroll and Fan Club (pres. 1985—86). Home: 3542 Wagon Trail Rd Greeley CO 80634-3405

MILLER, DON MAZ, literature and language professor; b. Raleigh, NC, Sept. 22, 1970; s. Donald Max and Lucie Howison Miller; m. Andrea Smith, July 9, 2005. MFA in Creative Writing, U. NC, Greensboro, 1998. English instr. Alamance CC, Graham, NC, 2001, distance learning coord., 2006—. Contbr. chapters to books. Discussion leader Bible Study Fellowship, Greensboro, 2006—09. Home: 1905 Fernwood Dr Greensboro NC 27408

MILLER, DON WILSON, nuclear engineering educator; b. Westerville, Ohio, Mar. 16, 1942; s. Don Paul and Rachel (Jones) M.; m. Mary Catherine Thompson, June 25, 1966; children: Amy Beth, Stacy Catherine, Paul Wilson Thompson. BS in Physics, Miami U., Oxford, Ohio, 1964, MS in Physics, 1966; MS in Nuc. Engring., Ohio State U., 1970, PhD in Nuc. Engring., 1971. Rsch. assoc. Ohio State U., Columbus, 1966-68, univ. fellow, 1968-69, tchg. assoc., 1969-71, asst. prof. nuc. engring., 1971—74, assoc. prof., 1974-80, chmn. nuc. engring. program, 1977-97, prof., 1980—2004, dir. nuc. reactor lab., 1977—2002, prof. emeritus, 2004—, dir. Advanced Sys. and Safety, 2005—08. Sec., treas. Cellar Lumber Co., Westerville, Ohio, 1972-84, 85—; cons. Monsanto Rsch. Corp., Miamisburg, Ohio, 1979, NRC, Washington, 1982-84, 99—2002, Scantech. Corp., Santa Fe, 1984-95, Neoprobe Corp., Columbus, 1990, Electric Power Rsch. Inst., Palo Alto, Calif., 1992-94; mem. adv. com. on reactor safeguards Nuc. Regulatory Commn., 1995-99. Patentee in field; contbr. articles to profl. jours. Mem. Westerville Bd. Edn., 1976-91, pres., 1977-78, 86-88; mem. Ohio Sch. Bd.'s Assn., Columbus, 1976-91; mem. fed. rels. com. Nat. Sch. Bd.'s Assn., Washington, 1984-86. With USAR, 1960-68. Named Tech. Person of Yr. Columbus Tech. Coun., 1979; named to All Region Bd. Ohio Sch. Bd's. Assn., 1981, 86, Westerville South H.S. Hall of Fame, 1996; recipient Achievement award Mid Ohio Chpt. Multiple Sclerosis Soc., 1988. Fellow Am. Nuc. Soc. (chmn. edn. divsn. 1986-87, bd. dirs. 1989-91, chair human factors divsn. 1993-94, v.p./pres. elect 1995-96, pres. 1996-97, Cert. Appreciation 1991); mem. IEEE (sr. mem.), Am. Soc. Engring. Edn. (chmn. nuc. engring. divsn. 1978-79, Glenn Murphy award 1989), Nuc. Dept. Heads Orgn. (chmn. 1985-86), Westerville Edn. Assn. (Friend of Edn. award 1992), Rotary (Courtright Cmty. Svc. award 1989), Kiwanis, Hoover Sailing Club, Alpha Nu Sigma (chmn. 1991-93). Avocations: American history, travel, amateur radio. Home: Friendship Village 5675 Ponderosa Dr Columbus OH 43231 Office: Ohio State U Dept Mech Engring Nuc Engring Program E430 Scott Lab 201 W 19th Ave Columbus OH 43210-1142 Home Phone: 614-891-1858; Office Phone: 614-292-7979. Business E-Mail: miller.68@osu.edu.

MILLER, DONALD EUGENE, anthropology educator; b. Hazard, Ky., Apr. 14, 1947; s. William Jr. and Margulee (Davis) M.; m. Tamsin Elaine Miller(Ledgerwood), Aug. 6, 1981; children: Susanna Cody, Rebekah Jody. BS in Youth Leadership, Brigham Young U., 1970, BA in Archaeology, 1973, MA in Archaeology, 1974; PhD in Edn. and Anthropology, U. Tenn., 1987. Cert. tchr., Tenn. Archaeologist Brigham Young U. New World Archaeol. Found., Provo, Utah, Comitan, Chiapas, Mex., 1975-78; tchr. Roane County Schs., Rockwood, Tenn., 1978-85; asst. prof. Coll. of DuPage, Glen Ellyn, Ill., 1985-86; prof. anthropology Roane State Community Coll., Harriman, Tenn., 1986—; cons. Brigham Young U. New World Archaeol. Found., Comitan, 1979—2009. Cons. Stearns-Roger Engring., Denver, 1981; adj. prof. Tenn. Technol. U., Cookeville, 1988. Contbr. articles to profl. jours. Commr. Roane County, Kingston, 1982-85; mem. policy coun. East Tenn. Human Resource Agy., Knoxville, 1982-85, 86-90; mem. Pvt. Industry Coun., Kingston, 1984-85, 88—99. Named Tchr. of Yr., Rockwood Jr. High Sch., 1982, Outstanding Young Secondary Educator, Kingston Jaycees, 1983. Mem. Soc. for Am. Archaeology, Southwestern Philosophy of Edn. Soc., So. History Edn. Soc., Coun. on Anthropology and Edn., Tenn. Anthrop. Assn., Nat. Eagle Scout Assn., Rotary Club Rockwood(Paul Harris fellowship), Masons, Order of the Arrow, Vigil Avocations: hiking, camping, skiing, travel. Home: 109 Coffey Cir Rockwood TN 37854-9103 Office: Roane State Community Coll 276 Patton Ln Rockwood TN 37854-2730 Office Phone: 865-882-4586. Business E-Mail: millerd@roanestate.edu.

MILLER, DONALD EUGENE, lawyer; b. Providence, Mar. 20, 1947; s. Meyer Samuel and Beatrice (Wattman) M.; m. Deborah Neary Miller, Mar. 14, 1987. BA, Boston U., 1968; JD, U. Pa., 1972. Law clk. Assoc. Justice Alfred H. Joslin Supreme Ct., Providence, 1972-73; prin., lawyer Temkin, Merolla & Zurier, Providence, 1973-81, Temkin & Miller, Ltd., Providence, 1981-91; exec. v.p., gen. counsel, cro, corp. sec. The Fairchild Corp., McLean, Va., 1991—. Author: (treatise) Buying and Selling a Small Business, 1987. Mem. RI Bar, Mass. Bar, DC Bar. Avocation: Shetland sheepdog breeding and exhibiting. Home: 10704 Riverwood Dr Potomac MD 20854-1332 Office: The Fairchild Corp 1750 Tysons Blvd Mc Lean VA 22102

MILLER, DONALD EUGENE, retired air traffic controller; b. Twin Falls, Idaho, Aug. 17, 1931; s. James Alonzo and Goldia Belle Miller; m. Betsy Jean Doty; children: Michelle Anne, Mileah Lynne. Studied, Aeronautical Acad., Okla. City, 1954—56. Lic. pilot FAA, 1977. Air traffic controller FAA, Des Moines, 1956—68, St. Louis, 1968—70; instr., air traffic control FAA Acad., Oklahoma City, 1970—74; automation specialist, air traffic control FAA Tower, Portland, Oreg., 1974—75, mgr., air traffic control Hillsboro, Oreg., 1975—77; liasion officer, air traffic control Marine Corps. Air Station, Yuma, Ariz., 1977—80; air traffic quality assurance FAA Regional Hdqs., LA, 1980—81, air traffic internat. br., 1985—90; air traffic mgr. FAA Radar Facility, Bakersfield, Calif., 1981—85; ret., 1990. Cons. Hughes Aircraft, Fullerton, Calif., 1991—. Author: (manual) Automated Radar Terminal System, 1971. County treas. Union County, Creston, Iowa, 1953—55. Staff sgt. USAF, 1949—52, Korea. Mem.: Air Traffic Control Assn. (bd. mem. 1980—82). Avocations: writing, golf, dance, travel. Home: 4963 Poseidon Way Oceanside CA 92056

MILLER, DONALD LESESSNE, publishing executive; b. NYC, Jan. 10, 1932; s. John H. and Mamie (Johnson) M.; m. Ann Davie, Aug. 12, 1951 (div. 1981); children: Lynn, Mark; m. Gail Aileen Wallace, June 27, 1981. BA, U. Md., 1967; cert., Harvard Grad. Sch. Bus. Adminstrn., 1969. Enlisted U.S. Army, 1948, advanced through grades to maj., 1966, ret., 1968; spl. asst. to pres., mgr. corp. recruitment Inmont Corp., NYC, 1968-70; v.p. indsl. relations Seatrain Shipbldg. Corp., NYC, 1970-71; dep. asst. sec. def. U.S. Dept. Def., Washington, 1971-73; v.p. personnel mgmt. Columbia U., NYC, 1973-78; dir. personnel devel. and adminstrn. Internat. Paper, NYC, 1978-79; v.p. employee relations Consol. Edison N.Y., NYC, 1979-86, Dow Jones & Co., Inc., NYC, 1986-95; CEO, pub. Our World News. Bd. dir. Bank NY, 1977—2002. Author: An Album of Black Americans in the Armed Forces, 1969. Chmn. bd. emeritus Associated Black Charities, N.Y.C., 1982-94; bd. dir. Schering-Plough, 1997-2004. Decorated Legion of Merit; decorated Army Commendation Medal; recipient Disting. Civilian Service medal Dept. Def., 1973, Disting. Alumnus award U. Md., 1977. Mem. Alpha Sigma Lambda, Pi Sigma Alpha, Phi Kappa Phi, Alpha Phi Alpha, Sigma Pi Phi.

MILLER, DONALD MAX, medical association administrator; b. Harrisburg, Pa., Jan. 15, 1945; s. Floyd Vernon and Ruth Steider Miller; m. Lucie Howison Miller, July 23, 1969; children: Donald Max, Samuel Scott, Virginia Holmes, Ruth Mae. BS, Fla. State U., Tallahassee, 1967; MD, Duke U., Durham, NC, 1973, PhD, 1967. Diplomate Am. Bd. Internal Medicine, 1979. Asst. prof. U. Mich., Ann Arbor, 1979—84; assoc. prof. to prof. U. Ala. at Birmingham, 1984—99; dir., assoc v.p. health affairs Brown Cancer Ctr., U. Louisvile, 1999—. Bd. mem. Leukemia Soc. America, Loiuisville, 1999—2009; grant dir. Komen Found., Louisville, 2001; bd. mem. Rudd Heart Lung Inst., Louisville, 2000—09, U. Louisville Hosp. Lt. comdr. PHS, 1975—78, Bethesda, MD. Recipient Founders' award, Southern Soc. Clin. Investigation, 2001, Lifetime Achievement award, Mint Jubilee, 2003. Mem.: Assn. Am. Physicians. Achievements include discovery of first oligonucleotide aptamer for cancer treatment. Avocations: photography, boating. Home: 537 Barberry Ln Louisville KY 40206 Office: Brown Cancer Ctr 529 S Jackson St Louisville KY 40202 Office Fax: 502-562-4368. Business E-Mail: donaldmi@ulh.org.

MILLER, DONNA REED, councilwoman; married; children: Tari McSween(dec.), Shakira. Mem. Dem. exec. com. 59th Ward, Phila., 1970—2005, leader, 1999—; councilwoman dist. 8 Phila. City Coun., 1996—. Chmn. disabled and handicapped com., pub. safety com. Phila City Coun., vice chmn. pub. health and human services com. Named one of 100 People to Watch, Phila. Bus. Mag., 1996. Office: Phila City Coun City Hall Rm 312 Philadelphia PA 19107-3201 Office Fax: 215-686-1937. Business E-Mail: donna.miller@phila.gov.*

MILLER, DOROTHY ANNE SMITH, retired cytogenetics educator; b. NYC, Oct. 20, 1931; d. John Philip and Anna Elizabeth (Hellberg) Smith; m. Orlando Jack Miller, July 10, 1954; children: Richard L., Cynthia K., Karen A. BA in Chemistry magna cum laude, Wilson Coll., Chambersburg, Pa., 1952; PhD in Biochemistry, Yale U., 1957. Rsch. assoc. dept. ob-gyn Columbia U., NYC, 1964-72, from rsch. assoc. to asst. prof. dept. human genetics-devel., 1973-85; prof. dept. molecular biology and genetics Wayne State U., Detroit, 1985-94, prof. dept. pathology, 1985-96, prof. Ctr. for Molecular Medicine and Genetics, 1994-96. Vis. scientist clin. and population cytogenetics unit Med. Rsch. Coun., Edinburgh, Scotland, 1983-84; vis. prof. dept. genetics and molecular biology U. la Sapienza, Rome, 1988; vis. disting. fellow La Trobe U., Melbourne, Australia, 1992. Contbr. numerous articles to sci. jours. Grantee March of Dimes Birth Defects Found., 1974-93, NSF, 1983-84; recipient Disting. Cytogeneticist award Am. Cytogeneticist Conf., 2008. Mem. Am. Soc. Human Genetics, Genetics Soc. Am., Genetics Soc. Australia, Phi Beta Kappa. Presbyterian. Home: 19365 Cypress Ridge Terr #817 Lansdowne VA 20176 Personal E-mail: damiller@smartneighborhood.net.

MILLER, DOROTHY ELOISE, education educator; b. Ft. Pierce, Fla., Apr. 13, 1944; d. Robert Foy and Aline (Mahon) Wilkes. BS in Edn., Bloomsburg U., 1966, MEd, 1969; MLA, Johns Hopkins U., 1978; EdD, Columbia U., 1991. Tchr. Cen. Dauphin East H.S., Harrisburg, Pa., 1966-68, Aberdeen (Md.) H.S., 1968-69; asst. dean of coll., prof. Harford C.C., Bel Air, Md., 1969—. Owner Ideas by Design, 1995—; mem. accreditation team Mid. States Commn., 1995—; statewide writing skills assessment com., statewide English stds. com. Md. Higher Edn. Commn. 1997-2001, English composition com., 1997—, English alignment com., 2002—; adj. prof. U. Balt., 2001. Editor: Renewing the American Community Colleges, 1984; contbr. articles to profl. jours. Pres. Harlan Sq. Condominium Assn., Bel Air, 1982, 90-96, Md. internat. divsn. St. Petersburg Sister State Com., 1993-2001; edn. liaison AAUW, Harford County, Md., 1982-92; cen. com. mem. Rep. Party, Harford County, 1974-78; crusade co-chair Am. Cancer Soc., Harford County, 1976-78; mem. faculty adv. com. Md. Higher Edn. Commn., 1993-96; people's adv. coun. Harford County Coun., 1994-2003. Recipient Nat. Tchg. Excellence award Nat. Inst. for Staff and Orgn. Devel., U. Tex.-Austin, 1992. Mem. Nat. Mus. Women in the Arts (charter). Republican. Methodist. Avocations: skiing, swimming, golf, reading, image consulting. Office: Harford Community Coll 401 Thomas Run Rd Bel Air MD 21015-1627 Business E-Mail: demiller@harford.edu.

MILLER, DOUGLAS LINN, lawyer; b. Reading, Pa., Nov. 17, 1950; BA, MA, Yale U., 1972; JD, Harvard U., 1975. Bar: Ga. 1975. Lawyer Troutman Sanders, Atlanta, 1975—99, mng. ptnr. having oversight of the Project Develop. and Fin. Practice Group Hong Kong, China, 1997—99; sr. v.p., gen. counsel, chief compliance officer Mirant Corp., Atlanta, 1999—2005. Miller acted as lead counsel in state regulatory rate case proceedings, as well as fuel cost recovery and demandside cost recovery riders, prudence reviews of nuclear power plant construction, nuclear power plant ops., fossil plant construction, and coal procurement practices. Mem. ABA, State Bar Ga. Office: Mirant Corp 1155 Perimeter Ctr W Atlanta GA 30338 Office Phone: 678-579-7924. Business E-Mail: douglas.miller@mirant.com.

MILLER, DUANE KING, health and beauty care company executive; b. NYC, Mar. 1, 1931; s. Henry Charles and Helen Marion (King) M.; m. Nancy L. Longley, June 6, 1954; children: Cheryl L., Duane L. AB in Econs. and Fin., NYU, 1951. V.p. mktg. Warner-Chilcott divsn. Warner Lambert Co., Morris Plains, NJ, 1970-72, pres. divsn., 1973-77; exec. v.p. Am. Optical div., pres. Am. Optical Internat div. Warner Lambert Co., Southbridge, Mass., 1978; pres. biol. and proprietary products divsn., v.p. Revlon Health Care Group, Revlon Corp., Tuckahoe, NY, 1978-80, pres. ethical, proprietary and vision care divsns., 1981-82, corp. v.p. parent co., 1982, pres. Revlon Health Care Group, 1983-92, corp. exec. v.p. parent co., 1984-92, pres. Revlon Health Beauty Care and Internat. Group, 1988-92, ret., 1992; pres. DKL Properties, health care cons., Promedex Techs., 1992—. Author: (with others) Marketing Planning for Chief Execs. and Planners, 1966. Mem. Rep. Nat. Com. Mem. Princeton Club NY, Masons, Shriners. Home: 9 Winding Way Greenville DE 19807

MILLER, DWIGHT RICHARD, professional hair care industry executive, cosmetologist, consultant; b. Johnstown, Pa., Jan. 24, 1943; Grad., Comer & Doran Sch., San Diego; DSc (hon.), London Inst. for Applied Rsch., 1973. Cert. aromatherapist; lic. cosmetologist., instr.; Brit. Mastercraftsman. Styles dir. Marinello-Comer, Hollywood, Calif., 1965-67; expert Pivot Point Internat., Chgo., 1967-68; styles dir. Lapins, LA, 1969; dir. Redken, LA, 1970, Vidal Sassoon, London, 1971-74; world amb. Pivot Point, New Zealand and Australia, 1974-75, internat. artistic dir. Chgo., 1975-78; internat. dir., co-founder Hair Artists Inst. & Registry, 1978-81; internat. artistic dir. Zotos Internat., Darien, Conn., 1981-87, Matrix Essentials, Inc., Solon, Ohio, 1987-92; bd. dirs., founder, v.p. creative Anasazi Exclusive Salon Products, Inc., Dubuque, Iowa, 1992-96; pres. Anasazi Salon Sys., Santa Fe, 1996-98; cons., 1998—; pres. Sahag Products, 2004—06; owner Salon Sante Fe, 2004—06; internat. creative dir. Sudzz FX, 2006—07; CEO VLVT Cos., VLVT Slutions (Hair Care), VLVT Acads. Asia, Europe, N.Am. Judge hairdressing competitions Norwegian Masters, Australian Nat. Championships, N.Am. Hairstyling Awards; pres. Intercrimpers, London, 1974-75; celebrity stylist Doris Day, Juliet Prowse, Cindy Crawford, Monica Seles; co-founder VLVT AAIR Care Acads., Savannah, Toronto, Seoul, Rome, 2007-; cons. in field. Author: Sculptic Cutting Pivot Point 75, Prismatics, 1983, Milady's Standard System of Salon Skills, 1998, Amos Master Cutting System, 2000; prodr.(and dir.): (documentaries, 15), (numerous tech. and industry videos); contbr. articles and photographs to popular mags.; mem. editl. bd.: Shades mag., Launchpad mag. With USMC, 1960—64. Named Artistic Dir. Yr. Am. Salon mag., Intercoiffure Educator of the Century; presented with Order of White Elephant, 1976; recipient London Gold Cup for Best Presentation London Beauty Festival, 1982, Dr. Everett G. McDonough award for Excellence in Permanent Waving, World Master award Art and Fashion Group, 1992, N.Am. Hairstylist of the Yr. award, 2000, Life Time Achievement award Neill Corp. Aveda, 2008, LEO award, 2009 Mem. Cercle des Arts et Techniques de la Coiffure, Intercoiffure, Haute Coiffure Franchaise, Soc. Cosmetic Chemists, Hair Artists Great Britain, Internat. Assn. Trichogists, Nat. Cosmetologists Assn. (HairAmerica, cert. instr.), Am. Soc. Phytotherapy and Aromatherapy, HairChicago (hon.), Art and Fashion Group (pres. 1993), 'Dressers MC (pres. 1990—), London's Alternative Hair Club (patron), Salon Assn., Am. Beauty Assn., Profl. Beauty Assn., Alternative Hair Club North Am. (hon. pres. 2003—). Achievements include development of several profl. product lines including Vidal Sassoon-London, Design Freedom, Bain de Terre, Ultra Bond, Vavoom!, Systeme Biolage, Anasazi, Sheer Blonde. Home and Office: 707 Don Gaspar Ave Santa Fe NM 87505-2629 Business E-Mail: dwight@dwightmiller.com, dwightrmiller@aol.com.

MILLER, EDMUND KENNETH, retired electrical engineer, educator; b. Dec. 24, 1935; s. Edmund William and Viola Louise (Ludwig) M.; Patricia Ann Denn, Aug. 23, 1958; children: Kerry Ann, Mark Christopher. BSEE, Mich. Tech. U., 1957; MS in Nuclear Engring., U. Mich., 1958; MSEE, 1961, PhD in Elec. Engring., 1965. Rsch. assoc. U. Mich., Ann Arbor, 1965-68; sr. scientist MB Assocs., San Ramon, Calif., 1968-71; group leader engring. rsch. div. Lawrence Livermore Lab., Livermore, Calif., 1971-78; leader engring. rsch. div., 1978-83; leader nuclear energy sys. div., 1983-85; regents prof. elect. and computer engring. U. Kans., 1985-87; mgr. electromagnetics Rockwell Sci. Ctr., Thousand Oaks, Calif., 1987-88; dir. electromagnetics rsch. op. Gen. Rsch. Corp., Santa Barbara, Calif., 1988-89; group leader MEE div. Los Alamos (N.Mex.) Nat. Lab., 1989-93; ret., 1993. Editor: Time Domain Measurements in Electromagnets, 1986; past assoc. editor Radio Sci.; assoc. editor IEEE Potentials, 1985-91, 94-96, 97—, editor, 1992-94; assoc. editor IEEE AP-S mag.l co-editor (with L. Medgyesi-Mitschang and E.H. Newman) Computational Electromagnetics, 1991; edtl. bd. Internat. Jour. Numerical Modeling, 1990—, Computer Applications in Engring. Edn., 1992-2000; editorL Jour. Electromagietic Waves and Applications, 1991—, Jour. of Applied Computational Electromagnetics Soc., IEEE Computer Soc. Mag. Computational Scu. and Engring., 1994-2000; contbr. 150 articles to profl. jours. Stocker vis. prof. of elec. and computer engring., Ohio U., Athens, 1994-95. Fellow IEEE (mem. pres. bd. 1991-93); mem. Optical Soc. Am., Acoustical Soc. Am., Am. Soc. Engring. Edn., Internat. Sci. Radio Union (past chmn. U.S. Commn. A), Applied Computational Electromagnetics Soc. (past pres., past bd. dirs., IEEE Third Millennium medal 2000). Home Phone: 916-408-0915; Office Phone: 916-408-0916. E-mail: e.miller@ieee.org.

MILLER, EDWARD DORING, anesthesiologist, hospital administrator, dean; b. Rochester, NY, Feb. 1, 1943; s. Edward D. and Natalie (Sidam) Miller; m. Leslie Coombs, June 15, 1968 (dec. Apr. 1987); children: Sara Davenport, Katherine Coombs; m. Lynne Root, Apr. 30, 1988; children: Lawrence Root, Elizabeth Root Fusco. AB, Ohio Wesleyan U., 1964; MD, U. Rochester, 1968. Diplomate Am. Bd. Anesthesiology, Am. Coll. Anesthesiology; cert. critical care medicine. Surg. intern Univ. Hosp., Boston, 1968-69; anesthesia resident Peter Bent Brigham Hosp., Boston, 1969-71; fellow in physiology Harvard Med. Sch., Boston, 1971-73; dir. anesthesia research Brooke Army Med. Ctr., Ft. Sam Houston, Tex., 1973-75; asst. prof. anesthesiology U. Va. Med. Ctr., Charlottesville, 1975-79, assoc. prof. anesthesiology, 1979-82, prof. anesthesiology, 1982-83, prof. anesthesiology, surgery, 1983-86; E.M. Papper prof. anesthesiology, chmn. dept. Columbia U. Coll. Physicians and Surgeons, NYC, 1986-94; Mark C. Rogers prof., chmn. dept. anesthesiology Johns Hopkins U., Balt., 1994—; interim dean med. faculty, v.p. medicine Johns Hopkins U. Sch. Medicine, Balt., 1996-97, dean, CEO, vice chmn., 1997—. Sr. scientist physiology, pharmacology Hosp. Necker, Paris, 1981-82; examiner Am. Bd. Anesthesiology; v.p. clin. faculty U. Va., 1983-85, pres. 1985-86. Editor Anesthesia and Analgesia, 1982-92; contbr. numerous articles to profl. jours. Pres. Barracks-Rugby-Preston Neighborhoods, Va., 1977-79;

vestry Christ Episc. Ch., Va., 1985-86. Served to maj. M.C., U.S. Army, 1973-75. Recipient Rsch. Career Devel. award Nat. Inst. Gen. Med. Scis., 1978-83; NIH grantee, 1977-87, Inst. Nat. de la Sante et de la Recherche Medicale grantee, 1981-82. Mem. Assn. U. Anesthetists (sec. 1984-87), Am. Soc. Anesthesiologists, Am. Physiol. Soc., Internat. Anesthesia Research Soc. (trustee 1988—), Soc. Critical Care Medicine, Soc. Cardiovascular Anesthesiologists, Assn. Univ. Anesthesiologists (pres. 1990-92), Found. for Anesthesia Edn. and Rsch. (bd. dirs. 1986—), Up Med. Bd. Presbyn. Hosp. Office: Johns Hopkins U Sch Med Adminstrn 733 N Broadway Ste 100 Baltimore MD 21205-2196 Office Phone: 410-955-3180. Business E-Mail: emiller@jhmi.edu.

MILLER, ELIZABETH ANN, mathematician, human services manager; b. Alexandria, La., Sept. 11, 1939; d. Brice Turrentine and Thelma Elizabeth (Stalsby) Harrison; m. Tilton Anthony Auenson, Nov. 26, 1957 (div. Oct. 1963); children: Rebecca Ann Auenson Issa, David Brice Auenson; m. Donald Keith Miller, Nov. 17, 1984. BS, La. Coll., 1962; MS, Northwestern State U., Natchitoches, La., 1964. Cert. tchr., La. Tchr. Rapides Parish Schs., Alexandria, La., 1964-65, 67-69; instr. Itawamba Jr. Coll., Fulton, Miss., 1965-66, Jefferson State. Jr. Coll., Birmingham, Ala., 1966-67; human svc. worker II Rapides Parish Office Human Devel., Alexandria, 1969-82; substitute tchr. various Alexandria schs., 1982-87; instr. Comm. Coll. Alexandria, 1987-88; substitute tchr. Rapides Parish Schs., Alexandria, 1989—, Holy Savior Menard Ctrl. H.S., Alexandra Country Day Sch., 1993—98; tchr. Forest Hill Acad., 2000. Grad. teaching asst. Northwestern State U., 1963-64.; adj. instr. St. Leo Coll., England AFB, La., 1990-92, La. Coll., Pineville, 1992, La. State U., Alexandria, 2002, La. C.C. and Tech. Coll. Sys., Ctrl. La. State Hosp, La. Cmty. and Tech. Coll., 2003. Mem. AAUW (sec. Alexandria-Pineville br. 1990-92, 2002-04, parliamentarian 2004—), DAR (Am. History Month chair 1991-94). Democrat. United Methodist. Home: 5821 Starling Cir Alexandria LA 71301-2641

MILLER, ELIZABETH GAMBLE, literature and language professor, translator; b. Boston, May 31, 1926; d. Fred Ridley and Leona Aileen (Crain) Gamble; m. Frederick James Miller, Jr., July 15, 1949 (dec. Jan. 17, 1997); children: Frederick James III, Janice Elaine Miller Jones, David Earl. BA, Tex. Christian U., 1946; MA, So. Meth. U., 1965; PhD, U. Tex., Dallas, 1981. Instr. So. Meth. U., Dallas, 1947-49, 62-72, asst. prof., 1972-84, assoc. prof. Spanish lang. and lit., 1984—, prof. emeritus, 2002—. Lectr. in field; translator in field. Translator: Sólo la voz/Only the Voice (Hugo Lindo), 1984, Fábulas/Fables (David Escobar Galindo), 1985, The Ways of Rain and Other Poems by Hugo Lindo, 1986, Ten Poems (Antonio Porpetta), 1994, Only Rage Will Rot (Carlos Ernesto Garcia), 1994, En las noches que desvisten otras noches/During Nights that Undress Other Nights (Nela Rio), 2003, Sosteniendo la mirada:cuando las imágenes tiemblan/Sustaining the Gaze/Soutenant le regard: quand les images tremblent, 2004, The Space of Light/El espacio de la luz, (short stories and poems), Nela Rio, 2004 (finalist Tex. Inst. Letters Soeurette Diehl Fraser award for best book of transl. for 2004); (short stories) The Enchanted Raisin (Jacquelin Balcells), 1988; trans. more than 30 authors of numerous poems, short stories and essays in various pubs.; contbr. articles to profl. jours. Named Académica Correspondiente, Acad. Lengua, El Salvador, 1985. Mem. Am. Lit. Translators Assn. (charter, editor newsletter 1983-2006, mem. editorial bd., sec.-treas. 1983-85), Translation Review (editl. bd.), Acad. Iberoamericana de Poesia, S.W. Coun. Latin Am. Studies, Latin Am. Studies Assn., Registro Creativo Canadian Hispanist. Mem. Christian Ch. (Disciples Of Christ). Avocations: boating, reading, travel. Office Phone: 214-768-2316. Business E-Mail: emiller@mail.smu.edu.

MILLER, ELIZABETH JOAN, artist, guidance counselor; b. Vienna, Austria, Nov. 2, 1925; arrived in U.S., 1941; d. Joseph Ronald Ehrlich and Martha Eleanor Lamm-Ehrlich; m. Alfred Abraham Miller; children: Mark M., Steven H. B in Chem. Engring., City Coll., NYC, 1947, MA in Math. Edn., 1965; MEd in Human Devel., Tchrs. Coll., Columbia U., NYC, 1977. Asst. to chief physicist Air Reduction Co., NYC, 1947—53; tchr. HS math. NYC Bd. Edn., 1960—77, guidance counselor, 1977—90; represented by High Studio Art Gallery, Moorpark, Calif. One-woman shows include Camarillo Ctr. for Spiritual Living, Calif., 2006, 2007, Harbor Village Gallery, Ventura, Calif., 2006, 2007, Thousand Oaks Botanic Gardens, 2006, 2007, Leisure Village, 2007, Buena Ventura Art Gallery, Ventura, Calif., 2007, Westlake Libr., 2007—, Seven Oaks Rehab. & Fitness Ctr., Westlake Vill., Calif., 71 Palms Restaurant Gallery, Ventura, Represented in permanent collections City of Oxnard. Mem. Westlake Village Art Guild, 1992—; pres. (sisterhood) Riverdale Temple, Bronx, NY, 1988—90; sec., pres. Soc. Women Engrs., NE Region, 1950—56. Mem.: Ventura County Maritime Mus., Calif. (mem., exhibiting artist), Buena Ventura Art Assn., Calif. Gold Coast Watercolor Soc., Peripheral Neuropathy Support (recording sec. 2000—06). Achievements include patents for visually learning mathematical operations with signed numbers. Home and Office: 2478 Chaucer Pl Thousand Oaks CA 91362 Office Phone: 805-493-2698. Personal E-mail: arliese@verizon.net.

MILLER, ELLEN S., marketing executive; b. Indpls., June 28, 1954; d. Harold Edward and Lilian (Gantner) M. BA, DePauw U., 1976; postgrad., Sch. Visual Arts, NYC, 1981-82. Editorial asst. Daisy mag., NYC, 1976-77; asst. dept. mgr., Christmas hiring mgr. Bloomingdale's, NYC, 1978; sales rep. Rosenthal USA Ltd., NYC, 1979, mktg. asst., 1980-81, dir. mktg. comms., 1982-90; mgr. consumer mktg. Creamer Dickson Basford, Providence, 1990, v.p., 1991-94; prin. E.S. Miller Comm., Providence, 1994—. Instr. Learning Connection. Editor Community Prep. Sch. newsletter, 1993. Trustee Cmty. Prep Sch., Providence, 1993—, mem. exec. com., 1997—. Recipient Bell Ringer award New Eng. Pub. Club, 1992, 93, Iris award N.J. chpt. Internat. Assn. Bus. Communicators, 1993, Silver Quill award Dist. I, 1993, Holland award Ctrl. Mass. Advt. Club, 1997. Mem. Pub. Rels. Soc. Am., Nat. Tabletop Assn. (com. chair 1989), Internat. Tabletop Awards (bd. dirs. 1989), Rotary Club. Republican. Presbyterian. Office Phone: 401-724-3773. Personal E-mail: ellensmiller@att.net.

MILLER, ELLIOTT CAIRNS, retired bank executive, lawyer; b. Cambridge, Mass., May 4, 1934; s. James Wilkinson and Mary Elliott (Cairns) M.; m. Mary Killion, July 2, 1960; children: Jonathan Vaill, Stephen Killion. AB, Harvard Coll., 1956; JD, U. Mich., 1961; LLM, Boston U., 1970. Bar: Conn. 1962. Assoc. Robinson & Cole, Hartford, Conn., 1961-66, ptnr., 1967-72; v.p., counsel Soc. for Savs., Hartford, Conn., 1972-73, sr. v.p., 1973-78, exec. v.p., 1978, pres., CEO, dir., 1979-90; pres., CEO Soc. for Savs. Bancorp Inc., 1987-90. Bd. dirs. nat. council Savs. Inst., Washington, 1984-88. Trustee, chmn. Kingswood-Oxford Sch., West Hartford, 1977-87; trustee Coordinating Coun. on Founds., 1987-90; bd. dirs. Downtown Coun., Hartford, 1975-90; trustee Greater Hartford Arts Coun., 1980-88; trustee Wadsworth Atheneum, 1990-99; trustee Hartford Stage Co., 1973-85; corporator Hartford Hosp., Inst. of Living; mem. transition com. Conn. State Treas. Denise Nappier, 1998-99. With U.S. Army, 1956-58. Mem. Conn. Bar Assn., 1893 Club (Hartford), Monday Evening Club (Hartford), Dauntless Club (Essex, Conn.), Ferrari Club Am., Bernese Mountain Dog Club. Methodist. Home: 9 Champlin Sq Essex CT 06426-1101 E-mail: soleoak@aol.com.

MILLER, EMILIE F., former state senator, consultant; b. Chgo., Aug. 11, 1936; d. Bruno C. and Etta M. (Senese) Feiza; m. Dean E. Miller; children: Desireé M., Edward C. BSBA, Drake U., 1958. Asst. buyer Jordan Marsh Co., Boston, 1958-60, Carson, Pirie, Scott & Co., Chgo., 1960-62; dept. mgr., asst. buyer Woodward & Lothrop, Washington, 1962-64; state labor coord. Robb Davis Daliles Joint Campaign; legis. aide Senator Adelard Brandt, Va., 1980-83; fin. dir. Saslaw for Congress, 1984; legis. cons. Va. Fedn. Bus. Profl. Women, 1986-87, 98-00; senator Va. Gen. Assembly, Richmond, 1988-92; cons. apptd. by Gov. Wilder to bd. dirs. Innovative Tech. Authority, 1992-94, Ctr. for Innovative Tech., 1992-94; sr. mgr. Thompson, Cobb, Bazilio & Assocs., 1999—2006; bd. visitors Mt. Vernon, 2009—. Bus. tng. seminars, Moscow, Nizhny Novgorod, Russia, 1993, Novgorod, St. Petersburg, 95; cons. in field. Guest editl. writer No. Va. Sun, 1981; host, prodr. weekly TV program, Channel 61. Active State Ctrl. Com. Dem. Party Va., Richmond, 1974—2005, steering com., 2000-05, chair 11th congrl. dist., 2001-05; mem. Fairfax County Dem. Com., 1968—, chair, 1976-80, 98-2000, Presdl. Inaugural Com., 1977, 1992 Dem. Nat. Platform Com., Va., Dem. Adv. Com. Robb-Spong Commn., 1978-79; chair 11th Congrl. Dist. Dem. Com., 2001—; founder, chair Va. Assoc. Dem. County and City Chmn., 1976-80; chmn. Fairfax County Dem. Com., 1976-80, 1998-00; security supr. 1980 Dem. Nat. Conv.; v.p. Va. Fedn. Dem. Women, 1992-94; bd. dirs. Stop Child Abuse Now, 1988, Ctr. Innovative Tech., 1992-94, Ct. Apptd. Spl. Advs., 1993-96; nat. alumni bd. J.A. Achievement, BRAVO adv. com. for the first Gov.'s Awards for Arts in Va., 1979-80; lay tchr. St. Ambrose Cath. Ch., 1963-80; del. to White House Conf. on Children, 1970; chair Va. Coalition for Mentally Disabled, 1992-94; com. of 100, Va. Opera Bd., 1994-99, guest lect., Osher Inst. GMU, 2006; bd. dirs. Social Action Linking Together; chair Women for Warner, 2009. Recipient Disting. Grad. award Jr. Achievement, 1973, Woman of Achievement award Fairfax (Va.) Bd. Suprs. and Fairfax County Commn. for Women, 1982, Cmty. Svc. award Friends of Victims Assistance Network, 1988, Founders award Fairfax County Coun. of Arts, 1989, Mental Health Assn. of Northern Va. Warren Stambaugh award, 1991, Ann. Svc. award Va. Assn. for Marriage and Family Therapy, 1991, Psychology Soc. of Washington Cmty. Svc. award, 1993, pacesetter award So. Women in Pub. Leadership Conf., 1996. Mem. NOW, Nat. Mus. Women in the Arts, Va. Assn. Female Execs. (adv. bd., bd. dirs., v.p. 1992-99), Va. Assn. Cmty. Svc. Bds. (chmn. 1980-82), North Va. Assn. Cmty. Bds. (chmn. 1978-79, 95-98), Fairfax County Coun. Arts (v.p. 1980—, mem. exec. com. internat. children's festival, Founders award 1989), Fairfax County C. of C. (legis. com.), Greater Merrifield Bus. and Profl. Assn., Mental Health Assn. No.Va. (bd. dirs.), Ctrl. Fairfax C. of C., Falls Church C. of C., Bus. and Profl. Women's Fedn. Va., Mantua Citizens Assn. (exec. bd.), Bus. and Profl. Women's Club (pres. Falls Church chpt. 1994-96, 2007—09, Woman of Yr. award 1990), Women's Nat. Dem. Club (past v.p., bd. govs.), Va. Assn. Female Execs. (bd. dirs. 1992-99), Phi Gamma Nu. Democrat. Roman Catholic. Avocations: tennis, art, baseball. Home: 8701 Duvall St Fairfax VA 22031-2711 Office Phone: 703-560-0291. Personal E-mail: emiliemiller9@cs.com, emiliemiller1@cox.net.

MILLER, ERNEST CHARLES, management consultant; b. Bronx, NY, July 14, 1925; s. Ernest Philip and Elizabeth (Hellwig) M.; m. Edith Grosvenor Porterfield, Nov. 11, 1947 (div. Oct. 3, 1963); children: Laura Lee, Marcy Rogers, Ernest Charles; m. Tung-fen Lin, Jan. 8, 1985. AB, Yale U., New Haven, 1945; MA, U. Pa., Phila., 1949. Lic. psychologist, N.Y. Instr. U. Pa., 1947-51, cons., 1950-53; br. mgr., bd. dirs. Richardson, Bellows, Henry & Co., Inc., 1953-55; mgr. personnel tech. Am. Standard, Inc., 1955-59; mng. prin. Hellwig, Miller & Assos., Westport, Conn., 1959-61; sr. assoc. Cresap, McCormick & Paget, Inc., NYC, 1961-63; with Am. Mgmt. Assns., NYC, 1964-83, pres. AMACOM div., 1978-81, group v.p. AMA Publs. Group, 1981-83; pres. Miller, Hellwig Assocs., 1984—. Author works in strategic planning, orgn. devel., human resources, exec. compensation and mgmt. Bd. dirs. La Jolla Inst. Allergy & Immunology; chmn. Compensation Com., Audit Com., 1989-07; assoc. Columbia U. All-Univ. Seminar Orgn & Mgmt. NEH fellow, 1980 Mem. APA, Soc. Indsl. and Orgnl. Psychology. Episcopalian. Office: Miller Hellwig Assocs 150 W End Ave New York NY 10023-5713

MILLER, EUGENE, business educator, consultant; b. Chgo., Oct. 6, 1925; s. Harry and Fannie (Prosterman) M.; m. Edith Sutker, Sept. 23, 1951 (div. Sept. 1965); children: Ross, Scott, June; m. Thelma Gottlieb, Dec. 22, 1965; stepchildren: Paul Gottlieb, Alan Gottlieb. BS, Ga. Inst. Tech., 1945; AB magna cum laude, Bethany Coll., 1947, LLD, 1969; diploma, Oxford U., Eng., 1947; MS in Journalism, Columbia U., 1948; MBA, NYU, 1959; postgrad., Pace U., 1973—. Reporter, then city editor Greensboro (N.C.) Daily News, 1948-52; S.W. bur. chief Bus. Week mag., Houston, 1952-54, assoc. mng. editor NYC, 1954-60; dir. pub. affairs and communications McGraw-Hill, Inc., 1960-63, v.p., 1963-68; sr. v.p. pub. rels. and investor rels., exec. com. N.Y. Stock Exch., NYC, 1968-73; sr. v.p. CNA Fin. Corp., Chgo., 1973-75; chmn. Eugene Miller & Assos., Glencoe, Ill., 1975-77; v.p. USG Corp., Chgo., 1977-82, sr. v.p., 1982-85, mem. mgmt. com., 1982-91, exec. v.p., CFO, 1985-87, elected vice chmn., CFO, 1987-91, mem. exec. com., also bd. dirs.; prof., exec.-in-residence Coll. Bus. Fla. Atlantic U., Boca Raton, 1991—; chmn., CEO Ideon Group, Inc., Jacksonville, Fla., 1996. Campaign speechwriter Pres. Dwight Eisenhower, 1956; adj. prof. mgmt. NYU, 1963-65; prof. bus. adminstrn. Fordham U., 1969-75; prof. fin., chmn. dept. Northeastern Ill. U., 1975-78; lectr. to bus. and ednl. groups; bd. dirs. MRFI, Inc., Chgo., 1990-, bd. dirs., mem. adv. bd. dirs. Nationwide Acceptance Corp., Chgo.; cons. to sec. Dept. Commerce, 1961-66; editor-in-residence U. Oreg., 1992; exec.-in-residence U. Ill., 1991, U. Wis., 1991, U. Toronto, 1992; exec.-in-residence, POHL fellow U. Wyo., 1992; mem. adv. bd. CFO mag., 1991-99; bd. dirs. The Strive Group, Chgo., 2000-; cons. Arthur Andersen & Co., Chgo., 1992-97; arbitrator NYSE, 2002—, NASD, 2005-. Author: Your Future in Securities, 1974, Barron's Guide to Graduate Business Schools, 1977, 15th edit., 2007; contbg. editor: Public Relations Handbook, 1988, Boardroom Reports, 1986—; writer syndicated bus. column., 1964-86; mem. editl. bd. IRQ mag., 1997—. Trustee Bethany Coll., 1970—; mem. alumni bd. Columbia U. Sch. Journalism. Comdr. USNR, World War II, ret. Recipient outstanding achievement award Bethany Coll., 1963, 50th anniversary award Sch. Journalism Columbia U., also honors award, 1963, Sch. Journalism Ohio U., 1964, disting. svc. award in investment edn. Nat. Assn. Investment Clubs, 1980, Roalman award Nat. Investor Rels. Inst., 1987; honored with Eugene Miller Bd. Rm. Bethany Coll., 1999, Eugene Miller Bd. Rm. Coll. Bus. Fla. Atlantic U., 2007. Fellow Pub. Rels. Soc. Am.; mem. Soc. Am. Bus. Editors and Writers (founder, Pres.'s award 2003), Fin. Execs. Inst., St. Andrew's Country Club, Sigma Delta Chi, Alpha Sigma Phi. Home: 7351 Ballantrae Ct Boca Raton FL 33496-1423 Office: Fla Atlantic U Coll Business 777 Glades Rd Boca Raton FL 33431-6424 Office Phone: 561-297-3630. Personal E-mail: Gene160@aol.com.

MILLER, EWING HARRY, retired architect; b. Toledo, Ohio, Oct. 5, 1923; s. Ewing Harry and Esther Alice (Graves) M.; children: Victoria Alice, Paul Ewing; m. Donna Barnard Ari. BA, U. Pa., 1947, MA, 1948. Draftsman Harbeson, Hough, Livingston & Larson, Phila., 1948; designer Nolen & Swinburne, Phila., 1950-52; project architect Gilboy & O'Malley, London, 1953-55; partner Miller, Vrydagh & Miller, Terre Haute, Ind., 1955-65; pres. Ewing Miller Partnership, Terre Haute, 1965-70, Archonics Corp., 1970-76, chmn. bd., 1976-79; sr. ptnr. for design Archonics Design Partnership, Indpls., 1979-84; prin. and dir. architecture eastern region U.S. Howard Needles, Tammen & Bergendoff, 1985-92; archtl. cons., 1992—2005; gen. ptnr. Lockerbie Devel. Co., 1978-86, Lockerbie Glove Devel. Co., 1983-86, East St. Devel. Co., 1979-86. Contbr. articles to profl. jours.; archtl. critic Indpls. Monthly Mag.; major archtl. works include: various bldgs. Ind. U., including grad. biology lab., Ind. State U., master plan and edn. bldgs., residence halls and sci. bldg., libr. and various classroom bldgs., Southwestern Ind. U., master plan and edn. bldgs., Ind. and Ohio Laborers Tng. Ctrs., master plan U. San Diego. Westin Conv. Hotel; various office parks, Indpls. Pub. Transp. Corp. facility, addition to Duesenberg Factory; master plan Ind. State Govt. Complex, State of Ind. and design of new state office bldg.; prin. in charge printing facility Ho. of Rep. Architect of the Capitol, prin. in charge of Mastser Plan for design and restoration of Old Exec. Office Bldg., Washington; master plan for remodeling The Pentagon, Washington; prin. in charge design for remodeling Dept. of State, Washington; client rep. for remodeling Midwest Direct Mktg. Ctr., B.M.G., Inc., N.Y. Mem. Ind. Gov.'s Commn. on Aging, 1959-62; pres. Gov.'s Commn. on Comprehensive Health Planning, Ind., 1970-75, Behavioral Research Found., 1965-85; bd. mgrs. Sheldon Swope Art Gallery, 1965-80, pres., 1965-73; bd. dirs. Center for Exploration of Values and Meaning, 1978-85, Herron Art Gallery, 1980-88; chmn. Indpls. Arts and Cultural Alliance, 1983; v.p. Am. Chestnut Land Trust, Port Republic, Md.; chmn. bd. Cove Point Natural Heritage Trust, Lusby, Md., 1995—, bd. mem. The Enviromnmental Fund of Maryland. Recipient design citation, biennial awards program Ind. Soc. Architects; Honor awards, triennial design awards East Central Region AIA; Nat. Archtl. award of excellence Am. Inst. Steel Constrn.; 1st Honor award and winner Internat. Competition for Housing, Indpls.; nat. award of excellence for univ. bldgs. Am. Sch. and Univ. Mag.; Am. Inst. Arch. Regional Honor award restoration of Circle Theater, various office bldgs. Fellow AIA (mem. com. on design, chmn. com. on architecture for edn., mem. Vision 2000 study, architecture in coming decade), Cove Point Natural heritage Trust (chmn. bd.), Downtown Neighborhood Assn. (bd. dirs. Penn Quater Wash. DC chpt.), Lambda Alpha Hon. Soc., Wash. DC chpt. Home: 601 Pennsylvania Ave NW Apt 1202 Washington DC 20004-2644

MILLER, FLEMON MARSHALL, public works manager; b. LA, Sept. 15, 1942; s. Flemon Harris Miller and Claudia Marshall; m. Peggy Ann Torres, Mar. 14, 1992; children: Diane Barboza, Anthony Barboza; m. Louida Jarmon Penland (div.); 1 child, Marguet Marshall. Cert. course instr. in supplier diversity 2000, hazardous waste mgr. Dept. Transp. Warehouse man City of LA, 1969—75, auto parts storekeeper, 1975—77, storekeeper dept. water and power, 1977—89, sr. storekeeper dept. power and water supply supr., 1989—92, sr. storekeeper dept. power and water, 1992—99, sr. storekeeper dept. power and water and supr. investment recovery, 1999—; owner, operator The Miller Method Indsl. Metal Recyclers. Chmn. adv. coun. Normandie Ave. Elem. Sch., LA, 1972—77. Recipient Recycler of Yr., City of LA, 2006, Law Enforcement Hero award, Nat. Assn. Police Orgns., 2006. Office: Investment Recovery 11797 Truesdale St Sun Valley CA 91352 Office Phone: 818-581-8918.

MILLER, FORREST E., telecommunications industry executive; BS in acctg., Univ. So. Calif.; MBA, Stanford Univ. CPA. Acct. Coopers & Lybrand; sr. assoc. Marakon Assoc.; mgmt. positions through pres. Pacific Bell directory Pacific Telesis, 1984—97; pres., CEO SBC directory ops. SBC Comm., 1997—99, pres., CEO SNET, 1999, pres., CEO Southwestern Bell, group pres. corp. planning, group pres. external affairs & planning, 2004; group pres. AT&T Comm. Corp. AT&T Inc. (merger of SBC Comm. with AT&T Corp.), San Antonio, 2005—06; group pres. strategic initiatives & HR AT&T Inc., San Antonio, 2006—07, group pres. corp. strategy & develop., 2007—. Office: AT&T Inc 175 E Houston San Antonio TX 78205 Mailing: AT&T Inc PO Box 2933 San Antonio TX 78299-2933*

MILLER, FRANK LOUIS, school psychologist; b. Flushing, NY, Nov. 28, 1949; s. Glen Robert and Joan Ann (Jockers) M.; m. Coletta Jean Cassel, Sept. 3, 1983; children: Adrian Mark, Monica Michelle, Sade Alexandra. BA in English Edn., Va. Poly. Inst. & State U., 1972; MS in Psychology, Radford U., Va., 1974, EdS in Sch. Psychology, 1990. Cert. sch. psychologist. Va., W.Va., Md., Del, sch. psychologist, NCSP. Sch. psychologist Montgomery County Schs., Christiansburg, Va., 1974-79, Salem (Va.) City/Roanoke County, 1979-80, Caroline County Schs., Denton, Md., 1988-97, Lake Forest Sch. Dist., Felton, Del., 1997—; sch. psychologist, dir. spl. svcs. Taylor County Schs., Grafton, W.Va., 1980-88. Pres. Caroline County Tchrs. Assn., Denton, 1992-93, Caroline County Coun. PTAs, Denton, 1992-94, Delware Assn. Sch. Psychologists, 2000-014; mem. state bd. Md. COngress Parents & Tchrs., Balt., 1992-94. Avocations: skiing, refinishing antiques, classic cars, gardening. Home: 8559 Dogwood Blossom Ln Denton MD 21629-2336 Personal E-mail: flmiller9@hotmail.com.

MILLER, FRED HEINS, lawyer, retired educator; s. Fred H. and Marian B. Miller; m. Marcia Henry, June 20, 1959; children: Frederick Clayton, Robert Henry. BA, U. Mich., Ann Arbor, 1959, JD, 1962. Bar: Ohio 1962, Okla. 1968. Assoc. Dunbar, Kienzle & Murphy, Columbus, Ohio, 1962—66; prof. U. Okla. Law Sch., Norman, 1966—2006, George L. Cross rsch. prof., 1989—2006, Kenneth McAfee chmn. law, centennial prof., 1991—2006; of counsel Phillips, Murrah, Oklahoma City, 2006—. Pres. Nat. Conf. Com. Uniform State Laws, Chgo., 2003—05; cons. Fed. Res. Bd., Washington, 1975—76, mem. consumer adv. coun., 1983—85. Author: Truth in Lending, 2000, Law Modern Payment Systems, 2002; author, editor: Hawkland UCC Series, 2005—. Recipient Svc. award, Oklahoma City U., 2002, Senator William Proxmire Lifetime Achievement award, 2005, UCC Exceptional Svc. award, ABA Bus. Sect., 2005. Mem.: ABA, Okla. Bar Assn., Am. Law Inst., Order of Coif, Phi Beta Kappa. Avocations: antiques, history. Office: U Okla Coll Law 300 Timberdell Rd Norman OK 73019

MILLER, FREDERICK, pathologist; b. NYC, Apr. 5, 1937; s. Alex and Sarah Miller; m. Emilie J Kronish, June 2, 1962; children: David, Allison. BS, U. Wis., 1956; MD, N.Y. U., 1961. Diplomate Am Bd Pathology. Intern Bellevue Hosp., NYC, 1961-62, resident, 1962-63; practice medicine specializing in pathology, 1965—; clin. assoc., attending physician Nat. Inst. Arthritis and Metabolic Diseases, 1963-65; resident chief pathology dept. NYU Med. Ctr., 1965-67; attending pathologist Bellevue and Univ. Hosps., NYC, 1967; asst. prof. pathology NYU, 1967-70, assoc. prof., 1970, SUNY, Stony Brook, 1970-75, prof., 1975—, chmn. dept. pathology, 1973-2000, Marvin Kuschner prof. pathology, 1991—, dir. lab. for arthritis and related diseases, 1976—; dir. labs. Univ. Hosp., Stony Brook, 1978—2003, assoc. dir. labs., 2003—, pathologist-in-chief, 1979—2003. Mem. Nat. Bd. Med. Examiners in Pathology, 1996—98. Contbr. articles to profl jours. With USPHS, 1963—65. Recipient Bausch and Lomb Medal for Research, 1961, Pres's Award, SUNY, Stony Brook, 1990, Chancellor's Award, 1990, Aesculapius Award, 1993, Golden Apple Award, ASMA, 1995; grantee

NIH, 1963—87. Mem.: AAAS, Am. Orchid Soc, Am. Assn. Immunologists, N.Y. Acad. Sci., Internat. Acad. Pathology, Am. Soc. Clin. Pathologists (award 1961), Harvey Soc., Alpha Omega Alpha (counselor 2000—03), Sigma Xi. Home: 46 Manchester Ln Stony Brook NY 11790-2826 Office: Univ Hosp USB L2-743B Stony Brook NY 11794-7025 Office Phone: 631-444-2222.

MILLER, FREDERICK EDWIN, JR., history professor, government agency administrator; b. Stamford, Conn., Jan. 27, 1939; s. Frederick Edwin and Florence Baker Miller; m. Louise Ellen Wood, July 20, 1985. B of Social Sci. in Edn. cum laude, Fairfield U., 1960; MA in History, Boston U., 1961; postgrad., NYU, 1965—67; JD, Fordham U., 1976. Tchr. dept. spl. pupil svcs. Stamford Pub. Schs., Conn., 1961—62; tchr. social studies Stamford Cath. High Sch., 1965—67; lectr. history and govt. CUNY, NYC CC, 1966—73; lectr. CUNY Queens Coll., 1968—69; state rep. Conn. Ho. Reps., Hartford, 1971—73; asst. clk. Superior Ct. Jud. Dist. Stamford-Norwalk, 1976—95; justice of peace Fairfield. Ajd. prof. Norwalk C.C., Concordia Coll., Bronxville, NY, Coll. New Rochelle, St. Basils Coll., Stamford, Fairfield U., Sacred Heart U.; incorporator Stamford Hosp., Stamford, Conn.; mem. bd. Drug Liberation Inc, Stamford, Conn., Stamford Forum for World Affairs, Stamford, Conn., South End Cmty. Ctr., Stamford, Conn., Spanish Internat. Ctr., Stamford, Conn.; mem. bd. trustees Catholic Charities, Diocese Bridgeport, Conn. Mem. adv. task force desegregation Stamford Pub. Schs., 1971—72; mem. Bd. Assessment Appeals, Fairfield, 1995—99, chmn., 1997—99; mem. Stamford Bd. Reps., 1967—77, pres., 1973—77. Mem.: AAUP, Am. Polit. Sci. Assn., Am. Cath. Hist. Assn., Am. Hist. Assn., Ancient Order Hibernians, KC 4th Degree, Fairfield U. Honor Soc., Phi Alpha Theta. Democrat. Roman Catholic. Home: 167 Rock Major Rd Fairfield CT 06824 Personal E-mail: miller.frederick@att.net.

MILLER, GALE TIMOTHY, lawyer; b. Kalamazoo, Sept. 15, 1946; s. Arthur H. and Eleanor (Johnson) M.; m. Janice Lindvall, June 1, 1968; children: Jeremy L., Amanda E., Timothy W. AB, Augustana Coll., 1968; JD, U. Mich., 1971. Bar: Mich. 1971, Colo. 1973, U.S. Dist. Ct. Colo. 1973, U.S. Ct. Appeals (10th cir.) 1979, U.S. Supreme Ct. 1997. Trial atty. FTC, Washington, 1971-73; assoc. Davis Graham & Stubbs LLP, Denver, 1973-77, ptnr., 1978—2008, chmn. exec. com., 1998—2001; judge Colo. Ct. Appeals, 2009—. Bd. dirs. Colo. Jud. Inst., 1999—, v.p., 2005—06, chair, 2006—08, Colo. Lawyers Com., 1989—91, bd. dirs., 1987—2006, mem. exec. com., 2004—06. Recipient Cmty. Svc. award Colo. Hispanic Bar Assn., 1996: named Individual Lawyer of Yr. Colo. Lawyers Com., 1994, Outstanding Sustainal Contbn., 2005. Mem. ABA (antitrust sect. task force on model civil antitrust jury instrns. 1985-87), Colo. Bar Assn. (mem. bd. govs., 2007-09, chair antitrust sect. 1996-98), Denver Bar Assn. Democrat. Lutheran. Office: Colo Ct Appeals 2 E 14th Ave Denver CO 80203 Office Phone: 303-861-1111.

MILLER, GARY C., lawyer; b. Little Rock, May 23, 1955; s. William Scott, Jr. and Margaret Imogene (Puckett) M.; m. Mary Catherine Miller, Oct. 23, 2000; children: Daniel, Sarah. BA in Econs. and Managerial Studies, Rice U., 1977; JD, U. Tex., 1980. Bar: Tex. 1980, US Dist. Ct. (so. dist.) Tex. 1981, US Dist. Ct. (no. and we. dists.) Tex. 1991, US Dist. Ct. (ea. dist.) Tex. 1993, US Ct. Appeals (5th cir) 1980, US Supreme Ct. 1995, 2008, US Dist. Ct. (ea. & we. dist.) orleans, 2008. Atty. Wood, Campbell, Moody & Gibbs, Houston, 1980-83, Gibbs & Ratliff, Houston, 1983-85, Andrews & Kurth LLP and prececessor, Houston, 1985—2008. Contbr. articles to profl. jours. Co-chair Ark. Bar. Assoc. Legal Svcs. Coms., 2009—; chmn. Westminster Weekday Sch., Houston, 1993—96; chmn., bd. trustees Westminster United Meth. Ch., Houston, 1996—98; bd. dirs. Houston Vol. Lawyers Program, 2000—04, Houston Lawyer Referral Svc., 2004—05; co-chair HBA Legalines, 2002—03. Mem. Houston Bar Assn., Order of Coif, Phi Beta Kappa. Office: 214 Hobson Ave Hot Springs AR 71913 Office Phone: 501-620-4949. Personal E-mail: garycmillerlaw@gmail.com.

MILLER, GARY EVAN, psychiatrist, mental health services professional; b. Cleve., Aug. 19, 1935; s. Henry M. and Mollie (Price) M.; m. Karen Ann Marie Barrett, Sept. 16, 1972; children: Anna Charis, Rebecca Elizabeth. MD, U. Tex., Galveston, 1960. Diplomate in psychiatry, addiction psychiatry, and geriatric psychiatry Am. Bd. Psychiatry and Neurology. Intern Montefiore Hosp., NYC, 1960-61; resident in psychiatry U. Hosp. Cleve., 1961-62, Austin State Hosp., Tex., 1963-65; dep. commr. mental health services Dept. Mental Health and Mental Retardation, Tex., 1967-70; dir. Rio Grande State Ctr. for Mental Health and Mental Retardation, Dept. Mental Health, Harlingen, Tex., 1966-67; asst. commr., dir. Rochester regional office State Dept. Mental Hygiene, NY, 1970-72; clin. asst. prof. psychiatry U. Rochester Sch. Medicine and Dentistry, 1970-72; asst. clin. prof. psychiatry SUNY, Buffalo, 1970-72; cons. mental health Ga. Dept. Human Resources, Atlanta, 1972, dir. div. mental health, 1972-74; clin. prof. psychiatry Emory U. Sch. Medicine, Atlanta, 1972-74; vice chmn. Ga. State Planning and Adv. Coun. for Devel. Disabilities Services and Constrn., 1972-73; cons. mental health services orgn. and adminstrn., 1974-76; dir. mental health and devel. services State of NH Concord, 1976-82; commr. Tex. Dept. Mental Health and Mental Retardation Austin, 1982-88; clin. prof. psychiatry U. Tex. Health Sci. Ctr., Houston, adj. assoc. prof. psychiatry San Antonio, 1984-95; dir. profl. svcs. HCA Gulf Pines Hosp., Houston, 1988-94, chief of staff, 1993; clin. dir. adult psychiatry Cypress Creek Hosp., Houston, 1994-2000, med. dir., 2000—03, pres. med. staff, 1996; assoc. clin. psychiatry Post Oak Psychiatry Assoc., Houston, 1988-90; pres. Alternative Svc. Network, Houston, 1990—; chief of staff Kingwood (Tex.) Pines Hosp., 2003—04, dir. Psychiatric Svcs., 2004—08, med. dir., 2008—. Dir. state alcoholism program in South Tex. region, 1966—67; dir. state alcoholism program in Ga., 1972—74; mem. faculty U. SC Sch. Alcohol and Drug Studies, 1975; mem. quality assurance com. Aetna US Healthcare Pharmacy, 1999—2001. Contbr. articles to profl. jours. Served as capt. M.C., US Army, 1962-63. Recipient Cert. Recognition, Ga. Psychol. Assn., 1973, Resolution Commendation, Assn. Retarded Citizens Tex., 1990, Helen Farabee Cmty. Leadership award, Mental Health Assn. Greater Houston, 1993, Pres.'s award, 1990, Elected Top Docs Houston, H Tex. Mag., 2004. Fellow Am. Psychiat. Assn. (disting. life; cert. in adminstrv. psychiatry, com. on psychiat. adminstrn. and mgmt. 1999-2002); mem. AMA, Am. Soc. Clin. Psychopharmacology (cert.), Am. Soc. Addiction Medicine (cert. alcoholism and other drug dependencies), Am. Acad. Addiction Psychiatry, NH Psychiat. Soc. (pres. 1981-82), Nat. Assn. State Mental Health Program Dir. (bd. dir. 1984-88, sec. 1986-88), NH Med. Soc., Am. Acad. Psychiatry and the Law, Am. Assn. Psychiat. Adminstr. (pres. Tex. chpt. 1986), Tex. Med. Assn., Tex. Soc. Psychiat. Physicians (chair socioecons. com. 2006—), Mental Health Assn. Greater Houston (bd. dir. 1989-95, v.p. advocacy 1990-95, adv. coun. 1999—), Alpha Omega Alpha. Home: 5314 Westminster Ct Houston TX 77069-3338 Office: 530 Wells Fargo Dr Ste 110 Houston TX 77090-4026 Office Phone: 281-440-6899. Personal E-mail: gemhou@yahoo.com.

MILLER, GARY G., United States Representative from California; b. Huntsville, Ark., Oct. 16, 1948; m. Cathy Miller, 1972; children: Matt, Brian, Elizabeth, Loren. Student, Mt. San Antonio CC. Founder G. Miller Devel. Co., 1970—; mem. Diamond Bar City Council, 1989—95, mayor, 1993—94; mem. Calif. State Assembly, 1995—98, US Congress from 42nd Calif. dist., Washington, 1998—, asst. whip, mem. budget com., fin. svcs. com., sci. com., trans. & infrastructure com. Mem. Nat. Guard & Reserve Components Caucus, Rep. Study Com.; chair Highway, Infrastructure & Transp. Caucus, Building a Better America Caucus, 2001—. Bd. dirs. Sunrise Christian Sch., 1982—90. Served with US Army, 1967—68. Mem.: Diamond Bar C. of C., Building Industry Assn. Republican. Achievements include proposing 24 bills signed into law; negotiating funding of 1st class size reduction program, producing a balanced budget that reduced bus. tax. to 1973 levels while maintaing a $310 million reserve. Office: US Ho Reps 1037 Longworth Ho Office Bldg Washington DC 20515-0542*

MILLER, GARY H., lawyer; b. New Orleans, Mar. 11, 1957; s. Leo Jr. and Suzanne Robinowitz (Meltzer) M.; m. Ellen Baldwin Hoffman, Oct. 18, 1986; children: Matthew Hilliard, Katherine Elise. BA magna cum laude, New Eng. Coll., 1979; JD cum laude, Tulane U. Sch. Law, 1982. Assoc. Jones Walker Weachter, Poitevent Carrere & Denegre LLP, New Orleans, 1982—89, 1990—2002, ptnr., 2002—04; shareholder Lugenbuhl, Wheaton Peck Rankin & Hubbard PC, New Orleans, 2004—05, counsel, 2005—; prin. Gary H. Miller, Atty.-at-Law New Orleans, Bryson City, NC; lectr. in field, bd. dir. Golden Retriever Club Greater New Orleans, 1980; bd. dir. Burtheville Cmty. Assn. Inc., 1997—2003; class agt. New Eng. Coll.; bd. dirs. Vill. View Homeowners Assn., 2005—07. Mem. La. Bar Assn. (treas.1990-91, chmn. Consumer Protection, Lender Liability and Bank Sect. 1991-92), NC Bar Assn., ABA, Phi Tau Beta. Democrat. Jewish. Office: PO Box 2667 Bryson City NC 28713 Office Phone: 828-488-0173. E-mail: gary@gmillerlaw.com.

MILLER, GAY DAVIS, lawyer; b. Florence, Ariz., Dec. 20, 1947; d. Franklin Theodore and Mary Davis; 1 child, Katherine Alexandra BA, U. Colo., 1969; JD, Am. U., Washington, DC, 1975. Bar: DC 1975. Atty., spl. asst. to gen. counsel, sr. counsel corp. affairs Inter Am. Devel. Bank, Washington, 1975—78, 1983—2004; atty. Intelsat, Washington, 1978-80. Articles editor: Am. U. Law Rev., 1974—75, contbg. author: The Inspection Panel of the World Bank: A Different Complaints Procedure, 2001. Bd. dirs. Hist. Mt. Pleasant, Inc., Washington, 1985-86, Washington Bridle Trails Assn., 1992—2004, Beulah Ambulance Dist., Colo. (bd. dir. 2007). Personal E-mail: gaydavismiller@socolo.net.

MILLER, GENEVIEVE, retired medical historian; b. Butler, Pa., Oct. 15, 1914; d. Charles Russell and Genevieve (Wolford) Miller. AB, Goucher Coll., Balt., 1935; MA, Johns Hopkins U., Balt., 1939; PhD, Cornell U., Ithaca, NY, 1955. Asst. in history medicine Johns Hopkins Inst. History of Medicine, Balt., 1943—44, instr., 1945—48, rsch. assoc., 1979—94; asst. prof. history of sci. Case Western Res. U. Sch. Medicine, Cleve., 1953-67, assoc. prof., 1967-79, assoc. prof. emeritus, 1979—; rsch. assoc. med. history Clevel. Med. Libr. Assn., 1953-62; curator Howard Dittrick Mus. Hist. Medicine, 1962-67, dir., 1967-79. Author: William Beaumont's Formative Years: Two Early Notebooks 1811-1821, 1946; The Adoption of Inoculation for Smallpox in England and France, 1957 (William H. Welch medal Am. Assn. History Medicine 1962), Bibliography of the History of Medicine of the U.S. and Canada, 1939-1960, 1964, Bibliography of the Writings of Henry E. Sigerist, 1966, Letters of Edward Jenner and Other Documents Concerning the Early History of Vaccination, 1983; assoc. editor Bull. of History of Medicine, 1944-48, acting editor, 1948, mem. adv. editl. bd., 1960-92; mem. bd. editors Jour. History of Medicine & Allied Scis., 1948-65; editor Newsletter Am. Assn. History of Medicine, 1986-96; contbr. articles to profl. jours. Alumna trustee Goucher Coll., Balt., 1966-69; trustee Judson Retirement Cmty., Clevel., 1993-99, Am. Coun. Learned Socs. fellow, 1948-50, Dean Van Meter fellow, Goucher Coll., 1953-54. Fellow Cleve. Med. Libr. Assn. (hon.); mem. Am. Assn. History Medicine (pres. 1978-80, mem. coun. 1960-63, Lifetime Achievement award 1999), Am. Hist. Assn., Internat. Soc. History of Medicine, Soc. Archtl. Historians, Phi Beta Kappa. Democrat. Home and Office: 1890 E 107th St Apt 220 Cleveland OH 44106

MILLER, GEORGE, III, United States Representative from California; b. Richmond, Calif., May 15, 1945; s. George and Dorothy (Rumsey) Miller; m. Cynthia Caccavo, 1964; children: George, Stephen. BA in Am. Problems, San Francisco State U., 1968; JD, U. Calif., Davis, 1972. Legis. counsel to Senator George Moscone Calif. State Senate, 1969—74; mem. US Congress from 7th Calif. dist., 1975—, US House Nat. Resources Com., chmn., 1991—94, US House Edn. & Labor Com., 2007—, US House Democratic Steering & Policy Com., 2003—. Founding mem. Progressive Caucus. Author: Giving Children A Chance: The Case for More Effective National Politics, 1989. Recipient Excellence in Pub. Svc., Am. Acad. Pediatrics, 1984, Cleve. Armory Capitol Courage award, Fund for Animals, 2002, William Steiger Meml. award, Am. Conf. Govt. Industrial Hygienists, 2002, Farmworker Justice award, Farmworker Justice Fund, Inc., 2003, N.Am. Govt. Leadership award, Global Semiconductor Industry Assn., 2007. Mem.: Davis Law Sch. Alumni Assn., Calif. Bar Assn., Martinez Dem. Club. Democrat. Roman Catholic. Office: US Congress 2205 Rayburn House Office Bldg Washington DC 20515-0507 also: 375 G St Ste 1 Vallejo CA 94592*

MILLER, GEORGE ARMITAGE, psychologist, educator; b. Charleston, W.Va., Feb. 3, 1920; s. George E. and Florence (Armitage) M.; m. Katherine James, Nov. 29, 1939 (dec. Jan. 1996); children: Nancy, Donnally James. BA, U. Ala., 1940, MA, 1941; AM, Harvard U., 1944, PhD, 1946; PhD (hon.), U. Louvain, 1976; D Social Sci. (hon.), Yale U., 1979; DSc (hon.), Columbia U., 1980, U. Sussex, 1984, New Sch. Social Rsch., 1993; LittD (hon.), Charleston U., 1992; DSc (hon.), DSc (hon.), New Sch. Social Rsch., 1993, Princeton U., 1996, Williams Coll., 2000; DSc (hon.), Carnegie Mellon U., 2003. Instr. psych. U. Ala., 1941-43; rsch. fellow Harvard Psycho-Acoustic Lab., 1944-48; asst. prof. psych. Harvard U., 1948-51, assoc. prof., 1955-58, prof., 1958-68, chmn. dept. psych., 1964-67, co-dir. Ctr. for Cognitive Studies, 1960-67; prof. Rockefeller U., NYC, 1968-79, adj. prof., 1979-82; prof. psych. Princeton U., 1979-90, James S. McDonnell Disting. prof. psych., 1982-90, James S. McDonnell Disting. prof. psych. emeritus, 1990—, prog. dir. McDonnell-Pew Prog. in Cognitive Neurosci., 1989-94; assoc. prof. MIT, 1951-55. Vis. Inst. for Advanced Study, Princeton, 1972-76, 82-83, mem., 1950, 70-72; vis. prof. Rockefeller U., 1967-68, MIT, 1976-79, grp. leader Lincoln Lab., 1953-55; fellow Ctr. Advanced Study in Behavioral Scis., Stanford U., 1958-59; Fulbright rsch. prof. Oxford (Eng.) U., 1963-64; Sesquicentennial prof. U. Ala., 1981. Author: Language and Communication, 1951, (with Galanter and Pribram) Plans and the Structure of Behavior, 1960, Psychology, 1962, (with Johnson-Laird) Language and Perception, 1976, Spontaneous Apprentices, 1977, Language and Speech, 1981, The Science of Words, 1991; editor: Psychol. Bulletin, 1981-82. Recipient Disting. Service award Am. Speech and Hearing Assn., 1976, award in behavioral scis. N.Y. Acad. Scis., 1982, Hermann von Helmholtz award Cognitive Neurosci. Inst., 1989, Nat. Medal Sci. NSF, 1991, Gold Medal Am. Psychol.Found. 1990, Nat. Medal of Sci. 1991, Louis E. Levy medal Franklin Inst., 1991, John P. Govern award, Am. Assn. for Advancement of Sci., 2000; Guggenheim fellow, 1986, William James fellow Am. Psychol. Soc., 1989; Fondation Fyssen Priz Internat. for cognitive sci., 1992. Fellow Brit. Psychol. Assn. (hon.); mem. NAS, AAAS (chmn. sect. J 1981, John P. McGovern award 2000), APA (pres. 1968-69, Disting. Sci. Contbn. award 1963, William James Book award divsn. gen. psych. 1993, Outstanding Lifetime Contbn. to Psych. award 2003), Eastern Psychol. Assn. (pres. 1961-62), Acoustical Soc. Am., Linguistic Soc. Am., Am. Statis. Assn., Am. Philos. Soc., Am. Physiol. Soc., Psychometric Soc., Soc. Exptl. Psychologists (Warren medal 1972), Am. Acad. Arts and Scis., Psychonomic Soc., Royal Netherlands Acad. Arts and Scis. (fgn.), Sigma Xi. Office: Princeton Univ Dept Psychology Green Hall Princeton NJ 08544 Home: PO Box 228 Spring Lake NJ 07762-0228

MILLER, GEORGE DAVID, retired military officer, not-for-profit executive; b. McKeesport, Pa., Apr. 5, 1930; s. George G. and Nellie G. (Cullen) M.; m. Barbara Aex; 1 child from previous marriage: George David Jr.; stepchildren: Jason Dunn, Elizabeth Dunn. BS, US Naval Acad., Annapolis, MD, 1953; MS in Aerospace Engring, Air Force Inst. Tech., Wright Patterson AFB, Dayton, Ohio, 1966; postgrad., Nat. War Coll., Fort Leslie J. McNair, Washington, 1970—71. Commd. 2d lt. US Air Force, 1953, advanced through grades to lt. gen., 1981; ops. officer, comdr. 22d Spl. Ops. Squadron, Nakhon Phanom Royal Thai AFB, Thailand, 1969—70; dep. comdr. for ops., vice comdr., comdr. 55th Strategic Reconnaissance Wing, Offutt AFB, Nebr., 1971-74; comdr. 17th Air div., 307th Strategic wing, U-Tapao Airfield, Thailand, 1974-75; comdr. 57th Air Div. Minot AFB, ND, 1975-76; asst. dep. chief staff ops. hdqrs. SAC, Offutt AFB, Nebr., 1976-77; dir. single integrated operational plan Joint Strategic Target Planning Staff, Joint Chiefs of Staff, 1977-79; dir. plans USAF, Washington, 1979-80, asst. dep. chief staff ops., plans and readiness, 1980-81; vice comdr.-in-chief SAC, Offutt AFB, Nebr., 1981-84; exec. dir., sec.-gen. U.S. Olympic Com., 1984-87; pres. exec. dir. Morris Animal Found., 1987—92; pres., CEO The Nat. Fire Protection Assoc., 1992—2002; pres. Miller Assocs. Consulting. Chmn. bd. dirs. RJA Group Inc.; bd. dirs. Target Safety Inc. Decorated Def. D.S.M., Air Force DSM, Legion of Merit, D.F.C. with 3 oak leaf clusters Air medal with 18 oak leaf clusters, others. Mem.: VFW, World Orgn. of Bldg. Ofcls. (pres. 2003—), Confedn. of Fire Protection Assns. Internat. (chmn. 1992—2005), Metro Fire Chiefs Assn., Nat. Fire Protection Assn. (pres. emeritus), Mil. Officers Assn., Air Force Assn., Daedalians, Shriners, Scottish Rite, Masons, Sojurners Am. Legion. Lutheran. Home: 20 Phillips Pond Natick MA 01760-5643 Office Phone: 508-380-9218. Business E-Mail: george.d.miller@comcast.net.

MILLER, G(ERSON) H(ARRY), science administrator, mathematician, computer scientist, chemist; b. Phila., Mar. 2, 1924; m. Mary Alexa Heath, Jan. 28, 1961; children: Byron, Alexandra. BA, Pomona Coll., 1949; MEd in Counseling and Pers., Temple U., 1951; PhD. in Ednl. Psychology, U. So. Calif., 1957; MS in Math., U. Ill., 1962, postgrad., 1963-65. Jr. high sch. and jr. coll. instr. math. L.A. Sch. Dist., 1953-57; assoc. prof. Western Ill. U., Macomb, 1957-60; prof. Towson State U., Balt., 1960-61; prof. math. and edn. Parsons Coll., Fairfield, Iowa, 1961-65; prof. Tenn. Technol. U., Cookeville, 1966—68; prof. math. and computer sci. Edinboro (Pa.) U., 1968-71, 81-89, asst. dir. Institutional Rsch., 1972-80, emeritus prof., 1989—; dir. Studies On Smoking, Inc. and SOS Stop Smoking Clinic, Edinboro, 1972—. Dir. Nat. Study Math. Requirements for Scientists and Engrs., 1966-73; condr. Nat. Symposium for Am. Inst. Biol. Scis., Am. Chem. Soc. and Am. Soc. Engring. Educators, 1970-75; dir. Math. for Industry Confs.; spkr., presenter in field Contbr. numerous articles to profl. jours. Pres. Edinboro YMCA, 1972-83; bd. dirs. Common Cause, Harrisburg, Pa., 1975-80; Sgt. USAAF, 1943-46, PTO. Grantee U.S. Office Edn., 1968, 70, No Other World, 1973, NAS, 1980, ITT Life Ins. Corp., 1983, Erie County Found., 1987. Fellow Am. Inst. Chemists (cert. profl. chemist), AAAS; mem. APHA, Am. Assn. World Health, Am. Chem. Soc., Am. Soc. Engring. Edn., Internat. Assn. Pure and Applied Chemists, Internat. Soc. for Preventive Oncology, Math. Assn. Am., Am. Diabetes Assn., Sch. Sci. and Math. Assn., N.Y. Acad. Scis. (hon.), Acad. Sr. Profls. (hon.). Personal E-mail: drghmiller@aol.com.

MILLER, GRAY HAMPTON, federal judge, lawyer; b. Houston, Dec. 9, 1948; Student, US Merchant Marine Acad.; BA, U. Houston, 1974, JD, 1978. Bar: Tex. 1978. Assoc. Fulbright & Jaworski LLP, Houston, 1978—86, head admiralty dept, 1996—2004, ptnr., 1986—2004, sr. ptnr., 2004—06; judge US Dist. Ct. (so. dist.) Tex., Houston, 2006—. Mem. ABA, Maritime Law Assn. U.S., State Bar Tex., Houston Bar Assn., Southeastern Admiralty Law Inst. (bd. dirs. 1989-91), Order of Barons. Office: US Dist Ct 515 Rusk Ave Houston TX 77002

MILLER, GREEN RUSSELL, economist, educator; b. Kenvir, Ky., Mar. 10, 1939; s. Clifford Wesley and Lorene (Farmer) M.; m. Carolyn Sue Blackburn, Oct. 7, 1966; children: Laura Marie, Russell Wesley. BA, U. Tex., El Paso, 1969; MA, U. Oreg., 1971; PhD, U. Ky., 1985. Instr. Transylvania U., Lexington, 1973—79; asst. prof. Sch. Pub. Affairs Ky. State U., Frankfort, 1977; prof. econs. Morehead State U., Ky., 1979—, dir. Ctr. for Econ. Edn., 1979—96. Bd. dirs. Ky. Coun. Econ. Edn., Louisville, 1979-96; cons. to various law firms, Ky., 1973—; supr. Cash-Fiscal Agy, El Paso Br. Fed. Reserve Bank of Dallas, 1959-1969; lectr. Beijing U. Coll. Arts and Scis., 1998, 2000. Contbr. numerous articles to profl. jours. Coach Little League Baseball, Morehead, 1982-85, Youth Soccer League, 1985-86; bd. dirs. St. Albans Ch., Morehead, 1979-82, Gethsemane Luth. Ch., 1989-97; vol. One-on-One program Dept. of Corrections, Lexington, 1973-82, Morehead Cmty-.Fed. Credit Union (treas. 1999-). With inf. U.S. Army, 1957-59. Mem. Midwest Econ. Assn., Ky. Econs. Assn., Internat. Bus. and Econ. Rsch. Assn. (Best Paper award, 2003), Mo. Valley Econ. Assn. (Jerome F. Schwier meritorious svc. award 1997), So. Econ. Assn., Ky. Assn. Ednl. Opportunity Program Pers., Joint Coun. on Econ. Edn., Nat. Assn. Econ. Educators, Ky. Coun. on Econ. Edn. (Outstanding Ctr. Dir. 1981-82), Assn. Ky. Econ. Educators (charter, original bylaws com., nominating com. 1985-93), Nat. Assn. Forensic Econs. (charter, bd. dirs. 1986-87, bus. editor Jour. Econs. 1990-97, chair acctg.-econs.-fin. 1988-2002), Southeastern Ky. Econ. Assn. (charter, pres. 2004-06), Internat. Acad. Bus. and Pub. Rels. Adminstrn. Disciplines. Democrat. Lutheran-Episcopal. Avocations: hiking, reading. Home: 1240 Rodburn Hollow Rd Morehead KY 40351-9092 Office: Morehead State U UPO 1280 150 University Blvd Morehead KY 40351 Business E-Mail: g.miller@moreheadstate.edu.

MILLER, GREG, photographer; b. Nashville, Tenn., 1967; married. BFA in Photography, Sch. Visual Arts, NYC, 1990. Asst. to photographer Bob Schatz, Nashville; comml. photographer, 1988—. Clients include Hewlett Packard, IBM, Truth/American Legacy, Movieline, Seagate, Esquire, Life, ExxonMobil, Smithsonian, Greater Bay Bancorp, Mastercard, Fortune, Washington Post Mag., 3Com, Nikon, Fast Co., Tyson, Details, Pillsbury Wintrhop, Sunny Delight, NarWest Bank, Vibe, Outside, and others. One-man shows include Primo Amore, Redux Gallery, NYC, 2004, exhibited in group shows at Three Generations of Nashville Photographers, The Arts Co., Nashville, 2008. Fellow John Simon Guggenheim Meml. Found., 2008. Office: Greg Miller Ste 456 55

Washington St Brooklyn NY 11201 also: Julian Richards & Assocs 2nd Fl 9 Desbrosses St New York NY 10013 Office Phone: 718-625-8938. Office Fax: 718-625-8927. E-mail: greg@gregmiller.com.*

MILLER, GREG, professional sports team executive; s. Larry H. and Karen Gail (Saxon) Miller. CEO Larry H. Miller Group Companies (owner of more than 40 auto dealerships, the Utah Jazz, Salt Lake Bees and Miller Motorsports Pk.), 2008—. Office: Larry H Miller Group Companies 9350 S 150 E Ste 1000 Sandy UT 84070 also: Utah Jazz 301 W South Temple Salt Lake City UT 84101*

MILLER, GREGORY R., retired prosecutor; BA, Drew U.; JD, Ohio No. U. Chief asst. US atty. (no. dist.) Fla. US Dept. Justice, Tallahassee, US atty. (no. dist.) Fla., 1993-98, asst. US atty. (no. dist.) Fla., 2000—02; US atty (no. dist.) Fla. US Dept Justice, Tallahassee, 2002—08; assoc. Fowler, White, Gillen, Boggs, Villareal and Banker, PA, Tallahassee, 1998-2000; ptnr. Beggs & Lane, RLLP, Tallahassee, 2008—. Office: 215 S Monroe St Ste 710 Tallahassee FL 32301 Office Phone: 850-391-0001. Business E-Mail: grm@beggslane.com.

MILLER, H. TODD, lawyer; b. Buffalo, Sept. 19, 1947; s. Henry Opel and Irene Teresa (Hauck) M.; m. June Diehl Lancaster, Aug. 1, 1970; children: Catharine Maclay, Todd Lancaster, Peter Hanes. BA, SUNY, Buffalo, 1969; JD, Duke U., 1971. Bar: NC 1971, DC 1973. Jud. clerk to Hon. Charles R. Simpson US Tax Ct., Washington, 1971-73; assoc. atty. Hogan & Hartson LLP, Washington, 1973-78, ptnr., 1979—. Mem. Phi Beta Kappa, Order of the Coif. Episcopalian. Office: Hogan & Hartson Columbia Sq 555 13th St NW Ste 9W-312 Washington DC 20004-1161 Home Phone: 301-657-6223; Office Phone: 202-637-5667.

MILLER, HAROLD EDWARD, retired manufacturing conglomerate executive, consultant; b. St. Louis, Nov. 23, 1926; s. George Edward and Georgenia Elizabeth (Franklin) M.; m. Lilian Ruth Gantner, Dec. 23, 1949; children— Ellen Susan, Jeffrey Arthur. BSBA, Washington U., St. Louis, 1949. Vice pres. Fulton Iron Works Co., St. Louis, 1968-71, pres., 1971-79, chmn. bd., 1979-90; v.p. Katy Industries Inc., Elgin, Ill., 1976-77, exec. v.p., 1978-90, also dir., to 1990; pres. HM Consulting, Palatine, Ill., 1990—. Internat. cons. Vigel Spa, Italy; v.p. Vigel U.S.A. Inc., 1996—. Served with U.S. Army, 1945-46. Mem. Barrington Tennis Club, Inverness Golf Club. Presbyterian. Office Phone: 847-991-7852. Personal E-mail: hmillercons84@sbcglobal.net.

MILLER, HARRIET SANDERS, former art center director; b. Apr. 18, 1926; m. Milton H. Miller, June 27, 1948; children: Bruce, Jeffrey, Marcie. BA, Ind. U., 1947; MA, Columbia U., 1949; MS, U. Wis., 1962, MFA, 1967. Dir. art sch. Madison (Wis.) Art Ctr., 1963-72; acting dir. Ctr. for Continuing Edn., Vancouver, B.C., Canada, 1975-76; mem. fine arts faculty Douglas Coll., Vancouver, 1972-78; exec. dir. Palos Verdes (Calif.) Arts Ctr., 1978-84; dir. Jr. Arts Ctr., LA, 1984-98. One woman exhibits at Gallery 7, Vancouver, 1978, Gallery 1, Toronto, Ont., Can., 1977, Linda Farris Gallery, Seattle, 1975, Galerie Allen, Vancouver, 1973.

MILLER, HARRISON STEWART, history professor; b. Balt., June 22, 1966; s. Gordon Elliott and Deanna Pilzer Miller; m. Yuka Oda, Nov. 1, 2001; children: Kasumi Oda, Yosuke Oda, Aliceanna. PhD, Columbia U., NY, 2001. Assoc. prof. U. South Ala., Mobile, 2002—; vis. asst. prof. Colo. Coll., Colorado Springs, 2001—02. Author: (non-fiction book) State versus Gentry in Late Ming Dynasty China, 1572-1644. Office: Univ S Alabama History Dept Humb 344 Mobile AL 36688 Business E-Mail: hsmiller@jaguar1.usouthal.edu.

MILLER, HARRY FREEMAN, university administrator; b. Vallejo, Calif., Aug. 27, 1946; s. Theodore Harry and Grace (Eubank) M.; 1 child, Charissa Rainie. BA, Howard U., 1969; JD, U. Calif., Davis, 1972; cert., Harvard U., 1989, U. Chgo., 1998. Cert. fund raising exec. Grad. legal counsel Office of Calif. Atty. Gen., San Francisco, 1972—73; assoc. gen. sec. Stanford U., Palo Alto, Calif., 1973-79; asst. dean, lectr. law Syracuse (N.Y.) U., 1979-81; dir. devel. Georgetown U. Law Ctr., Washington, 1981-83; v.p. instnl. advt. Morgan State U., Balt., 1983-91; assoc. v.p., dir. planned giving U. South Fla., Tampa, 1991-95; assoc. v.p. devel. Tex. So. U., Houston, 1996—2000; dir. devel. Tex. A&M Inst. Bioscis. and Tech., Houston, 2001—. Host Lou Rauls Telethon for United Negro Coll. Fund, Syracuse, 1981, adv. com., Tampa, 1993-95; active Nat. Sports Festival Com., Syracuse, 1981; unit chmn. Tex. State Employees Charitable Campaign, 2003-06. Mem. Nat. Soc. Fund Raising Execs., Assn. Fund Raising Officers (bd. dirs. 1984-90), Assn. Fundraising Profls., Am. Inst. Parliamentarians, Assn. for Healthcare Philanthropy, Leadership Tampa, Tampa Urban League (bd. dirs. 1993-95), Phi Alpha Delta. Office: Tex A&M U Sys 2121 W Holcombe Blvd Houston TX 77030

MILLER, HARVEY R., lawyer, bankruptcy reorganization specialist; b. Bklyn., Mar. 1, 1933; married AB, Bklyn. Coll., 1954; LLB, Columbia U. Law Sch., 1959. Bar: NY 1959, US Supreme Ct., US Ct. Appeals (2nd, 3rd, 4th, 5th and 9th cirs.), US Dist. Ct. (so. and ea. dists. NY). Ptnr. Seligson & Morris, 1963—70, Weil, Gotshal & Manges, LLP, NYC, 1970—2002, sr. ptnr., chair bus. financing & restructuring group, 2007—; mng. dir., vice chmn. Greenhill & Co., 2002—07. Adj. assoc. prof. law NYU Law Sch., 1974—76, adj. prof. law, 1976—; vis. lectr. Yale Law Sch., 1983—84; lectr. law Columbia U. Sch. Law, 2000—. Bd. visitors Columbia U. Sch. Law. Fellow: Am. Bar Found., Am. Coll. Bankruptcy. Office: Weil Gotshal & Manges LLP 767 5th Ave Fl 29 New York NY 10153-0023 Office Phone: 212-389-1580, 212-310-8000. Office Fax: 212-389-1780, 212-310-8007.*

MILLER, HARVEY S. SHIPLEY, foundation trustee, philanthropist; b. Phila., Sept. 28, 1948; s. Frank Leroy and Betty Charlotte (Elfont) M. BA, Swarthmore Coll., 1970; JD, Harvard U., 1973, postgrad. Bar: N.Y. 1973. Assoc. Debevoise & Plimpton, NYC, 1973-75; curator and dir. dept. collections and spl. exhbns. Franklin Inst., Phila., 1975-81; v.p. Energy Solutions, Inc., NYC, 1982-84; pres., chief exec. officer, dir. Daltex Med. Scis., Inc., NYC, 1983-86, dir. exec. com., 1983-94, chief operating officer, vice chmn., 1986-91, pres., chief operating officer, 1991-93; trustee The Judith Rothschild Found., NYC, 1993—. Author: Milton Avery: Drawings and Paintings, 1976, It's About Time, 1979; author, editor: New Spaces: Exploring the Aesthetic Dimensions of Holography, 1979; co-author: Rapid Inactivation of Infectious Pathogens by Chlorhexidine-coated Gloves, 1992; contbr. articles to profl. jours. Mem. vis. com. on photography George Eastman House, Rochester, N.Y., 1976-78; trustee Milton and Sally Avery Arts Found., N.Y.C., 1983—, sec., 1996—; trustee The Franklin Inst., Phila., 1993-95, Phila. Mus. Art, 1985—, exec. com., 1993-96; assoc. trustee U. Pa., 1981-95; trustee Arcadia U., 2002-2005; bd. govs. Print Club, Phila., 1976-87; bd. overseers U. Pa. Sch. Nursing, 1981—, Edith C. Blum Art Inst. Bard Coll., 1984-87; bd. dirs., mem. corp. MacDowell Colony, N.Y.C., 1982-85; exec. bd. dirs. Fabric Workshop, Phila., 1976-86, hon. trustee, Miami Mu. Modern Art, 2004—; mem. prints and drawings and photographs trustees adv. com. Phila. Mus. Art, 1974—, trustee, 1985—, vice chmn., 2004—, investment com., 1989-95, exec., devel. and exhbn. coms., 1993-96, chair 125th ann. campaign, 1999-2002; mem. vis. com. 19th-century, modern, and contemporary art Met. Mus. Art, 1998—; bd. assocs. Swarthmore Coll. Librs., Phila., 1978-86; treas., dir. Arcadia Found., Norristown, Pa., 1981—; chmn. adv. bd. Inst. Contemporary Art U. Pa., 1982-84; trustee, vice chmn. coms. on instrn. Pa. Acad. Fine Arts, 1982-91, trustee emeritus, 1991—, chmn. collections and exhbns. com., 1985-87; trustee N.Y. Studio Sch., 1974-80, U. of the Arts, 1979-86; mem. exec. bd. Citizens for Arts in Pa., 1980; adv. bd. The Highlands Hist. Soc., 1999—; bd. dirs. Once Gallery, Inc., 1974-75, Wildlife Preservation Trust Internat., Inc., 1990-95; mem. Mayor's Cultural Adv. Coun., Phila., 1987-91; founding chair Mayor's Art-in-City Hall Program, Phila., 1992-94; trustees coun. Nat. Gallery Art, Washington, 1995-2000, 2001—06; mem. collections com. Hist. Soc. Pa., 1991-93, councilor trustee, 1992-93; mem. vis. com. photographs Met. Mus. Art, 1996—, vis. com. modern art, 1998—; mem. trustees' com. on drawings Mus. Modern Art, 1996—, trustee, 2003—, Prints and Illustrated Books, Museum of Modern Art, 2001—, vice chmn. Prints and Illustrated Books Comm., 2007-; mem. photography accessions com. San Francisco Mus. of Modern Art, 1997-2002; arts adv. com. Fund for the Waterworks, 1999-2001; founding mem., bd. trustees Maltz Jupiter (Fla.)Theatre, 2001—06; bd. dirs. Am. Patrons of the Tate Gallery, 2003—06; charter mem. The Drawings Group, L.A. County Mus. Art, 2003—; mem. drawings com. L.A. Mus. Contemporary Art, 2003—; bd. trustees Whitney Mus. Am. Art, 2004—; mem. Commn. on Drawing, 2005—, chmn. com. on drawings, 2004; bd. overseers Hammer Mus., L.A., 2004—06; trustee Ursinus Coll., 2004—, Point Found., 2004—08; collections com. Harvard U. Art Mus; bd. dirs. Salzburg Festival Soc., 2006—; trustee Rema Hort Mann Found.; collection com. Morgan Library & Museum, 2007-. Recipient Disting. Civic Svc. award, City Phila., 1997, Hon. Alumni award, U. Pa. Sch. Nursing, 2005; named 1st non-Russian recipient of Diploma of Merit, Russian Ministry of Culture, 2002. Fellow The Pierpont Morgan Libr., Coll. Physicians Phila.; mem. ABA, Assn. of Bar of City of N.Y., Athenaeum, Libr. Co. Phila., Am. Philos. Soc., Hist. Soc. Pa., Phila. Art Alliance, Union League of Phila., Harvard Club of N.Y.C., Swarthmore Club Phila., Palm Beach Yacht Club, Sunnybrook Golf Club, Phi Sigma Kappa. Republican. Home: Plumlyn 7036 Sheaff Ln Fort Washington PA 19034-2017 Office: 535 West 23rd St Ste S 3k New York NY 10011

MILLER, HARVEY WILLIAM, retired military officer; b. LaCrosse, Wis., Nov. 20, 1919; s. Carl William and Charlotte (Lumley) Miller; m. Marylin Buck Grindle, May 16, 1995; m. Daphne Olive Roddy, Dec. 29, 1942 (dec. Jan. 1995); children: Charlene, David, Peggy. BS with honors, U. Wis., Madison, 1941; MS, Mont. State Coll., Bozeman, 1942. Cert. tchr. history and bus. econs. grades 9-12 Va. Officer and pilot to lt. comdr. US Navy, 1943—65, prof. naval scis., 1955—58; mideast navy intelligence officer Morocco, 1959—61; intelligence officer USS Enterprise CVA(N) 65, 1961—63, Def. Intelligence Agy., Arlington, Va., 1963—65; indusl. intelligence CIA, Langley, Va., 1965—76. Mgr. officers club, Honolulu, 1947. Pres. Country Club Hills Civic Assn., Fairfax City, Va., 1968—74; mgr. Little League, Port Lyautey, Morocco, 1960—61; chmn. Hawaiian Island Luth. Evang. Inst.; mem. sch. bd. Lutheran Sch., Richfield, Minn., 1956—58; tchr. adult Bible sch. base chapel Port Lyautey, Morocco, 1959—61. Mem.: Mil. Officer Assn. Am., Nat. Active and Ret. Fed. Employees Assn. (pres. Va. Chpt. 1885 1985—, pres. Fla. Chpt. 583 2005—06). Democrat. Lutheran. Avocations: bowling, golf, softball, dance. Home: 6332 Lomand Ave New Port Richey FL 34653 also: 1201 Eastover Pky Locust Grove VA 22508 Personal E-mail: harlinmill@juno.com.

MILLER, HEIDI GOLDBERG, diversified financial services company executive; b. 1953; m. Brian Miller; 2 children. BA in History, Princeton U., 1974; Ph.D in History, Yale U., 1979. Various positions to mng. dir. emerging markets structured finance group Chemical Bank, 1979—92; v.p. planning and analysis, asst. to pres. Travelers Group, 1992—95, exec. v.p., CFO, 1995—98, Citigroup (merger of Citibank and Travelers Group), NYC, 1998—2000; CFO, sr. exec. v.p. strategic planning and adminstrn. Priceline.com, Norwalk, Conn., 2000; vice chmn. Marsh & McLennan Co., Inc., NYC, 2001—02; exec. v.p. strategy and devel., CFO Bank One Corp., 2002—04; exec. v.p., CEO, treasury & securities divsn. J.P. Morgan Chase & Co., NYC, 2004—. Bd. dirs. General Mills Inc., 1999—, Merck & Co., Inc., 2000—04, Bank One Corp., 2000—02, Local Initiatives Support Corp., 2004—. Trustee Princeton U., NYU Med. Sch. Named one of 50 Most Powerful Women in Bus., Fortune mag., 2006—08, 25 Most Powerful Women in Banking, US Banker, 2006—08, 100 Most Influential Women in NYC Bus., Crain's NY Bus., 2007, 100 Most Powerful Women, Forbes mag., 2009. Democrat. Avocation: yoga. Office: JP Morgan Chase & Co 270 Park Ave New York NY 10017*

MILLER, HELEN ELIZABETH, art and adult education educator, artist; d. David Allen and Judith Busch (Stepmother), Ronald Raymond (Stepfather) and Christine Delores Mistarz; m. Todd Charles Miller, Aug. 8, 1998; 1 child, Samantha Alexandria. BA magna cum laude, Calumet Coll., 1995; MA, Ind. U., 1999; post-grad., U. Phoenix. Tchr. art Waukegan Sch. Sys., Ill., 2002—03, 2004—07, lead art tchr., 2005—; tchr. art Round Lake HS, Round Lake, 2003—04. Organizer clothing drive Carman Buckner Sch., Waukegan, Ill., 2004. Prin. works include 11 murals, Waukegan Sch. Sys. Grantee, Walmart, 2004. Green Party. Roman Catholic. Avocations: painting, drawing, scuba diving, bicycling, ceramics. Home: 330 Greenview Ln Lake Villa IL 60046 Office: Waukegan Sch Dist 60 Sheridan Rd Waukegan IL 60085 Office Phone: 847-360-5478. Personal E-mail: helenemiller@yahoo.com.

MILLER, HENRY FRANKLIN, lawyer; b. Phila., May 19, 1938; s. Lester and Bessie (Posner) M.; m. Barbara Ann Gendel, June 20, 1964; children: Andrew, Alexa. AB, Lafayette Coll., 1959; JD, U. Pa., 1964. Bar: Pa. 1965. Law clk. U.S. Dist. Ct. Del., Wilmington, 1964-65; assoc. Wolf, Block LLP, Phila., 1965—71, ptnr., 1971—2005; counsel Cozen O Connor, 2009—. Pres. Soc. Hill Synagogue, Phila., 1978-79, Big Brothers/Big Sisters Assn. of Phila., 1980-81, Jewish Family & Children's Agy., Phila., 1986-88. 1st lt. U.S. Army, 1959-60. Mem. Am. Coll. Real Estate Lawyers. Avocations: swimming, hiking, bicycling, reading. Office: Cozen O'Connor 1900 Market St Philadelphia PA 19103 Home Phone: 215-925-6408; Office Phone: 215-665-2133. Business E-Mail: hmiller@cozen.com.

MILLER, HERBERT DELL, petroleum engineer; b. Oklahoma City, Sept. 29, 1919; s. Merrill Dell and Susan (Green) M.; m. Rosalind Rebecca Moore, Nov. 23, 1947; children: Rebecca Miller Wheeler, Robert Rexford. BS in Petroleum Engring., Okla. U., Norman, 1941. Registered profl. engr., Okla., Tex. Field engr. Amerada Petroleum Corp., Hobbs, N.Mex., 1947—48, Houston, 1948—49, dist. engr. Longview, Tex., 1949—57, sr. engr. Tulsa, 1957—62; petroleum engr. Moore & Miller Oil Co., Oklahoma City, 1962—78; owner Herbert D. Miller Co., Oklahoma City, 1978—. Maj., F.A. AUS, 1941—47, ETO. Decorated Bronze Star with oak leaf cluster, Purple Heart (U.S.); Croix de Guerre (France). Mem. AIME, Oklahoma City Golf. Republican. Episcopalian (pres. Men's Club 1973). Home and Office: 1819 W Wilshire Blvd Oklahoma City OK 73116-4115

MILLER, HERBERT ELMER, accountant; b. DeWitt, Iowa, Aug. 11, 1914; s. Elmer Joseph and Marian (Briggs) M.; m. Lenore Snitkey, July 1, 1938; 1 dau., Barbara Ruth. AB, State U. Iowa, 1936, MA, 1937; PhD, U. Minn., 1944; Dr. h.c., Free U. Brussels, 1982; D.H.L. (h.c.), De Paul U., 1983. C.P.A., Iowa. Acctg. prof. U. Minn., U. Mich., Mich. State U., 1938-70; ptnr. Arthur Andersen & Co., Chgo., 1970-78; dir. Sch. Acctg., U. Ga., Athens, 1978-83. Co-author: Finney-Miller accounting series, 1950-70; editor, contbr.: C.P.A. Rev. Manual, 1951-79. Mem. AICPA (bd. dirs. 1968-70), Am. Acctg. Assn. (pres. 1965-66), Federated Schs. Acctg. (pres. 1982), Beta Gamma Sigma, Beta Alpha Psi (nat. pres. 1961-62) Home: 145 S Stratford Dr Athens GA 30605-3025

MILLER, I. GEORGE, physician, educator, researcher; b. Chgo., Apr. 18, 1937; s. Irving George and Florence (Levy) M.; m. Arlette Goldmuntz, Mar. 25, 1962; children: Lisa, John, David. AB, Harvard U., 1958, MD, 1962. Intern Univ. Hosp., Western Res, U., Cleve., 1962-63; resident Univ. Hosp., Western Res., U., Cleve., 1963-64; epidemiology intelligence officer Communicable Disease Ctr. USPHS, Atlanta, 1964-66; rsch. fellow in medicine Harvard U. Med. Sch., Boston, 1966-69; asst. prof. pediat., epidemiology, biophysics and biochemistry Yale Sch. Medicine, New Haven, 1969-72, J.F. Enders prof., 1979—. Mem. exptl. virology study sect. NIH, 1974-77; mem. sci. adv. com. Damon Runyon Fund, 1979-85, dir., 1985-94; Leukemia Soc. Am., 1976-81. Contbr. numerous articles, chpts. to profl. publs.; editl. bd. Jour. Virology, 1981-87, Virology, 1982-86. Recipient epidemic Intelligence Svc. Alumni Assn. prize, 1967; Macy faculty scholar, 1977, Am. Cancer Soc. scholar, 1990; Howard Hughes Med. Inst. investigatorship, 1972-80 Fellow Infectious Diseases Soc. (Squibb award 1982, Enders award 1989), AAAS, Am. Acad. Microbiology.; mem. Am. soc. Clin. Investigation, Am. Pediatric Soc., Am. Soc. Virology, Assn. Am. Physicians, Inst. Medicine. Jewish. Office: Yale U Sch Medicine Pediatrics Infectious Diseases PO Box 208064 New Haven CT 06520-8064 Home Phone: 203-389-6621; Office Phone: 203-785-4758. Business E-Mail: george.miller@yale.edu.

MILLER, IRVING FRANKLIN, chemical and biomedical engineer, academic administrator, educator; b. NYC, Sept. 27, 1934; s. Sol and Gertrude (Rochkind) M.; m. Baila Hannah Milner, Jan. 28, 1962; children: Eugenia Lynne, Jonathan Mark. BS in Chem. Engring., NYU, 1955; MS, Purdue U., 1956; PhD, U. Mich., 1960. Rsch. scientist United Aircraft Corp., Hartford, 1959-61; from asst. prof. to prof., head chem. engring. Poly. Inst. Bklyn., 1961-72; prof. bioengring., head bioengring. program U. Ill., Chgo., 1973-79, acting head sys. engring. dept., 1978-79, assoc. vice chancellor rsch., dean Grad. Coll., 1979-85, prof. chem. engring., head chem. engring., 1986-95, dir. Ctr. Advanced Edn. and Rsch., 1989-90, dir. Office Spl. Projects, 1990-92, dir. bioengring. program, 1992-95; dean Coll. Engring. U. Akron, Ohio, 1995-98, prof. biomed. engring., 1998-2000; dir. corp. ops. BioTechPlex Corp., 2002—06. Cons. to industry; cons. NAS, NIH, Exec. Svc. Corps, Chgo., 2007—; dir. distance learning programs Ohio Aerospace Inst., 1998—2000. Editor: Electrochemical Bioscience and Bioengineering, 1973; contbr. articles profl. jours. Mem. AIChE, AAAS, Am. Chem. Soc., Biomed. Engring. Soc., N.Y. Acad Scis. Home: 1746 N Larrabee St Chicago IL 60614-5634 Office Phone: 312-266-1728. Personal E-mail: ifmiller@sbcglobal.net. Business E-Mail: ifmiller@uic.edu.

MILLER, IVAN WILFRED, psychologist, educator; AB with Hons., Brown U., Providence, 1972; PhD, U. Maine, Orono, 1980. Cert. psychologist RI, 1981. Prof. Brown U. Med. Sch., Providence, 1995—. Dir. psychosocial rsch. program Butler Hosp., Providence, 2002—. Office: Butler Hosp 345 Blackstone Blvd Providence RI 02906

MILLER, J. ALLEN, lawyer; b. July 21, 1951; BA cum laude, U. NH, 1972; JD, Cornell U., 1979. Bar: NY 1980. Ptnr., chmn. Corp. Dept. Chadbourne & Parke LLP, NYC, co-coord., Latin Am. Practice Group. Spkr. in field; contbr. articles to profl. jour.; note & comment editor Cornell Internat. Law Jour., 1978—79. Mem.: ABA, NY State Bar Assn. Office: Chadbourne & Parke LLP 30 Rockefeller Plz New York NY 10112 Office Phone: 212-408-5454. Office Fax: 212-541-5369. Business E-Mail: amiller@chadbourne.com.

MILLER, JACK (JOHN PETER MILLER), journalist; b. Aug. 3, 1928; s. Wesley and Margaret (Baker) M.; m. Helen DeMars, July 30, 1949 (dec.); children: Candice(dec.), Gregory(dec.). Student, Welland and Toronto. From sports page editor to front page editor Welland Evening Tribune, 1949—53; with Hamilton (Ont.) Spectator, 1953—71, radio and TV columnist, 1955—71; with Toronto Daily Star, 1971—91, radio and TV columnist, 1971—78, comm. editor, 1979—85, sci. columnist, 1982—85, sci. writer, 1985—89, sci. editor, 1989—91, sci. corr., 1991—95; prof. journalism Niagara Coll., 1996—99. Frequent TV and radio appearances. Contbr. stories to mags. Mem.: Can. Sci. Writers Assn. (2 writing awards 1985, writing award 1987, 2 writing awards 1988, writing award 1989). Office: 162 Martindale Rd Apt 501 Saint Catharines ON L2S 3S4 Canada E-mail: jackasinmiller@yahoo.com.

MILLER, JACK DAVID R., radiologist, physician, educator; b. Johannesburg, Apr. 15, 1930; s. Harold Lewis and Inez (Behrman) M.; m. Miriam Sheckter, Dec., 1988. B.Sc., M.B., Ch.B., U. Witwatersrand, Johannesburg, 1956. Diplomate: Am. Bd. Radiology. Intern Coronation Hosp., Johannesburg, 1957-58; resident in radiology Passavant Meml. Hosp., Chgo., 1959-62, Wesley Meml. Hosp., Chgo., 1959-62; fellow in radiology Northwestern U. Med. Sch., 1962-63; chmn. dept. radiology U. Hosp., Edmonton, Alta., Canada, 1971-83; radiologist, dept. radiology U. Alta Hosp., 1963—2004, head, dir. neuroradiology, 1984—92; prof. emeritus radiology U. Alta., 1997—. Clin. prof. radiology U. Alta., 1971— Fellow Royal Coll. Physicians Can., Am. Coll. Radiology. Personal E-mail: miribud@shaw.ca.

MILLER, JACKIE DEAN, I, genealogist, historian; b. Cleve., Sept. 6, 1959; s. Lloyd Keith Miller and Lou Eva Isaacs; m. Mary Margaret Diachar, Apr. 23, 1991; children: Sheila Florencie, Jackie Herman II. Student, Sch. Paralegal Studies-PSCDI, Atlanta, 1996—97, Union Inst. and Colls., 1998—2002; M, Grand Canyon U., 2008, attending. Boy's adventure corp leader/local officer The Salvation Army - Citadel/Price Hill Corp, Cin., 1986—91; treas. Hamblen County Hist. Soc., Morristown, Tenn., 1995—96. Editor/founder/owner The Country Peddler Newspaper, Cin., 1983—86; radio dj WAIF Radio 88.5 FM, Cin., 1986—88; columist Ask the Col. The Appalachian Connection Newspaper, Cin., 1999—2000; rep. S.W. Ohio State of Ohio - We Care Network, Cin. Author: (book family genealogy history) The Isaacs Family of Kentucky 1600's-1991, (book of poems) On Gossamer Wings, (book family genealogy history) The English Bates to America 1415-1994, Johnson Family of Kentucky, Martin Family of Floyd County, Kentucky, (book genealogy family history) Miller Family in Search of Pocahontas, Hugh Arbuthnot & Margaret Keith, Rev. Samuel Walker 1586-2003, James Bane & Elizabeth Clark, poems. With USN, 1977—78. Recipient Key To the City of Morristown, Tenn., Mayor John R. Johnson for the City of Morristown, Tenn., 1994, Key to the City of Johnson City, Tenn., Reece Sexton for the City of Johnson City, Tenn., 1994, Rank of Col., N.Mex Gov. Bruce King for the State of N.Mex., 1994, Proclamation declaring a day in my honor, Mayor Jean Dean for

City of Huntington, W.Va., 1995, Key to the City Elsmore, Ky., Key to the City Nashville, Tenn., Proclamation honors, Bridgeport, Conn., Anaheim, Calif.; named Ky. Col., Ky. Gov. Ned McWherter, 1990. Mem.: Ky. Soc. Sons Am. Revolution (elected geniologist Simon Kenton chptr. 2009, membership com.). Republican. Baptist. Home: 162 Hawk Dr Elsmere KY 41018-1905 Home Phone: 859-342-0959; Office Phone: 859-609-8262. Personal E-mail: hillbillie_jack@yahoo.com. Business E-Mail: bigdiddymiller@juno.com. E-mail: thekeithfamilyus@yahoo.com.

MILLER, JACQUELINE WINSLOW, library director; b. NYC, Apr. 15, 1935; d. Lynward Roosevelt and Sarah Ellen (Grevious) W.; 1 child, Percy Scott. BA, Morgan State Coll., 1957; MLS, Pratt Inst., 1960; grad. profl. seminar, U. Md., 1973. Cert. profl. libr. With Bklyn. Pub. Libr., 1957-68; head ext. svcs. New Rochelle (N.Y.) Pub. Libr., 1969-70; br. adminstr. Grinton Will Yonkers (N.Y.) Pub. Libr., 1970-75; dir. Yonkers Pub. Libr., 1975-96. Mem. adj. faculty grad. libr. studies Queens Coll., CUNY, 1989, 90. Mem. commr.'s com. Statewide Libr. Devel., Albany, N.Y., 1980; mem. N.Y. Gov.'s Commn. on Librs., 1990, 91; bd. dirs. Cmty. Planning Coun., Yonkers, N.Y., 1987; mem. Yonkers Black Women's Polit. Caucus, 1987; pres. bd. Literacy Vols. of Westchester County, 1991-92; mem. fair campaign practices com. LWV, 1996—. Recipient Yonkers Citizen award Ch. of Our Saviour, 1980, 2d Ann. Mae Morgan Robinson award Yonkers chpt. Westchester Black Women's Polit. Caucus, 1992, 3d Ann. Equality Day award City of Yonkers, 1992, African-Am. Heritage 1st award YWCA, 1994; named Outstanding Profl. Woman Nat. Assn. Negro Bus. and Profl. Women's Clubs Inc., 1981. Mem. ALA (councilor 1987-91), N.Y. State Libr. Assn., Pub. Libr. Dirs. Assn. (exec. bd.), N.Y. State Pub. Libr. Dirs. Assn., Westchester Libr. Assn., Yonkers C. of C. (bd. dirs. 1992-95), Educate the Girls, Inc. (bd. dirs., 2003-04) Rotary (Yonkers chpt.). Personal E-mail: miatagurl@gmail.com.

MILLER, JAMES FORREST, lawyer; b. Sioux City, Iowa, Jan. 28, 1952; AB magna cum laude, Dartmouth Coll., 1974; JD, Columbia Univ., 1977. Bar: DC 1978. Litigator, tax divsn. US Dept. Justice; sp. counsel US Dept. Treasury, 1989—93; ptnr., regulated industries, govtl. rels. Hunton & Williams LLP, Washington. Recipient Stone Scholar. Office: Hunton & Williams LLP 1900 K St NW Washington DC 20006-1109 Office Phone: 202-955-1934. Office Fax: 202-778-2201. Business E-Mail: jfmiller@hunton.com.

MILLER, JAMES GEGAN, research scientist; b. St. Louis, Nov. 11, 1942; s. Francis John and Elizabeth Ann (Caul) M.; m. Judith Anne Kelvin, Apr. 23, 1966; 1 child, Douglas Ryan. AB, St. Louis U., 1964; MA, Washington U., 1966, PhD, 1969. Asst. prof. physics Washington U., St. Louis, 1970-72, assoc. prof., 1972-77, prof. physics, 1977—, dir. lab. for ultrasonics, 1987—, rsch. asst. prof. medicine, 1976-81, rsch. assoc. prof. medicine, 1981-88, rsch. prof. medicine, 1988-2000, prof. biomed. engring., 1998—, Albert Gordon Hill prof. physics, 1999—, prof. medicine, 2000—. Contbr. articles to profl. jours.; patentee in field. Recipient I-R 100 award, Indsl. Research Devel. Mag., 1974, 1978, Merit award, NIH, 1998, Tchg. award, Emerson U., 2004; grantee, NIH, NASA. Fellow IEEE (sr., gov. com. Ultrasonics, Ferroelectrics and Frequency Control Soc. 1978-80,86-88, 92-94, Achievement award 2006), Am. Inst. Ultrasound in Medicine, Acoustical Soc. Am. (Silver medal 2004), Am. Inst. Med. and Biol. Engring.; mem. Am. Phys. Soc., Sigma Xi (nat. lectr. 1981-82). Office: Washington Univ St Louis Physics Dept CB 1105 One Brookings Dr Saint Louis MO 63130 Business E-Mail: james.g.miller@wustl.edu.

MILLER, JAMES H., electric power industry executive; BSEE, U. Del. Plant engr. Pub. Svc. Electric & Gas, Salem, NJ; various Delmarva Power & Light Co.; v.p. ops., constrn. and engring. ABB Resource Recovery Sys., pres., 1990-93, U.C. Oper. Svcs., 1993-94, ABB Envrion. Sys. Inc., Birmingham, Ala., 1994-95; exec. v.p. prodn., nuc. regulatory and environ. affairs USEC Inc., Bethesda, Md., 1995—99, exec. v.p., COO, 1999—2001; pres. PPL Generation PPL Corp., Allentown, Pa., 2001—04, exec. v.p., COO, 2004—05, pres., COO, 2005—06, chmn., pres., CEO, 2006—. With USN. Office: PPL Corp 2 N 9th St Allentown PA 18101-1179

MILLER, JAMES N., JR., federal agency administrator; BA in Economics, Stanford U.; MA in Pub. Policy, Ph.D in Pub. Policy, John F. Kennedy Sch. Govt., Harvard U. Profl. staff mem. US House Armed Services Com., 1988—92; asst. prof. Duke U., 1992—97; dep. asst. sec. for requirements, plans & counterproliferation policy US Dept. Def., 1997—2000; v.p. Hicks & Associates, Inc., 2000—03, sr. v.p., 2003—07; sr. v.p., dir. studies Ctr. for a New Am. Security, 2007—09; prin. dep. under sec. for policy US Dept. Def., Washington, 2009—. Mem. Inst. for Strategic Studies; sr. assoc. Ctr. for Strategic & Internat. Studies, St. Antony's Coll.; adv. Combating WMD Panel Threat Reduction Advisory Com. Recipient Medal for Outstanding Pub. Svc., US Dept. Def., 2000. Office: US Dept Defense 2000 Def Pentagon Rm 3E634 Washington DC 20301*

MILLER, JAMES RUMRILL, III, finance educator; b. Phila., Dec. 21, 1937; s. James Rumrill and Elizabeth Pleasants (King) M.; m. Bettie M. Studer, May 1, 1989 (div. Jan. 2007); children from previous marriage: Elizabeth, Katharine, Kerry. AB, Princeton U., 1959; MBA (Woodrow Wilson fellow), Harvard U., 1962; PhD, MIT, 1966. Sys. analyst MITRE Corp., Bedford, Mass., 1962—67; asst. prof. bus. adminstrn. Stanford U., Calif., 1967—69, assoc. prof., 1970—73, prof., 1973—97, Walter and Elise Haas prof. bus. adminstrn., 1977—97, assoc. dean Bus. Sch., 1974—76, Walter and Elise Haas prof. bus. adminstrn. emeritus, 1997—. Cons. in field. Author: Professional Decision Making, 1970; contbr. numerous articles to profl. jours. Mem. Phi Beta Kappa. Republican. Episcopalian. Office: 16641 W Loma Verde Trail Surprise AZ 85387 E-mail: mdmsinc@aol.com.

MILLER, JAMES VINCE, university president; b. Waynetown, Ind., July 16, 1920; s. J. Vince and Hazel B. (Spore) M.; m. Mildred Mae Hockersmith, June 13, 1943; children: Maryllyn Jean, Rachel Katherine. BA in Philosophy and English, U. Indpls., 1942; M.Div. in History and Lit., United Sem., Dayton, Ohio, 1945; postgrad., Earlham Coll., 1945-46; PhD in Philosophy, Boston U., 1955; LL.D. (hon.), Otterbein Coll., 1971, U. Indpls., 1979. Ordained to ministry Evang. United Brethren Ch., 1945; pastor Greensfork, Ind., 1944-46, Stow, Mass., 1946-48; faculty dept. philosophy and religion Bates Coll., Lewiston, Maine, 1950-64, prof., 1960-64, chmn. dept., 1958-64; acad. dean Otterbein Coll., Westerville, Ohio, 1964-68, v.p. for acad. affairs, acad. dean, 1968-71; pres. Pacific U., Forest Grove, Oreg., 1971-83, pres. emeritus, 1983—; pres. Nat. Coll. of Naturopathic Medicine, Portland, Oreg., 1989-93, pres. emeritus, 1993—. Adj. prof. Union Grad. Sch., 1970-78, San Francisco Theol. Sem., 1979-86; chmn. N.W. Assn. Pvt. Colls. and Univs., 1974-76; treas. Oreg. Ind. Coll. Assn., 1974-75, 76-78, chmn., 1978-79; adv. com. Oreg. Ednl. Coordinating Commn., 1976-79; chmn. council for higher edn. United Ch. Bd. Homeland Missions, 1975-76; former mem. adv. com. Gov.'s Listening Post; former mem. spl. com. on future of edn. in Oreg., Oreg. Ednl. Coordinating Commn.; former mem. Oreg. Bd. Optometry, 1988-92. Methodist. Address: 1633 Mowry Sq Richland WA 99354-2612

MILLER, JAMES W. (JIM MILLER), federal agency administrator; m. Sandy Miller; children: Matt, Adam. BBA, Washington State U. Pres. Washington Assn. Wheat Growers, 1982—83, Nat. Assn. Wheat Growers, 1987—88, v.p. govt. rels., 1995—99; sr. analyst for agrl. & trade US Senate Budget Com.; chief economist Nat. Farmers Union (NFU), chief of staff, 2005—09; under sec. for farm & fgn. agrl. services USDA, Washington, 2009—. Mem. Agrl. Policy Advisory Com., 1986—92; co-chmn. Canada-US Joint Commn. on Grains. Democrat. Office: USDA Jamie L Whitten Fed Bldg 1400 Independence Ave SW Rm 205-E Washington DC 20520*

MILLER, JAMIE S., corporate financial executive; married; 3 children. BS in Acctg., Miami U., Oxford, Ohio, 1990. CPA. Contr. GE Fin. Assurance (now Genworth Fin.), 2003—05, v.p. & chief acctg. officer, 2004—05; leader, fin. svcs. & ptnr. PricewaterhouseCoopers LLP, Chgo.; sr. v.p Wellpoint Inc, contr., chief acctg. officer; v.p., contr. & chief acctg. officer GE Co., 2008—. Mem.: AICPA. Office: General Electric Co 3135 Easton Turnpike Fairfield CT 06828*

MILLER, JAN DEAN, metallurgy educator; b. Dubois, Pa., Apr. 7, 1942; s. Harry Moyer and Mary Virginia (McQuown) M.; m. Patricia Ann Rossman, Sept. 14, 1963; children: Pamela Ann, Jeanette Marie, Virginia Christine. BS, Pa. State U., University Park, 1964; MS, Colo. Sch. of Mines, Golden, 1966, PhD, 1969; D (hon.), U. Pretoria, South Africa, 2007; prof. appointment (hon.), Ctrl. South U., Changsha, P.R. China, 2007. Rsch. engr. Lawrence Livermore Lab., Calif., 1972, Anaconda Co., Mont., 1966; asst. prof. metallurgy U. Utah, Salt Lake City, 1968-72, assoc. prof., 1972-78, prof., 1978-2000, Ivor D. Thomas prof., 2000—, dept. chmn., 2002—, disting. prof., metallurgical engring., 2008. Cons. on processing of mineral resources to various cos. and govt. agys. Editor: Hydrometallurgy, Research, Development, and Plant Practice, 1983, others; contbr. over 500 articles to profl. jours.; 25 patents in field. Recipient Marcus A. Grossman award Am. Soc. Metals, 1974, Van Diest gold medal Colo. Sch. of Mines, 1977, Student award excellence in tchg. metall. engring. U. Utah, 1978, 82, 94, Extractive and Processing Lectr. award The Minerals, Metals and Materials Soc., 1992, Disting. Achievement medal Colo. Sch. of Mines, 1994, Best Paper award for fundamental rsch. 2000 TAPPI Recycling Symposium, 2000, Oustanding Tchg. award Coll. Mines and Earth Scis. U. Utah, 2000, J.D. Miller Symposium honor for innovations in resource processing, SME Annual meeting, Salt Lake City, 2005, Spl. Meritorious Recognition medal Gdansk U. Tech., Poland, 2005, Utah Govs. medal award for sci. and tech., 2006; Centennial fellow Coll. of Earth and Mineral Scis., Pa. State U., 1996. Mem. NAE, AIME (Henry Krumb lectr. 1987, Richards award 1991, Mineral Industry Edn. award 1997, Aplan award 2003), Soc. Mining, Metallurgy and Exploration (chmn. mineral processing divsn. 1980-81, Disting. Mem. award 1992, Antoine M. Gaudin award 1992), Am. Chem. Soc., Soc. Mining Engrs. (bd. dirs. 1980-83, program chmn. 1982-83, Taggart award 1986, 05, Stefanko award 1988, 02, symposium honoring J.D. Miller, 2005), Metall. Soc. (Extractive Metallurgy Tech. award 1988), Salt Lake Swim and Tennis Club, U. Utah Faculty Club. Baptist. Office: U Utah Metall Engring 135 S 1460 E Rm 412 Salt Lake City UT 84112-0114 Office Phone: 801-581-5160. Business E-Mail: jan.miller@utah.edu.

MILLER, JANEL HOWELL, psychologist; b. Boone, NC, May 18, 1947; d. John Estle and Grace Louise (Hemberger) Howell; m. C. Rick Miller, Nov. 24, 1968; children: Kimberly, Brian, Audrey, Rachel. BA, DePauw U., 1969; postgrad., Rice U., 1969; MA, U. Houston, 1972; PhD, Tex. A&M U., 1979. Lic. clin. psychologist, sch. psychologist Tex. Assoc. sch. psychologist Houston Ind. Sch. Dist., 1971-74; rsch. psychologist VA Hosp., Houston, 1972; assoc. sch. psychologist Clear Creek (Tex.) Ind. Sch. Dist., 1974-76; instr. psychology, counseling psychology intern Tex. A&M U., 1976-77; clin. psychology intern VA Hosp., Houston, 1977-78; coord. psychol. svcs. Clear Creek Ind. Sch. Dist., 1978-81, assoc. dir. psychol. svcs., 1981-82; pvt. practice Houston, 1982—. Faculty U. Houston-Clear Lake, 1984—; adolescent suicide cons., 1984—; mem. DePaww U. Alumni Bd. Dirs., 2008-. DePauw U. Alumni scholar, 1965-69; NIMH fellow U. Houston, 1970-71. Mem. APA, Am. Assn. Marriage and Family Therapists, Soc. for Personality Assessment, Am. Coll. Forensic Examiners, Internat. Rorschach Soc., Tex. Psychol. Assn., Tex. Assn. Marriage and Family Therapists, Houston Psychol. Assn. (media rep. 1984-85), Houston Assn. Marriage and Family Therapists. Home: 806 Walbrook Dr Houston TX 77062-4030 Office: 16854 Royal Crest Dr Houston TX 77058-2529 Office Phone: 281-461-4098. Business E-Mail: shrinkskate@sbcglobal.net.

MILLER, JEANNE-MARIE ANDERSON (MRS. NATHAN J. MILLER), language educator, academic administrator; b. Washington, Feb. 18, 1937; d. William and Agnes Catherine (Johns) Anderson; m. Nathan John Miller, Oct. 2, 1960. BA, Howard U., 1959, MA, 1963, PhD, 1976. Instr. dept. English Howard U., Washington, 1963-76, asst. prof., 1976-79, assoc. prof., 1979-92, prof., 1992-97, prof. emeritus, 1997—, asst. dir. Inst. Arts and Humanities, 1973-75, asst. acad. planning, office v.p. for acad. affairs, 1976-90. Cons. Am. Studies Assn., 1972—75, Silver Burdett Pub. Co., NEH, 1978—; mem. adv. bd. D.C. Libr. for Arts, 1973—. Editor, Black Theatre Bull., 1977-86; Realism to Ritual: Form and Style in Black Theatre, 1983; assoc. editor Theatre Jour., 1980-81; contbr. articles to profl. jours., chpts. to books. Mem. Washington Performing Arts Soc., 1971—, Friends of Sta. WETA-TV, 1971—, Mus. African Art, 1971—, Arena Stage Assocs., 1972—, Washington Nat. Opera Guild, 1982—, Wolf Trap Assocs., 1982—, Drama League N.Y., 1995, Shakespeare Theatre, 2001—, Met. Opera Guild, 2002—, Solomon R. Guggenheim Mus., 2007—, Mus. Modern Art, 2008. Ford Found. fellow, 1970-72, So. Fellowships Fund fellow, 1973-74; Howard U. rsch. grant, 1975-76, 94-97, ACLS grant, 1978-79, NEH grant, 1981-84. Mem.: LWV, MLA, ACLU, AAUP, Nat. Archives Found., Folger Shakespeare Libr., Acad. Am. Poets, Am. Theatre and Drama Soc., Studio Mus. Harlem, Nat. Mus. Women in Arts, Nat. Bldg. Mus., Winterthur Guild, Hist. Soc. Washington, D.C. Preservation League, Nat. Trust Historic Preservation, Zora Neale Hurston Soc., Langston Hughes Soc., Ibsen Soc., Friends of Kennedy Ctr. for Performing Arts, Am. Assn. Higher Edn., Coll. Lang. Assn., Common Cause, Am. Assn. Higher Edn., Am. Studies Assn., Coll. English Assn., Nat. Coun. Tchrs. English, Sierra Club, Pi Lambda Theta. Democrat. Episcopalian. Home: 504 24th St NE Washington DC 20002-4818 E-mail: jmamiller@verizon.net.

MILLER, JEFF, United States Representative from Florida; b. St. Petersburg, Fla., June 27, 1959; m. Vicki Griswold; children: Scott, Clint. BA in Journalism, U. Fla., 1984. Exec. asst. to commr. agriculture Doyle Conner, Tallahassee, 1984—88; mem. Fla. Ho. of Reps., 1998—2001, US Congress from 1st Fla. Dist., 2001—, mem. armed svcs. com., vets. affairs com., appt. mem. subcom. readiness & terrorism, subcom. unconventional threats & capabilities. Mem. Environ. Land Mgmt. Study Commn., 1992; vice-chair Santa Rosa County Planning Bd., 1996—98; chmn. Escambia County Legis. Del., 1999—2000; mem. Rep. Study Com., TEAM Santa Rosa Econ. Devel. Coun. Mem. Elizabeth Chapel United Meth. Ch., Chumuckla; bd. dirs. West Fla. Hosp., Fla. FFA Found., Gulf Coast Coun. Boy Scouts America, Santa Rose County United Way; adv. bd. mem. Milton Pregnancy Resource Ctr. Mem.: Fla. Hist. Soc., Kiwanis Club Milton. Republican. Methodist. Office: US House of Reps 2439 Rayburn House Office Bldg Washington DC 20515-0901*

MILLER, JENNIFER L., elementary school educator, small business owner; d. Frank L. and Patricia M. Warfel; m. Ryan G. Miller, July 2, 1994; children: Calleigh L., Garrett R., Trevor R. BA in Elem. Edn. (hon.), U. Portland, 1992. Cert. tchr. A-regular classroom Alaska, spl. edn. endorsement. Dir. summer recreation City of Wrangell, 1990—91; summer acad. tchr. geology; pvt. tutor Wrangell, 1991—92; 1st grade tchr. Wrangell City Schs., 1992—95, asst. coach h.s. girls basketball, 1993—94, multiage tchr. 1-2, 1995—96, multiage tchr. 2-3, 1996—2002; substitute tchr., 1998—92; multiage tchr. 1-2-3 Wrangell City Schs., 2002—03, multiage tchr. 2-3, 2003—04; tchr. 3rd grade Wrangell (Alaska) City Schs., 2004—; co-owner Clearwater Packing. Benchmark cut score com. dept. edn. State of Alaska, benchmark test bias com. edn. and early devel., stds. based assessment validation com., 2004—, content rev. com., 2005—, mem. dept. edn. data review com., 2006; adv. bd. Evergreen Elem., 2002—. Co-founder Evergreen Agtrl. Testing Site; leader Girl Scouts, Wrangell, 2002; active Friends of the Libr., Wrangell, Master Gardener's, Alaska; cmty. fair vendor Alaska, 1997; vol. Wrangell Little League, 2002, Alaskans for Drug Free Youth, Alaska, 1991, Hershey Track and Field, Alaska, 1990—91, Stikine River Rats Swim Team, Alaska, 1992; judge Wrangell H.S. Cheerleaders, Alaska, 1990—92. Recipient Youth Garden grant, Nat. Gardening Assn., 1999, Clay Muralist grant, Alaska Arts in Edn. Mem.: ASCD, NEA, NSTA, Alaska State Literacy Assn., Alaska Coun. Tchrs. Math., Internat. Reading Assn., Wrangell Tchr.'s Assn. (sec. 2000—, negotiations com., bldg. rep., Tchr. of Yr. 1997, 2001, 2006), Nat. Coun. Tchrs. English, Assn. for Childhood Edn. Internat., Juneau-Haines Reading Coun., Nat. Coun. Tchrs. Math., Elk. Home: PO Box 1899 25 Mile Zimovia Hwy Wrangell AK 99929 Home Fax: 907-874-3182. Personal E-mail: rjcgmill@aptalaska.net.

MILLER, JERRY HUBER, retired university chancellor; b. Salem, Ohio, June 15, 1931; s. Duber Daniel and Ida Claire (Holdereith) M.; m. Margaret A. Setter, 1958; children: Gregory, Joy, Carol, Beth, David. BA, Harvard U., 1953; MDiv., Hamma Sch. Theology, 1957; DD (hon.), Trinity Luth. Sem., 1981. Ordained to ministry Luth. Ch., 1957. Research assoc., intern Cornell U., Ithaca, NY, 1955-56; instr. Wittenberg U., Springfield, Ohio, 1956-57; parish pastor Ch. of Good Shepherd, Cin., 1957-62; asst. to pres. Ohio Synod Luth. Ch. Am., 1962-66; sr. campus pastor, dir. campus ministry U. Wis., Madison, 1966-69; regional dir. Nat. Luth. Campus Ministry, Madison, 1969-76, exec. dir. Chgo., 1977-81; pres. Calif. Luth. U., Thousand Oaks, 1981-92, chancellor, 1992-94, pres. emeritus, 1994—; ret. Ventura County Maritime Mus., Channel Islands Harbor, Calif., 1993-95. Chmn. Los Robles Bank, Thousand Oaks, 1987-2000; mem. exec. com. Coun. Ind. Colls., Washington, Assn. Ind. Calif. Colls. and Univs., 1981-92, Coun. Luth. Colls., Luth. Edn. Conf. N.Am., 1977-94; vice chair bd. behavioral sci. State Calif.; bd. dirs. Santa Barbara Bank and Trust. Editor: The Higher Disciplines, 1956; contbr. articles to profl. jours. Bd. dirs. Wittenberg U., Augustana Coll., Rock Island, Ill., United Way, Thousand oaks, Ventura County chpt. ARC, Thousand Oaks, YMCA; chmn. bd. dirs. Los Robles Hosp.; vice chair Stagecoach Inn Mus. Found., 1998—2003; bd. trustees Ventura County Maritime Mus., 1993—; bd. govs. Thousan Oaks Civic Arts Plaza, 2005—. Recipient Patrick Henry medal, Mil. Order of World Wars, 1992; named Man of Yr., Salem, 1975, Man of Yr. Conejo Valley, 1999; Siebert Found. fellow, 1975. Mem. Am. Assn. Higher Edn., Council Advancement and Support Edn., Harvard Alumni Assn., Western Coll. Assn. (bd. dirs.), Conejo Valley C. of C. (bd. dirs.), Conejo Symphony Orch. (bd. dirs.), Conejo Valley Hist. Soc. (bd. dirs. 1995—), Sr. Concerns Conejo Valley. Clubs: Harvard (Ill., Ohio, Wis., Calif.), YMCA (regional bd. dirs., vice chair 1996-99), Rotary. Avocations: skiing, golf, hiking, travel. Personal E-mail: msmjhm@aol.com.

MILLER, JO CAROLYN DENDY, family and marriage counselor, educator; b. Gorman, Tex., Sept. 16, 1942; d. Leonard Lee and Vera Vertie (Robison) Dendy; m. Douglas Terry Barnes, June 1, 1963 (div. June 1975); children: Douglas Alan, Bradley Jason; m. Walton Sansom Miller, Sept. 19, 1982. BA, Tarleton State U., Stephenville, Tex., 1964; MEd, U. North Tex., Denton, 1977; PhD, Tex. Woman's U., Denton, 1993. Tchr. Mineral Wells H.S., Tex., 1964-65, Weatherford Mid. Sch., Tex., 1969-74; counselor, instr. psychology Tarrant County Jr. Coll., Hurst, Tex., 1977-82; pvt. practice Dallas, 1982—. Author: (with Velma Baker, Jeannene Ward) Becoming: A Human Relations Workbook, 1981. Mem. ACA, Tex. State Bd. Examiners Profl. Counselors, Tex. State Bd. Marriage and Family Therapists, Tex. Counseling Assn., North Ctrl. Tex. Counseling Assn., Dallas Symphony Orch. League, Nat. Coun. Family Rels., Tex. Mental Health Counselors Assn., Internat. Assn. for Marriage and Family Counselors. Methodist. Office: 8222 Douglas Ave Ste 777 Dallas TX 75225-5938 Office Phone: 214-691-0400. Personal E-mail: jcdmphd@sbcglobal.net.

MILLER, JOHN, federal agency administrator, former news correspondent; married. Grad., FBI Nat. Exec. Inst. Correspondent WNEW-TV, 1973, WNBC-TV, 1988—94, ABCNEWS Law & Justice Unit, 1997—2002; co-anchor 20/20 ABC, 2002—03; dep. police commr., chief spokesman for commr. NYC Police Dept., 1994—95; bur. chief, counter-terrorism 7 criminal intelligence bur. LA Police Dept., 2003—05; asst. dir. pub. affairs FBI, Washington, 2005—. Co-author (with Michael Stone & Chris Mitchell): The Cell: Inside the 9/11 Plot, And Why the FBI and CIA Failed to Stop It, 2003. Recipient Emmy awards for broadcast journalist (9), Peabody awards (2), Dupont-Columbia award. Mem.: Internat. Assn. Police Chiefs, Internat. Assn. Bomb Technicians. Office: FBI 950 Pennsylvania Ave NW Washington DC 20535*

MILLER, JOHN GRIDER, writer; b. Annapolis, Md., Aug. 23, 1935; s. John Stanley and Ruby Corinne (Young) M.; m. Susan Bradner Bailey, Oct. 26, 1974; children: Kerry, John, Alison. BA, Yale U., 1957. Commd. 2d lt. USMC, 1957, advanced through grades to col., inf./ops. advisor Vietnamese Marine Corps., 1970-71, prin. speechwriter for Commandant Washington, 1971-76, commd. officer Battalion Landing Team, 1977-78, asst. chief of staff ops. and plans III Amphibious Force Okinawa, 1982-83, dep. dir. Marine Corps History Washington, 1983-85, ret., 1985; mng. editor Procs. and Naval History U.S. Naval Inst., Annapolis, Md., 1985-2000. Author: The Battle to Save the Houston, 1985, (Pocket Books edit., 1992, Bluejacket edit., 2000), The Bridge at Dong Ha, 1989, (Dell edit. 1990, Bluejacket edit., 1996, Audiobook edit., 1997), Punching Out: A Guide to Post-Military Transition, 1994, The Co-Vans: U.S. Marine Advisors in Vietnam, 2000; contbf. author: The Marines, 1998, Commandants of the Marine Corps, 2004. Decorated Legion of Merit with gold star, Bronze Star with combat V, Cross of Gallantry, Vietnamese Marine Corps.; recipient Author of Yr. award Naval Inst., 1990, Alfred Thayer Mahan award Navy League of U.S.,

2002, Brig. Gen. Robert L. Denig jr. award, Us Marine Corps Combat Correspondents Assn., 2009. Mem. Marine Corps. Hist. Found. (bd. dirs., Gen. Wallace M. Greene Jr. Book award 1989, Disting. Svc. award 1998), Mil. Order of World Wars (past chpt. comdr., chmn. nat. mag. com.), Civitan Internat. (past chpt. pres.), Washington Naval and Maritime Corrs.' Cir., New Providence Club, Annapolis Chorale. Avocations: music, piano, choral singing, boating. Home: 21 Sands Ave Annapolis MD 21403-4426 E-mail: millerjohng@comcast.net.

MILLER, JOHN LESTER, electro-optical physicist; b. Pitts., July 6, 1959; s. John Albert and Anna May (Bolinsky) M.; m. Corinne Leslie Foster, Dec. 22, 1985. BS in Physics, U. So. Calif., LA, 1981; MBA in Ops. Mgmt. with honors, Regis Coll., Denver, 1988. Telescope operator Griffith Obs., LA, 1980-84; optical tech. Mt. Wilson & Palomar Obs., LA, 1980-81; electro-optical engr. Rockwell Internat., LA, 1981-84; research assoc. U. Hawaii, Mauna Kea Obs., Hilo, 1984-85; lead engr., program mgr., IR sys. engring. mgr. Martin Marietta Astronautics, Denver, Utica, Orlando, 1985-96. Cons. in field. Author: Principles of Infrared Technology, Photarics Rules of Thumb; contbr. more than 50 articles to sci. jours. Active vol. Planned Parenthood. Recipient Bausch & Lomb Sci. award, 1976. Mem. Soc. Photo-Optical Instrumentation Engrs., Optical Soc. Am. Avocations: scuba and sky diving, skeptical inquries, himalayan hiking, kyaking.

MILLER, JOHN ROBERT, oil industry executive; b. Lima, Ohio, Dec. 28, 1937; s. John O. and Mary L. (Zickafoose) M.; m. Karen A. Eier, Dec. 30, 1961; children: Robert A., Lisa A., James E. BSChE with honors, U. Cin., 1960, D.Comml. Sc. hon., 1983. With Standard Oil Co., Cleve., 1960-86, dir. fin., 1974-75, v.p. fin., 1975-78, v.p. transp., 1978-79, sr. v.p. tech. and chems., 1979-80, pres., COO, bd. dirs., 1980—86; chmn., CEO TBN Holdings, Cleve., 1986—2000, Petroleum Ptnrs., Cleve., 2000—03; chmn. SIRVA, Inc., 2006—08. Bd. dirs. Eaton Corp., Blacklight Power, Inc.; chmn. Graphic Packaging Corp., 2006—, Cambrex Corp, 2008-; former chmn. Fed. Res. Bank, Cleve. Mem. Pepper Pike Club, The Country Club, Chagrin Valley Hunt Club, Tau Beta Pi. Home: 37300 Fairmount Blvd # 5 Chagrin Falls OH 44022-6618 Office Phone: 440-247-2096. Business E-Mail: office@johnrmiller.com.

MILLER, JOHN T., JR., lawyer, educator; b. Waterbury, Conn., Aug. 10, 1922; s. John T. and Anna (Purdy) M.; children: Kent, Lauren, Clare, Miriam, Michael, Sheila, Lisa, Colin, Margaret. AB with high honors, Clark U., 1944; JD, Georgetown U., 1948; Docteur en Droit, U. Geneva, 1951; postgrad., U. Paris, 1951. Bar: Conn. 1949 (inactive), DC 1950, US Ct. Appeals (2d, 3d, 5th, 10th, 11th and DC cirs.), US Supreme Ct. 1952. With Econ. Cooperation Adminstn. Am. Embassy, London, 1950-51; assoc. Covington & Burling, 1952-53, Gallagher, Connor & Boland, 1953-62; pvt. practice Washington, 1962—2007. Adj. prof. law Georgetown U. Law Ctr., Washington, 1959-2009; mem. Panel on Future of Internat. Ct. Justice. Co-author: Regulation of Trade, 1953, Modern American Antitrust Law, 1958, Major American Antitrust Laws, 1965; author: Foreign Trade in Gas and Electricity in North America: A Legal and Historical Study, 1970, Energy Problems and the Federal Government: Cases and Material, 8th edit., 1996, Deregulated Natural Gas and Electric Power Industries Seminar: Case Material, 5th edit., 2006; contbr. articles to profl. jours. Trustee Clark U., 1970-76, De Sales Sch. of Theology, 1993-97; mem. bd. advisors Georgetown Visitation Prep. Sch., 1978-94, trustee, 1994-96, emeritus trustee, 1996—; former fin. chmn. troop 46 Nat. Capital Area coun. Boy Scouts Am.; pres. Thomas More Soc. Am., 1996-97. 1st lt. U.S. Army, 1943-46, 48-49. Decorated Bronze Star; recipient 10 yr. teaching award, Nat. Jud. Coll., 1983. Mem. ABA (coun., chmn. adminstrv. law sect. 1972-73, ho. dels. 1991-93), AAUP, D.C. Bar Assn., Energy Bar Assn. (pres. 1990-91), Congl. Country Club, Army and Navy Club (bd. govs. 2000-08), DACOR, Prettyman-Leventhal Am. Inn of Ct. (master 1988-99, pres. 1995-96), Sovereign Mil. Order of Malta (knight). Republican. Roman Catholic. Home: 4721 Rodman St NW Washington DC 20016-3234 Personal E-mail: jtmillerjresq@verizon.net.

MILLER, JOHN WINFIELD, language educator, researcher; b. Allentown, Pa., Oct. 3, 1949; s. George Joseph and Muriel Grace Miller; m. Sunhee Son, July 27, 1986. BA in English, Windener U., Chester, Pa., 1971; PhD, Ohio U., Athens, 1999—2006. Peace corps vol. US Peace Corps, Pleebo, Liberia, 1982—84; pre-svc. tng. dir. US Peace Corps Cuttington U., Liberia, 1983—84; dir., fgn. lang. inst. Kyungsung U., Pusan, 1985—88; assoc. dir. Ohio program English lang. tchg. Chubu U., Kasugai, Japan, 1990—92, dir. Ohio program English lang. tchg., 1996—99; assoc. peace corps dir. US Peace Corps, Kiev, Ukraine, 1993—96; dir. grad. writing program Ohio Program Intensive English, Athens, 2002—03; divsn. chair Lane CC, Eugene, Oreg., 2003—04; academic specialist Asian Sch. III Def. Lang. Inst., Monterey, Calif., 2004—. Tchr. trainer Def. Lang. Inst., 2004—; tchr. trainer for US dept. State Ohio Program Intensive English, Athens, 1990—2003. Recipient Comdts. Coin Excellence, Def. Lang. Inst., 2006; fellow, Internat. Acad. Intercultural Rsch., 2005. Mem.: Phi Beta Delta. Achievements include research in the interculturing cycle, a model for intercultural communicating. Home: 912 Legends Dr Montgomery AL 36116-6580 Business E-Mail: john.miller@monterey.army.mil.

MILLER, JONATHAN F., investment company executive, former Internet company executive; b. 1957; BA cum laude, Harvard Coll. V.p., programming and NBA entertainment NBA, NYC, 1987—93; launched Paramount Comedy Channel, London; CEO, mng. dir Nickelodeon UK, 1993; mng. dir. Nickelodeon Internat., 1993—97; pres., CEO USA Broadcasting, 1997—99, USA Electronic Commerce Solutions, 1999—2000, USA Info. & Services (USAIS), 2000—02; chmn., CEO Am. Online, Inc., Dulles, Va., 2002—06; adv. Gen. Atlantic LLC; founder, gen. ptnr. Velocity Interactive Group, 2007—09; chmn. OpenX Co., London, 2008—09; chmn., CEO Digital Media Group News Corp., NYC, 2009—, chief digital officer, 2009—. Bd. dirs. TM Entertainment & Media, Inc., 2007—, Premier Exhibitions, 2007—, Idearc Media, 2007—, Clickable, 2007—, OpenX Co., 2008—, Next New Networks, Mahalo.com Inc., Kosmix Corp., Hanley Wood, LLC, Am. Film Inst. Trustee Emerson Coll., WNYC Pub. Radio. Recipient Vanguard award, Producers Guild Am., 2006. Office: News Corp 1211 Ave of the Americas New York NY 10018*

MILLER, JONATHAN S., former state treasurer; b. Lexington, July 24, 1967; m. Lisa Miller; 2 children. BA, Harvard Coll., 1989; JD, Harvard Univ., 1992. Legis. dir. Congressman Jim Cape, 1994; dep. chief of staff US Dept. Energy, 1995—96; atty. Miller, Griffin, and Marks, 1997—99; with ETA Properties, 1999—; state treas. State of Ky., 1999—2008. Bd. dir. Lottery Corp., 2000—; vice chmn. State Investment Commn., 2000—; del. Nat.l Summit on Retirement Savings, 2002. Bd. dir. Lexington Urban League, 1999—. Ky. Teachers Retirement Sys., 2000—, Ky. Higher Edn. Assistance Authority, 2002—. Mem.: Ky. Bar Assn. Democrat.

MILLER, JORDAN D., physiologist; b. St. Paul, Minn. BS, Winona State U., Minn., 1998; MS, U. Wis., La Crosse, 2000; PhD, U. Wis., Madison, 2005. NHLBI pre-doctoral fellow U. Wis., Madison, 2000—05; NHLBI post-doctoral fellow U. Iowa, Iowa City, 2005—. Contbr. articles to profl. jours. Internat. young scientist mentor Am. Heart Assn., Dallas, 2006. Mem.: Am. Physiol. Soc. (Mil. Physiology Pre-doctoral award 2003, Proctor and Gamble Predoctoral award 2004, Mil. Physiology Pre-doctoral award 2005, Cardiovascular sect. rsc h. recognition award 2006), AAAS, Am. Heart Assn. Office: University of Iowa 340B Eckstein Medical Research Building Iowa City IA 52242 E-mail: jordan-miller@uiowa.edu.

MILLER, JOSEPH (BUZZ), lobbyist, nuclear energy industry executive; BSChemE, Auburn U., Montgomery, Ala., 1983. Various positions in oil/gas svcs. and utilities svcs. sectors, Houston; engr. chemistry/environ. support sect. nuc. generation Ala. Power (subs.) Southern Co., 1986, various assignments at Ala. Power and Southern Nuc. Oper. Co., 1987—93, fed. affairs mgr. Washington, 1993—98, asst. to CEO Atlanta, 1998—99, v.p. govt. rels. Washington, 1999—2006, sr. v.p. nuc. devel., 2006—, pres. (subs.) Southern Nuc. Devel., LLC, 2006—. Acting v.p. legis. affairs Nuc. Energy Inst., Washington, 1996—97. Office: Southern Co Hdqs 30 Ivan Allen Jr Blvd NW Atlanta GA 30308 Office Phone: 404-506-5000.*

MILLER, JOYCE CATHERINE, chemistry professor, research scientist; d. Richard Norman and Gretna Mae Jones; m. John E. Miller, June 30, 1973. BA, Olivet Nazarene U., Kankakee, Ill., 1973; MA, Ball State U., Muncie, Ind., 1975; PhD, Ohio State U., Columbus, 1999. Cert. medical technologist Am. Soc. Clin. Pathologists, 1976. Rsch. technician in organic chemistry Ball Corp., Muncie, 1973—74; med. technologist Ball Meml. Hosp., Muncie, 1975—76; chemistry supr. Knox Cmty. Hosp., Mount Vernon, Ohio, 1976—78; evening supr. clin. lab. Bethesda Hosp., Zanesville, Ohio, 1978—81; clin. lab. dir. Joel Pomerene Meml. Hosp., Millersburg, Ohio, 1982—95; med. technologist Wooster Cmty. Hosp., Ohio, 1995—; tchg. asst. Ohio State U., 1996—98; assoc. prof. chemistry Mt. Vernon Nazarene U., Ohio, 1998—. Ch. pianist, Sunday sch. tchr. Loudonville Ch. Nazarene, 1981—2006. Mem.: AAAS. Protestant. Avocations: golf, bicycling. Home: 874 Fairway Dr Howard OH 43028 Office: Mt Vernon Nazarene Univ 800 Martinsburg Rd Mount Vernon OH 43050 Business E-Mail: joyce.miller@mvnu.edu.

MILLER, JUDITH BRAFFMAN, writer; b. St. Louis, Feb. 21, 1947; d. William and Lorraine Shirley Braffman; m. Mark Ellis Miller, June 9, 1968. BA, U. Calif., Berkeley, 1969. Freelance writer, 1978—. Author: Wisps, Ashes, and Smoke. Active Amnesty Internat., NYC, 2002—, Am. Friends Svc. Com., 2005. Fellow: Royal Astron. Soc. Gt. Britain; mem.: AAUW, AIAA, ACLU, AAAS, Fedn. Am. Scientists, Can. Assn. Physicists, Royal Inst. Gt. Britan, Am. Assn. Variable Star Observers, Internat. Dark Sky Assn., Astron. Soc. of the Pacific, Nat. Space Soc., Planetary Soc., Am. Inst. Physics, Brit. Astron. Assn., Am. Astron. Soc., Am. Chem. Soc., NY Acad. Scis., Am. Soc. Journalists and Authors, Union Concerned Scientists, Americans for Peace Now. Avocations: naturalist, poetry, politics. Home and Office: 1149 Partridge Ave Saint Louis MO 63130 Office Phone: 314-725-7096. Personal E-mail: jbraffmanmiller@sbcglobal.net.

MILLER, JUDITH ELAINE, retired middle school educator, musician; d. Thomas Clifford and Beulah Mae Miller. BA in Math. with distinction, Ind. U., Bloomington, 1965, MAT in Math., 1968. Lic. life secondary math. tchr. Ind. Dept. Edn. Math. tchr. Greater Clark County Schs., Jeffersonville, Ind., 1965—2002, math. dept. chair Parkview Mid. Sch., 1975—84, team leader Parkview Mid. Sch., 1985—2002; ret., 2002. Co-sponsor Nat. Jr. Honor Soc.; coach Acad. Superbowl. Organist Corydon United Meth. Ch. Recipient Svc. Playing cert., Am. Guild Organists, 2008; finalist Presdl. Award for Excellence in Math. and Sci. Tchg., State of Ind., 2002. Mem.: Ind. Ret. Tchrs. Assn., Nat. Coun. Tchrs. Math., So. Ind. Chpt. Am. Guild Organists (sec., corr. sec.), Fellowship United Meth. in Music and Worship, Ind. U. Alumni Assn. (life), Ind. Organists United, Jennie Gebhart Hedden Music Study Club (sec. 2007—09), Delta Kappa Gamma (Beta Pi corr. sec.). Home: 470 Morris Ave Corydon IN 47112 Office Phone: 812-734-4502. Personal E-mail: jemiller@epowerc.net.

MILLER, KARL FREDERICK, insurance professional; b. White Plains, NY, Oct. 30, 1963; s. Robert Bernard Miller and Elizabeth Hendricks Miller; m. Corinne Simpson Miller, Oct. 20, 1990; children: Kevin, Bridget, Kerry. BA in History, U. Fla., 1985; MA in History, Fla. Atlantic U., 2002. Chartered property casualty underwriter; assoc. risk mgmt. Adjuster Prudential, Fort Lauderdale, Fla., 1987-94; supr. Transp. Fin. Group, Fort Lauderdale, 1994-97; supr., program mgr. CCC Consumer Svcs., Fort Lauderdale, 1997-2000; ins. mgr. Am. Household, Inc., Boca Raton, Fla., 2000—05; dir., corp. risk Jarden Corp., 2005—; pres. C3KB Solutions, Inc., 2005—. Author: A Warning, 1990; contbr. fiction and poetry to numerous periodicals; inventor. Committeeman Broward Dem. Exec. Com., Ft. Lauderdale, 1992-95; v.p. Coral Springs Improvement Dist., 1995-2003. Mem. CPCU Soc., Nat. Cath. Edn. Assn., Fla. Rosary (pres. 1991-99), Fla. Youth Soccer Assn., Dems. for Life of Am. Roman Catholic. Avocations: guitar, running, coaching soccer. Home: 1999 NW 83rd Dr Coral Springs FL 33071-6271

MILLER, KATHLEEN FAIRBROTHER, librarian; b. Ft. Monmouth, NJ, May 21, 1958; d. Robert Harold and Patricia Ann Fairbrother; m. William Miller, May 5, 2006; 1 child, Robert William Hoeth. BA in Polit. Sci., SUNY, Albany, 1979, MLS, 1981; EdD, U. Ctrl. Fla., Orlando, 2008. Reference libr. St. John's U., SI, NY, 1981—83; young adult svcs. libr. NY Pub. Libr., 1984—86, adult svcs. libr., 1986—88, asst. br. libr., 1988—89; info. specialist Find/SVP, NYC, 1983—84; reference libr. Lee County Libr. Sys., Ft. Myers, Fla., 1989—89, head reference, 1989—90, asst. dir. pub. svcs., 1991—93, dep. dir., 1993—97; assoc. dean, libr. svcs. Fla. Gulf Coast U., Ft. Myers, 1997—2000, dir., libr. svcs., 2000—08, dean, libr. svcs., 2008—. Pres. SW Fla. Libr. Network, Ft. Myers, 2005—07; contbg. editor Libr. Issues, Ann Arbor, Mich., 2005—. Mem.: ALA, Fla. Libr. Assn., Assn. Coll. and Rsch. Librs. Office: Fla Gulf Coast Univ 10501 FGCU Blvd South Fort Myers FL 33965-6501 Business E-Mail: kmiller@fgcu.edu.

MILLER, KENDRA DANETTE, art services business owner; b. Jackson, Miss., Jan. 24, 1970; d. William Jerome Miller and Linda B. Walker. BA, Northwestern U., 1992; MA in Arts Adminstrn., Sch. of Art Inst. Chgo., 1997. Cert. fine and decorative art appraisal studies George Wash. U. Ctr for Profl. Devel., D.C., 2004. External affairs dir. Pinchot Inst. for Conservation, Wash., 2000—04; prin. Strata Fine Art Svcs., Silver Spring, Md., 2004—. Docent Nat. Mus. Women in the Arts, Wash., 2000—07; vol. Nativity Youth Ctr., Wash., 2004—05; adv. bd. McClinton Musical Theatre Arts Found., Bucharest, Romania, 2003—05; bd. mem. Woman Made Gallery, Chgo., 1997—99, treas., 1999; bd. mem. Imani Found. & Art Gallery, Kent, Ohio, Better Existence with HIV, Evanston, Ill., 1992—94. Scholar, Assn. Fundraising Profls., Greater N.Y. chpt., 2000, Nat. Capital Gift Planning Coun., 2002. Mem.: Am. Soc. Appraisers (assoc.). Conservative. Avocations: scuba diving, tennis, reading, art, travel. Home: 8000 Greenwood Ave Takoma Park MD 20912-6847 Business E-Mail: info@stratafineartservices.com.

MILLER, KENNETH EDWARD, sociologist, educator; b. NYC, June 17, 1929; s. Joseph F. and Irene (Edersheim) M.; m. Andrée Nora Barthelemy, Feb. 14, 1959 (div. Nov. 1984); children: Jennifer Andrée, Christopher Kenneth; m. Janet Sue Daniels, May 21, 1990. BA, U. Ala., 1953, MA, 1956; PhD, Duke, 1965; MS, Drake U., 1986. Asst. to pres., dir. devel. Jacksonville (Fla.) U., 1957-60; dir. Health Council, asso. dir. Community Planning Council, Birmingham, Ala., 1960-62; asst. prof. sociology Emory U., Atlanta, 1966-70, acting chmn. dept., 1969-70; prof. sociology Drake U., Des Moines, 1970-96, chmn. dept., 1970-79, 82-88, asst. to dean for grad. studies, 1991-92, prof. emeritus, 1996—. Research sociologist U. Ala., 1956-57; research asso. U.S. Civil Service Commn., summer 1968. Served with USN, 1946-48. Postdoctoral research fellow Duke, 1965-66. Mem. Midwest Sociol. Soc. Home: 2129 NW 140th St Clive IA 50325-8730

MILLER, KENNETH LEE, counselor, educator; s. Arthur Jerome and Geraldine Marie Miller; m. Suellyn Mary Hetrick, May 28, 1983. BA in Sociology, Purdue U., 1979, MEd in Counseling, 1985, PhD, 1990. Diplomate Am. Bd. Med. Psychotherapists, 1988; profl. clin. counselor Ohio Counselor, Social Worker, and Marriage and Family Therapist Bd., 2002, nat. cert. counselor Nat. Bd. for Cert. Counselors, Inc./Va., 1988, approved clin. supr. Ctr. for Credentialing and Edn., Inc./N.C., 1998, life skills educator Teachers Coll., Columbia U., 1982, cert. in profl. counseler Am. Bd. Co-dir. gender equity grant Purdue U., West Lafayette, Ind., 1987—89; asst. prof. Calif. State U., San Bernardino, 1990—92; asst. prof., capt. The Citadel, Charleston, SC, 1992—93; asst. prof. U. Hawaii at Manoa, Honolulu, 1993—95; assoc. prof. Youngstown (Ohio) State U., 2000—. Dir. U. Counseling Ctr./Cmty. Counseling Clinic Youngstown State U., 2000—04, dept. chair counseling, 2003—05; cons. Hunt County Dept. Mental Health, Greenville, Tex., 1995—95. Co-author: Gender-fair Counseling Strategies, 1988, Working for Change: Planning a Gender Equity Workshop, 1988; contbr. chapters to books, articles to profl. jours.; co-developer (videotape) A Model for Gender-fair Counseling, Freedom, Fairy Tale, Assembly Line, Your Choice/Your Future, Comedian, Obsolete, Inequality: A Subtle Disaster. Mem. San Bernardino County Mental Health Assn., 1990—92; adv. com. mem. Tri-County Child Advocacy Ctr., Youngstown, 2000—02; mem. bd. mgrs. John Will Anderson Boy's Club, Gary, Ind., 1983—83; sec. Hawaii Multicultural Counseling and Devel. Assn., Honolulu, 1994—95; com. mem. Multicultural Ethics Rev. Com., ACA, Honolulu, 1994—94; western divsn. rep. Nat. Orgn. for Human Svc. Edn., Seattle, 1991—92; judge Calif. Academic Decathlons, San Bernardino, Calif., 1990—91. Recipient Disting. Professorship award, Youngstown State U., 2001—02. Mem.: APA, ACA, Am. Psychotherapy Assn., Ohio Assn. for Counselor Edn. and Supervision, East Ohio Counseling Assn., Ohio Counseling Assn., Soc. for the Psychol. Study of Social Issues, Am. Coll. Counseling Assn., Assn. for Counselor Edn. and Supervision (Robert Frank Outstanding Counseling Program award 2002—03), Am. Ednl. Rsch. Assn., Kappa Delta Pi, Pi Lambda Theta, Chi Sigma Iota. Avocations: swimming, tennis, scuba diving. Office: Youngstown State Univ One University Plaza Youngstown OH 44555

MILLER, KENNETH MICHAEL, electronics executive, director; b. Chgo., Nov. 20, 1921; s. Matthew and Tillie (Otto) M.; m. Dolores June Miller, Jan. 16, 1943 (dec. Dec. 1968); children: Barbara Anne Reed, Nancy Jeanne Hathaway, Kenneth Michael, Roger Allan; m. Sally J. Ballingham, June 20, 1970 (dec. Apr. 2002). Student, Ill. Inst. Tech., 1940-41, UCLA, 1961. Electronics engr. Rauland Corp., Chgo., 1941-48; gen. mgr. Lear, Inc., Santa Monica, Calif., 1948-59; v.p., gen. mgr. Motorola Aviation Electronics, Inc., Culver City, Calif., 1959-60; v.p., gen. mgr. instrument divsn. Daystrom, Inc., LA, 1961; gen. mgr. metrics divsn. Singer Co., L.A. and Bridgeport, Conn., 1962-65; v.p., gen. mgr. Lear Jet Corp., 1965-66; pres., dir. Infonics, Inc., 1967-68; v.p., gen. mgr. Computer Industries, Inc., 1968-69; dir. ops., tech. products group Am. Std. Corp., McLean, Va., also v.p., gen. mgr. Wilcox Elec. divsn. Kansas City, Mo., 1969-71; pres. Wilcox Elec., Inc. subs. Northrop Corp., Kansas City, 1971-72; v.p., dir. World Wide Wilcox, Inc. subs., McLean, 1971-72; pres., CEO, dir. Penril Corp., Rockville, Md., 1973-86; pres. K-M Miller and Assocs., Rockville, 1986—. Dir. George Mason Bank, NA, Washington, Palmer Nat. Bank, Washington. Mem. adv. bd. Washington Bus. Jour.; contbr. articles to profl. jours. Mem. regional planning coun. Cmty. Mental Health Svcs., Bridgeport, 1964; mem. Bridgeport Capital Fund Com.; trustee Park City Hosp.; vice dir. Montgomery County Arts Coun.; bd. dirs. U. Bridgeport; mem. Md. State Com. High Tech. Recipient Job Makers award Mfrs. Assn. Bridgeport, 1963. Fellow Radio Club Am. (dir., chmn grants-in-aid com.); mem. AIAA, IEEE, Aircraft Owners and Pilots Assn., Am. Mgmt. Assn., Armed Forces Comm. and Electronics Assn. (life), Electronic Industries Assn., Instrument Soc. Am. (life), Nat. Aero. Assn., Soc. Non-Destructive Testing, Soc. Automotive Engrs., Air Force Assn., Am. Radio Relay League (life), Amateur Satellite Corp. (life), Am. Def. Preparedness Assn. (life), Aero. Elec. Soc. (life), Nat. Capital DX Assn. (pres. 1987-88), Assn. Old Crows (life), Mfrs. Assn. Bridgeport (dir.), Bridgeport Engring. Inst., Bridgeport C. of C. (pres. 1964), Quarter Century Wireless Assn. (life, Disting. Svc. award 1994), Soc. Wireless Pioneers, Rolling Hills Country Club (Wichita), Algonquin Club (Bridgeport). Home and Office: 16904 George Washington Dr Rockville MD 20853-1128 Home Phone: 301-774-7709; Office Phone: 301-774-7709. Personal E-mail: kmm@prodigy.net.

MILLER, KENNETH RAYMOND, biologist, educator; b. Rahway, NJ, July 14, 1948; s. Claude Ray and Marion Ruth (Hamill) M.; m. Jody Annette Zanot, June 10, 1972; children: Lauren Beth, Tracy Erin. BS in Biology, Brown U., 1970; PhD, U. Colo., 1974. Asst. prof. Harvard U., Cambridge, Mass., 1974-80, Brown U., Providence, 1980-82, assoc. prof., 1982-86, prof., 1986—. Author: Biology: Discovering Life, 1991, 2d edit., 1994, Biology, 1991, 3d edit., 1995; contbr. articles to profl. jours. Grantee NIH, 1977—, NSF, 1982—. Mem. AAAS, Am. Soc. Cell Biology (chmn. edn. com. 1986-90). Office: Brown U PO Box G-b589 Providence RI 02912-0001

MILLER, KENNETH W., lawyer; b. Chgo., Oct. 25, 1960; BS, U. Ill., 1982; JD magna cum laude, Northwestern U., 1985. Bar: Ill. 1985. Ptnr., co-chmn. pvt. equity practice Katten Muchin Rosenman LLP, Chgo. Mem.: ABA, Am. Inst. of CPAs. Office: Katten Muchin Rosenman LLP 525 W Monroe St Chicago IL 60661 Office Phone: 312-902-5261. Office Fax: 312-577-8747. Business E-Mail: ken.miller@kattenlaw.com.

MILLER, KHADIJAH OLIVIA, education educator; d. Joseph Richard and Eunice Verdell Turner; m. L. Eric Miller, Oct. 26, 1997; children: Ericka Olivia, Erin Kayla. BA in Print Journalism, NYU, 1993; MA in African Am. Studies, Temple U., 1995, PhD in African Am. Studies, 2001. Dir. women's studies program and women's ctr. Rosemont Coll., Pa., 2000—02; asst. prof. Norfolk State U., Va., 2002—, dept. head, interdisciplinary studies, 2006—07. Female faculty mentor Norfolk State U. Recipient award for innovative excellence in tchg., learning and tech., 17th Internat. Conf. Coll. Tchg. and Learning, 2006; grantee, NEH, 2005. Mem.: AAUW, Am. Democracy Project (v.p. Norfolk State U. chpt. 2005—). Office: Norfolk State U 700 Park Avenue Norfolk VA 23504 Office Fax: 757-823-8602. Business E-Mail: komiller@nsu.edu.

MILLER, L. MARTIN, accountant, financial planner; b. NYC, Sept. 17, 1939; s. Harvey and Julia (Louis) M.; m. Judith Sklar, Jan. 21, 1962; children: Philip, Marjorie. BS, U. Pa., Phila., 1960; M in Taxation, Villanova U., Pa., 2001. CPA; CFP; accredited fin. planning specialist. Jr. acct. Deloitte, Haskins & Sells, NYC, 1960-62, sr. acct. Phila., 1962-64; mng. ptnr. Morison Cogen LLP, Phila., 1964—2005. Treas. Coronet Container Co., Inc., Phila., Val Mar Realty Corp., NYC; dir. Penn Internat. Trading Co., Phila.; mng. dir. CPA Tax Forum, 1966-69; underwriting mem. Lloyds of London, 1978-95, chmn. Mid-Atlantic region, 1991-92; faculty Wharton Sch. U. Pa., 1992-2004, Villanova U., 2003—; MBA program faculty LaSalle U., 2003—; continuing edn. faculty AICPAs, 2006; lectr. in field. Author: Accountants Guide to S.E.C. Filings, 1968, Salaries, Penn. Non-Profit Report, 1997, Worker Compensation, Practical Tax Strategies, 2000; contbr. articles to profl. jours. Mem. Phila. Rep. Com., 1963-67, treas. Daerr-Bannon for state rep. com., 1997; chmn. Lower Merion Twp. scholarship fund, 1975-78; bd. dirs. Main Line Br. ARC, 1997-2000; bd. dirs. Penn Valley Civic Assn., 1973-79, Gladwyne Civic Assn., 1992-95; mem. Lower Merion Planning Commn., 1978-82, Gov.'s Tax Study Commn.; pres. Mensa Edn. and Rsch. Found., 1984-86; mem. SEC Forum on Small Bus. Capital Formation, 1983, Pa. Impact, 1995; apptd. to Pa. State Bd. Accountancy, 1985-94, chmn., 1990-91; elected sch. bd. dir. Lower Merion Twp., 1993-97, also chmn. fin. com. Served with U.S. Army, 1961-62. Recipient Outstanding Achievement award Germantown Civic Assn., 1965. Mem. Nat. Assn. Securities Dealers (industry arbitrator 2005—)Pa. Inst. CPAs (edn. com. 1975-78, bd. dirs. 1979-81, by-laws chmn. 1980-83, mem. non-profit orgns. com. 1995-99, fin. planning com. 2002-2003), Nat. Assn. State Bds. Accountancy (edn. com. 1987, nominating com. 1989, experience com. 1990, continuing edn. com. 1995—), Am. Arbitration Assn. (mem. comml. panel, 2002—), Cert. Fin. Planner (bd. ethics 1995-97), AICPAs (nat. tax commn. 1979-82, exec. com. self regulation divsn. for CPA firms 1984-87, acctg. and rev. svcs. com., long range planning com., ethics divsn. 1985-88, specialization bd. 1989-90, ethics exec. com. 1990-93, mem. curriculum and acctg. edn. 1993-96, chmn. fin. assistance task force 1995, bd. dirs. Estate Planning Coun. 1998-2004, nomination com. 1999, discussion leader continuing edn. 2005), Little 10 Acctg. Assn. (edn. chmn. 1980-84), Main Line C. of C. (govt. affairs com. 1991-99), Mensa (internat. fin. officer 1970-74), Masons (past master), Plays and Players Club (treas. 1978-79), Beta Alpha Psi. Home: 204 Dove Ln Haverford PA 19041-1902 Office: Morison Cogen LLP 150 Monument Rd Bala Cynwyd PA 19004-1702

MILLER, LARRY G., professional sports team executive; b. Phila. BBA in Acctg., Temple U., Phila., 1982; MBA, La Salle U., Phila., 1987. Exec. v.p., contr. Jantzen, Inc., Portland, Oreg., pres., 1992—97; v.p. USA apparel Nike, Inc., Oreg., 1997—99, pres. Brand Jordan, 1999—2006, v.p., gen. mgr. basketball, 2006—07; pres. Portland Trail Blazers, 2007—. Bd. mem. Urban League Portland, Portland Sports Authority. Office: Portland Trail Blazers One Center Ct Ste 200 Portland OR 97227*

MILLER, LAURA ARIANE, lawyer; b. NYC, Apr. 26, 1954; d. Walter Hamilton and Phoebe Therese (Adil) M.; m. Glenn Richard Reichardt, Sept. 10, 1977 (div. Dec. 1984). BA, U. Mich., 1974; MPP, Harvard U., 1976; JD, Yale Law Sch, 1988. Bar: Va. 1988, DC 1989, US Dist. Ct. (ea. dist.) Va. 1989, US Dist. Ct. DC 1990, US Ct. Appeals (4th and DC cirs.) 1990. Assoc. ICF, Inc., Washington, 1976-77; special asst. Sec. HEW, Washington, 1977-79; depty commr. U.S. Adminstrn. Children, Youth, Families, Washington, 1979-81; pres. The Delta Corp., Washington, 1981-85; law clk. to Hon. Byron White US Supreme Ct., Washington, 1988-89; assoc. Cacheris & Towey, Washington, 1989; ptnr., chair Govt. Investigations and White Collar Defense practice Nixon Peabody LLP, Washington. Com. mem. Fairfax County (Va.) Democrats; del. Va. State Democratic Conv., 1982; mem. Govs. Adv. Com. Children, Va., 1984-85. Named one of The 50 Most Influential Women Lawyers in Am., Nat. Law Jour., 2007. Mem. ABA (co-chair criminal litig. com., mem. governing coun. litig. sect.), Am. Inn of Ct., Va. Women Attys. Assn., DC Women's Bar Assn., DC Bar Assn., Commonwealth of Va. Bar Assn., Am. Trial Lawyers Assn., Lawyers Club of DC, Yale Law Sch. Assn. Washington (treas. 1990). Avocations: tennis, racquetball, opera. Office: Nixon Peabody LLP 401 9th St NW Ste 900 Washington DC 20004 Office Phone: 202-585-8313. Office Fax: 866-947-3685. E-mail: lmiller@nixonpeabody.com.*

MILLER, LAURA M., former mayor, journalist; b. Balt., Nov. 18, 1958; m. Steven Wolens; children: Alex, Lily, Maxwell. BA, U. Wis., Madison, 1980. Mem. city coun. City of Dallas, 1998—2002, mayor, 2002—07. Columnist, investigative reporter Dallas Observer, metro columnist Dallas Times Herald, New York Daily News, The Dallas Morning News, The Miami Herald; freelance writer: The Miami Herald. Recipient H.L. Mencken Writing award, Balt. Sun, 1995, 6 Katie awards, Dallas Press Club, 2 Tex. Headliner awards, 2 Philbin awards, Dallas Bar Assn., cert. of merit, ABA.

MILLER, LEE TODD, pediatrician, educator; b. NYC, Aug. 1, 1957; BA, Bowdoin Coll.; MD, U. Va., 1982. Cert. Pediat., 1987. Intern pediat. U. Va. Med. Ctr., Charlottesville, 1982—83, resident, 1983—86, chief resident pediat.; vice chair edn., dept. pediat. Cedars-Sinai Med. Ctr., LA; prof. pediat. David Geffen Sch. Med., UCLA. Recipient Golden Apple Tchg. Award. Mem.: Assn. Pediat. Program Dirs., Ambulatory Pediat. Assn., Am. Acad. Pediat. Office: Cedars-Sinai Med Ctr 8700 Beverly Blvd Los Angeles CA 90048 Office Phone: 310-423-4467. Office Fax: 310-423-0145. E-mail: lee.miller@cshs.org.

MILLER, LEROY PAUL, JR., language educator; b. Holyoke, Mass., Feb. 21, 1949; s. Leroy Paul Sr. and Rose Marie (Danehey) Miller. AA, Northampton Jr. Coll., Mass., 1972; BA, U. New. Eng., Biddeford, Maine, 1974; MEd, Springfield Coll., Mass., 1977; postgrad., Am. Internat. Coll., Springfield. Cert. elem. tchr., English tchr., history tchr., guidance counselor Mass. Sch. adjustment counselor Holyoke Pub. Schs., 1978-79, ednl. programmer, 1979-80, tutor Chpt. I, 1980-81; tutor Amherst (Mass.) Pub. Schs., 1982-84; tchr. West Springfield (Mass.) Pub. Schs., 1985-86; tchr. English Springfield Pub. Schs., 1986—. Fundraiser M. Marcus Kiley Mid. Sch., Commerce HS; alumni counselor U. New Eng., 1977—. Mem. NEA, ASCD, Nat. Coun. Tchrs. English, Mass. Tchrs. Assn., Springfield Edn. Assn. (faculty rep. 1986—), U. New Eng. Alumni Assn. (v.p. 1990—), Elks, Psi Chi. Democrat. Roman Catholic. Avocations: reading, bowling. Office: Commerce HS 180 Cooley St Springfield MA 01128 Home: 121 Wolcott Woods Rd Simsbury CT 06070 Home Phone: 860-306-2665. Personal E-mail: lmill55169@aol.com.

MILLER, LESLIE BETH, judge; b. NYC, Oct. 29, 1951; d. Frederic Joel and Elayne Miller. BA, Goucher Coll., 1973; JD, St. Louis U., 1976. Bar: Ariz. 1976, US Dist. Ct. Ariz. 1977. Law clk. Office of County Atty., Tucson, 1976; assoc. Whitehall, Berger, Karp & West, Tucson, 1977; asst. pub. defender Pima County, Tucson, 1978-82, superior ct. judge, 1985—, assoc. presiding judge, 1993—96, 1999—2001; city magistrate City of Tucson, 1982-85. Mem. Ariz. Commn. on Cts., 1988-89. Bd. dirs. Tucson Women's Found., 1982-84, Nat. Issues Forum, Tucson, 1984, Boys and Girls Club Tucson, 1985-, pres. 1999-2001; bd. dirs. Tucson Internat. Mariachi Conf., 1985—2005, Women's Studies Adv. Coun., 1988-91, La Frontera, 1986-93, v.p., 1990-91, pres., 1991-92; mem. Exec. Women's Coun., 1981-89, pres., 1984-86; mem. exec. constrn. com. Tucson Bicentennial, 1986-91, chair, 1988-91, Women on the Move Leadership Program, 1988-97, facilitator, 1989-91; mem. United Way Cmty. Profile Coun., 1992-94; bd. dirs. Susan G. Komen Breast Cancer Found., 2005-. Mem. ABA (nat. conf. state trial judges, chair 2000-01, mem. house dels. 2002-, jud. divsn., vice chair 2004-05, chair-elect 2005-, chair 2006-, jud. mem.-at-large bd. govs. 2009-), Ariz. Women Lawyers, State Bar Assn. Ariz. (bd. govs. 1983-85, pres. young lawyers divsn. 1983-84), Pima County Bar Assn. (bd. dirs. 1982-91, 93-2002, pres. 1989-90), Ariz. Judges Assn. (pres. 1992-93), Ariz. Assn. Drug Ct. Profls. (pres. 2000-02, exec. com. 2002-04). Office: Pima County Superior Ct 110 W Congress St Tucson AZ 85701-1331*

MILLER, LINDA B., political scientist; b. Manchester, NH, Aug. 7, 1937; d. Louis and Helene (Chase) M. AB cum laude, Radcliffe Coll., 1959; MA, Columbia U., 1961, PhD, 1965. Asst. prof. Barnard Coll., 1964-67; rsch. assoc. Princeton U., 1966-67, Harvard U., 1967-71, 76-81, lectr. polit. sci., 1968-69; assoc. prof. Wellesley (Mass.) Coll., 1969-75, prof. polit. sci., 1975—2004, chmn. dept., 1985-89. Vis. prof. rsch. Watson Inst., Brown U., 1997, adj. prof. internat. rels., 1998—2000, 2003—, sr. fellow, 2000—03; vis. prof. polit. sci. Brown U., 1997. Author: World Order and Local Disorder: The United Nations and Internal Conflicts, 1967, Dynamics of World Politics: Studies in the Resolution of Conflicts, 1968, Cyprus: The Law and Politics of Civil Strife, 1968; co-author, co-editor: Ideas and Ideals: Essays on Politics in Honor of Stanley Hoffmann, 1993, Argentia, 2007—; editor Internat. Studies Rev., 1999-2002; contbr. articles to profl. jours. Internat. Affairs fellow Coun. Fng. Rels., 1973-74, Rockefeller Found. fellow, 1976-77, Oceanographic Instn. sr. fellow, 1979-80, 82-83, NATO social sci. rsch. fellow, 1982-83. Mem. Inst. Strategic Studies, Internat. Studies Assn., Coun. Fgn. Rels., Phi Beta Kappa. Home: PO Box 415 South Wellfleet MA 02663-0415 Office: Watson Inst Brown U PO Box 1970 Providence RI 02912-1970 Office Phone: 401-863-1997. Business E-Mail: Linda_Miller@brown.edu.

MILLER, LISA ANN, lawyer; b. Bayshore, NY, Dec. 23, 1959; d. Harold Douglas and Joan Marie Miller; m. Michael E. Millhoan (div.); children: Shane E. Millhoan, Clayton W. Perry. BA in Polit. Sci., Ohio No. Coll., Ada, 1998; JD, U. Toledo, Toledo, Ohio, 2002. Bar: Ohio, Ohio (Supreme Ct.) 2002. Asst. to advertising dir. Good Housekeeping Mag., NY, 1985—88; asst. mktg. dir. Family Circle Mag., NY Times, NY, 1988—90; assoc. atty. Wise & Dorner LLC, Toledo, 2000—03; staff atty. Seneca County Dept. Family Svcs., Tiffin, Ohio, 2003—04; pvt. practice Findlay, Ohio, 2004—. Pres. Seneca County Bar Assoc., Tiffin, Ohio, 2006, v.p., 2004—05; law libr. trustee Seneca County Law Libr. Assoc., Tiffin, Ohio, 2004—06. Atty. advisor St. Wendelin HS Mock Trial Team, Fostonia, Ohio, 2006; voting rights staff Voter Protection Program, Fostonia, Ohio, 2004. Mem.: Southern Poverty Law Ctr., Ohio Assn. Criminal Defense Atty., Ohio State Bar Assn. Office Phone: 419-424-5553.

MILLER, LYNN FIELDMAN, lawyer; b. Newark, Oct. 9, 1938; d. George Martin and Helene G. (Friedman) Fieldman; m. Arthur Harold Miller, Aug. 24, 1958; children: Jennifer Lyn, Jonathan Daniel. BA in English, Barnard Coll., NYC, 1959; MLS, Rutgers U., New Brunswick, NJ, 1971, MA in Theater Arts, 1977; JD, Rutgers U., Newark, 1990. Bar: N.J. 1990, U.S. Dist. Ct. N.J. 1990, U.S. Ct. Appeals (3d cir.) 1992. Head libr. Alma White Coll., Zarapheth, N.J., 1971; reference libr. Douglas Coll., New Brunswick, N.J., 1971-79; media libr. Rutgers U., New Brunswick, 1979-87; intern Hon. Anne E. Thompson Fed. Dist. Ct., Trenton, NJ, 1988; assoc. Wilentz, Goldman & Spitzer, Woodbridge, NJ, 1989, Greenbaum, Rowe, Smith, Woodbridge, 1990-91, Miller & Littman, New Brunswick, 1991-93; ptnr. Miller & Miller, New Brunswick, 1993-2001, Miller, Miller & Tucker, P.A., 2001—. Editor in chief: (jour.) Women's Rights Law Reporter, 1989-90. Active Highland Park (NJ) Environ. Commn., 1991-97, Supreme Ct. Com. on Women in the Cts.; trustee Middlesex County Bar Found., 2002-2008. Mem. NJ State Bar Assn. (trustee 2000-06, individual rights com. 1989-95, chair individual rights com. 1995-97, dir. entertainment and arts law sect. 1992-96, bd. trustees Women in the Profession sect. 1997-98, sec. 1998-99, chmn. 2000-01, chair spl. com. consumer protection law 2002-2004), Middlesex County Bar Assn. (chair women lawyers sect. 1995-96, bd. trustees 1996-2002, treas. 2003-04, 2d v.p. 2004-05, 1st v.p. 2005-06, pres.-elect 2006-07, pres. 2007-08). Avocations: walking, bicycling. Office: 96 Paterson St New Brunswick NJ 08901-2109 Office Phone: 732-828-2234. Business E-Mail: lmiller@millerandmiller.com.

MILLER, MALCOLM HENRY, manufacturing sales executive, real estate developer; b. Elgin, Ill., Feb. 6, 1934; s. Carl Theodore and Alice Lucy (Garbisch) M. BA, U. Wis., Madison, 1957; postgrad., Am. Inst. Fgn. Trade, 1961, U. N.Mex., Albuquerque, 1963. Sales engr. Fairbanks Morse Corp., Beloit, Wis., 1962; pvt. practice real estate Albuquerque, 1964-75; supt., v.p. Walworth Foundries, Inc., Darien, Wis., 1959-61, exec. v.p. sales, co-owner, 1975—; v.p. sales, co-owner Waukesha Specialty Co., Inc., Darien, 1975—. Treas. Fastcast, Inc., Albuquerque, 1993—. Loan advisor, developer Community Assn. for Sr. Housing, Albuquerque, 1967-70; Rep. candidate for state senator N.Mex., 1970; active fin. com. Bernalillo County Reps., N.Mex., 1970-80, Walworth County Reps., Wis., 1976-77; mem. Congressman Ryan's 1st Dist. Small Bus. Adv. Com. Served to 1st lt. US Army, 1957-59. Mem. Am. Foundrymen's Assn., Dairy Food Industries Supply Assn., Dairy Food Industries Supply Assn. (bd. dir. 1992-95), Santa Fe Opera Guild, Big Foot Country Club, Nat. "W" Club, Masons, The Madison Club, Sigma Alpha Epsilon. Republican. Episcopalian. Avocations: exercise, films, opera, fly fishing. Home: 223 Fremont St PO Box 37 Walworth WI 53184-0037 Office: Walworth Foundries Inc PO Box 160 Hwy 14 and I-43 Interchange Darien WI 53114 Office Phone: 262-724-3600.

MILLER, MARGERY, psychologist, educator, speech pathology/audiology and mental health services professional, university administrator, academic administrator; m. Donald F. Moores; children: Kip Lee, Tige Justice. BA, Elmira Coll., 1971; MA, NYU, 1972; EdS, MS, SUNY, Albany, 1975; MA, Towson State U., 1987; PhD, Georgetown U., 1991. Lic. speech pathologist Md., psychologist Md., diplomate neuropsychologist, sch. neuro-psychologist; cert. tchr. nursery-6th grades, spl. edn. NY, nationally cert. sch. psychologist. Speech and lang. pathologist Mental Retardation Inst. Flower and Fifth Ave. Hosp., NYC, 1971—72; cmty. speech/lang. pathologist, dir. speech and hearing svc. NY State Dept. Mental Hygiene, Troy, 1972—74; instr. comm. disorders dept. Coll. St. Rose, Albany, NY, 1975—77; clin. supr. U. Md., College Park, 1978; speech/lang. pathologist Md. Sch. for Deaf, Frederick, 1978—84; auditory devel. specialist Montgomery County Pub. Schs., Rockville, Md., 1984—87; coord. Family Life program Nat. Acad. Gallaudet U., Washington, 1987—88, interim dir., 1988—89; dir. Counseling and Devel. Ctr. N.W. Campus, Washington, 1989—93; prof. psychology, coord. psychology internship program, dir. undergrad. psychology program Gallaudet U., Washington, 1993—2006, dean enrollment, mgmt., 2006—; lic. practicing psychologist Bethesda, Md., 1998—. Instr. sign-lang. program Frederick CC; dance instr. for deaf adolescents; diagnostic cons. psychology and speech pathology; presenter at confs.; profl. coaching, Md., Fla., 2002—. Author: It's O.K. to be Angry, 1976; co-author: Cognition, Education and Deafness: Directions for Research and Instruction, 1985; mem. editl. rev. com. Gov.'s Devel. Disabilities Coun., Md.; contbr. articles to profl. jours. Vol., choreographer Miss Deaf Am. Pageant, 1984. Office Edn. Children's Bur. fellow, 1971. Mem.: APA, Montgomery County Md. Mental Health Assn., Am. Assn. Higher Edn., Nat. Assn. Sch. Psychologists, Nat. Assn. Deaf, Am. Speech, Lang. and Hearing Assn. (cert. clin. competence in speech/lang. pathology). Office: Gallaudet U 800 Florida Ave NE Washington DC 20002-3660 Office Phone: 202-651-5540. Business E-Mail: margery.miller@gallaudet.edu.

MILLER, MARILYN LEA, library and information scientist, educator; AA, Graceland Coll., 1950; BS in English, U. Kans., 1952; AMLS, U. Mich., 1959, PhD of Librarianship and Higher Edn., 1976. Bldg.-level sch. libr. Wellsville HS, Kans., 1952-54; tchr.-libr. Arthur Capper Jr. HS, Topeka, 1954-56; head libr. Topeka HS, Topeka, 1956-62; sch. libr. cons. State of Kans. Dept. of Pub. Instrn., 1962-67; from asst. to assoc. prof. Sch. Librarianship Western Mich. U., Kalamazoo, 1967-77; assoc. prof. libr. sci. U. NC, Chapel Hill, 1977-87, prof., chair dept. libr. and info. studies Greensboro, 1987-95, prof. emeritus, 1996—. Vis. faculty Kans. State Tchrs., Emporia, 1960, 63, 64, 66, U. Minn., Mpls., 1971, U. Manitoba, Winnipeg, Can., 1971; vis. prof. Appalachian State U., Boone, NC, 1987; adv. bd. sch. libr. media program Nat. Ctr. for Ednl. Stats., 1989, user rev. panel, 1990; chair assoc. dean search com. Sch. Edn., 1988, coord. Piedmont young writers conf., 1989-94, 97-99, chair race and gender com., 1990-93, SACS planning and evaluation com., 1990-91, learning resources ctr. adv. com., 1991-93; hearing panel for honor code U. NC Greensboro, 1988-91, assn. women faculty and administrv. staff, 1987-95, faculty coun., 1987-95, chair, 1994-95, univ. libr. com., 1987-88, com. faculty devel. in race and gender scholarship, 1990-92; lectr. and cons. in field. Editor: Pioneers and Leaders in Library Service to Youth, 2003; mem. editl. bd. The Emergency Librarian, 1981-97, Collection Building: Studies in the Development and Effective Use of Library Resources, 1978-96; contbr. chpt. to books, articles to profl. jour. Children's libr. specialists to visit Russian sch. and pub. libr., book publs., Moscow, Leningrad, Tashkent, 1979; hon. del. White House Conf. on Libr. and Info. Svcs., Washington, 1991; head del. Romanian Summer Inst. on Librarianship in U.S., 1991; citizen amb. People to People Internat. Program, People's Republic of China, 1992, Russian and Poland, 1992, Russia, 1994, Barcelona, 1995; exec. bd. dirs. Friends of Greensboro Pub. Libr., 1996-99, chair Booklovers' Shop adv. com., 1996-2002, v.p., 2003-05, pres. 2005—, past pres., 2006-08; chair Citizens Materials Adv. com., 1999-; chair Citizens Strategic Long Range Planning com., 1994-95, 2001-03, chair, 2003, 06, Sch. Pub. Libr. com., 2002—, chair, 2003—; pub. libr. trustee, 2005-, NC State Libr. Commn., 2006-. Recipient Freedom Found. medal, 1962, Disting. Svc. to Sch. Librs. award Kans. Assn. Sch. Librs., 1982, Disting. Svc. award Graceland Coll., 1992, Disting. Alumnus award Sch. Libr. and Info. Studies, U. Mich., 1988, Contribution to Libr. Info. Sci. award Assn. Libr. Info. Sci., 1999; Delta Kappa Gamma scholar, 1972. Mem.: ALA (awards com. 1971—72, chair Chgo. conf. resolutions 1972, chair 1973—75, resolutions com. 1976—78, adv. com. Nat. Ctr. Ednl. Stats. 1984, standing com. libr. edn. 1987—91, yearbook adv. com. 1988—90, chair 1989—90, pres. 1992—93, exec. dir. 1994, chair rsch. com., chair search com., Disting. Svc. award Am. Assn. Sch. Librs. 1993), Friends of N.C. Pub. Librs. (bd. dirs. 2000—), So. Assn. Colls. and Schs. (accreditation team 1988), Southeastern Libr. Assn. (chair libr. educators sect. 1990—92), N.C. Assn. Sch. Librs. (Disting. Svc. award 2004), Assn. Libr Svc. to Children (bd. dirs. 1976—81, pres. 1979—80, rsch. com. 1982—85, chair 1984—85, Disting. Svc. award 2005), Assn. Ednl. Comms. and Tech., Am. Assn. Sch. Librs. (nominating com. 1980, pub. com. 1981—82, chair search com. exec. dir. 1985, v.p., pres.-elect 1985—86, pres. 1986—87, coord. coms. nat. stds. vision and implementation 1995—98), N.C. Libr. Assn. (life; edn. libr. com. 1978—80, 1982—86, bd. dirs. 1987—99, exec. bd. status women roundtable 1989—2003, chmn.-elect 1995—97, chmn. 1997—99, commn. on status of sch. librs. 1999—2000). Personal E-mail: mmiller023@triad.rr.com.

MILLER, MARK DAVID, orthopedist, surgeon, educator; b. Mesa, Ariz., July 18, 1957; m. Brenda Barker; children: Mason, Melissa, Michael, Matthew. BS, USAF Acad., 1979; MD, Uniformed Svcs. U., 1987. Diplomate Am. Bd. Orthopaedic Surgery. Resident Willford Hall USAF Med. Ctr., 1992; fellow U. Pitts., 1993; asst. clin. prof. U. Colo. Health Sci. Ctr., Denver, 1995—97; clin. assoc. prof. orthopaedic surgery U. Tex. Health Sci. Ctr., San Antonio, 1997—99, clin. asst. prof. orthopaedic surgery Dallas, 1999—2000; assoc. prof. orthopaedic surgery U. Va. Sch. Medicine, Charlottesville, 2000—03, co-dir. sports medicine, 2002—, assoc. prof. orthopaedic surgery, 2003—. Reviewer Jour. Connective Tissue Rsch., 2002—; mem. editl. bd. Am. Jour. Sports Medicine, 2003—, Trans Con Pocket Orthopedica, 2004; splty. rev. editor Jour. Bone and Joint Surgery, 2003—; mem. editl. adv. bd. Jour. of Knee Surgery, 2003—; spkr. in field. Author: (textbook) Surgical Atlas of Sports Medicine, Textbook of Arthroscopy, Review of Orthopaedics 4th Ed; contbr. articles to profl. jours. Adult Sunday sch. tchr., 2004; team physician US Olympic Com. Tng. Facility, 2002, James Madison U., Harrisonburg, Va., 2003. Decorated Meritorious Svc. medal USAF, Def. Meritorious Svc. Meritorious Svc. medal; recipient Founders Award, Eastern Orthopaedic Soc., 2004, Albert Trillat Young Investigator's award, International Soc. Arthroscopy, Knee Surgery and Orthopaedic Sports Medicine, 2003, Resident Tchg. award, U. Va., 2002, Golden Apple award for Outstanding Orthopaedic Resident Educator, USAF Medical Center, 1999. Achievements include research in meiscal repair, including three separate animal studies and numerous cadaver studies that have direct clinical application; hamstring tendon regeneration following harvesting for ACL reconstruction.

MILLER, MARK KARL, journalist, editor; b. Meadville, Pa., Aug. 5, 1953; s. Richard Karl and Ellener Louise (Zimber) M. BA in Comms. and Journalism, Shippensburg U. of Pa., 1975. Editl. asst. Broadcasting mag., Washington, 1975, staff writer, 1976—77, asst. editor, 1977—80, sr. news editor, 1980—87, asst. mng. editor, 1987—91; mng. editor Broadcasting & Cable mag., Washington, 1991—98, Digital TV mag., Washington, 1999; freelance editor, writer, photographer, rschr., 2000—; mng. editor TVNewsday.com, 2006—. Mem. editl. adv. bd. Shippensburg U. of Pa., 1989-94, mem. profl. adv. bd. comm./journalism dept., 1994-96. Recipient Outstanding Alumnus award Shippensburg U., 1992. Mem. Soc. Profl. Journalists, Art Deco Soc. of Washington (bd. dirs., publs. chair 1986-97), Nat. Press Club. Home and Office: 2425 Valley Way Cheverly MD 20785-2956 Office Phone: 301-773-0058. Business E-Mail: mkmiller@tvnewsday.com.

MILLER, MARSHALL LEE, lawyer; b. Chattanooga, Tenn., Oct. 18, 1942; BA, Harvard U., 1964; student, Oxford U., Eng., Heidelberg U., Germany; JD, Yale U., 1970. Bar: D.C. 1971, U.S. Supreme Ct. 1979. Spl. asst. to adminstr. U.S. EPA, 1971-73; assoc. dep. atty. gen. U.S. Dept. Justice, 1973-74; asst. sec. labor (acctg.), dep. adminstr. OSHA,

1975-76; ptnr. Baise & Miller, Washington. Bd. editors: Yale Law Jour.; Soviet Mil. editor: Armed Forces Jour., 1983-87; author books internat. and environ. topics. Bd. dirs. Bulgarian-Am. Enterprise Fund, Electronic Warfare Assocs., Am. Coun. of Internat. Living, Am. Assn. Advancement Sci. Home: PO Box 1311 Bethany Beach DE 19930-1311 Office: Baise Miller Pc PO Box 14368 Washington DC 20044-4368

MILLER, MARTIN EUGENE, management labor negotiator, lobbyist; b. Decatur, Ill., May 14, 1945; s. Floyd Homer and Vivian LaVerne (Gould) M.; m. Sherry Kay Bandy, May 25, 1968; children: Liane, Laura. BS, U. Ill., Champaign-Urbana, 1968; MEd, U. North Fla., Jacksonville, 1974. Cert. math. tchr.; cert. ednl. adminstrn. and supervision. Tchr. Decatur Pub. Schs., Ill., 1968, Clay County Sch. Bd., Green Cove Springs, Fla., 1970—74, coord. cert. pers., 1974—77, dir. instrnl. pers., 1977—78, dir. pers. svcs., 1978—81, asst. supt. for human resources and labor rels., 1981—93, dir. cmty. and govtl. rels., 1993—97; gen. dir. govtl. rels. Duval County Pub. Schs., Jacksonville, Fla., 1997—2001; pres. Miller Consulting Group, Inc., 2001—. Past mem. Edn. Stds. Commn., Tallahassee, 1985-93, vice chmn., 1988-92; past mem. Blue Cross-Blue Shield Adv. Coun., Jacksonville, Fla.; past mem. Fla. Ednl. Leaders Forum. Served as staff sgt. USAF, 1968-70. Mem.: Fla. Ednl. Legis. Liaisons (past pres.), Fla. Edn. Negotiators (past pres.), Fla. Assn. Sch. Adminstrs., Am. Assn. Sch. Adminstrs., Phi Delta Kappa. Republican. Presbyterian. Avocations: home computers, music, swimming, photography. Home: 1612 Bay Cir W Orange Park FL 32073-4746 Office: 1612 Bay Circle West Orange Park FL 32073

MILLER, MARY HELEN, retired state government administrator; b. Smiths Grove, Ky., June 30, 1936; d. Walter Frank and Lottie Belle (Russell) Huddleston; m. George Ward Wilson, Sept. 12, 1958 (div. Sept. 1973); children: Ward Glenn, Amy Elizabeth Huddleston; m. Francis Guion Miller Jr., June 6, 1981. BA, Western Ky. U., 1958. Tchr. Fayette County Schs., Lexington, Ky., 1958-60, Seneca High Sch., Louisville, 1960-63, Shelby County High Sch., Shelbyville, Ky., 1963-69; rsch. analyst Legis. Rsch. Com., Frankfort, Ky., 1973-79, asst. dir., 1979-83, 90-91; chief exec. asst. Office Gov., Frankfort, 1983-87, 93-95, legis. liaison, 1991-93; cabinet sec. Natural Resources and Environ. Protection Cabinet, Frankfort, 1987-88; sales assoc. W. Wagner, Jr. Comml. Real Estate, Louisville, 1989-91; ret., 1996. Author: (constl. revision) Citizens Guide To/Perspective, 1978, (booklet) A Look at Kentucky General Assembly, 1979, A Guide to Education Reform, 1990, (handbook) Gubernatorial Transition in Kentucky, 1991. Mem. Leadership Ky. Alumni, Frankfort, 1986, Waterfront Devel. Corp. Bd., Louisville, 1986—87, Greater Louis Partnership Econ. Devel., 1988—92, Shelbyville 2000 Found. Bd., 1991—92; mem., sec. Regional Airport Authority Bd., Louisville, 1986—89; mem. Shelby County Cmty. Theatre Bd., Shelbyville, 1978—83, 1988—91, treas., 1979—83, pres., 1989—91; chair Shelby County Cmty. Found., 1995—2000; mem. Ky. Long Term Policy Bd., 1992—99, chair, 1995; mem. Ky. Hist. Properties Commn., 1995—99; exec. com. Ky. Hist. Soc., 2002—07, v.p., 2004—07; mem. Shelby Devel. Found., 2003—05; bd. dirs. Women's Initiative Networking Group, 1996—99, pres., 1998. Recipient Vic Hellard Jr. Pub. Svc. in Ky. award, 1999; named Shelbyville Citizen of Yr., 1998. Mem. Caryatid Book Club (pres. 1999, 2009), Western Ky. U. Alumni Assn. (bd. dirs. 1992-95). Democrat. Episcopalian. Avocations: reading, theater, gardening, antiques. Home: 1116 Main St Shelbyville KY 40065-1420 Personal E-mail: mhmll6@aol.com.

MILLER, MATTHEW JASON, science educator, director; s. Herb and Patricia Barbara Miller. BS, Yale U., New Haven, 1983, MD, 1987; MPhil, Harvard U., Boston, 1998, ScD, 1999. Asst. prof. Harvard U., Sch. Pub. Health, 2003—; assoc. dir. Harvard Injury Control Rsch. Ctr., 2000—. Contbr. articles to profl. jours.

MILLER, MAX DUNHAM, JR., lawyer; b. Des Moines, Oct. 17, 1946; s. Max Dunham and Beulah (Head) M.; m. Melissa Ann Dart, Jan. 10, 1969 (div. July 1975); 1 child, Ann Marie Victoria; m. Caroline Jean Armendt, Sept. 19, 1981 (div. Dec. 2001); children: Alexander Bradshaw, Benjamin Everrett; m. Marion Beall Nadolny, June 27, 2004. BS with high honors, Mich. State U., 1968; postgrad., George Washington U., 1970-71; JD, U. Md., 1975. Bar: Md. 1976, U.S. Dist. Ct. Md. 1976, U.S. Ct. Appeals (4th cir.) 1981, U.S. Supreme Ct. 1982. Engr. U.S. Dept. of Def., Aberdeen Proving Ground, Md., 1968-72; law clk. to presiding judge Md. Cir. Ct., Higinbothom in Bel Air, Md., 1975-76; asst. county atty. Harford County, Bel Air, 1976-79; assoc. Lentz & Hooper P.A., Balt., 1979-81; ptnr. Miller, Olszewski & Moore, P.A., Bel Air, 1981-94; prin. Law Offices of Max D. Miller, P.A., 1994—. County atty. Harford County, Md., 1983-88. Named Superlawyers, 2008. Mem. Md. Bar Assn., Harford County Bar Assn., Phi Kappa Phi, Phi Eta Sigma. Avocations: golf, sailing, canoeing, bicycling. Office: 5 S Hickory Ave Bel Air MD 21014-3732 Office Phone: 410-879-3300.

MILLER, MAXINE LYNCH, retired home economist, interior designer, educator; b. Ellensburg, Wash., Feb. 15, 1921; d. Ralph A. Lynch and Bertha Sorenson; m. Harlan LeRoy Miller, Aug. 29, 1950 (div. June 1965). BA in Home Econs., Wash. State U., Pullman, 1942; MA in Home Econs., U. Wash., Seattle, 1959. Asst. prof. to prof. Calif. State U., LA, 1955—80; prof. emeritus, 1980. Chair program accreditation team, nat. treas. Interior Design Educators Coun., Inc. Recipient Interior Design Educators Coun. Emeritus Letter of Commendation award, Found. Interior Design Edn. Rsch., 1959; scholar, Am. Soc. Interior Design, 1968. Mem.: Nat. Soc. DAR. Avocations: genealogy, photography, art, crafts. Home: 913 Chamith Ln Ellensburg WA 98926

MILLER, MAYNARD MALCOLM, geologist, educator, geoscience institute director, former state legislator; b. Seattle, Jan. 23, 1921; s. Joseph Anthony and Juanita Queena (Davison) M.; m. Joan Walsh, Sept. 15, 1951; children: Ross McCord, Lance Davison. BS magna cum laude, Harvard U., 1943; MA, Columbia U., 1948; PhD, St. John's Coll., Cambridge U., 1957; student, Naval War Coll., Air War Coll., Nat. Def. U., Oak Ridge Inst. Nuc. Sci.; DSc (hon.), U. Alaska, 1990. Registered profl. geologist, Idaho. Asst. prof. naval sci. Princeton U., NJ, 1946; organizer, dir. Office Naval Rsch., Juneau Icefield Rsch. project Am. Geog. Soc., NYC, 1946—55, rsch. assoc., 1948—55; geologist Gulf Oil Co., Cuba, 1947; staff scientist Swiss Fed. Inst. for Snow and Avalanche Rsch., Davos, 1952—53; instr. dept. geography Cambridge U., 1953—56; assoc. prodr., field project dir. film Seven Wonders of the World Cinerama Corp., Europe, Asia, Africa, Mid. East, 1954—55; rsch. assoc. Lamont Geol. Obs., NYC, 1955—59; sr. scientist dept. geology Columbia U., NYC, 1957—59; asst. prof. geology Mich. State U., East Lansing, 1959—61, assoc. prof., 1961—63, prof., 1963—75; dean Coll. Mines and Earth Resources U. Idaho, Moscow, 1975—88, dean emeritus, prof. geology, dir. Glaciological and Arctic Scis. Inst., 1975—2009; dir., state geologist Idaho Geol. Survey, 1975—88, dir. emeritus; rep. Legislature of State of Idaho, Boise, 1992—2000. Geophys. cons. Nat. Park Svc., NASA, USAF, NAS; mapping expdn. Brady Icefield and Glacier Bay, Alaska, 1940-41; leader Mt. St. Elias Expdn. USAF-Harvard Mountaineering Club, Alaska, 1946; geologist Am. Mt. Everest Expdn., Nepal, 1963; dir. Nat. Geog. Soc. Alaskan Glacier Commemorative Project, 1964—; organizer leader Nat. Geog. Soc. Joint U.S.-Can. Mt. Kennedy Yukon Meml. Mapping Expdn., 1965; leader Muséo Argentino de Ciencias Naturales, Patagonian expdn. and glacier survey for Inst. Geologico del Peru and Am. Geog. Soc., 1949-50; adv. missions People's Republic of China, 1981, 86, 88, 98; geol. expdns. Himalaya, Nepal, 1963, 84, 87; USAF ice survey mission to Ellesmere Land, North Pole and Polar Sea, 1951; organizer, ops. officer USN-LTA blimp geophysics flight to Ice Island T-3 and North Pole area Office Naval Rsch., 1958; ONR-LTA coord. SS Nautilus First Transit North Pole; prin. investigator U.S. Naval Oceanog. Office sea and pack ice rsch. Ice Island T-3 Polar Sea, 1967-68, 70-73; dir. lunar field sta. project Mt. Rainier summit simulation USAF-Boeing Co., 1959-60; prin. investigator Nat. Geog. Soc. 30 Yr. Remap of Lemon, Taku and Cathedral Massif Glaciers, Juneau Icefield, 1989-2005; dir. Found. for Glacier and Environ. Rsch., Pacific Sci. Ctr., Seattle, 1955-95, 97—, chmn., 1992—, pres., 1955-85, trustee, 1960—, cons. Dept. Hwys. State of Alaska, 1965; chmn., dir. World Ctr. for Exploration Found., NYC, 1968-71; dir., adv. bd. Idaho Geol. Survey, 1975-88; chmn. nat. coun. JSHS program U.S. Army Rsch. Office and Acad. Applied Sci., 1982-90; sci. dir. U.S. Army Rsch. Office and DOD Nat. Sci. and Humanities Symposia programs, 1991—; disting. guest prof. China U. Geoscis., Wuhan, 1981—, Changchun U. Earth Scis., People's Republic of China, 1988—; adj. prof. U. Alaska, 1986-. Author: Field Manual of Glaciological and Arctic Sciences; co-author books on Alaskan glaciers and Nepal geology; contbr. articles to profl. jours., chpts. to books. Past mem. nat. exploring com., nat. sea exploring com. Boy Scouts Am.; past mem. nat. adv. bd. Embry Riddle Aero. U.; bd. dirs. Idaho Rsch. Found.; pres. state divsn. Mich. UN Assn., 1970-73; mem. Centennial and Health Environ. Commns., Moscow, Idaho, 1987—. With USN, 1943-46, PTO. Decorated 11 campaign and battle stars; Fulbright scholar Cambridge U., 1951-53; named Leader of Tomorrow Seattle C. of C. and Time mag., 1953, one of Ten Outstanding Young Men U.S. Jaycees, 1954; recipient commendation for lunar environ. study USAF, 1960, Hubbard medal Nat. Geog. Soc., 1963, Elisha Kent Kane Gold medal Geog. Soc. Phila., 1964, Karo award Soc. Mil. Engrs., 1966, Franklin L. Burr award Nat. Geog. Soc., 1967, Nat. Commendation Boy Scouts Am., 1970, Disting. Svc. plaque UN Assn. U.S., Disting. Svc. commendation State of Mich. Legis., 1975, Outstanding Civilian Svc. medal U.S. Army Rsch. Office, 1977, Outstanding Leadership in Minerals Edn. commendations Idaho Mining Assn., 1985, 87, Nat. Disting. Tchg. award Assn. Am. Geographers, 1996; grantee NSF, Nat. Geog. Soc., NASA, ARO, M.J. Murdock Trust, Dept. of Interior, others, 1948—. Fellow Geol. Soc. Am., Arctic Inst. N.Am., Explorers Club; mem. AAAS (councilor, Pacific divsn. 1978-80), AIME, ASME (hon. nat. lectr.), Am. Geophys. Union, Internat. Glaciological Soc. (past councilor), Assn. Am. State Geologists (hon.), Am. Legis. Exch. Coun., Am. Assn. Amateur Oarsmen (life), Am. Alpine Club (hon., life), Fulbright Assn., Alpine Club (London), Appalachian Club (hon. corr.), Brit. Mountaineering Assn. (hon., past v.p.), The Mountaineers (hon.), Cambridge U. Mountaineering Club (hon.), Himalyan Club (Calcutta), English Speaking Union (nat. lectr.), Naval Res. Assn. (life), Dutch Treat Club, Circumnavigators Club (life), Adventurers Club N.Y. (medalist), Am. Legion, VFW, Harvard Club (N.Y.C. and Seattle), Sigma Xi, Phi Beta Kappa (past pres. Epsilon chpt.), Phi Kappa Phi. Republican. Methodist. Avocations: skiing, mountaineering, photography. Home: 514 E 1st St Moscow ID 83843-2814 Address: Found Glacier & Environ Rsch 4470 N Douglas Hwy Juneau AK 99801-9403 Office Phone: 208-882-1237. Office Fax: 208-882-6207. Business E-Mail: jirp@foundglres.edu, jirp@fger.edu.

MILLER, MERRILL ANTHONY, JR., energy executive; b. Burlington, Iowa, July 4, 1950; s. Merrill Anthony Sr. and Florence Mae (Douglas) M.; m. Diana Sue Wagner, June 17, 1972; 1 child, Paul. BS in Engring., U.S. Mil. Acad., 1972; MBA, Harvard U., 1980. Team mgr. Procter & Gamble, Mehoopany, Pa., 1977-78; asst. to pres. Helmerick & Payne, Tulsa, 1980-82, v.p. and gen. mgr. no. div. Okla. City, 1982; with Nat. Oilwell Varco, Houston, 1996—, pres., 2000—, COO, 2000—05, CEO, 2001—, chmn., 2002—. Bd. dirs. Internat. Computer Exchange, Inc., Boulder, Colo. Mem. Internat. Assn. Drilling Contractors (bd. dirs. 1985—, chmn. midcontinent chpt. 1986-87). Roman Catholic. Avocations: sports, reading. Office: National Oilwell Varco 10000 Richmond Ave Houston TX 77042-4200

MILLER, MICHAEL, physician, educator; b. Queens, NY, June 19, 1957; s. Irving Maltz and Lenore (Goldstein) Miller; m. Lisa L. Miller; children: Avery Lauren, Ilana Frieda, Myles Solomon. BA, Rutgers U., 1979; MD, Robert Wood Johnson Med. Sch., 1983. Diplomate Am. Bd. Internal Medicine, Am. Bd. Cardiovascular Disease, Nat. Bd. Med. Examiners. Intern dept. medicine Med. Ctr. U. Cin., 1983-84, resident internal medicine, 1984-86; lipoprotein metabolism fellow Sch. Medicine Johns Hopkins U., Balt., 1986-89, cardiovascular disease fellow, 1988-91; dir. ctr. preventive cardiology U. Md. Med. Sys., Balt., 1991—; assoc. prof. medicine divsn. cardiology Sch. Medicine U. Md., Balt., 1991—; asst. prof. medicine divsn. cardiology Sch. Medicine Johns Hopkins U., Balt., 1997—2009, prof. medicine epidemiology & preventive medicine, 2009—; adj. asst. prof. dept. medicine Baylor Coll. Medicine, Houston, 1992—. Tchr. Sch. Medicine U. Md., 1994—, Johns Hopkins U., 1993—, Balt. Pub. Sch. Sys., 1991—; lectr. in field. Author: The Practice of Coronary Disease Prevention, 1996, The Cholesterol Planner, 3d edit., 2004, 5th edit., 2006; contbr. chpts. to books and articles to profl. jours.; reviewer numerous jours.; featured in ednl. recordings, 1990—; co-author: The AMA Guide to Preventing and Treating Heart Disease, 2008. Mem. Gov.'s Task Force Cardiovasc. Disease Prevention. Grantee NIH/Am. Heart Assn., 1989—, Bristol-Myers Squibb, 1991-93, Sandoz, 1992-93, Pfizer, 1992—, Merck, 1997—; recipient Robert Galbraith award, 1979, William F. Grupe award, 1983, Samuel Kaslev award, 1994, Named Most Influencial Drs., UJA, 2009, USA Today, 2009. Fellow Am. Coll. Cardiology (co-author Preventive Cardiology, 1998—), Am. Heart Assn. Coun. Arteriosclerosis; mem. AAAS, Am. Soc. Preventive Cardiology (past pres. 2007), Am. Heart Assn. Coun. Epidemiology, Phi Beta Kappa. Jewish. Avocations: skiing, tennis, hiking. Home: 5 Green Heather Ct Baltimore MD 21208 Office: U Md Divsn Cardiology 22 S Greene St Baltimore MD 21201-1544 Office Phone: 410-328-6299. E-mail: mmiller@medicine.maryland.edu.

MILLER, MICHAEL CAMPION, lawyer; AB cum laude, Boston Coll., 1982; JD, Georgetown U. Law Ctr., Washington DC, 1985. Bar: NY 1986, US Dist. Cts. (so. and ea. dists.) NY 1993, US Ct. Appeals (1st and 2nd cirs.). Prosecutor Manhattan Dist. Attys. Office; ptnr. Steptoe & Johnson LLP, NYC, 2007—. Adj. prof. Benjamin N. Cardozo Sch. Law, NYC, 1992—2002. Contbr. articles to profl. jours. Mem.: ABA, NY Coun. Def. Lawyers (bd. dirs. 2004—07), Nat. Assn. Criminal Def. Lawyers, NY County Am. Inns of Ct. (pres.), NY County Lawyers Assn., Bar Assn. NY (mem. criminal adv. com. 2007—). Office: Steptoe & Johnson LLP 750 7th Ave Ste 1900 New York NY 10019 Office Phone: 212-506-3955. Office Fax: 212-506-3950. E-mail: mmiller@steptoe.com.

MILLER, MICHAEL D., mathematics educator; BS, SW Bapt. U., Bolivar, Mo., 1976; MEd, U. Tex., Tyler, 1992. Secondary tchg. cert. State Ill., 1976. Math. dept. chair Galesburg HS, Ill., 2001—; adj. faculty Carl Sandburg Coll., Galesburg, 2002—. Mem.: NCTM. Baptist. Home: 1665 W North Galesburg IL 61401 Office: Galesburg HS 1135 W Fremont Galesburg IL 61401 Personal E-mail: mdmiller54@hotmail.com. Business E-Mail: mmiller@galesburg205.org.

MILLER, MICHAEL JEFFREY, editor, analyst; b. Chgo., Dec. 10, 1958; s. Kenneth Maynard and Joan (Callner) Miller; m. Joan A. Slobin, Oct. 18, 1987. BS in Computer Sci., Rensselaer Poly., Troy, NY, 1979; MS in Journalism, Northwestern U., Evanston, Ill., 1980. Sr. editor Bldg. Design and Constrn., Chgo., 1980—83; west coast bur. chief Popular Computing, San Francisco, 1983—85; exec. editor InfoWorld, Menlo Park, Calif., 1985—89, editor, 1989—90, editor-in-chief, 1991, PC Mag., NYC, 1991—2005; exec. v.p., editl. dir. Ziff-Davis Pub., 1997—2005; chief content officer Ziff-Davis Media, 2005—06; sr. v.p. tech. strategy Ziff Brothers Investments, 2006—. Mem.: Soc. Profl. Journalists, Am. Soc. Technion. Office: Ziff Broachers Investments 350 Park Ave New York NY 10022

MILLER, MILTON ALLEN, lawyer; b. LA, Jan. 15, 1954; s. Samuel C. and Sylvia Mary Jane (Silver) Miller; m. Mary Ann Toman, Sept. 10, 1988; 1 child, Mary Ann. AB in Econs. with distinction and honors, Stanford U., 1976; JD with honors, Harvard U., 1979. Bar: Calif. 1979, US Ct. Appeals 9th cir.) 1979, US Supreme Ct. 1989, Calif. (US Dist. Ct. (cen., no. and so. dists.)) 1981. Law clk. US Ct. Appeals (9th cir.), Sacramento, 1979—80; assoc. Latham & Watkins, LA, 1979—87, ptnr., 1987—. Chmn. global ethics com. Latham & Watkins, LA, 1986—. Author: (non fiction) Attorney Ethics, 1993; editor: (articles) Harvard Law Rev., 1978—79; contbr. articles to profl. jours. Mem.: ATLA, ABA, Royal Shakespeare Com., LA County Bar Assn. (chmn. profl. responsibility and ethics com.), Calif. State Bar Assn. (mem. com. on profl. responsibility), Harvard Club (Boston and NY), Phi Beta Kappa. Office: Latham Watkins 355 S Grand Ave Los Angeles CA 90071-1560 Office Phone: 213-485-1234. Business E-Mail: milt.miller@lw.com. *Notable cases include Medavoy vs. Klein and Raquel Welch vs. MGM Corp.; served as trial and insurance counsel in San Juan Dupont Plaza Hotel Fire litigation.*

MILLER, MORRIS HENRY, lawyer; b. Thomasville, Ga., June 14, 1954; s. Gibbes Ulmer and Marianne (Morris) M.; m. Anita Carol Payne, Mar. 23, 1985; children: Morris Payne, Rose Elizabeth, David Gibbes, Paul Louis Henry, John Henry. BS in Acctg. summa cum laude, Fla. State U., 1976; JD, U. Va., 1979. Bar: Fla. 1979. Assoc. Holland & Knight, Tampa, Fla., 1979-84, ptnr. Tallahassee, 1985, chmn. health law practice, 1989—2001, knowledge mgmt. ptnr., 2001—04, CLE ptnr., 2004—05. Of counsel Seminole Boosters, Inc., 2006—. Dist. fin. chmn. Gulf Ridge coun. Boy Scouts Am., 1988-89, mem. pack com., cubmaster Pack 23, Suwannee River Area coun., 1995-98, scoutmaster Troop 182, 1997-99, scoutmaster Troop 10, 2000-01, asst. scoutmaster, 2002-06, scoutmaster Troop 50, 2006—, dist. nominating com., exec. bd., 2005-; mem. Leadership Tampa, 1986, Leadership Tampa Bay, 1989; bd. dirs. John G. Riley House Mus. Ctr. for African-Am. History and Culture, 1998-99, Tallahassee YMCA, 1994-2002, chmn. long range planning com., 1997; founder, chmn. Tampa Bus. Com. for Arts, Inc., 1988-89; elder Presbyn. Ch. Mem. ABA (health and bus. law sects.), Fla. Bar (chmn., vice chmn. computer law com. 1983-89, Fla. corp. law revision com. 1986-89, health and bus. law sects.), Tallahassee Bar Assn. Office: Holland & Knight 315 S Calhoun St Ste 600 Tallahassee FL 32301-1897 Home Phone: 850-668-4193; Office Phone: 850-425-5655. Business E-Mail: morris.miller@hklaw.com.

MILLER, NANCY ELLEN, computer scientist, consultant; b. Detroit, Aug. 30, 1956; d. George Jacob and Charlotte M. Miller. BS in Computer and Comm. Scis., U. Mich., 1978; MS in Computer Scis., U. Wis., 1981. Automotive engr. Ford Motor Co., Dearborn, Mich., 1977; computer programmer Unique Bus. Sys., Inc., Southfield, Mich., 1978; tchg. asst. U. Wis., Computer Scis. Dept., Madison, 1978—82; computer scientist Lister Hill Nat. Ctr. Biomed. Commns., Nat. Libr. Medicine, NIH, Bethesda, Md., 1984—88; pvt. practice West Bloomfield, Mich., 1993—. Recipient Jour. of Am. Soc. for Info. Sci. Best Paper award, 1988. Mem. Assn. for Computing Machinery (sec. S.E. Mich. spl. interest group on artificial intelligence 1993-94), Am. Assn. for Artificial Intelligence, Assn. for Logic Programming, U. Wis. Alumni Assn. (life), U. Mich. Alumni Assn. (life), Am. Contract Bridge League, Nat. Women's Polit. Caucus, NARAL Pro-Choice Am., Jewish Fedn. Met. Detroit, Planned Parenthood Fed. Am., Hadassah: The Women's Zionist Orgn. Am. (life). Democrat. Jewish. Address: PO Box 4224 Southfield MI 48037-4224

MILLER, NANCY LOIS, senior pastor; b. Lancaster, Pa., July 20, 1954; d. William Martin and Dorothy DeBoer Miller. BA, Lebanon Valley Coll., 1976; MDiv, Garrett-Evangelical Theol. Sem., 1980. Cert. deacon Ea. Pa. Ann. Conf. United Meth. Ch., 1977, elder Ea. Pa. Ann. Conf. United Meth. Ch., 1981, basic quarter clin. pastoral edn. Rush Presbyn. St. Luke's Med. Ctr., Ill., 1979. Student asst. pastor Cmty. Ch. Wilmette, Ill., 1977—78; vesper intern Vesper Soc., San Leandro, Calif., 1978—79; sr. pastor Milton Grove United Meth. Ch., Mount Joy, Pa., 1980—82, Bellegrove United Meth. Ch., Annville, Pa., 1992—94, Water Works United Meth. Ch., Cleona, Pa., 1992—94, Radnor United Meth. Ch., Rosemont, Pa., 1994—98, Coventryville United Meth. Ch., Pottstown, Pa., 1998—2003, Messiah United Meth. Ch., Lafayette Hill, Pa., 2003—; assoc. in resident svs., assoc. chaplain Cornwall Manor Retirement Cmty., Pa., 1983—84; founding pastor Faith United Meth. Ch., Lititz, Pa., 1984—92. Mem. dist. com. min. Lancaster Dist. United Meth. Ch., Pa., 1981—83; chairperson Evaluation Com. Conf. Coun. on Mins. of The Ethnic Minority Local Ch. Task Force, Valley Forge, Pa., 1982—82; chairperson, mem. commn. Comission on Status & Role Women Ea. Pa. Ann. Conf. The United Meth. Ch., Valley Forge, Pa., 2000—; mem. United Meth. Ch. Camp Pocono Plateau Site Com., Cresco, Pa., 1981—85; co-chair Harry Hosier Dist. Ministerium of The United Meth. Ch., Phila., 1994—96; chair worship com. & retreat com., mem. of steering com. Women of Faith (sub-com. The Met. Christian Coun. of Phila.), 1994—98. Actor: (plays) Musical Carnival. Founding pastor Faith United Methodist Ch. Mem.: EPA Conf. United Meth. Ch. Women Profl. Ministry, Conshohocken Bus. and Profl. Women, Whitemarsh Twp. Bus. Assn. Democrat. Avocations: travel, camping, needlework, singing, piano. Office: Messiah United Meth Ch 527 Ridge Pike Lafayette Hill PA 19444 Personal E-mail: nancylmiller@verizon.net.

MILLER, NEIL STUART, advertising executive; b. NYC, July 30, 1958; s. Irving Israel Maltz and Lenore (Goldstein) M.; m. Karen Joyce Salomon, Nov. 22, 1987; children: Lindsay Alexandra, Jacqueline Olivia, Sara Allison. BS, SUNY, Buffalo, 1980; MBA, SUNY, Binghamton, 1982. CPA, N.Y. Staff auditor Peat Marwick Mitchell & Co., NYC, 1982-83; ops. auditor Gulf & Western Industries, NYC, 1983-84; spl. projects acct. Mickelberry Comms., NYC, 1984-86; v.p. fin. Ptnrs. & Shevack Inc. (subs. Mickelberry Comms. Inc.), NYC, 1986-87, sr. v.p. fin., 1987-89, exec. v.p., CFO, 1989-96, exec. v.p., COO, 1996-98; sr. v.p., fin. dir. McCann Erickson New York (subs. Interpublic Group of Cos.), NYC, 1998-2000; CFO N.Am. MindShare (subs. WPP Group PLC), NYC, 2000; COO TN Media (subs. True North

Comm./Interpublic Group of Cos.), NYC, 2000—01; CFO N.Am. Foote, Cone & Belding (subs. Interpub. Group of Cos.), NYC, 2001—04; exec. v.p., CFO N.Am. McCann Erickson, NYC, 2004—07; global CFO DraftFCB, NYC, 2007—. Mem. AICPA, N.Y. State Soc. CPAs (past mem. com. CFOs and advt.). Avocations: skiing, motorcycling, golf. Home: 594 W Saddle River Rd Upper Saddle River NJ 07458-1115 Office: DRAFT FCB 100 W 33rd St New York NY 10001 Office Phone: 212-885-2880.

MILLER, NICOLE JACQUELINE, fashion designer; b. Ft. Worth, Mar. 20, 1951; d. Grier Bovey and Jacqueline (Mahieu) M.; m. Kim Taipale; 1 child, Palmer BFA, RISD, 1973; cert. de coursspeciale, École de la Chambre Syndicale de la Couture Parisienne, Paris, 1971. Opened boutique Gamine, Stockbridge, Mass., 1973—74; asst. designer Clovis Ruffin, NYC, 1974; designer Raincheetahs, NYC, 1974—75, P.J. Walsh, NYC, 1975-82, Nicole Miller, NYC, 1982—, millergirl sportswear line, 2003—, Nicole by Nicole Miller, J.C. Penney, 2005—. Mem. Sports Commn. of NY, Commn. of Status of Women; bd. trustees RI Sch. of Design. Bd. dirs. Smith's Food and Drug. Recipient Dallas Fashion award, 1991, Earnie award for children's wear, Michael award for fashion. Mem. Fashion Group, Fashion Roundtable, Coun. Fashion Designers of Am., NY Athletic Club. Avocations: skiing, ice skating, waterskiing, wind surfing. Office: 525 7th Ave Fl 20 New York NY 10018-4901*

MILLER, NOELLE CHRISTINE, librarian; b. Johnstown, Pa., June 22, 1973; d. Edward John and Paulette Ann Fedorko; m. Jason Paul Miller, Aug. 10, 1996; children: Christauna Noelle, Annastasia Angelica, Parker Edward. BA in Elem. Edn., U. Pitts., Johnstown, 2000; MS in Libr. Sci. and Media Tech., Clarion, Pa., 2003. Elem. libr. Forest Hills Elem. Sch., Sidman, Pa., 2001—. Office: Forest Hills Elem 487 Locust St PO Box 290 Sidman PA 15955 Business E-Mail: noemil@mail.fhsd.k12.pa.us.

MILLER, NORMAN CALVIN, economist; b. Greensburg, Pa., May 28, 1939; s. Harold C. and Helen (Kovaleski) M.; m. Patricia Luan, Dec. 27, 1977; children: Doug, Scott, Craig, Pamela, Joshua. BS, St. Vincent Coll., 1961; MA, U. Pitts., 1964, PhD, 1966. Asst. prof. econs. Bowling Green (Ohio) U., 1966-67, Carnegie-Mellon U., Pitts., 1967-71; cons. U.S. Treasury Dept., Washington, 1971-72; prof. econs. U. Pitts., 1972-85; Lange prof. econs. and Am. enterprise Miami U., Oxford, Ohio, 1985—. Author: Macroeconomics, Balance of Payments and Exchange Rate Theories; editor: Open Economy Macroeconomics, International Reserves in Developing Countries; contbr. more than 30 scholarly articles to profl. jours. Grad. fellowship NSF, 1963-66, grantee NSF, 1967-69, U.S. State Dept., 1972. Mem. Am. Econ. Assn. Office: Miami U Laws Hall Oxford OH 45056-3628 Home Phone: 513-774-8523; Office Phone: 513-529-2836. E-mail: millernc@muohio.edu.

MILLER, NORMAN CHARLES, JR., editor, reporter; b. Pitts., Oct. 2, 1934; s. Norman Charles and Elizabeth (Burns) M.; m. Mollie Rudy, June 15, 1957; children— Norman III, Mary Ellen, Teri, Scott. BA, Pa. State U., 1956. Reporter Wall Street Jour., San Francisco, 1960-63, reporter NYC, 1963-64, bur. chief Detroit, 1964-66, Washington corr., 1966-72, Washington Bur. chief, 1973-83; nat. editor Los Angeles Times, 1983-97; lectr. journalism U. So. Calif., 1997—2001; ret., 2001. Author: The Great Salad Oil Swindle, 1965 Served to lt. (j.g.) USN, 1956-60. Recipient Disting. Alumnus award Pa. State U., 1978; George Polk Meml. award L.I. U., 1963; Pulitzer Prize, 1964 Mem.: Gridiron (Washington). Roman Catholic. Avocation: tennis.

MILLER, NORMAN RICHARD, lawyer; b. Oak Ridge, Tenn., Apr. 4, 1948; s. Francis J. and Sylvia R. Miller; children: Russell, Adam, Jordan. BA with distinction, Northwestern U., 1970; JD, Harvard U., 1973. Bar: Tex. Law clk. to Judge Latham Castle U.S. Ct. Appeals (7th cir.), Chgo., 1973-74; ptnr. Akin, Gump, Strauss, Hauer & Feld, Dallas, 1980-90, Kirkpatrick & Lockhart LLP, Dallas, 1995, Patton Boggs LLP, Dallas. Trustee Temple Shalom. Hon. Woodrow Wilson fellow. Mem. ABA (task force securities law opinions, com. fed. regulation securities, com. negotiated acquisitions), State Bar Tex. (securities com.), Dallas Bar Assn.; fellow Tex. Bus. Law Found., Phi Beta Kappa. Office: Patton Boggs LLP 2001 Ross Ave Ste 3000 Dallas TX 75201 Office Phone: 214-758-6630. Office Fax: 214-758-1550. E-mail: nmiller@pattonboggs.com.

MILLER, ORLANDO JACK, obstetrician, gynecologist, educator, geneticist; b. Okla. City, May 11, 1927; s. Arthur Leroy and Iduma Dorris (Berry) M.; m. Dorothy Anne Smith, July 10, 1954; children: Richard Lawrence, Cynthia Kathleen, Karen Ann. BS, Yale U., 1946, MD, 1950. Intern St. Anthony Hosp., Okla. City, 1950-51; asst. resident in obstetrics and gynecology Yale-New Haven Med. Center, 1954-57, resident, instr., 1957-58; vis. fellow dept. obstetrics and gynecology Tulane U. Service, Charity Hosp., New Orleans, 1958; hon. research asst. Galton Lab., Univ. Coll., London, 1958-60; instr. Coll. Physicians and Surgeons Columbia U., NYC, 1960, asso. dept. obstetrics and gynecology, 1960-61, asst. prof., 1961-65, asso. prof., 1965-69, prof. dept. human genetics and devel., dept. obstetrics and gynecology, 1969-85; asst. attending obstetrician, gynecologist Presbyn. Hosp., NYC, 1964-65, assoc., 1965-70, attending obstetrician and gynecologist, 1970-85; prof. molecular biology, genetics and ob-gyn. Wayne State U. Sch. Medicine, Detroit, 1985-94, prof. Ctr. for Molecular Medicine and Genetics, 1994-96, prof. emeritus, 1996—, chmn. dept. molecular biology and genetics, 1985-93, dir. Ctr. for Molecular Biology, 1987-90. Bd. dirs. Am. Bd. Med. Genetics, 1983-85, v.p., 1983, pres., 1984, 85. Author: (with E. Therman) Human Chromosomes, 2000; editor Cytogenetics, 1970-72; assoc. editor: Birth Defects Compendium, 1971-74, Cytogenetics and Cell Genetics, 1972-97; mem. editl. bd. Cytogenetics, 1961-69, Am. Jour. Human Genetics, 1969-74, 79-83, Gynecologic Investigation, 1970-77, Teratology, 1972-74, Cancer Genetics and Cytogenetics, 1979-84, Jour. Exptl. Zoology, 1989-92, Chromosome Rsch., 1994-99; mem. editl. bd. com. Genomics, 1987-93, assoc. editor, 1993-96; mem. adv. bd. Human Genetics, 1978-98; cons. Jour. Med. Primatology, 1977-94; consulting editor McGraw-Hill Yearbook of Sci. and Tech., 1995-2007, Encyclopedia of Science and Technology, 1997-2007; contbr. chpts. to textbooks and articles to med. and sci. jours. Mem. sci. adv. com. on rsch. Nat. Found. March of Dimes, 1967-96, mem. sci. com., 1996—; mem. sci. rec. com. Basil O'Connor starter grants, 1973-77, 86-94; mem. human embryology and devel. study sect. NIH, 1970-74, chmn., 1972-74; mem. com. for study of inborn errors of metabolism NRC, 1972-74; mem. sci. adv. com. virology and cell biology Am. Cancer Soc., 1974-78, mem. sci. adv. com. cell and devel. biology, 1986-90; mem. human genome study sect. NIH, 1991-94; U.S. rep. permanent com. Internat. Congress of Human Genetics, 1986-91. With AUS, 1951-53. James Hudson Brown Jr. fellow Yale U., 1947-48; NRC fellow, 1953-54; Population Council fellow, 1958-59; Josiah Macy Jr. fellow, 1960-61; NSF sr. postdoctoral fellow U. Oxford, 1968-69; vis. scientist U. Edinburgh, 1983-84; Disting. vis. fellow, Fogarty Internat. fellow LaTrobe U., Melbourne, Australia, 1992; recipient Pres. Disting. Scientist award Soc. for Gynecol. Investigation, 1999, Disting. Cytogeneticist award Am. Cytogeneticist Conf., 2008. Fellow AAAS; mem. AAAS, Am. Soc. Human Genetics (bd. dirs. 1970-73, 86-90), Genetics Soc. Am., Acad. Scholars, Wayne State U. (life, pres. 1996-97), Sigma Xi. Home: 19365 Cypress Ridge Terr # 817 Lansdowne VA 20176 Office: 540 E Canfield St Detroit MI 48201-1928 E-mail: ojmiller@smartneighborhood.net.

MILLER, PAMELA GUNDERSEN, retired mayor; b. Cambridge, Mass., Sept. 7, 1938; d. Sven M. and Harriet Adams Gundersen; m. Ralph E. Miller, July 7, 1962; children: Alexander, Erik, Karen. AB magna cum laude, Smith Coll., 1960. Feature writer Congl. Quar., Washington, 1962-65; dir. cable TV franchising Storer Broadcasting Co., Louisville, Lexington, Ky., 1978—80; mem. 4th dist. Lexington Fayette County Urban Coun., 1973-77; councilwoman-at-large, 1982-93; vice mayor, 1984-86, 89-93; mayor, 1993—2003. Dep. commr. Ky. Dept. Local Govt., Frankfort, 1980-81; pres. Pam Miller, Inc., 1984-94, Cmty. Ventures Corp., 1985-95. Mem. Fayette County Bd. Health, 1975—77, Downtown Devel. Commn., 1975—77; bd. dirs. YMCA, Lexington, 1975—77, 1985—90, Fund for the Arts, 1984—93, Coun. of Arts, 1978—80, Sister Cities, 1978—80; chmn. Prichard Com. for Acad. Excellence, 2004—09; treas. Planned Parenthood, 2003—08, Fayette Edn. Found., 2005—07; pres. Lexington Opera Soc., 2007—; mem. KY. Coun. Post Secondary Edn., 2008—; alt. del. Dem. Nat. Com., 1976; bd. dirs. Lexington Opera Soc., 2003—; chair Fund for Arts Campaign, 2003—04. Named woman of achievement YWCA, 1984, outstanding Woman of Blue Grass AAUW, 1984. Mem. LWV (dir. 1970-73), Profl. Women's Forum. Home: 140 Cherokee Park Lexington KY 40503-1304

MILLER, PATRICIA A., music educator, opera and concert artist; b. Washington, June 16; d. Robert Lee and Bernice (Echols) Miller. MusB, Boston U.; MusM, New Eng. Conservatory; artist's diploma, Accademia di Santa Cecilia, Rome; postdoctoral diploma, Mozarteum, Salzburg. Artist Thea Dispeker Artist's Mgmt., Inc., NYC, 1981—95; assoc. prof. music, artist-in-residence U. Mo., Columbia, 1983—85; prof. music, dir. vocal studies, artist-in-residence George Mason U., Fairfax, Va., 1991—, dir. Vocal Inst. Seoul, Republic of Korea, 2005—, artistic dir. Vocal Inst., 2009; prof. voice Oberlin Coll. Conservatory, Oberlin, Ohio, 2000—01. Dir. vocal studies George Mason U., 1995—, prodr. opera theater, 2000—, dir. Inst. Vocal Arts, 2004—; lectr. Smithsonian, Wash., DC, 2000—02; artist faculty Amalfi Coast Music Festival, Italy, 2008—09; artistic bd. dirs. Amadeus Concerts, Great Falls, Va., 2006—; pvt. practice, Va. Performer: (Operas) ERCOLE Amante, 1986, Carmen, 1981, 1985, Porgy & Bess, 1996,; concert/recital artist Kennedy Ctr., Washington, 2000, Kiev, 2002, Austrian Embassy, 2003, Salzburg, Austria, 2004, Kaynon Concert Hall, Seoul, Korea, 2005; performer (soloist): Schloss Leopololskron Great Hall, 2004, 2006, Lincoln Ctr.'s Alice Tully Hall, Kiev Philharmonic Orch., 2004, New Strathmore Music Ctr., 2005, Nat. Philharmonic Orch. and Chorus, 2005, 2007, Moscow State U., 2006, Pushkin Mus. and Concert Hall, 2006, Schloss Leopoldskron, 2006, Internat. Conf. on Edn., Health, Culture, Pub. Opinion, 2006; guest artist Philharmonic Hall, TULA, Moscow, 2007. Mem. opera panel Nat. Endowment Arts, 2003—04, 2006; mem. panel Va. Commn. for the Arts, 2004—05. Recipient Shining Star Cmty Svc. award, Nat. Urban League, Sojourner Truth Leadership award, George Mason U., 2004, Disting. Prof., 2007—08; grantee, Am. Embassy, 2002; Fulbright scholar, Rome. Mem.: Fulbright Assn. (bd. dirs. Nat. Capitol area), Nat. Assn. Tchrs. Singing (state bd. dirs.), Sigma Alpha Iota (Alumni Artistry Leadership award 2004, Outstanding Artist award 2004). Methodist. Avocations: travel, walking, swimming, cooking. Office: George Mason Univ Dept Music MSN-3E3 4400 University Dr Fairfax VA 22030-4444 Office Phone: 703-993-1382. Personal E-mail: labellavoce1@aol.com. Business E-Mail: pmilleb@gmu.edu.

MILLER, PATRICK WILLIAM, research scientist, educator; b. Toledo, Sept. 1, 1947; s. Richard William and Mary Olivia (Rinna) M.; m. Jean Ellen Thomas, Apr. 5, 1974; children: Joy, Tatum, Alex. BS in Indstrl. Edn., Bowling Green State U., 1971, MEd in Career Edn. and Tech., 1973; PhD in Indstrl. Tech. Edn., Ohio State U., 1977; Master's cert. Govt. Contract Adminstrn., George Washington U., 1995. Tchr. Montgomery Hills Jr. High Sch., Silver Spring, Md., 1971-72, Rockville (Md.) High Sch., 1973-74; asst. prof. Wayne State U., Detroit, 1977-79; assoc. prof., grad. coord. indstrl. edn. and tech. Western Carolina U., Cullowhee, NC, 1979-81; assoc prof. U. No. Iowa, Cedar Falls, 1981-86; dir. grad. studies practical arts and vocat.-tech. edn. U. Mo., Columbia, 1986-89; devel. editor Am. Tech. Pubs., Homewood, Ill., 1989-90; proposal mgr. Nat. Opinion Rsch. Ctr. U. Chgo., 1990-96; dir. grants & contracts City Colls. Chgo., 1996-99; assoc. v.p. acad. affairs Prairie State Coll., 1999—2001, also dean workforce devel. and career edn., 1999—2001; prof. Govs. State U., University Park, Ill., 2001—. Pres. Patrick W. Miller and Assocs., Munster, Ind., 1981—; presenter, cons. in field Author: Nonverbal Communication: Its Impact on Teaching and Learning, 1983, Teacher Written Tests: A Guide for Planning, Creating, Administering and Assessing, 1985, Nonverbal Communication: What Resarch Says to the Teacher, 1988, How To Write Tests for Students, 1990, Nonverbal Communication in the Classroom, 2000, Nonverbal Communication in the Workplace, 2000, Grant Writing: Strategies for Developing Winning Proposals, 2d edit., 2002, Test Development: Guidelines, Practical Suggestions and Examples, 2001, Body Language: An Illustrated Introduction for Teachers, 2005, Body Language on the Job, 2006, measurement and tchg., 2008, Grant Writing: Strategies for Developing Winning Government Proposals, 3rd edit., 2009; mem. editl. bd. Jour. Indsl. Tchr. Edn., 1981-88, Am. Vocat. Edn. Rsch. Jour., 1981-85, Tech. Tchr., 1982-84, Jour. Indsl. Tech., 1984—90, Jour. Vocat. and Tech. Edn., 1987-90, Human Resource Devel. Quar., 1989-93; contbr. articles to profl. jours. Sec. U. No. Iowa United Faculty, Cedar Falls, 1983-84, pres., 1984-86. Lance cpl. USMC, 1966-68, Vietnam. Recipient editl. recognition award, Jour. Indsl. Tchr. Edn., 1984, 1986, 1988; named one of Accomplished Grads. of Coll. Tech., Bowling Green State U., 1995. Mem. ASTD, Am. Ednl. Rsch. Assn., Assn. for Career and Tech. Edn., Am. Vocat. Edn. Rsch. Assn., Nat. Assn. Indsl. Tech. (chmn. rsch. grants 1982-87, pres. industry divsn. 1991-92, chmn. exec. bd. 1992-93, past pres. 1993-94, Leadership award 1992, 93), Nat. Assn. Indsl. and Tech. Tchr. Educators (pres. 1988-89, past pres. 1989-90, trustee 1990-93, Outstanding Svc. award 1988, 90), Internat. Tech. Edn. Assn., Coun. Tech. Tchr. Edn., Epsilon Pi Tau, Phi Delta Kappa.

MILLER, PAUL ALLEN, literature educator; b. Kansas City, Nov. 7, 1959; s. Melvin Joe and Mary Ellen (Testerman) M.; m. Ann Louise Poling, Aug. 15, 1958. BA summa cum laude, Washington U., 1982; MA, U. Tex., 1985, PhD, 1989. Asst. prof. Drury Coll., Springfield, Mo., 1989-91, Tex. Tech U., Lubbock, 1991-96, assoc. prof., 1996—; dir. comparative lit., 1995—. Beta tester Perseus Project, Cambridge, Mass., 1990-94; vis. prof. Hamilton Coll., Clinton, N.Y., 1996. Author: (poetry) Lyric Texts and Lyric Consciousness, 1994; editor Intertexts; contbr. articles to profl. jours. Recipient Honorable Mention award U. Paris, 1986; grantee Tex. Tech. U., Lubbock, Tex., 1992. Mem. MLA, Renaissance Soc., Am. Philol. Assn., Classical Assn. of Mid. West and South. Avocations: cooking, music, travel, gardening, racquetball. Office: Tex Tech U Dept Classical Modern Lang & Lit Lubbock TX 79409

MILLER, PAUL AUSBORN, adult education educator; b. East Liverpool, Ohio, Mar. 22, 1917; s. Harry A. and Elizabeth (Stewart) M.; m. Catherine Spiker, Dec. 9, 1939 (dec. Dec. 1964); children— Paula Kay, Thomas Ausborn; m. Francena Lounsbery Nolan, Jan. 15, 1966. BS, U. W.Va., 1939; MA, Mich. State U., 1947, PhD, 1953. County agrl. agt. in, W.Va., 1939-42; extension specialist sociology and anthropology Mich. State U., East Lansing, 1947-55, asst. prof., 1947-52, assoc. prof., 1953, prof., 1953-61, dir. coop. ext. svc., 1954-58, provost Morgantown, 1959-61; pres. W.Va. U., Morgantown, 1962-66; asst. sec. for edn. HEW, Charlotte, 1966-68; disting. prof. edn., dir. univ. planning studies U. N.C., Charlotte, 1966-68; prof. adult edn. N.C. Sate U. at Raleigh, 1668-69; pres. Rochester (N.Y.) Inst. of Tech., 1969-79, pres. emeritus, 1979—, prof., 1979-83. Sr. program cons. W.K. Kellogg Found., 1979-83; adj. prof. rural sociology U. Mo.-Columbia, 1994—. Author: Community Health Action, 1953; co-author: Patterns for Lifelong Learning, 1973; contbr. to publs. in field. Mem. Colombian Commn. Higher Edn., 1960-61. Served as 1st lt. USAAF, 1942-46. Named to the Internat. Adult and Continuing Edn. Hall of Fame. Fellow Am. Sociol. Assn.; mem. Rural Sociol. Soc., Phi Kappa Phi, Epsilon Sigma Phi. Home: 1909 Walden Ct Columbia MO 65203-5407

MILLER, PAUL SAMUEL, lawyer; b. Paterson, NJ, Apr. 8, 1939; s. Louis and Etta (Wolff) M.; m. Carol Plesser, Mar. 26, 1961; children: Nicole F., Margo H., Jason E. BA, Rutgers U., 1960, JD magna cum laude, 1962. Bar: N.Y. 1963. Assoc. Kaye, Scholer, Fierman, Hayes & Handler, NYC, 1962-63, Rubin, Baum & Levin, NYC, 1964; ptnr. Fishman, Miller & Zimet, NYC, 1964-70; counsel Leasing Cons., Inc., Rosyln, N.Y., 1970-71; with Pfizer Inc., NYC, 1971—2002, assoc. gen. counsel, v.p., gen. counsel, 1986-92, sr. v.p., gen. counsel, 1992-99, exec. v.p., gen. counsel, 1999—2002; spl. counsel Kaye Scholer LLP, NYC, 2002—. Ofcl. corr. Pharm. Mfrs. Assn., mem., chmn. exec. com. law sect., 1989-90. Mem. United Jewish Appeal Com., Essex County, 1981-83, co-chmn. Livingston sect., 1982; former chmn. bd. dirs. Citizens Crime Commn. of N.Y.C., Inc.; bd. dirs. Am. Israel Pub. Affairs Com., Am. Jewish Congress, Jewish Theol. Sem., U.S. C. of C., chmn. Nat. Chamber Litigation Coun.; mem. bus. adv. coun. Touro Law Sch.; mem. bd. overseers Inst. Civil Justice, RAND. Albert Einstein Coll. Medicine, Jaffee Inst. Strategic Studies at Tel Aviv U. Recipient Jerusalem Humanitarian award, Shaare Zedek Medical Ctr., 1999, Louis Marshall Award, Jewish Theological Seminar, 2001. Mem. ABA (antitrust law sect., corp. banking and bus. law sect., natural resources law sect., sci. and tech. sect., mem. health law forum com.), N.Y. State Bar Assn. (antitrust law sect., food and drug law sect.). Office: Kaye Scholer LLP 425 Park Ave New York NY 10022 Business E-Mail: pmiller@kayescholer.com.

MILLER, PAULA J., library director; m. Jay Miller; children: Jason, Jon, James. BA in Psychology, Kent State U.; MLIS, U. Md. Positions including head circulation, reference libr., children's asst. and adminstrv. coord. Kent Free Libr., Ohio; dir. Dover Pub. Libr., Del., Westlake Porter Pub. Libr., Ohio, 1992—2006; adminstr. Eastern Shore Regional Libr., Md.; exec. dir. Pikes Peak Libr. Dist., Colorado Springs, 2006—. Office: Pikes Peak Libr Dist PO Box 1579 Colorado Springs CO 80901 Office Phone: 719-531-6333 ext. 2010.

MILLER, PEGGY GORDON ELLIOTT, retired academic administrator; b. Matewan, W.Va., May 27, 1937; d. Herbert Hunt and Mary Ann (Renfro) Gordon; m. Robert Lawrence Miller, Nov. 23, 2001; stepchildren: Rohn J., Robert K.;children from previous marriage: Scott Vandling Elliott III, Anne Gordon Elliott. BA, Transylvania Coll., 1959; MA, Northwestern U., 1964; EdD, Ind. U., 1975; DHL (hon.), Transylvania U., 1993; degree (hon.), Chungnam Nat. U., Korea, 2000; D in Pub. Svc., SD State U., 2006. Tchr. Horace Mann H.S., Gary, Ind., 1959-64; instr. English Am. Inst. Banking, Gary, 1969-70, Ind. U. N.W., Gary, 1965-69, lectr. Edn., 1973-74, asst. prof. edn., 1975-78, assoc. prof., 1978-80, supr. secondary student tchg., 1973-74, dir. student tchg., 1975-77, dir. Office Field Experiences, 1977-78, dir. profl. devel., 1978-80, spl. asst. to chancellor, 1981-83, asst. to chancellor, 1983-84, acting chancellor, 1983-84, chancellor, 1984-92; pres. U. Akron, Ohio, 1992-96, SD State U., 1998—2006, pres. emeritus, 2006—. Sr. fellow Nat. Ctr. for Higher Edn., 1996-97; vis. prof. U. Ark., 1979-80, U. Alaska, 1982; bd. dirs. Lubrizol Corp., A. Schulman Corp., Commn. on Women in Higher Edn., SD Mus. Art, Akron Tomorrow, Ohio Aerospace Consortium, Ohio Super Computer Com., Brookings C. of C.; holder VA Harrington disting. chair in edn., 1994-96, Charles G. Herbrich chair in leadership mgmt., 1996—; chmn. Growth partnership Rsch. Pk. Author: (with C. Smith) Reading Activities for Middle and Secondary Schools: A Handbook for Teachers, 1979, Reading Instruction for Secondary Schools, 1986, How to Improve Your Scores on Reading Competency Tests, 1981, (with C. Smith and G. Ingersoll) Trends in Educational Materials: Traditionals and the New Technologies, 1983, The Urban Campus: Educating a New Majority for a New Century, 1994, also numerous articles. Bd. dirs. Am. Humanics Meth. Hosp., N.W. Ind. Forum, N.W. Ind. Symphony, S.D. Art Mus., Boys Club N.W. Ind., Akron Symphony, NBD Bank, John S. Knight Conv. Ctr., Inventure Pl., Akron Roundtable, Cleve. Com. Higher Edn., 4-H Found., S.D. Art Mus., S.D. Value. Recipient Authority Disting. Alumni award, Northwestern U., UA Hon. Alumni award, 1994, Dist. Alumni award, Ind. U., 2004, Disting. Hon. Alumni, S.D. State U.; numerous grants; Am. Council on Edn. fellow in acad. adminstrn. Ind. U., Bloomington, 1980-81. Mem. Assn. Tchr. Educators (nat. pres. 1984-85, Disting. Mem. 1990), Ind. Assn. Tchr. Educators (past pres.), North Ctrl. Assn. (mem. commn. at large), Am. Assn. State Colls. and Univs. (acting v.p. divsn. acad. and internat. programs 1997, bd. dirs., treas., chmn. global priorities commn.), Am. Coun. Edn. (bd. dirs., exec. com.), Leadership Devel. Coun. ACE, Office Women Higher Edn. (mem. emerita of exec. bd), Am. Humanics (bd. dirs.), Ohio Inter Univ. Coun. (chairperson), Internat. Reading Assn., SD Women's Exec. Leadership Coalition, Akron Urban League (bd. dirs.), P.E.O., Cosmos Club, Phi Delta Kappa (Outstanding Young Educator award), Delta Kappa Gamma (Leadership/Mgmt. fellow 1980), Pi Lambda Theta, Pi Kappa Phi, Chi Omega. Episcopalian. Avocation: music. Home: 4836 Sweet Meadow Cir Sarasota FL 34238 Office Phone: 605-691-7391. Business E-Mail: peggy.miller@sdstate.edu.

MILLER, PETER KARL, music educator; b. York, Pa., Sept. 11, 1959; s. Paul Wilson and Gertrud Dorothea Miller; m. Mary Elizabeth Feldmann, Oct. 16, 1982; children: Emily Elizabeth, Christina Anna, Marissa Allison. BS in music edn., Ind. U. Pa., 1981; MusM in vocal performance, Cleve. Inst. Music, 1983, MusM in organ performance, 1994. Cert. state tchr. Ohio, 1994, Ill., 2006. Dir. of music St. Ignatius of Antioch Ch., Cleveland, Ohio, 1983—91; organist, choir dir. Temple Emanu-El, University Heights, Ohio, 1983—96; dir. of music ministries St. Dominic Ch., Shaker Heights, Ohio, 1991—96; min. of music Grace United Meth. Ch., Decatur, Ill., 1996—2001; asst. adj. prof. of music Millikin U., Decatur, 1999—2002; elem. string tchr. Decatur Pub. Sch. Dist. 61, Decatur, Ill., 2001—02; asst. prof. music Ind. Wesleyan U., Marion, Ind., 2002—09, assoc. prof. music, 2009—. Music faculty Cuyahoga CC, Cleve., 1983—87; artistic dir. Sacred Madrigal Singers, Decatur, Ill., 1996—. Musician: various faculty recitals, 2003—; jr. and sr. recital vocal teacher, coach, accompanist:; presenter (discipline music) Intellect Base Internat. Consortium Conf., Dallas, 2009. Dir. Sons of Harmony Barbershop Chorus, Marion, Ind.; guest vocalist, bassoonist Decatur Mcpl. Band; with Organ Concert Series Recitals Westminster Prebyterian Ch., Ill., 2009; pianist, worship leader, choir dir., soloist Imboden Creek Gardens United Meth. Worship. Svc.; supply organist St. John's Episcopal Ch., Decatur, Ill., Gethsemane Episcopal Ch., Marion, Ind.; guest musician, organ dedications; recitals mem. Various Ch., Ohio. Mem.: Soc. for Preservation and Encouragement of Barbershop Quartet Singing in Am., Music Tchrs. Nat. Assn., Am. Guild Organists (assoc.), Music Educators Nat. Conf. (assoc.), Nat. Assn. Tchrs. Singing (assoc.), Decatur Running Club, Nat. Scholars Honor Soc., Phi Mu Alpha. Conservative. Luth. Avocations: running, bicycling, numismatics, philatelics, travel. Home: 413 W Decatur St Decatur IL 62522 Office: Ind Wesleyan U 4201 S Washington St Marion IN 46953 Office Fax: 765-677-2620. Personal E-mail: mepkmiller@comcast.net. Business E-Mail: peter.miller@indwes.edu.

MILLER, R. CHARLES, lawyer; BA cum laude, Harvard U., 1980; JD cum laude, U. Pa., 1985. Bar: D.C. 1989, US Supreme Ct. Law clk. Judge Spottswood W. Robinson III, US Ct. Appeals (D.C. cir.), Chief Justice William H. Rehnquist, US Supreme Ct.; spec. counsel Office of the Gen. Counsel, SEC, Washington, 1992—95; regional atty. Dole presidential campaign, 1996; adminstrv. ptnr. & mem. mgmt. com. Kirkpatrick & Lockhart Nicholson Graham LLP, Washington. Editor (in chief): Univ. Pa. Law Rev.; co-author: Mutual Fund Regulation - An A to Z Workshop; contbr. articles to profl. jours. Mem.: Am. Law Inst., Order of the Coif.

MILLER, R. TERRY, lawyer; b. San Jose, Calif., Feb. 28, 1947; BA, U. Calif., Berkeley, 1968; JD, So. Meth U., 1971. Bar: Tex. 1971. Sr. ptnr. Fulbright & Jaworski LLP, Dallas; now ptnr., co-chair real estate and fin. practice group and mem. mgmt. com. Akin Gump Strauss Hauer & Feld LLP, Dallas. Mem. ABA, State Bar Tex., Dallas Bar Assn., Phi Alpha Delta. Office: Akin Gump Strauss Hauer & Feld LLP ste 4100 1700 Pacific Ave Dallas TX 75201-4675 Office Phone: 214-969-4237. Office Fax: 214-969-4343. Business E-Mail: tmiller@akingump.com.

MILLER, R. WARBURTON, psychologist, farmer; b. Bellefonte, Pa., Nov. 23, 1921; s. Joseph Frederick and Mary (Warburton) Miller; m. Joyce Larayne Miller; children: Pamela Joyce, Page Layne. AB, Pa. State U., State College, 1942; MA, U. Redlands, Calif., 1951; PhD, U. So. Calif., LA, 1957; postgrad., San Bernardino Valley Coll., Calif., Columbia U., NYC, U. Mich., Ann Arbor, U. Minn., Mpls., LA State Coll., U. Internat., Saltillo, Coah, Mex., Inst. Mex. Cultura Internat., Guadalahara; JD, Loma Linda Coll. Law, 1985. Lic. clin. psychologist, marriage, family and child counselor, clin. speech pathologist. Capt. USN, 1942—44, 1951—53; officer USNR, 1942—74; staff psychologist San Bernardino County Med. Ctr., 1968—74; forensic psychologist/clin. psychologist; pvt. practice with Dr. Joyce Miller. Mem. psychology examining com. State Bd. Med. Examiners, 1970—74; dir. Mojave Valley Coordinating Coun. Family Mental Health, 1971—72; lectr. U. So. Calif., U. Redlands, Loma Linda U.; bd. dirs., v.p. E. Pioneer Mut. Water Co.; expert witness in forensic psychology; chmn. bd. dirs. AVORA Corp. Author (with Joyce Miller): Dealing with the Behavioral Problems in the Elementary School, 1968, A Layman's Handbook for Aphasic Rehabilitation, 1973; contbr. articles to profl. jours. Bd. dirs. State of Calif. Psychologists Polit Action Com.; past pres. Carriage Club, Civic Light Opera Assn., San Bernardino chpt. City of Hope Hosp. # 434, San Bernardino County Navy League; bd. dirs., past pres. Goodwill Industries Inland Counties; pres. San Bernardino Libr. Found., 1995—. Recipient George Washington medal, Freedoms Found. Valley Forge, 1970, 1972, 1973, honor cert., 1974, Disting. citizens Lifetime Achievement award, Calif. Inland Empire Coun., Boy Scouts Am., 2000. Fellow: Am. Assn. Marriage Counselors; mem.: SAR (nat. trustee 1970—74, chmn. nat. soc. Ind. Day com. 1971—73, v.p. gen. nat. soc. we. dist. 1972—74, nat. exec. com. 1973—74, sec. gen. nat. soc. 1974—76, past pres. So. Calif. chpt. Riverside, past pres. State of Calif.), Inland So. Calif. Soc. Clin. Psychologists, Calif. Sate Psychol. Assn., San Bernardino Area C. of C. (bd. dirs., pres. 1999), Naval Res. Assn., Rotary (Paul Harris award), Hon. Order Ky. Cols., Masons, Kappa Sigma, Pi Delta Sigma, Tau Kappa Alpha. Avocation: travel. Home and Office: 6836 Palm Ave Highland CA 92346-2513 Office Phone: 909-881-2786.

MILLER, RAYMOND EDWARD, computer science educator; b. Bay City, Mich., Oct. 9, 1928; s. Martin Theophil and Elizabeth Charlotte (Zierath) M.; m. Marilyn Lueck, June 18, 1955; children: Patricia Ann, Laura Jean, Donna Lyn, Martha Eileen. BS in Mech. Engring., U. Wis., 1950; BEE, U. Ill., 1954, MS in Math., 1955, PhD in Elec. Engring., 1957. Design engr. IBM, Endicott, Poughkeepsie, NY, 1950—51, mem. rsch. staff Yorktown Heights, NY, 1957—81; dir., prof. Ga. Inst. Tech., Atlanta, 1980—89, prof. emeritus, 1989—; dir. Ctr. Excellence in Space Data and Info. Scis. NASA, Greenbelt, Md., 1988—93; prof. U. Md., College Park, 1989—2001, prof. emeritus, 2002—. Pres. Computing Scis. Accreditation Bd., N.Y.C., 1985-87. Author: Switching Theory, Vols. I and II, 1965; editor: (with J.W. Thatcher) Complexity of Computer Computation, 1972; patentee in field. Lt. USAF, 1951-53. Fellow, Computing Sci. Accreditation Bd., 2003. Fellow AAAS, IEEE; Assn. for Computing Machinery, IEEE Computer Soc. (v.p. edn. acts 1991-92). Lutheran. Avocations: tennis, fishing. Office: U Md Dept of Computer Sci A V Williams Bldg College Park MD 20742-0001

MILLER, REBECCA LYNN, software engineer; b. Jasper, Tex., Feb. 9, 1948; d. Estelleen Odom Miller. BA, Lamar U., Beaumont, Tex., 1992. Lead software engr. GE Healthcare (formerly IDX Sys.), Dallas, 1994—. Singer: Sweet Adelines Internat. (2d pl. Internat. medal, 1989). Ct. apptd. child adv. CASA, Sherman, Tex., 2003—05. Mem.: Mensa (life). R-Conservative. Methodist. Avocation: travel. Home: 201 S College Dr Keene TX 76059 Personal E-mail: bebbaboo@hotmail.com.

MILLER, RHODA, academic administrator; d. Irving H. and Sylvia Salowe; m. Jay A. Miller, June 26, 1966; children: Suzanne Brunelli, Jessica Phipps. BA in Elem. Edn., Queens Coll., Flushing, NY, 1966; MS in Edn., Bklyn Coll., 1970; EdD, Dowling Coll., Oakdale, NY, 2006. Cert. Bd. Genealogists, 1998, in sch. dist. adminstr. NY State, 2004. Dir. student support svc. Dowling Coll., 1987—, adj. assoc. prof., 1993—, dir. GEAR UP, 2005. Pres. Jewish Genealogy Soc. LI, Dix Hills, NY, 2008; member-at-large Literacy Suffolk, Inc., Bellport, NY, 1984, Suffolk Cmty. Coun., Hauppauge, NY, Assn. Equality and Excellence Edn., NYC. Mem.: Nat. Geneal. Soc., Assn. Profl. Genealogists, Nat. Assn. Devel. Edn., Am. Ednl. Rsch. Assn. Jewish. Avocation: genealogy. Office: Dowling Coll 150 Idle Hour Blvd Oakdale NY 11769 Office Fax: 631-244-1035. Business E-Mail: millerr@dowling.edu.

MILLER, RHONDA KAY, food scientist, educator; b. Haxtun, Colo., Oct. 29, 1955; d. Gerald LaVern and Beulah Elizabeth Miller; m. Gordon Eugene Carstens, Dec. 22, 1984; children: Lauren Kay Carstens, Garret Paul Carstens. BS, MS, Colo. State U., Fort Collins, PhD, 1983. Instr. Colo. State U., Fort Collins, 1982—83; dir. rsch. Monfort Colo., Inc., Greeley, 1983—88; prof. Tex. A&M U., Coll. Sta., 1988—. Named Outstanding Tchr. Mem.: Am. Soc. Testing Materials, Inst. Food Sci., Am. Soc. Animal Sci. Achievements include research in identfied sodium lactate as an effective antimicrobial agent for beef products. Office: Tex A&M Univ 2471 Tamu College Station TX 77843-2471 Office Fax: 979-845-9454. Business E-Mail: rmiller@tamu.edu.

MILLER, RICHARD ALAN, retired economist, educator; b. Springfield, Ohio, Feb. 25, 1931; s. Ross and Beatrice Miller; m. Joan Taylor Walton, July 7, 1956; children: Carol Elizabeth, Jean Anne, Eric Ross. BA, Oberlin Coll., 1952; MA, Yale U., 1957; MA (hon.), Wesleyan U., 1972; PhD, Yale U., 1962. Mem. faculty Wesleyan U., Middletown, Conn., 1960—2006, chmn. dept. econs., 1968-69, 71-73, 75-76, 92-94, Andrews prof., 1995-98, Woodhouse/Sysco prof., 2002—06, Woodhouse/Sysco prof. emeritus, 2006—. Vis. prof. Wesleyan U. 2008-09, vis. lectr. Yale U., New Haven, 1961-62, vis. assoc. prof., 1967-68, vis. prof., 1973, 83, 85, 95; vis. assoc. prof. U. Calif., Berkeley, 1969-70; vis. prof. U. Adelaide, Australia, 1981; vis. lectr econs. U. Conn., Storrs, 1983; economist Econ. Policy Office, Antitrust Div., U.S. Dept. Justice, Washington, 1973-74, cons., 1974-75; cons. antitrust sect. State Conn., 1980, 82; dir. Kawanhee, Inc., Maine, 1975-81, 82-86 Contbr. articles on indsl. orgn. and antitrust econs. to profl. jours. Mem. cert. adv. coun. Dept. Edn., State Conn., 1982-86; mem. coms. Bd. for State Acad. Awards. State Conn., 1978-97; dean faculty of Cons. Examiners., 1985-87; trustee Conn. Joint Coun. Econ. Edn., 1982-85. Served to lt. (j.g.) USNR, 1952-55. Ford Found. fellow Yale U., 1958-59; NSF fellow MIT, 1964-65, Wesleyan U., 1965-69; Shelby Cullom Davis Found. grantee Wesleyan U., 1979-82; Fulbright fellow N.Z. Inst. Econ. Research, 1986, 88. Mem. Am. Econs. Assn., Indsl. Orgn. Soc. Congregationalist. Home: 83 Paterson Dr Middletown CT 06457-5138 Office Phone: 860-685-2354. E-mail: ramiller@wesleyan.edu.

MILLER, RICHARD ALLEN, lawyer; b. East Chgo., Ind., Nov. 22, 1945; s. Ernest R. and Sophie D. (Kurmis) M.; m. Patricia Annette Bratton, July 26, 1969 (div. May 1974); 1 child, Jason Todd; m. Kathleen Patrice Sills, Jan. 3, 1976; children: Andrew Christian, Caroline Grace. BS, Ind. U., 1967; JD, Valparaiso U., 1973. Bar: Ind. 1974, U.S. Dist. Ct. (no. dist.) Ind. 1974, U.S. Supreme Ct. 1985, U.S. Ct. Appeals (7th cir.) 1987, U.S. Claims Ct. 1990. Assoc. Owen W. Crumpacker & Assocs., Hammond, Ind., 1974-76, Benjamin, Greco & Gouveia, Gary, Ind., 1976-77; ptnr. Greco, Gouveia, Miller & Pera, Gary, 1978-79, Greco, Gouveia, Miller, Pera & Bishop, Merrillville, Ind., 1979-85, Gouveia & Miller, Merrillville, 1985—2004, Richard A. Miller & Assocs., Merrillville, Ind., 2004—07, MillerFisher Law LLC, 2007—. Spl. counsel City of Hammond, 1974-76; trial counsel Ind. Toll Rd. Com., South Bend, 1981-82, Ind. Dept. Highways Toll Rd. Div., Granger, 1982-87; spl. asst. U.S. Rep. Peter J. Visclosky, Gary and Washington, 1985-86. Author: Indiana Rules of Evidence Applying to Expert Testimony, 1991. Campaign mgr. Visclosky for U.S. Congress, 1st Congl. Dist., Ind., 1983-88; dist. coordinator Nat. Bicentennial Competition on U.S. Constitution and Bill of Rights, 1st Congl. Dist., Ind., 1987-88. Mem. Ind. Bar Assn., AAJ, Ind. Trial Lawyers Assn., Am. Assn. for Justice Democrat. Lutheran. Avocations: fly fishing, walking dog, writing. Home: 1018 Sterling Ct Crown Point IN 46307-2686 Office: 8927 Broadway Merrillville IN 46410-7039 Office Phone: 219-769-0783. Business E-Mail: ram@millerfisherlaw.com.

MILLER, RICHARD GLEN, financial planning executive; b. Plainfield, NJ, Dec. 28, 1949; s. James John and Agnes Margaret (Bergner) M.; m. Bonnie Joy Kunkle, Mar. 6, 1971 (div. 1980); children: Douglas, Daniel; m. Roxanne Louise Wackenhuth, Oct. 14, 1985 (div. 1996). BS in Plastics Engring., N.J. Inst. Tech., 1976; MS in Microbiology, U. S.C., 1983, PhD in Biomed. Engring., 1984; M in Hypnotherapy, 1990. Cert. tax profl. Engr. C.R. Bard, Inc., Murray Hill, NJ, 1968—86; fin. planner First Investors Corp., NYC, 1986—88; CEO Miller Assocs., Internat., Edison, NJ, 1988—. Appointee N.J. Gov.'s Childcare Legislation Commn.; v.p. bd. dirs. Mount Olive Child Devel. Ctr., Flanders., N.J., chmn. pers. com.; com. Morris Sussex coun. Boy Scouts Am.; mem. Morris County Zoning Legislation Bd., N.J. Childcare Advocacy Taskforce, Morris County Childcare Advocacy Taskforce, Citizen's Adv. Com., Twp. West Orange, N.J. Lt. Col. USAR. Named Businessman of Yr., N.J., 2003. Mem. AUSA, Am. Soc. Microbiology, Soc. Plastics Engrs., Soc. Pharm. Engrs., Theobold Smith Soc., VFW (Man of Yr.), Am. Legion, Mil. Officers Assn. Am., Res. Officers Assn., Mil. Order Fgn. Wars U.S., Vet. Corps of Arty. SNY, Order of Arrow, Mil. Order World Wars, Internat. Massage Assn., Internat. Assn. Colon Hydrotherapists, Am. Soc. Tax Profls., Am. Soc. Homeopaths, BPOE. Avocations: photography, travel, target shooting, outdoor activities, italian sportscars.

MILLER, RICHARD HARRY, philosopher, educator; b. Akron, Ohio, Feb. 28, 1944; m. Nola Gould, Aug. 20, 1966; 1 child, Benjamin. PhD, Columbia U., NY, 1971. Tchr. philosophy and history of ideas NC Sch. Arts, Winston-Salem, 1972—, interim dean undergraduate academic and grad. programs, 2006—. Leader soup kitchen team Samaritan Inn, Winston-Salem, 1985—2007. Recipient Excellence in Tchg. award, U. NC Bd. Govs., 1991. Office: NC Sch Arts 1533 S Main St Winston Salem NC 27117 Business E-Mail: millerr@ncarts.edu.

MILLER, RICHARD KEITH, academic administrator, engineering educator; b. Fresno, Calif., June 12, 1949; s. Albert Keith and Gloria Mae (Pittman) M.; m. Elizabeth Ann Parrish, July 10, 1971; children: Katherine Elizabeth, Julia Anne. BS in Aerospace Engring., U. Calif., Davis, 1971; MS in Mech. Engring., MIT, 1972; PhD in Applied Mechanics, Calif. Inst. Tech., Pasadena, 1976. Asst. prof. mech. engring. U. Calif., Santa Barbara, 1975-79; assoc. prof. civil engring. U. So. Calif., LA, 1979-85, prof., 1985-92, assoc. dean engring., 1989-92; prof., dean Coll. Engring., U. Iowa, 1992-99; first pres., prof. mech. engring. Franklin W. Olin Coll. Engring., Needham, Mass., 1999—. Cons. Astro Aerospace Corp., The Aerospace Corp., Jet Propulsion Lab. Contbr. numerous articles to sci. and profl. jours. Mem. AIAA, ASME, ASCE, Am. Soc. Engring. Edn. Office: Franklin W Olin Coll Engring Office of Pres Olin Way Needham MA 02492-1200 Office Phone: 781-292-2301. Office Fax: 781-292-2314. E-mail: richard.miller@olin.edu.

MILLER, RICHARD KIDWELL, artist, actor, educator; b. Fairmont, W.Va., Mar. 15, 1930; s. Maurice Entler and Lillian (Reed) M.; m. Teresa Marie Robinson, Apr. 27, 1957. Student, Pa. Acad. Fine Arts, 1948-49; BA, Am. U., 1953; MFA, Columbia U., 1956. Asst. prof. Kansas City Art Inst., 1968-69; instr. painting Scarsdale (N.Y.) Community Sch., 1970-75. Participated extensively in profl. theater as actor and singer including roles in Broadway Prodn. Baker Street, Oliver, Funny Girl, Wonderful Town, Illya, Darling, Indians, Rise and Fall of the City of Mahogonny; actor stock cos. including Fiddler on the Roof; one-man art shows include Trans-Lux Gallery, Washington, 1951, Bader Gallery, Washington, 1954, Balt. Mus. Art, 1955, Graham Gallery Ltd., N.Y.C., 1960, 62, 65, Argas Gallery, Madison, N.J., 1966, Jefferson Place Gallery, Washington, 1966, Albrecht Kemper Mus. Art, St. Joseph, Mo., 1969, L.I. U., 1973, Aaron Berman Gallery N.Y.C., 1983, Westbeth Gallery, N.Y.C., 1982, John Jay Gallery, N.Y.C., 1998, 2000, JCC of Mid-Westchester, 2001, Retrospective Exhbn., U. W.Va., 2004, John Jay Gallery, N.Y.C., 2006; group shows include Corcoran Gallery Art., 1950-51, 53, Pa. Acad. Fine Arts, 1951, 64, Carnegie Internat., 1961, Salon de National, Paris, 1954, Whitney Mus., 1958, U. Nebr., 1963, Martha Jackson Gallery, N.Y.C., 1973, Nat. Acad. Design, N.Y.C., 1996, 2002, 04, Art of the Northeast, New Caanan, Conn., 1996, Nat. Acad. Mus., N.Y.C., 2007, others; represented in permanent collections Albrecht Kemper Mus. of Art, St. Joseph, Mo., Hirshorn Mus. and Sculpture Garden, Washington, Phillips Collection, Washington, Rochester Mus. Art, U. Ariz. Mus. of Art, Tucson, Watkins Gallery Collection, Washington, U. W.Va., Morgantown, NAD Mus., also numerous private collections; featured in Jan. edit. Am. Artist Mag., 1988, Christian Sci. Monitor, 1990, World Artists (Claude Marks), 1991. Washington Times Herald scholar, 1944, 45, 46; Gertrude Whitney scholar, 1948-53, 55-56; Fulbright fellow, 1953-54 Mem.: Nat. Acad. Design Mus. Address: 222 W 83d St Apt 8C New York NY 10024-4913 Office Phone: 914-472-3300. *I have an insatiable need to express myself— I suppose I was born with it. I was given more than one talent to satisfy this need, and for that I thank God. I have endeavored to use these talents to the absolute best of my ability. I can do no more than that. Some times I have succeeded, and many times I have failed, but the real joy and meaning is in the doing. All the pain has been worth it.*

MILLER, RICHARD L., architectural executive; b. Salina, Kans., Jan. 31, 1941; s. L. William and Inez Corine (DeMars) M.; m. Sharalena Miller, June 22, 1963; children: Lora Miller Vinson, Scott Miller. Student, Kansas Wesleyan U., 1959-61; BArch, U. Kans., 1966, postgrad., 1966-67. Registered architect, 38 states and V.I. Assoc. Earl Swensson Assocs., Nashville, 1967-73, pres., 1973—. Mem. hosp. licensure task force State of Tenn. Dept. Pub. Health, 1975, Ambulatory Surg. Treatment Ctr. Act Task Force, 1976-77, SCARAB, Hon. Archtl. Frat., Nursing Home Task Force, 1977-78; participant Internat. Pub. Health Seminar, Budapest, 1984; speaker Fla. HRS seminars, 1986, 90; mem. ann. faculty health care forum on health facilities design, 1990; speaker numerous confs. in field, including World Workplace, 1995, NeoCon '95 World's Trade Fair, 1995, Health Facility Inst. Fifth Ann. Conf., 1994. Co-author: New Directions in Hospital and Healthcare Facility Design, 1995. Mem. Leadership Nashville, 1993-94. Fellow AIA (com. architecture for health 1980), Tenn. Soc. Architects (ad hoc fire com. 1975). Mem. Christian Ch. Avocations: golf, kite flying, sailing. Office: Earl Swensson Assocs 2100 W End Ave Ste 1200 Nashville TN 37203-5239

MILLER, RICHARD LEE, psychology professor, department chairman; b. Houston, Oct. 14, 1945; s. Fred and Ida Lois (Kerby) M.; m. Beth Vivian Lyons, (div. 1972); 1 child, Nathaniel; m. Jeanne Marie Butler. BS, Weber State U., Ogden, Utah, 1968; MA, Northwestern U., Evanston, Ill., 1970, PhD, 1974. Asst. prof. Georgetown U., Washington, 1973-75; dir. HumRRO, Heidelberg, Germany, 1975-82; adj. assoc. prof. U. Cologne, Germany, 1978-84; dir. Communit Learning Ctr., Mallorca, Spain, 1984-89; vis. prof. U. Ark., Monticello, 1989-90; prof., chmn. psychology dept. U. Nebr., Kearney, 1990--. Co-editor: Social Comparison Process, 1977; editor Jour. of Psychol. Inquiry; editor Developing, Promoting, and Sustaining the Undergraduate Research Experience in Psychology, 2008. Ensign USNR, 1968—70. Recipient Outstanding Tchg. and Instrnl. Activity award, U. Nebr., 1997, Disting. Svc. award, Rocky Mountain Psychol. Assn., 2003, Tchg. Excellence award, Soc. Tech. Psychology, 2009. Fellow APA, Am. Psychol. Soc.; mem. Sigma Xi (chpt. pres. 1991-94, chair Institutional Review Bd.). Office: U Nebr Dept Psychology Kearney NE 68849-0001 Home Phone: 308-234-4264; Office Phone: 308-865-8235. E-mail: millerrl@unk.edu.

MILLER, RICHARD OWEN, history professor; b. Rockville Centre, Ny, Mar. 23, 1949; s. Robert Everett and Virginia Ann Miller; m. Maryvonne Annie Leguilly, Dec. 1, 2005; children: Erin Christopher, Madaleine Catherine, Nicholas Evenett. PhD, U.Mo., Columbia, 1981. History prof. Austin CC, Tex., 1988—, Westminster Coll., Fulton, Mo., 1987—88. Contbr. articles. Home: 136 S Mockingbird Cir Cedar Creek TX 78612 Office: Austin CC 1020 Grove Blvd Austin TX 78741-3337 Business E-Mail: rmiller1@austincc.tx.us.edu.

MILLER, RICHARD SHERWIN, law educator; b. Boston, Dec. 11, 1930; s. Max and Mollie Miller; m. Doris Sheila Lunchick, May 24, 1956 (dec. April 23, 2005); m. Betty L. Sugarman; children: Andrea Jayne Armitage, Matthew Harlan; life ptnr. Betty L. Sugarman. BSBA, Boston U., 1951, JD magna cum laude, 1956; LLM, Yale U., New Haven, Conn., 1959. Bar: Mass. 1956, Mich. 1961, Hawaii 1977. Pvt. practice law, Boston, 1956—58; assoc. prof. law Wayne State U., Detroit, 1959—62, prof., 1962—65; prof. law Ohio State U., Columbus, 1965—73, dir. clin. and interdisciplinary programs, 1972—73; prof. U. Hawaii, Honolulu, 1973-95, prof. emeritus, 1995—, dean, 1981-84, dir. summer externship program, 2006—. Vis. prof. law USIA/U. Hawaii, Hiroshima U. Affiliation Program, Japan, 1986, Victoria U., Wellington, New Zealand, 1987; del. Hawaii State Jud. Conf., 1989-92 Author: Courts and the Law: An Introduction to our Legal System, 1980; editor: (with Roland Stanger) Essays on Expropriations, 1967; editor-in-chief: Boston U. Law Rev., 1955-56; contbr. articles to profl. jours. Mem. Hawaii Substance Abuse Task Force, 1994-95; mem. Hawaii Patients Rights Task Force, 2005-06; arbitrator Hawaii Ct. Annexed Arbitration Program, 1995-99; bd. dirs. Drug Policy Forum Hawaii, 1996—, Kokua Coun., 2007—; mem. Save our Star-Bulletin Com., 1999-2001, Citizens for Competitive Air Travel, 2002, Citizens Against Gasoline Price Gouging, 2003-; cons. Hawaii Coalition for Health, 1997-. 1st Lt. USAF, 1951—53. Sterling-Ford fellow Yale U., 1958-59; named Lawyer of Yr. Japan-Hawaii Lawyers Assn., 1990; recipient Cmty. Svc. award Hawaii Med. Assn. Alliance, 1999. Mem. ABA, Hawaii State Bar Assn., Hawaii ACLU, Am. Inn of Ct. IV (emeritus founding mem., master of the bench), Am. Law Inst., Honolulu Cmty.-Media Coun. (chair 1994-89, treas. 2000-02, vice chair 1998-2000), Yale Club of Hawaii., Am Humanist Assoc. 2007- Democrat. Office: U Hawaii Richardson Sch Law 2515 Dole St Honolulu HI 96822-2328 Office Phone: 617-208-3653. Business E-Mail: rmiller@aya.yale.edu.

MILLER, RICHARD STEVEN, lawyer; b. Mt. Vernon, NY, Dec. 5, 1951; s. Norman and Mildred (Curtis) M. BA, U. Pa., 1974; JD, NYU, 1977. Bar: N.Y. 1978, U.S. Dist. Ct. (so. and ea. dists.) N.Y. 1978, U.S. Ct. Appeals (2d cir.) 1978. Asst. dist. atty. Kings County, NY, 1977-79; with Hahn & Hessen, NYC, 1979-82, Levin & Weintraub & Crames, NYC, 1982-87; counsel, then ptnr. Rogers & Wells, NYC, 1987-91; ptnr. Dewey Ballantine LLP, NYC, 1991-2001; prin. shareholder Greenburg Traurig LLP, NYC, 2001—, co-chmn. nat. reorgn., bankruptcy and restructuring practice, 2001—07; ptnr. K&L Gates, NYC, 2007—. Mem. ABA, Internat. Bar Assn., Am. Bankruptcy Inst. Office Phone: 212-536-3922.

MILLER, RICHARDS THORN, naval architect, engineer; b. Jan. 31, 1918; s. Herman Geistweit and Helen Buckman (Thorn) M.; m. Jean Corbat Spear, Sept. 13, 1941 (dec.); children: Patricia (Mrs. Charles G. Fishburn), Linda (Mrs. John X. Carrier); m. Alice Johnson Houghton, May 19, 1984. BS in Naval Arch. and Marine Engring., Webb Inst. Naval Arch., Glen Cove, NY, 1940; Naval Engr., MIT, Boston, 1951. Registered profl. engr. Commd. ensign USN, 1940, advanced through grades to capt., 1960; head preliminary design br. Bur. Ships, 1960-63;

dir. Mine Def. Lab., Panama City, Fla., 1963-66; dir. ship design Naval Ship Engring. Ctr., 1966-68; specialized work design oceanographic rsch. ships, mine sweepers, torpedo boats, destroyers; ret., 1968. Mgr. ocean engring. Oceanic divsn. Westinghouse Electric Corp., 1969-75, adv. engr., 1975-79; cons. naval arch. and engr., 1968—; arbitrator admiralty and ship bldg. contract cases, 1978—; mem. com. naval arch. Am. Bur. Shipping, 1960-63, mem. tech. com., 1978-92; mem. ship structure com., 1966-68. Author: (with R.G. Henry) Sailing Yacht Design, 1963, (with K.L. Kirkman) Sailing Yacht Design—A New Appreciation, 1990; also sects. in books, articles. Decorated Navy Legion of Merit; recipient William Selkirk Owen award Webb Alumni Assn., 1983. Fellow Soc. Naval Archs. and Marine Engrs. (chmn. S.E. sect. 1965-66, chmn. marine sys. com. 1970-77, chmn. tech. and rsch. steering com. 1977-78, chmn. small craft com. 1983-87, v.p. tech. and rsch. 1979-81, hon. life v.p. 1981—, mem. coun. 1976—, mem. exec. com. 1977-81, Capt. Joseph H. Linnard prize 1964, Disting. Svc. award 1988); mem. Am. Soc. Naval Engrs. (mem. coun. 1976-78), U.S. Naval Inst., Christie Soc., Md. Bd. for Profl. Engrs., N.Y. Yacht Club, Annapolis Yacht Club, Sailing Club of the Chesapeake, (Chesapeake Sailing Yacht Symposia co-founder, 1971), Sigma Xi. Home and Office: BayWoods of Annapolis 7101 Bay Front Drive Apt 316 Annapolis MD 21403-3701

MILLER, RITA, personnel consultant, diecasting company executive; b. Bklyn., Jan. 15, 1925; d. Joseph and Etta M.; BA, Bklyn. Coll., 1947; MA, Boston U., 1949; children: Erika Greenwald, Roy Barnet Glickman. Personnel officer, sec. to pres. Marine Elec. Corp., Bklyn., 1943-47; script writer Song Debut, Boston, 1949-50; dir. Writers' Workshops, interviewer pub. opinion surveys, New Rochelle, N.Y., 1962-64; dir. pers. and indsl. rels. Dynacast divsn. Coats & Clark, Inc., Yorktown Heights, 1966-89. Mem. Am. Soc. Personnel Adminstrn., Westchester Personnel Mgmt. Assn. (dir.), Personnel Council New Rochelle, Bus. and Profl. Women U.S.A., Nat. Sociology Hon. Soc. Editor: The Management Consultant (George Kenning), 1965; contbr. articles to profl. jours. Home and Office: 29-I Windsor Ct Keene NH 03431 Office Phone: 603-352-7636.

MILLER, ROBERT, advertising executive; b. NYC, June 2, 1923; s. Samuel and Adele (Elswit) M.; m. Frances Fitzgerald, June 10, 1944 (dec. 1978); children: Marc Robert, William Fitzgerald, Daniel Bates, Ellen Minette (Mrs. John Meyer); m. Sandra Gold, 1980; 1 child, Richard Scott. Student, NYU, 1940-42, Syracuse U., 1943. Newsroom employee N.Y. Daily Mirror, 1942; with Miller Advt. Agy., Inc., NYC, 1946—, v.p., 1948-54, chmn. bd., 1954-57, pres., 1958—, Miller Advt. Service Corp., 1956-62, Miller Advt. Agy. Ill., Inc., 1965-73, also bd. dirs. Bd. dirs. Hereford Ins. Co., Inc., 1988-94. Author: Clash of Cultures, 2003; Contbg. editor Madison Avenue mag., 1975-78. Bd. govs. Roslyn Democratic Club, 1957-61, 68-73; mem. Nassau County Dem. Com., 1958-61, 68-73; Bd. dirs. Shalom Peace Found., 1970-89. Served to 1st lt. USAAF, 1942-46. Mem.: VFW, Jewish War Vets., Am. Legion. Home: 301 E 52nd St New York NY 10022-6319 also: 17 Shelly Dr Ellenville NY 12428-1809 Office: Miller Advt Agy Inc 71 Fifth Ave New York NY 10003-3004

MILLER, ROBERT, retired military officer; b. Charleston, SC, Aug. 28, 1974; m. Shane Miller, 1997; 1 child. Attended, Coll. Charleston; BA in Criminal Justice, U. SC; M Justice Adminstrn., Norwich U. Sch. Grad. Studies, 2008. Grad. Marine Corps Close Combat Instrs. Course, 1995, 2nd Spl. Ops. Tng. Group Scout Skier Package, 1996, Corporals Leadership Course, 1996, Marine Corps Close Combat Instr. Tng. Course, 1997, Inf. Squad Leaders Course, 1997, Tactical Recovery Aircraft Personnel Course, 2002, Expeditionary Warfare Sch. Seminar, 2006. Enlisted USMC, 1995, advanced through grades to capt., 2005; basic infantryman 2nd Bn. 8th Marines, 2D Marine Divsn.; mem. Bn. Landing Team 2/8, 24th Marine Expeditionary Unit deployed to Mediterranean, Operation Decisive Endeavor, 1996—98; bn. planning officer, bn. comdr. U. SC Naval Res. Officers Tng. Corps, 1998; inf. rifle platoon comdr. for 1st Platoon, inf. platoon comdr., weapons platoon comdr., fire support team leader Charlie Co., 1st Bn. 8th Marines, 2D Marine Divsn., Camp Lejeune, NC; deployed aboard USS Iwo Jima, Bn. Landing Team 1/8, 26th Marine Expeditionary Unit, Operation Iraqi Freedom, Operation Sheltering Sky, 2003; deployed with Bn. Combat Team 1/8 Operation Iraqi Freedom II, Operation Phantom Fury; series comdr. for Charlie Co. Marine Corps Recruit Depot, Parris Island, SC, 2005—06, comdr. Company A, First Recruit Training Battalion, 2006—07, hdqs. co. comdr., ops. officer for 1st Recruit Tng. Bn., 2007; ret., 2007. Decorated Navy and Marine Corps Commendation medal with Combat Distinguishing Device, Navy and Marine Corps Achievement medal, Combat Action Ribbon, Navy Unit Commendation, Good Conduct medal (X2), Nat. Def. medal (X2), Armed Forces Expeditionary medal, Iraqi Campaign medal, Global War on Terrorism Expeditionary medal, Global War on Terrorism Svc. medal, Armed Forces Svc. medal, Humanitarian Svc. medal, Sea Svc. Deployment Ribbon (X3), Marine Corps Drill Instr. Ribbon, NATO medal. Democrat. Office: 219 Scotts St Beaufort SC 29902 Office Phone: 843-522-6841. Business E-Mail: info@robmillerforcongress.com.*

MILLER, ROBERT CHARLES, retired physicist; b. State College, Pa., Feb. 2, 1925; s. Lawrence P. Miller and Eva Mae (Gross) Wiedemann; m. Virginia Callaghan, Aug. 30, 1952; children: Robin Miller Storey, Jeffrey Lawrence Miller, Lauren Miller Lynch. AB, Columbia U., 1948, MA, 1952, PhD, 1956. Staff mem. Johns-Manville Research Ctr., Finderne, NJ, 1948-49; teaching asst. in physics Columbia U., NYC, 1949-51, lectr. in physics, 1951-53; mem. tech. staff Bell Telephone Labs., Murray Hill, NJ, 1954-63, head solid state spectroscopy research dept., 1963-67; staff mem. Inst. Defense Analyses, Arlington, Va., 1967-68; head optical elec. research dept. Bell Telephone Labs., Murray Hill, 1968-77; mem. tech. staff AT&T Bell Labs., Murray Hill, 1977-84, disting. mem. tech. staff, 1984-88, ret., 1988. Cons. Office of Sec. Def., Arlington, Va., 1968-75. Inventor (with Dr. J.A. Giordmaine) Optical Parametric Oscillator, 1965 (co-recipient R.W. Wood prize, 1986); contbr. articles to profl. jours. Served with U.S. Army, 1943-46, ETO. RCA predoctoral fellow Columbia U., 1953-54. Fellow Am. Phys. Soc.; mem. AAAS, N.Y. Acad. Scis., Sigma Xi. Avocation: sports cars. Home: 65 Eaton Ct Cotuit MA 02635-2908 E-mail: rvcmiller@prodigy.net.

MILLER, ROBERT G., drug store chain company executive; b. 1944; With Albertson's Inc., 1961-89, exec. v.p. retail ops., 1989-91; chmn. bd., pres., CEO Fred Meyer Inc., Portland, Oreg., 1991—98, vice chmn. bd., CEO, 1998—99; vice chmn., COO Kroger Co., Cin., 1999; CEO Rite Aid Corp., Camp Hill, Pa., 1999—2003, chmn., 1999—2007. Dir. Harrah's Entertainment Inc., 1999—, Rite Aid Corp., 1999—; dir., non-exec. chmn. Wild Oats Markets Inc., 2004—06; dir. Nordstrom Inc., 2005—, Food Mktg. Inst., 2008—; chmn. Distbn. Trucking Co. Inc. Office: Rite Aid Corp 30 Hunter Ln Camp Hill PA 17011-2410*

MILLER, ROBERT HAROLD, otolaryngologist, educator; b. Columbia, Mo., July 2, 1947; s. Harold Oswald and Ruth Nadine (Ballew) M.; m. Nancy Eaves, Aug. 19, 2007; children: Morgan Guillory, Reed Thurston. BS in Biology, Tulane U., 1969, MD, 1973, MBA, 1996. Diplomate Am. Bd. Otolaryngology. Resident otolaryngology, head/neck surgery UCLA, 1978; from asst. prof. to assoc. prof. otolaryngology-head and neck surgery Baylor Coll. Medicine, Houston, 1978—87; prof., chmn. otolaryngology-head and neck surgery Tulane Sch. Medicine, New Orleans, 1987—98, vice-chancellor for clin. affairs, 1997—99; dean U. Nev. Sch. Medicine, 1999—2001, prof., 1999—2002; prof. otolaryngology-head and neck surgery Tulane Sch. Medicine, New Orleans, 2002—03; exec. dir. Am. Bd. Otolaryngology, Houston, 2004—. Bd. dirs. Am. Bd. Otolaryngology; chief of staff Tulane Hosp., 1995-96; vis. prof. otolaryngology Baylor Coll. Medicine, Houston, Tex., 2004—. Mem. editl. bd. Archives of Otolaryngology, 1986-05, Head & Neck Surgery, 1987-03, Laryngoscope, 1996-, ENToday, chmn., 2006-. Named Outstanding Young Man, Houston C. of C., 1980; Robert Wood Johnson Health Policy fellow, 1996-97. Fellow ACS, Am. Soc. Head & Neck Surgery, Am. Acad. Oto-Head & Neck Surgery (Disting. Svc. award 1994, Honor award 1991), Triological Soc. (exec. sec. 1992-97, treas. 1997-2004). Avocations: tennis, computers. Home: 2616 Wroxton Rd Houston TX 77005 Office: Am Bd Otolaryngology 5615 Kirby Dr 600 Houston TX 77005 Office Phone: 713-850-0399. Business E-Mail: rmiller@aboto.org.

MILLER, ROBERT JAMES, lawyer; b. Dunn, NC, Jan. 14, 1933; s. Robert James and Edith (Crockett) M.; m. Patricia L. Shaw, Sept. 29, 1984; children: Patricia Ann, Susan Ballantine, Nancy Crockett. BS, N.C. State U., 1956; M.F., Yale U., 1962, MS, 1965, PhD, 1967; JD, N.C. Central U., 1984. Registered land surveyor. Forester W.Va. Pulp & Paper Co., 1956-59, Tilghman Lumber Co., 1959-61; asst. in instrn. and research Yale U., New Haven, 1962-65; assoc. prof. biology Radford (Va.) Coll., 1965-67, prof., chmn. biology dept., 1967-68, dean div. natural scis., 1968-71, v.p. for acad. affairs, 1971-73; prof. law, dean of coll. St. Mary's Coll., Raleigh, N.C., 1973-85; atty. Patton, Boggs & Blow, Raleigh, N.C., 1985-89; pvt. practice, 1989—; mediator N.C. Gen. Ct. of Justice. Ecol. cons.; arbitrator Am. Arbitration Assn., Better Bus. Bur.; lectr. comml. law Tomsk (Russia) State U.; gen. counsel The Wetlands Group, 1998—; pres. Atlantic Dispute Resolution Assocs., 1998—. Author: The Assimilation of Nitrogen Compounds by Tree Seedlings, 1967, Some Ecological Aspects of Dry Matter Production, 1962, Liberal Arts and the Individual, 1972, Liberal Arts: An Educational Philosophy, 1973, Laboratory Notebook: General Biology, 1976, Educational Malpractice, 1984, Issues in International Commercial Mediation, 1995. Mem. Am. Soc. Plant Physiologists, Ecol. Soc. Am., ABA, Am. Immigration Lawyers Assn., N.C. Acad. Trial Lawyers, N.C. Bar Assn., Sigma Xi, Phi Kappa Phi, Xi Sigma Pi. Lodges: Masons; Shriners. Episcopalian. Home: 3404 Lake Boone Trl Raleigh NC 27607-6756 Personal E-mail: drmiller@nc.rr.com.

MILLER, ROBERT JAMES, education association administrator; b. Mansfield, Ohio, Jan. 27, 1926; s. Dennis Cornelius and Mabel (Snyder) M.; m. Jerri Ann Burran, June 5, 1952; children: Robert James Jr., Dennis Burran. Student, Heidelberg Coll., 1946-47; BS, U. N.Mex., 1950, MA, 1952; postgrad., Miami U., Oxford, Ohio, 1951-55; MBA, Fla. Atlantic U., 1978. Asst. exec. sec. Phi Delta Theta Hdqrs., Oxford, Ohio, 1951—54, adminstrv. sec., 1954—55, exec. v.p., 1955—91; pres. Phi Delta Theta Found., Oxford, 1984—96, historian, 2006—; bus. mgr. The Scroll, Oxford, 1955—91; cons., 1997—. Editor: Phikeia—The Manual of Phi Delta Theta, 1951, 19 edits., 1989, Phis Sing, 1958, Constitution and General Statutes of Phi Delta Theta, Fraternity Education Foundations, 1962, Directory of Phi Delta Theta, 1973. Chmn. United Appeal, Oxford, 1960; bd. dirs. Interfrat. Found., 1995—, Oxford Cmty. Arts Ctr., 2005-06; bd. dirs. Knolls Oxford, 2008; pres. Miami U. Art Mus., 1993-94, McCullough-Hyde Hosp., Oxford, 1966, chmn. endowment adv. com., 1988-89; vol. leader Boy Scouts Am., Oxford, 1966-79 Named Citizen of Yr., City of Oxford, 1968; recipient citation Theta Chi, 1967, Order of Interfrat. Svc. Lambda Chi Alpha, 1994, Interfrat. Leadership award Sigma Nu, 1994, accolate for intrafraternity svc. Kappa Alpha, Meritorious Svc. award Boy. Scouts Am., 1977, others; Interfrat. Inst. fellow Ind. U., 1988. Mem. Nat. Intrafraternity Conf. (com. mem. 1954-96, Gold medal 1992), Am. Soc. Assn. Execs. (cert.), Cin. Soc. Assn. Execs. (pres. 1982-83), Fraternity Execs. Assn. (pres. 1962-63, Disting. Svc. award 1991), Edgewater Conf. (pres. 1978-79), Summit Soc., Country Club Oxford (bd. dirs.), Work Devel. Assn. (pres. 1999—), Order of Symposiarchs, Order of Omega, Rotary (founder Oxford club 1965, pres. 1966, Merit award 1974, dist. gov. S.W. Ohio 1978-79, study group exch. leader South Africa 1992), Blue Key, Phi Delta Kappa, Omicron Delta Kappa Home: 15 Woodcrest Way Oxford OH 45056-9485 Office: Phi Delta Theta Edn Found 2 S Campus Ave Oxford OH 45056-1801 Office Phone: 513-523-6966.

MILLER, ROBERT JOSEPH, lawyer, former governor; b. Evanston, Ill., Mar. 30, 1945; s. Ross Wendell and Coletta Jane (Doyle) Miller; m. Sandra Ann Searles, Oct. 17, 1949; children: Ross, Corrine, Megan. BA in Polit. Sci., U. Santa Clara, 1967; JD, Loyola U., 1971. First legal advisor Las Vegas (Nev.) Met. Police Dept., 1973—75; justice of the peace Las Vegas Twp., 1975—78; dep. dist. atty. Clark County, Las Vegas, 1971—73, dist. atty., 1979—86; lt. gov. State of Nev., 1987—89, gov., 1989—98; sr. ptnr. Jones Vargas, Las Vegas, 1999—2005; prin. Dutko Worldwide, Las Vegas, Nev., 2005—. Bd. dir. Newmont Mining Corp., Zenith Nat. Ins. Corp., Wynn Resorts Ltd. Chmn. Nev. Commn. on Econ. Devel., Carson City, 1987—91, Nev. Commn. on Tourism, Carson City, 1987—91; mem. Pres. Reagan's Task Force on Victims of Crime, 1982; chmn. Nev. divsn. Am. Cancer Soc., 1988—90. Res. E-6 USAF, 1967—73. Recipient Nat. Advisor on Victim's Rights award, Nat. Org. for Victim Assistance, 1982, Life Achievement award, 1999, Women's Dem. Club award, 1983, Appreciation award, Am. Cancer Soc., 1983—84, Excalibur award, 1997, Silver Lily award, Easter Seals, 1985, Common Cause Ethics in Govt. award, 1990, Inaugural award for State Art Leadership, Americans for Arts, 1997, Breaking the Glass Ceiling award, Women Exec. in State Govt., 1997, Pres.'s medal, Claremont Grad. U. Ctr. for Edn. Studies, 1998, Monarch award, Nathan Adelson Hospice, 1998, Cmty. Hero Medallion, Nat. Conf. Cmty. and Justice, 1998, Life Achievement award, Nev. Mining Assn., 1998; named Law Enforcement Man of Yr., Downtown Optimist Club, Nev., 1980, Man of Yr., B'nai B'rith, 1985. Mem.: Nev. Dist. Attys. Assn. (pres. 1979, 1983), Nat. Govs. Assn. (vice chmn. exec. com. 1995—96, chmn. 1996—97, past chmn. com. on justice and pub. safety, chmn. legal affairs com. 1992—94, lead gov. on transp. 1992—, Bldg. Block award for Progress in Edn. 1998), Western Govs. Assn. (chmn. 1993—94), Nat. Dist. Attys. Assn. (pres. 1984—85, Pres.'s award 1983). Democrat. Roman Catholic. Office: Dutko Worldwide 900 S Pavilion Ctr Dr Las Vegas NV 89144 Office Phone: 702-240-0831.

MILLER, ROBERT L., JR., (BOB MILLER), federal judge; b. 1950; m. Jane Woodward. BA, Northwestern U., 1972; JD, Ind. U., 1975. Law clk. to Hon. Robert A. Grant U.S. Dist. Ct. (no. dist.) Ind., 1975; judge St. Joseph Superior Ct., South Bend, Ind., 1975-86, chief judge, 1981-83; judge US Dist. Ct. (no. dist.) Ind., South Bend, Ind., 1985—, chief judge, 2003—. Mem. US Jud. Panel on Multidistrict Litig., 2003—. Office: US Dist Ct 325 Robert A Grant Fed Bldg 204 S Main St South Bend IN 46601-2122

MILLER, ROBERT NOLEN, lawyer; b. Monmouth, Ill., May 30, 1940; s. Robert Clinton and Doris Margaret (Nolen) M.; m. Diane Wilmarth, Aug. 21, 1965; children: Robert Wilmarth, Anne Elizabeth. BA, Cornell Coll., Mt. Vernon, Iowa, 1962; JD, U. Colo., 1965. Bar: Colo. 1965. Assoc. firm M. Quiat, Denver, 1965-66, Fischer & Beaty, Ft. Collins, Colo., 1969-70; dist. atty. Weld County Dist. Atty's. Office, Greeley, Colo., 1971-81; U.S. atty. U.S. Dept. Justice, Denver, 1981-88; chief counsel litigation and security US West Inc., Englewood, Colo., 1988-93; of counsel Patton, Boggs & Blow, Denver, 1993-94; ptnr., head litig. LeBoeuf, Lamb, Greene & Mac Crae, Denver, 1994—2003; mng. ptnr. Perkins Coie, Denver, 2003—. Instr. bus. law Am. U., U. SC, Myrtle Beach, 1966-69; mem. Gov.'s Commn. for Columbine and Civil Justice Reform, 1999-2000; mem. Supreme Ct. Nominating Commn., 1999-2005; bd. dir., pres. Colorado Judicial Inst. 2004-. Co-author: Deathroads, 1978; White Color Law, 2007. Bd. dirs. Boys Club, Greeley, 1974-78, 1st Congl. Ch., Greeley, 1975-78; Rep. candidate for atty. gen. Colo., 1977-78. Capt. USAF, 1966-69. Recipient Citizen of Yr. award Elks Club, Greeley, Colorado Super Lawyer, Best Lawyers Am. Mem. Denver Bus. Jour., Fed. Bar Assn. (pres. Colo. chpt. 1983-84), Colo. Dist. Atty's Coun. (pres. 1976-77), Colo. Bar Assn., Weld County Bar Assn., Rotary (pres. local chpt. 1980-81). Republican. Avocations: fishing, hunting, reading. Office: Perkins Coie 1899 Wynkoop Ste 700 Denver CO 80202-1043 Home Phone: 970-330-4664; Office Phone: 303-291-2313, 303-291-2300. Business E-Mail: rmiller@perkinscioe.com.

MILLER, ROBERT SCOTT, clinical social worker, project manager; b. Seattle, Dec. 12, 1947; s. Bert Lester and Carol Theresa (Gustafson) M.; m. Karen Ann Staake, Nov. 12, 1977; children: Sarah, Megan, Emily. BA in Sociology cum laude, Seattle Pacific U., 1970; AM in Social Work, U. Chgo., 1972; MA in Human Resources Mgmt., Pepperdine U., Malibu, Calif., 1977; diploma in life skills coaching, Stonebridge Associated Colls., UK, 2002; DBA, Calif. Pacific U., Escondido, 2006; cert. in Aging, Inst. for Geriatric Social Work, Boston U., 2009. LCSW, cert. in aging Inst. Geriat. Social Work, Boston U., 2009. Br. supr. Wash. State Dept. Social and Health Svcs., Oak Harbor and Anacortes, 1975—78, supr. casework Everett, 1973—75; lectr., coord. rural cmty. mental health project U. Wash., Seattle, 1978—83; exec. dir. Armed Svcs. YMCA, Oak Harbor, 1984—86; area dir. United Way of Island County, 1986—88, exec. dir., 1988—92, Saratoga Cmty. Mental Health, Coupeville, 1992—93; outpatient therapist, attention-deficit/hyperactivity disorder mental health specialist Cath. Cmty. Svcs. Northwest, Oak Harbor, 1993—96; dir. Cath. Cmty. Svcs. NW, 1996—2001, Mount Vernon, 1996—99, clin. dir. Everett, 1998—2004; privacy officer Health Ins. Portability and Accountability Act, 2001—04; pvt. practice counselor, 2001—08; psychiat. hosp. surveyor, quality control reviewer Ascellon Corp., Landover, Md., 2004—07, project mgr. psychiatric hosp. fed. monitoring oversight & HIPAA privacy officer, 2008—; supr., mgr. skill cert. Rutgers U., 2007, project mgr. skill cert., 2007. Internship supr. counseling program, Seattle U., 1998-99, Bastyr U., 2000-01; instr. sociology and psychol. Chapman U. Naval Air Sta. Whidbey Island, Orange, Calif., 1988-95, 2004; practicum instr. sch. social work Ea. Wash. U., 2003. Contbr. articles to profl. jours. Pres. Wash. Assn. Social Welfare, 1975-76; bd. dir. Puget Sound chpt. Huntington's Disease Soc. Am., 1989-93, pres., 1991, fundraising chmn., 1989-91, v.p., 1990; adv. bd. United Ways Wash., 1991-92; chmn. Island County bd. emergency food and shelter program Fed. Emergency Mgmt. Agy.; vice chmn. Cmty. Resource Network, Oak Harbor, 1991; steering com. Greater Oak Harbor Econ. Summit, 1991; strategic planning com. Whidbey Gen. Hosp., Coupeville, 1992-93; exec. com. Mt. Baker coun. Boy Scouts Am., 1993; bd. dir. Opportunity Coun., Bellingham, 1993-94, Concerts on the Cove, Coupeville, 1993-96, v.p., 1994-95; active Oak Harbor Citizen's Comprehensive Plan Task Force, 1994, Readiness to Learn Coupeville Cmty. Team, 1996; risk mgmt. subcom. chair Assoc. Provider Network, 1997-98; child study team Island County, 1996-99, child protective team, 1997-99; health adv. bd. Head Start, Mt. Vernon, Wash., 1999-2002. Recipient outstanding svc. award Armed Svcs. YMCA of US, Dallas, 1985, two program merit awards McDonald's Corp., Oak Harbor, 1986; named Alumni of a Growing Vision, Seattle Pacific U., 1991, Diplomat of Yr. Greater Oak Harbor C. of C., 1991, Celebrating Excellence award, Ascellon Corp., 2005. Mem. NASW (bd. dirs. Wash. chpt. 1982-85), Acad. Cert. Social Workers, Greater Oak Harbor C. of C., Soc. Mayflower Descendants. Democrat. Roman Catholic. Avocations: kayaking, genealogy, fishing, 3rd degree mason. Home: 2450 Rocky Way Coupeville WA 98239-9610 Office: Ste B206 275 SE Cabot Dr Oak Harbor WA 98277 Office Phone: 240-487-3028.

MILLER, ROBERT STEVENS, JR., (STEVE MILLER), automotive parts company executive; b. Portland, Oreg., Nov. 4, 1941; s. Robert Stevens and Barbara (Weston) Miller; m. Margaret Rose Kyger, Nov. 9, 1966 (dec. Aug. 11, 2006); children: Christopher John, Robert Stevens, Alexander Lamont. AB with distinction, Stanford U., 1963; LLB, Harvard U., 1966; MBA, Stanford U., 1968. Bar: Calif. 1966. Fin. analyst Ford Motor Co., Dearborn, Mich., 1968-71, spl. studies mgr. Mexico City, 1971-73; dir. fin. Ford Asia-Pacific, Inc., Melbourne, Australia, 1974-77, Ford Motor Co., Caracas, Venezuela, 1977-79; v.p., treas. Chrysler Corp., Detroit, 1980-81, exec. v.p. fin., 1981-90, vice chmn., 1990-92; sr. ptnr. James D. Wolfensohn, Inc., NYC, 1992-93; chmn. Morrison Knudsen, 1995—96; chmn., CEO Waste Management, 1997—99, Fed. Mogul Corp., Smithfield, Mich., 1999—2000, 2004—05, non-exec. chmn., 2001; chmn., CEO Bethlehem Steel Corp., Pa., 2001—03, Delphi Corp., Troy, Mich., 2005—06, exec. chmn., 2007—. Bd. dirs. Symantec Corp., 1994—, Waste Mgmt. Inc., 1997—2005, Reliance Group Holdings Inc., 1999—2000, UAL Corp., 2003—, Delphi Corp., 2005—, Am. Internat. Group Inc. (AIG), 2009—. Author: The Turnaround Kid: What I Learned Rescuing America's Most Troubled Companies, 2008. Office: Delphi Corp 5725 Delphi Dr Troy MI 48098 Office Phone: 248-813-2000. Office Fax: 248-813-2673.*

MILLER, ROBERTA DORIS, elementary school educator; b. Lynn, Mass., May 14, 1940; d. Morris and Lorraine. BS in Edn. cum laude, Lesley Coll., Cambridge, Mass., 1961; M in Edn., Salem Coll., Mass., 1964; postgrad., Boston U. Tchr. Brookline (Mass.) Pub. Schs., 1968—. Pilot math. programs Ednl. Devel. Corp., Newton, Mass., 1988-89; pilot sci. programs TV series 3! 2! 1! Contact!, 1991; developer curriculum materials in math. and lang. arts Brookline Pub. Schs., 1969—; participant Math for Tomorrow program NSF, 1994; faculty Suffolk U., Boston, 2000—; presenter in field. Coord. presentation of programs to nursing homes and vets. hosps.; coord. fundraising victims and schs. of Hurricane Andrew, 1992; chair, coord. fundraising for victims of the Midwest floods, 1993. Mem.: MATSOL (Mass. Assn. Tchrs. of Speakers Other Langs., Inc.), NEA, Mass. Tchrs. Assn. Avocations: travel, reading, music. Personal E-mail: bobdorrob@yahoo.com.

MILLER, ROGER ALLEN, physicist; b. Chillicothe, Ohio, June 27, 1934; s. Joseph Perrin and Mary Josephine (Sowers) M.; m. Barbara Pauline Rice, Aug. 31, 1957; children: Erich Rice, Gretchen Rice, Carl Rice. BS, Ohio U., 1956; PhD, Case Inst., 1963. Rsch. assoc. Case Inst., Cleve., 1963-64; rsch. physicist Corning (N.Y.) Inc., 1964-71, sr. rsch. physicist, 1971-79, devel. assoc., 1979-87, sr. rsch. assoc., 1987—. Spl.

lectr. physics Elmira Coll., N.Y., 1966-69; mem. edit. bd. Fiber and Integrated Optics, Pasadena, Calif., 1976-86, mem. adv. bd. 1986-88. Contbr. articles to profl. jours. AART award Assn. for the Advancement Radiation Tech., 1990. Mem. Am. Phys. Soc., Optical Soc. Am., Am. Assn. Physics Tchrs., Sigma Xi, Phi Beta Kappa, Phi Kappa Phi. Achievements include contributions to the development of lead free Steuben crystal; development of optical waveguide coatings and coating applicators; design and development of the first, all dielectric, low-loss optical waveguide cable; patentee in field. Office: Corning Inc Sullivan Pk Sp Fr 03 # 1 Corning NY 14831-0001 Personal E-mail: ramiller@localnet.com.

MILLER, RONALD BAXTER, language educator, writer; b. Rocky Mount, NC, Oct. 11, 1948; s. Marcellus Cornelius and Elsie (Bryant) M.; m. Jessica Garris, June 5, 1971 (div. Dec. 1998); 1 child, Akin Dasan; m. Diana L. Ranson, Sept. 3, 2000. BA magna cum laude, N.C. Ctrl. U., 1970; AM, Brown U., 1972, PhD, 1974. Asst. prof. English Haverford Coll., Haverford, Pa., 1974-76; assoc. prof. English, dir. Black lit. program U. Tenn., Knoxville, Tenn., 1977-81, prof. English, dir. Black lit. program, 1982-92, Lindsay Young prof. liberal arts and English, 1986-87; prof. English, dir. Inst. for African Am. Studies U. Ga., Athens, 1992—2006, prof. English, African Am. studies, 2006—. Instr. summer sch. Roger Williams Coll., Bristol, R.I., 1973; lectr. SUNY, Oneonta, 1974; Mellon prof. Xavier Univ., New Orleans, 1988; Irvine Found. visiting scholar Univ. San Francisco, 1991. Author: (reference guide) Langston Hughes and Gwendolyn Brooks, 1978, The Art and Imagination of Langston Hughes, 1989, 2d. edit., 2006 (Am. Book award, 1991); editor, contbr.: Black American Literature and Humanism, 1981, Black American Poets Between Worlds, 1940-60, 1986; co-author, co-editor: Call and Response The Riverside Anthology of African American Literary Tradition, 1998, ed., "The Short Stories", Collected Works of Langston Hughes 15, 2002, Artistry of memory: Collected Essays of R. Baxter Miller; mem. editl. bd. Tenn. Studies in Lit., 1991-93, Black Fiction Project (Yale-Cornell-Duke-Harvard), 1985—, U. Ga. Press, 1994-97; contbr. articles to profl. jour. Recipient award Am. Coun. of Learned Soc., 1978, Golden Key Faculty award Nat. Golden Key, 1990, 95, Alpha award for disting. svc. U. Ga. Athens, 1993, Am. Book award, 1991; Sr. Tchg. fellow U. Ga. Athens, 1994, Langston Hughes prize, 2001, Outstanding Tchg. award Student Govt. Assn., 2005-06; Nat. Rsch. Coun. sr. fellow, 1986-87, NDEA fellow, 1970-72, Ford Found. fellow, 1972-73, NEH fellow, 1975; Nat. Fellowships Fund dissertation grant, 1973-74, ACLS Conf. grantee, 1978. Mem. MLA (exec. com. Afro-Am. Lit. Discussion Group 1980-83, chair 1982-83, mem. del. assembly 1984-86, 97-99, com. on langs. and lits. of Am. 1993-97, chair 1996), Langston Hughes Soc. (pres. 1984-90, exec. editor Langston Hughes Review 1993—). Office: U Ga Inst African Am Studies Athens GA 30602 Office Phone: 706-583-0328. Business E-Mail: rbmiller@uga.edu.

MILLER, RONALD K., real estate broker, educator; b. Penn Yan, Ny, Apr. 8, 1948; s. Harold and Helen Miller; m. Marguerite Miller, July 16, 2001; children: Jennifer McKay, Kristoffer; m. Jane Miller, Jan. 2, 1970 (div. May 1, 2001). BA, MacMurray Coll., Jacksonville, Illinois, 1970; MA, Elmira Coll., Elmira, NY, 1975. Educator Canandaigua Schools, Canandaigua, NY, 1970—71, Dundee Schools, Dundee, NY, 1972—. Assoc. broker Finger Lakes Properties, Penn Yan, NY, 1992—. Choir dir. First Presbyn. Ch., Penn Yan, NY, 1970—2002. Avocations: gardening, woodworking. Office: Dundee Central School 55 Water Street Dundee NY 14837

MILLER, RONALD LYNN, director; b. Pitts., Sept. 1, 1950; s. Calvin John and Virginia (Ricca) Miller; children: Veronica Lynn, Maria Eileen. B, Westminster Coll., 1972; M in religion, Pitts. Theol. Sem., 1975; vis. scholar, U. Oxford, 1990—92; PhD in sociology and internat. studies, U. Pitts., 1994. Prof., sociology U. Pitts., 1980—88, prof., religion, 1988—92, prof., global studies, 1992—96; founder to dir. Ctr. Global Studies Internat. Interdisciplinary, Pitts., 1995—. Lectr. various Universities; with Physics Textbook Com. Pitts. Pub. Schs., 2007, with Parent Sch. Cmty. Coun., 2007—08, with U. 6-12 Sch. Commn., 2008. Author: Introduction to Global Studies, 2003, Revolution in Japan and England, 1996, Individual Identity Formation, 1984; prodr.: Pitts. Cmty. TV, 2008. Mem.: Somatics Soc., Somatics Soc., World Hist. Assn., Am. Sociol. Assn., Am. Acad. of Religion, Assn. for Psychol. Sci., Am. Polit. Sci. Assn., Am. Phys. Soc., Am. Philos. Assn., Internat. Neural Network Soc., Assn. for the Study of Ethnicity and Nationalism, Am. Musicolog. Soc., Am. Math. Soc., Linguistics Soc. Am., Law and Soc. Assn., Modern Lang. Assn., Internat. Studies Assn., Am. Hist. Assn., Geol. Soc. Am., Internat. Geog. Union, Assn. Am. Geographers, Coun. for European Studies, Am. Econ. Assn., Econ. Soc. Am., Communal Studies Assn., Internat. Soc. for Comparative Study of Civilizations, Internat. Union of Pure and Applied Chemistry, Am. Chem. Soc., Genetics Soc. of Am., Am. Soc. for Micro., Am. Astron. Soc., Assn. for Asian Studies, Am. Assn. for Artificial Intelligence, Am. Anthrop. Assn., Am. Studies Assn., African Studies Assn. Achievements include patents pending for a module for doing global studies at the university level. Office: Ctr Global Studies Internat Interdisciplinary 40 Beltzhoover Ave Pittsburgh PA 15210 Office Phone: 412-381-3753. Business E-Mail: ronaldlynnmiller@centerforglobalstudies.com.

MILLER, RONALD MELLADO, education educator; b. El Paso, Texas, Nov. 3, 1970; s. Donald Hale and Corina Mellado Miller; m. Patricia Marie Addicks, Feb. 4, 1995; children: Hannah Aurora, Gideon McKay, Shiloh Marie, Eve Asenath. MS, Purdue Univ., 1997—99, PhD, 2000—03. Sci. rschr. Purdue Univ., West Lafayette, Ind., 1997—2003; prof. Brigham Young Univ., Laie, Hawaii, 2003—. Statis., human factors engrng. cons. Miller Consulting, West Lafayette, Ind., 1995; human factors engrng. cons. Purdue Univ. Human Factors in Aviation Rsch. Group, West Lafayette, Ind., 1998—; statis., human factors engrng. cons. Miller Consulting, Laie, Hawaii, 2003—. Internat. cmty. activist Purdue Univ., West Lafayette, Ind., 1998—2003, Brigham Young U., Hawaii, Laie, Hawaii, 2003. Grantee Rsch. Grant, Purdue U., 2002; scholar Mosell-Watt Bell Scholarship, Brigham Young U., 1995—97; Grad. Fellowship, Purdue Univ., 1997—2003. Mem.: APA, Psychonomic Soc., Am. Statis. Assn., Human Factors and Ergonomic Soc. Lds Ch. Achievements include research in refuting the fundamental theoretical difference between pavlovian and instrumental conditioning; co-author of the only current theory how mental chunking operates. Avocations: travel, swimming, surfing. Office: Brigham Young Univ Hawaii 55-220 Kulanui St BYUH Box #1970 Laie HI 96762 Home: 55-457 Moana St Laie HI 96762 Office Phone: 808-293-3831. Business E-Mail: millerr@byuh.edu.

MILLER, RONALD STUART, lawyer; b. Chgo., Sept. 28, 1931; s. Manuel and Ruth (Romack) M.; m. Patricia Ann Murphy, Dec. 14, 1962; children: Michelle Ann, Lynn Elizabeth. BS, U. Ill., 1953, LLB, 1955. Bar: Ill. 1955, NY 1960. Assoc. Devoe, Shadur & Mikva, Chgo., 1961-65; ptnr. Miller, Shakman & Beem, Chgo., 1965—. Adv. bd. Northwestern Law Sch. Inst. for Human Rights, 1998—2005; bd. dirs. Lawyers Com. for Civil Rights, Washington, 1977—2007, Chgo. Lawyers Com. for Civil Rights, 1974—2006, chmn., 1977—78; mem. Ill. Speakers Task Force, Springfield, 1984; convenor, moderator Pub. Affairs Roundtable, 1995—; sr. coun. pro bono affairs Ctr. for Disability and Elder Law, 2001—07. Bd. vis. U. Ill. Law Sch., Champaign, 1984-90, pres., 1988; bd. adv. DePaul Law Sch., Chgo., 1987-94; adv. com. Ctr. Civil and Human RTB, N. Dame Law Sch., chmn. Human Behavior Found., 1998-2001. Recipient Lifetime Achievement award, Chgo. Lawyers Com. for Civil Rights, 1997, Spl. Recognition award, Nat. Lawyers Com. Civil Rights, 2003, Chgo. Legal Legends award, Am. Constrn. Soc., 2007, Social Justice award, Jewish Coun. on Urban Affairs, 2007, Pickering Achievement award, Am. Bar Assn., 2007, Ill. Alumni Humanitarian award, 2009. Mem. ABA (Award of Achievement 2007), ACLU (co-chmn. adv. bd. Ill. chpt. 1998—, Civil Liberties award, 2006), Ill. Bar Assn. (Laureate Ill.Acad., 2002), Chgo. Bar Assn., Chgo. Coun. Lawyers. Jewish. Home: 330 W Diversey Pkwy Chicago IL 60657-6231 Office: Miller Shakman & BEEM 180 N La Salle St Ste 3600 Chicago IL 60601 Office Phone: 312-263-3700.

MILLER, ROSS HAYS, retired neurosurgeon; b. Ada, Okla., Jan. 30, 1923; s. Harry and Helen (Rice) M.; m. Catherine Railey, May 2, 1943; children— Terry Hays, Helen Stacy. BS, East Central State Coll., Ada, 1943; MD, U. Okla., 1946; MS in Neurosurgery, U. Minn., 1952. Diplomate: Am. Bd. Neurol. Surgery (chmn. exam. com. 1978-84). Intern St. Luke's Hosp., Cleve., 1946-47; fellow in neurosurgery Mayo Clinic, Rochester, Minn., 1950-54; instr. in neurosurgery Mayo Med. Sch., 1954-63, asst. prof. neurosurgery, 1963-73, asso. prof., 1973-75, prof., chmn. dept. neurosurgery, from 1975, now ret. Vis. prof. neurol. surgery Med. Coll. Ga., Augusta Contbr. articles to profl. jours. Trustee East Central State U. Found. Served as capt., M.C. U.S. Army, 1947-49, Korea. Named to Okla. Hall of Fame, 1977, Athletic Hall of Fame, East Central U. Okla., 1977; recipient Disting. Alumnus award East Central U. Okla., 1974, Mayo Found. Disting. Alumnus award, 1992. Mem. AMA, ACS, Am. Assn. Neurol. Surgeons (chmn. com. profl. practice 1976-79, dir. 1976-79, v.p. 1979, rep. to Council Med. Splty. Socs. 1980-84), Congress Neurol. Surgeons (exec. com. 1963-65), Minn. Soc. Neurol. Scis., Neurosurg. Soc. Am. (v.p. 1975), Soc. Neurol. Surgeons (v.p. 1983), Sigma Xi.

MILLER, ROSS JAMES, secretary of state; b. Las Vegas, Mar. 26, 1976; s. Bob and Sandy Miller; m. Lesley Miller; children: Cameron Elise, Geneva Layne. BA in English, Stanford U., Calif., 1999; student, Monterrey Technol. Inst., Mex.; JD/MBA, Loyola Marymount U., LA, 2002. Dep. dist. atty. Clark County, Nev.; sec. state State of Nev., Carson City, 2007—. Past pres. Citizen Alert, Nev.; bd. mem. HELP of So. Nev.; bd. mem. Legacy Soc. Boys and Girls Clubs. Democrat. Office: Office Sec State 101 N Carson #3 Carson City NV 89701 Office Phone: 775-684-5708. Business E-Mail: sosexec@sos.nv.gov.

MILLER, RUSH GLENN, JR., library director; b. Atlanta, Mar. 13, 1947; s. Rush Glenn and Gene (Ramsey) M.; m. Katherine Graves Miller, 2004; children: Lisa, Glenn, John, Edward; stepchildren: Hart, Megan. BA in History, Delta State Coll., Cleveland, Miss., 1969; MA in History, Miss. State U., 1971, PhD in Medieval History, 1973; MLS, Fla. State U., 1974. Asst. prof. U. Miss., Oxford, 1974-75; dir. libr. svcs. Delta State U., 1975-82; dir. libr. Sam Houston State U., Huntsville, Tex., 1982-86; dean librs. Bowling Green State U., 1986-94; dir. univ. libr. sys. U. Pitts., 1994—. Del. White House Conf. Librs., Washington, 1979; users coun. del. Online Computer Libr. Ctr., Inc., Dublin, Ohio, 1992-94; bd. mem. Assn. Rsch. Librs., 2003-06. Co-author: Beyond Survival: Managing Academic Libraries in Transition, 2007; contbg. author: Diversity and Multiculturalism in Libraries, 1994, others; editor: Miss. Librs., 1982-84; mem. editl. bd. Jour. Academic Leadership; contbr. articles to profl. jours. Recipient Past President's award Miss. Libr. Assn., 1976. Mem. ALA (various coms. 1976—), Southeastern Libr. Assn. (exec. bd. 1976-82), Acad. Libr. Assn. Ohio. Republican. Methodist. Avocations: golf, reading. Office: U Pitts Hillman Libr 3960 Forbes Ave Pittsburgh PA 15260 Office Phone: 412-648-7710, 412-648-7747. Office Fax: 412-648-7887. Business E-Mail: rgmiller@pitt.edu.

MILLER, RYAN, professional hockey player; b. East Lansing, Mich., July 17, 1980; Attended, Mich. State U., 1999—2002. Goalie Rochester Americans, 2002—05, Buffalo Sabres, 2003—. Player NHL YoungStars Game, 2003. Recipient Hobey Baker Meml. Award, 2001, Baz Bastien Meml. Trophy, Am. Hockey League, 2005; named to NHL All-Star Game, 2007. Office: Buffalo Sabres HSBC Arena One Seymour H Knox III Plaza Buffalo NY 14203-3096

MILLER, SABRINA WARES, librarian; d. Margaret Ann Bonds and Edson Brigham Wares; children: Adrian Matthew, Brandon Thomas. BA, Sul Ross State U., Alpine, Tex., 1992; MLS, NC Ctrl. U., Durham, 2000. Cert. health info. profl. Med. Libr. Assn., 2005. Med. libr. intern Laupus Libr., East Carolina U. Sch. of Medicine, Greenville, NC, 2000—00; edn. ctr. libr. Mid-Am. Cancer Ctr., Springfield, Mo., 2000—01; pub. svcs. med. libr. John B. Coleman, M.D., Health Scis. Libr., Houston CC, 2001—06; tech. libr. Champion Techs., Fresno, Tex., 2006—07; sci. and tech. info. officer Patrick AFB, Fla., 2007—. Accreditation cons. Acad. of HealthCare Professions, Houston, 2004—07. Vol. Poe Elem. Sch., Houston, 2003; vol. charity work Salvation Army. Bedichek Faculty Devel. grant, Houston C.C. Sys., 2001, 2003. Mem.: Spl. Libr. Assn., Mensa Internat., Acad. Health Info. Profls., Tex. Med. Ctr. Health Scis. Libr. Consortium, Med. Libr. Assn. Democrat. Office: PO Box 450499 Houston TX 77245

MILLER, SAM SCOTT, lawyer; b. Ft. Worth, July 26, 1938; s. Percy Vernon and Mildred Lois (MacDowell) M.; m. Mary Harrison FitzHugh, May 10, 1969. BA, Mich. State U., 1960; JD, Tulane U., 1964; LLM, Yale U., 1965. Bar: La. 1965, N.Y. 1966, Minn. 1969. Assoc. Simpson Thacher & Bartlett, NYC, 1965-68; sr. counsel Investors Diversified Services, Mpls., 1968-73; ptnr. Ireland Gibson Reams & Miller, Memphis, 1973-74; gen. counsel Paine Webber Group, Inc., NYC, 1974-87, sr. v.p., 1976-87; ptnr. Orrick, Herrington & Sutcliffe, NYC, 1987—2009. Adj. prof. NYU Law Sch., 1986-90; vis. lectr. Yale Law Sch., 1980-85, Inst. Internat. Econs. and Trade, Wuhan, China, 1983, U. Calif., 1986; trustee Omni Mut., Inc., 1988-90, ombudsman Charles Schwab & Co., 1991-. Contbr. articles to profl. jours.; editor-in-chief: Tulane Law Rev, 1964-65; bd. editors Securities Regulation Law Jour., 1982—. Bd. dirs. Guthrie Theatre Found., Mpls., 1971-74; bd. dirs. Minn. Opera Co., 1971-74, Yale U. Law Sch. Fund., 1981-1991; bd. govs. Investment Co. Inst., 1980-87, deans coun., Tulane Law Sch., 2004-, adv. coun. Atlantic Legal Found., 2008-. Fellow Fgn. Policy Assn.; mem. ABA (chmn. subcom. market regulation 1985-93, vice chmn. com. fed. regulation securities 1995-98, chmn. subcom. electronic comm. 1999-02), Assn. Bar City NY (treas. and mem. exec. com. 1994-96, chmn. broker-dealer investment co. and regulations subcom. 1982-83), Internat. Bar Assn., Securities Industry Assn. (chmn. fed. regulation com. 1976-78), Down Town Assn., Knickerbocker Club, Order of Coif, Omicron Delta Kappa. Democrat. Baptist. Office: Orrick Herrington & Sutcliffe 666 5th Ave Rm 203 New York NY 10103-1798

MILLER, SARABETH, secondary school educator; b. Apr. 6, 1927; d. Clayton Everett and Margaret (Noland) Reif; m. Lloyd Melvin Miller, Dec. 2, 1944; children: Virginia, Shirley, Judith, John, Nola, Steven. BA, Valparaiso U., 1972, MA in L.S, 1977; postgrad., Purdue U., 1983, Ind. U., 1986, postgrad., 1991, Art Inst. Ft. Lauderdale, Fla., 1992, Ind. State U., 1996, postgrad., 1997, St. Joseph U., 1998. Lic. tchr. Ind., cert. data processing. Office employee Porter County Herald, Hebron, Ind., 1954—55, Little Co. of Mary Hosp. and Home, San Pierre, Ind., 1960—65, Jasper County Co-op, Tefft, Ind., 1965—69, Hannon's, Valparaiso, 1969—72; tchr. art DeMotte (Ind.) elem. sch., 1972—76, Kankakee Valley High Sch., Wheatfield, Ind., 1976—. Participant Lilly Creative Tchr.'s Workshop. Participant (art and lit. mag.) Mirage, No. Region Artists Invitational; contbr. articles and photographs to local newspapers (50 Yrs. 4-H Leader award). Leader 4-H Club, Kouts; participant North Ctrl. Regional Forum, 1991, 1992, 1993; participant archeol. dig K.V. Hist. Soc. and Notre Dame; mem., elder Kouts Presbyn. Ch.; mem. adv. com. secondary sch. showcase Valparaiso U. Recipient various prizes, Lake Ctrl. (Ind.) Fair, 1975, 1980, photography award, Ind. Dept. Tourism, 1976, Porter County Fair, 1989, 1996, 1998, 2000, 2001, 2004, Gainer Bank Calendar award, 4-H Alumni award, 2002, 4-H 47 yr. leader tenure award, 1994; grantee, Nat. Gallery of Art, 1993; Lilly Endowment fellow, Lilly Extending Tchr. Creativity Inst., 1987, 1994, 1995, 1996, 2002, 2003, 2004, 2005, 2007—08. Mem.: AIA, NEA, North Ctrl. Assn. Secondary Schs. (mem. evaln. team), Kankakee Valley Tchrs. Assn., Ind. Art Edn. Assn., Ind. Tchrs. Assn., Nat. Art Edn. Assn., Nat. Mus. American Indians, Smithsonian Instn., Hist. Landmarks, Kankakee Valley Hist. Soc. Presbyterian. Home: 1056 S Baums Bridge Rd Kouts IN 46347-9712 Personal E-mail: smiller@kv.k12.in.us.

MILLER, SARAH GRAY, editor-in-chief; Joined Garden Design mag.; launch editor Organic Style mag., 2001; founding editor in chief Budget Living mag., 2002—05; cons. Entertainment Weekly, 2005—06; editor special issues Weddings, Home and Makeover InStyle mag., 2006—07; editor in chief O at Home mag. Hearst Corp., 2007—08, editor in chief Country Living mag., 2008—. Office: Country Living 300 W 57th St New York NY 10019-3788 Office Phone: 212-649-3500.*

MILLER, SCOTT EUGENE, legislative staff member; Legis. dir., Rep. Todd Platts US House of Reps., Washington, 2001—03, chief of staff to Rep. Todd Platts, 2003—. Republican. Office: 2455 Rayburn House Office Bldg Washington DC 20515 Office Phone: 202-225-5836. Office Fax: 202-226-1000.*

MILLER, SEAN, men's college basketball coach; b. Pa., Nov. 17, 1968; B, U. Pitts., 1992. Asst. coach U. Wis. Badgers, 1992—93, Miami U. Red Hawks, Ohio, 1993—95, U. Pitts. Panthers, 1995—96, NC State U. Wolfpack, 1996—2001; assoc. head coach Xavier U. Musketeers, 2001—04, head coach, 2004—09, U. Ariz. Wildcats, 2009—. Named Dist. 10 Coach of Yr., Nat. Assn. Basketball Coaches. Office: Univ Ariz Athletics McKale Ctr 1 National Championship Dr PO Box 210096 Tucson AZ 85721-0096*

MILLER, SHANNON, Olympic athlete; b. Rolla, Mo., Mar. 10, 1977; Grad., Boston Coll. Law Sch. Gymnist U.S. National Gymnastic Team, 1990—97. Named Female Athlete of Yr., Nat. March of Dimes Found., 1993; named to U.S. Olympic Hall of Fame, 2005, Internat. Gymnastics Hall of Fame, 2006. Achievements include being the most decorated gymnast in US history; won a total of 58 international and 49 national competition medals; won 9 World Championship medals including two back-to-back All-Around Gold medals; won a Silver medal for All-Around and Silver medal for the balance beam at the Barcelona Olympic Games, 1992; was a member of the Bronze medal team and won the Bronze medal for floor exercise and uneven bars at the Barcelona Olympic Games, 1992; was a member of the Gold medal team and won the Gold medal for balance beam at the Atlanta Olympics Games, 1996.

MILLER, SIENNA, actress; b. NYC, Dec. 28, 1981; d. Ed and Jo Miller. Attended, Lee Strasberg Inst. Rep. advertising campaign Tod's fashion house, 2007. Actor: (films) South Kensington, 2001, High Speed, 2002, Layer Cake, 2004, Alfie, 2004, Casanova, 2005, Interview, 2007, Stardust, 2007, The Mysteries of Pittsburgh, 2008, G.I. Joe: The Rise of Cobra, 2009; (TV series) Bedtime, 2002, Keen Eddie, 2003; guest appearance Late Night with Conan O'Brien, 2003. Recipient Elle Style Icon award, Elle Mag., 2009. Office: c/o Endeavor Talent Agency 9701 Wilshire Blvd, 3rd Fl Beverly Hills CA 90212

MILLER, STEPHANIE KATHERINE, radio personality, comedian; b. Lockport, NY, Sept. 29, 1961; Degree in Theatre, U. So. Calif. Stand up comedian Laugh Factory, Hollywood, Calif.; talk show host radio station WLVL, WCMF, Brother Wease Show, Rochester, NY, 1985, WCKG, Chgo., KFI, LA, 1993—95; late night TV talk show host The Stephanie Miller Show, Buena Vista TV, 1995; talk show host KTZN, KABC, LA, 1997; co-host Equal Time, CNBC, 1997—2000; game show host I've Got a Secret, Oxygen cable TV network, 2000—01, co-host Pure Oxygen, 2001—04; host The Stephanie Miller Show, 2004—. Regular panelist Balderdash, PAX-TV. Avocation: dogs. Office: Jones Radio Networks Inc 133 Ave Americas 11th Fl New York NY 10036 E-mail: stephanie@stephaniemiller.com.*

MILLER, STEPHEN HERSCHEL, surgeon, educator; b. NYC, Jan. 12, 1941; s. Morris Louis and Mildred Lily (Beller) M.; children: Mark, David. MD, UCLA, 1964; MPH, San Diego State, 1996. Diplomate Am. Bd. Surgery, Am. Bd. Plastic Surgery (mem. exec. com. 1985—, chmn. written examination sect. 1985—, bd. dirs. 1984—, chmn. 1989-90). Asst. prof. surgery U. Calif., San Francisco, 1973-74; from assoc. prof. to prof. surgery Milton S. Hershey Med. Ctr., Hershey, Pa., 1974—78; chief div. plastic surgery Oreg. Health Scis. U., Portland, 1979-88, Staff Scripps Clinic, La Jolla, Calif., 1988—98; clin. prof. surgery U. Calif., San Diego, 1989—98; adj. prof. surgery Northwestern U., Evanston, Ill., 1998—; pres., CEO Am. Bd. Med. Specialities, Evanston, Ill., 2004—07. Bd. dirs. Edn. Commn. for Foreign Med. Grads. Editor-in-chief Yearbook of Plastic, Reconstructive and Aesthetic Surgery, 1988-95, 2007. Physician advisor Boy Scouts Am., dist. chmn. scoutmaster exec. coun., 1983-84; bd. dirs. Temple Beth Israel, Portland, 1984-86. Recipient Physician Recognition award, 1976; grantee Med. Rsch. Found. of Oreg., 1980, Oreg. Health Scis. U., 1980. Mem. ACS (chmn. program com. 1983-87), Am. Soc. Plastic and Reconstructive Surgery (bd. dirs. 1980-89, v.p. 1985-86, pres.-elect 1986-87, pres. 1987-88, grantee 1976), Am. Assn. Plastic Surgeons (chmn. rsch. com. 1983-84, trustee 1988-91, sec. 1990-93, pres. 1994-95), Assn. Acad. Chmn. Plastic Surgery (sec./treas. 1985—); Am. Bd. Med. Specialites (sect., exec. v.p., 1998). Avocations: reading, golf. Office: 39289 Beringer Dr Murrieta CA 92563

MILLER, STEPHEN M., economics professor; s. Charles R. and C. Marjorie Miller; m. Leticia Nuesa, Aug. 27, 1977; 1 child, Alexandria. MA, SUNY, Buffalo, 1969, PhD, 1972; BS, Purdue U., LaFayette, Ind., 1967. Instr. economics U. Conn., Storrs, 1970—72, asst. prof. economics, 1972—76, assoc. prof. economics, 1976—81, prof. economics, 1981—2001, emeritis prof. economics, 2001—, prof. economics, chair, U. Nev., Las Vegas, 2001—; vis. economist Fed. Res. Bank Boston, 1978; prin. analyst., fiscal analysis Congl. Budget Office, Washington, 1987—88. Founder U. Conn. Quar. Review. Contbr. articles to profl.

jours. Mem. Conn. Econ. Conf. Bd., Hartford, 1991—2001, Nev. Coun. Economics Edn., Las Vegas, 2001. Mem.: Eastern Economics Assn., Western Economics Assn., Southern Economics Assn., Am. Economics Assn. Office: Univ Nev Las Vegas Box 456005 4505 S Maryland Pky Las Vegas NV 89154-6005 Business E-Mail: stephen.miller@unlv.edu.

MILLER, STEPHEN RALPH, lawyer; b. Chgo., Nov. 28, 1950; s. Ralph and Karin Ann (Olson) Miller; m. Sheila L. Krysiak, Feb. 2, 1998; children from previous marriage: David Williams, Lindsay Christine. BA cum laude, Yale U., 1972; JD, Cornell U., 1975. Bar: Ill. Assoc. McDermott, Will & Emery, Chgo., 1975-80, income ptnr., 1981-85, equity ptnr., 1986—2006, mgmt. com. mem., 1992-95, counsel, 2006—. Mem. spl. task force on post-employment benefits Fin. Acctg. Stds. Bd., Norwalk, Conn., 1987—91. Contbr. articles to profl. jours. Trustee Police Pension Bd., Wilmette, Ill., 1992—98; mem. Chgo. Coun. Fgn. Rels., 1978—, mem. devel. com., 1997—2002, chair devel. subcom., 1999—2002, mem. external rels. com., 2002—03, mem. pres.'s cir. steering com., 2005—; trustee Seabury Western Theol. Sem., Evanston, Ill., 1994—2002, chancellor, 1996—97, 2004—05, chair trusteeship com., 2000—02; mem. Seabury Coun., 2004—07. Mem.: ABA, Worldwide Employee Benefits Network, Chgo. Bar Assn. (assoc.), Hundred Club Cook County, Cornell Club Chgo., Lawyers' Club Chgo., Yale Club Chgo. Avocations: sailing, water-skiing, cross country skiing. Office: McDermott Will & Emery 227 W Monroe St Ste 4700 Chicago IL 60606-5096 Office Phone: 312-984-7634. Business E-Mail: smiller@mwe.com.

MILLER, STEVEN H., museum director; b. Phila., 1947; m. Jane McClure Pelson; children: Andrew Steven, Katherine Ann. BA, Bard Coll., 1970. Cert. in Conservation Sci. Internat. Ctr. for the Study of Preservation and Restoration of Cultural Property, Rome, 1978. Asst. to sr. curator Mus. of City of NY, NYC, 1971-72, asst. curator paintings, prints and photographs, 1973-77, curator prints and photographs, 1977-79, curator, dept. head fine art collections, history and spl. collections, 1979-85, sr. curator, 1985-87; asst. dir. Maine State Mus., 1987-91; dir. of mus. Western Res. Hist. Soc., Cleve., 1991-95; exec. dir. The Bennington Mus., Vt., 1995—2001, Morris Mus., Morristown, NJ, 2001—; exec. v.p. Morris Mus. Found., Morristown, NJ, 2001—. Adj. prof. mus. studies Case Western Res. U., 1991—94, Seton Hall U., 2001—; lectr. NYU, 1978—87, Columbia U., NYC, 1981, 82, New Sch. for Social Rsch., NYC, 1978, 83, Maine State Mus., 1987—91. Author catalogs; contbr. articles to profl. jours. Charter and former mem. hist. preservation com. City of Gardiner, Maine; mem. Williamstown Art Conservation Ctr.; bd. trustees ArtPride, NJ; bd. govs. Bard-St. Stephen's Alumni Assn.; past bd. dirs. Vt. Mus. and Gallery Alliance; former mem. landmarks preservation com. Shaker Heights, Ohio; former mem. adv. com. Blaine House Restoration, Maine; former mem., art adv. com. Gracie Mansion Conservancy, NYC; former mem. adv. coun. Mus. Moving Image, Astoria, NY; trustee ARTPride, NJ. Named John Cotton Dana award, NJ Assn. Mus., 2008. Mem.: NARAS (assoc.), Century Assn., Am. Assn. Mus. (mem. mus. advocacy team, mem. mus. accreditation vis. com.), Park Ave. Club (Morristown). Home: 45 Washington Ave Morristown NJ 07960-5622 Office: Morris Mus 6 Normandy Heights Rd Morristown NJ 07960 Office Phone: 973-971-3702. Business E-Mail: smiller@morrismuseum.org.

MILLER, STEVEN L., oil industry executive; b. Kansas City, Mo., Oct. 23, 1945; s. Irvin Earl and Betty Jane (Scharbach) M.; m. Sheila Margaret Porn, July 7, 1945; children: Steven Louis Jr., Ashley Margaret. BSChemE, U. Ill., 1967. Various engring. assignments Shell Oil Co., Houston, 1966-73; spl. assignment SIPM-Shell Internat., The Hague, The Netherlands, 1973-74; various mgmt. positions Shell Oil Co., Houston, Norco, La., 1974-92, Shell Internat. Petroleum Co., London, 1992-96; mng. dir. Royal Dutch/Shell Group Cos., London, 1996-99; chmn., pres., CEO Shell Oil Co., Houston, 1999—2002; chmn., pres. SLM Discovery Ventures, 2002—; chmn. RRI Energy, Houston, 2009—. Bd. dirs. Applied Materials Inc., Santa Clara, Calif., Am. Petroleum Inst., Washington, Coun. of the Ams., N.Y.C.; bd. advisors James A. Baker Inst. Pub. Policy, Houston, 1999—. Bd. dirs. Greater Houston Partnership, 1999, World Golf Found., St. Augustine, Fla., 1999; trustee United Way Tex.-Gulf Coast, Houston, 1999, George C. Marshall Found. Mem. Nat. Petroleum Coun., Bus. Roundtable, Gov.'s Bus. Coun. Presbyterian. Avocations: golf, american history, antiques. Office: RRI Energy 1000 Main St Houston TX 77002*

MILLER, STEVEN MAX, humanities educator; b. Portland, Ind., Feb. 9, 1950; s. J. Max and Belva Kathryn (Kitty Booher) M.; m. Fran Felice Koski, May 30, 1985 (div. 1992). BA in English with high honors, Coll. of William and Mary, 1972; MA in English Lang. and Lit., Ind. U., 1975, PhD in English Lang. and Lit., 1985. Sr. libr. asst. cataloger rare books and spl. collections Lilly Libr., Bloomington, Ind., 1972-76; prof. English Millersville U., Pa., 1985—, dir. univ. honors program, 1999-2001, dir. Honors Coll., 2001—06. Cons. women writers project Brown U., Providence, 1990-95. Contbr. articles to profl. jours. Grantee NEH, 1991, 92. Mem. MLA, John Donne Soc. Am., Spenser Soc., Bronte Soc. Episcopalian. Avocation: gardening. Office: Millersville U Dept English PO Box 1002 Millersville PA 17551-0302 Office Phone: 717-872-3121.

MILLER, STUART A., construction executive; s. Leonard and Sue Miller. Grad., Harvard U.; JD, U. Miami, 1982. Various positions homebuilding divsn. Lennar Corp., Miami, Fla., v.p., 1988—97, bd. dirs., 1990—, pres. homebuilding divsn., 1991—97, pres. prin. real estate and mgmt. divsn., 1995—97, pres., CEO Miami, Fla., 1997—; chmn. bd. Riley Property Holdings, LLC (formerly LNR Property Corp.), 1997—2005. Bd. dirs. Union Bank Fla.; mem. Harvard U. Joint Ctr. Housing Studies Policy Adv. Bd. Named one of 50 Most Generous Philanthropists, BusinessWeek, 2005. Office: Lennar Corp 700 NW 107th Ave Ste 400 Miami FL 33172-3154 Office Phone: 305-559-4000.

MILLER, SUSAN ANN, retired school system administrator; b. Cleve., Nov. 24, 1947; d. Earl Wilbur and Marie Coletta (Hendershot) M. BS in Edn., Kent State U., 1969; MEd, Cleve. State U., 1975; PhD, Kent State U., 1993. Cert. supt.; cert. elem. prin., cert. elem. supervisor; cert. Learning Disabled/Behavior Disabled tchr.; cert. tchr. grades 1-8; cert. sch. counselor; lic. counselor. Tchr., guidance counselor, interim prin. North Royalton City Schs., Ohio, 1969-84; dir. elem. and spl. edn., acting supt., asst. supt. Ednl. Svc. Ctr. of Cuyahoga County, Valley View, Ohio, 1984—2004. Contbr. articles to profl. jours. Grantee Latchkey Program, State Dept. Edn., North Coast Leadership Forum, Peer Assistance and Rev., Entry Yr. Program, Alt. H.S. Mem. ASCD, Coun. Exceptional Children, Phi Delta Kappa. Home: 7216 Morning Star Trail Sagamore Hills OH 44067 Personal E-mail: sumrtoi47@yahoo.com.

MILLER, SUSAN CALABRESE, lawyer, consumer products company executive; b. Groton, Conn., June 5, 1959; AB summa cum laude, Duke Univ., 1980; JD, Harvard Univ., 1984. Bar: Pa. 1984, Calif. 1985. Assoc. Latham & Watkins, LA; sr. counsel Avery Dennison, Pasadena, Calif., 1991—95, sr. counsel Asia Pacific Hong Kong, 1995—98, asst. gen. counsel Pasadena, Calif., 1998—2007, v.p., gen. counsel, 2007—08, sr. v.p., gen. counsel, 2008—. Mem.: ABA, LA County Bar Assn., Phi Beta Kappa. Office: Avery Dennison Corp 150 N Orange Grove Blvd Pasadena CA 91103

MILLER, SUSAN L., social services administrator; Student, Santa Monica Coll., 1980—85; cert. in mktg. and advt., Loyola Mount U., 1994; BA in Sociology and Mgmt., Eckerd Coll., 2006. Comptr., dir. fin. and adminstrn. Westside Ctr. for Ind. Living, Inc., LA, 1979—85; exec. dir. Placer Ind. Resource Svcs., Inc., Auburn, Calif., 1995—. Bd. dirs. Auburn Area Access, Inc. dba Auburn Cmty. TV, treas., 2000—. Bd. dirs. Capital Unity Coun., 2001—04, program adv. coun., 2004—; bd. dirs. Golden Sierra Workforce Investment, 2001—, v.p., 2004—06; treas. CA Found. for Ind. Living Ctrs., 2004—08; chair Golden Sierra Workforce Investment, 2006—; sec. CA Found. for Ind. Living Ctrs., 1999—2004; adv. coun. Placer County Social Svcs. Transp., 1997—, chair, 1998—99, Tahoe regional planning agy. com, 2001—, adv. coun. Alpine County, 2001—; chair adv. coun. Alpine County IHSS, 2004; client, family rels. com., cultural competency com. Placer County Health & Human Svcs., 2001—; bldg., fire and other codes adv. com. Calif. State Bldg. Commn., 1999—2002; active Tahoe Area Coord. Coun. on Disability, 1999—; treas. CA Found. for Ind. Living Ctrs., 1996—99, bd. dirs., 1995—; steering com. Best Step Trans. Collaborative, 1996—; bd. dirs. Foothill Employers Adv. Coun., 2003—05, mem., 2002—; steering com. Vision 2020 for Greater Auburn, 1998—2003; bd. dirs. Assn. Programs Rural Independent Living, 2003—, internal v.p., 2009—. Avocations: genealogy, painting, reading. Office: Placer Ind Resource Svcs Inc 11768 Atwood Rd Ste 29 Auburn CA 95603

MILLER, SUZANNE MARIE, library director, educator; b. Feb. 25, 1954; d. John Gordon and Dorothy Margaret (Sabatka) M.; 1 child, Altinay Marie. BA in English, U. S.D., 1975; MA in Library Sci., U. Denver, 1976, postgrad. in law, 1984. Librarian II Law Sch. U. SD, Vermillion, 1977-78; law libr. U. LaVerne, Calif., 1978-85, law instr., 1980-85; asst. libr. tech. svcs. McGeorge Sch. Law, Calif., 1985-99, prof. advanced legal rsch., 1994-99; libr. SD State Library, Pierre, 1999—2004, Minn. State Libr. Svcs. and Sch. Tech., Roseville, 2004—. Co-author (with Elizabeth J. Pokorny) U.S. Government Documents: A Practical Guide for Library Assistants in Academic and Public Libraries, 1988; contbr. chapters to book, articles to profl. jours. Pres. Short Grass Arts Coun., 2001—03; bd. dirs. Black Hills Playhouse Bd., 1999—2004, S.D. Ctr. for the Book Bd., 2002—04. Recipient A. Jurisprudence award Bancroft Whitney Pub. Co., 1983. Mem.: ALA, Minn. Ednl. Media Orgn., Minn. Libr. Assn., Western Coun. State Librs. (sec. 2001—02), Chief Officers of State Libr. Agys. (sec. 2002—04, chair Rsch. & Stats. com. 2004—06), Western Pacific Assn. Law Librs. (sec. 1990—94, pres. elect 1994—95, pres. 1995—96, local arrangements chair 1997), No. Calif. Assn. Law Librs. (mem. program com., inst. 1988), Mt. Plains Libr. Assn. (S.D. rep. to exec. bd. 2001—04), So. Calif. Assn. Law Librs. (arrangements com. 1981—82), Am. Assn. Law Librs., S.D. Libr. Assn. Roman Catholic. Office: Minn Dept Edn 1500 Hwy 36 West Roseville MN 55113-4266 Office Phone: 651-582-8251. Business E-Mail: suzanne.miller@state.mn.us.

MILLER, TED ROBERT, management consultant; b. Sept. 17, 1947; s. Marvin Lester and Carolyn Ruth Miller; m. Valerie Sue Nelkin. BS in Engring., Case Western Res. U., 1968; MS in Ops. Rsch., U. Pa., 1971, M in City Planning, 1970, PhD in Regional Sci., 1975. Ops. rsch. analyst U.S. Dept. Commerce, Nat. Bur. Stds. and HEW, Washington, 1971-75; staff dir. task force on Nat. Blood Data Ctr. Am. Blood Commn., Rosslyn, Va., 1975-77; asst. dir. urban and econ. devel. Nat. Inst. Advanced Studies, Washington, 1977-78; v.p. Granville Corp., Washington, 1978-84; sr. rsch. assoc. Urban Inst., Washington, 1984-93; dir. Children's Safety Network Econ. and Ins. Rsch. Ctr., 1992—. V.p. Nat. Pub. Svcs. Rsch. Inst., Calverton, Md., 1993-96, pres., 1997-2002; prin. rsch. scientist Pacific Inst. Rsch. and Evaluation, Calverton, 1997—. Mem. editl. bd. Jour. Safety Rsch., 1991—, Jour. Forensic Econs., 1991-2004, Acc. Analysis and Prevention, 1993—, Inj. Prev., 2002-; contbr. articles to profl. jours. Mem. Bd. Proprs. Ea. N.J., 1974-98; pres. Adelphi Ter. Condo. Assn., 1979-81. Recipient Nationwide on Your Side Hwy. Safety award, 1996, State and Territorial Injury Prevention Dirs. Assn. Vision award, 2005. Fellow Assn. Advt. Automotive Medicine, Am. Inst. Cert. Planners; mem. AAAS, APHA (Excellence in Sci. award injury control sect. 1999), So. Regional Sci. Assn. (exec. coun. 1990-92), Am. Econ. Assn., Pi Delta Epsilon. Democrat. Office: 11701 Beltsville Dr Ste 300 Beltsville MD 20705

MILLER, TERRY ALAN, chemistry professor; b. Girard, Kans., Dec. 18, 1943; s. Dwight D. Miller and Rachel E. (Detjen) Beltram; m. Barbara Hoffmann, July 16, 1966; children: Brian, Stuart. BA, U. Kans., 1965; PhD, Cambridge U., Eng., 1968. Disting. tech. staff Bell Telephone Labs, 1968-84; vis. asst. prof. Princeton U., 1968-71; vis. lectr. Stanford U., 1972; vis. fgn. scholar Inst. Molecular Sci., Okazaki, Japan, summer 1983; Ohio eminent scholar, prof. chemistry Ohio State U., Columbus, 1984—. Chair Molecular Spectroscopy Symposium, Columbus, 1992—. Mem. editl. bd. Jour. Chem. Physics, 1978-81, Laser Chemistry, 1986—, Rev. of Sci. Instruments, 1986-89, Jour. Phys. Chemistry, 1989-95, Jour. Optical Soc. Am., 1989-95, Chemtracts, 1989-90, Ann. Revs. Phys. Chemistry, 1989-94, Jour. Molecular Structure, 1996-; mem. editl. bd. Jour. Molecular Spectroscopy, 1982-87, editor 2005-; contbr. articles to profl. jours. Recipient Bourke medal Royal Soc. Chemistry, 1998; Marshall fellow Brit. Govt., 1965-67, NSF fellow, 1967-68. Fellow Optical Soc. Am. (Meggars award 1993), Am. Phys. Soc. (H.P. Broida award 1999, Earle K. Plyler prize 2009), AAAS; mem. Am. Chem. Soc. (councilor, cleve. sect., Edward W. Morley medal), Coblentz Soc. (Bomen-Michaelson award 1995). Office: Ohio State U 120 W 18th Ave Columbus OH 43210-1106 Office Phone: 614-292-2569.

MILLER, TERRY MORROW, lawyer; b. Columbus, Ohio, Mar. 11, 1947; s. Robert E. and Elizabeth Jane (Morrow) M.; m. Martha Estella Johnson, Mar. 20, 1976; 1 child, Timothy. BS, Ohio State U., 1969, JD, 1975. Bar: Ohio 1975, U.S. Ct. Appeals (6th cir.) 1979, U.S. Supreme Ct. 1980. Asst. atty. gen. State of Ohio, Columbus, 1975—77; ptnr. Miller & Noga, Columbus, 1977—81; assoc. Vorys, Sater, Seymour and Pease, Columbus, 1981—85, ptnr., 1986—. Trustee Columbus Lit. Coun., 1997—2004. Sgt. U.S. Army, 1969-71, Okinawa. Mem. Am. Bankruptcy Law Forum, Columbus Bar Assn., Lakes Golf and Country Club, Rattlesnake Ridge Golf Club. Avocations: golf, Ohio history. Home: 288 E North Broadway Columbus OH 43214-4114 Office: Vorys Sater Seymour et al PO Box 1008 52 E Gay St Columbus OH 43216-1008 Home Phone: 614-263-7670; Office Phone: 614-464-5645. Business E-Mail: tmmiller@vorys.com.

MILLER, THEODORE NORMAN, lawyer; b. Chgo., Oct. 9, 1942; s. Alexander Hyman and Bertha Helen (Swidler) Miller; m. Marylyn Sue Zax, June 21, 1964; 1 child, Amy. BA, U. Mich., 1964; LLB, Yale U., 1967. Bar: Ill. 1967, Calif. 1991, US Dist. Ct. (no. dist.) Ill. 1967, US Ct. Appeals (7th cir.) 1968, US Supreme Ct. 1972. Law clk. US Ct. Appeals (7th cir.), 1967—68; assoc. Sidley & Austin, Chgo., 1968—73, ptnr., 1973—, now mng. ptnr. NYC office, vice chmn. mgmt. com. and mem. exec. com. Mem.: ABA, Chgo. Coun. Lawyers, Chgo. Bar Assn., Order of Coif, Phi Beta Kappa. Office: Sidley Austin Brown & Wood LLP 787 Seventh Ave New York NY 10019-6018 Office Phone: 212-839-5886. Office Fax: 212-839-5599. Business E-Mail: tmiller@sidley.com.

MILLER, THERESA L., library director; b. Port Huron, Mich., Apr. 2, 1959; d. David R. Miller and Mary Louise Preininger. AA, AS, St. Clair County C.C., Port Huron, Mich., 1990; BS, Wayne State U., 1992, MLIS, 1994. Support tutor St. Clair County C.C., 1988-89, master tutor, 1989-91; circulation supr. Baker Coll. of Port Huron, 1992-95, faculty math., 1998, faculty blackboard, ethics, libr., computers, 2005—, co-chair pres. adv. coun., 2005—07; pub. spkr. Mich., 1988—; investigative asst. Huffmaster Cos., Port Huron, 1998-2000; libr. dir. Baker Coll. of Pt. Huron, 1995—; judge Bus. Profs. of Am., St. Clair County, 1994—2000, 2003—04, 2008—. Baker coll. rep. County Tech. Adv. Com., St. Clair County, 1997—2003; mem. adv. bd. Baker Coll. of Port Huron Career Svcs., 1997—2003; judge Port Huron HS Writing Competition, 1997—2001. Editor: (newsletter) Baker Beacon, 1997; author: (newsletter) LUC News, 1993-96; author: (book) A Reference Librarians User Guide to the Internet, 1993. Recorder for the Blind Libr. of Mich., Lansing, 1996-2004; mem. gov. bd. Seaway Cmty. Freenet, St. Clair County, 1995-96; pres., founding bd. dirs. First Night of Port Huron, 2001-04; bd. dirs. Girl Scouts Mich. Waterways Council, 2006-09. Mem.: ALA, Internat. Libr. Support Group (founder 1999—2005, chmn.), Librs. Using Computers/Mich. (chair 1994—96), Mich. Libr. Assn., Optimists (Port Huron bd. dir. 1997—99, pres. Pt. Huron chpt. 2000—01, lt. gov. Mich. 2001—04, Port Huron bd. dir. 2004—05), St. Clair County Pub. Libr. Friends, Phi Theta Kappa (treas. 1989—90, founding alumni pres. St. Clair C.C. chpt. 1991). Avocations: singing professionally, collecting jewelry, auctions, theater, investing. Office: Baker Coll Port Huron Libr 3403 Lapeer Rd Port Huron MI 48060 Office Phone: 810-989-2122. Business E-Mail: theresa.miller@baker.edu.

MILLER, THOMAS EUGENE, lawyer, writer; b. Bryan, Tex., Jan. 4, 1929; s. Eugene Adam and Ella Lucille (Schroeder) M. BA, BS, Tex. A&M U., 1950; MA, U. Tex., 1956, JD, 1966; postgrad., U. Houston, 1956-58, U. Calif., 1983. Bar: Tex. 1966. Rsch. technician M.D. Anderson Hosp., Houston, 1956-58; claims examiner trainee Social Security Adminstrn., New Orleans, 1964; trademark examiner U.S. Patent and Trademark Office, Washington, 1966; editor Bancroft-Whitney Co., San Francisco, 1966-92; ret., 1992. Author: (under pseudonym Millard Thomas) Home From 7-North, 1984; contbr. to numerous legal publs. Mem. Dem. Nat. Com., 1981—; mem. Celebrate Bryan Com., chmn. Bryan Med. Heritage Com. Mem. ABA, World Lit. Assn., World Inst. Achievement, United Writers Assn. India, Nat. Trust for Hist. Preservation, Tex. Bar Assn., U. Tex. Sch. of Law, Non-practicing Alumni Adv. Coun., African Wildlife Found., World Wildlife Fund, Internat. Platform Assn., Nat. Writers Assn., Scribes, Acad. Polit. Sci., Press Club, Commonwealth Club, Westerners Internat., Rotary Club (Paul Harris fellow, Found. fellow), Menninger Soc., Tex. A&M U. Club, Phi Kappa Phi, Psi Chi, Phi Eta Sigma. Methodist. Home: 3265 Minglewood Dr Beaumont TX 77703-2761 *Personal philosophy: Use your experience and abilities not only to understand life and to succeed, but also to help others' journeys through life.*

MILLER, THOMAS J., state attorney general; b. Dubuque, Iowa, Aug. 11, 1944; s. Elmer John and Betty Maude (Kross) Miller; m. Linda Cottington, Jan. 10, 1981; 1 child, Matthew. BA, Loras Coll., Dubuque, 1966; JD, Harvard U., 1969. Bar: Iowa 1969. With VISTA, Balt., 1969—70; legis. asst. to US Rep. John C. Culver, 1970—71; legal edn. dir. Balt. Legal Aid Bur., part-time faculty U. Md. Sch. Law, 1971—73; pvt. practice McGregor, Iowa, 1973—78; city atty., 1973—79, Marquette, Iowa; atty. gen. State of Iowa, 1978—90, 1994—; ptnr. Faegre & Benson, Des Moines, 1991—95. Chmn. Microsoft case exec. com.; co-chmn. Airline Competition Working Grp.; pres. 2nd Dist. New Dem. Club, Balt., 1972. Mem.: ABA, Nat. Assn. Attys. Gen. (pres. 1989—90, chmn. consumer protection, ins., budget, and antitrust coms., Wyman award 1990), Iowa Bar Assn., Common Cause. Democrat. Roman Catholic. Office: Office of Atty Gen Hoover State Office Bldg 1305 E Walnut St Des Moines IA 50319-0112 Office Phone: 515-281-5164.*

MILLER, THOMAS JAMES, biology professor; b. London, Apr. 25, 1960; s. Thomas Arthur and Gladys Margaret Miller; m. Gail Taylor Miller; children: Emma Taylor, Rose Taylor. BSc with honors, U. York, England, 1981; MS, NC State U., Raleigh, 1984, PhD, 1990. Sch. tchr. Bexley London Borough, Sidcup, Kent, England, 1984—86; postdoc. fellow McGill U., Montreal, Quebec, Canada, 1990—94; asst. prof. Chesapeake Biol. Lab., U. Md. Ctr. Environ. Sci., Solomons, Md., 1994—2000, assoc. prof., 2000—06, prof., 2006—. Sci. and statis. com. Mid Atlantic Fishery Mgmt. Coun., Dover, Del., 2001—; recruitment processes workgroup chair Internat. Coun. Exploration Sea, Copenhagen, 2002—; sci. advisor Potomac River Fisheries Commn., Colonial Beach, Va., 2005—; mgmt. and sci. com. Atlantic States Marine Fisheries Commn., Washington, 2005—. Named Outstanding Grad. Educator, MEES Program, U. Md. College Park, 1998, 2008. Mem.: Ecoloigcal Soc. United Kingdom, Am. Fisheries Soc. (assoc. editor 1998—2008). Office: Chesapeake Biological Lab 1 Williams St Solomons MD 20688 Business E-Mail: miller@cbl.umces.edu.

MILLER, THORMUND AUBREY, lawyer; b. Pocatello, Idaho, July 14, 1919; s. Roy Edmund and Lillian (Thordarson) Miller; m. Hannah A. Flansburgh, Feb. 10, 1946 (dec. Jan. 2003); children: Karen Lynette Van Gerpen, Christine Alison Westall; m. Barbara Cornell Singelyn, May 8, 2004. BA, Reed Coll., 1941; LLB, Columbia U., 1948; grad., Advanced Mgmt. Program, Harvard Bus. Sch., 1961. Bar: Calif. 1949, D.C. 1951, U.S. Supreme Ct. 1960. Assoc. McCutchen, Thomas, Matthews, Griffiths & Greene, San Francisco, 1948-50; atty. So. Pacific Transp. Co., Washington, 1950-56, asst. gen. atty., 1956-59, gen. atty., 1959—66, sr. gen. atty. San Francisco, 1966—75, gen. solicitor, 1975—79, gen. commerce counsel, 1979—83, dir., mem. exec. com., 1983—87, v.p., gen. counsel, 1983—89; gen. counsel So. Pacific Comms. Co., San Francisco, 1970—79, dir., 1970—81. Pres. Wood Acres Citizens Assn., Bethesda, Md., 1955-56; exec. com. Holbrook Palmer Recreation Park Found., 1979—, pres., 1982-84; bd. dirs. Atherton Civic Interest League, 1981-2008, pres., 1992-94; mem. Atherton Park and Recreation Commn., 1991-95, Atherton Waste Reduction Commn., 1999-2005, San Mateo Civil Grand Jury, 1997; alumni bd. Reed Coll., 1971-72, trustee, 1987-2002, campaign com., 1995-2000; joint donor Thormund A. Miller/Walter Mintz chair in econ. history; bd. dirs. Assocs. U. Calif. Press, 1994—2006. Lt. USNR, 1942-46. Mem.: ABA, Calif. Bar Assn. Presbyterian. Home: 57 Bay Tree Ln Los Altos CA 94022

MILLER, TIMOTHY ALAN, religion educator; b. Wichita, Kans., Aug. 23, 1944; s. Paul Alfred and Margaret Jean (Thompson) M.; m. Tamara Lea Dutton, Aug. 11, 1982; children: Jesse Dutton Miller, Abraham Dutton Miller. BA, U. Kans., 1966; MDiv, Crozer Theol. Sem., 1968; MA, U. Kans., 1969, PhD, 1973. Lectr. religious studies U. Kans., Lawrence, 1969-88, asst. prof. religious studies, 1988-93, assoc. prof., 1993—98, prof., 1998—; vis. prof. Dartmouth Coll., 1995. Chair Lawrence Unitarian Fellowship, 1989-90. Author: Following in His

Steps, 1987, American Communes 1860-1960, 1990, the Hippies and American Values, 1991, The Quest for Utopia in Twentieth-Century America, 1998, The 60's Communes, 1999; co-author: The Sauna Book, 1977; editor: When Prophets Die, 1991; editor: America's Alternative Religions, 1995; co-editor Am.Studies, 1982-86; contbr. articles to profl. jours.; editor Plumber's Friend, 1981-89. Mem. Communal Studies Assn. (bd. dirs. 1988-92), Am. Acad. Religion (chair new religious movements group, 1983-93), Internat. Communal Studies Assn. (pres., 2001-04). Office: U Kans Dept Religious Studies 103 Smith Hl Lawrence KS 66045-0001 Office Phone: 785-864-7263. Business E-Mail: tkansas@ku.edu.

MILLER, VINCENT PAUL, JR., geography and regional planning educator; b. Swissvale, Pa., May 11, 1932; s. Vincent Paul and May Eleanor Miller; m. Alida Field Ward, July 23, 1960; 1 child, Bradley Cleland. BS, Muskingum Coll., 1954; MS, Pa. State U., 1957; PhD, Mich. State U., 1970. Social sci. asst. Quartermaster R&D Comdt., Natick, Mass., 1957-59; instr. Coll. of Wooster, Ohio, 1959-60; asst. instr. Mich. State U., East Lansing, 1961; assoc. prof. Indiana (Pa.) U., 1962-70, prof., 1970-98, prof. emeritus, 1999—. Author: Project Ebenezer: Modeling Holistic Missions, 1981, Central Place Hierarchy & Access to Services, 1985; editor/author: The Future at the Bicentennial, 1977, Planning Issues in Marginal Areas, 1991, Technology, Landscape, and Arrested Development: Essays on the Geography of Marginality, 1997; asst editor The Pa. Jr. Geographer, 1965-66, editor, 1966-75. Dir. rsch. Ministries in Action, Miami, Fla., 1980—, dir. holistic curriculum devel., 1999—; bd. mem. Birthright, Indiana, United Ministry Indiana U. of Pa., pres. bd. 1997; mem. com. Diaconal Ministries Com., Kiskiminitas Presbytery, chair self-devel. of people com., 2002—; cons. Iona Study Ctr., Ministries in Action, Calvin Coll., Grand Rapids, Mich., 2006; co-founder PIMA (Planning Marginal Areas), 1989 Ctrl. Pl. Rsch. grantee, 1985, Travel grantee U. Presbyn. Ch., 1995. Mem. AAAS, Assn. Am. Geographers (bd. rural devel. splty. group 1984-88, sec. treas. 1984-86, pres. 1986-88), Assn. Pub. Justice, Pa. Geog. Soc. (pres. 1979-80), Soc. for Advancement of Scandinavian Studies, Ctrl. Ind. Model R.R. Club (pres. 2002, Sigma Xi (pres. Ind. chpt. 1977-78), Ctrl. Ind. Model RR Club (sec., 2007-). Avocations: music, writing, photography, yard work, model railroading. Home: 111 View St Indiana PA 15701-1547

MILLER, W. THADDEUS, energy executive; BS, US Merchant Marine Acad.; JD, St. John's Sch. Law. Atty., NYC; v.p. Goldman Sachs & Co., 1994—99; exec. v.p., chief legal officer Orion Power Holdings, Inc., 1999—2002; cons. Tex. Pacific Group, 2002—04; exec. v.p., chief legal officer Tex. Genco LLC, 2004—06; exec. v.p., chief legal officer, sec. Calpine Corp., 2008—. Officer USCG. Office: Calpine Corp Ste 1000 717 Texas Ave Houston TX 77002*

MILLER, WAENARD LIVINGSTON, cardiologist; b. Greenville, SC, Mar. 1, 1947; s. Waenard Livingston and Margaret Evelyn (Burns) M.; m. Sheila McLawhorn, Dec. 20, 1969; children: Waenard Livingston III, Bernyrd Carlysle. BS in Physics, Clemson U., 1969; MS in Nuclear Physics, U. Tenn., 1970; MS in Biology, Wright State U., 1974; MD, Med. U. S.C., 1978; MS in Med. Mgmt., U. Tex., 2000. Diplomate Am. Bd. Internal Medicine, subspecialty of cardiovascular disease. Intern in internal medicine Southwestern Med. Sch., Dallas, 1978-79, resident in internal medicine, 1979-81, fellow in cardiology, 1981-83; pvt. practice cardiology Plano, Tex., 1983—; lab. dir. Cardiac Catheterization HCA Med. Ctr., Plano, 1994; co-founder Legacy Heart Ctr. Trustee Bayler Healthcare Sys., 2004. 1st lt. USAF, 1971-74. Fellow Am. Coll. Cardiology, Am. Coll. Cardiology (councilor Tex. divsn., 2004-05), Am. Heart Assn. Avocations: travel, golf. Office: Legacy Heart Ctr 6601 Preston Rd Plano TX 75024 Office Phone: 469-326-3400.

MILLER, WALTER JAMES, retired literature educator, writer; b. McKee City, NJ, Jan. 16, 1918; s. Walter Theodore and Celestia Anna (Simmons) Miller; m. Mary T. Hume; children: Naomi, Jason, Robin, Jared, Elizabeth. BA, CUNY, 1941; MA, Columbia U., 1952. Instr. English Poly. Inst. Bklyn., 1946—53, asst. prof., 1953—55; asst. prof. English and modern langs. Colo. State U., Ft. Collins, 1955—56; assoc. prof. English NYU, 1958—66, prof. English, 1966—84, prof. emeritus, 1984—. Dir. Summer Writers Conf. Hofstra U., Hempstead, NY, 1972—79, NYU, NYC, 1983—85. Author: Engineers as Writers, 1953, Making an Angel: Poems, 1977, 1001 Ideas for English Papers, 1994, Love's Mainland: New and Selected Poems, 2001, Joseph in the Pit: A Verse Drama, 2002, Essential Vonnegut: Interviews Conducted by Walter Miller, CDI, 2006; author, translator: Annotated Jules Verne, 1995; editor, translator: Verne's 20,000 Leagues Under the Sea, 1993, The Meteor Hunt, 2006; contbg. editor Simon and Schuster, 1969-97. Pub. relations officer US Infantry, 1943—46. Recipient Spl. award, Engrs. Coun. Profl. Devel., 1966, Charles Angoff award, The Lit. Rev., 1983, Gt. Tchr. award, NYU Alumni Assn., 1980, Fisher Second Harvest award, CUNY Alumni Assn., 1997; fellow, Ruttenberg Found., 1999—2006. Home: 686 Rugby Rd Brooklyn NY 11230-1702 Home Phone: 718-859-4371; Office Phone: 212-998-7120. Business E-Mail: wjm2@nyu.edu.

MILLER, WALTER LUTHER, scientist, pediatrician, educator; b. Alexandria, Va., Feb. 21, 1944; s. Luther Samuel and Beryl (Rinderle) M. SB, MIT, 1965; MD, Duke U., 1970. Diplomate Am. Bd. Pediatrics. Intern, then resident Mass. Gen. Hosp., Boston, 1970-72; staff assoc. NIH, Bethesda, Md., 1972-74; sr. resident U. Calif., San Francisco, 1974-75, rsch. fellow, 1975-78, asst. prof. pediatrics, 1978-83, assoc. prof., 1983-87, prof., 1987—2008, dir. Child Health Rsch. Ctr., 1992—2003, faculty biomed. scis. grad. program, 1982—, faculty genetics grad. program, 1998—, dir. pediat. endocrinology tng. program, 1994—, chief divsn. endocrinology, 2000—, assoc. prof. metabolic rsch. unit, 1983-87, prof., 1987—. Bd. scientific counselors Nat. Inst. of Child Health & Human Devel., 2004—09. Editor DNA and Cell Biology Jour., 1983-2006; mem. editl. bds. numerous sci. jours.; contbr. articles to profl. jours., chpts. to books. Del. Dem. Nat. Conv., NYC, 1976. Served with USPHS, 1972-74. Recipient Nat. Rsch. Svc. award NIH, 1975, Clin. Investigator award, 1978, Albion O Bernstein award NY Med. Soc., 1993, Clin. Endocrinology Trust medal Brit. Endocrine Soc., 1993, Henning Andersen prize European Soc. Pediatric Endocrinology, 1993, Samuel Rosenthal Found. prize for excellence in acad. pediatrics, 1999. Fellow: AAAS, Molecular Medicine Soc.; mem.: Androgen Excess Soc. (founding mem., bd. dirs. 2002—05), Am. Soc. Biochem. Molecular Biology, Lawson Wilkins Pediat. Endocrine Soc. (edn. com. 1992—96, coun. 1995—96, corp. adv. bd. 1998—2002, program dirs. com. 2004—), Am. Soc. Clin. Investigation, Am. Soc. Human Genetics, Endocrine Soc. (fin. com. 1999—2002, annual meeting steering com. 2005—07, Edwin B. Astwood lecture award 1988, Clin. Investigator Lectr. award 2006), European Soc. for Paediatric Endocrinology (hon.), Japanese Soc. for Pediat. Endocrinology (hon.), We. Soc. Pediat. Rsch. (Ross Rsch. award 1982), Soc. Pediat. Rsch., Am. Pediat. Soc., Am. Acad. Pediats., Assn. Am. Physicians, Am. Soc. for Microbiology, Theta Delta Chi. Achievements include patents in field; published in over 340 publs. Office: U Calif Med Ctr Dept Pediat Rm 672 S San Francisco CA 94143-0978

MILLER, WALTER NEAL, insurance company consultant; b. NYC, Nov. 26, 1929; s. Morton and Kathryn (Gersten) M.; m. Nancy Louise Clapp, Sept. 11, 1954; children— Scott, Timothy, David, Kathryn Wallace, Amy Tully. BA, Swarthmore Coll., 1951. With N.Y. Life Ins. Co., NYC, 1951-86; sr. v.p., actuary Prudential Ins. Co., Newark, 1986-93; sr. v.p., chief actuary Prudential Preferred Fin. Svcs., Liberty Corner, NJ, 1993-94; pvt. practice cons., 1994—. Author: (with others) Analysis of Actuarial Theory for Variable Life Insurance, 1969; contbr. articles to profl. jours. Mem. Soc. Actuaries (bd. dirs.), Am. Acad. Actuaries (bd. dirs., v.p.), Actuarial Stds. Bd. (chmn.), Estuary Coun. Srs. (pres. bd. dirs.). Home: 48 Eagle Ridge Dr Essex CT 06426-1370 Personal E-mail: walterm746@aol.com.

MILLER, WAYNE CLAYTON, academic administrator; b. Columbus, Ohio, Feb. 23, 1949; s. Eugene H. and Beulah M. (Stoll) M. BA, Owosso Coll., 1971; MA, Mich. State U., 1979. Mgr. adminstrv. svcs. John Wesley Coll., Owosso, Mich., 1972-75, instr., social sci., 1975-78, dir., career planning, 1978-79; acad. advisor Spring Arbor (Mich.) Coll., 1979-81, instr., history, 1979-81; from acad. counselor to instr., asst. v.p. acad., asst. provost, chief enrollment mgmt. officer Franklin U., Columbus, 1981—85, instr. film appreciation and leadership philosophies, 1985—, asst. v.p. acad., 2004—08, chief enrollment mgmt. officer, 2004—08, asst. provost, 2008—. Advisor Franklin U. Student Senate, Columbus, 1982-84; inst. creative activities program Ohio State U., Columbus, 1990-98; discussion panelist Educable TV-25 Worl d Film Classics series, 1990-2002; juror social issues category The Columbus Internat. Film and Video Festival, 1994, chair edn. category, 1995—; mem. spkrs. bur. Franklin U. Editor: (newsletter) New Directions, 1985-91, Student Success Handbook, 2005; assoc. editor: Movies on Media Handbook. Co-host Columbus Mus. Art Film Series, 1996; scholar, rschr. Westerville Civic Symphony, 1997; judge Miss East-Ctrl. Ohio Scholarship program, 2000, Bus. and Profl. Women of Ohio State Speakoff Competition, 2001, Miss Mansfield Scholarship Program, 2001, Miss Ctrl. Ohio Scholarship Program, 2004, Miss Greater Dayton Scholarship Program, 2004, Teen Miss Ohio Program, 2004, Miss Greater Cleve. Scholarship Program, 2006, Miss North Coast Scholarship Program, 2007; mem. nat. nominating com. Outstanding Young Women am. and Young Men Am., 1997; exec. sec., 2008; bd. trustees Film Coun. Gtr. Columbus, chmn., 2005—08, exec. sec., 2008—. Named one of Outstanding Young Men in Am., 1982, 85; recipient Commitment to Excellence medallion Pres. Franklin U., 2005 Mem.: Ctr. Academic Integrity, Future Bus. Leaders Am. (competition judge state conf. 1997—), Ohio Coll. Pers. Assn., Am. Film Inst., Nat. Acad. Advising Assn. (Cert. of Merit award 1986, Outstanding Instnl. Advising award 1994), Nat. Film Soc. (life), Nat. Euchre Players Assn. (dir. adminstrn.), KIwanis Club Columbus, Phi Beta Lambda. Avocations: film studies, history, Sherlock Holmes memorabilia, charitable activites, playing cards. Home: 2729 Brittany Oaks Blvd Hilliard OH 43026-8575 Office: Franklin U 201 S Grant Ave Columbus OH 43215-5399

MILLER, WEBB C., computer scientist, biology professor; PhD, U. Wash., Seattle. Faculty mem. U. Ariz., U. Calif., Santa Barbara; permanent staff mem. IBM T. J. Watson Rsch. Ctr.; computer sci. and engring. prof. Pa. State U., 1985—, biology prof. Contbr. scientific papers; editor-in-chief: Collected Algorithms of the ACM, mem. editl. bd.: Genome Rsch., Jour. Computational Biology, Bioinformatics. Named one of The World's Most Influential People, TIME mag., 2009; grantee, NIH, 1989—. Achievements include research in algorithms and software for molecular biology. Office: Pa State Univ Dept Computer Sci & Engring 208 Mueller Lab University Park PA 16823 Business E-Mail: webb@cse.psu.edu.*

MILLER, WENDY A., elementary school educator; b. NC; BA in Spl. Edn., Univ. NC; MA in Curriculum/Adminstrn., E. Carolina Univ. Cert. Nat. Bd. Tchg. Standards 2002. Tchr., 1987—, James W. Smith Elem. Sch., Cove City, NC, 1998—. Featured in (TV spl.) Heroes in the Classroom, ABC, 2003, spl. guest (Wayne Brady Show) Salute to America's Best Teachers, 2003. Recipient Disney Am. Tchr. of Yr. Honoree, 2003; named Craven County Schs.' Tchr. of Yr./Tchr. Ambassador, 2004, SE Region Tchr. of Yr., 2005, NC Tchr. of Yr., 2006. Mem.: Internat.Reading Assn., Coun. for Exceptional Children, NC Assn. Educators. Office: James W Smith Elem Sch 150 Koonce Town Rd Cove City NC 28523 Business E-Mail: wendy.miller@craven.k12.nc.us.

MILLER, WILBUR RANDOLPH, academic administrator; b. Elsberry, Mo., Nov. 12, 1932; s. Charles Clifton and Pauline Jean (Dryden) M. Student, SE Mo. U., 1951-53; BEd, U. Mo., 1954, MEd, 1955, EdD, 1960. Cert. secondary tchr., Mo. Tchr. indsl. arts Hazelwood Sch. Dist., St. Louis, 1955-56, U. Lab. Sch., Columbia, Mo., 1956-60; indsl. tchr. educator Purdue U., West Lafayette, Ind., 1960-63; asst. prof. U. Mo., Columbia, 1963-67, assoc. prof. and chmn. dept. coll. edn., 1967-76, prof. and assoc. dean coll. edn., 1976-86, dean coll. edn., 1986-91, prof., dean emeritus, 1992; cons. Rep. of Turkey, 1993, 94; assoc. v.p. devel. Auburn U., Ala., 1996—2007; ret., 2007. Chmn. adv. coun. Fed. Rsch. Ctr. in Vocat. Edn., Ohio State U., Columbus, 1981-84; internat. edn. cons. 1992—; edn. adv. bd. DeVry Inc., Oakwood Terrace, Ill., 1986—; mem. pvt. post-sec. tech. sch. accreditation commn. Accrediting Commn. Career Schs. and Colls. Tech., 1994-98. Author: Teaching Children Through Construction Activities, 1985, Instructors and Their Jobs, 1998, 4th edit., 2009, The Golf Primer, 1991, Handbook for College Teaching, 2d edit., 2003; editor: (series) Basic Industrial Arts, 1978; contbr. more than 40 articles to profl. jours. Pres., bd. dirs. Lenoir Inc., Columbia, 1977-84; mem. Woodhaven Sch. Bd., Columbia, 1982-83. With USNR, 1955-63. Recipient U. Mo. Faculty/Alumni award, 1985. Mem. Nat. Assn. Indsl. Tchr. Educators (pres., officer 1965-74), Am. Indsl. Arts Assn. (v.p. 1980), Mo. Vocat. Assn. (pres. 1974-75), Mo. Assn. Colls. for Tchr. Edn. (pres. 1987-90), Am. Vocat. Assn. (Outstanding Svc. award 1979), U. Mo. Faculty Club (officer 1977-82), Kiwanis. Mem. Christian Ch. (Disciples Of Christ). Avocations: golf, travel, home maintenance. Office: PO Box 2683 Auburn AL 36831-2683 Office Phone: 334-332-7125.

MILLER, WILLIAM CHARLES, theological educator, anglican priest; b. Mpls., Oct. 26, 1947; s. Robert Charles and Cleithra Mae (Johnson) M.; m. Brenda Kathleen Barnes, July 24, 1969; children: Amy Renee, Jared Charles. BA, Ind. Wesleyan U., 1968; MLS, Kent State U., 1974, PhD, 1983; postgrad., U. Kans., 1984; MA in Religious Studies, Ctrl. Bapt. Theol. Sem., 1988; MBA, MidAm. Nazarene U., 1997; STM, Nashotah House, 2001. Ordained to ministry Ch. of Nazarene, 1986, ordained deacon Episcopal Ch., 2006, ordained priest Episcopal Ch., 2007. Libr. technician Kent State U., 1972—74; catalog libr. Mt. Vernon Nazarene Coll., Ohio, 1974—76, libr. catalog and acquisitions, 1976—78; dir. libr. svcs., prof. theol. bibliography Nazarene Theol. Sem., Kansas City, Mo., 1978—2005, dean adminstrn., 1996—98, 1999—2005; dir. accreditation Assn. Theol. Schs., Pitts., 2005—. Adj. rsch. assoc. U. Kans., 1984-85; adj. prof. MidAm. Nazarene U., Olathe, Kans., 1994-2000, Ind. Wesleyan U., 2005, Nazarene Theol. Sem., 2005-07; bd. dirs. Small Libr. Computing Inc.; pres. Mo. Libr. Network Corp., St. Louis, Mo., 1998-2001. Author: Holiness Works: A Bibliography, 1986; editor TUG Newsletter, 1984-87, bd. dirs., 1985-88; editor Jour. Religious and Theol. Info., 1990-98. With U.S. Army, 1968-72. Mem. Evangelical Theol. Soc., Assn. Study Higher Edn., Am. Theol. Libr. Assn. (bd. dirs. 1985-88), Wesleyan Theol. Soc., Ch. Eng. Record Soc., Beta Phi Mu. Office: Assn Theol Schs 10 Summit Park Dr Pittsburgh PA 15275-1103 Home: 727 Lincoln Highlands Dr Coraopolis PA 15108 Office Phone: 412-788-6505. Business E-Mail: miller@ats.edu.

MILLER, WILLIAM CHARLES, lawyer; b. Jacksonville, Fla., Aug. 6, 1937; s. Charles and Mary Elizabeth (Kiger) M.; m. Hadmut Gisela Larsen, June 10, 1961; children: Monica Lee, Charles Andreas. BA, Washington and Lee U., 1958, LLB, 1961; LLM, NYU, 1963; postgrad., Harvard U., 1978. Bar: Fla. 1961, Calif. 1984, Ind. 1987, US Supreme Ct. 1968. Counsel to electrochem., elastomers and internat. depts. E.I. duPont de Nemours & Co., Wilmington, Del., 1963-66; counsel S. Am. ops. Bristol-Myers Co., NYC, 1967-69; internat. counsel Xerox Corp., Stamford, Conn., 1969-79, assoc. gen. counsel, 1979-80; v.p., gen. counsel, sec. Max Factor & Co., Hollywood, Calif., 1981-85, Boehringer Mannheim Corp. (now Roche Diagnostics), Indpls., 1985-92; v.p., gen. counsel Collagen Corp., Palo Alto, Calif., 1992-95, GenProbe Inc., San Diego, 1995-96, Safeskin Corp., San Diego, 1996-98; exec. v.p. Lipomatrix Inc., Neuchatel, Switzerland, 1998-99; gen. counsel Turbostar Comm. Corp., 2000—02, exec. v.p., gen. counsel, 2002—03; exec. v.p., dir., gen. counsel Aesthetic and Reconstructive Techs., Inc., 2002—. Bd. dirs. Southwestern Legal Found., 1975-85. Fulbright scholar, 1959-60; Ford Found. fellow, 1961-62; Hague Acad. fellow, 1963; German Govt. grantee, 1962-63; Kappa Sigma scholar, 1959. Mem. Internat. Bar Assn., ABA, Calif. Bar Assn., Fla. Bar Assn., Ind. Bar Assn., Masons, Elks, Phi Beta Kappa, Phi Eta Sigma, Delta Theta Phi. Republican. Mem. Christian Ch. Home: 4521 Randag Dr North Fort Myers FL 33903-4731 Personal E-mail: wcmesq@comcast.net.

MILLER, WILLIAM CHARLES, architect, educator; b. San Francisco, May 11, 1945; s. Francis Leland and Ethel Lorene (Britt) M.; m. Beverly Jean McConnell, Dec. 22, 1968; children: Britt A., David A. BArch, U. Oreg., 1968; MArch, U. Ill., 1970. Cert. arch. Nat. Coun. Archtl. Registration Bds., Ariz., Kans., Utah. Asst. prof. Coll. Architecture U. Ariz., Tucson, 1970—77; assoc. prof. dept. architecture Kans. State U., Manhattan, 1977-86, prof., 1986-92, head dept., 1990-92; prof. Coll. of Architecture and Planning U. Utah, Salt Lake City, 1992—, dean, 1992—2002; architect various firms. Guest lectr. in field; presenter numerous profl. socs. and orgns.; dir. west ctrl. region Assn. Collegiate Schs. Architecture, 1988-91, chair theme paper sessions ann. meeting, San Francisco, 1990, chair regional paper sessions ann. meeting, Washington, 1991, co-chair adminstrv. conf., Milw., 1995; bd. dirs. Nat. Archtl. Accrediting Bd., 1996-99; mem. Utah Architects Lic. Bd., 2000-08; chair edn. com. NCARB, 2005-08; vis. disting. prof. U. Ill., Urbana Champain, 2003; chair nomenclature commn., NAAB, 2003. Author: Alvar Aalto: An Annotated Bibliography, 1984; co-editor: The Architecture of the In-Between, 1990, Architecture: Back to Life, 1991; contbr. over 60 articles to profl. jours., chpts. to books. Bd. dirs. Assist, Inc., 1992-2002, Artspace, Inc., 1997-2002, Contemporary Arts Group, 1992-96, Salt Lake City Art Design Bd., 1995-2003. Recipient Disting. Prof. award Assn. Collegiate Schs. Architecture, 2004, Svc. awards Nat. Coun. Archtl. Registration Bds., Nat. Archtl. Accrediting Bd. Fellow AIA (ALA Utah Bronze medal award, 2007, pres-elect Flint Hills, treas. Utah, exec. com., treas., exec. com. Western Mountain region, elected coll. of fellows 1997, EP/N adv. com. 2007—09); mem. Am.-Scandinavian Found., Soc. for Advancement Scandinavian Studies, Tau Sigma Delta, NCARB(chair com. edu.) Office: U Utah Coll Architecture & Planning Salt Lake City UT 84112 Office Phone: 801-581-8254. Business E-Mail: miller@arch.utah.edu.

MILLER, WILLIAM FREDERICK, research and development company executive, educator, financial consultant; b. Vincennes, Ind., Nov. 19, 1925; s. William and Elsie M. (Everts) M.; m. Patty J. Smith, June 19, 1949; 1 son, Rodney Wayne. Student, Vincennes U., 1946-47; BS, Purdue U., 1949, MS, 1951, PhD, 1956; DSc (hon.), 1972. Mem. staff Argonne Nat. Lab., 1955-64, assoc. physicist, 1956-59, dir. applied math. div., 1959-64; prof. computer sci. Stanford U., Palo Alto, Calif., 1965-97, Herbert Hoover prof. pub. and pvt. mgmt. emeritus, 1997—, assoc. provost for computing, 1968-70, v.p. for rsch., 1970-71, v.p., provost, 1971-78; mem. Stanford Assocs., 1972—; pres emeritus., CEO SRI Internat., Menlo Park, Calif., 1979-90; chmn. bd., CEO SRI Devel. Co., Menlo Park, David Sarnoff Rsch. Ctr., Inc., Princeton, NJ, 1987—90. Chmn. emeritus bd. dirs. Borland Software, Sentius Corp.; founder, chmn. Nanostellar, Inc.; professorial lectr. applied math. U. Chgo., 1962-64; vis. prof. math. Purdue U., 1962-63; vis. scholar Ctr. for Advanced Study in Behavioral Scis., 1976; mem. adv. coun. BHP Internat., 1990-97; computer sci. and engring bd. NAS, 1968-71; mem. Nat. Sci. Bd., 1982-88; corp. com. computers in edn. Brown UU., 1971-79; mem. policy bd. EDUCOM Planning Coun. on Computing in Edn., 1974-79, chmn., 1974-76; mem. ednl. adv. bd. Guggenheim Meml. Found., 1976-80; com. postdoctoral and doctoral rsch. staff NRC, 1977-80, computer sci. and telecom.; dir. Fund Am., 1977-91, Fireman's Fund Ins., 1977-91, Wells Fargo Bank and Co., 1996-97, Varian Assocs. Inc., 1973-96, hon. dean Wiiliam F. Miller Sch. Mgmt. Tech. Konkuk U. Seoul, Republic of Korea. Mem. editl. bd. Pattern Recognition Jour, 1968-72, Jour. Computational Physics, 1970-74. Served to 2d lt. F.A. AUS, 1943-46. Recipient Frederic B. Whitman award United Way Bay Area, 1982, Sarnoff Founders medal, 1997, David Packard Civic Entrepreneurship Team award, 1998, Robert K. Jaedicke Silver Apple award Stanford U. Bus. Sch. Alumni, 1998, The Dongbaeg medal Order of Civil Merit, The Rep. of Korea, 2000, The Okawa prize, The Okawa Found. for Info. and Telecoms., 2000, Most Mentor award Internat. Angel Investors, 2002; named to Silicon Valley Engring. Hall of Fame, 2001, Jr. Achievement Bus. Hall of Fame, 2002. Fellow IEEE (life), Am. Acad. Arts and Scis., AAAS; mem. Soc. Indsl. and Applied Math., Assn. Computing Machinery, Nat. Acad. Engring., Sigma Xi, Tau Beta Pi (Eminent Engr. 1989). Office: Stanford U Grad Sch Bus Stanford CA 94305

MILLER, WILLIAM GREEN, former ambassador; b. NYC, Aug. 15, 1931; m. Suzanne Lisle; 2 children. BA, MA, Oxford U., UK; postgrad., Harvard U. Tutor Winthrop House Harvard U., 1956-59; with Fgn. Svc., 1959; vice consul, polit. officer Isfahan, Iran, 1959-62; polit. officer Tehran, Iran, 1962-64; line officer, exec. secretariat Dept. of State, 1965-66; mem. Sr. Interdepartmental Group, 1966-67; spl. asst. fgn. affairs and def. Senator John Sherman Cooper, 1967-73; staff dir. Senate Select Com. Emergency Powers, 1973-75, Senate Select Com. to Study Govtl. Ops. with Respect to Intelligence Communities, 1975-76, Senate Select Com. Intelligence, 1976-81; assoc. dean, adj. prof. internat. politics Fletcher Sch. Law and Diplomacy, 1981-83, rsch. assoc., 1983-85; faculty assoc. Harvard Ctr. Middle Eastern Studies, 1983-86; pres. Am. Com. U.S.- Soviet Rels., 1986-92; U.S. amb. to Ukraine, 1993-98. Cons. D.H. Sawyer and Assocs., Ltd., N.Y.C., 1985; bd. dirs. Internat. Found., pres. 1986-92; pres. Com. Am.- Russian Rels., cons. Catherine T. MacArthur Found., 1992-93. Contbr. articles to profl. jours. Bd. mem. UN Assn., 2002—; co-chmn. bd. Myiv-Mohyla U. Found., 2002—; bd. dirs. The Andrei Sakharov Found., 1998—, Inst. Soc. Action and Renewal in Eurasia, 1998—; bd. mem. US - Ukraine Found., 2002—. Rsch. fellow Harvard Ctr. Sci. and Internat. Affairs, 1984-86,

John F. Kennedy Sch. of Govt. fellow Harvard U., 1986. Fellow Rsch. Inst. of Politics; mem. Nat. Acad. Pub. Diplomacy, Nat. Acad. Pub. Adminstrn., Internat. Inst. Strategic Studies, Coun. Fgn. Rels., Children of the 21st Century, Middle East Inst., Soc. Iranian Studies, Search For Common Ground. Office: Woodrow Wilson Internat Ctr Scholars 1 Woodrow Wilson Plaza 1300 Pennsylvania Ave NW Washington DC 20004-3002 Office Phone: 202-691-4000. Business E-Mail: wmiller@igc.org.

MILLER, WILLIAM HUGHES, theoretical chemist, educator; b. Kosciusko, Miss., Mar. 16, 1941; s. Weldon Howard and Jewel Irene (Hughes) M.; m. Margaret Ann Westbrook, June 4, 1966; children: Alison Leslie, Emily Sinclaire. BS in Chemistry, Ga. Inst. Tech., 1963; AM, Harvard U., 1964, PhD in Chemical Physics, 1967. Jr. fellow Harvard U. Soc. Fellows, 1967-69; NATO postdoctoral fellow Freiburg U., Germany, 1967-68; asst. prof. chemistry U. Calif., Berkeley, 1969-72, assoc. prof., 1972-74, prof., 1974—, dept. chmn., 1989-93, chancellor's prof., 1998—2001, Kenneth S. Pitzer disting. prof., 1999—. Fellow Churchill Coll., Cambridge (Eng.) U., 1975-76; hon. prof. Shandong U., People's Republic of China, 1994. Alfred P. Sloan fellow, 1970-72; Camille and Henry Dreyfus fellow, 1973-78; Guggenheim fellow, 1975-76, Christensen fellow St. Catherine's Coll., Oxford, 1993; recipient Alexander von Humboldt-Stiftung U.S. Sr. Scientist award, 1981-82, Ernest Orlando Lawrence Meml. award, 1985, Hirschfelder prize in theoretical chemistry, U. Wis., 1996, Alumni Achievement award Ga. Inst. Tech., 1997, Spiers medal Faraday divsn. Royal Soc. Chemistry, London, 1998. Fellow AAAS, Am. Acad. Arts and Scis., Am. Phys. Soc. (Irving Langmuir in Chem. Physics award 1990); mem. NAS, Am. Chem. Soc. (Theoretical Chemistry award 1994, Ira Remsen award 1997, Peter Debye award 2003), Internat. Acad. Quantum Molecular Sci. (Ann. prize 1974), Herschbach award in chem. dynamics 2007, Welsh award in chemistry 2007). Office: U Calif Dept Chemistry Berkeley CA 94720-0001

MILLER, WILLIAM IAN, law educator; b. 1946; BA, U. Wis., 1969, M of Philosophy, 1973, PhD, 1975; JD, Yale U., 1980. Bar: Wis. 1980. Assoc. prof. U. Houston, 1981-85; prof. U. Mich. Law Sch., Ann Arbor, 1984—, Thomas G. Long Prof. Law. Vis. assoc. prof. U. Mich., An Arbor, 1984-85; vis. prof. Yale U., fall 1988. Author: Bloodtaking and Peacemaking: Feud, Law, and Society in Saga Iceland, 1990, Humiliation, 1993, The Anatomy of Disgust, 1997, The Mystery of Courage, 2000, Faking It, 2003, An Eye for an Eye, 2006. Mem. Law and Soc. Assn., Am. Soc. Legal History, Am. Hist. Assn. Office: U Mich Law Sch 411 Hutchins Hall 625 S State St Ann Arbor MI 48109-1215 Office Phone: 734-763-9014. Office Fax: 734-763-9375. E-mail: wimiller@umich.edu.

MILLER, WILLIAM IRWIN, finance company executive; b. Columbus, Ind., Apr. 30, 1956; s. Joseph Irwin and Xenia Ruth (Simons) M.; m. Lynne Marie Maguire, Oct. 29, 1983; children: Katherine Maguire, Laura Marie, Emily Elizabeth. BA, Yale U., 1978; MBA, Stanford U., 1981. Sect. mgr. Cummins Engine Co., Inc., Charleston, SC, 1978-79; assoc. Warburg Pincus Capital Corp., NYC, 1981-83; pres. Irwin Mgmt. Co., Inc., Columbus, 1984-90, also bd. dirs.; chmn. Irwin Fin. Corp., Columbus, 1990—. Chmn. Irwin Mgmt. Co. and Tipton Lakes Co., Columbus, 1984—; bd. dirs. Cummins Inc., Irwin-Sweeney-Miller Found., Columbus, New Perspective Fund, LA, New World Fund, LA. Trustee The Taft Sch., Watertown, Conn., 1979-2006, Christian Theol. Sem., Indpls., 1988-94, Europacific Growth Fund, L.A., 1992—, Yale U., New Haven, 2005—; bd. dirs. Cummins Found., Columbus, Ind., 1989—, Irwin Fin. Found., Columbus, 1991—, Tennant Co., 1993-2005, The Heritage Fund of Bartholomew County, Columbus, 1998-2006, John D. and Catherine T. MacArthur Found., 2005—; mem. investment com. Yale U., New Haven, 1995-99, 2000—; mem. Ctrl. Ind. Corp. Partnership, Indpls., 1999—, Nat. Bldg. Mus., 2001-06. Fellow: Am. Acad. Arts and Sciences. Office: Irwin Fin Corp 500 Washington St PO Box 929 Columbus IN 47202-0929

MILLER, WILLIAM NAPIER CRIPPS, lawyer; b. Long Branch, NJ, June 7, 1930; adopted s. Julia (Erwin) M.; m. Carolyn Anderson, Jan. 19, 1951 (div. 1963); children: Bruce Douglass, Jennifer Erwin; m. Hannelore Steinbeck, Dec. 4, 1970 AA, Coll. Marin, 1949; student, U. Calif.-Berkeley, 1949-51, JD, 1955. Bar: N.Y., Calif. 1956, U.S. Supreme Ct. 1983. Assoc. Mudge, Stern, Baldwin & Todd, NYC, 1955-58, Pillsbury, Madison & Sutro, San Francisco, 1959-65; ptnr. Pillsbury, Winthrop Shaw Pittman LLP, San Francisco, 1966—; staff NYU Law Sch., 1957-58; ct. adv. com. Calif. State Assembly Judiciary Com., 1979-80. Author: Long Pig, 2002. Bd. dirs. Laguna Honda Hosp., San Francisco, 1966—; bd. visitors U. Calif.-Hastings Law Sch. Served with USAF, 1951-52. Served USAF, 1950—52. Recipient Bur. Nat. Affairs award U. Calif.-Hastings, 1955; recipient Thurston Soc. award, 1953. Fellow Am. Coll. Trial Lawyers; mem. ABA, San Francisco Bar Assn., Order of Coif, St. Francis Yacht Club. Home: 16 George Ln Sausalito CA 94965-1890 Office: Pillsbury Winthrop Shaw Pittman LLP PO Box 7880 San Francisco CA 94120-7880 Home Phone: 415-332-6665; Office Phone: 415-983-1464. Business E-Mail: william.miller@pillsburylaw.com.

MILLER, WILLIAM RICHEY, JR., lawyer; b. Oklahoma City, Apr. 4, 1947; s. William Richey and Edna Rosalind (Nielsen) M.; m. Susan Hammond, Aug. 2, 1970; children: Brooke, Karen. BA, Pomona Coll., Claremont, Calif., 1969; MA, Claremont Grad. Sch., 1972; JD, Lewis and Clark Coll., 1975. Bar: Oreg. 1975, U.S. Dist. Ct. Oreg. 1976, U.S. Ct. Appeals (9th cir.) 1976. Staff atty. Oreg. Ct. Appeals, Salem, 1975-76; with firm Griffith, Bittner, Abbott & Roberts, Portland, Oreg., 1976-83; ptnr. Davis Wright Termaine, Portland, 1983—. Adj. prof. Lewis and Clark Law Sch., 1975-78. Bd. dirs. Portland Civic Theatre, 1988-91, Am. Lung Assn. Oreg., Portland, 1985-88, Oreg. Bus. Com. for the Arts, Portland, 1991-93. Mem. Oreg. State Bar (sect. chair 1990-91), Comml. Fin. Assn., Oreg. Bankers Assn., Lewis and Clark Alumni Assn. (bd. dirs. 1989-92). Presbyterian. Home: 843 Lakeshore Rd Lake Oswego OR 97034-3704 Office: Davis Wright Tremaine 1300 SW 5th Ave Ste 2300 Portland OR 97201-5682 Office Phone: 503-778-5304.

MILLER, ZELL BRYAN, former senator, governor; b. Young Harris, Ga., Feb. 24, 1932; s. Stephen Grady and Birdie (Bryan) M.; m. Shirley Carver, Jan. 14, 1954; children: Murphy Carver, Matthew Stephen. Student, Young Harris Coll., 1951; AB in History, U. Ga., 1957, MA in History, 1958. Dir. Ga. Bd. Probation, 1965-66; dep. dir. Ga. Dept. Corrections, 1967-68; exec. sec. to gov. Ga., 1968-71; mem. State Bd. Pardons and Paroles, Atlanta, 1973-75; lt. gov. State of Ga., 1975-90, gov., 1990-98; prof. polit. sci. and history U. Ga., 1999; U.S. senator from Ga., 2000—05; sr. advisor McKenna Long & Aldridge LLP, Atlanta, 2005—. Prof. Young Harris Coll., 1959-64, Emory U., Young Harris Coll., U. Ga.; bd. dirs. various corps., including Overseas Pvt. Investment Corp. (OPIC), Ga. Power, Gray Comms., Ezgov.com, Post Properties, Kollmann USA; keynote speaker Democratic Nat. Convention, NYC, 1992, Republican Nat. Convention, NYC, 2004; retired Jan. 2005; commr., Am. Battle Monuments Commn., 2005-, part-time commentator, Fox News Channel, 2005-. Author: The Mountains Within Me, 1985, Great Georgians, 1983, They Heard Georgia Singing, 1996, Corps Values: Everything You Need to Know I Learned in the Marines, 1996, Listen to this Voice: Selected Speeches of Governor Zell Miller, 1998, A National Party No More: The Conscience of a Conservative Democrat, 2003, Deficit of Decency, 2005. Mem. Ga. Senate, 1960-64; mayor Young Harris, 1959; exec. dir. Democratic Com. Ga., 1971-72; pres. Coun. State Govts., 1991; vice chmn. So. Gov.'s Assn., 1991; bd. dirs. Towns County Hosp. Authority. Served with USMC, 1953-56. Mem. Ga. Sch. Food Services Assn. (life), Ga. Peace Officers Assn. (life), Gridiron Soc. U. Ga., Blue Key, Lions Club. Democrat. Meth. Office: McKenna Long & Aldridge LLP 303 Peachtree St NE Ste 5300 Atlanta GA 30308 also: Am Battle Monuments Commn 2300 Clarendon Blvd Ste 500 Arlington VA 22201

MILLER, ZOYA DICKINS, civic worker, consultant; b. Washington, July 15, 1923; d. Randolph and Zoya Pavlovna (Klementinovska) Dickins; m. Hilliard Eve Miller, Jr., Dec. 6, 1943; children: Jeffrey Arnot, Hilliard Eve III. Grad., Stuart Sch. Costume Design, Washington, 1942; student, Cochran Galleries of Fine Arts, 1942, Sophie Newcomb Coll., 1944, New Eng. Conservatory Music, 1946, Colo. Coll., 1965; grad., Internat. Sch. Reading, 1969; student, Cochran Galleries of Fine Arts, 1942. Lic. pvt. pilot. Instr. Stuart Summer Sch. Costume Design, Washington, 1942; fashion coord. Julius Garfinckel, Washington, 1942-43; fashion coord., cons. Mademoiselle mag., 1942-44; star TV show Cowbelle Kitchen, 1957-58, Flair for Living, 1958-59; model mags. and comml. films, also nat. comml. recs., 1956-80; dir. rsch. devel. Webb-Waring Inst. Cancer, Aging and Antioxidant Rsch., Denver, 1973—2006, devel. cons., 2006—. Contbr. articles, lectrs. on health care sys. and fund raising. Mem. exec. com., bd. dirs. El Paso County chpt. Am. Lung Assn. Colo., 1965—84, bd. dirs., 1965—87, chmn. radio and TV coun., 1963—70, mem. med. affairs com., 1965—70, pres., 1965—66, procurer found. funds, 1965—70; developer nat. radio ednl. prodns. for internat. use Am. Lung Assn., 1963—70, coord. statewide pulmonary screening programs Colo., other states, 1965—72; chmn. benefit fund raising El Paso County Cancer Soc., 1963; co-founder, coord. Colorado Springs Debutante Ball, 1967—; coord. Nat. Gov.'s Comprehensive Health Planning Coun., 1967—74, chmn., 1971—72, Colo. Chronic Care Com., 1969—73, chmn. fund raising, 1970—72, chmn. spl. com. conl. studies on nat. health bills, 1971—73; mem. Colo.-Wyo. Regional Med. Program Adv. Coun., 1969—73, Colo. Med. Found. Consumers Adv. Coun., 1972—78; mem. decorative arts com. Colorado Springs Fine Arts Ctr., 1972—75; founder, state coord. Nov. Noel Pediat. Benefit Am. Lung Assn., 1973—87; founder, chmn. bd. dirs. Newborn Hope, Inc., 1987—; mem. adv. bd. Wagon Wheel Girl Scouts, 1991—94; mem. cmty. adv. coun. Beth-El Nursing Sch., 1998—; chmn. Colo. Festival World Theatre Gala, 2005; gala chmn. Colorado Festival World Theatre, 2005; maj. donor devel. dir. Meml. Health Sys., Colorado Springs, 2006—; bd. dirs. Episcopal Columbarium Assn., 2001, The Family Attachment Ctr., Inc., Meml. Hosp. Found., Colo. Springs, Colo., 2004; hon. bd. mem. KCME 88.7 FM, Colorado Springs, Colo., 2004; gala chmn. Colo. Festival of World Theatre, 2005; maj. donor devel. dir. Meml. Health Sys., Colo. Springs, 2006—. Zoya Dickins Miller Vol. of Yr. award established Am. Lung Assn. of Colo., 1979; recipient James J. Waring award Colo. Conf. on Respiratory Disease Workers, 1963, Nat. Pub. Rels. award Am. Lung Assn., 1979, Gold Double Bar Cross award, 1980, 83, Jefferson award Am. Inst. Pub. Svc., 1991, Thousand Points of Light award The White House, 1992, Recognition award So. Colo. Women's C. of C., 1994, Silver Spur Cmty. award Pikes Peak Range Riders, 1994, Silver Bell award Assistance League Colorado Springs, 1996, Svc. to Mankind award Centennial Sertoma Club, 1997, Help Can't Wait award Pikes Peak chpt. ARC, 1997, Cmty. Weaver award The Independent News, 1997, Apgar award Colo. March of Dimes, 1998; named Humanitarian of Yr., Am. Lung Assn. of Colo., 1987, El Pomar Found. award for Excellence, Russell Tutt Leadership award, 2004. Mem.: Nat. Soc. Fund Raising Execs., Denver Round Table for Planned Giving, Colo. Assn. Fund Raisers, Nat. Soc. Colonial Dames, The Family Attachment Ctr., Nat. Cowbell Assn. (El Paso county pres. 1954, TV chmn., chmn. nat. Father of Yr. contest Colo. 1956—57), Broadmoor Garden Club, Garden of the Gods Club, Cheyenne Mountain Country Club. Home: PMB 110 1837 S Nevada Ave Colorado Springs CO 80905-2516 E-mail: hope4455@adelphia.net.

MILLER-LANE, BARBARA See LANE, BARBARA

MILLER-LERMAN, LINDSEY, state supreme court justice; b. LA, July 30, 1947; BA, Wellesley Coll., Mass., 1968; JD, Columbia U., NYC, 1973; LHD (hon.), Coll. St. Mary, Omaha, 1993. Bar: NY 1974, US Dist. Ct. (so. dist.) NY 1974, US Ct. Appeals (2d cir.) 1974, Nebr. 1976, US Dist. Ct. (ea. dist.) NY 1975, US Dist. Ct. Nebr. 1976, US Ct. Appeals (8th cir.) 1979, US Supreme Ct. 1982, US Ct. Appeals (6th cir.) 1984, US Ct. Appeals (10th cir.) 1987. Law clk. U.S. Dist. Ct., NYC, 1973-75; from assoc. to ptnr. Kutak Rock, Omaha, 1975-92; judge Nebr. Ct. Appeals, Lincoln, 1992-98, chief judge, 1996-98; justice Nebr. Supreme Ct., 1998—. Contbr. articles to profl. jours. Office: Nebr Supreme Ct State Capitol Rm 2222 Lincoln NE 68509 Office Phone: 402-471-3734. Business E-Mail: lmiller-lerman@nsc.state.ne.us.*

MILLER-MEEKS, MARIANNETTE JANE, ophthalmologist; b. Herlong, Calif., Sept. 6, 1955; d. Fred and Annette Miller; m. Curt Miller-Meeks; children: Jonathan, Taylor. BS in Nursing, Tex. Christian U.; MS in Edn., U. So. Calif.; MD, U. Tex. Faculty mem. U. Mich.; prof. Dept. Ophthalmology U. Iowa; pvt. practice Ottumwa, Iowa. Lt. col. USAR. Recipient Charles Phelps Award, 1995. Mem.: Iowa Med. Soc. (pres. 2006), Am. Bd. Ophthalmology (examiner), Am. Acad. Ophthalmology (AAO) (councilor for Iowa), Wapello County Medical Soc. (former pres.), Alpha Omega Alpha. Republican. Catholic. Office: 11674 90th St Ottumwa IA 52501 Office Phone: 641-226-0967. Office Fax: 641-683-7551. E-mail: mjmillermeeks@awsllc.net.*

MILLER-SYDNEY, AUDREY YVONNE, music educator; d. Joseph Horace Miller and Edith Mae Gibson-Miller. BA, Va. State U., Petersburg, 1960; MusM, Manhattan Sch. Music, NYC, 1966. Cert. tchr. NY. Choral and music instr. Irving N. Taylor Jr. HS, Danville, Va., 1960—62, NYC Pub. Schs., NYC, 1963—65; vocal and instrumental tchr. Union Settlement Music Sch., NYC, 1963—67; music tchr. Joan of Arc Jr. HS, NYC, 1967—68; project coord. Salem Crescent Learning Ctr., NYC, 1979—80; chmn. music, magnet coord. Dr. Alfred M. Franko Magnet Sch., Mt. Vernon, NY, 1978—97; adj. prof. music appreciation Coll. New Rochelle, NY, 2002—. Home: Apt 4B 730 Riverside Dr New York NY 10031-2444 E-mail: amsydney02@verizon.net.

MILLETT, PETER J., orthopedist; b. Reading, Pa., Dec. 31, 1967; s. James P. and Anne H. Millett; m. Sarah M. Malloy; children: Rosemary, Barbara, Sarah, James. BS, U. Scranton, Pa., 1990; MSc, U. Cambridge, Eng., 1995; MD, Dartmouth Med. Sch., Hanover, 1995. Cert. MD Colo., Mass., NY. Resident Hosp. Spl. Surgery, NYC, 2000; asst. prof. Harvard Med. Sch., Boston, 2001—05; ptnr. Steadman Hawkins Clinic, Vail, Colo., 2005—08; sci. adv. bd. Steadman Hawkins Rsch. Found., Vail, 2006—08, bd. mem., 2008—. Cons. Arthrex, Naples, 2003—; pres. ALM Rsch. LLC, Edwards, 2004—08; sci. adv. bd. Cool Systems, San Fransisco, Calif., 2006—, IVY Capital, NYC, 2007—. Contbr. articles to med. papers (ISAKOS award, 2005, AADS Sci. award, 2005). Recipient Zimmer award, ADA, 1999, Craige Davis award, JOSPT, 2005, Lewis Clark Wagner award, NYC, 1999—2000. Fellow: Am. Acad. Orthop. Surgeons; mem.: Am. Orthop. Soc. Sports Medicine, Am. Shoulder and Elbow Surgeons. Avocations: fly fishing, skiing. Office: Steadman Hawkins Clinic 181 W Meadow Dr Vail CO 81657 Office Phone: 970-476-1100.

MILLETTE, LEROY F., JR., state supreme court justice; b. Pa. m. M. Elizabeth O'Brien Millette; children: Lauren Elizabeth, LeRoy F. III. Degree in Economics, Coll. William and Mary, JD, 1974. Assoc. prof. Northern Va. Cmty. Coll., 1976—; asst. commonwealth atty. Prince William County; sole practitioner Compton, Latimer, Compton & Compton; judge Va. 31st Jud. Cir., 1993—98, chief judge, 1998—2000, 2006; judge Va. Ct. of Appeals, 2007—09, Va. Supreme Ct., 2009—. Office: Va Supreme Ct PO Box 1315 Richmond VA 23219-1315 Office Phone: 804-786-2251.*

MILLGATE, MICHAEL (HENRY), retired literature educator; b. Southampton, Eng., July 19, 1929; arrived in Can., 1964; s. Stanley and Marjorie Louisa Millgate; m. Jane Barr, Feb. 27, 1960. BA, Cambridge U., 1952, MA, 1956; postgrad., U. Mich., Ann Arbor, 1956-57; PhD, U. Leeds, 1960. Tutor Workers' Ednl. Assn., Eng., 1953-56; lectr. English lit. U. Leeds, 1958-64; prof., chmn. dept. English York U., Ont., Can., 1964-67; prof. English U. Toronto, 67-94, univ. prof., 87-94, univ. prof. emeritus, 1994—. Carpenter lectr. Ohio Wesleyan U., 1978; vis. scholar Meiji U., 1985. Author: William Faulkner, 1961, American Social Fiction, 1964, The Achievement of William Faulkner, 1966, Thomas Hardy: His Career as a Novelist, 1971, Thomas Hardy: A Biography, 1982, Testamentary Acts: Browning, Tennyson, James, Hardy, 1992, Faulkner's Place, 1997, Thomas Hardy: A Biography Revisited, 2004; editor: Tennyson: Selected Poems, 1963, Thomas Hardy: The Life and Work of Thomas Hardy, 1985, William Faulkner Manuscripts, 20 (4 vols.), 21 (2 vols.), 22 (4 vols.), 23 (2 vols.), 1986, New Essays on Light in August, 1987, Thomas Hardy: Selected Letters, 1990, Letters of Emma and Florence Hardy, 1996, Thomas Hardy's Public Voice, 2001; co-editor: Transatlantic Dialogue, 1966, Lion in the Garden, 1968, The Collected Letters of Thomas Hardy, Vol. I, 1978, Vol. II, 1980, Vol. III, 1982, Vol. IV, 1984, Vol. V, 1985, Vol. VI, 1987, Vol. VII, 1988, Thomas Hardy's Studies, Specimens, Etc. Notebook, 1994, Thomas Hardy's Poetical Matter Notebook, 2009. Mem. ednl. adv. bd. John Guggenheim Meml. Found., 1994—2005. Can. Coun. leave fellow, 1968-69, S.W. Brooks fellow U. Queensland, 1971; Killam sr. rsch. scholar, 1974-75; John Simon Guggenheim Meml. fellow, 1977-78, Connaught sr. fellow, 1979-80; Social Sci. and Humanities Rsch. Coun. Can. leave fellow, 1981-82, grantee, 1977—2006; Can. Coun. grantee, 1973-77; Killam rsch. fellow, 1986-88. Fellow Royal Soc. Lit., Royal Soc. Can. (Pierre Chauveau medal 1999); mem. MLA (adv. com. Ctr. for Edit. Am. Authors 1971-74, com. on scholarly edits. 1985-89), Victorian Studies Assn. Ont. (pres. 1970-72), Thomas Hardy Soc. (v.p. 1973—), Tennyson Soc. Home: 1 Balmoral Ave Apt 809 Toronto ON Canada M4V 3B9 E-mail: michael.millgate@utoronto.ca.

MILLIAN, JOHN C., lawyer; b. Jan. 30, 1958; BA in Econ., Univ. Calif., Berkeley, 1980; JD, Yale Univ., 1983. Bar: Wash. 1984, Calif. 1987, DC 1988. Law clk. Judge Gerhard A Gesell US Dist. Ct., Washington, 1983—84; ptnr. litig. dept. Gibson Dunn & Crutcher LLP, Washington, 1991—, former ptnr.-in-charge DC office. Pro bono atty. Wesley Theol. Sem.; bd. dir. Wesley Sem. Found.; former mem. exec. com. Gibson Dunn & Crutcher. Mem.: ABA, Coun. for Ct. Excellence (bd. dir.). Office: Gibson Dunn & Crutcher LLP 1050 Connecticut Ave NW Washington DC 20036 Office Phone: 202-955-8213. Business E-Mail: jmillian@gibsondunn.com.

MILLICHAP, JOSEPH GORDON, neurologist, educator; b. Wellington, Eng., Dec. 18, 1918; came to U.S., 1956, naturalized, 1965; s. Joseph P. and Alice (Flello) M.; m. Mary Irene Fortey, Feb. 25, 1946 (dec. Oct. 1969); children: Martin Gordon, Paul Anthony; m. Nancy Melanie Kluczynski, Nov. 7, 1970 (dec. Apr. 1995); children: Gordon Thomas, John Joseph. MB Surgery honors, St. Bartholomew's Med. Coll., U. London, 1946, MD Internal Medicine, 1951, diploma child health, 1948. Diplomate Am. Bd. Pediat., Am. Bd. Neurology and Child Neurology, Am. Bd. Electroencephalography. Intern, resident St. Bartholomew's Hosp., 1946—49, Hosp. Sick Children, London, 1951—53, Mass. Gen. Hosp., Boston, 1958—60; pediat. neurologist NIH, 1955—56; USPHS fellow neurology Mass. Gen. Hosp., Boston, 1958—60; cons. pediat. neurology Mayo Clinic, 1960—63; pediat. neurologist Children's Meml. Hosp., Northwestern Med. Ctr., Chgo., 1963—; prof. neurology and pediat. Northwestern U. Med. Sch., 1963—. Cons. surgeon gen. USPHS; mem. med. adv. bds. Ill. Epilepsy League, Muscular Dystrophy Found., Cerebral Palsy Found., 1963—; vis. prof. Gt. Ormond St. Hosp., U. London, 1986-87 Author: Febrile Convulsions, 1967, Pediatric Neurology, 1967, Learning Disabilities, 1974, The Hyperactive Child with MBD, 1975, Nutrition, Diet and Behavior, 1985, Dyslexia, 1986, Progress in Pediatric Neurology, 1991, Vol. II, 1994, Vol. III, 1997, Environmental Poisons in Our Food, 1993, A Guide to Drinking Water, Hazards and Health Risks, 1995, Attention Deficit Hyperactivity and Learning Disorders, 1998, (with G.T. Millichap) The School in a Garden, 2000; editor Jour. Pediatric Neurology Briefs; contbr. articles to profl. jours., chpts. to books Chmn. rsch. com. med. adv. bd. Epilepsy Found., 1965—. Served with RAF, 1949-51 Named New Citizen of Year in Met. Chgo., 1965; recipient Americanism Medal DAR, 1972, Brennemann award Chgo. Pediat. Soc., 1998; USPHS rsch. grantee, 1957 Fellow Royal Coll. Physicians; mem. AMA, Am. Neurol. Assn., Am. Pediat. Soc., Am. Soc. Pediat. Rsch., Am. Acad. Neurology, Am. Soc. Pharmacology and Exptl. Therapeautics, Soc. Exptl. Biology and Medicine, Am. Bd. Psychiatry and Neurology (asst. examiner 1961—) Episcopalian. Office: Children's Meml Hosp Box 51 2300 N Childrens Plz Chicago IL 60614-3394 Office Phone: 773-880-4352.

MILLIGAN, CYNTHIA HARDIN, dean, lawyer; BA, U. Kans., 1967; JD, George Washington U., 1970. Bar: D.C. 1970, Nebr. 1977. Assoc. Arent, Fox, Kintner, Plotkin & Kahn, Washington, 1970-77; ptnr. Rembolt, Ludtke, Milligan & Berger, Lincoln, Nebr., 1977-87; dir. Nebr. Dept. Banking and Fin., Lincoln, 1987-91; pres. CMA, Lincoln, 1991-98; dean U. Nebr. Coll. Bus. Adminstrn., Lincoln, 1998—2009, dean emeritus, 2009—. Bd. dirs. Wells Fargo & Co., San Francisco, Gallup Orgn., Washington, DC, Calvert Funds, Bethesda, Md. Trustee W.K. Kellogg Found., Battle Creek, Mich. Fellow Nebr. Bar Found.; mem. Nebr. Bar Assn.

MILLIGAN, JOHN DRANE, retired historian, educator; b. NYC, Oct. 11, 1924; s. Carl Glover and Hazel Gray (Drane) M.; m. Joyce Mary Jervis, Nov. 16, 1946; children: Jacqueline M., Paula J., Mary M., Elizabeth Y. BA, U. Mich., 1952, MA, 1953, PhD, 1961. Tchg. asst. U. Mich., 1951-52, tchg. fellow, 1954-56; from asst. prof. to prof. history SUNY, Buffalo, 1962-2000, dir. grad. programs in history, 1963-68, 94-95, dir. undergrad. programs in history, 1979-86, acting dept. chmn., summers, 1977, 78-80, 88, prof. emeritus, 2000. Vis. prof. McMaster U., Hamilton, Ont., Can., 1964, 69-70 Author: Gunboats Down the Mississippi, 1965, From the Fresh-Water Navy, 1861-1864, 1970; also chpts. in books, articles in jours., encys. Mem. Ann Arbor chpt. NAACP, exec. bd., 1956-61; mem. ACLU, exec. bd., 1959-61; mem. campaign coms. for various candidates for local and nat. office, 1960-76; mem. Buffalo NAACP, Buffalo Housing Opportunities Made Equal, Citizens Council on Human Relations, Physicians for Social Responsibility, Common Cause, Amnesty Internat.; faculty chmn. United Fund dr., 1977; active Foster Parents Plan, 1955-70; adoptive parent Internat. Social Services; founder charitable trust for minority coll. scholarships. Served with USAAF, 1943-46, USAFR, 1946-56. James B. Angell scholar U. Mich.; grantee Rsch. Found. SUNY, US Naval Inst.; Citation of Civil War Round Table; Moncado Award of Am. Mil. Inst. Mem.: Soc. Civil War Historians, Afro-Am. Hist. Soc., Buffalo and Erie County Hist. Soc., So. Hist. Assn., Assn. Am. Historians, Am. Hist. Assn., SUNY Buffalo Founders' Soc., Buffalo Coun. for Responsibility in Fgn. Policy, SUNY Buffalo Pres.'s Assocs., Civil War Round Table, Silver Wings Assn., Cambria Flying Soc., Niagara Soaring Club, Aircraft Owners and Pilots Assn., Soaring Soc. Am., Exptl. Aircraft Assn., Phi Alpha Theta, Phi Kappa Phi, Tau Sigma Delta. Home: 21 Allenhurst Rd Buffalo NY 14214-1201 Home Phone: 716-836-5534. *If an individual cannot influence for the better the course of humankind, one can sometimes influence for the better the life of another individual.*

MILLIGAN, JOHN F., information technology executive; PhD in Biochemistry, U. Ill. Rsch. scientist Gilead Sciences, Inc., 1990—96, dir. project mgmt., project team leader, Gilead Hoffmann-La Roche Tamiflu collaboration, 1996—98, corp. devel., 1998—2000, v.p. corp. devel., 2000—02, sr. v.p., 2002—03, prin. acctg. officer, CFO, 2002—08, exec. v.p., 2003—08, COO, 2007—, pres., 2008—. Named Bay Area CFO of Yr., 2006, Top Biotech. Industry CFO in the US, Instl. Investor mag., 2006—08; Am. Cancer Soc. postdoctoral fellow, U. Calif. San Francisco. Office: Gilead Sciences Inc 333 Lakeside Dr Foster City CA 94404 Office Phone: 650-574-3000. Office Fax: 650-578-9264.*

MILLIGAN, ROBERT S., business association administrator; m. Cynthia Milligan; 9 children. BA in Vocational Agr. & Agrl. Economics, U. Nebr.; JD, George Washington U. Dep. asst. sec for policy devel. US C. of C., midwest regional vice. chmn., mem. exec. com., chmn. bd. dirs.; chmn. M.I. Industries, Lincoln, Nebr. Mem. White House Office of Trade Negotiations; internat. pres. CBMC. Mem. World Pres. Org., CEO Org. Mem.: Nat. Assn. Mfrs. (pres. coun.), Boy Scouts of America (nat. adv. coun.). Office: US Chamber of Commerce 1615 H St NW Washington DC 20062-2000 Office Phone: 202-659-6000.*

MILLIGAN, VICTOR, consulting engineer; b. Belfast, No. Ireland, Nov. 11, 1929; arrived in Can., 1956; s. Albert and Margaret (Walker) M.; m. Mary Ann Pelikan, July 20, 1955 (dec. 1988); children: Jeffrey, Michael; m. Audrey Morrow, Oct. 9, 1990 (dec. Oct 2003); m. Donna Tigert, Sept. 30, 2006. BS, Queen's U., No. Ireland, 1951, MS, 1952, DSc (hon.), 1993; D Engring. (hon.), Waterloo U., Ont., Can., 1990. Registered profl. engr. Ont., Alta., Nfld. Asst. engr. James Williamson & Ptnrs., Glasgow, Scotland, 1952-54; rsch. fellow Purdue U., Lafayette, Ind., 1954-55; tech. officer Imperial Chem. Industries Ltd., Cheshire, England, 1955-56; from dist. to asst. chief engr. Geocon, Ltd., Toronto, Ont., Canada, 1956-60; prin. Golder Assocs., Toronto, 1960-74, pres., CEO, chmn., 1974-84, sr. prin., chmn., cons., 1984-94. Mem. faculty engring. sci. adv. com. U. Western Ont., 1973-76; adj. prof. dept. geol. engring. U. Toronto, 1980-83; pres. Consulting Engrs. Ont., 1982-83; chmn. assoc. com. on geotechnical rsch. NRC, 1984-89. Co-author: Stability in Open Pit Mining, 1971, Geotechnical Practice in Open Pit Mining, 1972; founding editor Can. Geotechnical Jour., 1963-68; contbr. over 60 sci. papers. King George VI Meml. Rsch. fellow 1954-55; recipient Engring. Excellence medal Assn. Profl. Engrs. Ont., 1988, Beaubien award Assn. Consulting Engrs. Canada Outstanding Excellence, 1997. Fellow Can. Acad. Engring., ASCE, Instn. Civil Engrs. (hon.), Geol. Soc. Can., Engring. Inst. Can. (Julian C. Smith medal 1991, K.Y. Lo medal 1998, Sir John Kennedy medal, 2005), Royal Acad. Engring., FICE (hon.); mem. Can. Geotech. Soc. (R.F. Legget award 1973), Internat. Soc. Soil Mechanics and Geotech. Engring.

MILLIKAN, DIANE LINDA, insurance company executive; b. Evanston, Ill., Oct. 14, 1954; d. Allen Frederick and Ruth Alice (Powell) Millikan; m. Charles Jackson Heckman II, Aug. 31, 1980; children: Heather Millikan Heckman, Laurel Millikan Heckman. BA, Oberlin Coll., Ohio, 1976; MBA, Harvard U., Boston, 1978. CPA, Ill. Cons., staff acct. Price Waterhouse, Seattle, 1978-80; sr. cons. Compass Cons. Group, Bellevue, Wash., 1980-81; dir. HMO divsn., asst. dir. fin., contr. Virginia Mason Med. Ctr., Seattle, 1981-86; sr. mgr. Ernst & Young/Ernst & Whinney, Chgo. and Balt., 1986-90; v.p. fin. Michael Reese Health Plan, Chgo., 1990-91; sr. mgr. Ernst & Young, Chgo., 1991-92; sr. v.p. fin. Celtic Group Inc., Chgo., 1992—2004; tchr. HS math. Frederick Douglass Acad., Chgo., 2005—06, Collins HS, 2005—06. Adv. bd. Tiber Group, Chgo., 1993-95. Contbr. articles to profl. jours. Bd. dirs. Children's Home Soc. of Wash. and/or Gallery, Seattle, 1980; 1976 class pres. 25th reunion Oberlin Alumni Coun., 1996—. Margaret E. Smith fellow Harvard Bus. Sch., 1976-77. Mem. Fin. Execs. Inst., Healthcare Fin. Mgmt. Assn., Chgo. Fin. Exchange Avocations: aerobic dance, water gardening, choreography, theater, cross country skiing. Personal E-mail: d_millikan@comcast.net.

MILLIKAN, KEITH WILLIAM, surgeon, educator; b. Chicago, Ill., Jan. 15, 1958; s. John William and Joanne Elizabeth Millikan; m. Janet Sue Deselich, Mar. 20, 1993; children: Samantha Elizabeth, Keith William, John Patrick, Michael Robert, Kyle John, Kameron Joseph; m. Michelle Krzeboit, May 19, 1984 (div. Feb. 3, 1993). BA in Chemistry, U. Chgo., Ill., 1980; MD, Rush Med. Coll., Chgo., Ill., 1984. Diplomate Am. Bd. Surgery, 1990. Asst. prof. Rush U., Chgo., 1989—96, dir. surg. undergrad. edn., 1989—2003, assoc. prof., 1996—2003, prof. surgery, 2003—, assoc. dean surgery, 2004—. Office: Univ Surgeons 1725 W Harrison Ste 810 Chicago IL 60612 Office Fax: 312-563-2080. Business E-Mail: keith_millikan@rush.edu.

MILLIKAN, LARRY EDWARD, dermatologist; b. Sterling, Ill., May 12, 1936; s. Daniel Franklin and Harriet Adeline (Parmenter) M.; m. Jeanine Dorothy Johnson, Aug. 27, 1960; children: Marshall, Rebecca. BA, Monmouth Coll., 1958; MD, U. Mo., 1962. Intern Great Lakes Naval Hosp., Ill., 1962-63; housestaff in tng. U. Mich., Ann Arbor, 1967-69, chief resident, 1969-70; asst. prof. dermatology U. Mo., Columbia, 1970-74, assoc. prof., 1974-81; chmn. dept. dermatology Tulane U., New Orleans, 1981—, chair/prof. emeritus, 2006—. Cons. physician Charity Hosp., New Orleans, Tulane U. Hosp., New Orleans, Riley Hosp., Anderson Hosp., Rush Hosp., all Meridian, Miss.; mem. bd. trustees Sulzberger Inst. for Dermatological Edn., 1995-99; chmn. cont. med. edn. com. La. State Med. Soc., 1994-97. Assoc. editor Internat. Jour. Dermatology, 1980-99, Clinics in Dermatology, 1999—; mem. editl. bd. Current Concepts in Skin Disorders, Am. Jour. Med. Scis.; mem. editl. bd. Clinics in Dermatology, 1985—, assoc. editor, 1999—; contbr. articles to med. jours. Bd. dirs. Women's Dermatol. Assn., 1994-99. With USN, 1960-67. Recipient Andres Bello awrd Govt. of Venezuela, 1989, citation of merit Sch. Medicine, U. Mo., 1993, Faculty Alumnus award U. Mo., 1997; named Disting. Alumnus, Monmouth Coll., 1990; Nat. Cancer Inst. grantee, 1976-84. Fellow ACP; mem. AAAS, AMA, Am. Acad. Dermatology (bd. dirs. 1986-90), Am. Dermatol. Assn., Am. Dermatol. Soc. for Allergy and Immunology (pres., bd. dirs.), Soc. for Investigative Dermatology (past pres. South sect.), So. Med. Assn. (vice chmn. dermatology sect. 1984, chmn. 1994), Coll. Physicians Phila., Assn. Profs. Dermatology (bd. dirs. 1984-86), Orleans Parish Med. Soc., La. Med. Soc., Pan Am. Med. Assn., Internat. Soc. Dermatology (dep. sec. gen. 1989-99), Mo. Allergy Assn. (past pres.), Am. Coll. Cryosurgery, Assn. Acad. Dermatol. Surgeons, Internat. Soc. Dermatol. Surgery, Internat. Acad. Cosmetic Dermatology (sec. gen. 1996-), Dermatol. Found. Leaders Soc. (state chmn. 1993-97). Office: Tulane Univ Sch Medicine Dept of Dermatology 1430 Tulane Ave TB36 New Orleans LA 70112-2699

MILLIKEN, GARRETT WILSON, psychology professor; s. Robert Lee and Bessie Jane Milliken; m. Susan Gail Bennett, Apr. 15, 1995; children: Joel Garrett, Max Robert. BA, Ohio U., Athens, 1984; MS, Memphis State U., Tenn., 1987; PhD, U. Memphis, Tenn., 1991. Cert. town planner Mcpl. Assn. SC, 2006. Postdoc. rsch. fellow U. Tex. Med. Sch., Houston, 1991—94, Baylor Coll. Medicine, Houston, 1994—95; vis. asst. prof. Auburn U., Ala., 1995—97; asst. prof. Coll. Charleston, SC, 1997—2002, dir., animal care & use program, 1998—, assoc. prof., 2002—. Contbr. articles to profl. sci. jours. Chair planning and zoning commn., Town of James Island, SC, 2006—08. Office: Coll Charleston Dept Psychology 66 George St Charleston SC 29424 Office Phone: 843-953-5443. Office Fax: 843-953-7151. Business E-Mail: millikeng@cofc.edu.

MILLIKEN, JOHN GORDON, research economist; b. Denver, May 12, 1927; s. William Boyd and Margaret Irene (Marsh) M.; m. Marie Violet Machell, June 13, 1953 (dec. 2004); children: Karen Marie, Douglas Gordon, David Tait, Anne Alain. BS, Yale U., 1949, BEng, 1950; MS, U. Colo., 1966, PhD, 1969. Registered profl. engr., Colo. Engr. U.S. Bur. Reclamation, Denver, 1950-55; asst. to plant mgr. Stanley Aviation Corp., Denver, 1955-56; prin. mgmt. engr., dept. mgr. Martin-Marietta Aerospace Divsn., Denver, 1956-64; mgmt. engr. Safeway Stores, Inc., Denver, 1964-66; sr. rsch. economist, prof., assoc. div. head U. Denver Rsch. Inst., 1966-86; pres. Univ. Senate, 1980-81; prin. Milliken Chapman Rsch. Group, Inc., Littleton, Colo., 1986-88, Milliken Rsch. Group, Inc., Littleton, 1988—. Vis. fellow sci. policy rsch. unit U. Sussex, Eng., 1975-76; cons. mgmt. engr. Author: Aerospace Management Techniques, 1971, Federal Incentives for Innovation, 1974, Recycling Municipal Wastewater, 1977, Water and Energy in Colorado's Future, 1981, Metropolitan Water Management, 1981, Technological Innovation and Economic Vitality, 1983, Water Management in the Denver, Colorado Urban Area, 1988, Benefits and Costs of Oxygenated Fuels in Colorado, 1990, Water Transfer Alternatives Study, 1994, Colorado Springs Water Resources Plan Alternative Assessment Study, 1995, Colorado Springs Utilities Wastewater Infrastructure Alternatives Study, 1998; contbr. articles to profl. jours. Bd. dirs. S.E. Englewood Water Dist., 1963—, South Englewood San. Dist., 1965—; bd. dirs. South Suburban Pk. and Recreation Dist., 1971-96, chmn., 1990-92; v.p. South Suburban Land and Facilities Corp., 2001—; chmn. Dem. Com. of Arapahoe County, 1969-71, 5th Congl. Dist. Colo., 1972-73, 74-75; mem. exec. com. Colo. Faculty Adv. Coun., 1981-85; mem. Garrison Diversion Unit Commn., 1984; trustee Colo. Local Govt. Liquid Asset Trust, 1986-2005, chmn., 1991-93; bd. dirs. Colo. Spl. Dist. Assn. Property and Liability Pool, 1989-2006, pres. 1997-98. With M.C., U.S. Army, 1945-46. Decorated WWII Vietnam medal; recipient Adlai E. Stevenson Meml. award, 1981, cert. of Appreciation for svc. to Nation, U.S. Sec. Interior, 1984, hon. title "Amicus Universitatis," U. Denver, 1994, Disting. Svc. award Spl. Dist. Assn. Colo., 1995; Milliken Park named in his honor for svcs. to Littleton/Centennial Cmty., 1996. Mem. Acad. Mgmt., Nat. Assn. Bus. Economists, Yale Sci. and Engring. Assn., Am. Water Works Assn., Sigma Xi, Tau Beta Pi, Beta Gamma Sigma, Sigma Iota Epsilon. Congregationalist. Home and Office: Po Box 200850 Denver CO 80220-0850 Personal E-mail: jgordonmil@aol.com.

MILLIKEN, MARY SUE, chef, television personality, writer; Former mem. staff Le Perroquet, Chgo., Restaurant d'Olympe, Paris; formerly chef, co-owner City Cafe, LA; chef, co-owner CITY, LA, 1985—94, Border Grill, LA, 1985—91, Santa Monica, 1990—, Las Vegas, 1999—, Ciudad, LA, 1998—. Co-host (TV series) Too Hot Tamales, 1995—, Tamales' World Tour, (radio show) Good Food; co-author: City Cuisine, 1989, Mesa Mexicana, 1994, Cantina, 1996, Cooking with Too Hot Tamales, 1997, Mexican Cooking for Dummies; guest appearances (TV series) Oprah Winfrey Show, Maury Povich, Today Show, Sabrina the Teenage Witch, featured in USA Today, People Mag., Entertainment Weekly. Active Scleroderma Rsch. Found. Named Chef of Yr., Calif. Restaurant Writers, 1993. Mem.: Chef's Collaborative 2000, Women Chefs and Restaurateurs. Office: Border Grill Santa Monica 445 S Figueroa St Ste 2950 Los Angeles CA 90071-1634

MILLIKEN, ROGER, textile and chemical company executive; b. NYC, Oct. 24, 1915; s. Gerrish and Agnes (Gayley); m. Justine V. R. Hooper, June 5, 1948 (dec.); children: Justine, Nancy, Roger, David, Weston. AB, Yale U., New Haven, Conn., 1937; LLD (hon.), Wofford Coll., Spartanburg, SC, Rose-Hulman Inst. Tech., Terre Haute, Ind., Phila. Coll. Textiles and Sci., Brenau U., Gainsville, Ga., The Citadel, Charleston, SC; D. Textile Industry (hon.), Clemson U., SC; DHL (hon.), Converse Coll., Spartanburg; D. Bus. Adminstrn. (hon.), U. SC, Spartanburg; LLD (hon.), LaGrange Coll., Ga., Furman U., Greenville, SC; HHD (hon.), Presbyn. Coll., Clinton, SC; DSc, NC State U., 2007. Bd. dirs. Milliken & Co. (formerly Deering Milliken), Spartanburg, SC, 1941—, pres., 1947-83, chmn., CEO, 1983—2005, chmn., 2006—. Chmn. bd. Inst. Textile Tech., 1948—97, chmn. emeritus, 1997—; bd. dirs. SC Textile Mfrs. Assn. Chmn. Greenville-Spartanburg Airport Commn.; trustee Wofford Coll., SC. Recipient Neville Holcombe Disting. Citizenship Award, Spartanburg Area C. of C., 1985, Lifetime Achievement award, No. Textile Assn., 1999, Buck Mickel Leadership award, Greenville C. of C., 2006; named Businessman of Yr., SC C. of C., 1981, Citizen of the Carolinas, NC C. of C., 1991, Leader of the Century, Textile World Mag., 1999; named to SC Bus. Hall of Fame, 1985, SC Hall of Fame, 1998, Nat. Bus. Hall of Fame, 2000. Mem.: AIA (hon.), Am. Soc. Landscape Architects (hon.), Garden Club Am. (mem.-at-large), Yeamans Hall, Augusta Nat. Golf Club, Links, Union League. Office: Milliken & Co PO Box 3167 Spartanburg SC 29304

MILLIKIN, MARSHA, finance educator; d. Francis X. (Stepfather) and Doris Marcoux; children: Kevin Scott, Eric Allan, Christine Shannon Weatherall. BS, U. Tex.-Tyler, 1994; MA, Tex. A&M-Commerce, 2006. Prof. Saginaw Valley State U., U. Ctr., Mich., 2005—. Achievements include research in rhetoric of lynching. Office: Saginaw Valley State Univ 7400 Bay Rd University Center MI 48710

MILLIKIN, MICHAEL P., lawyer, automotive executive; b. Battle Creek, Mich., Aug. 18, 1948; BS, Mich. State U., East Lansing, 1970; JD, Wash. U. Sch. Law, 1973. Law clk., Judge Vincent J. Brennan Mich. Ct. Appeals, 1973—75; asst. US atty. US Attorney's Office, Detroit, 1975—77; joined legal staff holding various positions Gen. Motors Corp., 1977—81, mem. overseas legal matters practice area, 1981—87, head, in-house litig. practice area, 1987—97, v.p., gen. counsel, GM Internat. Ops., GM Europe Zurich, Switzerland, 1997—2000, coord. legal services, GM global ops. Detroit, 2000—05, assoc. gen. counsel, 2005—. Mem. strategy bd. GM Internat. Ops., GM Europe, 1997—2000; supr. bd. mem. Adam Opel GmbH, 1998—; bd. dirs. GM Daewoo Auto and Tech. Co., 2002—. Mem.: Order of the Coif. Office: Gen Motors Corp PO Box 33170 Detroit MI 48232-5170*

MILLIMET, ERWIN, lawyer; b. NYC, Oct. 7, 1925; s. Maurice and Henrietta (Cohen) Millimet; children: Robert, James, Rachel, Sarah. BA magna cum laude, Amherst Coll., 1948; LLB cum laude, Harvard U., 1951. Bar: NY 1952. Formerly sr. ptnr., chmn. exec. com. Stroock & Stroock & Lavan, NYC; ret., 1991. Mem. faculty Grad. Sch. Mgmt., U. Mass. Mem. bd. visitors U. San Diego Law Sch.; mem. Five Coll. LIR (learning in retirement), Northhampton, Mass.; active Nat. Support Group for Africa; founder Citizens for Am., Washington, 1984; mem. Rep. Presdl. Task Force, 1948. Fellow, Amherst Coll., Boston Globe. Mem. NY State Bar Assn., Assn. of Bar of City of NY, Fed. Bar Assn., Rep. Club (NYC and Washington), Phi Beta Kappa. E-mail: emill@gis.net.

MILLIN, LAURA JEANNE, museum director; b. Elgin, Ill., June 11, 1954; d. Douglas Joseph and Patricia Ruth (Feragen) M. BA in Interdisciplinary Studies, The Evergreen State Coll., 1978. Dir. On The Boards, Seattle, 1979; art dir. City Fair Metrocenter YMCA, Seattle, 1980; dir. Ctr. on Contemporary Art, Seattle, 1981; co-owner Art in Form Bookstore, Seattle, 1981-89; co-dir. 3d internat festical of films by women dirs. Seattle Art Mus. & 911 Comtemporary Arts, 1988; auction coord. Allied Arts of Seattle, 1989; exec. dir. Missoula Mus. of Arts, Mont., 1990—. Dir. Visual AIDS Missoula Mus. of the Arts, 1989; curator Radio COCA, Ctr. on Contemporary Art, Seattle, 1986, co-curator, 1981, 83; lectr. in field. Co-editor: Another (ind. feminist newspaper), Seattle, 1989, editor: (exhibition catalog) James Turrell: Four Light Installations, 1981. Bd. dirs. Internat. Festival of Films by Women Dirs., Seattle, 1987, 89, Nine One One Comtemporary Arts Ctr., Seattle, 1981-87, bd. chmn. 1981-85; bd. advisors REFLEX (art mag.), Seattle, 1988-89, Ctr. on Contemporary Art, Seattle, 1983-86; state vis. Mont. Arts. Coun., Missoula, 1991, NEA, Mpls., 1988, Chgo., 1987; panelist Mont. Arts Coun., Helena, 1990; cons. Seattle Arts Commn., 1989, juror, 1985. Home: 1721 S 9th St W Missoula MT 59801-3432 Office: Missoula Art Mus 335 N Pattee St Missoula MT 59802-4520 Office Phone: 406-728-0447.

MILLIRON, NATHAN JOSEPH, lawyer; b. DuBois, Pa., Jan. 16, 1979; s. Joseph Ellsworth and Jill McFadden Milliron. BA, Seton Hall U., South Orange, NJ, 2001; JD, U. Houston, 2004. Bar: Tex. 2004, US Dist. Ct. (so dist.) Tex. 2005. Atty. Fahl & Takeuchi, P.C., Houston, 2004—05, Alonso, Cersonsky & Garcia, P.C., Houston, 2005. Mem.: ABA, Houston Bar Assn. R-Consevative. Methodist. Home: 1111 Post Oak Blvd Apt 432 Houston TX 77056-3118 Office Fax: 713-840-0038. Personal E-mail: nathan.milliron@sbcglobal.net. E-mail: nmilliron@law-acg.com.

MILLIS, ROBERT LOWELL, astronomer, science observatory director; b. Martinsville, Ill., Sept. 12, 1941; m. Julia Drean, 1965; children: David, Daniel. BA, Ea. Ill. U., 1963; PhD in Astronomy, U. Wis., 1968. Staff astronomer Lowell Obs., Flagstaff, Ariz., 1967—86, assoc. dir., 1986—90, acting dir., 1989—90, dir., 1990—. Bd. dir. Mus. of No. Ariz., United Way of No. Ariz. Mem. Am. Astron. Soc., Internat. Astronomy Union, Divsn. Planetary Sci. (sec.-treas. 1985-88, chmn. 1994-95). Achievements include discovery of the Rings of Uranus (with J.L. Elliot); research in planetary satellites and ring systems; the occultation studies of solar system objects; comet and Kuiper belt objects. Office: Lowell Observatory 1400 W Mars Hill Rd Flagstaff AZ 86001-4499 Office Phone: 928-774-3358. Business E-Mail: rim@lowell.edu.

MILLISOR, KENNETH RAY, lawyer; b. Belle Center, Ohio, Jan. 31, 1937; s. Darrel R. and Clara Sue (Miller) M.; m. Annette M. Seifert Ross, June 7, 1985. BA, Ohio Wesleyan U., 1959; JD, Ohio State U., 1960. Bar: Ohio 1960, US Dist. Ct. (no. dist.) Ohio, 1965, US Ct. Appeals (6th cir.) 1965, US Ct. Appeals (DC cir.) 1975, US Supreme Ct. 1970. Ptnr. Poetzel & Andress, Akron, Ohio, 1960-74, Millisor & Nobil, Akron and Cleve., 1975—. Past v.p. Akron Area coun. Boy Scouts Am.; active United Way. Mem. ABA, Ohio Bar Assn., Cleve. Bar Assn., Order of Coif, Shoreby Club (pres. 2000-03). Democrat. Home: 864 Beach Rd Lakewood OH 44107 Office: Millisor & Nobil Co 9150 S Hills Blvd Ste 300 Cleveland OH 44147-3599 Home Phone: 216-226-4868; Office Phone: 440-838-8800. E-mail: KMillisor@millisor.com.

MILLMAN, RICHARD GEORGE, architect, educator; b. St. Johns, Mich., Feb. 12, 1925; s. Harold Fildew and Elizabeth Hill (Van Deusen) M.; m. Mary Louise Manley, June 17, 1950; childen: John Richard, Ruth Barbara. BArch, U. Mich., 1951, MArch, 1962. Registered arch., Mich., Ohio, Ala. Job capt. Smith Hinchman & Grylls, Detroit, 1951-52; designer assoc. Eliot Robinson, AIA, Birmingham, Mich., 1952-55; designer Eero Saarinen Assocs., Bloomfield Hills, Mich., 1955-56; assoc. Chas. W. Lane Assocs. Inc., Ann Arbor, Mich., 1956-59; prin. Kainlauri, MacMullan, Millman, Ann Arbor, 1959-62; assoc. prof. Ohio U., Athens, 1962-68; prof. Auburn (Ala.) U., 1968—, head architecture dept., 1968-73, 84-85, head indsl. design dept., 1988-89. Prof. Mid. East Tech. U., Ankara, Turkey, 1966-67, King Faisal U., Dammam, Saudi Arabia, 1979-81. One man shows include Dhahran Art Group, Saudi Arabia, 1981, Peet Gallery, Auburn U., 1983, 91, Heritage Hall Mus., Talladega, Ala., 1998; author: Washtenaw Community College, 1962, Auburn U. Tour Guide, 1990. With U.S. Army, 1943-46, ETO, PTO. Decorated Bronze Star; recipient Cert. of Honor Ala. Hist. Commn., 1977; Alumni scholar U. Mich., 1961; Fulbright lectr. Exch. Com., Mid. East Tech. U., 1966. Mem. AIA (treas. Ala. coun. 1969, v.p. 1970, pres. 1972, emeritus 1990, Auburn chpt. pres. 1970, emeritus), Nat. Coun. Archtl. Registration Bd. (cert.), Auburn Arts Assn., Ga. Watercolor Soc. (signature mem.), Watercolor Soc. Ala. (signature mem.; pres. 2003), So. Watercolor Soc. (signature mem.). Avocations: painting, photography. Home: 736 Brenda Ave Auburn AL 36830-6038 Office Phone: 334-887-6428. E-mail: millmmm@charter.net.

MILLMAN, ROBERT A., lawyer; b. Chgo., Mar. 16, 1945; JD with honors, John Marshall Law Sch., Chgo., 1971. Bar: US Dist. Ct. Colo. 1973, US Ct. Appeals (10th cir.) 1991, Supreme Ct. Ill. 1971, Supreme Ct. Colo. 1973. Law clerk for Justice George N. Leighton Ill. Appellate Ct., Chgo., 1971—72; instr. legal rsch. & writing The John Marshall Law Sch., Chgo., 1971—72; atty. Robert A. Millman, PC, Colo. Springs, 1972—; pvt. practise, 1972—; commr. Colo. Ltd. Gaming Control Commn., 1999—2006; bd. mem. atty. discipline cases Colo. Supreme Ct. Hearing, 1999—. Lectr. at Bar Assn. & Trial Lawyers Assn. seminars. Exec. editor The John Marshall Law Review, 1970—71; contbr. articles to profl. jours.; editor, advisor, contb. author (book) Court Is In Session, 1990. Mem. Fourth Judicial Dist. Performance Evaluation Commn., 1988; commnr. Colo. Limited Gaming Control Commn., 1999—2006, vice-chair, 2004—. Mem.: ABA, El Paso County Bar Assn. (pres. professionalism com. 1988—89, founder Pro Bono Com.

1988—89, organizer & administer Trial Advocacy Sch. 1988—89, founder 2002), Colo. Trial Lawyers, Colo. Bar Assn. (bd. govs. 1987—93, mem. grants com. 1988, pres. Continuing Legal Edn. Colo., Inc. 1989—95, bd. dirs. Continuing Legal Edn., Colo., Inc. 1989—95, mem. criminal justice task force 1990, v.p., mem. exec. council 1992—93, creator & dir. mandatory course in professionalism 1994—95, chmn. professionalism com. 1994—95). Office: Robert A Millman PC 128 S Tejon Ste 402 Colorado Springs CO 80903

MILLNER, RACHEL ERIN, psychology educator, occupational therapist; b. Phila., Oct. 12, 1977; d. Martin S. and Jane Cohen Millner. D of Psychology magna cum alude, Alliant Internat. U., San Diego, Calif., 2004. Practicum student Calif. State U., San Marcos, Calif., 2000—01; intern Interfaith Cmty. Svcs., Escondido, 2001—03; internapa approved U. Buffalo Counseling and Psychol. Svcs., Buffalo, 2003—04; psychology fellow U. Pa. Counseling and Psychol. Svcs., Philadelphia. Supervision group leader U. of Pa., Philadelphia, Pa., 2004—; lectr. U. of Pa.- Sch. of Edn., Philadelphia, Pa., 2005—; vol. Healing Connections, San Diego, 1999; admissions interviewer Calif. Sch. of Profl. Psychology, San Diego; presenter in field. Vol. Sunshine Lady Found., 1998—2005. Recipient Outstanding Vol. Award, Healing Connections, 1999. Mem.: APA (assoc.), Psi Chi. Democrat. Jewish. Achievements include research in Poster Presentation at the Am. Psychol. Assn. Nat. Conf., 2004. Home: 943 Randolph Dr Yardley PA 19067 Personal E-mail: drmillner@rachelmillner.com.

MILLNER, THOMAS L., retail executive; Pres. The Pilliod Cabinet Co., High Point, N.C., Pilliod Holding Co., Swanton, Ohio, Remington Arms Co., Inc., Madison, Wis., 1994—2007, CEO, 1999—2009, Freedom Group, Inc., 2008—09; CEO, pres. Cabela's, Inc., Sidney, Nebr., 2009—. Bd. dirs. Remington Arms Co., Inc., 1994—2009, Cabela's, Inc., 2009—, Stanley Furniture Co., Inc., Lazy Days' R.V. Ctr., Inc. Office: Cabela's Inc 1 Cabela Dr Sidney NE 69160*

MILLON, HENRY ARMAND, art educator; b. Altoona, Pa., Feb. 22, 1927; s. Henri Francois and Louise (de Serent) M.; m. Emily Dees, June, 1953; m. Judith Rice, Dec. 27, 1966; children: Henri, Hadrian, Phoebe, Aaron. BA, Tulane U., 1947, BS, 1949, BArch, 1953; AM, Harvard U., 1954, MArch, 1955, PhD, 1964; LHD (hon.), Tulane U., 1995. Asst. prof. MIT, Cambridge, 1960-69, prof., 1969-80, vis. prof., 1981—2004, pres. univ. Film Study Ctr., 1972-73, trustee Film Study Ctr., 1967-73; dean Ctr. for Advanced Study in Visual Arts, Nat. Gallery Art, Washington, 1979-2000, dean emeritus, 2000—. Mem. bd. visitors Fine Arts Sch. Boston Mus., 1972-78; mem. rsch. grants panel NEH, 1972-73, rsch. tools panel, 1983; dir. Am. Acad. in Rome, 1974-77, trustee, 1977-96, vice chmn., 1982-96; mem. adv. coun. Sch. Architecture, Princeton U., 1970-73, 97—, adv. coun. dept. art and archeology, 1972-73, 80-84; mem. cons. com. Nat. Survey Historic Sites and Bldgs., Nat. Pk. Svc. div. U.S. Dept. Interior, 1969-80; vice chmn. Boston Landmarks Commn., 1970-73; panelist Gladys Krieble Delmas Found., 1979—; chmn. adv. bd. architecture and design TV series Guggenheim Prodns., 1980-88; vis. com. Dept. Fine Arts Harvard U., 1982-84, Sch. Hist. Studies Inst. Advanced Study, 1978, Arthur M. Sackler Gallery Smithsonian Instn., 1986-92; mem. U.S. Nat. Com. History of Art, 1980-2000; alt. del. Internat. Com. History of Art, 1981-85, del., 1985-96, sci. sec. working group Thesaurus Artis Universalis, 1983-89; hon. mem. Boston Archtl. Ctr., 1982—; chmn. sr. fellows com. history of landscape architecture program Dumbarton Oaks, 1983-89, convenor archtl. drawing adv. group, 1983-87; mem. adv. com. Getty Art Hist. Info. Program, 1983-91, mem. internat. repertory of lit. of art history, 1985-90, adv. com. Bibliography of the History of Art, 1986-2002; vice chmn. Coun. Am. Overseas Rsch. Ctrs., 1984-90; pres. Found. for Documents of Architecture, 1987-93; trustee Nat. Bldg. Mus., 1988-94. Author: Baroque and Rococo Architecture, 1962, Key Monuments in the History of Architecture, 1964; author: (with Andreina Griseri, Sarah McPhee, Mercedes Viale Ferrero) Filippo Juvarra: Drawings from the Roman Period, 1704-1714, Part I, 1984, Part II, 1999; author: (with Craigh Hugh Smyth) Michelangelo Architect, 1988; author: (with Linda Nochlin) Art and Architecture in the Service of Politics, 1978; editor: Studies in Italian Art and Architecture 15th through 18th Centuries, 1980, Triumph of the Baroque-Architecture in Europe, 1999, Circa 1700-Architecture in Europe and the Americas, 2005; co-editor: The Renaissance from Brunelleschi to Michelangelo, 1994. Trustee Clark Art Inst., 1996—2004, Phillips Collection, 2001—04, St. Paul's Ch., Rome, 2000—. With USNR, 1944—46. Recipient citation for excellence Internat. Archtl. Book Publ., AIA, 1994, Prix Hercule Catenacci, Inst. de France, 1995, A.H. Barr award Coll. Art Assn., 1996, Centennial medal Am. Acad. in Rome, Sesquicentennial medal Tulane U., 1997, Charles Homer Haskins lectr. Am. Coun. of Learned Societies, 2002; Hon. Mem. Accademia di San Luca, 1995; Fulbright fellow, Italy, 1957, Am. Acad. Rome fellow, 1957-60. Mem. Soc. Archtl. Historians (pres. 1968-70), Coll. Art Assn. (bd. dirs. 1982-85), Renaissance Soc., Am. Acad. Arts and Scis., Am. Philos. Soc. (curator 1998—), Deputazione Subalpina di Storia Patria, Soc. Preservation New Eng. Antiquities, Am. Inst. Archeology, Am. Soc. 18th Century Studies, Academia delle Scienze di Torino, Am. Co. Learned Soc. (fellows' adv. coun. 1998-2000). E-mail: judithmil@aol.com.

MILLOY, FRANK JOSEPH, JR., surgeon; b. Phoenix, June 26, 1924; s. Frank Joseph and Ola (McCabe) M. BS, Notre Dame U., 1946; MS, Northwestern U., 1949, MD, 1948. Diplomate Am. Bd. Surgery and Thoracic Surgery. Intern Cook County Hosp., Chgo., 1947-49, resident, 1953-57; practice medicine, specializing in surgery Lake Forest, Ill., 1958—. Hon. attending staff Presbyn.-St. Lukes Hosp.; former mem. attending staff Cook County Hosp.; mem. staff U. Ill. Rsch. Hosp.; clin. assoc. prof. surgery, U. Ill. Med. Sch.; assoc. prof. surgery Rush Med. Sch. Contbr. articles to profl. jours., chapters to books. Cons. West Side Vet. Hosp. Served as apprentice seaman USNR, 1943-45; lt. M.C., USNR, 1950-52; PTO. Mem.: ACS, Soc. Med. History Chgo. (pres.), Cook County Hosp. Surg. Alumni Assn., Karl Meyer Surg. Soc. (sec.), Warren Cole Surg. Soc. (past sec.), Ill. Thoracic Surg. Soc. (past pres.), Soc. Thoracic Surgeons, Am. Coll. Chest Physicians, Internat. Soc. Surgery, Chgo. Surg. Soc., Univ. Club (Chgo.), Met. Club, Knights of Malta, Phi Beta Pi. Home: 574 Jackson Ave Glencoe IL 60022-2036 Home Phone: 847-835-5578.

MILLS, BARRY, academic administrator, lawyer; b. Providence, Sept. 8, 1950; m. Karen Gordon Mills; 3 children. BA in Biochemistry and Govt. cum laude, Bowdoin, 1972; PhD, Syracuse U., 1976; JD, Columbia U., 1979. Bar: NY 1980. Mem. Debevoise & Plimpton, NYC, 1979—86, ptnr., 1986—2001; pres. Bowdoin Coll., Brunswick, Maine, 2001—. Bd. trustees Bowdoin Coll., Brunswick, Maine, 1994—2000. Harlan Fiske Stone scholar, Columbia Law Sch., 1979. Mem.: Assn. of Bar of City of NY. Office: Bowdoin Coll Hawthorne-Longfellow Hall 5700 College Station Brunswick ME 04011-8448 Office Phone: 207-725-3221.*

MILLS, BRADFORD, merchant banker; b. NYC, Dec. 16, 1926; s. Dudley Holbrook and Louise (Morris) M.; children: Elizabeth Lee, Bradford Alan, Barbara Louise, Ross Dudley. BA cum laude in Econs, Princeton U., 1948; postgrad., Oxford U., Eng., 1950-51. Asst. to dir. overseas pers. divsn. ECA, Paris, 1948-50; assoc. corp. fin. dept. F. Eberstadt & Co., NYC, 1954-62, ptnr., 1960-62; mng. ptnr. N.Y. Securities Co., 1962-70; chmn., dir. Specialized Svcs., Inc., Atlanta, 1968-85; pres., CEO Overseas Pvt. Investment Corp., Washington, 1971-73, dir., 1971-75; chmn. bd., dir. F. Eberstadt & Co. Internat., 1973-74; mng. ptnr. Bradford Assocs., 1974-92; ltd. ptnr. Bradford Investment Ptnrs. Ltd., 1992-96. Past chmn. Diamond Glass, MMX Corp., HWC Corp., Chgo. Stock Tab Corp., O.S. Kelly Co., Filtration Scis., Overseas Pvt. Investors Ltd., Overseas Pvt. Equities, Overseas Equity Investors, Inc., Specialized Svcs., Inc., U.S. Precision Glass, Inc., Amwell Valley Conservancy, Bradford Ventures, Stonecare Internat.; chmn. Bradford Investment Group, HDMR Discovery Inc., Wordsmith Media Ventures LLC; bd. dirs. The Princeton Packet, Pulsed Instruments, TF Instruments, Inc. Pres. Mills Found.; trustee, vice chmn. Millbrook Sch., NY, 1978-05; sec., trustee,mem. exec., 1995-2008, mem. fin. investment, 1995, Princeton Healthcare Sys.; trustee SAVE/Friends of Homeless Animals, 2006-, Am. Mus. of Fly Fishing. Mem. Coun. Fgn. Rels., Blooming Grove Club (Pa.), Links Club, Leash Club, Anglers Club N.Y., Nassau Club (trustee 1998-04), Bedens Brook Club, Amwell Valley Conservancy, Inc., Amwell Conservancy Found. (chmn.) Office: 2ND FL 92 Nassau St Princeton NJ 08542-4519 Office Phone: 609-921-3880. Personal E-mail: patchesteddy@msn.com.

MILLS, CHRISTOPHER JAMES, neurophysiologist, electroneurodiagnostic technologist; b. Ontario, Calif., Mar. 15, 1975; s. James Shultz Mills and Patricia Ann Patterson-Foged. BS in Biology, Calif. State U., San Marcos, 1998; ScD, Buxton Coll. Pub. Health, Vancouver, B.C., Can., 2004. Cert. clin. neurophysiologist Am. Coll. Surg. Neurophysiologists. Rsch. assoc. Oreg. Health and Sci. U., Portland, 2000—03, polysomnography technologist, 2001—04; neurophysiologist VSL Neuro Labs, Palm Beach Gardens, Fla., 2005—. Bd. dirs. Physicians Health Orgn., Miami. Fund raiser Physicians Health Orgn., Miami, 2004—. Fellow: Am. Coll. Neurophysiologists; mem.: Am. Soc. Neurophysiol. Monitoring, Am. Soc. Electroneurodiagnostic Technologists (licentiate). Liberal. Achievements include research in neurophysiological function during acute osmotic stimulation; role of vasopressin in regulation of blood pressure and oxytocin release. Avocations: golf, private pilot, travel, painting. Office: Neurosurg Diagnostics PA 3355 Burns Rd Ste 200 Palm Beach Gardens FL 33410 Home: 406 Victory Circle Boynton Beach FL 33436 Business E-Mail: millscj@neuroiom.net. E-mail: cmills@neurosed.us.

MILLS, CORINNE C., music educator; d. William P. and Cynthia L. Channon; children: Kristen Danielle, Pamela Dawn. MusB, Hartt Sch., West Hartford, Conn., 1977; MS in Ednl. Leadership, Ctrl. Conn. State U., 2007. Cert. Conn. Dept. Edn., adminstrn. cert. Conn. State U., 2007. Traffic coord. Fafair Bearing Co., New Britain, Conn., 1980—82; cello tchr. U. Conn. Cmty. Sch. Arts, Storrs, 1990—93; music tchr., 2007—, Hartford (Conn.) Pub. Sch., 1995—2001, dist. music coach, 2001—07; cello tchr., ensemble coach Hartford Conservatory, 1992—2000; music tchr. prek-8 Hartford Public Schs, 2007—. Tchr., coach, dir. summer program Hartford Conservatory, Conn., 1992—2000. Musician (asst. prin. cellist): Ea. Conn. Symphony Orch., 1982—; musician: (cellist) Chevrolet Music Theater, 1991—, Andrea Bocelli Am. Tour, 2001; co-author: Teaching Music in the Urban Classroom: A Guide to Survival, Success and Reform, 2006. Bd. trustees Hartford Conservatory, 2007—. Mem.: Music Educators Nat. Conf., Am. Orff Schulwerk Assn., Am. Fedn. Tchrs., Am. Fedn. Musicians, Phi Delta Kappa, Alpha Chi. Democrat. Avocation: gardening. Office Phone: 860-695-3021. Personal E-mail: corrinnemills@sbcglobal.net. Business E-Mail: millcool@hartfordschools.org.

MILLS, DALE DOUGLAS, journalist; b. Seattle, Oct. 4, 1930; d. Donald Emery and Antoinette (Kinleyside) Douglas; m. William Russell Mills, Aug. 13, 1955; children: Lida Susan, William Tad Jr., Peter Donald, Jane Douglas. BA, U. Wash., Seattle, 1952. Reporter Seattle Times, 1954-55, 74-83; asst. libr. Harvard U., 1955-56; editor Puget Soundings mag., 1968-71. Author: Deliver Us From Squid Roe, 1995. Mem. com. sign control Seattle City Coun., 1970-72; rsch. dir. City Coun. campaign; bd. mgrs. King County Juvenile Ct.; trustee Allied Arts Seattle; bd. dirs. King County Coun. for Prevention of Child Abuse and Neglect. Recipient awards for excellence in journalism Wash. Press Assn., Nat. Fedn. Press Women, Allied Daily Newspapers, C.B. Blethen Meml. award for disting. investigative reporting, Excellence award Soc. Profl. Journalists/Sigma Delta Chi; named Disting. Alumnus Lakeside-St. Nicholas Sch., 1984. Mem.: Jr. League Seattle, Helen T. Bush Children's Hosp Guild, Earthjustice, Sunset Club, Seattle Yacht Club, Kappa Kappa Gamma. E-mail: ddmills@comcast.net.

MILLS, DANIEL QUINN, business educator, consultant, author; b. Houston, Nov. 24, 1941; s. Daniel Monroe and Louise (Quinn) M.; children: Lisa Ann, Leandra, Shirley Elizabeth, Eliza Day, Sargent; m. Elizabeth Moore. BA, Ohio Wesleyan U., 1963; MA, Harvard U., 1965, PhD, 1968. Prof. MIT, Cambridge, 1968-75, Harvard Bus. Sch., Boston, 1976—. Impartial umpire Plan to Settle Disputes in Constrn., 1973-79, Trans-Alaska Pipeline, 1975-78, AFL-CIO Internal Disputes Plan, 1975-82; commr. Nat. Commn. on Employment Policy, Washington, 1982-86. Author: Industrial Relations in Construction, 1971, Labor, Government and Inflation, 1975, Labor-Management Relations, 1978, 5th edit., 1993, The New Competitors, 1985, Not Like Our Parents: The Baby-Boom Generation, 1987, The IBM Lesson, 1988, The Rebirth of the Corporation, 1990, The GEM Principle, 1994, Broken Promises: What Went Wrong at IBM, 1996, e-Leadership, 2000, Buy, Lie and Sell High: How Investors Lost Out on Enron and The Internet Bubble, 2002, Wheel, Deal and Steal: Deceptive Accounting, Deceitful CEO's and Ineffective Reforms, 2003, Having It All, 2004, How to Lead-How to Live, 2005, Principles of Management, 2005, Masters of Illusion, 2006. Mem. Am. Econ. Assn., Indsl. Rels. Rsch. Assn., Phi Beta Kappa Office: Harvard U Harvard Bus Sch Soldiers Field Rd Allston MA 02163 Office Phone: 617-495-6206. Business E-Mail: dmills@hbs.edu.

MILLS, DAVID L., retired electrical engineer, computer scientist, educator; b. Oakland, Calif., June 3, 1938; s. Richard A. and Adele E. Mills; m. Beverly J. Csizmadia, Feb. 8, 1965; children: Eileen E., Keith D. BS in Engring. Sci., U. Mich., Ann Arbor, 1960, BS in Engring. Math., 1961, MS in Elec. Engring., 1962, MS in Comm. Scis., 1964, PhD in Computer Sci., 1971. Lectr. U. Edinburgh, 1971—72; asst. prof. U. Md., College Park, 1972—77; sr. scientist M/A-COM Linkabit, Inc., Vienna, Va., 1977—86; prof. elec. and computer engring. U. Del., Newark, 1986—2008; ret. Author: (book) Computer Network Time Synchronization, 2006. Fellow: IEEE, Assn. Computing Machinery; mem.: Nat. Acad. Engring. Avocation: archaeology.

MILLS, DOROTHY JANE (DOROTHY Z. SEYMOUR, DOROTHY SEYMOUR MILLS), writer, editor, consultant; b. Cleve., July 5, 1928; d. Henry Zander and Katherine Helen Reinert; m. Harold Seymour, May 21, 1949 (dec. Sept. 25, 1992); m. Roy Elburt Mills, Feb. 15, 1995. Student, Cleve. State U., 1946—49; BS, Case-Western Res. U., 1950, MA, 1952. Cert. elem. and H.S. tchr. Ohio, N.Y. Tchr. Cleve. Pub. Schs., 1950—54, Parma Heights (Ohio) Pub. Schs., 1955—57, Pelham (N.Y.) Pub. Schs., 1957—63, Warwick (N.Y.) Pub. Schs., 1963—66; sr. editor Ginn & Co., Pubs., Boston, Lexington, Mass., 1967—73, Lexington, 1979—81; freelance writer, editor, cons., 1981—; owner Patrician Publs., Naples, Fla., 1998—. Cons. Stillpoint Pub., Walpole, NY, 1987—; freelance editor, 1987—95; lectr. in field. Author: (children's textbooks) Bill and the Fish, 1965, Brad and Nell, 1965, Stop Pretending, 1965, Ballerina Bess, 1965, Ann Likes Red, 1965, The Rabbit, 1965, The Tent, 1965, The Sandwich, 1965, Big Beds and Little Beds, 1965, (edn. text) Toad Charts, 1987, (novels) The Sceptre, 1998, 1999, The Labyrinth, 2003, The Treskel, 2005, (cookbook) Meatless Meat: A Book of Recipes for Meat Substitutes, 2001; co-author, editor: Fear Not to Sow Because of the Birds, 1988; co-author (with Harold Seymour): Baseball: The Early Years, 1960, Baseball: The Golden Age, 1971, Baseball: The People's Game, 1990; co-author: (edn. text) Word Recognition, 1987; author: (autobiography) A Woman's Work: Writing Baseball History with Harold Seymour, 2004, short stories; contbr. articles to publs. Named to Women's Baseball League Hall of Fame, 1996. Mem.: NASSH, AAUW, Soc. Am. Baseball Rsch. (Dr. Harold and Dorothy Seymour medal 1996). Democrat. Unitarian Universalist. Achievements include recognition as the first woman to write scholarly baseball history. Avocations: piano, singing, travel. Home: 6935 Carlisle Ct Apt C 142 Naples FL 34109 Office Phone: 239-596-2842.

MILLS, EDWIN SMITH, economics professor; b. Collingswood, NJ, June 25, 1928; s. Edwin Smith and Roberta (Haywood) M.; m. Barbara Jean Dressner, Sept. 2, 1950; children: Alan Stuart, Susan Dorinda; m. Margaret M. Hutchinson, Jan. 22, 1977. BA, Brown U., 1951; PhD, U. Birmingham, Eng., 1956. Asst. lectr. Univ. Coll. North Staffordshire, Eng., 1953-55; instr. MIT, 1955-57; mem. faculty Johns Hopkins, Balt., 1957-70, prof. econs., 1963-70, chmn. dept. econs., 1966-69; prof. econs. and pub. affairs, Gerald L. Phillippe prof. urban studies Princeton U., 1970-75, prof. econs., 1975-87, chmn. dept., 1975-77; Gary Rosenberg prof. real estate and fin. Kellog Sch. Mgmt. Northwestern U., Evanston, Ill., 1987—96, emeritus prof., 1996—. Vis. rsch. fellow Cowles Found., Yale, 1961; sr. profl. staff Coun. Econ. Advisers, 1964—65. Author: Urban Economics, 1972, The Burden of Government, 1986; editor: Jour. Urban Econs., 1973—90; contbr. articles to profl. jours. 2d lt. US Army, 1946—48. Recipient numerous rsch. grants and contracts, 1960—95. Mem.: Am. Econ. Assn., Phi Beta Kappa. Home: 1 Calvin Cir Apt A413 Evanston IL 60201-1953 Office: Northwestern U Ctr Real Estate Rsch Kellogg Graduate School 2001 Sheridan Rd Evanston IL 60208-2001 Home Phone: 847-491-2830; Office Phone: 847-491-8340. Business E-Mail: e_mills@kellogg.northwestern.edu.

MILLS, ELIZABETH SHOWN, historical writer, genealogist; b. Cleve., Miss., Dec. 29, 1944; d. Floyd Finley Shown and Elizabeth Thulmar (Jeffcoat) Carver; m. Gary B. Mills, 1963; children: Clayton Bernard, Donna Rachal, Daniel Garland. BA, U. Ala., Tuscaloosa, 1980. Cert. genealogist, geneal. lectr. Hist. writer, educator, 1972—; editor Nat. Geneal. Soc. Quar., Arlington, Va., 1987—2002. Faculty Samford U. Inst. of Genealogy and Hist. Rsch., Birmingham, Ala., 1980—; contract dir., cons. U. Ala., 1985-92; faculty Nat. Inst. of Geneal. Rsch., 1985-97. Author, editor, translator Cane River Creole Series, 6 vols.; author: Evidence: Citation and Analysis for the Family Historian, 1997, Professional Genealogy: A Manual for Researchers, Writers, Editors, Lecturers, and Librarians, 2001, Isle of Canes: A Historical Novel, 2004, QuickSheet Citation Series, 2005-09, Evidence Explained: Citing History Sources from Artifacts to Cyberspace, 2007, Libr. Jour. Best Reference, 2007, Quick Sheet: Citing Ancestry. Com Databases & Indexes, 2009; contbr. articles to acad. and profl. jours. Trustee Nat. Bd. Certification Genealogists, 1984—, v.p., 1989-94, pres., 1994-96; trustee Assn. Profl. Genealogists, 1984-90, 92-94, regional v.p., 1988-89; trustee Assn. Promotion Scholarship in Genealogy, 1984-90 Named Outstanding Young Women of Am. Jaycees, Gadsden, 1976, Outstanding Alumna award U. Ala. New Coll., Tuscaloosa, 1990. Fellow Am. Soc. Geneal. (sec. 1992-95, v.p. 1995-98, pres. 1998-2001), Nat. Geneal. Soc. (councilor 1987-92), Utah Geneal. Assn., Grady McWhiney Rsch. Found. (sr.); mem. Assn. Profl. Genealogists (Smallwood Svc. award, 1989). Republican. Roman Catholic.

MILLS, EUGENE SUMNER, academic administrator; b. West Newton, Ind., Sept. 13, 1924; s. Sumner Amos and Lela (Weatherly) M.; m. Dorothy Frances Wildman, Oct. 22, 1945; children: David Walden, Sara Anne. AB, Earlham Coll., 1948; MA, Claremont Grad. U., 1949, PhD, 1952; Spl. Postdoctoral Auditor, Harvard, 1958-59; LLD (hon.), So. NH U., 1979, U. N.H., 1988; LHD (hon.), Earlham Coll., 1987. From instr. to prof. psychology Whittier (Calif.) Coll., 1950—60, prof., 1960—62, chmn. dept. psychology, 1952—62; pres. Whittier (Calif.) Coll. and Whittier Coll. Sch. of Law, 1979-89; prof. psychology Whittier (Calif.) Coll., 1979-89, emeritus prof. psychology, pres. emeritus, 1989—; faculty U. NH, Durham, 1962—79, dean Grad. Sch., 1963—67, dean Coll. Liberal Arts, 1967—70, acad. v.p., 1970—71, provost, 1971—74, pres., 1974—79. Vis. prof. U. Victoria, B.C., 1958, 60; bd. dirs. Elderhostel, Inc., 1977-97, chmn., 1984-90, vice chmn., 1996-97; vice chmn., bd. dirs. Fedco Inc., 1996-98; interim pres. Earlham Coll., 1996-97; mem. NH Psychol. Assn., 1962-79, pres., 1969-70, bd. dirs., 1967-70; trustee Earlham Coll., 1966-69, 96-97, hon. lifetime trustee, 1997—. Author: George Trumbull Ladd: Pioneer American Psychologist, 1969, The Story of Elderhostel, 1993; contbr. articles to profl. jours. Bd. dirs. LA County coun. Boy Scouts Am., 1981—89; bd. dirs. Fedco Charitable Found., 2001—, UNH Mus. Art, 2004—. Danforth Found. grantee; NSF grantee. Fellow Am. Psychol. Assn.; mem. Western Psychol. Assn., Sigma Xi, Phi Kappa Phi., Omicron Delta Kappa Mem. Soc. Of Friends. E-mail: dottymills25@yahoo.com.

MILLS, GEORGE MARSHALL, risk management consultant; b. Newton, NJ, May 20, 1923; s. J. Marshall and Emma (Scott) M.; m. Dorothy Lovilla Allen, Apr. 21, 1945; children: Dianne (Mrs. Thomas McKay III), Dorothy L.A. (Mrs. Edward Sphatt). BA, Rutgers U., 1943; MA, Columbia U., 1951. CLU, CPCU; chartered fin. cons.; cert. govt. fund mgr. Pres. George M. Mills Inc., North Brunswick, NJ, 1946—75; pres. CORECO, Inc., Newark, 1960-78; risk mgr. N.J. Hwy. Authority, Woodbridge, 1976-95; pres. Assoc. Risk Mgmt., North Brunswick, NJ, 1995—. Cons. Govs.'s Com. on Bus. Efficiency in Pub. Schs., 1979-80; cons. Risk Mgmt. Ins., Real Estate. Bd. dirs. Alpha Chi Rho Ednl. Found., vice-chmn. 1991-95; workshop Easter Seal Soc.; mem. Gov.'s Task Force on Sound Mcpl. Govt., 1981-82; pres. Nat. Interfrat. Conf., 1979-80. With USNR, 1943-46. Recipient Congl. Order of Merit, 2006—09, Congl. Distinction medal, 2006—07. Mem. Congl. Bus. Adv. Coun. (chmn. 2003-09, co-chair Presdl. Inauguration Com. 2005), Am. Coll. Life Underwriters, Am. Coll. Property Liability Underwriters, Internat. Bridge Tunnel and Turnpike Assn. (chmn. risk mgmt. com. 1980-95, bus. ins. risk mgmt. bd. 1988-95, chair Congress Bus. Adv. Coun. 2003-09, co-chair presdl. inaugeration com. 2005, Matthew J. Lenz Jr. medal 1989, Paul K. Addams award 1992, Businessman of Yr., US Congress, 2003-06, Ronald Reagan Gold medal 2007-08, Rutgers Club (trustee), Alpha Chi Rho (nat. councillor 1964-70, nat. pres. 1970-73, nat. treas. 1975-78), Kappa Kappa Psi, Tau Kappa Alpha, Phi Delta Phi. Mem. Reformed Ch. Am. Home: 1054 Hoover Dr New Brunswick NJ 08902-3244

MILLS, HELENE AUDREY, retired education educator; b. Oct. 6, 1933; d. Paul Albert and Mabel Meister; m. Ray Mills, Apr. 17, 1954; children: Keith, Katherine(dec.), Kevin. BS in Family Life Edn., Wayne State U., Detroit, 1954; MEd in Human Resources, Wayne State U., 1965, EdD in Gen. Adminstrn., 1980. Supr., instr. Wayne State Coll. Edn., 1958-67; tchr. life studies, health edn. Seaholm HS, Birmingham, Mich., 1967-72, 74-77, asst. to prin., 1974-77, asst. prin., 1978-79, prin., 1990-97, Derby Mid. Sch., Birmingham, 1980-90; asst. prof. Oakland U., Rochester Hills, Mich., 1997—2002; ret., 2002. Adj. prof. Oakland U., Rochester, 1985—89, Wayne State U., Detroit, 1989—91; consulting editor Clearing Ho., 1985—97. Contbr. articles to profl. jours. Mem. steering com. Meadowbrook Leadership Acad., 1984—87; mem. Detroit Strategic Planning Task Force, 1986—88; mem. exec. bd. Oakland County Youth Assistance, 1987—90; v.p. Cmty. Ho. Sr. Women's Club, Birmingham, Mich., 2004—; program chairperson women's group Northbrooke Ch., 1997—99, mem. adult ministries purpose com., 1998—99. Recipient PTSA Coun. Pres. award, 1982, Celebration of Women award, Greater Detroit Coun. NA'AMAT U.S., 1986, Exemplary Secondary Sch. award, State of Mich., 1991. Mem.: NASCD, Oakland County Secondary Prins. Assn. (pres. 1983—85, Prin. of the Yr. 1991), Mich. Secondary Prins. Assn., Mich. Coun. Family Rels., Mich. Assn. Supervision and Curriculum Devel., Nat. Secondary Prins. Assn., Nat. Staff Devel. Assn., Birmingham Area Sr. Citizens Assn. (bd. mem., program chair 2003—), Phi Delta Kappa (chmn. mem. Oakland br. 1998—2002). Home Phone: 248-645-2738.

MILLS, HUGH HARRISON, III, geologist, educator; b. Rocky Mt., NC, Mar. 20, 1941; s. Hugh H. and Dorothy Zerbach Mills; m. Tu Anh Tran Mills, Sept. 14, 1970; children: Richard Tran, Katherine Tran. PhD, U. Wash., Seattle, 1975. Asst. prof. geology Clemson U., SC, 1976—77; asst. prof. to prof. Tenn. Technol. U., Cookeville, 1977—. Rschr. US Geol. Survey, Blacksburg, Va., 1978—81; assoc. editor Geol. Soc. Am. Bull, Boulder, Colo., 1989—95. Contbr. scientific papers. 1st lt. Signal Corps US Army, 1965—69, Fort Knox, Vietnam. Recipient Rsch. award, Tenn. Tech U., 2005; grant, NSF, 1987—88, 1991—93. Fellow: Geol. Soc. Am. Independent. Avocations: mountain climbing, travel. Home: 945 E Sixth St Cookeville TN 38501-2828 Office: Tenn Technol Univ 815 Quadrangle Dr Cookeville TN 38505 Office Phone: 931-372-3521. Business E-Mail: hmills@tntech.edu.

MILLS, HUGH MILTON, JR., retired college president; b. Albany, Ga., Oct. 24, 1922; s. Hugh Milton Mills Sr. and Johnie Lamar West; m. Evelyn Heath, Oct. 6, 1944 (dec. Aug. 1994); children: Hugh Milton III, Ralph West, Rebecca Ann; m. Patsy Faulkner Howell, May 30, 1998 (dec. May 29, 2009). AA, N. Ga. Coll., 1943; BS in Edn., U. Ga., 1945, MEd, 1947, EdD, 1956; LLD (hon.), Brenau Coll., 1983. Cert. profl. tchr., Ga. Tchr., coach Rockmart (Ga.) H.S., 1945-47, Albany (Ga.) H.S., 1947-48; from instr. to asst. prof. U. Ga., Athens, 1948-51, from asst. prof. to assoc. prof., 1953-65; supervising prin. Rockmart Pub. Schs., 1951-53; pres. Gainesville (Ga.) Jr. Coll., 1965-84; interim pres. Brenau Coll., Gainesville, 1985; pres. emeritus Gainesville Coll., 1985—. Cons. Ga. Dept. Vocat. Rehab., Atlanta, 1955-65. With USAAC, 1942-43. Named Ga. Man of the Yr. Conservation Dist. Ga., 1986. Mem. Phi Beta Kappa, Phi Kappa Phi, Kappa Delta Pi, Phi Delta Kappa. Baptist. Avocation: woodworking. Office: Gainesville Coll PO Box 1358 Gainesville GA 30503

MILLS, JANET TRAFTON, state attorney general, former state representative; b. Farmington, Maine, Dec. 12, 1947; d. S. Peter and Katherine Coffin Mills; m. Stanley Kuklinski; 5 stepchildren. BA, U. Mass., Boston; JD, U. Maine. Asst. atty. gen. State of Maine, 1976—80, atty. gen., 2009—; dist. atty. Androscoggin, Franklin and Oxford Counties, 1980; atty. Wright & Mills, PA, 1995—2008; mem. Maine House of Reps. from Dist. 78, 2002—08, mem. Judiciary Com., Criminal Justice and Pub. Safety Com. and the Appropriations Com. Mem.: Assn. Criminal Defense Lawyers (bd. dirs. 1996), Trial Lawyers Assn. (bd. dirs. 1996), Maine Coun for Humanities, Maine Civil Liberties Union (bd. dirs. 1978—80), Maine Prosecutors Assn. (bd. dirs. 1980—94, pres. 1984, 1988—92), League of Women Voters. Democrat. Avocations: poetry, fishing, cooking, reading. Office: Office of Atty Gen 6 State House Station Augusta ME 04333*

MILLS, JAN-RUTH, history professor; b. Reno, Dec. 10, 1957; d. WIlliam Charles William and Shirley Jane Bianchi; m. Dennis Charles Mills, Apr. 21, 2001. MFA, Columbia U., NYC, 1983. Instr. writing and holocaust history Pima CC, Tucson, 2005—; english tchr. St. Augustine HS, Tucson, 2007—08. Poetry editor Quar. West, Salt Lake City, 1991—93; english tchr. Miss. Tchr. Corps Yazoo City HS, 1993—94, Beulah HS, Beulah, Ala., 1997—2000, Auburn HS, Ala., 1999—2000; assoc. instr., writing U. Utah Writing Program, Salt Lake City, 1995—96; classroom tchr. Lee County Youth Devel., Opelika, Ala., 2000—01; adj. instr., writing Okaloos Walton CC, Niceville, Fla., 2002—05. Author: (book) St. Georgen-Gusen-Mauthausen: The History of Mauthausen Concentration Camp Reconsidered. Mem.: Gusen Meml. Com., Sunbelt Writing Project (tchr. cons. 1999—). Democrat. Office: Pima CC 8181 E Irvington Rd Tucson AZ 85709-4000 Business E-Mail: jan.mills@pima.edu.

MILLS, JON, dean emeritus, law educator; b. Miami, Fla., July 24, 1947; s. Herb J. and Marguerite (Sweat) M.; m. Beth Bechard; children: Marguerite St. Amand, Elizabeth Buchanan Mills. BA in Economics, Stetson U., 1969, LLD (hon.), 1986; JD with honors, U. Fla., 1972. Bar: U.S. Ct Appeals (11th Cir.). Jud. clerk 2nd Dist. Ct. Appeals, Fla., 1972; spl. asst. State Atty. Rolling vs. State, 1990; ptnr. McGalliard, Mills, DeMontomollin, Smith, Monaco & Sieg, 1980—86, Consel, Boies, Schiller & Flexner LLP, 2008—; mem. Fla. Ho. of Reps., 1978-88, majority leader, 1985—86, speaker, 1987-88; mem. faculty U. Fla., Gainesville, 1973—80; prof. law U. Fla., Coll. Law, Gainesville, 1995—, founding dir., Ctr. for Governmental Responsibility, 1973—80, 1988—, dir., Ctr. for Governmental Responsibility, 2003—, interim dean, 1999—2001, dean, 2001—03, dean emeritus, 2003—. Mem. Fla. Constitution Revision Commn., 1987—88, Commn. on the Future of the South, State Comprehensive Plan Com., 1985, Fla. Motion Picture, TV, and Recording Industry Bd.; adv. coun., bd. dir. State Legis. Leaders Found.; chair Fla. Coun. on Far East R&D; com. privacy and ct. records Fla. Supreme Ct., 2003—05; spkr. in field. Author: Privacy: The Lost Right, 2008; co-author: Voting Rights and Democracy: The Law and Politics Districting, 1996; prodr., moderator, Florida Forum, 1989; exec. prodr., moderator, Sunshine Showdown, 1991; co-editor, moderator, Common Ground, 1995 (recipient 1998 Suncoast Regional Emmy award for Common Ground TV program "Whose Water Is It Anyway?"; contbr. articles to profl. jours. Del., Dem. Nat. Convention, 1984; chair, State Dem. Convention, 1987; founding chmn., Fla. Chpt. Dem. Leadership Coun., 1987; pres., Fla. Chpt. Dem. Leadership Coun., 1993-; mem. Coun. Internat. Administrative Units, Office of Internat. Studies and Programs, Governor's Growth Mgmt. Adv. Com., 1993, U. Fla. Found. Investment Com., 1998-2002; founding pres. bd. dirs., So. Legal Coun., Fla. Arts Celebration; former mem. exec. com. Fla. Dem. Party; chair, U. Fla. President's External Rels. Com.; trustee, Fla. Nature Conservancy Bd., 1988-; bd. dir. U. Fla. Ctr. for Performing Arts, Save our Everglades, 1996-, Internat. Computer and Automated Rsch. 1st lt. USAR. Decorated Order of Coif; recipient Allen Morris award, 1979-80, 1985-86, Outstanding Legis. award Fla. Health Care Assn., 1982, Legis. award, Fla. Audubon Soc., 1983, Sierra Club Fla. Chpt., 1983, 1984, Fla. C.ofC. Legis. award for Leadership in Quality of Life Legislation, 1984, Dept. Health and Human Services Commissioner's award for Outstanding Leadership Services in Prevention of Child Abuse and Neglect, 1985, League of Women Voters Outstanding Elected Official, 1985, Nature Conservancy Pub. Svc. award, 1986, President's 1997 Conservationist of Yr. award, Fla. Audubon Soc., 1998, Spl. Recognition award, Fla. Assn. Countries for outstanding work as a mem. of the Constitution Revision Commn., 1998, Conservation Civic Leader of Yr., Fla. Wildlife Fedn., 1998, Bd. Regents Disting. Cmty. Svc. award, 1998; named Rep. of Yr. Assn. Retarded Citizens Fla., 1981, Most Effective Mem. of the House, 1985, 1986, Gainesville Sun 1998 Person of Yr. for Govt., 1998, Most Valuable Mem., Fla. Constitutional Revision Commn., 1998. Fellow Am. Bar Found.; mem. ABA (adv. com. World Justice Project, 2007-), Fla. Bar Assn., Fla. Supreme Ct. Hist. Soc., Pi Kappa Alpha, Fla. Blue Key, Fla. Supreme Ct. Professionalism Commn. Methodist. Avocations: flying, scuba diving, skiing, photography, Karate. Home: 2727 NW 58th Blvd Gainesville FL 32606-8516 Office: U Fla Coll Law 230 Bruton-Geer Hall Gainesville FL 32611 also: PO Box 117625 Gainesville FL 32611 Office Phone: 352-273-0835. Office Fax: 352-392-1457.

MILLS, KAREN GORDON, federal agency administrator, venture capitalist; b. 1953; d. Melvin J. and Ellen R. Gordon; m. Barry Mills, 1983; children: William, Henry, George. BA in Economics, Harvard U., 1975, MBA, 1977. With Gen. Foods; cons. McKinsey & Co.; pres. MMP Group, Inc., Brunswick, Maine, 1993—2009; founding ptnr. Solera Capital, LLC, NYC, 1999—2007; adminstr. US Small Bus. Adminstrn. (SBA), Washington, 2009—. Chairwomen Maine Gov.'s Coun. on Competitiveness and the Economy; chair Coun. on Jobs, Innovation and the Economy, 2006; bd. dirs. Arrow Electronics, Inc., 1994—, Latina Media Ventures LLC, Annie's Homegrown, The Scotts Miracle-Grow Co. Trustee Radcliffe Coll., 1985—93, bd. overseers, 1999; bd. mem. Maine Tech. Inst., Nature Conservancy (Maine chap.). Office: US Small Business Administration 409 3rd St SW Rm 7000 Washington DC 20416*

MILLS, KEVIN LEE, computer scientist, researcher; b. Frederick, Md., Oct. 21, 1951; s. John Lee and Doris Jean (Comer) M.; m. Karen June Davis, Dec. 30, 1972; children: Colin Walter, Elizabeth Anne. BS in Polit. Sci. and Econs., Frostburg State U., Md., 1973; MS in Tech. Mgmt., Am. U., 1979; PhD in Info. Tech., George Mason U., 1996. Sr. computer analyst System Devel. Corp., McLean, Va., 1976-81; project mgr. Tesdata Systems Corp., McLean, 1981-82; computer scientist Nat. Bur. of Stds., Gaithersburg, Md., 1982-84, group leader, 1984-87; divsn. chief Nat. Inst. Stds. and Tech., Gaithersburg, 1987-95; program mgr. Def. Advanced Rsch. Projects Agy., Arlington, Va., 1996-98; adj. prof. George Mason U., 1996—2006; divsn. chief Nat. Inst. Standards & Technology, Gaithersburg, Md., 1999-2001, sr. rsch. scientist, 2001—. Cons. in field, 1980-82. Contbr. articles to jours. With USMC, 1972—78. Mem. IEEE (sr.). Avocations: hiking, writing, reading, photography. Office Phone: 301-975-3618. E-mail: kmills@nist.gov.

MILLS, LAWRENCE, lawyer, business and transportation consultant; b. Salt Lake City, Aug. 15, 1932; s. Samuel L. and Beth (Neilson) M. BS, U. Utah, 1955, JD, 1956. Bar: Utah 1956, ICC 1961, U.S. Supreme Ct. 1963. With W.S. Hatch Co. Inc., Woods Cross, Utah, 1947-89, gen. mgr., 1963-89, v.p., 1970-89, also dir. Bd. dirs. Nat. Tank Truck Carriers, Inc., Washington, 1963—, pres., 1974-75, chmn. bd., 1975-76; mem. motor carrier adv. com. Utah State Dept. Transp., 1979—2007; keynote speaker Rocky Mountain Safety Suprs. Conf., 1976, 1996. Contbr. articles to legal and profl. jours. and transp. publs. Del. to County and State Convs., Utah, 1970-72; v.p. Utah Safety Coun., 1979-82, bd. dirs., 1979—, pres., 1983-84; mem. Utah Gov's Adv. Com. on Small Bus.; capt. Easter Seal Telethon, 1989, 90; state vice chmn. High Frontier, 1987—; mem. adv. com. Utah State Indsl. Commn., 1988—, chmn. com. studying health care cost containment and reporting requirements 1990—; mem. expdn. to Antarctica, 1996, Titanic '96 expedition, Iceland expedition, 2001, Greenland expedition, 2001. Recipient Safety Dir. award Nat. Tank Carriers Co., 1967, Outstanding Svc. and Contbn. award, 1995, Trophy award W.S. Hatch Co., 1975, Disting. Svc. award Utah State Indsl. Commn., 1992, Outstanding Svc. award Utah Safety Coun., 1994. Mem. Utah State Bar, Salt Lake County Bar Assn., Utah Motor Transport Assn. (dir. 1967—95, pres. 1974-76, Outstanding Achievement Award 1989), Utah Hwy. Users Assn. (dir. 1981—98), Indsl. Rels. Coun. (dir. 1974—94), Salt Lake City C. of C., U.S. Jaycees (life Senator 1969—, ambassador 1977—, pres. Utah Senate 1979-80, 2008-, Henry Giessenbier fellow 1989), Nat. Petroleum Coun., Utah Associated Gen. Contractors (assoc. 1975-77, 88—), Silver Tank Club, Hillsdale Coll. President's Club, Traveler's Century Club, U. Utah Pres. Club. Home: 119 Adams Ct Kamiah ID 83536-9410 *Personal philosophy: Excessive government regulation stifles individual initiative. We should learn from the downfall of communism & beware of the rise of Islam.*

MILLS, LINDA A., aerospace transportation executive; B in Math., Santa Clara U.; M in Computer Sci., U. Ill. Mgmt. positions in missions systems sector Northrop Grumman Corp., 1979—2003, v.p., mission assurance & six sigma, mission sys. sector, 2003—05, v.p., ops. & processes, info. tech. sector, 2005—07, pres., civilian agencies bus. group, IT sector, 2007—08, corp. v.p., pres., info. tech. sector, 2008—09, corp. v.p., pres. info. systems, 2009—. Recipient CEO Leadership Award, 2000, 2001, 2005; named one of Women Worth Watching, Diversity Journal, 2007. Mem.: corp. policy coun. Northrop Grumman Corp. (assoc.), Northern Va. Tech. Coun (assoc.), Fairfax Symphony Orchestra (assoc.). Office: Northrop Grumman Corp 1840 Century Park East Los Angeles CA 90067 Office Phone: 310-553-6262. Office Fax: 310-553-2076.*

MILLS, LINDA LOU, media specialist; b. Valporasion, Ind., May 23, 1951; d. Harry Eugene and Billie Ann Reinholt; m. Steven Allen Mills, Aug. 11, 1973. BS, Ball State U., Muncie, Ind., 1973; MLS, Ind. U., Bloomington, 1978. Cert. libr. media specialist Ind. Dept. Edn., 1973. Libr. media specialist Sunman Elem., Ind., 1973—86, Greensburg Elem., Ind., 1986—. Recipient Peggy L. Pfiffer award, Assn. Ind. Media Educators, 2004. Home: 913 Locust Batesville IN 47006 Office: Greensburg Elem Schs 900 N Big Blue Greensburg IN 47240 Business E-Mail: lmills@greensburg.k12.in.us.

MILLS, MARSHA LEE, retired secondary school educator; b. Independence, Kans., Dec. 28, 1948; d. Arthur Robert and Thelma Louise (Esch) M. BS in Edn., Truman U., 1970, MA, 1974; real estate cert., Ind. Career Inst., Westport, Mo., 1991. Part time tchr. NMSU Mo. U., Kirksville, 1970-72; jr. high art educator Lincoln County R-3 Schs., Troy, Mo., 1972—2005; ret., 2005; realtor assoc. Century 21 Coose, Troy, 1991—2002, Prudential Patterson Realtors, Troy, 2002—. Exhibitor: (ceramics) Mo. Coll. Art Students, 1969, Mo. Artists and Coll. Educators, 1970 (hon. mention), (multi media) N.E. Mo. U., 1974. Mus. friend St. Louis Art Mus., 1978—; badge cons. Boy Scouts Am., St. Louis Coun., 1978—; trustee Moscow Mills (Mo.) Meth. Ch., 1992—. Recipient I Dare You award Purina, 1966, Regents scholarship NMSU, Kirksville, 1966, Art Guild scholarship NMSU Art Guild, Kirksville, 1969. Mem. Mo. State Tchrs. Assn. (state retired tchrs. com. mem. 2008-, exe. bd. 2003-05, v.p., pres., dist. officer 1987-93), Greater St. Louis Tchrs. Assn. (2nd v.p. 1994, 95, pres. 1996-1998), Nat. Art Edn. Assn. (coun. 1978—), East Ctrl. Bd. Realtors, Alpha Delta Kappa (Beta Chi chpt. treas., sec., v.p. 1987-93, pres. 1994-2000), Delta Kappa Gamma, Multi-Million Dollar Producer. Democrat. Avocations: investments, computers, fine arts, baseball, walking. Home: 444 Highway Mm Moscow Mills MO 63362-1502 Office: 15 Sydnorville Rd Ste 2 Troy MO 63379 Home Phone: 636-366-4553; Office Phone: 636-462-8924, 636-474-6762. Personal E-mail: mmills@prupat.com.

MILLS, MIKE, musician; b. Calif., Dec. 17, 1958; 1 child, Julian. Student, U. Ga. Bass guitarist R.E.M., 1980—. Rec. albums include Chronic Town, 1982, Murmur, 1983 (Rolling Stone Album of Yr. 1983), Reckoning, 1984, Fables of the Reconstruction, 1985, Life's Rich Pageant, 1986, Dead Letter Office, 1987, Document, 1987, Eponymous, 1988, Green, 1988, Out of Time, 1991 (Group Grammy award, Best Alternative Music Performance, 1992), Automatic for the People, 1993 (4 Grammy nominations), Monster, 1994, Murmur, 1995, New Adventures in Hi-Fi, 1996, Up, 1998, Reveal, 2001, Around the Sun, 2004, Live, 2007, Accelerate, 2008; songs include The One I Love, Orange Crush (MTV Video Music award for Best Post Modern Video, 1990), Losing My Religion, 1991 (6 MTV Video Music Awards, 1991, 2 Grammy awards: Best Group Pop Vocal Performance, Best Short Form Music Video, 1992), Everybody Hurts, 1992 (4 MTV Video Music Awards, 1994), Man on the Moon, The Great Beyond, Imitation of Life, It's the End of the World As We Know It; appeared on Robbie Robertson's album, Storyville, 1991, Backbeat soundtrack, 1994, Man on the Moon soundtrack, 1999. Recipient Top Modern Rock Artist, Top World Album awards, Billboard Music Awards, 1991, 3 Grammy awards for Best Group Pop Vocal Performance, Best Alternative Music Performance, and Best Short Form Music Video, 1992, Best Internat. Group, Brit Awards, 1992, 1993, Patrick Lippert award, Rock the Vote, 1994, Video Vanguard award, MTV Video Music Awards, 1995; named to Rock & Roll Hall of Fame, with R.E.M., 2007. Office: REM PO Box 8032 Athens GA 30603-8032

MILLS, NICHOLAS JOHN, biology educator; b. St. Albans, Herts, Eng., Jan. 14, 1954; came to U.S., 1990; s. John Linton and Kathleen Iris (Moody) M.; m. Alison Mary Chambers, July 3, 1976; children: Rosie, Hester, Isobel. BSc in Biol. Scis., U. East Anglia, Norwich, Eng., 1975, PhD in Insect Ecology, 1979. Jr. rsch. fellow Oxford (Eng.) U., 1978-82; sr. forest entomologist European Sta. Internat. Inst. Biol. Control, Delemont, Switzerland, 1982-88, scientist-in-charge U.K. sta. Ascot, Eng., 1988-90; asst. prof. U. Calif., Berkeley, 1990—. Co-editor: Individuals, Populations and Patterns in Ecology, 1994; contbr. articles to sci. jours. Fellow Royal Entomol. Soc. London; mem. Entomol. Soc. Am., British Ecol. Soc., Ecol. Soc. Am., Internat. Orgn. Biol. Control. Office: U Calif 1050 San Pablo Ave Albany CA 94706-2256

MILLS, NICOLAUS, American studies educator, writer; b. Cleve., Dec. 2, 1938; s. Nicolaus and Muriel Mills. AB, Harvard U., 1960; PhD, Brown U., 1966. Asst. prof. English. U. Mich., Ann Arbor, 1965-70; rschr. Ctr. for Urban and Minority Studies Columbia U. Tchrs. Coll., NYC, 1970-72; prof. Am. studies Sarah Lawrence Coll., Bronxville, N.Y., 1972—. Author: American and English Fiction in the Nineteenth Century, 1973, The Crowd in American Literature, 1986, Like a Holy Crusade: Mississippi 1964, 1992, The Triump of Meanness: America's War Against Its Better Self, 1997, Their Last Battle: The Fight for the National World War II Memorial, 2004, Winning the Peace: The Marshall Plan and America's Coming of Age as a Superpower, 2008; Editor: Comparisons: A Short Story Anthology, 1972, The Great School Bus Controversy, 1973, The New Journalism, 1974, Busing USA, 1979, Culture in the Age of Money, 1990, Forty Years of Dissent, 1994, Agruing Immigraton, 1994, Debating Affirmative Action, 1994; co-editor: The New Killing Fields: Massacre and the Politics of Intervention, 2002, 50 Years of Dissent, 2004, Getting out: Historical Perspectives on Leaving Iraq, 2009; mem. editl. bd. Dissent, 1980-; Sunday mag. columnist Cleve. Plain Dealer, 1998-99; contbr. articles to mags. and newspapers, including N.Y. Times, L.A. Times, Newsday, Chgo. Tribune, San Francisco Chronicle, Nation, New Republic, Yale Rev., Dissent, Boston Globe, Am. Heritage. Woodrow Wilson fellow, 1960, Rockefeller Found., 1980; grantee Am. Coun. Learned Socs., 1971, Hewlett-Mellon grantee Sarah Lawrence Coll., 1996; sr. scholar Woodwor Wilson Internat. Ctr., Washington, 2001-2002. Mem.: PEN. Democrat. Office: Sarah Lawrence Coll One Mead Way Bronxville NY 10708

MILLS, OLAN, II, photography company executive; b. 1930; married. Grad., Princeton U., 1952. With Olan Mills, Inc., Chattanooga, 1955—, now chmn. Office: Olan Mills Inc Gen Offices 4325 Amnicola Hwy Chattanooga TN 37406-1014

MILLS, RICHARD HENRY, federal judge; b. Beardstown, Ill., July 19, 1929; s. Myron Epler and Helen Christine (Greve) M.; m. Rachel Ann Keagle, June 16, 1962; children: Jonathan K., Daniel Cass. BA, Ill. Coll., 1951; JD, Mercer U., 1957; LLM, U. Va., 1982. Bar: Ill. 1957, U.S. Dist. Ct. Ill. 1958, U.S. Ct. Appeals 1959, U.S. Ct. Mil. Appeals 1963, U.S. Supreme Ct. 1963. Legal advisor Ill. Youth Commn., 1958-60; state's atty. Cass County, Virginia, Ill., 1960-64; judge Ill. 8th Jud. Cir., Virginia, 1966-76, Ill. 4th Dist. Appellate Ct., Springfield, Ill., 1976-85, U.S. Dist. Ct. (cen. dist.) Ill., Springfield, 1985—. Adj. prof. So. Ill. U. Sch. Medicine, 1985-06; mem. adv. bd. Nat. Inst. Corrections, Washington, 1984-88, Ill. Supreme Ct. Rules Com., Chgo., 1963-85. Contbr. articles to profl. jours. Pres. Abraham Lincoln coun. Boy Scouts Am., 1978-80. With U.S. Army, 1952-54, Korea, col. res.; maj. gen. Ill. Militia. Recipient George Washington Honor medal Freedoms Found., 1969, 73, 75, 82, Disting. Eagle Scout Boy Scouts Am., 1985. Fellow Am. Bar Found.; mem. ABA, Nat. Conf. Fed. Trial Judges (chmn. 1999-00), Ill. Bar Assn., Chgo. Bar Assn., Cass County Bar Assn. (pres. 1962-64, 75-76), Sangamon County Bar Assn., 7th Cir. Bar Assn., Am. Law Inst., Fed. Judges Assn., Army and Navy Club (Washington), Illini Country Club, Sangamo Club, Masons (33 degree), Lincoln-Douglas Am. Inn of Ct. 150 (founding, pres. 1991-93). Republican. Office: US Dist Ct 600 E Monroe St Ste 117 Springfield IL 62701-1659

MILLS, RICHARD PAUL, former state official, school system administrator; b. Paris, Nov. 28, 1944; m. Judith Mills. BA with honors, Middlebury Coll., 1966; MA in Am. History, Columbia U., 1967, MBA, 1975, EdD, 1977. Tchr. history Dalton Sch., NYC, 1967—71; creator with others Elizabeth Seeger Sch., NYC, 1971—73; planning assoc. NJ Dept. of Edn., 1975-78, dir. policy analysis, 1978-80, dep. asst. commr., 1980-82, spl. asst. to the commr., 1982-84; spl. asst. to Gov. Thomas H. Kean State of NJ, 1984-88; commr. of edn. State of Vt., 1988-95, State of NY, 1995—2009; pres. Univ. of the State of NY, 1995—2009. Adj. asst. prof. Columbia Univ. Tchrs. Coll., 1977; adj. assoc. prof. Rider Coll., N.J., 1979; cons. task force to oversee fiscal reform in Newark, 1975; tchr. The Dalton Sch., N.Y.C., 1967-71, Elizabeth Seeger Sch., N.Y.C., 1971-73; mem. Carnegie Task Force on Learning in the Primary

Grades; chair mgmt. group Nat. Alliance for Restructuring Edn.; bd. New Stds. Project; mem. bd. Nat. Ctr. on Edn. and the Economy. Contbr. articles to profl. jours. U.S. rep. to standing com. European Ministers of Edn., 1987.*

MILLS, RICHARD PENCE, ophthalmologist; b. Evanston, Ill., Sept. 13, 1943; s. Glen Earl and Ruth Arlene (Pence) M.; m. Catherine Louise Baily, June 1, 1966 (div. Sept. 1975); 1 child, Lianne Louise; m. Karen Elisabeth, Aug. 1, 1976; children: Elisabeth Ruth, Emily Carole. BA magna cum laude, Yale U., 1964, MD cum laude, 1968. Clin. instr. dept. ophthalmology U. Wash., Seattle, 1972-75, clin. asst. prof., 1975-80, clin. assoc. prof. depts. ophthalmology, medicine, 1980-84, assoc. prof. dept. ophthalmology, 1984-87, prof., vice-chmn. dept. ophthalmology, 1987-97, acting chmn. dept. ophthalmology, 1997—99; prof. U. Ky., 1999—2003, chmn., 1999—2003; pvt. practice Glaucoma Cons. NW, Seattle, 2003—. Adj. prof. depts. medicine and neurol. surgery, U. Wash., 1987-99; pres. St. Peter Hosp. Med. Staff, Olympia, Wash., 1982; trustee Bishop Found., Seattle, 1996-99; trustee Prevent Blindness Am., 1998-2000. Author: (books) Glaucoma Surgical Techniques, 1991, Perimetry Update: 1990-91, 1991, Perimetry Update: 1992-93, 1993, 94-95, 95. Surgeon USPHS, 1969-73. Recipient Optic Neuritis Treatment Trial award Nat. Eye Inst., Washington, 1988-91, Collaborative Initial Glaucoma Treatment Study, 1993-97, Collaborative Normal Tension Glaucoma Study award Glaucoma Rsch. Found., San Francisco, 1988-97. Fellow AMA (del. 1996-2001), Am. Acad. Ophthalmology (pres. 1995, Honor award 1989, Sr. Honor award 1996, Lifetime Lectr. Honor award 2007), Found. Am. Acad. Ophthalmology (adv. bd. 2007-, chief eye com. Care America, 2007-), Am. Bd. Ophthalmology (bd. dirs. 1998-2005), Wash. Acad. Eye Physicians and Surgeons (pres. 1983, Spl. Honor 1993), Wash. State Med. Assn. (trustee 1996), Am. Glaucoma Soc. (dir. 1993-94, sec. 2006-), No. Am. Neuro-Ophth. Soc., Internat. Perimetric Soc. (sec. 1988-94, treas. 1997-2005). Avocations: piano, hiking. Office: Glaucoma Cons NW 1221 Madison St Ste 1124 Seattle WA 98104 Personal E-mail: rmillswa@comcast.net.

MILLS, STEPHEN, performing company executive; Prin. dancer Ballet Austin, 1987, choreographer, 1988, resident choreographer, 1992, assoc. artistic dir., 1999—2000, artistic dir., 2000—. Instr. Internat. Theatrical Inst., Cyprus; master tchr. Booker T. Washington H.S. for the Performing Arts, Dallas, Va. Sch. of the Arts, New Orleans Ctr. for Creative Arts, Stephens Coll., Mo., Point Park Coll., Pitts., Ballet Austin. Choreographed works have been shown at Ballet Builders at Lincoln Ctr., 1998, Rencontres Chorégraphiques Internat. des Seine-Saint-Denis, Paris, Cuballet, Havana, The Dayton Ballet, The Sarasota (Fla.) Ballet, Ballet Pacifica, Dallas Black Dance Theatre, Dance Kaleidoscope, Ontario Ballet Theatre, Toronto, Icelandic Ballet Co., Reykjavik; performing mem. Harkness Ballet, Am. Dance Machine, Cin. Ballet, Indpls. Ballet Theatre, Balanchine Repertoire. Bd. trustees Dance USA. Recipient Humanitarian award, Austin Anti-Defamation League, 2006. Home: 501 W 3rd St Austin TX 78701-3807*

MILLS, STEVEN A., information technology executive; Sales trainee, mktg. rep. IBM, NYC, 1974—80, mem. bus. planning staff divsn. data processing, 1981—82, mgr. bus. planning staff, 1982—84, adminstrv. asst. to v.p. and asst. group exec. plans and controls, 1984—85, dir. planning info. sys. and comm. group, 1985—88, dir. fin. planning, 1988—89, dir. ops. programming sys., 1989—90, asst. gen. mgr. fin. and planning, 1990—92, gen. mgr. Santa Teresa lab., 1992—95, gen. mgr. software group strategy and solutions, 1995—2000, sr. v.p., group exec. software group, 2000—. Mem. ops. com. IBM, mem. worldwide mgmt. coun., mem. corp. tech. com.*

MILLS, STEVEN R., agricultural company executive, accountant; b. July 12, 1955; BS in Mathematics, Ill. Coll, 1977. CPA 1981. Acct. State Farm Ins., Bloomington, Ind., 1977—79; joined Archer Daniels Midland Co., 1979—, contr., 1994—2000, v.p., contr., 2000—02, group v.p., contr., 2002—06, sr. v.p. strategic planning, 2006—08, exec. v.p., CFO, 2008—. Bd. dirs. Kirby Coll.; bd. trustees Ill. Coll. Office: Archer Daniels Midland Co 4666 Farus Pkwy Decatur IL 62526*

MILLS, SUSAN WILSON, music educator; b. Louisville, Nov. 12, 1962; d. William Johnson II and Linda Lee Wilson; m. Dennis Richard Mills, Oct. 25, 1997. BA, Rollins Coll., Winter Park, Fla., 1984; MA, U. Ctrl. Fla., Orlando, 1990, EdD, 1999. Cert. profl. educator, music Fla., 1989, NC, 2007. Dir. sch. music St. Margaret Mary Sch., Winter Park, 1990—98; vis. asst. prof. U. Ctrl. Fla., Orlando, 1999—2000; assoc. chair performing arts Frostburg State U., Md., 2000—06; assoc. prof., coord. music edn. Appalachian State U., Boone, NC, 2006—. Mem. exec. bd. Md. Music Educators Assn., Balt., 2003—06; grant reviewer Md. Arts Coun., Balt., 2003—04. Contbr. chapters to books; performer: Master Musicians Festival, 2003. Grantee Umcolo: The Kimberley Project, Eastman Sch. Music, 2001; Summer Music fellow, Northwestern U., 1994, Appalachian Music fellow, Berea Coll., 2006. Mem.: Am. Orff Schulwerk Assn., Coll. Music Soc., Music Educators Nat. Conf., NC Music Educators Assn. Avocations: sailing, swimming, dance, reading, cooking. Office: Appalachian State U Hayes Sch Music ASU Box 32096 Boone NC 28608 Office Phone: 828-262-6441.

MILLS, WILLIAM HAROLD, JR., construction executive; b. St. Petersburg, Fla., July 24, 1939; s. William Harold and Caroline (Bonfoey) M.; m. Sylvia Ludwig, Jan. 4, 1962 (div. 1975); children—William Harold III, Robert Michael, Leslie Anne; m. Kimberly Keyes, May 4, 1985 (div. 1988); m. Gigi Alice Schmidt, Aug. 1, 1990. Grad., Woodberry Forest Sch., 1954-57; BS in Civil Engring., U. Fla., 1961. Cert. Class A gen. contractor, Fla. V.P. bus. devel. Mills & Jones Constrn., St. Petersburg, Fla., 1964-68; v.p. Wellington Corp., Atlanta, 1968-71; exec. v.p. Mills & Jones Constrn., St. Petersburg, Fla., 1971-79; pres., chmn. Federal Constrn. Co., St. Petersburg, 1979-88, vice chmn., 1988—; pres., chair Univ. Housing Svcs., Inc., St. Petersburg. Mem. adv. com. St Petersburg Port, 1993—. Pres. St. Petersburg Progress, Inc., 1986-87; active mem. Suncoasters, St. Petersburg, 1974—, St. Anthony's Devel. Found., St. Petersburg, 1983-86; past chmn. Pinellas Marine Inst., St. Petersburg, Blue Ribbon Zoning Com., City of St. Petersburg; mem. Tony Janus Award Com.; former mem. Pinellas County Constrn. Licensing Bd., Tampa Bay Aviation Adv. Com., United Fund Pinellas County; former mem. U. South Fla. Campus Adv. Bd. Served with USPHS, 1962-64. Named Hon. Royal Navy Liaison officer Her Majesty's Royal Navy, 1984. Mem. ASCE, NSPE, Am. Mgmt. Assn., Mensa, St. Petersburg Area C. of C. (bd. govs. 1983-85), Fla. Sports Adv. Coun., Order of Salvador/Salvador Dali Mus., St. Petersburg Yacht Club, Dragon Club, Les Ambassadeurs Club (London), Annabel's Club (London), Useppa Island Club (past bd. govs.), Sigma Alpha Epsilon, U.S. Croquet Assn., Univ. Fla. Pres.'s Coun. (life). Republican. Episcopalian. Home: 1260 Brightwaters Blvd NE Saint Petersburg FL 33704-3728 E-mail: wmillsjr@uhsi.com.

MILLS, WILLIAM HAYES, lawyer; b. Gordo, Ala., Mar. 30, 1931; s. Early S. and Bama (Cameron) M. LLB, U. Ala., 1956. Bar: Ala. 1956. Pvt. practice, Birmingham, Ala.; ptnr. Rogers, Howard, Redden & Mills, 1961—79, Redden, Mills & Clark, 1979—. Arbitrator Fed. Mediation and Conciliation Svc., Am. Arbitration Assn. Served with AUS, 1948-50, 50-51. Mem. ABA, Ala. Bar Assn., Birmingham Bar Assn. Baptist. Home: 2105 Williamsburg Way Birmingham AL 35223-1740 Office: Redden Mills & Clark 940 Financial Ctr Birmingham AL 35203 Home Phone: 205-870-4139; Office Phone: 205-322-0457. Business E-Mail: whm@rmclaw.com.

MILLS, WILLIAM J., bank executive; Grad., Denison U. V.p., mem. Structured Finance Rating Com. Standard & Poor's Corp.; joined Smith Barney, 1982, co-head fin. institutions divsn., head Debt Origination/Securitization Group, co-head global investment banking divsn. NYC, 1994—99; CEO Asia Pacific, mem. mgmt. com. Salomon Smith Barney; chmn., CEO Europe, Middle East and Africa (EMEA) Citi Markets & Banking; CEO Western Europe, Middle East and Africa (WEMEA) Citigroup Inc., chair CitiDifference Diversity Steering Com. Office: Citigroup Inc 399 Park Ave New York NY 10043*

MILLS, WILLIAM JAMES, JR., orthopedist, surgeon, researcher; b. San Francisco, Calif., July 7, 1918; s. William James Mills and Rose Lena Conrad; m. Elaine Mary Nagelvoort, Aug. 23, 1952; children: Sarah, Janet, William, Martha, Mary, John, Matthew. BA, U. Calif., 1942; MD, Stanford U., 1950; LittD (hon.), U. Alaska, 2003; DSc (hon.), U. Man., 2006. Cert. Am. Coll. Surgery, Am. Acad. Orthopedic Surgery, Am. Orthopedic Assn., Arctic Inst. N. Am. Intern U. Mich. Hosp., Ann Arbor, Mich., 1949—51, resident, 1951—54; pvt. practice orthopaedist Anchorage, 1955—66; pvt. practice orthop. surgeon, 1968—; surgeon US Naval Hosp., DaNang, Vietnam, 1966—67; asst. prof. Vanderbilt U. Hosp., Nashville, 1967—68. Founder, dir. Alaska Arctic Med. Rsch. Found., Anchorage, 1978—; adj. prof. U. Alaska, Anchorage, 1980—; clin. prof. dept. orthop. surgery U. Wash. Editor-in-chief: Alaska Medicine Jour., 1959; contbr. scientific articles, photographs to jours. Rear admiral USNR, 1942—78, WWII, Vietnam, ret. USNR, 1978. Recipient Dr. Helen Whaley award, Alaska Treatment Ctr., Alpine Team medal, City of Lecco, Italy, 1961, Disting. Achievement award, U. Mich., 2002, Jack Hildes medal, Circumpolar Health Soc., 2003, Disting. Achievement, U. Mich., 2001. Fellow: ACS, Am. Orthop. Assn., Am. Acad. Orthop. Surgeons. Avocations: camping, fly fishing, reading, stamp collecting/philately, gardening. Home and Office: 1544 Hidden Lane Anchorage AK 99501

MILLS-KOONCE, WILLIAM ROGER, psychologist, director; b. Washington, Sept. 19, 1978; s. William Roger and Brenda Mills (Stepmother), Zachary Taylor (Stepfather) and Peggy Koonce; m. Cathi Barbra Propper, Apr. 1, 2006; 1 child, Liam Zachary. PhD, UNC Chapel Hill, 2005. Rsch. scientist UNC Chapel Hill, 2005—. Asst. dir. Ctr. Devel. Sci., UNC CH, 2007—; dir. Family Life Project, Chapel Hill, 2005—. Contbr. scientific papers. Recipient Rsch. award, NIH, 2007—. Mem.: Soc. Rsch. Child Devel. Liberal.

MILLSPAUGH, MARTIN LAURENCE, real estate developer, consultant; b. Columbus, Ohio, Dec. 16, 1925; s. Martin Laurence and Elisabeth (Park) M.; m. Meredith Plant, May 10, 1952; children: Elisabeth, M. Laurence, Meredith, Thomas. AB summa cum laude, Princeton U., 1949. Reporter, columnist Richmond News Leader, Va., 1949-53; urban affairs writer Balt. Evening Sun, 1953-57; asst. commr. Urban Renewal Adminstrn., Washington, 1957-60; dep. gen. mgr. Charles Ctr., Balt., 1960-65; pres., chmn., CEO Charles Ctr.-Inner Harbor Mgmt., Inc., 1965-85; exec. v.p., pres., vice chmn. Enterprise Devel. Co., Columbia, Md., 1985—2005; pres. Enterprise Internat. Devel. Co., Columbia, 1988-91, vice chmn., 1991—2005, Enterprise Real Estate Svcs., Inc., 1996—2005; chmn. Global Harbors Documentary Inc., 2004—; pvt. practice Balt., 2005—. Conducted seminars in Nagasaki and Kagoshima, Japan, 1991-92; lectr. Columbia U., Princeton U., Johns Hopkins U., U. Md., U. New Orleans, NYU, Acad. Polit. Sci., AAAS, Lambda Alpha Internat. Urban Land Inst., 1985-95, U.K. Inst. Travel and Tourism, 1993, Can. Water Resources Assn., 1991, Nat. Bldg. Mus., 1995, Internat. Property Market, Cannes, 1996, others; appeared on USIA Worldnet TV Dialogue, Montevideo, Uruguay, 1990, Recife and Rio de Janeiro, 1995; cons. in field. Author: (with others) The Human Side of Urban Renewal, 1958; author (newspaper series) Design for Living (hon. mention Heywood Broun award 1957);City Alive, 2007, profl. appearances include VOA, 1994, CBS Sunday News, 1994; contbr. articles to profl. jours. Trustee Enoch Pratt Free Libr., Balt., 1965-85, Gilman Sch., 1975-80, Bryn Mawr Sch. for Girls, 1978-81; bd. dirs. Planned Parenthood Assn. Md., 1962-65, Roland Park Civic League, 1962-64, sec., 1963-64, Blue Cross of Md., Inc., 1970-80, Balt. Symphony Orch. Assn., 1974-78, YMCA Greater Balt. area, 1977-81; Md. Internat. Coun., Balt., 1992-96, mem. long range planning com., 1994-96, sec., 1995-96; chair nominating com. World Trade Ctr. Inst., 1996-01; task force Twentieth Century Fund, NYC, 1984-85; adv. coun. real estate devel. program Columbia U. Grad. Sch. Architecture and Planning, 1985-94; bd. advisors Fight-Blight Fund, Balt., 1961-62, Waterfront Ctr., Washington, 1987-90; adv. bd. Nat. Aquarium, Balt., 1988-2001, Sch. Bus. Mgmt. Morgan State U., 1993-94, Real Estate Inst., Sch. Profl. and Bus. Studies Johns Hopkins U., 1994-2006, chair, 2000-2002; pres.'s adv. bd. U. Md. Balt. County, 1989-94; adv. bd. Ctr. for Balt. Studies/U. Balt., 2001-02; adv. panel Ctr. Strategic and Internat. Studies, Washington, 1993-94; mem. Md. Transp. Real Estate Adv. Group, 1996; mem. U.S. Senate Productivity Award Selection Com. for Md., 1987. Sgt. USAF, 1944-46, PTO. Recipient Disting. Svc. award U.S. Housing and Home Fin. Agy., Washington, 1960, Excellence award Urban Land Inst., 1980, Civic Accomplishment award Greater Balt. Comm., 1981, Urban Planning award The Waterfront Ctr., 1995, Prix d'Excellence Awd. Internat. Real Estate Fedn., 1997. Mem. Urban Land Inst. (hon., exec. group internat. coun., 1989-97, vice chmn. internat. coun. 1995-96, chair adv. panel for city of Harrisburg, Pa., 1984, internat. com. 1987-88, Balt. dist. coord. 1987-91, vice-chmn. dist. coun. com. 1991-94, Balt. dist. coun. exec. com. 1992—, adv. panel for Oklahoma City, 1995, chair Project Analysis Chattanooga, 1999, awards com. 1995-97), Internat. Real Estate Fedn. Greater Balt. Com. (urban affairs coun. 1982-87), Coun. on Urban Econ. Devel., Internat. Downtown Assn., Internat. New Town Assn. (adv. panel for waterfront devel. for City of Malmo, Sweden 1987), Phi Beta Kappa, Lambda Alpha. Clubs: Center, Balt., 14 W Hamilton St (Balt.); Ivy (Princeton, NJ). Democrat. Episcopalian. Home: 203 Ridgewood Rd Baltimore MD 21210-2538 E-mail: mmillsii@aol.com.

MILLSTEIN, IRA M., lawyer, educator; b. NYC, Nov. 8, 1926; s. Harry M. and Birdie E. (Rosenbaum) M.; m. Diane G. Greenberg, July 3, 1949; children: James Eliot, Elizabeth Jane. BS, Columbia U., 1947, LL.B., 1949. Bar: NY 1949, US Supreme Ct. 1973. Atty. antitrust div. Dept. Justice, Washington, 1949-51; assoc. firm Weil Gotshal & Manges LLP, NYC, 1951-57, ptnr., 1957—. Fellow faculty govt. John F. Kennedy Sch. Govt., Harvard U., 1983-87; Yale Sch. Mgmt. sr. assoc. dean for corp. governance 2005-, Eugene F. Williams Jr. vis. prof. in competetive enterprise and strategy 1996—; adv. bd. mem.Millstein Ctr. for Corp. Govt. and Performance; chmn. pvt. sector adv. group of Global Corp. Governance Forum sponsored by World Bank/OECD-Paris, Washington, 1999-2005, chmn. emeritus 2005-; counsel, bd. dirs. Lower Manhattan Devel. Corp., 2002-07; bd. mem. World Trade Ctr. Meml. Found.; chmn. NY State Commn. Pub. Authority Reform, 2004-06. Author: (with Katsh) The Limits of Corporate Power, 1981, (with MacAvoy) The Recurrent Crisis in Corporate Governance, 2003; contbr. articles to profl. jours. Mem. Nat. Commn. on Consumer Fin., 1969-72, chmn., 1971-72; chmn. exec. com. bd. overseers Albert Einstein Coll. Medicine, Yeshiva U., Bronx, NY, 1981—, chmn., 2004-07; chmn. bd. trustees Cen. Pk. Conservancy, 1990-99; co-chair NYSE, NASD Blue Ribbon com. on improving audit coms., 1999. Named one of the 100 Most Influential Lawyers, Nat. Law Jour., 2006; recipient: Lifetime Achievement award, The Am. Lawyer mag., 2007; Decorated chevalier Nat. Order of Merit, France. Mem. Am. Acad. Arts and Scis. (elected), ABA (chmn. antitrust law sect. 1977-78), NY State Bar Assn. (chmn. antitrust law sect. 1967-68), Nat. Assn. Corp. Dirs. (bd. dirs. 1994—2004, 2007-, governance coun. 2004-07), Met. Club, Quaker Ridge Golf Club. Home: 1240 Flagler Dr Mamaroneck NY 10543-4601 Office: Weil Gotshal & Manges LLP 767 5th Ave Ste 3201 New York NY 10153-0023 Business E-Mail: ira.millstein@weil.com.

MILLSTEIN, LINCOLN, media company executive; BA in Polit. Sci., U. Conn.; postgrad., Stanford U., 1980—81. Reporter, editor The Hartford Courant, 1973—83, bus. editor, 1981—83; varous editor positions The Globe, 1983—85; v.p. new media The Boston Globe, 1995—99; CEO Boston.com, 1998—99; group v.p., pub. N.Y. Times Digital, N.Y. Times Co., NY, 1999—2000, exec. v.p. NY, 2000—04; sr. v.p., dir. digital media Hearst Newspapers, 2005—. Profl. Journalism fellow, NEH, 1980—81. Achievements include development of and introduction of The Globe 100 list of the top companies in Massachusetts in 1989. Office: Hearst 300 W 57TH ST New York NY 10019-3790

MILLSTONE, DAVID JEFFREY, lawyer; b. Morgantown, W.Va., 1946; AB, Johns Hopkins U., 1968; JD, W.Va. U., 1971. Bar: Ohio 1971. Ptnr. Squire, Sanders & Dempsey LLP, Cleve. Co-author: Wage Hour Law--How to Comply, 2001; editor: Ohio and Fed. Employment Law Manual, 2001; contbr. chapters to books. Past chair regional bd., nat commr., nat. exec. com. mem., chair edn. com. Anti-Defamation League, 2006—09. Mem.: ABA, Ohio Bar Assn., Ohio Mgmt. Lawyers Assn., Cleve. Bar Assn. Office: Squire Sanders & Dempsey 4900 Key Tower 127 Public Sq Ste 4900 Cleveland OH 44114-1304 Office Phone: 216-479-8574. E-mail: dmillstone@ssd.com.

MILLWOOD, KENNETH ANDREW, university librarian; s. Earl Andrew Millwood and Minette; m. Linda Gail Oaks, June 9, 1985; children: Andrew, David, Danielle. AS, Hiwassee Coll., Madisonville, TN, 1974; BA in Communicatons, U. Tenn., Knoxville, 1976; MA in Libr. Sci., U. Tenn., 1986; MA in Edn., Mid. Tenn. State U., Murfreesboro, 1978. Dir. libr. svcs. Hiwassee Coll., 1979—88, Anderson U., SC, 1988—. Pres. Kiwanis, Madisonville, 1987—87. Mem.: SC. Libr. Assn., Assn. Librarians and Archivists Bapt. Instns. (pres. 2008—), Am. Library Assn. Methodist. Office: Anderson Univ 316 Boulevard Anderson SC 29621 Personal E-mail: kmillwood@gmail.com.

MILMAN, NATALIE BORDELON, education educator; BA in English and Spanish, Tulane U., 1991; MA in Multicultural Edn., Calif. State U., Dominguez Hills, 1994; PhD in Instructional Tech., U. Va., Charlottesville, 2000. Tchr. Long Beach (Calif.) Unified Sch. Dist., 1991—96; assoc. prof. George Washington U., Washington, 2008—. Author: The Digital Teaching Portfolio Handbook: A How-To Guide for Teachers, 2003, What Every School Leader Should Know About Digital Teaching Portfolios, 2003, The Digital Teaching Portfolio Workbook: Understanding the Digital Teaching Portfolio Process, 2005, Digital teaching portfolios: Catalysts for Fostering Authentic Professional Development, 2005. Recipient Outstanding Grad. Tchg. Asst. award, U. Va., 1999; named Luminary, Gelman Libr., George Wash. U., 2005; Curry Ctr. for Tech. and Tchr. Edn. fellow, U. Va., 1997—2000. Mem.: Am. Ednl. Rsch. Assn. (officer spl. interest group 2005—). Office: George Washington U 2134 G St NW Washington DC 20052

MILMOE, J. GREGORY, JR., lawyer; b. White Plains, NY, Nov. 16, 1947; AB, Cornell U., 1970; JD, Fordham U., 1975. Bar: NY 1976. Joined Skadden, Arps, Slate, Meagher & Flom, NYC, 1971—, mailroom asst., 1971, ptnr., co-leader corp. restructuring. Lectr. on fiduciary and restructuring issues for legal and business audiences. Articles editor Fordham Law Rev., 1974—75. Named a Dealmaker of Yr., Am. Lawyer mag., 2007. Office: Skadden Arps Slate Meagher & Flom 4 Times Sq New York NY 10036 Office Phone: 212-735-3770. Office Fax: 917-777-3770. Business E-Mail: jmilmoe@skadden.com.

MILNE, CHRISTOPHER-PAUL, medical association administrator; b. Chgo., July 30, 1952; s. James Toner and Helen Matic Milne; m. Deborah Laurence, June 18, 1977; children: Vanessa Maria, Andrew Laurence, James Maxwell. DVM, U.N.P.H.U., Sto. Dgo., Dom. Rep., 1982; M in Pub. Health, Johns Hopkins U., Balt., 1988; JD, Franklin Pierce Law Ctr., Concord, NH, 1997. Bar: NH State Bar Assn. (law atty.) 1997; cert. Fla. Bd. Vet. Medicine, 1984. Pub. response program mgr. NJ State Dept. Health, Trenton, 1988—94; assoc. dir. Tufts Ctr. Study Drug Devel., Boston, 1997—. Vis. fellow U. Edinburgh Innogen Ctr., 2008—. Contbr. articles to profl. jours., chapters to books. Recipient Outstanding Achievement award, Drug Devel. Assn., 2004. Independent. Roman Catholic. Avocations: travel, hiking. Office: Tufts Univ 75 Kneeland St Ste 1100 Boston MA 02111 Office Fax: 617-636-2425. Business E-Mail: christopher.milne@tufts.edu.

MILNE, KAREN LOUISE, retired science educator; b. Phoenix, Apr. 26, 1947; d. Jean Raisch Stewart; children: Jamie Barbara Roberson, Benjamin Morrison. BA in Edn., Ariz. State U., Tempe, 1972. Sci./math tchr. 5th grade Manzanita Sch., Phoenix, 1969—74; sci./math tchr. 8th grade Cactus Wren Sch., Phoenix, 1980—84; sci. tchr. 7th grade Cholla Mid. Sch., Phoenix, 1984—96; sci. tchr. 7th and 8th grade Sweetwater Sch., Glendale, Ariz., 1996—2009. Mid. sch. biology instr. Woodrow Wilson Nat. Fellowship Found., Princeton, NJ, 1995—98. Student coun. advisor Sweetwater Sch., 1996—2006; treas. Cholla Sch. PTO, Phoenix, 1984—85; sec. Sweetwater PTO, Glendale, 1997—98, Sweetwater Site Coun., Glendale, 2000—02, mem., 2002—04; yearbook advisor Sweetwater Sch., 1996—2006; v.p. Sweetwater PTO, Ariz., 2007—. Recipient Sci. Tchr. of Yr., Ariz. Sci. Tchrs. Assn., 1994, Team That Makes Difference award, Arz. Middle Level Assn., 2009; grantee, Woodrow Wilson Nat. Fellowship Found., 1994, Ariz. Game and Fish Dept., 1994. Mem.: Ariz. Profl. Educators, NEA, Nat. Biology Tchrs. Assn., Nat. Sci. Tchrs. Assn. Office: Sweetwater Sch 4602 W Sweetwater Ave Glendale AZ 85304 Office Phone: 602-896-6555. Business E-Mail: karen.milne@wesdschools.org.

MILNER, BRENDA ATKINSON LANGFORD, neuropsychologist; b. Manchester, Eng., July 15, 1918; arrived in Can., 1944; d. Samuel and Leslie (Doig) Langford. BA, Cambridge U., Eng., 1939, MA, 1949, DSc, 1972; DSc (hon.), McGill U., 1991, U. Man., 1982; PhD, McGill U., 1952; DSc (hon.), Wesleyan U., 1991, Acadia U., 1991, U. St. Andrews, 1992, U. Hartford, 1997, McMaster U., 1999, Meml. U., 2002; LLD (hon.), Queen's U., 1980, U. Lethbridge, 1986, Mt. Holyoke Coll., 1986, U. Laval, 1987, U. Toronto, 1987, Cambridge U., 2000; LHD (hon.), Mt. St. Vincent U., 1988; Doctorate (hon.), U. Montréal, 1988, U. Ottawa, 2004; ScD (hon.), Columbia U., 2002, U. Naples II, 2002; ScD,

Am. Jour. Med. Genetics, 1977-94, Bioethics Digest, 1977-78, Prenatal Diagnosis, 1980-90, 92—, Intelligence Reports in Ob-Gyn., 1982-88, Fetal Therapy, 1986—; peer reviewer New England Jour. Medicine, Pediatrics, Am. Jour. Med. Genetics, Am. Jour. Ob-Gyn., Am. Jour. Law and Medicine, Am. Jour. Pub. Health, Prenatal Diagnosis, Fetal Therapy, Ob-Gyn., Epidemiology, Jour. Pediatrics; contbr. over 300 articles to profl. jours. Recipient First Place Film award Nat. Coun. Family Rels. Media Awards Co., 1990, Tinsley Harrison award So. Soc. for Clin. Investigation, 1991; Aubrey Milunsky Endowed Chair in Human Genetics named in his honor Boston U., 1991. Fellow Am. Coll. Med. Genetics (founding), Royal Coll. Physicians (diploma in child health 1965); mem. Am. Pediat. Soc., Am. Soc. Human Genetics (social issues com. 1983-87), Am. Soc. Law and Medicine (v.p. 1982-83, pres.-elect 1983-85, pres. 1985-86, bd. dirs. 1986-88, 90-93), Soc. for Pediat. Rsch., Mass. Med. Soc. Office: Boston U Sch Medicine Ctr for Human Genetics 715 Albany St Boston MA 02118-2307

MILUTINOVIC, MILAN A., former President of the Republic of Serbia; b. Belgrade, Yugoslavia, Dec. 19, 1942; s. Aleksandar Milan Milutinovic and Ljubica Vladimir Jokic; m. Olga Branko Sapasojevic, Dec. 6, 1970; 1 son, Veljko. LLM, U. Belgrade, 1965. Mem. presidency Yugoslav Socialist Youth Union, Belgrade, 1969-71; M.P. Belgrade, 1969-74; sec. Communal Com. of League of Communists, 1972-74; sec. for ideology City Com. of League of Communists of Belgrade, 1974-77; Republican sec. for edn. and sci. Govt. of Serbia, 1977-82, dir. Nat. Library of Serbia, 1983-87; ambassador, head sector for press info. and culture Fed. Secretariat for Fgn. Affairs, 1987-89; mem. fgn. affairs com. Fed. Assembly, 1969-74; ambassador to Greece Fed. Republic of Yugoslavia, 1989-95, minister for fgn. affairs, 1995-97; pres. Republic of Serbia, 1997—2002. Mem., chief 90 Yugoslav meetings and dels. to UN, OECD, UNESCO. Author: University__Eppur si muove, 1985; also articles. Decorated Order of Merit with Silver Star, 1974, medal for work with gold coronet, 1980. Avocation: stamp collecting/philately. Home: Koste Glavinica 9 11000 Belgrade Serbia E-mail: bel6radek6@yahoo.com.

MILWAY, PHYLLIS LOUISE, human services manager; b. Wathena, Kans., Apr. 25, 1937; d. Leslie Lauern and Lula Belle Lehman; m. James Terrill Milway; children: Teri, Richard. Degree, Arapahoe CC,U. Colo. Mgr. Gates Rubber Co., Denver, 1966—92. Mgr. Gates Career Ctr. Co., 1987—92; bd. mem. Treasurer Compsych, Calif., 1992—; cons. Compsyck, 1970—, Poland Consulting Co., 2009—. Contbr. articles. Trustee PED, 2004—08; bd. mem. Woman Sch. Lakewood, 1980; com. mem. DU Bus. Sch., 1980—90. Recipient Outstanding award, Dex. U., 1980—90, award, ASID, 1988, Woman's Achievement award, YWCA, 1980. Avocation: reading.

MIMS, JULIAN L., III, history professor, archivist; s. M. Hansford and Nancy Crockett Mims; m. Paulette C. Champy, Dec. 30, 1966 (div.); children: Stuart C., Julian L. Mims. IV, Florence A. MA, U. SC, Columbia, 1969, PhD, 2002. Cert. social studies tchr. SC State Dept. Edn., 1966, Inst. Cert. Records Mgrs., 1981, Acad. Cert. Archivists, 1988. History prof. U. SC Distance Edn., 1973—, Augusta State U., 2001—, Morehouse Coll., Atlanta, 2008—. Mem. history adv. com. SCITV, Columbia, 1970. Elder Presbyn. Ch. US, Phila., 1973—. Recipient Award of Merit, ARMA Internat., 1979. Mem.: Ga Assn. Historians. Episcopalian. Avocations: music, camping, travel, writing. Home: 290 Miles Ashley Rd Trenton SC 29847

MIMS, NATHALIA REGINA, music educator; b. Bay Minette, Ala., Feb. 24, 1959; d. Leroy Roland and Helen Durant Mims; 1 child, Anais Chanel Downs. MusB in Mus. Edn., U. Ariz., Tucson, 1992. Mid. sch. chorus tchr. TUSD, Tucson, 1992—. Dir. music Prince Chapel African Methodist Episcopal Ch., Tucson, 2000—. Asst. dir. music Tucson chpt. Gospel Music Workshop Am., 2002—. Mem.: Zeta Phi Beta. Democrat. Methodist. Home: 1872 W Camelot Rd Tucson AZ 85713 Office: Booth Fickett Math Sci Magnet 450 S Montego Dr Tucson AZ 85713 Personal E-mail: nrmims@gmail.com.

MIMS, WILLIAM CLEVELAND, state attorney general, lawyer; b. Harrisonburg, Va., June 20, 1957; s. David Lathan and Lurleen Shirley (Stovall) M.; m. Jane Ellen Rehme, Dec. 20, 1980; children: Katherine Grace, Emily Anne, Sarah Joy. AB, Coll. of William & Mary, 1979; JD, George Washington U., 1984; LLM, Georgetown U., 1986. Bar: Va. Legis. asst. Congressman Paul Trible, Washington, 1981-82; dep. legis. dir. Senator Paul Trible, Washington, 1983-85; chief of staff Congressman Frank Wolf, Washington, 1986-87; atty. Hazel & Thomas, P.C., Leesburg, Va., 1987-91, Worcester, Mims & Atwill, P.C., 1993—2002, Mims, Atwill & Leigh, P.C., Leesburg, 2002—05; mem. Va. Gen. Assembly, Richmond, 1991—2006, del., 1992-98, senator, 1998—2005; chief deputy atty. gen. State of Va., 2006—09, atty. gen., 2009—. Adj. prof. law George Mason U., 2002-05; mem. Va. Housing Commn., 1994-2005, chmn. 2000—2003; mem. Va. Code Commn., 2000, 05, chmn., 2003—. Active Nat. Eagle Scout Assn., 1992--. Mem. Va. Bar Assn. (Boyd-Graves Conf. 1996—, bd. govs. 2002—). Republican. Presbyterian. Office: Office of Atty Gen 900 E Main St Richmond VA 23219*

MIN, JAMES B., legislative staff member; Legis. aide to congressman Bill Thomas US House of Reps., Washington, 2001—02, legis. asst., 2002—03, chief of staff, 2003—07, chief of staff to congressman Kevin McCarthy, 2007—. Republican. Mailing: US House Reps 1523 Longworth House Office Bldg Washington DC 20215 Office Phone: 202-225-2915. Office Fax: 202-225-2908.*

MIN, JANICE BYUNG, former editor-in-chief; b. Atlanta, Aug. 13, 1969; d. Hong Min; m. Peter Sheehy, 1997; children: Will, Tate. BA in Journalism, Columbia U., NYC, 1990. Reporter, Westchester County, NY, 1990—92; writer to sr. editor People mag., NYC, 1992—97; with Life mag., NYC, 1997—98; asst. mng. editor In Style mag., NYC, 1998—2001; exec. editor Us Weekly mag., NYC, 2002—03, editor-in-chief, 2003—09. Recipient Editor of Yr., AdWeek mag., 2005; named one of 40 Under 40, Crain's NY Bus., 2006, The 50 Most Powerful Women in NYC, NY Post, 2007.*

MIN, MISUN, mathematician; b. Chungju, Republic of Korea, Nov. 23, 1968; d. Kyung Won Min and Jae Myung Um. PhD in Applied Math., Brown U., Providence, 2002. Rsch. engr. Hynix Semiconductor Inc., Icheon, Kyungki-Do, Republic of Korea, 1994—96; asst. computational scientist Argonne Nat. Lab., Ill., 2003—.

MIN, SOO BONG, bank executive; b. Hwanghae Province, Korea, 1938; BA in Economics, Seoul U. Various positions including COO, pres. Comml. Bank Korea, Seoul, Republic of Korea, 1959—94; pres., CEO Hanmi Bank, 1995—99; pres., CEO, dir. Wilshire Bancorp, LA, 1999—. Office: Wilshire Bancorp Inc 3200 Wilshire Blvd Los Angeles CA 90010 Office Phone: 213-387-3200. Office Fax: 213-427-6584.

MIN, SUN-JOON, research scientist, educator; s. Sang-Ki Min and Bun-Nam Kwon; m. Soohyun Lee, Dec. 27, 2000; children: Andrew Jaeyeon, Irene Suyeon. PhD, UCLA, 2005. Postdoc. rsch. assoc. Columbia U., NYC, 2005—08; sr. rsch. scientist Korea Inst. Sci. & Tech., Seoul, Republic of Korea, 2008—. Adj. assoc. prof. U. Sci. & Tech., Daejeon, Republic of Korea, 2008—. Contbr. scientific papers. Mem.: Korean Chem. Soc., Am. Chem. Soc. Achievements include research in natural product synthesis; development of new synthetic methodology. Office: Korea Inst Sci & Tech 39-1 Hawolgok-dong Seongbuk-gu Seoul 136-791 Republic of Korea Office Fax: 82-2-958-5189. Personal E-mail: smin92@gmail.com. Business E-Mail: sjmin@kist.re.kr.

MINA, JOHN LOUIS (IVAN MINEA), religious studies educator, archivist; b. Nancy, France, Jan. 31, 1950; came to U.S. 1951; s. Albert and Mila (Koenig) M. BA with highest honors, U. Calif., Santa Barbara, 1972; MA, U. Calif., Berkeley, 1974, PhD, 1979. Lectr. Centre D'Etudes Russes, Meudon, France, 1984—85; vis. asst. prof. U. Ky., Lexington, 1987—88; prof. Sts. Cyril and Methodius Sem., Pitts., 1990—95; archivist Met. Archdiocese of Pitts., Byzantine Rite, 1997—. Contbr. articles to profl. jours. Mem. Cath. Hist. Soc. West Pa., Pitts.; rep. theol. com. Christian Assocs. S.W. Pa. Recipient Dobro Slovo, U. Calif., Berkeley, 1980; U. Calif. Regents scholar, 1968; Fulbright fellow, 1972. Mem. KC (4th degree), Phi Beta Kappa. Byzantine Catholic. Avocations: travel, foreign affairs. Home: 318 Park Ave Clairton PA 15025-1758 Personal E-mail: ivanmina@verizon.net.

MINAGAWA, TEIICHI, molecular biologist; b. Kamo, Niigata, Japan, Oct. 28, 1924; s. Ryozo Taguchi and Tatsu Minagawa; m. Sachiko Isahaya, Apr. 13, 1952; 1 child. BS, Kyoto U., Japan, 1947, MS, 1949, DSc, 1957. Assoc. prof. Kobe U., 1953-64; postdoctoral Syracuse (N.Y.) U., 1957-58; rsch. assoc. Carnegie Inst. Wash. (Cold Spring Harbor), 1958—60; assoc. prof. Kyoto U., 1965-70, prof., 1970-88, emeritus prof., 1988—. Author: T-Phages, 1991, Genetics and Evolution, 1995, Dictionary of Molecular Cell Biology, 1997, Virology, 1997 and other works on molecular biology. Recipient KunSanto Kyokujitsu Chuju-sho (Rising Sun) from Japan Govt., 2003, Forty Yr. Membership award, Am. Soc. Microbiology, 2007. Avocations: gardening, listening to classics.

MINAHAN, DANIEL FRANCIS, lawyer, retired manufacturing executive; b. Orange, NJ, Dec. 3, 1929; s. Alfred A. and Katherine (Kelly) M.; m. Mary Jean Gaffney, May 2, 1953; children: Daniel F. Jr. (dec.), John A. AB magna cum laude, U. Notre Dame, 1951; JD magna cum laude, U. Conn., 1964; grad., Advanced Mgmt. Program, Harvard, 1975. Bar: Conn. 1964, U.S. Supreme Ct 1969, U.S. Ct. of Appeals (2d cir.), U.S. Dist. Ct. Conn. 1971. Mgr. indsl. engring. Uniroyal, Inc., Naugatuck, Conn., 1952-59, mgr. indsl. relations, 1959-64, dir. labor relations NYC, 1964-66; v.p. indsl. relations and labor counsel Phillips Van Heusen Corp., NYC, 1966-69; v.p. personnel-adminstrn. Broadway-Hale Stores, Inc., LA, 1969-70; v.p. employee relations, sec. Magnavox-N.Am., Philips Corp., 1970-73, v.p. ops., group exec., 1973-83, sr. v.p. adminstrn., 1984-89, exec. v.p., 1989-93, vice-chmn., 1991-93; vice-chmn. nat. found. bd. Robert Anderson Sch. Mgmt., U. N.Mex., 1993-98; pvt. practice, 1998—. Trustees adv. coun., Fairfield U., mem. dean's coun. Grad. Sch. Bus. Co-author: The Developing Labor Law, 1971. Chmn. bd. Internat. Fedn. Keystone Youth Orgns., London and Chgo., 1984-88; vice-chmn. nat. found. bd. Anderson Sch. Mgmt., U. N.Mex., 1993-98. With USMC. Mem. The Forum for World Affairs, Conn. Bar Assn., Harvard Club, Club Internat. (Chgo.).

MINAI, ALI, engineering educator; married. PhD, U. Va., Charlottesville, 1991. Rsch. assoc. U. Va., 1991—93; asst. prof., ECE dept. U. Cin., 1993—2000, assoc. prof., ECE dept., 2000—. Editor: (book) Complex Engineered Systems: Science Meets Technology, Unifying Themes in Complex Systems III, Unifying Themes in Complex Systems II; contbr. articles to profl. jours. Grant, NSF, 1996—98, 1998—2000, 2007—. Mem.: IEEE, Internat. Neural Networks Soc. (sec. 2006—), Sigma Xi, Soc. Neurosci., Eta Kappa Nu, Tau Beta Pi. Office: Univ Cin Dept Elec & Computer Engring Cincinnati OH 45221-0030

MINAI, OMAR AHMAD, physician; b. Lahore, Pakistan; s. Idris Ahmad and Riaz Fatima Minai; m. Beena Ahmad, Dec. 7, 1998. MB BS, Aga Khan U., Karachi, Pakistan, 1990. Diplomate Am. Bd. Internal Medicine, Am. Bd. Pulmonary Medicine, Am. Bd. Critical Care Medicine, Am. Bd. Sleep Medicine. Intern in internal medicine U. Conn., Farmington, 1992-93, resident in internal medicine, 1992-96; fellow in pulmonary and critical care medicine Cleve. Clin. Found., 1996-99, staff physician in pulmonary and critical care medicine, 1999—. Contbr. Mem.: ACP, Am. Thoracic Soc., Am. Coll. Chest Physicians. Office: Cleve Clinic Found 9500 Euclid Ave Ste A-90 Cleveland OH 44195-0001 Office Phone: 216-445-2610. E-mail: minaio@ccf.org.

MINAR, PAUL G., interior designer, consultant; b. Phoenix, July 12, 1932; s. Aaron Crowther and Ione Anna (Schmid) Mortensen. Student, Ariz. State U., 1950-54, John F. Kennedy U., 1978-80, Antioch West U., 1980. Sound effects technician, TV stage mgr. Sta. KHJ-AM-TV, LA, 1955-63; displayer W.&J. Sloane Furniture Co., Beverly Hills, Calif., 1963-66, Bullock's Dept. Store, LA, 1966-68, Macy's Dept. Store, San Francisco, 1968-70; interior designer Lloyd's Furniture Co., San Diego, 1970-71, Bonynge's Furniture Co., Oakland, Calif., 1971-72, Breuner's Furniture Co., Oakland, 1972-74; design cons. The Other Artist, San Francisco, 1974—. Archival rschr. and conservation Petaluma Hist. Mus., 1994—; cons. Human Svcs. Dept., Oakland, Calif., 2003—; profl. numerologist; lectr. in onomatology. Author: Numbers: The Energy Force in Your Name, 2006; writer, producer (documentary) The Modern Nursing Home, 1959. Vol. talent agt. San Francisco Symphony Black and White Ball, 1983; mem. Fine Arts Mus. of San Francisco. Mem. Inst. Noetic Scis., Petaluma Mus. Assn., Assn. Internationale de Numerologues, Calif. Soc. Psychical Study. Democrat. Roman Catholic. Avocations: wilderness exploration, tennis, classical music, parapsychology, world history. Office: The Other Artist 3200 Buchanan St San Francisco CA 94123-3517 E-mail: numbers@paulminar.com.

MINAYA, OMAR, professional sports team executive; b. Valverde Mao, Dominican Republic, Nov. 10, 1958; m. Rachel Albright. Scout Tex. Rangers, 1985—97, dir. pers. and internat. scouting, 1995—97; sr. asst. gen. mgr. NY Mets, 1997—2002, exec. v.p. baseball ops., gen. mgr., 2004—; v.p. Montreal Expos, 2002—04, gen. mgr., 2002—04. Recipient Hispanic Heritage in Sports award, Hispanic Heritage Found., 2003; named one of The Most Influential People in the World of Sports, Bus. Week, 2007. Office: c/o NY Mets Shea Stadium 123-01 Roosevelt Ave Flushing NY 11368*

MINC, HENRYK, mathematics professor; b. Lodz, Poland, Nov. 12, 1919; s. Izrael and Haja (Zyngler) M.; m. Catherine Taylor Duncan, Apr. 16, 1943; children: Robert Henry, Ralph Edward, Raymond. MA with honors, Edinburgh U., Scotland, 1955, PhD, 1959. Tchr. Morgan Acad., Dundee, Scotland, 1956-58; lectr. Dundee Tech. Coll., 1957-58, U. BC, Vancouver, Canada, 1958-59, asst. prof., 1959-60; assoc. prof. U. Fla., Gainesville, 1960-63; prof. U. Calif., Santa Barbara, 1963-90, prof. emeritus, 1990—. Vis. prof. Technion Israel Inst. Tech., Haifa, 1969-80. Author: A Survey of Matrix Theory and Matrix Inequalities, 1964, Russian translation, 1972, Chinese translation, 1990, Introduction to Linear Algebra, 1968, Spanish translation, 1968, Modern University Algebra, 1966, Elementary Linear Algebra, Spanish translation, 1971, New College Algebra, 1968, Elementary Functions and Coordinate Geometry, 1969, Algebra and Trigonometry, 1970, College Algebra, 1970, College Trigonometry, 1971, Integrated Analytic Geometry and Algebra with Circular Functions, 1973, Permanents, 1978, Russian translation, 1980, Chinese translation, 1991, Nonnegative Matrices, 1988, Chinese translation, 1991; contbr. over 80 rsch. articles to math. jours., 9 rsch. papers to archaeol. and ancient numismatic jours., 12 articles to Burns Chronicle; referee and reviewer math. jours. 2nd lt. Polish Army, 1940-48, France, UK. Recipient Lester Ford award Math. Assn. Am., 1966, rsch. contract Office Naval Rsch., 1985-88, Air Force Office Sci. Rsch. grantee, 1960-83, Lady Davis fellow, 1975-78. Mem.: Scottish Soc. Santa Barbara (past chieftain), Robert Burns World Fedn. (hon. pres.), Am. Math. Soc. Democrat. Home: 4076 Naranjo Dr Santa Barbara CA 93110-1213 Office: U Calif Dept Math Santa Barbara CA 93106 Home Phone: 805-687-1824. Personal E-mail: hmincburns@cox.net.

MINCE, CAROL KIRKHAM, history educator; b. Clarksville, Tenn., Aug. 1, 1961; d. Lawrence Ray and Mary Virginia Cox; m. John William Mince Jr., Apr. 23, 1992. BS, Austin Peay State U., 1982, MA in Edn., 1984. Cert. tchr. Tenn. Asst. mgr. Kelley's Food City, Clarksville, 1980—93; social studies tchr. New Providence Mid. Sch., Clarksville, 1993—2005; world history tchr. Montgomery Ctrl. HS, Cunningham, Tenn., 2005—06, Am. govt. and world geography tchr. and world history tchr., 2006—. Named Tchr. of Yr. at Bldg. Level, Tenn. Dept. Edn., 2000, 2004. Mem.: NEA, ASPCA, Tenn. Geog. Alliance, Nat. Coun. Social Studies., Clarksville-Montgomery County Edn. Assn. (Disting. Classroom Tchr. award 2000, 2004), Tenn. Edn. Assn., Nat. Humane Edn. Soc., Am. Humane Assn., Humane Soc. US, Phi Kappa Phi. Avocations: reading, hiking, antiques, photography. Office: Montgomery Ctrl HS 3955 Hwy 48 Cunningham TN 37052 Business E-Mail: carol.mince@cmcss.net.

MINCHEFF, DONNA CURRIE, special education educator; b. NYC, Nov. 24, 1969; m. Scott Mincheff, Apr. 8, 1995; children: Chandler Scott, Caleb Michael. BS in Spl. Edn., Old Dominion U., Norfolk, Va., 1992; MS in Sch. Counseling, Cambridge Coll., Chesapeake, Va., 2007. Spl. edn. tchr. Va. Beach Pub. Schs., 1992—2001, Cheaspeake Pub. Schs., Va., 2001—. Mem.: Coun. Exceptional Children. Office: Cheaspeake Pub Schs 1997 Hawk Blvd Chesapeake VA 23322 Personal E-mail: dmincheff@cox.net.

MINDEL, LAURENCE BRISKER, restaurateur; b. Toledo, Oct. 27, 1937; s. Seymour Stewart and Eleanor (Brisker) Mindel; m. Deborah Dudley, Oct. 20, 1978; children: Katherine Dudley, Nicolas Laurence; children: Michael Laurence, Laura Beth, Anthony Jay. BA, U. Mich., 1959. Gen. mgr. Western Coffee Instants Inc., Burlingame, Calif., 1962—64, dir. & ptnr., 1964; chmn. & dir. Caswell Coffee Co., San Francisco, 1964—70; pres. Coffee Instants Inc., Long Island City, NY, 1966—70, Restaurant Group Saga Corp., Menlo Pk., Calif., 1985—86; v.p. Superior Tea and Coffee Co., 1970—72; chmn. & CEO Spectrum Foods Inc., 1970—85. Founder Ill. Fornaio Am. Corp.; mem., adv. bd. Stanislaus Ptnrs.; chmn., trustees Branson Sch. Mem.: Inst. Am. Entrepreneurs, World Pres. Orgn. Home: 86 San Carlos Ave Sausalito CA 94965-2048 Office: Il Fornaio Am Corp 770 Tamalpais Dr Ste 400 Corte Madera CA 94925

MINDELL, EUGENE ROBERT, surgeon, educator; b. Chgo., Feb. 24, 1922; s. Leon and Tillie (Rosenthal) M.; m. June A. Abrams, Sept. 19, 1945; children: Barbara, Ruth, David, Douglas. BS, U. Chgo., 1943, MD, 1945. Diplomate Am. Bd. Orthopaedic Surgery (bd. dir. 1977-84, pres. 1983-84). Resident in orthopaedic surgery U. Chgo. Clinics, 1948-52; instr. U. Chgo., 1952; mem. faculty dept. orthopaedic surgery Sch. Medicine SUNY, Buffalo, 1953—, prof. Sch. Medicine, 1964—; chmn. dept. SUNY Sch. Medicine, Buffalo, 1964-88, dir. orthopaedic oncology Sch. Medicine, 1988—. Mem. bd. mgrs. Erie County Med. Ctr., 1990-96. Assoc. editor Jour. Bone and Joint Surgery, 1984-88, trustee, 1991—; dep. editor Clin. Orthopaedics and Related Rsch. representing Musculoskeletal Tumor Soc., 1997—; contbr. articles to profl. jours. Lt. (j.g.) M.C. USNR, 1946-48. Eugene R. Mindell Endowed Chair of Orthopaedic Surgery established in his honor SUNY, Buffalo, 1996, chair fully funded, 2008; recipient Disting. Svc. award Alumni U. Chgo. Sch. Medicine, 1990, award for achievement in health care D'Youville Coll., 2002, Lifetime Acheivement Excellence in Tchg. award, SUNY Buffalo Dept. Orthop. Surgery, 2002; NRC fellow, 1949-50. Fellow ACS; mem. Am. Acad. Orthopaedic Surgeons (bd. dirs. 1991-92), Am. Orthopaedic Assn. (v.p. 1990-91), Assn. Orthopaedic Chmn., Am. Assn. Surgery of Trauma, Am. Orthopaedic Rsch. Soc. (pres. 1972-73, residency rev. com. 1985-91), Musculoskeletal Tumor Soc. (pres. 1989-90), Coun. Musculoskeletal Specialty Socs. (chmn. elect 1991, chmn. 1992). Jewish. Office: 100 High St Buffalo NY 14203-1126 Home: 705 Renaissance Dr Apt T218 Williamsville NY 14221-8030 Home Phone: 716-929-5726. Business E-Mail: emindell@kaleidehealth.org.

MINDICH, ERIC M., hedge fund manager; b. Aug. 29, 1967; m. Stacey Okun Mindich; 3 children. BA in Economics, summa cum laude, Harvard U., 1988. Mem. equities arbitrage dept. Goldman Sachs Group Inc., 1988—92, head dept., 1992—2000, ptnr., 1994—2003, co-COO equities divsn., 2000—02, co-head equities divsn., mem. mgmt. com., 2002—03, sr. strategy officer, 2003; founder, chmn., CEO Eton Pk. Capital Mgmt., 2004—. Chair asset managers' com. Pres.'s Working Group Fin. Markets, US Dept. Treasury. Trustee Whitney Mus. Am. Art, Mt. Sinai Med. Ctr. Inc., NYC; bd. dirs. Havard Mgmt. Co., 1996—2004, Lincoln Ctr. Theatre, NYC, Horace Mann Sch., NYC. Mem.: Phi Beta Kappa. Office: Eton Park Captial Mgmt LP 399 Park Ave New York NY 10022 also: Eton Park Captial Mgmt 825 Third Ave New York NY 10022 Office Phone: 212-756-5300. Office Fax: 212-756-5361.*

MINDLIN, PAULA ROSALIE, retired reading educator; b. NYC, Nov. 27, 1944; d. Simon S. and Sylvia (Naroff) Bernstein; m. Alfred Carl Mindlin, Aug. 14, 1965; 1 child, Spencer Douglas. BA in Edn., Bklyn. Coll., 1965; MS in Edn., Queens Coll., 1970, Specialist Diploma in Sch. Adminstrn and Supervision, 1973. Tchr. Dist. 16 Pub. Sch., Bklyn., 1965—68; reading tchr. Dist. 29 Pub. Sch. and Dist. 16, Bklyn., 1968—85; instr. insvc. courses Cmty. Sch. Dist. 29, Queens Village, NY, 1984—93, reading coord. Reading/Comm. Arts Program, 1985—90, dir. reading, 1990—94. Adj. lectr. York Coll., 1989; dir. Chpt. 1 Program (Nat. Recognition 1994, U.S. Sec. of Edn.); curriculum cons., 1997—98. Sisterhood pres. Congregation Beth-El, Massapequa, 1999—2000, bd. trustees NY, 2006—08. Recipient svc. award NY State Reading Assn. Coun., 1996, Woman of Achievement award Jewish Theol. Seminary-Women's League for Conservative Judaism, 2001. Mem. Queensboro

Reading Coun. (pres. 1994-96, Educator of Yr. award 1994, bd. trustees, 2006-, sisterhood pres., 1999-2001),; congregation Beth el, massapequa, NY. Avocations: reading, gardening, travel.

MINEAR, RICHARD HOFFMAN, history professor; b. Evanston, Ill., Dec. 31, 1938; s. Paul S. and Gladys (Hoffman) M.; m. Edith C.; children: Robert C., Edward L. AB, Yale U., 1960; MA, Harvard U., 1962, PhD, 1968. Asst. prof. history Ohio State U., 1967-70; from assoc. prof. history to prof. history U. Mass., Amherst, 1970—. Author: Japanese Tradition and Western Law, 1970, Victors' Justice, 1971, Dr. Seuss Goes To War, 1999; editor: Through Japanese Eyes, 1974; translator: Requiem for Battleship Yamato, 1985, Hiroshima: Three Witnesses, 1990, Black Eggs, 1994, When We Say Hiroshima, 1999, Japan's Past, Japan's Future, 2000, The Scars of War, 2007. Mem. Amherst Town Mtg., 1976-91, Amherst Select Bd., 1981-90. Fulbright fellow, Kyoto, Japan, 1964-66, 70-71, Japan Found. fellow, Tokyo, Sapporo, 1992-93. Office: Dept History U Mass Amherst MA 01003

MINEHAN, CATHY ELIZABETH, retired bank executive; b. Jersey City, Feb. 15, 1947; d. Harry Manford Jones and Rita Jane (Decora) Jones Leary; m. Gerald Paul Minehan, July 18, 1970; children: Melissa Jane, Brian Patrick. BA, U. Rochester, 1968; MBA, NYU, 1977. Various positions to sr. v.p. Fed. Res. Bank NY, NYC, 1968—75, ops. analysis officer, 1975, mgr. mgmt. info. dept., 1976—78, asst. v.p., 1979—82, v.p., 1982—87, sr. v.p., 1987—91; COO Fed. Res. Bank Boston, 1991-94, pres., 1994—2007. Cons. IMF, Washington, 1990-91; bd. dirs. Boston Mcpl. Rsch. Bur., Park St. Corp., The New Eng. Coun., Visa Inc., 2007-, Becton Dickinson & Co., 2007-, Mass. Mutual Life Ins. Co., 2009-; mem. Gov.'s Coun. Econ. Growth and Tech. Bd. dirs. Boston Pvt. Industry Council, Boston Mcpl. Rsch. Bur., Jobs for Mass., New Eng. Council, Boston Pub. Libr. Found.; mem. Mass. Women's Forum, Boston, 1991—; bd. advisors Caroll Sch. Mgmt. Boston Coll.; trustee Bentley Coll., 1992—; trustee coun. U. Rochester, 1993—. Mem. Pub. Securities Assn. (ex officio, govt. ops. com. 1986-91), Beta Gamma Sigma. Democrat. Roman Catholic. Avocations: golf, skiing, jogging.*

MINER, CRAIG ALAN, special education educator; b. East St. Louis, Ill., May 3, 1956; s. Joseph Clifford and Manelle (Egmon) M.; m. Patricia Ann Stallings, Aug. 7, 1982 (div. Nov. 1987); 1 child, Joseph Michael; m. Shari Lee Errandi, Dec. 24, 1992; 1 child, Anthony Michael. BS, Milligan Coll., 1978; MS, So. Ill. U., 1985, PhD, 1994. State tech. cert. in trainable mentally handicapped, Ill. Tchr., adminstr. Mamie O. Stookey Sch., Belleville, Ill., 1979-86; ctr. coord. St. Louis (Mo.) ARC, 1986-87; tchr., program coord. BeDell Achievement Ctr., Wood River, Ill., 1987-91; lectr. So. Ill. U., Carbondale, summer 1994; instr. clin. psychiatry So. Ill. U. Sch. Medicine, Springfield, 1994—. Cons. BeDell Achievement Ctr., Wood River, 1991, St. Louis (Mo.) ARC, 1992, Alton (Ill.) Pub. Schs., 1994. Recipient Cmty. Bldg. Project award Ill. Planning Coun., Belleville, 1994. Mem. Coun. for Exceptional Children, Assn. for Persons with Severe Handicaps, Am. Assn. for Mental Retardation, Nat. Assn. for the Dually Diagnosed. Avocations: baseball coaching, playing guitar and mandolin. Home: 1027 N Stanford Ave Clovis CA 93611-6605

MINER, JACQUELINE, political consultant; b. Dec. 10, 1936; d. Ralph E. and Agnes (McGee) Mariani; m. Roger J. Miner, Aug. 11, 1975; children: Laurence, Ronald Carmichael, Ralph Carmichael, Mark. Ind. polit. cons., Hudson, NY; instr. history and polit. sci. SUNY, Hudson, 1974—79. Mem. nat. steering com. Fund for Am.'s Future, 2d cir. Hist. Com.; mem. White House Outreach Working Group on Central Am.; candidate for Rep. nomination U.S. Senate, 1982; co-chair N.Y. state steering com. George Bush for Pres. campaign, 1986—88; del. Rep. Conv., 1992, GOP Conv., 1992; Rep. county committeewoman, 1958—76; vice chmn. N.Y. State Ronald Reagan campaign, 1980, N.Y. State Rep. Com., 1991—93; co-chmn. N.Y. State Reagan Roundup Campaign, 1984—86; chmn. Coll. Consortium for Internat. Studies. Mem.: PEO, U.S. Supreme Ct. Hist. Soc. Address: 1 Merlins Way Hudson NY 12534-4157

MINER, JOHN BURNHAM, industrial relations educator, writer; b. NYC, July 20, 1926; s. John Lynn and Bess (Burnham) M.; children by previous marriage: Barbara, John, Cynthia, Frances; m. Barbara Allen Williams, June 1, 1979; children: Jennifer, Heather. AB, Princeton U., 1950, PhD, 1955; MA, Clark U., 1952. Lic. psychologist, N.Y. Rsch. assoc. Columbia U., 1956-57; mgr. psychol. svcs. Atlantic Refining Co., Phila., 1957-60; mem. faculty U. Oreg., Eugene, 1960-68; prof., chmn. dept. orgnl. sci. U. Md., College Park, 1968-73; rsch. prof. Ga. State U., Atlanta, 1973-87, Disting. prof., 1974; pres. Orgnl. Measurement Systems Press, Eugene, Oreg., 1976—; prof. human resources SUNY, Buffalo, 1987-94, chmn. dept. orgn. and human resources, 1989-92; profl. practice Eugene, Oreg., 1995—. Cons. McKinsey & Co., N.Y.C., 1966-69; vis. lectr. U. Pa., Phila., 1959-60; vis. prof. U. Calif., Berkeley, 1966-67, U. South Fla., Tampa, 1972; researcher on orgnl. motivation, theories of orgn., human resource utilization, bus. policy and strategy, entrepreneurship. Author: Personnel Psychology, 1969, Personnel and Industrial Relations, 1969, 1973, 1977, 1985, The Challenge of Managing, 1975; author: (with Mary Green Miner) Policy Issues Personnel and Industrial Relations, 1977; author: (with George A. Steiner) Management Policy and Strategy, 1977; author: (with M.G. Miner) Employee Selection Within the Law, 1978; author: Theories of Organizational Behavior, 1980, Theories of Organizational Structure and Process, 1982, People Problems: The Executive Answer Book, 1985, The Practice of Management, 1985, Organizational Behavior: Performance and Productivity, 1988, Industrial-Organizational Psychology, 1992, Role Motivation Theories, 1993; with Donald P. Crane Human Resource Management: The Strategic Perspective, 1995; author: The 4 Routes to Entrepreneurial Success, 1996; author: (with Michael H. Capps) How Honesty Testing Works, 1997; author: A Psychological Typology of Successful Entrepreneurs, 1997, Organizational Behavior: Foundations, Theories and Analyses, 2002, Organizational Behavior: Essential Theories of Motivation and Leadership, 2005, Organizational Behavior: Essential Theories of Process and Structure, 2006, Organizational Behavior: Historical Origins, Theoretical Foundations, and the Future, 2006, Organizational Behavior: From Theory To Practice, 2007, Organizational Behavior: From Unconscious Motivation to Role Motivated Leadership, 2008, many other books and monographs; contbr. numerous articles, papers to profl. jours. With US Army, 1944—46, ETO. Decorated Bronze Star, Combat Infantryman's badge. Fellow APA, Acad. of Mgmt. (editor Jour. 1973-75, pres. 1977-78), Soc. for Personality Assessment, Am. Psychol. Soc.; mem. Soc. for Human Resource Mgmt., Inst. Operations Rsch. Mgmt. Sci., Am. Sociolog. Assn., Indsl. Rels. Rsch. Assn., Internat. Coun. for Small Bus., Strategic Mgmt. Soc., Internat. Pers. Mgmt. Assn., Human Resource Planning Soc. Republican. Home and Office: 34199 Country View Dr Eugene OR 97408-9440 Office Phone: 541-484-2715.

MINER, ROBERT MATTHEW, orthodontist, educator; s. Robert Clarence and Jeanne Roberta Owens Miner; m. Lynn Ann Maconochie, Aug. 29, 1998; children: Carolyn Hilmer, Todd Winslow. BA, Colby Coll., Waterville, Maine, 1967; DDS, NY U. Sch. Dentistry, 1971. Diplomate Am. Bd. Orthodontics, 1989; cert. in gen. practice reisdency Englewood Hosp., Englewood, NJ, 1972, in orthodontic Harvard U. Sch. Dental Medicine, Boston, 1976. Asst. clin. prof. Harvard Sch. Dental Medicine, Boston, 1977—, dept. head, dept. orthodontics, 1995—98; pres. Edward H. Angle Soc. East Component, Boston, 2006—07; assoc. clin. prof. Tufts U. Dental Sch., Boston, 2009—. Dir. Dedham Med. Assocs., Mass., 1988—, pres., 1990—94; cons. Cadent Corp., Carlsbad, NJ, 2006—. Contbr. articles to profl. jours. Lt. USN, 1974—86, NAS Oceana, Va. Named Outstanding Tchr., Forsyth Dental Ctr., 1969. Mem.: Edward H. Angle Soc., Am. Lingual Orthodontic Assn., Am. Bd. Orthodontics, Am. Assn. Orthodontists, ADA, Omicron Kappa Upsilon. Achievements include research in new technological applications for othodontics. Office: Dedham Med Assocs One Lyons St Dedham MA 02026 Office Fax: 781-320-9087. Business E-Mail: minerortho@dedhammedical.com.

MINER, ROGER JEFFREY, federal judge; b. Apr. 14, 1934; s. Abram and Anne M. Miner; m. Jacqueline Mariani; 4 children. BS, SUNY; LLB cum laude, NY Law Sch., 1956; postgrad., Bklyn. Law Sch., Judge Advocate Gen.'s Sch., U. Va.; LLD (hon.), NY Law Sch., 1989, Syracuse U., 1990, Albany Law Sch./Union U., 1996; attended, Emory U. Bar: NY 1956, US Ct. Mil. Appeals 1956, Republic of Korea 1958, US Dist. Ct. (so. and ea. dists.) NY 1959. Ptnr. Miner & Miner, Hudson, NY, 1959—75; corp. counsel City of Hudson, 1961—64; asst. dist. atty. Columbia County, 1964, dist. atty., 1968—75; justice NY State Supreme Ct., 1976—81; judge US Dist. Ct. (no. dist.) NY, 1981—85; sr. judge US Ct. Appeals (2d cir.), Albany, NY, 1997—. Adj. assoc. prof. criminal law State U. Sys., NY, 1974—79; adj. prof. law NY Law Sch., 1986—96, Albany Law Sch. Union U., 1997—2002; faculty assoc. Ariz. State U. Coll. Law, 2004; lectr. state and local bar assns.; lectr. SUNY, Albany, 1985; with NY Law Sch. Bd. Trustees, 1991—96; hon. trustee NY Law Sch. bd. trustees, 1996—; chmn. 2d Cir. Com. on Hist. and Commemorative Events, 1989—94; mem. jud. coun. 2d Cir., 1992—96; with No. Dist. Hist. Com., 1981—85, State, Fed. Jud. Coun. of N.Y., 1986—91, Cameras in the Courtoom Com., 1993—96; chmn. Jud. Conf. on US com. on fed.-state jurisdiction, 1987—92, State, Fed. Jud. Coun. of N.Y., 1990—91; trustee Practicing Law Inst., 1995—2002. Mng. editor: NY Law Sch. Law Rev.; contbr. articles to law jours. 1st lt. JAGC US Army, 1956—59, capt. USAR, ret. Recipient Dean's medal for disting. profl. svc., NY Law Sch., Disting. Alumnus award, Charles W. Froessel award for Valuable Contbn. to Law, Albany Jewish Fedn. award, Abraham Lincoln award, Cmty. Svc. award, Kiwanis, others, Ellis Island medal of honor; named Columbia County Man of Yr., 1984. Mem.: ATLA, ABA, Columbia County Magistrates Assn., Am. Soc. Writers on Legal Subjects, Fed. Bar Coun., Fed. Judges Assn., Am. Judicature Soc., Am. Law Inst., Columbia County Bar Assn., Assn. of Bar of City of NY, NY State Bar Assn., B'nai Brith, NY Law Sch. Alumni Assn. (hon.; bd. dirs.), Supreme Ct. Hist. Soc., Columbia County Hist. Soc., Elks (past exalted ruler). Jewish. Office: US Ct Appeals 445 Broadway Ste 414 Albany NY 12207-2926*

MINER, THOMAS HAWLEY, entrepreneur; b. Shelbyville, Ill., June 19, 1927; s. Lester Ward and Thirza (Hawley) M.; m. Lucyna T. Minciel, July 22, 1983; children: Robert Thomas, William John. Student, U.S. Mil. Acad., 1946—47; BA, Knox Coll., 1950; JD, U. Ill., 1953. Bar: Ill. 1954. Counsel Continental Ill. Nat. Bank & Trust Co., Chgo., 1953—55; pres. Harper-Wyman Internat. S.A., Venezuela and Mex., 1955—58, Hudson Internat. S.A., Can. and Switzerland, 1958—60, Thomas H. Miner & Assoc., Inc., Chgo., 1960—; chmn. Miner, Fraser & Gabriel Pub. Affairs, Inc., Washington, 1982—88, Miner Sys., Inc., 1981—; internat. dir. Urban Retail Properties Inc., 2005—; chmn., CEO Ill. Global Partnership, Inc., 2005—; dir. US-China C. of C., 2007—. Bd. dirs. Lakeside Bank, Worldschool, Bright Oceans Internat. Corp.; chmn. Ill. dist. export coun. U.S. Dept. Commerce, 1971—; sec. Consular Corps. Chgo., 1986—88; chmn. Mid-Am. China Mgmt. Tng. Ctr., Global Software Source, Geo Vision, Inc., U.S.-Iraq Bus. Alliance; dir. Global Heavy Lift Holdings LLc. Chmn. bd. dirs. Sch. Art Inst. Chgo., 1977-81; bd. govs., life mem., sustaining fellow Art Inst. Chgo.; former chmn. UN Assn., Chgo.; founder, chmn. Mid-Am. Com., 1968—; former mem. bd. dirs. UNICEF, NAM, Internat. Trade Policy Com. and Working Group on Commonwealth of Ind. States and Ea. Europe; trustee 4th Presbyn. Ch., Chgo., Roosevelt U., Chgo., 1996; bd. advisors Mercy Hosp.; vice chmn. Chgo. Sister Cities; mem. adv. bd. Internat. Inst. Edn.; bd. dirs. Internat. Sister Cities. With USNR, 1945-46; mem. Pres. Coun. U. Ill. Found.; dir. Internat. Urgan Retail Properties Co.; chmn. Ill. Global Partnership, Inc. Capt. U.S. Army, 1946-47. Decorated comdr. Crown of the Kingdom of Belgium, 2003, commendatore Ordine al Merito della Repubblica Italiana; recipient Alumni Achievement award Knox Coll., 1974, Gold Medallion award Internat. Visitors Ctr. Chgo., 1989; named One of Chgo.'s 10 Outstanding Young Men, 1962, Chicagoan of Year Chgo. Assn. Commerce and Industry, 1968, Alumni of Month Coll. Law U. Ill., Nov. 1970, Aug. 1984; hon. consul Republic of Senegal, 1970-88. Mem. Am. Mgmt. Assn., Chicagoland C. of C., Mid-Am. Arab C. of C. (founder, former pres.), Chgo. Bar Assn., Chgo. Com., Chgo. Coun. Fgn. Rels. (past dir.), Coun. of the Ams., Internat. Trade Club (past dir., pres.), Japan-Am. Soc., Nat. Coun. U.S.-China Trade, Nat. Acad. Scis. (pres. coun.), English Speaking Union (dir., past chmn.) Trade and Econs. Coun. USA-CIS (dir.), U.S.-Russia Bus. Coun., Mus. Contemporary Art, Newcomen Soc. N.Am., U.S.-China Bus. Coun., U.S.-Arab C. of C. (bd. dirs.), U.S.-Mex. C. of C. (bd. dirs.), Thomas Minor Soc., Chgo. Club, Econ. Club, Grant Park Concerts Soc., Chgo. Farmers Club, Mid-Am. Club, Univ. Club (Washington), Univ. Club (Milw.), Hillsboro Club (Fla.), Tryall Golf and Beach Club (Jamaica), Rotary, Phi Delta Phi, Phi Gamma Delta. Office: 900 N Michigan Ave Ste 900 Chicago IL 60611 Home Phone: 312-944-2453; Office Phone: 312-915-3336. Personal E-mail: ltminer@aol.com. Business E-Mail: minert@urbanretail.com.

MINER, TRACY A., lawyer; b. 1958; BA in Psych., U. Notre Dame, 1980; JD summa cum laude, Boston Coll., 1985. Bar: Mass. 1985, US Ct. Appeals (DC cir.). Atty., chair white collar def. grp. Mintz, Levin, Cohn, Ferris, Glovsky & Popeo, P.C., Boston. Bd. advs. Sentencing Project Am. Law Inst.; mem. adv. com. US Ct. Appeals (1st cir.). Contbr. chapters to books. Named a Mass. Super Lawyer, 2004—09. Mem.: Boston Bar Assn. (mem. criminal law steering com.), Mass. Assn. Criminal Def. Lawyers (bd. dirs., past pres.), NACDL. Office: Mintz Levin Cohn Ferris Glovsky & Popeo PC 1 Financial Ctr Boston MA 02111 Office Phone: 617-348-1694. Office Fax: 617-542-2241. E-mail: taminer@mintz.com.

MINETA, NORMAN YOSHIO, consulting firm executive, former United States Secretary of Commerce and Transportation; b. San Jose, Calif., Nov. 12, 1931; s. Kay Kunisaku and Kane (Watanabe) M.; m. Danealia; children: David, K., Stuart S.; stepchildren: Robert M. Brantner, Mark Brantner. BS, U. Calif.-Berkeley, 1953; D of Pub. Svc., Santa Clara U., 1989; HHD (hon.), Rust Coll., 1993. Agt./broker Mineta Ins. Agy., San Jose, 1956-89; mem. adv. bd. Bank of Tokyo, Calif., 1961-75; mem. city coun. City of San Jose, 1967-71, vice mayor, 1969-71, mayor, 1971-75; mem. US Congress from 13th (now 15th) Calif. dist., 1975-95, mem. subcom. surface transp., 1989-92, chmn. pub. works. & transp. com., 1992—95; sr. v.p., mng. dir. transp. sys. & services Lockheed Martin, Washington, 1995-2000; sec. US Dept. Commerce, Washington, 2000-2001, US Dept. Transp., Washington, 2001—06; vice chmn. global comm. consultancy Hill & Knowlton, Inc., Washington, 2006—; sr. adv. Credit Suisse, 2008—. Chmn. fin. com. Santa Clara County (Calif.) Council Chs., 1960-62; commr., San Jose Human Relations Commn., 1962-64, San Jose Housing Authority, 1966-67; delegate, state convention Calif. Dem. Party, 1971-74, Dem. Nat. Convention, 1972, 1976, 1980, 1984; chmn. Nat. Civil Aviation Review Commn., 1997-2000; bd. dirs. Nat. RR Passenger Corp.(AMTRAK), 2001-06; mem. Homeland Security Coun., 2001-06, Nat. Econ. Coun., 2001-06, Fed. Coun. on the Arts & Humanities, 2001-06, Nat. Sci. & Tech. Coun., 2001-06, Advisory Coun. on Historic Preservation, 2001-06, Gulf Coast Recovery & Rebuilding Coun., 2005-06; bd. dirs. AECOM Tech. Corp. 2007-, SJW Corp. 2008-; mem. advisory bd. Carolinks 2006- Precinct chmn. Community Theater Bond Issue, 1964; mem. spl. gifts com. Santa Clara County Coun. Boy Scouts Am., 1967; sec. Santa Clara County Grand Jury, 1964; bd. dirs. Wesley Found., San Jose State Coll., 1956-58, Pacific Neighbors, Community Council Cen. Santa Clara County, Japan Soc., San Francisco, Santa Clara County chpt. NCCJ, Mexican-Am. Community Services Agy.; mem. exec. bd. No. Calif.-Western Nev. dist. council Japanese Am. Citizens League, 1960-62, pres. San Jose chpt., 1957-59; bd. regents Smithsonian Instn., 1979-95; chmn. Smithsonian vis. com. for Freer Gallery, 1981-95, mem. Smithsonian Nat. Bd., 1996—; mem. bd. regents Santa Clara U.; chmn. Nat. Civil Aviation Rev. Commn., 1997; Served to lt. AUS, 1954-56. Recipient Golden Plate award, Acad. Achievement, 2005, Presdl. Medal of Freedom, The White House, 2006. Mem. Greater San Jose C. of C., Nat. Assn. Indsl. Ins. Agts., Calif. Assn. Indsl. Ins. Agts., San Jose Assn. Ind. Ins. Agts. (dir. 1960-62), North San Jose Optimists Club (pres. 1956-58), Jackson-Taylor Bus. and Profl. Assn. (dir. 1963). Democrat. Meth. Office: Hill & Knowlton Inc 607 14th St NW Ste 300 Washington DC 20005-2000 *Personal philosophy: My two greatest responsibilities are accountability and accessibility to everyone I represent, and to anyone who comes to me for help.**

MING, SI-CHUN, pathologist, educator; b. Shanghai, Nov. 10, 1922; arrived in US, 1949, naturalized, 1964; s. Sian-Fan and Jan-Teh (Kuo) M.; m. Pen-Ming Lee, Aug. 17, 1957; children: Carol, Ruby, Stephanie, Michael, Jeffrey, Eileen. MD, Nat. Ctrl. U. Coll. Medicine, China, 1947. Resident in pathology Mass. Gen. Hosp., Boston, 1952-56; assoc. pathologist Beth Israel Hosp., Boston, 1956-67; asst. prof. pathology Harvard U. Med. Sch., 1965-67; assoc. prof. U. Md., 1967-71; prof. Temple U., Phila., 1971-93, prof. emeritus, 1993—, acting chmn. dept. pathology, 1978-80, dep. chmn. dept. path., 1980-86. US rep. WHO Collaborating Ctr. for Primary Prevention, Diagnosis and Treatment of Gastric Cancer, 1984-98; hon. prof. Tianjin Med. Coll., Shanghai Second Med. U., Fourth Mil. Med. U., China, 1988—. Author: Tumors of the Esophagus and Stomach, 1973, supplement, 1985, Precursors of Gastric Cancer, 1984, Pathology of the Gastrointestinal Tract, 1992, 2d edit., 1998; mem. editl. bd. World Jour. Gastroenterology, 1998-05, Gastric Cancer, 1998-05. Nat. Cancer Inst. sr. fellow Karolinska Inst. Stockholm, 1964-65. Mem. AAAS, US Canadian Acad. Pathology, Am. Soc. Investigative Pathology, Am. Gastroenterol. Assn., NY Acad. Scis. Achievements include development of classification method for stomach carcinoma based on the growth pattern of the cancer; establishment of pathological criteria for the diagnosis of premalignant lesions of the digestive tract. Office: 3401 N Broad St Philadelphia PA 19140-5104 Business E-Mail: ming@temple.edu.

MING, YAO, professional basketball player; b. Shanghai, Sept. 12, 1980; s. Yao Zhie Yuan and Fang Feng Di; m. Ye Li, Aug. 6, 2007. Student, Shanghai Phys. & Sport Technic Edn. Inst., Shanghai Fgn. Lang. Inst. Player Shanghai Sharks, Chinese Basketball Assn., 1997—2002, Houston Rockets, NBA, 2002—. Mem. Chinese Olympic Men's Basketball Team, Athens, 2004, Beijing, 08. Author: Yao: A Life in Two Worlds, 2004; film appearances The Year of the Yao, 2004, guest appearances (TV series) The Simpsons (voice only), 2005. Founder The Yao Ming Found., 2008—; environment champion UN Environment Programme, 2008—. Recipient Laureus World Newcomer of Yr. award, 2003; named NBA All-Rookie First Team, 2002; named one of 100 Most Influential People, People mag., 2004, The Most Influential People in the World of Sports, Bus. Week, 2007; named to Western Conf. All-Star Team, NBA, 2003—09. Achievements include being the first international player to be the first overall pick in the NBA Draft, 2002. Avocation: computer games. Office: Houston Rockets 1510 Polk St Houston TX 77002*

MINGER, TERRELL JOHN, public administration and natural resource institute executive; b. Canton, Ohio, Oct. 7, 1942; s. John Wilson and Margaret Rose M.; m. Judith R. Arnold, Aug. 7, 1965; 1 child, Gabriella Sophia. BA, Baker U., 1966; MPA, Kans. U., 1969; postgrad., MIT, 1975; Loeb fellow, Harvard U., 1976-77; postgrad, Stanford U., 1979; MBA, U. Colo., 1983. Asst. dir. admissions Baker U., 1966-67; asst. city mgr. City of Boulder, Colo., 1968-69; city mgr. City of Vail, Colo., 1969-79; pres., CEO Whistler Village Land Co., Vancouver, B.C., Can., 1979-81; v.p., gen. mgr. Cumberland S.W. Inc., Denver, 1981-83; exec. asst. dep. chief of staff to Gov. Colo., 1983-87; pres., CEO Sundance Inst. for Resource Mgmt., Utah, 1986—, Sundance Enterprises Ltd., 1988-91. Adj. prof. grad. sch. pub. affairs U. Colo., 1983—, Sch. Bus. U. Denver, 1992—; bd. dirs. Colo. Open Lands, Inc.; participant UN Conf. on Environment and Devel., Rio de Janeiro, 1992; chmn. environ. adv. bd. Wal-Mart, Inc., 1990—; co-chmn. task force sustainable consumption World Bus. Coun. Sustainable Devel.; co-chmn. N.Am. Telecom./Environ. Taskforce; dir. Stapleton Found. Sustainable Cities, 2000-; chmn. Environ. Excellence Task Force Telecomm. Industry; environ. advisor Salt Lake City Olympic Com.; bd. chmn. Three Sisters Mountain Village, Canmore, Aberta, 2002-. Editor: Greenhouse/Glasnost-The Global Warming Crisis, 1990, Val Symposium Papers, 1970-79; author, editor: Growth Alternatives for Rocky Mountain West, 1976, Future of Human Settlements in the West, 1977. Spl. del. UN Habitat Conf. Human Settlements, spl. rep. to UN Environ. Program, 1992, coord. UN Global Youth Forum, 1993-94, co-chmn. conf. on environ. and mktg., N.Y.C., 1993; founder Vail Symposium, advisor UN Environ. Program Telecom. Charter, Nairobi, Kenya, 1999; co-founder, bd. dirs. Colo. Park Found., 1985—; chair World Alpine Championship Conf., Vail, Colo., 1999; founding mem. Greenhouse/Glasnost U.S./USSR Teleconf. with Soviet Acad. Scis., 1989—; mem. pres. task force Commn. on Sustainable Devel., 1994—; co-chmn. Golf and Environ. Conf., Pebble Beach, Calif., 1995; founder, pres. Western Rendezvous, 1995—; bd. dirs. Piton Found., 1996; co-chair UN Sustainability Roundtable for Europe and No. Am., 2002. Nat. finalist White House Fellowship, 1978; recipient Colo. Soc. Landscape Arch. award, 1999, Sacred Mountain Gold medal, Taos, N.Mex., 2005; named one of B.C.'s Top Bus. Leaders for the '80s, 1980. Mem. Urban Land Inst., Colo. Acad. Pub. Adminstrn. (charter, founding mem. 1988), Colo. City Mgmt. Innovation award 1974-76), Western Gov.'s Assn. (staff coun., chmn. adv. com. 1985-86), Flatirons Athletic Club, Lewis and Clark Nat. Bicentenial Commn. (commr. 2000-2005). Home: 785 6th St Boulder CO 80302-7416 Office: Ctr for Resource Mgmt 1030 13th St Ste 100 Boulder CO 80302 Business E-Mail: tminger@crm.org.

MINGES WOLS, HEATHER ANN, biology professor; PhD in Microbiology,Immunology, Loyola U. Chgo., Maywood, Ill., 2003. Asst. prof. Barat Coll. DePaul U., Lake Forest, Ill., 2003—05, Columbia Coll. Chgo., 2005—. Contbr. articles to profl. jours. Faculty Devel. grant, Columbia Coll. Chgo., 2006, 2008. Mem.: Nat. Assn. Biology Tchrs., Am. Assn. Microbiologists. Office: Columbia Coll Chgo 600 S Michigan Ave Chicago IL 60605

MINGLE, JOHN ORVILLE, engineer, educator, lawyer, consultant; b. Oakley, Kans., May 6, 1931; s. John Russell and Beulah Amelia (Johnson) M.; m. Patricia Ruth Schmitt, Aug. 17, 1957; children: Elizabeth Lorene, Stephen Roy. BS, Kans. State U., Manhattan, 1953, MS, 1958; PhD, Northwestern U., 1960; JD, Washburn U., 1980. Bar: Kans., Wyo., U.S. Patent Office; registered profl. engr., Kans. Tng. engr. Gen. Electric Co., Schenectady, 1953-54; mem. faculty Kans. State U., 1956-90, prof. nuclear engring., 1965-90, prof. emeritus, 1990—, Black & Veatch Disting. prof., 1973-78; dir. Inst. Computational Research Engring., 1969-88; exec. v.p., patent counsel Kans. State U. Research Found., 1983-88. Instr. Northwestern U., 1958-59; vis. prof. U. So. Calif., 1967-68; cons. govt. and industry; engring. legal cons. 1990—. Author: The Invarient Imbedding Theory of Nuclear Transport, 1973; also articles. Bd. dirs. Laramie Regional Airport, 1994-97. Officer AUS, 1954—56, lt. US Army, 1954—56. Mem. ABA (chairperson sci. and tech. phys. scis. com. 1982-92), NSPE (sect. exec. com. 1985-87, chmn. 1985-86), Am. Nuclear Soc. (sect. pres. 1976-77), Am. Inst. Chem. Engrs. (profl. devel. com. 1982-95), Am. Soc. Engring. Edn. (chmn. Midwest sect. 1985-86, exec. com. 1984-87), Profl. Engrs. in Edn. (vice chmn. 1978-80, workshop chairperson 1983), Kans. Engring. Soc. (past chpt. pres.), Kans. Bar Assn., Licensing Execs. Soc., Sigma Xi (past chpt. pres., lectr.), Soc. Univ. Patent Adminstrs. (exec. com. 1985-87, v.p. cen. region 1985-87). Home: 1409 Downey St Laramie WY 82072-1867 Office Phone: 307-742-0171. *In times past workaholic behavior produced prudent contributions. Now in our world of paradox, the philosophy has been turned on its head, and an iota of "wisdom work" often overshadows everything else.*

MINICHELLO, DENNIS, lawyer; b. Cleve., June 9, 1952; s. Ernest Anthony and Mary Theresa (Rocci) M.; m. Janine Stevens, Feb. 14, 1987. BA in Econs., MA in Econs., Ohio U., 1974; JD, Northwestern U., 1978. Bar: U.S. Dist. Ct. (no. dist.) Ill., U.S. Ct. Appeals (7th cir.), Supreme Ct. Ill., U.S. Supreme Ct. Assoc. Haskell & Perrin, Chgo., 1978-84; ptnr. Tribler & Marwedel, Chgo., 1984-89, Keck, Mahin & Cate, Chgo., 1989—97; shareholder Marwedel, Minichellot & Reeb, P.C., 1997—. Contbr. articles to profl. jours. Bd. dirs. Great Lakes Naval and Maritime Mus. Fulbright scholar, 1974-75. Mem. ABA, Ill. State Bar Assn., Chgo. Bar Assn. (mem. transp. com.), Maritime Law Assn. (proctor, com. chair, 2008), The Propeller Club US (pres. 1983-84), Port Chgo., Transp. Lawyers Assn., Conf. Freight Counsel, Midwest High Speed Rail Coalition (pres. 2000—08), Def. Rsch. Inst., Leading Lawyers Network., Ohio U. Alumni Assn.(chair bd. dirs., 2008-) Roman Catholic. Avocations: reading, exercise. Office: Marwedel Minichello & Reeb PC 10 S Riverside Plz Ste 720 Chicago IL 60606-3709 Office Phone: 312-902-1600 ext. 5065. Business E-Mail: dminichello@mmr-law.com.

MINICK, MICHAEL, publishing executive; b. Albany, NY, Mar. 26, 1945; s. Jason and Ruth Isabelle (Solomon) M. Student, U. Va., 1963-66; BA in History, L.I. U., 1968. Editorial dir. Mag. Mgmt., NYC, 1969-73; mng. editor Gentlemen's Quarterly, NYC, 1975-76; pub., ptnr. Beauty Digest, NYC, 1978-90; pub. Pa. Ofcl. Wine and Liquor Quar., NYC, 1985—, Ohio Liquor Quar., 1990—. Adj. prof. NYU Sch. Journalism. Author: The Kung Fu Exercise Book-Health Secrets of Ancient China, 1974, The Wisdom of Kung Fu, 1974; contbr. numerous articles to popular mags. Mem.: Pa. Wine and Spirit Assn., Sir Harold Actors Soc., 25 Yr. Club of Ind. Distbrs. Democrat. Home: 440 W 22nd St New York NY 10011-2526

MINICUCCI, RICHARD FRANCIS, lawyer, former hospital administrator; b. NYC, Jan. 16, 1947; s. Daniel Michael and Marie Felice (Trotta) M.; m. Nancy Jean Moran, Aug. 16, 1969; children: Jonathan, Elizabeth, Richard. BA, Rutgers U., 1969; MHA, Duke U., 1971; JD, Memphis State U., 1976. Bar: Tenn. 1977, N.Y. 1978. Adminstrv. asst. Duke Hosp., Durham, NC, 1971; health planner Mid-South Med. Ctr. Coun., Memphis, 1971-73; dir. adminstrn. Memphis & Shelby County Hosp. Authority, 1973-77; assoc. Hayt Hayt & Landau, Great Neck, NY, 1977-81, ptnr., 1981-89, Nixon Peabody LLP (Nixon Hargrave Devans & Doyle, LLP), Garden City, NY, 1989—. Lectr. various health law assns. Editor: New York Environmental Law Handbook, 2d edit.; author: Residency Training Program Accreditation, 1st-5th edits., Mastering the Accreditation Process, 1999; editor-in-chief Accreditation Alert, Trouble in Academia: Ten Years of Litigation in Medical Education, 2003; contbr articles to profl. jours. Co-chmn. fund raising Luth. High Sch., Brookville, N.Y., 1991. Capt. U.S. Army, 1971-79. Mem. Am., Nassau Bar Assn., Am. Health Lawyers Assn. Republican. Roman Catholic. Avocations: tennis, skiing, hockey, travel. Office: Nixon Peabody LLP 50 Jericho Quadrangle STE 300 Jericho NY 11753-2728

MINIKES, NEIL IRA, pediatrician, allergist, immunologist; b. NYC, 1951; MD, Columbia U. Coll. Physicians & Surgeons, 1980. Diplomate Am. Bd. Pediat., 1986, Am. Bd. Allergy & Immunology. Resident in pediat. Columbia Presbyn. Med. Ctr., NYC, 1980—83; fellow in allergy & immunology LI Jewish Med. Ctr., New Hyde Park, NY, 1986—90; pvt. practice pediat. and adult allergy immunology, Teaneck, NJ, Closter, NJ. Asst. clin. prof. pediat. Columbia U. Coll. Physicians & Surgeons. Named one of America's Top Doctors, Castle Connolly Med. Ltd., 2006. Mem.: NJ Allergy Soc., Am. Coll. Allergy & Immunology, Am. Acad. Pediat., Am. Acad. Allergy & Immunology. Office: Met Pediat N 570 Peirmont Rd Ste 17 Closter NJ 07624 also: 704 Palisade Ave Teaneck NJ 07666-3144 Office Phone: 201-836-4301, 201-768-8811. Office Fax: 201-768-7316.

MINIKES, STEPHAN MICHAEL, ambassador, lawyer, banker; b. Berlin, Aug. 29, 1938; came to U.S., 1949; naturalized, 1957; married; 1 child. BS, Cornell U., 1961; JD, Yale U., 1964. Bar: N.Y. State 1965, U.S. Ct. Appeals 2nd Circuit, 1967, U.S. Supreme Ct. 1972, U.S. Ct. Mil. Appeals, 1973, D.C. 1977. Assoc. firm Milbank, Tweed, Hadley & McCloy, NYC, 1964-68, Borden & Ball, NYC, 1968-72; counsel to spl. cons. for energy Pres. U.S., 1973; counsel to chief Naval Ops., Washington, 1972-74; sr. v.p. Export-Import Bank of U.S., Washington, 1974-77; resident mng. partner firm Butler & Binion, Houston and Washington, 1977-84, Thelen Reid & Priest, NY, LA, San Francisco, and Wash., 1984—2001; amb. Org. Security and Coop. in Europe, Vienna, 2001—05; chmn. global affairs and pub. policy Xenophon Strategies, San Francisco, 2006—, Wash., 2006—. Bd. dirs. A.T. Kearnery Pub. Scetor and Def. Svcs. LLC; spl. ptnr. RPM Ventures; bd. advisors Riverglass, Inc.; of counsel Xenophon Strategies; ltd. ptnr. Wilbanks Res. Contbr. articles to profl. jours. Mem. exec. com. Yale U. Law Sch., 1979-82, 86-89, 93-97; trustee, chmn. fin. com. Washington Opera, 1979-84. Mem. ABA, Fed. Bar Assn., D.C. Bar Assn., Assn. of Bar of City of N.Y., Am. Soc. Internat. Law, Am. Coun. Germany (bd. dirs., 1994-2001), Cornell U. Alumni Assn., Yale U. Alumni Assn. (law sch. rep. 1981-83, 86-90), Yale Law Sch. (Exec. Com., 1986-90), Internat. Rep. Inst. (bd. dirs.), Yale Club (Washington), Metropolitan Club (Washington). Home: 419 Walker Rd Great Falls VA 22066 Office Phone: 202-289-4001.

MINKEL, HERBERT PHILIP, JR., lawyer; b. Boston, Feb. 11, 1947; s. Herbert Philip and Helen (Sullivan) M. BA, Holy Cross Coll., 1969; JD, NYU, 1972. Bar: Mass. 1973, US Dist. Ct. Mass. 1973, NY 1976, US Dist. Ct. (so. dist.) NY 1978. Law clk. U.S. Dist. Ct. Mass., Boston, 1972-73; assoc. Milbank, Tweed, Hadley & McCloy, NYC, 1973-79; ptnr. Fried, Frank, Harris, Shriver & Jacobson, NYC, 1979-94; mem. adv. com. on bankruptcy rules Jud. Conf. U.S., 1987-93; sr. ptnr. Minkel and Assoc., NYC and Boston, 1994—. Adj. assoc. prof. NYU Law Sch., 1987-94. Contbg. author: American Bankers Assn. Bankruptcy Manual, 1979; contbg. editor: Collier on Bankruptcy, 15th edit., 1979-96; contbr. articles to profl. jours. Bd. advisors Internat. Yacht Restoration Sch., Newport, R.I., internat. coun., Mystic Seaport, Conn. Root-Tilden scholar NYU, 1969-72. Mem. ABA, Nat. Bankruptcy Conf., Assn. Bar City of N.Y. Home: 68 Bumps River Rd Osterville MA 02655-1525 Office: Minkel and Assocs 131 E 62d St New York NY 10021 Business E-Mail: hminkel@nyc.rr.com.

MINKEL, JUSTIN, elementary school educator; s. Dan and Julie M.; m. Karen Minkel. BA, Cornell Univ.; MA, Univ. Calif., Berkeley. Former tchr. Teach for Am., NY, Calif., Texas, Senegal, W. Africa; tchr. Harvey Jones Elem. Sch., Springdale, Ark., 2003—. Named Ark. Tchr. of Yr., 2007; finalist Nat. Tchr. of Yr., 2007. Achievements include being fluent in Spanish, French, two African languages. Office: Jones Elem Sch 900 S Powell St Springdale AR 72764 Business E-Mail: justinmink@yahoo.com.

MINKER, JACK, computer scientist, educator; b. Bklyn., July 4, 1927; s. Harry and Rose (Lapuck) M.; m. Rita Goldberg, June 24, 1951 (dec. Oct. 11, 1988); children: Michael Saul, Sally Anne; m. Johanna Cartee Weinstein, Jan. 19, 1997. BA cum laude with honors in Math., Bklyn. Coll., 1949; MS in Math., U. Wis., 1950; PhD in Math., U. Pa., 1959. Grad. teaching asst. U. Wis., 1949-50; tchr. math. Erasmus Hall HS, Bklyn., 1950-51; engr. Bell Aircraft Corp., Buffalo, 1951-52; mgr. info. tech. sect. RCA, Bethesda, Md., 1952-63; dir. tech. staff Auerbach Corp., Washington, 1963-67, tech. cons., 1967-72; mem. Faculty NIH Grad. Sch., 1965-66; vis. mem. faculty U. Md., 1967-68, assoc. prof. computer sci., 1968-71, prof., 1971-98, prof. emeritus, 1998—, 1st chmn. dept. computer sci., 1974-79; cons., speaker, lectr. in field; cons. NSF, 1979-82, chmn. adv. bd. on computer sci., 1980-82. Prof. Inst. Advanced Computer Studies, 1986-1998; vice-chmn. Com. Concerned Scientists, 1973—; past mem. US Nat. Com. for Fedn. Info. Documentalists. Author: (with H. Gallaire and J.M. Nicolas) Logic and Data Bases a Deductive Approach, 1984; editor: (with H. Gallaire and J.M. Nicholas) Advances in Data Base Theory, vol. 1, 1980, vol. 2, 1984, (with H. Gallaire) Logic and Data Bases, 1978, Foundations of Deductive Databases and Logic Programming, 1988, (with J. Lobo and A. Rajasekar) Foundations of Disjunctive Logic Programming, 1992; editor: Logic-Based Artificial Intelligence, 2000; founding editor-in-chief Theory and Practice of Logic Programming, 2000-2001; contbr. articles to profl. jours.; publs. reviewer; mem. editl. bd. numerous jours. With US Army, 1945—46. Recipient U. Md. Presdl. medal, 1996, Allen Newell award ACM/AAAS, 2005; named Disting. Scholar-Tchr. U. Md., 1997-98, fellow Acad. Excellence in Tchg. and Learning, 2002—. Fellow: IEEE (editl. bd. Expert Info.Sys. jour.), ACM, AAAS, Am. Assn. Artificial Intelligence; mem.: Assn. Computing Machinery (chmn. nat. program com. 1968—69, vice chmn. com. on sci. freedom and human rights 1979—89, founding, Outstanding Contbn. award 1985). Jewish. Office: U Md Dept Computer Sci Dept and Inst Advanced Computer College Park MD 20742-0001

MINKIEWICZ, ARLENE FRENCH, computer scientist; d. Francis Gilbert and Janice French; m. Victor Minkiewicz, Apr. 13, 1985; children: Andrew Joseph, Nicholas James. BS, Lehigh U., Bethlehem, Pa., 1982; MS, Drexel U., Phila., 1988. Control sys. engr. Bechtel Power Corp., Gaithersburg, Md., 1983—84; software developer PRICE Sys. LLC, Mt. Laurel, NJ, 1984—88, engr. software devel., 1988—92, sr. engr., 1992—97, dir. product devel., 1997—98, chief scientist, 1998—. Comm. chair Merchanrtville Jr. Woman's Club, NJ, 2005—08; v.p. St. Stephens PTA, Pennsuaken, NJ, 1998—2001. Achievements include patents for methodology for estimating object oriented software applications. Office: PRICE Sys LLC 17000 Commerce Pky Ste A Mount Laurel NJ 08054 Office Fax: 856-608-7247. Business E-Mail: arlene.minkiewicz@pricesystems.com.

MINKKINEN, ARNO RAFAEL, photographer, educator; b. Helsinki, Finland, June 4, 1945; s. Reino Johannes and Riitta Ali Minkkinen; m. Sandra Jean Hughes; 1 child, Dan Hughes. BA, Wagner Coll., Staten Island, NY, 1967; MFA, RI Sch Design, Providence, 1974. Vis. lectr. Taideteollinen Korkeakoulu, Helsinki, 1974—76; asst. prof. Mass. Inst. Tech., Cambridge, 1977—81; vis. prof. U. Arts, Phila., 1981—82; vis. lectr. Lahti Inst. Design, Finland, 1975—76, 1984—86; vis. prof. U. Art & Design Helsinki, 1984—86, docent, 1991—; prof. U. Mass., Lowell, 1987—; vis. prof. École d'Arts Appliqués, Vevey, Vaud, Switzerland, 1995—2005; grad. faculty Maine Media Coll., Rockport, Maine, 2001—. Bd. mem. Soc. Photographic Edn., Cleve., 2008—. Exhibitions include; contbr. to monographs (Book of Yr., 1994). Recipient Art prize, Finnish Govt., 2006, Scritture d'Acqua prize, Salsomaggiore Terme, Italy, 1996; named Knighthood Order of Lion, Finnish Govt., 1992; fellowship, Nat. Endowment Arts New Eng. Region, 1991. Mem.: Photographic Resource Ctr. Boston, Soc. Photographic Edn. (bd. mem.). Avocations: sailing, skiing, hiking, rowing. Office: Univ Mass Lowell 77 Wilder St Lowell MA 01852 Business E-Mail: arno_minkkinen@uml.edu.

MINKOFF, JACK, retired economics professor; b. NYC, Jan. 29, 1925; s. Isidore and Yetta (Fine) M.; m. Anne B. Johnson, June 19, 1948; children— Ellen, Paul. AB, Cornell U., 1948; A.M., Columbia U., 1950, PhD (Ford Found. fellow), 1960. Instr. econs. Western Res. U., 1952-53; instr. econs. Sarah Lawrence Coll., 1959-60; prof. econs., chmn. dept. social sci. Pratt Inst., Bklyn., 1960—, acting dean Sch. Liberal Arts and Scis., 1985-86, dean, 1986-93, acting provost, 1993-95, prof. econs., 1996—2002, ret., 2002. Served with USAAF, 1943-45. Social Sci. Rsch. Coun. fellow, 1950-51. Mem. Phi Beta Kappa. Home: 57 Ruxton Rd Great Neck NY 11023-1528

MINKOFF, JOHN, applied mathematics educator; b. Bklyn. s. Alvin Minkoff and Mollie Schwartz; m. Susan Alder, Nov. 19, 1966; 1 child, John. BSEE, Columbia U., 1962, MSEE, 1963, PhD, 1967. Rsch. engr. Columbia U., NYC, 1964-67, rsch. assoc., 1967-73; mgr. analysis activities Riverside Rsch. Inst., NYC, 1973-77; mem. tech. staff Bell Tel. Labs., Whippany, NJ, 1977-86; disting mem. tech. staff ATT/Lucent Techs. Bell Labs., Whippany, 1986—2001; staff scientist space sys. divsn. ITT, 2001—. Adj. prof. elec. engring. Polytech. U. NY, 1989-90; adj. prof. applied math. NYU, NYC, 1990-95. Author: Signals Noise and Active Sensors, 1992, Signal Processing Fundamentals and Applications for Communications and Sensing Systems, 2002; contbr. articles to profl. jours. Music dir. Hawthorne (NJ) Symphony Orch. NSF grantee, 1975. Mem. Am. Phys. Soc. Jewish. Avocation: music. Home: 578 Jones Rd Englewood NJ 07631 Office Phone: 973-284-2011. Office Fax: 973-284-3414. Business E-Mail: john.minkoff@itt.com.

MINKOWITZ, MARTIN, lawyer, former state government official; b. Bklyn., 1939; s. Jacob and Marion Minkowitz; m. Carol L. Ziegler; 1 son from previous marriage, Stuart Allan. AA, Bklyn. Coll., 1959, BA, 1961; JD, Bklyn. Law Sch., 1963, LLM, 1965. Bar: NY 1963, US Supreme Ct. 1967, US Tax Ct. 1974, all four US Dist. Cts. NY. Ptnr. Minkowitz, Hagen & Rosenbluth, NYC, 1964—76; gen. counsel State of N.Y. Workers' Compensation Bd., 1976—81; dep. supt. and gen. counsel State of N.Y. Ins. Dept., 1981—88; instr. CUNY, 1975; ptnr. Stroock & Stroock & Lavan, 1988—. Cons. City Coun. NYC 1969; hearing officer NYC Transp. Dept., 1970-75; adj. prof. law NY Law Sch., NYC, 1982—; adv. bd. Coll. Ins., 1987-90; lectr. ABA, NY C. of C., Practicing Law Inst., NY State Bar Assn., Nat. Assn. Ins. Commrs., Nat. Conf. Ins. Legis. Author: West's New York Workers' Compensation, 2003-; (with others) Rent Stabilization and Control, 1973, Handling the Basic Workers' Compensation Law Case, 1996, West's New York General Practice; co-author: Workers Compensation, Insurance and Law Practice-The Next Generation, 1989; commentaries to McKinney's Consol. Laws, 1982—; mem. editl. bd. Jour. Occupl. Rehab. U. Rochester, 1991—; contbr. articles to profl. jours. Bd. dir., sec. Kingsbay YM-YWHA, Bklyn., 1978-99, elected dir. emeritus, 1999—2007; pres. bd. dir. Shore Terrace Co-op., Bklyn., 1982-83; co-chmn. exec. bd., met. coun., nat. v.p. Am. Jewish Congress, N.Y.C., 1983-91; bd. dir. Met. Coord. Coun. on Jewish poverty, 1993—, Nat. Conf. Cmty. and Justice (bd. dir. N.Y. divsn. 1994-2001, nat. bd. trustees 1995-2001, chair N.Y. divsn. 1998-2001); bd. Am. Soc. Workers Compensation, 2003—. Recipient cert. meritorious svc. Bklyn. Law Sch., Outstanding Pub. Svc. award Ind. Ins. Agt. Assn., Legends award Am. Co., citation outstanding performance State of N.Y. Workers' Compensation Bd., Disting. Leadership award N.Y. Claims Assn., City of Peace award State of Israel Bonds, Brotherhood award NCCJ, Man of Yr. awards Congregation B'Nai Avraham, Bklyn., Kingsbay YM-YWHA. Fellow NY State Bar Found.; mem. (life) Fed. Bar Coun. Com. 2d Cir., NY County Lawyers Assn. (chmn. unlawful practice of law com. 1982-86, mem. profl. ethics com. 1985-91, chair worker's compensation com. 1988-91, bd. dir. 1997-2006, chair profl. ethics com. 2001-2006, bd. dir., exec. bd. 2003-05, 2006-07), NY State Bar Assn. (mem. house of dels. 1999-2003, 2004-08, 09, com. access to justice, 2008-, chmn. unlawful practice of law com. 1981-83, mem. com. on profl. ethics 1981-84, chmn. com. profl. discipline, mem. com. on jud. nominations, chair elect gen. practice sect., 2008-09, chair 2009-, editor One on One publ. 2001—, Sustaining Mem. of Yr. award 1995), Soc. Ins. Receivers, Bklyn. Law Sch. Alumni Assn. (v.p. bd. dir. 1984-92, pres. elect 1993-94, pres. 1995-96). Office: Stroock Stroock & Lavan 180 Maiden Ln Fl 17 New York NY 10038-4937 Office Phone: 212-806-6256. Business E-Mail: mminkowitz@stroock.com.

MINKOWYCZ, W. J., mechanical engineering educator; b. Libokhora, Ukraine, Oct. 21, 1937; came to U.S., 1949; s. Alexander and Anna (Tokan) M.; m. Diana Eva Szandra, May 12, 1973; 1 child, Liliana Christine Anne BS in Mech. Engring., U. Minn., 1958, MS in Mech. Engring., 1961, PhD in Mech. Engring, 1965. From asst. prof. to James P. Hartnett prof. U. Ill., Chgo., 1966—2006, James P. Hartnett prof., 2006—. Cons. Argonne Nat. Lab, Ill., 1970-82, U. Hawaii, Honolulu, 1974-94. Founding editor-in-chief (jour.) Jour. Numerical Heat Transfer, 1978—; editor-in-chief: Internat. Jour. Heat and Mass Transfer, 1968-, Rheologically Complex Fluids, 1972, Internat. Comms. in Heat and Mass Transfer Jour., 1974-, 1988, Handbook of Numerical Heat Transfer, 2006; editor: (book series) Computational and Physical Processes in Mechanics and Thermal Sciences, 1979—, Advances in Numerical Heat Transfer, 1996—, Vol. 1, 1997, Vol. 2, 2000, Vol. 3, 2009; contbr. articles to profl. jours. Recipient Silver Circle for Excellence in Teaching, U. Ill.-Chgo., 1975, 76, 81, 86, 90, 94, Harold A. Simon award Excellence in Teaching, 1986, Ralph Coats Roe Outstanding Tchr. award Am. Soc. Engring. Edn., 1988, U. Ill. Disting. Tchr. award, 1989. Fellow: ASME (Heat Transfer Meml. award 1993, Classic Paper award 2006); mem.: Pi Tau Sigma, Sigma Xi. Republican. Ukrainian Catholic. Office: U Ill Dept Mech Engring Mail Code 251 842 W Taylor St Chicago IL 60607-7021 Office Phone: 312-996-3467. Business E-Mail: wjm@uic.edu.

MINNELLI, LIZA, singer, actress; b. Los Angeles, Mar. 12, 1946; d. Vincente and Judy (Garland) M.; m. Peter Allen, Mar. 3, 1967 (div. June 24, 1972); m. Jack Haley Jr., Sept. 15, 1974 (div. 1979); m. Mark Gero, Dec. 4, 1979 (div. 1992); m. David Gest, Mar. 16, 2002 (div. 2003). Appeared in Off-Broadway revival of Best Foot Forward, 1963; appeared with mother at London Palladium, 1964; nightclub debut at Shoreham Hotel, Washington, 1965; appeared in Flora, the Red Menace, 1965 (Tony award), The Act, 1977 (Tony award), The Rink, 1984, Victor Victoria; films include Charlie Bubbles, 1967, The Sterile Cuckoo, 1969, Tell Me That You Love Me, Junie Moon, 1970, Cabaret, 1972 (Golden Globe award, Acad. award, BAFTA award), That's Entertainment, 1974, Lucky Lady, 1975, A Matter of Time, 1976, Silent Movie, 1976, New York, New York, 1977, Arthur, 1981, Rent A Cop, Arthur on the Rocks, 1988, Stepping Out, 1991, The OH in Ohio, 2006; recorded You Are For Loving, 1963, Tropical Nights, 1977, Liza Minnelli at Carnegie Hall, 1987, Results, 1989, Maybe This Time, 1996, Gently, 1996, Minnelli on Minnelli, 2000, (with Herbie Hancock, Johnny Mathis, Donna Summer), Liza's Back!, 2003; (TV films) Parallel Lives, 1994, The West Side Waltz, 1995, Jackie's Back!, 1999; appeared on TV in own spl. Liza With a Z, 1972 (Recipient Emmy award); other TV appearances include Goldie and Liza Together, 1980, Baryshnikov on Broadway, 1980, The Princess and the Pea, Showtime, 1983, A Time to Live, 1985, Sam Found Out, 1988, Liza Minnelli Live from Radio City Music Hall, PBS (Emmy nomination, Music Program Performance, 1993), The Wonderful World of Oz: 50 Years of Magic, 1990, A Century of Cinema, 1994, My Favorite Broadway: The Leading Ladies, 1999, (TV series) Arrested Development, 2003-05; guest appearance Law & Order: Criminal Intent, 2006; internat. tour with Frank Sinatra, Sammy Davis Jr., 1988. Recipient Italy's David di Donatello award (twice), the Valentino award, Drama Desk award, 2009, Tony award for Best Spl. Theatrical Event, 2009. Address: Capitol Records Inc 1750 Vine St Hollywood CA 90028-5209 Office: EMI MUSIC 900 PLAZA TEN Jersey City NJ 07311-4008*

MINNEMAN, KENNETH PAUL, pharmacology educator; b. Sacramento, Calif., Sept. 1, 1952; s. John Jesse and Esther Annette Minneman; children: Jennifer, Rebecca, Jeffrey. BS, MIT, 1974; PhD, U. Cambridge, England, 1977. Asst. prof. pharm. Emory U., Atlanta, 1980-85, assoc. prof. pharm., 1985-90, prof. pharm, 1990-2000, Charles Howard Candler prof. pharm., 2000—. Editor: Brody's Human Pharmacology: Molecular to Clinical, 2005 Undergrad. fellowship, NSF, 1970-74; biomed. rsch. grantee NIH, 1981-2005; postdoctoral fellow U. Colo. Med. Ctr., Denver, 1977-80; John Jacob Abel award, 1986, Award for Excellence in Basic Pharmacology, PhRMA Found., 2000. Mem. AAAS, Am. Soc. Pharm. & Exptl. Therapeutics (exec. coun. 1999-02, pres.-elect 2006-07, pres. 2007-08), Soc. Neurosci., Internat. Soc. Neurochem. Office: Emory U 1510 Clifton Rd Atlanta GA 30322 Office Phone: 404-727-5985. Office Fax: 404-727-0365. Business E-Mail: kminneman@pharm.emory.edu.

MINNER, RUTH ANN, former Governor of Delaware; b. Melford, Del., Jan. 17, 1935; m. Frank Ingram (dec. 1967); children: Frank, Wayne, Gary; m. Roger Minner (dec. 1991). Student, Del. Tech. and CC. Office receptionist to Gov, State of Del., Dover, 1972—74; mem. Del. Ho. of Representatives, Dover, 1974—82, Del. State Senate, Dover, 1982—92; lt. gov. State of Del., Dover, 1993—2001, gov., 2001—09. Recipient Legislator of Yr., Del. Wildlife Fedn., 1989, Outstanding Environmentalist, Coalition for Natural Stream Valleys Inc., 1990, Alexis I. Bayard Award, Del. Dem. Party, 1991, Environ. Award, Del. Sierra Club, 1991, Mother of Yr., Del. Assn. Am. Mothers Inc., 1993; named to Del. Women's Hall of Fame, 1995. Mem.: Dem. Nat. Com., Capitol City Bus. & Profl. Women's Club, Milford New Century Club. Democrat.*

MINNERLY, ROBERT WARD, retired headmaster; b. Yonkers, NY, Mar. 21, 1935; s. Richard Warren and Margaret Marion (DeBrocky) M.; m. Sandra Overmire, June 12, 1957; children: Scott Ward, John Robert, Sydney Sue. AB, Brown U., Providence, 1957; MAT, U. Tex., Arlington, 1980. Tchr., coach Rumsey Hall Sch., Washington, Conn., 1962—64, Berkshire Sch., Sheffield, Mass., 1964—70, asst. head, 1969—70, headmaster, 1970—76; dir. Salisbury Summer Sch. Reading and English, Conn., 1970; prin. upper sch. Ft. Worth Country Day Sch., 1976—86; headmaster Charles Wright Acad., Tacoma, 1986—96; ednl. cons. The Edn. Group, 1996—2000; interim dir. Harold E. LeMay Mus., 2001—02; exec. dir. R. Merle Palmer Minority Students Scholarship Found., 2004—06. Cons. Tarrant County Coalition on Substance Abuse, 1982-84; mayor's task force Tacoma Edn. Summit, 1991-92; bd. dirs. World Cultural Interaction, Gig Harbor, Wash. Contbr. articles to profl. jours. Bd. dirs. Tacoma/Pierce County Good Will Games Art Coun., 1989, Multicare Found., Tacoma, 2002, Tacoma Baseball Found., 2003—05; mem. exec. com. Am. Leadership Forum, 1991-95; bd. dirs. Broadway Ctr. for Performing Arts, Tacoma, 1988-94, 96-98, mem. exec. com., 1990-93; elected Wash. State Bd. Edn., 1996-2001; bd. dirs. Tacoma Youth Choir, 2000-03. Named Adminstr. of Yr. Wash. Journalism Edn. Assn., 1991; recipient Columbia award, Wash. Fedn. Ind. Schs., 2000. Mem. Pacific N.W. Assn. Ind. Schs. (chmn. long-range planning com. 1989-92, exec. com. 1990-92, 91, v.p. 1994). Presbyterian. Home: 6204 Waterview Dr Arlington TX 76016 Personal E-mail: bobmin7309@sbcglobal.net.

MINNERS, HOWARD ALYN, federal agency administrator, researcher, preventive medicine physician; b. Rockville Center, NY, Sept. 1, 1931; s. Howard A. and Marie Henriette (Soberski) M.; m. Gretchen Paffenbarger, Oct. 25, 1958; children: Todd, Bradford. AB, Princeton U., 1953; MD, Yale U., 1957; MPH, Harvard U., 1960. Diplomate Am. Bd. Preventive Medicine, Nat. Bd. Med. Examiners. 2d. lt. USAF, 1956; intern Wilford Hall USAF Hosp., San Antonio, 1957-58; resident Sch. of Aerospace Medicine, USAF, Brooks AFB, Tex., 1960-62; advanced through grades to maj. USAF, 1966; advanced through grades to rear adm. USPHS, ret., 1987; dir. office rsch. promotion and devel. WHO, Geneva, Switzerland, 1977-80; dir. Office of Sci. Advisor Agy. Internat. Devel., Washington, 1981-91; dep. dir. Office Internat. Health USPHS and Asst. Surgeon Gen., 1980-81. Assoc. dir. NIH NIAID, 1966-77; astronaut flight surgeon NASA, Houston, 1962-66; mem. Dean's Coun. Yale Med. Sch., 2007-. Pres. Model A Ford Found., 1994-2000. Fellow World Acad. Art and Sci., Am. Coll. Preventive Medicine; mem. AAAS, Internat. Found. Sci. Stockholm (pres., chmn. bd. trustees 1991-97), Yale Med. Alumni Fund (chmn. bd. trustees 2003-06). Avocations: Model A Ford restoration, history.

MINNESTE, VIKTOR, JR., retired engineering executive; b. Haapsalu, Estonia, Jan. 15, 1932; s. Viktor and Alice (Lembra) M. BSEE, U. Ill., 1960. Elec. engr. Bell & Howell Co., 1960-69; microstatics divsn. A-M Co., 1969-71, multigraphics divsn., 1972-73; elec. engr. bus. products group Victor Comptometer Co. (merged with Walter Kidde Corp.), Chgo., 1973-74, svc. mgr. internat. group, 1974-75, supr. elecs. desing group, 1975-82; project engr. Warner Electric, 1982-84; systems engr. Barrett Elecs., 1984-85; phone engr. Williams Elecs., 1986-88; cons. engr., 1988-92; ind. contractor, 1993-95; ret., 1995. Pub. Motteid/Thoughts, 1962-68. Chmn. Estonian-Ams. Polit Action Com., 1968-72. With AUS, 1952-54. Home and Office: 3134 N Kimball Ave Chicago IL 60618-6856

MINNICH, DONNA, social sciences educator; Sociology prof. George Wash. U., Wash., DC, 2002—. Mem.: ASA (life).

MINNICK, BRUCE ALEXANDER, lawyer; b. New London, Conn., Apr. 16, 1943; s. Robert Wood Minnick and Nedra Louise (Alexander) Wiesman; m. Judith Anita Saxon, Sept. 23, 1967 (div. 1981); children: Audra Anne, Lisa Michelle; m. Charlotte Ann Springfield, Apr. 10, 1983 (div. 1991); 1 child, Matthew Alexander; m. Debra C. Williams, July 3, 1997; 1 stepchild, Brandy Michelle Williams. AA, Broward Community Coll., 1970; BS with honors, Fla. State U., 1971, JD, 1977. Bar: Fla. 1978, U.S. Dist. Ct. (no. dist.) Fla. 1979, U.S. Dist. Ct. (mid. and so. dists.) Fla. 1982, U.S. Supreme Ct. 1981, U.S. Ct. Appeals (11th cir.) 1982, U.S. Tax Ct. 1983, U.S. Ct. Claims 1983, U.S. Dist. Ct. (ea. dist.) Mich. 1990; cert. Expert in Labor and Employment Law, The Fla. Bar, 2003-08. Asst. v.p., asst. comptroller Pan Am. Bank Miami, 1971—74; staff dir., counsel rules com. Fla. Ho. Reps., Tallahassee, 1976-78; v.p., gen. counsel Fla. Credit Union League, Tallahassee, 1978-80; asst. atty. gen. dept. legal affairs State of Fla., Tallahassee, 1981-86; ptnr. Mang, Rett & Collette, P.A., Tallahassee, 1986-93, Mang, Rett & Minnick PA, Tallahassee, 1994-95; pvt. practice Bruce A. Minnick PA, Tallahassee, 1996—; resident ptnr. Kahn & Assocs., LLC, Cleve., 2005—08. Chief advocate Fla. Commn. on Ethics, 1985—86; lectr. state agys., 1982—, Fla. Bar, 1986—; pres. Civil Rights Dispute Resolution Ctr., 2002—07. Mem. Leon County Dist. Adv. Com., 1980—82, 1992—94; mem. exec. com. Leon County Dems., 1984—2000, 2001—05. Commd. officer field arty. US Army, 1967—69. Mem.: ABA (labor sect., local govt. and law sect.), Fed. Bar Assn. (pres.-elect Tallahassee chpt. 1995, pres. 1996), Fla. Women Lawyers Assn., Fla. Govt. Bar Assn., Tallahassee Bar Assn., Fla. Bar Assn. (chmn. com. labor sect. 1987—91, exec. coun. labor sect. 1989—93, founding chmn. Fed. Ct. practice com. 1990—92, del. to 11th Cir. Jud. Conf. 1990—92, rep. mem. pub. rels. com. 1991—93, com. chmn. govt. lawyer sect. 1991—2000, ann. meeting com. 2004—06, Super Lawyer Fla. 2006—), Golden Eagle Country Club, Calvary Chapel Tallahassee, Phi Alpha Delta. Avocations: golf, astronomy, writing. Home and Office: 9017 Eagles Ridge Dr PO Box 15588 Tallahassee FL 32312-4046 Office Phone: 850-386-9444. Personal E-mail: bam@minnicklaw.com. Business E-Mail: clients@minnicklaw.com.

MINNICK, MALCOLM DAVID, lawyer; b. Indpls., July 5, 1946; s. Malcolm Dick and Frances Louise (Porter) M.; m. Heidi Rosemarie Klein, May 24, 1972. BA, U. Mich., 1968, JD, 1972. Bar: Calif. 1972, U.S. Dist. Ct. (ctrl. dist.) Calif. 1972, U.S. Ct. Appeals (9th cir.) 1984, U.S. Dist. Ct. (no. dist.) Calif. 1986, U.S. Supreme Ct. 1986. Assoc. Lillick McHose & Charles, LA, 1972-78; ptnr. Lillick & McHose, LA, 1978-91, Pillsbury Winthrop Shaw Pittman LLP, San Francisco, 1991—. Group mgr. Creditors Rights and Bankruptcy Group, 1993-98; panelist Calif. Continuing Edn. of Bar, LA, 1982-86, 88, San Francisco, 2005, Practicing Law Inst., 1992, 93, 94, Banking Law Inst., 1999, 2000; bd. govs. Fin. Lawyers Conf., LA, 1981-84; mem. exec. com. Lillick & McHose, 1982-85. Co-author: Checklist for Secured Commercial Loans, 1983. Pres. Ross Sch. Found., 1997-98. Mem. ABA (corp., banking and bus. law sect.), Am. Bankruptcy Inst., Calif. Bar Assn. (Uniform Comml. Code com. 1983-86), LA County Bar Assn. (exec. com. comml. law and bankruptcy sect. 1987-90), Bar Assn. San Francisco (comml. law and bankruptcy sect., panelist 2004), LA Country Club, Univ. Club (bd. dirs. 1983-86, pres. 1985-86). Avocation: golf. Office: Pillsbury Winthrop Shaw Pittman LLP 50 Fremont St San Francisco CA 94105-2230 Office Phone: 415-983-1351. Business E-Mail: dminnick@pillsburylaw.com.

MINNICK, MARY E., investment company executive, former beverage company executive; b. Evanston, Ill., Nov. 27, 1959; BS in Bus., Bowling Green St. U., 1981; MBA, Duke U., 1983. With fountain sales, bottle/can divsn. Coca-Cola USA; asst. v.p., dir non-carbonated beverages The Coca-Cola Co., 1993—95, v.p., Middle & Far East mktg., 1996—97, pres. South Pacific divsn., 1997—2000, pres., Coca-Cola Japan, 2000—01, pres., COO, Asia Group, 2001—05, exec. v.p., 2002—07, pres. mktg., strategy & innovation, 2005—07; ptnr. Lion Capital, London, 2007—. Mem. Dean's Coun. John F. Kennedy Sch. Bus., Harvard U.; bd. visitors Fuqua Sch. Bus. Named one of 50 Most Powerful Women in Bus., Fortune mag., 2005, 2006, 100 Most Powerful Women in World, Forbes mag., 2005, 25 Masters of Innovation, BusinessWeek, 2006, 50 Women to Watch, Wall St. Jour., 2006, Next 20 Female CEOs, Pink Mag. & Forté Found., 2006. Office: Lion Capital 21 Grosvenor Place London SW1X 7HF England Office Phone: +44 (0) 20 7201 2200. Office Fax: +44 (0) 20 7201 2222.

MINNICK, WALTER CLIFFORD, United States Representative from Idaho, former building materials company executive; b. Walla Walla, Wash., Sept. 20, 1942; s. Walter Lawrence and Dorothy (Waldron) M.; children from previous marriage: Amy Louise, Adam Wade; m. A.K. Lienhart. BA summa cum laude in Econs., Whitman Coll., 1964; MBA with high distinction, Harvard U., 1966, JD magna cum laude, 1969. Bar: Oreg. and Wash. bars. Assoc. firm Davies, Biggs, Strayer, Stoel & Boley, Portland, Oreg., 1969-70; staff asst. to pres. Domestic Council, Washington, 1971-72; dep. asst. dir. Office Mgmt. and Budget, Washington, 1972-73; with T.J. Internat., Boise, Idaho, 1974-95, v.p. div. ops., 1976-79, pres., COO, 1979-95, pres., CEO, 1986-95, also past chmn. bd. dirs., trustee; mem. US Congress from 1st Idaho Dist., 2009—. Bd. dir. Eljer Corp., MacMillan Bloedel, Ltd.; chmn. Bogus Basin Ski Area Chmn. Albertson Coll. of Idaho, 1989-1993; Served to 1st Lt. U.S. Army, 1970-72. Named Idaho Bus. Leader of Yr., 1992. Mem. Wash. State Bar Assn., Oreg. State Bar Assn., Idaho Conservation League, Nature Conservancy, Boise Fgn. Affairs Soc. (mem. exec. com.), Bogus Basin Recreation Assn. (past chmn.). Democrat. Unitarian Universalist. Office: US Congress 1517 Longworth House Office Bldg Washington DC 20515-1201 also: Dist Office 802 W Bannock Ste 101 Boise ID 83702 Office Phone: 202-225-6611, 208-336-9831. Office Fax: 202-225-3029, 208-336-9891.*

MINNIGH, JOEL DOUGLAS, library director; b. Greenville, Pa., Apr. 9, 1949; s. Wendell Ellsworth and Frances Alene (Hyde) M.; m. Margaret Beth Crowther, Dec. 26, 1972; children: Bradley Dean, Douglas Knox. BA, Allegheny Coll., 1971; MLS, U. Pitts., 1975. Cert. libr., Pa. Asst. libr. Wilkinsburg (Pa.) Pub. Libr., 1976-77, head libr., 1977—. Bd. dirs. Goodwill Industries Pitts., 1980-90, Mulberry Sr. Citizens Ctr., Wilkinsburg, Pa., 2001-09; vice chmn. bd. dirs. Bach Choir Pitts., 1984-87; sec., bd. dirs. United Meth. Ch. Union, Pitts., 1987-88; elder, deacon Fox Chapel Presbyn. Ch., 1987—, soloist, 1998—. Recipient honor Goodwill Industries Pitts., 1990, citation Pa. Senate, 1991. Mem. Pa. Libr. Assn. (treas. S.W. chpt. 1988-89, 2004-05), Allegheny County Libr. Assn. (pres. librs. adv. coun. 2001-02, bd. dirs. 2002-05), Wilkinsburg C. of C. (dir. 1998-03, sec. 1999-2003). Republican. Avocations: travel, cooking, gardening, music, reading. Home: 1009 Blackridge Rd Pittsburgh PA 15235-2719 Office: Wilkinsburg Pub Libr 605 Ross Ave Pittsburgh PA 15221-2145

MINNILLO, VANESSA JOY, news correspondent; b. Pampanga, Philippines, Nov. 9, 1980; d. Vince Minnillo and Helen Berecero, Donna (Stepmother). News correspondent Entertainment Tonight, 2005—08. Appearances on (TV series) That's Life, 2001, City Guys, 2001, Bold and the Beautiful, 2001, Maybe it's Me, 2002, How I Met Your Mother, 2008, host Top of the Pops, 2002, MTV's Prom Date, 2004, The Road to Stardom with Missy Elliott, 2005, co-host Total Request Live, 2003—07, correspondent Entertainment Tonight, 2005—08, host (TV films) The Break, 2003, (TV spl.) 2 Punk Rock 4 This: The Real World San Diego Reunion, High School Stories, Spring Break Celebrity Fantasies, Miss Teen USA, 2004, correspondent 50th Ann. Miss USA Pageant, 2001, judge Miss Teen USA, 2003, 2007, co-host Miss Universe Pageant, 2007, actress (films) Fantastic Four: Rise of The Silver Surfer, 2006, Disaster Movie, 2008. Named Miss Teen USA, 1998, Miss Congeniality, 1998. Avocations: Flag Football, tennis, volleyball. Office: c/o Adam Sher William Morris Agy LLC 151 El Camino Dr Beverly Hills CA 90212

MINOGUE, ROBERT BROPHY, retired nuclear engineer; b. Covington, Ky., Jan. 31, 1928; s. Joseph and Catherine Ann (Brophy) M.; m. Marie Joan Clarke, June 12, 1954; children: Patrick, Margaret, Marie, Francis. BS, Thomas More Coll., 1949; MS, U. Cin., 1951; grad., Oak Ridge Sch. Reactor Tech., 1952. Nuclear engr., then head nuclear tech. sect. naval reactors br. AEC, Washington, 1952-56; head research reactor design and enngring., then head nuclear power plant engring. sect. Gen. Atomic div. Gen. Dynamics Corp., 1957-67; chief spl. projects br. div. reactor standards AEC, Washington, 1967-72, asst. dir., then dep. dir. regulatory standards, 1972-74; dir. office standards devel. Nuclear Regulatory Commn., Washington, 1975-80, dir. office research, 1980-86; pvt. practice, 1986—. U.S. mem. sr. adv. group Safety Standards IAEA, 1974-86; mem. Com. on Interagy. Radiation Research and Policy Coordination, 1982-86. Author: Reactor Shielding Design Manual, 1956; patentee: Triga Research Reactor. Served with AUS, 1946-48. Recipient Bernard F. Langer award, ASME, 1982. Roman Catholic. Home and Office: 16 Pico Vista Novato CA 94947

MINOR, GEORGE GILMER, III, drug and hospital supply company executive; b. 1940; married. BA, Va. Mil. Inst., 1963; MBA, U. Va., 1966. With Owens & Minor, Inc., Richmond, Va., 1963—, mgr. sales Acme Candy Co. div., 1966-68, mgr. retail mktg., 1968-73, div. mgr. wholesale drug br., 1973-77, v.p., 1977-80, exec. v.p., 1980-81, pres., 1981—99, CEO, 1984—2005, chmn., 1994—. Bd. dir. SunTrust Banks Inc. Bd. dir. Va. Biotechnology Rsch. Park Authority, Richmond Renaissance; v.p. bd. vis. Va. Mil. Inst.; chmn. bd. trustees Va. Health Care Found.; mem. adv. bd. Univ. Va. Sch. Nursing. Named Va. Industrialist of the Year, 2001; named to Greater Richmond Bus. Hall of Fame, 2003. Office: Owens & Minor Inc 9120 Lockwood Blvd Mechanicsville VA 23116*

MINOR, JOSEPH EDWARD, civil engineer, educator; b. Corpus Christi, Tex., June 2, 1938; s. William Smoot Jr. and Irene (Schiller) M.; m. Treva Ann Edmiston, Sept. 3, 1960; children: Joseph Edward Jr., Sharon Diane. BSCE, Tex. A&M U., 1959, M of Engring., 1960; PhD, Tex. Tech U., 1974. Registered profl. engr., Tex., Mo., Fla. Sr. rsch. engr. Southwest Research Inst., San Antonio, 1962-69; P. Whitfield Horn prof. Tex. Tech U., Lubbock, 1969-88; emeritus prof., 2008; Thomas Reese prof., chmn. dept. civil engring. U. Mo., Rolla, 1988-93, rsch. prof., 1993—. Pres. Insulating Glass Cert. Council, N.Y., 1986-89; vis. prof. Tex. A&M U., Kingsville, 2003-. Contbr. articles to profl. jours. Served with USAR, Recipient Disting. Engr. award Tex. Tech U., 1989, Disting. Svc. award Nat. Hurricane Conf., 1999; Nat. Def. fellow, 1959-60; Fulbright scholar, 1978. Fellow ASCE (pres. Tex. sect. 1984-85, award of honor 2003); mem. NSPE, Tex. Soc. Profl. Engrs. (Engr. of Yr. Nueces chpt. 2006). Presbyterian. Avocation: fishing. Office: Joseph E Minor PE Consulting Engineer PO Box 603 Rockport TX 78381-0603 E-mail: josephminor@sbcglobal.net.

MINOR, ROBERT ALLEN, lawyer; b. Washington, Oct. 20, 1948; s. Robert Walter and Joan (Allen) M.; m. Sue Ellyn Blose, June 13, 1981; children: Robert Barratt, Sarah Allen. AB in English, Duke U., 1970; JD, Ohio State U., 1975. Bar: Ohio 1975, US Dist. Ct. (so. dist.) Ohio 1976, DC 1979. Assoc. Vorys, Sater, Seymour & Pease, LLP, Columbus, Ohio, 1975-82, ptnr., 1982—. Author seminar articles. With U.S. Army, 1970-72. Mem. Ohio Bar Assn., Columbus Bar Assn., Scioto Country Club. Republican. Presbyterian. Office: Vorys Sater Seymour & Pease LLP PO Box 1008 52 E Gay St Columbus OH 43215-3161 Office Phone: 614-464-6410. Business E-Mail: raminor@vssp.com.

MINOR, RONALD RAY, minister; b. Aliceville, Ala., Nov. 3, 1944; s. Hershel Ray and Minnie Ozell (Goodson) M.; m. Gwendolyn Otella Newsome, July 25, 1970; 1 child, Rhonda Davis. BA in Ministerial, Southeastern U., 1971, BA in Secondary Edn., 1973; DDiv, So. Bible Coll., 1984. Ordained to ministry Pentecostal Ch. of God, 1968. Gen. sec. Pentecostal Ch of God, Joplin, Mo., 1979—2005, dist. supt. Miss., 1975-79, pastor LaBelle, Fla., Bartow, Fla., Orient Park Tabernacle, Tampa, Fla., Lafayette (Ind.) Pentecostal Ch. of God. Pres. Pentecostal Young People's Assn., Fla. and Miss.; sec. Gen. Bd. Pentecostal Ch. of God, Joplin, 1979-2005; bd. dirs. Nat. Assn. Evangs., Wheaton, Ill., 1981-96; adv. coun. Am. Bible Soc., N.Y.C., 1979-2003; sec. Commn. Chaplains, Washington, 1991-95. Office: Christ Ch Lafayette 3616 S 9th St Lafayette IN 47909 Home Phone: 765-477-9803. Personal E-mail: ronaldminor@gmail.com.

MINOT, STEPHEN, writer; b. Boston, May 27, 1927; s. William and Elizabeth Howard Chapman M.; m. Mollie Minot, 1949 (div. 1952); 1 child, Reid; m. Virginia S. Minot, Feb. 18, 1955; children: Nicholas William, Chrystos Bailey. AB, Harvard Coll., 1951; MA, Johns Hopkins U., 1955. Instr. Bowdoin Coll., Brunswick, Maine, 1955-57, asst. prof., 1957-58; vis. asst. prof. U. Conn., Hartford, 1958-59, Trinity Coll., Hartford, 1959-61, lectr., 1961-65, asst. prof., 1965-69, adj. assoc. prof., 1969-72, assoc. prof. part-time, 1972-77, prof. part-time, 1977-89; prof., chair U. Calif., Riverside, 1990-95, prof. emeritus, 1995—. Author: Chill of Dusk, 1964, Three Genres, 1965, 8th edit., 2006, Ghost Images, 1979, Surviving the Flood, 1981, Reading Fiction, 1984; co-editor: Three Stances of Modern Fiction, 1965, Literary Nonfiction, 2002; author many short stories; contbr. articles to profl. jours. With Army Air Corps, 1945-46. Recipient Atlantic First The Atlantic Monthly, 1962; Saxton Meml. fellowship Eugene F. Saxton Meml. Found., 1963, fellowship for writing Nat. Endowment for the Arts, 1976-77, 81-82. Mem. Authors Guild. Democrat. Avocations: forest management, boating. Home: 2225 Mt Vernon Ave Riverside CA 92507 Office: Dept Creative Writing U Calif Riverside CA 92521 Personal E-mail: minot3@gmail.com. E-mail: s.minot@juno.com.

MINOT, WINTHROP GARDNER, lawyer; b. Greenwich, Conn., Jan. 27, 1951; s. William Amory Gardner Minot and Molly (Cummings) Cook; children: Hilary Russell, Amory Cummings, Constance Gardner. AB magna cum laude, Harvard U., 1973, MPA, JD magna cum laude, 1979; MA, University Coll., Oxford, Eng., 1975. Bar: Mass. 1979. Assoc. Ropes & Gray, Boston, 1979-87, ptnr., 1987—. Bd. dirs. Beacon Hill Civic Assn., Boston, 1981-88; trustee Mass. Eye and Ear Infirmary, Boston, 1987—, Boston Chamber Music Soc. Mem. ABA, Boston Bar Assn., Phi Beta Kappa. Editor Harvard U Law Rev., 1978-79. Office: Ropes & Gray 1 International Pl Fl 4 Boston MA 02110-2624 Office Phone: 617-951-7364. Office Fax: 617-235-0076. Business E-Mail: winthrop.minot@ropesgray.com.

MINOW, JOSEPHINE BASKIN, civic volunteer; b. Chgo., Nov. 3, 1926; d. Salem N. and Bessie (Sampson) Baskin; m. Newton N. Minow, May 29, 1949; children: Nell, Martha, Mary. BS, Northwestern U., Evanston, Ill., 1948. Asst. to advt. dir. Mandel Brothers Dept. Store, Chgo., 1948-49; tchr. Francis W. Parker Sch., Chgo., 1949-50; vol. in civil and charitable activities, 1950—; bd. dirs. Juvenile Protective Assn., Chgo., 1958—, pres., 1973-75. Bd. dirs. Parnham Trust, Beaminster, Dorset, England. Author: Marty the Broken Hearted Artichoke, 1997. Founder, coord. Children's divsn. Hospitality and Info. Svc., Washington, 1961-63; mem. Caucus Com., Glencoe, Ill., 1965-69; co-chmn. spl. study on juvenile justice Chgo. Cmty. Trust, 1978-80; chmn. Know Your Chgo., 1980-83; bd. dirs. Chgo. Coun. Fgn. Rels., 1977-2003, hon. life mem., 2003; life trustee Chgo. Hist. Mus., Ravinia Festival Assn.; mem. women's bd. Field Mus., U. Chgo.; founding mem., v.p. women's bd. Northwestern U., 1978; bd. govs. Chgo. Symphony, 1966-73, 76-; mem. Citizens Com. Juvenile Ct. of Cook County, 1985-96; exec. com. Northwestern U. Libr. Coun., 1974-96; co-chair grandparents' adv. com. Chgo. Children's Mus., 1999; bd. dirs. Jane Addams Juvenile Ct. Found.; dir. Abraham Lincoln Presdl. Libr. and Mus., 2005—. Recipient spl. award Chgo. Sch. and Workshop for Retarded, 1975, Children's Guardian award Juvenile Protective Assn., 1993, Peacemoleer award The Cath. Theol. Union, 2009 Mem. Hebrew Immigrant Aid Soc. (bd. dirs. 1977-98, award 1988), Friday Club, The Arts Club. Democrat. Jewish. Office: Chgo Hist Museum Clark St at North Ave Chicago IL 60614

MINOW, MARTHA LOUISE, dean, law educator; b. Highland Pk., Ill., Dec. 6, 1954; AB in History, U. Mich., 1975; EdM, Harvard U., 1976; JD, Yale U., 1979; EdD (hon.), Wheelock Coll., 1998. Bar: Mass. 1981. Law clk. to Judge David L. Bazelon US Ct. Appeals DC Cir., 1979-80; law clk. to Assoc. Justice Thurgood Marshall US Supreme Ct., 1980-81; asst. prof. law Harvard Law Sch., Cambridge, Mass., 1981-86, prof., 1986—, William Henry Bloomberg prof. law, 2003—04, Jeremiah Smith, Jr. prof. law, 2005—, dean, 2009—. Sr. fellow Harvard Soc. Fellows, 1997—; acting dir. Safra Found. Ctr. for Ethics Harvard U., 1993—94, 2000—01, co-chair Project on Justice, Welfare & Economics, 2001—03; co-chair curriculum reform com. Harvard Law Sch., 2003—06. Author: Making All the Difference: Inclusion, Exclusion, and

American Law, 1990, Not Only For Myself: Identity, Politics, and Law, 1997, Between Vengeance and Forgiveness: Facing History After Genocide and Mass Violence, 1998, Breaking the Cycles of Hatred: Memory, Law & Repair, 2002, Partners, Not Rivals: Privatization and the Public Good, 2002; co-author: Teacher's Manual, Civil Procedure: Doctrine, Practice, and Context, 2004; editor: Family Matters: Readings on Family Lives and the Law, 1993; co-editor: Narrative, Violence, and the Law, 1992, The Free Exercise of Culture, 2001, Imagine Coexistence: Restoring Humanity After Violent Ethnic Conflict, 2003, Mary Joe Frug's Women and the Law, 2004; co-editor: (with Gary Bellow) Law Stories: Law, Meaning, & Violence, 1996; co-editor: (with Richard Shweder & Hazel Rose Markus) Engaging in Cultural Differences, 2002, Just Schools: Pursuing Equality in Societies of Diffence, 2008; co-editor: (with Jody Freeman) Government By Contract: Outsourcing and American Democracy, 2009. Trustee emeritus Judge Baker Children's Ctr.; trustee William T. Grant Found.; bd. dirs. Judge David L. Bazelon Ctr. for Mental Health Law, The Covenant Found.; bd. mem. Charles H. Revson Found.; mem. Ind. Internat. Commn. on Kosovo. Recipient Sacks-Freund award for Teaching Excellence, Harvard Law Sch., 2005. Mem.: Am. Bar Found. (bd. dirs. 1985—94), Law and Soc. Assn. Office: Harvard Law Sch Griswold 200 Cambridge MA 02138 Office Phone: 617-495-4601. Office Fax: 617-495-5115. Business E-Mail: minow@law.harvard.edu.*

MINOW, NELL, financial analyst, editor; b. Washington, Feb. 23, 1952; d. Newton Norman and Josephine (Baskin) M.; m. David Brown Apatoff, Aug. 7, 1977; children: Benjamin, Rachel. BA, Sarah Lawrence Coll., 1974; JD, U. Chgo., 1977. Bar: Ill. 1977, D.C. 1978. Atty. EPA, Washington, 1977-81, Office Mgmt. & Budget, Exec. Office of the Pres., Washington, 1981-85, US Dept. Justice, Washington, 1985-86, Instnl. Shareholder Svcs., Washington, 1986-92; prin. Lens, Inc., 1990—2000; co-founder, editor The Corporate Library, 1999—; movie critic, columnist Belief.net, 2007—. Prof. corp. goverance George Mason U. Co-author: (with Robert A.G. Monks) Power and Accountability, 1991, Corporate Governance, 1995, Watching the Watchers: Corporate Governance for the 21st Century, 1996; author: The Moviemom's Guide to Family Movies, 1997. Trustee Washington Ednl. Television Assn., 1986-92, 93—. Recipient Internat. Corporate Governance Network award, 2008; named one of The 20 Most Influential People in Corporate Governance, Directorship mag., 2007. Office: The Corporate Library 1200 G St NW Washington DC 20005 Office Phone: 202-434-8723.*

MINOW, NEWTON NORMAN, lawyer, educator; b. Milw., Jan. 17, 1926; s. Jay A. and Doris (Stein) Minow; m. Josephine Baskin, May 29, 1949; children: Nell, Martha, Mary. BS, Northwestern U., 1949, JD, 1950, LLD (hon.), 1965, U. Wis., Brandeis U., 1963, Columbia Coll., 1972, Govs. State U., 1984, De Paul U., 1989, RAND Grad. Sch., 1993, U. Notre Dame, 1994, Roosevelt U., 1996, Barat Coll., 1996, Santa Clara U. Sch. Law, 1998, Cath. Theol. Union, 2001. Chmn. RAND Corp.; with firm Mayer, Brown & Platt, Chgo., 1950-51, 53-55; law clk. to chief justice U.S. Supreme Ct., 1951-52; asst. counsel to Ill. Gov. Stevenson, 1952-53; spl. asst. to Adlai E. Stevenson in presdl. campaign, 1952, 56; ptnr. firm Stevenson, Rifkind & Wirtz, Chgo., NYC and Washington, 1955-61; chmn. FCC, Washington, 1961-63; exec. v.p., gen. counsel, dir. Ency. Brit., Chgo., 1963-65; ptnr. Sidley Austin LLP, Chgo., 1965—91, sr. counsel, 1991—. Former trustee, past chmn. bd. dirs., adv. trustee Rand Corp.; past chmn. Chgo. Ednl. TV; chmn. pub. rev. bd. Arthur Andersen & Co., 1974—83; trustee Carnegie Corp. N.Y., 1987—97, chmn. bd. trustees, 1993—97; Annenberg prof. comm. law and policy Northwestern U., 1987—2003, prof. emeritus, 2003—, hon. trustee, 2007—; dir. Annenberg Washington Program, 1987—96; chmn. tech. and privacy adv. com. Sec. Def., 2003—04. Author: (book) Equal Time: The Private Broadcasters and the Public Interest, 1964; co-author: Presidential Television, 1973, Electronics and the Future, 1977, For Great Debates, 1987, Abandoned in the Wasteland: Children, Television, and the First Amendment, 1995, As We Knew Adlai. Bd. govs. Pub. Broadcasting Svc., 1973—80; chmn. The World Health Imaging Alliance, 2009—; chmn. bd. dirs. Pub. Broadcasting Svc., 1978—80; chmn. Carnegie Found.; vice chmn., commn. Presidential Debates; vice chmn. presdl. debates LWV, 1976, 1980, 1993—; chmn. bd. overseers Jewish Theol. Sem., 1974—77; trustee Notre Dame U., 1964—77, 1983—96, life trustee, 1996; trustee Mayo Found., 1973—81, Northwestern U., 1975—87, life trustee, 1987—. With US Army, 1944—46. Recipient George Foster Peabody Broadcasting award, 1961, Ralph Lowell award, 1982, Lifetime Achievement award, The Am. Lawyer mag., 2004, Woodrow Wilson award for Pub. Svc., 2006, Legal Legend award, Am. Constitution Soc., 2006, Lifetime Achievement award, Common Sense Media, 2006, Paul Simon award for Pub. Svc., 2006; named one of Am.'s 10 Outstanding Young Men, 1961. Fellow: Am. Acad. Arts and Scis., Am. Bar Found.; mem.: Northwestern U. Alumni Assn. (medal 1978), Century Club (N.Y.C.), Chgo. Club, Comml. Club (pres. 1987—88). Democrat. Office: Sidley Austin LLP One S Dearborn St Chicago IL 60603 Office Phone: 312-853-7555.

MINSHALL, GREG, computer programmer; b. Carmel, Calif., Apr. 21, 1952; s. Glenn Almon and Martha Jane (Hardesty) M.; m. Maria Concepción Gonzalez, Dec. 30, 1976 (div. Jan. 1984); children: Matthew, Cecilia; m. Carol Ann Mendel, Oct. 4, 1987 (div. Feb. 1992); children: Oriana, Jacob. BA in Math., U. Calif., Berkeley, 1985. Computer programmer Stanford Linear Accelerator Ctr., Menlo Park, Calif., 1969-70, 72-73; computer programmer/engr. Inst. for Advanced Computation, Sunnyvale, Calif., 1978-80; computer programmer U. Calif., Berkeley, 1980-88; cons., 1984-88; computer programmer Novell, Inc., Walnut Creek, Calif., 1988-95, Ipsilon Networks, Inc., Mountain View, Calif., 1995—97; founder Siara Sys., 1998—2002; mem. tech. adv. bd. Netillion, 2004—05. Bd. dirs. Kronos Quartet. Mem. Assn. for Computing Machinery, Usenix

MINSHEW, NANCY J., neurologist, educator; MD, Wash. U. Sch. Medicine, 1974. Prof. psychiatry & neurology U. Pitts. Office: 811 O'Hara St Webster Hall Ste 300 Pittsburgh PA 15213 Office Phone: 412-246-5485. Office Fax: 412-246-5470. E-mail: minshewnj@upmc.edu.*

MINSKOFF, EDWARD J., architectural firm executive; s. Leo Minskoff and Isabelle; m. Julie Minskoff. Grad., Mich. State U.; MBA, U. Calif., LA. CEO Olympia & York; founder, chmn. Edward J. Minskoff Equities Inc. Chair endowment, pediatric oncology NYU Med. Ctr. Trustee NYU Med. Ctr.; bd. dirs. NYU Med. Ctr. Cancer Inst.; vice chmn. bd. trustee NYU Sch. Medicine Found. Named one of Top 200 Collectors, ARTnews Mag., 2006—08. Mem.: Assn. for a Better NY (exec. com.), Real Estate Bd. NY (gov.). Avocations: squash, golf, exercise. Office: 1325 Ave of Americas 53rd St New York NY 10019

MINSKY, MARVIN LEE, mathematician, educator; b. NYC, Aug. 9, 1927; s. Henry and Fannie (Reyser) M.; m. Gloria Anna Rudisch, July 30, 1952; children: Margaret, Henry, Juliana. BA in Math., Harvard U., 1950; PhD in Math., Princeton U., 1954; PhD (hon.), Free U. of Brussels, 1986, Pine Manor Coll., 1987. Jr. fellow Harvard Soc. Fellows, 1954-57; staff mem. Lincoln Lab., MIT, 1957-58, asst. prof. math., 1958-61, founder, co-dir. artificial intelligence lab., 1959—74, dir., artificial intelligence group MAC project, 1959, prof. elec. engring., 1974, Donner prof. sci., 1974—89; Toshiba prof. media arts and sciences MIT, 1990—, prof. emeritus, media arts and sciences. Dir. Info. Internat., Inc., 1961—84; fellow Walt Disney Imagineering; founder Thinking Machines, LOGO Computer Systems, Inc. Author: Computation: Finite and Infinate Machines, 1967, Semantic Information Processing, 1968, Robotics, 1986, The Society of Mind, 1987; co-author (with S. Papert) Perceptrons, 1969, rev. edit., 1988, Artificial Intelligence, 1972, with H. Harrison) The Turning Option, 1992. Served with USN, 1944-45; bd. advisor, Nat. Dance Inst., Planetary Soc.; bd. governor, Nat. Space Soc.; mem. awards coun. Am. Acad. Achievement; mem. League for Programming Freedom. Recipient Turing award Assn. Computing Machinery, 1970, Japan prize Sci. and Tech. Found., Japan, 1990, Rsch. Excellence award Internat. Joint Conf. on Artificial Intelligence, 1991, Joseph Priestley award Dickinson Coll., 1995, Rank prize, Royal Soc. Medicine, 1995, Computer Pioneer award, IEEE Computer Soc., 1995, R.W. Wood prize, Optical Soc. Am., 2001, Benjamin Franklin medal, Franklin Inst, 2001, In Praise of Reason award, World Skeptics Congress, 2002. Fellow IEEE, Am. Acad. Arts & Sciences, Com. for the Scientific Investigation of Claims of the Paranormal; mem. NAE, NAS, Argentine NAS, Am. Assn. for Artificial Intelligence (pres. 1981-82). Achievements include SNARC: First Neural Network Simulator in 1951; Confocal Scanning Microscope in 1955; First head-mounted graphical display in 1963; Concept of Binary-Tree Robotic Manipulator in 1963; Serpentine Hydraulic Robot Arm in 1967; The "Muse" Musical Variations Synthesizer (with E. Fredkin) in 1970; First LOGO "turtle" device (with S. Papert) in 1972. Office: MIT Media Lab Bldg E15 77 Massachusetts Ave Cambridge MA 02139-4307 Office Phone: 617-253-5864. E-mail: minsky@media.mit.edu.

MINSON, ARTHUR, Internet company executive; b. 1970; married; 3 children. BSBA, Georgetown Univ., 1992; MBA, Columbia Univ., 1997. CPA. Acct. in audit practice Ernst & Young; dir. fin. spl. projects Time Warner Inc., 1998—99; exec. dir. fin. & bus. devel. Time Warner Digital Media, 1999—2000; sr. v.p. Rainbow Media Holdings, Inc., 2000—04; sr. v.p. corp. fin. & develop. AOL, 2004—06; sr. v.p. fin. Time Warner Cable, 2006—07, exec. v.p., dep. CFO, 2007—09; exec. v.p., CFO AOL (after spinoff from Time Warner), 2009—. Office: AOL LLC 770 Broadway New York NY 10003*

MINTEER, DANIEL C., lawyer; b. Pasadena, Calif., Sept. 20, 1949; BA with high honors, San Diego State U., 1971; JD Order of the Coif, UCLA Sch. Law, 1974. Bar: Calif. 1974, US Dist. Ct. (Colo.), US Ct. Appeals (fed. cir.). Ptnr. Pillsbury Winthrop Shaw Pittman LLP, San Diego, 1974—2005, Duane Morris LLP, San Diego, 2005—. Past pres. San Diego Jr. C. of C. Mem.: ABA, State Bar Calif., Am. Arbitration Assn., Assn. Trial Lawyers (San Diego chpt.), San Diego County Bar Assn. Office: Duane Morris LLP 101 W Broadway Ste 900 San Diego CA 92101 Office Phone: 619-744-2286. Office Fax: 619-923-3554. Business E-Mail: DMinteer@duanemorris.com.*

MINTEL, RICHARD WALTER, chemistry professor; b. Ann Arbor, Mich., May 1, 1938; s. Walter Otto and Frances Wiley Mintel; m. Judith Ann King, July 24, 1971; children: Josephine Therese, Mark Owen; m. Marcia Louise Borst, Aug. 25, 1961 (div. June 10, 1966). SB, U. Chgo., Ill., 1960, PhD, 1965. Asst. prof. biochemistry Johns Hopkins U. Sch. Medicine, Balt., 1974—76; asst. prof. biology U. Va., Charlottesville, 1976—79; assoc. prof. biochemistry U. Ill. Coll. Medicine, Urbana, 1979—; asst. prof. biochemistry U. Chgo.; assoc. scientist Argonne Cancer Rsch. Hosp., U. Chgo., Chgo. Pres. Parents Assn. U. Chgo. Lab. Schs., Chgo., 2007—08; rec. engr. Music Baroque, 1974—, Grand Teton Music Festival, Wyo., 1985—. Author: (book) Student's Companion to Stryer's Biochemistry; prodr.: (syndicated radio broadcasts) Music of the Baroque, (nat. radio broadcasts) Grand Teton Music Festival. Recipient Lewellyn John & Harriet Manchester Quantrell award, U. Chgo., 1972. Mem.: U. Club Chgo. Liberal. Baptist. Avocations: mountain climbing, bicycling, sailing, flying. Home: 4950 S Chicago Beach Dr Chicago IL 60615 Office: Univ Ill 504 S Mathews Ave Urbana IL 61801 Office Fax: 217-333-8868. Business E-Mail: dick@mintel.org, r-mintel@uiuc.edu.

MINTER, DAVID LEE, English literature educator; b. Midland, Tex., Mar. 20, 1935; s. Kenneth Cruse and Frances (Hennessy) M.; m. Cynthia Caroline Sewell, Dec. 22, 1957; children: Christopher Sewell, Frances Elizabeth. BA, N. Tex. State U., 1957, MA, 1959; BD, Yale U., 1961, PhD, 1965. Univ. lectr. Hamburg (W. Ger.) U., 1965-66; lectr. Yale U., 1966-67; asst. prof. Rice U., Houston, 1967-69, assoc. prof., 1969-74, prof., 1974-80; prof. English Emory U., Atlanta, 1981-89, Asa G. Candler prof. Am. lit., 1989-90, dean Coll. Arts and Scis., 1981-90, v.p. arts and scis., 1984-90; Libbie Shearn Moody prof. English Rice U., Houston, 1990-99, interim vice provost, univ. libr., 1995-96, interim provost, 1999-2000, Bruce and Elizabeth Dunlevie prof. English, 1999—2002. Author: The Interpreted Design as a Structural Principle in American Prose, 1969, William Faulkner: His Life and Work, 1980, 82, 91, 97, French edit., 1984, Korean edito., 1999, A Cultural History of the American Novel: Henry James to William Faulkner, 1994, 96, Faulkner's Questioning Narratives: Fiction of the Major Phase, 2001, 04; editor: Twentieth-Century Interpretations of Light in August, 1969, The Norton Critical Edit. of The Sound and the Fury, 1987, 93; co-editor: The Harper American Literature, 1986, 93, 96, 97, The Columbia Literary History of the United States, 1987 (Italian edit. 1990, Chinese edit. 1994, Japanese edit. 1997); also articles and revs. Fulbright Travel fellow, 1966; Nat. Endowment for Humanities fellow, 1969-70; Am. Council Learned Socs. grantee, 1975; Fred Harris Daniels fellow, 1980 Mem. MLA, Am. Lit. Group, Am. Studies Assn., Phi Beta Kappa. Methodist. Home: 2145 Swift Houston TX 77030-1215 E-mail: dcmint@rice.edu.

MINTER, KAREN CELESTE, music educator; b. Marietta, Ga., Oct. 30, 1950; d. Gerald Hollis and Mary Patricia Minter; 1 child, Jamey Andrew Garner. BS Music Edn., Piano and Voice, U. Tenn.Chattanooga, 1972; MA Music, Vocal Performance, U. Denver, Colo., 1984; DMA in Music, Vocal Performance, U. Mo., Kans. City, 1993. Asst. prof. music Truman State U., Kirksville, Mo., 1988—89; prof. music Benedictine Coll., Atchison, Kans., 1990—. Singer Kans. City Lyric Opera, Mo., 1986—. Singer opera. Vol. and youth bd. mem. Village Presbyn. Ch., Prairie Village, Kans., 1988—95. Mem.: Nat. Assn. Tchrs. Singing (kans. city chpt. mem. at large, v.p., and pres. 1993—96). Achievements include 3 world premieres. Avocations: travel, gardening, needlecrafts, cooking. Office: Benedictine Coll 1020 N 2nd St Kansas City KS 66002 Business E-Mail: kminter@benedictine.edu.

MINTER, PHILIP CLAYTON, retired communications company executive; b. Sydney, Aug. 9, 1928; came to U.S., 1957; s. Roy Dixon and Adeline Claire (Bradly) M.; m. Mary Bashford Schettler, Jan. 24., 1959 (dec. July 1999); children: Elizabeth C., Margaret S. BSc with honours, U. Sydney, 1951; MS, U. Wyo., 1958; PhD, U. Wis., 1960. Tchr. King's Sch., Parramatta, Australia, 1951-57; mng. dir. Motivational Rsch. Assocs., Sydney, 1960-62; dir. rsch. Nat. Fund Raising Coun., Sydney, 1962-65; project dir. USDA, Ft. Collins, Colo., 1965-67; chief info. pesticides program USPHS, Atlanta, 1967-68; mgr. data bases div. Pa. Rsch. Assocs., Phila., 1968-70; pres. Ednl. Communications Inc., King of Prussia, Pa., 1970-94; v.p. Medication Mgmt. Systems Internat., LLC, 2001—; dir. Unmaned Ocean Vehicles, 2005—. Pres. Svc. Tng. Ltd., Kenilworth, Eng., 1976-88; cons. Westinghouse Learning Corp., 1972. Author: Handbook for Pesticide-Chemicals Program Coordinators, 1967. Recipient Terry Magill award Australia Soc., N.Y., 1994. Mem. Soc. Automotive Engrs., Sci. Rsch. Soc. Am., Royal Heritage Soc. (bd. dirs.), U. Wis. Alumni Assn. (bd. dirs. Delaware Valley br.), Sydney U. Grads. Union N.Am. (pres. 2006-08), Australian/Am. C. of C. Phila. (pres.), Union League, Brit. Officers Club Phila. (pres. 1992-93), The Order of Autralia, Sigma Xi. Republican. Episcopalian. Home: 1576 Stapler Dr Yardley PA 19067-4214

MINTON, DWIGHT CHURCH, manufacturing executive; b. North Hills, NY, Dec. 17, 1934; s. Henry Miller and Helen Dwight (Church) M.; m. Marian Haven Haines, Aug. 4, 1956; children: Valerie Haven, Daphne Forsyth, Henry Brewster. BA, Yale U., 1959; MBA, Stanford U., 1961. With Church & Dwight Co., Inc., Princeton, N.J., 1961—, asst. v.p., 1964-66, v.p., 1966-67, bd. dir., 1966—2006, chem., 1981—2001, chem. emeritus, 2001—, pres., 1967-81, chief exec. officer, 1969-95, chmn., 1981—, chmn. bd., 1966—2001, chmn. emeritus Princeton, NJ, 2001—. Bd. dirs. Crane Corp. Trustee Atlanta U., 1971-88, Morehouse Coll., 1971—2008, Spelman Coll., 1971-80; Greater Yellowstone Coalition, 1991-99, Nat. Parks Conservation, With U.S. Army, 1956-57. Mem. Chem. Mfrs. Assn. (bd. dirs. 1980-83), Grocery Mfrs. Am. (dir. 1983-87). Clubs: Racquet and Tennis, Yale, Lotos. Office: 120 W Cleveland St PO Box 4727 Bozeman MT 59715 Office Phone: 406-551-2018.

MINTON, HARVEY STEIGER, lawyer; b. Columbus, Ohio, Dec. 16, 1933; s. Harvey Alan and Elsie (Steiger) M.; m. Jane Rickey Grimm, July 21, 1956; children: Harvey Randall, Jennifer Thelma. BS, Ohio State U., 1956, JD, 1962. Bar: Ohio 1956, NY 1985. Atty. Shumaker, Loop & Kendrick, Toledo, 1962-65; asst. sec. Owens Ill., Toledo, 1965-82; pres. Sun Master (subs. of Owens, Ill., Corning, NY), 1983-84; v.p. Leeward Capital, Columbus, Ohio, 1985-87; v.p. counsel, sr. ptnr. Harvey S. Minton & Assocs., Worthington, Ohio, 1987--; mayor City of Worthington, Ohio, 1999—. Pres. bd. trustees Toledo Symphony, 1973-76; chmn. Law Week, Toledo, 1964, Jail Action Improvement League, Toledo, 1973; vice chair Worthington Zoning Bd. Appeals, 1992. Capt. USAF, jet pilot, 1956-59. Mem. Dublin-Worthington Rotary (named Man of Yr. 1988). Republican. Presbyterian. Home: 617 Hartford St Worthington OH 43085-4119 Office: 6641 N High St Worthington OH 43085-4038 Office Phone: 614-848-9600. E-mail: hsminton@justee.com.

MINTON, HENRY LEE, psychology professor; b. NYC, Nov. 20, 1934; s. Irving and Sophie (Shapiro) M.; m. Sheila Gay Cohen, Jan. 27, 1963 (div. Dec. 1983); 1 child, Gregory. BA, NYU, 1956; MA, So. Ill. U., 1958; PhD, Pa. State U., 1962. Asst. prof. Calif. State U., LA, 1963-65, SUNY, Albany, 1965-67; assoc. prof. Miami U., Oxford, Ohio, 1967-70; prof. psychology U. Windsor, Ont., Can., 1970-2000, prof. emeritus, 2000—. Author: Differential Psychology, 1980, Lewis M. Terman, 1988, Currents of Thought in American Social Psychology, 1991, Departing from Deviance, 2002. Grantee Social Sci. and Humanities Rsch. Coun., Ottawa, Ont., 1995-98. Fellow APA; mem. Cheiron Soc. Avocations: painting, travel. Home: 670 Camden Ct Rochester Hills MI 48307-4590 E-mail: hlminton@aol.com.

MINTON, JERRY DAVIS, retired banker, lawyer; b. Ft. Worth, Aug. 13, 1928; s. Robert Bruch and Anna Elizabeth (Davis) M.; m. Martha Drew Fields, Nov. 28, 1975; children: Marianne, Martha, John Morgan. BBA, U. Tex., Austin, 1949, JD, 1960; grad. cert., Nat. Trust Sch., Northwestern U., 1960. Of counsel Michener, Larimore, Swindle, Whitaker, Flowers et al., 1991—96; adv. dir. Kanaly Trust Co., Houston, 1992-2000. Vice chmn. 1st Nat. Bank Ft. Worth, 1982-84; chmn., CEO 1st City Nat. Bank Ft. Worth, 1986-91. Pilot USAF, 1951-55, pilot Tex. Air N.G., 1955-57; capt. USAFR Ret. Decorated D.F.C., Air medal with 3 oak leaf clusters. Mem. Air Force Assn., State Bar Tex., Tarrant County Bar Assn., Soc. Descs. of Washington's Army at Valley Forge, SAR, Mil. Order World Wars, D.F.C. Soc., Order Quiet Birdmen, Order of Daedalians, River Crest Country Club, Sigma Iota Epsilon, Phi Delta Phi. Episcopalian. Home: 5404 El Dorado Dr Fort Worth TX 76107-3236

MINTON, JOHN DEAN, JR., state supreme court chief justice; b. Ky., Mar. 19, 1952; s. John Dean and Betty Jo (Redick) Minton; m. Susan Lenell Page; children: Page Sullivan, John Dean III. BA in English & History, Western Ky. U., 1974; JD, U. Ky. Coll. of Law, 1977. Assoc. Cole, Harned & Broderick, 1977—88; ptnr. Cole, Broderick, Minton, Moore & Thornton, Ky., 1988—91, Cole, Minton & Moore, Ky., 1991—92; judge Divsn. 2 Warren County Cir. Ct., Ky., 1992—2003; chief administrative judge Green River Region Judicial Circuits, Ky., 1996—2003; judge Second Appellate Dist. Ky. Ct. of Appeals, 2003—06; justice Ky. Supreme Ct., 2006—, chief justice, 2008—. Leader Ky. Conf. of United Methodist Church, 1996—2004. Mem.: Ky. Bar Assn. (Outstanding Judge award 2003). Office: Ky Supreme Ct 231 Capitol Bldg 700 Capital Ave Frankfort KY 40601 Office Phone: 270-746-7867 ext. 103. E-mail: johnminton@kycourts.net.*

MINTON, JOSEPH PAUL, retired safety organization executive; b. Houston, Oct. 20, 1924; s. Joseph Marion and Stella (Fite) M.; m. Nancy Fettig, June 19, 1948; children: Joan M., Michael J., Jean A., Mary B., John E., Diane C. BS in Air Transp., Purdue U., 1949; Grad., U.S. Air Force Air Command and Staff Coll., 1958. Commd. 2d lt. USAF, 1944, advanced through grades to col., 1966, combat Burma, World War II, assignments in crew, staff and command, ret., 1967; v.p. Purdue Airlines Inc., Lafayette, Ind., 1967-68, pres., CEO, 1969-71; mng. dir., chief exec. officer Saber Air Ltd., Singapore, 1971-73; sr. v.p. Brit. Caledonian Airways, NYC, 1974-76; mng. dir. Nat. Transp. Safety Bd., Washington, 1977-78; exec. dir. Nat. Safety Coun., Washington, 1978-88. Decorated D.F.C. with oak leaf cluster, Air medal with 3 oak leaf clusters, 3 battle stars, Air Force Commendation medal with oak leaf cluster. Roman Catholic. Address: Joe & Nancy Minton 46996 Eaker St Potomac Falls VA 20165

MINTON, MARK C., United States Ambassador to Mongolia; BA in Lit., Columbia U., NYC; MA in History, Yale U., New Haven. Polit. officer, US Fgn. Svc. US Dept. State, Tokyo, 1977, mem., policy planning staff Washington, assigned to office Soviet Union affairs, consul gen. Sapporo, Japan, US Senate Pearson fellow with the exec. secretariat, dep. dir. Japanese affairs Washington, min. counselor polit. affairs, US Embassy Seoul, Republic of Korea, dir. Korean affairs Washington, min. counselor polit. affairs, US Mission to the UN NYC, dep. chief of mission, charge d'affaires ad interim Seoul, US amb. to Mongolia Ulaanbaatar, 2006—. Diplomat-in-residence City Coll. NY. Served with US Army. Office: DOS Amb 4410 Ulaanbaatar Pl Washington DC 20521-4410*

MINTON, YVONNE FAY, mezzo-soprano; b. Sydney; d. Robert Thomas and Alice Violet M.; m. William Barclay, Aug. 24, 1965; children— Malcolm Alexander, Alison Elizabeth. Student, Sydney Conservatorium Music, 1960-61. Mezzo-soprano with all maj. orchs. in, Australia, 1958-61; moved to, London, 1961, joined, Royal Opera House, Covent Garden, 1965-70, guest artist, Cologne (Germany) Opera, 1969—, U.S. debut as Octavian in Der Rosenkavalier, 1970; appeared, with Lyric Opera, Chgo., 1970, Met. Opera, N.Y.C., 1973, San Francisco Opera, 1974, Paris Opera, 1974, Bayreuth, 1974, Salzburg, 1978; sang regularly with maj. symphony orchs. throughout world, 1968—; recs. include The Knot Garden, 1970, Cosi Fan Tutte, 1971, Lulu, 1979; maj. vocal works include Mahler songs with, Chgo. Symphony; condr. master classes across Europe and vocal coach in London. Comdr. Order Brit. Empire, 1980 Hon. mem. Royal Acad. Music. Office: care Ingpen & Williams 7 St Georges Ct 131 Putney Bridge Rd London SW15 2PA England

MINTON-MCNEILL, DORIS, councilwoman; Adminstr., Ctr. Profl. Growth Indpls. Pub. Schools; councillor, dist. 15 Indpls.-Marion County City-County Coun. Democrat. Office: Indpls Marion County City County Coun 241 City County Bldg 200 E Washington St Indianapolis IN 46204 Office Phone: 317-327-4242. Business E-Mail: dmmcneil@indygov.org.*

MINTZ, DOUGLAS N., radiologist; b. NYC, Sept. 6, 1062; s. Norman N. and Marcia Belford Mintz. AB, Columbia U., NY, 1984, MD, 1988. Cert. radiologist Am. Bd. Radiology, 1997, lic. NY, Ohio, Conn., 1993. Resident surgery U. Minn. Hosp. and Clinics, Mpls., 1988—90; attending physician Kaiser Permanente Med. Group, San Diego, 1990—92; rsch. assoc. Scripps Rsch. Inst., La Jolla, Calif., 1990—92; resident radiology Lenox Hill Hosp., 1993—97; attending radiologist Hosp. for Spl. Surgery, NYC, 1998—, fellow musculoskeletal radiology, 1997—98; attending radiologist NY Presbyn. Hosp., 1998—; asst. prof. radiology Weill Med. Coll., Cornell U., 1998—2004, assoc. prof. clin. radiology, 2004—. Author: (scientific exhibit) Load Dependence of the Thumb and Carpal Bone Configuration during Static Pinch; contbr. scientific papers to profl. pubs. and confs., chapters to books; co-author: Orthopedic Pathology. Grantee, NYPH Inst. of Aging, 2002—05, NIH, 2002—05, Bayer Found., 2005—07. Mem.: Argentina Assn. Orthops. and Trauma (hon.), Oxford/ Cambridge Club. Jewish. Achievements include patents for methods of identifying inhibitors of LPS-mediated LBP binding. Office: Hospl for Spl Surgery 535 East 71st St New York NY 10021 Business E-Mail: mintzd@hss.edu.

MINTZ, KEITH PETER, research scientist; b. Bronx, NY, Mar. 10, 1956; s. William and Susan Lenore Mintz; m. Debra Devon Stenner. PhD, U. Vt., 1989. Intramural rsch training fellow NIH/Nat. Inst. of Dental & Craniofacial Rsch., Bethesda, Md., 1989—91; rsch. assoc. U. Vt., Burlington, 1991—2000, rsch. asst. prof., 2001—. Grantee R01, NIH, 2001—. Mem.: Am. Soc. Microbiology, Internat. Assn. Dental Rsch. Office: U Vt 95 Carrigan Dr Burlington VT 05405 Home: 17493 Via Capri Boca Raton FL 33496-1645 Business E-Mail: kmintz@zoo.uvm.edu.

MINTZ, M. J., lawyer; b. Phila., Oct. 29, 1940; s. Arthur and Lillian (Altenberg) Mintz; m. Judith E. Held; children: Robert A., Christine L. BS, Temple U., 1961, JD, 1968. CPA Pa., D.C.; bar: D.C. Atty. adv. to judge U.S. Tax Ct., Washington, 1968-70; asst. gen. counsel Cost of Living Coun. Exec. Office of Pres., Washington, 1971-73; ptnr. Dickstein, Shapiro & Morin, Washington, 1973—2005, M.J. Mintz, P.C., Washington, 2006—. Adj. prof. George Mason U. Law Sch., Va., 1974—78; advisor U.S. Sec. Labor, Employee Ret. Income Security Act, 1974, Adv. Coun., Washington, 1982—85. Contbr. articles to profl. jours. Apptd. by Pres. Ronald Reagan to adv. com. Pension Benefit Guaranty Corp., 1987, reapptd. and designated chmn. by Pres. George Bush; apptd. by Gov. George Allen of Va. Bd. Va. Pub. Bldg. Authority, 1996—2001, reapptd. by Gov. James Gilmore, 2001—06; Rep. candidate Fairfax County Bd. Suprs., 1971. Fellow: Nat. Assn. Watch & Cook Collectors (star), Freeman of the Worshipful Co. of Clockmakers (London); mem.: Antiquarian Horological Soc. (London), Naval Club (London), Chappaquiddick Beach Club, Met. Club (Washington), Belle Haven Country Club, Cosmos Club. Avocation: antiquarian horologist.

MINTZ, MARILYN D., artist, writer; b. Phila., Mar. 18; d. Milton A. and Mildred L. Mintz. Attended, U. Calif., Santa Barbara, 1968—70; BFA in Theater, Calif. Inst. of Arts, 1972; MA in Film and TV, U. Calif., LA, 1975. Founder, pres., CEO M.D.M. Co., Studio City, Calif., 1981, The Sweetheart Arts Co., Inc., Los Gatos, Calif., 1990—. Actor: Calif. Shakespeare Festival, 1970; author: (play) A Man (adaptation of Shakespeare's Julius Caesar), 1972, The Martial Arts Films, 1978, 2nd edit., 1983; scriptwriter, creator: Cartoon Pictures, 1979, The Cartoonist, 1980, columnist: Images, 1967—68. Achievements include patents for doll and associated products. Office: The Sweetheart Arts Co Inc PO Box 1411 Los Gatos CA 95031

MINTZ, MORTON ABNER, writer, reporter; b. Ann Arbor, Mich., Jan. 26, 1922; s. William and Sarah (Solomon) M.; m. Anita Inez Franz, Aug. 30, 1946; children— Margaret Ruth, Elizabeth Diane (dec.), Roberta Joan, Daniel Robert. AB in Econs, U. Mich., 1943. Reporter St. Louis Star-Times, 1946-50; reporter, asst. city editor St. Louis Globe-Democrat, 1951-58; reporter Washington Post, 1958-88. Former chair Fund for Investigative Journalism; sr. advisor niemanwatchdog.org; dir. Project on Govt. Oversight, 1997—. Author: The Therapeutic Nightmare, 1965, By Prescription Only, 1967, The Pill: An Alarming Report, 1969, At Any Cost: Corporate Greed, Women, and the Dalkon Shield, 1985, (with Jerry S. Cohen) America, Inc.: Who Owns and Operates the United States, 1971, Power, Inc.; Public and Private Rulers and How to Make Them Accountable, 1976, (with others) In the Name of Profit: Profiles in Corporate Irresponsiblity, 1972, More Bucks, Less Bang: How the Pentagon Buys Ineffective Weapons, 1983. Recipient Heywood Broun, Raymond Clapper, George Polk awards for journalism, 1962, A.J. Liebling award, 1974, Worth Bingham Meml. award, 1976, Columbia Journalism award, 1983, Hugh M. Hefner First Amendment award for lifetime achievement, 1996. Mem.: Com. Concerned Journalists. E-mail: mintzm@earthlink.net.

MINTZ, NORMAN NELSON, investment banker, educator, retired academic administrator; b. NYC, Sept. 18, 1934; s. Alexander and Rebecca (Nelson) M.; m. Marcia Lynn Belford, Aug. 27, 1960; children: Geoffrey Belford, Douglas Nelson. AB, Bucknell U., Lewisburg, Pa., 1955; PhD, NYU, NYC, 1966. Asst. gen. mgr. Ross Products Inc., NYC, 1957-59; media analyst Benton & Bowles Inc., NYC, 1960; asst. prof. fin. Syracuse (N.Y.) U., 1965-69; asst. prof. econs. Columbia U., NYC, 1968-72, assoc. dean Grad. Sch. Arts and Scis., 1972-77, dep. provost, 1977-80, acting provost, 1978-79, sr. v.p., 1980-82, exec. v.p. for acad. affairs, 1982-89, exec. v.p., ret., 1990—; mng. dir. Loeb Ptnrs. Corp., 1990—. Economist U.S.-P.R. Commn. on Status of P.R., 1965-66; bd. dirs. Loeb Holding Corp., Loeb Ptnrs. Corp., Sr. Network, Inc., KmX Corp., Intersections, Inc., Loeb Arbitrage Fund., Ultramercial, LLC, Virtualscopics, Inc. Author: Monetary Union and Economic Integration, 1970; contbr. articles to profl. jours. Dir. Citizens Budget Commn., Conf. on Jewish Social Studies, 1975—94, N.Y.C. Coun. on Econ. Edn., 1993—. 1st lt. Signal Corps. US Army, 1955—57. Earhart Found. fellow, 1963-65. Mem. Am. Econ. Assn., Am. Fin. Assn., Royal Econ. Soc., India House Club, Phi Beta Kappa, Omicron Delta Epsilon. Office: care Loeb Ptnrs 61 Broadway New York NY 10006-2701 Home Phone: 212-749-8043; Office Phone: 212-483-7041. E-mail: nmintz@loebpartners.com.

MINTZ, PAUL DAVID, pathologist; b. NYC, Sept. 17, 1948; s. Bernard Jacod and Alene Paula (Lowenstein) M.; m. Susan Joyce Levy, June 3, 1973; children: Jeremy, Emily. AB in Philosophy with high distinction, U. Rochester, 1970, MD with honors, 1974. Lic. physician, N.Y., Pa., Va., Nat. Bd. Med. Examiners. Summer oncology fellow Boston U. Sch. Medicine, 1972; resident clin. pathology SUNY, Upstate Med. Ctr., Syracuse, 1974-77, chief resident, 1976-77; fellow clin. coagulation U. N.C. Sch. Medicine, Chapel Hill, 1977-78; fellow Specialized Ctr. Thrombosis Rsch. Temple U. Health Scis. Ctr., 1978-79; ast. prof. pathology U. Va. Sch. Medicine, Charlottesville, 1979-85, assoc. prof., 1985-88, assoc. prof. pathology and internal medicine, 1988-94; prof. pathology and internal medicine, 1994—; assoc. dir. Blood Bank and Transfusion Svcs. U. Va. Med. Ctr., Charlottesville, 1979-82, dir., 1982—. Cons. lab. svc. VA Hosp., Salem, Va., 1979—; chmn. continuing med. edn. com. Transfusion Medicine Acad. Awardees, 1986-88; mem. planning com. Nat. Blood Resources Edn. Program, Nat. Heart, Lung and Blood Inst., 1987, spl. grant rev. com. transfusion medicine acad. award, 1991; mem. blood svcs. com. Red Cross Blood Svcs., Charlottesville chpt., Washington region; mem. hosp. transfusion com. Health Scis. Ctr., 1979—, faculty grievance com. Sch. Medicine, 1992—, continuing med. edn. com., 1993—. Mem. editl. bd. Am. Jour. Clin. Pathology, 1991—; contbr. articles to profl. jours. Bd. dirs. ARC, Ctrl. Va. chpt., 1984-90, Hillel Found., U. Va., 1986-88, Va. Discovery Mus. Recipient Charles E. Walter Meml. award Mid-Atlantic Assn. Blood Banks, 1992; grantee NIH, 1978-79, Ciba-Geigy Corp., 1979-82, Nat. Heart, Lung and Blood Inst., 1985-90, Am. Assn. Blood Banks Found., 1986-88, IVAC Corp., 1986, 88, 89, 91, 93, Baxter Healthcare Corp., 1990, ARC Jerome Holland Rsch. Lab., 1991, IBG Corp., 1991, Cobe Labs., 1991, 92, Va. Blood Svcs., 1992. Mem. Am. Assn. Blood Banks (chair subcom. on immunohematology com. on stds. 1989-93, transfusion quality assurance com. 1992—), Mid-Atlantic Blood Banks (pres. 1986-87, chair awards com. 1992—), Internat. Soc. Blood Transfusion, Assn. Clin. Scientists (coun. on immunohematology 1983—), Am. Soc. Apheresis, Acad. Clin. Lab. Physicians and Scientists, Internat. Soc. Hematotherapy and Gene Engring., B'nai B'rith (pres. Thomas Jefferson Lodge 1985-86). Office: U Va Health Scis Ctr PO Box 286 Charlottesville VA 22902-0286

MINTZ-HITTNER, HELEN ANN, physician, researcher; b. Houston, Aug. 12, 1944; d. Bert and Jeanette (Haydis) Mintz; m. David Hittner, Sept. 8, 1968 (div. May 11, 1989); children: Miriam Annette Hittner Tondera, Susan Michelle Hittner, George Jacob Hittner. BA, Rice U., 1965; MD, Baylor Coll. Medicine, 1969. Lic. Tex. Bd. of Med. Examiners, 1969. Intern pediat. Baylor Affiliated Hosps., Houston, 1969—70, resident ophthalmology, 1970—73; fellow pediat. ophthalmology Tex. Children's Hosp., Houston, 1973—74; pediat. ophthalmologist Houston, 1974—95; Alfred W. Lasher III prof. pediat. ophthalmology U. Tex. Houston Med. Sch., 1995—. Prin. investigator clin. trial Beracizumab Eliminates the Angiogenic Threat of Retinopathy Prematurity. Author: several rsch. reports and jour. articles; contbr. articles to profl. sci. jours. Fellow: Am. Acad. Ophthalmology (Honor award 1986, Sr. Honor award 2005); mem.: N.Y. Acad. Medicine, N.Y. Acad. Sci., Ciba Found., Soc. Heed Fellows (life), Assn. Rsch. in Vision and Ophthalmology, Am. Assn. Pediat. Ophthalmology and Strabismus, Phi Beta Kappa (life), Alpha Omega Alpha (life). Liberal. Jewish. Achievements include discovery of Primary etiology of retinopathy of prematurity; research in Genetic linkage of aniridia to chromosome 11p13 (PAX6); Genetic identification of anterior segment dysgenesis on chromosomes 10q25 (PITX3), 1p32 (FOXE3), 20p11.2 (VSX1); FDA. Home: 2400 N Braeswood Blvd #125 Houston TX 77030-4357 Office: U of Tex-Houston Med Sch 6410 Fannin St #920 Houston TX 77030-5204 Personal E-mail: mintzhittner@aol.com. Business E-Mail: helen.a.mintz-hittner@uth.tmc.edu.

MIOLI, JOSEPH S., state legislator; b. Santa Teresa di Riva, Italy, Mar. 18, 1938; children: Frank, Rae Monique. With transit dept. County Trust Co. (now Bank of NY), 1964—68; co-owner Westport Pizzeria/Mioli Brothers, Inc., 1968—2002, ret., 2002; mem. Dist. 136 Conn. House of Reps., 2005—, mem. commerce com., transp. com. Rep. Westport Town Meeting, 2003—05. Served with US Army, 1962—64. Mem.: Assn. Advancement Retired Persons, Westport Downtown Merchants Assn. (founding mem.), US Power Squadron (life), Am. Legion Post #143 (life), Minuteman Yacht Club, Fayerweather Yacht Club (life). Democrat. Roman Catholic. Mailing: Legis Office Bldg Rm 4032 Hartford CT 06106 Office: Dist Address 90 Main St Unit 6 Westport CT 06880 Office Phone: 203-226-9166. Office Fax: 860-240-8585. Business E-Mail: Joe.Mioli@cga.ct.gov.*

MIQUELON, MIRIAM F., former prosecutor, lawyer; b. Elmhurst, Ill. children: Aaron, Rachel. Grad., U. Ariz., 1975, DePaul U., 1978; LLM in Taxation, Chgo.-Kent Coll. Law; postgrad. in Taxation, DePaul U.; postgrad. in History, Northwestern U. Lawyer, Houston, Stone, McGuire, Benjamin & Kocoras, Miquelon and Assocs., 1981—88, Keck, Mahin & Cate, Chgo., 1988—91; asst. U.S. atty. Ea. Dist. N.Y., Bklyn., 1991—93, So. Dist. Ill., 1993—99; asst. spl. counsel to Spl. Counsel John C. Danforth, 1999—2000; asst. U.S. atty. So. Dist. Ill., 2000—02, U.S. atty., 2002—03. Adj. prof. law Washington U. Sch. Law, St. Louis; adj. faculty Northwestern U. Coll. Law, Chgo. Recipient Chief Postal Inspector's award, U.S. Postal Inspection Svc., 2001, Spl. commendations, FBI, Drug Enforcement Adminstrn., U.S. Customs Svc., IRS. Avocations: volunteering, sports activities.

MIQUELON, WADE D., retail executive; b. Oct. 28, 1964; BS in Civil Engring., Purdue U., 1987; MBA, Washington U., St. Louis, 1989. Fin. dir. SE Asian Beauty Care bus. Procter & Gamble, CFO Thailand, Myanmar, Cambodia and Laos subsidiaries, CFO, sr. dir. ASEAN, Australia and India region Singapore, 2001—03, CFO Western European bus. Geneva, 2003—06; exec. v.p., CFO Tyson Foods, Springdale, Ark., 2006—08; sr. v.p., CFO Walgreen Co., Deerfield, Ill., 2008—09, exec. v.p., CFO, 2009—. Office: Walgreen Co 200 Wilmot Rd Deerfield IL 60015*

MIR, ALEKSANDRA, artist; b. Lubin, Poland, 1967; Communication & Media studies, Schillerska/Gothenburg U., Gothenburg, 1986—87; BFA in Media Arts, Sch. Visual Arts, NY, 1992; Grad. Faculty Cultural Anthropology, New Sch. Social Rsch., NY, 1994—96. One-man shows include Life is Sweet in Sweden, Trixter, Gothenburg, 1995, Pick UP (oh baby), Lyd/Galerie, Copenhagen, 1997, City Forest (prototype), Tompkins Sq. Pk., NY, 1998, Conspiracy Night, Swiss Inst., NY, 1999, Gavin Brown's enterprise, NY, 2001, Corp. Mentality, Lukas & Sternberg, NY, 2002, Naming Tokyo (part II), Swiss Inst., NY, 2003, Happy Holidays, The Wrong Gallery, NY, 2003, The Big Umbrella (NY), PS1 Contemporary Art Ctr., NY, 2004, New Commission, Fundacion NMAC, Montenmedio, 2005, exhibited in group shows at Empires without States, Swiss Inst., NY, 1999, Democracy!, Royal Coll. Art, London, 2000, COPY, Roth Horowitz Gallery, NY, 2002, The Twentieth Anniversary Show, Gavin Brown's enterprise, NY, 2003, Sandwiched, Jacob Fabricius, NY, 2003, Power, Corruption & Lies, Roth Horowitz, NY, 2004, Calif. Earthquakes, Daniel Reich Gallery, NY, 2004, Whitney Biennial, Whitney Mus. Am. Art, 2004. Mailing: c/o Andrew Roth 160 A East 70th St New York NY 10021 E-mail: aleksandra_mir@hotmail.com.

MIR, MONTSERRAT, education educator; PhD, U. Ill., Urbana-Champaign, 1994. Assoc. prof. Ill. State U., Normal, 1997—.

MIRABITO, ANTHONY JASON, lawyer, educator; b. NYC, Jan. 29, 1948; s. Anthony Joseph Mirabito and Jean Theresa (Cultrone) Mirobito; m. Marjorie Rose Berger, July 7, 1974; children: Katherine Rose, Andrew. BS in Engring. Physics, NYU, 1965—69; JD, Am. U., 1973; LLM in Patent/Internat. Law, Georgetown U., 1975. Bar: Pa. 1974, DC 1975, Mass. 1981, registered: US Patent & Trademark Office 1977. Patent examiner, atty. US Patent & Trademark Office, Arlington, Va., 1969—75; atty. US Dept. Commerce, Washington, 1975—77, US Internat. Trade Commn., Washington; in-house counsel Westinghouse Electric Co., Pitts., 1979—80; legal cons. Mass. computer & software cos., Boston area, 1980—; of counsel Gaston Snow & Ely Bartlett, Boston, 1984, head, patent dept.; ptnr., Intellectual Property Law Wolf, Greenfield & Sacks; founding ptnr., co-chmn., Intellectual Property Law Sect. Mintz Levin Cohn Ferris Glovsky & Popeo PC, Boston. Assoc. prof. law Suffolk U. Law Sch., Boston, 1980—; lectr. in field. Contbr. articles to law reviews; editor: Foreign Investment in US, 1977. Mem.: Pa. Bar Assn., Mass. Bar Assn., ABA, DC Bar Assn. (Internat. Law Sect.), Boston Bar Assn., Small Bus. Assn. of New Eng., Boston Patent Law Assn. (former pres.), Winchester Boat Club (Mass.). Achievements include patents in field. Office: Mintz Levin Cohn Ferris Glovsky & Popeo PC One Financial Ctr Boston MA 02111 also: Suffolk U Law Sch 41 Temple St Boston MA 02114-4241 Office Phone: 617-348-1805. Office Fax: 617-542-2241. Business E-Mail: jmirabito@mintz.com.

MIRACLE, DORIS JEAN, retired medical/surgical nurse; b. Louisville, July 23, 1931; d. Bernard Louis and Catherine Federle; m. Earl Miracle, Aug. 31, 1951; 1 child, David. Surg. nurse Norton Hosp., Louisville, 1951, Norton-Children's Hosp., Louisville, 1969—86; ret., 1986. Poetry (albums) Sounds of Poetry, 2003; author: (poetry) Silver Music Box, 2009, Springtime in the City, 2009, Shark, 2009, The Sunshine Cart, 2009, numerous poems; contbr. articles to profl. jours.;, author poetry to anthology. Recipient Editors Choice award, Internat. Libr., 2003, 2006, 2007. Mem.: Wilderness Rd. Writers, Gaslight Writers, Ky. Writers Coalition, Internat. Soc. of Poets, Soc. Children's Book Writers and Illustrators, Louisville Astronomical Soc. Avocations: reading, poetry, astronomy, art, music. Personal E-mail: doriskitm@aol.com.

MIRACLE, GORDON ELDON, advertising educator; b. Olympia, Wash., May 28, 1930; s. Gordon Tipler and Corine Adriana (Orlebeke) M.; m. Christa Stoeter, June 29, 1957; children: Gary, Gregory, Glenn. BBA, U. Wis., 1952, MBA, 1958, PhD, 1962. Case officer, civilian intelligence analyst U.S. Army, Fed. Republic Germany, 1955-57; instr. commerce U. Wis. Grad. Sch. Bus., Madison, 1958-60; instr., then asst. prof. mktg. U. Mich., Ann Arbor, 1960-66; assoc. prof. advt. Mich. State U., East Lansing, 1966-70, chmn. PhD program in mass media, 1973-74, chmn. dept., 1974-80, prof. advt., 1970-99, prof. emeritus, 1999—. Vis. prof. mktg. mgmt. N. European Mgmt. Inst., Oslo, 1972-73; dir. InterSIP World Wide Student Internship Program, 2007—; cons., lectr. in field. Author: Management of International Advertising, 1966; co-author: International Marketing Management, 1970, Advertising and Government Regulation, 1979, Instructor's Manual for International Marketing Management, 1971, European Regulation of Advertising: Supranational Regulation of Advertising in the European Economic Community, 1986, Voluntary Regulation of Advertising: A Comparative Analysis of the United Kingdom and the United States, 1987, (in Korean) Cultures in Advertising: Advertising in Cultures, 1990; contbr. articles to scholarly and profl. jours.; editor: Marketing Decision Making: Strategy and Payoff, 1965, Sharing for Understanding, Proc. Ann. Conf. Am. Acad. Advt., 1977. Served with AUS, 1952-55. Recipient first Biennial Excellence in Advt. award, U. Ill., 1995; Ford Found. fellow, 1961-62, 64, Am. Assn. Advt. Agys. fellow Marsteller, Inc., 1967, Advt. Ednl. Found. fellow McCann-Erickson Hakuhodo, 1985, Fulbright rsch. fellow Waseda U., Tokyo, 1985; recipient numerous grants; recipient Viktor-Mataja medal Austrian Advt. Rsch. Assn., Vienna, 1999. Fellow: Am. Acad. Advt. (treas., exec. com. 1978—79); mem.: Internat. Advt. Assn., Internat. Advt. Assn. ((ednl. accreditation com. 1993—95, internat. advt. edn. group 1996—2001), Am. Mktg. Assn., Acad. Internat. Bus. (sec., exec. com. 1973—75), Adcraft Club Detroit. Home: 10025 Oak Island Dr Laingsburg MI 48848-8718 Office: Mich State U Dept Advt East Lansing MI 48824 Business E-Mail: miracle@msu.edu.

MIRAKIAN-ESCOBAR, RACHEL ANN, language educator; b. Cleve., July 21, 1966; d. Nazar Mirakian and Mary Hazarian, Lucy Baboyan (Stepmother); m. Ebert Eduardo Escobar, Jan. 22, 2005. Bachelor, SUNY, Purchase, 2005. Tchg. asst. Souther Westchester Boces, Valhalla, NY, 1996—99; freelance writing tutor self-employed, New Rochelle, NY, 1996—2005; English lang. instr. Pace U., Pleasantville, NY, 2006—; adj. instr. Westchester CC, Valhalla, NY, 2006—. Student workshop devel. Westchester CC, 2003—06, editor/proofreader ann. report, 2005, author student devel. handbooks, 2005—06. Designer (computer game) Symmetry;, author short stories. Mem. United Ch. Christ, Pelham, NY, 2005—, Empty Hand Zen Ctr., New Rochelle, 2006. Mem.: Avant Guard, Bookbuilders, Purchase Alumni Assn., Mensa. Liberal. Christian-Buddhist. Avocations: writing, meditation, reading, films, travel. Office: Pace U 861 Bedford Rd Pleasantville NY 10570 Personal E-mail: rme580@optonline.net.

MIRAN, PATRICIA MARIE, art educator; b. Seattle, Apr. 6, 1951; d. Robert Glenroy Hancock and Bernice Iris Brisky; m. Maynard Alvin Miran, May 1, 1983; children: Maxwell, Jacob, Emma. Diploma in fine arts, Art Students League, NYC, 1974; BS in Psychology cum laude, Excelsior Coll., Albany, NY, 2001. Childrens story hr. dir. Sayre Libr., 1989—95; exec. dir. Lincoln Acad., Waverly, NY, 1998—2004; tchr. Jewish Cmty. Sch., Elmira, NY, 1999—. Libr. dir. Cady Libr., Nichols, NY, 1996; remedial reading tutor M-G Edn., Elmira, 2001—08; instr. Elmira Bus. Inst., 2005, pvt. painting lessons, 2006—. Exhibitions include oil paintings Ann. Exhbn., Art Students League, NYC, 1970—74, Vet. Artist Outdoor Exhbn., Lincoln Ctr., 1971, Ann. Exhbn., Salmagundi Club, 1975, Ctr. for Arts Homer, NY, 2008, Bank Show, Tioga County Coun. on Arts, 2008, Arts Coun. Southern Finger Lakes, Corning, NY, 2009, exhibited in group shows at Whitney Mus. Am. Art, 1975. Bd. mem., vol. Susquahanna River Archeological Ctr., Waverly, NY, 2008—; vol. Meadowgate, Equine Rescue & Rehab. Facility, Newfield, NY, 2009; rep. 4-H Cornell Coop. Ext., Owego, NY, 1989—2001; active Tioga County Coun. on the Arts. Grantee, N.Y. State Coun. on Arts, 1994—96; scholar, Calif. Coll. Arts and Crafts, 1969—70, Art Student League, 1971. Mem.: Art Coun. Southern Finger

Lakes, The Am. Artists Profl. League, Tioga County Coun. on the Arts, Arnot Art Mus. Avocations: gardening, painting, dance, horseback riding, fencing. Home and Studio: 21 Lincoln St Waverly NY 14892 Office: Jewish Cmty Sch PO Box 3087 1008 W Water St Elmira NY 14905 Office Phone: 607-732-7410. Personal E-mail: mmiran@stny.rr.com.

MIRANDA, CARLOS SA, food products company executive; b. Fall River, Mass., Nov. 16, 1929; s. Carlos Sa and Annette (Pratt) M.; m. Natalie Cardoso, Jan. 5, 1949; children: Carla, Lucy, John. BS in Mech. Engrng., Marquette U., 1956. With internat. divsn. Kellogg Co., Battle Creek, Mich., 1964—65; gen. mgr. Kellogg Co. Brazil, 1965—80; v.p. Kellogg Internat., Battle Creek, 1980—89; gen. mgr. Kellogg's Spain, 1983—84; country dir. internat. exec. svc. corps. Costa Rica, 1990—91; mediator Fla. County Cts., 1994—2008. Recipient Pero Vaz Caminha award, Brazil, 1976; conferred title Comdr. of Legion of Honor of Marshal Rondon, Brazil, 1971. Mem. ASME. Independent. Roman Catholic. Home: 8949 Wildlife Loop Sarasota FL 34238

MIRANDA, HERMES, school counselor; b. LA, Aug. 24, 1958; s. Henrietta Collins; m. Patricia Salazar, Feb. 4, 1971; children: Naomi Ruth Cross, Isaac Keith. MS, LI U., NY, 1996. Cert. sch. counselor NY, 1997. Enlisted US Army, 1976, advanced to master sgt., 1995, ret., 1997; counselor Newburgh Enlarged Sch. Dist., NY, 1997—. Decorated Meritorious Svc. medal with Oak Leaf Cluster US Army. Mem.: Newburgh Tchrs. Assn., Orange County Counselor's Assn. (assoc.). Republican. Home: 9 Princeton Dr Walden NY 12586

MIRANDA, LEOPOLDO, zoologist, director; m. Jesica Soto, Dec. 21, 2002. MS in Wildlife Mgmt. & Zoology, NC State U., Raleigh, 1995. Nat. program leader US Fish & Wildlife Svc. Chesapeake Bay Office, Arlington, 2003—08, dir., 2008—. Pvt. lands program coord. US Fish & Wildlife Svc. Caribbean Office, Boqueron, PR, 1998—2003. Home and Office: US Fish & Wildlife Svc 177 Admiral Cochrane Dr Annapolis MD 21401 Business E-Mail: leopoldo_miranda@fws.gov.

MIRANDA, LIN-MANUEL, actor, composer, lyricist; b. NYC, Jan. 16, 1980; Attended, Wesleyan U. Composer, lyricist, performer: (Broadway plays) In the Heights, 2008— (Theatre World award, 2007, Drama Desk award for Outstanding Ensemble Performance, 2007, Outer Critics Cir. award for Outstanding Musical, 2007, Lucille Lortel award for Outstanding Musical, 2007, Obie award for Music & Lyics, 2007, Best Musical, Best Original Score, Tony Awards, 2008, Grammy award for Best Musical Show Album, 2009); traslator West Side Story, 2009. Office: c/o Richard Rodgers Theatre In the Heights 226 W 46th St New York NY 10036*

MIRANDA, ROBERT, psychologist, researcher; Asst. rsch. prof. Brown U., Providence, 2001—. Grantee, NIH. Achievements include research in addictive behavior among adolescents and young adults. Office: Brown U 121 South Main St Rm 510 Providence RI 02912 Office Fax: 401-863-6697. Business E-Mail: robert_miranda_jr@brown.edu.

MIRANDA, ROBERT NICHOLAS, publishing executive, director; b. Bklyn., July 9, 1934; m. Marilyn H. Pils, May 25, 1958; children: Marilyn, Robert, Susan, Lori, Jennifer. AA in Acctg. and Bus. Adminstrn., SUNY, Farmingdale, 1967. Pres. Pergamon Press, Inc., Elmsford, NY, 1965—92; chmn., CEO Cognizant Communication Corp., Elmsford, 1992—; owner Miranda Press, 2002. Bd. dirs., exec. v.p., vice chmn. Soc. and Assoc. Svc. Corp., McLean, Va., 1979-82; bd. dirs., chmn. electronics com. Copyright Clearance Ctr., 1984-93. Pub. Acupuncture and Electro Therapeutics Rsch., Analgesia, Bird Behavior, Cancer Prevention Internat., Cell Transplantation, Festival Mgmt. and Event Tourism, Gene Expression, Info. Tech. and Tourism, Life Support and Biosphere Sci., Oncology Rsch., Tourism Analysis, Technology: Jour. of Regulatory Sci., Failure and Lessons Learned in Info. Tech., Pacific Tourism Rev., Tourism, Culture and Comm., Tourism Dynamic Book Series, Tourism in Marine Environments, Habitation: An Internat. Jour., Revs. in Analgesia, Event Mgmt., Tourism Rev. Internat., Info. Tech. in Hospitality. Served with USNR, 1954-59. Mem. Internat. Soc. Intelligent Sys. (founder, bd. dirs., fin. dir. 1992—). Avocations: hunting, fishing, horseback riding. Office: Cognizant Comm Corp 3 Hartsdale Rd Elmsford NY 10523-3701 Office Phone: 914-592-7720. Personal E-mail: cogcomm@aol.com.

MIRANDA-EVANS, VALETTA LEE, social worker, human services manager; d. Leland James and Mary Miranda; m. Bruce Claude Evans, Aug. 23, 1986; children: Darcel Lynette Murray, Adam Bruce Evans, Kristina L. Evans. BA, Boston U., 1977; MSW, Boston Coll., 1979. LCSW 1986, Cert. Employee Assistance Prof. 1983, Prof. Human Resources 2000. Program specialist Nat. Clearinghouse for Alcohol/Drug Info., Rockville, Md., 1979—82; employee assistance counselor Prince George's County Health Dept., Beltsville, Md., 1982—84; substance abuse program coord. Social Security Adminstrn., Balt., 1984—88; dir. employee assistance program ARC, Washington, 1988—92; employee assistance cons. DuPont, Richmond, Va., 1992—96, human resource mgr., 1996—2002, employee assistance cons. Wilmington, Del., 2002—. Office: DuPont Rte 141 CRP 700/32 Wilmington DE 19808

MIRANDA-LEVI, JASON, film producer, writer; arrived in US, 1939, naturalized, 1957; s. Jose Antonio Miranda and Mercedes Bertolin-Levi; m. Maria L Maria Luisa Echaurren, Nov. 24, 1962. BS, Fordham U., 1954—58; JD, St. Johns U., 1958—61. Lic.: NY (Attorney) 1963. Pvt. law practice, NYC, 1964—74. Prodr.: (film and telvision) Han Matado a Un Cadaver; (TV series) Cara a Cara; author: (novels) The Spanish Enigma, The Vitruvian Sequence, Manhattan Serenade, Dancer in the Dark; exhibitions include Photographic Surrealism, Toledo Art Mus., Ohio. Lance cpl. USMC, 1951—53, Korea. Recipient Dama del Paraguas, City of Barcelona, Spain, 1973, La Font de Canaletas, City Coun. of the City of Barcelona, Spain, 1973, Medal of San Jordi, Province of Barcelona, Barcelona, Spain, 1976, Font de Canaletas, City Coun. of Barcelona, Spain, 1975. Mem.: SAG, NY Bar. Republican. Jewish. Avocations: antique watch collector, travel, reading, haute cuisine, flute. Personal E-mail: jmlevi@sbcglobal.net.

MIRANTE, THOMAS ANTHONY, retired secondary education educator; b. Utica, NY, Oct. 11, 1931; s. John and Catherine (Cerro) M.; m. Lucy Fiore, Aug. 11, 1962; children: Anne Catherine, Mary Jo. BS in Music, SUNY, Potsdam, 1954; MS in Music, Ithaca Coll., 1955; postgrad., Colgate U., 1964; studies with Earl George, David Diamond. Cert. music tchr., guidance counselor, N.Y. Pianist 6th Infantry div. Band U.S. Army, Ft. Ord, Calif., 1955-56; choral dir. 1st Infantry div. Post Chapel U.S. Army, Ft. Riley, Kans., 1956-57; tchr. music Port Leyden (N.Y.) Cen. Sch., 1957-60; dir. music, tchr. Oneida (N.Y.) City Schs., 1960-92. Music critic Oneida Dispatch, 1972; composer: Piano Sonata, 1964, Symphony 1, 1968, Viola Concerto, 1971, numerous other works, 1968-87; author: Voices Amid the Thunder, 1989, Song of Evil, 1996; contbr. articles to profl. jours. Trustee Canastota (N.Y.) Library Bd., 1986. Rockefeller grantee Am. Music Ctr., 1975, grantee N.Y. State Council of Arts, 1975. Mem. BMI, Madison County Music Tchrs. Assn. Democrat. Roman Catholic. Avocation: walking. Home: 208 N Main St Canastota NY 13032-1033

MIREAU, JENNIFER LYN, band director, gymnastics coach; b. Phoenix, Dec. 29, 1975; d. Dottie and Larry Richard Daniels; m. Sean Michael Mireau, June 22, 2002; 1 child, Marcus Amadeus. MusB, Northern Ariz. U., Flagstaff, 1998. K-12 music cert. Ariz. Dept. Edn., 1998. Band dir. Shadow Mountain HS, Phoenix, 1998—2004, Chaparral HS, Scottsdale, 2004—. Mem.: Scottsdale Edn. Assn. Conservative. Avocations: gymnastics, singing, travel, flute, trumpet. Office: Chaparral HS 6935 E Gold Dust Ave Scottsdale AZ 85253 E-mail: jmireau@susd.org.

MIRELS, HAROLD, aerospace engineer; b. NYC, July 29, 1924; s. Hyman and Lily (Efron) M.; m. Nell Segal, Oct. 4, 1953; children: Lily, Laurence Franklin, Jeremy Mark. BSME, Cooper U., 1944; MSME, Case Inst. Tech., 1949; PhD in Aero. Engring., Cornell U., 1953. Sect. head NACA, Cleve., 1944-57; br. chief NASA, Cleve., 1957-61; dept. head Aerospace Corp., El Segundo, Calif., 1961-78, assoc. dir., 1978-84, prin. scientist, 1984-93; cons., 1993—. Co-inventor continuous wave chem. laser. Recipient Tech. Achievement award Cleve. Tech. Socs., 1960. Fellow AIAA (Fluid and Plasmadynamics award 1988), Am. Phys. Soc.; mem. Nat. Acad. Engring. Home: 3 Seahurst Rd Palos Verdes Peninsula CA 90274-3700

MIRENBURG, BARRY LEONARD, publishing executive, educator; b. NYC, Feb. 16, 1952; s. Fred and Mildred (Solomon) M. BS, Mercy Coll., 1979; BFA, Cooper Union, 1980; MBA, N.Y. Inst. of Tech., 1983; MA, Columbia U., 1983, postgrad., 1983—; MFA, Syracuse U., 1990; postgrad., Columbia U. Tchrs. Coll., 1997. Pres., pub. Barlenmir House, NYC, 1972—; pres., owner Barlenmir House Theatres, Inc., NYC, 1978—; head Design Graphics N.Y. Inst. of Tech., NYC, 1979—; pres., creative dir. The Corp. Communications Group, NYC, 1985—, Mirenburg & Co., NYC, 1985—. Instr. unranked Parsons Sch. of Design, N.Y.C., 1979—, coord. computer graphics, 1990-91; asst. prof. Fashion Inst. of Tech., N.Y.C., 1979-81; corp. art dir. Music Sales/Quick Fox, N.Y.C., 1982-85; adj. assoc. prof. Grad. Sch. Coll. of New Rochelle, N.Y., 1985—; founder, exec. dir. Am. Health and Fitness Alliance, 1998—. Recipient more than 125 awards and honors for art and design; Fulbright scholar, 1991. Mem. AAUP, Nat. Coun. Art Adminstrs., Am. Inst. Graphic Arts, Soc. Publ. Designers, Am. Ctr. for Design, Art Dirs. Club, Soc. Indsl. Designers, Coll. Art Assn., Mensa. Home and Office: 404 E 79th St New York NY 10021

MIRES, CHARLENE, historian, educator; b. Wilmington, Ohio, Sept. 11, 1957; d. Charles W. and Jane D. Mires. BS, Ball State U., Muncie, Ind., 1979; MLA, U. Pa., Phila., 1992; PhD, Temple U., Phila., 1997. Reporter Mich. City News Dispatch, Ind., 1979—80; reporter, sect. editor Ft. Wayne News Sentinel, Ind., 1980—84; editor Phila. Inquirer, 1984—92; asst. prof. history Villanova U., Pa., 1997—2004, assoc. prof. history, 2004—. Editl. bd. mem. Jour. Am. History, Bloomington, Ind., 2007—, Pub. Historian, Santa Barbara, Calif., 2003—, Pa. Mag. History and Biography, Phila., 2005—; editor Pa. History Studies Series, Mansfield, 2004—08. Author: (book) Independence Hall in American Memory (Phila. Athenaeum Lit. award, 2004). Mem. City Phila. Oversight Com. Pre. Home Commemoration, Phila., 2005—08. Office: Villanova Univ 800 E Lancaster Ave Villanova PA 19106

MIRFAKHRAIE, KOOROSH, systems engineer, educator; s. Ali Mirfakhraie and Sorayya-Banou Mansour; m. Denise H. Sparrow, Apr. 27, 1996; children: Kamyar A. M., Arman A. C., Lily S., Daria D. children: Isabel H. BME, George Washington U., Washington, 1982; MS in Aerospace Engring., U. Minn., Mpls., 1984; PhD in Aero. and Astronautical Engring., U. Ill., Urbana-Champaign, 1990. Trajectory analyst Analex Corp., Brookpark, Ohio, 1990—96; sr. sys. engr. Lockheed Martin Missiles & Space, East Windsor, NJ, 1996—98, INTELSAT, Washington, 1998—2001, Augusta Sys., Morgantown, W.Va., 2004—08; chief sys. engr. Titan Corp., Fairmont, W.Va., 2001—04; prin. sys. engr. Raytheon Missile Sys., Tucson, 2008—.

MIRIAM, FRAZURE AMANDA, research scientist; d. Billy Gene and Cathy Meggs Frazure. AS, Holmes CC, Goodman, Miss., 2000; BS, U. Southern Miss., Hattiesburg, 2003, MS, 2005. Vis. faculty U. Southern Miss., Hattiesburg, 2007—08; sr. visualization rschr. Ctr. Higher Learning @NASA Stennis Space Ctr., Stennis Space Center, 2008. Author: (poem) Life.

MIRICK, JOHN O., lawyer; b. Worcester, Mass., Nov. 27, 1946; s. Richard W. and Margaret (Whittemore) M.; m. Diane Kay Lohman, Aug. 2, 1969; children: Christopher R., Seth H. BA magna cum laude, Amherst Coll., Mass., 1968; MA, University Coll., London, 1969; JD cum laude, Harvard U., 1972. Bar: Mass. 1972, U.S. Dist. Ct. Mass. 1973, U.S. Ct. Appeals (1st cir.) 1974, U.S. Ct. Appeals (2nd cir.) 1979, U.S. Supreme Ct. 1980, U.S. Ct. Appeals (fed. cir.) 2006. Assoc. Hale & Dorr, Boston, 1972-76; ptnr. Mirick, O'Connell, DeMallie & Lougee, Worcester, Mass., 1976—. Trustee Mass. Continuing Legal Edn., 1988-92. Trustee Dynamy, Inc., Worcester, 1979—89, Mass. Bd. Bar Overseers, 1999—2002, chair, 2001—02; mem. Mass. Jud. Nominating Commn., 2003—06. Fulbright scholar, 1969. Mem. ABA, Mass. Bar Assn, Mass. Acad. Trial Attys., Assn. Trial Lawyers Am., Am. Antiquarion Soc., Phi Beta Kappa. Office: Mirick O'Connell DeMallie & Lougee 100 Front St Worcester MA 01608 Office Phone: 508-791-8500. Business E-Mail: jomirick@modl.com.

MIRIPOL, JERILYN ELISE, poet, writer, writing therapist; b. Chgo., Jan. 22; d. Albert and Janice (Tuchin) M.; m. Richard Palmer Van Duyne, Dec. 30, 1986. BA in English Lit., Northeastern Ill. U., 1974. Writing therapist Northshore Retirement Hotel, Evanston, Ill., 1983; creative writing tchr. Oakton Community Coll., Evanston, 1985—; writing therapist St. Francis Hosp., Evanston, 1989—. Artist-writer-in-residence Dawes Sch., Evanston, 1985; artist-in-residence Evanston Twp. High Sch., 1988; writing facilitator for individual students, Chgo., 1987—; tchr. writing therapy to mental health profls. and caregivers U. Wis., Milw., 1989; presenter writing therapy workshop, 1990, Nat. Assn. Poetry-Therapy, Chgo., 1991. Author: Discovering Self-Awareness Through Poetry, 1987, (poetry) The Sounds Were Distilled, 1977; author numerous poems; contbr. articles to profl. jours. Vol. Ridgeview Nursing Home, Evanston, 1982-83; advocate of children of abuse, human and civil rights. Talent scholar in creative writing Northeastern Ill. U., Squaw Valley Community Writers scholar, 1980, Radgale Found. scholar, 1985, Aspen Writer's Workshop Breadloaf Writer's Conf. scholar; Danforth fellow nominee; Dawes Sch. grantee, 1987. Mem. NOW, PEN, UNICEF, ACLU, Nat. Assn. Poetry Therapy, Women's Internat. League for Peace, Humanitas Internat. (human rights com.), Amnesty Internat., Am. Acad. Poets, Ill. Alliance of Arts, Pan Pacific Southeast Asia Women's Assn. (v.p.), 11th Ann. Poetry Therapy Conf. (keynote speaker), Greenpeace, Death Penalty Foes. Avocations: music, dance, art, reading, drama, films. Home: 1520 Washington Ave Wilmette IL 60091-2417 Home Phone: 847-251-6721. Personal E-mail: jmiripol@webtv.net.

MIRISOLA, LISA HEINEMANN, program supervisor; b. Glendale, Calif., Mar. 25, 1963; d. J. Herbert and Betty Jane (Howson) Heinemann; m. Daniel Carl Mirisola, June 27, 1987; 1 child, Ian Cataldo. BSME, UCLA, 1986. Cert. engr.-in-tng., Calif. Program supr. South Coast Air Quality Mgmt. Dist., Diamond Bar, Calif., 1988—. Chancellor's scholar UCLA, 1981. Mem. ASME, SAE, Soc. Women Engrs. Office: South Coast Air Quality Mgmt Dist 21865 Copley Dr Diamond Bar CA 91765-4178 Office Phone: 909-396-2638. E-mail: lmirisola@aqmd.gov.

MIRKARIMI, ROSS, city supervisor; b. Chgo., Aug. 4, 1961; s. Hamid Mirkarimi and Nancy Kolman. B in Polit. Sci., St. Louis U.; M in Internat. Econs. and Affairs, Golden Gate U., San Francisco; MS in Environ. Sci., U. San Francisco; grad., San Francisco Police Acad. Cert. Commn. on Peace Officer Standards & Training (POST). Formerly with San Francisco Dist. Atty.'s Office; supr., Dist. 5 San Francisco Bd. Supervisors, 2004—, chair govt. audits & oversight com., Transp. Authority, vice-chair budget & fin. com., pub. safety com. Dir. San Francisco Nuclear Freeze Zone Coalition; mem. exec. bd. Assn. Bay Area Govt.'s; mem. Children & Families First Commn., Local Agy. Formation Commn.; co-founder Calif. Green Party, 1990; coord. Ralph Nader Presdl. Campaign, Calif., 2000; campaign mgr. Harry Britt for State Assembly, San Francisco, 2002, Matt Gonzalez for Mayor, San Francisco, 2003. Mem.: NOW, Iranian-Am. C. of C., Harvey Milk Lesbian/Gay/Bisexual/Transgender Dem. Club. Green Party. Office: City Hall 1 Dr Carlton B Goodlet Pl Rm 244 San Francisco CA 94102-4689 Office Phone: 415-554-7630. Fax: 415-554-7634. E-mail: ross.mirkarimi@sfgov.org.*

MIRKIN, CHAD A., chemistry professor; b. 1963; BS in Chemistry, Dickinson Coll., 1986; PhD, Pa. State U., 1989; doctorate (hon.), Dickinson Coll. Asst. prof. chemistry Northwestern U., Evanston, Ill., 1991-95, assoc. prof. chemistry, 1995-97, prof. chemistry, 1997-2000, George B. Rathmann prof. chemistry, dir. Internat. Inst. Nanotechnology, 2000—. Contbr. articles to profl. jours. NSF postdoctoral fellow MIT, 1989-91; recipient Beckman Young Investigators award, 1992-94, Disting. New Faculty award Camille and Henry Dreyfus Found., 1991-96, Young Investigator Rsch. award NSF, Young Prof. award DuPont, Young Investigator award ONR, Inventors award B.F. Goodrich, Wilson prize, Award in Pure Cemistry Am. Chem. Soc., Nobel Signature award, Am. Chem. Soc., Collegiate Inventors award, Nat. Inventors Hall of Fame, 2003, 04, Pioneer award, NIH, 2004, Lemelson-MIT prize, 2009; grantee USN. Mem. Am. Chem. Soc., NAE Achievements include research nanotechnology biosensors and new ligand design in synthetic organometallic chemistry; over 50 patents in field. Office: Northwestern U Dept Chemistry 2145 Sheridan Rd K111 Evanston IL 60208-3113 E-mail: chadnano@northwestern.edu.*

MIRKIN, GABE BARON, physician, medical educator, writer, radio personality; b. Brookline, Mass., June 18, 1935; s. Mitchell and Vera (Baron) M.; children: Gene, Jan, Jill, Geoffrey, Kenny; m. Diana Purdie Rich, 1998. BA, Harvard U., 1957; MD, Baylor U., 1961. Diplomate Am. Bd. Pediatrics, Sub Bd. Allergy, Am. Bd. Allergy and Immunology, Am. Bd. Sports Medicine. Resident in pediatrics Mass. Gen. Hosp., Boston, 1961-63; fellow allergy, immunology, dermatology Johns Hopkins Hosp., Balt., 1963-65; allergy, immunology, dermatology, sports medicine pvt. practice, Silver Spring, Md., 1966—. Tchg. fellow pediat. Harvard Med. Sch., 1962-63; tchg. fellow allergy and immunology Johns Hopkins Med. Sch., 1963-65; asst. prof. dept. phys. edn. U. Md., College Park, 1976-83; assoc. clin. prof. dept. pediat. Georgetown U. Sch. of Medicine, 1984—. Author: The Sportsmedicine Book, 1978, Getting Thin, 1983, Dr. Gabe Mirkin's Fitness Clinic, 1986, The Complete Sportsmedicine Book for Women, 1985, 2d rev. edit. 1991; (with Shangold) Women and Exercise, 1988, Dr. Gabe Mirkin's Fatfree, Flavorfull Book, 1995; (with Diana Mirkin) The 20 Gram Diet, 1995, The 20/30 Fat and Fiber Diet Plan, Dr. Gabe Mirkins Pocket Guide to Fitness & Sports; (with Rich) The Whole Grains Cookbook, 1997, The Good Food Book, 2001, Healthy Heart Miracle, 2004; author (newsletter) The Mirkin Report, 1990—; columnist: N.Y. Times, 1978-89, United Features, 1989-94, Washington Post, 1976, Singer Media Corp., 1994-99; appearances on P.M. Mag. WDVM-TV, Washington, 1979, House Party, NBC TV, 1990, The Learning Channel; host internationally syndicated radio talk show, 1996-2003; daily radio spots on fitness and nutrition, CBS Radio Stations News Svc., 1979—; host talk show on health fitness and nutrition, KMOX Radio, St. Louis, 1982-98; nightly talk show host NBC Washington, WRC, 1982-84, 87—, WNTR, 1984-86; weekly spots for Physicians Radio Network, 1984-85; daily talk show syndicated by Sun Radio Network, 1992; weekly talk show WEEI, Boston, 1993-94, others; columnist and contbg. editor to health and fitness mags.; contbr. articles to profl. jours., chpts. to books. Major USAF, 1968-70. Fellow Am. Coll. Allergists, Am. Assn. Cert. Allergists, Am. Assn. for Clin. Immunology and Allergy, Am. Acad. Pediatrics, Am. Acad. Allergy and Immunology. Avocation: bicycle tandem racing. Home: 2001 Hartford Path The Villages FL 32162 Office Phone: 301-942-7900. Business E-Mail: gabe@drmirkin.com.

MIRMAN, JOEL HARVEY, lawyer; b. Toledo, Dec. 3, 1941; s. Benjamin and Minnie Mirman; children: Lisa, Julie, Benjamin. BBA, Ohio U., 1963; JD, Ohio State U., 1966. Bar: Ohio 1966, U.S. Dist. Ct. (so. dist.) Ohio 1966, U.S. Supreme Ct. 1972. Ptnr. Topper, Alloway, Goodman, DeLeone & Duffey, Columbus, Ohio, 1966-85, Benesch, Friedlander, Coplan & Aronoff, 1986-93, Gamble Hartshorn, LLC, Columbus, 2004—07, Adams, Babner and Gen. Counsel, Gosh Enterprises, Inc., 2008—09; shareholder Buckingham, Doolittle & Burroughs, Columbus, 1994—2003; ptnr. Gitlitz, LLC, 2008—09, of counsel. Lectr. Ohio CLE Inst., Columbus, 1972—; former mem. Supreme Ct. of Ohio Commn. on Certification of Specialists. Author direct examination CLE materials; contbr. articles to profl. jours. Mem. Ohio Elections Commn., 1976-80, vice-chmn. 1980. Named Ohio Super Lawyer, 2003—; named one of Best Lawyers in Am., 2003—, Ohio's Top 100 Super Lawyers, 2004, Top 50 Lawyers in Columbus, Ohio Super Lawyers, 2005. Mem. Ohio State Bar Assn. (coun. of dels.), Worthington Hills Civic Assn. (pres. 1992-93). Office: Adams Babner Gitlitz LLC 5003 Horizons Dr Ste 200 Columbus OH 43220 Office Phone: 614-324-5985, 614-360-1056. Business E-Mail: jhm@abglawyers.com.

MIRNAJAFIZADEH, SEYED ALI, engineering educator, researcher; b. Tehran, Iran, Jan. 21, 1962; s. Javaad Mirnajafizadeh and Ozra Nakhaee; m. Hamideh Hosseini, Dec. 19, 1985; children: Zahra, Hossein, Mahdi, Zeynab. PhD, Flinders U. South Australia, Adelaide, 2001. Rsch. asst. prof. U. Pitts., 2001—04; adj. asst. prof. U. Calif., Irvine, 2006—. R & D prin. engr. Edwards Lifescis., Irvine, 2005—. Recipient Best Grad. Student Presentation award, Inst. Engrs. Australia,

1998. Mem.: ASME. Achievements include patents for a novel method of developing heart valve leaflets with better longevity. Home: 10 Clover Irvine CA 92604 Office: Edwards Lifesci 1 Edwards Way Irvine CA 92604 Office Fax: 1-949-250-2501.

MIROWSKI, PHILIP EDWARD, economics professor; b. Jackson, Mich., Aug. 21, 1951; s. Edward and Elizabeth Mirowski. BA, Mich. State U., 1973; MA in Econs., U. Mich., 1976, PhD in Econs., 1979. Asst. prof. U. Santa Clara, Calif., 1978-81, Tufts U., Medford, Mass., 1981-84, assoc. prof. econs., 1984-90; Carl Koch prof. econs. and history and philosophy of sci. U. Notre Dame, Ind., 1990—. Vis. assoc. prof. Yale U., New Haven, 1987-88; vis. prof. Tinbergen Inst., Erasmus U., Rotterdam, Holland, 1991, U. Paris, 1997, U. Modena, Italy, 1998, Santa Fe Inst., 2001; Fulbright sr. fellow, 2003, Internat. Ctr. for Advanced Studies, NYU, 2004,fellow, All Souls Oxford, 2008. Author: Reconstruction of Economic Theory, 1986, Against Mechanism, 1988, More Heat Than Light, 1989, Machine Dreams, 2002, Science Bought and Sold, 2002, Effortless Economy of Science, 2004; editor: Natural Images in Economics, 1994, Edgeworth on Chance, 1994, Collected Works of William Thomas Thornton, 1999, Agreement on Demand, 2006, The Road From Mount Peltrew, 2009; mem. editl. bd. History Polit. Econ., Duke U., 1986—, Social Concept, 1988-94, Jour. Instnl. Econs., 2004—, Jour. History of Econ., 2001—; contbr. articles to profl. jours. Mem. AAAS, Am. Econs. Assn., History Sci. Soc., History Econs. Soc., Soc. for Social Studies of Sci. (Ludwig Fleck prize 2006), Philosophy of Sci. Assn. Office: U Notre Dame 400 Decio Hall Notre Dame IN 46556 E-mail: mirowski.1@nd.edu.

MIROWSKI, PIOTR, medical researcher; MSc in Computer Sci., Ecole Nat. Supérieure ENSEEIHT, Toulouse, France, 2002; MSc Applied Math.; PhD in Computer Sci., NY U., 2005—. Cert. in diplôme d'ingénieur des grandes ecoles, ENSEEIHT, 2002. Software engr. intern Schlumberger, Clamart, France, 2001—02; rsch. engr. Schlumberger Cambridge Rsch., 2002—03, Schlumberger Doll Rsch., Ridgefield, Conn., 2003—05; rsch. assoc. NYU Med. Ctr., 2006—; software engr. intern Google, NYC, 2008. Co-dir. N7 Projets Jr. Venture, Consulting, Toulouse, France, 1999—2002. Recreational therapist Cherub Improv. Recipient Henry McCracken award, NYU. Mem.: IEEE Computer, NY Acad. Scis. Achievements include patents for the application of machine learning to geology & medicine. Office: Courant Institute NY Univ 719 Broadway New York NY 10003 Business E-Mail: piotr.mirowski@computer.org.

MIRR, JOSEPH R., lawyer; b. Ladysmith, Wis., July 27, 1956; s. Ralph B. and Margaret R. Mirr; m. Judy M. Mirr; children: Paul J., Brian P. BA in Bus. Adminstrn., U. Wis., Eau Claire, 1978; JD, U. Wis., Madison, 1981. Bar: Wis. 1981, U.S. Dist. Ct. (we. dist.) Wis. 1981. Atty. Ruder Ware LLSC, Eau Claire, 1981—. With U. Wis. Eau Claire Found., 1991—98; bd. dirs., pres. Eau Claire YMCA, 1993—99, pres., 1999; bd. dirs. Eau Claire Area Econ. Devel. Corp., 2009—. Mem.: ABA, Eau Claire County Bar Assn., State Bar Wis. Roman Catholic. Avocations: running, golf, softball. Office: Ruder Ware LLSC PO Box 187 402 Graham Ave Eau Claire WI 54702-0187 Home Phone: 715-831-0527. Business E-Mail: jmirr@ruderware.com.

MIRRA, SUZANNE SAMUELS, pathologist; BA, Hunter Coll., 1962; MD, SUNY, Bklyn., 1967. Instr. pathology Yale U. Sch. Medicine, New Haven, 1971-73; staff pathologist Atlanta VA Med. Ctr., Decatur, Ga., 1973-97; asst. prof. pathology Emory U. Sch. Medicine, Atlanta, 1973-80, assoc. prof. pathology, 1981-93, prof. pathology, 1993-97; prof., chair dept. pathology SUNY Health Sci. Ctr., Bklyn., 1997—. Dir., prin. investor Emory Alzheimer's Disease Ctr., Atlanta, 1991—97. Mem. editl. bd. Arch Pathol. Lab. Med., 1988-2000, Jour. Neuropathology Exptl. Neurology, 1991-95, Brain Pathology, 1995-99, Alzheimer's Disease Reviews, 1995-2000. Recipient Albert E. Levy Sci. Faculty Rsch. award Emory U., 1987, Disting. Alumnus Achievement award SUNY, 1992; named to Hunter Coll. Hall of Fame, 1996. Fellow Coll. Am. Pathologists (Presdl. award 1987,89, Herbert Lansky award 1990, chair neuropathology commn. 1992-95); mem. Am. Assn. Neuropathologists (v.p. profl. affairs 1992-97, pres. 1999-2000, Meritorious Contributions to Neuropathology award, 2005), Alzheimer's Assn. (bd. dir. Atlanta chpt. 1987-97, nat. bd. dir. 1997-05), Alpha Omega Alpha. Office: SUNY Health Sci Ctr 450 Clarkson Ave Brooklyn NY 11203-2056 Office Phone: 718-270-4599. Business E-Mail: suzanne.mirra@downstate.edu.

MIRREN, HELEN (ILYNEA LYDIA MIRONOFF), actress; b. London, Eng., July 26, 1945; d. Basil and Katherine Mirren; m. Taylor Hackford, Dec. 31, 1997. Joined Royal Shakespeare Co., 1967; with Peter Brook's Ctr. Internat. de Recheres Theatrales, Africa, US, 1972—73. Actor: (theatre) Nat. Youth Theatre, Antony and Cleopatra, 1965, Royal Shakespeare Co., 1967, The Revenger's Tragedy, All's Well That Ends Well, Much Ado About Nothing, 1968, Batholomew Fair, 1969, Richard III, Hamlet, The Two Gentlemen of Verona, 1970, Enemies, 1971, Lady McBeth, 1974—75, Teeth 'n' Smiles, 1975, The Bed Before Yesterday, 1975, The Roaring Girl, Henry VI, 1977—78, Measure for Measure, 1979, The Duchess of Malfi, 1980—81, Faith Healer, 1981, Barbican, 1983, Extremities, 1984, Madame Bovary, 1987, Two Way Mirror, 1988, Sex Please We're Italian, 1991, A Month in the Country, 1994 (Tony nominee Lead Actress in a Play, 1995); (films) Herostratus, 1967, A Midsummer Night's Dream, 1968, Red Hot Shot, 1969, Age of Consent, 1969, Miss Julie, 1972, Savage Messiah, 1972, O Lucky Man!, 1973, Hamlet, 1976, The Quiz Kid, 1979, Caligula, 1979, The Hussy, 1980, The Fiendish Plot of Dr. Fu Manchu, 1980, The Long Good Friday, 1980, Excalibur, 1981, Cal, 1984 (Best Actress Cannes Film Festival, 1984), 2010, 1984, White Nights, 1984, Coming Through, 1985, Heavenly Pursuits, 1985, The Mosquito Coast, 1986, Pascali's Island, 1987, When the Whales Came, 1988, The Cook, the Thief, His Wife, and Her Lover, 1989, Bethune, The Making of a Hero, 1990, The Comfort of Strangers, 1990, Where Angels Fear to Tread, 1991, The Gift, 1991, The Hawk, 1991, The Prince of Jutland, 1991, The Madness of King George, 1994 (Acad. award nominee for Best Supporting Actress), The Snow Queen, 1995, Some Mother's Son, 1996, Critical Care, 1997, Teaching Mrs. Tingle, 1998, Greenfingers, 2000, The Pledge, 2001, No Such Thing, 2001, Last Orders, 2001, Gosford Park, 2001, Calendar Girls, 2003, The Clearing, 2004, Raising Helen, 2004, Shadowboxer, 2005, The Queen, 2006 (Volpi award for Best Actress, Best Actress award Venice Film Festival, NY Film Critics Circle award & LA Film Critics Assn., Nat. Bd. Rev., Fla. Film Critics Cir., African-Am. Film Critics Assn., Nat. Soc. of Film Critics, 2007, Critics Choice award, Broadcast Film Critics Assn., Best Performance by an Actress in a Motion Picture Drama, Golden Globe award, Hollywood Fgn. Press. Assn., 2007, Outstanding Performance by Female Actor in a Leading Role & Outstanding Performance by a Female Actor in a TV Movie or Miniseries, SAG, 2007, Actress in a Leading Role, British Acad. Film and TV Arts, 2007, Acad. award Best Actress in a Leading Role, 2007), National Treasure: Book of Secrets, 2007, Inkheart, 2008, State of Play, 2009; actor, dir.: Happy Birthday, 2001; actor: (TV films) Bellamira, 1974, Caesar and Claretta, 1974, The Philanthropist, 1975, The Collection, 1976, As You Like It, 1978, S.O.S. Titanic, 1979, Mrs. Reinhardt, 1981, A Midsummer Night's Dream, 1981, Cymbeline, 1982, Soft Targets, 1982, Faerie Tale Theatre, 1987, Red Kind White Knight, 1988, Prime Suspect, 1991 (Best Actress award BAFTA), Prime Suspect 2, 1992 (Best Actress award BAFTA), Prime Suspect 3, 1993 (Best Actress award BAFTA), Prime Suspect 4: The Lost Child, 1995 (Emmy award Best Actress, 1996), Prime Suspect 4: Inner Circles, 1995, Prime Suspect 4: Scent of Darkness, 1995, Losing Chase, 1995, Prime Suspect 5: Errors of Judgement, 1996, The Passion of Avn Road, 1999, On the Edge, 2001, Georgetown, 2002, Door to Door, 2002, The Roman Spring of Mrs. Stone, 2003, Prime Suspect 6: The Last Witness, 2003, Elizabeth I, 2005 (Emmy award for Outstanding Lead Actress in a Miniseries or Movie, 2006, Best Performance by an Actress in a Miniseries or Motion Picture Made for TV, Golden Globe award, Hollywood Fgn. Press Assn., 2007), Prime Suspect 7: The Final Act, 2006 (Primetime Emmy for Outstanding Lead Actress in a Miniseries or Movie, Acad. TV ARts and Scis., 2007), (voice only): (films) Prince of Eqypt, 1998, The Hitchhiker's Guide to the Galaxy, 2005, Pride, 2004,: (TV miniseries) Cousin Bette, 1971, Oresteia, 1979, Painted Lady, 1997, (TV appearances): Thriller, 1974, Play of the Month, 1974, 1975, 1977, Play for Today, 1979, 1982, The Hidden Room, 1993, Tracey Takes On, 1998, French and Saunders, 1999, Frasier, 2004, Third Watch, 2005; author: In the Frame: My Life in Words and Pictures, 2008. Recipient Distinction in Theatre award, Geffen Playhouse, 2007; named Dame, Brit. Empire, 2003. Mem.: PTO.*

MIRRER, LOUISE, professional society administrator, former language educator; b. NYC, Apr. 27, 1953; d. Gerald Paul and Mildred (Friedelbaum) M.; m. Philip Singer, Sept. 1, 1974 (div. Nov., 1984); 1 child, Philip Mirrer-Singer; m. David Halle, Mar. 6, 1947; children: Carla, Malcolm. BA in Spanish magna cum laude, U. Pa., 1973; diploma in Linguistics, Cambridge U., Eng., 1975; MA, Stanford U., 1977, PhD in Spanish and Humanities, 1980. Asst. prof. Spanish and Portugese Fordham U., NYC, 1979-86, assoc. prof., 1986-91, prof. and dept. chair, 1991-94; prof. and chair Spanish & Portuguese dept. U. Minn., Mpls., 1994—95, prof. Spanish & Portuguese, 1994—99, vice provost arts, sci. & engring., 1995—97; vice chancellor for academic affairs CUNY, NY, 1997—2004, prof. Hispanic & Luso-Brazilian studies & medieval studies NY, 1997—2004; pres., CEO NY Hist. Soc., 2004—. Bd. advisors Medieval Feminist Newsletter, 1991—; project dir. Japan Found. Grant, 1992-94; editorial bd. mem. Hispanic Issues U. Minnesota Press, 1995-. Author The Language of Evaluation: A Sociolinguistic Approach to the Story of Pedro el Cruel in Ballad and Chronicle, 1986, Women, Jews, and Muslims in the Texts of Reconquest Castile, 1996; co-author (with David Halle) Prints of Power, 1991; editor Upon My Husband's Death: Widows in the Literature and Histories of Medieval Europe, 1992; contributor Medieval Crime and Social Control, 1999, Women in Medieval Western European Culture, 1999, Charting Memory: Recalling Medieval Spain, 1999. Recipient McKnight fellowship, U. Minn., 1995, YWCA Women Achievers award, 2000, Leadership award Asian-Am. Rsch. Institution, 2003; grantee Littauer Found., 1993, NY Coun. for Humanities, 1994, fellow council on Institutional Cooperation, 1995-96; named one of 50 Most Influential Women in NY, NY Post, 2003. Mem. Governor's Interagency Council on Women, NY State Commissioner's Policy Advisory Com. Governing Bd. (vice chair), Alliance for Minority Participation, NY Acad. of Sci. Working Group for NY Tech. Council, Exec. Com. Modern Language Assn. Div. on Medieval Spanish Literature (chair 1999-2000, mem. delegate assembly 1988-91), Nominating Com. Internat. Assocn. of Hispanists, 1999-, bd. dirs. NY Structural Biology Ctr., bd. advisors Gateway Inst. for Pre-Coll. Edn., Asian-Am. Rsch. Inst., Soc. Medieval Feminist Scholarship, 1991-. Achievements include application of sociolinguistic methodology to orally composed texts; feminist approaches to medieval Spanish literature. Office: NY Hist Soc 170 Ctrl Pk W New York NY 10024 Office Phone: 212-873-3400.

MIRRLEES, SIR JAMES ALEXANDER, economics professor; b. Minnigaff, Scotland, July 5, 1936; s. George Barlas MacNab and Nan Lindsay (Purdie) M.; m. Gillian Marjorie Hughes, July 29, 1961 (dec. 1993); children: Catriona, Fiona; m. Patricia Wilson, May 12, 2001. MA, Edinburgh U., Scotland, 1957; BA, Cambridge U., Eng., 1959, PhD, 1963; DLitt (hon.), Warwick U., Eng., 1982, Portsmouth U., 1997, Brunel U., 1997, Edinburgh U., Scotland, 1997, Oxford U., 1998. Lectr. in econ. U. Cambridge, England, 1963-68; Edgeworth prof. econs. U. Oxford, England, 1968-95; prof. polit. economy U. Cambridge, 1995—2003, emeritus prof. polit. economy, 2003—, fellow Trinity Coll., 1995—; disting. prof.-at-large Chinese U. of Hong Kong, 2002—; disting. prof. U. Macau, 2005—; vis. prof. Peking U.; vis. laureate prof. U. Melbourne, Australia, 2005—. Vis. prof. MIT, 1968, 70, 71, 76, U. Calif., Berkeley, 1986, Yale U., 1989. Co-author: (with Little) Project Appraisal and Planning for Developing Countries, 1974, Welfare, Incentives and Taxation, 2006; contbr. articles to profl. publications. Recipient Nobel Prize in Econ. Sciences, 1996; Knighted for contributions to econ. sci., Eng., 1997. Fellow Brit. Acad., Roy. Soc. of Edinburgh, Econometric Soc. (pres. 1983-84); mem. NAS (fgn. mem.), Royal Econ. Soc. (pres. 1989-92), Am. Econ. Assn. (hon.), Am. Acad. Arts and Sci., Assn. Univ. Tchr. Econ. (chmn. 1983-87). Office: Morningside Coll 3/F Mong Manwai Bldg Shatin Hong Kong Office Phone: 88226961404.

MIRRO, JOHN, engineering company executive; Student, MIT, Cambridge, Mass. Pres. Conmec, Inc., Bethlehem, Pa. Office: Conmec Inc 1480 Valley Center Pky Bethlehem PA 18017-2264

MIRSKI, MAREK ALEXANDER, anesthesiologist, educator; b. Wash., May 6, 1958; s. Jerzy Zapadko Mirski and Janina Lutyk; m. Lenore Tomoye Nii, May 31, 1986; children: Kara Tomoye, Erin Alexis. BS in Chemistry & Biology, MIT, Cambridge, 1980; PhD, Wash. U., St. Louis, 1986. MD Wash. U. St. Louis, 1986, diplomate Anesthesiology & Critical Care Medicine Am. Bd. Med. Specialties, 1991, Neurology Am. Bd. Med. Specialties, 1995. Intern Wash. U. St. Louis Med. Ctr., 1986—87; assoc. prof. medicine & surgery John Burns Sch. Medicine, Honolulu, 1996—99; med. dir. - neuroscience inst. Queen's Med. Ctr., Honolulu, 1996—99; prof. anesthesiology & critical care medicine, neurology, neurosurgery Johns Hopkins Medicine, Balt., vice-chair, dept. anesthesiology & critical care medicine, 2004—, dir. - neuroscience critical care divsn., 1999—, chief - neuroanesthesiology, 1999—, resident - neurology, 1987—91, resident - anesthesiology & critical care medicine, 1989—91, fellow- neuroanesthesiology, 1991—92, fellow - neurocritical care, 1991—93, asst. prof. - anesthesiology & critical care medicine, neurology, neurosurgery, 1993—95, assoc. prof. anesthesiology & critical care medicine, neurology, neurosurgery, 1999—2008, dir. - anesthesiology clin. rsch. program, 2008—, dir. - percutaneous tracheostomy program, 2004—. Bd. dir. NeuroCritical Care Soc., Minn. Contbr. articles to numerous profl. jours. Bd. mem., head fin. com. Soc. NeuroCritical Care, Minn., 2004—08. Grantee Grant, NIH, 2000—08; Med. Scientist Tng. Program grant, 1980—86, Grant, Am. Epilepsy Found., 1993—95, Investigator-sponsored rsch. grant, Hospira, 2005—08. Mem.: Am. Acad. Neurology, Am. Neurol. Assn., Soc. Critical Care Medicine, Am. Epilepsy Soc., Am. Soc. Anesthesiology, NeuroCritical Care Soc. (bd. dir. 2004—08). Democrat. Roman Catholic. Achievements include discovery of novel neuroanatomical pathway in brain important in propagation of seizures; leading to successful clinical trials of deep brain stimulation in anterior thalamus for refractory epilepsy; first to laboratory and clinical research validating the now common therapy of hypertonic saline for the treatment of severe brain swelling following stroke or trauma; medical program for the comprehensive percutaneous tracheostomy program for intensive care units; development of First Neuroscience Intensive Care Unit in Hawaii & Pacific Rim. Avocations: bicycling, travel, tennis, backpacking. Office: Johns Hopkins Medicine 600 N Wolfe St Meyer 8-140 Baltimore MD 21287 Business E-Mail: mmirski@jhmi.edu.

MIRSKY, ARTHUR, retired geologist, educator; b. Phila., Feb. 8, 1927; s. Victor and Dorothy M.; m. Patricia Shorey, Dec. 22, 1961; 1 dau., Alexis Catherine. Student, Bklyn. Coll., 1944, student, 1946—48; BA, U. Calif., LA, 1950; MS, U. Ariz., 1955; PhD, Ohio State U., 1960. Cert. geologist, Ind. Field uranium geologist AEC, S.W. U.S., 1951-53; cons. uranium geologist Albuquerque, 1955-56; asst. dir. Inst. Polar Studies, Ohio State U., 1960-67; adj. asst. prof. geology Ohio State U., 1964-67; from asst. prof. geology to prof. Ind. U.-Purdue U., Indpls., 1967-94, prof. emeritus, 1994—, coord. geology, 1967-69, chmn. dept. geology, 1969-93. Contbr. articles to profl. jours. Served with USN, 1944-46. Mem. AAAS, AAUP, Am. Inst. Profl. Geologists, Geol. Soc. Am., Nat. Assn. Geosci. Tchrs., Am. Geol. Inst., Soc. Sedimentary Geology, Ind. Acad. Sci., Sigma Xi. Office: Indiana U-Purdue U Dept Earth Scis 723 W Michigan St Indianapolis IN 46202-5132 Office Phone: 317-278-0229. E-mail: amirsky@iupui.edu.

MIRVAHABI, FARIN, lawyer; b. Tehran, Iran; d. Ali and Azar Mirvahabi; m. Richard C. Powell; children: Bobby Naemi, Jimmy Naemi. Degree in Law, Tehran U., Iran, 1968; M of Comparative Law, Georgetown U., 1972; LLM, George Washington U., 1976; JSD, NYU, 1978; diploma, The Hague Acad. Internat. Law, 1983. Bar: Va. 1989, U.S. Dist. Ct. (ea. and we. dists.) Va. 1990, D.C. 1990, U.S. Dist. Ct. D.C. 1990, U.S. Supreme Ct. 1997. With Gold & Cutner, NYC, 1979-80; in-house counsel IRA Engring. and Constrn., Tehran, London, 1981-82; legal advisor Bank Markazi, Tehran, 1981-82; practiced law The Hague, The Netherlands, 1982-87; arbitrator Iran Air-Pan Am Arbitration Tribunal, Paris, 1984-87; legal cons. Rooney, Barry & Fogerty, Washington, 1987-88; atty. sole practice, Washington, 1989—. Law prof. No. Va. Law Sch., Alexandria, 1989-90; instr. Paralegal Inst., Arlington, Va., 1988-89; prof. Tehran U., 1982; panelist Am. Arbitration Assn.; guest speaker in field; life dep. gov. Am. Biog. Inst. Rsch. Assn., 19995—. Contbr. numerous articles to profl. jours. Named Maxplank fellow Maxplank Inst. of Internat. Law, 1986; recipient Clyde Eagleton award NYU, 1977, Woman of Yr. medallion honoring Cmty. Svc. and Profl. Achievement, 1995, Spl. Merit award DC Bar, 2005. Mem. ABA, Internat. Bar Assn., Arbitration Forum Inc., D.C. Bar Assn. (panelist client-atty. arbitration bd. 1990—), D.C. Bar & Lawyers Assn., Trial Lawyers Assn., Va. Bar Found., Am. Soc. Internat. Law, Am. Film Inst. The Kennedy Ctr. Avocations: reading, writing, Broadway shows, picnic, swimming. Office: 1629 K St NW Ste 300 Washington DC 20006 Office Phone: 703-534-6677.

MIRZA, LEONA LOUSIN, elementary school educator, director; b. Chgo., July 1, 1944; d. Max B. and Opal Lousin; m. David B. Mirza; children: Sara Anush, Elizabeth Ann. BA in Math., North Park Coll., Chgo., 1965; MA in Edn., Western Mich. U., Kalamazoo, 1967, EdD in Edn., 1972; cert. in computer studies, North Park Coll., 1983. Specialist in elem. curriculum and adminstrn. Tchr. Kalamazoo Pub. Schs., 1965-69; prof. math. edn. North Park U., Chgo., 1969-2001, asst. acad. dean, 1999—2001, chair dept. stats., 2004—; dir. Inst. for Internat. and Cultural Studies, 2001—06. Editor The Ill. Math. Tchr., 1992-95; contbr. articles to profl. jours. Chmn. adv. com. on edn. in Ill., 1975-77. Mem. Nat. Coun. Tchrs. Math., Ill. Coun. Tchrs. Math., Ill. Assn. Colls. of Tchr. Edn., Ill. Assn. Tchrs. Edn. in Pvt. Colls. (officer 1974-86). Home: 5241 N Sawyer Ave Chicago IL 60625-4715 Office: 3225 W Foster Ave Chicago IL 60625-4823 Business E-Mail: lmirza@northpark.edu.

MIRZA, MANSHA PARVEN QAMAR HUSAIN, public health service officer, consultant; MS in Occupl. Therapy, U. Ill., Chgo., 2004. Info. access cons. U. Ill., 2006—, postdoc. fellow, 2006—. Human rights educator Amnesty Internat., Chgo., 2004—04; Schweitzer fellow Health & Medicine Policy Rsch. Group, Chgo., 2008—; steering com. mem. Access Living Immigrants Disabilities Rights Project, Chgo., 2009—. Contbr. articles to profl. jours. (Chancellors Student Svc. award, 2005, Provosts award, 2008). Recipient Silver Jubilee Cash prize, Seth G.S. Med. Coll. & K.E.M. Hosp., 2002. Mem.: Soc. Disability Studies (Outstanding Svc. award 2005—07), Soc. Study Social Problems. Office: Univ Ill Chgo 1200 W Harrison St Ste 1190 Chicago IL 60607 Business E-Mail: mmirza2@uic.edu.

MIRZA, SOHAIL K., orthopedist, educator; MD, U. Colo. Sch. Medicine, 1989; MPH, U. Wash. Sch. Pub. Health, 2005. Cert. orthopaedic surgery 1994. Intern U. Wash. Hosp., 1989—90, resident, 1990—94; fellow Beth Israel Deaconess Med. Ctr., 1994—95; vice chmn. dept. orthopaedics Dartmouth-Hitchcock Med. Ctr. Office: Dartmouth-Hitchcock Medical Center Orthopaedic Surgery One Medical Center Dr Lebanon NH 03756 Office Phone: 603-650-2225. Office Fax: 603-650-6322.*

MIRZA, ZAKIR HUSSAIN, aerospace company consultant; b. Jullundar, India, Dec. 15, 1947; arrived in Can., 1971; came to US, 1977, naturalized, 1984. s. Mohammad Hussain and Kaniz Fatima Mirza; m. Naveeda J. Mirza, Aug. 26, 1977; children: Noreen, Hassan, Nadeem. BSc in Physics/Maths., U. Panjab, Lahore, Pakistan, 1968, MSc in Physics, 1970. Cert. pvt. pilot FAA, in project mgmt. Calif. Inst. Tech. Test engr. Bendix Corp., Windsor, Ont., Can., 1971-79; mgr. instrumentation engring. Nat. Tech. Sys., Saugus, Calif., 1979-82; sr. instrumentation engr. Wyle Labs., Norco, Calif., 1982-84; sr. test engr. Rohr Corp., Chula Vista, Calif., 1984-87; cons. various clients Hughes Space and Comm., El Segundo, Calif.; cons. Ledtronics, Torrance, Calif., Teledyne Continental Motors, Muskegon, Mich., FMC Corp., San Jose, Calif., Stewart and Stevenson, Houston, Thiokol Corp., Brigham City, Utah, 1987—2001; sr. staff engr. Boeing Satellite Devel. Ctr., El Segundo, 2001—. Fellow AIAA (assoc., past chmn. LA chpt.), Inst. Advancement Engring. Dfl. Muslim. Avocations: flying fixed wing aircraft, swimming. Office Phone: 310-416-3917. Business E-Mail: zakir.h.mirza@boeing.com.

MIRZADEH, SAED, nuclear scientist, researcher; BS in Chemistry, Nat. U. Iran, 1969; PhD in Phys. Chemistry, U. N.Mex., Albuquerque, 1978. Rsch. assoc. Med. Radioisotope Program Los Alamos Nat. Lab., N.Mex., 1979; rsch. assoc. Chemistry Dept. Brookhaven Nat. Lab., Upton, NY, 1980—81, asst. scientist, 1981, scientist Med. Dept., 1982—87; adj. assoc. prof. chemistry Natural Scis. Divsn. LI U., 1985—87; scientist radiation oncology NIH Nat. Cancer Inst., Bethesda, Md., 1987—89; sr. rschr. Nuc. Sci. and Tech. Divsn. Oak Ridge Nat. Lab., Tenn., 1989—. Vis. scientist Australian Nuc. Sci. and Tech. Orgn., 1993. Contbr. articles to sci. jours. Recipient Seaborg medal, Am. Nuc.

Soc., 2007. Office: Oak Ridge Nat Lab PO Box 2008 MS6229 Oak Ridge TN 37831-6229 Office Phone: 865-574-8399. Office Fax: 865-574-6226. E-mail: mirzadehs@ornl.gov.

MIRZAEI, AHMAD, electrical engineer; s. Safarali Mirzaei and Farkhondeh Abdollahi; m. Mercedeh Khajavikhan, Feb. 14, 2006. MS in Elec. Engring., Sharif U. Tech., 2002; PhD, UCLA, 2006. Sr. analog design engr. Novin Computer Co., Tehran, Iran, 2000—02; rsch. tchg. asst. UCLA, 2002—06; sr. RF analog engr. Wilinx Co., LA, 2005—06; staff scientist Broadcom Corp., Irvine, Calif., 2007—08, sr. staff scientist, 2008—. Contbr. articles to profl. jours. Recipient Silver medal in Nat. Math. Olympiad, Min. Edn., 1996, Outstanding Student Designer award, Analog Devices, Inc., 2003. Mem.: IEEE. Achievements include patents for more than 25 issued and pending patent applications; development of new methods to analyze locked and coupled oscillators; discovery of multiple-node injection to widen lock-range of injection-locked dividers; invention of a novel second-order anti-aliasing pre-filter for SDR receivers and new technique to integrate SAW filter function inside ICs.

MIRZAEI, SHAHNAM, engineering educator; m. Farahnaz Nezhad; 1 child, Viyana. BSc, U. Thhran, 1993; PhD, U. Calif., Santa Barbara, 2008. Field applications engr. Nu Horizond Electronics, Westlake Village, Calif., 1999—2005; lectr. Calif. State U., Northridge, 2003—. Recipient 2nd prize, Calif. State U., 1999. Home: 19200 Hamlin St 1 Reseda CA 91335

MIRZAI, PIROOZ (VICTOR MIRZAI), architect, educator, consultant; b. Tehran, Feb. 3, 1953; came to U.S., 1971; s. Ahmad and Akhtar Mirzai; m. Sepideh Kardar; children: Arman, Shawyan. BArch, So. U., 1977; BS in Architecture and Art, La. State U., 1977; MArch, Tulane U., 1980, postgrad.; cert. in photography, N.Y. Inst., 1980. Registered architect; lic. architect in Middle East. Architect August Perez & Assocs., New Orleans, 1977-78; resident architect, project mgr. Charity Hosp., New Orleans, 1978-79; architect Daniel, Mann, Johnson, Mendenhall, New Orleans, 1981-83; program dir., instr. Meadows Draughon Coll., New Orleans, 1977-83; chmn., instr. Cameron Coll., New Orleans, 1983-87; prin. PVM Cons., New Orleans, 1985—; prof., head dept. architecture Delgado Community Coll., New Orleans, 1983—. Faculty senator, Delgado Community Coll. Project dir. bldg. design/planning Home Builders New Orleans, 1990, Preservation Resource Orgn., 1989; author, editor Delarchi News, 1988; contbr. artiles to profl. jours. Recipient Archtl. Design Honor award AIA/La. Archtl. Assn., 1975, Excellence in Tch. award/Disting. Professorship (DCC), 1991, Home Builders award, 1990, Prince Charles Found. cert., 2008; nominee US Prof. Delagdo. Mem. AAUP (founder Delgado chpt., pres. 1987-89, exec. mem., historian La. State conf. 1989-91), Assn. Coll. Schs. Architecture, Constrn. Specification Inst., Nat. Assoc. Home Builders (Outstanding Educator award 2003), Soc. Archtl. Historians, Nat. Trust for Hist. Preservation, Am. Tech. Edn. Assn. (La. Educator, Meritorious Commendation Professorship Delgado CC, Constrn. Spesification Inst. Merit award, New Orleans Mayor Commendation award, Build award Am. Inst. Archs. Constrn. Design), Preservation Resource Ctr. Avocations: photography, writing, sports. Home: PO Box 6016 Metairie LA 70009-6016 Home Phone: 504-975-5631; Office Phone: 504-671-6184. Home Fax: 504-483-1847. Personal E-mail: pvictormirzai@yahoo.com. Business E-Mail: pmirza@dcc.edu.

MIRZAKHANI, MARYAM, mathematician; b. Tehran, Iran, May 1977; BS in Math., Sharif U. Tech., Tehran, Iran, 1999; PhD in Math., Harvard U., Cambridge, Mass., 2004. Postdoctoral rschr. dept. math. Harvard U., Cambridge, Mass.; rsch. fellow Clay Math. Inst., Cambridge, Mass., 2004—; asst. prof. math. Princeton U., NJ. Contbr. articles to profl. jours. Recipient Blumenthal award, Am. Math. Soc., 2009; named one of Brilliant 10, Popular Sci. mag., 2005. Office: Dept Math Princeton U 904 Fine Hall Princeton NJ 08544 Office Phone: 609-258-4236. E-mail: mmirzakh@princeton.edu.*

MISA, KENNETH FRANKLIN, management consultant; b. Jamaica, NY, Sept. 24, 1939; s. Frank J. and Mary M. (Soszka) M. BS in Psychology cum laude, Purdue U., 1963; PhD in Psychology, St. John's U., 1966. Cert. mgmt. cons.; lic. psychologist, Calif. Staff psychologist Rohrer, Hibler & Replogle, LA, 1966-67; assoc. A.T. Kearney, Inc., LA, 1968-71, sr. assoc., 1972-74, prin., 1975-78, v.p., ptnr., 1979-86; pres. HR Cons. Group, 1987—. Mem. APA, Am. Psychol. Soc., Calif. State Psychol. Assn., Soc. for Human Resources Mgmt., Human Resources Planning Soc., Indsl. Rels. Rsch. Assn., Soc. for Indsl. and Orgnl. Psychology, World Affairs Coun. L.A., Town Hall So. Calif., Glendale C. of C., Jonathan Club. Republican. Roman Catholic. Home: One Bristol Ct Rancho Mirage CA 92270 Home Phone: 818-261-9972; Office Phone: 818-241-0060. Home Fax: 323-254-8553. Personal E-mail: kfmhrcg@aol.com.

MISAKIAN, JO ELLEN PRIEST, school librarian; d. Frederick and Velma Priest; m. John L. Misakian, Nov. 3, 1956; children: Johnny Lee, Jeffrey Dale, James Kevin. BS, N.Y. Inst. Tech., NYC, 1992; MLS, San Jose State U., 1993; cert. in tchg., Nat. U., Fresno, Calif., 1994; cert. in libr. media svc., San Jose State U., 1994. Libr. technician Sanger (Calif.) Unified Sch. Dist., 1970—94; libr. media coord. Fresno County Office of Edn., 1994—99; libr. media program dir. Fresno Pacific U., 9999—, interim dean Sch. Edn., 2005—08. Mem. adv. bd. Infopeople, Calif., 2002—, Ame Nixon Ctr. for Study of Children's Lit., Fresno, 2002—. Mem. adv. bd.: Tchr. Libr. Jour., 2002—; author: The Essential School Library Glossary, 2004; contbr. articles to profl. jours. Chair Ctrl. Valley Libr. Com., 2000—, Fresno Reads Roundtable, 2001—04; ex-dir. Heartland Regional Libr. Network, 2002—, William Saroyan Soc. Bd., 2006—. Mem.: ALA, Calif. Sch. Libr. Assn. (pres. 2000—01, chair libr. standards task force 2002—04, Profl. Svc. award 2005). Republican. Protestant. Home: 253 N DeWolf Fresno CA 93727 Office: Fresno Pacific Univ Sch Edn 1717 S Chestnut Fresno CA 93702 Office Phone: 559-453-2291. Office Fax: 559-453-7168. Business E-Mail: jmisakian@fresno.edu.

MISAWA, MITSURU, finance educator; b. Ina-shi, Japan, Sept. 18, 1936; came to U.S., 1996; s. Fukuji and Kaneyo (Haba) M.; m. Kuniko Ishii, Mar. 6, 1965; children: Anne Megumi, Marie Lei. LLB, Tokyo U., 1960; LLM, Harvard U., 1964; MBA, U. Hawaii, 1965; PhD, U. Mich., 1967. Officer Indsl. Bank Japan, Tokyo, 1960-89; dir. IBJ Lease, Tokyo, 1989, pres. NYC, 1989—; prof. fin. U. Hawaii, Honolulu, 1996—, dir. ctr. Japanese global investment fin., 1998—. Mem. Waialae Country Club, Tokyo Am. Club. Avocation: golf. Home: Imperial Plaza 725 Kapiolani Blvd Apt 811 Honolulu HI 96813 Office: Univ Hawaii Dept fin Econs Instn 2404 Maile Way Honolulu HI 96822-2223 E-mail: misawa@busadm.cba.hawaii.edu.

MISCHKA, JAMES, fashion designer; b. Burlington, Wis., Dec. 23, 1960; BA in Mgmt. and Art Hist., Rice Univ., Houston, 1982; BFA in Fashion Design, Parsons Sch. Design, NYC, 1985. Apprenticeship with Yves St. Laurent, Paris; apprenticeship with Willi Smith NYC, 1985—88; co-founder, ptnr. Badgley Mischka, NYC, 1985—; ptnr. Badgley Mischka Dress, NYC. Recipient Mouton Cadet Young Designers award, 1989, Dallas Internat. Apparel Rising Star award, 1992; named Designer of Yr., Am. Apparel and Footwear Assn., 2008; named one of Top 10 American Designers, Vogue. Office: c/o Ogan Dallal Assocs 1185 Ave of Americas 20th Fl New York NY 10036

MISCHKE, FREDERICK CHARLES, retired manufacturing executive; b. Benton Harbor, Mich., Sept. 21, 1930; s. Fred William and Clara Adeline (Ruhno) M.; m. Kathleen Ann Schultz, Nov. 19, 1955 (dec. Aug. 1980); children: Stephanie Ann, Michael Frederick (dec. Oct. 12, 1996), Eric William; m. Lori Ann Leonard, Dec. 23, 1983. AA, Lake Mich. Coll., 1956; BBA, Western Mich. U., 1958. CPA, Ind., Mich. Staff acct. Lybrand, Ross Bros. & Montgomery, Chgo., 1958-63, supr. acctg. Niles, Mich., 1963-65; v.p., treas. Skyline Corp., Elkhart, Ind., 1965-91, ret., 1991. Vol. Svc. Corps. Ret. Execs., 1992-2007, local v.p., 1993-99, treas. 2000-2006; chmn. Meml. Endowment Fund Luth. Ch., 1995-2006. Mem. AICPA, Ind. Assn. CPAs (Civic Achievement award, 1976), Mich. Assn. CPAs, Fin. Execs. Inst. (Michiana chpt. pres. 1974-75), Elcona Country Club (pres. 1975), Rotary (local pres. 1976-77). Republican. Lutheran. Avocations: photography, boating, golf. Home: 23322 Greenleaf Blvd Elkhart IN 46514-4508 Personal E-mail: freddycm@aol.com.

MISCIK, JAMI A., diversified financial services company executive, former federal agency administrator; b. Chgo., 1958; BA in Polit. Sci. & Economics with honors, Pepperdine U., Malibu, Calif., 1980; MA, U. Denver Sch. Internat. Studies. Joined as econ. analyst CIA, 1983, exec. asst. to dep. dir. ctrl intelligence, 1996—97, dep. dir. nonproliferation ctr., 1998—99, dir. office transnational issues, 1999—2001, assoc. dep. dir. intelligence, 2001—02, dep. dir. intelligence, 2002—05; mng. dir., global head sovereign risk Lehman Brothers Holdings, Inc., NYC, 2005—08; global head sovereign risk Barclays Capital, 2008—. Dir. intelligence progs. Nat. Security Coun., Washington, 1995—96. Bd. dirs. Am. Ditchley Found. Recipient Disting. Intelligence medal, Def. Intelligence Agy. Dir.'s medal, Directorate Ctrl. Intelligence Dir.'s medal, Intelligence Commendation madal. Mem.: Coun. Fgn. Rels. (bd. dirs.), UN Assn.-USA (bd. dirs.). Office: Barclays Capital Inc N Am Hdqs 200 Park Ave Fl 35 New York NY 10166*

MISE, JESSE SHERDEN, structural engineer, consultant; b. Jonesville, Va., July 13, 1933; s. Clabe Moss and Gladys Elizabeth (Orr) M.; m. Betty Joy Curtiss, July 8, 1984; children: Nancy Miller, Linda Andrews, Doug Hinshaw. BS in Math., Tenn. Tech., 1957. Registered profl. engr., Tenn., Mo. Road designer Va. Dept. Hwys., Petersburg, 1958-64; structural designer various archtl., engring. firms, 1964-67; structural engr. Combustion Engring., Windsor, Conn., 1967-72, Tenn. Eastman, Kingsport, 1973-76, TVA, Knoxville, 1976-87, ABB Environ., Knoxville, 1988-91; cons. Jesse S. Mise, P.E., Knoxville, 1992—; chief engr. James Thomas Engring., Knoxville, 1992—. Author: Engineers Guide to Unusual Opportunities, 1972. Mem. Patriots of East Tenn., Knoxville, 1996—. Mem. ASCE, Nat. Coun. of Examiners for Engring. and Surveying, 1993—. Home and Office: 5704 Melstone Rd Knoxville TN 37912-4629 Personal E-mail: alt2000tec@aol.com, jessemise@aol.com.

MISEMER, SARAH M., theater educator; b. Kans. City, Mo., Oct. 15, 1972; d. Kent A. and Cathy S. Misemer; life ptnr. John P. Seigler. BA, U. Kans., Lawrence, 1994, MA, 1997, PhD, 2001. Vis. asst. prof. U. Puget Sound, Tacoma, 2001—04; asst. prof. Tex. A&M U., Coll. Sta., 2004—. Contbr. articles to profl. publs. Bd. mem. Pk. Meadow Subdivsn., Bryan, Tex., 2008; mem. adv. com. Melbern G. Glasscock Ctr. Humanities, Coll. Sta., 2007. Mem.: MLA. Office: Tex A&M Univ 4238 Tamu College Station TX 77843-4238

MISER, ANN, retired government researcher; b. Balt., Jan. 29, 1935; d. Robert and Lucile Miser; 1 adopted child, Janna. BS in Fine Arts and Edn., U. NC, Chapel Hill, 1956; student, Earlham Coll., Richmond, 1952—54, Johns Hopkins U., Balt., 1960. Art tchr. Md. State Dept. Edn., Balt., 1958—60, NY State Dept. Edn., NYC, 1961—62; owner Lady Balt. Temporary Agy. and Miss Liberty Inc., London, 1963—75; US govt. rschr. Commerce Dept., Phila., 1975—2005; ret., 2005. Mem.: U. NC Alumni Assn., Multiple Myeloma Soc. Democrat. Avocations: travel, reading, sports. Home: 6101 Allwood Ct Baltimore MD 21210

MISHAAN, EMILIO, transplant surgeon, educator; b. Guatemala, Guatemala, Aug. 20, 1960; s. Ezra Mishaan and Ivonne Smeke; 1 child, Isabella. BS, U. del Valle, Guatemala, 1981; MD, U. Francisco Manoquin, Guatemala, 1985. Chief resident surgery Hosp. San Juan de Dios, Guatemala, 1989—90, emergency surgeon, 1992—94; gen. surgeon Hosp. Militar, Guatemala, 1990—99; prof. surgery U. Francisco Marroquin, Guatemala, 1992—; transplant surgeon Hosp. San Juan de Dios, 1994—. CEO Venoclinic, Guatemala, 2001—06, Guatemala Laser Inst. Fellow: ACS, SAGES. Jewish. Avocations: running, hunting, fishing. Home: Km 19 9 Carretera El Salvador Guatemala City Guatemala Office: Gae 3-22 Z10 of 403 CMII Guatemala City Guatemala Personal E-mail: emishaans@yahoo.com.

MISHCHENKO, EUGENE, physics professor; b. Barnaul, Russia, 1974; PhD, Landau Inst. Theoretical Physics, Moscow. Rsch. assoc. Leiden U., Netherlands, 1998—2000, Harvard U., Cambridge, Mass., 2002—04; postdoc. rschr. U. Colo. Bell Labs., Boulder, 2000—02; assoc. prof. physics U. Utah, Salt Lake City, 2004—, assoc. chair, 2008—. Achievements include research in condensed matter physics. Office: Univ Utah Dept Physics 115 S 1400 E Salt Lake City UT 84112 Personal E-mail: eugene.mishchenko@gmail.com.

MISHEL, LAWRENCE, think-tank executive, economist, researcher; BA, Pa. State U., 1974; MA, Am. U., 1977; PhD in Econs., U. Wis., 1982. Prof. of Econs. Cornell U., Ithaca, N.Y., 1982-83; economist UAW, Detroit, 1983-85, IUD, AFL-CIO, Washington, 1986-87; rsch. dir. Econ. Policy Inst., Washington, 1987, v.p., pres., 2002—. Spkr. in field. Co-author: The State of Working America, 1991; contbr. articles to profl. jours. Office: Econ Policy Inst Ste 300, East Tower 1333 H St, NW Washington DC 20005-4707 Office Phone: 202-775-8810. Office Fax: 202-775-0819.*

MISHELEVICH, DAVID JACOB, medical products executive; b. Pitts., Jan. 26, 1942; s. Benjamin and Sarah (Bachrach) M.; m. Bonnie Gray McKim, Dec. 6, 1981; 1 child, Cory Jane. BS in Physics, U. Pitts., 1962; MD, Johns Hopkins U., 1966, PhD in Biomed. Engring., 1970. Lic., Md., Tex. Intern in medicine Balt. City Hosps. (now The John Hopkins Bayview Med. Ctr.), 1966-67; active duty USPHS, 1967—69, inactive reserve, 1969—; staff assoc. Nat. Inst. Neurol. Diseases and Stroke, NIH, Bethesda, Md., 1967-69; exec. v.p. Nat. Ednl. Consultants, Balt., 1971-72; prof., dept. chairperson, dir. med. computing resources ctr. U. Tex. Health Sci. Ctr., Dallas, 1972-82; attending physician/sr. attending physician internal med. Dallas County Hosp., Dist. Parkland Meml. Hosp., 1973-82; v.p. computer and software tech. EAN-TECH, Mountain View, Calif., 1983-84; CEO Garden Gate Software, Cupertino, Calif., 1984-86; dir., then v.p. and gen. mgr. applications and rsch. divsn. IntelliCorp, Inc., Mountain View, 1986-89; v.p. mktg. and sales Viewpoint Engring., Mountain View, 1989-90; v.p. engring. AirWays Med. Techs., Inc., Palo Alto, Calif., 1991-93; dir., then v.p. R&D, chief tech. officer Circadian, Inc., San Jose, Calif., 1993-95, v.p., gen. mgr. AirWays Asthma Ctrs. divsn., 1995-96; CEO Sterling Healthcare Outcomes, Inc., Cupertino, 1996—2002, Playa del Rey, Calif., 2002—; founder, exec. v.p., chief tech. officer QENM.com, 1999-2001; chief tech. officer HealthShore, Inc., 2001—04; lead technologist Outbreak! Music Sys., 2002—; chief tech. officer TeleCath, 2003—05. Pres. Mishelevich Assocs., Dallas, 1982-83, Cupertino, 1990-91, cons. prof. of neurosurgery Stanford U. Sch. Medicine, 2003-; dir. biomed. engring. and med. affairs Aubrey Group, Inc., Irvine, Calif., 2005—; mem. biomed. libr. rev. com. NIH-Nat. Libr. Medicine, 1978-82; cons. in field. Former tech. reviewer IBM Sys. Jour., Jour. of AMA; rev. IEEE computer Soc. Internet, 2001-03; contbr. numerous articles to profl. jours.; patentee in field. V.p. Dallas chpt. Am. Jewish Congress, 1980-84, Am. Jewish Fund, 1980-81; pres. Westport Bch. Club Villas, Homeowners Assn., 2003-06. Fellow Am. Coll. Med. Informatics; mem. AAAS, IEEE, IEEE Computer Soc. (exec. bd. tech. com. on computational medicine 1981-83), Am. Assn. for Artificial Intelligence, Assn. for Computing Machinery (chair Dallas chpt. 1974-75), Am. Med. Informatics Assn., Internat. Tandem Users Group (past pres.), Model T Ford Club of Am., Am. Radio Relay League (life), Phi Beta Kappa, Omicron Kappa. Democrat. Jewish. Home and Office: 7301 Vista del Mar #B111 Playa Del Rey CA 90293 Office Phone: 310-305-2791. Personal E-mail: david@mishelevich.com. *Working with computers for some forty-five years has made me particularly sensitive to human needs and productivity. Two principles in which I believe are the human resources principle (maximize people's strengths and minimize or neutralize their weaknesses so they perform personally and professionally better than they would otherwise expect of themselves), and the optimality principle (I would rather do a 92% job in two weeks than a 97% job in 2 years).*

MISHIN, EVGENY VILENOVICH, physicist; b. Irkutsk, Russia, Mar. 16, 1948; s. Vilen Moiseevich and Ninel Alekseevna (Kiseleva) M.; m. Lyubov Petrovna Maksimova, July 8, 1967; children: Dmitrii, Anna. MSc in Physics, Novosibirsk State U., Russia, 1971; PhD, Izmiran, Troitsk, Russia, 1974, DrSc, 1985, prof., 1991. Jr. scientist Izmiran, 1974-82, sr. scientist, 1982-86, head lab., 1986-92; vis. prof. Max Planck Inst. Aeronomie, Lindau, Germany, 1992—99. Chmn. Ionosphere sect. Geophys. Com., Moscow, 1989-93; mem. Coun. Radiowave Propagation, Russian Acad. Scis., 1989-93; vis. scholar MIT Haystack observatory, Mass., 1999-2001; sr. scientist Boston Coll., 2001-08; sr. physicist Air Force Rsch. Lab., 2008-. Author: Interaction of Electron Beams with the Ionospheric Plasma, 1989, Plasma Effects of Suprathermal Electrons in the Ionosphere, 1990; contbr. articles to profl. jours. Mem. European Geophys. Soc., Polish Soc. Applied Electromagnetism, Am. Geophys. Union. Avocation: tennis.

MISHKIN, BARBARA FRIEDMAN, lawyer; b. Phila., Feb. 19, 1936; d. Maurice Harold and Gertrude (Sanders) F.; m. Martin S. Thaler, Mar. 22, 1958 (div. 1970); children: Diane Sanders, Paul Sanders, David Emile, Amy Suzanne; m. Mortimer Mishkin, May 27, 1971. AB, Mount Holyoke Coll., 1957; MA, Yale U., 1958; JD, Am. U., 1981. Bar: D.C. 1982, U.S. Supreme Ct. 1989, U.S. Ct. Appeals (4th cir.) 1995. Rsch. psychologist NIMH, Bethesda, Md., 1968-69; spl. asst. to chief judge U.S. Ct. Appeals (D.C. cir.), Washington, 1970-71; spl. asst. to scientific dir. Nat. Inst. Child Health, Bethesda, 1971-74; asst. staff dir. Nat. Commn. for the Protection of Human Subjects, Washington, 1974-78; staff dir. Ethics Adv. Bd. HEW, Washington, 1978-80; dep. dir. Pres.' Commn. on Ethics in Medicine and Rsch., Washington, 1980-83; assoc. Hogan and Hartson, Washington, 1983-89, counsel, 1990-93, ptnr., 1994—2006, of counsel, 2006—. Cons. Ctr. for Law and Health Scis., Boston, 1970-73; cons., lectr. Johns Hopkins U. Sch. of Medicine, Balt., 1971-73; bd. dirs. Bon Secours Health Systems, Inc., Columbia, Md., 1984-90. Contbr. numerous articles on health law, med. ethics and biomed. research to jours. in field. Mem. policy bd. Legal Counsel for the Elderly, Washington, 1984-88, vice chair, 1988-90; trustee Mt. Holyoke Coll., 1985-90; mem. Mayor's Adv. Task Force on Hospice Licensure, Washington, 1985-87; bd. dirs. Hebrew Home Greater Washington, 1987-91. Recipient Lifetime Achievement award, Health Improvement Inst., 2004. Mem. ABA (chair sect. on health and environment 1988-92, chair com. on regulating rsch. 1996-98), D.C. Bar Assn. (subcom. rights of the elderly and the handicapped 1985-92, Pro Bono Atty. Yr. 1988), AAAS (com. on sci. freedom and responsibility 1986-92, AAAS/ABA Nat. Conf. Lawyers and Scientists 1992, ABA co-chair 1993-97), Am. Soc. Law, Medicine and Ethics (bd. dirs. 1995-98). Home: 5610 Wisconsin Ave Apt 402 Chevy Chase MD 20815-4429 Office: Hogan & Hartson Columbia Sq 555 13th St Washington DC 20004-1109 Home Phone: 301-652-0490; Office Phone: 202-637-5680. Business E-Mail: bfmishkin@hhlaw.com.

MISHKIN, FREDERIC STANLEY, economics professor, former federal official; b. NYC, Jan. 11, 1951; s. Sidney and Jeanne (Silverstein) M.; m. Sally A. Hammond; children: Matthew, Laura. Student, Oxford U., Eng., 1971-72; BS in Economics, MIT, 1973, PhD in Economics, 1976. Tchg. asst. MIT, 1974—76; asst. prof. U. Chgo., 1976-81, assoc. prof., 1981-83; vis. assoc. prof., dept. economics and dept. fin., Kellogg Grad. Sch. Mgmt. Northwestern U., Evanston, Ill., 1982-83; faculty rsch. fellow Nat. Bur. Econ. Rsch., Cambridge, Mass., 1979—80, rsch. assoc., 1980—83; prof. economics Columbia U. Grad. Sch. Bus., NYC, 1983-91, A. Barton Hepburn prof. econs., 1991—99, Alfred Lerner prof. Banking and Fin. Institutions, 1999—; exec. v.p. and dir. rsch. Fed. Res. Bank NY, NYC, 1994—97; mem. bd. govs. Fed. Res. Sys., Washington, 2006—08. Economist, bd. govs., Fed. Res. System, Washington, 1977, acad. cons. bd. govs., 1993, vis. scholar, Divsn. Internat. Fin., bd. govs., 1993; mem. Conf. on Income and Wealth, 1984-; vis. scholar, Inst. for Fiscal and Monetary Policy, Ministry of Fin., Japan, Tokyo, 1986, Res. Bank of Australia, 1994, Bank of Eng., 2001; mem. Brookings Panel on Econ. Activity, Washington, 1977-78; mem. acad. adv. panel Fed. Res. Bank of N.Y., NYC, 1990-94, 1997-, academic cons., 1997-; vis. prof. Princeton U., 1990-91; mem., Ctr. for Latin Am. Economics, Fed. Res. Bank Dallas, 1996-; Harry Johnson Lecture, Money Macroeconomics and Finance Rsch. Group Annual Conf., 1993; hon. prof. Renmin (Peoples) U. China, 1999; Homer Jones Lecture, 2000; Henry George Lecture, Univ. Scranton, 2004; John Kuszczak Meml. Lecture: Bank of Can., 2005; JMCB-FDIC invited lecture, 2005; chmn., External Evaluation Com. for Rsch. Activities, Internat. Monetary Fund, 1999; advisor, Inst. Contemporary Fin., Shanghai Jiao Tong U., 2000-, Bank of Korea, Inst. for Monetary and Econ. Rsch., 2005-06; mem. Financial Economists Roundtable, 2001-04; mem. internat. adv. bd., financial supervisory svc., S. Korea, 2000-01; vis. rsch. fellow, The World Bank, 2000-01; sr. fellow, FDIC Ctr. for Banking Rsch., 2003-. Author: A Rational Expectations Approach to Macroeconometrics, 1983, The Economics of Money, Banking and Financial Markets, 1986, 4th edit. 1995, Money, Interest Rates and Inflation, 1993, Financial Markets, Institutions and Money, 1995, also articles; mem. editl. bd. American Economic Review, 1982-85, journal of International Money and Finance, 1992-, Fianance India, 1999-, Ctrl. Bank of Chile Series, Central Banking Analysis, and Economic Policy, 2001-; assoc. editor Journal of Business and Economic Statistics, 1986-93, Journal Applied Econometrics, 1985-2000, Journal Money, Credit and Banking, 1992-, Journal

Economic Perspectives, 1994-2004; mem. adv. bd. International Finance, 1997-, Macroeconomics and Monetary Economics Abstracts, 1996-; editor Fed. Res. Bank NY, Economic Policy Review, 1994-97, mem. editl. bd., 1997- NSF Grad. Fellowship, 1973—76, Alfred P. Sloan Found. Fellowship, 1982—86. Mem. Am. Econ. Assn., Am. Fin. Assn., Ea. Econ. Assn. (v.p., 2002-03, pres.-elect, 2003-04, pres. 2004-05), Phi Beta Kappa, Sigma Xi. Avocations: sailing, cross country skiing, long distance cycling, reading. Office: Columbia U Grad Bus Sch 3022 Broadway Uris Hall 619 New York NY 10027 Business E-Mail: fsm3@columbia.edu.

MISHKIN, MICHAEL LAWRENCE, psychologist, educator; b. Staten Island, NY, Feb. 24, 1951; s. Arthur E. and Arlene Rubinstein Mishkin. BS in Psychology, U. Fla., Gainesville, 1972; MS in Psychology, U. Ala., Birmingham, 1978; EdS in Sch. Psychology, U. Fla., Gainesville, 1981, PhD in Sch. Psychology, 1987. Lic. psychologist Fla., cert. Fla., nat. cert. sch. psychologist. Ednl. diagnostician Marion County Pub. Schs., Ocala, Fla., 1976, 1978—80, sch. psychologist, 1980—; pvt. practice psychologist NCS Counseling and Devel. Ctr., Tavares, Fla., 2005—. Adj. prof. Argosy U., Sarasota, Fla., 2005—. Homeless children's tutor Marion County Pub. Schs., 2002—; mem. leadership coun. Take Stock in Children, Ocala, 1997—; pres. bd. dirs. Cornerstone Sch., Ocala, 1990. Named Student Svcs. Worker of Yr., Marion County Sch. Sys., 1980. Mem.: Internat. Assn. Sch. Psychologists, Nat. Assn. Sch. Psychologists, Fla. Assn. Sch. Psychologists, Marion Counseling Assn. (sec., treas. pres., Sch. Psychologist of Yr. 1986—87). Republican. Jewish. Avocations: reading, games, theater. Home: 2325 SE 19th Cir Ocala FL 34471 Office: Marion County Pub Schs 1517 SE 30th Ave Ste 5 Ocala FL 34471

MISHKIN, MORTIMER, neuropsychologist; b. Fitchburg, Mass., Dec. 13, 1926; AB, Dartmouth Coll., 1946; MA, McGill U., Montreal, Can., 1949, PhD, 1951; DSc (hon.), McGill U., 2004. Asst. in research and physiology and psychiatry Yale U. Med. Sch., New Haven, 1949-51; research assoc. Inst. of Living, Hartford-Conn. and NYU Bellevue Med. Ctr., NYC, 1951-55; research psychologist, sect. on neuropsychology NIMH, Bethesda, Md., 1955-75, research physiologist, Lab. of Neuropsychology, 1976-78, chief sect. cerebral mechanisms Lab. of Neuropsychology, 1979-80, chief Lab. of Neuropsychology, 1980-97, assoc. dir. basic rsch. DIRP, 1994-97, chief sect. cognitive neuroscience, 1997—, acting chief, lab neuropsychology, 2005—. Part-time instr. psychology Howard U., 1956-58; vis. scientist Nencki Inst. Exptl. Biology, Warsaw, Poland, winter 1958, 68, Tokyo Met. Inst. Neuroscis., summer 1978, Oxford U. Dept. Exptl. Psychology, summer 1979, Inst. Child Health U. Coll. London, 1993, vis. prof., 2000-; mem. psychol. scis. panel NIH, 1959-61, exptl. psychology study sect., 1965-69; mem. NIMH Assembly of Scientists Council, 1962-64, 72-74; mem. NIMH Scientist Promotion Rev. Com., 1984-86; mem. adv. com. Cognitive Neurosci. Inst., 1982-86; mem. NIH Fogart Internat. Scholars-in-Residence Adv. Panel, 1985-89, McDonnell Found. Study panel, 1987-89; adv. bd. McDonnell-Pew Program Cognitive Neurosci., 1989-94; cons. Developmental Cognitive Neurosci. Unit, Inst. Child Health, U. Coll. London, 1990—, vis. prof., 2000—; active Human Frontier Sci. Program, 1992-94, chmn. 1993; adv. bd. Ctr. for the Neural Basis of Cognition, U. Pitts. and Carnegie Mellon U., 1994-96, chair, 1999, 2004; adv. bd. La. State U. Neurosci. Ctr., 1994-96, Frontier Rsch. Program, RIKEN, Japan, 1994-96, Zanvyl Krieger Mind-Brain Inst., Johns Hopkins U., 1994-2000, Cognitive and Behavioral Neurosci. Panel, SUNY, Stony Brook, 1996, Mental Health and Neurosci. Clin. Rsch. Ctr., U. N.C., Chapel Hill, 1996-98, Krasnow Inst., George Mason U., Fellow Mentor Program, 1997-2002. Cons. editor Jour. Comparative and Physiol. Psychology, 1963-73, Exptl. Brain Rsch., 1965—, Brain Rsch., 1974-78, Neuropsychologia, 1963-92, Human Neurobiology, 1981-87, Jour. Cognitive Neurosci., 1989—, Jour. NIH Rsch., 1989-97, Cerebral Cortex, 1990-95, Advances in Neurobiology, 1990—, Handbook Behavioral Neurology, 1991—, Current Opinion in Neurobiology, 1991—, Neurobiology of Learning and Memory, 1992—, Learning and Memory, 1993—, Jour. Internat. Neuropsychol. Soc., 1995-99, Internat. Encyclopedia of the Social and Behavioral Scis., 1998-2002; reviewing editors Sci., 1985-93; assoc. editor Neuroreport, 1990-2000; contbr. numerous articles to profl. jours., also abstracts and book revs. Served to lt. (j.g.) USNR. Recipient U.S. Presdl. Disting. Rank award, 1992, Karl Spencer Lashley prize Am. Philos. Soc., 1996, Found. Ipsen Neuronal Plasticity prize, 1995, Med. Rsch. award Met. Life Found., 2000. Fellow AAAS (chair-elect 1990-91, chair 1991-92, past chair 1992-93), APA Assn. (officer, divsn. 6 mem. at large 1964-66, coun. rep. 1967-69, pres. 1968-69, Disting. Scientific Contribution award, 1985); mem. NAS (officer, sect. 52 chmn. 1989-92), Ea. Psychol. Assn., Internat. Brain Research Orgn. (officer, rep.-at-large governing coun. 1993-98), Internat. Neuropsychol. Soc., Internat. Neuropsychol. Symposium, Internat. Primatological Soc., Internat. Soc. Neuroethology, Cognitive Neuroscience Soc. (Hermann von Helmholtz award, 1989) Soc. Exptl. Psychologists (Howard Crosby Warren medal 1998), Soc. Neurosci. (officer, pres.-elect 1985-86, pres. 1986-87, past pres. 1987-88), Inst. Medicine, Brazilian Acad. Sci., Sigma Xi, Phi Beta Kappa. Achievements includes research in behavioral and cognitive neuroscience in primates. Office: NIMH Lab Neuropsychology 49 Convent Dr Msc 4415 Bldg 49 Bethesda MD 20892-0001 Business E-Mail: mishkinm@mail.nih.gov.

MISHLER, CLIFFORD LESLIE, publisher; b. Vandalia, Mich., Aug. 11, 1939; s. Nelson Howard and Lily Mae (Young) M.; m. Sandra Rae Knutson, Dec. 21, 1963 (dec. July 8, 1972); m. Sylvia M. Leer, Feb. 27, 1976; children: Sheila, Sharon, Susan. Student, Northwestern U., 1957-58. Author, pub. ann. edits. Ann. Studies U.S. and Can. Commemorative Medals and Tokens, 1958-63; assoc. editor Numismatic News, Krause Publs., Iola, Wis., 1963-64, editor, 1964-66, numismatic editor all publs., 1966-75, exec. v.p., pub. all numismatic publs., 1975-78, exec. v.p., pub. all products, 1978-88, sr. v.p., pub. all Numismatic products, 1988-89, sr. v.p. ops., 1989-90; pres. Krause Publs., Iola, Wis., 1991-99, chmn. bd. dir., 2000—02, numismatic cons., 2002—05; dir. numismatic devel. Whitman Pub., 2005—. Bd. dirs. First State Bank Iola, 1972-83, Scandinavia Telephone Co., 1981-97, TDS Telecom cmty. bd., 1997-2000; mem. coins and medals adv. panel Am. Revolution Bicentennial Commn., 1970-75; mem. ann. assay commn. U.S. Mint, 1973. Co-author: Standard Catalog of World Coins, ann. 1972-2005; contbr. articles New Book Knowledge, ann. 1969-81. Co-founder Iola Old Car Show, Inc., 1972, ex-officio dir., 1985—2003; mem. Wis. Commemorative Quarter Coun., 2001—03; bd. dirs. William R. Higgins, Jr. Found., 1991—; chmn. fund drive Iola-Scandinavia Cmty. Fitness and Aquatic Ctr., 1999—2001. Recipient The Internat. Vreneli Preistrager: The "Friendly Prize" for lifetime numismatic achievements, Munzen-Revue, Basel, Switzerland, 2001, Numis. Amb. award, Numis. News/Balt., Md., 2003. Fellow Am. Numismatic Soc. (life, coun. mem. 1997-2003, trustee 2003—); mem. Am. Numismatic Assn. (life, bd. govs. 2007—, Merit medal 1983, Farran Zerbe Meml. Disting Svc. award 1984, Glen Smedley meml. dedicated svcs. award 1991, Lifetime Achievement award 1997, named Numismatist of Yr. 2002, named to Hall Fame 2004, Burnett Anderson Meml. award for Excellence in Numismatic writing, 2005), Token and Medal Soc. (life, pres. 1976-78, editor jour. 1964-68, Disting. Svc. award 1966, 80), Numismatists of Wis. (life, pres. 1974-76, Meritorious Svc. award 1972), Soc. Internat. Numismatics (award of excellence 1981), Blue Ridge Numismatic Assn. (life, hall of fame 1994), Tex. Numismatic Assn. (life, hall of fame 1993), Ind. State Numismatic Assn. (life, founders award 1993), Ctrl. States Numismatic Soc. (life, medal of merit 1984), Ancient Coin Collectors Guild (Exceptionally Meritorious Recognition award, 2008), Iola Lions (Melvin Jones fellow 1996). Home: N 2253 Butternut Rd Waupaca WI 54981 Office: 105 N Main St Iola WI 54945-0001 Office Phone: 715-445-5050. Personal E-mail: mish@electicpursuitsiola.com.

MISHLER, JOHN MILTON (YOCHANAN MENASHSHEH BEN SHAUL), science educator, artist; b. Cairo, Ill., Sept. 25, 1946; s. John Milton and Mary Jane (Woodbury) Mishler; m. Mary Therese Stember, Apr. 15, 1972 (div. Nov. 1981); m. Sigrid Ruth Elizabeth Fischer, Dec. 15, 1981; 1 child, Joshua Evan. AA with honors, Orange Coast Coll., Costa Mesa, Calif., 1966; AB in Molecular Biology, U. Calif., San Diego, 1969, ScM in Engring. Scis., 1971; DPhil in Immunohematology, St. John's Coll., Oxford U., 1978. Cert. cmty. coll. instr. Calif. Clin. coord. McGaw Labs., Costa Mesa, 1972-78; rsch. fellow Royal Postgrad. Med. Sch., Eng., 1977-78, Med. U., Cologne, Fed. Republic Germany, 1978-80; br. chief Nat. Heart, Lung and Blood Inst. NIH, Bethesda, Md., 1980-82; prof. med., basic life scis. and pharmacol. U. Mo., Kansas City, 1983-89, asst. vice chancellor, 1983-85, dir. div. basic med. scis., 1985-86, assoc. vice chancellor, 1985-89; prof. nat. scis. U. Md. Ea. Shore, Princess Anne, 1989-94, dean grad. studies and rsch., 1989-91; prof. biology Delaware Valley Coll. Sci. and Agrl., Doylestown, Pa., 1994—, dean of Coll., 1994-95. Frequent nat. and internat. lectr.; chmn. 13 nat. and internat. meeting sects. Author: Pharmacology of Hydroxyethyl Starch. Use in Therapy and Blood Banking, 1982; mem. editl. bd. Jour. Soc. Rsch. Adminstrs., 1987-91; book rev. editor Grants Mag., 1987-89; contbr. over 100 articles to profl. jours. Bd. dirs. Ctr. for Bus. Innovation, Inc., 1987, Bucks Assn. for Retarded Citizens, 1995-96; v.p. Artsbridge, 1999-2000. Recipient Outstanding Adminstrn. Svc. award U. Mo., Kansas City, 1987, Excellence award Soc. Rsch. Adminstrn., 1989, Cert. Appreciation, 1991, Silver and Bronze awards Artist Guild of Delaware Valley, 1998, Second prize Chester County Art Assn., 1998, Bd. Dirs. award Gtr. Norristown Art League, 1998, Award of Merit Westmoreland Art Nats., 1998, Perkins Ctr. for Arts, 2000, Robert Ransley Outstanding Talent award, 1999, 2d prize drawing Ctr. for the Creative Arts, 1999, 1st prize graphics Perkiomen Valley Art Ctr., 1999, 2d prize, 2002, Wayne Art Supply award Wayne Art Ctr., 2002, Pres.'s award Salmagundi Club, 2002, Honorable Mention, 2008; Best of Show/1st Pl. award Louisville Art Assn., 2003, Jerry's Artarama award Montana Watercolor Soc., 2003, honorable mention Associated Artists Southport, 2004, Franklin Square Gallery, 2004, hon. mention Taos Nat. Watercolor Soc., 2004, Winston Churchill award Mo. Watercolor Soc., 2005, Ursus Abstract award Tubac Ctr. of Arts, 2006, 3rd prize Conneaut Cmty. Ctr. for Arts, 2006, Art student League NY award, Audubon Artists Inc., 2007, Arches Paper award, Oklahama watercolor Assn., 2007; Sr. rsch. fellow Alexander von Humboldt Foun.,Germany, 1978-80. Fellow Internat. Soc. Haematology, Royal Coll. Pathologists; mem. Am. Soc. Hematology, German Soc. Hematology, Nat. Coun. Univ. Rsch. Adminstrn., Nat. Assn. State Univs. and Land-Grant Colls. (mem. exec. com. coun. on rsch. policy and grad. edn. 1990-91), Coun. Grad. Schs., N.Y. Acad. Scis., Sigma Xi. Jewish. Avocations: reading, abstract art painting, writing, music. Home: 475 North St Apt 6F Doylestown PA 18901-3863 Office: Delaware Valley Coll 700 E Butler Ave Doylestown PA 18901-2607 Office Phone: 215-489-2351. Business E-Mail: mishlerj@devalcol.edu.

MISHRA, BUD, science educator; b. s. Purna Chandra and Baidehi Mishra; m. Jane Mishra; 1 child, Bud. Degree in Physics, Utkal U.; degree in Electronics, Communication Engring., Indian Inst. Tech., Kharagpur; PhD, Carnegie Mellon, Pitts., 1985. Prof., computer sci., math. NYU, Courant Inst. Math. Scis., 1985—; prof., human genetics Mt. Sinai Sch. Medicine; prof., cell biology NYU Sch. Medicine. Office: NYU 715 Broadway Rm 1002 New York NY 10003

MISHRA, LOPA, gastroenterologist, educator; b. Kenya, Nov. 29, 1957; m. Bibhuti Bushan Mishra, June 12, 1985; children: Ekavali, Viveka. MBBS, U. London, 1982. Diplomate Am. Bd. Internal Medicine, 1987, in gastroenterology 1989. Rsch. assoc. Johns Hopkins Sch. Medicine, Balt., 1988—91, instr. gastroenterology and medicine, 1990—91; staff gastroenterologist Vets. Affairs Med. Ctr., Washington, 1990—2002; asst. prof. medicine Georgetown U., Washington, 1992—96, vice-chair rsch., 2005—, assoc. prof. medicine and cell biology, 2002—03, dir. cancer genetics, 2003—, prof. surg. scis., 2003—; assoc. prof. biochemistry and cell biology Temple U., Fels Cancer Inst., Phila., 1997—2002. Recipient Stuart Mill prize, Royal Free Hosp. Med. Sch., 1981, Industry New Investigator award, USV, 1995, Elisabeth and John Cox award for Innovative Clin. Therapy Esophageal Cancer, 1996, Betty and Harry Myerberg award, 1998; Rsch. grant, Nat. Cancer Inst., 2006—, NIH, 2008—. Mem.: Georgetown U. GCRC Rsch. Adv. Com., Georgetown U. Med. Ctr., Dept. Medicine Rsch. Com., Georgetown U. Faculty Adv. Com., AASLD Rsch. Com., Rsch. Com., Surgery Dept. GUMC (chair 2005), Joint Oversight Clin. Rsch. Com., Georgetown U., NIH, DDIC, Liver Subcom., NIH Devel. Biology Interest Group. Office: Georgetown Univ Med-Dent Bldg NW 212 3900 Reservoir Rd Washington DC 20007 Office Fax: 202-687-0992. Business E-Mail: lm229@georgetown.edu.

MISHRA, PRACHI, economist; b. Patna, Bihar, India; PhD, Columbia U., NY, 2004. Economist IMF, Washington, 2004—. Office: IMF 700 19th St NW Washington DC 20431

MISHRA, RAJIV SHARAN, metallurgical engineer, educator; b. Chapra, Bihar, India, July 15, 1961; s. Shambhu Sharan and Indu Mishra; m. Sarita Trivedi; children: Mayank, Rajit. B. Engring., U. of Rajasthan, Jaipur, India, 1982; M.Tech., Indian Inst. of tech., Kanpur, India, 1985; PhD, U. Seffield, Eng., 1988. Scientist, group leader Def. Metall. Rsch. Lab., Hyderabad, Andra Pradesh, India, 1988—94; postgrad. rsch. engr. U. Calif., Davis, 1994—97, adj. asst. prof., 1997—99; asst. prof. U. Mo., Rolla, 1999—. Mem. mfg. edn. exec. com. U. Mo., Rolla, 1999—; vice-chmn. Joint ASM/TMS Com. on Mech. Behavior of Materials, Warrendale. Editor: (proceedings) Creep Behavior of Advanced Materials for the 21st Century, 1999, Ultrafine Grained Materials, 2000, Friction Stir Welding and Processing, 2001; contbr. over 115 articles to profl. jours. Recipient Faculty Excellence award, U. Mo.i-Rolla, 2001, Young Metallurgist award, Indian Inst. of Metals, India, 1993, Brunton Medal, University of Sheffield, UK, 1988, ORS award, Com. of Vice-Chancellors and Prins. of UK, 1985—88; fellow Firth Pre-doctoral fellowship, U. of Sheffield, UK, 1985—88. Mem.: Am. Welding Soc., Soc. Mfg. Engrs., The Minerals, Metals and Materials Soc., Am. Soc. Metals, Indian Inst. of Metals (life). Achievements include patents for include nanocrystalline alumina-diamond composites. Office: Univ of Missouri Dept Metall Engring 1870 Miner Cir Rolla MO 65409 Business E-Mail: rsmishra@umr.edu.

MISHRA, SHRI KANT, neurologist, educator, neuroscientist; s. Jai Gopal and Dil Raji Mishra; m. Ann Mishra, Mar. 3, 1968; children: Alok Kumar, Arvind Kumar. ABMS, Ims BHU, Varanasi, India, 1964; MD, U. Toronto, Canada, 1971; MS, U. Wis., Maddison, 1990. Cert. neurologist ABPN, 1976, in neuromuscular medicine ABPN, 2008. Prof. neurology Keck Sch. Medicine, U. Southern Calif., Los Angeles, 1987—; dir. neuromuscular Va Gla, Los Angeles, 1998. Prof. neurology UCLA, 2007. Bd. dir. Health World on Line, Los Angeles, 2004. Colonel Army Med. Core Res. US Army, 2000—04, Los Angeles. Recipient Best tchr. award, David Geffen Sch. Medicine UCAL, 2004, Lifetime achievement award, AINA, 2009. Office: Univ Southern Calif 1100 N State st 4th fl Clinic Tower Neurology Los Angeles CA 90033 Home Phone: 818-895-9473. Home Fax: 818-895-5801. Business E-Mail: smishra@usc.edu.

MISHRA, SUDIB KUMAR, research scientist; b. Kolkata, West Bengal, India, June 1, 1981; s. Suniti Kumar and Sadhana Mishra. Attending, U. Ariz., Tucson, 2009. Rsch. assoc. U. Ariz., 2006—, U. Calif., Irvine, 2009. Author: Post Modern Poetry. Organizer Rural Devel., Kolkatta, 2004—. Achievements include research in multiscale modeling. Home and Office: Univ Ariz Dept Civil Engring 1209 E 2 nd St Tucson AZ 85721 Business E-Mail: sudib@email.arizona.edu.

MISKIMEN, THERESA MARIE, psychiatrist, educator; b. Mayaguez, P.R., Sept. 5, 1964; d. George William and Carmen M. (Rivera) M.; m. Juan Carlos Ortiz. BS in Biology magna cum laude, U. P.R., 1986, MD, 1990. Diplomate Am. Bd. Psychiatry and Neurology. Instr. psychiatry U. Medicine and Dentistry N.J., Newark, 1994-97, asst. prof. psychiatry, 1997—2000; assoc. prof. psychiatry Robert Wood Johnson Med. Sch., Piscataway, 2000—. Med. dir., acute inpatient unit, U. Behavioral Health Care, 2004-, v.p., med. svcs., 2006-. Am. Assn. Med. Colls. fellow, 1997, Disting. fellow. Mem. Am. Psychiat. Assn. (disting. & fellow-chairperson early career psychiatry com. 1997-98); mem. N.J. Psychiat. Assn. (treas. 2004-06, v.p. 2006-08, pres. elect 2008-), Beta Beta Beta. Business E-Mail: miskimtm@umdnj.edu.

MISKIOGLU, IBRAHIM, engineering educator; PhD, Iowa State U., Ames, 1981. Lab. asst. Bogazici U., Istanbul, Turkey, 1973—76; tchg. asst. Miss. State U., 1976—77, Iowa State U., Ames, 1977—81, temp. instr. and rsch. assoc., 1981—82, vis. asst. prof., 1984—85; project engr. Turkish Land Forces Command, Ankara, Turkey, 1983—84; asst. prof. Mich. Technol. U., Houghton, 1985—92, assoc. prof., 1992—. Assoc. tech. editor Exptl. Techniques, 1991—95, tech. editor, 1995—97. Grant, Mich. Materials and Processing Inst., 1994, Chrysler, 1996—2000, NSF, 1999—2002. Mem.: ASME, Soc. Exptl. Mechanics (mem. editl. coun. 1993—97, mem. xec. bd. 1999—2001), Am. Soc. Composites. Office: Mich Technol Univ ME-EM Dept Houghton MI 49931-1295 Office Fax: 906-487-2822. Business E-Mail: imiski@mtu.edu.

MISKOLCZI, FERENC MARK, research scientist; b. Budapest, Hungary, Apr. 20, 1947; m. Ferencne Anna Szabari; children: Ferenc, Mark. MS in Physics, Eotvos Lorand U., Budapest, 1971, PhD in Physics, 1975; PhD n Earth Scis., Hungarian Acad. Scis, Budapest, 1981. Sr. prin. scientist Analytical Svcs. & Materials Inc., Hampton, Va., 2001—06. Contbr. articles to profl. sci. jours. Home: 3 Holston Ln Hampton VA 23664 Personal E-mail: fmiskolczi@cox.net.

MISKUS, MICHAEL ANTHONY, electrical engineer; b. East Chicago, Ind., Dec. 10, 1950; s. Paul and Josephine Miskus. BS, Purdue U., 1972, AAS in Elec. Engring. Tech., 1972; cert. mgmt., Ind. U., 1972, Ind. Ctrl. Coll., 1974; MA in Orgnl. Mgmt., U. Phoenix, 1996, postgrad., 1997; PhD in Orgnl. Behavior, Columbia U., 1998. Cert. plant engr. IIPFE; registered environ. assessor REA, Calif. Svc. engr. Reliance Electric & Engring. Co., Hammond, Ind., 1972-73; maintenance supr., maintenance mgr. Diamond Chain Co./AMSTED Industries, Indpls., 1973-76; primary and facilities elec. engr. Johnson & Johnson Baby Products Co., Park Forest South, Ill., 1976-81; prin. Miskus Cons., indsl./comml. elec. cons., 1979—; plant and facilities engring. mgr. Sherwin Williams Co., Chgo. Emulsion Plant, 1981-85; with Miscon Assocs., Riverside, Calif., 1985—; acting dir. plant and facilities engring. Bourns Inc., 1982-90; facility mgr. Cardiovascular Devices Inc., 3M Healthcare, 1990—; mgr. Metrology and Corp. Metrology Lab. & ISO 9000, 3M, St. Paul; facilities ops. mgr. Press Enterprise, Riverside, 1997-2001; dir. facilities and plant engring. Shell Solar Industries LP, Camarillo, Calif., 2001—; project mgr. Devel. mktg. svcs. tng. sales tools Siemens, Power Conversion Divsn., NYC, 2002—. Instr., lectr. EET program Moraine Valley CC, Palos Hills, Ill., 1979; instr. cert. program plant engring. U. Calif.; lectr. energy engring., bldg. automation sys. Prairie State Coll., Chicago Heights, Ill., 1980—; mem. adj. faculty, faculty adv. bd. Orange Coast Coll., Costa Mesa, Calif.; bd. dirs., v.p. adminstrn. Internat. Inst. Plant & Facilities Engring.; commr., chmn. Riverside Energy Commn., 1988—; mem. Elec. Industry Evaluation Panel; siemens project mgr. Siemens Energy and Automation LD Motors, 2002—; chief cons. Miscon Cons. Productivity, Improvement Sys. Self Elec. Use Sys. Author: (text) The New Business Society. Mem. faculty adv. bd. Moraine Valley CC, 1980—. Mem. IEEE, Am. Inst. Plant Engrs. (pres. Pomona chpt. 1989—, chmn. western region VI membership, chmn. nat. coun. stds. labs. region II Twin Cities sect. 1995—), Assn. Facility Engrs. (pres. Inland Empire chpt. III 1997—), Assn. Energy Engrs. (sr., So. Calif. chpt.), Assn. Profl. Energy Mgrs. (bd. dirs. Orange County chpt. 1992), Internat. Inst. Plant and Facilities Engring. (dir. tech. 1999—), Illuminating Engring. Soc. N.Am., Internat. Platform Assn., Riverside C. of C., Purdue Alumni Orgn. LA (v.p. Inland chpt.), Purdue Club LA (v.p. Inland Empire sect.). Personal E-mail: columbia303@yahoo.com, jakeyboy@ez2.net.

MISLOVE, MICHAEL WILLIAM, mathematics educator, theoretical computer scientist; b. Washington, Feb. 8, 1944; s. Rhoda Frank and Ellsworth Herman Grell (Stepfather); m. Marilyn Burrus, Apr. 12, 1975; children: Alan, Caroline. BA in Math., U. of the South, 1965; PhD in Math., U. Tenn., 1969. Vis. asst. prof. U. Fla., Gainesville, 1970; asst. prof. Tulane U., New Orleans, 1970—75, assoc. prof. math., 1975—79, prof. math., 1979—, Pendergraft Herbert Buchanan Prof. of Math., 2006—. Alexander von Humboldt rsch. fellow Math. Inst., U. Tübingen, Tübingen, Germany, 1976, Technische Hochschule Darmstadt, Germany, 1978, 82; vis. faculty Math. Inst. U. Oxford, England, 1984, vis. prof. programming rsch. group, 91; vis. prof. U. Paris VII, 1995, 97, 98, 99, 2001, 02, U. Udine, Italy, 2003; summer faculty Thomas Watson Rsch. Ctr. IBM, Yorktown Heights, NY, 1988, 89, 90. Editor: Semigroup Forum, 1975—; co-author: A Compendium of Continuous Lattices, 1980, Continuous Lattices and Domains, 2003; mng. editor, founder: jour. Electronic Notes in Theoretical Computer Sci., 1995—; editor: Theoretical Computer Sci., 1994—, Mathematical Structures in Computer Science, 2007—. Named Astor Vis. Lectr., U. Oxford, 1998; grantee, NSF, 1971—81, 1998—2006, Office of Naval Rsch., 1988—; Travel scholar, Fulbright Commn., 1975. Master: jjj; mem.: hhhh. Avocation: sailing. Office: Tulane Univ Dept Math 6823 St Charles Ave New Orleans LA 70118 Business E-Mail: mislove@tulane.edu.

MISLOW, KURT MARTIN, chemist, educator; b. Berlin, June 5, 1923; came to U.S., 1940, naturalized, 1946; s. Max and Ida (Bingen) M.; m. Jacqueline Ford, 1966; children: Christopher, John. BS, Tulane

U., 1944, DSc (hon.), 1975; PhD, Calif. Inst. Tech., 1947; Doctorate (hon.), Free U., Brussels, 1974, Uppsala U., 1977, Düsseldorf U., 1994, Zurich U., 2004. Instr. NYU, 1947-51, asst. prof., 1951-56, asso. prof., 1956-60, prof., 1960-64; Hugh Stott Taylor prof. chemistry Princeton, 1964-88, chmn. dept. chemistry, 1968-74, prof. emeritus, 1988—. Vis. prof. Stanford U., 1960, Calif. Inst. Tech., 1994; M.S. Kharasch vis. prof. U. Chgo., 1989; Univ. lectr. U. London, 1965; J.A. McRae Meml. lectr. Queen's U., 1967; H.A. Iddles lectr. U. N.H., 1972; Solvay lectr. and medalist Free U. Brussels, 1972; E.C. Lee lectr. U. Chgo.; A.A. Vernon lectr. Northeastern U., 1976; PPG lectr. Ohio U., 1977; J. Musher Meml. lectr. Hebrew U. Jerusalem, 1978; North Country lectr., 1978; Honor lectr. Ariz. State U., 1981; E. Ritchie meml. lectr. Sydney U., 1983; Fuson lectr. U. Nev., 1983; Research Scholar lectr. Drew U., 1983; McGregory lectr. Colgate U., 1984; Sandia lectr. U. Alta., 1984; Purves lectr. McGill U., 1985; Arnold lectr. So. Ill. U., 1985; Bergmann lectr. Yale U., 1986; H.C. Brown lectr. Purdue U., 1988; Irvine lectr. U. St. Andrews, 1988; Eyring lectr. Ariz. State U., 1989; Disting. Scientist lectr. Bard Coll., 1991; Syntex Disting. lectr. Colo. State U., 1991; Disting. scientist lectr. Bard Coll., 1991; J.W.T. Spinks lectr. U. Saskatchewan, 1992; Bristol-Myers-Squibb disting. lectr. Syracuse U., 1992; Churchill fellow Cambridge U., 1974-75; mem. adv. panel chemistry NSF, 1963-66; mem. panel medical and organic chemistry NIH, 1963-66. Author: Introduction to Stereochemistry, 1965; also numerous articles; bd. editors: Jour. Organic Chemistry, 1965-70; mem. editl. adv. bd. Monatshefte für Chemie, Topics in Stereochemistry, Accounts of Chem. Rsch., Chem. and Engring. News, Bull des Sociétés Chimiques Belges, Symmetry, Jour. Math. Chemistry. Recipient Solvay medal Free U. Brussels, 1972, Prelog medal, ETH Zurich, 1986, W.H. Nichols medal, 1987, Sci. Achievement award medal CCNY, 1988, Disting. Alumni award Calif. Inst. Tech., 1990, Chirality medal, 1993, Sesquicentennial medal Tulane U., 1997, Arthur C. Cope Scholar award Am. Chem. Soc. 1995; Guggenheim fellow, 1957-58, 74-75, Alfred P. Sloan fellow, 1959-63, Sherman Fairchild disting. scholar Calif. Inst. Tech., 1990, 91, 94. Fellow AAAS, Am. Acad. Arts and Scis.; mem. NAS, AAUP, Am. Chem. Soc. (James Flack Norris award 1975), Academia Nazionale dei Lincei (fgn. mem.), Phi Beta Kappa, Sigma Xi. Personal E-mail: kmislow@princeton.edu.

MISRA, AMIT, materials scientist, researcher; b. India, Sept. 28, 1969; PhD, U. Mich., Ann Arbor, 1994. Rsch. fellow U. Mich., Ann Arbor, 1995—96; mem. tech. staff Los Alamos Nat. Lab, N.Mex., 1996—. Contbr. over 170 articles to profl. jours., chapters to books. Recipient Outstanding Materials Divsn. Paper award, NASA Glenn Rsch. Ctr., Cleve., 1992, Los Alamos Achievement award, Los Alamos Nat. Lab, 1999, Employee Recognition award, 2003, Teamwork award, 2006, Outstanding Innovation award, 2006, Outstanding Rsch. LANL Fellows Prize, 2008. Mem.: Bohmische Phys. Soc. (sci. mem. 1999), Minerals, Metals and Materials Soc. (chmn. nanomechanical behavior com. 2007—), Materials Rsch. Soc. Achievements include patent for high strength nanometer scale twinned coatings and foils. Office: Ctr Integrated Nanotechnologies Ms K771 Los Alamos NM 87545 Office Fax: 505-665-9030. Business E-Mail: amisra@lanl.gov.

MISRA, RAGHUNATH PRASAD, physician, educator; b. Calcutta, West. Bengal, India, Feb. 1, 1928; came to U.S., 1964; s. Guru Prasad and Anandi M.; m. Therese Rettenmund, Sept. 13, 1963; children: Sima, Joya, Maya, Tara. BSc honors, Calcutta U., 1948; MBBS, Med. Coll., Calcutta, 1953; PhD, McGill U., Montreal, Que., 1965. Diplomate Am. Bd. Anat. and Clin. Pathology. Asst. prof., dir. kidney lab. U. Louisville Sch. Medicine, 1964—68; assoc. investigator and dir. kidney lab Mt. Sinai Hosp., Cleve., 1968—73; asst. prof. Case We. Res. Med. Sch., Cleve., 1973—76; asst. prof., dir. kidney lab. Sch. Medicine La. State U., Shreveport, 1976—80, assoc. prof. Sch. Medicine, 1990—96, prof. Sch. Medicine, 1986—98, emeritus prof. Sch. Medicine, 1998—. Cons. VA Med. Ctr., Shreveport, 1977-98, EA Conway Meml. Hosp., Monroe, La., 1980-98; dir. Ocular Pathology Lab. Sch. Medicine La. State U., Shreveport, 1988— Author: Atlas of Skin Biopsy, 1983 Pres. India Assn. of Shreveport, 1979, 81 Tallisman fellow Mt. Sinai Hosp., 1970-73. Fellow Am. Coll. Pathologists, Am. Soc. Clin. Pathologists, Am. Coll. Internat. Physicians, U. Calcutta Med. Alumni Assn. Am. (pres. 1992-93), Sigma Xi (pres. 1987-89) Democrat. Hindu. Avocations: photography, travel. Office: La State U Sch Medicine 1501 Kings Hwy Shreveport LA 71103-4228 Home Phone: 318-865-9092; Office Phone: 318-675-5012. Business E-Mail: rmisra@lsuhsc.edu.

MISRACK, TANA MARIE, counselor, minister, writer; b. Toledo, July 25, 1954; d. Anthony James and Isabelle (Drinkhouse) Richards; m. Robert Aaron Misrack, June 30, 1996. AS in Interior Design, West Valley Coll., 1979. Ordained to ministry Universal Ch. of Master, 1986. Owner, designer Interiors by Tana Marie, Saratoga, Calif., 1979-88; min., profl. intuitive counselor Monterey, Calif., 1988—; CEO, cons. Strategies for Success, Monterey, Calif., 1994—; CEO, Tana Marie's Passion Island, 2002—; owner Passion Island Travel. Lectr., seminar leader, Monterey, 1988—; radio personality Sta. KNRY-1240 Cannery Row, Monterey, 2000—; profl. intuitive counselor. Author: Isle of Fantasies, 1995, Mating Games: Stop Playing and Start Loving, 1999, Guy Code: Understand Your Man, 2000, Care and Feeding of a Heart, 2001, The Dream Keeper, 2007; contbr. articles to profl. jours. Amb. San Jose (Calif.) C. of C., 1993-2000; mem. Mountain View (Calif.) Chamber, 1994-98. Recipient Oustanding Woman award, Monterey County Commn. on Status of Women, 2006. Mem. Women's Fund (1st v.p. 1994-98, pres. 1998-2000), Monterey C. of C. Avocations: bicycling, photography, writing. Office Phone: 831-646-1137. Personal E-mail: TM@Tanamarie.com.

MISRA-HEBERT, ANITA DIANA, physician; married. Cert. physician Ohio. Staff physician U. Chgo., 1995—99, Cleve. Clinic, 2000—. Office: Cleve Clinic 9500 Euclid Ave A11 Cleveland OH 44195

MISRAN, JENNIFER, language educator; b. Thionville, Moselle, France, Mar. 12, 1981; d. Pascal and Marlene Erna Anne Misran. PhD, U. Wis. Madison, 2008. Tchg. asst. U. Wis. Madison, 2006—. Achievements include research in francophone african literature. Office: French and Italian Dept UW-Madison 1220 Linden Dr Madison WI 53706

MISSAR, CHARLES DONALD, retired librarian; b. Cleve., July 16, 1925; s. Charles Frank and Genevieve Catherine (Buechele) M.; m. Margaret Mary du Fief, Feb. 17, 1962 (dec.); children: Charles David, Stephen du Fief. Student, Sacred Heart Sem., Detroit, 1943-45, St. Mary's Sem., Cleve., 1945-49; BA, John Carroll U., 1951; MLS, Cath. U. Am., 1960. Referral specialist Libr. of Congress, Washington, 1963-66; ERIC info. specialist U.S. Office Edn., Washington, 1966-72; head Ednl. Reference Ctr. Nat. Inst. Edn., Washington, 1973-78, supervisory libr., 1978-85; sr. libr. U.S. Dept. Edn., 1985-86; sr. editor Computer Scis. Corp. Profl. Svcs. Group, 1986-94, Missar Assocs., Washington, 1994—2001. Agy. rep. Fed. Libr. Com., Washington, 1978-86; ann. lectr. Fed. Libr. Resources Workshop, Catholic U. Am., Washington, 1981-96. Editor: Management of Federally Sponsored Libraries: Case Studies and Analysis, 1995; compiler, author: A Checklist of Ohio Imprints From 1821 to 1825, 1960; editor monthly jour. Tech. Abstract Bull., 1958-60; mem. editl. bd. Online Mag., 1977-80 Bd. dirs. Shrine of the Most Blessed Sacrament St. Pius X Libr., 1995-2000. Recipient Superior Svc. Group award U.S. Office Edn., 1968, Superior Performance award Nat. Inst. Edn., 1974, 84; inductee Spl. Libraries Assn. Hall of Fame, 1991. Mem. ALA, D.C. Libr. Assn. (treas. 1972-74), Spl. Librs. Assn. (chmn. edn. divsn. 1980-81, chmn. 1989-90), Am. Soc. Info. Sci. (chmn. info. svcs. for edn. group 1984-86), John Carroll Soc., Cleve. Club, Serra Club (pres. 1992-93, 94-96), Cosmos Club. Roman Catholic. Home: 5617 32nd St NW Washington DC 20015-1622

MISSICK, LAMONT S., literature and language professor; BA in English, Fla. A & M U., Tallahassee, 1995; MA, U. Miami, Coral Gables, Fla., 1998. Grad. tchr. U. Miami, 1996—2007, Fla. State U., Tallahassee, 1999—2002; adj. prof. English Miami Dade Coll., Fla., 1999—, Barry U., Miami Shores, 2006—, St. Thomas U., Miami, 2007, Fla. Internat. U., North Miami, 2007. Activist NAACP, Miami-Dade, Fla., 2007—08. Mem.: Non Verba Opera, Golden Key. Office: Barry Univ Dept English 11300 NE 2nd Ave Miami Shores FL 33161 Office Fax: 305-899-3445. Business E-Mail: l.missick@umail.miami.edu, lmissick@mail.barry.edu.

MISSICK, PATRICIA ANN, secondary school educator; b. NYC, July 26, 1950; d. Rudolph and Evangeline (Hicks) Corbett; m. John Missick, Mar. 12, 1972; 1 child, Kareeta Sonika. BA, CCNY, 1973; MA, NYU, 1975, PhD, 1995; MEd, Columbia U., 1978. Ordained minister Bapt. Ch., 1986; cert. adminstr., supr. Broadcast mgr. S. Kleins Dept. Store, NYC, 1968-70; recreation therapist Queens State Sch. for the Mentally Retarded & Brain Damaged, NYC, 1971-72; dir. Salvation Army/Sr. Citizen Day Camp, NYC, 1974-75, Sr. Citizen Programs and Day Camp, NYC, 1976, Langston Hughes Library Homework Program, NYC, 1979-80; tchr. N.Y.C. Bd. Edn., 1968—. Adj. prof. Rust Coll., Miss., 1983, N.Y. Theol. Sem., N.Y.C., 1983-85, Ahmadu Bello U., Zairo, Nigeria, 1984; adminstr., singer NYU Fellowship Program, 1981; vocal artist Pub. Sch. Dist. 127 and Steinway Jr. High Sch., N.Y.C., 1982-83, Resurrection Day Care Ctr., N.Y.C.; asst. minister Ebenezer Bapt. Ch. Author: Walking in Gods Love, 1979, Powerful & Positive Living, 1982. Founder, dir. Tchrs. Mag./Evangelyn, Queens Coll., 1985, host TV prograrm, 1989—; adminstr. Success & Religious Edn. Jour., 1987; concert artist Tribute to God Concert, Carnegie Hall, 1989—. Mem. Gerontol. Soc., Nation Coun. of Negro Women, Am. Bapt. Assn. (soloist), World Bapt. Alliance, Women's Nat. Evangelistic Conf. (speaker). Office: Tchrs Mag PO Box 315 Flushing NY 11369-0315

MISTACCO, VICKI E., foreign language educator; b. Bklyn., Nov. 18, 1942; d. Anthony Sebastian and Lucia (Lalli) M. BA, NYU, 1963; MA, Middlebury Coll., 1964; M of Philosophy, Yale U., 1968, PhD, 1972. Instr. French Wellesley Coll., Mass., 1968-72, asst. prof. French, 1972-78, assoc. prof. French, 1978-84, prof. French, 1984—, chmn., 1978-81. Nat. adv. bd. Sweet Briar Jr. Yr. in France, Va., 1978—. Author: Women and Literary Tradition: Anthology from The Middle Ages to the Present, 2006, vol. 2, 2007; contbr. articles to profl. jours. Fulbright fellow, 1963-64, Woodrow Wilson fellow, 1964-67; NEH fellow, 1983-84, 94-95. Mem.: North East MLA, MLA, Soc. Internat. pour l'Etude des Femmes de l'Ancien Régime, Women in French, Am. Assn. Tchrs. French, Phi Beta Kappa. Democrat. Roman Catholic. Avocations: photography, travel. Office: Wellesley Coll Dept French 106 Central St Wellesley MA 02481-8268 Office Phone: 781-283-2406. Business E-Mail: vmistacco@wellesley.edu.

MISTRANO, JOSEPH, lawyer; b. Phila., Feb. 7, 1934; s. Samuel and Dora Mistrano; children: Marsha Faass, Samuel A., Albert. BS, Temple U., Phila., 1956, JD, 1959. Bar: Pa. 1960, US Dist. Ct. (ea. dist.) Pa. 1960, US Ct. Appeals (3d cir.) 1972, cert.: Phila. (judge pro tem) 1990, US Dist. Ct. (ea. dist.) Pa. (mediator) 1992. Assoc. Gerber & Galfand, Phila., 1960—64; assoc. gen. counsel Phila. Housing Authority, 1964—67, acting gen. counsel, 1967—72, Phila. Housing Devel. Corp., 1967—72; prin. Mistrano, Jacobs & Levin, Phila., 1972—81, Joseph Mistrano & Assocs., P.C., Phila., 1981—; with Am. Arbitration Assn. Freelance arbitrator, 1965—. Vol. Judicare, Phila., 1980—, Com. Seventy, Phila., 1960—; program mgr. Lawyers Voter Protection; vol. Dem. Party, Phila., 1960—; fundraiser Presdl. Campaign, Phila., 2000, 2004. Mem.: ATLA, ABA, Pa. Trial Lawyers Assn., Phila. Trial Lawyers Assn., Patrial Lawyers Assn., Pa. Bar Assn., Phila. Bar Assn., Lawyer's Club Phila. Avocations: travel, sports, running, walking, theater. Office: Joseph Mistrano & Assocs PC 1500 Walnut St Ste 1900 Philadelphia PA 19102 Office Phone: 215-985-2020. Business E-Mail: jmistrano@mistranolaw.com.

MISTRY, BHARGAV MANGALDAS, surgeon, director; s. Mangaldas and Kamlaben Mistry; m. Bhanu Odedra-Mistry; children: Satyam, Karishma. MBBS, MR Med. Coll., Gulbarga, India, 1983. Cert. in abdominal transplant surgery United Network Organ Sharing, 1998, in surgery Am. Bd. Surgery, 2001, in critical care Am. Bd. Surgery, 2001. Dir., transplantation svc. Merit Care Hosp., Fargo, ND, 2000—, attending physician, 2000—. Clin. assoc. prof. U. ND Sch. Medicine, Grand Forks, 2006—. Contbr. scientific papers. Mem., exec. bd. LifeSource, St. Paul, 2001—07, pres., 2005—06, med. dir., 2004—06. Fellow: ACS, Royal Coll. Surgeons Engr. (London), Royal Coll. Physicians & Surgeons (Dublin); mem.: ND Med. Assn., Soc. Am. Gastrointestinal Endoscopic Surgeons, Soc. Surgery Alimentary Tract, Am. Soc. Transplant Surgeons. Office: Merit Care Hosp 736 Broadway Fargo ND 58122 Office Fax: 70123438686; Home Fax: 701-234-3868. Personal E-mail: bmistr@gmail.com. Business E-Mail: bhargavmistry@meritcare.com.

MISTRY, PERCY SHIAVAK, investment banker; b. Bombay, July 22, 1947; arrived in UK, 1987; s. Shiavak P. and Banoo S. (Engineer) M.; m. Pauline Earnshaw, Oct. 15, 1969. B of Tech. with honors, Loughborough U., Eng., 1969; MBA, U. Toronto, 1970, MPhil, 1971. Sr. advisor to exec. v.p. Internat. Fin. Corp., Washington, 1977-78; mng. dir. SGV-SUN Hung Kai Corp. Fin., Hong Kong, 1978-81; dir., sr. fin. advisor The World Bank, Washington, 1981-87; sr. fellow Oxford (Eng.) U., 1987-92; chmn. Oxford Internat. Assoc., 1988—, Oxford Internat. Fin., 1992-97; CEO Synergy Power Corp., 1998-2000, Acad. Coun. Willon Park, 1999—2004. Chmn. Ukraine Fin. Corp., 1995-98, D.C. Gardner & Co., London, 1992-93; bd. dirs. Indsl. Credit & Investment Corp. India, Bombay, 1993-97, Forum on Debt & Devel., The Hague, Holland, 1988-98, Synergy Power Corp., Hong-Kong, 1987-2003, Small Enterprises Assistance Funds; columnist The Banker, 1987-91; advisor DBSA, UN-ECA, 1999—, Commonwealth Secretariat on Internat. Fin. Svcs., 2005, Govt. of Mauritius, 2005-08; chmn. high-level expert com. on making Mumbai an IF Ctr., 2006; sr. advisor Europa Ptnrs. Ltd., 2007-; chmn., CEO India Infrastructure Fund; non-exec. dir. J.P. Morgan Emerging Markets Investment Trust, London; emeritus vis. prof. Adminstrv. Staff Coll. India, Hyderabad. African Debt: The Case for Relief, 1988, African Debt Revisited: Procrastination or Progress?, 1991, Inflation in Ethiopia, 1992, Economic Integration in Southern Africa, 1993, The Financial Condition of the African Development Bank, 1993, Multilateral Debt: An Emerging Crisis, 1994; author: Multilateral Development Banks, 1995, Resolving Africa's Multilateral Debt Problem, 1996, Regional Integration and Economic Development, 1996, Adjustment, Investment and Development Finance in Southern Africa, 2000, Role of the Commonwealth in International Negotiations, 2001, Mobilizing Support and Resources for the UN, 2001, Financing for Development, 2001, Regulation of International Financial Service in Mauritices: Cost/Benefit Study, 2006, Mitigating Risks for Foreign Investments in Least Developed Countries, 2003, Cost-Benefit Study of AML-CFT Regulations in Commonwealth Countries, 2006, Making Mumbai an International Financial Center, 2007; co-author: Development Finance in Southern Africa, 1989, Zambia: Exchange Rate Policy, 1989, Financing the Multilateral System, 1991, The Conversion of Official Bilateral Debt, 1992, Adjusting Privatization, 1992 (Acad. Book of Yr., 1993), Considering The Consequence, 2008, Export of Services: The Case of Mauritius, 2009. Dir. US-Caresbac, Atlanta, 1988-92; trustee The P.C. Mistry Found., Bombay, 1987—, F.S. Mistry Found. Mem. The Reform Club, The Willingdon Club, Cricket Club of India, The Royal Western India Turf Club. Avocations: thoroughbred racehorse owning and breeding, swimming, squash, tennis, reading. Office Phone: 4419 9383 1567, 44 20 7440 3529. Personal E-mail: OxfordIntluk@aol.com, percysmistryuk@aol.com. Business E-Mail: pmistry@europapartners.com.

MITAKIDES, JANE, corporate communications specialist; b. Ohio; m. John Mitakides; children: Katie, Andrew. Attended, Wright State U., Ohio. Founder Helsley Advertising; dir. mktg. Dental Recycling NA. Founding mem. Women's Coun. the Dem. Senatorial Campaign Com., Small Business Coun. the Dem. Nat. Com.; mem. devel. bd. St. Elizabeth Hosp.; bd. mem. Friends the Dayton Ballet and Opera Guild, NAACP, Dayton Chpt., Women in Leadership. Recipient ANDY award, ADDY award, CLIO award, Leadership award, Nat. Coordinated Effort of Hellenes, 2008. Mem.: EMILY's List, Women's Leadership Forum. Mailing: PO Box 29-3039 Dayton OH 45429

MITAL, AMIT, computer software company executive; MS in Engring., Dartmouth Coll., Hanover, NH. Various positions in technical leadership, field and customer engagement, tech. devel. and acquisition mgmt. Microsoft Corp., Redmond, Wash., gen. mgr. BizTalk server product group, gen. mgr. Office Live Meeting, gen. mgr. Live Mesh and Developer Platform orgn., corp. v.p. unlimited potential group and start-up bus. accelerator, 2009—. Achievements include patents in field. Office: Microsoft Corp One Microsoft Way Redmond WA 98052-6399*

MITAL, ANIL, engineering educator; b. Barabanki, India, Nov. 13, 1951; came to US, 1975; s. Virendra Nath and Malti (Gupta) Mital; m. Chetna Gupta, June 12, 1981; children: Anubhav, Aashi. BE, Allahabad U., 1974; MS, Kans. State U., Manhattan, 1976; PhD, Tex. Tech. U., Lubbock, 1980. Asst. prof. indsl. engring. U. Wis., Platteville, 1979—80, assoc. prof., 1984—92, prof. indsl. engring. and phys. med. and rehab., 1993—; coord. human factors engring. grad. U. Cin., 1981—. Dir. Ergonomics Rsch. Lab., 1981—. Editor-in-chief Internat. Jour. Indsl. Ergonomics, 1986-2003, Internat. Jour. Indls. Engring.-Theory Applications and Practice, 1994—, Elsevier Book Series in Ergonomics; founding editor-in-chief Emeritus Internat. Jour., 2004—; exec. editor: Internat. Jour. Human Resource Devel. and Mgmt., 1999—; gen. editor: Trends in Ergonomics/Human Factors I, 1984, Applications of Fuzzy Set Theory in Human Factors, 1986, Manual Materials Handling, 1989, A Guide to Manual Materials Handling, 1993, 2nd edit., 1997, Handbook of Expert Systems in Manufacturing and Production Engring., 1994, numerous other ergonomics jours.; contbr. numerous articles to profl. jours. Mem. Big Bros.-Big Sisters, Lubbock, Tex., 1977—. Grantee Nat. Inst. Occupl. Safety and Health, 1982-85, NSF, 1993-96; rsch. grantee Nat. Inst. Disability and Rehab., 1993-97; recipient Gold Medal for performacnce Allahabad U., 1974, David F. Baker Disting. Rsch. award Inst. Indsl. Engrs., 2007; named Young Engr. Yr. Engrs. and Scientists Cin., 1984; Jr. Morrow Rsch. Chair, 1982-83. Fellow Human Factors and Ergonomics Soc. (Paul M. Fitts award 1996), Inst. Indsl. Engrs. (treas. Cin. chpt. 1983-84, ergonomics divsn. 1987-88, Ergonomics award 1989, Eugene L. Grante award 1988, David F. Baker Disting. Rsch. award 2007); mem. Am. Indsl. Hygiene Assn. (chmn. nat. ergonomics com. 1984-85), Human Factors Soc. Am. (editl. bd., chmn. indsl. ergonomics tech. group 1985-86, Outstanding Contbns. award Tri-State chpt. 1984), Human Factors Soc. Greater Cin. (pres. 1983-84), Soc. Automotive Engrs. (faculty advisor 1987-88, Ralph R. Teetor award 1985), Internat. Soc. Occupl. Ergonomics and Safety (Disting. Accomplishment award 1993), 100 Mile Joggers, Pi Tau Sigma, Alpha Pi Mu, Tau Beta Pi (faculty advisor 1981-85), Phi Kappa Phi, Omicron Delta Kappa, delta Phi Epsilon, Sigma Xi (Disting. Rsch. award 1984). Home: 7242 Cascade Dr West Chester OH 45069-2291 Office: Univ Cin Mech Engring Dept Cincinnati OH 45221-0072 Office Phone: 513-556-2652.

MITARAI, FUJIO, electronics company executive; b. Sept. 23, 1935; Grad., Chuo U., 1961. Joined Canon Inc., 1961, pres. Canon USA Inc., 1979—89, dir., 1981, mng. dir., 1985, chief adminstrv. officer, 1989, sr. mng. dir., 1989, exec. v.p., 1993, pres., CEO Tokyo, 1995—2006, chmn., CEO, 2006—. Chmn. Japan Bus. Fedn., Tokyo. Named one of World's Top 25 Managers, BusinessWeek mag., 2001. Office: Canon Inc 30-2 Shimomaruko 3-chome Ohta-ku Tokyo 146-8501 Japan Office Phone: +81-3-3758-2111.

MITAU, LEE R., lawyer, bank executive; b. Oct. 17, 1948; AB cum laude, Dartmouth Coll., 1969; JD magna cum laude, U. Minn., 1972. Bar: Minn. 1972, NY 1973. Law clk. to Hon. George E. MacKinnon US Ct. Appeals (DC cir.), 1972-73; assoc. Cleary, Gottlieb, Steen & Hamilton, 1973—79; ptnr. Oppenheimer, Wolff & Donnelly, 1979—83, Dorsey & Whitney, Mpls., 1983—95, mem. policy com., 1988—99, chmn. corp. dept., 1989—95; exec. v.p., gen. counsel US Bancorp, Mpls., 1995—. Adj. prof. law William Mitchell Coll. Law, 1982—83; bd. dirs. H.B. Fuller Co., St. Paul, 1996—, Graco Inc., Mpls., 1990—, chmn., 2002—. Trustee Mpls. Inst. Arts, Minn. Pvt. Coll. Coun.; bd. govs. Mpls. Club. Office: US Bancorp US Bancorp Ctr 800 Nicollet Mall Minneapolis MN 55402*

MITCHAM, JULIUS JEROME, accountant; b. Pine Bluff, Ark., Jan. 2, 1941; s. James Vernon and Bertha Lee (Robertson) M.; m. Janet Claire Berry, Mar. 31, 1970 (div. Sept. 1981); m. Marsha Lee Henderson, Oct. 22, 1983; 1 child, Timothy John. BBA, U. Cen. Ark., 1971. CPA Ark., Okla.; cert. healthcare fin. mgr. Br. mgr. Comml. Nat. Bank, Little Rock, 1961-66; auditor, acctg. supr. Ark. Blue Cross and Blue Shield, Little Rock, 1971-77; contr. Riverview Hosp., Little Rock, 1977-81; pvt. practice acctg. Little Rock, 1981-82; contr. Henryetta Med. Ctr., Okla., 1982-83; fin. report supr. Am. Med. Internat., Inc., Houston, 1983; dir. corp. acctg. Ft. Myers Cmty. Hosp., Fla., 1984-86; contr. Med. Ctr. of Southeast Okla., Durant, 1986-87; CFO Gulf Coast Cmty. Hosp./Qualicare of Miss., Inc., 1987-88; asst. adminstr. fin. S.W. Gen. Hosp., San Antonio, 1988-89; pvt. practice San Antonio, 1989-90; CFO Bapt. Meml. Hosps. of Mississippi County, Blytheville, Ark., 1991-94, Med. Arts Hosp., Texarkana, Tex., 1994-96, Healthsouth Rehab. Hosp., Texarkana, Tex., 1997-98; pres. Mitcham & Assocs., 1998—2001; CFO Muscogee (Creek) Nation Divsn. Health Adminstrn., Okmulgee, Okla., 2002—04, Booneville Meml. Hosp., Ark., 2004—05, Okmulgee Meml. Hosp., 2005—. With USN, 1959—61. Mem. AICPA, Ark. Soc. CPAs,

Okla. Soc. CPAs, Healthcare Fin. Mgmt. Assn. (cert. fellow), Lions (sec. 1985-86, 2d v.p. 1995-96), Masons. Republican. Baptist. Office: PO Box 1038 Okmulgee OK 74447 Office Phone: 918-758-3102. Personal E-mail: jmitch41@aol.com.

MITCHELL, ALICE JOYCE JONES, retired secondary school educator, dietician; b. W.Va., Jan. 27, 1936; d. Edgar Dunbar and Mildred Edna Jones; m. Ernest Lopez Mitchell. BS in Home Econs., W.Va. State Coll., Institute, 1957; degree in Higher Edn. Adminstrn., N.Y.U., Hofstra U. Dietician Kings County Hosp., Bklyn., 1957—58, Montefiore Hosp., Bronx, 1958—66; substitute tchr. home econs. Bd. Edn. Bronx, 1966—68; tchr. home econs. NYC Bd. Edn., 1968—91; ret., 1991. Chairperson home econs. dept. Jr. HS 117, Bklyn., 1971—75, Bklyn., 1979—85, dean of girls, 1976—79; tchr. mentor 117 Intermediate Sch., Bklyn., 1989—91. Served Coast Guard Aux., 1977—78, Bayside, N.Y. Named Master Tchr., Prin. 117 Bklyn., 1971, 1972, 1973, 1974, 1975, 1979, 1980, 1981, 1982, 1985. Mem.: Sr. Coalition, TREA Sr. Citizens League, W.Va. State U. Alumni Club, Acorn, 55+ Club. Republican. Catholic. Avocations: sewing, gardening, travel. Home: 572 S Main St Freeport NY 11520

MITCHELL, ALISON N., newspaper reporter, editor; b. Bay Shore, NY, May 2, 1954; d. Sidney L. and Audrey (Auerhahn) M. BA, Radcliffe Coll., 1976. Reporter The Record, Bergen County, NJ, 1976-77; reporter Newsday, Melville, NY, 1977-81, Capital bur. chief, 1981-84, Congl. corr., Capital Bureau chief, fgn. correspondent Washington & Moscow, 1985—91; reporter, White House correspondent, Washington bureau chief New York Times, Washington & NYC, 1991—2003, dep. nat. editor, 2003, edn. editor. Recipient Walter Brown award for coverage of state govt., Legis. Corr. Assn., 1983, Everett McKinley Dirksen award, Nat. Press Found., 1999. Mem. N.Y. Legis. Corr. Assn. Office: New York Times 620 8th Ave New York NY 10018-1405 Office Phone: 212-556-7356. Office Fax: 212-556-7614.

MITCHELL, ANDREA, journalist, television news anchor; b. NYC, Oct. 30, 1946; d. Sydney and Cecile Mitchell; m. Alan Greenspan, Apr. 6, 1997. BA in English Lit., U. Pa., 1967. Polit. reporter KYW Newsradio, Phila., 1967-76; polit. corr. Sta. KYW-TV, Phila., 1972-76; corr. Sta. WTOP-TV, Washington, 1977-78; gen. assignment and energy corr. NBC News, Washington, 1978-81, White House corr., 1981-88, chief congl. corr., 1989-92, chief White House corr., 1993-94, chief fgn. affairs corr. Washington, 1995—. Regular appearances on Hardball with Chris Matthews, The Rachel Maddow Show; regular guest host Meet the Press. Author: Talking Back: ...to Presidents, Dictators, and Assorted Scoundrels, 2005. Trustee U. Pa., 1995—. Recipient Pub. Affairs Reporting award, Am. Polit. Sci. Assn., 1969, AP Pub. Affairs Reporting award, 1976, AP Broadcast award, 1977, Lucretia Mott award, Woman's Way, 1991, Welles Hangen award for superior achievement in journalism, Brown U., 2003, Lifetime Achievement award, Radio-TV News Directors Assn., 2004, Goldsmith Career Achievement prize, Harvard U., 2005; named Communicator of Yr., Women in Comm., 1976, Woman of Yr., Am. Women in Radio & TV, 1989. Office: NBC News 4001 Nebraska Ave NW Washington DC 20016-2733*

MITCHELL, ANN MARGARET, psychiatric nurse practitioner, educator; b. Pitts. d. John G. and Joan M. RN diploma, Pa. State U., 1974, BS, 1976, MS, 1979; PhD, U. Pitts., 1987. Clin. nurse specialist Western Psychiat. Inst. and Clinic, Pitts., 1985-89; pvt. practice, traveling nurse, cons. Pa., Calif, 1989-91; rsch. asst. prof. U. Pitts. Sch. Nursing, Pitts., 1991-95, asst. prof. nursing & psychiatry, 1995—. Bd. trustees Mayview State Hosp., 2001—. Collaborator: Interpersonal Relationship Skills Tng. Program, 1978, Rels. Tng., 1984. Mem. Exec. Women's Coun., Greater Pitts., Inc., 1992. Recipient traineeship Pa. State U., University Park, 1976-78, scholarship U. Pit ts., Pa., 1980-82; grantee faculty scholar Uppsala U., Sweden, 1996, Keio U., Tokyo, 1998. Mem. ANA, Am. Assn. Suicidology, Am. Found. Suicide Prevention (bd. dirs. Pitts. chpt.), Psychiat. Nurse Mgrs. Pa., Inc. (hon.), Assn. Clin. Nurse Specialists, Sigma Theta Tau, Kappa Delta Pi. Home: 5826 Nicholson St Pittsburgh PA 15217-2341 Office: Univ Pitts Sch Nursing # 415 Victoria Bldg 3500 Victoria St Pittsburgh PA 15261 Business E-Mail: ammi@pitt.edu.

MITCHELL, ARTHUR, dancer, choreographer, performing company executive, educator; b. NYC, Mar. 27, 1934; s. Arthur and Willie Mae Mitchell. Student, Sch. Am. Ballet.; D. Arts (hon.), Columbia Coll., Chgo., 1975; cert. of competence, Peter U., 1978; DFA (hon.), City Coll., CUNY, 1979, N.C. Sch. Arts, 1981, L.I. U. Sch. Bus. Pub. Adminstrn., 1982, Fordham U., 1983, Princeton U., 1986, Williams Coll., 1986, Juilliard Sch., 1990; DHS (hon.), Urbana Coll., 1979; DA (hon.), Harvard U., 1987. With William Dollar's Ballet Theatre Workshop, 1954, John Butler Co., 1955; prin. dancer NYC Ballet, 1955-72; artistic dir., founder Am. Negro Dance Co., NYC, 1966—; founder, dir., choreographer Dance Theatre of Harlem, NYC, 1969—2009, artistic dir. emeritus, 2009—; former resident choreographer, artistic dir. Nat. Ballet Co., Brazil. Tchr. dance Karel Shook Studio, Melissa Hayden Sch., Cedarhurst, NY, Jones-Haywood Sch. Ballet, Washington. Dancer Kiss Me Kate, Orpheus, Carmen Jones, Allegro, Creation of the World, Episodes, House of Flowers, choreographer with Rod Alexander Newport Jazz Festival, Rhythmetron, 1971, Ode to Otis, 1969, Lil' Gal, 1969, Tones, 1970, Biosfera, 1970, Fun and Games, 1970, Holberg Suite, 1970, Manifestations, 1975, Concerto for Jazz Band and Orch., 1971, Fête Noire, 1971, Spiritual Suite: Dance In Praise of His Name, 1976, Breezin', 1977, The Greatest, 1977, El Mar, 1977, Doin' It, 1978, Porgy and Bess, 1985, Phoenix Rising, 1987, John Henry, 1988, Ribbon in the Sky, 1990, Bach Passacaglia, 1993; co-choreographer Broadway prodn. Shinebone Alley, dancer, choreographer, actor Spoleto Festival of Two Worlds, 1960; dancer tv prodns. A Streetcar Named Desire, PBS dance prodn. Songs of Mahler, Dance in America: Dance Theatre of Harlem, Stravinsky's Firebird, NBC prodn. Creole Giselle, A&E prodn. Fall River Legend. Active Nat. Conf. on Social Welfare, 1973, U.S. Dept. State Dance Adv. Panel; pres. Task Force on Arts and Humanities, 1981; mem. Commn. for Cultural Affairs, NYC, 1982; mem. adv. bd. Arts and Entertainment, NYC; mem. Partnership, Inc., 1983, Nat. Coun. Arts, 1987, Pres. Commn. on White House Fellowships, 1991. Recipient Changers award, Mademoiselle Mag., 1970, award, North Shore Commn. Arts Ctr., 1980, Capezio Dance award, 1971, Ann. Excellence award, John F. Kennedy Ctr. for Performing Arts, 1980, award, Am. Dance Guild, 1982, Am. Black Achievement award, Ebony Mag., 1983, Pres.'s Cabinet award, U. Detroit, 1982, Paul Robeson award, Actors Equity Assn., 1986, Lion of the Performing Arts award, NY Pub. Libr., 1986, Arnold Gingrich Meml. award, 1987, Banquet of Golden Plate, 1989, Harkness Disting. Artist award, Adelphi U., 1990, Disting. Svc. to Arts award, Am. Acad. Arts and Letters, 1994, Zenith award for Fine Arts, 1994, Handel Medallion, NYC, 1993, Barnard Medal of Distinction, Barnard Coll., 1994, Lifetime Achievement award, Sch. Am. Ballet, 1995, Nat. Medal of Arts, Nat. Endowment Arts, 1995, Living Landmarks award, NY Landmarks of Conservancy, 1995, Kennedy Ctr. Honor, 1993, Honors, Dance USA, 2004; named to Hall of Fame, NAACP Image Awards, 1986; grantee Fletcher Fellowship, Fletcher Found.; Conroy fellow, St. Paul's Sch., Concord, N.H., 1982, MacArthur fellow, 1994. Office: Dance Theatre Harlem 466 W 152nd St New York NY 10031-1896

MITCHELL, BETTY JO, publishing executive, writer; b. May 2, 1931; d. Edith Darrah McWilliams. BA, S.W. Mo. State U., Springfield, 1952; MSL, U. So. Calif., 1967; MBA, PhD, Calif. Coast U., 2002. Asst. acquisitions libr. Calif. State U., Northridge, 1967—69, libr. for pers. and fin., 1969-71, acting assoc. libr. dir., 1971-72, assoc. dir. univ. librs., 1972-81; mgr. info. sys. City Santa Monica Rent Control, Calif., 1984-93; owner Viewpoint Press, Tehachapi, Calif. Cons. We. Interstate Commn. for Higher Edn. USOE Inst. for Tng. in Staff Devel. Problem Solving; participant workshops in field; spkr. at profl. confs. in field; bd. dirs. Tehachapi Cmty. Orch. Author: ALMS: A Budget Based Library Management System, 1982, The Secret of Hilhouse: An Adult Book for Teens, 1993, The Huckenpuck Papers: The Tale of a Family's Secret and a Young Girl's Search for Self-Esteem, 2001, Seeds of Violence, 2005; co-author: Cost Analysis of Library Functions: A Total System Approach, 1978, How to See the U.S. on $12 a Day; contbr. writings to profl. publs.; editor Staff Development column in Spl. Librs., 1975-76. Bd. dirs. San Fernando Valley coun. Girl Scouts U.S., 1974-77, employed pers. com., 1979-81; bd. dirs. Bear Valley Springs Condominium Owners Assn., 1978, Empyrean Found., 1978-81, Tehachapi Cmty. Orch. Found., 1998—, Tehachapi Performing Arts Ctr. Found., 2003—, Tehachapi Heritage League, 2005— Mem. AAUP, AAUW, ALA (chmn. various coms.), Assn. Women in Computing (bd. dirs. 1987-89), Nat. Libr. Assn., Author's Guild, Calif. Libr. Assn., Assn. Calif. State U. Profs. (sec., exec. com. 1971-72), Phi Beta Chi, Alpha Mu Gamma. Office: PMB 400 785 Tucker Rd Ste G Tehachapi CA 93561-2523 Personal E-mail: joie99@aol.com.

MITCHELL, BEVERLY SHRIVER, hematologist, oncologist, educator; b. Balt., May 14, 1944; m. John Robert Pringle; children: Robert Mitchell, Elizabeth Greene. AB summa cum laude in Biochemistry, Smith Coll., 1965; MD, Harvard U., 1969. Hematology fellow U. Mich., Ann Arbor, 1975-77, from instr. to asst. prof. internal medicine, 1977-81, assoc. prof., 1981-87, prof. internal medicine and pharmacology, 1987-91, U. N.C., Chapel Hill, 1991—, divsn. chief hematology/oncology, 1994—2003; assoc. dir. Lineberger Cancer Ctr., Chapel Hill, 1994—2005; deputy dir. Stanford Cancer Ctr., Stanford U., 2005—. Mem. bd. sci. counselors Cancer Treatment divsn. Nat. Cancer Inst. Vice chair med. and sci. affairs Leukemia and Lymphoma Soc., 2003—05. Recipient Stohlman award Leukemia Soc., 1988. Mem. Am. Soc. Hematology (treas. 1991-96, v.p. 1998, pres. 2000), Phi Beta, Inst. Medicine. Achievements include research in nucleotide metabolism and the development of novel therapies for hematologic malignancies. Office: Stanford Blood Center 3373 Hillview Ave Palo Alto CA 94304-1204 Office Phone: 650-736-7716. Business E-Mail: bmitchell@stanford.edu.

MITCHELL, BRIAN CHRISTOPHER, academic administrator; b. Lowell, Mass., Feb. 23, 1953; s. Christopher Joseph and Doris Katherine (McEvoy) M.; m. Maryjane Murphy, June 28, 1975; children: Jeffrey Ryan, Patrick Joseph. BA, Merrimack Coll., 1974; MA, U. Rochester, 1976, PhD, 1981. Chair history dept. Anna Maria Coll., Paxton, Mass., 1982-85; program officer Nat. Endowment Humanities, Washington, 1985-91; pres. Commn. Ind. Colls. and Univs. Pa., Harrisburg, 1991-98, Washington and Jefferson Coll., Washington, Pa., 1998—2004, Bucknell U., Lewisburg, Pa., 2004—. Instr. U. Mass., Lowell, 1977-85; adj. prof. George Mason U., Fairfax, Va., 1988-91; cons. Lowell Nat. Hist. Park, 1977-81, Lowell Heritage State Park, 1977-78. Author: The Paddy Camps: The Irish of Lowell, 1821-1861, 1988, On The North Bank, 1984; editor: Building the American Catholic City, 1986; contbg. author: From Paddy to Stud, 1986. Mem. Pa. Humanities Coun.; mem. Pa. Hist. and Mus. Commn.; chair Pa. selection com. Rhodes Scholarship Trust. Grantee Am. Coun. Learned Socs., 1985, NEH. Mem. Am. Hist. Assn. (Albert J. Beveridge award), Orgn. Am. Historians, Nat. Assn. Ind. Colls. and Univs. Roman Catholic. Office: Off of President Bucknell U Box A0527 Lewisburg PA 17837 Office Phone: 570-577-1511. E-mail: bmitchel@bucknell.edu.*

MITCHELL, BRIAN STOKES, actor; b. Seattle, Oct. 31, 1958; s. George Thomas and Lillian (Stokes) M. Prin. actor 12th Night Repertory Co., San Diego, 1977-80; co-star Roots: The Next Generations, LA, 1980, Trapper John, M.D., LA, 1980-86, The Good War, LA, 1987, The Fresh Prince of Bel Air, 1993, In the House, 1996, Crossing Jordan, 2002, Frasier, 2002—03; co-star Mail Kennedy Ctr., Washington, The Music Box Theatre, Broadway, N.Y.C., and Pasadena, Calif., 1987-88; star David Merrick's Broadway play Oh Kay Richard Rodgers Theatre, 1990. Guest tchr., speaker San Diego Jr. Theater, 1984; guest star The White Shadow, 227, Houston Knights, Alf, Night Court, L.A., 1987; voice-over actor, series reg. California Raisins, New Kids on the Block, Kid 'n Play, 1988—; trustee Actor's Fund, 1999—, pres. 2004-07; mem. honors artists com. Kennedy Ctr., 2001, 02, 04; pres. Actors Fund Am., 2004; mem. artist's com. Ams. for the Arts, 2004. Appeared in Broadway prodn. Jelly's Last Jam, 1992, Kiss of the Spider Woman, 1994-95, Ragtime, Ford Theater for Performing Arts, 1996 (Drama League Disting. Performance award, Can.'s Dora award, Drama League award), Shubert Theatre, L.A., 1997 (L.A. Critics award), Kiss Me Kate, 1999-2001 (Tony Award, 2000, Drama Desk award, Outer Critics Circle award), Do Re Mi, 2000, Carnival, 2001, King Hedley II, 2001, Sweeney Todd, 2002, South Pacific, 2005; appeared in National Theater prodn. Man of La Mancha, 2002 (Helen Hayes award), National Symphony Orchestra Pops: An Evening with Brian Stokes Mitchell, 2005; composer: (symphonic suite) 3 Scenes for Clipper Ships, 1983; (Trapper John, M.D. TV scores) The Wunderkind, Friends and Lovers, I Only Have Ice For You, 1984; film work includes Ghost Dad, 1990, (voice) The Prince of Egypt, 1998, Ruby's Bucket of Blood, 2000, Call me Clause, 2001; composer (CD) Brian Stokes Mitchell, 2006. Ambassador March of Dimes, U.S. Tour, 1984-85; performer USO, European Tour, 1984, Far East/Middle East Tour, 1985, Calif. Orgn. of Police and Sheriffs, L.A., 1986. Recipient Best Pop Song and Composer of Yr. awards Los Angeles Songwriters Showcase, 1986, Drama League Distinguished Performance Award, 1998, Nightlife award, outstanding cabaret male vocalist in a major engagement, 2006. Mem. Acad. of TV Arts and Scis. (blue ribbon panelist 1987), ASCAP, Screen Actors' Guild, AFTRA, Actors Equity Assn. Avocations: flying, skiing, composing.

MITCHELL, BRUCE TYSON, lawyer; b. San Francisco, Nov. 6, 1928; s. John Robert and Lorraine C. (Tyson) M.; m. Adrienne Means Hiscox, Oct. 14, 1951; 1 son, Mark Means. AB with great distinction, Stanford U., Calif., 1949, JD, 1951. Bar: Calif. 1952, US Dist. Ct. (no. dist.) Calif 1952, US Ct. Appeals (9th cir.) 1952, US Supreme Ct. 1971. Estate adminstr. Crocker Nat. Bank, San Francisco, 1955-57; atty. Utah Internat. Inc., San Francisco, 1957-87, sec., 1974-87, sr. counsel, 1961—87, ret., 1987; pvt. practice securities arbitrator. Mem. non-securities panel arbitrators NY Stock Exch., NASD Bd. Arbitrators; mem. adv. bd. archaeology, 2005-09, Stanford U. Chmn. San Mateo County Rep. Ctrl. Com., 1964-70; mem. Calif. Rep. Ctrl. Com., 1964-74, 77-83; alt. del. Rep. Nat. Conv., 1968; co-chmn. San Mateo (Calif.) County Pres. Ford Com., 1976; mem. bd. visitors sch. law Stanford U., 1980-83; exec. v.p., bd. dirs. San Francisco Jr. C. of C., 1961; bd. dirs. No. Calif. chpt. Arthritis Found., 1972-85, 1987-92, St. Francis Hosp. Found., San Francisco, 1992-98, 99—, hon. dir., 1998-99—. Lt. (j.g.) USNR, 1952-55, Japan. Mem. ABA, Calif. Bar Assn., San Francisco Bar Assn., Am. Judicature Soc., Am. Soc. Corp. Secs. (v.p. 1976-77, dir. 1976-79), Assn. Former Intelligence Officers, Commonwealth Club of Calif. (pres. San Francisco 1973), Stanford Assocs., Pacific Union Club, Olympic Club, Capitol Hill Club, Travelers Century Club, Masons. Congregationalist. Home: 165 Redwood Dr Hillsborough CA 94010-6971 Office: 165 Redwood Dr Hillsborough CA 94010

MITCHELL, BURLEY BAYARD, JR., lawyer; b. Oxford, NC, Dec. 15, 1940; s. Burley Bayard and Dorothy Ford (Champion) M.; m. Mary Lou Willett, Aug. 3, 1962; children: David Bayard (dec.), Catherine Morris. BA with honors, N.C. State U., 1966, DHL (hon.), 1995; JD, U. N.C., 1969; LLD (hon.), Campbell U., 1998. Bar: N.C. 1969, U.S. Ct. Appeals (4th cir.) 1970, U.S. Ct. Appeals (3d cir.) 2002, U.S. Supreme Ct. 1972. Asst. atty. gen. State of N.C., Raleigh, 1969-72, dist. atty., 1973-77, judge Ct. Appeals, 1977-79, sec. crime control, 1979-82; justice Supreme Ct. N.C., Raleigh, 1982-94; chief justice Supreme Ct. of N.C., Raleigh, 1995-99; ptnr. Womble Carlyle Sandridge and Rice, Raleigh, 1999—. Served with USN, 1958-62, Asia. Recipient N.C. Nat. Guard Citizen Commendation award, 1982 Mem. ABA, VFW, N.C. Bar Assn., Mensa, Am. Legion, Phi Beta Kappa. Democrat. Methodist. Home: 4301 City of Oaks Wynd Raleigh NC 27612-5316 Office: Wacovia Capital Ctr 150 Fayetteville St Mall Ste 2100 PO Box 831 Raleigh NC 27602-0831 Office Phone: 919-755-8166.

MITCHELL, CARMENCITA C., literature and language professor; b. NYC, Dec. 27, 1969; BA in Humanities, NYU, 1998; MA in English, St. John's U., 2001; student, Fla. Atlantic U., 2003—. Admissions clerk, receptionist NYU, NYC, 1996—99; grad. tchg., rsch. asst. St. John's U., Jamaica, NY, 1999—2001; adj. asst. prof. English Hofstra U., Hempstead, NY, 2001—03, writing ctr. tutor, 2001—03; instr. English Fla. Atlantic U., Boca Raton, Fla., 2003—. Freelance ESL tutor, 2000—; adj. instr. English, speech St. John's U., Jamaica, NY, 2002—03; presenter in field. Poet (collections in field). Vol. career mentor Girl Scouts Am., Bklyn., 2000—. Mem.: Nat. Women's Studies Assn. (25th ann. conf. presenter 2004, Travel award 2004). Roman Catholic. Avocations: Middle Eastern dance, fashion design, writing, opera. Office: Fla Atlantic Univ 777 Glades Rd Boca Raton FL 33431

MITCHELL, CAROL ANN, nursing educator; b. Portsmouth, Va., Aug. 31, 1942; d. William Howell and Eleanor Bertha (Wesarg) M.; m. David Alan Friedman, June 17, 1971 (div. 1988). Diploma, NYU, 1963; BS, Columbia U., 1968, MA, 1971, EdM, 1974, EdD, 1980; MS, SUNY, Stony Brook, 1990. Charge nurse Nassau County Med. Ctr., East Meadow, N.Y., 1963-65; staff nurse Meml. Hosp., NYC, 1965-68; head nurse, supr. Cmty. at Glen Cove (N.Y.), 1969-71; assoc. prof. dept. nursing Queensborough C.C. CUNY, Bayside, 1971-80; assoc. prof. Marion A. Buckley Sch. Nursing Adelphi U., Garden City, N.Y., 1981-88; ednl. cons. Nat. League for Nursing, NYC, 1980-81; prof. sch. nursing SUNY, Stony Brook, 1988-92, chmn. adult nursing, 1988-92; prof. chair Coll. Nursing East Tenn. State U., 1992-95, mem faculty, 1995-96; geriat. nurse practitioner, dir. geriat. evaluation unit Vet. Affairs Med. Ctr., Mountain Home, Tenn., 1997—2004; tchr. Therapeutic Yoga & Taichi. Mem. faculty Regents Coll. degrees in nursing program USNY, Albany, 1978-91, cons., 1978—; faculty cons. geriats. Montefiore Med. Ctr., 1991-93. Editor emeritus: Scholarly Inquiry in Nursing Practice, 1983—; contbr. articles to profl. jours. Robert Wood Johnson clin. nurse scholar postdoctoral fellow U. Rochester (N.Y.), 1983-85. Mem.: Am. Geriatrics Soc., Am. Nurses Assn. Avocations: reading, gardening, bicycling, travel, cooking.

MITCHELL, CHRIS, publishing executive; m. Pilar Guzman; 2 children. BA in English, U. Calif. Berkeley; MA in Publishing, NYU. Sales representative to advertising dir. Wired mag. Conde Nast, 1996—2000, assoc. publisher The New Yorker, 2001—04, v.p., publisher Details mag., 2004—08, v.p., publisher Wired Media, 2008—09; v.p., publisher Conde Nast Traveler, 2009—. Office: Conde Nast 4 Times Sq New York NY 10036*

MITCHELL, CRANSTON J., commissioner; b. St. Louis, Aug. 25, 1946; s. Monroe M. and Elizabeth Mitchell; m. Aleta Grimes, July 8, 1983; children: Leslie Barnes, Catherine J., Christie J. BA in Polit. Sci., U. Mo. St. Louis, 1973; attended, John F. Kennedy Sch. Govt., Harvard U. Police officer St. Louis Police Dept., 1967—74; mktg. rep. Mitchum-Thayer Inc., 1974—75; counselor, adminstr. Dept. Elem. and Secondary Edn., Div. Vocational Rehab., 1975—83; chmn., dir. bd. probation and parole Mo. Dept. Corrections, 1985—2000; correctional prog. specialist Nat. Inst. Corrections (NIC), Washington, DC, 2000—03; commr. U.S. Parole Commn., 2003—. Mem. Am. Probation & Parole Assn., 1984—, Am. Corrections Assn., 1984—; charter v.p. Nat. Assn. Blacks in Criminal Justice, 1984—; regional v.p. Assn. Paroling Authorities Internat., 1988—90; commr. Jefferson City Housing Authority, 1990—. Recipient Danforth Fellowship, Vincent O'Leary Award, Jonathan Jasper Wright Cmty. Leadership Award, Nat. Assn. Blacks in Criminal Justice. Office: US Parole Commission Park Pl Bldg 5550 Friendship Blvd Rm 420 Chevy Chase MD 20815 Office Phone: 301-492-5990.*

MITCHELL, DAVID BENJAMIN, lawyer, arbitrator, mediator; b. Miami Beach, Fla., Nov. 3, 1950; s. Quintus Eugene and Gertrude (Ziegler) M.; m. Lynn Stewart, Dec. 11, 1993. BA, U. Miami, Coral Gables, Fla., 1973; JD, Stetson U., 1978. Bar: Fla. 1979, U.S. Dist. Ct. (so. dist.) Fla. 1979, U.S. Tax Ct. 1987, U.S. Supreme Ct. 2004; cert. family mediator; cert. arbitrator; cert. ins. mediator. Assoc., sr. assoc. Semet, Lickstein, Morgenstern & Berger, P.A., Coral Gables, 1987-90; pres. David B. Mitchell, P.A., Coral Gables, 1990—. Pres. South Fla. Mediation Assocs., Inc., Coral Gables, 1990-92. Author: Magna Carta: It's American Legacy, 2005. Active Coral Gables Cmty. Found., 1996—; grad. Leadership Miami, 1987; bd. dirs. Ponce de Leon Devel. Assn., pres., 1992-93; bd. dirs. Internat. Zen Found. of Fla., 1997—, Coral Gables Citizens Crime Watch, 1998-2006, pres., 2001-03; vice chmn. Coral Gables City-Wide Anti-Crime Com., 2002-05, chmn., 2005-06; active Coral Gables Emergency Ops. Dept., 2005; chmn. Coral Gables Pub. Safety Com., 2006—. Recipient Key to the City of Coral Gables, 1993, 2006. Mem. The Fla. Bar (family law sect.), Dade County Bar Assn. (family law com., county cts. com., vice chair, 2004, Cert. of Appreciation 1994-95), Coral Gables Bar Assn. (law day com. 1996, scholarship com. 1996, bd. dirs. 1997-2005, pres. 2003-04), Fla. Acad. Profl. Mediators, U. Miami Alumni Club of Greater Miami (sec., dir. 1996-98), 200 Club Greater Miami (dir. 2009), Republican Nat. Lawyers Assn., Federalist Soc., SAR (chpt. pres., 2005-06), Jamestown Soc., Soc. Descs. of Knights of the Garter, Order of Crown of Charlemagne, Baronial Order of Magna Carta, Rotary Club Coral Gables (dir. 2001-03, pres. 2007-08), Royal Soc. St. George, Mil. Order Crusades, Order Mergovinian Dynasty, Order Founders and Patriots Am., Son Confederate Vets, Mil. Order of the Stars and Bars. Republican. Buddhist. Office Phone: 305-461-5015. Personal E-mail: mitchellesq@aol.com.

MITCHELL, DAVID WALKER, lawyer; b. Oakland, Calif., Nov. 11, 1935; s. Theodore Boyd and Helen Louise (Walker) M.; m. Carolyn Hilliard Graves, July 29, 1961; children: Sarah, Betsy. AB in History, Stanford U., 1957; JD, Harvard U., 1960. Bar: Calif. 1961. Assoc. Kindel & Anderson, LA, 1961-65, Weir, Hopkins, Donovan, San Jose, Calif., 1965-68; ptnr. Hopkins, Mitchell & Carley, San Jose, 1968-87, McCutchen, Doyle, Brown & Enersen, San Jose, 1987-93, Hoge, Fenton, Jones & Appel, San Jose, 1993-2000, of counsel, 2001—. Bd. dirs. Peninsula Open Space Trust, Menlo Park, Calif., 1982—2005, pres., 1984-92; bd. dirs. Cmty. Found. Silicon Valley, San Jose, 1977-94, 99-2003; chair bd. trustees United Way Santa Clara County, 1983-85. Fellow Am. Bar Found., Am. Leadership Forum (sr.); mem. Santa Clara County Bar Assn. (trustee 1972-75), San Jose C. of C. (bd. dirs. 1975-80). Mem. United Ch. of Christ. Avocations: music, hiking. Office: Hoge Fenton Jones Appel 60 S Market St Ste 1400 San Jose CA 95113-2396 Office Phone: 408-287-9501. Business E-Mail: dwm@hogefenton.com.

MITCHELL, EARL WESLEY, clergyman; b. Excelsior Springs, Mo., Mar. 16, 1931; s. Earl Van and Ora Leah (Butterfield) M.; m. Mary Lou Bell, June 8, 1956; children: Susan Yvonne, Randall Bruce. Ordained to ministry Christian Union Ch., 1971. Min. Vibbard (Mo.) Christian Union Ch., 1962-69, Liberty (Mo.) Christian Ch., 1969—77, Barwick Christian Union Ch., Cameron, Mo., 1977-80, Independence (Mo.) Christian Union Ch., 1980—95; assoc. pastor Flack Meml. Christian Union Ch., Excelsior Springs, Mo., 1995—2009. Former mem. state exec. bd. Christian Union Mo., 1995-98; area rep. Mo. Christian Union USA; former mem. gen. exec. bd., former editor C.U. Witness. Sgt USAF, 1951—55. Avocations: music, woodworking, painting, photography. Home and Office: 618 Henrie St Excelsior Springs MO 64024-2022

MITCHELL, EDWARD JOHN, economist, retired educator; b. Newark, Aug. 15, 1937; s. Edward Charles and Gladys (Werner) M.; m. Mary Josephine Osborne, June 14, 1958; children: Susan, Edward. BA summa cum laude, Bowling Green State U., 1960; postgrad., Oxford U., Eng., 1963-64; PhD in Econs., U. Pa., Eng., 1966. Lectr. in econs. Wharton Sch., U. Pa., 1964-65; economist Rand Corp., 1965-68; mem. Inst. Advanced Study, Princeton, NJ, 1968-69; sr. economist Pres.'s Council Econ. Advs., Washington, 1969-72; vis. assoc. prof. econs. Cornell U., 1972-73; assoc. prof. bus. econs. U. Mich., 1973-75, prof., 1975-88, prof. emeritus bus. econs. and pub. policy, 1988—; pres. Edward J. Mitchell Inc., Ann Arbor, 1977—94. Dir. nat. energy project Am. Enterprise Inst., 1974-76; pres. Fountainhead Investment Co., 1984—94. Author: U.S. Energy Policy: A Primer, 1974, Dialogue on World Oil, 1974, Financing the Energy Industry, 1975, Vertical Integration of the Oil Industry, 1976, The Deregulation of Natural Gas, 1983; contbr. articles to profl. jours. Home: 310 Penny Ln Santa Barbara CA 93108-2601 Office: Grad Sch Bus U Mich Ann Arbor MI 48109 Home: 1 Ct House Ln Apt 3401 Auckland 1141 New Zealand Personal E-mail: ejmitchell@xtra.co.nz. Business E-Mail: edward.john.mitchell@gmail.com.

MITCHELL, ELIZABETH H. (LIBBY MITCHELL), state legislator; b. SC, June 22, 1940; m. Jim Mitchell, 1965; children: J. Elizabeth, Will, Charlie, Emily BA, Furman U.; MA, U. NC, Chapel Hill; JD, U. Maine Sch. Law. Assoc. Mitchell & Davis, Augusta, Maine; mem. Maine State House Reps., 1974—84, 1991—98, majority leader, 1980—84, spkr., 1997—98; mem. Dist. 24 Maine State Senate, 2005—, pres., 2009—. Bd. mem. Maine Gen. Health, Jobs for Main's Graduates, Maine Coalition for Excellence in Edn.; mem. Kennebec Valley Cmty. Coll. Advisory Coun., New England Bd. Higher Edn., Jobs for Maine Graduates. Distinguished Alumna award, Furman U. Maine Women's Lobby; Vassalboro Historical Soc. Democrat. Office: Maine State Senate 3 State House Station Augusta ME 04333 also: 277 Cushnoc Rd Vassalboro ME 04989*

MITCHELL, GEOFFREY SCOTT, Spanish language educator; b. Ann Arbor, Mich., Mar. 4, 1964; s. Leonard Louis and Judith Rae (Stutzman) M. BA in Spanish, Hillsdale Coll., 1987; MA in Spanish, U. Mo., 1992. Spanish and history tchr. Lenawee Christian Sch., Adrian, Mich., 1987-89; Spanish instr. U. Mo., Columbia, 1989-92; Spanish tchr. Wichita (Kans.) Pub. Schs., 1992-93; Spanish instr. Wichita State U., 1993, Butler County C.C., Wichita, 1993, U. So. Miss., Hattiesburg, 1993—, editor fgn. lang. newsletter, 1993—, dir. summer study program in Mex., 1993—. Translator Howard Industries, Laurel, Miss., 1994—. Mem. Christian Coalition, Virginia Beach, Va. Mem. MLA, Am. Assn. Tchrs. Spanish and Portuguese, Sigma Delta Pi, Alpha Tau Omega. Republican. Home: 617 Walnut St Hattiesburg MS 39401-3959

MITCHELL, GEORGE JOHN, diplomat, former United States Senator from Maine; b. Waterville, Maine, Aug. 20, 1933; s. George J. and Mary (Saad) Mitchell; m. Heather MacLachlan; children: Andrea, Andrew, Claire. BA, Bowdoin Coll., Brunswick, Maine, 1954; LLB, Georgetown U., DC, 1960. Bar: Maine 1960, DC 1960. Trial atty. anti-trust divsn. US Dept. Justice, Washington, 1960-62; exec. asst. to Senator Edmund Muskie US Senate, 1962-65; ptnr. Jensen, Baird, Gardner & Henry, Portland, Maine, 1965-77; US atty. Dist. Maine US Dept. Justice, 1977-79; judge US Dist. Ct. Maine, 1979-80; US Senator from Maine, 1980-95; majority leader, 1988-95; mem. environ. and pub. works com., 1980-95; mem. vet. affairs com., fin. com., 1981-95; mem. nat. ocean policy study group, arms control observer group; ex officio mem. intelligence com.; chmn. Dem. Senatorial Campaign Com., 1984-86; spl. counsel Verner, Liipfert, Bernhard, McPherson and Hand, Washington, 1996—2002, Preti, Flaherty, Beliveau, Pachios & Haley, Portland, Maine, 1997—2005; ptnr. Piper Rudnick, Washington, 2002—04; ptnr., chmn. global bd., co-chmn. Govt. Controversies practice group DLA Piper, 2005—, now chmn. emeritus; chmn. The Walt Disney Co., Burbank, Calif., 2004—06; spl. presdl. envoy to the Middle East The White House, Washington, 2009—; with, US Spl. Envoy Mid East Pl. US Dept. State, Washington. Chmn. Maine Democratic Com., 1966—68; nat. committeeman Maine, 1969—77; dep. dir. Edmund S. Muskie presdl. campaign, 1968, 1972; asst. county atty. Cumberland County, 1971; spl. adv. to Pres. and Sec. of State for Econ. Initiatives in Ireland, 1995—2000; chmn. Sharm el-Sheikh Internat. Fact-Finding Com. to Examine Crisis in Middle East, 2000—01; head Investigation Steroid Abuse in Major League Baseball, 2006—07; bd. dirs. Boston Red Sox, The Walt Disney Co., 1995—2006. Author: World on Fire: Saving an Endangered Earth, 1990, Not For America Alone: The Triumph of Democracy and The Fall of Communism, 1997, Making Peace, 1999; co-author (with William S. Cohen): Men of Zeal: A Candid Inside Story of the Iran-Contra Hearings, 1988. Overseer Red Cross 9-11 Disaster Fund. Served with US Army, 1954—56. Recipient Phila. Liberty medal, 1998, Presdl. Medal of Freedom, The White House, 1999, Truman Inst. Peace Prize, German Peace Prize, UNESCO Peace Prize, Harry Hopkins medal, Harry S. Truman Good Neighbor award, Harry S. Truman Good Neighbor Award Found., 2007; named one of the 100 Most Influential People in the World, TIME mag., 2008. Democrat. Achievements include chaired Northern Ireland peace talks which led to the Good Friday Agreement, 1998; released the Mitchell Report naming major league baseball players involved with possible steroid usage, 2007. Office: US Dept State Washington DC 20004 Office Phone: 202-647-2021. Business E-Mail: mitchell.g@state.gov.

MITCHELL, HARRY E., United States Representative from Arizona, former state legislator; b. Tempe, July 18, 1940; s. Harry Casey and Irene Gladys (Childres) M.; m. Marianne Prevratil, May 5, 1962; children: Amy, Mark. BA, Ariz. State U., 1962, MPA, 1981. Tchr. Tempe (Ariz.) H.S., 1964—; city councilman City of Tempe, 1970—76, vice mayor, 1976—78, mayor, 1978—94; mem. Ariz. State Senate, 1999—2006, US Congress from 5th Ariz. dist., 2007—, mem. sci. & tech. com., transp. & infrastructure com., vets affairs com. Chmn., Ariz. Dem. Party, 2005-06; Bd. dirs. Tempe Sister City; trustee Tempe St. Lukes Hosp., Rio Salado Devel. Dist.; state rep. Sister Cities Internat., Washington; mem. Ariz. State U. Liberal Arts Alumni Adv. Bd., Adv. Council Ctr. Pub. Affairs, Ariz. Commn. Post Secondary Edn.; mem. Nat. League Cities Resolutions Com.; exec. com. League Ariz. Cities; bd. dirs. Ariz. Mcpl. Water Users. Recipient Disting. Svc. award Tempe Jaycees, Pub. Programs Disting. Achievement award, Ariz. State U. Mem. Ariz. State U. Alumni Bd. (chmn.), Ariz. State U. Advanced Pub. Exec. Program. Democrat. Roman Catholic. Office: 2434 Rayburn House Office Bldg Washington DC 20515 also: 7201 E Camelback Rd Ste 335 Scottsdale AZ 85253*

MITCHELL, HELEN BUSS, philosophy educator; b. NYC, July 17, 1941; d. Joseph William and Helen Ruth (Fitz) Buss; m. Joseph Rocco Mitchell, June 20, 1964; 1 child, Jason Christopher. AB, Hood Coll., Frederick, 1963; MEd, Loyola Coll., Balt., 1974, MMS, 1978; PhD, U. Md., 1990. Tchr. Howard County Pub. Sch., Ellicott City, Md., 1963-67; freelance writer Balt. News Am., Balt., 1972-75; columnist Cen. Md. News, Ellicott City, 1972-77; coord. adult basic edn. Howard Community Coll., Columbia, Md., 1974—77, asst. dir. continuing edn., 1977-79, dir., 1979-83, exec. dir., 1983-86, assoc. dean, continuing edn., 1986-93, chmn. instnl. self study, 1988—90, prof. philosophy, dir. women's studies, 1993—. Coach Howard Com. Coll. Ethics Bowl Team, 2002—. Author: History of the Orton Society, 1974, Roots of Wisdom 5th edit., 2007, 4th edit. retranslation, 2007, Readings From the Roots of Wisdom, 1997, 3d edit., 2002, Taking Sides: Clashing Views in World History, 1998, 3rd edit., 2005, The Holocaust: Readings And Interpretations, 2001. Mem. Mid-Md. Pvt. Industry Coun., 1991-93, Howard County study Commn. on Status of Women, 1972, Leadership Howard County, 1987-88; bd. dirs. Howard County Hist. Soc., 1989-92. Recipient Excellence award Nat. Inst. for Staff and Orgnl. Devel., 1997-98; named Outstanding Faculty Mem., Howard C.C., 1996, Distance Educator of the Yr., PBS, 1999; named to Howard County Women's Hall of Fame, 1999 Mem. Am. Philos. Assn., Nat. Women's Studies Assn., Md. Deans Continuing Edn. (pres. 1983-84, 92-93), Alpha Sigma Nu, Phi Kappa Phi. Achievements include development of For the Love of Wisdom telecourse. Avocations: travel, reading, music, yoga, tai chi. Office: Howard Community Coll 10901 Little Patuxent Pkwy Columbia MD 21044-3197

MITCHELL, HOMER, marketing executive; b. Ithaca, NY, Mar. 30, 1941; s. Edwin G. and Elizabeth (Pritchard) M.; m. Susan Reid, Feb. 1, 1964 (div. 1988); children: Margaret E., Homer D.; m. Lynne Luan Sechrist, Aug. 15, 1988. Student, Alfred U., NY, 1960-64; BA, N.Y. State Regents, 1983; MFA, Goddard Coll., 1992. Advt. mgr. Custom Foods, Inc., Binghamton, N.Y., 1968-70; dir. Upstate N.Y. mktg. Ky. Fried Chicken, Syracuse, 1970-78; mktg. specialist St. Lawrence County Econ. Devel., Canton, N.Y., 1978-86; mktg. mgr. Carthage (N.Y.) Machine Co., 1986-90; mktg. communications cons., 1991—. Cons. in field. Avocations: photography, writing. Home: 5 Willard St Willimantic CT 06226-3329

MITCHELL, JAMES ANDREW, education educator; b. Fort Campbell, Ky., Feb. 16, 1953; s. James Andrew and Joyce Anne (Smith) M.; 1 child, Magdalena Amelie. AB, Vassar Coll., 1975; MA, Princeton U., 1979, PhD, 1985. Instr. Princeton U., Princeton, NJ, 1981—82; asst. prof. Haverford Coll., Pa., 1981—82, U. Redlands, Calif., 1982—85; escort/interpreter U.S. Dept. State, Washington, 1983—86; project mgr. Delphi Internat. Group, Washington, 1986—89; asst. prof. Mt. Vernon Coll., Washington, 1990—94; assoc. prof. Calif. State U., Northridge, 1994—2003, prof., 2003—. Vis. faculty fellow Am. U. in Kygyzstan, 2001, U. Bucharest, 2001; bd. dirs. South East European Inst. of Internat. Affairs; Am. fgn. policy adv. bd. Dushkin Publ., 2006—. Contbr. articles to profl. jours. Mem. African policy issues group George Bush for Pres. Campaign, Washington, 1988. J. William Fulbright fellow CIES and USIA, U. Bucharest, 1977, NEH fellow, Washington, 1989, John Parker Compton pre-doctoral fellow Ctr. for Internat. Studies, Princeton U., 1981; Rsch. grantee Woodrow Wilson Sch., Princeton U., 1989 Mem.: Princeton Club of N.Y. Avocations: exercise, aerobics. Office: Dept Polit Sci/Calif State 18111 Nordhoff St Northridge CA 91330-0001 Office Phone: 818-677-3488. Business E-Mail: james.mitchell@csun.edu.

MITCHELL, JAMES B., medical researcher; PhD in cellular radiation biology, Colo. State U., 1978. Joined Radiation Br. Nat. Cancer Inst., NIH, 1979, independent investigator, 1984, past chief Radiobiology Sect., past dep. chief Radiation Oncology Br., chief Radiation Biology Br. Ctr. Cancer Rsch., 1993—, head Tumor Biology Sect., acting chief Radiation Oncology Br. Office: Ctr Cancer Rsch 10 Center Dr Bldg 10 Rm B3B69 9000 Rockville Pike Bethesda MD 20892 Office Phone: 301-496-7511. Office Fax: 301-480-2238. E-mail: jbm@helix.nih.gov.*

MITCHELL, SIR JAMES FITZALLEN, former Prime Minister of Saint Vincent and The Grenadines, agronomist, hotelier; b. Bequia, Grenadines, May 15, 1931; s. Reginald Fitzgerald M. and Lois Gooding Baynes; divorced; children: Sabrina, Gretel, Louise, Gabija. Grad., Imperial Coll. of Tropical Agr., Trinidad, 1954, U. B.C., 1954-56. Cocoa agronomist, St. Lucia, 1957; agrl. rsch. officer St. Vincent, 1958-61; sci. lectr. various schs., Eng., 1962-64; tech. editor on pest control Ministry of Overseas Devel., London, 1964-65; elected mem. St. Vincent Labour Party, 1966-67, elected as ind., 1972-74, premier, 1972-74; founder New Dem. Party, 1975, pres., 1975-2000; min. trade, agr., labor and tourism Govt. St. Vincent and the Grenadines, 1967—72, prime min., 1972—74, 1984—2000, former min. fin., planning and fgn. affairs. Chmn. Hotel Frangipani, Plumeria Investments; lectr. Cornell U., Ind. U., Princeton U. Author: Caribbean Crusade, 1989, Guiding Change in the Islands, 1996, A Season of Light, 2001, Beyond the Islands, 2006. Pres., founder New Dem. Party, privy councillor, 1985; chmn. Caribbean Dem. Union, Caribbean Cmty. Heads of Govt., 2000; vice chmn. Internat. Dem. Union. Decorated Order of Liberator (Venezuela), 1972, Knight Commdr. of Order of St. Michael and St. George, 1995, Chevalier d'Honneur, 1995, Order of Propitious Clouds, 1995, Order of the Great Cross of Infante Dom Henrique (Portugal), 1998; recipient Alumni award of distinction U. B.C., Can., 1988, Centennary award, 2008. Mem. Bequia Sailing Club, St. Vincent Nat. Trust (life), Interaction Coun. Anglican. Avocations: sailing, planting trees. Address: Villa Helianthus Bequia Saint Vincent and the Grenadines Home Phone: 1784-458-3263; Office Phone: 1784-458-3255. Personal E-mail: frangi@caribsurf.com.

MITCHELL, JAMES KENNETH, civil engineer, educator; b. Manchester, NH, Apr. 19, 1930; s. Richard N. and Henrietta (Moench) M.; m. Virginia D. Williams, Nov. 24, 1951; children: Richard A., Laura K., James W., Donald M., David L.; m. Holly R. Taylor, May 19, 2007. BCE, Rensselaer Poly. Inst., 1951; MS, MIT, 1953, DSc, 1956. Mem. faculty U. Calif., Berkeley, 1958-93, prof. civil engring., 1968-89, chmn. dept., 1979-84, Edward G. and John R. Cahill prof. civil engring., 1989-92, Edward G. and John R. Cahill prof. civil engring. emeritus, 1993—; Via prof. civil engring. Va. Poly. Inst. and State U., Blacksburg, 1994-99, Univ. Disting. prof., 1996-99, Univ. Disting. prof. emeritus, 1999—. Geotech. cons., 1960—. Author: Fundamentals of Soil Behavior, 1976, 3d edit., 2005; contbr. articles to profl. jours. Asst. scoutmaster Boy Scouts Am., 1975-82; mem. Moraga (Calif.) Environ. Rev. Com., 1978-80. Served to 1st lt. AUS, 1956-58. Recipient Exceptional Sci. Achievement medal NASA, 1973, Berkeley citation, 1993, Chief of Engrs. Outstanding Svc. award U.S. Army Corps Engrs., 1999, Rensselaer Alumni Assn. Fellows award, 2006, Dept. of Army Outstanding Civilian Svc. medal, 2007. Mem. ASCE (hon., Huber prize 1965, Disting. Middlebrooks award 1962, 70, 73, 01, Norman medal 1972, 95, Terzaghi lectr. 1984, Terzaghi award 1985, H. Bolton Seed medal 2004, Outstanding Projects and Leaders award in edn., 2006, pres. San Francisco sect. 1986-87), NAS, Nat. Acad. Engring. (vice chair civil engring. sect. 2001-03, chair 2003-05), Am. Soc. Engring. Edn. (We. Electric Fund award 1979), NRC (geotech. bd. chmn. 1990-94, bd. on infrastructure and constrn. environ. 1994-96, transp. rsch. bd. exec. com. 1983-87, mem. water sci. and tech. bd. 2005—08), Internat. Soc. Soil Mechanics and Geotech. Engring. (v.p. N.Am. 1989-94, Kevin Nash Gold medal 2001), Earthquake Engring. Rsch. Inst., Japanese Geotech. Soc. (internat. hon. mem.), Brit. Geotech. Soc. (Rankine lectr. 1991), Sigma Xi, Tau Beta Pi. Office: Va Tech Dept Civil Engring Blacksburg VA 24061-0105 Office Phone: 540-231-7351. Business E-Mail: jkm@vt.edu.

MITCHELL, JAMES KENNETH, geography educator; b. Londonderry, No. Ireland, Apr. 5, 1943; came to U.S., 1965; s. James and Sarah Ethel (Orr) M.; m. Elizabeth Jean McConaghy, Aug. 12, 1966; children: James Alexander, Patrick Alan. BSc with honors, Queens U. Belfast, No. Ireland, 1965; MA, U. Cin., 1965-67, M of Cmty. Planning, 1967; PhD in Geography, U. Chgo., 1973. Lectr. environ. resources Cook Coll., Rutgers U., New Brunswick, N.J., 1970-73, asst. prof., 1973-75, assoc. prof., 1975-80; chair dept. geography Rutgers U., 1994—96, 1988—91, 2003—05, prof. geography, 1980—, dir. grad. program in geography, 1977-85, 88-91, 99-01; mem. NJ Govs. Fl. Mitigation Task Force, 2005—06; fellow Am. Assoc. Advancement Sci., 2005—. Chair U.S. Sci. Com. on the Outer Continental Shelf, Washington, 1979-82; mem. com. on natural disasters NRC, Washington, 1982-86; expert witness. Author: Community Response to Coastal Erosion, 1974; author, editor: The Long Road to Recovery, 1996, Crucibles of Hazard: Megacities and Disasters in Transition, 1999; founding editor Global Environ. Change, 1990-93, Environ. Hazards, 1999—. Mem. curriculum adv. com. South Brunswick (N.J.) H.S., 1986-89. Recipient Presdl. award for disting. pub. svc. Rutgers U., 1984; East-West Ctr. fellow Environment and Policy Inst., 1987; Ctr. for Critical Analysis of Contemporary Culture fellow, 1991-92. Mem.: AAAS, Internat. Geog. Union (chair study group on the disaster vulnerability of megacities 1993—97), Internat. Rsch. Com. on Disasters, Inst. Brit. Geographers, Royal Geog. Soc., Assn. Am. Geographers, Am. Geog. Soc. (coun. 1984—93), Am. Conf. for Irish Studies. Presbyterian. Office: Rutgers U Dept Geography 54 Joyce Kilmer Ave Dept Piscataway NJ 08854-8045 E-mail: jmitchel@rci.rutgers.edu.

MITCHELL, JASON WAYNE, interventional radiologist; b. Passaic, NJ, Dec. 29, 1976; s. William Steven and Diane Lee (Brum) Mitchell; m. Amy Michelle Morin, July 10, 1999; 1 child, Caoilfhionn Lynn. BS, Boston Coll., Chestnut Hill, 1994—98; MD, UMDNJ-NJMS, Newark, 2000—04. Intern transitional program St. Barnabas Med. Ctr., Livingston, NJ, 2004—05; resident diagnostic radiology UMDNJ, 2005—09; fellow interventional radiology Northwestern Meml. Hosp., Chgo., 2009—. Mem.: Soc. Interventional Radiology, Radiologic Soc. N.Am., Am. Coll. Radiology, Am. Mensa. Conservative. Roman Catholic. Achievements include research in diagnostic and interventional radiology with a focus in hepatic pathology and the treatment of hepatocellular carcinoma. Office: UMDNJ 150 Bergen St C-320 Newark NJ 07103 Home: 457 Old Surrey Rd Hinsdale IL 60521 Office Phone: 973-972-5188. Personal E-mail: mitchejn@gmail.com.

MITCHELL, JERE HOLLOWAY, physiologist, researcher, medical educator; b. Longview, Tex., Oct. 17, 1928; s. William Holloway and Dorothea (Turner) M.; m. Pamela Battey, Oct. 1, 1960; children: Wendy Mitchell O'Sullivan, Laurie Mitchell Woods, Amy Mitchell Poeppel. BS with honors, Va. Mil. Inst., 1950; MD, Southwestern Med. Sch., 1954; PhD (hon.), U. Copenhagen, 2000. Intern Parkland Meml. Hosp., Dallas, 1954-55; resident in internal medicine, 1955-56; cardiology fellow U. Tex. Southwestern, 1956—58; with, pub. health svc. Lab. Cardiovasc. Physiology, Nat. Heart Inst., Bethesda, Md., 1958—62; asst. prof. medicine and physiology U. Tex. Southwestern Med. Ctr., Dallas, 1962-66; dir. Weinberger Lab. Cardiopulmonary Rsch., 1966—99; assoc. prof., 1966-69; prof., 1969—; dir. Harry S. Moss Heart Ctr., 1976—2000; holder Frank M. Ryburn Jr. chair in heart rsch., 1982—2000; holder Carolyn P. and S. Roger Hochow chair in cardiac rsch., 1989—; attending physician Parkland Meml. Hosp., 1963—, St. Paul Med. Ctr., 1966—, VA Med. Ctr., Dallas, 1969—; mem. courtesy staff Zale-Lipshy U. Hosp., 1990—. Pfizer vis. prof. Pa. State U., 1990; Percy Russo lectr. prof. U. Sydney, Cumberland Coll., 1991; established investigator Am. Heart Assn., 1962-67; mem. applied physiol. orthopedic sutdy sect. NIH, 1979-81, respirat. appl physiol. studysect., 1981-82; mem. sci. adv. bd. USAF, 1988-90, rsch. rev. com. A-NHLBI, 1992-97. Mem. editl. bd. Am. Jour. Physiology, 1972-76, Circulation, 1978-81, 1993-2004, Am. Jour. Cardiology, 1965-74, 82-84, Cardiovasculatr Rsch., 1979-87, Jour. Cardiopulmonary Rehab, 1981-91, Clin. Physiology and Functional Imaging, 1981—, Exptl. Physiology, assoc. editor, 1993-2000, Jour. Applied Physiology, 1978-82, 84-89, assoc. editor, 1990-93. Recipient Career Devel. award USPHS, 1968-73, Donald W. Seldin rsch. award U. Tex. Southwestern, 1978. Fellow Am. Coll. Cardiology (Young Invetigator award 1961, Disting. Scientist award 1999), Am. Coll. Sprots Medicine (Citation award 1983, Honor award 1988, Joseph B. Wolffe lectr. 1989); mem. AAAS (med. sci. com. 1988—), Internat. Union Physiol. Soc. (commn. on cardiovascular physiology 1977—), Internat. Soc. & Fed. Cardiol. (mem. coun. cardiac rehab. 1981—), Am. Heart Assn. (Award of Merit 1984, pres. Dallas divsn. 1977-78, pres. Tex. affil. 1983-84, nat. v.p. 1990-91), Am. Fedn. Clin. Rsch. (emeritus), Am. Soc. Clin. Investigation (emeritus), Assn. Am. Physicians, Am. Physiol. Soc. (cardiovascular sect.-Carl J. Wiggers award 1992, environ. and exercise physiology sect.-Edward Adolph Disting. Lectr. 2003, honor award 2007), Assn. Univ. Cardiologists, Alpha Omega Alpha. Office: Univ Tex Southwestern Med Ctr Cardiology Divsn 5323 Harry Hines Blvd Dallas TX 75390-9174 Home Phone: 214-369-1199; Office Phone: 214-648-3424. Business E-Mail: jere.mitchell@utswithwestern.edu.

MITCHELL, JEREMY NEIL, geologist, materials scientist; b. Cleve., Nov. 11, 1963; s. Terence Edward and Marion (Wyatt) M.; m. Melissa Anne Brown. BA in Geol. Sci., Case Western Res. U., 1986; MS in Geology, Miami U., Oxford, Ohio, 1989; PhD in Geology and Geophysics, U. Wyoming, Laramie, 1993. Postdoctoral rsch. assoc. U. Tenn., Knoxville, 1994-95, Los Alamos (N.Mex.) Nat. Lab., 1995-98, tech. staff mem., 1998—. Contbr. articles to profl. jours. Recipient Philips Petroleum scholarship U. Wyo., Laramie, 1993, S.H. Knight scholarship Wyo. Geol. Assn., Casper, 1991, J. David Love Field fellowship, 1990, Presdl. scholar Microscopy Soc. of Am., 1986. Mem. Am. Geophys. Union, Mineral. Soc. Am., Geol. Soc. Am. Office: Los Alamos Nat Lab Mail Stop G721 Los Alamos NM 87545-0001 E-mail: jeremy@lanl.gov.

MITCHELL, JERRY, reporter; b. Texarkana, Tex., 1959; BA, Harding U., Ark., 1982; MA, Ohio State U., Columbus, 1997. Spl. projects reporter Clarion-Ledger, Jackson, Miss., 1986—. Author: The Preacher & the Klansman, 1998; cons. (documentaries) Killed by the Klan, 1999. Recipient Kennedy Ctr. honors, ADL, 1998, Heywood Broun award for disting. journalism, 1999, Outstanding Alumnus award, Harding U., 1999, Nat. Assn. Black Journalists award, 1999, newspaper award, Sidney Hillman Found., 1999, Sigma Delta Chi award for pub. svc. in journalism, Soc. Professional Journalists, 1999, 2 Best of Gannett awards, 1999, Silver Em award, U. Miss. Dept. Journalism, 2000, Outstanding Achievement Award of Excellence, Gannett Co., 2002, John Chancellor award for Excellence in Journalism, Columbia U., 2005, Pres.'s medal, CUNY Queen's Coll., 2005, Vernon Jarrett award, NC Agricultural & Technical State U. Inst. Advanced Journalism Studies, 2006, Tom Renner medal for outstanding crime reporting, Investigative Reporters & Editors, 2006, George Polk award for Justice Reporting, 2006, George Polk award for State Reporting, 2007; finalist Pulitzer Prize, 2006. Achievements include investigative reporting leading to the prosecution and conviction of white supremacists who had committed murders in the 1960s; including the murders of civil rights activists in Mississippi and the 1963 bombing of a church in Birmingham that killed four girls. Office: Clarion-Ledger PO Box 40 Jackson MS 39205 Office Phone: 601-961-7064. Office Fax: 601-961-7211. E-mail: jmitchell@clarionledger.com.

MITCHELL, JOAN LAVERNE, research scientist; b. Palo Alto, Calif., May 24, 1947; d. William Richardson and Doris LaVerne (Roddan) M. BS in Physics, Stanford U., 1969; MS in Physics, U. Ill., 1971, PhD in Physics, 1974. Rsch. staff mem. T.J. Watson Rsch. Ctr. IBM, Yorktown Heights, NY, 1974-88, 96-98, mgr. T.J. Watson Rsch. Ctr., 1979-88, image tech. cons. mktg. White Plains, NY, 1989-91, rsch. staff mem. T.J. Watson Rsch. Ctr. Hawthorne, NY, 1991-94, mgr. T.J. Watson Rsch. Ctr., 1992-94, supplemental employee Burlington, NY, 1994-96; vis. prof. U. Ill., Urbana, 1996; with IBM Printing Systems Divsn., Boulder, Colo., 1999—2007, IBM fellow, 2001—07; InfoPrint Solutions Co. fellow InfoPrint Solutions Co., 2007—09. Del. CCITT Study Group XIV, 1978-79, ISO JPEG Com., 1987-94, ITU-T Study Group 16 Working Party 3, 2005-07. Co-author: JPEG Still Image Data Compression Standard, 1993, MPEG Video Compression Standard, 1997, (mentoring book) Straight Talk About Talking Change Of Your Career, 2007; contbr. articles to profl. jours. Recipient U. Ill. Coll. Engrng. Disting. Alumni Svc. award, 2006, Leadership award Internat. Multimedia Telecoms. Consortium, 2006; Xerox Indsl. fellow, 1970-71. Fellow IEEE; mem. NAE, Am. Phys. Soc., Soc. for Imaging Sci. and Tech., Sigma Xi (chpt. sec. 1976, v.p. 1977, pres. 1978), Phi Beta Kappa, Phi Kappa Phi. Democrat. Achievements include co-inventor on numerous patents. Home: 1200 Woodrow Ave Apt 9B Modesto CA 95351 Home Phone: 209-523-5917; Office Phone: 720-663-3525. Business E-Mail: joan.mitchell@infoprint.co, joan.mitchell@stanfordalumni.org.

MITCHELL, JOHN CHARLES, marketing professional; b. Bedford, Ind., May 25, 1947; s. John Lewis and Mary Ellen (Rowe) M.; m. Marie Elizabeth Bruland, Aug. 21, 1971; 1 child, Allison Anne. BA in Econs., Va. Mil. Inst., 1969; MBA, JD, Ind. U., 1975. Bar: Ind., 1975, Fed. Cts., 1975. Brand mgr. Procter and Gamble Co., Cin., 1975-82; group product mgr. RJR/Del Monte, San Francisco, 1982-84; dir. mktg. RJR/Nabisco, Parsippany, NJ, 1984-87, v.p. mktg., 1987-88, v.p., gen. mgr., 1988-90, pres. sales and logistics co., 1991-94, pres. Planters, Lifesavers co. Winston-Salem, NC, 1994-96; pres. bus. printer divsn. Lexmark Internat., Inc., Lexington, Ky., 1997-99; founder Collaborative Leaders, Inc., Chapel Hill, NC, 2001—. 1st lt. US Army, 1969-71. Inductee Va. Mil. Inst. Sports Hall of Fame, 1981. Republican. Methodist. Avocations: golf, skiing. E-mail: jandmmitchell@nc.rr.com.

MITCHELL, JONI (ROBERTA JOAN ANDERSON), singer, songwriter, artist; b. Ft. Macleod, Alta., Can., Nov. 7, 1943; d. William A. and Myrtle M. (McKee) Anderson; m. Chuck Mitchell (div.); m. Larry Klein, Nov. 21, 1982. Student, Alta. Coll. Albums Song to a Seagull, Clouds, Ladies of the Canyon, Blue, For the Roses, Court and Spark, 1974, Miles of Aisles, The Hissing of Summer Lawns, 1975, Hejira, 1976, Don Juan's Reckless Daughter, 1979, Mingus, 1979 (Jazz Album of Year and Rock-Blues Album of Year, Downbeat mag., 1979), Shadows and Light, 1980, Wild Things Run Fast, 1982, Dog Eat Dog, 1985, Chalk Mark in a Rainstorm, 1988, Night Ride Home, 1991, Turbulent Indigo, 1994 (Grammy award for Best Pop Vocal Album, Best Album Package, 1996), Hits, 1996, Taming the Tiger, 1998, Both Sides Now, 2000 (Grammy award for Best Traditional Pop Vocal Performance, 2001), Travelogue, 2002, Shine, 2007 (Grammy award for Best Pop Instrumental Performance, 2008), screenwriter/actor (films) Love, 1982; contbr. album dog Eat Dog/Wild Things Run Fast, 1996; co-creator (Operas) The Fiddle and the Drum, 2007; exhibitions include Green Flag Song, 2006, Flag Dance, 2007. Recipient Grammy award for Best Folk Performance, 1969, Grammy award for Best Arrangement Accompanying Vocalists (with Tom Scott), 1974, Grammy awards for Best Album Package & Best Pop Vocal Album, 1996, Grammy award for Best Traditional Pop Vocal Performance, 2001, Century award, Billboard, 1995, Polar Music prize, 1996; named one of 100 Greatest Guitarists of All Time, Rolling Stone, 2003; named to Rock and Roll Hall of Fame, 1997. Office: c/o Sam Feldman SL Fedlman & Assocs 1505 W 2nd Ave Ste 200 Vancouver BC V6H 3Y4 Canada

MITCHELL, JOSEPH PATRICK, architect; b. Bellingham, Wash., Sept. 29, 1939; s. Joseph Henry and Jessie Delila (Smith) Mitchell; m. Marilyn Ruth Jorgenson, June 23, 1962; children: Amy Evangeline, Kirk Patrick, Scott Henry. Student, Western Wash. State Coll., 1957-59; BA, U. Wash., 1963, BArch, 1965. Assoc. designer, draftsman, project architect Beckwith Spangler Davis, Bellevue, Wash., 1965-70; prin. J. Patrick Mitchell, AIA & Assocs./Architects/Planners/Cons., Kirkland, Wash., 1970—. Del. various internat. confs.; charter mem. Northshore Bapt. Ch., 1969, elder, 1984—90; bd. ext. and ctrl. com. Columbia Bapt. Conf., 1977—83, vice-moderator, 1995—96, moderator, 1996—97, overseer ch. ministries bd., pres., 1997—99; charter mem. Cascade Cmty. Ch., 1997—; trustee Bakke Libr./Cultural Ctr., 1994—96; chmn. long range planning com. Lake Retreat Camp, 1965—93; active Deming Hist. Cemetery Assn., 1997—. Recipient Internat. Archtl. Design award, St. John Vianney Parish, 1989. Mem.: AIA, Christian Camp and Conf. Assn., Wash. Farm Forestry Assn., Internat. Conf. Bldg. Ofcls., Nat. Coun. Archtl. Registration Bds., Nat. Fedn. Bus., Interfaith Forum Religion, Art, and Architecture (arch. edn. tour Finland, St. Petersburg, Russia 1998, Japan 2000, edn. tour China 2001, Spain, Portugal, Scandanavia, Estonia, Russia 2002, Switzerland, France 2004, Eng., Scotland, Ireland 2005, France 2006, Peru, Equador, Costa Rica 2007, Italy 2008—), Constrn. Specification Inst., Woodinville C. of C. Office: 12620 120th Ave NE Ste 208 Kirkland WA 98034-7511

MITCHELL, KAREN LEE, special education educator, consultant; b. Hudson, Mass., Nov. 23, 1949; d. Leon E. and Barbara V. (Jusseaume) LaFlamme; m. Ernest L. Mitchell, July 24, 1971; 1 child, Jeremy R. BS in Edn., Fitchburg U., Mass., 1971; MA in Psychology, Anna Maria Coll., 1982. Cert. spl. edn. tchr., elem. tchr., sch. guidance counselor. Tchr. spl. needs Quaboag Regional Jr./Sr. High Sch., Warren, Mass., 1971-73; specialize care foster parent Mass. Dept. Social Svcs., 1973-81; tchr. gifted and talented Oxford Acad., Northborough, Mass., 1981-89, test adminstr., cons., 1985-89; tchr. Here We Grow Pre-Sch., Auburn, Mass., 1990—94; tchr. spl. edn. Bartlett Jr./Sr. H.S., Webster, Mass., 1994—. Pvt. practice edn. cons., Auburn, 1989—90. Sunday Sch. tchr. First Congl. Ch., Auburn, 1974-78, trustee, 1980; den leader Boy Scouts Am., Auburn, 1982-85. Avocations: photography, cross country skiing, biking, swimming, camping. Home: 71 Hill St Auburn MA 01501-3335 Personal E-mail: teachem_1@msn.com. E-mail: teachem_1@charter.net.

MITCHELL, KENNETH DAVID, physiologist, educator; b. Musselburgh, Scotland, Mar. 5, 1959; children: Elaine J., Fraser K., Keith J. BSc with upper 2d class honors, U. Edinburgh, Scotland, 1981, PhD in Physiology, 1986. Physiology tutor Univ. Med. Sch., Edinburgh, 1981-84; rsch. assoc. dept. physiology and biophysics Nephrology Rsch. and Tng. Ctr. U. Ala., Birmingham, 1984-86, postdoctoral rsch. fellow, 1986-87, rsch. instr., 1987-88, scientist I, 1987-88; asst. prof. dept. physiology Tulane U. Sch. Medicine, New Orleans, 1988-95, assoc. prof., 1995—. Contbr. articles to profl. jours. Fellow Am. Heart Assn. (fellow Coun. High Blood Pressure Rsch. 1993—, Established Investigator award 1995-2000), Am. Soc. Nephrology; mem. Am. Physiol. Soc., Internat. Soc. Nephrology. Office: Tulane U Sch Medicine Dept Physiology SL39 1430 Tulane Ave New Orleans LA 70112-2699 Office Phone: 504-988-2593. Business E-Mail: kdmitch@tulane.edu.

MITCHELL, KOSSUTH MAYER, business educator; b. Thomasville, Ala., Aug. 10, 1942; s. Zadock and Carrie Bell (Harvel) M.; m. Sandra Shafer Mitchell; children: Sherry Roy, Kossuth II, Lenore Pollard, Christie Snyder, Maribeth. AA, Monterey Peninsula Coll., 1975; BBA, James Madison U., 1982, MBA, 1984; D in Bus. Adminstrn., Nova Southea. U., 1993. Enlisted U.S. Army, 1960, advanced through grades to sgt. maj., ret., 1983; prof. bus. adminstrn., bus. program coord. Alice Lloyd Coll., Pippa Passes, Ky., 1984—. Dir. Ctry. for Econ. Edn., Alice Lloyd Coll., 1988-92, founder Students in Free Enterprise team, 1988, faculty sponsor Bapt. Student Union, 1985-88, guest spkr., 1985—, workshop leader Mission Project, spring 1993; presenter edn1., profl., civic and ch. orgns. Bd. dirs. Our Lady of the Way Hosp., Martin, Ky., 1993—; mem. adv. bd. Caney Creek Mental Rehab. Complex, Pippa Passes, 1994—; active Gideons, 1995—. Decorated Bronze Star with two bronze oak leaf clusters; Kossuth M. Mitchell scholarship endowed in his name Alice Lloyd Coll., 1996. Mem. Acad. Mgmt., Midwest Acad. Mgmt., Ky. Bus. Soc., Acad. Fin. Mgmt., Noncommd. Officers Assn. (life), Am. Fedn. Police (Am. Patriotism award 1996), VFW (life), DAV (life), Kiwanis (lt. gov. divsn. 8 Ky.-Tenn. dist. 1993-94, pres. Knott County club 1991-92, club sec., treas. 1990-91, 94-95), Ky. Cols., Alpha Chi (v.p. region V 1990-92, pres. 1992-94, inaugurator Ky. Eta chpt Alice Lloyd Coll. 1988, inaugurator Caney Creek Cmty. Ctr. alumni chpt. 1993), Phi Beta Lambda (founder, primary advisor Omega Alpha Tau chpt. 1986-88, asst. advisor 1988—, advisor Alice Lloyd Coll. bus. club 1984-86). Baptist. Avocations: reading, running, shopping. Home and Office: Alice Lloyd Coll 100 Purpose Rd # 28 Pippa Passes KY 41844-9005

MITCHELL, LANCE BERNARD, social worker; b. Rochester, NY, Dec. 3, 1964; s. Bernard and Mary Frances Mitchell; m. Deborah Lynn Joynt, July 16, 1988; children: Sierra Lynn, Morgan Maxfield, Darcy James, Reegan Ashley. BSc, Roberts Wesleyan Coll., North Chili, NY, 1988, MS in Social Work, 1997. Adolescent chem. dependency counselor Unity Health Sys., Rochester, 1988—97; sch. social worker Spencerport High Sch., Rochester, 1997—2000; prevention intervention youth specialist Brighton Ctrl. Schs., Rochester, 2000—, sch. social worker, 2000—. Outreach addiction therapist 4 Unity Health Sys., Rochester, 1997—. Head coach Genesee Valley Youth Hockey Club, River Cats, Rochester, 2000—08; youth min. Powerhouse Youth, Parkridge Free Meth. Ch., Rochester, 1997—2008; pee wee hockey Genesee Valley Youth Hockey Club, River Cats, 2008—; alumni coll. pres. Roberts Wesleyan Coll., Rochester, 1998—2004. Recipient Grad. Last Decade award, Roberts Wesleyan Coll., 1998; named Helen Gunther Counselor of Yr., Nat. Coun. Alcoholism, 2001, MSW of Yr., Roberts Wesleyan Coll., 2008. Mem.: Rochester Youth Hockey Assn. (asst. head coach), Brighton Task Force Healthy Youth. Home: 83 Donna Marie Circle Rochester NY 14606 Office: Brighton Ctrl Schs 1150 Winton Rd South Rochester NY 14618 Office Phone: 585-242-5012. Office Fax: 585-242-7364. Personal E-mail: roctekoa@yahoo.com. Business E-Mail: lance_mitchell@bcsd.org.

MITCHELL, LEE MARK, private equity investor, executive; b. Albany, NY, Apr. 16, 1943; s. Maurice B. and Mildred (Roth) M.; m. Barbara Lee Anderson, Aug. 27, 1966; children: Mark, Matthew. AB, Wesleyan U., 1965; JD, U. Chgo., 1968. Bar: Ill. 1968, D.C. 1969, U.S. Supreme Ct. 1972. Assoc. Leibman, Williams, Bennett, Baird & Minow, Chgo. and Washington, 1968-72, Sidley & Austin, Washington, 1972-74, ptnr., 1974-84, 92-94; exec. v.p. and gen. counsel Field Enterprises, Inc., Chgo., 1981-83, pres., CEO, 1983-84, Field Corp., 1984-92; prin. Golder, Thoma, Cressey, Rauner, Inc., Chgo., 1994-98; mng. ptnr. Thoma Cressey Bravo, Inc., Chgo., 1998—. Chmn. Chgo. Stock Exch., Inc., 2000—04. Author: Openly Arrived At, 1974, With the Nation Watching, 1979; co-author: Presidential Television, 1973. Bd. visitors U. Chgo. Law Sch., 1984—86, Medill Sch. Journalism, Northwestern U., 1984—91; pres. bd. govs. Chgo. Met. Planning Coun., 1988—91; mem. midwest regional adv. bd. Inst. Internat. Edn., 1987—99; trustee Ravinia Festival Assn., 1989—97, Northwestern U., Northwestern Meml. Hosp.; U.S. del. Brit. Legis. Conf. on Govt. and Media, Ditchley Park, England, 1974; adv. com. LWV Presdl. Debates, Washington, 1979—80, 1982; vice chair Chgo. Met. Planning Coun., 1999—2005, chair, 2005—. Mem.: Econ. Mid-Am. Club, ABA, Comml. Club Chgo. Home: 135 Maple Hill Rd Glencoe IL 60022-1252 Office: Thoma Cressey Bravo Inc Sears Tower Ste 9200 233 S Wacker Dr Chicago IL 60606-6331 Business E-Mail: lmitchell@tcb.com.

MITCHELL, MARY JENKINS, public health service officer; b. Rochester, NY; d. Hudson and Clara May Jenkins; m. Floyd Mitchell, Aug. 24, 1991; 1 child, Derek Scot. B Cmty. Health, St. Joseph's Coll., Bklyn., 1984; MPA, LI U., Bklyn., 1999. Cert. non-profit mgmt. Columbia U., 1986. Asst. to pres. Bklyn. Borough Pres.' Office, 1987—95; dir., health careers inst. LI U., 1995—2000; regional v.p. Am. Cancer Soc., Bklyn., 2000—03; exec. dir. MSI Area Health Edn. Ctr., NYC, 2004—. Adj. prof. LI U., Brooklyn, NY, 1998—2000; student cons. Pub. Svc. Commn., Pretoria, South Africa, 1998. V.p. Justice Works Cmty., Inc., Bklyn., 1995—2000; deaconess Flatbush Tompkins Congl. Ch., Bklyn., 1997—2004; bd. dirs. NY Women's Found., NYC, 1993—95. Recipient Ability, Accomplishment and Cmty. Svc. award, Outstanding Young Women Am., 1986, Cmty. Leadership award, Bklyn Exec. Bus. Women's Assoc., 2004. Mem.: Pi Alpha Alpha (life). Office: Manhattan-State Area Health Educ Ctr 43 Central Park North New York NY 10026 Personal E-mail: mljm1@excite.com. Business E-Mail: mary@msiahec.org.

MITCHELL, MARY NIALL, history professor; married. BA in Fine Arts, Vanderbilt U., Nashville, 1991; MA in Journalism, NYU, NYC, 1993; PhD in History, NYU, 2001. Assoc. prof. history U. New Orleans, 2001—. Author: (book) Raising Freedom's Child: Black Children and Visions of the Future After Slavery. Rsch. fellowship, Gilder Lehrman Inst. Am. History, 2008, Andrew Oliver fellowship, Mass. Hist. Soc., 2008, Oscar Handlin fellowship, Am. Coun. Learned Socs., 2004—05. Mem.: Orgn. Am. Historians, Am. Studies Assn. (Constance Rourke prize 2003), Am. Hist. Assn. Office: Univ New Orleans Dept of History New Orleans LA 70148 Business E-Mail: mnmitche@uno.edu.

MITCHELL, MELVIN CLIFFORD, music educator; b. Talihina, Okla., Dec. 1, 1942; s. Lem Granville Mitchell and Evelyn Irene Gale, J. E. Gale (Stepfather); m. Joyce Elaine Anglin, June 23, 1962; children: Matthew Clark, Daniel Dale. MusB in Edn., Okla. State U., 1964; MEd, Southwestern Okla. State U., 1975. Cert. vocal music dir. K-12 Okla. State U. Vocal music dir. Shelbyville (Mo.) Sch. Sys., 1964—65, Littleton (Colo.) Sch. Dist., 1965—66, Lone Wolf (Okla.) Pub. Sch. Sys., 1967—70, Woodward (Okla.) Pub. Sch. Sys., 1970—75; chmn. and vocal music dir. Ea. Okla. State Coll., Wilburton, 1975—83; vocal music dir. Lewisville (Tex.) Ind. Sch. Dist, 1986—. Musical cast mem. and soloist Okla. State U., Stillwater, 1961—64; contest chmn. N.W. Okla Vocal Music Dist., Woodward, 1970—75; vocal music adjudicator/clinician, Okla., 1970—83; mem. all-state music com. Okla. Music Educators Assn., Oklahoma City, 1972—75; dir. sweepstakes choirs Woodward choral orgns., Enid, Okla., 1973—75; dir. musicals Woodward Pub. Schs., 1973—75; vocal music dir. Okla. State 4-H Round-Up, Stillwater, 1975—79; dir. musicals Ea. Okla State coll., 1975—83; vocal choral arranger Griffin Mid. Sch. A cappella Choir, The Colony, Tex., 1998—. Fellow: Phi Delta Kappa (assoc.; found. rep. 1998—2004); mem.: Tex. Choral Dirs. Assn. (assoc.), Tex. Music Educators Assn. (assoc.), Am. Choral Dirs. Assn. (life). Republican. Baptist. Avocation: golf. Home: 2216 Swallow Ln Lewisville TX 75077 Office: Griffin Mid Sch 5105 N Colony Blvd The Colony TX 75056 Home Fax: 972-317-9863. Business E-Mail: mitchellmc@lisd.net.

MITCHELL, MOZELLA GORDON, language educator, minister; b. Starkville, Miss., Aug. 14, 1936; d. John Thomas and Odena Mae (Graham) Gordon; m. Edrick R. Woodson, Mar. 20, 1951 (div. 1974); children: Cynthia LaVern, Marcia Delores Woodson Miller. AB, LeMoyne Coll., 1959; MA in English, U. Mich., 1963; MA in Religious Studies, Colgate-Rochester Divinity Sch., 1973; PhD, Emory U., 1980. Instr. in English and Speech Alcorn A&M Coll., Lorman, Miss., 1960-61; instr. English, chmn. dept. Owen Jr. Coll., Memphis, 1961-65; asst. prof. English and religion Norfolk State Coll. U. Norfolk, Va., 1965—81; assoc. prof. U. South Fla., Tampa, 1981—93, prof., 1993—, chmn.-elect religious studies dept., 2005—; chair religious studies dept., 2006—; pastor Mount Sinai AME Zion Ch., 1982—89; presiding elder Tampa dist. AME Zion Ch., 1988—; pastor, founder Love of Christ AME Zion Tabernacle, Branden, 1993—; candidate for bishop AME Zion Ch., 2003—04, presiding Elder, 1998—2004. Vis. assoc. prof. Hood Theol. Sem., Salisbury, N.C., 1979-80, St. Louis U., 1992-93; vis. asst. lectr. U. Rochester, N.Y., 1972-73; co-dir. Ghent VISTA Project, Norfolk, 1969-71; cons. Black Women and Ministry Interdenominational Theol. Ctr; lectr. Fla. Humanities Coun., 1994-95; Meml. lectr. Mordecai Johnson Inst., Colgate Rochester Div. Sch., 1997. Author: Spiritual Dynamics of Howard Thurman's Theology, 1985, Howard Thurman and the Quest for Freedom, Proc. 2d Ann. Howard Thurman Convocation (Peter Lang), 1992, African American Religious History in Tampa Bay, 1992;, New Africa in America: The Blending of African and American Religious and Social Traditions Among Black People in Meridian, Mississippi and Surrounding Counties (Peter Lang), 1994, Crucial Issues in Caribbean Religions (Peter Lang), 2006, Crucial Issues in Caribbean Religion, 2006; editor: Martin Luther King Meml. Series in Religion, Culture and Social Devel.; editorial bd. Cornucopia Reprint Series; contr. articles and essays in field. Mem. Tampa-Hillsborough County Human Rels. Coun., 1987—; founder Women at the Well, Inc.; del. 7th assembly World Coun. Chs., Canberra, Australia, 1991, 17th World Meth. Coun., Rio de Janiero, 1996; del. 18th World Meth. Coun., Brighton, England, 2001; mem. connectional coun. A.M.E. Zion Ch., Charlotte, 1984—, staff writer Sunday sch. lit., 1981—, mem. jud. coun., candidate for bishop, 2002—04; pres. Fla. Coun. Chs., Orlando, Fla., 1988—90, pres.-elect, 1998—, pres. exec. bd., 2000. Recipient ecumenical leadership citation Fla. Coun. Chs., 1990, Inaugural lectr. award Geddes Hanson Black Cultural Ctr. Princeton Theol. Sem., 1993; fellow Nat. Doctoral Fund, 1978-80; grantee NEH, 1981, Fla. Endowment for Humanities, 1990—, U. South Fla. Rsch. Coun., 1990—. Mem. Coll. Theology Soc., Am. Acad. Religion, Soc. for the Study of Black Religion (pres. 1992-96), Joint Ctr. for Polit. Studies, Black Women in Ch. and Soc., Alpha Kappa Alpha. Phi Kappa Phi. Democrat. Methodist. Avocations: piano, poetry, tennis, bicycling, Scrabble. Office: Univ South Florida Religious Studies Dept CPR 107 Tampa FL 33620 Office Phone: 813-974-1852. Personal E-mail: mozellam@aol.com. Business E-Mail: mmitchel@acas.usf.edu. *In my estimation, people are people, whatever the race, class or status. Between the front yard and the back porch of each individual dwells the real person, to whom I like to direct my approach.*

MITCHELL, NORMA TAYLOR, history professor; b. Norfolk, Va., Nov. 14, 1936; d. Orville Carson Sr. and Emma (Heal) Taylor; m. Frank Joseph Mitchell, Sept. 5, 1959; 1 child, Anne Mitchell Whisnant. BA in History, Coll. William and Mary, 1958; MA, Duke U., 1962, PhD, 1967. Assoc. prof. history Troy (Ala.) State U. (now Troy U.), 1970—84, prof. history, 1984—99, prof. emerita, 1999—. Instr. history and polit. sci. Union Coll., Barbourville, Ky., 1962-64; dean women Ctrl. Meth. Coll., Fayette, Mo., 1968-70; gen. commn. on archives and history United Meth. Ch., 1972-80, chair women's history project, 1977-80; vice chair nat. planning com. Bicentennial of Methodism in Am., 1979-80; lectr., presenter in field. Contbr. chpts. in books; author articles and revs. Lay leader United Meth. Ch., local, state and nat. levels, 1960—, including bd. dirs. United Meth. Bd. Pastoral Care and Counseling, 1984-92, bd. dirs. United Meth. Children's Homes, Ala.-West Fla., 1989-99; del. Southeastern Jurisdictional Confs., 1980; United Meth. Women conf. officer, 1976-80; conf. chair Commn. on Status and Role of Women, 1976-80; bd. dirs. Scarritt-Bennett Ctr., 2003—. Recipient awards and honors; So. Fellowships Fund grantee, 1958-61; Cokesbury Tchg. fellow, 1964-65. Mem. AAUP, NEA, NOW, AAUW (v.p. for membership Troy br. 1995-99, honoree Ednl. Found. 1998-99), Ala. Edn. Assn., Am. Hist. Assn., So. Hist. Assn. (membership com. 1992), So. Assn. Women Historians, Ala. Assn. Historians, Ala. Hist. Assn., North Ala.

United Meth. Hist. Soc., Bread for the World, Amnesty Internat., Humane Soc. U.S., Phi Beta Kappa, Phi Kappa Phi, Phi Alpha Theta, Omicron Delta Kappa. Democrat. Avocation: children's and animal rights advocacy. Home: 7 Vandora Pl Durham NC 27705-5481 Office: Troy U Dept History Bibb Graves Hall 305 Troy AL 36082-0001 Office Phone: 919-402-0984. E-mail: ntmitchell@earthlink.net.

MITCHELL, OWEN ROBERT, dean, electrical engineering educator; b. Beaumont, Tex., July 4, 1945; s. Owen Robert and Ruth Wilmeth (Briley) M.; m. Gloria Jane, Dec. 27, 1968; children: Amy Kathleen, Russell David, Ryan Thomas. BS, Lamar U., 1967; MS, MIT, 1968, PhD, 1972. Registered profl. engr., Mo., Ind. Prof. elec. engring. Purdue U., Lafayette, Ind., 1972-88; chmn. elec. engring. dept. U. Tex., Arlington, 1988-94; dean engring. U. Mo., Rolla, 1994—. Assoc. dir. Purdue U. engring. Rsch. Ctr., 1985-88; dir. Ctr. Advanced Electron Devices, Arlington, 1991-94. Contbr. articles to profl. jours. NSF fellow, 1967. Mem. IEEE (sr.). Mem. Ch. of Christ. Office: U Mo 101 Erl Rolla MO 65409-0001

MITCHELL, PAMELA R., speech professional, educator; BA, Ohio State U., Columbus, 1976, MA, 1978; PhD, U. Wisconsin, Madison, 1988. Cert. Speech-language pathologist Am. Speech Lang. Hearing Assn., 1978. Assoc. prof. W.Va. U., Morgantown, 1984—90, Marshall U., Huntington, W.Va., 1990—91; dir., speech pathology Columbus Speech & Hearing Ctr., 1992—93; assoc. prof. Kent State U., Ohio, 1993—. Cons., rsch. inst. Hattie Larlham Found., Mantua, Ohio, 2003—06. Mem. Celtic Music group Kent State U., Ohio, 1998. Mem.: Coun. Academic Programs Communication Scis. & Disorder (editor 2006—09), Am. Assn. Intellectual & Devel. Disabilities, Ohio Speech Lang. Hearing Assn., Am. Speech Lang. Hearing Assn. Achievements include design of educational activities in second life virtual world. Office: Kent State Univ A107 MSP Sch SP&A Kent OH 44242-0001 Personal E-mail: mitchmail06a@yahoo.com.

MITCHELL, PATRICIA, finance educator, director; b. Buchanan, Mich. d. Harold and Allegra Boyce; children: Thomas, Allegra Matthews. PhD, U. Ga., Athens, 2001. Bd. edn. Gwinnett County GA Pub. Schs., Lawrenceville, Ga., 1991—94; dir. Tal Inc., Lawrenceville, 1995—98. Faculty East Carolina U., Greenville, NC, 2001—; adj. faculty Appalachian State U., Boone, NC, 2002—; dir. econ. devel. Ashe County Govt., Jefferson, NC, 2004—; adj. faculty Nova Southeastern U., Ft. Lauderdale, Fla., 2008—. Steering com. Nat. Assn. Counties, Washington, 2005—; legis. com. NC Econ. Developers Assn., Raleigh, NC, 2005—; mem. Ashe County C. of C., West Jefferson, NC, 2004—08, NC Rural Devel. Ctr., Raleigh, 2007—. Independent. Methodist. Avocation: antiques. Office: Ashe County Govt 150 Govt Circle Ste 2500 Jefferson NC 28640 Home Fax: 336-846-5516. Business E-Mail: pmitchell@ashecountygov.com.

MITCHELL, PATRICIA EDENFIELD, broadcast museum administrator; b. Swainsboro, Ga., Jan. 20, 1943; d. James Otis and Bernice Tucker Edenfield; m. Jay Addison Mitchell, Aug. 20, 1964 (div. June 1970); 1 child, Mark Addison. BA magna cum laude, U. Ga., 1964, MA, 1965. English instr. U. Ga., Athens, 1965—69; English, drama instr. Va. Commonwealth U., Richmond, 1969—70; rschr., writer LOOK Mag., NYC, 1970; speech writer Garth Assocs., NYC, 1970—71; TV prodr., reporter WB2-TV, Boston, 1971—77; anchor, talk show host WTTG-TV, Washington, 1977—79; corr. Today Show, NYC, 1984—89, Sunday Morning, NYC, 1989—90; co-founder, exec. prodr., writer documentaries VU Prodns., LA, 1990—92; prodr. CNN Prodns., 1992—95, pres., 1995—2000; pres., CEO PBS, 2000—06; pres. Paley Ctr. for Media (formerly Mus. TV & Radio), 2006—. Spkr., conf. leader on women's issues, 1973—; creator, prodr., host, owner Woman to Woman (nationally syndicated program), LA, 1983—; bd. dirs. Bank of America Corp., 2001—09. Mem. adv. com. Nat. Coun. on Rsch. on Women, NYC, 1990—92; mem. adv. bd. Schlesinger Libr. on History of Women, Radcliffe Coll., Cambridge, Mass., 1985—92; media com. Hollywood Women's Polit. Com., LA, 1989—92; former trustee Metro Atlanta YMCA, High Mus. Art, Atlanta; mem. adv. bd. Santa Barbara Sch. Comm. U. Calif.; pres. Global Green USA (Am. affiliate Mikhail Gorbachev's worldwide conservation orgn.); nat. bd. mem. Girls Inc. Recipient Emmy for Best Daytime Program, TV Acad., 1984, Emmy for Best Host-Daytime, 1971, numerous film festival awards, 1989—92, Women in Cable & Broadcasting Woman of the Year, CINE Golden Eagle for Lifetime Achievement, Sandra Day O'Connor award for Leadership; named One of the 100 Most Powerful Women in Television, The Hollywood Reporter. Mem.: Internat. Documentary Assn. (bd. dirs.). Avocations: hiking, bicycling, horseback riding, reading. Office: Paley Ctr for Media 25 W 52nd St New York NY 10019 Office Phone: 212-621-6800.*

MITCHELL, PATSY MALIER, religious school founder, administrator; b. Greenwood, Miss., Aug. 28, 1948; d. William Lonal and Lillian (Walker) Malier; m. Charles E. Mitchell, Apr. 20, 1970; children: Christopher, Kara, Angela. BS in Edn., Delta State U., 1970, MEd, 1974, Edn. Specialist, 1979; MA in Ch. Ministries, Ch. of God Sch. Theology, 1990; PhD in Psychology and Counseling, La. Bapt. U., 1994; D in Edn. Christian Sch. Adminstrn., Baptist Christian U., 1992. Cert. sch. adminstr. Youth, Christian edn. dir. Ch. of God, Minter City, Miss., 1975—, teen talent dir., 1983—, missions rep., 1975—, dist. Christian edn. dir. Cleveland, Miss., 1983-85, sch. adminstr., 1985—. Del. Ch. of God Edn. Leadership, Cleveland, Tenn., 1990; del., spkr. Christian Sch. Internat., Chattanooga, 1991. Prodr.: (TV and radio program) Maranatha Live, 1994; contbr. articles to profl. jours. Dir. St. Jude Children's Hosp., Memphis, 1991; vol. 4-H Club, Greenwood, Miss., 1985—91. Recipient Cmty. Pride award, Chevron, 1988, Internat. Woman of Yr. award, 1993, One of One Thousand Greatest Ams., 2004, Top 100 Educators in the World, 2005—06, Internat. Educator of Yr., 2004, 2005, 2006, 2007, 2008; named Outstanding Young Women of Am., 1983, Top 10 of 50 Leading Bus. Women in Miss., 2001. Mem.: NAFE, Ch. of God Edn. Assn., Christian Schs. Internat., Christian Sch. Adminstrs., Gospel Music Assn., Ch. of God Sch. of Theology Alumni assn., Delta State Alumni Assn. Republican. Home: 5642 County Rd 544 Minter City MS 38944 Office Phone: 662-299-4592. *The greatest gift that God has given mankind is the capacity to love and encourage others. It is God's gift to us and our gift to others.*

MITCHELL, PAULA RAE, nursing educator, dean; b. Independence, Mo., Jan. 10, 1951; d. Millard Henry and E. Lorene (Denton) Gates; m. Ralph William Mitchell, May 24, 1975. BS in Nursing, Graceland U., Lamoni, Iowa, 1973; MS in Nursing, U. Tex., 1976; EdD in Ednl. Adminstrn., N.Mex. State U., 1996. RN, Tex., Mo. Instr. nursing El Paso C.C., Tex., 1979-85, dir. nursing Tex., 1985—2003, acting divsn. chmn. health occupations Tex., 1985-86, divsn. dean Tex., 1998-99, dean health occupations Tex., 1999-2000, curriculum facilitator Tex., 1984—85, dean health occupations, math and sci., campus dean Rio Grande, 2000—08, dean health career tech. edn. Math and sci. campus dean rio grade, 2008—. Ob-gyn. nurse practitioner Planned Parenthood, El Paso, 1981-86, med. com., 1986-98; cons. in field, army med. dept. officer Acad. Health Scis.Ft. Author: (with Grippando) Nursing Perspectives and Issues, 1989, 93; contbr. articles to profl. jours. Founder, bd. dirs. Health-CREST, El Paso, 1981—85; mem. pub. edn. com. Am. Cancer Soc., El Paso, 1983—84, mem. profl. activities com., 1992—93; mem. El-Paso City-County Bd. Health, 1989—91; mem. Govt. Applications Rev. Com. Rio Grande Coun. Govts., 1989—91; mem. collaborative coun. El Paso Magnet H.S. for Health Care Professions, 1992—94; co-chair health and human svcs. task force Unite El Paso Health, 1996—98, mem. steering com., 1999—2000; co-chair health taskforce El Paso Cmty. Legis. Agenda, 1997—99; mem. adv. com. Ctr. for Border Health Rsch., Paso del Norte Health Found., 1998—2004; mem. Leadership El Paso, 1999; mem. health profl. shortage task force Greater El Paso C. of C., 2001—, mem. health care coun., 2002—; mem. star adv. com. Canutillo Tex. Ind. Sch. Dist., 2003—05; mem. El Paso County Civil Svc. Commn., 2006—, chair, 2009—; coord. West Tex. Med. Res. Corps, 2006—; bd. dirs. Border Health Inst., El Paso, 2001—08, sec.-treas., 2003—08; mem. cmty. adv. bd. Victory Warriors Drill and Dance Acad., El Paso, 2001—; mem. governing bd. Mesa Hills Specialty Hosp., 2002—09. Capt. US Army, 1972—78, capt. USAR, 1978—98, ret. USAR, 1998. Decorated Army Commendation medal, Meritorious Svc. medal; named to Women's Hall Fame, El Paso Commn., 1999; named Outstanding Alumni, N.Mex. State U. Dept. Edn. Mgmt. and Devel., 2002-03; recipient Unite El Paso Legacy award 1997, Merit and Svc. cert. Victory Warriors Drill and Dance Acad., 2003, Outstanding Cmty. Svc. award, 2003, Appreciation and Cmty. Responsibility cert., 2005, Appreciation cert., 2006. Mem. Nat. League Nursing (resolutions com. Assocs. Degree coun. 1987-89, accreditation site visitor, AD coun. 1990—, Tex. edn. com. 1991-92, Tex. 3d v.p. 1992-93, Tex. 1st v.p. 1997-99, nominating com. 1999-2000), Am. Soc. Psychoprophylaxis Obstetrics (cert. childbirth educator 1978), Nurses Assn. Am. Coll. Ob-Gyn. (cert. in ambulatory women's healthcare, 1983, chpt. coord. 1979-83, nat. program rev. com. 1984-86, corr. 1987-89), Advanced Nurse Practitioner Group El Paso (coord. 1980-83, legis. com. 1984), Am. Phys. Therapist Assn. (commn. on accreditation, site visitor for phys. therapist asst. programs 1991-), Orgn. Assoc. Degree Nursing (Tex. membership chmn. 1985-89, chmn. goals com. 1989-2004, nat. bylaws com. 1990-95), Am. Vocat. Assn., Am. Assn. Women Cmty. and Jr. Colls., Tex. Orgn. Nurse Execs., Nat. Coun. Workforce Edn. (articulation task force 1986-89, program standards task force 1991-93), Nat. Coun. Instrnl. Adminstrs., Tex. Soc. Allied Health Profls. (sec. 2004-2007, elect pres. 2007-08, pres. 2008-), Tex. Nurses Assn. (pres. elect dist. one 2002-03, pres. 2003-05, past pres. 2005-06, bd. mem., 2008-09, com. mem. 2009-), Am. Soc. Allied Health Profls. (edn. com. 1993-96), El Paso C. of C. (healthcare coun. 2001-05), El Paso Commn. for Women (treas. 2007—), Am. Legion, Mil. Order World Wars (staff officer 2007-08, jr. vice comdr., 2008-) (award, 2008, Silver Patrick Henry, 2009), Sigma Theta Tau, Phi Kappa Phi. Mem. Christian Ch. (Disciples Of Christ). Home: 4616 Cupid Dr El Paso TX 79924-1726 Office: El Paso C C PO Box 20500 El Paso TX 79998-0500 Office Phone: 915-831-4030. Business E-Mail: paulam@epcc.edu.

MITCHELL, PETER J., legislative staff member; b. Mt. Vernon, NY, Mar. 24, 1952; m. Ann Carter, Jan. 2, 1981; 3 children. BA, U. Fla., Gainesville, 1975; MS, Fla. State U., Tallahassee, 1981. Staff dir. Fla. House of Reps., 1988—94; chief of staff Office of the Fla. State Treas., 1994—99; spl. cons., 1999—2002; chief of staff to Senator Bill Nelson US Senate, Washington, 2001—. Mem. adv. com. Leon County Sch. Dist., 1990; mem. Fla. Health Kids Corp., 1999. Democrat. Avocations: fishing, sports, music, reading. Office: 716 Hart Senate Office Bldg Washington DC 20510-0905 Office Phone: 202-224-5274.*

MITCHELL, PETER KENNETH, educational consultant; b. Bklyn., June 12, 1949; s. Peter Kenneth and Joan Marie (Hayes) Mitchell; 1 child, Elyse Alexandra. Cert. in French lang. proficiency, U. de Neuchatel, Switzerland, 1969; BA, SUNY, Geneseo, 1970; MS in French, L.I. U., 1975. Tchr. French, Spanish and English Mid. Country Sch. Dist., Selden, NY, 1972-81; tech. asst. to dir. internat. affairs dept. Am. Fedn. Tchrs., Washington, 1981—90; asst. to gen. sec. Internat. Fedn. Free Tchrs. Unions, Amsterdam, Netherlands, 1986—91; exec. dir. Internat. Reading Assn., Newark, Del., 1990-91; owner Insights Out Assocs., Newark, Del., 1992—97. Dir. mktg. Jr. Achievement Del., 1994—99. Contbr. articles to profl. jours. Recipient Father of the Yr. award, Nat. Multiple Sclerosis Soc., 1998. Mem.: Amnesty Internat., Washington U. Club, Blue and Gold Club. Avocations: reading, music. Home and Office: 6525 Lancaster Pike Hockessin DE 19707-9582

MITCHELL, RIE ROGERS, psychologist, counselor, educator; b. Tucson, Feb. 1, 1940; d. Martin Smith and Lavaun (Peterson) Rogers; m. Rex C. Mitchell, Mar. 16, 1961; 1 child, Scott Rogers. Student, Mills Coll., 1958-59; BS, U. Utah, 1962, MS, 1963; postgrad., San Diego State U., 1965-66; MA, PhD, UCLA, 1969. Diplomate Am. Bd. Psychology; registered play therapist, supr.; cert. sandplay therapist. Tchr. Coronado (Calif.) Unified Sch. Dist., 1964-65; sch. psychologist Glendale (Calif.) Unified Sch. Dist., 1968-70; psychologist Glendale Guidance Clinic, 1970-77; asst. prof. ednl. psychology Calif. State U., Northridge, 1970-74, assoc. prof., 1974-78, prof., 1978—. Chmn. dept. ednl. psychology, 1976-80, 2000—06, acting exec. asst. to pres. Calif. State U., Dominguez Hills, 1978-79; cons. to various Calif. sch. dists.; pvt. practice psychology, Calabasas, Calif. Author: Sandplay: Past Present & Future, 1994, Supervision of Sandplay Therapy, 2008; contbr. numerous articles to profl. jours. Recipient Outstanding Educator award Maharishi Soc., 1978, Woman of Yr. award U. Utah, 1962, Profl. Leadership award Western Assn. Counselor Edn., 1990, Disting. Tchg. award Calif. U. Northridge, 1994. Mem. APA, Calif. Assn. Counselor Edn., Supervision and Adminstrn. (dir. 1976-77), Western Assn. Counselor Edn. and Supervision (officer 1978-82, pres. 1980-81), Assn. Counselor Edn. and Supervision (dir. 1980-81, program chmn. 1981-82, treas. 1983-86, Presdl. award 1986, Leadership award 1987), UCLA Doctoral Alumni Assn. (pres. 1974-76), Am. Ednl. Rsch. Assn., Calif. Women in Higher Edn. (pres. chpt. 1977-78), Calif. Concerns (treas. 1984-86), Sandplay Therpists of Am. (pres., 2008, fin. officer 1996-2000, bd. mem. 1993—, exceptions com. chair, 1995-96), Internat. Soc. Sandplay Therapy (bd. mem., 2004-, v.p., 2006-), Pi Lambda Theta (pres. chpt. 1970-71, chairwoman nat. resolutions 1971-73). Home: 4503 Alta Tupelo Dr Calabasas CA 91302-2516 Office: Calif State U Counselor Edn Dept Northridge CA 91330-0001 Office Phone: 818-677-4976. Business E-Mail: rie.mitchell@csun.edu.

MITCHELL, ROBERT D., lawyer; b. Phoenix, June 21, 1959; m. Lisa B. Mitchell, Dec. 17, 1983. BS in Acctg., Ariz. State U., Tempe, 1984, JD, 1987. Bar: Ariz. 1988, Calif. 1988, US Ct. Appeals (9th cir.) 1988, Utah 1999. Atty. and ptnr. Mitchell & Forest, P.C., Phoenix, Ariz., 1993—. Master: Am. Inns of Ct.; mem.: Ariz. State U. Alumni Assn. Office: Mitchell & Assocs 1850 N Central Ave Ste 1715 Phoenix AZ 85004-4634 Business E-Mail: robertmitchell@mitchell-attorneys.com.

MITCHELL, ROGER LOWRY, retired agronomy educator; b. Grinnell, Iowa, Sept. 13, 1932; s. Robert T. and Cecile (Lowry) M.; m. Joyce Elaine Lindgren, June 26, 1955; children: Laura, Susan, Sarah, Martha. BS in Agronomy, Iowa State Coll., 1954; MS, Cornell U., 1958; PhD in Crop Physiology, Iowa State U., 1961. Mem. faculty Iowa State U., 1959-69, prof. agronomy, 1966-69, prof. charge farm operation curriculum, 1962-66; prof. agronomy, chmn. dept. U. Mo., Columbia, 1969-72, 81-83, emeritus prof., 1998—, dean agr., dir. expt. sta., 1983-98, dean extension, 1972-75, emeritus dean, 1998—; v.p. agr. Kans. State U., Manhattan, 1975-80; exec. dir. Mid-Am. Internat. Agrl. Consortium, 1981; ret., 1998. Exec. bd. divsn. agr. Nat. Assn. State Univs. and Land Grant Colls., 1978-80, 85-90, chmn., 1988-89; mem. bd. agr. NRC/NAS, 1983-86. Author: Crop Growth and Culture, 1970; co-author: Physiology of Crop Plants, 1985 Served to 2d lt. USAAF, 1954-56. Danforth fellow, 1956-61; Acad. Adminstrn. fellow Am. Council Edn., 1966-67; recipient Henry A. Wallace award Iowa State U., 1993, Sec.'s Honor award USDA, 1998, Cardinal Key Disting. Alumni award, 2009. Fellow AAAS (chmn. sect. O 1980-81), Am. Soc. Agronomy (pres. 1979-80), Crop Sci. Soc. (pres. 1975-76); mem. Soil Sci. Soc. Am., Coun. Agrl. Sci. and Tech., Sigma Xi, Gamma Sigma Delta, Alpha Zeta, Phi Kappa Phi. Home: 502 W Lathrop Rd Columbia MO 65203-2804 Business E-Mail: mitchellrj@missouri.edu.

MITCHELL, RONALD K., finance educator; s. John and Bertha Mitchell; m. Cynthia Kay Terry, Aug. 23, 1974; children: Seth, Rob, Ben, Tanner. BS in Commerce, U. Calgary, 1976; PhD in Bus. Adminstrn., U. Utah, 1994. CPA Utah, 1978. Cert. profl. acct. Deloitte Haskins & Sells, 1976—80; exec., mgmt. cons., entrepreneur U. Utah, 1980—90, mgmt. cons., 1990—93, vis. asst. prof., 1993—94; asst. assoc., prof. U. Victoria, BC, Canada, 1994—2005; pursuant to meeting bd. regents Tex. Tech. U., 2005—, Jean Austin Bagley Regents chair mgmt., Rawls Coll. Bus., 2005. Contbr. articles to numerous profl. jours., chapters to books. Recipient Outstanding Excellence Rsch. award, U. Victoria, Faculty Bus., 2003—04, Best Conceptual Conf. Paper award, USASBE, San Antonio, 2006; nominee Dean Ali Dastmalchian Academic of Yr., U. Victoria, Faculty Bus., 2003, Best Paper award, USASBE, Ann. Meeting, 2008. Avocations: music, keyboards. Office: Tex Tech Univ Rawls Coll Bus PO Box 42101 Lubbock TX 79409-2101 Office Fax: 806-742-3848. Business E-Mail: ronald.mitchell@ttu.edu.

MITCHELL, SAM, former professional basketball coach; b. Sept. 2, 1963; m. Anita Mitchell; children: Morgann, Maya, Rhagan, Rhana. Student, Mercer U. Draft pick NBA Houston Rockets, 1985; player Continental Basketball Assn. Rapid City Thrillers, SD, 1985—87; profl. basketball player France, 1987—89, NBA Minn. Timberwolves, 1989—92, 1995—2002, NBA Ind. Pacers, 1992—95; asst. coach NBA Milw. Bucks, 2002—04; lead asst. coach NBA Charlotte Bobcats, 2004; head coach NBA Toronto Raptors, 2004—08. Named NBA Coach of Yr., 2007.*

MITCHELL, SHAMIKA ANN, literature and language professor; d. Carolyn L. Britton Mitchell and John H. Mitchell. BA, U. Mich., Ann Arbor, 1996, Syracuse U., NY, 1999; MA, Seton Hall U., South Orange, NJ, 2001; PhD, Temple U., Phila., 2002. Resident adviser Syracuse U., 1998—99; grad. asst. Seton Hall U., 1999—2000, tchg. asst., 2000—01, writing instr., 2001—02; grad. extern Temple U., 2002—05, adj. instr., 2004—05; adj. asst. prof. SUNY Rockland CC, Suffern, NY, 2005—07, instr., 2007—; adj. asst. prof. Pace U., Pleasantville, NY, 2007. Contbr. articles to profl. jours. Mem. Dem. Congressional Campaign Com., Washington, 2007—09. Mem.: Soc. Study Multi-Ethnic Lit. US, NJ. Coll. English Assn. (grad. liaison 2005—07), Coll. Lang. Assn., MLA, Am. Studies Assn., Golden Key Internat., Phi Sigma Pi. Office: SUNY Rockland CC English Dept 145 College Rd Suffern NY 10901 Office Fax: 845-574-4173. Business E-Mail: smitchel@sunyrockland.edu.

MITCHELL, STACY MARIE, medical transcriptionist; b. Lakewood, Calif., June 11, 1973; d. Jerry Layne and Mary Anne Barbour; m. Sean Thomas Mitchell, Aug. 12, 2000; children: Marshal Sean, Molly Marie. BS in Office Adminstrn., Bob Jones U., Greenville, SC, 1991—95. Sr. mktg. specialist World Class Promotions/Internat., Englewood, Colo., 1995—2000; dist. compression adminstr. J-W Oper. Co., Wray, Colo., 2000—01; phys. therapy sec. Melissa Meml. Hosp., Holyoke, Colo., 2001—05; freelance med. transcriptionist Holyoke, 2005—07, Sterling, Colo., 2007—. Mem.: Am. Assn. Med. Transcriptionist, Nat. Assn. Self-Employed. Conservative-R. Non-Denominational. Avocations: walking, reading. Home and Office: 1171 Westview Dr Sterling CO 80751 Office Fax: 970-522-2418. Personal E-mail: jeepmom812@yahoo.com.

MITCHELL, STEPHEN RAY, dean, rheumatologist; Practicing adult and pediatric rheumatologist; faculty mem. Georgetown U. Sch. Medicine, Washington, 1988—, program dir. Internal Medicine Residency Program, 1992—99, assoc. dean clinical curriculum, 1998—2000, sr. assoc. dean undergrad. acad. affairs, 2000, Joseph J. Butenas prof. med. edn., dir. medicine/pediatric program, assoc. program dir. medicine/pediatrics, dean med. edn. Recipient Upjohn Young Investigator award. Office: Georgetown Univ Sch Med Box 570417 Medical & Dental Bldg Rm 106 Washington DC 20057-0417 Office Phone: 202-687-3922. Office Fax: 202-687-2792. E-mail: mitchelr@georgetown.edu.*

MITCHELL, STEVE HAROLD, psychologist; b. Madison, Tenn., Nov. 28, 1954; s. Ralph and Doris Mitchell. BS, Tenn. Tech. U., 1977; MS, U. Ala., 1978; PhD, OH State U., 1983. Assoc. prof. psychology Cumberland Coll., Williamsburg, Ky., 1986-92; asst. prof. Ball State U., Muncie, Ind., 1983-86; behavior specialist, 1989-99; assoc. prof. psychology Somerset CC, Ky., 1999—. Author: Conception Through Adolecence: Research, Theories, and Applications; contbr. articles to profl. jours. Recipient Nat Excellence Tchg. award. Mem.: Soc. Rsch. Child Devel., Coun. Children Behavior Disorders, Coun. Exceptional Children, Lions (pres. Somerset chpt. 2002—05). Achievements include research in sexual attitudes of college students in the 21st Century.

MITCHELL, STUART, medical entomologist, consulting physician; m. Martha Mitchell. BS in Physics, Iowa State U., Ames, 1981, BS in Forensic Psychology, 2007; PhD in Entomology, Trinity Coll., 2000, PhD in Zoology, 2002, PhD in Biology, 2003, PhD in Naturopathy, 2005, D of Naturopathy; PhD (hon.), Breyer State U., 2006; DSc in Osteo. Medicine, Des Moines U., 2005, MPH, 2007. Cert. in traditional naturopathy; bd. cert. entomologist, cert. in homeland security, wildlife control profl., trainer in food safety Nat. Environ. Health Assn., med. investigator. Cons. physician, med. entomologist Springer Svcs., Des Moines, 1996—. Tchr., food mgr. NSF Internat., Des Moines, 2002—, tchr. HACCP, 2002—; cons. Whitmire Micro-Gen Labs., 2003. Author: (pest mgmt. tng. manual) Guidelines On Training; contbr. articles to profl. jours. Developer Quality Pro Inst.; mem. Des Moines Parks Bd., 2002—03; bd. dirs. Blank Pk. Zoo, Des Moines, 2002—03, Des Moines Bot. Ctr., 2002—03. Fellowship, Am. Assn. Integrative Medicine. Mem.: AAAS, Entomol. Soc. Am., Am. Inst. Baking, Phi Chi Omega (BCE dir. 2009). Democrat. Lutheran. Avocations: science, walking. Office: Springer Svcs 5360 NE 14th Str Ste A Des Moines IA 50313-2002 Office Fax: 515-262-9149. Personal E-mail: docmitchell@me.com.

MITCHELL, SUSAN LISA, geriatrician; b. Montreal, Canada; BS, McGill U., 1984; MD cum laude, U. Ottawa, 1988; MPH, Harvard U., 1996. Lic. Buffalo, NY, 1988, Commonwealth of Mass., 1992, cert. Coll. Physicians and Surgeons Ont., 1989, Med. Coun. Can., 1989, Royal Coll. Physicians and Surgeons of Canada, 1994, diplomate Am. Bd. Internal Med. Intern in internal medicine Ottawa Civic Hosp., 1988—89; resident in internal medicine Ottawa Civic and Gen. Hospitals, 1989—91, staff physician, 1997—98; clin. fellow in medicine, aging divsn. Harvard Med. Sch., 1992—94, rsch. fellow in medicine, aging divsn., 1994—95; staff geriatrician Hebrew Rehab. Ctr. Aged, Boston, 1994—97, med. dir. Agewell Sr. Services Outpatient Clinic, 1995—96, staff physician, 2000—, assoc. scientist, 2002—05; asst. prof. medicine U. Ottawa, 1997—2000, asst. prof. epidemiology and cmty. medicine, 1999—2000; dir. rsch., geriatrics divsn. Ottawa Hosp., 1997—2000; instr. medicine Harvard Med. Sch., 2000—01, assoc. dir. fellowship in geriatric medicine, 2000—, asst. prof. medicine, 2001—05, assoc. prof. medicine, 2005—; assoc. dir. Harvard Geriatric Medicine Fellowship Prog., Boston, 2000—05, assoc. dir. rsch. training, 2005—; assoc. scientist Hebrew Sr. Life Inst. Aging Rsch., Boston, 2001—05, sr. scientist, 2006—. Affiliate mem., clin. epidemiology unit Loeb Health Rsch. Inst., Ottawa, 1997—2000. Recipient Career Scientist award, Ont. Ministry Health, 1998—2000, NIH-NIA K23 Mentored Clin. Scientist award, 2001—04; fellow Charles A. King Trust, 1995—97. Fellow: Royal Coll. Physicians and Surgeons of Canada; mem.: Nat. Alzheimer's Assn. (grant reviewer 2005—, abstract review com. 2006—), Gerontological Soc. America, Physicians for Human Rights, Am. Geriatrics Soc. (ethics com. 2004—07, Best Paper in Biol. Sciences 2003, Best Paper in Health Services Rsch. 2006), Am. Coll. Physicians, Coll. Physicians and Surgeons Ont. Office: Hebrew Senior Life 1200 Centre St Boston MA 02131 Office Phone: 617-363-8626. Office Fax: 617-363-8936. E-mail: smitchell@hrca.harvard.edu.*

MITCHELL, TEDDY LEE, physician; b. Columbia, La., Feb. 24, 1962; s. Oliver Clayton nad Mary Elizabeth (Johnston) M.; m. Janet Luisa Tornelli, Apr. 9, 1988; children: Mary Katherine, Oliver Charles, Christopher Tornelli. BS in Biology, Stephen F. Austin State U., 1983; MD, U. Tex. Med. Br., 1987. Diplomate Am. Bd. Internal Medicine, Cert. of Added Qualification-Sports Medicine. Intern U. Tex. Med. Br., Galveston, 1987-88, resident, 1988-90, 90-91; med. dir. wellness program Cooper Aerobics Ctr., Dallas, 1991—2006, pres., med. dir., 2006—, pres. & CEO, 2008—. Mem. Rep. Sen. Inner Cir., Washington, 1993, Heritage Found., Washington, 1993. Capt. U.S. Army Res. Med. Corps, 1988-96. Fellow ACP (cert. Merit 1990), Am. Coll. Sports Medicine; mem. AMA, Tex. Med. Assn., Dallas County Med. Soc. Methodist. Avocations: exercise, travel, music. Home: 3224 Lovers Ln Dallas TX 75225-7626 Home Phone: 214-750-1278; Office Phone: 972-560-2667.

MITCHELL, THEODORE REED, educational association administrator, former academic administrator; b. San Rafael, Calif., Jan. 29, 1956; s. Theodore Robert and Genevieve Dolores (Doose) Mitchell; m. Christine M. Beckman, July 8, 1995; children: Caroline Mitchell Beckman, Theo Beckman. BA, Stanford U., 1978, MA, 1980, PhD, 1983. Asst. prof. Dartmouth Coll., Hanover, NH, 1981—86, assoc. prof., 1986—87, chair dept. edn., 1987—91; dep. to pres. and provost Stanford U., Calif., 1991—92; dean Sch. Edn. and Info. Studies UCLA, 1992—96, vice chancellor, 1996—98; v.p. for edn. and strategic initiatives The J. Paul Getty Trust, 1998—99; pres. Occidental Coll., 1999—2005; CEO NewSchools Venture Fund, San Francisco, 2005—. Trustee Stanford U., 1985—90, Thetford Acad., Vt., 1989—91; bd. dirs. L.A. Edn. Partnership, L.E.A.R.N. Author: Political Education, 1985, Sociology of Education, 1998. Bd. dirs. Children Now, Oakland, Calif., 1994—, Gateway Learning Corp., 1996—. Office: NewSchools Venture Fund 49 Stevenson St, Ste 575 San Francisco CA 94105 Office Phone: 415-615-6860. Fax: 415-615-6861.

MITCHELL, TODD (JAMES TODD MITCHELL), legislative staff member; m. Mara Mitchell. Legis. dir., Rep. Rob Simmons US House of Reps., Washington, 2001—02, chief of staff to Rep. Rob Simmons, 2002—07, legis. dir., Rep. Vern Buchanan, 2007—08, chief of staff to Rep. Leonard Lance, 2009—. Republican. Office: 114 Cannon House Office Bldg Washington DC 20515 Office Phone: 202-225-5361. Office Fax: 202-225-9460.*

MITCHELL, WAYNE LEE, retired health administrator; b. Mar. 25, 1937; s. Albert C. and Elizabeth Isabelle (Nagel) M.; m. Marie Galletti. BA, U. Redlands, Calif., 1959; MSW, Ariz. State U., 1970, EdD, 1979. Social worker various county, state, and fed. agys., 1962-70; social worker Bur. Indian Affairs, Phoenix, 1970-77, USPHS, 1977-79; asst. prof. Ariz. State U., 1979-84; with USPHS, Phoenix, 1984—2003, ret., 2003; pvt. practice cons. Phoenix, 2003—. Lectr. in field. Contbr. articles to profl. jours. Bd. dirs. Phoenix Indian Cmty. Sch., 1973-75, ATLATL, 1994-98, Partnership for Cmty. Devel. Ariz. State U.-West, 1996-99, Cen. Ariz. Health Sys. Agy., 1982-85; mem. Phoenix Area Health Adv. Bd., 1975, Cmty. Behavioral Mental Health Bd., 1976-80, Fgn. Rels. Com., Phoenix; trustee Heard Mus. Anthropology, Phoenix, 1996; apptd. Ariz. State Bd. Behavioral Health Examiners, 2000-2002. With USCG, 1960-62. Recipient Comty. Svc. award, Ariz. Temple of Islam, 1980, Ariz. State U., 1996, Dir. Excellence award, Phoenix Area IHS Dir., 1992, 1993, Nat. IHS Dir.'s award for outstanding svc., 2001, NARD Lifetime Achievement award, 2005; named in Voices and Faces, 2003. Mem. NASW (Lifetime Achievement award 2003), Fgn. Rels. Coun., U.S.-China Assn., Kappa Delta Pi, Phi Delta Kappa, Chi Sigma Chi. Democrat. Congregationalist. Home: PO Box 9592 Phoenix AZ 85068-9592 Personal E-mail: drwlmitch@cox.net.

MITCHELL, WILFRID BEDE, librarian, library association executive; b. Bloomington, Ind., Nov. 5, 1953; s. W. Bede and Barbara Plumb Mitchell; m. Carrie N. Cornejo, May 30, 1992. BA in Philosophy, U. Mich., 1975, MLS, 1977; EdD, Mont. State U., 1989. Circulation and reserve libr. Mont. State U., Bozeman, 1978-85; head circulation libr. U. N.C., Greensboro, 1985-90; assoc. univ. libr. Appalachian State U., Boone, N.C., 1990-99; dean libr. Ga. So. U., Statesboro, 1999—. Contbr. articles to profl. jours. Mem. ALA, Assn. Coll. and Rsch. Librs. (chair acad. status com. 1995-96, chair instnl. priorities and faculty rewards task force, 1996-98, bd. dirs. 2002—06), Libr. Adminstrn. Mgmt. Assn. (chair publs. and bibliography com. sys. and svcs. sect. 1997-98, strategic planning implementation com. 2001-03, pres.-elect, 2006-07, pres. 2007-08, past pres. 2008-09), Ga. Libr. Assn. (chmn. academic libr. divsn. 2001-02, chmn. adminstrv. svcs. com. 2003), Southeastern Libr. Assn. (chmn. legis com. 2005-06). Office: Ga So U Henderson Libr PO Box 8074 Statesboro GA 30460-8074 Office Phone: 912-478-5115. Office Fax: 912-478-0093. Business E-Mail: wbmitch@georgiasouthern.edu.

MITCHELL, WILLIAM D. (BILL MITCHELL), lawyer; b. Great Falls, Mont., June 15, 1947; s. William Howard and Dorothy Elizabeth (Lane) Mitchell; m. Mary Claire McDonough, Aug. 15, 1973; children: James Edward, Andrew Elliott, Thomas Michael. BA cum laude, U. Wash., Seattle, 1969; MA in Econs., U. Calif., Berkeley, 1976, JD, 1976; MLT, Georgetown U., DC, 1982. Bar: Calif. 1977, DC 1978, Mont. 1981, Del. 1982, Fla. 1983, US Dist. Ct. Mont. 1981, US Dist. Ct. (mid. dist.) Fla. 1984, US Dist. Ct. (so. dist.) Fla. 1986, US Dist. Ct. (no. dist.) Fla. 1992, US Ct. Appeals (11th cir.) 1994, US Tax Ct. 1992. Atty. Fed. Trade Commn., Washington, 1976-79; assoc. Koteen & Burt, Washington, 1979-80, Tipp, Hoven & Skjelset, Missoula, Mont., 1980-81, Murdoch & Walsh, Wilmington, Del., 1982-83, Carlton, Fields, Ward, Smith & Cutler, Tampa, 1983-88; of counsel Foley & Lardner, Tampa, 1988-90; ptnr. Langford, Hill, Mitchell, Trybus & Whalen, Tampa, Fla., 1991-92; pres. Mitchell Law Group, Tampa, 1992—. Author: Estate and Retirement Answer Book, 1994; co-author: Employee Fringe and Welfare Benefit Plans, 1988; contbr. articles to profl. jours. Mem. devel. bd. Suncoast Alzheimer & Gerentology Ctr., Tampa; adv. Cmty. Found. Tampa Bay; mem. Grace Luth. Ch. Lt. USN, 1969—72. Mem.: ABA, Mensa, Tampa Bay Writers Alliance, Greater Tampa Sertoma Club (dir. 1993—96, pres. 1996—97). Democrat. Lutheran. Avocations: creative writing, acting, golf, weightlifting, auto sports.*

MITCHELL, WILLIAM EDMUND, electronics executive; b. LA, Mar. 13, 1944; s. John Stewart and Helen (Fine) M.; m. Jan Marie Scheyer, Feb. 16, 1969; children: Alden, Amanda, Alyssa. BS in Engring., Princeton U., NJ, 1966; MS in Engring., U. Mich., Ann Arbor, 1967. Analyst Exxon Corp., NYC, 1969-72, dept. mgr. Baton Rouge, 1972-73; ops. mgr. Raychem. Corp., Menlo Park, Calif., 1973-76; regional mgr. Raychem Internat., Menlo Park, Calif., 1977-85, v.p., 1985-88; sr. v.p. Raychem Corp., Menlo Park, 1988-93; pres., CEO Nashua Corp., NH, 1993—95; chmn., pres., CEO Sequel Inc., 1995—99; pres. Solectron Global Svcs., 1999—2002; exec. v.p. Solectron Corp., 1999—2003; pres., CEO Arrow Electronics Inc., Melville, NY, 2003—06, chmn., pres., CEO, 2006—08, chmn., CEO, 2008—09, exec. chmn., 2009—. Bd. dirs. Rogers Corp., Conn., bd. dirs. Humana Inc., bd. dirs. Brown-Forman Corp., 2009- Mem. Orgn. Corp. Growth, Am. Electronics Assn. (bd. dirs. 1993—), Ladera Oaks Club. Republican. Avocations: swimming, tennis, literature. Office: Arrow Electronics Inc 50 Marcus Dr Melville NY 11747-4210 Office Phone: 631-847-2000.*

MITCHELL, WILLIAM H., computer software company executive; BS in Computer Sci., U. Minn.; M in Computer Sci., PhD in Computer Sci., Ariz. State U. CAD engr. Intel Corp.; co-founder software startup Tempe, Ariz.; application arch. Microsoft Corp., Redmond, Wash., 1992, co-founder Windows CE, Handheld PC projects, 1993, dir. handheld PC group, 1996, gen. mgr. mobile electronics group, 1998—2000, founder smart personal objects team, 2000—03, corp. v.p. PC 3 effort, 2003—07, corp. v.p. PC 3 platform, components, creation & collaboration, 2007—. Office: Microsoft Corp One Microsoft Way Redmond WA 98052-6399*

MITCHELL, WILLIAM JOHN, mathematics educator; b. Mpls., Dec. 30, 1943; s. John Edwards and Jane (Cavert) M.; m. Jean Ann Larson, Oct. 1, 1988. Student, Carleton Coll., 1961-63; BA, U. Wis., 1965; PhD, U. Calif., Berkeley, 1970. Lectr. U. Chgo., 1970-72; asst. prof. Rockefeller U., NYC, 1972-77; from assoc. prof. to prof. Pa. State U., State College, 1979-89; prof. U. Fla., Gainesville, 1989—. Office: U Fla Dept Math Gainesville FL 32611

MITCHELL, WILLIAM MARVIN, pathology educator; b. Atlanta, Mar. 3, 1935; s. William Joseph and Marvin Eugenia (Peavy) M.; m. Shirley Ann Crowell, Dec. 22, 1959; children: Alexander James, Keith Townsend, Derek Loren. BA, Vanderbilt U., 1957, MD, 1960; PhD, Johns Hopkins U., 1966. Diplomate Am. Bd. Pathology. Asst. prof. microbiology and medicine Vanderbilt U., Nashville, 1966-70, assoc. prof. pathology, 1970-78, prof., 1978—. Med. dir. Specialized Assays, Nashville, 1981-91; med. dir. Vanderbilt Pathology Lab. Svcs., 1994—; med. dir. Home Health Care Am., 1998—; planning dir. Vanderbilt Cancer Rsch. and Treatment Ctr., 1971-72; founder ActivBiotics, Inc., Boston, Genocyte, Inc., Nashville; cons. NIH, DuPont Co., Smith Kline, others. Patentee in field; contbr. articles to profl. jours. Bd. dirs. St. Augustine's Chapel, Nashville, 1981-86, Hemispherx Biopharma, Inc., Phila., 1998—, Chronix Biomedical, Inc., 2006-; judge Regional Sci. and Engring. Fair, Nashville, 1985, 88; judge Internat. Sci. Engring. Fair, Nashville, 1992, Birmingham, 1994. Eleanor Roosevelt Internat. Cancer fellow Internat. Union Against Cancer, 1976-77; grantee NIH. Mem. AAAS, Am. Assn. Pathology, Am. Chem. Soc., Am. Soc. Biol. Chemists, Am. Soc. Microbiology, Internat. Acad. Pathology, Am. Soc. Interferon Rsch., Am. AIDS Soc., Sigma Xi. Episcopalian. Avocations: skiing, crafts, music. Home Phone: 615-297-6308; Office Phone: 615-322-3238. E-mail: bill.mitchell@vanderbilt.edu.

MITCHELL, WILLIAM P. (BILLY), arbitrator; b. Fairmont, NC, Apr. 5, 1930; s. Julius Pender Mitchell and Dolibel Mitchell Caudell; m. Jerry Stevenson Mitchell (div.); children: Sharon Lynne Huggins, Steven Lee, Amy Elizabeth Harrison; m. Rebecca Burroughs, Apr. 2, 1983. AB, Duke U., 1953. Exec. v.p. Gainesville (Fla.) Area C. of C., 1961—70, Greater Macon (Ga.) C. of C., 1970—80; pres. Metro Jackson (Miss.) C. of C., 1980—82; mgr. chamber rels. U.S. C. of C., Washington, 1982—95; pres. Arlington Mediation Svc., Hendersonville, NC, 1994—. Bd. dirs. Carolina Forum, Hendersonville, 2002—. Aviation cadet USAF, 1953—55. Mem.: N.C. Bar Assn. (dispute resolution sect.), N.C. Assn. Profl. Family Mediators (pres. 2002). Republican. Lutheran. Office: Arlington Arbitration Svc 29 Hunters Ln Hendersonville NC 28791 Home Phone: 828-890-5461. Personal E-mail: bmitch@bellsouth.net.

MITCHELL-BOYASK, ROBIN NORMAN, classics educator; b. Cambridge, Eng., May 20, 1961; came to U.S. 1963; s. Terence Edward and Marion (Wyatt) M.; m. Amanda Caroline Boyask, Mar. 18, 1990; 1 child, Nina Miriam. BA, U. Chgo., 1982; MA, Brown U., 1985, PhD, 1988. Asst. prof. Temple U., Phila., 1993—. Vis. asst. prof. Temple U., 1988-93, Haverford (Pa.) Coll., 1989. Contbr.: (book) Read Freud Reading, 1993; contbr. articles to profl. jours. Mem. Young Adult Congregation, Ralph Shalon, Phila., 1989—. Fellow Ctr. for Hellenic Studies, Washington, 1993; participant NEH summer seminar/Cornell U., London, 1991, NEH summer inst./U. Calif., Santa Cruz, 1992. Mem. Am. Philol. Assn. (com. on the classical tradition 1993-95), Modern Lang. Assn., Classical Assn. Atlantic States, Philol. Assn. of the Pacific Coast. Democrat. Jewish. Avocations: classical music, bicycling, gardening, reading. Home: 7431 Sprague St Philadelphia PA 19119-1037 Office: Temple Univ 12th And Berks Philadelphia PA 19122

MITCHELSON, MARY SUE, federal agency administrator, lawyer; b. Joplin, Mo., Mar. 17, 1951; d. L. R. and Mildred (Mathes) M. BA, U. Kans., 1973; JD, Georgetown U., 1976. Asst. dean Georgetown U. Law Ctr., Washington, 1976-78; law clk. to Hon. Harold Greene US Dist. Ct. DC, Washington, 1978-79; trial atty. civil div. comml. litigation br. US Dept. Justice, Washington, 1979-86, asst. dir. civil div. comml. litigation br., 1986-89, asst. dir., dep. dir. comml. litigation br. Civil Divsn., 1990-91, 1991-95; asst. general counsel Clarke Cons. Group, 1989-90; dep. general counsel Office of the General Counsel, Office of Pers. Mgmt., Washington, 1995-2000; asst. inspector gen. analysis and inspection US Dept. Edn., Washington, 2000—02, counsel to inspector gen., 2002—08, dep. inspector gen., 2008—, acting inspector gen., 2009—. Office: US Dept Edn Office of Inspector Gen 400 Maryland Ave, SW Washington DC 20202*

MITCHEM, ALLEN P., lawyer; b. Burley, Idaho, Oct. 30, 1918; s. James Edgar and Adah Elizabeth (Allen) Mitchem; m. Katherine I. Webber, Aug. 21, 1993; children: Allen P., James E., Lowell E. AB, Ft. Hays State U., Kans., 1940; JD magna cum laude, Washburn U., Kans., 1947; LLM, Columbia U., NYC, 1948. Bar: Kans. 1947, Colo. 1949, US Supreme Ct. 2004. Assoc. prof. Coll. Law, U. Denver, 1948—53; pvt. practice law Denver, 1953—60, 1963—; minority counsel interior and insular affairs com. U.S. Senate, Washington, 1961—62. Vis. lectr. Sch. Law U. Colo., Boulder, 1954, 57, 59; lectr. Coll. Law U. Denver, 1953—63; arbitrator, Denver, 1965—. Contbr. articles to legal rev. Dist. gov. Civitan Internat., 1957—58, judge adv., 1958—59; pres. Denver Execs. Club, 1986—88; chmn. gen. bd. Ctrl. Christian Ch., 1963—65, 1975—76; trustee Endowment Assn. Ft. Hays State U., 1968—78; dir. Colo. Christian Home, Denver, 1974—80; pres. Denver Civitan Club, 1955—56; dir. Denver Area Coun. Chs., 1955, 1957. Capt. USMC, 1942—45. Recipient Alumni Achievement award, Ft. Hays State U., 1970. Mem.: ABA, Denver Bar Assn., Colo. Bar Assn. Home: 420 S Marion Pkwy Apt 2002 Denver CO 80209-5526 Personal E-mail: apmitchem@msn.com.

MITCHEM, CHERYL E., accounting educator; b. South Bend, Ind., June 24, 1947; d. Roy Francis and Marcella Evelyn (Chryst) Drake; m. Allen Pershing Mitchem, Jr., Nov. 28, 1969; children: Michael, Marlo, Megan, Melissa. BA, Tex. Christian U., 1969; MBA, San Diego State U., 1980; PhD, Va. Commonwealth U., 1990. CPA, Va.; cert. mgmt. acct. Vis. prof. acctg. Coll. William and Mary, Williamsburg, Va., 1986-88; adj. prof. acctg. Va. Commonwealth U., Richmond, 1988-89; asst. prof. acctg. Christopher Newport U., Newport News, 1989-91; asst. prof. Va. State U., Petersburg, 1991—98, chair acctg., 1993—2003, assoc. prof., 1998—, acting asst. dean Sch. Bus., 2004—. Contbr. articles to profl. jours. Mem. AICPA, Am. Acctg. Assn., Inst. Mgmt. Accts, USCPA, Va. Soc. CPAs. Mem. Christian Ch. (Disciples Of Christ). Avocations: travel, reading.

MITCHINER, JAMES C., emergency physician; b. Ft. Wayne, Ind., 1953; BS & BSME, Purdue U., 1975; MD, U. Ill., 1979; MPH, U. Mich., 1996. Intern U. Ill./Cook County Hosp., Chgo., 1979-80, resident, 1980-81, Denver Gen. Hosp., 1981-83; with St. Joseph Mercy Hosp., Ann Arbor, Mich. Clin. asst. prof. emergency medicine. U. Mich. Med. Sch. Mem. APHA, Am. Coll. Emergency Physicians, Soc. Acad. Emergency Medicine, Mich. State Med. Soc., Am. Health Quality Assn. Office: St Joseph Mercy Hosp 5301 E Huron River Dr Ann Arbor MI 48106 Office Phone: 734-712-1343.

MITCHISON, TIMOTHY JOHN, cell biologist, pharmacology educator; b. Edinburgh, July 20, 1958; came to US, 1980; s. Avrion and Lorna (Martin) M. BA in Biochemistry, Oxford U., Eng., 1980; PhD in Biochemistry, U. Calif., San Francisco, 1984. Asst. prof. U. Calif., San Francisco, 1987-92, assoc. prof., 1992—97; co-dir. Harvard Med Sch. Inst. Chem. and Cell Biology, Boston, 1997—2005; prof. cell biology Harvard Med Sch., Boston, 1997—2003, Hasib Sabbagh prof., 1999—, prof. systems biology, 2003—. Contbr. numerous sci. articles to profl. publs. Rsch. grantee NIH, 1987; fellow Packard Found., Searle Found. Fellow Am. Acad. Arts and Sciences, Royal Soc.; mem. Am. Soc. Cell Biology. Avocations: dog-walking, fishing. Office: Harvard Med Sch Dept Systems Biology Alpert 536 200 Longwood Ave Boston MA 02115 Office Phone: 617-432-3805. Office Fax: 617-432-5012. E-mail: timothy_mitchison@hms.harvard.edu.

MITELMAN, SERGE A., researcher; married. MD, Saratov Med. Sch., Russia, 1990. Assoc. prof. Mt. Sinai Sch. Medicine, NYC, 2000—; chief, child psychiatry inpatient svcs. Elmhurst Hosp. Ctr., NY, 2002—. Contbr. articles to profl. jours. Recipient Young Investigator award, NARSAD, 2006—08; grantee, NIMH, 2006—. Office: Mt Sinai Sch Medicine One Gustave L Levy Pl Box 1505 New York NY 10029 Business E-Mail: serge.mitelman@mssm.edu.

MITMAN, MEGHAN FEHLIG, transportation engineer; BSE in Ops. Rsch. and Fin. Engring., Princeton U., NJ, 2002; MCE, U. Calif., Berkeley, 2007, MA in City and Regional Planning, 2007. Cert. AICP Am. Planning Assn., 2008. Transp. engr. Parsons Brinckerhoff, Princeton, 2002—05; sr. transp. engr. Fehr & Peers, San Francisco, 2007—. Eisenhower fellowship, FHWA, 2005—07, fellow, Eno Transp. Found., 2007. Mem.: Inst. Transp. Engrs. (sec., pedestrian-bicycle coun.), Women's Transp. Seminar (bd. mem.). Business E-Mail: m.mitman@fehrandpeers.com.

MITRA, ABHIJIT, chemistry professor; s. Kalyan Ananda Mitra and Neera Sarkar. MA, MS, MPhil, Columbia U., NYC, PhD, 1977; BSc with honors, St. Xavier's Coll., Calcutta U., Kolkata, 1967; MSc, Calcutta U., 1969. Cert. radiation officer Radiation Acad., Rockville, MD, 2001. Assoc. prof. Coll. Mt. St. Vincent, Riverdale, NY, 1988—. Fellow: Indian Chem. Soc.; mem.: Am. Chem. Soc., Sigma Xi (pres.). Business E-Mail: a.mitra@mountsaintvincent.edu.

MITRA, AMLAN, economics professor, researcher; married. PhD in Economics, Northern Ill. U., DeKalb. Assoc. prof. economics Purdue U. Calumet, Hammond, Ind., 2004—. Mem., exec. com., transp. and econ. devel. Transp. Rsch. Bd., Wash., 2008—. Contbr. scientific papers to profl. jours. Grant, Ind. Dept. Workforce Devel., 2004—06. Mem.: Global Rev. Bus. and Econ. Rsch. (mem. editl. bd. 2005—08), Internat. Rev. Bus. and Economics (mem. editl. bd. 2005—09), Pub. Fin. and Mgmt. (mem. editl. bd. 2005—08), Southern Econ. Assn., Am. Econ. Assn. Achievements include research in transportation. Office: Purdue Univ Calumet 2200 169th St Hammond IN 46323-2094 Office Fax: 219-989-3158; Home Fax: 630-961-6588. Business E-Mail: mitra@calumet.purdue.edu.

MITRA, ASOKE NATH, retired physicist, educator; b. Rajshahi, India, Apr. 15, 1929; s. Jatindra Nath and Rama Rani (Bose) M.; m. Anjali Ghosh, Nov. 27, 1956; children: Bani, Gargi. BA with honors in Math., Ramjas Coll., Delhi, 1947, MA in Math., 1949; PhD in Physics, Delhi U., 1952, Cornel U., 1955. Lectr. physics U. Delhi, 1949-52; ctrl. states scholar Govt. India, Cornell U., Ithaca, N.Y., 1952-55; reader in physics Aligarh Muslim U., India, 1955-60, Delhi U., 1960-62; vis. prof. physics Ind. U., Bloomington, 1962-63; prof. physics Delhi U., 1963-69, sr. prof., 1969-89; Einstein rsch. prof. U. Delhi, 1989—94; slet freelance writer-rschr., 1996—. Profl. cons. Rutherford Lab., 1968; vis. scientist UCLA, 1967, CERN, 1968, 83, 85, U. Tex.-Austin, 1971, Bonn, 1974, U. Paris, 1977, Deutsche Elektronen Synchrotron, 1979, Internat. Ctr. for Theoretical Physics, Trieste, 1962, 65, 67, 68, 69, 70, 71, 74, 77, 83, Tubingen, 1985, Ind U., Bloomington, 1986; nat. lectr. Univ. Grants Commn., India, 1973; vis. prof. U. Ill., Chgo., 1986-87, Nat. Inst. Adv. Studies, Bangalore, 1995; vis. lectr. Nuffield Found., Australia, 1973; mem. internat. adv. coms. for successive internat. conf. series on few body problems in nuc. and particle physics and other internat. confs.; convenor, organizer 7th Internat. Conf. on Few Body Problems, Delhi U., 1975-76; sr. exch. visitor U.S. univs., Indo-U.S. Joint Program, 1976; sr. exch. visitor Brit. univs., Indian Nat. Sci. Acad. Royal Soc. Exch. Programme, 1979. Editor: Few Body Dynamics, 1976, Niels Bohr-A Profile, 1985, Quantum Field Theory, 2000, India in the World of Physics: Then and Now, 2008; bd. editors: Few Body Systems, 1985-2000; contbr. over 220 articles to revs. to profl. jours. Mem. physics panel Univ. Grants Commn., India, New Delhi, 1974-76, 80-82; mem. coun. Raman Rsch. Inst., Bangalore, India, 1978-88; mem. Nat. Bd. for Higher Maths., Bombay, 1982-88; mem. phys. adv. com. dept. sci. and tech. Govt. India, 1982-87; mem. physics coms. Coun. for Sci. and Indsl. Rsch., New Delhi, 1974-78, 81-91; mem. nat. accelerator com. Dept. Atomic Energy, India, 1979-83. Recipient S.S. Bhatnagar award Coun. for Sci. and Indsl. Rsch. India, New Delhi, 1969, Megh Nad Saha award Univ. Grants Commn., New Delhi, 1975, S.K. Mitra Birth Centenary medal Indian Sci. Congl. Assn., 1999; nat. fellow Univ. Grants Commn., 1975-78; assoc. Internat. Ctr. for Theoretical Physics, Trieste, 1967-70, sr. assoc., 1972-77, hon. assoc., 1978-83. Fellow Third World Acad. Scis., Indian Nat. Sci. Acad. (sec. 1975-79, editor publ. 1983-86, Albert Einstein rsch. prof. 1989-94, S.N. Bose medal 1986), Indian Acad. Sci. (coun. 1975-78), Am. Phys. Soc., Nat. Acad. Sci. India. Avocations: stamp collecting/philately, philosophy of science. Home: 244 Tagore Park New Delhi 110009 India Home Phone: 91-11-27444731; Office Phone: 91-11-27446153. Personal E-mail: ganmitra@nde.vsnl.net.in.

MITRA, JOYDEEP, electrical engineer, educator; PhD, Tex. A & M U., Coll. Station, 1997. Sr. cons. engr. LCG Consulting, Los Altos, Calif., 1997—2000; asst. prof. ND State U., Fargo, 2000—03, N.Mex State U., Las Cruces, N.Mex., 2003—04, 2003—04; assoc. prof. Mich. State U., East Lansing, Mich., 2008—. Assoc. dir. Electric Utility Mgmt. Program, Las Cruces, 2003—08. Contbr. articles to profl jours. Recipient Career award, NSF, 2002. Mem.: IEEE. Achievements include patents for standby generator integration system. Office: Michigan State Univ Dept ECE 2120 Engineering Bldg East Lansing MI 48824 Office Fax: 517-353-1980. Business E-Mail: mitraj@msu.edu.

MITRA, MAUTUSI, biologist; b. Kolkata, West Bengal, India, Feb. 14, 1968; d. Subir Kumar and Jaya Mitra. PhD, La. State U., US, 2003. Postdoc. scholar U. Calif., Berkeley, 2004—08, instr., 2008, assoc. specialist, 2008—. Mem.: Am. Soc. Plant Biologists, Internat. Soc. Photosynthesis Rsch. Achievements include patents for application of the TLA1 gene in chlorophyll antenna size regulation. Office: Univ Calif 111 Koshland Hall Berkeley CA 94720 Office Fax: 510-642-4995. Business E-Mail: mmitra@nature.berkeley.edu.

MITRA, PRITHA, economist; PhD, Columbia U., NYC, 2005. Sr. economist Arthur Andersen, NYC, 1998—2001; economist Internat. Monetary Fund, Washington, 2005—. Project coord. Asha Edn., NYC, 2000—05.

MITRA, RAJA, electronics engineer; b. Calcutta, West Bengal, India, Dec. 23, 1973; s. Sanat Kumar and Aparna Mitra; m. Joyeeta De, June 10, 1998; 1 child, Rimjhim. B Tech., Indian Inst. Tech., Kharagpur, 1996; DSc, Washington U., St. Louis, 2000. Cert. in fin. markets, India Nat. Stock Exchange Ltd., 2007; MCSD Microsoft Inc., 1999; project mgmt. profl. 2006, Internat. Project Mgmt. Assn., 2006. Software cons. G.A. Sullivan Software Devel. Solutions, St. Louis, 1999; vis. faculty mem. elec. engring. dept. Indian Inst. Tech., Kharagpur, 2000—01; sr. engring. mgr. Cadence Design Sys., Noida, India, 2001—. Contbr. articles to profl. jours. Fundraiser Make A Child Smile, Noida, India, 2007. Recipient Intel award for porting Cadence Virtuoso tools, 2002. Mem.: Soc. Industry Leaders, IEEE CAS (sec. and treas. 2007—07). Hindu. Avocation: guitar. Home: A 503 Kesar Garden Sector 48 Uttar Pradesh Noida 201305 India Office: Cadence Design Sys Pvt Ltd 57 A&B NSEZ Uttar Pradesh Noida 201305 India Personal E-mail: rajajoy2001@yahoo.com.

MITRA, RUPAK, molecular biologist; s. Sunil and Chabi Rani Mitra; m. Aditi Chatterjee, July 19, 1999; 1 child, Aurek. PhD, Calcutta U., India, 2000. Rsch. specialist HHMI, Balt., 2006—. Achievements include research in DNA transposition & recombination.

MITRA, SANJIT KUMAR, electrical and computer engineering educator; b. Calcutta, West Bengal, India, Nov. 26, 1935; came to U.S., 1958; MS in Tech., U. Calcutta, 1956; MS, U. Calif., Berkeley, 1960, PhD, 1962; D of Tech. (hon.), Tampere U. Tech, Finland, 1987; Academician, Acad. Finland, 2000; D in Tech. (hon.), Tech. U. Bucharest, Romania, 2004; D in Tech., U. Iasi, Romania, 2007. Asst. engr. Indian Statis. Inst., Calcutta, 1956-58; from teaching asst. to assoc. Univ. Calif., Berkeley, 1958-62; asst. prof. Cornell U., Ithaca, NY, 1962-65; mem. tech. staff Bell Telephone Labs., Holmdel, NJ, 1965-67; prof. U. Calif., Davis, 1967-77, prof. elec. and computer engring. Santa Barbara, 1977—, chmn. dept. elec. and computer engring., 1979-82; dir. Ctr. for Info. Processing Rsch., 1993-96. Cons. Lawrence Livermore (Calif.) Nat. Lab., 1974-95; cons. editor Van Nostrand Reinhold Co., N.Y.C., 1977-88; mem. adv. bd. Coll. Engring. Rice U., Houston, 1986-89; mem. adv. coun. Rsch. Inst. for Math. and Computing Sci., U. Groningen, The Netherlands, 1995—; mem. adv. bd. Internat. Signal Processing Ctr., Tampere U. of Tech., Finland, 1997—; external assessor Faculty of Engring., U. Putra Malaysia, Serdang, 1997—2000; hon. prof. No. Jiatong U., Beijing, China, 1985, Tech. U. Cluj-Napoka, 2005. Author: Analysis and Synthesis of Linear Active Networks, 1969, Digital and Analog Integrated Circuits, 1980; co-editor: Modern Filter Theory and Design, 1973, Two-Dimensional Digital Signal Processing, 1978, Miniaturized and Integrated Filters, 1989, Multidimensional Processing of Video Signals, 1992, Handbook for Digital Signal Processing, 1993, Digital Signal Processing: A Computer-Based Approach, 1997, 3d edit., 2005, Nonuniform Discrete Fourier Transform and Its Signal Processing Applications, 1998, Digital Signal Processing Laboratory Using MATLAB, 1999, Nonlinear Image Processing, 2000. Recipient F.E. Terman award, 1973, award, AT&T Found., 1985, Edn. award, Am. Soc. Eng. Edn., 1988, U. medal, Tech. U. Slovakia, 2005; named Disting. Fulbright Prof., Coun. for Internat. Exch. of Scholars, 1984, 1986, 1988, Disting. Sr. Scientist, Humboldt Found., 1989, Hon. Citizen, Cluj-Napoca, Romania, 2007. Fellow: IEEE (Tech. Achievement award 1996, Mac Van Valkenburg award 1999, Millennium medal 2000, McGraw-Hill/Jacob Millman award 2001, Best Paper award 2002, James H. Mulligan Jr. Edn. medal 2006, Soc. award 2006, Edn. award 2006), AAAS, Internat. Soc. Optical Engring. (Tech. Achievement award 2005); mem.: India NAS, Indian Nat. Acad. Engring., IEE UK (Blumlein-Browne-Wilans premium 2000), Acad. Engring. Mex., US Nat. Acad. Engring., Norwegian Acad. Technol. Scis., Croatian Acad. Arts and Scis., Acad. of Finland, European Assn. for Signal Processing (Tech. Achievement award 2001). Achievements include patents for two-port networks for realizing transfer functions; non-reciprocal wave translating device; discrete cosine transform-based image coding and decoding method; method and apparatus for multipath channel shaping; method for embedding and extracting digital data in images and videos. Office: Univ Calif Dept Elec and Computer Engring Santa Barbara CA 93106-9560

MITRA, SOPHIE, economics professor; b. Arcachon, France; m. Joydeep Mitra; children: Leela L., Alain D., Neel P. PhD in Economics, U. Pantheon-Sorbonne, Paris, 2001. Rsch. analyst Rutgers, State U., New Brunswick, NJ, 2002—05; asst. prof. Fordham U., Bronx, 2005—. Contbr. articles to profl. jour. on economics. Mem.: Am. Econ. Assn. Office: Fordham Univ 441 East Fordham Rd Bronx NY 10458 Business E-Mail: mitra@fordham.edu.

MITRA, SUNANDA DATTA, engineering educator; d. Suresh Chandra and Navamallika Datta; m. Arun Kumar Mitra, May 8, 1960; children: Atindra Kumar, Rita Mitra Oberdier. BS in Physics with honors, Presidency Coll., Calcutta U., India, 1955; MS in Physics, Calcutta U., 1957; DSc, Marburg U., Republic of Germany, 1966. Cert. in nuclear physics Saha Inst. Nuc. Physics, 1959. Lectr. Lady Brabourne Coll., Calcutta U., 1959—64; rsch. assoc., dept. ECE Tex. Tech. U., Lubbock, 1969—73, rsch. assoc. Sch. Medicine, 1974—75, rsch. scientist, 1977—83, asst. prof., dept. ECE, 1984—90, dir., computer vision and image analysis lab., 1988—, assoc. prof., dept. ECE, 1990—93, prof. dept. ECE, 1993—2008, P. W. Horn prof., 2005—. Mem. bd. sci. counselors Nat. Libr. Medicine, NIH, Bethesda, Md., 1997—2001; assoc. editor Jour. Electronic Imaging. Contbr. articles to profl. jours. (Barnie E. Rushing, Jr. Faculty Disting. Rsch. award, 2002). Mem.: SPIE, IEEE. Achievements include patents for adaptive vector quantization, quantizer. Office: Tex Tech Univ 19th at Boston Ave Mail Stop 3102 Lubbock TX 79409-3102 Business E-Mail: sunanda.mitra@ttu.edu.

MITRASINOVIC, PETAR M., chemistry professor, engineer, research scientist; b. Valjevo, Serbia, Nov. 15, 1968; permanent resident, Can. s. Milorad P. and Milena M. Mitrasinovic. BSc in Control Engring., MSc in Control Engring., U. Belgarde, Serbia, D in Materials Sci. and Nanotechnology; PhD in Phys. Chemistry, Fla. State U. Process control engr. Sumerbank Holding, Izmir, Turkey, 1991—93; tchg. instr., rsch. fellow Molecular Machines Rsch. Ctr., U. Belgrade, Serbia and Montenegro, 1993—96; rsch. and tchg. asst. Dept. Chemistry, Fla. State U., 1997—2002; European Union postdoctoral rsch. assoc. Ctr. Rsch. Molecular Electronics and Photonics, U. Mons-Hainaut, Mons, Wallona, Belgium, 2002; Izaak Walton Killam postdoctoral assoc. Dept. Chemistry, Dalhousie U., Halifax, Canada, 2003—04; rsch. scientist for IBM Molecular Enzymology Lab., Henri Poincaré U., Nancy, France, 2005; sr. sci. assoc. Dept. Info. Tech., Ctr. Multidisciplinary Studies, U. Belgrade, 2006—. Assoc. prof. Dept. Biophysics, Ctr. Multidisciplinary Studies, U. Belgrade, 2007—; prof. U. Banja Luka; lectr. in field. Contbr. (chapter to book) World of Chemistry, 40 papers to profl. jours.; reviewer: Jour. Mass Spectrometry, Current Radiopharmaceuticals, Jour. Am. Chem. Soc., Jour. Phys. Chemistry A/B, IEEE Computer Soc. Proceedings and IEEE Control Sys. Soc. Proceedings, Current Process Chemistry; rsch. reviews Biosciences, India, 2007—. Mem. Greek Orthodox Ch., Tallahasse, 1994—; sci. fair judge Tallahassee Region, 1997—. Grantee Grad. Studies Rsch. grant, Dalhousie U., Can., 2003—04, Congress Grad. Studies Rsch. grant, Fla. State U., 2000—01; Internat. Assn. for Exch. of Students of Tech. Experience fellowship, 1991, Yugoslavian Nat. Sci. Found. fellowship, 1993—96, Young Scientists fellowship, 1993—95, Fla. State U. Grad. fellowship, 1997—2002, European Union SANEME fellowship, Belgium, 2002, Izaak Walton Killam Meml. fellowship, Dalhousie U., Can., 2003—04. Mem.: Serbian Chem. Soc., Foresight Inst. Molecular Nanotechnology, European Soc. Computational Methods in Sci. and Engring. (peer elected full mem., award 2005), Can. Soc. Chemistry, Am. Chem. Soc. Achievements include research in bioinformatics, medicinal chemistry, systems biology, computational chemistry and materials science. Avocations: foreign languages, cooking, travel, history, literature. Mailing: Ivana Djaje 5-22 11000 Belgrade Serbia

MITROFF, IAN I., finance educator; s. Joseph Mitroff and Mabel Sacks; m. Donna Drevenak, Dec. 20, 1964; 1 child, Dana Mitroff-Silvers. PhD, U. Calif., Berkeley, 1967; PhD (hon.), U. Stockholm, 2000. Prof. Marshall Goldsmith Sch. Bus., San Francisco, 2006—; vis. prof. Collaborative Catastrophic Risk Mgmt., UC Berkeley, 2006—, sr. inverstigator, 2006—. Pres. Comprehensive Crisis Mgmt., Oakland, Calif., 2006—. Contbr. articles to numerous profl. jours. Fellow: AAAS, Am. Acad. Mgmt. Liberal. Avocation: harmonica.

MITSCHER, LESTER ALLEN, chemist, educator; b. Detroit, Aug. 20, 1931; s. Lester and Mary Athelda (Pounder) M.; m. Betty Jane McRoberts, May 29, 1953; children: Katrina, Kurt, Mark. BS, Wayne U., 1953, PhD, 1958. Rsch. scientist, group leader Lederle Labs., Pearl River, NY, 1958-67; prof. Ohio State U., Columbus, 1967-75, U. Kans., Lawrence, 1975—, chmn. dept. medicinal chemistry, 1975-92; intersearch prof. Victorian Coll. of Pharmacy, Monash U., Melbourne, Australia, 1975—. Author: (with D. Lednicer) The Organic Chemistry of Drug Synthesis, Vol. 1, 1976, Vol. 2, 1980, Vol. 3, 1984, Vol. 4, 1990, The Chemistry of the Tetracycline Antibiotics, 1978; co-author: The Green Tea Book, 2nd edit., 2007; editor-in-chief Medicinal Research Reviews, 1995-99; contbr. over 270 articles to profl. jours. Recipient Disting. Alumnus award Sch. Pharmacy, Wayne State U., 1980, 97, Rsch. Achievement award Acad. Pharm. Scis., 1980, 97, Volweiler Rsch. award Am. Assn. Colls. Pharmacy, 1985, Higuchi-Simmons award U. Kans., 1986. Fellow AAAS; mem. Am. Soc. Pharmacognosy (pres. 1992-93, Rsch. Achievement award 2007), Am. Chem. Soc. (former chmn. councilor medicinal chemistry divsn., Bristol-Myers Smissman rsch. award 1989, Med. Chemistry award 2000, Medicinal Chemistry Hall of Fame medicinal chemistry divsn. 2007), Norman Fern Worth Rsch. award, Am. Soc. Pharmacology, 2007, Japanese Antibiotics Assn., Soc. Heterocyclic Chemistry, Internat. Orgn. for Chemistry in Developing Countries (steering com.). Presbyterian. Office: Dept Medicinal Chemistry U Kans Lawrence KS 66045 Office Phone: 785-864-4562. Business E-Mail: lmitscher@ku.edu.

MITSEFF, CARL, lawyer; b. Detroit, Nov. 16, 1928; s. Frank H. and Katherine M.; m. Phyllis Schlitters, June 28, 1952; children: C. Randall, Bradley Scott, Julie, Emily, Faye. BS, Wayne State U., 1952, JD, 1955. Bar: Mich. 1956. Practiced in Detroit, 1956—; staff atty. Burroughs Corp., 1955-60; mem. firm LeVasseur, Mitseff, Egan & Capp, 1960-80, Mitseff & Baril, 1980-85, Fitzgerald, Hodgman, Cox, Cawthoren & McMahon, 1986-90, Cox & Hodgman, 1990—, mitseff, assoc., 2007—. Spl. asst. atty. gen. State of Mich.; lectr. in field. Named to Mich. Workers Compensation Hall of Fame, 2000. Mem. ABA, State Bar Mich., Internat. Assn. Ins. Counsel, Internat. Assn. Indsl. Accident Bds. and Commns., Detroit Athletic Club (bd. dirs.), Beavers (pres.), Exec. Club (pres.), Bus. Round Table (chmn.), Lochmoor Club, Grosse Pointe Yacht Club, Pi Kappa Alpha, Delta Theta Phi. Home: 612 N Brys Dr Grosse Pointe Woods MI 48236-1247 Office: 20789 Harper Ave Harper Woods MI 48225 Home Phone: 313-882-2302; Office Phone: 313-963-3210, 313-881-3030. Office Fax: 313-640-5934. Personal E-mail: c.mitseff@aol.com.

MITSUYASU, RONALD T., physician, researcher, medical educator; b. Berkeley, Calif., Feb. 12, 1952; s. Kiyoshi and Hisako (Sato) M.; m. Sharon R., June 23, 1984. BA in Biochemistry, U. Calif., 1973; MD, UCLA, 1978. Diplomate Am. Bd. Internal Medicine. Intern internal medicine Rush-Presbyn.-St. Luke's, Chgo., 1978, resident internal medicine, 1978-81; fellow in hematology, oncology Sch. Medicine UCLA, 1981-84, asst. prof. medicine Sch. Medicine, 1984-90, prof. medicine Sch. Medicine, 1990—, dir. CARE Ctr. Sch. Medicine, 1991—. Group chair AIDS Malignancy Consortium, 2006-, assoc. dir. UCLA AIDS Inst. Contbr. over 400 articles to profl. jours., chpts. to books. Fellow Am. Coll. Physicians; mem. Am. Soc. Clin. Oncology, Am. Soc. Hematology, Internat. AIDS Soc. Office: 9911 W Pico Blvd Ste 980 Los Angeles CA 90035-2703

MITTAL, BANWARI, finance educator, entrepreneur; s. Rameshwer Mittal; m. Meena Tandon, Dec. 8, 1975; children: Pratik, Mayank. PhD, U. Pitts., 1982. Faculty mem. SUNY, Buffalo, 1982—87; prof. mktg. Northern Ky. U., Highland Heights, 1988—; vis. prof. U. Miami, Fla., 1994—95, U. NSW, Sydney, 2004. Pres. and entrepreneur-at-large Valuespace, Inc., Cin., 2001—. Author: (books) Valuespace-Winning the Battle for Market Leadership, Customer Behavior: Consumer Behavior and Beyond, Consumer Behavior-How Humans Think, Feel, and Act in the Marketplace; contbr. articles to profl. jours. Named Keynote Spkr., IPAM Porto Portugal, 2008. Mem.: AMA. Liberal. Avocations: travel, reading, yoga, music. Office: Northern Ky Univ Nunn Dr Highland Heights KY 41099 Personal E-mail: ban@myvaluespace.com. Business E-Mail: mittal@nku.edu.

MITTAL, SANDEEP, neurosurgeon, director; b. Bareilly, Uttar Pradesh, India, Mar. 30, 1973; s. Khyali Ram and Maya Devi Mittal; m. Monika Mittal, Dec. 23, 2002; children: Priya, Adesh. MD, McGill U., Montreal, Quebec, Canada, 1997. Lic. Med. Coun. Can., 1998. Chief, neuro-oncological surgery Karmanos Cancer Ctr., Detroit, 2006—, co-director, dir., 2008—; asst. prof., dept. neurosurgery Wayne State U., Detroit, 2006—, chief, epilepsy surgery, faculty dept. physiology, 2007—. Contbr. scientific papers, chapters to books. Recipient Gov. Gen. Medal, Goverment Can., 1992, Merck, Sharp & Dohme award, McGill U., 1994, H.L. Teuber prize, 1999, Wilder Penfield award, 2004, Upjohn Achievement award, 1993, 1994, 1995, ANCQ prize, Que. Assn. Neurol. Surgeons, 1998, 2001, 2000; fellowship, McGill U., 2003, 2004, 2005, Brain Sci. Found., 2005—06, FRSQ, Que., Can., 1993, 1996, 2001—03, Brigham Women's Hosp., Harvard Med. Sch., 2006, Muscular Dystrophy Assn. Can., 1995, Med. Rsch. Coun. Can., 1996. Fellow: Royal Coll. Physicians Surgeons (Can.); mem.: Mich. Assn. Neurol. Surgeons, Can. Neurosurg. Soc., Internat. League Against Epilepsy, Soc. Neuro-Oncology, Am. Epilepsy Soc., Congress Neurol. Surgeons, Am. Assn. Neurol. Surgeons. Achievements include research in neuro-oncology, epileptogenesis, neuro-imaging. Office: Wayne State Univ 4160 John R St Ste 930 Detroit MI 48201 Office Fax: 313-966-0368. Business E-Mail: smittal@med.wayne.edu.

MITTELDORFER, SHIRLEY JUSTIS, education educator, consultant; b. Richmond, Va., Nov. 14, 1939; d. Thomas R. and V. Marian Justis; m. Marx E. Mitteldorfer; children: James N. McGinnis, C. David McGinnis, Michael T. Hoerter. BS, MEd, Va. Commonwealth U., Richmond, 2008. Cert. collegiate profl. Va., 2007. Classroom tchr. Chesterfield County Pub. Schs., Va., 1976—82, instrnl. tech. integrator, 1983—2004; tchr. J. Sergeant Reynolds CC, Richmond, 1984—; prof. U. Richmond, 1997—; instrnl. tech. cons. Va. Commonwealth U., 2004—. Named Disting. Faculty of Yr., U. Richmond, Apple Nat. Computer Contest Winner, 1984.

MITTELSTAEDT, ROBERT E., JR., dean; married; 3 children. BS in Mech. Engring., Tulane U., 1965; MBA, U. Pa., 1971. Founder, pres. Intellego, Inc., 1985—89; mem. faculty Wharton Sch. of U. Pa., Phila., 1973—2004, vice dean exec. edn., 1990—2004, vice dean Wharton West, 2000—01; dean Ariz. State U. W.P. Carey Sch. Bus., Tempe, Ariz., 2004—. Bd. dirs. Lab. Corp. of Am., 1996—, HIP Found., Inc., 1997—, IS&S Inc., 1988—, chmn., 1988—97. Served USN, 1965—70. Office: Ariz State U WP Carey Sch Bus Main Campus PO Box 873506 Tempe AZ 85287-3506 Office Phone: 480-965-2468. Office Fax: 480-965-5539. E-mail: Robert.Mittelstaedt@asu.edu.*

MITTEN, L. RUSSELL, lawyer, former telecommunications industry executive; BA, Southeast Mo. State U.; JD, Wash. U., St. Louis. Bar: Conn., Mo., Tex., Wash., Hawaii, US Supreme Ct., US Ct. of Appeals, U.S. Dist. Ct. Gen. counsel Missouri Public Service Commn., Gen. Telephone Co. of Southwest, Gen. Telephone Co. of Northwest, GTE Service Corp.; v.p., gen. counsel, sec. GTE Hawaiian Telephone; gen. counsel Citizens Communications, 1990—91, v.p., gen. counsel, asst. sec., 1991—2000, v.p., gen. counsel, sec., 2000—02, sr. v.p., gen. counsel, sec., 2002—06; atty. Brydon, Swearengen & England PC, Jefferson City, Mo., 2006—. Office: Brydon, Swearengen & England PC 312 E Capitol Ave PO Box 456 Jefferson City MO 65102 Office Phone: 573-635-7166 160. Office Fax: 573-635-0427. E-mail: rmitten@brydonlaw.com.

MITTENDORF, KIMBERLY ANN, retired secondary school educator, real estate consultant; d. K. A. and Jo Mittendorf. BS in Edn., Murray State U., 1980, MA in Edn., 1987. Cert. career and tech. edn. Nat. Bd. Tchr. Certification, 2004, lic. real estate Paducah C.C., 1990. Tchr. McCracken County Pub. Schs., Paducah, Ky., 1982—2009; real estate specialist Prudential Real Estate, Paducah, 1990—99. Mem. Paducah Bd. Realtors, 1990—2001; mem. edn. com. Challenger Learning Space Ctr., Paducah, 2001—03; mem. fed. res. economics edn. com. Fed. Res., Louisville, 2005—. Affiliate Hon. Order of Ky. Cols., Louisville, 1996—; inductee Paducah C. of C. Leadership Class, 1995—96; mem. Paducah C. of C., 1995—98; mem. funds distbn. com. United Way, Paducah, 1996—97. Recipient Invitation to China, People to People Amb. -Edn. Del. to China, 2005. Mem.: NEA (assoc.), Ky. Edn. Assn. (assoc.), Ky. Assn. Career and Tech. Edn. (assoc.), Pi Lambda Theta. Avocations: literature, architecture and design, fitness, cuisine. Home Phone: 270-442-4149. Business E-Mail: mitten@vci.net.

MITTERMILLER, JAMES JOSEPH, lawyer; b. Washington, Apr. 13, 1953; s. Jack and Alice Marie (Froeba) M.; m. Elizabeth Gaillard Simons, June 23, 1979; children: Samuel Stoney, Paul Andrew, Laurie Alice, Claire Mary. Student, U. Heidelberg, 1973-74; BA, Claremont McKenna Coll., 1975; JD, U. Calif. Berkeley, 1978. Bar: Calif., U.S. Dist. Ct. (so., ctrl. and ea. dists.) Calif., U.S. Ct. Appeals (9th cir.), U.S. Supreme Ct. Assoc. Sheppard, Mullin, Richter & Hampton, LA, 1978-86, ptnr., 1986—. Panelist Calif. Continuing Edn. of Bar, L.A. and San Diego, 1984—. Dir. Legal Aid Soc. of San Diego, 1990—, pres., 1998-2000; bd.dirs., LaJolla YMCA, 2001-04. Recipient Wiley Manuel Pro Bono award Calif. State Bar, 1992, 2001. Mem. Assn. Bus. Trial Lawyers (bd. dirs. 1998-2001), Am. Inns of Ct., Claremont McKenna Coll. Alumni Assn. San Diego (bd. dirs.). Avocations: swimming, surfing. Office: Sheppard Mullin Richter & Hampton 501 W Broadway Fl 19 San Diego CA 92101-3536

MITTLEBERG, ERIC MICHAEL, pharmaceutical executive; b. NYC, Nov. 7, 1951; s. Irving Ralph and Rose (Schnieder) M.; m. Jane Susan Baumoehl, Dec. 25, 1977; children: Scott, Alyson, Lauren. BS in Pharmacy, St. Johns U., Jamaica, NY, 1974, MS in Ind. Pharmaceutics,

1978, PhD in Pharmaceutics, 1982. Registered pharmacist, N.Y. Assoc. scientist Hoffmann-LaRoche Inc., Nutley, NJ, 1974-78; dept. head process improvement Lederle Labs, Pearl River, NY, 1978-83; mgr. mfg. devel. Key Pharm., Miami, Fla., 1983-86; dir. prodn. and tech. svcs. Schering Labs, Miami, 1986-89; sr. dir. pharm. devel. and tech. svcs. worldwide R.W. Johnson Pharm. Rsch. Inst., Raritan, NJ, 1989-97; v.p. sci., med. affairs Ivax Corp., 1997—2006; exec. v.p. pharm. R&D Par Pharm., Inc., Spring Valley, NY, 2006—09, Sandoz Pharm, NJ, 2009—. Mem. Internat. Soc. Pharm. Engrs., Acad. Pharm. Sci., Am. Pharm. Assn. Office: Sandoz Pharm 506 Carnegie Ctr Princeton NJ 08540 Office Phone: 609-627-8841. Business E-Mail: eric.mittleberg@sandoz.com.

MITTLEIDER, REBECCA ANN, elementary school educator; d. Leslie Earl and Bonnie Kay Johnson; m. Randy Wayne Mittleider, Aug. 20, 1988; 1 child, Megan Kate. B Sociology, Western Wash. U., 1988; M Tchg., Wash. State U., 1995. Cert. tchr. Wash. Cmty. corrections officer Dept. Corrections, Kennewick, Wash., 1988—95; mid. sch. tchr. Kennewick (Wash.) Sch. Dist., 1995—96; elem. sch. tchr. Richland Sch. Dist., West Richland, Wash., 1996—. Sci. curriculum coord. Tapteal Elem. Sch., Richland, 2004—05; presenter in field. Vol. pet therapist with miniature horses at local nursing homes, Wash., 2004—05; vol. horse therapist Handicapped Equestrian Riding Team, Kennewick, 1995—95. Recipient Excellence in Tchg. award, KEPR News, 2001; Tchr. Leadership Project grantee, Bill and Melinda Gates Found., 2000. Mem.: NAST, Wash. Orgn. Reading Devel., Am. Miniature Horse Registry (Nat. Top-Ten All Star in Roadster and Obstacle 2004), Columbia Basin Bass Club (bd. dirs., newsletter editor 1998—99), Ctrl. Wash. Miniature Horse Club (Yr. End High Point awards 2004—05), Franklin County Saddle Club.

MITTLER, DIANA (DIANA MITTLER-BATTIPAGLIA), music educator, pianist; b. NYC, Oct. 19, 1941; d. Franz and Regina (Schilling) Mittler; m. Victor Battipaglia, Sept. 5, 1965 (div. 1982). BS, Juilliard Sch., 1962, MS, 1963; DMA, Eastman Sch. Music, 1974. Choral dir. William Cowper Jr. H.S. and Springfield Gardens Jr. H.S., Queens, NY, 1963-68; coord. music Flushing H.S., Queens, 1968-79; asst. prin. music Bayside H.S., Queens, 1979-86; assoc. prof. music Lehman Coll., CUNY, 1986-87, prof., 1987—, choral dir., 1986—. Cons. ednl. projects New World Records, 1987—; ednl. cons. Flushing Coun. on Culture and the Arts; cons. Sta. WNET; assoc. condr. Queens Borough-Wide Chorus, 1964-70; pianist, founder Con Brio Chamber Ensemble, 1978; faculty So. Vt. Music Festival, 1979-83; soloist with N.Y. Philharm., 1956; examiner NYC Bd. Edn. Bd. Exams., 1985—. Author: 57 Lessons for the H.S. Music Class, 1983, Franz Mittler: Austro-American Composer, Musician and Humorous Poet, 1993; contbr. articles to profl. jours.; performance Internat. Summer acad. Mozarteum, Salzburg, Austria, 1995, Weill Recital Hall, 1996, Merkin Hall, 1997, Herbert von Karajan Centrum, Vienna, Austria, 1998; rec. Franz Mittler., Preiser Records, Trio and Piano Pieces, 2003; featured in Last Stop, Kew Gardens, 2007; featured on Study with the Best Series, CUNY TV, 2005. Choral dir., accompanist various charitable, religious, mil., civic holiday functions. N.Y. State Regents scholar, 1958-62; scholarships Juilliard Sch. and Eastman Sch. Music; recipient Excellence in Tchg. award, 1993, Prism award, 1996, Proclamation Lifetime Musical Achievement award NY State Assembly, 2009. Mem. Am. Choral Dirs. Assn., Music Edn. Nat. Conf., Golden Key Soc. Democrat. Home: 10857 66th Ave Forest Hills NY 11375-2247 Office: Lehman Coll Music Dept Bedford Pk Blvd W Bronx NY 10468 Home Phone: 718-459-1277; Office Phone: 718-960-7795. Personal E-mail: dianamittler@aol.com.

MITTLER, MARK A., neurosurgeon; b. NYC, May 24, 1965; MD, U. Rochester, NY, 1991. Diplomate Am. Bd. Neurol. Surgery, Am. Bd. Pediatric Neurol. Surgery. Intern neurol. surgery Brown U./RI Hosp., Providence, 1991—92, resident pediatric neurology; chief resident Hasbro Children's Hosp., RI; fellow pediatric neurol. surgery Children's Hosp. LA, 1998—99; staff LI Neurosurgical Assoc., New Hyde Park, NY, 1999—; co-chief divsn. pediatric neurosurgery LI Jewish Health Sys./Schneider Children's Hosp., Manhasset, NY, 2002—. Clin. asst. prof. NYU. Contbr. articles to profl. jours., chapters to books. Mem.: AMA, Nassau County Med. Soc., NY State Med. Soc., Am. Soc. Pediatric Neurosurgeons, Congress Neurol. Surgeons, Am. Assn. Neurol. Surgeons. Office: LI Neurosurgical Assoc 410 Lakeville Rd Ste 204 New Hyde Park NY 11042 Office Phone: 516-354-3401. Office Fax: 516-354-8597.*

MITTMAN, NEAL, nephrologist, medical educator; b. NYC, Jan. 24, 1953; s. Arnold and Tess (Blumenthal) M.; m. Candace Clark (Martin), Sept. 21, 1980; children: Alexander Clark and Zachary Wade. BA, Queens Coll., CUNY, 1973; MD, N.Y. Med. Coll., 1977. Diplomate Am. Bd. Internal Medicine and Am. Bd. Nephrology. Intern N.Y. Med. Coll., Met. Hosp. Ctr., 1977-78, resident, 1978-80; resident nephrologist Albert Einstein Coll. Medicine, Bronx, NY, 1980-82; asst. prof. medicine Mt. Sinai Sch. Medicine, 1982-86; assoc. chief nephrology Beth Israel Med. Ctr., NYC, 1982-86, L.I. Coll. Hosp., Bklyn., 1986—, program dir. nephrology fellowship, 2005—; assoc. prof. clin. medicine State Univ. of N.Y. Health Sci. Ctr., Bklyn., 1993—; med. dir. Atlantic Hemodialysis, 2000—. Med. adv. bd. Nat. Kidney Found. NY, NJ, and N.Y.C., 1994-2002; grants and fellowship rev. com., 1995-2002; sec. med. adv. bd., chmn. corp. partnerships com. Kidney and Urology Found. Am., 2002-; Bd. of trustees, Kidney and Urology Found. Am., 2003-. Co-editor: Ambulatory Peritoneal Dialysis, 1990; contbg. articles to med. jour. Recipient Clin. Rsch. Award NIH, 1980-82; named NY Met. Best Dr., Castle, Connolly Med., Ltd., 1997-; named one of NY Times Super Drs., 2008-09. Fellow ACP, Am. Soc. Nephrology, Royal Coll. Medicine (London); mem. Am. Soc. Artificial Internal Organs, Am. Soc. Hypertension, Internat. Soc. Nephrology, NY Soc. Nephrology (sec. treas. 1996-97, v.p. 1997-98, pres. 1998-99), Met. Renal Care Network (bd. dir., sec.). Avocations: country living, opera, gourmet cooking. Office: LI Coll Hosp 339 Hicks St Brooklyn NY 11201-5509 Office Phone: 718-780-1248. Personal E-mail: nmittman@aol.com. Business E-Mail: nmittman@chpnet.org.

MITTS, EMMA, alderwoman; b. Elaine, Ark., June 12, 1955; 2 children. Attended, Phillip County CC, U. Ark., Triton Coll., Melrose Pk., Ill. Parking aide Chgo. Dept. Revenue; acctg. tech Chgo. Dept. Streets and Sanitation; coord. spl. projects Chgo. Bur. St. Ops.; with workforce devel. program Office of the Mayor, Chgo.; alderwoman, 37th ward Chgo. City Coun. Former Sunday sch. instr. Henry Horner Boys & Girls Club; mem. 1st Bapt. Congl. Ch.; founder, former pres. Cmty. Action Coun., Chgo. Democrat. Office: 5344 W North Ave Chicago IL 60639 also: City Hall 121 N LaSalle St Rm 300 Chicago IL 60602 Office Phone: 773-745-2894, 312-744-8019. Office Fax: 773-745-3749. Business E-Mail: emitts@cityofchicago.org.

MITZNER, KENNETH MARTIN, electrical engineer, consultant; b. Bklyn., May 7, 1938; s. Louis Bernard and Dora (Sandler) Mitzner; m. Ruth Maria Osorio, Dec. 26, 1968; children: Camille Lorena Mitzner Zeiter, Esther Jeannette Mitzner Lin, Sharon Michelle Mitzner Mentkowski. BS, MIT, 1958; MS, Calif. Inst. Tech., 1959, PhD, 1964. Mem. tech. staff Hughes Aircraft, Malibu, Calif., 1959-64; prin. engr. B-2 divsn. Northrop Corp., Pico Rivera, Calif., 1964-94; owner Mitzner Sci. and Tech., Oceanside, Calif., 1995—. Instr. U. Calif., Santa Barbara, 1964—65; lectr. in field. Author: (handbook) Demonstrations Against Abortion & Death Selection, 1970; contbr. chapters to books, articles to profl. jours. Bd. dirs. Nat. Right to Life Com., 1980—81; pres. Mobilization for Unnamed, Oceanside, 1970—; bd. dirs. Ams. United for Life, 1971—94; sec. Calif. Pro Life Coun., Sacramento, 1972; mem. Los Angeles County Select Citizens Com. Life Support Policies, LA, 1983—85; bd. dirs. Jewish Life Issues Com., Solana Beach, 1983—. Recipient Pres.'s award, 1979; named Patron of Life, Calif. Pro Life Coun., 1976; Howard Hughes fellow, 1959—64, Fulbright Found. grantee, Govt. of Italy, 1961—62. Fellow: IEEE (life); mem.: Electromagnetics Acad., U.S. Nat. Commn. Internat. Union Radio Sci. (del. 20th gen. assembly). Jewish. Avocations: history, stamp collecting/philately, birdwatching. Personal E-mail: kmitzner@aol.com.

MIURA, MASAKO KUSAYANAGI, retired dermatologist; b. Pasadena, Calif., June 29, 1914; d. Takejiro Kusayanagi and Matsu Hoshizaki; m. Kiyoshi Miura, June 29, 1955; m. James Mitsuo Goto (div.); children: Denise Goto Kodani, Hans Masaji Goto. AB, U. So. Calif., LA, 1936, MD, 1941. Resident dermatology LA County Hosp., 1941—42, 1945—49; physician War Relocation Authority, Manzanar, 1942—43, Topaz, 1943—45; sch. physician LA Bd. Edn, 1951—54; physician US Army, Oakland, 1954—55, Monterey, 1955—81; ret., 1981; supervising physician Project Scout, Santa Cruz County, 1983—88. Fellow: Pacific Dermatology Assn. (nominating com. 1987); mem.: Internat. Soc. Dermatology, San Francisco Dermatol. Soc., Nat. Assn. Ret. Fed. Employees (program chair 2000), Half-Century Club, Japanese Am. Citizens League, 4-H (10 year gold pin for tchg. fgn. foods), Phi Kappa Phi, Phi Beta Kappa. Methodist. Home: 2917 Crocker Ct Aptos CA 95003

MIURA, ROBERT MITSURU, mathematician, researcher, educator; s. Richard Katsuki and Frances Yoneko Miura; m. Kathryn Bannai; children: Derek Katsuki, Brian Robert, Jared Bannai Nagae, Sean Takeo. BS, U. Calif.-Berkeley, 1960, MS, 1962; MA, Princeton U., 1964, PhD, 1966. Rsch. assoc. Princeton U. Plasma Physics Lab., 1965-67; assoc. rsch. scientist Courant Inst. Math. Sci., NYC, 1967-68; asst. prof. math. NYU, 1968—71; assoc. prof. math. Vanderbilt U., Nashville, 1971—75; assoc. prof. to prof. math. U. BC, Vancouver, Canada, 1975—2001; prof. math. sci. and biomed. engring. NJ Inst. Tech., Newark, 2001—07, disting. prof., 2007—. Assoc. chmn. math. sci. NJ Inst. Tech., 2003—05, dir. divsn. biol. scis., 2004—05, acting chmn. math. sci., 2005—06; co-program dir., program in Quantitative Neurosci. Howard Hughes Med. Inst., 2006—09. Editor: Backlund Transformations, 1976, Nonlinear Phenomena in Physics and Biology, 1981, Some Mathematical Questions in Biology-Neurobiology, 1982, Muscle Physiology, 1986, DNA Sequence Analysis, 1986, Plant Biology, 1986; mem. editl. bd. Can. Applied Math. Quar., 1991—; co-editor-in-chief: Analysis and Applications, 2000—, editl. bd.: Integrative Neurosci., 2001—06, SIAM J. Appl. Math., 2009—, mem. editl. bd.: SIAM Book, SIAM Book Series on Math Modeling and Computation; contbr. articles to profl. jours. Mem. steering com. Ctr. Math. Rsch., U. Montreal, 1990-94; mem. sci. adv. panel Fields Inst., Toronto, 2002-06, mem. sci. nominating com., 2003, chair Bd. Trustees Math. Biosciences Inst. John Simon Guggenheim fellow, 1980-81; U. B.C. hon. Killam fellow, 1980-81. Fellow AAAS (nominating com., math. sect.), Royal Soc. Can.; mem. Am. Math. Soc. (Leroy P. Steele prize-Seminal Contribution to Rsch., 2006), Soc. Indsl. and Applied Math. (chmn. joint com. on math. in life scis. 1981-84; vice chair, chair, activity group on the life scis. 2005-06, 2007-08, fellow 2009-), Can. Math. Soc. (internat. affairs com.), Soc. Math. Biology (bd. dirs. 1995-98, nominating com. 1998), Pacific Inst. Math. Sci. (interim exec. bd. 1996), Sigma Xi. Office: NJ Inst Tech Dept Math Sci Univ Hgts Newark NJ 07102 Business E-Mail: miura@njit.edu.

MIVILLE, NINA DECARIO, management consultant, educator; b. Coral Gables, Fla., Dec. 10, 1964; d. Vincent Francis and Adolfina Grau DeCario; m. George Joseph Miville, Oct. 18, 1997; 1 child, Katerina Marina. BSIE, U. Miami, Coral Gables, 1986, MBA, 1991; M, George Washington U., Washington, 2000; DBA, Nova Southeastern U., Ft. Lauderdale, Fla., 2005. Mgmt. intern Am. Bankers Ins. Group, Miami, 1986—87, supr. mgmt. sys., 1987—97, bus. sys. analyst, 1991—94; dir. mgmt. sys. Mercy Hosp., Miami, 1994—2005; sr. mgmt. cons. Mt. Sinai Med. Ctr., Miami Beach, 2005—07; adj. faculty Am. Intercontinental U., Chgo., 2005—; lectr. U. Miami, 2007—. Mem.: Inst. Indsl. Engrs. Home: 8190 SW 184 Ln Cutler Ridge FL 33157 Office: Univ Miami 1251 Memorial Dr Coral Gables FL 33146 Office Fax: 305-284-4040. Business E-Mail: ndecario1@miami.edu.

MIX, JILL KAYE, secondary school educator, artist; b. Oshkosh, Wis., Apr. 12, 1947; d. Emil Frank and Faye Ione (Wegner) Mix; m. Daniel Charles Knoop (div.); children: Victoria Mae Gonzalez, Valorie Faye Knoop. AA, Riverside CC, 1981; BA, Calif. State U., 1997. Cert. tchr. Calif. Advt. staff Moreno Valley (Calif.) News; pub. rels. staff, photographer Moreno Valley C. of C.; art and art history tchr. Ramona HS, Riverside, Big Bear HS, Big Bear Lake, Calif. Represented in permanent collections Sugar Loaf Park, Grant Elem. Sch., Ramona HS. Sec. Moreno Valley C. of C., 1987. Grantee, Steven G. Mihaylo Edn. Found., 2004. Mem.: NEA, Calif. Tchrs. Assn., Phi Kappa Phi. Avocations: interior decorating, photography, painting. Office: Big Bear High Sch PO Box 1708 Big Bear Lake CA 92315

MIX, VICKIE LYNN, school librarian, educator; d. James B. and Isabel L. Tischler; m. Mickey Charles Mix, July 18, 2003; m. Thomas Jon Salonen, Dec. 20, 1980 (div. July 5, 2002); children: Jamie Lee Salonen, Laura Mae Salonen, Leslie Ann Salonen. BA in Comm., SD State U., Brookings, 1978, MEd, 2005; MLIS, U. North Tex., Denton, 2003. Reference libr. SD State U. H. M. Briggs Libr., 2003—06, docs. libr., asst. prof., 2006—. State edn. chair AAUW, SD, 2007—. Mem.: ALA, Govt. Docs. Roundtable, Assn. Coll. and Rsch. Librs., SD Libr. Assn. (academic sect. chair 2005—06, Profl. Devel. grant 2006), Mountain Plains Libr. Assn. (Leadership Inst. fellow 2006). Democrat. Office: HM Briggs Libr N Campus Dr Box 2115 Brookings SD 57007 Office Fax: 605-688-6133.

MIXDORF, JON, science educator; b. Waverly, Iowa, Dec. 11, 1945; s. Albert and Ruby Mixdorf. MS in Engring. Mgmt., Milw. Sch. Engring., 1999. Lic. State of Iowa, Ins. Dept., 1980. Instr. Hawkeye CC, Waterloo, Iowa, 1995—. Del. NEA. Office: Hawkeye CC 1501 E Orange Rd Waterloo IA 50704 Business E-Mail: jmixdorf@hawkeyecollege.edu.

MIXON, AARON MALACHI, III, medical products executive; b. May 22, 1940; m. Barbara Weber; 2 children. BA, Harvard U., 1962, MBA, 1968. CEO, chmn. Invacare Corp., Elyria, Ohio, 1979—. Chmn. bd. trustees Cleve. Clinic Found., Cleve. Inst. Music. Recipient Alumni Achievement award, Harvard Bus. Sch., 2007. Office: Invacare Corp 1 Invacare Way PO Box 4028 Elyria OH 44036-2125 Office Phone: 440-329-6000. Office Fax: 440-366-9008.

MIXON, VICTORIA, writer; B of English, Cal Poly San Luis Obispo State U., 1992. Tchr. children's art Child Arts Presch., Bellingham, Wash., 1984-85; tech. writer IPT, San Luis Obispo, Calif., 1990, IBM, Santa Teresa, Calif., 1992-93, Cygnus Support, Mountain View, Calif., 1995-96. Co-author: Children and the Internet: A Zen Guide for Parents and Educators, 1996. Child Advocate Battered Women's Shelter, San Luis Obispo, 1988-90; nuclear free zone legis. Whatcom County Nuclear Free Zone, Bellingham, 1984-85. NCR scholar, 1990-91. Avocations: children's education and pacificst social development, travel, literature.

MIXSON, ARCHIBALD JAMES, research scientist, internist, endocrinologist; b. Louisville, Oct. 25, 1952; s. James Goodwin and Loraine Lyle Mixson; m. Nancy Ruth Gavin, Oct. 3, 1981; children: Claire Loraine, James Gavin. BA in Math., Vanderbilt U., Nashville, 1974; MD, Emory Sch. Medicine, Atlanta, 1979. Lic. internal medicine ACP, 1983. Post-doctoral fellow NIH, Bethesda, Md., 1986—89, sr. staff fellow, 1989—95; rsch. asst. prof. U. Md., Balt., 1995—98, asst. prof., 1998—2006, assoc. prof., 2006—. Named to America's Top Physicians, Consumer's Rsch. Coun. of Am., 2003—07; grantee, NIH, Nat. Cancer Inst., 1997—2002, 2004—10, 2009—13, Md. Indsl. Partnerships, 2002—05, 2008—11. Achievements include patents for carrier: DNA complexes containing DNA ecoding anti-angiogenic peptides and their use in gene therapy; histidine copolymers and methods for using same; branched histidine copolymers and methods for using same; cationic vehicle: DNA complexes and their use in gene therapy; branched cationic copolymers & methods for antimicrobial use. Avocations: tennis, travel. Office: U Md 10 South Pine St Bldg MSTF Rm 759 Baltimore MD 21201

MIYAGAWA, ICHIRO, physicist; b. Hiratsuka, Kanagawa, Japan, Mar. 5, 1922; s. Shigejiro and Tsuma (Itoh) M.; m. Mitsuko Yamada, Feb. 10, 1950; children: Shigeru, Haruyo, Mari. BS, Nagoya U., Japan, 1945; DSc, U. Tokyo, 1954. Asst. prof. U. Tokyo, 1959-62; vis. asst. prof. Duke U., Durham, NC, 1963-65; asst. prof. physics U. Ala., Tuscaloosa, 1965-66, assoc. prof., 1966-70, prof., 1970-80, Univ. Research prof. physics, 1980-92, prof. emeritus, 1992—. Contbr. articles to profl. jours. Recipient Samuel Ullman award, 1998; USPHS grantee; EPA grantee; NIH grantee. Fellow Am. Phys. Soc.; mem., AAAS, Sigma Xi. Home: 6434 Misty Ridge Dr Birmingham AL 35235- *Finding truth in any work or in any matter, however simple, is rewarding, although painful in many cases. Successful people in every spectrum of society are master discoverers of truth.*

MIYAKE, ISSEY, fashion designer; b. Hiroshima, Japan, Apr. 22, 1938; BA in Graphic Design, Tama Art U., Tokyo, 1959—64; studies at, La Chambre Syndicale de la Couture Parisienne, Paris, 1965—68. Began making clothing, 1962; presented first collection in, 1963; asst. designer Guy Laroche, Paris, 1965—68, Hubert de Givenchy, Paris, 1968-69; designer Geoffrey Beene, NYC, 1969-70; founder Miyake Design Studio, NYC, 1970—, Issey Miyake, Inc., NYC, 1971—. Started working on the pleats series, 1988; launched the line Pleats Please Issey Mikake, 93; presented A-POC line (A Piece of Cloth), 98; established Mikake Issey Found., 2004. Exhbns. of work include: exhbns. in NY and Paris in 1971-73, Issey Miyake and a Piece of Cloth Seibu Mus. Art, Tokyo, 1977, East Meets West, Internat. Design Conf., Apsen, Colo., 1979, Musee des Arts Decoratifs, Paris, 1978, Costumes for Maurice Béjart's ballet, Casta Diva, performed at IRCAM, Centre Pompidou, Paris in collaboration with Tomio Mohri, 1980, MIT, Cambridge, 1982, San Francisco Mus. Modern Art, 1983, Issey Miyake Bodyworks, Victoria and Albert Mus., London, 1985, Energies exhbns. Stedelijk Mus., Amsterdam, 1990, Touko Mus. of Contemporary Art, Tokyo, 1990, Costume for the Loss of Small Details William Forsythe & Frankfurter Ballet, 1991, Issey Miyake Making Things exhbn., found. Cartier pour l'art contempo-rain Paris, ACE Gallery, NY, Mus. Contemporary Art, Tokyo, 1998-2000, A-POC Making Issey Miyake & Dai Fujiwara exhbn. Vitra Design Mus. Berlin, 2001, Big Bang exhbn. Centre Pompidou Paris, 2005; represented in permanent collections: Met. Mus. Art, NYC, Victoria and Albert Mus., London. Author: Issey Miyake: East Meets West, 1978, Issey Miyake: Bodyworks, 1983. Recipient Japan Fashion Editor's Club award, 1974, Mainichi Design award, 1977, 1984, 1996, Pratt Inst. NY award for Creative Design, 1980, Internat. award, Coun. Am. Fashion Designers, 1984, Neiman-Marcus award, 1984, Best Collection presented by a Fgn. Designer award of Les Oscars 1985 de la Mode, Paris, 1985, award of the Japanese mag. for the textile industry Senken Shimbun, 1986, Asahi award, 1992, Chevalier de l'ordre Nat. de la Légion d'Honneur, 1993, Georg Jensen award, Denmark, 1999, Wexner prize, U. Ohio, 2004, Praemium Imperiale award for sculpture, Japan Art Assn., 2005, Kyoto prize (Arts and Philosophy Category), Inamori Found., 2006; named Person of Cultural Merit, Japan Govt., 1998. Office: Issey Miyake USA Corp 3 W 18th St Fl 7 New York NY 10011-4610 Address: Miyake Design Studio 1-23 Ohyama-cho Shibuya-ku Tokyo 151 Japan*

MIYAKE, STEPHANIE ANN, psychology professor, director, marriage and family therapist; b. Tulsa, Okla., Feb. 8, 1953; d. Thomas Wayne and Thelma Ann Shank; m. Thomas Masami Miyake, Mar. 19, 1988; children: Jan, Amber, Diann, Chris, Lance. BA, U. Ark., 1988; MA, Phillips Grad. Inst., 1994. Lic. marriage and family therapist Calif., Tex. Bus. mgr., therapist Angeles Cmty. Counseling Ctr., Monrovia, Calif., 1994—2002; marriage and family therapist self employed, 1994—; PsyD program admin. Azusa Pacific U., Azusa, Calif., 1999—2003, dir. MA clin. psych. program, 2001—05, dir. clin. training, 2005—07, PsyD adminstrv. faculty, 2007—. Trea., bd. mem. Angeles Cmty. Counseling Ctr., Monrovia, Calif., 1998—2002; adv. So. Calif. Consortium of Marriage and Family Therapist Educators, Encino, Calif., 2002—. Editor: Skilled Empathy, 2004; author: Clinical Placement Manual, 2000. Chairperson Claremont HS Grad. Night 2000, Claremont, Calif., 1999—2000; bd. pres. San Gabriel Valley Choral Co., Monrovia, Calif., 1997—99, bd. sec., 2000—03; 1st. v.p. Parent Faculty Assn., Claremont, Calif., 1998—99. Recipient Pres. award, Phillips Grad. Inst., 1994. Mem.: Tex. Assn. of Marriage and Family Therapists, Calif. Assn. of Marriage and Family Therapists, Am. Assn. of Marriage and Family Therapists, Phi Kappa Phi. Achievements include built MA program to be nationally recognized in a 3 year period. Avocations: gardening, singing. Office: Azusa Pacific U Dept of Grad Psych 701 E Foothill Blvd Azusa CA 91702 Office Fax: 628-815-5015. Business E-Mail: smiyake@apu.edu.

MIYAKE, YASUJI, computer science educator; b. Nagoya, Aichi Pref, Japan, Nov. 28, 1936; m. Sugako Yamada, Apr. 29, 1971; 1 child, Shigemitsu. B in Engring., Nagoya U., 1960, M in Engring., 1962, DEng, 1968. Rsch. assoc. Nagoya U., 1965-68, asst. prof., 1968-69, assoc. prof., 1969-78; prof. engring. Mie U., Japan, 1978-2000, prof. emeritus, 2000—; prof., computer sci. dept. engring. Chubu U., Japan, 2000—07, chairperson computer sci. dept. engring., 2000—03, chairperson computer sci. dept. Grad. Sch., 2004—07, vis. prof., 2007—08. Dir. Computation Ctr. Mie U., 1982-87, senator, 1997-99. Inventor, patentee in field; contbr. articles to profl. jours. Recipient 1st prize Inst. for character recognition technique contests, Inst. Posts and Telecom., Ministry of Posts and Telecom. Japan, 1992, 93, 94, commendation from dir. Tokai Elec. Comm. Control, 1997. Mem. Inst. Electronics, Info. Comm. Engrs. Japan, Info. Processing Soc. Japan, Japanese Soc. Med. Electronics Biol. Engring. Buddhist. Avocations: photography, collecting cameras, driving. Personal E-mail: y-miyake@u01.gate01.com.

MIYAMORI, KEIKO, artist; b. Yokohama, Kanagawa, Japan, Jan. 14, 1964; arrived in U.S., 1998; d. Yukio and Yuriko Miyamori. BFA, U. Tsukuba, Japan, 1993, MFA, 1995. Adj. faculty Pa. Acad. Fine Arts, Phila., 2000—. Artist-in-residence U. Pa., Phila., 1998—99, Soc. Contemporary Craft, Pitts., 2003. Recipient Sculputre Competition award, Frederik Meijer Gardens and Sculpture Park, 2004; grantee, Leeway Found., 2003, 2008. Office: PO Box 11771 Philadelphia PA 19101 Office Phone: 215-888-3245. Business E-Mail: info@princewoods.com.

MIYASAKI, DONOVAN, philosopher, educator; b. Idaho Falls, Idaho, Oct. 14, 1975; s. Fred Sakaguchi and Angela Miyasaki; life ptnr. Barbara Hansen. PhD in Philosophy, U. Toronto, Ont., Can., 2004. Vis. asst. prof. philosophy U. Wis. Milwaukee, Honors Coll., 2006—07; asst. prof. philosophy Wright State U., Dayton, Ohio, 2007—. Contbr. chapters to books, articles to profl. jours. Recipient J. Glenn Gray award in Philosophy, Colo. Coll., 1997; Postdoc. fellowship in Humanities, U. Toronto, 2004, Rsch. Travel grant, Coll. Liberal Arts, Wright State U., 2008. Mem.: North Am. Nietzsche Soc., Friedrich Nietzsche Soc., Am. Philos. Assn., Phi Beta Kappa. Home: 335 Union St Yellow Springs OH 45387 Office: Wright State Univ 370 Millett Hall 3640 Colonel Glenn Hwy Dayton OH 45435 Office Fax: 937-775-2892. Business E-Mail: d.miyasaki@wright.edu.

MIYASAKI, GEORGE JOJI, artist; b. Kalopa, Hawaii, Mar. 24, 1935; BFA, Calif. Coll. Arts and Crafts, 1957, MFA, 1958. Asst. prof. art Calif. Coll. Arts and Crafts, Oakland, 1958-64; mem. faculty dept. art U. Calif., Berkeley, 1964-94, prof. emeritus, 1994—. Grantee John Hay Whitney fellow, 1957—58; Tamarind printing fellow, 1961, Guggenheim fellow, 1963—64, Nat. Endowment for Arts fellow, 1980—81, 1985—86. Mem.: NAD. Home: 2844 Forest Ave Berkeley CA 94705-1309

MIYAZAKI, KOICHI, economics professor; b. Yokohama, Japan, Dec. 7, 1949; s. Yoshikazu and Teruko (Inukai) M.; m. Mizuyo Muto, Jan. 16, 1993. BA, Yokohama Nat. U., 1972; MA, U. Tokyo, 1974. Prof. dept. econs. Hosei U., Tokyo, 1986—. Author: Elucidating the Hellish Trap of Commodity Futures - A Proposal of a Fundamental Reform to Rescue Victims and Revitalize the Japanese Economy, revised edit., 2006; contbr. articles to profl. jours. Mem. Am. Econ. Assn., Tokyo Ctr. for Econ. Rsch., Japanese Econ. Assn. Avocation: walking. Home: 350-1-108 Katakura-Machi Hachioji 192-0914 Japan Office: Hosei U Dept Econs 4342 Aihara-Machi Machida 194-0298 Japan E-mail: koichi@m.email.ne.jp.

MIYAZATO, AI, professional golfer; b. Okinawa, Japan, June 19, 1985; Profl. golfer JLPGA Tour, 2004—05, LPGA Tour, 2006—. Achievements include winning 12 JLPGA Tour events, 2004-2005; youngest golfer (at age 20) to win JLPGA Major, Japan Open, 2005; first Japanese Woman to compete in domestic men's competition, Okinawa Open, 2005. Office: LPGA 100 International Golf Dr Daytona Beach FL 32124-1092

MIZE, GERALD L., JR., lawyer; b. Atlanta, Aug. 14, 1958; Student, Phillips Universität, Marburg an der Lahn, W. Germany, 1978, Ludwig Maximillans Universität, Munich, 1979; AB in Polit. Sci. and German, Univ. Ga., 1980, JD, 1984. Bar: Ga. 1984. Ptnr. in charge, internal comm. Alston & Bird LLP, Atlanta, co-chair, bus. devel. com. Office: Alston & Bird LLP One Atlantic Ctr 1201 W Peachtree St NW Atlanta GA 30309-3424 Office Phone: 404-881-7579. Office Fax: 404-881-7777. Business E-Mail: gmize@alston.com.

MIZE, JOE HENRY, industrial engineer, educator; b. Colorado City, Tex., June 14, 1934; s. Kelly Marcus and Birtie (Adams) M.; m. Betty Bentley, Mar. 16, 1966; 1 dau., Kelly Jean. BS in Indsl. Engring, Tex. Tech. Coll., 1958; MS (Research Found. grantee) in Indsl. Engring, Purdue U., 1963, PhD, 1964. Registered profl. engr., Ala., Okla. Indsl. engr. White Sands Missile Range, N.Mex., 1958-61; grad. research asst. Purdue U., Lafayette, Ind., 1961-64; asso. prof. engring. Auburn (Ala.) U., 1964-69; dir. Auburn (Ala.) U. (Computer Center), 1965-66; prof. engring. Ariz. State U., Tempe, 1969-72; prof., head Sch. Indsl. Engring. and Mgmt. Okla. State U., Stillwater, 1972-80, dir. Univ. Ctr. for Energy Research, 1980-83, Regents prof., 1982-94; v.p. Hong Kong U. of Sci. and Tech., 1994-98; prof., v.p. Hong Kong U. Sci. & Tech., 1994-98; rsch. affiliate engring. sys. divsn. MIT, 1998—. Cons. to Air War Coll., 1968-69, U.S. Army, Ops. Analysis Standby Unit, U. N.C., 1965-69, various mfg. firms, 1964—; program adv. Office of Mgmt. and Budget, Exec. Office of the President, Washington, 1974-79; adv. to NSF, 1974-94, Nat. Center for Productivity and Quality of Work Life, 1973-78; chmn. tech. adv. council So. Growth Policies Bd., 1975-77; accrediting visitor Engrs. Council for Profl. Devel., 1973-80 Author: (with J.G. Cox) Essentials of Simulation (translated into Japanese 1970), 1968, Prosim V.: Instructor's Manual, 1971, Student's Manual, 1971, (with C.R. White and George H. Brooks) Operations Planning and Control, 1971, (with J.L. Kuester) Optimization Techniques with Fortran, 1973, (with W.C. Turner and K.E. Case) Introduction to Industrial and Systems Engineering, 3d edit., 1993 (named Book of Yr., Am. Inst. Indsl. Engrs. 1979), Guide to Systems Integration, 1991; contrbr. articles to profl. jours., more. Recipient Disting. Engring. Alumnus award Purdue U., 1978 Mem. Am. Inst. Indsl. Engrs. (exec. v.p. 1978-80, pres. 1981-82, H.G. Maynard Innovative Achievement award 1977, Gilbreth Indsl. Engring. award 1990), Am. Soc. for Engring. Edn. (sec. govt. rels. com. 1975-76), Nat. Soc. Profl. Engrs., Okla. Soc. Profl. Engrs. (Outstanding Engring. Achievement award 1977, Outstanding Engr. in Okla. 1981), Inst. Mgmt. Scis., Coun. Indsl. Engring. Acad. Dept. Heads (chmn. 1975-76), NAE, Nat. Rsch. Coun., Sigma Xi, Tau Beta Pi, Alpha Pi Mu. Office: Oklahoma State U Dept Indsl Engring Stillwater OK 74078-0001

MIZE, RONALD L., social studies educator; s. Ronald L. and Veronica E. Mize; m. Christine G. Batman; children: Tori E., Theo S. BS, U. Colo., Boulder, 1991; MA, Colo. State U., Fort Collins, 1994; PhD, U. Wis., Madison, 2000. Asst. prof. U. St. Francis, Fort Wayne, Ind., 2001—04, Cornell U., Ithaca, NY, 2004—. Assoc. dir. Nat. Latino Rsch. Ctr., San Marcos, Calif., 2000—01. Contbr. articles to profl. jours. Bd. mem. Fall Creek Elem. Sch. SAP, Ithaca, 2008—. Head Start Tng. grant, ACYF DHHS, 2000—04. Mem.: Taskforce Institutionalizing Pub. Sociology. Roman Catholic.

MIZEL, LARRY A., housing construction company executive; b. 1942; married. BA, U. Okla., 1964; JD, U. Denver, 1967. Founder, dir. MDC Holdings Inc., Denver, 1972—, pres., 1996—99, chmn. bd., CEO, 1999—. Past trustee Marsico Investment Fund; dir. Richmond Am. Homes. Chmn. bd. Simon Weisenthal Ctr., 2003—. Office: MDC Holdings Inc 4350 S Monaco St Denver CO 80237-1867

MIZELLE, NANCY BATSON, education educator, consultant; b. Wilmington, NC, July 20, 1946; d. Harvey Lee and Elizabeth Hamilton Batson; m. William Otha Mizelle, Jr., Aug. 28, 1966; children: Susan Mizelle Wright, Heather Mizelle Pittman, Sarah Elizabeth, William Otha III. BA in English, Meredith Coll., Raleigh, NC, 1968; MEd in Reading Edn., Clemson U., SC, 1971; EdD in Elem. Edn., U. Ga., Athens, 1992. Elem. edn. tchg. cert. NC, 1968, SC, 1970, mid. grades cert. Profl. Standards Commn., Ga., 1997. Tchr. Wake County Sch. Sys., Raleigh, 1968—70; sch. libr. grades 1-6 Pickens County Sch. Sys., SC, 1970—71; grad. tchg. asst. U. Ga., Athens, 1988—92, rsch. asst., 1990—92, temp. asst. prof. dept. elem. edn., 1992—97, dir. N.E. ctr. Ga. Initiative Math. and Sci., 1993—97; acting assoc. dir. ops. Nat. Reading Rsch. Ctr. U. Ga., U. Md. Consortium, Athens, 1994—95, asst. dir. Nat. Reading Rsch. Ctr., 1995—96; tchr. Clarke County Sch. Sys., Athens, 1997—98; asst. mentor leader dept. early childhood and mid. grades edn. Ga. Coll. & State U., Milledgeville, 1999—2004, assoc. prof., mentor leader for mid. grades cohort, 2004—, chair early childhood and middle grades edn., 2007—, prof. mentor leader middle grades edn., 2009—, assoc. prof., 2004—09, prof. middle grades edn., 2009—. Cons. Charles Dana Ctr., Austin, 2001—02, Wyo. Collaborative Mentorship Acad., Casper, Wyo., 2005, Hechinger Inst. Edn. and the Media, Columbia U., NYC, 2005, Oconee Regional Ednl. Svc. Agy., Sandersville, Ga., 2006; visit evaluator Ga. Lighthouse Schs. to Watch Site, 2003—. Co-author: Professional Community/Agency/Empowerment, Research and resources in support of This We Believe, Motivation to Read and Learn from Text, Transition Into and Out of Middle School; guest co-editor: Mid. Sch. Jour., collaborative editor: Becoming a Mentor Leader in a Professional Community, reviewer: Rsch. Mid. Level Edn. Quar., 1996—, Mid. Sch. Jour., 1998—; mem. editl. bd. Handbook of Research in Middle Level Education, 2000—, Middle Grades Rsch. Jour., 2006—; contbr. articles to profl. jours. Neighborhood chairperson Leukemia and Lymphoma Soc., Milledgeville, Ga., 2005—06; team organizer, leader Relay for Life, Milledgeville, 2005—06. Grantee, Title II Eisenhower Act, US Dept. Edn., 1994—96; Re-visioning Mid. Sch. Tchr. Edn. grantee, POET Profl. Devel. Program, 1995—97, Literacy Learning Young Adolescents grantee, Nat. Reading Rsch. Ctr. U. Ga. and U. Md., 1996—97, Oconee RESA Tchr. Recruitment and Induction Initiative grantee, Profl. Stds. Commn. Ga., 2005—06. Mem.: ASCD, Nat. Coun. Accreditation Tchr. Edn., Mid. Level Edn. Rsch. of Am. Ednl. Rsch. Assn. (treas. 2000), Assn. Childhood Edn. Internat., Nat. Profs. Mid. Level Edn., Nat. Mid. Sch. Assn. (rsch. com. mem. 1998—2003, program reviewer 2007—), Ga. Assn. Tchr. Educators (bd. dirs. 2005—), Ga. Professors Mid. Level Edn. (liaison with Ga. Mid. Sch. Assn. 2005—), Ga. Mid. Sch. Assn. (bd. dirs. 2005—), Am. Ednl. Rsch. Assn. Home: 185 Admiralty Way NW Milledgeville GA 31061 Office: Ga Coll and State U Cbx 071 Milledgeville GA 31061 Office Fax: 478-445-6695. Business E-Mail: nancy.mizelle@gcsu.edu.

MIZGALA, HENRY F., physician, consultant, retired medical educator; b. Montreal, Can., Nov. 28, 1932; s. Louis and Mary (Ropeleski) M.; m. Pauline Barbara Delaney, Oct. 26, 1957; children: Paul Stephen, Cynthia Louise, Liane Mary Mizgala Sizemore, Melanie Frances Mizgala Dressler, Nancy Elizabeth Mizgala Lewis. BA magna cum laude, Loyola Coll., Montreal, 1953; MD, CM, McGill U., 1957. Rotating intern, then resident in medicine St. Mary's Hosp., Montreal, 1957—59, asst. physician, 1963—66; resident in medicine Royal Victoria Hosp., Montreal, 1959—60; Dazian fellow cardiology Mt. Sinai Hosp., NYC, 1960—61, USPHS fellow cardiology, 1961—62; resident in cardiology Montreal Gen. Hosp., 1962—63, assoc. physician, 1966—74; asst. physician, cons. cardiology Lachine Gen. Hosp., Que., 1964—80; mem. faculty McGill U. Med. Sch., Montreal, 1968—74, assoc. prof. medicine, 1973—74; assoc. prof., then prof. Montreal U. Med. Sch., 1974—81; cardiologist Montreal Heart Inst., also dir. CCU, 1974—80; prof. medicine U. B.C., 1980—87, prof. medicine, head divsn. cardiology, 1980—87, prof. medicine emeritus, 1998—; hon. attending med. staff, cardiologist Vancouver Hosp. and Health Scis. Ctr. Cons. Centre Hosp. Baie des Chaleurs, Gaspe, Que., 1975—80, B.C. Cancer Agy., Vancouver, 1981—; cons. staff Univ. Hosp., U. B.C. site, 1981—94; hon. cons. Montreal Heart Inst., 1980—. Mem. editl. bd. Can. Jour. Cardiology, 1988-99, Jour. Am. Coll. Cardiology, 1992-95; contbr. articles to profl. jours. Fellow Royal Coll. Physicians and Surgeons Can., Am. Coll. Cardiology, Am. Heart Assn. (coun. clin. cardiology); mem. Can. Med. Assn., Can. Cardiovasc. Soc. (treas. 1974-90), Que. Med. Assn., B.C. Med. Assn., B.C. and Yukon Heart and Stroke Found. (bd. dirs., sr. bd. dirs.), Alpha Omega Alpha. Office: UBC Hosp Dept Cardiology Rm S110 UBC Hosp 2211 Wesbrook Mall Vancouver BC V6T 2B5 Canada Office Phone: 604-822-1747.

MIZIORKO, HENRY M., research scientist, educator; PhD, U. Pa. Prof., biochemistry Med. Coll. Wis., Milw., 1977—2004; prof. molecular biology & biochemistry U. Mo., Kans. City, 2004—. Recipient Rsch. Career Devel. award, NIH, 1978—83; fellowship, Alexander von Humboldt Stiftung, 1983. Mem.: NIH (Merit award).

MIZRACH, BRUCE, economics professor; b. Coral Gables, Fla., June 23, 1960; AB, Tufts U., Medford, Mass., 1981; PhD, U. Pa., Phila., 1987. Asst. prof. economics Boston Coll., Chestnut Hill, Mass., 1987—90; sr. economist Fed. Res. Bank NY, NYC, 1992—95; assoc. prof. economics Rutgers U., NB, NJ, 1995—. Prin. Nonlinear Analysis Group, Westfield, NJ, 1998—; vis. assoc. prof. fin. Stern Sch. Bus., NYC, 2005; vis. asst. prof. fin. Wharton Sch., Phila. Mem.: Soc. Nonlinear Dynamics and Econometrics (bd. mem. 1992—2007). Office: Rutgers Univ 75 Hamilton St New Brunswick NJ 08901 Business E-Mail: mizrach@econ.rutgers.edu.

MIZRAHI, ABRAHAM MORDECHAY, retired health products executive, pediatrician; b. Jerusalem, Apr. 16, 1929; came to U.S., 1952, naturalized, 1960; s. Solomon R. and Rachel (Haliwa) M.; m. Suzanne Eve Glasser, Mar. 15, 1956; children: Debra, Judith, Karen. BS, Manchester Coll., 1955; MD, Albert Einstein Coll. Medicine, 1960. Diplomate: Am. Bd. Pediatrics, Nat. Bd. Med. Examiners. Intern U. N.C., 1960-61; pediatric resident Columbia-Presbyn. Med. Center, NYC, 1961-63, NIH fellow in neonatology, 1963-65; assoc. dir. Newborn Service Mt. Sinai Hosp., NYC; also dir. Newborn Service Elmhurst Med. Center, 1965-67; staff physician Geigy Pharm. Corp., NYC, 1967-69, head cardio-pulmonary sect., 1969-71; sr. v.p. corp. med. affairs USV Pharm. Corp., Tuckahoe, NY, 1971-76; v.p. health and safety Revlon, Inc., NYC, 1976-89, sr. v.p. human resources, 1989-94; ret., 1994. Assoc. in pediatrics Columbia U., 1963-67; cons. in neonatology Misericordia-Fordham Med. Ctr., 1967-89; clin. affiliate N.Y. Hosp.; clin. asst. prof. Cornell U. Med. Coll., 1982—. Contbr. articles to profl. jours. Trustee Westchester (N.Y.) Jewish Center. Mem. AMA, N.Y. State and County Med. Soc., Am., N.Y. acads. medicine, Am. Soc. Clin. Pharmacology and Therapeutics, Am. Pub. Health Assn., Am. Occupational Med. Assn. Home: 7 Jason Ln Mamaroneck NY 10543-2108 *The principles that have guided my life are old Biblical concepts. Firstly, that God had created Adam and Eve and all Men are, therefore, brothers and sisters. Secondly, God created Man and, therefore every human being has a spark of God in him. It, therefore, follows that killing diminshes God's presence on earth and saving of a human being increases His presence.*

MIZRAHI, ISAAC, fashion designer; b. Bklyn., Oct. 14, 1961; s. Zeke and Sarah M. Attended, Parsons Sch. Design, 1982. Design asst. Perry Ellis, 1982-84, Jeffrey Banks, 1984-85, Calvin Klein, 1985-87; founder, ready-to-wear line Isaac Mizrahi, 1987—98, added menswear line, added eyewear, 1990—98; designer, Isaac Mizrahi for Target Target Corp., 2002—; designer, Isaac By Isaac Mizrahi; creative dir., Liz Claiborne brand Liz Claiborne Inc., NYC, 2008—. Subject: (documentaries) Unzipped, 1995; costume designer: Twyla Tharp's Ballet Brief Fling, Am. Ballet Theatre.; costume designer The Women, Roundabout Theatre Co., 2002 (Costume Design, Drama Desk award, 2002), Barefoot In the Park, Cort Theatre, NYC, 2006, The Threepenny Opera, Roundabout Theatre Co., 2006, English National Opera's-King Arthur, 2006, creator (series of comic books) The Adventures of Sandee the Supermodel, 1997, one man show (off broadway) Les Mizrahi, host (TV series) The Isaac Mizrahi Show, Oxygen Network, 2001—03, Isaac, Style Network, 2005—, The Fashion Show, 2009—. Recipient Perry Ellis new fashion talent award Coun. Fashion Designers Am., 1989; named Best Womenswear Designer 1989 Coun. Fashion Designers Am., 1990. Jewish. Office: Liz Claiborne Inc 1441 Broadway New York NY 10018*

MIZROCH, JOHN F., lawyer, former federal agency administrator; b. Norfolk, Va., Sept. 28, 1948; s. Solomon B. and Muriel G. Mizroch; m. Martha Melissa Bankston; children: Zachary, Elliott, Brandon, Marissa. BA, U. Va., 1970, MA, 1972; JD, Coll. of William and Mary, 1975. Bar: Va. 1975, D.C. 1977, Colo. 1980, Tex. 1985. Asst. commonwealth atty. Commonwealth Atty. Office, Arlington, Va., 1975-76; fgn. svc. officer USIA, Washington, 1976-79; pvt. practice real estate devel., Winter Park, Colo., 1980-84; v.p., counsel VCMI, Dallas, 1984-86; gen. counsel W.O. Bankston, Enterprise, Dallas, 1986-87; dep. asst. sec. commerce Office of Trade Devel., Washington, 1987-89; advisor to minority Joint Econ. Com. of Congress, Washington, 1989-90; mng. dir., gen. coun. R.J.M. Internat., Washington, 1991-93; exec. dir. US Environ. Tech. Export Coun.; CEO World Environment Ctr.; prin. dep. asst. sec. for energy efficiency & renewable energy US Dept. Energy, Washington, 2006—09, acting asst. sec., 2009; of counsel Wilson Sonsini Goorich & Rosati, 2009—. Mem. Trade & Environ. Policy Advisory Com. Office US Trade Representative, 1999—2006; mem. Cleaner Fossil Fuel Systems Advisory Com. World Energy Coun., 1999—2006; mem. Task Force Sustainable Industrial Devel., China Coun. for Internat. Cooperation on Environment & Devel., 2003. Town councilman Winter Park Town Council, 1982-84. Mem. ABA., State Bar Va., DC Bar Assn. Office: Wilson Sonsini Goorich & Rosati 1700 K St NW Fifth Fl Washington DC 20006 Office Phone: 202-973-8800. Office Fax: 202-972-8899. E-mail: jmizroch@wsgr.com.*

MIZRUCHI, MARK SHELDON, sociology professor, business administration professor; b. New Haven, Dec. 10, 1953; s. Ephraim Harold and Ruth M.; m. Katherine Teves, June 1981 (div. June 1995); 1 child, Joshua; m. Gail Schulman, Nov. 2006. BA, Washington U., 1975; MA, SUNY, Stony Brook, 1977, PhD, 1980. Statis. analyst Albert Einstein Coll. of Medicine, Bronx, NY, 1980-83, asst. prof. psychiatry, 1981-87, supr. statis. svcs., 1983-87; asst. prof. sociology Columbia U., NYC, 1987-89, assoc. prof. sociology, 1989-91; prof. sociology and bus. adminstrn. U. Mich., Ann Arbor, 1991—. Author: The American Corporate Network, 1904-1974, 1982, The Structure of Corporate Political Action, 1992; editor (with M. Schwartz) Intercorporate Relations, 1987. Recipient Presdl. Young Investigator award NSF, 1988-93, Excellence in Edn. award U. Mich., 2004, Dist. Grad. Mentoring award, 2008; grantee NSF, 1987-88, 93-95, 99-2000, 2002-03, 09-; invited fellow Ctr. for Advanced Study in the Behavioral Scis., 1989. Mem. Am. Sociol. Assn., Acad. Mgmt., Internat. Network for Social Network Analysis, Sociol. Rsch. Assn. Office: Dept Sociology Univ Mich Ann Arbor MI 48109-1382 Office Phone: 734-764-7444. Office Fax: 734-763-6887. Business E-Mail: mizruchi@umich.edu.

MIZUKOSHI, KOSHI, metal products executive; b. Seoul, Korea, Sept. 1, 1938; Grad., Univ. Tokyo, 1961. Positions in corp. planning & econ. rsch. Kobe Steel Ltd., Kobe, Japan, 1961—73, mgr. iron & steel sector corp. planning dept., 1973—78, asst. to pres., 1978, gen. mgr. planning & adminstrn. iron & steel div., 1983—89, dir., gen. mgr. planning & adminstrn. iron & steel div., 1989—91, mng. dir., gen. mgr. planning & adminstrn. iron & steel div., 1991—93, sr. mng. dir., gen. mgr. tech. adminstrn. dept., 1993—96, exec. v.p., 1996—99, pres., CEO, 1999—2004, chmn., 2004—. Office: Kobe Steel Ltd Shinko Bldg 10-26 Wakinohamacho 2-chome Chuo-ku Kobe 651-8585 Japan Office Phone: 81-78-261-5111. Office Fax: 81-78-261-4123.

MIZUMORI, SHERI J.Y., psychology professor, department chairman; BS in Psychology, U. Wash., Seattle, 1977; MA in Psychology, U. Calif., Berkeley, 1983, PhD in Psychology, 1985. Postdoctoral fellow U. Colo., 1985—89; asst. prof. U. Utah, 1989—92, assoc. prof., 1992—2000, acting chair psychology dept., 1995; assoc. prof. U. Wash., 2000—03, prof. psychology, 2003—, chair psychology dept., 2005—, co-dir. grad. program in neurobiology and behavior, 2007—. Contbr. articles to profl. jours. Office: Univ Wash Psychology Dept Box 351525 Seattle WA 98195-1525 Office Phone: 206-543-2699. Business E-Mail: mizumori@u.washington.edu.*

MIZUNO, ATSUSHI, economist; b. Handa, Aichi, Japan, Aug. 18, 1959; came to U.S., 1984; s. Yosei and Kimiko (Nagasaka) M. BA in Econs., Waseda U., Tokyo, 1984; postgrad., Brown U., 1984-85; MPhil in Econs., CUNY, 1988, PhD in Econs., 1989. Postdoc. vis. scholar Nat. Bur. Econs. Rsch., NYC, 1989; sr. economist The Nomura Securities Co., Ltd., Tokyo, 1989-94, chief strategist, 1995-97; chief fixed income strategist Deutsche Morgan Grenfell Capital Markets Ltd., Tokyo Br., 1997—, Deutsche Securities Ltd. Tokyo Br., 1998—, mng. dir., chief fixed income strategist, chief economist, 1999—, vice chmn. global markets, 2004; chief fixed income strategist Credit Suisse First Boston Securities (Japan), 2004; mem. policy bd. Bank of Japan, 2004—. Adj. instr. Baruch Coll., N.Y.C., 1987, Rutgers U., Newark, 1987, Manhattan Coll., Riverdale, N.Y., 1988. Mem. Found. Japan Post, 2002—03. Named #1 Ranked Fixed Income Strategist, Nikkei Newsletter on Bond and Money, 1996-99, #2 Ranked Fixed Income Strategist, 2000-01, 03; CUNY fellow, 1985-87; first team of Japanese fixed-income strategy/1997-99; All-Asia Rsch. Team, 2d team, 2000 Avocations: tennis, golf. Home: 5-2-5-1006 Minami-Azabu Minato Japan Office: Bank of Japan 2-1-1 Nihonbashi Hongckucho Chuo-ku Tokyo 103-8660 Japan

MKRYAN, SONYA, geophysicist, educator, research scientist; b. Beyrouth, Lebanon, Mar. 1, 1935; arrived in U.S., 1979; d. Vahram and Marie (Topalian) Faradjian; m. Karapet Mkryan, Apr. 11, 1970; children: Marine, Anahit, Lusine. MS in Physics, Pedagogical Inst., 1956; PhD in Tech. Scis., Tbilicy State U., 1970. Physics, math. tchr. HS, Ghaltakchi, 1956-57; libr. Ores Dept., Leninakan, Armenia, 1957-60; geophycist, rschr. Inst. Geophysics Engring. Seismology, Leninakan, 1960-70; assoc. prof. physics Polytech. Inst., Kirovakan, Armenia, 1970-79; mech. insp. Robertshaw Co., Anaheim, Calif., 1980-82; tchr. Pasadena (Calif.) Sch. Dist., 1983-86; eligibility worker, acting supr. Dept. of Pub. Svcs., Glendale, Calif., 1986-97; social worker home supportive svcs. Glendale, 1997—. Author: (poetry) Ups and Downs of Life, 1987, Incessant Melodies, 1992, Light and Darkness, 1997, (novels) Eternities Travelers, 1998, Man and Its Time, 2006, Paradoxical Reality and My Heartbeats, 2006; one-woman shows include Tekeyan Gallere, Pasadena, Calif., 1989, Pasadena Union of Marash Armenians Hall, 1982—95, exhibited in group shows at Altadena, Pasadena, Downey, Glendale, Ambassador Hotel, L.A. (2d prize, 1987), Wilshir Ebel, 1988. Bd. dirs. Sahag-Mesrob Armenian Christian Sch. Named Women of Yr. Mem.: Armenian Radio and TV Com., Armenian Allied Arts Assn. (1st prize 1982, 1984, 1985, 1987, 1991), Nat. Libr. Poets, Internat. Soc. Poets, Armenian Writers Union Calif. Avocations: writing, walking, reading, cooking, dance. Home: 2723 N Lake Ave Altadena CA 91001-1903

MLADICK, RICHARD ANTHONY, plastic surgeon; b. Melrose Park, Ill., May 28, 1934; s. Edward Anthony and Gladys Jane (Castens) M.; m. Elly Dalgas Jensen, Aug. 13, 1966; children: Kristen, Richard. BA, Northwestern U., 1955, MD, 1959. Diplomate Am. Bd. Plastic Surgery, Am. Bd. Surgery. Intern Cook County Hosp., 1959—60, resident in gen. surgery, 1960—64; resident in plastic and reconstructive surgery Duke U. Med. Ctr., 1965—68; asst. prof. plastic surgery Duke U. Med. Sch., Durham, N.C., 1968-69; prof. plastic surgery Eastern Va. Med. Sch., Norfolk, 1969-75; dir. Ctr. for Cosmetic Plastic Surgery, Virginia Beach, Va., 1975—. Guest editor: Clinics in Plastic Surgery, 1989; contbr. articles, chpts. to profl. publs. Bd. dirs. Va. Orchestral Assn., Virginia Beach; mem. Orgn. Pub. Safety. Fellow Am. Coll. Surgeons; Mem. AMA, Am. Assn. Plastic Surgeons, Am. Soc. Aesthetic Plastic Surgery, Lipoplasty Soc. N.Am. (bd. dirs., past pres.), Med. Soc. Va., Seaboard Med. Assn., Am. Soc. Plastic and Reconstructive Surgeons, Va. Soc. Plastic and Reconstructive Plastic Surgeons (pres. 1973-74), Southeastern Soc. Plastic Surgeons, So. Med. Assn., Va. Beach Med. Soc. Virginia Beach Rotary Club. Presbyterian. Avocations: running, tennis, gardening, biking. Office Phone: 757-481-5151.

MLAKAR, ROY A., former professional sports team executive; b. 1953; m. Tamera Mlakar; children: Tracy, Jill, Michelle, Nicolle. Student, Cuyahoga Western Coll., 1968-69, Kent State U., 1970-72; grad., U. Akron, 1972. With sales, promotions, pub. rels. Cleve. Barons, 1969-73; merchandising and promotions dir. Cleve. Cavaliers and Cleve. Indians, 1969-73; exec. dir. pub. rels. Providence Reds, 1973-78; from pub. rels. dir. to dir. ops., pres. New Haven Nighthawks, 1978-88; gen. mgr. New Haven Night Hawks, 1983-88; exec. v.p. LA Kings, 1988-92, pres., 1992—94; COO Pitts. Penguins; pres., CEO Ottawa Senators, 1996—2009, Scotiabank Place, 1998—2009. Recipient Hendy award as League Exec. of Yr., Am. Hockey League Bd. Govs., 1983; named Am. Hockey League Publicist of Yr., The Hockey News, 1978.

MLAY, MARIAN, retired government official; b. Pitts., Sept. 11, 1935; AB, U. Pitts., 1957; postgrad., Princeton U., 1969-70; JD, Am. U., 1977. Mgmt. intern HEW, Washington, 1961-70, dep. dir. Chgo. region, 1971-72, dir. divsn. consol. funding, 1972-73; dep. dir. office policy devel. and planning USPHS, Washington, 1973-77; dir. program evaluation EPA, Washington, 1978-9, dep. dir. office of drinking water, 1979-84; sr. fed. exec., 1979—97; dir. office of ground water protection EPA, Washington, 1984-91, dir. oceans and coastal protection, 1991-95; sr. rsch. assoc. Nat. Acad. Pub. Adminstrn., 1995-97; ret., 1997. Contbr. articles to profl. jours., chpts. to books. Bd. dirs. DC United Fund, 1979-80, New Dominion Chorale, 2001-04, Davis Meml. Goodwill Book Com., 1999-02; mem. Woman's Nat. Dem. Club, 2005, sec. bd. govs., 2007. Princeton U. fellow, 1969-70; recipient Career Edn. award Nat. Inst. Public Affairs, 1969. Mem. DC Bar Assn. (co-chair steering com. energy, environ. and natural resources sect., Best Section award, 1986-87). Achievements include development of a ground-water protection strategy for EPA establishing a national program to support related state and local efforts and to define a common ground-water protection policy for EPA. Home: 3146 Gracefield Rd Apt 417 Silver Spring MD 20904 Home Phone: 301-890-8525. Personal E-mail: mmlay@comcast.net.

MNUCHIN, ALAN GEOFFREY, investment banker; b. 1960; s. Robert Mnuchin and Elaine Terner Cooper; m. Kimberly Kassel, Feb. 11, 1995. BS, U. Pa., 1982; MBA, U. Chgo., 1984. Various positions to v.p., comm., media, tech. divsn. Goldman Sachs, NYC, 1984—96; sr. mng. dir. Bear Stearns Co., NYC, 1996—99; co-head, media banking Lehman Brothers, NYC, 1999—2003; founder, mng. dir. AGM Ptnrs. LLC, NYC, 2003—. Named a Top Dealmaker, Dealmaker mag., 2006. Office: AGM Ptnrs LLC 767 5th Ave New York NY 10153 Office Phone: 212-812-7878.

MO, JIANWEI, research scientist; 1 child. MS, Wuhan U., China, 1988; PhD, Nat. Inst. Chemistry, Lubljana, Slovenia, 2000. Lectr. Wuhan U., 1988—92; lectr. assoc. prof. Shantou U., Guangdong, China, 1992—97; postdoc. rschr. N.Mex. State U., Las Cruces, 2000—01; v.p. tech. and strategy, sr. dir., chief scientist Kumetrix, Inc., Union City, Calif., 2001—. Mng. editor Jour. Frontiers in Biosci., 2004—05; fund reviewer NIH, NIAID, Bethesda, Md., 2007—07. Recipient Devel. Sci. and Tech. award, State Dept. Edn. China, 1992; grantee, NSF, 2006, NIH, 2002—04. Mem.: Am. Chemistry Soc. Achievements include patents pending for painfree platform biosensors in single-use and continuous monitoring self-testing blood constitutes; development of noninvasive alcohol monitoring patches with excellent immunity, wide dynamic range and high sensitivity, applicable in anti-drug compliance testing for drivers; disposable self contained bioassay chip and handheld meter, provide painless, automated easy to use, rapid on-site assays for versatile blood analytes. Office: Kumetrix Inc 29524 Union City Blvd Union City CA 94587 Office Fax: 510-476-0953. Business E-Mail: jmo@kumetrix.com.

MO, LUKE WEI, physicist, researcher; b. Shangtung, China, June 3, 1934; s. Si-leng and Shu-feng (Lo) M.; m. Doris Chang, Dec. 31, 1960; children: Curtis L., Alice. BSEE, Nat. Taiwan U., 1955; MS in Physics, Nat. Tsinghua U., 1959; PhD, Columbia U., 1963. Rsch. assoc. Columbia U., NYC, 1963—64; rsch. physicist Stanford Linear Accelerator, Calif., 1965—69; asst. prof. physics U. Chgo., 1969—76; prof. physics Va. Poly. Inst. and State U., Blacksburg, 1976—. Contbr. articles to profl. jours. Served with Taiwan Air Force, 1955-56. Recipient Alumni Research Excellence award Va. Poly. Inst. and State U., 1980, Guggenheim fellow, 1981. Fellow Am. Phys. Soc. Office: Va Poly Inst Dept Physics Blacksburg VA 24061-0435 Business E-Mail: lmo@vt.edu.

MO, YI-LUNG, structural engineer, educator; b. Taichung, Taiwan, Aug. 28, 1955; s. Tzai-Nan and In-Fang (Teng) M.; m. Grace H.C. Wu, Sept. 26, 1985; children: Steven, Sophia. BS, Nat. Cheng Kung U., 1977; MS, Nat. Taiwan U., 1979; PhD, U. Hannover, Germany, 1982; MS, DePaul U., 1989. Assoc. prof. Nat. Cheng Kung U., Tainan, 1991—94, prof., 1994—2000; rsch. asst. Nat. Taiwan U., Taipei, 1977—79, U. Hannover, 1979—82; postdoctoral rsch. assoc. U. Houston, 1982—84, rsch. prof., 1999—2000, prof. dept. civil and environ. engring., 2000—; structural engring. designer Sargent & Lundy Engrs., Chgo., 1984—89, engring. analyst, 1989—91. Alexander von Humboldt vis. prof. U. Hannover, 1995; vis. engr. Korean Power Engring. Co., Seoul, 1990; vis. scholar Stanford U., 1998; dir. Thomas T.C. Hsu Structural Rsch. Lab., Cullen Coll. Engring. Author: Dynamic Behavior of Concrete Structures, 1994. Recipient Disting. Rsch. award Nat. Sci. Coun., Taiwan, 1999, Rsch. Creativity award, 2000; scholar Friedrich Ebert Stiftung, 1982, Prestressed Sys. Inc., 1982-84; Alexander von Humboldt Rsch. fellow, Germany, 1995. Fellow Am. Concrete Inst., Alexander von Humboldt Stiftung, Germany; mem. ASCE, Am. Concrete Inst., Am. Biog. Inst. Rsch. Assn., Internat. Assn. for Bridge and Structural Engring., Internat. Biog. Assn. Eng., NY Acad. Sci. Office: Dept Civil Environ Engring U Houston Houston TX 77204-4003 Home Phone: 713-666-7986; Office Phone: 713-743-4274. Business E-Mail: ymo@uh.edu.

MOAG, RODNEY FRANK, language educator, country and bluegrass singer, musician, record producer; b. Warsaw, NY, Oct. 15, 1936; s. Hugh Alexander and Imogene (Hodges) Moag; m. Rachel Ann Foley, Feb. 9, 1964 (div. Aug. 1974); children: Robin Gray, Hugh Daniel, Jeffrey Lee. BS, Syracuse U., 1961; MA, U. Wis., 1966, PhD, 1973. Instr., asst. prof. U. Mo., Columbia, 1968—74, dir. college preparatory program for visually impaired, 1974; vis. Fulbright prof. U. S. Pacific, Suva, Fiji, 1975-78; vis. assoc. prof. U. Mich., Ann Arbor, 1978-80, adj. prof., 1981, vis. assoc. prof., 1982; sr. lectr. U. Tex., Austin, 1981, 83-90, assoc. prof., 1990—2004, prof. emeritus, 2004—. Author: (reference grammar) Fiji Hindi, 1977, Malayalam, 1986, singer (country music artist) 6 albums. Mng. dir. Amateur Radio Repeaters Washtenaw, 1984—86; pres. Mich. Repeater Coun., 1985—88; vol. programmer KO-OP, 1995—. Mem.: Austin Repeater Orgn., Tex. VHF FM Soc., Ctrl. Tex. Bluegrass Assn., Austin Amateur Radio Club (v.p. 1993—94). Avocations: amateur radio, music. Home: 6909 Miranda Dr Austin TX 78752-3119 Office Phone: 512-467-6825. Personal E-mail: rodmoag@texas.net.

MOAK, REX R., psychology educator; Physics instr. Miss. Gulf Coast CC, Gautier, 1997—. Office: Miss Gulf Coast CC PO 100 Gautier MS 39553

MOATS, LOUISA COOK, educational consultant, researcher; d. Thomas Poultney and Mildred Benedict Cook; m. Stephen Dennis Mitchell, May 23, 2003; 1 child, Charlotte Cook. EdD, Harvard Grad. Sch. Edn., Cambridge, Mass., 1982. Lic. psychologist Upper Valley Assos., East Thetford, Vt., 1984—96; expert advisor reading rsch. Reading Lions Ctr., Sacramento County Office Edn., 1996—97; co-prin. investigator, NICHD EArly interventions project U. Tex., Houston, Health Sci. Ctr., 1997—2001; consulting advisor Sopris West Ednl. Svcs., Longmont, Colo., 2001—. Author: Language Essentials for Teachers of Reading and Spelling, Speech to Print: Language Essentials for Teachers, STraight Talk about Reading (Margot Marek Book award, NY Internat. Dyslexia Assn., 2000). V.p. Internat. Dyslexia Assn., Balt., 2006—. Office: Sopris West 4093 Specialty Pl Longmont CO 80504 Business E-Mail: louisam@sopriswest.com.

MOAVENZADEH, FRED, engineering educator; BS, Teheran U., 1958; MS, Cornell U., 1960; PhD, Purdue U., 1962. Asst. prof. MIT, Cambridge, Mass., 1965—66, assoc. prof., 1966—72, prof., 1972—, dir. tech. & devel. program, 1973—, dir. Ctr. for Tech., Policy & Indsl. Devel., 1998—, James Mason Crafts prof. systems engring. Cons. in field; mem. rsch. ctr. coun. CII, 1992—. Author: (book) Future Cities: Dynamics and Sustainability, 2002, Global Construction and the Environment: Strategies and Opportunities, 1994; author: (with David Geltner) Transportation, Energy and Economic Development: A Dilemma in the Developing World, 1984; author: over 300 profl. publs. and reports; editor: Concise Encyclopedia of Building & Construction Materials, 1990, Proceedings of the Conference on Science, Technology and Development in Latin America, 1986; editor-in-chief: Construction Business Review, mem. editl. bd.: Jour. Urban Tech. Recipient deFleury Medal, U.S. Army Corps Engrs., 2001. Mem.: NAE (Transp. Rsch. bd., Bldg. Rsch. Inst.), ASCE (mem. editl. bd. Jour. Infrastructure Systems), AAAS, Soc. Internat. Devel. Sci. Office: MIT Bldg E40-231 77 Massachusetts Ave Cambridge MA 02139-4307 also: MIT 1-175 77 Massachusetts Ave Cambridge MA 02139-4307 Office Phone: 617-253-8973. Office Fax: 617-253-7140. Business E-Mail: ctpidcom@mit.edu.

MOAZED, KHOSROW L., retired engineering educator; b. Meshed, Iran, Sept. 14, 1930; arrived in U.S., 1943; s. Mohammed and Forough Moazed; m. Carolyn Turner Green, Nov. 14, 1953; children: David Charles, Steven Darius, Elizabeth Ashraf, Maryam Leela. BSc, Rensselaer Poly., 1953, MSc, 1956, Carnegie Mellon U., 1958, PhD, 1959. Registered profl. engr., N.C. Rsch. assoc. Rensselaer Poly. Inst., Troy, NY, 1953—56; GE fellow Carnegie-Mellon U., Pitts., 1956—59; asst. prof. Ohio State U., Columbus, 1959—65, assoc. prof., 1965—68; prof. N.C. State U., Raleigh, 1968—91, prof. emeritus, 1991—, chmn. faculty senate, 1982—83. Prin. sci. officer Nat. Phys. Lab., Teddington, England, 1966; vis. prof. Naval Ocean Sys. Ctr., San Diego, 1985—90. Contbr. scientific papers to profl. jours. Capt., mission pilot CAP, 1995—2002. Grantee, NSF, USAF Office Sci. Rsch., U.S. Army Rsch. Office, Office Naval Rsch. Avocations: flying, art, writing, skiing.

MOBASSER, ANTHONY, cosmetic dentist; B in Math. and Engring., Cerritos Coll., 1974; BS in Biochemistry, UCLA, 1976; DMD, U. Pa., 1980. Cert. Calif., Nev., Pa. Founder, dentist Beverly Hills Dental Specialist Network. Contbr. articles to profl. jours. Mem.: ADA, Pa. Dental Assn., Calif. Dental Assn., LA Dental Soc., Am. Acad. Cosmetic Dentistry. Office: Sunset Med Tower 9201 Sunset Blvd Ste 618 Los Angeles CA 90069 Office Phone: 310-550-0383. Office Fax: 310-860-0486. Business E-Mail: anthony@drmobasser.com.

MOBBERLEY, JAMES, music educator, composer; b. Des Moines, June 10, 1954; s. David and Marjorie Mobberley; m. Laura Moore, June 3, 1989; children: Lucas, Jacob. BA in Music, U. N.C., 1978, MusM, 1980; DMA, Cleve. Inst. of Music, 1982. Mem. composition faculty U. Mo. Conservatory of Music, Kans. City, 1983—99, curators' prof. music, 1999—, interim dean, 2008; composer in residence Kans. City (Mo.) Symphony, 1991—99, newEar Ensemble, 1999—2002; vis. prof. Ind. U. Sch. of Music, Bloomington, 1998. Composer: TNT, 1994—2001 (Nat. Endowment for Arts Composers Fellowship, 1993), Soggiorno (Rome Prize Fellowship, 1989), Give 'em Hell!, 2000 (Van Cliburn Composers Invitational, 2001), Concerto #1 for Piano and Orch. (Guggenheim Fellowship, 1992), Vox Inhumana, 2003 (Commns. from Koussevitzky and Barlow Founds., 2001), (ballets) Arena, 1996. Bd. mem. Walden Sch., San Francisco, 2003—. Recipient Lee Ettelson Composers award, Composers, Inc., 1991, Kazimierz Serocki Competition, League-ISCM (Polish Sect.), 1993, Disting. Composer of Yr., Music Tchrs. Nat. Assn., 1998, Walter Hinrichsen award, AAAL, 2008; fellow Guggenheim Found., 1992—93; Composers fellowship, Nat. Endowment Arts, 1993—94. Mem.: ASCAP (Std. award 1988—). Avocation: bicycling. Office: Univ Mo Kans City Conservatory of Music 4949 Cherry Kansas City MO 64110 Office Fax: 816-235-5265. E-mail: mobberleyj@umkc.edu.

MOBERG, DAVID OSCAR, sociology educator; b. Montevideo, Minn., Feb. 13, 1922; s. Fred Ludwig and Anna E. (Sundberg) M.; m. Helen H. Heitzman, Mar. 16, 1946 (dec. Oct. 16, 1992); children: David Paul, Lynette, Jonathan, Philip; m. Marlys Taege, July 23, 1994. AA, Bethel Jr. Coll., 1942; AB, Seattle Pacific Coll., 1947; MA, U. Wash., 1949; PhD, U. Minn., 1952. Assoc. instr. U. Wash., Seattle, 1948-49; faculty Bethel Coll., St. Paul, 1949-68, prof. sociology, 1959-68, chmn. dept. social scis., 1952-68; prof. sociology Marquette U., Milw., 1968-91, prof. emeritus, 1991—, chmn. dept. sociology and anthropology, 1968-77. Cons. Nat. Liberty Found., 1970-71, Fetzer Inst., 1995-96; rsch. cons. Internat. Luth. Women's Missionary League, 1997-99, Bonnie Walker & Assocs., 1997-99; cons. Nat. Interfaith Coalition on Aging, 1973-75, mem. nat. adv. bd., 1980-89; guest rschr. Sociology of Religion Inst., Stockholm, Sweden, summer 1978; adj. prof. San Francisco Theol. Sem., 1964-73, McCormick Theol. Sem., 1975-78, 81-82; vis. prof. U. So. Calif., 1979, Princeton Theol. Sem., 1979, So. Bapt. Theol. Sem., 1982, Soc. for Care of the Handicapped in the Gaza Strip of Palestine, 1995; mem. adv. bd. Ecumenical Ministry with Mature Adults, 1983-92; resource scholar Christianity Today Inst., 1985; mem. bd. adv. editors Haworth Pastoral Press, 1998-2007. Author: The Church as A Social Institution, 1962, 2d edit. 1984, (with Robert M. Gray) The Church and the Older Person, 1962, 2d edit., 1977, Inasmuch: Christian Social Responsibility in the 20th Century, 1965, White House Conference on Aging: Spiritual Well-Being Background and Issues, 1971, The Great Reversal: Evangelism and Social Concern, 1972, 2d edit, 1977, 3d edit., 2007, Wholistic Christianity, 1985, Woman of God: An Assessment of the Spirituality of Women in the LCMS, 1999; also articles, chpts. in symposia.; editor: International Directory of Religious Information Systems, 1971, Spiritual Well-Being: Sociological Perspectives, 1979, Rev. Religious Research, 1968-72, Jour. Am. Sci. Affiliation, 1962-64, Adris Newsletter, 1971-76, Aging and Spirituality: Spiritual Dimensions of Aging Theory, Research, Practice, and Policy, 2001; co-editor Research in the Social Scientific Study of Religion, 1986-04; assoc. editor: Social Compass, 1968-2003; mem. editl. bd. Christian Univ. Press, 1979-84, Perspectives on Sci. and Christian Faith, 1988—07, Jour. of Religion, Spirituality and Aging, 2006—; cons. editor Calif. Sociologist, 1982-96. Fulbright lectr. U. Groningen, Netherlands, 1957-58, Fulbright lectr. Muenster U., West Germany, 1964-65. Fellow Am. Sci. Affiliation (editor jour. 1962-64, publs. com. 1984-91, social ethics com. 1985-88, program chair 1995-96), Gerontol. Soc. Am.; mem. Am. Sociol. Assn., Internat. Sociol. Assn. (sociology of religion rsch. com. 1972—), Wis. Sociol. Assn. (pres. 1969-71), Midwest Sociol. Assn. (Wis. bd. dirs. 1971-73), Assn. Devel. Religious Info. Sys. (coord. ADRIS 1971—98, editor ADRIS newsletter 1971-76), Religious Rsch. Assn. (editor Rev. Religious Rsch. 1968-72, contbg. editor 1973-77, assoc. editor 1983-2000, bd. dirs. 1959-61, 68-72, pres. 1981-82, H. Paul Douglass lectr. 1986), Assn. for Sociology of Religion (exec. coun. 1971-73, pres. 1976-77), Soc. for Sci. Study Religion (exec. coun. 1971-74, sr. editl. cons. SSSR-RRA History Project 1995-99), Evangelicals for Social Action (planning com. 1973-75), Christian Sociol. Soc. (steering com. 1973-81, newsletter lit. reviewer 1981-93), Family Rsch. Coun. (assoc. 1985-88, rsch. network 1989-98), Internat Rsch. Found. Devel. (adv. bd. 1994-), Psychologists Interested in Religious Issues (profl. affiliate 1984-99), Univ. Faculty for Life, Midwest Coun. Social Rsch. on Aging (fellow 1961-64, 87—), Am. Soc. Aging, Village at Manor Pk. Ethics Com.2007-, CPE (profl. consultation com. 2005-), Forum on Religion, Spirituality and Aging, Fairview Elder Enterprises (bd. dirs. 1989-), Vibrant Living Elder Enterprises. Home and Office: 7120 W Dove Ct Milwaukee WI 53223-2766 *As I try to live with eternity's values in view, my entire lifetime seems to grow ever briefer, not longer.*

MOBLEY, BARBARA JEAN, former state legislator, lawyer; b. Dec. 1, 1947; m. James L. Savage, Jr. BS, Savannah State Coll.; MSW, U. Ill.; JD, So. Meth. U. Atty.; mem. Ga. Ho. of Reps. from 69th Dist., 1992—2002; mem. higher edn. com., chair ethics com. Ga. Ho. of Reps., mem. pub. safety com., mem. judiciary com., 1999; mem. Ga. Ho. of Reps. from 58th Dist., 2003—05. Flemming fellow. Mem.: Delta Sigma Theta. Democrat. Baptist. Home: 3009 Miriam Ct Decatur GA 30032

MOBLEY, CLARENCE FOWLER, retired civil engineer; b. Johnston, SC, Apr. 24, 1921; s. Clarence Fowler Mobley and Anna Juanita (Williams) Mobley McCreight; m. Hazel Cleo Shankel, May 28, 1948 (dec. Feb. 1976); children: Richard Alan, Robert Steven; m. Annie Long Smith, Dec. 19, 1986 (dec. Apr. 1990). BSCE, U. S.C., Columbia, 1942; cert. in mgmt., USN Postgraduate Sch., Monterey, Calif., 1958; MBA, U. San Francisco, 1978. Registered profl. engr., Calif. Jr. civil engr. U.S. Tenn. Valley Authority, Knoxville, Tenn., 1942; commd. ensign USN, 1943, advanced through grades to comdr., 1968; pub. works officer Civil Engr. Corps, USN, Hawthorne, Nev., 1955-58; exec. officer USN Housing Activity, Yokohama, Japan, 1960-63; asst. pub. works officer San Francisco Bay Naval Shipyard, 1965-68; asst. engr. City of Daly City, Calif., 1968-69, engr., supr. water divsn. Calif., 1969-70, city engr. Calif., 1977-78, city engr., pub. works dir. Calif., 1979-82, ret. Calif., 1982. Contbr. articles to We. Constrn., USN Civil Engr. Corps Bull., Engring. News Record, The Rocket. Mem. ASCE, Soc. Am. Mil. Engrs. (treas. Seattle chpt. 1959-60), Calif. Soc. Profl. Engrs. (sec. 1970-72), Masons, Toastmasters Internat. Democrat. Home: 91 Fairmont Dr Daly City CA 94015-3072 Home Phone: 650-992-0324.

MOBLEY, DAWN KELLY, legislative staff member; B, JD, U. NC, Chapel Hill. Bar: NC, Ohio. Trial lawyer Office of the Dist. Atty., NC, Cuyahoga County Prosecutor's Office, Ohio, supr., felony and juvenile justice sections; sixth dist. cmty. prosecutor US Dept. Justice, US Atty. Office; counsel, Rep. Stephanie Tubbs Jones US House of Reps., Washington, 2007—08, atty., ethics com., 2007—, chief of staff to Rep. Marcia Fudge, 2008—. Coord. Project Safe Neighborhoods. Recipient Sixth Dist. Outstanding Svc. & Litig. awards, 2005, Cmty. Justice Adv. Network award, 2005, 2006. Office: 1513 Longworth House Office Bldg Washington DC 20515 Office Phone: 202-225-7032. Office Fax: 202-225-1339.

MOBLEY, EMILY RUTH, library director, educator, dean; b. Valdosta, Ga., Oct. 1, 1942; d. Emmett and Ruth (Johnson) M. AB in Edn., U. Mich., 1964, AM in Libr. Sci., 1967, postgrad., 1973-76. Tchr. Ecorse (Mich.) Pub. Schs., 1964-65; adminstrv. trainee Chrysler Corp., Highland Park, Mich., 1965-66, engring. libr., 1966-69; libr. II Wayne State U., Detroit, 1969-72, libr. III, 1972-75; staff asst. GM Rsch. Labs. Libr., Warren, Mich., 1976-78, supr. reader svcs., 1978-81; libr. dir. GMI Engring. & Mgmt. Inst., Flint, Mich., 1982-86; assoc. dir. for pub. svcs. & collection devel., assoc. prof. libr. sci. Purdue U. Librs., West Lafayette, Ind., 1986-89, acting dir. librs., assoc. prof. libr. sci., 1989, dean librs., prof. libr. sci., 1989—2004; Esther Ellis Norton Disting. Prof. Libr. Sci. Purdue U., West Lafayette, Ind., 1997—. Adj. lectr. U. Mich. Sch. Libr. Sci., Ann Arbor, 1974-75, 83-86; grants reader Libr. of Mich., 1980-81; project dir. Mideastern Mich. Region Libr. Cooperation,

1984-86; cons. Libr. Coop. of Macomb, 1985-86, Clark-Atlanta U., 1990-91; search com. for new dir. of libr. Smithsonian Instn., 1988; mem. GM Pub. Affairs Subcom. on Introducing Minorities to Engring.; presenter in field. Author: Special Libraries at Work, 1984; mem. editl. bd. Reference Svcs. Rev., 1989-2004, Infomanage, 1993-97. Corp. vis. com. for libr. MIT, 1990-2004, Carnegie-Mellon U., 1998—; mem. Ind. Statewide Libr. Automation Task Force, 1989-90; state tech. strategy subcom. on info. tech. and telecomms. Ind. Corp. for Sci. & Tech., 1989; nat. adv. com. Libr. of Congress, 1988; trustee Libr. of Mich., 1983-86, v.p., 1986, long range plan com., 1979-82, task force on document access and delivery, 1977-79; info. project mem. Rep. Nat. Conv., 1980; bd. dirs. Small Farms Assn., Southfield, Mich., Lafayette Symphony Orch., YWCA. Recipient Bausch & Lomb award, 1960, Cert. for Outstanding Performance in Acad. Achievement State of Mich. Ho. of Reps., 1976, Spl. Tribute for Outstanding Contbns. Libr. of Mich. Bd. Trustees, 1986, Disting. Alumnus award U. Mich. Sch. Info. & Libr. Studies, 1989; U. Mich. Regents Alumni scholar, 1960-64; CIC doctoral fellow in libr. sci., 1973-76. Mem. ALA (com. on accreditation, subcom. to rev. 1972, standards for accreditation 1988-89, OLOS minority internship com. 1988-89, nominating com. 1992-93, mem. coun. resolutions com. 1993-97), Assn. Coll. & Rsch. Librs. (task force on libr. sch. curriculum 1988-89, com. on profl. edn. 1990-92), Libr. Adminstrn. & Mgmt. Assn., Assn. Rsch. Librs. (bd. dirs. 1990-93), Spl. Librs. Assn. (pres. 1987-88, fellow 1991, com. mem.), Alpha Kappa Alpha, Phi Kappa Phi, Sigma Xi, Iron Key. Office: Purdue U Librs Stewart Ctr Lafayette IN 47907 Business E-Mail: emobley@purdue.edu.

MOBLEY, JAMES ROBERT, dentist; b. Sedalia, Mo., Oct. 25, 1944; s. Howard Holman and Esther Pauline (Webb) M.; m. Terrell Elizabeth Kirk, June 3, 1967 (div.); children: John Kirk, Joshua Scott. DDS, U. Mo., Kansas City, 1969. Intern U.S. Army Hosp., Honolulu, 1969-70; gen. practice dentistry Kansas City, 1972—. Asst. prof. dentistry U. Mo., Kansas City, 1972-76; vol. dentist Kans. Sch. for Deaf, Olathe, 1983-86. Served to capt. USAR, 1969-72. Mem. ADA, Greater Kansas City Dental Soc. (chmn. continuing edn. com. 1975). Clubs: Carriage (Kansas City), Hockey. Avocations: tennis, golf, windsurfing. Office: 315 Nichols Rd Ste 201 Kansas City MO 64112-1565

MOBLEY, JOHN HOMER, II, lawyer; b. Shreveport, La., Apr. 21, 1930; s. John Hinson and Beulah (Wilson) Mobley; m. Sue Lawton, Aug. 9, 1958; children: John Lawton(dec.), Anne Davant. AB, U. Ga., 1951, JD, 1953. Bar: Ga. 1952, U.S. Dist. Ct. D.C. Ptnr. Kelley & Mobley, Atlanta, 1956-63, Gambrell & Mobley, Atlanta, 1963-83; sr. ptnr. Sutherland Asbill & Brennan, Atlanta, 1983—. Founding chmn. Cmtys. in Schs. of Ga.; bd. dirs. Nat. Cmtys. in Schs.; former mem. bd. visitors Emory U.; trustee emeritus Canterbury Ct. Episcopal Retirement Home of Atlanta; trustee Episcopal Diocese of Atlanta Fund; twice sr. warden All Saints Episcopal Ch. Capt. JAGC USAF, 1953—55. Recipient Disting. Svc. Scroll, U. Ga. Law Sch., 2003. Mem. ABA, D.C. Bar, State Bar Ga., Atlanta Bar Assn., Am. Judicature Soc., Atlanta Lawyers Club, Atlanta Country Club, Piedmont Driving Club, NY Athletic Club, Met. Club of Washington, Phi Delta Phi. Office: Sutherland Asbill & Brennan 999 Peachtree St NE Ste 2300 Atlanta GA 30309-3996 Home: 3750 Peachtree Rd NE #77 Atlanta GA 30319 Home Phone: 404-201-7077; Office Phone: 404-853-8128. Business E-Mail: john.mobley@sutherland.com.

MOBLEY, NANCY ELIZABETH, artist, educator; b. San Angelo, Tex, July 29, 1940; d. William Carl and Mary Elizabeth Fox; m. Billy Jack Wimberley, Aug. 2, 1958 (div. 1972); children: Billy Carl, John Wayne, James Bryan; m. Thomas Howard Mobley, Sept. 28, 1974. BA, Angelo State U., San Angelo, 1990. Draftsman Gen. Tele. Co., San Angelo, 1965-68, William E. Fox & Assoc., San Angelo, 1970-74; draftsman, archtl. estimator Burk Constrn. Co., San Angelo, 1974-76; illustrator Helenikon Air Base, Athens, Greece, 1977-80, Bitburg Air Base, Germany, 1980-82, publicity writer, editor, 1982-83; jewelry designer Jeweler's Workshop, San Angelo, Tex., 1985-87; part-time artist, art tchr. San Angelo, Tex., 1976—. Vol. art tchr. Children's Art Mus., San Angelo, 1995-98; tchr. watercolor Kendall Gallery, San Angelo, 2004—. One-woman shows include Art Gallery in Athens, 1979, Bitburg (Germany) Am. Express Bank, 1980, Houston Harte U. Ctr. Gallery, San Angelo, Tex., 1984-85, 88, 96, 2007, Tom Green County Libr., San Angelo, 2000, 04, Houston Harte U. Ctr. Gallery, 2007; exhibited in group shows at Tom Green County Libr., San Angelo, 1984, Breckenridge (Tex.) Fine Arts Ctr., 1996-99, Soc. Watercolor Artists, Ft. Worth, 1997, Watercolor Art Soc. Houston, 1998, Shannon Hosp., San Angelo, 1999; paintings in J.Walker Gallery, San Angelo, Tex., 2001—, Gallery One Fine Arts, Brownwood, Tex., 2004, 05; represented in pub. and pvt. collections. Docent San Angelo Mus. Fine Art, San Angelo, 1995-99; bd. dirs. Hospice of San Angelo, 2004—. Bertha B. Becton scholar Angelo State U., San Angelo, 1988, Charles Wendell Art scholar Angelo State U., San Angelo, 1990, Carr acad. scholar Angelo State U., San Angelo, 1988-90, 1st pl. watercolors Breckenridge (Tex.) Arts Nat. Competition, 1996, 1st pl. alumni art competition Angelo State U. Alumni Assn., San Angelo, 1998, Best of Show Zeta Phi's 2nd Internat. Art Competition, San Angelo, Tex. 1st pl. Marcia Williams Art Comp., 2003, 1st pl. watercolors Fine Arts of Coleman, 2003, Russel C. Myers competition, 2004, others. Mem. San Angelo Art Club (3rd v.p. 1997-98, 2006—, 1st v.p. 1998-99, 2nd v.p. 1999-02, Artist of Yr. 1998).mem. Friends Book Club, 2000—.chmn. of Art Auction to benfit Hospice of San Angelo,2003 Baptist. Avocations: reading, writing, exercising, collecting antiques. Home: 106 Churchill Blvd San Angelo TX 76903-8613

MOBLEY, TONY ALLEN, foundation administrator, former dean, recreation educator; b. Harrodsburg, Ky., May 19, 1938; s. Cecil and Beatrice (Bailey) M.; m. Betty Weaver, June 10, 1961; 1 child, Derek Lloyd. BS, Georgetown Coll., 1960; MS, Ind. U., 1962, D Recreation, 1965; MRE, So. Sem., Louisville, 1963. Chmn. dept. recreation and pks. Western Ill. U., Macomb, 1965-72, Pa. State U., University Park, 1972-76; prof., chmn. recreation and pks., dean Sch. Health, Phys. Edn. and Recreation Ind. U., Bloomington, 1976—; exec. dir. Ind. U. Found., Bloomington, 2002—. Chair health adv. coun. White River Park Commn., State of Ind., 1979—; v.p Ind. Sports Corp., Indpls., 1983-89; bd. dirs. Nat. Inst. for Fitness and Sport, Indpls., 1984-93; J.B. Nash scholar, lectr. Am. Assn. Leisure and Recreation, Reston, Va., 1985. Contbr. over 50 articles to profl. jours. Bd. dirs. Monroe County YMCA, Bloomington, 1984-88, United Way, Bloomington, 1994—; mem. Gov.'s Coun. for Phys. Fitness and Sport, 1991—. Am. Coun. Edn. adminstrv. internship fellow, N.C. State U., 1970-71. Fellow Am. Acad. Pk. and Recreation Adminstrn. (pres. 1985-86); mem. Nat. Recreation and Pk. Assn. (pres. 1978-79, Nat. Disting. Profl. award 1981), Assn. Rsch., Adminstrn., Profl. Couns. and Socs. (pres. 1986-87, award 1987), Am. Alliance Health, Phys. Edn., Recreation and Dance (Coll. and Univ. Adminstrs. Coun. Honor award 1986, R. Tait McKenzie award 1996), Soc. Pk. and Recreation Edn. (pres. 1974-75, award 1978), Ind. Pk. and Recreation Assn. (pres. 1979-80, Outstanding Profl. award 1985). Avocations: golf, travel. Office: Ind U Found PO Box 500 Bloomington IN 47402

MOBLEY, WILLIAM HODGES, management consultant, educator, writer, researcher; b. Akron, Ohio, Nov. 15, 1941; BA, Denison U., 1963; PhD, U. Md., 1971. Registered psychologist, Hong Kong. Mgr. employee rels. rsch. PPG Industries, Pitts., 1971-73; prof. U. SC, Columbia, 1973-80; head dept. of mgmt. Tex. A&M U., College Station, 1980-83, dean. Coll. of Bus. Adminstrn., 1983-86, exec. dep. chancellor, 1986-88, pres., 1988-93; chancellor Tex. A&M U. Sys., College Station, 1993-94; prof. mgmt. Tex. A&M U., Coll. Sta., 1980—94; pres. Mobley Group Pacific Ltd., Shanghai, 2001—; CEO William Global Investment Ptnrs. Ltd., Hong Kong, 2007—. Vis. fellow Cornell U., 1994, vis. prof. Hong Kong U. Sci. and Tech., 1995-97, U. Hong Kong, 1998; prof. mgmt. China Europe Internat. Bus. Sch., Shanghai, 2002-09, prof. emeritus, 2009-. Author: Employee Turnover, 1982, Advances in Global Leadership, vol. I, 1999, vol. II, 2001, vol. III, 2003, vol. IV, 2006, vol. V, 2009. Bd. dirs. Internat. Food and Agrl. Devel. and Econ. Coop., U.S. AID, 1992-94; mem. tri-lateral task force on N.Am. Higher Edn. Coop., USIA, 1993-95; trustee SIOP Found., 1998-2001, AMMA Found., Denison U., 2000-2002; mem. Pres. Bush's Commn. on Minority Bus. Devel., 1990-92, U.S. Com. of the Pacific Econ. Coop. Coun., 1995—. Sr. Fulbright scholar Found. for Scholarly Exchange, Republic China, 1978-79; fellowship DAAD, Rep. Germany, 1984; Fellow NDEA U.S. Dept. of Edn., 1968-71. Fellow APA, Am. Psychol. Soc. Business E-Mail: williamm@mobleygrouppacific.com.

MOCH, PEGGY L., mathematics professor; d. Edward J. and Elma M. Moch; 1 child, Julie A. Weinbloom. AA, Valencia C.C., 1994; BS in Math Edn., U. Ctrl. Fla., 1996, MEd in Math Edn., 1999, PhD in Curriculum and Instrn., 2002. Cert. lab. tech. Colo., 1978, med. tech. Fla., 1979. Mgr. Orlando Plasma Ctr., Fla., 1979—81; med. technologist Orlando Gen. Hosp., 1981—90, Princeton Hosp., Orlando, 1990—96; math. tchr. Maynard Evans HS, Orlando, 1996—99; grad. tchg. asst. U. Ctrl. Fla., Orlando, 1999—2002; assoc. prof. math. Valdosta State U., Ga., 2002—. Math. cons. Lee County Pub. Sch., Ft. Myers, Fla., 2000, Valdosta City Schs., 2007; math. writer Math. and Sci. Profl. Devel. Project, Orlando, 2001, math. cons., Brevard and Orange County, Fla., 02; logo designer U. Ctrl. Fla. Holmes Partnership, Orlando, 2002; math. & sci. cons. Math. & Sci. Partnership Ctrl. Plains RESA, Ga., 2005—07, Pace HS, Cin., 2006—07. Author: Mathematics Content for Elementary Teachers, 2005. Recipient Scholars Outstanding Tchr. award, Radio Shack and Tandy, 1998—99. Mem.: Am. Soc. Clin. Pathologists, Sch. Sci. and Math. Assn., Am. Assn. for Tchg. and Curriculum, Math. Assn. Am., Kappa Delta Pi (co-chair convocation com. 2001, mem. convocation com. 2004—05, Alpha Beta Kappa counselor 2004—, Outstanding Svc. to Chpt. award Omicron Lambda chpt. 1997, 1999). Republican. Avocations: guitar, writing poems, songs, and stories. Office Fax: 229-219-1257. E-mail: plmoch@valdosta.edu.

MOCHALIN, VADYM N., research assistant professor, consultant; s. Nikolai V. Mochalin and Valentina D. Mochalina; 1 child, Eduard V. MS in Biochemistry, Donetsk State U., Ukraine, 1993; PhD in Phys. Chemistry, Inst. Phys. Organic & Coal Chemistry NAS Ukraine, Donetsk, 2001. Rschr. Inst. Phys. Organic & Coal Chemistry NAS Ukraine, 1993—2005; postdoc. rschr. Drexel U., Phila., 2005—07, sr. rschr., 2007—09, rsch. asst. prof., 2009—. Cons. NanoBlox Inc., Boca-Raton, Fla., 2005—. Contbr. articles to profl. jours. Recipient 1st prize, Am. Ceramic Soc., 2006; named Hot Paper, Thomson Sci., 2006; Personal fellowship, Presidium NAS Ukraine, 1996, NAS Ukraine, 1999, Rsch. grants, Ben Franklin Tech. Partners South Eastern Pa., 2005—08. Mem.: Materials Rsch. Soc., Am. Chem. Soc. Achievements include patents for purifying nanodiamond compositions and applications; carbon composite materials based on exfoliated graphite and amorphous carbon, exfoliated graphite and TiO_2; patents pending for modified ultradisperse diamonds as non-toxic quantum dots for biomedical applications; chemical functionalization of nanodiamond; polymer matrix composites with covalently bonded diamond particles. Avocations: travel, computers, reading, music. Office: Drexel Univ Dept Material Sci & Engring 3141 Chestnut St Philadelphia PA 19104 Office Phone: 215-895-6211. Office Fax: 215-895-1934.

MOCHIDA, PAULA T., library director; Reference libr. to head Sinclair Libr. U. Hawaii, Manoa, 1974—98; spl. asst. distance learning U. Hawaii Sys., 1998—2005; interim assoc. univ. libr. adminstrn. and pub. svcs. U. Hawaii, Manoa, 2006, acting univ. libr., 2006—. Mem. adv. bd. U. Hawaii Libr. and Info. Sci. prog. Editor: Ke Kukini Library Newsletter. Office: U Hawaii Manoa Libr 2550 McCarthy Mall Honolulu HI 96822 Office Phone: 808-956-2472. E-mail: paula@hawaii.edu.

MOCK, BEVERLY A., geneticist, researcher; children: Alex, Chris; m. Douglas Lowy. MS, U. Md., 1980, PhD in zoology, 1983. Studies on the genetics of susceptibility to parasitic diseases Dept. Immunology Walter Reed Army Inst. Rsch.; assoc. dir. sci. programs Ctr. Cancer Rsch., Nat. Cancer Inst., NIH, 1999—2007, chief Lab. Genetics, 2004—06, dep. chief Lab. Cancer Biology and Genetics. Office: Lab Cancer Biology and Genetics 37 Convent Dr Bldg 37 Rm 3146 Bethesda MD 20892-4258 Office Phone: 301-496-2360. Office Fax: 301-402-1031. E-mail: bev@helix.nih.gov.*

MOCK, DAVID CLINTON, JR., internist; b. Redlands, Calif., 1922; s. David Clinton and Eithel (Benson) Mock; m. Marcella Enriqueta Fellin, 1952. AB, U. So. Calif., 1944; MD, M.H.D., Hahnemann Med. Coll., 1948. Intern Hahnemann Hosp., Phila., 1948-49; resident San Mateo (Calif.) County Hosp., 1949-51, 54, VA Hosp., Oklahoma City, 1954-55; research fellow in exptl. therapeutics U. Okla., Oklahoma City, 1956-57, L.N. Upjohn fellow, 1958, dir. exptl. therapeutics unit, 1959-62; dir., preceptorship program, 1968-76; assoc. prof. medicine U. Okla., Oklahoma City, 1963-72, prof., 1972-84, prof. emeritus medicine, 1984—, assoc. dean med. student affairs, 1970-76, assoc. dean postdoctoral edn., 1976-82, dir. continuing med. edn., 1980-83, dir. Transitional Yr. program, 1980-84, dir. History of Medicine program, 1982-84. Chief med. svc., Navajo Base Hosp., Ft. Defiance, Ariz., 1951-53; assoc. faculty homeopathy Royal London Homeopathic Hosp. Capt. USPHS, 1951-99, res.; now ret. Fellow: ACP; mem.: N.Y. Acad. Scis., Am. Fedn. Medical Rsch. Unitarian Universalist. Home: 570 Alameda Blvd Coronado CA 92118-1617

MOCK, FRANK MACKENZIE, lawyer; b. South Bend, Ind., May 17, 1944; s. Frank Carlton and Julia (Baughmann) M.; m. Virginia Johns, Dec. 31, 1974 (div. Feb. 1991); children: Shannon, John, Bridget; m. Christine Mall, June 1995; 1 child, Mackenzie Ann. BA, Duke U., 1966, JD, 1969. Bar: Fla. 1969. Assoc. Mahoney, Adams, Criser, Jacksonville, Fla., 1969-74, ptnr., 1977-92; gen. counsel Builders Investment Group, Valley Forge, Pa., 1974-77; ptnr. Baker & Hostetler, Orlando, Fla., 1992—2006, Ruden McClosky, Orlando, Fla., 2006—08. Mem. ABA, Am. Coll. Mortgage Lawyers, Duval County Bar Assn., Orange County Bar Assn., Dade County Bar Assn., Palm Beach County Bar Assn., Turnaround Mgmt. Assn. Republican. Episcopalian. Avocations: hiking, fishing, reading. Home: 2147 Santa Antilles Rd Orlando FL 32806-1533 Home Phone: 407-894-6402; Office Phone: 407-244-8001, 407-418-6211. Business E-Mail: frank.mock@lowndes-law.com.

MOCK, JOAN BODET, music educator; b. Houston, Dec. 3, 1937; d. Edward Bodet and Dorothy Crawford; m. Donald P. Garrett, 1966 (dec. 1985); children: William Clifford Garrett, Christopher Paul Garrett; m. Raymond Cecil Mock, July 7, 2002; 1 child from previous marriage, Charles H. Edwards II. B Music Edn., Ind. U., 1960; postgrad., U. N.Mex. Cert. tchr. N.Mex. Tchr. Espanola (N.Mex.) H.S., 1963—66, Hope H.S., Albuquerque, 1978—79; tchr. group piano lessons Piano Store Orgn., Colorado Springs, 1969—70; pvt. tchr. Garrett's Sch. Piano and Voice, Albuquerque; substitute tchr. Albuquerque Pub. Schs. Soloist for Ed Sullivan, Houston, 1956. Performer: Houston Little Theater, 1954—56, Acola Theater, 1970—79, The Ballad Hunter TV Program, 1954—56; dir.: O.P.E.R.A., 1978; contbr. poems to lit. publs. Soloist Christ Unity Ch., Albuquerque, 1988—92. Inst. Work scholar, Ind. U., 1957—60. Mem.: Albuquerque Music Tchrs. Assn., Nat. Music Tchrs. Assn., Nat. Fedn. Music Clubs. Home and Office: 10401 Crosscut Dr NW Albuquerque NM 87114 Office Phone: 505-350-7612.

MOCKABEE, M(ARION) EUGENE, minister; b. Concordia, Kans., June 17, 1940; s. Owen Eugene Brewer and Velda Evon (Cherington) Mockabee; m. Sondra Sue Stanton, June 8, 1963; 1 child, Tabitha Joy Mockabee Coykendall. BSEE, Kans. State U., 1963; MDiv, Lexington Theol. Sem., 1967, D Ministry, 1977. Ordained min. Christian Ch. Pastor First Christian Ch., Dos Palos, Calif., 1967-71, Plattsmouth, Nebr., 1971-79; talk show host Radio KOTD, Plattsmouth, Nebr., 1976-78; sr. pastor Ctrl. Christian Ch., Kalispell, Mont., 1980-88; owner, software developer Nova Computers, Kalispell, Mont., 1984-89; sr. pastor Wyatt Pk. Christian Ch., St. Joseph, Mo., 1989—2006. Moderator Christian Ch. Mont., Great Falls, 1984-86, NW Area Christian Chs., 2003-06; mem. gen. bd. Christian Ch. in U.S. & Can., Indpls., 1985-90, adminstrv. com., 1988-90, fin. commn., 1990-96. Chaplain Flathead County Sheriff's Dept., Kalispell, 1985-86, Kalispell Police Dept., 1987-88. Decorated Admiral Nebr. Navy, 1979. Mem. High Twelve Club (chaplain 1993—), Freemasons (Scottish rite), Shriners, Rotary (chaplain 1984-90). Democrat. Avocations: amateur radio, computers, astronomy, travel, golf. Office: Wyatt Pk Christian Ch 2623 Mitchell Ave Saint Joseph MO 64507-1639 Home: 12 Ivy Ln Plymouth NH 03264-4009 Office Phone: 816-232-3374. Personal E-mail: genemockabee@yahoo.com.

MOCKAPETRIS, PAUL V., computer scientist, information technology executive; BS in Physics and Elec. Engring., MIT, 1971; PhD in Info. and Computer Sci., U. Calif., Irvine, 1982. Rschr. Info. Scis. Inst., U. So. Calif., dir. High Performance Computing and Comm. Div.; program mgr. networking Advanced Rsch. Projects Agency (ARPA); with @Home, Software.com (now OpenWave), Fiberlane (now Cisco), Siara (now Redback Networks); chmn., chief scientist Nominum Inc., Redwood City, Calif. Chair Internet Engring. Task Force, 1994—96; mem. adv. bd. Staccato Comms., 2005—. Mem.: NAE. Achievements include invention of Domain Name System (DNS). Office: Nominum 2000 Seaport Blvd Ste 400 Redwood City CA 94063-5584

MOCKFORD, EDWARD LEE, retired educator biology; b. Indpls., June 16, 1930; s. Harry Grover and Helen (Lewis) M. A.B., Ind. U., 1952; M.S., U. Fla., 1954; Ph.D., U. Ill.-Urbana, 1960. Grad. asst. biology U. Fla., Gainesville, 1952-54; research asst. Ill. Natural Hist. Survey, Champaign, 1956-60; asst. prof. to prof. biol. scis. Ill. State U., Normal, 1960-86; research assoc. Fla. Dept. Agr., Gainesville, 1959—; coop. scientist U.S. Dept. Agr., Washington, 1960—; vis. prof. Inst. Technologico, Monterrey, Mex., 1963-64. Contbr. articles to profl. jours. Served with U.S. Army, 1954-56. Am. Mus. Natural History Travel grantee, 1959; NSF Research grantee, 1961, 63, 65, 67, 83; recipient Disting. Prof. award Ill. State U., 1984. Mem. Ill. Acad. Sci., Entomol. Soc. Am., Sociedad Mex. de Entomologia, Soc. Systematic Zoology, Soc. Tropical Biology. Democrat. Avocations: hiking; bird watching; swimming; fishing; fiction reading. Office: Ill State U Dept Biol Scis Normal IL 61790 Home: 505 Bowles St Normal IL 61761-1519 Office Phone: 309-438-2666. Business E-Mail: elmockf@ilstu.edu.

MOCKLER, JOLEE MARIE, art educator; b. Kenosha, Wis., June 21, 1957; d. Frank A. and Josephine (Pavelich) Bobusch; m. John R. Mockler, Feb. 20, 1982. BA in Art Edn., Carthage Coll., 1979; MS in Secondary Edn., U. Wis., 2000. Lic. Art Edn. K-12 Wis. Elem. art tchr. Kenosha Unified Sch., Kenosha, Wis., 1979—80; adj. prof. Edgewood Coll., Art Edn. Dept., Madison, Wis., 2003—; art instr., chairperson Reedsburg Area HS, Wis., 1988—; bus. owner Homeworks Furniture and Accents, Reedsburg, Wis., 1991—98. Supr. student tchrs. Edgewood Coll., Madison, Wis., 1996—; art dept. chairperson Reedsburg Sch. Dist., Reedsburg, Wis., 1998—; supr. student tchrs. Luther Coll., Decorah, Iowa, 2000; judge art shows Sauk County Art Assn., Baraboo, 2006; liason US Army recruiter Reedsburg Area HS, 2006—; mem. Sauk County Arts and Humanities Com., 2008—. Co-author: Reedsburg Sch. Dist., K-12 Art Curriculum, 1988—89. Judge for rep. Tammy Baldwin's Congressional Art Competition 2nd Congressional, Madison, Wis., 2003; active Sauk County Basset Hound Rescue. Recipient Top Notch Tchr. award, Wis. TV Channel 3, 2003, Excellence in Edn. award, Reedsburg BOE, 1999, Tchr. of Month award, Reedsburg Area HS, 1998, 2003, 2007, Outstanding Am. Tchrs. award, Nat. Honor Roll, 2005—06. Mem.: NEA, Sauk County Arts, Humanities and Hist. Preservation Com., Reedsburg Edn. Assn., Wis. Edn. Assn. Home: PO Box 243 La Valle WI 53941 Office: Reedsburg Area HS 1100 S Albert Ave Reedsburg WI 53959 Office Phone: 608-524-4327 ext. 1134. Business E-Mail: jmockler@rsd.k12.wi.us.

MOCKO, GEORGE PAUL, minister; b. Little Falls, NY, Feb. 15, 1934; s. George and Anna (Swancara) M.; m. Elizabeth Carol Davidson, Sept. 2, 1956 (dec); children: David (dec.), Paul, Kristopher, Elissa; m. Delores Hay, Oct. 16, 2004. BA, Hartwick Coll., 1956; BD, Phila. Sem., 1959, STM, 1972; DD (hon.), Gettysburg Coll., 1978. Ordained to ministry Evang. Luth. Ch. in Am., 1959. Pastor Jacob's and Outwood Chs., Pine Grove, Pa., 1959-62; assoc. pastor St Mark's Ch., Wilmington, Del., 1962-65, sr. pastor, 1965-78, Ascension Evang. Luth. Ch., Towson, Md., 1978-91; bishop Del.-Md. Synod Evang. Luth Ch. in Am., Towson, 1991-2000, ret., 2000. Author books; contbr. articles to profl. jours. Mem. Evang. Luth. Ch. Home: 501 Sussex Rd Baltimore MD 21286-7609 Home Phone: 410-296-7136. Personal E-mail: GPmocko@aol.com. *Colossians speaks of Christ as the one in whom "all things hold together". I know that Christ is the one who holds me together. Proclaiming and living his life, the church holds our society together.*

MOCZYDLOWSKI, EDWARD GERARD, biologist, researcher; b. Pitts., Sept. 18, 1953; s. Edward J. and Adele (Shumovich) M.; m. Stephenie K. Lemmon, June 27, 1981; children: Seth R. and Laurel A. BA summa cum laude, Cornell U., 1975; PhD, U. Calif., San Diego, 1980. Asst. prof. physiology U. Cin., 1984-86; asst. prof. pharmacology Yale U. Sch. Medicine, New Haven, Conn., 1986-89, assoc. prof. pharmacology, 1989-98, prof. pharmacology, 1998—. Mem. editorial bd. Jour. of Gen., Physiology, 1989—. Named Searle scholar, 1985. Mem. Biophysical Soc., Soc. for Neuroscience, Soc. Gen. Physiologists, Internat. Soc. on Toxinology, Phi Beta Kappa. Unitarian Universalist.

Achievements include notable findings in electrophysiological analysis of biological ion channels in reconstituted lipid bilayers. Office: Yale U Sch Medicine Dept Pharmacology PO Box 208066 New Haven CT 06520-8066

MODABBER, ZIA F., lawyer; b. Jan. 9, 1962; BA, U. Calif., Berkeley, 1984; JD, Loyola Law Sch., 1988. Bar: Calif. 1988, US Dist. Ct. (ctrl. dist.) Calif., US Dist. Ct. (no. dist.), US Ct. Appeals (9th cir.). Assoc. Wyman Bautzer Kuchel & Silbert, LA; ptnr. Katten Muchin Rosenman, LA. Mem.: ABA, LA County Bar Assn., St. Thomas More Law Honor Soc. Office: Katten Muchin Rosenman Ste 2600 2029 Century Park E Los Angeles CA 90067 Office Phone: 310-788-4627. Office Fax: 310-712-8462. Business E-Mail: zia.modabber@kattenlaw.com.

MODANO, MIKE, professional hockey player; b. Livonia, Mich., June 7, 1970; m. Willa Ford, Aug. 25, 2007. Center Minn. North Stars, 1988—93, Dallas Stars, 1993—. Mem. Team USA, Canada Cup, 1991, Team USA, World Cup of Hockey, 1996, 2004, US Olympic Hockey Team, Nagano, Japan, 1998, Salt Lake City, 2002, Torino, Italy, 06. Named to NHL All-Star Game, 1993, 1998—2000, 2003, 2004, 2009. Achievements include being the first overall draft pick in NHL entry draft, 1988; being a member of World Cup Champion Team USA, 1996; being a member of Stanley Cup Champion Dallas Stars, 1999; being a member of silver medal winning USA Hockey Team, Salt Lake City Olympics, 2002; being captain of USA Olympics Hockey Team, 2006; being the second US-born player to score 500 goals, 2007; becoming the highest-scoring American in NHL history, 2007. Office: c/o Dallas Stars 2601 Avenue of the Stars Frisco TX 75034*

MODD, LAWRENCE R., surgeon; b. Evanston, Ill., Mar. 24, 1960; s. Laura Corse; m. Kristine Ann Schmidt, Sept. 11, 1993; children: Jackson R. Moss, Kristine Sierra Moss, Ruby Mckayla Moss. BA English Lit., Stanford U., Palo Alto, CA, 1982; MD, U. Calif, San Diego, 1986; MS (hon.), Yale U., New Haven, 1979. Diplomate Am. Bd. Surgery,Pa., 1993. Surgeon-in-chief Yale New Haven Children's Hosp., 2002—; chief, pediatric surgery Yale U. Sch. Medicine, New Haven, vice chair, surgery, 2002—. Office: Yale Univ School Medicine 333 Cedar St FMB 132 Box 208062 New Haven CT 06520-8062 Office Fax: 203-785-3820.

MODDELMOG, HALA, medical association administrator; b. Ga., Jan. 3, 1956; BA in English, Ga. Southern U.; MA in Journalism & Mass Comm., U. Ga. Pres. Church's Chicken, 1995—2004; founder Catalytic Ventures, 2004—; pres., CEO Susan G. Komen for the Cure, Dallas, 2006—. Bd. dirs. Fiesta Brands, Inc., 2006—08, HyperActive Technologies, 2006—07, AMN Healthcare Services, Inc., 2008—, AMERIGROUP Corp., 2009—. Bd. trustees Ga. Southern U. Found., 2005—08, Clark Atlanta U., 2004—06. Recipient Rising Star award, Restaurant Hospitality, Pacesetter award, Roundtable for Women in Food Svc. Mem.: Internat. Franchise Assn. (Bonny LeVine award). Office: Susan G. Komen for the Cure 5005 LBJ Freeway Ste 250 Dallas TX 75244*

MODE, CHARLES J., mathematician, educator; b. Bismarck, ND, Dec. 29, 1927; s. Charles and Fannie E. (Hansen) M.; m. Eleanore L. Perdelwitz; 1 dau., Martha Lisa. BS in Genetics, N.D. State U., 1952; MS in Genetics, Kans. State U., 1953; PhD in Genetics, U. Calif., Davis and Berkeley, 1956; postgrad. in stats. (Univ. fellow), N.C. State U., 1956-57. Asst. prof. math. Mont. State U., 1957-59, asso. prof., 1960-62, prof., 1963-66, mem. genetics group, 1957-66; asso. prof. math. stats. SUNY, Buffalo, 1966-70; prof. math. Drexel U., 1970—. Cons. to industry. Author: (books) Multitype Branching Processes - Theory and Applications, 1971, Stochastic Processes in Demography and Their Computer Implementation, 1985, Stochastic Processes in Epidemiology, HIV/AIDS, Other Infectious Diseases and Computers, 2000; contbr. articles to profl. pulbs.; editor (assoc.): (jour.) Math. Bioscis., 1975—. Mem. Inst. Math. Stats., Biometric Soc., Am. Math. Soc., AAAS, Population Assn. Am., Sigma Xi, Phi Kappa Phi, Pi Mu Epsilon. Lutheran. Office: Drexel U Dept Math Philadelphia PA 19104 Home: 422 Freedom Blvd Coatesville PA 19320 Business E-Mail: cmode@math.drexel.edu.

MODELL, JEROME HERBERT, anesthesiologist, educator; b. St. Paul, Sept. 9, 1932; s. William and Frieda (Singer) M.; m. Shirley Graves, Nov. 25, 1977; children— Charles, Jack, Julie. BA, U. Minn., 1954, BS, MD, U. Minn., 1957; DSc (hon.), U. Fla., 2004. Intern U.S. Naval Hosp., St. Albans, NY, 1957-58, resident, 1958-60; practice medicine specializing in anesthesiology Gainesville, Fla., 1969—; attending staff U.S. Naval Hosp., St. Albans, 1960-61, chief anesthesiology Pensacola, Fla., 1961-63; asso. prof. dept. anesthesiology U. Miami (Fla.) Sch. Medicine, 1963-69; prof., chmn. dept. anesthesiology U. Fla. Coll. Medicine, Gainesville, 1969-92, sr. assoc. dean clin. affairs, 1990-95, exec. assoc. dean, 1996-97, interim dean, 1997; assoc. v.p. U. Fla. Health Sci. Ctr. Affiliations, 1992-96. Assoc. v.p. U. Fla. Health Sci., 1998-2000, emeritus prof. 2000—, courtesy prof. large animal scis., 1999—. Author: The Pathophysiology and Treatment of Drowning and Near-Drowning, 1971, (with others) Introduction to Life Support, 1973; also numerous scientific articles. Served to lt. comdr. USN, 1957-63. Recipient Rsch. Career Devel. award, NIH, 1967—69, Lifetime Achievement award, Am. Soc. Critical Care Anesthesiologists, 1991. Mem. AMA, AAAS, Assn. U. Anesthetists, Am. Soc. Anesthesiologists (Disting. Svc. award, 2005), N.Y. Acad. Scis., Am. Coll. Chest Physicians. Home: PO Box 14347 Gainesville FL 32604-2347 Office: U Fla Coll Medicine PO Box 100254 Gainesville FL 32610-0254 Office Phone: 352-265-8076. Business E-Mail: modeljh@shands.ufl.edu.

MODELL, STEPHEN MARK, medical researcher, educator; b. Detroit, June 22, 1958; s. Richard Martin and Sola Jane (Hamburger) M.; m. Wanpen Prasoptham, Jan. 14, 1988; 1 child, Marrisa Lynne. AB in Philosophy, Stanford U., 1980; MD, Med. Coll. Ohio, 1984; MS in Clin. Rsch. Design/Statis. Analysis, U. Mich., 1991. Asst. coord. The Resource for Pub. Health Policy U. Mich. Sch. Pub. Health, Ann Arbor, 1987-89; rsch. asst., dept. psychiatry U. Mich., Ann Arbor, 1989-90, Genome Ethics Com. rsch. assoc., 1992-94, Coun. Genetics and Soc. rsch. assoc. dept. health mgmt. and policy, 1995-98, rsch. dir. genetics policy dept. health mgmt. and policy, 1999—2001; dir. dissemination Mich. Ctr. for Genomics and Pub. Health, 2001—. Mem. pres.'s coun. Med. Coll. Ohio, 1992—2003. Genome studies sect. editor Ultimate Reality and Meaning, 1995—; editor Studies in Biophilosophy, 1997, Studies in Medicine and Health, 2006, co-editor jour. 2009-. Recipient honorable mention Nellie Westerman prize competition in clin. rsch. ethics, Am. Fedn. Clin. Rsch., 1995. Mem. AMA, Am. Fedn. Med. Rsch., N.Y. Acad. Scis., Maimonides Soc., Internat. Soc. Study of Human Ideas on Ultimate Reality and Meaning (bd. dirs. 1994—, treas. 1999-2000, v.p. 2001-02, pres. 2003-04), Rotary (hon.), Am. Pub. Health Assn & Fedn. Avocations: book discussion groups, water sports, jogging, hiking, travel. Office: U Mich Sch Pub Health 4605 SPH-I Tower 109 S Observatory St Ann Arbor MI 48109-2029 E-mail: mod@umich.edu.

MODEN, JOLEEN, communications executive; B in Bus. Adminstrn. and Acctg., Kans. State U. CPA. Ptnr. Coopers & Lybrand; v.p., CFO, treas. Signature Home Care Grp.; dir. corp. audit PepsiCo Inc.; asst. contr. internal audit GTE, 1998—2000; sr. v.p. internal auditing Verizon Comm. Inc., NYC, 2000—. Office: Verizon Comms Inc Verizon Ctr VC44E227 One Verizon Way Basking Ridge NJ 07920-1997 E-mail: joleenmoden@verizon.com.

MODESITT, CAROL ANN, vocalist, music educator, opera director; b. Mar. 6, 1947; BA, Utah State U., Logan, 1968; MusM, Ea. Ky. U., Richmond, 1973. Asst. prof. Utah State U., Logan, 1978-84; vis. asst. prof. U. Colo., Boulder, 1984-90; artist in residence Plymouth (N.H.) State Coll., 1990-93; prof. voice and opera So. Utah U., Cedar City, 1993—2006, chair music dept., 2005—06, prof., 2006—. Author: (ednl. software) Reindeer Ednl. Network, 1999; book reviewer: Nat. Opera Assn. Jour., 1998—; performer (debut recital): Carnegie Hall, 2002. Pres. Cedar City (Utah) Music Arts, 1999—2002, Cedar City Arts Coun., 2002—05. Recipient Contribution to Arts award, Cedar City C. of C., 2001. Mem.: NOW, Nat. Opera Assn. (west ctrl. region gov. 1997, bd. mem. 2008—), Music Tchrs. Nat. Assn. (pres. Cedar City 1997—), Nat. Assn. Tchrs. of Singing (pres. Las Vegas chpt. 2005—06). Home: 255 Sunnyview Rd Cedar City UT 84720-2897 Office Phone: 435-865-8166. Home Fax: 435-865-1732. Business E-Mail: modesitt@suu.edu.

MODESITT, LELAND EXTON, JR., (L.E. MODESITT JR.), consultant, writer, poet; b. Denver, Oct. 19, 1943; s. Leland Exton and Nancy Lila (Evans) M.; m. Virginia Dale Eschenburg, Sept. 16, 1964 (div. 1977); m. 2d, Christina Alma Gribben, Oct. 22, 1977 (div. 1991); children— Leland Exton, Susan Carnall, Catherine Grant, Nancy Mayo, Elizabeth Leanore, Kristen Linnea; m. Carol Ann James Hill, Jan. 4, 1992; step-children: Lara Beth Hill, Kevin L. Hill. BA, Williams Coll., 1965; postgrad. U. Denver, 1970-71. Rsch. analyst C.A. Norgren Co., Littleton, Colo., 1969-70; assoc. Koelbel & Co., Denver, 1970-72; rsch. dir. Armstrong for Congress, Aurora, Colo., 1972; legis. asst. US Rep. William Armstrong, Washington, 1973-78; adminstrv. asst. US Rep. Ken Kramer, Washington, 1979-81; dir. legislation US EPA, Washington, 1981-84, spl. asst. external affairs, 1984-85; mem. Multinat. Bus. Svcs., 1985—91; instr. Georgetown U., 1980-81; lectr. Plymouth State U., 1990-93. Author: (novels) The Fires of Paratime, 1982 (main selection Sci. Fiction Book Club, May, 1982), The Hammer of Darkness, 1985, The Ecologic Envoy, 1986, Dawn For a Distant Earth, 1987, The Silent Warrior, 1987, In Endless Twilight, 1988, The Magic of Recluce, 1991, The Towers of the Sunset, 1992, The Magic Engineer, 1994, The Order War, 1995, The White Order, 1998, Scion of Cyador, 2000, Legacies, 2002, Scepters, 2004, Flash, 2004, Wellspring of Chaos, 2004, Ordermaster, 2005, Alector's Choice, 2005, The Eternity Artifact, 2005, Cadmian's Choice, 2006, Soarer's Choice, 2006, The Elysium Commission, 2007, Natural Ordermage, 2007, Viewpoints Critical, 2008, Mage-Guard of Hamor, 2008, The Lord-Protector's Daughter, 2008, Imager, 2009, Haze, 2009, Imager's Challenge, 2009; author short stories and poetry; contbr. articles to profl. jours. With USN, 1965-69, SE Asia. Republican. Home: 255 Sunnyview Rd Cedar City UT 84720-2897 Personal E-mail: lmodesitt@aol.com.

MODESITT, SUSAN CARNALL, oncologist, director; d. Leland Exton Modesitt and Virginia Dale Eschenburg; m. Kacy Scott Burnsed, Sept. 26, 1998; children: Ava Modesitt Burnsed, Adaire Modesitt Burnsed. BS, Emory U., Atlanta, 1991; MD, U. Va., Charlottesville, 1995. Diplomate Am. Bd. Ob-Gyn., 2003, in gynecologic oncology Am. Bd. Ob-Gyn., 2005. Resident ob-gyn.dept, U. NC, Chapel Hill, 1995—99; fellow gynecologic oncology, M.D. Anderson Cancer Ctr., Houston, 1999—2002; asst. prof. gynecologic oncology, U. Ky., Lexington, 2002—06; assoc. prof. gynecologic oncology, U. Va., Charlottesville, Dir. gynecologic oncology divsn., 2007—. Contbr. articles to numerous profl.jours., chapters to books. Mentor Girls in Sci., Lexington, Ky., 2002—06. Recipient Outstanding Resident Tchg. award, Coun. Resident Edn. Ob-Gyn., 2006, Excellence in Tchg. award, Assn. of Profs. Ob-Gyn., 2005, Excellence Resident Tchg., Berlex, 1996, Diver of Yr., U. Athletic Assn., 1989, Hon. Mention All Am. in Diving, NCAA, 1989, Shannon Award, U. Va., 1991; Rsch. grant, Ctr. Rsch. on Violence Against Women, 2003, Rsch. Scholar, Bldg. Interdisciplinary Rsch. in Women's Health, 2003—06, Research grants, from numerous U. Fellow: Am. Coll. Ob-gyn. (task force mem. 2008—), ACS; mem.: Gynecologic Oncology Group (com. mem. and prin. investigator 2004), Mid Atlantic Gynecologic Oncology Soc. (pres. elect ii 2008—), Soc. Gynecologic Oncologists (task force chair 2006—07). Avocations: sports, gymnastics, diving, triathlon. Office: Divsn Gynecologic Oncology Box 800712 Univ Va Charlottesville VA 22908-0712 Office Phone: 434-924-5197. Office Fax: 434-982-1840.

MODEST, MICHAEL FRITZ, mechanical engineering educator; b. Berlin, Mar. 1, 1944; arrived in U.S., 1969; s. Fritz Ulrich and Ella (Weiss) M.; m. Ellen J. Peterson, June 1974 (div. 1979); m. Monika Klara Graf, Aug. 11, 1984; children: Mara Claudia, Michelle Rebecca. Diploma in engring., Tech. U. Munich, 1968; MS, PhD, U. Calif., Berkeley, 1972. Postdoctoral rsch. asst. Johnson Space Ctr. NASA, Houston, 1972-74; lectr. in engring. San Francisco State U., 1974-75; from asst. to assoc. prof. mech. engring. Rensselaer Poly. Inst., Troy, NY, 1975—80; from assoc. prof. to prof. mech. engring. U. So. Calif., LA, 1980-86; prof. mech. engring. Pa. State U., University Park, 1987—2009; Shaffer & George prof. engring. U. Calif., Merced, 2009—. Cons. Lawrence Berkeley Lab., 1975, GE, Schenectady, N.Y., 1975-76, 80-84, HUD, Albany, N.Y., 1978, and others. Author: Radiative Heat Transfer, 2003; assoc. tech. editor Jour. Quant. Spectr. Rad. Transfer; assoc. tech. editor Jour. Heat Transfer; editor several conf. procs.; contbr. articles to profl. jours. Recipient Outstanding Rsch. award Pa. State Engring. Soc., 2000, Premier Rsch. award 2003; grantee NSF, NASA, NIH, Dept. Energy, and others. Fellow ASME (Heat Transfer Meml. award 2005, U. Disting. prof. 2007), AIAA (assoc., Thermophysics award 2008); mem. Laser Inst. Am., Sigma Xi. Office: Pa State U 301C Reber Bldg University Park PA 16802-1414 Business E-Mail: mfmodest@psu.edu, mfmodest@ucmerced.edu.

MODI, KALPEN SURESH See PENN, KAL

MODIC, MICHAEL, radiologist, educator; MD, Case Western Reserve U. Sch. Medicine, 1975. Resident in radiology Cleveland Clinic, fellow in neuroradiology, neuroradiologist, 1980—82, head magnetic resonance, 1982—85, chmn. radiology, 1989—2000, bd. govs., 2000; asst. prof. radiology Cleveland U. Hosp., 1979—80; dir. magnetic resonance & neuroradiology Case Western U. Reserve Sch. Medicine, 1985—89; prof. radiology Ohio State U., 1993—, Cleveland Clinic Lerner Coll. Medicine, 2004—07; chmn. Neurological Inst., 2007—. Editorial bd. Radiology, Am. Jour. Neuroradiology, Neurology, Magnetic Resonance in Medicine, Magnetic Resonance Imaging. Fellow: Am. Coll. Radiology; mem.: Am. Stroke Assn., Am. Heart Assn., Am. Soc. Spine Radiology, Am. Soc. Neuroradiology, Radiological Soc. North America, Soc. Magnetic Resonance Imaging (bd. dirs.), Soc. Magnetic Resonance in Medicine (pres. 1992—93, former bd. trustees, Gold Medal in Clinical Sci. 1991). Office: Cleveland Clinic Main Campus 9500 Euclid Ave MC-T13 Cleveland OH 44195 Office Phone: 216-444-9308.*

MODICA, ROBERT L, IV, humanities educator; ABD in History, U. Ariz., Tucson, 1975. Humanities faculty Pima CC, Tucson, 1973—. Chair Volleyball Advisor Bd., Tucson, 1980—87. Office: Pima CC 8181 E Irvington Rd Tucson AZ 85709 Business E-Mail: rmodica@pima.edu.

MODIN, FREDRIK, professional hockey player; b. Sundsvall, Sweden, Oct. 8, 1974; Left wing Brynas IF, Toronto Maple Leafs, 1996—99, Tampa Bay Lightning, 1999—2006, Columbus Blue Jackets, 2006—. Player NHL All-Star Game, 2001. Achievements include being a member of Stanley Cup Champion Tampa Bay Lightning, 2004; being a member of gold medal winning Swedish Hockey Team, Torino Olympics, Italy, 2006. Office: Columbus Blue Jackets Nationwide Arena 200 W Nationwide Blvd Columbus OH 43215

MODISHER, MELVIN WAYNE, obstetrician, gynecologist, educator; b. Sharpsville, Pa., May 9, 1916; MD, Temple U., Phila., 1943. Diplomate Am. Bd. Ob-Gyn. Intern Abington Meml. Hosp., 1944; resident in ob-gyn. Bethesda Hosp., Cin., 1946-49; mem. staff U. Hosp. Vol., San Diego. Assoc. clin. prof. reproductive medicine Med. Sch. U. Calif. San Diego. Fellow ACS. Personal E-mail: melandcorla@san.rr.com.

MODJTABAI, AVID, bank executive; b. 1961; 1 child. BS in Indsl. Engring., Stanford U.; MBA in Fin., Columbia U. With McKinsey & Co.; exec. v.p., dir. Internet svcs. Wells Fargo, San Francisco, head online personal fin. svcs., exec. v.p., dir. HR, 2005—07, exec. v.p. tech. & ops., CIO, 2007—, head, ops. group, 2009—. Active The B.A.Y. Fund. Named one of 100 Most Influential Women in Bay Area Bus., San Francisco Bus. Times, 2004—05, 25 Most Powerful Women in Banking, US Banker, 2004, 25 Women to Watch, 2006—08. Office: Wells Fargo 420 Montgomery St San Francisco CA 94104*

MODJTAHEDI, BAGHER, economist, educator; PhD, U. Calif., Davis, 1984. Lecturer, dept economics U Calif. Author: (textbook) Microeconomics, Macroeconomis: Theory and Policy. Office: Dept Economics UC Davis One Shields Ave Davis CA 95616 Office Phone: 530-752-0741. Business E-Mail: bmodjtahedi@ucdavis.edu.

MODLA, VIRGINIA BORDONARO, education educator; b. Syracuse, Ny, May 10, 1946; d. James Joseph and Grace Lenore Bordonaro; m. Andrew Anthony Modla; 1 child, Jennifer Kathryn. BA, Douglass Coll., New Brunswick, NJ, 1968; MEd, Temple U., Phila., 1974, PhD, 1980. Cert. in supt.'s letter of eligibility Pa., 1998, reading supervisor Pa., NJ., 1979, reading specialist Pa., 1974, NJ, 1976, cert. in elementary edn. Pa., 1970. Tchr. Collegeville-Trappe Sch. Dist., Pa., 1970—73; reading specialist Hamilton HS East, NJ, 1979—81; reading curriculum assoc. Cheltenham Twp. Sch. Dist., Elkins Pk., Pa., 1982—87; reading supr., dir curriculum Upper Dublin Sch. Dist., Dresher, Pa., 1987—98; dir. curriculum & instrn. Wissahickon Sch. Dist., Ambler, Pa., 1998—2001; prof. Lincoln U., Oxford, Pa., 1981—82, La Salle U., Phila., 2001—. Contbr. articles to profl. jours. Chair, clin. divsn. Assn. Literacy Educators & Rschr., 2007—09. Recipient Doctoral award, Phi Delta Gamma, 1980. Mem.: Del. Valley Reading Assn. (pres. 1982—84, rsch. chair. 2001—), Alpha Delta Kappa (chpt. pres. 1986—88, state pres. 2004—06, PA Gamma Chpt. 1986—88, Edn. award 2008). Avocations: travel, reading, yoga, knitting, bicycling. Office: La Salle Univ 1900 W Olney Ave Philadelphia PA 19141 Office Fax: 215-951-5029. Business E-Mail: modla@lasalle.edu.

MODLIN, ADAM D., real estate company executive; b. NY, Feb. 28, 1973; s. Joe and Sylvia Modlin; m. Wendy Modlin. BBA in Mktg., CUNY, 1996. With Bergdorf; co-founder, owner Modlin Group, 1999—. Bd. dirs. Baruch Coll. Real Estate Sch., CUNY, Cobble Hill Health Ctr. Mem.: Real Estate Bd. NY. Office: Modlin Group 200 W 57th St Ste 308 New York NY 10019 Office Phone: 212-974-0740. Office Fax: 212-974-0625. Business E-Mail: adam@modlingroup.com.

MODLIN, HOWARD S., lawyer; b. NYC, Apr. 10, 1931; s. Martin and Rose Modlin; m. Margot S. Modlin, Oct. 18, 1956; children: James, Laura, Peter. AB, Union Coll., Schenectady, 1952; JD, Columbia U., 1955. Bar: N.Y. 1956, D.C. 1973. Assoc. Weisman, Celler, Spett & Modlin, P.C., NYC, 1956-61, ptnr., 1961-76, mng. ptnr., 1976-95, pres., 1996—. Chmn. bd. dirs., sec. Gen. DataComm Industries, Inc., Naugatuck, Conn.; bd. dirs. Am.-Book-Stratford Press, Inc., NYC, Trans-Lux Corp., Norwalk, Conn. Chmn. bd. dirs. Daus. of Jacob Geriat. Ctr., Bronx, N.Y. Mem. ABA, Assn. of Bar of City of N.Y., D.C. Bar Assn. Office: Weisman Celler Spett & Modlin PC 445 Park Ave New York NY 10022-2606 Office Phone: 212-371-5400.

MODNY, CYNTHIA JEAN, dermatologist; b. Jan. 23, 1945; d. Michael Theodore and Mary (Tabaka) M. BA, Mt. Holyoke Coll., 1967; MD, U. Va., Charlottesville, 1971. Diplomate Am. Bd. Dermatology. Intern Lenox Hill Hosp., NYC, 1971-72; resident N.Y. Hosp./Cornell Med. Ctr., NYC, 1972-75, instr. dermatology, 1976—81; practice medicine specializing in dermatology Montclair, N.J., 1976-92, Phoenix, 1994—2006. Pvt. practice cons. undersea medicine, Montclair, 1982-92; clin. instr. dermatology Skin and Cancer Unit, NYU Med. Ctr., N.Y.C., 1981-92; participant Physicians' Undersea Medicine Tng., NOAA, Miami, Fla., 1982; dir. Skin Cancer Inst., Montclair, 1984. Med. editor Dive Travel Report (monthly), 1983-92; contbr. article to Skin Diver mag. Bd. dirs. Montclair Sr. Citizens, 1984. Fellow Am. Acad. Dermatology; mem. Undersea Med. Soc., Am. Soc. Dermatologic Surgery, Princeton Club, Mt. Holyoke Club (N.Y.C.).

MODRELL, COREY JOHN, educator; b. Battle Creek, Iowa, Mar. 6, 1979; s. John Samuel Modrell III and Julie Anne Modrell. B, Grand View Coll., Des Moines, Iowa, 2002. Cert. in chiropractic Colo., 2006. Chiropractor Modrell Family & Sports Chiropractic, Montrose, Colo., 2006—; prof. biology Mesa State Coll., Montrose, Colo., 2006—. Chiropractic sports physician Am. Chiropractic Bd. Sports Physicians, 2007—. Home: 713 S Forty Dr Montrose CO 81401 Office: Modrell Family & Sports Chiropractic 100 Tessitore Ct Ste B Montrose CO 81401 Office Fax: 970-240-4897.

MOE, ANDREW IRVING, veterinarian; b. Tacoma, Jan. 2, 1927; s. Ole Andrew and Ingeborg (Gordham) M.; m. Dorothy Clara Becker, June 25, 1950 (dec. Nov. 30, 2001); children: Sylvia Moe McGowan, Pamela Moe Barker, Joyce. BS in Biology, U. Puget Sound, 1949; BA, Wash. State U., 1953, DVM, 1954. Meat cutter Art Hansen, Tacoma, 1943—48; gen. practice as vet. Baronti Vet. Hosp., Eugene, Oreg., 1956-57; vet. regulatory Calif. Animal Health br., resident vet. II Calif. Dept. Food & Agr., Modesto, 1957-64, acting vet.-in-charge Modesto Dist. office, vet. III, 1976-77, ret., 1990—. Watersafety instr. ARC, 1958-61. Capt. Vet. Corps., 1954-56, 62; lt. col. Biomed Scis. Corps. USAF, ret., 1982. Recipient Chief Vet. badge, 1975. Mem. VFW (life, comdr. post 4144 1998-2001, quartermaster 2000-02, trustee post 3199, 2004-08), No. San Joaquin Vet. Med. Assn. (pres. 1979), Calif. Acad. Vet. Medicine (charter), Mil. Officers Assn. of Am. (charter), Res. Officers Assn. (life), Ret. Officers Assn. (life), Assn. Mil. Surgeons U.S. (life), Sons of Norway, Am. Legion (life), Shriners (bd. dirs. Modesto Shrine 1995), Masons (life), (Illustrious Master Modesto chpt. 1983, Allied Masonic degrees, pres. Modesto Masonic Luncheon Club 1991, 98, Meritorious Svc. medal 1992, Man of Yr. award 1999), Scottish Rite (life, pres. Ctrl. Valley 1997, bd. dirs. 1998-2008), Presido Yacht Club Sausalito, Theta Chi, Alpha Psi. Lutheran. Home: 161 Norwegian Ave Modesto CA 95350-3542

MOE, KARI J., legislative staff member; BA in Urban History and Sociology, Carleton Coll., Northfield, Minn., 1974; M in City Planning, Urban Planning and Pub. Policy, Mass. Inst. Tech., Cambridge, 1982; PhD in Pub. Adminstrn. and Pub. Policy, George Wash. U., Washington, 2005. Sr. exec. positions City of Chgo., 1983—89; chief of staff to Senator Paul Wellstone US Senate, Washington, 1991—97, sr. policy advisor, Senator Paul Wellstone, 1998—2001; dir. leadership tng. George Wash. U. Ctr. Excellence in Pub. Leadership, 1999—2005; chief of staff to Rep. Keith Ellison US House of Reps., Washington, 2007—. Democrat. Office: 1122 Longworth House Office Bldg Washington DC 20515 Office Phone: 202-225-4755. Office Fax: 202-225-4886. Business E-Mail: kari.moe@mail.house.gov.*

MOE, LONN ANDRE, state revenue official; b. Springfield, Minn., Nov. 18, 1958; s. Roy Melvin and Margaret Joy Moe. BS in Agrl. Econs. and Agrl. Bus. Adminstrn., U. Minn., St. Paul, 1981, MS in Agrl. Bus. Mgmt., 1984. Rsch. analyst Minn. Dept. Revenue, St. Paul, 1985—87, rsch. analyst intermediate, 1987, rsch. analyst specialist, 1987—92, rsch. analyst specialist sr., 1992—99, revenue ops. specialist, 1999—. Study leader Grace Ch. Roseville, Minn., 1988—. Recipient Achievement award, Minn. Dept. Revenue, 1989, 1995, 2005, 2007. Mem.: Landscape Plant Devel. Ctr. Avocations: horticulture, horseback riding. Office Phone: 651-556-6144.

MOE, RICHARD PALMER, lawyer; b. Duluth, Minn., Nov. 27, 1936; s. Russell James and Virginia Mary (Palmer) M.; m. Julia Neimeyer, Dec. 26, 1964; children— Eric Palmer, Andrew Neimeyer, Alexandra Julia. BA, Williams Coll., 1959; LL.B., U. Minn., 1966. Bar: Minn. 1967, D.C. 1979, N.Y. 1991. Adminstrv. asst. to mayor, City of Mpls., 1961-62; to lt. gov. Minn., 1963-66; fin. dir. Minn. Democratic Farmer-Labor Party, 1967-69, chmn., 1969-72; adminstrv. asst. to Sen. Walter F. Mondale of Minn., Washington, 1972-76; chief of staff Vice Pres. Walter F. Mondale, 1977-81; counsel Davis Polk & Wardwell, Washington, 1981-85, ptnr., 1985-92; pres. Nat. Trust for Hist. Preservation, Washington, 1992—. Trustee Ford Found., 1998—. Office: Nat Trust for Hist Preservation 1785 Massachusetts Ave NW Washington DC 20036-2117

MOE, STANLEY ALLEN, architect, consultant; b. Fargo, ND, May 28, 1914; s. Ole Arnold and Freda Emily (Pape) Moe; m. Doris Lucille Anderson, July 25, 1937 (dec. 2000); children: Willa Moe Crouse, Myra Moe Galther; m. Reiko Izuno, Nov. 11, 2001. BArch, U. Minn., Mpls., 1936; DEng (hon.), U. ND, Grand Forks, 1993. lic. arch. several states; cert. Nat. Coun. Archtl. Registration Bds. Project arch. various firms, 1936—42, U.S. Army Corps Engrs., Africa, 1942—43; ptnr. H.S. Starin, Archs. & Engrs., Duluth, Minn., 1943—47; sr. ptnr. Moe & Larsen, Archs. & Engrs., LA, 1947-54; ptnr., gen. mgr., exec. v.p. Daniel, Mann, Johnson & Mendenall, LA, 1954-71, corp. v.p., 1972-79; prin. Stanley A. Moe, AIA, LA, 1979—. Dir. design of major mil. projects in Eritrea, Sudan, Egypt, Yemen for Allied Forces, 1942-43; chmn. control com. DMJM & Assocs., dir. design prototype, tng. & operational facilities Titan I Intercontinental Ballistic Missiles Program USAF, 1958-63; project dir. Space Shuttle facilities Kennedy Space Ctr., 1973; project dir. for design of aircraft maintenance complex Iranian Aircraft Industries, 1978; project mgr. for design of major med. facility program Min. of Def. and Aviation, Saudi Arabia, 1975-76; project mgr. design of Boufarik Internat. Airport, Algeria, 1983. Pres. San. Fernando Valley Young Reps., 1952, Van Nuys (Calif.) Jaycees, 1950. Recipient Disting. Svc. award for cmty. svc., Van Nuys Jaycees, 1949, Sioux award, U. ND Alumni Assn., 1985, Trustees Soc. award, U. Minn., 1992; inducted into ND Entrepreneur Hall of Fame, 2000. Mem. AIA (Calif. coun.), Rotary, Delta Tau Delta. Republican. Presbyterian. Avocations: world travel, hunting, fishing, historic restoration, woodworking. Home and Office: 447 S Plymouth Blvd Los Angeles CA 90020-4706

MOEHLMAN, MICHAEL SCOTT, lawyer; b. Columbus, Ohio, Apr. 11, 1938; s. Arthur Henry and Marguerite Caroline M.; m. Carol Jean Shafer, Sept. 28, 1963; 1 son, Matthew. BA, Harvard U., 1960; LLB, U. Tex., 1963. Bar: Tex. 1963. With Strasburger & Price, Houston. Bd. dirs. St. Martin's Episcopal Children's Ctr. Fellow Tex. Bar Found.; mem. ABA (com. bank securities), Internat. Bar Assn., Tex. Bar Assn. (com. revision corp. law), Houston Bar Assn. (judicature com.), Tex.-Mex. Bar Assn., Am. Judicature Soc., Houston Bar Found. (chmn. bd. dirs.), Phi Delta Phi. Clubs: Houston (chmn. fin. com., bd. dirs., pres.), Houston Racquet, Houston Yacht, Harvard (Boston), Harvard (NYC), St. Charles Bay Hunting. Episcopalian. Office: Strasburger & Price 1401 McKinney St Ste 2200 Houston TX 77010-4035 Office Phone: 713-951-5684. Business E-Mail: michael.moehlman@strasburger.com.

MOEHRING, GREGORY, chemistry professor, department chairman; b. Watertown, SD, Dec. 26, 1958; s. Harold and Bernice Moehring; m. Miyoko Tsuchida; children: Peter, Christopher. AS, Centralia Coll., Wash., 1979; BS, Western Wash. U., Bellingham, 1981; PhD, Purdue U., West Lafayette, Ind., 1987. GS-5 chemist Naval Med. Rsch. Inst., Bethesda, Md., 1982—82; chemist DuPont, New Johnsonville, Tenn., 1987—88; postdoc. fellow U. BC, Vancouver, Canada, 1988—89; asst. prof., chemistry U. La., Lafayette, 1989—90; prof., inorganic chemistry Govs. State U., U. Pk., Ill., 1990—2006; prof., chair, chemistry Tex. A&M U., Kingsville, Tex., 2006—. Contbr. articles to profl. jours. Grant, NSF-CCLI, 1999—2000, Ill. Bd. Higher Edn., 2000, NSF-STEP, 2008—, Robert A. Welch Found., 2009—. Mem.: Am. Chem. Soc. (chair elect, South Tex. Local Sect. 2009—). Office: Tex A&M Univ 900 Univ Blvd Kingsville TX 78363

MOELDERS, CARMEN NICOLE (NICOLE MÖLDERS), science educator, researcher; arrived in US, 2001, naturalized, 2007; d. Hermann Wilhelm and Ilse Hedwig Mölders; m. Gerhard Kramm, Aug. 13, 1992. BS in Meteorology, U. Cologne, Germany, 1983, MS in Meteorology, 1988, PhD in Geophysics, 1992; postgrad., SUNY, Albany, 1989; Habilitation in Meteorology, U. Leipzig, Germany, 1999. Scholar U. Clermont-Ferrand, France, 1985—86; rsch. asst. U. Cologne, 1984—93; rschr. assoc. Fraunhofer Inst., Garmisch-Partenkirchen, Bavaria, Germany, 1993; rsch. assoc., instr., scholar U. Leipzig, Saxonia, Germany, 1994—99, Heisenberg prof. phys. hydrology, 1999—2001; assoc. prof. atmospheric sci. U. Alaska, Fairbanks, 2001—06, chair atmospheric sci. program, 2005—08, prof. atmospheric sci., 2006—, chair dept. atmospheric scis., 2008—; mem. UCAR Nomination Com., 2007—, UCAR U. Relationship Com., 2008—; fin. and budget com. mem. Am. Geophys. Union, 2008—; nomination com. mem. U. Cooperation for Atmosphere Rsch., 2007—, univ. relation com., 2008—. Intern Nuc. Rsch. Ctr. Juelich, Germany, 1986—90; vis scientist Nat. Ctr. Atmospheric Rsch., Boulder, Colo., 2000. Recipient Merit award, Geophys. Inst., U. Alaska, 2003, NSF, 2006, Advising & Mentoring award, Coll. Natural Sci. & Math., 2009, Faculty Bonus award, 2009, Outstanding Grad. Student Mentoring and Adv. award, 2009. Mem.: US Permafrost Assn., Am. Geophys. Union, U. Cooperation for Atmospheric Rsch. (mem. rep. 2005—), Am. Meteorol. Soc., U. Women Assn. Avocation: ballroom dancing. Office: U Alaska Geophysical Inst Coll Natural Sci & Math 903 Koyukuk Dr Fairbanks AK 99775-7320 Office Fax: 907-474-7290. Business E-Mail: cmoelders@alaska.edu.

MOELHMAN, AMY JO, social worker; b. Lafayette, Ind., Mar. 18, 1954; d. Charles and Marian (Young) Moelhman. BS, Ball State U., 1976; MSW, U. Denver, 1979. Lic. clin. social worker, Ind. Social worker Adolescent Crisis Team, Adams County Social Svc., Denver; counselor adolescent boys prog. Pleasant Run Children's Home, Indpls.; group therapist Mothers of Victims of Sexual Abuse, Mid-Town Mental Health, Indpls.; supr. foster care and counseling prog. Children's Bur., Indpls.; mgr. Family Connection Ctr., 1989-90; dir. family programs Vis. Nurse Svc., Indpls., 1990-96; dir. Holy Family Svcs., Cath. Social Svcs., Indpls., 1996—2001; cons. Brown County Family Access Ctr., 1999—; supr. cmty. programs Indpls. Transition Ctr. Casey Family Programs, 2001—03; exec. dir. Ind. Alliance Human Svcs., Indpls., 2004—. Chair Ind. Coalition of Family-based Svcs., 1992-94; co-chair family preservation com. Marion County Stepahead; part-time faculty masters in social work program Ind. U.-Purdue U., Indpls. Contbr. articles to profl. jours. Mem. NASW, Acad. Cert. Social Workers. Home: 818 E 53rd St Indianapolis IN 46220-3104 Office Phone: 317-603-6866. Personal E-mail: amoelhman@aol.com.

MOELING, WALTER GOOS, IV, lawyer; b. Quantico, Va., Feb. 16, 1943; s. Walter Goos III and Dorothy M.; m. Nell Frances Askew, Aug. 27, 1965; children: Charles H., Christine E. BA, Duke U., 1965, JD, 1968. Bar: Ga. 1968. Assoc. Bryan Cave, Atlanta, 1968-75, ptnr., 1975—. Bd. dirs. So. Banking Law and Policy Conf., 1989-96, Southeastern Conf. for Bank Dirs., 1996—, Children's Rehab. Ctr., Atlanta, 1982—, Gatchell Home, Atlanta, 1983-99; bd. dirs. Frazer Ctr., 1989—, chmn. bd. dirs., 1993. Mem. ABA (mem. banking com. 1986—), Ga. C. of C. (bd. dirs. 1998-2000), Ga. Bar Assn., Ga. Bankers Assn. (assoc., chairperson bank counsel sect. 1992-95, bd. dirs. 1998-2000), Cmty. Bankers Assn. (assoc.), Capital City Club, Willow Point Country Club. Democrat. Unitarian Universalist. Avocations: golf, fly fishing. Office: Bryan Cave LLP One Atlantic Ctr 1201 W Peachtree St Atlanta GA 30309-1740 Office Phone: 404-572-6629. Business E-Mail: watt.moeling@bryancave.com.

MOELLEKEN, BRENT RODERICK WILFRED, plastic surgeon; b. Vancouver, BC, Can., Apr. 19, 1960; m. Dayna Devon; 2 children. BA, Purdue U., 1979; MD, Yale U., 1985; postgrad., Harvard U., 1980-81. Diplomate Am. Bd. Surgery, Am. Bd. Plastic Surgery. Intern U. Calif., San Francisco, 1985-86, resident in gen. surgery, 1986-92, rsch. fellow in plastic surgery, 1988-90, resident in plastic surgery, 1992-94; fellow in aesthetic surgery UCLA, 1994-95; pvt. practice Beverly Hills, Calif., 1995—, Santa Barbara, Calif., 1995—. Attending surgeon UCLA Hosp., Cedars-Sinai Hosp., LA; instr. U. Calif. Sch. Medicine, San Francisco, 1992-94, clin. instr. UCLA, 1994-99, assoc. clin. prof., 1999-2007; surgeon ABC-TV Extreme Makeover, Oprah, Discovery Channel, E!, CNN, NBC. Plastic surgery before and after lead surgeon: (TV series) Discovery Health Channel; contbr. several articles to profl. jours.; appeared in: over 60 TV shows. Founder About Face surg. found. Fellow ACS; mem. AMA, AAAS, Am. Soc. Plastic Surgeons, Am. Soc. Aesthetic Plastic Surgery, Calif. Med. Assn., Calif. Soc. Plastic Surgeons, Santa Barbara County Med. Soc., LA County Med. Assn., LA Soc. Plastic Surgeons, LA Surg. Soc., Wound Healing Soc. (founding mem.), Lipoplasty Soc. N.Am. Achievements include invention of Livefill graft; superficial cheek lift operation; hybrid abdominoplasty 360 facelift. Office: 120 S Spalding Dr Ste 340 Beverly Hills CA 90212 Office Phone: 310-273-1001. Office Fax: 310-205-4881. Personal E-mail: drbrent@drbrent.com. Business E-Mail: info@drbrent.com.

MOELLENBERNDT, SCOTT D., principal; b. Denison, Iowa, Dec. 21, 1961; s. James D. Moellenberndt and Patricia L. Riley, Delbert Riley (Stepfather); m. Lori A. Madigan, Mar. 30, 1985; children: Lindsay R., Melissa A., Emily R. BEd, Ariz. State U., Tempe, 1981—83, MEd, 1987—88; EdS, We. Mich. U., Kalamazoo, 1998—2004. Cert. sch. adminstr. Mich., 1996. Tchr., coach Nadaburg Elem. Sch. Dist. #81, Wittmann, Ariz., 1983—87; athletic dir., coach Wickenburg Cmty. Schs., Ariz., 1988—91; prin. Edwardsburg Pub. Schs., Mich., 1991—. Bd. mem. Jr. Achievement Michiana, St. Joseph, Mich., 2003—. Mich. Assn. Mid. Sch. Educators, Lansing, 1999—2003. Recipient Mich. Golden Apple award, Mich. Dept. Edn., 2001—02, Mich. Blue Ribbon Sch. Recognition award, 2002—03; Mich.'s Best award, Mich. Assn. Sch. Bds., 1996—97. Mem.: Mich. Elem. & Mid. Sch. Prins. Assn., St. Peter's Lodge #106. Avocations: golf, travel, exercise. Office: Edwardsburg Pub Schs 69410 Section St Edwardsburg MI 49112 Office Fax: 269-663-6156. Business E-Mail: smoellen@remc11.k12.mi.us.

MOELLER, AUDREY CAROLYN, retired energy company executive, corporate secretary; b. Pitts., May 10, 1935; d. Nicholas William and Edith Tecla (Russman) M. Grad. high sch., Pitts. Legal sec. Equitable Resources Inc., Pitts., 1955-72, asst. corp. sec., 1972-80, corp. sec., 1980-86, v.p., corp. sec., 1986-99; also corp. sec. Equitable Resources Inc. subs.; ret., 1999. Com. mem. United Way Allegheny County, Pa., 1978, United Way Southwestern Pa., 1984. Mem.: Am. Soc. Corp. Secs. (chmn. membership and asst. sec. Pitts. chpt. 1995, treas. 1996, v.p and program chmn. 1997, pres. 1998), Loyal Christian Benefit Assn. (nat. coun. 1993, pres. br. 331 2000—09, nat. auditor 2001—04). Democrat. Roman Catholic. Avocations: singing, golf, travel. Home: 1003 Cherry Hill Dr Presto PA 15142

MOELLER, DADE WILLIAM, environmental engineer, educator; b. Grant, Fla., Feb. 27, 1927; s. Robert A. and Victoria (Bolton) M.; m. Betty Jean Radford, Oct. 7, 1949 (dec. Oct. 1998); children: Garland Radford, Mark Bolton, William Kehne, Matthew Palmer, Elisabeth Anne. BSCE, Ga. Inst. Tech., 1947, MS in Environ. Engring., 1948; PhD in Nuc. Engring., N.C. State U., 1957. Commd. jr. asst. san. engr. USPHS, 1948, advanced through grades to san. engr. dir., 1961; rsch. engr. Los Alamos (N.Mex.) Sci. Lab., 1949-52; staff asst. Radiol. Health Program, Washington, 1952-54; rsch. assoc. Oak Ridge Nat. Lab., 1956-57; chief radiol. health tng. Taft San. Engring. Ctr., Cin., 1957-61; officer charge Northeastern Radiol. Health Lab., Winchester, Mass., 1961-66; assoc. dir. Kresge Ctr. Environ. Health, Harvard Sch. Pub. Health, 1966-83, prof. engring. in environ. health, head dept. environ. health scis., 1968-83, dir. Office of Continuing Edn., 1982-84, assoc. dean continuing edn., 1985-93; environ. cons., 1993—; pres. Dade Moeller & Assocs., Inc., 1993—2003, chmn. bd., 2005—; prof. emeritus Harvard Sch. Pub. Health, 2006—. Cons. radiol. health. Author: (textbook) Environmental Health, 3rd edit., 2005; contbr. articles to profl. jours. Chmn. Am. Bd. Health Physics, 1967-70; mem. com. 4 Internat. Commn. on Radiol. Protection, 1978-85; chmn. nat. air pollution manpower devel. adv. com. U.S. EPA, 1972-75; mem. adv. com. reactor safeguards U.S. NRC, 1973-88, chmn., 1976, chmn. adv. com. nuc. waste, 1988-93; chmn. sci. and tech. rev. panel Office of Civilian Radioactive Waste Mgmt., U.S. Dept. Energy, 2003-. Recipient Disting. Engring. Alumnus award, N.C. State U., 2001, Disting. Prof. Emeritus award of merit, Sch. Pub. Health, Harvard U., 2006, honored, Nat. Coun. Radiation Protection and Measurement, 2008; named to Ga. Inst. Tech. Engring. Hall of Fame, 1999. Fellow Am. Pub. Health Assn., Am. Nuc. Soc.; mem. AAAS, Am. Acad. Environ. Engrs., Nat. Coun. Radiation Protection and Measurements (hon.), NAE, Am. Acad. Health Physics Soc. (pres. 1971-72, Robley D. Evans Commemorative medal 2003, William McAdams Outstanding Svc. award 2005). Home and Office: 257 River Island Rd New Bern NC 28562-3669

MOELLER, JAMES CHARLES, writer, educator; b. Alameda, Calif, June 7, 1954; s. Wayne Jack Bowen and Barbara Ann (Herrick) Moeller; m. Diana E. Moeller, Feb. 18, 1984; children: Jennifer M., Emmeline J., Abigail C., Clara G. BA in Gen. Studies, Univ. of NE, Omaha, NE, 1987, MA, 1997. First Date Res. Sup. First Data Res., Omaha, 1984—87; trainer Marriott Res. Ctr., Omaha, 1989—2003; adj. prof. Grace Univ., Omaha, 2000—02, Iowa Western C.C., Council Bluffs, 2003—, Met. CC, Omaha, 2007—, Buena Vista U., Coun. Buffs, Iowa, 2009—. Publications: jour. Answering the Call: Omaha Jewry and the War Effort, 1941-1945, 1995, Memories of the Jewish Midwest, 1995; author: (jour. article) Memories of the Jewish MW, 1997, The Death of Raymond Yellow Thunder, 2002; author: Jour. of the West, 2002; publications: jour. Nebr. Life, 2003, In Nebr. with Lewis & Clark, 2003; author: (mag. article) Nebr. Life, 2003. Del. Rep. Party of Nebr., Lincoln, Nebr., 1996, Rep. Party of Douglas County, Omaha, 1996. Mil. police US Army, 1977—80, Europe. Recipient deans list, Coll. of Arts & Sci./Univ. Nebr., Omaha, 1987. Mem.: Phi Alpha Theta Honors Soc. Republican. Lutheran. Avocations: deer, golf, auto restoration, Star Trek & Sci-Fi, Indian. Home: 4717 N 131st St Omaha NE 68164 Office: Iowa Western Cmty Coll 2700 College Rd Box 4-C Council Bluffs IA 51503 Office Phone: 712-325-3311. Business E-Mail: jcneriecmoeller@tconl.com.

MOELLER, JOHN, biology professor; b. San Fransisco, May 14, 1964; s. Robert John and Elsie Rose Moeller. PhD, U. Calif., Santa Barbara, 1995. Asst. prof. St Andrews Presbyn. Coll., Laurinburg, NC, 2000—; assoc. prof. Wofford Coll., Spartanburg, SC, 2007—. Office: Biology Dept Wofford Coll 429 N Church St Spartanburg SC 29304 Business E-Mail: moellerjf@wofford.edu.

MOELLER, JON R., consumer products company executive; b. Chgo., June 11, 1964; BS, Cornell Univ., 1986, MBA, 1988. Cost analyst Procter & Gamble Co., Cin., 1988—89, asst. plant acctg. mgr., 1989—90, food & beverage forecaster, 1990—91, sr. fin. analyst juice products, 1991—93, group mgr. salted snacks fin., 1993—94, assoc. dir. salted snacks fin., 1994—96, fin. mgr. & fin. dir. China laundry, Asia salted snacks Guangzhou, China, 1996—99, fin. dir. corp. forecast & analysis Cin., 1999—2002, mgr. fin. global beauty care, feminine care & health care, 2002—05, v.p. fin. & acctg. global beauty care & global health, 2005—07, v.p. fin. & treas., 2007—09, CFO, 2009—. Mem. Cin. Bus. Adv. Council Fed. Reserve Bank Cleve.; mem. Conf. Bd. Council for Treas.; lectr. Johnson Grad. Sch. Mgmt., Cornell Univ. Author: Art in Life, The Discovery of Regional Furniture in China. Mem. bd. ethics City of Covington, Ky.; trustee, mem. exec. com. Visiting Nurse Assn. Office: Procter & Gamble Co 1 Procter & Gamble Plz Cincinnati OH 45202-3393 Mailing: Procter & Gamble Co PO Box 599 Cincinnati OH 45201-0599*

MOELLER, JOSEPH JOHN, JR., university official; b. Jersey City, Feb. 1, 1946; s. Joseph John and Paula (Huneke) M.; m. Linda Lee Recksiek, Aug. 8, 1971. BEng, Stevens Inst. Tech., 1967, MEng, 1969, PhD, 1975. Instr. Stevens Inst. Tech., Hoboken, N.J., 1970-75, asst. prof., 1975-77, dean ednl. devel., 1977-85, mgr. personal computer program, 1983-85, assoc. provost for computing and info. systems, 1985-88, v.p. for info. systems, 1988-92, v.p. for adminstrv. and info. sys., 1992-94, v.p. grad. sch. and rsch., 1994—. Adminstr. N.J. Bus.-Industry-Sci. Edn. Consortium, Hoboken, 1985-92; adminstr. N.J. Intercampus Network, Inc., Steering Com. Adminstr., Hoboken, 1990-93, pres. 1993-97, bd. trustees, 1990—; chmn. Newark Remote Access Ctr., Hoboken, 1988-93. Contbr. articles to profl. jours., chpt. to book. Dir. Hudson County chpt. United Way, 1992-94. Named Outstanding Tchr. of Yr., Stevens Inst. Tech., 1973; honored by N.J. Gen. Assembly for meritorious svc. to edn., 1997. Mem. Assn. Ind. Colls. and Univs. (dir. 1993—), Am. Soc. for Engring. Edn., N.J. Soc. for Info. Mgmt., Sigma Xi, Tau Beta Pi (mem. adv. bd.). Avocations: travel, music.

MOELLER, JOSEPH W., forest products company executive, former chemicals executive; b. Holdenville, Okla., 1943; m. Mary Fellers; children: Suzanne, Sherri, Jason. BS in Bus. Adminstrn., Aarhus U., Denmark; BS in Petroleum Mktg., U. Tulsa, 1966. Various positions Koch Industries, Wichita, Kans., 1966—80, pres., refined products group, 1980—92, pres., petroleum group, 1992—95, pres., Koch Industries Internat., 1995—98, pres., Koch Ventures, Inc. Scottsdale, Ariz., 1998—99, pres., COO Wichita, 1999—2005; pres., CEO Georgia-Pacific Corp., Atlanta, 2005—06, chmn. bd., pres., CEO, 2006, chmn. bd., CEO, 2006—. Bd. dirs. Koch Industries, 1986—2005, Georgia-Pacific Corp., 2005. Bd. trustees U. Tulsa, 1994—98, 2000—. Named Outstanding Alumnus, U. Tulsa, Coll. Bus. Adminstrn., 1995—96, Disting. Alumnus, U. Tulsa, 2004. Mem.: Am. Petroleum Inst. (mem. 25 yr. club), Beta Gamma Sigma (Bus. Achievement award). Avocation: golf. Office: Georgia-Pacific 133 Peachtree St NE Atlanta GA 30303 Office Phone: 404-652-4000.

MOELLER, JUDITH STONE, reading educator, consultant; d. Francis Richard and Helen Mae Bradshaw; m. Roger W. Moeller, Apr. 17, 2004; children: Kristin, Allyson; m. Robert Mark Stone (div.); 1 child, Kelly Stone. BA in Elem. and Spl. Edn., Kean U., 1977, MA in Reading Recovery, 1982; student, So. Conn. State U.; degree in Reading Recovery (hon.), U. Conn., 1995. Spl. edn. tchr. Hopewell Elem., NJ, 1977—79, Pennington Grammar Sch., NJ, 1979—80; reading recovery cons. North Branford Dist., Conn., 1992—95; reading recovery tchr., cons. Sandy Hook Elem., NJ, 1995—99; reading recovery cons., staff developer Bethel Dist., Conn., 1999—2003, Watertown Dist., Conn., 2002—, reading and language arts coord., 2002—08; arts edn. specialist k-12 ACES, 2008—. Cons. in field; mem. Reading Recovery Coun. N. Am., 1995—, Nat. Coun. Tchrs. of English, 1999—. Leader, coord. Brownie/Girl Scouts, Newtown, 1989—90. Mem.: Conn. Assn. Reading, Conn. Reading Rsch. Assn., Assn. Supervision & Curriculum Devel., Internat. Reading Assn. Avocations: travel, arts, theater. Home: PO Box 386 Bethlehem CT 06751 Office: ACES 350 State St North Haven CT 06473 Business E-Mail: jmoelle@aces.org.

MOELLER, PHILIP D., commissioner; b. Chgo., 1960; BA in Polit. Sci., Stanford U., 1983. Staff coord. com. energy, utilities and telecom. Washington State Senate; energy policy advisor to Senator Slade Gordon US Senate, 1997—2000; dir. fed. rels. Capline Corp., Wash.; commr.

Fed. Energy Regulatory Commn. (FERC), Washington, 2006—. Head fed. office Alliance Energy Corp. Office: Fed Energy Regulatory Commn 888 First St NE Washington DC 20426 Office Phone: 202-502-8852. Office Fax: 202-502-6400.*

MOELLERING, JOHN HENRY, aviation maintenance company executive; b. Ft. Wayne, Ind., Feb. 4, 1938; s. Robert Charles and Irene Pauline (Nolde) M.; m. Karla Louise Fritzsche, Dec. 21, 1963; children: John Henry, Matthew C., Ann Elizabeth. BS, U.S. Mil. Acad., 1959; MS, U. Calif., Berkeley, 1962; postgrad., Army Command and Gen. Staff Coll., 1971-72, Army War Coll., 1976-77. Registered profl. engr., La. Commd. 2d lt. U.S. Army, 1959, advanced through grades to lt. gen., 1985; aide de camp Combat Devel. Command, 1961-63; command and staff 24th Inf. Div., Fed. Republic Germany, 1964-67; ops. officer Engr. Group, Vietnam, 1967-68; instr. civil engring., asst. prof. history U.S. Mil. Acad., 1968-71; with Office Army Chief of Staff, Pentagon, 1972-73; White House staff, 1973-74; bn. comdr. 101st Airborne Div., 1974-76; dist. engr. Vicksburg, Miss., 1977-79; exec. to Army Chief of Staff, Pentagon, 1979-81; asst. div. comdr. 9th Inf. Div., Ft. Lewis, Wash., 1981-82; commandant West Point, NY, 1982-84; comdg. gen. Ft. Leonard Wood, Mo., 1984-85; asst. to chmn. Joint Chiefs of Staff, Pentagon, Washington, 1985-87; corp. v.p. Automatic Data Processing, Inc., San Ramon, Calif., 1987-90; pres., chief exec. officer Lear Siegler Mgmt. Svcs. Corp., Oklahoma City, 1990-93; pres. UNC Aviation Svcs., Annapolis, Md., 1993-97; pres., CEO Lear Siegler Svcs., Inc., Annapolis, Md., 1997—2002, JM Assocs., Chapel Hill, NC, 2002—. Bd. dirs. USAA, 1996—, chmn., 2007—; bd. dirs. Lear Sigeler Svcs., Inc., Indsl. Coll. of the Armed Forces; frequent lectr. Nat. Def. U.; mem. adv. bd. Sch. Bus. Adminstrn. The Citadel; adj. faculty Kenan-Flagler bus. sch. U. NC, 2006—. Editor, contbr.: Evolution of Modern Warfare, 1969, Battalion Commanders Speak Out, 1977. Mem. Sci. Def. Bd., The Pentagon; chmn. Class of '59 fund com. U.S. Mil. Acad., 1984—89. Decorated Def. DSM, Army DSM, Legion of Merit, Bronze Star; White House fellow, 1973-74. Mem.: Nat. Def. Indsl. Assn. (bd. dirs.), Phi Kappa Phi. Office: 50130 Manly Chapel Hill NC 27517-8565 Personal E-mail: johnmoellering@hotmail.com.

MOELLERING, ROBERT CHARLES, JR., internist, educator; b. Lafayette, Ind., June 9, 1936; s. Robert Charles and Irene Pauline (Nolde) M.; children: Anne Elizabeth, Robert Charles, Catherine Irene; m. Mary Jane Ferraro, July 11, 1987. BA, Valparaiso U., 1958, DSc, 1980; MD cum laude, Harvard U., 1962; DPH (hon.), St. Elizabeth U., 2005. Diplomate: Am. Bd. Internal Medicine. Intern Mass. Gen. Hosp., Boston, 1962-63, resident, 1963-64, postdoctoral fellow in infectious diseases, 1967-70, resident, 1966-67, mem. infectious disease unit and asst. physician, 1970-76, assoc. physician, 1976-83, hon. physician, 1983—, cons. bacteriology, 1972-87; instr. medicine Harvard U. Med. Sch., Boston, 1970-72, asst. prof., 1972-76, assoc. prof., 1976-80, prof., 1980—; chmn. dept. medicine, physician-in-chief New Eng. Deaconess Hosp., 1981-96; pres., CEO Deaconess Profl. Practice Group, 1995-98; Shields Warren-Mallinckrodt prof. rsch. Harvard U. Med. Sch., Boston, 1981-89, Shields Warren-Mallinckrodt prof. med. rsch., 1989-99, 2005—, Herrman Blumgart prof. medicine, 1999—2005; assoc. physician-in-chief Beth Israel Deaconess Med. Ctr., 1996—98, physician-in-chief, 1998—2005, pres., CEO, Harvard Med. Faculty physician, 1998—2003, chmn. bd. dirs., pres., trustee, 2003—05; vis. prof. infectious diseases Catholic U. Rome, 2003—. Mem. subcom. on susceptibility testing Nat. Com. for Clin. Lab. Standards, 1976-88; mem. subcom. on antimicrobial agts. and chemotherapy, 1978-80; subcom. on antimicrobiol disc. diffusion suceptibility testing, 1980-88; chmn. data safety monitoring bd. Nat. Inst. Allergy and Infections Disease, NIH, 1997—2002; trustee Caregroup, 1998-2005, BIDMC, 1998-2005; bd. dirs. NanoBio Corp., Nabriva Therapeutics Forschungs GmBH. Mem. editl. bd. Antimicrobial Agts. and Chemotherapy, 1977-81, editor, 1981-85, editor-in-chief, 1985-95; editor European Jour. Clin. Microbial Infectious Diseases, 1990-2007; consulting. editor Infectious Disease Clinics N.Am., 1986—; editor Les Infections, 1983; editl. bd. New Eng. Jour. Medicine, 1977-81, European Jour.Clin. Microbiology, 1981—, Jour. Infectious Diseases, 1981-85, 89-93, Infectious Disease Alert, 1981-92, Pharmacotherapy, 1982—, Antimicrobial Agts. Ann., 1984-87, Zentralblatt Fur Bacteriologie, Microbiologie and Hygience, 1984—, Jour. of Infection, 1986—, Innovations, 1986-90, Residents Forum in Internal Medicine, 1988-90, Diagnostic Microbiology and Infectious Disease, 1989-90, Internat. Jour. Antimicrobial Agts., 1990—, Infectious Diseases in Clin. Practice, 1991-92, Jour. Infection and Chemotherapy, 1995—, Clin. Infectious Disease, 1999-2004, jour. Inf.Public Health, 2008-. Served with USPHS, 1964-66. Grantee USPHS, NIH. Master ACP, Am. Acad. Microbiology, Infectious Diseases Soc. Am. (v.p. 1988-89, pres. elect 1989-90, pres. 1990-91, past pres. 1991-92); fellow Royal Coll. Physicians (hon.); mem. Am. Soc. Microbiology, Am. Clin. and Climatol. Assn., Internat. Soc. Chemotherapy, Am. Soc. Clin. Investigation, Assn. Am. Physicians, European Soc. Clin. Microbiology, Am. Fedn. Clin. Rsch., Assn. Profs. Medicine, Roxbury Clin. Records Club, Mass. Med. Soc. (councilor), Brit. Soc. Antimicrobial Chemotherapy, Coun. Biology Editors, Alpha Omega Alpha, Phi Kappa Psi. Home: 49 Longfellow Rd Wellesley MA 02481-5220 Office: Beth Israel Deaconess Med Ctr Dept Medicine 110 Francis St Boston MA 02215-5501 E-mail: rmoeller@bidmc.harvard.edu.

MOELY, BARBARA E., psychologist, educator; b. Prairie du Sac, Wis., July 17, 1940; d. John Arthur and Loretta Ruth (Giese) M.; children: John Jacob Moely Wiener, David Andrew Moely Wiener. Student, Carroll Coll., 1958-60; BA, U. Wis., 1962, MA, 1964; PhD, U. Minn., 1968. Asst. prof. U. Hawaii, Honolulu, 1967-71; rsch. psychologist UCLA, 1971-72; asst. prof. Tulane U., New Orleans, 1972-75, assoc. prof. psychology, 1975-85, prof., 1985—2004, prof. emerita, 2004—, dept. chmn., 1992-96, dir. Office of Svc. Learning, 1999—2004. Contbr. articles to profl. jours. Grantee U.S. Office Edn., Handicapped Pers. Preparation, 1977-80, Tulane U., 1973, 75, 77-78, 83-84, Inst. for Mental Hygiene, City of New Orleans, 1983-84, 2000, Nat. Inst. Edn., 1983-84, La. Edn. Quality Support Fund, 1988-89, 91-92, 96, HUD, 1997-2003, Annenberg, 1997, HHS, 1997-2002, US Dept. Edn., 1999-2002, Fund for Improvement Post-Secondary Edn., 2000-03, Corp. Nat. and Cmty. Svc., 2003-08. Mem. AAUP (v.p. La. conf. 1992-93, sec. 1993-97, v.p. 1998-2000, pres. Tulane 1992-94), Southwestern Soc. Rsch. Human Devel. (pres. 1986-88), Phi Beta Kappa (pres. Alpha chpt. La. 1981-82, sec. 1995-99) Office: Tulane Univ Ctr Pub Svc 327 Gibson Hall New Orleans LA 70118 Business E-Mail: moely@tulane.edu.

MOENSSENS, SANDRA BIRKELBACH, licensed marriage and family therapist, licensed mental health counselor; d. Carl Birkelbach and Diane Pery; life ptnr. Noel Moenssens; children: Nicole, Sophia. BA, Am. U., DC, 1987; MS, Barry U., Orlando, Fla., 2006. Case mgr., child specialist Mental Health Svcs. Orange County, Orlando, 1988—89; admissions officer Orlando Coll., Orlando, Fla., 1990—94; leaders-in-tng. Lake Sumter CC, Leesburg, Fla., 2006—, tchr.; mental health therapist Ctrl. Fla. Mental Health, 2007—09. Cons., presenter in field, 2007—; owner, therapist Counselling For Your Success, 2009—. Author: (book) Testing Success: Learning to Control Your Anxiety. Bd. mem. BETA Ho., Orlando, 1997; sustaining mem. Jr. League Greater Orlando, 1998—99, bd. mem.; bd. cert. prof. counselor Am. Psychotherapy Assn. Mem.: Ctrl. Fla. Assn. Marriage Family Therapists (bd. mem.), Assn. Play Therapy, Am. Assn. Marital & Family Therapists. Avocations: travel, swimming. Personal E-mail: sandra@counselingforyoursuccess.com.

MOERDLER, CHARLES GERARD, lawyer; b. Paris, Nov. 15, 1934; came to the U.S., 1946, naturalized, 1952; s. Herman and Erna Anna (Brandwein) M.; m. Pearl G. Hecht, Dec. 26, 1955; children: Jeffrey Alan, Mark Laurence, Sharon Michele. BA, L.I.U., 1953; JD, Fordham U., 1956. Bar: NY 1956, U.S. Supreme Ct. 1962. Assoc. Cravath, Swaine & Moore, NYC, 1956-65; spl. counsel coms. City of N.Y. and judiciary N.Y. State Assembly, 1960-61; commr. bldgs. City of N.Y., 1966-67; sr. ptnr., chmn. litigation dept. Stroock & Stroock & Lavan, NYC, 1967—. Bd. dirs., gen. counsel, dir. N.Y. Post Co., Inc., 1987-92; cons. housing, urban devel. and real estate to Mayor of N.Y.C., 1967-73; mem. com. on character and fitness of applicants for admission to Bar, Appellate divsn. 1st Dept., N.Y., 1977—, vice chmn. 1998—; mem. disciplinary com. appellate divsn. 1st Dept., N.Y., 1998—2004, 06—, commr. N.Y. State Ins. Fund, 1978-97, vice chmn., 1986-94, chmn., 1995-97; mem. Mayor's Com. on Judiciary, 1994-2001; mem. N.Y.C. Housing Devel. Corp., 1997—; bd. dirs. N.Y.C. Residential Mortgage Ins. Corp., 1997—; chmn. bd. dirs. Bank Austria Creditanstalt LLC, 1999-2001; mem. N.Y.C. Bd. Collective Bargaining, 2000—. Mem. editorial bd. N.Y. Law Jour., 1985—; assoc. editor Fordham Law Rev., 1956. Asst. dir. Rockefeller nat. presdl. campaign com., 1964; adv. bd. Sch. Internat. Affairs Columbia U., 1977-80; bd. govs. L.I.U., 1966, trustee, 1985-91; chmn. Cmty. Planning Bds. 8 and 14, Bronx County, 1977-78; sr. v.p., mem. exec. com. Am. Jewish Congress, 2005—; bd. overseers Jewish Theol. Sem. Am., 1993-95; trustee St. Barnabas Hosp., Bronx, N.Y., 1985—. Recipient Walker Metcalf award L.I. U., 1966, Castle award Manhattanville Coll., 2005. Mem. Am. Bar Assn., N.Y. State Bar Assn., N.Y. County Lawyers Assn., Internat. Bar Assn., Assn. of Bar of City of N.Y., Metro. Club. Home: 7 Rivercrest Rd Bronx NY 10471-1236 Office: Stroock & Stroock & Lavan 180 Maiden Ln New York NY 10038 Office Phone: 212-806-5648. Business E-Mail: cmoerdler@stroock.com.

MOERNER, WILLIAM ESCO, physical chemist, educator; b. Pleasanton, Calif., June 24, 1953; s. William Alfred and Bertha Frances M.; m. Sharon Judith Stein, June 19, 1983; 1 child, Daniel Everett. BS in Physics and Elec. Engring., Washington U., St. Louis, 1975, AB in Math., 1975; MS in Physics, Cornell U., 1978, PhD in Physics, 1982. Langsdorf engring. fellow Washington U., St. Louis, 1971-75; NSF grad. fellow Cornell U., Ithaca, N.Y., 1975-78, rsch. asst., 1978-81; mem. rsch. staff IBM Almaden Rsch. Ctr., San Jose, Calif., 1981-88, mgr. Laser-Materials Interactions, 1988-89, rsch. staff mem. and photorefractive polymer project leader, 1989-95; prof. and disting. chair phys. chemistry and biochemistry U. Calif., San Diego, 1995-98; prof. chemistry Stanford U., Calif., 1998—, Harry S. Mosher prof. chemistry Calif., 2002, prof. applied physics Calif., 2005. Gen. chair Topical Meeting on Persistent Spectral Hole-Burning, 1991; Samuel L. McElvain lectr., dept. chemistry, U. Wis., 1993; Ehrenfest Colloquium lectr., U. Leiden, The Netherlands, 1994; vis. guest prof., lab. for phys. chemistry, Swiss Inst. Tech., Switzerland, 1993-94; A.D. Little Lectr., Dept. Chemsitry, MIT, 1995; Robert Burns Woodward vis. prof. Harvard U., 1997-98. Author, editor: Persistent Spectral Hole-Burning: Science and Applications, 1988, Single Molecule Optical Detection, Imaging, and Spectroscopy, 1997; guest editor, spl. issue, Accounts of Chem. Rsch. on Single Molecules and Atoms, 1996; adv. editor Chemical Physics Letters, Chem. Phys. Chem.; contbr. articles to tech. publs. Tenor San Jose Symphonic Choir, 1983-91, Stanford Symphonic Chorus, 2000—; ofcl. observer Am. Radio Relay League, Santa Clara Valley, Calif., 1987-88, asst. tech. coord., 1990-95, asst. emergency coord., 2000—08. Named Wilkinson Outstanding Young Elec. Engr. award, Nat. Winner Eta Kappa Nu, 1984; recipient IBM Outstanding Technical Achievement awards for Photon-Gated Persistent Spectral Hole-Burning, 1988, Single-Molecule Detection and Spectroscopy, 1992, Earle K. Plyler prize for molecular spectroscopy, 2001; co-recipient Wolf Found. prize in Chemistry, Israel, 2008, Irving Langmuir prize, 2009. Fellow Am. Phys. Soc.(symposium organizer, laser sci. topical group, 1992, March mtg., 1993), Optical Soc. Am.(chair fundamental and applied spectroscopy technical group, 1992-94, gen. chair and founder, adv. chair topical conf. on persistent spectral hole-burning sci. and applications, 1991, 1993, 1994, co-editor), Am. Acad. Arts and Scis., AAAS, Geoffrey Frew Fellow Australian Acad. Scis.,; mem. IEEE (sr. mem., asst. treas. Lasers and Electro-Optics Soc. ann. meeting 1988, 1989, symposium organizer, ann. mtg. 1989), Am. Chem. Soc. (organizer, symposium on chemistry of single molecules, 1997), Biophys. Soc., IBM Amateur Radio Club (pres. 1987-88), Materials Rsch. Soc. (symposium organizer, 1991), Soc. Photo-Optical Instrumentation Engrs. (mem. program com., 1996-98), NAS. Achievements include single molecule detection and spectroscopy being a patentee in strain-sensitive spectral features detection method, device, photorefractive polymers. Office: Dept Chemistry, M/C 5080 Stanford Univ 375 N-S Mall Stanford CA 94305-5080 Office Phone: 650-723-1727. Office Fax: 650-725-0259. Business E-Mail: wmoerner@stanford.edu.

MOESCHL, STANLEY FRANCIS, electronics and electrical engineer, management consultant; b. Cin., Mar. 14, 1931; s. Stanley F. and Matilda F. (Trenkamp) M.; m. Kathleen K. Koebel, Aug. 21, 1954; children: Stanley, Melissa, Deborah, Karen. BSEE, Purdue U., 1957. Engr. Honeywell Space Div., St. Petersberg, Fla., 1957-60, engring. mgr., 1960-69, program mgr., 1969-77; dir. engring. Honeywell Avionics Div., Mpls., 1977-80; v.p. gen. mgr. Honeywell Space Div., St. Petersberg, 1980-82, Honeywell Avionics Div., Mpls., 1982-88; pres. Sundstrand Data Control, Redmond, Wash., 1988-92. Bd. mem. Com. of 100, St. Petersberg, 1980-82, Wash. Round Table, Seattle, 1989-92. Bd. dirs. Jr. Achievement, Mpls., 1983-86, Seattle, 1989-92. With USCG, 1951—54, Korea. Mem.: IEEE, Am. Assn. Individual Investors, Tau Beta Pi, Eta Kappa Nu. Home: 12826 Yacht Club Cir Fort Myers FL 33919-4635 Personal E-mail: sfmoeschl@aol.com.

MOESER, JAMES CHARLES, music educator, former academic administrator; b. Colorado City, Tex., Apr. 3, 1939; s. Charles Victor and Virginia (James) M.; m. Jesse Kaye Edwards, Jan. 26, 1963 (div. July 1984); children: James Christopher, Kathryn Carter; m. Susan Kay Smith Dickerson, June 21, 1987. B.Mus., U. Tex., 1961, M.M., 1964; postgrad. (Fulbright grantee), Hochschule fur Musik, Berlin, 1961-62; D.MA (Univ. fellow), U. Mich., 1966. Chmn. dept. organ, asst. prof. organ U. Kans., 1966-69, assoc. prof., 1969-74, prof., 1974-86, dean Sch. Fine Arts, 1975-86, Carl and Ruth Althaus disting. prof. organ, 1985-86; organist, choirmaster Plymouth Congl. Ch., Lawrence, Kans., 1987-86; organist nat. conf. Music Tchrs. Nat. Assn., Portland, Oreg., 1972, LA, 1974; dean Coll. Arts and Architecture, Pa. State U., State College, 1986—91; v.p., academic affairs & provost U. SC, 1991—96; chancellor U. Nebr., Lincoln, Nebr., 1996—2000, U. NC, Chapel Hill, 2000—08; prof. music Inst. for Arts and Humanities, U. NC, 2008—. Concert organist, on tour, W. Ger., 1977, Lisbon (Portugal) Festival, 1978, 81, recitals for, Musica Festiva da Costa Verde, Portugal, 1981; organist concerts, W. Ger., 1982, 86, 87; world premier Paul Creston's 3d Symphony for Organ and Orchestra, Kennedy Ctr., Washington, 1982. Bd. govs. Josephson Inst. Ethics, 1998-2002; trustee N.C. Symphony Soc., Inc., 2001—09; mem. vis. com. Meml. Ch., Harvard U. Recipient Palmer Christian award U. Mich., 1981, Disting. Alumnus awrd Grad. Sch. U. Tex., 2001; Kent fellow Danforth Found.; Danforth Assoc. Mem. Am. Guild Organists (past dean chpt., nat. dir. student groups 1973-75, nat. chmn. com. on profl. edn. 1983—, chmn. 2d nat. conf. on organ pedagogy 1984, 3d nat. conf. 1986, v.p. 1986—), fellow Am. Acad. Arts & Scis. Episcopalian. Office: Inst Arts and Humanities Campus Box 3322 Chapel Hill NC 27599-3322 Home: 505 N Boundary St Chapel Hill NC 27514 Office Phone: 919-843-2558. E-mail: james_moeser@unc.edu.

MOFFA, JOHN L., media specialist, director; b. Camden, NJ, Jan. 10, 1954; s. Anthony E. and Edith H. Moffa; m. Linda L. Sampaio, Dec. 2, 1978; children: Morgan A., Daniel J., Jesse L. A, New Eng. Inst. Tech., Warwick, RI, 1993. Cert. tech. specialist Infocomm Internat., Va., 2005. Profl. musician The Visitors-Rock Band, San Francisco, 1977—81; equipment operator R. E. Dir. Ship Bldg., Middletown, RI, 1982—88; dir., media svcs. Roger Williams U., Bristol, RI, 1993—. Forensic videography analyst (confidential), RI, 2006—08. Office: Roger Williams Univ 10 Metacom Ave Bristol RI 02809 Office Fax: 401-254-4642. Business E-Mail: jmoffa@rwu.edu.

MOFFAT, CHARLES GORDON, history professor, department chairman; b. Union City, Tenn., Oct. 21, 1940; s. Gordon Steele and Beulah Montgomery Moffat; m. Jerrie Hollingsworth Hollingsworth, June 8, 1963; children: Charles Gordon, Samuel Montgomery. PhD, U. Tenn., Knoxville, 1974. Prof. history, dept. chmn. Carson Newman Coll., Jefferson City, Tenn., 1969—. Fellow, Van Lunen Found., 2002—08. Liberal. Presbyterian. Home: 1308 Russell Gap Rd New Market TN 37820 Office: Carson-Newman Coll Box 71914 Jefferson City TN 37760 Business E-Mail: cmoffat@cn.edu.

MOFFAT, MARYBETH, consulting company executive; b. Pitts., July 25, 1951; d. Herbert Franklin and Florence Grafe (Knerem) M.; m. Brian Francis Soulier, Nov. 30, 1974 (div.). BA, Carroll Coll., Waukesha, Wis., 1973. Indsl. engring. technician Wis. Centrifugal Co., Waukesha, Wisc., 1976-77; indsl. engr. Utility Products, Inc., Milw., 1977-79; mgr. indsl. engring. Bear Automotive (divsn. SPX Corp.), Bangor, Pa., 1980-90; program mgr. Toyota Johnson Controls, Inc. Automotive Systems Group, 1990-2001; pres., CEO Moffat Enterprises, Inc., 2001—. Group home house parent Headwaters Regional Achievement Ctr., Lake Tomahawk, Wis., 1974. Mem. Am. Inst. Indsl. Engrs., MTM Assn. for Standards Rsch., Indsl. Mgmt. Soc., Alpha Gamma Delta (standards chmn. 1971-72). Republican. Methodist. Avocations: skiing, horseback riding, swimming, reading. Personal E-mail: m.moffat@insightbb.com.

MOFFAT, ROBERT W., JR., information technology executive; b. 1956; BS in Economics, Union Coll., 1978; MBA in Mgmt. Info. Sys., Iona Coll. Various mgmt. positions including gen. mgr. personal sys. group, gen. mgr. fin., planning, and bus. sup. IBM Europe IBM Corp., 1978—, sr. v.p., integrated supply chain, 2003—05, sr. v.p. integrated ops., 2005—08, sr. v.p., group exec systems & tech. group, 2008—. IBM ptnr. exec. Bell South, Aetna, Carolina Power & Light, Ingram Micro, Progress Energy, CDW, Insight Direct. Bd. trustees The Manufacturing Inst. Recipient Franz Edelman award, 1999. Office: IBM Corp 1133 Westchester Ave White Plains NY 10604*

MOFFAT SALANT, MARILYN, physical therapist, educator; d. Daniel and Georgina Moffat; m. Robert S. Salant, Sept. 12, 1970 (dec. Jan. 28, 1979); children: Susan Salant Wierdsma, Margaret Earle Vickery, Robert Stephen Salant. BS, Queens Coll., New York, 1962; MA, NY U., NYC, 1964, PhD, 1973; D Phys. Therapy, Mass. Gen. Hosp. Inst. Health Professions, Boston, 2006; DSc (hon.), U. Scis., Phila., 2009. Cert. physical therapy N.Y., 1963. Staff mem. to supr. phys. therapist Inst. of Rehab. Medicine, NYC, 1963—71; pvt. practitioner Locust Valley and NYC, 1964—; instr. Queens Coll., 1967—67, co-dir. inst. devel. human resources, 1967—67; instr. to assoc. prof. N.Y. U., 1967—82; editor Jour. of the Am. Phys. Therapy Assn., 1968—70; adj. faculty U. of Del., Newark, Del., 1975—84; cons. phys. therapist Profl. Exam. Svc., NYC, 1976—83, N.Y.C. Police Dept., 1980—85; prof. N.Y. U., 1982—. Spkr. in field. Mem. The Nat. Inst. of Social Scis., NYC, 1993—2003; mem. benefit com. Helping Hands, Conn., 1998—98, Nassau County Mus. of Fine Arts, Roslyn, NY, 1980—80; mem. Howard A Rusk rehab. medicine campaign com. N.Y. U. Med. Ctr., NYC, 1984—85; mem. benefit com. Planned Parenthood of LI, Hempstead, 1991—91; founding mem. and mem. of adv. bd. Women's Optimum Wellness Now - N.Y. U. Med. Ctr., NYC, 1996—2003; mem. fund raising ball ARC (Nassau County chpt.), Locust Valley, 1998—2003; bd. dirs. and exec. com. World Rehab. Fund, NYC, 1998—; mem. Four Oaks Found., Princeton, NJ, 1979—82; mem. bd. dirs. Children's Village, Dobbs Ferry, NY, 1983—93; mem. exercise rm. com. Piping Rock Club, Locust Valley, 2002—03. Recipient Founder's Day award, N.Y. U., 1973, Sawadi Skulkai Lecture award, Mahidol U., Bangkok, 1986, commendation, Mahidol U., Bangkok Thailand, 1987, Phys. Therapy Assn. of the Republic of China, 1987, Barbara C. White Lecture award, U. of Fla., Gainesville, 1990, Howard A Rusk Humanitarian award, World Rehab. Fund, N.Y.C., 1998, Disting. Faculty award, Dept. of Phys. Therapy, N.Y. U., 2002, Amb. award, Nat. Strength and Conditioning Assn., 2003, Mildred Elson award for internat. leadership in phys. therapy, World Confederation for Phys. Therapy, 2003. Mem.: Chartered Soc. Physiotherapists (Alan Walker Meml. Lectr. award 2005), World Confederation for Phys. Therapy (pres. 2007—), TriAlliance of Rehab. Professionals (chair 1996), Found. for Phys. Therapy (vice chair 1990—91, trustee 1990—91, 2003—), N.Y. Phys. Therapy Assn. (pres. 1978—82, Disting. Svc. award 1994), Am. Phys. Therapy Assn. (exec. coun. sect. for edn. 1980—82, bd. dirs. 1983—89, pres. 1991—97, adv. panel on minority affairs, Highest Commendation bd. dirs. svc. 1986, 1989, Catherine Worthingham fellow 1990, Highest Commendation bd. dirs. svc. 1994, 1997, Diversity 2000 award 1999, R. Charles Harker Policy Maker award 2000, recipient first Marilyn Moffat Leadership award 2003, Mary McMillan Lectr. 2004), Kappa Delta Phi, Pi Lambda Theta. Avocations: travel, golf, reading, bridge, exercise. Home: Ludlam Lane Locust Valley NY 11560 Office: NY U Physical Therapy Dept 4th Floor 380 Second Ave New York NY 10010 Business E-Mail: mm8@nyu.edu.

MOFFATT, HENRY KEITH, science educator; b. Edinburgh, Apr. 12, 1935; s. Frederick Henry and Emmeline Marchant (Fleming) M.; m. Katharine Stiven, Dec. 17, 1960; children: Fergus (dec. 1987), Peter, Hester, Penelope. Attended, George Watson's Coll., Edinburgh, 1943—53, Edinburgh U., 1953—57, BSc Math. Sci. with honors, 1957; BA, Trinity Coll., Cambridge, 1959, PhD in Magnetohydrodynamic Turbulence, 1962; ScD, 1987; DSc (hon.), Inst. Nat. Polytechnique Grenoble, 1987, SUNY, 1990, Edinburgh U., 2001, Eindhoven Tech. U., 2005, Glasgow U., 2007. Fellow, lectr., dir. studies in Math. Trinity Coll., Cambridge, 1961—76, tutor, 1970—74, sr. tutor, 1975—76, fellow, 1980—; asst. lectr., dept. applied math. and theoretical physics Cambridge U., 1961—64, lectr., 1964—76, prof. math. physics, 1980—2002, head dept. applied math. and theoretical physics, 1983—91, emeritus prof., 2002—; prof., chair, applied math. Bristol,

1977—80; vis. professorship Ecole Polytechnique, Palaiseau, 1992—99; dir. Isaac Newton Inst. Math. Sciences, Cambridge, 1996—2001, sr. fellow, 2001—; Blaise Pascal prof., chair Ecole Normale Superieure, Paris, 2001—03, Leverhulme emeritus prof., 2003—05. Trustee, mem. coun. African Inst. for Math. Sciences, Muizenberg, South Africa, 2003; mem. bur. Internat. Union of Theoretical and Applied Mechanics, 1996—2000, pres., 2000—04, v.p., 2004—. Author: Magnetic Field Generation in Electrically Conducting Fluids, 1978; co-editor: Topological Aspects of the Dynamics of Fluids and Plasmas, 1991; editor Jour. Fluid Mechanics, 1966-83; contbr. articles to profl. jours. Officier des Palmes Academiques, France, 1998. Fellow Royal Soc., Nat. Acad. Sci., USA, Royal Soc. Edinburgh; mem. Royal Netherlands Acad. (fgn. mem.), Acad. des Scis. (Paris), Acad. Lincei (Rome), Acad. Europeae. Office: Dept Applied Math and Theoretical Physics U Cambridge Wilberforce Rd Cambridge CB3 OWA England Office Fax: 44 0 1223 765 900. Business E-Mail: H.K.Moffatt@damtp.cam.ac.uk.

MOFFATT, JOYCE ANNE, performing company executive; b. Grand Rapids, Mich., Jan. 3, 1936; d. John Barnard and Ruth Lillian (Pellow) M. BA in Lit., U. Mich., 1957, MA in Theatre, 1960; HHD (hon.), Profl. Sch. Psychology, San Francisco, 1991. Stage mgr., lighting designer Off-Broadway plays; costume, lighting and set designer, stage mgr. stock cos., 1954-62; nat. subscription mgr. Theatre Guild/Am. Theatre Soc., NYC, 1965-67; subscription mgr. Theatre, Inc.-Phoenix Theatre, NYC, 1963-67; cons. NYC Ballet and NYC Opera, 1967-70; asst. house mgr. NY State Theater, 1970-72; dir. ticket sales City Ctr. of Music and Drama, Inc., NYC, 1970-72; prodn. mgr. San Antonio's Symphony/Opera, 1973-75; gen. mgr. San Antonio Symphony/Opera, 1975-76, 55th St. Dance Theater Found., Inc., NYC, 1976-77, Ballet Theatre Found., Inc./Am. Ballet Theatre, NYC, 1977-81; v.p. prodn. Radio City Music Hall Prodns., Inc., NYC, 1981-83; artist-in-residence CCNY, 1981—; propr. mgmt. cons. firm for performing arts NYC, 1983—; exec. dir. San Francisco Ballet Assn., 1987-93; mng. dir. Houston Ballet Assoc., 1993-95; gen. mgr. Chgo. Music and Dance Theater, Inc., 1995—2004. Cons. Ford Found., NY State Coun. on Arts, Kennedy Ctr. Performing Arts., Lensic Performing Arts Ctr., Santa Fe, Bloomington Cultural Dist., Ill., Sheboygan Theater Found., Wis., The Arts Partnership Spartanburg, SC; mem. dance panels NY State Coun. on Arts, 1979-81; mem. panels for Support to Prominent Orgns. and Dance, Calif. Arts Coun., 1988-92. Appointee San Francisco Cultural Affairs Task Force, 1991; chmn. bd. dir. Tex. Inst. Arts in Edn., 1994—; trustee Internat. Alliance of Theatrical Stage Employees Local 16 Pension and Welfare Fund, 1991-94; bd. dir. Rudolf Nureyev Dance Found., Chgo., 1998—. Mem. Assn. Theatrical Press Agts. and Mgrs., Actors Equity Assn., United Scenic Artists Local 829, San Francisco Visitors and Conv. Bur. (bd. dirs.), Argyle Club (San Antonio). Office Phone: 864-457-4575.

MOFFATT, KATY (KATHERINE LOUELLA MOFFATT), musician, lyricist, vocalist; b. Ft. Worth, Nov. 19, 1950; d. Lester Huger and Sue-Jo (Jarrott) M. Student, Sophie Newcomb Coll., 1968, St. John's Coll., 1969-70. Rec. artist Columbia Records, 1975-79, Permian/MCA Records, 1982-84, Enigma Records, LA, 1985, Wrestler Records, LA, 1987-88, Red Moon Records, Switzerland, 1988-93, Philo/Rounder Records, 1989-96, Round Tower Music, U.K., Ireland, Europe, 1993-96, Watermelon Records, U.S., 1994-96, Panther City Records, New Zealand, 1998, Hightone/HMG Records, 1998-2001, Western Jubilee/Dualtone Records, 2001—, Demon/Westside Records, 2002, Fuel Records/Universal Records, 2005, Zeppel in Records, 2008, Floating World Evangeline Records, 2009. Folksinger, Ft. Worth, 1967-68; musician, vocalist, songwriter, rec. artist: (films) Billy Jack, 1970, Hard Country, 1981, The Thing Called Love, 1993; prodn. asst. film, Sta. KIII-TV, Corpus Christi, 1970, audio engr., Sta. KRIS-TV, Corpus Christi, 1970; musician, vocalist in blues band, Corpus Christi, 1970; receptionist, bookkeeping asst., copywriter, announcer, Sta. KFWT, Ft. Worth, 1971, musician, vocalist, songwriter, Denver, 1971-72, on tour, 1973, 75—, Denver, 1974, on tour, 1976-79, European tour, 1977, Can. tour, 1984-85, on tour in Europe, U.S., Can., Asia and Australia, 1985—; albums include Katy, 1976, Kissin' In The California Sun, Am. release, 1977, internat. release, 1978, A Town South of Bakersfield, 1985, Walkin' on the Moon, European release, 1988, U.S. release, 1989, Child Bride, 1990, (duet album with brother Hugh) Dance Me Outside, 1992, (Switzerland only) Indoor Fireworks, 1992, The Greatest Show On Earth A.K.A. The Evangeline Hotel, 1994, Hearts Gone Wild, 1994, Tulare Dust, 1995, (duet album with Kate Brislin) Sleepless Nights, 1996, Midnight Radio, 1996, Angel Town, 1998, Loose Diamond, 1999, Cowboy Girl, 2001, (reissue on CD) Katy/Kissin' in the California Sun, 2002, Up Close & Personal, 2005, Fewer Things, 2008, Trilogy, 2009; songs include The Magic Ring, 1971; Gerry's Song, 1973, Kansas City Morning, 1974, Take Me Back To Texas, 1975, (Waitin' For) The Real Thing, 1975, Didn't We Have Love, 1976, Kissin' in the California Sun, 1977, Walkin' on the Moon, 1989. Recipient Record World Album award, 1976; named one of 4 Top New Female Vocalists, Cashbox Singles Awards, 1976; nominee for Top New Female Vocalist, Acad. Country Music, 1985; winner best singer-songwriter category Ft. Worth Weekly Mag. Music awards, 1997. Mem. AFTRA, SAG, Am. Fedn. Musicians.

MOFFATT, LAURIE NORTON, museum director, curator; BA, Conn. Coll., 1978; MMI, Mus. Mgmt. Inst., U. Calif., Berleley, 1987; MBA, U. Mass., Amherst, 1998. Docent Old Corner House, Stockbridge Hist. Soc., Mass., 1977—78, rschr., asst. to dir., 1978—81; curator Norman Rockwell Mus. at Old Corner House, 1982—86; dir., CEO Norman Rockwell Mus., Stockbridge, 1986—. Contbr. articles to profl. jours. Mem.: Mass. Advocates for Arts, Scis. and Humanities, New England Mus. Assn., Am. Assn. Mus., Assn. Art Mus. Dirs. Office: Norman Rockwell Mus PO Box 308 Stockbridge MA 01262 Office Phone: 413-298-4140. Office Fax: 413-298-4142. E-mail: lmn@nrn.org, lnmoffatt@aol.com.

MOFFETT, DAVID MCKENZIE, former mortgage company executive, retired bank executive; b. Daytona Beach, Fla., Feb. 22, 1952; s. James Denny Jr. and Dorothy McCall (McKenzie) M.; m. Cynthia Ann Daugherty, Aug. 25, 1973 (div. Oct. 1977); m. Katherine Ann Martin, May 26, 1979 (div.); children: Jeffrey Martin, Layne McCall, Hilary Marie; m. Mary M. McCall, Oct. 8, 1988 (div. June 15, 2007); children: James McCall, John McKenzie; m. Lori B. Appelbaum, 2008 BA, Okla. U., 1974; MBA, So. Meth. U., 1975; grad. Stonier Sch. Banking, Rutgers U., 1981. Planning analyst First Nat. Bank & Trust Co., Tulsa, 1975-76, fin. analyst, 1978, v.p., 1978-80, sr. v.p., 1981-86, exec. v.p., 1987—93; CFO Star Banc Corp. (merged with Firstar Corp.), 1993—98; vice chmn., CFO Firstar Corp. (merged with US Bancorp), Milw., 1998—2001, US Bancorp, Mpls., 2001—07; sr. advisor The Carlyle Group, Washington, 2007—08; chmn., CEO Freddie Mac (Fed. Home Loan Mortgage Corp.), McLean, Va., 2008—09, cons., 2009—. Bd. dirs. Bldg. Materials Holding Corp. (BMHC), 2006-; Ebay Inc., 2007-, MBIA Ins. Corp., 2007-08, The E.W. Scripps Inc., 2007-; faculty grad. sch. banking U. Wis., 1986; adj. prof. U. Tulsa; past chmn CFO Council, Fin. Services Roundtable; past fin. services adv., Standard & Poors; mem. CFO Roundtable Bank Adminstrn. Inst. Chgo.; mem. bd. adv. Price Sch. Bus. U. Okla. Bd. dirs. Leadership Tulsa, Inc., 1985-87, Arts & Humanities Council, Tulsa, 1986, Salvation Army, 1986, St. John's Episc. Ch., Tulsa, 1987. Recipient Chmn.'s award bd. dirs. First Nat. Bank, 1980. Mem. Nat. Asset/Liability Mgmt. Assn. (charter), Bank Adminstrn. Inst. (treasury mgmt. com. 1984, investment banking com. 1987). Republican. Epsicopalian. Clubs: Tulsa, Cedar Ridge Country (Tulsa). Avocations: running, golf, skiing, scuba diving, bicycling.*

MOFFETT, JAMES ROBERT, mining executive; b. Houma, La., Aug. 16, 1938; s. Robert E. and Mary G. (Pollack) M.; m. Louise C. Hohmann, June 5, 1960; children: Crystal Louise, James R. BS, U. Tex., 1961; MS, Tulane U., 1963. Cons. geologist oil and gas industry, New Orleans, 1964-69; v.p. founding ptnr. McMoRan Exploration Co., New Orleans, 1969-74; pres., chief exec. officer McMoRan Oil & Gas Co., New Orleans, 1974-81, 81-85, chmn., chief exec. officer, 1985—97, dir., from 1974; vice-chmn. Freeport McMoRan Inc., New Orleans, 1981-85, chmn., chief exec. officer, 1984—97, chmn., 1997—; co-chmn. McMoRan Exploration Co. Mem. Nat. Petroleum Council, Washington, 1979, Commn. on the Future of South, 1986; bd. dirs. La. Energy Nat. PAC, Metairie, La., 1979, World Trade Ctr., New Orleans, Am. Cancer Soc. Greater New Orleans, Bus. Task Force Edn., Inc.; chmn. bd. La. Coun. Fiscal Reform; chmn. bus. coun. New Orleans and River Region, 1985-87. 2nd lt. U.S. Army, 1961-68, capt. Res. ret. Recipient T award Ex Students Assn. U. Tex., 1960, Hornblower Yr. award Pub. Relations Soc. Am., 1986, Vol. Yr. award Urban League Greater New Orleans, 1987; Minnie Stevens Piper Found. scholar U. Tex., 1960, Jacques E. Yenni, S.J. award Loyola U. of New Orleans for Outstanding Community Svc., Jr. Achievement Bus. Hall of Fame award, 1987, Loyola U. of New Orleans' Integritas Vitae award, 1988; named One of Ten Outstanding Persons of 1985 Inst. for Human Understanding, New Orleans Mem. All Am. Wildcatters, New Orleans Geol. Soc., Petroleum Club New Orleans, Greater New Orleans Mktg. Com. (exec. com. 1987), Geology Found U. Tex. (adv. council 1972-85), Devel. bd. U. Tex., La. Ind. producers Royalty Owners Assn. South La. Mid-Contintent Oil Gas Assn. (v.p.), Dinner Steering Com. (Disting, Citizen award 1983, 85 Boy Scouts Am. New Orleans div.), Green Wave Club. Republican. Mailing: Freeport-McMoRan Copper & Gold Co PO Box 61119 New Orleans LA 70161*

MOFFETT, JOE, literature and language professor; PhD, W.Va. U. English prof. Ky. Wesleyan Coll., Owensboro, Ky., 2004—. Author: (book) The Search for Origins in the Twentieth-Century Long Poem, Understanding Charles Wright. Office: Ky Wesleyan Coll 3000 Frederica St Owensboro KY 42301 Business E-Mail: jmoffett@kwc.edu.

MOFFETT, KENNETH LEE, superintendent; b. Mt. Vernon, Wash., May 6, 1935; s. Charles R. and Edith May Moffett; m. Diane Muriel Buckley, July 30, 1966; children: Kendis Charlene, Patrick Charles. BA, Western Wash. State U., 1957; MA, Calif. State U., LA, 1958—60; EdD, U. So. Calif., 1972. Tchr. pub. schs., Inglewood, Calif., 1957—61, 1963—65; asst. prin., 1965—69; prin., 1969—73; tchr. U.S. Dependent Sch., Pirmasens, Fed. Republic Germany, 1961—62; asst. prin. Erlangen, Fed. Republic Germany, 1962—63; asst. supt. Inglewood Sch. Dist., Calif., 1973—76; supt. Lennox Sch. Dist., Calif., 1976—86, ABC Unified Sch. Dist., Cerritos, Calif., 1986—96; interim supt. Oak Pk. Unified Sch. Dist., Calif., 2003, Pleasant Valley Sch. Dist., Calif., 2006—. Mem. adv. bd. Ad Hoc Com. on Mental Health for Tchrs., LA, 1980—81; chmn. scholarship com. Bank of Am., 1979—84; educator in residence Pepperdine U., 1994—2001. Mem. adv. com. LA Area coun. Boy Scouts Am., 1981—83; mem. support group for U. So. Calif., 1978—84; bd. dirs. Centinela Valley Guidance Clinic, Inglewood, 1978—82. Recipient Svc. awards, PTA, Inglewood, 1973, Lennox, 1982; named Nat. Supt. of the Yr., Am. Assn. School Adminstrators, 1994. Mem.: Centinela Valley Trustees and Adminstrs. Assn. (sec.-treas. 1977—78), Centinela Valley Supts. Group (chmn. 1980—84), Assn. Calif. Sch. Adminstrs. (region chmn. 1980—82, Svc. award 1982), Centinela Valley Adminstrs. Assn. (charter pres. 1979—80). Republican. Methodist. Office: Pleasant Valley School Dist 600 Temple Ave Camarillo CA 93010

MOFFETT, MONDRE, musician, educator; b. Tex., July 19, 1953; s. Charles Mack Moffett and Louis Natalie Wilson; m. Diane L. Moffett; children: Marchelle, Marchon, Eustacia, Jessica, Kayla. BA in Music, New Coll. Calif., San Francisco, 1983; MA in Performance & Composition, NYU, 1999; candidate, Boston U., 2006—. With Moffett Family Jazz Band, NYC, 1973—94, trumpeter, 1973—94, Duke Ellington Orch., NYC, 1996—99; music educator NYC Bd. Edn., Bklyn., 1999—2005; band dir. LI U., Bklyn., 2003—05; dir. jazz NC A & T State U., Greensboro, 2005—, asst. prof. music, 2005—. Composer: (symphony) The Wishbone Suite. Mem.: African Am. Jazz Caucus, Am. Soc. Composers and Arrangers, Local 802 Musicians Union, MENC. Home: PO Box 911 Jamestown NC 27282 Office: NC A&T State Univ 1601 E Market St Greensboro NC 27411 Personal E-mail: cmondre@aol.com. Business E-Mail: cmmoffet@ncat.edu.

MOFFITT, CHARLES WILLIAM, owner servello gallery art; b. Altoona, Pa., Mar. 24, 1932; s. Charles William and Beatrice Jeanette (Shellenberger) Moffitt; m. Virginia Colyer, July 26, 1956 (dec.); m. Marianne Foley Potter, May 23, 1980 (dec.); children: Michelle Ann Hunt, Charles William III, Deborah K. Moffitt Russell; m. Mary Lou Herold, Nov. 24, 2001; stepchildren: Sherry Marshall, Heather Clayton, Kristin Pfauser. BA, Pa. State U., 1957. Examiner Pa. R.R., Buffalo, 1957-62; asst. to pres. White Cross Stores, Inc., Monroeville, Pa., 1962-65, sec., 1965-70, v.p. adminstrn., sec., 1970-72; dir. labor relations and legal affairs Revco D.S., Inc., Cleve., 1972-75, asst. v.p. personnel, 1974-75; pres. Fashion Wearhouse, Inc., Altoona, Pa., 1975-87; dir., ptnr. Servello Gallery Art, 2002—. Owner Omega Advt. Co.; pres. Olympus I, Inc., 1980-87; agt. Prin. Fin. Group, 1988-90, Variable Annuity Life Ins. Co., 1990-2001. Co-author: Mincemeat Cartoons, Altoona Mirror Newspaper. Bd. dirs. Bedford Springs Music Festival, 1984-87, Blair County Arts Found., 1987-91, Blair Concert Chorale, 2005-07. Republican. Roman Catholic. Home: RR 5 Box 2324 Altoona PA 16601 Office Phone: 814-946-8922. E-mail: monkmoffitt@hotmail.com.

MOFFITT, ROBERT ALLEN, economics educator; b. Houston, Aug. 10, 1948; s. Herbert Franklin and Evelyn (Sinderson) M. BA, Rice U., 1970; MA, Brown U., 1972, PhD, 1975. Rsch. economist Mathematica, Inc., Princeton, N.J., 1975-78; asst. prof. econs. Rutgers U., New Brunswick, N.J., 1978-83, assoc. prof., 1983-84; assoc. prof. econs. Brown U., Providence, 1984-87, prof., 1987-95; prof. econs. Johns Hopkins U., Balt., 1995—. Editor: Jour. Human Resources, 1985-91, Am. Econ. Review, 2004-; co-editor: Rev. Econs. and Statistics, 1991—1998; contbr. articles to profl. jours. Mem. Am. Econ. Assn., Econometric Soc., Population Assn. Am. Office: Johns Hopkins U Dept Econs Baltimore MD 21218

MOGABGAB, ROSE-WARREN BERRYMAN, academic administrator, writer; b. Richmond, Va., Mar. 13, 1940; d. Maynard Warren Berryman and Bessie Virginia Edwards; m. William Joseph Mogabgab, July 15, 1988 (dec.); children: Robert Mogabgab Berryman, William Joseph Mogabgab Berryman. AB, Randolph-Macon Woman's Coll., 1962. From mgr. lab. Sch. Medicine to rsch. assoc. Tulane U., New Orleans, 1965—81, rsch. assoc. Sch. Medicine, 1981—92; freelance med. writer and cons. New Orleans, 1993—. Presenter in field. Contbr. articles to profl. jours. Recipient 25 Yr. Svc. award, Tulane U. Sch. Medicine, 1980, Civc award, Mayor New Orleans, 1982. Mem.: Lake Ponchartrain Basin Found., Wyes TV, New Orleans Mus. Art, Women for a Better La., Randolph Macon Woman's Coll. Alumnae (pres. New Orleans chpt. 1990—2001), Southern Yacht Club, Kappa Alpha Theta. Avocations: antiques, gardening, travel. Home: 7442 Canal Blvd New Orleans LA 70124 Home Phone: 504-286-1620.

MOGAE, FESTUS GONTEBANYE, former president of Botswana; b. Serowe, Botswana, Aug. 21, 1939; s. Dithabano and Dithunya M.; m. Barbara Gemma Modise, 1968; 3 children. MA, Univs. Oxford and Sussex, UK; LLD (hon.), Howard U., 2009. Planning officer Ministry of Devel. Planning, Botswana, 1968-69, Ministry of Fin. and Devel. Planning, Botswana, 1970-71, sr. planning officer, 1971-72, dir. econ. affairs, 1972-74, permanent sec., 1975-76, min., 1989—; alt. exec. dir. IMF, 1976-78, exec. dir., 1978-80; gov. Bank of Botswana, 1981-82; permanent sec. to pres. Office of Pres. Govt. of Botswana, 1982-89, min. fin. and devel. planning, 1989-92, pres., 1992—2008. Chmn. SADC Coun. of Ministers, 1992—; mem. Global Coalition for Africa, Washington, 1992—; mem. internat. adv. bd. Transparency Internat., Berlin, 1993—; dir. ECCO Cold Stores Ltd., Allied Meat Importers Ltd., DeBeers Botswana Mining Co. (Pty) Ltd., Botswana RST Ltd., Bangwato Concessions Ltd., BCL Sales Ltd., Bank of Botswana; leader of hours Botswana nat. Assembly. Rep. Commonwealth Fund for Tech. Cooperation, 1971—; bd. mem. Water Utilities, Botswana Housing Corp., Botswana Meat Commn., Botswana Meat Commn. (UK) Holdings; m. Botswana Dem. Party Ctrl. Com., chmn. fin. and econ. com., mem. ctrl. com. responsible for Letswapo Region, 1992-95; mem. Parliamentarians for Global Action, Global Coalition for Africa; active Kalahari Conservation Soc.; pres. Botswana Soc. for Deaf, Botswana Soc.; patron Jr. Achievement Botswana. Recipient Presdl. Order of Honour of Botswana, 1989, Officier de l'Order Nationale D'e Cote d'Ivoire, 1979, L'Order Nationale du Mali and the HATAB's Award for outstanding contbn. to Botswana's Tourism Industry, 1997, Global Marketplace award Corp. Coun. on Africa, Houston, 1999, Disting. Achievement award for AIDS leadership in So. Africa, Medunsa Trust, Washington, 2000, Harvard Aids Inst., 2001, Golden Plate award, Acad. Achievement, 2005, Mo Ibrahim Prize for Achievement in African Leadership, 2008. Fellow Botswana Inst. Bankers (hon.); mem. Commonwealth Parliamentary Assn. Avocations: reading, tennis, music.

MOGEL, LEONARD HENRY, writer; b. Bklyn., Oct. 23, 1922; s. Isaac and Shirley (Goldman) M.; m. Ann Vera Levy, Oct. 23, 1949; children: Wendy Lynn, Jane Ellen. BBA, CCNY, 1947. Salesman N.Y. Printing Co., NYC, 1946-48; sales mgr. Pollak Printing Co., NYC, 1948-52; advt. dir. Diners Club, Inc., NYC, 1952-56; pub. Diners Club for Signature and Bravo mags., 1956-67; pres. Leonard Mogel Assos., Inc. (nat. advt. reps.), NYC, 1952-67; prin. owner San Francisco Warriors Profl. Basketball Team, 1963-64; pres. Twenty First Century Comm. Inc., NYC, 1967-72; pub. Cheetah and Weight Watchers mags., 1967-75; dir. Regents Pub. Co. divsn. Simon & Schuster, 1960-67; advt. cons. Harvard Lampoon, 1968; pub. Nat. Lampoon, 1970-86, Liberty mag., 1971-73, Ingenue mag., 1973-75, Heavy Metal mag., 1977-86. Adj. prof. NYU Sch. Continuing Edn., 1973—78; panelist Folio Mag. Pub. Conf., 1975—76. Exec. prodr.: (feature films) Heavy Metal, 1981; author: Everything You Need to Know to Make It in the Magazine Business, 1979, Making It in the Media Professions, 1988, Making It in Advertising, 1993, Making It in Public Relations, 1993, Making It in Broadcasting, 1994, Making It in Book Publishing, 1996, Creating Your Career in Communications, the Media and Entertainment, 1998, The Newspaper: Everything You Need to Know to Make It in the Newspaper Business, 2000, This Business of Broadcasting, 2004. Sponsor Albert Einstein Med. Coll., Birch Wathen Sch., N.Y.C. Served with AUS, 1942-46, CBI. Personal E-mail: mogelpub@aol.com.

MOGEL, WILLIAM ALLEN, lawyer; b. NYC, Mar. 7, 1942; s. Harry H. and Therese M.; m. Judith; children: Elisabeth, Andrew. BA cum laude, Hobart Coll., 1963; LLB, U. Pa., 1966. Bar: D.C. 1967, Md. 1971. Ptnr. Saul Ewing, 2005. Adj. instr. Am. U., Washington, 1982—, editor Regulation Gas Industry. Author: Transportation & Marketing of Natural Gas, 1985, 86, Natural Gas: Current Federal and State Developments, 1987; editor: Natural Gas Yearbook, 1988-92; co-editor: Energy Law & Transactions; emeritus editor-in-chief Energy Law Jour.; contbr. articles to profl. jours. Trustee Hobart Coll., 1983-88. Capt. U.S. Army, 1966-69. Mem. Energy Bar Assn. Home: 5812 Madaket Rd Bethesda MD 20816-3201 Home Phone: 301-642-5804; Office Phone: 202-295-6612. Business E-Mail: wamogel@gmail.com.

MOGG, JIMMY W., gas industry executive; b. Hydro, Okla., 1949; m. Freda Mogg; 2 children. B in Math., Southwestern Okla. State U., 1971; grad. advanced mgmt. program, Harvard U. With gas supply dept. Panhandle Ea. Pipe Line Co., Liberal, Kans., 1973—80; mgr. forcasting and ops. Panhandle Ea., Kansas City, 1980—86; gen. mgr. gas supply Trunkline Gas Co., Houston, 1986—88; gen. mgr. contracts and ops., gas supply Panhandle Ea., Trunkline, 1988; v.p. gas supply Panhandle Ea., Trunkline, Tex. Ea. Transmission Corp., 1989—91; sr. v.p. Panhandle Ea., 1991; pres. Centana Energy Corp., 1992—94; pres., CEO Duke Energy Field Svcs. LP, Denver, NC, 1994—99, chmn., pres., CEO, 1999—2004; group v.p. Duke Energy, Charlotte, NC, 2004—06, chief devel. officer, 2004—06, advisor to chmn., 2006; chmn. DCP Midstream Ptnrs; various exec. and sr. mgmt. positions Pan Energy; chmn. TEPPCO, 2002—05, Wind Holdings, Inc. Chmn. bd. dirs. TEPPCO Ptnrs. LP, 1997—2005; bd. dirs. Bill Barrett Corp., ONEOK Ptnrs., L.P., 2009—. Bd. Trustees Southwestern Oklahoma State U.'s Found., bd. trustees; bd. dirs. Rocky Mountain chpt. Jr. Achievement. Mem.: Gas Processors Assn. (past pres.), Soc. Petroleum Engrs. Office: DCP Midstream Partners 370 17th St Ste 2775 Denver CO 80202 also: First Wind Holdings Inc Ste 305 85 Wells Ave Newton Center MA 02459 Office Phone: 617-964-3340. Office Fax: 617-964-3342.*

MOGGE, HARRIET MORGAN, educational association executive; b. Cleve. d. Russell VanDyke and Grace (Wells) Morgan; m. Robert Arthur Mogge (dec.); 1 child, Linda Jean. BME, Northwestern U.; postgrad., Ill. State U. Instr. piano, Evanston, Ill., 1954-58; instr. elem. music pub. schs., Evanston, 1959; editl. asst. archivist Summy-Birchard Co., Evanston, 1964-66, asst. to editor-in-chief, 1966-67, cons., 1968-69, ednl. dir., 1969-74, also historian, 1973-74; supr. vocal music jr. high sch., Watseka, Ill., 1967-68; asst. dir. profl. programs Music Educators Nat. Conf., Reston, Va., 1974-84, dir. meetings and convs., 1984-94, mgr. direct mktg. svc., 1981-89; sr. cons. Conv. Cons. Svc., 1993—2003, ret., 2003—. Mng. editor Am. Suzuki Jour., 1972-74, Gen. Music Today, 1987-91; mgr. display advt. Model T Times, 1971—2006; vice chair editl. bd. Exposition Mgmt., 1991-93. Active various cmty. drives; parish bd. clerk, United Christian Parish, 2001—08; sec., bd. dirs. Reston Cmty. Orch., 2006-08. Mem. Music Educators Nat. Conf., Am. Choral Dirs. Assn., In and About Chgo., Music Educators Assn. (bd. dirs.1973-74), Suzuki Assn. Ams. (exec. sec. 1972-74, Disting. Svc. award 1996), Internat. Assn. Exposition Mgmt. (cert., mem. edn. com.

1979-88, chmn. edn. com. 1985-87, bd. liaison edn. com. 1987-88, bd. dirs. Washington chpt. 1983-85, nat. bd. dirs. 1986-91, nat. v.p. 1989, nat. pres. 1990, Disting. Svc. award 1996), Bus. and Profl. Women's Club Watseka (bd. dirs. 1968-70), Antique Automobile Club (registrar ann. meeting 1961-86), Model T Ford Club Internat. (v.p. 1971-72, 76-77, pres. 1981, treas. 1983-87, bd. dirs. 1971-87), Mu Phi Epsilon, Kappa Delta (province pres. 1960-66, 72-76, regional chpts. dir. 1976-78, nat. dir. scholarship 1981-84). Republican. Presbyterian. Home and Office: 1919A Villaridge Dr Reston VA 20191-4824 Office Phone: 703-201-1281.

MOGHADAM, VALENTINE M., sociology professor; m. Karshenas Massoud. PhD, Am. U., Wash., 1986. Sr. rschr. UN U., Wider Inst., Helsinki, Finland, 1990—95; dir. women's studies Ill. State U., Normal, 1996—2005; chief gender equality and devel. UNESCO, Paris, 2004—06; dir. women's studies and prof. sociology Purdue U., West Lafayette, Ind., 2007—. Cons. in fields, NYC, 1996—96. Contbr. to numerous profl. jours. Mem. and former pres. Assn. Mid. East Women's Studies, LA, 1993—. Recipient Victoria Schuck award, Am. Polit. Sci. Assn., 2005; Pub. Policy Fellowship, Woodrow Wilson Internat. Ctr. Scholars, 2001—02. Mem.: Internat. Sociol. Assn., Am. Sociol. Assn. (rep. internat. sociol. assn. 2006—). Avocations: reading, music, jogging, aerobics, movies. Office: Purdue Univ 100 N University St West Lafayette IN 47907-2098 Business E-Mail: moghadam@purdue.edu.

MOGHIMZADEH, MAHMOOD, economics professor; PhD in Economics, West Va. U., Morgantown, 1982. Assoc. prof. PVCC, Charlottesville, Va., 2001—. Personal E-mail: mmoghimzadeh@yahoo.com.

MOGILNICKI, ERIC J., legislative staff member; b. New Bedford, Mass., Sept. 5, 1960; s. Robert and Georgette Mogilnicki; m. Peggy Dotzel; children: Annie, Sam. BA, Yale U., New Haven, 1982, JD, 1986. Legis. asst., Rep. Gerry Studds US House of Reps., Washington; asst. atty. gen., chief elections counsel State of Mass, Boston, 1987—91; atty. Wilmer, Cutler, Pickering, Hale & Dorr Law Firm, Washington, 1991—2006; chief of staff to Senator Edward Kennedy US Senate, Washington, 2006—09. Democrat.*

MOGK, JOHN EDWARD, law educator, association executive, consultant; b. Detroit, Feb. 10, 1939; s. Clifford Anthony and Evelyn Lenore (Paselk) M.; m. Lylas Heidi Good, Aug. 23, 1964; children: Marja, Tenley, Matthew. BBA, U. Mich., 1961, JD with distinction, 1964; diploma in comparative law, U. Stockholm, 1965. Bar: N.Y. 1966, Mich. 1970. Assoc. atty. Shearman & Sterling, NYC, 1964-68; mem. faculty Wayne State U. Sch. Law, 1968—, dir. grad. studies, 1990-95. Pres. MERRA Rsch. Corp., 1974-94; cons. econ. and urban devel., arbitrator; vis. prof. U. Utrecht, The Netherlands, 2000. Editor Michigan International Lawyer and Utilities Law Rev.; contbr. articles to profl. jours. Chmn. Mich. TOP Task Force, 1972; vice chmn. Mich. Constrn. Code Commn., 1973; mem. exec. com. Southeastern Mich. Coun. Govts., 1970; chmn. Detroit Sch. Boundary Commn., 1970, Downtown Detroit Vacant Bldg. Com., 1991-93; mem. Detroit Bd. Edn., 1970; mgr. Detroit Empowerment Zone Proposal, 1994; project exec. New Detroit Stadium, 1995; pres. Habitat for Humanity Detroit, 1999-2006; chmn. Mich. Coun. Labor and Econ. Health, 2009. Named Outstanding Wayne State U. Assoc. Prof., 1971, Outstanding Wayne Law Sch. Prof., 1977, 83, 93, 97, 2003, Outstanding Young Man in Detroit, 1972, One of Ten Outstanding Young Men in U.S., 1973, One of Four Outstanding Vols. in U.S., 1974; recipient Presdl. citation Wayne State U., 1977, State of Mich., 1988, 94; Am.-Scandinavian fellow, 1965; vis. fellow U. Warwick, Eng., 1985-86. Mem. ABA, Mich. Bar Assn. (Outstanding Achievement award Internat. Law Sect. 2001). Home: 1000 Yorkshire Rd Grosse Pointe Park MI 48230-1432

MOGLIA, JOSEPH H., brokerage house executive; b. Apr. 1, 1949; m. Amy Jardine; 4 children from previous marriage. BA, Fordham U., 1971; MA, U. Del., 1974. Def. coord. Dartmouth Coll. football team, 1981—83; with Merrill Lynch & Co., Inc., 1983—97, head global fixed income inst. sales, head mcpl. div., sr. v.p., head investment performance & product group, 1997—2001; CEO TD Ameritrade Holding Corp., Omaha, 2001—08, non exec. chmn., 2008—. Bd. dirs. TD Ameritrade Holding Corp., 2001—. Author: Perimeter Attack Offense, 1981. Bd. dirs. Creighton Univ., Nat. Italian Am. Found., 2005—, AXA Fin., 2002—. Office: TD Ameritrade Holding Corp 4211 S 102nd St Omaha NE 68127-1031 Mailing: PO Box 2760 Omaha NE 68103-2760 Office Phone: 402-331-2744. Business E-Mail: jmoglia@ameritrade.com.

MOGOL, ALAN JAY, lawyer; b. Balt., July 29, 1946; s. Jesse and Kitty (Stutman) m.; m. Ellen Epstein, June 19, 1969; children: Andrew Stephen, Jonathan David. BA with distinction, U. Va., 1968, JD, 1971. Bar: Md. 1972, U.S. Dist. Ct. Md. 1972, U.S. Ct. Appeals (4th cir.) 1972, U.S. Supreme Ct. 1978. Assoc. Ober, Kaler, Grimes & Shriver, Balt., 1971-77, ptnr., 1978—. Chmn. comml. finance Ober, Kaler, Grimes & Shriver, Balt., 1980-81, 84-85, 91-97, 2002—, chmn. comml. Fin. practice group, 1998—; lectr. on continuing edn. Md. Inst. Continuing Profl. Edn. for Lawyers, 1988-92, trustee, 1990-93; spkr. seminars Nat. Health Lawyers Assn., Washington, 1986-87, Rocky Mountain Mgmt., Denver, 1987, Med. Imaging Expo., 1995, Washington, 1995. Co-author: In Structuring the Secured Loan Agreement, 1991, Commercial Finance Guide, 1997, Equipment Leasing, 2007; contbr. articles to profl. jours. and local newspapers. Bd. dirs. Transitional Living Coun., Balt., 1972-92; bd. trustees Md. Inst. of Continuing Profl. Edn. for Lawyers, 1990-93. Fellow Md. Bar Found., Inc., Am. Bar Found., Inc.; mem. ABA, Equipment Leasing and Fin. Assn. (lawyers com. 1986-89, program com. 1986-91, speaker seminars), Md. Bar Assn. (uniform comml. code com. 1988—, chmn. 1991-93, vice chmn. bus. sect. 1995-96, chmn. bus. sect. 1996-97). Avocation: tennis. Office: Ober Kaler Grimes & Shriver 120 E Baltimore St Ste 800 Baltimore MD 21202-1643 E-mail: ajmogol@ober.com.

MOHAGHEGHI, ALI, chemical engineer; b. Zanjan, Iran, Apr. 4, 1947; m. Manijeh Taherynia. PhD, Colo. Sch. Mines, Golden, 1985. Instr. Sharif U. Tech., Tehran, Iran, 1970—76, rsch. staff, 1970—76; sr. biochem. engr. Nat. Renewable Energy Lab., Golden, 1983—. Mem.: Jour. Indsl. Microbiology & Letters Applied Microbiology (editor 1990—2008), Soc. Indsl. Microbiology. Office: Nat Renewable Energy Lab 1617 Cole Blvd Golden CO 80401

MOHAIDEEN, A. HASSAN, surgeon, consultant, health products executive; b. Ramanathapuram, India, Aug. 14, 1940; s. Abdul and Mariam (Pitchai) Kader; m. Zarina M. Meera, May 30, 1965 (dec. July 1986); children: Ahamed, Mariam, Najeeba, Azeema; m. Laurie J. Kucich, June 23, 1989; children: Yasmin Sara, Leila Jahan. MD, U. Madras, India, 1965; MBA, Wagner Coll., 1996. Diplomate Am. Bd. Surgery, Am. Bd. Quality Assurance and Utilization; cert. physician exec. Am. Coll. Physician Execs. Intern Govt. Stanley Hosp., Madras, 1965-66, Good Samaritan Hosp., West Islip, NY, 1967-68; resident in gen. and vascular surgery L.I. Coll. Hosp., Bklyn., 1968-73, asst. attending surgeon, 1973-76, assoc. attending surgeon, 1976-78, attending surgeon, 1978—, chief divsn. vascular surgery, 1980-93, dir. vascular lab., 1981-93; v.p. Bklyn.-Caledonian Hosp. Ctr. (affiliate of NYU), 1994-95; sr. v.p., managed care and exec. vice-chmn. dept. surgery The Bklyn.-Caledonian Hosp. Ctr. (affiliate of NYU), 1995-96; pres., CEO, Health Plan Systems, Inc., Rochelle Park, NJ, 2001—. Asst. surgeon G.H.Q. Hosp., Ramnad, India, 1966-67; assoc. attending surgeon Meth. Hosp., Bklyn., 1982-90, attending surgeon, 1991-97; asst. attending surgeon Bklyn. Caledonian Med. Ctr., 1973-85, mem. courtesy staff, 1985-94, 97—, attending surgeon, 1994-96; attending surgeon Victory Meml. Hosp., Bklyn., 1982—; vis. physician Kings County Hosp. Ctr., Bklyn., 1973-94; clin. instr. in surgery Downstate Med. Ctr., SUNY, Bklyn., 1973-78, clin. asst. prof. surgery, 1978—; mem. exec. com. of med. staff L.I. Coll. Hosp., Bklyn., 1979-93, treas. med. staff, 1982-85, pres., 1985-87, med. chmn. Guild Ball com., 1981, mem. quality assurance com. dept. surgery, 1988-94, chmn. credentials com., 1990-93, quality assurance and risk mgmt. com., 1990-93; bd. dirs. Aetna Health Plans of N.Y., AIDS adv. com., 1987-93, stds. com., 1986-94, quality assurance com.; bd. dirs. Aetna-U.S. Healthcare, 1997; mem. credentials com. Prucare, 1988-92; sr. v.p. managed care Bklyn. Hosp., 1995-96; mem. quality mgmt. com. Oxford Health Plans, 1995-2002; mem. quality improvement com. Chubb Health, N.Y., 1994-96, Cigna (HealthSource), 1997-2003; mem. credentials com. United Healthcare, 1997—; exec. dir. Mayan Health, PPO, Atlantic Med. Assocs. IPA; pres. Health Plan Sys., Inc. Contbr. articles to med. jours. Fellow ACS (com. on Long Island dist. applicants, 1988-99, bd. dirs. Bklyn.-L.I. chpt.), Royal Coll. Physicians and Surgeons Can. (cert.), Internat. Coll. Surgeons; mem. AMA (Physician's Recognition award), AAAS, Am. Coll. Physician Execs., Med. Soc. of State of N.Y., N.Y. State Soc. of Surgeons, N.Y. Acad. of Scis., Med. Soc. of County of Kings (mediation com., 1979-85), Bklyn. Surg. Soc., Soc. for Non-Invasive Vascular Technicians, Kings Physicians I.P.A. (pres./med. dir., 1985-95), Bklyn. Physicians I.P.A. (v.p., 1985-96, pres.). Avocations: photography, computers, walking. Home Phone: 718-816-8866; Office Phone: 201-556-9430. E-mail: hassan@mohaideen.com.

MOHAJER IRAVANI, BAHARAK, engineer; b. Tehran, Tehran, Iran, Sept. 8, 1975; d. Parviz Mohajer Iravani and Hilda Kayvanmahd; m. Mahmoud Amin EL Sabbagh, Jan. 16, 2008. BS, Sharif U. Tech., Tehran, Iran, 1998; MS, AmirKabir U. Tech., Iran, 2001, U. Md., Coll. Pk., 2004, PhD, 2007. Grad. rsch. asst. U. Amirkabir, Tehran, Iran, 1998—2001; grad. rsch., tchg. asst. U. Md., Coll. Pk., 2001—06, grad. rsch. asst., 2007; vis. scholar U. Waterloo, Ontario, Canada, 2006—07; sr. rf engr. Rayspan Corp., San Diego, Md., 2008—. Contbr. articles to profl. pubs. Mem.: IEEE, IEEE Woman in Engring. Achievements include design and development of electromagnetic bandgap structures applicable in IC packages; research in the development of simple equivalent circuit model to predict the location of bandgap in the procedure of design of planar EBG structures. Avocations: dance, travel. Personal E-mail: bmohajer@ieee.org.

MOHAMADI, MASOUD, retired surgeon; b. Tehran, Iran, June 8, 1937; arrived in U.S., 1962; children: Hooman, Michele, Robert; m. Soheila Emami, 1990. MD, U. Tehran, 1961. Diplomate Am. Bd. Surgery. Intern Coney Island Hosp., NYC, 1962-63; resident in gen. surgery Maimonides Med. Ctr., Bklyn., 1963-67; fellow in vasc. surgery SUNY, Bklyn., 1967-68. Mem. AMA. Personal E-mail: mmohamadi@tampabay.rr.com.

MOHAMED, JABARI, language educator; b. Ait Zoli Kelaa Mgouna, Ourzazate, Morocco, Apr. 10, 1971; MBA, Nat. U., La Jolla San Diego, 2006. Lectr. arabic Palomar Coll., San Marcos, Calif., 2005—. Office: Palomar Cmty Coll 1140 West Mission Rd San Marcos CA 92069 Home: 4462 Estada Dr Oceanside CA 92057-6637 Office Fax: 760-729-8219. Business E-Mail: mjabari@palomar.edu.

MOHAMED BEN-RUWIN, MOHAMED A., political science professor; m. Amal M. Abouhgar, Aug. 21, 1987; children: Zakaria Ben-Ruwin, Yusef Ben-Ruwin. PhD, U. N. Tex., Denton, 1993. Dept. chair Tex. A&M Internat. U., Laredo, 2007—08, prof., 1993—. Office: Tex A&M Internat Univ 5201 University Blvd Laredo TX 78041 Office Fax: 956-326-2464. Business E-Mail: mbenruwin@tamiu.edu.

MOHAMMAD, ASIF IQBAL, algorithms engineer, researcher; s. Iqbal Mohammad and Ameerunnisa Begum. BS in Elec. Engring., Osmania U., Hyderabad, India, 2001; MS in Elec. Engring., U. Mo., Rolla, 2003, PhD, 2007. Rsch. asst. U. Mo., Rolla, 2001—07; rsch. intern. Microsoft Rsch., Redmond, Wash., 2006; dsp engr. Aware, Inc, Bedford, Mass., 2007; sr. systems engr. Qualcomm, San Diego, 2007—. Contbr. over 12 articles to profl. jours. Recipient Best Paper award, IEEE Internat. Conf. on Multimedia and Expo, 2007. Mem.: IEEE (assoc-.mem.). Achievements include patents pending for providing true full-duplex echo-free communication over mobile phones and teleconferencing devices.

MOHAMMADPOUR VELNI, JAVAD, research scientist; b. Gonbadekavoos, Golestan, Iran, Oct. 30, 1977; m. Mona Meisami-Azad. BS in Elec. Engring., Sharif U. Tech., Tehran, 1999; MS in Elec. Engring., U. Tehran, 2002; PhD in Mech. Engring., U. Houston, Tex., 2007. Process control engr. Tavaan Azmayan Co., Tehran, Iran, 2000—02; rsch. assoc. Concordia U., Montreal, Que., Canada, 2003—04, U. Houston, 2008, rsch. asst., 2004—07, asst. prof. mech. engring., 2008—; rsch. controls engr. Cummins Inc., Columbus, Ind., 2005—06. Recipient Instrumentation, Sys. and Automation award, 2006; Presdl. fellowship, U. houston, 2004—06. Mem.: SIAM, IEEE, Sigma Xi. Office: U Houston 4800 Calhoun Rd Engring Bldg 1 Houston TX 77204 Business E-Mail: jmohammadpour@uh.edu.

MOHAMMED, HAMISH, epidemiologist, educator; BSc, Morehouse Coll., Atlanta, 2000; MPH, Tulane U. Sch. Pub. Health & Tropical Medicine, New Orleans, LA, 2002; PhD, 2005. Epidemic intelligence svc. officer Ctrs. fDisease Control & Prevention Dengue Br., San Juan, 2007, epidemiologist, 2007—08; asst. prof. Ross U. Sch. Vet. Medicine, Basseterre, 2008—. Office: Ross Univ Sch Vet Med PO Box 334 Basseterre Saint Kitts and Nevis

MOHAMMED, NAZR, professional basketball player; b. Sept. 5, 1977; m. Mandy Mohammed; children: Amani, Nasir. Student in bus. mgmt., U. Ky., Lexington, 1995—99. Center Phila. 76ers, Pa., 1999—2001, Atlanta Hawks, Ga., 2001—03, NY Knicks, NY, 2003—04, San Antonio Spurs, Tex., 2004—06, Detroit Pistons, 2006—07, Charlotte Bobcats, 2007—. Achievements include member of NCAA Final Four championship winning University of Kentucky Wildcats, 1996, 1998; member of NBA Finals championship winning San Antonio Spurs, 2005. Office: Charlotte Bobcats 333 E Trade St Charlotte NC 28202*

MOHAN, JOHN J., lawyer; b. St. Louis, May 22, 1945; s. John Joseph and Virginia Loretta (Durkin) M.; m. Elaine Bronwyn Lipe, May 29, 1982; children: Bryn Elizabeth, John Burke. BS Indsl. Engring., St. Louis U., Sch. Engring. and Earth Scis., 1967; JD, St. Louis U., 1971. Bar: Mo. 1971, Ill. 1971, U.S. Dist. Ct. (we. dist.) Mo. 1971, U.S. Dist. Ct. (ea. dist.) Mo. 1980, U.S. Dist. Ct. (so. dist.) Ill. 1981, U.S. Ct. Appeals (8th cir.) 1987. Asst. prosecuting atty. St. Louis County, 1971-72; asst. cir. atty. St. Louis Cir. Atty's. Office, 1972-74; spl. asst. state's atty. St. Clair County Atty's. Office, Belleville, Ill., 1974—; assoc. Lashley, Caruthers, Theis, Rava & Hamel, St. Louis, 1979-80; ptnr. Schreiber, Tueth & Mohan, Clayton, Mo., 1981-83, Danis, Reid, Murphy, Tobben, Schreiber & Mohan, Ladue, Mo., 1983-87, Hinshaw & Culbertson, St. Louis, 1987-97, Blackwell, Sanders, Peper, Martin, St. Louis, 1998-2000, Tueth, Keeney, Cooper, Mohan & Jackstadt, P.C., 2000—; mcpl. judge City Wildwood, Mo., 2004—07. Mem. U. Mo. Law Sch. Found. Scholarship. Mem. ABA, Am. Arbitration Assn. (cert. mediator, arbitrator 1988—), Ill. State Bar Assn., Mo. Bar, Bar Assn. Met. St. Louis, St. Clair County Bar, St. Louis County Bar, Def. Rsch. Inst., Mo. Orgn. Def. Lawyers, Pinnacle Arbitration and Mediation Svcs. (cert. mediator, arbitrator 1997—), Phi Delta Phi. Home: 529 Big Horn Basin Ct Wildwood MO 63011-4818 Office: Tueth Keeney Cooper Mohan Jackstadt PC Ste 600 34 N Meramec Clayton MO 63105

MOHAN, JYOTI, history professor; b. Nagpur, Maharashtra, India, Mar. 7, 1976; d. Mohan Srinivasan and Kamala Mohan; m. Mahesh Valiya Naduvath, Jan. 21, 2002; children: Nandika Mahesh, Arjun Mahesh. MA, Delhi U., 1998, U. Md., Coll. Pk., 2000, PhD, 2009. Instr. U. Md., 2003—; lectr. Morgan State U., Balt., 2006—. Editor H-Net.org. Contbr. articles to profl. jours.

MOHAN, RAM VASU, engineering educator, researcher; MS in Mech. Engring., W.Va. U., Morgantown, 1987; MS, U. Ill., Urbana Champaign, 1990; PhD, U. Minn., Twin Cities, 1997. Assoc. prof. NC A&T State U., Greensboro, 2003—. Contbr. articles to sci. and engring. jours. Mem.: Am. Soc. Mech. Engrs. (assoc.; chair, materials processing tech. com. 2005—). Office: NC A&T State Univ 1601 E Market St Greensboro NC 27411

MOHAN, SUBBURAMAN, biochemist, educator; b. Salem, India, June 15, 1951; came to U.S., 1979; s. Subburama and Pavayee Gounder; children: Shilpa, Ashwin. BSc, Bangalore U., India, 1972, MSc, 1974, PhD, 1978. CSIR rsch. fellow Bangalore U., 1974-78, CSIR postdoctoral fellow, 1978-79; Am. Heart Assn. rsch. fellow U. So. Calif., LA, 1979-80; lectr., rsch. assoc. Calif. Poly. U., Pomona, 1980-82; asst. rsch. prof. Loma Linda (Calif.) U., 1982-87, assoc. rsch. prof., 1987-91, rsch. prof., 1991—, asst. dir. molecular genetics divsn., 2000—; dir. Musculo Skeletal Disease Ctr., 2008—. Lectr. in field; presenter symposia. Mem. editl. bd. Endocrinology, 1993—96, Jour. Bone Mineral Rsch., Faculty 1000 Biology; contbr. numerous articles to sci. publs. Mem. Am. Soc. Biochemistry and Molecular Biology, Am. Soc. Cell Biology, Am. Soc. Clin. Rsch., Am. Soc. Bone and Mineral Rsch., Sigma Xi (Rsch. Merit award Loma Linda chpt. 1990). Avocations: tennis, hiking, reading. Office: Pettis Vets Hosp 151 11201 Benton St Loma Linda CA 92357-1000 Office Phone: 909-825-7084. E-mail: subburaman.mohan@va.gov.

MOHAN, TUNGESH NATH, television and film producer, film educator; b. Lucknow, India, Oct. 30, 1949; arrived in U.S., 1979; s. Bhola Shambu and Saraswati P. (Devi) Nath; m. Annette Gonsalves Mohan; 1 child, Lathika. BS, Kalyani U., India, 1969; diploma in Cinema, Film and TV Inst. India, Poona, 1972; MA, Andrews U., 1980. Prodr. Bombay TV, 1972-75, 77-79; asst. prof. Film and TV Inst. India, Poona, 1975-77; TV prodr. 700 Club, Virginia Beach, Va., 1980-82; prodr. spl. projects Christian Broadcasting Network, Virginia Beach, 1982-86, Christian Broadcasting Network Cable Prodns., Inc., Virginia Beach, 1986-87; dir. Internat. CBN Prodrs. Group, 1987-89, Internat. NorthStar Entertainment Group, LA, 1989-92; mgr. Adventist Comm. Network, Silver Spring, Md., 1992-93; pres. TriAngel Media Corp., Thousand Oaks, Calif., 1992-94; dir. Digital Video Ctr., Samford U., Birmingham, Ala., 2005—09. Adj. prof. Film and TV Inst. India, Poona, 1975—79, Spicer Coll., Poona, 1975—79, Hampton U., Va., 1980—92; pres. Prodrs. Unit One, Virginia Beach, 1982—, L.I.F.E. Inc., 1993—; cons. Global Comm. Assocs., Virginia Beach, 1987—88, Global TV Syndication, 1998—; dir. Telecom. Ctr., Huntsville, Ala., 1998—2000. Prodr., dir.: (films) Even So, 1972; Dishantar, 1975 (cert. Proficiency, 1975); Raktajeevee, 1977 (Golden Lion award, 1977); (documentaries) Afghanistan: Under the Iron Claw, 1982; Here I Stand, 2001; In the Footsteps of Martin Luther, 2001; Revolution of Conscience, 2001; A Heart Set Free!, 2007; prodr., dir., writer: (films) U-Turn, 1973 (Garima award, 1973); exec. prodr.: Stand at Ease, 1989—90, A Father of Preachers, 2001; co-exec. prodr.: Rin Tin Tin K-9 Cop, 1988—89; prodr.: Touching the Supernatural, 1992, Midnight Cry, 1994, Master Control, 1994, The Way We Were, 1995, Bought at a Price, 1996, Hanged on a Twisted Cross, 1996 (Chris award for best film, Bronze medal for screenplay Columbus Film Festival, 1996), Inn Keeper, 1996, The Invitation, 1997, The Gift, 1997 (Bronze Plaque for 2d pl. Columbus Internat. Film Fest, 1997); prodr., dir.: Reaalizing the Vision, 2001; The Hymnmaker, 2002; For One English Officer, 2002; The Dawning, 2002; Thank You, Mr. Hodges, 2003; The Invitation, 2003; Truth to Tell, 2003; Christianity & Islam: A Dialogue, 2004; The 51st State, 2006; Born With a Wooden Spoon, 2006; Life is Calling, 2007; Called, 2007; Truth Matters, 2008; A Heart Set Free, 2008. Mem.: NATAS, Dirs. Guild Am., Writers Guild Am., Lions. Mem. Seventh-Day Adventist. Avocation: Avocations: collecting stamps, music, camping, travel, tennis. Home Phone: 256-852-4054; Office Phone: 205-422-6798. Personal E-mail: lifeincva@aol.com.

MOHANAKUMAR, THALACHALLOUR, medical educator, director; m. Tattamangalam Chandrika; children: Sunil Kumar, Anil Kumar. PhD, Duke U., Durham, NC, 1974. Cert. Am. Soc. Histocompatibility & Immunogenetics, lab. dir. Am. Bd. Bioanalysis, 1993, Am. Bd. Histocompatibility and Immunogenetics, 1996. Dir. histocompatibility & immunogenetics Barnes-Jewish Hosp., St. Louis, 1987—; prof. surgery, immunology & pathology Wash. U. Sch. Medicine, St. Louis, 1988—, dir. Islet core facility, 1996—, Maritz chair immunology & oncology, 1998—. Cons. HLA lab. William Beaumont Hosp., Royal Oak, Mich., 2007—. Recipient Mary Jane Kugel award, JDRF, 2005. Mem.: Xenotransplantation Assn., Transplantation Soc., Am. Soc. Transplantation (chair basic sci. com. 2003—04, Fujisawa Career Basic Sci. award 2001, Astellas Basic Sci. Established Investigator award 2008), Am. Soc. Histocompatibility & Immunogenetics (bd. dirs. 2005, Disting. Scientist award 2003), Am. Assn. Immunology. Office: Washington Univ Sch Medicine Box 8109 660 S Euclid Ave Saint Louis MO 63110

MOHANTY, AARON, neurosurgeon, educator; b. Cuttack, Orissa, India, June 30, 1962; s. Upendra Narayan and Girishbala (Pattnaik) M.; m. Mary Reeni Mathew George, Feb. 28, 1992; 1 child, Alina. Intermediate degree in sci., Ravenshaw Coll., Cuttack, India, 1979; MB BS, SCB Med. Coll., Cuttack, 1986; MCh in Neurosurgery, Nat. Inst. Mental Health, Bangalore, India, 1991. Sr. resident in neurosurgery Nat. Inst. Mental Health and Neuro Scis., Bangalore, 1991-93, asst. prof. neurosurgery, 1993-97, fellow in pediat. neurosurgery, 1997-99; assoc. prof. neurosurgery Nat. Inst. Mental Health & Neurosci., Bangalore, 1997—2001, prof. neurosurgery, 2001—. Contbr. articles to profl. jours. Mem. Congress Neurol. Surgeons, Asian Soc. Stereotactic and Functional Neurosurgery, Indian Soc. Stereotactic and Functional Neurosurgery, Indian Soc. Pediat. Neurosurgery. Avocations: cricket, indian music. Office: Univ Texas Medical Branch 301 University Blvd Route 0517 Galveston TX 77555-0517

MOHANTY, DILLIP K., chemistry professor, researcher; b. Baripada, Orissa, India, Nov. 13, 1956; s. Nabakishore and Subarna Mohanty; m. Padmashree Roy-Choudhray, Sept. 17, 1988; children: Ankita, Arpita. BS, Ravenshaw Coll., Cuttack, India, 1974; MS, Indian Inst. Tech., Kharagpur, India, 1976, Diploma in Rubber Tech., 1977; MS, Stony Brook U., NY, 1979; PhD, Va. Tech, Blacksburg, 1983. Sr. rsch. scientist Air Products, Allentown, Pa., 1983—85; rsch. scientist Va. Tech, 1985—88; asst. prof. Ctrl. Mich. U., Mt. Pleasant, 1988—93, prof. chemistry, 1997—, assoc. prof., 1993—97. Rschr. Ctrl. Mich. U., 1988—. Donations to charitable orgns. Salvation Army, Doctors without Borders, Mt. Pleasant, 1989—2006. Grantee, Army Rsch. Office, Mich., Petroleum Rsch. Fund, NIH, Mich. U. Challenge Initiative, State of Mich., USN. Mem.: Am. Soc. Microbiology, Am. Soc. Materials. Achievements include discovery of new reaction; vicarious Michael additions; patents for plasticization of poly (vinyl alcohol); cross linking of poly (ary ether phosphine oxides); patents pending for inert polymers; pegylation; vicarious Michael reaction; dendrimer cores; cross linking of poly(phenylene sulfide)s; polymeric vasodialtor. Avocations: gardening, reading, walking. Office: Ctrl Mich U Dow 254 Mount Pleasant MI 48859 Office Fax: 989-774-3883. Business E-Mail: mohan1dk@cmich.edu.

MOHANTY, SARAJU P., computer scientist, educator; B Tech Elec. Engring., Coll. Engring. and Tech., Bhubaneswar, Orissa, India, 1995; ME Systems Sci. and Automation, Indian Inst. Sci., Bangalore, 1999; PhD in Computer Sci. and Engring., U. South Fla., 2003. Asst. prof. U. North Tex., Denton, 2004—. Contbr. over 90 articles to profl. jours.; author conf. procs. Mem.: ACM, IEEE. Achievements include research in power leakage performance modelling and optimization for nanoscale VLSI circuits; design and CAD for nanoscale digital and analog/mixed-signal circuits; algorithms and architecture for multimedia processing. Business E-Mail: smohanty@cs.unt.edu.

MOHAPATRA, SURYA N., laboratory executive; PhD in Med. Physics, U. London; MSEE, Sambalpur Univ., India. Sr. v.p. Picker Internat., 1981—99; sr. v.p., COO Quest Diagnostics, Teterboro, NJ, 1999, pres., COO, 1999—2004, chmn., pres., CEO, 2004—. Bd. dirs. Vasogen Inc., 1999—. Contbr. articles to profl. jours. Mem.: Royal Coll. Surgeons Eng. (hon.). Achievements include patents in field. Office: Quest Diagnostics One Malcolm Ave Teterboro NJ 07608*

MOHIELDIN, AHMED NADER, electrical engineer; b. Cairo, Feb. 23, 1974; arrived in US, 1999; s. Nader Mohieldin Rizk and Inas Hassan Abuzaid; m. Marwa Aly Mahmoud Aly, Sept. 24, 2003; 1 child, Abdelrahman Ahmed Nader. BS, Cairo U., 1996, MS, 1998; PhD in Elec. Engring., Tex. A&M U., 2003. Tchg. asst. Cairo U., 1996—98; rsch. asst. Tex. A&M U., Coll. Sta., Tex., 1999—2003; integrated circuits design engr. Tex. Instruments Inc., Dallas, 2003—. Reviewer Transactions on Cirs. and Sys., 2001—06. Contbr. articles to profl. jours. Mem.: IEEE. Achievements include patents pending for digital compensation of continuous-time sigma-delta converter; digital blockers detection for wireless receiver; patents for high frequency tunable filter. Home: PO Box 742731 Dallas TX 75374 Personal E-mail: anader2000@yahoo.com.

MOHIELDIN, TAJ OSMAN, engineering educator; s. Osman Mohieldin El-Imam and Fatima Hassan Ahmed; m. Sumia Imam Mohieldin, Mar. 5, 1990; children: Ahmed T.O., Daniah T.O. PhD, Old Dominion U., Norfolk, Va., 1989. Assoc. prof. Old Dominion U., 1995—2000, prof., 2001—. Home: 5413 Wallingford Arch Virginia Beach VA 23464 Office: Old Dominion Univ Hampton Blvd Norfolk VA 23529 Office Fax: 757-683-5655. Business E-Mail: tmohield@odu.edu.

MOHIUDDIN, SYED MAQDOOM, cardiologist, educator; b. Hyderabad, India, Nov. 14, 1934; came to US, 1961, naturalized, 1976; s. syed Nizamuddin and Amat-Ul-Butool Mahmoodi Mohiuddin; m. Ayesha Sultana Mahmoodi, July 16, 0961; children: Sameena J., Syed R., Kulsoom S. MB, BS, Osmania U., 1960; MS, Creighton U., Omaha, 1967; DSc, Laval U., Que., Can., 1970. Diplomate in internal medicine and cardiovasc. disease Am. Bd. Internal Medicine. Intern Altoona Gen. Hosp., Pa., 1961-62; resident in cardiology Creighton Meml. Hosp., also St. Joseph Hosp., Omaha, 1963-65, mem. staff, 1965—; prof. adjoint Laval U. Med. Sch., 1970; practice medicine specializing in cardiology Omaha, 1970—; prof. Creighton U. Med. Sch., 1977—, assoc. dir. div. cardiology, 1983-96; prof. pharmacy practice Creighton U. Sch. Pharmacy, 1986—, dir. divsn. cardiology, 1996—2007, assoc. chair for acad. affairs dept. medicine, 1998—2007, Richard W. Booth MD prof. cardiology, 2005—, chair dept. medicine, 2007—. Cons. Omaha VA Hosp. Rsch. fellow Med. Rsch. Coun. Can., 1968; grantee Med. Rsch. Coun. Can., 1970, NIH, 1973, 2000-03. Fellow ACP, Am. Coll. Cardiology (gov. for Nebr. 1987-90), Am. Coll. Clin. Pharmacology, Am. Coll. Chest Physicians; mem. AAAS, Am. Heart Assn. (fellow coun. clin. cardiology, bd. dirs. 1973-75), Am. Fedn. Clin. Rsch., Nebr. Heart Assn. (chmn. rsch. com. 1974-76, dir. 1973—), Gt. Plains Heart Com. (Nebr. rep. 1976-84, pres. 1977-78), N.Y. Acad. Scis., Nebr. Cardiovasc. Soc. (pres. 1980-81), Creighton Med. Assn. (v.p. 2005-07), Am. Inst. Islamic Study & Culture(pres. 2007-). Democrat. Muslim. Home: 12531 Shamrock Rd Omaha NE 68154-3529 Office: Cardiac Ctr Creighton U 3006 Webster St Omaha NE 68131-2027 Office Phone: 402-280-4566. Business E-Mail: smm@cardiac.creighton.edu.

MOHL, NORMAN DAVID, dental educator; b. Paterson, NJ, May 15, 1931; s. Irving and Fannie (Weiss) M.; m. Eldene Jaffe, Dec. 27, 1953; children: Ilana, Lawrence, Daniel, Steven. DDS, U. Buffalo, 1956; MA, SUNY, Buffalo, 1968, PhD, 1971. Dentist, pvt. practice, Buffalo, 1958-67; from prof. to disting. svc. prof. SUNY, 1971—2005, emeritus, 2005—, assoc. dean acad. affairs, 1972-87, dir. oral sci. grad. program, 1977-94. Coun. mem. on dental materials, instruments and equipment ADA, Chgo., 1987-92; cons. NIH, Washington, 1988-92, FDA, Washington, 1989-97; chmn. dept. oral diagnostic scis., SUNY, Buffalo, 1994-2004. Author, editor: A Textbook of Occlusion, 1988, TMJ and Masticatory Muscle Disorders, 1995; contbr. articles to profl. jours. Lt. USNR, 1956-58. Named Disting. Svc. Prof., SUNY, 1971—2005. Mem. Internat. Assn. for Dental Rsch., Neuroscis. TMJ-Orofacial Pain Programs (pres. 1991-92), Am. Coun. on Edn. (fellow Acad. Adminstrn., spl. asst. v.p. for health scis. 1975-76). Avocations: bicycling, reading. Home: 7631 Uliva Way Sarasota FL 34238-4797 Home Phone: 941-929-9507. Personal E-mail: ndmohl@comcast.net.

MOHLER, BRIAN JEFFERY, diplomat; b. Niskayuna, NY, May 28, 1948; s. Donald and Rosemary (Brown) M. BA, Johns Hopkins U., 1970, MA, 1972. Economist Congl. Rsch. Svc. Libr. of Congress, Washington, 1973-74; commd. fgn. svc. officer U.S. Dept. State, 1974, staff asst. Bur. Econ. Affairs Washington, 1974-76, economist Bur. Econ. Affairs, 1979-82, desk officer European cmty. affairs Bur. European Affairs, 1982-84, desk officer Japanese affairs Bur. East Asian and Pacific Affairs, 1984-86, dep. dir. of econs. for Japanese affairs Bur. East Asian and Pacific Affairs, 1993-95, dir. econ. sanctions policy Bur. Econ. Affairs, 1999-2001, dir. Japanese affairs Bur. East Asian and Pacific Affairs, 2001—03, sr. adviser for Iraq Econ. Reconstrn. Bur. Econ. Affairs, 2003—04, sr. insp. Office of the Insp. Gen., 2004—05; consul Am. Consulate Gen., Strasbourg, France, 1976-78; petroleum attache Am. Embassy, Riyadh, Saudi Arabia, 1986-88, counselor for econ. affairs, 1988-90, dep. chief of mission Abu Dhabi, United Arab Emirates, 1990-93; counselor for econ. affairs Am. Embassy, Tokyo, 1995-99; minister counselor econ. affairs Am. Embassy, Ottawa, Canada, 2005—. 2d lt. U.S. Army, 1972, capt. USAR, 1972-85. Recipient Superior Honor award Dept. of State, 1993, 98, 2003, 04, Meritorious Honor award, 1987, 2004, award Sec. of Transp., 1998. Mem.: Japan-Am. Soc. of Washington DC, Am. Fgn. Svc. Assn., Can. Club Ottawa, Sigma Nu. Roman Catholic. Home: 18 Maple Lane Ottawa ON K1M 1G7 Canada Office Phone: 613-688-5214. Personal E-mail: bjmohler@hotmail.com. Business E-Mail: mohlerbj@state.gov.

MOHLER, MARY GAIL, magazine editor; b. Milaca, Minn., Dec. 15, 1948; d. Albert and Deane (Vedders) M.; m. Paul Rodes Trautman, June 5, 1976 (div. 1994); children: Elizabeth Deane, David Albert Rodes, Theodore DeForest Lloyd. BA, U. Calif.-Davis, 1974; MA in Lit., SUNY-Stony Brook, 1976. Asst., then editor-reporter Family Circle Mag., NYC, 1979-81; editorial coordinator Ladies' Home Jour., NYC, 1981, assoc. articles editor, 1982, mng. editor, 1982-93, sr. editor, 1994-98; editor in chief Ladies' Home Jour. Parent's Digest; mng. editor Parents Mag., 1999—2001, editor at large, freelance writer, 2001—. Co-author: Those Who Can...Teach, 1999. Medieval philosophy fellow SUNY-Binghamton, 1978 Mem. MLA, Am. Soc. Mag. Editors, Phi Beta Kappa Clubs: Medieval; Overseas Press. Office: Parents Mag 375 Lexington Ave New York NY 10017-5514

MOHLER, RICHARD ALBERT, JR., academic administrator, theologian; b. Lakeland, Fla., Oct. 9, 1959; s. Richard Albert Sr. and Janet Rae (Johnson) M.; m. Mary Ann Kahler, July 16, 1983; children: Mary Katherine, Christopher Albert. BA magna cum laude, Samford U., 1980; MDiv, So. Bapt. Theol. Sem., Louisville, 1983, PhD, 1989; postgrad., St. Meinrad Sch. Theology, 1985, Oxford U., Eng., 1986. Ordained min. So. Bapt. Ch. Pastor Union Grove Bapt. Ch., Bedford, Ky., 1982-87; asst. to pres., coord. found. support, dir. capital funding So. Bapt. Theol. Sem., Louisville, 1983-89, pres., 1993—; editor The Christian Index, Atlanta, 1989-93, prof. christian theology, 1996—, Joseph Emerson Brown prof. Christian theology, 2005—. Assoc. dir. The So. Sem. Found., 1983-89; rsch. fellow Ethics and Religious Liberty Commn., 1998—; bd. dirs. Focus on the Family; lectr. in field. Assoc. editor Preaching, 1985-93, contbg. editor, 1993—; gen. editor: The Gods of the Age of the God of the Ages?, 1993; editor-in-chief The So. Bapt. Jour. Theology, 1997—; columnist Religion News Svc., 1998—; sr. corr. World Mag., 1997—; mem. editl. bd. Salem Broadcasting, 1999—; host (radio programs) Truth On the Line, 2001—, The Albert Mohler Program; author daily Crosswalk Commentaries, Engaging Current issues with Timeless Truth, 2008, A Christian Confronts the New Atheists, 2008, Desire & Deceit: The Real Cost of New Sexual Tolerence, 2008, He is not Silent: Preaching in a Postmodern world, 2008, The Dissappearance of God: Dangerous Beliefs in the New Spiritual Openness, 2009; contbr. articles to profl. jours. Pres., chmn. Coun. of Sem. Pres. of So. Bapt. Conv., 1996—, chmn., Greater Louisville Billy Graham Crusade, 2001. Named one of 40 Rising Evang. Leaders, Christianity Today, 1996, one of 96 Southerners to Watch, Atlanta Jour. and Constitution, 1996, one of 50 Young Leaders Under 40 years of age TIME Mag., one of Emerging Leaders in Edn. CHANGE Mag., 1998. Mem. Am. Acad. Religion, Soc. Biblical Lit., Evang. Theol. Soc., Evang. Philos. Soc., So. Bapt. Hist. Soc., Bapt. Pub. Rels. Assn., So. Bapt. Press Assn., Evang. Press Assn., Nat. Assn. Evangs., Ga. Bapt. Hist. Soc., Rotary Internat., Phi Kappa Phi, Omicron Delta Kappa. Achievements include being named one of 50 young leaders under 40 years of age TIME Mag. Office: So Bapt Theol Sem 2825 Lexington Rd Louisville KY 40280-0001 Home Phone: 502-897-4121; Office Phone: 502-897-4121. Personal E-mail: mail@albertmohler.com. Business E-Mail: presoffice@sbts.edu, mohler@sbts.edu.

MOHLER, RONALD RUTT, electrical engineering educator; b. Ephrata, Pa., Apr. 11, 1931; s. David Wealand and Elizabeth (Rutt) M.; m. Nancy Alice Strickler, May 6, 1950; children: Curtis Gene, Pamela Louise, Susan Lynn, Anita Marie, John Scott, Andrew Thomas, Jennifer Lee, Lisa Nancy. BS (scholarship), Pa. State U., 1956; MS, U. So. Calif., 1958; PhD, U. Mich., 1965. Designer, trainee Textile Machine Works, Rockwell Internat. Corp., Reading, Pa., 1949-56; staff mem. Hughes Aircraft Co., Culver City, Calif., 1956-58, Los Alamos Sci. Lab., 1958-65; asso. prof. elec. engring. U. N.Mex., Albuquerque, 1965-69; prof. elec. engring./aerospace, mech. and nuclear engring. U. Okla., 1969-72, prof., chmn. info. and computing scis., 1970-72; dir. Systems Research Center, 1969-72; adj. prof. elec. engring. and nuclear engring. U. N.Mex., Los Alamos Grad. Center, 1959-65; cons. Sandia Corp., Albuquerque, 1966-69, Aerojet-Gen. Corp., Sacramento, 1966; vis. assoc. prof. system sci. UCLA, 1968-69; cons. community health project OEO, Oklahoma City, 1970-71; prof. elec. and computer engring. Oreg. State U., Corvallis, 1972-98, prof. emeritus, 1998—, head dept., 1972-79, 90; pres. Pace Tech., Inc., 1982-97. Vis. prof. U. Rome, 1973, 75, Imperial Coll., London, 1978-79, U.S. Naval Postgrad. Sch., 1983-85, Australian Nat. U., 1988, Sydney U., 1995, 98; cons. Optimization Software, L.A., 1973—, Bonneville Power Adminstrn., 1975—, Internat. Inst. Applied Systems Analysis, 1988—. Author: Optimal Control of Nuclear Reactors, 1970, Bilinear Control Processes, 1973, Nonlinear Systems: Dynamics and Control, vol. 1, 1991, Applications to Bilinear Control, vol. II, 1991, Disease Dynamics, 1993; editor: Theory and Application of Variable Structure Systems, 1972, Variable Structure Systems with Application to Biology and Economics, 1975, Recent Developments in Variable Structure Systems, Economics and Biology, 1979, Nonlinear Time Series and Signal Processing, 1988, assoc. editor Annals of Nuclear Energy, 1973-97; contbr. jours. Chmn. St. Stephens Sch. Bd., Norman, 1970-72. Recipient NATO award, 1979; rsch. grantee NSF, 1966-99, Sandia Labs., 1966-68, 96-97, ONR, 1981-92, NASA, EPRI, BPA, 1990-97; AEC fellow, 1961-65, Hughes fellow, 1956-58; Acad. Sci. exch. scientist to USSR and China, 1980, US-CIS (USSR) Commn. on Engring. Edn., 1991—. Fellow IEEE (life, local chmn. 1975); mem. Control System Soc., Sigma Xi, Tau Beta Pi, Pi Tau Sigma. Democrat.

MOHLER, STANLEY ROSS, preventive medicine physician, educator; b. Amarillo, Tex., Sept. 30, 1927; s. Norton Harrison and Minnie Alice (Ross) M.; m. Ursula Luise Burkhardt, Jan. 24, 1953; children: Susan Luise, Stanley Ross, Mark Hallock. BA, MA, U. Tex., 1953, MD, 1956. Diplomate Am. Bd. Preventive Medicine. Intern USPHS Hosp., San Francisco, 1956-57; med. officer Center Aging Research, NIH, Bethesda, Md., 1957-61; dir. Civil Aeromed. Rsch. Inst., FAA, Oklahoma City, 1961-66, chief aeromed. applications divsn. Washington, 1966-78; prof., vice chmn. dept. community medicine, dir. aerospace medicine Wright State U. Sch. Medicine, Dayton, Ohio, 1978—. Rsch. assoc. prof. preventive medicine and pub. health U. Okla. Med. Sch., 1961—; vice-chmn. Am. Bd. Preventive Medicine, 1978—, sec.-treas., 1980—. Co-editor: Space Biology and Medicine (5 vols.), 1995 (Life Scis. Book award Internat. Acad. Astronautics); contbr. articles to profl. jours. Bd. dirs. Sr. Citizens Assn. Oklahoma City, 1962—, Flying Physicians Assn., 1961—. Served with AUS, 1946-48. Recipient Gail Borden Rsch. award, Boothby award Aerospace Med. Assn., 1966, Henry L. Taylor award, 2008, FAA Meritorious Svc. award, 1974, Cecil A. Brownlow Publ. award Flight Safety Found., 1998, Marie Marvingt award French Soc. Aerospace Medicine and Aerospace Med. Assn., 2006; co-recipient Life Scis. Book award in space, biology and medicine Internat. Acad. Astronautics, 1995. Fellow Geriatrics Soc., Aerospace Med. Assn. (pres. 1983, Harry G. Moseley award 1974, Lyster award 1984, Louis H. Bauer Founders award 1998), Am. Coll. Preventive Medicine, Gerontol. Soc.; mem. AMA, Aircraft Owners and Pilots Assn. (Sharples award 1984, Hubertus Strughold award 1991), Alpha Omega Alpha. Home: 6539 Reigate Rd Dayton OH 45459-3214 Office: Wright State U Sch Medicine PO Box 927 Dayton OH 45401-0927

MOHLING, CHARLOTTE, middle school educator; BA in Home Econ. Edn., ND State Univ. Tchr. Wessington Springs (SD) Sch. Dist., 1975—. Bd. visitors ND State Univ. Recipient Wessington Springs Disting. Svc. award (three times); named ESA Region 3 Tchr. of Yr., 2007, SD Tchr. of Yr., 2007; named to USA 2004 All-USA Tchr. Team. Mem.: Nat. Coalition of Family and Consumer Sci., Assn. Edn. Comm. and Tech. Project, Assn. Career and Technical Edn. (pres., Family & Consumer Sci. Divsn.). Office: Wessington Springs Sch Dist 301 Dakota North PO Box 449 Wessington Springs SD 57382 Business E-Mail: charlotte.mohling@k12.sd.us.

MOHN, MELVIN PAUL, anatomist, educator; b. Cleve., June 19, 1926; s. Paul Melvin and Julia (Jacobik) M.; m. Audrey Faye Lonergan, June 28, 1952; children— Shorey Faye, Andrew Paul AB, Marietta Coll., 1950; Sc.M., Brown U., 1952, PhD in Biology, 1955. Instr. SUNY Downstate Med. Ctr., Bklyn., 1955-59, asst. prof., 1959-63; asst. prof. anatomy U. Kans. Sch. Medicine, Kansas City, 1963-65, assoc. prof., 1965-72, prof., 1972-89, prof. emeritus, 1989—. Cons. Nat. Med. Audiovisual Ctr., Atlanta, 1972; vis. lectr. U. Miami Sch. Medicine, Fla., 1966. Bd. dirs. U. Kans. Med. Ctr. Credit Union, 1968-77, Kansas City Youth Symphony, 1972-77; mem. U.S. Pony Club, 1964-71, Med. Arts Symphony, 1965-71, 90—, Spring Hill Chorale, 1990-96, Spring Hill Hist. Soc., 1997—. Served with USN, 1944-46, PTO. McCoy fellow, 1950, Arnold biology fellow, 1954 Fellow AAAS; mem. Am. Soc. Zoologists, Am. Assn. Anatomists, Am. Inst. Biol. Sci., Masons, Lions, Rotary, Ruritan, Olathe Trail Riders, Phi Beta Kappa, Sigma Xi, Beta Beta Beta. Republican. Methodist. Home: Yankee Bit Farm 23595 W 223rd St Spring Hill KS 66083-4029 Office: U Kans Med Ctr Dept Anatomy 39th and Rainbow St Kansas City KS 66103

MOHON, EARLENE MANN, counselor; b. Jackson, Tenn., Sept. 22, 1939; d. German Earl and Lillie Frances (Graves) Mann; m. Robert Troy Mohon, Apr. 21, l961; children: David, Chad. BS, Miss. U. for Women, 1960; MEd in Counseling and Guidance, Miss. Coll., 1968; attended, Miss. State U., 1958, U. So. Miss., 1960, E. Tex. U., 1964—65, Stephen Austin U., 1964—65, So. Methodist U., 1964, U. Ala., Birmingham, 1979—89. Tchr. Natchez Pub. Schs., Miss., 1960-61, Leesville Pub. Schs., La., 1961-62, Chapel Hill Pub. Schs., Tex., 1962-63, Judson Pub. Schs., Longview, Tex., 1963-65, Jackson Pub. Schs., Miss., 1965-69; substitute tchr. Mountain Brook Pub. Schs., Ala., 1981-83; counselor Birmingham City Schs., Ala., 1987—2003; ret. Recipient citation for drug free program Mayor of Birmingham, citation for drug free progam in elem. sch. Birmingham Sch. Bd. Mem. NEA, Am. Assn. for Counseling and Devel., Ala. Assn. for Counseling and Devel., Ala. Edn. Assn., Birmingham Edn. Assn., Chi Sigma Iota (sponsor Just Say No Club Ala., 1989), Pi Tau Chi. Republican. Baptist. Avocations: painting, needlecrafts, gardening. Home: 3516 Crest Brook Rd Birmingham AL 35223-1510

MOHR, DANIEL REED, electronics engineer; b. Phila., Feb. 3, 1952; s. Charles Napoleon and Florence Claire (Reed) M.; m. Cynthia Anne Maurer, May 6, 1978. Student, Drexel U., 1970-71. Electronic engr. R&D dept. Princeton (N.J.) Applied Rsch. Corp., 1973-95; sr. engr. Egerton Germershausen & Grier, Princeton, 1995—. Design engr. Princeton Deisgn Group, 1981-86. Patentee in field. Elim fellow. Avocations: photography, singing, motorcycles. Home: 192 Route 526 Allentown NJ 08501-2018 Office: EG&G PARC 375 Phillips Blvd Trenton NJ 08618-1428

MOHR, JAY, comedian, actor; b. Verona, NJ, Aug. 23, 1970; m. Nicole Chamberlain, 1998 (div. 2004); 1 child, Jackson; m. Nikki Cox, Dec. 29, 2006. Actor: (films) For Better or Worse, 1996, Jerry Maguire, 1996, The Brave Little Toaster to the Rescue, 1997, Picture Perfect, 1997, Suicide Kings, 1997, Paulie, 1998, Small Soldiers, 1998, Jane Austen's Mafia!, 1998, Playing By Heart, 1998, 200 Cigarettes, 1999, Go, 1999, Cherry Falls, 2000, Pay It Forward, 2000, Speaking of Sex, 2001, The Adventures of Pluto Nash, 2002, Simone, 2002, Seeing Other People, 2004, Are We There Yet?, 2005, King's Ransom, 2005, Even Money, 2006, The Groomsmen, 2006, Lonely Street, 2006, Street Kings, 2008; (TV films) The Barefoot Executive, 1995, Olive, the Other Reindeer, 1999, Black River, 2001, Community Service, 2006, A Salute to the Troops and USO, 2006, Christmas Do-Over, 2006; (TV series) Saturday Night Live, 1993—95, Local Heroes, 1995—96, The Jeff Foxworthy Show, 1996, From the Earth to the Moon, 1998, Ghost Whisperer, 2006; guest appearances (TV series) Action, 1999, The Simpsons, 2000, Nights Visions, 2001, Scrubs, 2003, Fastlane, 2003, CSI: Miami, 2003, The West Wing, 2004, Las Vegas, 2005, Family Guy, 2000, 2005.

MOHR, JAY PRESTON, neurologist, educator; b. Mar. 5, 1937; s. John G. and Marguerite F. Mohr; m. Joan L. Seal, Mar. 10, 1962; children: Thea, Gregory. AB, Haverford Coll., 1958; MS, MD, U. Va., 1963. Diplomate Am. Bd. Neurology and Psychiatry. Intern then asst. resident Mary Imogene Bassett Hosp., Cooperstown, NY, 1963-65; asst. resident N.Y. Neurol. Inst., Columbia-Presbyn. Med. Ctr., NYC, 1965-66; instr. neurology Johns Hopkins U. Med. Sch., U. Md. Med. Sch., 1969-71; assoc. neurologist Mass. Gen. Hosp., Boston, 1972-78; asst. prof. Harvard U. Med. Sch., 1972-78; prof. neurologi, chmn. dept. U. South Ala. Med. Sch., Mobile, 1978-83; Sciarra prof. clin. neurology Columbia U. Coll. Physicians & Surgeons, NYC, 1983—. Dir. cerebrovascular research N.Y. Neurol. Inst., N.Y.C., 1983—; dir. Doris and Stanley Tananbaum Stroke Ctr., 2003—. Contbr. articles to med. jours. Mag. M.C., U.S. Army, 1969-72. Recepient Johan Josef Wepfer award European Stroke Soc., 2009; Neurology fellow Mass. Gen. Hosp., 1966-69. Fellow Am. Acad. Neurology; mem. Am. Neurol. Assn., Am. Heart Assn. (Stroke coun., named Disting. Scientist 2006), Sigma Xi. Democrat. Mem. Soc. Of Friends. Office: Doris & Stanley Tananbaum Stroke Ctr NY Neurol Inst 710 W 168th St New York NY 10032-2603 also: Presbyn Hosp Columbia-Presbyn Med Ctr New York NY 10032-3784 Office Phone: 212-305-8033. Business E-Mail: jpm10@columbia.edu.

MOHR, LAWRENCE CHARLES, physician; b. S.I., NY, July 8, 1947; s. Lawrence Charles Sr. and Mary Estelle (Dawsey) M.; m. Linda Johnson, June 14, 1970; 1 child, Andrea Marie. AB with highest honors, U. N.C., 1975, MD, 1979. Diplomate Am. Bd. Internal Medicine. Commd. 2d lt. U.S. Army, 1967, advanced through grades to col., 1989; med. intern Walter Reed Army Med. Ctr., Washington, 1979-80, resident in medicine, 1980-82, chief resident, 1982-83, attending physician, 1984-86, pulmonary fellow, 1986-87; command surgeon 9th Inf. Div., Ft. Lewis, Wash., 1983-84; med. cons. Madigan Army Med. Ctr., Tacoma, 1983-84; White House physician Washington, 1987-93; asst. prof. medicine Uniformed Svcs. U. of the Health Scis., Bethesda, Md., 1984-91; assoc. prof. medicine Uniformed Svcs. U. Health Scis., Bethesda, Md., 1991-94; assoc. clin. prof. medicine George Washington U., Washington, 1990-94; prof. medicine Med. U. S.C., Charleston, 1994—, dir. environ. bioscis. program, 1995—. Attending physician Med. U. Hosp., Charleston, 1994—, Charleston Meml. Hosp., 1994—; mem. Working Group on Disability in U.S. Presidents, 1995—. Editor: International Case Studies in Risk Assessment and Magagement, 1997, Biomarkers, Medical and Workplace Applications, 1998; contbr. articles to profl. jours. and books. Bd. dirs. Internat. Lung Found., Washington; mem. adv. bd. Nat. Mus. Health and Medicine, Washington; mem. sci. adv. bd. Consortium in Environ. Risk Evaluation; prin. investigator Consortium in Molecular Epidemiology and Biomarker Rsch. Decorated Silver Star, Bronze Star with 2 V devices and 3 oak leaf clusters, Purple Heart, Meritorious Svc. medal with oak leaf cluster, Air medal, Army Commendation medal with oak leaf cluster, D.S.M.; recipient Erskine award Walter Reed Army Med. Ctr., 1982; named Outstanding Med. Resident, 1982. Fellow ACP, Am. Coll. Chest Physicians; mem. AMA, Army and Navy Club, Order Mil. Med. Merit, Harbour Club, Phi Beta Kappa. Episcopalian. Avocations: mountain climbing, skiing. Home: 673 Lake Francis Dr Charleston SC 29412-4345 Office: Med U S C Environ Bioscis Program 171 Ashley Ave Charleston SC 29425-0001

MOHR, MICHAEL ARTHUR, lawyer; b. Ft. Monmouth, NJ, 1950; m. Denise Mohr; children: Julia, Amy, Ian. BSME, Tex. A&M U., 1972; JD, Georgetown U., 1977. Bar: Mich. 1977. Design engineer Gen. Electric Co., 1972—73, patent agent, 1973—77; ptnr. Price, Heneveld, Huizenga & Cooper, 1977—87; with Amway Corp. (subsidiary of Alticor Inc.), Ada, Mich., 1987—2001, v.p., gen. counsel, 2001—. Office: Alticor Inc Legal Dept 7575 E Fulton Rd Ada MI 49355 Office Phone: 616-787-8457. Office Fax: 616-787-4000. E-mail: mike.mohr@alticor.com.*

MOHR, ROGER JOHN, retired advertising agency executive; b. Milw., Sept. 8, 1931; s. Reinhold and Clara (Meissner) M.; m. Pauline Spicuzza, Oct. 18, 1958; children: Gregory, Mary Margaret, Kristin, Thomas, Kathleen. BS in Speech, Marquette U., 1953; postgrad. radio and TV, Northwestern U., 1955-56. Staff announcer radio sta. WBKB, West Bend, Wis., 1952, WCAN, Milw., 1952-54; with Arthur Meyerhoff Assos., Inc., Chgo., 1956-80, pres., 1965-80, BBDO, Chgo., 1980-82, chmn., 1982-90, vice chmn. internat., 1991-93; ret., 1993. Chmn. Lake Bluff (Ill.) Plan Commn., 1972-75; mem. Lake Forest (Ill.) Plan Commn., 1994-2000, chmn., 1999-2000; bd. dirs. Chgo. City Ballet, 1982-84, Off the Street Club, 1976-78; mem. adv. coun. Marquette U. Sch. Comm., 1993-99; alderman Lake Forest City Coun., 2000-06; mem. Lake Forest Sr. Resources Commn., 2006—, chmn., 2008-. Served with AUS, 1954-55. Mem. Am. Assn. Advt. Agys. (chmn. Chgo. coun. 1966-67, sec., treas., nat. bd. dirs. 1976-77), Evans Scholars Alumni Assn. (pres. 1964-65), Western Golf Assn. (bd. dirs. 1980-2000, v.p. 1994-2000, trustee 2000—, vice-chmn. 2008-), Knollwood Club (bd. govs. 1980-85, 89-92), Tavern Club (bd. govs., v.p. 1988-94). Home: 2000 Knollwood Rd Lake Forest IL 60045-1137 Home Phone: 847-234-5853. Personal E-mail: rogermohr@sbcglobal.net.

MOHRIG, JERRY R., chemistry professor, researcher; BS, U. Mich., Ann Arbor, 1957; PhD in Chemistry, U. Colo., Boulder, 1962. Asst. prof. chemistry Hope Coll., Holland, Mich., 1964—67; prof. chemistry Carleton Coll., Northfield, Minn., 1967—2003, emeritus prof. Pres. Coun. on Undergrad. Rsch., Washington, 1983—87; cons. NSF, Washington, 1985—88; corp. vis. com., chemistry MIT, Cambridge, 1990—2002. Recipient Catalyst award, Chem. Manufacturers Assn., 1978, James Flack Norris Outstanding Achievement award, 1989, CUR Fellow award, 2004; petroleum rsch. fund, Am Chem. Soc., 1967—2002, rsch. grant, NSF, 1984, 2001, NIH, 1988, 2001. Mem.: Am. Chem. Soc. (petroleum rsch. fund adv. com. 1984—87, com. on profl. tng., chair 1997—2000, Brasted award 2008). Office: Carleton Coll Dept Chemistry 1 North College St Northfield MN 55057

MOHRMAN, KATHRYN J., academic administrator; BA, Grinnell Coll., 1967; MA, U. Wis., 1969; PhD, George Washington U., 1982. Dean undergrad. studies U. Md., College Park, 1988—93; pres. The Colo. Coll., Colorado Springs, 1993—2002; exec. dir. Hopkins-Nanjing Ctr. for Chinese and Am. Studies, Johns Hopkins U., 2003—08; dir. Inst. Univ. Design, prof. sch. pub. affairs Ariz. State U., 2008—. Office: 1619 Massachusetts Ave NW Washington DC 20036 Office Phone: 202-496-0463. Business E-Mail: kmohrman@asu.edu.

MOHSENI LANGURI, EHSAN, mechanical engineer, researcher; b. Babol, Mazandaran, Iran, May 7, 1982; s. Ali Mohseni Langouri and Mahdokht Tirgar Bahnamiri. Student, U. Wis. Milw., 2007—. Contbr. scientific papers to jours. Mem.: ASME.

MOIDEEN, RAFEEQ, dermatologist, consultant; b. Cochin, India, May 19, 1967; s. N. Moideen and P. Sulaikha; m. Saira Banu; children: Farah Rafeeq, Fardeen Rafeeq. MBBS, Jawaharlal Nehru Med. Coll., Aligarh, India, 1991; MD, Kuvempu U., India, 1996. Sr. cons. dermatologist Nat. Hosp., Calicut, India, 1996—; dir., dermato-cosmetologist Dr. Rafeeq's Skin & Cosmetic Surgery Rsch. Ctr., Calicut, 2006—. Organizer Muslim Edn. Soc., Calicut, 1996. Named Outstanding Young Person, Jr. Chamber Internat., 2006. Fellow: Am. Acad. Dermatology; mem.: Indian Red Cross Soc., Indian Assn. Cosmetic Laser Surgeons, Indian Med. Assn. (life), Indian Assn. Neuroscience, Indian Assn. Dermatologist, Venerologist and Leprologist, Rotary Club Calicut Metropolis (dir. 2002), Rotary Club Calicut Metropolis, Malabar Dermatology Club. Office: Dr Rafeeq's Skin & Cosmetic Surgery Rsch Ctr E Nadakkav Kolkata 673006 India Business E-Mail: drrafeeqskincosme@gmail.com.

MOISE, CLAUDIA, finance educator; BS, U. Bucharest, Romania, 1990, MS, 1991, U. SC, Columbia, 1997; MBA, U. Chgo., Booth Sch. Bus., Ill., 2005, PhD, 2006. Asst. prof. banking and fin. Case Western Res. U., Cleve., 2006—. Contbr. scientific papers. Mem.: Soc. Fin. Econometrics, Western Fin. Assn., Am. Fin. Assn., Mu Sigma Rho. Office: Case Western Reserve Univ WSOM 10900 Euclid Ave 369 PBL Bldg Cleveland OH 44106

MOISE, KENNETH JOSEPH, JR., medical educator; b. New Orleans, July 28, 1955; s. Kenneth Joseph and Beverly Moise; m. Karen Yvette Massey, Apr. 6, 1985; children: Rachael Kathryn, Kaitlyn Anne, Erin Elizabeth. BS in Zoology, La. State U., Baton Rouge, 1977; MD, La. State U., New Orleans, 1981. Diplomate in ob-gyn. Am. Bd. Ob-Gyn., 2008, in maternal-fetal medicine 2008. Asst. prof. ob-gyn. Baylor Coll. Medicine, Houston, 1987—90, assoc. prof. ob-gyn, 1990—96, prof. ob-gyn., 1996—98, 2008—, dir. maternal-fetal medicine fellowship, 1991—98, 2000—05, dir., fetal intervention fellowship, 2008; prof. ob-gyn. U. NC, Chapel Hill, 1998—2006, dir. divsn. maternal-fetal medicine, 1998—2005. Contbr. articles to numerous profl.jours. Bd. mem. Habitat for Humanity, Houston, 1996—98. Recipient Excellence Tchg. award, Baylor Coll. Medicine, 2007; named Am. Prof. Ob-Gyn., 2007. Mem.: Soc. Maternal-Fetal Medicine (bd. dir. 1999—2002), N.Am. Fetal Treatment Network (bd. dir. 2005—08), Internat. Fetal Medicine and Surgery Soc. (sec., treas. 2007—08). Achievements include patents for Rh blood group antigen compositions and methods of use. Office: Baylor Coll Medicine 6620 Main St Ste 1100 Houston TX 77030 Office Fax: 713-798-2809.

MOISES, ALFONSO ARTURO, communications educator; b. San Salvador, El Salvador, Nov. 16, 1950; s. Alfonso Moises and Ruth Calderon; m. Martha Alicia Martha Arevalo; children: Samadhy, Sidharta, David Alfonso. PhD, Northwestern U., Evanston, Ill., 1988. Asst. prof. Calif. State U., Chico, 1985—90; assoc. prof. U. Ariz., Tucson, 1990—97; communication cons. UNICEF, San Salvador, 1998—2002; dir. grad. studies U. Don Bosco, San Salvador, 2002—06; assoc. prof. and coord. mass communication program Albany State U., Ga., 2007—. Dir.: (interactive multimedia) The Mesoamerican Cultural Code. Home: 201 Holly Dr Apt J-4 Albany GA 31705 Office: Albany State University Albany GA 31705 Business E-Mail: alfonso.moises@asurams.edu.

MOJTABAI, ANN GRACE, author, educator; b. NYC, June 8, 1937; d. Robert and Naomi (Friedman) Alpher; m. Fathollah Mojtabai, Apr. 27, 1960 (div. 1966); children: Chitra, Ramin. BA in Philosophy, Antioch Coll., 1958; MA in Philosophy, Columbia U., 1968, MS in Libr. Sci., 1970. Lectr. philosophy Hunter Coll., CUNY, 1966-68; libr. CCNY, 1970-76; fellow Radcliffe Inst. Ind. Study, Cambridge, Mass., 1976-78; Briggs-Copeland lectr. on English Harvard U., 1978-83; writer-in-residence U. Tulsa, 1983—2005, Yaddo Found., Saratoga, NY, 1975, 76. Author: Mundome, 1974, The 400 Eels of Sigmund Freud, 1976, A Stopping Place, 1979, Autumn, 1982, Blessed Assurance, 1986, Ordinary Time, 1989, Called Out, 1994, Soon: Tales From Hospice, 1998, All That Road Going, 2008. Recipient Richard and Hinda Rosenthal award Am. Acad. and Inst. Arts and Letters, 1983, Lillian Smith award So. Regional Coun., 1986, Lit. Acad. award AAAL, 1993; Guggenheim fellow, 1981-82 Mem.: PEN, Mark Twain Soc., Tex. Inst. Letters, Phi Beta Kappa. Home: 2329 Woodside Drive Amarillo TX 79124-1036 Personal E-mail: agmojtabai@aol.com.

MOK, CARSON KWOK-CHI, structural engineer; b. Canton, China, Jan. 17, 1932; came to U.S., 1956, naturalized, 1962; s. King and Chi-Big (Lum) M.; m. Virginia Wai-Ching Cheng, Sept. 19, 1959. BSCE, Chu Hai U., Hong Kong, 1953; M.C.E., Cath. U. Am., 1968. Registered profl. engr., Md., D.C. Structural designer Wong Cho Tong, Hong Kong, 1954-56; bridge designer Michael Baker Jr., Inc., College Park, Md., 1957-60; structural engr., chief design engr., assoc. Milton A. Gurewitz Assocs., Washington, 1961-65; ptnr. Wright & Mok, Silver Spring, Md., 1966-75; owner Carson K.C. Mok, Cons. Engr., Silver Spring, 1976-81, pres., 1982—. Facility engring. cons. Washington Met. Area Transit Authority, 1985-86; pres. Transp. Engring. and Mgmt. Assocs., P.C., Washington, 1986-2002; adj. asst. prof. Howard U., Washington, 1976-79, adj. assoc. prof., 1980-81. Contbr. articles to profl. jours. Bd. dirs. U.S. Pan Asian Am. C. of C. Sec.; N.Am. trustee China Grad. Sch. Theology, Wayne, Pa., 1972-74, pres., 1975-83, v.p., 1984-91, dir., 1992—; elder Chinese Bible Ch. Md., Rockville, 1978-80; chmn. Chinese Christian Ch. Greater Washington, 1958-61, 71, elder, 1972-76; dir. Evergreen Family Friendship Svc., Inc., A Pub. Benefit Corp., Colorado Springs, 1993—. Recipient Outstanding Std. of Tchg. award Howard U., 1980, Nat. Merit award U.S. Dept. Transp., 2000. Mem. ASCE, ASTM, Nat. Assn. Corrosion Engrs., Concrete Reinforcing Steel Inst., Am. Inst. Steel Constrn., Am. Concrete Inst., Am. Welding Soc., Prestressed Concrete Inst., Post-Tensioning Inst., Soc. Exptl. Mechanics, Internat. Assn. Bridge and Structural Engring., Pui Ching Mid. Sch. Alumni Assn. (pres. nation's capital chpt. 1991-97). Home: 4405 Bestor Dr Rockville MD 20853-2137 Office: 9001 Ottawa Pl Silver Spring MD 20910-2257 Office Phone: 301-587-3448. E-mail: ckm9001@aol.com.

MOK, SAMUEL TINSING, management consultant, former federal agency administrator; b. Shanghai, 1944; m. Nancy H. Mok; 2 children. BS in Acctg., Fordham U., 1968; MA in Auditing, Cath. U., Washington, 1982; grad., US Army Inst. Adminstrn., Ft. Benjamin Harrison, US Fgn. Svc. Inst., Rosslyn, Va. Cert. Internal Auditor, Govt. Fin. Mgr. Auditor Main & Hurdman; sr. auditor Parnell Kerr & Forster; dir. acctg. Time-Life Books, 1976—82; contr. then corp. treasurer US News & World Report, 1982—86; foreign svc. officer Bur. East Asian & Pacific Affairs US Dept. of State, 1986; mem. fed. sr. exec. svc., CFO, comptr. US Dept. Treasury, 1988—92; CEO GL Assocs., 1992—96; mng. mem. Condor Cons., LLC, 1996—2002; CFO US Dept. Labor, Washington, 2002—07; mng. ptnr. Condor Internat. Advisors, LLC (formerly Condor Cons., LLC, Washington, 2007—. Mem. Nat. Adv. Coun. Pub. Svc.; vice chmn. bd. trustees Acad. Govt. Accountability; Disting. practitioner in residence U. Ky. Martin Sch. Pub. Policy & Adminstrn., 2006—. Mem. Rep. Marshall Islands Trust Fund Com., Gen. Adminstrn. Bd., USDA Grad. Sch. Served in US Army, 1971—76. Decorated Meritorious Unit Citation, Meritorious Svc. medal; recipient AGA Disting. Nat. Leadership award, Assn. Govt. Accountants (AGA), 2005, Donald L. Scantlebury Meml. award for Disting. Leadership in Fin. Mgmt. Improvement, 2006, Einhorn/Gary award, Assn. Govt. Accountants (AGA), Ellis I. Medal of Honor, 2007; named one of "The Fed 100", Fed. Computer Week; fellow Nat. Acad. Pub. Adminstrn. Mem.: Assn. Govt. Accountants (AGA) (nat. pres.-elect 2007—).

MOKHATAB, SAEID, gas industry technical consultant; BS in Gas-Engineering, Tehran U., Iran, 1998; MS in Chem. Engring., Tarbiat Modarres U., Iran, 2000. Internat. rsch. assoc. David Wood & Assoc., Lincoln, England, 2006—09; tech. advisor Prodn. & Lift Tech. LLC, Lubbock, Tex., 2007—. Rsch. advisor natural gas engring. projects U. Wyo., Laramie, 2005—07; mem. SPE London Sect. Bd. Soc. Petroleum Engrs., 2003—05, mem. SPE Disting. Achievement Petroleum Engring. Faculty Award Com., 2006—; mem. Gas Processors Assn. Europe, 2003—06. Contbr. articles to profl. jours. Mem.: ASME, Mo. Acad. Sci., Asian Inst. Tech. (editl. adv. bd. mem. 2007—), Gulf Profl. Pub. (chmn. natural gas engring. editl. adv. bd. 2006—07), Gulf Pub. Co. (editl. advisor 2007—), Sigma Xi.

MOKRASCH, LEWIS CARL, neurochemist, educator; b. St. Paul, May 9, 1930; s. Lewis and Anna (Dvorak) M.; m. Jane Carolyn Church, Apr. 20, 1974. BS magna cum laude, Coll. St. Thomas, 1952; PhD, U. Wis., 1955. Rsch. assoc. dept. psychiatry and neurology La. State U. Med. Center, New Orleans, 1956-57, assoc. prof. dept. biochemistry, 1971-76, prof., 1976-92, prof. emeritus, 1992—, acting head dept., 1978-79. Instr. medicine U. Kans. Med. Center, Kansas City, 1957-59, assoc. in medicine, dir. neurochemistry lab., 1959-62; asst. biochemist McLean Hosp., Belmont, Mass., 1960-64, assoc. biochemist, 1964-71; assoc. dept. biol. chemistry Harvard Med. Sch., Boston, 1964-67; asst. prof., 1967-71; adj. assoc. prof. biology Hellenic Coll., Brookline, Mass., 1969-71; staff scientist Neurosciences Rsch. Programs, Brookline, 1970-71; vis. prof. neurology Duke U. Med. Ctr., 1981-82; grant reviewer neurological diseases and blindness NIMH, 1969-92; lectr. in field Co-author: Myelin, 1971; contbr. articles to profl. jours., 1952-94; reviewer: jours. Sci., FASEB, 1956-92. Pres. Belmont Preservation Soc., 1969; candidate Bd. Selectman, Belmont, 1969; active Forsyth County Adult Care Home Cmty. Adv. Com., Hospice, Sr. Fin. Care, Winston-Salem, Sr. Svcs. Program, Winston Salem, 1992-, Citizens Quality Nursing Home Care, New Orleans, 1987-92; sr. leader Duke Long Term Care Program Edn. Com., 1999; edn. com. Shepherd Ctr., 1996; Reynolda House Mus. Am. Art, 2007-, Reynolda Gardens. Grantee NIMH, 1973-74, Nat. Inst. Neurol. Disability and Blindness, 1957-90, Schlieder Found., 1971-72, 83-84, La. Bd. Regents, 1986-88. Fellow Am. Assn. Clin. Chemists; mem. Am. Soc. Neurochemistry (local chmn. 1974), Am. Soc. Biol. Chemists, Soc. Neurosci. (founder, pres. local chpt. 1974-75), Soc. Rsch. Adminstrs. (membership chmn. New Eng. sect.), Nat. Citizens Coalition Nursing Home Reform, Am. Assn. Individual Investors (founder, past pres., sec. Piedmont chpt.). Libertarian. Achievements include first demonstration of adaptive enzyme regulation in animals and allosteric control of fructose bisphosphatase, of incorporation of hydrouracil into transfer RNA, of thermogenic mechanism for arousing hibernators, of metabolic control in hibernation, of altered hydrophobic proteins in neurological disorders, of biosynthesis of hydrophobic proteins and mitochondrial proteins in brain in vitro, of altered transport processes in cells of neurological disease victims, of defective transport of acetylcholine precursors into cells of Alzheimer's victims and that such transport is modulatable; development of coestimation method for ketoses, aldoses, and pentoses; first isolation in pure form of receptor hydrophobic proteins from mammalian brain. Home: 2711 Pilgrim Ct Winston Salem NC 27106 Personal E-mail: drlcmokrasch@bellsouth.net. *Before I entered Science, I regarded it as a Priesthood of individuals dedicated to the service of humanity, whose common goal was the enhancement of human life and the remedying of its ills. After 50 years in Science, I hold this thesis more strongly and have found many colleagues who agree with it. I am certain now that the failures and abuses of Science derive from the use of it for the goals of wealth, fame and power.*

MOL, GRETCHEN, actress; b. Deep River, Conn., Nov. 8, 1972; d. Janet Mol; m. Tod Williams, June 1, 2004; 1 child, Ptolemy John. Grad., Am. Musical & Dramatic Acad. Actor: (films) Girl 6, 1996, The Funeral, 1996, Donnie Brasco, 1997, The Last Time I Committed Suicide, 1997, The Deli, 1997, Bleach, 1998, Too Tired to Die, 1998, Rounders, 1998, New Rose Hotel, 1998, Celebrity, 1998, Finding Graceland, 1998, Music from Another Room, 1998, The Thirteenth Floor, 1999, Cradle Will Rock, 1999, Sweet & Lowdown, 1999, Forever Mine, 1999, Just Looking, 1999, Attraction, 2000, Get Carter, 2000, The Shape of Things, 2003, Heavy Put-Away, 2004, The Notorious Bettie Page, 2005, Puccini for Beginners, 2006, Trainwreck: My Life as an Idiot, 2007, The Ten, 2007, 3:10 to Yuma, 2007; (TV films) Calm at Sunset, 1996, Subway Stories: Tales from the Underground, 1997, Picnic, 2000, Freshening Up, 2002, The Magnificent Ambersons, 2002, The Memory Keeper's Daughter, 2008; (TV miniseries) Dead Man's Walk, 1996; (TV series) Girls Club, 2002, Life on Mars, 2008—09. Office: c/o William Morris Agy 1 William Morris Pl Beverly Hills CA 90212 Office Phone: 310-859-4000.

MOLANDER, DEBORAH JEAN, special education educator; d. William Lawrence and Yvetta Jean Paine; m. Danny Howard Molander, Sept. 25, 1971; 1 child, Christopher Clayton. BA in Edn., Ctrl. State U., Edmond, Okla., 1974; M in Spl. Edn., East Ctrl. U., Ada, Okla., 1981. Cert. autism State Okla., 2005, other health impaired State Okla., 2004, spl. edn. State Okla., 2004, traumatic brain dysfunction State Dept. Okla., 2006. Tchr. Healdton Pub. Schs., Okla., 1974—75; spl. edn. instr. Pauls Valley Pub. Schs., Okla., 1976—79; tchr. Whitebead Ind. Sch. Dist., Okla., 1980—81; spl. edn. instr. Duncan Pub. Schs., Okla., 1981—97, inclusion facilitator, network provider, 1998—99; spl. edn. instr. Grand Prarie Pub. Schs., Tex., 2000—01; spl. edn. coord., instr. Ardmore Pub. Schs., Okla., 2001—03, spl. edn. instr., 2004—, homebound instr., 2005—. Contbr. articles to newspapers. Officer DAR, Duncan, 1984—2000; power hours instr. Wilson-Ardmore Boys and Girls Club Am., 2004—. Mem.: Kappa Kappa Iota (past pres.), Delta Kappa Gamma Zi Chpt. (past pres.). Democrat. Presbyterian. Avocations: sculpting, swimming. Office: Ardmore Mid Sch 511 Veteran's Blvd Ardmore OK 73401

MOLD, JAMES WILLIAM, geriatrician, preventive medicine physician, educator; b. Detroit, Oct. 29, 1948; MD, Duke U., 1974; MPH in biostatistics, U. Okla. Coll. Medicine, 1999. Cert. Family Medicine, 1978, Geriatric Medicine, 1988. Resident in family medicine U. Rochester, NY, 1974—77; fellow in geriatrics U. NC, Chapel Hill, 1986—87; asst. prof. family and preventive medicine U. Okla. Health Sciences Ctr., Oklahoma City, 1984—90, assoc. prof. family and preventive medicine, 1990—96, prof. and dir. rsch. family and preventive medicine, 1996—, adj. prof. geriatric medicine, 1997—; Smock endowed chair U. Louisville, Ky., 1992—93. Mem.: Inst. Medicine. Office: Family Medicine Ctr 900 NE 10th St Oklahoma City OK 73104-5420*

MOLDENHAUER, KAREN ANN KUENZEL, agriculturist, educator; d. Norris Herman and Zella Ruth Kuenzel; m. Paul M. Moldenhauer, June 15, 1985; children: Jonathan Christian, Henry Harold Madison. BS, Iowa State U., Ames, 1975, PhD, 1982; MS, NC State U., Raleigh, 1977. Asst. prof. U. Ark., Fayetteville, 1982—87, assoc. prof., 1987—92, prof., 1992—, prof. & rice industry, chair variety devel., 2002—, prof. & interim dir. rice res. & ext. ctr., divsn. Agr. Stuttgart, 2001—02; interim dir. Rice Res. & Ext. Ctr. Divsn. Agr. Stuttgart, 2001—02. Recipient Riceland Friend Farmer award, Riceland Foods Inc., 2001, Disting. Rsch. & Edn. award, Rice Tech. Working Group, 2002, Disting. Rice Rsch. & Edn. Team award, 2004; Fellowship, Crop Sci. Soc. Am., 1998, Am. Soc. Agronomy, 1999, AAAS, 2007. Lutheran. Achievements include patents for 5 rice varieties wells, ahrent, francis, banks, & spring; patents pending for rice variety CL171AR. Office: Univ Ark Rice Res & Ext Ctr 2900 Hwy 130 E Stuttgart AR 72160

MOLDENHAUER, WILLIAM CALVIN, soil scientist; b. New Underwood, SD, Oct. 27, 1923; s. Calvin Fred and Ida (Killam) M.; m. Catherine Ann Maher, Nov. 26, 1947; children— Jean Ann, Patricia, Barbara, James, Thomas BS, S.D. State U., 1949; MS, U. Wis., 1951, PhD, 1956. Soil surveyor S.D. State U., Brookings, 1948-54; soil scientist U.S. Dept. Agr., Big Spring, Tex., 1954-57, Ames, Iowa, 1957-72, Morris, Minn., 1972-75; rsch. leader Nat. Soil Erosion Rsch. Lab., Agrl. Rsch. Svc. U.S. Dept. Agr., West Lafayette, Ind., 1975-85; prof. dept. agronomy Purdue U., West Lafayette, 1975-85, prof. emeritus, 1985—. Contbr. articles to profl. jours. Served with U.S. Army, 1943-46 Fellow Am. Soc. Agronomy, Soil Sci. Soc., Soil Conservation Soc. Am. (pres. 1979), World Assn. Soil and Water Conservation (pres.

1983-85, exec. sec. 1985-2003, asst. treas. 2003-08). Home and Office: 2400 Sunrise Ridge Cir #107 Brookings SD 57006 Home Phone: 605-697-6470; Office Phone: 605-697-6470. E-mail: moldwc@itctel.com.

MÖLDERS, NICOLE, environmental scientist, educator; d. Hermann Wilhelm and Ilse Hedwig Mölders; m. Gerhard Kramm, Aug. 13, 1992. BS in Meteorology, U. zu Köln, Cologne, Germany, 1983, MS in Meteorology, 1988, PhD in Geophysics, 1992; habilitation in Meteorology, U. Leipzig, Saxony, Germany. Postdoc. rschr. Fraunhofer Inst. Environ. Rsch., Garmisch-Partenkirchen, Bavaria, Germany, 1993; rsch. assoc. U. Leipzig, Saxony, Germany, 1994—97, habiltanden scholar, 1997—99, heisenberg fellow, 1999—2001; assoc. prof. U. Alaska Fairbanks, 2001—06, chair, atmospheric scis. program, 2005—08, prof. atmospheric scis., 2006—, dept. chair, 2008—. Vis. scientist SUNY, Albany, 1989, Nat. Ctr. Atmospheric Rsch. Boulder, 2000. Recipient DFQ Travel award, 1985—86, Extraordinary Performance award, Geophys. Inst., U. Alaska Fairbanks, 2003, Travel award, NSF, 2006, Outstanding Grads. Mentor & Advisor award, CNSM, 2009; Vis. Scholar, U. Clermont-Ferrand, France, 1985—89. Mem.: UCAR (mem. rep. 2005, mem. nomination comm. 2007—, com. mem. u. relation 2008—), U. Women Assn. (chair, scholarship com. 2002—03), Am. Geophys. Union (mem. fin. & budget com. 2008), US Permafrost Assn., Am. Meteorol. Soc. Achievements include research in air quality modeling, land atmosphere interaction modeling. Avocation: ballroom dancing. Office: Univ Alaska Fairbanks 903 Koyukuk Dr Fairbanks AK 99775 Office Fax: 907-474-7379.

MOLEN, JOHN KLAUMINZER, lawyer; b. Gary, Ind., June 13, 1952; s. Franklin B. and Jane Anne (Klauminzer) M.; m. Susan Wilson Blair, Aug. 10, 1985; children: Mary Wilson, Elisabeth Blair. AB with honors, U. NC, 1974, MBA, 1978, JD with honors, 1978. Bar: Ala. 1978. Assoc. Bradley Arant Boult Cummings LLP, Birmingham, Ala., 1978—84, ptnr., 1984—. Mem. Rotary Club Birmingham-Sunrise. Presbyterian. Avocations: sailing, swimming. Office: Bradley Arant Boult Cummings LLP One Federal Pl 1819 5th Ave N Birmingham AL 35203-2104 Office Phone: 205-521-8238. Business E-Mail: jmolen@babc.com.

MOLER, EDWARD HAROLD, retired lawyer; b. Oklahoma City, May 26, 1923; s. Harold Stanley and Rosemary (Callahan) M.; m. Donna Blocksom Cram, Sept. 12, 1964; children: John Frederick, Shelley Elizabeth, Christopher Bryan. BA, U. Okla., 1947, LLB, 1948. Bar: Okla. 1948, U.S. Supreme Ct. 1951. Pvt. practice law, Oklahoma City, 1948-52, 61—; asst. mcpl. counselor, 1952-59; mcpl. counselor, 1959-61; spl. justice Okla. Supreme Ct., 1977. Trustee Oklahoma City Mcpl. Improvement Authority, 1960-61, Dolese Found, 2007-; bd. dirs. Mummers Theatre, Inc., 1969—; bd. dirs. Greater Oklahoma City YMCA, 1981-91. 2d lt. USAAF, 1943-45. Mem. ABA, Okla. Bar Assn., Oklahoma County Bar Assn. (bd. dirs. 1963-67, pres. 1968), Rotary, Phi Delta Phi, Phi Gamma Delta (pres. local chpt. 1946, pres. Nu Omega Housing Assn. 1963-65). Home: 2540 NW Grand Blvd Oklahoma City OK 73116-4110 E-mail: demoler@cox.net.

MOLER, ELIZABETH ANNE, utilities executive; b. Salt Lake City, Jan. 24, 1949; d. Murray McClure and Eleanor Lorraine (Barry) M.; m. Thomas Blake Williams, Oct. 19, 1979; children: Blake Martin Williams, Eleanor Bliss Williams. BA, Am. U., 1971; postgraduate student, Johns Hopkins U., Balt., 1972; JD, George Wash. U., 1977. Bar: DC 1978. Chief legis. asst. Senator Floyd Haskell, Washington DC, 1973-75; law clk. Sharon, Pierson, Semmes, Crolius & Finley, Washington DC, 1975-76; profl. staff mem. com. on energy and natural resources US Senate Com. on Energy and Natural Resources, Washington DC, 1976—77, counsel, 1977—86, sr. counsel, 1987-88; mem. FERC, Washington DC, 1988-93, chair, 1993-97; dep. sec. Dept. Energy, Washington DC, 1997-98, acting sec., 1998; ptnr. Vinson & Elkins, Washington DC, 1999; sr. v.p. govt. affairs and policy Unicom Corp. (now Exelon Corp.), 2000—02, exec. v.p., 2002; exec. v.p. govt. and environ. affairs and pub. policy, mem. exec. com. Exelon Corp., Washington DC. Bd. dirs. Henry M. Jackson Found. Recipient Disting. Svc. award, Nat. Energy Resources Orgn., Energy Daily Ann. Pub. Policy Leadership award, Woman of Yr. award, Women's Coun. Energy and the Environment. Mem. ABA, DC Bar Assn. Democrat. Office: Exelon Corp Suite 400 East 101 Constitution Ave NW Washington DC 20001 Office Phone: 202-347-7500.

MOLESKY, MARK, history professor; b. Balt., Feb. 16, 1967; s. Thomas Joseph and Mary Jane Molesky. BA, U. Mich., Ann Arbor, 1990; MA, Harvard U., Cambridge, MA, 1991; PhD, Harvard U., 2000. Lectr. history & lit. Harvard U., 2000—03; asst. prof. history Seton Hall U., South Orange, NJ, 2004—. Author: (book) Our Oldest Enemy: A History of America's Disastrous Relationship with France. Recipient Phi Beta Kappa, U. Mich., Ann Arbor, 1990, Nat. Endownment, 2009; Rsch. grant, Earhart Found., 2007—08, Seton Hall U., 2008. Mem.: Am. Hist. Assn. Office: Seton Hall Univ History Dept 400 S Orange Ave South Orange NJ 07079

MOLHO, EMANUEL, publisher; b. NYC, Jan. 27, 1936; s. Isaac Emanuel and Alvira (Altchek) M.; m. Brenda Nadel, Sept. 25, 1965; children— Deborah Rochelle, Brian Emanuel. BA, NYU, 1957; MBA, Wharton Sch., U. Pa., 1960. Pres. French & European Publs., Inc., NYC, 1961—, French & Spanish Book Corp., 1967—. Pres. Librairie de France, Inc., 1961—. Recipient Orden de Merito Civil Spain, 1975 Mem. Am. Booksellers Assn., French-Am. C. of C. in US (exec. com.), Paris Am. Club. Office: Librairie de France Rockefeller Center Promenade 610 5th Ave New York NY 10020-2497 Personal E-mail: livresny@gmail.com.

MOLHO, ERIC STEVEN, neurologist, researcher; b. NYC, Nov. 6, 1961; s. Roeben and Roslyn Molho. AB, Vassar Coll., Poughkeepsie, NY, 1983; MD, Albany Med. Coll., NY, 1987. Intern Albany Med. Ctr., 1987—88, resident in neurology, 1988—91, fellow in movement disorders, 1991—92, asst. prof. neurology, 1992—98, assoc. prof., 1998—, Rilay family chair in Parkinson's Disease, 2005—. Fellow: Am. Acad. Neurology. Avocation: birdwatching. Office: Albany Med Ctr Parkinsons Disease and Movement Disorder 215 Washington Ave E Albany NY 12205

MOLHOEK, KERRINGTON RAMSEY, research scientist; d. Carlton Lee and Linda Ford Ramsey; m. Charles Conrad Molhoek, June 12, 2004. PhD, U. Va., Charlottesville, 2004. Rsch. faculty U. Va. Sch. Medicine, Charlottesville, 2004—. Mem.: U. Va. Alumni Assn. (life), Colonnade Club (life), Nat. Soc. Collegiate Scholars (life), Delta Delta Delta (life). Office: U Va 409 Lane Rd MR-4 Rm 3038 Charlottesville VA 22908 Business E-Mail: klr5w@virginia.edu.

MOLHOLM, KURT NELSON, retired federal agency administrator; b. Denver, June 24, 1937; s. Ervin Maurice and Helen Pauline (Nelson) M.; m. Sonja Dell Williams, Aug. 17, 1967; children: Kevin William, Paul Nelson. BS, U. Oreg., 1959; MS, George Washington U., 1974; grad., Indsl. Coll. Armed Forces, 1974. Computer specialist D.L.A. Adminstrv. Support Ctr., Alexandria, Va., 1963-65; with Hdqrs. Def. Logistics Agy., Alexandria, 1965-85, chief planning and policy office, 1975-76, chief ADP/T tech. div., 1984-85; adminstr. Def. Tech. Info. Ctr., Alexandria, 1985—2005; ret., 2005; pvt. practice, 2007—. Pres. Nat. Fedn. Abstracting and Info. Svcs., Phila., 1993-94, treas., 1990-93; del. Va. Govs. Conf. Librs. Info. Svcs., 1990, Fed. Libr. Pre-White House Conf. On Librs. Info. Sci., 1990; vice chmn. Fed. Libr. and Info. Ctr. Com., 1992-93, 2002-03; chmn. CENDI Group, 1991-94, 99-2001; mem. NATO Agard Tech. Info. Panel, 1985-91, Internat. Coun. Sci. and Tech. Info., 1993—, treas., 1998-2001, chair editl. bd., 1999-2001, pres. 2001—04; mem. Info. Infrastructure Task Force, 1993-97; chair panel 2 U.S. Nat. Commn. on Librs. and Info. Sci. Comprehensive Assessment of Pub. Info. Dissemination, 2000; mem. Handle Sys. Adv. Com., 2001-; NFAIS Conrad Meml. lectr., 2003; cons. in field, 2006-. 1st lt. U.S. Army, 1960-63. Recipient Meritorious award William A. Jump Meml. Found., 1973, Civilian Svc. award, Def. Logistics Agy., 1991, Exceptional Civilian Svc. award, DLA, 1985, Exceptional Civilan Svc. award, Def. Info. Systems Agy., 2005. Methodist.

MOLINA, JOSEPH MARIO (MARIO MOLINA), medical administrator; b. Long Beach, Calif., May 16, 1958; s. C. David and Mary R. (Salandini) M.; m. Therese Ann Flynn; children: Carley, Colleen, David, Mary Clare. BA, Calif. State U., Long Beach, 1980; MD, U. So. Calif., 1984. Diplomate Am. Bd. Internal Medicine. Intern and residency Johns Hopkins U., 1984—87; assoc. investigator VA, San Diego, 1988-90; asst. clin. prof. U. So. Calif., LA, 1990-91; med. dir. Molina Healthcare, Inc., Long Beach, 1991-94, v.p. HMO, 1994—96, chmn., pres., CEO, 1996—. Bd. dirs. New Am. Alliance. Nat. trustee Boys and Girls Club Am. Recipient Ernst & Young Gr. L.A. Entrepreneur of Yr. award, 2002; named one of Top 10 Latinos in Healthcare, LatinoLeaders mag., 2004, 25 Most Influential Hispanics, Time Mag., 2005; named to Hall of Fame, Long Beach Cmty. Coll., 2002. Mem. ACP, Am. Diabetes Assn., Calif. Med. Assn. Avocation: collecting antique medical books. Office: Molina Health Care 200 Oceangate Ste 100 Long Beach CA 90802-4317 Office Phone: 562-435-3666. Business E-Mail: mario.molina@molinahealthcare.com.

MOLINA, MARIO JOSE, physical chemist, educator; b. Mexico City, Mar. 19, 1943; arrived in U.S., 1968; s. Roberto Molina-Pasquel and Leonor Henríquez; m. Alvarez Guadalupe, Feb. 11, 2006; 1 child, Felipe. Bachillerato, Acad. Hispano Mexicana, Mexico City, 1959; Ingeniero Químico, U. Nacional Autónoma de México, 1965; postgrad., U. Freiburg, Fed. Republic Germany, 1966—67; PhD, U. Calif., Berkeley, 1972. Asst. prof. U. Nacional Autónoma de México, 1967—68; research assoc. U. Calif.-Berkeley, 1972—73, U. Calif.-Irvine, 1973—75, asst. prof. phys. chemistry, 1975—79, assoc. prof., 1979—82; sr. rsch. scientist Jet Propulsion Lab., 1983—89; prof. dept. earth, atmospheric and planet sci., dept. chemistry MIT, Cambridge, 1989—96, Martin prof. atmospheric chemistry, 1997—2004, Inst. prof., 1997—2004; prof., chemistry and biochemistry Univ. Calif., San Diego, 2004—; faculty, Ctr. for Atmospheric Sci. Scripps Inst. of Oceanography, 2004—. Bd. dirs. MacArthur Found. Recipient Tyler Ecology award, 1983, Esselen award for chemistry in pub. interest, 1987, Max-Planck-Forschungs-Preis, Alexander von Humboldt-Stiftung, 1994, Nobel Prize in Chemistry, 1995, Sasakawa prize, UNEP, 1999; named a Trailblazer in Sci., Sci. Spectrum Mag., 2005; named one of 50 Most Important Hispanics in Govt., Edn., Hispanic Engineer and Info. Tech. mag., 2005. Mem.: NAS, Pontifical Acad. Sci., Inst. of Medicine, Am. Geophys. Union (Pres.'s Com. on Advisors on Sci. and Tech. 1994—2000), Am. Phys. Soc., Am. Chem. Soc. Achievements include discovery of the theory that fluorocarbons deplete ozone layer of stratosphere. Office: Dept Chem & Biochem UCSD 3050-E 9500 Gilman Dr La Jolla CA 92093-0356 Office Phone: 858-534-1696. *We have to understand our environment to find out if we are tampering with it. One of our accomplishments has been to call attention to society's potential altering of the atmosphere.*

MOLINA, YADIER B., professional baseball player; b. Bayamon, PR, July 13, 1982; m. Wanda Molina; 1 child, Yanuell Benjamin. Catcher St. Louis Cardinals, 2004—. Mem. Puerto Rican nat. team World Baseball Classic, 2006, 09. Recipient Fielding Bible award, 2007, 2008, Gold Glove award, 2008; named to Nat. League All-Star Team, Maj. League Baseball, 2009. Achievements include member of the World Series Championship winning St. Louis Cardinals, 2006. Office: St Louis Cardinals 700 Clark St Saint Louis MO 63102*

MOLINARI, SUSAN, lobbyist, former congresswoman; b. Staten Island, NY, Mar. 27, 1958; d. Guy V. and Marguerite (Wing) Molinari; m. Bill Paxon; 2 children. BA, SUNY, Albany, 1980, MA, 1982. Former intern for State Senator Christopher Mega; former rsch. analyst NY State Senate Fin. Com.; former fin. asst. Nat. Rep. Gov.'s Assn.; ethnic community liaison Rep. Nat. Com., 1983-84; minority leader NYC Coun., 1986-90; mem. US Congress from 14th (now 13th) NY dist., 1990-97, vice-chair House Rep. Conf.; anchor CBS News Sat. Morning, NYC, 1997-98; chmn., CEO The Washington Group, 2001—; pres. Ketchum Pub. Affairs, 2004—. Author: (book) Representative Mom: Balancing Budgets, Bill and Baby in the U.S. Congress, 1998. Recipient 50 Top Lobbyists, Washingtonian mag., 2007. Roman Catholic. Office: c/o The Washington Group 601 13th St NW Ste 410S Washington DC 20005-3864*

MOLINARO, JAMES P., city official; b. NYC, Mar. 11, 1931; m. Carol E. Molinaro (dec. 1990); 2 children. Chief of staff to Congressman Guy. V. Molinari 14th Congl. Dist., NY; dep. borough pres. Staten Island, NY, 1990—2001; borough pres., 2002—. With NY State Conservative Party, 1964—, chmn. Richmond County, 1974—89, exec. vice chair, 1989—. Bd. dirs. Heart Inst. Staten Island, Sisters of Charity Health Care Corp.; founder Staten Island AIDS Day Care Ctr. and AIDS med. care facility; chmn. St. Elizabeth Anne's Health and Rehab. Ctr., 1993—99. Republican. Office: Borough Pres 120 Borough Hall Staten Island NY 10301*

MOLINARO, JOSEPH DANIEL, dentist, director; b. Phila., May 4, 1969; s. Daniel Joseph and Antoinette Marie (Napolio) Molinaro; m. Ellen Catherine Frank, June 14, 2003. BS in Biology, Villanova U., Pa., 1991; DMD, Temple U., Phila., 1995; MS in Oral Biology, George Washington U., Washington, 2001. Diplomate Fed. Svcs. Bd. Gen. Dentistry, 2002, Am. Bd. Gen. Dentistry 2002. Gen. dentist U.S. Naval Dental Ctr. USN, Agana, Guam, 1995—97, dental clinic divsn. officer, 1996—97, gen. dentist USS George Washington CVN 73 Norfolk, Va., 1997—99, dental clinic divsn. officer, 1998—99, resident, comprehensive dentistry Nat. Naval Dental Ctr. Bethesda, Md., 1999—2001, comprehensive dentist, dental clinic dept. head dental annex br. Indian Head, Md., 2001—04, dep. sr. dental surgeon pers. exch. program Portsmouth, England, 2004—06; operative dentistry dept. head Dental Clinic MC Recruit Depot, 2006—07; dir. advanced edn. gen. dentistry program Branch Dental Clinic, San Diego, 2007—. Contbr. articles to profl. jours. Comdr. Dental Corps USN, 1995—, Dental Corps. Decorated Navy and Marine Corps Commendation medal, Navy and Marine Corps Achievement medal, Humanitarian Svc. medal USN; recipient Martin I. Munin award, Temple U. Sch. Dentistry, 1995, Comdg. Officer's award for excellence, Nat. Naval Dental Ctr., 2000, Chief of the Dental Corps award, 2001; Health Profls. scholar, USN, 1994—95. Fellow: Acad. Gen. Dentistry; mem.: ADA, Acad. Operative Dentistry, Edward C. Penick Endodontic Study Club. Roman Catholic. Achievements include completed a study comparing the influence of various dental restorative materials on tooth cusp stiffness. Avocations: travel, reading, sports. Personal E-mail: joeandellen@molinaro.us.

MOLINARO, SAMUEL L., JR., diversified financial services company executive; b. Binghamton, NY, Dec. 30, 1957; m. Lisa Melino; children: Danielle Anne, Alexa Nicole. BBA in Acctg., St. Bonaventure U., Olean, NY, 1980. CPA, NY. Mgr. Price Waterhouse, NYC, 1980-86; sr. v.p. fin. Bear Stearns Companies Inc., NYC, 1986-96, sr. v.p., CFO, 1996—2001, exec. v.p., CFO, 2001—07, exec. v.p., CFO, COO, 2007—. Office: Bear Stearns 383 Madison Ave New York NY 10179

MOLINARO-THOMPSON, DAVID ROBERT, secondary school educator; b. Washington, Pa., May 18, 1962; s. Robert David and Ellen Bennington Thompson; m. Jacqueline Anne Molinaro, Oct. 13, 1990; 1 child, Ian David. BA, Coll. Wooster, Ohio, 1985; MS in Edn., Duquesne U., Pitts., 1994. Polit. cons., organizer, various locations, 1986—92; history and humanities tchr. Bethelehem Ctr. Sch. Dist., Fredericktown, Pa., 1996—, chmn. sch. renewal team, 2002—06. Cert. mem. Student Assistance Team, Fredericktown, 1999—. Exhibitions include Mt. Lebanon Pub. Libr., 2006. Vol. Mt. Lebanon Libr., Pitts., 2002—; vol. various polit. candidates Pitts., 1992—. Mem.: NEA, Pa. State Edn. Assn., Bethlehem Ctr. Tchrs.' Assn. Avocations: bicycling, reading, photography, hiking, movies. Office: Bethlehem Ctr Sch Dist 179 Crawford Rd Fredericktown PA 15333

MOLINA_FIGUEROA, SINTIA E., language educator; d. Felix Antonio Molina-Delgado and Consuelo Molina; m. Pedro J. Figueroa, Aug. 24, 1980; children: Elizabeth Dianne Figueroa, Cristina Leonor Figueroa. PhD, Grad. Ctr. CUNY, 1995. Latin Am. and latino studies prof. St. Francis Coll., Brooklyn, NY, 2001—. Bd. mem. Caribbean Jour., Mass., 2007—. Contbr. articles to profl. publs. Mem. Nat. Women Orgn., NY, 2003. Recipient Faculty Rsch. award, 2002, 2005, 2007. D-Liberal. Roman Catholic. Office: St Francis Coll 180 Remsen St Brooklyn NY 11201 Business E-Mail: smolina@stfranciscollege.edu.

MOLINDER, JOHN IRVING, engineering educator, consultant; b. Erie, Pa., June 14, 1941; s. Karl Oskar and Carin (Ecklund) M.; m. Janet Marie Ahlquist, June 16, 1962; children: Tim, Karen. BSEE, U. Nebr., 1963; MSEE, Air Force Inst. Tech., 1964; PhD EE, Calif. Inst. Tech., 1969. Registered profl. engr., Calif. Project officer Ballistic Systems Div., Norton AFB, Calif., 1964-67; sr. engr. Jet Propulsion Lab., Pasadena, Calif., 1969-70; prof. engring. Harvey Mudd Coll., Claremont, Calif., 1970—; prin. engr. Qualcomm Inc., 1996-97; contractor Boeing Satellite Systems, 2000—02. Part-time lectr. Calif. State U., L.A., 1970-74; mem. tech. adv. panel Kinematics, Pasadena, 1985-86; part-time mem. tech. staff Jet Propulsion Lab., Pasadena, 1974-97, rep. NASA Hdqrs., Washington, 1979-80; vis. prof. elec. engring. Calif. Inst. Tech., 1982-83. Contbr. articles to profl. jours. Served to capt. USAF, 1963-67. Mem.: IEEE (sr.). Avocations: bicycling, reading, computers. Office: Harvey Mudd Coll Dept Engring 301 Platt Blvd Claremont CA 91711-5901 Home Phone: 909-593-0982. Business E-Mail: John_Molinder@hmc.edu.

MOLINE, JACQUELINE, occupational physician; b. Buffalo, Nov. 10, 1962; d. Sheldon Walter and Gloria Bettina Moline; m. Antoine Drye, Nov. 17, 2001. BA, U. Chgo., 1984, MD, 1988; MsC, Mt. Sinai Sch. Medicine, 1993. Diplomate Nat. Bd. Med. Examiners, Am. Bd. Internal Medicine, Am. Bd. Preventive Medicine. Resident in internal medicine Yale U./New Haven Hosp., 1988—91; resident in occupl. medicine Mt. Sinai Sch. Medicine, 1991—93, residency dir. occupl. medicine NYC, 1998—2006, vice chmn. dept. cmty. and preventive medicine, 2002—, assoc. prof. community and preventative medicine, assoc. prof. gen. internal medicine; dir. NY NJ Edn. & Rsch. Ctr., 2006—. Cons. United Fedn. Tchrs., NYC, 1992—; med. core dir. WTC Worker and Vol. Screening Program, NYC, 2002—06; dir. WTC Med. Monitoring & Treatment Program Clin. Ctr., Mt. Sinai, 2006—. Bd. dirs. JazzReach, NYC, 2002—. Recipient fellowship award, Found. for Occupl. Medicine, 1993, Laborer's award, NY-NJ Laborers, 1999. Mem.: ACP, Am. Coll. Occupl. and Environ. Medicine (bd. dirs. NY 2001—). Office: Mt Sinai Sch Medicine 1 Gustave Levy Pl New York NY 10029 E-mail: jacqueline.moline@mssm.edu.*

MOLINE, JENNIFER M., corporate financial executive; Various positions up to v.p., treas. Tupperware Corp., 1989—2000; v.p. acctg. svcs. ANC Rental Corp., 2000—03; v.p. US fin. ops., dir. fin. integration DHL Express, 2003—06; sr. v.p., contr. Office Depot, Inc., Delray Beach, Fla., 2006—08.

MOLINEAUX, CHARLES BORROMEO, lawyer, arbitrator, columnist, poet; b. NYC, Sept. 27, 1930; s. Charles Borromeo and Marion Frances (Belter) M.; m. Patricia Leo Devereux, July 2, 1960; children: Charles, Stephen, Christopher, Patricia, Peter, Elizabeth. BS cum laude, Georgetown U., 1950; JD, St. Johns U., 1959. Bar: N.Y. 1959, Mass. 1981, D.C. 1988. From assoc. to ptnr. Nevius, Jarvis & Pilz and successor firms, NYC, 1959-77; ptnr. Gadsby & Hannah, NYC, 1978-80; v.p., gen. counsel Perini Corp., Framingham, Mass., 1980-87; pvt. practice Washington, 1987—. Adj. faculty Internat. Law Inst., Washington, 1989—. Author numerous poems. Mem. adv. bd. Inst. for Transnat. Arbitration; committeeman Rep. Party, Nassau County, NY, 1965—71, mem. exec. com., committeeman Fairfax County, Va., 1989. 1st lt. US Army, 1954—56. Fellow Am. Bar Found.; mem. ASCE, Am. Arbitration Assn. (constrn. ADR task force 1994—), Chartered Inst. Arbitrators, Fedn. Internat. Engrs.-Conseils (Assoc. Gen. Contractors del. constrn. contract com., Louis Prangey award for svc. to profession cons. engring. 1996), Soc. Constrn. Arbitrators London, Del. Hist. Soc., London Ct. Internat. Arbitration, Fellowship Cath. Scholars. Roman Catholic. Home: 8321 Weller Ave Mc Lean VA 22102-1717 Office: 1660 International Dr Ste 400 Mc Lean VA 22102 Office Phone: 703-287-4232. Personal E-mail: cmlnx@aol.com.

MOLITERNO, DAVID J., cardiologist, educator; b. Flint, Mich., Oct. 29, 1960; m. Judith Ann Delp; children: Nathaniel, Benjamin. BS with honors, U. Mich., 1982; MD, Med. Coll. Va., 1987. Diplomate Am. Bd. Internal Medicine, Am. Bd. Cardiovascular Medicine, Am. Bd. Interventional Cardiology. Intern Vanderbilt U. Hosps., Vanderbilt U. Med. Ctr., Nashville, 1987—88; resident Vanderbilt U. Hosps. and Nashville VA Med. Ctr., 1988—90; fellow Parkland Meml. Hosp. and Dallas VA Med. Ctr., U. Tex. Southwestern Med. Ctr., 1990—93; fellow in interventional cardiology The Cleve. Clinic Found., 1993—94, staff physician sect. interventional cardiology dept. cardiovascular medicine, 1994—2003; vice chmn., internal medicine, chief, divsn. cardiology, Jefferson M. Gill prof. cardiology Univ. Ky., 2003—. Contbr. numerous articles to profl. jours.; reviewer: jours. in field, sect. editor: Jour. Thrombosis and Thrombolysis, mem. editl. bd.: Jour. Am. Coll. Cardiology. Named one of Best Doctors in Am., 2007. Fellow: ACP, European Soc. Cardiology, Am. Coll. Cardiology; mem.: AMA, Am. Heart Assn. Office: Gill Heart Inst U Ky HealthCare 800 Rose St Lexington KY 40536 Address: U Ky Divsn Cardiovascular Medicine Wethington Bldg Rm 317 900 S Limestone St Lexington KY 40536-0200 Office Phone: 859-323-5843. Office Fax: 859-257-3537. Business E-Mail: moliterno@uky.edu.

MOLITOR, GRAHAM THOMAS TATE, lawyer; b. Seattle, Apr. 6, 1934; s. Robert Franklin and Louise Margaret (Graham) M.; m. Carlotta Jean Crate, July 30, 1960; children: Graham Thomas Tate, Anne Therese, Christopher Robert. BS, U. Wash., 1955; LLB, Am. U., 1963. Bar: D.C. 1963. Rsch. asst. U. Wash., Seattle, 1957; bailiff U.S. Criminal Ct. D.C., 1958-59; legis. counsel U.S. Ho. of Reps., Washington, 1961-63; dir. candidate rsch. Rockefeller for Pres. Com., 1963-64, 68; D.C. counsel, asst. dir. govtl. rels. Nabisco, Inc., Washington, 1964-70; dir. govtl. rels. Gen. Mills, Inc., Washington, 1970-77; pres., CEO Pub. Policy Forecasting, Inc., Potomac, Md., 1977—2004; prin. ptnr. Pub. Policy Communicators, 1989-91. Prin., ptnr. Pub. Policy Action Inst., Potomac; adv. bd. Creative Bus. Strategies, Inc.; adj. prof. Grad. Sch. Bus. Am. U., Washington, 1969—75, Washington, 1979—85, Montgomery Coll., Rockville, Md., 1987—88; dir. rsch. White House Conf. on Indsl. World Ahead, 1971—72; mem. White House Adv. Com. on Social Indicators, 1975—76; chmn. Commn. on the Future of Montgomery County, 1986—88; guest lectr. numerous univs.; mem. White House Confs. on Food, Nutrition and Health, 1969—71, White House Conf. on Youth, 1970; bd. dirs. First Global Conf. on the Future, Inc., Can., 1980—; organizing com. Found. for the Future, 1997—, bd. advisors, 1999—, mem. scholar adv. bd., 2001—. Contbg. editor Food Tomorrow Newsletter, 1976-77; co-editor, chmn. editl. bd. Ency. of the Future, 1991-96; cons. editor Hist. Guide to Am. Govt., 1995-97, McMillan Compendium of the Twenty-First Century, 1998-99; editl. adv. bd. Technol. Forecasting and Social Change, 1999—; chmn. editl. bd. Future Survey, 1995-97, World Ency. of Police Forces and Correctional Systems, 2003-05; mem. editl. bd. Hudson Inst. Study of World Food Problems, 1975-77, bd. Bus. Tomorrow Newsletter, 1977-79, Jour. Futures Studies, 2001—; bd. advisors New Mktg. Techs. Monitor, 1983-85; polit. editor On the Horizon, 1993-95; contbr. articles to profl. jours. Mem. Food Adv. Bd., N.Y.C., 1980-86. Served to 1st lt. U.S. Army, 1958-61. Recipient Disting. Service award Grocery Mfrs. Am., 1973-74, Disting. Service award Nat. Consumer Info. Center, 1974, Disting. Service award Am. Mgmt. Assn., 1975. Fellow: World Acad. Art and Sci. (exec. com. 2000—, chmn. com. on yr. 3000 2001—, bd. trustees); mem.: World Future Soc. (gen. chmn. 2d Gen. Assembly 1975, v.p., dir. 1981—94, v.p., legal counsel 1994—2004, Disting. Svc. award 1975, 2004), E.D. Export Coun., Washington Indsl. Roundtable, Washington Bus.-Govt. Rels. Coun., Univ. Club, Phi Alpha Delta, Phi Kappa Sigma. Republican. Presbyterian. Home and Office: 6343 Saucon Valley Dr Fayetteville PA 17222-9242

MOLL, DAVID CARTER, civil engineer; b. Ames, Iowa, Aug. 5, 1948; s. Dale Curtis and Virginia (Carter) Moll; m. Margaret E. Newman (div. 1989); 1 child, Megahn Elizabeth; m. Melanie G. Harding, 2004 (div. 2006). BSCE, Iowa State U., 1971; cert. advanced study, Am. Grad. Sch. Internat. Mgmt., 1983; MBA with distinction, U. Mich., 1984; advanced masters cert. in project mgmt., George Washington U., 2006. Engr. in tng., Iowa; field engr. Chgo. Bridge & Iron Co., 1971; subcontract supr., field engr. Morrison-Knudsen Internat. Co., Inc., Surinam and Panama, 1976; site supt. engring., asst. supt. constrn. Fluor Corp., Saudi Arabia, 1977-82; group mgr. Cummins Engine Co., Columbus, Ind., 1984-85; mgr. spl. projects Kerr-McGee Coal Corp., Oklahoma City, 1985-88; project mgr. Kerr-McGee Corp., Oklahoma City, 1989, 1993—98, London, 1989-90, Saudi Arabia, 1990—92, Kerr-McGee Environ. Mgmt. Corp., Oklahoma City, 1998—2004; pres. Integrated Solutions Inc., 2005—. Lt. USN, 1971—75. Mem.: AGSIM (leadership cir.), ASCE, Project Mgmt. Inst. (Red Earth chpt. dir. fin., cert. project mgmt. profl.), NY Acad. Scis., Am. Soc. Quality Control (mem. constrn. tech. com.), Civil Engr. Corps (Meritorious Svc. medal), Marston Club, Order of the Knoll (Campanile Guild), Am. Legion, Chi Epsilon. Avocations: cross country skiing, jogging, golf, travel.

MOLL, GEORGE WILLIAM, pediatrician, educator; b. Milw., Nov. 23, 1947; s. George William, Sr. and Laverne Delores (Klein) M.; m. Susana Valdez Ramos, June 24, 1978; children: Christina, Teresa. BA in Chemistry cum laude, Carleton Coll., 1969; PhD in Biochemistry, U. Chgo., 1975, MD, 1977. Diplomate Nat. Bd. Med. Examiners; diplomate in pediatrics and pediat. endocrinology Am. Bd. Pediatrics; cert. PALS, CPR. Pediatric resident Mott Children's Hosp., U. Mich., Ann Arbor, 1977-79; pediatric endocrinology fellowship Wyler Children's Hosp., U. Chgo., 1979-81; asst. prof. pediatrics U. Chgo., 1981-85, Emory U. Sch. Medicine, Atlanta, 1985-87; assoc. prof. pediatrics U. Miss. Med. Ctr., Jackson, 1987-93, prof. pediatrics, 1993—; assoc. staff pediatric endocrinology Little Co. of Mary Hosp., Evergreen Park, Ill., 1981-85, The Meth. Hosps., Gary and Merrillville, Ind., 1981-85; staff pediatric endocrinologist The Emory Clinic, Atlanta, 1985-87, Henrietta Egleston Hosp. for Children, Atlanta, 1985-87, Grady Meml. Hosp., Atlanta, 1985-87; staff Emory Univ. Hosp., 1987, dir. pediatric endocrinology; staff U. Miss. Med. Ctr., Jackson, 1987—. Contbr. articles to profl. jours. Active Diabetes Found. of Miss., Inc., 1998, Juv. Diabetes Found. Internat., 1998, Filipino-Am. Assn. of Miss., 1990—, Chronic Disease Coalition of Miss., 1996—. Recipient med. scientist NIH scholarship/grant U. Chgo., 1970-77, Andrew Mellon Found. fellowship, 1981-82, Med. Excellence award So. Med. Assn., 1995; grantee Am. Lung Assn., 1987-89, Eli Lilly Co., Mobil Oil Co., 1991, Diabetes Rsch. and Edn. Found., Inct., 1992, Pharmacia & Upjohn, 1998, others. Fellow Am. Acad. Pediatrics, Am. Coll. Endocrinology; mem. AAAS, Nat. Bd. Med. Examiners (comprehensive task force for reprodn./endocrinology 1989-90), Chgo. Endocrine Club (sec. 1984-85), N.Y. Acad. of Sci., Am. Fedn. for Med. Rsch., Lawson Wilkins Soc. for Pediat. Endocrinology, Midwest and So. Soc. for Pediatric Rsch., Miss. State Med. Assn., Cen. Miss. Med. and Pediatric Soc., The Endocrine Soc. (regional rep. U.S. Pharmacopeia Quinquennial), Am. Diabetes Assn., Juv. Diabetes Found., Sigma Xi, others. Achievements include isolation of a bovine brain protein kinase and establishment of a protein kinase assay employing a novel PEI-cellulose thin-layer system as part of a PhD Biochemistry; established a novel modified flow-dialysis system for steady state hormone action studies; assisted the delineation of a LH-receptor defect related to precocious puberty and a novel genetic mutation in thyroid binding globulin in males; novel genetic mutation in succinate dehydrogenase subunit B gene for malignant paraganglioma. Avocations: carpentry, general handicrafts, electronics, computer repair work. Office: Univ Miss Med Ctr 2500 N State St Jackson MS 39216-4500 Business E-Mail: gmoll@ped.umsmed.edu.

MOLL, JOHN LEWIS, retired electronics engineer; b. Wauseon, Ohio, Dec. 21, 1921; s. Samuel Andrew and Esther (Studer) M.; m. Isabel Mary Sieber, Oct. 28, 1944; children: Nicolas Josef, Benjamin Alex, Diana Carolyn. B.Sc., Ohio State U., 1943, PhD, 1952; Dr. h.c., Faculty Engring., Katholieke U. Leuven, (Belgium), 1983. Elec. engr. RCA Labs., Lancaster, Pa., 1943-45; mem. tech. staff Bell Telephone Labs., Murray Hill, N.J., 1952-58; mem. faculty Stanford U., 1958-69, prof. elec. engring., 1959-69; tech. dir. optoelectronics Fairchild Camera and Instrument Corp., 1969-74; dir. integrated circuits labs. Hewlett-Packard Labs., Palo Alto, Calif., 1974-80, dir. IC structures research, sr. scientist, 1980-87, dir. Superconductivity Lab., 1987-90, mem. tech. staff, 1990-96; ret., 1996. Author: Physics of Semi Conductors, 1964; co-author Computer Aided Design and VLSI Device Development, 1985, rev. edit., 1988; inventor (with Ebers) first analytical transistor model, 1953, still valid and useful for circuit design. Recipient Howard N. Potts medal Franklin Inst., 1967, Disting. Alumnus award Coll. Engring., Ohio State U., 1970, Benjamin C. Lamme medal Coll. Engring., Ohio State U., 1988, Vladimir Karapetoff award Eta Kappa Nu, 1995; Guggenheim fellow, 1964, C&C Award, NEC Fund Integration Comm. and Computers, 1997. Fellow IEEE (Ebers award 1971, Thomas A. Edison medal 1991), Am. Acad. Arts and Scis.; mem. Am. Phys. Soc., Nat. Acad. Engring., Nat. Acad. Scis. Home: 600 Sand Hill Rd Apt 201H Palo Alto CA 94304-2635

MOLL, LLOYD HENRY, retired bank executive; b. Reading, Pa., June 26, 1925; s. Lewis J. and Katie (Rothermel) M.; m. Luise G. Keiper, Oct. 25, 1947; children: Lloyd E., Darryl M. BA, Albright Coll., Reading, 1952. Aircraft engine installer War Dept., 1942-47; tire inspector Firestone Tire & Rubber Co., Pottstown, Pa., 1947-48; asst. mgr. Household Fin. Corp., Reading, Pa., 1952—57; v.p. Meridian Asset Mgmt. Inc. and Meridian Trust Co. (formerly Am. Bank & Trust Co. of Pa.), Reading, 1957—94; v.p. sales and mktg. Investors Trust Co., Wyomissing, Pa., 1995—2005; ret., 2005. Co-founder, past dir. Estate Planning Council of Berks County. Served with AUS, 1945-47. Mem. Am. Inst. Banking. (dir., chmn. bank relations Berks County chpt., pres. 1972-73), Toastmasters (pres. Reading club 1992), Optimists (pres. Reading club 1978-79). Democrat. Home Phone: 610-779-2705. *Although it has been known to fail me on occasion I try to live by my understanding of the "Golden Rule". When it does fail me I'm usually able to discount such failure by recounting in my mind the many times it has been a two-way street or by convincing myself that I didn't try hard enough in this particular instance. All too often it comes to me much later that the other fellow's interpretation of the "Golden Rule" was far superior to mine. When this happens I have added to my learning. When it does not happen, it forces me to try that much harder to avoid "PERFECTION".*

MOLL, MARYANN ELIZABETH, education educator; b. Buffalo, Apr. 1, 1943; d. Bernard J. and Jean Moll; children: Mark D. Szczepanik, Nancy J. Szczepanik. AA in Paralegal with honors, Erie C.C., Buffalo, 1998; BA in Legal Studies and History, SUNY, Buffalo, 2000; MEd with hon. summa cum laude, Ottawa U., Phoenix, 2008. Cert. social studies tchr. Ariz., 2001, endorsed ESL tchr. Ariz., 2006, cert. English tchr. Ariz., 2009. Copyright asst. U. Buffalo Law Sch., 1998—2000; sub. tchr. Mesa Pub. Schs., Ariz., 2001—03; tchr., ESL coord. Ombudsman Ednl. Svcs., Phoenix, 2004—. Vol. Make A Difference, Phoenix, 2003—. Roman Catholic. Avocations: embroidery, sewing, reading, crocheting.

MOLL, STEPHAN, medical educator; b. Wuppertal, German, Sept. 22, 1959; married; 4 children. Cert. in internal medicine 2002, Germany, Norway, 1998, in hematology, lic. NC. Fellow and head clin. lab. Dept. Cardiology Humboldt U. Charite, Berlin, 1997—99; assoc. prof. Dept. Medicine, Divsn. Hematology-Oncology, U. NC. Bd. mem. Anticoagulation Forum, 2006—; bd. dir., chmn. med. and sci. adv. bd. Nat. Allaince Throntbosis and Thrombophilia, 2007—. Contbr. articles to jours., chapters to books. Recipient Recognisation award, UNC Dept. Medicine, 2006; grant, Bldg. Interdisciplinary Rsch. Ctr. Mem.: Am. Soc. Hematology (bd. mem. 2008—), Internat. Soc. Thrombosis and Haemostasis. Avocations: hiking, bicycling, travel. Office: Univ NC Sch Medicine Dept Medicine Divsn Hematology Oncology CB 7035 Chapel Hill NC 27599 Office Fax: 919-966-7369. Business E-Mail: smoll@med.unc.edu.*

MOLLA, AHMED ABDIN, surgeon; b. Al Madinah, Saudi Arabia, Oct. 15, 1929; s. Abdin Amin Molla and Azeeza Mustafa Khalil; m. Fayza Niazi, 1956 (div. 1961); 1 child, Nadia; m. Roberta Jean Sadowski, June 1962 (div. 1981); children: Nezar, Dina, Nora, Sara; m. Sarah Hamed Al Abbadi, Feb. 8, 1983; children: Amr, Asem, Adnan, Azeez, Ola. MB, BChir, Cairo U., 1954; diploma, Coll. Med. Evangelist, LA, 1960. Diplomate Am. Bd. Surgery. Dir. Sch. Health, Madinah, Saudi Arabia, 1956-59; head sch. health Almadina, 1960—61; resident St. Francis Gen. Hosp., Pitts., 1961—66; chief surgery King's Hosp., Madinah, 1966-74, Mil. Hosp., Jeddah, Saudi Arabia, 1975-87; vol. free cons. to the poor Al Madina, 1987—. Contbr. articles to newspapers. Recipient Al Istihkak medal Syrian Pres., Damascus, 1973. Fellow ACS, Internat. Coll. Surgeons. Muslim. Avocations: reading, travel. Home: PO Box 2528 Al Madinah Saudi Arabia Office Phone: 96648481675. Home Fax: 96648485096.

MOLLEN, EDWARD LEIGH, pediatrician, allergist, clinical immunologist; b. Richmond, Va., May 13, 1946; s. Irving Roth and Ruth (Damsky) M.; m. Mary Viola Jeffrey, Dec. 14, 1975; children: Shawn, Michael, Eric, Christopher. BS in Chemistry, Coll. William and Mary, 1968; MD, Med. Coll. Va., 1972. Diplomate Am. Bd. Pediatrics, Am. Bd. Allergy and Immunology. Resident in pediatrics Med. Coll. Va., Richmond, 1972-75, fellow in allergy and immunology, 1975-77; practice allergy and pediatric allergy and clin. immunology Allergy Assocs. of Richmond, 1977-85; pvt. practice allergy/pediatric allergy and clin. immunology Richmond, 1985—. Fellow Am. Acad. Allergy, Asthma and Immunology, Am. Acad. Pediatrics; mem. Med. Soc. Va., Richmond Acad. Medicine, Asthma and Allergy Soc. Va. Avocations: bicycling, running. Office: 5855 Bremo Rd Ste 702 Richmond VA 23226-1926 Home Phone: 804-353-8353; Office Phone: 804-288-5216. E-mail: elmollenmd@aol.com.

MOLLENAUER, LINN FREDERICK, retired physicist, writer; b. Washington, Pa., Jan. 6, 1937; B of Engring. Physics, Cornell U., 1959; PhD in Physics, Stanford U., 1965. Asst. prof. physics U. Calif., Berkeley, 1965—72; rsch. staff Bell Labs./Lucent Techs., Holmdel, NJ, 1972—2003; ret., 2003. Author (with J.P. Gordon): Solitons in Optical Fibers: Fundamentals and Applications, 2006; co-editor (with J.C. White): Tunable Lasers, 1987. Recipient Ballantine medal, Franklin Inst., 1986, Rank prize in Photonics, 1991; fellow, Bell Labs., 2000. Fellow: IEEE (LEOS Disting. Lectr. award 1991, LEOS Quantum Electronics award 2001), AAAS, Optical Soc. Am. (R.W. Wood prize 1982, Charles Hard Townes award 1997); mem.: NAE. Achievements include first to demonstrate optical soliton propagation, leading to the realization of soliton-based, ultra-high-capacity lightwave communication. Personal E-mail: linnm@optonline.net.

MOLLER, JAMES HERMAN, pediatrician, educator; b. Fresno, Calif., Aug. 12, 1933; s. Leonard Hansen and Eloise Jean (Hunter) M.; m. Carol Suzanne Eymann, Sept. 8, 1957; children: James, Elizabeth. AB, Stanford U., 1954, MD, 1958. Instr. pediat. U. Minn., Mpls., 1965-66, asst. prof., 1966-70, assoc. prof., 1970-73, prof., 1973—, Dwan prof., 1975—2005, interim head pediat., 1976-78, 97-99, chief pediat., 1976-78, head pediat., 1999—2003; chief of staff U. Minn. Hosp., Mpls., 1984-89. Vis. prof. Nat. Heart & Lung Inst., London, 1989-90, Inst. Child Health, London, 1989-90. Contbr. over 200 sci. articles to profl. jours. Bd. dirs. U. Minn. Hosp., 1984-89, Mpls. Children's Health Ctr., 1975-78, Children's Hosp., St. Paul, 1975-78, Minn. Assn. Pub. tchg. Hosps., Mpls., 1984-89, Variety Club Heart Assn., Mpls., 1980-83. Capt. U.S. Army, 1961-63. Fellow Am. Acad. Pediat. (exec. bd. 1991-92, dist. chmn. 1991-92, alternate dist. chmn. 1985-91, Ross Edn. award 1989), Am. Coll. Cardiology; mem. Am. Heart Assn. (pres. 1993-94, v.p. 1986-91, bd. dirs. 1986-95, award of Merit 1989), Am. Fedn. Clin. Rsch., Am. Pediatric Soc., Am. Bd. Pediat. Nat. Bd. Med. Examiners, Midwest Soc. Pediatric Cardiology Soc., Minn. Med. Assn. (intersplty. coun. 1979-82, resource group child health 1980-82), Minn. Acad. Medicine, Mpls. Met. Pediatric Soc, No. Pediatric Cardiology Soc. (pres. 1978-79), Midwest Soc. Pediatric Rsch. Soc. Pediatric Rsch., Hennepin County Med. Soc. (bd. dirs. 1986-89), Irish Am. Paediatric Soc., British Paediatric Cardiac Assn., Coun. Med. Splty. Socs. (bd. dirs., 1991—), Sub-bd. Pediatric Cardiology (chmn. 1992-94), Internam. Heart Found. (pres. 1997-98), World Heart Fedn. (bd. dirs. 1999). Independent. Congregationalist. Avocations: gardening, travel, oriental carpets, reading. Home: 4816 Sheridan Ave S Minneapolis MN 55410-1917 Office: U Minn 420 Delaware St SE Minneapolis MN 55455-0374 Office Phone: 612-626-2790. Business E-Mail: molle002@umn.edu.

MOLLER, MAERSK MC-KINNEY, shipowner; b. July 13, 1913; s. Arnold Peter and Chastine Estelle Mc-Kinney M.; m. Emma Mc-Kinney Moller, 1940 (dec. 2005); children: Leise, Kirsten, Ane. Ptnr. A.P. Møller, Copenhagen K, Denmark, 1940-65, sr. ptnr., 1965—. Chmn. A/S Dampskibsselskabet Svendborg, 1965-2003, chmn. Dampskibsselskabet af 1912 A/S, 1965-2003, A.P. Moller-Maersk A/S, 2003, Odense Steel Shipyard Ltd., A.P. Møller and Chastine Mc-Kinney Møller Found.; bd. dirs. Maersk Olie og Gas AS; mem. Internat. Coun. Morgan Guaranty Trust Co. N.Y, 1967-84; mem. adv. bd. IBM Corp., 1984-93, bd. dirs. 1970-84. Decorated Danish Order of the Elephant, Grand Cross of Order of Dannebrog; named Hon. Knight Brit. Empire, 1990, Hon. Mem. Baltic Exch., London, 1991; recipient Peace and Commerce medal US Dept. Commerce, 1991, Internat. Gold Medal award Kennedy Ctr., 2005. Address: 50 Esplanaden DK-1098 Copenhagen K Denmark

MOLLER, PATRICIA NEWTON, United States Ambassador to Burundi; m. Gilbert Sperling. Investment banker, tax specialist Smith Barney, 1977—87; US fgn. svc. officer US State Dept., 1987—, with consular sect. Munich, mgmt. officer Madras, India, 1989—91, watch officer, staff aide to the asst. sec. intelligence and rsch., Vietnam desk officer Washington, 1991—96, mgmt. officer Belgrade, Serbia, dep. mission chief Yerevan, Armenia, 2000—02, Tbilisi, Georgia, 2002—05, US amb. to Burundi, 2006—. Recipient Superior Honor award, US State Dept., Leamon R. Hunt award for adminstrn. excellence, 2000. Office: 2100 Bujumbura Pl Washington DC 20521*

MOLLICA, JOSEPH A., pharmaceutical executive; b. 1940; Various positions, sr. v.p. drug devel. Ciba-Geigy, Ardsley, NY, 1966—86; v.p. med. products E.I. Du Pont De Nemours & Co., Inc., Wilmington, Del., 1987—90; CEO Du Pont Merck Pharm. Co., Wilmington, Del., 1991—93; CEO, chmn. Pharmacopeia, Princeton, NJ, 1994—2004, chmn., 2004—, Neurocrine Biosciences, Inc., San Diego. Office: Neurocrine Biosciences Inc 12790 El Camino Real San Diego CA 92130 also: Pharmacopeia Inc 3000 Eastpark Blvd Cranbury NJ 08512-3516 Business E-Mail: mollica@pcop.com.

MOLLINS, GREGG J., metal products executive; b. 1955; Divsn. mgr. Santa Clara divsn. Reliance Steel & Aluminum Co., 1986—92, v.p., 1992—94, v.p., COO, 1994—95, COO, 1995—, exec. v.p., 1995—2002, bd. dirs., 1997—, pres., 2002—. Bd. dirs. Earle M. Jorgensen Co. Office: Reliance Steel & Aluminum Co 350 S Grand Ave Los Angeles CA 90071*

MOLLIS, A. RALPH, Secretary of State, Rhode Island, former mayor; b. Providence, May 24, 1961; s. Joseph Gregory Jr. and Gloria Louise (Stone) Mollis; children: Michael, Angelo, Briana; m. Laurie Ranaldi; 1 stepchild Gian Piscione. BA in Polit. Sci., St. Anselm Coll., 1983; student, So. New Eng. Sch. Law, 1983—85. Registered investment adv. 1996. V.p., dir. office ops. LAMCO Pension and Investment Adv. Firm, Worwick, RI, 1983—94; acting mayor Town of North Providence, RI, 1994, mayor RI, 1997—2007; bus. mgr. AAT Restaurant Corp., Providence, 1994-95; inst. & investment rep. NY Life, Providence, 1995-96; asst. property mgr., budget cons. Ferland Property Mgmt., RI, 1996; sec. state State of RI, Providence, 2007—. Coun. mem. Town of North Providence, 1986-96, coun. pres., 1992-94, HS bldg. com., 1991—. Recipient Environ. Merit award, US EPA, 2000, Giovanni Da Verrazzano award for Outstanding Svc. to RI Cmty., 2002, Portuguese Am. Citizens Com. of RI Govt. award, 2005. Mem. Lions, Italia-Am. Club (Outstanding Pub. Svc. award 2000), Sons of Italy. Democrat. Roman Catholic. Avocations: coaching, golf. Office: Office Sec State 82 Smith St State House Rm 217 Providence RI 02903

MOLLMAN, JOHN PETER, publishing executive; b. Belleville, Ill., Feb. 8, 1931; s. Kenneth John and Maurine (Farrow) M.; m. Carol J. Piper, Apr. 4, 1998; children: Sarah Chase Underhill, Eric Cleburne. BA, Washington U., St. Louis, 1952; cert. in advanced mgmt. program, Harvard Bus. Sch., 1986. Advt. specialist Gen. Electric Co., Schenectady and Boston, 1952-54; mgr. Enterprise Printing Co., Millstadt, Ill., 1956-66; dir. prodn. Harper & Row Pubs., NYC, 1967-74; pub. Harper's Mag. Press, NYC, 1971-74; v.p. prodn. Random House Inc., NYC, 1974-81; sr. v.p. World Book-Childcraft Inc., Chgo., 1981-88; pres. World Book Pub., 1988-91; pub. cons., 1991-92; dir. intellectual property devel. Multimedia Publishing Microsoft, 1992-96; cons. in electronic pub. Carmel, Calif., 1996—. Mem. vis. com. Washington U.; mem. pub. com. Art Inst. Chgo.; bd. dirs. Yerba Buena Ctr. for the Arts, San Francisco; pres. Internat. ebook Award Found., NY; dir. Carmel Pub.Libr. Found.,Calif. Mem. Golf Club at Quail Lodge, Phi Delta Theta, Sigma Delta Chi, Omicron Delta Kappa. Unitarian Universalist. Home: 25340 Vista Del Pinos Carmel CA 93923-8804 Office Phone: 831-622-7532. Personal E-mail: pmollman@msn.com.

MOLLOHAN, ALAN BOWLBY, United States Representative from West Virginia; b. Fairmont, W.Va., May 14, 1943; s. Robert H. and Helen (Holt) Mollohan; m. Barbara Whiting, Aug. 7, 1976; children: Alan, Robert, Andrew, Karl, Mary Kathryn. AB in Polit. Sci., Coll. William and Mary, 1966; JD, W.Va. U. Coll. Law, 1970. Assoc. law firm, 1970-82; mem. US Congress from 1st W.Va. dist., 1983—, mem. appropriations com., ranking minority mem. sci., state, justice, commerce and related agencies subcommittee, mem. mil. constrn., veterans affairs, and related agencies subcommittee, mem. interior, environ., and related agencies subcommittee. Served in USAR, 1970—83. Mem.: ABA, W.Va. Bar, Elks, Moose. Democrat. Baptist. Office: US Ho Reps 2302 Rayburn Ho Office Bldg Washington DC 20515-0001 Office Phone: 202-225-4172.*

MOLLOI, SABEE, medical educator; PhD, UW-Madison, Wis., 1987. Prof. U. Calif., Irvine, 1988—. Contbr. articles to numerous profl. jours. Recipient Outstanding Sr. award, Mankato State U., Minn., 1980; grant, NIH, 1989—2008. Mem.: Am. Assn. Physicist Medicine. Achievements include patents for automatic x-ray beam equalizer. Office: Univ CA Med Scis I B-140 Irvine CA 92697

MOLLOY, DAVID SCOTT, JR., labor relations educator; b. Providence, Aug. 17, 1946; s. David Scott and Miriam Virginia (Handy) Molloy; children: Kelsey Allende Molloy, Cady Larkin Molloy. BA, RI Coll., Providence, 1970; MA, U. NH, Durham, 1972; PhD, Providence Coll., 1991. Bus driver RI Pub. Transit Authority, Providence, 1973-81; bus. agt. Amalgamated Transit Union, Providence, 1981-84; chief-of-staff US Congresswoman Schnieder, Cranston, RI, 1984-86; prof. U. RI, Kingston, 1986—. Lectr. various labor unions, 1980—; intern dir. Labor Rsch. Ctr., U. RI, Kingston, 1986—; radio commentator Voice of America, Washington, 1992—. Author: (book) Trolley Wars, 1996, Irish Titan, Irish Toiler, 2008; contbr. articles to profl. jours.; contbg. editor: Two-Volume Historical Encyclopedia of American Labor, 2004. Mem. exec. bd. Providence Heritage Commn., 1982—92, Leadership RI, Providence, 1987—90; bd. dirs. RI State Humanities Coun., Providence, 1985—95; chmn. Libr. RI Hist. Soc., Providence, 1987—93. Recipient Achievement medal, City of Providence, 1986, Scott Molloy Labor Collection award, Smithsonian Instn., 1990, Tchg. Excellence award, Indsl. Rels. Rsch. Assn., 2000, Inst. Labor Studies, 2001; named RI Prof. of Yr., Carnegie Found. and CASE, 2005; named to Rhode Island Heritage Hall Of Fame, 2009. Mem.: AAUP (U. RI chmn. PAC 1994—96), Inst. Labor Studies (bd. dirs. 1987—), RI Indsl. Rels. Assn. (pres. 1995—96), Am. Fedn. Labor and Congress of Indsl. Orgn. (RI adv. exec. bd. 1981—84, Achievement award 1995), RI Irish Famine Meml. (edn. dir. 1996—2007), Blackstone Valley Heritage Corridor (commr. 1988—98), RI Labor History Soc. (founder, 1st pres. 1987—2000). Avocations: collecting labor and industrial artifacts, weightlifting. Home: 550 Usquepaugh Rd West Kingston RI 02892-1924 Office: Labor Rsch Ctr 36 Upper College Rd Kingston RI 02881-2005 Home Phone: 401-782-3614; Office Phone: 401-874-2569. Business E-Mail: molloy@uri.edu.

MOLNAR, GREG ROBERT, science educator; s. Robert Gerald Molnar and Priscilla Mitchell; m. Karla Anne Engel, Mar. 22, 1993; children: Seth Orion, Atticus Carter. BS, U. Fla., Gainesville, 1985; MS, U. Wyo., Laramie, 1989; PhD, Wash. State U., Pullman, 1993. Rsch. A.I. DuPont Children's Hosp., Wilmington, 1994—98; sci. instr. Ft. Myers High, Fla., 1998—2002, Valdosta HS, Ga., 2002—03, North Fla. CC, Madison, 2003—. Culture Satellite Cells grant, NASA, 1994—98. Mem.: Phi Theta Kappa. Achievements include research in isolate and characterize muscle stem cells in vitro; growth of muscle cells in simulated microgravity. Home: 958 NE Rocky Springs Church Rd Madison FL 32340 Office: N Fla CC 325 Turner Davis Dr Madison FL 32340 Business E-Mail: molnarg@nfcc.edu.

MOLNAR, VIOLET, mental health nurse; b. Budapest, Hungary; arrived in U.S., 1960; d. Janos Molnar and Erzsebeth Krekacs. ADN, Atlantic Union Coll., 1967; BSN, Walla Walla Coll., Wash., 1973. RN Mass., Calif. Staff nurse New Eng. Meml. Hosp., Stoneham, Mass., 1968—70; IV therapist Loma Linda U. Med. Hosp., Calif., 1970—72; psychiat. nurse St. Bernardines Med. Ctr., San Bernardino, Calif., 1974—89, Corona Regional Med. Ctr., San Bernardino, 1990—. Pub. spkr. Pres. Lady's Club Friendly Cir., Loma Linda, 1997—99, pres., 2006—; elder, deaconess, greeter Seventh Day Adventist Ch. Loma Linda U., 1975—. Mem.: Rotary Club San Bernardino/Highland (Paul Harris fellow 2001). Avocations: travel, reading, church activities. Home: 11422 Benton St Loma Linda CA 92354 Personal E-mail: imolnar@juno.com, ibimolnar@verizon.net.

MOLNAU, CAROL L., Lieutenant Governor of Minnesota; b. Waconia, Minn., Sept. 17, 1949; m. Steven F. Molnau, 1971; children: Heather, Kristen, Megan Attended, U. Minn. Mem. Chaska City Coun., 1989—92, Minn. Ho. of Reps., 1992—2003; commr. Minn. Dept. Transportation, 2003—08; lt. gov. State of Minn., St. Paul, 2003—. Active Corn Growers, Farm Bur., Soybean Growers, Norseland Ch. Mem. Agrl. Com., Econ. Devel., Infrastructure & Regulation Fin.-Transportation Fin. Divsn., Fin. Inst. & Ins.: Internat. Trade & Economic Devel. Republican. Lutheran. Office: Office Lt Governor 130 State Capitol 75 Rev Dr Martin Luther King Jr Blvd Saint Paul MN 55155 Office Phone: 651-296-3391. Office Fax: 651-296-2089.

MOLONEY, DANIEL M., electronics executive; BSEE, U. Mich.; MBA in Mgmt., U. Chgo. Joined Gen. Instrument Corp. (merged with Motorola), 1983; sr. v.p., gen. mgr. IP sys. group Motorola, Inc., Schaumburg, Ill., 2000—02, exec. v.p., pres., CEO broadband comm. sector, 2002—05, exec. v.p., pres. connected home solutions Horsham, Pa., 2005—. Contbr. articles to profl. jours. Office: Motorola Inc 1295 E Algonquin Rd Schaumburg IL 60196 also: Motorola Inc 101 Tournament Dr Horsham PA 19044-3603*

MOLONEY, STEPHEN MICHAEL, lawyer; b. LA, July 1, 1949; s. Donald Joseph and Madeline Marie (Sartoris) M.; m. Nancy Paula Barile, Jan. 15, 1972; children: Michael, John, Kathleen. Student, St. John's Sem., Camarillo, Calif., 1967-69; BS, U. Santa Clara, 1971, JD, 1975. Bar: Calif. 1975, U.S. Dist. Ct. (cen. dist.) Calif. 1976, U.S. Supreme Ct. 1990. Assoc. Gilbert, Kelly, Crowley & Jennett, LA, 1975-80, from ptnr. to sr. ptnr., 1980—. Arbitrator, settlement officer Los Angeles Superior Ct., 1985—. Contbr. articles to profl. jours. Dir. Calif. Def. Polit. Action Com., Sacramento, 1991—. With USAR. Recipient Svc. award to Pres. of So. Calif. Def. Counsel, Def. Rsch. Inst., Chgo., 1992. Mem. Assn. So. Calif. Def. Counsel (pres. 1992-93), Calif. Def. Counsel (dir. 1991—), L.A. County Bar Assn. (vols. in parole, 1976-77, exec. com. alternative dispute resolution com. 1992-96), Oakmont Country Club, La Quinta Resort and Club. Democrat. Roman Catholic. Avocations: politics, golf, reading, travel. E-mail: smm@gilbertkelly.com.

MOLONEY, THOMAS E., lawyer; b. Rockville Ctr., NY, Jan. 9, 1949; BS, U. Dayton, 1971; JD, U. Notre Dame, 1974. Bar: Ohio 1974. Prin. Am. Energy Svcs., Inc., Columbus, Ohio. Office: Am Energy Svcs Inc 1105 Schrock Rd Ste 602 Columbus OH 43229-1174 Office Phone: 614-885-1901. E-mail: amtem@sbcglobal.net.

MOLONEY, THOMAS JOSEPH, lawyer; b. Bklyn., Oct. 14, 1952; s. Thomas J. and Grace (Nelson) M.; m. Molly K. Heines, Dec. 26, 1976. AB, Columbia U., 1973; JD cum laude, NYU, 1976. Bar: NY 1977, US Dist. Ct. (so. dist.) NY 1977, US Dist. Ct. (ea. dist.) NY 1978, US Ct. Appeals (2d cir.) 1981, US Dist. Ct. (no. dist.) NY 1988, US Ct. Appeals (4th cir.) 1989, US Supreme Ct. 1991. Assoc. Cleary, Gottlieb, Steen & Hamilton, NYC, 1976—84, ptnr., 1984—. Bd. dirs. NY Lawyers for Pub. Interest, NYC, 1986-91; mediator US Bankruptcy Ct. for So. Dist. NY, 1995. Asst. counsel Gov.'s Jud. Nominating Com., NYC, 1981-85; chmn. bus. adv. coun. Washington Irving High Sch., 1994—. Mem. ABA, Am. Bankruptcy Inst., Assn. of Bar of City of NY (bankruptcy, corp. reorganization coms. 1983-86, chair com. legal assistance 1995-97), Order of Coif. Avocations: chess, golf, dance, travel, wine. Office: Cleary Gottlieb Steen & Hamilton 1 Liberty Plz Fl 38 New York NY 10006-1470

MOLONEY, WILLIAM J., former state official, school system administrator; BA in History and Polit. sci., MA in History and Polit. sci., Harvard U.; PhD in Ednl. Mgmt., Harvard U., Cambridge, Mass.; postgrad. studies in Slavic History, Oxford and U. of London. Served as a tchr., asst. prin., prin. Prin., headmaster, asst. supt., & supt. Mass., RI, NY, Pa. and Md.; dir. Am. Sch., London; supt. Calvert county pub. schools, Prince Frederick, Md., 1993—97; commr. edn. Colo. Dept. Edn., Denver, 1997—2007; sec. Colo. Bd. Edn., 1997—2007. Chmn. Edn. Leaders Coun., Washington; adj prof. Various Univs.; bd. dirs. Bds. of the Ctr. for Workforce Preparation, Ednl. Excellence Network; spkr. in field; cons. in field. Co-author: (Books) The Content of America's Character, Education Innovation: An Agenda to Frame the Future; newspaper columnist:.

MOLPUS, DICK H., investment company executive; b. Philadelphia, Miss., Sept. 7, 1949; s. Richard and Frances (Blount) M.; m. Sally Nash, May 27, 1971; children— Helen Nash, Richard Gregory BBA, U. Miss., 1971. V.p. mfg. Molpus Co., Phila., 1971-80; exec. dir. Gov's Office Fed.-State Programs, Jackson, Miss., 1980-83; sec. of state State of Miss., Jackson, 1984-96; pres., chmn. Molpus Co., Phila., 1996—; pres., dir. Molpus Woodlands Group, Jackson, Miss., 1996—; pres. Timberland Mgmt. Investment Orgn., Jackson, Miss. Dir. Citizens Bank and Trust Co. Vice pres. Miss. Agr. and Forestry Mus., 1979; campaign dir., chmn. bd. United Givers Fund, Nehshoba County, Miss., 1979-80; bd. dirs. Miss. PTA, 1980—; founder Parents for Pub. Schs. orgn., 1989. Recipient Friends of Children award Miss. Assn. Elem. Sch. Adminstrs., 1984, Pub. Ofcl. of Yr. award Miss. chpt. Am. Soc. for Pub. Adminstrn., 1985 Mem. Miss. Forestry Assn. (bd. dirs. 1980-87), Nat. Assn. Secs. of State (pres. 1992), Nature Conservancy (bd. dirs. Miss. chpt.), Sigma Chi, Omicron Delta Kappa, Pi Sigma Alpha (Theta Beta chpt.). Avocations: hiking, tennis, running, reading. Office: 654 N State St Jackson MS 39202

MOLSON, ANDREW T., management consultant; AB, Princeton U.; JD, Laval U.; MSc in Corp. Governance and Ethics, U. London. Ptnr., vice chmn. Res Publica Consulting Group, Monteal, Canada; vice chmn. bd. Molson Coors Brewing Co., 2008—. Bd. dirs. McCord Mus. of Can. History, Montreal Fluency Centre, Ste-Justine Hosp. Found., Concordia U.; v.p. Molson Found. Fellow: Inst. of Chartered Secretaries and Administrators (profl. adminstr.). Office: Res Publica Cons Group 2001 McGill College Ave, Ste 800 Montreal PQ H3A 1G1 Canada*

MOLSON, GEOFFREY ERIC, brewery company executive; s. Eric and Jane (Mitchell) Molson; m. Katherine Brigid Finn, May 30, 1998. BA in Econs., Saint Lawrence U., 1992; MBA, Babson Coll., 1996. Media asst. Coca Cola Co.; sr. strategy cons., CSC Consulting (formerly The Kalchas Group), NYC; key account mgr. Molson Canada; dir. field mktg. Molson USA, v.p. quality and distributor devel., v.p. sales and mktg.; v.p. customer mktg. Molson Coors Brewing Co., Quebec, Canada, 2006—07, v.p. mktg., 2007—. Bd. dirs. Montreal Canadiens. Bd. dirs. St. Mary's Hosp. Found., St. Lawrence U. Office: Molson Coors Brewing Co 1555 Notre-Dame Est Montreal PQ H2L 2R5 Canada*

MOLTENI, AGOSTINO, pathology educator; b. Como, Lombardy, Italy, Nov. 12, 1933; came to U.S., 1963; s. Enrico and Antonia (Signorini) M.; m. Loredana Brizio, Sept. 5, 1963; children: Claudio Enrico, Ronald Stephen. MD, U. Milan, Italy, 1957; PhD in Pathology, SUNY, Buffalo, 1970. Lic. Italian Bd. Internal Medicine, 1963. Intern and resident in internal medicine U. Milan (Italy), 1957-62; asst. prof. U. Milan, 1957-63; chief rsch. sect. Farmitalia Drug Co., Milan, 1963-65; rsch. assoc. SUNY, Buffalo, 1965-69, asst. prof., 1969-71; assoc. prof. U. Kans., Kansas City, 1971-76; prof. pathology Northwestern U., Chgo., 1976-96, prof. emeritus, 1996—; prof. pathology and pharmacology U. Mo., Kansas City, 1996—, adj. prof. basic med. scis. Vis. prof. Harvard U., 1983-84; dir. med. students rsch. program U. Mo. Kansas City, 2004-; adj. prof. anesthesia, U. Mo., Kansas City, 2007-. Editor, author: Endocrinology and Thermal Trauma, 1990, Menopause Update, 1992; exec. editor Current Pharmaceutical Design, 2000—, Nutrition Rsch., 2003, PPAR Rsch., 2005; contbr. articles to profl. jours., chpts. to books. Recipient Sharer in Lasker award Lasker Found., N.Y.C., 1983, Rsch. Career Devel. award NIH, Washington, 1970, award Am. Heart Assn., Chgo., 1982. Fellow Am. Acad. Clin. Biochemistry; mem. Am. Acad. Pathology, Am. Soc. Investigative Pathology, Clin. Chemistry Soc., Endocrine Soc. (emeritus), Am. Assn. Clin. Chemistry (emeritus). Achievements include patent for captopril as a cancer chemo-preventive agent; research on hypertension and hormonal regulation of cancer. Office: U Mo Truman Med Ctr 2301 Holmes St Kansas City MO 64108-2640 Office Phone: 816-235-5604. Business E-Mail: moltenia@umkc.edu.

MOLTZ, JAMES EDWARD, brokerage house executive; b. Williamsport, Pa., July 25, 1932; s. George N. and Margaret L. (Abell) M.; m. Barbara Vance, Sept. 8, 1956; children: George Wilson, James Clay, John Thomas. BS, Williams Coll., 1954; MBA, Wharton Sch., U. Pa., 1956. Chartered fin. analyst. Fin. analyst Cyrus J. Lawrence Inc., NYC, 1957-62, rsch. dir., 1962-64, gen. ptnr., 1964-71, mng. ptnr., 1971-73; chmn., pres. C.J. Lawrence/Deutsche Bank Securities Corp., NYC, 1973-95; chief investment officer Deutsche Bank Securities, 1996-99; vice chmn. ISI Inc., NYC, 1999—. Mem. adv. fin. com. Williams Coll.; trustee Sterling and Francine Clark Art Inst.; chmn. Woods Hole Oceanographic Inst., hon. trustee; trustee Rockefeller Bros. Fund, Edna McConnell Clark Found Mem. Fin. Analysts Fedn., N.Y. Soc. Security Analysts (former dir.), Union League Club (N.Y.C.), Wee Burn Country Club (Darien), Windsor Club (Vero Beach), The Links (N.Y.C.), The Blind Brock Club Home: 29 Indian Spring Trl Darien CT 06820-2109 Office: ISI Inc 40 W 57th St New York NY 10019 E-mail: jmoltz@isimgt.com.

MOLTZ, JOHN HENRY, III, biology professor; b. San Antonio, Aug. 4, 1949; s. John Henry and Verna Lee Moltz; m. Candace Carson Carson, Dec. 12, 1972; children: John Henry, Heidi Lee. PhD, U. Tex. Grad. Sch. Biomed. Scis., Southwestern Me, Dallas, 1977. Prof. basic sci., dir. rsch. Parker Coll., Dallas, 1989—2000; sr. lectr. U. Tex. Dallas, 1995—. Bd. trustees Midlothian ISD, Tex., 1983—94. Home: 2431 Clearview Midlothian TX 76065 Office: Univ Tex Dallas 800 W Campbell Rd Richardson TX 75083 Home Fax: 972-723-3281. Personal E-mail: jmoltz@aol.com.

MOLZ, REDMOND KATHLEEN, public affairs educator; b. Balt., Mar. 5, 1928; d. Joseph T. and Regina (Barry) M. BS, Johns Hopkins U., Balt., 1949, MA, 1950; MALS, U. Mich., Ann Arbor, 1953; DLS, Columbia U., NYC, 1976. Librarian I and II Enoch Pratt Free Library, Balt., 1953-56; pub. relations officer Free Library of Phila., 1958-62; editor Wilson Library Bull. H.W. Wilson Co., Bronx, NY, 1962-68; chief planning staff Bur. Libraries and Learning Resources U.S. Office Edn., Washington, 1968-73; prof. library sci. Sch. Library Service Columbia U., NYC, 1976-80, Melvil Dewey prof., 1980-93; prof. pub. affairs Sch. Internat. and Pub. Affairs, Columbia U., NYC, 1993-99, prof. emeritus, 2000—. Cons. U.S. Nat. Commn. Librs. and Info. Sci., Washington, 1974-75, U.S. Adv. Commn. Intergovtl. Relations, Washington, 1979-80; mem. nat. adv. coun. The Sheridan Librs., Johns Hopkins U., 1997—. Author: Federal Policy and Library Support, 1976 (Ralph R. Shaw award 1977), National Planning for Library Service, 1935-75, 1984, Library Planning and Policy Making: The Legacy of the Public and Private Sector, 1990, The Federal Roles in Support of Public Library Services, 1990, The Federal Roles in Support of Academic and Research Libraries, 1991; co-author (with Phyllis Dain) Civic Space/Cyberspace: The American Public Library in the Information Age, 1999; co-editor: The Metropolitan Library (anthology), 1972; author TV script Portraits in Print, 1959. Recipient Leadership Tng. award Fund for Adult Edn., 1956-57; recipient Disting. Alumnus award Sch. Library Sci. U. Mich., 1969, George Virgil Fuller award Columbia U., 1975, Johns Hopkins U. scholar, 1949-50, Horace H. Rackham fellow U. Mich., 1952-53, Columbia U. scholar, 1974-76, Tangley Oaks fellow, 1975-76; Council Library Resources Inc. Officers' grantee, 1974 Mem. ALA (councilor 1972-74, 76-80, exec. bd. 1976-80, chmn. legis. com. 1985-86), Freedom to Read Found. (dir. 1972-79, pres. 1977-79)

MOMADAY, NAVARRE SCOTT, writer, poet; b. Lawton, Okla., Feb. 27, 1934; s. Alfred Morris and Natachee (Scott) M.; m. Gaye Mangold, Sept. 5, 1959; children: Cael, Jill, Brit; m. Regina Heitzer, July 21, 1978; 1 dau., Lore. AB, U. N.Mex., 1958; AM, Stanford U., 1960, PhD, 1963. Asst. prof. U. Calif., Santa Barbara, 1963-65, assoc. prof. English, 1968-69, assoc. prof. English and comparative lit. Berkeley, 1969-73; prof. English and comparative lit. Stanford U., 1973—82, U. Ariz., Tucson, 1982—85, Regents prof. English; staff scholar Sch. Am. Rsch., Santa Fe. Cons. Nat. Endowment for Humanities, Nat. Endowment for Arts, 1970—. Author: Owl in the Cedar Tree, 1965, The Journey of Tai-me, 1967 (pub. as The Way to Rainy Mountain, 1969), House Made of Dawn, 1968 (Pulitzer Prize for fiction 1969), Colorado: Summer/Fall/Winter/Spring, 1973 (Western Heritage award 1974), Angle of Geese and Other Poems, 1974, The Gourd Dancer, 1976, The Names: A Memoir, 1976, The Ancient Child, 1989, In the Presence of the Sun, 1991, Circle of Wonder: A Native American Christmas Story, 1993, The Native Americans: Indian Country, 1993, The Man Made of Words: Essays, Stories, Passages, 1997, In the Bear's House, 1999, Three Plays, 2007; co-author: American Indian Photographic Images, 1868-1931, 1982; editor: The Complete Poems of Frederick Goddard Tuckerman, 1965, American Indian Authors, 1972. Founding trustee Mus. of Am. Indian, 1978-; founder and dir. Buffalo Trust. Named Poet Laureate of Okla., 2007-08; named to Acad. Achievement, 1993; named an Artist for Peace, UNESCO, 2004; recipient Acad. Am. Poets prize for "The Bear", 1962, Pulitzer Prize for Fiction, 1969, Premio Letterario Internazionale Mondello Italy, 1979, Nat. Medal Arts, 2007; Guggenheim fellow, 1966-67, Nat. Inst. Arts and Letters grantee, 1970. Mem. MLA, Am. Studies Assn., PEN; fellow AAAS. Office: Sch Am Rsch PO Box 2188 Santa Fe NM 87504-2188

MOMAND, ELIZABETH BLANTON, singer, music educator; b. Miss., Oct. 10, 1963; d. Dorothy Case and Clarence Hix Blanton; m. Mohammad Isa Momand, June 21, 1986; children: Maleka Elizabeth Rosella, Bilal Hassan. MusB, Miss. Coll., Clinton, 1986; MusM, Miss. Coll., 1991; D of Musical Arts, U.Tex., Austin, 2001. Dir. vocal studies Power Academic and Performing Arts Complex, Jackson, Miss., 1990—97; dir. fine arts Lanier H.S., Austin, Tex., 2001—03; assoc. prof. music U. of Ark., Ft. Smith, 2003—. Fulbright Hays fellowship, Fulbright Assn., 1994, German Exch. scholarship, Miss. Coll., 1985. Mem.: Nat. Assn. of Teachers of Singing, Fulbright Assn. Avocations: travel, music. Office: Univ of Ark 5210 Grand Ave Fort Smith AR 72903 Personal E-mail: elimom@hotmail.com.

MOMBOULI, SERGE, ambassador; b. Pointe-Noire, Republic of Congo, 1959; married; 6 children. Corp. sales Air Afrique, Paris; v.p. A.W.E. Grp., Houston; v.p. internat. ops. and project devel. Transworld Consortium Corp., Houston, 1995—97; Congolese presdl. spokesman in US, 1997; chargé d'affaires Embassy of Republic of Congo, 1997—2001; Congolese amb. to the US, 2001—. Office: Embassy of Republic of Congo 4891 Colorado Ave NW Washington DC 20011 Home Phone: 301-765-5931; Office Phone: 202-726-5500. E-mail: smombouli@hotmail.com.

MOMENI, ARASH, plastic surgeon; b. Dubai, United Arab Emirates, Nov. 18, 1978; BS, Baylor Coll. Medicine, 2002; MS, Stanford U. Sch. Medicine, 2007; MD magna cum laude, Johannes Gutenberg U., Mainz, Germany, 2004. Plastic surgery resident U. Freiburg Med. Ctr., Germany, 2004—. Contbr. articles to profl. jours. Mem.: German Soc. Plastic, Reconstructive, and Aesthetic Surgeons (assoc.). Office: Stanford Univ Medical Ctr 300 Pasteur Dr Stanford CA 94305 Personal E-mail: arash.momeni@googlemail.com. Business E-Mail: arash.momeni@uniklinik-freiburg.de, amomeni@stanford.edu.

MOMENI, REZA, plastic surgeon; BA, Haverford Coll., 1990—94; MD, Med. Coll. of Pa., 1994—98. Diplomate Am. Bd. Plastic Surgery. Resident in gen. surgery Yale U., New Haven, 1998—2001, resident in plastic surgery, 2001—04, chief resident in plastic surgery, 2003—04; plastic, reconstructive, & hand surgeon Summit Med. Group, Summit, NJ, 2004—. Cons. MedSN.com, Santa Monica, Calif., 1998—2000; sci. reviewer Med. Sci. Monitor, Old Westbury, NY; med. illustration J/B Woolsey, Conshohocken, Pa., 1998—99. Nat. splty. rep. Am. Assn. of Med. Colleges - Orgn. of Resident Representatives, Washington, 2003—. Recipient Phi Beta Kappa, Haverford Coll., 1994, 1st Pl., US Pharmacopaeia Competition, 1996, Nat. Pathology Honor Soc., Med. Coll. of Pa., 1996, Alpha Omega Alpha, 1998; named Top Doc, NJ Monthly, 2007, America's Top Plastic Surgeons, 2008; scholar Class of 1934 scholarship, Haverford Coll., 1992; Howard Hughes Med. Inst. Rsch. scholarship, Howard Hughes Inst., 1993, Med. Coll. of Pa., Haverford Coll., 1995, Class of 1910 scholarship, Med. Coll. of Pa., 1995, Huldah Kerner scholarship, 1996, Ruth Weil Meml. scholarship, 1997, Weston Ellsworth scholarship, 1997, William Goldman scholarship, William Goldman Found., 1996—98, Yale Plastic Surgery Scholastic award, Yale Univ., 2002. Fellow: ACS; mem.: AMA, Am. Soc. Aesthetic Plastic Surgery, NJ Soc. Plastic Surgeons, NY Regional Soc. Plastic Surgery, Am. Soc. Plastic Surgeons (amb. surgeon 2007—), Union County Med. Soc., NJ Med. Soc., Phi Beta Kappa, Alpha Omega Alpha, Yale Surg. Soc. Achievements include research in cranial reconstruction after dural complications; pulse oximetry in melanoma sentinel node dissection may be false; frontal sinus fractures: an institutional review. Avocations: travel, sailing, skiing, snowboarding. Office: Summit Plastic Surgery 1 Diamond Hill Rd Berkeley Heights NJ 07922

MOMIN, ALHAJ BABUL AHMED, investigation bureau director, poet, writer; b. Dhaka, Bangladesh, Jan. 1, 1956; arrived in The Netherlands, 1978. s. Sultan Ahmed Shorkar and Begum Ahmed (Rohisunnesa) Sultan; m. Begum Sheila Anwara, Apr. 12, 1990; children: Sultana Beatrix Ahmed, Atiqul Alexander Ahmed. BS, Dhaka U., 1975; postgrad. in agrl. engring., Nat. Aq. Coll., The Netherlands, 1983; D in Advance Thought, Internat. Acad. Planetary, 1985; D in Internat. Politics, Internat. Yorker U., Milan, Italy, 2006. Gen. sec. Social Welfare Assn., Bangladesh, 1975-77; telex and microwave radio comm. specialist The Royal Dutch Army, The Netherlands, 1987-89; with comms. UN Peace Keeping Force, Israel and Egypt, 1989-90; security planning officer to advisor Randstad Bewaking BV, The Netherlands, 1990-92; civil servant The Royal Dutch Marine, The Netherlands, 1993-94; investigator Amsterdam Onderzoek Bur., The Netherlands, 1996—. Vice chmn. Found. Anjuman, The Netherlands, 1994; adminstrv. exec. Content Profl. BV, The Netherlands, 1995; 3rd World Agrl. advisor Stichting Vrijheid Matschapij, The Netherlands, 1985; journalist News Net-Work, 1997; chief advisor NGO-Prova; A-status mem. UN Geneva Convention of Human Rights; peace man Al-Momin, Sultan Peace Trust Bd., 2006; mem. peace force UN Multinational Forces Observer, Mid. East, 1990. Author, editor: (documentary) Cry for One World, 1980, Cry Humanity, 1998, Cry Peace, 2001, Press Card Journalist, bonafied mem., Int. Press Corps., AGORO Int., USA, 1999—. Active Bangladesh Embassy Cmty. Ctr., Dhaka, 1989; minority rights advisor Progressive Minority, The Netherlands, 1993; founding chmn. Dutch Human Rights Party; elected mem. N.H. Province for Partÿ van de Mensenrechten; mem. Provincial Govt. North Holland for Dutch Water Bd. Authority, 1997—; chmn. St. Bangladesh Vrÿheid Soc., Dutch Bangla Friendship Soc., Matschapÿ, 2000—, Federatic Mensenrechten Platform; human rights rschr. Amnesty Internat., The Netherlands, 1979; referee FIFA/KNVB, Royal Dutch Football; PvdM human rights comnr. NL vet. UN/MFO Peace Mission to Mid. East Isral and Palestain, 1989—90, Sinai, Egypt. Decorated NL medal Nat. Honor for Peace Svc. in Middle East in Respect to NL Minister of Def. and her highness Queen Beatrix His Excellency Amb. Bangladesh in The Hague. Mem. VISA (sec. push in push back berodi com. Bangladesh Freedom Fighter Assn. (Liberation War of Bangledash 1971, human rights negotiator 1980), Stichting Freedom Soc. (mem. restoration of democracy in Bangladesh), Royal Air Force Assn. (life), Internat. Assn. for Identification, Oxford Club. Avocations: speaker human rights and peace, travel, football referee, first aid and swimming. Office: Amsterdam Onderzoek Bur PvdM Postbus 12592 1100 AN Amsterdam Netherlands Home Phone: 0031614807662; Office Phone: 0031641128854. Personal E-mail: drmominmfo@yahoo.co.uk, mab4hr@yahoo.com.

MOMIN, SHAMIM, curator; BA, Williams Coll., 1995; PhD, CUNY. Assoc. curator Whitney Museum Am. Art, NYC, 2003—; co-curator Whitney Biennial, 2004, 2008. Co-author: Alex Katz: Small Paintings, 2001, Sue De Beer, 2005, Zak Smith: Pictures Of Girls, 2005, Ellen Harvey: Mirror, 2006, Terence Koh, 2007. Named one of The 50 Most Powerful Women in NYC, NY Post, 2007. Office: Whitney Museum 945 Madison Ave New York NY 10021

MOMJIAN, ARTHUR JAMES, lawyer; b. Atlantic City, Feb. 28, 1952; s. James H. and Mary K. (Kalajian) Momjian; m. Lucy Susan Giragosian, July 30, 1983; children: Ani, Talene. BA, Columbia U., NYC, 1974; JD, Rutgers Sch. Law, Newark, 1978; LLM in Taxation, Temple U. Sch. Law, Phila., 1982. Bar: NJ 1978, Pa. 1985, NY 2001, US Dist. Ct. (NJ), US Tax Ct., Supreme Ct. NJ, Supreme Ct. Pa. Assoc. Cooper, Pevskie, April, Neidelman & Wagonheim, Atlantic City, 1978—81, ptnr., 1982—84; assoc. Mesirov, Gelman, Jaffe, Cramer & Jamieson, Phila., 1984—87, ptnr., 1988—98, Duane Morris LLP, Phila., 1998—. Vice chmn. Armenian Sisters Acad., Radua, Pa., 1986—92; mem. adv. bd. First Comml. Bank Phila., 1991—. Contbr. articles to profl. jours. Bd. dirs. People's Emergency Ctr., Phila.; chmn. bd. dirs. People's Emergency Ctr. Cmty. Devel. Corp. Mem.: ABA, Pa. Bar Assn., NJ State Bar Assn. Office: Duane Morris LLP 30 S 17th St Philadelphia PA 19103 Office Phone: 215-979-1521. Office Fax: 215-689-3604. Business E-Mail: AJMomjian@duanemorris.com.*

MOMMSEN, KATHARINA, retired literature and language professor, foundation administrator; b. Berlin, Sept. 18, 1925; came to U.S., 1974, naturalized, 1980; d. Hermann and Anna (Johannsen) Zimmer; m. Momme Mommsen, Dec. 23, 1948. DPhil, U. Tübingen, 1956; Dr. habil., Berlin Free U., 1962. Collaborator Acad. Scis., Berlin, 1949—61; assoc. prof. Free U., Berlin, 1962—70; prof. German Carleton U., Ottawa, Canada, 1970—74; Albert Guerard prof. lit. Stanford U., 1974—94, ret., 1995. Vis. prof. U. Giessen, Tech. U. Berlin, 1965, State U. N.Y., Buffalo, 1966, U. Calif., San Diego, 1973; pres. Mommsen Found. Author over 200 publs. on 18th-20th century German and comparative lit.; editor: Germanic Studies in America. Mem. Goethe Soc. Home: 980 Palo Alto Ave Palo Alto CA 94301-2223 Business E-Mail: katmom@stanford.edu. E-mail: k.mommsen@comcast.net.

MOMTAHEN, AMIR JAVAD, radiologist; b. Iran, July 3, 1977; married. MD, Tehran U. Med. Scis., Iran, 2003. Physician Firoozkooh Med. Ctr., Tehran, 2003—04; rsch. fellow Parto Tashkhis Med. Imaging Ctr., 2005—06, St. Louis U., 2006—08, radiology resident, 2008—. Editor: (book) Hypertension: Pathophysiology, Diagnosis, and Treatment; contbr. articles to profl. jours., to profl. publs. Mem.: Am. Coll. Radiology, Am. Soc. Emergency Medicine, Am. Roentgen Ray Soc., Radiol. Soc. N.Am. (Roentgen Resident Fellow Rsch. award 2008). Office: St Louis Univ 3635 Vista Ave Saint Louis MO 63144 E-mail: momtahen@yahoo.com.

MONACO, CHRIS, historian, writer, documentary filmmaker; b. Ann Arbor, Mich., June 7, 1950; s. John Monaco and Marilyn Hermine Meeks; life ptnr. Rose Widman. BA, U. of Fla., 1973; MFA, U. of South Fla., 1977; PhD, Oxford Brookes U., 2007. Adv. bd. mem. Conservation Trust for Fla., 2001—. Editor: (book) A Plan for the Abolition of Slavery; dir./writer/prodr. (films) The Far Frontier (Outstanding Achievement, Fla. Trust for Hist. Preservation, 1999), (TV series) Education Showcase (Beacon Award, Nat. Cable TV Pub. Affairs Assn., 1994); author: Moses Levy of Florida: Jewish Utopian and Antebellum Reformer (Presdl. Award of Distinction, Fla. Hist. Soc., 2006). Bd. mem. Plan Bd., Micanopy, Fla., 1997—99. Recipient Hampton Dunn award, Fla. Hist. Soc., 1998, Flori award, Fla. Ind. Filmmakers Festival, 1979, Award of Excellence, Nat. Cable TV Advt. and Mktg., 1986—87; Faculty-Staff scholarship, U. of South Fla., 1976—77, Individual Artist fellowship, Fla. Fine Arts Coun., 1978. Mem.: So. Jewish Hist. Soc., Fla. Hist. Soc., Orgn. of Am. Historians. Achievements include discovery of the earliest and most important antislavery publication by an American Jew; identifying the earliest Jewish communal settlement in the United States, M. E. Levy's Pilgrimage Plantation (1822-1835); establishing Moses Elias Levy as one of the most significant figures in early American Jewish history. Avocations: graphic arts, photography. Personal E-mail: csmonaco@cs.com.

MONACO, JULIE, bank executive; 1 child. BA in Internat. Rels., George Wash. U., Washington; MBA in Fin., NYU. Key mgmt. positions in product sales, product mgmt., and ops. mgmt. Bankers Trust, 1985—93, head strategy and product mgmt., 1993—99, Deutsche Bank, 1999—2001; sr. v.p., mng. dir. treasury and trade services divsn. JP Morgan Chase, 2001—07; mng. dir., head global transactions services, North America Citigroup, Inc., NYC, 2007—. Bd. mem. ECCHO, 1995—97; mem. AFP Payments Adv. Group. Active Children's Hope Found. Named one of 25 Women to Watch, US Banker, 2008. Office: Citigroup Inc 388 Greenwich St New York NY 10013 Office Phone: 212-816-5340. Business E-Mail: julie.monaco@citi.com.*

MONACO, ROBERT ANTHONY, radiologist; b. NYC, July 5, 1945; s. Edmond V. and Jean M.; m. Susan Margaret Thompson; children: Kevin, Robert, Christopher, Sarah. BS, Siena Coll., 1967; MD, N.J. Coll. Medicine, 1971. Diplomate Am. Bd. Radiology, Am. Bd. Nuclear Medicine. Radiology resident N.J. Coll. Medicine, Newark, 1971-75; fellow in nuclear medicine med. ctr. NYU, NYC, 1975-76; attending radiologist Med. Ctr. Ocean County, Point Pleasant, NJ, 1976-87, dir. dept. radiology, 1987—, sec. med. staff, 1998-2000. Gen. ptnr Point Pleasant Radiology Group, 1987—; sec. bd. dirs. Found. Med. Ctr. Ocean County, Mid-Coastal IPA, 1997; mng. ptnr. Open MRI of Wall, 1999—. Capt. USAR, 1972-76. Mem. Am. Coll. Radiology, Am. Coll. Nuc. Medicine, Radiol. Soc. NJ (exec. com. 2005-). Roman Catholic. Avocations: tennis, fishing, swimming. Home: 13 Bretwood Dr Colts Neck NJ 07722 Office: Open MRI of Wall Rt 34 Wall NJ 07719 Office Phone: 732-974-8060. Personal E-mail: rammdo1@aol.com.

MONAGHAN, CRAIG THOMAS, automotive executive; b. Phila., Feb. 16, 1957; m. Mary Lou Murphy, Jul. 25, 1981; children: Shannon, Connor, Rand. BS industrial engr., Lehigh U., 1980; MBA in fin., Wharton U. Pa., 1985. Cert. mgmt. acct. Financial analyst General Motors Corp., NYC, 1985-87, mgr. overseas fin., 1987-88; dir. corp. fin. Squibb, Princeton, NJ, 1988-90; dir. internat. fin. Bristol-Myers Squibb, NYC, 1990-91; asst. treas. Reader's Digest, Pleasantville, NY, 1991-92, controller europe, 1992—98; CFO iVillage.com, 1998-2000; exec. v.p., CFO AutoNation, Inc., Fort Lauderdale, Fla., 2000—06; CFO Sears Holdings Corp., Hoffman Estates, Ill., 2006—07; sr. v.p., CFO Asbury Automotive Group, NYC, 2008—. Capt. US Army, 1980—83. Mem.: Inst. Mgmt. Accts. Avocations: fishing, golf, reading. Office: Asbury Automotive Group 622 3d Ave New York NY 10017

MONAGHAN, DOMINIC, actor; b. Berlin, Dec. 8, 1976; Actor: (TV series) Hetty Wainthropp Investigates, 1996—98, Lost, 2004— (Outstanding Performance by an Ensemble in a Drama Series, Screen Actors Guild award, 2006); (TV films) Hostile Waters, 1997, This Is Personal: The Hunt for the Yorkshire Ripper, 2000; (TV miniseries) Monsignor Renard, 2000; appeared: I Love the 90's, 2005; I Love the 90's: Part Deux, 2005; actor: (films) The Lord of the Rings: The Fellowship of the Ring, 2001, The Lord of the Rings: The Two Towers, 2002, The Lord of the Rings: The Return of the King, 2003, An Insomniac's Nightmare, 2003, Spivs, 2004, The Purifiers, 2004, Shooting Livien, 2005, I Sell the Dead, 2008, X-Men Origins: Wolverine, 2009. Office: c/o ABC 77 W 66th St New York NY 10023*

MONAGHAN, KATHLEEN M., art museum director; b. Waterville, Maine, Sept. 6, 1936; d. Russell Vernon and Gloria Beatrice (LeClair) M. BA in Art History, U. Calif.-Santa Barbara, 1979, MA in Art History, 1981. Curatorial fellow Whitney Mus., NYC, 1979, dir. Equitable Br., 1985-93; asst. curator Santa Barbara Mus., Calif., 1980-81, curator of art Calif., 1983-84; curator, dir. Akron Art Mus., Ohio, 1984-85; dir. The Hyde Collection, Glens Falls, NY, 1994—99; exec. dir. Fresno Metropolitan Museum, Fresno, Calif., 1999—. Mem. Internat. Com. on Mus., Coll. Art Assn. Office: Fresno Metropolitan Museum 1540 Fulton St Fresno CA 93721-1612

MONAGHAN, MICHELLE, actress; b. Winthrop, Iowa, Mar. 23, 1976; d. Robert John and Sharon Monaghan; m. Peter White, Aug. 2005; 1 child, Willow Katherine White. Studied Journalism, Columbia Coll., Chgo. Model. Actress (films) Perfume, 2001, Unfaithful, 2002, It Runs in the Family, 2003, Winter Solstice, 2004, The Bourne Supremacy, 2004, Constantine, 2005, Kiss Kiss Bang Bang, 2005, Mr. & Mrs. Smith, 2005, North Country, 2005, Mission: Impossible III, 2006, Gone Baby Gone, 2007, The Heartbreak Kid, 2007, Trucker, 2008, Made of Honor, 2008, Eagle Eye, 2008, (TV series) Boston Public, 2002—03, guest appearances include Young Americans, 2000, Law & Order: Special Victims Unit, 2001, Hack, 2002. Named Hottest Breakout Star, Giant Mag., 2005. Office: c/o Widescreen Mgmt 270 Lafayette St Ste 402 New York NY 10012

MONAHAN, MARTIN J., social studies educator; b. Troy, NY, Aug. 29, 1947; s. Sylvester F. and Catherine E. Monahan; m. Patricia C. Clancy, July 10, 1982; children: Stephen F., Conor T. BA cum laude, Siena Coll., Loudonville, NY, 1969; MA, NY U., 1971, PhD, 1991. Social studies tchr. Averill Pk. HS, NY, 1970—2003; tchr. Siena Coll., Loudonville, NY, 1979—80, dept. chair; adj. instr. Hudson Valley CC, Troy, 1996—. Bd. edn. mem. Troy Sch. Bd., 2000—02. Fellow Pennfield, NY U., 1977—78. Roman Catholic. Avocations: reading, travel, swimming, walking, writing. Home: 33 N Colonial Hts Troy NY 12180 Office: Hudson Valley CC 80 Vandenburgh Ave Troy NY 12180 Personal E-mail: mmonahan@nycap.rr.com. Business E-Mail: m.monahan@hvcc.edu.

MONAHAN, MICHAEL, manufacturing executive; BS & MS, SUNY, Albany. CPA. Former sr. auditor Price Waterhouse; mgr. corp. acctg. Pitney Bowes Inc., 1988—95, dir. investor rels., 1995—98, v.p. finance & info. technol. Production Mail Divsn., 1998—99, v.p. investor rels. & fin. rsch., 1999—2001, v.p. corp. devel., 2001—08, exec. v.p. & CFO, 2008—. Former bd. chmn. Urban League Southwestern Conn.; bd. mem. Armed Svcs. YMCA, Sherman Higher Edn. Fund. Office: 1 Elmcroft Rd Stamford CT 06926-0700 Office Phone: 203-356-5000.*

MONAHAN, THOMAS PAUL, accountant; b. Pitts., Feb. 27, 1951; s. Thomas Andrew and Patricia (Tompkins) M.; m. Ellen McKeithan Easterby, Aug. 2, 1975; children: Kelley Kathleen, Thomas Patrick, Kyle Easterby, Tessa Elizabeth. BS in Acctg., U. S.C., 1073. CPA SC. Staff acct. Rogers, Brigman, Peterson & Co., Columbia, S.C., 1972-75, ptnr., 1975-82; chmn., treas., prin. GMK Assocs., Columbia, 1982—. Chmn., bd. dirs., treas. Devel. Properties, Inc.; trustee, pres. Town Theater Trust, 2000—. Mem. bus. coun. S. Dems., 1986—; bd. dirs. Cultural Coun. of Richland and Lexington Counties; pres. Town Theatre Trust; active Com. of 100. Mem. AICPA, S.C. Assn. CPAs, Columbia Stage Soc. (trustee, bd. dirs.), Spring Valley Country Club, Capital City Club, Palmetto Club, Zeta Beta Tau (trustee emeritus). Home: 1117 Adger Rd Columbia SC 29205-1942 Office: GMK Assoc Ste 2100 1201 Main St Columbia SC 29201-3263 Office Phone: 803-256-0000. Business E-Mail: tmonahan@gmka.com.

MONALISA, MITALI, application developer; d. Pravakar and Sukanti Dash; m. Pranabesh Dash, Dec. 2, 2003. MTech, Indian Inst. Tech., Kharagpur, 1999. Software developer Wipro Techs., Bangalore, Karnataka, India, 1999—2003, Intel Corp., Hillsboro, Oreg., 2005—. Contbr. articles to profl. jours. Home: 14535 NW Weible Way Beaverton OR 97006

MONAN, JAMES DONALD, university chancellor; b. Blasdell, NY, Dec. 31, 1924; s. Edward Roland and Mary Gertrude (Ward) M. AB, Woodstock Coll., 1948, PhL, 1949, STL, 1956; PhD, U. Louvain, 1959; post-doctoral research, Munich, Oxford, Paris; LHD (hon.), Le Moyne Coll., 1973, St. Joseph's Coll., 1973, New Eng. Sch. Law, 1975, Northeastern U., 1975, U. Mass., 1984; LLD (hon.), Harvard U., 1982, Loyola U., Chgo., 1987, Nat. U. Ireland, 1991, Boston Coll., 1996, U. Mass., 1997, Western New Eng. Coll., 2000, Xavier U., 2001. Prof. philosophy Le Moyne Coll., Syracuse, N.Y., 1960-68, v.p., acad. dean, 1968-72; pres. Boston Coll., Chestnut Hill, Mass., 1972-96, chancellor, 1996—. Cons. to N.Y. Jesuit Provincial for Higher Edn., 1966-72; dir. First Nat. Bank Boston, Bank of Boston Corp., 1976-96; interim pres. Assn. Jesuit Colls. and Univs., 1996-97. Author: The Philosophy of Human Knowing, 1952, A Prelude to Metaphysics, 1967, Moral Knowledge and Its Methodology in Aristotle, 1968. Chmn. edn. div. Boston United Way, 1974; chmn. steering com. of coll. pres. under phase II of ct.-ordered desegregation Boston Pub. Sch. System, 1974-76, Coun. for Aid to Edn., 1985-96, The Partnership, 1984-94, Sr. Thea Bowman Black Cath. Ednl. Found., 1989-96, Gov.'s Internat. Trade Adv. Bd., 1992; bd. dirs. Nat. Mentoring Partnership, 1991—, Naval Acad. Endowment Trust, 1998-2003; co-chair Mass. Mentoring Partnership, 1992-2001, bd. dirs., 1992—; co-chmn. Mass. Summit for Promise of Our Youth, 1997; trustee Le Moyne Coll., 1961-69, 1995-2004, Fordham U., 1969-75, Boston Coll., 1972-96, Canisius Coll., 1976-82, Georgetown U., 1979-84, Sta WGBH, 1972-96; exec. com. Boston Higher Edn. Ptnrship, 1988-96; mem. com. to Review and Implement Apostolic Constitution Ex Corde Ecclesiae, 1991-96. Mem. Assn. Jesuit Colls. and Univs. (dir., chmn. exec. com. 1983-86), Assn. Ind. Colls. and Univs. Mass. (exec. com. 1988-91, chmn. 1977-78), Nat. Assn. Ind. Colls. and Univs., Harvard Bd. Overseers (com. to visit grad. sch. bus. adminstrn., 1987-93), Nat. Collegiate Athletic Assn. (pres.'s commn. 1984-88), Metaphys. Soc. Am., Jesuit Philos. Assn., Soc. Phenomenology and Existential Philosophy, Soc. Ancient Greek Philosophy. Home: Boston Coll Chestnut Hill MA 02467 Office Phone: 617-552-2128. Business E-Mail: monan@bc.edu.

MONASSAR, HISHAM M.A., language and linguistics educator; s. Muhammad Ali Al-Qershi and Musk Abdulkhaleq Assaqaf; children: Jamaladdean Hisham, Leila Ione. BA in English, Sana'a U., Yemen, 1989; MA, Ball State U., Muncie, Ind., 1995, MS, 2001, MA, 2003, PhD, 2005. Tchg. asst. Ball State U., 1996—2001; prof. linguistics and Arabic Ga. Ctr. for Lang., Ft. Gordon, Ga., 2005—. Rsch. asst. Ball State U., 1997—98; presenter INTESOL, Indpls., 2004, TESOL, Seattle, 2007; freelance translator, interpreter. Fulbright scholar, USIS, 1993—95. Mem.: TESOL (assoc.). Home: 1129 Bison Way Grovetown GA 30813 Personal E-mail: monassar@hotmail.com.

MONAT, WILLIAM ROBERT, university official; b. Biwabik, Minn., Oct. 9, 1924; s. William Stephen and Milda Aleta (Sundby) M.; m. Josephine Ann Sclafani, Sept. 9, 1951; children: Lise Ann, Kathryn, Margaret, William Michael, Eric. AA, Virginia Jr. Coll., Minn., 1947; BA magna cum laude, U. Minn., 1949, PhD, 1956; postgrad., Wayne U., 1949-50. Asst. prof. Wayne U., 1954-57; exec. asst. to Gov. Mich., 1957-60; assoc. prof. Pa. State U., 1960-65, prof. polit. sci., 1965-69; asso. dir. Inst. Pub. Adminstrn., 1962-69; majority budget dir. Pa. Ho. of Reps., 1968-69; prof., chmn. dept. polit. sci. No. Ill. U., De Kalb, 1969-71, provost, 1976-78, Regency prof., 1986-92; Regency prof. emeritus, 1992—; pres. No. Ill. U., De Kalb, 1978-84; chancellor Ill. Bd. Regents, 1984-86; prof., dean faculties Baruch Coll., City U. N.Y., 1971-74, v.p. acad. affairs, 1974-76. Cons. USPHS, 1958, Office of Sec. Dept. Labor, 1963-64, Bur. Labor Stads., 1966, Office of Gov. Pa., 1968; bd. dirs. 1st Nat. Bank DeKalb, Castle Bancgroup, Inc. Author: Labor Goes to War, 1965, The Public Library and its Community, 1967, Politics, Poverty and Education, 1968; Editor: Public Adminstration in Era of Change, 1962, The Achieving Institution, 2000; contbr. articles to profl. jours. Mem. Gov.'s Commn. on Sci. and Tech., 1983-87; trustee Grad. Sch. Polit. Mgmt., NY, 1986-95; chmn. City of Dekalb Plan Commn.; trustee DeKalb Sanitary Dist., 2005. With AUS, 1943-46. Recipient Outstanding Achievement award U. Minn., 1981, named Alumni of Notable Achievemnet Coll. Liberal Arts U. Minn., 2008; decorated Bronze Star medal. Mem. Am. Polit. Sci. Assn., Am. Soc. Pub. Adminstrn., Phi Beta Kappa. Home: 1605 Mayflower Dr Dekalb IL 60115-1723 Business E-Mail: wmonat@niu.edu.

MONCRIEF, JACQUELINE C., retired state agency administrator; b. Cin., Ohio, Apr. 27, 1940; d. John L. Craddock and Novella D. Noble; children: David, Vanessa, Orlando. Student, Cen. State U., Wilberforce, Ohio, 1958—61; BA, Capital U., Columbus, Ohio, 1991. Cert. Gospel Lighthouse Sch. Ministry, lic. missionary Bishop Ross, Triedstone Ch. Monetary supr. Ohio Bur. Employment Svcs., Columbus, 1974—2001, initial claims supr., 1974—2001; compliance auditor Ohio Dept. Job and Family Svcs., Columbus, 1974—2001; ret. Mem. various planning teams ODJFS, Columbus. Vol. United Way; tutor, mentor Adopt-a-Sch. program Starling Sch., 1996—99; tutor, mentor Ohio Reads program Sedalia Sch., 1999—2000. Recipient Outstanding Svc. award and trophy, GMWA, 1988, plaque, Luth. Social Svcs., 1985. Mem.: Gospel Music Workshop of Am. Baptist. Avocations: singing in choir, dance, travel, games. Home: 1858 Riverdale Rd Columbus OH 43232

MONCRIEF, MICHAEL JOSEPH, Mayor, Fort Worth, former state legislator; b. Houston, Sept. 5, 1943; s. Richard Barto Sr. and Mary Daisy (Wiley) M.; m. Rosemary Brewer, Dec. 31, 1980; children: Troy L., Mitchell K. BS, Tarleton State U., 1968. Ind. oil prodr., Ft. Worth, 1969—; mem. Tex. Ho. of Reps., 1971—72, mem. appropriations com., 1970-72; judge Tarrant County, Tex., 1974—86; mem. Tex. State Senate, 1991—2003; pres. pro tempore Tex. Senate, 2001; mayor City of Ft. Worth, 2003—. Past mem. Tarrant County Drug Abuse Bd., Lone Star Transp. Authority, N. Central Tex. Council of Govts., Appropriations Com.; mem. Gov.'s Blue Ribbon Commn. on Criminal Justice, many other groups. Bd. dirs. Assn. Retarded Citizens (hon. chmn.), chmn. Neighborhood Resources Devel. Coun., Tarrant County Med., Edn. and Rsch. Found., Tarrant County Mental Health Assn., Drug Treatment Ctr., Tarrant County Juvenile Bd., Ft. Worth State Sch., Inst. Pub. Svc. Tarleton State U., Tex. Affiliate Adv. Com., AHA, Alliance for Children (hon.), Paul Quinn Coll., Tex. Preservation Bd., US Olympic Com., and several others; pres. Neighborhood Health Horizons; past bd. dirs. Gill Children Svcs., Inc., Ft. Worth Libr. Bd., Longhorn Coun. Boy Scouts Am., Tex. Soc. for Prevention of Blindness, North Tex., many others; dir. North Tex. Commn., 2003-; affiliated with Ft. Worth C. of C., Tex. Arts Alliance, Muscular Dystrophy Assn., Inc. and several others. Named Outstanding Cmty. Leader Am., 1970, Outstanding Young Man Am., 1971, Newsmaker of Yr., 1974, 78, Freshman Legislator of Yr., Tex. Legislature, 1971, AARP award, 1997, Common Cause Star of Tex. Pub. Svc. award, 2000, Kiwanis Club ' Community Builder" award, 2002, many other honors. Mem. Tarleton Alumni Assn. (Disting. Alumni 1977), Ind. Petroleum Assn. Am., Am. Judicature Soc., Nat. Coll. Probate Judges, Ft. Worth Res. Police Officers, other profl. orgns. Avocations: skiing, tennis, golf, hunting rattlesnakes and alligators. Office: Office of Mayor 1000 Throckmorton St Fort Worth TX 76102 Business E-Mail: Mayor@fortworthgov.org.*

MONCRIEFF, MITCHELL WILLIAM, atmosphere physicist researcher; arrived in US, 1986, naturalized, 1999; s. Mitchell James and Eliza Agnes Moncrieff; m. Patricia Margaret Nicolson; 1 child, Kerri Elizabeth. BS in Math., Aberdeen U., Scotland, 1967; PhD in Atmospheric Physics, Imperial Coll., London, 1970. Post doctoral fellow Imperial Coll., 1972—79, lectr., 1972—86, reader, 1987—88; sr. scientist Nat Ctr. Atmospheric Rsch., Boulder, Colo., 1988—, group head, 1994—. Head, Mesoscale Interactions Sect. Convective Storms Divsn. Nat. Ctr. Atmospheric Rsch., 1986, vis. scientist, 87; head Atmospheric Physics Group, Imperial Coll., 1988. Contbr. chapters to books, over 100 articles to profl. jours. Bus. amb. Highlands and Islands Enterprise, Scotland. Recipient of various acad. awards, Aberdeen U., 1964, 1966, Cert. of Excellence, Nat. Ctr. Atmospheric Rsch., 1999. Fellow: Royal Meteorol. Soc. (Buchan prize 1974), Am. Meteorol. Soc. Achievements include development of models of atmospheric convection; numeric models of cloud systems; research in climate and atmospheric sci. Office Fax: 303-497-8181. Business E-Mail: moncrief@ucar.edu.

MONCURE, ASHBY CARTER, surgeon, educator; b. Richmond, Va., Dec. 27, 1934; s. Powhatan and Maude Leah (Carley) M.; m. Patricia Juanita Leighton, June 21, 1960 (dec. Oct. 2001); children: Diana, Ann Marie, Ashby, Elizabeth; m. Margot Graham Lord, June 19, 2004. MD, U. Va., 1960. Diplomate Am. Bd. Surgery, Am. Bd. Thoracic Surgery, Am. Bd. Vascular Surgery. Intern Mass. Gen. Hosp., Boston, 1960-61, resident, 1961-62, 64-68; practice medicine specializing in surgery Boston, 1969—. Instr. surgery Harvard Med. Sch., Boston, 1969-71, asst. prof. surgery, 1971-77, asst. clin. prof. surgery, 1977-86, assoc. clin. prof. surgery, 1986—2000, clin. prof. surgery, 2000-03, clin. prof. surgery emeritus, 2003; assoc. vis. surgeon Mass. Gen. Hosp., Boston, 1973-79, vis. surgeon, 1980—2003, sr. surgeon, 2003—. Editor: MGH Textbook of Emergency Medicine, 1978, 2d edit., 1983, 3d edit., 1989, Complex Operations at the Mass. Gen. Hospital, 1983. Capt. U.S. Army, 1962-64. Fellow ACS; mem. New Eng. Surg. Soc. (pres. 2000), Ea. Surg. Soc. (pres. 2004), Am. Surg. Assn., Soc. Thoracic Surgeons, Internat. Cardiovascular Soc., Am. Assn. Thoracic Surgery, Soc. Vascular Surgery, Boston Surg. Soc. (pres. 1995). Clubs: Union Boat, Weston Golf. Episcopalian. Home: 3 Glen Oak Dr Wayland MA 01778 Home Phone: 508-358-2378; Office Phone: 617-724-3760.

MONCURE, JOHN LEWIS, lawyer; b. Houston, Nov. 4, 1930; s. Walter Raleigh Daniel and Margaret (Atkins) M.; m. Norma Steed, Dec. 29, 1954 (dec. June 1982); children: John Carter, Michael Lewis, Douglas Lee, Stuart Richard, Mary Margaret; m. Margaret Edmonston, Nov. 12, 1983. BBA, U. Houston, 1953; JD, U. Tex., 1956. Bar: Tex. 1956. Assoc. Butler, Binion, Rice, Cook & Knapp, Houston, 1956-68; ptnr. Prappas, Moncure & Eidman, Houston, 1969-86, John L. Moncure and Assocs., Houston, 1987—. Lectr. bus. law U. Houston, 1958-59, 68-69 Mem. sch. bd. St. Thomas Episcopal Sch., Houston, 1965-78; mem. vestry St. Thomas Episc. Ch., 1975-78. Named Distinguished Alumni Coll. Bus., U. Houston, 1968 Fellow Am. Coll. Probate Counsel; mem. Am., Tex., Houston bar assns., Assn. Christian Schs. (trustee), Coll. Bus. Alumni Assn. U. Houston (pres., dir.), U. Houston Alumni Fedn. (treas., dir.), Sigma Alpha Epsilon. Republican. Home: 1220 W Clay Houston TX 77019 Office: 1200 River Oaks Tower 3730 Kirby Dr Houston TX 77098-3905 Home Phone: 713-528-9870; Office Phone: 713-831-6821. Personal E-mail: johnmoncure@abby.com.

MONDALE, JOAN ADAMS, wife of former Vice President of United States; b. Eugene, Oreg., Aug. 8, 1930; d. John Maxwell and Eleanor Jane (Hall) Adams; m. Walter F. Mondale, Dec. 27, 1955; children: Theodore, Eleanor Jane, William Hall. BA, Macalester Coll., 1952. Asst. slide librarian Boston Mus. Fine Arts, 1952-53; asst. in edn. Mpls. Inst. of Arts, 1953-57; weekly tour guide Nat. Gallery of Art, Washington, 1965-74; hostess Washington Whirl-A-Round, 1975-76; amb. to Japan, 1993-96. Author: Politics in Art, 1972, Letters from Japan, 1998. Bd. govs. Women's Nat. Dem. Club; hon. chmn. Fed. Coun. on Arts and Humanities, 1978-80; bd. dirs. Associated Coun. of Arts, 1973-75, Reading Is Fundamental, Am. Craft Coun., NYC, 1981-88, J.F.K. Ctr. Performing Arts, 1981-90, Walker Art Ctr., Mpls., 1987-93, 97-03, Minn. Orch., Mpls., 1988-93, 97-2003, St. Paul Chamber Orch., 1988-90, Northern Clay Ctr., 1988-93, St. Paul, 1988-93, Nancy Hauser Dance Co., Mpls., 1989-93, Minn. Landmarks, 1991-93; trustee Macalester Coll., 1986—08; mem. commn. Nat. Portrait Gallery, 1997—; chair Hiawatha Light Rail Transit Pub. Art and Design com., 2000-04; active Walker Art Ctr., 2003—07, Minn. Orch., 1997—; citizen's stamp adv. com. US Postal Svc., 2005— Mem.: Phi Beta Kappa Epsilon. Democrat. Presbyterian. Home: 600 2nd St S #405 Minneapolis MN 55401 E-mail: joan.mondale@mac.com.

MONDALE, WALTER FREDERICK, former Vice President of United States, lawyer; b. Ceylon, Minn., Jan. 5, 1928; s. Theodore Sigvaard and Claribel Hope (Cowan) M.; m. Joan Adams, Dec. 27, 1955; children: Theodore, Eleanor, William. BA cum laude, U. Minn., 1951, LLB cum laude, 1956. Bar: Minn. 1956. Law clk. Minn. Supreme Ct.; pvt. practice law, 1956-60; atty. gen. State of Minn., 1960-64; US Senator from Minn., 1964-77; v.p. U.S., 1977-81; mem. NSC, 1977-81; mem. firm Winston & Strawn LLP, 1981-87; US amb. to Japan US Dept. State, Tokyo, 1993-96, presdl. envoy to Indonesia, 1998; ptnr. Dorsey & Whitney LLP, Mpls., 1987—93, ptnr., internat. corp. practice group, sr. counsel, 1997—. Chmn. Nat. Democratic Inst. for Internat. Affairs, 1986—93. Author: The Accountability of Power*Toward a Responsible Presidency, 1975; mem. Minn. Law Rev. Dem. nominee for Pres. U.S., 1984; hon. consul gen. to Norway Norwegian Ministry Fgn. Affairs, Mpls., 2008—. With U.S. Army, 1951-53. Named Disting. Univ. Fellow in law and pub. affairs, Hubert H. Humphrey Inst. of Pub. Affairs, Univ. Minn. Democrat. Presbyterian. Office: Dorsey & Whitney 50 S 6th St Ste 1500 Minneapolis MN 55402-1498 Office Phone: 612-340-2600. Office Fax: 612-340-2868.

MONDELLO, JOSEPH N., political organization administrator; b. Bklyn., Feb. 13, 1938; s. Joseph and Rose Martin Mondello; m. Linda Elisabeth Crabtree; children: Joseph, Elizabeth, Lisa. BA, Hofstra Coll.; JD, New England Sch. of Law; DA (hon.), Five Towns Coll., 1995. Tchr. East Meadow Sch. Dist.; probation officer Nassau County; ptnr. Flaum, Imbarrato & Mondello, Levittown, NY, 1975-87; councilman Town of Hempstead, NY, 1979-87; asst. atty. gen.; counsel NY State Legis.; spl. agent US Office Naval Intelligence; vice chmn. Nassau County Bd. of Suprs., Mineola, NY, 1987-93; presiding supr. Town of Hempstead, 1987-93; Rep. nat. committeeman NYC, 1992—2004, Washington, 1992—; chmn. Nassau County Rep. com., Westbury, 1983—, NY Rep. Party, Albany, 2006—09; counsel Berkman, Henoch, Peterson and Peddy, 2003—; adj. prof. Hofstra U. Chmn., pres. Nassau Downs, 1993—97. Maj. gen. NY Guard, Albany; dist. chmn. Boy Scouts Am., coord. Cath. Charities Decorated Cert. of Merit Veterans of Fgn. Wars US; recipient President's award, LI Hispanic C. of C., Good Scout award for Cmty. Svc., Nassau County Coun. Boy Scouts Am., Law Enforcement Man of Yr. award, Detective's Assn. Nassau County Police Dept., Youth Svc. award, Levittown Athletic Club, Merit award, Hispanic Com. Nassau County, Cert. Achievement, Am. Com. on Italian Migration, Frank A. Gulotta Criminal Justice award, Torch of Freedom award, Nassau Conservative Com., Christian Family award, Roman Cath. Diocese of Rockville, Justice Frank A. Gulotta/Justice Marcus Christ award. Mem. Nassau Country Bar Assn., Dist. Attorneys' Assn., Nassau Lawyers' Assn., Columbian Lawyers' Assn. (Disting. Svc. award), NY State Dist. Attorneys' Assn., Criminal Bar Assn., LI Area Devel. Assn., Uniondale Hispanic Assn., Nassau County Heart Assn., Knights of the Holy Sepulcher, KC, Marco Polo Lodge, Order of Sons of Italy (Cmty. Svc. recognition), Levittown Kiwanis Club, Am. Vets., Am. Legion, Ushers Soc. St. Bernard Ch. Republican. Roman Catholic. Avocations: fishing, tennis. Office: Nassau County Rep Com 164 Post Ave Westbury NY 11590-3170*

MONDELLO, LISETTE MCSOUD, legislative staff member, former federal agency administrator; b. 1956; d. Rosemary C. Elizondo; m. Joseph Nestor Mondello Jr., Aug. 9, 1997. BA, Trinity Coll., 1978; Certificate in Fin., Cox Sch. Bus., So. Methodist U., 1993. Campaign mgr. Sam Johnson for Congress; sr. v.p. Spaeth Communications, Inc., Dallas, 1989—94; dir. comm. for Senator Al D'Amato US Senate, 1995—98, dir. comm. for Senator Kay Bailey Hutchison, 1999—2003; sr. advisor Office Comm. & Outreach US Dept. Edn., 2003—05; asst. sec. for pub. & intergovernmental affairs US Dept. Veterans Affairs, 2005—09; sr. adv. for Senator Kay Bailey Hutchison US Senate, 2009—. Bd. trustees Am. Folklife Ctr., Library of Congress. Republican. Office: US Senate 284 Russell Senate Office Bldg Washington DC 20510*

MONDELLO, MARK T., electronics executive; BSME, U. South Fla. Former project mgr. on comml. and def.-related aerospace programs Moog, Inc.; prodn. line supr. Jabil Cir., St. Petersburg, Fla., 1992—93, project mgr., 1993—97, v.p. bus. devel., 1997—99, sr. v.p. bus. devel., 1999—2002, COO, 2002—. Bd. dirs. All Children's Hosp. Office: Jabil Cir 10560 9th St N Saint Petersburg FL 33716

MONDINO, BARTLY J., ophthalmologist; b. Sacramento, May 24, 1945; married; children: Kara, Kristen. BA in Med. Scis., Stanford U., 1967, MD, 1971. Diplomate Am. Bd. Ophthalmology. Intern Stanford (Calif.) U. Hosp., 1971-72; ophthalmology resident N.Y. Hosp., Cornell U., NYC, 1972-75; fellow in cornea, external disease U. Pitts. Sch. Medicine - Eye and Ear Hosp., Pitts., 1975-76, asst. prof. ophthalmology, 1976-79, assoc. prof. ophthalmology, 1979-82; dir. Charles T. Campbell Microbiology Lab. Eye and Ear Hosp., Pitts., 1978-82; assoc. prof. ophthalmology UCLA - Jules Stein Eye Inst., LA, 1982-83, prof. ophthalmology, 1983—, Wasserman Endowed chair dept. ophthalmology, 1988—; chief cornea-external disease divsn. UCLA, 1991-99, chmn. dept. ophthalmology, 1994—; dir. UCLA - Jules Stein Eye Inst., 1994—; with exec. program for acad. healthcare mgmt. The John E. Anderson Grad. Sch. Mgmt./UCLA, 1992. Bd. dirs. Charles R. Drew U. of Medicine and Sci., L.A., Braille Inst., L.A.; mem. adv. com. Rsch. Study Club, Murrieta, Calif., 1994—, scientific adv. panel on ophthalmology Calif. Med. Assn., San Francisco, 1994—. Editl. bd.: Am. Jour. Ophthalmology, Chgo., 1992—, ophthalmic Surgery and Lasers, 1995—, Ophthalmology Times, 1996—, Ophthalmic Practice (Can.), 1996—; editor-in-chief: EYE Newsletter, 1994—; co-chair corneal diseases program planning panel of Nat. Eye Inst.'s Vision Rsch. Program Planning Subcom., Bethesda, md., 1997—, others. Recipient scholarship Stanford U. Sch. Medicine, Rsch. to Prevent Blindness Manpower award 1983-84, Rsch. to Prevent Blindness Sr. Scientific Investigator's award 1994, various lectureships, others. Mem. AMA, Assn. for Rsch. in Vision and Ophthalmology, Assn. Univ. Profs. of Ophthalmology, Am. Acad. Ophthalmology, Calif. Assn. Ophthalmology, Calif. Cornea Club, Calif. Med. Assn., Contact Lens Assn. of Ophthalmologists, Eye Bank Assn. of Am., L.A. County Med. Assn., L.A. Soc. Ophthalmology, Ophthalmology Rsch. Found., Ophthalmic Surgery and Laser Therapy, Rsch. Study Club. Office: 100 Stein Plz # 2-142 Los Angeles CA 90095-7000 Business E-Mail: mondino@jsei.ucla.edu.

MONDLIN, MARVIN, publisher, appraiser, consultant; b. Bklyn., July 1, 1927; s. Samuel and Thelma (Schultz) M.; m. Phyllis Grossman, Oct. 23, 1962 (div. 1968); 1 child, Gerri; m. Irene Szmulewicz, Sept. 4, 1970. Student, Cornell U., 1945; student of Aesthetic Realism, with Eli Siegel, 1945—68; student, CCNY, 1948, Bklyn. Coll., 1969—71. Ptnr. Amory Books, NYC, 1953-59; clk. Strand Book Store, NYC, 1951, estate book buyer, 1959-71, 74-76, sr. exec. v.p., 1976—2004; proprietor Am. Sunbeam Pub., NYC, 1996—. Bus. mgr. Definition Press., NYC, 1957; cataloger U. Cath. de Louvain, Belgium, 1972. Author: Appraisals: A Guide for Bookmen, 1997; co-author: Book Row, An Anecdotal and Pictorial History of the Antiquarian Book Trade, 2003; proofreader, copy editor Dover Publs., NYC, 1958; editor Yearbook of Internat. Assocs., 1974; pub. Robert Clairmont's Quintillions, 2006. Mem.: Typophiles, Ephemera Soc. Am., European Soc. History of Phtography, Am. Photog. Hist. Soc., Bibliog. Soc. London, Bibliog. Soc. Am., Appraisers Assn. Am., Camera Club. Avocation: photography. Home Phone: 212-982-8189; Office Phone: 212-982-8189. E-mail: marvinmondlin@verizon.net.

MONDRY, LAWRENCE N., automotive executive; V.p., nat. mdse. mgr. Highland Superstones, Inc., 1983-88, 88-90; sr. v.p., gen. mdse. mgr. CompUSA, Inc., Dallas, 1990-93, exec. v.p. merchandising, 1993—2000, pres., COO, 2000—03, CEO, 2003—06; pres., CEO CSK Auto Inc., Phoenix, 2007—. Bd. dir. Micron Technology, Golfsmith Inc. Office: CSK Auto Inc 645 E Missouri Ave Phoenix AZ 85012

MONDUL, DONALD DAVID, patent lawyer; b. Miami, Fla., Aug. 24, 1945; s. David Donald and Marian Wright (Heck) M.; children: Alison Marian, Ashley Megan; m. Anna Marie Towle, Oct. 12, 1996. BS in Physics, U.S. Naval Acad., 1967; MBA, Roosevelt U., 1976; JD, John Marshall Law Sch., 1979. Bar: Ill. 1979, Fla. 1980, Tex. 1998; U.S. Patent Office 1980; U.S. Ct. Appeals (fed. cir.) 1982; U.S. Supreme Ct. 1990. Commd. ensign USN, 1967, advanced through grades to comdr., 1977; mktg. rep. Control Data Corp., Chgo., 1977-79; patent atty. Square D Co., Palatine, Ill., 1979-81; group patent counsel Ill. Tool Works Inc., Chgo., 1981-87; assoc. Cook, Wetzel & Egan, Chgo., 1987-89; ptnr. Foley & Lardner, Chgo. and Milw., 1989-95; sr. patent atty. IBM, East Fishkill, NY, 1995-96; gen. patent counsel Ericsson, Inc., Richardson, Tex., 1996-99; pvt. practice Dallas, 1999—. Comdr., USNR, 1967-87. Achievements include patents for Electrical Encoding Device; Method and Apparatus for Determining the Product of Two Numbers; Apparatus for Providing Power to Selected Portions of a Multiplying Device; Method and Apparatus for Multiplying a Plurality of N Numbers; Method and for Establishing an Operating Parameter for a Power Supply Device; Apparatus and Method for Locating Objects in a Three-Dimensional Space; Air Baffle Apparatus. Home and Office: 3060 Bonsai Dr Plano TX 75093 Personal E-mail: dmondul@aol.com.

MONE, LAWRENCE J., think-tank executive; BA summa cum laude, Coll. of the Holy Cross; MA in pub. policy, U. Calif., Berkeley, 1982. Tchr. history, Cambridge, Mass.; joined Manhattan Inst., 1982, pub. policy specialist, program dir., v.p., pres., 1995—. Adv. bd. mem. Common Good. Contbr. articles to profl. jours. Office: Manhattan Inst 52 Vanderbilt Ave New York NY 10017 Office Phone: 212-599-7000. Office Fax: 212-599-3494. E-mail: lmone@manhattan-institute.org.*

MONE, PETER JOHN, lawyer; b. Brockton, Mass., Apr. 8, 1940; s. Edward Patrick and June E. (Kelliher) M.; m. Sharon Lee Bright, Oct. 9, 1965; children: Kathleen, Peter. AB, Bowdoin Coll., 1962; JD, U. Chgo., 1965. Ptnr. Baker & McKenzie, Chgo., 1968—. Active Winnetka Caucus, Ill., 1984-85. Capt. U.S. Army, 1966-67, Vietnam. Decorated Purple Heart, Bronze Star, Air medal. Fellow Am. Coll. Trial Lawyers, Internat. Acad. Trial Lawyers; mem. Soc. Trial Lawyers, Internat. Assn. Def. Counsel, Skokie Country Club. Democrat. Roman Catholic. Avocations: photography, golf. Home Phone: 847-446-4149. Personal E-mail: psm4840@comcast.net.

MONE, ROBERT PAUL, lawyer; b. Columbus, Ohio, July 23, 1934; s. Henry P. and Ann E. (Freedlund) M.; m. Lucille L. Willman, May 3, 1960; children: Robert, Maria, Andrew, Richard. BA, U. Dayton, 1956; JD, U. Notre Dame, 1959. Bar: Ohio 1959. Law clk.to presiding judge U.S. Dist. Ct. (no. dist.) Ohio, Cleve., 1960-62; assoc. George, Greek, King, et al, Columbus, 1962-66, ptnr., 1966-79, McConnaughey, Stradley, et al, Columbus, 1979-81, Thompson Hine LLP, Columbus, 1981—. Cpl. U.S. Army, 1959-60. Mem. ABA, Ohio State Bar Assn., Energy Bar Assn., Columbus Bar Assn., Nat. Generation and Transmission Coop. Lawyers Assn. (1st pres.), Rotary. Office: Thompson Hine LLP 41 South High St Columbus OH 43215-6101 Home: 1998 Cardigan Ave Columbus OH 43212-2717

MONEGRO, FRANCISCO, alternative medicine consultant, psychology professor; b. La Vega, Dominican Republic, Apr. 20, 1949; s. Francisco Monegro-Fdez and Ana A. (Pena) Monegro. Grad. cum laude, Pontifical U., Santiago, Dominican Republic, 1973; grad. psychology, Autonomous U. Santo Domingo, 1978, MD, 1986; MA in Ednl. Psychology, Tech. Inst. Santo Domingo, 1981; PhD in Nutrition, LaSalle U., Mandeville, La., 1993. Cert. natural health profl., hypnotherapist, profl. biofeedback profl.; diplomate in behavioral medicine, diplomate in pain mgmt.; lic. in psychology Autonomous U. Santo Domingo, 1978. Tchr. Peace H.S., Santo Domingo, Dominican Republic, 1975-76; dir. dept. psychology Holy Trinity Ednl. Ctr., Santo Domingo, 1978-80; prof. Sch. Medicine Tech. Inst. Santo Domingo, 1986-87; dir. dept. psychology Interam. U., Santo Domingo, 1988-89; prof. psychology and medicine Autonomous U. Santo Domingo, 1978-89, psychologist, counseling dept., 1979-84; staff mem. spl. edn. Bd. Edn. Dist. X, Bronx, NY, 1991-93; founder, chmn. N.Y. Inst. for Holistic Life, NYC, 1991—; prof. psychology CUNY at HCC, Bronx, 1990—. Founder, pioneer in behavioral medicine Behavioral Medicine Clinic, Santo Domingo, 1987-94. Author: Biofeedback-Bio-retroalimentacion, 1988, Holistic Behavioral Medicine, 1993, Biomagnetic Medicine: Secrets and Power of Magnetic Energy, 1996, Psychology and Life Mind, Body and Society, 1997, Commonly Prescribed Psychiatric Drugs. A Guide for Clinicians and Care Takers, 2003, A Guidebook for Behavioral Evaluators, 2003, (interactive CD-ROMs) Psychology and Life, 2000, Developmental Aphasia, 2002, Commonly Prescribed Psychiatric Drugs. A Guide for Clinicians and Care Takers, 2003, A Guide for Behavioral Evaluators, 2003; editor, pub.: BOEST, 1978, Dominican Bull. Behavioral Medicine, 1987, Holistic Life/Vida Holistica, 1991, others. Mem. Dominican Psychol. Assn. (treas. 1978-79), Soc. Behavioral Medicine, Assn. for Advancement of Behavior Therapy, Am. Acad. Pain Mgmt., Assn. for Applied Psychophysiology and Biofeedback. Democrat. Roman Catholic. Avocations: computers, golf, basketball, swimming, travel. Home: PO Box 302 Bronx NY 10458-0302 Office: NY Inst for Holistic Life 976 Mclean Ave Ste 370 Yonkers NY 10704-4105 Office Phone: 718-364-2202. Personal E-mail: holisticlife@msn.com.

MONES, STUART MATTHEW, lawyer; b. Port Jefferson, NY, June 20, 1976; s. Herbert and Gretchen Mones; m. Kathleen Elizabeth Geary, May 27, 2000. BA magna cum laude in Law and Society, SUNY, Albany, 1998; JD, Emory U., Atlanta, Ga., 2001. Bar: Ga. 2001, U.S. Dist. Ct. (no. dist.) Ga. 2001, U.S. Dist. Ct. (so. dist.) Ga. 2005, U.S. Dist. Ct. (mid. dist.) Ga. 2006, U.S. Ct. Appeals (11th cir.) 2004. Law clk. Hon. Judge Robert E. McDuff, Marietta, Ga., 2001—02; atty. Drew, Eckl & Farnham, Atlanta, 2002—03, Stuart M. Mones, P.C., 2003—. Mem.: ABA, Cobb County Bar Assn., Atlanta Bar Assn., Ga. Assn. Criminal Def. Lawyers, Nat. Assn. Criminal Def. Lawyers. Office: Stuart M Mones PC 146 Nassau St Atlanta GA 30303 Office Fax: 404-681-3953. Business E-Mail: smm@moneslaw.com.

MONEY, DAVID R., lawyer, information technology executive; BS, MBA, U. Utah, Salt Lake City; student, U. Oreg. Sch. Law; JD, U. Utah, Salt Lake City. Ptnr. Jones, Waldo, Holbrook and McDonough, Salt Lake City; dep. gen. counsel First Data Corp., Greenwood Village, Colo., 2004—07, exec. v.p., gen. counsel, sec., 2007—. Mem.: Utah Bar Assn., Colo. Bar Assn. Office: First Data Corp 6200 S Quebec St Greenwood Village CO 80111 Office Phone: 303-488-8000.

MONEYPENNY, EDWARD WILLIAM, retail executive; b. Long Branch, NJ, Jan. 28, 1942; s. Edward Henry and Eleanor Kathleen (O'Hagan) M.; m. Connie Wills, Feb. 19, 1966; children: Matthew, Jonathan, Christopher. BS in Acctg., St. Joseph's U., 1964; MS in Acctg. Sci., U. Ill., 1967. CPA, Pa. Audit mgr. Coopers & Lybrand, Phila., 1970-76; mgr. corp. acctg. Sun Co., Inc., Radnor, Pa., 1976-78; v.p. fin. adminstrn. Sun Prodn. Co., Dallas, 1978-81; v.p. fin., CFO Oryx Energy Co. (formerly Sun Exploration and Prodn. Co.), Dallas, 1981-91; sr. v.p. fin., CFO Oryx Energy Co., Dallas, 1992-94, exec. v.p. fin., CFO, bd. dirs., 1994-99; sr. v.p. fin., CFO Fla. Progress Corp., St. Petersburg, Fla., 1999-2000; exec. v.p. fin., CFO Covanta Energy Corp., Fairfield, NJ, 2001; sr. v.p. fin., CFO 7-Eleven, Inc., Dallas, 2002—05. Chmn. dean's bus. coun. U. Ill. Sch. Bus., 2000-01, mem. exec. com., dean's bus. coun., 2002-07; bd. dirs., chmn. Audit Com., mem. Compensation Com. The Timberland Co., Stratham, NH, 2006-, bd. dirs., mem. Audit com. NY and Co., N.Y.C., 2006-2007, mem. bd. trustee and strategic planning Com., St. Joseph U., Phila. 1st lt. U.S. Army, 1967-70. Home: 149 White St Southampton NY 11968 Home Phone: 631-287-7112.

MONG, ROBERT WILLIAM, JR., editor, publishing executive; b. Fremont, Ohio, Jan. 22, 1949; s. Robert William and Betty (Dwyer) M.; m. Carla Beth Sweet, July 25, 1975 (div. 1979); m. Diane Elizabeth Reischel, Jan. 23, 1988; children: Eric Robert, Elizabeth Diana. BA, Haverford Coll., Pa., 1971; graduate exec. bus. program, Stanford U., 1997. Reporter Cin. Post, 1973-75, Capital Times, Madison, Wis., 1975-77; city editor Madison Press Connection, 1977-79; asst. city editor Dallas Morning News, 1979-80, bus. editor, 1980-81, projects editor, 1981-83, asst. mng. editor, 1983-88, dep. mng. editor, 1988-90, mng. editor, 1990-96; pub. Owensboro Messenger-Inquirer, 1996-97; exec. v.p. A.H. Belo Corp., Dallas, 1997-98; pres., gen. mgr. The Dallas Morning News, Dallas, 1998-2001, pres., editor, 2001—. Recipient J.B. Buck Marryat award for meritorious svc., Dallas Press Club, 2005. Mem. Am. Soc. Newspaper Editors, Newspaper Assn. Am., Southern Newspaper Pubs. Assn., Am. Press Inst. (bd. dirs.). Office: The Dallas Morning News PO Box 655237 508 Young St Dallas TX 75202-4828 Home Phone: 214-521-1952; Office Phone: 214-977-8222. Business E-Mail: bmong@dallasnews.com.*

MONGA, MANOJ, medical educator; b. Belfast, Northern Ireland, May 4, 1965; s. Trilok Nath and Uma Monga Monga; m. Mary McGinnis, May 29, 1995; children: Nathan Joseph, Miles Manoj, Natalie Marie. BS with honors, Queen's U., Kingston, Ont., 1986; MD, Chgo. Med. Sch., 1990. Asst. prof. U. Calif., San Diego, 1997—2001; assoc. prof. U. Minn., Mpls., 2001—04, prof., 2004—. Dir. urology residency program U. Minn., Mpls., 2005—; co-dir., Ctr. Systematic Reviews Urologic Surgery VAHCS Mpls., Mpls., 2005—; dir. endourology & urologic laparoscopy fellowship U. Minn., 2002—, mem. biomedical engring. inst., 2002—. Contbr. articles to profl. jours., chapters to books. Vol. surg. missions Internat. Volunteers Urology, Bhopal, India, 2002. Recipient Disting. Alumni award, Chgo. Med. Sch., 2006. Fellow: ACS, Am. Urol. Assn.; mem.: R.O.C.K. Soc., Endourologial Soc. Achievements include patents for percutaneous plug; guide wire engaging ureteroscope; 4 patents pending in medical devices. Office: U Minn 420 Delaware St SE MMC 394 Minneapolis MN 55455 E-mail: monga002@umn.edu.

MONGAN, JAMES JOHN, healthcare system administrator; b. San Francisco, Apr. 10, 1942; s. Martin and Audrey Vera (Cunningham) M.; m. Jean Trotter Holmes, Apr. 22, 1972; children: John Holmes, Sarah Holmes. Student, U. Calif., Berkeley, 1959-62; BA, Stanford U., 1963, MD, 1967. Intern Kaiser Found. Hosp., San Francisco, 1967-68; med. officer USPHS, Denver, 1968-70; profl. staff mem. U.S. Senate Fin. Com., Washington, 1970-77; dep. asst. sec. for health HEW, Washington, 1977-79; assoc. dir. human resources Domestic Policy Staff, White House, 1979-81; asst. surgeon gen. USPHS, 1979-81; exec. dir. Truman Med. Center, U. Mo., Kansas City, 1981-96; dean sch. medicine U. Mo., Kansas City, 1987-96; pres. Mass. Gen. Hosp., 1996—2002; pres., CEO Partners HealthCare Sys. Inc, Boston, 2003—. Prof. healthcare policy, prof. medicine Harvard Med. Sch.; mem. com. on consequences of uninsured Inst. Medicine; chair adv. com. Commonwealth Fund Task Force; mem. Kaiser Commn. on Medicaid and the Uninsured. Trustee Kaiser Family Found., 1993—2001; chmn. Greater Boston C. of C., 2004—. Mem. NAS, Inst. Medicine (coun. mem. 2006-), Am. Hosp. Assn. (trustee 1988-91), Am. Assn. Teaching Hospitals. (bd. dirs. coun. tchg hospitals. 1984-90). Office: Partners HealthCare Sys Inc Prudential Tower 800 Boylston St Ste 1150 Boston MA 02199-8001*

MONGIARDO, DANIEL (FRANK DANIEL MONGIARDO), Lieutenant Governor of Kentucky, state senator, otolaryngologist; b. Hazard, Ky., July 4, 1960; m. Alison Mongiardo. BA, Transylvania U., 1982; MD, U. Ky., 1986. Resident McGill U., Can., 1987-91; staff mem. Hazard Appalachian Regional Med. Ctr., 1991—; chief of staff Hazard Appalachian Regional Hosp., 1999—; mem. Ky. State Senate from 30th dist. (formerly 17th dist.), Frankfort, 2001—07; lt. gov. State of Ky., Frankfort, 2007—. Bd. dirs. Rotary Free Clinic, 1999—, Hazard-Perry County Indsl. Devel., 2000—. Democrat. Roman Catholic. Office: Office Lt Gov 700 Capitol Ave Ste 142 Frankfort KY 40601

MONGIN, ALEXANDER ANATOLIEVICH, neuroscientist, educator; b. Minsk, Belarus, Mar. 9, 1965; arrived in U.S., 1997; s. Anatoli I. and Tamara N. Mongin; m. Alena Rudkouskaya, July 22, 1987; children: Feodor, Anton, Katrine. MS, Belarussian State U., 1989; PhD, Acad. Scis. Belarus, 1995. Rsch. fellow Acad. Scis. Belarus, Minsk, 1995-97, sr. scientist, 1997; Fogarty fellow Albany (N.Y.) Med. Coll., 1997-99, asst. prof., 1999—2009, assoc. prof., 2009—. Contbr. chpts. to books, articles to profl. jours. Recipient award Fedn. European Societies Biochemistry, 1995, 1st prize European Soc. Neurochemistry, 1997, prize and medal European Acad., 1997, Career Devel. award APS, 2008; Fogarty fellowship NIH, 1997, Wiggers fellowship, 2005. Mem.: Am. Heart Assn., Am. Soc. Neurochemistry, N.Y. Acad. Scis., Soc. Neuroscience, Am. Physio. Soc. Office: Albany Med Coll MC136 47 New Scotland Ave Albany NY 12208 Business E-Mail: MonginA@mail.amc.edu.

MONGKHONVANIT, PORNCHAI, academic administrator; b. Phyatai, Bangkok, Thailand, Nov. 25, 1958; s. Narong and Kasalai Mongkhonvanit; m. Chollada Jungprasert, July 14, 1993; children: Kritphong, Chutiporn, Nichapha. B in Engring., Kasetsart U., 1981; MBA, U. Wis.-Madison, 1982; D in Ednl. Mgmt. (hon.), Angeles U., 2004. Inst. Ednl. mgmt. Grad. Sch. Edn., Harvard U., 2000. Pres. Siam U., Phasicharoen, Bangkok, Thailand, 1984—, Assn. Pvt. Higher Edn. Instn., Bangkok, 1997—99, Internat. Assn. U. Pres., Bangkok, 2005—. Pres. Phi Delta Kappa, Thailand chpt., Bangkok, 1996—97. Author: (academic article) Knowledge Mgmt. in Higher Edn. at the dawn of 21st century. Recipient Hon. Prof., Autonomous U. Guadarajala, 1987, Medal of Honor, Internat. Assn. U. Presidents, 1996, Disting. Alumni award, Kasetsart U., 2000, Disting. Alumni Award, St. GabrielS Coll., 2001. Master: Phi Delta Kappa, Thailand Chpt.; mem.: Internat. Assn. Univ. Pres. (pres. 2005—), Engring. Coun. Thailand. Home: 343/12 Charansanitwong 12 Bangkok Bangkokyai 10600 Thailand Office: Siam Univ Petkasem Rd Bangkok Phasicharoen 10163 Thailand Office Fax: 662-868-6879; Home Fax: 662-412-9861. Business E-Mail: pornchai@siam.edu.

MONGKOLRATTANOTHAI, KANOKPORN, medical educator; Diplomate Am. Bd. Pediat. Asst. prof. U. Ill. Coll. Medicine, Peoria, 2005—. Office: Univ Ill Coll Medicine 530 NE Glen Oak Ave Peoria IL 61637

MONGO, KAREN MATHIS, speech educator; BA in Comm., U. Ark., Fayetteville, MA. Speech comm. prof. El Centro Coll., Dallas, 2002—; human resources Home Dept.; lectr. Tex. Woman's U., Denton, Tex. Svc. learning coord. Varied, Dallas, 2002. Avocations: acting, reading, dance.

MONHEIT, ALAN GOODMAN, obstetrician, gynecologist; b. Phila., Apr. 5, 1949; s. Richard S. and Jane G. Monheit; children: Robin, Jeffrey, Daniel. BSc, Muhlenberg Coll., 1971; MD, U. Pa., 1975. Intern U. Calif., San Diego, 1975-76, resident physician dept. ob-gyn., 1975-79, fellow, maternal/fetal medicine, 1979-81; attending physician U. Hosp., Stony Brook, 1981—; clin. assoc. prof. SUNY, Stony Brook, 1981—. Tchr. medicine, specialist in high risk pregnancy SUNY, Stony Brook, 1981—. Contbr. articles to profl. jours. Recipient Tchg. award Coun. on Resident Edn. in Ob-gyn., 1997. Mem. ACOG, Assn. Profs. Ob-Gyn., Soc. Perinatal Obstetricians (poster prize 1987), Suffolk County Ob-Gyn. Soc., Phi Beta Kappa. Avocations: bicycling, hiking, space exploration, meteorology. Office: SUNY Dept Obstetrics Gynecology HSC T-9 Stony Brook NY 11794 Office Phone: 631-444-7650.

MONHEIT, MOLLY JANE, artist; b. Yakima, Wash., Aug. 5, 1922; d. Laurel LaVergne and Edna (Bracewell) Lugar; m. John Palmer Ruckel (dec. 1952); children: Gail Ruckel, Andrew Ruckel; m. George Monheit, Dec. 7, 1962 (dec. 2007); 1 child, William. Student, Art Ctr. Sch., Calif., 1942; BA magna cum laude, Wash. State U., 1944; MA, Mills Coll., 1947. Clk., artist, cons. Papyrus, Lafayette, Calif., 1976-97; ret., 1997. Exhibited paintings in Wash., Tex., and Calif.; prin. works represented in permanent collections in pvt. homes and museums in 38 countries; contbr. articles to Bird Watchers Digest. Precinct chmn. Reps., Lafayette, 1954-70; social chmn. Valley View Estates, Lafayette, 1954-80. Recipient fellowship Aurelia Reinhart, 1945-47. Mem. Soc. Western Artists, Am. Women Artists, East Bay Watercolor Soc., Audubon Soc., Am. Field Svc. (pres. 1970), Diablo Art Assn. (pres.), Alpha Gamma Delta. Presbyterian. Avocations: birding trips, track and field. Home: 950 Diablo Rd Apt 147 Danville CA 94526-1928

MONIÉ, ALAIN, information technology executive; Degree in automation engring. studies with high honors, Ecole Nationale Supérieure d'Arts et Metiers, France; MBA, Institut Supérieur des Affaires, Jouy en Josas, France. Civil constrn. engr., Mexico City; contr. Renault, France; gen. mgmt. positions Sogitec Inc.; regional sales mgr. to head of Asia-Pacific ops. Allied Signal; pres. Latin Am. divsn. Honeywell Internat.; exec. v.p. Ingram Micro, Inc., Santa Ana, Calif., 2003—04, pres. Asia-Pacific region, 2004—07, pres., COO, 2007—. Office: Ingram Micro 1600 E St Andrew Pl PO Box 25125 Santa Ana CA 92799 Office Phone: 714-566-1000.*

MONISMITH, CARL LEROY, civil engineering educator; b. Harrisburg, Pa., Oct. 23, 1926; s. Carl Samuel and Camilla Frances (Geidt) M. BSCE, U. Calif., Berkeley, 1950, MSCE, 1954; D of Engring. (hon.), Carleton U., Ottawa, 2004. Registered civil engr., Calif., 1961. From instr. to prof. civil engring. U. Calif., Berkeley, 1951—, chmn. dept. civil engring., 1974-79, Robert Horonjeff prof. civil engring., 1986—, prof. emeritus, 1996: Cons. Chevron Rsch. Co., Richmond, Calif., 1957-93, U.S. Army CE Waterways Expt. Sta., Vicksburg, Miss., 1968-00, B.A. Vallerga, Inc., Oakland, Calif., 1980-98, ARE, Austin, Tex. and Scotts Valley, Calif., 1978-92; cons. Bechtel Corp., San Francisco, 1982-86; keynote speaker Hoover Mentoring Workshop, Iowa State U., 2007. Contbr. numerous articles to profl. jours. Served to 2d lt. C.E., U.S. Army, 1945-47. Recipient Rupert Myers medal U. NSW, 1976; named Henry M. Shaw Lectr. in Civil Engring., N.C. State U., 1993, First Paul Kraser Kent lectr. dept. civil and environ. engring. U. Ill., Urbana-Champaign, 2007; sr. scholar Fulbright Found., U. NSW, 1971, Nat. Asphalt Pavelent Assn. R.D. Kenyon Rsch. and Edn. award for Outstanding Contbns. for Hot Mix Asphalt Tech., 2002, Hall of Fame, 2005; named Disting. Engring. Alumnus, Coll. Engring., U. Calif., Berkeley, 1996 Fellow: AAAS; mem.: ASTM, NAE, NRC (assoc.), NAS (assoc.), ASCE (hon.; pres. San Francisco sect. 1979—80, ednl. activities com. 1989—91, State of Art award 1977, James Laurie prize 1988), Nat. Assn. of the Nat. Acads., Asphalt Inst. (Roll of Honor 1990), Calif. Asphalt Pavement Alliance (award 2002), Am. Soc. Engring. Edn., Internat. Soc. Asphalt Pavements (hon.; chmn. bd. dirs. 1988—90, Disting. Lectr. 2004), Assn. Asphalt Paving Technologists (hon.; pres. 1968, W.J. Emmons award 1961, 1965, 1985), Transp. Rsch. Bd. (assoc.; chmn. pavement design sect. 1973—79, K.B. Woods award 1972, 1st disting. lectureship 1992, Roy W. Crum award 1995). Avocation: stamp collecting/philately. Office: U Calif Dept Civil Engring 215 Mclaughlin Hall Berkeley CA 94720-1712 Office Phone: 510-665-3560. Business E-Mail: clm@maxwell.berkeley.edu.

MONJAN, ANDREW ARTHUR, retired neuroscientist; b. NYC, Feb. 9, 1938; s. Victor Momjian and Sonia (Sherinian) Dardarian; m. Susan Vollenweider, July 1961 (div. Nov. 1965); m. Usha Bose, Aug. 14, 1969; children: Matthew, Vanessa. BSc, Rensselaer Poly. Inst., 1960; PhD, U. Rochester, 1965; MPH, Johns Hopkins U., 1970. Rsch. asst. Sterling-Winthrop Rsch. Inst., Rensselaer, NY, 1960; USPHS rsch. fellow Ctr. for Brain Rsch. U. Rochester, NY, 1964-66; asst. prof. depts. psychology and physiology U. Western Ont., London, Canada, 1966-69; from asst. prof. to assoc. prof. dept. epidemiology Sch. Hygiene and Pub. Health Johns Hopkins U., Balt., 1971-83; expert epidemiology extramural programs br. NIH, Bethesda, Md., 1983-85, chief neurobiology/immunology programs physiology aging br., 1985-87, acting assoc. dir., 1987, chief neurobiology, 1987—2009; exec. sec. Nat. Commn. on Sleep Disorders Rsch., 1990-92. Presenter in field. Contbr. articles to profl. jours. N.Y. State Regents scholar, 1955-59; N.Y. State Regents Grad. Tchg. fellow, 1960-62, USPHS rsch. fellow, 1962-64, 69-70. Office Phone: 410-496-9350. Personal E-mail: amonjan@verizon.net.

MONK, CARL COLBURN, law educator, former legal association administrator; b. Sept. 11, 1942; BA in Polit. Sci., Okla. State U., 1965; JD, Howard U., 1971. Bar: DC 1971, NY 1973. Assoc. Simpson, Thacher & Bartlett, NYC, 1971—74; asst. prof. to assoc. prof. Washburn U. Sch. Law, Topeka, 1974—78, assoc. dean to dean, prof., 1976—88, disting. prof. law, 1988—. Dep. dir. Assn. Am. Law Schs., Washington, 1988-90, exec. dir., exec. v.p., 1992-2008; vis. scholar Bklyn. Law Sch., 1985-86; vis. prof. law W.S. Richardson Sch. Law U. Hawaii Manao, 1990-91; lit. cons. Contbr. articles to profl. jours. Bd. dirs. Kans. Civil Liberties Union. Office: Washburn U Sch Law 1700 SW College Ave Topeka KS 66621 Office Phone: 202-296-1526. Office Fax: 202-296-8869. E-mail: cmonk@aals.org.

MONK, DIANA CHARLA, small business owner; b. Visalia, Calif., Feb. 25, 1927; d. Charles Edward and Viola Genevieve (Shea) Williams; m. James Alfred Monk, Aug. 11, 1951; children: Kiloran, Sydney, Geoffrey, Anne, Eric. Student, U. Pacific, Stockton, Calif., 1946-47, Sacramento Coll., 1947-48, Calif. Coll. Fine Arts, San Francisco, 1948-51, Calif. Coll. Arts & Crafts, Oakland, 1972. Art tchr. Mt. Diablo Sch. Dist., Concord, Calif., 1958-63; pvt. art tchr. Lafayette, Calif., 1963-70; gallery dir. Jason Aver Gallery, San Francisco, 1970-72; owner, mgr. Monk & Lee Assocs., Lafayette, 1973-80; stable owner, mgr. Longacre Tng. Stables, Santa Rosa, Calif., 1989—. One-person shows include John F. Kennedy U., Orinda, Calif., Civic Arts Gallery, Walnut Creek, Calif., Vallery Art Gallery, Walnut Creek, Sea Ranch Gallery, Gualala, Calif., Jason Aver Gallery, San Francisco; exhibited in group shows at Oakland (Calif.) Art Mus., Crocker Nat. Art Gallery, Sacramento, Le Salon des Nations, Paris. Chair bd. dirs. Walnut Creek (Calif.) Civic Arts, 1972-74, advisor to dir., 1968-72; exhibit chmn. Valley Art Gallery, Walnut Creek, 1977-78; juror Women's Art Show, Walnut Creek, 1970, Oakland Calif. Art. Home and Office: Longacre Tng Stables 1702 Willowside Rd Santa Rosa CA 95401-3922 Office Phone: 707-544-7030. Personal E-mail: longacrestables@msn.com.

MONK, MEREDITH JANE, artistic director, composer, choreographer, filmmaker; b. NYC, Nov. 20, 1942; d. Theodore G. and Audrey Lois (Zellman) Monk. BA, Sarah Lawrence Coll., 1964; ArtsD (hon.), Bard Coll., 1988, U. of the Arts, 1989, Juilliard Sch. Music, 1997, San Francisco Art Inst., 1998, Boston Conservatory, 2001, Bennington Coll., 2002, Cornish Coll. Arts, 2002. Artistic dir., founder Ho. Found. Arts, NYC, 1968—. Bd. dirs. Am. Music Ctr., The Kitchen. Prin. works include 16 Millimeter Earrings, 1966, Vessel, 1971, Quarry, 1976, Recent Ruins, 1979, Turtle Dreams, 1983, The Games, 1983, Book of Days, 1988, Facing North, 1990, Atlas, 1991, Three Heavens and Hells, 1992, Volcano Songs, 1994, American Archeology, 1994, The Politics of Quiet, 1996, Magic Frequencies, 1998, Mercy, 2001, Possible Sky, 2003, Impermanence, 2004, Stringsongs, 2005, Basket Rondo, 2007, Song of Ascension, 2008, exhibitions include Libr. of Performing Arts, Lincoln Ctr., 1996, Walker Art Ctr., Mpls., 1998, Whitney Mus. Art, 2002, Exit Art, 2002. Recipient Obie award, Village Voice, 1972, 1976, 1985, Creative Arts award, Brandeis U., 1974, Villager award, 1980, 1983, Deutches Kritiker preis, 1981, 1986, Bessie award, 1985, Nat. Music Theatre award, 1986, 2005, Dance Mag. award, 1993, John D. and Catherine T. MacArthur award, 1995, Sarah Lawrence Disting. Alumna award, 1996, Samuel Scripps award, 1996, Sigma Phi Omega award, 1987, USA Avist award, 2006, Demetrio Stratos award, 2007, L'Arlecchino d'oro di Mantova, 2008; fellow Guggenheim, 1972, 1982, Norton Stevens, 1993—94, MacDowell Colony. Fellow: Am. Acad. Arts and Scis. (USA Artist award 2006); mem.: ASCAP (award 1980—2000, Concert Music award 2005, Bessie award 2005, Classical Music award 2006). Office: House Found for Arts 260 West Broadway Ste 2 New York NY 10013

MONK, SHARON ANNE, special education educator; b. Boulder City, Nev., Dec. 9, 1948; d. Earl Robert Oxtoby and Katherine Francis Brazil; m. Michael Arthur Monk, July 20, 1968; children: Robert Lee, John Patrick, James Michael. BA with spl. distinction, U. So. Colo., 1979; MA in Spl. Edn. summa cum laude, Azusa Pacific U., Calif., 2004. Cert. elem. sch. tchr. Colo., elem. sch. tchr. regular edn. Calif., regular edn. K-12, early childhood tchr. Calif., No Child Left Behind Act highly qualified tchr. cert. Calif., cert. cross-cultural and academic devel. Calif. Instrnl. asst. Harrison Sch. Dist., Colorado Springs, Colo., 1977—78; preschool tchr. YMCA/La Petite Acad., Sacramento, 1987—89; children's after-sch. tchr. San Juan Unified Sch. Dist., Carmichael, Calif., 1989—94; early intervention tchr. V.I.P.-Tots Presch., Hemet, Calif., 2002—03; primary spl. edn. tchr. Perris (Calif.) Elem. Sch. Dist., 2003—. Profl., parent advocate Parent Helping Parents, Sacramento, 1992—94, Parents of Children with Disabilities, Sacramento, 1992—94. Apple grantee, Calif. Commn. on Tchr. Credentialing, 2002, 2004, 2005, 2006. Mem.: NEA, Calif. Edn. Assn., Coun. on Exceptional Children, Pi Lambda Theta. Avocations: travel, writing, music, research, reading. Office: 250 'D' S Lyon Ave PMB 212 Hemet CA 92543

MONK, SUSAN MARIE, pediatrician, educator; d. John Spotz and Mary Elizabeth (Shelly) M.; m. Jaime Pacheco, June 5, 1971; children: Benjamin Joaquin, Maria Cristina. AB, Colby Coll., Waterville, Maine, 1967; MD, Jefferson Med. Coll., Phila., 1971. Diplomate Am. Bd. Pediatrics. Pediatrician Children's Med. Ctr., Dayton, Ohio, 1975—; asst. clin. prof. pediat. Wright State U., Dayton, 1976—83, assoc. clin. prof. pediat., 1983—2000, asst. prof. pediat., 2000—08, assoc. proff. pediat., 2008—. Mem. bd. dirs. Children's Med. Ctr., Dayton, 1991-96, chief-of-staff, 1992-94. Mem. Am. Acad. Pediatrics, We. Ohio Pediatric Soc., Pediatric Ambulatory Care Soc. Avocations: reading, gardening, travel, movies, theater. Office: Childrens Health Clinic 730 C Valley St Dayton OH 45404-1845 Office Phone: 937-641-5355.

MONK, SUZANNE RENEE, academic administrator; d. Samuel William and Evelyn Sue Monk. M, Ohio U., Athens, 1986. Mng. editor Meridian Star, Miss., 1998—2007; dir. pub. info. East Miss. CC, Scooba, 2007—. Pvt. practise, Miss., 2007—. Recipient numerous awards, Miss. Press Assn., 1994—2008. Office: East MS CC 1512 Kemper St Scooba MS 39358 Business E-Mail: smonk@eastms.edu.

MONKELIEN, SHERYL L., music educator; MusB, Iowa State U., Ames, 1980; MusM, U. Nebr., Lincoln, 1995, PhD, 2001. Assoc. prof. music Mansfield U., Pa., 2001—. Office: Mansfield Univ 18 Campus View Dr Butler Mansfield PA 16933 Business E-Mail: smonkeli@mansfield.edu.

MONK KIDD, SUE, writer; b. Sylvester, Ga., Aug. 12, 1948; m. Sandy Monk Kidd; children: Bob, Ann. BS in Nursing, Tex. Christian U., Fort Worth, 1970; student, Emory U., Atlanta. Nurse St. Joseph's Hosp., Fort Worth, Tex. Writer in residence Phoebe Pember House, Charleston, SC. Former contbg. editor Guideposts mag.; author: God's Joyful Surprise, 1988, When the Heart Waits: Spiritual Direction for Life's Sacred Questions, 1990, The Dance of the Dissident Daughter: A Woman's Journey from Christian Tradition to the Sacred Feminine, 1996, The Secret Life of Bees, 2002 (SEBA Book of Yr. award, 2003, Publishers Weekly bestseller, 2003, 2004, 2008), The Mermaid Chair, 2005 (Publishers Weekly bestseller, 2005, Quills award for gen. fiction, 2005); contbr. essays to mags. Recipient Fiction Projectaward, SC Arts Commn., 1993, 1995, 1997, Isak Dineson Creative Non-Fiction award, 1994; fellow, SC Arts Commn., 1993—94, 1994, 1996; scholar, Bread Loaf Writers Conf., 1995. Office: c/o Carolyn Coleburn Viking Penguin 375 Hudson St New York NY 10014*

MONK-TUTOR, MARY R., pharmacist, educator; b. Birmingham, Ala. m. Terry M. Tutor. BS in Pharmacy, Auburn U., 1984; MS in Hosp. Pharmacy, U. Miss., 1989, PhD in Pharmacy Adminstrn., 1993. Pharmacy mgr. Response Oncology, Inc, Memphis, 1994—96; asst. prof. pharmacy adminstrn. Sch. Pharmacy Samford U., Birmingham, 1996—2001, vice-chair pharmacy practice Sch. Pharmacy, 2001—02, assoc. prof., Sch. Pharmacy, 2002—07, dir., assessment, Sch. Pharmacy, 2007—. Home care surveyor Joint Commn. on Accreditation of Healthcare Orgn. (JCAHO), Chgo., 1990—2002; pres. Monk-Tutor Consulting, Birmingham, 1995—. Contbr. articles to profl. jours. Profl. adv. com. Alacare Home Health, Birmingham, 1997—. Grantee, Nat. Home Infusion Assn., 2002—05. Fellow: Am. Soc. Health Sys. Pharmacists (dir. at-large home care sect. 1997—99); mem.: Ala. Soc. Health Sys. Pharmacists (home care com. chair 2000—01), Am. Assn. Colls. Pharmacy (Social and Admin. Sci. com. mem. 2000—06). Office: Samford U Sch Pharmacy 800 Lakeshore Dr Birmingham AL 35229 Office Phone: 205-726-2876. Business E-Mail: mrmonktu@samford.edu.

MONKUL, MEHMET MURAT, geotechnical engineering researcher; b. Istanbul, Turkey, Oct. 4, 1980; s. Rifat Osman and Havva Suna Monkul; m. Bahar Ozmen-Monkul. BS, Mid. East Tech. U., Ankara, 2002; MSc, Dokuz Eylul U., Izmir, 2005; PhD. candidate, Oreg. State U., Corvallis, 2005. Grad. rsch. asst. Oreg. State U., 2005—08, grad. tchg. asst., 2008—. Contbr. scientific papers to profl. jours. (Oreg. State U. Coll. Engring. Fellowship, 2005, 2006). Cultural OSU Turkish Student Assn., Corvallis, 2006—08. Office: Oregon State Univ 220 Owen Hall Corvallis OR 97331

MONNET, JACQUES CHARLES LOUIS, automotive executive; b. Paris, Oct. 15, 1951; s. Pierre Louis Gabriel Monnet and Denise Marie-Thérèse Jacques; m. Isabelle Andree Moreau, Feb. 27, 1978; children: Christophe, Kimberley. MSME, Ecole Ctrl De Lyon, France, Tech. U. Damstadt, Germany, 1974; general mgmt. program, Insead, Fontainebleau, 1990. Export sales engr. Valeo Climate Control, Paris, 1976—80; v.p. gen. mgr. Valeo Climate Control North Am., Detroit, 1980—87, pres., 1994—95; v.p. sales, mktg. strategic planning Valeo Climate Control, 1987—93; CEO Valeo Seiko Compressors, Paris, 1993; gen. mgr. TRW Auto., Paris, 1995—2000; CEO Fed. French Auto. Equip. Ind., Paris, 2000—. V.p. Societe Des Ingenieurs De L'Automobile, Paris, 2003; bd. mem. Union Technique Auto., Motorcycle, Cycle, Paris, 2000, Afnor Cet., Paris, 2002. Mem.: Auto. Club De

France. Catholic. Avocations: golf, cooking, skiing. Home: 1 Impasse Des Acacias 78112 Fourqueux France Office: Fiev 79 Rue Jean-Jacques Rousseau 92158 Suresnes France Office Phone: 331 46250253. Business E-Mail: jmonnet@fiev.fr.

MONROE, CARL DEAN, III, lawyer; b. Birmingham, Ala., Sept. 15, 1960; s. Carl D. and Martha Jo M. BA, Birmingham-So. Coll., 1982; JD, Georgetown U., Washington, DC, 1985. Bar: Ala. 1986, US Ct. Appeals (11th cir.) 1988. Scheduler Siegelman for Atty. Gen., Montgomery, 1986; legal rsch. aide Office of Sec. of State State of Ala., Montgomery, 1986; asst. atty. gen., adminstrv. asst. Office of Atty. Gen., Montgomery, 1987-89; atty.-advisor Office Gen. Counsel US Dept. Energy, Washington, 1989—. Mem. panel of judges Georgetown Law Ctr. Moot Ct., 1991, 92, CIA Environ. Roundtable; lectr. waste mgmt. Johns Hopkins U., natural resources George Washington U. Mem. panel of judges Ala. YMCA Youth Legislature, Montgomery, 1979, 87, 88, 89; office coord. blood dr. ARC, Montgomery, 1987, 88; com. mem. Georgetown Alumni Admissions, Washington, 1986-91; mem. Nat. Trust for Hist. Preservation, Beahrs Environ. Leadership Seminar, U. Calif.-Berkeley, 2001. Mem. ABA (author environ. law sect. newsletter Looking Ahead), Acad. Polit. Sci., Ala. Bar Assn., Birmingham-So. Alumni (alumni leader 1986—), Phi Beta Kappa, Am. Soc. Internat. Law. Democrat. Presbyn. Avocations: water-skiing, tennis, horseback riding. Home Phone: 202-629-4248; Office Phone: 202-586-2948. Personal E-mail: rufkdlk@gmail.com. Business E-Mail: dean.monroe@hq.doe.gov.

MONROE, CRAIG (KEYSTONE), professional baseball player; b. Texarkana, Tex., Feb. 27, 1977; s. Marilyn Monroe; m. Kasey Monroe; 1 child, Morgan. Outfielder Tex. Rangers, 2001, Detroit Tigers, 2002—07, Chgo. Cubs, 2007, Minn. Twins, 2008—. Outfielder Puerto Rican Winter League, 2003—04. Achievements include tying for second among all American League outfielders with 12 assists, 2006. Mailing: c/o Minnesota Twins Metrodome 34 Kirby Puckett Pl Minneapolis MN 55415

MONROE, DAN L., museum director; Dep. dir. Alaska State Mus. System, 1974—84; dir. Portland Art Mus., 1984—92; exec. dir., CEO Peabody Essex Mus., Salem, Mass., 1994—. Mem. Lijang Studio. Achievements include winning various awards in filmmaking. Office: Peabody Essex Mus 134 Essex St Salem MA 01970

MONROE, EVELYN JONES, retired librarian; d. Freeman B. Jones Sr. and Emma Bush Jones; m. Ralph B. Benbow (div.); m. Robert Aaron Monroe, June 6, 1966; 1 child, Cheryl Denise. BS, Ala. State Coll., Montgomery, 1955; MS in Libr. and Info. Scis., U. Wis., Madison, 1964. Cert. life and health ins. agt. Va., 1995. Tchr., libr. Mobile County Sch. Bd., Mobile, Ala., 1955—66; sch. libr. Norfolk Pub. Sch. Sys., Va., 1966—67; adminstrv. libr. Fleet Combat Direction Sys. Support Activity, Virginia Beach, Va., 1967—84; tech. libr. Virginia Beach, 1984—94; benefit coord. Benefit Assn., Virginia Beach, 1995—96; asst. instr. Donovan Agy., Virginia Beach, 1996—97; asst. registrar Portsmouth, Va., 1999—2000; ret., 1994. Chmn., tng. coord. Coun. Navy Sci. and Tech. Librs., Dept. Navy, 1987—92; counselor, coord. FCDSSA, Virginia Beach, 1976—86; supr. tech. writers, editors Computer Program Documentation for Delivery to Ship and Shore Activities, 1984—94. Chmn. bd. trustees Hist. Third Bapt. Ch., Portsmouth, Va., 2003—. Recipient Excellence award, Naval Sea Sys. Command, 1984. Mem.: Am. Contract Bridge League, Am. Bridge Assn. (club point coord. 1987—2006), Delta Sigma Theta. Democrat. Avocation: bridge. Home: 37 Lantern Way Portsmouth VA 23703 E-mail: monroeejn@aol.com.

MONROE, FREDERICK FALES, geologist, oceanographer; b. Washington, May 3, 1936; s. Sheldon McKinley and Fredericka Fales Monroe; m. Lori Rose Farquharson, June 11, 1988; m. Patricia Ann Lynch, July 11, 1971 (dec.); m. Sue Ellen Reeves, Oct. 7, 1963 (div. Oct. 7, 1970); children: Elizabeth Carmela, Patricia Alexis(dec.), Calli Grace, Victoria Michelle, John Scott, Lisa Diane Buyan, Christina Lee. BA, Amherst Coll., 1958; MS, The Am. U., 1970; MA, U. Miami, 1977; PhD, The Am. U., 1989. Profl. geologist Va., 1983. Geologist King & Gavaris, Cons. Engrs., NYC, 1960—62; phys. sci. aide US Geol. Survey, Denver, 1962; oceanographer US Army Corps Engrs., Washington, 1962—67; ass't. prof ocean engring. Fla. Atlantic U., Boca Raton, 1967—71; oceanog. cons. Arthur Strock, Inc., 1971—75; fgn. affairs officer US Dept. State, Washington, 1975—. Adj. asst. prof. No. Va. CC, Alexandria, 2002—05; professorial lectr. The Am. U., Washington, 1989—93. Recipient Meritorious Honor award, US Dept. State, 1983, Career Achievement medal, 2001. Fellow: The Explorers Club; mem.: Marine Tech. Soc. (founding). Achievements include research in marine resource potential of US Exclusive Economic Zone; co-founded US Army Corps of Engrs. Coastal Engring Rsch. Ctr. Underwater Ops. Group; provided tech. support on deep seabed mining to US delegation to the UN Law of the Sea Convention; wrote Coastal State Control and the Global Ocean Harvest UMI, Ann Arbor, 1989. Personal E-mail: ffmonroe@hotmail.com.

MONROE, FREDERICK LEROY, chemist; b. Redmond, Oreg., Oct. 13, 1942; s. Herman Sylvan Monroe and Mary Roberta (Grant) Emery. BS in Chemistry, Oreg. State U., Corvallis, 1964; MS in Environ. Engring., Wash. State U., Pullman, 1974. Control specialist Air Pollution Control Authority, Centralia, Wash., 1969-70; asst. chemist Wash. State U., 1970-74; environ. engr. Ore-Ida Foods, Inc., Idaho, 1974-77; cons. Idaho, 1977-78; applications engr. AFL Industries, Riviera Beach, Fla., 1979-80; mgr. chem. control PCA Internat., Matthews, NC, 1980—85; quality assurance mgr. Stork Screens Am., Charlotte, NC, 1985—99; grade IV NC wastewater treatment operator. Pres. Unity Ch., 1982-84. Served with USAF, 1964-68, maj. Res. ret.; served with N.G., 1973-78. Decorated Air Force Commendation medal, Vietnam Era Svc. Commemorative medal; recipient Blue Thumb award Charlotte-Mecklenburg Utility Dist., 1993. Fellow AIChE. Republican. Home and Office: 207 Summermore Dr Charlotte NC 28270 Home Phone: 541-728-5485. Personal E-mail: fredmonroe@aol.com.

MONROE, HASKELL MOORMAN, JR., chancellor emeritus, retired history professor, dean; b. Dallas, Mar. 18, 1931; s. Haskell M. and Myrtle Marie (Jackson) Monroe; m. Margaret Joan Phillips, June 15, 1957; children: Stephen, Melanie, Mark, John. BA, Austin Coll., Tex., 1952, MA, 1954; PhD, Rice U., Houston, 1961; D (hon.), Austin Coll., 1984. From instr. to prof. Tex. A&M U., 1959-80, asst. dean Grad. Sch., 1965-68, asst. v.p. acad. affairs, 1972-74, dean faculties, 1974-80, assoc. v.p. acad. affairs, 1977-80, dean faculties emeritus College Station, 1997—; pres. U. Tex., El Paso, 1980-87; chancellor U. Mo., Columbia, 1987-91, prof. history, 1987-97, chancellor emeritus, prof. history, 1997—. Instr. Schreiner Inst., Kerrville, Tex., 1959; vis. lectr. Emory U., 1967, 72; faculty lectr. Tex. A&M U., 1972; alumni lectr. Austin Coll., 1980; bd. dirs. City Nat. Bank, Southwestern Bell Corp., Boone County Nat. Bank, SBC Comms., Inc.; history adv. com. Sec. Air Force, 1987; orientation com. Dept. Def.-Joint Chiefs, 1986. Contbr. articles, revs. to profl. jours.; editor: Papers of Jefferson Davis, 1964—69; adv. editor: Texana, 1964—71; mem. bd. editl. advisers Booker T. Washington Washington Papers, 1965—85. Bd. dirs. Brazos Valley Rehab. Ctr., 1975-77, Salvation Army, El Paso, 1984-87, Columbia, Mo., 1988-97, Crime Stoppers of El Paso, United Way Columbia, 1988-94, Keep Brazos Beautiful, 1999-2003, Washington-on-the-Brazos State Park Assn., 2002-; trustee Bryan Hosp., 1976-79, chmn., 1979; bd. ch. visitors Austin Coll., 1977-78; deacon First Presbyn. Ch., Bryan, 1961-63, elder, 1965-67, 69-71, 73-74, clk. of session, 1973-74, chmn. pulpit nominating com., 1971-72; mem. presbytery's coun. Presbytery of Brazos, 1969-71, mem. resources for the 80s steering com., 1978-80; elder 1st Presbyn. Ch., El Paso, 1984-87, 1st Presbyn. Ch., Columbia, 1994-96; mem. exec. bd. Great Rivers coun. Boy Scouts Am., 1990-97; mem. Pres. Coun. NCAA, 1986-87; chmn. Jefferson Davis award com. Confederate Mus., 1996-97; bd. dirs. Salvation Army, 1989-97, Schreiner U., 1998-2007 Recipient Citation of Appreciation, LULAC, 1982, Honor award Salvation Army, 1997, Faculty Disting. Achievement award Tex. A&M U., 1964, U. Mo. Alumni award for tchg., 1995, also numerous achievement awards; grantee Social Sci. Rsch. Coun., Tex. A&M U., Huntington Libr., Intrafraternity and Sorority Outstanding Tchr. award, U. Mo., 1997; named Ky. Col., 1967; named to Legends of Aggieland, 1998. Mem. Am. Hist. Assn., Orgn. Am. Historians, So. Hist. Assn. Hist. Found. Presbyn. and Reformed Chs. (pres. 1970-72), Coll. Football Assn. (chmn. bd. 1989-90, bd. dirs.), Truman Scholarship Panel, Soc. Conf. Deans Faculties and Acad. V.P.s (pres. 1978), Rotary (El Paso, hon. Columbia, Mo., Bryan, Tex., Paul Harris fellow 1986, 2000). Home: 1005 Sonoma Cir College Station TX 77845-7907 Office: Tex A&M U 6B15 Evans Libr College Station TX 77843 Office Phone: 979-324-4546. Business E-Mail: hmonroe@tamu.edu.

MONROE, JAMES WALTER, retired corporate financial executive; b. Fairfax, SD, Feb. 13, 1936; s. Sherman William and Frances (Burnett) M.; m. Dorothy Lou Gillette, Apr. 1, 1961; children— Steven James, David Walter, Melody Anne, Andrew Scott. Student, Huron Coll., SD, 1954-56, U. Nebr., 1956-57; BA, Nebr. Wesleyan U., 1960. Mgr. Belleville (Kans.) C. of C., 1960-61, Concordia (Kans.) C. of C., 1961-62; asst. chief Div. Nebr. Resources, 1962-65; dir. S.D. Indsl. Devel. Expansion Agy., 1965-67, Nebr. Dept. Econ. Devel., 1967-71; sec. Nebr. Resources Found., 1967-71; exec. dir. Omaha Econ. Devel. Council, 1971-76; pres. Kansas City (Mo.-Kans.) Area Devel. Council, 1976-90; pres., chief exec. officer New Orleans and the River Region C. of C., 1990-96, Metrovision Found., Econ. Devel. Coun. Metro, New Orleans; ret., 1996. Mem. Am. Indsl. Devel. Council, 1965—, chmn. certification bd., 1981-82; sec. labor mgmt. council Greater Kansas City, 1979-90; mem. exec. com. Gov.'s Econ. Devel. Adv. Council, 1979-81. Bd. dirs. Am. Econ. Devel. Coun., 1992—. Served with AUS, 1957-59. Independent. Congregationalist. Home: 19015 84th Ave W Edmonds WA 98026

MONROE, JOHN B., history professor; b. Moscow, Idaho, Dec. 11, 1945; s. Ervin Monroe and Shirley Jones; m. Earlene N. Rayment; children: John Earl, Michael Lee, Berton John. MA in History, Eastern Wash. U., Cheney, 1995. With USMC, Calif., 1966—70; medic 1st sgt. USAF, Fairchild, Wash., 1971—91; history tchr. IEL, Colville, Wash., 1997—. Decorated MSM USAF. Home: 12516 E 27th Ave Spokane WA 99216-0230 Office: Inst Extended Learning 955 S Elm St Colville WA 99114-2662

MONROE, JOHN WARNE, history professor; b. Palo Alto, Calif., Feb. 22, 1973; s. John William and Margaret Warne Monroe; m. Wendie Ellen Schneider, Oct. 15, 2003. AB in History, Princeton U., NJ, 1995; PhD, Yale U., New Haven, Conn., 2002. Assoc. prof. history Iowa State U., Ames, 2002—. Contbr. monograph (Theron Rockwell Field prize, 2002). Office: IA State Univ Dept History 603 Ross Hall Ames IA 50011 Business E-Mail: jmonroe@iastate.edu.

MONROE, JOSEPH M., oil industry executive; B in Chem. Engring., NC State U.; M in Chem. Engring., U. Calif., Berkeley; MBA, U. So. Calif. V.p. pipelines and terminals, pres. Unocal Pipeline Co. Unocal Corp., 1999—2002; sr. v.p. supply and distbn. Tesoro Refining and Mktg. Co. Tesoro Corp., San Antonio, 2002—04, sr. v.p. strategic planning and bus. devel., sr. v.p. orgnl. effectiveness, sr. v.p. bus. intergration & analysis, sr. v.p. bus. devel. & logistics, sr. v.p. corp. devel. Office: Tesoro Corp 300 Concord Plz San Antonio TX 78216-6999 Office Phone: 210-283-2464.*

MONROE, JUDITH A., state agency administrator, public health service officer; m. Robert Lubitz; 3 children. B, Ea. Ky. Univ., 1975; MD, Univ. Md., 1983. Residency Univ. Cin., 1983—86; physician Nat. Health Svc. Corps, Morgan County, Tenn., 1986—90; dir. clinics Dept. Family Med., Ind. Univ., 1990—92; dir. primary care ctr. & family med. residency prog. St. Vincent Hosp. & Health Svc., Indpls., 1992—2005; commr. Ind. Dept. Health, Indpls., 2005—. Chairwoman Tobacco Prevention and Cessation Exec. Bd.; mem. Ind. Health Info. Exch. Bd.; pres. Assn. State and Territorial Health Officials. Fellow, Ea. Tenn. State Univ., 1990, Univ. Wis., 1993. Office: Ind State Dept Health 2 N Meridian St Indianapolis IN 46204*

MONROE, KELVIN JONATHAN, musician, educator; b. Sparta, Ga., Aug. 18, 1974; s. Herbert and Linda Monroe. MusB, Valdosta State U., Ga., 2000; student, Wash. State U., Pullman, 2001—. Instr. comparative ethnic studies Wash. State U., Pullman, 2003—, grad. tchg. asst., 2006—. Contbr. articles to profl. jours. Educator/activist MOVE, Valdosta, Ga., 1998—2000. Mem.: Phi Mu Alpha Inc. (assoc.). Communist. Office: Dept Comparative Ethnic Studies PO Box 644010 Pullman WA 99164-4010

MONROE, KENDYL KURTH, retired lawyer; b. Clayton, N.Mex., Sept. 6, 1936; s. Dottis Donald and Helen (Kurth) Monroe; m. Barbara Sayre, Sept. 12, 1956; children: Sidney, Dean, Loren. AB, Stanford U., Calif., 1958, LLB, 1960. Bar: NY 1961, Calif. 1961. Assoc. Sullivan & Cromwell, NYC, 1960-67, ptnr., 1968-94; ret., 1994. Chmn. TEB Charter Svcs., Inc., Teterboro, NJ, El Valle Escondido Ranch Ltd. Co., Seneca, N.Mex., Eklund Assn. Clayton, N.Mex. Chmn. adv. coun. Mandala Ctr., Des Moines, N.Mex.; mem. adv. com. Cornerstones Cmty. Partnerships, Santa Fe; pres-elect., bd. dirs. Clan Munro Assn., Great Falls, Va.; chmn. Union County Med. Found., Clayton, N.Mex.; bd. dirs. Union County Water Bd., Clayton, N.Mex. Water Dialogue, Santa Ferim, NY Chamber Soloists, NYC. Mem.: Assn. Bar City of NY, State Bar Calif., Met. Club. Home: 189 Sayre Rd Seneca NM 88415 Personal E-mail: kkmonroe@bacavalley.com.

MONROE, LOREN, lobbyist; BA in Polit. Sci., U. Vt. Legis. staff mem. to Senator Pete Domenici US Senate, Washington; bus. devel. coord. Cassidy & Assocs., Washington; COO BGR Holding, Washington, 2005—. Fundraising aide Fin. Dept. Nat. Rep. Congl. Com., 1994; mem. fin. com. Rep. Govs. Assn., Rep. Attys. Gen. Assn. Office: BGR Holding The Homer Bldg, Eleventh Fl S 601 Thirteenth St NW Washington DC 20005 Office Phone: 202-333-4936. Office Fax: 202-833-9392. E-mail: LMonroe@bgrdc.com.*

MONROE, MELROSE, retired bank executive; b. Flowery Branch, Ga., Apr. 13, 1919; d. Willis Jeptha and Leila Adell Cash; m. Lynn Austin, June 14, 1942. AB in Edn., Ga. State U., 1968. Negotiator Trust Co. Bank, Atlanta, 1962-89, ret., 1989. Mem. Nat. Women's C. of C. (pres. 1987-88), Atlanta Women's C. of C. (dir. 1965-66, pres. Fidelis SS class 1962-63), Nat. Am. Legion Aux. (so. divsn. chmn. aux. Americanism 1995-96, so. divsn. chmn. aux. emergency fund 1996-97, cmty. svc. com.), Am. Legion Aux. (pres. 5th dist. 1986-87, Ga. state chaplain 1989-90, state historian 1991-92, state 2d v.p. 1992-93, 1st v.p. 1993-94, pres. 1994-95, Americanism chmn. so. divsn. 1995-95, chmn. emergency fund 1996-97, mem. cmty. svc. com. 1997-98, nat. historian 1999-00, v. chmn. nat. poppy com. 2000-01), Order Ea. Star (worthy matron 1951-52). Democrat. Home and Office: 6250 Spout Springs Rd Flowery Branch GA 30542-5031 Office Phone: 770-967-2992.

MONROE, RICHARD W., university professor; s. Aubrey W. Monroe and Margie N. Reed; m. Christine M. Bowler, Apr. 2, 1986; 1 child, Kevin R. BS, So. Tech. Inst., Marietta, Ga., 1975; MS, We. New Eng. Coll., Springfield, Mass., 1990; PhD, Old Dominion U., Norfolk, Va., 1997. Cert. in six sigma green belt Am. Soc. Quality, 2006, in supply chain Profl. APICS, 2006, in production and inventory Mgmt. APICS, 2005. Chief indsl. engr. Stanadyne Automotive Corp., Windsor, Conn., 1987—92; grad. asst. Old Dominion U., Norfolk, Va., 1992—97, adj. instr., 1992—97; asst. prof. Kennesaw State U., Ga., 1998—2001, So. Poly. State U., Marietta, Ga., 2001—04, Coastal Carolina U., Conway, SC, 2007—; assoc. prof. East Carolina U., Greenville, NC, 2004—07. Cons. PaperPak Inc., Greenville, NC, 2005—06, trainer, 2005—06. Contbr. articles to profl. jours. Youth soccer coach YMCA, Woodstock, Ga., 2002. Recipient Outstanding Instr. O&P Program, Kennesaw State U., 2001, Outstanding Student Adviser, 2001. Mem.: APICS (chpt. pres. 2006—07), Am. Soc. Quality. Office: Coastal Carolina Univ PO Box 261954 Conway SC 29528-6054

MONROE, ROBERT RAWSON, national security consultant; b. Oakland, Calif., Sept. 25, 1927; s. Robert Ansley and Muriel Estelle (Burnham) M.; m. Charlotte Boies Anderson, Oct. 16, 1951; children: Robert Anderson, Nancy Lynn Monroe Sims, Susan Leslie Monroe Gordon. BS in Naval Sci., U.S. Naval Acad., 1950; MA in Internat. Rels., Stanford U., Calif., 1962. Commd. ensign USN, 1950, advanced through grades to vice-admiral, 1977; dir. Navy Systems Analysis, 1972-73; comdr. South Atlantic Force, 1973-74; comdr. Operational Test and Evaluation Force USN, 1974-77; dir. Def. Nuclear Agy., 1977-80; dir. Navy Rsch., Devel., Test and Evaluation, 1980-83; ret., 1983; joined Bechtel Nat., Inc., San Francisco, 1984, mgr. def. and space, 1984-89, v.p., 1985, sr. v.p., ptnr., 1987, mgr. mktg. and govt. ops., 1989-91, mgr. spl. projects, 1992-93, mgr. govt. ops. Washington, 1993—2002, sr. counselor, 2002—05; ret., 2005; nat. security cons., 2006—. Mem. nat. security adv. bd. Los Alamos (N.Mex.) Nat. Lab., 1983—88; mem. tech. evaluation panel U.S. Dept. Energy, 1983—88; mem. engring. adv. com. Oak Ridge Nat. Lab., 1986—89, Rensselaer Poly. Inst., 1990—91; mem. bd. advisors Office Tech. Assessment, Washington, 1987—89, Nat. Contract Mgmt. Assn., 1986—91; mem. task forces Def. Sci. Bd., Washington, 1983—89; corp. mem. Charles Stark Draper Lab., Cambridge, Mass., 1983—; affiliate mem. Ctr. for Internat. Security and Cooperation, Stanford U., 1989—93; chmn. space transp. subcom. NASA's Adv. Coun., 1995—2001; mem. strategic adv. bd. Nev. Test Site, 1995—99; mem. Nat. Security adv. panel Sandia Nat. Labs., 1996—; mem. threat reduction adv. com. (nuc. panel) Dept. Def., 1998—; mem. Enhanced Test Readiness External Rev. Group, 2002—03; mem. threat reduction adv. com. (sys. & tech. panel) Dept. Def., 2004—, mem. U.S. Nuc. Strategy Forum, 2004—; mem. mil. com. Ctr. for Security Policy, 2004—; mem. adv. bd. arms control and nonproliferation State Dept., Washington, 2005—06, chmn. task force on nat. strategy to combat weapons of mass destruction, 2006—07, mem. internat. security adv. bd., 2006—; pres. US Naval Acad. Class 1950, 2009—. Decorated Def. DSM, Navy DSM, Legion of Merit, Bronze Star medal with combat device, Joint Svcs. Commendation medal, USN Commendation medal with combat device; Legion of Honor (France). Avocations: tennis, golf, hiking, reading. Home: 2313 Sawdust Rd Vienna VA 22181-3044 Personal E-mail: rrmonroe@cox.net.

MONROE, STEPHANIE JOHNSON, lobbyist, former federal agency administrator; b. 1958; BA in Govt. & Politics, U. Md., 1980; JD, U. Balt., 1985. Legis. asst. to Senator Gordon Humphrey US Senate, 1987—89; chief counsel, staff dir. US Senate Com. on Labor & Human Resources, Children, Families, Drugs & Alcoholism Subcommittee, 1989—2001; chief counsel US Senate Com. on Health, Education, Labor & Pensions, 2001—05; profl. staff mem. US Senate Budget Com.; asst. sec. for civil rights US Dept. Edn., Washington, 2005—09, acting asst. sec. for congressional & legis. affairs, 2008; founder, pres. The Wrenwood Group, LLC, 2009—. Head Start Quality & Expansion adv. com. US Dept. Health & Human Services, 1993—.*

MONROE, THOMAS EDWARD, business and financial executive; b. Ironton, Mo., Nov. 19, 1947; s. Donald Mansfield and Edwina Frances (Carr) M.; children: Thomas Edward II, Katherine Jenna. BA, Drury U., 1969; postgrad., Washington U. Sch. Bus. Adminstrn., St. Louis, 1970. Acctg. mgr., asst. contr. Am. Transit Corp., St. Louis, 1970-74; mgr. corp. devel., asst. treas. Chromalloy Am. Corp., St. Louis, 1974-77, v.p. fin., 1977-78, exec. v.p., 1978-82; dir. Chromalloy Fin. Corp., 1976-82, Am. Universal Ins. Co., 1978-82; chmn. Capital Assocs. Corp., 1982—, Fed. Air Ambulance, The Safe Deposit Co., CompuVault, Inc., James Flying Svc., Inc., Lindbergh Leasing, Inc., Vault II, LLC. Trustee Kingsbury Pl. Assn.; former trustee 2d Presbyn. Ch. With USMC, 1969—75. Mem. Algonquin Club. Presbyterian. Office: Capital Assocs Corp 515 S Lindbergh Blvd Saint Louis MO 63131-2731 Office Phone: 314-991-3130.

MONROE, WILLIAM LEWIS, human resources executive; b. Detroit, May 11, 1941; s. Lewis Stewart and Ada Jeanette (Williams) Monroe; m. Sharon Lynne Kahal, June 30, 1967; children: Andrea M. Dunk, William J. BA, Western Mich. U., 1963, MA, 1964. Rsch. analyst Chrysler Corp., Detroit, 1965-72, labor economist, 1972-77, mgr. retirement, savs. and unemployment benefit plans, 1977-81; dir. employee benefits W. R. Grace & Co., NYC, 1981-87, v.p. human resources, 1987-2001, bd. trustee, v.p. coun. on employee benefits, 1989-2001, pres. coun. on employee benefits, 1995-96; cons. AON, Boca Raton, 2001—02. Adj. prof. mgmt. FAU Univ., Boca Raton, 2001; corp. bd. dirs. Internat. Found. Employee Benefits, 1986—88; mem. bus. rsch. adv. coun. U.S. Dept. Labor/Bur. Labor Stats., 1987—96; mem. Human Resources Policy Inst. Boston U., 1993—96. Co-chmn. closing com. PTSA Sch., Birmingham, Mich., 1977; chmn. pers. com. Wilton Presbyn. ch., Wilton, Conn., 1982—86; officer, bd. dirs. Forest Hills Property Owners Assn., Birmingham, 1974—80; mem. exec. bd. Gulf Stream coun. Boy Scouts Am., 1993—99. Served USAR, 1965—71. Mem.: Soc. for Human Resources & Mgmt., Boca Raton Resort and Club, Royal Palm Yacht & Country Club. Independent. Presbyterian. Avocations: tennis, golf. Personal E-mail: billmonroe03@yahoo.com.

MONSELL, EDWIN, otolaryngologist, educator; b. Tulsa, Okla., Mar. 1, 1948; s. Edwin M. and Marguerite Monsell; m. Wendy S. Sheine, Dec. 23, 1978; children: Sarah E., Susan A. BA with Honours, Williams Coll., Williamstown, Mass., 1971; PhD, Duke U., Durham, NC, 1976; MD, U.

NC, Chapel Hill, 1979. Diplomate Am. Bd. Otolaryngology, 1984, neurotology Am. Bd. Otolaryngology, 2005. Sr. staff physician Henry Ford Health Sys., Detroit, 1988—2000; prof. Wayne State U. Sch. Medicine, 2000—. Chair, com. hearing & equilibrium Am. Acad. Otolaryngology-Head & Neck Surgery, Alexandria, Va., 1992—94, coord. rsch. & bd. dirs., 1996—2002; pres. Assn. Rsch. Otolaryngology, 2003. Named one of Best Doctors, Woodward & White, 1994—. Fellow: Am. Neurotology Soc., Am. Acad. Otolaryngology-Head & Neck Surgery (disting. svc. award 2004); mem.: AMA, Soc. U. Otolaryngologists, Am. Triological Soc. (excellence award 2003), Am. Otol. Soc., Politzer Internat. Ear Surg. Soc., Chgo. Laryngologic & Otologic Soc., Sigma Xi. Avocations: travel, bicycling. Office: Univ Physicians Otolaryngology 27177 Lahser Rd Ste 203 Southfield MI 48034

MONSEN, ELAINE RANKER, nutritionist, educator, editor; b. Oakland, Calif., June 6, 1935; d. Emery R. and Irene Stewart (Thorley) Ranker; m. Raymond Joseph Monsen, Jr., Jan. 21, 1959; 1 dau., Maren Ranker Grainger-Monsen. BA, U. Utah, 1956; MS (Mead Johnson grad. scholar), U. Calif., Berkeley, 1959, PhD (NSF fellow), 1961; postgrad. NSF sci. faculty fellow, Harvard U., 1968-69. Dietetic intern Mass. Gen. Hosp., Boston, 1956-57; asst. prof. nutrition, lectr. biochemistry Brigham Young U., Provo, Utah, 1960-63; mem. faculty U. Wash., 1963—, prof. nutrition, adj. prof. medicine, 1976-84, prof. nutrition and medicine, 1984—2004, prof. emeritus, 2004—, chmn. div. human nutrition, dietetics and foods, 1977-82, dir. grad. nutritional scis. program, 1994-99, mem. Council of Coll. Arts and Scis., 1974-78; chmn. Nutrition Studies Commn., 1969-83; bd. dirs. U. Wash. Found., 2007—. Vis. scholar Stanford U., 1971-72; mem. sci. adv. com. food fortification Pan-Am. Health Orgn., São Paulo, Brazil, 1972; tng. grant coordinator NIH, 1976-97. Editor-in-chief Jour. Am. Dietetic Assn., 1983-2003; Editor Emeritus, Jour. Am. Dietetic Assn., 2003—; mem. editorial bd. Coun. Biology Editors, 1992-96; author rsch. papers on lipid metabolism, iron absorption, Research: Successful Approaches, 3rd edit., 2008. Bd. dirs. A Contemporary Theatre, Seattle, 1969-72; trustee, bd. dirs. Seattle Found., 1978-95, vice chmn., 1987-91, chmn., 1991-93; pres. Seattle bd. Santa Fe Chamber Music Festival, 1984-85; mem. Puget Sound Blood Ctr. Bd., 1996-99. Grantee Nutrition Found., 1965-68, Agrl. Rsch. Svc., 1969-84; recipient Disting. Alumnus award U. Utah, F. Fischer Meml. Nutrition Lectr. award, 1988, L.F. Cooper Meml. Lectr. award, 1991, L. Hatch Meml. Lectr. award, 1992, Goble Lectr. award Purdue U., 1997. Fellow: Am. Soc. Clin. Nutrition (sec. 1987—90), Am. Inst. Nutrition; mem.: Wash. Heart Assn. (nutrition coun. 1973—76), Am. Soc. Parenteral and Enteral Nutrition (found. bd. mem. U. Wash. 2006—), Soc. Nutriton Edn., Am. Dietetic Assn.

MONSER, EDWARD L., electronics executive; BA, Ea. Mich. U., 1972; BS in Elec. Engring., Ill. Inst. Tech., 1980. Sr. engr. Rosemount divsn. Emerson, 1981, dir. tech., 1987—89, dir. new products and tech., 1989, v.p. pressure ops., v.p. pressure and temperature, 1994—95, v.p. and gen. mgr. pressure and temperature, 1995—96, pres., 1996—2001; COO Emerson Electric Co., St. Louis, 2001—. Office: Emerson Electric Co 8000 W Florissant Ave Saint Louis MO 63136

MONSKY, JOHN BERTRAND, investment company executive; b. Montgomery, Ala., May 17, 1930; s. Harry and Belle (Golding) M.; m. Joan Gilbert, June 8, 1952; children: Leslie Joy, John Richard, Harry Robert. BA, Yale, 1952; MBA, Harvard, 1954. Sec. Devoe & Raynolds Co., Inc., Louisville, Ky., 1956-65; v.p., dir. Universal Marion Corp., Jacksonville, Fla., 1965-69, pres., chmn. bd., chief exec. officer, 1969-71, cons., 1971—; vice chmn. ServAmerica, Inc., Jacksonville, 1972-74, co-chmn. bd. dirs., 1974-80, chmn. bd. dirs., 1980—; pres., chmn. bd. dirs. First Fla. Capital Corp., 1985—. Dir. Fla. Wire & Cable Co., Jacksonville, 1975-82 Past pres. bd. trustees Jacksonville Country Day Sch. Prior Affiliations Include; bd. dirs. Jacksonville Art Mus.; trustee Bolles Sch., Jacksonville, Jacksonville Symphony Assn. Served with USAF, 1954-56. Mem. Jacksonville Area C. of C. (com. of 100), Jackson County Citizen Involvement Clubs, Harvard Bus. Sch. Club of Ky. (exec. com. 1964-65), Phillips Acad. Andover Alumni Club of Ky. (pres. 1963-64), Epping Forest Cmty. Master Assn. (bd. dirs. 1994—), Yale Club N.E. Fla. (bd. dirs. 1987—), Yale Club of NYC, Harvard Club (Jacksonville), Assn. Yale Alumni (del. 1996—, schs. com.), AYA (sch. com.), River Club, Ponte Vedra Club, Epping Forest Yacht Club, Harvard Bus. Sch. Alumni Club (Jacksonville, bd. dirs.) Home: Epping Forest 7015 Gaines Ct Jacksonville FL 32217-2672 Office: 300 Wharfside Way # B Jacksonville FL 32207-8153 Office Phone: 904-396-0348. Personal E-mail: jbmonsky@aol.com. Business E-Mail: jbmonsky@firstfloridacapital.com.

MONSON, CAROL LYNN, osteopath, psychotherapist; b. Blue Island, Ill., Nov. 3, 1946; d. Marcus Edward and Margaret Bertha (Andres) Monson; m. Frank E. Warden, Feb. 28, 1981. BS, No. Ill. U., 1968, MS, 1969; D.O., Mich State Coll. Osteo. Medicine, 1979. Lic. physician Mich., diplomate Am. Bd. Osteo., Am. Bd. Family Physicians, Am. Bd. Osteo. Gen. Practice. Expeditor-psychotherapist H. Douglas Singer Zone Ctr., Rockford, Ill., 1969—71; psychotherapist Tri-County Mental Health, St. Johns, Mich., 1971—76; pvt. practice psychotherapy East Lansing, Mich., 1976—80; intern Lansing Gen. Hosp., Mich., 1979—80, residency dir. family practice, 1988—97; pvt. practice osteo. medicine Lansing, 1980—2002; mem. staff Ingham Regional Med. Ctr., chmn. family practice, 1987—89. Field instr. Sch. Social Work U. Mich., 1973—76; clin. instr. Ctrl. Mich. Dept. Psychology, 1974—75; clin. prof. Mich. State U., 1980—88, asst. prof., 1988—2003, assoc. prof., 2003—06, prof., 2006—, tng. supr. family medicine residency, 1988—97, faculty devel. fellow, 1994—95, chair dept. family and cmty. medicine, 2005—, residency dir. family medicine, 1994—97; mem. adv. bd. Substance Abuse Clearinghouse, Lansing, 1983—85, Kelly Health Care, Lansing, 1983—85, Americor Health Svcs., Lansing, 1984—88, Lansing Home Care, Lansing, 1988—94. Fellow: Am. Coll. Family Practice (osteo.); mem.: Coun. Med. Splty. Socs. (mem. conjoint com. 2005—), Am. Coll. Family Physicians (residency insp. 1991—), Mich. Assn. Osteo. Family Physicians (pres.-elect 1994, pres. 1995—96), Nat. Assn. Career Women (conv. com. 1984—), Ingham County Osteo. Assn. (pres. 1993—95, 1996—97), Mich. Osteo. Assn. (program com. 1992—, governance coun. 1996—97, bd. trustees 1997—2004, pres.-elect 2001—02, pres. 2002—03), Internat. Transactional Analysis Assn., Am. Acad. Family Practice, Am. Osteo. Assn. (del. 1994—, health policy fellow 1997—98, bd. trustees 2003—, chair membership 2004—), Mich. Coun. Grad. Med. Edn. (appointee 1998—, pres. 1999—2002), Lansing Assn. Career Women, Soc. Tchrs. of Family Medicine, Zonta (chmn. service com. Mid Mich. Capital Area chpt.). Avocations: gardening, orchid growing, antique collecting. Office: B201E West Fee Hall East Lansing MI 48824-1316

MONSON, DAN, men's college basketball coach; b. Spokane, Wash., Oct. 6, 1961; BS in Math., U. Idaho, 1985; MS in Athletic Adminstrn., U. Ala., 1988. Asst. coach Oregon City HS, 1985—86; grad. asst. U. Ala., Birmingham, 1986—88; asst. coach Gonzaga U., Spokane, 1988—94, assoc. head coach, 1994—97, head coach, 1997—99, U. Minn., 1999—2006, Long Beach State U., Calif., 2007—. Dir. Gopherball Basketball Camp, Mpls.; asst. coach World Univ. Games, 1999, USA Basketball's 20-and-under team, 2004. Named Coach of Yr., 1998, Nat. Rookie Coach of Yr., Basketball Times, 1998. Achievements include coaching the West Coast Conf. Champions, 1998; reached NCAA Sweet 16, 1998-99. Office: Long Beach State U Mens Basketball Athletic Dept 1250 Bellflower Blvd Long Beach CA 90840

MONSON, DAVID CARL, state legislator; b. Langdon, ND, July 30, 1950; s. Carl and Shirley; m. Mary Monson; 3 children. AA, U. ND, Williston, 1970; BS, U. ND, Grand Forks, 1972, MEd, 1983. Cert. tchr. ND; adminstr. ND. Sci. tchr. Hankinson Pub. Sch., 1972-75; farmer Osnabrock, 1975—; tchr. Nekoma Pub. Sch., 1975-76; tchr. & prin. NeKoma Pub. Sch., 1976-79; tchr. & supt. Nekoma Pub. Sch., 1979-80; tchr. & prin. Milton Osnabrock High Sch., 1981-84; supt. Adams Pub. Schs., 1984-88; ins. agt. N.Y. Life, Fargo, ND, 1988-95; self-employed ins. agt., Osnabrock, 1988—2003; mem. Dist. 10 ND House of Reps., Bismarck, 1993—, asst. majority leader, 1998—2008, spkr. of the house, 2008—; supt. Edinburg Pub. Schs., 1995—2007; tchr. & prin. Edinburg Sch., 2007—08. Dir. Cavalier County Mut. Ins. Co., Osnabrock, N.D., 1990-98, Northeast Mut. Ins. Co., Cando, N.D., 1998-, N.Am. Indsl. Hemp Coun., 1999—. Leader Bobcats 4-H Club, 1988—2001; pres. Dovre Luth. Ch., Osnabrock, 2002—; mem. sch. bd. dirs. Osnabrock Sch. Bd., 1989—2001. Fellow (life) NRA, Nat. Wildlife Fedn.; Mem. N.D. Farm Bur., Eagles, KP (grand sec. N.D. and Sask. 1985-93, award 1990), Retired Tchrs. Assn. Republican. Lutheran. Avocations: skiing, gardening, hunting, coin collecting/numismatics. Office: PO Box 8 Osnabrock ND 58269-0008 also: State Capitol 600 E Blvd Bismarck ND 58505 Office Phone: 701-496-3394, 701-328-3373. Business E-Mail: dmonson@nd.gov.

MONSON, DIANNE LYNN, literacy educator; b. Minot, ND, Nov. 24, 1934; d. Albert Rachie and Iona Cordelia (Kirk) M. BS, U. Minn., 1956, MA, 1962, PhD, 1966. Tchr. Rochester (Minn.) Pub. Schs., 1956-59, U.S. Dept. Def., Schweinfurt, West Germany, 1959-61, St. Louis Park (Minn.) Schs., 1961-62; instr. U. Minn., Mpls., 1962-66; prof. U. Wash., Seattle, 1966-82; prof. literacy edn. U. Minn., Mpls., 1982-97, prof. emeritus, 1997—. Chmn. curriculum and instrn. U. Minn., 1986—89. Co-author: Scott Foresman Reading, 2000, New Horizons in the Language Arts, 1972, Children and Books, 6th edit., 1981, Experiencing Children's Literature, 1984, Language Arts: Teaching and Learning Effective Use of Language, 1988, Reading Together: Helping Children Get A Good Start With Reading, 1991; assoc. editor: Dictionary of Literacy, 1995; mem. editl. bd. Five Owls Mag., 1997-2005. Bd. adv. Kerlan Collection, 2001—04, Minn. Humanities Commn., 2004—05; bd. dirs. Friends of Kerlan Collection, 2000—04. Recipient Outstanding Educator award U. Minn. Alumni Assn., 1983, Alumni Faculty award U. Minn. Alumni Assn., 1991. Fellow Nat. Conf. Rsch. in English (pres. 1990-91); mem. ALA, Nat. Coun. Tchrs. English (exec. com. 1979-81), Internat. Reading Assn. (dir. 1980-83, Arbuthnot award 1993, Reading Hall of Fame 1997), U.S. Bd. Books for Young People (pres. 1988-90). Lutheran. Home: 515 S Lexington Pkwy # 604 Saint Paul MN 55116 Business E-Mail: monso001@tc.umn.edu.

MONSON, INGRID, musicologist; BA, U. Wis., Madison, 1978; MusB with honors, New England Conservatory of Music, 1982; MA in musicology, NYU, 1989, PhD in musicology, 1991. Asst. prof. music U. Chgo., 1991—95; vis. asst. prof. music U. Mich., 1995—96; Quincy Jones vis. asst. prof. Afro-Am. studies and music Harvard U., 1999; asst. prof. music Washington U., St. Louis, 1996—99, assoc. prof. music, 1999—2001; Quincy Jones prof. African Am. music Harvard U., 2001—. Author: Saying Something: Jazz Improvisation and Interaction, 1996 (Irving Lowens prize for best monograph in Am. music, Sonneck Soc., 1996), Freedom Sounds: Jazz, Civil Rights, and Africa, 1950-1967, 2005; editor: The African Diaspora: A Musical Perspective, 2000. Fellow Nat. Endowment for the Arts, 1985—86, Am. Assn. U. Women, 1990—91, Chgo. Humanities Inst., 1992, 1993, Am. Coun. Learned Societies, 1994—95, John Simon Guggenheim Meml. Found., 2009; Langley fellow, 1985—86, Earl H. and Suzanne S. Harbison faculty fellow, Washington U., 1996—99. Mem.: Phi Kappa Lambda, Phi Beta Kappa. Office: Harvard U Dept African and African Am Studies 12 Quincy St Cambridge MA 02138 Office Phone: 617-495-2791. Office Fax: 617-496-8081. E-mail: imonson@fas.harvard.edu.*

MONSON, JAMES EDWARD, electrical engineer, educator; b. Oakland, Calif., June 20, 1932; s. George Edward and Frances Eleanor M.; m. Julie Elizabeth Conzelman, June 25, 1954; children: John, Jamie, Jennifer BSEE, Stanford U., 1954, MSEE, 1955, PhD in Elec. Engring., 1961. Mem. tech. staff Bell Telephone Labs., Murray Hill, NJ, 1955-56; devel. engr. Hewlett-Packard Co., Palo Alto, Calif., 1956-61; Robert C. Sabini prof. engring. emeritus Harvey Mudd Coll., 1961—. Governing bd. Claremont Unified Sch. Dist., 1966—71, pres., 1969—70, Claremont Civic Assn., 1974—75; bd. dirs. Claremont YMCA, 1978—82, Coastal Health Alliance, 1999—2006, West Main Sr. Svcs., 2007—. Fellow NSF, 1954-55, Japan Soc. Promotion Sci., 1984; Fulbright Rsch. grantee, 1975-76; Fulbright sr. lectr., 1980. Fellow IEEE (life); mem. Phi Beta Kappa, Sigma Xi. Home: PO Box 1029 Point Reyes Station CA 94956-1029 Office: Harvey Mudd Coll 301 E 12th St Claremont CA 91711-5901 Personal E-mail: j.monson@ieee.org.

MONSON, LARRY LEE, music educator; b. Grand Island, Nebr., Oct. 17, 1942; s. Owen H. and Glenna Imojene Monson; m. LaVonne Elise Havekost, Mar. 21, 1964; children: Martin Laurence, Ann Elise, Eric Lee. BA, Midland Luth. Coll., 1965; MA, U. Iowa, 1966. Cert. tchr. Iowa. Dir. music 1st Luth. Ch., Sioux Falls, SD, 1969—72, St. Paul Luth. Ch., Davenport, Iowa, 1972—79; choral dir. City HS, Iowa City, 1979—89; dir. choral activities Doane Coll., Crete, Nebr., 1989—, ret. prof. choral music, 2004; vis. dir. ch. activities U. Ctrl. Mo., 2007—08. Bd. dirs. Polley Music Libr., Lincoln, 1989—95. Recipient Outstanding Alumni Achievement award, Midland Luth. Coll., 2001, Zenon R. Hansen Leadership award, Doane Coll., 2004; named to Hall of Fame, CSD Barbershop Harmony Soc., 2002. Mem.: Barbershop Harmony Soc., MENC, Internat. Fedn. Choral Music, Am. Choral Dirs. Assn. Avocations: biking, travel, coaching quartets, gardening. Home: 611 W Water St Decorah IA 52101 Home Phone: 563-382-6255. E-mail: larry.monson@doane.edu.

MONSON, MICHAEL JAMES, economist, consultant; b. Webster City, Iowa, Aug. 15, 1956; s. James Ernest and Glenda Jean Monson; m. Sandra Johnson; children: Jeffery James, Steven Michael. PhD, U. Fla., Gainesville, 1986. Dept. chair Agrl. Economics, UMC, Columbia, Mo., 2006—. Office: Univ Missouri 218 Mumford Hall UMC Columbia MO 65211

MONSON, NANCY PECKEL, writer, editor, book collaborator, spokesperson; b. NYC, Mar. 11, 1959; m. John C. Monson, June 18, 1988 (div. 2000). BS magna cum laude, Boston U., 1979. Actress, 1979-86; adminstrv. asst. MIT, Cambridge, 1981; assoc. editor Profl. Postgrad. Svcs., Secaucus, N.J., 1984-87; assoc. editor, reporter The Convention Reporter Group, Secaucus, 1985-88, editor, 1988-90; freelance consumer & med. edn. writer, editor, book collaborator, spokesperson Shelton, Conn., 1984—. Author: The Smart Guide to Boosting Your Energy, 1999, Craft to Heal: Soothing Your Soul with Sewing, Painting and Other Pastimes, 2005; past columnist First for Women, Bottom Line/Personal, Quilter's Home; contbr. articles to mags. including Family Circle, Fitness, Glamour, McCall's More, New Woman, Reader's Digest, Redbook, Shape, Today's Health & Wellness and Woman's Day; contbr. to book: The Vitamin Book, 1998. Mem. AFTRA, SAG (inactive), Am. Soc. Journalists and Authors. Avocations: quilting, movies, tennis.

MONSON, ROBERT JOSEPH, education educator; b. St. Paul, July 2, 1947; s. Robert Joseph and Lorraine (Pieruccioni) M.; m. Tracey Monson, Dec. 18, 1970 (dec. 1986); 1 child, Ashley Taylor. BA, St. Thomas Coll., St. Paul, 1969, MA, 1971; PhD, St. Louis U., 1975. Tchr. St. Bernards Schs., St. Paul, 1969-71; asst. prin. Mamaroneck (N.Y.) High Sch., 1975-78; prin. Chapel Hill (N.C.) High Sch., 1978-81; asst. sch. supt. Sch. Dist. South Orange-Maplewood (N.J.), 1981-85; supt. schs. Beachwood (Ohio) pub. schs., 1985-87, Westwood (Mass.) pub. schs., 1987-94, Mendota Heights, Minn., 1994-99; sr. lectr. Lesley Coll., 1990-2000; sr. lectr. Tchrs. Coll. Columbia U., NYC, 1999—. Rsch. cons. NSF, 1975. Contbr. articles to profl. jours. Named Educator of Yr., AGPA, 1981; postdoctoral fellow Harvard U., 1977. Mem. Prins Ctr. Harvard U. (bd. dirs. 1989-91). Roman Catholic. Home: 150 South Field Ave#2213 Stamford CT 06902 also: 40 Memorial Hwy 17P New Rochelle NY 10801 Office Phone: 212-678-8118. Business E-Mail: rjm210@columbia.edu.

MONSON, THOMAS SPENCER, religious organization administrator, retired publishing executive; b. Salt Lake City, Aug. 21, 1927; s. George Spencer and Gladys (Condie) M.; m. Frances Beverly Johnson, Oct. 7, 1948; children Thomas L., Ann Frances, Clark Spencer. BS with honors in mktg, U. Utah, 1948; MBA, Brigham Young U., 1974, LLD (hon.), 1981; D in Bus. (hon.), U. Utah, 2007. With Deseret News Press, Salt Lake City, 1948-64, mgr., 1962-64; mem., Coun. Twelve Apostles Ch. of Jesus Christ of Latter-day Saints, 1963-85, bishop, Coun. Twelve Apostles, 1950-55, second counselor in the first presidency, 1985—95, first counselor to ch. pres. Gordon B. Hinckley, simultaneously becoming Pres. of the Quorum of the Twelve Apostles, 1995—2008, pres., 2008—, Canadian Mission, 1959-62; chmn. bd. Deseret News Pub. Co., 1977-96. Vice chmn. Deseret Mgmt. Corp.; pres. Printing Industry Utah, 1958; bd. dirs. Printing Industry Am., 1958-64; mem. Utah exec. bd. U.S. West Comm.; bd. dir. KSL-TV, Beneficial Life Ins. Co. Author Be Your Best Self, 1979, Inspiring Experiences That Build Faith: From the Life and Ministry of Thomas S. Monson, Favorite Quotations from the Collection of Thomas S. Monson, Live the Good Life, Faith Rewarded: A Personal Account of Prophetic Promises to the East German Saints, Christmas Gifts, Christmas Blessings, The Search for Jesus, Meeting your Goliath, A Christmas Dress for Ellen, Invitation to Exaltation, Pathways to Perfection. Mem. Utah Bd. Regents; mem. nat. exec. bd. Boy Scouts Am.; trustee Brigham Young U. With USNR, 1945-46. Recipient Recognition award, 1964, Disting. Alumnus award U. Utah, 1966; Silver Beaver award Boy Scouts Am., 1971; Silver Buffalo award, 1978; Bronze Wolf award World Orgn. of the Scout Movement, 1993. Mem. Utah Assn. Sales Execs., U. Utah Alumni Assn. (dir.), Salt Lake Advt. Club, Alpha Kappa Psi. Clubs: Exchange (Salt Lake City). Mem. Lds Ch. Office: LDS Ch 47 E South Temple Salt Lake City UT 84150-9701 Office Phone: 801-240-2181.

MONTAG, THOMAS K. (THOMAS KELL MONTAG), bank executive; b. 1957; m. Janet Montag. BA, Stanford U., 1979; MBA, Northwestern U., 1982. Mgmt. positions First Nat. Bank of Chgo.; pres., dir. Goldman Sachs Mitsui Marine Derivative Products, 1993, ptnr., exec. v.p., 1996; gen. ptnr., v.p. Goldman Sachs & Co., mng. dir., co-pres. Japanese Ops., 2001—06, co-head global securities bus., 2007; exec. v.p., head global sales & trading Merrill Lynch & Co., 2008; pres., global corp. & investment banking, global markets Bank of America Corp., 2009—. Dir. Goldman Sachs Fin. Products US Co.; gen. ptnr. Goldman Sachs Fin. Products US LP; mgmt. com. Goldman Sachs Grp. Inc.; chmn. Internat. Swaps Derivatives Assn., Inc. Bd. trustees Riverdale Country Sch. Office: Bank of America Corp 100 N Tryon St Charlotte NC 28202 Office Phone: 704-386-5681. Office Fax: 704-386-6699.*

MONTAGNIER, LUC ANTOINE, virologist; b. Chabris, Indre, France, Aug. 18, 1932; 3 children. Cert. of Studies on Natural Scis., U. Poitiers, France, 1953, BS, 1955; MD, U. Paris, 1960. Asst. Faculté des Scis, Paris, 1955-60; attaché de recherche Nat. Ctr. Sci. Rsch., Paris, 1960-63, chargé de recherche, 1963-67, maitre de recherche, 1967-72, dir. research, 1974—, head lab. Orsay, France, 1965-72; head viral oncology unit Institut Pasteur, Paris, 1972—, head virology dept., 1982-85, prof., 1974—, head dept. AIDS and Retroviruses, 1990-96; disting. prof., dir. Ctr. for Molecular and Cellular Biology Queens Coll. of the CUNY, 1997-2001. Dir. virology course Institut Pasteur, 1980-85, head dept. AIDS and Retrovirus, 1991-97; mem. responsible research team CNRS; discovered HIV-1 virus, 1983 and HIV-2 virus, 1985; pres. adminstrv. coun. European Fed. for AIDS Rsch., 1988. Author: Vaincre le Sida, 1987, Des virus et des hommes, 1994, AIDS, Oxidative Stress and Cancer, 1997, Virus, in English, 2000. Pres. World Found. for AIDS Rsch. and Prevention, Paris, 1993—. Decorated comdr. Legion of Honor, comdr. Ordre Nat. du Mérite; recipient: Lasker prize, 1986, Gairdner prize, 1987, Japan prize, 1988, Warrent Alpert Found. prize, 1998, Prince of Asturias prize, 2000; co-recipient: Nobel Prize in Physiology or Medicine, 2008; named to Nat. Inventor Hall of Fame, 2004. Mem. Acad. Nat. de Médecine, French Acad. Scis. Co-discoverer (with Robert Gallo) of the AIDS virus, 1983. Office: World Found AIDS Rsch and Prevention 1 rue Miollis F-75015 Paris France*

MONTAGUE, BRIAN JOHN, consulting company executive; b. Washington, Oct. 9, 1951; s. H.C. and Dorothy (Brand) M.; m. Kathryn Valente, Oct. 2, 1993. BA, Bridgewater Coll., 1973; student, St. Mary's Coll., Md., 1975, George Washington U., 1980, Miss. State U., 1981. Toxicology technician Hazelton Labs., Vienna, Va., 1973-74; asst. mgr. Chesapeake Sea Farms, Ridge, Md., 1974-76; tng. instr., program coord. Natural Resources Dept., Annapolis, Md., 1976-77; fishery biologist Nat. Aquarium, U.S. Fish and Wildlife Svc., Washington, 1977-82, curator aquarium, 1982-88; pres. Aquatic Images, Annapolis, 1989—. Lectr. local interest groups, 1990—; fisheries biologist, ecol. risk assessment specialist U.S. EPA, Washington.

MONTAGUE, DEBORAH MARIE, elementary school and music educator, consultant; b. Cin., July 2, 1953; d. Charles Jay and June Marie Henry; m. Steven A. Montague, Aug. 17, 1979; children: Sarah, Benjamin. BA in Music Edn., Ctrl. Wash. U., 1974; MA in Music Edn., U. Wash. Music educator grades 3-6 Northshore Sch. Dist., Bothell, Wash., 1974—79; music educator grades 5-9 Sumner (Wash.) Sch. Dist., 1979—88; freelance music educator/cons. Alta Loma, Calif., 1988—90; music educator grades 5-9 Northshore Sch. Dist., Kenmore, Wash., 1990—. Dist. honor band chair Northshore Sch. Dist., Bothell, 1990—; member-at-large Cascade Youth Orch. Symphony, Bothell, 1999—; performer N.W. Music Educator's Conf., 1993, 2001, 03, Nat. Music Educator's Conf., 2002. Mem.: NEA, West Ctrl. Music Educators Nat. Conf. (band rep. 1984—85), Music Educators Nat. Conf. Lutheran. Office: Kenmore Jr High 20323 66 Ave NE Kenmore WA 98028

MONTAGUE, DROGO K., urologist; b. Alpena, Mich., Dec. 11, 1942; s. Frank Wright and Susan Alice (Kidder) M.; children: Mark Andrew, Lisa Joy. Student, U. Mich., 1960—63, MD cum laude, 1968. Diplomate Am. Bd. Urology. Intern Cleve. Clinic Hosp., 1968-69, resident in gen. surgery, 1969-70, resident in urology, 1970-73; assoc. staff urologist Cleve. Clinic Found., 1973-75, staff urologist, 1975—, head sect. prosthetic surgery, 1981—, urology residence program dir., 1985—2006, dir. Ctr. for Sexual Function, 1987—; prof. surgery Cleve. Clinic Lerner Coll. Medicine Case Western Res. U., 2004—. Trainee cardiovascular rsch. tng. program NIH, 1962-68; trustee Am. Bd. Urology, 1989-95, mem. examination com., 1975-80, examiner cert. exam., 1980-88, rep. to Am. Bd. Med. Specialties, 1989-95. Reviewer various publs. in field; contbr. numerous articles to profl. publs., chpts. to books; editor: Disorders of Male Sexual Function, 1988, Surgical Treatment of Erectile Dysfunction, 1993, Textbook Reconstructive Urologic Surgery, 2008; author audiovisual tapes in field; mem. editl. bd. Jour. Urology. James B. Angell scholar, 1961, 62, Nat. Found. scholar, 1963-68; recipient Russell and Mary Hugh Scott Edn. award, 1989, Iowa Rsch. award, 1967, Parker J. Palmer Courage to Teach award ACGME, 2009. Fellow ACS; mem. Am. Urolog. Assn. (chmn. sci. exhibits com. North Cen. sect. 1977, mem. residency edn. com. 1979-83, vice chmn. audio visual com. 1989-95, mem. various coms., editor Am. Urolog. Assn. Video Libr. 1995-2000, chmn. audio visual com. 1996-2002, chmn. erectile dysfunction guidelines panel 1999—), Am. Assn. Genitourinary Surgeons, Cleve. Urolog. Soc. (sec.-treas. 1978-80, v.p. 1980-81, pres. 1981-82, 94-95), Soc. for Study of Impotence (pres. 1995). Office: Cleve Clinic Glickman Urol & Kidney Inst A/100 9500 Euclid Ave Q10-1 Cleveland OH 44195-0001 Home Phone: 216-831-9937; Office Phone: 216-444-5590. Business E-Mail: montagd@ccf.org.

MONTAGUE, EDGAR BURWELL, III, (MONTY MONTAGUE), industrial designer; b. Charlotte, NC, Aug. 6, 1958; s. Edgar B. Jr. and Mary Sue (Calhoun) M.; m. Nancy Oliver Stallworth, Feb. 25, 1984; children: Nancy Lea, Edgar Eubank. B Environ. Design cum laude, N.C. State U., 1980. Indsl. designer Design/Joe Sonderman, Inc., Charlotte, 1980-85; design prin. Bolt Group (formerly Machen Montague, Inc.), Charlotte, NYC, 1985—, BOLT, Charlotte, 1994—. Holder over 15 design and/or utility patents; work published in Product Design 1-6, Design for Humanity. Designer corp. identity program Habitat for Humanity, Charlotte, 1987 (logo design now used throughout world). Recipient ann. design award Internat. Design mag., 1988-93, ID-40 ID Mag., 1994, Disting. Alumni award N.C. State U., 1999. Mem. Indsl. Designer Soc. Am. (co-founder Carolina chpt., program chmn. 1981-83, vice chmn. 1984, 93, Kudo award for chpt. svc. 1982, Indsl. Design Excellence awards 1990-2000). Avocations: travel, art, coaching soccer. Office: BOLTgroup 1415 S Church St Ste S Charlotte NC 28203-4124 Office Phone: 704-372-2658. Business E-Mail: monty@boltgroup.com.

MONTAGUE, MICHELLE LOUISE, geologist, educator; m. Monty Montague. BS in Earthsci. Edn., U. Ariz., Tucson, 1999, MA in Geosci. Edn., 2001. Sci. tchr. Globe High Sch., Ariz., 2002—08; prof. geology Glendale CC, Ariz., 2006—. Geologist Freeport McMoran, Miami, Ariz., 2008—. Tchr. LDS Ch., Globe, 2002—08. Recipient Excellence Edn. award, Gila County, 2007. Mem.: Nat. Sci. Tchrs. Assn., Soc. Mining Metallurgy and Exploration, Delta Kappa Gamma. Conservative. Mem. Lds Ch. Avocations: travel, sewing. Home: 1174 E Blazer Dr Globe AZ 85501 Office: Glendale CC 6000 W Olive Ave Glendale AZ 85302 Business E-Mail: michelle.montague@gcmail.maricopa.edu.

MONTAGUE, ROBERT LATANE, III, lawyer; b. Washington, Sept. 18, 1935; s. Robert Latane and Frances Breckinridge (Wilson) M.; m. Prudence Darnell, June 20, 1964; children: Anne Steele Mason Montague Bavin, Robert Latane IV. BA, U. Va., 1956, LLB, 1961. Bar: Va. 1961, D.C. 1966, U.S. Supreme Ct. 1966. Asst. atty. gen., Ky., 1961-64; pres. Historic Alexandria Found., 1968-70; chmn. Alexandria Environ. Policy Commn., 1970-74; pres. Conservation Coun. Va., 1978-80; chmn. Alexandria Commn. on Bicentennial of U.S. Constitution, 1987-91, Alexandria Historical Restoration and Preservation Commn., 1988—2001; trustee Assn. for Preservation of Va. Antiquities, 1990-96. Chmn. Bd. of Vis. of Gunston Hall, 1987-92; del. Moscow Conf. on Law and Econ. Coop., 1990. Comdr. USNR, 1956-79. Mem. Va. Bar Assn., Va. State Bar (chmn. environ. law sect. 1973-74), Alexandria Bar Assn. Office: 1007 King St Alexandria VA 22314-2922

MONTALVO, ELBA, social services administrator; b. San Sebastian, Puerto Rico, Oct. 27, 1947; d. Isidro and Severina (Rodriguez) M.; m. Zenon Arribalzaga, June 5, 1976; children: Luis, Amanda. BA, St. Joseph's Coll., 1968; MA, Hunter Coll., 1975. Lic. early childhood tchr. Tchr. Bd. Edn., NYC, 1968-73; ednl. dir. Assn. Day Care, NYC, 1974-77; dir. Coun. Adoptable Children, NYC, 1978-82; exec. dir. Com. Hispanic Children & Families, Inc., NYC, 1982—. Bd. dirs. Child Welfare League, 1990—, Judl. Comm. Children, N.Y., 1991—, Children of Bellvue, N.Y.C., 1996—; chairperson Coun. Latino Execs., 1992—. Recipient Bklyn. History Maker award Bklyn. Hist. Soc., 1991, KOOL Achiever award Brown and Williamson Tobacco Corp., 1991, Nat. Hispana Leadership Inst. award, 1995, Women of Influence award YWCA of Bklyn., 1996, Latina Excellence award Hispanic Mag., 1996, I Have a Dream award Gov. George Pataki, N.Y., 1998. Democrat. Roman Catholic. Avocations: reading mysteries, jogging, dance, travel. Office: Com Hispanic Children & Families Inc 110 William St Ste 1802 New York NY 10038

MONTALVO-RODRIGUEZ, RAFAEL R., microbiologist, educator; s. Rafael Montalvo and Leyda Rodriguez; m. Yadhira Quiles, July 9, 1994; children: Rafael Montalvo, Mario Montalvo. PhD, U. Nebr., Lincoln, 2003. Assoc. prof. U. PR, Mayaguez, 2006—. Named one of Top Outstanding Young People in Rsch. Mem.: Am. Soc. Microbiology. Office: Univ PR Biology Dept PO Box 9012 Mayaguez PR 00681 Personal E-mail: titomontal@yahoo.com.

MONTANA, HANNAH See CYRUS, MILEY

MONTANDON, MICHAEL, Mayor, North Las Vegas, Nevada; m. Antoinette Montandon; 5 children. BS in Fin., Ariz. State U., Tempe; completed Harvard Univ. Sr. Exec. Program, John F. Kennedy Sch. Govt., Cambridge. Treas. Appraisal Inst., Las Vegas Chpt., 1995—96; pres. Hidden Canyon Homeowners Assn., 1995—97; current bus. devel. consultant Nev. Constrn. Svcs., Core Constrn.; mayor City of North Las Vegas, Nev., 1997—. Served on North Las Vegas Mayor's Task Force for Wages, Benefits and Fin. Vol. leader Boy Scouts; exec. bd. mem. Civilian Military Coun. Southern Nev.; mem. Clean Water Coalition, Las Vegas Conv. and Visitors Authority, North Las Vegas Redevelopment Agy., North Las Vegas Housing Authority; rep. Clark County Debt Mgmt. Commn.; chmn. Southern Nev. Regional Planning Coalition Fed. Lands Subcommittee; ex-officio mem. Deferred Compensation Adv. Com. Republican. Avocations: dirt bike riding, racquetball. Office: 2200 Civic Center Dr North Las Vegas NV 89030 Office Phone: 702-633-1007.*

MONTANER, SILVIA, medical educator, researcher; b. Murcia, Spain; Assoc. prof. U. Md., Balt., 2004—. Office: Univ MD 650 W Balt St Rm 7263 Baltimore MD 21201

MONTANEZ-JOHNER, NANCY, federal agency administrator; With profl. ptnrs. program region III behavioral health svcs. Health and Human Svcs. Sys. State of Nebr., 1995—99, adminstr. S.W. svc. area, 1999—2001, CEO We. svc. area, 2001—04, dir., 2004—06; under sec. agr. food, nutrition & consumer services USDA, Washington, 2006—. Bd. dirs. Commodity Credit Corp. USDA, 2006—. Office: USDA Whitten Bldg 1400 Independence Ave SW Rm 240-E Washington DC 20250 Office Phone: 202-720-7711. Office Fax: 202-690-3100.*

MONTANO, GLORIA I., legislative staff member; Grad., U. Ariz., 2003. Dist. aide, Rep. Raul Grijalva US House of Reps., Ariz., 2003—06, chief of staff to Rep. Raul Grijalva Washington, 2006—. Democrat. Office: 1440 Longworth House Office Bldg Washington DC 20515 Office Phone: 202-225-2435. Office Fax: 202-225-1541. Business E-Mail: gloria.montano@mail.house.gov.*

MONTAVON, VICTORIA A., university librarian, dean; b. Cin. m. James M. Myers; 3 children. Libr. Rider U., Temple U., Lindenwood Coll., Carlow Coll., Notre Dame Coll., Ohio, St. Joseph 's U., Phila., 1990—96, Wright State U., 1996—2001; dean, libr. U. Cin., 2001—. Recipient Pres. Quality Svc. award, 2003. Office: U Cin U Librs PO Box 210033 Cincinnati OH 45221-0033 Office Phone: 513-556-1515. E-mail: Victoria.Montavon@uc.edu.

MONTE, SCOTT VINCENT, medical researcher, director; b. Buffalo, Dec. 20, 1982; s. Kerry Charles and Barbara Judith Monte. D in Pharmacy, U. Buffalo Sch. Pharmacy, 2006. Clin. asst. prof. U. Buffalo Sch. Pharmacy, 2007—; dir. diabetes & cardiovasc. rsch. CPL Assocs. LLC, Amherst, NY, 2007—. Mem.: APHA. Home: 43 Nina Ter Buffalo NY 14224 Office: CPL Assocs LLC Sheridan Dr Amherst NY 14226 Office Fax: 716-839-5138. Business E-Mail: smonte@cplassociates.com.

MONTEIRO, ANTÓNIA, biology professor; b. Glasgow, Mar. 18, 1969; d. Luís and Maria de Lourdes Fraser Monteiro; m. William H. Piel; 1 child, Florence M. Piel. PhD, Edinburgh U., 1997. Asst. prof. Yale U., New Haven, 2006—. Achievements include research in evolution of development of butterfly wing patterns. Office: Yale Univ 165 Prospect St New Haven CT 06511

MONTEITH, LARRY KING, chancellor emeritus; b. Bryson City, NC, Aug. 17, 1933; s. Earl and Essie (King) M.; m. Nancy Alexander, Apr. 19, 1952; children: Larry, Carol, Steve. BSEE, N.C. State U., 1960; MSEE, Duke U., 1962, PhD in Elec. Engring., 1965. Registered profl. engr., N.C. Mem. tech. staff Bell Tel. Labs., Burlington, NC, 1960-62, Rsch. Triangle Inst., Raleigh, NC, 1962-66, group leader rsch. sect., 1966-68; adj. asst. prof. elec. engring. N.C. State U., Raleigh, 1965-68, assoc. prof., 1968-72, prof., 1972—, head dept. elec. engring., 1974-78, dean of engring., 1978-89, interim chancellor, 1989-90, chancellor, 1990-98, chancellor emeritus, 1998—. Contbr. articles to profl. jours. With USN, 1952-56. Recipient Disting. Engring. Alumnus award Duke U., 1984, Outstanding Engring. Achievement award N.C. Soc. Engrs., 1990, Disting. Engring. Alumnus award N.C. State U., 1999. Fellow IEEE, Am. Soc. for Engring. Edn.; mem. NSPE (edn. adv. group), Raleigh C. of C. (bd. dirs.), Rotary Internat. (Paul Harris fellow Rotary Found. 1991), Phi Beta Kappa, Sigma Xi, Sigma Iota Rho, Phi Kappa Phi, Eta Kappa Nu, Tau Beta Pi, Sigma Beta Delta. E-mail: lmonteith@nc.rr.com.

MONTEITH, MATTHEW, photographer; b. Howell, Mich., 1974; Student, Internat. Ctr. Photography, NYC, 1995; MFA, Yale U., 2004. One-man shows include Galerie de la Butte, Cherbourg-Octeville, France, 2002, 779 Galerie + Editions, Paris, 2003, Prinz Galerie, Kyoto, Japan, 2004, Hotel Nord Pinus, Arles, 2005, exhibited in group shows at Small Works, P.S. 122, NYC, 1999, Ville/Visages, Regional Ctr. Cherbourg-Octeville, France, 2000, Advance Notice, Internat. Ctr. Photography, NYC, 2002, Pictures for People Like Us, Wallspace Gallery, NYC, 2003, Emerging Photographers Festival, NYC, 2004, Stilled Life, Placemaker Gallery, Miami, 2004, Let's Talk About, Larissa Goldston Gallery, NYC, 2006, Clinic, Les Nuits Blanches and Paris Photo, Paris, 2006. Recipient Abigail Cohen Rome prize, Am. Acad. Rome, 2008. Mailing: 140 16th St Brooklyn NY 11215 Office: Rosier Gallery 98 San Pablo Ave San Francisco CA 94127*

MONTELEONE, PATRICIA L., dean; MD, St. Louis U., 1961; MBA, MHA. V.p. med. affairs Cardinal Glennon Children's Hosp., 1986—93; prof. pediatrics St. Louis U. Sch. Medicine, 1967—, dean, 1994—. Office: St Louis U Sch Medicine 1402 S Grand Blvd Saint Louis MO 63104-1004

MONTELONGO, MICHAEL D., marketing executive, former civilian military employee; b. NYC, Aug. 20, 1955; m. Debra Tenison; 1 child, Amanda. BS in Gen. Engring., U.S. Mil. Acad., 1977; MBA in Corp. Strategy and Fin., Harvard U., 1988; grad., Command and Gen. Staff Coll., 1992. Commd. 2d lt. U.S. Army, 1977, advanced through grades to lt. col.; asst. prof. social scis. dept. U.S. Mil. Acad., West Point, NY, 1988; adv., spl. asst. to comdr.-in chief U.S. So. Command, 1989; bn. exec. officer, bn. and brigade ops. officer U.S. Army, 1993—94, spl. asst. to chief of staff, 1994—95; legis. asst. U.S. Senate, 1995—96; dir. BellSouth Small Bus. Svcs., 1996—98; sales exec. and cons. Cap Gemini Ernst & Young, 1998—2001; asst. sec. for fin. mgmt. & comptr., Dept. of Air Force US Dept. Def., Washington, 2001—05; sr. v.p. for strategic mktg. Sodexho Inc., Gaithersburg, Md., 2005—. Bd. dirs. Denny's Corp., 2005—. Trustee Unite El Paso, 1993; mem. Leadership El Paso Program, 1999. U.S. Army Advanced Civil Schooling fellow, 1986, Inter-Univ. Seminar on Armed Forces and Soc. fellow, 1990, Congl. Hispanic Caucus Inst. fellow, 1992, Army Congl. fellow, 1995. Mem.: Am. Soc. Mil. Comptrollers (pres. 2004), Nat. Soc. Hispanic MBAs (sec.), Assn. West Point Grads. (minority outreach com. 1999—, bd. dirs. Ga. Hispanic voter registration campaign 2000).

MONTER, E. WILLIAM, retired history professor; b. Cin., Sept. 22, 1936; s. Edward W. and Florence S. Monter; m. Barbara Heldt, June 18, 1963 (div. Aug. 2, 1976); children: Andrea, Gustav C. Heldt, Elizabeth A. Heldt(dec.); m. Rosellen E. Engstrom, July 22, 1978. BA, Wabash Coll., Crawfordsville, Ind., 1958; PhD, Princeton U., 1963. Prof. of history Northwestern U., Evanston, Ill., 1972—2002, prof. emeritus, 2002—. Sec., program on cultural exch. in Europe, 1400-1700 European Sci. Found., Strasbourg, 1997—2004; cons. 2000 papal jubilee Office of Papal Theologian, Vatican City, 1998; mem. editl. bd. Ency. of Witchcraft ABC-Clio Pub., Santa Barbara, Calif., 1999—; vis. prof. history U. Chgo., 2005—06. Author: Calvin's Geneva (also Japanese ed.), 1967, (book) Witchcraft in France and Switzerland, 1976, Ritual, Myth and Magic (also Italian ed.), 1983, Frontiers of Heresy (Spanish ed.), 1990, Judging the French Reformation, 1999, Bewitched Duchy: Lorraine, 2007. Grantee, Am. Coun. of Learned Societies, 1969, 1972; fellow, NEH, 1974-75, 1992-93, 1999-2000, Camargo Found. (France), 1994, 2001;, Social Sci. Rsch. Coun., 1966—67, Guggenheim fellow, 1994, Richardson fellow, Inst. for Advanced Study, 1987—88, CIES (Fulbright) fellow, CCHN, Spain, 1985—86, Mellon Emeritus fellowship, 2008—. Mem.: Am. Hist. Assn. (com. on coms. 1984—87), Am. Soc. for Reformation Rsch. (pres. 1980), Soc. d'Histoire de Genève (corr.). Home: 829 Linden Ave Wilmette IL 60091 Personal E-mail: monter@northwestern.edu.

MONTERO, JOSÉ THIER, state agency administrator, public health service officer; MD, Universidad Nacional de Colombia, 1986; degree in epidemiology, Pontificia Universidad Javeriana, Bogota, Colombia, 1992. Chief, communicable disease sect. NH Dept. Health and Human Services, state epidemiologist, dir., divsn. pub. health services. Bd. dir. ex-officio NH Pub. Health Assn. Office: NH DHHS Divsn Pub Health Services 29 Hazen Dr Concord NH 03301-4604 Office Phone: 603-271-4501. Office Fax: 603-271-4827. Business E-Mail: jmontero@dhhs.state.nh.us.*

MONTERO, SYLVIA, former pharmaceutical executive; b. PR; BA, Columbia U. Barnard Coll., 1972; MA, CUNY Queens Coll., 1976. HS tchr. Spanish and bilingual studies, NYC; prof. lit. Interamerican U., PR; with Pfizer Puerto Rico, 1978—82, Pfizer, Inc., NYC, 1982—2007, v.p. human resources Animal Health Grp., 1994, sr. v.p. human resources Global Rsch. and Devel., 2003—05, sr. v.p. human resources, 2005—07. Bd. mem. Grand St. Settlement. Recipient Orgullo Latino award, 100 Hispanic Women orgn., 2005; named one of Top 50 Hispanic Bus. Women, Hispanic Bus. Mag., 2001, 80 Elite Women, 2002, 20 Corp. Elite in US, 2006. Mem.: Hispanic Fedn.

MONTERO ALPÍREZ, GISELA, chemical engineer, researcher; d. Juan Ricardo Montero Trujillo and Joaquina Alpírez Fernández. BS in Chem. Engring., U. Nat. Autónoma de México, 1985, PhD in Chem. Engring., 2006; MS in Thermodynamics Engring., U. Autónoma de Baja Calif., Mex., 1997. Project engr. Assn., Mexico, 1980—82; assoc. prof. chem. engring. U. Nat. Autónoma Mex., 1980—85, prof. chem. engring., 1985—87; rschr. energy area Engring. Inst. U. Autónoma de Baja California, Mexico, 1987—2008, coord. geothermal diploma program, 1992—95, coord. chem. engring area, 2006—08, grad. coord., 2009. Project engr. combustion divsn. Mex. Petroleum Inst., 1984—87, rschr., 1998. Recipient Nat. prize of saving elec. energy, Fed. Commn. Electricity, 1992; scholar, Secretariat Pub. Edn., 1994, Programa de Mejoramiento de Personal Académico, 1999—2002, Nat. Coun. Sci. and Tech., Mex., 1999—2002. Mem.: Mex. Inst. Chem. Engrs. Avocations: movies, travel, music, reading. Office: Instituto de Ingeniería UABC Benito Juarez y Calle de la Normal S/N Col Insurgentes Este Mexicali Baja California 21280 Mexico Office Fax: 52+686-566-4150. Personal E-mail: gmontero4@yahoo.com. Business E-Mail: gmontero@iing.mxl.uabc.mx.

MONTEROS, MARIA, biochemist and plant breeder, educator; d. Jose Ricardo and Martha Isabel Monteros; m. Clyde F. Hardin, Nov. 9, 2007. BS cum laude, U. Valle, Guatemala, 2000, Licentiate, 2001; PhD, U. Ga., Athens, 2006. Biochemistry lectr. U. del Valle, 1999—2000, rsch. asst., 2000—01; grad. rsch. asst. U. Ga., 2001—06; asst. prof. Samuel Roberts Noble Found., Ardmore, Okla., 2007—; adj. faculty Inst. Plant Breeding, Genetics & Genomics, Athens. Participating scientist Convercciencia, Guatemala City, 2007. Translator: Principles of Turfgrass Management. Recipient Gerald O. Mott award, Crop Sci. Soc. of Am., 2005; Rsch. Travel grant, Tinker Found., 2004, Travel grant, Grad. Sch. U. Ga., 2004, Coll. Ag and Environ. Sci., U. Ga., 2004. Mem.: AAAS, Nat. Coun. Sci. and Tech. (Guatemala), Crop Sci. Soc. America, Am. Soc. Agronomy, Gamma Sigma Delta (Agronomy), Phi Kappa Phi. Achievements include patents pending for plant transcription factors as molecular markers; research in mapping and confirmation of the 'Hyuuga' red-brown lesion resistance gene for Asian soybean rust. Office: Samuel Roberts Noble Found 2510 Sam Noble Pky Ardmore OK 73401

MONTES, INGRID, chemistry professor; d. Carlos Enrique Montes and Carmen Ana González; m. José Antonio Prieto, Jan. 2, 2005; children: Gerardo José López-Cepero, Mariana Del Carmen López-Cepero. PhD, U. Puerto Rico-Río Piedras, San Juan, PR, 1985. Prof. dept. chemistry U. Puerto Rico-Río Piedras, 1998—. Fellowship, Internat. Pure and Applied Chemistry, 2006. Fellow: Internat. Union Pure and Applied Chemistry; mem.: Am. Chem. Soc. (Washington) (pres. 2005, chair, adv. bd. Chemmatters Mag. 2007—, chair, com. cmty. activities 2007—, Outstanding Vol. Svc. Plaque 2005, Leonardo Igaravidez award. PR Sect. 2006, Nominated Vol. Svc. award 2008, Salute to Excellence award, Com. Cmty. Activities, NCW Coord. 2004). Office: Univ Puerto Rico-Rio Piedras Dept Chemistry PO Box 23346 San Juan PR 00931-3346 Office Fax: 787-764-1588. Business E-Mail: imontes@uprrp.edu.

MONTES, LEOPOLDO FELICIANO, dermatologist, educator; b. Buenos Aires, Nov. 22, 1929; came to U.S., 1955, naturalized, 1974; s. Leopoldo A. and Celia (Gaztambide) M.; m. Maria Mercedes Pfeiffer, Nov. 25, 1961; children: Carolina, Mercedes, Ana, Leopoldo, Teresa, William. MD, U. Buenos Aires, 1954; MS, U. Mich., 1959. Intern City of Buenos Aires Hosps., 1954-55; resident in dermatology Pa. Hosp., Phila., 1955-56; resident in dermatology, then instr. U. Mich. Med. Center, Ann Arbor, 1956-60; practice medicine specializing in dermatology Buenos Aires, 1960-63, 82—, Houston, 1963-66, Birmingham, Ala., 1966-81; dermatologist U. Ala., Eye Found.; asst. prof. Baylor U. Coll. Medicine, Houston, 1963—66; mem. faculty U. Ala. Med. Ctr. and Med. Coll. Ala., Birmingham, 1966—, prof. dermatology, 1969—81, assoc. prof. microbiology, 1968—91, prof. emeritus, 1982—; dermatologist Birmingham Dermatology Ctr., 1985—; clin. prof. dermatology U. South Ala., 2002—03; dermatologist Inst. Argentino de Diagnostico & Tratamiento, 1995—. Adj. prof. anatomy Coll. Medicine, U. South Ala., Mobile, 1981-89; adj. prof. large animal surgery and medicine Auburn U. Sch. Veterinary Medicine, 1977—; dir. Dermatology Rsch. Structural Rsch. Ctr., Mobile, 1990—, Vitiligo Unit, 1990; cons. Johnson & Johnson, Del-Ray Lab., Procter & Gamble, Upjohn Co., Delbay Co., Bayer, Warner, Lambert, Westwood Pharms., Tex. Pharm., Alcon, Owen Lab., Hoffman-La Roche, 1963—; CEO Westhoven Press. Author: Atlas of Skin Diseases of the Horse, 1983, Vitiligo-Nutritional Therapy, 1999, Scanning Electron Microscopy of Normal and Abnormal Skin, 1985, Vitiligo-Current Knowledge and Nutritional Therapy, 2006; founding editor Jour. Cutaneous Pathology, 1973-83. Mem. internat. adv. bd. Nat. Vitiligo Found., 2002—. Recipient Rsch. Career Devel. award USPHS, 1965-70; grantee USPHS, NSF, Kresge Found., John A. Hartford Found., NASA. Fellow Am. Acad. Dermatology, Am. Acad. Microbiology, Royal Coll. Physicians and Surgeons Can. (life); mem. AAAS, Am. Soc. Microbiology, Soc. Investigative Dermatology, Histochem. Soc., Am. Soc. Cell Biology, Am. Fedn. Clin. Rsch., Electron Microscope Soc. Am., Internat. Soc. Tropical Dermatology (Asst. sec. gen. 1969-74), Am. Dermatol. Assn., Am. Soc. Dermatopathology, Nat. Acad. Medicine Buenos Aires (life), Jockey Club Argentina (life), Sigma Xi. Achievements include patents in field. Home: Suipacha 1308 1011 Buenos Aires Argentina Office: Paraguay 2302 1121 Buenos Aires Argentina also: Structural Rsch Ctr 120 Novatan Rd Mobile AL 36608

Home Phone: 54149624289; Office Phone: 011-5411-4962-4684. Fax: 011-5411-4314-4328. E-mail: leopoldo_montes@hotmail.com. *While taking care of a patient I always considered it indispensable to study and research as much as I could about the disease I was treating, to feel I was perhaps the only one in a position to help, to put myself-as Lord Lister said- in the patient's place.*

MONTES-PIZARRO, ERROL L., mathematician, researcher; PhD, Cornell U., Ithaca, NY. Prof. U. PR, Cayey, 1994—. Prodr.(host): (radio program on African music) Rumba Africana; contbr. scientific papers. Rsch. grant, NIH, 2004—. Mem.: Math. Assn. America. Office: Univ Puerto Rico Cayey Antonio R Barcelo Ave Cayey PR 00736 Home Fax: 787-263-1625. Business E-Mail: emontes@caribe.net.

MONTFORD, JOHN THOMAS, communications executive, lawyer, former state legislator; b. Ft. Worth, June 28, 1943; s. Thomas L. and Jewell F. (Coursey) M.; m. Pamela Jacobs, June 3, 1966 (div.); 1 child, Melinda; m. Debra Kay Mears, Dec. 24, 1975; children: Melonie, John Ross. BA, U. Tex., Austin, 1965, JD, 1968; LLD (hon.), Lubbock Christian U., Tex., 1989. Bar: Tex. 1968. Pvt. practice, Lubbock, 1971-78; criminal dist. atty. Lubbock County, 1979-82; state sen. Dist. 28, Lubbock, 1983-96; chancellor Health Scis. Ctr. Tex. Tech. U., 1996—2001; sr. v.p. legislative and political affairs SBC Southwestern Bell, 2001—02, pres. external affairs, 2002—04; sr. v.p. western region legislative and regulatory affairs AT&T, Inc. Adj. faculty Tex. Tech. Coll. of Edn., High Edn. Adminstrn. Program, 1999; founding pres. South Plains Pub. Sch. Found.; bd. dirs. Fleetwood Enterprises, 1999-, Trustee S. Park Hosp., Lubbock, 1981-82; bd. dirs., trustee Tex. Boys Ranch, Lubbock, 1982-2005; chmn. profl. divsn. United Way, Lubbock, 1980; energy com. So. Legis. Conf., 1983; senate appointee So. Growth Policies Bd., 1983; chmn. adv. coun. Lubbock Substance Abuse Prevention Partnership; mem. bd. govs. West Tex. chpt. Multiple Sclerosis; mem. Dean's Roundtable U. Tex. Sch. Law, 1988; mem. Lubbock Symphony Orch. Bd., 1997-2005; v.p. Jaycees, 1974; adv. group Am. Heart Assn. Tex. affiliate, 1999; co-chmn., adv. coun. Tex. LWV Edn. Fund, 1999; bd. trustees The Nature Conservancy of Tex., 1999. Maj. USMC, 1968-71. Recipient Outstanding Young Man of Lubbock award Jaycees, 1973, Headliner of Yr. award Greater Lubbock Press Club, 1979, Man of Yr./Law Enforcement award Lubbock Optimist Club, 1979, Boss of Yr. award Legal Secs. Assn., 1980, Exec. of Yr., Lubbock Sales Exec. Assn., 1981; named Finest Freshman Tex. Bus. Mag., 1983, Outstanding State Sen. Tex. Youth Commn., 1988, Legislator of Yr. Tex. Pub. Health Assn., 1988, Legislator of Yr. Tex. Pub. Employees Assn. and State Employees, 1989, Outstanding Tex. Leader award John Ben Shepperd Pub. Leadership Forum, 1989, Best New Legislator award Tex. Monthly mag., 1983, Disting. Alumni, L.D. Bell H.S., 1984, Lubbock's Man of the Yr. LWV and Am. Diabetes Assn,. 1987, Disting. Svc. award Tex. C. of C., 1989, Outstanding Legislator in State of Tex., Epsilon Sigma Phi, 1989, Legislator of Yr. award Tex. Soc. Profl. Surveyors, 1989, Legislator of Yr. award 71st Legis., Tex. Mcpl. League, 1989, Tree of Life award Jewish Nat. Fund, 1989; named one of the Ten Best Legislators 71st Legis., Dallas Morning News, Tex. Monthly, 1989, 72d Legis., 1991, Tex. Monthly, 1989, 91, Outstanding Legislator Epsilon Sigma Phi, 1989, Tex. Mcpl. League, 1989; recipient Outstanding Svc. award Tex. Electric Coops., 1989, Pub. Ofcl. award Tex. Pub. Power Assn., 1990, George Woods award in politics NAACP, 1990, Legis. Leadership award 72d Legislator Tex. C. of C., 1992, One of the Seven Best Legislators 73d Legis. Dallas Morning News, 1993, 74th Legis. Dallas Morning News, 1995, One of the Ten Best Legislators 73d Legis. Tex. Monthly, 1993, 74th Legis. Tex. Monthly, 1995, Legislator of Yr. Tex. Pub. Employees Assn., 1993, award Lubbock arts Festival, 1994, award Tex. Mental Health Assn., 1994, honor award Tex. Commn. on the Arts, 1994, Cmty. Statesman award Heritage of Odessa Found., 1995, Legislator of Yr. award Tex. Game Warden's Assn., 1995, Judy coyle Tex. Liberty award Assn. Tex. Profl. Educators, 1995, Man of Yr. in Tex. Colls. & Univs., 1995, Outstanding Legislator award Tex. Police chiefs Assn., 1995, One of Top Ten, Harte-Hanks CComm., Inc., 1995, Newsmaker of 1995, Lubbock Avalanche Jour., One of Friends of Bus. 74th Legis., Tex. Bus. Mag., 1995, Outstanding Legislator, Tex. Jr. Coll. Tchrs Assn., 1995, Integrated Pest Mgmt. award in Excellence, Nat. Found. Integrated Pest Mgmt. Edn., 1996, Paul Harris fellow Rotary Internat., 1997, Founders award Ind. Coll. and Univ. Tex., 1997, Tex. most powerful citizen Lubbock Avalanche-Jour., 1999, Road Hand award Tex. Good Roads Assn., 1999, Declaration of Gratitude Tex. Tech. Sch. Pharmacy, 2000 and numerous others. Mem. State Bar Tex. (com. admissions), Tex. Criminal Def. Lawyers Assn., Tex. Dist. and County Attys. Assn. (life, legis. com.), Western State Water Coun., Tex. Assn. Cmty. Schs. (hon. life), Tex. Heart Inst. (nat. adv. coun. 1991), Lubbock C. of C. (Disting. Svcs. award 1996), Tex. Bar Found., Order of Coif (hon.), Rotary, Lions (Lubbock club), Omicron Delta Kappa, Delta Theta Phi, Phi Kappa Phi, Kappa Sigma (Pres. Commn. 2000), Phi Beta Delta.

MONTGOMERIE, COLIN STUART, professional golfer; b. Glasgow, Troon, Ayrshire, Scotland, June 23, 1963; children: Olivia Rose, Venetia, Cameron. Mem. Walker Cup Team, 1985, 87, Ryder Cup Team, 1991, 93, 95, 97, 99, 2002, 2004, 2006, Dunhill Cup Team, 1988, 91-2000, World Cup Team, 1988, 91-93, 97-99, 2007, UBS Cup Team, 2003, 2004. Decorated European Order of Merit; winner Scottish Stroke Play, 1985, Scottish Amateur Championship, 1987, European Tour Rookie of Yr., 1988, Portuguese Open, 1989, Scandinavian Masters, 1991, 99, 2001, Heineken Dutch Open, 1993, Volvo Masters, 1993, 2002, Spanish Open, 1994, English Open, 1994, Volvo German Open, 1994-95, Alfred Dunhill Cup, 1995, Trophee Lancome, 1995, Dubai Desert Classic, 1996, Murphy's Irish Open, 1996-97, 2001, Canon European Masters, 1996, Million Dollar Challenge, 1996, Compaq European Grand Prix, 1997, World Cup Individual, 1997, Andersen Cons. World Champion, 1997, King Hassan II Trophy, 1997, Brit. Masters, 1998, German Masters, 1998, Benson & Hedges Internat. Open, 1999, BMW Internat. Open, 1999, Std. Life Loch Lomond, 1999, Volvo PGA Championship, 1998-2000, Cisco World Matchplay Championship, 1999, The Skins Game (USA), 2000, Novotel Perrier Open de France, 2000, Ericsson Australian Masters, 2001, European Open, 2007; 2d pl. US Open, 1994, 97, TCL Classic 2002, Macau Open, 2003, Caltex Singapore Masters, 2004, Hong Kong Open, 2005, Smurfit Kappa European Open, 2007; leader European Tour Merit, 1993-99, 2005. Avocations: music, cars, films. Mailing: PGA Tour 112 PGA Tour Blvd Ponte Vedra Beach FL 32082

MONTGOMERY, BETTY DEE, former state attorney general, state legislator; b. Apr. 3, 1948; BA, Bowling Green State U.; JD, Coll. Law U. Toledo, 1976. Criminal clk. Lucas County Common Pleas Ct.; asst. pros. atty. Wood County, Ohio, 1977—78, pros. atty. Ohio, 1980—88, City of Perrysburg, Ohio, 1978—81; mem. Ohio State Senate, Columbus, 1988—95; atty. gen. State of Ohio, Columbus, 1994—2002, auditor, 2002—06. Bd. dirs. Dominion Homes, Inc., 2007—. Mem. bd. dirs. Ohio Sch. Bd. Atty. Assn. Recipient Women of Achievement award, Toledo Women in Comms., 1984, Govt. Leaders Against Drunk Drivers, MADD, 1990, Senator of the Year, Ohio Hospice Assn., 1991, Disting. Svc. award, Ohio State Bar Assn., 1992, Ohio Women Hall of Fame award, 1996, Public Svc. award, Ohio Assn. of Big Brothers/Big Sisters, 1999, Advocacy award, Ohio Soc. Healthcare Consumer Advocacy, 1999, Child Adv. of the Year, Ohio Ct. Appointed Spl. Advs./Guardian Ad Litem Assn., 1999, Toledo YWCA Milestones award, Women in Govt., 2001, Presdl. award for Pro Bono Svc., The Ohio Legal Assistance Found., 2002, ABA Pro Bono award, to the Office of the Atty. Gen., 2002, Disting. Alumnus award, Bowling Green State Univ., 2003. Mem.: Ohio Prosecuting Atty. Assn. (mem. 1984), Legis. Com., Internat. Prosecutors Assn., Wood County Bar Assn., Alternative Edn. Adv. Com. (former chmn.), Wood County Child Abuse & Neglect Adv. Bd. (former vice-chmn., chmn.), Sexual Abuse Prevention Project, Wood County Sch. (mem. 1981—), Bowling Green C. of C. Republican.

MONTGOMERY, CHARLES BARRY, lawyer; b. Latrobe, Pa., Apr. 17, 1937; BA cum laude, Muskingum Coll., 1959; JD, U. Mich., 1962. Bar: Ill. 1962, U.S. Dist. Ct. (no. dist.) Ill. 1982, U.S. Supreme Ct. 1971. Atty. Jacobs & McKenna, 1962-67; founder, ptnr. Jacobs, Williams and Montgomery, Ltd., 1967-85; sr. ptnr., comml. and class action litig. and profl. liability litig. Williams Montgomery & John Ltd., Chgo., 1985—. Instr. advocacy inst. U. Mich., Ann Arbor, 1985, advanced program Nat. Inst. Trial Advocacy, 1986, trial acad. Internat. Assn. Def. Counsel, 1987, law inst. program Def. Rsch. Inst; pub. spkr. litigation. Contbr. articles to profl. jours. Fellow Internat. Acad. Trial Lawyers, Internat. Soc. Barristers; mem. ABA (vice-chair medicine and law com. 1989-90), Am. Bd. Trial Advs., Am. Arbitration Assn., Chgo. Bar Assn., Def. Rsch. Inst., Ill. Assn. Def. Trial Counsel, Ill. Assn. Hosp. Attys., Ill. State Bar Assn., Internat. Assn. Def. Counsel, Soc. Trial Lawyers, Legal Club of Chgo., Trial Lawyers Club of Chgo. Office: Williams Montgomery & John Ltd Ste 2100 20 N Wacker Dr Chicago IL 60606-3094 Office Phone: 312-443-3200, 312-443-3242. Office Fax: 312-630-8542. Business E-Mail: cbm@willmont.com.

MONTGOMERY, CHARLES HARVEY, lawyer; b. Spartanburg, SC, Jan. 28, 1949; s. Dan Hugh and Ann Louise (Gasque) M.; m. Renée Jean Gubernot, Mar. 27, 1971; children: Charles Scott, Marie Renée. BA, Duke U., 1971; JD, Vanderbilt U., 1974. Bar: N.C. 1974, U.S. Dist. Ct. (ea. dist.) N.C. 1974, U.S. Supreme Ct. 1979, U.S. Dist. Ct. (mid. dist.) N.C. 1991; cert. family law specialist, N.C., 1995. Assoc. Jordan Morris & Hoke, Raleigh, NC, 1974-75; atty. Wake County Legal Svcs., Raleigh, 1975-76; pvt. practice, Raleigh, 1977; ptnr. Montgomery & Montgomery, Cary, NC, 1978-79, Sanford Adams McCullough & Beard, Raleigh, 1979-86, Adams McCullough & Beard, Raleigh, 1986-88, Toms Reagan & Montgomery, Cary, 1989-92, Toms & Montgomery, Cary, 1992-93; pvt. practice, Cary, 1993—. NC super lawers 2009,bd. dirs. Br. Bank and Trust, Cary, 1978-; pres. Family Law Mediation, Inc. Councilman Town of Cary, 1977-81, 83-87; vice-chmn. Wake County Dem. party, Raleigh, 1991-92; commr. Wake County, Raleigh, 1992; bd. dirs. East Cen. Cmty. Legal Svcs., Inc., 1997-2003, State Capitol Found., 1994—. Mem.: ABA, Cary Bar Assn. (organizer 1993—), N.C. Acad. Trial Lawyers (chair family law sect. 1996—98), Wake County Bar Assn. (bd. dirs. 1999—2001), N.C. Bar Assn. (chmn. pub. info. com. 1994—96, dir. family law coun. 1994—97, 2006—09). Methodist. Avocation: sailing. Office: PO Box 1325 Cary NC 27512-1325 also: 590 New Waverly Pl Ste 110 Cary NC 27512-1325 Office Phone: 919-816-9002. Business E-Mail: charles@montylaw.com.

MONTGOMERY, CHARLES HOWARD, retired bank executive; b. Bloomington, Ill., Mar. 23, 1930; s. Dewey H. and Madeline (Wonderlin) M.; m. Diane Dickerson Cohen, Aug. 30, 1978 (dec. Oct. 1996); children: Alison, Douglas; m. Katharine Yang, Oct. 4, 1997. AB, Ill. Wesleyan U., 1951; MS, U. Ill., 1960. CPA, Ill. Auditor Lybrand Ross Bros. & Montgomery, Rockford, Ill., 1955-59; with Abbott Labs., North Chicago, Ill., 1959-67, controller, 1965-67; v.p. finance Anchor Coupling Co., Libertyville, 1967-69; v.p., comptroller First Nat. Bank Chgo., 1969-73, sr. v.p., 1973-75, exec. v.p., 1976-88, comptroller, 1973-88, First Chgo. Corp.; ret. Past chmn. Inter-Assn. Com. Bank Acctg. With US Army, 1952—53. Mem. Fin. Execs. Inst., AICPA, Ill. Soc. CPAs, Tau Kappa Epsilon, Phi Kappa Phi, Univ. Club (Chgo.) Home: 6321 N Avers Ave Chicago IL 60659-1001 Personal E-mail: chmonty@att.net.

MONTGOMERY, CLEOTHUS, minister; b. Henderson, Tex., Dec. 6, 1926; s. Lewis and Amanda (Waters) M.; m. Emma Agusta Tinch (dec. Aug. 23, 1987); children: Michael Dennis, Debra Marie, Pamela Key, Diane Renea, Anthony Cleothus (dec.). BS in Drafting, Calif. Coll., 1951; B in Theology, Union Bapt. Theol. Sem., 1962; M in Theology, Inter Bapt. Theol. Sem., 1965, DD, 1973; D in Sacred Theol. (hon.), Mt. Hope Bible Coll., 1973; M in Ministry, Trinity Theol. Sem., 1990, D in Ministry, 1993. Cert. christian counselor, Tex. Minister Northside Missionary Bapt. Ch., Houston, 1962—. Counselor Chemical Dependency, Houston, 1989-97, Internat. Christian Isnt., 1990-97; invited pastor by Campus for Christ to Israel, 1987, Africa, 1990, Russia, 1995-97. Pres. World Christian Tng. Ctr., Houston, 1985-90, Houston Minister Christian Fellowship, 1992-97; chmn. Minister Network Life Gift, Houston, 1988-90, Ministers Against Crime, Houston, 1989-97; treas. Life Investment for Tng., Houston, 1990-97; v.p. Ministerial Adv. to Mayor, Houston, 1995-97; trustee bd. of regency, adv. bd. Coll. of Biblical Studies. With U.S. Army, 1945-46. Mem. NAACP, Am. Assn. Christian Counselors (chemical dependency counselor 1993-97). Democrat. Baptist. Avocations: reading, devotional writings, bowling, travel, jogging. Home: 1407 Laurentide St Houston TX 77029-3411 Office: Northside Missionary Bapt Ch 3202 Bennington St Houston TX 77093-9222

MONTGOMERY, CLIFF WILSON, journalist, writer, researcher; b. Cumberland, Md., Aug. 13, 1965; s. Clifford Ray and Elizabeth Ann Montgomery. European Lit. (hon.), Ed. by pvt. tutor, Charlotte, NC, 1983—91, Am. Lit. (hon.), 1994—98. East coast polit. corr. 3 AM Mag., Kirkland, Wash., 2000—07; editor, pub. The Am. Spark, 2006—. Media cons. Sierra Club, Charlotte, NC, 1998. Freelance journalist Washington Spectator, In These Times, Working for Change, Alternet and Political Affairs. Active Nat. Trust for Hist. Preservation, 1996—99, Archaeol. Inst. Am., 1999—2000; activist Amnesty Internat., 1992—96; active Pub. Concern Found., 1994—. Independent. Avocations: history, travel, motorcycling. Personal E-mail: clifmn@aol.com. Business E-Mail: cmont@americanspark.com.

MONTGOMERY, DAVID BRUCE, marketing educator; b. Fargo, ND, Apr. 30, 1938; s. David William and Iva Bernice (Trask) Montgomery; m. Toby Marie Franks, June 11, 1960; children: David Richard, Scott Bradford, Pamela Marie. BSEE, Stanford U., 1960, MBA, 1962, MS in Stats., 1964, PhD in Mgmt. Sci., 1966; D honoris causa, Limburgs U. Centrum, Belgium, 1998. Asst. prof. mgmt. MIT, 1966-69, assoc. prof., 1969-70; assoc. prof. mktg. and mgmt. sci. Stanford U., 1970-73, prof., 1973-78, Robert A. Magowan prof. mktg., 1978-92, Sebastian S. Kregge prof. mktg. strategy, 1992-99, prof. emeritus, 1999—; dean Sch. Bus. Singapore Mgmt. U., 2003—05, cons. and vis. prof., mktg. and mgmt., 2006—. Prin. MAC Group, Inc., 1969-91; adv. bd. LEK Partnership, London; sci. adv. bd. Univ. Connection, Bonn, Germany; acad. trustee Mktg. Sci. Inst., 1994-2000, exec. dir., 1995-97; exec. dir. coun., 2000-; cons. Mktg. & Mgmt. Singapore Mgmt. U., 2006-, vis. prof., 2006-; chair mktg. dist. scholar Hong Kong Poly.U., 2008. Author: (with Glen L. Urban) Management Science in Marketing, 1969, (with Massy and Morrison) Stochastic Models of Buying Behavior, 1970, (with Day et al) Planning: Cases in Computer and Model Assisted Marketing, 1973, (with others) Consumer Behavior: Theoretical Sources, 1973, (with G. J. Eskin) Data Analysis, 1975; editor 5 books; editor: Management Science, Marketing Department; cons. editor Jour. Internat. Mktg., 2000-03; mem. editl. bd. Mgmt. Sci., Jour. Mktg., Jour. Mktg. Rsch., Mktg. Sci., Jour. acad. of Mktg. Sci., Jour. Internat. Mktg.; contbr. more than 100 articles and tech. reports to sci. and profl. jours. Trustee Family Service Assn. of Mid Peninsula, 1972-73. Recipient citation for outstanding contbns. to use of computers in mgmt. edn. Hewlett Packard, 1977, Best Paper award Strategic Mgmt. Soc., 1996. Fellow: INFORMS Soc. Mktg. Sci. (inagural fellow 2008); mem.: Am. Mktg. Assn. (Contribution to Mktg. Strategy award 2002), Inst. Mgmt. Scis., Tau Beta Pi. Presbyterian. Office: Stanford U Grad Sch Bus Stanford CA 94305 Home: 2462 Mountain Dr Lenoir City TN 37772 Business E-Mail: montgomery_david@gsb.stanford.edu.

MONTGOMERY, DAVID CAMPBELL, retired physics professor; b. Milan, Mo., Mar. 5, 1936; s. Merrill Edward and Ruth E. (Campbell) Montgomery; m. Shirley Arlene Imig, July 20, 1957; children: Kathleen Montgomery Sutton, Elizabeth. Student, U. Mo., 1953-55; BS, U. Wis., 1956; MA, Princeton U., 1958, PhD, 1959; D honoris causa (hon.), Eindhoven U. Tech., The Netherlands, 1996. Research assoc. Princeton U., 1959-60; instr. U. Wis., 1961-62; asst. prof. U. Md., 1962-65; assoc. prof. U. Iowa, Iowa City, 1965-70, prof., 1970-77; prof. physics Coll. William and Mary, Williamsburg, Va., 1977-84; prof. Dartmouth Coll., Hanover, NH, 1984—2004, rsch. prof., prof. emeritus, 2004—. Vis. prof., rschr. U. Colo., 1966, U. Alaska, 1968, U. Calif., Berkeley, 1969—70, Bell Labs., 1971; lectr. Internat. Summer Sch. Theoretical Physics, Les Houches, France, 1972, U. Wis., Madison, 1973, vis. prof., rschr., 89; vis. prof. Hunter Campus CUNY, 1973—74, U. Nagoya, Japan, 1983, Columbia U., NYC, 1985, Tech. U., Eindhoven, Netherlands, 1992; vis. scientist Nat. Ctr. Atmospheric Rsch., Boulder, Colo., 1975—76, Boulder, 1979, Boulder, 87, Boulder, 2002, Boulder, 2004—07, Riso Nat. Lab., Roskilde, Denmark, 2001; cons. NASA Hdqs., Washington, 1977—82, JET Joint Undertaking, Culham, England, 1991; vis. rsch. prof. U. Md., 1977—84; vis. staff Los Alamos Sci. Lab., 1977—81, 1986, 1991—92, 1994, cons., collaborator, vis. staff; former cons. Oak Ridge Nat. Lab., NASA; vis. rschr. Los Alamos Nat. Lab., 1987—88, cons., 1998—2000; J. M. Burgers prof. Eindhoven Tech. U., Netherlands, 1995—98, Netherlands, 2000—01, U. Md., 1997; vis. rschr. Courant Inst. NYU, 1997. Former assoc. editor: Physics of Fluids, Internat. Jour. Engring. Sci.; contbr. articles to profl. publs. and monographs. Fellow: Am. Phys. Soc.; mem.: NY Acad. Scis., Sigma Xi, Phi Beta Kappa, Phi Mu Alpha, Pi Mu Epsilon. Achievements include introduction of modern fluid turbulence methods into space and controlled fusion theory; development of maximum entropy, or "most probable" states, method of describing coherent structures achieved as a product of turbulent relaxation. Office: Dartmouth College Physics Dept Hanover NH 03755 Office Phone: 603-646-3219.

MONTGOMERY, DAVID R., geologist, educator, writer; b. Stanford, Calif., Sept. 7, 1961; s. Bruce David and Toby Marie (Franks) Montgomery. BS in Geology, Stanford U., 1984; PhD in Geomorphology, U. Calif., Berkeley, 1991. Faculty mem. U. Wash., Seattle, 1991—, prof. Dept. Earth and Space Scis. Author: King Of Fish: The Thousand-Year Run of Salmon, 2003, Dirt: The Erosion of Civilizations, 2007; contbr. articles to profl. jours. Named a MacArthur Fellow, The John D. and Catherine T. MacArthur Found., 2008. Mem.: Geol. Soc. Am., Am. Geophys. Union. Office: Geomorphological Rsch Group Dept Earth and Space Scis / U Wash Box 351310 Seattle WA 98195-1310 Office Phone: 206-685-2560. Office Fax: 206-543-3836. E-mail: dave@ess.washington.edu.

MONTGOMERY, DAVID SCOTT, physicist, director; s. Richard Allen Montgomery and JoAnn J. Foster; m. Cindy Marie Romero, Dec. 3, 1994; children: Jessica Marie, Christina Elisia, Daniel Adam, Rachel Elisabeth Goodman. BSc, Northeastern State U., Tahlequah, Okla., 1984. Physicist Lawrence Livermore Nat. Lab., Calif., 1984—96, Los Alamos Nat. Lab., N.Mex., 1996—, dir., trident laser facility, 2008—. Contbr. articles to profl. jours. Fellow: Am. Phys. Soc. Office: Los Alamos Nat Lab Los Alamos NM 87545

MONTGOMERY, DENISE KAREN, nurse; b. NYC, Dec. 23, 1951; d. Thomas Cornell and Dorothy Marie (Castine) Simons; m. Timothy Bruce Montgomery, July 19, 1974 (div. Feb. 1981); m. Joseph Samuel Montgomery, Aug. 20, 1983. A in Nursing, San Jacinto Coll., 1971. RN, Tex. Charge nurse Aarons Womens Clinic, Houston, 1977; rsch. asst. dept. ob-gyn. Baylor Coll. Medicine, Houston, 1977-81, nursing supr., 1979-81, program coord. population control program, 1979-81; nurse Dr. Eric J. Haufrect, Houston, 1982-83; office mgr., supr. Dr. Samuel Law, Houston, 1983-84, Dr. J.S. Montgomery III, 1987—. Contbr. articles to profl. jours. Recipient Disting. Pub. Svc. award Am. Heart Assn., 1976; numerous rsch. grants. Mem. Nat. Assn. Coll. Ob-Gyn. Republican. Mem. Christian Ch. Home: 8202 N Tahoe Dr Houston TX 77040-1256 Office Phone: 281-955-5330. E-mail: denmnt@hotmail.com.

MONTGOMERY, DILLARD BREWSTER, musician, educator; b. Memphis, Jan. 1, 1936; s. Mary Joyce Montgomery; m. Joyce Helena Beale, Dec. 9, 1965; 1 child, Lisa Jenean. BS, Tenn. State U., 1962, MA, 1968. Profl. musician Nashville Assn. Musicians, 1958—; band dir., keyboardist The New Imperials, Nashville, 1962—; tchr. Met. Nashville Schs., 1962-94, ret., 1994; asst. prin. W.A. Bass Middle Sch., 1984-93, prin., 1993-94. Choir dir. John Wesley United Meth. Ch., Nashville, 1958—, Dixon United Meth. Ch., 1970-71, Braden United Meth. Ch., 1985-2002; profl. model Terrance Hurd Agy., 1999—. Served with USAF, 1955-58. Mem. NEA, Tenn. Edn. Assn., Met. Nashville Edn. Assn., Nat. Musicians Union, Tenn. State U. Alumni Assn. (life), Alpha Phi Alpha (life). Democrat. Methodist. Avocations: computers, collecting old music, collecting old movies, recording and transferring old albums and tapes to CD, recording old movies to video and DVD. Home: 638 W Nocturne Dr Nashville TN 37207 Office Phone: 615-650-3232. E-mail: dmontgo1@bellsouth.net.

MONTGOMERY, DOUGLAS CARTER, industrial engineering educator; b. Roanoke, Va., June 5, 1943; s. Gordon Ashby and Gladys (Reed) M.; m. Martha Ellen Price, Aug. 7, 1965 (div. July 1982); children: Meredith, Colin, Neil. BSIE, Va. Poly. Inst., 1965, MS, 1967, PhD, 1969. Prof. indsl. systems engring. Ga. Inst. Tech., Atlanta, 1969-84; prof. mech. engring., dir. indsl. engring. U. Wash., Seattle, 1984-88, John M. Fluke disting. prof. mfg. engring., 1985-88; regents prof. indsl. engring and stats. Ariz. State U., Tempe, 1988—. Cons. IBM, various locations, 1979—, Coca-Cola Co., Atlanta, 1970-94, Boeing, Seattle, 1984, Motorola, 1990—, other mfg. cos. Author eleven books, including: Introduction to Statistical Quality Control, 6th edit. 2008, design and Analysis of Experiments, 7th edit. 2001. Fellow Am. Soc. Quality Control, Am. Stats. Assn., Inst. Indsl. Engrs.; mem. Internat. Stats. inst., internat. Acad. Quality. Avocation: golf. Home: 3841 E Talowa St Phoenix AZ 85044-3017 Office: Ariz State U/Fulton Sch Engring Dept Indsl Engring Tempe AZ 85287

MONTGOMERY, EDWARD BRUCE, federal official, former dean, economics professor; b. NYC, July 3, 1955; s. David and Martel Laneda (Wilcher) M.; m. Kari Lynn McPeck, Oct. 7, 1994; children: Elizabeth Joan, Lindsay Martel, Edward Julius. BS, Pa. State U., 1976; MA, Harvard U., 1980, PhD, 1982. Estimator, planner Eastman Kodak Co., Rochester, NY, 1976-77; teaching fellow Harvard U., Cambridge, Mass., 1979-81; rsch. assoc. Fed. Res. Sys., Washington, 1980; asst. prof. economics Carnegie Mellon U., Pitts., 1981-86; assoc. prof. economics Mich. State U., East Lansing, 1986-90, U. Md., College Park, 1990-92, prof. economics, 1992—2009, sr. assoc. dean, 2002—03, dean, 2003—09; chmn. Barack Obama's Presdl. Transition Labor Review Team, 2008—09; chief economist US Dept. Labor, 1997—98, asst. sec. for policy, 1999—2000, dep. sec., 2000—01; dir. Recovery for Auto Communities & Workers The White House, Washington, 2009—. Vis. scholar Bd. Govs. Fed. Res., 1983-84; Ameritech fellow Case Western Res. U., Cleve., 1988; Ford Found. scholar Nat. Bur. Econ. Rsch., Cambridge, 1989; cons. Fed. Res. Bank Cleve., 1985-86, Urban League Pa., Pitts., 1986, Friend of the Ct.-Mich., Lansing, 1988-89, Mich. Dept. Transp., 1989 Contbr. articles to profl. publs. Mem. Am. Econ. Assn., Nat. Econ. Assn., Midwest Econ. Assn., Phi Kappa Phi, Omicron Delta Kappa. Avocations: scuba diving, rugby, squash, running, reading. Office: US Dept Labor 200 Constitution Ave NW Washington DC 20057 Office Phone: 202-693-6000.

MONTGOMERY, HENRY EDWARD, chemistry professor; b. Lexington, Ky., July 7, 1946; s. Henry Edward and Agnes Luella Montgomery; m. Ruth Graham; children: Allison Krista Gray, Robert Henry Graham. BA, Berea Coll., Ky., 1968; PhD, U. Ky., Lexington, 1971. Capt. USN, 1971—99, supr. shipbuilding Groton, Conn., 1994—97; chief staff Naval Undersea Warfare Ctr., Newport, 1997—99; prof. Ctr. Coll., Danville, Ky., 2000—. Chmn., bd. dirs. Garrard County Long Term. Lay leader Lancaster United Meth. Ch., Ky., 2004—05. Decorated Legion of Merit Pres. Conservative. Home: 260 Richmond Loop One Lancaster KY 40444 Office: Ctr Coll 600 W Walnut St Danville KY 40422 Personal E-mail: montgomery2@windstream.net. Business E-Mail: ed.montgomery@centre.edu.

MONTGOMERY, HUBERT THERON, JR., physician, health care administrator; b. Birmingham, Ala., July 29, 1935; s. Hubert Theron and Edna M. (Morrison) M.; m. Sarah Diane Bryans, Sept. 19, 1969; children: Alfred Peter, Melanie Anne, Laurel Elaine, Amy Diane. AB, Birmingham So. Coll., 1957; MD, Tulane U., 1961. Diplomate Am. Bd. Surgery, Am. Bd. Plastic Surgery. Rotating intern St. Vincent Hosp., Birmingham, 1961-62; resident surgery Lloyd Noland Hosp., Fairfield, Ala., 1964-68; pvt. practice, Montgomery, Ala., 1968-73, 75—; resident plastic surgery U. Tenn., Memphis, 1974-75; pres., CEO Med One Inc., Montgomery, 1983—96; exec. v.p., chief exec. officer Central Ala. Preferred Provider, Inc., Montgomery, 1984-96; sec.-treas. Montgomery Surg. Ctr., Inc., 1984-85; pres. Bodegas de Mendoza, Inc., 2001—; pres., CEO Crux Imports, Inc., 2005—. Sect. chief plastic surgery Bapt. Med. Ctr., Montgomery, 1976-78, St. Margaret's Hosp., Montgomery, 1987-89. Sec.-treas. Ala. Soc. Plastic Surgeons, 1990-92, pres. 1994-96; mem. Hitchcock Award Com., Montgomery, 1985. Maj. U.S. Army, 1963-69. Named New Bus. of Yr., Ala. Bus. Rev., Montgomery, 1985. Fellow: ACS; mem.: Soc. Latin Am. Plastic Surgeons (treas. 1997—98, v.p. 1999—2001, pres. 2002—04), Am. Cancer Soc. (dir. Montgomery chpt. 2002—), Newcomen Soc. N.Am., Wynn Lakes Country Club, Montgomery Country Club, Capitol City Kiwanis (dir. 1987—88). Baptist.

MONTGOMERY, JERRY LYNN, retired education educator; b. Owensville, Ind., Apr. 21, 1935; s. Philip Matthew and Lois Caroline (Anderson) M.; m. Murelyn Ann Rogers, Sept. 21, 1957 (div. Apr. 1976); stepchildren: Rebecca Williams Slominski, Matthew Williams; m. Gretchen Wendelroth Golzè, May 14, 1977; children: Robin Schneider, Lori Abbott, Vicki Randolph. BS, Purdue U., West Lafayette, Ind., 1957; MA, Ball State U., Muncie, Ind., 1964, EdD, 1969. Vocat. agrl. Milton (Ind.) Pub. Schs., 1957-58, Carthage (Ind.) Pub. Schs., 1958-61; sci. tchr. Angola (Ind.) City Schs., 1961-66; grad. asst. Ball State U., 1966-69, asst. prof. biology, 1969; edn. prof. Marietta (Ohio) Coll., 1969—2001; sci. educator Project Discovery, Athens, Ohio, 1994-99; Discovery dir. Dist. #11, 1997-98. Goal #4 com. Marietta City Schs., Ohio, 1993-96, grade 4 sci. profiency test content rev. and rangefinder coms. Ohio Dept. of Edn., Columbus, Ohio, 1994-2002; mem. young engrs. and scientists Marietta Telesis Group, 1992-96; vis. prof. physics Ohio State U., 1994; grant evaluator Wash. State C.C. and Regional Profl. Devel. Ctr., 1999-2003; Praxis III evaluator State of Ohio, 1997—; mem. exec. bd. Ohio Math. and Sci. Coalition, 2001-05; reviewer Sci. Program Improvement, NSTA, 2005-. Recipient Outstanding Educator Martha Holden Jennings Found., 1989. Mem. Assn. Tchr. Educators (credentials com. 1991-2000), Nat. Sci. Tchrs. Assn., Sci. Edn. Coun. Ohio, Ohio Acad. of Sci., Phi Delta Kappa. Avocations: reading, canoeing, travel, fishing, golf. Home: 105 Rathbone Ter Marietta OH 45750-1443 Office: Marietta Coll 215 5th St Marietta OH 45750-4033 Business E-Mail: montgomj@marietta.edu.

MONTGOMERY, JOHN A., physicist; b. Memphis, Jan. 2, 1944; s. John and Mary Emma (Pittman) Montgomery; m. Cathi Montgomery. B in Physics, North Tex. State U., 1967, M in Physics, 1969; PhD, Catholic U. Am., 1982. Rsch. physicist advanced techniques br. electronic warfare divsn. Naval Rsch. Lab., 1968—80, head off-board countermeasures br., 1980—85, superintendent Tactical Electronic Warfare Divsn. (TEWD), 1985—2002, dir. rsch, 2002—. U.S. nat. leader Tech. Cooperation Program Multinat. Group on Electronic Warfare, 1987—. Mem.: Sr. Exec. Svc. (Presdl. Rank Meritorious Exec. award 1988, Presdl. Rank. Disting. Exec. award 1991, Presdl. Rank Meritorious. Exec. award 1999, Presdl. Rank. Disting. Exec. award 2002), Sigma Xi. Achievements include development of new electronic warfare technologies; more than 80 systems approved for operational use by the Navy and other services. Office: Naval Rsch Lab 4555 Overlook Ave SW Washington DC 20375

MONTGOMERY, JOHN HAROLD, psychiatrist; s. Joseph and Jane Montgomery; m. Heather Montgomery, July 17, 1999; children: Abigail, Blake, Zachary. DO, Nova Southeastern U., 1998. Diplomate Psychiatry and Forensic Psychiatry, Am. Bd. Psychiatry and Neurology. Forensic psychiatrist Miss. State Hosp., Whitfield, 2003—, svc. chief female line, 2004—. Asst. clin. prof. dept. psychiatry U. Miss. Med. Ctr., Jackson, 2003—. Contbr. articles to profl. jours. Recipient Young Investigator award, Am. Acad. of Psychiatry and the Law, 2003, Rosner award, Am. Acad. Forensic Scis., 2004; Steinberg Fellowship in Psychiatry and the Law, U. Rochester Sch. Medicine and Dentistry, 2002—03. Office: MS State Hospital Whitfield MS 39193 Personal E-mail: jmontgo651@yahoo.com. Business E-Mail: montgjo@msh.state.ms.us.

MONTGOMERY, JOHN RICHARD, pediatrician, educator; b. Burnsville, Miss., Oct. 24, 1934; s. Guy Austin and Harriet Pauline (Owens) M.; m. Dottye Ann Newell, June 26, 1965; children: John Newell, Michelle Elizabeth. BS, U. Ala., 1955, MD, 1958. Cert. Am. Bd. Pediat. Intern U. Miss., Jackson, 1958-59, resident in pediat., 1959-60, Baylor Coll. Medicine, Houston, 1960-61, fellow in pediat. infectious diseases and immunology, 1964-66, asst. prof. pediat., 1966-70, assoc. prof., 1970-75; chief pediat. programs U. Ala. Sch. Medicine, Huntsville, 1975-95, prof., 1975-97, prof. emeritus, 1997—. Bd. dirs. State Bd. Health, Ala. Bd. Med. Examiners; adv. com. Ala. EMS for Children. Contbr. articles to books and profl. jours. With AUS, 1961—62, Korea, ret. col. USAR, 1999. Mem. Soc. Pediat. Rsch., Am. Assn. Immunologists, Infectious Diseases Soc., N.Y. Acad. Scis., Am. Acad. Pediats. (pres. Ala. chpt. 1991-93), Sigma Xi, Phi Beta Kappa. Achievements include assisting in development of germ-free invironmental bubble to protect patient with no natural immunity (patient later subject of movie The Boy in the Plastic Bubble, 1976 and PBS documentary on American Experience, 2006). Home Phone: 256-883-9029; Office Phone: 256-551-4600. Personal E-mail: dnjrmont@bellsouth.net.

MONTGOMERY, JOHN T., lawyer; BA, U. Mich., 1969; JD, Boston Coll., 1975. Bar: Mass. 1975, US Dist. Ct. (Mass., ea. Mich.), US Ct. Appeals (1st, 2d, 3d, 4th & D.C. cir.). Asst. atty. gen. Commonwealth of Mass.; assoc. Ropes & Gray, Boston, 1982—85, ptnr. litigation dept., 1985—90; first asst. atty. gen. Commonwealth of Mass., 1990—92; ptnr. litigation dept. Ropes & Gray, Boston, 1992—, mng. ptnr. & mem. mgmt. com. Named one of Top Ten Lawyers, Mass. Lawyers' Weekly, 1998. Fellow: Am. Coll. Trial Lawyers; mem.: New England Legal Found. (dir.). Office: Ropes & Gray 1 International Pl Boston MA 02110-2624 Office Phone: 617-951-7565. Office Fax: 617-951-7050. Business E-Mail: john.montgomery@ropesgray.com.

MONTGOMERY, JOHN WARWICK (BARON OF KILTARTAN AND LORD OF MORRIS, COMTE DE ST. GERMAIN DE MONTGOMMERY), law educator, theologian; b. Warsaw, NY, Oct. 18, 1931; s. Maurice Warwick and Harriet (Smith) M.; m. Lanalee de Kant, Aug. 26, 1988; 1 adopted child, Jean-Marie. AB in Philosophy with distinction, Cornell U., 1952; BLS, U. Calif., Berkeley, 1954, MA, 1958; BD, Wittenberg U., 1958, MST, 1960; PhD, U. Chgo., 1962; Docteur de l'Université, mention Théologie Protestante, U. Strasbourg, France, 1964; LLB, LaSalle Extension U., 1977; diplôme cum laude, Internat. Inst. Human Rights, Strasbourg, 1978; MPhil in Law, U. Essex, Eng., 1983; Dr. (hon.), Inst. Religion and Law, Moscow, 1999; LLM, Cardiff U., Wales, 2000; LLD, Cardiff U., 2003. Bar: Va. 1978, Calif. 1979, D.C. 1985, Wash. 1990, U.S. Supreme Ct. 1981, Eng. 1984, Paris 2003; lic. real estate broker Calif.; cert. law librarian, fraud examiner; advanced cert. Heraldry Soc.; diplomate Med. Library Assn.; ordained to ministry Luth. Ch., 1958. Librarian, gen. reference service U. Calif. Library, Berkeley, 1954-55; instr. Bibl. Hebrew, Hellenistic Greek, Medieval Latin Wittenberg U., Springfield, Ohio, 1956-59; head librarian Swift Libr. div. and Philosophy, mem. federated theol. faculty U. Chgo., 1959-60; assoc. prof., chmn. dept. history Wilfred Laurier U. (formerly Waterloo Luth. U.), Ont., Can., 1960-64; prof., chmn. div. ch. history, history of Christian thought, dir. European Seminar program Trinity Evang. Div. Sch., Deerfield, Ill., 1964-74; prof. law and theology George Mason U. Sch. Law (formerly Internat. Sch. of Law), Arlington, Va., 1974-75; theol. cons. Christian Legal Soc., 1975-76; dir. studies Internat. Inst. Human Rights, Strasbourg, France, 1979-81; founding dean, prof. jurisprudence, dir. European program Simon Greenleaf U. Sch. Law, Anaheim, Calif., 1980-88; lic. disting. prof. theology and law, dir. European program Faith Evang. Luth. Sem., Tacoma, 1989-91; from prin. lectr. to reader in law Bedfordshire U., England, 1991-93, prof. law and humanities, dir. Ctr. Human Rights, 1993-97, emeritus prof., 1997—; disting. prof. apologetics, law, and history of Christian thought, v.p. acad. affairs U.K. and Europe Trinity Coll. and Theol. Sem., Newburgh, Ind., 1997—2007; disting. prof. law Regent U., Va., 1997-99; sr. counsel European Ctr. Law and Justice, 1997-2001; founding dir. Internat. Acad. of Apologetics, Evangelism and Human Rights, Strasbourg, France, 1997—; disting. rsch. prof. philosophy and Christian thought Patrick Henry Coll., Purcellville, Va., 2007—. Vis. prof. Concordia Theol. Sem., Springfield, Ill., 1964-67, DePaul U., Chgo., 1967-70, Concordia U., Irvine, Calif., 2006; hon. fellow Revelle Coll., U. Calif., San Diego, 1970; rector Freie Fakultaten Hamburg, Fed. Republic Germany, 1981-82; lectr. Rsch. Scientists Christian Fellowship Conf. St. Catherines Coll., Oxford U., 1985, Internat. Anti-Corruption Conf., Beijing, China, 1995; Pascal lectr. on Christianity and the Univ., U. Waterloo, Ont., Can., 1987; A. Kurt Weiss lectr. biomed. ethics U. Okla., 1997; adj. prof. Puget Sound U. Sch. Law, Tacoma, 1990-91; founding dir. Internat. Acad. Apologetics, Evangelism and Human Rights, Strasbourg, France, 1997—; Worldwide Adv. Conf. lectr. Inns of Ct. Sch. Law, London, 1998; law and religion colloquium lectr. U. Coll. London, 2000, IVR World Congress on Philosophy Law, Crakow, Poland, 2007, Shanghai, 2009; hon. chmn. academic bd. Internat. Inst. Religious Freedom, World Evangel. Fellowship, 2005-. Author: The Writing of Research Papers in Theology, 1959, A Union List of Serial Publications in Chicago Area Protestant Theological Libraries, 1960, A Seventeenth-Century View of European Libraries, 1962, 1962, Chytraeus on Sacrifice: A Reformation Treatise in Biblical Theology, 1962, The Shape of the Past: An Introduction to Philosophical Historiography, 1962; author: (rev. edit.), 1975; author: The Is God Dead Controversy, 1966; author: (with Thomas J.J. Altizer) The Altizer-Montgomery Dialogue, 1967; author: Crisis in Lutheran Theology, 2 vols., 1967; author: (rev. edit.), 1973; author: Es confiable el Christianismo?, 1968, Ecumenicity, Evangelicals, and Rome, 1969, Where is History Going?, 1969, (Romanian edit.) 2004, History and Christianity, 1970, Damned Through the Church, 1970, The Suicide of Christian Theology, 1970, Computers, Cultural Change and the Christ, 1970, In Defense of Martin Luther, 1970, La Mort de Dieu, 1971; author: (with Joseph Fletcher) Situation Ethics: True or False?, 1972; author: The Quest for Noah's Ark, 1972; author: (rev. edit.), 1974; author: Verdammt durch die Kirche, 1973, Christianity for the Toughminded, 1973, Cross and Crucible, 2 vols., 1973, Principalities and Powers: The World of the Occult, 1973, (rev. edit.), 1975, (Romanian edit.), 2004, How Do We Know There is a God?, 1973, Myth, Allegory and Gospel, 1974, God's Inerrant Word, 1974, Jurisprudence: A Book of Readings, 1974; author: (4th edit.), 1992; author: The Law Above the Law, 1975, Cómo Sabemos Que Hay un Dios?, 1975, Demon Possession, 1975, The Shaping of America, 1976, Faith Founded on Fact, 1978, Law and Gospel: A Study for Integrating Faith and Practice, 1978; author: (3rd edit.), 1994; author: Slaughter of the Innocents, 1981, The Marxist Approach to Human Rights: Analysis & Critique, 1984, Human Rights and Human Dignity, 1987, (Romanian edit.) 2004, Wohin marschiert China?, 1991, Evidence for Faith: Deciding the God Question, 1991, Giant in Chains: China Today and Tomorrow, 1994, Law and Morality: Friends or Foes?, 1994, Jésus: La Raison Rejoint L'Histoire, 1995; author: (with C.E.B. Cranfield and David Kilgour) Christians in the Public Square, 1996; author: Conflicts of Law, 1997, The Transcendent Holmes, 2000, The Repression of Evangelism in Greece, 2001, Tractatus Logico-Theologicus, 2002, Christ Our Advocate, 2002, History, Law and Christianity, 2002, Heraldic Aspects of the German Reformation, 2003, The Church: Blessing or Curse?, 2004; editor: Lippincott's Evangelical Perspectives, 7 vols., 1970-72, 1970—72, International Scholars Directory, 1973, Simon Greenleaf Law Rev., 7 vols., 1981—88, Global Jour. Classical Theology, 1998—; contbg. editor: Christianity Today, 1965—84, New Oxford Review, 1993—95; author: (films) Is Christianity Credible, 1968, In Search of Noah's Ark, 1977, Defending the Biblical Gospel (11 videocassette series), 1985, (TV series) Christianity on Trial, 1987—93; contbr. articles to acad., theol., legal encys. and jours., chapters to books. Nat. Luth. Edni. Conf. fellow, 1959-60; Can. Council postdoctoral sr. research fellow, 1963-64; Am. Assn. Theol. Schs. faculty fellow, 1967-68; recipient Angel award Nat. Religious Broadcasters, 1989, 90, 92, Patriarch's Medal, Romanian Orthodox Church, 2003. Fellow Trinity Coll. (Newburgh, Ind.), Royal Soc. Arts (Eng.), Victoria Inst. (London) (hon. v.p.; essay prize 2003-04), Soc. Advanced Legal Studies (U.K.), Acad. Internat. des Gourmets et des Traditions Gastronomiques (Paris), Am. Sci. Affiliation (nat. philosophy sci. and history sci. commn. 1966-70); mem. ALA, European Acad. Arts, Scis. and Humanities (corr. mem., Paris), Acad. Lit. France (titulary mem.), Lawyers' Christian Fellowship (hon. v.p. 1995—), Nat. Conf. U. Profs., Calif. bar Assn. (human rights commn. 1980-83), Internat. Bar Assn., World Assn. Law Profs., Mid. Temple and Lincoln's Inn (barrister mem.), Am. Soc. Internat. Law, Union Internat. des Avocats, Nat. Assn. Realtors, Tolkien Soc. Am., N.Y. C.S. Lewis Soc., Am. Hist. Assn., Soc. Reformation Rsch., Creation Rsch. Soc., Tyndale Fellowship (Eng.), Stair Soc. (Scotland), Presbyn. Hist. Soc. (North Ireland), Heraldry Soc. (advanced cert.), Soc. Genealogists, Irish Geneaol. Soc., Am. Theol. Libr. Assn., Bibliog. Soc. U. Va., Evang. Theol. Soc., Internat. Wine and Food Soc., Soc. des Amis des Arts (Strasbourg), Chaîne des Rôtisseurs (commandeur), Athenaeum (London), Players' Theatre Club (London), Sherlock Holmes Soc. London, Soc. Sherlock Holmes de France (hon.), Club des Casseroles Lasserre (Paris), Club Prosper Montagné (Paris), Ordre des chevaliers du Saint-Sepulcre Byzantin (commandeur), Freeman of City of London, Freeman and Liveryman of Scriveners' Co., Phi Beta Kappa, Phi Kappa Phi, Beta Phi Mu. Mailing: 2 rue de Rome 67000 Strasbourg France Office: No 9 4 Crane Ct Fleet St London EC4A 2EJ England Office Fax: 33-3-88057294. Personal E-mail: 106612.1066@compuserve.com.

MONTGOMERY, JOSEPH WILLIAM, financial consultant; m. Linda Montgomery; children: Joseph, Madeline. BBA, Coll. William and Mary, Williamsburg, Va., 1974. CFP; cert. portfolio mgr. Account exec. Wheat, First Securities, Inc., Lynchburg, Va., 1975-79, Williamsburg, Va., 1979-81, v.p., investment officer, 1981-82, sr. v.p., investment officer, 1982-90; mng. dir. investments Wells Fargo Advisors (formerly Wachovia Securities), Williamsburg, Va., 1990—, head Optimal Svc. Group. Mem. nat. nominating com. Outstanding Young Am. Program, 1998; bd. dirs. Future Hampton Roads, Inc., 1995—; mem. nat. campaign steering com. Campaign of 4th Century, William & Mary, 1992, United Way Williamsburg, 1993-95; bd. vis., 1995-99; mem. commn. tercentenary observanced Coll. William & Mary, 1992; sec. William & Mary Endowment Assn., 2000-05; mem. nat. campaign steering com. William & Mary, 2001; mem. adv. coun. Peninsula White Sox, 1986; bd. dirs. Nat. Conf. Christians & Jews, peninsula chpt., 1986-91; mem. Williamsburg Cmty. Health Found., 1998; dir., treas. Franklin & Gladys Clark Found.; mem. Greater Williamsburg Cmty. Trust, 1999-; mem. Jamestown Yorktown Found., 1999-, v.p., 2000, sr. v.p., 2001; bd. trustees Hamptons Rds. Acad., 2003-; mem. nat. adv. coun. Colonial Williamsburg, 2006-; mem. adv. com. Va. Retirement System, 2001-05. Named one of Top 300 Fin. Advisors in Country, Worth Mag., 1998, Top 100 Fin. Advisors, Worth Mag., 1999-, Top 10 Ace Advisers, Ticker Mag., 2000, Nation's 100 Most Exclusive Wealth Advisors, 2004, Worth Mag., Top Ranked Teams in Am. Rsch. Mag., 2004, 05, 06, 07, 08, Top 100 Brokers Barron's Mag., 2004-, Top 100 Wealth Advisors Worth Mag., 2005, 06, 07; named to Broker Hall of Fame, Rsch. mag., 1996, The Chancellor's Cir., Coll. William and Mary, 1998; recipient Best Brokers in Am. award Reg. Rep. Mag., 2002, Am. Top 50 Brokers award Reg. Rep. Mag., 2003, 05, Top Wirehouse Rep. Am., 2007, 08; named State of Va. Top Fin. Advisor Va. Bus. Mag., 2005-08, 09; featured advisor The Winner's Cir. Book, 2002, Winner's Cir. IV Book, 2005. Mem. Internat. Assn. Fin. Planning, Inst. Cert. Fin. Planners, Investment Mgmt. Cons. Found., 1998, Soc. of Alumni William & Mary (pres. 1992, treas. 1991, sec. 1990, bd. dirs. 1989, Alumni Medallion 1996, Wachovia Way award, 2004). Office: Wells Fargo Advisors 428 McLaws Cir Williamsburg VA 23185 Office Phone: 757-220-1782.

MONTGOMERY, KAREN E., retired library and information scientist; b. Madison, Wis., May 25, 1939; d. Guerdon Morris and Mildred Nelson Matthews; m. William Darrell Montgomery, June 17, 1961; children: Anne Elizabeth, Jon Nelson. BA in English Edn., St. Olaf Coll., 1961; postgrad., U. Wis., River Falls, 1977—79. Cataloging asst. U. Calif. Libr., Berkeley, 1962; circulation supr. U. Minn. Libr., Mpls., 1963—64; libr. So. St. Paul (Minn.) Pub. Schs., 1964—65; libr. asst. Am. Bankers Assn., NYC, 1965—66; choir dir. Ezekiel Luth. Ch., River Falls; owner, technician Piano Works, River Falls, 1980—95; asst. cataloger U. Wis. Libr., River Falls, 1989—2005; ret., 2005. Mem. River Falls Pub. Libr. Found. Bd., 2002—, v.p., 2005—. Mem., treas. River Falls Pub. Sch. Band Boosters, 1982—87; treas. St. Croix Valley Summer Theatre Friends, River Falls; mem. Cmty. Arts Base, River Falls, 1999—. Mem.: AAUW (pres. River Falls Br. 1995—97, Wis. state bd. 1995—97, treas. River Falls Br. 1997—2002, Wis. state bd. 2003—04, pres. River Falls Br. 2005—07, fin. v.p Wis. 2006—), Luth. Office Pub. Policy WI Coun., Wis. Assn. Acad. Librs., Wis. Libr. Assn. Democrat. Evangelical Lutheran. Avocations: gardening, reading, volunteering, antiques, interior decorating. Home: 75 Woodridge Dr East River Falls WI 54022

MONTGOMERY, LANI LYNN, art educator; b. Oceanside, NY, Sept. 24, 1950; d. Warren Andrew and Lucy Marie; m. Bruce Montgomery, Dec. 18, 1976; children: Colin, Kirstin, Kerrin. AA, Suffolk County C.C., NY, 1972; BA, Dowling Coll., Oakdale, NY, 1976; MA, Montclaire State U., NJ, 1997. Tchr. art Bridgewater-Raritan Schs., NJ, Abington Sch. Dist., Pa. Recipient Disting. Tchr. award, Bridgewater-Raritan Schs., 2003, Golden Apple award, 1990, 1993. Fellow: Nat. Art Edn. Assn., NJ Art Edn. Assn.; mem.: NEA, Am. Canoe Assn. (instr. 1999—). Episcopalian. Avocations: kayaking, white-water rafting, cross country skiing, bicycling, hiking.

MONTGOMERY, LARRY (R. LAWRENCE MONTGOMERY), retail executive; b. 1949; BS in Math., Ferris State U., Mich., 1969. Pres., CEO Black's divsn. Allied Store Corp., 1985-87; sr. v.p., dir. stores, gen. mdse. mgr. Softlines, L.S. Ayres divsn. May Dept. Stores, 1987-88; sr. v.p., dir. stores Kohl's Corp., Menomonee Falls, Wis., 1988-93, exec. v.p., 1993-96, vice chmn., 1996—2000, CEO, 1999—2002, chmn., CEO, 2002—08, chmn., 2008—09. Bd. dirs. Kohl's Corp., 1994—. Republican. Office: Kohls Corp N56 W17000 Ridgewood Dr Menomonee Falls WI 53051-5660 Office Phone: 262-703-7000.*

MONTGOMERY, LYNN MARIE, educational consultant; b. Faribault, Minn., July 13, 1955; d. Wilford C. and Marian Margaret Campbell; m. Daniel Dale Montgomery, June 12, 1976; children: Kristi Lynn, Ryan Lee. BS, Coll. of St. Benedict, St. Joseph, Minn., 1976; MA, U. St. Thomas, St. Paul, 1994. Elem. tchr. Anoka-Hennepin # 11, Coon Rapids, Minn., 1977-98; exec. dir. Assn. Tchr. Educators, Reston, Va., 1998—2003; tchg. and learning specialist Anoka-Hennepin, Coon Rapids, Minn., 2003—05, asst. dir. for student svcs., 2005—. Greater Minn. facilitator Destination Imagination, 1999-2007, Odyssey of the Mind, 1986-98; chair Adams Environ. Edn. Com., Minn., 1994—. Mem. AAUW, ASCD, Assn. Tchr. Educators (pres. 1998-99, Disting. Clinician

1995, Pres.'s Svc. award 1997), Minn. Assn. Tchr. Educators (bd. dirs. 1990-2000), Anoka-Hennepin Edn. Found. (bd. dirs. 1995-2000). Office: Anoka Hennepin 11 11299 Hanson Blvd Minneapolis MN 55433

MONTGOMERY, MICHAEL DAVIS, research and development company executive, real estate investor; b. San Luis Obispo, Calif., June 4, 1936; s. Harold Ray and Elva Dee (Davis) M.; m. Rita Martin, Dec. 28, 1957 (div. Sept. 1975); children: Jeanne, Gwen, Michele. MSEE, Stanford U., 1959; PhD, U. N.Mex., 1967. Group leader Max Planck Inst. for Astrophysics, Munich, 1974-76; group leader advanced concepts Los Alamos (N.Mex.) Nat. Labs., 1976-83; program mgr. for simulation Maxwell Labs. Inc., San Diego, 1983-84, dep. for DNA programs, 1984-85, v.p. rsch. and devel., 1986-91, sr. v.p. applied tech., 1991-92, sr. cons., 1992—97; owner Casa Del Mar Inn, Santa Barbara, Calif., 1991-97; real estate investor Montgomery Investments, LLC, 1997—. Owner and cons. All Santa Fe Reservations Assoc., 1999—2005. Assoc. editor Jour. Geophys. Research; contbr. articles to sci. jours. Served to lt. comdr. USN, 1959-62. Recipient (charter) Sr. Scientist award Alexander Von Humboldt Found., 1972. Mem. AAAS, Am. Phys. Soc., Phi Beta Kappa, Sigma Xi, Tau Beta Pi. Avocation: amateur radio. Home and Office: 872 Muirfield Dr Oceanside CA 92058 Home Phone: 760-231-9225. Personal E-mail: mikedmont@cox.net.

MONTGOMERY, MIKE, men's college basketball coach; b. Long Beach, Calif., Feb. 27, 1947; m. Sarah Montgomery; children: John, Anne. BA in Phys. Edn., Long Beach State U., Calif., 1968; MS in Phys. Edn., Colo. State U., 1976. Asst. coach U. Fla. Gators, The Citadel Bulldogs, Colo. State U. Rams, USCG Acad., Boise State U. Broncos, U. Mont. Grizzlies, 1975—77, head coach, 1977—86, Stanford U. Cardinal, Calif., 1986—2004, asst. to athletic dir., 2007—08; head coach Golden State Warriors, 2004—06, U. Calif. Golden Bears, 2008—. Head coach USA Basketball 22-and-Under Select Team, 1996; asst. coach USA Basketball, 2002. Named Devel. Coach of Yr., USA Basketball, 1996, US Olympic Com. 1996, Pac-10 Coach of Yr. 1999, 2000, 03, 04, Nat. Coach of Yr. Basketball Times 2000, 04; named to Long Beach State Hall of Fame; recipient John R. Wooden Legends of Coaching Lifetime Achievement award, 2004. Office: U Calif c/o Dept Athletics University Ave Berkeley CA 94720

MONTGOMERY, REX, biochemist, educator; b. Halesowen, Eng., Sept. 4, 1923; came to U.S., 1948, naturalized, 1963; s. Fred and Jane (Holloway) M.; m. Barbara Winifred Price, Aug. 9, 1948 (dec.); children: Ian, David, Jennifer, Christopher. BSc, U. Birmingham, Eng., 1943, PhD, 1946, DSc, 1963. Rsch. assoc. U. Minn., 1951-55; mem. faculty U. Iowa, Iowa City, 1955—2005, prof. biochemistry, 1963—2005, assoc. dean U. Iowa Coll. Medicine, 1974-95, v.p. rsch., 1989-90, prof. emeritus, 2005—. Vis. prof. Nat. Australian U., 1969-70; mem. physiol. chemistry study sect. NIH, 1968-72; mem. drug devel. contract rev. com., 1975-87; chmn. com. biol. chemistry NAS, 1961-64; pesticide and fertilizer adv. bd. Iowa Dept. Agr., 1990-91; bd. dirs. Wallace Tech. Transfer Found., 1989-93; chmn. bd. dirs. Neurotron Inc., 1990-95; mem. rsch. com. Iowa Corn Promotion Bd., 1995-2001; rsch. dir. Biotech. Byproducts Consortium, 1989—; cons. in field. Author: Chemical Production of Lactic Acid, 1949, Chemistry of Plant Gums and Mucilages, 1959, Quantitative Problems in Biochemical Sciences, 2d edit., 1976, Biochemistry: A Case-Orientated Approach, 6th edit., 1996; mem. editl. adv. bd. Carbohydrate Rsch., 1968-80; mem. editl. bd. Molecular Biotherapy, 1988-92; contbr. articles to profl. jours. Postdoctoral fellow Ohio State U., 1948-49; fellow Sugar Research Found., Dept. Agr., 1949-51 Fellow: Royal Soc. Chemistry. Home: 1 Oaknoll Ct Iowa City IA 52246-5168 Office: U Iowa Coll Medicine Dept Biochemistry Iowa City IA 52242 Business E-Mail: rex-montgomery@uiowa.edu.

MONTGOMERY, ROBERT AVERY, transplant surgeon; b. Buffalo, Jan. 22, 1960; MD, U. Rochester, 1987; PhD, Oxford U., Eng.; DSc honoris causa, St. Lawrence U. Intern John Hopkins Hosp., Balt., 1987—88, resident, 1988—89, fellow, 1997, asst. surgeon, 1995—97; assoc. prof. surgery John Hopkins Univ. and Hosp., Balt., dir., Incompatible Kidney Transplant Program, chief, divsn. transplantation, dir., Comprehensive Transplant Ctr., 2003—. Pres., med. advisor Montgomery Heart Found. for Cardiomyopathy. Fulbright Scholar, Thomas J. Watson Fellow. Mem.: Alpha Omega Alpha, Phi Beta Kappa. Achievements include being part of the team that performed the world's first live donor kidney removal using minimally invasive techniques; led the team that performed the first triple domino kidney transplant in 2005; being part of the team the performed historic domino donor quintuple kidney transplant in 2006; led the team that performed the first 6-way kidney transplant in 2008; considered a world's expert on kidney transplantation for highly-sensitized and ABO incompatible patients; led the team that removed a donor kidney through the vagina for the first time in 2009; orchestrated nation's first multi-center six-way kidney transplant involving 12 patients at three different hospitals, nine surgeons and a team of nearly 100 people in 2009. Office: Johns Hopkins Comprehensive Transplant Ctr Incompatible Kidney Transplant Program 720 Rutland Ave Turner 76 Baltimore MD 21205*

MONTGOMERY, ROY DELBERT, retired gas industry executive; b. Indpls., Apr. 24, 1926; s. Lloyd Sipes and Nona Mae (Brummett) M.; m. Barbara Ann Reno, Apr. 21, 1946; children: Stephanie, Rebecca, Jeffrey, Laura. Student, Purdue U., 1950-51; M.E., Internat. Corr. Schs., 1953; A.S. in Mgmt. and Adminstrn., Ind. U., 1973. Registered profl. engr. Ind. Engr. Citizens Gas & Coke Utility, Indpls., 1952-59, supt., 1959-60, dir., 1960-73, exec. dir., 1973-78, v.p., 1978-82, sr. v.p., 1982-86, cons., 1986-88. Mem. adv. bd. AdvancedMgmt. Conf., I.U. Grad. Sch. Bus., 1974—78. Contbr. articles to profl. jours. V.p. exploring Crossroads Am. Coun. Boy Scouts Am., Ind., 1978; corp. rep. Jr. Achievement Ind., 1970-82; pres. Fairway Trace at Pendia I, 1994—, Fairway Trace Home Owners Assn., 1995-99. Recipient Bronze Big Horn award Boy Scouts Am. Explorer Div., Ind., 1978 Mem. Am. Gas Assn. (merit award 1966), Ind. Gas Assn., Scientec Club Ind., Kiwanis. Republican. Avocations: painting, golf, genealogy. Personal E-mail: roydmon@comcast.net.

MONTGOMERY, THEODORE ASHTON, physician; b. LA, Oct. 27, 1923; s. Wayne A. and Hazel (Osmer) M. MD, U. So. Calif., 1947; MPH cum laude, Harvard U., 1955. Diplomate: Am. Bd. Preventive Medicine, Am. Bd. Pediatrics. Intern Los Angeles County Gen. Hosp., 1946-48; intern L.A. Children's Hosp., 1948, resident, 1950-51, St. Louis Children's Hosp., 1951-52; asst. in pediatrics Washington U., St. Louis, 1951-52; instr. pediatrics U. So. Calif., 1952-55; practice medicine specializing in pediatrics, LA, 1952-54; lectr. pub. health U. Calif., Berkeley, 1960-83. Cons. child health Calif. Dept. Pub. Health, 1954-60, chief maternal and perinatal health, 1960-61, acting chief bur. maternal and child health, 1961-63, asst. chief div. preventive med. services, 1963-66, chief, 1966-68, chief preventive medicine program, 1966-69, dep. dir. of Dept., 1969-73; mem. mental retardation projects rev. com. USPHS, 1965-66, charter mem. surgeon gen.'s adv. com. on immunization practices, 1964-66; mem. task force on alcoholism, drug and narcotic abuse Calif. Commn. on Criminal Justice, 1968-70; chief div. disease control Alameda County Health Care Svcs. Agy., 1973-74; cons. maternal and child health Calif. Dept. Health, Berkeley, 1974-78; chief maternal and child health br. No. Calif. Regional Office, Calif. Dept. Health Svcs., 1978-83; WHO fellow med. care adminstrn., Europe, 1966; co-chmn. Calif. Inter-agy. Council on Tb, 1966-72; vice chmn. Calif. Drug Rsch. Adv. Panel, 1969-70; participant White House Conf. Mental Retardation, 1963, White House Conf. on Mental Retardation Cmty. Ctrs., 1965; Gov's. chmn. Calif. Regional Hemodialysis Rev. Com., 1968-73; exec. sec. Gov.'s Population Study Commn., 1966; mem. com. on Tb, Calif. Lung Assn., 1973-74 Author: (with others) Standards and Recommendations for Public Prenatal Care, 1960, Guide to Hearing Testing of School Children, 1961; contbr. articles to med. jours. Bd. dirs. Calif. Interagy. Coun. on Family Planning, 1970-73; chmn. Calif. State Interdepartmental Com. on Food and Nutrition, 1977-79, pres. Clan Montgomery Soc. Internat., 1981-84, regional commr., 1985-91. With M.C. AUS, 1948-50. Fellow Am. Acad. Pediatrics (chmn. Calif. com. Indian health 1973-76, mem. nat. com. on Indian health 1963-79, vice chmn. 1977-79), Am. Pub. Health Assn. (chmn. task force on population policy 1971-72); mem. Alpha Epsilon Delta, Delta Omega. Home: 85 Wildwood Gdns Piedmont CA 94611-3831

MONTGOMERY, THOM MATHEW, health program administrator, counselor; b. Delaware, Okla., Dec. 30, 1942; s. Francis Thomas and Ellen Grace (Whelan) M.; m. Dinah Lee Hicks, Feb. 4, 1961 (div. 1964); children, Laura Diane, Raymond Hunter; m. A.N.D. Miller (dec. 2006). Degree, Highlands U., 1966; student, Tulsa U., 1961-64, U. Calif., Irvine, 1980-81, Glenn U., Dublin, Ireland, 1993—2002. Brokerage mgr. John Hancock Life Ins. Co., Boston, 1964-70; mng. editor Renown Publs., Reseda, Calif., 1970-77; publs. dir. Am. Pub. Health Found., Corona Del Mar, Calif., 1977-79; program adminstr. Life Plus Martin Luther Hosp., Anaheim, Calif., 1979-92; dir. rsch. Brookside Inst., Irvine, Calif., 2001—. Pres. Montgomery Counseling Assocs., Fullerton, 1986—. Author: Ennobled Blood: The Heiresses of Monkstown Castle, 2002, Naltrexone: Pulling Back the Curtain, 2004; contbr. articles to profl. jours. Founding mem. Task Force on Alcohol & Drug Abuse for Disabled, Orange County, 1981, Sobriety Faire, Orange County, 1982; bd. dirs. Mid Valley Cmty. Police Coun., San Fernando Valley Employee Assistance Programs. Fellow Am. Pub. Health Found.; mem. Nat. Assn. Alcohol and Drug Abuse Counselors, Internat. Assn. Alcohol and Drug Abuse Counselors, Calif. Assn. Alcohol and Drug Abuse Counselors. Republican. Presbyn. Avocations: chess, hiking, swimming, poetry, drama. Home: 35167 El Diamante Dr Wildomar CA 92595 Office: 16587 Brookhurst St Fountain Valley CA 92708 Office Phone: 310-413-4672.

MONTGOMERY, WILL S., lawyer; b. Dallas, Jan. 8, 1958; BA, Stanford U., 1980, MA, 1981; JD, U. Chgo., 1984. Bar: Tex. 1984. Shareholder Jenkens & Gilchrist, P.C., Dallas, 1992—2007, firm leader litig. practice group; ptnr. Hunton & Williams LLP, Dallas, 2007—. Mem.: ABA, Dallas Bar Assn., Tex. State Bar. Office: Hunton & Williams LLP Ste 3700 1445 Ross Ave Dallas TX 75202 Office Phone: 214-468-3361. Office Fax: 214-468-3599. Business E-Mail: wmontgomery@hunton.com.

MONTGOMERY, WILLIAM ADAM, lawyer; b. Chgo., May 22, 1933; s. John Rogerson and Helen (Fyke) Montgomery; m. Jane Fauver, July 28, 1956 (div. Dec. 1967); children: Elizabeth, William, Virginia; m. Deborah Stephens, July 29, 1972; children: Alex, Katherine. AB, Williams Coll., 1955; LLB, Harvard U., 1958. Bar: D.C. 1958, Ill. 1959, U.S. Ct. Appeals (7th cir.) 1959, U.S. Supreme Ct. 1977. Atty. civil divsn., appellate sect. Dept. Justice, Washington, 1958—60; assoc. Schiff Hardin LLP, Chgo., 1960—68, ptnr., 1968—93, 1999—; v.p., gen. counsel State Farm Ins. Cos., Bloomington, Ill., 1994—97, sr. v.p., gen. counsel, 1997—99. Author: (39 corp. practice series) Tying Arrangements, 1984; co-author: Insurance Antitrust and Unfair Trade Practices Law, 2002; contbr. articles to profl. jours. Fellow: Am. Coll. Trial Lawyers; mem.: ABA (coun. antitrust sect. 1989—92), Seventh Cir. Bar Assn. (pres. 1988—89), Chgo. Bar Assn., Lawyers Club Chgo. Avocations: skiing, woodturning. Office: Schiff Hardin LLP 6600 Sears Tower Chicago IL 60606 Business E-Mail: wmontgomery@schiffhardin.com.

MONTGOMERY, WILLIAM E., biology professor, department chairman; s. Leo S. and Violet A. Montgomery; m. Susan K. Hershey. MS, U. Md., coll. Pk., 1969. Prof. biology Coll. Southern Md., LaPlata, 1971—83, chair, biol., phys. sci., 1983—. Office: Coll Southern Md Box 910 La Plata MD 20646 Business E-Mail: billm@csmd.edu.

MONTGOMERY, WILLIAM LAYTON, musician, educator; b. Waco, Tex., Mar. 28, 1934; s. Layton Edmond and Fey Ruth (Fomby) M.; children: Layton Howard, Scott Lewis, Claudia Cathleen. B Mus. Edn., Cornell Coll. Iowa, 1953; postgrad., Curtis Inst. Music, 1953-54; MusM, Cath. U. Am., Washington, 1957, PhD, 1975. Prin. flutist Nat. Gallery of Art Orch., Washington, 1965-88, Theater Chamber Players of Kennedy Ctr., Washington, 1968—2004; prof. music U. Md., College Park, 1964, chair instrumental, wind and percussion divsns., 1972—91, dir. grad. studies, 1991—99, mem. univ. senate exec. com., 2005—07, chair univ. senate core com., 2005—07, chair univ. senate, 2007—08. Bd. advisors Flute Talk Mag., Northbrook, Ill., 1982-95, Instrumentalist Mag., Northbrook, 1978-95; adv. cons. Libr. Congress, Music Div., Washington, 1978, 79, 84; mem. Fulbright selection com. in music, 1995-98. Prin. flutist U.S. Marine Band, 1954-63. Mem. Nat. Flute Assn. (pres. 1976-77, program chair 1976, 1985), Flute Soc. Washington (pres. 1978-80, 82-84), Arts Club Washington (music chmn. 1990—, prodr. weekly Friday noon concert series 1992—). Home: 4616 Harvard Rd College Park MD 20740-3753 Office: Univ Md Sch Music College Park MD 20742-0001 Business E-Mail: wlm@umd.edu.

MONTILLA, VICTOR JAVIER, broadcast executive; b. Santurce, PR, May 26, 1970; s. Fernando J. Montilla and Mitza Elena Torres; m. Mari Carmen Serrano, Aug. 26, 1995; children: Victor Alfonso, Paola Sofia. BA in Telecom., Loyola U., New Orleans, 1992. Pres. PR Corp. Pub. Broadcasting, San Juan, 2005—. V.p. NATAS Suncoast Chpt., Miami, Fla., 2001—06. Dir. Latino Pub. Radio Consortium, Denver, 2007—. Recipient Governor's award, NATAS, 2006; named TV Exec. of Yr., Ad Notas, 2006. Mem.: Pub. Broadcasters Mgmt. Assn., Puerto Rican Assn. Radio Broadcasters, Nat. Assn. Broadcasters, Nat. Assn. Tv Programming Execs., PR Conv. Bur., PR Chamber Commerce, Sales & Mktg. Exces. Assn. PR, Corp. Pub. Broadcasting Pub. Awareness Initiative Bd. Achievements include Puerto Rico's inclusion in the NATAS. Office: PR Corporation Public Broadcasting Ave Hostos 570 Urb Baldrich San Juan PR 00918-9918 Office Fax: 787-753-9846. Business E-Mail: vmontilla@cprdp.gobierno.pr.

MONTJOY, RICHARD WILSON, II, lawyer; b. Greenwood, Miss., Oct. 15, 1953; s. Paul Dyche and Dorothy (Sabin) M.; married. BA, U. Miss., 1975, JD, 1978. Bar: Miss. 1978, U.S. Dist. Ct. (no. and so. dists.) Miss. 1978, U.S. Ct. Appeals (5th and 11th cir.) 1978, U.S. Ct. Appeals (10th cir.) 1985, U.S. Supreme Ct. 1984. Mem. Brunini, Grantham, Grower & Hewes, Jackson, Miss., 1978—. Articles editor U. Miss. Law Rev., 1977-78. V.p. bd. dirs. Grace House, Inc., 1988—98; jr. warden St. Andrew's Cathedral, 2001—03, sr. warden, 2003—05, chair search com., 2006—07; corp. mem. St. Andrew's Episcopal Sch., 2002—08, bd. mem., 2009—; wedding lawyers Bus. Corp. Commercial Chambers USA, 2008, Energy Chambers USA, 2009. Recipient Corp. Commercial award, Chambers USA Leading Lawyers Bus., 2008, Energy award, 2009. Fellow Am. Bar Found.; mem. ABA (bd. govs. 1997-2000, nominating com. 1996-97, house of dels. 1990-92, 1995-97, 2000, sec. energy, environ. and resources budget officer, coun. 1995-96, strategic planning com., energy policy com., pub. svc. task force, ADR com. oil and natural gas com., standing com. on CLE, young lawyers divsn., assembly clk. 1987-88, assembly spkr. 1988-89, fellow, dir. mem. suport network, sec. environ., energy, resources, budget dir., 2001-03), Miss. Bar Assn. (bd. dirs. young lawyers divsn. 1986-88), Jackson Young Lawyers Assn., Inc. (bd. dirs. 1980-82, treas. 1984-85, sec. 1985-86, pres.-elect 1986-87, pres. 1987-88), Hinds County Bar Assn. (bd. dirs. 1987-89), Inst. Profls. Taxation Chambers USA (Am. Leading Lawyers Bus. Energy and Natural Resources), Omicron Delta Kappa, Phi Kappa Phi. Episcopalian. Avocations: golf, travel. Home: 2218 Sheffield Dr Jackson MS 39211-5852 Office Phone: 601-960-6856. Business E-Mail: wmontjoy@brunini.com.

MONTO, ARNOLD SIMON, epidemiology educator; b. Bklyn., Mar. 22, 1933; s. Jacob and Mildred (Kaplan) M.; m. Ellyne Gay Polsky, June 15, 1958; children: Sarah D. Monto Maniaci, Jane E., Richard L., Stephen A. BA in Zoology, Cornell U., Ithaca, NY, 1954; MD, Cornell U., NYC, 1958. Diplomate Am. Coll. Epidemiology. Intern, asst. resident in medicine Vanderbilt U. Hosp., Nashville, 1958—60; USPHS postdoctoral fellow in infectious disease Stanford U. Med. Ctr., Palo Alto, Calif., 1960—62; mem. staff virus diseases sect. mid. Am. rsch. unit Nat. Inst. Allergy and Infectious Disease, Panama, 1962—65; assoc. prof. U. Mich. Sch. Pub. Health, Ann Arbor, 1965—76, prof., 1976—, chmn. dept. population planning and internat. health, 1993—97, dir. Ctr. for Population Planning, 1993—97, dir. U. Mich. Bioterrorism Preparedness Initiative, 2002—04. Vis. scientist Clin. Rsch. Ctr., Northwick Park Hosp., Harrow, Eng., 1976; scholar-in-residence bd. on sci. and tech. for internat. devel. NAS and Inst. Medicine, Washington, 1983-84; vis. scientist div. communicable diseases WHO, Geneva, 1986-87; mem. pulmonary diseases adv. com. Nat. Heart, Lung and Blood Inst., Bethesda, Md., 1979-83; mem. nat. adv. coun. Nat. Inst. Allergy and Infectious Diseases, Bethesda, 1989-93; mem. WHO Influenza Pandemic Task Force, 2006—. Contbr. articles to med. jours. Recipient career devel. award NIH. Fellow Am. Coll. Epidemiology, Infectious Diseases Soc. Am.; mem. APHA (governing coun. 1978-80), Am. Epidemiol. Soc. (pres. 2004-05). Achievements include research on respiratory viral infections in the community; demonstration of effectiveness of influenza vaccine in severe disease in the elderly; prevention of spread of influenza virus and treatment of illness, occurrence, causes and treatment of common cold. Office: U Mich Sch Pub Health I 109 Observatory St Ann Arbor MI 48109-2029 Office Phone: 734-764-5453. Business E-Mail: asmonto@umich.edu.

MONTONE, KATHLEEN T., pathologist; MD, Pa. State U., Hershey, 1989. Diplomate Am. Bd. Pathology, 1993. Asst. prof. U. Pa., Phila., 1993—98, assoc. prof., 2006—; staff pathologist Abington Meml. Hosp., Pa., 1998—2005. Office: Univ Pa 3400 Spruce St 6 Founders Philadelphia PA 19104 Office Fax: 215-349-5910. Business E-Mail: kmontone@mail.med.upenn.edu.

MONTOYA, GONZALO, chemical engineer, educator; b. Lima, Peru, Aug. 27, 1966; s. Jorge Montoya and Ines Ramsay; m. Wendy Baldwin. MA, U. Wash., Seattle, 2004. Cert. chem. engring., U. Simon Bolivar, 1992. Lectr. Seattle U., 2005—. Office: Seattle Univ 901 12th Ave Seattle WA 98122 Business E-Mail: montoyag@seattleu.edu.

MONTOYA, JUAN PABLO, professional race car driver; b. Bogota, Colombia, Sept. 20, 1975; m. Connie Freydell; children: Sebastian, Paulina. Race car driver Formula One Williams, 2001—04, McLaren, 2005—06; race car driver NASCAR Chip Ganassi Racing, 2007—. 2nd pl. Spanish Grand Prix, 2001, 02, European Grand Prix, 2001, 03; 1st pl. Italian Grand Prix, 2001, 05, 2nd pl., 03, Japanese Grand Prix, 2001, Australian Grand Prix, 2002, 03, Malaysian Grand Prix, 2002, 04; 3rd pl. Austrian Grand Prix, 2002, Brit. Grand Prix, 2002, 2nd pl., 03, 1st pl., 05; 2nd pl. German Grand Prix, 2002, 05, 1st pl., 03; 3rd pl. Belgian Grand Prix, 2002; 1st pl. Monaco Grand Prix, 2003, 2nd pl., 06; 3rd pl. Can. Grand Prix, 2003; 2nd pl. French Grand Prix, 2003; 3rd pl. Hungarian Grand Prix, 2003, San Marino Grand Prix, 2004, 06; 1st pl. Brazilian Grand Prix, 2004, 05; 3rd pl. Turkish Grand Prix, 2005; 1st pl. Toyota/Save Mart 350 Infineon Raceway, 2007; 2nd pl. Allstate 400 Indpls. Motor Speedway, 2007. Founder Formula Smiles Found.; goodwill amb. UN. Recipient Lorenzo Bandini trophy, 2002; named Newcomer of Yr., Laureus World Sports Awards, 2002, NASCAR Nextel Cup Rookie of Yr., 2007. Avocations: video games, snowboarding, golf. Mailing: Ganassi Racing 8500 Westmoreland Dr Concord NC 28027

MONTOYA, REGINA T., lawyer; b. Tucumcari, N.Mex., Dec. 25, 1953; d Fred and Rosa (Meraz) M.; m. Paul E. Coggins, June 12, 1976; 1 child, Jessica. BA, Wellesley Coll., 1975; JD, Harvard U., 1979. Bar: Tex. 1979. Law clk. to US Dist. Judge Sarah T. Hughes, Dallas, 1979—80; ptnr. Akin, Gump, Strauss, Hauer & Feld, Dallas, 1980-90; shareholder Godwin, Carlton & Maxwell, Dallas, 1990-93; asst. to pres., dir. Office of Intergovernmental Affairs, Washington D.C., 1993; v.p. Westcott Comm., 1994—95; panelist Between the Lines KERA-TV, 1994; public delegate UN Gen. Assembly, 1998; pres. WORKRules, 1995—2005; CEO New Am. Alliance, 2005—08; sr. v.p., gen. counsel Children's Med. Ctr., Dallas, 2009—. Bd. dirs. Wash. Mut. Inc., 2006-. Trustee Emerita Wellesley Coll.; chair bd. Parkland Found., 2005-09; bd. dirs. Mexican Am. Legal Def. and Ednl. Fund, 2009-. Mem. Student Loan Mktg. Assn. (bd. dirs. 1994-2001). Democrat. Roman Catholic. Office Phone: 214-456-0367. Personal E-mail: rtmontoya@gmail.com. Business E-Mail: regina.montoya@childrens.com.

MONTOYA, VELMA, economist, consultant; b. LA, Apr. 9, 1938; d. Jose Gutierrez and Consuelo (Cavazos) Montoya; m. Earl A. Thompson; 1 child, Bret L. Thompson. BA in Diplomacy and World Affairs, Occidental Coll., 1959, MA in Internat. Rels., 1960; MS in Econs., Stanford U., 1965; PhD in Econs., UCLA, 1977. Asst. prof. econs. Calif. State U., LA, 1965-68; vis. assoc. prof. U. So. Calif., 1979; instr. UCLA, 1981-82; staff economist The Rand Corp., Santa Monica, Calif., 1973-82; asst. dir. for strategy, White House Office of Policy Devel. Exec. Office of the Pres., 1982-83; expert economist Office Regulatory Analysis, OSHA, U.S. Dept. of Labor, 1983-85; dir. of Studies in Pub. Policy and Assoc. Prof. of Political Economy, Sch. of Bus. Mgmt. Chapman U., 1985-87; adj. prof. Sch. Bus. Mgmt. Pepperdine U., 1987-88; pres. Hispanic-Am. Pub. Policy Inst., 1984-90; assoc. prof. fin. Sch. Bus. Adminstrn., Calif. State Poly. U., Pomona, 1988-90; mem. Occupl. Safety and Health Rev. Commn., 1990-97; cons. on regulatory and econ. policy, 1997—. Cons. Urban Inst., 1974, Mexican-Am. Study Project UCLA, 1966, Grad. and Profl. Fellowships to the Office of Post Secondary Edn., U.S. Dept. Edn.; editl. referee Contemporary Policy Issues, Economic Inquiry, Policy Analysis, Jour. Econ. Lit.; discussion leader Am. Assembly on Rels. Between the U.S. and Mex.; pres. del. White House Conf. on Aging, 1981; reader of 1988 proposals for the U.S. Dept Edn. for the Improvement and Reform of Schs. and Tchg.;

rsch. participant U.S. Dept. Edn. Delphi Assessment of Drug Policies for Use in Minority Neighborhoods, 1989; mem. Hispanic adv. panel Nat. Commn. for Employment Policy, 1981-82; lectr. Brookings Inst. Seminars for U.S. Bus. Leaders; bd. adv. Close-Up Found., 1982-83; discussant Western Econ. Assn. Meetings, 1985, 93; bd. adv. Nat. Rehab. Hosp., 1991-94; nat. exec. adv. bd. Harvard Jour. Hispanic Policy, 1993-95; reader proposals for Hispanic Serving Instns., U.S. Dept. Edn., 2001-2004; regional panel to select White House Fellows, 2002—, hon. coun. U. Calif. Press, 2007-. Mem. census adv. com. on hispanic population for 1990 census, 1988—93; mem. adv. com. Senate Rep. Conf. Task Force on Hispanic Affairs, Washington, 1991—; bd. regents U. Calif., 1994—2005; program rev. com. Los Alamos (N.Mex.) Nat. Lab.; mem. steering com. GetSmarter.org, 1998—99; mem. outreach adv. bd. U. Calif., 1998—2005, mem. coun. friends Bancroft Libr. Berkeley, 2005—; commr. Calif. Postsecondary Edn. Commn., 2000—01, 2004—05; mem. Am. Coun. Trustees and Alumni, Inst. Effective Governance Adv. Bd., 2003—, White Ho. Fellows Regional Selection Panel, 2002—; mem. Calif. state adv. com. US Commn. Civil Rights, 2007—. Named One of the 100 U.S. Hispanic Influentials Hispanic Bus. Mag., 1982, 90, 97, Woman of the Yr. Mex.-Am. Oportunity Found., 1983, The East L.A. Com. Union, 1979, one of 80 Elite Hispanic Women, Hispanic Bus. Mag., 2002, 03; recipient Freedom Found. at Valley Forge Honor Econ. Edn. Excellence Cert., 1986, Profl. Achievement award S.E. L.A. Lincoln Club, 2002, Hispanic Leadership award Minorities in Bus. Mag., 2001; Univ. fellow Stanford U., Internat. Rels. fellow Calif. PTA, John Hay Whitney Opportunity fellow; Calif. State Univ. Found. Faculty Rsch. grantee; Marshall scholar, Fulbright scholar. Mem. ASTM (com. on rsch. and tech. planning 1985-87), Am. Econ. Assn. (session chair ann. meetings 1995), Nat. Coun. Hispanic Women (pres. 1997—), Am. Soc. Hispanic Econimists, State Bar of Calif., Calif. State Bar Ct. (exec. com. 1987-89, disciplinary bd. 1986-89), Western Econ. Assn., Indsl. Rsch. Inst. for Pacific Nations (adv. bd. 1988-89), Salesian Boys and Girls Club (bd. dirs. 1989—), Vets. in Com. Svc. (adv. com. 1989-94), Phi Beta Kappa, Omicron Delta Epsilon, Phi Alpha Theta. Home: 6970 Los Tilos Rd Los Angeles CA 90068-3107 Office Phone: 213-427-8048.

MONTROLL, ANDREW H., lawyer, councilman; b. Washington, Apr. 11, 1957; s. Elliott W. and Shirley A. Montroll; m. Barbara Anne Komons, July 7, 1996; children: Sarah D., Elliott G. BS in Optics, U. Rochester, 1975—80, MS in Optics, 1980—81; JD summa cum laude, Vt. Law Sch., 1986—89. Bar: Vt. Supreme Ct. 1990. Engr. MRJ, Inc, Oakton, Va., 1981—86; jud. law clk. Vt. Supreme Ct., Montpelier, 1989—90; atty. Burak & Anderson, Burlington, 1990—96; counsel Riser Mgmt. Systems, Burlington, Vt., 1997—2004; atty. Law Offices of Andrew H. Montroll, Burlington, 2004—. Editor in chief The Vermont Law Review, 1988—89; hearing officer Vt. Dept. Edn., 2006—. Author: (book) Critical Connections, Wired for Profit. Mem. Chittenden County Met. Planning Orgn., 2005—; pres. Burlington City Coun., 2001—05, city councilor, 1994—; mem. Bd. Civil Authority, Burlington, 1994—; examiner Vt. Bd. Bar Examiners, Montpelier. Recipient Vt. Legal Scholar, Vt. Law Sch., 1989. Achievements include patents for Monolithic semiconductor laser and optical amplifier; semiconductor laser and optical amplifier. Avocation: photography. Office: Law Offices Andrew H Montroll 200 Church St Burlington VT 05401

MONTRONE, PAUL MICHAEL, former scientific instruments company executive; b. Scranton, Pa., May 8, 1941; s. Angelo H. and Beatrice M. (Giancini) M.; m. Sandra G. Gaudenzi, May 30, 1963; children: Michele Marie Cogan, Angelo Henry, Jerome Lawrence. BS in Accounting magna cum laude, U. Scranton, 1962; PhD in Fin., Econs. and Ops. Research, Columbia U., 1965. Ops. analyst Office Sec. Def., Washington, 1965-67; exec. v.p., chief fin. officer Wheelabrator-Frye Inc., Hampton, NH, 1970-83; exec. v.p. Signal Cos., Inc., La Jolla, Calif., 1983-85, pres. Engineered Products Group Hampton, NH, 1983-85; exec. v.p. fin. and adminstrn. AlliedSignal Inc., Morristown, NJ, 1985-86; pres. The Henley Group Inc., Hampton, NH, 1986-92, bd. dirs.; chmn., CEO Wheelabrator Techs. Inc., Hampton, NH, 1987-90; pres., co-owner The Gen. Chem. Group Inc., 1989-94, chmn. bd., 1994-96; vice chmn. Abex Inc., 1992-95; pres. Fisher Sci. Internat., Inc., Hampton, NH, 1991—98, CEO, 1991—2006, chmn., 1998—2006. Bd. dirs. Waste Mgmt.; mem. adv. bd. Sintokogio, Ltd. Pres. emeritus Met. Opera Assn.; bd. dir. Wang Ctr. for Performing Arts; dir. & treas. Found. for NIH; trustee Healthcare Leadership Council; mem. bd. overseers The Bus. Roundtable, Bus. Sch. Columbia U., N.Y.C.; adv. com. Consumer Protection and Quality in the Health Care Industry, Washington. Capt. U.S. Army, 1965-67. Mem.: Brook, University (N.Y.C.); Bald Peak Colony (Melvin Village, N.H.); Lyford Cay (Nassau, Bahamas). Roman Catholic.

MONTROSE-GRAEM, DOUGLASS, poet-painter, music-man, museum director, bank executive; b. Budapest, Hungary, July 6, 1924; came to U.S., 1954, naturalized, 1965; s. Hugh Merton and Ellen Charlotte (Baroness Podmaniczky) G.; children: Robert, Christopher, Anabel, Ian, Isis Marina. BA, Piarist Fathers Coll., 1944; MBA, NY Inst. Fin. (now NYU), 1958. Lic. real estate broker Acad. Real Estate Denver, 1975. Various position through ptnr. R.W. Pressprich; ptnr. Mitchell, Hutchins & Co., NYC; co-founder William D. Witter Inc., NYC; founder, dir. Turner Mus., Denver, 1973—. Bank owner, Lafayette, Colo.; organizer, govt. securities com. Investment Assn. NY, 1955; non-exec. dir. Midwestern Fin., Denver, exec. bd. chmn.; organizer Internat. Bank Colo.; bd. dirs. Turner Soc. London. Author: Durer and Domjan, 1972, Turner's Cosmic Optimism, 1990, Turner's Angels, 1991, Turner's Rainbows, 1992, Turner's Children--So Much Love, 1993, Turner's Powerful Allegories, 1994, Ascendent Turner, 2002, Triple Turner Treat, 2003. Patron H.R.H. The Prince of Wales, 1978—. With Brit. Army, 1942—60. Cited as founder of one of Am.'s 99 Finest Museums, 1973, founder of first virtual art mus. in the world, 2001; recipient Papal Blessing, Pope John 23. Mem.: DAV (life nominated Disabled Am. Vet. of Yr. 2004), St. Andrew's Soc. Colo. (life). Office: Turner Mus PO Box 11073 Sarasota FL 34278-1073 Office Phone: 941-365-1649. Business E-Mail: curator@turnermuseum.org.

MONTROSS, FRANKLIN, IV, (TAD MONTROSS), reinsurance company executive; b. Jan. 12, 1956; s. Franklin and Joan Oliver Montross; m. Laura Lee Eifert, Apr. 20, 1991. BA in Econs., Harvard U., Cambridge, Mass. Joined Gen. Re Corp., Stamford, Conn., 1978, exec. v.p., chief underwriting officer, 2000—01, pres., 2001—08, chmn., CEO, 2008—. Chmn. Herbert Clough, Inc., Ardent, Inc.; mem. Vorstand Cologne Re. Republican. Office: Gen Re Corp 695 E Main St Stamford CT 06904-0300 Office Phone: 203-328-5575. Office Fax: 203-328-6423.

MONTS, STEPHEN LEE, retired chemistry professor; b. Tuscola, Ill., Oct. 28, 1949; BS, Northern Ill. U., DeKalb, 1971, MS in Chemistry, 1974; PhD, Ill. State U., Normal, 1985. Chemistry instr. Kankakee CC, Ill., 1974—84, chairperson, math., sci., and engring. divsn., 1984—2008. Fin. com. chairperson Asbury United Meth. Ch., Kankakee, 2008. Mem.: Am. Chem. Soc. (chairperson Joliet sect. 1987). Home: 351 Kristina Dr Bourbonnais IL 60914

MONTY, JULIE ANNE, language educator; b. Sacramento, Jan. 4, 1965; d. Dewey Edwin and Dorothy May Monty; m. Gregory Hansell Monty, Sept. 28, 1996; children: Matisse Ondine, Camille Roxanne; m. Farzad Sabet (div.); 1 child, Hannah Meenou Sabet. PhD in French and Francophone Lit., U. Tex., Austin, 2006. Asst. instr. U. Tex., 1998—2003; asst. prof. French U. Ctrl. Ark., Conway, 2007—. Film Festival grant, French Am. Cultural Exch., 2008. Mem.: MLA, Ark. Fgn. Lang. Tchrs. Assn., Am. Assn. Tchrs. French, Women French. Avocations: travel, reading, yoga. Home: 4665 Sawgrass Cove Conway AR 72034 Office: Univ Ctrl Ark 201 Donaghey Ave Conway AR 72035 Business E-Mail: jmonty@uca.edu.

MONZON, CARLOS MANUEL, physician; s. Carlos Manuel and Amparo (Letona) Monzon; children: Carlos Rodolfo, Juan Pablo. MD, U. San Carlos, Guatemala, 1976; MSc, U. Minn. Campus, 1982. Diplomate Am. Bd. Pediat., Am. Bd. Pediat. Hematology and Oncology. Resident in pediat. U. San Carlos, 1976-77, U. Mo., Columbia, 1977-80; fellow in pediat. hematology and oncology Mayo Grad. Sch. Medicine, Rochester, Minn., 1980-82; instr. pediat. U. Mo., Columbia, 1982-83, asst. prof. child health, 1983-89; clin. asst. prof. in pediatrics Kansas U. Sch. Medicine, Kans. City, 1992—2003. Contbr. articles to med. jours. Recipient Fritz Kenny Meml. award in pediat. rsch. Midwest Soc. Pediat. Rsch., 1981. Fellow Am. Acad. Pediat. Home: 14201 Melrose St Overland Park KS 66221 Office: 20375 W 151st St Olathe KS 66061-7218

MOOD, FRANCIS P., JR., lawyer, utilities executive; BA, The Citadel, 1960, LLD (hon.), 1985; LLB, U. Va., 1963; LLD (hon.), U. SC, 2004. Bar: SC 1963. Ptnr. Haynsworth Sinkler Boyd, Columbia, SC, 1967—2004, pres., 1984—92; sr. v.p., gen. counsel, asst. sec. SCANA Corp., Columbia, SC, 2005—. Permanent mem. Judicial Conf., US Ct. Appeals (4th cir.); interim dean Univ. SC Sch. Law, 2003; chmn. SC Bd. Law Examiners, 1973—82. Mem. bd. vis. The Citadel, 1973—79, 1994—2000, chmn., 1997—2000; bd. dir. The Citadel Develop. Found., 1980—88, 1990—94, 2001—, pres., 1982—86; mem. Univ. SC Sch. Law Partnership Bd., 1991—94, pres., 1991—93; mem. Ctrl. Carolina Cmty. Found., 1992—98, pres., 1995—97; bd. dir. Liberty Fellowship, 2004—, Columbia Urban League. Served US Army, 1964—66. Mem.: ABA, State Bar SC, Richland County Bar Assn. Office: SCANA Corp 1426 Main St Columbia SC 29218

MOODY, DIXON MCGUIRE, radiologist; b. Tyler, Tex., Jan. 12, 1937; s. Dwight Lyman Moody and Helen Blaine McGuire; m. Lucinda L. Blitz, Aug. 15, 1964; children: Abigail Ann (Moody) Sinwell, Susan Eloise (Moody) Prieto, Sarah Katherine (Moody) Bialas. MD, U. of Tex. Southwestern, Dallas, 1963. Diplomate Diagnostic Radiology Am. Bd. of Radiology, 1971, Neuroradiology Am. Bd. of Radiology, 1995. Resident physician Stanford U. Sch of Medicine, Palo Alto, Calif., 1963—70; asst. physician Cornell U. Sch of Medicine, NYC, 1970—71; asst. prof. U. of N.Mex Sch Medicine, Albuquerque, 1971—73; prof. and chief of neuroradiology Wake Forest U. Sch. Medicine, Winston-Salem, NC. Mem. Nat. Adv. Coun. NINDS, NIH, Bethesda, Md., 1994—97, Ctr. for Sci. Rev., NIH, Bethesda, Md., 1998—2004; mem., sci. program com. Radiol. Soc. of N.Am., Oak Brook, Ill. Capt. US Army, 1966—67. Decorated Bronze Star Medal US Army; recipient Established Investigator, Clin. Sci. Award, Wake Forest U. Sch. of Medicine, 2002; grantee Jacob K Javits Neurosci. Investigator, NIH, 1984—2008, Clin. Hypotheses in Neuroscience Imaging Rsch., Charles A Dana Found., 1996-1999. Fellow: Am. Coll. of Radiology; mem.: Am. Soc. of Neuroradiology (Outstanding Contributions in Rsch. award 2005), Soc. for Neurosci., Radiol. Soc. of N.Am. (Outstanding Rschr. award 2005), Forsyth Country Club, Hillsboro Club, Alpha Omega Alpha. Achievements include research in Brain injury during heart surgery due to fat emboli; brain hemorrhage in neonates due to rupture of veins; dementia due to obstruction of veins and loss of capillaries; significant vascular disease in Alzheimer's brains; cause and prevention of brain injury during cardiopulmonary bypass. Avocation: tennis. Office: Wake Forest University School Medicine Medical Center Blvd Winston Salem NC 27157-1088 Business E-Mail: dmmoody@wfubmc.edu.

MOODY, JACQUELINE ELAINE, music educator; d. Roberta Anita Foster; m. Christopher Moody, Dec. 29, 1981; children: Dominique Elaine, Crystal Simone. BS, Fisk U., Nashville, 1978; MusM, Boston Conservatory of Music, 1980; EdS, U. of Miami, Coral Gables, Fla., 1992. Tchr. Fla. Dept. of Edn. Music instr. Elaine Sch. of Music, Miami, 1988—; music tchr. Perrine Elem., Miami, 1997—; music prof. Miami Dade Coll., Miami, 2006—. Singer Conn. Opera Co., Hartford, 1982—88, Fla. Grand Opera, Miami, 1989—90. Vol. Sweet Home Missionary Bapt., Perrine, Fla., 2003—06. Recipient Presdl. scholarship, Fisk U., 1974—75, Minority scholarship, U. of Miami, 1988—89, Champion of the Arts award, Nat. Bus. and Profl. Women, 2005; named Educator of Note, Young Patronesses of the Opera, 2000, Outstanding Educator, Delta Sigma Theta, 2000. Mem.: Jack and Jill of Am., Inc (corr.; chaplain, chairperson for children's cluster 2002—), Sigma Alpha Iota (corr.; corr. sec. 1999—2000), Delta Sigma Theta (corr. Outstanding Educator 2000). Democrat. Baptist. Avocations: playing the piano, singing, cooking, travel, sewing. Office: Perrine Elem Sc 8891 SW 168 St Miami FL 33157

MOODY, LIZABETH ANN, lawyer, educator; b. Johnson City, Tenn., July 11, 1934; d. Robert Alexander and Clara Pauline (Fine) M.; m. Alan Paul Buchmann, Sept. 5, 1959. AB, Columbia U., 1956; LLB, Yale U., 1959. Bar: Conn. 1959, Ohio 1960, U.S. Dist. Ct. Conn. 1960, U.S. Supreme Ct. 1977, U.S. Dist. Ct. (no. dist.) Ohio 1961. Assoc. Goldstein & Peck, Bridgeport, Conn., 1959-60, Slough & Slough, Cleve., 1960-61, 63-66, Ginsberg, Guren & Meritt, Cleve., 1962; ptnr. Metzenbaum, Gaines, Finley & Stern, Cleve., 1967-71; assoc. prof. Cleve. State U., 1970-73, prof., 1973-94, interim dean and prof., 1987-88; vis. prof. U. Toledo, 1976-77; v.p., dean Coll. Law, prof. Stetson U., 1994-99, Disting. univ. prof., 1998—. Rev. authority on civil rights HEW, Washington, 1973—79; vis. prof. Nat. Law Ctr. George Washington U., 1981—82, U. Hawaii, Honolulu, 1988, So. Meth. U., 2004, Bklyn. Law Sch., 2007; Wallace S. Fugiama Disting. prof. U. Hawaii, Honolulu, 2002; CEO Law Sch. Admission Svcs., Newtown, Pa., 1991—93; v.p. Stetson U., 1994—99; dir., sec., mem. exec. com. Fla. Health Scis. Ctr., Tampa Gen. Hosp., Fla., 1998—2002; chair drafting com. to revise MoDel Non-Profit Corp. Act, 2009. Author: Smith's Review of Corps, 1987, Smith's Review of Estates, 1987; contbr. articles to profl. jours. Pres. Cuyahoga County Econ. and Cmty. Devel., Cleve., 1984-88, Task Force on Violent Crime, Cleve., 1987-88; chmn. audit com. Law Sch. Admission Coun., New Town, Pa., 1988-89, bd. trustees Law Sch. Admission Coun., 1989-94, exec. dir., 1991-93, pres., CEO, dir. Law Sch. Admission Svc., 1991-93; commr. Ohio Ethics Commn., Columbus, Ohio, 1988-91, Ohio Pub. Defender Commn.; v.p., trustee Gt. Lakes Theatre Festival, Cleve., 1972-90; dir., sec. exec. com. Fla. Health Scis. Ctr., 1997—; dir. Cleve. Growth Assn., 1987-88; trustee Acad. Prep., St. Petersburg, Fla., 1999—; lay reader Cathedral Ch. of St. Peter's, St. Petersburg, Fla., 2000— Recipient New Frontier award Ams. for Dem. Action, 1977, YWCA Women of Distinction award, 1988, Josephine Irwin award, 1990, award for Excellence in Governance Fl. Health Sci. Ctr., 2002; Day named in her honor, May 8, 1990, Cleve. Mem.: AAUP, ABA (chair bus. law sect., non-profit corp. com. 1987—91, bus. law sect. coun. mem. 1993—94, house of dels. 1994—99, mem. accreditation com. 1994—2000, chair internat. programs com. 1995—99, sr. lawyers divsn. coun. 1997—2001, chair accreditation com. 1999—2000, sect. legal edn. coun. 2000—, specialization standing com. 2001—04, chair sr. lawyers divsn. coun. 2003—04, chair 2003—04, standing com. libr. mem., Congress Law Libr., Glass Cutter award 1997), English Speaking Union (trustee 1986—89), Cleve. Bar Assn. (pres. 1987—88, meritorious svc. award 1987), Ohio State Bar Assn. (coun. of dels. 1981—91, Ohio Bar medal 1992), Am. Law Inst. (ALI-ABA com. 1998—2001, adv. com. 2001—, elected mem.), Assn. Am. Law Schs. (exec. com. 1977—81), St. Petersburg Yacht Club (Stetson U. Hall of Fame). Office: 1401 61st St S Saint Petersburg FL 33707-3246 Office Phone: 727-562-7848. Business E-Mail: moody@law.stetson.edu.

MOODY, MARILYN LEAVITT, retired special education educator; b. Lowell, Mass., Dec. 18, 1937; d. Thomas and Lillian Leavitt; m. Paul Elliot Moody, Mar. 14, 1959; children: Kristann Lee, Paul Elliot Jr., Kathleen Ann. BS in Elem. Edn., U. Mass., Lowell, 1959; student, Brown U., Providence, U. RI. Cert. tchr. RI, Mass. Tchr. Lexington Pub. Schs., Mass., 1959, Lowell Pub. Schs., 1959, Barrington Pub. Schs., RI, 1974—78, RI Coll., Providence, 1984—91; head tchr. Children's Perceptual Achievement Ctr., Rumford, RI, 1978—2008. Author: (booklets) Consumers - Are You Aware of Your Rights?, 1978, Chisanbop - Math Finger Calculation, 1990. Mem. Golden Retriever Rescue Inc., Hudson, Mass., 2001—. Recipient Cert. of Appreciation, Barrington Pub. Schs., 1978. Mem.: Stevenson Reading Prog., Sci. Rsch. Assn., Nat. Wildlife Fedn., Smithsonian Instn., Nat. Trust Hist. Preservation, Orton Gillingham Soc. Roman Catholic. Avocations: reading, cooking, antiques, dogs, birdwatching. Home: 6 Lafayette Rd Barrington RI 02806

MOODY, MARY ELIZABETH, speech pathology/audiology services professional; d. George Albert Berley and Mullen; m. Michael Jarrett Moody, Mar. 28. MA, Cath. U., Washington. Cert. speech-language pathologist Am. Speech-Language-and Hearing Assn. Prof. George Wash. U., Washington; pvt. practice Speech Voice Pathology, Kentlands, Md., 1970—. Asst. prof. Montgomery Coll., Rockville, Md.; dirs. in fields. Contbr. articles. Pres. Speech and Hearing Discussion Group Greater Met. Area, Md.; with St. Raphael's Nursery Sch., Md.; profl. representation Adventist Home Health Agy., Md. Recipient Exellence award, Coll. New Rochelle; fellow Grad. fellowship, Cath. U. Am. Mem.: Am. Speech-Language and Hearing Assn. Avocations: tennis, crafts. Office: Private Practice: Voice and Speech 308 Inspiration Lane The Kentlands MD 20878

MOODY, MYRIAM SYLVIE, mathematics professor; b. Worcester, Mass., July 29, 1965; d. Violette Anais and George Louis Haddad. BA in Math., Calif. State U., Fullerton, 1989, MA in Math., 1991. Math. instr. San Diego Mesa Coll., 2001—07, Southwestern Coll., Chula Vista, 2003—, Grossmont C.C., El Cajon, 2003—07. Vol. ARC, San Diego, 2003, 2007. Recipient Math. Instr. of Yr., Riverside C.C. Dist. Personal E-mail: msm@cox.net.

MOODY, ROBERT ADAMS, neurosurgeon; b. Swampscott, Mass., Oct. 1, 1934; s. George F. and Florence P. M.; m. Claudia; children: Robert Adams, II, Cathy, Paul, Lisa, Sherri. BA, U. Chgo., 1955, BS, 1956, MD, 1960. Intern Royal Victoria Hosp., Montreal, Que., Canada, 1960-61; resident in neurosurgery U. Vt. Affiliated Hosps., 1961-66; fellow Lahey Clinic, Boston, 1963-64; asst. prof. neurol. surgery U. Chgo. Med. Sch., 1966-71; sr. clin. instr., then asst. clin. prof. Tufts U. Med. Sch., 1972-74; prof. neurosurgery Abraham Lincoln Med. Sch., U. Ill., Chgo., 1975-81; chmn. div. neurosurgery Cook County Hosp., Chgo., 1974-81, assoc. chmn. dept. surgery, 1976-81; clin. prof. neurosurgery SUNY-Binghamton, 1983—2005; chmn. neurosurgery Guthrie Clinic, Sayre, Pa., 1981-95; ret., 1995. Contbr. articles med. jours. USPHS fellow, 1957-58 Mem. ACS, Am. Assn. Neurol. Surgeons, Pa. Neurosurg. Soc. (councillor 1986-87, pres.-elect 1988, pres. 1989), Mid-Atlantic Neurosurg. Soc., Ctrl. Neurosurg. Soc. (pres. 1978-79), Alumni Assn. Lahey Clinic Found., Sigma Xi. Office: Guthrie Clinic Guthrie Sq Sayre PA 18840 Business E-Mail: rcmoody@cqservices.com.

MOODY, ROBERT LEE, insurance company executive; b. 1936; Chmn., chief exec. officer Nat. Western Life Ins. Co., Austin, Tex., also bd. dirs.; pres. Am. Nat. Ins. Co., Galveston, Tex., 1995—2000, chmn., CEO, 2000—, also bd. dirs.; also pres. Moody Bankshares, Inc., Galveston, Tex. Pres. Moody Investments, Galveston. Office: Am Nat Ins Co 1 Moody Plz Galveston TX 77550

MOODY, RON, actor, writer; b. London, Jan. 8, 1924; s. Bernard and Kate (Ogus) Moodnick. BSc in Econs., U. London, 1953. Appeared in plays: 6 Years Revue, 1959, Candide, 1960, Oliver, as Shylock in Merchant of Venice, 1967, as Polonius in Hamlet, 1972, as Richard in Richard III, 1978, Iago in Othello, 1981, as Harpagon in Moliere's The Miser, Peter Pan, 2000, 05, The Sunshine Boys, 2001, Comedians, 2001, Oliver, 2003, Peter Pan, Malvern, 2005, Scrooge in A Christmas Carol, 2006-07; (films) Oliver, 1967, Twelve Chairs, 1970, Dogpound Shuffle, 1973, Wrong is Right, 1981, Where is Parsifal?, 1983, Ghost in Monte Carlo, 1989, Kid at King Arthur's Court, 1995, The Three Kings, 1999, Paradise Grove, 1999, Chopsticks, 2000, Steps, 2000, Revelation, 2001, Lost Dogs, 2004, Moussaka and Chips, 2005, The Lizard Boy, 2006, The Legion of Fire, 2007; stage musicals: USA tour HMS Pinafore, 1987, Sherlock Holmes, 1989, Streets of Dublin, 1992, Bertie, 1993, Peter Pan, 1995, The Canterville Ghost, 1998; on TV as Inspector Hart in Nobody's Perfect, ABC-TV, 1980, Dial M for Murder, 1981, Keen Eddie, 2003, The Bill, 2003, Holby City, 2005, Celebration of Oliver, 2005; dir. (play) Kafka In Love, 1991; author-composer musical comedies Joey, 1966, Saturnalia, 1970, Move Along Sideways, 1971, The Showman, 1976, Nine Lives, 1991; touring Move Along Sideways, 1991, Monologues, 2003; author: (books) The Devil You Don't, 1980, Very Very Slightly Imperfect, Off the Cuff, 1987, The Amazon Box, 1998. Served with RAF, 1943-48. Recipient Golden Globe award, 1968, Moscow Golden Bear award as best actor, 1970, Coco Trophy award, Clowns Internat., 1999; nominated Oscar, 1968. Mem. Am. Acad. Motion Picture Arts and Scis., Variety Club of Great Brit., Actors Equity, Screen Actors Guild, Clowns Internat. (life pres.), Performing Rights Soc. Writers, Soc. Authors. Home: Ingleside 41 The Green Southgate London N14 6EN England Office: Eric Glass Ltd 25 Ladbroke Crescent Notting Hill London WII IP5 England also: The Barry Freed Co 468 N Camden Dr Ste 201 Beverly Hills CA 90210

MOODY-ADAMS, MICHELE MARCIA, dean, philosophy professor; b. Chgo., Aug. 31, 1956; d. Harold Lee and Shirley (McDonald) Moody; m. James Eli Admas, June 16, 1984; 1 child, Katherine Claire. BA, Oxford U., 1980; BA in Philosophy with highest honors, Wellesley Coll., 1978; MA, PhD, Harvard U., 1986. Tchg. fellow Harvard U., Mass., 1982—84; instr. Wellesley Coll., 1984—86, asst. prof. philosophy, 1986—88; asst. prof. U. Rochester, Rochester, NY, 1988—91, Ind. U., Bloomington, Ind., 1991—96, assoc. prof., 1996—2000, assoc. dean undergraduate edn. Coll. Arts and Scis., 1998—2000; prof. philosophy Cornell U., 2000—09, dir. and Hutchinson prof. Program on Ethics and Pub. Life, 2000—09, vice provost undergraduate edn., 2005—09; dean Columbia Coll. Columbia U., NYC, 2009—, Henry L. and Lucy G. Moses prof., Joseph Straus prof. polit. philosophy and legal theory, v.p. undergraduate edn., 2009—. Mem. Marshall Scholarship Selection Com., Boston, 1987—90, Chgo., 1993. Mem. editl. bd. Pub. Affairs Quarterly, 1992—94; author: Fieldwork in Familiar Places: Morality, Culture, and Philosophy, 1997; contbr. articles to profl. jours. Recipient Marshall scholarship, British Marshall Commn., 1978—80; fellow Nat. Endowment For Humanities, U. Tchrs., 1991—92. Mem.: Internat. Soc. for Value Inquiry, Am. Soc. Value Inquiry, Am. Assn. Univ. Women, N.E. Victorian Studies Assn., Hume Soc., Soc. Philosophy & Pub. Affairs, Am. Philos. Assn. Office: Columbia Coll 208 Hamilton Hall / Mail Code 2805 1130 Amsterdam Ave New York NY 10027 Office Phone: 212-854-2441. E-mail: moody-adams@columbia.edu.*

MOOERS, CHRISTOPHER NORTHRUP KENNARD, physical oceanographer, educator; b. Hagerstown, Md., Nov. 11, 1935; s. Frank Burt and Helen (Miner) M.; m. Elizabeth Eva Fauntleroy, June 11, 1960; children: Blaine Hanson MacFee, Randall Walden Lincoln. BS, U.S. Naval Acad., 1957; MS, U. Conn., 1964; PhD, Oreg. State U., 1969. Postdoctoral fellow U. Liverpool, Eng., 1969-70; asst. prof. U. Miami, Fla., 1970-72, assoc. prof., 1972-76, U. Del., Newark, 1976-78, prof., 1978-79; prof., chmn. dept. oceanography Naval Postgrad. Sch., Monterey, Calif., 1979-86; dir. Inst. for Naval Oceanography, Stennis Space Ctr., Miss., 1986-89; sci. advisor to dir. Inst. for Naval Oceanography, 1989; rsch. prof. U. N.H., Durham, 1989-91; prof., chmn. divsn. applied marine physics U. Miami, 1991—2008, dir. Ocean Pollution Rsch. Ctr., 1992—2002, dir. Ocean Prediction Exptl. Lab., 1993—. Coord. Coastal Ocean Sci. Program, 1991—2008; chmn. modeling and analysis steering team Integrated Ocean Observing Sys., 2006—08; rsch. prof. Portland State U., Dept. Civil Environ. Engring., Oreg., 2008—. *My central goal is to understand the ocean as a physical system by combining the interpretation of observations with dynamical theory and numerical models. Special emphasis has been on the dynamics of coastal oceans (continental shelf regions) and then forming the scientific basis for practical mesoscale ocean prediction applied to coastal oceans and semi-enclosed seas and pioneering the development of operational oceanography. Most recently, I have been strategizing the integration of observing, modeling, and information management subsystems synergistically in R&D and operational modes to foster and facilitate sustained ocean state estimation for both scientific and societal purposes.* Editor Jour. Phys. Oceanography, 1991-96; mng. editor Coastal and Estuarine Studies, 1978-99. With USN, 1957-64. NSF fellow, 1964-67; NATO fellow, 1969-70; Sr. Queen Elizabeth fellow, 1980 Mem.: AAAS, Coastal Estuarine Res. Fedn., Marine Tech. Soc., Am. Meteorol. Soc. (chmn. sci.and tech. com. meterology and oceanography of Coastal Zone 1996—2002), U. Nat. Oceanog. Lab. Sys./Fleet Improvement Com. (chair 1994—97), U.S. Nat. Com. Internat. Union Geodesy and Geophysics (chmn. 1995—99), Ea. Pacific Oceanic Conf. (chmn. 1979—86), Am. Geophys. Union (pres. ocean sci. sect. 1982—84), The Oceanography Soc. (interim councilor 1987—88), Sigma Xi (U. Miami chpt. pres. 2006—08). Achievements include pioneering direct observation of transient coastal ocean currents and fronts plus mesoscale and coastal ocean prediction rsch. Home: 2520 NE Siskiyou St Portland OR 97212-2565 Office: Dept Civil & Environ Engring Portland State Univ PO Box 751 Portland OR 97207-0751 Office Phone: 503-954-2772. Business E-Mail: cmooers@rsmas.miami.edu, cmooers@cecs.pdx.edu.

MOOK, HERBERT ARTHUR, research scientist; b. Meadville, Pa., Apr. 17; s. Herbert Arthur and Elizabeth Mary Mook; m. Barbara Jane Vose, Oct. 8, 1965. PhD, Harvard, Cambridge, Mass., 1965. Staff scientist Oak Ridge Nat. Lab., 1965—75, sr. corp. fellow; corp. fellow Oak Ridge, Tenn., 1985—95; sr. corp. fellow ORNL, Tenn., 1985—, corp. fellow, 1975—85; dir. Ctr. Neutron Rsch., 1985—95; sci. dir. Spallation Neutron Source. Contbr. scientific papers. Oak Ridge Boys Club, Tex., 1975—85. Fellow: AAAS, Am. Soc. Advancement Sci., Neutron Scattering Soc. America, Am. Phys. Soc. (Beams award for Scientist 2008). Achievements include patents for polarizer for neutron scattering and ultrasonic neutron spectrometer. Avocation: golf. Office: Oak Ridge Nat Lab Oak Ridge TN 37830-8631 Home: Guinn Rd Oak Ridge TN 37931 Office Fax: 865-574-6268. Business E-Mail: mookhajr@ornl.gov.

MOOK, SARAH, retired chemist; b. Bklyn., Oct. 29, 1929; d. Wong and Lie Won (Woo) M. BA, Hunter Coll., NYC, 1952; postgrad., Columbia U., NYC, 1954—57, postgrad., 1962—65, U. Hartford, Conn., 1958—59; grad., N.Y.C. Citizens Police Acad., 2001. Cartographic aide U.S. Geol. Survey Dept. of Interior, Washington, 1952-54; rsch. asst. Mineral Beneficiation Lab. Columbia U., NYC, 1954-57; analytical chemist nuc. divsn. Combustion Engring., Inc., Windsor, Conn., 1957-59; rsch. scientist Radiations Applications Inc., Long Island City, NY, 1959-62; chemist Marks Polarized Corp., Whitestone, NY, 1962-64; sr. chemist NRA Inc. subs. Nuc. Rsch. Assoc., Inc., New Hyde Park, NY, 1964-75; clin. chemist Coney Island Hosp., Bklyn., 1974-84, cmty. bd., 1978-80; assoc. chemist Bellevue Hosp. Ctr., 1984-89, prin. chemist, 1989-95; ret., 1995. Instr. ESL Homecrest Cmty. Svcs., Inc., Bklyn., 1999—2005, Jay Sr. Ctr., Bklyn., 2006—; patient safety com. Coney Island Hosp., NY, 2007—. Contbr. articles to profl. jours. Mem. adv. com. to state assemblyman State of NY, 1970-72; trustee Park Ave. Christian Ch., 1973-82, sec., 1973-80, vice-chair, 1980-81, chair bd. trustees, 1981-82, pres. Christian Women's Fellowship, 1962-65, elder, 1982—; mem. Neighborhood Adv. Bd. for Cmty. Devel., 1996—, sec., 1996-99, chair 2000-02; mem. Cmty. Bd., 2002-04; mem. cmty. adv. bd. Coney Island Hosp., 2004—. Recipient Margaret M. McCord Woman of Yr. Meml. award, Sheepshead Bay Hist. Soc., 2004, Woman of Yr. Humanitarian award, NY State Senate, 2004, Disting. Leadership in Cmty. award, NYC Office of Comptr., Marjorie Matthews Cmty. Advocate Recognition award, Com. NYC Health & Hosp. Corp., 2008; named Woman of Yr., N.Y.C. Coun., 2004. Mem. Am. Assn. Clin. Chemistry (sec. NY Met. sect. 1999—), AAAS, Am. Chem. Soc., NY Acad. Sci., Van Slyke Soc., Citizens Police Acad. Alumni Assn. (publicity com. 2004—). Republican. Home: 2042 E 14th St Brooklyn NY 11229-3314

MOOKHERJEE, REETABRATA, computer scientist; s. Amitava and Rita Mookherjee; m. Dipanwita Batabyal, May 8, 2008. BE, Jadavpur U., Kolkata, 2001; MS in Systems Engring., Boston U., 2003; PhD in Indsl. Engring., Pa. State U., Univ. Pk., 2006. Cert. in six sigma green belt, Am. Soc. Quality, 2003. Grad. fellow Boston U., 2001—02; quality sys. co-op Axcelis Tech., Beverly, Mass., 2002—03; grad. rsch. asst. Pa. State U., Univ. Pk., 2003—06; scientist, retail sci. Oracle Corp., Cambridge, Mass., 2006—07; sr. scientist, pricing sci. group Zilliant Inc., Austin, Tex., 2007—. Contbr. articles to profl. jours. Recipient People Choice Value award, Zilliant Inc., 2008; Outstanding Grad. Tchg. fellow, Boston U., 2002, CMEI fellowship, Pa. State U., 2003. Mem.: INFORMS, Sigma Xi. Achievements include research in price list optimization for B2B companies; simultaneous estimation of price elasticity and seasonality from retail transaction history; patents pending for method and system for estimating demand model parameters when losses are unobserved. Home: 8515 Brodie Ln Apt 921 Austin TX 78745 Office: Zilliant Inc 3815 S Capital Texas Hwy Ste 300 Austin TX 78704

MOOMAW, SALLY COUP, education educator; b. Mt. Vernon, Ohio, Oct. 15, 1948; d. William Baldwin and Audrey Lazear Coup; m. Charles Jay Moomaw, Nov. 28, 1970; children: Peter William, Jeffrey Charles. BM, U. Cin., 1971, MEd, 1972, EdD, 2008. Lic. tchr. k-3 Ohio, 1987. Early childhood edn. specialist Arlitt Ctr. U. Cin., 1978—2000, assoc. direc. profl. devel., 2000—06; ann. adj. instr. U. Cin., 2007—08, asst. prof. education, 2008—. Cons. Ohio Dept. Educ. State Support Teams, Columbus, 2000—; reading faculty Nat. Head Start and RISE, Cin., 2002—04; faculty cons. Ohio State U. Rsch. Found., Columbus, 2004—07; ednl. cons. Ohio Dept. Edn., Columbus, 2005—06. Author: 12 books on early childhood education; contbr. articles to profl. jours. Pres. Cin. Pub. Sch. Clifton Elem. PTA, 1983—84; with Miami Valley Coun. Native Americans, Dayton, Ohio, 1997—2006; bd. mem. Fairview German Bilingual Sch., Cin., 1985—88. Mem.: Ohio Assn. Edn. Young Children (v.p. bus. 2004—08), Coun. Exceptional Children, Assn. Childhood Edn. Internat., Am. Ednl. Rsch. Assn., Nat. Coun. Teachers Math., Nat. Assn. Edn. Young Children. Avocations: horseback riding, music. Home: 3169 State Rt 133 Bethel OH 45106 Office: Univ Cin One Edwards PO Box 210105 Cincinnati OH 45221-0105 Office Fax: 513-556-3764; Home Fax: 513-734-1927. Business E-Mail: sally.moomaw@uc.edu.

MOON, BARBARA G., lawyer; d. Thomas Hassell Cook and Mable Ruth Head; children: Shane Brock, Angie Moon Eidschun. BA in Polit. Sci., Ga. State U., Atlanta, 1985, JD, 1988. Bar: Ga. 1991, South Fulton County 1991, Atlanta 1991, Fayette 1991, DC 1991, US Dist. Ct. (no. and mid. dists.) Ga. 1989, US Ct. Appeals (11th cir.) 1989, US Ct. Appeals (DC cir.) 1992, Ga. Supreme Ct. 1989, US Supreme Ct. 1992. Pvt. practice, def. atty. Barbara G. Moon, Esq., Jonesboro, Ga., 1992—. Spkr. in field; pro hac magistrate judge Clayton County Magistrate Ct., 1993—97. Mem.: Assn. Nat. Criminal Def. Lawyers, Ga. Assn. Criminal Def. Attys. (v.p. 1995—97), Henry County Bar Assn., Clayton County Bar Assn., Atlanta Bar Assn. Family Law, Criminal Law Sects., South Fulton Bar Assn. (v.p. 1993—94, pres. 1995—97), Phi Alpha Delta. Baptist. Avocations: swimming, skiing, reading, exercise. Office Phone: 678-583-9205. Business E-Mail: bgm2000@bellsouth.net.

MOON, CHEIL, neuroscientist, researcher; married. BSc, Yonsei U., Seoul, Republic of Korea, 1989; MSc, Imperial Coll. Sci. Tech. & Med., London, 1990, PhD, 1994. DIC Imperial Coll., U. London, 1990. Rsch. fellow Johns Hopkins U. Sch. Medicine, Balt., 1995—2005, instr., 2005; prof. Kyungpook Nat. U., Daegu, Republic of Korea, 2005—. Contbr. articles to sci. jours. Rsch. grant, NIDCD, 1996—2001, KSEF, 2006—, MOEHRD, 2006—08. Mem.: Soc. Neurosci. Office: Johns Hopkins Univ Sch Medicine 855 N Wolfe St Baltimore MD 21205

MOON, CRAIG A., retired publishing executive; b. Jamestown, NY; m. Patricia Moon; children: Kelly, Jeffrey, Taylor. Student, St. Petersburg Coll., U. South Fla. Mgmt. positions in adv. and circulation Tampa Tribune, Phila. Inquirer, Yakima Herald-Republic, Wash.; advt. dir. Modesto Bee, Calif.; v.p. advt. The Cin. Post, 1985—88, The Cin. Enquirer, 1985—88; pres. & pub. The News-Press, Ft. Myers, Fla., 1988—89, Ark. Gazette, Little Rock, 1989—91; pres. The Tennessean, Nashville, 1991—2002, pub., 1992—2002; pres. Piedmont Newspaper Group Gannett Co., Inc., 1999—2002, exec. v.p. Newspaper Divsn. McLean, Va., 2002—03, pres. & pub., USA Today, 2003—09, ret., 2009.*

MOON, DEOK HYUN, research scientist, educator; arrived in U.S., 1991; s. Dae Ju Moon and Chun Ja Go; m. Mun Jung Kang, Aug. 4, 1968. BE in Environ. Engring., Chosun U., 1991; ME in Environ. Engring., Stevens Inst. Tech., 1994; PhD, Stevens Inst. Tech., 2003. Postdoctoral rsch. assoc. Stevens Inst. Tech., Hoboken, 2003—06, rsch. asst. prof., 2006—. Office: Dept Environ Engring Chosun Univ Gwangju 501-759 Republic of Korea Office Fax: 201-216-8212. Business E-Mail: dmoon10@hotmail.com.

MOON, HOJIN, statistician, educator; m. Elizabeth K. Hyunju; children: Mark (Ki Sung), Christopher K. PhD, SUNY, Stony Brook, 1999. Instr. U. Tex., M. D. Anderson Cancer Ctr., Houston, 1999—2003; math. statistician Nat. Ctr. for Toxicological Rsch., U.S. FDA, Jefferson, Ark., 2003—07; assoc. prof. Calif. State U.- Long Beach, Dept. Math. & Stats., 2007—. Scientist Instl. Animal Care and Use Com., Nat. Ctr. for Toxicological Rsch., US FDA, Jefferson, Ark., 2004—07. Contbr. articles to profl. jours., chapters to books. Recipient Academic Excellence award, Han Yang U., 1987, Disting. Student Paper award, Internat. Biometric Soc., Ea. NAm. Region, 1999, award, US FDA, 2004, Outstanding Svc. award, 2004, 2006, award, Calif. State U., Long Beach, 2008. Mem.: Scholar and Creative Activities Com., Soc. for Risk Analysis, Am. Statis. Assn. (Ctrl. Ark. chpt. rep. 2004—), FDA Statis. Assn. (ctr. rep. 2005—), Am. Assn. for Cancer Rsch., Internat. Biometric Soc. Presbyterian. Achievements include research in attribution of tumor lethality for occult tumors in the absence of cause-of-death information; development of improved survival-adjusted tests for animal carcinogenicity/tumorigenicity data; estimation of lag time between onset of and death from an occult tumor via attribution of tumor lethality; dose-response modeling for microbial risk assessment; optimal tree-based ensemble methods for class prediction and classification by ensembles from radom partitions; high-dimensional biomarkers in personalized medicine. Office: Calif State Univ- Long Beach 1250 Bellflower Blvd Long Beach CA 90840-1001 Business E-Mail: hmoon@csulb.edu.

MOON, IL-JU, meteorologist; b. Busan, Busansi, Republic Of Korea, May 20, 1968; s. Hong-Rae Moon and In-Sik Kim; m. Hyunjoo Lee, June 30, 2002; 1 child, Hannah. PhD Oceanography, Seoul Nat. U., Korea, 2000. Postdoctoral rsch. scientist U. RI, Narragansett, 2000—03, marine rsch. assoc., 2003—05; asst. prof. Cheju Nat. U. Contbr. articles to profl. jours. Grantee Rsch. grant, NSF, 2004—07, Ctr. Atmospheric Sci. & Earthquake Rsch., 2006—07. Mem.: Korean Meteorol. Soc. (jour. editor 2006—), Korean Oceanogrphy Soc. (life). Achievements include development of coupled hurricane-wave-ocean model; new momentum flux parameterization under strong wind speeds.

MOON, JAMES RUSSELL, retired technology education educator; b. St. Cloud, Minn., Apr. 12, 1950; s. Glenn Howard and Audrey Katherine (Berg) M.; m. Corrine Mae St. Aubin, July 14, 1978; children: Sheri Ann, Brian Michael. BS, St. Cloud State U., 1972; MS, Bemidji State U., 1975. Tech. edn. tchr. Minnetonka Pub. Schs., Minn., 1972—2005, dist. dept. chmn. tech. edn., 1993-95; ret., 2006. Voc. standards com. Minn. Dept. Edn., 1995; mem. State Planning Com., 1989-2005. Designer/engr.: Row Crop Tractor, 1975; contbr. articles to profl. jours. Recipient Anchor award Minn. Pub. Schs., 1991, Tchr. Excellence award Internat. Tech. Edn. Assn., 1994, Disting. Tech. Educator Citation, 2002, Minnetonka Co-curricular Advisor of Yr., 2001, Tchr. of Yr. Optimist Club of Glen Lake, 2005; named Disting. Tech. Educator, Internat. Tech. Edn. Assn., 2002. Mem. Minn. Valley Tech. Edn. Assn. (sec. 1974), Minn. Tech. Edn. Assn. (mem. supermileage state competition com. 1989-2005, Tech. Edn. Tchr. of Yr. 1993, Disting. Svc. award 1991, 92, 94, Joyce Gustafson Meml. award, 2003). Presbyterian. Avocations: auto restoration, outdoor activities. Home: 2037 20th St SE Buffalo MN 55313-4813 Home Phone: 763-682-3679.

MOON, JANE ANDERSON, systems engineer, consultant; b. Bryn Mawr, Pa., Feb. 6, 1938; d. Karl Leopold and Louise Laylander (Fowler) Anderson; m. Marion Francis Moon, June 28, 1965; children: Douglas Charles Moon, Cary Moon Gordon, Diana Moon Robinson BSc cum laude, U. Calif., Irvine, 1972, MSc, 1976. Programmer Collins Radio Co., Newport Beach, Calif., 1960-63; engring. programmer Hughes Aircraft Co., Fullerton, Calif., 1963-66; software engr. Calif. Computer Products, Anaheim, Calif., 1966-69; prin., owner Moon Mgmt. Consulting, Orange, Calif., 1972-76; lectr. U. Calif., Irvine, 1973-75; software engring. mgr. Burroughs Corp., Santa Ana, Calif., 1976-81; sr. prin. scientist Hughes Aircraft Co., Fullerton, 1981-98; engring. tech. dir., engring. process group Raytheon Co., Fullerton, 1998—, sr. staff to dir. engring., 1999—2004, sr. staff to dir. sys. engring., 2004—. Prin. Moon Mgmt. Consulting, Orange, Calif., 1985—; adv. bd. Software Engring. Inst., Pitts., 1993-96, lead assessor, 1996-2004, lead appraiser, 2000—; mem. Capability Maturity Model Integration Product Devel. Team, 1998; lectr., presenter in field Author: Hughes Aircraft's Widespread Deployment of a Continuously Improving Software Process; contbr. articles to profl. jours Vol. Loma Linda (Calif.) U. Med. Ctr. Children's Hosp., 1996—. Recipient Outstanding Achievement award, Hughes Aircraft Co., 1986, 1990, 1992, 1994, Summit award, 1996, Outstanding Achievement award, Raytheon Co., 1998, One Co. award, 2003. Mem. Internat. Council Systems Engring., Orange County Philharmonic Soc. Avocations: gardening, art quilting, restoring old houses.

MOON, JOHN ELLIS VAN COURTLAND, retired historian; b. Geneva, Oct. 25, 1929; arrived in US, 1940; s. Carlyle van Courtland and Marie Edmée (Choisy) Moon; m. Palma Roberge (div.); children: John Albert van Courtland, Margaret Hames, Laurelle Conte; m. Joan Mary Farrell, July 24, 1971. AB in History and Lit., Harvard U., 1952, PhD in Am. Civilization, 1968; MA in English and Comparative Lit., Columbia U., 1953. Instr. English Merrimack Coll., North Andover, Mass., 1953—55, Boston U., 1957—58; from instr. to prof. history Boston State Coll., 1958—82; prof. Fitchburg State Coll., Mass., 1982—93, prof. emeritus, 1993—. Chmn. com. Coun. Pres., Mass. State Coll. Sys., 1990; presenter in field; vis. prof. Kings Coll., U. London, 1994—95, 2008—09. Author: Confines of Concept: American Strategy in World War II, 1988; co-editor: Biological and Toxin Weapons: Research, Development and Use from the Middle Ages to 1945, 1999; contbr. articles to profl. jours. Grantee, John Kittredge Fund, 1994, John D. and Catherine MacArthur Found., 1994. Mem.: Mass. State Coll. Assn. (pres., Boston State Coll. chpt. 1980—82), Am. Assn. Univ. Profs. (pres., Boston State Coll. chpt. 1970—72, pres. Mass. state conf. 1982—84, William S. Tacey award 1998). Avocations: mountain climbing, book collecting, trekking, travel. Home and Office: 11 Monmouth Ct Brookline MA 02446 Personal E-mail: jevcm@comcast.net.

MOON, JOHN HENRY, SR., banker; b. Van Buren, Ark., Aug. 19, 1937; s. B.R. and Alma (Witte) M.; m. Agnes Rose Dickens, Aug. 16, 1958; children: John Henry, Randall Allen. AA, Delmar Coll., Corpus Christi, Tex., 1956; BBA cum laude, Tex. A&M U., Kingsville, 1958. Sr. acct. Tex. Eastern Transp. Co. and subs., 1958-63; exec. v.p., dir. Houston Rsch. Inst., 1963-68; sr. v.p., asst. to chmn. bd., dir. Main Bank, 1968—69; vice chmn. bd., dir. N.E. Bank, 1969; CEO, chmn. bd., dir. Pasadena Nat. Bank, Tex., 1970-81; gen. ptnr. Moon and Assocs., Ltd., 1977—. Chmn. bd., pres. Interservice Life Ins. Corp., Phoenix, Cmty. Bank, Houston, 1975-81, Interstate Bank, Houston, 1977-81, Moon Credit Corp., Pasadena, 1975—, Peoples Bank, Houston, 1983-93; chmn. bd. Cmty. Nat. Bank, Friendswood, Tex., 1981-93, Peoples Nat. Bank, Pasadena, Tex., 1984-93; chmn., pres. Sam Houston Pky. Transp. Corp., 1991-93; bd. dirs. Quality Wire Rope Corp., chmn., 1999-2005; pres. Sure Found. Inc., 1987—. Past bd. dirs. Pasadena Heart Assn., Salvation Army, Tex. Assn. Prevention of Blindness; past chmn. City of Pasadena Bd. Devel.; past chmn. adv. bd. Pasadena Civic Ctr.; past dir. S.E. Econ. Devel., Inc.; bd. dirs. Sure Found., Tex. Rangers Law Enforcement Assn., San Jacinto Coll. Found., 2000-03, chmn., 2002-03. Named Outstanding Young Man of Yr., Pasadena Jr. C. of C., 1973; named to Pasadena Hall of Fame, 1988. Mem. AICPA, Pasadena C. of C. (bd. dirs. S.E. Econ. Devel., CCC Club, Citizen of Yr. 1994), Tex. Soc. CPAs, Tex. Bankers Assn., Rotary (pres. Pasadena Rotary found. 2001-07). Home: 310 Del Monte Dr Friendswood TX 77546 Office: PO Box 3487 Pasadena TX 77501 Office Phone: 713-943-7777. Business E-Mail: jhmoon@mooncapitalcorp.com.

MOON, KATHLEEN K., language arts educator; m. Gary F. Moon. BA in Elem. Edn. with honors, Georgian Ct. Coll., Lakewood, NJ, 1971. Cert. reading recovery Rutgers U., New Brunswick, 2002. Tchr. grade 3 John Adams Elem. Sch., North Brunswick, 1973—74; tchr. grade 1 Parsons Elem. Sch., North Brunswick, 1971—73, 1974—2001, tchr. reading recovery, 2001—02, tchr. lang. arts academic support, 2002—. Chair TV-Turn-Off Week, NBTEA scholarship com. Parsons Elem. Sch. Mem. Literacy Vols. Am., 1991—; vol. Elijah's Promise Soup Kitchen, New Brunswick; usher Ch. of the Assumption, New Egypt, NJ, 2005—, St. Thomas Acquinas Ch., Beach Haven, NJ, 2007—. Recipient and honored, Gov.'s Tchr. Recognition Program, 2003. Mem.: NJEA, Georgian Ct. U. (class agent), North Brunswick Twp. Ednl. Assn., Middlesex County Ednl. Assn., N.J. Reading Assn., Middlesex Reading Assn., NEA, Georgian Ct. U. Alumni Assn., Delta Tau Kappa, Phi Delta Phi. Avocations: reading, walking, boating, cross stitch, kayaking. Office: Parsons Elem Sch 899 Hollywood St North Brunswick NJ 08902

MOON, KYOUNG-SIK, research scientist; b. Seoul, Republic Of Korea, Dec. 20, 1967; s. Tae Moon and Jung Lee; m. Hyun-joo Hwang, May 23, 1998. BS, Mateirals Sci. and Engring., Korea U., Seoul, 1993, MS, 1995; PhD, Korea U., 1999. Postdoc. fellow Ga. Inst. Tech., Atlanta, 1999—2003. Contbr. scientific papers; author: (book) Nano & Bio Electronics Packaging Springer, 2009. Recipient Best Poster Paper, IEEE Internat. Symposium on Advanced Packaging Materials, 2001, Best Paper award, 2004. Achievements include invention of use of sacrificial anode materials in electrically conductive adhesives for corrosion control; ultra high conductivity of isotropic conductive adhesives; ESD protection of WLP devices via polymer composites; abrasion resistant superhydrophobic coatings via the combination of epoxy and inorganic nanoparticles; patents pending for electrically conductive adhesives using copper fillers; patents for electrically conductive adhesives and methods of making it; invention of aldehyde for high performance ECAs. Home: 6039 Chinarose Ln Duluth GA 30097 Office: Ga Inst Tech Schl Mtrls Sci & Engring 771 Ferst Dr NW Atlanta GA 30332-0245 Office Phone: 678-369-5725. Personal E-mail: jack.moon@gmail.com. Business E-Mail: jack.moon@gatech.edu.

MOON, LLOYD N., chemicals executive; BS, La. State U.; postgraduate studies in biochemistry, Northwestern U.; postgraduate studies in bus., Tulane U. Positions with New Orleans C. of C.; sales & mktg.

positions Xerox Corp., Johnson & Johnson; mgmt. positions in govt. affairs & comm. Tulane Univ., La. State Univ.; mgmt. positions through v.p. global govt. affairs & comm. Chemtura Corp., 1996—. Mem. Pub. Affairs Rsch. Coun., NAM, CEFIC, various state chem. industry councils. Past bd. dir. United Way, Greenwich, Conn., Boy Scouts America. Mem.: Am. Chemistry Coun. Office: Chemtura Corp 199 Benson Rd Waterbury CT 06749 Office Phone: 203-573-2000. Office Fax: 203-353-5424.*

MOON, LORETTA MARIE, recreational therapist; b. Spokane, Wash., Jan. 22, 1952; d. George Edmond and Eva Louise Moon; m. William Roy Rose, 1976 (div. 1989); children: Charlie Ann, Julie Lynn, Jennifer Rene, Nicolle Louise. AS, AA, Big Bend C.C., Moses Lake, Wash., 1974; BA in Recreation Adminstrn., Ea. Wash. U., Cheney, 1976. Cert. recreation therapist Nat. Coun. Therapeutic Recreation, 1989. Lifeguard Spokane County Parks Dept., Wash., 1971—76; recreation leader 2 Interlake Sch. Severe and Profound, Medical Lake, 1989—92; instr. adult swimming class YWCA, Spokane, 1990—92, coord. adaptive aquatic, 1992—94; recreation therapist geriatric unit Ea. State Hosp., Medical Lake, 1992—94; recreation therapist, aquatic therapy specialist Ea. State Hosp./ Wash. State Therapy Pool, 1994—; lifeguard, instr. water safety YWCA, 2002—05; nurse asst. Carol's Adult Family Home, Nine Mile Falls, 2004—06; lifeguard instr. Lakeland Village, 2005—09. Mem., pres. Med. Lake Mid. Sch., 2001—02; leader, outdoor chmn. Inland North West Campfire, Spokane, 1983—91; tchr. LDS Ch., 1980—. Mem.: US Water Fitness Assn. (Top 100 Aquatic Dirs. US 1997—2009, Top Aquatic Therapy Ctr. US 2003—09), Am. Assn. Phys. Activity (master tchr. 2000—), Am. Therapeutic Recreation Assn. Mem. Lds Ch. Avocations: swimming, embroidery, crocheting, gardening. Business E-Mail: moonlore@dshs.wa.gov.

MOON, MARILYN LEE, economist; b. El Dorado, Kans., July 7, 1947; d. Jesse Morris and Shirley Lois M.; m. Douglas Gomery, Jan. 13, 1973. BA in Econs., Colo. Coll., 1969; MS in Econs., U. Wis., 1972, PhD in Econs., 1974. Rsch. assoc. Inst. for Rsch. on Poverty U. Wis., Madison, 1973-74; asst. prof. econs. U. Wis., Milw., 1974-80, assoc. prof. econs., 1980-81; sr. analyst human resources and cmty. devel. divsn. The Congl. Budget Office, Washington, 1981-83; sr. rsch. assoc. Health Policy Ctr. The Urban Inst., Washington, 1983-86; dir. pub. policy inst. AARP, 1986-89; sr. rsch. assoc. The Urban Inst., 1989-94, sr. fellow, 1994—2003; v.p. Am. Insts. for Rsch., 2003—, dir. health program. Cons. The Pepper Commn., 1989. Author: The Meaurement of Economic Welfare: Its Application to the Aged, 1977, Medicare Now and in the Future, 1993, 2d edit., 1996, Medicare: A Policy Primer, 2006; co-author: Balancing Access, Cost and Politics: The American Context for Health System Reform, 1991, Entitlements and the Elderly: Protecting Promises, Recognizing Realities, 1995; editor: Economic Transfers in the United States, vol. 49, 1984; co-editor: Improving Measures of Economic Well-Being, 1977; columnist The Washington Post, 1993-00; contbr. articles to profl. jours. Pub. trustee social security and Medicare trust funds, 1995-00. Ford Found. fellow, 1971-73. Mem. Nat. Acad. Social Ins. (bd. dirs. 1993-00, pres. 2005-), Medicare Rights Ctr. (bd. dirs. 1998, pres. 2005-), Inst. Medicine, Phi Beta Kappa. Avocations: photography, hiking, reading. Office: Am Insts for Rsch 10720 Columbia Pike Silver Spring MD 20901 Home Phone: 301-951-4385; Office Phone: 301-592-2101. E-mail: mmoon@air.org.

MOON, RONALD T.Y., state supreme court chief justice; b. Sept. 4, 1940; m. Stella H. Moon. B in Psychology and Sociology, Coe Coll., 1962, LLD (hon.), 2001; LLB, U. Iowa, 1965; LLD (hon.), Inha U., Incheon, Korea, 2003. Bailiff, law clk. to Chief Judge Martin Pence U.S. Dist. Ct., 1965-66; dep. prosecutor City and County of Honolulu, 1966-68; assoc. Libkuman, Ventura, Ayabe, Chong & Nishimoto (predecessor firm Libkuman, Ventura, Moon & Ayabe), Honolulu, 1968-72, ptnr., 1972-82; judge 9th div. 1st cir., Cir. Ct., State of Hawaii, Honolulu, 1982-90; assoc. justice Hawaii Supreme Ct., Honolulu, 1990-93, chief justice, 1993—. Bd. dirs. Nat. Consortium on Racial and Ethnic Fairness in Ctr., 2004—; adj. prof. law U. Hawaii, 1986—88; lectr., guest spkr. numerous events. Recipient Disting. Svc. award, Nat. Ctr. for State Cts., 2003, Grand Prize award, Kyungmin Mission Schs., Korea, 2003, Light of Orient award, Korean Am. Found., Hawaii, 2008, Order of Civil Merit Moran medal, Korean Govt., 2008, Light of Orient award, Korean Am. Found., Hawaii, 2008, Moran medal, Korean Govt., 2008; named Order of Merit. Mem. ABA (Pursuit of Justice award tort, trial and ins. practice sect. 2006), ATLA, Hawaii Bar Assn. (Golden Gavel award 2001), Am. Bd. Trial Advocates (pres. 1986-93, nat. sec. 89-91), Am. Inns of Cts. IV (bencher 1983—, bd. trustees 2004—), Am. Judicature Soc., Hawaii Trial Judges' Assn., Conf. Chief Justices (bd. dirs.). Office: Supreme Ct Hawaii 417 S King St Honolulu HI 96813-2902 Office Phone: 808-539-4700. Business E-Mail: ronald.t.moon@courts.state.hi.us.*

MOON, SANGKIL, finance educator; b. Kyungsan, Kyungpook; s. Myungsool Moon and Okhae Keum; married. PhD in Mktg., U. Iowa, Iowa City, 2003. Asst. prof. NC State U., Raleigh, 2003—. Office: NC State Univ Coll Mgmt Raleigh NC 27695-7229 Business E-Mail: smoon2@ncsu.edu.

MOON, TODD KAY, engineering educator; b. Provo, Utah, Aug. 1963; s. Harold Kay and Mayva Ann Moon; m. Barbara Jo Rytting, Apr. 24, 1986; children: Leslie Diane, Kyra Michelle, Kaylie Rebecca, Jennie Marissa, Kiana Camille, Spencer Todd. PhD, U. Utah, Salt Lake City, 1991. Prof. and head, ECE dept. Utah State U., Logan, 2006—. Adj. mem. Ctr. Comm. Rsch., Princeton, NJ, 2000—. Author: (grad. textbook) Mathematical Methods and Algoritms for Signal Processing, Error Correction Coding: Mathematical Methods and Algorithms; contbr. scientific papers. Mem.: IEEE. Home: 450 E 125 N Providence UT 84332 Office: Utah State Univ Elec and Computer Engring 4120 Old Main Hill Logan UT 84322-4120 Office Fax: 435-797-2970. Business E-Mail: todd.moon@usu.edu.

MOONEN, RICK, chef, restaurant owner; b. Sept. 12, 1956; Grad., Culinary Inst. Am., 1976—78. Saucier La Cote Basque, 1980; chef Le Cirque, NYC; exec. chef Le Relais, Century Café, Chelsea Central, The Water Club, NYC, 1988, Oceana, NYC; owner, exec. chef rm, NYC, 2002—05, Branzini, NYC, 2002—05, RM Seafood, Las Vegas, 2005—. Mem. Corp. Culinary Inst. Am., Am. Inst. Wine Food Day's of Taste children's prog.; mem. restaurant com. Share Our Strength; mem. bd. adv. French Culinary Inst.; founding mem. Seafood Choices Alliance, Chef's Coalition; Am. rep. Oliviers & Co.; chef's adv. bd. mem. Ecofish. Contbg. editor: Food & Wine Mag.; guest appearances include (TV series) Today, Good Morning Am., The Early Show, Cooking Live with Sara Moulton, Lou Dobbs Tonight; author: (cookbooks) Fish Without a Doubt, 2008. Recipient Chef of Yr. award for Northeast Region, Chefs in Am., 1993, Epicurean award for Best Seafood in Las Vegas, Las Vegas Life Mag., 2007. Mem.: Wildlife Conservation Soc. Office: RM Seafood Mandalay Bay Resort & Casino 3950 Las Vegas Blvd S Las Vegas NV 89119 Office Phone: 702-795-7155.

MOONEY, BETH, bank executive; BA, U. Tex., 1977; MBA, So. Meth. U., Dallas, 1983. Sec. First Republic Bank, Dallas, bank mgr., 1980, Citicorp; line assignments of increasing responsibility Citicorp Real Estate, Inc., Hall Fin. Group, Bank One Corp., regional pres. Akron, Dayton, Ohio, pres. Ohio; head banking group AmSouth Bank, Tenn., No. La., 2000—04, sr. exec. v.p., CFO Birmingham, 2004—06; vice chairwoman cmty. banking KeyCorp, 2006—. Active Cleve. Orch.; bd. dir. United Way Met. Nashville, 2001—, Vanderbilt Univ. Med. Ctr. Recipient Women of Achievement award, YWCA, 2008; named Disting. Alumni, So. Meth. U. Cox Sch. Bus., 2007—08; named one of 25 Most Powerful Women in Banking, US Banker, 2005, 2008, Top 10 CFOs in Banking, 2006, 25 Women to Watch, 2006, 2007. Office: KeyCorp 127 Public Sq Cleveland OH 44114 Office Phone: 615-748-2214. Office Fax: 205-326-4072.*

MOONEY, BRIAN JOSEPH, lawyer; b. Hayward, Calif., July 28, 1963; s. Robert and Patricia Mooney; m. Ann McDonald Mooney, Oct. 12, 1991; children: Hannah, Sarah. BA, U. Calif., Davis, 1985; JD, UCLA, 1989. Bar: Calif. 1989, US Dist. Ct. (central dist.), Calif. 1991, US Dist. Ct. (no., so. and ea. dists.), Calif. 1992, US Ct. Appeals (9th cir.) 1989, US Supreme Ct. 2008. Assoc. Allen Matkins Leck Gamble & Mallory, LA, 1989—91, Gordon & Rees, LLP, San Francisco, 1992—96, ptnr., 1996—. Chmn. Drug & Medical Device Grp. Gordon & Rees, San Francisco, 2003—. Del. to bd. Alta Bates, Berkeley, Calif., 2003—04. Named Super Lawyer, San Francisco Mag., 2006—07, 2007—08. Mem.: Defense Rsch. Inst. Office: Gordon & Rees LLP 275 Battery St Ste 2000 San Francisco CA 94111 Office Phone: 415-986-5900. Business E-Mail: bmooney@gordonrees.com.

MOONEY, DAVID PATRICK, surgeon; b. St. Louis, June 23, 1959; MD, St. Louis U., 1985. Intern Med. Ctr. Hosp. Vt., Burlington, 1985-86, resident in surgery, 1986-87, 88-91; resident in pediatric surgery Children's Mercy Hosp., Kansas City, Mo., 1991-93; fellow in surg. rsch. U. Vt., Burlington, 1987-88; staff physician Mary Hitchcock Meml. Hosp., Lebanon, N.H., 1993—. Asst. prof. pediatric surgery Dartmouth Med. Sch., Lebanon, 1993—, Harvard Med. Sch., 1999-, trauma program dir. Childrens Hosp. Boston, 1999-. Office: Childrens Hospital Boston 300 Longwood Ave Boston MA 02115 Office Phone: 617-355-0535.

MOONEY, DENNIS M., automotive executive; b. 1956; BS in Mech. Engring., U. Mich., 1978; MS in Natural Resource Strategy, Nat. Def. U., 1998. Joined Oldsmobile, Lansing, Mich., 1978, detail engr., 1978, project engr., 1980, sr. project engr., 1983, asst. staff engr., 1986, bus. team mgr.-compact and midsize cars, 1989, bus. team mgr.-large/luxury cars, 1991; dir. N-car planning Lansing Automotive Divsn. Buick-Oldsmobile-Cadillac Group, 1992, dir. projects for future programs, 1993, vehicle chief engr.-compact cars Small Car Group, 1996; engring. dir. chassis, electrical HVAC, interiors Midsize and Luxury Car Group GM Corp., Flint, Mich., 1998, engring. dir. interior sys. N.Am. Car Group, 1999, engring. dir. electrical sys., 1999, exec. dir. vehicle performance GM N.Am. Engring., 2001, exec. dir. vehicle integration, 2001, chmn., mng. dir. Holden, 2003—07, v.p. global vehicle sys. and integration, 2007—. Office: GM Corp PO Box 33170 Detroit MI 48232-5170*

MOONEY, ELIZABETH KAATZ, adult education educator; d. Theodore James Katz and Eliza Faust. BA, Beloit Coll., Wis., 1948; MS, U. Wis., Madison, 1950; ArtsD (hon.), Inst. Advanced Study Human Sexuality, San Francisco, 2006. Cert. sexuality educator Am. Assn. Sexuality Educators, Counseors and Therapists, 1976; LCSW Mich. and Ind., 1976. Tchr. North HS, Sheboygan, Wis., 1950—55; therapist Houfek Mooney Med. Office, Sheboygan, 1960—67, social worker, 1960—67; rsch. assoc. Kinsey Inst., Bloomington, Ind., 1967—75; lectr. Sch. Edn., Ind. U., Bloomington, 1967—75, Sch. Social Work, Western Mich. U., Kalamazoo, 1975—79, sociology dept., Ind. U. South Bend, Ind., 1983—; dir. ednl. svcs. Planned Parenthood, Kalamazoo, 1975—79, asst. exec. dir. Chgo., 1979—83, exec. dir. South Bend, Ind., 1983—94. Treas. Am. Assn. Sexuality Educators, Counselors and Therapists, Richmond, Va., 1977—85; bd. mem. YWCA, South Bend, 1985—90; fin. com. LaSalle Coun., Boy Scouts America, South Bend, 1993—2008. Recipient Disting. Svc. award, Beloit Coll., 1973, Merit Status, Ind. U., South Bend, 1999, Tchg. Excellence Recognition award, 2000, Disting. Tchg. award, Ind. U., Bloomington, 2005, Ind. U., South Bend, 2008; grant, Ford Found., H. Hefner Found. Mem.: Am. Assn. Sexuality Educators, Counselors and Therapists. Independent. Avocations: travel, reading. Office: Ind Univ South Bend 1700 Mishawaka Ave South Bend IN 46634

MOONEY, JAMES F., telecommunications industry executive; With IBM Corp., 1980—99; COO Baan Co.; CEO, COO Tradeout Inc.; exec. v.p., COO Nextel Comms.; non-exec. chmn. Virgin Media Inc, NYC, 2003—. Bd. dir. NTL Europe. Office: NTL Europe Inc 22 Suffolk St London SW1Y 4HG England also: Virgin Media Inc Ste 2863 909 3rd Ave New York NY 10022

MOONEY, JEROME HENRI, lawyer; b. Salt Lake City, Aug. 7, 1944; s. Jerome Henri and Bonnie (Shepherd) M.; m. Carolyn Lasrich, Aug. 10, 1965 (div. Dec. 1978); 1 child, Dierdre Nicole; m. Kaitlyn Cardon, Sept. 23, 1995. BS, U. Utah, 1966, JD, 1972. Bar: Utah 1972, Calif. 1998, U.S. Ct. Appeals (10th cir.) 1974, U.S. Supreme 1984, U.S. Ct. Appeals (7th cir.) 1999, U.S. Ct. Appeals (9th cir.) 2001, U.S. Ct. Appeals (4th cir.) 2002. Sole practice, Salt Lake City, 1972-75, 79-83; sr. ptnr. Mooney, Jorgenson & Nakamura, Salt Lake City, 1975-78, Mooney & Smith, Salt Lake City, 1983-87, Mooney & Assoc., Salt Lake City, 1987-94, Mooney Law Firm, Salt Lake City, 1995—98, 2001—06, Larsen & Mooney Law, Salt Lake City, 1999—2001, Weston, Garrou, Walters & Mooney, 2007—. Bd. dirs. Mooney Real Estate, Salt Lake City; mem. Active Music, Calif. Copyright Conf. Active Gov.'s Coun. on Vet. Affiars, Salt Lake City, 1982-89; trustee Project Realty, Salt Lake City, 1976—; SAMHSA sponsor Project Reality, 1994—; vice-chair State Mil. Acad. Assoc. With U.S. Army N.G., 1992-93. Mem. ABA (criminal justice sect. U.S. Sentencing Commn. com.), Utah Bar Assn. (chmn. criminal bar sect. 1987-88), Beverly Hills Bar Assn., Nat. Assn. Rec. Industry Profls., Utah NG Assn. (trustee 1976), 1st Amendment Lawyers Assn. (v.p. 1986-88, pres. 1988-89), Nat. Assn. Criminal Def. Lawyers, Families Against Mandatory Minimums (adv. coun.), VFW. Democrat. Jewish. Avocations: sailng, computers. Office: 50 W Broadway Ste 1000 Salt Lake City UT 84101-2066 Office Phone: 801-364-5635, 310-442-0072. Business E-Mail: jerrym@mooneylaw.com.

MOONEY, JUSTIN DAVID, motel executive, consultant; b. Kansas City, Mo., Feb. 21, 1932; s. J.L. and Phoebe (Lighton) M.; m. Alayne I. Kohn, June 15, 1958; children: Jo Ann, David Alan. BBA, U. Mich., 1954, MBA, 1957. Cert. hotel administr. Mich. State U., 1982, advacned hotel administr. Am. Hotel and Lodging Sch., Fla., 1991. Mgr., women's divsn. Woolf Bros., Kansas City, 1958-66, asst. to pres., 1967-70; pres. Mission Inn Motel, Inc., Overland Park, Kans., 1970-90, J & A Ventures, Inc., Leawood, Kans., 1990—. Bd. dirs. Nat. Fedn. of Ind. Bus., 1989-95, vice chmn. State of Kans., 1994-95. Mem. C. of C., Greater Kans. City, 1965-71, life mem. 1968-70, chmn. membership dept., 1970-71; chmn. Hwy. 56 Bus. Dist., 1984-87, bd. dir., 1984-90; bd. dir. hospitality divsn. Johnson County C.C., 1982-2005, chmn. bd., 1986-2005; bd. dir. Overland Park Conv. and Visitors Bur., 1983-90, v.p., 1987-90; bd. dir. Temple B'nai Jehudah, 1972-83, 86-93, hon. bd. dir. 1995-, pres. Men's Club, 1972-74; bd. dir. 1965-90, pres. Catalina Bay, 1990-95, bd. dir. 1987-95, Heart Am. Jewish Hist. Soc., 1991-93, treas., 1991-93; bd. dir., exec. com., pres. Spindrifter, 1990-95; bd. mem. Pavilions Property, 2000-06, treas 2005-06; exec. bd., treas. Nat. Coun. Jewish Women, 2003-07. With Army Intelligence US Army, 1954—56. Recipient Lifetime award Jewish Chautauqua, 1979, Hannah G. Solomon award Nat. Coun. Jewish Women, 2003, Cmty. Sect.2009; named to Men's Club Hall of Fame, 1978. Mem. Am. Hotel and Motel Assn. (bd. dirs. 1983-89, small properties adv. com., 1985-89, chmn. small properties adv. com., 1988-89, exec. com. 1987-89, vice-chmn. small properties adv. coun. 1985-88, chmn. 1988-89), Kansas City C. of C. (Hall of Fame Man of Yr. 1971), Kans. Hotel Motel Assn. (bd. dirs. 1972-84, pres. 1982-84, Hotel Man of Yr. 1981, 82), Greater Kans. City Hotel/Lodging Assn. (bd. dirs. 1973—, pres. 1982-84, chair 1985, Life Time Achievement award 1998), Greater Kansas City Hotel and Lodging Found. (bd. dir. 2000-2009), Kans. Lodging Assn. (bd. dir. 1983-1990, Hotel Man of Yr. 1981, 82, 83, 84, chmn. bd. 1985-86), Kansas City Athletic Club (treas. 1971-72, 1992, 2009, bd. dirs. 1969-72), Temple Sisterhood (life). Avocations: antiques, sports. Home and Office: J&A Ventures Inc 14701 Delmar Leawood KS 66224-9545

MOONEY, KRISTA MICHELE, academic administrator; b. Tallahassee, Fla., Jan. 4, 1973; d. Dennis Robert and Mary Ann Mooney. Student, Auburn U., 1990—91; AA, Tallahassee CC, 1990, AA, 1992; BA in Psychology, Fla. State U., 1995, JD, 1998, PhD in Higher Edn., 2005; Cert. of Completion law program, Oxford U., Eng., 1996. Head coach all-star squad Fla. Cheer Gyms, Inc., Tallahassee, 1993—94; instr. Nat. Cheerleaders Assn., Tallahassee, 1993—95; Fla. Supreme Ct. cert. legal intern Leon County Attorney's Office, Tallahassee, 1997; dir. alumni devel. Fla. State U. Coll. Law, Tallahassee, 1998—99; rsch. asst., academic and student affairs, bd. regents State U. Sys. Fla., Tallahassee, 1999—2000, sr. ednl. policy analyst, academic student affairs, bd. govs., 2003—06, assoc. dir. bd. gov., 2006—; cons. MGT Am., Inc., Tallahassee, 2000—02; sr. ct. analyst Office of State Courts Adminstr., Supreme Ct. Fla., Tallahassee, 2002—03. Participant and grad. Opportunity Tallahassee, 2005—05; vol. Guardian ad Litem, Tallahassee, 1995—99, Ronald McDonald Ho., Tallahassee, 1992—2002, Habitat for Humanity, Tallahassee, 1992—98, Meals on Wheels, Tallahassee, 1992—2002, Children's Miracle Network, Tallahassee, 1992—95; sec. Tallahassee 25, 2004—05, internat. v.p., 2005—06, tutoring/mentoring chmn., 2003—04, pres., 2006—; vol. fundraiser and booster Seminole Boosters, Tallahassee, 1992—2006. Recipient Follow the Leader Leader Vol. of the Yr., Tallahassee 25, 2004, Disting. Pro Bono Svc. award, Fla. State U. Coll. Law, 1998; named one of Top Twenty-Five Instr., Nat. Cheerleaders Assn., 1993—94; scholar, Auburn U., 1990—94. Mem.: ASTD, So. Assn. Coll. Student Affairs, Nat. Assn. Student Pers. Adminstrs., Nat. Assn. Grad.-Profl. Students, Hardee Ctr. Women in Higher Edn., Edn. Law Assn., Am. Ednl. Rsch. Assn., Fla. State U. Alumni Assn. (life), U. Ctr. Club, Capital Tiger Bay Club, Fla. State U. Varsity Club (life), Seminole Torchbearers (life), Alpha Delta Pi Alumni Assn., Phi Alpha Delta. Office: Florida Bd Govs 325 West Gaines Street Suite 1601-A Tallahassee FL 32399-0400 Home: 5355 Carisbrooke Ln Tallahassee FL 32309-6807 Personal E-mail: fsujdphd@aol.com.

MOONEY, MARILYN, lawyer; b. Pitts., July 29, 1952; d. James Russell and Mary Elizabeth (Cartwright) M. BA summa cum laude, U. Pa., 1973, JD, 1976. Bar: Mass. 1977, D.C. 1985, Pa. 1990, U.S. Dist. Ct. D.C. 1985, U.S. Ct. Appeals (D.C. cir.) 1985, U.S. Supreme Ct. 1986. Atty. E. I. du Pont de Nemours & Co., Wilmington, Del., 1976-84, Washington, 1985; assoc. Fulbright & Jaworski L.L.P., Washington, 1985—89, ptnr., 1990—, ptnr. in charge corp. and securities practice Washington Office, 2005—. Contbr. articles to profl. jours. Mem.: ABA (fed. regulation securities com.), D.C. Bar (corp. fin. and securities law and internat. sections), Internat. Bar Assn. (issues and trading in securities com.), Am. Soc. Corp. Secs. (securities law com.). Office: Fulbright & Jaworski LLP 801 Pennsylvania Ave NW Washington DC 20004-2615 Home Phone: 202-468-7070; Office Phone: 202-662-4678. E-mail: mmooney@fulbright.com.

MOONEY, MICHAEL C., academic administrator, coach; b. College Park, Md., Nov. 14, 1961; s. James J. and Beverly K. (Lauer) M.; m. Jean W. Barnett, Aug. 2, 1986; children: Trevor, Allison. BS, U. Buffalo, 1983; MS, Canisius Coll., Buffalo, 1985. Residence hall dir. SUNY, Geneseo, 1985-86, dir. intramurals and recreation, 1986-91, facility mgr. sports and recreation, 1991-99, men's varsity soccer coach, 1985—, asst. dir. athletics, 1999—2003, assoc. dir. athletics and recreation, 2003—. Chair all-conf. com. SUNY Athletic Conf., Fredonia, NY, 1987-2004, soccer guide editor, 1989-2006; mem. men's divsn. III soccer com. NCAA, 1999-2005, nat. com. chair, 2001-04; mem. scheduling com. SUNYAC Conf., 2002—, mem. fin. com., eligibility com., 2002-2004, chair championships com., 2005-08; mem. soccer All-Am. com. NSCAA, 1992—; referee USSF, 1983—. Recipient SUNYAC Men's Soccer Coach Yr., 1989, 1997, 2006, 2008, NSCAA Men's Soccer Regional Coach Yr., 2004. Mem. Am. Alliance Health and Phys. Edn., Nat. Soccer Coaches Assn. Am. (all-Am. com. 2001, divsn. III nat. chair all-am. com.), Nat. Intramurals/Recreation Sports Assn., Nat. Ski Patrol (patroller 1978—, asst. patrol dir. 2003-), US Tennis Assn. Avocations: golf, tennis, skiing. Office: SUNY Geneseo 1 College Cir Geneseo NY 14454-1401 Office Phone: 585-245-5343. Business E-Mail: mooney@geneseo.edu.

MOONEY, MICHAEL EDWARD, lawyer; b. Beloit, Wis., Jan. 21, 1945; s. William C. and Edith (Slothower) M. BA in Econs., St. Norbert Coll., 1966; JD, Boston Coll., 1969. Bar: Mass. 1969, Maine 1969, US Tax Ct. 1975, US Ct. Internat. Trade 1986. Assoc. Nutter, McClennen & Fish, LLP, Boston, 1969—77, sr. ptnr., 1978—, now mng. ptnr. V.p., exec. dir. Fed. Tax Inst. New Eng.; spkr., lectr. numerous seminars. Co-editor: Considerations in Buying or Selling a Business, 1985; mem. bd. editors Accounting and Financial Planning for Law Firms, 1988—. Co-chmn. Metro One Divsn. United Way, 2003—06; chmn. A Better City; bd. dirs. Filene Found., Jobs for Mass. Fellow Am. Coll. Tax Counsel; mem. Boston Bar Assn. (chmn. tax highlights com. 1986-95, fin. com. 1990-92, founder, chmn. summer jobs program, co-chair Diversity Task Force 2007-08), Boston Tax Forum. Office: Nutter McClennen & Fish World Trade Ctr West 155 Seaport Blvd Boston MA 02210-2604 Office Phone: 617-439-2000. Personal E-mail: mmooney@nutter.com.

MOONEY, MICHAEL JOSEPH, university professor; b. Evansville, Ind., Dec. 15, 1942; s. Joseph Thomas and Marie Louise (DeJean) Mooney; children: Susanne, Julia. AB summa cum laude, St. Meinrad Coll., 1964; STL magna cum laude, Univ. Innsbruck, Austria, 1968; M in Philosophy, Columbia U., NYC, 1973, PhD, 1982; DHL (hon.), Kyoto U. Fgn. Studies, 1991, Waseda U., Japan, 1999. Lectr. dept. religious studies, St. Mary's U., Halifax, Nova Scotia, Canada, 1968-70; project coord. Columbia U., NYC, 1973-74, preceptor dept. religion, 1975-76, spl. asst. to exec. v.p. for acad. affairs, 1976-77, asst. provost, 1977-79, assoc. provost, 1979-82, dep. provost, 1982-89; pres. Lewis and Clark Coll., Portland, Oreg., 1989—2003; prof. Waseda U., Tokyo, 2003—, spl. advisor to pres., 2004—. Bd. dirs. Reid Hall, Inc., NYC and Paris,

1977—89, v.p., 1983—89; trustee Jour. Philosophy, 1982—; bd. dirs. Roothbert Fund, 1980—92; visitor Inst. for Advanced Study, Princeton, NJ, 1984; bd. dirs. Nat. Assn. Ind. Colls. and Univs., 1995—99, Waseda USA, 2008—; mem. exec. com. Nat. Assn. Ind. Colls. and Univs., 1997—99, sec., 1998—99; mem. commn. on internat. edn. Am. Coun. Edn., 1993—95, mem. com. women in higher edn., 1997; mem. Truman Scholarship Finalists Selection Com., 2001—04. Author: Vico in the Tradition of Rhetoric, 1985 (Gottschalk prize Am. Soc. 18th Century Studies 1985); editor: Renaissance Thought and Its Sources, 1979; co-editor: Toward a Theology of Christian Faith: Readings in Theology, 1968, Vico and Contemporary Thought, 1976, Small Comforts for Hard Times: Humanists on Public Policy, 1977. Trustee Scuola d'Italia, NYC, 1986—89, World Affairs Coun., Oreg., 1992—2001, pres., 1999—2000; trustee Oregon Ballet Theatre, 1992—2004; advisor Portland Opera Assn., 1992—93; bd. advisors Music Performance Trust Fund, 2002—04. Recipient Rome prize Am. Acad. in Rome, 1989, Internat. Citizen award Oreg. Consular Corps., 2002; Roothbert Fund fellow, 1972, Kent fellow Danforth Found., 1972, Woodrow Wilson fellow, 1972, Presdl. fellow Columbia U., 1972, F.J.E. Woodbridge Disting. fellow Columbia U., 1973; NEH grantee, 1984; Cavaliere Ufficiale, Order Merit, Republic of Italy, 1991. Fellow Italian Acad. for Advanced Studies in Am. (sr.); mem. Phi Beta Kappa (hon.).

MOONEY, PATRICIA KATHRYN, business owner, video producer, writer, philanthropist; b. Galesburg, Ill., July 1, 1955; d. Joseph Edmond and Magi (Richard) M.; m. Mark Levon Schulze, July 23, 1987. Student, Mich. State U., East Lansing, 1973-75. Freelance writer, San Diego, 1975—; office mgr. REGAIN, San Diego, 1977-80; owner A-Action Typing and Writing Svc., San Diego, 1980-82; COO Crystal Pyramid Prodns., San Diego, 1982—, New & Unique Videos, San Diego, 1984—. Author of poetry; prodr.: (broadcast interviews) Hillary Clinton, Hilary Swank, Toby Maguire, Kirsten Dunst, Topher Grace, Lucy Liu and numerous others. Recipient Women Who Mean Bus. award San Diego Bus. Jour., 2005, San Diego's Top 100 Fastest-Growing Companies award, 2007; Outstanding Cmty. Involvement Micro Bus. award SD C. of C., 2008; YWCA TWIN (Tribute to Women in Industry) award, 2008, internat. awards for ednl. videos produced and edited and for poetry. Democrat. Avocations: travel, mountain biking, photography, surfing, art. Office: Crystal Pyramid Inc 7323 Rondel Ct San Diego CA 92119-1530 Office Phone: 619-644-3000. E-mail: patty@crystalpyramid.com.

MOONEY, RICHARD EMERSON, writer; b. Plainfield, NJ, Mar. 31, 1927; s. Wandell M. and Alice (Joy) M.; m. Elizabeth B. Coleman, Oct. 30, 1954; children: James C., Stephen E., John B. BA, Yale U., 1947; postgrad. (Nieman fellow), Harvard U., 1955-56. Writer United Press, NYC, 1948-51, econ. reporter Washington, 1951-56, N.Y. Times, Washington, 1957-63, European econ. correspondent Paris, 1963-67, econ. reporter NYC, 1967, asst. to exec. editor, 1968, asst. to mng. editor, 1969, dep. fgn. editor, 1970-72, asst. fin. editor, 1972-76, mem. editl. bd., 1982-95; contbg. editor, 1995-96; v.p. Hartford Courant, 1976-81, exec. editor, 1976-81, dir., 1977-81. Author: (with Edwin L. Dale, Jr.) Inflation and Recession, 1959. Trustee Hartford Courant Found., 1977-81. Served with USNR, 1944-48. Mem. Soc. Silurians (bd. govs. 1998-2004), Yale Club, The Coffee House, Century Assn. Home and Office: 130 E 67th St New York NY 10065-6136 Personal E-mail: remooney@aol.com.

MOONEY, ROBERT THURSTON, healthcare educator; b. Bryan, Tex., Jan. 5, 1935; s. Archie T. and Eda Belle (Arrington) M.; m. Jean Russell, June 24, 1955; children: Cynthia Mooney Conyers, Sandra Mooney Cook. BS, Tex. A&M U., College Station, 1958, MEd, 1963. Cert. trainer. Tchr. Navasota (Tex.) Ind. Sch. Dist., 1958-61, Bay City (Tex.) Ind. Sch. Dist., 1961-65, dir. audio-visual instrn., 1965-66; ednl. media specialist Ednl. Media Labs., Austin, Tex., 1967-68; dir. edn. and tng. Bexar County Hosp. Dist., San Antonio, 1968-75; asst. prof. Southwest Tex. State U., San Marcos, 1974-80, assoc. prof., 1980—, chmn. allied health scis., 1976-81, dir. health svcs. mgmt., 1988-90, dir. Health Resource Ctr., 1981-82; mayor pro tem City of San Marcos, San Marcos, 1995-96; dir. undergraduate studies Tex. State U., San Marcos, 2003—. Dir. Sch. Paramed. Tng., Bexar County Hosp. Dist., San Antonio, 1970-72; cons. pvt. contractor, San Marcos, 1975—; mem. community/environ. task force Cen. Tex. Health Systems Agy., 1977; mem. health occupations edn. adv. com. Tex. Edn. Agy., 1989-91; mem. summer games organizing com. Tex. Spl. Olympics, 1990-91, security chmn., 1990; mem. health occupations projects adv. com. U. Tex., Austin, 1990-91. Author: Overhead Projection, 1968; (with Sister Rene Fisher and Beth Knox) Guidelines for the Development of a Hospital-Wide Education Service, 1979; contbr. articles to profl. jours. Chmn. disaster svc. Hays County Red Cross, San Marcos, 1988-89, bd. dirs., 1986-89; res. comdr. San Marcos Police Res., 1984-85; treas. Hays/Caldwell Counties Alcohol and Drug Abuse Coun., 1984-85, exec. bd. mem., 1984-85; res. dep. Hays County Sheriffs Dept., 1985-86, San Marcos Police Dept., 1986-87; zoning commr. City of San Marcos, 1991-93, city councilman, 1993-96; bd. dirs. Hays County Ctrl. Appraiser Dist., 1994-97; bd. pres. San Marcos/Hays County EMS; planning and zoning commr. City of San Marcos, 1997-2001; v.p. Hays County Appraisal Dist. Bd., 1996-98; chair Planning and Zoning Commn., City San Marcos, 1998-2000; pres. San Marcos Coun. Neighborhood Assns., 2001-02; pres.-elect Heritage Assn. San Marcos, 2002-03. Mem. ASTD, Am. Coll. Healthcare Execs., Soc. Human Resource Mgmt., Am. Soc. Healthcare Edn. and Tng. (bd. mem. 1971-72), Am. Hosp. Assn., Tex. Soc. Healthcare Educators (pres. 1971-72, pres. 1991-92, disting. svc. and achievement award 1989), Bay City Classroom Tchrs. Assn. (pres.), Navasota Classroom Tchrs. Assn. (pres.), Alamo Tng. and Insvc. Coun. Hosp. and Allied Health Educators (pres. 1969-71), Internat. Personnel Mgmt. Assn. (publs. adv. bd. 1988), Tex. Hosp. Assn., Assn. of Univ. Programs in Health Adminstrn., Soc. for Human Resource Mgmt. (reviewer HR magazine 1990-96), Heritage Assn. San Marcos (pres.-elect 2002-03), Kiwanis, Hays County A&M Club (pres. 2002-03). Avocations: hunting, fishing. Office Phone: 512-245-3511. Business E-Mail: rm02@txstate.edu.

MOONEY, TED (EDWARD COMSTOCK MOONEY), editor, art critic, writer; b. Dallas, Tex., Oct. 19, 1951; s. Booth and Elizabeth (Comstock) M. Student, Columbia U., 1969-71; BA, Bennington Coll., 1973. Mng. editor Fiction mag., NYC, 1975-77; sr. editor Art in Am. mag., NYC, 1977—2009. Author: (novels) Easy Travel to Other Planets, 1981 (Sue Kaufman prize for 1st fiction AAAL 1981), Traffic and Laughter, 1990, Singing Into the Piano, 1997; contbr. short stories in Esquire, Am. Rev., Granta, Seattle Review articles to L.A. Times, Vogue, Harper's Bazaar, Artforum; lectr. in field. Fellow Creative Artists Pub. Svc. Award, 1977, Ingram Merrill Found., 1978, 80, Guggenheim fellow, 1983. Fellow N.Y. Inst. for Humanities; mem PEN Am. Center. Democrat. Episcopalian. Home Phone: 212-316-1747. Personal E-mail: tedmooney1@gmail.com.

MOONEY, WILLIAM PIATT, actor; b. Bernie, Mo., May 2, 1936; s. Lowell E. and Louise S. M.; m. Valorie Shaw Goodall, Jan. 13, 1962; children: Sean Goodall, William Norvell. Student Am. theater wing, U. Colo., Boulder, Doctorate (hon.). Pres. William Mooney Assocs., cons. to industry for exec. presentations. Appeared in continuing role of Paul Martin on TV series All My Children, 1972-85 (2 Emmy nominations); one-man show Half Horse, Half Alligator, 1964, Damn Everything But the Circus, 1980, They All Wanted in the Act (The Lindbergh Kidnapping and Trial), 2004, Tonight! Buffalo Bill!, 2006, Code Trackers & Long Walkers, 2007, The Jim beam story- America's Top Sparkled Whiskey, 2008; stage appearances: Brownsville Raid, We, A Man for All Seasons, 1965,Lolita, 1981; films: The Next Man, Network, A Flash of Green, Beer, Second Sight, C.A.T. Squad; author/star mus. play Banjo Reb and the Blue Ghost; co-author: ASAP-The Fastest Way to Create a Memorable Speech, 1992, Ready-to-Tell Tales, 1994, A Storyteller's Guide, 1995, Spiders in the Hairdo, 1999, (Grammy nominee 1998), (PBS) With a Dog's Eyes, 1997; recording artist: Why the Dog Chases the Cat, 1997 (ALA Notable Parent's Choice Gold and Naird awards), Spiders In The Hairdo, 1997, More Ready-To-Tell Tales From Around The World, 2000, The Exploding Toilet, 2004. Dir. jazz mus. Jam, 8 yrs. Colo. Univ. Opera Theater, others. Recipient Regents' Disting. Svc. award, U. Colo., Boulder, 2007; nominee Grammy award, 1995, 1998. Address: 2879 Shadow Creek Dr #105 Boulder CO 80303 E-mail: bmooney303@aol.com.

MOONVES, LESLIE, broadcast executive; b. NYC, Oct. 6, 1949; s. Herman and Josephine (Schleifer) Moonves; m. Nancy Wiesenfeld, Dec. 17, 1978 (div.); children: Adam, Sara, Michael; m. Julie Chen, Dec. 23, 2004. BA, Bucknell U., Lewisburg, Pa., 1971. Devel. exec. Catalina Prodns., Burbank, Calif., 1980—81; v.p. devel. Saul Ilson Prodns. Columbia Pictures TV, Burbank, 1981—82; v.p. movies and mini-series 20th Century Fox, LA, 1982—85, Lorimar, Inc., Culver City, Calif., 1985—88; exec. v.p. creative affairs Lorimar-Telepictures, Culver City, 1988—90; pres. Lorimar TV, Burbank, 1989—93, Warner Bros. TV, Burbank, 1993—95, CBS Entertainment, LA, 1995—97; exec. v.p. CBS/Broadcast Group, 1995—97; pres., CEO CBS TV, 1998—2003, chmn., CEO, 2003—04; co-pres., co-COO Viacom Inc., NYC, 2004—06; pres., CEO CBS Corp., 2006—. Bd. dirs. KB Home, 2004—. Developer, prodr. (TV series) Dallas, Dark Justice, Guns of Paradise, Knots Landing, Midnight Caller, Sisters, Family Matters, Full House, Perfect Strangers, Family Man, I'll Fly Away, Reasonable Doubts, Step by Step, Hangin' with Mr. Cooper, The Jackie Thomas Show, Crossroads, Homefront, Going to Extremes, Shaky Ground, It Had To Be You, Time Trax, Against the Grain, Lois & Clark: The Adventures of Superman, Cafe Americain, How'd They Do That, Living Single, Family Album, Getting By. Bd. dirs. LA Free Clinic; co-chair LA bd. govs. Mus. TV and Radio; bd. trustees Entertainment Industries Coun.; trustee Nat. Coun. for Families and TV, Am. Film Inst.; mem. adv. bd. NCAA. Recipient Gold Medal award, Internat. Radio and TV Soc., 2003, Career Achievement award, Casting Soc. Am., Sherrill Corwin award, Am. Jewish Com.; named Showman of Yr., Variety, Most Powerful Man in Hollywood, Entertainment Weekly. Mem.: NATAS (exec. com.), Hollywood Radio & TV Soc. (bd. dirs. 1988—91, pres. 1991). Democrat. Jewish. Office: CBS Corp 51 W 52nd St New York NY 10019-6188 Office Phone: 212-975-4321.

MOONWALKER, TU, minister, counselor, artist; b. Feb. 9, 1948; BA, Calif. State U., Sacramento, 1972; BS, U. Calif., Davis, 1973; MA, Tex. Tech. U., 1978, MS, 1979; postgrad., So. Meth. U., 1979. Chef Fairmont Hotel, San Francisco, 1971—72; rsch. and biopsy technician Tex. Tech. U. and Med. Ctr., Lubbock, 1974—78; Native Am. artist Santa Fe, 1979—87; cons. Am. Indian art Wheelwright Mus., Santa Fe, 1984—87; spiritual counselor, tchr. Ctr. for Universal Beingness, Moriarty, N.Mex., 1988—; min., canon Brigade of Light Ch., Cedar Mountain, NC, 1991—. Tech. advisor Am. Playhouse PBS Spl., Crestone, Colo., 1987; chmn., bd. dirs. Crystal Found., Denver, 1988—92, Profit from the Sun, Moriarty, 1999—2001; co-founder Ctr. for Universal Beingness; cons., spkr. in field. Dir.(writer): Karen Lee Dance Theater, 2000—02; author: Business Revolution Through Ancestral Wisdom, 2008. Chmn., bd. dirs. Ednl. Opportunity Program Calif. State U., Sacramento, 1971; mem. art com. chair, bd. dirs. YWCA, Lubbock, 1976—77; coun. mem. Sacramento Indian Ctr., 1971; vol. Talking Talons Youth Group, Tijeras, N.Mex., 2000. Recipient Humanitarian award, Friends for Life, Albuquerque, 1996; named Outstanding Young Woman Am., 1982; finalist Next Generation Indie Book awards, 2009; Wetlands Devel. Fed. grant, U.S. Wildlife, N.Mex., 1999. Mem.: Inst. Noetic Scis., Astron. Soc. Pacific, N.Y. Acad. Scis., Defenders of Wildlife (Wildlife Guardian), Acad. Am. Poets. Avocations: crafts, woodworking, stained glass, poetry, writing. Office: 30-A Steeldust Ave Moriarty NM 87035

MOOR, KRISTIAN P., insurance company executive; b. NYC, 1959; BS in Fin., Bryant Coll., 1981; MBA, Pace U. Joined American Internat. Group, Inc., NYC, 1981, pres. Nat. Union's Mgmt. Liability Divsn., 1995—97, sr. v.p. domestic gen. ins., 1997—98, exec. v.p. domestic gen. ins., 1998—2008, mem. exec. com., 2002—, pres., CEO AIG Property Casualty Group NYC, 2008—. Bd. trustees Bryant Coll. Office: American Internat Group Inc 70 Pine St New York NY 10270*

MOOR, ROB, professional sports team executive; b. Geneva; came to US, 1966; Grad., U. Calif., Irvine. Distbn. staff MGM Studios; mem. staff royalties, licensing and profits 20th Century Fox Studios; exec. v.p. NHL LA Kings; pres. Minn. Timberwolves, 1994—2005, CEO, 2005—; pres. Midwest Entertainment Grp. Bd. mem. Greater Mpls. Conv. and Visitors Assn., Downtown Coun. Mem. Greater Mpls. C. of C. (bd. dirs.). Office: Minn Timberwolves 600 First Ave N Minneapolis MN 55403-1416*

MOORAD, JEFF, professional sports team executive; b. Modesto, Calif., 1956; m. Jan Moorad; 3 children. AA, Modesto Jr. Coll., 1976; BA in Polit. Sci., UCLA, 1978; JD, Villanova U. Sch. Law, Pa., 1981. Founder, pres., CEO Moorad Sports Mgmt., 1983—2004; gen. ptnr., CEO Ariz. Diamondbacks, 2004—09; co-owner Hall of Fame Racing, 2007—; vice chmn., CEO San Diego Padres, 2009—. Tech. cons., cameo appearance: (films) Jerry Maguire, 1996; For Love of the Game, 1999. Named one of The 100 Most Powerful People in Sports, The Sporting News. Office: San Diego Padres 9449 Friars Rd San Diego CA 92108*

MOORADIAN, ARSHAG DERTAD, internist, educator; b. Aleppo, Syria, Aug. 20, 1953; arrived in U.S., 1981; s. Dertad and Araxi (Halajian) Mooradian; m. Deborah Lynn Miles, June 25, 1985; children: Arshag Dertad, Jr., Ariana Araxie. BS, Am. U., Beirut, 1976, MD, 1980. Diplomate Am. Bd. Internal Medicine. Asst. prof. medicine UCLA, 1985-88; assoc. prof. U. Ariz., Tucson, 1988-91; prof. St. Louis U., 1991—2006; prof. medicine, chmn. dept. medicine U. Fla., 2006—. Contbr. articles to profl. jours. Grantee VA, 1985—97. Mem.: Am. Diabetes Assn. (chmn. task force micronutrients 1990—91, chmn. coun. nutrition and metabolism 2000—02), Endocrine Soc., Gerontol. Soc. Am., Am. Fedn. Clin. Rsch., Phi Kappa Phi, Alpha Omega Alpha. Mem. Armenian Orthodox Ch. Achievements include identification of a potential biomarker of aging; research in on age-related changes in the blood-brain barrier; on age-related changes in thyroid hormone action; on diabetes related changes in the central nervous system. Office: U Fla Coll Medicine Dept Medicine 653-1 West Eighth St Jacksonville FL 32209 Business E-Mail: arshag.mooradian@jax.ufl.edu.

MOORADIAN, GEORGE T., lawyer; BA with high distinction, U. Mich., 1976; JD, U. Mich. Law Sch., 1978; LLM, NYU, 1980. Bar: DC 1979, Mich. 1979, Calif. 1983. Ptnr.-in-charge Baker & Hostetler, Costa Mesa, Calif., coord., tax, personal planning and employee benefits. Office: Baker & Hostetler LLP 600 Anton Blvd Ste 900 Costa Mesa CA 92626-7221

MOORADIAN, PATRICIA, museum administrator; b. 1960; BFA, Tex. Christian U. Regional dir. mktg. Taubman Co.; COO The Henry Ford, Dearborn, Mich., 2000—05, pres., 2005—. Mem. bd. dirs. Henry Ford Health System Detroit Campus, Henry Ford Learning Inst., Arab Cmty. Ctr. for Econ. and Social Issues. Mem. bd. dirs. Mich. Travel Commn., Cult. Alliance Southeast Mich., Detroit Metro Conv. & Visitor's Bur.; mem. adv. coun. US Cult. & Heritage Tourism Summit; mem. citizens adv. coun. U. Mich.-Dearborn; leadership policy conf. com. Detroit Regional Chamber. Office: The Henry Ford 20900 Oakwood Blvd Dearborn MI 48124-4088

MOORCROFT, WILLIAM HERBERT, retired bio-psychologist, educator, researcher; b. Detroit, Feb. 1, 1944; s. Leonard and Elsie Moorcroft; m. Christina Louise Perrin, Nov. 27, 1971; children: Marcile Louise Cappel, Partick Richard, Andrew William. PhD, Princeton U., 1970. Prof. psychobiology Luther Coll., Decorah, Iowa, 1971—2002; adj. prof. psychology Colo. State U., Ft. Collins, Colo., 2001—04. Cons. No. Colo. Sleep Consultants, Fort Collins, 2005—. Author: (textbook) Understanding Sleep and Dreaming. Mem.: APA, Am. Acad. Sleep Medicine, Phi Beta Kappa. Democrat. Episcopalian. Avocations: sailing, internationaltravel. Home: 4443 Vista Dr Fort Collins CO 80526 Office: 4500 E 9th Ave Ste 550 Denver CO E-mail: bill@sleeplessincolorado.com.

MOORE, ALAN, writer; b. Northampton, England, Nov. 18, 1953; m. Phyllis Moore (div.); children: Amber, Leah; m. Melinda Gebbie. Authored numerous issues of 2000AD, Captain Britain, Dark Star, Doctor Who, Marvelman, Warrior, Swamp Thing, WildC.A.T.S, Spawn, Supreme, Taboo. Author: (comic books and graphic novels) V for Vendetta, 1982—88, Swamp Thing, 1983—87, Watchmen, 1986—87 (Hugo award, 1988, named one of All-Time 100 Novels, Time mag., 2005), Batman: The Killing Joke, 1988, From Hell, 1991—98, 1963, 1993, From Hell: The Compleat Scripts, 1994, The League of Extraordinary Gentlemen, 1999—2000, Promethea, 1999—2005, Tomorrow Stories, 1999—2002, Tom Strong, 1999—2006, Top 10, 1999—2001, The League of Extraordinary Gentlemen, Volume II, 2002—03, Terra Obscura, 2003—05, Alan Moore's Yuggoth Cultures and Other Growths, 2003, DC Universe: The Stories of Alan Moore, 2003, The Extraordinary Works of Alan Moore, 2003, Smax, 2003—04, Top 10: The Forty-Niners, 2005, Lost Girls, 2006, Alan Moore's Complete WildC.A.T.S, 2007, Alan Moore: Wild Worlds, 2007, The League of Extraordinary Gentlemen: Black Dossier, 2007. Recipient Best Writer, Jack Kirby Awards, 1985, 1986, 1987, Will Eisner Comic Industry Awards, 1988, 1989, 1995, 1996, 1997, 2000, 2001, 2004, 2006.*

MOORE, ALBERT CUNNINGHAM, lawyer, insurance company executive; b. Miami, Fla., May 31, 1931; s. Elias Richard and Virginia Adelaide (Thompson) Moore; m. Anne Cambreleng Bonynge, Aug. 24, 1957; children: Emily Robinson French, Barbara Raffield, Catherine Anne Bonygne Wells. AB, U. N.C., 1953; JD, U. Va., 1959. Bar: N.Y. 1960. Atty. White & Case, NYC, 1959-69; corporate sec. Studebaker-Worthington, Inc., NYC, 1969-72; sr. v.p., gen. counsel Crum & Forster, 1973-87. Former trustee N.J. Shakespeare Festival; former bd. dirs. DeBordieu Property Owners Assn., DeBordieu Arch. Rev. Bd. With USNR, 1953—56. Mem.: Wilton Ctr. Tennis Club (NH), Chi Phi, Phi Alpha Delta. Home: 529 Cedar Club Cir Chapel Hill NC 27517

MOORE, ALECIA BETH See PINK

MOORE, ALMA C., publishing executive, consultant; b. Cin. d. Henry Paul and Helena Anne (Link) Clausing; m. Roy Moore. Student, Stephens Coll., Parsons Sch. Design, New Sch. Social Rsch., NYC. Women's editor TV Guide mag., NYC, 1962-70; dir. advt., promotion and pub. rels. Yves Saint Laurent Parfums, 1971-72; v.p., promotion and editl. dir. Viva/Omni mags., 1974-80; dir. mktg. comm. Redbook mag., 1980-83; editor, pub. Women Entrepreneur mag., 1983-85; pres. Alma C. Moore & Assocs. Mag. Cons., NYC, 1983—95. Photographer: (with Roy Moore) Thomas Jefferson's Journey to the South of France, 1999. Mem. ind. jud. screening panel N.Y.C. Civil Ct. Judges Dem. Com., 1985, Emily's List, Eleanor Roosevelt Legacy Com., Children's Aid Soc. Mem. ACLU, NOW, LWV, Nat. Trust Hist. Preservation, Advt. Women N.Y., Women's City Club of N.Y. Home and Office: 1040 Park Ave New York NY 10028-1032

MOORE, AMANDA LEIGH See MOORE, MANDY

MOORE, ANDREW GIVEN TOBIAS, II, investment banker, law educator; b. New Orleans, Nov. 25, 1935; m. Ann Elizabeth Dawson, June 5, 1965; children— Cecily Elizabeth (dec.), Marianne Dawson. BBA, Tulane U., 1958, JD, 1960. Bar: La. 1960, Del. 1963. Law clk. to chief justice Del., Dover, 1963; assoc. firm Killoran & Van Brunt, Wilmington, Del., 1964-70, partner, 1971-76; partner firm Connolly, Bove & Lodge, Wilmington, 1976-82; justice Del. Supreme Ct., Wilmington, 1982-94; sr. mng. dir. Wasserstein Perella & Co., Inc., NYC, 1994—2001, Drsdner Kleinwort Wasserstein, Inc., NYC, 2001—. Mem. Del. Bar Examiners, 1975-82; mem. Del. Gen. Corp. law com., 1969-83; chmn. joint com. Del. Bar Assn.-Del. Bankers Assn., 1978-79; chmn. Del. Jud. Proprieties Com., 1983-94, Del. Bench and Bar Conf., 1988-94; trustee Del. Bar Found., 1984-94; faculty Tulane Inst. European Legal Studies, Paris Inst., 1990-96, 99; adj. prof. law Georgetown U. Law Ctr., Widener U. Sch. Law, U. Iowa Coll. Law; guest lectr. law Columbia U., Tulane U., U. Toronto, Can., U. Tex., Villanova U., Washington U., St. Louis, U. Iowa, George Mason U., DeVrije U. van Brussel, Cath. U. Louvain La Neuve; mem. pres.'s coun. Tulane U., 1990-96; chmn. Tulane Corp. Law Inst., 1988-95; Lehmann disting. vis. prof. law Washington U., St. Louis, 1994, 96; Mason Ladd disting. vis. prof. U. Iowa, 1995; disting. vis. prof. law St. Louis U., 1995, 96, 99; bd. dirs. Am. Lawyer Media, Inc. Trustee Del. Home and Hosp. for Chronically Ill, Smyrna, 1966-70, chmn., 1966-69; mem. New Castle County Hist. Rev. Bd., Wilmington, 1974-82; mem. Del. Cts. Planning Com., 1982-94; dean's coun. Tulane U. Law Sch., 1988-96; bd. visitors Walter F. George Sch. Law, Mercer U., 1985-91, chmn., 1988-90. With JAGC, USAF, 1960-63. Mem. ABA, La. Bar Assn., Del. Bar Assn. (v.p. 1976-77, exec. com. 1982-83), Am. Judicature Soc. (bd. dirs. 1982-86), Order Barristers, Phi Delta Phi, Delta Theta Phi (hon.), Omicron Delta Kappa Democrat. Presbyterian.

MOORE, ANDREW TAYLOR, JR., banker; b. Tarboro, NC, June 17, 1940; s. Andrew Taylor and Mary Dare (Allsbrook) M. BA in History, Duke U., 1962; LLB, U.Va., Charlottesville, 1965. Asst. sec. Signet Banking Corp., Richmond, 1965-71, asst. v.p., corporate sec., 1971-75, v.p., corporate sec., 1975-82, sr. v.p., corporate sec., 1982-94. Bd. dirs. Theatre IV, Richmond, Va., 1981-97, Va. State YMCA adv. coun.,

Lynchburg, 1988-96; trustee Hist. Richmond Found., 1993-98; mem. presidents coun. Va. Hist. Soc., 1996-2004. Presbyterian (elder 1996—). Avocations: jogging, gardening, travel. Home: 2011 Hanover Ave Richmond VA 23220-3539 Office Phone: 804-353-5039. Personal E-mail: atmjr01@aol.com.

MOORE, ANN S., publishing executive; b. McLean, Va., 1950; d. Monty and Bea Sommovigo; m. Donovan Moore; 1 child, Brendan. BA in Polit. Sci., Vanderbilt U., Nashville, 1971; MBA, Harvard U., Cambridge, Mass., 1978. Corp. fin. analyst Time, Inc., NYC, 1978—83, gen. mgr. Sports Illustrated, 1983—89, founding pub. Sports Illustrated for Kids, 1989-91, pub. People mag., 1991—93, pres. People mag., 1993—98, pres. People Mag. Grp. (renamed People/In Style Mag. Grp., 2001), 1998—2001, exec. v.p., 2001—02, chmn., CEO, 2002—. Bd. dirs. Avon Products Inc., 1993; spkr. in field. Hon. bd. mem. Gilda's Club, NYC; founder Time to Give Back; bd. dirs. Wallace Found. Recipient Civic Leadership award, AOL Time Warner, 2003, Alumni Achievement award, Harvard Bus. Sch., 2006; named Pub. Exec. of Yr., Adweek, 1998; named a Bus. Statesman, Harvard Bus. Sch., 2004; named one of 50 Most Powerful Women in Bus., Fortune mag., 1998—2008, 100 Most Powerful Women, Forbes mag., 2005—09, 50 Women to Watch, The Wall St. Jour., 2005, 2008, Next 20 Female CEOs, Pink Mag. & Forté Found., 2006, The 50 Most Powerful Women in NYC, NY Post, 2007. Achievements include guiding People magazine to spin off several popular titles including In Style (domestic and international), Teen People, People en Español, and Real Simple. Office: Time Inc 1271 Ave Americas New York NY 10020*

MOORE, ANNE, physician; b. NYC, Apr. 28, 1944; d. John D.J. and Mary Foote Moore; m. Arnold L. Lisio, Sept. 6, 1969; children: Philip Moore, Mary Foote. BA, Smith Coll., 1965; MD, Columbia U., 1969. Diplomate Am. Bd. Internal Medicine, Am. Bd. Hematology (chmn. 1996), Am. Bd. Oncology. Intern dept. medicine N.Y. Hosp., NYC, 1969-73, assoc. attending physician, 1981-95, attending physician, 1996—; postdoctoral fellow Rockefeller U., 1972-73, hematology-oncology fellow, 1973-75; asst. prof. medicine Cornell U. Med. Coll., NYC, 1975-91, assoc. prof. clin. medicine, 1981-95, prof. clin. medicine, 1996—. Cons. Strang Cancer Prevention Ctr.; lectr., cons., in field. Author: Patient's Guide to Breast Cancer Treatment, 1992, rev. edit., 1997; ad hoc reviewer Am. Jour. Clin. Oncology, 1994, New Eng. Jour. Medicine, 1994, 96, 97; contbr. articles to profl. jours., chpts. to books. Trustee St. David's Sch., 1983-89, HealthCare Chaplaincy, Inc., 1991—; bd. dirs. Camilli Found., 1990—, Cure Myeloma Fund, 1988-98, N.Y. Community Trust. Recipient award SHARE, 1992, Wholeness of Life award Hosp. Chaplaincy, 1992, Alumnae award Oak Knoll Sch., 1994, Eileen Dreyer Meml. Lectureship award Sass Found. for Med. Rsch., 1996, Commendation award Office of Exec. Nassau County, 1996, award Artists for Breast Cancer Survival, Inc., 2000. Mem. Am. Bd. Internal Medicine (bd. dirs. 1996—), Am. Soc. Hematology, Am. Soc. Clin. Oncology, N.Y. Acad. Scis., Soc. for Study of Blood (membership chmn. 1979-80), N.Y. Met. Breast Cancer Group (membership chmn. 1992-93, sec.-treas. 1993-95, v.p. 1995-96, pres. 1997-99), Soc. for Study of Breast Disease, N.Y. Cancer Soc., N.Y. Acad. Medicine (trustee 1998-2006). Office: Weill Cornell Breast Ctr 425 E 61st St 8th Fl New York NY 10065

MOORE, BARBARA C., fraternal organization administrator; b. Columbia, SC, Dec. 27, 1949; d. Albert and Wilhelmina Crockett; m. Norman Moore, 1971; 1 child, Walletta. BS in Biology, Benedict Coll., Columbia, SC, 1971; MS in Edn., U. Chgo., 1986. With Benedict Coll., 1975—, admissions counselor, recruiter, dir. alumni affairs, current v.p. institutional advancement; internat. pres. Zeta Phi Beta Sorority, Inc., 2002—. Bd. dirs. Midlands YWCA, Richland County Nat. March of Dimes Found. Named one of Most Influential Black Americans, Ebony mag., 2006; named to Power 150, 2008. Mem.: Nat. Polit. Congress of Black Women, Inc., Coun. Advancement and Support of Edn., Nat. Assn. Female Execs., Nat. Coun. Negro Women (Living the Legacy Award 1983), Top Ladies of Distinction, Inc., Zeta Phi Beta Sorority (life; nat. first v.p., chair nat. exec. bd., chmn. Nat. Capital Campaign, Grand Basileus, nat. pres. 2002—). Baptist. Office: Zeta Phi Beta Sorority, Inc 1734 New Hampshire Ave, NW Washington DC 20009 also: 2nd Fl 145 Kennedy St, NW Washington DC 20011

MOORE, BEATRICE, religious organization administrator; b. Somerville, Mass., Oct. 6, 1928; d. George and Christina Turner; m. Wendell Moore, May 9, 1953; children: Karl C., Linda Moore Flewelling, Diane Pearl, Larry. BA in Theology and English, Berkshire Christian Coll., Lenox, Mass., 1950. Pres. The Woman's Home and Foreign Mission Soc., Loudon, NH, past nat. pres. Charlotte, NC, 1987—96, nat. spiritual life chmn., 1997—2005. Sunday sch. tchr., deaconess Loudon Ridge Family Bible Ch.; chair Concord Christian Women's Club, 2002-03, 05-06; prayer coord. Ladies Bible Study leader, 1998-05, Concord Christian Women's Club, 2003-04; active Women's Home and Fgn. Mission Soc., Loudon, past pres. NH Soc., past pres. ea. region; hostess, contact chmn., prayer adv., Bible club guide Stonecroft Ministries, Friendship Bible Study Guide; past leader 4-H Club. Mem.: Friendship Bible Studies (Coord. 2007—08), Concord Christian Womens Club (chair 2005—). Office: Woman's Home & Foreign Mission 845 Loudon Ridge Rd Loudon NH 03307-1712

MOORE, BETTY JO, retired legal assistant; b. Medicine Lodge, Kans., July 10, 1921; d. Joseph Christy and Helen Blanche (Hubbell) Sims; m. Harold Frank Moore, June 19, 1941 (dec.); children: Terrance C., Harold Anthony, Trisha Jo. Cert., U. West L.A., 1978; student, Wichita U., Kans., 1940-41. Cert. legal asst./escrow officer. Sec. UCLA, 1949-59; escrow officer Security Pacific Nat. Bank, LA, 1959-62, Empire Savs. & Loan Assn., Van Nuys, Calif., 1962-64; escrow supr. San Fernando Valley Bank, Van Nuys, 1964; escrow officer Heritage Bank, Westwood, Calif., 1964-66; escrow coord. Land Sys. Corp., Woodland Hills, Calif., 1966-67; senior escrow officer/asst. mgr., real estate lending officer Security Pacific Nat. Bank, LA, 1967-80; real estate paralegal Pub. Storage, Pasadena, 1980-81; asst. mgr. escrow dept. First Beverly Bank, Century City, Calif., 1982-84; escrow trainer/officer Moore's Tng. Temps Inc., Canoga Park, Calif., 1984—92, legal asst., 1992—. Participant People to People Amb. Program/Women in Mgmt. to USSR, 1989; observer Internat. Fedn. Bus. and Profl. Women's Congress, Washington, 1965, 81, Nassau, Bahamas, 1989, Narobi, Kenya, 1991, Havana, Cuba, 2004. Adv. bd. escrow edn. Pierce Coll., Woodland Hills, Calif., 1968-80. Recipient Cert. of Appreciation, Pierce Coll., 1979, Calif. Fedn. Bus. and Profl. Women, 1989, Nat. Women's History Project, 1995. Mem. Nat. Fedn. Bus. and Profl. Women's Clubs, Calif. Fedn. Bus. and Profl. Women (pres. dist. 1987-88, Calif. Found. chmn. 1988-89, internat. concerns chmn. 1996-97, 2003), Woodland Hills Bus. and Profl. Women ((pres. 1991-92, 94-95), Valley/Sunset Dist. BPW (v.p. legislation/pub. policy 1997-98, 2001-02, 03, Cert. of Appreciation 2002), Tri Valley Dist. Bus. and Profl. Women (legis. chair 1992-93, exec./corr. sec. 1993-94, 94-95), Internat. Fedn. Bus. and Profl. Women, Nat. Women's Polit. Caucus (coord., sec. San Fernando Valley caucus 1986-87, sec. 1990-2003, legis. co-chair 1991-93), Women's Orgn. Coalition San Fernando Valley (pres. 2002-, exec. com. L.A. Women's Equality Day 1995), San Fernando Valley Escrow Assn. (bd. dirs. 1962-64), L.A. Women's Family Equity Coalition, U. West L.A. Alumni Assn., Rotary, U.N. Assn. (v.p. San Fernando Valley), League of Women Voters. Democrat. Methodist. Avocations: reading, musical theater.

MOORE, BILLY DON, scriptwriter, film producer; b. Oklahoma City, Dec. 26, 1956; s. Orval L. and Mary E. (Perry) M.; m. Donna M. Lovelace; stepchildren: Derek, Ryan. BA in Journalism, U. Okla., 1979, MA in Journalism, 1993. Prodn. asst. FAA, Oklahoma City, 1979-81; media technician, supr. Oklahoma City C.C., 1981-85; video prodn. specialist Okla. Dept. Transportation, Oklahoma City, 1985-99; motion picture and broadcast archivist Okla. Hist. Soc., Oklahoma City, 1999—2009. Owner BVC Video. Editor, photographer (cable series) Connecting, 1983-85; prodr. pub. svc. announcements, (aviation video mag.) Okla. Approach, 1995-99; prodr. documentaries Okla. Pub. TV; prodr., editor, photographer: (TV) Yesterday; author: (book) The Oklahoma Aviation Story, 2005, Norick: The Mayors of Oklahoma City, 2006. Recipient Crystal award The Communicator, 1998, Telly award excellence, 1998, Aegis award, 1999, Videographer award excellence, 1999, 20th Anniversary Classic Telly award, 1999, Disting. Alumni award Okla. U. Coll. Journalism, 2003. Democrat. Baptist. Avocation: writing. Home Phone: 405-691-5927. E-mail: okvideobill@aol.com.

MOORE, BOB STAHLY, communications executive; b. Pasadena, Calif., July 3, 1936; s. Norman Hastings and Mary Augusta (Stahly) M. Student, U. Mo., 1954-58, MIT, 1958-62. Dir. news WPEO, Peoria, Ill., 1958—60, KSST, Davenport, Iowa, 1960—62, WIRE, Indpls., 1962—64, WCFL, Chgo., 1964—67; White House corr. Metromedia, Inc., Washington, 1967—71; dir. news Gateway Comm., Altoona, Pa., 1972—74; chief Washington Bur. MBS, 1974—76, v.p. news Arlington, Va., 1976—78, White House corr., 1978—81; dir. comm. Fed. Home Loan Bank Bd., Washington, 1981—85; spl. asst. to bd. govs. Fed. Res. Sys., Washington, 1985—. Active ARC. Served with USAF, 1961-63. Recipient profl. awards Ind. News Broadcasters, 1963, Ill. News Broadcasters, 1965, UPI, 1960, 63, 65, AP, 1956, 58, 61, 65, 67, Mo. News Broadcasters, 1956, 61. Mem. Radio and TV News Dirs. Assn. (Profl. award), White House Corrs. Assn., State Dept. Corrs. Assn., Radio-TV Corrs. Gallery (U.S. Capitol), Chgo. Coun. on Fgn. Rels., Pub. Rels. Soc. Am., Nat. Press Club, Washington Press Club, Chgo. Press Club, Mo. C. of C., Ill. C. of C., Sigma Delta Chi. Home: 114 W Arlington Ave Vandalia MO 63382 Office: 20th And Constitution NW Washington DC 20551-0001

MOORE, BRIAN P., health care professional; b. June 8, 1943; s. Nicholas and Rose Moore; m. Peggy Espejo, 2003; stepchildren: Andrea, Emily. Student in liberal arts & great books, St. Mary's Coll., Moraga, Calif., 1961—62; attended, Franciscan Theol. Sem., Calif., 1962—67; BA in Philosophy, Mission San Luis Rey Coll., Calif., 1966; grad. student, Calif. State U., LA, 1968; student in health care mgmt., UCLA, 1973; MPA, Ariz. State U., Tempe, 1976. Vol. US Peace Corps, Latin America, 1969—72; health care exec., managed care/HMO pioneer, internat. health cons., 1973—92; program fundraiser INMED, 1992—97; internat. cons. in pub. health projects thru pub. & pvt. partnerships, 1992—97; health principle, exec. recruitment firm, 1998—. V.p. Fedn. 69 Civic Assns., Washington, 1996—98; Fla. heritage mem. State of Fla.; supporter Flagler Mus.; pres. Good Govt. League, Hernando County, Fla., 2003, 2004; chair, co-founder Nature-Coast Coalition Peace & Justice, 2002—07; del. DC Constl. Convention, 1981; ind. city coun., mayoral candidate Washington, 1984—98; ind. US Congl. candidate, Fla. 5th dist., 2002, 2004; ind. US Senate candidate Fla., 2006; US presdl. candidate Socialist Party, 2008; Civil War re-enactor, 14th Bklyn. unit; player, mgr. NatureCoast Adult Baseball League, 2000—07. Named Man of Yr., Fedn. 69 Civic Assns., 1997. Mem.: Irish-Am. Soc., Hernando County (pres. 2002, 2003), Hernando County Hist. Soc. Socialist. Office: c/o Socialist Party USA 339 Lafayette St #303 New York NY 10012*

MOORE, C. BRADLEY, chemistry professor; b. Boston, Dec. 7, 1939; s. Charles Walden and Dorothy (Lutz) Moore; m. Penelope Williamson Percival, Aug. 27, 1960; children: Megan Bradley, Scott Woodward. BA magna cum laude, Harvard U., 1960; PhD, U. Calif., Berkeley, 1963. Predoctoral fellow NSF, 1960-63; asst. prof. chemistry U. Calif., Berkeley, 1963-68, assoc. prof., 1968-72, prof., 1972-2000, prof. emeritus, 2000—, vice chmn. dept., 1971-75, chmn. dept. chemistry, 1982-86, dean Coll. Chemistry, 1988-94; v.p. rsch. Ohio State U., Columbus, Disting. prof. math. and phys. sci., prof. chemistry, 2000—03, prof. emeritus, 2003—; prof. chemistry Northwestern U., 2003—08, v.p. rsch., 2003—07, prof. emeritus, 2008—. Assoc. prof. Faculty Scis., Paris, 1970, 75; Miller Rsch. Prof. U. Calif., Berkeley, 1972-73, 87-88, mgr. strategy & planning energy biosci. inst., 2008-; vis. prof. Inst. for Molecular Sci., Okazaki, Japan, 1979, Fudan U., Shanghai, 1979, adv. prof., 1988—; vis. fellow Joint Inst. for Lab. Astrophysics, U. Colo., Boulder, 1981-82; vis. prof., U. Göttingen, 1994, University Heidelberg, 1994, Max Planck Inst. L.C. Quantum Optics, 1997; faculty sr. scientist (Chemical Sci. Div.) Lawrence Berkeley Nat. Lab., 1974-2000, divsn. dir., 1998-2000: mem. editl. bd. Jour. Chem. Physics, 1973-75, Chem. Physics Letters, 1980-85, Jour. Phys. Chemistry, 1981-87, Laser Chemistry, 1982—; mem. Basic Energy Scis. adv. com. Office Sci. U.S. Dept. Energy, 2000-03; mem. gov. bd. Fermi Nat. Accelator Lab., 2006-07; mem. bd. Chgo. Coun. Sci. & Tech., 2006-08 Editor: Chemical and Biochemical Applications of Lasers; assoc. editor Annual Review of Physical Chemistry, 1985-90; contbr. articles to profl. jours. Trustee Sci. Svc., 1995-2007, Sci. and Tech. Campus, 2000-03; mem. bd. govs. Ohio Supercomputer Ctr., 2000-03; rsch. officer Coun. of Ohio Bd. of Regents, 2000-03; pres., chmn. bd. Ohio State U. Rsch. Found., 2000-03; mem. governing bd. Argonne Nat. Lab., 2005-07, mem. sci. policy coun., 2005-07. Recipient Coblentz award, 1973, E.O. Lawrence Meml. award U.S. Dept. Energy, 1986, Lippincott award, 1987, 1st award Inter-Am. Photochem. Soc., 1988; nat. scholar Harvard U., 1958-60; fellow Alfred P. Sloan Found., 1968, Guggenheim Found., 1969, Humboldt Rsch. award for Sr. U.S. Scientists, 1994. Fellow AAAS (coun. 2007-, com. coun. affairs, 2008-), Am. Acad. Arts and Scis., Am. Phys. Soc. (Plyler award 1994); mem. NSF adv. com. for education and human resources directorate, chair subcom. policy and planning 1997-99, NAS (chmn. com. undergrad. sci. edn. 1993-97, class I membership com., 1998-2000, 2002, 2000 nominating com.), Am. Chem. Soc. (past chmn. divsn. phys. chemistry, Calif. sect. award 1977). Avocation: bicycling. Office: Univ Calif Dept Chemistry Consulting Univ Rsch Program Devel Infrastructure Berkeley CA 94720-1460 Office Phone: 510-206-1409. Business E-Mail: moorecb@berkeley.edu.

MOORE, CALVIN C., mathematics professor, academic administrator; b. NYC, Nov. 2, 1936; s. Robert A. and Ruth (Miller) M.; m. Doris Lienhard, Sept. 14, 1974. AB summa cum laude, Harvard U., 1958, MA, 1959, PhD in Math., 1960. Research instr. U. Chgo., 1960-61; asst. prof. U. Calif. at Berkeley, 1961-65, asso. prof., 1965-66, prof. math., 1966—, dean phys. scis., 1971-76, chair dept. math., 1996—2002; dir. Center Pure and Applied Math, 1977-80; dep. dir. Math. Scis. Research Inst., 1981-85; asst. v.p. acad. planning and personnel U. Calif. Systemwide Adminstrn., 1985-86, assoc. v.p. acad. affairs, 1986-94. Mem. Inst. for Advanced Study, 1964-65; mem. at large NRC, 1971-73; mem. Math. Sci. Edn. Bd., 1991-93, mem. exec. com.; mem. Pres.'s Com. on Nat. Medal Sci., 1979-81; chair task force on rewards and recognition in math. scis. Joint Policy Bd. for Math., 1993-95. Chmn. bd. govs.: Pacific Jour. Math., 1972-76; editor: Mathematische Zeitschrift, Ill. Jour. Math, Pacific Jour. Math.; exec. editor research announcements; mng. editor: Bull. Am. Math. Soc.; contbg. editor: Advances in Mathematics; contbr. articles to profl. jours. Recipient Berkeley Citation award, 2003, Oliver Johnson award, 2004, Berkeley Faculty Svc. award, 2005. Fellow Am. Acad. Arts and Scis., Am. Assn for Advancement Sci.; mem. Am. Math. Soc. (exec. com., council mem. at large, v.p., chmn. bd. trustees, com. on sci. policy). Home: 1408 Eagle Point Ct Lafayette CA 94549-2328 Office: U Calif at Berkeley Dept Math Evans Hall Berkeley CA 94720

MOORE, CARLETON BRYANT, geochemistry educator; b. NYC, Sept. 1, 1932; s. Eldridge Carleton and Mabel Florence (Drake) M.; m. Jane Elizabeth Strouse, July 25, 1959; children: Barbara Jeanne, Robert Carleton; m. Diane Beets, Apr. 23, 2000. BS, Alfred U., 1954, DSc (hon.), 1977; PhD, Cal. Inst. Tech., 1960. Asst. prof. geology Wesleyan U., Middletown, Conn., 1959-61; mem. faculty Ariz. State U., Tempe, 1961—; nat. rsch. coun. rsch. assoc. NASA Ames Rsch. Ctr., 1974; prof., founding dir. Ctr. for Meteorite Studies Ariz. State U., Regents' prof., 1988—. Vis. prof. Stanford U., 1974; Prin. investigator Apollo 11-17; preliminary exam. team Lunar Receiving Lab., Apollo, 12-17. Author: Cosmic Debris, 1969, Meteorites, 1971, Principles of Geochemistry, 1982, Grundzügeder Geochemie, 1985; editor: Researches on Meteorites, 1961, Jour. Meteoritical Soc.; contbr. articles to profl. jours. Asteroid 5046 named Carletonmoore in his honor, 2000. Fellow Am. Geophys. Union, Ariz.-Nev. Acad. Sci. (pres. 1979-80), Meteoritical Soc. (life hon., pres. 1966-68), Geol. Soc. Am., Mineral. Soc. Am., AAAS (council 1967-70); mem. Geochem. Soc., Am. Chem. Soc., Am. Ceramic Soc., Sigma Xi. Office: Ariz State U Ctr Meteorite Studies Tempe AZ 85287-2504 Address: PO Box 26137 Tempe AZ 85285 Home Phone: 480-838-3353; Office Phone: 480-965-3576. Business E-Mail: cmoore@asu.edu.

MOORE, CAROLE IRENE, librarian; b. Berkeley, Calif., Aug. 15, 1944; AB, Stanford U., 1966; MLS, Columbia U., 1967. Reference libr. Columbia U., NYC, 1967-68, U. Toronto, Can., 1968-80, head cataloging, 1980-85, assoc. libr., 1985-86, chief libr., 1986—. Mem. nat. adv. bd. Nat. Libr. Can., Ottawa, 1991-94; bd. dirs. Rsch. Librs. Group. 1994-2000, U. Toronto Press, 1994—. Recipient Disting. Alumni award Columbia U., 1989. Mem. ALA, Can. Libr. Assn., Can. Assn. Rsch. Librs. (pres. 1989-91, bd. dirs. 1996-98). Avocation: gardening. Office: U Toronto Libr 130 Saint George St Toronto ON Canada M5S 1A5

MOORE, CASSANDRA CHRONES, policy analyst; b. Oneonta, NY, June 14, 1935; d. Constantine John and Antonia (Laskaris) Chrones; m. Thomas Gale Moore, Dec. 28, 1958; children: Charles Godwin, Antonia Laskaris. BA summa cum laude, Radcliffe Coll., Cambridge, Mass., 1956; MA, Harvard U., 1958; PhD, U. Mich., 1975. Lic. real estate broker Calif. Lectr. Duquesne U., Pitts., 1962-65, Mich. State U., East Lansing, 1966-68; broker, owner Moore Assocs., Palo Alto, Calif., 1983-85; dir. state and mcpl. legislation Nat. Assn. Realtors, Washington, 1985-87; exec. dir. Fed. Interagy. Coun. on Homeless, Washington, 1987-89; adj. scholar Competitive Enterprise Inst., Washington, 1989—, mem. adv. bd., 1995—; adj. scholar Cato Inst., Washington, 1996—. Author: Haunted Housing, 1997. Co-chmn. Radcliffe Alumnae Lectureship Com., Palo Alto and San Francisco, 1984-2000; mem. nat. com. Radcliffe Alumnae Professorship Fund, 2001-02. Recipient Fulbright fellowship U.S. Govt., Washington, 1956-57. Mem.: Calif. Assn. Scholars (mem. adv. bd. 2005—), Palo Alto Bd. Realtors (dir. 1984, 1985), Tsintzinian Soc. (bd. mem. 1999—, alt. bd. mem. 2001—02), Am. Assn. Small Property Owners (bd. mem. 1997—), Radcliffe Club Peninsula (pres. 1980—82), Phi Beta Kappa. Avocations: hiking, swimming, skiing. Office: 415 Cambridge Ave Palo Alto CA 94306 Office Phone: 650-853-0798. Personal E-mail: ccmassoc@comcast.net.

MOORE, CHARLES EDWARD, lawyer, political organization administrator; b. Jenkins, Ky., Aug. 29, 1948; s. Charles Foster and Belle (Elliott) M.; m. Deborah Jane Howes (div. 1970); 1 child, Andrea Belle; m. Mary O'Brien Hoge, Aug. 3, 1974 (dov. Dec. 1992); 1 child, Lacy O'Brien; m. Brucie Waggoner Hooks, Oct. 1, 1994. BS, Pikeville Coll., 1971; JD, U. Louisville, 1974. Bar: Ky. 1974, US Ct. Appeals (6th cir.), US Ct. Appeals, (8th cir.), US Supreme Ct., cert.: Nat. Bd. Trial Advocacy (civil trial advocate) 1982, Am. Bd. Trial Advocates (advocate) 1990. Atty., mng. ptnr. Moore, Malone & Burlew, Owensboro, Ky., 1974—; chmn. Ky. Dem. Party, 2009—. Tchr. trial advocacy U. Ky. Coll. Law, Lexington, 1986; spl. justice Supreme Ct. Ky., Frankfort, 1991. Recipient Disting. Alumni award, U. Louisville Louis D. Brandeis Sch. Law, 2003; named one of Best Lawyers in America. Mem. ABA, Am. Assn. Justice, Ky. Justice Assn. (treas. 2000, sec. 2001, v.p. 2002, pres.-elect 2003, pres. 2004; Peter Perlman Outstanding Trial Lawyers award 2005), Ky. Bar Assn. (bd. govs. 2001-06, conv. spkr.), Daviess County Bar Assn. (pres. 2000). Democrat. Office: Moore Moore & Malone 104 E 4th St PO Box 549 Owensboro KY 42302-0549 also: Ky Dem Party 190 Democrat Dr PO Box 694 Frankfort KY 40602 Office Phone: 502-695-4828.*

MOORE, CHARLES HEWES, JR., manufacturing executive; b. Coatesville, Pa., Aug. 12, 1929; s. Charles Hewes and Jane Richards (Scott) M.; m. Judith L. McClellan, June 23, 1971; children: Charles Hewes III, James, David, Susan, Kevin, Christopher, Margery, Brian, Amanda. BME, Cornell U., 1952. With Lenape Forge Co. div. Gulf & Western Industries, West Chester, Pa., 1952-73; pres. Lapp div. Interpace Corp., Le Roy, NY, 1973—78; pres., chief exec. officer Allied Thermal Corp. subs. Interpace, 1978-79; sr. v.p., dir. Interpace, 1979-80; exec. v.p., dir. Interpace Corp., Parsippany, NJ, 1980-81; pres., chief exec. officer, dir. Clevepak Corp., 1981-83, 84-86, chief exec. officer, vice chmn. bd., dir., 1983-84; mng. dir. Peers & Co., 1987-88; chief exec. officer Peers Mgmt. Resources, Inc., 1987-88; pres., chief exec. officer Ransburg Corp., Indpls., 1988-92; pres. ITW Finishing Systems and Products, Indpls., 1990-92; exec. v.p. Ill. Tool Works Inc., Glenview, 1991-92; vice-chmn. Advisory Capital Ptnrs., Inc., Greenwich, Conn., 1992—94; chmn. bd. dirs. Xpander Pak Inc., 1994—2000; dir. athletics Cornell U., 1994—99. Dep. to chairs Com. Encouraging Corp. Philanthropy, NY, 1999—2000, exec. dir., NY, 2000—; mem. Pres. Coun. on Phys. Fitness and Sports, 2002—. Commr. Smithsonian Am. Art Mus., 2000—09; chmn. audit com., pub. sector dir. U.S. Olympic Com., 1992—2000; mem. nat. bd. Smithsonian Instn., 2001—06. Recipient Gold medal in 400 meter hurdles, 1952 Olympics, Herbert Adams Meml. award for advancement of Am. sculpture, Nat. Sculpture Soc., 1985. Mem. Pine Valley Golf Club (N.J.), Royal and Ancient Golf Club St. Andrews (Scotland), Blind Brook Golf Club (N.Y.). Republican. Episcopalian. Office: Com Encouraging Corp Philanthropy 110 Wall St Ste 2-1 New York NY 10005 Office Phone: 212-825-1254.

MOORE, CHARLES WILLARD, music educator; b. Indpls., Jan. 25, 1930; s. Carl B. and Mildred (Schmedel) M.; m. JoAnn Strebe; children: Carol Diann Moore Wright, Amy Michele Moore Keusink. MusB, Jordan Coll. Music, 1955; MS, Butler U., 1958; MusD, Ind. U., 1967. Pub. sch. tchr. Greenfield (Ind.) City Schs., 1955-56; pub. sch. tchr.

Harry Wood High Sch., Indpls. Pub. Schs., 1956-58, Warren Cen. High Sch., Indpls., 1960-63; prof. and chmn. vocal music East Carolina U., Greenville, N.C., 1965-92, ret., 1992. Author: IvorGurney: Poet & Songwriter, 1973; contbr. articles to profl. jours. Founder Pitt-Greenville Arts Adv. Coun., Greenville, 1976, chmn., 1980-88; pres., treas. Eastern Carolina Orch. Assn., Greenville, 1976-91; pres., treas. Operation Sunshine, Greenville, 1976-92; bd. dirs. E. Carolina U. Retired Faculty, 1994-96; mem. com. on drugs and crime Greenville City Coun., 1992-96; active Radio Reading for Blind and Disabled, 2000—. Named Foundateur, Les Amis de Francis Poulenc, Paris, 1965. Mem. Music Tchrs. Nat. Assn. (v.p. N.C. chpt. 1980-82), Am. Choral Dirs. Assn. (life), Nat. Assn. Tchrs. Singing (N.C. state pres. 1983-85, mid-atlantic regional lt. gov. 1983-89), Music Educators Nat. Conf., Ivor Gurney Soc. (founding mem. 1965). Episcopalian. Home: 1600 Brownlea Dr Greenville NC 27858-4632 E-mail: cmoore92@suddenlink.net.

MOORE, CHERYL (MILKES) JEROME, lawyer; b. Dallas, Jan. 10, 1951; d. Dean and Marjorie (Wolens) Milkes; m. Edward Jerome, Aug. 21, 1976 (div. 1986); 1 child, Elizabeth Milkes; m. David Moore, Feb. 25, 1995. Student, Tulane U., 1969-70; BA and BSW, Syracuse U., 1972, JD, 1976. Bar: N.Y. 1977, Tex. 1978, U.S. Dist. Ct. (no. dist.) N.Y., U.S. Dist. Ct. (all dists.) Tex., U.S. Ct. Appeals (5th cir.). Law clk. Bogart & Andrews, Syracuse, NY, 1975-76; assoc. Law Office Louis Tarantelli, Horseheads, NY, 1976-78, Glast, Miller & Allen, Dallas, 1985-86; sr. planner, adminstrn. asst. County of Dallas, 1977—78, chief commr. fraud, Dist. Atty.'s Office, 1979-85; ptnr. Hewitt, Jerome & Armstrong, Dallas; ptnr., Securities, Oil & Gas Law, Comml. & Transactional Litigation Patton Boggs LLP, Dallas, dep. chmn. litigation dept., mem. mgmt. com. Adj. prof. So. Meth. U. Coll. Law, Dallas, 1986-2000; tchg. staff Nat. Inst. Trial Advocacy. Contbr. articles to profl. jours. Bd. dirs. Cmty. Homes Adults, Inc., Dallas, 1987-2004; bd. dirs. Jewish Fedn. Dallas; chair Legacy Sr. Communities Inc., 2004—. Mem. N.Y. Bar Assn., Tex. Bar Assn., Dallas Bar Assn. Democrat. Jewish. Office: Patton Boggs LLP Suite 3000 2001 Ross Ave Dallas TX 75201-8001 Office Phone: 214-758-3504. Office Fax: 214-758-1550. Business E-Mail: cmoore@pattonboggs.com.

MOORE, CHESTER, engineering educator; s. Robert and Ella Moore; m. Elnore Davis, Aug. 28, 1971; 1 child, Angela Regina Moore-Jones. BS, Athens State Coll., Ala., 1990. Owner & CEO Moore's Plumbing and Electric Co., Dixons Mills, Ala., 1974—88; tchr. Ala. Southern CC, Thomasville, 1985—. Asst. scout master Boy Scouts America Troop 253, Dixons Mills, 1983—2008, unit commr., 2002; deacon and sunday sch. tchr. Shiloh Primitive Bapt. Ch., Dixons Mills, 1978—2008; chmn. bd. Dixons Mills Vol. Fire Dept., 1990—98; bd. mem. Marengo County Communication Dist., Demopolis, Ala., 1992—2000. Mem.: ASME. Home: PO Box 295 Dixons Mills AL 36736 Office: Ala Southern CC PO Box 2000 Thomasville AL 36784

MOORE, CHRISTOPHER, writer; b. Toledo, 1957; Student, Ohio State U., Brooks Inst. Photography, Santa Barbara. Author: (novels) Practical Demonkeeping, 1992, Coyote Blue, 1994, Bloodsucking Friends: A Love Story, 1995, Island of the Sequined Love Nun, 1997, The Lust Lizard of Melancholy Cove, 1999, Lamb: The Gospel According to Biff, Christ's Childhood Pal, 2002, Fluke: or I Know Why the Winged Whale Sings, 2003, The Stupidest Angel: A Heartwarming Tale of Christmas Terror, 2004, A Dirty Job, 2006 (Quill Award for General Fiction, 2006), You Suck: A Love Story, 2007, Fool, 2009 (Publishers Weekly bestseller), (short stories) Our Lady of the Fishnet Stockings, 1987, Cat's Karma, 1987; co-author: (screenplays) The Griff, 2001. Office: HarperCollins 10 E 53rd St New York NY 10022*

MOORE, CHRISTOPHER HUGH, writer; b. Stoke-on-Trent, Eng., June 9, 1950; arrived in Can., 1954; s. M. Vincent and Kathleen A. (Lennox) M.; m. Louise A. Brophy, May 7, 1977; children: Elizabeth, Kate. BA with honors, U. B.C., Vancouver, 1971; MA, U. Ottawa, Ont., Can., 1977. Staff historian Nat. Historic Pks. Svc., Louisbourg, N.S., Can., 1972-75; sec. to bd. Heritage Can. Found., Ottawa, 1977-78; writer, historian Toronto, Ont., 1979—; dir. Access Copyright Licensing Agy., 2001—07. Author: Louisbourg Portraits, 1982, 2000, The Loyalists, 1984, 94, Eighteen Sixty-Seven, 1997, The Big Book of Canada, 2002; co-author: Illustrated History of Canada, 1987, The Story of Canada, 1992, Canada: Our Century, 1999. Recipient Gov. Gen.'s Lit. award Can., 1983, Sec. of State Prize Govt. Can., Ottawa, 1985, Mr. Christie's Prize Christie-Brown Ltd., Toronto, 1993. Mem. Writers' Union of Can. (chair contracts com. 1990-94, mem. nat. coun. 1995-97, nat. chair, 1999-00), Can. Hist. Assn. Office: 70 Woodside Ave Toronto ON Canada M6P 1M1 E-mail: cmed@sympatico.ca.

MOORE, CHRISTOPHER M., lawyer; b. LA, Oct. 12, 1938; s. Prentiss Elder and Josephine (French) M.; m. Gillian Reed, Sept. 29, 1965; children: Stephanie Kia Conn, Carrie Christine McKay. AB, Stanford U.; JD, Harvard U. Dep. county counsel L.A. County Counsel, 1965-66; ptnr. Burkley & Moore, Torrance, Calif., 1969-74; pvt. practice Law Offices of Christopher Moore, Torrance, 1974-81; ptnr. Burkley, Moore, Greenberg & Lyman, Torrance, 1981-90; prin. Christopher M. Moore & Assoc., Torrance, 1990-2000, Moore, Bryan & Schroff, Torrance, 2000—. Mem. bd. edn. Palos Verdes (Calif.) Peninsula Unified Sch. Dist., 1972—77. Fellow: Am. Acad. Matrimonial Lawyers, Am. Coll. Trust and Estate Counsel; mem.: Palos Verdes Golf Club, L.A. Yacht Club. Avocations: sailing, golf. Office: Moore Bryan & Schroff Ste 490 21515 Hawthorne Blvd Torrance CA 90503-6525 Home Phone: 310-375-4967; Office Phone: 310-540-8855. E-mail: chris@mbslawcorp.com.

MOORE, CHRISTOPHER ROBERTSON KINLEY, energy industry consultant; b. Manchester, Eng., Sept. 28, 1954; came to U.S., 1989; s. James Robertson Kinley and Irene (Mason) M.; m. Marian Isabel Pope, Sept. 3, 1977 (div.); children: Andrew Christopher, Scott David. BA, U. Cambridge, 1975, MA, 1979. Geologist Brit. Petroleum Co., Scotland, England, Tunisia, 1975-80; sr. geologist Tricentrol Oil Corp., London, 1980-88; planning mgr. ARCO Brit. Ltd., London, 1988-89; from exploration planning advisor to dir. exploration ARCO Internat. Oil & Gas Co., Plano, Tex., 1989-98; Bohai Bay asset mgr. ARCO China Inc., Plano, 1998-99, mgr. China ADT, 1999-2000; mng. dir. Moyes & Co., Inc., Dallas, 2000—; dir. Brit. Am. Nat. Gas Corp., 2007—; non exe. dir. Black Rock Oil & Gas Plc., 2007—09. Fellow Geol. Soc. London; mem. Am. Assn. Petroleum Geologists, Soc. Petroleum Engrs., Internat. Assn. Petroleum Negotiators. Home: 4544 Siena Dr Frisco TX 75034 Office: Moyes & Co Inc 8235 Douglas Ave Ste 1221 Dallas TX 75225-6012 Home Phone: 214-618-3504; Office Phone: 214-363-9020. Business E-Mail: cmoore@moyesco.com.

MOORE, CLAYBOURNE MAUNSELL, biology professor; b. Lafayette, Ala., Dec. 23, 1964; s. James Olice and Dorothy Gabbett Moore; m. April Dawn Alexander; children: Stephen Alexander Ziembroski, Ernest John Ziembroski II. BS, Jacksonville State U., Ala., 1986, MS, 1988. Instr. biology Ala. State U., Montgomery, 1995—2002; prof. biology St. Johns River CC, Palatka, Fla., 2002—. Mem.: Phi Theta Kappa Internat. Honor Soc. (advisor 2003—). Office: St Johns River CC 5001 St Johns Ave Palatka FL 32177

MOORE, CLEMMIE ARCHER, retired elementary school educator; b. Ahoskie, NC, Dec. 3, 1949; d. Everette Warren and Mary (Daniels) Archer; m. Bernard Moore, Nov. 23, 1972 (dec. Jan. 2005); children: Marlo Oweita, Amber Crystal. BS, Elizabeth City State U., 1971; MA in Edn., E. Carolina U., 1987. Cert. elem. edn. mentor. Tchr. 2d grade, instrnl. specialist Hertford County Bd. Edn., Winton, NC, 1971—2002; ret. Mem. NC Tchg. Excellence and Math. Project. Mem. NC Coun. Tchrs. Math., NC Assn. Educators, NC Ret. Sch. Personnell. Home: PO Box Y Winton NC 27986-0325 Personal E-mail: viking_lady71@yahoo.com.

MOORE, CORNELL LEVERETTE, financial services executive, lawyer; b. Tignall, Ga., Sept. 18, 1939; s. Jesse Lamar and Luetta (Leverette) M.; m. Wenda Lee Weekes, June 27, 1965; children: Lynne M., Jonathon C. Meredith L. AB, Va. Union U., 1961; JD, Howard U., 1964. Bar: Minn. 1964, U.S. Dist. Ct. Minn. 1977. Atty. US Treasury, various locations, 1965-68; asst. v.p., legal officer N.W.N. Bank, Mpls., 1968-70; pres. Leverette, Weekes, Mpls., 1970—; exec. v.p. Shelter Mfg. Co., Mpls., 1970-74; pres., chief exec. officer Lease Moore Equipment, Inc., Mpls., 1977-86; sr. v.p., gen. counsel Miller and Shroeder Fin. Inc., Mpls., 1987—95. Bd. dirs. Golden Valley (Minn.) Bank, Ward & Assocs., Inc., Atlanta, bd. mem. Johnson C. Smith U., Nat. Underground freedom Ctr., ptnr. Dorsey & Whitney LLP. Trustee Mpls. Soc. Fine Arts, 1986, Va. Union U., Richmond, 1986, Dunwoody Inst., Mpls. 1986, chmn. bd. vis., John H. Johnson Sch. Comm. Howard Univ. Named to Power 150, Ebony mag., 2008. Member African Methodist Epicopal. Club: Minneapolis.

MOORE, DALE, lobbyist, former federal agency administrator; b. Copeland, Kans. BS in Animal Sci., Fort Hays State U. Agr. legis. asst. to Rep. Pat Roberts US House of Reps., Washington, 1985—91; minority counsel, subcommittee of ops. rsch. & fgn. agr. US House Agrl. Com., Washington, 1991—93, Rep. legis. coord., 1993—94, legis. dir., 1995—96; exec. dir. legis. affairs Nat. Cattlemen's Beef Assn. (NCBA), Washington, 1997—2001; chief of staff USDA, Washington, 2001—09; v.p. Policy Directions Inc., 2009—. Office: Policy Directions Inc 818 Connecticut Ave NW Ste 950 Washington DC 20006 Office Phone: 202-776-0071. Office Fax: 202-776-0083.*

MOORE, DANIEL CHARLES, retired anesthesiologist; b. Cin., Sept. 9, 1918; s. Daniel Clark and May (Strebel) M.; m. Betty Maxine Tobias, Aug. 5, 1945 (div. 1988); children: Barbara, Nancy, Daniel, Susan. Grad., Amherst Coll., Mass., 1940; MD, Northwestern U., 1944. Diplomate Am. Bd. Anesthesiologists. Intern Wesley Meml. Hosp., Chgo., 1944, resident, 1945; dir. anesthesia Va. Mason Hosp., Seattle, 1947-72; anesthesiologist (Mason Clinic), 1947-72, sr. cons. in anesthesia, 1972-83. Clin. prof. U. Wash. Sch. Medicine, 1963—89. Author: Regional Block, 1953, Stellate Ganglion Block, 1954, Complications of Regional Anesthesia, 1955, Anesthetic Techniques for Obstetrical Anesthesia and Analgesia, 1964, also papers. Served as capt. M.C. AUS, 1945-47. Recipient Ralph M. Waters award Ill. Soc. Anesthesiologists, Carl Koller Gold medal European Soc. Regional Anaesthesia, 1995, Eagle Scout, 1930. Mem. Am. Soc. Anesthesiologists (1st v.p. 1953-54, 2d v.p. 1954-55, pres. 1958-59, distinguished service award 1976), AMA (sec. anesthesiology sect. 1956-58), Am. Acad. Anesthesiology, Am. Soc. Regional Anesthesia (adv. bd., Gaston Labat award 1977), Wash. Soc. Anesthesiologists (pres. 1949-50), Wash. Med. Soc., King County Med. Soc., Faculty Anaesthetists Royal Coll. Surgeons (hon.), Northwest Forum, Beta Theta Pi, Nu Sigma Nu. Home: Madison Park Pl # 103 2000 43rd Ave E Seattle WA 98112-2704 Office: PO Box 900 Seattle WA 98111-0900 Home Phone: 206-726-9832; Office Phone: 206-223-6980. Fax: 206-223-6982. E-mail: daniel.moore@vmmc.org.

MOORE, DANIEL EDMUND, psychologist, educator, retired educational administrator; b. Pitts., Dec. 31, 1926; s. John Daniel and Alma Helen (Goehring) M.; m. Rose Marie Blunkosky, Nov. 11, 1949; children: Catherine Chiodo, Claire Marie Moore Caveney, Mary Moore Brilmyer, Suzanne Moore Gray, Elizabeth Moore Sullivan. BSEd, Duquesne U., 1949, MEd, 1952; postgrad., California State Coll., Pa., 1954-56, U. Pitts., 1958-59, Mt. Mercy Coll., 1959-60, Cath. U. Am., 1966, W.Va. U., 1970-72. Lic. psychologist; cert. sch. psychologist. Tchr. math. Cecil Twp. Sch. Dist., McDonald, Pa., 1949-52, Pitts. Public Schs., 1952-53; with Mt. Lebanon Twp. (Pa.) Sch. Dist., 1953-88, psychologist, 1954-71, dir. pupil personnel svcs., 1988; psychol cons. Peters Twp. Sch. Dist., McMurray, Pa., 1961-88; psychol. cons. Blackhawk Sch. Dist., Beaver, Pa., 1989—98; psychol cons. Quaker Valley Sch. Dist., Sewickley, Pa., 1989-90; lectr., supr. Grad. and Undergrad. Sch. Edn. Duquesne U.; psychologist DePaul Inst., Pitts., 1992—98. Lectr. ednl. psychology Grad. Sch. Edn., Duquesne U., 1957-92, supr. student tchrs., 1989-92; ednl. cons. St. Francis Schs. Nursing, New Castle and Pitts., 1959-91; mem. test adv. bd. Ednl. Records Bur., 1976-86; hearing officer Right to Edn. Office, Dept. Edn., Harrisburg, Pa., 1975—; in-svc. adv. bd. Pa. Dept. Edn. Hearing Officers; clients assessment Pa. Bur. Disability(BDD), 1988-, Attys. Law, 1990-. Mem. Chartiers Valley Sch. Dist. Bd., 1963-94, pres., 1971, v.p., 1991; mem. Pkwy. West Tech. Sch. Bd. 1965-67; bd. dirs. secondary sch. rsch. program Ednl. Testing Svc., Princeton, 1971-85; bd. dirs. Robert E. Ward Home for Children, 1975-87, St. Agatha Parish Coun., 1988—, Pathfinder Sch., 1989, v.p., 1990-94, pres. sch. bd., 1991-92; vol. Bridgeville Area Food Bank, 1988—; chairperson Parish 100 Jubilee Ceremony, Goodwill Villa Bd., Goodwill Plaza, Inc., Goodwill Villa Bd. of Incorporators, 1992—; pres. bd. dirs. Goodwill Plaza, 1992—; active assessment Psychol. Corp. Harcourt Assessment, 2002-; jubilee chairperson St. Agatha's, Bridgeville, Pa. With USNR, 1945-48. Henry C. Frick grantee, 1970, 73; named Jaycee Educator of Yr. for South Hills Area, Ward Home Outstanding Community Leader, 1984, Outstanding Cmty. Leader, Chartiers Valley Human Rels. Coun., 1998; recipient Human Rels. award Chartiers Valley Inter-relationships Soc., 1998, Key award Harcourt-Brace Psyschol. Testing Svc., Outstanding Achievement Pearson Testing Program award, 2008. Mem. Am., Pa. psychol. assns., Coun. Exceptional Children (pres. 1957), Phi Delta Kappa (pres. chpt. 1974-75, chmn. lay awards com. 1979-2001, Svc. Key award 1985). Roman Catholic. Home: 213 Station St Bridgeville PA 15017-1806 Office Phone: 412-221-5217.

MOORE, DAVID C., tobacco company executive; Various fin. & mgmt. positions Universal Corp., Richmond, Va., 1978—99; sr. v.p. services Universal Leaf Internat., 1999—2002, mng. dir., 2002—05; sr. v.p. Universal Leaf Tobacco Co., Richmond, Va., 2005—06; v.p., chief adminstrv. officer Universal Corp., Richmond, Va., 2006—08, sr. v.p., CFO, 2008—. Bd. dir., treas. Va. Manufacturers Assn. Office: Universal Corp 1501 N Hamilton St Richmond VA 23230 Mailing: Universal Corp PO Box 25099 Richmond VA 23260 Office Phone: 804-359-9311. Office Fax: 803-254-3582.

MOORE, DAVID HARRY, medical educator; b. Lake Charles, La., Sept. 19, 1955; s. Harry Albert Moore and Loretta Lou Sperry; m. Mary Kristine Beckwith, May 3, 1986; children: Harry William, Aaron Lester. BA, Wabash Coll., Crawfordsville, Ind., 1978; MD, Ind. U. Sch. Medicine, 1982. Asst. prof. ob-gyn. U. NC, Chapel Hill, 1988—93; assoc. prof. ob-gyn. Ind. U. Sch. Medicine, Indpls., 1993—99, prof. gynecologic oncology, 1999—2006, mary fendrich hulman prof. gynecologic oncology, 2004—06. Mem.: ACS, Phi Rho Sigma Med. Soc., Minimally Invasive Robotic Assn., Am. Coll. Obstetricians and Gynecologists, Am. Soc. Clin. Oncology, Internat. Soc. Gynecologic Oncologists, Soc. Gynecologic Oncologists (chair, clin. practice com. 2008—), Gynecologic Oncology Group (chair, co-chair cervix and vulva com. 1994—2007). Presbyterian. Avocations: golf, bicycling. Office: Gynecologic Oncology Ind 5255 E Stop 11 Rd Ste 310 Indianapolis IN 46237 Office Fax: 317-851-2566; Home Fax: 317-823-2626. Personal E-mail: dhrrym@aol.com. Business E-Mail: david.moore@ssfhs.org.

MOORE, DAWSON, performing company executive, playwright; b. Ithaca, NY, July 26, 1970; s. Judith Moore. BA in Theatre, U. Alaska, Anchorage, 1997. Artisitc dir. Three Wise Monkeys Theatre Co., San Francisco, 2000—03; Last Frontier Theatre conf. coord. Prince William Sound CC, Valdez, Alaska, 2003—. Playwright (one-act play) Bile in the Afterlife. Bd. mem. Advs. Victims Violence, Valdez, Alaska, 2007—. Mem.: Dramatists Guild America. Home: PO Box 3505 Valdez AK 99686 Business E-Mail: dmoore@pwscc.edu.

MOORE, DEBORAH DASH, religion educator; b. NYC, Aug. 6, 1946; d. Martin and Irene (Golden) Dash; m. MacDonald Smith Moore, June 15, 1967; children: Mordecai, Mikhael. BA, Brandeis U., 1967; MA, Columbia U., 1968, PhD, 1975. Asst. prof. Vassar Coll., Poughkeepsie, N.Y., 1976-84, assoc. prof., 1984-88, profl., 1988—. Author: At Home in America, 1981, B'Nai Brith and the Challenge of Ethnic Leadership, 1981; editor Yivo Annual, 1990-96, To the Golden Cities, 1994; co-editor Jewish Women in America, 1997. NEH fellow, 1979, 89, Meml. Found. fellow, 1983, Fulbright Found. fellow, 1984; Littauer Found. grantee, 1990. Mem. Nat. Found. for Jewish Culture (acad. adv. panel), Immigration History Soc. (bd. dirs. 1983-86), Assn. for Jewish Studies (bd. dirs. 1981-85, 1999—), Am. Jewish Hist. Soc. (acad. coun. 1977—). Democrat. Home: 620 Fort Washington Ave New York NY 10040-3929 Office: Vassar Coll Dept Religion Poughkeepsie NY 12601

MOORE, DEMI (DEMI GUYNES, DEMETRIA GENE GUYNES), actress; b. Roswell, N.Mex., Nov. 11, 1962; d. Danny and Virginia Guynes; m. Freddy Moore, 1980 (div. 1984), m. Bruce Willis, Nov. 21, 1987 (div. 2000); 3 daughters: Rumer Glenn, Scout LaRue, Tallulah Belle; m. Ashton Kutcher, Sept. 24, 2005. Studies with Zina Provendie. Owner Moving Pictures. Actress: (feature films) Choices, 1981, Parasite, 1981, Young Doctors in Love, 1982, Blame it on Rio, 1984, No Small Affair, 1984, Master Ninja 1, 1984, St. Elmo's Fire, 1985, About Last Night..., 1986, Wisdom, 1986, One Crazy Summer, 1987, The Seventh Sign, 1988, We're No Angels, 1989, Ghost, 1990, Mortal Thoughts, 1991 (also co-producer), The Butcher's Wife, 1991, Nothing But Trouble, 1991, A Few Good Men, 1992, Indecent Proposal, 1993, Disclosure, 1994, The Scarlet Letter, 1995, Now and Then, 1995 (also prodr.), Undisclosed, 1996, Striptease, 1996, The Juror, 1996, G.I. Jane, 1997 (also prodr.), Deconstructing Harry, 1997, Passion of Mind, 2000, Charlie's Angels: Full Throttle, 2003, Half Light, 2006, Bobby, 2006, Mr. Brooks, 2007, Flawless, 2007; (TV series) General Hospital, 1982-83; (TV movies) If These Walls Could Talk, 1996 (also exec. prodr.), (voice) The Magic 7, 2006; (voice) Beavis and Butt-Head Do America,1996, The Hunchback of Notre Dame, 1996, The Hunchback of Notre Dame II, 2002; Producer: Austin Powers: International Man of Mystery, 1997, Austin Powers: The Spy Who Shagged Me, 1999, Austin Powers in Goldmember, 2002; guest appearances on Saturday Night Live (host), 1988, Moonlighting, 1989, Tales of the Crypt, 1990, Will & Grace, 2003. Named one of 50 Most Beautiful People in the World, People, 1996.

MOORE, DENNIS, United States Representative from Kansas; b. Anthony, Kans., Nov. 8, 1945; m. Stephene Moore; 7 children. BS, U. Kans., 1967; JD, Washburn U., 1970. Bar: Kans. 1970. Asst. atty. gen. State of Kans., 1971-73; pvt. practice, 1973-76; dist. atty. Johnson County, 1977-89; ptnr. Erker & Moore, LLC, 1991-98, Smith, Gill, Fisher & Butts, 1989-91; mem. US Congress from 3d Kans. Dist., 1999—, US House Financial Services Com., US House Small Bus. Com. Elected to Johnson County C.C. bd. trustees, 1993; re-elected, 1997; bd. dirs. Johnson County Safehome, Coalition for Prevention of Child Abuse, Kans. Child Abuse Prevention Coun., CASA (Ct. Appointed Spl. Advocate), United Cmty. Svcs., Cmty. Corrections Adv. Bd.; unsuccessful Dem. candidate for state atty. gen., 1986. With U.S. Army, U.S. Army Res. Mem.: Blue Dog Coalition. Democrat. Protestant. Achievements include personally prosecuting more than 25 felony jury trials; led Consumer Protection Divsn. in the investigation and successful prosecution of a nat. oil co. charged with rigging gas pumps to cheat consumers; established a victim assistance unit; was cited by an ind. cons. hired by the Johnson County Bd. Commrs. as running the most efficient office in Johnson County govt.; served as pres. Kans. County and Dist. Atty.'s Assn. Office: US Congress 1727 Longworth House Office Bldg Washington DC 20515-1603 also: 8417 Santa Fe Dr #101 Overland Park KS 66212*

MOORE, DERRICK LANIER, military officer; b. Buffalo, Jan. 6, 1960; s. Willis Carl Moore and Catherine Hill; m. Jacqueline Lewis (div.). BS in Criminal Justice, Grambling State U., LA, 1983; MS in Pub. Adminstrn., Chaminade U., 1987; AS in Criminology, C.C. of the Air Force, Cheyenne, Wyo., 1999. Flight chief-security forces USAF, Washington, 1984—, manpower and orgn. project mgr. Panama City, Fla., 2000—03; min. Full Gospel Bapt. Ch. Fellowship, Howell, NJ, 1998—. Asst. flight chief, dir. deployed forces USAF, FE Warren AFB, Wyo., 1998, flight chief, dir. deployed forces, Tyndall AFB, 2004—05, lead mil. war planner, 2000—03; security coord. Russian START treaty 90th Space Wing, FE Warren AFB, 1999. Actor: (movie) The Sitting Place, 2000. Project coord. Ronald McDonald Ho., Pensacola, Fla., 2002—04; lay min., coord. Tyndall AFB Chapel, Panama City, 2003—; v.p. Tyndall Parish Coun., 2003—05. Master sgt. USAF, 1984—. Decorated Commendation medals (6) USAF. Mem.: VFW, Am. Legion, Wyo. Buffalo Soldier Assn. (pres.). Democrat. Avocations: military history, sports memorabilia, Biblical history, singing, songwriting.

MOORE, DONALD EMERSON, III, zoological park administrator, curator, wildlife biologist; b. Syracuse, NY, Jan. 9, 1954; s. Donald Emerson and Ruth Hodge (Steinhilber) M.; m. Adrienne Rose Whiteley (div.); children: Jessie Rose, Caitlin Grace; m. Suzanne L. Daley. BS in Environ. Sci. and Forestry, SUNY, Syracuse, 1976; MPA, Syracuse U., 1990; PhD, SUNY, Syracuse, 2001. Cert. biologist. Edn. asst. Burnet Park Zoo, Syracuse, 1976-77, technician animal care, 1977-79, zoologist, 1980-83, curator mammals, 1984-93; dir. Thompson Park Conservancy, 1993-95; curator Wildlife Conservation Soc., NYC, 1997—2002, dir., 2003—06; adj. prof. Hunter Coll. Animal Behavior and Conservation Focus, 2005—07; assoc. dir. Smithsonian Nat. Zoo, 2006—. Sci. adviser Thompson Park Zoo, Watertown, N.Y., 1984-2006, Polar Bears Internat., 1998-; mem. master plan team A New Breed of Zoo, 1980-86, Springdale Farm Park, 1985-88; exploring adviser, 1989-96. Author: (mgmt. format) Species Mgmt. Plan, 1978, Disney's Wonderful World of Animals, 2006; contbr. articles to sci. jours. Instr. ARC, Syracuse, 1978-87; mem. master plan team Millbrook Sch., 1988-89. Fellow: Am. Zoo and Aquarium Assn. (prof.); mem.: NY Acad. Sci., Internat. Soc.

Behavioral Ecology, Soc. Conservation Biology, Internat. Union Conservation Nature and Natural Resources (deer specialist group, mustelid/viverrid specialist group, reintroduction specialist group), Wildlife Soc., Am. Soc. Mammalogists, Explorers Club (nat. fellow), Sigma Xi. Presbyterian. Avocations: skiing, hiking, canoeing, canning jams and jellies, photography. Office: Smithsonian Nat Zoo 3001 Connecticut Ave NW Washington DC 20010 Office Phone: 202-633-3241.

MOORE, DONALD L., finance educator; b. Blythedale, Mo., Feb. 16, 1932; s. Harry Leonard and Bessie Lee (Hale) Moore. BS, N.W. Mo. State U., 1958; MA, U. Northern Colo., 1965; PhD, 1972. Cert. tchr. Colo., Mo. Instr. bus. Corning HS, Iowa, 1958—59; instr. bus., prin. Edison Sch., Yoder, 1959—61; tchr. Sch. Dist. 11, Colorado Springs, 1961—2004; instr. bus. Pikes Peak CC., Colorado Springs, 1972—. Lectr. edn. Colo. Coll., Colorado Springs, 1975—; tchr. corps vol. NEA/AID, Addis Ababa, Ethiopia, 1970, Kathmandu, Nepal, 75; sec.-treas. Policies Comm. Bus. & Econ. Edn., 1983—86; asst. venue coordinator-volleyball Nat. Sports Festival V, 1983; vol. Nat. Sports Festivals I and II, Colorado Springs, 1979—80. With US Army, 1952—54. Mem.: Colorado Springs Edn. Assn., Colo. Edn. Assn., Colo. Assn. Career & Tech. Edn., Nat. Edn. Assn., Assn. Career & Tech. Edn., Internat. Soc. Bus. Edn., Colo. Assn. Career & Tech. Edn. (Hall of Fame award 2007), Colo. Educators for/about Bus. (pres.-elect 1977—78, pres. 1978—79, Svc. award 1981, Merit award 1984, Donald L. Moore Bus. Edn. Outstanding Svc. award 2003), Mountain-Plains Bus. Edn. Assn. (Colo. rep. 1983—86, treas. 1986—88, pres.-elect 1988—89, pres. 1989—90, Colo. rep. 2000—01, Secondary Tchr. of Yr. 1988, Leadership award 1991), Nat. Bus. Edn. Assn., NEA (state membership dir. 1983—86, nat. conv. registration chmn. 1983—98, nat conv. program dir. 1988, Mountain Plains rep. 1990—91, pres. elect 1991—92, pres. 1992—93, Named Secondary Tchr. of Yr. 1990), Delta Pi Epsilon (chpt. pres. 1970—72, advisor 1972—2002), Phi Delta Kappa. Democrat. Mailing: PO Box 1122 Colorado Springs CO 80901-1122 Office: 1590 W Fillmore St Colorado Springs CO 80904-1198

MOORE, DONALD WALTER, retired academic administrator; b. Culver City, Calif., June 9, 1942; s. Raymond Owen and Jewel Elizabeth (Young) M.; m. Dagmar Ulbrich, Mar. 28, 1968; 1 child, Michael. AA, L.A. Valley Coll., 1967; BA in History, Calif. State U., Northridge, 1970; MA in Learning Disability, Calif. State U., 1973; MLS, U. So. Calif., 1974. Asst., adj. prof. L.A. Pierce Coll. Libr., 1974—; instr. reading L.A. Trade Tech. Coll., 1978—80, pres.'s staff asst., 1983—87, adj. computer prof., 1983—; instr. learning skills L.A. City Coll., 1987—88, dir. amnesty edn., 1988—92, dir. English and citizenship program, 1992—2003, ret., 2003. Adj. instr. computer sci. LA Trade-Tech. Coll., 1983-. Author: A Guidebook to US Army Dress Helmets, 2000, Custer's Ghosts and Custer's Gold, 2007; contbr. fiction, articles, revs. to various publs. Mem. Little Big Horn Assn., The Co. Mil. Historians, Western Writers Am., Mystery Writers Am., Custer Battlefield Hist. and Museum Assn., Inc. (Custer Battlefield Preservation Com.). Republican. Roman Catholic. Avocations: writing, collecting Indian war memorabilia, reading, photography. Personal E-mail: writer99@ca.rr.com. *Personal philosophy: To survive in this world you must believe in yourself and know what's worth fighting for and what's not. But never despair, despair is the greatest sin.*

MOORE, DONNICA LAUREN, physician, medical writer; b. Queens, NY, May 14, 1961; d. Dennis Brian and Toby (Lapkin) M.; m. Stanley Bernard Jr. BA cum laude, Princeton U., 1981; MD, SUNY, Buffalo, 1986. Diplomate Am. Bd. Med. Examiners. Resident in ob-gyn Temple U. Hosp., Phila., 1986-88; resident in family medicine Meml. Hosp., Mount Holly, NJ, 1988-89; assoc. dir. med. ops. Sandoz Pharmaceuticals, Hanover, NJ, 1989-90, dir. med. edn. ctr., 1990-93, assoc. dir. profl. rels., med. edn. ctr., 1993; founder, pres. Sapphire Women's Health Group LLC, DrDonnica.com, 2000—. Freelance med. writer, 1986-90; adj. clin. prof. dept. physiology U. Medicine and Dentistry NJ, 1990-92; attending physician Planned Parenthood NJ, 1991; editl. bd. Jour. Women's Health; columnist First for Women mag. Co-auth: (with Sarah Jarvis) Women's Health for Life, 2009; women's health contbr.: NBC's Weekend Today Show, NBC's Later Today, 1999-2000; guest contbr.: The Oprah Winfrey Show, ABC's The View, Good Morning America, CNN-Internat., others; radio host: Dr. Donnica's Women's Health Report, 2000-2002. Named one of The Most Influential Forces in Healthcare Info. Tech., Advance for Healthcare Tech. Mag., 2000; recipient Alumnae Leadership award, Princeton U. Women's Ctr., Connie Woodruff award, NJ Commn. on the Status of Women's Health, 1999; Rotary scholar U. Coll., Dublin, Ireland, 1981-82. Mem. AMA, Am. Med. Women's Assn. (v.p., bd. dirs.), NJ Med. Soc., Am. Med. Writers Assn., Soc. for Advancement of Women's Health Rsch. (past pres. corp. adv. coun.), Coalition for Women's Health, Nat. Coun. Women's Health (bd. dirs.), Research! America (bd. dirs.), Nat. Acad. Women's Health Med. Edn. (bd. dirs.), Am. Coll. Physician Execs. Jewish. Avocations: swimming, writing.*

MOORE, DOUGLAS T., retail executive; B, MBA, U. Va. Operational and consumer mktg. positions Carnation Co., A.H. Robins Co., Inc., AMF Bowling, Inc.; sr. leadership positions in sales, ops. and installation Circuit City Stores, Inc., exec. v.p., chief merchandising officer; sr. v.p. hardlines merchandising Sears Holdings Corp., 2007—08, sr. v.p., pres. appliances, 2008—. Bd. dirs. Lumber Liquidators, 2006—. Office: Sears Holdings Corp 3333 Beverly Rd Hoffman Estates IL 60179*

MOORE, DUNCAN THOMAS, optics scientist, educator; b. Biddeford, Maine, Dec. 7, 1946; s. Thomas Fogg Moore and Virginia Robinson Wing; m. Gunta Liders, July 1995. BA in Physics, U. Maine, 1969, DSc (hon.), 1995; MS in Optics, Rochester U., NY, 1970, PhD in Optics, 1974. Asst. prof. U. Rochester, 1974-78, assoc. prof., 1978-86, prof., 1986—, Kingslake prof., 1993—, dean engring. and applied sci., 1995-97, prof. biomed. engring., 2001—, prof. bus. adminstrn., 2005—, vice provost entrepreneurship, 2007—; pres. and founder Gradient Lens Corp., Rochester, 1980—97; dir. N.Y. State Ctr. Advanced Optical Tech., Rochester, 1987—94; assoc. dir. technology White House Office Sci. & Technology Policy, Washington, 1997—2000; CEO Infotonics Tech. Ctr. Inc., 2002—04. Vis. scientist Nippon Schlumberger, Tokyo, 1983; Congl. fellow Am. Phys. Soc., Washington, 1993—94; sci. advisor Sen. John D. Rockefeller IV, W.Va., 1993—94; exec. dir. Univ. Industry and Govt. Partnership Advanced Photonics, 2001—02; mem. environ. and energy svc. rev. com. Idaho Nat. Engring. and Environ. Lab., 2001—02; mem. bd. assessment for Nat. Inst. Stds. and Tech. programs NRC, 2001—05, mem. panel for physics, 2001—05, chmn. panel for physics, 2002—05, chmn., 2002—05, mem. adv. coun. US commn. optics, 2006—, mem. com. sci., tech. and law, 2006—; mem. engring. vis. com. NASA-Goddard Space Flight Ctr., 2002—06, chair applied engring. and tech. directorate vis. com., 2002—06, mem. James Webb Space Telescope product integrity team, 2002—; mem. nat. innovation initiative Coun. on Competitiveness, 2004; v.p. Internat. Commn. Optics, 2008—; lectr. in field. Contbr. articles to profl. jours. Chmn. Hubble Ind. Rev. Panel, 1990—91. Recipient Disting. Inventor of Yr. award, Rochester Intellectual Property Law Assn., 1993, Grin Optics award, Japanese Applied Physics Soc., 1993, Sci. and Tech. award, Greater Rochester C. of C., 1992, Gold medal, Internat. Soc. Optical Engring., 2006, Edwin H. Land medal, Soc. Imaging Sci. and Tech. and, 2009; named Engr. of the Yr., Rochester Engring. Soc., 1999. Mem.: AAAS (mem. com. sci. engring. and pub. policy 2005—, fellow 2004), NAE, IEEE Lasers and Electro-Optics Soc. (govt. fellows selection com. 2005—), Am. Inst. Physics (state dept. fellowship selection com. 2001—02), Coalition Photonics and Optics (chair 1996—97), Forum Physics and Soc. (exec. com. 1996—97), Coun. Sci. Soc. (co-chair govt. affairs com. 1996—97), Materials Rsch. Soc., Am. Assn. Engring. Soc. (bd. govs. 1995—97, Nat. Engring. award 1999), Optical Soc. Am. (bd. dirs. 1987—89, editor Applied Optics 1990—92, bd. dirs. 1992—97, v.p. 1994, pres. 1996, adv. coun. homeland security 2004—, Leadership award 2001), Am. Soc. Precision Engring., Am. Ceramic Soc. (Edward Orton, Jr. Meml. lectr 2002). Achievements include patents in field. Home: 4 Claret Dr Fairport NY 14450-4610 Office: The Inst Optics U Rochester Rochester NY 14627-0186 Office Phone: 585-275-5248. Business E-Mail: moore@optics.rochester.edu.

MOORE, EDDIE N., JR., college president; BS, Pa. State U., 1968; MBA, U. Pitts., 1975; HDL (hon.), Va. State U. Cert. acct., Tex., Va. Various acctg. positions, 1971-85; asst. comptroller Commonwealth of Va./Dept. of Accounts, Richmond, 1985-88; asst. treas., registered agt. Endowment Assn./Coll. of William and Mary, Inc., 1988-90; comptroller Coll. of William and Mary, Williamsburg, Va., 1988-90; state treas. Commonwealth of Va./Dept. of Treasury, Richmond, 1990-93; pres. Va. State U., Petersburg, Va., 1993—. Bd. dirs. Universal Corp., Richmond, Va., 2000—, Owens & Minor, Mechanicsville, Va. 1st lt. U.S. Army. Recipient Key to the City of Phila., Mayor W. Wilson Goode, others; decorated Bronze Star, Meritorious Achievement award, Army Commendation medal. Mem. Fiscal Officers of Colls. and Univs. (former v.p.). Office: Va State Univ PO Box 9085 Petersburg VA 23806-0001*

MOORE, EDGAR ALLAN, music educator; b. Galveston, Tex., Aug. 28, 1946; s. John Allan and Win Moore; m. Gretchen York, July 31, 1999. MusB, North Tex. State U., Dentoen, 1969; MusM in Voice & Conducting, U. Houston, 1993. Prof. music San Jacinto Coll., Houston, 1993—. Dir. music Atascocita Presbyn. Ch., Houston, 1989—2000; founder, artistic dir. Sons Orpheus Men's Chorus, Houston, 2000—. Mem.: Tex. Two Year Coll. Choral Dirs. Assn. (past pres. 2002—02, exec. bd. mem. 2002—08), Omicron Delta Kappa, Pi Kappa Lambda. Independent. Avocations: travel, music, model building. Home: 626 Columbia Houston TX 77007 Office: San Jacinto Coll 5800 Uvalde Houston TX 77049

MOORE, EDWARD WARREN, lawyer; b. Odessa, Tex., July 21, 1959; s. Edward Warren and Gloria (Schroeter) M.; m. JoAnne Bisso; children: Peggy, Barbara. BA in Econs., Princeton U., 1981; JD, So. Meth. U., 1984. Bar: Tex. 1984, US Dist. Ct. (no. dist.) Tex. 1984, US Dist. Ct. (we. dist.) Tex. 2003, US Ct. Appeals (5th cir.) 1984, US Ct. Appeals (10th cir.) 1985. Sec., dir. Tissue Gen, Inc., E.N. Bisso & Son, Inc.; dir. Edward W. Moore Law Office, PPLC. Mentor North Tex. Enterprise Ctr. for Med. Tech.; expert witness N. Mex. State Senate; sec. U. Park Comty. League; coord. Leadership U. P. Mem. Princeton U. Class Alumni Giving Com.; auction host, annual convention Safari Club Internat.; chmn. exhbitor registration com. Dallas Safari Club. Fellow Am. Bar Found.; mem. AAAS, ABA (litigation sect., bus. law sect. and com., intellectual property sect.), State Bar Tex., Dallas Bar Assn., Dallas Country Club, Safari Club Internat. (life), Dallas Safari Club (life), DSC 100 (vol.), Order of Flags, Salesmanship Club (Dallas) Roman Catholic. Home: 7044 Turtle Creek Blvd Dallas TX 75205-1254 Home Phone: 214-369-2636; Office Phone: 214-706-9040. Business E-Mail: eddymoore@ewmpllc.net.

MOORE, EMMETT BURRIS, JR., physical chemist, educator; b. Bozeman, Mont., June 14, 1929; s. Emmett Burris and Iris Marie (Brown) M.; m. Diane Elizabeth Girling, Oct. 1, 1960; children: Karen Elizabeth, Robin Diane. BS in Chemistry with honors, Wash. State U., 1951; PhD in Phys. Chemistry (Shell fellow), U. Minn., 1956. Teaching asst. U. Minn., Mpls., 1951-55, asst. prof. physics Duluth, 1957-59; staff scientist Boeing Sci. Research Labs., Seattle, 1959-73. Lectr. chemistry Seattle U., 1973; dir. power plant siting Minn. Environ. Quality Bd., St. Paul, 1973-76; gen. mgr. Richland (Wash.) Divsn. Olympic Engring. Corp., 1976-78; staff scientist Pacific N.W. Nat. Lab., 1978-96; mem. environ. engring. rev. panel EPA, 1989-95; alt. mem. Hanford Adv. Bd., 1995-2000, 2007-; adj. prof. environ. sci. Wash. State U., 1990—. Author: (book) The Environmental Impact Statement Process and Environmental Law, 1997, 2d edit., 2000, An Introduction to the Management and Regulation of Hazardous Waste, 2000, 2nd edit., 2007; contbr. articles to profl. jours. Trustee Mid-Columbia Symphony Soc., 1978-85, v.p., 1980-81, pres., 1981-83; trustee Richland Light Opera Co., 1984-88, bus. mgr., 1984-88. Recipient Land Grant Faculty Excellence award Wash. State U., 1999. Fellow AAAS; mem. Am. Phys. Soc., Am. Chem. Soc. (chmn. Pauling award com. 1971, sec. Puget Sound sect. 1971-73, mem. energy panel of com. on chemistry and pub. affairs 1983-86), Am. Assn. Physics Tchrs. (v.p. Wash. sect. 1965-66, pres. 1966-67), Phi Beta Kappa, Phi Kappa Phi, Phi Eta Sigma, Alpha Chi Sigma, Phi Lambda Upsilon, Sigma Alpha Epsilon (v.p. province 1972-73) Episcopalian (vestryman 1967-69, 76-79, 91, sr. warden 1969, del. diocesan conv. 1969-72). Home: 2323 Greenbrook Blvd Richland WA 99352-8427 Office: Wash State U 2710 University Dr Richland WA 99354-1671 Office Phone: 509-372-7276. Business E-Mail: ebmoore@wsu.edu.

MOORE, FAY LINDA, systems engineer; b. Houston, Apr. 7, 1942; d. Charlie Louis and Esther Mable (Banks) Moore; m. Noel Patrick Walker, Jan. 5, 1963 (div. 1967); 1 child, Trina Nicole Moore. Student, Prairie View Agrl. and Mech. Coll., 1960-61, Tex. So. U., 1961, Our Lady Lake U., 1993, U. Phoenix, 2003. Cert. ISO 9001 Internal Auditor, 1994-97. Instr. Internat. Bus. Coll., Houston, 1965; keypunch operator IBM Corp., Houston, 1965-67, sr. keypunch operator, 1967-70, programmer technician, 1970-72, asst. programmer, 1972-73, assoc. programmer, 1973-74, sr. assoc. programmer, 1984-87, staff programmer, 1987-92, staff sys. analyst, 1992-96; sr. software quality engr. Loral Space Info. Sys., Houston, 1994—96; owner, pres. AFT Co., Houston, 1993—; sr. software quality engr. Lockheed Martin Corp., Houston, 1996-97; software quality engr. Motorola, Inc., Austin, 1998-2001, quality sys. rev. assessor, 1998-2001, info. tech. quality engr., 2000-2001; prin. sys. engr. L-3 comms. Titan Corp., Houston, 2001—, ISO 9001 lead internal auditor, 2005—; software quality engr. Software Engring. Inst. Space shuttle flight support team IBM, 1985—92, mem. space sta. team, 1992—93. Recipient Apollo Achievement award, NASA, 1969, Quality and Productivity award, 1986, 1992, Cert. of Recognition, NASA Office of Space Flight, 2004. Democrat. Roman Catholic. Avocation: personal computing.

MOORE, FAYE HALFACRE, jewelry manufacturer; b. Granville, Tenn., Oct. 16, 1941; d. Benton Mack and Dora Mai (Carter) Halfacre; m. Travis Edward Halford, Jan. 2, 1965; children: Kristi Faye, Trent Edward; m. Charles Harold Moore, Jan. 23, 1989. BSBA, Tenn. Technol. U., 1963. Exec. sec. E.I. du Pont de Nemours, Old Hickory, Tenn., 1963-65, Amoco, New Orleans, 1965-66; adminstrv. asst. Thompson & Moss, Atlanta, 1967-72; founder, owner Strictly Natural, Ltd., Atlanta, 1975—, Elegant Accessories, Internat., Atlanta, 1980—. Pres. Sandy Springs Arts and Heritage Soc., Atlanta, 1986; founding dir. Leadership Sandy Springs, 1987; bd. dirs. Lindsey-Wilson Coll., Columbia, Ky., 1989, Cardinal Hill Hosp., Lexington, 1989, Ky. Ednl. TV Authority, vice chmn. 1992; bd. dirs. Ky. Literacy Commn., Ky. Literacy Found., chmn. 1991; bd. dirs. Lexington Philharm. Found., 1989, chmn. 1991—; adv. bd. Marco Cmty. Banks, 2003-; trustee Tenn. Technol. U., 2005—. Named Citizen of Yr. Sandy Springs Jr. Women's Club, 1976. Mem. Women Bus. Owners, Assn. Women Entrepreneurs (founder), Women's Commerce Club, Marco Island Woman's Club (pres., 2003), Remax, 100% Club, Rotary. Democrat. Avocations: harp, piano, reading, painting, gardening. Home: 5900 Russell Cave Rd Lexington KY 40511-8441 Office: 847 N Collier Blvd Marco Island FL 34145 Home: 840 S Collier Marco Island FL 34145 Personal E-mail: marcofaye@aol.com.

MOORE, GEORGE CRAWFORD JACKSON, lawyer; b. Tenn. BA, U. Fla., 1963; PhB in Soviet Law, U. St. Andrews, Scotland, 1966; MA in English Law with honors, Cambridge U., Eng., 1968, LLM in Internat. Law, 1969. Bar: Eng. (Barrister, Inner Temple) 1970, Jamaica 1971, Fla. 1973, Turks & Caicos Islands 1974, U.S. Supreme Ct. 1976, Antigua and Barbuda, Brit. V.I., Grenada, Montserrat, St. Lucia 1977, Anguilla 1999. Legis. asst. to U.S. sen., Washington, 1970-72; asst. pub. defender Palm Beach County, Fla., 1973; pvt. practice West Palm Beach, Fla., 1973—. Founding pres. World Trade Coun. of Palm Beach County, 1981—; chmn. Fla. Coun. Internat. Devel., 1983—84, 2000—03, Fla. Gov.'s Conf. on World Trade and Investment, 1989, Fla. Export Coun. of U.S. Dept. Commerce, 1991—92, Free Trade Agreement of Americas. Editor spl. issues Fla. Bar Jour., 1982, 87, chmn. editorial bd., 1988-89; mem. editorial bd. The Internat. Lawyer jour. of ABA, 1979-84; contbr. articles to profl. jours. Chmn. Fla. Econ. Growth and Internat. Devel. Commn., 1989-90. Fellow: Ctr. Internat. Legal Studies, Soc. Internat. Bus. Fellows (v.p.); mem.: ABA, Fla. Bar (chmn. internat. law sect. 1994—95, bd. cert. specialist in internat. law 1999—, chmn. internat. law cert. bd. 2004—). Office: 105 S Narcissus Ave Ste 812 West Palm Beach FL 33401-5530 also: 11 King's Bench Walk, Temple London EC4Y 7EQ England Office Phone: 561-833-9000, 44-20-7632-8500. Business E-Mail: barrister@barrister.law.com.

MOORE, GEORGE DAVID, physics professor, researcher; b. Kans. City, Mo., Aug. 2, 1940; m. Sharon Ann Ward, June 20, 1959; children: David Scott, Dana Lynn Teegardin. PhD in Physics, U. Mo., Columbia, 1972. Pres. Moore Assocs. Consulting Ltd., Cumming, Ga., 1995—2004; asst. prof. physics Reinhardt Coll., Waleska, Ga., 2004—. Cpl. USMC, 1955—61, San Diego. Home: 2325 Hampton Trail Cumming GA 30041 Office: Reinhardt Coll 7300 Reinhardt College Cir Waleska GA 30183 Personal E-mail: gdm369@comcast.net. Business E-Mail: gdm@reinhardt.edu.

MOORE, GEORGE EMERSON, JR., geologist, educator; b. Lebanon, Mo., Jan. 2, 1914; s. George Emerson and Dorothea Louisa (Niewohner) M.; m. Wilma Corrine Leonard, May 20, 1939; children: George E. III, Dana Corinne, Craig G. AB, U. Mo., 1936, MA, 1938; PhD, Harvard U., 1947. Instr. U. Mo., 1938-39; teaching asst. Harvard U., 1940-42, 1946-47; geologist A.P. Green Fire Brick Co., Mexico, Mo., 1942-46; instr. Ohio State U. at Columbus, 1947-48, asst. prof., 1948-57, assoc. prof., 1957-64, prof., 1964-84, prof. emeritus, 1984—. Geologist U.S. Geol. Survey, 1952-83 Fellow Geol. Soc. Am.; mem. Phi Beta Kappa, Sigma Xi. Home: 58 Mulberry Dr Wakefield RI 02879-1416

MOORE, GORDON E., electronics executive, researcher; b. San Francisco, Jan. 3, 1929; s. Walter Harold and Florence Almira (Williamson) Moore; m. Betty I. Whittaker, Sept. 9, 1950; children: Kenneth, Steven. BS in Chemistry, U. Calif., Berkeley, 1950; PhD in Chemistry and Physics, Calif. Inst. Tech., 1954. Tech. staff Shockley Semicondr. Lab., 1956—57; mgr. engring. Fairchild Camera & Instrument Corp., 1957—59, dir. R & D, 1959—68; co-founder Intel Corp., Santa Clara, Calif., 1968, exec. v.p., 1968—75, pres., CEO, 1975—79, CEO, 1979—87, chmn., 1979—97, chmn. emeritus, 1997—. Bd. dirs. Varian Assocs. Inc., Transamerica Corp., Gilead Sciences, Inc. Founder, chmn. Gordon & Betty Moore Found.; bd. trustee Calif. Inst. Tech., 1995—2001, sr. trustee, 2001—. Recipient Nat. Medal Tech., President George Bush, 1990, Fellow award, Computer History Mus., 1998, Bower award for Bus. Leadership, Franklin Inst., 2002, Presdl. Medal of Freedom, The White House, 2002, Perkin medal, Soc. Chem. Industry, 2004; named one of Forbes' Richest Americans, 1999—, World's Richest People, Forbes mag., 2001. Fellow: IEEE (Founders medal 1977, Medal of Honor 2008); mem.: Am. Phys. Soc., NAE. Achievements include having a pygmy owl named after him for his donations to environ. rsch. Avocations: fishing, golf. Office: Intel Corp 2200 Mission College Blvd Santa Clara CA 95054-1549 also: Betty & Gordon Moore Library Wilberforce Rd Cambridge CB3 0WD England*

MOORE, GREGORY L., editor; b. Cleve., Sept. 16, 1954; m. Nina Henderson Moore; children: Michael Langston, Jasmine Henderson. B. Journalism & Polit. Sci., Ohio Wesleyan U., 1976. Reporter Dayton Journal Herald, 1976—80, Cleveland Plain Dealer, 1980—83, political editor, 1983—86; asst. metro editor Boston Globe, 1986—94, mng. editor, 1994—2002; editor Denver Post, 2002—. Mem. Pulitzer Prize Bd., 2004—; mem. bd. trustees Ohio Wesleyan U. Recipient Lifetime Achievement award, Colo. Assn. Black Journalists, 2009; named Journalist of Yr., New Eng. ch., Nat. Assn. Black Journalists, 1996. Mem.: Am. Soc. Newspaper Editors, Nat. Assn. Black Journalists. Office: Denver Post 101 W Colfax Ave Denver CO 80202-5177 Office Phone: 303-820-1400. E-mail: gmoore@denverpost.com.*

MOORE, GREGORY T., civil rights association executive; children: Gregory Jr., Jelani. BS, Coll. Comm., Ohio U. Sr. v.p., govt. rels. TriCom Assocs. Advertising Firm; founder, pres., CEO GTM Consulting Svcs.; exec. dir. Citizenship Edn. Fund Nat. Rainbow Coalition, 1987—92; dep. polit. dir., liaison to tng. divsn. Dem. Nat. Com., Washington, DC, 1994—97, cons., 2006; chief staff to Rep. John Conyers US Congress, Washington, 1993; exec. dir. Nat. Voter Fund NAACP, Washington, 2001—. Adv. bd. Progressive Democrats Abroad. Named one of The Power 150, Ebony mag., 2008; named to Power 150, 2008. Office: NAACP Nat Voter Fund 1200 G St NW Ste 800 Washington DC 20005 Office Phone: 202-898-0969. Office Fax: 202-898-1397.

MOORE, GUY WILL, retired public information officer, historian, writer; b. Retta, Okla., June 19, 1922; s. Guy Thomas Moore and Pearl Grace Glasgow; m. Hazel Avenell Cartwright, Aug. 31, 1948 (dec. June 18, 1986); children: Anne Elizabeth Tarquinio, March Victoria Dodge. BA in Journalism, U. Okla., 1950, MA in History, 1952. News writer Office of the Army Surgeon Gen., Washington, 1956—57, info. specialist, 1957—59; info. specialist (first) US Army Rsch. and Devel. Command, Washington, 1959—60; dep. info. officer, divsn. gen. med. scis. NIH, Bethesda, Md., 1960—61, staff asst., office of dir. pub. affairs, 1961—64, chief pub. info. sect. office of rsch info., chief supervisory pub. info. specialist, news br., office of comm., 1967—79; ret., 1979. Chmn. pub. info. intern recruitment tng. com. NIH, 1961—79, spkr.

grants assoc. seminar, 1971—72; spkr. Am. Coll. Pub. Rels. Assn., Washington, 1970. Author: The Case of Mrs. Surratt, 1954, The NIH: How it Works, 1981; contbg. author: The Surratt Society's In Pursuit of..., 1990; contbr. articles to astronomy jours. Contr. project feeder watch Cornell Lab of Ornithology, 1987—. Mem.: No. Va. Astronomy Club, Nat. Capitol Astronomers, Surratt Soc. Avocations: astronomy, birdwatching. Home: 224 N Nelson St Arlington VA 22201 Home Phone: 703-525-6446.

MOORE, GWENDOLYNNE S. (GWEN MOORE), United States Representative from Wisconsin; b. Racine, Wis., Apr. 18, 1951; 3 children. BA in Polit. Sci., Marquette U., Milw., 1978. Mem. Wis. State Assembly, 1989—92, Wis. State Senate from 4th dist., Madison, 1992—2004, US Congress from 4th Wis. dist., 2005—, mem. small bus. com., mem. fin. svcs. com. Named one of Most Influential Black Americans, Ebony mag., 2006; named to Power 150, 2008. Democrat. Office: US House Reps 1408 Longworth House Office Bldg Washington DC 20515-4904 Office Phone: 202-225-4572.*

MOORE, HAL G., retired mathematician, educator; b. Vernal, Utah, Aug. 14, 1929; s. Lewis Henry and Nora (Gillman) M.; m. D'On Empey, July 20, 1956; children: David, Nora (Mrs. Bret C. Hess), Alison (Mrs. Samuel M. Smith). BS, U. Utah, 1952, MS, 1957; PhD, U. Calif., Santa Barbara, 1967. Tchr. Salt Lake City Pub. Schs., 1952-53; instr. math. Carbon Jr. Coll., also Carbon H.S., Price, Utah, 1953-55, Purdue U., Lafayette, Ind., 1957-61, adminstrv. asst. dept. math, 1960-61; from asst. prof. math. to assoc. prof. math. Brigham Young U., Provo, Utah, 1961-71, prof., 1971-95, prof. emeritus, 1995—, assoc. chmn. dept. math., 1986-89. Author: Precalculus Mathematics, 2d edit., 1977, (with Adil Yaqub) Elementary Linear Algebra With Applications, 1980, College Algebra and Trigonometry, 1983, A First Course in Linear Algebra, 1992, 3d edit., 1998; contbr. articles to profl. jours. Mem. High Coun., LDS Ch., 1985-91, MTC br. pres., 1991-94, Bishop, 1958-61, 78-82. NSF faculty fellow, U. Calif., Santa Barbara, 1964—66. Mem. Am. Math. Soc., Math. Assn. Am. (bd. govs. 1989-92), Utah State Math. Coalition (planning dir. 1990, bd. dir. 1991-92), Sigma Xi (dir. 1974-80, 82-85, com. chmn. 1982-90), Phi Kappa Phi. Home and Office: 631 W 650 S Orem UT 84058-6027 Home Phone: 801-225-7125. Personal E-mail: mooreh@math.byu.edu. *Revelation and reason can work together to bring human beings closer to the truth of their existence and place in the universe. But charity and love and dedication are as necessary to the success of this union as they are to all others.*

MOORE, HUBERT, JR., retired addictions counselor, consultant; b. Oklahoma City, Jan. 2, 1932; s. Hubert and Goldie Edith Moore; m. Mary Alene Jarnet, Dec. 9, 1958 (div. Oct. 1959); 1 child, LeAnne; m. Shirley M. Mumchuck, Apr. 1978 (dec. Nov. 8, 1985); children: Peggy, JoAnn, Lisa, Sharon. AA in Counseling, U. Alaska, 1986, BA in Human Svcs., 1992, BA in Psychology, 1992, BA in Sociology, 1996; MA in Anthropology, U. Mindanao, Philippines, 1998. Cert. addictions counselor II Alaska, Nat. Assn. Alcohol and Drug Abuse Counselors, master forensic counselor and criminal justice specialist Nat. Assn. Forensic Counselors, Nat. Register Addiction Counselors, Calif. Registry Addiction Specialists. Health and safety insp. Alaska Offshore Drilling, 1968—77; substance abuse counselor II No. Regional Ctr. for Addictions, Fairbanks, Alaska, 1977—85; forensic counselor Fairbanks Correction Facility, 1995—96; addictions cons. Soldotna, Alaska, 1991—2005; owner, operator (daycare ctr.) Papa's Playhouse, Soldotna, 1998—2006; ret., 2006. Campaign vol. Rep. Caucus, Soldotna, 1991—. Mem.: Phi Theta Kappa (bd. mem., Aurora Borealis Charter Sch.). Republican. Muslim. Avocations: philosophic studies, demographic research, motorcycling, moutain climbing, social research. Home and Office: PO Box 1057 Soldotna AK 99669 Home Phone: 907-262-3512.

MOORE, HUGH LESLIE, retired pediatrician; b. Dallas, Jan. 6, 1939; s. Robert Leslie and Maybeth (Thompson) Moore; m. LeAnn Kridelbaugh, May 25, 1996; children: Gwen Moore Holliday, Carolyn Moore Becker, Hugh Samuel. BA, U. Colo., 1960; MD, U. Tex.Southwestern Med. Sch., 1964. Diplomate Am. Bd. Pediat., Am. Bd. Pediat. Nephrology. Resident in pediat. Cin. Children's Hosp., Cin., 1964—67; fellow in pediat. nephrology U. Minn. Hosp., Mpls., 1969—71; pediatrician Clin. Pediat. Assoc., Dallas, 1971—; clin. prof. pediat. U. Tex. Southwestern Med. Sch., Dallas, 1982—2005; ret. Pediat. tchr. Childrens Med. Ctr., Dallas, 1971—, bd. trustees, 1984—. Lt. comdr. USN, 1967—69. Recipient Outstanding Tchr. award, Children's Med. Ctr.; named one of Top Doctors, D Mag., 1992, 1996, 1999, 2002, Best Doctor's in Am., 2000—01, 2001—02, 2003—04, 2004—05. Mem.: Tex. Pediat. Soc., Am. Soc. Pediat. Nephrology, Am. Soc. Nephrology, Dallas County Med. Soc., Tex. Med. Assn. Avocations: travel, photography, bird watching, motorcycles. Office: 7547 Greenbrier Dr Dallas TX 75225

MOORE, J. STROTHER, computer scientist, educator; s. J. Strother and Jessie Louise Moore; m. Jo Anne O'Neil; children: Lisa, Jonathan, Chris. BS in Math., MIT, Cambridge, 1970; PhD in Computational Logic, U.Edinburgh, Scotland, 1973. Programmer, dept. computational logic U. Edinburgh, Scotland, 1971—72, rsch. fellow, 1973; rsch. mathematician, Computer Sci. Lab. Xerox Palo Alto Rsch. Ctr., Calif., 1973—76, SRI Internat., Menlo Park, Calif., 1976—78, sr. rsch. mathematician, 1979—81, staff scientist, 1981; assoc. prof., dept. computer scis. U. Tex., Austin, 1981—84, Gottesman Family Centennial prof., 1985—88, Adm. B.R. Inman prof. computing theory, 1997—, chair, dept. computer scis., 2001—. Founder, bd. dirs. Computational Logic, Inc., 1987—, chief scientist, 1987—96; lectr. in field. Co-author: (software) Boyer-Moore Theorem Prover, 1971, A Computational Logic, 1979, A Computational Logic Handbook, 1988, Computer-Aided Reasoning: An Approach, 2000; co-editor: The Correctness Problem in Computer Science, 1981; mem. editl. bd.: Jour. Automated Reasoning, Formal Methods in Sys. Design; contbr. articles to profl. jours. Co-recipient John McCarthy prize for program verification, 1983, Current prize in automatic theorem proving, Am. Math. Soc., 1991, Herbrand award, Conf. on Automated Deduction, 1999. Fellow: Assn. Computing Machinery (Software Sys. award 2005), Am. Assn. Artificial Intelligence; mem.: NAE. Avocations: rock climbing, backpacking. Office: U Tex Dept Computer Sci Taylor Hall 2-124 Austin TX 78712-1188 also: Computational Logic Inc 1717 W Sixth St Ste 290 Austin TX 78712 Office Phone: 512-471-9590. Office Fax: 512-471-8885. Business E-Mail: moore@cs.utexas.edu.

MOORE, JACK B., oil industry executive; b. 1953; BBA in Fin. and Mktg., U. Houston, 1977; grad. Advanced Mgmt. Program, Harvard Bus. Sch. Dir. materials Baker Hughes Inc., dir. market rsch., dir. HR, v.p. Latin Am. Ops., v.p. Eastern Hemisphere, v.p. Western Hemisphere; v.p., gen. mgr. western hemisphere Cameron Internat. Corp. (formerly Cameron Cooper Corp.), 1999—2002, pres., Drilling and Prodn. Sys. Group Houston, 2002—06, pres., COO, 2007—08, pres., CEO, 2008—. Exec. adv. bd. CT Bauer Coll. Bus.; dir., mem. audit com. Maverick Tube Corp., 2005—; bd. dirs. Cameron Internat. Corp. (formerly Cooper Cameron Corp.), 2007—. Office: Cameron Internat Corp 1333 W Loop S Ste 1700 Houston TX 77027-9109 Office Phone: 713-513-3300. Office Fax: 713-513-3355.

MOORE, JACQUELYN CORNELIA, retired labor union administrator, editor; b. Dec. 25, 1929; d. James C. and Harriette I. Thomas; m. Clarence Carbin Moore, Jan. 19, 1947 (dec. Feb. 1970); children: Clarence Joseph, Janet Elizabeth Moore Marshall. Mail clk. U.S. P.O., Phila., 1966—93; editor Local 509 Newsletter Nat. Alliance of Postal and Fed. Employees, Washington, 1969—74, editl. newsletter chmn., 1969—74, sec. dist. 5, 1972—74, nat. editor Nat. Alliance, 1974—2004, mem. exec. bd., 1974—, union photographer, 1974—2004, ret., 2004. Sec. supervisory com. Nat. Fed. Credit Union, 1977—82, 1984—94, chair, 2009. Vol. D.C. Voting Rights Corp., Washington, 1979—2004; sustaining mem. Dem. Nat. Com., 1977—2009. Mem.: Nat. Alliance Postel and Fed. Employees. Roman Catholic. Home: 1640 11th St NW 202 Washington DC 20001 E-mail: jacmar5362@aol.com.

MOORE, JAMES ALFRED, chemist, educator; b. Bklyn., Aug. 30, 1939; s. Joseph Alfred and Henrietta (Utzig) M.; m. Lotte Wiechert, Jan. 15, 1966; children: Martina, Christopher. BS, St. John's U., 1961; PhD, Poly. Inst. Bklyn., 1967. Postdoctoral fellow U. Mainz, Fed. Republic of Germany, 1967-68; rsch. assoc. U. Mich., Ann Arbor, 1968-69; asst. prof. Rensselaer Poly. Inst., Troy, N.Y., 1969-75, assoc. prof., 1975-84, prof., 1984—. Cons. Arco Chem. Co., Newtown Square, Pa., 1990—. Contbr. articles to more than 150 profl. jours. Mem. Am. Chem. Soc. Avocations: hunting, fishing, skiing, target shooting. Office: Rensselaer Poly Inst Dept Chemistry Troy NY 12180-3590 Business E-Mail: moorej@rpi.edu.

MOORE, JAMES CONKLIN, lawyer; b. Albany, NY, Dec. 20, 1939; s. James Alexander and Doris Virginia (Conklin) M.; m. Shirley Jean Mitchell, June 17, 1961; children: James, Jennifer, David, Eliza. BS, Cornell U., 1961, LLB, 1964. Bar: NY 1964, U.S. Dist. Ct. (we. dist.) NY 1966, U.S. Dist. Ct. (mid. dist.) Pa. 1981, U.S. Dist. Ct. (no. dist.) NY 1980, U.S. Ct. Mil. Appeals 1965. Assoc. Wiser, Shaw, Freeman, VanGraafeiland, Harter & Secrest, Rochester, NY, 1966-74; ptnr. Harter, Secrest & Emery, Rochester, 1974—2003, counsel, 2004—, mediator, arbitrator. Bd. dirs. Empire Justice Ctr., chmn., 2007—. Contbr. articles to profl. jours., chapters to books. Trustee, pres. Friends of Rochester (N.Y.) Pub. Libr., 1993—98; trustee Nat. Equal Justice Libr., 2006—08; bd. dirs. Geva Theater, Inc., 2002—09; pres. Legal Connection, Inc., 2002—04; coun. mem. Cornell U., 1997—2002; bd. dirs. Monroe County Bar Found., 2002—04; chmn. bd. trustees NY Lawyer Assistance Trust, 2001—04. Capt. US Army, 1964—66, Vietnam. Adv. bd. Rochester Area Ednl. TV, 1981-87; elder, trustee Third Presbyn. Ch., Rochester. Fellow: ABA (ho. of dels. 1998—2006, standing comm. on legal assistance to indigent defendants), N.Y. Bar Found. (bd. dirs. 1997—2000), Am. Coll. Trial Lawyers; mem.: Union Internat. Advocate (US pres. 2005—07, exec. com. 2007—), Am. Arbitration Assn. (panel neutral), Nat. Conf. Bar Pres. (exec. com. 1999—2002), Monroe County Bar Assn. (chmn. judiciary com. 1982—85, trustee 2004—06, chmn. com. on lawyer advt. 2006), N.Y. State Bar Assn. (chmn. ins. sect. 1984—85, chmn. task force on liability ins. 1986—87, 1986—87, chmn. com. ins. programs 1988—94, exec. com. 1992—2000, ho. del. 1993—, v.p. 1994—97, pres. 1998—99, chmn. nominating com. 2001, chmn. com. on ADR 2006—08, com. on jud. nominations 2006—), Am. Inst. Law (elected). Avocations: history, restoring old furniture. Home: 251 Windemere Rd Rochester NY 14610-1342 Office: Harter Secrest & Emery 1600 Bausch & Lomb Pl Rochester NY 14604-2711 Office Phone: 585-231-1124. Business E-Mail: jmoore@hselaw.com.

MOORE, JAMES E., former state supreme court justice; b. Laurens, SC, Mar. 13, 1936; s. Roy Ernest and Marie (Hill) M.; m. Mary Alicia Deadwyler, Jan. 27, 1963; children: Erin Alicia, Travis Warren. BA, Duke U., 1958, JD, 1961; D of Humanities (hon.), Lander Univ., 1997. Bar: S.C. 1961, U.S. Dist. Ct. S.C. 1961. Pvt. practice, Greenwood, S.C., 1961-76; mem. SC Ho. of Reps., Columbia, SC, 1968—76; cir. judge 8th Jud. Cir. SC, Greenwood, 1976-91; assoc. justice SC Supreme Ct., 1992—2008. Supreme ct. liaison S.C. Bd. of Law Examiners, Bd. of Commn. on Jud. Conduct, Bd. of Commn. on Atty. Conduct; chmn. Chief Justice's Commn. on Profession. Recipient Outstanding Contribution to Justice award, S.C. Trial Lawyers Assn., 1996. Mem. S.C. Bar Assn., ABA, Am. Judicature Soc.; First Baptist Church of Greenwood. Baptist. Home: 148 Amherst Dr Greenwood SC 29649-8901 Office Phone: 864-942-8559.

MOORE, JAMES L., III, counselor, educator; b. Lyman, SC, Dec. 29, 1971; s. James L. Jr. and Edna M. Moore; m. Stephanie M. Moore, Mar. 10, 2006; 1 child, James L. IV. BA in English Edn., Del. State U., Dover, 1995; MAEd in Counselor Edn., Va. Inst. Tech. and State U., Blacksburg, 1997, PhD in Counselor Edn., 2000. Cert. sports counselor Del., English tchr. grades 7-12, sch. counselor Va. Asst. dir. Va. Inst. Tech. and State U., 1996—97, dir., 1997—2000; asst. prof. U. SC, Columbia, 2000—02, Ohio State U., Columbus, 2002—06, assoc. prof., 2006—. Recipient Disting. Scholar award, Ohio State U. Coll. Edn., 2003, Rsch. award, Ohio Sch. Counselor Assn., 2004, George E. Hill Counselor Educator award, Ohio Sch. Counselors Assn., 2005, Deanna Hawes Outstanding Mentor award, N. Ctrl. Assn. for Counselor Edn. and Supervision, 2005, Ohana award, Counselors for Social Justice, 2006, Jr. Scholar award, Nat. BOTH, 2003; Laser scholar, U. South Fla., Tampa, 2004—, affiliated scholar, John Glen Inst., Ohio State U., 2004—, Ohio Collaborative, Columbus, 2004—. Mem.: Nat. Assn. for Gifted Children, Am. Sch. Counselor Assn., Am. Ednl. Rsch. Assn. (Early Career award Divsn. E 2004). Avocations: reading, writing, solving problems, jazz. Home: 6105 Bristol Way Alexandria VA 22310 Office: Ohio State U Coll Edn and Human Ecology A444 PAES Bldg 305 W 17th Ave Columbus OH 43210 Personal E-mail: jlmoemoe@aol.com. Business E-Mail: moore.1408@osu.edu.

MOORE, JAMES R., lawyer; b. Longview, Wash., Sept. 14, 1944; s. James Carlton and Virginia (Rice) M.; m. Patricia Riley, Aug. 25, 1967 (div. 1978); 1 child, Katherine M.; m. Christine M. Monkman, July 14, 1979 (div. 1996); stepchildren: Amy McKenna, John McKenna; 1 foster child, Zia Sunseri; m. Kathryn Lindquist, Aug. 26, 1996; stepchildren: Matthew Elggren, Adam Elggren, Erin Elggren, David Heilner. BA, Whitman Coll., 1966; JD, Duke U., 1969. Bar: Wash. 1970, U.S. Ct. Appeals (4th cir.) 1972, U.S. Supreme Ct. 1973, U.S. Ct. Appeals (9th cir.) 1974, D.C., 1995. Law clk. to Hon. J. Barnes U.S. Ct. Appeals (9th cir.), LA, 1969-70; trial atty. pollution control, land/natural resources div. U.S. Dept. Justice, Washington, 1970-74; asst. U.S. atty. U.S. Atty.'s Office, Seattle, 1974-82; regional counsel U.S. EPA Region 10, 1982-87; counsel Perkins Coie, 1987-88, ptnr., 1989-98; sr. environ. counsel, v.p. Huntsman Corp., Salt Lake City, 1999—; dep. gen. counsel Huntsman Internat., 2002—04, Huntsman LLC, Salt Lake City, 2004—, Huntsman Corp., Salt Lake City, 2005—. Spkr. in field. Contbr. articles to profl. jours. Bd. dirs. Environ. Law Inst., 1995-2000; chmn. audit com. Whitman Coll., 1994-2007, ethics com. Bd. Environ. Auditors Cert., 1998—, bd. overseers 2003—; mem. Athlete's Hall of Fame Com., 2003—; pres. W Club, 2008-. Mem. ABA (sect. environ., energy and resources 1987—, vice chmn. in-house counsel com., 2003-04, chmn. 2004-06), Wash. State Bar Assn. (environ. and land use sects. 1974—, spl. dist. coun. 1988-95), DC Bar, Utah Bar. Democrat. Office: Huntsman Corp 500 Huntsman Way Salt Lake City UT 84108-1235 Home Phone: 801-583-0830; Office Phone: 801-584-5828. Business E-Mail: jim_moore@huntsman.com.

MOORE, JANE ROSS, librarian, educator; b. Phila., Apr. 24, 1929; d. John William and Mary M. Ross; m. Cyril Howard Moore, Jr., June 1, 1956 (div. Mar. 1967). AB, Smith Coll., 1951; MLS, Drexel U., 1952; postgrad., Columbia U.; MBA with distinction, NYU, 1965; PhD, Case Western Res. U., 1974. Cataloguer Yale U. Libr., 1952-54; chief tech. processes libr. Lederle Labs., Am. Cyanamid Co., Pearl River, NY, 1954-58; chief serials catalog libr. Bklyn. Coll. Libr., 1958-65, asst. prof., chief catalog divsn., 1965-70, assoc. prof., chief catalog divsn., 1971-73, asso. prof., assoc. libr. adminstrv. svcs., 1973-76; prof., chief libr. Mina Rees Libr., Grad. Ctr., CUNY, 1976-91, prof., chief libr. emerita, 1991—. Lectr. Syracuse U. Grad. Sch. Libr. Sci., 1967, 69, Queens Coll. Grad. Sch. Libr. and Info. Studies, 1967—69, adj. assoc. prof., 1974—76, adj. prof., 1977—86; HEW Title IIB fellow Case Western Res. U. Sch. Libr. Sci., 1970—72; mem. chancellor's task force librs. CUNY, 1979—81; trustee N.Y. Met. Reference and Rsch. Libr. Agy., 1984—93, 2d v.p., 1985—88, v.p., 1988—90, treas., 1991—93. Elder Presbyn. Ch., clk. session, pres. corp.; bd. dirs. Vis. Nurse Assn. Bklyn., 1984—2006, mem. exec. com., 1987—2006, vice chmn., 2001—06; bd. dirs., mem. exec. com., sec. Vis. Nurse Regional Health Care Sys., Inc., 2001—06. Mem.: AAUW, AAUP, ALA (life; membership com. 1967—71, chmn. coun. regional groups, resources and tech. svcs. divsn. 1968—69, dir. divsn. 1968—70, 1975—76, chmn. divsn. cataloging and classification sect. 1975—76), The Typophiles (sec.-treas. 1996—2006), N.Y. Tech. Svcs. Librs. (pres. 1963—64), Spl. Librs. Assn., Am. Printing History Assn., OCLC Users Coun. (SUNY del. 1981—85), Assn. Coll. and Rsch. Librs. (chmn. univ. librs. sect. 1983—84), N.Y. Libr. Assn. (pres. resources and tech. svcs. sect., councilor 1966—67, sec.-treas. acad. and spl. librs. sect. 1973—75, councilor 1975—76, 1978—81, pres. 1979—80), Chartered Inst. Libr. and Info. Profl. Gt. Britain (life), NYU Grad. Sch. Bus. Adminstrn. Alumni Assn. (rec. sec. 1967—69, dir. 1969—70, 1975—79), Princeton Club N.Y., Smith Coll. Club Bklyn. (pres. 1966—68, class treas. 1976—81), N.Y. Libr. Club (sec. 1964—66, coun. 1966—70, 1973—77, 1979—82, pres. 1980—81), Smith Coll. Club N.Y., Grolier Club, Colophon, Phi Kappa Phi. Home: 103 Kendal Dr Oberlin OH 44074-1905

MOORE, JANET L.S., music educator, dean; d. Wallace Milton and Roberta Lee Schulze; m. Marvin Lynn Moore; children: Gregory Scott, Kellia Lynne. MusB, Ea. Ky. U., 1974; MusM, U. N.C., Greensboro, 1977, EdD, 1984. Choral and keyboard instr. Rockingham County Sr. H.S., Wentworth, NC, 1977—80; fine arts supr., cultural arts coord. Rockingham County Schs., Wentworth, 1978—80; elem. music specialist Price Traditional Sch., Greensboro, 1984; asst. prof. music edn. Rutgers U., New Brunswick, NJ, 1985—88, Northwestern U., Evanston, Ill., 1988—89; asst. prof. music Sch. Music U. South Fla., Tampa, 1989—95, coord. music edn., 1995—98, assoc. prof. music, 1995—, assoc. dean Coll. Visual and Performing Arts, 1998—2003, assoc. dean undergrad. studies, 2003—. Pres. faculty senate U. South Fla., Tampa, 1997—99; external evaluator Hillsborough County Sch. Sys., Tampa, 2002—07. Author: (music textbook) Understanding Music Through Sound Exploration and Experiments; contbr. music textbook On the Nature of Musical Experience; editor: (state curriculum guide) Introduction to Music Performance. Recipient Tchg. Incentive Program award, Fla. State Legislature and State U. Sys., 1994; grantee, U. South Fla. Rsch. Coun., 1990—97, U. South Fla. Ctr. Tchg. Enhancement, 1998; internat. travel grantee, Inst. on Black Life, U. South Fla., 1993, 1997, summer fellow, Rutgers U. Rsch. Coun., 1987. Mem.: Coun. Colls. Arts and Scis., Fla. Music Educators Assn. (Leadership award 1998), Am. Orff Schulwerk Assn., Internat. Soc. Music Edn. (nat. adv. bd. 1991—94, world conf. adv. bd. 1991—94), Soc. Gen. Music, Soc. Rsch. in Music Edn., Music Educators Nat. Conf. (nat. mem.-at-large Soc. Gen. Music 1997—99, editor Gen. Music Today jour. 2000—03, editl. bd. Soc. Gen. Music), Phi Kappa Phi (life), Pi Kappa Lambda (life; founding pres., Eta Lambda chpt. 1992—94). Office: U South Fla 4202 E Fowler Ave UGS SVC 2002 Tampa FL 33620-6920

MOORE, JASON, theater director; b. Fayetteville, Ark., Oct. 22, 1970; Grad., Northwestern U. Dir.: (Broadway plays) Avenue Q, 2003, Steel Magnolias, 2005, Shrek The Musical, 2008; (plays) The Crumple Zone, 2000, Guardians, 2006, Jerry Springer: The Opera. Mailing: PO Box 1252 New York NY 10113-1252*

MOORE, JEAN E., social worker, academic administrator, educator, radio personality; d. Hugh Huriel and Theodora H. Buchanan Campbell; m. Robert M. Moore, Jr.; children: Robert M. III, Doreen R. Moore Closson. BA, Hunter Coll., 1947; M of Social Svc., Bryn Mawr Coll., 1949; EdD, Temple U., 1978. Cert. social worker Acad. Cert. Social Workers, LSW Pa., 1989. Social worker Children's Svc., Inc., Phila., 1949—52; asst. chief clin. social work svcs. Med. and Mental Hygiene Clinic Region 10 U.S. VA, Phila., 1952—60; social work specialist Ctrl. Relocation Bur., Phila. Redevel. Authority, 1962—67; social work/human svcs. adviser for Model Cities Region III U.S. Dept. Housing and Urban devel. for 6 states and D.C., 1967—69; assoc. prof., grad. faculty, dir. new career ladders Temple U., Phila., dir. program devel. Office of Rsch. and Program Devel., 1969—89, assoc. prof. emerita, 1989—; exec. asst. to pres. Cheyney U. of Pa., 1985—91; v.p. instnl. advancement U. Md. Ea. Shore, Princess Anne, Md., 1991—97; host, Univ. Forum WESM, 1994—97; host, exec. prodr. Univ. Forum Temple U. Pub. Radio, Phila., 1997—. Mem. internat. bd. advisors Radio for Peace Internat.; bd. dirs., club dir. Gundaker Found., Inc.; cons., spkr., presenter, lectr. Contbr. articles to profl. publs. Past bd. trustees Lackawanna Jr. Coll., C.C. of Phila.; past pres. Fair Housing Coun. Suburban Phila.; chair vis. accreditation teams Mid. States Assn. Colls. and Schs. Commn. on Higher Edn.; past bd. pres. Spectrum Health Svcs., Inc.; chair State Bd. Pvt. Corresp. Schs.; elder Lansdowne First Presbyn. Ch.; bd. dirs. Children's Svc., Inc. Recipient Documentary Gold award, Internat. Assn. Audio Visual Commns., 1999, Crystal awards of Excellence, The Communicator Awards, 1999, 2000, 2002, 2003, 2004, 2005, 2006, 2008, 1st pl. radio/ednl., Broadcast Edn. Assn., 2000, Documentary award, 2000, Achievement in Radio award, March of Dimes, 2000—04, Gold Cindy award, Internat. Assn. Audio Visual Communicators, 2000, 2002, 2003, Undoing Racism Unity award, Radnor Twp., 2002, Media award, Kelly Anne Dolan Meml. Fund, 2003, Martin Luther King Jr. Humanitarian award, Upper Merion, 2004, Mayor's Fire Prevention medal, City of N.Y., Outstanding Contbn. in Edn. award, Theta Nu Sigma, Image award, Black Women in Sport Found., Radio Program awards, Best Coverage Maternal Health Issues/Problems Risk Pregnancies, numerous academic awards, Alumni Lifetime Achievement award, Bryn Mawr Coll. Grad. Sch. Social Work and Social Rsch., 2008; named Paul Harris fellow, Rotary Found., 2005, Guy Gundaker fellow, Gundaker Found. Rotary Internat. Dist. 7450, 2006; named to Hall of Fame, Hunter Coll., 1999. Mem.: NASW (charter mem. 1955, Golden Membership Disting. Svc. award 2005), Broadcast Pioneers of Phila., Inc., Pa. Abolition Soc. (bd. mgrs.), Darby

Lansdowne Club, Rotary Club Upper Darby-Lansdown (bd. dirs. 2001—05), Phi Delta Kappa, Alpha Chi Alpha, Phi Beta Kappa, Delta Sigma Theta. Avocations: international travel, writing, poetry. Office Phone: 215-204-4376.

MOORE, JEFFREY SCOTT, chemist, materials scientist, educator; b. Sept. 15, 1962; BS, U. Ill., 1984, PhD, 1989. NSF postdoctoral fellow Calif. Inst. Tech., 1989-90; asst. prof. U. Mich., Ann Arbor, 1990-93; assoc. prof. chemistry and materials sci. and engring. U. Ill., Urbana-Champaign, 1993-95, prof. materials sci. and engring., 1995—, Murchison-Mallory prof. chemistry, 2007—, William H. and Janet G. Lycan prof. chemistry, 2000—07. Mem. faculty Beckman Inst., U. Ill., Frederick Seitz Materials Rsch. Libr., U. Ill. Mem. editl. adv. bd. Chemistry of Materials, Macromolecular Synthesis; contbr. numerous articles to profl. jours. Recipient Bronze Tablet Univ. Acad. award, 1984, Sch. Chem. Sciences Teaching award, 2002, Prof. of Yr., Alpha Epsilon Delta Pre-Health Honors Soc., 2003; NSF Young Investigator, 1992-97, Office Naval Rsch. Young Investigator, 1994-97, Camille Dreyfus Tchr.-Scholar, 1994, Arthur C. Cope scholar, 1996, Univ. scholar, 1996-98, Alfred P. Sloan fellow, 1997 Fellow AAAS, Am. Acad. Arts and Sciences; mem. Am. Chem. Soc. (assoc. editor Jour. Am. Chem. Soc.), Materials Rsch. Soc. Office: U Ill Dept Chemistry 268 Roger Adams Lab 600 S Mathews Ave Urbana IL 61801 Office Phone: 217-244-4024. Office Fax: 217-244-8024. E-mail: moore@scs.uiuc.edu.

MOORE, JERRY JAY, sales executive, retired archaeologist; b. Ft. Sam Houston, Tex., Jan. 29, 1960; s. Richard Vernal and Irmgard Ludwiga Ottilia (Bennewitz) Moore. Student, Ea. Ill. U., 1980—83. Lab. asst. Archaeol. Investigations Ctr. So. Ill. U., Carbondale, 1979; field/lab. technician Ill. State Mus. Soc., Springfield, 1980; asst. lab. supr. Ill. State Mus. Soc., Dickson Mounds Mus., Havana, 1980—81, Am. Resources Group, Ltd., Carbondale, 1983—86; archaeol. technician Midwestern Archaeol. Rsch. Ctr. Ill. State U., Normal, 1986—93; archaeol. asst. U. Ill., Urbana, 1993—94; archaeol. asst. Inst. Archaeology and Anthropology U. S.C., Columbia, 1993—94; merchandising asst. J.C. Penney Co., Champaign, Ill., 1994—2000; sales profl. Bergner's/Saks Inc., Urbana, 2000—02, Dick's Sporting Goods, Inc., Champaign, 2002—. Co-author: monographs; contbr. articles to profl. jours. Founding mem. Nat. Campaign for Tolerance, Civil Rights Meml. Ctr., Wall of Tolerance, Montgomery, Ala., 2004; founding sponsor Martin Luther King Jr. Nat. Meml., Washington, 2006. Named to Wall Tolerance, So. Poverty Law Ctr. Civil Rights Meml. Ctr., 2004; scholar, State of Ill., 1978—82. Mem.: SAR, Soc. Collegiate Journalists, Iroquois County Hist. and Geneal. Soc., Soc. of the War of 1812 (U.S. Army Mil. Uniform Ft. Dearborn, Ill. Project 1999—2000, sgt. at arms 2000—), Sons of the Revolution, Sons of Union Vets. of the Civil War (dept. of Ill. genealogist 1998—2007, Ill. dept. ordnance assessment 2004—05), Phi Theta Kappa. Republican. Roman Catholic. Avocations: history, antiques, genealogy. Home: 590 S Park St Paxton IL 60957 Office: 2113 N Prospect Ave Champaign IL 61822 Office Phone: 217-352-4173.

MOORE, JOHN EDDY, former lieutenant governor; b. Charleston, W.Va., July 13, 1943; s. George Roy and Alvaretta (Hoskins) M.; m. Martha Clay Spangenberg, Aug. 7, 1966; children— Brian Clay, Stacia Hoskins BS in Comemrce, Washington and Lee U., 1965; JD, U. Ky., 1968. Group dir. Rockwell Internat., Cedar Rapids, Iowa, 1974-80, v.p. Dallas, 1980-81; v.p., ptnr. Korn/Ferry Internat., Dallas, 1981-82; sr. v.p. Cessna Aircraft, Wichita, Kans., 1982—2002; lt. gov. State of Kansas, 2003—07. Dir. Health Care Plus, Wichita, Kans., Riverside Hosp., Wichita; former mem. Spl. Commn. on Pub. Agenda for Kans.; sec. Kans. Foodbank Warehouse, Wichita; bd. dirs. Booth Meml. Residence, Wichita Mem. Midwest Aerospace Indsl. Relations Council, Machinery and Allied Products Inst. (human resources council), Wichita C. of C. (chmn. state legis. com.), Kans. C. of C. and Industry (bd. dirs.) Republican. Methodist. Avocation: golf.

MOORE, JOHN HARTWELL, anthropology educator, consultant; b. Williston, ND, Feb. 27, 1939; s. William Andrew and Mary Montgomery Moore; m. Shelley Ann Arlen, June 6, 1981; children: Jeremiah, Jessica, Alexandra. BS in Chem. Engring., U. of Ark., Fayetteville, AR, 1962; PhD in Anthropology, NYU, New York, NY, 1974. Anthropology educator U. Okla., Norman, 1977—93, Albion Coll., Mich., 1972—77, U. Fla., Gainesville, 1993—. Cons. Native Am. Rights Fund, Boulder, Colo., 1979—, Sand Creek Massacre Descendants Trust, Anadarko, Okla., 1991—, Sawridge Indian Band, Slave Lake, Alberta, Canada, 1992—; pres. U. Fla. Faculty, 2006—. Author: (book) The Cheyenne, The Cheyenne Nation: A Social and Demographic History, History of the Pamunkey Nation, Identifying the Sand Creek Descendants; editor: (book) Political Economy of North American Indians, Interstellar Travel and Multi-Generation Space Ships; editor-in-chief: Macmillan, Encyclopedia of Race and Racism, 2007. Del. to state conv. Dem. Party, Oklahoma City, 1991—91; chpt. pres. Vietnam Veterans Against the War, West Orange, NJ, 1968—69; state com. Rainbow Coalition, Oklahoma City, 1987—93. Second Lt. US Army, 1962—64, East Asia. Decorated UN Peacekeeping Medal, Armed Forces Expeditionary Medal US Army, US Nat. Def. medal, Good Conduct medal, Korea Nat. Def. medal; recipient Governor's Cmty. Svc. Award, State of Okla., 1990. Fellow: AAAS, Ctr. for Advanced Study in the Behavioral Sciences, Am. Assn. for the Advancement of Science (chair of anthropology sect. 1997—98); mem.: Human Genome Diversity Project (chair north am. cmty. 1998). Democrat. Ethical Culture. Achievements include research in role of ethnogenesis in human evolution; rates of gene flow from ethnic inter-marriage; demographic requirements for interstellar space travel; correlations between genetic and linguistic changes. Home: 3328 North West 18 Avenue Gainesville FL 32605 Office: University of Florida 1112 Turlington Gainesville FL 32611

MOORE, JOHN MORTON, biology professor, consultant; s. Edward Horace and Marguerite Jenette Moore; m. Cathy Lynne Hinkley. BS in Biology, Taylor U., Upland, Ind., 1972; MA in Biology, Ball State U., Muncie, Ind., 1978, EdD in Biology, 1989. Tchr. Marion Com. Schs., Ind., 1973—92; prof. Taylor U., 1992—, dept. chair, 1992—. Pres. Ind. Assn. Biology Tchrs., W. Lafayette, Ind., 1993—93; bd. dirs. Hossier Assn. Biology Tchrs., Inc., Indpls., 2000—07; region iii coord. Nat. Assn. Biology Tchrs., Reston, Va., 2001—, pres. elect, 2008—; faculty cons. Coll. Bd. Biology, Princeton, NJ. Contbr. articles to profl. jours. Bd. mem. water safety ARC, Marion, Ind., 1974—89. Mem.: NSTA, Nat. Assn. Biology Tchrs. (pres. elect 2008), Ind. Assn. Biology Tchrs. (pres. 1993—94), Alpha Chi, Phi Delta Kappa. Independent. Avocations: hiking, travel, camping. Office: 236 W Reade Ave Upland IN 46989-1001 Office Phone: 765-998-4994.

MOORE, JOHN NORTON, lawyer, educator, diplomat; b. NYC, June 12, 1937; s. William Thomas and Lorena (Norton) M.; m. Barbara Schneider, Dec. 12, 1981; children: Victoria Norton, Elizabeth Norton. AB in Economics, Drew U., 1959; LLB with honors, Duke U., 1962; LLM, U. Ill., 1965; postgrad., Yale U., 1965-66. Bar: Fla. 1962, Ill. 1963, Va. 1969, D.C. 1972, U.S. Supreme Ct. 1972. Tchg. fellow U. Ill., 1962—63; asst. prof. U. Fla., 1963—65, assoc. prof., 1965—66, asst. dean, 1964—66; assoc. prof. U. Va. Sch. Law, Charlottesville, 1966—69, prof., 1969—76, Walter L. Brown prof. law, 1976—, dir. grad. program, 1968—93, dir. Ctr. Oceans Law and Policy, 1976—, dir. Ctr. Nat. Security Law, 1984—. Counselor on internat. law Dept. State, Washington, 1972-73; chmn. Nat. Security Coun. Task Force on Law of Sea and dep. spl. rep. of Pres. and amb. Law of Sea Conf., 1973-76; fellow Woodrow Wilson Internat. Ctr. for Scholars, Washington, 1976; adj. prof. Georgetown Law Ctr., 1978—; mem. Nat. Adv. Com. on Oceans and Atmosphere, 1984-85; mem. U.S. del. Conf. Security and Coop. in Europe, 1984; spl. counsel, dep. agt. for U.S. to World Ct.; former cons. to the Pres.'s Intelligence Oversight Bd., Arms Control and Disarmament Agy., U.S. Info. Agy.; chmn. bd. dirs. U.S. Inst. Peace, 1985-91; co-chmn. with the U.S. dep. atty. gen. Moscow Seminar on the Rule of Law, 1990; legal advisor during Gulf crisis Kuwait's Amb. to U.S., Kuwait Rep. to UN Boundary Commn., 1991-94. Author: Law and the Indo-China War, 1972 (Phi Beta Kappa award); editor: Law and Civil War in the Modern World, 1976, Readings in International Law, 1979, The Arab-Israeli Conflict, 3 vols., 1976, 4th vol., 1991, Nat. Security Law, 1990, 2d edit., 2005, Crisis in the Gulf, 1992, Nat. Security Law Documents, 1995, Treaty Interpretation, The Constitution and the Rule of Law, 2001, The National Law of Treaty Implementation, 2001, Solving the War Puzzle, 2003; editor: The Real Lessons of the Vietnam War, 2002, Civil Litigation Against Terrorism, 2003; mem. editl. bd. Am. Jour. Internat. Law; contbr. articles to profl. jours. Sesquicentennial assoc. Ctr. Advanced Studies, U. Va., 1971-72; adv. bd. law of sea State Dept., 1977-80, adv. bd. internat. law, 1982; chmn. bd. dirs. U.S. Inst. Peace, 1986-89, 89-91; chmn. oceans policy com. Rep. Nat. Com.; com. on exploration of the seas Nat. Acad. Nat. Rsch. Coun., 2002; active Consortium on Intelligence. Recipient Alumni award in arts Drew U., 1976; Compass Disting. Achievement award for significant contbns. to art and sci. of oceanography and marine tech., 1994; NIH fellow Yale U., 1965-66. Mem. ABA (past vice-chmn. sect. internat. law, past 4-term chmn. com. on law and nat. security), Am. Law Inst., Am. Oceanic Orgn. (past exec. coun.), Marine Tech. Soc. (past exec. coun.), Rhodes Acad. Oceans Law and Policy (founding dir.), Coun. Fgn. Rels., Order of Coif, Cosmos Club, N.Y. Yacht Club, Freedom House (bd. dirs., sec., governance and ethics com. mem., exec. com. mem. 2008-), Phi Beta Kappa. Republican. Episcopalian. Office: U Va Sch Law 580 Massie Rd Charlottesville VA 22903-1789 Office Phone: 434-924-7441. E-mail: jnm9s@virginia.edu. *Life offers opportunity to pursue many worthwhile interests. In selecting among them it has seemed most useful to focus on those issues of sufficiently broad general significance as to justify the efforts of a lifetime. For me that has meant focus on promoting democracy and the rule of law, improving the functioning of government, controlling and reducing war, and the policy choices of the ocean frontier.*

MOORE, JOHN PLUNKETT DENNIS, publisher; b. Mexico, Mo., Mar. 2, 1931; s. Dennis Talmage and Vona Mae (Vance) M.; m. Lydia Benz Ahern, Aug. 15, 1959; children: Alison Ahern, Lydia Benz, John Talmage, Maude Ahern, Meredith Coleman. Student, Princeton U., 1948-51, U.S. Naval Acad., 1951-53; BA, U. Mo., Columbia, 1953; postgrad., Harvard Law Sch., 1955-56. Coll. traveler The Dryden Press, Inc., NYC, 1957-59; coll. traveler The Macmillan Co., NYC, 1959-60, editor, 1960-67; assoc. exec. editor Columbia U. Press, NYC, 1968-74, editor in chief, 1974-80, pres., 1980-97, also bd. dirs. Bd. dirs., pres. Columbia U. Music Press; bd. dirs. Univ. Presses of Calif., Columbia and Princeton, Chichester, West Sussex, Eng., 1979-97, chmn., 1981-83, 85-87, 96-97; trustee Composer's Recordings, Inc., 1984-97. Author: Columbia University Press: A Historical Sketch, 1893-1993; mem. editl. bd. N.Y. Acad. Scis., 1993-01. Bd. dirs. Greenwich (Conn.) Health Assn., 1970-75; bd. dirs. assoc. Family Ctr., Greenwich, Stamford, 1975—; trustee Princeton Libr. in N.Y.C., 1984—; mem. vestry St. Barnabas Ch., Greenwich, 1995-98. With U.S. Army, 1953-55. Mem. Assn. Am. Univ. Presses (chair internat. com. 1994-96, bd. dirs. 1996-97). Clubs: Publishers Lunch (admissions com. 1996-99), Princeton Club NY (mem. sr. com. 2006—, Faculty House Columbia U., Century Assn.; Nassau, the Book Table, The Ch. Club N.Y., Princeton Club So. Calif., The English Speaking Union, The Mystery Club (pres. 2006-07), mem. exec. com. Princeton class 1952-2007, Royal Oak Found., Friends Canterbury Cathedral, US, NW Greenwich Assn. (bd. mem. 2009-). Episcopalian. Home: 321 Riversville Rd Greenwich CT 06831-3228 Home (Winter): 1912 Kelton Ave Los Angeles CA 90025 E-mail: jdm123@aol.com.

MOORE, JOHN RONALD, manufacturing executive; b. Pueblo, Colo., July 12, 1935; s. John E. and Anna (Yesberger) M.; m. Judith Russelyn Bauman, Sept. 5, 1959; children: Leland, Roni, Timothy, Elaine. BS, U. Colo., 1959; grad. advanced mgmt. program, Harvard Grad. Sch. Bus., 1981. Mgmt. trainee Montgomery Ward & Co., Denver, 1960-65; distbn. mgr. Midas Internat. Corp., Chgo., 1965-71; v.p., gen. mgr. Midas, Can., Toronto, Ont., 1972-75; pres. Auto Group Midas Internat. Corp., Chgo., 1976-82, pres., chief exec. officer, 1982-98. Bd. dirs. Lake Forest Grad. Sch. Mgmt.; dir. Chgo. Crime Commn.; trustee U. Colo. Found. Mem. Harvard Bus. Sch. Alumni Assn., U. Colo. Alumni Assn., Chgo. Coun. Global Affairs, Econ. Club Chgo., Comml. Club Chgo. Republican. *There is very little we accomplish in our lifetime that results from effort we alone expend. All of us should have the wisdom to express our appreciation to our families and associates who have helped us attain our goals and accomplishments— for failure to do so tarnishes our successes and breeds selfishness.*

MOORE, JOHN THOMAS, chemistry professor, writer; b. McCormick, SC, Apr. 7, 1947; s. John Reuben Moore and Grace Elizabeth Forrester; m. Robin Kay Lewis, May 21, 1986; children: Jason Scott, Matthew Neil. BA, Asheville-Biltmore Coll., 1968; MS, Furman U., Greenville, SC, 1969; EdD, Tex. A&M U., Coll. Sta., 1991. Regents prof. chemistry Stephen F. Austin State U., Nacogdoches, Tex., 1971—, co-director, tchg. excellence ctr., 2006—. Author: (text) Chemistry for Dummies, Chemistry Made Simple; co-author: 5 Steps to a 5 AP Chemistry, (book) Chemistry for the Utterly Confused, (text) Biochemistry for Dummies. Mem.-officer Kiwanis, Nacogdoches, Tex., 1998—2008. Eisenhower Grants, State Tex. Higher Edn. Coordinatiung Bd., 1998—2002. Mem.: Am. Chem. Soc. Democrat. Presbyterian. Avocations: travel, woodworking. Home: 3821 Maid Marion Ln Nacogdoches TX 75965 Office: Stephen F Austin State Univ Box 13006 SFA Sta Nacogdoches TX 75962 Office Fax: 936-468-7634. Business E-Mail: jmoore@sfasu.edu.

MOORE, JOSEPH ARTHUR, alderman, lawyer; b. Chgo., July 22, 1958; s. Max Dale and Marilyn Ruth (Herzog) Moore; children: Nathan Alexander, Zachary Arthur. BA, Knox Coll., Galesburg, Ill., 1980; JD, DePaul U., Chgo., 1984. Bar: Ill. Atty. City of Chgo. Dept. Law, 1984-91; alderman, 49th ward Chgo. City Coun., 1991—. Mem. adv. bd. Dev Corp., Chgo. Pres. Network 49, Chgo., 1987-90; bd. dirs. Citizen Action, Washington, 1994-97, Ill. Pub. Action, Chgo., 1991-97, Ind. Voters Ill., Chgo., 1986-97, Citizen Action Ill., 1998—, Nat. League of Cities, former chair energy, environment and natural resources steering com., advocacy com., ctrl. cities coun., mem. adv. coun.; chmn. Nat. Dem. Mcpl. Officials Conf., 2004-06; mem. exec. com. Dem. Nat. Com., chmn. budget & fin. com., 2004-06, chmn. cities progress, 2003-. Dan Coman scholar, DePaul U. Coll. Law, 1984. Democrat. Roman Catholic. Office: 7356 N Greenview Ave Chicago IL 60626-1924 also: City Hall 121 N Lasalle St Chicago IL 60602 Office Phone: 773-338-5796, 312-744-3067. Business E-Mail: aldmoore@aol.com.

MOORE, JOSEPH PATRICK, medical researcher, educator; PhD in Anatomy & Neurobiology, U. Ky., Lexington, 1997. Tchg. asst., dept. anatomy & neurobiology U. Ky., 1993—97; IRTA postdoc. fellow Nat. Insts. Health NINDS, Bethesda, Md., 1997—2000. Asst. prof. U. Louisville, Sch. Medicine, 2000—. Office: Univ Louisville- ASNB 500 S Preston St Louisville KY 40202 Business E-Mail: jpmoor03@louisville.edu.

MOORE, JOY JITTAUN, dean; d. Ruth Moore. BA, Nat. Louis U., Evanston, Ill.; MDiv, Garrett-Evangelical Theol. Sem., Evanston, Ill.; PhD, Brunel U., London, 2007. Dir. student life Asbury Theol. Sem., Wilmore, Ky., 1998—2000, prof. preaching, 2000—07; sr. pastor First United Meth. Ch., Greenville, Mich., 2007—08; assoc. dean Duke U. Div. Sch., Durham, NC, 2008—. Jurisdictional mem. UMC Gen. Commn. Christian Unity & Interreligious Concerns, NYC, 2000—08. Mem.: Am. Acad. Religion, Soc. Bibl. Lit., Acad. Homiletics. Office: Divinity Sch Duke Univ 2 Chapel Dr Box 90966 Durham NC 27708

MOORE, JUANITA, museum administrator; Grad., NC Ctrl. U. Exec. dir. Nat. Civil Rights Mus., Memphis, Am. Jazz Mus., Kans. City, Mo.; pres., CEO Charles H. Wright Mus. African Am. Hist., Detroit, 2006—. Mem.: Kans. City Conv. and Visitors Assn. (bd. mem.), African Am. Museums Assn. (former pres.). Office: Charles H Wright Mus African Am Hist 315 E Warren Ave Detroit MI 48201

MOORE, JULIANNE (JULIE ANNE SMITH), actress; b. Fayetteville, NC, Dec. 3, 1960; m. Sundar Chakravarthy, Nov. 21, 1983 (div. Oct. 12, 1985); m. John Gould Rubin, May 3, 1986 (div. Aug. 25, 1995); m. Bart Freundlich, Aug. 23, 2003; 2 children. BFA, Boston Univ. With The Guthrie Theater, 1988-89. Actress: (theatre) Serious Money, 1987, Bone-the-Fish, 1988, Ice Cream with Hot Fudge, 1990, Uncle Vanya; (Broadway) The Vertical Hour, 2006; (TV soap operas) As the World Turns (Emmy award outstanding ingenue in daytime drama series 1988), The Edge of Night; (TV films) Money, Power, Murder, 1989, Lovecraft, 1991; (feature films) The Hand That Rocks the Cradle, 1992, The Gun in Betty Lou's Handbag, 1992, Body of Evidence, 1993, Benny & Joon, 1993, The Fugitive, 1993, Short Cuts, 1993, Vanya on 42nd Street, 1994, Roommates, 1995, Nine Months, 1995, Safe, 1995, Assassins, 1995, Surviving Picasso, 1996, The Myth of Fingerprints, 1997, The Lost World: Jurassic Park, 1997, Hellcab, 1997, Boogie Nights, 1997, Chicago Cab, 1998, The Big Lebowski, 1998, Psycho, 1998, Map of the World, 1999, Magnolia, 1999, Cookie's Fortune, 1999, An Ideal Husband, 1999, The End of the Affair, 1999, Hannibal, 2001, Evolution, 2001, The Shipping News, 2001, Far From Heaven, 2002, The Hours, 2002, Marie and Bruce, 2004, Laws of Attraction, 2004, The Forgotten, 2004, The Prize Winner of Defiance, Ohio, 2005, Freedomland, 2006, Children of Men, 2006, Next, 2007, I'm Not There, 2007, Savage Grace, 2007, Blindness, 2008. Office: c/o Kevin Huvane Creative Artists Agy 9830 Wilshire Blvd Beverly Hills CA 90212-1825

MOORE, JULIE L., writer, director, poet; d. Paul Wesley and Doris Marie Stackhouse; m. John Andrew Moore, June 13, 1987; children: Ashley Lauren, Alex Wesley. MA in English, U. Dayton, Ohio, 1989. Writing ctr. dir. Cedarville U., Ohio, 1999—. Author: (poetry Chapbook) Election Day. Nominee Pushcart prize, 2008. Office: Cedarville Univ English Dept 251 N Main St Cedarville OH 45314

MOORE, KAREN NELSON, federal judge; AB magna cum laude, Radcliffe Coll., 1970; JD magna cum laude, Harvard U., 1973. Bar: DC 1973, Ohio 1976, US Ct. Appeals (DC cir.) 1974, US Supreme Ct. 1980, US Ct. Appeals (6th cir.) 1984. Law clk. to Hon. Malcolm R. Wilkey US Ct. Appeals (DC Cir.), Washington, 1973—74; law clk. to Hon. Harry A. Blackmun US Supreme Ct., Washington, 1974—75; assoc. Jones, Day, Reavis & Pogue, Cleve., 1975—77; asst. prof. Case Western Res. Law Sch., Cleve., 1977—80, assoc. prof., 1980—82, prof., 1982—95; judge US Ct. Appeals (6th cir.), Cleve., 1995—. Vis. prof. Harvard Law Sch., 1990—91. Mem. Harvard Law Rev., 1971—73; contbr. articles to profl. jours. Trustee Lakewood Hosp., Ohio, 1978—85, Radcliffe Coll., Cambridge, 1980—84. Fellow: Am. Bar Found.; mem.: Harvard U. Alumni Assn. (bd. dirs. 1984—87), Am. Law Inst., Phi Beta Kappa. Office: US Ct Appeals 6th Cir Carl B Stokes US Courthouse 801 W Superior Ave Cleveland OH 44113-1831*

MOORE, KELLY ANN, secondary school educator; b. Holyoke, Mass., Mar. 31, 1966; d. Timothy and Dianne Moore. BS, Am. Internat. Coll., Springfield, Mass.; M in Spl. Edn., Westfield State Coll., Mass. Lic. tchr. Mass. Tchr. spl. needs Westfield Mid. Sch., Westfield, Mass., 1993—94; tchr. history West Springfield H.S., 1994—. Advisor and head Ceili Crew, West Springfield, Mass., 2003—; bd. dir. Irish Cultural Ctr., Chicope, Mass., sec., 1998—. Recipient Tchg. Excellence award, Westfield State Coll., 2006. Mem.: Irish Cultural Ctr., John Boyle O'Reilly, Alpha Delta Kappa. Office: W Springfield HS 425 Piper Rd West Springfield MA 01089 Business E-Mail: moore@wsps.org.

MOORE, KENNETH CAMERON, lawyer; b. Chgo., Oct. 25, 1947; s. Kenneth Edwards and Margaret Elizabeth (Cameron) M.; m. Karen M. Nelson, June 22, 1974; children: Roger Cameron, Kenneth Nelson, Kristin Karen. BA summa cum laude, Hiram Coll., 1969; JD cum laude, Harvard U., 1973. Bar: Ohio 1973, U.S. Dist. Ct. Md. 1974, U.S. Ct. Appeals (4th cir.) 1974, D.C. 1975, U.S. Dist. Ct. (no. dist.) Ohio 1976, U.S. Ct. Appeals (6th cir.) 1977, U.S. Ct. Appeals (D.C. cir.) 1979, U.S. Supreme Ct. 1980. Law clk. to judge Harrison L. Winter U.S. Ct. Appeals (4th cir.), Balt., 1973-74; assoc. Squire, Sanders & Dempsey LLP, Washington, 1974—75, Cleve., 1975-82, ptnr., 1982—, profl. ethics ptnr., 1996—, mem. fin. com., 1990—, chair profl. ethics com., 2003—. Chmn. Ohio Fin. Com. for Jimmy Carter presdl. campaign, 1976; del. Dem. Nat. Conv., 1976; chief legal counsel Ohio Carter-Mondale Campaign, 1976; trustee Hiram Coll., 1997—, mem. exec. com., 1999, vice chair bd. trustees, 2000—, chair bd. trustees, 2009, mem. bd. Laurel Sch., mem., 2005-, exec. com., 2006-, chair elect, 2006-, vice chair, 2007—. With AUS, 1970—76. Mem. ABA, Fed. Bar Assn., Ohio Bar Assn., Cleve. Bar Assn., Cleve. City Club. Home: 15602 Edgewater Dr Cleveland OH 44107-1212 Office: Squire Sanders & Dempsey LLP 4900 Key Ctr 127 Public Sq Ste 4900 Cleveland OH 44114-1304 Office Phone: 216-479-8500.

MOORE, KENNETH JAMES, agronomist, educator; b. Phoenix, June 6, 1957; s. George Taylor and Barbara Joyce (Amy) M.; m. Gina Marie McCarthy Aug. 11, 1979; children: Ellyn Elizabeth, David Taylor, Mark Daniel. BS in Agr., Ariz. State U., 1979; MS in Agronomy, Purdue U., 1981, PhD in Agronomy, 1983. Asst. prof. agronomy U. Ill., Urbana, 1983-87; assoc. prof. N.Mex. State U., Las Cruces, 1988-89; rsch. agronomist Agrl. Rsch. Svc., USDA, Lincoln, Nebr., 1989-93; prof. Iowa State U., Ames, 1993—. Adj. assoc. prof. U. Nebr. Lincoln, 1989-93, prof., 1993-96; sr. rsch. fellow Ag Rsch. Grasslands, New Zealand, 1998; dir. MS in Agronomy Distance Edn. program Iowa State

U., 1995—, dir. Crop Advisor Inst., 2000—. Founding editor Crop Mgmt., 2001-02; assoc. editor Agronomy Jour., 1989-93, tech. editor, 1994-97; assoc. editor Crop Sci., 1994; editor: Forages: An Introduction to Grassland Ag, 2003, Forages: The Science of Grassland Agriculture, 2007, Native-Warm Season Grasses: Research Trends and Issues, 2000, Post-Harvest Physiology and Preservation of Forages, 1995; contbr. chpts. to books. Bd. dirs. Lincoln Children's Mus., 1991-93, Children's Svcs. of Ctrl. Iowa, 1996-97; bd. dirs. Children's Mus. Ctrl. Iowa, 1997-2002, pres., 2000-01; mem. mgmt. com. N.E. YMCA, Lincoln, 1991-93; mem. youth policy forum Lincoln YMCA, 1991-92. Recipient Point of Light award USDA, 1991. Fellow Am. Soc. Agronomy (bd. dirs. 2002-05 06-09, pres. 2008), Crop Sci. Soc. Am. (divsn. chmn. 1990-92, pres. 2003-04, exec. com. and bd. dirs. 2002-05, Young Crop Scientist award 1993), Am. Assn. Advancement Scis.; mem. Am. Forage and Grassland Coun. (Outstanding Young Scientist award 1982, merit award 1991). Independent. Methodist. Avocations: swimming, fishing, music, diving, sailing. Office: Iowa State U Agronomy Dept 1571 Agronomy Hall Ames IA 50011-0001 Office Phone: 515-294-5482. Business E-Mail: kjmoore@iastate.edu.

MOORE, KIMBERLY ANN, federal judge; b. Baltimore, Md., June 15, 1968; BS in Electrical Engring., MIT, 1990, MS, 1991; JD, Georgetown U., 1994. Bar: Md. 1995, DC. Assoc. Kirkland & Ellis LLP, DC & L.A., 1994—95; law clk. to Hon. Glenn L. Archer Jr. US Ct. Appeals (fed. cir.), Washington, 1995—97, judge, 2006—; asst. prof. law Chgo.-Kent Coll. Law, 1997—99, assoc. dir., Intellectual Property Law Program, 1998—99; asst. prof. law U. Md. Sch. Law, 1999—2000; counsel Morgan, Lewis & Bockius LLP, 2000—03; assoc. prof. law George Mason U. Sch. Law, 2000—04, prof. law, 2004—06. Assoc. editor Fed. Cir. Bar Journ., 1997—98, editor-in-chief, 1998—2006. Named one of 100 Most Influential Lawyers in America, Nat. Law Jour., 2006. Office: US Ct Appeals Fed Cir 717 Madison Pl NW Washington DC 20439*

MOORE, LAURENCE JOHN, business educator; b. Greeley, Colo., May 7, 1938; s. John Harold and Ruth Anderson M.; m. Nancy Kay Hibbert, Aug. 31, 1963 (div. Apr. 1996); children: Rebecca Ann, John Andrew, Stefani Ruth. BA in Econs., Monmouth Coll., Ill., 1962; MS in Econs., Ariz. State U., 1965, DBA in Mgmt. Sci., 1970. Dist. mktg. rep. Standard Oil Co. (Ind.), Chgo., 1962-63; sr. analyst long range and capital planning, 1964-66; head quantitative studies Continental Ill. Bank, Chgo., 1966-67; mem. faculty dept. mgmt. sci. Coll. Bus. Va. Poly. Inst. and State U., Blacksburg, 1970—2007, prof. Coll. Bus., 1977-85, C&P Disting. prof. bus., 1985-96, head dept. Coll. Bus., 1976-83, dir. univ. fin. planning and analysis, 1983-84, dir. univ. planning, 1988-89, Bell Atlantic-Va. prof. of bus., 1996—2002, Verizon prof. bus., 2002—07, emeritus, 2007. Cons. in field. Author: (with S.M. Lee, B.W. Taylor) Management Science, 1981, 4th edit., 1993, (with S.M. Lee) Introduction to Decision Sciences, 1975, (with E.R. Clayton) GERT Modeling and Simulation: Fundamentals and Applications, 1976. Served with U.S. Army, 1957-59. Recipient Disting. Service award SE region Am. Inst. Decision Scis., 1977 Fellow Am. Inst. Decision Scis. (pres. 1983-84, Disting. Svc. award 1986); mem. Inst. Mgmt. Sci. (Disting. Svc. award SE region), Inst. for Ops. Rsch. and Mgmt. Sci., Alpha Iota Delta, Beta Gamma Sigma, Omicron Delta Epsilon, Sigma Iota Epsilon. Presbyterian. Home: 1013 Chateau Ct Blacksburg VA 24060-3676 Business E-Mail: ljmoore@vt.edu.

MOORE, LINDA A., art dealer, curator; b. Janesville, Wis., Aug. 2, 1947; d. Evert August Frederick and Helen Marilyn Anderson; m. Terry Douglass Moore, Mar. 22, 1969; children: Adrienne Jean, Craig William. Fgn. study program, U. Madrid, 1968; BA magna cum laude, U. of Calif., Santa Barbara, 1969; MA, Stanford U., Palo Alto, 1970; MHA, U. of Wash., 1976. Adminstr. U. of Calif. Student Health Svc., Irvine, 1972—75; v.p. Children's Hosp. and Health Ctr., San Diego, 1976—78; asst. hosp. adminstr. Kaiser Permanente, San Diego, 1978—83, asst. med. group adminstr., 1983—88; owner Linda Moore Gallery, San Diego, 1983—. Bd. dirs. Mus. of Photographic Arts, San Diego; adv. bd. Lux Art Inst., San Diego, 2004—; mem. Latin Am. arts com. San Diego Mus. of Art, 1990—. Contbr. book; author: (exhbn. catalogue) Iturria (Best Art Catalogue, Cleo Design award, 1992), Drowned Ophelia, Lo Maravilloso; editor: DEfining A Vision, 2006. Mem. Presidio Pk. Adv. Coun., San Diego, 2004—07, Patrons of the Prado, Balboa Pk., San Diego, 2005—07. Recipient TWIN - honoring Women Profls. award, YWCA, 1979, Top Women Hosp. Adminstrs., Calif. Hosp. Forum Mag., 1980, grad. study grant, Kellogg Found., 1975—76; fellow, Ford Found., 1969—70. Mem.: Francis Parker Sch. (bd. mem., chair ann. fund 1988—89), Young Hosp. Adminstrs. of San Diego (pres. 1981—82), Am. Coll. of Health Care Adminstrs. (chair young adminstrs. forum 1980—81), Jeanie Anderson Meml. Fund (bd. mem. 1972—2006), LEAD San Diego (bd. mem. 1986—87), ZLAC Rowing Club, Jr. League of San Diego (bd. mem. 1984—85, Best Project Video Employer Sponsored Child Care Project award 1986), Rotary Club 33 of San Diego, Phi Beta Kappa. Avocations: travel, writing, bridge. Office: Linda Moore Gallery 4244 Altamirano Way San Diego CA 92103 Personal E-mail: lmooregal@aol.com.

MOORE, MALCOLM FREDERICK, manufacturing executive; b. Kankakee, Ill., Sept. 19, 1950; s. Robert Dunham and Josephine Frances (Jones) M.; m. Patricia Claudine Bennert, June 13, 1971; children: Michael Dunham, Emily Woodhull, Marjorie Nicoll. BSBA, Am. U., 1972; M of Mgmt., Northwestern U., 1982. Internat. mktg. mgr., product mgr. FMC Corp., Chgo., 1973-84, mktg. and engring. mgr., 1985-90; cons. Frank Lynn & Assoc., Chgo., 1984-85; v.p., gen. mgr. Lindberg unit of Gen. Signal, Watertown, Wis., 1990-93; pres. Abar Ipsen Industries, Inc., Bensalem, Pa., 1993-96, Centorr Vacuum Industries, Nashua, NH, 1993-96, Linac Holdings, Inc., Rockford, Ill., 1994-96; pres., CEO Pangborn Corp., Hagerstown, Md., 1996-98; pres. Gehl Co., West Bend, Wis., 1999—2009; CEO & pres. Mavzron Americas, West Bend, 2009—. Bd. dirs. Twin Disc, Inc.; bd. mem. Skylight Opera Theatre Milw. Yacht Club. Inventor material handling equipment. Episcopalian.

MOORE, MANDY (AMANDA LEIGH MOORE), actress, singer; b. Nashua, NH, Apr. 10, 1984; d. Don and Stacy Moore; m. Ryan Adams, Mar. 10, 2009. Host MTV show, Mandy, 2000. Actor: (films) Street Rats, 1996, Magic Al and the Mind Factory, 2000, (voice only) Dr. Doolittle 2, 2001, The Princess Diaries, 2001, A Walk to Remember, 2002 (MTV Movie award breakthrough performance-female, 2002, Teen Choice awards choice breakout performance-actress, with Shane West Teen Choice awards choice chemistry, 2002), Try Seventeen, 2002, How to Deal, 2003, Chasing Liberty, 2004, Saved!, 2004, (voice only) Racing Stripes, 2005, Romance & Cigarettes, 2005, American Dreamz, 2006, Southland Tales, 2006, (voice only) Brother Bear 2, 2006, Dedication, 2007, Because I Said So, 2007, License to Wed, 2007; (TV films) Summer Music Mania 2001, 2001, (TV appearances) Touched by an Angel, 1997, Entourage, 2005, Scrubs, 2006, How I Met Your Mother, 2007, (voice only) The Simpsons, 2006; singer: (albums) So Real, 1999, I Wanna Be With You, 2000, Mandy Moore, 2001, Coverage, 2003, The Best of Mandy Moore, 2004, Candy, 2005, Wild Hope, 2007, Amanda Leigh, 2009. Recipient Fashion Innovator award, Accessories Coun. of Excellence, 2007. Office: c/o William Morris Agy One William Morris Pl Beverly Hills CA 90212*

MOORE, MARLA W., school librarian; d. Charles and Sarah Cearley Whitworth; m. Michael W. Moore, Aug. 4; children: Whitney, Landon, Sarah Grace. BSE, Ouachita Bapt. U., Arkadelphia, Ark., 1984; MSE, Henderson State U., Arkadelphia, Ark., 1986, U. Ctrl. Ark., Conway, 1988. Cert. in English Ark. Dept. Edn., 1984, in elem. counseling 1986, in libr. media 1988. English tchr. Amity HS, Ark., 1984—85; elem. counselor East End Elem., Little Rock, 1985—93; libr. media specialist Sheridan Mid. Sch., Ark., 1993—. Pres. P.E.O., Sheridan, 1998—2000; youth leader First Bapt. Ch., Sheridan, 1985—2008. Mem.: Ark. Assn. Instrnl. Media. Democrat. Southern Baptist. Avocations: reading, camping, sports.

MOORE, MARVELENE C., music educator; b. Franklin, Tenn., Sept. 13, 1944; d. Frank and Sadie Gibson Moore. BA, Talladega Coll., 1966; M in Music Edn., George Peabody Coll., 1970, edn. specialist, 1971; PhD, U. Mich., 1977. Music specialist Decatur Pub. Sch., Ala., 1966—69; prof., music edn. U. Tenn., Knoxville, 1978—; asst. prof., music edn. Savannah State Coll., Ga., 1977—78; admin. asst. U. Mich., Ann Arbor, 1974—77. Chair, music in sch. and tchr. edn. Internat. Soc. for Music Edn., Nedlands, Australia, 2004—; mem. Jour. for Arts Edn., Hong Kong. Author: Making Music Series, 2002—05, The Music Connection Series, 1995—, Making Music with Movement and Dance, 2005—, Classroom Managment in the General Choral and Instrumental Programs, 2002—. Instr., children's classes in movement U. Tenn., Knoxville, 1985—95; min. of music United Methodist Ch., Knoxville, 1980—87, Redemption Internat. Ctr., Knoxville, 1987—95; adv. bd. Tenn. Alliance for Arts Edn., Nashville. Recipient James A. Cox Endowed Chair, U. Tenn., 2002—05, Hall of Fame, Tenn. Music Edn. Assn., 2005. Mem.: Internat. Assn. Jazz Edn. Resource Team, Music Educators Nat. Conf. (gen. music chair 1998—2000). Presbyterian. Home: 1256 Halifax Rd Knoxville TN 37922 Office: U Tenn 1741 Vol Blvd Knoxville TN 37922 Office Phone: 865-974-7515. Business E-Mail: mmoore7@utk.edu.

MOORE, MARY FRENCH (MUFFY), potter, advocate; d. John and Rhoda French; m. Barry Corbet, 1959; m. Alan Baird Minier, 1982; children: Jonathan Corbet, Jennifer Corbet, Michael Corbet. BA cum laude, Colo. U., 1964. Ceramics mfg., Wilson, Wyo., 1969-82, Cheyenne, Wyo., 1982—. Commr. County Teton (Wyo.), 1976-83, chmn. bd. commrs., 1981, 83, mem. dept. pub. assistance and social svc., 1976-82, mem. recreation bd., 1978-81, water quality adv. bd., 1976-82. Bd. dirs. Teton Sci. Sch., 1968-83, vice chmn., 1979-81, chmn., 1982; bd. dirs. Grand Teton Music Festival, 1963-68, Teton Energy Coun., 1978-83, Whitney Gallery of Western Art, Cody, Wyo., 1995—, Opera Colo., 1998—, Opera Colo. Found., 2005-06; mem. water quality adv. bd. Wyo. Dept. Environ. Quality, 1979-83; Dem. precinct committeewoman, 1978-81; mem. Wyo. Dem. Ctrl. Com., 1981-83; vice chmn. Laramie County Dem. Ctrl. Com., 1983-84, Wyo. Dem. nat. committeewoman, 1984-87; chmn. Wyo. Dem. Party, 1987-89; del. Dem. Nat. Conv., 1984, 88, mem. fairness commn. Dem. Nat. Com., 1985, vice-chair western caucus, 1986-89; chmn. platform com. Wyo. Dem. Conv., 1982; mem. Wyo. Dept. Environ. Quality Land Quality Adv. Bd., 1983-86; mem. Gov.'s Steering Com. on Troubled Youth, 1982, dem. nat. com. Compliance Assistance Commn., 1986-87; exec. com. Assn. of State Dem. Chairs, 1989; mem. Wyo. Coun. on the Arts, 1989-95, chmn., 1994-95, Dem. Nat. Com. Jud. Coun., 1989—; legis. aide for Gov. Wyo., 1985, 86; project coord. Gov.'s Com. on Childrens' Svcs., 1985-86; bd. dirs. Wyo. Outdoor Coun., 1984-85; polit. dir., dep. mgr. Schuster for Congress, 1994-95; adminstrv. dir. Freudenthal for Gov., 2002, pers. coord., 2002; mem. pres.' adv. com. on the performing arts John F. Kennedy Ctr. for the Performing Arts, 1999-2001. Recipient Woman of Yr. award Jackson Hole Bus. and Profl. Women, 1981, Dem. of Yr. Nellie Tayloe Ross award Wyo. Dems., 1990. Mem. Alden Kindred of Am., Jackson Hole Art Assn. (bd. dirs., vice chmn. 1981, chmn. 1982), Assn. State Dem. Chairs, Soc. Mayflower Descendents, Pi Sigma Alpha. Home: 8907 Cowpoke Rd Cheyenne WY 82009-1234

MOORE, MARY JOHNSON, retired community health nurse; b. West Point, NY, Feb. 8, 1940; d. Robert Phillip and Edith Virginia (Carr) Johnson; m. Prentis Monroe Moore, Dec. 28, 1960 (dec. Jan. 1990); children: Carol Edith, Tracey Marie. Diploma, Boston City Hosp. Sch. Nursing, 1960. RN. Clinic nurse in pediat. and obstetrics Harris County Health Dept./Lyons Clinic, Houston, 1982—85; clinic nurse Tex. Sch. for Deaf, Austin, 1986—87; staff nurse pediat. Ben Taub Hosp., Houston, 1989—92; telephone triage nurse, ob-gyn. McGregor Clinic, Houston, 1992—93; staff nurse pediat. Grant Hosp., Chgo., 1994—96; clinic nurse Columbus-Maryville Hosp., Chgo., 1996—2002; travel nurse Star-Med Profl. Staffing, 2002—03; case mgr. Brockton Neighborhood Health Ctr., Mass., 2003—04; ret., 2004. Active Sr. Chorus Massasoit C.C., 2006—; bd. dirs. Boston City Hosp., Sch. Nursing Alumnus, 2008; mem. vol. choir St. Chrysostoms Episcopal Ch., 1997—2002; lay reader Trinity Episcopal Ch., Brockton, 2006—. George Monks Meml. scholar, 1960. Democrat. Avocations: art, music, poetry, collecting unicorns, angels and lighthouses. Home: 72 Pine St Brockton MA 02302 Home Phone: 508-584-4594. Personal E-mail: mryjrn@yahoo.com.

MOORE, MCPHERSON DORSETT, lawyer; b. Pine Bluff, Ark., Mar. 1, 1947; s. Arl Van and Jesse (Dorsett) M. BS, U. Miss., 1970; JD, U. Ark., 1974. Bar: Ark. 1974, Mo. 1975, U.S. Patent and Trademark Office 1977, U.S. Dist. Ct. (ea. dist.) Mo. 1977, U.S. Ct. Appeals (8th, 10th and fed. cirs.). Design engr. Tenneco, Newport News, Va., 1970-71; assoc. Rogers, Eilers & Howell, St. Louis, 1974-80; ptnr. Rogers, Howell, Moore & Haferkamp, St. Louis, 1981-89, Armstrong, Teasdale, Schlafly & Davis, St. Louis, 1989-95, Polster, Lieder, Woodruff & Lucchesi, St. Louis, 1995—. Engr. City of Ladue, Mo., 1998-2000; mem. intellectual property adv. bd. Washington U. Bd. dirs. Legal Svcs. Ea. Mo.; mem. Ladue Zoning and Planning Commn., 1998—; chmn. St. Michael's Houses, Ch. St. Michael and St. George. With USAR, 1970-76. Mem. ABA, Bar Assn. Met. St. Louis (chmn. young lawyers sect. 1981-82, sec. 1984-85, v.p. 1985-86, chmn. trial sect. 1986-87, pres. 1988-89), Ark. Bar Assn., St. Louis Bar Found. (sec. 1984-85, v.p. 1988-89, pres. 1989-90), The Mo. Bar (chmn. patent, trademark and copyright law com. 1992-94, co-chmn. 1994-95), St. Louis County Bar Assn., Women Lawyers Assn., Am. Intellectual Property Law Assn., Mound City Bar Assn., Phi Delta Theta Alumni (treas. St. Louis chpt. 1987-88, sec. 1988-89, v.p. 1989-90), St. Louis County Club. Home: 3 Mayfair Rd Saint Louis MO 63124-1663 Office: Polster Lieder Woodruff & Lucchesi Ste 200 12412 Powers Ct Dr Saint Louis MO 63131-3615 Office Phone: 314-238-2400.

MOORE, MECHLIN DONGAN, communications executive, marketing consultant; b. NYC, May 21, 1930; s. Albere Ethier and Pamela (Robinson) M.; m. Elizabeth Ann Tonkin, Feb. 11, 1956 (dec. 1992); children: Lansing, Pamela; m. Valery Ann Shields, July 14, 1995. AB, Harvard U., 1952. Reporter Washington Post, 1955-59; dir. build Am. better com. Nat. Assn. Real Estate Bds., D.C., 1960-64; dir. info. Urban Land Inst., D.C., 1964-66; exec. v.p. Ctrl. Assn. Seattle, 1966-70; asst. to pres. United Airlines, Inc., Chgo., 1971-72, sr. v.p. external affairs, 1972-74, group v.p. mktg., 1975-76, sr. v.p. pub. affairs, 1976-79; pres. Ins. Info. Inst., NYC, 1979-91; chmn., CEO Informatrix Worldwide SuperSite Devel., 1996-98; pvt. practice Rye, NY, 1991—; advisor Vertical Net, Inc., 1998-2001; project planning dir. Fla. Gulf Coast Univ. Found., 2004—05. Pres. Eagles Mere Water Co., 1993-96; bd. electors Ins. Hall of Fame; feature editor Risk Retention Reporter 2008-. Author publs. Nat. Assn. Real Estate Bds.; assoc. editor Jour. Property Mgmt. Adv. bd. mem. Traffic Inst. Northwestern U.; past mem. St. George's Vestry, N.Y.C. 1st lt. U.S. Army, 1952-54. Recipient Commendation Ribbon with Metal Pendant U.S. Army, 1954, Disting. Svc. award Central Assn. Seattle, 1972 Mem. Univ. Club, Shenorock Shore Club. Independent. Episcopalian. Home: 720 Milton Rd 1BW Rye NY 10580 Office Phone: 239-777-1595. E-mail: mmoore7412@aol.com.

MOORE, MELISSA, professional society administrator; BA in Polit. Sci., Wells Coll., Aurora, NY. Washington liaison Am. Nuc. Soc.; mng. dir. Am. Assn. Engring. Societies; asst. dir. govt. rels., dir. pub. affairs devel. ASME; exec. dir., bd. dirs., mem. exec. com. Assn. for Advancement of Cost Engring. Internat.; exec. v.p. Soc. Engring. in Agr., Food and Biol. Systems Am. Soc. Agrl. and Biol. Engrs. (formerly Am. Soc. Agrl. Engrs.), exec. v.p. Mem.: Am. Soc. Assn. Execs., Coun. Engring. and Sci. Soc. Execs. Office: Am Soc Agrl and Biol Engrs 2950 Niles Rd Saint Joseph MI 49085 Office Phone: 269-428-6321. Office Fax: 269-428-3852. E-mail: moore@asabe.org.

MOORE, MELISSA J., diversified financial services company executive; Fin. svcs. audit and bus. adv. ptnr. PricewaterhouseCoopers; corp. controller Bank One, 2001; chief adminstrv. officer treasury and securities svcs. JP Morgan Chase & Co., pres., COO treasury svcs., pres., CEO treasury svcs., 2008—. Office: JPMorgan Chase & Co 270 Park Ave New York NY 10017*

MOORE, MICHAEL, filmmaker, writer; b. Flint, Mich., Apr. 23, 1954; s. Frank and Veronica Moore; m. Kathleen Glynn, 1991; 1 stepchild, Natalie. Studied Journalism, U. Mich.-Flint. Founder, editor The Mich. Voice (formerly The Flint Voice), 1976—86; editor Mother Jones, 1986. Founder Traverse City Film Festival, Mich., 2005. Dir., writer, prodr. (documentaries) Roger & Me, 1989, Bowling for Columbine, 2002 (Academy award for Best Documentary Feature, 2003), Fahrenheit 9/11, 2004 (Palme d'Or, Cannes Film Festival, 2004), Sicko, 2007 (2007 Critics Choice award for Best Documentary Feature, Broadcast Film Critics Assn., 2008, named Best Documentory Film, Producers Guild of America, 2008), Slacker Uprising, 2008, actor, dir. prodr., writer (films) Canadian Bacon, 1994, dir., creator, host: TV Nation, 1994—95 (Emmy award for Outstanding Informational Series, 1995), The Awful Truth, 1999—2000 (Hugh M. Hefner First Amendment award in Arts & Entertainment, 1999), Michael Moore Live, 1999; dir.: (films) Two Mikes Don't Make a Wright, 1992, The Big One, 1997; actor: EdTV, 1999, Lucky Numbers, 2000, The Fever, 2004; author: Downsize This! Random Threats from Unarmed America, 1996, Adventures in a TV Nation, 1998, Stupid White Men and Other Sorry Excuses for the State of the Nation!, 2002, Dude, Where's My Country?, 2003, Will They Ever Trust Us Again? Letters From the War Zone, 2004, The Official Fahrenheit 9/11 Reader, 2004. Named one of 100 Most Influential People, TIME mag., 2005, 50 Smartest People in Hollywood, Entertainment Weekly, 2007.*

MOORE, MIKE (MICHAEL C.), lawyer, former state attorney general; b. Pascagoula, Miss. m. Tisha R. Moore; 1 child, Kyle. Grad., Jackson County Jr. Coll., 1972; BA, U. Miss., 1974, JD, 1976. Asst. dist. atty. State of Miss., Jackson, Miss., 1977—78, dist. atty., 1979, atty. gen., 1988—2004; gen. counsel Phelps Dunbar LLP, Jackson, Miss., 2004—; pvt. practice Mike Moore Law Firm. Chmn. Partnership for a Greater Miss. Recipient Wyman award; named Lawyer of Yr., Nat. Law Jour., 1998; named one of Ten Most Outstanding Young Americans, Young Jaycees, 1992. Democrat.

MOORE, MITCHELL JAY, lawyer, educator; b. Lincoln, Nebr., Aug. 29, 1954; s. Earl J. and Betty Marie (Zimmerlin) M.; m. Sharon Lea Campbell, Sept. 5, 1987. BS in Edn., U. Mo., Columbia, 1977, JD, 1981. Bar: Mo. 1981, U.S. Dist. Ct. (we. dist.) Mo. 1981, Tex. 1982, U.S. Ct. Appeals (8th cir.) 1998. Tchr. Clinton Mid. Sch., 1978; sole practice Columbia, Mo., 1981—. Coordinating atty. student legal svcs. ctr. U. Mo., Columbia, 1983-89. Mem. Columbia Substance Abuse Adv. Commn., 1989—; bd. dirs. Planned Parenthood of Ctrl. Mo., Columbia, 1984-86, Opportunities Unltd., Columbia, 1984-86, ACLU of Mid-Mo., 1991-98; Libertarian candidate for Atty. Gen. of Mo., 1992, 2000, for 9th congl. dist. U.S. Ho. of Reps., 1994, 96, for Mo. State Rep. 23d dist., 1998, mem. Probation and Parole Citizens Adv. Bd., 1997-99. Recipient Pro Bono Publico award, Mid-Mo. Legal Svcs. Corp. Mem.: Nat. Assn. Consumer Bankruptcy Attys., Tex. Bar Assn., Mo. Bar Assn., Boone County Bar Assn., Phi Delta Phi. Libertarian. Unitarian Universalist. Avocations: softball, camping, Tae Kwon Do, gardening. Office: 1210 W Broadway Columbia MO 65203-2126 Office Phone: 573-449-3318.

MOORE, NANCEY FAY, history educator; d. George Thomas and Mildred Fay Moore. BA in Polit. Sci., U. Charleston, W.Va., 1979, BA in European History, 1979; MA in Am. History., NC State U., Raleigh, 1994. Cert. PPI Inc., NC, 1998. History instr. Wake Tech CC, Raleigh, 1994—; computer instr. Durham Tech CC, NC, 2001—02. Mem. polit. sci. search com. Wake Tech CC, 2005—05; com. rep. U. Ulster, Raleigh, 2006; mem. history search com. Wake Tech. CC, 2008. Election return rep. WCHS TV sta., Charleston, W.Va., 1980—80. Mem.: Am. Assn. Women in CC's, So. Assn. Women Historians (life), Phi Alpha Theta (life; pres. 1975—79), Pi Gamma Mu (life; v.p. 1975—79). Democrat. Baptist. Office: Wake Tech Bookstore 8109 Fayetteville Rd # 129 Raleigh NC 27603-5635 Business E-Mail: nfmoore@waketech.edu.

MOORE, NANCY M., secondary school educator; PhD, Capella U., St. Paul, 2005. Tchr. Nassau County Schs., Callahan, Fla., 1999—2008; adj. instr. FCCJ, Jacksonville, Fla., 2001—08.

MOORE, OLIVER SEMON, III, publishing executive, consultant; b. Jersey City, July 26, 1942; s. Oliver S. and Ann Loy (Spies) M.; m. Dina Downing DuBois, Feb. 23, 1961 (div. 1974); 1 child, Deborah; m. Christine Laine Meyers, May 12, 1990; 1 child, Kathryn Laine. BA, U. Va., 1964. Chief bur. Richmond (Va.) Times-Dispatch, 1964-66; corr. Time mag., NYC, 1966-67, contbg. editor, 1967-68; assoc. editor Newsweek, NYC, 1969-71; freelance writer, 1972-75; mng. editor Motor Boating and Sailing, NYC, 1976-78, editor, 1980-82; exec. editor US Mag., N.Y. Times Co., 1978-80; dep. editor Town & Country Mag., NYC, 1982-84; editor Sci. Digest Mag., NYC, 1984-86; pub. dir. Yachting Mag., NYC, 1986-95; editorial dir. Outdoor Life, NYC, 1993-95; v.p. The Outdoor Co., NYC, 1994-95; editor-at-large Motor Boating & Sailing, 1995—2001; pres. Alamo Pub. Svcs., Inc., Detroit, 1995—. Co-founder, chmn. bd. Corp! (Mag.), 1998. Author: (poems) Voices International, 1969; contbg. editor Sports Afield, 1996—; photographer (mags.) Motor Boating and Sailing, Yachting, Working Woman Corp! (books) Lines to a Little Girl, Rancho Paradiso. Recipient Merit award Art Dirs. Club, 1981, award of merit Soc. Publ. Designers, 1981, Excellence in Media award Nat. Arbor Day Found., 1985. Mem. Am. Soc. Mag. Editors, Mag. Pubs. Assn. (nat. mag. award 1995), N.Y. Yacht Club, Grosse Pointe (Mich.) Club, Bayview (Mich.) Yacht Club, Wyndemere Country Club (Fla.). Republican. Episcopalian. Avocations: sailing, antique cars. Home and Office: 604 Courtside Dr Naples FL 34105-7133 Personal E-mail: omoore@comcast.net.

MOORE, PAMELA GAY, retired music educator; b. Eugene, Oreg., Dec. 31, 1945; d. John Robert and Alta Rachel Wetzel; m. Glen Eugene Moore; children: Sean Eugene, Connemara Heather Pursley. BA in Music, Seattle Pacific U., 1968; MA in Edn., U. Wash., Seattle, 1971. Cert. tchr. Wash., Yamaha Music Sch., Wash. Profl. musician, entertainer, Port Angeles and Seattle, Wash.; tchr.'s asst. Sharples Jr. HS, Seattle, 1971—72; preschool music tchr. Yamaha Music Sch., Seattle and Port Angeles, 1972—82; tchr. parent presch. coop. Peninsula Coll., Port Angeles, 1975—76; pvt. piano tchr. Seattle and Port Angeles, 1973—85; elem. gen. music tchr. Port Angeles Pub. Schs., 1977—85, mid. sch. choral tchr. gen. music, 1985—97, k-5 elem. gen. music tchr., 1997—2007; ret., 2007. Music entertainer, Oregon, Washington, Idaho, 1979—; choral dir. Holy Trinity Luth. Ch., Port Angeles, 1980—81; coord., dir. mid. sch. mass choir North Olympic Music Educators, Wash., 1986—88; music dir. musicals Port Angeles Cmty. Players, 1985—; site team mem. Franklin Elem. Sch., Port Angeles, 2003—. Composer scripts, musical arrangements, musicals for children, adult scripts, arrangements, songs; developer: curriculum in group music education, music composition. Women's retreat music dir. Holy Trinity Luth., Sequim Cmty. Ch., Port Angeles, Sequim, Wash., 1987—2006; mem. contemporary svc. worship team Sequim Cmty. Ch., 2002—06. Grantee, Port Angeles Pub. Schools, 1996; scholar, Seattle Pacific U., 1964. Mem.: Delta Kappa Gamma. Democrat. Avocations: painting, music synthesizers, reading, travel, sports.

MOORE, PAT HOWARD, engineering and construction executive, educator; b. Laredo, Tex., Sept. 16, 1930; s. Howard Warren and Odette Evelyn (Bunn) M.; m. Elsie Mae Crossman, Mar. 23, 1954; children: Linda Marie Ford, Margaret Ann, Andrew Patrick. BA, Rice U., Houston, 1952, BS in Civil Engring., 1953; postgrad., Tulane U., New Orleans, 1956-58. Registered profl. engr., Tex., La. Div. engr. McDermott Inc., Morgan City, La., 1956-58; pres., dir. Navasota Tel. Co., Tex., 1958-63; project mgr. Brown & Root, Inc., Houston, 1963-67, exec. v.p., dir., 1990-95; pres., dir. Fluor Ocean Svcs., Houston, 1968-80; sr. v.p. Raymond Internat., Inc., Houston, 1980-86; pres., dir. Martin Moore Inc., Bellaire, Tex., 1986-90; mgmt. cons. Bellaire, 1996—2003. Adv. dir. Tex. Commerce Bank, Houston, 1979-86, Third Tech. Inc., Ft. Worth, 2004-06; bd. govs. Rice U., 1984-88, lectr. ethics 1996-03, adj. prof. civil and environ. engring., 2003-; bd. dirs. SGB, Inc., Houston, 1986-90, Charter Builders, Inc., Dallas, 1988-90, Versar, Inc., Springfield, Va., 1998-02, XServ, Inc., Houston, 1997-2007. Spl. investigator US Army Counter Intelligence, 1954—56, hon. discharge, 1962. Named Outstanding Engring. Alumnus, Rice U., 2005. Fellow ASCE(life mem. 1995); mem. Chi Epsilon (hon. mem. 1995), Kiwanis (pres. 1960). Methodist. Home: 124 Chuckwagon Trail Georgetown TX 78633-4598 Business E-Mail: moore@rice.edu.

MOORE, PATRICK J., paper company executive; b. Sept. 7, 1954; m. Beth Moore; 3 children. BSBA, DePaul U., Chgo. Asst. treas. Jefferson Smurfit Corp., St. Louis, 1987-90, treas., 1990-93, v.p., treas., 1993-94; v.p., gen. mgr. Indsl. Packaging divsn. Indsl. Packaging divsn., St. Louis, 1994-96; v.p., CFO Jefferson Smurfit Corp., St. Louis, 1996—98, Smurfit-Stone Container Corp., Chgo., 1998—2002, pres., CEO, 2002—03, chmn., pres., CEO, 2003—06, chmn., CEO, 2006—. Serves on NASDAQ CEO Coun.; bd. dir. Am. Forest & Paper Assn., JP Morgan Nat. Adv. Bd., Intern. Corrugated Case Assn., Archer Daniels Midland. Mem. Civic Progress, St. Louis, Comml. Club, Chgo., Wash. U. John M. Olin Sch. Bus. Nat. Coun.; bd. dir. Met. YMCA, St. Louis, Boys Hope/Girls Hope, Big Shoulders Fund, Chgo. Office: Smurfit-Stone Container Corp 150 N Michigan Ave Chicago IL 60601-7568

MOORE, PAUL D., lawyer; b. 1951; BS summa cum laude, Boston Coll., 1973; JD cum laude, Boston Coll. Law Sch., 1976. Bar: Mass. 1977, US Dist. Ct. (Mass.), US Ct. Appeals (1st cir.), US Supreme Ct. Assoc. Testa, Hurwitz & Thibeault, Boston, 1976—76, Foley, Hoag & Eliot, Boston, 1979—82, ptnr., 1982—90, Choate, Hall & Stewart, Boston, 1990—99, Duane Morris LLP, 1999—. Contbr. articles to profl. jours. Named a SuperLawyer, Boston mag.; named one of America's Leading Bus. Lawyers, Chambers USA. Mem.: ABA, Assn. Insolvency & Restructuring Advisors (bd. dirs. 2006—), Am. Bankruptcy Inst., Boston Bar Assn., Mass. Bar Assn. Office: Duane Morris LLP 470 Atlantic Ave Ste 500 Boston MA 02210 Office Phone: 857-488-8230. Office Fax: 857-401-3057. Business E-Mail: PDMoore@duanemorris.com.*

MOORE, PEARL B., retired nursing educator; b. Pitts., Aug. 25, 1936; d. Hyman and Ethel (Antis) Friedman; 1 child, Cheryl. BS in Nursing, U. Pitts., 1968, M in Nursing, 1974. Staff nurse Allegheny Gen. Hosp., Pitts., 1957-60; instr. Liliane S. Kaufman Sch. Nursing, Pitts., 1960-70, asst. dir., 1970, dir., 1970-72; cancer nurse specialist Montefiore Hosp., Pitts., 1974-75; coord. Brain Tumor Study Group, Pitts., 1975-83; adj. asst. prof. U. Pitts., 1983—. Contbr. articles in field to profl. publs. Fellow Am. Acad. Nursing; mem. ANA, Oncology Nursing Soc. (exec. dir. 1983—, CEO 1999-2007, Disting. Svc. award 1995), Am. Soc. Clin. Oncology, Am. Soc. Assn. Execs., Nurses Alumnae U. Pitts., Sigma Theta Tau. Home: 5701 Centre Ave Pittsburgh PA 15206

MOORE, PETER BARTLETT, biochemist, educator; b. Boston, Oct. 15, 1939; s. Francis Daniels and Laura Benton (Bartlett) M.; m. Margaret Sue Murphy, Jan. 30, 1966; children: Catherine, Philip. BS, Yale U., 1961, MA (hon.); PhD, Harvard U., 1966. Postdoctoral fellow U. Geneva, 1966-67, MRC Lab. of Molecular Biology, Cambridge, Eng., 1967-69; asst. prof., then assoc. prof. dept. molecular biophysics Yale U., New Haven, 1969-76, assoc. prof. dept. of chemistry, 1976-79, prof., 1979—2002, Sterling prof., 2002—, chmn. dept. chemistry, 1987-90. Contbr. articles to profl. jours. Guggenheim Found. fellow, 1979-80. Fellow AAAS; mem. Am. Chem. Soc., Am. Soc. Biol. Chemists and Molecular Biologists, Nat. Acad. Scis., Am. Acad. Arts and Scis., Biophys. Soc. (editor Biophys. Jour. 1997-2002) Office: Yale U Dept of Chemistry 225 Prospect Ave New Haven CT 06512-1958

MOORE, POWELL ALLEN, former federal agency administrator; b. Milledgeville, Ga., Jan. 5, 1938; s. Jere N. and Sarah (Allen) Moore; m. Pamla Hill Prochnow, Sept. 29, 2001; children: Frances Moore Preston, Powell Allen Jr. BA in Jounalism, U. Ga., 1959. Press sec. to Senator Richard Russell US Senate, Washington, 1966-71; dep. dir. pub. info. US Dept. Justice, Washington, 1971-72; dep. spl. asst. to Pres. for legis. affairs The White House, Washington, 1973-75, cons. pub. affairs, 1975-81, dep. asst. to Pres. for legis. affairs, 1981-82; asst. sec. for congl. rels. US Dept. State, Washington, 1982-83; v.p. legis. affairs Lockheed Corp., Washington, 1983-85, Ginn, Edington, Moore and Wade, Washington, 1985-90; pres. ASL Internat., Washington, 1990-93; sr. prin., mng. dir. Capitoline, MS&L, Washington, 1993-98; chief of staff to Senator Fred Thompson US Senate, Washington, 1998-2001; asst. sec. for legis. affairs US Dept. Def., Washington, 2001—05; mng. dir., fed. govt. relations McKenna Long & Aldridge LLP, Washington, 2005—. Dir. press Com. to Re-elect the Pres., Washington, 1972; cons. Pres. Ford Com., 1976, Reagan-Bush Com., 1980. Served to capt., inf. U.S. Army, 1959-62. Recipient Def. Dept.'s medal for Disting. Pub. Svc., 2005. Mem. Belle Haven Country Club, Met. Club. Republican. Episcopalian. Office: McKenna Long & Aldridge LLP 1900 K St NW Washington DC 20006 E-mail: pmoore@mckennalong.com.

MOORE, RICHARD HANCOCK, lawyer, former state treasurer; b. Oxford, NC, Aug. 30, 1960; s. Graham Tingley and Lucy Landis (Hancock) M.; m. Noel Crook, May 18, 1985; 3 children. BA cum laude, Wake Forest U., 1982, JD, 1986; postgrad. degree, London Sch. Econs and Polit. Sci., 1984. Bar: NC 1986, DC 1987, US Claims Ct. 1988, US Dist. Ct. DC 1988. Clk. to presiding justice U.S. Dist. Ct. (so. dist.) Tex., Corpus Christi, 1986-87; assoc. Finley, Kumble, Wagner, Washington DC, 1987-88, Laxalt, Washington, Perito & Dubuc, Washington DC, 1988; chief exec. Dept. Crime Control and Pub. Safety, 1996; atty. Zolicoffer and Long Law; fedl. prosecutor Ea. NC; state treas. State of NC, 2001—09. NC State Ho. of Reps., 1992-94. Co-author: Faces from the Flood: Hurricane Floyd Remembered Mem. ABA, N.C. Bar Assn., D.C. Bar Assn., Order of Barristers, Phi Alpha Theta. Democrat. Episcopalian. Office Phone: 919-508-5176. Office Fax: 919-508-5167.

MOORE, RICHARD KERR, electrical engineering educator; b. St. Louis, Nov. 13, 1923; s. Louis D. and Nina (Megown) M.; m. Wilma Lois Schallau, Dec. 10, 1944 (dec. 1999); children: John Richard, Daniel Charles. BS, Washington U. at St. Louis, 1943; PhD, Cornell U., 1951. Test equipment engr. RCA, Camden, NJ, 1943-44; instr. and rsch. engr. Washington U., St. Louis, 1947-49; rsch. assoc. Cornell U., 1949-51; rsch. engr., sect. supr. Sandia Corp., Albuquerque, 1951-55; prof., chmn. elec. engring. U. N.Mex., 1955-62; Black and Veatch prof. U. Kans., Lawrence, 1962-94; prof. emeritus, 1994—; dir. remote sensing lab. U. Kans., 1964-74, 84-93. Pres. Cadre Corp., Lawrence, 1968-87; cons. cos., govt. agys. Author: Traveling Wave Engineering, 1960; co-author: (with Ulaby and Fung) Microwave Remote Sensing, Vol. I, 1981, Vol. II, 1982, Vol. III, 1986; contbr. to profl. jours. and handbooks. Lt. (j.g.) USNR, 1944-46. Recipient Achievement award Washington U. Engring. Alumni Assn., 1978, Outstanding Tech. Achievement award IEEE Geosci. and Remote Sensing Soc., 1982, Louise E. Byrd Grad. Educator award U. Kans., 1984, Irving Youngberg Rsch. award U. Kans., 1989, Australia prize, 1995. Fellow AAAS, IEEE (sect. chmn. 1960-61, Outstanding Tech. Achievement award coun. oceanic engring. 1978); mem., NAE, AAUP, Am. Soc. Engring. Edn., Am. Geophys. Union, Internat. Sci. Radio Union (chmn. U.S. commn. F 1984-87, internat. vice chmn. commn. F 1990-93, chmn. 1993-96), Kiwanis, Sigma Xi, Tau Beta Pi. Presbyterian (past elder). Achievements include research in submarine communications, radar altimetry, radar as a remote sensor, radar oceanography; patent for polypanchromatic radar. Home: 1712 Carmel Dr Lawrence KS 66047-1840 Office: U Kans R S & Remote Sensing Lab 2335 Irving Hill Rd Lawrence KS 66045-7612 Personal E-mail: rmoore@sunflower.com.

MOORE, RICHARD LAWRENCE, structural engineer, consultant; b. Rocky Ford, Colo., Feb. 7, 1934; s. Lawrence and Margaret Kathryn (Bolling) M.; m. Donna St. Clair, Mar. 26, 1972 (div. 1983); 1 child, Andrew Trousdale; m. Margaret Ann Guthrie, May 4, 1984. BSCE, U. Colo., 1957; MS, Princeton U., 1963; PhD, Calif. Western U., Santa Ana, 1975. Registered profl. engr., Mass., Maine, Colo., Pa., Iowa, Nebr., N.Mex., Wyo., Ill., Ark., Mo., ND, Mich., Okla., Mont., N.H. Structural engr. Cameron Engrs., Denver, 1964-66; v.p. Moore Internat., Jeddah, Saudi Arabia, 1967-78; asst. to pres. C.H. Guernsey Co., Oklahoma City, 1979-82; pres. R.L. Moore Co., Boston, 1983—; v.p., dir. Isolink Ing., Basel, Switzerland, 1990—. Nat. chmn. Roof Cons. Inst., Raleigh, N.C., 1988-92; prof. Episcopal Sch. Theology, Denver, 1967-71. Patentee in field. Member Mound City (Mo.) Libr. Bd., 1963-64; pres. Dist. Rep. Party, Boston, 1988—; sr. warden St. John Chrysostom Epis. Ch., Denver, 1966-71. Danforth Found. scholar, 1962. Mem. ASCE, NSPE, Am. Concrete Inst., Nat. Forensic Ctr. Avocations: golf, travel, antique pocket watch collecting. Home and Office: 350 W 4th St 308 Boston MA 02127

MOORE, RICHARD THOMAS, state legislator; b. Milford, Mass., Aug. 7, 1943; s. Thomas James and Helen Eliza (Andrew) M.; m. Joanne Bednarz, May 26, 1979. BA in History, Clark U., 1966; MA in Student Pers., Colgate U., 1967; postgrad., Clark U., 1967-70, U. Mass., 1981-85. Cert. tchr. secondary level social studies. Assoc. dean students Assumption Coll., Worcester, Mass., 1967-69; asst. to pres. Bentley Coll., Waltham, Mass., 1969-77; mem. Mass. House of Reps., 1977-94; assoc. dir. mitigation Fed. Emergency Mgmt. Agy., Washington, 1994-96; mem. Worcester & Norfolk Dist. Mass. State Senate, 1996—, chmn. senate com. on pub. svc., 1997-98, chmn. senate com. healthcare, 1999—. Pres. Mass. Selectmen's Assn., Boston, 1975-76; chmn. House Com. on Election Laws, Boston, 1992-94, House Com. on Taxation, Boston, 1983-85, House Com. on State Adminstrn., Boston, 1983. Chmn. Blackstone Nat. Heritage Corridor Commn., Uxbridge, Mass., 1988-90, 2000—; presdl. elector Mass. Electoral Coll., Boston, 1992; chmn. Mass. Dem. Leadership Coun., Boston, 1990-93; trustee Nichols Coll., 1997—, Named Outstanding Legislator Mass. Town Clks. Assn., Boston, 1993, New Dem. of Yr. Mass. Dem. Leadership Coun., Boston, 1994; recipient Disting. Svc. award Fed. Emergency Mgmt. Agy., 1996. Mem. ASPA (bd. dirs. Mass. chpt. 1981-85, chpt. v.p. 1999-2000, pres.-elect 2000-2001, pres. 2001—03, mem. nat. coun., 2003—, Disting. Pub. Adminstrn. award 1997, Coun. State Govt.'s 2000 Toll fellow), Nat. Conf. State Legislatures (exec. com.), Nat. Emergency Mgmt. Assn., Knights Holy Sepulchre. Democrat. Roman Catholic. Avocations: politics, collecting political items. Office: State House Rm 111 Boston MA 02133 E-mail: Richard.Moore@state.ma.us.*

MOORE, RICHARD WAYNE, electric power industry executive, former prosecutor; b. Bartow, Fla., Dec. 5, 1952; s. James Ferrell and Mary Etta (Carlisle) M.; m. Elizabeth Ann Mitchell, Sept. 1, 1984; children: Michaelan Susan, John Mark. BS summa cum laude, Spring Hill Coll., 1974; JD, Samford U., 1977. Bar: Ala. 1977, U.S. Dist. Ct. Ala. 1977. Assoc. Marr & Friedlander, Mobile, Ala., 1977-79; ptnr. Sherling, Drinkard & Moore, Mobile, Ala., 1979-81; assoc. Gibbs & Craze, Cleve., 1981-85; sr. litigation counsel U.S. Atty.'s Office, Mobile, 1985—2003; insp. gen. TVA, Knoxville, Tenn., 2003—. Atlantic fellow in Pub. Policy U.K., Oxford, Eng., 1997. Mem. Mobile County Bar Assn., Paul Brock Mobile Inn of Ct. Anglican. Office: TVA E Tower 400 W Summit Hill Dr Rm 4C Knoxville TN 37902 Office Phone: 865-632-4120.

MOORE, ROBERT H., pediatrician, educator; married. MD, U. Tex. Med. Br., Galveston, 1980. Lic. Tex. State Bd. Med. Examiners, 1980, cert. Am. Acad. Pediat., 1985, pulmonologist 1995. Assoc. prof. pediat. Baylor Coll. Medicine, Houston, 1993—. Office: Baylor Coll Medicine 6621 Fannin CCC1040 Houston TX 77030 Office Fax: 832-825-3308. Business E-Mail: rmoore@bcm.tmc.edu.

MOORE, ROBERT HENRY, writer, editor, communications consultant; b. Madisonville, Ky., Sept. 16, 1940; s. William Lee Moore and Robbie (Pritchett) Ruby; m. Diana Churchill, Aug. 17, 1963 (div. 1978); children: Randall Lee, Robin Churchill; m. Patricia Mary George, Oct. 4, 1981; 1 child, Christopher Robert. BA, Davidson Coll., NC, 1962; MA, U. N.C., 1964; PhD, U. Wis., 1972. Asst. dir. admissions Davidson Coll., 1963-64; teaching asst. U. Wis., Madison, 1965-68; staff and faculty U.S. Mil. Acad., West Point, NY, 1968-70; lectr., asst. prof. U. Md., College Park, 1970-76, assoc. prof., 1976; cons. U.S. Congress, Washington, 1976-77; emerging issues coordinator The Conf. Bd., NYC, 1977-79; dir. govt. relations Benefacts, Inc., Washington, 1977-78; v.p. Alexander & Alexander, Inc., Washington, 1978-81, Alexander & Alexander Svcs. Inc., NYC, Washington, 1981-85, sr. v.p. corp. rels., 1985-95, sr. v.p. (inactive), 1995-97; chmn., pres. A & A Govt. and Industry Affairs Inc., Washington, 1990-94, Aon Corp., Vienna, Va., 1997—2005; pres. PMR Comm. Group, Vienna, Va., 2005—, sr. editor. Del. Nat. Security Affairs Conf., Washington, 1978-82; mem. adv. bd. Career Opportunities Inst., U. Va., Charlottesville, 1982-86, Ctr. for New Am. Work Force, 1992-96; mem. corp. adv. bd. Queens Coll., CUNY, 1985-96; mem. V.P.'s Forum, 1989-94; mem. coun. Conf. Bd. Corp. Comm. Execs., 1990-94; mem. Pub. Rels. Sem., 1993-97; editl. advisor Ctr. for Mind-Body Medicine, Washington, 1998-2000; adv. coun. Mindfulness Practice Ctr. of Fairfax, 1998—; bd. visitors Dictionary of Am. Regional English, 1999—; adv. to chmn. NEH, 1999-2001; expert commentator IRMI Com., 2003-. Co-author: (with others) School for Soldiers: West Point and the Profession of Arms, 1974 (NYT award 1974), Spreading the Risks: Insuring the American Experience, 2003 (Washington Book Pubs. award 2003), Risk Management, 2004 (Book of the Year), Revised Edit., 2005; columinist Raleigh Telegram, 2008-; contbr. articles to profl. jours.; contbr. interviews to nat. mags., newspapers, radio and TV. Mem. kitchen cabinet Points of Light Found., 1991-95. With U.S. Army, 1968-70, capt. USAR, 1970-72. Ops. Crossroads Africa fellow, 1960; U. Md. rsch. grantee, 1972, 76. Mem. Nat. Assn. Ins. Brokers (exec. com., bd. dirs., pres. 1985-86, chmn. past presidents adv. coun. 1989-93).

MOORE, ROBERT MADISON, food products executive, lawyer; b. New Orleans, June 21, 1925; s. Clarence Greer and Anna Omega (Odendahl) M.; m. Evelyn Eileen Varva, Apr. 11, 1953; children: Eileen Alexandria Moore Wynne, John Greer. BBA, Tulane U., 1947; JD, U. Va., 1952; LLM (Food Law Inst. fellow), NYU, 1953. Bar: La. 1956, Calif. 1972. Asst. to pres., gen. counsel Underwear Inst., NYC, 1953-55; pvt. practice law New Orleans, 1955-56; asst. gen. atty., dir. Legal services, sec. and gen. atty. Standard Fruit & Steamship Co., New Orleans, 1957-72; v.p., gen. counsel Castle & Cooke Foods, 1972-81, Castle & Cooke, Inc., 1973-81, sr. v.p. law and govt., 1981-82; pres. Internat. Banana Assn., 1983-98; acting exec. dir. Pan Am. Devel. Found., 1999. Dir. Ferson Optics of Del., Inc., 1958-69, Baltime Securities Corp., Pan American Devel. Found. Asst. atty. gen., La., 1960-66. Served with AUS, 1943-46. Mem. ABA, Calif. Bar Assn., La. Bar Assn., SAR (sec. 1960-61), KM, Cosmos Club, Phi Delta Phi, Alpha Tau Omega. Democrat. Roman Catholic. Home: 3323 R St NW Washington DC 20007-2310 Personal E-mail: rmevmoore@aol.com.

MOORE, ROBERT WILLIAM, professional organization executive; b. Claysburg, Pa., June 4, 1924; s. Frank B. and Sarah A. (Edelbute) M.; m. Helen Lingenfelter, July 17, 1948; children: Thomas R., Priscilla Jane. BA, Pa. State U., 1948. With Price Waterhouse & Co., Pitts., 1948-62, mgr., 1955-62; asst. contr. Con-Gas Svc. Corp., Pitts., 1962-65, Consol. Natural Gas Svc. Co., Inc., Pitts., 1966-72, contr., 1972-78, Consol. Natural Gas Co., Pitts., 1972-78; pres. Fin. Execs. Inst., Morristown, NJ, 1978-89, pres. emeritus, 1989—. Mem. Fin. Acctg. Standards Adv. Coun., 1978-89. Bd. dirs. Central Blood Bank, Pitts., 1960-78, treas. corp., 1962-68, chmn. finance com., 1962-68, chmn. bd., 1969-72; mem. exec. bd. Pa. State U. Alumni Council, 1975-83; mem. exec. com. Campaign for Pa. State U., bd. vis.; pres. Pa. State Coll. Bus. Adminstrn. Soc., 1981-83. Served with AUS, 1943-45. Named to Inaugural Class of Fin. Execs. Inst. Hall of Fame. Mem. Am., Pa. insts. C.P.A.s, Inst. of Mgmt. Acct., Fin. Execs. Inst., Pa. State U. Alumni Assn., Pa. Soc., Beta Alpha Psi (nat. forum), Delta Tau Delta. Clubs: University (dir., pres. 1975-76), Valley Brook Country (dir. 1968-70, v.p. bd. 1970), Duquesne (Pitts.), St. Clair Country. Episcopalian. E-mail: rmoorepgh@msn.com.

MOORE, RODERICK W., United State Ambassador to Montenegro; BA in Russian Studies and Internat. Rels., Brown U., Providence, 1986, MA in Slavic Linguistics, 1987. Embassy postings US Dept. State, Port-au-Prince, Haiti, 1988—89, Sofia, Bulgaria, 1990—92, with ops. ctr. Washington, 1992, rep. Skopje, Macedonia, 1992—93, polit.-mil. officer, Ctrl. and Ea. Europe Washington, 1993—95, sr. polit. advisor, Office Security and Cooperation in Europe Sarajevo, Bosnia-Herzegovina, 1996, polit.-econ. counselor Zagreb, Croatia, 1996—99, fellow, Fletcher Sch. Law and Diplomacy Washington, 1999—2000, dep. chief of mission Sofia, 2000—03, Belgrade, Montenegro, 2004—07, US amb. to Montenegro, 2007—. Office: DOS Amb 5070 Belgrade Pl Washington DC 20521-5070*

MOORE, RODNEY GREGORY, lawyer; b. Birmingham, Ala., Sept. 1, 1960; s. Jethroe and Tommie (Feagin) M.; m. Yalsyn Moore; children: Nyosha, Rodney II, Imari. BA, U. Wash., 1982; JD, Santa Clara U., Calif., 1985. Bar: Calif. 1987, Ga. 2000, US Ct. Appeals (9th, 11th cir.), US Supreme Ct. Concert promoter Clanagan & Moore/Class "A", Seattle and San Jose, Calif., 1984-87; ptnr. Williams, Robinson & Moore, San Jose, 1987-89; prin. Moore Law Firm, San Jose, 1989-97; gen. counsel East Side Union HS Dist., San Jose, 1997-2000; gen. counsel, chief legal officer Atlanta Pub. Schs., 2000—05; of counsel Greenberg Traurig LLP, Atlanta, 2005—08; ptnr. Adorno & Yoss, Atlanta, 2008—. Disc jockey Sta. KCMU, Seattle, 1980-82; assoc. prof. contract law Lincoln Law Sch., 1992-94. Assoc. editor: Santa Clara U. Computer Law Jour., 1984—85, chmn. editl. bd.: Nat. Bar Assn. Jour., 1997—99. Mem. sch. bd. East Side Union HS Dist. Named one of Best Lawyers in America, 2007—, 50 Most Influential Minority Lawyers in America, Nat. Law Jour., 2008; scholar, Santa Clara U., 1982—85. Mem. Nat. Bar Assn. (chpt. pres. 1989, gen. counsel 1997-99, v.p. 2002-04, pres. 2008-09), Santa Clara County Bar Assn. (trustee 1990), Assn. Trial Lawyers Am., NY Sports and Entertainment Soc., Santa Clara County Black Lawyers Assn. (pres. San Jose chpt. 1989-90), Calif. Assn. Black Lawyers (pres. 1993-94, Loren Miller Atty. of Yr., 1997), Calif. Sch. Lawyers Assn., Ga. Sch. Lawyers Assn., Nat. Alliance Black Sch. Educators, Nat. Coun. Sch. Attys. Office: Adorno & Yoss Two Midtown Plz 1349 W Peachtree St Ste 1500 Atlanta GA 30309 Office Phone: 404-347-8108. Business E-Mail: rmoore@adorno.com.*

MOORE, ROGER ADDISON, pediatrician, anesthesiologist; b. Portsmouth, Va., 1948; MD, U. Va., Charlottesville, 1973. Diplomate Am. Bd. Pediat., Am. Bd. Anesthesiology. Intern, resident pediat. U. Colo., Denver, 1974—77; resident anesthesiology U. Pa. Hosp., Phila., 1977-

79; fellow pediatric anesthesia/intensive care Children's Hosp., Phila., 1979; chmn. anesthesiology dept. Deborah Heart & Lung Ctr., Browns Mills, NJ, 1993—2005, chair emeritus, 2005—; clin. assoc. prof. anesthesiology U. Medicine & Dentistry NJ, Newark, 1998—. Named a Top Doc, South Jersey Mag., 2006—08. Mem.: AMA, Med. Soc. NJ, NJ State Soc. Anesthesiologists (v.p. 1987—89, pres. 1989—91, treas. 1999—), Soc. Cardiovasc. Anesthesiologists (v.p. 1999—2001, pres. 2001—03), Am. Soc. Anesthesiologists (NJ dir. 1995—96, sec.-treas. 1996—99, asst. treas. 1999—2003, treas. 2004—06, v.p. 2007, pres. 2008—), Am. Assn. Pediat., Alpha Omega Alpha. Office: Deborah Heart & Lung Ctr 200 Trenton Rd Browns Mills NJ 08015 Office Phone: 609-893-6611. Personal E-mail: rogermoore435@yahoo.com.*

MOORE, RONALD LEE, physicist; b. Fort Wayne, Ind., Mar. 30, 1942; s. Akin E. and Vernice Marjorie Moore; m. Barbara Joyce Welenc, Apr. 22, 1972; children: Heather Grace Goethert, Shannon Jean Cronin, Megan Elliott Smith. BS in Aero. Engring., Purdue U., West Lafayette, Indiana, 1964; MS in Aero. and Astron. Sci., Stanford U., Palo Alto, Calif., 1965, PhD in Aero. and Astron. Sci., 1972. Rsch. fellow in solar astronomy Calif. Inst. Tech., Pasadena, Calif., 1972—75, sr. rsch. fellow iolar astronomy, 1975—81; astrophysicist solar studies NASA Marshall Space Flight Ctr., Huntsville, Ala., 1981—. Mem.: Internat. Aston. Union, Am. Geophys. Union, Am. Aston. Soc.

MOORE, ROSA-LEE, information technology executive; b. Aurora, Ill., Sept. 8, 1973; d. General Arwood Moore, Jr. and Wanda Kay Moore; m. Jerry Lee Cooke. AAS in Environ. Sci., Mountain Empire CC, Big Stone Gap, Va., 1999; student in Natural Resources, Oreg. State U., 2007—. Cert. Tchr. Mountain Empire CC, 2004. Info. tech. specialist Mountain Empire CC, 1999—, web designer, 1999—, water treatment instr., 2004—. Mem.: Va. Operator Certification Stakeholders. Office: Mountain Empire CC 3441 Mountain Empire Rd Big Stone Gap VA 24219 Business E-Mail: rmoore@me.vccs.edu.

MOORE, ROY DEAN, retired judge; b. Chickasha, Okla., Jan. 15, 1940; s. Frank B. and Delia Pauline (Morgan) M.; m. Carolyn Kaye Wood, Aug. 10, 1962; children— Darla Kaye, Jared Dean, Amy Darise. BA, Central State U., 1962, M. Teaching, 1966; JD, Oklahoma City U., 1970; grad., Nat. Coll. State Trial Judges, 1972. Bar: Okla. 1970. Coach debate, instr. dramatics Kingfisher (Okla.) High Sch., 1962-67; instr. English and journalism, head dept. lang. arts. Jarman Jr. High Sch., Midwest City, Okla., 1967-70; pros. atty. City of Lawton, Okla., 1970; spl. dist. judge 5th Jud. Dist. Okla., 1971-72; pvt. practice law Lawton, 1973-90; dist. judge 5th Jud. Dist. Okla., 1990—2002. Pres. Swinney PTA, 1975-76; Editor: Problems in Teaching in the Secondary School, 1966. Pres. Comanche County Mental Health Assn., 1973-74, bd. dirs., 1972-76; co-chmn. Kingfisher County Reps. for Congressman James V. Smith, 1966; mem. state exec. com. Okla. Republican Com., 1973-74, chmn. auditing com., 1977-78; del. Rep. Nat. Conv., 1976; chmn. cts. com. Assn. South Central Okla. Govts. Crime Commn.; chmn. Comanche County Reps. for Reagan for Pres., 1973-83; mem. adv. bd. Jim Taliferro Mental Health Center, 1977-78; del. Nat. Mental Health Assn. Conv., 1975; bd. dirs. Lawton Campfire Girls; elder N.W. Ch. of Christ, 1977-2004; dir. Back to Bible Campaigns, 1976-2002. Named Outstanding Dist. Judge in State of Okla., Okla. Trial Lawyers Assn., 1999. Mem. Am., Okla., Comanche County bar assns., Okla. Trial Lawyers Assn., Lawton Antique Auto Club, Ford Retractible Club Am., Alpha Psi Omega, Delta Theta Phi. Republican. Mem. Ch. of Christ (elder). Clubs: Fraternal Order of Police, Lion. Home: 2114 NW Atlanta Ave Lawton OK 73505-3923

MOORE, RYAN NATALIE, creative director; b. Redlands, Calif., Sept. 14, 1977; d. Robert Willard Moore and Cynthia Moon. BA, U. Calif., San Diego, 1998. Assoc. writer, prodr. KGTV, McGraw-Hill Broadcasting Group, San Diego, 1997—2000; dir. creative svcs. Disney-ABC Domestic TV, Burbank, Calif., 2000—. Mem.: PROMAX, Acad. TV Arts Scis., Mensa. Office: Disney ABC Domestic TV 500 S Buena Vista St Burbank CA 91521-4220 Personal E-mail: ryannatalie@earthlink.net.

MOORE, SHERRY MILLS, lawyer; b. 1951; m. Tim Moore; 2 children. BA, Beloit Coll.; JD, Univ. ND, 1979. Bar: ND 1979. Pvt. practice, Bismarck, ND. Bd. mem. Mental Health Assn. of ND, Prevent Child Abuse ND; pres. Bismarck Library Bd.; chair Mayor's Task Force on Methamphetamine. Named Vol. Lawyer of Yr., Big Muddy Bar Assn., 2000. Mem.: State Bar Assn. ND (pres. 2004). Avocations: photography, reading, jetskiing. Office: Atty-at-Law 300 N 4th St PO Box 4144 Bismarck ND 58502-4144 Office Phone: 701-222-4777. Office Fax: 701-222-8502.

MOORE, STANLEY RAY, lawyer; b. Dallas, July 20, 1946; s. Elzey and Heloise M.; m. Sherri Boren; children: Natalie, William, Julie, Colin, Brendan. BSME, So. Meth. U., 1969, JD, 1973. Bar: Tex. 1973, U.S. Dist. Ct. (no. dist.) Tex. 1974, U.S. Ct. Appeals (fed. cir.). Assoc. Clegg, Cantrell, Crisman, Dallas, 1973-75; ptnr. Crisman & Moore, Dallas, 1975-80, Schley Cantrell & Moore, Dallas, 1980-83, Schley, Cantrell, Kice & Moore, Dallas, 1983-87, Johnson & Wortley, P.C., Dallas, 1987-94, Jenkens & Gilchrist, Dallas, 1995—, head IP dept., 2005. Patentee in field. Foster parent Hope Cottage, Dallas, 1982-90; fund raiser Am. Heart Assn., YMCA, rep. Orgn. Recipient Outstanding Leadership commendation ASME, 1969. Mem. ABA, IAPLA, INTA, Dallas Bar Assn. (chair IP sect. 2004) Home: 1 Victoria Cir Rowlett TX 75088-6059 Office: Jenkens & Gilchrist 1445 Ross Ave Ste 3200 Dallas TX 75202-2785 Home Phone: 972-475-3945; Office Phone: 214-855-4713. E-mail: smoore@jenkens.com.

MOORE, STANLEY WAYNE, retired political science professor; b. Camden, NJ, Feb. 11, 1937; s. Frank Stafford and Alma Beatrice (Law) M.; m. Nancy Joan Crawford, Sept. 1, 1961; children: David Crawford, Andrea Katrina, Stanley Edward Stafford Moore, Sonia Elizabeth. AB magna cum laude, Wheaton Coll., 1959; MA and PhD in Govt., Claremont Grad. U., 1971. Asst. prof. polit. sci. Calif. State U.-Stanislaus, Turlock, 1967—69, Monterey Inst. for Internat. Affairs, Calif., 1969—72; vis. assoc. U. Redlands, Calif., 1972—73; assoc. prof. Pepperdine U., Malibu, Calif., 1973—79, prof. polit. sci., 1979—, 2006—, emeritus prof. polit. sci. Pres. Calif. Ctr. for Edn. in Pub. Affairs, Inc., 1981-2002. Author: A Child's Political World: A Longitudinal Perspective, 1985; contbr. articles to profl. jours. Scoutmaster troop 761 Boy Scouts Am., 1981-92, adv. bd. LA Area Coun., 1993-1999, chair advancement com., 1994-98; vice chmn. Ventura County Air Pollution Control Bd., 1981-92; mem. Ventura County Beyond the Yr. 2000 Commn., 1988-90, Nat. Dem. Com., Calif. Dem. Com., Christians in Polit. Sci.; bd. dirs. Calif. Bicentennial Found. for US Constn., 1987-91; moderator Camps and Conf. Ministry Bd., 1998-2004; bd. dir. Friends Southwest Mus. Coalition; bd. Staff of Hope, 2003—; elder Presbyn. Ch., USA, del. Gen. Assembly, 2000; San Gabriel Presbytery, Com. on Preparation for Ministry, 2005-; elected to Hist. Highland Pk. Neighborhood Coun., 2002—, treas. 2006-, v.p. 2008-; mem. Congress LA Neighborhood Couns., 2006—, steering com. mem., Peace Northeast, 2008,2009, Friends SW Mus. Colition, 2008-, Dept. Water and Power Oversight Com., 2006-, steering com. Peace Northeast March, 2008-. Recipient Medal of Honor, Boy Scouts Am., 1989; grantee Spencer Found. Chgo., 1979, 81. Fellow Am. Sci. Affiliation; mem. Am. Polit. Sci. Assn., We. Polit. Sci. Assn., So. Calif. Polit. Sci. Assn. (pres. 1988-2002), So. Calif. Soc. for Internat. Devel. (pres. 1988-98), Coun. Soc. for Internat. Devel., Sierra, Aubudon Soc., Nat. Wildlife Fedn., Highland Pk. C. of C. (bd. dirs., sec. 2003-), Kiwanis (bd. dirs. 2003—, pres.elect 2007-). Presbyterian (elder). Avocations: backpacking, fishing, photography, community activity.

MOORE, STEPHEN JAMES, lawyer; b. Kansas City, Mo., Aug. 9, 1947; s. James Andrew and Frances Clare (Kennedy) M. BSBA, Rockhurst U., 1969, BA, 1975; JD, U. Mo., Kansas City, 1977, LLM, 1997. Bar: Mo. 1978, U.S. Dist. Ct. (we. dist.) Mo. 1978, U.S. Ct. Appeals (8th cir.) 1980, U.S. Ct. Appeals (10th cir.) 1981, U.S. Ct. Fed. Claims 1991, U.S. Ct. Appeals (6th cir.) 1997. Law intern Mo. Atty. Gen.'s Office, Kansas City, 1976-77, asst., 1978; assoc. Popham, Conway, Sweeny, Fremont & Bundschu PC, Kansas City, 1978-84, Freilich, Leitner & Carlisle, PC, Kansas City, 1985, Freilich, Feinstein, Kansas City, 1985-86, Freilich, Leitner, Carlisle & Shortlidge, Kansas City, 1986-90; ptnr. Freilich, Leitner & Carlisle, Kansas City, Dallas, L.A., 1987-2000, Aspen, Colo., 1997-2000, Peters, Moore & Jones, LLC, Kansas City, Mo., 2001—02, Peters & Moore, L.L.C., 2002—04; pvt. law firm Stephen J. Moore, PC, 2005—. Adj. prof. law U. Mo., Kansas City, 1995—. Mem. Friends of Art, Nelson-Atkins Mus. Art, Kansas City, 1988—, Smithsonian Inst., Washington, 1985—, Nat. Trust for Historic Preservation, Washington, 1988—, Libr. of Congress Assocs., The Federalist Soc., Nat. Audubon Soc. Mem. ABA, Assn. Trial Lawyers Am., Kansas City Metro Bar Assn., Sports Car Club Am., Am. Mus. Nat. History, Porsche Club Am., Lake Ozarks Yacht Assn., Boat Owners Assn. U.S., Ancient Order of Hibernians, Delta Theta Phi, Tau Kappa Epsilon. Roman Catholic. Avocations: vintage sportscars, boating. Home: 5840 McGee St Kansas City MO 64113-2132 Office: 1500 Traders on Grand Bld 1125 Grand Ave Kansas City MO 64106 Office Phone: 816-777-1012. Business E-Mail: stephen@moorelandlaw.com.

MOORE, STEVEN E., legislative staff member; BJ, U. Okla., 1990; attended, Thunderbird, The Am. Grad. Sch. Internat. Mgmt., 1999—2000. Comm. coord. First Virtual Holdings, 1996—97; resident program officer Internat. Republican Inst., Indonesia, 2002—03, Iraq; ptnr. Gorton Moore & Mulanix Internat., 2004—05; pub. opinion rschr. & strategic effects analyst Coalition Forces, Iraq, 2005—06; of counsel Roskam for Congress Com., 2006; chief of staff to Rep. Peter Roskam US House of Reps., Washington, 2006—. Polit. cons. Boris Yeltsin's Presdl. Campaign, Russia, 1996; cons. Arthur D. Little, 2001. Republican. Office: 507 Cannon House Office Bldg Washington DC 20515 Office Phone: 202-225-4561. Office Fax: 202-225-1166.*

MOORE, TERRY LYNN, physician, researcher; s. Kenneth Clyde and Mary Elizabeth Moore; m. Carol Louise Miller, July 9, 1971; children: Heather Elizabeth Baldanza, Tara Ellen Medlock, Misti Louise Benson, Kendra Lauren McNichols. AB, U. Mo., Columbia, 1968; MD, St. Louis U., 1972. Diplomate in rheumatology Am. Bd. Internal Medicine, 1976. Prof. internal medicine, pediat., molecular biology and immunology St. Louis U. Med. Ctr., 1976—, dir. adult and pediatric rheumatology, 1976—, 1983—. Contbr. articles to over 170 med. publs. Recipient Rsch. Juvenile Arthritis award, NIH, Am. Coll. Rheumatology, Campbell-Avery Trust Found. Fellow: ACP, Am. Coll. Rheumatology, Am. Acad. Pediat. Achievements include research in juvenile arthritis; systemic lupus erythematosus; other immunological topics. Avocations: softball, soccer. Office: Saint Louis Univ Medical Ctr 1402 S Grand Blvd Saint Louis MO 63104 Office Phone: 314-977-8838. Office Fax: 314-977-8818. Business E-Mail: mooretl@slu.edu.

MOORE, THOMAS, museum director, retired accountant; b. Bellefontaine, Ohio, May 25, 1946; m. Lillie Moore, 1972; 2 children. BS in Bus. Adminstrn., Franklin U., Columbus, Ohio, 1968. Accountant Quaker Oats Co., ret., 2003; interim exec. dir. African Am. Hist. Mus. and Cultural Ctr., 2003, exec. dir., 2004—. Co-founder African Am. Heritage Found., 1993, bd. v.p., 1994—96, 2001—03, bd. pres., 1996—2000. Various positions including tchr., choir mem., historian and trustee Mt. Zion Missionary Bapt. Ch., Cedar Rapids, Iowa; bd. dirs. New Bohemia, United Way of East Ctrl. Iowa, First Light Ministries. With USAF, 1969—73. Mem.: Iowa Mus. Assn. (bd. dirs.). Office: African Am Hist Mus and Cultural Ctr 55 12th Ave SE Cedar Rapids IA 52401 Office Phone: 319-862-2101 ext. 13. Business E-Mail: director@blackiowa.org.

MOORE, THOMAS A., lawyer; b. Waterford, Ireland, May 2, 1942; STL, Cath. U., 1968; JD, Fordham U., 1972. Bar: N.Y. 1973, U.S. Dist. Ct. (so. and ea. dists.) N.Y. 1973, U.S. Supreme Ct. 1991. Atty. Kramer, Dillof, Livingston & Moore, NYC, 1973—, sr. ptnr. Lectr. in field. Named one of Best Lawyers in NY, NY mag., Super Lawyers mag. Fellow: Internat. Acad. Trial Lawyers; mem.: ATLA (nat. bd. dirs. 1992), Internat. Soc. Barristers, Inner Circle of Advocates, Am. Bd. Trial Advs., N.Y. State Trial Lawyers Assn. Office: Kramer Dillof Livingston & Moore 217 Broadway New York NY 10007*

MOORE, THOMAS ANDREW, biotechnology executive; b. Cambridge, Mass., Jan. 28, 1951; s. Leo B. and Christine (Banios) M.; m. Avril Barton, Nov. 8, 1975; children: Thomas, Diana, Juliet. BA in History, Princeton U., 1973. Brand asst. Procter & Gamble Co., Cin., 1973-84, advt. mgr. Beauty Care, 1984-86, gen. mgr. Vidal Sassoon LA, 1986-88, v.p. Health Care Cin., 1988-91; pres. Procter & Gamble Can., Toronto, Ont., Can., 1991-92; pres. Health Care Procter & Gamble USA, Cin., 1992-96; group v.p. Procter & Gamble Co., Cin., 1992-96; pres., CEO Nelson Communications, 1996—2002; CEO Biopure Corp., Cambridge, Mass., 2002—04; chmn., CEO Advaxis Corp., New Brunswick, NJ, 2006—. Bd. mem. Alteon Inc., 2001—07, El Dorado Mktg., 2004—, MD Offices Inc., Kingston, NY, 2006—; chmn. of bd. Ashanti Vineyards, Paarl, South Africa, 2005—, Mayan Pigments Inc., El Paso, Tex., 2006—. Treas. Alliance Drug Free Can., Toronto, 1991, 92; chmn. Cin. Ballet Co., 1986-91; bd. dirs. Am. Health Found., NYC, 1989-2004, Mercy Hosp., Anderson, Ohio, 1993-96, D&R Greenway Land Trust, 2000-06, Nat. Pub. Radio Found., 2002-06, Sound Portraits Prodn., 2004-. Mem. Non Prescription Drug Mfrs. Assn. (vice chmn. 1992—96), Princeton Club, Union Club, Jasna Polana. Avocations: fly fishing, wine collecting, consumption. Office Phone: 617-331-4872. Business E-Mail: mooringsllc@aol.com.

MOORE, THOMAS DAVID, academic administrator; b. Rochester, NY, July 26, 1937; s. Robert Franklin and Hilda (Kennedy) M.; m. Virginia Muller, June 13, 1959; children: Kathleen Mary, Michael David, Thomas David. BSS, St. John Fisher Coll., 1959; MS, SUNY, Brockport, 1962; EdD, Rutgers U., 1966. Tchr. Rochester City Schs., 1959-62; grad. asst. Rutgers U., New Brunswick, NJ, 1963-65; from asst. to full prof. Kent (Ohio) State U., 1965-93, asst. v.p. acad. affairs, 1976-83, v.p. faculty affairs and personnel, 1984-86, provost, v.p. acad. and student affairs, 1987-91, prof. emeritus ednl. philosophy, 1991—; provost, v.p. acad. affairs Ctrl. Washington U., 1993-97, prof. edn. and philosophy, 1997—. Roman Catholic. Avocations: sports, films, public affairs, music. Office Phone: 330-524-0688. Personal E-mail: vmoore4860@sbcglobal.net.

MOORE, THOMAS EDWIN, biologist, educator, museum director; b. Champaign, Ill. s. Gerald E. and Velma (Lewis) M.; m. E. Eleanor Sifferd, Feb. 4, 1951; children: Deborah S., Melinda S. BS, U. Ill., 1951, MS, 1952, PhD, 1956. Tech. asst. Ill. Natural History Survey, Urbana, 1950-56; instr. zoology U. Mich., Ann Arbor, 1956-59, asst. prof. zoology, 1959-63, assoc. prof. zoology, 1963-66, prof. biology, 1966—2000, curator insects, 1956—2000, dir. exhibit mus., 1988-93. Vis. prof. Orgn. Tropical Studies, San Jose, Costa Rica, 1970, 72; bd. dir. Orgn. Tropical Studies, San Jose, 1968-79; mem. steering com. tropical biome US Internat. Biol. Program, 1969-72; mem. conf. planning com. Nat. Inst. Environment, 1991-92; mem. steering com. Univ. Colloquium on Environ. Rsch. and Edn., 1991-93, grievance com. U. Mich., 1997-98, faculty handbook com., 1997-98. Co-editor: Lectures on Science Education, 1991, 92, 93; Cricket Behavior and Neurobiology, 1989; author movie 17-Year Cicadas, 1975, TV, 1998; co-author: Singing Insects of N.Am. Website, 2003—. County rep. Huron River Watershed Coun., Ann Arbor, 1987-95; mem. Mich. H.S. Accreditation Adv. Com., Ann Arbor, 1988-92; mem. U. Mich. Senate Adv. Com. on Univ. Affairs, 1993-96, vice chair, 1995-96, Provost's Task Force Grievance Policies, U. Mich., 2008; bd. mem. U. Mich. Acad. Freedom Lecture Fund, 1995—, treas., 1995-98; vol. Kempf House Ctr. for Local History, Ann Arbor, Mich.; cons. NSF Visual Tech. in Environ. Curricula, 1994-97; cons. Misery Bay exhibits Ont. ParksCanada, 2005-, bd. mem. Friends Misery Bay, 2007-. Rsch. grantee NSF, 1963-66, 66-69, 96-97, rsch. equipment grantee, 1984-86, rsch. grantee Def. Advanced Rsch. Project Agy./Office of Naval Rsch. 1998—2001. Fellow AAAS, Royal Entomol. Soc. London, Linnaen Soc. London; mem. Assn. Tropical Biology & Conservation(pres. 1973-75), Sigma Xi (pres. U. Mich. chpt. 1994-96, coun. 1993-98) Home: 4243 N Delhi Rd Ann Arbor MI 48103-9485 Office: Mus of Zoology U Mich Ann Arbor MI 48109-1079 Office Phone: 734-764-0471. Business E-Mail: temoore@umich.edu.

MOORE, THOMAS HILL, commissioner; m. Adrienne Moore; children: Carlton, Phyllis. BS in Acctg., Jacksonville U., 1971; JD, U. Fla., Gainesville, 1974. Govt. rels. cons.; legis. affairs dir. Allen, Rovin & Assocs.; staff atty. Nat. Consumer Law Ctr.; asst. dean U. Fla. Coll. Law, 1974—77; exec. v.p. Nat. Med. Assn.; legis. asst. to Senator Richard Stone US Senate, legis. counsel to Senator John Breaux, 1988—95; commr. US Consumer Product Safety Commn., Bethesda, Md., 1995—. Mem.: Comm. Bar Assn., DC Bar Assn., Fla. Bar Assn. Office: US Consumer Product Safety Commn 4330 East West Hwy Bethesda MD 20814 Office Phone: 301-504-7902. Office Fax: 301-504-0121.*

MOORE, THOMAS HOLMES, retired school administrator; b. Grafton, NH, June 14, 1920; s. Thomas R. and Lillian Alice (Thompson) M.; m. Norma Jean Smith, Sept. 9, 1944; children: Thomas, Andrew, Jamyn, Robinson, Elibet. Grad., New Hampton Sch., 1938; AB, Middlebury Coll., 1946; postgrad., Breadloaf Sch. English, 1948; PhD (hon.), Franklin Pierce Coll., 1977. With New Hampton Sch., NH, 1946—92, instr. English, head dept., registrar NH, 1946-53, dir. admissions summer session NH, 1949-53, exec. headmaster NH, 1954-59, headmaster NH, 1959-72, 90-92, pres. NH, 1972-90; headmaster emeritus, 1992—. Chmn. bd. Bristol Bank, 1982-83, 85—92; dir. Concord Group Ins. Co.; pres. NH Ednl. Broadcasting Coun., 1963-68, treas., 1964—, sec., 1970—; mem., chmn. commn. ind. schs. New Eng. Assn. Schs. and Colls., 1970-71, mem. exec. com., 1972—, interim exec. dir., 1973, treas., 1974, v.p., 1975, pres., 1976; chmn. NH Non-Pub. Sch. Adv. Coun.; mem. NH Libr. Commn.; chmn.-elect dist. 1 Coun. Advancement and Support of Edn. Bd. dirs. N.H. Music Festival (pres. 1966, 88), Laconia Hosp., Gordon-Nash Library; pres. No. New Eng. Found. Served to lt. (s.g.), AC USNR, 1941-45. Decorated Air medal, Peitee medal; recipient: Granite State award. Mem. Ind. Schs. Assn. No. New Eng. (pres. 1966), N.H. Library Trustees Assn. (chmn. legislative com.), Bristol C. of C. (dir. 1958) Home Phone: 603-744-2765. Personal E-mail: bujimoo@metrocast.net.

MOORE, THOMAS JOSEPH, finance company executive; b. Kalamazoo, Jan. 5, 1943; s. John Joseph and Bernita (Ryan) M.; m. Laura Leigh Johnson, Aug. 1, 1975; children: Ryan Michael, Janelle Marie, Darcie Kathleen. BBA, Western Mich. U., 1965; MBA, So. Meth. U., 1990. Various sales and mktg. positions IBM Corp., Southfield, Mich., 1968-79; exec. v.p., owner Carsonville (Mich.) Metal Products Corp., 1976-79; assoc. prof. Oakland Coll., Farmington Hills, Mich., 1977-78; group mgr. industry mktg. Recognition Equipment Inc., Dallas, 1979-81; mgmt. cons. APC Skills div. Alexander Proudfoot Co., Palm Beach, Fla., 1982-83; pres., chief exec. officer Lumentech of Am., Inc., Dallas, 1983-85; v.p., prin. Capital Alliance Corp., Dallas, 1985-2001; ptnr. EquiCap Ptnrs., LLC, Dallas, 2001—; mgr. EquiCap Investments, LLC, Dallas, 2003—; ptnr. Cunningham Partnership LLP, Houston, 2003—. Chmn., CEO, Laura Leigh Stores, Inc., Plano, Tex., 1993-2006; chmn. Luxury Baths by Arrow, Houston, 2003—; vis. lectr. Baylor U., Waco, Tex., 1986-89, sponsor, CEO roundtable, 1989-93; bd. dirs. MJ Designs, Inc., Coppell, Tex., 1997-98; co-CEO Arrow Marble LLC, Houston, 2003—, Designer Bath and Kitchen, LLC, 2005—07, Luxury Baths of San Antonio, LLC, 2005—, Luxury Baths of Dallas, LLC, 2005—. Pres. Bent Tree Homeowners Assn., Dallas, 1981-83; co-chair Jesuit Coll. Prep. Sch. Challenge Dr., 1992-95; chair car raffle Ursuline Acad. of Dallas, chmn. maj. donor campaign, 1994-95, co-chair bridge the gap campaign, 1995-96, chair underwriting, 1996; chmn. adv. coun., chmn. fin. com. John Paul II HS, Plano, Tex., 2004-2006; adv. coun. Cath. Found., 2008-; trustee, Holy Trinity Sem., Seminarian Scholarship Trust, 2008-, John Paul II HS Trust, 2008-. Mem. So. Meth. U. Exec. MBA Alumni Assn. (bd. dirs. 1990-92), Legatus, Serra Club Dallas (pres. 2008-09). Republican. Roman Catholic. Avocations: walking, reading, racquetball, cooking, wine tasting. Home: 5418 Westgrove Dallas TX 75248-2039 Office: EquiCap Ptnrs LLC Ste 1000 Two Galleria Tower 13455 Noel Rd Dallas TX 75240 Office Phone: 972-233-8282. Business E-Mail: tmoore@equicappartners.com.

MOORE, THOMAS PAUL, retired broadcast executive; b. Danville, Ill., Feb. 29, 1928; s. Lester Rufus and Mabel Ellen (Jackson) M.; m. Jean LaVonne Sather, Aug. 31, 1952; children: Randyl Ellen, Patricia Kay, Gregory Sather. BA, North Cen. Coll., Naperville, Ill., 1952; postgrad., Denver U., 1952-53. Newscaster Sta. KFEL-AM-FM-TV, Denver, 1952-54; sales rep. Sta. KGMC, Englewood, Colo., 1954-56; sales mgr. Sta. KDEN-AM-FM, Denver, 1956-62; pres. Stas. WBCO, WQEL, Bucyrus, Ohio, 1962-98; ret., 1998. Hon. dir. First Fed. Cmty. Bank, 2001—. Lay leader, mem. program coun. Ohio Sandusky Conf., United Meth. Ch., 1966-69 (pres. gen. laity bd. and laymen's found. 1968-72); mem. Gen Coun. on Ministries, 1980-84, N.W. Ohio Water Devel. Adv. Com., 1967-69, Sandusky River Basin Water Pollution Study Com., 1968-69; v.p., bd. mgrs. EUB Men, Evang. United Brethren Ch., 1958-68; pres. Rocky Mountain Conf., 1957-61; mem. gen. bd. Nat. Coun. Christian Chs. Am., 1968-72; charter pres. Bucyrus Bratwurst Festival, Inc., 1968; adv. bd. Bucyrus Salvation Army, 1964-68; mem.

planning com. East Ohio Conf., 1972-76 (chmn. commn. on minimum salaries, 1968-72, lay leader, 1972-76); vice chmn. coun. ministries, mem. episcopal com., 1972-76, head. del. to gen. conf., Portland, Oreg., 1976, Balt., 1984; head del. to Jurisdictional Conf., Sioux Falls, 1976, Duluth, Minn., 1984; pres. United Meth. Comms., 1972-76, mem. gen. coun. fin. and adminstrn., 1976-80; mem. comms. commn. Nat. Coun. Chs., 1972-76; mem. comms. con. Ohio Coun. Chs.; mem. Episc. com., chmn. New Vision Task Group, both East Ohio Conf., North Cen. Jurisdiction, United Meth. Ch.; mem. exec. com. Coun. on Ministries, 1980-86; mem. World Meth. Coun., 1986-91, World Meth. Conf., 1996; trustee United Theol. Sem., 1972-80; trustee Ohio No. U., 1986-2007, life trustee, 2007-, mem. exec. com., 1991-2003, chair student affairs com., 1991-95, chair, 1995-2007; mem. exec. com. East Ohio del. to United Meth. Gen. Conf. and Jurisdictional Conf., 1987-91; sec. Cmty. Improvement Corp., Bucyrus, 1989-91; mem. Overall Econ. Devel. Com. of Crawford County, 1992-96; chmn. Crawford County Traffic Safety Coun., 1979-89, 96-98; pres. Crawford County Econ. Devel. Adv. Coun., 1992-96; mem., sec. Crawford County Devel. Bd., Inc., 1997-2000; mem. exec. com. of del. to 1988 Gen. Conf. United Meth. Ch., St. Louis; bd. dirs. Bucyrus Cmty. Hosp., 1992-, mem. fin. com., 1993-96, chmn., 2004-2007, chmn. nominating com., 1993-96, campaign dir., chair fundraising com., 1993-96, v.p. bd. dirs., 1994-96; chmn. North Ctrl. Ohio Health Sys., 1996-98; mem. Crawford County Rep. Ctrl. Com., 1998-2001; mem. City of Bucyrus Bd. of Zoning Appeals, 1998-2001; pres. Crawford County Devel. Bd., 2000—; chmn. City of Bucyrus Bd. Zoning Appeals, 2000-01; sec. Bucyrus Pub. Libr Bd., 2004—. Served with USN, 1946-48. Named a Civic Leader of Am., 1968. Mem. Nat. Assn. Broadcasters (legis. liaison 1984-91, mem. small market radio com.), Ohio Assn. Broadcasters (pres. 1982-85), North Ctrl. Ohio Broadcasters Assn. (pres. 1983-84, 96-98, v.p. 1985-96), Bucyrus Area C. of C. (chmn. airport study com. 1967-68, bd. dirs. 1964-67, pres. 1989-91), Rotary (pres. Bucyrus chpt. 1992-93). Personal E-mail: tommoore@wavelinc.com. E-mail: ccdb@bucyruscrossroads.org.

MOORE, THOMAS RONALD (LORD BRIDESTOWE), lawyer; b. Duluth, Minn., Mar. 27, 1932; s. Ralph Henry and Estelle Marguerite (Hero) M.; m. Margaret C. King, Sept. 10, 1955 (dec. May 10, 2003); children: Willard S., Clarissa, Charles R.H. BA magna cum laude, Class Marshall, Yale U., 1954; JD, Harvard U., 1957. Bar: N.Y. 1958, U.S. Supreme Ct. 1965. Instr. Harvard Law Sch., 1956-57; with Dewey Ballantine, NYC; ptnr. Breed, Abbott & Morgan, NYC, Law Offices of Thomas R. Moore, NYC. Lectr. Harvard U. Law Sch., Cornell Law Sch., NYU Law Sch., Practising Law Inst., NYC, Las Vegas, New Orleans; lectr. Oxford U. Author: Plantagenet Descent, 31 Generations from William the Conqueror to Today, 1995; co-author: Estate Planning and the Close Corporation; editor-in-chief: Gastronome, bd. editors: The Tax Lawyer; contbr. articles to profl. jours.; numerous interviews in popular press and TV commentaries. Bd. dirs. exec. com. Citymeals on Wheels; pres. bd. dirs. Nat. Soc. to Prevent Blindness; sec.-treas., trustee A.D. Henderson Found., Del., trustee, Fla.; bd. dirs. Phoenix Theatre Inc., Inst. Aegean Prehistory, Found. Future of Man, Am. Friends of Victoria and Albert Mus., London; conservator NY Pub. Libr.; trustee Found. for Renaissance of St. Petersburg (Russia), Malcolm Wiener Found.; pres. bd. dirs. Laurence Levine Charitable Fund., Inc.; vice chmn. NY Hist. Soc.; hon. chmn. Youth America Grand Prix; bd. dirs. Gov.'s Commn. on Scholastic Achievement; constl. advisor to Pres. George H. W. Bush; advisor to King Michael of Romania. Decorated Knight, Queen Elizabeth II; recipient Coat of Arms, Order of Crown of Charlemagne, Order of Plantagenet, Order of Barons of Magna Charta, Order of Descendants Knights of the Garter, Thomas R. Moore Disting. Pub. Servant award, Nat. Soc. to Prevent Blindness; Scholar of House, Yale. Mem.: St. Andrews Soc., St. George Soc., Confrerie de la Chaine des Rotisseurs (nat. pres., dir., exec. com. world coun. Paris), Robert Burns Soc., Nat. Wine Coalition (bd. dirs.), Chevalier du Tastevin, The Pilgrims, Church Club, Univ. Club, Delta Sigma Rho. Republican. Episcopalian. Office: 590 Madison Ave Ste 2100 New York NY 10022 Office Phone: 212-333-8630.

MOORE, THURSTON ROACH, lawyer; b. Memphis, Dec. 10, 1946; s. Richard Charlton Moore and Halcyon Hall (Roach) Lynn; m. Corell Luckhardt Halsey, Sept. 26, 1998. BA with distinction, U. Va., 1968, JD, 1974. Bar: Va. 1974. Rsch. analyst Scudder, Stevens & Clark, NYC, 1968—71; ptnr. Hunton & Williams LLP, Richmond, Va., 1974—91, mng. partner, 1991—2006, chmn., 2006—. Mem.: ABA (chmn. ptnrs. com. 1992—96, bus. law sect., fed. regulation security com., bus. law coun.), Colonial Williamsburg Found. (trustee, bd. dirs.), Va. Performing Arts Founds. (dir.), Richmond Bar Assn., Va. State Bar, Va. Bar Assn., Va. Commwealth U. Sch. Bus. Found. (trustee, bd. dirs.), Nature Conservancy Va. (chmn., trustee, bd. dir.), Va. Found. Ind. Coll. (trustee, bd. dirs.), Met. Bus. Found. (pres. 1995—2001, dir.), Mary Morton Parsons Found. (trustee, bd. dir. 1992—2009), Va. Mus. Fine Arts (trustee), Phi Beta Kappa. Office: Hunton & Williams Riverfront Plz E Tower 951 E Byrd St Richmond VA 23219-4074 Office Fax: 804-788-8218. Business E-Mail: tmoore@hunton.com.

MOORE, TIM, lawyer; b. Lafayette, La., Sept. 4, 1957; BS in geology, Stephen F. Austin State U., 1979; JD summa cum laude, U. Houston, 1990. Bar: Tex. 1990. Geologist Placid Oil Co., New Orleans, 1980—84, Jackson, Miss., 1980—84; regional geologist Gulf Coast Kaiser Energy Inc., New Orleans, 1984—87; assoc. Weil, Gotshal & Manges, Houston, 1990—94; gen. counsel - corp. TransTex. Gas Corp., 1994—2000; v.p., gen. counsel, sec. Plains Resources, 2000—01, Plains All Am. Pipeline, Houston, 2000—. Mem.: Am. Corp. Counsel Assn., State Bar Tex., Order of the Barons, Order of the Coif, Omicron Delta Kappa. Office: Plains All Am Pipeline 333 Clay St Ste 1600 PO Box 4648 Houston TX 77210-4648*

MOORE, TIRIN, neuroscientist, educator; b. Oakland, Calif., June 12, 1969; s. Walter Peter Moore and Mary Lucille Salmon; m. Giovanna Ceserani, June 21, 2003; 1 child, Emilia T. PhD, Princeton U., NJ, 1995. Asst. prof. neurobiology Stanford U., Calif., 2003—. Mem. Bio-X. Contbr. several articles to profl. jours. Recipient Nat. Rsch. Svc. award, NIH, 1999—2002, Early Career award, NSF, 2006—; co-recipient Troland Rsch. award, NAS, 2009; fellow, Alfred P. Sloan Found. fellow, 2004—06; scholar, Pew Charitable Trust, 2004—08, McKnight Endowment Fund Neurosci., 2006—;, NSF fellow, 1990—93, MIT fellow, 1995—99, Princeton U. fellow, 1999—2003. Mem.: Soc. Neurosci. Achievements include research in neurophysiology of vision, movement and cognition. Avocations: travel, movies. Office: Stanford U Sch Medicine 300 Pasteur Dr Stanford CA 94305 Business E-Mail: tirin@stanford.edu.*

MOORE, VICTORIA, artist; b. San Diego, 1956; d. Howard Thornton and Jeanne Fuller M. Co-owner, v.p. prodn. Yellow Pages Publs., Inc.-Fla. Author: Inspired Art of Danny Hahlbohm. Mem. NAFE, Nat. Women in the Arts Found. Republican. Office: Yellow Page Publishers Inc 1906 Hollywood Blvd Hollywood FL 33020-4524

MOORE, VIRGINIA BRADLEY, librarian; b. Laurens, SC, May 13, 1932; d. Robert Otis Brown and Queen Esther (Smith) Bradley; m. David Lee Moore, Dec. 27, 1957 (div. 1973). BS, Winston-Salem State U., 1954; MLS, U. Md., 1970. Cert. in libr. sci. edn. Tchr. John R. Hawkins H.S., Warrenton, NC, 1954-55, Happy Plains H.S., Taylorsville, NC, 1955-58, Young and Carver elem. schs., Washington, 1958-65; libr. Davis and Minor elem. schs., Washington, 1965-72, Ballou Sr. H.S., Kramer Jr. H.S., Washington, 1972-75, 78-80, Anacostia Sr. H.S., Washington, 1975-77, 80-95; libr. I, adult svcs. Greenbelt (Md.) Br. Libr., 1997—. Dir. ch. libr. workshops Asbury United Meth. Ch., Washington, 1972—74, 1976; spkr., presenter Ch. and Synagogue Libr. Assn., 1975, 80, 83, spkr. spring workshop, 99, presenter, 2000; mem. serials com. Prince George's County Meml. Libr. Sys., 2000—05; chair-competency based curriculum D.C. pub. schs., 1978—93; chair local arrangements launching Nat. Sch. Libr. Media Month U.S. Capitol, 1985; mem. 1st libr. and info. sci. del. to People's Republic China, 1985; mem. faculty 1st established pub. svc. acad. in nation Anacostia Sr. H.S., 1990—95; coord. Nat. Libr. Week workshop Greenbelt Libr. Prince George's County Meml. Libr. Sys., 2002; presenter in field; host ch. chair spring workshops Ch. and Synagogue Libr. Coun., Nat. Capital Area, 2004. Author: (bibliography) The Negro in American History, 1619-1968, 1968; (with Helen E. Williams) Books By African-American Authors and Illustrators for Children and Young Adults, 1991; TV script for vacation reading program, 1971, sound/slide presentation D.C. Church Librs.' Bicentennial Celebration, 1976; video script and tchr.'s guide for Nat. Libr. Week Balloon Launch Day, 1983; bibliography Black Literature/Materials, 1987; contbr. articles to profl. jours. Co-chmn. nat. libr. involvement com. Martin Luther King, Jr. Fed. Holiday Commn., 1990—99, chmn., 1996—99; trustee LeRoy C. Merritt Humanitarian Fund, 2002—06; libr. Mt. Carmel Bapt. Ch., Washington, 1984, chair ch. libr. com., 2000—05, ad hoc com. for churchwide programs, 2001—05, libr. Sunday Sch. Mother's Day coord., 1990—94, jr. ch. pianist, 1994—97, Sunday Sch. adult dept. pianist, 1984—, co-chmn. African-Am. History Mo. commn., 1996—2005, chmn. publicity com., 1996—99, com. renovation of Rev. Arthur H. Pace Libr. Multipurpose Rm., vice-chair publicity liaison com., 1999—2005, soprano sanctuary choir, 1995—, soprano soloist women's day and tribute commemoration, 1998, music com., 1998—2005; chmn. social responsibilities roundtable Martin Luther King Jr. holiday task force Am. Libr. Assn., 1999—; rec. sec. Washington Pan-Hellenic Coun., 1975. Recipient Outstanding Congl. Libr., Ch. and Synagogue Libr. Assn., 2001, certs. of award, D.C. Pub. Libr., 1980, D.C. Pub. Schs., 1983; named outstanding educator, Mt. Carmel Bapt. Ch., 1984; fellow Grad. fellow, U. Md., 1969; scholar NDEA scholar, Central State Coll., Edmond, Okla., 1969, U. Ky., 1969, Ball State U., 1969. Mem. ALA (councilor-at-large 1983-91, 96—, com. on coms. 2005, Freedom to Read Honor Roll, 1999), LWV (sec. Prince George's County, Md. 1997-99, v.p. 1999-2000, pres. 2000-05, mem. lobby corps. 2004-, nominations chair Nat. Capital area 2005—2006), AARP, Internat. Assn. Sch. Librs., NEA (life), Am. Assn. Sch. Librs. (coms. 1973-83, 1987—), D.C. Assn. Sch. Librs. (pres. 1971-73, citation 1973, newsletter editor 1971-75, 83), Intellectual Freedom Com. (chmn. 1983-99), Freedom to Read Found., Soc. Sch. Librs. Internat. (charter), Intellectual Freedom Roundtable (bd. dirs. exec. com. 1989-91), D.C. Libr. Assn., Md. Libr. Assn., Md. Ednl. Media Orgn., Internat. Platform Assn., S.E. Neighbors Club, Am. First Day Cover Soc., Nat. Coun. Negro Women, Zeta Phi Beta (v.p. chpt. 1972-74), Delta Kappa Gamma (v.p. Alpha chpt. 1990-92, pres. 1992-95, Nu State D.C. membership chmn. 1991-92, 2002-, v.p. 1994-95, pres. 1995-97, liaison U.S. Forum 1995-97, 99—, spkr., state pres. 1997-99, steering com. spkr. Soc. Internat. Legis. seminar 1998, D.C. state del. Nat. Legis. Seminar 2006). Democrat. Achievements include being First Lady Laura Bush's guest at White House to launch Nat. Libr. Week, 2003. Home: 2100 Brooks Dr Apt 721 Forestville MD 20747-1016 Personal E-mail: vbmoore_99@yahoo.com.

MOORE, WARD WILFRED, medical educator; b. Cowden, Ill., Feb. 12, 1924; s. Cecil Everett and Velma Leona (Frye) M.; m. Frances Laura Campbell, Jan. 29, 1949; children— Scott Thomas, Ann Gail, Brian Dean, Kevin Lee. AB, U. Ill., 1948, MS, 1951, PhD, 1952; DSc (hon.), Mahidol U., Bangkok, 2001. Instr., rsch. assoc. U. Ill., 1952-54; asst. prof. Okla. State U., Stillwater, 1954-55, Ind. U., Bloomington, 1955-59, assoc. prof., 1959-66, prof. physiology, 1966-89, prof. physiology and biophysics emeritus, 1989—, acting chmn. dept. anatomy, 1971-73, assoc. dean basic med. scis., 1971-89, assoc. dean, dir. med. scis. program, 1976-89. Vis. prof. Postgrad. Med. Center, Karachi, Pakistan, 1963-64; staff mem. Rockefeller Found., 1968-71; vis. prof., chmn. dept. physiology, faculty sci. Mahidol U., Bangkok, Thailand, 1968-71 Served with U.S. Army, 1943-46. Mem. Am. Physiol. Soc., Endocrine Soc., Am. Soc. Nephrology, Soc. Study Reproduction, Am. Assn. Anatomists, Soc. Exptl. Biology and Medicine, Am. Assn. Med. Colls., AAAS, Am. Inst. Biol. Scis., AAUP, Ind. Acad. Sci., Ind. Hist. Soc., Shelby County (Ill.) Hist. Soc., Monroe County (Ind.) Hist. Soc., Soc. Sons of Am. Revolution, Sigma Xi, Phi Sigma. Home: 3500 E Bradley St Bloomington IN 47401-4201 Office: Indiana U Jordan Hall # 105 Bloomington IN 47405 Business E-Mail: moorew@indiana.edu.

MOORE, WESLEY SANFORD, vascular surgeon; b. San Bernardino, Calif., Aug. 1, 1935; s. Louis and Anna M.; m. Patricia Lorenz, Oct. 25, 1960; children: Edward Lorenz, Michael Robertson. BS, U. So. Calif., 1955; MD, U. Calif., 1959. Diplomate: Am. Bd. Surgery (examiner 1980). Intern U. Calif., San Francisco, 1959-60; asst. resident gen. surgery U. Calif. Hosps., San Francisco, 1960-63, chief resident, 1963-64; chief vascular surgery VA Hosp., 1966-77, asst. chief surgery service, 1975-77; asst. prof., surgery U. Calif. Sch. Medicine, San Francisco, 1968—73, assoc. prof., 1973—77; practice medicine specializing in vascular surgery San Francisco, 1966-77; chief, vascular surgery sect. Ariz. Health Scis., 1977—80, VA Hosp., 1977—80; prof. surgery U. Ariz. Coll. Medicine, Tuscon, 1977—80; chief vascular surgery section UCLA Sch. Medicine, 1980—96, chief emeritus, div. vascular surgery, 1996—2004, prof. surgery, 1980—2004; prof., chief emeritus David Geffen Sch. Medicine UCLA, divsn. vascular surgeon, 2004—. Cons. Blue Cross of Calif., Med. Policy Com., 1987—96. Mem. editorial bd. Stroke, 1981—, Jour. Vascular Surgery, 1983—, Annals of Vascular Surgery, 1985—; assoc. editor Vascular Surgery; contbr. over 290 articles on vascular surgery to profl. jours., 195 chpts. to med. texts; editor or co-editor: Vascular Surgery, 1977, 3d edit. 1989, Vascular Surgery: A Comprehensive Review, 1983, 2d edit., 1986, 3rd edit, 1991, 4th edit. 1993, 5th edit. 1998, 6th edit. 2001,Surgery for Cerebrovascular Disease, 1987, 2d edit., 1996, Lower Extremity Amputation, 1989, Endovascular Surgery, 1989, 2d edit., 1992, Cerebrovascular Iscnaemia: Investigation and Management, 1992, Vascular and endovascular Surgery, A Comprehensive Review, 7th edit., 2006 Served to capt., M.C. U.S. Army, 1964-66. Capt. Army Med. Corps, 1964—66, Germany. NIH grantee, 1973-76 Fellow A.C.S. (sec. treas. No. Calif. chpt. 1971-77), Am. Heart Assn. (council on cerebrovascular disease), Am. Surg. Assn.; mem. Internat. Cardiovascular Soc. (membership com. 1977—), Soc. for Vascular Surgery (sec. 1980, pres. 1986-87), Assn. Acad. Surgery, Western Vascular Soc. (founder 1985, pres. 1991-92), San Francisco Surg. Soc., Los Angeles Surg. Soc., Soc. of Univ. Surgeons, Assn. VA Surgeons, Pacific Coast Surg. Assn., Bay Area Vascular Soc. (sec. 1967-77), Rocky Mountain Vascular Soc. (founding mem. 1979, pres. 1979-80), Phi Beta Kappa. Office: David Geffen Sch Medicine at UCLA 200 Medical Plaza Rm 510-6 Los Angeles CA 90095

MOORE, WILLARD S., oceanographer, educator; s. Ross H. and Alice Sutton Moore; m. Virginia Saunders, June 13, 1980. BS, Millsaps Coll., Jackson, 1962; MA, Columbia U., NYC, 1965; PhD, SUNY Stony Brook, 1969. Oceanographer US Naval Oceanog. Office, Chesapeake Beach, Md., 1969—76; post-doc. fellow Tata Inst. Fundamental Rsch., Bombay, 1970—71; prof. U. SC, Columbia, SC, 1976—2000, rsch. prof., 2000—, disting. prof. emeritus, 2000—; adj. scientist Woods Hole Oceanog. Instn., Mass., 2001—04; faculty mem. Semester Sea, Pitts., 2004. Dept. chair U. SC, 1980—84; sci. steering com. NSF Future Ocean Chemistry in US, Arlington, Va., Coastal Ocean Processes, Washington; advisor IAEA, Vienna; com. reference materials ocean sci. Nat. Acad. Sci., Washington. Contbr. articles to profl. jours. Recipient B.H. Ketchum award, Woods Hole Oceanog. Instn., 1999, Disting. Alumni, SUNY, Stony Brook, 2007, Edn. Found. award, U. SC, 1993; Fellow, Am. Geophys. Union, 2006, Hanse-Wissenschaftskolleg, 2008—, Rsch. Grants, NSF, 1975—2008. Fellow: Am. Geophys. Union, Explorers Club (chair, greater piedmont chpt. 1995—96); mem.: AAAS, Geol. Soc. Am., Oceanog. Soc. (life), Geochem. Soc. Achievements include patents for fibrous filtering material and preparation thereof. Home: 1300 Louis LeConte Rd Hopkins SC 29061 Business E-Mail: moore@geol.sc.edu.

MOORE, WILLIAM B., energy executive; m. Shelly Moore; 2 children. BBA, Wichita State U., 1974. Fin. asst. Westar Energy, Inc., Topeka, 1978, v.p. fin., 1985, exec. v.p., CFO, treas, 1998—2000, exec. v.p., COO, 2002—06, pres., COO, 2006—07, pres., CEO, 2007—; sr. mng. dir., sr. adv. Saber Ptnrs., LLC, 2000—02. Chmn. bd., v.p. electric divsn. KGE. Mem. exec. bd. Wichita Area C. of C.; chair Goodwill Industries, Easter Seals Kans., United Way Plains, 2004; mem. exec. com. of bd. dirs. Wichita State U. Found.; bd. dirs. Kans. Sports Hall of Fame, Intrust Fin. Corp., Shocker Athletic Scholarship Orgn., Wichita Insight. Office: Westar Energy Inc 818 S Kansas Ave Topeka KS 66612 Office Phone: 785-575-6300.

MOORE, WILLIAM HENRY, radiologist; b. Pompton, NJ, Dec. 6, 1973; m. Rebecca Anne Case, May 30, 1999; 1 child, Charlotte Catherine. MD, Albany Med. Coll., N.Y. 1999. Diplomate Am. Bd. Radiology. Intern Albany Med. Ctr., 1999—2000; resident in radiology U. Hosp., Stony Brook, NY, 2000—04, chief thoracic imaging, 2004—; vis. fellow thoracic imaging NYU, NYC, 2003—04; dir. med. student edn., dept. radiology Stony Brook U. Med. Ctr., 2005—, med. dir., dept. radiology, 2007—, radiology program dir., residency tng. radiology. Contbr. articles to profl. jours. Recipient Roentgen Rsch. award, 2003, Outstanding Tchr., Stony Brook Med. Sch., 2008; named Tchr. of Yr., 2005, Outstanding Tchr., Stony Brook Med. Sch., 2006. Mem.: Soc. Thoracic Radiologist (sr.), Alpha Omega Alpha, A3CR2 (assoc.; vice chair problem solving 2002—03). Office Fax: 631-444-7538. Business E-Mail: william.moore@stonybrook.edu.

MOORE, WILLIAM VEGH, sports medicine physician; b. Berkeley, Calif., Apr. 26, 1974; s. Raymond Houston Moore, Jr. and Letitia Mary Moore; m. Patricia Ann Ash, Mar. 19, 2005; 1 child, Stephen Raymond. BS in Biol. Scis. cum laude, U. Calif., Davis, 1996; MD, Tulane U., New Orleans, 2001. Diplomate Am. Bd. Phys. Medicine and Rehab., 2007. Internship Tucson Hosps. Med. Edn. Program, 2001—02; resident physician, dept. functional restoration, divsin phys. medicine and rehab. Stanford U., Calif., 2002—05; fellow sports medicine, dept. phys. medicine and rehab. Johns Hopkins, Balt., 2005—06; spine and sports physician Mission Peak Orthop. Med. Group, Fremont, Calif., 2006—07; sports medicine physician Kaiser Permanente, Union City, Calif., 2007—. Contbr. chapters to books, articles to profl. jours. Vol. League Volunteers Newark, Calif., 1994—95; co-chmn. young democrats U. Calif., Davis, 1993—94. Recipient Outstanding Performance in Biol. Scis. award, U. Calif., 1996; named Resident of Yr., Stanford U., 2005. Mem.: Am. Coll. Sports Medicine, Phi Kappa Phi, Phi Sigma, Golden Key. Democrat-Npl. Roman Catholic. Avocations: tennis, weightlifting, reading.

MOORE, WILLIS HENRY ALLPHIN, history educator; b. NYC, Dec. 14, 1940; s. Carl Allphin and Mary Catherine (Moody) M.; children: Patrick Kakela, Michael Kirby, Catherine Malia. BA Letters, U. Okla., 1962; MEd in Adminstrn., U. Hawaii, 1971. Teaching asst. dept. history U. Hawaii, 1962-64; dir. edn. Bernice P. Bishop Mus., Honolulu, 1967-76; pres. Hawaii Geog. Soc., Honolulu, 1976-78, exec. sec., editor, 1978—. Mem. Hawaii Com. for Humanities, 1976—78; producer, narrator film-lecture programs Nat. Audubon Soc. and travelogue forums; instr. in history, religion and polit. sci. Chaminade U. of Honolulu, 1986—; instr. Hawaii Prison Sys. Co-author/co-editor Hawaii Parklands, Sociological History of Honolulu, Total Solar Eclipse Over Hawaii, 1991, Christmas Comes to Hawaii; contbr. articles to newspapers and other publs. Mem. Am. Mus. Assn., Pacific Sci. Assn., Hawaii Mus. Assn. (pres.), Hawaii Pub. Radio, Am. Guild Organists, Sierra Club (chmn. Hawaii chpt. 1973-75), Hawaiian Hist. Soc., Nat. Soc. Arts and Letters, Hawaii Chpt. (pres. 2009-), Nat. Episcopal Historians and Archivists (pres., editor), Historical Soc. Episcopal Ch. (bd. trustees). Office: PO Box 1698 Honolulu HI 96806-1698 Home Phone: 808-521-7779; Office Phone: 800-538-3950, 808-538-3952. Personal E-mail: profwillishamoore@gmail.com.

MOORE, WISTAR, cardiovascular surgeon; b. Feb. 16, 1959; BA, U. N.C., 1981, MD, 1985. Bd. cert. gen. surgery, thoracic surgery. Gen. surgery resident Mass. Gen. Hosp., 1985-90; cardiothoracic resident The Emory Clinic, 1990-93; cardiovasc. surgeon Watson Clinic, Lakeland, Fla., 1993-2000; chief divsn. cardiovasc. thoracic surgery Lakeland Regional Med. Ctr., 1996-2000; cardiovasc. surgeon Cardiovasc. Surgeons, Orlando, Fla., 2000—04, Leesburg-Ocala Heart Inst., 2004—. Fellow ACS, Am. Coll. Chest Physicians; mem. Fla. Soc. Thoracic and Cardiovasc. Surgeons, So. Thoracic Surg. Assn., Soc. Thoracic Surgeons. Office: 700 Doctors Ct Leesburg FL 34748

MOORE-JUMONVILLE, KIMBERLY, literature educator; b. Lubbock, Tex., Oct. 7, 1958; d. Darrell Paul and Donna (Browning) Moore; m. Robert Stuart Moore-Jumonville, Jan. 1, 1982; 1 child, Annesley. BA in English, Seattle Pacific U., 1981; MPhil in 19th Century Studies, Drew U., 1987, PhD in 19th Century Studies, 1991. Asst. prof. English Taylor U., Upland, Ind., 1992—98, assoc. prof. English, 1998—2001, Spring Arbor (Mich.) U., 2001—09, chmn. English Dept., 2002—. Mem.: Modern Lang. Assn., Christianty and Lit., Dorothy Sayers Soc. Office: Spring Arbor Univ English Dept 106 E Main St Spring Arbor MI 49283 Office Phone: 517-750-6692.

MOORER, ANNETTE JOHNSON See WYNDEWICKE, KIONNE

MOORER, DOUGLASS CHARLES, educator; b. Birmingham, Ala., May 5, 1951; s. Charles and Lou Ethel (Thornton) M.; BS, Ala. State U., 1975; MS US Sports Acad., 1987. Cert. Level I coach, USA Volleyball,

1994; ordained Roman Catholic deacon, Ala., 2005. Instr., Lawson State Community Coll., Ala., 1974-76; Tchr. Corps Project community coord. Miles Coll., Fairfield, Ala., 1976-77; elem. sch. tchr. Birmingham Bd. Edn., 1977—; athletic trainer Summer Youth Sports program, Miles Coll., 1977-82, G.W. Carver High Sch., 1978—. Vol. water safety instr. ARC, 1969-82, CPR instr., 1980—, instr., trainer water safety, lifeguarding, first aide and CPR; Boys' Club worker, 1969-73, 78-81; vol. Epiphany Ministries, 1992-, Kiaros Ministries Ala., 1997-. Recipient Vol. Service award ARC, 1980, 81, 85, 86, Svc. award Upward Bound Program, 1979; named Volleyball Coach of Yr., Birmingham City Schs., 2005. Mem. Assn. for Secondary Curriculum Devel., Nat. Assn. Sports Ofcls., Nat. Fedn. Interscholastic Ofcls. Assn., Nat. Athletic Trainers Assn. (assoc.), Am. Volleyball Coaches Assn., AAHPERD, Ambitious Adults, Foresters, Knights of St. Peter Claver, Knights Columbus Coun. (3rd degree mem.), Omega Psi Phi, Alpha Kappa Mu. Republican. Roman Catholic. Home: 3140 Spaulding St SW Birmingham AL 35221-1919 Office: Birmingham Bd Edn 4811 Court J Birmingham AL 35208-1720 Office Phone: 205-427-7885. Personal E-mail: dougmoorer@hotmail.com. Business E-Mail: dougmoor@bellsouth.net.

MOORER, EMILY HALL, literature and language educator; d. William H. and Mary R. Hall; m. William Louis Moorer; children: William Chadwick, Gregory Alan. MA, U. Ala., Tuscaloosa. Cert. profl. tchr. Nat. Bd., 1999, tchr. Miss. English instr. Hinds CC., Raymond, Miss., 2002—.

MOORE-SICKMANN, SUSAN, psychologist; d. Carl Henry and Sue Watkins Moore; m. Thomas William Sickmann, June 22, 1986; children: Zachary Thomas Sickmann, Matthew William Sickmann. BA, Baylor U., Waco, Tex., 1977; MA, U. Tex., San Antonio, 1984. Tchr. Wash. Irving Jr. Sch., San Antonio, 1978—78; sch. counselor Rose Garden Schertz Elem. Schs., Universal City, 1986—88, Oak Grove Elem. Sch., San Antonio, 1988—90, St. Mary's Hall, 1990—; journalism Samuel Clemens H.S., Schertz, english tchr., 1978—86. Christian. Avocations: cycling, reading, parenting, living, laughing. Home: 234 Devonshire San Antonio TX 78209 Office: St Mary's Hall 9401 Starcrest San Antonio TX 78217 Office Fax: 210-655-3000. Business E-Mail: smoore@smhall.org.

MOORE-WLEKLINSKI, PATRICIA MARIE, secondary school educator; b. Syracuse, NY, Oct. 10, 1956; d. John William and Mary Jane Moore; m. John Joseph Wleklinski, Aug. 18, 1984; 1 child, Alyssa Jane Wleklinski. BS in Elem. Edn., SUNY, Cortland, 1978, MEd, 1990. Cert. elem. tchr. NY. Elem. tchr. St. Ann's Sch., Syracuse, 1982—85; English tchr. Christian Bros. Acad., Syracuse, 1985—2005. Varsity cheerleading coach West Genesee Sr. HS, Camillus, NY, 1978—85; majorette instr. Liverpool HS, NY, 1975—78, Cicero-North Syracuse HS, Cicero, NY, 1978—81, Syracuse U., 1981—83, West Genesee Alumni Bd., 2001, Genesee Alumni Bd., 2006. Basketball support chmn. Empire State Games, Syracuse, 1982—2006; religious edn. tchr. St. Joseph's Ch., Camillus, 2001—08, eucharistic min. and lector, 2001—04. Recipient Outstanding Educator for a Merrill Presdl. scholar, Cornell U., 2005, Coach's Achievement award, Onondaga HS League, 1994. Mem.: Nat. Cath. Educators Assn., NY State English Coun., Nat. Coun. Tchrs. English. Roman Catholic. Avocations: reading, music, puzzles, twirling. Personal E-mail: pmmw10@twcny.rr.com.

MOORHEAD, ALAN R., internal auditor; BS, Drake U.; MS, Troy State U. CPA, cert. info. sys. auditor. V.p., audit dir. Assurant Inc.; dir., internal audit HNI Corp., 2006—08, v.p., internal audit, 2008—. Office: HNI Corp 408 E Second St Muscatine IA 52761 Office Phone: 563-272-7400. Office Fax: 563-272-7655.*

MOORHEAD, GERALD LEE, architect; b. Davenport, Iowa, Feb. 18, 1947; s. Wayne Lee and Marilou (George) M. BA, Rice U., 1969, BArch, 1971. Arch. Middleton & Statton, El Paso, Tex., 1967, MA Floyd Assocs., Houston, 1968, CRS Design Inc., Houston, 1969-70, Phillips & Peterson AIA, Houston, 1969-73; arch., v.p. Charles Tapley Assocs., Houston, 1973-83; propr. Lloyd Jones Fillpot Assocs., 1986-87, Gerald Moorhead, Arch., 1983-98; sr. assoc. Bailey Archs., 1998—. Photography exhibited in group shows at Galveston Arts Coun., Tex., 1976, Jewish Cmty. Ctr., Houston, 1977, Cronin Gallery, Houston, 1977; one-man photog. exhbns. include Autry Ho. Gallery, Houston, 1979; editor, photographer: Houston Architectural Guide, 1999, Buildings of Texas; editor: Houston Architectural Ballade, 2000; contbg. editor Tex. Arch., Arthtl. Record; contbr. articles on architecture to profl. publs.; exhbn. curator Houston Mus. Natural Sci., 1990, Mus. Fine Arts, Houston, 1991, FotoFest, Houston, 1996. Treas. Houston Ctr. for Photography, 1985-87. Recipient Spl. award Houston AIA/Houston Home & Garden, 1979, Internat. prize Union Archs. Kazakstan, 1991; named Arch. Laureate of Kazakstan, 1992. Fellow AIA (Honor award Houston chpt. 1979, Young Arch. award Houston chpt. 1985); mem. Soc. Archtl. Historians, Nat. Trust for Hist. Preservation, Tex. Soc. Archs. (1st Honor award 1976, Interiors award 1986, Flowers Journalism award 1995), Rice Design Alliance. Home: 1755 W Main Ave Houston TX 77098-3607

MOORHEAD, LUCY GALPIN, writer; b. NYC, Jan. 24, 1926; d. Perrin Comstock and Stephanie (English) Galpin; m. William S. Moorhead, Jr., 1946 (dec. 1987); children: William S., Lucy Perrin M. Grayson, Stephen G., James B. BA, Vassar Coll., Poughkeepsie, NY, 1946. Author: Entertaining in Washington, 1978, Dolly Appleton, (a novel) In the Town and In the Country (a memoir), 2004. Mem. Chevy Chase Club, Dau. of the Cin. Episcopalian. Avocations: fox-hunting, painting.

MOORHEAD, SYLVESTER ANDREW, retired education educator; b. Denver, Feb. 23, 1920; s. Ray Rodney and Cora Margaret (Payne) M.; m. Katherine May Schlessman, July 21, 1945; children: Rodney A., Sylvia Kay, Kent A., Pamela Ann. BA, U. No. Colo., 1942; PhD, Stanford U., 1950. Tchr. secondary sch., Redwood City, Calif., 1947-48, Sunnyvale, Calif., 1948-49; mem. faculty U. Miss., 1949—, prof. edn., 1955—, dean U. Sch. Edn., 1961-85, dean emeritus, 1985—. Contbr. articles profl. jours. Served with USAAF, 1942-45. Mem. NEA (life), Kappa Delta Pi, Phi Delta Kappa. Lodges: Rotary. Baptist. Home: 211 Vivian St Oxford MS 38655-2719

MOORING, F. PAUL, physics editor; b. Pitt County, NC, Feb. 6, 1921; s. Benjamin Arthur and Amanda Elizabeth (Congleton) M.; m. Jean Louise Carpenter, Aug. 28, 1948; children: Cecily Hamm, Carol Larson, Margaret Calderon. BA, Duke U., 1944; PhD, U. Wis., 1951. Instr. Duke U., Durham, NC, 1943-46; teaching asst. U. Wis., Madison, 1946-50, rsch. asst., 1950-51; physicist Argonne (Ill.) Nat. Lab., 1951-83; editor, cons. Am. Inst. Physics, Argonne, 1983—. Adj. prof. St. Louis U., 1966-83. Contbr. articles to profl. jours. Pres. The Ill. Prairie Path, Wheaton, Ill., 1971-93, Ill. Audubon Soc., Wayne, Ill., 1978-81. Fulbright Rsch. fellow U. Helsinki, 1962-63. Mem. AAAS, Am. Phys. Soc, DuPage County Environ. Commn. Democrat. Home: 295 Abbotsford Ct Glen Ellyn IL 60137-4803 E-mail: fmooring@aol.com.

MOORMAN, CHARLES W., transportation executive; b. Hattiesburg, Miss. Grad., Ga. Tech. Univ., Harvard Bus. Sch. With Norfolk Southern Corp., 1970—, v.p. employee rels., 1992—93, v.p. info. tech., 1993—99; pres. Thoroughbred Tech. & Telecommunications, 1999—2003; sr. v.p. corp. planning & svc. Norfolk Southern Corp., 2003—04, pres., 2005—, CEO, 2005—, chmn., 2006—. Office: Norfolk Southern Corp 3 Commercial Pl Norfolk VA 23510-2191

MOORMAN, RICHARD HAL, IV, lawyer; b. Waco, Tex., Mar. 2, 1950; s. George R. and Billie (Scoggin) M.; m. Lucy Baker, May 24, 1974; children: Theodore Clark, Lydia Anne, Peter Baker. BCE, MIT, 1971; JD, So. Meth. U., 1976. Bar: Tex. 1976, U.S. Dist. Ct. (so. dist., we. dist., ea. dist.) Tex. 1976, U.S. Ct. Appeals (5th cir.) 1976; Bd. Cert. Civil Trial Law and Estate Planning and Probate Law, Tex. Bd. of Legal Specialization. Engr. Turner Collie & Braden, Houston, 1971-72, P.G. Bell Co., Houston, 1972-73; ptnr. Moorman Tate Moorman Urquhart & Haley L.L.P., Brenham, Tex., 1976—. Bd. dirs. Washington County Abstract Co., Brenham; bd. mem. Trinity Med. Ctr. Hosp.; past examiner (2002) Tex. Bd. of Legal Specialization; course dir. State Bar of Tex. Advanced Estate Planning and Probate Seminar. Editor: Real Property Probate and Trust Law Jour. Mem. Tex. Air Control Bd., Austin, 1980-86; past pres. Washington on Brazos State Pk. Assn., Brenham, Brenham Downtown Assn. Named one of Tex. Superlawyers. Fellow Am. Coll. Trust and Estate Counsel, State Chair Tex. Bar Found.; mem. ABA (estate gift tax com.), State Bar of Tex. (coun. mem. real estate probate and trust sect.), Washington County C. of C. (pres.); Main Street Bd, Elder: Brenham Bible Ch. Avocations: antiques, hunting, fishing, theology. Office: Moorman Tate Moorman Urquhart Haley LLP 207 E Main St Brenham TX 77833-3754 Office Phone: 979-836-5664. Business E-Mail: hmoorman@moormantate.com.

MOORMAN, TED, finance educator; b. Brenham, Tex., Jan. 4, 1979; s. Richard Hal and Lucy Baker Moorman; m. Sara Lynn Eisenbarth, Aug. 21, 2004; children: Evelynn Elizabeth, Della Grace. BA in Bus. Economics, Wheaton Coll., Ill., 2001; PhD in Fin., Tex. A&M U., College Station, 2005. Vis. asst. prof., fin. U. NH, Durham, 2005—06; asst. prof., fin. Northern Ill. U., DeKalb, 2006—. Contbr. articles to profl. jours. Steering com. mem., DeKalb. Finalist Wheeler award, Numeric Investors, Boston, 2008. Mem.: Western Fin. Assn., Fin. Mgmt. Assn., Am. Fin. Assn. Office: Northern Ill Univ Dept Fin Dekalb IL 60115 Office Fax: 815-753-0504. Business E-Mail: tmoorman@niu.edu.

MOORMAN, WILLIAM A., federal judge, retired career military officer; b. Chgo. BA in History and Econs., U. Ill., 1967, JD, 1970; Grad., Air Command. & Staff Coll., Maxwell AFB, 1980; student Nat. War Coll., 1988—89. Commd. 2d lt. USAF, 1970, advanced through grades to maj. gen., 1999, ret., 2002; chief of contracts Air Force Comm. Svc., Richards-Gebaur AFB, Mo., 1971—74; chief of claims 475th Air Base Wing and 5th Air Force, Yokota AB, Japan, 1974-77; dep. staff judge advocate then staff judge advocate 31st Tactical Fighter Wing, Homestead AFB, Fla., 1977-79; staff judge advocate 832nd Air Divsn., Luke AFB, Ariz., 1980-83; chief preventive law and legal air group, then chief Office of the Judge Advocate Gen., Washington, 1983-88; staff judge advocate 12th Air Force/US Southern Command Air Forces, Bergstrom AFB, Tex., 1989-91; dep. staff judge advocate Strategic Air Command, Offutt AFB, Nebr., 1991-92, staff judge advocate, 1992-93, Hdqrs. USAF Europe, Ramstein AB, Germany, 1993-95; comdr. Air Force Legal Svcs. Agy., Bolling AFB, D.C., 1995-96; staff judge advocate Hdqs. Air Combat Command, Langley AFB, Va., 1996—99; judge JAG Hdqs., USAF, Washington, 1999—2003, US Ct. Appeals Veterans' Claims, Washington, 2004—. Decorated Legion of Merit with oak leaf cluster. Office: US Ct Appeals Veterans Claims 625 Indiana Ave NW Ste 900 Washington DC 20004*

MOOS, H. WARREN, physicist, educator, astronomer, director; b. NYC, Mar. 26, 1936; s. Henry H. and Dorothy E. (Warren) M.; m. Doris Elaine McClure, July 13, 1957; children: Janet, Paul, Daniel, David. BS, Brown U., 1957; MA, U. Mich., 1959, PhD, 1962. Rsch. assoc. Stanford (Calif.) U., 1961-63; acting asst. prof. Johns Hopkins U., Balt., 1963-64, asst. prof., 1964-68, assoc. prof., 1968-71, prof., 1971—2008, dir. Ctr. for Astrophys. Scis., 1988-93, chmn. Physics & Astronomy, 1993-96, res. prof., 2008—. Cons. in field; mem. com. on planetary and lunar exploration NRC/Nat. Acad. Sci., Washington, 1982-86; mem. space and earth sci. adv. com. NASA, Washington, 1984-87; vis. fellow Joint Inst. for Lab. Astrophysics, 1972-73, 80-81. Co-editor Optical Properties of Ions in Crystals, 1967, Astrophysics in the Far Ultraviolet: Five Years of Discovery with Fuse, 2006, Future Directions in Ultraviolet Spectroscopy, 2009; contbr. over 300 articles to profl. jours. Trustee Associated Univs., Inc., 2002—, chair bd. trustees, 2004—08. Sloan Found. fellow, 1965-69. Fellow Am. Phys. Soc.; mem. Am. Astron. Soc., Internat. Astron. Union. Achievements include prin. investigatorof far ultraviolet spectroscopic explorer; co-investigator of Apollo 17 ultraviolet spectrometer, of Hopkins Ultraviolet Telescope, of Voyager ultraviolet spectrometer, of space telescope imaging spectograph; research on astrophysics and fusion plasma diagnostics. Office: Johns Hopkins U Dept Physics & Astronomy 34th & Charles Sts Baltimore MD 21218

MOOS, RUDOLF H., psychologist, researcher; b. Berlin, Sept. 10, 1934; s. Henry R. and Herta M. (Ehrlich) M.; m. Bernice Schradski, June 9, 1963; children: Karen, Kevin. BA in Psychology, U. Calif., Berkeley, 1956, PhD, 1960. Mem. faculty psychiatry Stanford (Calif.) U., 1962—, dir. psychiatry research tng. program, 1967-92, prof. psychiatry, 1972—, dir. social ecology lab., 1967-92; sr. rsch. career scientist VA Med. Center, Palo Alto, Calif., 1981—, dir. Ctr. for Health Care Evaluation, 1984—2002, dir. Program Evaluation and Resource Ctr., 1990-99. Vis. prof. Inst. Psychiatry, also Maudsley and Royal Bethlem Hosp., London, 1969-70 Author: Issues in Social Ecology, 1974, Evaluating Treatment Environments, 1974, Health and the Social Environment, 1974, Evaluating Correctional and Community Settings, 1975, Human Adaptation Coping with Life Crises, 1976, The Human Context, 1976, Environment and Utopia, 1977, Coping with Physical Illness, 1977, Evaluating Educational Environments, 1979, Coping with Physical Illness: New Perspectives, 1984, Coping with Life Crises: An Integrated Approach, 1986, Alcoholism Treatment: Content, Process and Outcome, 1990, Group Residential Facilities for Older Adults, 1994, Evaluating Residential Facilities, 1996; mem. editl. bd. Jour. Behavioral Medicine, 1984-04, Internat. Jour. Therapeutic Cmtys., Prevention in Human Svcs., Psychosomatic Medicine, Evaluation and Program Planning, 1977-99, Jour. Personality and Social Psychology, 1985-91, Health Psychology: An Internat. Jour., 1985-97, Violence, Agression, and Terrorism, 1985-94, Jour. Substance Abuse, 1986-2001, Jour. Applied Gerontology, 1988-2005, Jour. Cmty. and Applied Social Psychology, Psychology and Aging, 1986-91, Environ. and Behavior, 1987-91, Indian Jour. Clin. Psychology, 1996-2002, Jour. Studies Alcohol, 1997, Am. Jour. Cmty. Psychology, 1998—, Pakistan Jour. Psychol. Rsch., 2005, Internat. Jour. Clin. and Health Psychology, 2006; assoc. editor: Ency. of Psychological Assessment. Fellow APA, Acad. Clin. Psychology, Acad. Behavioral Medicine, Soc. Behavioral Medicine, Am. Orthopsychiat. Assn., Nat. Inst. on Alcohol Abuse and Alcoholism (mem. coun.); mem. Am. Sociol. Assn., Am. Psychosomatic Assn. (mem. coun.). Home: 25661 W Fremont Rd Los Altos CA 94022-1600 Office: Stanford U Dept Psychiatry MC 5550 Palo Alto CA 94305

MOOSA, AHMED SHAFEEQ IBRAHIM (SAPPÉ), journalist; b. Maldives, Nov. 4, 1968; arrived in UK, 2003; m. Miranda Moosa, 1993 (div. 2002); 3 children; m. Fathimath Moosa, 2002; 2 children. BEng with honors, U. Glasgow, 1995; MPhil Eng., U. Birmingham, 1997. Mktg. exec. Travelin Maldives Pvt. Ltd., mktg., rsch. & devel. cons.; sr. engr. Maldives Transport & Contracting Co.; founding chmn., mng. dir. A Co. Pvt. Ltd., 1999—2003; dir. bus. devel. & e-commerce Sun Travels & Tours Pvt. Ltd.; mgr. Haruge Café, Malé, 2001—03, Dhiraagu Cyber Café, Malé, 2002; dir. Horizon Fisheries Pvt. Ltd., Malé, 2003; founder, editor-in-chief Dhivehi Observer, 2003—. Mem. gen. council Maldivian Democratic Party, 2003—. Office: c/o Dr DJ Balance University of Glasgow Glasgow G12 8QQ Scotland Office Phone: 44-7932-939-103. E-mail: amoosa@gmail.com, asimoosa@hotmail.com, dhivehiobserver@gmail.com.

MOOSSA, A. R., surgeon, educator; b. Port Louis, Mauritius, Oct. 10, 1939; s. Yacoob and Maude (Rochecoute) M.; m. Denise Willoughby, Dec. 28, 1973; children: Pierre, Noel, Claude, Valentine. BS, U. Liverpool, Eng., 1962, MD (hon.), 1965; postgrad., Johns Hopkins U., 1972—73, U. Chgo., 1973—74. Intern Liverpool Royal Infirmary, 1965—66; resident United Liverpool Hosps. and Alder Hey Children's Hosp., 1966—72; from asst. prof. surgery to assoc. prof. U. Chgo., 1975-77, prof., dir. surg. rsch., chief gen. surgery svc., vice chmn. dept., 1977-83; chmn. dept. surgery U. Calif.-San Diego Med. Ctr., 1983—2004, disting. prof., surgery, emeritus chmn., assoc. dean, spl. counsel clin. affairs, 2004—. Litchfield lectr. U., Oxford, Eng., 1978; praelector in surgery U. Dundee, Scotland, 1979; Hampson Trust vis. prof. U. Liverpool, 1992, G.B. Ong. vis. prof. U. Hong Kong, 1993, Philip Sandblon vis. prof. U. Lund, Sweden. Editor: Tumors of the Pancreas, 1982, Essential Surgical Practice, 1983, 4th edit., 2000, Comprehensive Textbook of Oncology, 1985, 2d edit., 1991, Gastrointestinal Emergencies, 1985, Problems in General Surgery, 1989, Operative Colorectal Surgery, 1993. Fellow Royal Coll. Surgeons (Hunterian prof. 1977); mem. ACS, Am. Surg. Assn., Soc. Univ. Surgeons, Am. Soc. Clin. Oncology, European Surg. Assn. Office: U Calif San Diego Thornton Hosp 9300 Campus Point Dr 7212 La Jolla CA 92037 Office Phone: 858-657-6112. Business E-Mail: amoossa@ucsd.edu.

MOOSSY, JOHN, neurologist, consultant, pathologist; b. Shreveport, La., Aug. 24, 1925; s. John Yazbeck and Rose (Ferris) M.; m. Yvonne Reese, Mar. 15, 1951; children: John Jefferson, Joan Marie. MD, Tulane U., 1950. Intern Charity Hosp. of New Orleans, 1950-51, neurology resident, 1951-53; neuropathology fellow Columbia U. Coll. of Physicians and Surgeons, NYC, 1953-54; assoc., lectr. in neuropathology Tulane U. Sch. Medicine, New Orleans, 1954-57; asst. to prof. in pathology, neurology La. State U., New Orleans, 1957-65; prof. pathology, grad. faculty U. Pitts., 1965-67; prof. pathology neuropathology Bowman Gray Sch. of Medicine, Winston-Salem, NC, 1967-72; prof. pathology and neurology, dir. div. neuropathology U. Pitts., 1972-93, emeritus prof., 1993—. Dir. Cerebrovascular Disease Study, World Fedn. of Neurology, Antwerp, Belgium, 1960-61; cons. Armed Forces Inst. of Pathology, Washington, 1977—, mem. sci. adv. bd., Washington, 1984-86. Editor: Cerebral Vascular Disease Seventh Conference, 1970, Cerebrovascular Diseases 12th Research Conference, 1981; editor-in-chief Jour. Neuropathology and Exptl. Neurology, 1981-91; mem. editorial bd. Archives Neurology, 1982-92. Recipient Excellence in Teaching award U. Pitts. Sch. of Medicine, 1987-88; named Commencement Speaker U. Pitts. Sch. of Medicine, 1989. Mem. Am. Acad. Neurology (sec.-treas. 1963-655), Am. Neurol. Assn. (v.p. 1977-78), Am. Assn. Neuropathologists (pres. 1974-75, Neuropathology award 1992), Internat. Soc. Neuropathology, Coun. Biology Editors.

MOOTE, A. LLOYD, history professor; b. Hamilton, Ont., Can., Mar. 22, 1931; s. Stanley Alanson and Esther Grace (Wood) M.; m. Barbara Brown, Dec. 27, 1956 (div. 1982); children: Karen, Peter, Daphne, Robert; m. Dorothy Carter May, May 30, 1986. BA, U. Toronto, 1954; MA, U. Minn., Mpls., 1956, PhD, 1958. Tchg. asst. U. Minn., Mpls., 1955-58; lectr. U. Toronto, 1958-61; asst. prof. U. Cin., 1961-62; from asst. prof. to prof. history U. So. Calif., LA, 1962-92, prof emeritus, 1993—. Vis. prof. Queen's U., Kingston, Ont., 1965-66; chmn. gen. edn. program U. So. Calif., 1978-81; mem. Inst. Advanced Study, Princeton, 1988-89; affiliated prof. Rutgers U., 1994—. Author: The Seventeenth Century, 1970, The Revolt of the Judges, 1971, The World of Europe: The Seventeenth Century, 1973, 2d edit., 1979, Louis XIII: The Just, 1989, paperback edit., 1991, (with Dorothy C. Moote) The Great Plague: The Story of London's Most Deadly Year, 2004, paperback edit., 2006 (nominated Pulitzer prize); co-editor, contbr. issue of French hist. studies on biography, 1996; mem. editl. bd. French Hist. Studies, 1971-74; internat. adv. bd. European History Quar., 1983—. Founder, convener So. Calif. Early Modern French Studies Group, 1980-93, Rutgers, Princeton and Phila. Early Modern History Group, 1994—. Recipient William Koren prize Soc. French Hist. Studies, 1962, creative scholarship award U. So. Calif. Assocs., 1973, faculty book award U. So. Calif. chpt. Phi Kappa Phi, 1990; younger scholar NEH, 1969; grantee Am. Philos. Soc., 1962, Haynes Found., 1973, Wellcome Inst. for History Medicine, 1993-94, Burroughs-Wellcome Fund, 1996; Guggenheim fellow, 1976, fellow U. Essex, Eng., 1993-94, Rutgers Ctr. for Hist. Analysis, 1995-97. Mem. Am. Hist. Assn., Soc. French Hist. Studies (pres. 1984-85), Soc. for Study French History (U.K.), Sixteenth-Century Studies Conf. Home: 149 Meaowbrook Dr Princeton NJ 08540-3664 Home Phone: 609-252-0224. Personal E-mail: dlmoote@verizon.net.

MOOTHA, VAMSI KRISHNA, biomedical researcher, educator; BS, Stanford U., 1993; MD, Harvard U, 1998; internship and residency in Internal Med., Brigham and Women's Hospital, 1998—2001; postdoctoral fellowship, Whitehead and Broad Institutes, 2004. Asst. prof. sys. biology Harvard Med. Sch., Boston; also asst. prof. med. Mass. Gen. Hosp., Boston. Author: numerous articles in jour. such as Proceedings of the Nat. Acad. of Sci. USA, Cell, and Nature Genetics. Named a MacArthur Fellow, 2004. Mem.: Broad Inst. (assoc.). Achievements include pioneering powerful, adaptable computational strategies for mining data collected in laboratories throughout the world, as well as for fundamental insights in seritochondrial biology. Office: Dept Systems Biology Broad Inst 2 Cambridge Ctr Cambridge MA 02142-1401 Address: Ctr for Human Genetic Rsch Simches Rsch Bldg 185 Cambridge St Boston MA 02114 Office Phone: 617-252-1672. Office Fax: 617-252-1902. E-mail: vamsi@hms.harvard.edu.

MOOTY, JOHN WILLIAM, lawyer; b. Adrian, Minn., Nov. 27, 1922; s. John Wilson and Genevieve (Brown) M.; m. Virginia Nelson, June 6, 1952 (dec. 1964); children: David N., Bruce W., Charles W.; m. Jane Nelson, Jan. 15, 1972. BSL, U. Minn., 1943, LLB, 1944. Bar: Minn. 1944. Ptnr. Gray, Plant, Mooty & Bennett, Mpls., 1945—. Bd. dirs. Culligan Water Conditioning Co., Bur. of Engraving, Inc., Riverway Co. and subs.; chmn. Rio Verde Svcs., Inc., Ariz. Author (with others):

Minnesota Practice Methods, 1956. Chmn. Gov.'s Task Force on Edn., 1981; pres. Citizens League Mpls., 1970; acting chmn. Republican Party of Minn., 1958. Named to Minn. Bus. Hall of Fame, 2003. Mem. ABA, Minn. Bar Assn., Hennepin County Bar Assn., U. Minn. Alumni Assn. (pres. 1982), Tonto Verde Country Club, Minikahda (Mpls.) Club, Mpls. Club. Home: 8106 Highwood Dr Apt Y232 Bloomington MN 55438-1054 Office Phone: 612-632-3200. Business E-Mail: john.mooty@gpmlaw.com.

MORA, ALBERTO J., retail executive, lawyer; b. Boston, 1952; BA with honors, Swarthmore Coll., 1974; JD, U. Miami, 1981. Bar: Fla., D.C. Fgn. svc. officer US Dept. State, 1975—78; gen. counsel US Info. Agy., 1989—93, mem. broadcasting bd. governors, 1995—2001; counsel internat. law Greenberg Traurig LLP, Washington; gen. counsel, Dept. Navy US Dept. Def., Washington, 2001—05; v.p., gen. counsel, internat. divsn. Wal-Mart Stores, Inc., 2006—. Bd. dirs. Nat. Coun. for Internat. Visitors, Radio Free Asia, Radio Free Europe/Radio Liberty. Editor-in-chief: Law of the Ams.: U. Miami Jour. of Internat. Law; appeared in (documentaries) Taxi to the Dark Side, 2008. Recipient John F. Kennedy Profile in Courage award, John F. Kennedy Library Found., 2006; fellow, Orgn. of Am. States. Mem.: Coun. Fgn. Rels. Office: Wal-Mart Stores Inc 702 SW 8th St Bentonville AR 72716 Office Phone: 479-204-9027.

MORA, ELIZABETH, comptroller, academic administrator; B, U. Calif. Berkeley; MBA, Simmons Grad. Sch. Mgmt. CPA. Mgr. nat. regulatory cons. Coopers & Lybrand (now PricewaterhouseCoopers), 1987—97; dir. cost analysis and compliance Harvard U., 1997—2000, dir. office sponsored programs, 2000—04, assoc. v.p. for sponsored programs, 2004—06, acting v.p. fin., 2006, v.p. fin., CFO, 2006—. Office: Harvard U Massachusetts Hall Harvard Yard Cambridge MA 02138 E-mail: elizabeth_mora@harvard.edu.

MORA, JIM (JAMES LAWRENCE MORA), professional football coach; b. LA, Nov. 19, 1961; s. James Earnest and Connie Beatrice Mora; m. Shannon Mora; children: Cole, Lillia, Ryder, Trey. Grad., U. Wash., Seattle, 1983. Asst. coach U. Wash. Huskies, 1984; secondary asst. San Diego Chargers, 1985—88, secondary coach, 1989—91, New Orleans Saints, 1992—96, San Francisco 49ers, 1997—98, defensive coord., 1999—2003; head coach Atlanta Falcons, Flowery Br., Ga., 2004—07; asst. head coach/secondary Seattle Seahawks, 2007—08, head coach, 2009—. Office: Seattle Seahawks 12 Seahawks Way Renton WA 98056-1572*

MORA, PAT, writer, speech professional; b. El Paso, Tex., Jan. 19, 1942; d. Raul Antonio and Estella (Delgado) Mora; m. William H. Burnside, July 27, 1963 (div. Aug. 1981); children: William, Elizabeth, Cecilia; m. Vernon L. Scarborough, May 25, 1984. BA, Tex. Western Coll., 1963; MA, U. Tex., El Paso, 1967. Lectr. English U. Tex., El Paso, 1979-81, asst. to v.p. for acad. affairs, 1981-89, mus. dir., asst. to pres., 1987-89; cons. W.K. Kellogg Found., Battle Creek, Mich., 1989-91. Adv. Kellogg Nat. Fellowship Program, 1991—93. Author: (poetry) Chants, 1984 (SW Book award, 1985), Borders, 1986 (SW Book award, 1987), Communion, 1991, A Voice, 1991, Sonrisas, 1994, Agua Santa: Holy Water, Aunt Carmen's Book of Practical Saints, 1997, Uncoiling, 2001, (children's books) Tomas and the Library Lady, 1989, A Birthday Basket for Tía, 1992 (SW Book award, 1993), Pablo's Tree, 1994, The Desert is My Mother, 1995, The Big Sky, 1998, The Rainbow Tulip, 1999, Love to Mama, 2001, The Bakery Lady, 2002, A Library for Juana: The World of Sor Juana Inez, 2003 (Tomás Rivera Mexican Am. Children's Book award, 2002), Maria Paints the Hills, 2003, Dona Flor: A Tall Tale About a Giant Woman with a Great Big Heart, 2005, The Song of Francis and the Animals, 2006, Confeti: Poemas para Niños, 2006, (nonfiction) Nepantla: Essays from the Land in the Middle, 1993, House of Houses, 1997. Recipient Creative Writing award, Nat. Assn. Chicano Studies, 1983, Poetry award, Conf. Cin. Women, 1990, Ohioana award for children's lit., 2000, Lit. award, Nat. Hispanic Cultural Ctr., 2006, Roberta Long Medal for distinguished contributions, 2007; named to Writers Hall of Fame, El Paso Herald Post, 1988; fellow W.K. Kellogg Found., 1986, Nat. Endowment Arts, 1994. Mem.: ALA (hon. Pura Belpre award 2006), Poetry Soc. America, Soc. Children's Book Writers & Illustrators (Golden Kite award 2006), Nat. Coun. Tchrs. English, Acad. Am. Poets, Tex. Inst. Letters. Democrat. Avocations: reading, walking, travel. Home: 1817 Calle De Sebastian Santa Fe NM 87505-7307

MORABITO, ENZO C., real estate broker; b. Italy, 1946; arrived in US, 1958; Lifeguard Cupsogue Beach, Westhampton, NY, 1972; Jr. HS tchr. Patchogue-Medford Sch. Dist., LI, NY; owner The Barge, East Quogue, NY, Summers Beach Club, East Quogue, NY; co-owner Quogue Polo Club, 1981; owner Sagaponack Real Estate, NY; assoc. broker Dunemere Assoc. Real Estate, Southampton, NY, 2000; assoc. broker, exec. v.p. Prudential Douglas Elliman Real Estate, Bridgehampton, NY, 2003—. Office: Prudential Douglas Elliman 2488 Main St Bridgehampton NY 11932 Office Phone: 516-695-3433.*

MORACA-SAWICKI, ANNE MARIE, oncology nurse; b. Niagara Falls, NY, Sept. 28, 1952; d. Joseph R. and Joan (Forgione) Moraca; m. Richard L. Sawicki, Sept. 15, 1979. BSN, D'Youville Coll., 1974; MS in Nursing, SUNY at Buffalo, 1977. Asst. prof. nursing D'Youville Coll., Buffalo, 1977-81; clin. editor Springhouse (Pa.) Corp., 1981-82; charge nurse Mt. St. Mary's Hosp., Lewiston, N.Y., 1982-84; surg. coord., adminstrv. asst. Dr. Richard L. Sawicki, Niagara Falls, N.Y., 1983—. Clin. cons., externship site supr. Niagara County C.C., Sanborn, N.Y.; bd. dirs. Health Assn. Niagara County, Inc., adult day care program Health Assn. Niagara County Inc. Contbr.: Nurses Legal Handbook, 1985, Pharmacotherapeutics: A Nursing Process Approach, 1986, 2d edit., 1990, 3rd edit., 1994, 4th edit., 1998; clin. editor, contbr. Nurses Ref. Libr. Series Vols. on Drugs, Definitions, Procedures and Practices; clin. reviewer Manual of Med./Sug. Nursing, 1995, contbr., 1996; clin. reviewer Critical Care Handbook and IV Drug Handbook, 1995; clin. cons. Critical Care Plans, 1987, Taber's Cyclopedic Med. Dictionary, 16th edit., 1989; grant writer LaSalle Bus. and Profl. Assn. Mem. Niagara Falls Cmty. Devel. Bd.; bd. dirs. Barbara Zimmer Holiday Wish Show, Barbara Zimmer Holiday Wish Breast Cancer Fund Raiser; co-chairperson LaSalle Bus. and Profl. Cmty. Devel. Fund Raising Com. Recipient Cert. of Appreciation Niagara County C.C., 1988, 91, 92, Cmty. Svc. award Am. Cancer Soc., 1978, Miss Hope award, 1977, Am. Cancer Soc. Nursing Fellowship Grant, 1977, Good Neighbor award Niagara Falls Meml. Med. Ctr., 2003, LaSalle Bus. and Profl. Assn. Cmty. Svc. award, 2003, Pres.'s award, HANEI, 2004; Grad. fellow SUNY, Buffalo, 1976-77; grantee mulitple grants for cmty. devel., beautification and health and safety, LaSalle. Mem. AAUP, N.Y. State Nurse's Assn., Health Assn. Niagara County (chairperson 1995—, bd. dirs. adult day care program), LaSalle Bus. and Profl. Assn. (publicity chairperson), Am. Bus. Women's Assn., Sigma Theta Tau. Home: 4658 Vrooman Dr Lewiston NY 14092-1049 Home Phone: 716-754-4413. E-mail: ams928@webtv.net.

MORADI, AHMAD F., software company executive; b. Tehran, Persia, Mar. 21, 1955; arrived in US, 1973; s. Akbar and Afsar (Mokaram) M.; m. Lourdes Pernas; 1 child, Aimee. AS, Broward Community Coll., 1978; BA, Fla. Atlantic U., 1980; PhD, LaSalle U., 1989. Advisor restaurant industries, Miami, Fla., 1974-78; pres. Octa-8, Inc., Ft. Lauderdale, Fla., 1980-82; mgmt. cons. MGI-MCG, Boca Raton, Fla., 1982-83; dir. ops. Datamation, Hollywood, Fla., 1983-85; pres. Software Intelligence Corp., Ft. Lauderdale, 1985—; with ARM Financial Corp., 1987-89; MIS dir., CIO Churchill Tech., Inc., Davie, Fla., 1992—; MIS dir. Westmack Group Holding Co., Delray Beach, 1995—; prin. G4, Inc., Ft. Lauderdale, 1992—; CEO Futuretrak Internat. OTC BB:FTRK, 1998-99, Worldcast Interactive Inc.; with Biomed. Rsch. Techs., 1997—, Interchange Med., Inc., 1999—, Maxwell Rand Inc., 1999—, Netstairs.com, 2000—. Lectr. South Fla. Bus. Jour., 1984-85, Victoria Hosp., Miami, Fla., 1985, Mt. Sinai Hosp., Miami, Fla., 1985, U. Miami, Fla., 1986, Chiropractic Today, 1989; cons., bus., mktg., internat. mktg. and telemarketing mgmt. Software Intelligence Corp., 1985—; systems analyst Softway, Inc., Ft. Lauderdale, 1986; hon. co-chmn. bus. adv. coun. Nat. Leadership Coun.and Nat. Rep. Bus. Commn.; hon. chmn. U.S. Presdl. Bus. Commn., 2002. Recipient Gold medal, U.S. Presdl. Bus. Commn., 2002; named Businessman of Yr., 2003. Mem. Data Processing Mgmt. Assn., Small Bus. Inst. Office Phone: 954-229-0900. Personal E-mail: amoradi@g41.com.

MORAK, GLENN H., lawyer; b. Bklyn., June 19, 1957; d. Arnold Aaron and Janice Esther Morak; m. Marsha Nathan Morak, Apr. 5, 1986; children: Jessica, Jeremy, Jonathan. BA, Boston U., 1978; JD, Am. U., Washington, 1981. Bar: NY 1982, US Dist. Ct. (ea. dist.) NY 1985, US Dist. Ct. (so. dist.) NY 1986. Atty. Legal Aid Soc., Bklyn., 1981—87, supr., 1987—88; sr. trial atty. Sandback & Birnbaum, Mineola, NY, 1988—93; sr. assoc. Law Office Michael J. Ross, NY, 1993—94; sr. ptnr. Abramson & Morak, NY, 1994—. Mem.: NY State Defenders, NY City Criminal Bar Assn., NY State Bar Assn. Democrat. Jewish. Avocations: history, baseball, reading, movies, music. Office: Abramson & Morak 35 Worth St New York NY 10013

MORALES, CARLOS M., lawyer; b. NY, 1953; JD, Columbia Law Sch., NYC. Bar: NY 1980. With Mktg. Regulation Divsn. SEC; with Merrill Lynch & Co., NYC, 1986—, mem., Equity Trading Counsel Grp., 1989—92, mem., Debt and Equity Markets Counsel Grp., 1992; sr. v.p., assoc. gen. counsel Merrill Lynch Internat., NYC; chief legal officer, dir. Merrill Lynch Pierce, Fenner & Smith. Co-founder Merrill Lynch Hispanic Employee Network. Mem. bd. dirs. Hispanic Fedn. Named one of Corp. Elite, Hispanic Bus. Mag., 2007. Office: Merrill Lynch & Co 222 Broadway 4th Fl New York NY 10038 Office Phone: 212-236-1000. Office Fax: 212-670-4446.

MORALES, HECTOR ELIAS, JR., ambassador, former bank executive; b. 1963; m. Selden Wallace. BA in History, Columbia Coll.; JD, U. Tex. Pvt. practice Graves, Dougherty, Hearon & Moody, Austin, Tex., Crain, Caton, & James, Houston; atty. internat. law Reliant Energy, Houston, 1993—97; pres., gen. mgr. Reliant Energy Argentina, 1997—2000; sr. v.p. Viamericas Corp., 2000—03; alt. exec. dir. US Inter-Am. Devel. Bank, 2003, acting exec. dir., 2003—04, exec. dir., 2004—08; US amb. to OAS US Dept. State, 2008—. Bd. dirs. Inter-Am. Found., 2007—. Office: US Dept State Bur We Hempishere Affairs Rm 5914 Washington DC 20520

MORALES, MARIA ISABEL, language educator; b. San Fernando, Cadiz, Spain, June 25, 1980; d. Francisco Morales and Isabel Martinez; m. Alvaro Garcia, Nov. 22, 2006. Bachelor of Humanities, U. Cadiz, Spain, 2002, PhD attending, 2002—. Instr. Kenosha Unified Sch. Dist., Wis., 2003—06; prof. Carthage Coll., Kenosha, 2006—. Office: Carthage Coll 2001 Alford Pk Dr Kenosha WI 53140 Business E-Mail: mmorales@carthage.edu.

MORALES-PALIZA, MANUEL ANGEL, electronic engineering educator; b. Cuzco, Peru, Oct. 9, 1967; s. Manuel Morales and Raquel Paliza Morales. BSc in Electronic Engring., Nat. U. of Engring., 1990, profl. title, 1993; MSc in Physics, Vanderbilt U., 1997. Teaching and rsch. asst. Cath. Univ of Peru, Lima, 1990-91, asst. prof., 1991—. Cons. comm. Cath. U. of Peru, Lima, 1991-94; rschr. in microelectronics Cath. U. of Peru, Lima, 1992-94. Fulbright scholar Vanderbilt U. Mem. IEEE, N.Y. Acad. Scis., Inst. Ecol. of Lima (Conimera Nat. prize 1993, Technol. Innovation Concytec Nat. prize 1994). Avocations: music, movies. Home: 1203 17th Ave S Apt 2 Nashville TN 37212-2820 Office: Vanderbilt U Dept Physics and Astronomy PO Box Sta B 1807 Nashville TN 37235

MORALES-PITA, ANTONIO EVARISTO, economics professor; b. Havana, Cuba, Oct. 26, 1940; s. Florentino Silvestre Morales-Morales and Siria Pita-Allende; m. Gladys Eusebia Nunez - Diaz, Jan. 21, 1976; children: Rosa Morales - Pacheco, Antonio Morales - Pacheco. BS in Economics, U. Havana, 1967; MS in Operational Rsch., Strathclyde U., Glasgow, Scotland, 1971; PhD in Economics, Inst. Economics Ukrainian Acad. Sci., Kiev, 1990. Invited prof. Inst. Tech., Merida, Mexico, 1993—96; asst. prof. economics St. Augustine Coll., Chgo., 1996—97, bus. dept. chmn., 1997—2002, spl. asst. to pres., 2002—04, asst. dean academic affairs, 2004—06; adj. faculty economics & internat. studies DePaul U., Chgo., 1998—. Prof. operational rsch. & rsch. methodology U. de la Habana, 1965—81, rsch. team leader & prof., 1982—93, Inst. Tech. de Merida, 1994—96; rsch. team leader U. Autonoma de Yucatan, Merida, 1993—94; motivational spkr. Chgo. Pub. Sch., 2007—. Author: (novels) Havana-Merida-Chgo. A journey to freedom; contbr. scientific papers to profl. jours. Eucharistian min. St. Paul's-by-the-Lake, Chgo., 2008. Recipient Outstanding prof., Republic of Cuba, 1985, Outstanding Scientist, 1990. Episcopalian. Achievements include research in method of optimal programming of the sugar cane. Office: DePaul Univ 1 E Jackson Boulevard Chicago IL 60604 Personal E-mail: amoralespita@hotmail.com. Business E-Mail: amorale1@depaul.edu.

MORALES-ZENO, ANA J., literature and language professor; d. Jorge Morales-Yordán and Carmen Zeno Puente. BA magna cum laude, U. PR, San Juan, 1982; MA in Romance Studies, Cornell U., Ithaca, NY, 1989, PhD in Romance Studies, 1993. Tchg. asst. Cornell U., Ithaca, 1983—86; instr. U. PR, Bayamón, 1994—2001, asst. prof., 2001—02, assoc. prof., 2002—. Coord. fed. programs Coun. on Higher Edn. U. PR, Rio Piedras, 1986—88, del. Coun. on Higher Edn., Washington, 1987; vis. prof. U. Montreal, Canada, 2002; chair Instnl. Reading Group U. PR, 2001—06; spkr. Nat. Assembly Profl. Real Estate Women, San Juan, 2005; facilitator yoga and meditation workshops, Bayamón, 00, Bayamón, 01, Bayamón, 05; presenter papers in field; chair seminars and panels in field. Editor: Milenio Jour. Arts and Scis., 1998—2006; evaluator, editor: PR Nat. Found. for Humanities, 2006—07; contbr. articles to profl. jours. Recipient Cornell Grad. fellowship, Cornell U., 1983—84, Presdl. fellowship, U. PR, 1987—89. Mem.: MLA, Assn. Profs. of Spanish, Feministas Unidas. Avocations: yoga, meditation, French language and culture. Home: Duke 251 University Gardens San Juan PR 00927 Office: U PR Recinto Bayamón Parque Industrial MinillasCarr 174 # 170 Bayamon PR 00959

MORALEZ, JOSELYN HOPE, special education educator; b. Lordsburg, N.Mex., July 7, 1966; d. Mary Lou Chavez. BS, N.Mex. State U., 1988. Instr. elem. spl. edn. Animas Pub. Schs., N.Mex., 1988—90, Lordsburg Pub. Schs., 1990—2008. Mem. Nat. Edn. Assn., 2007—. Mem. NEA, Coun. Exceptional Children, Delta Kappa Gamma, Office: Southside Elem Sch 200E 9th St Lordsburg NM 88045 Personal E-mail: gg_m@hotmail.com.

MORAN, CESAR A., pathologist, educator; s. Rigoberto and Leticia Moran; m. Susan L. Spradling; children: Kate L., Jean E. MD, San Carlos U., Guatemala, 1981. Diplomate Am. Bd. Pathology, 1992. Pathology resident Mt. Sinai Hosp., NYC, 1984—88; chief resident Yale U., New Haven, 1988—89; assoc. chmn. Armed Forces Inst. Pathology, Washington, 1989—98; maj. USAF, Washington, 1990—98. Contbr. articles to sci. jours. Recipient Tri-Svc. medals, Armed Forces Inst. Pathology, 1996—97. Fellow: Am. Soc. Clin. Pathologists (ednl. com. mem.). Office: M D Anderson Cancer Ctr 1515 Holcombe Blvd Houston TX 77030 Office Fax: 713-563-1848. Business E-Mail: cesarmoran@mdanderson.org.

MORAN, CHARLES A., security firm executive, educator; b. Chgo., Feb. 7, 1943; s. Charles W. and Rose B. M.; m. Donna L. Orbach, Sept. 3, 1967; children: Scott Alan, Erin Lizabeth. AB, Princeton U., 1964; JD, U. Mich., 1967; postgrad. advanced mgmt., Harvard U., 1982. CFPR CFP Bd. Stds., 1996, cert. employee benefit specialist Internat. Found. and Wharton Sch. U Pa., 2003. With Chase Manhattan Bank, NYC, 1967-70; pension trust officer, adminstrv. officer, officer in charge new bus. devel., pension div. Mfrs. Hanover Trust Co., NYC, 1970-87, sr. v.p., officer-in-charge employee benefit trust div., 1979-80; chmn. bd., pres., CEO, MH/Edie Investment Counsel (formerly Lionel D. Edie & Co.), NYC, 1980-82, officer-in-charge corp. trust div., 1982-83, officer in charge-global securities group, 1983-87; pres. Govt. Securities Clearing Corp., NYC, 1987-96, Strategic Fin. Adv., Montclair, NJ, 1996—; asst. prof., faculty fellow, faculty senate Coll. of NJ, Trenton, 1996—99; prof. Harvard U., Summer Sch. Arts & Scis., Cambridge, Mass., 1997—; asst. prof., residential coll. adv. bd. Bucknell U., 1999—2003; prof. dir. fin. planning program SUNY, Cobleskill, 2003—; dir. Ctr. for Collaborative Sustainability NYU, 2006—. Bd. dirs. Cert. Fin. Planner Bd. Std., Inc.,2008-, chmn. Audit Fin. Investment Com.; chmn. bd. dirs. Inform, Inc.; cons. Urban Vol. Cons. Group, Inc.; adv. coun. US Dept. Labor; adv. bd. BNA Pension Reporter; mem. Employees Retirement Income Security Act of 1974 Roundtable; industry adv. com. Future Electronic Funds Payments Svcs. Fed. Res.; lectr. in field. Adv. bd. mem., Jour. Fin. Planning; contbr. articles to profl. jours. Mem. Am. Inst. Banking, Am. Employee Benefits Inst. (treas. 1976-79), NY State Bankers Assn. (employees trust com.), Assn. Pvt. Pension and Welfare Plans (dir., mem. exec. com.), ERISA Industry Com. (pres., dir., mem. exec. com., treas.), Am. Bankers Assn. (chmn. employee benefit trust com. 1977-82), Internat. Found. Pension and Welfare Plans, Bank Adminstrn. Inst. (mem. tech. commn.), NY C. of C. (task force on pub. pensions), Fin. Planning Assn. (dir., chmn. govt. rels. com., chmn. ethics com.), The Inst. of Cert. Fin. Planners (bd. dirs., com. on career devel.), NJ Soc. Inst. Cert. Fin. Planners (bd. dirs., sec., treas.), World Future Soc., Internat. Soc. Cert. Employee Benefit Specialists, Am. Acad. Mgmt., Am. Soc. Fin. Svcs. Profls., Strategic Mgmt. Soc., Internat. Soc. Cert. Employee Benefit Specialist, Princeton Club, Harvard Bus. Sch. Club NY-Cmty. Ptnrs. (cons., bd. dir.).

MORAN, DANIEL THOMAS, dentist, poet; b. NYC, Mar. 9, 1957; s. Thomas Daniel and Jean Elizabeth Moran; m. Karen Kay; children: Lindsay Alison, Ashley Zurl, Gregory Riordan. AS, Nassau Coll., 1977; BS, SUNY, Stony Brook, 1979; D in Dental Surgery, Howard U., 1983. Staff assoc. Southhampton (N.Y.) Hosp., 1988-94; host L.I. Radio mag., Southampton, NY, 1994—99; literary corr. L.I. Pub. Radio, Southampton, NY, 1994—2001; pvt. practice Shelter Island, N.Y., 1987—; v.p. Ludwig Vogelstein Found., 2007—; clin. instr. Boston U. Sch. Dental Medicine, 2008—. Author: Dancing for Victoria, 1991, Gone to Innisfree, 1993, Sheltered by Islands, 1995, In Praise of August, 1999, From Hilo to Willow Pond, 2002, Looking for the Uncertain Past, 2006, The Light of City and Sea, 2006; contbr. poetry to profl. publs. Trustee Shelter Island chpt. ARC; dir. Gardiner's Bay Country Club, 1993-98, historian 1993—, tournament chmn., 1993-96); v.p. Walt Whitman Birthplace Assn., Huntington, N.Y., 1997-2005, v.p., 2001-05; hon. dir. Wildlife Rescue Ctr. of the Hamptons. Grantee Poets and Writers, Inc., 1996-2007; named Poet Laureate Suffolk County Legislature, NY, 2005-07, Humanist Celebrant Am. Humanist Assn; named to Dean's Coun., Melville Libr., Stonybrook U., 2005, Named to Hall Of Fame Massapegua, NY, 2007. Mem. Poetry Soc. of Am., Irish Am. Writers Assn., Assn. Literary Scholars & Critics, Pen Am. Ctr., New England Poetry Club, Avocations: harmonica, drums, piano. Home: PO Box 2008 Shelter Island NY 11964-2008 Address: 515 Shawmut Ave Boston MA 02118 Home Phone: 857-350-3338; Office Phone: 631-749-0539. E-mail: dan@danielthomasmoran.net.

MORAN, EILEEN A., utilities executive; BSBA, Seton Hall U., South Orange, NJ; M in Econs., D in Econs., Fordham U., NY; grad. Mgmt. Devel. Program, Harvard Grad. Sch. Bus. Adminstrn. With Pub. Svc. Electric. & Gas Co., 1977, various fin. and investment positions including asst. treas.; v.p. investments PSEG Resources, 1986—90, pres., 1990—, Enterprise Group Devel. Corp., 1997—; mem. exec. officers group Pub. Svc. Enterprise Group Inc., 1997—, sr. v.p. for strategic initiatives, 2008—. Bd. mem. Duff & Phelps Utility and Corp. Bond Trust, Duff & Phelps Utilities Tax Free Income Fund, Phoenix Duff & Phelps Instnl. Mut. Funds. Mem. adv. bd. Benedictine Acad. Office: PSEG PO Box 570 Newark NJ 07101 Office Phone: 973-430-7000.

MORAN, ELLEN, federal agency administrator; b. Troy, NY, May 1, 1966; m. Kirk Fabel. BA in English Lit. & Polit. Sci., Wheaton Coll., Norton, Mass., 1988. Nat. campaign staff Senator Tom Harkin US Senate, 1992; dir. issue advocacy Dem. Congl. Campaign Com. (DCCC), 2000; mgr. Wal-Mart corp. accountability campaign, voter contact coord. AFL-CIO, Washington; dir. ind. expenditures Dem. Nat. Com., 2004; exec. dir. EMILY's List, Washington, 2005—08; comm. dir. The White House, Washington, 2009; chief of staff US Dept. Commerce, Washington, 2009—. Internat. democracy work US Agy. Internat. Devel. (USAID), Indonesia; campaign mgr. various gov., US Senate and US House of Reps. elections; overseer EMILY's List into voter mobilization, 1994. Democrat. Office: US Dept Commerce 1401 Constitution Ave NW Washington DC 20230*

MORAN, JAMES JOSEPH, JR., insurance company executive; s. James J. and Marilyn A. (Sullivan) M.; m. Mary Therese Stevens, Oct. 6, 1979; children: Sean M., James E., Matthew S. AB cum laude, Boston Coll., 1975, JD, 1978. Bar: Mass. 1978, U.S. Ct. Appeals (1st cir.) 1979, U.S. Dist Ct. Mass. 1979, U.S. Tax Ct. 1979, U.S. Supreme Ct. 1982; CPCU; Assoc. in reins. Assoc. Haussermann, Davison & Shattuck, Boston, 1978-84, Morrison, Mahoney & Miller, Boston, 1984—87, ptnr., 1988—98; pres. Eastern Casualty Ins. Co., Marlborough, Mass., 1998—2001; sr. v.p., sec., gen. counsel Quincy (Mass.) Mutual Fire Ins. Co., 2001—. V.p., gen. counsel Ind. Property-Casualty Insurers Mass.

Inc., 1991-98; bd. dirs. R.I. Insurers Insolvency Fund, 2003-06; bd. dirs. Mass. Insurers Insolvency Fund, 2004—, Liquor Liability Joint Underwriting Assn. Mass., 2006-08; counsel Mass. Assn. Ins. Agts., 1985-96; ins. broker, Mass.; New Eng. regional regulatory counsel Alliance Am. Insurers, 1994-98; trustee New Eng. Coll. Fin., 1998-2000. Bd. dirs. (gubernatorial appointee) Mass. Pollution Liability Reinsurance Corp., 1988-90. Recipient Econ. Leadership award Orgn. New Equality, 1997. Mem. Internat. Assn. Def. Coun., CPCU Soc. (pres. Boston chpt. 1993-94), Fedn. Ins. Corp. Coun., Ins. Libr. Assn. Boston (trustee 1983-2004, pres. 1989-90) Roman Catholic. Home: 15 Bramel Cir Walpole MA 02081-2043 Office: Quincy Mutual Fire Ins Co 57 Washington St Quincy MA 02169-9155

MORAN, JAMES MICHAEL, JR., astronomer, educator; b. Plainfield, NJ, Jan. 3, 1943; s. James Michael and Martha (Algermissen) M.; m. Barbara Putney Smith, Nov. 30, 1974; children: Susan Harrison, Michael Putney. BS, U. Notre Dame, 1963; SM, MIT, 1965, PhD, 1968. Mem. staff MIT Lincoln Lab., Lexington, 1968-70; sr. radio astronomer Smithsonian Astrophys. Obs., Cambridge, Mass., 1970—; prof. practice of astronomy Harvard U., Cambridge, 1979-89, Donald H. Menzel prof. astrophysics, 2001—, chmn. astronomy dept., 2006—; assoc. dir. Harvard-Smithsonian Ctr. Astrophysics, Cambridge, 1987-92, dir. Submillimeter Array Project, 1996—2005. Jansky lectr. Nat. Radio Astronomy Obs., 1996; trustee N.E. Radio Obs. Corp., Cambridge, 1983—, Associated U. Inc., Washington, 2005-, Murchison Widefield Array. Contbr. numerous articles on radio astronomy to profl. publs. Co-recipient Rumford prize Am. Acad. Arts and Scis., 1971; recipient Sr. award Alexander von Humboldt Soc., 1993. Fellow AAAS, IEEE; mem. NAS, Am. Astron. Soc. (Pierce prize 1978), Explorers Club. Achievements include development of technique of very long baseline interferrometry; research in study of black holes. Home: 93 Anson Rd Concord MA 01742-5704 Office: Harvard-Smithsonian Center for Astrophysics 60 Garden St Cambridge MA 02138-1516 Office Phone: 617-495-7477. Business E-Mail: moran@cfa.harvard.edu.

MORAN, JERRY, United States Representative from Kansas; b. Great Bend, Kans., May 29, 1954; m. Robba A. Moran; 2 children. BS, Kansas U., 1976, JD, 1981. Senator dist. 37 State of Kans., 1989—96, sen. majority leader, 1994—96; mem., asst. majority whip US Congress from 1st Kans. dist., 1997—, mem. agr., transp., infrastructure, vets. affairs coms., chmn. subcom. on gen. commodities; chmn. Rural Health Care Coalition. Republican. Office: US House Reps 1519 Longworth House Office Bldg Washington DC 20515-1601 Office Phone: 202-225-2715. Office Fax: 202-225-5124.*

MORAN, JIM (JAMES PATRICK MORAN JR.), United States Representative from Virginia, stock broker; b. Buffalo, May 16, 1945; s. James Patrick and Dorothy (Dwyer) Moran; m. Mary Craig, Dec. 27, 1967 (div. 1974); children: Jimmy, Mary; m. Mary Howard; children: Michael, Patrick, Dorothy. BA in Econs., Coll. Holy Cross, Worcester, Mass., 1967; postgraduate student, CUNY, 1967-68; MPA, U. Pitts., 1970. Comptr., budget analyst US Dept. Health, Edn. and Welfare, Washington, 1968—74; budget and fiscal policy specialist Congl. Rsch. Svc. Libr. Congress, Washington, 1974-76; sr. staff mem. appropriations com. US Senate, Washington, 1976-79; investment broker A.G. Edwards & Sons, Alexandria, Va., 1979; mem. City Coun., Alexandria, Va., 1979—82; vice mayor Alexandria, Va., 1982-84; mayor, 1985—90; mem. US Congress from 8th Va. dist., 1991—, mem. appropriations com. Chmn. No. Va. Transp. Bd., 1988, United Way, 1977-79; vice chmn. Mental Health Retard and Substance Abuse Bd., 1976-78, vice chmn. D.E.O., 1976-78; dir. Met. Area Coun. Govts., dir. No. Va. Transp. Commn., 1985. Recipient Outstanding Citizenship award, YMCA, 1983. Mem. C. of C. (dir. 1985-86). Democrat. Roman Catholic. Office: US House Reps 2239 Rayburn House Office Bldg Washington DC 20515-4608 Office Phone: 202-225-4376.*

MORAN, JOAN JENSEN, physical education and healthcare educator; b. Chgo., Sept. 25, 1952; d. Axel Fred and Mary J. (Maes) J.; m. Gregory Keith Moran. BS in Edn., Western Ill. U., Macomb, 1974; MS in Edn., No. Ill. U., DeKalb, 1978. Cert. tchr. Ill. Tchr., coach East Coloma Sch., Rock Falls, Ill., 1974—2007; ret., 2007; adj. faculty Sauk Valley C.C., 2007—. Recreation specialist Woodhaven Lakes, Sublette, Ill., 1975-79; cons. Ill. State Bd. Edn., Springfield, 1984—; instr. NDEITA, Ill., 1988—; facilitator Project Wild, Ill., 1990—; part-time worker, Fitness Ctr., Sauk Valley CC, part-time adj. faculty. Instr. ARC, Rock Falls, 1978—, Am. Heart Assn., Rock Falls, 1978—; exec. bd. East Coloma Cmty. Club; fitness del. to Russia and Hungary, 1992; cons. Alcohol Awareness & Occupant Restraint Ill. State Bd. Edn., Substance Abuse Guidance Edn. Com., Rock Falls Drug Free Cmty. Grant com., Whiteside County CPR Coord. com. Recipient Western Ill. U. Alumni Achievement award, 1993, Western Ill. Master Tchr. award, 1993, Svc. award Ill. Assn. Health, Phys. Edn., Recreation and Dance, 1991, 92, Outstanding Young Woman award, 1986, Phys. Educator of Yr. award, 1988; named Mid. Sch. Phys. Edn. Tchr. of Yr. Midwest AAHPERD, 1993, Ill. Assn. Health, Phys. Edn., Recreation and Dance, 1992, Gov.'s Coun. Health and Phys. Edn. award, 1991, Am. Tchr. of Yr. award Walt Disney Co., 1993, Excel award Ill. State Bd. Edn., 1995, finalist Ill. Tchr. of Yr., 1996, Milkin Nat. Educator award, 1997, Health Edn. award and Quarter Century award Ill. Assn. Health, Phys. Edn., Recreation and Dance, 1999, Presidential citation, 1998; named to USA Today Tchr. Team, 2000. Mem.: AAHPERD (Health Tchr. of Yr. midwest chpt. 2001), Environ. Edn. Assn. Ill., East Coloma Edn. Assn. (pres., pub. rels., v.p. 1993—94), Ill. Edn. Assn., No. Dist. Ill. Assn. Health, Phys. Edn., Recreation and Dance (newsletter editor 1984—85, exec. bd. 1985—90, treas. 1985—90), Ill. Assn. Health, Phys. Edn., Recreation and Dance (v.p. teenage youth 1988—90, pres. 1994, past pres., conv. coord. 1995, Honor Fellow award 1996). Democrat. Lutheran. Avocations: skiing, hiking, biking, reading, travel. Home: 1903 E 41st St Sterling IL 61081-9449 Personal E-mail: moran@essex1.com.

MORAN, JOHN FRANCIS, cardiologist; b. Chgo., Sept. 5, 1938; MD, Loyola U., Stritch Sch. Medicine, 1964. Cert. cardio. disease 1973. Office: Loyola U Med Ctr 2160 S 1st Ave Maywood IL 60153 Office Phone: 708-327-2784.

MORAN, JUSTIN LOUIS, retired management consultant; b. Portland, Oreg, Oct. 2, 1932; s. Louis Hunt and Effie Adeline (Carr) Moran; m. Carol Elizabeth Graham, Oct. 6, 1956; children: M. Elizabeth, Louis H. II, Susan C. AB, U. Notre Dame, 1954. Salesman Moran Oil Co., Portland, 1956—62; account exec. NW Ayer & Son, Detroit, 1962—67, Grey Advt. Co., Detroit, 1967—70; v.p. Bank of Commonwealth, Detroit, 1972—75; dir., comm. Motor Vehicle Mfrs., Detroit, 1976—77; pres. & cons. Justin L. Moran Inc., Grosse Pointe, Mich., 1977—96; ret., 1996. Author: Strategic Marketing for Community Banks, 1987; contbr. over 200 articles to mags. & trade publs.; spkr. in field. Dir. Sterling Bank and Trust Southfield, 1990—98, Hanson's Landing Assn., Stuart, Fla., 1996—99, 2005—, pres., 1999, 2006—, sec., 1996—98, v.p., 2005. Served to 1st lt. US Army, 1954—56, PTO. Mem.: Great Lakes Cruising Club (rear commdr. 2003—06), Miles Grant Country Club (Fla.), Grosse Pointe Yacht Club (Mich.), Adcraft Club Detroit. Republican. Roman Catholic. Home and Office: 658 N Rosedale Ct Grosse Pointe MI 48236-1141

MORAN, KEVIN J., publishing operations director; s. Thomas F. and Loraine Moran; m. Gail Anne Iskra, Dec. 23, 1983; children: Thomas F., Nora K., Conor G., Kevin. BA (hon.), SUNY, 1976. Pub. Hatherleigh Press, Long Island City, NY, 1995—2008; pub. ops. dir. Overlook Press, NY, 2008—. Mng. editor (non-fiction book) Living with Hepatitis C: A Survivor's Guide, 2006, The Arab Mind, 2007; contbr. Dictionary of American Biography. Coach Cath. Youth Orgn., New York, NY, 1993—2004. Mem.: Regis Alumni Assn. (assoc.). Democrat. Roman Catholic. Avocations: fishing, bird watching, hiking. Office Phone: 212-673-2480. Business E-Mail: kmoran@overlookny.com.

MORAN, KIMBERLY DIANNE, secondary school educator, artist; b. Kingsport, Tenn., Apr. 3, 1959; d. Talmadge Atlee and Alma Irene Archer; m. M. G. Moran, May 26, 1990; 1 child, Nathaniel T.; 1 child, Jamie C. BS, East Tenn. State U., 1981. Bank teller First Atlanta Bank, 1984—87; art tchr. Sullivan County Schs., Kingsport, Tenn., 1987—89, Crestview HS, Fla., 1989—95, W.C. Pryor Mid. Sch., Fort Walton Beach, Fla., 1995—2006, Fort Walton Beach HS, 2006—. Tchr. adult and children Sunday Sch.; art coord. Okaloosa Dist. Art Show. Named Tchr. of Yr., Pryor Middle Sch., 1999—2000. Mem.: Okaloosa County Edn. Assn., Nat. Edn. Assn., Nat. Art Edn. Assn. Republican. Presbyn. Avocations: reading, walking, sewing, board games, painting, drawing, working with clay. Home: 210 Baker Ave Fort Walton Beach FL 32548-4318 Office: Fort Walton Beach HS 400 Hollywood Blvd Fort Walton Beach FL 32548

MORAN, MARISSA J., law educator; b. Bklyn. m. James Moran; children: James, JonPaul, Justin. JD, Bklyn. Law Sch. Law clk. Hon. Burton R. Lifland, Chief Judge US Bankruptcy Ct. So. Dist. NY, 1989—91; assoc. Kaye, Scholer, Fierman, Hays & Handler, Emmet, Marvin & Martin; prof. dept. law & paralegal studies NYC Coll. Tech., Bklyn.; adj. prof. Leonard N. Stern Sch. Bus. NYU. Chair legis. com., faculty-student disciplinary com., guest spkr., conf. organizer NYC Coll. Tech. Contbr. articles to profl. jours.; co-author: Technology in the Law Office. Mem.: ABA, Alpha Sigma Nu, Bkln. Bar Assn., Columbian Lawyers Assn., NY State Bar Assn., Am. Assn. Paralegal Educators, Alpha Sigma Nu, Jesuit. Office: NYC Coll Tech Dept Law & Paralegal Studies 300 Jay St N622 Brooklyn NY 11201 Business E-Mail: mmoran@citytech.cuny.edu.

MORAN, MARK J., air transportation executive; married; 4 children. B in Engring., Marquette U., Milw., 1979. Registered profl. engr. Design engr. Boeing Co., 1979; with Piedmont Airlines; dir. engring. US Airways; with Continental Airlines, Inc., Houston, 1994—, sr. v.p. tech. ops. and purchasing, exec. v.p. ops., 2004—. Office: Continental Airlines Inc PO Box 4607 Houston TX 77210

MORAN, MARTIN JOSEPH, fundraising company executive; b. Bklyn., Nov. 3, 1930; s. Dominick and Mary (Lydon) Moran; m. Mary Therese Schofield, June 5, 1954; children: Martin Joseph, John P., Maureen M., Thomas S., Robert P., William M., Maria M. BA, St. John's U., 1952. Profl. fundraising cons., 1956—; founder Martin J. Moran Co., Inc., NYC, 1964, pres., 1964—74, chmn. bd., 1974—. Mem. Am. Revolution Bicentennial Commn., Oyster Bay, NY, Massapequa Park Ethics Commn., 1969—72; trustee Notre Dame Coll., SI, NY, 1969—72, La Salle Acad., NYC, 1971—87; mem. pres.'s coun. Cath. U. P.R., Ponce, 1966—71; mem. Cardinal's Com. for Edn., NYC, 1970—79, Cardinal's Com. for Laity Archdiocese NY, 1979—98, Massapequa Park (NY) Bd. Zoning Appeals, 1972—84, chmn., 1978—84; bd. councilors, sec., treas. Equestrian Order Holy Sepulchre of Jerusalem, 1990—, sec.-treas., 1990—93, pres., 1993—. Served as aviator USNR, 1952—56. Decorated knight Grand Cross Order Holy Sepulchre, Pope Paul VI, Knight of Malta Pope Paul VI, papal Knight of Order of St. Gregory the Gt. Pope John Paul II, knight comdr.; recipient Pietas medal, St. John's U., NY, 1988. Mem.: Am. Assn. Fundraising Counsel (bd. dirs. 1970—75), Navy Hist. Assn., Navy League, Friendly Sons of St. Patrick, St. John's U. Alumni Assn. (pres. 1987—94), Nassau County Hist. Soc., KC. Home: 1300 Lakeshore Dr Massapequa Park NY 11762-1764 Office: Martin J Moran Company 11 Penn Plz Fl 5 New York NY 10001-2003

MORAN, MICHAEL E., urologist; married. MD, Southern Ill. U., Springfield, 1983. Diplomate in urology Am. Bd. Urology, 1990. Surgeon dept. urology, Albany, NY, 1993—2007; owner Renaissance Urology, Stuart, Fla., 2008—. Assoc. prof. dept. surgery, Albany, 1992—2007. Recipient McCarthy prize, Western Sect. AUA, 1989, Alumni of Yr., SIU Sch. Medicine, 2006. Mem.: Am. Urol. Assn., ROCK Soc. (past pres. 2004—05, Golden Apple award 2005). Achievements include research in robotics, kidney stone disease. Office: Renaissance Urology 509 SE Riverside Dr Ste 202 Stuart FL 34994

MORAN, PAUL JAMES, journalist, columnist; b. Buffalo, July 20, 1947; s. Paul James and Frances (Sciortino) M.; m. Kim Maldiner, Mar. 17, 1975 (div. July 1979); m. Colette Stass (div. Jan. 1997). Student, SUNY, Buffalo, 1965-67, Millard Fillmore Coll., 1971-73. Sports editor Tonawanda News, North Tonawanda, NY, 1972-75; writer/columnist Fort Lauderdale (Fla.) News/Sun Sentinel, 1975-85, N.Y. Newsday, Melville, 1985—2007; columnist Florida Horse ESPN.com. Cons. Green Country Racing Assn., Tulsa, 1983-85. Author: (with others) Crown Jewels of Thoroughbred Racing; contbr. articles to mags. and newspapers. Sgt. USAF, 1967-71. Recipient Eclipse award Thoroughbred Racing Assn., 1985, 90, Disting. Writing award Am. Soc. Newspaper Editors, 1990, Deadline Writing award Soc. Silurians, 1990, Deadline Reporting award L.I. Press Club, 1991, Disting. Sports Writing award N.Y. Newspaper Pubs. Assn., 1992, (with others) Journalism collection Best Newspaper Writing 1991, Media award L.I. Vet. Med. Assn., 1997, excellence in continuing feature Fla. Mag. Assn., 1999, Best of Manhattan award N.Y. Press, 2002. Mem. N.Y. Turf Writers' Assn. (pres. 1990-92, sec.-treas. 1992-94), Nat. Turf Writers' Assn. (bd. dirs. 1987-90). Republican. Avocations: photography, art collecting. Home: 12 Ascot Cir Saratoga Springs NY 12866 Personal E-mail: pmoran1686@aol.com.

MORAN, PHILIP DAVID, lawyer; b. Lynn, Mass., June 3, 1937; s. J. Francis and Margaret M. (Shanahan) M.; m. Carole A. Regan, May 12, 1962; children: Maura F., Philip David. AB, Holy Cross Coll., 1958; EdM, Salem State Coll., 1961; JD, Suffolk U., 1968. Bar: Mass. 1968, US Dist. Ct. Mass. 1972, US Supreme Ct. 1988, US Ct. Appeals (1st cir.) 1993, US Ct. Appeals (fed. cir.) 2006. House counsel Viatron Computer Systems Corp., Burlington, Mass., 1968-71; ptnr. Kane & Moran, Lynn, Mass., 1972-78; pvt. practice law Salem, Mass., 1978—; propr. Law Offices of Philip D. Moran P.C., 1993—. Asst. dist. atty. Essex County (Mass.), 1974-78; mem. pres.'s coun. Holy Cross Coll., 1985—, Nat. Inst. Trial Advocacy U. Colo., 1973; gen. chmn. bicentenary com. Maynooth Coll., Boston, 1994-96. Contbg. author: Encyclopedia of Biomedical Policy, 1995. Bd. dirs. Nat. Right to Life Inc., 1977-83, 87—, treas., 1981-83; bd. dirs. Mass. Citizens for Life, 1973—, pres. 1979-80, chmn. 1991-93; chmn. Salem Con Con, 1982-89; active Salem Bd. Voter Registration, 2005; pastoral coun. Archdiocese Boston, 2006—; bd. dirs. Cath. Citizenship, 2004-, treas., 2004-. With US Army, 1960—66. Recipient Ignatius O'Connor Pro Life award, 1994, Gold medatl St. Patrick Maynooth Coll., Irelnd, 1996, Knight of Malta, 1997, Family, Faith and Freedom award Family Rsch. Coun., 1997, Citizenship award Mass. Family Inst., 1997, Leadership award, Nat. Rep. Cong. Com., 2003. Mem. Mass. Bar Assn., Salem Bar Assn., Lynn Bar Assn., Am. Trial Lawyers Assn., Nat. Acad. Elder Law Attys., Murray Inn of Ct., Pro Life Legal Def. Fund (pres. 1997), Hibernian Civil Rights Coalition (bd. dirs. 1997, pres. 1997), Irish Am. Partnership, Nat. Coalition of Pro Life Dems. (bd. dirs., treas. 1999-2001), Dem State Com., Catholic Alliance (bd. dirs., gen. coun. 1999-2001), Internat. Soc. Photographers. Roman Catholic. Avocations: swimming, reading, gardening, boating, photography. Home: 415 Lafayette St Salem MA 01970-5337 Office: 265 Essex St Salem MA 01970-3419 Office Phone: 978-745-6085. Personal E-mail: philipmoranesq@aol.com.

MORAN, RACHEL, law educator; b. Kansas City, Mo., June 27, 1956; d. Thomas Albert and Josephine (Portillo) Moran. AB, Stanford U., 1978; JD, Yale U., 1981. Bar: Calif. 1984. Assoc Heller, Ehrman, White & McAuliffe, San Francisco, 1982-83; prof. law U. Calif., Berkeley, 1984—, Robert D. and Leslie-Kay Raven prof. law, 1998—. Vis. prof. UCLA Sch. Law, 1988, 2002, Stanford (Calif.) U. Law Sch., 1989, NYU Sch. Law, 1996, U. Miami Sch. Law, 1997, U. Tex. Law Sch., 2000, Fordham Law Sch., 2005, UC Irvine, 2008—; chair Chicano/Latino Policy Project, 1993—96; dir. Inst. for Study Social Change, 2003—08. Contbr. articles to profl. jours. Recipient Disting. Tchg. award, U. Calif. Mem.: Assn. Am. Law Schs. (pres.), Calif. Bar Assn., Am. Law Inst., Phi Beta Kappa. Democrat. Unitarian Universalist. Avocations: jogging, aerobics, reading, listening to music. Office: U Calif Sch Law Boalt Hall Berkeley CA 94720 Home Phone: 510-420-0992; Office Phone: 510-643-6351. Business E-Mail: moran@law.berkeley.edu.

MORAN, ROBERT F., retail executive; BS in Acctg., Villanova U. Fin. & mgmt. positions Sears Roebuck & Co.; CFO, exec. v.p. Galerias Preciados, 1991—93; mgmt. positions through pres., CEO, Sears de Mexico Sears, Roebuck & Co., 1993—98; pres. Toys R Us Ltd. Canada, 1998—99; pres., stores, N.Am. PetSmart Inc., 1999—2001, pres., COO, 2001—09, pres., CEO, 2009—. Bd. dirs. Collective Brands Inc., 2007—, PetSmart Inc., 2009—, Med. Mgmt. Internat. Inc., PetSmart Charities Inc. Mem.: Retail Industry Leaders Assn. (bd. dirs.). Office: PetSmart Inc 19601 N 27th Ave Phoenix AZ 85027*

MORAN, SUZANNAH, social sciences educator; b. Evanston, Ill. MS in Geoenviron. Studies, Shippensburg U., Pa. Geography prof. Hagerstown C.C., Md., 1998—. Office: Hagerstown Cmty Coll 11400 Robinwood Dr Hagerstown MD 21742 Office Phone: 301-790-2800 302. Business E-Mail: morans@hagerstowncc.edu.

MORAN, THOMAS HARRY, retired academic administrator; b. Milw., Oct. 21, 1937; s. Harry Edward and Edna Agnes Moran; m. Barbara Ellen Saklad, June 10, 1969; children: David Thomas, Karen Ellen. BS, U. Wis., Madison, 1964, MA, 1972, PhD, 1974. Dir. capital budgeting Wis. Dept. Adminstrn., 1962-64; exec. dir. Wis. Higher Ednl. Aids Bd., 1964-69; spl. cons. tax policy Wis. Dept. Revenue, 1973-74; dep. dir. Wis. Manpower Coun., Office of Gov., 1974-76; v.p. bus. and fin., treas. U. Detroit, 1976-78; exec. assoc. v.p. health affairs U. So. Calif., LA, 1979-87, v.p. bus. affairs, 1988—2002, v.p. emeritus, 2002—. USN fellow, 1957-59, U.S. Office Edn. rsch. fellow, 1973. Mem. Am. Assn. Higher Edn., Phi Kappa Phi. Personal E-mail: moranthm@aol.com.

MORAN, THOMAS J., insurance company executive; BS in Math., Manhattan Coll.; JD (hon.), Nat. Univ. Ireland. Pension underwriter through exec. v.p. Mutual of America Life Ins. Co., NYC, 1975—90, pres., COO, 1992—94, pres., CEO, 1994—. Bd. dir. Life Ins. Coun. NY, Genovese Drug Stores. Bd. mem. Manhattan Coll., United Way NYC, Nat. Ctr. for Disability Services, Nat. Com. on American Fgn. Policy, Univ. Coll. Dublin Graduate Sch. Bus. Recipient Medal of Honor, Cavalry Hospital, Humanitarian Award, NYC Fire Dept., Concern Worldwide, Ellis Island Medal of Honor, Terence Cardinal Cooke award. Office: Mutual of America Life Ins Co 320 Park Ave New York NY 10022 Office Phone: 212-224-1600. Office Fax: 212-224-2539.

MORAN, WENDY JACQUELINE, musician, educator; b. Chappaqua, NY, Jan. 16, 1952; d. Edward Albert and Gladys (Dildarian) Hamilton; m. Brian Vincent Moran, Aug. 5, 1979; children: Melissa Kathleen, Kevin William. Attended, U. N.C., Greensboro, 1970—72; MusB Edn., Westminster Choir Coll., Princeton, NJ, 1975; grad. student in Musicology, NYU, 1978—80. Cert. music specialist Pre-K-12 Dept. Edn. Mass., 2000, N.J., 1975. Music specialist Westminster Choir Coll. (Conservatory divsn.), Princeton, 1975; pvt. instrn. (voice/flute/recorder/eurhythmics) Holliston, Mass., 1975—; music specialist Montessori Children's Rm., Armonk, NY, 1975—83, various Montessori schs., music schs., pub. schs., pvt. schs., Md., Mass., and NY, 1983—89, Christian Family Montessori Sch., Holliston, 1989—2006, Hopkinton Pub. Schs., Mass., 1996—. Flute soloist in field, 1975—; soprano soloist in field, 1975—; student Kodaly Music Tchrs. Workshops, Princeton, 1975; participant/student Music Educator Workshops/Chamber Music Workshops:Dalcroze Sch. of Music/Mannes Coll. of Music, NYC, 1978—89; participant master class with Jean-Pierre Rampal, NYC, 1979, Montessori Music Teacher's Workshop Whitby Sch., Greenwich, Conn., 1980; flutist Southeastern Mass. Concert Band, Medway, Mass., 1990—; singer Berkshire Choral Inst., Sheffield, Mass., 1996—; profl. devel. mgr., exec. bd. New Eng. chpt. Am. Orff-Schulwerk Assn., Lexington, Mass., 1999—2003; singer Heritage Chorale, Framingham, 1999—, chorus rep. bd. dirs., 2003—07; singer/flutist Composer's Conf.: Chamber Music Ctr. and Singer's Workshop, Wellesley, Mass., 2003—. Author (co-author): (guidebook) Curriculum Guide for Hopkinton, Mass. Dept. Music; singer: (concerts) choral concerts under the direction of Leonard Bernstein, Pierre Boulez, Antal Dorati, (concert) under Robert Shaw in Mostly Mozart Festival, Lincoln Ctr. Music specialist, volunteered classes in music to support funding for town playground Town of Annapolis, Md., 1988; membership chmn. Medway Newcomer's Club, Mass., 1988—89. Recipient numerous monetary awards given to Hopkinton Edn. Found. in name of Ms. Moran for fostering excellence in edn., Hopkinton, Mass., 1999—2008. Mem.: Am. Orff-Schulwerk Assn., Nat. Assn. Tchrs. Singing, Mass. Music Educators Assn., Music Educators Nat. Conf., Soc. Gen. Music (Mass.), Gone with the Winds woodwind quintet, Cmty. Orch., Arundel Vocal Arts Soc. (Md.), Westchester Choral Soc., Somer's Chorale, Bach Choral Soc., Pleasantville Cantata Singers (N.Y.), Broadmoor Chamber Singers. Achievements include developing a system for music education based upon Kodaly/Orff/Dalcroze methods; researching and developing methods for ear-training and pitch understanding for young children; thirty years of studying and implementing creative approaches of music education based upon the Dalcroze, Kodaly, Orff methods of music learning. Avocations: yoga, swimming, cross-country skiing, hiking, dance. Home: 267 Norfolk St Holliston MA 01746 Office: Hopkinton Public Schools Haydn Rowe St Hopkinton MA 01748 Home Phone: 508-429-1949. Personal E-mail: wenmora@aol.com. Business E-Mail: wmoran@hopkinton.k12.ma.us.

MORANT, BLAKE, dean, law educator; b. Hampton, Va. m. Paulette Morant. BA, U. Va., Charlottesville, 1975, JD, 1978. Legal intern NASA Office the Gen. Counsel, Hampton, 1976, Washington, 1977; atty., 18th Airborne Corps US Army Judge Advocate Gen., Ft. Bragg, NC, 1979—82, atty., Corps Profl. Recruiting Office Ft. Belvoir, Va., 1982—84, adminstrv. law atty. Washington, 1984—85; faculty mem. Campbell U., 1980—82; sr. assoc. Marguiles & Rephan, Washington, 1985—87; asst. gen. counsel Washington Met. Transit Authority, 1987—92; faculty mem. Am. U. Washington Coll. Law, 1988—92, U. Toledo Coll. Law, 1992—94, 1995—96, 1997, U. Mich. Law Sch., 1994; Roy L. Steinheimer prof. law, dir. Frances Lewis Law Ctr. Wash. and Lee U. Sch. Law, 1997—2007, assoc. dean academic affairs; faculty mem. U. Ala. Sch. Law, 2002; dean, prof. law Wake Forest U. Sch. Law, Winston-Salem, NC, 2007—. Mem., past chmn. com. on diversity ABA; mem. profl. devel. com. Assn. Am. Law Schools; mem. task force to study gender bias in Va. courts Va. Supreme Ct.; vis. fellow Oxford U., England, 2001. Mem. editl. bd.: Jour. Legal Edn.; contbr. articles to profl. jours. 2d. lt. US Army, capt. US Army Judge Advocate Gen. Corps. Decorated Meritorious Svc. medal 1st Oak Leaf Cluster US Army. Office: Wake Forest Sch Law 1834 Wake Forest Rd Winston Salem NC 27109 Office Phone: 336-758-5435. Business E-Mail: morantbd@wfu.edu.*

MORANT, RICARDO BERNARDINO, psychology professor; b. New Britain, Conn., Feb. 13, 1926; s. J. Ramon and Rosario (Ciscar) M.; m. G. Francisca Giner, Dec. 26, 1955; children— Ramon, Francisca, Dolores, Ricardo. AB, Harvard, 1948; postgrad., Wesleyan Coll., Middletown, Conn., 1948-49; MA, Clark U., 1950, PhD, 1952. From faculty to prof. Brandeis U., Waltham, Mass., 1952—91, Minnie and Harold L. Fierman prof. psychology, 1991—2005, prof. Volen Nat. Ctr. for Complex Sys., 1994—2005, prof. emeritus, 2005—. Prin. investigator NIMH, Spencer Found., Rothman Found. 1960—; spl. research space perception, body orientation. Bd. dirs. Coun. Pub. Schs., 1970-73; mem. steering com. Sensory Aid Eval. and Devel. Ctr., MIT, 1963-67; chmn. bd. trustees Hiatt Ednl. Programs, 1982-94. Served with USNR, 1946-48. Fellow APA; mem. Psychonomic Soc. Home: 35 Cliff Rd Wellesley MA 02481-3001 E-mail: morant@brandeis.edu.

MORARI, MANFRED, chemical engineer, educator; b. Graz, Austria, May 13, 1951; came to U.S., 1975; s. Manfred and Hilde M.; m. Marina Korchynsky, May 12, 1984. Diploma Chem. Engring., Eidgenoessische Technische Hochschule, Zurich, Switzerland, 1974; PhD in Chem. Engring., U. Minn., 1977; Dr h c, Babes Bolyai U., 2003. Asst. prof. U. Wis., Madison, 1977-81, assoc. prof., 1981-83; prof. chem. engring. Calif. Inst. Tech., Pasadena, 1983-94, McCollum-Corcoran prof., 1991-94, exec. officer, 1990-93, prof. control and dynamical sys., 1993-94; exec. officer, 1993-94; head automatic control lab. ETH. Gulf vis. prof. chem. engring. Carnegie Mellon U., 1987. Contbr. articles to profl. jours. Recipient D.P. Eckman award Am. Automatic Control Coun., 1980, J.R. Ragazzini award Am. Automatic Control Coun., 2007. Fellow: AIChE (A.P. Colburn award 1984, Profl. Progress award 1995, Computing in Chem. Engring. award 2002), IEEE (George S. Axelby Outstanding Paper award 1990, Control Sys. Field award 2005), Am. Soc. Engring. Edn. (Curtis W. McGraw rsch. award 1989), Am. Chem. Soc.; mem.: NAE. Home: Laerchentobelstrasse 22 CH-8700 Kusnacht Switzerland Office: Automatic Control Lab ETH-Z ETL I 29 CH-8092 Zurich Switzerland Business E-Mail: morari@control.ee.ethz.ch.

MORATH, MAX EDWARD, entertainer, composer, writer; b. Colorado Springs, Colo., Oct. 1, 1926; s. Frederic Palmer and Gladys Hester Nancy (Ramsell) M.; m. Norma Loy Tackitt, Oct. 23, 1953 (div. 1992); children: Kathryn, Christine, Frederic; m. Diane Fay Skomars, May 24, 1993. BA in English, Colo. Coll., 1948; postgrad., Stanford NBC-Radio-TV Inst., Palo Alto, Calif., 1951; MA in Am. Studies, Columbia U., 1996. Touring nationally in concerts and theater, 1961-2005; writer, host (radio series WFMT Radio) Ragtime to the Max, 2006; recs. on Epic, RCA, Vanguard, SoloArt, Omega, Premier; author: The Road to Ragtime, 1999, The NPR Curious Listener's Guide to Popular Standards, 2002, I Love You Truly, 2008; playwright, prodr., composer. Mem. Broadcast Music, Inc. Home and Office: 463 Hartley Place Duluth MN 55803 Office Phone: 218-724-5886. Personal E-mail: rathmo@gmail.com.

MORAWETZ, CATHLEEN SYNGE, mathematician; b. Toronto, Ont., Can., May 5, 1923; arrived in U.S., 1945, naturalized, 1950; d. John Lighton and Elizabeth Eleanor Mabel (Allen) Synge; m. Herbert Morawetz, Oct. 28, 1945; children: Pegeen Morawetz Rubinstein, John Synge, Lida Morawetz Jeck, Nancy. BA, U. Toronto, 1945; SM, MIT, 1946; PhD, NYU, 1951; degree (hon.), Ea. Mich. U., 1980, Smith Coll., 1982, Brown U., 1982, Princeton U., 1986, Duke U., 1988, N.J. Inst. Tech., 1988, U. Waterloo, 1993, U. Dublin, 1996, U. Toronto, 1996, NYU, 2007. Research assoc. Courant Inst., NYU, 1952—57, asst. prof. math., 1957—60, assoc. prof., 1960—65, prof., 1965—, assoc. dir., 1978—84, dir., 1984—88. Chmn. bd. Sch. Theoretical Physics Dublin Inst. for Advanced Studies, 1995—2000. Contbr. articles to profl. jours. Trustee Princeton U., 1973—78, Sloan Found., 1980—94. Recipient Nat. medal of Sci., NSF, 1998; grantee Office of Naval Rsch., 1975—90; fellow Guggenheim, 1967, 1979. Fellow: AAAS, Royal Soc. Can.; mem.: NAS, London Math. Soc., Royal Irish Acad., Soc. Indsl. and Applied Math., Am. Philos. Soc., Am. Acad. Arts and Scis., Am. Math. Soc. (term trustee 1975—85, pres. 1995—97, George David Birkhoff prize in Applied Math. (awarded jointly by Am. Math. Soc. and Soc. for Indsl. and Applied Math.) 2006, Steele prize 2004). Achievements include research in applications of partial differential equations, especially transonic flow and scattering theory. Office: CIMS 251 Mercer St New York NY 10012-1110 Office Phone: 212-998-3297. Business E-Mail: morawetz@cims.nyu.edu.

MORCHIO, RENZO GIULIO, retired biophysicist, researcher, educator; b. Genoa, Italy, Dec. 7, 1924; s. Rocco and Leontina (Vildosi) M.; m. Ada Mussi, May 3, 1952. D in Scis., U. Genoa, 1947; PhD, U. Rome, 1971. Trainee Inst. Zoology U. Genoa, 1948-49, trainee Inst. Theoretic Physics, 1959, asst. prof., 1960, prof., 1962-97; ret., 1997. Guest Harvard U., Boston, 1956-57; pres. Comitate Nazionale U., U. Genoa, 1970-84; pres. Commn. of the Faculty, U. Genoa, 1977-78. Author: Fondamenti Della Biofisica, 1982, Una Biografia Della Scienza, 2005, others; mem. adv. bd. Rivista di Biologia/Biology Forum, 1997, asst. editor, 1999-2000, co-editor, 2000; contbr. over 90 articles to profl. jours. Mem. NY Acad. Scis. Avocations: music, astronomy. Home: Via Canevari 24 16137 Genoa Italy Home Phone: 39-10-8397255; Office Phone: 39 10 3536267.

MORCOTT, SCOTT M., physician, health facility administrator; MD in Family Medicine, U. South Carolina, 1993; studied, U. Pa., 1983—87. Cert. Family Medicine. Assoc. fellowship in integrative medicine U. Ariz.; with Condell Med. Ctr., Lake Forest Hosp.; dir. Northshore Health & Wellness Ctr.; co-dir. Alitus Integrative Health & Wellness Ctr.; med. dir. Passport Health Chgo., 1999—; chief med. officer PathFinder Health. Served in USN, naval flight surgeon USMC. Office: PathFinder Health 250 E Center Dr Ste 201 Vernon Hills IL 60061 Office Phone: 847-686-7284.*

MORCOTT, SOUTHWOOD JELKS (WOODY MORCOTT), retired automotive parts company executive; b. 1939; BA, Davidson Coll., 1960; MBA, U. Mich. Sales engineer, plant mgr. Dana Corp., Tyston, Ind., 1963-75, v.p. ops. Hayes Dana Ltd., 1975-77, exec. v.p., gen. mgr., 1977-78, pres. Hayes-Dana Ltd., 1978-80, group v.p. Dana svc. parts group, 1980-84, pres. N.Am. ops., 1984-86, pres., COO, 1986-89, CEO, 1989-99, chmn., 1990-2000. Bd. dirs. CSX Corp., 1990—, Phelps Dodge, 1991—2003, Johnson Controls, Inc., 1993—, Navistar Internat. Corp., 2000—. Bd. dirs. Meml. U. Med. Ctr., 2003—. Recipient Automotive Industry Leader of Yr. award, Automotive Hall of Fame, 1998.

MORD, IRVING CONRAD, II, lawyer; b. Mar. 22, 1950; s. Irving Conrad and Lillie Viva (Chapman) M.; m. Julia Ann Russell, Aug. 22, 1970 (div. Apr. 1980); children: Russell Conrad, Emily Ann; m. Kay E. McDaniel, Aug. 31, 1985; children: Kurt August, Clayton Troy. BS, Miss. State U., 1972; JD, U. Miss., 1974. Bar: Miss. 1974, U.S. Dist. Ct. (no. dist.) Miss. 1974, U.S. Dist. Ct. (so. dist.) Miss. 1984. Counsel to bd. suprs. Noxubee County, Miss., 1976-80, Walthall County, Miss., 1980—, Bd. Edn., Walthall County, 1982—. County pros. atty. Noxubee County, Macon, Miss., 1974—80, Walthall County, Tylertown, Miss., 1982—88, Tylertown, 1991—96. Bd. dirs. East Miss. Coun., Meridian, 1978-80, Trustmark Nat. Bank, Tylertown, 1986—, chmn., 2002-; v.p. Macon coun. Boy Scouts Am., 1978, mem. coun., 1979; county crusade chmn. Am. Cancer Soc., Macon, 1976-78, county pres., 1979; chmn. fund dr. fine arts complex Miss. State U., Macon, 1979; Walthall County family master, 1996—, Walthall County Youth referee, 1996—; mem. Local Workforce Investment Bd., 2000—. Recipient Youth Leadership award Miss. Econ. Coun., 1976. Mem. Miss. Assn. Bd. Attys. (v.p. 1985, pres. 1986), Miss. Assn. Sch. Bd. Attys., Miss. State Bar, Am. Judicature Soc. (Torts award 1972), Nat. Fed. Ind. Bus., Miss. State U. Alumni Assn., Walthall County C. of C., Phi Kappa Tau (bd. govs. 1976-80, grad. coun. 1972—, pres. grad. coun. 1977-80, pres. house corp. 1977-80, Alumnus of Yr. Alpha Chi chpt. 1979), Rotary (sec.-treas. 1977, v.p. 1978, pres. Macon 1979, pres. Tylertown club 1986-87), Phi Delta Phi. Office: 729 Beulah Ave Tylertown MS 39667-2709 Office Phone: 601-876-2611. E-mail: icmord@bellsouth.net.

MORDAUNT, OWEN GLEN, literature and language professor, director; s. Walter W. Mordaunt and Paulina G. Anderson; m. Beverly J. Moolenaar; children: Alycia G., Austin T. BEd, U. Botswana, Roma, Lesotho, Swaziland, 1966; MS, Ind. U., Bloomington, 1971, PhD, 1981. Cert. in edn. UBLS, Swaziland Govt., 1970, AID, 1983. Tchr. Our Lady Sorrow's HS, Hluti, Swaziland, 1967—70, Kankakee Valley HS & Sch. Dist., Wheatfield, Ind., 1985—86; assoc. instr. Ind. U., Ctr. English Lang. Tng., 1971—73, 1977—79, rsch. asst., 1974—75; instr. William Pitcher Tchr.'s Coll., Manzini, Swaziland, 1975—77; sr. insp. schs. English Swaziland Ministry Edn., Mbabane, 1981—85; instr. English U. Swaziland, Kwaluseni, 1985—85, asst. prof., 1984—85; liaison English dept. and internat. studies, cons. ESL U. Nebr., Omaha, 1986—, asst. prof., 1986—92, assoc. prof., 1992—2001, prof., 2001—, dir. TESOL certs., 2005—. Contbr. articles to profl. jour. Chaplain Alegent Health Sys., Omaha, 2002. Mem.: TESOL, Global Studies Adv. Com., U. Nebr., Dana Coll., Creighton U., MIDTESOL, Western Lit. Assn., Coll. English Assn. Avocations: gardening, piano, singing. Office: Univ Nebr at Omaha 60th & Dodge Sts Omaha NE 68182-0175

MORDEN, ANNETTE SONJA KNUDSON, retired education educator; b. Phoenix, Mar. 17, 1940; d. Maynard Wold and Mertie Lucille Knudson; m. Robert Dean Morden, Aug. 5, 1962; children: Kristina, Shauna. BA, U. No. Iowa, 1962, MA in edn., 1966. Math tchr. Rockford Roosevelt, Ill., 1962—65; benthic biologist U. Wis., 1972, 1975, sr. lectr. and dir. math tutoring lab, 1982—2005. Unit leader and budget, audit and fin. com. League of Women Voters, 1971—73; brownie and girl scout leader Girl Scouts Am., 1963—64, 1977—82; bd. dirs. and exec. bd. YMCA, 1976—81; mem. founding com. and exec. bd. Habitat for Humanity, 1991—94. Mem.: Assn. U. Wis. Profls. Lutheran. Avocations: reading, travel, snorkeling. Home: 1422 N 21st St Superior WI 54880

MORDEN, JOHN REID, security-international relations consultant; b. Hamilton, Ont., Canada, June 17, 1941; s. Warren Wilbert and Isabelle Gemmell (Reid) M.; m. Margaret Keens, June 27, 1964; children: Michael, Geoffrey. BA, Dalhousie U., 1962; postgrad., Dalhousie Law Sch., 1962-63; LLD (hon.), Dalhousie U., 2003. With Can. Dept. External Affairs, various worldwide cities, 1963-84; asst. dep. min. native claims Dept. Indian & Northern Devel., Canada, 1984-85; trade and econ. policy Can. Dept. External Affairs, 1985-86; asst. sec. to cabinet Fgn. and Def. Affairs, Can., 1986-87; dir. Can. Security Intelligence Svc., 1987-91; dep. min. fgn. affairs Govt. Can., 1991-94; pres, CEO, Atomic Energy of Can., Ltd., Ottawa, Ont., Canada, 1994-98; mng. dir. Kroll Asocs. Can., Toronto, 1999-2000; chmn. KPMG Corp. Intelligence Inc., Toronto, 2000—02; pres. RM & A, Inc., 2002—; exec. dir. Independent Inquiry UN Iraq Oil for Food Programme, 2004—06. Mem. Can. com. Coun. Security and Cooperation in Asia and Pacific; security advisor CARE Can.; adv. bd. Homeland Security Alliance, 2003—05; sr. rsch. fellow Can. Def. and Fgn. Affairs Inst.; mem. audit com. Dept. Fgn. Affairs & Internat. Trial. Chair bd. govs. Trent U., 2002—08; mem. internat. adv. coun. York U., 1993—2006; chair Coun. Chairs Ont. Univs., 2004—06; bd. dirs. Nat. Assn. U. Bd. Chairs, 2007—08. Decorated Order of Can.; Order of So. Cross (Brazil); recipient Ian L. Macrae award, 1998. Mem.: Nat. Club, Toronto Hunt Club. Avocations: photography, music, ballet, reading. Office Phone: 416-486-3520. Business E-Mail: reidmorden@rogers.com.

MORDEN, ROBERT DEAN, biology professor; b. Jefferson, Iowa, Mar. 16, 1939; s. Bert E. and Ruth Agnus Morden; m. Annette Sonja Knudson, Aug. 5, 1962; children: Kristina Kay, Shauna Suzanne. BA, U. Northern Iowa, Cedar Falls, 1962, MA, 1966; PhD, U. Ill., Champaign, 1971. Lic. med. technologist AMA, 1977. Chmn. dept. sci. Dysart HS, Iowa, 1962; sci. tchr. Auburn HS, Rockford, Ill., 1962—65; fellow U. Northern Iowa, 1965—66, U. Ill. Nat. Inst. Health, Urbana, 1966—71; faculty U. Wis., Superior, 1971—, chmn. dept. biology and med. tech., 1989—92. Mem. clin. faculty St. Lukes Hosp., Duluth, Minn., 1977—83. Contbr. articles to profl. jours. Recipient Tchg. Excellence award, Regents of Wis., 1993—94, Chancellor's Exemplary Advising award, 1996—97, 1997—98, Faculty Achievement award, Burlington Northern Found., 1996—97. Avocations: travel, golf. Business E-Mail: rmorden@uwsuper.edu.

MORDOHAI, PHILIPPOS, engineering educator; b. Thessaloniki, Greece, Oct. 27, 1975; Diploma in Elec. and Computer Engring., Aristotle U., Thessaloniki, 1998; MS in Elec. Engring., U. Southern Calif., LA, 2000, PhD in Elec. Engring., 2005. Postdoc. rsch. assoc. U. NC, Chapel Hill, 2005—07; postdoc. rschr. U. Pa., Phila., 2007—08; asst. prof. Stevens Inst. Tech., Hoboken, NJ, 2008—.

MORDUCH, JONATHAN, economist, educator; b. London, Oct. 3, 1963; married. BA, Brown U., Providence, 1985; PhD, Harvard U., Cambridge, Mass., 1991; PhD (hon.), U. Libre de Bruxelles, Brussels, 2008. Asst. prof. Harvard U., 1991—95, assoc. prof., 1995—98; rsch. fellow Princeton U., NJ, 1998—2000; assoc. prof. NYU, 2000—06, prof., 2006—. Mng. dir. Fin. Access Initiative, NYC, 2006—. Author: (book) Economics of Microfinance, Portfolios of the Poor: How the World's Poor Live on $2 a Day. Mem. UN Advisors Group Inclusive Fin. Sectors, NYC, 2006—08, World Econ. Forum Global Agenda Coun., Geneva, 2008. Grant, NSF, 1993—96, Nat. fellowship, Hoover Instn., Stanford U., 1997—98, Abe fellowship, Ctr. Global Partnership, 2002—03, grant, Bill and Melinda Gates Found., 2006—. Mem.: Am. Econ. Assn.

MORDY, JAMES CALVIN, retired lawyer; b. Ashland, Kans., Jan. 3, 1927; s. Thomas Robson and Ruth (Floyd) M.; m. Marjory Ellen Nelson, Nov. 17, 1951; children: Jean Claire Mordy Jongeling, Rebecca Jane Mordy King, James Nelson. BA in Chemistry, U. Kans., 1947; JD, U. Mich., 1950; postgrad., George Washington U., 1952—53. Bar: Kans. 1950, Mo. 1950, cert.: Am. Bankruptcy Bd. (in bus. bankruptcy law). Assoc., Morrison, Hecker, Buck, Cozad & Rogers, Kansas City, Mo., 1950—59; ptnr. Morrison & Hecker LLP, Kansas City, 1959—96, sr. counsel, 1996—97, of counsel, 1997—2000; ret., 2000. Mem. Mich. Law Rev., 1948-49; contbg. author: Missouri Bar Insurance Handbook, 1968, Missouri Bar Bankruptcy Handbook, 1991, also supplements; contbr. articles to profl. jours. Chmn. bd. Broadway United Meth. Ch., Kansas City, 1964-70, chmn. bd. trustees, chmn. fin. com., 1988-90, 94, 2000-2002; bd. dirs. Broadway Child Enrichment Ctr., 1980-2006; bd. dirs., exec. com. Della Lamb Neighborhood House, Kansas City, 1973-80; bd. dirs., treas. Friends of Sacred Structures, Kansas City, 2000-2007; coun. mem. St. Paul Sch. Theology, Kansas City, 1986-; bd. dirs. Kingswood Sr. Living Cmty., Kansas City, 2004—, vice chmn., 2005-; del. 17th World Meth. Conf., Rio de Janeiro, 1996; ranger Rocky Mountain Nat. Park, 1948-1949. With USN, 1945-46, 51-53, comdr. USNR, ret. Recipient Shepherd of the Lamb award, Della Lamb Neighborhood House, 1980; Summerfield scholar, 1943—47. Fellow Am. Coll. Bankruptcy, Am. Bar Found. (life); mem. ABA, Am. Judicature Soc., Am. Bankruptcy Inst., Mo. Bar Assn., Kansas City Met. Bar Assn., Lawyers Assn. Kansas City, Workout Profs. Assn. Kansas City, Univ. Club (v.p., bd. dirs. 1983, 86), Barristers Soc., Phi Beta Kappa, Delta Tau Delta (pres. Kansas City alumni chpt. 1965-72, pres. U. Kans. House Corp. 1966-72), Alpha Chi Sigma, Phi Alpha Delta. Avocations: travel, geography (maps), history, music, theology. Office: Stinson Morrison Hecker LLP 1201 Walnut St Kansas City MO 64106-2150 Home: 10000 Wornall Rd Apt 1412 Kansas City MO 64114

MORE, DOUGLAS MCLOCHLAN, lawyer; b. NYC, Apr. 21, 1926; s. Morgan Berkeley and Lucinda (Bateson) M.; m. Pamela Bennett Marr, Aug. 6, 1954; children— Robin Maclachlan More Eddy, Alison Marr More Davies. Grad., Phillips Exeter Acad., 1943; BA, Harvard U., 1947; LL.B., Columbia U., 1950. Bar: N.Y. State bar 1950, Conn. bar 1981, Fla. bar 1983. With N.Y. Trust Co., 1950-51; assoc. firm Bigham, Englar, Jones & Houston, NYC, 1951-53; fin. analyst Johns-Manville Corp., 1953-54; assoc. firm Kissam & Halpin, NYC, 1954-59; assoc. counsel Hooker Chem. Corp., 1959-63, gen. counsel, 1963-72, v.p., 1967-72; v.p. law Airco, Inc., 1972-75; gen. counsel Beker Industries Corp., 1975-81, v.p., 1975-78, sr. v.p., 1978-81; ptnr. firm More Phillips & Duncan, P.C., Greenwich, Conn., 1981-88. Served to lt. (j.g.) USNR, 1943-46. Mem. ABA, Conn. Bar Assn., Phi Delta Phi, Phoenix S-K Club, Hasty Pudding Inst. 1770 (Harvard). Home and Office: 27 Skylark Rd Greenwich CT 06830-4624 Office Phone: 203-869-0663.

MORE, PHILIP HARVEY BIRNBAUM, business administration educator; b. San Diego, Jan. 21, 1944; s. Louis and Ruth Laureen (Bay) B.; m. Marlin Sue Van Every, Dec. 26, 1964; 1 child, Brian Philip. BA, U. Calif., Berkeley, 1965; PhD, U. Wash., 1975. Internal cons./analyst Los Angeles County Civil Svc. Commn., 1965-67; tchg. assoc. U. Wash., Seattle, 1972-74; asst. prof. bus. adminstrn. Ind. U., Bloomington, 1975-80, assoc. prof., 1980-85, prof., 1986—. Resident dir. J.F.K. Int., Tiburg U., The Netherlands; vis. scholar Polish Acad. Scis., Hungarian Acad. Scis., Tokyo U., SDA Bocconi, Milan, Italy, Seoul Nat. U., Korea, Dartmouth Coll. Co-author: Organization Theory: Structural and Behavioral Analysis, Modern Management Techniques for Engineers and Scientists, International Research Management: Studies in Interdisciplinary Methods From Business, Government and Academics, 1990; assoc. editor IEEE Transaction on Engring. Mgmt. jour.; contbr. articles to profl. jours., book revs., chpts. to books. With USAF, 1967—71. NSF fellow, 1974-75, NY Acad. Scis. fellow, 1981; U. Hong Kong Sr. Fulbright scholar, 1981-82. Mem. Acad. Mgmt. (pres. tech. and innovation mgmt. divsn. 1989-90), Engring. Mgmt. Soc., Inst. Ops. Rsch. and Mgmt. Scis., Internat. Assn. for Study of Interdisciplinary Rsch., Beta Gamma Sigma, Beta Alpha Psi, Sigma Iota Epsilon, Sigma Chi. Methodist Rotarian. Office: Univ So Calif Marshall Sch Bus Los Angeles CA 90089-0808 Office Phone: 213-740-0744. Business E-Mail: phbmore@marshall.usc.edu.

MOREAU, CLAUDE P., oil industry executive; Degree in fin., Laval U., Quebec, Can. Mktg. and bus. devel. positions Texaco Can., Inc., Texaco Internat. Ltd., Alimentation Couche Tard Inc.; v.p. mfg. & mktg. Chevron Texaco Latin America Products Co., 2001—03; chief comml. officer, the Americas Trafigura AG, 2003—07; v.p. mktg. Tesoro Corp., San Antonio, 2007—. Office: Tesoro Corp 300 Concord Plz Dr San Antonio TX 78216 Office Phone: 210-828-8484.

MOREAU, ETHAN, professional hockey player; b. Huntsville, Ont., Can., Sept. 22, 1975; m. Ornella Moreau; children: Trey, Mia. Left wing Chgo. Blackhawks, 1996—99, Edmonton Oilers, 1999—, capt., 2007—. Active in Oilers Cmty. Found. Recipient King Clancy Trophy, 2009. Office: Edmonton Oilers Hockey Club 11230 - 110 St Edmonton AB T5G 3H7 Canada*

MOREAU, NANCY A., physics professor; d. Cyril and Rose Harvilchuck; m. Wayne Martin Moreau, Nov. 10, 1967; children: David, Deborah. BS, EdM, Pa. State U., 1966; PhD, Capella U. Nat. bd. cert. physics tchr. Rsch. physicist IBM, Yorktown Heights, NY; physics tchr. Wappingers Sch., NY, 1975—2005; physics prof. Dutchess CC, Poughkeepsie, NY, 1980—2005; edn. prof. Northampton CC, Bethlehem, Pa., 2005—. Physics tchr., rsch. agent Am. Assn. Physics Tchrs., Coll. Pk., Md., 1986—; cons. Coll. Bd., Phila., 1986—. Author: (chemistry book) General Chemistry Review, 1985, (algebra book) Math A and Math B, 2004—. Trustee Wappingers Presbyn. Ch., 1990, United Meth. Ch., Gouldsboro, Pa., 2006. Engring. Grant, Dartmouth Coll., 2000. Mem.: Am. Assn. Physics Tchrs. (HS chair 1995—2002), Trout Unlimited (chpt. organizer 2005—). Avocations: trout fishing, watercolors. Business E-Mail: nmoreau@northampton.edu.

MOREHOUSE, DAVID, professional sports team executive; m. Vanessa Morehouse; children: Jackson, Mackenzie. Attended, CC of Allegheny County, Duquesne U.; MPA, Harvard U., 1999. Dep. dir. D.A.R.E. America, 1997—98; sr. counselor to v.p. Al Gore The White House, 1999—2001, dep. dir. presdl. advance, dir. strategic planning Nat. Drug Control Policy; spl. asst. legis. affairs US Dept. Defense; dep. dir. exec. edn. John F. Kennedy Sch. Govt., Harvard U., 2001—03; sr. advisor, traveling chief of staff John Kerry for Pres. campaign, 2004; sr. cons. Pitts. Penguins, 2004—07, pres., 2007—. Achievements include being the president of Stanely Cup Champion Pittsburgh Penguins, 2009. Office: Pittsburgh Penguins 66 Mario Lemieux Pl Pittsburgh PA 15219

MOREHOUSE, DAVID FRANK, geologist; b. Charles City, Iowa, Dec. 8, 1943; s. Neal Francis and Florence E. (Schwendener) M. BS in Gen. Scis., State U. Iowa, 1967; MS in Geology, Iowa State U., 1970; postgrad., Pa. State U., 1970-74. Staff geologist Nat. Gas Survey and Planning and Spl. Projects Div., FPC, Washington, 1974-78; dir. Info. Processing and Interpretation and Analysis Divs. Oil and Gas Info. System, Energy Info. Adminstrn., Washington, 1978-80, sr. supervisory geologist, 1980-95, sr. petroleum geologist, 1996—. Advisor petroleum data sys. U. Okla., Norman, 1975-86; Energy Info. Adminstrn. rep. Am. Gas Assn. Com. on Natural Gas Res., Washington, 1991-95, Potential Gas Com., Boulder, Colo., 1991—; Dept. of Energy rep. Fed. Geog. Data Com. Coordination Group, 1997—; Nat. Critical Infrastructure Task Force Energy Group, 1998—. V.p. Iowa Jr. Acad. Sci., 1961. Recipient awards for outstanding performance Fed. Govt., Washington, 1974—. Fellow Nat. Speleological Soc.; mem. AAAS, AIME, AGI, Am. Geophys. Union, Internat. Assn. Math. Geology, N.Y. Acad. Scis. Congregationalist. Achievements include first evidence that sulfuric acid can be important to speleogenesis; exercising the prin. responsibility for design and establishment of fed. govts. domestic oil and gas reserves estimation and analysis program. Office: Energy Info Adminstrn EI-46 1000 Independence Ave SW Washington DC 20585-0644 E-mail: david.morehouse@eia.doe.gov.

MOREHOUSE, LAWRENCE GLEN, veterinarian, educator, academic administrator; b. Manchester, Kans., July 21, 1925; s. Edwy Owen and Ethel Merle (Glenn) M.; m. Georgia Ann Lewis, Oct. 6, 1956; children: Timothy Lawrence, Glenn Ellen. BS in Biol. Sci., Kans. State U., 1952, DVM, 1952; MS in Animal Pathology, Purdue U., 1956, PhD, 1960. Lic. vet. medicine. Veterinarian County Animal Hosp., Des Peres, Mo., 1952-53; supr. Brucellosis labs. Purdue U., West Lafayette, Ind., 1953-60; staff veterinarian lab. svcs. USDA, Washington, 1960-61; discipline leader in pathology and toxicology, animal health divsn. USDA Nat. Animal Disease Lab., Ames, Iowa, 1961-64; prof., chmn. dept. vet. pathology U. Mo. Coll. Vet. Medicine, Columbia, Mo., 1964—69, 1969—86, dir. Vet. Med. Diagnostic Lab., 1968-88, prof. emeritus, 1986—. Cons. USDA, to comdg. gen. U.S. Army R&D Command, Am. Inst. Biol. Scis., NAS, to Surg. Gen., Miss. State U., St. Louis Zoo Residency Tng. Program, Miss. Vet. Med. Assn., Okla. State U., Pa. Dept. Agr., Ohio Dept. Agr. Co-editor: Mycotoxic Fungi, Mycotoxins, Mycotoxicoses: An International Encyclopedic Handbook, 3 vols., 1977; contbr. articles on diseases of animals to profl. jours. Active Trinity Presbyn. Ch., Columbia, 1964-2002; bd. dirs. Mo. Symphony Soc., Columbia, 1989-92. Pharmacists mate second class USNR, 1943-46, PTO; 2d. lt. U.S. Army, 1952-56. Recipient Outstanding Svc. award USDA, 1959, merit cert., 1963, 64, Disting. Svc. award U. Mo. Coll. Vet. Medicine, 1987, Dean's Impact award, 1996, Kans. State U. Alumni award, 2004. Fellow Royal Soc. Health London; mem. AAAS, Am. Assn. Vet. Lab. Diagnosticians (E.P. Pope award 1976, chmn. lab. accreditation bd. 1972-79, 87-90, pres. 1979-80, sec.-treas. 1983-87), World Assn. Vet. Lab. Diagnosticians (bd. dirs. 1984-94, dir. emeritus 1994—), N.Y. Acad. Sci., U. S. Animal Health Assn., Am. Assn. Lab. Animal Sci., Mo. Soc. Microbiology, Am. Assn. Avian Pathologists, N.Am. Conf. Rsch. Workers in Animal Diseases, Mo. Univ. Retirees Assn. (pres. 1996-99). Presbyterian. Avocations: classic cars, boating, genealogy. Home: 916 Danforth Dr Columbia MO 65201-6164 Office: U Mo Vet Med Diagnostic Lab PO Box 6023 Columbia MO 65205-6023 Office Phone: 573-442-7069. Personal E-mail: gmoreho@att.global.net. Business E-Mail: lmorehou@coin.org.

MOREHOUSE, RICHARD EDWARD, psychology professor; b. LaCrosse, Wis., May 21, 1941; s. Ervin Lenard and Anna Martha (Weiland) Morehouse; m. Rita Spangler, Aug. 20, 1966; 1 child, Lyda Ann. BS, U. Wis., 1971, MST, 1973; PhD, Union Inst., 1979. Teaching asst. U. Wis., LaCrosse, 1971-72; ednl. cons. Coop. Ednl. Svcs. Agy., LaCrosse, 1972-80; dir. coop. edn. Viterbo U., LaCrosse, 1980-85; from asst. to prof. psychology Viterbo Coll., LaCrosse, 1985—. Dept. chmn. Viterbo U., LaCrosse, 1986—93, chair, 1995—2000; vis. scholar Tex. Wesleyan U., Ft. Worth, 1993—94; vis. prof. Glyndwr U., Wrexham, 2008—. Co-author: Student Study Guide for Human Development Across the Lifespan, 1991, 1994, Beginning Qualitative Research, 1994; co-editor: Analytic Teaching, 1991—96; editor, 1996—; mem. editl. bd. Curriculum Jour., 1997—99, cons. editor Alta. Jour. Edn. Rsch., 2000—, Can. Jour. Edn., editl. bd. mem. Jour. Pedagogical Rsch. & Scholarship. Grantee Gifted Edn., Elem. and Secondary Edn. Act, 1976—79, Tchr. Tng., Cmty. Awareness, Wis. Humanities, 1982, Coll., Cmty. Symposium, 1983. Mem.: Am. Psychol. soc. (charter), N.Am. Assn. for Cmty. Inquiry (founder, 1st pres. 1994). Democrat. Unitarian Universalist. Home: 1131 Charles St La Crosse WI 54603-2508 Office: Viterbo Coll 815 9th St S La Crosse WI 54601-4777 Office Phone: 608-782-4041. Business E-Mail: remorehouse@viterbo.edu.

MOREHOUSE, SARAH MCCALLY, retired political science professor; b. Boston, Jan. 15, 1927; d. Ralph Dewey and Eugenia Whitehead (Norris) Powell; m. Richard Kenyon McCally June 25, 1949 (div. Sept. 1969) m. W. Bradley Morehouse, Nov. 8, 1969 (div. Nov. 1986); children: Richard, John, Catherine, David; m. Malcolm Edwin Jewell, Dec. 28, 1991. BA in Polit. Sci., Wellesley Coll., 1948; PhD in Polit. Sci., Yale U., 1964. Instr. Conn. Coll., New London, 1964-66; lectr. Hunter Coll., Bronx, NY, 1966—69; assoc. prof. Manhattanville Coll., Purchase, NY, 1969—75; prof. U. Conn., Stamford, 1976-92, prof. emerita, 1992—. Univ. senator U. Conn., 1982-85, assoc. dir., 1990-91. Author: State Politics, Parties and Policy, 2nd. Edit. 2003, The Governor as Party Leader, 1998; contbr. various articles to profl. jours. Sec. Charter Revision Commn. Fairfield, Conn., 1960, mem., 2006; chmn. Ethics Commn., Fairfield, 1984-88; pres. LWV, 1996-98; state LWV sec. bd. dirs. 1998-2001. Vis. professorship for women NSF, 1991; fellow Danforth Found., 1960; rsch. grantee Russell Sage Found., 1983; vis. scholar U. Calif, Berkeley, 1991-92, Career Achievement award in State Politics and Policy, Am. Political Sci. Assn. 1999. Mem. Wellesley Club. Home: 242 Somerset Ave Fairfield CT 06824-4935 Office Phone: 203-486-2440. Personal E-mail: macsarahj@worldnet.att.net.

MOREHOUSE, VALERIE JEANNE, librarian; b. Taft, Calif., Jan. 30, 1947; d. Gordon Stanley and Cloe Ozelle (Reed) Hogue; m. Keith Herbert Morehouse, Aug. 22, 1968 (div. 1994); 1 child, Gordon. AA, Taft Coll., 1966; AB in English, U. Calif., Berkeley, 1968; MSLS, Simmons Grad. Sch. Libr. Sci., 1977. Cert. profl. librarian, Mass. Asst. libr. dir. Plymouth (Mass.) Pub. Librs., 1977—82; asst. exec. dir. Southeastern Librs. Coop., Rochester, Minn., 1982—84; libr. automation cons. N.D. State Libr., Bismarck, 1984—89; dist. libr. media dir. Bismarck Pub. Sch. Dist., 1989—97; sys. adminstr. MARINet, San Rafael, Calif., 1997—2000; libr. Temple Isaiah of Contra Costa County, Lafayette, 2001—. Adv. panelist for literature Mass. Coun. on Arts and Humanities, Boston, 1980-82. Editor, writer Libr. A Word to the Wise, 1995-97; author: Anthology: A Collection of Cape Cod Poets, 1974, Pleasanton Poetry, 2008. Legis. chair, membership chair N.D. Libr. Assn., 1987-93; mem. N.D. Gov.'s Adv. Libr. Vision 2004 Com., Bismarck, 1995-96; mem. Ctrl. Dakota Libr. Network Bd., Bismarck, 1992—. Recipient Capewide 1st prize for poetry Provincetown Assn. for Living Arts, 1972, Spl. Recognition award COSMEP, 1977, Pres.' award for svc. to librs. N.D. Libr. Assn., 1994. Mem. ALA (chair publs. com. 1985-87, columnist, reviewer The Book List 1977-79), Beta Phi Mu. Avocations: gardening, travel. Office: Temple Isaiah Libr 3800 Mt Diablo Blvd Lafayette CA 94549 Office Phone: 925-283-8575. E-mail: val@valmorehouse.info.

MOREIRA, MARCIO MARTINS, advertising executive; b. Sao Paulo, Brazil, Nov. 20, 1947; arrived in US, 1980, naturalized, 1990; s. Guido Martins and Maria Rosa Macrine; m. Maria Auxiliadora Godinho, Oct. 18, 1981; children: Eliana, Maria, Godinho; children: Joaquim, Pedro, Rezende. Ed., U. Sao Paulo, Brazil, 1970. TV producer-copywriter McCann-Erickson, Sao Paulo, Brazil, 1967-71, creative dir., 1974-77, group creative dir. London, Lisbon and Frankfurt, 1971-74, executive creative dir. Latin America, 1977-80, internat. creative dir. NYC, 1980-88; vice chmn., chief creative officer McCann Erickson Worldwide, NYC, 1988—; vice chmn., regional dir. Asia-Pacific McCann-Erickson Worldwide, NYC, 1995-99, chief creative officer, dir. global brands, 1999; vice-chmn., profl. mgmt. McCann Worldgroup. Bd. mem. Brazilian-Am. C. of C.; chmn. bd. judges NY Festivals; US judge, pres. jury Cannes Film Festival, 1989. Contbr. articles to profl. jours. Recipient Clio award, 5 time winner, 1976—89, H.K. McCann award, 1977, Paul Foley award, Interpub. Group, 1983, Gold Lion award, Silver Lion award, Bronze Lion award, AdColor Legend award, 2007. Republican. Roman Catholic. Avocations: cinema, songwriting, cars, speedwalking. Office: McCann Erickson Worldwide Hdqs 622 3rd Ave New York NY 10017-2703

MORELAN, PAULA KAY, choreographer; b. Lafayette, Ind., Nov. 24, 1949; d. Dickie Booth and Marian Maxine (Fetterhoff) M.; m. Kerim Sayan, Aug. 10, 1974. Student, U. Utah, 1968-69; BFA, Tex. Christian U., 1972; postgrad., El Centro Coll., 1969-70. Tchr. Rosello Sch. Ballet, Dallas, 1972-74; mgr., tchr. Ballet Arts Ctr., Dallas, 1974-76; owner, tchr. Ballet Classique, Garland, Tex., 1976-87, Garland Ballet Acad., 1977-87; resident choreographer Garland Civic Theatre, 1988—, lifetime mem., 1998. Asst. to Mythra Rosello Tex. Civic Ballet, Dallas, 1972—74; assoc. artistic dir. Dance Repertory Theatre Dallas, 1974—75, artistic dir., 1975—76, Garland (Tex.) Ballet Assn., 1977—90, Classical Ballet Acad., Performing Arts Sch., 1987—90, Aerial Work, 1988—2004, Metropex Gynyuatium, 2005—07, Elite Champion Gymnatics, 2009; artistic dir. musical theatre dept. KD Actors Conservatory, 2005—; founder, chairperson Act IV Guild, 2002—05. Bd. dirs. Garland Civic Theatre, 2000—05. Recipient Leon Rabin award Best Choreography, Dallas Theatre League, 1996, 1998, 2000—01, 2004, Choreographer of Yr. award, 2001—04, Best Choreographer award, 2003, Column award, 2004; nominee Best Choreography award, 2006, Best Choreographer award, 2006. Personal E-mail: pkm@worldnet.att.net.

MORELAND, DONALD EDWIN, physiologist; b. Enfield, Conn., Oct. 12, 1919; s. Albert Sinclair and Ruth (Cowan) M.; m. Verdie Brown Stallings, Nov. 6, 1954; 1 child, Donna Faye; stepchildren: Frank C., Paul Ziglar. BS in Forestry, N.C. State U., 1949, MS in Plant Physiology, 1950, PhD in Plant Physiology, 1953. Plant physiologist SUNY Coll. Forestry, Syracuse, 1952-53, USDA-Agrl. Rsch. Svc., Raleigh, NC, 1953-71, rsch. leader, 1972-78, sr. exec., 1979-95, collaborator, 1996—; asst. prof. to prof. N.C. State U., Raleigh, 1953-95, prof. emeritus, 1996—. Mem. toxicology study sect. NIH, USPHS, Bethesda, Md., 1963-67. Editor: Biochemical Responses Induced by Herbicides, 1982; mem. editorial bd. Pesticide Biochemistry and Physiology, 1971-97, Pesticide Sci., 1987-96; contbr. articles to profl. jours. 1st lt. U.S. Army, 1941-46. AEC predoctoral fellow, 1950-52. Fellow AAAS, Weed Sci. Soc. Am. (outstanding rsch. award 1973); mem. Am. Chem. Soc., Plant Growth Regulator Soc. Am., Am. Soc. Plant Physiologists, So. Weed Sci. Soc., Sigma Xi. Avocations: woodworking, surf fishing, square dancing. Home: 1508 Pineview Dr Raleigh NC 27606-2562 Office: NC State U USDA-Agrl Rsch Svc Dept Crop Sci 3127 Ligon St Raleigh NC 27607-5376

MORELAND, RICHARD PAUL, musician, educator; b. Hastings, Nebr., Aug. 15, 1946; s. Robert Howard Moreland and Marjorie Ellen Musick-Moreland; m. Marian Hope Snyder, Aug. 24, 1968; children: Laurel Ann Moreland-Graves, Randall Scott. BS in Music Edn., Bob Jones U., Greenville, SC, 1969. Cert. tchr. Mich. Tchr. Covert Pub. Schs., Mich., 1969—70, Swartz Creek Pub. Schs., Mich., 1970—97; dir. music United Meth. Ch. of Swartz Creek, 1972—. Part-time tchr. Montrose Cmty. Schs., Mich., 2002—06; chmn. divsn. interpretation Bd. Diaconal Ministry, Mich., 1986—94; ann. conf. choir dir. United Meth. Ch., Mich., 2005. Composer choral anthems; author: (children's plays) The Not-So-Silent Night, 1998—, Wee Three Kings, 1999—; orchestrater: online orchestrations cokesbury.com. Avocations: model railroading, hiking.

MORELAND, VICKI ANN, education educator; b. Middletown, Ohio, Nov. 19, 1957; d. Rodney Clifford and Phyllis Marie Clippinger; m. Roy Allen Moreland, Dec. 28, 1995; children: Adam Bowling, Bradley Bowling, Carrie Bowling, Jeffery, Randy. BS in Consumer Homemaker Edn., Miami U., Oxford, Ohio, 1979, MS in Family and Child Studies, 1996. Nutrition educator Cooperative Ext., Hamilton, Ohio, 1987—89; family and child studies tchr. Preble Shawnee Schs., Camden, Ohio, 1990—2004; career technical instr. Butler Tech. and Career Devel. Schs., Fairfield Twp., Ohio, 2004—. Cons. Miami U., Oxford, Ohio, 2000—03, Ohio Dept. Edn., Columbus, 2001—06. Mem.: Ohio Assn. Tchrs. Family and Consumer Scis. (profl. devel. chair 2000—05, pres. 2006). Assembly Of God. Avocations: writing, singing. Office: Fairfield Sr HS 8800 Holden Blvd Fairfield OH 45014

MORELL, MICHAEL J., federal agency administrator; Joined CIA, Washington, 1980, head, regional office in the directorate of intelligence, head, President's daily brief prodn. unit, presdl. briefer, exec. asst. to the dir., assoc. dep. dir. intelligence, strategic programs, dep. dir. intelligence, nat. counter-terrorism ctr., assoc. dep. dir., 2006—08, dir. intelligence, 2008—. Office: Ctrl Intelligence Agency Office of Dir Intelligence c/o Office Pub Affairs Washington DC 20250*

MORELL, WILLIAM NELSON, JR., retired foreign trade association executive, government agency administrator; b. July 13, 1920; s. William N. and Louise (Cox) M.; m. Patricia Leonhard, Apr. 3, 1943; 1 child, Lynn Noble. Student, Coll. William and Mary, 1938—40; AB, George Washington U., 1942; MA, U. Pa., 1948; postgrad., Am. U., 1950—51; grad., Nat. War Coll., 1956. Jr. economist Bur. Labor Stats., 1941; asst. to prof. fin. George Washington U., 1941; naval mem. U.S. mil. mission to Moscow, 1944-46; asst. prof. Drexel Inst. Tech., 1946-48; instr. U. Pa., 1947-48; with CIA, 1949-68, staff mem. Office Nat. Est., 1950-52, mng. dir. U.S. econ. intelligence com., 1955-65, chmn., 1966-67; chmn. spl. study group NSC Planning Bd., 1960; econ. counselor Am. Embassy, Moscow, 1960-61; dep. dir. office rsch. and reports CIA, 1962-66, dir. Office Econ. Rsch., 1966-67, mem. U.S. econ. def. adv. com., adv. com. export policy, 1966-67; lectr. on Communist econs., 1960-68; faculty Nat. War Coll., 1968; econ. counselor Am. Embassy, Taipei, Taiwan, 1968-73, nat. security advisor to sec. treasury, 1973—77; treasury mem. U.S. Nat. Intelligence Bd., 1973-77; mng. dir. USA-ROC Econ. Coun., Crystal Lake, Ill., 1977-78, pres., 1979-90; ret. U.S. Taiwan Trade Coun., 1990. Author, lectr. on Taiwan economy. Eucharistic min. Episc. ch. Lt. USNR, 1942-46. Decorated Order Brilliant Star Taiwan, Order Brilliant Star with Violet Grand Cordon; recipient Superior Achievement award, medal of merit CIA, Exceptional Svc. medal Treasury Dept., U.S. Nat. Intelligence Disting. Svc. award, Taiwan Econ. Ministry medal. Mem. Artus, Econ. Soc. (hon.). Home: 340 S Berkshire Dr Lake Forest IL 60045-4823

MORELLA, CONSTANCE ALBANESE, former United States Representative from Maryland; b. Somerville, Mass., Feb. 12, 1931; d. Salvatore and Mary Christine (Fallette) Albanese; m. Anthony C. Morella, Aug. 21, 1954; children: Paul, Mark, Laura; guardians of: Christine, Catherine, Louise, Rachel, Paul, Ursula. AA, Boston U., 1950, AB, 1954; MA, Am. U., 1967, D of Pub. Svc. (hon.), 1988, Norwich U. and Dickinson Coll., 1989, Mt. Vernon Coll., 1995, U. Md. U. Coll., 1996, USUHS, 1997, U. Md., 1997, Elizabethtown Coll., 1999. Tchr. Montgomery County (Md.) Pub. Schs., 1956-60; instr. Am. U., 1968-70; prof. Montgomery Coll., Rockville, Md., 1970-86; mem. Md. Ho. Dels., Annapolis, 1979-86, U.S. Congress from 8th Md. dist., 1987—2003; mem. sci. com., tech. subcom., basic rsch. subcom., govt. reform com., chair D.C. subcom., mem. civil svc. subcom.; visiting fellow Kennedy School, Harvard, 2003; U.S. permanent rep. to Orgn. for Econ. Co-operation & Devel. U.S. Dept. State, Paris, 2003—07. Mem. civil svc., adv. bd. Am. Univ., Washington Mem. adv. coun. Montgomery County Hospice Soc.; hon. bd. mem. Nat. Kidney Found; active Human Rights Caucus; Congressional Women's Caucus, Older Ams. Caucus, Population and Devel. Caucus; mem. Bd. Cafritz Found. Named Glamour Woman of Yr. Glamour mag. 1995, Washingtonian of Yr. 1991; named to Md. Women's Hall of Fame, Md. Women's Hall of Fame, 1994. Republican. Avocations: theater, tennis, reading.

MORELLI, JAMES KEVIN, biochemist; b. Bangor, Maine, May 22, 1963; s. Louis Vincent Morelli and Irma Avis Smith. BS in Biology, U. Maine, Orono, 1985, MS in Biochemistry, 1996. Rsch. asst. U. Maine, 1991—96; molecular toxicologist Astrazeneca Phams., Wilmington, Del., 1997—2008. Personal E-mail: i1335@msn.com.

MORELLO, CANDIS MARGUERITE, pharmacist, educator; b. Lynwood, Calif., May 5, 1969; d. Albert James and Darcy Lovgren Pavich (Stepmother), Keith R. (Stepfather) and Claire Barragan Kerr; m. Christopher Salvatore Morello; children: Joseph Salvatore, Lucas Sebastian. BA, U. Calif., Davis, 1991; PharmD, U. Calif., San Francisco, 1996. Cert. Diabetic educator Nat. Cert. Bd. Diabetes Educators, 1999. Ambulatory care pharmacist specialist Vets. Affairs San Diego Healthcare Sys., 1997—99; ambulatory care pharmacist specialist Spectrum Healthcare Resources Naval Med. Ctr. San Diego Ambulatory Care Clinics, 1999—2002; affiliate faculty mem. dept. pharmacy Idaho State U., Pocatella, 1999—2002; clin. asst. prof. Sch. Pharmacy Western U. Health Scis., Calif., 1999—2002; asst. clin. prof. Sch. Pharmacy U. Calif., San Francisco, 2000—08, asst. prof., clin. pharmacy Skaggs Sch. Pharmacy and Pharm. Scis. San Diego, 2002—08, assoc. prof. clin. pharmacy Skaggs Sch. Pharmacy and Pharm. Scis., 2008—; ambulatory care pharmacist specialist, vets. affairs San Diego Healthcare Sys., 2008—. Co-author: A Process Guide for Pharmacists, 3rd ed.; contbr. articles to profl. jours. Clin. pharmacist vol. Various Cmty. Outreach Projects, San Diego, 1996—, Taking Control of Your Diabetes, San Diego, 1996; clin. pharmacist vol. Free Med. Clinic Project U. Calif, San Diego, 2000—; co-chair and coord., Ask a Pharmacist session Taking Control of Your Diabetes Conf., San Diego, 2002—; clin. pharmacist vol., Project Stand Down Vetrans Village, San Diego, 2002—03. Recipient Faculty Excellence award, U. Calif., San Diego, 2003, Excellence in Tchg. award, 2005, 2006. Fellow: Calif. Soc. Health-Sys. Pharmacists (assoc.; del. 1997, co-chair continuing edn. com. 1998—99, faculty student liason 2003—, Practitioner Recognition Program award 2003); mem.: Am. Pharm. Assn. (assoc.), Am. Soc. Health-Sys. Pharmacists (assoc.; student faculty liason 2003—05), San Diego Soc. Health-Sys. Pharmacists (assoc.; sec., mem. cmty. outreach com. 1998—2001, del. seminar meetings 1999—2005, bd. dirs. 2002—05, Pharmacist of the Yr. 2002, Dena L. Barker Meml. award 2002), Am. Coll. Clin. Pharmacy (assoc.), Am. Assn. Colls. Pharmacy (assoc.), Phi Lambda Sigma (assoc.), Rho Chi (assoc.), Phi Delta Chi (assoc.; v.p. 1993—94). Office: U Calif San Diego Skaggs Sch Pharmacy, PharmSci 9500 Gilman # 0719 La Jolla CA 92093-0719 Office Fax: 858-822-5624. Business E-Mail: candismorello@ucsd.edu.

MORELLO, DANIEL CONWAY, plastic surgeon; b. Vineland, NJ, Nov. 12, 1943; s. John B. and Mina M. (Conway) M.; m. Mona L. Comras; children: Amy, Elise, Kate. BS, U. Notre Dame, 1965; MD, Georgetown U., 1969. Diplomate Am. Bd. Plastic Surgery, Am. Bd. Surgery, Nat. Bd. Med. Examiners. Intern Hahnemann Med. Coll. Hosp., Phila., 1969-70, surgery resident to chief resident, 1970-74; plastic surgery resident to chief resident NYU Med. Ctr. Inst. for Reconstructive Plastic Surgery, NYC, 1974-76; attending surgeon White Plains (N.Y.) Hosp. Med. Ctr., 1976—, chief of plastic surgery, 1992-98; pvt. practice in plastic surgery White Plains, 1976—, emeritus chief, 1999—; attending surgeon Mank Eye, Ear and Throat Hosp., 1999—. Asst. attending surgeon Bellevue Hosp., Manhattan VA Hosp., Manhattan Eye, Ear and Throat Hosp., N.Y.C., 1976-85; attending surgeon No. Westchester (N.Y.) Hosp. Ctr., 1976—; cons. Burke Rehab. Ctr., 1977-81; asst. instr. surgery, Hahnemann Med. Coll., 1973-74, clin. instr. plastic surgery, NYU Sch. Medicine, 1974-78, clin. asst. prof. plastic surgery, 1978-86. Contbr. numerous articles to profl. jours., chpts. to books; presenter in field, including co-chair symposia 1993, 95. Bd. dirs., golf chmn. Whippoorwill Club, 1989-95, extensive com. work 1988-95. Fellow: ACS; mem.: Nat. Endowment for Plastic Surgery (bd. govs. 2005—08), Westchester County Med. Soc. (bd. dirs. 1986—88, med.-legal rels. com. 1988—98, numerous other coms.), Med. Soc. State of NY, NY Regional Soc. Plastic Surgery (membership com. 1978—80, chair program com. 1987—88, sec. 1988—90, bd. dirs. 1988—91), Am. Assn. for Accreditation of Ambulatory Surgery Facilities (bd. dirs. 1989—98, strategic planning com. 1991—2004, pres. 1994—98, trustee 1998—, other offices, coms.), Am. Soc. Plastic and Reconstructive Surgeons (ofcl. spokesperson 1992—, pub. edn. com. and sci. program subcom. 1994—99, other coms.), Am. Soc. Aesthetic Plastic Surgery (ofcl. spokesperson 1988—, bd. dirs. 1990—, chair pub. edn. com. and internat. task force 1994—97, treas. 1995—98, v.p. 1998—99, 1999—2000, pres. 2000—01, chair bd. trustees 2001—02, trustee 2001—04, chair nominating com. 2003—04, trustee 2005—08, chair nominating com. 2009, other offices and coms.). Avocations: golf, travel, reading. Office: 10 Chester Ave White Plains NY 10601-5112 also: 531 E 88th St New York NY 10128 Home: 18525 SE Village Cir Tequesta FL 33469 Office: 641 University Blvd Jupiter FL 33458 Office Phone: 914-761-8667. Business E-Mail: info@drmorello.com.

MORELLO, DEBRA A., dean; MBA, Binghamton U., NY, 1981. Dean, continuing edn. Broome CC, Binghamton, 1992—; adj. prof. Binghamton U., 1998—. Cons. Debra Morello, Binghamton, 1981—. Illustrator. Chair, grantwriting Southern Tier Opportunity Coalition, Binghamton, 2005—08. Home: 6 Bedford St Binghamton NY 13903 Office: Broome CC 1017 Front St Binghamton NY 13901

MORELLO, JOSEPH ALBERT, musician, educator; b. Springfield, Mass., July 17, 1928; s. Joseph Charles and Lilia (LaPalme) M.; m. Jean Ann Mehnert. Grad. high sch., Springfield. Ind. drummer, Springfield, 1945-49; drummer Gil Melé, Stan Kenton, Tal Farlow, Johnny Smith, NYC, 1953-55, Dave Brubeck Quartet, touring worldwide, 1955-68; clinician Selmer Ludwig Drum Co., Elkhart, Ind., 1957-92; leader Joe Morello Quartet, 1979—; clinician DW Drums, Oxnard, Calif., 1993—; rec. artist Digital Music Products Inc., 1993—. Rec. artist Savoy, Capitol, Norgran, Blue Note, Columbia, RCA labels; innovator finger control in jazz drumming; author: Joe Morello Drum Method, The Natural Approach to Technique, 1993, Joe Morello Drum Method 2, 1994, also New Directions in Rhythm, Rudimental Jazz, Off the Record, Master Studies, Master Studies II, 2006 (voted number one technical snare drum studies), Modern Drummer Mag., 2007, releases include (with Joe Morello Quartet) Going Places, 1993, Morello's Standard Time, 1994, Marion Mc Partland's Hickory House Trio, 1999, Marion McPartland Trio with Joe Morello, 2002, Rufus Reid Live at Shanghai Jazz, 2002. Recipient New Star award, Downbeat mag., 1955, Melody Maker mag. award, 1963—67, Jazz mag. award, 1964—67, Thomas A. Edison Lifetime Achievement award, 1990, Lifetime Achievement award, Jersey Shore Jazz and Blues Found., 1996, 2008, Publs. award, Staff Modern Drummer, Recognition of Outstanding Leadership award, Kosa Internat. Percussion Workshops, 2002, Lifetime Achievement award, Montreal Drum Festival, 2002, poll winner, Downbeat mag., 1963—65, Playboy mag., 1963—67, Lifetime Achievement award, Sabian Ltd., 2003; named to Hall of Fame, Modern Drummer mag., 1988, Percussive Arts Soc. Hall of Fame, 1993, Am. Jazz Hall of Fame, 2001, Trumpets Jazz Hall of Fame, 2002. Mem.: N.J. Jazz Soc. Avocation: photography.

MORELLO, TOM, musician; b. NYC, May 30, 1964; s. Mary Morello and Ngethe Njoroge. B in polit. sci., Harvard Coll. Band mem. Lock Up; guitarist Rage Against the Machine, 1991—2001, Audioslave, 2001—; solo artist (as The Night Watchman), 2007—. Played at Lollapalooza, 1992, Latinpalooza, 1994, Tibetan Freedom Concert, San Francisco, 1996, Lollapalooza, 1996, Tibetan Freedom Concert, East Troy, Wis., 1999, Woodstock 99, Coachella Festival, Indio, Calif., 1999, Indio, 2007. Musician: (albums) (with Lock Up) Something Bitchin' This Way Comes, 1989, (with Rage Against the Machine) Rage Against the Machine, 1992, Evil Empire, 1996, The Battle of Los Angeles, 1999, Renegades, 2000, Live at the Grand Olympic Auditorium, 2003, (with Audioslave) Audioslave, 2002, Out of Exile, 2005, Revelations, 2006, (as The Nightwatchman) One Man Revolution, 2007, (songs) (with Rage Against the Machine) Tire Me, 1996 (Grammy award for Best Metal Performance, 1997), Guerilla Radio, 2000 (Grammy award for Best Hard Rock Performance, 2001); actor: (films) Made, 2001, Berkeley, 2005. Co-founder Axis of Justice; co-host Axis of Justice Radio Network. Recipient Best Guitarist award, Calif. Music Awards, 1997—2001; named one of 100 Greatest Guitarists of All Time, Rolling Stone, 2003.

MORELOCK, JASMINE CRAWFORD, artist; b. Boise, June 30, 1925; d. Graydon Clemson and Doris Cecile (Dinwiddie) Crawford; m. Max Maurice Morelock, Apr. 8, 1950; 1 child, Maurice Max. AA, Stephens Coll., Columbia, Mo., 1945; BA, La. State U., 1948; MA, La. Sch. Tech., 1979; MFA cum laude, Inst. Allende, San Miguel Allende, Guanajuato, Mexico, 1978. Cert. tchr. speech and art, La. Advtsg. writer programming dept. KRMD Radio Sta., Shreveport, La., 1946—47; with Bozell and Jacobs Nat. Advt. Agy., 1949—50; with comml. design Glen Mason Advt. Agy.; asst. prof. fine arts La. State U., Baton Rouge, 1948-49; head art dept. Southfield Sch., Shreveport, La., 1972-74; tchr. portrait classes Bossier C. C., Bossier City, La., 1989-91; tchr. art Caddo Parish Sch. Bd., Shreveport, La., 1975-80; represented by Gallery on the Green, Lexington, Mass., Juleaux Gallery of Fine Arts, Kansas City, WLR Design Co., Shreveport, La., Lytle's, Shreveport, La., Riverwalk Gallery, New Orleans. Presenter workshops Barnwell Art Ctr., Shreveport, La., J&M Studio Groups, Shreveport, Women's Dept. Club, Shreveport, Springhill Art Assn., La., 1993. One woman exhbns. include La. State U. Shreveport Gallery, 1992, Cambridge Club, Shreveport, 1993, The Glen Gallery, Shreveport, 1995, Shreve Meml. Libr., Shreveport, 1995, numerous others; group exhbns. include Valerie Originals, KJ's Antiques and Silks, Hot Springs, Ark., 1986, Women Artists of La., Baton Rouge, 1987, Boots Pharmaceutical Co., Cambridge Club, Shreveport, La., 1988, 90, 92, Stoner Arts Ctr., Shreveport, 1989, 90, Gallery on the Green, Lexington, Mass., 1989, Simmers Gallery, Shreveport, 1989, La. Artist Group Show, 1990, Barksdale Air Base, 1990, Turner Art Ctr., 1990, Artport, 2002-09, Shreveport, 1990-2001, Riverside Galleries, Shreveport, Lytles Galleries Shreveport, 2009, Southwestern Watercolor Soc., 1992, 94, Nat. Mus. Art, Washington, 1993, Still River Artists, Danbury, Conn., 1993, Okla. 12th Annual Juried Show, 1995, Shreveport Art Port, 2004-06, 2007-, Northwest La. Triennial Competition, Meadows Mus., 2006, numerous others including online galleries; represented in pvt. and pub. collections La. State U. Ctr., St. Luke's Hosp., St. Vincent's Acad., U. Club, Seagull Cos., McGoldrick Oil Co., numerous others; featured in (cover) (Goodloe Stuck) The Shreveport Madam, 1986, Boots Pharm. Art Catalogue, 1990, Behold, I Make All Things New, 1991, Artists of La. Catalogue, 1991, (t.v. show) Focus on the Arts, The Shreveport Times, 1995. Recipient Special Selection award Ark. Arts Ctr., Little Rock, 1984, First Purchase Prize Izora and Thilo Steinschulte Meml. award First Meth. Ch. Alexandria (La.), 1984, First Place Ark-La-Tex-Okla Competition First Meth. Ch., Shreveport, 1984. Mem. Nat. Watercolor Soc., Nat. Assn. Women Artists, Southwestern Watercolor Soc. (Elizabeth Shanon Meml. award 1991), La. Watercolor Soc. Soc. Exptl. Artists, Hoover Watercolor Soc. (v.p., First Place 1984, H.M. award 1993), Registry of La. Artists, La. Artists, Inc., Southeastern Ctr. for Contemporary Art, Coalition of Women's Art (nat., Dallas). Home: 427 Monrovia St Shreveport LA 71106-1607 Home Phone: 318-861-3773. Personal E-mail: jcmore@bellsouth.net.

MORELOS-ZARAGOZA, ROBERT HENRY, communications engineer; b. Houma, La., May 16, 1959; s. Jorge Rafael and Sandra Lola (Ascanio) Morelos-Z.; m. Naoko Tawara; children: Kai, Len. BSEE, Nat. Autonomous U. of Mexico, 1985, MSEE, 1987; PhD in Elec. Engring., U. Hawaii, 1992. Cons. engr. Tevescom, Mexico City, 1987-88; rsch. asst. U. Hawaii, Honolulu, 1988-92; asst. prof. Tec. Monterrey, Mexico, 1992-93; rsch. assoc. Osaka U., Japan, 1993-94; rsch. fellow Nara Inst. of Sci. and Technology, Japan, 1994-95; rsch. assoc. U. Tokyo, 1995-97; staff engr. LSI Logic Corp., Milpitas, Calif., 1997—. Vis. rsch. assoc. Osaka U., Japan, 1993-94; rsch. asst. U. Hawaii, Manoa, 1988-92, tchg. asst., 1986-87. Contbr. articles to profl. jours. Mem. IEEE (sr.), Eta Kappa Nu. Office: San Jose Univ 1 Washington Sq San Jose CA 95192-0084 Personal E-mail: morelos_zaragoza@yahoo.com.

MOREL-SEYTOUX, HUBERT JEAN, civil engineer, educator; b. Calais, Artois, France, Oct. 6, 1932; came to U.S., 1956; s. Aimé and Suzanne Claire (Rousseau) M.-S.; m. Margery K. Keyes, Apr. 16, 1960; children: Aimée, Claire, Sylvie, Marie-Jeanne. BS, Ecole St. Genevieve, Versailles, France, 1953; MS, Ecole Nationale des Ponts et Chaussées, Paris, 1956; PhD, Stanford U., 1962. Research engr. Chevron Oil Field Research Co., La Habra, Calif., 1962-66; prof. Colo. State U., Ft. Collins, 1966-91, prof. emeritus, 1991—; chargé de recherches U. Grenoble, France, 1972-73; maitre de recherches Ecole des Mines de Paris, Fontainebleau, France, 1982; directeur de recherches ORSTOM, Montpellier, France, 1991—; cons. hydrology Atherton, Calif., 1992—. Cons. AID, Dakar, Senegal, 1985-86, 88, Ministry of Agriculture and Water, Riyadh, Saudi Arabia, 1978-83, City of Thornton, Colo., 1986-88, King Abdulaziz U., Jeddah, Saudi Arabia, 1987, 89, Ford Found., India, 1976, 79, South Fla. Water Mgmt. Dist., West Palm Beach, 1991-93, Battelle Pacific Northwest Labs., Richland, Wash., 1991-94, City of Paris, France, 1992—, Agence de l'Eau Seine-Normandie, 1992-2000, Utah State U., Logan, 1994-95, Reservoir Engring. Rsch. Inst., Palo Alto, 1994-95, Bay Delta Modeling forum, 1997—, U.S. Bur. Reclamation, 1998-2006, Stockholm Environment Inst., 2006-07; vis. prof. Ecole Polytechnique Federale de Lausanne, 1987; vis. scholar Stanford U., 1992-96, 2006-; adj. prof. U. Colo., Boulder, 1992—; lectr. U. Calif., Berkley, 1993. Editor: Hydrology Days, 1981—2000, 3d Internat. Hydrology Symposium, 1977, Unsaturated Flow in Hydrologic Modeling, 1989. Pres. Internat. Ctr., Ft. Collins, 1984-86. Served to lt. French Army Marine Corps Engrs., 1959-62. Sr. Fulbright scholar, France, 1972-73; recipient Abell Faculty Rsch. award Colo. State U. Coll. Engring., 1985. Mem. Am. Geophys. Union, ASCE (best paper award, Water Resources Planning and Mgmt., 1999), Soc. Petroleum Engrs., Am. Meteorol. Soc., Am. Soc. Agrl. Engrs. Home: 57 Selby Ln Atherton CA 94027-3926 Office: Hydroprose Internat Cons Hydrology Days Publs 57 Selby Ln Atherton CA 94027-3926 Office Phone: 650-365-4080. Personal E-mail: hydroprose@batnet.com. Business E-Mail: hydroprose@sbcglobal.net.

MORENCY, PAULA J., lawyer; b. Oak Park, Ill., Mar. 13, 1955; AB magna cum laude, Princeton U., 1977; JD, U. Va., 1980. Bar: Ill. 1980, U.S. Dist. Ct. (no. dist.) Ill. 1980, U.S. Ct. Appeals (7th cir.) 1981, U.S. Ct. Appeals (5th cir.) 1990, U.S. Dist. Ct. (ctrl. dist.) Ill. 1999, U.S. Dist. Ct. (ea. dist.) Wis. 2000. Assoc. Mayer, Brown & Platt, Chgo., 1980-86, ptnr., 1987-94, Schiff Hardin LLP, Chgo., 1994—; practice group leader Intellectual Property, 2005—. Adj. prof. trial advocacy Northwestern U. Sch. Law, Chgo., 1997--; faculty Midwest Regional, Nat. Inst. for Trial Advocacy, 1988—; mem. pres.'s coun. Dominican U., 1998-2002. Author: Cross-Examination of a Franchise Executive, 1995, Insurance Coverage Issues in Franchise and Intellectual Property Litigation, 1996, Re-Emergence of Franchise Class Actions, 1997, Judicial and Legislative Update: ABA Forum on Franchising, 1999, How to Find, Use and Defend Against the Expert Witness, 2000, Dealing With System Change in a High-Tech World, 2001, A Decade After Daubert, 2004. Mem. ABA (forum franchising, governing com. 2001-04, litig. sect., antitrust sect., intellectual property sect.), Chgo. Coun. of Lawyers (bd. govs. 1989-93), Constnl. Rights Found. Chgo. (chair 2001, bd. dirs. 1994-). Office: Schiff Hardin LLP 6600 Sears Tower Chicago IL 60606 Office Phone: 312-258-5549.

MORENO, ALBERT F., lawyer, former apparel executive; b. Dec. 1943; BA in economics, San Diego State U., 1966; M in L.Am. econ. studies, U. Madrid, 1967; JD, U. Calif., Berkeley, 1970. Bar: Calif. 1970. Regional dir. Legal Svcs. Corp., San Francisco; asst. gen. counsel Levi Strauss & Co., San Francisco, 1978—81, assoc. gen. counsel, 1981—85, dep. gen. counsel, 1985—94, chief counsel Levi Strauss N.Am., 1994—96, sr. v.p., gen. counsel, 1996—2006. Bd. dirs. New Century Energies Inc., 1999—2000, Xcel Energy Inc., 2000—. Dean's adv. coun. San Diego State U. Coll. Arts and Letters; chmn. bd. trustees Rosenberg Found., 2003—. Recipient Monty Alumni Award, San Diego State U., 2001.

MORENO, ARTURO (ARTE MORENO), professional sports team executive, former advertising executive; b. Tucson, 1946; s. Arturo and Mary Moreno; m. Carol Moreno, 1986; 3 children. BS in Mktg., U. Ariz., 1973. With Eller Outdoor, 1973—84; pres., COO Outdoor Systems Inc., 1984—99; former owner Salt Lake Trappers minor league baseball club; former minority owner Arizona Diamondbacks, Phoenix Suns; owner, pres. L.A. Angels of Anaheim, 2003—. Bd. dir. Nelnet. Cofounder (with Carol Moreno) Moreno Family Found. Served US Army, 1966—68, Vietnam. Named one of Forbes' Richest Americans, Forbes mag., 2006, The Most Influential People in the World of Sports, Bus. Week mag., 2007. Office: Los Angeles Angels of Anaheim 2000 Gene Autry Way Anaheim CA 92806

MORENO, CARLOS R., state supreme court justice; b. L.A., Nov. 4, 1948; m. Christine Moreno; children: Keiko, Nicholas. BA in Polit. Sci., Yale U., 1970; JD, Stanford U., 1975. Dep. city atty. L.A. City Atty.'s Office; atty. Mori & Ota (now known as Kelley, Drye & Warren), 1979; justice Mcpl. Ct., 1986—93, L.A. County Superior Ct., 1993—97, US Dist. Ct. (ctrl. dist.) Calif., 1998—2001; assoc. justice Supreme Ct. Calif., 2001—. Bd. visitors Stanford Law Sch.; bd. govs. Assn. Yale Alumni; dir. Arroyo Vista Family Health Ctr. Recipient Criminal Justice Superior Ct. Judge of Yr. award, L.A. County Bar Assn., 1997, For God, For Country and For Yale award, Yale U., 2001. Mem.: Municipal Ct. Judges Assn., Presiding Judges Assn., Calif. Judges Assn., Mexican Am. Bar Assn. (past pres.). Avocations: theater, opera, crossword puzzles. Office: Calif Supreme Ct 350 McAllister St San Francisco CA 94102-4783*

MORENO, CARLOS SANCHEZ, aerospace engineer; b. East Point, Ga., Sept. 28, 1964; s. Hugo Sanchez and Alida (Smith) M.; m. Genevieve Lucy Fairbrother, June 22, 1991. BS, MIT, 1986, MS, 1988. Teaching asst. MIT Aeronaautics & Astronomics Dept., Cambridge, Mass., 1986; staff engr. NASA Jet Propulsion Lab., Pasadena, Calif., 1988-90, C.S. Draper Lab. Inc., Cambridge, Mass., 1990—. Editor concepts & tech. catalog, 1990. Summer fellow, U. Space Rsch. Assn., NASA, 1986, Draper fellow, 1987. Mem. AIAA, Sigma Gamma Tau, Tau Beta Pi. Avocations: reading, scuba diving, skiing, percussion instruments, gourmet cooking.

MORENO, HELENA, newscaster; b. Xalapa, Veracruz, Mex. d. Felix Moreno and Nancy Pearson. Grad. in Journalism, So. Meth. U., Dallas. Intern for Hillary Clinton White House, Washington; gen. assignment reporter, fill-in anchor WTOC-TV, Savannah, Ga.; reporter WDSU-TV, New Orleans, 2000—08, mem. investigative reporting team. Named Broadcaster of Yr., La. Fedn. of Teachers, Newscaster of Yr., Victims and Citizens Against Crime, Reporter of Yr., Gambit Weekly. Democrat. Office: 3337 Magazine St New Orleans LA 70115*

MORENO, JAIME, professional soccer player; b. Santa Cruz, Bolivia, Jan. 19, 1974; Grad., Tahuichi Acad., Santa Cruz. Mem. Middlebrough, English Premier League, 1995—96, DC United Major League Soccer, 1996—2002, NY/NJ MetroStars, Major League Soccer, 2003; forward DC United, Washington, 2004—, Bolivia Nat. Soccer Team, 1999—. Named Most Valuable Player, Major League Soccer, 1999, AT&T Best XI, 1999. Mem., DC United, Major League Soccer Cup Champions, 1996, 1997, & 1999; mem. DC United, Major League Soccer, US Open Cup Champions, 1996; mem. DC United, Major League Soccer, CONCACAF Champions Cup Winners, 1998; Winner, Golden Boot award, Major League Soccer (16 goals), 1997. Mailing: RFK Stadium 2400 East Capital St, SE Washington DC 20003

MORENO, LUIS ALBERTO, bank executive; m. Gabriela Febres-Cordero; children: Nicolas, Natalia. B in Bus. Adminstrn. and Econs., Fla. Atlantic U., 1975; MBA, Thunderbird U., 1977. Divisional mgr. Praco, 1977—82; exec. prodr. TV Hoy, 1982—90; pres. Instituto de Fomento Industrial, Colombia, 1991—92; min. econ. devel., 1992—94; chair Andres Pastrana presdl. campaign, 1994; sr. advisor Luis Carlos Sarmiento Orgn., 1994—97; rep. for Andean Region WestSphere Capital, 1997—98; Colombian amb. to the US, 1998—2005; pres. Inter-Am. Devel. Bank, Washington, 2005—. Recipient King of Spain prize for journalism, Orden al Mérito Civil Ciudad de Bogotá, en el Grado de Gran Cruz, Mayor of Bogotá, 1990, Orden al Mérito Industrial — José Gutiérrez Gómez, Colombian Nat. Bus. Assn., 2002, Orden de Boyacá en el Grado de Gran Cruz, Pres. of Colombia, 2002. Office: Inter-Am Devel Bank 1300 New York Ave NW Washington DC 20577*

MORENO, PATRICIA FRAZIER, lawyer; b. Lebanon, Pa. d. Joseph James and Cariella Agnes (Rothermel) Frazier; m. Camille Quijada Moreno, Dec. 4, 1982; children: William David, Helen Grace, Camille Fitzcarraldo. Student, Millersville U., 1969-71, Cochise Coll., 1992-93; BA in Polit. Sci., U. Ariz., Sierra Vista, 1997; JD, U. Ariz., 2001. Cert.: Nat. Assn. Legal Secs. (profl. legal sec.), Nat. Assn. Legal Assts. (legal asst.), bar: Ariz. 2002. Law clerk John F. Kelliher, Jr. PC, Sierra Vista, Ariz., 1999-2001, assoc., 2002—04; spl. asst. atty. gen. State of Ariz., 2005, assoc. atty. gen., 2007. Assoc. faculty Cochise Coll., Sierra Vista, 1996—97, U. Ariz. S., 2003—; with Policy-Studies, Inc., 2005. Mem. human rels. commn. City of Sierra Vista, 1982—83; mem. adv. bd. Salvation Army, Sierra Vista, 1988—92; gov. bd. Ariz. Family Support Coun., 2006. Named Sec. of the Yr., S.E. Ariz. Legal Secs. Assn., 1993, Lawyer of the Yr., Ariz. Vol. Lawyers Program, Alumnus of the Yr., U. Ariz. S., 2006; named one of Top 50 Pro Bono Lawyers, Ariz. Legal Svcs. Found., 2005. Mem.: ACLU, Borderline Mensa (officer 1987—93, scholar 1992). Democrat. Avocations: cyberculture, film history, politics, writing. Office: Child Support Svcs Ariz 7 Bisbee Rd Bisbee AZ 85603 Office Phone: 520-432-3161. Business E-Mail: patricia.moreno@azbar.org.

MORENO, RITA (ROSITA DOLORES ALVERIO), actress; b. Humacao, PR, Dec. 11, 1931; m. Leonard I. Gordon, June 18, 1965; 1 child, Fernanda Luisa. Spanish dancer since childhood, night club entertainer; appeared on Broadway in The Sign in Sidney Brustein's Window, 1964-65, Gantry, 1969-70, The Last of the Red Hot Lovers, 1970-71, The National Health, 1974, The Ritz, 1975, Wally's Cafe, 1981, The Odd Couple, 1985; (off Broadway) After Play, 1995, (London prodn.) Sunset Blvd., 1996; (films) Singin' in the Rain, 1952, The King and I, 1956, West Side Story, 1961 (Acad. Award for Best Supporting Actress, 1962), Night of the Following Day, 1968, Carnal Knowledge, 1971, The Four Seasons, 1981, I Like It Like That, 1994, Angus, 1995, Wharf Rat, 1995, Slums of Beverly Hills, 1998, Carlo's Wake, 1999, Blue Moon, 2000, Pinero, 2001, King of the Corner, 2004, Lolo's Cafe, 2006, Play It By Ear, 2006; (TV series) Oz, 1997-2003; (TV appearances) The Rockford Files: If It Bleeds...It Leads, 1999, Strong Medicine, 2003, The Guardian, 2003, Copshop, 2004, Law and Order, 2005, American Family, 2002. Recipient Grammy award for best rec., 1973, Antoinette Perry award for best supporting actress Broadway play, 1975, Emmy award, 1977, 78, award Nat. Osteoporosis Found., 2000, Presdl. Freedom medal, 2005; named to The Calif. Hall of Fame, 2007 Achievements include being in the Guinness Book of World Records as the only female performer to win Acad., Grammy, Tony and Emmy awards.*

MORENO, WILLIAM A., museum director; Degree in bus. mgmt., St. Mary's Coll., 1989. Dir. sales & mktg., mgr. staff devel. Citibank; founder William Moreno Fine Art, 1998—2001; dir. Aguirre Gallery, San Mateo, Calif., 2001—03; exec. dir. Mex. Mus., San Francisco, 2003—06, Claremont Mus. Art, Claremont, Calif., 2007—. Mem.: Calif. Assn. Museums (bd. dirs.). Office: Claremont Mus Art 536 W 1st St Claremont CA 91711 Office Phone: 909-621-3200 ext. 101. Office Fax: 909-625-1629. E-mail: wm@claremontmuseum.org.

MORENO-ASPITIA, ALVARO, physician, researcher; s. Ricardo Moreno-Azorero and Susana Aspitia; m. Maga; children: Sebastian, Camila, Pablo. MD, U. Nacional de Asuncion, Paraguay, 1991. Diplomate Internal Medicine Am. Bd. of Internal Medicine, PA, 1997, Medical Oncology Am. Bd. of Internal Medicine, 2000, Hematology Am. Bd. of Internal Medicine, 2000, Pediatrics Am. Bd. of Pediat., 1997, Am. Bd. of Pediat., 2004. Resident internal medicine/pediat. Scott and White Hosp. Tex. A&M Coll. of Medicine, Temple, Tex., 1993—97, chief resident, 1996—97; fellow Mayo Clinic Grad. Sch. Medicine, Jacksonville, Fla., 1997—2000; cons., asst. prof. medicine Mayo Clinic and Mayo Grad. Sch. of Medicine, Jacksonville, Fla., 2000—. Assoc. dir. clin. studies unit Mayo Clinic, Jacksonville, Fla., 2001—, assoc. dir. multidisciplinary breast clinic, 2005—; assoc. program dir. hematology & oncology fellowship Mayo Grad. Sch. of Medicine, Jacksonville, Fla., 2005—. Contbr. scientific papers. Recipient, Alpha Omega Alpha Honor Med. Soc., 1997, Sr. yr. gold medal, Coll. Internat., 1985, 2000 Shahin Award for Rsch., DCMS, 2000, Tchr. of the Yr. (Hematology/Oncology), Dept. of Internal Medicine, 2004; scholar Oncology Fellow Scholarship Methods in Clin. Cancer Rsch., AACR-ASCO, 1998. Fellow: ACP, Am. Acad. of Pediat.; mem.: Am. Assn. for Cancer Rsch., Am. Soc. of Hematology, Am. Soc. of Clin. Oncology, Alpha Omega Alpha Honor Med. Soc. Achievements include research in Clinical trials in the treatment of hematologic and solid malignancies. Office: Mayo Clinic 4500 San Pablo Rd Jacksonville FL 32224

MORENS, DAVID MICHAEL, epidemiologist, tropical medicine investigator; b. Detroit, Mar. 7, 1948; s. Ralph Michael and Martha Louise (Wright) M.; m. Darlene Lin Sun Luke, May 26, 1974 (div. Sept. 1977); children: Bryan Scott Kum Chan, Benjamin Michael Kum Chin; m. Ratna Soetjahja, Dec. 22, 1987. AB, U. Mich., 1969, MD, 1973. Epidemic Intelligence Service officer U.S. Ctrs. Disease Control, Atlanta, 1976-78, med. officer Bur. Labs. Atlanta, Ga. and Sierra Leone, 1978-81, chief respiratory and spl. pathogens br., 1981-82; assoc. prof. tropical medicine U. Hawaii, Honolulu, 1982-86, prof., chmn. dept. community medicine, 1987-92, prof. pub. health, 1987—, prof. tropical medicine, 1987—, Nat. Inst. Allergy and Infectious Disease, NIH, Bethesda, Md., 1998—. Cons. WHO, govts. Bangladesh, Egypt, Israel, Sierra Leone, Liberia, Indonesia, Vietnam, Papua New Guinea, and various Pacific Island jurisdictions; med. dir. labs. Leahi Hosp., Honolulu, 1982-91; lab. dir. Diamond Head Health Ctr., 1993-98. Co-author textbook chpts.; contbr. over 300 articles to profl. jours. Served to commdr. USPHS, 1976-82. Grantee NIH, WHO, Rockefeller Found., others. Fellow Am. Coll. Epidemiology; mem. Am. Assn. for History of Medicine, Am. Epidemiol. Soc., Soc. Epidemiologic Rsch., Am. Com. Arthropod-Borne Viruses, Am. Soc. Tropical Med. Hygiene. Avocations: music, hiking, travel. Home: 4624 Nottingham Dr Chevy Chase MD 20815-5345 Office: Nat Inst Health 6700-B Rockledge Dr Bethesda MD 20892-7630 E-mail: dm270q@nih.gov.

MORET, JEANINE, film educator; b. Bethesda, Md., June 15, 1954; d. Alfred Theophile Moret and Mary Jean McAllister; m. Wayne Douglass Goldwyn. BA in Visual Arts, U. Calif. San Diego, La Jolla, 1979; MFA in Theater Arts, UCLA, 1987. Video prodn. staff Neuropsychiat. Inst. UCLA, 1987—91, filmmaker, prod., dir. Latin Am. Ctr., 1990—91; adj. faculty screen writing Chapman U., Palm Desert, 1995—97; tenured faculty dept. fine arts Allan Hancock Coll., Santa Maria, 2001—. Media edn. initiative region 6 implementation team South Coast Media Edn. Ctr., Santa Barbara, 2002—. Editor: (book) A Traveler's Guide to California's Scenic Highway 33, 2004; prodn. mgr.: (films) Conocer Mexico, 1985; Monopoly, 1987; location mgr., prodn. asst. Powaqqats, 1986—87; prodr., dir.: (documentary film) Banderani, 1987; co-prodr., videographer Song Journey, 1995. Bd. dirs. Los Padres Forest Assn., Santa Barbara, 2000—02. Recipient Dir.'s Internship award, UCLA, 1986, Elaine Stanley award, 1987; Prodn. grant, Independent TV Svc., 1993. Mem.: Siggraph Forest Watch, Nat. Resources Defence Coun., Forest Watch Defenders Wildlife. Avocations: art, horseback riding, backpacking. Office: Allan Hancock Coll 800 Southern Coll Dr Santa Maria CA 93454 Office Phone: 805-922-6966 ext. 3389. Business E-Mail: jmoret@hancockcollege.edu.

MORÉTEAU, OLIVIER, law educator; DEA in Comparative Law, Université Jean Moulin, 1978, DEA in French Pvt. Law, 1981, PhD summa cum laude, 1990. Tchg. and rsch. asst. Université Jean Moulin, Lyon, France, 1980—90, dir. internat. rels., 1993—95, v.p. internat. rels., 1997—99, assoc. dir. Edouard Lambert Institute of Comparative Law, 1985—2000, dir., 2000—05, assoc. prof., 1990—98, prof. comparative law, 2000—05; prof. pvt. law Université Pierre Mendes, Grenoble, France, 1998—2000; prof. law, Russell B. Long Eminent Scholars Academic Chair, dir. Ctr. of Civil Law Studies La. State U., Baton Rouge, 2005—. Vis. prof. U. Minn., 1992, Boston U., 1993—2000, 2002—04, U. Melbourne, 2002, 04. Contbr. articles to profl. jours. Mem.: Am. Law Inst., Société de Législation comparée, European Centre of Tort and Insurance Law, European Group on Tort Law, Internat. Acad. Comparative Law. Office: La State U Paul M Herbert Law Ctr W323 Law Ctr Baton Rouge LA 70803-1000 Office Phone: 225-578-0067. Office Fax: 225-578-3677. Business E-Mail: moreteau@lsu.edu.

MORETTI, AUGUST JOSEPH, pharmaceutical executive, lawyer; b. Elmira, NY, Aug. 18, 1950; s. John Anthony and Dorothy M. (De Blasio) M.; m. Audrey B. Kavka, Nov. 8, 1981; children: David Anthony, Matthew Alexander. BA magna cum laude, Princeton U., 1972; JD cum laude, Harvard U., 1975. Assoc. Heller, Ehrman, White and McAuliffe, San Francisco, 1976-82, ptnr., 1982-2000; CFO, gen. counsel Surro Med, Inc., 2001—05; CFO Alexza Pharms., 2005—. Lectr. bus. adminstrn. U. Calif. Berkeley, 1977-79; bd. dirs. AviGenics. Bd. dirs. Ann Martin Children's Ctr.; mem. adv. panel U. Calif. Berkeley Entrepreneur Program. Mem. ABA.

MOREY, CARL REGINALD, musicologist; b. Toronto, Ont., Can., July 14, 1934; s. Reginald Donald and Julia Beatrice (Mabey) M.; m. Lorna Ann Dalton, June 2, 1960 (dec.); 1 child, Rachel Adriana MusB, U. Toronto, 1957; MusM, Ind. U., 1961, PhD, 1965. Asst. prof. Wayne State U., Detroit, 1962-63; assoc. prof. U. Windsor, Ont., 1964-70; prof. music U. Toronto, 1970-2000, dean faculty of music, 1984-90, Jean A. Chalmers prof., dir. Inst. for Can. Music, 1991-2000. Author: Music in Canada: A Research and Information Guide, 1997; MacMillan On Music, 1997, An Opera Sampler, 1998, Opera Viva, 2000; editor: (musical) Works of Glenn Gould (Schott), 1995, 96, 97, 99, 2004. Avocation: swimming. Office: U Toronto Faculty of Music Toronto ON Canada M5S 2C5 Home: 907 77 Carlton St Toronto ON Canada M5B 2J7 Business E-Mail: carl.morey@utoronto.ca.

MOREY, DARYL R., professional sports team executive; b. Sept. 14, 1972; m. Ellen Morey; children: Karen, Scott. BS in Computer Sci., Northwestern U., 1996; MBA, MIT, 2000. Statis. cons. STATS, Inc.; prin. cons., dir. knowledge mgmt. Parthenon Grp.; tech. lead MITRE Corp.; sr. v.p. ops. & info. Boston Celtics, 2003—06; asst. gen. mgr. Houston Rockets, 2006—07, gen. mgr., 2007—. Tchr. MIT Sloan Sch. Mgmt. Contbr. articles to profl. publs. Office: Houston Comets 1730 Jefferson St Houston TX 77003-5028*

MOREYRA, ABEL E., medical educator; b. Mar del Plata, Argentina, Dec. 2, 1941; came to U.S., 1972; s. Genaro and Emilia (Basso) M.; m. Maria Elena Moreyra; children: Maria Eugenia, Maria Evelina, Fernando Abel. MD, U. Nacional de La Plata, Argentina, 1967. Fellow Cleve. Clinic Found., 1972-75; asst. prof. medicine UMDNJ-Robert Wood Johnson Med. Sch., New Brunswick, NJ, 1975-83, assoc. prof., 1983-95, prof., 1995—. Fellow ACP, Am. Coll. Cardiology; mem. Am. Coll. Angiology. Office: UMDNJ-RW Johnson Med Sch CN-19 Rm 582A New Brunswick NJ 08903 Office Phone: 732-235-7851. E-mail: moreyrae@umdnj.edu.

MORFORD, CRAIG S., health products executive, former prosecutor; b. Schenectady, NY, Feb. 10, 1959; married; 4 children. BA in Econ., Hope Coll., 1981; JD, Valparaiso U. Sch. Law, 1984. Trial atty. Office Chief Counsel IRS, 1984—87; spl. trial atty. Cleve. Organized Crime Taskforce US Dept. Justice, 1986—89, asst. US atty. (no. dist.) OH, 1989—2002, interim US atty. (ea. dist.) Mich., 2004—05, spl. atty. to US atty. gen. heading investigation into first major US post Sept. 11th trial, 2004, 1st. US atty. (no. dist.) Ohio, 2005—06, interim US atty. (mid. dist.) Tenn., 2006—07, acting dep. atty. gen., 2007—08; chief compliance officer Cardinal Health, Inc., Dublin, 2008—. Recipient Dir. award for Superior Performance, US Dept. Justice, 1996, 2000, Atty. Gen. Disting Svc. award, 2003, 2005; named Outstanding Asst. US Atty., Nat. Assn. Former US Attorneys, 2005. Fellow: Am. Coll. Trial Lawyers. Office: Cardinal Health Inc 7000 Cardinal Pl Dublin OH 43017*

MORGA BELLIZZI, CELESTE, editor; b. NYC, Mar. 8, 1921; d. Louis and Emma (Macari) Morga; m. John J. Bellizzi, Sept. 1, 1942; children: John J., Robert F. Student, Columbia U., 1940-41, SUNY, Albany, 1970. Cert. med. lab. technician. Medical lab. technician USMC Hosp., NYC, 1942, Woman's Hosp., NYC, 1942-52; spl. investigator N.Y. State Atty. Gen.'s Office, Albany, 1958-65; editor Internat. Drug Report publ., The Narc Officer publ. Internat. Narcotic Enforcement Officers Assn., Albany, 1965—2004. Dir. Albany Inst. History and Art, 1988-90, N.Y. State Press Women, Albany, 1987; advisor UN Non-govtl. Orgns. Drug Com., N.Y.C., 1980-90, White House Conf. Drug Free Am., Washington, 1987; mem. com. Bethlehem Drug Prevention Program, Delmar, N.Y., 1987-90, Action Commn. Narc Edn., Delmar, 1984-90; v.p. Women's Rep. Party Albany, 1972 Recipient Pres.'s award INEOA, 1982, Disting. Svc. award Houston Police Dept., 1981. Mem. Nat. Fedn. Press Women, Nat. Press Club, Univ. Club, Albany Country Club, Aberdeen Country Club. Avocations: painting, golf, tennis. Office: Internat Narcotic Enforcement Officers Assn 112 State St Albany NY 12207-2079 Home Phone: 518-439-5129.

MORGAN, ALFRED VANCE, management consulting company executive; b. Liberal, Kans., Apr. 13, 1936; s. Forest Francis and Gertrude Irene (Henning) M.; m. Peggy Ann Riley, June 29, 1960; children: Trudie Marie, Vance Riley, Allen Forest, Bradley Augustus, Kelly James. BBA, U. Kans., 1958; MBA, U. So. Calif., 1966; postgrad., Am. Inst. Banking, 1965. Asst. mgr. Fruehauf Trailer Co., LA, Calif., 1960-61; asst. mktg. dir. Security Pacific Nat. Bank, 1961-65; mktg. exec. Doyle, Dane, Bernbach Advt., 1965-66; cons. Harbridge House, Inc., Boston, 1966-71; pres. Morgan Bus. Assocs., Inc., Santa Barbara and Boston, 1971—; instr. bus. L.A. City Coll., 1971-72; instr. mgmt. Santa Barbara City Coll., 1973. Pres. Exptl. in Internat. Living, 1980-81. Contbr. articles to profl. publs. Mem. Lobero Theatre Bd., 1984-88; mem. vestry All Saints Espiscopal Ch., 2003-06, jr. warden, fin. com. 2006-; v.p. El Escorial Condo Assn., 2003-08. With AUS, 1958-60. Mem. ASTD, Am. Mktg. Assn. L.A., Am. Soc. Profl. Cons., U. So. Calif. Grad. Sch. Bus. Alumni Assn. Office: Morgan Bus Assocs 8096 Puesta del Sol Carpinteria CA 93013 Office Phone: 805-684-6191. Personal E-mail: almorgan@morganba.com.

MORGAN, ANDREW LANE, urologist, educator; b. May 13, 1920; s. James Albert and Elsie Edna (Johnson) M.; m. Miriam Cleary, June 9, 1951; children: Andrew Lane, Christine, Martha, James. Exch. fellowship, St. John's U., Shanghai, China, 1939—40; BA, Dartmouth Coll., 1942; MD, Cornell U., 1945. Diplomate Am. Bd. Urology. Intern Lenox Hill Hosp., NYC, 1945—46; resident Queen's Med. Ctr., Honolulu, 1948—50, Yale U., 1950—52; practice medicine, specializing in urology Honolulu, 1952—87; ret., 1987. Chmn. dept. surgery Queen's Med. Ctr., 1979; clin. prof. urology John Burns Sch. Medicine, U. Hawaii; mem. renal transplant team St. Francis Med. Ctr.; past pres. Hawaii Med. Libr., 1957-58 Served to capt., AUS, 1946-48 Fellow ACS; mem. AMA, Am. Urol. Assn. (past pres. We. sect.), Hawaii Med. Assn., Societe Internationale d'Urologie, Honolulu County Med. Soc. (bd. govs. 1970-76, treas. 1978-79), Pacific Club Honolulu Episcopalian. Home: 44 Puako Beach Dr Kamuela HI 96743-9707

MORGAN, ANDREW WESLEY, artist, educator; b. Cleve., July 29, 1922; s. John B. and Bertha (Amersbach) M.; m. Dahlia Kaplow, May 18, 1973; children from previous marriage— Alexander, Vincent, Nicholas. BA, Kenyon Coll., 1948; M.F.A., U. N.C., 1952; postgrad., N.Y.U., 1955-57; L.H.D. (hon.), Tarkio Coll. Head art dept. Greenwich (Conn.) Country Day Sch., 1952-59; chmn. dept. art, dir. gallery U. Miss., 1959-60; pres. Kansas City (Mo.) Art Inst., 1960-70; prof., chmn. art dept. U. Miami, Fla., 1970-87. Commr. Municipal Art Commn., Kansas City, 1965-70; co-chmn. Mid-Am. Urban Design Conf., 1966 One-man shows include Stanford (Conn.) Mus., 1958, Pietrantonio Gallery, N.Y.C., 1960, Lowe Mus., 1980, Viscaya Mus., Miami, Fla., 1984, Leedy-Voulkos Art Ctr., Kansas City, Mo., 1990, Polk Mus., Lakeland, Fla., 1991, New World Sch. for Arts Gallery, Miami, 1992, U. Miami, 1993, Art Mus. No. Ariz. U., 1993-94, one-person show Ctr. for Visual Comm., Coral Gables, Fla., 1995, Leedy-Voulkes Gallery, Kansas City, 1998; groups shows include Boston Arts Festival, 1960, Mid-South Annual, Memphis, 1961, Roko Gallery, N.Y.C., 1960, U. Miss., 1959, N.E. Ann. (Jury award oil prize), Silver Mine, Conn., 1958, Ctr. for Contemporary Art, 1989, Six Miami Painters, 1st Ave. Gallery, Sarasota, Fla., 1993, Fla. Landscape, painters, travel exhibit States of Ga. and Fla., 1994. Active Com. Econ. Devel., Kans., 1965-70; bd. dirs. Kansas City Regional Coun. Higher Edn.; pres. bd. dirs. Union Ind. Colls. Art, 1967-70; mem. visual arts bd. Nat. Found. for Arts, Miami, 1988; adv. bd. Vt. Studio Ctr., Johnson, 1989. With AUS, 1942-46. Mem. Nat. Assn. Schs. Art (dir.), Coll. Art. Assn. Home: 10331 SW 59th Ave Miami FL 33156-4114

MORGAN, ANITA L., academic librarian; b. Chgo., June 23, 1950; d. LaVelle Margaret Geer; m. Robert Andrew Morgan, Aug. 20, 1994; 1 child, Laura Michele Attebery. BA, Rosary Coll., River Forest, Ill., 1971; MLIS, Dominican U., River Forest, 2002. Devel. asst. Field Mus., Chgo., 1984—85, vol. coord., 1984—96, adminstrv. asst., 1985—91; assoc. dir. devel. Dominican U., River Forest, 1996—2002; tech. svc. libr. St. Xavier U., Chgo., 2002—. Sec. Ill. OCLC Users Group, Springfield, 2005—07, vice-chair, chair-elect, 2007—08, chair, 2008—. Vol. Barack Obama Presdl. Campaign, Chgo., 2008. Home: 32 Lathrop River Forest IL 60305 Office: St Xavier Univ 3700 W 103rd St Chicago IL 60655 Office Fax: 773-779-5231. Business E-Mail: amorgan@sxu.edu.

MORGAN, ANNE MARIE G., broadcast journalist, educator; b. Paducah, Ky., Apr. 23, 1955; d. Ralph Edward and Vera Christine Gill; m. Michael William Morgan, Nov. 19, 1977; children: Deborah, Jon, James. BA in Govt. and Psychology, Coll. William and Mary, 1976; MA in Polit. Sci., U. Richmond, 1997; postgrad. in Pub. Policy, Va. Commonwealth U., 1998. HS tchr. James-City County Sch., Williamsburg, Va., 1977, Colonial Hts. Sch., Va., 1977-79; TV and radio journalist Va. Capitol News Network, Richmond, Va., 1984—, Va. Pub. Broadcasting, Richmond, Va., 1987—, WRIC-TV, Richmond, 1994—96, WTVR-TV, Richmond, 1996—2000; broadcast news anchor Va. News Network, Richmond, Va., 2000—02; journalist WVTF Radio, Roanoke, 2002—, Va. Pub. Radio, 2002—. Prof. polit. sci. U. Richmond, Va., 1998—. Author: (with others) Controversies in American Public Polity, 1999, Opposing Viewpoints Series, 1991. Sec. Parents' Guidance/Pupil Pers. Guidance Com., Powhatan, Va., 1996—98; state bd. dirs. Va. Pub. Broadcasting, Richmond, 2000—02; bd. dirs. Va. Adv. Coun. Adult Edn. and Literacy, Richmond, 1999—2002, Coun. Child Care and Early Childhood Devel., Richmond, 1995—96; chair bd. dirs. State Bd. for Cmty. Colls., Richmond, 1997—2002; chair Va. Coun. Status of Women, Richmond, 1994—2002. Recipient Meritorious award, Va. Assoc. Press Broadcasters, 2002, Disting. Faculty award, U. Richmond Sch. Contg. Studies, 2005, 1st Pl. award, Nat. Fedn. Press Women, 2005; Gov. proclamation Anne Marie Morgan Day in Commonwealth Va., Gov. Va., 1997. Mem.: Soc. Profl. Journalists, Soc. Profl. Journalists (Va. profl. chpt.), Nat. Fedn. Press Women (1st Pl. Prepared Radio Report award 2005), Va. Press Women (1st Pl. award 2005, 1st Pl. Scene Report Radio award 2006, 1st Pl. Spl. Radio Programming award 2007, 2009, 1st Pl. Prepared Radio Report award 2007—08), Capitol Corrs. Assn., Am. Polit. Sci. Assn., Pi Sigma Alpha. Avocations: music, singing, mentoring.

MORGAN, ARDYS NORD, school improvement consultant; b. South Bend, Ind., Nov. 1, 1946; d. Arthur August and Janet Ardis (Eide) Nord; children: Elizabeth Elayne, Matthew Richard. BS in Elem. Edn., Ind. U., Bloomington, 1968; MS in Elem. Edn., Ind. U., Indpls., 1972; reading cert., Ind. U., South Bend, 1982; EDS, Ind. U., Bloomington, 1992; adminstr. lic., Ind. U.-Purdue U., Indpls., 1989; EdD in Curriculum and Sch. Adminstrn., Ind. U., 1994. Tchr., South Bend, 1968-69, 73-87; adminstr. dept. instrn. and curriculum, 1987-90; tchr. Indpls., 1969-70; resident lectr. Ind. U./Purdue U., Indpls., 1970-73, adminstr., 1989; mem. adj. faculty Ind. U., South Bend, 1985-90, acting program dir. elem. and secondary edn., 1990-92; asst. supt. schs. Michigan City (Ind.) Area Schs., 1992-94; supt. Union North United Schs. Corp., 1994-96; ednl. cons., tech. and staff devel. in curriculum Lightspan Partnership, San Diego, 1997-99; pres. Sch. Improvement Partnership, Inc., Granger, Ind., 1999—. Cons. in field. Recipient Disting. Alumni award div. edn. Ind. U., South Bend, 1990. Lilly Endowment fellow, 1987. Home: 51550 Stratton Ct Granger IN 46530-8342 Office: Sch Improvement Partnership 51550 Stratton Ct Ste 300 Granger IN 46530-8342

MORGAN, BARBARA R., science educator, former astronaut; b. Fresno, Calif., Nov. 28, 1951; m. Clay Morgan; 2 children. BA in Human Biology with distinction, Stanford U., 1973; tchg. credential, Coll. Notre Dame, Belmont, Calif., 1974; PhD (hon.), Boise State U., 2008. Tchr. remedial reading and math Flathead Indian Reservation Arlee Elem. Sch., Mont., 1974; tchr. remedial reading/math McCall-Donnelly Elem. Sch., Idaho, 1975—78, tchr., 1975—78, 1979—85, 1986—98; tchr. elem. English and sci. Colegio Americano de Quito, Ecuador, 1978—79; astronaut, educator mission specialist candidate NASA, Johnson Space Ctr., Houston, 1998—2008; disting. educator-in-residence Boise State U., 2008—. Backup candidate for Tchr. in Space Program NASA, 1985, mem. edn. divsn., office human resources and edn.; mem. fed. task force for women and minorities in sci. and engring. NSF; worked with NASA, speaking to ednl. organizations throughout the country, 1986; crew mem. STS-118 mission (Endeavour), 2007. Recipient Citizen of Yr. award, USA Today, 1986, Edn. award, Women in Aerospace, 1991, Wright Bros. "Kitty Hawk" Sands of Time Edn. award, L.A. C. of C., 1991, Space Pioneer award for edn., Nat. Space Soc., 1992, Pres.'s Medallion award, U. Idaho, 1998, Idaho Fellowship award, 1998, Women in Aerospace award, 2003. Mem.: NEA, Challenger Ctr. for Space Sci. Edn. (Challenger 7 award 1995), Internat. Tech. Edn. Assn. (Lawrence Prakken Profl. Cooperation award 1996), Internat. Reading Assn., Nat. Sci. Tchrs. Assn., Nat. Coun. Tchrs. Math., Idaho Edn. Assn., Nat. PTA (hon.; hon. life mem.), Phi Beta Kappa. Avocations: playing the flute, reading, hiking, swimming, skiing. Office: Boise State U 1910 University Dr Boise ID 83725

MORGAN, BETSY ELIZABETH ROBISON, biology professor; married. BS, Tex. A & M U., Coll. Sta., 1983, MEd, 1990. Honors biology tchr. John Jay HS, San Antonio, 1983—88; adj. biology prof. Bakersfield Coll., Calif., 1991—93; honors biology tchr. Kingwood HS, Tex., 1998—2002; adj. biology prof. Kingwood Coll., Tex., 1994—2002; freshman biology programs tchg. supr. Tex. A & M U., 2002—03; biology prof. Lone Star Coll. Kingwood, 2003—. Vol. Sci. Mus., Bakersfiled, 1990—93. Pres. Swim Team, Kingwood, 1997—2002. Recipient Faculty Excellence award, Kingwood Coll., 2009; TxCETP Inquiry Activities grant. Mem.: NSTA, NABT. Office: Lone Star Coll 20000 Kingwood Dr Kingwood TX 77339

MORGAN, BETSY L., former publishing executive; b. Aug. 10, 1968; d. Jasper W. Morgan Jr. and Jacqueline W. Morgan; m. Clarence H. Gifford III, June 6, 1998. BA in Polit. Sci. & Economics, Colby Coll., Waterville, Maine, 1990; MBA, Harvard U., Cambridge, Mass., 1995. With Schroders and Co. (now Salomon Smith Barney), Fed. Res. Bank, Am. Sky Broadcasting; dir. Strategic Mgmt. Group CBS Corp.; exec. dir., bus. devel. CBS News, 1998, v.p., bus. devel., digital media, new ventures; gen. mgr. CBSNews.com, 2005—08; sr. v.p. CBS Interactive, 2005—08; CEO Huffington Post, 2008—09. Bd. overseers Colby Coll.; mem. Coun. on Fgn. Rels. Mem.: NY Women in Comm. Found. (pres. bd. dirs.).*

MORGAN, BETSY STELLE, lawyer; b. Terre Haute, Ind., Mar. 15, 1963; BA, DePauw U., 1985; JD, John Marshall Law Sch., 1988. Bar: Ill. 1989. With Baker & McKenzie, Chgo., 1988—, counsel, 1997—2002, ptnr., 2002—07, prin., 2007—. Co-chair N.Am. Pro Bono Initiative Baker & McKenzie, Chgo. Author: United States Business Immigration Manual, 2003. Office: Baker & McKenzie One Prudential Plz 130 E Randolph Dr Chicago IL 60601

MORGAN, BEVERLY CARVER, pediatrician, educator; b. NYC, May 29, 1927; d. Jay and Florence (Newkamp) Carver; children: Nancy, Thomas E. III, John E. MD cum laude, Duke U., 1955. Diplomate Am. Bd. Pediat. (oral examiner 1984-90, mem. written examination com. 1990—), Nat. Bd. Med. Examiners. Intern, asst. resident Stanford U. Hosp., San Francisco, 1955-56; clin. fellow pediat., trainee pediatric cardiology Babies Hosp.-Columbia Presbyn. Med. Ctr., NYC, 1956-59; rsch. fellow cardiovasc. diagnostic lab. Columbia-Presbyn. Med. Ctr., NYC, 1959-60; instr. pediat. Coll. Physicians and Surgeons, Columbia U., NYC, 1960; dir. heart sta. Robert B. Green Meml. Hosp., San Antonio, 1960-62; lectr. pediat. U. Tex., 1960-62; spl. rsch. fellow in pediatric cardiology Sch. Medicine, U. Wash., Seattle, 1962-64, from instr. to prof. pediat., 1962-73, chmn. dept. pediat., 1973-80; mem. staff U. Wash. Hosp., chief of staff, 1975-77; mem. staff Harborview Med. Ctr., Children's Orthop. Hosp. and Med. Ctr., dir. dept. medicine, 1974-80; prof., chmn. dept. pediat. U. Calif., Irvine, 1980-88, prof. pediat. and pediatric cardiology, 1980—; pediatrician in chief Children's Hosp. Orange County, 1988. Mem. pulmonary acad. awards panel Nat. Heart and Lung Inst., 1972-75; mem. grad. med. edn. nat. adv. com. to sec. HEW, 1977-80; mem. Coun. on Pediatric Practice; chmn. Task Force on Opportunities for Women in Pediat., 1982; mem. nursing rev. com. NIH, 1987-88. Contbr. articles to profl. jours.; mem. editl. bd. Clin. Pediat., Am. Jour. Diseases of Children, Jour. of Orange County Pediatric Soc., Jour. Am. Acad. Pediat., LA Pediatric Soc. Recipient Women of Achievement award Matrix Table, Seattle, 1974; Disting. Alumnus award Duke U. Med. Sch., 1974; Ann. award Nat. Bd. Med. Coll. Pa., 1977; Career Devel. award USPHS, 1966-71; Moseby scholar, 1955. Mem. Am. Acad. Pediat. (chmn. com. on pediat. manpower 1984-86), Am. Coll. Cardiology, Soc. for Pediat. Rsch., Am. Fedn. Clin. Rsch., Am. Pediat. Soc., Assn. Med. Sch. Pediat. Dept. Chmn. (sec.-treas. 1981-87), Western Soc. for Pediat. Rsch., Alpha Omega Alpha. Office: U Calif Irvine Med Ctr Dept Pediatrics 101 The City Dr S Orange CA 92868-3201 Office Phone: 714-456-6483. Business E-Mail: bcmorgan@uci.edu.

MORGAN, CATHERINE MARIE, psychologist, writer; b. Duluth, Minn., Mar. 27, 1947; m. Ralph Morgan, 1967; 1 child, Andrew. BS, U. Nebr., 1968; MEd, U. Okla., 1973; PhD, Okla. State U., 1987; postgrad. Menninger Found., Psychotherapy Tng. Program, 1987-89. Child devel. specialist Southwest Guidance Ctr., Wheatland, Okla., 1973-74; pvt. practice Family Counseling Assocs., San Antonio, 1974-75; psychol. asst. Edmond Guidance Ctr., Okla., 1975-82; psychol. asst. supr. Southeast Guidance Ctr., Del City, Okla., 1982-86; psychol. intern Cleve. County Health Dept., Moore, Okla., 1986-87; psychologist Cen. State Hosp., Norman, Okla., 1987-89; pvt. practice assocs. in psychology Edmond, Okla.; vice chair bd. mgrs. Integris Mental Health; pres. Assocs. in Psychology, 1988—. Mem. AAUW, APA, Okla. Psychol.

Assn., Am. Bus. Women's Assn., P.E.O., Kappa Delta Pi. Avocations: writing, reading, knitting, racquetball. Office: 11212 N May Ste 302 Oklahoma City OK 73120 Office Phone: 405-753-9009.

MORGAN, CHRISTOPHER DONALD, mechanical engineer, consultant; b. South Bend, Ind., June 4, 1965; s. George Henry and Janis Sue Morgan; m. Catherine Elizabeth Foley, Nov. 21, 1991; children: Caitlin Elizabeth Barbara, Christopher Robert. BSME, Purdue U., 1988, MSME, 1991; PhD, U. Akron, 1996. Registered profl. engr., Ohio, Mich., Md., Va. and DC; bd. cert. noise contol engr. Inst. Noise Control Engrs. Engring. intern AC Rochester, Flint, Mich., 1985-91; advanced tire engr. Bridgestone/Firestone, Inc., Akron, Ohio, 1992-96; rsch. engr. Kumho Tires, Akron, Ohio, 1996-2000, SuperTrapp Industries, Inc., Cleve., 2000-01; prin. engr. noise and vibration control Key Safety Sys., Inc. (formerly Breed Techs., Inc.), Sterling Heights, Mich., 2001—05. Propr., cons. H&P Engring., Akron, 1996—2007; instr. Project Focus: HOPE, Detroit, 2002—08; proprietor Morgan Vibro Acoustics, 2008—; sr. vibrations and acoustics cons. Polysonics Corp, Warrenton, Va., 2008—. Coach Sci. Olympiad, Sterling Heights, 2007—08. Mem.: ASHRAE, IEEE, ASME, Inst. Noise Control Engrs., Assn. Computing Machinery, Acoustical Soc. Am., Soc. Indsl. Applied Math., Soc. Exptl. Mechanics, Soc. Auto. Engrs. (mem. at large engring. tech. stds. bd., Forest R. McFarland award 2007). Avocations: software development, soccer, triathlon, bicycling. Office Phone: 540-341-4988. Business E-Mail: chrism@polysonics-corp.com.

MORGAN, CLAIRE MARIE, elementary school educator; BA in English, SUNY, Geneseo, 1974; MA in Policies Studies, Empire Coll., Saratoga Springs, NY, 1994. Provisional cert. tchr. NY, 1994, permanent cert. tchr. NY, 1999. Adult protective case worker Wyo. County Dept. Social Svcs., Warsaw, NY, 1977—85; county coord. Ednl. Opportunity Ctr., Wyo. County, NY, 1985—93; substitute tchr. Bd. Coop. Ednl. Svcs. Dist. Schs., Genesee, 1995—2009; tchr. elem. sch. Genesee Wyo. Cath. Sch., Attica, NY, 2001—; tchr. Holy Family Cath. Sch. Adv. bd. office aging Wyo. County Bd. Suprs., Warsaw, 1981; Temp. Corrections Counselor Wyo Correctional Facility, Attica; tchr. Alexander & Wyo. Ctrl. Schs. Scrabble Inst. Vol. Literacy Vols. Am., Warsaw, 1989—. Home: 1343 Beck Rd Attica NY 14011 Office: Genesee Wyoming Cc School 106 Main St Attica NY 14011-1244

MORGAN, CLYDE NATHANIEL, dermatologist; b. Bell County, Tex., Nov. 2, 1923; s. Xenophen William and Rhoda Ella (Deck) M.; m. Birdie Joyce Rich, Mar. 3, 1951; children: Clyde Nathaniel Jr., Reinette Jean, Nancy Elaine. BS, Abilene Christian Coll., 1948; MD, U. Tex., Galveston, 1953. Cert. Bd. of Am. Acad. Cryosurgery, 1978. Assoc. prof. biology Abilene (Tex.) Christian Coll., 1954-56; pvt. practice Abilene, 1954-67; dermatologist, 1969—. Contbr. articles to profl. jours. Chmn. Taylor County Republican Party, 1965—70; delegate Republican Nat. Convention, 1968, 1980, alt. delegate, 1976. 1st lt. air corps US Army, 1943—46. Recipient Med. Econs. award, 1963; named Disting. Pres., Greater Abilene Kiwanis Club, 1979. Fellow Am. Acad. Family Practice; mem. AMA, SAR (chpt. pres. 1997-99, past pres. Big Country chpt., award 1995), Am. Coll. Cryosurgery, Internat. Soc. Cryosurgery, Tex. Med. Assn., So. Med. Assn., Tex. Dermatologic Soc., Taylor-Jones-Haskell County Med. Soc., Indian Coun. on Cryogenics (hon. fellow). Republican. Mem. Ch. Of Christ. Avocations: golf, fishing, hunting, cryogenics research. Home: 1718 Cedar Crest Dr Abilene TX 79601-3228 Office: 1166 Merchant St Abilene TX 79603-5014 Home Phone: 325-673-3848; Office Phone: 325-673-4242. Personal E-mail: clybird@juno.com.

MORGAN, COLBY SHANNON, JR., lawyer; b. Marshalltown, Iowa, Mar. 29, 1949; s. Colby Shannon and Elizabeth Perkinson (Robertson) M.; m. Leslie Marmon, Apr. 5, 1975; children: Colby Shannon III, Jeffrey Michael, Sarah Elizabeth. AB cum laude, Dartmouth Coll., 1971; JD, Vanderbilt U., 1974. Bar: NY 1975, US Dist. Ct. (so. and ea. dists.) NY 1976, Tenn. 1977, US Dist. Ct. (we. dist.) Tenn. 1978, US Ct. Appeals (6th cir.) 1980, US Dist. Ct. (ea. and we. dists.) Ark. 1983, US Ct. Appeals (8th cir.) 1987, US Dist. Ct. (no. dist.) Calif. 1994, US Ct. Appeals (3d cir.) 1995, US Ct. Appeals (9th cir.) 1996, US Ct. Appeals (4th cir.) 1996, US Supreme Ct. 1998, US Dist. Ct. (no. dist.) NY 1998, US Dist. Ct. (we. dist.) Mich. 2001, US Dist. Ct. (ctrl. and no. dists.) Ill. 2001, US Ct. Appeals (2d cir.) 2004. Assoc. Crowe, McCoy, Agoglia & Zweibel, Mineola, N.Y., 1974-78, Rosenfield, Borod & Kremer, Memphis, 1978-83, Apperson, Crump, Duzane & Maxwell, Memphis, 1983-86, Shuttleworth, Smith, Young & Webb, Memphis, 1986; sr. atty. Holiday Inns, Inc., Memphis, 1986-91; assoc. Petkoff & Lancaster, Memphis, 1991-92; sr. counsel Fed. Express Corp., Memphis, 1992. Chancellor, bd. dirs. Memphis Boys Town, 1979-86; chmn. Memphis Civil Svc. Commn., 1980-83; bd. dirs., chmn. bd. dirs. Memphis Emmaus Cmty., 1983—; bd. dirs. Christ Meth. Adminstrv. Bd., Memphis, 1984-86; Leadership Memphis, 1984—; cubmaster Pack 241 Boy Scouts Am., Memphis, 1992-93; treas., bd. dirs. Memphis Symphony Chorus, 1981-85. Recipient FedEx Five Star award, 1997, Campaign Leadership award, United Way of the Mid South, 2000. Mem. ABA, FBA, Assn. Corp. Counsel, Dartmouth Lawyers Assn., Federalist Soc., Order of the First Families of Tenn., Gen. Soc. Colonial Wars, NY Sons of the Revolution, Mil. Order of the Stars and Bars (lt. comdr. 1994—), Tenn. Geneaol. Soc., Jamestowne Soc., Hereditary Order of Families of the Presidents, Clan Donnachaidh Soc., Mensa, SAR (chancellor, past pres. Memphis soc., v.p. West Tenn. 1992—, pres.-elect, past registrar, past chancellor, bd. govs. Tenn. chpt. 1994—), Scottish Rite. Republican. Methodist. Avocations: genealogy, marathon runner, tennis, golf, reading. Home: 5521 Fiesta Dr Memphis TN 38120-2826 Office: Fed Express Corp 3620 Hacks Cross Rd Memphis TN 38125 Office Phone: 901-434-8545. E-mail: csmorgan@fedex.com.

MORGAN, DAVID RAYMOND, financial consultant, retired bank executive; b. Melbourne, Australia, Mar. 14, 1947; s. Raymond K. and Verna Morgan; m. Roslyn Joan Kelly; 2 children. B in Econs. with honors, La Trobe U., Australia, 1970; MSc, PhD, U. London; AMP, Harvard U. Sr. economist, fiscal affairs dept. IMF, U.S., 1976-79; asst. sec. Fgn. Investment br. Treasury, 1980-81; sec. govt. task force Australian Fin. Sys. Inquiry, 1981; asst. sec. Fiscal and Monetary Policy br. GFEP Treasury, 1982-83; mem. taxation policy div. Treasury Dept. Canberra, 1983-85; 1st asst. sec. gen. fin. and econ. policy Commonwealth Treasury, 1986-87, dep. sec. fin., 1987, dep. sec. econs., 1989; dep. mng. dir. Westpac Fin. Svcs. Group, 1990—; chief gen. mgr. Asia Pacific div. Westpac, Sydney, 1990, mng. dir. Westpac Fin. Svcs. Group, 1990-91; group exec., retail banking group Westpac Banking Corp., Sydney, 1992—94, group exec. instnl. and internat., 1994—97, exec. dir., 1997—98, CEO, 1999—2008; operating ptnr., chmn. Australian ops. J.C. Flowers & Co., NYC, 2008—. Bd. dir. BHP Billiton. Mem. MCC, Union Club. Avocations: wine, tennis, classical music. Mailing: JC Flowers & Co 717 Fifth Ave New York NY 10022

MORGAN, DENNIS R., telecommunications industry executive; BSEE, U. Cin., 1965; MSEE, Syracuse U., NY, 1968, PhD in Elec. Engring., 1970. Cert. PE, Ohio, 1965. Sr. engr. Gen. Electric, Electronics Lab., Syracuse, 1965—84; disting. mem. tech. staff Bell Labs., Alcatel-Lucent, Murray Hill, NJ, 1984—. Contbr. articles to profl. jours. Achievements include patents in field. Office: Alcatel-Lucent 700 Mountain Ave 1C-260 New Providence NJ 07974

MORGAN, DENNIS RICHARD, lawyer; b. Jan. 3, 1942; s. Benjamin Richard and Gladys Belle (Brown) Morgan. BA, Washington and Lee U., 1964; JD, U. Va., 1967; LLM in Labor Law, NYU, 1971. Bar: Ohio 1967, Va. 1967, U.S. Ct. Appeals (4th cir.) 1968, U.S. Ct. Appeals (6th cir.) 1971, U.S. Supreme Ct. 1972. Law clk. to chief judge U.S. Dist. Ct. (ea. dist.) Va., 1967—68; mem. Marshman, Snyder & Seeley, Cleve., 1971—72; dir. labor rels. Ohio Dept. Adminstrv. Svcs., 1972—75; asst. city atty. Columbus, Ohio, 1975—77; dir. Ohio Legis. Reference Bur., Columbus, 1979—81; assoc. Clemans, Nelson & Assocs., Columbus, 1981; pvt. practice Columbus, 1978—92. Lectr. in field; guest lectr. Cen. Mich. U., 1975; judge moot ct. Ohio State U. Sch. Law, 1981, 83, grad. divsn., 73, 74, 76; guest lectr. Baldwin-Wallace Coll., 1973; legal counsel Dist. IV Comms. Workers Am., 1982—88; pers. dir. Pub. Utilities Commn., Ohio, 1989—91; asst. atty. gen. State of Ohio, 1991—2003. Negotiator Franklin County United Way, 1977—81; regional chmn. ann. alumni fund-raising program U. Va. Sch. Law, 1976—2007; mem. Greater Hilltop Area Commn., 1989—2006; pres. Woodbrook Village Condominium Assn., 1985—2005, v.p., 2005—; vice-chmn. Franklin County Dem. Party, 1976—82; dem. com. person Ward 58, Columbus, 1973—2006; chmn. rules com. Ohio State Dem. Conv., 1974; co-founder, trustee Greater West Side Dem. Club; bd. dirs. Hilltop Civic Coun., Inc., 1997—99. Capt. US Army, 1968—70. Recipient Am. Jurisprudence award, 1967; scholar Robert E. Lee Rsch., 1965. Mem.: Am. Judicature Soc., Fed. Bar Assn., Indsl. Rels. Rsch. Assn., Pi Sigma Alpha. Roman Catholic. Home: 21320 Lancaster Run Unit 1116 Estero FL 33928 Personal E-mail: wahoos1967@yahoo.com.

MORGAN, DONNA EVENSEN, lawyer; b. Bklyn., Feb. 28, 1957; d. Edward Ivar and Judith (Larsen) Evensen; m. Charles S. Morgan, Sept. 3, 1988. BA, Colgate U., 1979; JD, U. Mich., 1984. Bar: Ill. 1985. Assoc. Chapman and Cutler, Chgo., 1985-86, Kirkland and Ellis, Chgo., 1987-89, Mayer Brown LLP, Chgo., 1989—. Address: Mayer Brown LLP 71 S Wacker Dr Chicago IL 60606-4637 Home Phone: 630-887-0192; Office Phone: 312-701-7138. Business E-Mail: dmorgan@mayerbrown.com.

MORGAN, DOROTHY ANN, literature and language educator; b. Gary, Ind., May 28, 1946; d. Horace and Annie Ruth Morgan; m. Jacob A. Rhodes (div.). BS in Bus. Edn., Knoxville Coll., Tenn., 1970; MS in Vocat. Bus. Edn., Kent State U., Ohio, 1976; MA in Theology, Chgo. Theol. Sem., 1993. Cert. Nat. Bd. for Profl. Tchg. Stds., mentor State of Ind. Bus. tchr. Gary Pub. Schs., Ind., 1970—72; bus. edn. tchr. Canton City Schs., Ohio, 1972—75; adj. bus. tchr. Ind. U. NW, Gary, 1976—78; bus. edn. tchr. Westville Cmty. Ctr., Ind., 1978—88; English tchr. gifted and talented program West Side HS, Gary, Ind., 1992—. Part-time English tchr. Ind. Wesleyan, Merrillville, 2002; advanced placement reader and table leader Edn. Testing Svc./Coll. Bd., Daytona Beach, Fla., 1997—; faculty cons. Coll. Bd., NYC, 1998—. Contbr. articles to profl. jours., poetry to anthologies. Recipient Nat. Youth Leadership Forum cert., 2000, Mellon fellowship, Coll. Bd. Advanced Placement Program, 1997, Creative Writing scholarship, Purdue U., 1997. Mem.: Nat. Coun. Tchrs. English, Am. Fedn. Tchrs. Avocations: sewing, photography, travel, theater. Home: PO Box 646 612 Fernway Rd Kingsford Heights IN 46346 Office: West Side H S 8th Ave at Gerry St Gary IN 46406 Personal E-mail: dor_mor@msn.com.

MORGAN, DOUGLAS F., public service educator; b. Rupert, Idaho, Jan. 15, 1943; s. Dallas Y. and Marguerite Gladys Morgan; m. Candace Dunn, Aug. 3, 1963; children: Cheryl, Kari Brenk. PhD, U. Chgo., 1969. Prof. Lewis and Clark Coll., Portland, Oreg., 1978—96, Portland State U., 1996—, dir., Exec. Leadership Inst., 1996—. Author: (textbook) Foundations of Public Service. Bd. ofcl. Portland Pub. Schs., 2004—08. Tchg. and Rsch. fellowships, Nat. Endowment Humanities, 1978, 1981. Mem.: ASPA (state pres. 1989—90, Brownlow award 1996). Liberal. Achievements include research in role of career administrators in local Government. Avocations: fly fishing, backpacking, travel. Home: 707 SW Dolph St Portland OR 97219 Office: Portland State Univ 500 Mill St Portland OR 97207 Business E-Mail: morgandf@pdx.edu.

MORGAN, EDMUND SEARS, retired history professor; b. Mpls., Jan. 17, 1916; s. Edmund Morris and Elsie Sears (Smith) Morgan; m. Helen Theresa Mayer, July 7, 1939; children: Penelope, Pamela; m. Marie Caskey, July 22, 1983. AB, Harvard U., 1937, PhD, 1942. Instrument maker Radiation Lab., MIT, 1942-45; instr. U. Chgo., 1945-46; asst. prof. Brown U., 1946-49, asso. prof., 1949-51, prof., 1951-55, acting dean grad. sch., 1951-52; prof. Yale U., 1955-65, Sterling prof., 1965-86, prof. emeritus, 1986—. Rsch. fellow Huntington Libr., 1952—53; Johnson rsch. prof. U. Wis., 1968—69; trustee Smith Coll., Northampton, Mass., 1984—89. Author: The Puritan Family, 1944, Virginians at Home, 1953, The Stamp Act Crisis (with Helen M. Morgan), 1953, The Birth of the Republic, 1956, The Puritan Dilemma: The Story of John Winthrop, 1958, The American Revolution: A Review of Changing Interpretations, 1958, The Mirror of the Indian, 1958, Visible Saints: The History of a Puritan Idea, 1963, Roger Williams: The Church and the State, 1967, So What About History?, 1969, American Slavery, American Freedom: The Ordeal of Colonial Virginia, 1975, The Challenge of the American Revolution, 1976, The Meaning of Independence: John Adams, George Washington, and Thomas Jefferson, 1976, The Genius of George Washington, 1980, The Gentle Puritan: A Life of Ezra Stiles, 1727-1795, 1984, Inventing the People: The Rise of Popular Sovereignty in England and America, 1988, Benjamin Franklin, 2002, The Genuine Article: A Historian Looks at Early America, 2004, Not Your Usual Founding Father, 2006; editor: Prologue to the Revolution: Sources and Documents on the Stamp Act Crisis, 1764-1766, 1959, The Founding of Massachusetts: Historians and the Sources, 1964; mem. editl. bd.: N.E. Quar.; contbr. articles and revs. to hist. jours. Recipient Nat. Humanities medal, 2000, Pulitzer Prize for hist., 2006, Gold medal History, Am. Acad. Arts and Letters. Mem.: Am. Acad. Arts and Scis., Orgn. Am. Historians (pres. 1971—72), Royal Hist. Soc., Brit. Acad., Am. Philos. Soc., Am. Antiquarian Soc., Mass. Hist. Soc., Colonial Soc. Mass. Office Phone: 203-777-1933.

MORGAN, EDWARD A., oil industry executive; BS in acctg., Miss. State Univ.; M in acctg., Univ. Tenn. CPA. Acctg. positions Deloitte & Touche, 1993—97; dir. treas. ops. Am. Homepatient Inc., 1997—2002; fin. mgmt. positions Delek US Holdings, Brentwood, Tenn., 2002—03, treas., 2003—05, v.p., treas., 2005—06, v.p., CFO, 2006—09; CFO, treas. CVR Energy Inc., CVR Partners LP, Sugar Land, Tex., 2009—. Mem.: Am. Inst. CPAs, Assn. Fin. Professionals, Tenn. Soc. CPAs. Office: CVR Energy Inc Ste 500 2277 Plaza Dr Sugar Land TX 77479*

MORGAN, ELAINE R., hematologist, oncologist, medical educator; b. Phila., May 22, 1946; d. Bernard and Sadie Jean (Blackman) Morgan; children: Brandon, Kerry David, Ari, Erin, Katelyn. BA, U. Pa., Phila., 1967, MD, 1971; cert. in Clin. Bioethics, Med. Coll. Wis., Milw., 2001. Diplomate Am. Bd. Pediat. Hospice and Palliative Medicine, 2008. Resident pediat. Children's Hosp. of LA, 1971—74; fellow pediat. oncology Children's Hosp. Med. Ctr., Boston, 1974—75; attending physician Children's Meml. Hosp., Chgo., 1976—. Co-dir. pediat. hospice Horizon Hospice; med. advisor Make A Wish Found., Ill.; med. dir. Parent to Parent Children's Meml. Hosp., Chgo., 1995—; mem. faculty Feinberg Sch. Medicine, Northwestern U., 1978—, prof. pediat., 2005—; co med. dir. Palliative Care Team, Children Meml. Hosp. Contbr. articles to profl. jours. Recipient Tchr. of Yr., Children's Meml. Hosp., 1987; grantee, Leukemia Rsch. Found., 1978—79. Fellow: Am. Acad. Pediat.; mem.: AAHPM, Am. Soc. Bioethics and Humanities, Am. Acad. Pediat. Hematology-Oncology, Am. Soc. Clin. Oncology, Am. Soc. Hematology, Phi Beta Kappa. Avocations: reading, children's issues, crafts. Office: Children's Meml Hosp 2300 Children's Plz Chicago IL 60614 Office Phone: 773-880-4562. Business E-Mail: emorgan@northwestern.edu.

MORGAN, ELIZABETH K., retired critical care nurse; b. Lansdowne, Pa., Feb. 18, 1951; d. Charles Knight and Marian Swope (Wing) Morgan; m. James Tracy Grey III, Dec. 27, 1980 (div. 2002); children: Michael Grey, James Tracy IV Grey, Joshua S. Grey. AA, Elmira Coll., NY, 1976; grad. in practical nursing, Upper Bucks Voc-Tech, Perkasie, Pa., 1979; AA in Nursing, Bucks County Community Coll., Newtown, Pa., 1989; student, LaSalle U., 1992—96. Cert. health profl. paramedic, Pa.; cert. CPR, ACLS, TNCC. Paramedic Warminster Ambulance, Pa., 1986; staff practical nurse Warminster Gen. Hosp., 1986—89; ICU/CCU staff nurse Nazareth Hosp., Phila., 1989—96, coord. cardiac rehab., 2001—02, staff to charge nurse telemetry stroke fl., part-time nurse IV team, 2002—. Mem. Warrington Ambulance Corps. Mem. AACN. Home: 4345 Teesdale St Philadelphia PA 19136

MORGAN, FRANK, mathematics professor; BS, MIT, 1974; MA, Princeton U., 1976, PhD, 1977; ScD (hon.), Cedar Crest Coll., 1995. C.L.E. Moore instr. to assoc. prof., Green prof. MIT, Cambridge, 1977—79, chmn., undergraduate math. office, 1979—82, Cecil and Ida Green Career Develop. Chair, 1985—86; chmn. Dept. Math. Williams Coll., 1988—94, Dennis Meenan 1954 Thrid Century prof., 1997—2003, Webster Atwell Class of 1921 prof. math., 2003—. Vis. asst. prof. Rice U., Houston, 1982-83; vis. assoc. prof. Stanford U., 1986-87; mem. Inst. Advanced Study, Princeton, N.J., 1990-91; vis. prof., Queens Coll. CUNY, 1994; Princeton 250-Anniversary vis. prof. disting. tchg. Princeton U., 1997-98; adj. prof. U. Mass., 1992-; NSF math adv. com. 1987-90, 1994-97; chair Hudson River Undergraduate Math. Conf., 1997; spkr. in field. Author: Geometric Measure Theory, 1988, 3rd edit., 2000, Riemannian Geometry, 1993, revised edit., 2001, Calculus Lite, 1995, 2nd edit., 1997, The Math Chat Book, 2000, Real Analysis, 2005, Real Analysis and Applications, 2006; contbr. several articles to profl. jours. Recipient First Nat. Disting. Tchg. award, 1992, Disting. Alumnus award, William Allen HS, 1995; NSF Fellow, 1976, 1977; NSF rsch. grants 1977-2006, 2008-. Mem.: Am. Math. Soc. (coun. 1994—97), Math. Assn. Am. (2nd v.p. 2000—02, Haimo award for disting. coll. or univ. tchg. of math. 1993). Office: Williams Coll Dept of Mathematics and Statistics Bronfman Science Center Williamstown MA 01267 Office Phone: 413-597-2437. Office Fax: 413-597-4061. Business E-Mail: Frank.Morgan@williams.edu.*

MORGAN, GEORGE ARTHUR, psychologist; b. Chgo., 1936; s. George Arthur and Josephine Read Morgan; m. Hildegarde Swanson, June 9, 1962; children: Arthur Swanson, Lisa Morgan Heimer. BA, DePauw U., Greencastle, Ind., 1958; MA, Harvard U., Cambridge, Mass., 1959; PhD, Cornell U., Ithaca, N.Y., 1965. Instr. psychology Washington and Jefferson Coll., Washington, Pa., 1959—61; human factors psychologist IBM Space Guidance Ctr., Owego, NY, 1962—62; asst. prof. psychology Hiram Coll., Ohio, 1964—71; health scientist adminstr. Nat. Inst. Child Health and Human Devel., Bethesda, Md., 1971—73, rsch. psychologist, 1973—76; asst. acad. v.p. and assoc. prof. psychology Coll. Charleston, SC, 1976—79; prof. human devel. and family studies Colo. State U., Fort Collins, 1979—2001, prof., sch. edn., 1992—2001, prof. emeritus edn. and human devel., 2001—. Asst. dir. Upward Bound project Hiram Coll., Ohio, 1966—69, asst. dean, dir. instl. rsch., 1967—71; assoc. dean Colo. State U., Fort Collins, 1979—84, head dept. of design, merchandising and consumer scis., 1984—92, coord. Sch. Edn., Office Rsch. Support, 2001—; clin. prof. psychiatry U. Colo. Sch. Medicine, Denver, 1999—. Editor (author): (scholarly book) Mastery Motivation: Origins, Conceptualizations, and Applications, 1995; author: (text book) Research Methods in Applied Settings: An Integrated Approach to Design and Analysis, (2nd Edit.), 2009, Understanding and Evaluating Research in Applied and Clinical Settings, 2006, SPSS for Introductory Statistics: Use and Interpretation (3rd ed), 2007, SPSS for Intermediate Statistics: Use and Interpretation (3rd ed), 2008; contbr. over 60 articles to profl. jours. Chair Western Home Econs. Rsch. Administrs., 1983—85; bd. mem. Colo. Home Econs. Assn., 1984—85; resource allocation panel Ft. Collins United Way, Colo., 1984—86; treas. Friends of Gustafson Gallery, Fort Collins, Colo., 1986—91; textiles com. Gov.'s Execs. for Econ. Opportunity, Colo., 1990—92; cons. Larimer County Index of Cmty. Well-Being Project, Fort Collins, Colo., 2002—02. Recipient Scholarly Excellence award, Coll. Applied Human Scis., Colo. State U., 2000; fellowship, Woodrow Wilson Found., 1958-1959, Grad. fellowship, Danforth Found., 1958-1964, Acad. Adminstrn. fellow, Am. Coun. Edn., 1969-1970, Curriculum Evaluation grant, US Office of Edn., 1969-1971, Curriculum Devel. grant, NEH, 1969-1971, Faculty Devel. grant, Lilly Endowment, 1978-1979, Rsch. on Mastery Motivation grant, Devel. Psychobiology Rsch. Group, 1979-2000, Mastery Motivation Rsch. grant, MacArthur Found. Rsch. Network, 1982-1987. Mem.: APA (life), Devel. Psychobiology Rsch. Group (exec. com. 1997—2004), Soc. Rsch. Child Devel. (emeritus), Phi Beta Kappa. Achievements include research in mastery motivation in infants and toddlers; development of dimensions of mastery questionnaire. Avocations: family genealogy, travel. Home: 4824 Regency Dr Fort Collins CO 80526-3810 Office: Colo State Univ 233 Edn Bldg Fort Collins CO 80523-1588 Personal E-mail: george.morgan@colostate.edu. Business E-Mail: gmorgan@cahs.colostate.edu.

MORGAN, GREGORY PAUL, financial investment advisor; b. Cocoa Beach, Fla., Sept. 9, 1958; s. Paul Leo and Mickey Maxine (Cooper) M. BS in Psychology magna cum laude, Pepperdine U., 1980. Cert. fin. planner. Fin. analyst Williams & McCombs, Inc., Arlington, Tex., 1980-83; fin. advisor Balanced Fin., Dallas, 1983-86; ptnr. Strategic Fin. Group, Arlington, 1986—. Chmn. coun. Lowry Fin. Svcs.; pres. Strategic Fin.Mgmt., 1989; lectr. numerous orgns. Big Bros. Am. United Way, Dallas, 1986—. Recipient Bloomberg Top 200 Wealth Mgrs., 2007, 2008; named Best Fin. Planners, Dallas Mag., 2003, 2004, 2005; named to Bloomberg Top 200 Wealth Mgrs., 2003, 2004, 2005, 2006. Mem.: Fin. Planners Assn. Avocations: tennis, running, snow-skiing. Office: 5310 Harvest Hill Rd Ste 226 Dallas TX 75230-5893 Home: 403 Rockcrest Dr Coppell TX 75019 Office Phone: 972-960-6460 Ext.2. Business E-Mail: gmorgan@sfmgadvisors.com, greg@sfmg.com.

MORGAN, JACQUI, illustrator, painter, art educator, writer; b. NYC, Feb. 22, 1939; d. Henry and Emily (Cook) Morganstern; m. Onnig Kalfayan, Apr. 23, 1967 (div. 1972); m. Tomás Gonda, Jan. 1983 (dec. 1988). BFA with honors, Pratt Inst., Bklyn., 1960; MA, CCNY, 1978.

Textile designer M. Lowenstein & Sons, NYC, 1961-62, Fruit of the Loom, NYC, 1962; stylist-design dir. Au Courant, Inc., NYC, 1966—; assoc. prof. Pratt Inst., Bklyn., 1977—, Fashion Inst. Tech., NYC. Guest lectr. U. Que., Syracuse U., Warsaw TV & Radio, Poland, NYU, Parsons Sch. Design, N.Y.C., Sch. Visual Arts, N.Y.C., Va. Commonwealth U., Fashion Inst. of Tech., others; mem. profl. juries; curator Tomás Gonda retrospective exhbn.; condr. workshops. One-person shows include Soc. Illustrators, NYC, 1977, 2005, 2008, Art Dirs. Club, NYC, 1978, Gallerie Nowe Miasto, Warsaw, 1978, Gallerie Baumeister, Munich, 1978, Hansen-Feuerman Gallery, NYC, 1980, Krannert Mus./U. Ill., 1998, Art Gallery at Marywood U., Scranton, Pa., 1998, Spring Studio, 2006; group shows include Mus. Contemporary Crafts, NYC, 1975, Smithsonian Instn., Washington, 1976, Mus. Warsaw, 1976, 78, Mus. Tokyo, 1979, Nat. Watercolor Soc., 1989, Salmagundi Club, 1990, New Eng. Watercolor Soc. Open, 1990, Miss. Watercolor Grand Nat., 1990, Illustration West 29, 1990, Adirondack Nat., 1990, Die Verlassenen Schuhe, 1993, N.Y. restaurant Sch., 1994, Lizan-Tops Gallery, 1996, 2005, The Art Club, 2000, Mus. at Fashion Inst. Am., 2003, Soc. Illustrators, NYC, 2004, The Hopper Ho., 2006, Spring Studio, 2007, NY Soc. Illustrators, 2008; represented in permanent collections: Smithsonian Instn., Mus. Warsaw; author, illustrator: Watercolor for Illustration; produced 3 instrnl. watercolor videos; series of prints pub., 1995; series of plates publ., 1995; co-curator Tomas Gonda Retrospective, Va. Commonwealth U., Rutgers U., Carnegie Mellon U., others in U.S., Mus. Modern Art, Buenos Aires, Ulmer Mus., Ulm, Germany; illustrator Lights Along the Path, 1999, The Healing Garden, 1999; contbr. articles to profl. jours. Recipient more than 200 awards from various orgns. including Soc. Illustrators, Fed. Design Coun., Comm. Arts Mag., Am. Inst. Graphic Arts, N.Y. Art Dirs. Club, Print Design Ann. Mem.: Graphic Artists Guild (dir. 1975—79), Soc. Illustrators, Women Artists of the West, Pa. Watercolor Soc. Studio: 6940 Yellowstone Blvd 515 Forest Hills NY 11375-3400 *I understand that it's the pleasure of the process and the satisfaction of improvement that gives satisfaction.*

MORGAN, JAMES C., retired manufacturing executive; b. 1938; BSME, MBA, Cornell U.; DEng (hon.), De Anza Coll., 1994. Corp. staff Textron Inc., 1963—72; sr. ptnr. West Ven Mgmt., San Francisco, 1972—76; pres. Applied Materials, Inc., Santa Clara, Calif., 1976—87, CEO, 1977—2003, chmn., 1987—2009, chmn. emeritus, 2009—. Apptd. by Pres. Clinton to Commn. U.S.-Pacific Trade and Investment Policy, 1996; mem. Nat. Adv. Com. Semiconductors, 1988—92; bd. dirs. Cisco Sys.; apptd. to U.S.-Japan Sector Govt. Commn., 2002; adv. bd. mem. Ctr. Sci. Tech. &: Soc. Santa Clara U., Calif.; vice-chmn. Presdl. Export Council, 2003—. Co-author: Cracking the Japanese Market: Strategies for Success in the New Global Economy. Bd. gov. Nature Conservancy; trustee Nature Conservancy Calif. Recipient Cmty. Svc. award, NCCJ, 1995, Nat. Medal of Tech., Pres. Clinton, 1996, Global Humanitarian Award, Tech. Mus. Innovation, Cmty. Svc. Award, Nat. Conf. Cmty. & Justice; named Internat. Citizen of Yr., World Forum of Silicon Valley, 1995; named to Jr. Achievement Hall of Fame, 1991. Mem.: Semiconductor Equipment and Materials Internat. (dir. emeritus, past pres.), Pacific Basin Econ. Coun. (chmn.'s circle), Coun. Competitiveness, Nat. Ctr. Asia-Pacific Econ. Cooperation (bd. dirs.), Congrl. Econ. Leadership Inst. (bd. dirs.), World Presidents Orgn., Semiconductor Equipment and Materials Internat./SEMATECH (past bd. dirs., Global Pioneer Award), Am. Electronics Assn. (past bd. dirs.). Office: Applied Materials Inc 3050 Bowers Ave Santa Clara CA 95054-3298*

MORGAN, JAMES H., food services company executive, former investment company executive; m. Peggy Morgan. Grad., Vanderbilt U., 1969. With Hornblower & Weeks, Bach Halsey Stuart Shields, Interstate/Johnson Lane, Charlotte, NC, 1986-89; pres. Morgan Investments, Inc., 1989—90; pres., COO Interstate/Johnson Lane, Charlotte, NC, 1990-94, pres., CEO, 1994-99, Wachovia Securities, Inc., 1999, cons. Winston-Salem, NC, 2000—01; chmn., chief investment officer Covenant Capital, LLC (formerly Morgan Semones Associates, LLC), 2001—08; vice chmn. Krispy Kreme Doughnuts, Inc., Winston-Salem, 2004—05, chmn., 2005—, pres., CEO, 2008—. Bd. dirs. Krispy Kreme Doughnuts, Inc., Winston Salem, NC, 2000—. Lt. USN. Recipient One-Yr. Investing Derby, Smart Money mag. Office: Morgan Semones Assocs 4201 Congress St #155 Charlotte NC 28209 Mailing: Chairman of the Bd Kripsy Kreme Doughnuts Inc 370 Knollwood St Ste 500 Winston Salem NC 27103

MORGAN, JAMES PHILIP, pharmacology and cardiology educator; b. Cin., Jan. 13, 1948; s. James Weldon and Dorcas Adele (Meyer) M.; m. Kathleen Greive, Dec. 22, 1973; children: James Patrick, Jonathan Michael. BS, U. Cin., 1970, PhD, 1974, MD, 1976. Diplomate Am. Bd. Internal Medicine, Am. Bd. Cardiovascular Disease. Fellow internal medicine Mayo Clinic, Rochester, Minn., 1976—79, fellow cardiovascular disease, 1979—83; asst. medicine Beth Israel Hosp., Boston, 1983—. Instr. pharmacology U. Cin., 1975—76; asst. prof. pharmacology, instr. medicine Mayo Clinic, 1981—83; asst. prof. medicine Harvard U., Boston, 1983, assoc. prof., 1988—96, Herman Dana prof. medicine, 1996—2005; affiliate faculty, dept. pharmacology Harvard Med. Sch., 1986—2000; chief and program dir. cardiovascular divsn. Beth Israel Hosp., 1994—2001, vice chmn. medicine, 2000—05; chief cardiovasc. medicine St. Elizabeth's Med. Ctr., Boston, 2005—08, dir. Caritas Christi Cardiovasc. Ctr., 2006—08; chief cardiovasc. medicine Caritas Carney Hosp.; med. dir. cardiovasc. svcs. Carney Hosp., 2008—. Contbr. articles to profl. jours. Recipient Young Investigators award Am. Coll. Cardiology, 1982, Balfour award Mayo Clinic, 1983, Advanced Cardiac Life Support Spl. Recogition award Mayo Clinic, 1983, Rsch. Career Devel. award NIH, 1985-90. Mem. AMA, Am. Heart Assn., Biophys. Soc. Am. Soc. Pharmacology and Exptl. Therapeutics, Masons. Avocation: philatelics. Office: Caritas St Elizabeth's Med Ctr 736 Cambridge St Boston MA 02135-2997 Office Phone: 617-789-2226. Business E-Mail: james.morgan@caritachristi.org.

MORGAN, JANE HALE, retired library director; b. Dines, Wyo., May 11, 1926; d. Arthur Hale and Billie (Wood) Hale; m. Joseph Charles Morgan, Aug. 12, 1955; children: Joseph Hale, Jane Frances, Ann Michele. BA, Howard U., 1947; MA, U. Denver, 1954. Staff Detroit Pub. Libr., 1954-87, exec. asst. dir., 1973-75, dep. dir., 1975-78, dir., 1978-87; ret., 1987. Mem. Mich. Libr. Consortium Bd.; exec. bd. Southeastern Mich. Regional Film Libr.; vis. prof. Wayne State U., 1989—. Trustee New Detroit, Inc., Delta Dental Plan of Mich., v.p. Delta Dental Fund, Delta Dental Plan of Ohio; v.p. United Southwestern Mich.; pres. Univ.-Cultural Ctr. Assn.; bd. dirs. Rehab. Inst., YWCA, Met. Affairs Corp., Literacy Vols. Am., Detroit, Mich. Ctr. for the Book, Interfaith Coun.; bd. dirs., v.p. United Comty. Svcs. Met. Detroit; chmn. Detroiters for Adult Reading Excellence; chmn. adv. coun. libr. sci. U. Mich.; mem. adv. coun. libr. sci. U. Mich., mem. adv. coun. libr. sci. Wayne State U.; dir. Met. Detroit Youth Found.; chmn. Mich. LSCA adv. coun.; mem. UWA Literacy Com., Attys. Grievance Com., Women's Commn., Mich. Civil Svc. Rev. Com.; vice-chair Mich. Coun. for Humanities; v.p. Commn. for the Greening of Detroit; adv. com. Headstart; mem. Detroit Women's Com., Detroit Women's Forum, Detroit Exec. Svc. Corps.; sec., treas. Delta Dental Fund, pres., 1999. Recipient Anthony Wayne award Wayne State U., 1981, Summit award Greater Detroit C. of C.; named Detroit Howardite of Year, 1983 Mem. ALA, AAUW, Mich. Libr. Assn., Women's Nat. Book Assn., Assn. Mcpl. Profl. Women, NAACP, LWV, Women's Econ. Club (bd. dirs.), Sorosis Club (v.p.), Alpha Kappa Alpha (pres.). Democrat. Episcopalian. Home: 7473 N Brynmawr Ct West Bloomfield MI 48322-3542

MORGAN, JEAN ELIZABETH, plastic surgeon; b. Washington, July 9, 1947; d. William James and Antonia (Bell) Morgan; 1 child, Elena. BA magna cum laude, Harvard U., 1967; postgrad. (fellow), Oxford U., 1967, postgrad. (fellow), 1970; MD, Yale U., 1971; PhD in Psychology, U. Canterbury, Christchurch, New Zealand, 1995; MPH in Health Scis., UCLA, 2009. Cert. Am. Bd. Plastic Surgery, Am. Bd. Surgery, 1988. Intern Yale-New Haven Hosp., 1971-72, resident, 1972-73, 76-77, Tufts-New Eng. Med. Center, Boston, 1973-76, Harvard-Cambridge Hosp., Mass., 1977-78; columnist Cosmopolitan mag., 1973-80; pvt. practice specializing in cosmetic plastic surgery Washington, 1978-87, McLean, Va., 1998—2006, Chevy Chase, Md., 1998—2006; chief plastic surgery Beverly Hills Physicians, Calif., 2006—07; asst. clin. prof. dept. plastic surgery UCLA, 2006—09. Faculty dept. psychology U. Md., 1995; assoc. faculty dept. law, justice and soc. Am. U., 1998. Author: The Making of A Woman Surgeon, 1980, Solo Practice, 1982, Custody, A True Story, 1986, The Complete Book of Cosmetic Surgery for Men, Women and Teens, 1988. Fellow: ACS, Am. Soc. Plastic Surgeons; mem.: APA, APA, Am. Pub. Health Soc., Am. Soc. Aesthetic Plastic Surgery. Episcopalian. Avocations: ballet, opera, exercise, writing, travel. Office: 333 S Doheny Dr 202 Los Angeles CA 90048-3527 Home Phone: 310-858-1561; Office Phone: 310-858-1561. Business E-Mail: morgan52650@gmail.com.

MORGAN, JEFF, literature and language professor; s. George Morgan and Mabel Ensign; m. Dana Lodge; 1 child, Colin. PhD, Case Western Res. U., Cleve. English dept. chair Lynn U., 2000—08, assoc. prof. English, 2004—. Editor Fla. English, Internat. Jour. Soc. Scis. and Quest. Author: (book) Sarah Orne Jewett's Feminine Pastoral Vision: The Country of the Pointed Firs. Mem. Boynton Beach Hist. Soc. Named Faculty Mem. of Yr., 2003. Mem.: Fla. Coll. English Assn. and the Ralph Waldo Emerson Soc.

MORGAN, JOE LELAND, physician, psychiatrist; b. Augusta, Ga., June 5, 1955; s. Robert Leland and Jozette Morgan; m. Debra Baily Morgan, July 10, 1993; children: Robert, David 1 stepchild, Tonya. BS, Valdosta State Coll., Valdosta, Ga., 1976; MS, Univ. Ga. Vet Sch., Athens, Ga., 1979; MD, Med. Coll. of Ga., Augusta, Ga., 1987. Cert. Am. bd. of Psychiatry and Neurology, 1993. Rsch. asst. Med. Coll. of Ga., Augusta, Ga., 1979—83, med. sch., 1983—87, med. resident, 1988—89, psychiatry resident, 1989—90, chief resident psychiatry, 1990—91, asst. prof. psychiatry, 1991—95; pvt. practice Valdosta Psychiatric Assoc., Valdosta, Ga., 1995—. Chief psychiatry svc. South Ga. Med. Ctr., Valdosta, Ga., 2000—, Parkwood Devel. Ctr., Valdosta, Ga., 1999—. Contbr. chapters to books, articles pub. to profl. jour. Recipient Vet. Adminstrn. Special Performance Award, 1993; grantee Dean's Summer Rsch. Grant, Med. Coll. og Ga., 1984; Disting. fellow, Am. Psychiatric Assn., 2007. Mem.: APA, Med. Ass. of Ga., Ga. Psychiatric Physicians Assn. (pres. 2008, Psychiatrist of Yr. 2004). Republican. Meth. Avocations: fishing, tennis, snorkeling, scuba diving, baseball. Office: Valdosta Psychiatric Asso PO Box 3229 Valdosta GA 31604-3229 Office Phone: 229-244-4200. Business E-Mail: 244200@bellsouth.net.

MORGAN, JOHN DAVIS, government agency administrator, consultant; b. Newark, Feb. 14, 1921; s. John Davis and Caroline Frommel (Schaller) M.; m. Leta Maude Bretzinger, June 27, 1953; children: John Davis III, Bret Zinger. BS, Pa. State U., 1942, MS, 1947, PhD, 1948, E.M., 1950; grad. extension course, Indsl. Coll. of Armed Forces, Washington, 1953. Asst. for materials and stockpile policies Nat. Security Resources Bd., Washington, 1948-51; dir. materials rev. div. DPA, Washington, 1951-53; materials expert ODM, Washington, 1953-56; mem. staff President's Cabinet Com. on Mineral Policy, 1953-54; cons. bus. and def. problems in metals, minerals and fuels Washington, 1956-71; mem. nat. def. exec. res. for ODM, 1956-58, OCDM, 1958-61, Office Emergency Planning, 1961-71, Emergency Minerals Adminstrn., 1972-95; mem. spl. stockpile advisory com. to ODM, 1957-58; com. on scope and conduct of materials research NAS, 1959-60, then, mem. com. on mineral sci. and tech., 1966-70; mem. Interagy. Adv. Com. on Mining and Mineral Research, 1977-95. Head dept. sci. and math. Daytona Beach C.C., Fla., 1961-71; asst. dir. mineral position analysis U.S. Bur. Mines, Dept. Interior, Washington, 1971-74, acting dir. bur., 1973-74, 77-78, assoc. dir. mineral and materials supply/demand analysis, 1974-79, chief staff officer, 1979-95, Interior Dept. liaison to Com. Internat. Econ. Policy Staff, 1973-77, to Econ. Policy Bd. Staff, 1974-77, to Dept. Def. Materials Steering Group, 1975-78, to FPA-FEMA Stockpile Com., 1975-88, to Winter Energy Emergency Planning Group of Dept. of Energy, 1977-81; alt. Interior rep. Trade Policy Rev. Group, 1975-81; chmn. minerals rev. com. Non-Fuel Minerals Policy Study, 1978; chmn. materials supply task force NSC Stockpile Study, 1983-87; liaison to Dept. Def. Stockpile Com., 1988-95; mem. Def. Logistics Agy. Market Impact Com., 1988-95; mem. Def. Dept. Adv. Com. Operation and Modernization of Stockpile, 1993-95; invited reviewer, NMAB-NAS Report "Managing Materials for a 21st Century, 2007; U.S. rep. UN Sci. Conf. on Resources, 1949; lectr. numerous univs. including Nat. Def. U., War Coll., Indsl. Coll., Def. Intelligence Coll., Army War Coll., 1949—; hon. prof. Indsl. Coll., 1983—; invited spkr. nat. meetings sci. and engring. socs., 1949—. Author: Domestic Mining Industry of the U.S. in World War II, 1949; corr.: Mining Ann. Rev., London, 1958-95; contbr. articles to profl. jours. Served from 2d lt. to maj. Corps Engrs. AUS, 1942-46. Decorated Bronze Star; recipient Distinguished Service gold medal Interior Dept., 1976; named Meritorious Exec. Sr. Exec. Service, 1983. Fellow Soc. Am. Mil. Engrs.; mem. Sci. Research Soc. Am., Soc. Mining Engrs. (Disting. mem.), AIME (nat. Krumb lectr. 1973, Legion of Honor 1989), Sigma Xi, Tau Beta Pi, Sigma Tau, Pi Mu Epsilon, Phi Lambda Upsilon, Phi Kappa Phi, Phi Eta Sigma, Sigma Gamma Epsilon. Clubs: Cosmos (Washington). Home: 5013 Worthington Dr Bethesda MD 20816-2748

MORGAN, JOHN DERALD, foundation director, electrical engineer, educator, writer, researcher; b. Hays, Kans., 1939; s. John Baber and Avis Ruth (Wolf) M.; m. Elizabeth June McKneely, 1962; children: Laura Elizabeth, Kimberly Ann, Rebecca Ruth, John Derald. BSEE, La. Tech. U., Ruston, 1962; MS, U. Mo., Rolla, 1965, Degree (hon.) in Elec. Engring., 1987; PhD in Engring., Ariz. State U., Tempe, 1968. Registered profl. engr. Mo., N.Mex., Ala., SC; bd. cert. engr. in forensic engring. Elec. engr. Tex. Eastman div. Eastman Kodak Co., 1962-63; instr. U. Mo., Rolla, 1963-65, Ariz. State U., 1965-68; asso. prof. elec. engring. U. Mo., Rolla, 1968-72, Alcoa Found. prof. elec. engring., 1972-75, chmn. elec. engring., 1978-85, assoc. dir. Ctr. Internat. Programs, 1970-78, Emerson Electric prof., 1975-85; dean engring. N.Mex. State U., 1985-99; v.p. univ. advancement U. Ala. in Huntsville, 1999—2007; exec. sec. U. Ala. Huntsville Found., 1999—2008; pres. J. Derald Morgan and Assoc., Inc.; ptnr. Morgan-Morris Devel. Co. LLC; mng. ptnr. Morgan Travel, LLC. Nat. adv. com. Engring. Exploring; cons. to industry. Author: Power Apparatus Testing Techniques, 1969, Computer Monitoring and Control of Electric Utility Systems, 1972, Control and Distribution of Megawatts Through Man-Machine Interaction, 1973, Electromechanical and Electromagnetic Machines and Devices, 1986, Wolf Brethren, 2003, Macy Friends, vols. I and II, 2004; also articles; mem. editl. bd. McMillan Publishers Engring. Divsn. Pres. bd. trustees First United Meth. Ch., Rolla, 1971-73, pres. adminstrv. bd., 1978-79; v.p., mem. bd. adminstrn. People to People, 1976; bd. dirs., cubmaster Ozarks dist. Boy Scouts Am., 1968-79, asst. dist. commr., 1971-73, cubmaster Yucca coun., 1986-90, coun. commr., 1989-90, asst. scout master, 1990-99, dist. com. Sunshine Dist., dist. chmn. Meramec dist., 1978-80, engring. exploring nat. com.; chmn. Creek Dist., 2000—05, bd. dirs. Greater Ala. Coun. No. Svc. Dist., 2000—09; bd. dirs. Mo. Ptnrs. of the Americas; external adv. com. mem. for engring. rsch., Wash. U., St. Louis; adv. bd. Nat. Pollution Prevention Ctr.; mem. tech. com. NASULGC; coord. 27th Nat. Engring. Deans' Inst.; mem. Engrs. Club St. Louis; treas. Mo. Incutech Found. (bd. dir., founding mem.); mem. tech. adv. com. N. Mex. Rsch. Devel. Inst.; com. mem. N. Mex. Commn. Higher Edn.; mem bd. dir. N. Mex. INC, Quatro, MESA, ASEE (by-laws com. mem.), US West; task force mem. EDC/NSPE; bd. dir. Order of the Engr. Recipient Scouters Key award and Scouter Tng. award Ozarks coun., Boy Scouts Am., 1971, Dist. award of merit 1977, Silver Beaver award, 1982, Cub Leader award, Webelos Leader award, Dist. Com. Key award, James West Soc. award, Sunshine Dist. Yucca coun.; T.H. Harris scholar, 1959-61; John H. Horton scholar, 1961-62; Exec. of Yr. Messila Valley Profl. Sec. Assn.; Pres. Svc. award, N. Mex. State U., 1990; Disting. Engr. award, N.Mex. Engring. Found.; Engr. Yr., NMSPE, 1993. Fellow: IEEE (chmn. internat. practices subcom. 1972—79, v.p. midwest power symposium advisory bd. 1973—74, chmn. ednl. resources subcom. 1973—78, chmn. 1979—85, sec. PSE com., chmn. internat. practices subcom., sec. power sys. engring. com., mem. standards com. on dielectric testing, chmn. power sys. engring. com., chmn. ednl. resources subcom., vice chmn., mem. power sys. engring. standards com., PES ednl. com., midwest power symposium adv. bd., IEEE Centennial award 1984, award of Merit St. Louis sect., Educators award St. Louis sect., honor award St. Louis sect.), Nat. Acad. Forensic Engrs.; mem.: PSI, ASTM, NSSAR (Robert E. Burt Boy Scout Vol. award), ALSSAR (Eaglescout award Com, Meritorious Svc. medal), Nat. Soc. Engring. Profls. (mem. com., edn. adv. group, nomination com., vice chair, nat. dir., PEE mem. com. chair, PEE chair, edn. found. fin. devel., bd. dir.), Order of the Engr. (nat. bd. govs. 1996—, sec., vice chair, chair), Am. Soc. Engring. Edn. (chair bylaws com. 1999—2001), N.Mex. Soc. Profl. Engrs. (N.Mex. Engr. of Yr. 1993), NSPE (bd. govs., nat. dir., vice chmn., S.W. chmn. Profl. Engrs. in Edn. v.p., mem. Steinman Coun.), SAR (Tenn. Valley chpt. sec., treas., v.p., pres., Bronze Good Svc. award medal), Rotary Internat. (Paul Harris fellow 1997), Phi Kappa Phi, Omicron Delta Kappa, Eta Kappa Nu, Tau Beta Pi, Sigma Xi, Epsilon Gamma (grand master, grand procurator), Kappa Sigma (faculty and alumni advisor, Hall of Fame Beta Chi Chpt.). Republican. Methodist. Achievements include patents in field. Home: 113 Lansdowne Dr Madison AL 35758-7613 Personal E-mail: jdm@knology.net, jderaldmorgan@hotmail.com.

MORGAN, JOHN RICHARD, writer, publishing executive; b. Torrington, Conn., Sept. 28, 1953; s. John Brechin Morgan and Alice May (Getchell) Morris; m. Barbara Ann Walsh, Oct. 5, 2002; children: John Ashworth, Charles Nicholas. BA in English Lit., U. Conn., Storrs, 1978; MAT English, Brown U., Providence, 1981. Mgr. real estate test devel. Assessment Svcs., Inc., Bala Cynwyd, Pa., 1994—98, database mgr. and test specialist ins. programs Phila. and Bala Cynwyd, 1991—94; owner Morgan Testing Svcs., New London, Conn., 1998—. Instr. mythology and Shakespeare, The Am. Sch. in Switzerland, Thorpe, Surrey, England, 1981—83; editor, writer SAT/AP programs Ednl. Testing Svcs., Princeton, NJ, 1986—90; rhetoric instr. U. Iowa, Iowa City, 1986—87; real estate sales Coldwell-Banker, Tucson, 1990—91. Author: Real Estate Exam Prep (PSI), 2005, Real Estate Exam Prep (Promissor), 2007, Real Estate Exam Prep: Connecticut Regs, 2007, Real Estate Exam Prep: Conn Combo, 2007, Bermuda Real Estate, 2007, Real Estate Exam Prep (AMP), 2008. Founder and donor Getchell Legacy scholarship fund Lyme Acad. Coll. Fine Arts, Old Lyme, Conn., 2004—. With USCGR, 1979—86, Pt. Judith, RI and Nashville. Grantee Nashville's Parthenon's East & West Pediments Mythology Rsch., Nashville Coun. on the Arts, 1983. Mem.: Real Estate Educators Assn., Assn. Real Estate Lic. Law Ofcls. (assoc.), Mensa, Mystic Seaport, Am. Legion. Achievements include 17 marathons completed nationwide. Home: Box 231 Waterford CT 06385 Office Fax: 860-447-0757. Business E-Mail: jmorgan@morgantestingservices.com.

MORGAN, JOSEPH GERARD, history professor; b. Chgo., July 9, 1953; s. James Paul Morgan and Joan Margaret Fitzgerald. PhD, Georgetown U., Washington, 1993. Secondary sch. tchr. Bishop Hendricken HS, Warwick, RI, 1978—85; assoc. prof. history Iona Coll., New Rochelle, NY, 1989—. Author history monograph. Brother Congregation Christian Bros., New Rochelle, 1971—. Mem.: Assn. Asian Studies, Soc. Historians Am. Fgn. Rels., Am. Hist. Assn. Roman Catholic. Office: Iona Coll 715 North Ave New Rochelle NY 10801 Office Phone: 914-633-2698. Business E-Mail: jmorgan@iona.edu.

MORGAN, JOYCE ELIZABETH, retired elementary school educator; b. Pitts., June 8, 1940; d. Richard Gailbreth and Pauline (Wasil) Cunningham; m. John R. Morgan; children: Janet Lynn, Jennifer Ann, Joy Ellyn, Jamie Elizabeth. BS, Calif. State U., 1962. Elem. tchr. Chartiers Valley Sch. Dist., Pitts., 1971—99; ret., 1999. Mem. Tchrs. & Adminstrs. for Better Schs. Com., 1993-94. Facilitator Our Lady of Grace Bible Sch., Scott Twp., 1975-78, CCD tchr., 1978-82, mem. choir, 1982-85, mem. folk group choir, 1990-93, tchr. children's liturgy, 1993-94; mem. Eucharistic Ministry, 1994—2009. Republican. Roman Catholic. Avocations: reading, landcaping, plants, travel, golf. Personal E-mail: joyce6840@aol.com.

MORGAN, JOYCE KAYE, social worker; b. Acme, Pa., July 17, 1941; d. Jesse Gray and Lillian (Kubick) Hoyman; m. James Edward Morgan, Oct. 13, 1967 (dec. Nov. 2, 1996). BS in Secondary Edn., Calif. State Coll., 1963; MSW, W.Va. U., 1967. Cert. social worker; lic. social worker, Pa.; bd. cert. diplomate social work. Tchr. Scottdale (Pa.) Jr.-Sr. High Sch., 1963-64, Hempfield Jr. High, Greensburg, Pa., 1966; social worker, supr. Rosewood State Hosp., Owings Mills, Md., 1967-72, Latrobe (Pa.) Area Hosp., 1974-79; pvt. practice Mt. Pleasant, Pa., 1987-2000. Mem. Multi Disciplinary Team Child Abuse, Greensburg, Pa., 1978-79; sec. adv. bd. Westmoreland County Children's Bur., Greensburg, 1979-83. Avocations: gardening, crafts, painting. Home: Happy Hill Farm 113 Sunset View Ln Mount Pleasant PA 15666-8927

MORGAN, KATHRYN DIANE, criminology educator; b. Cameron, Tex., Aug. 14, 1953; children: Moya Elyse, Bria Kathryn. PhD, Fla. State U., Tallahassee, 1991. Assoc. prof. U. Ala., Birmingham, 1991—. Mem. bd., site-based coun. Tuscaloosa City Schs. PTSA, 2000. Patricia Harris fellow, 1986—91. Mem.: Acad. Criminal Justice Scis., Am. Soc. Criminology, Phi Kappa Phi. Baptist. Avocations: cooking, reading. Home: 4714 7th Ct E Tuscaloosa AL 35405 Office: U Ala 210 University Blvd Office Bldg Birmingham AL 35294-4562 Office Fax: 205-934-2067; Home Fax: 205-934-2067. Personal E-mail: kmorgan0853@comcast.net. Business E-Mail: kmorgan@uab.edu.

MORGAN, KERMIT JOHNSON, lawyer; b. Wales-Henderson, Iowa, Feb. 13, 1914; s. Samuel Jr. and Jennie Amelia Morgan; m. Georgina R. Wilson, Oct. 12, 1940 (dec. 1958); children: Georgina Morgan Street, Wilson S.; m. Ortrud Impol, Dec. 9, 1960. BA, U. Iowa, 1935; JD, U. So. Calif., 1937. Bar: Calif. 1939. Pvt. practice, LA, 1940—45, 1958—65, 1971—80, 1991—; ptnr. McBain & Morgan, LA, 1945—58, McBain, Morgan & Roper, 1965—71, Morgan & Armbrister, LA, 1980—91. Mem. ABA, Am. Bd. Trial Advs. (diplomate, nat. pres. 1973, pres. LA 1972, Inaugural Lifetime Achievement award local chpt. 2004, Nat. Lifetime Achievement award 2005), Assn. Def. Trial Attys. (bd. dirs. 1982-85), Internat. Assn. Ins. Counsel, Hon. Order of Blue Goose, Calif. State Bar, Assn. So. Calif. Def. Counsel (bd. dirs. 1966-67), LA Bar Assn. Republican. Congregationalist. Avocation: golf. Home: 2108 Stradella Rd Los Angeles CA 90077-2325 Office: 3420 Ocean Pk Blvd Santa Monica CA 90405 Office Phone: 310-314-4764, 310-476-6648, 213-241-0900. E-mail: lamarb@cableone.net.

MORGAN, LARRY RONALD, minister; b. Springhill, La., Mar. 12, 1936; s. Woodrow Wilson Morgan and Alma Elizabeth (Dunn) Burch; m. Elizabeth Dianne Baker, May 24, 1958; children: Elizabeth Denise Morgan Davis, Dennis Kevin. ADiv, Bapt. Missionary Assn. Theol. Sem., Jacksonville, Tex., 1990. Ordained to ministry Bapt. Ch., 1971. Clk., carrier U.S. P.O., Springhill, La., 1956-71; assoc. pastor Webb Chapel Bapt. Ch., Dallas, 1971-72, pastor, 1972-99, First Bapt. Ch., Springhill, La., 1999—. Clk., trustee Bapt. Missionary Assn. Sem., Jacksonville, 1983-86; chmn. bd. trustees Bapt. Progress, Dallas, 1984-87. Pres. PTA Browning Elem. Sch., Springhill, 1969-70. With USAR, 1959-66. Mem. Bapt. Missionary Assn. Am. (v.p. hdqrs. Little Rock 1985-86, pres. 1986-88, v.p. Am. 1996-98, pres. 1998-2000), Dallas County Bapt. Assn. (moderator 1982-84), Bapt. Missionary Assn. of La. (moderator 2000—)., Springhill Baptist Assn. (moderator 2001-). Baptist. Home: 611 Butler St Springhill LA 71075-2519 Office Phone: 318-539-2610. Personal E-mail: ronaldmorgan1@cmaaccess.com.

MORGAN, LEON ALFORD, retired utilities executive; b. Washington, Dec. 29, 1934; s. Albert Lewis and Alice Viets (Alford) M.; children: David Richard, Sherry Alice; m. Jacqueline Jamieson, Feb. 14, 1993. BSEE, Worcester Poly. Inst., Mass., 1957. Registered profl. engr., Conn. With United Illuminating Co., New Haven, 1957-94, gen. ops. mgr., then v.p. ops., 1973-76, exec. v.p., 1976-83, sr. v.p. fin., 1984-94. Episcopalian. Home: 43 Forest Brook Rd Guilford CT 06437-2245

MORGAN, LEON TERRELL, environmental health services specialist; b. Spartanburg, SC, Oct. 9, 1957; s. Leon W. and Helen K. Morgan; m. Susan Elaine Morgan, Aug. 28, 1999. AA, Anderson Coll., 1960; BS, East Tenn. State U., 1982. Registered environ. health specialist, reg. sanitarian Nat. Environ. Health Assn., 2001. Environ. health officer USPHS, Rockville, Md., 2001—03; investigator/ life safety surveyor SC. Dept. of Health & Environ. Control, Columbia, 2005—. State dir. US Jr. C. of C., Spartanburg, SC, 1990—95, v.p.-cmty. devel. Boiling Springs, SC, 1995—97; fire fighter Seneca Fire Dept., SC, 1978—84; firefighter/med. first responder North Spartanburg Fire Dept., SC, 1990—95. Lt. USPHS, 2001—03. Decorated Nat. Def. medal USAF. Mem.: Nat. Environ. Health Assn. (licentiate), Am. Soc. of Safety Engrs. (assoc.). Home: PO Box 91 Fort Defiance AZ 86504-0091

MORGAN, LUCY WARE, senior correspondent, journalist; b. Memphis, Oct. 11, 1940; d. Thomas Allin and Lucile (Sanders) Keen; m. Alton F. Ware, June 26, 1958 (div. Sept. 1967); children: Mary Kathleen, Andrew Allin; m. Richard Alan Morgan, Aug. 9, 1968; children: Lynn Elwell, Kent Morgan AA, Pasco Hernando C.C., New Port Richey, Fla., 1975; student, U. South Fla., 1976-80. Reporter Ocala Star Banner, Fla., 1965-68, St. Petersburg Times, Fla., 1967-86, capitol bur. chief, 1986—2006, sr. corr., 2006—. Assoc. editor and bd. dirs. Times Pub. Co., 1991—2006. Recipient Paul Hansel award Fla. Soc. Newspaper Editors, 1981, First in Pub. Service award Fla. Soc. Newspaper Editors, 1982, First Place award in pub. service Fla. Press Club, 1982, Pulitzer award for investigative reporting Columbia U., 1985, First Place award in investigative reporting Sigma Delta Chi, 1985; named to Kappa Tau Alpha Hall of Fame, 1992, Fla. Women's Hall of Fame, 2006; named Fla. Senate Press Gallery in Morgan's honor, 2005, 1st Pl. Non deadline Reporting, Sigma Delta Chi, 2009. Home: 7030 Spencer Dr Tallahassee FL 32312-3548 Office: St Petersburg Times 336 E College Ave Tallahassee FL 32301-1551 Home Phone: 850-668-8817; Office Phone: 850-224-7263. Personal E-mail: lucytimes@aol.com.

MORGAN, LYLE WARNER, II, medical educator; b. Fremont, Nebr., Apr. 5, 1947; s. Lyle W. and Ione E. Morgan. AB, Doane Coll., 1969; MEd, Fla. Christian U., 1970; MA, Wayne State Coll., Nebr., 1973, MS in Edn., 1976; PhD, U. Nebr., 1980; D in Homeopathic Medicine, Internat. U., Brussels, Belgium, 1984. Prof. Pittsburg State U., Kans., 1984—, chmn. pre-medicine & health scis. program, 2000—04. Dir. composition Pittsburg State U., 1984—, dir. English edn., 1984—; sachem Tribe of Mic-O-Say, 1980; chieftain Tribe of Lone Bear, Mo., 2005. Author: Homeopathic Treatment of Sports Injuries, 1988, Homeopathic Medicine: First-Aid & Emergency Care, 1989, Treating Sports Injuries the Natural Way, 1990, Homeopathy and Your Child, 1992. Mem. Ozark Trails Coun. Boy Scouts of Am., Springfield, Mo., 1984—, exec. bd. mem., v.p., 1994—. Recipient Vigil Honor award, Order of the Arrow, 1979, Silver Beaver award, Boy Scouts Am., 1983, Distinguished Eagle Scout award, 1995, Silver Antelope award, 1997; fellow, Coll. Preceptors, UK, 1993. Mem.: SAR, Rockefeller Family and Assocs. Republican. Office: Pitts State U 1701 S Broadway Pittsburg KS 66762-7515

MORGAN, M. JANE, computer systems consultant; b. Washington, July 21, 1945; d. Edmond John and Roberta (Livingstone) Dolphin (dec.); 1 child, Sheena Anne. Student, U. Md., 1963-66, Montgomery Coll., 1966-70; BA in Applied Behavioral Sci with honors, Nat.-Louis Univ., 1987, MS in Mgmt., 1991; postgrad. diploma in info. resource mgmt, Am. U., 1995; cert., USDA Grad. Sch., 2000; postgrad. diploma, State U. Calif., Northridge, 2002. With HUD, Washington, 1965-84, computer specialist, 1978-84; pres., CEO Systems and Mgmt. Assocs., 1983-91; dir. systems engring. Advanced Tech. Systems, Inc., Vienna, Va., 1984-86, sr. cons., 1989; chief tech. staff Tech. and Mgmt. Svcs., Inc., 1986-89; sr. computer scientist Integrated Systems divsn. Computer Scis. Corp., 1989-90; computer systems specialist gen. svcs. adminstrn. U.S. Govt., 1991—2001; divsn. dir. U.S. Gen. Svcs. Adminstrn., 2001—06. Mgmt. cons. Author: Rapid Identification of Critical Staff, 1991. Bd. dirs. PL Active. Mem. Federally Employed Women (life, webmaster, 1996-, nat. exec. v.p. 1998-2000), Order Eastern Star. Episcopalian.

MORGAN, MAGGIE, costume designer, design educator; d. Monroe and Ann Betts Morgan. BA, U. Calif., Davis, 1984; MFA, Yale U., Sch. Drama, New Haven, 1992. Costume designer Pvt. Practice, LA, 1992—; prof. U. Calif., Davis, 2002—. Costume designer (theatre) The Heiress, South Coast Repertory, (theatre (world premiere) Mask: A New Musical, Pasadena Playhouse, Sleeping Beauty Wakes, Kirk Douglas Theatre, (theatre (west coast premiere) Bach at Leipzig, South Coast Repertory, (theatre) Enchanted April, Arizona Theatre Company. Mem.: Costume Deisgners Guild, United Scenic Artists. Office: Univ Calif Davis 1 Shields Ave Davis CA 95616 Personal E-mail: maggiemorgan@aol.com. Business E-Mail: mjmorgan@ucdavis.edu.

MORGAN, MARCYLIENA, sociologist, educator; b. 1950; m. Lawrence D. Bobo. BA in Comm. and Anthropology, U. Ill., Chgo., 1972, MA in Comm., 1973; MA in Theol. Linguistics, U. Essex, Eng., 1978; PhD, U. Pa. Grad. Sch. Edn., 1989. Instr. dept. speech comm. No. Ill. U., 1972—77; lectr. black studies prog. U. Ill., Chgo., 1974—76; instr. lang., linguistics U. Pa., 1980—85; asst. prof. linguistics Pomona Coll., Calif.; asst. prof. dept. anthropology UCLA, 1990—2002; assoc. prof. dept. African Am. studies, dir. Hip-Hop Archive Harvard U., 2002—05; assoc. prof. dept. comm. Stanford U., 2005—07; prof. African and African Am. studies Harvard U., 2008—. Founding dir. Hip-Hop Archive, W.E.B. Du Bois Inst. Harvard U.; vis. prof. linguistics, Ctr. African Studies St. Hughes Coll., Oxford, 1990; vis. assoc. prof. Harvard U. Grad. Sch. Edn., 1999—2001. Editor: Language and the Social Construction of Identity in Creole Situations, 1994; author: Language, Discourse and Power in African American Culture, 2002; contbr. articles to profl. jours., chapters to books. Recipient Rsch. award, Pomona Coll., 1990, Faculty Career Devel. award, UCLA, 1993, Dean's award, Harvard U. Grad. Sch. Edn., 2000. Mem.: Assn. Black Anthropologists, Am. Ethnological Soc., Soc. Cultural Anthropology, Soc. Caribbean Linguistics, Internat. Pragmatics Assn., Am. Edn. Rsch. Assn., Am. Anthrop. Assn. Office: Harvard U Afro-Am Studies 12 Quincy St-Barker Ctr Cambridge MA 02138 Office Phone: 617-496-6621. Office Fax: 617-496-2871. E-mail: mmorgan@fas.harvard.edu.

MORGAN, MARLENE, education educator, consultant; b. Aug. 01; AAS, Lower Columbia Coll., 1992; BA in Human Devel., Wash. State U., 1996; MS in Early Childhood, U. Houston, 2004. Cert. ESL, GT, EC-4 tchr. 2008; master trainer Tex. Head Start State Collaboration Office, 2005. Tchr., spl. edn. coord. Lower Columbia Coll. Head Start, Longview, Wash., 1991—99; trainer, tech. asst. Tex. Tech U. Head Start Quality Info. Ctr., Lubbock, 2000—03; literacy mentor tchr. Galveston Head Start and Cir. Program; early childhood cons. pvt. practice, Houston, 2001—; nat. literacy head start trainer Ctr. Improving Readiness Children Learning and Edn., U. Tex. Med. Br., 2002—02; early head start, head start fed. program reviewer Danya Internat., Washington, 2002—; instr. edn. Lee Coll., Baytown, 2005—; pre-kindergarten tchr., Bay Area charter elem. instr. U. Houston-Clear Lake, 2007—09, advisor, Assn. Childhood Edn. Internat., 2006—, Lee Coll., 2006—. Summer program dir. Kids Coll., Galveston Coll., 2000—00; ednl. sci. intern Space Ctr. Houston, 2004—04; profl. devel. lab instr. Environ. Inst. Houston, Houston, 2003—05. Leader, organizer Apple Ln. Task Force, Kelso, Wash., 1998—99. Recipient Significant Svc. award Head Start, Lower Columbia Coll., 2000, Presdl. award, U. Houston Clear Lake, 2002—04, Silver medal, Freedoms Found., Valley Forge, 2008, Best Global award, 2008, Outstanding Mem. Svc. award, Assn. Childhood Edn. Internat., 2008, Best Children's Event, Com.outreach; named Internat. Student Leader Yr., Assn. Childhood Edn. Internat., 2004, Orientation Leader Yr., U. Houston Clear Lake, 2005; grantee, Lakeshore Learning Materials, 2000, Software Edn. Future Tchrs., 2006; grant, Galveston Coll., 2008. Mem.: ASCD (assoc.), Assn. Childhood Edn. Internat. (assoc.; pres., advisor 2003—06), Nat. Assn. Edn. Young Children (assoc.; sec. 1993—2006), Tex. Head Start Assn. (assoc.), Nat. Head Start (assoc.), Kappa Delta Pi (sec., pres. 2004—06), Omicron Delta Kappa (pres. 2004—06, Cir. Leader Yr. 2005), Phi Theta Kappa (life; v.p. 2003—05). Achievements include development of a collaborative program with three diverse education organizations to reach out to low income familes called Reading Parties: Sharing the Joy of Literacy; a warehouse clearance book fair twice a year to raise funds to help at risk children in the local community; an educational professional development organization at Lee College for students majoring in edcuation; connecting students and organizations at the University of Houston Clear Lake with children orphaned by AIDS in Kenya to help with their educational needs called Starfish Kenya. Avocation: gardening.

MORGAN, MARY ANN, lawyer; b. Orlando, Fla., Mar. 12, 1955; d. Charles Clayburn and Eileen Louise (Mutzbauer) M.; m. Patrick Thomas Burke, Dec. 12, 1992. BS in Criminology, Fla. State U., 1978, JD, 1986. Bar: Fla. 1986, U.S. Dist. Ct. (mid. dist.) Fla. 1986, U.S. Supreme Ct. Investigator Auditor Gen.'s Office State of Fla., Orlando, 1979-83; staff analyst criminal justice com. Fla. Ho. of Reps., Tallahassee, 1985-86; ptnr. Billings, Cunningham, Morgan & Boatwright, Orlando, 1986—2005; mng. ptnr. Billings, Morgan & Boatwright LLC, Orlando, 2005—. Chmn. renovation com. Orange County Hist. Mus., Orlando, 1995—; spkr. Physician/Lawyer Drug Awareness Program, Orange County Schs., Orlando, 1997. Mem. ABA, ATLA, Fla. Bar Assn. (spkrs. bur. 1997, chair grievance com. 1993-96, vice chair 9th jud. cir. fee arbitration com., bd. govs. 2009-), Orange County Bar Assn. (exec. coun. 1991—, chmn. renovation com. 1995—, del. ABA 1989, 90, pres. young lawyers sect. 1990-91, pres. 2001-02), Acad. Fla. Trial Lawyers, Ctrl. Fla. Assn. for Women Lawyers (bd. dirs. 1990-92), Fla. State U. Alumni Assn. (bd. dirs. 1996—), Orange County Legal Aid Soc. (bd. dirs. 1997—, pres.-elect 1998-99, pres. 1999-2000), Nat. Assn. Women Lawyers, Am. Inns of Ct., Tiger Bay Club, Million Dollar Advs. Club. Avocations: waterskiing, golf, boating. Office: Billings Morgan Boatwright & Herandez LLC 399 Carolina Ave Winter Park FL 32789 Office Phone: 407-679-9900. Business E-Mail: maryann@billingslawfirm.com.

MORGAN, MARY DAN, librarian; b. Tallulah, La., Nov. 30, 1943; d. Daniel Boone and Mary Louise (McLeod) M.; m. William Jefferson Day (div. Dec. 1995); 1 child, Forrest Jefferson Day. BA, La. Coll., 1965; MLS, La. State U., 1968; MA Edn., Murray State U., 1976; MSW, U. Louisville, 1992. Cert. social worker, Ky., Ind. Libr. Ascension Parish Schs., Donaldsonville, La., 1966—68, Jefferson County Schs., Louisville, 1968—75; tchr. Webster County Schs., Dixon, Ky., 1975—79, Hardin County Schs., Elizabethtown, Ky., 1979—82, dir. media ctr. & cert. social worker, 1982—87, tchr. day and residential juvenile facilities, 1987—91, tchr. mid. and sr. high alt. schs., 1991—93; social worker Hospice of Ctrl. Ky., Elizabethtown, 1993—2000, Gentiva Health Svcs., Louisville, 1995, Lincoln Trail Dist. Home Health, Elizabethtown, 1997—98; libr. Luther Luckett Correctional Complex, La Grange, Ky., 2000—. Pres. Webster County Tchrs. Assn., Dixon, Ky., 1977-78; sec. Ky. Libr. Network Bd., Frankfort, 1986-87. Mem.: ALA, AAUW, NASW, NEA (life), Correctional Peace Officers Found., Filson Hist. Soc. Office: Luther Luckett Correctional Complex PO Box 6 La Grange KY 40031 Office Phone: 502-222-0363.

MORGAN, MARY E., publishing executive; married; 1 child. B, SUNY Binghamton. Various positions including beauty dir., NY mgr., assoc. advt. dir. Ladies Home Jour. Meredith Corp.; adv. dir. Fitness mag., 1992—94; assoc. grp. pub. parenthood divsn. Gruner & Jahr, 1994—95; assoc. pub. Ladies Home Jour., 1995—97; pub. Health mag. Time Inc., 1997—99, v.p., pub., 1999—2003; v.p., pub. Redbook Hearst Corp., 2003—. Mem. editl. bd. Pharm. Exec. mag. Mem.: Nat. Assn. Chain Drug Stores, Cosmetic Exec. Women (philanthropy com.), Advt. Women NY (mem. bd. dirs.), Advt. Club NY. Office: Redbook 300 West 57th St New York NY 10019 Home: Chatham MA Office Phone: 212-649-3450.*

MORGAN, MARY JO, school system administrator; b. West Point, NY, Aug. 19, 1948; d. William Burbridge and Phyllis VanderFehr Yancey; m. Joe Howard Morgan, Nov. 25, 1976; children: Phyllis Ruthann(dec.), Marian Amanda, Elizabeth Darbonne. Master's degree, George Wash. U., 1972; PhD, U. ND, 1993. H.s. prin. Norman County West Schs., Halstad, Minn., 1993—98; chief ops. officer Little Falls (Minn.) Cmty. Schs., 1999—. Asst. dir. Bur. of Ed Rsch., U. N.D., Grand Forks, 1990—93. Mem.: AAUW (pres. 2004), ASCD, Soc. for Human Resource Mgmt. Dfl. Roman Catholic. Avocation: community theater. Home: 1109 Celebration Dr Sartell MN 56377 Office Fax: 320-632-2010; Home Fax: 320-632-2010. Business E-Mail: mjmorgan@lfalls.k12.mn.us.

MORGAN, MICHAEL BREWSTER, publishing executive; b. LA, Dec. 30, 1953; s. Brewster Bowen and Eleanor (Boysen) M.; m. Debra Hunter, July 20, 1986. BA, Conn. Coll., 1975. Coll. sales rep. Addison Wesley Pub. Co., Chapel Hill, NC, 1977—81, sponsoring editor Reading, Mass., 1981—84; CEO Morgan Kaufmann Pubs., San Francisco, 1984—2002, Morgan and Claypool Pubs., San Rafael, Calif., 2002—. Mem. Am. Assn. Artificial Intelligence, Assn. Computing Machinery. Office: Morgan and Claypool Pubs 40 Oak View Dr San Rafael CA 94903 Home Phone: 415-492-9415. Business E-Mail: morgan@morganclaypool.com.

MORGAN, M(ILLETT) GRANGER, electrical engineering educator, researcher; b. Hanover, NH, Mar. 7, 1941; s. Millett G. M. and Eleanor (Walbridge) M.; m. Elizabeth Nichols, Aug. 10, 1963; children: Kristiana L., Frederick M. AB, Harvard U., 1963; MS, Cornell U., 1965; PhD, U. Calif., San Diego, 1969. Rsch. asst., grad. rsch. asst., NASA fellow Dartmouth Coll., Jicamarca Radar Obs./Cornell U./Arcibo Obs. and U. Calif.-San Diego, 1959—69; dir. computer jobs thru tng. project U. Calif., San Diego, 1969—72, lectr., 1970—71, acting asst. prof., 1971—72; assoc. prog. dir., prog. dir. divsn. computer rsch. NSF, Washington, 1972—74; vis. assoc. physicist Brookhaven Nat. Lab., Upton, NY, 1974; from asst. prof. elec. engring.-engring. and pub. policy, coord. grad. program in EEP to prof. Carnegie-Mellon U., Pitts., 1974—81, prof. engring., 1981—, head dept. engring. and pub. policy, 1980—, Lord chair prof. engring., 1996—, univ. prof., 2003—. Chmn. sci. adv. bd. EPA; chmn. adv. bd. Elec. Power Rsch. Inst.; environ. tech. adv. bd. Alcoa; chmn. sci. and tech. coun. Internat. Risk Governance Coun.; assoc. Nat. Acad., 2002—; cons. in field. Author: (with Max Menrion) Uncertainty: A Guide to Dealing with Uncertainty in Quantitative Risk and Policy Analysis, 1990, paperback edit., 1992; (with others) Risk Communication: A Mental Model Approach, 2002; (with John Peha) Science and Technology Advice for Congress, 2003; mem. editl. bd. Environ. Sci. and Tech.; contbr. articles to profl. jours. Fellow IEEE, AAAS, Soc. Risk Analysis (editl. bd., Disting. Achievement award 1995); mem. Am. Geophys. Bioelectromagnetics Soc., Sci. Am. (bd. advisors, 2007—), NAS, Sigma Xi. Office: Carnegie Mellon U Dept Engring and Pub Policy Baker Hall 129 Pittsburgh PA 15213 Office Phone: 412-268-2672. E-mail: granger.morgan@andrew.cmu.edu. *My primary professional objective is to improve education and practice related to policy research on problems that involve science and technology.*

MORGAN, NEIL, editor, journalist, writer; b. Smithfield, NC, Feb. 27, 1924; s. Samuel Lewis and Isabelle (Robeson) M.; m. Caryl Lawrence, 1945 (div. 1954); m. Katharine Starkey, 1955 (div. 1962); m. Judith Blakely, 1964; 1 child, Jill. AB, Wake Forest Coll., 1943. Columnist San Diego Daily Jour., 1946-50; columnist San Diego Evening Tribune, 1950-92, assoc. editor, 1977-81, editor, 1981-92; assoc. editor, sr. columnist San Diego Union-Tribune, 1992—2004. Syndicated columnist Morgan Jour., Copley News Service, 1958—; sr. editor, dir., commentator KPBS, 2004—; cons. on Calif. affairs Bank of Am., Sunset mag.; lectr. in field. Author: My San Diego, 1951, It Began With a Roar, 1953, Know Your Doctor, 1954, Crosstown, 1955, My San Diego, 1959, 1960, Westward Tilt, 1963, Neil Morgan's San Diego, 1964, The Pacific States, 1967, The California Syndrome, 1969; author: (with Robert Witty) Marines of Margarita, 1970; author: The Unconventional City, 1972; author: (with Tom Blair) Yesterday's San Diego, 1976; author: This Great Land, 1983, Above San Diego, 1990; author: (with Judith Morgan) Dr. Seuss & Mr. Geisel, 1995, Roger: The Biography of Roger Revelle, 1997; author: (forewords) Under Cover for Wells Fargo, 1999, San Diego's Navy, 2001; contbr. non-fiction articles to Nat. Geog., Esquire, Redbook, Reader's Digest, Holiday, Harper's, San Diego Mag., Travel and Leisure, Ency. Brit., commentator KPBS, 2004—, sr. editor Voice of San Diego website, 2005—. Lt. USNR, 1943-46. Recipient Ernie Pyle Meml. award, 1957, Bill Corum Meml. award, 1961, Disting. Svc. citation, Wake Forest U., 1966, Grand award for travel writing, Pacific Area Travel Assn., 1972, 1978, Fourth Estate award, San Diego State U., 1988, The Morgan award, Leadership Edn. Awareness Devel. San Diego, 1993, Chancellors medal, U. Calif., San Diego, 2000, News Editors award for best column, AP Mng. Editors, 2004; co-recipient Ellen and Roger Revelle award, 1986; named Outstanding Young Man of Yr., San Diego, 1959, 1st place news commentary, Calif. News Pub. Assn., 1993, Harold Keen award, 1996, Mr. San Diego, Rotary, 1999. Mem. Authors Guild, Soc. Profl. Journalists (award for best column 1999), Soc. of Am. Travel Writers, Bohemian Club, Phi Beta Kappa. Home: 7930 Prospect Pl La Jolla CA 92037-3721 Personal E-mail: nmorgan@san.rr.com. Business E-Mail: neil.morgan@uniontrib.com.

MORGAN, OLIVER WC, epidemiologist; BS in Environ. Engring. with honors, U. Newcastle-upon-Tyne, 1995; MSc in Environ. Epidemiology, London Sch. Hygiene and Tropical Medicine, 2001; PhD in Epidemiology, Imperial Coll., 2007. Cert. in med. toxicology Cardiff U. Sch. Medicine, 2003. Pub. health engr. Oxfam, MSF, Christian Aid, Mozambique, 1995—2000, India, 1995—2000, Peru, 1995—2000, Honduras, 1995—2000, Dominican Republic, 1995—2000, Guatemala, 1995—2000; pub. health analyst Kensington & Chelsea and Westminster Health Authority, London, 2001—02; pub. health specialist NHS Postgrad. Deanery Med. and Dental Edn., London, 2002—06; regional epidemiologist East Eng. Health Protection Agy., Cambridge, England, 2006—07; epidemic intelligence officer Ctrs. Disease Control and Prevention, Atlanta, 2007—. Cons. WHO, Sudan, 2004, Sri Lanka, 05. Author: (book) Management of Dead Bodies after Disasters: A Field Manual for First Responders; contbr. articles to profl. jours. Recipient Rsch. award, Health Improvement Network, 2005; grantee Bygott studentship, U. London. Mem.: Faculty Pub. Health, UK, Royal Inst. Pub. Health, UK. Achievements include research in infectious disease risks from dead bodies after natural disasters and their management; epidemiology of drug poisoning mortality in England and Wales; investigation of numerous public health threats and outbreaks in England; operational research during humanitarian disasters (e.g. Darfur, Sudan and Tsunami affected countries); provision of public health engineering services (water and sanitation) following humanitarian disasters including natural disasters and civil conflicts; providing public health response during terrorist incidents in England (London bombings in 2005 and Polonium radioactive contamination in London in 2006).

MORGAN, PATRICIA ANN, nursing educator; b. Providence, Aug. 19, 1953; married, Sept. 9, 1978; children: Jesse William, Steven Anthony. BSN, U. RI, Kingston, 1976; MS, U. NH, Durham, 2001. Cert. nursing educator, Nat. League Nursing, 2008. RN Wentworth Douglass Hosp., Dover, NH, 1976—91, York Hosp., Maine, 1990—99, York Women's Care, 1998—2001; asst. prof. U. New Eng., Portland, Maine, 2001—, assoc. degree coord., 2004—, assoc. chair UNE nursing, 2009. Contbr. articles to profl. jours. Recipient Outstanding Faculty Mem. award, UNE Student Govt. Assn., 2005—06; Pres.'s Faculty Mini grant, UNE Rsch. com., 2005—07. Mem.: Women Health Obstetric & Neonatal Nurses, Assn. Women's Health (maine state chair 2007—, AWHONN Sect. grant 2007). Independent. Office: Univ New Eng 716 Stevens Ave Portland ME 04103 Office Fax: 207-221-4895. Business E-Mail: pamorgan@une.edu.

MORGAN, RAYMOND F., plastic surgeon; b. Pitts., Apr. 24, 1948; s. Edwin J. and Alberta (Hirt) M.; m. Sue Ann; children: Ryan Frederic, Alexander Evan, Elizabeth Anne. BS, U. Pitts., 1969, MEd, DMD, U. Pitts., 1972; MD, W.Va. U., 1976. Diplomate Am. Bd. Plastic Surgery, Am. Bd. Hand Surgery. Intern Johns Hopkins U. Hosp., Balt., 1976-77, resident surgery, 1977-80, resident plastic surgery, 1980-82; resident hand surgery Union Meml. Hosp., Balt.; staff U. Va. Health Scis. Ctr., Charlottesville, M.T. Edgerton prof., chmn. dept. plastic surgery, 1988, prof. plastic maxilofacial surgery, clin. orthopedic surgery, and chair, dept. plastic maxillofacial surgery. Fellow ACS, Soc. Univ. Surgeons, So. Surg. Assn., Am. Soc. for Surgery of the Hand, Am. Assn. Plastic Surgeons. Office: U of Va Dept Of Plastic Surgery PO Box 800376 Charlottesville VA 22908-0376 Business E-Mail: rfm9u@virginia.edu.

MORGAN, RAYMOND FRANKLIN, education educator; b. Crisfield, Md., Dec. 19, 1943; s. Raymond Franklin and Anna Marie (Evans) M.; m. Susan Morgan, July 1, 1978; children: Jonathan, Christopher. BA, Randoph-Macon Coll., 1966; MEd, U. Va., 1970, EdD, 1974. Tchr. English and reading Chesterfield Pub. Schs.; English tchr. York Acad. and Miller Sch. of Albemarle; asst./assoc. prof. grad. program dir. in reading, then prof. edn. Old Dominion U., Norfolk, Va., 1974—2009. Presenter, spkr., cons. in field. Co-author: The Psychology of Human Development, 2d edit., 1985, 3rd edit., 1993, Reading to Learn in the Content Areas, 7th edit., 2009; mem. editl. bd. Reading in Va., Reading Improvement; contbr. over 60 articles to profl. jours Recipient Tonelson award Darden Coll. Edn.; NSF grantee. Mem.: Nat. Soc. for the Study of Edn., Phi Kappa Phi. Avocation: golf. Home: 5298 W Valleyside Ct Virginia Beach VA 23464-2606 Personal E-mail: rmorgvbva@aol.com. Business E-Mail: rmorgan@odu.edu.

MORGAN, RAYMOND VICTOR, JR., mathematics professor; b. Brownwood, Tex., May 10, 1942; s. Raymond Victor and Lovey Lucile (Tate) M.; m. Mary Jane Folks, Aug. 13, 1967; children: Jason Wesley (dec.), Jeremy Victor. BA, Howard Payne U., 1965; MA, Vanderbilt U., 1966; PhD, U. Mo., 1969. Asst. prof. So. Meth. U., Dallas, 1969-75; assoc. prof. Sul Ross State U., Alpine, Tex., 1975-82, math. dept. chmn., 1976-85, prof., 1982—, dean of scis., 1979-86, exec. asst. pres., 1985-90, pres., 1990—. Author textbook: Agricultural Mathematics, 1978; author articles. Bd. dirs. Texas Rural Cmtys., 1998-2006, chair, 2003—04, Marfa Pub. Radio, 2005-, Tex. Internat. Edn. Consortium; founder regional commr. Alpine Soccer League, 1984; v.p. coach Alpine Baseball League, 1983; pres. Alpine PTA, 1982-83; founder, pres. So. Meth. U. Faculty Club, 1973-75; mem. exec. com. Tex. Assn. Coll. and Univ. Student Pers. Adminstrs., 1990-92; commr. So. Assn. Colls. and Schs., 1999-2003, mem. commn. on colls. class of 2003, 2003. NSF grantee, 1979. Mem. Am. Assn. Higher Edn., Tex. Assn. Coll. Tchrs. (chpt. v.p. 1978-79), Math. Assn. Am. (chmn. Tex. sect. 1985-86), Chihuahuan Desert Rsch. Inst. (bd. dirs.), Lions Club (pres. 1979-80, Lion of Yr. 1980, 83), Alpine Country Club. Republican. Mem. Ch. Of Christ. Avocations: motorcycling, golf, hunting, sports. Home: PO Box 1341 Alpine TX 79831-1341 Office: Sul Ross State U E Highway 90 PO Box C114 Alpine TX 79831-0114 Home Phone: 432-837-8245, 432-837-5739; Office Phone: 432-837-8032. Business E-Mail: rvmorgan@sulross.edu.

MORGAN, RICHARD J., law educator, dean; JD, UCLA, 1971. Bar: Calif. Assoc., ptnr. Krueger & Marsh, LA, 1972-80; dean, prof. U. Wyo. Coll. Law, 1987-89; assoc. dean Ariz. State U. Coll. Law, Tempe, 1983-87, dean, prof., 1990-97, U. Nev. William S. Boyd Sch. Law, Las Vegas, 1997—2007, dean emeritus, 2007—. Office: c/o Univ Nev Las Vegas William S Boyd Sch Law 4505 S Maryland Pkwy Las Vegas NV 89154-9900*

MORGAN, ROBERT MARION, educational research educator; b. Ponca City, Okla., Feb. 5, 1930; s. Perry Harrison and Velma Beatrice (Stowe) M.; m. Constance Louise Claus, Jan. 3, 1963; children—Stephen, Melayne. BS, Okla. State U., 1955, MS, 1956; PhD, Ohio State U., 1958; LLD, Dongah U., Pusan, Korea. Asst. prof. U. N.M., 1958-62; pres. Gen. Programmed Tchg. Corp., Palo Alto, Calif., 1961-64; v.p. Ranchers Corp., Albuquerque, 1962-64; dir. ednl. systems Litton Industries, College Park, Md., 1964-66; dep. dir. divsn. vocational rsch. U.S. Office Edn., Washington, 1966-68; prof., head dept. ednl. rsch. Fla. State U., Tallahassee, 1968-74; dir. Center for Ednl. Tech., 1968-75, Learning Systems Inst., 1975—2003, prof. emeritus, 2003. Lectr. Catholic U. Am., 1966-68, Seoul (Korea) Nat. U., 1970-71; cons. AID, Republic of Brazil, Korea, Italian Air Force, Navy Dept., U.S. Naval Acad.; Chmn. Fla. R & D, Council, 1969—; sch. bd. U. Sch., Tallahassee, 1969-74. Author: Programmed Instruction-A Concept of Learning, 1963, An Educational Systems Analysis for the Republic of Korea, 1970; contbr. articles to profl. jours. Bd. dirs. U.S. Coalition for Edn. for All, 1992—; trustee Aerospace Ednl. Found. With AUS, 1949-52. Fellow Royal Soc. Arts; mem. Am. Ednl. Research Assn., Am. Psychol. Assn., Nat. Soc. for Programmed Instrn., Am. Mgmt. Assn., Sigma Xi. Republican. Episcopalian. Home: 144 Bellevalley Ln Columbia SC 29223 Home Phone: 803-788-1981. E-mail: rmorgan32@sc.rr.com.

MORGAN, RUBY NORRIS, musician, educator; b. Charleston, SC, Feb. 5, 1943; d. William Lee Morgan and Ruby Emma Norris; m. Douglas Malcolm MacDonald, Dec. 10, 1983. DMA, Fla. State U., Tallahassee; MM, 1966; BS, Winthrop U., Rock Hill, SC, 1965—65; Degree in Profl. Studies, The Juilliard Sch., NYC, 1978. Piano prof. Furman U., Greenville, SC, 1968—. Pianist Heritage Chamber Players, 1980—2000. Musician violinist. Recipient Hon. Life Membership award, Greenville Woman's Music Club, 2006. Mem.: Coll. Music Soc., SC Music Tchrs. Nat. Assn. (competitions chair), Crescent Music Club, Phi Kappa Phi, PEO. Avocations: cooking, travel. Home: 418 Patrol Club Rd Greenville SC 29609 Office: Furman Univ Greenville SC 29609 Business E-Mail: ruby.morgan@furman.edu.

MORGAN, RUTH PROUSE, academic administrator, educator; b. Berkeley, Calif., Mar. 30, 1934; d. Ervin Joseph and Thelma Ruth (Prcesang) Prouse; m. Vernon Edward Morgan, June 3, 1956; children: Glenn Edward, Renée Ruth. BA summa cum laude, U. Tex., 1956; MA, La. State U., 1961, PhD, 1966. Asst. prof. Am. govt., politics and theory So. Meth. U., Dallas, 1966-70, assoc. prof., 1970-74, prof., 1974-95; prof. emeritus, 1995—; asst. provost So. Meth. U., Dallas, 1978-82, assoc. provost, 1982—86, provost ad interim, 1986-87, provost, 1987-93, provost emerita, 1993—; v.p. Chem. Abatement Tech., Inc., 1995—. Tex. state polit. analyst ABC, N.Y.C., 1972-84. Author: The President and Civil Rights, 1970, Governance By Decree: The Impact of the Voting Rights Act in Dallas, 2004; mem. editl. bd. Jour. of Politics, 1975-82, Presdl. Studies Quar., 1980-2006; contbr. articles to profl. jours. Active Internat. Women's Forum, 1987—, City of Dallas Redistricting Commn., 2001, Greater Dallas Planning Coun, 1997—; trustee Hockaday Sch., 1988-94, Kilby Awards Found., 1993-95; bd. dirs. United Way, Met. Dallas, 1993-99; adv. com. US Army Command and Gen. Staff. Coll., 1994-97; founder Archives of Women of the Southwest, 1992, chmn. adv. com. 1995-99; mem. Dallas Women's Found.; adv. bd. Cary M. Maguire Ctr. for Ethics and Pub. Responsibilty, 1998—; mem., Photographic Soc. America. Mem. Am. Polit. Sci. Assn., So. Polit. Sci. Assn. (exec. coun. 1979-84), Southwestern Polit. Sci. Assn. (pres. 1982-83, exec. coun. 1981-84), The Dallas Assembly, The Dallas Forum of Internat. Women's Forum (pres. 1996-97), Charter 100 Club (pres. 1991-92), Ctr. for the Study of the Presidency, The Women's Mus (charter), Dallas Summit Club (pres. 1992-93), Phi Beta Kappa, Pi Sigma Alpha, Phi Kappa Phi, Theta Sigma Phi. Avocations: photography, travel. Personal E-mail: morgan_ruth@yahoo.com.

MORGAN, SAMUEL P(OPE), physicist, applied mathematician; b. San Diego, July 14, 1923; s. Samuel Pope and Beatrice Marie (Summers) M.; m. Mary Caroline Annin, Jan. 23, 1948; children: Caroline Gail, Lesley Anne, Alison Lee, Diane Elizabeth. BS, Calif. Inst. Tech., 1943, MS, 1944, PhD in Physics, 1947. Mem. tech. staff AT&T Bell Labs., Murray Hill, NJ, 1947-59, head dept. math. physics, 1959-67, dir. computing tech., 1969-70, dir. computing sci. research center, 1967-82, disting. mem. tech. staff, 1982-95, Lucent Tech./Bell Labs., 1996-98, ret., 1998. Research, publs. on electromagnetic theory, applied math., queueing theory; patentee in field. Fellow IEEE (life); mem. AAAS, Am. Phys. Soc., Sigma Xi. Home: 4113 Fellowship Rd Basking Ridge NJ 07920-3906

MORGAN, SANDRA, science educator; b. Houston, Aug. 7, 1952; d. Louis and (Regine) Muras; m. Russell Morgan, Jan. 2, 2005; children: William, Ann, Eric. BS, U. Houston, MEd, 1976, ABD, 1982. Phys. edn. tchr. Houston Ind. Sch. Dist., 1974—76; prof. fine arts and phys. edn. San Jacinto Coll. Ctrl., Pasadena, Tex., 1976—. Business E-Mail: sandi.morgan@sjcd.edu.

MORGAN, STEPHEN CHARLES, academic administrator; b. Upland, Calif., June 2, 1946; s. Thomas Andrew and Ruth Elizabeth (Miller) M.; m. Ann Marie McMurray, Sept. 6, 1969; 1 child, Kesley Suzanne. BA, U. La Verne, 1968; MS, U. So. Calif., 1971; EdD, U. No. Colo., 1979. Devel. officer U. La Verne, Calif., 1968-71, asst. to pres. Calif., 1971-73, dir. devel. Calif., 1973-75, v.p. devel. Calif., 1975-76, pres. Calif., 1985—; dir. devel. U. So. Calif., LA, 1976-79; exec. dir. Ind. Colls. No. Calif., San Francisco, 1979-85. Dir. Ind. Colls. So. Calif., L.A., 1985—. Bd. dirs. Mt. Baldy United Way, Ontario, Calif., 1988-98, McKinley Children's Ctr., San Dimas, Calif., 1989-99, LeRoy Haynes Ctr. for Family and Children's Svcs., 2000—; chair nat. com. on higher edn. Ch. of Brethren, Elgin, Ill., 1988-90; dir. Pomona Valley Hosp. Med. Ctr., 1992-98, 99—, Inter Valley Health Plan, 1992-97, PFF Bank and Trust, 2001—. Mem. Assn. Ind. Calif. Colls. and Univs. (exec. com. 1989—, vice-chmn. 1996-2000, chmn. 2000-2002), L.A. County Fair Assn. (bd. dirs., chmn. 2002—), Western Coll. Assn. (exec. com. 1992-98, pres. 1996-98), Western Assn. Schs. and Colls. (sr. accrediting commn. 1996-2001), Pi Gamma Mu. Avocations: orchid culture, gardening, travel. Home: 2518 N Mountain Ave Claremont CA 91711-1579 Office: U LaVerne Office Pres 1950 3rd St La Verne CA 91750-4401 E-mail: morgans@ulv.edu.

MORGAN, STEVEN R., computer game company executive; Various exec. mgmt. positions May Dept. Stores, Federated Dept. Stores; regional v.p. Filene's Dept. Stores, 1988—96, sr. v.p., dir. stores, 1996—98; pres., CEO Millennium Futures, Inc., 1998—2001; sr. v.p. stores Electronics Boutique, 2001—02, pres. stores N.Am., pres. Can., sr. v.p., 2002—05; pres. GameStop Corp., 2005—. Office: GameStop Corp 625 Westport Pky Grapevine TX 76051 Office Phone: 817-424-2000. Office Fax: 817-424-2002.

MORGAN, SUANN LEE, information technology manager, consultant; b. New Brunswick, NJ, June 25, 1954; d. George and Helen Mahilo; 1 child, Melanie Morgan Thumm. Grad. H.S., Somerville, NJ. Project mgr. AT&T, NYC, 2001—. Office: AT&T 225 Liberty St New York NY 10080 Business E-Mail: suann_morgan@ml.com.

MORGAN, TIMI SUE, lawyer; b. Parsons, Kans., June 16, 1953; d. James Daniel and Iris Mae (Wilson) Baumgardner; m. Rex Michael Morgan, Oct. 28, 1983; children: Tessa Anne, Camma Elizabeth. BS, U. Kans., 1974; JD, So. Meth. U., 1977. Bar: Tex. 1977, U.S. Dist. Ct. (no. dist.) Tex. 1978, U.S. Ct. Appeals (5th cir.) 1979, U.S. Tax Ct. 1980; cert. tax law specialist. Assoc. Gardere & Wynne, Dallas, 1977-79, Akin, Gump, Strauss, Hauer & Feld, Dallas, 1979-83, ptnr., 1984-86; of counsel Stinson, Mag & Fizzell, Dallas, 1986-88; sole practice Dallas, 1988—. Adj. lectr. law So. Meth. U., 1989-90, 92-98. Bd. dirs. Dallas Urban League Inc., 1987-91. Mem. State Bar Tex. (mem. taxation sect.), Dallas Bar Assn., So. Meth. U. Law Alumni Coun. (sec. 1985-86), Order of Coif, Beta Gamma Sigma. Republican. Episcopalian. Personal E-mail: tsmorganpc@aol.com.

MORGAN, TRACY, actor, comedian; b. Bronx, NY, Nov. 10, 1968; m. Sabina Morgan, 1985 (div. 2009); children: Tracy, Malcom, Gitrid. Actor: (TV series) Uptown Comedy Club, 1993—94, Martin, 1994—96, Saturday Night Live, 1996—2006, Late Night with Conan O'Brien, 2000—07, Crank Yankers, 2002, Totally Awesome, 2006, 30 Rock, 2006—; (films) A Thin Line Between Love and Hate, 1996, Half Baked, 1998, 30 Years to Life, 1999, Jay and Silent Bob Strike Back, 2000, How High, 2001, Frank McKlusky, C.I., 2002, Head of State, 2003, Are We There Yet?, 2005, The Longest Yard, 2005, Farce of the Penguins, 2006, Little Man, 2006, First Sunday, 2008, Superhero Movie, 2008; host (TV series) Comic Groove, 2002, actor, prodr., writer The Tracy Morgan Show, 2003. Mailing: c/o David Becky 3 Arts Entertainment Inc 9460 Wilshire Blvd Fl 7 Beverly Hills CA 90212

MORGAN, VICTORIA, performing company executive, choreographer; BFA, U. Utah, 1973, MFA magna cum laude, 1976. Prin. dancer Ballet West, 1969-78, San Francisco Ballet, 1978-87; resident choreographer San Francisco Opera, 1987—97; artistic dir. Cin. Ballet, 1997—, CEO, 2008—. Bd. trustees Dance USA; mem. adv. bd. Dance mag. Dancer with lead roles in numerous classical, neoclassical and modern ballets including works by George Balanchine, Forsythe, and Kudelka, lead roles for TV and films, choreographer creating over 40 works for 20 ballet and opera cos. across U.S. including Utah Ballet, Pacific Northwest Ballet, Glimmerglass Opera, N.Y.C. Opera and Cin. Opera; creator, prodr. Ballet CD-ROM, choreography featured in documentary The Creation of O.M.O. Named Woman of Yr. Non-Profit, Cin. Regional Chamber, 2008, Career Woman of Achievement, YWCA, 2009. Office: Cincinnati Ballet 1555 Central Pkwy Cincinnati OH 45214-2863*

MORGAN, VINCENT THOMAS, research scientist, consultant; b. London, May 10, 1923; arrived in Australia, 1964; s. David Luther and Julia (Bracken) M.; m. Jeanette Lilian Simmons, March 31, 1951; children: Carol, Andrew, Clare, Philip, Angela. Diploma in Elec. Engring., Borough Poly., London, 1943; BSc in Engring. (hon.), London U., 1950, PhD, 1971, DSc, 1994; PhD, U. Tech. Sydney, 2002. Rschr. Telcon, London, 1945-51; rschr. C.E.G.B., Leatherhead, England, 1951-56, group leader, 1956-64; sr. rsh. scientist C.S.I.R.O., Sydney, Australia, 1964-73, prin. rsch. scientist, 1973-84, sr. prin. rsch. scientist, 1984-88, hon. rsch. fellow, 1988—2004, Nat. Measurement Inst., Sydney, 2004—. Mem. Australian panel 22 of CIGRE, 1968—, Nat. Com. CIGRE, 1976—87, Australian Elec. Rsch. Bd., 1978—81; editor book series Rsch. Studies Press, Baldock, England, 1993—; vis. prof. McMaster U., 1989—90, 1994, 2001. Author: Overhead Line Charts, 1952, Thermal Behaviour of Electrical Conductors, 1991; contbr. many articles to sci. jour. Pres. St. Vincent de Paul Soc., Chatswood, 1979-82, 92-02; chmn. Festival of Light, Sydney, 1976-85, 88-96; pres. Found. Genesis, Sydney, 1985-97. Named Hooker Disting. Prof. McMaster U., Hamilton, Ont., Can., 1989-90, Disting. mem. CIGRE, 2002; participant Internat. Scientific Exch. NSERC, McMaster U., 1994. Fellow IEEE (Herman Halperin award 1998, Millennium medal 2000), IEE (chmn. NSW com. 1984-91), Australian Inst. Physics. Avocations: history, art. Home: 64 Clanville Rd Roseville NSW 2069 Australia Office: Nat Measurement Inst Bradfield Rd Lindfield NSW 2070 Australia Business E-Mail: Vincent.Morgan@measurement.gov.au. E-mail: vtmorgan@bigpond.net.au.

MORGAN, WAYNE JOSEPH, medical educator, medical association administrator; arrived in USA, 1980; DCS, McGill U., Montreal, 1971, MD, CM, McGill U., Montreal, 1976. Asst. prof., pediat., pediatric pulmonary sect. U. Ariz., Tucson, 1982—87, 1989—90, rsch. asst. prof., physiology dept., 1987—89, rsch. asst. prof., pediat., pediatric pulmonary sect., 1987—89, asst. prof., physiology dept., 1989—90, assoc. prof., physiology dept., 1990—97, assoc. prof., pediat., pediatric pulmonary sect., 1990—97, dir., Tucson Cystic Fibrosis Ctr., 1990—, chief, pediat., pediatric pulmonary sect., 1991—, prof., pediat., pediatric pulmonary sect., 1997—, prof., physiology dept., 1997—, assoc. head, academic affairs, dept. pediat., 1997—. Recipient Wood Gold medal, 1976, Alexander D. Stewart prize, 1976, Robert Forsyth prize, 1976, Clin. Investigator award, NIH-NHLBI, 1984, award, Am. Thoracic Soc., 1987, Coll. Medicine, U. Ariz., 1987—88, Vernon and Virginia Furrow award, 1989, Outstanding Lectr. award, U. Ariz., 2001, Vernon and Virginia Furrow award, 2005—06; named Best Dr. America, Woodward, White, 1994; Clin. fellow, Can. Cystic Fibrosis Found., 1980, Rsch. fellow, Med. Rsch. Coun. Can., 1981. Mem.: Royal Coll. Physicians & Surgeons Can., Am. Thoracic Soc. Office: Univ Ariz 1501 N Campbell Ave Tucson AZ 85724 Office Phone: 520-626-6754. Office Fax: 520-626-9465.

MORGAN, WILLIAM (BILL), telecommunications industry executive; B in Comm., St. Louis U. Various sr. mktg. positions D'Arcy Masius Benton & Bowles, Inc., Grey Advt., Hal Riney & Ptnrs., SBC Comm. Inc.; gen. mgr. Silicon Valley ops., chief mktg. officer TV divsn. Microsoft Corp.; chief strategy/mktg. officer Heller Ehrman LLP, San Francisco; v.p. brand/advt. Sprint Nextel Corp., 2006—07, sr. v.p. corp. mktg., 2007—. Named a Power Player, Advt. Age, 2008. Office: Sprint Nextel Corp Hdqs 6391 Sprint Pky Overland Park KS 66251 Office Fax: 913-794-1482.*

MORGAN, WILLIAM BRUCE, naval architect; b. Fairfield, Iowa, Dec. 20, 1926; s. Orville Burns and Mary Verle (Balderson) M.; m. Mary Maxine Gillam, June 21, 1950; children: Margaret Ann, Ann Elise. BS in Marine Engring., U.S. Mcht. Marine Acad., 1950; MS in Hydraulic Engring., U. Iowa, 1951; DEng in Naval Architecture, U. Calif., 1961. Hydraulic engr. David Taylor Model Basin, Bethesda, Md., 1951-52, naval architect, 1952-58, naval architect supr., 1958-62, head propeller br., 1962-70; head hydromechanics div. David Taylor Naval Ship R&D Ctr. (formerly David Taylor Model Basin), Bethesda, 1970-79, head hydromechanics directorate, 1979—2001; ret. Chmn. exec. com. Am. Towing Tank Conf., 1983-86; mem. exec. com. Internat. Towing Tank Conf., 1984-90. Co-inventor ventilated propeller, supercavitating propeller with air ventilation; contbr. articles to profl. jours. Recipient Navy Disting. Civilian Svc. award USN, 2000, Navy Superior Civilian Svc. award, 1974, Navy Meritorious Svc. award, 1967, Meritorious Exec. award Office of Pres., 1987, William Froude medal Royal Instn. Naval Architects, 1989, Capt. Robert Dexter Conrad award USN, 1993, Gibbs Bros. medal NAS, 1997; named to U. Iowa Disting. Engring. Alumni Acad., 1999, US Merchant Marine Acad. Hall Disting. Grad., 2008. Fellow Soc. Naval Architects and Marine Engrs. (hon. life; exec. com. 1985—, Davidson medal 1986), ASME (chmn. fluids engring. div. 1981-82); mem. NAE, Schiffbautechnische Gesellschaft, Am. Soc. Naval Engrs. (Gold Medal award 1993), Chinese Soc. Naval Architects and Marine Engrs. (hon.), Sigma Xi. Presbyterian. Home: 110 Upton St Rockville MD 20850-1836 Personal E-mail: wbmorgan@erols.com.

MORGAN, WILLIAM J., independent director, leadership development consultant and retired accounting company executive; b. Bklyn., Jan. 12, 1947; s. William J. and Emma T. (Kraft); m. Patricia A. Maltz, Mar. 23, 1968; children: Michele, Jennifer. BS, St. John's U., 1968. CPA, NY Conn. Ind. dir. Barnes Group Inc., PGT Inc.; ptnr. KPMG LLP, Stamford, Conn., ret. audit staff, 1968—72, audit supr., 1972—74, audit mgr., 1974—77, ptnr.-in-charge pvt. bus. adv. svc. NYC, 1977—79, nat. office, ptnr.-in-charge recruiting, 1979—82, ptnr. comml. health care practice Short Hills, NJ, 1982—91, ptnr.-in-charge N.J. audit practice, 1989—91, mng. ptnr. Fairfield/Westchester counties practice, 1991—94, ptnr. in charge met. N.Y. area mfg., retail and distbn. practice, 1993—96, ptnr. in charge global accts., 1996—98, mng. ptnr. Stamford office, 1996—2003, chmn. audit quality coun., mem. audit and risk adv. svcs. leadership team, 2004—06; ret., 2006. Mem. Bus. Unit Planning Task Force, 1987—90, compensation com., 1990—91, chmn. profit distbn. com., 1991—95, future direction com., 1991—93, pension task force, 1991—92, chmn. compensation com., 1997—2003, bd. process com., 1997—2002, nominating com., 2002—03, independence disciplinary com., 2000—06; bd. dirs. KPMG LLP, 1991—2003, KPMG Americas, 1997—2003, Barnes Group, Inc., 2006—, PGT, Inc., 2007—. Acctg. adv. bd. Grad. Sch. Bus. Fordham U., 1979—82; standardization com. Nat. Retail Mchts. Assn., 1979; trustee Tri County Scholarship Fund, 1984—91; v.p., exec. com., adv. bd. Fairfield coun. Boy Scouts Am., 1993—95; bd. dirs. Stamford Symphony, 1995—99; bd. dirs., chmn. bus. ops. com. heritage affiliate Am. Heart Assn., 1997—2000; chmn. Fairfield County Info. Exch., 1992—94; chmn. bd. SACIA, the Bus. Coun. of Fairfield Co., 2001—03, bd. dirs., 1993—2004, Inroads

Fairfield and Westchester County chpt., 1992—95; Ambs. Roundtable Bus. Execs. for Nat. Security, 1995—99; exec. com. Conn. Policy and Econs. Coun., 1995—99. Recipient Stamford Good Scout award, 1999, Walter H. Wheeler Disting. Leadership award, 2000, KPMG-Walter E. Hanson Lifetime Achievement award, 2004. Mem. AICPA (small bus. devel. com. 1979-81, acctg. lit. awards com. 1983-86), N.J. Soc. CPA (chmn. acctg. and auditing stds. com. 1988-90, trustee 1990-92, pub. rels. task force, 1987, subcom. health care acctg. 1983-86), N.Y. State CPA (retail acctg. com. 1975-78, com. on edn. in coll. and univs. 1978-82), Nat. Assn. Accts. (dir. manuscripts 1975-77, v.p. N.Y. chpt. 1977-81, pres. NY chpt. 1981-82, nat. publs. com. 1982-83, com. acad. rels. 1983-84, nat. dir. 1983-86, Disting. Svc. award 1975), Health Care Fin. Mgmt. Assn. (NJ chpt. chmn. auditing com. 1982-83, legis. task force com. 1985-86, chmn. joint ventures com., 1987-88), Swedish Am. C. of C. (bd. dirs., exec. com. 1993-2008), The Loxahatchee Club, Woodway Country Club. Roman Catholic.

MORGAN, WILLIAM NEWTON, architect, educator; b. Jacksonville, Fla., Dec. 14, 1930; s. Thomas and Kathleen (Fiske) M.; m. Bernice E. Leimback, July 31, 1954; children: William Newton, Dylan Thomas. AB magna cum laude, Harvard Coll., 1952, MArch Grad. Sch. of Design, 1958. Pres. William Morgan Architects, P.A., Jacksonville, Fla., 1961—. Critic various archtl. schs.; lectr. in field; adj. prof. of art history, Jacksonville U., 1995-96, U. North Fla., 1997; Beinecke-Reeves Disting. Prof. Architecture, U. Fla., 1998-99. Prin. works include Fla. State Mus., Jacksonville Police Meml. Bldg., Pyramid Condominium, Ocean City, Md., Fed. Cts. and Offices, Ft. Lauderdale, Fla., Westinghouse World Hdqs., Orlando, Fla., Neiman-Marcus store, Ft. Lauderdale, 1st Dist. Ct. Appeal, Tallahassee, Fla., Conf. Ctr., Tallahassee, U.S. Embassy, Khartoum, Sudan, U.S. Courthouse, Tallahassee; author: Prehistoric Architecture in the Eastern United States, 1980, Prehistoric Architecture in Micronesia, 1988, Ancient Architecture of the Southwest, 1994, Precolumbian Architecture in Eastern North America, 1999, Earth Architecture, 2008. Subject of The Architecture of William Morgan (Paul Spreiregen) 1987, Images Master Architect Series: William Morgan (Robert McCarter), 2002; Fulbright grantee to Italy, 1958-59; grantee Graham Found. Advanced Studies in the Fine Arts, 1973; Lehman fellow Harvard U., 1957, Wheelwright fellow 1964-65, fellow NEA, 1991; Sam Gibbons Eminent scholar Fla. A&M U. and U. South Fla.; recipient numerous nat. and regional awards for excellence in design. Fellow AIA (past chmn. com. design) AIA Inst. honor for rsch. into the beginnings of archtl. creativity 1998, Fla. 2000 Millenium award honor for design 2000). Office: William Morgan Architects 220 E Forsyth St Jacksonville FL 32202-3328 Office Phone: 904-356-4195. Personal E-mail: wnmorgan@aol.com.

MORGAN, WILLIAM RICHARD, mechanical engineer; b. Cambridge, Ohio, Mar. 27, 1922; s. Wilbur Alfred and Treva Beatrice (Minto) M.; m. Marjorie Eleanor Stevens, Feb. 17, 1946; children: Carol M. Morgan Dingledy, William R., Jr. BSME, The Ohio State U., 1944; MSME, Purdue U., 1950, PhD in Mech. Engring., 1951. Power plant design engr. Curtiss Wright Corp., Columbus, Ohio, 1946-47; instr., rsch. fellow Purdue U., West Lafayette, Ind., 1947-51; supr. exptl. mech. engring. GE, Cin., 1951-55, mgr. controls analysis, devel. Aircraft Gas Turbine Divsn., 1955-59, mgr. XV5A vertical take-off and landing aircraft program, 1959-65, mgr. acoustic engring. Flight Propulsion Divsn., 1965-69, mgr. quiet engine program Flight Propulsion Divsn., 1969-71; pres. Cin. Rsch. Corp., 1971-73; v.p., COO SDRC Internat., Cin., 1973-79; engring. and mgmt. cons. Cin., 1979—. Contbr. articles to profl. jours. Lt. j.g. USNR, WWII. Westinghouse Rsch. fellow Mem. ASME, Masons, Sigma Xi (emeritus), Pi Tau Sigma, Pi Mu Epsilon. Achievements include patents in Humidity Detection and Indicating Instrument, Stall Prevention/Acoustic Tip Treatment, Acoustic Treatment, Inlet Noise Reduction Configuration; research in geometric configuration factors in radiant heat transmission. Home and Office: 312 Ardon Ln Cincinnati OH 45215-4102

MORGAN-GRENVILLE, GEORGE S., travel company executive; With Abercrombie & Kent Inc., 1987, chief mktg. officer, mng. dir. London, pres., 2002—, dir., 2006—. Adv. bd. mem. Luxury Travel Expo, Las Vegas, Nev.; panelist Forbes Traveler 400. Office: Abercrombie Kent Inc 1411 Opus Pl Ste 300 Downers Grove IL 60515-1098 Office Phone: 630-954-2944, 800-554-7016. Office Fax: 630-954-3324.

MORGANROTH, MAYER, lawyer; b. Detroit, Mar. 20, 1931; s. Maurice Jack Morganroth and Sophie (Reisman) Blum; m. Sheila Rubinstein, Aug. 16, 1958; children: Lauri, Jeffrey, Cherie. JD, Detroit Coll. Law, 1954. Bar: Mich. 1955, US Dist. Ct. Mich. 1955, Ohio 1958, US Dist. Ct. (no. dist.) Ohio 1958, US Dist. Ct. DC 2002, US Ct. Appeals (6th cir.) 1968, US Supreme Ct. 1971, NY 1983, US Dist. Ct. NY 1985, US Tax Ct. 1985, US Ct. Appeals (4th cir.) 1985, US Ct. Claims 1986, US Ct. Appeals (2d cir.) 1986, US Ct. Appeals (fed. cir.), US Ct. Appeals (8th cir.) 1994, US Dist. Ct. Wash. DC, 2002. Sole practice, Detroit, 1955—, NYC, 1983—; ptnr. Morganroth & Morganroth, PLLC, 1989—. Cons. to lending instns.; lectr. on real estate NYU, 1980—, bus. entities and structures Wayne State U., 1981—; trial atty. in fed. and state jurisdictions, nationwide. Served with USN, 1948-50. Mem. ATLA, ABA, FBA, NY State Bar Assn., Southfield Bar Assn., Oakland Bar Assn., Assn. Trial Lawyers Mich., Am. Judicature Soc., US Supreme Ct. Hist. Soc., Nat. Assn. Criminal Def. Attys., West Bloomfield (Mich.) Club, Fairlane Club (Dearborn, Mich.), Knollwood Country Club, Edgewood Athletic Club (pres. 1963-65). Democrat. Jewish. Office: 3000 Town Ctr Ste 1500 Southfield MI 48075-1186 also: 156 W 56th St Ste 1101 New York NY 10019-3800 Office Phone: 248-355-3084. Business E-Mail: mmorganroth@morganrothlaw.com.

MORGENS, WARREN KENDALL, retired lawyer; b. Oklahoma City, May 25, 1940; s. Alvin Gustav and Helen Alene (McFarland) M. Student, Westminster Coll., Fulton, Mo., 1958-60; BSBA, Washington U., St. Louis, 1962, JD, 1964. Bar: Mo., 1964, US Supreme Ct. 1968, DC, 1981. Atty., gen. counsel's office SEC, Washington, 1968—69; asst. atty. gen. State of Mo., St. Louis, 1969-72; ptnr. Park, Craft & Morgens, Kansas City, Mo., 1973-76; pvt. practice law Kansas City, 1976-81; mng. atty. Hoskins. King, McGannon & Hahn, Washington, 1981-85; spl. ptnr. Barnett & Alagia, Washington, 1985-89; of counsel Anderson, Hibey, Nauheim & Blair, Washington, 1989-93; pvt. practice Washington, 1993—2003; property trustee Va., 2001—03; cons. trustee Ariz. and Calif., 2003—. Patron Nat. Symphony, Washington, 1966-68, 81-85, Washington Performing Arts Soc., 1989—93, Kansas City Philharm., 1974-80, Supreme Ct. Hist. Soc., Washington, 1982—93, The Williamsburg Found., Va., 1982—93, La Jolla Hist. Soc., 2007-. Lt. JAG Corps. USN, 1964—68, Washington. Named one of Outstanding Young Men Am., 1977. Mem. Mo. Bar Assn., DC Bar Assn.,U. Club St. Louis, Mo. Athletic Club (St. Louis). Republican. Presbyterian. Avocations: hiking, sailing, fishing, golf. Home: 5221 La Jolla Hermosa Ave La Jolla CA 92037 Personal E-mail: mogues@att.net.

MORGENSTEIN, WILLIAM, shoe company executive; b. Bklyn., Jan. 11, 1933; s. Samuel and Jeanne Marie (Mittentag) M.; m. Sylvia Dove, June 8, 1952; children: Lee Brian, David Barry. BS in Fin., U. Ala., 1955. Salesman Greenwald Shoe Co., Birmingham, Ala., 1954-56; sr. buyer Melville Shoe Corp., NYC, 1958-67; pres. Kitty Kelly Shoe Co., NYC, 1967-70; exec. v.p. A.S. Beck Shoes, NYC, 1970-71, Sandia Internat., Englewood Cliffs, NJ, 1971-75; pres., chief exec. officer Marquesa Internat. Corp., Englewood, NJ, 1975-95; sr. acct. mgr. Signature Group divsn. Montgomery Ward, 1995—99; v.p. Advanceme-.com Inc., 1999—; sr. v.p., nat. sales dir. Sterling Funding Corp., 2005—; CEO, pres. Marquesa Funding & Consulting Corp., 2009—. Internat. cons. footwear exporting, 1965—. Served with U.S. Army, 1956-58. Mem. Footwear Distbrs. and Retailers Am. (vice-chmn., bd. dirs., exec. com.), Internat. Footwear Assn. (vice-chmn., exec. com. 1986—, chmn. 1989—, pres.), 210 Assn. (Pres.' Circle 1987), Toastmasters (past pres. Teaneck, NJ chpt.). Republican. Jewish. Avocations: history, golf. Office Phone: 800-753-7840. Personal E-mail: bmorgens@aol.com. Business E-Mail: bill@marquesafunding.com.

MORGENSTERN, KENNETH E., plastic surgeon; 2 children. BS, Emory U., Atlanta, Ga., 1991; MD, Hahnemann U., Phila., 1995. Ophthalmology Am. Bd. of Ophthalmology, 2005, Orbital and Plastic Surgery Am. Soc. of Ophthalmic Plastic and Reconstructive Surgery, 2005. Categorical gen. surgery resident Med. Coll. of Pa., Hahnemann U., 1995—99; ophthalmology resident W.Va. U., Morgantown, 1999—2002, chief resident, 2001—02; asst/ clin. prof Ohio State U., Columbus, 2002—04; pediatric orbital and reconstructive surgery Children's Hosp. of Columbus, Ohio, 2002—04; facial cosmetic surgery Ctr. for Facial Rejuvination, Columbus, Ohio, 2003—04; asst. clin. prof Va. Commonwealth U., 2004—05, U. Pa., Phila., 2005—06; pres. Morgenstern Ctr. for Orbital and Facial Plastic Surgery, Phila., 2006—; dir. of orbital and facial plastic surgery Veterans Adminstrn. Med. Ctr., Phila., 2006—. Rsch. Morgenstern Ctr. for Orbital and Facial Plastic Surgery, Phila., 2002—; assoc. fellowship preceptor U. Pa., Phila., 2006—, Childrens Hosp. of Pa., Phila., 2006—; editl. com. BioMed Ctrl., Opthalmic Plastic and Reconstructive Surgery; resident rev. com. Am. Coll. of Gen. Med. Edn.; bd. mem. Resident Coun. of ACGME; pres. Honor Ct. of Med. Coll. of Pa. Dir.: (educational course) Ophthalmology for the Internist; contbr. educational course; dir.: (educational program) Talking with Patients in Difficult Situations; contbr. scientific papers, chapters to books. Recipient W.Va. U. Resident Rsch. award, Dept of Opthalmology, W.Va. U., 2002, Resident Rsch. Aaward, W.Va. Acad. of Opthalmology, 2002, Physician Humanitarian award, County Med. Soc. of Phila., 1998, Intern of Yr., Med. Coll. of Pa. and Hahnemann U., 1995—96, Cheif Resident, W.Va. U., 2002; grant, Nat. Inst. of Health, 1997—99, Am. Thyroid Cancer Assn. Rsch. grant, Am. thyroid Cancer Assn., 2002—04, Departmental grant, Dept Ophthalmolgy, W.Va. U., 2000—02, Rsch. Devel. grant, W.Va. U., 2000—01. Fellow: Am. Soc. of Ophthalmic Plastic and Reconstructive Surgery, Am. Bd. of Ophthalmology; mem.: AMA, Assn. Rsch. in Vision and Ophthalmology, Pa. Med. Soc., ARVO, W.Va. Acad. of Ophthalmology, Va. Acad. of Ophthalmology. Achievements include patents for blocking agent for I131 induced lacrimal injury. E-mail: kmorgenstern@pol.net.

MORGENSTERN, LEON, surgeon; b. Pitts., July 14, 1919; s. Max Samuel and Sarah (Master) M.; m. Laurie Mattlin, Nov. 27, 1967; 1 son, David Ethan. Student, CCNY, 1936—37; BA magna cum laude, Bklyn. Coll., 1940; MD, N.Y. U., 1943. Diplomate: Am. Bd. Surgery. Intern Queens Gen. Hosp., Jamaica, NY, 1943—44, fellow, asst. resident in pathology, 1947—48, resident in surgery, 1948—52; practice medicine, specializing in surgery LA, 1953—, Bronx, NY, 1959—60; dir. surgery Cedars of Lebanon Hosp., LA, 1960—73, Cedars-Sinai Med. Ctr., LA, 1973—88, emeritus dir. surgery, 1989—, dir. bioethics program, 1995—; prof. surgery UCLA Sch. Medicine, 1973-90, prof. surgery emeritus, 1990—. Asst. prof. surgery Albert Einstein Coll. Medicine, N.Y.C., 1959-60; adj. prof. bioethics U. Judaism, L.A., 1996—; dir. Ctr. Health Care Ethics Cedars-Sinai Med. Ctr., 1998-2004, emeritus dir. 2004-, sr. advisor 2008-. Assoc. editor Mount Sinai Jour. Medicine, 1984-88, Surg. Innovation, 2004-; contbr. articles to profl. publs. Served to capt. M.C. U.S. Army, 1944-46. Mem. Soc. for Surgery Alimentary Tract, Soc. Am. Gastrointestinal Endoscopic Surgeons (hon.), Am. Gastroent. Assn., L.A. Surg. Soc. (pres. 1977), ACS (sec.-treas. 1976-77, pres. 1978, bd. dirs. So. Calif. chpt. 1976-84, gov.-at-large), Internat. Soc. Surgery, Western Surg. Assn., Pacific Coast Surg. Assn., AMA, Calif. Med. Assn., L.A. County Med. Assn., Am. Surg. Assn., others. Home: 5694 Calpine Dr Malibu CA 90265-3812 Office Phone: 310-423-1630. Business E-Mail: morgenstern@cshs.org, lmorgenstern@verizon.net.

MORGENTHALER, ALISA, lawyer; b. St. Louis, June 3, 1960; d. Gerald Thomas and Mary Louise (Neece) M. BA, S.W. Mo. State U., 1982; JD, Cornell U., 1985. Bar: N.Y. 1986, D.C. 1988, Calif. 1990. Law clk. City of Springfield, Mo., 1981; atty. bd. govs. Fed. Res. Sys., Washington, 1984, staff atty., 1985-86; assoc. Kirkpatrick & Lockhart, Washington, 1986-88, Stroock & Stroock & Lavan, Washington, 1988-89; ptnr. Glaser, Weil, Fink, Howley, Jacobs & Shapiro, LLP, LA, 1989—. V.p., sec., bd. dirs. L.A. Retarded Citizens Found.; v.p., bd. dirs. Malibu Riviera III Homeowners Assn., 2000—04. Named one of So. Calif. Super Lawyers, 2006, 2007, 2008, 2009, Top 50 Women Lawyers So. Calif., 2007, 2009. Mem. ABA, Calif. Bar Assn. (del. to com. on adminstrn. justice), DC Bar Assn., NY Bar Assn., LA County Bar Assn. (jud. appts. com., 1999-2007, jud. profile com.), Beverly Hills Bar Assn., Century City Bar Assn., Women Lawyers Assn. of LA (bd. dirs.), 3019 Third St. Owners Assn. (v.p. bd. dirs. 1991-00), Order of Omega, Phi Alpha Delta, Rho Lambda, Phi Kappa Phi, Pi Sigma Alpha, Gamma Phi Beta. Business E-Mail: amorgenthaler@glaserueil.com.

MORGENTHALER, DAVID TURNER, venture capitalist; b. Chester, SC, Aug. 5, 1919; s. Henry W. and Elizabeth (Taylor) Morgenthaler; m. Lindsay Anne Jordan, May 17, 1945; children: David T., Gary J., Todd W., Gaye Elizabeth. BS in Mech. Engring., MIT, MS, 1941. Sales mgr. Ervite Corp., 1945—47; mech. engr. Copes Vulcan/Blaw-Knox Co., 1947—50; v.p., dir. sales Delavan Mfg. Co., Des Moines, 1950—57; pres. Foseco Inc., Cleve., 1957—68; chmn. bd. Foseco Technik Ltd., Birmingham, England, 1964—68, API Instruments Co., 1968—70, dir., 1968—70; chmn. bd. Mfg. Data Sys., Inc., Ann Arbor, Mich., 1969—81; chmn. exec. com., dir. LFE Corp., Waltham, Mass., 1970—85; founding ptnr. Morgenthaler Assocs.; mng. ptnr. Morgenthaler Ventures, 1981—. Dir. Hausermand, Inc., Cleve., Tartan Labs., Inc., Pitts., Three Phoenix Co.; bd. dirs. Ribozyme Pharmas., 1992—2002, chmn., 1995—2002; cons. Brentwood Assocs. Trustee Cleve. Clinic Found.; bd. overseers Case Western Res. U. Served to capt. AUS, 1941—45. Mem.: Young Pres. Orgn. (sr. v.p., bd. dirs.), Chief Execs. Orgn., Inc. (past pres.), Nat. Venture Capital Assn. (past pres.), Lyford Cay Club, Westwood Country Club, Union Club, Sigma Nu. Home: 13904 Edgewater Dr Cleveland OH 44107-1416 Office: 50 Public Sq Ste 2700 Cleveland OH 44113

MORGENTHAU, ROBERT MORRIS, prosecutor; b. NYC, July 31, 1919; s. Henry Jr. and Elinor (Fatman) M.; m. Martha Pattridge (dec.); children: Joan, Anne, Elinor, Robert P., Barbara; m. Lucinda Franks, Nov. 19, 1977; children: Joshua, Amy. BA, Amherst Coll., 1941, LLD (hon.), 1966; LLB, Yale U., 1948; LLD (hon.), NY Law Sch., 1968, Syracuse Law Sch., 1976, Albany Law Sch., 1982, Colgate U., 1988. Bar: N.Y. 1949. Assoc. Patterson Belknap & Webb, NYC, 1948-53, ptnr., 1954-61; US atty (so. dist.) NY US Dept. Justice, 1961-62, 62-70; dist. atty. NY County, New York County, 1975—. Former pres. N.Y. State Dist. Attys. Assn.; lectr. London Sch. Econs., 1993. Chmn. Police Athletic League; trustee Baron de Hirsch Fund; chmn. Gov.'s Adv. Com. on Sentencing, 1979; counsel N.Y. State Law Enforcement Coun.; chmn. A Living Meml. to the Holocaust-Mus. of Jewish Heritage; Dem. candidate for Gov. of N.Y., 1962; trustee Temple Emanu-El, NYC; bd. dirs. P.R. Legal Def. and Edn. Fund. Lt. comdr. USNR, 1940—45. Recipient Emory Buckner award Fed. Bar Coun., 1983, Yale Citation of Merit, 1982, Fordham-Stein prize, 1988, Thomas Jefferson award in law U. Va., 1991, Brandeis medal U. Louisville, 1995, Omanut award Yeshiva U., 1995, Trumpeter award Nat. Consumers League, 1995, Frank S. Hogan award N.Y. State Dist. Atty's. Assn., 2000, Lone Sailor award USN Meml. Found., 2000; named Man of Yr., Fed. Law Enforcement Assn. Found., 2004; Matheson-Morgenthau Disting. Professorship in Law named in his honor, Va. Law Sch. Fellow Am. Bar Found.; mem. ABA, N.Y. State Bar Assn. (award for Excellence in Pub. Svc. 2001), Assn. of the Bar of the City of N.Y., N.Y. County Lawyers Assn. (Disting. Pub. Svc. award 1993), Amherst Alumni Assn. (hon. pres. 2001), Phi Beta Kappa. Office: Office Dist Atty 1 Hogan Pl New York NY 10013-4311*

MORHAIME, MIKE, video game company executive; B, UCLA, 1990. Co-founder, pres. Blizzard Entertainment (originally Silicon & Synapse), Irvine, Calif., 1991—. Prodr.: (video games) The Lost Vikings, 1992, Orcs & Humans, 1994, The Death and Return of Superman, 1994, BlackThorne, 1994, Warcraft II: Tides of Darkness, 1995, Justice League Task Force, 1995, Diablo, 1997, Warcraft II: The Dark Saga, 1997, Norse by Norse West: The Return of the Lost Vikings, 1997, StarCraft: Brood War, 1998, StarCraft, 1998, Warcraft II: Battle.net Edition, 1999, StarCraft 64, 2000, Diablo II, 2000, Diablo II: Collector's Edition, 2000, Diablo II: Lord of Destruction, 2001, Warcraft III: Reign of Chaos, 2002, Warcraft III: Reign of Chaos Collector's Edition, 2002, Warcraft III: The Frozen Throne, 2003, Rock 'n Roll Racing, 2003, World of Warcraft, 2004, World of Warcraft: The Burning Crusade, 2007. Named one of 50 Who Matter Now, CNNMoney.com Bus. 2.0, 2006, 50 Most Important People on the Web, PC World, 2007. Office: Blizzard Entertainment PO Box 18979 Irvine CA 92623

MORI, ALLEN ANTHONY, retired academic administrator; b. Hazleton, Pa., Nov. 1, 1947; s. Primo Philip and Carmella (DeNoia) M.; m. Barbara Epoca, June 26, 1971; 1 child, Kirsten Lynn. BA, Franklin and Marshall Coll., Lancaster, Pa., 1969; MEd, Bloomsburg U. Pa., 1971; PhD, U. Pitts., 1975. Spl. edn. tchr. White Haven (Pa.) State Sch. and Hosp., 1969-70, Hazleton Area Sch. Dist., 1970-71, Pitts. Pub. Schs., 1971-74; supr. student tchrs. U. Pitts., 1974-75; prof. spl. edn. U. Nev., Las Vegas, 1975-84; dean coll edn. Marshall U., Huntington, W.Va., 1984-87; dean coll. edn. Calif. State U., LA, 1987—2003, provost, v.p. acad. affairs Dominquez Hills, 2003—07. Hearing officer pub. law 94-142 Nev. Dept. Edn., Carson City, 1978—; mem. Nev. Gov.'s Com. on Mental Health and Mental Retardation, 1983-84; cons. Ministry Edn., Manitoba, Can., 1980-82; pres. Tchr. Edn. Coun. State Colls. and Univs., 1993-94. Author: Families of Children with Special Needs, 1983; co-author: Teaching the Severely Retarded, 1980, Handbook of Preschool, Special Education, 1980, Adapted Physical Education, 1983, A Vocational Training Continuum for the Mentally and Physically Disabled, 1985, Teaching Secondary Students with Mild Learning and Behavior Problems, 1986, 93, 99; author numerous articles, book revs. and monographs. Bd. dirs. Assn. Retarded Citizens San Gabriel Valley, ElMonte, 1989—94. Recipient grants U.S. Dept. Edn., 1976-91, Nev. Dept. Edn., W.Va. Dept. Edn., Calif. State U. Chancellor's Office. Mem. Assn. Tchr. Educators, Coun. for Exceptional Children (div. on Career Devel. exec. com. 1981-83), Nat. Soc. for Study of Edn., Phi Beta Delta, Phi Delta Kappa, Pi Lambda Theta, Phi Kappa Phi. Avocations: wine collecting, travel. Home: 1761 Avenida Entrada San Dimas CA 91773 Business E-Mail: stelerfn1@roadrunner.com.

MORI, KENJI, chemistry professor; b. Seoul, Mar. 21, 1935; s. Sakuichi and Yoshi (Ayukawa) Mori; m. Keiko Suzuki, Nov. 4, 1962; 1 child, Nobuko. BSc, U. Tokyo, 1957, MSc, 1959, PhD, 1962. From asst. to prof. U. Tokyo, 1962-95, prof. emeritus, 1995; prof. Sci. U. Tokyo, 1995—2001; tech. cons. Fuji Flavor Co. Ltd., 2002—06; rsch. cons. Riken Inst. Phys. Chem. Rsch., 2003—; tech. cons. Toyo Gosei Co. Ltd., 2006—. Mem. Sci. Coun. Japan, 1988-91. Author: Total Synthesis of Natural Products, 1992. Pres. Internat. Soc. Chem. Ecology, 1992-93. Recipient Japan Acad. award, 1981, Agrl. Soc. prize Fedn. Agrl. Soc., 1992, silver medal Internat. Soc. Chem. Ecology, 1996, Ernest Guenther award Am. Chem. Soc., 1999, Šorm medal Acad. Sci. Czech Republic, 2003. Mem. Soc. Synthetic Organic Chemistry (pres. 1993-95, Spl. prize 2003), Japan Soc. Biosci., Biotech. and Agrochemistry (pres. 2001-03). Mem. Christian Ch. Avocation: collecting fossils. Home: 1-20-6-1309 Mukogaoka Tokyo Bunkyo 113-0023 Japan

MORIAL, MARC HAYDEL, civil rights association executive, former mayor; b. New Orleans, Jan. 3, 1958; s. Ernest and Sybil Haydel M.; m. Michelle Miller; 2 children, Mason and Margeaux; 1 child from previous marriage, Kemah. BS in Economics, Georgetown U., 1980; JD, Georgetown U. Law Ctr., 1983. Bar: La. Legis. intern to Senator Russell Long US Senate, Washington DC, 1979; dir. Office Supportive Services U. Pa., Phila., 1979-80; summer assoc. Office US Atty. (so. dist.) NY US Dept. Justice, 1982; legis. asst. to Rep. George T. Leland US Congress, Washington DC, 1983; atty. Barham & Churchill, New Orleans, 1983-85; pvt. practice New Orleans, 1985—94; mem. La. State Senate from Dist. 4, Baton Rouge, 1985—94, mem. revenue and fiscal affairs com., commerce com., labor and indsl. rels. com., select com. crime & drugs, intergovtl. rels. com., Pres. Clinton's action com. on crime & drugs, senate select com. on econ. devel.; mayor City of New Orleans, 1994—2002; ptnr. Adams & Reese, 2002—03; pres. Nat. Urban League, NYC, 2003—. Mem. Gov. Spl. Taskforce on Disparity in State Procurement, 1989-91; adj. prof. law & polit. sci. Xavier U., 1988-90. Del. Nat. Rainbow Coalition Conv., 1986, La. State Dem. Conv., 1986, Dem. Nat. Conv. Delegate, 1984,88,92,96,2000; cooperating atty. NAACP Legal Def. Fund, mem. nat., New Orleans br.; gen. counsel La. Assn. Minority and Women Owned Businesses, Inc., La. Voter Registration/Edn. Crusade; cooperating atty. Minority Bus. Enterprise Legal Def. and Edn. Fund; divestment coord., legal adv. New Orleans Anti-Apartheid Coalition, 1983—; bd. dirs. La. ACLU, La. Spl. Olympics, Milne Boys Home; mem. project steering com. Voting Rights Law Reporter; mem. Young Leadership Coun., Friend of New Orleans Ctr. for Creative Arts. Recipient La. NAACP Cmty. Svc. award, 1988, Chairman's award Congl. Black Caucus, 1989, Outstanding Svc. award Lutcher H.S., 1990, Nat. Pathfinder award, 1995; named Legis. Rookie of Yr. Baton Rouge Bus. Report, 1992, All Rookie Team by polit. columnist John Maginnis, 1993, Legis. Newcomer of Yr., 1992; named one of The Most Influential Black Americans Ebony mag., 1994-2008 Mem. ABA (standing com. on world order under law 1982-83), Nat. Bar Assn., La. State Bar Assn. (Pro Bono Pub. award, 1988), La. Assn. Criminal Def. Attys., Nat. Conf. Black Lawyers, Amnesty Internat. USA, Transafrica, Louis A. Martinet Legal Soc. New Orleans, La. Trial Lawyers Assn. (pres. adv. coun.), Nat. Black Law Students Assn. (nat. bd. dirs. 1981-83), US Conf. Mayors (pres. 2001-02), Alpha Phi Alpha. Democrat. Office: Nat Urban League 120 Wall St 8th Fl New York NY 10005*

MORIARTY, DONALD WILLIAM, JR., bank executive; b. Amarillo, Tex., Sept. 15, 1939; s. Donald William and Lorraine Julia (Walck) Moriarty; m. Rita Ann Giller, Nov. 28, 1964; children: Mary Kathleen, Jennifer Ann, Anne Marie, Kerry Lee, Erin Teresa. Student, St. Benedict's Coll., 1957-59, 60-61; BSc, Washington U., 1962; MSc, St. Louis U., 1965, PhD, 1970. Cost acct. Emerson Electric, St. Louis, 1959-63; grad. fellow in econs. St. Louis U., 1963-65, instr., 1965-68; asst. prof. U. Mo., St. Louis, 1968-70; with Fed. Res. Bank of St. Louis, 1968-83, v.p., 1971-74, sr. v.p., controller, 1974-77, 1st v.p., 1977-83; sr. v.p. Gen. Bancshares Corp., 1983-86; exec. v.p. Commerce Bancshares, Inc., 1986-87; bank cons., 1987-89; pres., CEO, bd. dirs. Duchesne Bank, St. Peters, Mo., 1989-95; sr. cons. Universal Fin. Group, Inc., 1996—2003; assoc. prof. bus. Fontbonne U., St. Louis, 1998—2005; bus. cons., 2005—. Vis. instr. Webster Coll., 1975—82; adviser City of Des Peres, Mo., chmn. fin. com., 1976—78, chmn. mgmt. com., 1978—81, mem. pers. commn., 1978—81, mem. planning and zoning com., 1981—83; bd. dirs. Mid-Am. Payments Exch., Duchesne Bank. Mem. parent's coun. Creighton U., Omaha, 1995—97; mem. adv. bd. St. Joseph Acad., 1982—86; mem. pres.'s coun. St. Louis U., 1983—; dist. chmn. Boy Scouts Am., 1991—93, vice chmn., 1994—2001; Arbitrator NASD, 2006, NYSE, 2007, FINRA, 2007—; trustee, chmn. St. Joseph Hosp., 1982—93; bd. dirs. ea. Mo. region NCCJ, 1987—93. Recipient Alumni Merit award, St. Louis U., 1979. Mem.: Nat. Assn. Securities Dealers (arbitrator 2006—), Alpha Kappa Psi, Beta Gamma Sigma.

MORIARTY, GEORGE MARSHALL, lawyer; b. Youngstown, Ohio, Sept. 16, 1942; s. George Albert Moriarty and Caroline (Jones) Bass; m. Elizabeth Bradley Moore, Sept. 11, 1965 (div. 1986); children: Bradley Marshall, Caroline Walden, Sarah Cameron; m. Phyllis A.N. Thompson, May 2, 1998. BA magna cum laude, Harvard U., 1964, LLB magna cum laude, 1968. Bar: Mass. 1969, U.S. Dist. Ct. Mass. 1973, U.S. Ct. Appeals (1st cir.) 1976, U.S. Ct. Appeals (D.C. cir.) 1984, U.S. Claims Ct. 1983, U.S. Supreme Ct. 1976, U.S. Ct. Appeals (2d cir.) 1997. Law clk. to Hon. Bailey Aldrich U.S. Ct. Appeals (1st cir.), Boston, 1968-69; law clk. to Hon. Warren Burger, Hon. Hugo Black, Hon. Potter Stewart, Hon. Byron White U.S. Supreme Ct., Washington, 1969-70; spl. asst. to Hon. Elliot L. Richardson, Dept. Health, Edn. & Welfare, Washington, 1970-71, exec. asst., 1971-72; assoc. Ropes & Gray, Boston, 1972-77, ptnr., 1977—2007, sr. counsel, 2008—. Bd. dirs. Ptnrs. Healthcare Sys. Pres. Boston Athenaeum; chmn. Brigham and Women's Hosp. Mem. ABA, Am. Law Inst., Boston Bar Assn., Somerset Club, Tavern Club, Met. Club. Office: Ropes & Gray 1 Internat Pl Boston MA 02110 Office Phone: 617-951-7513.

MORIARTY, JAMES FRANCIS, United States Ambassador to Bangladesh; m. Lauren Moriarty; children: Mana, Kate. BA in History, summa cum laude, Dartmouth Coll., Hanover, NH. Joined Fgn. Svc., 1975; consular officer US Embassy, Rabat, Morocco, polit., econ. officer Mbabane, Swaziland, dep. chief, polit. sect. Beijing, polit. min.-counselor, 1994—98; econ. officer, So. African affairs US State Dept., polit. officer Islamabad, Pakistan, dep. dir., UN polit. affairs, 1991—93, US amb. to Nepal, 2004—07, US amb. to Bangladesh, 2008—; diplomat-in-residence East-West Ctr., Honolulu, 1993—94; chief gen. affairs polit. sect. Am. Inst., Taiwan; spl. asst. to pres., dir. China affairs Nat. Security Coun., 2001—02. Recipient William R. Rivkin award, Am. Fgn. Svc. Assn., Dir. General's award, US State Dept., 1987, Superior Honor award, 1993, 2000, Presdl. Pay award, 2005. Office: DOS Amb 2130 Dakar Pl Washington DC 20521*

MORIARTY, JOHN, opera administrator, artistic director; b. Fall River, Mass., Sept. 30, 1930; s. John J. and Fabiola Marie (Ripeau) M. MusB summa cum laude, New Eng. Conservatory, 1952, DM, 1992. Artistic adminstr. Opera Soc. of Washington, 1960-62, Santa Fe Opera, 1962-65; dir. Wolf Trap Co., Vienna, Va., 1972-77; chmn. opera dept. Boston Conservatory, 1973-89, New Eng. Conservatory, 1989—. Prin. condr. Central City Opera, Denver, 1978—, artistic dir., 1982-98, artistic dir. emeritus, 1998—; panelist Nat. Inst. Music Theater, 1985, 86, 87, Conn. Arts Coun., 1982, 84; adjudicator various contests including Met. Opera auditions, 1965—. Author: Diction, 1975. Bd. dirs. Wm. Matheus Sullivan Found., Fall River Hist. Preservation Soc.; trustee Boston Concert Opera; recs. on Cambridge Records, Newport Classics, Parnassus Records; mem. adv. bd. Shoshana Found. Recipient Frank Huntington Beebe award, Boston, 1954, Disting. Alumni award New Eng. Conservatory Alumni Assn., 1982, Gold Chair award Central City Opera House Assn., 1988, Disting. Alumni award, River H.S. Alumni Assn., 2006. Mem. Nat. Opera Assn., Sigma Alpha Iota, Delta Omicron, Pi Kappa Lambda. Office: New Eng Conservatory 290 Huntington Ave Boston MA 02115-5018 also: Central City Opera House Assn 400 S Colorado Blvd Ste 530 Denver CO 80246-1255 Office Phone: 617-585-1100.

MORIARTY, JOHN KLINGE, electrical engineer, consultant; b. Washington, Feb. 6, 1956; s. John Klinge and Mary (Cozart) M.; m. Elizabeth Rouse, Dec. 31, 1987; children: Maire Elizabeth, John Lank, Harris James. BS in Physics, Va. Tech., Blacksburg, 1981; M of Engring. in Elec. Engring., Clemson U., SC, 1996. Project engr. Delco Electronics divsn. G.M.C., Kokomo, Ind., 1981-84; staff engr. Hekimian Labs., Gaithersburg, Md., 1984-85; sr. LSI design engr. Case Comms., Inc., Columbia, Md., 1985-86; ind. electronics cons. Gaithersburg, 1986-88; mem. tech. staff Bell Labs., Reading, Pa., 1988-97; ind. electronics cons. Reading, 1997—99; sr. prin. engr. Clare, Inc., 1999—2003; sr. mem. tech. staff Legerity, Inc., 2003—07, Zarlink, Inc., 2007—. Cons. Squire Comms., Miami, Fla., 1986, Delco Electronics Corp., Kokomo, 1986—88, Mfg. Networks Inc., San Francisco, CPClare Corp., Beverly, Mass., Wireless Sys. Techs., Inc., San Jose, Calif.; mem. tech. adv. bd. SOMA Networks, Inc., San Francisco; tutorial presenter West Med. Design and Mfg. Conf., Anaheim, Calif., 1991, East Med. Design and Mfg. Conf., NYC, 1991. Contbr. articles to profl. jours. including IEEE Jour. Solid State Cirs., Procs. IEEE Custom Integrated Cirs., Cons. Record of IEEE Indsl. Applications Soc., Cancer Treatment Reports, Procs. IEEE Internat. Conf. on Integrated Circuit Design & Tech. Recipient Supplier Recognition award Hughes Aircraft Corp., 1992. Mem. IEEE, IEEE Electron Device Soc., IEEE Solid State Cirs. Soc., IEEE Cirs. and Sys. Soc. Achievements include patents in field. Home: 2557 River Rd Reading PA 19605-2840 Office Phone: 610-929-7223. Personal E-mail: jmoriarty@ieee.org.

MORIARTY, THOMAS M., lawyer; b. Elizabeth, NJ, Apr. 19, 1963; m. Diane Moriarty; children: Connor, Matthew, Leigh. BA in Govt. & Law, Lafayette Coll., Easton, Pa., 1985; JD, U. Va. Sch. Law, 1989. Assoc. Mudge Rose Guthrie Alexander & Ferdon, 1989—93; asst. counsel Merck & Co., Inc.; asst. gen. counsel, pharma & North America Merial Ltd.; asst. counsel Medco Health Solutions, Inc., dep. gen. counsel, v.p. & mng. counsel, sr. v.p. bus. devel., 2006—07, gen. counsel, sec., sr. v.p. pharm. contracting, 2007—. Avocations: tennis, golf, basketball. Office: Medco Health Solutions Inc 100 Parsons Pond Dr Franklin Lakes NJ 07417 Office Phone: 201-269-3400.*

MORIARTY ADAMS, MARY BRIDGET, councilwoman, human resources specialist; b. Conneaut, Ohio, Aug. 17, 1954; d. Patrick Joseph and Margaret LaVerne (Potvin) Moriarty; m. Wilbur Franklin Adams, Jan. 22, 1994. BA in Polit. Sci. and History, I.U.P.U.I., 1978, MPA in Pub. Affairs, 2001. Cert. pub. mgmt. Phone clk. Sec. of State, Indpls., 1971-72, legis. proof reader, 1972-73, summer clk., 1976; data entry clk. State Land Office, Indpls., 1978-89; councillor, dist. 17 Indpls.-Marion County City-County Coun., 1987—; contr. Ind. Sec. of State, Indpls., 1989-91; former human resource supr. Ind. Housing Fin. Authority, Indpls.; human resources, office mgr. Nat. Multiple Sclerosis Soc. Chair pub. safety and criminal justice com. Indpls.-Marion County City-County Coun. Precinct committeewoman Marion County Dem. Party, 1974-97, ward chairwoman, 1991-97, pres. 1976-78; state del. State Dem. Party, Indpls., 1988-92; mem. pub. plicy com. United Way Ctrl. Ind.; mem. Little Flower Parish. Honoree Network of Women in Bus., 1994. Mem.: Women in Mcpl. Govt., Ind. Assn. Cities & Towns, Nat. League Cities, Southside Dem. Club, Warren Twp. Dem. Club, Ladies Ancient Order of Hibernians. Democrat. Roman Catholic. Avocations: travel, singing, reading, aerobics, walking. Office: 5256 E 13th St Indianapolis IN 46219-2966 also: Indpls Marion County City County Coun 241 City County Bldg 200 E Washington St Indianapolis IN 46204-3310 Office Phone: 317-359-6940, 317-327-4242. Business E-Mail: mmadams@iquest.net.*

MORIKAWA, SHUNICHI, medical educator; s. Masatoshi and Toshiko Morikawa; m. Ayumi Koga, Oct. 29, 1981. PhD in Human Scis., Waseda U., Saitama, 1999. Vis. rschr. Cardiovasc. Rsch. Inst., U. Calif., 1999—2001; asst. prof. dept. anatomy & devel. biology Tokyo Women's Med. U. Sch. Medicine, Shinjuku-ku, 2001—. Encouragement grant, Takeda Sci. Found., 2007. Conservative. Office: Tokyo Women's Med Univ 8-1 Kawada-cho Shinjuku Tokyo 162-8666 Japan Office Fax: 81-3-5269-7407. Business E-Mail: shun@research.twmu.ac.jp.

MORIKIS, JOHN G., manufacturing executive; BBA, St. Joseph's Coll.; MBA. Mgmt. trainee Sherwin-Williams Co., Cleve., 1984, sr. v.p., dir. mktg. Paint Stores Group, 1997—98, pres., gen. mgr. Ea. Divsn. Paint Stores Group, 1998—99, pres. Paint Stores Group, 1999—2006, pres., COO, 2006—. Bd. dirs. ARC Greater Cleve. chpt. Office: Sherwin Williams Co 101 Prospect Ave NW Cleveland OH 44115 Office Phone: 216-566-2000.

MORIMOTO, MASAHARU, chef, television personality; b. Hiroshima, Japan, May 26, 1955; Trained in Sushi and traditional Kaiseki cuisine, Hiroshima. Exec. chef Sony Club, NYC, 1993—94, Nobu Restaurant, NYC, 1994—99; chef, owner Morimoto Restaurant, Phila., 2001—, NYC, 2006—, Wasabi, Mumbai, India, 2004—, New Delhi, 2008—, Morimoto XEX, Tokyo, 2005—, Morimoto Sushi Bar, Boca Raton Resort & Club, Fla., 2008—. Iron chef Japan Iron Chef (Food Network), 1995—99, Iron Chef America, 2005—. Author: Morimoto: The New Art of Japanese Cooking, 2007 (2 Internat. Assn. Culinary Professionals Cookbook awards, 2008). Office: Morimoto Restaurant 723 Chestnut St Philadelphia PA 19102 also: 88 10th Ave New York NY 10011 Office Phone: 215-413-9070, 212-989-8883. Office Fax: 215-413-9075.*

MORIN, CHRISTOPHER JOSEPH, vascular surgeon; s. Louis Peter and Rosamond Agatha Morin; m. Christine Sotorp, Feb. 17, 1996; children: Colleen Campbell, Kelly Anne, Chrisotpher Jr. BA, Coll. the Holy Cross, Worcester, Mass.; MD, Brown U., Providence, RI; MBA, U.RI, Kingston. Lic. Vascular Surgery Am. Bd. Surgery, Clincial Instr. Surgery Harvard Med. Sch., cert. Vascular Surgery Bd., Am. Bd. Surgery, 2008. Chmn. dept. surgery St. Luke's Hosp. and Health Network, Bethlehem, Pa., 1997—2002; clin. asst. prof. surgery Brown U., 1982—97, U. Pa., 1998—2005; chmn. cardiovasc. ops. St. Francis Cardiac and Vascular Care Ctr., Indpls., 2002—06; vascular surgeon Brantigan and Morin, Denver, 2006—; cons. Heart Works Advisors, Indpls., 2006—; endovascular surgery cons. Internat. Hosp., Cairo, 2006—; chmn. dept. surgery PSL Med. Ctr. Denver, 2009—, Health One Network Rocky Vista U., 2009—; clin. prof. DeSales U., 1998—. Cons. DeSales U. Ctr. for Faith and Culture, Center Valley, Pa.; dir. Brown U. Med. Alumni Assn., Providence, 1980—97, pres., 1986—88; chair dept. surgery, PSL Presbyterian St. Lukes Med. Ctr., 2008—; chair dept. surgery St. Lukes Hosp. & Health Network, Bethlehem, Pa. Comdr. USNR, 1984—91. Named one of Top Surgeon in the US, Consumer Rsch. Concil. Fellow: ACS; mem.: Am. Coll. Physician Execs., Internat. Soc. for Vascular Surgery, European Soc. for Vascular Surgery, Soc. for Vascular Surgery. Office: Brantigan & Morin 2253 Downing St Denver CO 80205 Business E-Mail: vascsurg@aol.com.

MORIN, FREDERICK C., dean, pediatrician, educator; BS in Biology, U. Notre Dame; MD, Yale U. Asst. prof. pediat. U. Buffalo, 1986, assoc. prof. pediat. and physiology, 1989, prof. pediat., vice chmn. rsch. Pediat. Dept., 1994, chair Pediat. Dept., 1997, interim v.p. health affairs, 2005; chief neonatology divsn. Women and Children's Hosp. of Buffalo, 1989, pediatrician-in-chief, 1997; chief pediat. svc. Women and Children's Hops. of Buffalo and Kaleida Health; A. Conger Goodyear prof., chmn. Dept. Pediat. U. Buffalo Sch. Medicine and Biomedical Scis., interim dean, 2005; dean U. Vt. Coll. Medicine, 2007—. Contbr. articles to med. jours. Mem.: Nitric Oxide Soc., Am. Soc. Pediat. Dept. Chairs, Am. Physiological Assn., Am. Acad. Pediat., Am. Thoracic Soc., Am. Pediat. Soc., Soc. Pediat. Rsch. Office: U Vt Coll Medicine Office of Dean Given E Rm 126 Burlington VT 05405 Office Phone: 802-656-2156. E-mail: Frederick.Morin@uvm.edu.*

MORIN, JAMIE MICHAEL, civilian military employee; b. Mich., 1975; BS in Fgn. Svc., Georgetown U., Washington, 1996; MS in Pub. Adminstrn. & Pub. Policy, London Sch. Economics, 1998; PhD in Polit. Sci., Yale U., New Haven, 2003. Econ. devel. cons. J.E. Austin Assocs., Washington, 1995—97, economist, strategy specialist, 2000; policy intern Office of Under Sec. Def., Washington, 1999; vis. fellow Ctr. Strategic and Budgetary Assessments, Washington, 2001; nat. fellow pub. affairs U. Va. Miller Ctr. Pub. Affairs, Charlottesville, 2002—03; sr. def. analyst US Senate Budget Com., Washington, 2003—09; asst. sec. for fin. mgmt., comptr. Dept. Air Force, US Dept. Def., Washington, 2009—. Policy advisor Pres. Obama's def. transition team; term. mem. Coun. Fgn. Rels. Mem.: Air Force Assn., Am. Soc. Mil. Comptrs. Office: Dept of Air Force Dept Def 1690 Air Force Pentagon Washington DC 20330*

MORIN, JARED W., computer scientist, educator, technologist; s. Gerald and Lynn Morin. MEd, U. Hartford, 2002; MusB, Hartt Sch. Music, 2001. Cert. A+ Smart Certify Direct, FL, 2002; Professional Educator Conn. State Dept. Edn., 2001. Fieldwork coord. U. Hartford, West Hartford, Conn., 2001—02; music dir. Capitol Region Edn. Coun., Hartford, Conn., 2002—03, technologist, 2002—, team leader, 2002—. Technologist team leader Capitol Region Edn. Coun., Hartford, Conn., 2003. Mem. NEA, Washington, DC, DC, 2001, Music Educator Nat. Conf., Washington, 1997—2003, Conn. Educator Computer Assn., Hartford, Conn., 2001, Conn. Educator Assn., Hartford, Conn., 2001. Fellow $15, 000 Grad. Asst. Fellowship, U. Hartford, 2001-2002. Mem.: Music Educator Nat. Conf. (assoc.), Conn. Educator Computer Assn. (assoc.), NEA (assoc.), Conn. Educator Assn. (assoc.). Achievements include research in Educational Technology Integration. Office: Capitol Region Edn Council 111 Charter Oak Ave Hartford CT 06116 Home: 100 Brunswick Ave West Hartford CT 06107-1713 Home Fax: 860-290-5330. Personal E-mail: jmorin@crec.org.

MORIN, JOYANN HAUGE, education educator; d. Harry Adrian and Anna (Barnec) Hauge; m. Dale Arthur Morin, May 21, 1954; children: David Dale, Angelique Marie, Debra Kay(dec.). AA, ElCamino Coll., 1967; BA in History, Calif. State U., Dominguez Hills, 1969, MA, 1977; EdD in Curriculum and Instrn., U. So. Calif., 1986. Elem. tchg. credential Commn. on Tchr. Credentialing, Calif. Elem. tchr. St. Catherine Laboure Sch., Torrance, Calif., 1969—71, L.A. Unified Sch. Dist., 1971—77; curriculum coord. L.A. Sch. Dist., 1977—84; prof. Calif. State U., Northridge, 1984—93, LA, 1993—, prof. emeritus, 2002. Presenter in field. Author: Social Education Instruction, 2003; contbr. articles to profl. jours. Recipient Spl. Merit award, Edn. Jour., 1996; Innovative Tchg. grant, Calif. State U., L.A., 1994. Mem.: AAUP, Calif. Coun.on the Edn. Tchrs., Nat. Coun. for the Social Studies. Avocations: creative writing, researching. Home: PO Box 875 Wolf Point MT 59201 Office: Calif State Univ PO Box 875 6309 Rodeo Rd Wolf Point MT 59201

MORIN, LOUIS, lawyer; b. Que., Can., Sept. 29, 1941; s. Paul-Emile and Jeanne Dechene) M.; m. Marthe Champoux, Sept. 12, 1970; children: Francois, Antoine, Brigitte. BA, Coll. Jesuites, 1962; LLL, U. Laval, 1965. Atty. Grondin LeBel Morin, Que., Canada, 1966—77; judge Que. Labor Ct., 1977—2002, chief judge, 1990—98; pres. Que. Labour Rels. Bd., 2002—04; atty. Grondin Poudrier Bernier, Québec, Canada, 2004—. Mem. Que. Jud. Coun., Montreal, 1992-96; tchr. labor law U. Laval, Que., 1989. Mem. Can. Bar Assn., Que. Bar Assn., Que. Young Bar Assn. (pres. 1975-76), Que. Judge's Assn. (pres. 1989-90). Avocations: skiing, bicycling. Office: Grondin Poudrier Bernier 500 Grande Allée Est Bur 900 Quebec City PQ Canada G1R 2J7 Office Phone: 418-683-3000. Business E-Mail: lmorin@grondinpoudrier.com.

MORIN, LYNN P., music educator, director, secondary school educator; d. Marjorie Huber. BA in Voice and Theatre Performance, Rocky Mountain Coll., 1995; BA in Music Edn., U. Mont., 1996. Dir. band and choir St. Regis (Mont.) Sch., 1996—2001; dir. choral Richland (Wash.) H.S., 2001—04; choral dir. Torrington (Conn.) H.S., 2004—. Dir. Mineral County Choir, St. Regis, Mont., 1999—2001; soprano Mont. Chorale, Great Falls, Mont., 1998—2001, Hartford (Conn.) Chorale, 2004—05; vocal dir. Richland (Wash.) Light Opera Co., 2003—04. Actor: (plays). Praise team Southside Ch., Richland, 2001—04; bd. dirs. Richland (Wash.) Cmty. Concerts, 2002—03. Schieffelin scholar, Rocky Mountain Coll., 1992—95. Mem.: NEA, Music Educator's Nat. Conf., Am. Choral Dirs. Assn. (assoc.). Republican. Avocations: travel, acting, theater, scrapbooks.

MORIN, PIERRE JEAN, retired management consultant, social services administrator; b. Quebec City, Que., Can., Aug. 5, 1931; s. Augustin Norbert and Yvonne (Gaudry) M.; m. Colette Poulin, Apr. 3, 1954; children: Anne, Gilles, Louis. BS, Concordia U., Montreal, 1964; MS, Laval U., Que., 1970, D.Sc., 1973. Quality control technician Dow Brevery, Montreal, Que., 1952-56; research assoc. Royal Victoria Hosp., Montreal, 1957-67; coordinator of research Que. Heart Inst., 1967-73; dir. research labs. Laval Hosp., Que., 1973-80, lectr. dept. medicine Que., 1973-77; dir. gen. Community Service Ctr., 1980-88; mgmt. cons., 1988-91; ret., 1991. Cons. Que. Minister of Environ., 1975-84. Co-author: Artificial Lungs for Acute Respiratory Failure, 1976, Solid and Liquid Wastes, 1984, La Fluoration-Autopsie d'une Erreur Scientifique, 2005; contbr. articles to profl. jours. Schering Travelling fellow, 1971 Mem. AAAS Roman Catholic. Home: 336 Rg Castor Leclercville PQ Canada G0S 2K0 *Well assumed failure may be a must towards later success.*

MORIN, ROGER PAUL, bishop; b. Lowell, Mass., Mar. 7, 1941; BA, St. John's Sem. Coll., 1966; MDiv, Notre Dame Sem., 1970; MS, Tulane U., 1974. Ordained priest Archdiocese of New Orleans, La., 1971; ordained bishop, 2003; aux. bishop Archdiocese of New Orleans, La., 2003—09; bishop Diocese of Biloxi, Miss., 2009—. Roman Catholic. Office: Diocese of Biloxi PO Box 1189 1790 Popps Ferry Rd Biloxi MS 39533-1189 Office Phone: 228-702-2112. Office Fax: 228-702-2125.*

MORIS, FRANCISCO, senior analyst; BS in Chemistry, U. PR; MA in Internat. Sci. and Tech. Policy, George Wash. U., Wahington; MA in Econ., U. Md., College Pk. Cons. indicators & analysis sci., tech., & innovation OECD, Paris; sr. analyst NSF, Arlington, Va., 2000—. Economist Nat. Inst. Standards & Tech., Gaithersburg, Md., Bur. Labor Stats., Washington; rsch. assoc. U. S. Congl. Rsch. Svc., Washington. Computer instr. Computer Ministry, St. Anthony Padua, Falls Ch., Va., 2001—05. Office: Nat Sci Found 4201 Wilson Blvd Arlington VA 22230 Business E-Mail: fmoris@nsf.gov.

MORIS, LAMBERTO GIULIANO, architect; b. Siena, Tuscany, Italy, Mar. 29, 1944; arrived in US, 1972; s. Gualtiero Luigi and Giovanna (Avanzati) M.; m. Tracy P. Schilling, 1970 (div. 1985); children: Giacomo, Stefano; m. Beverly Chiang, Mar. 28, 1986; 1 child, Christopher. MA in Arch., U. Florence, Italy, 1970. Assoc. Marquis Assocs., San Francisco, 1972-78, prin., 1978-85, Simon Martin-Vegue Winkelstein Moris, San Francisco, 1985—2005, Moris/Marino and Assoc., San Francisco, 2005—. Tchr. San Francisco City Coll., 1982—84; juror DuPont Antron Design Awards, 1989, AIA Hon. Awards, 1995, AIA Interior Architecture Awards, Chgo. chpt., 1997; mem. interior design adv. coun. Acad. Art Coll., San Francisco, 1992—2001; lectr. AIA Nat. Conf., 1996, Aircraft Interiors Expo, Canne, France, 2000, Aircraft Interiors Conf. and Exhbn., Long Beach, Calif., 2001, AIA- Italy Summit, San Francisco, 2003. Mem. design com. Clairmont Pines Task Force, 1991; charter mem. Forecast 21 Principals Roundtable, 1993; mem. Bldg. Industry Conf. Bd. (BICB), 2001—; mem. bd. dirs. ItaLingua Inst., 1984—. Mem.: FAIA (mem. selection com. 2003), AIA (mem. internat. com. 2003), Interior Architecture, No. Calif. chpt., Am. Inst. Architects, Coll. Fellows, Am. Inst. Architects (corp. mem. 1979—), Am. C. of C. in Italy, Oakland Met. C. of C., Accademia Italiane della Cucina, Cath. Prof. Bus. Club, San Francisco Opera Assn., Il Cenacolo (bd. dirs. 1991), San Francisco Heritage Assn., Engr. Club. Roman Catholic. Avocations: coin collecting/numismatics, skiing, travel. Office: Page and Moris 48 2d St San Francisco CA 94105 Home Phone: 510-654-7581; Office Phone: 510-381-5083. Personal E-mail: lgmoris@mindspring.com.

MORISATO, SUSAN CAY, actuary; b. Chgo., Feb. 11, 1955; d. George and Jessie (Fujita) M.; m. Thomas Michael Remec, Mar. 6, 1981. BS, U. Ill., 1975, MS, 1977. Actuarial student Aetna Life & Casualty, Hartford, Conn., 1977-79; actuarial asst. Bankers Life & Casualty Co., Chgo., 1979-80, asst. actuary, 1980-83, assoc. actuary, 1983-85, health product actuary, 1985-86, v.p., 1986-95, sr. v.p., 1996—2004, also bd. dirs., 2000—04; COO, sr. and retiree svcs. Ovations Ins. Solutions (UnitedHealth Group Co.), 2005—07, pres., 2009—; pres., fed. programs United Health Group Alliances, 2007—08. Participant individual forum Am.'s Health Ins. Plans, 1983; spkr. in field. Adv. panel on long term care financing Brookings' Inst.; chair fin. com., treas. Minn. Zoo. Found. Bd., 2008—; trustee Minn. Zoo Found., 2005—. Fellow Soc. Actuaries (workshop leader 1990, 93, news editor health sect. news 1988-90, conf. spkr. 2001, 02); mem. Am. Acad. Actuaries, Am.'s Health Ins. Plans (long term care task force 1988-04, chair 1993-95, tech. adv. com. 1991-93, legis. policy com. 1996-99, nominating com. 1996-98, other coms., policy coord. coun. 1999-03, sr. mktg. task force chair 2000-01, chmn. task force on Medicare modernization 2002-04, exec. com. 2004, bd. dirs. 2004, policy com. 2004, medicare com. 2005-08, LTC leadership coun. 2006-08, medigap leadership coun., 2009-, product leadership coun., 2009-, Founders award 1996), Health Ins. Assn. Am. (conf. spkr. 2000), LIMRA Internat. (strategic mktg. ins. com. 2001-06, bd. dirs. 2003-07, chmn. compensation and benefits com. 2004-05, vice-chair bd. dirs. 2005-06, chair bd. 2006), Nat. Assn. Ins. Commrs. (ad hoc actuarial working group for long term care nonforfeiture benefits 1992), Am. Coun. Life Ins. (accelerated benefits/long term care com. 1997-01), Chgo. Actuarial Assn. (sec. 1983-85, program com. 1987-89), Phi Beta Kappa, Kappa Delta Pi, Phi Kappa Phi. Office: Ovations UnitedHealth Group MN006-E900 9701 Data Park Dr Minnetonka MN 55343 Home Phone: 847-299-0560; Office Phone: 952-931-4463. Business E-Mail: susan_c_morisato@uhc.com.

MORISEY, A. ALEXANDER, government agency administrator; b. Rocky Mt., NC, Sept. 10, 1940; MA in Govt. Adminstrn., U. Pa., Phila., 1964. Excutive dir. Lighthouse, Phila., 1981—86; ombudsman Mental Health Assoc. SEPA, Phila., 1986—. Chairperson human rights com. Norristown State Hosp., Pa., 2003—. Contbr. articles to profl. jour. Former bd. mem. Am. Friends Svc. Com., Phila., Friends Rehab. Project, Phila., Horizon House, Phila. Mem.: Mental Health Assn. Southeastern Pa. (bd. dirs., Exemplary Practice award). Democrat. Mem. Soc. Of Friends. Avocation: travel. Home: 4710 Locust St Apt 203 Philadelphia PA 19139 Office: Mental Health Assoc SEPA 1211 Chestnut St 11th Fl Philadelphia PA 19107 Office Fax: 215-636-6310. Business E-Mail: amorisey@mhasp.org.

MORISHIGE, TERUO TED, engineering educator; b. Sapporo, Hokkaido, Japan, June 11, 1926; arrived in US, 1956, naturalized; s. Shizuo and Tamako Morishige; m. Setsuko A. Morishige, Sept. 15, 1958; children: Nina Teresa, Sachi Johanna Lockwood. D in Mech. Engring., U. Tokyo, 1955. Dir., R & D lab. Ranco Inc., Tokyo, 1959—61; prof., engring. & physics U. Ctrl. Okla., Edmond, 1961—. Lang. specialist FBI, Washington, 1998—. Mem.: SPIE, Am. Assn. Physics Tchrs. Avocations: travel, reading, flower arranging. Home: 1117 N Washington St Edmond OK 73034 Office: Univ Ctrl Okla 100 N University Dr Edmond OK 73034 Business E-Mail: tmorishige@uco.edu.

MORISHITA, AKIHIKO, trading company executive; b. Osaka, Japan, Oct. 14, 1941; came to U.S., 1981; s. Sueyoshi and Toshiko Morishita; m. Fumiko Okamura; children: Shizuko, Kumiko, Okamura. BA in Econs., Wakayama U., Wakayama, Japan, 1965. Mgr. Hanwa & Co. Ltd., Osaka, 1965-80; cons. oil dept. Pacific Southwest Trading Co., San Diego, 1981-82; exec. Pacific Marine Bunkering, Inc., LA, 1982—. Mem.: Club Leconte. Home: 4610 Don Pio Dr Woodland Hills CA 91364-4205

MORISKY, DONALD E., director, medical educator; b. Kalamazoo, Mich., Dec. 30, 1945; m. Susan Magueflor Morisky, June 26, 1971; children: Philip M., Marty M. ScD, Johns Hopkins U., 1981. Asst. prof. UCLA Sch. of Pub. Health, LA, Calif., 1982—87, assoc. prof., 1987—94, prof., vice chair, 1994—2003, prof., 1994—, chair, 2004—. Vis. prof. Taipei Med. U., 2007, Yang Ming U., 2009. Recipient Disting. Career Fellow, Soc. of Pub. Health Edn. and Am. Acad. Health Behavior, 2003, Elizabeth Fries prize, 2006; grant, NIH Ctrs. for Disease Control, 1987—. Fellow: Am. Acad. Health Behavior, Coun. Epidemiology Rsch.; mem.: APHA (chairperson 1985—86, Early Career Award 1986), Delta Omega (pres. 2000—02). Achievements include research in longitudinal assessments of behavioral interventions on health status; self-reported medication taking behavior assessment tool; HIV/AIDS prevention interventions in the Philippines; tuberculosis control programs for Hispanic adults and adolescents. Office: UCLA 650 Charles E Young Dr S Los Angeles CA 90095-1772 Home: 2020 Glencoe Ave Venice CA 90291-4007 E-mail: dmorisky@ucla.edu.

MORISON, JOHN HOPKINS, casting manufacturing company executive; b. Milw., June 29, 1913; s. George Abbot and Amelia (Elmore) M. m. Olga de Souza Dantas, July 29, 1944; children: Maria de Souza Dantas, John Hopkins III. AB, Harvard U., 1935; LLD, New Eng. Coll., 1973. Various positions Bucyrus-Erie Co., South Milwaukee, Wis., U.S. and Latin Am., 1935-49; pres., dir. Hitchiner Mfg. Co., Inc., Milford, N.H., 1949-93, chmn. bd., 1973-93, chmn. emeritus, 1994—. Pres., treas. Upland Farm Inc., Peterborough, N.H., 1986-98, sec., 1967—; chmn. RiverMead Retirement Community, Peterborough, N.H., 1991-96, trustee 1991—. Commr. N.H. Commn. on Arts, 1967-77; mem. regional exec. com. Boy Scouts Am., Framingham, Mass., 1970-76; mem. exec. com., pres., N.H. Coun. on World Affairs, 1955-76; trustee Canterbury Shaker Village, 1982-96; trustee Land Use Found. N.H., 1970-75, World Peace Found., 1962-90, Currier Gallery Art, 1969-2000, trustee emeritus, 2000—; pres. bd. dirs. Matthew Thornton Health Plan, 1972-82; bd. dirs. Forum on N.H.'s Future, 1979-81; pres., distbg. dir. N.H. Charitable Fund, 1968-79; mem. corp. MacDowell Colony; v.p. bd. govs. N.H. Public TV, 1979-89. Lt. (j.g.) USNR, 1943-46. Recipient Lifetime Achievement award N.H. Bus. and Industry Assn., 1993, N.H. High Tech. Coun., 1996, Granite State award U. N.H., 1994. Unitarian Universalist. Home: PO Box 2001 Milford NH 03055-2001

MORISSEAU, CHRISTOPHE HENRI PIERRE, entomologist, researcher; s. Pierre and Louise Morisseau; m. Shu-yin Susan Chen, Feb. 16, 1999; children: Evelyne Falann Bernardette, Jasmine Falin Camille, Cedric Hengli Pierre. BS in Food Sci., U. Nantes, France, 1989; degree in Food Sci. Engr., ENSBANA, Dijon, France, 1992; PhD in Organic Chemistry, U. de la Mediteranee, Marseille, France, 1995. Postgrad. rschr. U. Calif., Davis, 1996—2000, asst. rsch. scientist, 2000—06, assoc. rsch. scientist, 2006—. Mem.: Am. Chem. Soc. Office: Univ Calif Dept Entomology One Shields Ave Davis CA 95616

MORISSETTE, ALANIS NADINE, singer; b. Ottawa, ON, Canada, June 1, 1974; d. Alan and Georgia Morissette. Singer: (albums) Alanis, 1991, Now is the Time, 1992, Jagged Little Pill, 1995 (Grammy award for Album of Yr., Best Female Rock Vocal Performance, Best Rock Song, Best Rock Album, 1996), Supposed Former Infatuation Junkie, 1998, Space Cakes, 1998, Alanis Unplugged, 1999, Under Rug Swept, 2002, Feast On Scraps, 2002, So-Called Chaos, 2004, Jagged Little Pill Acoustic, 2005, Alanis Morissette: The Collection, 2005, Flavors of Entanglement, 2008; actor: (films) Anything for Love, 1993, Dogma, 1999, Jay and Silent Bob Strike Back, 2001; (TV films) The Great Warming, 2003; (TV series) You Can't Do That on Television, 1986; actor, prodr., writer (TV series) We're with the Band, 2006; actor: (TV appearances) Sex and the City, 2000, American Dreams, 2004, Degrassi: The Next Generation, 2005, Nip/Tuck, 2006; (plays) The Exonerated, 2003. Recipient BRIT award for Best Internat. Newcomer, 1996, MTV European Music award for Best Female Artist, 1996, Juno award for Prodr. of the Yr., 2003. Achievements include inducted into Canadian Walk of Fame, 2005.

MORISUE, GLENN T., graphics designer; b. San Francisco, Nov. 22, 1940; BA, Art Inst. Pitts., 1962; BFA, Cleve. Inst. Art, 1964. Greeting card designer Am. Greetings Corp., Cleve., 1965—69; art dir. Schuckert Studio, Cleve., 1970—73; creative dir. Hauser King Marford Co., Cleve., 1974—76; v.p., design dir. Copper K Industries, Cleve., 1977—79; dean edn. Cooper Sch. Art, Cleve., 1980—82; free-lance illustrator, 1983—93. One-man shows include paintings Ashtabula Arts Ctr., Ohio, 2008; featured personality (premiere issue mag.) Shore Mag., 2007. Recipient numerous Best of Show awards, Nat. Drawing Competition award winner, Am. Artist Drawing Mag., 2004. Mem.: Pastel Soc. Am., Am. Soc. Portrait Artists, Meadville Coun. on the Arts. Home: 6201 1/2 Lake Rd W Ashtabula OH 44004-9757 Office Phone: 440-964-0250.

MORITA, KATSURA, chemical company executive; b. Osaka-fu, Japan, May 6, 1925; s. Keijiro and Sueno M.; m. Mitome Morita; children: Atsuko Matsumura, Hiroshi. BS, Kyoto U., Japan, 1948; PhD, Kyoto U., 1960. Mgr. new product planning and devel. div. Takeda Chem. Industries, Ltd., Japan, 1974-75; dir. cen. rsch. div. Medicinal Rsch. Labs., Takeda, 1975-81; gen. mgr. cen. rsch. div. Takeda Chem. Industries, Ltd., 1982-85, also bd. dirs., mng. dir., 1985-86, sr. mng. dir., 1986-89, exec. v.p., 1989-91; pres. Takeda Chem. Industries Ltd., Osaka-shi, Japan, 1991-93, CEO, chmn., 1993-97, of counsel, 1997—2005; pres. Inst. for Fermentation, Osaka, 1991—. Author: Discovery of Lenthionine, Tetrahedron Letters, 1966; Editor: Dictionary of Organic Compounds, The Soc. Synthetic Organic Chemistry, Japan, 1985. Recipient Yakuji-koro-sho, Osaka-fu, 1986, 2d Class Order of Sacred Treasure, Japan, 1997. Fellow Bioindustry Devel. Ctr.; mem. Chem. Soc. Japan, Pharm. Soc. Japan. Avocations: Go, golf. Home: 8-16-5 Minoo Minoo-shi Osaka 562-0001 Japan Office Phone: 06 6300 6555. Personal E-mail: morita@ifo.or.jp, k.morita@vanilla.ocn.nejp.

MORITA, LINA, pianist, educator; b. Sao Paulo, Brazil, Aug. 15, 1977; d. Yasuo and Nobuko Morita. MusB in Piano Performance, Ind. U., Bloomington, 1999; MusM in Piano Performance, Rice U., Houston, 2001; DMA in Piano Performance and Lit., Eastman Sch. Music, Rochester, NY, 2005. Instr. piano, Shepherd Sch. Music Prep. Program Rice U., 1999—2001, tchg. asst., 1999—2001, Eastman Sch. Music, 2001—04, instr. piano, Cmty. Music Sch., 2004—05; instr. piano Hochstein Sch. Music, Rochester, 2004—05, Levine Sch. Music, Washington, 2005—07; artist, asst. prof. piano McNeese State U., Lake Charles, La., 2007—. Judge Washington DC Music Tchrs. Nat. Assn. Competition, 2007. Soloist, pianist Lake Charles Symphony, 2008, Atlas Performing Arts Ctr., Washington, 2007, Ch. Epiphany, 2007, Washington Sinfonietta, 2008, Music Ctr. Strathmore, Women in the Arts Series, Rockville, Md., 2007. Pianist, organist Bergen 1st Presbyn. Ch., Rochester, 2003—05; pianist Atascocita Presbyn. Ch., Tex., 2000—01. Recipient Tchg. Asst. award, Eastman Sch. Music, 2004. Mem.: Coll. Music Soc., Lake Charles Piano Tchrs. Assn., Music Tchrs. Nat. Assn. Avocations: languages, travel. Business E-Mail: lmorita@mcneese.edu.

MORITA, NORIMASA, otolaryngologist, researcher; b. Kurashiki, Japan, Aug. 22, 1972; s. Morita; m. Mikiko Harada, Jan. 1, 1975; 1 child, Tetsushi. MD, Kawasaki Med. Sch., Kurashiki, 1999, PhD, 2005. Resident Kawasaki Med. Sch., Kurashiki, 1999—2002, 2006—07; tchg. staff U. Minn., Mpls., 2007—. Mem.: Oto-Rhino-Laryngological Soc. Japan. Avocation: golf. Office: Univ Minn Otolaryngology-Head and Neck Surgery 516 Delaware St SE 8-310 PWB Minneapolis MN 55455

MORITA, RICHARD YUKIO, microbiology and oceanography educator; b. Pasadena, Calif., Mar. 27, 1923; s. Jiro and Reiko (Yamamoto) M.; m. Toshiko Nishihara, May 29, 1926; children— Sally Jean, Ellen Jane, Peter Wayne BS, U. Nebr., 1947; MS, U. So. Calif., 1949; PhD, U. Calif., 1954. Microbiologist Mid-Pacific Expdn., 1950, Danish Galathea Deep-Sea Expdn., 1952, Trans-Pacific Expdn.; Postdoctoral fellow U. Calif., Scripps Inst. Oceanography, 1954-55; asst. prof. U. Houston, 1955-58; asst. prof., assoc. prof. U. Neb., 1958-62; prof. microbiology and oceanography Oreg. State U., Corvallis, 1962-89, prof. emeritus microbiology and oceanography, 1989—. Prog. dir. biochemistry NSF, 1968-69; Disting. vis. prof. Kyoto Univ.; cons. NIH, 1968-70; rschr. in field. Contbr. articles to sci. lit. Patentee in field. Served with US Army, 1944—46. Grantee NSF, 1962—, NIH, 1960-68, NASA, 1967-72, Office Naval Research, 1966-70, Dept. Interior, 1968-72, NOAA, 1975-82, Bur. Land Mgmt., 1982, EPA, 1986—; recipient awards including King Fredericus IX Medal and Ribbon, 1954, Sr. Queen Elizabeth II Fellowship, 1973-74, Hotpack lectr. and award Can. Soc. Fellow Japan Soc. for Promotion Sci.; mem. Am. Soc. Microbiology (Fisher award). Home: 1515 NW 14th St Corvallis OR 97330 Home Phone: 541-753-0337. Personal E-mail: dickmorita@aol.com.

MORITANI, TOSHIO, radiologist, educator; b. Okayama, Japan, Jan. 21, 1961; arrived in U.S., 1999; s. Hideo and Tomoko Moritani; m. Yumiko Moritani, June 8, 2003. MD, Showa U., Tokyo, 1987; PhD, Showa U., 1991. Cert. Edn. Commn. Fgn. Med. Grads. Head physician Saitama Children's Med. Ctr., Japan, 1993—99; asst. rsch. prof. U. Rochester, NY, 1999—2004; clin. assoc. U. Iowa, Iowa City, 2004—05, asst. prof., 2005—. Asst. prof. Showa U. Sch. Medicine, 1991—97, 1997—99, adj. assoc. prof., 2004—; vis. prof. U. Iowa, Iowa City, 2003; adj. asst. prof. U. Rochester, 2004—. Author: Diffusion-Weighted Imaging of the Brain, 2003, Japanese transl., 2005, 2nd edit., 2009; contbr. articles to profl. jours. Mem.: Japanese Coll. Radiology, Am. Soc. Neuroradiology (several citations 1999—2006), Radiol. Soc. N.Am. (several citations 1997—2005). Avocations: golf, tennis, travel, reading, shorinji. Office: U Iowa Dept Radiology 200 Hawkins Dr Iowa City IA 52242 Home: 221 E Coll St 1207 Iowa City IA 52240 Office Phone: 319-356-1177, 319-356-3767, 319-356-3676. Personal E-mail: moritani2001@yahoo.com.

MORITZ, A.F. (ALBERT FRANK), poet, educator; b. Niles, Ohio, Apr. 15, 1947; arrived in Toronto, Can., 1974; m. Theresa Moritz. Grad., Marquette U., Milw. Tchr. U. Toronto, 1986—. Author: (poetry) Here, 1975, Signs and Certainties, 1979, Black Orchid, 1981, Between the Root and the Flower, 1982, The Visitation, 1983, The Tradition, 1986, Song of Fear, 1992, The Ruined Cottage, 1993, Ciudad Interior, 1993, Phantoms in the Ark, 1994, Mahoning, 1994, A Houseboat on the Styx, 1998, Rest on the Flight into Egypt, 1999, The End of the Age, 2000, Conflicting Desire, 2000, Early Poems, 2002, Night Street Repairs, 2005 (ReLit award, 2005), The Sentinel, 2008 (Griffin Poetry prize, 2009), (non-fiction) The Pocket Canada: A Guidebook, 1982, Leacock: A Biography, 1985, The Oxford Literary Guide to Canada, 1987, Stephen Leacock: His Remarkable Life, 2000, The World's Most Dangerous Woman: A New Biography of Emma Goldman, 2002; contbr. works of poetry to numerous anthologies and mags.;, translator various works of poetry from fgn. lang. into English. Recipient Ingram Merrill Found. Fellowship, 1982, Guggenheim Fellowship, 1990, Award for Lit., AAAL, 1991, Bess Hokin prize, Poetry mag., 2004. Office: Victoria Coll U Toronto 73 Queens Pk Crescent #NF 206 Toronto ON M5S 1K7 Canada Business E-Mail: albert.moritz@utoronto.ca.

MORITZ, CHAD HENRY, research scientist; Grad. magna cum laude, U. Wis., 1977. Diagnostic radiographer Aurora Health Care, Milw., 1991—93, Covenant Health Care, Milw., 1993—94; MRI rsch. technologist Med. Coll. Wis., Milw., 1994—96; rsch. assoc. Dartmouth Coll., Hanover, NH, 1996—98; rsch. program mgr. radiology dept. U. Wis. Med. Sch., Madison, 1999—. Presenter in field. Contbr. chapters to books, articles to profl. jours. Recipient award for Excellence, St. Luke's Sch. Radiol. Tech., 1993; Profl. devel. grantee, U. Wis., 2003. Mem.: Am. Soc. Functional Neuroradiology, Soc. for Magnetic Resonance Technologists, Am. Soc. Radiol. Technologists (cert. radiologic technologist), Orgn. for Human Brain Mapping, Internat. Soc. for Magnetic Resonance in Medicine. Avocations: bicycling, accordion. Business E-Mail: cmoritz@uwhealth.org.

MORITZ, DONALD BROOKS, mechanical engineer, consultant; b. Mpls., June 17, 1927; s. Donald B. and Frances W. (Whalen) M.; m. Joan Claire Betzenderfer, June 17, 1950 (dec. Dec. 21, 2004); children: Craig, Pamela, Brian. BS in Mech. Engring., U. Minn., 1950; postgrad., Western Res. U., 1956-58. Registered profl. engr., Ill. Minn., Ohio. V.p., gen. mgr. Waco Scaffold Shoring Co., Addison, Ill., 1950-72; group v.p. Bliss and Laughlin Industries, Oak Brook, Ill., 1972-83; sr. v.p. AXIA Inc. (formerly Bliss and Laughlin Industries, Oak Brook, 1983-84, exec. v.p., chief operating officer, 1984-88; cons. Exec. Svc. Corps Chgo., 1988—; pres. Image-A-Nation, Unltd., 1988—. Bd. dirs. Am. Photographic Acad. Patentee in field. Served with USN, 1945-46. Mem. ASME, Scaffold and Shoring Inst. (founder, past pres.), Mensa, Five Seasons Country Club. Office: Moritz and Assocs PO Box 305 Clarendon Hills IL 60514-0305

MORITZ, MICHAEL J., venture capitalist; b. Cardiff, Wales, 1952; married; 2 children. MA in Hist., U. Oxford, 1976; MBA, U. Pa. Wharton Sch. Bus., 1978. Corr. TIME mag., 1979; with Time Warner; founder Technologic Partners; gen. ptnr., mng. dir. Sequoia Cap., 1986—. Mem. bd. dirs. Flextronics, 1993—2005, Yahoo!, 1995—2003, Google, Inc., 1999—2007. Author: The Little Kingdom: The Private Story of Apple Computer, 1986. Named one of The World's Most Influential People, TIME mag., 2007, 50 Who Matter Now, Business 2.0, 2007, The Richest People in Britain, London's Sunday Times. Office: Sequoia Capital Bldg 4 Ste 180 3000 Sand Hill Rd Menlo Park CA 94025 Office Phone: 650-854-3927. Office Fax: 650-854-2977. Business E-Mail: moritz@sequoiacap.com.

MORITZ, TIMOTHY BOVIE, psychiatrist; b. Portsmouth, Ohio, July 26, 1936; s. Charles Raymond and Elisabeth Bovie (Morgan) M.; m. Joyce Elizabeth Rasmussen, Oct. 13, 1962 (div. Sept. 1969); children: Elizabeth Wynne, Laura Morgan; m. Antoinette Tanasichuk, Oct. 31, 1981; children: David Michael, Stephanie Lysbeth. BA, Ohio State U., 1959; MD, Cornell U., 1963. Diplomate Am. Bd. Psychiatry and Neurology. Intern in medicine N.Y. Hosp., NYC, 1963-64, resident in psychiatry, 1964-67; spl. asst. to dir. NIMH, Bethesda, Md., 1967-69; dir. Community Mental Health Ctr., Rockland County, NY, 1970-74, Ohio Dept. Mental Health, Columbus, Ohio, 1975-81; med. dir. psychiatry Miami Valley Hosp., Dayton, Ohio, 1981-82; med. dir. N.E. Ga. Community Mental Health Ctr., Athens, Ga., 1982-83, Charter Vista Hosp., Fayetteville, Ark., 1983-87; clin. dir. adult psychiatry Charter Hosp., Las Vegas, Nev., 1987-94; pvt. practice psychiatry Las Vegas, 1987—; med. dir. Problem Gambling Cons., Las Vegas, 2000—. Prof. Wright State U., Dayton, Ohio, 1981-82; asst. prof. Cornell U., N.Y.C., 1970-73; mem. human subjects biomed. scis. rev. com. U. Nev., Las Vegas, 2000-2001; cons. NIMH, Rockville, Md., 1973-83. Author: (chpt.) Rehabilitation Medicine and Psychiatry, 1976; mem. editorial bd. Directions in Psychiatry, 1981-1993. Dir. dept. mental health and mental retardation Gov.'s Cabinet, State of Ohio, Columbus, 1975-81. Recipient Svc. award Ohio Senate, 1981, Svc. Achievement award Ohio Gov., 1981. Fellow Am. Psychiat. Assn. (disting. life, Disting. Svc. award 1981); mem. AMA, Nev. Assn. Psychiat. Physicians, Nev. State Med. Assn., Am. Assn. Chronic Fatigue Syndrome, Clark County Med. Soc., Cornell U. Med. Coll. Alumni Assn., Ohio State U. Alumni Assn. (life). Office: 2330 Paseo del Prado Ste C-109 Las Vegas NV 89102-4336 Office Phone: 702-363-3633.

MORIUCHI, K. DEREK, secondary school educator; b. LA, 1958; BA, UCLA, 1981; MA, Calif. State U., 1982; MA in Edni. Adminstrn., Calif. State U., LA, 2005. Cert. single subject tchg. credential in math., cross cultural lang. acquisition devel., nat. bd. cert. tchr., lic. in adminstrv. svcs. Tchr. math. Marshall Mid. Sch., 1986—90, Ganesha H.S., 1991—93; tchr. history Stevenson Middle Sch., LA, 1993—2003, chairdept. math.; secondary math. expert L.A. Unified Sch. Dist., LA, 2003—. Spkr. in field. Mem.: Calif. Math. Coun. (spkr. 2000—03), Nat. Bd. for Profl. Tchg. Stds. (bd. mem. 2001—), Pi Lambda Theta. Office: Local Dist 5 LA Unified Sch Dist 2151 N Soto St Los Angeles CA 90032 Office Phone: 323-224-3132. Personal E-mail: k12536@aol.com. E-mail: derek.moriuchi@lausd.net.

MORIYAMA, KAREN ITO, retired educational association administrator; d. Sadamu and Sumiko Honma Ito; children: Ryan M., Kristel S. BEd with high honors, U. Hawaii, Manoa, 1970, MEd, 1975. Lic. sch. adminstr. Dept. Edn., Hawaii, sch. counselor Dept. Edn., Hawaii, psychol. examiner Dept. Edn., Hawaii, cert. elem. tchr. Dept. Edn., Hawaii. Tchr. Red Hill Elem., Honolulu, 1971—73, Kipapa Elem. Sch., Mililani, Hawaii, 1973—82; counselor Solomon Elem. Sch., Wahiawa, Hawaii, 1982—85; counseling resource tchr. Dept. Edn., Central District, Hawaii, 1985—87; vice prin. Wheeler Intermediate Sch., Wahiawa, 1987—89; prin. Leihoku Elem. Sch., Waianae, Hawaii, 1989—94, Kanoelani Elem. Sch., Waipahu, Hawaii, 1995—2000; dist. dep. supt. Leeward Dist., Waipahu, 2000—02; complex area supt. Nanakuli-Pearl City, Waipahu, 2002—. Adv. mem. U. Hawaii Counseling and Guidance Adv. Com., Honolulu, 1986. Mem., sec. Waianae Mil./Civilian Adv. Coun., 1991—94; bd. dirs. Joint Venture Edn. Forum, Honolulu, 2002—05, YMCA, Mililani, Hawaii, 1997—2001. Mem.: NAESP (assoc. Leeward Dist. Disting. Prin. award 1994, 1999), Hawaii Assn. Supervision and Curriculum Devel. (assoc.), Delta Kappa Gamma (Beta chpt.) (assoc.; pres., v.p. 1996—2000).

MORJAN, WILMAR, entomologist, researcher; 1994, naturalized, 2005; AA in Agronomy, Panamerican Sch. Agr., Zamorano, Honduras, 1990, BS in Agronomy, 1993; MS in Entomology, Iowa State U., Ames, 1997, PhD in Entomology, Ecology and Evolutionary Biology, 2001. Entomology mgr. Monsanto Co., Waterman, Ill., 2002—07; tech. devel. lead for large seeds & processing Seminis, De Forest, Wis., 2007—. Recipient Comstock award, Entomol. Grad. Student Orgn., 2000, Tchg. Excellence award, Iowa Sate U., 2001; grantee Rsch. grant, Leopold Ctr., 2000—01. Mem.: Internat. Orgn. Biol. Ctrl., Fla. Entomologist, Entomol. Soc. Am., Gamma Sigma Delta (hon.). Office: Seminis 7202 Portage Rd De Forest WI 53532 Personal E-mail: wilmar_morjan@yahoo.com.

MORLEY, HARRY THOMAS, JR., real estate executive; b. St. Louis, Aug. 13, 1930; s. Harry Thomas and Celeste Elizabeth (Davies) M.; m. Nelda Lee Mulholland, Sept. 3, 1960; children: Lisa, Mark, Marci. BA, U. Mo., 1955; MA, U. Denver, 1959. Dir. men's student activities Iowa State Tchrs. Coll., 1955-57; dir. student housing U. Denver, 1957-60; pvt. practice psychol. consulting St. Louis, 1960-63; dir. adminstrn. County of St. Louis, Mo., 1963-70; regional dir. HUD, Kansas City, Mo., 1970-71, asst. sec. adminstrn., 1971-73; pres. St. Louis Regional Commerce and Growth Assn., 1973-78, Taylor, Morley, Inc., St. Louis, 1978—2005, Morley Investments, Inc., 2005—. Teaching cons., lectr. Washington U., St. Louis, 1962-70; bd. dirs. Mid-Am. Alliance Corp., Life Ins. Co. Bd. dirs., exec. com. St. Louis Coll. Pharmacy; past chmn. Better Bus. Bur.; chmn. Mo. Indsl. Devel. Bd., Mo. State Hwy. Commn.; bd. dirs. St. Luke's Hosps., St. Johns Hosp., Downtown St. Louis, Inc., Laclede's Landing Redevel. Corp. With USN, 1951-53. Mem. Am. Nat. Assn. Homebuilders, St. Louis Homebuilders Assn. (pres.), St. Louis Advt. Club, Mo. Athletic Club, St. Louis Club, Noonday Club, Castle Oak Country Club, Round Table Club, Sunset Country Club. Republican. Methodist. Home: 14238 Forest Crest Dr Chesterfield MO 63017-2818 E-mail: morleyh@charter.net.

MORLEY, JAMES THOMAS, philosopher, educator; b. Balt., Dec. 16, 1942; s. William Logan and Robertine Merle Morley; m. Charlotte May Holbroke. PhD, U. Tennesse, Knoxville, 1987. Philosophy instr. FTCC, 1997—. Mem.: Mind Assoc. Home: 206 Hull Rd Fayetteville NC 28303 Office: Fayetteville Tech CC PO Box 35236 Fayetteville NC 28303 Business E-Mail: morleyj@faytechcc.edu.

MORLEY, JEFFREY JOSHUA, dentist, educator; b. Los Angeles, Apr. 25, 1953; s. David and Reneé Morley. Student, San Francisco Art Inst., 1989-91, Calif. State U., Northridge, 1971-72; grad., Calif. State U., San Jose, 1973; DDS, U. Pacific, San Francisco, 1976. Pvt. practice dentistry, San Francisco, 1981—; founder San Francisco Inst. for Age Reversing Dentistry, 2003, Morley Seminars Tng., 2007. Dir. Advanced Esthetic Program, Baylor Coll. Dentistry, Dallas; vis. faculty U. Minn., U. Mo., Kansas City; adj. prof. esthetic dentistry U. Buffalo; co-director Advanced Restorative Esthetics Post Grad. Continuums, La. State U. and UCLA. Assoc. editor Jour. of the Am. Dental Assn., mem. editl. bd. Dentistry Today, Esthetic Dentistry Update; contbr. articles to profl. jours. Fellow: Am. Acad. Cosmetic Dentistry (pres.-elect, v.p. 1984—86, pres. 1987—89, bd. trustees, Charitable Found., accredited fellow, co-founder 1984); mem.: Esthetic Dentistry Rsch. Group., Am. Soc. for Dental Aesthetics. Office Phone: 415-474-1555. E-mail: drjeffmorley@mindspring.com.

MORLEY, JOHN EDWARD, physician; b. Eshowe, Zululand, South Africa, June 13, 1946; came to U.S., 1977; s. Peter and Vera Rose (Phipson) M.; m. Patricia Morley, Apr. 4, 1970; children: Robert, Susan, Jacqueline. MB, BCh, U. Witwatersrand, Johannesburg, South Africa, 1972. Diplomate Am. Bd. Internal Medicine, subspecialty cert. endocrinology and geriatrics. Asst. prof. Mpls. VA Med. Ctr. and U. Minn., 1979-81; assoc. prof. U. Minn., Mpls., 1981-84; prof. UCLA San Fernando Valley, 1985-89; dir. GRECC Sepulveda (Calif.) VA Med. Ctr., 1985-89; Dammert prof. gerontology, dir. div. geriatric medicine St. Louis U. Med. Ctr., 1989—; dir. geriatric rsch., edn. and clin. ctr. St. Louis VA Med. Ctr., 1989—. Author: (with others) Nutritional Modulation of Neuronal Function, 1988, Neuropeptides and Stress, 1988, Geriatric Nutrition, 1990, 2d edit., 1995, Medical Care in the Nursing Home, 1991, 2d edit., 1997, Endocrinology and Metabolism in the Elderly, 1992, Memory Function and Aging Related Disorders, 1992, Aging and Musculoskeletal Disorders, 1993, Aging, Immunity and Infection, 1994, Sleep Disorders and Insomnia in the Elderly, 1993, Quality Improvement in Geriatric Care, 1995, Focus on Nutrition, 1995, Applying Health Services Research to Long-Term Care, 1996, Cardiovascular Disease in Older People, 1997, Hydration and Aging, 1997, Advances in Care of Older People with Diabetes, 1999, Endocrinology of Aging, 1999, Science of Geriatrics, 2000, Subacute Care, 2000, Anti-Aging, 2004, Principles and Practices of Geriatric Medicine, 4th edit., 2006; The Sci. Staying Young, 2007; mem. editl. bd. Peptides, 1983—, Internat. Jour. Obesity, 1986-89, Jour. Nutritional Medicine, 1990—, Clinics in Applied Nutrition, 1990-92; editor geriatrics sect. Yearbook of Endocrinology, 1987-2001, Nursing Home Medicine, 1992-97, Clin. Geriatrics, 1992-97, Sandwich Generation, 1997, others; editor Jour. Gerontology: Med. Scis., 2000-06, Jour. Am. Med. Dirs. Assn., 2006—. Mem. adv. bd. Alzheimer's Assn., St. Louis, 1990-92; mem. adv. com. for physicians Mo. Divsn. Aging, Jefferson City, 1990-2001; bd. dirs. Mo. Assn. Long Term Care Physicians, 1991—, Long Term Care Ombudsman Program, St. Louis, 1992, Fund for Psychoneuroimmunology, 1990-2001, Hamilton Hts. Health Resource Ctr., 1992—. Recipient Mead Johnson award, Am. Inst. Nutrition, 1985, Cmty. Svc. award, BREM, 1997, Robert H. Bollinger Disting. Acad. award, U. Kans., 1997, Longevity prize, Ispen Found., 1999, Circle award, Am. Dietetics Assn., 2001, Marsha Goodwin-Beck Interdisciplinary award for excellence in geriatric leadership, Dept. Vets. Affairs, 2005. Mem. ACP (geriatrics subcom. 1991-92), Am. Geriatric Soc. (Nasher/Manning award 2002), Internat. Soc. Study-Aging Male, Am. Soc. Clin. Investigation, Endocrine Soc., Am. Fedn. Clin. Rsch., Am. Acad. Behavioral Sci., Gerontology Soc. Am. (Freeman award, 2004), Am. Diabetes Assn., Am. Soc. Pharmacy and Therapeutics, Soc. for Neurosci., La Asociacion de Gerontologica y Geriatrica, A.C. (hon.), Assn. Dirs. Geriatric Acad. Programs, Internat. Soc. Study Male Aging, Phi Beta Kappa. Office: Saint Louis U Sch Medicine 1402 S Grand Blvd Rm M238 Saint Louis MO 63104-1004 Office Phone: 314-977-8462. Business E-Mail: morley@slu.edu.

MORLEY, LLOYD ALBERT, electrical engineering educator; b. Provo, Utah, Oct. 28, 1940; s. John Jr. and Dorothea (Nielsen) M.; m. Jo Ann Bryant, Feb. 22, 1975; 1 child, Paul Loring. BS in Mining Engring., U. Utah, 1968, PhD in Mining Engring., 1972. Tchg. asst., rsch. assoc. U. Utah, Salt Lake City, 1968-71; asst. prof. mining engring. Pa. State U., University Park, 1971-75, assoc. prof., 1975-80, prof., 1980-85; prof., head dept. mineral engring. U. Ala., Tuscaloosa, 1985-93, endowed chair mining engring., 1993-99, prof. elec. engring., 1996—2006, assoc. dept. head elec. and computer engring., 1997-99, interim head, 1999-2000, head, 2000—04, prof. emeritus, 2007—. Cons. Jim Walter Resources, Inc., Brookwood, Ala., 1987-98, Pitts. and Midway Coal Mining Co., Englewood, Colo., 1990-98, Drummond Co., Inc., Birmingham, Ala., 1991-98. Author: Mine Power Systems, 1990; contbr. articles to profl. jours. Staff sgt. USNG, 1958-66. Recipient Wilson Outstanding Tchg. award Pa. State U., 1980; Outstanding Rsch. Report awards U.S. Bur. Mines, 1983-84, Hackney Faculty Leadership award, U. Ala., 2000, HKN Outstanding Tchg. award, U. Ala., 2004. Fellow IEEE (life) (bd. dirs. 1991-92, 94, 97-99, v.p. publs. 1994, 99, v.p. tech. activities 1997, 98, corp. integrity officer 2006—, Richard M. Emberson award 2005); mem. Industry Applications Soc. IEEE (Mining Best Paper awards 1984, 88, 90, pres. 1988, Disting. lectr. 1991, Disting. Svc. award 1995), Power Engr. Soc., Computer Soc., Phi Kappa Phi, Eta Kappa Nu. Avocations: high-fidelity systems, classic sports cars, rose growing, music. Home Phone: 205-758-8551. Business E-Mail: lmorley@eng.ua.edu.

MORLINO, ROBERT CHARLES, bishop; b. Scranton, Pa., Dec. 31, 1946; BA in Philosophy, Fordham U., 1969; MA in Philosophy, U. Notre Dame, 1970; MDiv, Weston Sch. Theology, Cambridge, Mass., 1974; STD, Pontifical Gregorian U., Rome, 1990. Ordained priest Soc. of Jesus, 1974; incardinated Diocese of Kalamazoo, 1983; ordained bishop, 1999; bishop Diocese of Helena, 1999—2003, Diocese of Madison, Wis., 2003—. Chmn. bd. dirs. Nat. Cath. Bioethics Ctr., 2005—. Mem.: US Conf. Cath. Bishops. Roman Catholic. Office: Diocese of Madison PO Box 44983 3577 High Point Rd Madison WI 53744 Office Phone: 608-821-3000. Office Fax: 608-821-3013.

MORNEAU, JUSTIN ERNEST GEORGE, professional baseball player; b. New Westminster, BC, Can., May 15, 1981; s. George and Audra Morneau. First baseman Minn. Twins, 2003—. Mem. Can. nat. team World Baseball Championship, 2001, World Baseball Classic, 2009. Recipient Silver Slugger award, 2006, 2008; named Am. League MVP, Maj. League Baseball, 2006; named to Am. League All-Star Team, 2007—09. Mailing: c/o Minn Twins Metrodome 34 Kirby Puckett Plc Minneapolis MN 55415*

MORNEAU, ROBERT FEALEY, bishop; b. New London, Wis., Sept. 10, 1938; s. Leroy Frederick and Catherine (Fealey) Morneau. MA, Catholic U., 1962; DD (hon.), 1979. Ordained priest Diocese of Green Bay, Wis., 1966; Instr. philosophy Silver Lake Coll., Manitowoc, Wis., 1966-78; dir. ministry to priests program Green Bay, Wis., 1979-85; aux. bishop Diocese of Green Bay, 1978—; ordained bishop, 1979. Chmn. commn. on prison reform, Wis. Cath. Conf.; lectr. in field. Author: Our Father Revisited, 1978, Trinity Sunday Revisited, 1980, Discovering God's Presence, 1980, Mantras for the Morning, 1981, Mantras for the Evening, 1982, Principles of Preaching, 1982, Seasonal Themes, 1984, Mantras for Midnight, 1985 and others; author tape series from Alba House; contbr. articles to profl. jours. Bd. trustees St. Norbert Coll. Mem. Nat. Conf. Cath. Bishops, Bishops Com. on Priestly Formation, Com. on Edn. US Cath. Conf. Roman Catholic. Office: PO Box 23825 Green Bay WI 54305-3825

MORNEAU, WILLIAM, pension and benefits company executive; BA, U. Western Ontario; MSc, London Sch. Econs.; MBA, INSEAD, France. Chmn., CEO Morneau Sobeco, Toronto. Apptd. bd. dirs. AGF Mgmt. Ltd., 2000. Involved with numerous charitable and community organizations. Named one of Canada's Top 40 under 40, 2001. Office: Morneau Sobeco 895 Don Mills Rd Ste 700 Toronto ON Canada M3C 1W3

MORNHINWEG, MARTY, professional football coach; b. Edmond, Okla., Mar. 29, 1962; m. Lindsay Mornhinweg; children: Madison, Skye, Molly, Bobby Cade. Coach U. Mont., 1985; grad. asst., quarterback coach U. Tex., El Paso, 1986—87; coach running backs No. Ariz. U., 1988; offensive coord./quarterbacks S.E. Mo. State U., 1989—90; coach offensive line, tight ends U. Mo., 1991—93; offensive coord. No. Ariz. U., 1994; offensive asst., quality control, quarterback coach Green Bay Packers, Wis., 1995—96; offensive coord. San Francisco 49ers, 1997—2000; head coach Detroit Lions, 2001—03; sr. asst coach Phila. Eagles, 2003—04, asst. head coach, 2004—, offensive coord., 2006—. Office: Phila Eagles NovaCare Complex 1 Novacare Way Philadelphia PA 19145*

MOROF, JEFFREY W., lawyer; AB, U. Mich, 1976; JD, Washington U., St. Louis, 1979. Bar: Calif., Mo., US Dist. Ct. (Ctrl. & No. dists.) Calif., US Dist. Ct. Colo., US Dist. Ct. (So. dist.) Fla., US Dist. Ct. NJ. With Bryan Cave LLP, Chgo., 1979—, ptnr., 1988—, mng. ptnr., mem. exec. com.; settlement conference atty. US Dist. Ct. (Ctrl. dist.) Calif., 1998—2000, 2001—03. Office Phone: 312-602-5045. Office Fax: 312-602-5045. E-mail: jwmorof@bryancave.com.

MOROLES, JESÚS BAUTISTA, sculptor; b. Corpus Christi, Tex., Sept. 22, 1950; AA, El Centro Coll., Dallas, 1975; BFA, No. Tex. State U., 1978. Bd. dirs. Internat. Sculpture Ctr., Washington, 1988-97; instr. Nat. Mus. Am. Art Symposium, 1992; bd. trustees, Art Mus. South Tex., Corpus Christi, 1993-96; bd. commrs., Nat. Am. Art Mus., Washington, 1996—; visual arts adv. bd., U. North Tex., Denton, 2001—. One-person exhibs include Arthur Roger Gallery, New Orleans, 2000, 2002, 2004, 2007, LewAllen Contemp, Santa Fe, 2000, 2001, 2002, 2003, 2004, 2005, 2007, Barbara Davis Gallery, Houston, 2000, 2002, McClain Gallery, Houston, 2001, 2003, (Untitled) Gallery, Okla City, 2001, 2006, Dallas Mus Art, 2004; commd. Tex. Commerce Bank, Dallas, 1983, Riata Devel., Houston, 1984, Siena Sq., Boulder, Colo., 1985, Nat. Health Ins. Co., Dallas, 1986, IBM, Raleigh, NC, 1986; represented in permanent collections Albuquerque Mus., Mus. Fine Arts, Santa Fe, Old Jail Art Ctr., Albany, Tex., U. Houston, Mint Mus., Charlotte, NC, Dallas Mus. Art, Nat. Mus. Am. Art, Smithsonian Inst., Washington. Visual Art fellow Southeastern Ctr. Contemporary Art, Winston-Salem, NC, 1982; grantee Nat. Endowment Arts, Birmingham Botanical Gardens, 1984; recipient Pres. Citation award, U. No. Tex., 1992, Martha Turner award, 2006, AIA award, 1995, 1998, Artist award, Multicultural Edn. Ctr. Arts, Houston, 1997, Landscape Arch. (Colo. chapt.) award, 1999, Outstanding Citizen award, Corpus Christi, Tex., 2004, Tex. Medal of Arts, 2007, Nat. Medal of Arts, 2008. Studio: 408 W 6th St Rockport TX 78382-4422*

MORONEY, JAMES M., III, publishing executive; b. 1957; s. Lynn Wilhoit Moroney and James M. Moroney, Jr.; m. Barbara Moroney; 5 children. BA in Am. Studies, Stanford U., 1978; MBA, U. Tex., 1983. Acct. exec. WFAA-TV, KFDM-TV, Beaumont, Tex., 1978—84; local sales mgr. WFAA-TV, Dallas-Ft. Worth, 1985; gen. sales mgr. KOTV, Tulsa, Okla., 1985—89, v.p., gen. mgr., 1992—93, pres., gen. mgr., 1993; with Belo Corp., Dallas, 1978—86, controller, 1989, asst. to pres. broadcast divsn., 1990—92, v.p. broadcast divsn., 1993—95, exec. v.p. TV Group, 1995—97, pres. TV Group, 1997—98, exec. v.p., 1998—99, 2007—; founding pres. Belo Interactive, Inc., Dallas, 1999—2001; pub. & CEO Dallas Morning News, 2001—. Bd. dirs. Newspaper Assn. Am. Mem. Dallas Citizens Coun.; mem. bd. dirs. TV Bur. Adv., Goodwill Industries, Dallas, Tulsa, United Way Tulsa, Cath. Charities Tulsa, Jr. Achievement Tulsa, Gilcrease Mus. Tulsa, Cistercian Prep. Sch. Dallas, Greater Dallas Chamber, State Fair Tex., U. Tex. Austin Coll. Comm., State Fair of Tex., Cistercian Prep. Sch., Dallas, Belo Corp. Named Pub. of Yr., Editor & Pub. mag., 2004. Office: Dallas Morning News 508 Young St Dallas TX 75202 also: Belo Corp PO Box 655237 Dallas TX 75265-7526 Business E-Mail: jmoroney@dallasnews.com.*

MORONEY, JOHN RODGERS, economist, educator; b. Dallas, Jan. 29, 1939; s. John Rodgers and Irene (Lewis) M.; m. Margaret Cecil Kearny, May 30, 1959; children: John Rodgers, Stephen Kearny, Helen, Michael Edward; m. Carmen Lambert, May 22, 1993 BA, So. Meth. U., Dallas, 1960; PhD, Duke U., Durham, NC, 1964. Asst. prof. econs. Fla. State U., 1964—66; assoc. prof. econs. Mich. State U., 1966—69; mem. exec. com. Inst. Pub. Utilities, 1968—69; prof. econs., chmn. dept. Tulane U., New Orleans, 1969—81; prof., head dept. econs. Tex. A&M U., College Station, 1981—. Vis. prof. econs. MIT, 1975-76; Schmidt internat. prof. A.B. Freeman Sch. Bus., Tulane U., New Orleans, 1998—; pres. Moroney Econ. Rsch. Assocs., 1992— Author: The Structure of Production in American Manufacturing, 1972, Exploration, Development, and Production: Texas Oil and Gas, 1997, Energy and Sustainable Development in Mexico, 2005, Power Struggle: World Energy in the 21st Century, 2008; editor, contbr.: Income Inequality: Trends and Internat. Comparisons, 1979, Economic Aspects of New Technology, 1980, Formal Energy and Resource Models, 1982; editor: Econometric Models of the Demand for Energy, 1984; editor, contbr.: Energy, Capital, and Technological Change, 1987, Energy, Growth, and the Environment, 1992, Energy Prices and Production, 1994, Sustainable Economic Growth, 1995, Energy Supply and Demand, 1997, Fuels for the Future, 1999; mem. editl. bd. Bus. Topics, 1968-69, So. Econ. Jour, 1975— Social Sci. Rsch. Coun. faculty rsch. fellow, 1969; NSF rsch. fellow, 1975-76, 77-79 Mem. Am. Econ. Assn., So. Econ. Assn. (exec. com. 1975—, v.p. 1980), Royal Econ. Assn., Econometric Soc., Phi Beta Kappa Home: 210 Fireside Cir College Station TX 77840-1877 Office: Dept Econs Tex A&M U College Station TX 77843-4228 Office Phone: 979-845-1363. Business E-Mail: jmoroney@econmail.tamu.edu.

MOROOKA, HIROSHI, neurosurgeon; b. Kurashiki, Okayama, Japan, Aug. 28, 1946; s. Shigeru and Akiko (Kobayashi) M.; m. Michiko Ninomiya, June 6, 1976; children: Takatoshi, Hanako, Teruko. MD, U. Okayama, 1971, PhD, 1978. Diplomate Japanese Bd. Neurol. Surgery. Clin. asst. neurosurgery U. Okayama Med. Sch., 1972—77, instr. neurosurgery, 1980-83, asst. prof. neurosurgery, 1984-86; rsch. assoc. neurology U. Miami Med. Sch., Fla., 1977-79; chief neurosurgery Okayama Rousai Hosp., 1987-92, Bizen City Hosp., 1993-95, Okayama Saidaiji Hosp., 1996—97, Morooka Neurosurg. and Pediat. Clinic, Okayama, 1998—. Author: Cytoprotection & Cytobiology, 1995-97, Medical Biochemical & Chemical Aspects of Free Radicals, 1989, Intracranial Pressure VII, 1989, Brain Edema IX, 1993. Recipient Disting. Prof. award, BWW Soc., Inst. Advancement of Positive Global Solutions, Calif., 2003, Legion of Honor award, United Cultural Conv., NC, 2005; Nat. Rsch. grantee, 1981. Mem. AAAS, Japan Neurol. Soc., Societas Neurologica Japonica, NY Acad. Scis., Am. Heart Assn., Am. Chem. Soc. Liberal Dem. Christian. Avocation: golf. Home: 880-165 Minato 703 8266 Okayama Japan Office: Morooka Neurosurgical & Pediatric Clinic 492-1 Kitajima Setouchi City Okayama 701-4232 Japan Office Phone: 086-943-1222. Business E-Mail: morooka@okym.enjoy.ne.jp.

MOROVICH, GEORGE L., rancher, contractor; b. Galveston, Tex., Jan. 22, 1956; s. Leo H. and Doris L. Morovich; m. Betsy Ann Craig, 1984; children: George, Camille. BS in Geography, Sam Houston State U., 1978. Rancher; with bus. devel., contracting, project mgmt. bus. Republican. Office: 130 N Washington St La Grange TX 78945*

MOROWITZ, HAROLD JOSEPH, biophysicist, educator; b. Poughkeepsie, NY, Dec. 4, 1927; s. Philip Frank and Anna (Levine) M.; m. Lucille Rita Stein, Jan. 30, 1949; children: Joanna Lynn, Eli David, Joshua Alan, Zachary Adam, Noah Daniel. BS, Yale U., 1947, MS, 1950, PhD, 1951. Physicist Nat. Bur. Stds., 1951-53, Nat. Heart Inst., Bethesda, Md., 1953-55; mem. faculty Yale U., 1955-88, assoc. prof. biophysics, 1960-68, prof. molecular biophysics and biochemistry, 1968-88, master Pierson Coll., 1981-86; mem. faculty George Mason U., Fairfax, Va., 1988—, Robinson prof. biology and natural philosophy, 1988—; dir. Krasnow Inst. for Advanced Study, 1993-98. Chmn. com. on models for biomed. rsch. NRC, 1983-85, mem. bd. on basic biology, 1986-92. Author: Life and the Physical Sciences, 1964, (with Waterman) Theoretical and Mathematical Biology, 1965, Energy Flow in Biology, 1968, Entropy for Biologists, 1970, (with Lucille Morowitz) Life On The Planet Earth, 1974, Ego Niches, 1977, Foundations of Bioenergetics, 1978, The Wine of Life, 1979, Mayonnaise and the Origin of Life, 1985, Cosmic Joy and Local Pain, 1987, The Thermodynamics of Pizza, 1991, Beginnings of Cellular Life, 1992, (with James Trefil) The Facts of Life, 1992, Entropy and the Magic Flute, 1993, The Kindly Dr. Guillotin, 1997, The Emergence of Everything, 2002; editor Complexity, 1994-2002; contbr. articles to profl. jours. Mem. sci. adv. bd. Santa Fe Inst., 1991-97, co-chmn. sci. adv. bd., 2000—06. Recipient Biol. Scis. award, Washington Acad. Scis., 2004. Mem. Biophys. Soc. (exec. com. 1965), Nat. Ctr. for Rsch. Resources (coun. 1987-92). Office: George Mason U Mail Stop 2A1 Krasnow Inst Advanced Study Fairfax VA 22030 Office Phone: 703-993-4334.

MORPHEW, CHRISTOPHER CLARK, education educator; b. Des Moines; s. Larry Dale and Susan Marie Morphew; m. Tanya Sue Kooi, May 28, 1994; children: Clora Kooi children: Anthony Kooi, Samuel Clark Kooi. BA, U. Notre Dame, Ind., 1990; MEd, Harvard U., Cambridge, Mass., 1991; MA, PhD, Stanford U., Calif., 1996. Asst. prof. U. Kans., Lawrence, 1997—2002, assoc. prof., 2002—05, Inst. Higher Edn. U. Ga., Athens, 2005—, 2005—09; prof. U. Iowa, 2009—. Office: Lindquist Ctr Coll Edn Univ Iowa Iowa City IA 52242 Business E-Mail: morphew@uiowa.edu.

MORPHEW, DOROTHY RICHARDS-BASSETT, artist, real estate broker; b. Cambridge, Mass., Aug. 4, 1918; d. George and Evangeline Booth Richards; children: Jon Eric Bassett, Marc Alan Bassett, Dana Kimball Bassett. Grad., Boston Art Inst., 1949. Draftsman United Shoe Machinery Co., 1937—42; blueprinter, advt. artist A.C. Lawrence Leather Co., Peabody, Mass., 1949—51; propr. Studio Shop and Studio Potters, Beverly, Mass., 1951—53; tchr. ceramics and art Kingston, NH, 1953—; real estate broker, 1965—81; two-man exhbn. Topsfield (Mass.) Libr., 1960; owner, operator Ceramic Shop, West Stewartstown, NH. With USNR, 1942—44. Recipient Profl. award, New Eng. Ceramic Show, 1975, also numerous certs. in ceramics. Mem.: Englewood (Fla.) Art Guild.

MORPHY, JAMES CALVIN, lawyer; b. Pitts., Jan. 16, 1954; s. Robert Samson and Autumn (Phillips) M.; m. Priscilla Winslow Plimpton, July 11, 1981; children: Calvin, Katherine, Victoria. BA, Harvard U., Cambridge, Mass., 1976, JD, 1979. Bar: NY 1980. Assoc. Sullivan & Cromwell LLP, NYC, 1979-86, ptnr., 1986—, mng. ptnr. com., 1992—95, mng. ptnr M&A group, 1995—2007, firm mng. ptnr., 2007—. Co-chmn. Tulane M&A Law Inst.; guest lectr. Harvard Law Sch.; mem. adv. bd. govs. Harvard Corp. Governance Program. Contbg. author: treatise New York and Delaware Business Entities: Choice Formation, Operation, Financing, and Acquisition, 1997, Transactional Lawyer's Deskbook, 2001. Trustee Greenwich Acad. Mem. ABA (com. on fed. securities law 1992—), Assn. Bar of City of NY, Wianno Club (bd. govs.), Greenwich Country Club, Harvard Club NY, Wianno Yacht Club, Phi Beta Kappa. Office: Sullivan & Cromwell LLP 125 Broad St New York NY 10004-2489 Office Phone: 212-558-4000. Office Fax: 212-558-3588. Business E-Mail: morphyj@sullcrom.com.

MORPURGO DAVIES, ANNA ELBINA, philologist, educator; b. Milan, June 21, 1937; d. Augusto Morpurgo and Maria Castelnuovo; m. John Kenyon Davies, Sept. 9, 1962 (div.). Dott. Lett. in Classics with Comparative Philology and Sanskrit, U. Rome, 1959, libera docenza in Glottologia, 1963; MA, U. Oxford, Eng., 1964; DLitt (hon.), U. St. Andrews, Scotland, 1981. Asst. classical philology U. Rome, 1959—61; jr. fellow Ctr. Hellenic Studies, Harvard U., Washington, 1961—62;

lectr. classical philology U. Oxford, England, 1964—71, prof. comparative philology, 1971—2003, Diebold prof. emeritus, 2003—04; fellow St. Hilda's Coll., Oxford, 1966—71, hon. fellow, 1972—; profl. fellow Somerville Coll., Oxford, 1971—2004, emeritus, 2004—. Vis. prof. U. Pa., 1971, Yale U., 1977, U. Pavia, 2005, U. Calif., Berkeley, 2006—07; Collitz prof. LSA, 1975, vis. prof. Ling Inst., 2009; prof. Stanford U., 1988; Sather prof., Berkeley, 2000; lectr. U. Cin., 1983, Jackson Harvard U., 1990; Sather, Berkeley, 2000. Contbr. articles to profl. jours.; author: (books) Mycenaeae Graecitatis Lexicon, 1963; editor (with W. Meid): Studies in Greek, Italic and Indo-European Linguistics. Festschrift for L.R. Palmer, 1976; author: La linguistica dell'Ottocento, 1996; editor: Nineteenth Century Linguistics, 1998; editor: (with Y. Duhoux) Linear B, a 1984 Survey, 1986, A Companion to Linear B, vol. I, 2008. Recipient Premio linceo per la linguistica, Accademia dei Lincei, 1996. Fellow: Brit. Acad., Linguistic Soc. America (hon.); mem.: Acad. Inscriptions et Belles Lettres, Academia Europea, Bayerside Acad. Wissenschaften (corr.), Oesterreichische Acad. Wissenschaften (corr.), Linguistic Soc. America (hon.), Am. Acad. Arts and Scis. (hon.), Dame Brit. Empire (hon.), Inst. France (corr.), Brit. Philol. Soc. (pres. 1976—80, hon. v.p. 1980—), Am. Philos. Soc. Home: 22 Yarnells Hill Oxford OX2 9BD England Office: Somerville Coll Oxford OX2 6HD England E-mail: anna.davies@some.ox.ac.uk.

MORRÉ, DOROTHY MARIE, nutrition educator, researcher; b. Bonnets Hill, Mo., Jan. 18, 1935; d. Conrad and Marie Wibberg; m. D. James Morré, Aug. 25, 1956; children: Connie, Jeffrey, Suzanne. BS, U. Mo., 1958; PhD, Purdue U., 1977. Asst. prof. Purdue U., West Lafayette, Ind., 1978-83, assoc. prof., 1983-89, prof., 1989—. Contbr. articles to profl. jours. Mem.: Am. Inst. Nutrition, Am. Soc. Cell Biologists, Sigma Xi. Office: Purdue U Dept Nutrition West Lafayette IN 47907

MORREALE, JOSEPH CONSTANTINO, academic administrator, educator, economist, consultant; b. Bronx, NY, Oct. 26, 1944; s. Joseph Vincent Morreale and Grace (Soricelli); m. Barbara McAdorey; children: Gwenn F., Margaret I., Adam J.; stepchildren: Neil J., Michael D., John D. BA, Queens Coll. CUNY, 1967; MA, SUNY, Buffalo, 1969, PhD in Econs., 1972; MS in Higher Ednl. Adminstrn., SUNY, Albany, 1989. Asst. prof. econs. Western Mich. U., Kalamazoo, 1970-74; rsch. assoc. U. Wis., Madison, 1974-75; asst. to assoc. prof. health svcs. adminstrn., econs. Grad. Sch. Pub. Health U. Pitts., 1975-79; assoc. to prof. econs., environ. studies Bard Coll., Annandale-On-Hudson, NY, 1979-88; vis. rsch. fellow Grad. Sch. Edn., H.E. Adminstrn. SUNY, Albany, 1988-89; prof., chmn. dept. pub. adminstrn. Grad. Sch. Pace U., White Plains, NY, 1989-96; vice provost for planning assessment and instnl. rsch. Pace U., NYC, Westchester, 1996-98, v.p. planning, assessment, rsch. and acad. support, 1998—2003, provost, 2003—. Health care and govt. fin. cons. to fed. agencies, state and local govts., pvt. firms, 1979—; adj. prof. law Pace U., 1990-96; adj. prof. pub. adminstrn. Grad. Sch. Pub. Affairs, SUNY-Albany, 1990-96; vis. prof. U. Lancaster, Eng., 1984-85; rsch. assoc., bd. dirs. Hudsonia Environ. Rsch., Annandale, 1985-95; fin. planner Prudential Fin. Svcs., Newburgh, N.Y., 1987-89. Author: Health Care Economics, 1977, Post Tenure Review and Renewal: Experienced Voices, 2002; editor: The U.S. Medical Care Industry, 1974, Post-tenure Review: Policies, Practices, Precautions, 1997; contbr. articles to profl. jours. Appoint pub. rep. Westchester County Deferred Compensation Bd., Mt. Kisco Planning Bd. Recipient NDEA fellowship, 1967-70, Pharm. Mfg. Assn. fellowship, 1969-70, post-doctoral fellowship Health Econ. Rsch. Ctr. U. Wis., 1974-75, rsch. fellowship Grad. Sch. Edn. SUNY-Albany, 1988-89, ACE fellowship UNC, Charlotte, 1995-96, sr. rsch. fellow Harvard IEM Inst., 2000. Mem. Am. Soc. for Pub. Adminstrn., Am. Econ. Assn., Am. Ednl. Fin. Assn., Assn. Instl. Rsch., Am. Assn. Higher Edn., Am. Coun. Edn. (fellow 1995-96). Mem. Soc. Of Friends. Avocations: photography, tennis, music. Office: Pace U VP 1 Pace Plz New York NY 10038-1598 Business E-Mail: jmorreale@pace.edu.

MORREIM, E. HAAVI, medical ethics educator; b. 1950; d. Paul and Florence Morreim. BA in Philosophy, St. Olaf Coll., 1972; MA in Philosophy, U. Va., 1976, PhD, 1980. Med. philosopher program in human biology and soc. U. Va. Sch. Medicine, Charlottesville, 1980-82, asst. prof. philosophy in medicine, 1982-84; from asst. to assoc. prof. dept. human values and ethics U. Tenn. Coll. Medicine, Memphis, 1988—93, prof. dept. human values and ethics, 1993—. Adj. prof. philosophy Va. Commonwealth U., Richmond, 1980; vis. prof. philosophy St. Olaf Coll., Northfield, Minn., 1982; Andrew Mellon vis. asst. prof. humanities and medicine Georgetown U. Sch. Medicine, Washington, 1983; sr. vis. rsch. scholar Kennedy Inst. Ethics, Georgetown U., 1983; manuscript reviewer; presenter and lectr. in field. Author: Balancing Act: The New Medical Ethics of Medicine's New Economics, 1991, Holding Health Care Accountable: Law and the New Medical Marketplace, 2001; bd. editors: Jour. Law, Medicine and Ethics, IRB: Ethics and Human Research, Accountability in Research; contbr. articles to profl. jours. Active Hastings Ctr. Mem. Am. Health Lawyers Assn., Am. Soc. Law, Medicine, and Ethics, Am. Soc. for Bioethics and Humanities, Phi Beta Kappa. Avocations: running, high-performance automobile driving, photography, skiing. Office: Univ Tenn Coll Medicine 910 Madison #314 Memphis TN 38163-2814 Office Phone: 901-448-5725. Business E-Mail: hmorreim@utmem.edu.

MORRELL, AYAKO M., language educator; d. Toshiyuki and Tei Matsukawa; m. Steven R. Morrell, July 10, 1983; children: Robert T., Sean T. MA, Am. U., Washington, 1981. Cert. tchr. Eichi U., Hyogo, Japan, 1971. Tchr. Berlitz Internat. Inc., Summit, NJ, 1993—95, Parsippany Adult & Cmty. Edn., NJ, 1994—96, Bernards Twp. Pub. Sch., Baskin Ridge, NJ, 2001—03; substitute tchr. Morris County Pub. Sch., Parsippany, 1998—2001; Japanese instr. County Coll. Morris, Randolph, NJ, 2005—; Montclair State U., NJ, 2008—. Translator: (children's book) Song of Life, 1992. Business E-Mail: morrella@mail.montclair.edu.

MORRELL, DEAN SCOTT, pediatric dermatologist; b. Norwich, NY, May 11, 1965; s. Edward Arthur and Clarissa (Hyuck) M.; m. Karen Anne Hendrix, Sept. 12, 1989. BS magna cum laude, Wake Forest U., Winston-Salem, NC, 1987; M Phys. Therapy, Hahnemann U., Phila., 1989; MD, U. NC Sch. Medicine, Chapel Hill, 1997. Lic. phys. therapist Md., cert. in dermatology 2001, in pediatric dermatology 2006. Staff phys. therapist Burch, Rhoads, Loomis, P.A., Balt.; internship in pediat. U. NC Hosps., Chapel Hill, 1997—98, residency in dermatology, 1998—2000; fellow in pediatric dermatology Children's Hosp. Wis., Med. Coll. Wis., Milw., 2000—01; asst. prof. dermatology U. NC Sch. Medicine, 2001—06, assoc. prof., program dir., dir. pediatric and adolescent dermatology, dept. dermatology, 2006—. Contbr. articles to profl. jours., chapters to books. Coach YMCA Ladies Baseball Team, Towson, Md., 1990. Mem. Am. Phys. Therapy Assn. Democrat. Methodist. Avocations: running, basketball, volleyball. Office: U NC Sch Medicine Dept Dermatology 3100 Thurston-Bowles Bldg CB 7287 Chapel Hill NC 27599-7287 Office Phone: 919-966-0785. Office Fax: 919-966-3898.

MORRELL, ROBERT HANLY, television producer, director; b. Fayetteville, Nc, Dec. 6, 1951; s. Robert Hanly and Kathleen Hook Morrell; children: Eden, Rebecca. BA, Columbia Coll., Hollywood, Calif., 1980. Dir. WLTX-TV, Columbia, SC, 1981—84; prodr. dir. SCETV, Spartanburg, SC, 1987—; sales rep. Paramount Pictures Corp., LA, 1980—81; adj. prof. USC Upstate, Columbia, 1995—2008. Bd. dirs. Carolina Foothills Artisan Ctr., Chesnee, SC, 2007—08; bd. advisors Swofford Career Ctr., Chesnee, 2000—. Prodr.(dir.): (TV series) Impressions; editor: (documentary) Gilliard's Charleston (Silver Addie, 2006). Episcopalian. Avocations: surfing, travel, baseball.

MORRICAL, ART ANDREW, communications engineer; b. Kankakee, Ill., Mar. 22, 1960; s. Victor and Helen Morrical; m. Rogene Kugler, June 9, 1984; children: Jeffery Ryan, Linda Ann. BS in Elec. Engring. Tech., Bradley U., Peoria, Ill., 1982; MSc in Computer Sci., North Ctrl. Coll., Naperville, Ill., 1989. Cert. quality engr., Am. Soc. Quality, 1989, lead assessor, Brit. Standards Instn., London, 1995, project mgemt. profl., Project Mgmt. Inst., 2007. Sr. engr. GTE Comm. Systems, Northlake, Ill., 1982—85; quality mgr. AT&T Bell Labs., Lucent Technologies/Alcatel-Lucent, Naperville, 1985—. Sec. N.Am. region QuEST Forum, 2007—08, founding contbr., 1997—2007; founder, chair Gt. Lakes TL 9000 Spl. Interest Group, Naperville, 2003—09; mem. leadership coun. QuEST Forum; vice chair Ams. Region QuESt Forum, 2008—09; trustee Sugar Grove Pub. Libr., Ill., 1996—97, v.p., 1997—99, pres., bd. trustees, 1999—. Recipient Leadership award, QuEST Forum, 2001, Outstanding Leadership and Contbn. award, 2005, 2007—08. Mem.: Ill. Libr. Assn., ALA, Project Mgmt. Inst., Am. Soc. Quality. Avocations: juggling, genealogy. Home: 225 Bastian Dr Sugar Grove IL 60554 Office Phone: 630-224-4158. Personal E-mail: tl9000guru@aol.com, art@artmorrical.com. Business E-Mail: art.morrical@alcatel-lucent.com.

MORRILL, ALLEN S., library director; b. Champaign, Ill., July 26, 1960; s. Walter D. and Marcia S. Morrill; m. Susan Carrigan, May 26, 1963; children: Thomas S., Madelene S., Annabelle L. BA, Hanover Coll., Ind., 1983; MLS, Ind. U., Bloomington, 1985. Libr. Nat. Soc. SAR, Louisville, 1985—89; libr. dir. Kans. City Art Inst., Mo., 1989—99; assoc. dean libr. and info. svc. Mass. Coll. Liberal Arts, North Adams, Mass., 1999—2007; dir. langenheim meml. libr. Thiel Coll., Greenville, Pa., 2007—. Pres. Mass. Conf. Chief Libr. Profl. Higher Ednl. Institutions MCCLPHEI, Mass., 2002—03, Ctrl. Western Mass. Automated Resource Sharing CWMARS, Worcester, Mass., 2004—05; boardmember Western Mass. Regional Libr. Sys., Hadley, 2004—07. Red feather soc. United Way, North Adams, Mass., 2005—07; moderator First Congl. Ch. North Adams, United Ch. Christ, North Adams, Mass., 2003—07; bd. mem. Berkshire Arts and Tech. Pub. Charter Sch., Adams, Mass., 2005—07. Mem.: ALA (clip note com. 1991—97). Mem. Christian Ch. Avocations: photography, fly fishing. Office: Thiel Coll 75 College Ave Greenville PA 16125 Office Fax: 724-589-2122. Business E-Mail: amorrill@thiel.edu.

MORRILL, DONALD, dean, director; b. Des Moines, Iowa, July 24, 1955; PhD, U. Fla., Gainesville, 1985. Interim dean Coll. Arts & Letters U. Tampa, Fla. Bd. dirs. Assn. Writers & Writing Programs, Fairfax, Va., 2006—. Author: (book) A Stranger's Neighborhood (Emerging Writer award, 1998), Sounding for Cool, The Untouched Minutes (River Teeth Lit. Nonfiction award, 2002), Impetuous Sleeper, At the Bottom of the Sky (award, 1998), With Your Back to Half the Day. Fulbright fellow, 1988. Office: Univ Tampa 401 W Kennedy Blvd Tampa FL 33606

MORRILL, JOYCE MARIE, social worker, educator, photographer; b. Rockland, Maine, Dec. 27, 1939; d. Henry Higgins and Julia Ellen (Philbrook) Thompson; m. Edward Morrill, Sept. 7, 1972; 1 son, Gregory Hodgeman; 1 stepchild, Shawn Morrill. BA, U. Hartford, 1964; MSW, Hunter Coll., 1972. Co-host Today in Conn. Program Sta. WHNB-TV, Hartford, 1964—65; clin. social worker, field instr. Rehab. Inst., NYC, 1972—78; dir., founder Wellness Svcs., Jamaica Estates, NY, 1979—95; pres. Morrill Support, 1996—. Photographer-artist. Mem.: NASW, Pen & Brush Inc., Inst. Noetic Scis., Alliance of Queens Artists, Profl. Woman Photographers. Home and Office: 181-38 Midland Pky Jamaica NY 11432 E-mail: joyce@morrillsupport.com.

MORRILL, NANCY PORTER, management consultant; b. Natick, Mass., Apr. 14, 1939; d. Rupert Felch and Vera (Richardson) Porter; m. William Ashley Morrill, Aug. 26, 1978; 4 stepchildren. AB in Polit. Sci., Bryn Mawr Coll., 1960. Sr. report specialist McKinsey & Co., Inc., San Francisco, 1960—61; pers. sec., confidential asst. Hon. Edward W. Brooke, Mass. State Atty Gen. and U.S. Senator, 1962—69; pers. asst. to chmn. Diebold Group, NYC, 1969—70; staff asst. Am. Revolution Bicentennial Commn., Washington, 1970—71; Washington rep. Girl Scouts U.S.A., Washington, 1971—73; spl. asst. to sec. HEW, Washington, 1973—77; owner, pres. New Perceptions, New Hope, Pa., 1977—. Commr. Am. Revolution Bicentennial Commn., 1971-73; mem. exec. com., bd. dir. Girl Scouts U.S.A., N.Y.C., 1974-78; NCO del. UN Conf. IWY, Mexico City, 1975; del.-at-large Women's Nat. Conf., Houston, 1977; pres., bd. dirs. Planned Parenthood Assn. Bucks County, 1981-86; founding pres. Bucks County Women's Fund, Pa., 1989-94, v.p. bd., 2006-; chair ann. fund com. Bryn Mawr Coll., 1990-93; co-founder, bd. dir. Bucks County Wine and Food Festival, 1992-97; mem. steering com. Bucks County Ops. and Rev. Evaluation Com., 1992; mem. Bucks County Adv. Coun. Human Svcs., 1992-98; coord. cmty. partnerships Pennsbury Sch. Dist., 1995-2005; bd. advisors leadership program Lower Bucks Chamber, 1999—; co-founder arts and cultural coun. Bucks County, 2002—, bd. dir. 2008-. Named Woman of Vision, Bucks County Women's Fund, 1994, Bucks County Women of Achievement in Pub. Svc., March of Dimes, 2007, Bucks County Womens History award, 2008. Democrat. Avocations: tennis, travel, food and wine, cooking, gardening. Home: N206 Pennswood Village 1382 Newtown-Langhorne Rd Newtown PA 18940 Personal E-mail: npmorrill@comcast.net.

MORRIS, AMY, biology professor; PhD, Idaho State U., Pocatello, 2001. Assoc. prof. biology Hastings Coll., Nebr., 2001—. Office: Hastings Coll 710 N Turner Ave Hastings NE 68901

MORRIS, ARLENE MYERS, biopharmaceutical company executive; b. Washington, Pa., Dec. 29, 1951; d. Frank Hayes Myers and Lula Irene (Slusser) Kolcun; m. John L. Sullivan, Feb. 17, 1971 (div. July 1982); m. David Wellons Morris, July 27, 1984. BA in Biology & Chemistry, Carlow Coll., 1974; postgrad., Western New England Coll., 1981-82. Sales rep. Syntex Labs., Inc., Palo Alto, Calif., 1974-77; profl. sales rep. McNeil Pharm., Spring House, Pa., 1977-78, mental health rep., 1978-80, asst. product dir., 1981-82, dist. mgr., 1982-85, new product dir., 1985-87, exec. dir. new bus. devel., 1987-89, v.p. bus. devel., 1989-93, Scios Inc., Mountain View, Calif., 1993-96; sr. v.p. bus. devel. Coulter Pharmaceutical, Inc., 1996—2001; pres., CEO Clearview Projects, 2001—03, Affymax, Inc., 2003—; chairperson Nuon Therapeutics, Inc., 2009—. Bd. dirs. Affymax, Inc., 2003—, Nuon Therapeutics, Inc., 2009—, MediciNova, Inc. Mem. Found. of Ind. Colls., Phila., 1989. Mem. Pharm. Advt. Coun., Am. Diabetes Assn., Am. Acad. Sci., Healthcare Bus. Womens Assn., Lic. Execs. Soc. Office: Affymax Inc 4001 Miranda Ave Palo Alto CA 94304*

MORRIS, BRAD, legislative staff member; B, George Wash. U., Washington, 1997; M, U. Miss., 1999; JD, U. Miss. Sch. Law, 2008. Chief of staff to Rep. Travis Childers US House of Reps., Washington, 2008—. Democrat. Office: 1708 Longworth House Office Bldg Washington DC 20515 Office Phone: 202-225-4306. Office Fax: 202-225-3549. Business E-Mail: brad.morris@mail.house.gov.*

MORRIS, BRENDA DENISE, music educator, director; b. Kansas City, Mo., Mar. 27, 1952; d. Clyde Edward and Irene Perdue; m. Casey Thomas Morris, June 1, 1991; m. Walter Edward Freeman (dec.); children: Kerri, Michelle, Derek, Jamie. At, U. Mo. Music Conservatory, Kansas City. Pvt. music tchr., 1967—2006; prin. tchr. Prodigy Sch. MusicArts, 2006—. Ch. musician First Assembly of God Ch., 1961—70; condr. 12th grade Lee's Summit H.S., 1969—70; music dir. Longview Christian Ch., 1989—99, Longview Bapt. Ch., 2000—02, One Spirit Meth. Ch., Kansas City, 2004—, Aldersgate Meth. Ch., Olathe, Kans.

MORRIS, BRIAN, state supreme court justice; b. Butte, Mont., Sept. 5, 1963; m. Cherche Prezeau; 3 children. BA in Economics, Stanford U., 1986, MA in Economics, 1987; JD, Stanford Law Sch., 1992. Law clerk for Judge John T. Noonan, Jr. U.S. Ct. of Appeals for Ninth Circuit, 1992—93; law clerk for Justice William H. Rehnquist U.S. Supreme Ct., 1993—94; legal asst. Iran-U.S. Claims Tribunal, The Hague, 1994—95; prtnr. Goetz, Gallik, Baldwin & Dolan, 1995—99; sr. legal officer UN Compensation Commn., 2000—01; state solicitor Mont. Dept. of Justice, 2001—04; justice Mont. Supreme Ct., 2005—. Author several law review and professional jour. articles. Office: Mont Supreme Ct PO Box 203003 Helena MT 59620-3003*

MORRIS, CHARLOTTE ANN, media specialist, school librarian; b. Tampa, Oct. 16, 1946; d. Frank A. and Charlotte C. Hutchinson; 1 child, Theresa M. BS in Edn., U. SC., Columbia, 1968; MLS, U. Ariz., Tucson, 1974. Cert. NBPTS, 2003. Media specialist Millwood Elem., Sumter, SC, 1968—70, Marshall Elem. Sch., Flagstaff, Ariz., 1970—73, Denny Terrace Elem., Flagstaff, 1985—2000; media specialist-ITS Caughman Rd Elem., Columbia, 2000—08. Children's libr. ABBE Regional Libr., Aiken, SC, 1974—76, Flagstaff City Coconino County Pub. Libr., 1976—85. Sunday sch. tchr. Greenlawn Bapt. Ch., Columbia, 1989—2006. Baptist. Achievements include Estabblished Children's Services division for ABBE Regional Library; Facilitated Puppet Power group in Northern Arizona; Helped write Information Literacy standards for Richland School District One. Avocations: camping, gardening. Office: Caughman Rd Elem 7725 Caughman Rd Columbia SC 29209 Business E-Mail: cmorris@richlandone.org.

MORRIS, DAVID, science educator; s. Charles Morris and Nancy Fiers; m. Adina Morris, Dec. 28, 1996; children: Dora, Athena. MS in Applied Geoscis., San Francisco State U., 1998. Instr. astronomy & geology Eastern Ariz. Coll., Thatcher, 1991—. Office: Eastern Ariz Coll 615 N Stadium Ave Thatcher AZ 85552 Business E-Mail: david.morris@eac.edu.

MORRIS, DESMOND (JOHN), zoologist, writer, artist; s. Harry Howe Morris and Dorothy Marjorie (Hunt) Fuller; m. Ramona Joy Baulch, July 30, 1952; 1 son, Jason. BSc, Birmingham U., Eng., 1951; DPhil, Oxford U., Eng., 1954; DSc (hon.), Reading U., Eng., 1998. Rsch. worker zoology U. Oxford, Eng., 1954-56; head Granada T.V. and Film Unit, Zool. Soc. London, 1956-59, curator mammals, 1959-67; dir. Inst. Contemporary Arts, London, 1967-68; rsch. fellow Wolfson Coll., Oxford, 1973-81. Author: Biology of Art, 1962, Apes and Monkeys, 1965, Big Cats, 1965, Mammals: A Guide to the Living Species, 1966, The Naked Ape, 1968, The Human Zoo, 1969, Intimate Behavior, 1971, Manwatching: A Field Guide to Human Behavior, 1977, The Soccer Tribe, 1981, The Book of Ages, 1983, The Art of Ancient Cyprus, 1985, Bodywatching: A Field Guide to the Human Species, 1985, The Illustrated Naked Ape, 1986, Catwatching, 1986, Dogwatching, 1986, The Secret Surrealist, 1987, Catlore, 1987, The Animals Roadshow, 1988, The Human Nestbuilders, 1988, Horsewatching, 1988, The Animal Contract, 1990, Animalwatching, 1990, Babywatching, 1991, Christmas Watching, 1992, The World of Animals, 1993, The Human Animal, 1994, Body Talk, A World Guide to Gestures, 1994, The Naked Ape Trilogy, 1994, Illustrated Cat Watching, 1994, Illustrated Babywatching, 1995, Illustrated Dogwatching, 1996, Catworld: A Feline Encyclopedia, 1996, The Human Sexes, 1997, Illustrated Horsewatching, 1998, Cool Cats: The 100 Cat Breeds of the World, 1999, Body Guards, 1999, Dogs: A Dictionary of Dog Breeds, 2001, Peoplewatching, 2002, The Nature of Happiness, 2004, The Naked Woman, 2004, Watching: Encounters With Humans and Other Animals, 2006, Fantastic Cats, 2006, The Naked Man, 2008, others; co-author: (with Ramona Morris) Men and Snakes, 1965, Men and Apes, 1966, Men and Pandas, 1966, The Giant Panda, 1981, Gestures: Their Origins and Distribution, 1979; autobiography Animal Days, 1979, The Naked Eye, 2000; editor: Primate Ethology, 1969, (fiction) Inrock, 1983; contbr. numerous articles to zool. jours.; one-man shows include Mayor Gallery, London, 1997, Pub. Art Gallery, Buxton, 1997, Keitelman Gallery, Brussels, 1998, Rossaert Gallery, Antwerp, 1998, Witteveen Gallery, Amsterdam, 1999, Mus. Modern Art, Ostend, 2002, others. Address: care Jonathan Cape RandomCH 20 Vauxhall Bridge Rd London SWIV 2SA England

MORRIS, DICK, columnist, political consultant; b. NY, Nov. 28, 1948; s. Eugene Morris; m. Eileen McGann. BA in Govt., Columbia U., NYC, 1967. Polit. cons. Bill Clinton Campaign for Gov., Ark., 1977, Ark., 1982, Bill Clinton Re-Election Campaign for Gov., Ark., 1984, Ark., 1986, Ark., 1990; presdl. adv. Clinton adminstrn., 1992—96; campaign mgr. Bill Clinton Re-Election Campaign for Pres., 1996; chief strategist presdl. campaign Argentina Pres. Fernando de la Rua, 1999, Uruguay Pres. Jorge Battle, 1999, Mexican Reformer Vicente Fox, 2000; commentator FOX News Channel; weekly columnist NY Post, The Hill (print/online). Founder, pres. Vote.com, 1999—; co-founder (with Eileen McGann) Legalvote.com, 2000. Author: Bum Rap on America's Cities - The Real Causes of Urban Decay, 1977, Behind the Oval Office: Getting Re-Elected Against All Odds, 1998, The New Prince: Machiavelli Updated for the 21st Century, 1999, Vote.com - A Guide to the Internet basted politics of the future, 2000, Power Plays: Win or Lose - How History's Great Polit. Leaders Play the Game, 2003, Off With Their Heads: Traitors, Crooks & Obstructionists in Am. Politics, Media & Bus., 2003; co-author (with Eileen McGann): Because He Could, 2004, Rewriting History, 2004, Condi vs. Hillary: The Next Great Presidential Race, 2005, Outrage: How Illegal Immigration, the United Nations, Congressional Ripoffs, Student Loan Overcharges, Tobacco Companies, Trade Protection, and Drug Companies Are Ripping Us Off..., 2007 (NY Times bestseller), Fleeced: How Barack Obama, Media Mockery of Terrorist Threats, Liberals Who Want To Kill Talk Radio, The Do-Nothing Congress, Companies That Help Iran, And Washington Lobbyists For Foreign Governments Are Scamming Us..., 2008 (NY Times bestseller), Catastrophe, 2009 (#1 Publishers Weekly bestseller).

Achievements include working as polit. cons. for winning campaigns of more than 30 senators or governors. Office: NY Post 1211 Avenue Of The Americas New York NY 10036 E-mail: dickmorris@dickmorris.com.*

MORRIS, DONNA JONES, library director; Dir. Ark. Valley Regional Libr. Svc. Sys., Pueblo, Colo., 1985—2004; state libr., dir. Utah State Libr., Salt Lake City, 2004—. Former pres. Colo. Assn. Librs. Recipient Francis Keppel award, 2005; named Colo. Libr. of Yr., 1992. Mem.: ALA (Nat. Advocacy Honor Roll 2000), Utah Libr. Assn., Chief Officers of State Libr. Agencies, Western Coun. State Librs., Utah Academic Libr. Consortium, Mountain Plains Libr. Assn. (Disting. award 2005). Office: Utah State Libr 250 N 1950 W Ste A Salt Lake City UT 84116-7901 Office Phone: 801-715-6770. Office Fax: 801-715-6767. E-mail: dmorris@utah.gov.

MORRIS, DOUG (DOUGLAS PETER MORRIS), recording industry executive; b. Far Rockaway, NY, Nov. 23, 1938; s. Walter and Mary (Lerner) Morris; m. Monique Jequel, Mar. 20, 1964; children: Walter, Peter. BA, Columbia Coll., 1960. Gen. mgr. Robert Mellin, Inc., NYC, 1964—65; writer. producer Laurie Records, Inc., NYC, 1965—69, v.p., gen. mgr.; owner Big Tree Records (acquired by Atlantic Records), NYC, 1970—78; pres. ATCO Records, Swan Song and Rolling Stones Records (subs. of Warner Music), 1978, Atlantic Records, NYC, 1980—90; co-chmn., co-CEO Atlantic Recording Group, NYC, 1990—94; chmn., COO, pres. Warner Music-U.S., 1994—95; chmn., CEO Universal Music Group (formerly MCA Music Ent.), NYC, 1995—. Cons. Ampex Records, 1968; bd. dirs. CBS Corp., 2007—. Composer: (songs) Sweet Talkin Guys, 1968, Smoking in the Boys' Room, 1970; prodr.: (song) Wave on Wave, 2003. Served in US Army, 1962—64. Named Man of Yr. in Record Industry, United Jewish Appeal, 1981; named one of 25 Most Influential People in Web Music, Powergeek 25, 2007; scholar, Paragon Oil, 1954, Columbia Coll., 1960. Mem.: ASCAP. Office: Universal Music Group 1755 Broadway Fl 7 New York NY 10019-3743

MORRIS, DOUGLAS CLAUDE, cardiologist, educator; b. Marietta, Ga., Apr. 18, 1942; BA in Chemistry, Duke U.; MD, Baylor Coll. Medicine, Houston, 1968. Cert. Internal Medicine, Cardiovascular Disease, Interventional Cardiology. Intern, internal medicine Vanderbilt U. Hosp., Nashville, 1968—69, resident, cardiology, 1969—70, 1972—73; fellow Emory U. Hosp., 1973—75; faculty staff mem., dept. medicine, divsn. cardiology Emory U. Sch. Medicine, 1973—, J. Willis Hurst prof. medicine, 1996—; dir., Carlyle Fraser Heart Ctr. Crawford Long Hosp., 1986; dir. Emory Heart Ctr., 1993; vice-chair, dept. medicine Emory U., 1999. Named one of Ten Best Doctors in Cardiovascular Disease, Atlanta Mag., 1999—. Mem.: Soc. Cardiac Angiography, Am. Coll. Cardiology (co-chair scientific sessions 1996—2000), ACP. Avocation: running. Office: Emory U Rm A2205 Emory Clinic 1365A Clifton Rd NE Atlanta GA 30322 Office Phone: 404-778-5310. Office Fax: 404-778-5320. Business E-Mail: douglas.morris@emoryhealthcare.org.

MORRIS, ERROL, filmmaker; b. Hewlett, NY, Feb. 5, 1948; s. Abner and Cinnabelle (Burzinsky) M.; m. Julia Bynum Sheehan; 1 child, Nathaniel Hamilton. BA, U. Wis., 1969; postgrad., Princeton U., 1970-71, U. Calif., Berkeley, 1972-76. Pres. Fourth Floor Prodns., Inc., Cambridge, Mass. Dir., prodr.: (documentaries) Gates of Heaven, 1978, Vernon, Florida, 1982, Fast, Cheap and Out of Control, 1997, Mr. Death: The Rise and Fall of Fred Leuchter, Jr., 1999, The Fog of War: Eleven Lessons from the Life of Robert S. McNamara, 2003 (Acad. award for Best Documentary Feature, 2004, Best Documentary of Yr. Nat. Bd. Review, LA Film Critics Assn.), Standard Operating Procedure, 2008 (Silver Berlin Bear award Berlin Internat. Film Festival, 2008); dir. only: The Thin Blue Line, 1988 (Edgar Allan Poe award for Best Motion Picture, Mystery Writers America, named Best Film of Yr. The Washington Post, named Best Documentary of Yr. NY Film Critics Cir., Nat. Soc. Film Critics), The Dark Wind, 1991, A Brief History of Time, 1992; (TV episodes) First Person, 2001; actor: Hotel New York, 1984 Guggenheim fellow, 1990, MacArthur fellow, 1990-94. Fellow Am. Acad. Arts & Scis.

MORRIS, FRANCIS LOCKWOOD, computer scientist; b. Washington, July 2, 1943; s. Charles Shiras Morris Jr. and Elizabeth Lockwood Morris; m. Diane E. Zimmerman, July 31, 1982. BA in Math., Harvard Coll., Cambridge, MA, 1964; PhD in Computer Sci., Stanford U., Palo Alto, CA, 1972; MS in Mfg. Engring., Syracuse U., NY, 1995. Temp. lectr. in computing sci. U. Essex, Colchester, England, 1969—71; rsch. fellow, computer sci. dept. U. Edinburgh, 1974—75; vis. rsch. fellow, programming rsch. group, vis. fellow Wolfson Coll. Oxford U., England, 1980—81; prof., sch. computer and info. sci. Syracuse U., 1975—93, prof. emeritus, dept. elec. engring. and computer sci. Mem.: Math. Assn. America. Avocations: literature, bridge. Office: Dept of EECS Syracuse Univ College Pl Syracuse NY 13244-4100

MORRIS, G. MICHAEL, science educator; BS in Engring. Physics with spl. distinction, U. Okla., 1975; MS in Elec. Engring., Calif. Inst. Tech., 1976, PhD, 1979. Scientist U. Rochester, Inst. of Optics, 1979—82; prof. of optics U. Roch., Inst. of Optics, 1982—2001; adj. prof. of optics U. Rochester, Inst. of Optics, 2001—; co-founder Rochester Photonics Corp. (RPC), 1989—. CEO Apollo Optical Systems LLC, Rochester Photonics Corp., 1989—. Recipient Rochester C. of C. Civic award for sci. and tech., 1997. Fellow: Optical Soc. of Am. (pres. 2003); mem.: Optical Soc. of Am., Rochester Sect. (hon.). Office: Optical Society of America 8SCR Lane Victor NY 14564

MORRIS, G. RONALD, automotive executive; b. East St. Louis, Ill., Aug. 30, 1936; s. George H. and Mildred C. M.; m. Margaret Heino, June 20, 1959; children: David, Michele, James. BS in Metall. Engring, U. Ill., 1959. Metall. engr. Delco-Remy divsn. Gen. Motors Corp., 1959-60; factory metallurgist Dubuque Tractor Works, John Deere Co., Iowa, 1960-66; with Fed.-Mogul Corp., 1966-79, v.p., group mgr. ball and roller bearing group, 1979; pres. Tenneco Automotive divsn. Tenneco, Inc., Deerfield, Ill., 1979-82; pres., CEO PT Components, Inc., Indpls., 1982-88; vice-chmn. Rexnord Corp., Indpls., 1988-89; chmn., pres., CEO CTP Holdings Inc., 1986-88; chmn. Integrated Technologies, Inc., Indpls., 1990-92, also bd. dirs.; pres., CEO Western Industries, Inc., Milw., 1991-99. Bd. dirs. NN, Inc., Erwin, Tenn., Prism Capital Inc. Mem. Pres.'s Coun., U. Ill., mem. sr. adv. bd. Sch. Materials Sci. and Engring, U. Ill.; mem. U. Ill. Found. Mem. ASM, SAE, The Landings Club (Savannah, Ga.), Masons, Scottish Rite, Kiwanis Internat. Republican. Presbyterian. E-mail: savannahronm@yahoo.com.

MORRIS, GERALD DOUGLAS, newspaper editor; b. Boston, May 7, 1937; s. George Christopher and Lucy Bell (MacPhee) M.; m. Elaine Louise Owen, Nov. 13, 1964 (div. 1976); children: Laura Louise, Douglas Owen; m. Mary Elizabeth Simpson Stevens, Apr. 15, 1977; children: Jeffrey David Stevens Morris, Wendy Elizabeth Stevens Morris. Student, Boston U., 1959. Reporter Patriot Ledger, Quincy, Mass., 1961-66; copy editor Boston Globe, 1966—, travel editor, 1989—. Syndicated columnist Globe-Trotting, 1970—. Author: Boston Globe Guide to Boston, 1989, New England under Sail, 1993, Guide to Cape Cod, 1999. Chmn. Canton (Mass.) Cable Adv. Bd., 1990-92; bd. dirs. Lowell Thomas Found., 1997. With U.S. Army, 1959-61. Mem. Soc. Am. Travel Writers (chmn. N.E. chpt. 2000—), Skal Club Boston, Lions (pres. Canton 1969-70, 80-81). Avocations: photography, travel. Office: Globe Newspaper Co 135 Morrissey Blvd Boston MA 02125-3310 Home: 165 Taylors Pond Rd South Chatham MA 02659-1643

MORRIS, GORDON JAMES, financial company executive, consultant; b. Mt. Vernon, Ohio, Oct. 6, 1942; s. R. Hugh and Betty Jane (Roberts) M.; m. Janet Ann Swanson, Aug. 28, 1965 (div. 1971); m. Nancy Joan Meyfarth, July 26, 1975 (div. Oct. 1998); 1 child, Lawrence Hugh; m. Phyllis J. Hersha, Jan. 1, 2000. Student, Ohio State U., 1960-61; BA, Otterbein Coll., 1966; postgrad. in law, Capital U., Bexley, Ohio, 1967-68; postgrad., Coll. Fin. Planning, Denver, 1983-90, Inst. Cert. Fund Specialists, 1991. Registered investment advisor; cert. fin. planner; cert. fund specialist; lic. loving trust advisor; cert. divorce planner; life lic., Fla., 1974—; security lic. NASD, 1976—; real estate lic., Fla., 1986—. Asst. to pres. Jaeger Machine Co., Columbus, Ohio, 1968-73; rep. Equitable Fin. Svcs., Sarasota, Fla., 1974-81; pres. Beacon Wealth Mgmt. (formerly Morris & Assocs., P.A.), Sarasota, 1981—; co-gen. ptnr. Beacon Bridge Loan Pool, Ltd., 1994-97. Chmn. bd. dirs. MAP Fin. Group, Inc., Sarasota, 1985-89; co-owner U.S.I.S.L. West Fla. Fury Soccer Team, 1996-98; bd. dirs., v.p. Soccer Resource Group, Sarasota, 1997-99, Radyx Capital Ptnr., Tampa, 1999-2003, seminar lectr. High Mark Ins. Svcs., Inc., Beacon Wealth Mgmt., 2003-09. Past columnist The Creative News. Past chmn. West Coast chpt. March of Dimes, Bradenton, Fla., bd. dirs., 1986-88; v.p. All Sch. Kids, Inc., 1998-99; pres. Epilepsy Found. S.W. Fla., Inc., 1986-87. Mem. Inst. Cert. Fin. Planners, Million Dollar Roundtable, Sertoma (pres. local club 1979-80). Republican. Methodist. Home and Office: 3822 Countryside Ln Sarasota FL 34233-2122 Personal E-mail: gim.buckeye@yahoo.com. Business E-Mail: beaconl@sigmarep.com.

MORRIS, GREG, director, former federal agency administrator; b. 1958; m. Karen Morris; 4 children. BS in Bus. Adminstrn., W.Va. Wesleyan Coll., 1980; MBA, W.Va. U., 1987. Exec. dir. W.Va. Health Care Authority, 1998—2001; chief of staff, sr. adv. to adminstr. Substance Abuse & Mental Health Services Adminstrn. (SAMSHA) US Dept. Health & Human Services, Rockville, Md., 2001—04; dir. Ctr. for Faith-Based & Comm. Initiatives (CFBCI) US Dept. Health & Human Services (HHS), Washington, 2004—07, dep. chief of staff, 2007—09; CEO PACE TEC (Tng. & Evaluation Ctr.), Inc. W.Va. Wesleyan Coll., Morgantown, W.Va., 2009—. Office: PACE Training & Evaluation Ctr 420 Pleasant Hill Ave PO Box 4241 Morgantown WV 26504 Office Phone: 304-599-0513. Office Fax: 304-598-2224.*

MORRIS, HENRY MADISON, III, minister, writer, speech professional, consultant; b. El Paso, Tex., May 15, 1942; s. Henry Madison and Mry Louis (Beach) M.; m. Janet Deckman, July 25, 1965; children: Henry M., Scotta Marie. BA summa cum laude, Christian Heritage Coll., 1976; MDiv, Luther Rice Sem., 1977; DMin, 1978; MBA, Pepperdine U., 1989. Ordained to ministry Bapt. Ch., 1968. Regional mgr. Integon Ins. Co., Greenville, SC, 1969-75; pastor Hallmark Bapt. Ch., Greenville, SC, 1969-75; assoc. prof. Bible Christian Heritage Coll., El Cajon, Calif., 1977-78; adminstrv. v.p., 1978-80; pastor First Bapt. Ch., Canoga Park, Calif., 1980-86; chief adminstrv. officer, CFO SunGard Fin. Sys. Inc., Canoga Park, 1986-94; v.p. sales and mktg., 1994-96; adminstrv. pastor Ch. at Rocky Peak, Chatsworth, Calif., 1996-99; regional sales mgr. SunGard Ins. Sys., 2000—06; exec. v.p. Inst. for Creation Rsch., Santee, Calif., 2002—07, CEO, 2007—. Cons. World Pubs., 1995; commr. Transitional Assn. Christian Colls. and Schs., 2003-08; lectr. in field. Author: Baptism: What is It?, 1977, Explore the Word, 1978, Churches: History and Doctrine, 1980, After Eden, 2003; co-author: Many Infallible Proofs, 1996, Sampling the Psalms, 1999, 5 Reasons to Believe in Recent Creation, 2008, Exploring the Evidence for Creation, 2009, The Big 3: Three Events That Charged All, 2009; contbg. editor: The Defenders Bible, 1995; contbr. articles to profl. publs. Served with U.S. Army, 1959-66. Republican. Office: Inst for Creation Rsch 1806 Royal Ln Dallas TX 75229 Office Phone: 214-615-8300. Business E-Mail: hmorrisiii@icr.org.

MORRIS, JAMES BRUCE, internist; b. Rochester, NY, May 13, 1943; s. Max G. and Beatrice Ruth (Becker) M.; m. Susan Carol Shencup, July 31, 1966; children: Carrie, Douglas, Deborah, Rebecca. BA, U. Rochester, 1964; MD, Yale U., 1968. Diplomate Am. Bd. Internal Medicine, Am. Bd. Infectious Diseases. Intern SUNY, Buffalo, 1968-69, resident, 1969-70, 72-73, chief resident, 1973; pvt. practice medicine & infectious diseases Plantation, Fla., 1974—. Chmn. infection control com. Lauderdale Lakes Gen. Hosp., 1974-76; chmn. infection control com. Plantation Gen. Hosp., 1976-80, 83-85, chmn. pharmacy com., 1980-81, chmn. tissue com., 1982; sec., program chmn. dept. medicine Bennett Community Hosp., 1978-80, chmn. dept. medicine, 1980-81, vice chief staff, 1981-83; chmn. infection control com. Fla. Med. Center, 1980-82; chief staff Humana Hosp. Bennett, 1983-85, trustee, 1983-88, chmn. infection control com., 1985-87; clin. assoc. prof. U. Miami Med. Sch., 1975—, bd. trustees Westside Regional Med. Ctr., 2008-. With USAR, 1970-72. Recipient Recognition, Town & Country Guide to Primary Care Physicians; named one of Top Docs in South Fla., Miami Metro; fellow, U. Miami, 1974. Fellow ACP; mem. AMA, Am. Soc. Microbiology, Infectious Diseases Soc. Am., Am. Soc. Internal Medicine, Fla. Med. Assn., Broward County Med. Assn. Office: Morris Sklaver Mestre & Perez MD PA 7353 NW 4th St Plantation FL 33317-2202 Office Phone: 954-584-9111.

MORRIS, JAMES CARL, architect; b. Richmond, Va., Sept. 2, 1930; s. James Carl and Florence Virginia (Hey) M.; m. Frances Parrott Wooten, June 9, 1952; children: James Carl Jr., David Palmer. Student, N.C. State U., 1948—50; BS in Bldg. Constrn., Va. Polytechnic Inst., Blacksburg, 1952. Cert. Nat. Coun. Archtl. Registration Bds. Archtl. draftsman Va. Electric & Power Co., Richmond, Va., 1955-56, Marcellus, Wright & Son, Richmond, 1956-57; architect C.W. Huff, Jr., Richmond, 1957; ptnr. to prin./owner Huff-Morris Architects, Richmond, 1966—2006. Ptnr. JCM Partnership, Chesterfield, 1988—; cons. to Huff-Morris Arch. PC, 2006-. Contbr. articles to profl. jours. Bd. dirs. Chesterfield Preservation Commn.; deacon Branch's Ch., Richmond, 1986-; mem. Va. Bapt. Extension Bd., Richmond, 1991-2001, 2004-; mem. 250th anniversary com. Chesterfield County, 1999. With U.S. Army, 1953-54. Recipient award of Merit S.S. Bd. of So. Bapt., Nashville, Excellence in Masonry Design award Va. Masonry Coun., Richmond. Mem. AIA (past pres. Richmond chpt.), Commonwealth Club of Va. Avocations: woodworking, fishing, hunting. Home: 5907 Village Lake Ct Richmond VA 23234-6945 Home Phone: 804-275-1782.

MORRIS, JAMES MALACHY, lawyer; b. Champaign, Ill., June 5, 1952; s. Walter Michael and Ellen Frances (Solon) M.; m. Mary Delilah Baker, Oct. 17, 1987; children: James Malachy Jr., Elliot Rice Baker, Walter Michael, Nicholas Aidan. Student, Oxford U., Eng., 1972; BA, Brown U., 1974; JD, U. Pa., 1977. Bar: NY 1978, US Dist. Ct. (so. and ea. dists.) NY 1978, Ill. 1980, US Tax Ct. 1982, US Supreme Ct. 1983; admitted to Barristers Chambers, Manchester, Eng., 1987. Assoc. Reid & Priest, NYC, 1977-80; sr. law clk. Supreme Ct. Ill., Springfield, 1980-81; assoc. Carter, Ledyard & Milburn, NYC, 1981-83; sole practice NYC, 1983-87; counsel FCA, Washington, 1987—2006; acting sec., gen. counsel FCS Ins. Corp., McLean, Va., 1990-98, exec. asst., bd. chmn., 2005—06, gen counsel, 2006—. Cons. Internat. Awards Found., Zurich, 1981—2002, Pritzker Architecture Prize Found., NYC, 1981—2002, Herbert Oppenheimer, Nathan & VanDyck, London, 1985—2004. Contbr. articles to profl. jours. Recipient FCA Trust award, 2001. Mem. ABA, Ill. Bar Assn., NY State Bar Assn., NY County Lawyers Assn., Assn. Bar City NY, Brit. Inst. Internat. and Comparative Law, Am. Inst. Parliamentarians, Lansdowne Club (London), Penn Club (NYC), Casanova (Va.) Hunt Club. Office: PO Box 1407 Mc Lean VA 22101-1407

MORRIS, JAMES T., insurance company executive; BA, UCLA, 1982. Asst. actuary, spl. mktg. Pacific Life Ins. Co., Newport Beach, Calif., 1982—86, asst. v.p. product rsch. & develop., 1986—87, 2d v.p. product design & develop., 1987—90, v.p. product design, 1990—93, v.p. m-ops., 1993—96, sr. v.p. m-ops., 1996—2002, exec. v.p. life ins. div., 2002—05, exec. v.p. chief ins. officer, 2005—06, COO, 2006—07, pres., CEO, 2007—08, chmn., pres., CEO, 2008—. Fellow: Soc. Actuaries; mem.: Am. Acad. Actuaries, LA Actuarial Club. Office: Pacific Life Ins Co 700 Newport Ctr Dr Newport Beach CA 92658-9030

MORRIS, JAMES THOMAS, former international organization official; b. Terre Haute, Ind., Apr. 18, 1943; s. Howard James and Kathlyne (Eastes) M.; m. Jacqueline Harrell, Apr. 2, 1965; children: John Timothy, Jeffrey Todd, Jennifer Lynn. BA in Polit. sci., geography, Ind. U., Bloomington, 1965; MBA, Butler U., Indpls., 1970; DBA (hon.), Vincennes U., 1978, Butler U., 1982, Ind. State U., 1985, U. So. Ind., 1987, Franklin Coll., 1987, Rose-Hulman Inst. Tech., 1990, Martin U., 1992. Trainee Am. Fletcher Nat. Bank, Indpls., 1966-67; adminstrv. asst., chief of staff Mayor Richard G. Lugar, Indpls., 1967-73; v.p. Lilly Endowment, Inc., Indpls., 1973-84, pres., 1984-89, Indpls. Water Co. and IWC Resources, 1989—2002; exec. dir. World Food Programme UN, Rome, 2002—06. Mem. U.S. del. NATO Com. on Challenges of Modern Soc., 1970-71; bd. dir., Am. Red Cross (treas. and chmn. audit and ethics com.); mem., US Olympics Com. Chmn. bd. trustees Marion County Health and Hosp. Corp., 1976-83; chmn., trustee Ind. State U., 1971-79; bd. dirs. Indpls. Conv. and Visitors Assn., United Way of Greater Indpls., 1980—, Goodwill Industries Ind., Greater Indpls. Progress com., YMCA of Greater Indpls., Boy Scouts Am.; mem. exec. bd. U.S. Olympic Com., 1985-92; trustee, vice chmn. U.S. Olympic Found., 1987-93, Butler U., Christian Theol. Sem.; mem. U.S. Olympic Oversight Commn., 1988; elder Second Presbyn. Ch.; trustee NCAA Found., 1990, Freedoms Found., 1990; apptd. dir. by Pres. Bush Environ. of The Americas Bd., 1991. Named Outstanding Young Man in Indpls., 1972, one of five Outstanding Young Hoosiers, 1973; recipient Disting. Eagle Scout award, 1985, Disting. Alumni award Butler U., 1986, Disting. Service award Ind. U., 1987, Disting. Alumni Svc. award Ind. U., 1991, Horatio Alger award 1992, Whitney Young award Indpls. Urban League, numerous awards received from various field. Mem. Indpls. C. of C. (bd. dirs. 1985-89), Meridian Clubs, One Am. Mut. Holding Co. (bd dirs.), Nat. Adv. Bd, Boy Scouts Am., NCAA (chmn.), NCAA Found. (bd. dirs.), NCAA Adv. Bd., Riley Children's Foundation (trustee) Republican. Office: Pacers Sports & Entertainment One Conseco Ct 125 South Pennsylvania St Indianapolis IN 46204 Home Phone: 317-917-2520. Office Fax: 317-917-2799.

MORRIS, JEFFREY BRANDON, law educator; b. NYC, Jan. 8, 1941; s. Richard B. and Berenice (Robinson) M.; m. Dona Gene Baron, July 9, 1972; children: David Brandon, Deborah Helaine. AB, Princeton U., 1962; JD, Columbia U., 1965, PhD in Polit. Sci., 1972. Bar: N.Y. 1967, U.S. Supreme Ct. 1970, D.C. 1978, U.S. Dist. Ct. D.C. 1978. Lectr., instr., asst. prof. CUNY, NYC, 1968-74; spl. asst. to provost Columbia U., NYC, 1974-76; jud. fellow U.S. Supreme Ct., Washington, 1976-77, rsch. assoc. adminstrv. asst. chief justice, 1977-81; asst. prof. polit. sci. U. Pa., Phila., 1981-88; vis. assoc. prof. Bklyn. Law Sch., NYC, 1988-90; from assoc. prof. to prof. law Touro Law Sch., Huntington, NY, 1990—. Rapporteur Nat. Conf. on Causes Population Dissatisfaction, with Popular Dissatisfaction Adminstrn. of Justice, St. Paul, 1976; cons. bicentennial exhibitions Independence Nat. Hist. Park, 1986. Author: Federal Justice in the Second Circuit, 1988, U.S. District Court Eastern District N.Y., 1965-90, 1992, Making Sure We are True to Our Founders, 1997, Brooklyn Law School: The First Hundred Years, 2001, History Of Courts District Of Columbia Court, Calmly to Poise the Scales of Justice, 2001, Establishing Justice In Middle America: A History Of The United States Court Of Appeals For The Eighth Circuit, 2007; co-author: A Pocket History of the United States, 9th rev. edit., 1992; editor: Encyclopedia of American History, 1982, 7th edit., 1996; assoc. editor Yearbook, Supreme Ct. Hist. Soc., 1979-83. Mem. Brookings Conf. on Interbr. Rels., Williamsburg, Va., 1980, 81. Jewish. Avocations: opera, dance, theater. Home: 234 Forest Rd Flushing NY 11363-1303 Office: Touro Law Sch 225 Eastview Dr Central Islip NY 11722 Business E-Mail: jeffreym@tourolaw.edu.

MORRIS, JOHN, composer, conductor, arranger; b. Elizabeth, NJ; s. Thomas Arthur and Helen (Sherratt) M.; m. Francesca Bosetti; children: Evan Bosetti, Bronwen Helen. Student, Julliard Sch. Music, 1946-48, U. Wash., 1947, New Sch. Social Research, 1946-49. Composer (film) The Producers, The Twelve Chairs, The Gamblers, Blazing Saddles (nominated Acad. award 1976), The Bank Shot, Young Frankenstein, Sherlock Holmes Smarter Brother, Silent Movie, The Last Remake of Beau Geste, The In-Laws, The World's Greatest Lover, In God We Trust, High Anxiety, The Elephant Man (nominated Acad. award 1981), Table for Five, History of the World Part I, Yellowbeard, The Doctor and the Devils, Clue, To Be or Not To Be, Woman in Red, Johnny Dangerously, Haunted Honeymoon, Dirty Dancing, Spaceballs, Ironweed, The Wash, Stella, Life Stinks; (Broadway stage plays) My Mother, My Father and Me, Doll's House, Camino Real; (mus.) A Time for Singing; (off-Broadway) Take One Step, Young Andy Jackson, N.Y. Shakespeare Festival Much Ado About Nothing, Peer Gynt, Richard III, Love's Labor's Lost, Electra, As You Like It, Comedy of Errors, Titus Andronicus, Henry IV Parts 1 and 2, Romeo and Juliet, Hamlet, The Cherry Orchard, Stratford Connecticut Shakespeare Festival The Tempest, Julius Caesar, Antony and Cleopatra, Measure for Measure, Twelfth Night, Lincoln Ctr. King Lear; (TV) Fresno, Katherine Anne Porter, Ghost Dancing, The Firm, The Mating Season, Splendor in the Grass, The Electric Grandmother, The Scarlet Letter, The Adams Chronicles, Georgia O'Keeffe, The Franken Project, The Tap Dance Kid (Emmy award 1986), Make Believe Marriage, ABC After Sch. Spl. Theme, Making Things Grow Theme, The French Chef Theme, The Desperate Hours, The Skirts of Happy Chance, Infancy and Childhood, The Fig Tree, The Little Match Girl, Our Sons, The Last to Go, The Last Best Year, The Sunset Gang, Coach Theme, Favorite Son, Journey Into Genius, When Lions Roared, Scarlett Mini Series, With God On Our Side, Ellen Foster, Murder in a Small Town, The Lady in Question, Tribute to Julie Harris, Only Love, Blackwater Lightship, From Kansas to Kandahar, documentary films; mus. supr., condr., arranger numerous TV spls., Broadway and off-Broadway shows and recs. including Anne

Bancroft Spl. #1 (Emmy award), 'S Lemmon 'S Gershwin 'S Wonderful (Emmy award), Hallmark Christmas Spls.; (Broadway) Peter Pan, Bells Are Ringing, Bye-Bye Birdie, All-American, Wild Cat, Kwanmina, Baker Street, Mack and Mabel, Much Ado About Nothing; (off-Broadway) Hair; (records) Wildcat, All-American, Bells Are Ringing, First Impressions, Bye-Bye Birdie, Kwamina, Baker Street, Rodgers and Hart, George Gershwin vols. I and II, Jerome Kern, Lyrics of Ira Gershwin, Cole Porter, Blazing Saddles, Young Frankenstein, Elephant Man, Dirty Dancing, Space Balls, others. Mem. ASCAP, Acad. Motion Picture Arts and Scis., Soc. Composers and Lyricists, Am. Fedn. Musicians. Personal E-mail: jmorris319@hotmail.com.

MORRIS, JOHN ALBERT, medical educator; b. NYC, Jan. 1, 1947; s. John Albert and Edna Brokaw Morris; m. Julia Caldwell Caldwell, July 10, 1976; children: Jessie Caldwell Adams, Sara Hennen, Miller Layson. BA, Trinity Coll., Hartford, Conn., 1969; MD, U. Ky., Lexington, 1977. Diplomate bd. cert. Am. Bd. Surgeons. Prof. surgery Vanderbilt U. Med. Ctr, Nashville, 1984—. Chief Divsn. Trauma, Nashville, 1984—; adv. bd. mem. Johns Hopkins Injury Prevention, 1988—; chmn. Sirrom Partners, Nashville, 1995—. Bd. trustees Nat. Outdoor Leadership, 1986—89, Harpeth Hall Sch., Nashville, 1996—2002; pres. Eastern Assn. Surgery Trauma, Nashville, 1997—98; exec. bd. mem. Mid TN Coun. Boy Scouts America, Nashville, 2006—07; chmn. Tenn. Com. on Trauma ACS, Nashville, 1989—95. Fellow: ACS; mem.: AMA, Am. Trauma Soc. Avocations: tennis, fly fishing, running. Office: Sirrom Partners 4015 Hillsboro Pike Ste 214 Nashville TN 37215 Office Fax: 615-665-4450.

MORRIS, JOHN CARL, neurologist, educator, researcher; b. Cleve., Feb. 13, 1948; s. Edward Francis and Eleanor Caroline (Pongratz) M.; m. Lucy Laub Babcox, Apr. 14, 1979; children: Carrie Laub, Edward Babcox, Mary Pongratz. BA, Ohio Wesleyan U., 1970; MD, U. Rochester Sch. Medicine and Dentistry, 1974. Diplomate Am. Bd. Internal Medicine, Am. Bd. Psychiatry and Neurology; cert. Nat. Bd. Med. Examiners. Intern San Francisco Gen. Hosp., 1974-75; pvt. practice Fairbanks (Alaska) Clinic, 1975-76, Carlsbad (N.Mex.) Regional Med. Ctr., 1976-77; asst. resident and sr. resident in medicine Akron (Ohio) Gen. Med. Ctr., 1977-79; asst. resident and sr. resident in neurology Cleve. Met. Gen. Hosp., 1979-81, resident in neuropathology, 1981-82; fellow in neuropharmacology Washington Univ. Sch. Medicine, St. Louis, 1982-85, rsch. instr. pharmacology, 1982-84, instr. neurology, 1983-85, asst. and assoc. prof. neurology and neuropathology, 1985-98, asst. prof. pathology and immunology, 1989-2000; Friedman prof. neurology Alzheimers Disease Rsch. Ctr., 2001—, prof. pathology and immunology, 2001—; dir. Alzheimer's disease rsch. ctr. Barnes-Jewish Hosp. St. Louis, 1989—, dir. ctr. aging., 1995—. Bd. dirs. Alzheimer Assn., Chgo., 1998—, Jewish Ctr. for the Aged, St. Louis, 2001—; sci. adv. bd. Inst. for the Study of Aging, Inc., 2000—, Leeza Gibbons Memory Found., 2005—; adv. bd. mem. St. Louis chpt. Alzheimer's Assn., Alzheimer Rsch. Forum, 2002—; lectr. in field. Editl. bd. mem. The Neurologist, 1992—; editor-in-chief: Alzheimer's Disease and Associated Disorders: An International Jour., 2001—; ad hoc reviewer and contbr. articles, chaps. to numerous profl. jours. Recipient Disting. Achievement Citation Ohio Wesleyan U., 2000, MetLife Found. award for rsch. in Alzheimer's Disease, 2004, Physician-Scientist Lifetime Achievement award, Barnes-Jewish Hosp. Found., 2005, Dr. Neville Grant award, 2006, Academic Women's Network Mentor award, Washington U., 2008. Fellow ACP, Am. Acad. Neurology (chair geriatric neurology section, Potamkin prize 2005); mem. Soc. for Neuroscience, Am. Neurol. Soc., Am. Geriatrics Soc., Ctrl. Soc. Neurological Rsch. (pres., 1995-96), Soc. Exptl. Neuropathology, Mo. State Neurological Assn., Am. Soc. Exptl. NeuroTherapeutics, Internat. Coll. Geriatric Psychoneuropharmacology, Rsch. Group on Dementia (exec. com., 2001—), World Fedn. Neurology, Asia-Pacific Internat. Working Group on Harmonization of Dementia Drug Guidelines (exec. com., 2001—) Office: Wash U Sch Medicine Dept Neurol Campus Box 8111-ADRC 660 S Euclid Ave Saint Louis MO 63110-1010 E-mail: morrisj@abraxas.wustl.edu.*

MORRIS, JOHN WILLIAM, JR., metallurgy educator; b. Birmingham, Ala., June 7, 1943; s. John William and Lillian Lucille (Burnette) M.; m. Pamela Mary Dryer, Dec. 30, 1966 (div. 1978); 1 child, McKinley Lee. BS in Metall. Engring., MIT, 1964, ScD in Materials Sci., 1969. Rsch. scientist Bell Aerospace Co., Buffalo, 1968-70, mgr. materials sci., 1970-71; sr. sci. faculty mem. Lawrence Berkeley Nat. Lab., 1971—; asst. prof. dept. materials sci. and mineral engring. U. Calif., Berkeley, 1971-74, assoc. prof., 1974-77, Miller rsch. prof., 1976-77, prof. metallurgy, materials sci. and mineral engring., 1977—. Prog. leader structural materials Ctr. Advanced Materials Lawrence Berkeley Lab., 1985—; lectr., chmn. various tech. confs. Author: The Structure and Propeties of Dual Phase Steels, 1979; patentee various steels and alloys; contbr. articles to profl. jours. Disting. exch. scholar Peoples Republic of China, 1985; recipient Materials Rsch. award US Dept. Energy, 1981, Tech. 100 Citation for advancement of tech. in US Tech. Mag., 1981, Disting. Tchg. award U. Calif. Berkeley, 1988. Fellow Am. Soc. Metals (chmn. Golden Gate chpt. 1979-80, edn. com., Bradley Stoughton Tchg. award 1975); mem. NAE, Metall. Soc.- AIME (chmn. chemistry and physics of metals com. 1978-80, chmn. publs. com. 1978-79, heat treatment com., Robert Lansing Hardy gold medal 1972), Am. Phys. Soc., Am. Soc. Engring. Edn. (AT&T Found. award 1989), Internat. Cryogenic Materials Conf. (bd. dirs.), Phi Delta Theta. Republican. Avocation: golf. Office: Dept Materials Sci and Engring U Calif Berkeley 210 Hearst Meml Mining Bldg Rm 228 Berkeley CA 94720 Office Phone: 510-486-6482. Office Fax: 510-643-5792. E-mail: jwmorris@berkeley.edu.

MORRIS, JOHN WOODLAND, II, retired engineering consultant, military officer; b. Princess Anne, Md., Sept. 10, 1921; s. John Earl and Allice (Cropper) M.; m. Geraldine Moore King, May 12, 1947; children: Susan K., John Woodland III. BS, U.S. Mil. Acad., 1943; MS, U. Iowa, 1948; postgrad., Army War Coll., 1961—62, U. Pitts., 1966. Commd. 2d lt. U.S. Army, 1943, advanced through grades to lt. gen., 1976; dep. dist. engr. Savannah, Ga., 1952-54; resident engr. Goose Bay, Labrador, 1955-57; staff officer Office Chief Engrs., 1957-60; comdg. officer 8th Engr. Bn., Korea, 1960-61; dist. engr. Tulsa, 1962-65; dep. comdt. U.S. Mil. Acad., 1965-67; dep. chief legis. liaison Office Sec. Army, Washington, 1967-69; comdg. gen. 18th Engr. Brigade, Vietnam, 1969-70; div. engr. Missouri River Div., Omaha, 1970-72; dir. civil works Office C.E., Washington, 1972-75; dep. chief engr. U.S. Army, 1975-76, chief engr., 1976-80; ret., 1980; exec. dir. Royal Volker Stevin, 1980-84; pres. J.W. Morris Ltd., 1981—2006; ret., 2006; prof. U. Md., 1983-86; chmn. bd., CEO PRC Engring., 1986-88. Engr. advisor, cons. Zorc, Rissetto, Weaver & Rosen, 1988-92; engr. advisor Seltzer & Rosen, 1992-98; bd. dirs. Air Water Tech., Morganti Constrn. Co., Search Techs. Inc., Thaco Rsch. Inc., Dutra Corp.; mem. adv. bd. AMEC Ltd. Mem. Indian Nations coun. Boy Scouts Am., 1962-65; chmn. Water Resources Congress, 1988-90; trustee U.S. Mil. Acad. Assn. Grads, 1986—98; advisor dean engring. and math. U. Vt., 1990-96. Decorated Legion of Merit with three oak leaf clusters, Army D.S.M., Def. D.S.M.; recipient Merit award Am. Cons. Engrs. Council; Palladium medal Audubon Soc.; Excellence award, Constrn. Industry Inst., 1997. Fellow ASCE (Disting. Constructor award 2000); mem. AIA (hon.), Internat. Navigation Congress (v.p.), U.S. Soc. Mil. Engrs. (pres.), Nat. Acad. Engrs. (Founders award 1996), U.S. Com. on Large Dams (named Constrn. Man of Yr. 1977, Navigation Hall of Fame 1990, Golden Beaver award for engring. 1995, Golden Eagle award, 1998, Acad. of Dist. Eng. U. Iowa, 1998, Dist. Grad. of U.S. Mil. Acad., 1998). Episcopalian. E-mail: morrisJ@aol.com.

MORRIS, JOSEPH WESLEY, physician assistant; b. Kansas City, Mo., Feb. 17, 1958; s. Glenn Wesley and Julia Ann (Witt) M.; m. Sharon Kennedy, Oct. 2, 1982 (div. Aug. 1989). A Engring., 1978; AAS, Penn Valley CC, Kansas City, Mo., 1980; BS, Physician Assoc. with distinction, U. Okla., Oklahoma City, 1989; MS in Med. Sci. emphasis in Emergency Medicine, Alderson-Broaddus Coll., Philippi, W.Va., 1995. Nat. cert. physician asst. in primary care and surgery. Firefighter/paramedic North Kansas City (Mo.) Fire Dept., 1981-89; residency for physician assts. in surgery St. Vincent's Med. Ctr., SI, NY, 1989-90, physician asst. ob-gyn., 1990-91, physician asst. in surgery & trauma, 1991-93, with, Students Med. Ctr.; physician asst. in ob-gyn. St. Vincents Hosp, SI; NY physician asst. in emergency medicine St. Joseph's Hosp., Parkersburg, W.Va., 1993-95; acad. coord., asst. prof. clin. medicine PA program Coll. W.Va., Beckley, 1995—96; physician asst. in emergency medicine Emergency & Acute Care Svcs., Inc., Gastonia, NC, 1996—2007, Carolina Urgent Care, 2007—08; active US Pub. Health Svc., 2008—. Emergency medicine svcs. instr., Kansas City, Mo., 1980-86; emergency medicine svcs. coord., Kansas City, 1981-86; bd. dirs. CPR Now!, Kansas City, 1981-86; asst. med. dir. emergency medicine svcs. St. Joseph's Hosp., Parkersburg, W.Va., 1993-95. Mem. dist. com. Boy scouts Am., Kansas City, 1979-86; mem. agrl. com. of Rep. Thomas Coleman, Kansas City, 1980-82; mem. planning com. W.Va. Managed Care Conf., Flatwoods, W.Va., 1996; mem. citizen issue com. of Rep. Sue Myrick, Gastonia, NC, 1997-2000. USMCR, 1977-81; with US Army NG, 1986-2008, US Pub. Svc., 2008-, Ops. Iraqi Freedom, 2003-05, Operation Enduring Freedom, 2005-06., 2003—05, Ops. Iraqi Freedom. Fellow: Am. Acad. Physician Assts. (disting. fellow), Am. Acad. Experts in Traumatic Stress; mem.: AAPA (life; mem. Vets Caucus), Undersea & Hyperbaric Soc., USPHS Soc. of PAS, Soc. Physician Assistants, Hawaii Acad. PAS, Internat. Soc. Travel Medicine, Nat. Assn. Search and Rescue, Am. Soc. Hygiene and Tropical Medicine, Wilderness Med. Soc., Am. Heart Assn., Am. Trauma Soc., Undersea and Hyperbaric Medicine Soc., Soc. Emergency Medicine Physician Assts., Soc. Army Physician Assts., NOAA Dive Med. Officer, Nat. Field Archery Assn. (life), Nat. Archery Assn. (life; level 3 coach), Nat. Eagle Scout Assn. (life). Avocations: archery, astronomy, painting, reading, scuba diving. Home: NOAA Ship Hi'ialakai 1897 Ranger Loop #184 Honolulu HI 96818-5072

MORRIS, KENDALL FRANCIS, psychology professor; b. Chester, Pa., July 29, 1951; s. Edna May Morris; m. Kendall Francis Wade; 1 child, Kendall David. PhD, U. South Fla., Tampa, 1993. Cert. State Tchr. Fla., 1973. Tchr. Hillsborough County Schs., Tampa, Fla., 1973—87; assoc. prof. U. South Fla. Health, Tampa, 1993—. Contbr. scientific papers. Web master Tampa Sailing Squadron, Apollo Beach, Fla., 2002—. Indepedent Rsch. grant, NIH Nhlbi, 2008—. Mem.: Soc. for Neurosci. Office: Univ S Fla Health 12901 Bruce B Downs Blvd MDC Box 8 Tampa FL 33612-4799 Business E-Mail: kmorris@health.usf.edu.

MORRIS, LEE C., federal agency administrator; BA in Lit., Am. U., 1993. Specialist US Army; legis. dir. Senator Don Nickles; fed. liaison legis. action NRA, 2005—07; dep. asst. sec. legis. affairs US Dept. Homeland Security, 2007—08, asst. sec. legis. affairs, 2008—. Office: US Dept Homeland Security 12th & C St SW Washington DC 20024*

MORRIS, LEIGH EDWARD, former mayor, retired health facility administrator; b. Hartford City, Ind., Dec. 26, 1934; s. Fredus Orlando and Martha (Malott) M.; m. Marcia Renee Meredith, Oct. 7, 1967; children: Meredith Anne, Curtis Paul. BS in Commerce, Internat. Coll., 1954; BSBA, Ball State U., 1958; M in Health Adminstrn., U. Minn., 1972. Mem. labor relations staff Borg-Warner Corp., Muncie, Ind., 1961-64; various positions then personnel mgr. Internat. Harvester Co., Ft. Wayne, Ind., 1964-70; pres. Huntington (Ind.) Meml. Hosp., 1972-78, La Porte (Ind.) Hosp., 1978-2000; ret., 2004—07; mayor City of LaPorte; exec. dir. Ind. Toll Rd.; chmn. Northern Ind. Regional Devel. Authority; dir. Meml. Health Found., South Bend. Bd. dirs. First of Am. Bank of Ind., Am. Hosp. Svcs., Inc., Health Forum, Inc.; chmn., bd. dirs. Am. Hosp. Pub. Co.; chmn. La Porte Devel. Corp., 1980-81; exec. dir. Ind. Toll Rd.; chmn. Northwest Ind. Regional Devel. Authority. Chmn. LaPorte chpt. ARC, 1984-86; bd. dirs., vice chmn. John G. Blank Ctr. for the Arts, Lubeznik Ctr. for the Arts, LaPorte County Symphony Orch. With U.S. Army, 1958-60. Recipient Disting. Alumni award Ball State U., Muncie, Ind., 1968, James A. Hamilton award U. Minn., Mpls., 1972, Trustees award Am. Hosp. Assn., 1996. Fellow Am. Coll. Healthcare Adminstrn. (life), Health Care Fin. Mgmt. Assn.; mem. APHA, Am. Hosp. Assn. (trustee, regional chmn. 1985-89), Soc. for Healthcare Planning and Mktg. (bd. dirs.), Soc. Ind. Pioneers (bd. dirs., pres.), Ind. Hosp. Assn. (chmn. 1980-81), La Porte C. of C. (chmn. 1981-82). Republican. Presbyterian. Avocations: classic cars, civic affairs. Home: 424 Upper Lake Shore Dr La Porte IN 46350-2917 Personal E-mail: lmorris@csinet.net. Business E-Mail: lmorris2@indot.in.gov.

MORRIS, LISSA CAMILLE, music educator; d. Thomas Melvin Melot and Audrey Camille LaCroix; m. Randall Wyatt Morris, Mar. 15, 1986; children: Thomas Zachary, Linday Alissa, Jesse Randall, Aaron Wyatt. BA, Excelsior Coll., 1995. Music tchr. Village Pkwy. Sch., San Antonio, 1996—97; dir. music St. Michael's Ch., San Antonio, 1997—98, St. George Ch., San Antonio, 1998—2004, ret., 2004; co-owner WOW Sci. Lab., San Antonio, 2003—. Founder Little Mozarts Music Camp, Nishnabec Organic Farm, 2005—06; pianist St. Mary's Ter. Cathedral, Guthrie, Okla.; master tchr. J. Rogers Performing Arts Studio; owner and dir. Allegro Music Studio Guthrie. Contbr. articles to profl. jours.; composer: On the Ledge, 2002. Mem.: Music Educators Nat. Conf., Nat. Piano Guild. Republican. Roman Catholic. Avocations: reading, dance. Home Phone: 405-260-0728. Personal E-mail: lissacamille@yahoo.com.

MORRIS, LOIS LAWSON, retired education educator; b. Antoine, Ark., Nov. 27, 1914; d. Oscar Moran and Dona Alice (Ward) Lawson; m. William D. Morris, July 2, 1932 (dec.); 1 child, Lavonne Morris Howell (dec.). BA, Henderson U., 1948; specialist degree, U. Ark., 1956, MS, 1951, MA, 1966; postgrad., U. Colo., 1954, Am. U., 1958, U. N.C., 1968. History tchr. Delight H.S., Ark., 1942-47; counselor Huntsville Vocat. Sch., 1947-48; guidance dir. Russellville Pub. Sch. Sys., Ark., 1948-55; asst. prof. edn. U. Ark., Fayetteville, 1955-82; prof. emeritus, 1982—. Ednl. cons. Ark. Pub. Schs., 1965—78. Author: Biographical Essays, 2000; contbr. book reviews and articles to mags. and profl. jours. including Ga. Hist. Quar., 1998, Ark. Biography, 2000. Mem. Hist. Preservation Alliance Ark.; pres. Washington County Hist. Soc., 1983-85, Pope County Hist. Assn.; mem. Ark. Symphony Guild; charter mem. Nat. Mus. in Arts; bd. dirs. Potts Inn Mus. Found. Named Ark. Coll. Tchr. of Yr., 1972; recipient Plaque for Outstanding Svcs. to Washington County Hist. Soc., 1984. Mem. LWV, AAUW, NEA, Washington County Hist., Soc. (exec. bd. 1977-80), Ark. Edn. Assn., Ark. Hist. Assn., Pope County Hist. Assn. (pres. 1991-92), The Ga. Hist. Soc., U. Ark. Alumni Assn., Sierra Club, Nature Conservancy, Ark. River Valley Arts Assn., Phi Delta Kappa, Kappa Delta Pi, Phi Alpha Theta. Democrat. Episcopalian. Address: 1601 W 3d St Russellville AR 72801-4725 Home Phone: 479-967-6714.

MORRIS, M. CATHERINE, electronics executive; B in Fin., Colo. State U., Ft. Collins; grad. Gen. Mgmt. Prog., Harvard Bus. Sch. V.p. fin., corp. contr. Anthem Electronics; with Arrow Electronics, Inc., Melville, NY, 1994, v.p. corp. devel., v.p. fin. and support svcs. Enterprise Computing Solutions, v.p. support svcs. N.Am., sr. v.p., pres. Enterprise Computing Solutions, sr. v.p., chief strategy officer, 2008—. Office: Arrow Electronics Inc 50 Marcus Dr Melville NY 11747-4210 Office Phone: 631-847-2000.*

MORRIS, MAC GLENN, advertising executive; b. Bessemer City, NC, Jan. 24, 1922; s. Manly T. and Erin C. (Cline) M.; m. Janelle Connevey, July 27, 1946; children— Robert S., Janelle C., Patricia A., John Logan. AB, Davidson Coll., 1942. Space salesman Progressive Farmer mag., NYC, 1946-52; exec. v.p., advt. dir. This Week mag., 1952-68; pres. Newspaper One, NYC, 1968-71; sr. v.p. nat. sales Newspaper Advt. Bur., NYC, 1972-87; proprietor MGM Assocs., Princeton, NJ, 1987—. Bd. dirs. Princeton Bank & Trust Co. divsn. Chem. Bank N.J., N.A., now owned by P.N.C. Bank, N.Y.C. Served to 1st lt., pilot USMCR, World War II. Decorated D.F.C. (2), Air medal (7). Mem. Newcomen Soc. in N. Am., Pi Kappa Phi. Presbyn. (deacon). Club: Springdale Golf (Princeton, N.J.) (bd. govs.). Home and Office: 383 Herrontown Rd Princeton NJ 08540 *I am always an optimist at my work, with friends, and with my family.*

MORRIS, MALCOLM STEWART, title company executive, lawyer; b. Houston, May 8, 1946; s. Carloss M.; m. Rebecca Ann Simmons, June 14, 1969; children: Matthew William, Andrew James. BBA, So. Meth. U., 1968; JD, U. Tex., 1970, MBA, 1972. Bar: Tex. 1970. Legis. aid State of Tex., Sen. Charles Wilson, Austin, 1969-70; examiner Stewart Title Austin Inc., 1970-71; analyst Bank of the S.W., Houston, 1973-74; bus. mgr. Richard Hogue Evangelism, Inc., Houston, 1974-75; cons. Morris, Lendais, Hollrah & Snowden, Houston; v.p. ops. Stewart Title Guaranty Co., Houston, 1975-87, sr. exec. v.p., asst. chmn., 1987-91, pres., CEO, 1991—; chmn. Stewart Title Co.; chmn., co-CEO Stewart Info. Services Corp., Houston, 2000—. Mem. bd. Stewart Title Ins. Co., N.Y.C., Stewart Title Ins. Co. U.K.; past pres. Tex. Land Title Assn., Am. Land Title Assn. Past chmn. Deacons, 1st Bapt. Ch., Houston; past chmn. Living Water Internat.; chmn. Millennium Water Alliance. Fellow Am. Bar Found., Houston Bar Assn.; mem. ABA, State Bar Tex., Houston Bar Assn., Phi Delta Phi. Baptist. Office: 1980 Post Oak Blvd Ste 800 Houston TX 77056-3826 also: Stewart Info Services Corp 1980 Post Oak Blvd Houston TX 77056

MORRIS, MARGRETTA ELIZABETH, conservationist; b. Oakland, Calif., Sept. 14, 1950; d. Joseph Francis and Mildred Ruth Madeo; m. Dennis W. Morris, July 22, 1972; children: Matthew B., Roseanna A. BA in Geography, Radford U., 1972. Paralegal Law Office of Henry F. Zwack, Stephentown, N.Y., 1980-91; exec. dir. Ea. Rensselaer County Waste Mgmt. Authority, Stephentown, 1991-97; v.p., founder ERC Cmty. Warehouse, 1996—; mgr. govt. programs EnergyAnswers, Albany, NY, 1997—2005, v.p. govt. programs, 2006—08; dir. environment sci. cmty. affair Covanta Energy Corp., 2008—. Co-founder MDM Prodns., Stephentown, 1986—. Councilperson Town of Stephentown, NY, 1987—92; treas. Stephentown Meml. Libr., 2002—03; bd. dir. Go Green, Inc., 2002—. Mem.: Mass. Recycle (bd. dir. 2009—), America Recycles (bd. dirs. 2002—07, chmn.), Fedn. N.Y. Solid Waste Assns. (chmn. 1997—), N.Y. State Assn. Reduction, Reuse and Recycling (treas. 1992—2008, bd. dir. 1992—), N.Y. State Assn. Solid Waste Mgmt. (rec. sec. 1992—94), Nat. Recycling Coalition (bd. dirs. 1999—2005, pres.), Antilles H.S. Alumni Assn. (treas. 2002—), Gamma Theta Upsilon. Republican. Roman Catholic. Avocations: cross country skiing, hiking, biking. Office: Covanta Energy Corp 749 columbia Tpk E East Greenbush NY 12061 Business E-Mail: mmorris@covantaenergy.com.

MORRIS, MARIA R., insurance company executive; BA, Franklin & Marshall Coll. With MetLife Ins. Co., NYC, 1984—2003, sr. v.p. group ins. sales, 2003—05, exec. v.p. employee benefits sales, 2005—08, exec. v.p., head tech. ops., 2008—. Bd. dir. MetLife Securities. Mem. nat. bd. INROADS; bd. mem. All Stars Project Inc. Named one of Women to Watch, Profiles in Diversity Jour., 2005; named to YWCA Acad. Women Achievers. Mem.: Phi Beta Kappa. Office: MetLife Ins Co 200 Park Ave New York NY 10166*

MORRIS, MARK WILLIAM, choreographer; b. Seattle, Aug. 29, 1956; s. William and Maxine (Crittenden) Morris. Studied with, Verla Flowers and Perry Brunson; D (hon.), Boston Conservatory of Music, Juilliard Sch., L.I. U., Pratt Inst., Bowdoin Coll. Artistic dir. Mark Morris Dance Group, NYC, 1980—, Théâtre Royal de la Monnaie, Brussels, 1988—91; co-founder White Oak Dance Project, 1990; owner Mark Morris Dance Ctr., Bklyn., 2001—. Performed with Lar Lubovitch Dance Co., Hannah Kahn Dance Co., Laura Dean Dancers and Musicians, Eliot Feld Ballet, Koleda Balkan Dance Ensemble. Choreographer Esteemed Guests, Joffrey Ballet, 1986, Nixon in China, Houston Grand Opera, 1987, L'Allegro, il Penseroso ed il Moderato, 1988, Drink to Me Only With Thine Eyes, Am. Ballet Theatre, 1988, Orféo et Euridice, Seattle Opera, 1988, Dido and Aeneas, 1989, Ein Herz, Paris Opera Ballet, 1990, The Death of Klinghoffer, Théâtre de la Monnaie, 1991, The Hard Nut, 1991, Great Performances/Dance in Am. The Hard Nut, 1992, Maelstrom, San Francisco Ballet, 1994, The Office, 1994, Lucky Charms, 1994, Pacific, San Francisco Ballet, 1995, Platée, Royal Opera Covent Garden, 1997, Sandpaper Ballet, San Francisco Ballet, 1999, Four Saints in Three Acts, 2000, Sang-Froid, 2000, A Garden, San Francisco Ballet, 2001, Gong, Am. Ballet Theatre, 2001; dir.: Die Fledermaus, 1988, Falling Down Stairs, 1997 (Emmy award, 1997), The Capeman, Kolam, 2002. Recipient Dance and Performance award, 1984, 1990, Mayor's award for arts and culture, NYC Dept. Cultural Affairs, 2006, Gramophone Spl. Recognition award, WQXR, Lifetime Achievement award, Samuel H. Scripps Am. Dance Festival, 2007; fellow, Guggenheim Found., 1986, MacArthur Found., 1991. Mem.: Am. Philos. Soc., Am. Acad. Arts and Scis. Office: Mark Morris Dance Group 3 Lafayette Ave Brooklyn NY 11217-1415 Office Phone: 718-624-8400. E-mail: info@mmdg.org.*

MORRIS, MARTIN W., legislative staff member; b. Feb. 10, 1956; m. Pamela Maloley, Nov. 9, 1985; 1 child. AB, Duke U., Durham, NC, 1978; JD, Cumberland Sch. Law, Birmingham, Ala., 1981. Bar: Ind. 1981, DC 1991. Polit. dir., Senator Richard Lugar US Senate, Washington, 1981—82, exec. asst., Senator Richard Lugar, 1982—84, counsel, Senator Richard Lugar, 1985—87, campaign mgr., Senator Richard Lugar, 1987—88, chief of staff to Senator Richard Lugar, 1990—; practicing atty., 1985—87; gen. mgr., Midwest divsn. SC Tees,

1988—90. Mem.: Phi Delta Phi, Phi Delta Theta. Republican. Office: 306 Hart Senate Office Bldg Washington DC 20510-1401 Office Phone: 202-224-4814. Business E-Mail: marty_morris@lugar.senate.gov.*

MORRIS, MELANIE R., legislative staff member; BA in Comm., Boston U., 2003. Press sec. for Rep. Allen Boyd, US House of Reps., Washington, 2006—09, dep. chief of staff, chief of staff, 2009—. Office: Office of Congressman Allen Boyd 1227 Longworth House Ofice Bldg Washington DC 20515 Office Phone: 202-225-5235. Office Fax: 202-225-5615.*

MORRIS, MICHAEL G., electric power industry executive; b. Fremont, Ohio, Nov. 11, 1946; married, Linda Lindstrom, 1970; two children. BS, Ea. Mich. U., MS, 1973; JD cum laude, Detroit Coll. Law, 1981. With environ. dept. Commonwealth Assocs., Jackson, Mich., 1973—76; pres. ANR Gathering Co.; exec. v.p. mktg., transp. and gas supply ANR Pipeline Co., 1982—87; pres. Colo. Interstate Gas Co., 1987—88; exec. v.p., natural gas & mktg. Consumers Energy subsidiary of CMS Energy Corp., 1988—92, COO, 1992—94, pres., CEO, 1994—97; chmn., pres., CEO Northeast Utilities, Berlin, Conn., 1997—2003; pres., CEO Am. Electric Power Co., Springfield, Mass., 2004—, chmn., 2004—. Past chmn. Conn. Bus. & Industry Assn.; chmn. Edison Electric Inst.; bd. dir. Nuclear Electric Ins. Ltd., Flint Ink Corp., Cincinnati Bell, Hartford Fin. Svc. Group Inc., Alcoa Inc., 2008—. Exec. com., trustee Inst. Gas Tech.; trustee Ea. Mich. U. Found.; trustee Detroit Coll. Law, Delta Sigma Phi Found.; mem. Olivet Coll. Leadership Adv. Coun.; US Dept. Energy, Electricity Adv. Bd.; Task Force Electricity Infrastructure, Nat. Gov. Assn.; Inst. Nuclear Power Ops.; Bus. Roundtable; Columbus Downtown Devel. Corp.; bd. dirs. Libr. Mich. Found.; bd. regents Ea. Mich. U., 1997—. Recipient Disting. Alumnus award Ea. Mich. U., 1995. Mem. Mich. Bar Assn., Delta Sigma Phi (pres.). Office: Am Electric Power Co 1 Riverside Plz Columbus OH 43215-2372

MORRIS, OWEN GLENN, engineering corporation executive; b. Shawnee, Okla., Feb. 3, 1927; s. Vestus and Myrtle (Lindsey) M.; m. Joyce Gast; children: Deborah Moree, Janine Inez. BS in Mech. Engring, U. Okla., 1947, M.Aero. Engring., 1948; postgrad., U. Va., 1952-53, Va. Poly. Inst., 1955-56, Coll. William and Mary, 1957-58. Aero., research scientist NASA, Langley Field, Va., 1948-61, mgr. lunar module, 1961—71, mgr. sys. integration space shuttle, 1974—80, mgr. Apollo spacecraft program, 1971—72; pres. Eagle Engring., 1980-86; pres., chief exec. officer Eagle Aerospace, Houston, 1987-90, chmn., chief exec. officer, 1990-93, chmn. bd., 1992—. Served with USNR, 1943-46. Recipient U.S. Medal of Freedom, 1972, NASA Distinguished Service medal, 1973, NASA Exceptional Service medal, 1969, Outstanding Leadership medal NASA, 1979. Asso. fellow Am. Inst. Aeros. and Astronautics; mem. Am. Astronautical Soc., Acad. Model Aeros., Tau Beta Pi, Tau Omega. Presbyterian (elder 1964—). Club: Rotary. Home: 14914 Timberland Ct Houston TX 77062-2922

MORRIS, PATRICK J., Mayor, San Bernardino, California; m. Sally Morris. Grad. cum laude, U. Redlands; JD, Stanford U. Dep. Office Dist. Atty., San Bernardino, Calif.; atty. pvt. practice San Bernardino, Calif.; supervising judge family law divsn. Superior Ct. Calif., 1978—81, presiding judge, 1981—84, presiding judge juvenile ct., 1984—89, supervising criminal law judge, 1990—96, presiding judge juvenile ct.; mayor City of San Bernadino, Calif., 2006—. Trustee U. Redlands; pres. bd. edn., San Bernardino; chmn. Jud. Coun. Task Force on Drug Cts.; chmn. bd. dirs. Nat. Assn. of Drug Ct. profl., 1998; chief justice Jud. Coun., 1991—93. Bd. mem. San Bernadino Assoc. Govts.; chmn. Planning and Productivity Com.; bd. dirs. Southern Calif. Regional Rail Authority; pres. San Bernadino Internat. Airport Authority; founder Children's Network, 1985; co-chmn. Inland Valley Devel. Agy. Recipient Meritorious Svc. award, Nat. Coun. Juvenile and Family Ct. Judges, 1991, Disting. Svc. award, 1994, Trial Jurist of Yr. award, Jud. Coun. of Calif., 1994; named a Inland Southern California's Trial Judge of Yr., 1981. Office: Office of Mayor 300 N D St 6th Fl San Bernardino CA 92418 Office Phone: 909-384-5133. Office Fax: 909-384-5067. E-mail: meier_sh@sbcity.org.*

MORRIS, PAUL, psychologist, educator; PhD, U. Southampton. Prin. lectr. dept. psychology U. Portsmouth. Office: University of Portsmouth Dept of Psychology King Henry Bldg King Henry 1 St Hampshire PO1 2DY England E-mail: paul.morris@port.ac.uk.*

MORRIS, RAHEEM, professional football coach; b. Irvington, NJ, Sept. 3, 1976; BS in Phys. Edn., Hofstra U., Hempstead, NY, 1998. Grad. asst. Hofstra U. Pride, 1998, defensive backs coach, 2000—01; defensive backs coach, spl. teams asst. Cornell U. Big Red, Ithaca, NY, 1999; defensive internship NY Jets, 2001; defensive quality control coach Tampa Bay Buccaneers, 2002, defensive asst., 2003, asst. defensive backs coach, 2004—05, defensive backs coach, 2007—08, head football coach, 2009—; defensive coord. Kansas State U. Wildcats, 2006. Achievements include member of Super Bowl XXXVII Championship winning Tampa Bay Buccaneers, 2003. Office: Tampa Bay Buccaneers One Buccaneer Pl Tampa FL 33607*

MORRIS, RANDY G., small business owner; b. Waynesboro, Tenn., Sept. 7, 1953; m. Katherine Morris; children: Julianne, Sarah. AS in Pre-Bus., Columbia State CC, 1977; BS in Accounting, Tenn. Technol. U., Cookeville, 1979. Accountant Tenn. Dept. Corrections, 1983—85; controller Wayne County Gen. Hosp., 1985—96; owner Shake Raq, Inc. (64-Mart), 1996—. Aircraft repairman USAF, 1971—75. Democrat. Mem. Christian Ch. (Disciples Of Christ). Office: Shake Raq Inc 64-Mart 1023 Savannah Hwy Waynesboro TN 38485 Office Phone: 931-722-6464.

MORRIS, REBECCA, painter; b. Honolulu, 1969; BA, Smith Coll., 1991; post-baccalaureate studio cert., Sch. Art Inst. Chgo., 1992, MFA, 1994; student, Skowhegan Sch. Painting and Sculpture, 1994. One-woman shows include Ten in One Gallery, NYC, 2001, Shane Campbell Gallery, Oak Park, Ill., 2001, Santa Monica Mus. Art, 2003, Susanne Vielmetter LA Projects, 2004, Renaissance Soc., U. Chgo., 2005, Galerie Barbara Weiss, Berlin, 2006, Samson Projects, Boston, 2006, Karyn Lovegrove Gallery, LA, 2007, exhibited in group shows at Post-Pop, Post-Pictures, Smart Mus. Art, U. Chgo., 1997, Cool Painting, Brian Gross Fine Art, San Francisco, 1998, Good Images and Objects, Donald Young Gallery, Chicago, 2001, Painting and Sculpture, Mark Moore Gallery, Santa Monica, 2004, Abstraktes, Galerie Barbara Weiss, Berlin, 2005, Figures in the Field, Mus. Contemporary Art, Chgo., 2006, Affinities: Painting in Abstraction, Hessel Art Mus, Annandale-on-Hudson, NY, 2007, Color Climax, James Graham & Sons, NYC, 2008. Recipient Biennial Competition artist award, Louis Comfort Tiffany Found., 1999; fellow Guggenheim Found., 2008. Office: c/o Shane Campbell Gallery 1431 W Chicago Ave Chicago IL 60622 also: c/o Galerie Barbara Weiss Zimmerstrasse 88-91 10117 Berlin Germany E-mail: rm@rebeccamorris.net.

MORRIS, ROBERT GEMMILL, retired foreign service officer; b. Des Moines, July 20, 1929; s. Robert William and Iva May (Gemmill) M.; m. Beverly Schupfer, July 3, 1955; children: Robert William II, John Schupfer, Richard Edward. BS, Iowa State U., 1951; postgrad., Charles Francis U., Graz, 1951—52; MS, Calif. Inst. Tech., 1954; PhD, Iowa State U., 1957. Asst. prof. S.D. Sch. Mines and Tech., Rapid City, 1958-59, assoc. prof., 1959-62, prof., head dept. physics, 1962-68; phys. sci. officer Office of Naval Research, Washington, 1968-73, dir. electronics program, 1973-74; U.S. fgn. service officer U.S. Dept. State, Washington, 1974-78; counselor for sci. and technol. affairs U.S. Mission to OECD, Paris, 1978-82, U.S. Embassy, Bonn, Fed. Republic Germany, 1982-85; dep. asst. sec. of state for sci. and tech. affairs Washington, 1985-87; fgn. svc. officer U.S. Embassy, Buenos Aires, 1987-90, Madrid, 1990-92. Contbr. articles to profl. jours. Fulbright scholar, Austria, 1951; Swiss govt. fellow, Zurich, 1957. Mem. APS. Personal E-mail: morrash@mind.net.

MORRIS, ROBERT TAPPAN, computer science educator, Internet company executive; b. 1965; s. Robert Morris. AB, Harvard U., 1987, PhD in Applied Scis., 1999. Co-founder Viaweb, 1995, Y Combinator, 2005, ptnr., 2005—; assoc. prof. computer sci. MIT, 1999—. Tech. advisor Meraki Networks, 2006—; spkr. in field. Contbr. articles to profl. jours. Recipient Career award, NSF, 2003; named one of 50 Most Important People on the Web, PC World, 2007. Mem.: Chaos Computer Club. Office: MIT Rm 32-G972 32 Vassar St Cambridge MA 02139 also: Y Combinator 320 Pioneer Way Mountain View CA 94041 Office Phone: 617-253-5983. Office Fax: 617-258-8607. Business E-Mail: rtm@csail.mit.edu.

MORRIS, ROLAND, lawyer; b. Feb. 18, 1933; s. Edward S. and Leslie H. (Hun) Morris; m. Sally J. Fageol, Jan. 29, 1955; children: Roland, Deirdre, Heather. BA, Princeton U., NJ, 1955; LLB, U. Pa. Law Sch., 1960; DSc (hon.), U. Scis. Phila. Bar: Pa. 1961, US Dist. Ct. (ea. and mid. dists.) Pa. 1961, US Dist. Ct. (NJ), US Dist. Ct. (ea. dist.) Wis., US Ct. Appeals (3rd. cir.) 1961, Supreme Ct. NJ, Supreme Ct. Pa., US Supreme Ct. 1975. Assoc. Duane Morris LLP, Phila., 1961—65, ptnr., 1965—99, of counsel, 2000—, mng. ptnr., 1983—89, vice chmn., 1989—93, chmn., 1993—97. Contbr. articles to profl. jours. Trustee Thomas Jefferson U., Phila., C. Herbert Bell Charitable Trust, Christian R. & Mary F. Lindback Found., Magee Rehabilitation Hosp., Phila., Dolfinger-McMahon Found.; dir. Citizens Crime Commn. Phila., Phila. Urban Coalition; bd. dirs. Big Brothers Assn. Phila., pres., 1975—87; bd. dirs. Legal Aid Soc. Phila., v.p., 1972—75. Mem.: ABA, Nat. Assn. Coll. & Univ. Attorneys, Am. Coll. Healthcare Attorneys, Pa. Soc. Healthcare Attorneys, Pa. Bar Assn., Phila. Bar Assn. Democrat. Office: Duane Morris LLP 30 S 17th St Philadelphia PA 19103 Office Phone: 215-979-1076. Office Fax: 215-689-3605. Business E-Mail: Morris@duanemorris.com.*

MORRIS, SARAH, literature and language educator; BA, MA, W.Va. Univ. Substitute tchr. Preston County Schs., W.Va., 2000—01; English tchr. Berkeley Springs (W.Va.) H.S., 2001—. Author: Burying Opal, Nantahala Rev., 2002, My Father Teaches Me to Fish, Gray's Sporting Jour., 2005. Recipient Mary Linn Fox First Year Tchr. award, 2002; named W.Va. Tchr. of Yr., 2007; grantee Japan Fulbright Meml. Fund Tchr. Program, 2006. Office: Berkeley Springs High Sch 149 Concord Ave Berkeley Springs WV 25411 Business E-Mail: srmorris@access.k12.wv.us.

MORRIS, SHARON LOUISE STEWART, emergency medical technician, paramedic; b. Washington, Feb. 9, 1956; d. George Arthur Jr. and Shirley Ann (Dickinson) S. (dec.); m. Brian Stanley Morris, Feb. 9, 1979 (div.); children: Jessica Kristin, Krystle Maria. BS, Atlantic Christian Coll., Wilson, NC, 1978; student, Wilson County Tech. Coll., 1998; paramedic stud., Nash C.C. Cert. tchr. elem. edn. and math., N.C., EMT paramedic, ACLS, Pediatric Advanced Life Support, pediat. edn. prehosp. profls., AHA CPR/BLS instr.; cert. pre-hosp. trauma life support Prehosp. Edn. for Prehosp. Profls.; automatic external defibrilator (AED) instr.; basic trauma life support (BTLS); farm medic. Cashier Safeway Fin., Wilson, 1980-81, Provident Fin., Wilson, 1981-85; mktg. svc. mgr. Beneficial of NC Inc., Wilson, 1985-91; ind. carrier Wilson Daily Times, 1991-94; child care provider Crestview Day Sch., Wilson, 1994-95; EMT vol. Elm City, NC, 1996—; EMT paramedic Wilson County Emergency Med. Svcs., 1998—2004, training office, 2003—04, shift asst. supr., 2004—. Agt. Cen. Nat. Life Ins., Wilson, 1988-91, Olde Republic, 1990; EMT Elm City Emergency Svcs., 1996, attendant, driver Am. Med. Response, 1997; Avon rep., 2005-; paramedic Sch. Nash Tech. CC, Wayne County EMS, 2006-. Notary pub. State of NC, 1986—2006; bd. dirs. Elm City, 1997, 99; full time paramedic for Johnston Ambulance Svc., 2002-07, first responder instr. EMT, 2003; paramedic Wayne County EMS, 2006-. Democrat. Methodist. Avocations: crocheting, cross-stitch, needlepoint, plants, baking. Home: PO Box 9053 Wilson NC 27895 Personal E-mail: emsbabygirl120@peoplepc.com.

MORRIS, STEPHEN, philosopher, educator; b. Miami, Fla., Oct. 22, 1970; s. Peter and Cheryl Morris; m. Lacey Sischo, June 14, 2007; 1 child, Zoe. PhD, Fla. State U., Tallahassee, 2004. Asst. prof., philosophy Coll. Staten Island, CUNY, 2009—. Mem. ethics com. Heartland Hosp., St. Joseph, 2005—. Recipient Disting. Prof. award, Mo. Western State U. Bd. Govs., 2008. Mem.: Fla. Philos. Assn., Philosophy Sci. Assn., Am. Philos. Assn. Liberal. Avocation: music. Office: Missouri Western State Univ 4525 Downs Dr Saint Joseph MO 64507 Personal E-mail: smorris@missouriwestern.edu.

MORRIS, STEPHEN BURRITT, marketing information company executive; b. Morristown, NJ, Aug. 13, 1943; s. Grinnell and Cornelia (Kellogg) M.; m. Victoria Ann French, Feb. 18, 1967; children: Christopher Jackson, Robin Taylor BA, Yale U., 1965; MBA, Harvard U., 1969. With product mgmt. Gen. Foods Corp., White Plains, NY, 1969—83, gen. mgr. Maxwell House Coffee div., 1983-85, v.p., 1983-87, pres. Maxwell House div., 1986-87; founder, dir. Spectra Mktg. Systems Inc., Chgo., 1987-90; pres., CEO Vid Code Inc., Waltham, Mass., 1990-92; chmn., pres., CEO Arbitron Inc., NYC, 1992—2009. Bd. dirs. John B. Stetson Co., Welch, Inc. Trustee David Parsons Dance Co., 2003. Served to 2d lt. USMCR, 1965-66. Avocations: travel, gardening. Home: 300 Mt Holly Rd Katonah NY 10536-3546

MORRIS, STEVEN LYNN, engineering consultant, retired military officer; b. Dallas, Dec. 7, 1952; s. William Ira and Alta Faye (McCarley) M.; m. Jacqueline Ann Fenter, July 30, 1977; children: Steven Sean, Michael Wayne. BS in Engring. Scis., USAF Acad., Colorado Springs, Colo., 1975; MS in Aero. Engring, Air Force Inst. Tech., Dayton, Ohio, 1980; PhD in Aerospace Engring., Tex. A&M U., College Station, 1989. Registered profl. engr., Tex., Colo. Commd. 2d lt. USAF, 1975, advanced through grades to lt. col., 1991, ret., 1999; assoc. prof., dep. head dept. aeronautics USAF Acad., Colo., 1989-99; engring. specialist SRS Techs., Colorado Springs, Colo., 1999-2000; sr. cons. Engring. Systems, Inc., 2000—. Named to Outstanding Young Men in Am., 1981. Fellow AIAA (assoc., flight mechanics tech. com. 1991-94, 98-01, mem. applied aerodynamics tech. com. 2003-06, 2008-, dep. dir. for edn. region V 1992-94, dep. dir. for precoll. outreach region V 1998-02 Sustained Svc. award 2005, Summerfield Book award 2006); mem. USAF Acad. Assn. Grads., Soc. Automotive Engrs. (mem. aircraft icing tech. com.), Air Force Assn., Tex. A&M U. Assn. Former Students, Tau Beta Pi, Sigma Gamma Tau. Baptist. Avocations: running, photography, hiking. Home: 5331 Wells Fargo Dr Colorado Springs CO 80918 Office: Engring Systems Inc Ste 106 4775 Centennial Blvd Colorado Springs CO 80919 Office Phone: 719-535-0400. Business E-Mail: slmorris@esi-co.com.

MORRIS, STEVLAND See WONDER, STEVIE

MORRIS, STEWART, JR., title insurance company executive; b. Houston, Oct. 14, 1948; s. Stewart Sr. and Joella (Mitchel) M. BA, Rice U., 1971; MBA, U. Tex., 1973. With Stewart Title Co., 1973—, v.p. Houston, 1975-87, sr. exec. v.p., asst. to pres., 1987-91, chmn., pres., 1991—; advisory dir. Stewart Information Services Corp., 1997—2000, bd. dir., pres., co-CEO, 2000—. Bd. dirs. Southern Nat. Bank, Houston. Bd. dirs. Houston chpt. Cystic Fibrosis Found., 1985—. Mem. Am. Land Title Assn., Am. Driving Soc. (bd. dirs. 1984—), Houston Area Carriage Assn. (pres. 1995—), Carriage Assn. Am. (pres. 1995—). Office: 1980 Post Oak Blvd Ste 800 Houston TX 77056-3826

MORRIS, TAMMY KAY, bank executive; d. George Allan and Harriet Nadine Zumwalt; m. Vincent Carl Morris, Sept. 14, 1985; children: Vincent Keath, Kerry Lashell. Mortgage banker Wells Fargo Home Mortgage, Show Low, Ariz., 1999—2004; banking ctr. mgr. Bank Am., 2004—. Pres., charter mem. Kiwanis Internat., Show Low, 2005—. Recipient Sales & Svc. Excellence award, Bank Am. Pacific SW Divsn., 2005—. Conservative. Evangelical. Avocation: reading.

MORRIS, THOMAS WILLIAM, symphony orchestra administrator; b. Rochester, NY, Feb. 7, 1944; s. William H. and Eleanor E. M.; m. Jane Allison, Aug. 7, 1965; children: Elisa L., Charles A., William H. AB, Princeton U., 1965; MBA, Wharton Sch. U. Pa., 1969. Adminstrv. asst., Ford Found. fellow for adminstrv. interns in arts Cin. Symphony, 1965-67; payroll clk. bus. office Boston Symphony Orch., 1969-71, asst. mgr. bus. affairs, 1971-73, mgr., 1973-78, gen. mgr., 1978-86, v.p. spl. projects and planning, 1986; pres. Thomas W. Morris and Co., Inc., Boston, 1986-87; exec. dir. Cleve. Orch., 1987—2004; artistic dir. Ojai Music Festival, 2004—. Chmn. policy com. Maj. Orch. Mgrs., 1977-79; chmn, orch. panel Nat. Endowment for Arts, 1979-80. Chmn. Cleve. Cultural Coalition, 1992-95; mem. Cleve. Bicentennial Commn., 1993-97; mem. bd. overseers Curtis Inst. Music, 1998—. Mem. Am. Symphony Orch. League (dir. 1977-79) Office: 2533 Fairmount Blvd Cleveland OH 44106

MORRIS, TONY RAY, literature and language professor, writer; b. Fayetteville, NC, July 3, 1958; s. Harold Lyndon and Dicy Kathryn Morris; m. Jill Cheree Kjos, Apr. 29, 2000; children: Morgan Ray, Isaac Henry. PhD, Fla. State U., Tallahassee, 2002. Asst. prof. Gardner Webb U., Boiling Springs, NC, 2002—04, Armstrong Atlantic State U., Savannah, Ga., 2004—. Contbr. articles to profl. jours. (Mary Beth Campbell Poetry Book award, 2004). Pres. Poetry Soc. Ga., Savannah, 2006—08; mng. editor Southern Poetry Rev., Savannah, 2004; poetry chair Savannah Book Festival, Savannah, 2007. Recipient La. Lit. Poetry prize, 2001, Tenn. Writer's Alliance Writer's award, 2003, Tenn. William's award, 2003. Mem.: MLA, Coun. Lit. Magazines and Presses, Assoc. Writers and Writing Programs, Assoc. Collegiate Press, Phi Kappa Phi. Office: Armstrong Atlantice State Univ 11935 Abercorn St Savannah GA 31419 Office Fax: 912-344-3494. Business E-Mail: tony@tonymorris.org.

MORRIS, WILLIAM CHARLES, investor; b. St. Louis, Apr. 15, 1938; s. Barney Lockhart and Kathryn (Evers) M.; m. Susan VanAvery Follett, Aug. 26, 1961; children: Edward F., David L., Kenneth V. SB in Chem. Engring., MIT, 1960; MBA, Harvard U., 1963. Assoc. Mobil Chem. Co., NYC, 1963-66; with Lehman Bros., NYC, 1967—84; chmn. Carbo Ceramics Inc., Dallas, 1987—, J&W Seligman & Co., Inc., NYC, 1988—2008. Mng. dir. Met. Opera Assn., NY, 1995—, pres., CEO NY, 2003—; trustee Woods Hole (Mass.) Oceanog. Instn., 2001—. Ensign USCGR, 1961. Office: 100 Park Ave New York NY 10017-5598 also: Cove Point Holdings LLC 100 Park Ave 16th Fl New York NY 10017 Office Phone: 212-850-1864.

MORRIS, WILLIAM CLINTON, JR., petroleum engineer; s. William Clinton and Willie D. Morris; m. Linda May Lang, Nov. 14, 2003; children: Courteney N., Ashley M. BS in Civil Engring. with high honors, U. Tex., Austin, 1990. EIT Tex., 1990. Project engr. drilling Exxon Co. USA, Houston, 1991—92, sr. project engr. drilling, 1992—96, sr. engr. reservoir, 1996—98, supervising engr. drilling New Orleans, 1998—2000; sr. supervising engr. drilling ExxonMobil Devel. Co., Houston, 2000—02; drilling advisor ExxonMobil Malaysia, Kuala Lumpur, 2002—05, engring. mgr. drilling, 2005—. Presdl. scholar, U. Tex. Austin Sch. Engring., 1988—90. Mem.: Soc. Petroleum Engrs. (assoc.), Tau Beta Pi (life), Chi Epsilon (life; pres. 1990—90). Conservative. Baptist. Achievements include patents pending for downhole opening drill bit nozzle. Avocation: golf.

MORRIS, WILLIAM OTIS, JR., lawyer, educator; b. Fairmont, W.Va., Dec. 2, 1922; s. William Otis and Flora Helois (Preston) M.; m. Hazel Irene Kolbus, May 28, 1948; children: Barbara Ann, Melinda Lou. Student, Fairmont State Coll., W.Va., 1940—41; AB, Coll. William and Mary, Williamsburg, Va., 1944; LLB, U. Ill., Champaign/Urbana, 1946; JD, U. Ill., Champaign, 1968; HDC, Nicholas Copernicus U., Torun, Poland, 1992; LLD, Fairmont State U., W.Va., 2003. Bar: Va. 1945, Ill. 1946, U.S. Supreme Ct. 1949. Prof. bus. law U. Ill., 1947-55; assoc. prof. law Stetson U., 1955-58; prof. law W.Va. U., Morgantown, 1958-94, prof. emeritus law, 1994—. Vis. U. Vienna, Austria, Nat. U., Singapore, Nat. U., Seoul, Korea, U. Sydney, Australia, East China Inst. Law and Politics, U. Thessaloniki, Greece; vis. prof. U. Tex., U. Miss., Baylor U., U. San Diego, Samford U., Stetson U., George Washington U., others. Author: Dental Litigation, 1972, 2d edit., 1977, The Law of Domestic Relations in West Virginia, 1975, Veterinarian in Litigation, 1976, Revocation of Professional License, 1985, Handbook of Dental Law, 1994, The Dentist's Legal Advisor, 1994; mem. bd. editors Jour. Law and Ethics in Dentistry, Med. Malpractice Prevention, Clin. Jour.; contbr. articles to profl. jours. With USAR, 1942—43, with Enlisted Reserve US Army, 1941—44. Decorated Merit medal (Poland); recipient Spl. award Nat. U. Seoul, Old Guard Medallion Coll. William and Mary, 1994, Lifetime Achievement Award Dentistry, 1994. Fellow Cleve. Clinic Med. Inst.; mem. ATLA, Va. Bar, Ill. Bar, W.Va. Trial Lawyers Assn., Order of Coif, Order of White Jackets, Sir Robert Boyle Soc. Republican. Lutheran. Home: 644 Bellaire Dr Morgantown WV 26505-2421 Home Phone: 304-599-2664; Office Phone: 304-599-2664. Personal E-mail: bajrmig@webtv.net, wmillini@aol.com.

MORRISETT, LLOYD N., retired foundation executive; b. Oklahoma City, Nov. 2, 1929; s. Lloyd N. and Jessie Ruth (Watson) M.; m. Mary Frances Pierre, June 10, 1952; children: Sarah, Julie. BA, Oberlin Coll.,

1951, LHD (hon.), 1971; postgrad., U. Calif., 1951-53; PhD, Yale U., 1956; degree (hon.), Northwestern U., 1975, RAND Grad. Sch., 1995. Instr. U. Calif., 1956-57, asst. prof., 1957-58; staff mem. Social Sci. Research Council, 1958-59; exec. asst. Carnegie Corp. of N.Y., 1959-61, exec. assoc., 1961-63, exec. assoc. and asst. to pres., 1963-65, v.p., 1965-69, Carnegie Found. for Advancement Teaching, 1965-69; pres. Markle Found., 1969-98; chair. Infonautics, Inc., NYC, 1998—. Trustee Sys. Devel. Found., 1970-88; trustee N.Y. Rand Inst., 1969-75, chmn. bd., 1972-75; trustee Riverside Rsch. Inst., 1971-74, Rsch. Triangle Inst., 1970-79, Ednl. Testing Svc., 1983-87; trustee Oberlin Coll., 1972-88, chmn. bd., 1975-81; trustee Rand, 1973-83, 85-95, 96—, chmn. bd., 1986-95; chmn. bd. trustees Children's TV Workshop, 1970—; bd. dirs. Infonautics Corp., chmn., 1998—; mem. adv. bd. Walt Whitman Ctr., Rutgers U., 1993—; mem. bd. WEBS, 1996—, overseers Darmouth Sch. Medicine, 1995-98. Mem. Coun. on Fgn. Rels., 1968—; mem. N.Y. State Commn. on Quality, Cost and Financing Elem. and Secondary Edn., 1969-72; bd. dirs. Sys. Devel. Corp., 1966-70; mem. vis. com. Office for Info. Tech., Harvard, 1974-80; mem. Am. Coun. on Germany, 1975-79; bd. dirs. Haskins Labs., 1976—; mem. steering com. NRC, 1994-95. Fellow NSF, 1953-56. Fellow APA, AAAS; mem. N.Y. Acad. Scis., Sigma Xi.

MORRISEY, MARENA GRANT, museum director; b. Newport News, Va., May 28, 1945; BFA in Interior Design, Va. Commonwealth U., 1967, MA in Art History, 1970. With Orlando (Fla.) Mus. Art, 1970—, exec. dir., 1976—. Former v.p., chmn. mus. svcs. com., mem. ad hoc com. on collections sharing and long range planning com., past chmn. exhbns. and edn. com. Am. Fedn. Arts; former mem. nat. adv. coun. George Washington U. Clearinghouse on Mus. Edn.; former mem. accreditation com. Nat. Found. for Interior Design Edn. Rsch. Former mem. strategic planning adv. coun. Orange County Sch. Dist.; former mem. advt. rev. bd. BBB; former mem. Orlando Pub. Art Adv. Bd., Orlando Leadership Coun., Orlando Hist. Bldg. Commn.; mem. art selection com. Orlando Internat. Airport, former chmn.; former mem. bd. dirs. Sta. WMFE-TV; bd. dirs. New World Sch. of Arts; vol. Sister Cities of Orlando; mem. internat. arts and culture com. Metro Orlando Internat. Affairs Commn.; pub. art review com. Orange County; exec. com. Uptown Dist. Named Orlando's Outstanding Woman of Yr. in Field of Art; recipient Fla. State of Arts award. Mem. Am. Assn. Mus. (former mem. governing bd., accreditation commn., profl. stds. and practices com., internat. coun. of mus.), Assn. Art Mus. Dirs. (comm. and publs. com.), Southeastern Mus. Conf. (past pres.), Fla. Art Mus. Dirs. Assn. (past pres.), Fla. Assn. Mus. (former bd. dirs.), Greater Orlando C. of C. (past mem. steering com. Leadership Orlando), Jr. League Orlando-Winter Park, Rotary Club Orlando (Paul Harris fellow). Office: Orlando Museum of Art 2416 N Mills Ave Orlando FL 32803-1483 Office Phone: 407-896-4231. Business E-Mail: mgmorrissey@omart.org.

MORRISON, BRENDAN, professional hockey player; b. Pitt Meadows, BC, Can., Aug. 15, 1975; m. Erin Morrison; children: Brayden, Makenna, Kailyn, Taylor. Grad., U. Mich., 1997. Center NJ Devils, 1997—2000, Vancouver Canucks, 2000—08, Anaheim Ducks, 2008—09, Dallas Stars, 2009, Washington Capitals, 2009—. Recipient Hobey Baker Meml. Award, 1997; named Championship Tournament MVP, NCAA, 1996; named to West First All-Am. Team, 1995, 1996, 1997, Championship All-Tournament Team, 1996. Achievements include being a member of NCAA National Championship Team, University of Michigan, 1996. Office: c/o Washington Capitals MCI Center 601 F St NW Washington DC 20004*

MORRISON, BRIGGS, pharmaceutical executive; BS in Biology, Georgetown U.; MD, U. Conn. Sch. Medicine. Sr. rsch. and clin. data mgmt. positions, including exec. dir. and v.p. clin. data mgmt. ops. Merck & Co., Inc., 1995—2004, spl. assignment to review and enhance the effectiveness rsch. ops., 2004—06, v.p., clin. scis., oncology, sr. v.p. rsch.; chief clin. develop., global R&D Pfizer, Inc., 2007—. Fellow, clin. oncology Dana-Farber Cancer Inst.; instr. medicine Harvard Med. Sch. Office: Pfizer Inc 235 E 42nd St New York NY 10017

MORRISON, BRUCE ANDREW, federal official, public affairs consultant; b. NYC, Oct. 8, 1944; s. George and Dorothea A. (Meyer) M.; m. Nancy A. Wanat, Sept. 22, 1991; 1 child, Drew. S.B., MIT, 1965; MS, U. Ill., 1970; JD, Yale U., 1973; LittD (hon.), Quinnipiac Coll.; LLD (hon.), U. Coll. Dublin. Staff atty. New Haven Legal Assistance Assn., 1973-74, mng. atty., 1974-76, exec. dir., 1976-82; mem. 98th-101st Congresses from 3d Conn. dist., 1983-91; chmn. LI Sound Caucus, chmn. Third World Debt Caucus. Chmn. judiciary subcom. on immigration, refugees, and internat. law U.S. Ho. of Reps.; chmn. Fed. Housing Fin. Bd., 1995-2000; co-chmn. ad hoc com. on Irish affairs; mem. U.S. commn. on immigration reform, 1991-97; chair Irish Ams. for Clinton-Gore, 1992, 96; chair Ams. for a New Irish Agenda, 1993-95; vice chmn. GPC Internat., 2000-2001; chmn. Morrison Pub. Affairs Group, 2001-. Mem. Nat. Dem. Ethnic Coordinating Com., Nat. Dem. Ethnic Leadership Coun.; bd. dirs. Alliance for Responsible Cuba Policy; bd. dirs. USA br. Internat. Social Svcs. Mem. ABA, Conn. Bar Assn., Am. Immigration Lawyers Assn. Democrat. Lutheran. Office: 6004 Onondaga Rd Bethesda MD 20816 Home Phone: 301-263-1140; Office Phone: 301-263-1142. Personal E-mail: b.a.m@att.net.

MORRISON, CHARLES EDWARD, think-tank executive; b. Billings, Mont., 1944; m. Chieko Hayashi; children: Karen, Erica, Kenneth, Douglas. BA in Internat. Studies, Johns Hopkins U., MA, PhD, Johns Hopkins U. Legis. asst. U.S. Senate, 1972-80; part-time sr. rsch. assoc. Japan Ctr. for Internat. Exch., 1980-92; asst. to pres. East-West Ctr., 1986-92, dir. program on internat. econs. and politics, 1992-95, pres., 1998—; chair U.S. Consortium of APEC Study Ctrs., 1996-98; internat. chair Pacific Econ. Cooperation Coun., 2006—. Author: wide range of books, papers and analyses; widely quoted by major news media on issues of regional cooperation, internat. rels., U.S. Asia policy and trade policies. Mem.: U.S. Asia Pacific Coun. (founding mem. 2003). Office: East West Ctr 1601 E West Rd Honolulu HI 96848-1601 Office Phone: 808-944-7111.

MORRISON, CRAIG O., chemicals executive; Grad., Ea. Ky. Univ.; MBA, Harvard Univ., 1987. Cons. Bain & Co., 1987—90; sr. operational and bus. mgmt. pos. GE Co., 1990—93; pres., gen. mgr. Van Leer, Inc., 1993—98, Alcan Pharm. and Cosmetic Packaging, divsn. Alcan, Inc., Millville, NJ, 1998—2002; pres., CEO Hexion Specialty Chemicals Inc., Columbus, Ohio, 2002—, chmn., 2005—. Office: Hexion 180 E Broad St Columbus OH 43215

MORRISON, DEBORAH K., medical researcher; PhD, Vanderbilt U. Postdoctoral fellow Harvard Med. Sch., U. Calif., San Francisco, rschr. Berkeley, 1996—97; joined ABL-Basic Rsch. Program Nat. Cancer Inst., NIH, Frederick, Md., 1990, head Cellular Growth Mechanisms Sect., 1995, chief Lab. Cell and Developmental Signaling, Ctr. Cancer Rsch., 1999—. Office: Nat Cancer Inst, NIH Bldg 560, Rm 22-90B NCI-Frederick Frederick MD 21702 Office Phone: 301-846-1733. Office Fax: 301-846-1666. E-mail: dmorrison@ncifcrf.gov.*

MORRISON, DEBRA LYNN, financial planner; b. Mercer, Pa., Mar. 26, 1956; d. Norman Lewis and Mary Boneta (Zahniser) M. BSBA, Messiah Coll., 1978; cert. fin. planner, Coll. for Fin. Planning, Denver, 1987. Cert. fin. planner. Claims adjuster Nationwide Ins., Harrisburg, Pa., 1978; spl. rep. John Hancock Life Ins., Camp Hill, Pa., 1978-79; ins. and investment cons. John Hancock Cos., Camp Hill, 1979-80; dir. tax-advantaged Manzi and Assocs., Ridgewood, NJ, 1980-86; cert. fin. planner The Fin. Network, Clifton, NJ, 1986-88; cert. fin. planner, stockbroker, gen. securities prin., dir. equity sales Lincoln Fin. Advisors, Fairfield, NJ, 1988—94; pres. Debra L. Morrison & Assocs., LLC, Fairfield, NJ, 1994—2001; ptnr. Regent Atlantic Capital, NJ, 2001—05; fee-only wealth mgr. Capital Fin. Advisors, LLC, NJ, 2005—; pres. Debra L. Morrison Speaks, LLC. Contbr. articles to profl. jours. including The Wall St. Jour., USA Today, Nation's Bus., Jour. Fin. Planning, Garden State Woman, Ladies Home Jour., Money, Investment News, Family Money, America's Online Money Wise and Readers Digest and Daily Record; guest appearances: CNN, ABC, MSG's Metro Money. Vol., donor Make-A-Wish Found., NJ, Spl. Olympics NJ, Piscataway; donor Habitat for Humanity, Americus, Ga.; mem. Evangelical & Ecumenical Woman's Caucus, Norfolk, Va.; bd. dirs. Philharmonic Orchestra NJ, Kirkridge Retreat Ctr. Named Top 50 Bus. Women, NJ Bus. Mem., NAPW, NAFE, NJ Assn. Women Bus. Owners, Inst. CFPs., Bus. and Profl. Women (Summit, NJ), Estate Planner's Coun. Bergen County (pres.), Fin. Planner Assn. (Denver), Nat. Assn. Personal Fin. Advisors (Arlington Heights, Ill.), Nat. Assn. Estate Planners & Couns. (Cleve.), Women Fund NJ, Pillar of Cmty. (Union, NJ), NJ 300 (Trenton). Democrat. Avocations: racquetball, water and snow skiing, golf. Home: 65 Gettysburg Way Lincoln Park NJ 07035-1817 Office: 101 Eisenhower Pkwy Ste 300 Roseland NJ 07068 Office Phone: 800-620-4232 ext. 705, 973-709-2244. Business E-Mail: debra.morrison@trovena.com, info@msmorrisonspeaks.com, debra@msmorrisonspeaks.com.

MORRISON, DELMAR R., chemical engineer; married. BA in Chemistry, Knox Coll., Galesburg, Ill., 1996; MS in Chem. Engring., Okla. State U., Stillwater, 1998; PhD, Ill. Inst.Tech., Chgo., 2008. Cert. profl. engr., Ill. Mng. engr. Exponent Inc., Lisle, Ill., 2003—. Frat. advisor Beta Theta Pi, Galesburg, Ill., 1999—2008. Mem.: AIChE, NFPA. Office: Exponent Inc 1011 Warrenville Rd Ste 215 Lisle IL 60532 Office Fax: 630-743-7799. Business E-Mail: tmorrison@exponent.com.

MORRISON, DENISE M., food products executive; b. Neptune, NJ, Jan. 13, 1954; d. Dennis J. and Constance R. (Shields) Sullivan; m. Barry J. Mullen, June 21, 1975, (div. Apr. 1984); 1 child, Michelle; m. Thomas C. Morrison, Oct. 26, 1985; 1 child, Kelly. BS in Economics & Psychology, Boston Coll., 1975. Unit sales mgr. Procter & Gamble, Boston, 1975-82; trade developer mgr. Pepsi, U.S.A., Purchase, NY, 1982-84; dir. conjections mktg. Nestle USA, Purchase, NY, 1984-89, west zone v.p. Bakersfield, Calif., 1991-95, v.p. impulse sales, 1995; area v.p. sales & logistics Nabisco, Inc., Pleasanton, Calif., 1995—98, sr. v.p., 1998—2000, gen. mgr. Down the Street divsn., 2000—01; exec. v.p., gen. mgr. Snacks and Confections divsn. Kraft Foods, 2001—03; pres.-global sales, chief customer officer Campbell Soup Co., Camden, NJ, 2003—05, pres. N.Am. Soup, Sauces, & Beverages, 2007—; pres. Campbell USA, Camden, NJ, 2005—07. Bd. dirs. The Goodyear Tire & Rubber Co., 2005—. Recipient Althea Gibson Beacon award for Bus. Leadership, 2003, Salute to Policy Makers, Exec. Women NJ, 2006, Aiming High award, Legal Momentum, 2007; named Exec. of the Year, Snack Food & Bakery mag., 2003; named a Woman of Influence, NJBiz mag., 2003; named one of The Most Powerful Women in Bus., Fortune mag., 1999—2006; named to NY YWCA Academy of Women Achievers, 2001. Mem. Republican Womens Club. Roman Catholic. Avocations: hiking, reading, boating, skiing, music. Office: Campbell Soup Co 1 Campbell Pl Camden NJ 08103*

MORRISON, DONALD FRANKLIN, statistician, educator; b. Stoneham, Mass., Feb. 10, 1931; s. Daniel Norman and Agnes Beatrice (Packard) M.; m. Phyllis Ann Hazen, Aug. 19, 1967; children: Norman Hazen, Stephen Donald. BS in Bus. Adminstrn, Boston U., 1953, AM, 1954; MS, U. N.C., 1957; PhD, Va. Poly. Inst. and State U., 1960; MA (hon.), U. Pa., 1971. Mem. staff Lincoln Lab., M.I.T., 1956; cons. math. statistician NIMH, Bethesda, Md., 1956-63; mem. tech. staff Bell Labs., Holmdel, NJ, 1967; mem. faculty, dept. stats. Wharton Sch., U. Pa., 1963-99, prof. stats., 1973-99, chmn. dept., 1978-85, prof. emeritus, 2000—. Author: Multivariate Statistical Methods, 4th edit., 2005, Applied Linear Statistical Methods, 1983; editor The Am. Statistician, 1972-75; assoc. editor Biometrics, 1972-74; contbr. articles to profl. jours. Served with USPHS, 1956-58. NSF grantee, 1966 Fellow Am. Statis. Assn., Inst. Math. Stats.; mem. Internat. Statis. Inst., B&M R.R. Hist. Soc., Nat. R.R. Hist. Soc., R.R. and Locomotive Hist. Soc., N&W Hist. Soc., Bridge Line Hist. Soc., N.E. Elec. Rwy. Hist. Soc. Democrat. Lutheran. Home: 118 E Brookhaven Rd Wallingford PA 19086-6327 E-mail: donaldm@wharton.upenn.edu.

MORRISON, DONALD WILLIAM, lawyer; b. Portland, Oreg., Mar. 31, 1926; s. Robert Angus and Laura Calista (Hodgson) M.; m. Elizabeth Margaret Perry, July 25, 1953; children: Elizabeth Laura, Carol Margaret. BSE.E., U. Wash., 1946; LL.B., Stanford U., 1950. Bar: Oreg. 1950, Calif. 1950, N.Y. 1967, Ill. 1968, Ohio 1974. Assoc. Pendergrass, Spackman, Bullivant & Wright, Portland, 1950-57, ptnr., 1957-60; gen. atty. Pacific N.W. Bell, Portland, 1960-66; atty. AT&T, NYC, 1966-68; counsel Ill. Bell Telephone Co., Chgo., 1968-74; v.p., gen. counsel Ohio Bell Telephone Co., Cleve., 1974-91; of counsel Arter & Hadden, Cleve., 1992—2003. Dir. Archael. Inst. Am.; trustee Cleve. Archaeol. Soc., Cleve. Chamber Music Soc., Cleve. Coun. on World Affairs, Apollo's Fire Baroque Orch.; mem. adv. com. Cleve. Bot. Garden; mem. Ohio adv. bd. Trust for Pub. Land. With USN, 1943—50. Recipient various bar and civic appreciation awards. Mem. ABA, Ohio State Bar Assn., Oreg. State Bar Assn., Calif. Bar Assn., Rowfant Club.

MORRISON, FRED LAMONT, law educator; b. Salina, Kans., Dec. 12, 1939; s. Earl F. and Madge Louise (Glass) M.; m. Charlotte Foot, Dec. 27, 1971; children: Charles, Theodore, George, David. AB, U. Kans., 1961; BA, Oxford U., Eng., 1963, MA, 1968; PhD, Princeton U., 1966; JD, U. Chgo., 1967. Bar: Minn. 1973. Asst. prof. law U. Iowa, Iowa City, 1967-69; counselor on internat. law U.S. State Dept., Washington, 1982-83; assoc. prof. law U. Minn., Mpls., 1969-73, prof. law, 1973-90, Oppenheimer Wolff and Donnelly prof., 1990-97, acting dean, 1994-95, Popham Haik/Lindquist & Vennum prof., 1998—, interim co-dean, 2006—08. Of counsel Popham, Haik, Schnobrich & Kaufman, Mpls., 1983-97. Dir. Am. Soc. for Comparative Study of Law; mem. adv. com. on internat. law U.S. Dept. State, Washington, 1987-89; mem. internat. adv. bd. Inst. on Internat. Law, Kiel, Germany, 1989—; mem. Am. Law Inst., bd. editors for Am. Jour. Comparative Law. Recipient President's Award for Outstanding Svc., U. Minn., 1997. Home: 1412 W 47th St Minneapolis MN 55419-5204 Office: U Minn Law Sch 229 19th Ave S Minneapolis MN 55455-0400 Office Phone: 612-625-0321. Business E-Mail: morrison@umn.edu.

MORRISON, GAIL, internist, nephrologist, educator; BA in Biology, Chemistry magna cum laude, Boston U., 1967; MD, U. Pa., 1971. Diplomate Am. Bd. Med. Examiners, Am. Bd. Internal Medicine, Am. Bd. Nephrology. Instr. dept. continuing edn. Boston U., 1966-67; clin. fellow Harvard U., Boston, 1971-72; intern Beth Israel Hosp., Boston, 1971-72; jr. asst. resident Georgetown U. Hosp., Washington, 1972-73; staff physician clin. ctr. NIH, Bethesda, Md., 1973-74, staff assoc. Nat. Heart & Lung Inst., 1973-74; fellow in nephrology renal electrolyte sect. U. Pa. Hosp., Phila., 1974-76, rsch. fellow in nephrology renal electrolyte sect. NIH, 1975-76, asst. prof. medicine, 1976—83; assoc. prof. medicine U. Pa. Sch. Medicine, Phila., 1984—94, prof. medicine, 1994—, vice dean edn., 1995—, dir. acad. programs, 1995—; attending Phila. Vets. Adminstrn. Med. Ctr., 1976-77, U. Pa. Health Sys., 1976—. Asst. dir. dialysis unit U. Pa. Hosp., Phila., 1976-77, assoc. dir., 1977-82, dir. renal outpatient prog., 1976-82, dir. outpatient dialysis unit, 1979-81, acting dir. dialysis prog. for inpatient and outpatient dialysis units, 1981-82, dir., 1982-86; acad. coord. dept. medicine U. Pa. Hosp., Phila., 1985-96; assoc. chmn. dept. medicine for student edn. U. Pa. Sch. Medicine, Phila., 1986-96, acting assoc. dean for clin. curriculum, 1991, assoc. dean for clin. curriculum, 1991-95, vice dean for edn., dir. acad. progs., 1995—, mem. numerous acad., search, planning, steering, alumni, budget, nutrition coms., others; cons., advisor in field; presenter, co-dir., tchr., leader workshops, symposiums, confs. Author: (with A. Goroll) Core Medicine Clerkship: A Curriculum Guide, Manual for Curriculum 2000, 1996; editor: (with others) Introduction to Clinical Medicine, 2d rev. edit., 1995, Concepts in Basic Science, 1995, Essentials of Nutrition: A Case-Based Approach; mem. editorial bd. Am. Jour. Medicine, 1996-99; author papers, reviews, abstracts, chpts. to books; contbr. articles to profl. jours. Recipient Daniel C. Tosteson award for leadership in med. edn., 2006, Disting. Aumni Svc. award U. Pa.; grantee Pa. Sch. Nursing, 1989-90, Heinz Endowment Fund, 1990-95, U. Pa. Sch. Medicine, 1993-95, 93-96, 97-98. Fellow ACP, Coll. Physicians of Pa. (mem. sect. on pub. health and preventive medicine 1995—); mem. AAAS, Internat. Soc. Nephrology, Am. Soc. Nephrology, Am. Fedn. for Clin. Rsch., Am. Assn. Med. Colls. Women's Liaison Officer, Pa. Soc. Nephrology (coun. mem. network #24 federally funded end-stage renal disease orgn. 1978-83, mem. facility planning bd. 1979-80, chmn. 1980-82, mem. exec. com. 1980-82, ad-hoc mem. med. review bd. 1980-82, mem. nomination and credential com. 1982-83), Southeastern Nat. Kidney Found. (bd. dirs. 1984-88), Phi Beta Kappa, Sigma Xi, Alpha Omega Alpha. Home: 1040 Stony Ln Gladwyne PA 19035-1136 Office Phone: 215-898-8034. Fax: 215-573-4289. Business E-Mail: morrisog@mailmed.upenn.edu.

MORRISON, GLENN LESLIE, minister; b. Cortez, Colo., Feb. 26, 1929; s. Ward Carl Morrison and Alma Irene (Butler) Anderson; m. Beverely Joanne Buck, Aug. 26, 1949; children: David Mark, Betty Jo Morrison Mullen, Gary Alan, Judith Lynn Morrison Oltmann, Stephen Scott. Student, San Diego State U., 1948-49, Chabot Coll., 1968-69. Ordained ministry Evang. Ch. Alliance, 1961. Dir. counseling follow-up Oakland (Calif.) Youth Christ, 1954-56; pres. Follow Up Ministries, Inc., Castro Valley, Calif., 1956—. Assoc. pastor 1st Covenant Ch., Oakland, 1956-58; exec. dir. East Bay Youth Christ, Oakland, 1960-66; supervising chaplain Alameda County (Calif.) Probation Dept., 1971-90; vol. chaplain Alameda County Sheriff's Dept., 1971—; founder, dir. God Squad Vol. Program Prison Workers, 1972—; seminar leader Calif. Dept. Corrections, Sacramento, 1978—, mem. chaplains coordinating com., 1988—. Author: Scripture Investigation Course, 1956, Tired of the Same Ol' Same Ol'? There is a Better Way, 1978. Mem. Am. Correctional Assn., Am. Protestant Correctional Chaplains Assn. (regional pres., sec. 1980-86, nat. sec. 1986-88, nat. 2nd v.p. 1996-98). Office: Follow Up Ministries Inc PO Box 2514 Castro Valley CA 94546-2514 Personal E-mail: fumi2000@cox.net.

MORRISON, HAROLD L., JR., insurance company executive; BA in History, Duke U., Durham, NC. Leadership positions in ops. The Chubb Corp., San Jose, Calif., San Francisco, Warren, NJ, mgr., dept. fin. institutions, mgr., northwest regional office Seattle, 1996—2001, NY brokerage zone officer, 2001—03, exec. v.p., US field ops. mgr., Chubb & Son, 2003—08, exec. v.p., chief global field officer, 2008—. Office: Chubb Group Ins Companies 15 Mountain View Rd Warren NJ 07059 Office Phone: 908-903-2000. Office Fax: 908-903-2027.

MORRISON, HARRY, chemistry professor; b. Bklyn., Apr. 25, 1937; s. Edward and Pauline (Sommers) M.; m. Harriet Thurman, Aug. 23, 1958; children: Howard, David, Daniel. BA, Brandeis U., 1957; PhD, Harvard U., 1961. NATO-NSF postdoctoral fellow Swiss Fed. Inst., Zurich, 1961-62; rsch. assoc. U. Wis., Madison, 1962-63; asst. prof. chemistry Purdue U., West Lafayette, Ind., 1963-69, assoc. prof., 1969-76, prof., 1976—, dept. head, 1987-92, dean Sch. Sci., 1992—2002. Mem. acad. adv. com. Indsl. Rsch. Inst., 1993-96. Contbr. numerous articles to profl. jours. Bd. fellows Brandeis U. Mem. Am. Chem. Soc., Am. Soc. Photobiology, Inter-Am. Photochem. Soc., Coun. for Chem. Rsch. (chmn. 1995), Phi Beta Kappa Office: Purdue Univ Dept Chemistry Brown Bldg West Lafayette IN 47907-2084 Office Phone: 765-494-5246. Business E-Mail: hmorrison@purdue.edu.

MORRISON, JAMES EMERSON, English language educator; b. Detroit, Oct. 16, 1960; s. James E. and Veronica (Dolan) M. BA, Wayne State U., 1983; MA, SUNY, Buffalo, 1987, PhD, 1988. Teaching fellow SUNY, Buffalo, 1983-88; lectr. Wayne State U., Detroit, 1988-89; asst. prof. English N.C. State U., Raleigh, 1990—. Contbr. fiction essays in profl. jours. NEH grantee, 1993. Office: NC State U Dept English PO Box 8105 Raleigh NC 27695-0001

MORRISON, JAMES V., biology professor; s. James V. and Mary E. Morrison; m. Louise V. Mottashed, Aug. 5, 1968; children: Jennifer Forte, James. BA in Biology, Kans. State U., Manhattan, 1968, MS in Zoology, 1971; MPH in Epidemiology, Loma Linda U., Calif., 1978. Assoc. prof. biology Riverside CC, Calif., 1971—. Mem.: Phi Kappa Phi, Delta Omega (life). Avocations: sailing, scuba diving, travel. Office: Riverside CC 2001 Third St Norco CA 92860-2600 Office Fax: 951-372-7050; Home Fax: 951-372-7050.

MORRISON, JAMES WILLIAM, JR., lobbyist, government agency administrator, consultant; b. Bluefield, W.Va., Jan. 14, 1936; s. James William and Winnie Ella (Hendricks) M.; m. Marva Elizabeth Tillman, Aug. 8, 1957 (div.); children: Traquita Renee, James William III; m. Jean Murray Barber, May 15, 2001; 1 stepchild, Susannah Claire. BA, W.Va. State Coll., 1957; MPA, U. Dayton, 1970. Inventory mgr. Dayton Air Force Depot/Def. Electronics Supply Ctr., 1959-63; mgmt. specialist Air Force Logistics Command, Dayton, 1963-72; exec. asst. to dir. mgmt. sys. NASA, Washington, 1972-74; sr. mgmt. assoc. Exec. Office of Pres. Office Mgmt. and Budget, 1974-79; asst. dir. econ. and govt. U.S. Office of Pers. Mgmt., 1979, dir. congl. rels., 1979-81, assoc. dir. compensation, 1981-87; sr. mgt. CNA Ins. Co., 1987-88; pres. Morrison Assocs., 1988—. Vis. lectr. pub. exec. project SUNY Albany, 1974-76. Contbr. articles to profl. jours. Mem. adv. com. Dayton Bd. Edn., 1971. With U.S. Army, 1957-59. Recipient Presdl. Rank award of Disting. Exec.,

1985. Mem. Alpha Phi Alpha, Pi Delta Phi, Pi Alpha Alpha. Independent. Presbyterian. Home: 35056 N 80th Way Scottsdale AZ 85266 Office Phone: 480-515-2859. Personal E-mail: jwmorrison@cox.net.

MORRISON, JEFFRY H., social sciences educator; s. Donald A. Morrison; children: Alexander L., Ella M., Evelyn C. BA, McDaniel Coll., Westminster, Md., 1983; MA, Boston Coll., Chestnut Hill, 1994; Ph.D., Georgetown U., Washington, DC, 1999. Asst. prof. USAF Acad., Colo. Springs, 1999—2001, Regent U., Va. Beach, 2001—03; grad. faculty James Madison Meml. Fellowship Found., Washington, 2002—; vis. asst. prof. Princeton U., NJ, 2003—04; assoc. prof. Regent U., Va. Beach, 2004—. Author: (book) The Political Philosophy of George Washington, John Witherspoon and the Founding of the American Republic; editor: The Founders on God and Government. Recipient Faculty of Yr., Regent U., 2006—07; Fellowship, Princeton U., 2003—04. Mem.: Am. Polit. Sci. Assn., Phi Sigma Tau. Office: Regent Univ 1000 Regent University Dr Virginia Beach VA 23464 Office Phone: 757-352-4309. Personal E-mail: morrisoj@georgetown.edu. Business E-Mail: jeffmor@regent.edu.

MORRISON, JOHN HORTON, lawyer, arbitrator; b. Sept. 15, 1933; BBA, U. N.Mex., Albuquerque, 1955; MA, U. Oxford, 1957; JD, Harvard U., Cambridge, Mass., 1962. Bar: Ill. 1962, US Supreme Ct. 1966. Assoc. Kirkland & Ellis, Chgo., 1962-67, ptnr., 1968-99. Named Hon. Officer Most Excellent Order Brit. Empire, 1994; Rhodes scholar. Mem. ABA, Internat. Bar Assn., Assn. Am. Rhodes Scholars (pres. 1998-2006), Chgo. Internat. Dispute Resolution Assn. (dir.). Home: 2550 Princeton Ave Evanston IL 60201-4941 Personal E-mail: johnhmorrison@post.harvard.edu. Business E-Mail: jmorrison@kirkland.com.

MORRISON, JOHN LEWIS, former food company executive, investor; b. Mpls., Apr. 6, 1945; s. John Washburn and Charlotte (Lewis) Morrison; m. Christine Anderson, June 23, 1967; children: Kelly, John. BA, Yale U., New Haven, 1967; MBA, Harvard U., Cambridge, Mass., 1971. V.p. Kidder, Peabody & Co., Inc., NYC, 1971-76; asst. treas. to CFO internat. grp. Pillsbury Co., Mpls., 1976-79, gen. mgr., pres. Mexico, 1979-81, group v.p. internat. grp. Mpls., 1981-84, pres. internat. grp., 1984-87, exec. v.p., chmn. US consumer foods, 1987—89; co-founder, mng. dir. Goldner Hawn Johnson & Morrison Inc., Mpls., 1989—. Mem. US Olympic Hockey Team, Grenoble, France, 1968, Fgn. Intelligence Adv. Bd., Washington, 2005—; bd. dirs. Hormel Foods Corp., 2003—, Diamond Brands Internat., Human Capital Corp., Anderson Windows Inc., Petermann Holding Co., Michael Foods Inc.; co-founder, chmn. Callanish Capital, LLC, Minnetonka, Minn., 2001—. Bd. dirs. Abbott-Northwestern Hosp., Mpls.; trustee Mpls. Inst. Arts, 1985—. Recipient All-Am. award in Hockey, NCAA, 1967, Mallory award, Yale U., 1967. Mem.: Links NYC, Woodhill Country Club (bd. dirs. 1984—). Republican. Presbyterian. Office: Goldner Hawn 3700 Wells Fargo Ctr 90 S Seventh St Minneapolis MN 55402-4304 Office Phone: 612-338-5912. Business E-Mail: morrison@goldnerhawn.com.*

MORRISON, JOHN MARTIN, lawyer, State Auditor Montana; b. McCook, Nebr., June 18, 1961; s. Frank Brennor and Sharon Romain (McDonald) M.; m. Catherine Helen Wright, Aug. 17, 1991; children: Allison Kay, Amanda Grace. BA, Whitman Coll., 1983; JD, U. Denver, 1986. Bar: Mont. 1987, U.S. Dist. Ct. Mont. 1988, U.S. Ct. Appeals (9th cir.) 1989, U.S. Supreme Ct. 1996. Legis. asst., legal counsel U.S. Senate, Washington, 1987-88; ptnr. Morrison Law Offices, Helena, Mont., 1988-93, Meloy & Morrison, Helena, 1994-2000; auditor State of Mont., 2000—, ins. and securities commr., 2001—08. Author: Mavericks: The Lives and Battles of Montana's Political Legends, 1997; contbr. articles to profl. jours. Del. Dem. Nat. Platform Com., 1992; Dem. candidate for U.S. Senate, 2006. Mem. Mont. Trial Lawyers Assn. (past pres., bd. dirs. 1991-2000), Western Trial Lawyers Assn. (bd. govs. 1990-95), Trial Lawyers Pub. Justice (chair 1989-90), Nat. Assn. Ins. Commn., N.Am. Assn. Securities Administrs. Avocations: skiing, fly fishing, mountain climbing, river rafting, running. Office: Office of the Mont State Auditor PO Box 4009 840 Helena Ave Helena MT 59604 also: Morrison Law Firm 805 Warren Helena MT 59601 Office Phone: 406-444-2040, 406-442-6922. Business E-Mail: jmorrison@mt.gov, jmmontana@msn.com.

MORRISON, KENDRA ANN, environmental scientist; b. Hugo, Colo., June 8, 1970; d. Kenneth Patrick and Judy Ann Morrison. BS in Environ. Health, Colo. State U., Ft. Collins, 1993; MS in Environ. Scis., U. Colo., 1999. Specialist consumer health and protection Colo. Dept. Pub. Health and Environ., Denver, 1993; specialist environ. health Tri-County Health Dept., Commerce City, Colo., 1993—98; scientist U.S. Environ. Protection Agy., Denver, 1998—. Rsch. asst. U. Colo., Denver, 2001; mem. adv. bd. Engrs. Without Borders, Longmont, Colo., 2003—05; intern, lab. and rsch. asst. MIT, Honolulu, 1994. Named Environ. Pub. Health Emerging Leader, U.S. Dept. Health and Human Svcs. Ctrs. Disease Control and Prevention, 2003; grantee, Colo. Leadership Devel. Program, 2007. Mem.: Colo. Hazardous Waste Mgmt. Soc., Air and Waste Mgmt. Assn., Nat. Environ. Health Assn. (registered environ. health specialist 2000, registered sanitarian 2000, Merit award 2004, scholar 1998). Avocations: travel, martial arts. Home: 180 Poplar St Unit G Denver CO 80220 Office: US EPA Region 8 1595 Wynkoop St Denver CO 80202

MORRISON, KENNETH DUNCAN, retired retail grocery executive; b. Bradford, England, Oct. 20, 1931; s. William Murdoch and Hilda Morrison; m. Lynne Morrison; 5 children. LLD (hon.), U. Leeds. With William Morrison Supermarkets PLC, Bradford, England, 1952—, chmn., mng. dir., 1956—97, chief exec., exec. chmn., 2006—08. Recipient Order of British Empire, 1990. Office: William Morrison Supermarkets PLC Hilmore House Gain Lane Bradford BD3 7DL England Office Phone: 44-845-611-5000.

MORRISON, MALCOLM CAMERON, engineering management professional; b. Pitts., Apr. 12, 1942; s. Malcolm Smith and Floy Alphine (Sample) M.; m. Julia Gertrude Collette, Dec. 30, 1960 (div. oct. 1972); 1 child, Malcolm Paul; m. Lois Roxane Florian, July 27, 1974; 1 child, Rachel Floy. BS, Caltech, Pasadena, Calif., 1964, PhD, 1969. Sr. scientist Havens Internat., San Diego, 1969-71; group leader Calgon Corp., San Diego, 1971-72; v.p. Chem. Systems, Irvine, Calif., 1972-79, Purolator Puropore, Tustin, Calif., 1979-82, Puropore, Inc., Tustin, 1982-85; dir. Microgon, Laguna Hills, Calif., 1985-95, Spectrum Cos., Laguna Hills, 1995-98; v.p. Spectrum Labs., Rancho Dominquez, Calif., 1998—2002; sr. process engr. Santa Fe Sci. and Tech., 2004—. Cons. in field, 1985—; v.p./owner OMMS Engrs., Inc., Santa Ana, Calif., 1982-2005. Contbr. articles to profl. jours. Dir. Santiago Sanitation Dist., Silverado, Calif., 1978-80. Mem. Am. Inst. Chem. Engrs., Orange County CAER (sec./treas. 1990-2005), Am. Filtration Soc. (pres. Golden State chpt. 1985-91), The Nature Conservancy. Republican. Roman Catholic. Avocations: horseback riding, gardening, birding, church activities. Home: Box 810 El Rito NM 87530-0810 Office: Santa Fe Sci and Tech 3216 Richards Ln Santa Fe NM 87507 Home Phone: 505-581-9115; Office Phone: 505-474-3500 ext. 22. Business E-Mail: morrison@sfst.net.

MORRISON, MARTIN, writer; b. Oakland, Calif., Mar. 28, 1947; s. Raymond Earl and June (Cabral) M. AB with distinction, U. Calif., Berkeley, 1967, MA, 1969, postgrad., 1969-73. Certified (life) nat. tournament dir.; cert. jr./community coll. tchr. (life), Calif. Instr. classics and English composition U. Calif. at Berkeley, 1967-73; instr. legal argument Boalt Hall Law Sch., 1972; with exec. office CF Air Freight, Inc., 1979-83, asst. to traffic mgr. for spl. projects, 1982-83, computer systems mgr., 1982-83; computer systems analyst Qantel Bus. Computers, 1983-86, sr. computer systems analyst, 1986-92; sr. tech. writer Shared Med. Systems, 1992-96, supr. tech. writing, 1996-98, mgr. tech. writing, 1998—2000; lead tech. writer Kaiser Permanent, 2001—. Mem. Amateur Chamber Music Players, 1978—. Author: Writing Argument, 1972, USCF Yearbooks, 1974-76, Official Rules of Chess, 1975, 77, Chess Competitor's Handbook, 1980, Latin Works for Transparent Language Computer Program, 1992-93; editor: Chess Voice, 1968-73, Keeping Ancient Rome Alive, 1987-89; contbg. author: Fundamentals of Management, 3d edit., 2000; chess editor: Oakland Tribune, 1965-66; columnist Via Lorenzo, 1987-88, Metric Today, 1985—; pub., bus. mgr. Chess Life & Rev., 1977-78, Bancroft Music Sch., 1958-60. Asst. concertmaster Berkeley Chamber Chorus and Orch., 1980-83; concertmaster Oakland Philharm., 1987-90, bd. dirs., corp. sec., 1988-90; 1st violin Albany Trio, 1987-91, Mostly Baroque Ensemble, 1999-2000; vol. staff Chabot Sci. Ctr., 1981-84, chmn. computer system mgmt. staff; sec., treas. AstroSoft, 1983-87. Schola Gregoriana San Francisco, 1989-92, Schola Cantemus, 1992-95; dir. St. John Schola, 1995—. Fellow U.S. Metric Assn. (life, chmn. consumer edn. com. 1984—, Spl. Citation 1986, cert. advanced metrication specialist 1987); mem. Am. Philol. Assn., Am. Classical League, Eastbay Astron. Soc. (bd. dirs. 1981-84, v.p. 1983-84), Internat. Assn. Chess Press (v.p. 1973-77), Soc. for Tech. Comm. (sr.), Chess Journalists Assn. (pres. 1972-75), World Chess Fedn. (internat. life arbiter, mem. rules com. 1973-78, chmn. 1976-78), U.S. Chess Fedn. (bd. dels. 1968-78, 1st v.p. Pacific Region 1972-73, nat. sec. 1972-75, tech. dir. 1973-76, exec. dir. 1976-78, Disting. Vol. award, 1982, Spl. citation, 1984, Disting. Svc. award 1995), Calif. Alumni Assn. (life, scholarship com., chmn. 1987-93, Disting. Chmn. award 1990), San Lorenzo Garden Homes Assn. (v.p./sec. 1985-86, pres. 1986-92), Mensa, Friends of the Alameda Free Library, Phi Beta Kappa.

MORRISON, MATTHEW, actor; b. Fort Ord, Calif., Oct. 30, 1978; Performer: (Broadway plays) Footloose, 1998—2000, The Rocky Horror Show, 2000—02, Hairspray, 2002—04, The Light in the Piazza, 2005, A Naked Girl on the Appian Way, 2005, South Pacific, 2008, (plays) 10 Million Miles, 2007, (TV films) Once Upon a Mattress, 2005; actor: (films) Marci X, 2003, Blinders, 2006, Music and Lyrics, 2007, Dan in Real Life, 2007; (TV series) As the World Turns, 2006, Glee, 2009; (TV films) Nice Girls Don't Get the Corner Office, 2007. Office: c/o Randi Goldstein The Gersh Agy 41 Madison Ave 33rd Fl New York NY 10010 also: The Gersh Agy 232 N Canon Dr Beverly Hills CA 90210

MORRISON, PATRICE BURGERT, lawyer; b. St. Louis, July 8, 1948; d. Frank J. and Loretta S. Burgert; m. William Brian Morrison; 1 child, W. Brett. AB, U. Miami, 1971, MA, 1972; JD, Am. U., 1975; LLM in Taxation, Georgetown U., 1978. Bar: Fla. 1975, DC 1977, NY 1983. Atty. US Dept. Treas., Washington, 1975-79; atty., ptnr. Nixon Hargrave Devans & Doyle, LLP, Palm Beach County, Fla., 1980-89, Nixon Peabody LLP (formerly Nixon, Hargrave, Devans & Doyle), Rochester, NY, 1989—. Bd. dirs. Rochester Friendly Sr. Svcs., Inc., 1996—. Bd. dirs. Alzheimer's Assn., Rochester, 1996—2001, Nat. Women's Hall of Fame, 1990—92; mem. exec. com. Estate Planning Coun. Rochester, 1992—95; bd. chair & dir. Cloverwood Sr. Living, Inc., 2000—. Mem.: Am. Immigration Lawyers Assn. Office: Nixon Peabody LLP 1100 Clinton Sq Rochester NY 14604

MORRISON, PATRICIA B., former electronics executive; BA in Math. & Stats. summa cum laude, Miami Univ., BS in Secondary Edn. Sys. mgmt., IT positions Procter & Gamble; CIO GE Indsl. Sys. Gen. Electric, 1997—2000; CIO Quaker Oats Co., Chgo., 2000—02; exec. v.p., CIO Office Depot, Inc., Delray Beach, Fla., 2002—05; sr. v.p., chief info. officer Motorola Inc., Schaumburg, Ill., 2005—07, exec. v.p., CIO, 2007—08. Bd. dir. Jo-Ann Stores, Inc., SPSS Inc., 2007—; mem. adv. bd. UST Global, 2009—. Bd. mem. Chgo. Symphony Orch., Lyric Opera Chgo. Named to CIO Hall of Fame, CIO Mag., 2008. Mailing: UST Global Ste 500 120 Vantis Aliso Viejo CA 92656*

MORRISON, PAUL J., former state attorney general, prosecutor; b. Dodge City, Kans., June 1, 1954; m. Joyce Morrison; 3 children. Student, Kans. State U.; BA in Criminal Justice, Washburn U., Topeka; JD, Washburn U. Sch. Law, Topeka, 1980. Asst. dist. atty. Johnson County, Kans., 1980—89, dist. atty. Kans., 1989—2005; atty. gen. State of Kans., Topeka, 2007—08. Vice chair Kans. Sentencing Commn. Chmn. fundraising effort Johnson County United Way, 2004; mem. Good Shepherd Cath. Ch.; pres., bd. mem. Sunflower House, SafeHome, Inc. Recipient Clarence M. Kelley award for Excellence in Criminal Justice Adminstrn., Lifetime Achievement award, Kans. County & Dist. Attorney's Assn., 2007; named Prosecutor of the Yr., 2001. Mem.: Johnson County Bar Found. (former pres.), Kans. County and Dist. Attys. Assn. (former pres.). Democrat. Roman Catholic.

MORRISON, PORTIA OWEN, lawyer; b. Charlotte, NC, Apr. 1, 1944; d. Robert Hall Jr. and Josephine Currier (Hutchison) M.; m. Alan Peter Richmond, June 19, 1976; 1 child, Anne Morrison. BA in English, Agnes Scott Coll., 1966; MA, U. Wis., 1967; JD, U. Chgo., 1978. Bar: Ill. 1978. Of counsel DLA Piper U.S. LLP, Chgo., 1978—. Lectr. in field. Past pres. Girl Scouts of Chgo. Fellow: Am. Coll. Real Estate Lawyers (past pres. bd. govs., bd. govs.); mem.: ABA, CREW Chgo. Office: DLA Piper US LLP 203 N La Salle St Chicago IL 60601-1210 Office Phone: 312-368-4013. Business E-Mail: portia.morrison@dlapiper.com.

MORRISON, RICHARD THANE, federal judge; b. Hutchinson, Kans., June 10, 1967; s. Robert and Wanda Morrison; m. Rebecca Yasmin Khamneipur; 2 children. BA, BS, U. Kans., 1989; JD, U. Chgo., 1993, MA, 1994. Rsch. asst. to Hon. Jerry E. Posner U. Chgo. Law Sch., 1991; summer assoc. Christy & Viener, NYC, 1991, Baker & McKenzie, Chgo., 1992, Fulbright & Jaworski, Houston, 1993; part-time clk. Baker & McKenzie, Chgo., 1993; law clk. to Hon. Jerry E. Smith US Ct. Appeals (5th circuit), Houston, 1993—94; assoc. Baker & McKenzie, Chgo., 1994—96, Mayer Brown & Platt, Chgo., 1996—2001; dep. asst. atty. gen. review and appellate matters, Tax Divsn. US Dept. Justice, Washington, 2001—07, acting asst. atty. gen., 2007—08; judge US Tax Ct., 2008—. Mem.: ABA Section on Taxation, The Federalist Soc. Office: US Tax Ct 400 Second St, NW Washington DC 20217 Office Phone: 202-521-0853.*

MORRISON, ROBERT SCHECK, former manufacturing executive, former food products executive; b. NYC, Apr. 4, 1942; s. Forrest John and Grayce Scheck (Hopkins) Morrison; m. Susan E. Brennan, Oct. 8, 1988; children: R. Scott, Stephen L., James F., Emily E., Catherine A. BS in English, Coll. Holy Cross, 1963; MBA, U. Pa., 1969. With Procter & Gamble, Cin., 1969—83; chmn., CEO Kraft Inc., Northfield, Ill., 1983—97; chmn., pres. CEO Quaker Oats Co., Chgo., 1997—2001; vice chmn. PepsiCo., Inc., Purchase, NY, 2001—03; interim chmn., CEO 3M Co., St. Paul, 2005. Bd. dirs. Aon Corp., 2000—, Tribune Co., 2001—, 3M Corp., 2002—, Ill. Tool Works Inc., 2003—, Grocery Mfrs. Am. Bd. trustees Lyric Opera Chgo., Mus. Sci. and Industry, Chgo., Rush Med. Ctr., Chgo. Capt. USMC, 1963—67. Decorated Silver Star, Purple Heart. Mem.: Onwentsia Club, Old Elm Club, Wianno Club, Red Stick Golf Club. Avocations: golf, tennis, skiing.

MORRISON, SCOTT DAVID, management consultant, small business owner; b. Duluth, Minn., May 8, 1952; s. Robert Henry and Shirley Elaine (Tester) M. (dec. 1990); m. Jana Louise Bergeron, May 29, 1976; chilren: Robert Scott (dec. 1999), Matthew John. Cert. in welding, Duluth Area Inst. Tech., 1971; student, U. Wis.-Superior, 1976-77; A in Mfg. Mgmt., N. Hennepin C.C., 1985; BA, Concordia Coll., St. Paul, 1988; MBA, St. Thomas U., St. Paul, 1991. Cert. in quality tech., Am. Soc. Quality, 1985, Dell Computer, Inc. instr. Six Sigma; lic. vocat. instr., Minn. Cert. welder Litton Ship Systems, Pascagoula, Miss., 1971-72, Barko Hydraulics, Superior, Wis., 1972-76, Am. Hoist and Derrick Co., Mpls., 1977-79, cert. level II non-destructive exam. insp., 1979-80; quality supr. Colight Inc., Mpls., 1980, Tol-O-Matic, Inc., Mpls., 1980-82; quality assurance engr. ADC Telecomm., Mpls., 1982-84, design assurance engr., 1985-86, product assurance engr., 1986-87, sr. product assurance engr., quality improvement facilitator, 1987-88, product engr. supr., 1988-90, mgr. design assurance, quality assurance, component engring., 1990-92; dir. quality and reg. affairs Waters Instruments, Inc., 1992-96, sr. quality engr., 1996, corp. quality sys. mgr., 1996-98; corp. mfg. and quality Compaq Computer Corp., Houston, 1996-98; sys. engr., sr. cons. Dimension Product Group, 1998—2001, Dell Computer Corp., Round Rock, Tex., 1998—, quality engr., sr. cons. Transactional Line of Bus., 1999—2000, mgr. quality sys. application team project, 2000, supplier quality engr., sr. cons., 2000—01; sr. cons. ABS Cons. Mgmt. Sys. divsns., Houston, 2001—03; mgr. Mgmt. Sys. Cons., 2002—03; owner Dimensions in Quality, LLC, 2003—; contract mgmt. sys. auditor Moody Internat., 2004—, auditor quality, environ. and health and safety mgmt. sys., 2006—; sr. cons. Sirius Solutions LLC, 2009—. Judge U.S. Amateur Boxing Fedn., Mpls., 1978-87, 95-97; examiner Minn. Quality Award Minn. Coun. for Quality, 1993, 95, Tex. Quality Award, 1997; mem. quality coun. Am. Electronics Assn., 1994-95; mem. bd. dirs. Rochester Quality Coun., 1994-95; examiner Malcolm Baldridge Nat. Quality award Nat. Inst. Standards and Technology, 1994-95, sr. examiner, 1996-97, alumni examiner, 1999-2000; reviewer fellowship grant applications ASQ, 1996; adj. instr. Riverland Tech. Coll., Rochester, Minn., 1995; lic. profl. boxing judge Tex. Dept. Licensing and Regulation, 1996—2008; cert. lead quality auditor Brit. Standards Internat., 1996, cert. lead environ. sys. auditor, 2001; facilitator Malcolm Bridge Nat. Quality Award Regional Conf., 1997; cons. in field. Recipient Tech. Excellence award ADC Telecoms., 1987, 88. Mem. ASTM, Am. Soc. Quality (cert. quality engr. cert. quality auditor, cert. quality mgr., cert. six sigma black belt, chmn. host and attendance subcom. 1986-87), Am. Welding Soc., Soc. Mfg. Engrs., Internat. Platform Assn. Roman Catholic. Home and Office: 18 Seneca Pl The Woodlands TX 77382-5353 Office Phone: 713-201-3725. E-mail: diming@att.net.

MORRISON, SHELLEY, actress; b. NYC, Oct. 26, 1936; d. Maurice Nissim and Hortense Mitrani; m. Walter R. Dominguez, Aug. 11, 1973. Student, L.A. City Coll., 1954—56. Presenter Alma awards, 2001—02, Imagan Awards, 2001, Nosotros Golden Eagle awards, 2002. Actress: (films) Interns, 1962, The Greatest Story Ever Told, 1964, Castle of Evil, 1965, Divorce, American Style, 1965, How to Save a Marriage, 1966, Funny Girl, 1967, Three Guns for Texas, 1969, Man and Boy, 1971, Blume in Love, 1972, McKenna's Gold, 1967, Breezy, 1973, People Toys, 1973, Rabbit Test, 1975, Max Dugan Returns, 1982, Troop Beverly Hills, 1988, Fools Rush In, 1996, Shark Tale, 2004, Food Fight, 2007, others, (TV movies) The Girl Who Came Giftwrapped, Three's a Crowd, 1969, Once an Eagle, 1974, The Night That Panicked America, 1975, Kids Don't Tell, 1984, Cries From the Heart, 1994, Columbo: It's All In the Game, Lassie: A New Beginning, others, (TV series) Laredo, 1965-67, The Flying Nun, 1966-70, First and Ten, 1987, I'm Home, 1990, The Fanelli Boys, 1990, Love, Lies and Murder, 1990, Playhouse 90, Dr. Kildare, The Fugitive, Gunsmoke, Marcus Welby, General Hospital, and many others, 1960-70, Man of the People, Sisters, 1991, 92, Murder She Wrote, 1992, Johnny Bago, 1993, Columbo, 1993, L.A. Law, 1994, Live Shot, 1995, Courthouse, Home Improvement, 1997, Nothing Sacred, 1997, Prey, 1997, Nearly Yours, 1998; recurring role in Will & Grace, 1998-, series regular 1999-06 (Diversity award 2004, People's Choice award 2005, nominee Golden Globe award 2005, nominee SAG award 2005); TV guest appearances include Prey, Nothing Sacred, L.A. Law, Busting Loose, Marcus Welby, M.D., Occasional Wife, Between the Lines, Home Improvement, Murder, She Wrote, The Bold Ones, Divorce Court, Soap, The Streets of San Francisco, Dr. Kildare, Man of the People, The Partridge Family, My Favorite Martian, The Outer Limits, The Robert Taylor Show, My Name is Earl, The Megan Mullally Show, (talk show) Wayne Brady, 2003-04, Ryan's Secret, 2003-04, Florence Henderson, 2006; (voice over animated cartoon comml.) Handy Manny, 2006, 07 (voice animated cartoon series), (A&E) Letters, 2003, numerous others, (stage prodns.) Pal Joey, 1956, Bus Stop, 1956, Only in America, 1960, Orpheus Descending, 1960, Spring's Awakening, 1962, over 65 other prodns., 1956-1970, also appeared in The Mikado, Pal Joey, Anastasia, Orpheus Descending, A Streetcar Named Desire, Sweet Bird of Youth, The Crucible, Zoo Story, Rashomon, Desk Set, Pygmalian, The Would-Be Gentleman, Comedy of Errors, Tiger at the Gates, The Rose Tattoo, Orpheus Descending, Come Back Little Sheba, The Odd Couple, Only in America, El Camino Real, Hamlet, Country Girl, Romeo and Juliet, Cotton Candy, Point of View, Coney Island of the Mind, Last of the Aztecs, numerous others; prodr., writer, 1975—; prodr. (with husband Walter Dominguez) documentary Mexican culture, 2003; game shows, "Hollywood Squares", 2004-06, "Pyramid", "Celebrity Black jack". Condr. seminars (with husband Walter Dominquez) about Native Americans to keep traditions and ceremonies flourishing. Honored (with husband Walter Dominguez) for work with homeless City of LA, 1985, for work during LA riots, 1992, Bronx Walk of Fame, 2004, Eternity award Women's Theater Group, 2004; nominated for Alma awards SAG, 2000, 01, 02, 06; recipient Emmy award Best Comedy for Will and Grace, 2000, SAG award for Will and Grace, 2002, Halo award, 2003, People's Choice award for Will and Grace ensemble, 2004, Gladd award for Will and Grace ensemble, 2004, Diversity award for Will and Grace ensemble, 2004. Mem. SAG, AFTRA, Actors Equity Assn. Democrat.

MORRISON, SHIRLEY MARIE, retired nursing educator; b. Stuttgart, Ark., June 13, 1927; d. Jack Vade Wimberly and Mabel Claire (Dennison) George; m. Dana Jennings, Mar. 12, 1951 (dec. Dec. 1995); children: Stephen Leslie, Dana Randall, William Lee, Martha Ann Morrison Comardo. Diploma, Bapt. Hosp. Sch. Nursing, Nashville, 1949; BSN, Calif. U., Fullerton, 1977; MSN, Calif. U., LA, 1980; EdD, Nova Southeastern U., 1987. RN, Tex., Calif.; cert. pub. health nurse, Calif.; cert. secondary tchr., Calif. Staff nurse perinatal svcs. Martin Luther Hosp., Anaheim, Calif., 1960-77, relief 11-7 house supr., 1960-77; dir. vocat. nursing program Inst. Med. Studies, 1978-81; mem.

faculty BSN program Abilene (Tex.) Intercollegiate Sch. Nursing, 1981-92, dir. ADN program, 1992-97; nursing educator Cisco Jr. Coll., Abilene, Tex., 1997—2008. Mem. profl. adv. bd. Nurse Care, Inc., Abilene, 1988-2003, bd. dirs. West Tarpas Rehab Ctr., 2000-. Mem. adv. bd. parent edn. program Abilene Ind. Sch. Dist., 1985-2000; active Mar. Dimes, Abilene, 1990—, Ednl. Coalition for Bob Hunter, Abilene, 1994; bd. dirs. Hospice Big Country, Abilene, 1987—, The House That Kerry Built, 2000—. Grantee NIH, 1992; recipient Nat. Humor Project award Jour. Nursing Jocularity, 1996. Mem. Nat. Orgn. Assn. Degree Nurses (mem. program com. 10th anniversary nat. conv.), Tex. Orgn. Assoc. Degree Nurses, So. Nursing Rsch. Soc. (rsch. presenter), Health Edn. Resource Network Abilene (founding mem., pres. elect, pres. 1995-96), Sigma Theta Tau (bd. dirs. 1999-2004, bd. dirs. Omicron Zeta chpt. 1999-2001), West Tex. Rehab. Ctr. (bd. dir. 2003-). Democrat. Methodist. Avocations: travel, reading. Home: PO Box 2583 Abilene TX 79604-2583 Home Phone: 325-691-0260; Office Phone: 325-669-6106. Personal E-mail: ShirleyfromAbilene@webtv.net.

MORRISON, STACY LYNNE, editor; b. Jenkintown, Pa., Jan. 17, 1969; d. Robert Isaac and Sharon Lee (Wiley) Morrison; m. Christopher Cole Shannon, Sept. 1, 1994. BA cum laude, Washington & Lee U., 1990. Editl. asst. Mirabella mag., NYC, 1991-92, asst. editor, 1992-93, assoc. features editor, 1993-95; mng. editor J. Crew Group Inc., NYC, 1995, Time Out New York, NYC, Conde Nast Sports for Women; editor-in-chief Modern Bride, 1998—2000, ONE, 2000—01; exec. editor Marie Claire Hearst Corp., NYC, 2001—04, editor-in-chief Redbook, 2004—. Office: Redbook 300 W 57th St New York NY 10019 Office Phone: 212-649-2000. Office Fax: 212-649-2108.*

MORRISON, THOMAS ALLEN, retired military officer, lawyer, dean; b. Oak Park, Ill., Mar. 25, 1947; s. Allen R. and Evelyn M. (Herbst) M.; m. Karen A. Petit, Oct. 28, 1972; children: Kelly, Douglas, James. BA, Marquette U., 1969, JD cum laude, 1977; LLM in Environ. Law with highest honors, George Washington U., 1984. Bar: Wis. 1977, U.S. Dist. Ct. (we. and ea. dists.) Wis. 1977, U.S. Ct. Appeals (9th cir.) 1978, U.S. Mil. Ct. Appeals 1988. Commd. ensign USN, 1969, intelligence, adminstrn. officer, 1969-71, computer maintenance officer, 1971-72, dept. head coll. programs recruiting command, 1972-74, atty. legal svcs. office Pearl Harbor, Hawaii, 1977-80; spl. asst. U.S. Atty., 1977-80; staff judge advocate sub. base USN, Pearl Harbor, Hawaii, 1980-81, dept. head procurement and plans JAG Alexandria, Va., 1981-83, legis. counsel, 1984-86, exec. officer legal svc. office Charleston, SC, 1986—89, advanced through grades to radm, 1989—, comdg. officer legal svc. office Long Beach, 1989-93, dept. asst. JAG for mil. pers. Alexandria, Va., 1993-95, asst. JAG for ops. and mgmt., 1995-98, ret., 1998; sr. assoc. dean George Washington Univ. Law Sch., 1998—. Office: George Washington Univ Law Sch 2000 H St NW Washington DC 20052 Home Phone: 703-440-8050; Office Phone: 202-994-6288. Business E-Mail: tmorrison@law.gwu.edu.

MORRISON, TIMOTHY M., prosecutor; BA in Polit. Sci., Ind. U., 1971; JD, Ind. U., Bloomington, 1974. Bar: Ind., US Dist. Ct. (so. dist.) Ind., Seventh Cir. Ct. Appeals, Chgo. Chief dep. prosecuting atty. Monroe County, Ind., 1975—81; supervising dep. prosecutor Marion County; first asst. US atty. (so. dist.) Ind. US Dept. Justice, 1988—2008, interim US atty. (so. dist.) Ind., 1993, 2000—01, acting US atty. (so. dist.) Ind., 2007—08, US atty. (so. dist.) Ind., 2008—. Mem.: Sagamore Inn of Ct., Nat. Assn. of Former US Attys., Seventh Cir. Bar Assn., Ind. State Bar Assn. Office: US Attys Office 10 W Market St, Ste 2100 Indianapolis IN 46204 Office Fax: 317-226-6125.*

MORRISON, TONI (CHLOE ARDELIA WOFFORD), writer, educator, editor; b. Lorain, Ohio, Feb. 18, 1931; d. George and Ella Ramah (Willis) Wofford; m. Harold Morrison, 1958 (div. 1964); children: Harold Ford, Slade Kevin. BA in English, Howard U., Washington, 1953; MA in Am. Lit., Cornell U., NYC, 1955; degree (hon.), Harvard U., U. Pa., Columbia U., Yale U., Georgetown U., Brown U., U. Mich., Dartmouth Coll., Sarah Lawrence Coll., Oberlin Coll., Universite Paris 7-Denis Diderot. Instr. English Tex. So. U., Houston, 1955-57, Howard U., 1957-64; assoc. editor Random House, Syracuse, NY, 1965—67, sr. editor NYC, 1967—83; assoc. prof. English SUNY, Purchase, 1971-72, Albert Schweitzer prof. humanities Albany, NY, 1984-89; Robert F. Goheen prof. humanities Princeton U., Princeton, NJ, 1989—2006, dir. Princeton Atelier, 1994—2006; ret., 2006. Vis. lectr. Yale U., New Haven, 1976—77, Bard Coll., NY, 1986—88; Obert C. Tanner lectr. U. Mich., Ann Arbor, 1988; Jeannette K. Watson disting. prof. Syracuse U., NY, 1988; presenter of Clark lectrs. Trinity Coll., 1990, Massey lectrs. Harvard U., 1990; internat. cordorcet chair Ecole Normale Superieure & Coll., France, 1994. Author: (novels) The Bluest Eye, 1970, Sula, 1974 (Ohioana Book award, 1975), Song of Solomon, 1977 (Nat. Book Critics Circle award, 1977), Tar Baby, 1981, Beloved, 1987 (Robert F. Kennedy Meml. Book award, 1988, Anisfield-Wolf Book award, 1988, Unitarian Universalist Assn.'s Frederic G. Melcher Book award, 1988, Pulitzer prize for fiction, 1988, named best Am. novel pub. in previous 25 yrs., NY Times Book Review, 2006), Jazz, 1992, Paradise, 1999, Love, 2003, A Mercy, 2008, (non-fiction) The Black Book, 1974, Playing in the Dark: Whiteness and the Literary Imagination, 1992, The Dancing Mind, 1996, Remember: The Journey to School Integration, 2004 (ALA's Coretta Scott King award, 2005), What Moves at the Margins: Selected Essays, Reviews and Speeches, 2008, (plays) Dreaming Emmett, 1986; co-author (with Slade Morrison): (children's lit.) The Big Box, 2002, The Book of Mean People, 2002, The Lion or the Mouse?, 2003, The Ant or the Grasshopper?, 2003, The Poppy or the Snake?, 2003; editor: Race-ing Justice, En-Gendering Power: Essays on Anita Hill, Clarence Thomas, and the Construction of Social Reality, 1992, To Die for the People: The Writings of Huey P. Newton, 1995; co-editor: Birth of a Nation'hood: Gaze, Script, Spectacle in the O.J. Simpson Case, 1997. Recipient Medal of Distinction, Barnard Coll., 1979, NY State Gov.'s Art award, 1986, Nobel Prize for Lit., 1993, Medal for Disting. Contbn. to Am. Letters, Nat. Book Found., 1996, Nat. Humanities Medal, 2000, Living Legends award, Libr. Congress, 2000, Elizabeth Cady Stanton award, NOW, Golden Plate award, Acad. Achievement, 2005; named one of 30 Most Powerful Women in America, Ladies' Home Jour., 2001; named to NJ Hall of Fame, 2007. Mem.: AAAL, Nat. Coun. Arts, Author's Guild. Achievements include becoming first African American woman to win the Nobel Prize in Literature.*

MORRISON, WINIFRED ELAINE HAAS, social sciences educator; b. Buffalo, Aug. 31; d. Edward Albert and Elaine Magdalene (McNamara) Haas; m. Robert Charles Morrison; children: Robert Edward, James Richard. BS in Edn., SUC, Buffalo, MS in Edn. magna cum laude, 1964, PhD, 1984, postgrad.; MLS, SUNY, Geneseo, 1969; postgrad., Harvard U., UCLA. Instr., Genesee Community Coll., 1972-78, 80, also asst. prof. State U. Coll., Buffalo, 1973-77; instr. corr. course Empire State Coll., Saratoga Springs, N.Y., 1975-78; dir. early edn. div. Park Sch., Buffalo, 1960-74, dir. lower sch., 1974-78; mem. grad. faculties ednl. studies & social scis., lectr., SUNY, Buffalo, also social scis. interdisciplinary studies faculty; coord. child care adv. service Early Childhood Research Ctr., Amherst campus, 1978-80; dir. children's services Erie County Assn. for Retarded Children, 1980-83, pres. Heritage Ctrs., 1983-95; chmn. early childhood com. Nat. Office Gifted and Talented, HEW, 1976; panelist symposium Chautauqua Inst., 1974; bd. dirs. Heritage-Oak Found., v.p., 1989-95. Author: This Book is About Your School, Early Education Unit, 1976, Primary Unit, 1977, You Are Your Child's First Teacher, 1974, (with Carol Woodard) You Can Help Your Baby Learn, 1979, (with Betty Jenkins) (screening materials) Kiddy Kards, 1982. Pres. bd. dirs. Day Care Coun. Western N.Y., 1971-72; adv. com. parenthood edn. project Buffalo and Erie County coun. Girl Scouts U.S., 1972-76; child adv. com. child/adult edn. project Western N.Y. div. Salvation Army, 1977-82; TV and reading com. WNED-TV Public Broadcasting, 1977-79; chmn. community com. Erie Community Coll., 1971-72; hon. chmn. Week of the Young Child; pres. Erie County Adv. Coun. on Disabled, 1986-88; bd. dirs. Heritage-Oak Found., 1987-95, v.p., 1990-95. Recipient Outstanding Svc. award Villa Maria Coll. Child Devel. Adv. Coun., 1979, 84, Outstanding Achievement award YWCA of Buffalo and Erie County, 1985, State Sr. Svc. award SLLC- Buffalo, 2008. Mem. AAUW, ALA, ASCD, Nat. Assn. Edn. of Young Children, Coun. Exceptional Children, World Orgn. Presch. Edn., Ctr. Women in Mgmt. (bd. dirs. 1983-92, Mgr. of Yr. award 1987), Am. Mgmt. Assn., N.Y. State Coun. for Children, Rotary (sec. Buffalo club 1991-92, bd. dirs. 1991-93, Paul Harris fellow), Zonta Internat. (pres. Cheektowaga-Lancaster Club 1989-91, area dir. 1992-94, area sec. 1994-96), Pi Lambda Theta (pres. Alpha Nu chpt. 1985-87, sec. N.E. region 1990-92, Outstanding Pi Lambda Thetan award 1987, Lillian and Henry Barry award 1989), Phi Delta Kappa (v.p. Alpha Psi chpt.). Home Fax: 716-929-5567. Personal E-mail: whm@buffalo.edu.

MORRISS, FRANK, writer, educator; b. Pasadena, Calif., Mar. 28, 1923; s. B. Gerard Morriss and Regina Spann; m. Mary Rita Moynihan, Feb. 11, 1950 (dec. Oct. 23, 1996); children: Patricia, Mary Ellen Hill, Regina Sister M. John, OSF(dec.), Gerard. BS in Philosophy magna cum laude, Regis Coll., Denver, 1943; JD, Georgetown U., 1948. Editor Register Newspapers, Denver, 1949—61, 1963—67; assoc. editor Vt. Cath. Tribune, Burlington, 1961—63; contbg. editor The Wanderer, St. Paul, 1967—2007; educator Colorado Cath. Acad., Wheat Ridge, Colo., 1973—. Bd. dirs. Wanderer Forum Found., St. Paul, 1969—; policy expert Heritage Found., 1995—. Author: Saints In Verse, Two Chapels, The Divine Epic, The Catholic as Citizen, The Conservative Imperative, Boy of Philadelphia, Alfred of Wessex, The Adventures of Broken Hand, Submarine Pioneer, (lectrs. on CD) Saints Speak to Modern World, Francis Thompson: A Reflection on the Poetic Vocation. Founder Colo. Cath. Acad., Wheat Ridge, 1970—2002. Sgt. US Army, 1943—45, PTO. Recipient Frederic Ozanam award, Soc. Cath. Social Scientists, 2003. Mem.: Fellowship of Cath. Scholars, VFW. Republican. Roman Catholic. Home: 3505 Owens St Wheat Ridge CO 80033 Home Fax: 303-422-1475.

MORRISS, FRANK HOWARD, JR., pediatrics educator; b. Birmingham, Ala., Apr. 20, 1940; s. Frank Howard Sr. and Rochelle (Snow) M.; m. Mary J. Hagan, June 29, 1968; children: John Hagan, Matthew Snow. BA, U. Va., 1962; MD, Duke U., 1966; MPH, Harvard U., 2006. Diplomate Am. Bd. Pediatrics, Am. Bd. Perinatal and Neonatal Medicine. Intern Duke U. Med. Ctr., Durham, NC, 1966-67, resident in pediatrics, 1967-68, fellow in neonatology, 1970-71, U. Colo., Denver, 1971-73; asst. prof. to prof. U. Tex. Med. Sch., Houston, 1973-86; prof. U. Iowa Coll. Medicine, Iowa City, 1987—, chmn. dept., 1987—2004. Editor: Role of Human Milk in Infant Nutrition and Health, 1986; contbr. numerous articles to profl. jours, chpts. to books. Lt. comdr. USN, 1968-70. Grantee, NIH, 1977—87, 1990—2004. Mem. Am. Pediatric Soc., Soc. Pediatric Rsch., Am. Acad. Pediatrics, Midwest Soc. Pediatric Rsch. Office: U Iowa Hosps & Clinics Dept Pediatrics Iowa City IA 52242 Office Phone: 319-384-6530.

MORRISSETTE, JERUSHA M., music educator; b. Putnam, Conn., Oct. 22, 1977; d. Donald R. and Susan C. Morrissette; m. Dan Arcamone, Jan. 8, 2000 (div. May 12, 2004); 1 child, Colby J. Arcamone. MusB, Western Conn. State U., Danbury, 2000; MA in Tchg., Sacred Heart U., Griswold, Conn., 2009. Cert. in elem. edn. Conn., 2009. Music tchr. Westport Music Ctr., Conn., 1998—2000, Norwalk Music Inc., Conn., 2000—03; shift supr. Rite Aide Pharmacy, Moosup, Conn., 2003—08; substitute tchr. Plainfield Pub. Schs., Conn., 2007—; with Sterling Cmty. Sch., Conn., 2007—08. Mem.: Conn. Reading Assn., Internat. Reading Assn., Phi Lambda Theta.

MORRISSEY, CHARLES THOMAS, historian, educator; b. Newton, Mass., Nov. 11, 1933; s. Leonard Eugene and Margaret (McCarthy) M. AB, Dartmouth Coll., 1956; MA, U. Calif., Berkeley, 1957. Instr. Dartmouth Coll., Hanover, N.H., 1961-62; oral historian Harry S. Truman Library, Independence, Mo., 1962-64; chief oral history project John F. Kennedy Libr., Washington, 1965-66; dir. Vt. Hist. Soc., Montpelier, 1966-71, 73-75; dir. oral history project Ford Found., 1971-73; adj. prof. history U. Vt., Burlington, 1969-73, 75-85; dir. Oral History and Archives Office Baylor Coll. Medicine, Houston, 1985—97, cons., 1997—. Vis. instr. oral and pub. history Portland State U., 1979—82, 1984—2001, 2003—05, Vt. Coll., Montpelier, 1985—2000, 2002—06; lectr. in field. Author: Vermont: A Bicentennial History, 1981, (with others) Vermont, 1985; editor: Oral History Assn. Newsletter, 1968-71, Vermont History, 1967-71, 73-76, Internat. Jour. Oral History, 1985-89; contbg. editor: Vermont Life mag., 1969-81, editor, 1982-83; contbr. chpts. to books; contbr. articles to profl. jours.; radio commentator Sta. WDEV, Waterbury, Vt., 1982—; columnist Hardwick (Vt.) Gazette, 1997—. Recipient Harvey Kantor award New England Assn. Oral History, 1980. Mem. Ctr. for Rsch. on Vt., Oral History Assn. (pres. 1971-72), Nat. Coun. on Pub. History (coun. 1980-82), Assn. Oral History Educators, Cosmos Club (Washington). Office Phone: 713-798-5130.

MORRISSEY, J. RICHARD, lawyer; b. LA, Jan. 8, 1941; BA, Santa Clara Univ., 1963; JD, Univ. Calif., Berkeley, 1966. Bar: Calif. 1966, US Ct. Mil. Appeals 1967, US Supreme Ct. 1980. Ptnr., co-leader Product Liability practice, head LA Litigation sect. Pillsbury Winthrop Shaw Pittman, LA. Mem.: ABA, LA County Bar Assn. Office: Pillsbury Winthrop Shaw Pittman Suite 2800 725 S Figueroa St Los Angeles CA 90017 Office Phone: 213-488-7525. Office Fax: 213-629-1033. Business E-Mail: richard.morrissey@pillsburylaw.com.

MORRISSEY, JOHN CARROLL, SR., lawyer; b. NYC, Sept. 2, 1914; s. Edward Joseph and Estelle (Caine) M.; m. Eileen Colligan, Oct. 14, 1950; children: Jonathan Edward, Ellen (Mrs. James A. Jenkins), Katherine, John, Patricia, Richard, Brian, Peter. BA magna cum laude, Yale U., 1937, LLB, 1940; JSD, N.Y. U., 1951; grad., Command and Gen. Staff Sch., 1944. Bar: N.Y. State 1940, D.C. 1953, Calif. 1954, U.S. Supreme Ct. 1944. Asso. firm Dorsey and Adams, 1940-41, Dorsey, Adams and Walker, 1946-50; counsel Office of Sec. of Def., Dept. Def., Washington, 1950-52; acting gen. counsel def. Electric Power Adminstrn., 1952-53; atty. Pacific Gas and Electric Co., San Francisco, 1953-70, assoc. gen. counsel, 1970-74, v.p., gen. counsel, 1975-80; individual practice law San Francisco, 1980-2000. Dir. Gas Lines, Inc. Bd. dirs. Legal Aid Soc., San Francisco; chmn. Golden Gate dist. Boy Scouts Am., 1973-75; commr. Human Rights Commn. of San Francisco, 1976-89, chmn., 1980-82; chmn. Cath. Social Svc. of San Francisco, 1966-68; adv. com. Archdiocesean Legal Affairs, 1981—; regent Archdiocesan Sch. of Theology, St. Patrick's Sem., 1994-99; dir. Presidio Preservation Assn., 1995-99. Served to col. F.A. U.S. Army, ETO, 1941-46. Decorated Bronze star, Army Commendation medal. Mem. NAS, AAAS, ABA, Calif. State Bar Assn., Fed. Power Bar Assn., N.Y. Acad. Scis., Calif. Conf. Pub. Utility Counsel, Pacific Coast Electric Assn., Pacific Coast Gas Assn., Econ. Round Table of San Francisco, World Affairs Council, San Francisco C. of C., Calif. State C. of C., Harold Brunn Soc. Med. Rsch., Electric Club, Serra Club, Commonwealth Club, Yale Club of San Francisco (pres. 1989-90), Pacific-Union Club, Sometimes Tuesday Club, Sovereign Mil. Order Malta, Phi Beta Kappa. Roman Catholic. Office: 1661 Pine St # 1135 San Francisco CA 94109-0426 Personal E-mail: dadjcm@aol.com.

MORRISSEY, LAWRENCE, Mayor, Rockford, Illinois; s. Joseph A. and Josephine (Matranga). Grad. magna cum laude, U. Notre Dame, 1991; JD cum laude, U. Ill., 1995. Bar: Ill. Atty. Morrissey Law Offices, 1997—2005; mayor City of Rockford, 2005—. Bd. mem. Rockford Area Econ. Devel. Coun., 2005—, Cmty. Collaboration Inc., 2007—, Rockford C. of C.; former bd. mem. Rockford Area Conv. and Visitor's Bur., Goodwill Industries & Abilities Ctr. Rep. Regional Transit Authority; former rep. Southwest Rockford Neighborhood Group; dir. Mayor's Youth Adv. Coun., Mayor's Minority Adv. Coun.; policy com. mem. Rockford Area Transp. Study (RATS); CEO mem. Workforce Investment Bd.; charter mem. Greater Rockford Transp. Coalition; founding mem. Winnebago County Crime and Pub. Safety Commn. Mem.: Am. Inst. Architects (Ill. Chpt.) (former pub. dir.), Northern Ill. Mayor's Assn., Nat. League Cities, US Coun. Mayors, Winnebago County Bar Assn., Ill. Trial Lawyers Assn., Ill. Bar Assn., Am. Assn. for Justice, ABA, River Dist. Assn (bd. mem. & pres. 1998—2001), Internat. Coun. Shopping Centers, Congress of New Urbanism, Midwest High Speed Rail Assn. Independent. Office: 425 E State St Rockford IL 61104 Office Phone: 815-987-5590. Office Fax: 815-967-6952. E-mail: Lawrence.Morrissey@rockfordil.gov.*

MORRISSEY, MICHAEL JOSEPH, finance executive; b. Mount Holly, NJ, June 26, 1947; s. Edward Francis and Winifred (Monahan) M.; m. Joanne Stone, June 5, 1982; children: Scott Christopher, Nathanial Joseph Cake. AB, Boston Coll., 1969; MBA, Dartmouth Coll., 1971; grad. Corp. Fin. Mgmt. Program, Harvard U., 1979. Security analyst Philo Smith & Co., Inc., Stamford, Conn., 1971-73, Kidder Peabody & Co., Inc., NYC, 1973-74, asst. v.p., 1974-76, v.p., 1976-77, Dean Witter Reynolds, Inc., NYC, 1977-78, Crum and Forster, Morristown, NJ, 1978-80, sr. v.p., 1980-83; pres. Firemark Investments, Morristown, NJ, 1983-85, chmn. bd., 1985—2009; exec. v.p. Manhattan Nat. Corp., NYC, 1985, pres., chief operating officer, 1985-86; mng. ptnr. Firemark Tiger Fund, 2005—09; pres. & CEO Internat. Ins. Soc., NYC, 2009—. Bd. dir. Selective Ins. Group, NJ, CGA Group Ltd., Bermuda. Vice chmn. Rep. Party Santa Fe County; bd. dirs. Boys & Girls Club, Santa Fe. Recipient CFA award, 1977. Mem. Internat. Ins. Soc., Young Pres.' Orgn., Dartmouth Club (N.Y.C.), Spring Brook Country Club, Boston coll. Wall St. Coun, Internat. Insurance Soc. (pres. & chief exe. officer 2009-). Republican. Episcopalian. Office: Internat Ins Soc 101 Murray St New York NY 10007 Office Phone: 212-815-9291. Business E-Mail: mmorrissey@iionline.org.

MORRISSEY, PATRICIA A., federal agency administrator; AA in Liberal Arts, Hartford CC, 1964; BA in Psychology, Stetson U., 1966; M.Ed. in Spl. Edn., Pa. State U., 1971, PhD in Spl. Edn., 1974. Positions with US Ho. of Reps. Com. on Edn. and Labor, Senate Com. on Health, Edn., Labor, and Pensions; sr. assoc. Booz Allen Hamilton, McLean, Va.; commr. Adminstrn. Devel. Disabilities Adminstrn. Children and Families, HHS, 2001—. Republican. Office: Adminstrn Children and Families Adminstrn Devel Disabilities 370 L'Enfant Promenade SW Washington DC 20447 Office Phone: 202-690-6590. Business E-Mail: pmorrissey@acf.hhs.gov.*

MORRONE, FRANK, electronics executive; b. Marano Marchesato, Cosenza, Italy, May 13, 1949; s. Luigi and Emma (Molinaro) M.; m. Katherine Ann Kuehn, Feb. 1, 1975; children: Louis H., Cecilia E., Joseph V. BSEE, U. Wis., 1972; MBA, Northwestern U., 1993. Project engr. 3M Co., St. Paul, 1972—73; product engr., mgr. Eaton Corp., Kenosha, Wis., 1973—79; chief elec. engr. Tree Machine Tool, Racine, Wis., 1979—80; v.p. engring. MacPower divsn. Manu-Tronics, Inc., Kenosha, 1980—84, exec. v.p., 1984—99, bd. dirs., sec., 1988—99; v.p. ops. Sanmina Corp., 1999—2001, sr. v.p., 2001—08, exec. v.p., 2008—. Exec. bd. Southeast coun. Boy Scouts Am., Racine, 1987—2005, adv. bd. 2005-; bd. dirs. Kenosha Libr., 1987-98, U. Wis.-Parkside Benevolent Found., 2000—2007; mgmt. coun. Lakeview Tech. Acad., 1997-99. Mem. IEEE, Kenosha County Club (bd. dirs.). Office: Sanmina-SCI Corp 8701 100th St Pleasant Prairie WI 53158-2202 Office Phone: 262-947-7700.

MORROW, BRADFORD, novelist, editor, educator; b. Balt., Apr. 8, 1951; s. Ernest Dean and Lois DeLaine Morrow; BA, U. Colo., Boulder, 1973. Vis. lectr. writing Princeton U., NJ, 1996—97, Columbia U., NYC, 1994—97; prof. lit., Bard Ctr. fellow Bard Coll., Annandale-on-Hudson, NY, 1990—; founder & editor Conjunctions, NYC, 1981—. Author: (novels) Come Sunday; editor: (anthology) Classics Revisited, by Kenneth Rexroth, More Classics Revisited, by Kenneth Rexroth; co-editor: The Complete Poems of Kenneth Rexroth; editor: Selected Poems of Kenneth Rexroth, World Outside the Window: Selected Essays of Kenneth Rexroth; co-editor: The New Gothic; author: (children's book) Didn't Didn't Do It, 2007, A Bestiary, (novels) The Almanac Branch (PEN Faulkner award, 1992), Trinity Fields (Am. Acad. award, 1998), Giovanni's Gift, Ariel's Crossing. Vol. Amigos de las Americas & Colo. Med. Soc., Honduras, 1967. Recipient CCLM Editor's award, Coordinating Coun. Lit. Magazines, 1984, 1988, Acad. award, AAAL, 1998; fellowship, Danforth Found., 1972, grant, NY Found. Arts, 1989, Lannan Found., 1995, fellowship, John Simon Guggenheim Meml. Found., 2007. Mem.: PEN Am. Ctr. (bd. trustees 1996—2001, PEN, Magid award 2007). Office: Bard Coll Conjunctions Annandale On Hudson NY 12504 Business E-Mail: morrow@mindspring.com.

MORROW, BRENDEN, professional hockey player; b. Carlyle, Sask., Can., Jan. 16, 1979; m. Anne-Marie Carbonneau; 1 child, Bryella Mackenzie. Left wing Dallas Stars, 1999—, capt., 2006—. Mem. Team Can., World Championships, 2001, 02, 04, 05, Team Can., World Cup of Hockey, 2004. Named to NHL YoungStars Game, 2002. Achievements include being a member of World Cup Champion Team Canada, 2004. Office: Dallas Stars 2601 Avenue of the Stars Frisco TX 75034

MORROW, BRUCE WILLIAM, academic administrator, management consultant; b. Rochester, Minn., May 20, 1946; s. J. Robert and Frances P. Morrow; m. Jenny Lea Morrow. BA, U. Notre Dame, 1968, MBA in Mgmt. with honors, 1974, MA in Comparative Lit., 1975; grad., U.S. Army Command and Gen. Staff Coll., 1978. Cert. project mgmt. profl. Project Mgmt. Inst., 2003. Chmn. elem. German U. Notre Dame, 1973—75; co-mgr. Wendy's Old Fashioned Hamburgers, South Bend, Ind., 1976—77; adminstrn. mgr. Ea. States Devel. Corp., Richmond, Va., 1977; v.p. JDB Assocs., Inc., Alexandria, Va., 1976—78; sr. cons. Data

Base Mgmt., Inc., Springfield, Va., 1979—80; owner Aardvark Prodns., Alexandria, Va., 1980—82; sys. analyst, staff officer Hdqrs., Dept. Army, Washington, 1980—84; chmn. bd. Commonwealth Dominion Corp., Sierra Vista, Ariz., 1982—. Strategic planner, dep. comdr. Fort Pickett, Blackstone, Va., 1986—89; dir. continuing edn. Southside Va. C.C., Alberta, 1989—91; co-founder S.W. Bus. Group, Tucson, 1995—99; pres. Sierra Vista Golf, Inc., Ariz., 1994—95; Cochise County team leader Ariz. Coun. Econ. Conversion, 1994—95; mem. com. Ariz. Small Bus. Initiative, 1994—99; internet webmaster, 1996—; exec. dir. Southea. Ariz. Contrs. Assn., 1997—98; corp. adminstr. Garcia Cos., Sierra Vista, Tucson, Phoenix, 1997—99; property adminstr. Brown & Root Svcs., Ft. Huachuca, Ariz., Land Between the Lakes, Ky., 1999—2000, logistics coord., 2000—02; dir. assessment ctr. Transport. Security Agy. NCS Pearson, Nashville and Fresno, 2002; project advisor Dyncorp Internat., Irving, Tex., 2004. Author: (radio series) Survival in the Computer Jungle, 1986, (classroom text) Introduction to Computers, 1988, 2d edit., 1993, Defense Conversion Handbook, 1995, Business Assessment Manual, 1996, Employee Manual Guide, 1996, Business Plan Guide, 1996, Marketing Plan Guide, 1996, (screenplay) Gray Rock, 2000; contbg. columnist Notre Dame mag., 1974—86; exec. prodr.: (motion picture) Beneath the Law, 1995—96; composer songs. Active Boy Scouts Am., 1960—69; firefighter Roanoke Wildwood Vol. Fire Dept., 1991—93. Lt. col. USAR, ret. Decorated Bronze Stars, Army commendation medals, Army Achievement medal, Meritorious Svc. medals, Parachutist's badge, Army Gen. Staff badge. Mem. VFW (life), Nat. Eagle Scout Assn., Lake Gaston C. of C. (bd. dirs.), Am. Legion, Sierra Vista Area C. of C., Lions (v.p. local club), Friends Internat. (Am. v.p. 1969-71, Boeblingen, Germany), Order of DeMolay, Beta Gamma Sigma, Delta Phi Alpha. Office: Commonwealth Dominion Corp 334 Landing Strip Rd Hardin KY 42048-9413 E-mail: cdc@theriver.com.

MORROW, CAROLINE DONOVAN, retired social worker; b. Houston, Tex., Dec. 11, 1937; d. Ira and Verda Ree Donovan; m. Leonard Emery Morrow, June 17, 1967; children: Emery Donovan, April Antionette. BS, Wiley Coll., 1960; MSW, Atlanta U., 1962. LCSW Colo. Counselor Ansel Rd. Golden Age Ctr., Cleve., 1962—67; vol. counselor Rhein Main AFB, Frankfurt, Germany, 1967—69; adminstr. Job Corp. YWCA, Denver, 1970—75; med. social worker Rose Med. Ctr., Denver, 1976—2003, ret., 2003; advocate, Civil Rights Movement, 1958—. Cons. in field. Vol. Village East Elem. Sch., Aurora, Colo., 2002—04; hon. mem. Pres. Barack Obama's Kitchen Cabinet; vol. presdl. election Dem Com., Denver, 2002, 2004; vol. presdl. connection AIN, 2008; vol. food bank Mt. Gilead Bapt. Ch., Denver, sec., 1999. Recipient Appreciation cert., USAF, 1978, Wall Tolerance, 2004, Am. Diabetes Assn., 2009, Recognition cert., NAACP, 2004; named Outstanding Vol., Meml. Sloan-Kettering Cancer Ctr., 2008—09. Mem.: ASA Med. Social Worker (Gold Card Membership), Nat. Assn. Social Workers, Order Ea. Star, Alpha Kappa Alpha. Democrat. Achievements include received award from Washington, DC for donations to the Dr. Martin Luther King Jr. Nat. Memorial Project Foundation, Inc. in 2006-08. Her name will also be published on one of the buildings. Avocations: reading, writing, puzzles, collecting recipes, decorating. Home: 1358 So Oswego Ct Aurora CO 80012

MORROW, GEORGE J., medical products executive; m. Katherine Morrow; 3 children. BA, Southampton Coll.; MA in Biochemistry, Bryn Mawr Coll., Pa.; MBA, Duke U., Durham, NC. V.p., gen. mgr. sales and mktg. divsn. Glaxo, Inc., 1992, group v.p. comml. ops., 1993—96; mng. dir. Glaxo Wellcome UK, 1997—98; pres., CEO Glaxo Wellcome Inc., Research Park Triangle, NC, 1999—2001; exec. v.p., worldwide sales and mktg. Amgen, Inc., Thousand Oaks, Calif., 2001—03, exec. v.p. global comml. ops., 2003—. Mem. adv. bd. Duke U. Fuqua Sch. Bus.; bd. visitors Duke U. Med. Ctr. Office: Amgen Inc 1 Amgen Ctr Dr Thousand Oaks CA 91320-1799 Office Phone: 805-447-1000. Office Fax: 805-447-1010.

MORROW, JAMES FRANKLIN, lawyer; b. Shenandoah, Iowa, Oct. 23, 1944; s. Warren Ralph and Margaret Glee (Palm) M. BS, Kans. State U., 1967; JD, U. Ariz., 1973. Bar: Ariz. 1973, U.S. Dist. Ct. Ariz. 1973. Ptnr. Bilby, Shoenhair, Warnock & Dolph, Tucson, 1973-83, Quarles & Brady Streich Lang LLP, Tucson, 1984—. Mng. editor U. Ariz. Law Rev., 1972-73. Past chmn. bd. trustees Palo Verde Mental Health Svcs.; past pres. U. Ariz. Alumni Assn.; past chmn. bd. Palo Verde Hosp., Ariz. Tech. Devel. Corp.; past pres. bd. Cath. Cmty. Svcs.; past chmn. bd. dirs. U. Ariz. Found. Capt. U.S. Army, 1967-70. Mem. Am. Coll. Real Estate Lawyers, Am. Coll. Mortgage Attys., State Bar Ariz. (cert. real estate specialist, adv. com. real estate specialists, past chmn. real estate property sect.), Pima County Bar Assn., Calif. Bar Assn. Democrat. Roman Catholic. Avocation: golf. Office: Quarles & Brady LLP Ste 1700 One South Church Ave Tucson AZ 85701

MORROW, JAMES THOMAS, energy executive; b. Seattle, Apr. 24, 1941; s. James Elroy and Helen Margaret (Helzer) M.; 1 child, Shannon F. BSEE, BS Gen. Sci., Oreg. State U., 1964; MBA, U. Santa Clara, 1966, PhD, 1973. Registered investment advisor, SEC; profl. engr., Calif., Oreg. Engr. GE Co., San Jose, Calif., 1964—66; mgr. engring. Beckman Instruments, Inc., Palo Alto, Calif., 1966—69; pres. MSA Cons., Inc., Portland, Oreg., 1969—75; mgr. A.T. Kearney, Inc., San Francisco, 1975—78; v.p. mktg. Pierce Pacific Mfg., Portland, 1978—79; chmn., CEO Lanco Internat., Inc., Clackamas, Oreg., 1979—81; regional mgr., v.p. Case & Co., Portland, 1981—82; chmn. bd., exec. v.p. Morley Fin. Svcs. Inc., 1982—94; exec. v.p., dir. Bioject Med. Tech. Inc., 1983—92; chmn., pres., CEO Capital Devel. Group, Inc., Portland, 1994—96; chmn., CEO Apollo Fin. Group, NYC, 1996—98, Olympic Healthcare Tech., Inc., Portland, NYC, 1998—2002; sr. v.p. El Rincon Resort, Cabo San Lucas, Mexico, 2002—03; pres., CEO, dir. Naanovo Energy, Inc., Calgary, Alta., Canada, 2003—07; CEO Naanovo Energy USA, Inc., Lincoln City, Oreg., 2003—07; pres., CEO Naanovo Internat. Free Zone N.V., Oranjestad, Aruba, 2005—07, Naanovo Internat. FZC, Dubai, United Arab Emirates, 2005—07, Caanov SA, Guatemala City, 2006—; mgr. T Squared LLC, Newport, Oreg., 2005—; pres., dir., CEO Green Energy 1 Inc., Newport, 2008—. Chmn. bd. dirs. Ship Harbor Resort and Marina, Inc., 1998-2004, Turtle Cove Resort, Inc., 1998, Olympic Capital, Inc., 1998-2003; bd. dirs. Naanove Energy, Accucom Data Network, Inc., Pierce Pacific Mfg., Lanco Internat., Energy Guard, Inc., G&R Devel. Co., Inc., MSA Cons., Inc.; sec.-treas. Everybody's Record Co., Inc. Contbr. articles to profl. jours., chpts. to textbooks Bd. dirs. Found. for Oreg. Rsch. and Edn., Jr. Achievement, First August Fin., Inc., Met. Youth Symphony; chmn. steering com. R.S. Dow Neurol. Scis. Inst.; mem. Russian ANT-25 Aviation Com. Mem.: Oreg. Pilots Assn. (pres. Beaverton chpt. 2001—02). Republican. Congregationalist. Achievements include patents for waste to energy technology; solar energy to electricity; biojector needleless syringe. Office: 1070 NE 7th Dr Newport OR 97365 Home: 515 NW Saltzman Rd Portland OR 97229 Office Phone: 971-223-0628. Business E-Mail: tmorrow@greenenergy1.com.

MORROW, JENNIFER LEIGH See **LEIGH, JENNIFER**

MORROW, MONICA, medical educator; b. Abington, Pa., Sept. 16, 1953; d. James Robert and Maxine Cooper Morrow; m. Virgil Craig Jordan, OBE, PhD, DSc. BS magna cum laude, Pa. State U., 1974; MD, Jefferson Med. Coll., 1976. Diplomate Am. Bd. of Surgery. Fellow in surg. oncology Meml. Sloan Kettering Cancer Ctr., New York, NY, 1981—83; asst. prof. surgery SUNY Health Sci. Ctr., Bklyn., 1983—88; assoc. prof. surgery U. Chgo., 1988—93, Northwestern U., Chgo., 1993—97, prof. surgery, 1997—2004; chmn. dept. surgical oncology and G. Willing Pepper chair cancer rsch. Fox Chase Cancer Ctr., Phila., 2004—08; chief breast surg. svc. Meml. Sloan Kettering Cancer Ctr.; prof. surgery Weill Cornell Med. Coll. Dir., cancer dept. ACS, Chgo., 1999—2001; exec. dir. Am. Joint Com. on Cancer, Chgo., 1999—2001; mem. Nat. Cancer Policy Bd., Inst. of Medicine, Washington, 1999—2002; co-chair Joint Com. of the ACS, Am. Coll. of Radiology, and Coll. of Am. Pathologists on Standards for Breast Conservation, 2000—02, 2005. Editor: (book) Managing Breast Cancer Risk, American Joint Committee on Cancer Staging Manual, sixth edition, Diseases of the Breast, Breast Diseases: A Problem Based Approach. Recipient Alumni Achievement award, Jefferson Med. Coll., 2006; named Distingushed Alumni, Pa, State U., 2002; Co-Principal Investigator, Specialized Program Rsch. Excellence in Breast Cancer grantee, Nat. Cancer Inst., 2000—05, Avon Found. Ctr. Excellence grantee prin. investigator, 2000—06. Fellow: Am. Coll. Surgeons, Royal Coll. Physicians and Surgeons Glasgow (hon.); mem.: Am. Surg. Assn., Am. Soc. Clin. Oncology (bd. dirs. 1998—2001), Soc. Surg. Oncology (exec. com. 1993—96, 2003—06, sec. 2007—). Avocations: travel, history, wine. Office: Meml Sloan Kettering Cancer Ctr MRI 1026 1275 York Ave New York NY 10021 Business E-Mail: morrowm@mskcc.org.

MORROW, RICHARD MARTIN, retired oil company executive; b. Wheeling, W.Va., Feb. 27, 1926; B.M.E., Ohio State U., 1948. With Amoco Corp., 1948-91; v.p. Amoco Prodn. Co., 1964-66; exec. v.p. Amoco Internat. Oil Co., 1966-70, Amoco Chem. Corp., 1970-74, pres., 1974-78, Amoco Corp., 1978-83, chmn. chief exec. officer, 1983-91; ret., 1991. Trustee U. Chgo. and Rush U. Med. Ctr. Office: 200 E Randolph Dr Ste 6952 Chicago IL 60601-7704

MORROW, ROB, actor; b. New Rochelle, NY, Sept. 21, 1962; s. Murray and Diane Francis (Markowitz) M; m. Debbon Ayer, 1988; 1 child. Mem. Ensemble Studio Theatre. Actor (TV series) Tattingers, 1988, Northern Exposure, 1990-94 (Lead Actor in TV Drama Emmy award nominee 1991, 92, 93, Lead Actor in TV Drama Golden Globe nominee 1991, 92, 93), Nearly Yours, 1999, Street Time, 2002-03, Numb3rs, 2005-, (TV films) The Day Lincoln Was Shot, 1998, Only Love, 1998, The Thin Blue Lie, 2000, Jenifer, 2001, (films) Private Resort, 1985, Quiz Show, 1994, Last Dance, 1996, Mother, 1996, Into My Heart, 1998, Other Voices, 2000, Maze, 2000, Sam the Man, 2000, Labor Pains, 2000, The Guru, 2002, The Emperor's Club, 2002, Night's Noontime, 2002, Going Shopping, 2004, The Bucket List, 2007; dir. (TV series) Oz, 2002, Street Time, 2003, Joan of Arcadia, 2004, (TV films) The Silent Alarm, 1993, (films) Maze, 2000; Stage appearances include Escape from Riverdale, 1984, The Return of Pinnochio, 1988, The Chosen, 1987-88, The Substance of Fire, 1990. Bd. dirs. Project ALS. Mem. Naked Angels (co-founder). Jewish.

MORROW, WALTER EDWIN, JR., electrical engineer, lab administrator; b. Springfield, Mass., July 24, 1928; s. Walter Edwin and Mary Elizabeth (Ganley) M.; m. Janice Lila Lombard, Feb. 25, 1951; children: Clifford E., Gregory A., Carolyn F. S.B., M.I.T., 1949, S.M., 1951. Mem. staff Lincoln Lab., MIT, Lexington, Mass., 1951-55, group leader, 1956-65; head div. communications MIT Lincoln Lab., 1966-68, asst. dir., 1968-71, asso. dir., 1972-77, dir., 1977-98, dir. emeritus, 1998—. Contbr. articles to profl. publs. Recipient award for outstanding achievement Pres. M.I.T., 1963, Edwin Howard Armstrong Achievement award IEEE Communications Soc., 1976 Fellow IEEE, Nat. Acad. Engring. Achievements include patent for synchronous satellite, electric power plant using electrolytic cell-fuel cell combination. Office: MIT Lincoln Lab PO Box 73 Lexington MA 02420-9108

MORROW, WILLIAM EARL, retired government official, law educator; b. Perryopolis, Pa., Oct. 22, 1923; s. Robert Ferguson and Daisy (Johnson) M.; m. Danna Katunaric, Apr. 26, 1958; children: Jamie Johnson, Tammara Marie, Kim Ina, William Joseph, Geoffrey Sean. BS in Psychology and Edn., Waynesburg U., 1948; MA in Human Resource Mgmt. and Industry, U. Pitts., 1953; LLD (hon.), U. Zagreb, 1958; postgrad., U. Md., 1969, Indsl. Coll. Armed Forces, 1969-70. With Survey Rsch. Ct. U. Mich., 1947; auditor, employment interviewer, then asst. dir. pers. Jones & Laughlin Steel Corp., 1948—54; exec. coord. Peoples Cab Co., 1954; labor-mgmt. adviser, policy coord. Arabian Am. Oil Co., Saudi Arabia, 1954—57; pers. expert UN/ILO, Geneva, Zagreb, Yugoslavia, 1957—58; cons., 1958—59; tng./program officer AID U.S. Dept. State, 1959—65; adminstrv. officer Bur. Internat. Labor Affairs U.S. Labor Dept., 1965—68; dep. divsn. chief Bur. Internat. Labor Affairs Labor Dept., 1968—72, projects dir. L.Am., Caribbean, 1973—80; asst. dir. Office Fgn. Rels., 1980—86; exec. sec. Employee Retirement Income Security Act Office of Sec. Labor U.S. Dept. Labor, 1986—95; ret., 1995. Guest prof. U. Coll. W.I., 1960-64; lectr. Prince George's Community Coll., 1965-97; lectr. U. Md., 1967-97; adj. prof. U. Md., 1997-2003. Mem. Tantallon (Md.) Citizens Assn. With USAF, 1942-44. Mem. Indsl. Rels. Rsch. Assn., Prince George's County Bd. Realtors, Am. Fedn. Govt. Employees, Am. Soc. Tng. Dirs., Am. Legion, D.A.V., Masons, Scottish Rite, Shriners, U. Md. Faculty Club, Dominion Valley Golf and Country Club, Tantallon-On-The-Potomac Golf and Country Club, Psi Chi Iota, Phi Alpha Theta, Delta Sigma Phi. Methodist. Home (Winter): Village Walk on Palmer Ranch 8308 Jesolo Ln Sarasota FL 34238 Home (Summer): Dominion Valley Golf and Country Club 5726 Wheelwright Way Haymarket VA 20169 Personal E-mail: willmorrow@aol.com.

MORROW, WINSTON VAUGHAN, financial executive; b. Grand Rapids, Mich., Mar. 22, 1924; s. Winston V. and Selma (von Egloffstein) M.; m. Margaret Ellen Staples, June 25, 1948 (div.); children: Thomas Christopher, Mark Staples; m. Edith Burrows Ulrich, Mar. 2, 1990. AB cum laude, Williams Coll., 1947; JD, Harvard U., 1950. Bar: RI 1950, US Dist. Ct., US Supreme Ct. Assoc. atty. Edwards & Angell, Providence, 1950-57; exec. v.p., asst. treas., gen. counsel, bd. dirs. Avis, Inc. and subs., 1957-61; v.p., gen. mgr. Rent A Car div. Avis, Inc., 1962-64, pres., bd. dirs., 1964-75; chmn., chief exec. officer, bd. dirs. Avis, Inc. and Avis Rent A Car System, Inc., 1965-77; chmn., pres., bd. dirs. Teleflorists Inc. and subs., 1978-80; pres. Westwood Equities Corp., LA, 1981-95, CEO, 1984-95, also bd. dirs.; chmn., pres., chief exec. officer Ticor Title Ins. Co., 1982-91, also bd. dirs.; chmn. TRTS Data Svcs. Inc., 1985-91; bd. dirs. AECOM Tech. Corp., LA, 1990-99. Mem. Pres.'s Industry and Govt. Spl. Travel Task Force, 1968, travel adv. bd. US Travel Svcs., 1968-76, LA City-wide Airport Adv. Com., 1983-85; co-chmn. LA Transp. Coalition, 1985-91. Mem. juvenile delinquency task force Nat. Coun. Crime and Delinquency, 1985-86, LA Mayor's Bus. Coun., 1983-86, Housing Roundtable, Washington, 1983-85, Calif. Bus. Roundtable, 1985-90; chmn., pres. Spring St. Found., 1991-2006; bd. dir. Police Found., Washington, 1983-91; trustee Com. Econ. Devel., Washington, 1987-91; trustee Adelphi U., 1970-75. Decorated Stella Della Solidarieta Italy, Gold Tourism medal Austria. Fellow The Huntington; mem. Car and Truck Rental Leasing Assn. (nat. pres. 1961-63), Am. Land Title Assn. (bd. govs. 1989-90), LA Area C. of C. (bd. dirs. 1983-90), Calif. Club, LA Tennis Club, Phi Beta Kappa, Kappa Alpha. Home: 4056 Farmouth Dr Los Angeles CA 90027-1314 also: Meadowview Farm 286 Cushing Corner Rd Freedom NH 03836

MORROW CAMPBELL, JULIETTE MICHELLE, lawyer; BS, SW Tex. State U., 1996, MEd in Elem. Edn., 1997; JD, Washburn U., Topeka, 2002. Bar: Kans. 2002, Colo. 2008, US Dist. Ct. Kans. 2002. 2nd grade tchr., 1996—97; tax rsch. atty. Sprint Nextel Corp., Overland Park, Kans., 2002—06, bankruptcy specialist Lone Tree, Colo., 2006—07; counselor, 2007—; 7th grade tchr., 1997—99. Office: Sprint Nextel Corp 10002 Park Meadows Dr Lone Tree CO 80124 E-mail: morrowsjuliette@yahoo.com.

MORSBERGER, ROBERT EUSTIS, English language educator; b. Balt., Sept. 10, 1929; s. Eustis Espey and Mary Virginia (Burgess) M.; m. Katharine Miller, June 17, 1955; 1 child, Grace Anne. BA, Johns Hopkins U., 1950; MA, U. Iowa, 1954, PhD, 1956. Instr., asst. prof. Miami U., Oxford, Ohio, 1956-59; asst. prof. English Utah State U., Logan, 1959-61; asst. prof., assoc. prof. Mich. State U., East Lansing, 1961-68; assoc. prof., dept. head U. Nigeria, Nsukka, 1964-66; prof. English Eastern Ky. U., Richmond, 1968-69; assoc. prof., prof. English, dept. head Calif. State Polytech U., Pomona, 1969—. Author: James Thurber, 1964, (with wife) Lew Wallace: Militant Romantic, 1980, McCulley The Mark of Zorro, 2005, Steinbeck, The Short Reign of Pippin IV, 2007; editor: Steinbeck, ZAPATA, 1993; co-editor: American Screenwriters, 1984, vol. 2, 1986; contbr. articles, books and short stories. Chmn. bd. dirs. Claremont (Calif.) Playhouse, 1978-81; bd. dirs. CAMASU, Claremont, 1992—. Mem. Modern Lang. Assn., Internat. John Steinbeck Soc. (edit. bd. 1970—, Burkhardt award Outstanding Contbn. 1991), Am. Assn. 18th Century Studies. Democrat. Avocations: fencing, acting, snorkeling. Home: 1530 Berea Ct Claremont CA 91711-3505 Office: Calif State Polytech U 3801 W Temple Ave Pomona CA 91768-2557 Home Phone: 909-626-8491. Personal E-mail: randkmorsberger@verizon.net.

MORSE, BARBARA, mathematics educator; BA, Univ. RI; Master's student in Tchg. Secondary Math, Providence Coll. Math tchr. Davisville Mid. Sch., N. Kingstown, RI, 1996—99, N. Kingstown (RI) H.S., 1999—, and math. dept. chair, 2003—. Named N. Kingstown Tchr. of Yr., 2005, RI Tchr. of Yr., 2006. Office: N Kingstown Sr High Sch 150 Fairway Dr North Kingstown RI 02852 Business E-Mail: Barbara_Morse@nksd.net.

MORSE, BARBARA JEANNE, library director; b. LA, Jan. 4, 1947; d. Joseph Emilio Consiglio and Therese Marie Burke; m. James Carlton Morse, May 6, 1967; children: James Joseph, Scott Anthony. BA in History, Westfield State Coll., 1986; MLS, SUNY, Albany, 1990. Teaching cert. State Mass., 1986. Libr. dir. Southwick Pub. Libr., Mass., 1982—94, West Springfield Pub. Libr., Mass., 1994—2000, City Leesburg Pub. Libr., Fla., 2002—; dir. libr. svcs. Beacon Coll., Leesburg, Fla., 2000—02. Exec. bd. dir. Fla. Libr. Assn., Lake City, Fla., 2004—06, Ctrl.-Western Mass Automated Resource Sharing Nework, Worcester, 1998; wmrls adv. coun. Western Mass. Regional Libr. Sys., Hatfield, Mass., 1993—94; long-range plan steering com. Mass. Bd. Libr. Commn., Boston, 1997—98. Recreation bd. mem. Town Southwick, Mass., 1977—80. Recipient Good Egg Award, Leesburg Area C. of C., 2007; named City Employee of Yr., Leesburg Partnership, Inc, 2007. Mem.: ALA, Fla. Libr. Assn. Roman Catholic. Avocations: reading, travel. Office: City of Leesburg Pub Lib 100 E Main St Leesburg FL 34748 Office Fax: 352-728-9794. Business E-Mail: barbara.morse@leesburgflorida.gov.

MORSE, CARMEL LEI, professor; b. Spokane, Wash., June 15, 1953; d. John Ola and Billie Jean (Garrett) Lindgren; m. John Christopher Keaton, Apr. 15, 1972 (div. Apr. 1977); 1 child, Theresa Jean; m. David Scott Morse, June 21, 1980. BA, U. Dayton, 1996; MA, Wright State U., 2003; attending, U. Nebr., Lincoln., 2009—. Cert. in women studies 2009. Adj. instr. English Women's Studies, Wright State U., Dayton, Ohio, 2009—. Author: (book) Audio-Visual Primer, 1983; (movie script) Murder Is A Negative Act, 1984; (poem) Storm Warning (2d place League Innovation Student Lit. contest). Democrat. Avocations: photography, reading. Business E-Mail: carmel.morse@wright.edu.

MORSE, DANIEL E., biochemistry educator, science administrator; b. NYC, May 20, 1941; BA, Harvard U., 1963; PhD in Molecular Biology, Albert Einstein Coll. Medicine, 1967. Fellow in molecular genetics Stanford U., 1967-69; from Silas Arnold Houston asst. prof. to Silas Arnold Houston assoc. prof. med. sch. Harvard U., 1969-73; prof. molecular genetics and biochemistry U. Calif., Santa Barbara, 1973—, chmn. sect. molecular biology and biochemistry dept. biol. sci., 1981-85, chmn. Marine Biotechnology Ctr., 1986—. Mem. NRC, U.S. Nat. Com. Internat. Union Biol. Sci., 1986—; chmn. task force biotechnology in ocean sci. NSF, 1987—. Fellow AAAS; mem. Am. Soc. Molecular Biology and Biochemistry, Am. Soc. Limnology and Oceanography, Am. Soc. Microbiology, Am. Soc. Zoology, N.Y. Acad. Sci., Internat. Soc. Chem. Ecology. Achievements include research on molecular mechanisms controlling reproduction, larval metamorphosis, development and gene expression; signal molecules, receptors, and transducers; molecular marine biology; molecular neurobiology; molecular chemosensory mechanisms. Office: U Calif Marine Biotech Ctr Dept Biology Santa Barbara CA 93106

MORSE, DAVID, actor; b. Hamilton, Mass., Oct. 11, 1953; s. Charles and Jacquelyn Morse; m. Susan Wheeler Duff, June 19, 1982; 3 children. Studied, William Esper Studio. Performer Boston Repertory Co., 1971—77, Circle Repertory Co. Actor: (films) Inside Moves, 1980, Max Dugan Returns, 1983, Personal Foul, 1987, Desperate Hours, 1990, The Indian Runner, 1991, The Good Son, 1993, The Getaway, 1994, Magic Kid II, 1994, The Taming Power of the Small, 1995, The Crossing Guard, 1995, Twelve Monkeys, 1995, The Rock, 1996, Extreme Measures, 1996, The Long Kiss Goodnight, 1996, George B., 1997, Contact, 1997, The Legend of Pig Eye, 1998, The Negotiator, 1998, Crazy in Alabama, 1999, The Green Mile, 1999, Dancer in the Dark, 2000, Bait, 2000, Proof of Life, 2000, Diary of a City Priest, 2001, Hearts in Atlantis, 2001, The Slaughter Rule, 2002, Shuang tong, 2002, Down in the Valley, 2005, Nearing Grace, 2005, Dreamer: Inspired by a True Story, 2005, A.W.O.L, 2006, 16 Blocks, 2006, Hounddog, 2007, Disturbia, 2007, Passengers, 2008; (TV films) Our Family Business, 1981, Prototype, 1983, Shattered Vows, 1984, When Dreams Come True, 1985, Place at the Table, 1987, Six Against the Rock, 1987, Downpayment on Murder, 1987, Winnie, 1988, Brotherhood of the Rose, 1989, Cross of Fire, 1989, Two-Fisted Tales, 1991, Cry in the Wild: The Taking of Peggy Ann, 1991, Dead Ahead: The Exxon Valdez Disaster, 1992, Miracle on Interstate 880, 1993, The Langoliers, 1995, Tecumseh: The Last Warrior, 1995, Murder Live!, 1997, Hack, 2002; (TV series) Big Wave Dave's, 1993, The New Adventures of Madeline, 1995, Action Man, 1995, Hack, 2002—04, House M.D., 2006—07; (TV miniseries) Abraham and Mary Lincoln: A House Divided, 2001, John

Adams, 2008; (plays) How I Learned to Drive, 1997 (Drama Desk award, The Obie); (Broadway plays) The Seafarer, 2008; actor, dir. (TV series) St. Elsewhere, 1987; dir.: (TV series) Friday the 13th, 1987. Recipient FirstGlance award, Phila. FirstGlance Film Festival, 2003. Office: c/o Mara Buxbaum ID PR 9 Desbrosses St 2nd fl New York NY 10013

MORSE, EDWARD LEWIS, energy economist, director; b. NYC, Jan. 5, 1942; s. Jonah Benjamin and Rebecca (Freiberg) M.; m. Linda Kasle Jones, Aug. 15, 1965; children: Michael Ari, Molly Rachel. BA, Johns Hopkins U., Balt., 1963; MA, Johns Hopkins U., Washington, 1966; PhD, Princeton U., 1969. Asst. prof. internat. politics Woodrow Wilson Sch. Princeton (N.J.) U., 1969-75; sr. rsch. fellow Coun. on Fgn. Rels., NYC, 1975-78; exec. asst. to undersec. econ. affairs U.S. Dept. State, Washington, 1978-79, dep. asst. sec. for internat. energy policy, 1979-81; dir. internat. affairs Phillips Petroleum Co., Bartlesville, Okla., 1981-84; mng. dir. Petroleum Fin. Co., Ltd., Washington, 1984-96; pres., publisher Petroleum Intelligence Weekly, NYC, 1988-99, The Oil Daily Co., NYC, 1996-99; exec. Hess Energy Trading Co., NYC, 1999—2006; mng. dir., chief energy economist Lehman Bros., NYC, 2006—08; mng. dir., head rsch. Louis Capital Markets, NYC, 2008—. Author: Foreign Policy and Interdependence in Gaullist France, 1973, Modernization and the Transformation of International Relations, 1976; contbr. articles to various publs. Office: Louis Capital Markets 500 5th Ave New York NY 10010 Office Phone: 212-651-3196. Personal E-mail: edmorse@aol.com. Business E-Mail: emorse@louiscapital.com.

MORSE, GAYLE SKAWENNIO, psychologist, consultant; d. Arthur T. Lamendola and Karonhiosta Thomas; children: Mark T., Catherine Ann, Alexander Granville(dec.). BA, Kennesaw U., Ga., 1992; PhD, SUNY, Albany, 2000. Lic. psychologist N.Y. State Bd. of Edn. Program dir. Crossroads/CDPC/NYS-OMH, Castleton, NY, 2004—06; psychologist, cons. mobil team, office of child and family svcs. Capital Dist. Psychiat. Ctr., Albany, NY, 2000—04; asst. prof. The Sage Colls., Albany, NY, 2005—. Adj. faculty SUNY, Albany, 1994—; med. cons. group NY State Police, Albany, 2000—06; with Consultation Ctr., 2007—; presenter in field. Contbr. articles to rsch. jours. and numerous nat. publs. and presentations. Mem. Foster Children Program Women's Club of Albany, 2005—. Mem.: ACA (mem. Native Am. concerns com. 1997—98, jour. reviewer Jour. Counseling and Devel. 2003—06, interim v.p. Assn. for Multicultural Counseling and Devel.), APA (mem. partnership com. 1999—2002, mem. working group Assn. Grad. Students and Bd. Ednl. Affairs 1999—2002). Achievements include research in relationships among culture, mental health and quality of life; impact of environmental toxins on health.

MORSE, JUDITH, music educator, conductor; MusB in Music Performance, Manhattan Sch. Music, 1982; MA in Music Edn., Columbia U., 1983, EdM in Music Edn., 1986. Tchg. asst. to Dr. Samuel Applebaum, 1977—80; music tchr., dir. mid. sch. and HS orchs. Hopewell Valley Regional Schs., Pennington, NJ, 1985—; condr., music dir. Edison (NJ) Symphony Orch., 2000—; faculty, violin & viola Westminster Conservatory, Princeton, NJ, 2007—, Carnegie Hall, 2008. Tour condr. Ann Jillian; condr. guitarist Celino Romero, von Trapp Children, Jack Jones, Ft. Worth Symphony Orch., Trenton Sister City Orch.; guest condr. NJ Region Orch., 1996. Condr.: Clay Aiken Christmas Concerts, 2006. Recipient Proclamation, NJ State Senate, 1987, Mayor of Edison, 2000, Nat. Gold Orch. award, Boston, 2004, Nat. Music Tchr. award, 2006; finalist Grammy Signature. Mem.: NJ Music Educators, Music Educators Nat. Conf. Personal E-mail: jmorse777@hotmail.com.

MORSE, LEONARD J., epidemiologist, public health service officer; MD, U. Md., 1955. Intern and resident in internal medicine, fellow in infectious diseases U. Md. Med. Sys.; resident in internal medicine New Eng. Med. Care Hosp.; pvt. practice Worcester, Mass.; ret., 1996; med. dir. New Bedford Cmty. Health Ctr., 1996—2001; prof. clin. medicine, family medicine, cmty. health U. Mass. Med. Sch., Worcester; pub. health commr. Worcester, 2001—. Mem.: AMA (past chair coun. ethical and jud. affairs, Pride in Profession award 2004), Am. Soc. History Medicine, Am. Soc. Microbiology, Infectious Diseases Soc. Am., Mass. Med. Soc. (pres. 1993—94, past chmn. com. ethics and discipline, Lifetime Achievement award 1997, Grant V. Rodkey award 1997), Am. Coll. Physicians (Named Internist of Yr. Mass. chpt. 1998). Office: Worcester Pub Health 25 Meade St Worcester MA 01610 Office Phone: 508-799-8531. Business E-Mail: morsel@ci.worcester.ma.us, lmorsemd@massmed.org.

MORSE, M. HOWARD, lawyer; b. Louisville, May 30, 1959; s. Marvin Henry and Betty Anne (Hess) M.; m. Laura E. Loeb, Apr. 17, 1988; children: Elizabeth L., Marni L. AB summa cum laude, Dartmouth Coll., 1981; JD cum laude, Harvard U., 1984. Bar: D.C. 1984, U.S. Ct. of Internat. Trade 1985, U.S. Ct. Appeals (fed. cir.) 1985, U.S. Dist. Ct. D.C. 1986, U.S. Ct. Appeals (D.C. cir.) 1986, U.S. Ct. Appeals (4th cir.) 1987. Assoc. Arnold & Porter, Washington, 1984-88; atty. FTC Bur. Competition, Washington, 1988-91, dep. asst. dir. for policy, 1991-93, asst. dir., 1993-97; ptnr., co-chair, antitrust group Drinker, Biddle & Reath LLP, Washington, 1998—. Adj. prof. law Georgetown Law Ctr., Washington, 1995—2000. Dist. enrollment dir. Dartmouth Coll., 2004—; bd. mem. Dartmouth Club, Washington, 2007. Mem.: ABA (chair computer industry com. 1996—99, chair intellectual property com. 1999—2002, coun. 2002—05, chair exemptions and immunities com. 2006—09, mem. antitrust sect.), Fed. Civil Enforcement Coun. (chair 2009—), D.C. Bar Assn., Intellectual Property Owners Assn. (vice chair antitrust and competition law com. 2004—07), Phi Beta Kappa. Office: Drinker Biddle & Reath LLP 1500 K St NW Ste 1100 Washington DC 20005-1209 Office Phone: 202-842-8883. Office Fax: 202-842-8465. Personal E-mail: morsemh@msn.com.

MORSE, MARVIN HENRY, retired judge; b. Mt. Vernon, NY, July 19, 1929; s. Frank Irving and Lillian (Seeger) M.; m. Betty Anne Hess, Dec. 27, 1953; children: Martin Albert, Michael Howard, Lee Anne. AB, Colgate U., 1949; LLB, Yale U., 1952. Bar: N.Y. 1952, Ky. 1956, Md. 1964, U.S. Supreme Ct. 1960, U.S. Ct. Appeals (6th cir.), U.S. Dist. Ct. (we. dist.) Ky., U.S. Ct. Mil. Appeals, U.S. Ct. Claims, U.S. Ct. Appeals (D.C. cir.), U.S. Ct. Appeals (fed. cir.), U.S. Dist. Ct. (no. dist.) Tex., U.S. Dist. Ct. Hawaii. Pvt. practice, Louisville, 1956-62; asst. counsel Office of Gen. Counsel Dept. Navy, Washington, 1962-65, Office of Gen. Counsel Office Sec. Def., Washington, 1965-68; asst. gen. counsel GSA, Washington, 1968-70, U.S. Postal Svc., Washington, 1970-73; adminstrv. law judge Fed. Energy Regulatory Commn., Washington, 1973-75, Postal Rate Commn., Washington, 1975-77, CAB, Washington, 1977-80; dir. adminstrv. law judges Office Pers. Mgmt., Washington, 1980-82; chief adminstrv. law judge SBA, Washington, 1982-87, asst. adminstr. hearings and appeals, 1985-87; adminstrv. law judge Exec. Office of Immigration Rev. Dept. Justice, Washington, 1987—2002; temp. mem. Bd. of Immigration Appeals, 1998—2002; ret., 2002. Mem. Adminstrv. Conf. of U.S., 1980-84, govt. mem., 1985-86, 87-95, liaison mem.; faculty and faculty coord. The Nat. Jud. Coll., 1977, 79-80. Author: (with S. Groner) ABA Handbook chpt. on adminstrv. law, 1981, (with Lucy Moran) Troubling the Waters: Human Cargos, 2002. Trustee Washington area chpt. Am. Digestive Disease Soc., 1976-87. With JAGC, USAF, 1952-56, to col. USAFR, ret. 1979. Decorated USAF Legion of Merit; recipient Disting. Svc. award Am. Digestive Disease Soc., 1980. Mem. ABA (exec. com. 1977-82, 84-87, chmn. 1980-81, conf. adminstrv. law judges, del. ho. of dels. 1984-87, lawyers in govt. com. 1985-86, jud. selection, tenure and compensation com. 1987-93, govt. pub. sect. lawyers divsn., coun. 1996-02), Fed. Bar Assn. (nat. coun. 1976—, chmn. career svc. sect. 1983-86, chmn. judiciary sect. 1986-88, sect. coord. 1988-90, sec. 1991-92, del. to ABA ho. of dels. 1992-93, 97-99, v.p. 1993-94, pres.-elect 1994-95, pres. 1995-96), Am. Law Inst., Fed. Adminstrv. Law Judges Conf. (exec. com. 1975-77, 82-96, 2000-01), Nat. Assn. Adminstrv. Law Judges (hon.), Fed. Am. Inn of Ct. (coun. 1990-92, pres. 1992-94), Longboat Key Democratic Club, Fla. (pres. 2006-08).: 2425 Gulf of Mexico Dr Apt 6A Longboat Key FL 34228-3287 Home Phone: 941-383-4707. Personal E-mail: bhmmhm@comcast.net.

MORSE, RICHARD JAY, human resources and organizational development specialist, consultant; b. Detroit, Mich., Aug. 2, 1933; s. Maurice and Belle Rosalyn (Jacobson) M. BA, U. Va., 1955; MA in Clin. Psychology, Calif. State U., LA, 1967. Area pers. adminstr. Gen. Tel. Co. of Calif., Santa Monica, 1957-67; sr. v.p. human resources The Bekins Co., Glendale, Calif., 1967-83; pvt. cons. human resources and orgn. devel. Cambria, 1983—. Contbr. articles to profl. jours. Fund raiser various orgns., So. Calif., 1970—. Mem. Internat. Soc. Performance Improvement (founding mem. 1958—). Democrat. Jewish. Avocations: travel, tennis, walking, swimming. Home and Office: 6410 Cambria Pines Rd Cambria CA 93428-2009 Office Phone: 805-927-3457. Personal E-mail: dickmorse@earthlink.net.

MORSE, ROBERT HARRY, lawyer; b. Bklyn., May 25, 1941; s. Soll and Rachel Morse; m. Sandra Goldstein, July 22, 1967; children: Lisa Jennifer, Eric Jeffrey. BSEE with honors, MIT, 1963, MSEE with honors, 1964; JD, Harvard U., 1967. Bar: N.Y. 1968, D.C. 1978, Md. 1985. Assoc. Kenyon & Kenyon, Reilly, Carr & Chapin, NYC, 1967-71; trial atty. antitrust divsn. Dept. Justice, Washington, 1971-74, sr. trial atty., 1974-78; ptnr. Peabody, Lambert & Meyers, Washington, 1978-82, Galland, Kharasch, Morse & Garfinkle, Washington, 1982-96, Ropes and Gray, Washington, 1997-2000; pres., CEO Esrom Consulting LLC, Rockville, Md., 2000—; ptnr. Farkas & Morse LLC, Washington, 2003—05. Dir. Earle Palmer Brown Cos., 1984-98. Mem. nat. capital area coun. Boy Scouts Am., gen. counsel, 1991-94, exec. bd. dirs., 1990—, pres. 2001-02, chmn., 2002-2003. Recipient Spl. Achievement award Dept. Justice, 1973, Meritorious award Dept. Justice, 1976, Silver Beaver award Boy Scouts Am., 1999. Mem.: ABA, Patent Bar, D.C. Bar Assn., Nat. Alumni Assn. MIT (bd. dirs. 1986—88), MIT Club Washington (sec. 1981—82, pres. 1983—84), Eta Kappa Nu, Tau Beta Pi, Sigma Xi. Avocation: tennis. Home Phone: 650-260-2601; Office Phone: 650-260-2603. Business E-Mail: rhmorse@alum.mit.edu.

MORSE, ROBERT PARKER, investment company executive; b. Nyack, NY, May 8, 1945; s. Robert Willard Parker and Julia (Larson) M.; m. Sarah Morgan Cumings, Sept. 23, 1978; children: Robert Bradley St. Clair, Parker Morgan, Sarah Spencer. BS in Econs., U. Pa., 1967; student in advanced currency theory, Adelphi Suffolk U., 1970-71. V.p. Am. Express/W.H. Morton Divsn., NYC, 1970-74; sr. v.p., ptnr. William G. Campbell & Co., Inc., NYC, 1975-80; chmn., CEO Morse, Williams & Co., Inc., NYC, 1981—. Bd. dirs. Dialog Comm., 2005—06, eLottery, Inc., 860 UN Plaza, Inc., Stowe, Vt., 2007—. Gov. emeritus Soc. Mayflower Descs., N.Y., 1993-98; trustee Plimoth Plantation, Mass., 1994-2000, Bermuda Biol. Sta. Rsch., 1983-2000, Gen. Svc. Bd., N.Y., 1981-93, trustee, chmn. fin. English Spkg. Union, 1998—, U.S. del. internat. coun., English Spkg. Union, London, 2002; bd. assocs. The Whitehead Inst., MIT, 1996—; bd. dirs. Arlington Inst., 1995-2001; chmn. bd. The Wall Street Fund, 1984—. Lt. USNR, 1967-78. Mem. Am. Def. Preparedness Assn., Pilgrims of U.S., River Club, Bond Club N.Y., U.S. Naval Inst., Union Club, N.Y. Yacht Club, Links Club, River Club. Episcopalian. Avocations: sailing, skiing, reading, golf, tennis. Home: 441 Lexington Ave Fl 17 New York NY 10017-3926 Office Phone: 212-856-8200. Business E-Mail: rpm@morsewilliams.com.

MORSE, SAUL JULIAN, lawyer; b. Jan. 17, 1948; s. Leon William and Goldie (Kohn) M.; m. Anne Bruce Morgan, Aug. 21, 1982; children: John Samuel, Elizabeth Miriam. BA, U. Ill., 1969, JD, 1972. Bar: Ill. 1973, U.S. Dist. Ct. (so. dist.) Ill. 1976, U.S. Ct. Appeals (7th cir.) 1983, U.S. Supreme Ct. 1979, U.S. Tax Ct. 1982. Law clk. State of Ill. EPA, 1971-72, Ill. Commerce Commn., 1972, hearing examiner, 1972-73, trial atty., 1973-75; asst. minority legal counsel Ill. Senate, 1975, minority legal counsel, 1975-77; mem. Ill. Human Rights Commn., 1985-91; dir., treas., chair grievance com. Ill. Comprehensive Health Ins. Plan, 1987—2002; gen. counsel Ill. Legis. Space Needs Commn., 1978-92; pvt. practice Springfield, Ill., 1977-79; ptnr. Gramlich & Morse, Springfield, 1980-85; prin. Saul J. Morse and Assocs., 1985-87; ptnr. Morse, Giganti and Appleton, 1987-92; v.p., gen. counsel Ill. State Med. Soc., 1992—2004; of counsel Brown, Hay & Stephens, LLP, Springfield, Ill., 2004—. Lectr. in continuing med. edn, 1986—90; counsel symposia; adj. asst. prof. med. humanities So. Ill. Univ. Sch. Medicine; adj. lectr. legal studies U. Ill., Springfield, 2004; pres. Springfield Profl. Baseball, LLC. Bd. dirs. Springfield Ctr. for Ind. Living, 1984-89, Ill. Comprehensive Health Ins. Plan Bd., 1987-02, United Way Ctrl. Ill., Inc., 1991-97, G.I.N.I. Inst., 2002, Hope Sch., Springfield, 1996-03, Springfield Jewish Fedn., 1992-95; mem. task force on transp. Rep. Nat. Com., 1979-80; mem. Springfield Jewish Cmty. Rels. Coun., 1976-79, 97-2002; bd. dirs. internat. Post Polio Health Internat., 2002—, treas.; bd. dirs. Springfield Jewish Fedn. Endowment; mem. spl. com. on zoning and land use planning Sangamon County Bd., 1978; treas. City of Leland Grove, 1999—; exec. com. AMA and State Med. Socs. Litig. Ctr., 1999-04, chmn. 2003-04; commr. Ill. Guardianship and Advocacy Commn., 2002-08, chmn., 2005-08; mem. chancellor's cmty. adv. coun. U. Ill., Springfield, 2002—; bd. dirs. Vis. Nurse Assn. Ctrl. Ill., 2004-07; vice chmn. United Cerebral Palsy Land of Lincoln, 2002-07, pres., 2006—; chmn. VCP Housing Corp., 2008, bd. dirs. Sangams County Cmty. Found., 2009. Named Disabled Adv. of Yr., Ill. Dept. Rehab. Svcs., 1985; recipient Chmn.'s Spl. award Ill. State Med. Soc., 1987, Susan S. Suter award as outstanding disabled citizen of Ill. Peers Leading Lawyers Network, 1990, 06. Mem. ABA (vice-chmn. medicine and law com. 1988-90, tort and ins. practice sect., forum com. on health law), Am. Assn. Health Lawyers, Am. Soc. Law and Medicine, Ill. State Bar Assn. (spl. com. on reform of legis. process 1976-82, spl. com. on the disabled lawyer 1978-82, young lawyers sect. com. on role of govt. atty. 1977-80, chmn. 1982, sect. coun. adminstrv. law, vice-chmn. 1981-82), Sangamon County Bar Assn., Am. Soc. Med. Assn. Counsel, Phi Delta Phi. Home: 1701 S Illini Rd Springfield IL 62704-3301 Office: Brown Hay Stephens LLC PO Box 2459 205 S Fifth St Ste 700 Springfield IL 62705 Office Phone: 217-241-5053. Personal E-mail: saulmorse@sbcglobal.net. Business E-Mail: smorse@bhslaw.com.

MORSE, STEPHEN SCOTT, virologist, epidemiologist, immunologist, educator; b. NYC, Nov. 22, 1951; s. Murray H. and Phyllis Morse; m. Marilyn Gewirtz, Feb. 1991. BS, CCNY, 1971; MS, U. Wis., 1974, PhD, 1977. NSF trainee dept. bacteriology U. Wis., Madison, 1971-72, rsch. asst., 1972-77; Nat. Cancer Inst. rsch. fellow Med. Coll. Va./Va. Commonwealth U., Richmond, 1977-80, instr. microbiology, 1980-81; asst. prof. microbiology Rutgers U., New Brunswick, NJ, 1981-85; rsch. assoc. Rockefeller U., NYC, 1985-88, asst. prof., 1988-96, adj. faculty, 1996—; program mgr. Def. Advanced Rsch. Projects Agy., 1996-2000; asst. prof. to prof. epidemiology, Mailman Sch. Pub. Health, Columbia U., 1996—2008, dir. Ctr. Pub. Health Preparedness, Mailman Sch. Pub. Health, 2000—05. Cons. US Congress Office Tech. Assessment, Washington, 1989; chair conf. on emerging viruses NIH, 1989; mem. com. microbial threats to health, chair subcom. on viruses Inst. Medicine-NAS, 1990—92, steering com. forum on emerging infections, 1996—, com. future biothreats, 2003—05; chair program for monitoring emerging diseases (ProMED) Fedn. Am. Scientists, 1993—99; mem. com. on biodef. analysis and countermeasures NAS-NRC, 2005—08. Author: Emerging Viruses, 1993, Evolutionary Biology of Viruses, 1994; editor-in-chief Pasteur Inst. Jour., 1996—99; sect. editor: Ctr. for Disease Control and Prevention Jour., Emerging Infectious Diseases, 1995—2002, mem. editl. bd.: Emerging Infectious Diseases, 2003—06, Biosecurity and Bioterrorism, 2003—. Fellow: NY Acad. Medicine, Am. Coll. Epidemiology, NY Acad. Scis. (vice chair microbiology sect. 1994—96, chair 1996—98), Am. Acad. Microbiology; mem.: Marine Biology Lab., Am. Assn. Immunologists, Am. Soc. Microbiology, Coun. on Fgn. Rels., Cosmos Club, Sigma Xi. Office: Columbia U Mailman Sch Pub Health 722 W 168th St New York NY 10032-3722 Business E-Mail: ssm20@columbia.edu.

MORSE, TIMOTHY R., Internet company executive; b. 1969; BS in Fin., Ops. & Strategic Mgmt., Boston Coll. Various positions GE Co., 1992—2007; CFO, gen. mgr. bus. devel. GE Plastics; sr. v.p., CFO Altera Corp., San Jose, Calif., 2007—09; CFO Yahoo! Inc., Sunnyvale, Calif., 2009—. Office: Yahoo! Inc 701 First Ave Sunnyvale CA 94086*

MORSE-MCNEELY, PATRICIA, poet, writer, retired secondary school educator; b. Galveston, Tex., Apr. 2, 1923; d. Bleecker Lansing Sr. and Annie Maud (Pillow) Morse; m. Chalmers Rankin McNeely, Mar. 22, 1949 (div. Aug. 1959); children: David Lansing McNeely, Timothy Ann McNeely Caldwell, Patricia Grace McNeely Dragon, Abigail Rankin McNeely. BS in Edn., U. Tex., 1972; LLD in Ednl. Psychology/Spl. Edn., U. Tex., San Antonio, 1976, MA in Ednl. Psychology/Counseling, 1981. Cert. tchr. Tex., profl. counselor. Sec. various cos., Galveston & Austin, Tex., 1941, 1945—49; sec. to dir. Parks and Recreation, Galveston, 1946—47; dep. clk. Ct. of Civil Appeals, Galveston, 1947-48; police stenographer Austin Police Dept., 1970-74; history and spl. edn. tchr. N.E. Ind. Sch. Dist., San Antonio, 1974-76; spl. edn. tchr. S.W. Ind. Sch. Dist., San Antonio, 1978-81; vocat. adjustment coord. East Ctrl. Ind. Sch. Dist., San Antonio, 1981-82; counselor, tchr. Stockdale Ind. Sch. Dist., Tex., 1982-84; clinic sec. Humana Hosp., Dallas, 1985-87; tchr. history, spl. edn. and lang. arts Dallas Ind. Sch. Dist., 1987-2000; ret., 2000. TSTA/NEA assn. rep. Hill Mid. Sch., Dallas, 1990—91, E.B. Comstock Mid. Sch., Dallas, 1991—2000. Author: (poet) Texas City, 1947 (awards poetry & other writing), A Gift of Love, 1978, The Key, 1991, The Gull's Quill, 2001, 2d edit., 2005, Pat's Portfolio, 2002, From Mother's Writings, 2005, My Counting Calendar, 2007, Ghostly Tales from Amer. Jails Anthology, 2007, The Inconstant Moon, 2008, numerous poems and short stories in lit. publs. and anthologies; contbr. articles to newsletters, newspapers and profl. jours. Internat. chmn. ad hoc com. for writing leadership tng. program Parents Without Ptnrs., Inc., Austin, 1968, v.p. zone, corr. sec., libr., various coms., 1965—74, Parents Without Ptnrs. Internat., Inc., 1976—78; newsletter editor Parents Without Ptnrs., Inc., Austin, 1967—72. Mem.: AARP, NEA (life), Hill County Book Festival, Acad. Amer Poets, San Gabriel Writers League, Soc. Children's Book Writers and Illustrators, Nat. Trust for Edn. (trustee), U. Tex. Austin Alumni Assn. (First Recipient Bernice Milburn Moore scholarship award 1972), Internat. Libr. Poetry (Hall of Fame 1997), Nat. Edn. Assn. Ret. (life), TSTA-R (life; del. to Tex. State Tchrs. Assn. Conf. 1978—81, 1991—97), Internat. Soc. Poets (life). Episcopalian. Avocations: reading, music, sewing/handcrafts, book collecting. Personal E-mail: pmmcneely@austin.rr.com.

MORSI, BADIE I., engineering educator, researcher; PhD, ENSIC-INPL, Nancy, France, DSc, 1982. Prof. U. Pitts., 1982—. Office: Univ Pitts 1249 Bendum Hall Pittsburgh PA 15261 Office Fax: 412-624-9639.

MORSY, MOHAMED NAGEEB, electrical engineering educator, researcher; b. Assiut, Egypt, Nov. 22, 1953; s. Morsy; m. Amal Kamel Morsy, Nov. 6, 1986; children: Amr, Khaled. BSc, Mil. Tech. Coll., Cairo, 1976; MSc in Elec. Engring., Assiut U., Assiut, Egypt, 1983; DSc in Elec. Engring. and Applied Sci., George Washington U., 1990. Multi-channel microwave comm. sys. Signal Corps, Cairo, 1976-80, comm. devices Assiut, Egypt, 1980-84; staff R&D dept. Armament Authority, Cairo, 1984—86, 1990—2001; staff engring. edn. dept. Mil. Acad., Cairo, 1986-87; part-time faculty George Washington U., 2002—03; chair Sch. Electronics Tech., ITT Tech. Inst., Springfield, Va., 2004—. Contbr. articles to profl. jours. Mem. IEEE (sr.). Office: ITT Tech Inst 7300 Boston Blvd Springfield VA 22153 Home: 3851 Aristotle Ct 319 Fairfax VA 22030-7492 Personal E-mail: m.morsy@ieee.org.

MORTENSEN, ERIC MICHAEL, medical researcher; m. Christine Mortensen, Aug. 16, 2008. MD, Med. Coll. Pa., Phila., 1996; MSc, U. Pitts., 2001. Diplomate Am. Bd. Internal Medicine, 1999. Assoc. prof., medicine U. Tex. Health Sci. Ctr. San Antonio, 2001—. Office: Audie L Murphy Va Hosp 7400 Merton Minter Blvd 11C6 San Antonio TX 78229 Business E-Mail: mortensene@uthscsa.edu.

MORTENSEN, GORDON LOUIS, artist, printmaker; b. Arnegard, ND, Apr. 27, 1938; s. Gunner and Otillia Ernestine (Reiner) M.; m. Phoebe Hollis Hansen, Apr. 10, 1965 (div. 1968); m. Linda Johanna Sisson, Dec. 7, 1969. BFA, Mpls. Coll. Art and Design, 1964; postgrad., U. Minn., 1969—72. One-man shows include Minn. Mus., St. Paul, 1967, Concept Art Gallery, Pitts., 1981, 1983, 1985, 1987, 1989, 1991, 1993, C.G. Rein Galleries, Mpls., 1978, 1980, 1985, 1989, 1991, 1993, others, exhibited in group shows at Miami U., Oxford, Ohio (1st pl. award, 1977), Phila. Print Club (George Bunker award, 1977), 12th Nat. Silvermine Guild Print Exhbn., New Canaan, Conn., 1976, 1978, 1980, 1983, 1986, 1994, 1996 (Hearsch Mag. award, 1978, Purchase award, 1983, 1986), 4th Miami Internat. Print Biennial (4th pl. award, 1980), Rockford Internat., 1981, 1985 (Juror's award, 1981), Boston Printmakers Nat. Exhbn., 1977, 1979—81, 1983, 1997, 2003 (Purchase award, 1977, 1979, 1983, Juror's Accomodation), 2007, others, Represented in permanent collections Achenbach Found. Graphic Arts at Palace Legion of Honor, San Francisco, Bklyn. Mus., Phila. Mus. Art, Libr. of Congress, Minn. Mus. Art, Met. Mus. and Art Ctr., Miami, Fla., Mus. Am. Art, Washington, Art Inst. Chgo., Mus. Art at Carnegie-Mellon Inst., Pitts., Walker Art Ctr., Mpls., Dulin Gallery Art, Knoxville, Tenn., Phila. Mus. Art, Tokyo Fuji Art Mus., numerous corp. collections; profiled in numerous art jours. Served with USMC, 1957-60. Mem. Boston Printmakers, Phila. Print Club, L.A. Printmaking Soc., Albany Print Club, Am. Print Alliance. Home and Office: 4153 Crest Rd Pebble Beach CA 93953-3052 Office Phone: 831-625-0960.

MORTENSEN, PAMELA S., retail executive; b. 1955; BS, U. Ark., Fayetteville, 1977. Buyer Federated Dept. Stores; sr. buyer Bailey, Banks, & Biddle (divsn. Zale Corp.), 1985—97; v.p., divisional mdse. mgr. svc. mdse., Home divsn. Wal-Mart Stores, Inc., 1997—2002, v.p., divisional mdse. mgr. Fine Jewelry & Watch divsn., 2002—09; sr. v.p., gen. mdse mgr. Fine Jewelry JC Penney Co., Inc., 2009—. Office: JCPenney Corp Hdqs PO Box 10001 Dallas TX 75301*

MORTENSEN, ROBERT HENRY, landscape and golf course architect; b. Jackson, Mich., June 9, 1939; s. Henry and Charlotte Marie (Brown) Mortensen; m. Linda McGinnis, 2005; children: Phillip, Paul, Susan, Julia. B in Landscape Architecture, Ohio State U., 1961; M in Landscape Architecture, U. Mich., 1965. Registered landscape arch., Va., Md. Landscape arch. various firms, Louisville, 1960, 61-63; with Ohio Divsn. Pks., Columbus, 1960-61; landscape arch. various firms, Toledo, 1963, 65-67; pvt. practice Ann Arbor, Mich., 1963-65; ptnr. firms Toledo, 1967-78; pres. Harvey Jones and Assocs., Clearwater, Fla., 1979-81; owner Mortensen Assocs., Toledo and Falls Church, Va., 1979-85; prin. Mortensen, Lewis & Scully, Inc., Vienna, Va., 1985-93; owner Mortensen Assocs., McLean, Va., 1993—. Assoc. prof. U. Mich. Grad. Sch., 1973; vis. lectr. Ohio State U., 1965—, Bowling Green State U., Ohio, 1969—, U. Mich., 1971, Purdue U., 1971, Mich. State U., 1973—, U. Mass., 1986—, U. Cath., Cordoba, Argentina, 2007, U. Buenus Aires, 2007, Beijing Forestry U., 2008; archtl. environ. rev. com. Ohio Arts Coun., 1974-78; adj. prof. Dept. Landscape Architecture, U. Md., 1992-96; chmn. Merrifield Master Plan Task Force, 1998-2001. Editor: Handbook of Professional Practice, 1972, Marketing Landscape Architectural Services to the Federal Government, 1974. Mem. Ohio Bd. Unreclaimed Strip Mined Lands, 1973-76; mem. Lucas County facilities rev. com. Health Planning Assn. N.W. Ohio, 1972-76, chmn. maternal and child health subcom., 1972-74; bd. dirs. No. Va. Cmty. Appearance Alliance, 1988-, chair, 1991, pres., 1994. Recipient Disting. Svc. award Health Planning Assn. N.W. Ohio, 1973, Disting. Alumni award U. Mich. Sch. Natural Resources, 1985, Disting. Alumnus award Ohio State U. Coll. Engring., 1985. Fellow Am. Soc. Landscape Architects (trustee 1977-82, v.p. 1982-83, pres.-elect 1983-84, nat. pres. 1984-85, del. to Internat. Fedn. Landscape Architects 1987-92, del. Internat. Landscape Alliance 1994-2000); mem. Ohio Soc. Landscape Architects (pres. 1969-74), Landscape Inst. U.K. (hon. corr.), Toledo C. of C. (chmn. sts. and hwys. transit com. 1972-73), Greater Merrifield Bus. and Profl. Assn. (bd. dirs. 1993-2002, chmn. bd. dirs. 1998, pres. 1997), Nat. Bldg. Stone Inst. (mem. adv. bd.), Va. Cmty. Revitalization & Reinvestment Adv. Group (Fairfax county bd. mem. 2009-), Washington Golf and Country Club (officer, bd. dirs. 1999-2003, pres. 2002-03), Sigma Phi Epsilon. Home: 6843 Churchill Rd Mc Lean VA 22101-2822 Office: Mortensen Assocs 6843 Churchill Rd Mc Lean VA 22101 Home Phone: 703-827-0995; Office Phone: 703-917-1515. Personal E-mail: rhmort@aol.com. *One of the best continuing educational experiences for a practising professional is to teach students what you have learned. They respond in a critical and ever-so-fresh "so what" atmosphere, and demand more of you sometimes than you demand of yourself. Thus, there is learning on both sides of the lectern.*

MORTENSEN, VIGGO, actor, writer; b. NYC, Oct. 20, 1958; s. Viggo P. and Grace Mortensen; m. Christine Cervenka, July 8, 1987 (div. Mar. 13, 1998); 1 child, Henry. BA in Govt. and Spanish, St. Lawrence U., Canton, NY, 1980; ArtsD (hon.), St. Lawrence U., 2006. Owner Perceval Press, 2002—. Actor: (films) Witness, 1985, Salvation!, 1987, Fresh Horses, 1988, Prison, 1988, Leatherface: Texas Chainsaw Massacre III, 1990, Young Guns II, 1990, Reflecting Skin, The, 1990, Tripwire, 1990, The Indian Runner, 1991, Boiling Point, 1993, Ruby Cairo, 1993, Carlito's Way, 1993, The Young Americans, 1993, Ewangelia wedlug Harry'ego, 1993, Desert Lunch, 1994, Floundering, 1994, The Crew, 1994, American Yakuza, 1994, Crimson Tide, 1995, Black Velvet Pantsuit, 1995, The Prophecy, 1995, Gimlet, 1995, Albino Alligator, 1996, The Portrait of a Lady, 1996, Daylight, 1996, G.I. Jane, 1997, La Pistola de mi hermano, 1997, A Perfect Murder, 1998, Psycho, 1998, A Walk on the Moon, 1999, 28 Days, 2000, Lord of the Rings: The Fellowship of the Ring, 2001, Lord of the Rings: The Two Towers, 2002, Lord of the Rings: The Return of the King, 2003, Hidalgo, 2004, A History of Violence, 2005, Alatriste, 2006, Eastern Promises, 2007, Appaloosa, 2008; (TV films) Once In a Blue Moon, 1990; (TV miniseries) George Washington, 1984; author: (poetry) Ten Last Night, 1993, (essays) I Forget You Forever, 2006; musician: (albums) One Man's Meat, 1999, One Less Thing to Worry About, 1999, The Other Parade, 1999, 3 Fools 4 April, 2008, Time Waits for Everyone, 2008.

MORTENSON, GREG, not-for-profit fundraiser, writer; b. Minn., 1957; m. Tara Bishop; 2 children. Grad., U. South Dakota, 1983. Co-founder Ctrl. Asia Inst., Pennies For Peace. Co-author (with David Oliver Relin): Three Cups of Tea: One Man's Mission to Promote Peace...One School at a Time, 2007 (No. 1 NY Times bestseller, TIME mag. Asia Book of Yr., Publishers Weekly bestseller, Kiriyama Prize Nonfiction award, PNBA Nonfiction Book of Yr.). Served with US Army, 1977—79, Germany. Decorated Commendation medal US Army; recipient David Brower Conservation award, Am. Alpine Club, 1998, Peacemaker award, Mont. Cmty. Mediation Ctr., 2002, Golden Piton award for humanitarian effort, Climbing mag., 2003, Vincent Lombardi Champion award for humanitarian svc., 2003, Free Spirit award, Nat. Press Club DC, 2004, Jeanette Rankin Peace award, Inst. for Peace, 2004, Golden Fleur-de-lis award, Comune Firenze, Italy, 2006, Paul Harris award for promoting friendly relations among people, Rotary Internat., 2007, Award for Excellence in mountain cmty. svc., Mountain Inst., 2007, Dayton Lit. Peace Prize, 2007; named Humanitarian of Yr., Red Cross Mont., 2005. Achievements include climbing Pakistan's K2, the world's second highest mountain in the Karakoram range; establishment of over 61 schools in rural regions of Pakistan and Afghanistan which provide education to over 25,000 children. Mailing: Ctrl Asia Inst PO Box 7209 Bozeman MT 59771 Office Phone: 406-585-7841. Office Fax: 406-585-5302.

MORTIER, GERARD, opera company director; b. Ghent, Belgium, Nov. 25, 1943; D (hon.), U. Antwerp, Belgium. Adminstr. asst. Flanders Festival, 1968—72; artistic planner Duetsche Oper am Rhein, Düsseldorf, 1972—73; asst. adminstr. Oper der Stadt Frankfurt am Main, 1973—77; dir. artistic prodn. Hamburg Staatsoper, 1977—79; tech. program cons. Théâtre Nat. de 'Opéra de Paris, 1979—81; gen. dir. Théâtre Royal de la Monnaie, Brussels, 1981—91, Salzburger Festspiele, Austria, 1990—2001; founding dir. Ruhr Triennial Arts Festival, Germany, 2001—04; gen. dir. Opéra National de Paris, 2004—09; gen. dir. designate NYC Opera, 2007—08, Teatro Real, Madrid, 2008—. Decorated Comdr. des Arts et des Lettres, France; recipient Nat. Medal of Honor, Belgium, Germany. Mem.: Acad. Arts Berlin. Office: Teatro Real Plaza Isabel II 28013 Madrid Spain Office Phone: 33-1-40-01-1789.*

MORTIMER, PETER MICHAEL, lawyer; b. Detroit, May 20, 1943; s. Robert J. and Harriet C. (Evenson) M.; m. Sharon M. Olson, Aug. 20, 1966; children: Katherine, Trever, Peter. AB magna cum laude, Cornell U., 1965; JD cum laude, Harvard U., 1968. Bar: D.C. 1968, N.Y. 1970. Atty. Office Legal Adviser, U.S. Dept. State, Washington, 1968; assoc. Milbank, Tweed, Hadley & McCloy, NYC, 1969-76, ptnr., 1977—2001, resident ptnr. Hong Kong, 1977-79, London, 1983-88, mem. compensation com. NYC, 1992—96, co-practice group leader banking & instnl. investment group and global corporate fin. group, 1995—2001, ret. ptnr., 2002—. Fellow Frick Collection, NYC, 1981-91, Pierpont Morgan Libr., NYC, 1980-91, mem. coun., 1981-83. Decorated Order of Francisco de Miranda 1st class (Venezuela). Mem. D.C. Bar, Assn. of Bar of City of NY, John's Island Club, Redstick Golf Club, Grolier Club, Short Hills Club (bd. govs. 1994-2000), Baltusrol Golf Club (bd. govs. 1998-2004), Phi Beta Kappa. Office: Milbank Tweed Hadley & McCloy 1 Chase Manhattan Plz Fl 47 New York NY 10005-1413 Home: 590 Indian Harbor Rd Vero Beach FL 32963

MORTIMER, RICHARD WALTER, mechanical engineer, educator; b. Phila., Dec. 7, 1936; s. Horace and Almira Duffield (Matthews) M.; m. Doris Claire Ridler, June 29, 1957; children: Patrick Lee, David Walter, James Matthew, Daniel Scott. BSME, Drexel U., 1962, MSME, 1964, PhD, 1967. Prof. Drexel U., Phila., 1967—2002, assoc. dean grad. sch., 1974-76, head dept. mech. engring., 1976-85, assoc. v.p. acad. affairs, 1985-89. Mem. exec. com. Engring. Accreditation Com., N.Y.C., 1986-91. Contbr. over 40 articles to profl. jours. Pres. Haverford (Pa.) Twp. Sch. Dist., 1980-83. With US Army, 1958—60. Recipient Achievement award Am. Soc. Nondestructive Testing, 1973, Best Tech. Paper award, 1973; fellow NASA, 1967, 68; grantee numerous orgns. including NASA, USAF, NSF, 1967-87; Fellow Members awd., Am. Soc. for Engineering Education, 1992. Fellow Am. Soc. Engring. Educators; mem. ASME (mem. numerous coms., bds. and chairs 1976-92). Republican. Episcopalian. Achievements include research in fields of structural dynamics and composite materials. Personal E-mail: tokeym@verizon.net.

MORTIMER, TINSLEY RANDOLPH, apparel designer; b. Richmond, Va., 1976; d. George R. and Dale Tatum Mercer; m. Robert Livingston Mortimer, May 4, 2002. BA in Art Hist., Columbia U., 1998. Asst. to Amy Astley Vogue Mag., NYC; account exec. Harrison & Shriftman; handbag designer Samantha Thavasa by Tinsley Mortimer, 2006; designer clothing line Riccimie by Tinsley Mortimer, 2007. Beauty amb. Christian Dior, 2007—. Named one of The Most Powerful Women in NYC, NY Post, 2008. Home: 66 E 79th New York NY 10021 Home Phone: 212-327-4841.

MORTIMER, WENDELL REED, JR., retired judge; b. Alhambra, Calif., Apr. 7, 1937; s. Wendell Reed and Blanche (Wilson) M.; m. Cecilia Vick, Aug. 11, 1962; children: Michelle Dawn, Kimberly Grace. AB, Occidental Coll., 1958; JD, U. So. Calif., LA, 1965. Bar: Calif. 1966. Trial atty. Legal div. State of Calif., LA, 1965-73; assoc. Thelen, Marrin, Johnson & Bridges, LA, 1973-76, ptnr., 1976-93; pvt. practice San Marino, Calif., 1994-95; judge L.A. Superior Ct., 1995—2008, mem. complex litigation panel, 2000—08; arbitrator & mediator ADR Svcs. Inc., 2008. With U.S. Army, 1960-62. Mem. ABA, Internat. Acad. Trial Judges, Los Angeles County Bar Assn., Calif. Judges Assn., Am. Judicature Soc., Am. Judges Assn., Legion Lex., Irish-Am. Bar Assn., Am. Bd. Trial Advocacy (nat. bd. dirs., exec. com. L.A. chpt.), San Marino City Club (past pres.), Pasadena Bar Assn., Balboa Yacht Club, San Gabriel Country Club Home: 1420 San Marino Ave San Marino CA 91108-2042

MORTIZ, JACQUES, obstetrician, gynecologist, educator; BS, U. Miami, 1981; MS in Biology, Barry U., 1983; MD, U. Miami Sch. Medicine, 1988. Cert. obstetrics & gynecology. Resident Columbia-Presbyterian Med. Ctr., 1988—92; asst. clinical prof. obstetrics & gynecology Columbia U. Coll. Physicians & Surgeons; dir. endoscopy section & divsn. gynecology St. Luke's-Roosevelt Hosp. Office: 315 W 57th St Ste 204 New York NY 10019 Office Phone: 212-603-4160.*

MORTON, ANDREW J., diversified financial services company executive; B.Math, Waterloo U.; PhD in Applied Probability, Cornell U. Rsch. prof. fin. math. U. Ill., Chgo., 1989—92; vis. rsch. prof. U. Mich., 1992—93; head fixed income derivatives rsch. Lehman Brothers Holdings, Inc., NYC, 1993—97, head US Dollar derivative trading, 1997—99, head European interest rate bus. London, 1999—2004, co-head European fixed income div., 2004—07, head European fixed income divsn., 2007, co-COO global fixed income divsn. NYC, 2007—08, head global fixed income divsn., 2008; mng. dir., head G-10 rates, risk treasury & fixed income fin. Citigroup Inc., 2008—. Office: Citigroup Inc 399 Park Ave New York NY 10043*

MORTON, D. HOLMES, physician; m. Caroline Smith; children: Mary Caperton, Sarah McRae, Paul Holmes. Grad., Trinity Coll., 1979; MD, Harvard Med. Sch., 1983. Resident Children's Hosp. Boston; conducted biochemical genetics rsch. John Hopkins U., Children's Hosp. Phila.; country doctor, rsch. physician, clinic dir., co-founder Clinic for Spl. Children, Strasburg, Pa., 1989—. Contbr. articles to Nature Genetics, American Journal of Medical Genetics, Pediatrics and others. Recipient Albert Schweitzer prize for humanitarianism, 1993; MacArthur fellow, John D. and Catherine T. MacArthur Found., 2006. being co-founder with wife of a non-profit medical and diagnostic service for children with inherited metabolic disorders in Lancaster County, Pennsylvania. The clinic was established to provide comprehensive medical care for children with chronic, complex medical problems due to inherited disorders. Office: Clinic for Special Children 535 Bunker Hill Rd Strasburg PA 17579

MORTON, DONALD CHARLES, astronomer; b. Kapuskasing, Ont., Can., June 12, 1933; s. Charles Orr and Irene Mary (Wightman) M.; m. Winifred May Austin, Dec. 12, 1970; children: Keith James, Christine Elizabeth. BA, U. Toronto, 1956; PhD, Princeton U., 1959. Astronomer U.S. Naval Rsch. Lab., Washington, 1959-61; from rsch. assoc. to sr. rsch. astronomer with rank of prof. Princeton (N.J.) U., 1961-76; dir. Anglo-Australian Obs., Epping and Coonabarabran, Australia, 1976-86; dir. gen. Herzberg Inst. Astrophysics, NRC of Can., Ottawa and Victoria, 1986—2000; rschr. emeritus NRC of Can., 2001—. Contbr. numerous articles to profl. jours. Fellow Australian Acad. Sci.; mem. Internat. Astron. Union, Royal Astron. Soc. (assoc. 1980), Astron. Soc. Australia (pres. 1981-83, hon. mem. 1986), Royal Astron. Soc. Can., Am. Astron. Soc. (councilor 1970-73), Can. Astron. Soc., Can. Assn. Physicists, U.K. Alpine Club, Am. Alpine Club, Alpine Club Can. Avocations: mountain climbing, rock climbing, ice climbing, marathon running. Office: Herzberg Inst Astrophysics NRC Can 5071 W Saanich Rd Victoria BC Canada V9E 2E7 Home Phone: 250-721-4942; Office Phone: 250-363-8313.

MORTON, DONALD JOHN, librarian; b. Bklyn., Jan. 11, 1931; s. Ellwood Stokes and Gladys (Hassler) M.; m. Ann Mayo Tilden, Aug. 16, 1958; children— Saundra Kay, Donald John, Mary Ann. BS, U. Del., 1952; MS, La. State U., 1954; PhD, U. Calif., Berkeley, 1958; MS in Libr. Sci., Simmons Coll., 1969, Dr. in Libr. Sci., 1976. Asst. prof. botany N.M. State U., Las Cruces, 1957-58; asst. prof. plant pathology N.D. State U., Fargo, 1959-61; plant pathologist Agr. Dept., Tifton, Ga., 1961-65; asso. prof. plant pathology U. Del., Newark, 1965-68; librarian Northeastern U., Boston, 1968-70; head librarian, asst. prof. history of medicine U. Mass. Med. Sch., Worcester, 1970—94, dir. libr., assoc. prof. libr. sci., 1974-94, libr. cons., 1994—; tchr. med. librarianship Worcester State Coll., 1974-94; libr. cons., 1994—; computer cons. Hampton Hist. Soc., 1995—2006; libr. advisor Exeter Hosp., NH, 1996—2006; libr. vol. Maine Med. Ctr., 2006—; libr. Oceanview Libr., Falmouth, Maine, 2007—; libr. vol. Mercy Hosp., Portland, Maine, 2008—. Cons. in field; mem. adv. com. med. librarianship Simmons Coll., 1972-94; mem. task force com. New Eng. Regional Libr. Svc., 1971-94; mem. cooperating staff Worcester Found. Exptl. Biology, 1972-94; chmn. Coun. Developing Med. Librs., 1974; pres. North Atlantic Health Scis. Librs., 1974-75, Worcester Area Coop. Librs., 1974-75. Contbr. articles to profl. jours. Mem. Oliver Wendell Holmes endowment com. Boston Med. Libr., 1973-74, U. Mass. Bicentennial Com., 1973-75. Mem. Am. Assn. Univ. Adminstrs., Simmons Coll. Libr. Sch. Alumni Assn. (pres. 1975-76), Worcester Art Mus., Worcester Hist. Soc., Northboro Hist. Soc., Hampton Hist. Soc., N.H. Hist. Soc., Am. Soc. Info. Sci., ALA, Mass. Libr. Assn., Med. Libr. Assn. (chmn. New Eng. group 1974-75), Mycol. Soc. Am., Spl. Librs. Assn., New Eng. Coll. Librarians, Piscatagua Pioneers Hereditary Soc., Sigma Xi, Phi Kappa Phi, Phi Sigma, Delta Tau Delta, Alpha Zeta. Personal E-mail: atmdjm@maine.rr.com.

MORTON, EDWARD JAMES, insurance company executive; b. Ft. Wayne, Ind., Nov. 8, 1926; s. Clifford Leroy and Clara Marie (Merklein) M.; m. Jean Ann McClernon, Apr. 30, 1949; children: Marcia Lynn, Anne; m. Matthild Schneider, Sept. 19, 1986; 1 child, Katherine. BA, Yale U., 1949. With John Hancock Mut. Life Ins. Co., Boston, 1949—, v.p., then sr. v.p., 1967-74, exec. v.p., 1974-82, pres., chief operating officer, 1982-86, chmn., chief exec. officer, 1987-92, also bd. dirs. Trustee Gettysburg Coll. 1990-2002, trustee emeritus, 2002—; hon. life overseer Children's Hosp. Fellow Soc. Actuaries; mem. Actuaries Club Boston, Comml. Club Boston, Phi Beta Kappa. Office: John Hancock Life Ins Co PO Box 111 C-01-03 Boston MA 02117-0111 Personal E-mail: ejmorton@potomacnet.com.

MORTON, FREDERIC, author; b. Vienna, Oct. 5, 1924; s. Frank and Rose (Ungvary) M.; m. Marcia Colman, Mar. 28, 1957; 1 dau., Rebecca. BS, Coll. City N.Y., 1947; MA, New Sch. Social Research, 1949. Author: The Hound, 1947, The Darkness Below, 1949, Asphalt and Desire, 1952, The Witching Ship, 1960, The Schatten Affair, 1965, Snow Gods, 1969, An Unknown Woman, 1976, The Forever Street, 1984, Crosstown Sabbath, 1987, (biography) The Rothschilds, 1962, A Nervous Splendor-Vienna 1888-89, 1979, Budapest 2007, Tokyo 2008, Thunder at Twilight-Vienna 1913/14, 1989, Runaway Waltz--A Memoir From Vienna To New York, 2005; books translated into 14 langs.; actor (documentary) Crosstown Sabbath, 1995; contbg. editor: Vanity Fair; contbr. to publs. including Best Am. Short Stories, 1965, Best Am. Essays of 2003, and other anthologies, N.Y. Times, Harper's mag., Atlantic mag., Nation, Playboy, Esquire, N.Y. Mag., Hudson Rev., Wall Street Jour., Vanity Fair, L.A. Times, others; columnist Village Voice, Conde-Nast Traveler, Wall Street Jour.3.2 Recipient Author of Year award Nat. Anti-Defamation League, B'nai B'rith; Hon. Professorship award Republic of Austria, 1980, Tom Osborne Disting. lectureship U. Nebr., 1989; Dodd, Mead Intercollegiate Lit. fellow, 1947; Yaddo residence fellow, 1948, 50; Breadloaf Writers' Conf. fellow, 1947; Columbia U. fellow, 1953; recipient Golden Merit award City of Vienna, 1986, City of Vienna medal of honor in gold, 2001, Cross of Honor for Achievements in Arts, Republic of Austria, 2003. Mem. Author's Guild (exec. coun.), P.E.N. Home: 110 Riverside Dr New York NY 10024-3715 Office: Sandra Diskstra Agy PMB 515 1155 Camino Del Mar Del Mar CA 92014 Office Phone: 212-721-6938. *As a writer I'm trying to tell the truth interestingly.*

MORTON, JAMES CARNES, JR., retired automotive executive; b. Duncan, Okla., May 8, 1945; s. James Carnes and Syble Lyda (Looney) Morton; m. Susan Phillips, May 25, 1968; children: James III, Terrissa Anne, Scott Thomas. BA, Westminster Coll., 1967; JD, U. Mo., 1972. Bar: Mo. 1972. Tax acct. Arthur Andersen Co., St. Louis, 1972—74; tax atty. Gen. Dynamics Corp., St. Louis, 1974—76; asst. gen. counsel Michelin Tire Corp., Greenville, SC, 1976—86; gen. counsel Michelin Tire Corp. and Michelin Tires (Can.) Ltd., Greenville, 1990—92; dir. pub. rels. and govt. affairs Michelin Tire Corp., Greenville, 1986—92; exec. dir. external rels. Michelin N.Am., Inc., Greenville, 1992—96, v.p. pub. rels. and govt. rels., 1996—2000; sr. v.p. fin. and adminstrn., bd. dirs., mem. mgmt. com. Nissan N.Am., Inc., LA, 2000—06, vice chmn. Nashville, 2006—07, asst. to CEO, sr. advisor govt. affairs, 2007—08; pres. Morton Consulting Inc., 2007—. Adv. bd. Trent Lott Leadership Inst., U. Miss., 2006—08, Hollings Cancer Ctr. Med. U. SC, 2005—, vice chmn., 2008—. Bd. dirs. Greenville Symphony Orch., 1986—89, United Way Greenville, 1987—88, Greenville YMCA, 1988—89, Greenville Tech Found., 2007—, vice chmn.; mem. S.C. Reorganization Commn., 1985—98; trustee S.C. Gov.'s Sch. Sci. and Math., 1996—99; mem. sch. bd. Christ Ch. Episcopal Sch., Greenville, 1997—2000; vice chmn. S.C. Ports Authority, 1999—2000; pres. Nissan Found., 2003—07; bd. trustees Greenville Hosp. Sys., 2008—. Lt. US Army, 1967—70, capt. Mo. Army N.G., 1970—72. Recipient Alumni Achievement award, Westminster Coll., 2003. Mem.: ABA, Mo. Bar Assn. (non-resident), Alliance Automobile Mfrs. (bd. dirs. 2000—03), Rubber Mfrs. Assn. (bd. dirs. 1995—2000, govt. affairs com., tire mgmt. com.), Assn. Internat. Automobile Mfrs. (exec. com. 2000—07, chmn. bd. dirs. 2005—07), Nat. Urban League (trustee 2004—07), S.C. C. of C. (exec. com. 1981—84, 1986—95, pres. 1993—94, chmn. 1994—95, bd. dirs.), Greater Greenville C. of C. (bd. dirs. 1990—93, chmn. legis. affairs com. 1996—98), L.A. Urban League (bd. dirs. 2001—05), Calif. C. of C. (bd. dirs. 2001—04), Kiawah Island Club, Greenville Country Club (bd. govs. 2008—, v.p. 2009). Presbyterian. Avocation: golf. Home Phone: 864-232-5841; Office Phone: 864-239-0616. Personal E-mail: jmorton5841@charter.net.

MORTON, JOHN M., surgeon, consultant; b. Montgomery, Ala. BS in Biology & English, Tulane U., 1988, MPH, MD, Tulane U., 1993; MHA, U. Wash., Seattle, 1997. Cert. Am. Bd. Surgery, 2002, lic. Calif. Resident Tulane Sch. Medicine, 1993—95, 1997—99, Swedish Med. Ctr., 1999—2001; fellow U. NC, 2001—03; asst. prof. dept. surgery Stanford U. Sch. Medicine, 2003—, dir. bariatric surgery, 2003—, med. dir. surgical sub-specialties clinic, 2005—, dir. minimally invasive surgery fellowship, 2005—, dir. Surgery Ctr. for Outcomes Rsch. & Evaluation, 2006—, dir. quality, surgery & surgical subspecialties, 2007—. Assoc. editor SOARD Jour. of Am. Soc. for Bariatric Surgery, 2004—; reviewer for various industry jours. Recipient Outstanding Resident award, Soc. Laparoscopic Surgeons, 2001, Excellence in Teaching award, Stanford Sch. Medicine, 2005. Fellow: Am. Coll. Surgeons; mem.: SAGES, AMA, Western Surgical Assn., Pacific Coast Surgical Assn., Assn. for Surgical Edn., Assn. for Acad. Surgery, Am. Soc. Bariatric Surgeons. Office: Stanford University School of Medicine 300 Pasteur Dr Rm H 3680 Stanford CA 94305-5655 Home: 735 Valparaiso Ave Menlo Park CA 94025-4244 Office Phone: 650-725-5247. Office Fax: 650-725-0791. E-mail: morton@stanford.edu.*

MORTON, JOHN TEMPLETON, federal agency administrator; b. 1966; m. Laura Morton; children: Olivia, Lucie. Trial atty. US Dept. Justice, 1994, spl. asst. to gen. counsel, Immigration & Naturalization Svc. (INS), then counsel to dep. atty. gen., 1996—99, asst. US atty. (ea. dist.) Va. major crimes & terrorism unit, 1999—2006, acting chief domestic security sect., sr. counsel to asst. atty. gen. criminal divsn., 2007—09, acting dep. asst. atty. gen. criminal divsn., 2009; asst. sec. for immigration & customs enforcement (ICE) US Dept. Homeland Security, 2009—. Office: US Dept Homeland Security 425 Eye St NW Rm 7100 Washington DC 20528*

MORTON, JOSEPH, state official, school system administrator; BS, Auburn U.; MS, U. Ala., PhD in Ednl. Adminstrn. Supt. of edn. Sumter County Schs., Ala., Sylacauga City Schs., Ala.; dep. state supt. edn. Ala. Dept. Edn., 1996—2004, interim state supt. edn., 2004, state supt. edn., 2004—. Founder Sylacauga City Schools Found. Founder Sylacauga City Schs. Found. Named one of Top 100 Sch. Executives in N.Am., Exec. Educator Mag. Office: Ala Dept Edn 50 N Ripley St PO Box 302101 Montgomery AL 36104 Office Phone: 334-242-9700. E-mail: jmorton@alsde.edu.*

MORTON, LINDA JUNE, academic administrator; b. Nashville, Jan. 21, 1943; d. William Taylor Morton and Ruby Grayson (Maiden name-Page) Morton. BA, George Peabody Coll., 1964, MS, 1976; PhD, Vanderbilt U., 1981. Cert. ednl. adminstr. Tenn., 1981, tchr. English 7-12 Tenn., 1964, tchr. music K-12 Tenn., 1964, career ladder III tchr. Tenn., 1985. Tchr. high sch. English, music Metro Nashville Pub. Schs., 1964—67, tchr. mid. sch. tchr. music, 1967—89, asst. prin., 1989—2000. Chair, McGavock cluster prins. Metro Nashville Pub. Schools, 1990—91, spl. edn. prins. adv. com. mem., 1992—94; chair curriculum com. 10 yr. sacs evaluation McGavock H.S., 1992—92. Wrote and compiled (7th grade music curriculum outline) 7th Grade Music Curriculum Outline. Dir. Jr. Dept. Woman's Club Nashville, 1972—74; vice-moderator, bd. trustees Memphis Theol. Sem., 1998—2003; mem., former trustee, elder, deacon, pianist, choir dir. West Nashville Cumberland Presbyn. Ch., established William Taylor Morton Endowment, 1998; established Ruby Page Morton endowment Memphis Theol. Seminary, 2001; mem. bd. dirs. Kidney Found. Mid. Tenn., 1981—83. Mem.: People-to-People, Fla. Oceanographic Soc., Aerospace Edn., Internat. Soc. Music Edn., U. Club Nashville, Woman's Club Nashville (life), Phi Delta Kappa, Alpha Delta Kappa. Presbyterian. Avocations: photography, swimming, travel, music, scuba diving. Home: 6740 Currywood Dr Nashville TN 37205 Personal E-mail: laquarius@aol.com.

MORTON, LOUIS GEORGE, retired social sciences educator; b. St. Louis, May 21, 1928; s. Louis George and Helen (Kesl) Morton; children: Robert, David, James. BS in Edn., Mo. U., 1953; MA, Western State Coll., Gunnison, Colo., 1966, cert. in edn. specialist, 1971. Tchr. history Ctrl. HS, Grand Junction, Colo., 1961—66; prof. polit. sci. Mesa State Coll., Grand Junction, 1966—95, prof. emeritus, 1995—, pres. faculty senate, 1988—90, dept. chmn. social scis., 1991—92. Pres. Ctrl. CEA, Grand Junction, 1965—66. Author: A Student's Guide to the U.S. Constitution, 1987, A Wandering Jew in Brazil, 1992, reprinted, 2006, A Citizen's Guide to the U.S. Constitution, 1993, The First 75 Years History Mesa State College, 2003, E Mail Humor, 2005, E Mail Humor Revisited, 2006, Faerie Queen, 2007, Tidbits, 2007. 1st lt. USAF, 1946—53. NSF grantee, U. Mo., 1966, U. Tex., 1975. Mem.: Nat. Ret. Tchrs. Assn. (nat. guidance com.), Mesa State Coll. Emeriti Assn. (pres. 1997—98), Colo. Ret. Sch. Employees Assn. (pres. 2004—06), Mesa County Ret. Sch. Employees Assn. (pres. 2000—01), Am. Legion. Democrat. Methodist. Avocations: coin collecting/numismatics, stamp collecting/philately, writing. Home: 1753 Ridge Dr Grand Junction CO 81506-4079 Personal E-mail: mtlou3@aol.com.

MORTON, NEWTON ENNIS, human geneticist; b. Camden, NJ, Dec. 21, 1929; arrived in U.K., 1988; s. Newton and Laura Rebecca (Jones) M.; m. Nancy Okazaki, Feb. 11, 1949 (div. Jan. 1972); children: Teru, Peter, Amy, John, Robert; m. Patricia Ann Jacobs, May 15, 1972. BA, U. Hawaii, 1951, MA, 1952; PhD, U. Wis., 1955; MD, Umea U., Sweden, 1976. Geneticist Atomic Bomb Casulty Commn., Japan, 1952-53; postdoctoral fellow U. Wis., 1955-56, asst. to assoc. prof., 1956-62; prof. U. Hawaii, 1962-85; dept. head Sloan Kettering Cancer Ctr., 1985-87; prof. U. Southampton, U.K., 1988—. Pres. 9th Internat. Congress Human Genetics, 1997. Mem. adv. bd. Jour. of Human Genetics, 1997—; author: Genetics of Interracial Crosses in Hawaii, 1967, Genetic Structure of Populations, 1973, Outline of Genetic Epidemiology, 1982; editor: Genetic Epidemiology, 1978; mem. editl. bd. Proc. NAS. Recipient Lederle Med. Faculty award, 1951, Allan award Am. Soc. of Human Genetics, 1963. Fellow: Royal Coll. of Physicians; mem.: Brazilian Acad. of Scis., Nat. Acad. of Sci. Avocations: tennis, walking, gardening, entomology. Office: Human Genetics U Southamptn Duthie Bldg Southampton SO16 6YD England Home Phone: 44-1722-710393; Office Phone: 44-23-8079-6536. Business E-Mail: nem@soton.ac.uk.

MORTON, PERRY WILLIAMS, investment banker; b. Lincoln, Oct. 17, 1939; s. Perry William and Faye Evelyn (Williams) M.; m. Virginia Louise Dow, July 16, 1966; children: Carolyn Faye, Christine Dow. BA, U. Mich., 1961; LLB, Harvard U., 1964. Bar: N.Y. 1965, Mass. 1974; cert. gen. securities prin. Fin. Industry Regulatory Authority. Atty. Debevoise & Plimpton, NYC, 1967-73; sr. v.p. Bay Fin. Corp., Boston, 1973-80; pres. The Morton Co., Marblehead, Mass., 1980—; mng. dir. Ulin, Morton, Bradley & Welling, Boston, 1984-92, Advest, Inc., Boston, 1990-92, Baldwin & Clarke Corp. Fin., Inc., Boston, 1993—. Bd. dirs. Citizens Scholarship Found., Financial Exec. Internat., Boston, Marblehead Cliffs Assn., NorthShore Alliance Econ. Devel.; Treas.'s Club, Boston, Marblehead Little Theatre, North Shore Tech. Coun., North Shore Alliance Econ. Devel. Capt. US Army, 1965-67. Mem. Tedesco County Club. Home: 17 Indianhead Cir Marblehead MA 01945-1218 Office: PO Box 285 Marblehead MA 01945 Office Phone: 617-697-7640. Business E-Mail: pwm@bcfinance.com.

MORTON, R. STEVEN, lawyer; b. Atlanta, Dec. 3, 1958; BS in Environ. Studies, Allegheny Coll., 1980; grad. studies in Hydrogeology, U. Tex.; JD, Vanderbilt U., 1984. Bar: Tenn. 1985, Tex. 1986. Ptnr. Brown McCarroll & Oaks Hartline, Austin, Tex.; shareholder Jenkens & Gilchrist, P.C., Austin, 1995—2007; ptnr. Moltz Morton O'Toole LLC, Austin, 2007—. Office: Moltz Morton OToole The Littlefield Bldg 106 E 6th St Ste 700 Austin TX 78701 Office Phone: 512-499-3856. Office Fax: 512-499-3810. Business E-Mail: smorton@jenkens.com.

MORTON, SAMANTHA, actress; b. Nottingham, Eng., May 13, 1977; d. Peter and Pamela Morton; children: Esme, Edie. Actor: (TV miniseries) Band of Gold, 1995, The History of Tom Jones, a Foundling, 1997; (TV series) Soldier Soldier, 1991, Max and Ruby, 2002; (TV films) The Token King, 1993, Emma, 1996, Jane Eyre, 1997, Longford, 2007 (Best Performance by an Actress in a Supporting Role in a Series, Mini-Series or Motion Picture Made for TV, Golden Globe award, 2008); (films) The Future Lasts a Long Time, 1996, Under the Skin, 1997, This is the Sea, 1998, Sweet and Lowdown, 1999 (Acad. award nomination for best supporting actress, 2000), Jesus' Son, 1999, The Last Yellow, 1999, Eden, 2001, Morvern Callar, 2002, Minority Report, 2002, In America, 2002 (Acad. award nomination for best actress, 2004), Code 46, 2003, The Libertine, 2004, River Queen, 2005, Lassie, 2005, Elizabeth: The Golden Age, 2007, Expired, 2007, Control, 2007, Mister Lonely, 2007. Mailing: c/o Creative Artists Agy 9830 Wilshire Blvd Beverly Hills CA 90212

MORTON, SOPHIE, literature and language professor; b. France; married. MA in French, UNT; U. Francois Rabelais. Lectr., coord. 1st & 2nd yr. French program UNT, Denton, Tex., 2006—. Office: Univ of North Tex Po Box 311127 Denton TX 76203-1127 Business E-Mail: smorton@unt.edu.

MORTON, STEPHEN DANA, chemist, consultant; b. Madison, Wis., Sept. 7, 1932; s. Walter Albert and Rosalie (Amlie) M. BS, U. Wis., 1954, PhD, 1962. Asst. prof. chemistry Otterbein Coll., Westerville, Ohio, 1962-66; postdoctoral fellow water chemistry, pollution control U. Wis., Madison, 1966-67; water pollution rsch. chemist WARF Inst., Madison, 1967-73, head environ. quality dept., 1973-76; mgr. quality assurance Raltech Sci. Svcs., 1977-82; pres. SDM Cons., 1982—. Author: Water Pollution-Causes and Cures, 1976. 1st lt. Chem. Corps, AUS, 1954-56. Mem. AAAS, Am. Chem. Soc. Home and Office: 1126 Sherman Ave Madison WI 53703-1620

MORTON, YU TONG, electrical engineer, educator; b. Wuhan, Hubei Province, China, Aug. 1, 1963; m. John Phillip Morton, June 19, 1988; children: James Tong, Rachael Jean. BS, Nanjing U., China, 1983; MSEE, Case Western Res. U., Cleve. Ohio, 1987; PhD, Pa. State U., State Coll., 1991. Asst. prof. Miami U., Oxford, Ohio, 2000—06, assoc. prof., 2006—09, prof., 2009. Office: Miami Univ Elec & Computer Engring Dept Oxford OH 45056 Office Phone: 513-529-0749. Business E-Mail: mortonyt@muohio.edu.

MORTON-YOUNG, TOMMIE, psychology professor, writer; b. Nashville; BA cum laude, Tenn. State U., Nashville, 1951; MA, Peabody Vanderbilt U., 1955; PhD, Duke U., Durham, NC, 1977; postgrad., U. Okla., Norman, 1967, U. Nebr., 1968. Coord. Young Adult Program Lucy Thurman br. YWCA, 1951-52; instr. edn. Tenn. State U., Nashville, 1956-59; instr. coord. media program Prairie View Coll., Tex., 1959-61; asst. prof. edn., assoc. prof. English, dir. IMC Ctr. U. Ark., Pine Bluff, 1965-69; asst. prof. English and edn., dir. learning lab NC Ctrl. U., Durham, 1969-74; prof., dir./chairperson libr. /dir. Afro-Am. Family Project, prof. philosophy sociol. found. NC Agrl. and Tech. State U., Greensboro, 1975—92; adj. prof. langs., lit. and philosophy, dir. schs. history project Tenn. State U., Nashville, 1994—. Dir. workshops, grants; pres., dir. Ednl. Cons. Svcs.; owner Historic Black Nashville Tours; with Tenn. Judicial Coun., 2008-. Author: Afro-Am. Genealogy Sourcebook, 1987, Oral Histories of Former All-Black Public Schs., 1991, After School Program for At-Risk Youth and Their Families, 1997, Sable Scenes, 1996, Genealogist's Guide to Discovering Your African Ancestors, 1997, A Sister Speaks, 1998, Nashville, Tennessee, 2000, Fabulous You: Women Celebrating the Fabulous Self, 2005, Ride a Dark Horse, 2007; contbr. poem to Poetry: American Heritage; contbr. rsch. papers, articles to profl. jours., pub. ten books. Nat. chmn. Com. to Re-Elect the Pres.; past sec. Fedn. Colored Women's Clubs; bd. dirs. Southwestern div. ARC, Nashville area, 1994-, dir. Volun-Teens; chairperson schs. div. Durham County Unit Am. Cancer Soc.; past adv. bd., bd. dirs. YMCA, Atlanta; chair Guilford County Commn. on Needs of Children; bd. advisors NIH, NC Coun. of the Arts; mem. Guilford County Involvement Coun.; chmn. NC adv. com. US Civil Rights Com.; exec. planning com. Greensboro; hon. staff 54th Legis. Dist., Nashville, 1996; pres. Davidson County Dem. Women, 2003-04; rep. dist. I exec. com. Davidson County Dem. Party; chair resolutions com. Nat. Fedn. Dem. Women. Recipient awards ARC, 1968, 73, NAACP, 1973, HEW, 1978, US Commn. on Civil Rights, 1982, cert. of Accomplishement Contributing to Youth Devel. Bus. and Profl. Women, 2000, Extraordinary Cmty. Svc. award Tenn. Coun. Women, 2005, Civic and Bus. Leaders Enterprising award, 2006, Civil Rights Leadership award Tenn. Dem. Party, 2006, Athena award Athena Powerlink, Nashville, 2006, others; named Disting. Alumni Tenn. State U., 1994, Peabody Colls. Gift to the World. Mem. AAUW (honor award 1983, pres. Greensboro br., chairperson internat. rels. com.), ALA (divsn. coll. and rsch. librs., past chair), NAACP (life, 1st v.p. Durham br., exec. bd. Greensboro br. dir. parent edn./child advocacy program, chair exec. com. Nashville, Woman of Yr. 1992, Dedicated Svc. to Civil Rights, 2005, President's award Nashville br. 2006), NEA, LWV (bd. dirs. Nashville), Assn. Childhood Ednl. Internat., Comperative and Internat. Edn. Assn., Archives Assoc., Internat. Platform Assn., Nat. Hist. Soc., Greenboro Jr. League (community adv. bd. 1991—), African Am. Gen. Soc. Tenn. (founder 1994), Zeta Phi Beta (chairperson polit. action com. eastern region, nat. grammateus, Polit. and Civic Svc. award 1974, Outstanding Social-Polit. Svc. award 1982, Woman of Yr. 1977), Comm. on Status of Women (Woman of Achievement 1991), Phi Kappa Phi (Disting. Alumni award Tenn. State U. 1994, Disting. Alumni NAFEO award, 1995, Carl Rowan-Oprah Winfrey lectr. Tenn. State U., 1995, Excellence in Journlism award SPJ, 1995, Tenn. Outstanding Achievement award, 1997), 100 Black Women, Steering Com., Tenn. Trust for Historic Preservation, 1999 (named Woman of Distinction Top Ladies, 2001, named Peabody/Vanderbilt Jnin Great, 2005, nominee Athena award 2005). Achievements include being the first African American to graduate from Peabody College (Vanderbilt University) 2006; having a community Service award named in her honor by Vanderbilt University, 2006. Home: PO Box 281613 Nashville TN 37228-8506

MORTVEDT, JOHN JACOB, soil scientist, researcher; b. Dell Rapids, SD, Jan. 25, 1932; s. Ernest R. and Clara M.; m. Marlene L. Fodness, Jan. 23, 1955; children: Sheryl Mortvedt Jarratt, Lori Mortvedt Klopf, Julie Mortvedt Stride. BS, SD State U., 1953, MS, 1959; PhD, U. Wis., 1962. Soil chemist TVA, Muscle Shoals, Ala., 1962-87, sr. scientist, 1987-92, regional mgr. field programs dept., 1992-93; ext. soils specialist Colo. State U., Ft. Collins, 1994-95, ext. environ. and pesticide edn. specialist, 1996. Agr. cons. U.S. Borax, 1997-2007. Co-author: Fertilizer Technology and Application, 1999; editor: Micronutrients in Agriculture, 1972, 2d edit., 1991; contbr. articles to profl. jours. 1st lt. U.S. Army, 1953-57. Fellow AAAS, Soil Sci. Soc. Am. (pres. 1988-89, editor-in-chief 1982-87, Profl. Svc. award 1991, Disting. Svc. award 1996), Am. Soc. Agronomy (exec. com. 1987-90, Agronomic Svc. award 2003); mem. Internat. Union Soil Sci., Colombian Soil Sci. Soc. (hon.), Exch. Club (pres. Florence, Ala. chpt. 1987-88), Toastmasters (pres. Florence chpt. 1964-65), Phi Kappa Phi. Avocations: photography, golf. Office: Colo State U Dept Soil And Crop Scis Fort Collins CO 80523-1170

MORVILLO, ROBERT GUY, lawyer; b. NYC, Jan. 22, 1938; s. M. Victor and Marie (Santeramo) M.; m. Catherine A. Shields, Apr. 20, 1963; children: Christopher, Gregory, Edward, Robert. AB, Colgate U., 1960; JD, Columbia U., 1963. Bar: N.Y. 1964, U.S. Dist. Ct. (so. dist.) 1966, U.S. Ct. Appeals (2nd cir.) 1964, U.S. Ct. Appeals (3rd cir.) 1979, U.S. Ct. Appeals (10th cir.) 1983, U.S. Supreme Ct. 1982. Law clk. to Hon. William B. Herlands U.S. Dist. Ct. (so. dist.), NYC, 1963-64, asst. U.S. atty., 1964-68, chief trial counsel fraud unit, 1970-71, chief criminal div., 1971-73; assoc. Reavis & McGrath, NYC, 1968-70; prin. Morvillo, Abramowitz & Grand, P.C. and predecessors, NYC, 1973—. Lectr. Columbia Law Sch., N.Y.C., 1973-85. Columnist, N.Y. Law Jour., N.Y.C., 1982—; editor, White Collar Crime: Business and Regulatory Offenses, 1990. Bd. dirs. South Nassau Cmty. Hosp., 2005—. Fellow Am. Coll. Trial Lawyers; mem. ABA, Assn. of Bar of City of N.Y., N.Y. State Bar Assn., N.Y. Coun. of Def. Lawyers (bd. dirs. 1987—91). Office: Morvillo Abramowitz Grand Iason Anello & Bohrer PC 565 Fifth Ave New York NY 10017 Home Phone: 516-766-3728; Office Phone: 212-880-9400. E-mail: rmorvillo@magislaw.com.

MORWAY, DAVID S., professional sports team executive; b. Bklyn., Nov. 9, 1959; s. Richard S. and Carol Morway; m. Karen E. Chellis, Oct. 10, 1996; children: Robbie, Michael. BS in Bus., U. Ariz., 1982; JD, U. San Diego, 1985. Bar: Calif. 1987. Asst. to pres. San Diego Padres, 1985—88; pres. Profl. Excellence in Sports, Inc., San Diego, 1989—95, DSM Inc., Salt Lake City, 1996—98; sr. v.p. basketball ops. Ind. Pacers, Indpls., 1999—2008, gen. mgr., 2008—. Mem.: Calif. Bar Assn. Avocations: tennis, golf. Office: Ind Pacers 125 S Pennsylvania St Indianapolis IN 46204-3610*

MORWITZ, VICKI GAIL, finance educator; d. Bernard William and Ruth Morwitz; m. Eric Andrew Greenleaf; children: Anna Sophie Greenleaf, Leo David Greenleaf. BS, Rutgers U., Cook Coll., New Brunswick, NJ, 1983; MS, Poly. U., Bklyn., 1996; PhD, U. Pa., Phila., 1991. Rsch. prof. Stern Sch. NYU, NYC, 1991—. Office: Stern Sch Bus NYU 40 W 4th St Ste 807 New York NY 10012

MOSAVIAN, PARISA, dentist; m. André Azarnifar. Grad., Karolinska Inst., Stockholm; DDS, Royal Caroline Medico-Sugico Univ., 1998. Private practice dentist Embarcadero Dental, San Francisco. Mem.: San Francisco Dental Soc., Calif. Dental Assn., Am. Dental Assn. Office: Embarcadero Dental 129 Sacramento St San Francisco CA 94111 Office Phone: 415-362-1850. Office Fax: 415-362-5912.*

MOSBACHER, ROBERT ADAM, SR., oil and gas industry executive, political organization executive, former United States Secretary of Commerce; b. Mt. Vernon, NY, Mar. 11, 1927; s. Emil and Gertrude (Schwartz) M.; children: Diane, Robert Jr., Kathryn, Lisa Mosbacher Mears. BS, Washington and Lee U., 1947, LLD (hon.), 1984. Independent oil and gas producer, 1948—; sec. US Dept. Commerce, Washington, 1989-92; gen. chmn. Pres. Bush's re-election campaign, 1992; gen. chmn. fin. Rep. Nat. Com., Washington, 1992; chmn. Mosbacher Energy Co., Houston, Mosbacher Power Group, Houston, 1995—. Former bd. dirs. Choate Sch., Wallingford, Conn.; dir. emeritus Aspen Inst., Ctr. for Strategic and Internat. Studies; chmn. bd. visitors M.D. Anderson Hosp.; nat. fin. chmn. George Bush for Pres.; chmn. Pres. Ford Fin. Com.; co-chmn. Republican Nat. Fin. Com.; dir. Tex. Heart Inst.; pres. Odyssey Acad., Galveston, 1998—. Mem. Am. Petroleum Inst. (dir., exec. com.), Nat. Petroleum Coun. (past chmn.), All Am. Wildcatters Assn. (past chmn.), Am. Assn. Petroleum Landmen (past pres.). Republican. Presbyterian. Address: Mosbacher Energy Corp 712 Main St Ste 2200 Houston TX 77002-3206

MOSBACHER, ROBERT ADAM, JR., former investment company executive; b. Houston, May 29, 1951; s. Robert Adam and Jane (Pennbacker) Mosbacher; m. Catherine Lyn Clark, 1980; children: Peter Clark, Jane Marion, Meredith Bess. Student, U. Tex., 1969—71; BA, Georgetown U., 1973; JD, So. Methodist U., 1977. Legis. asst. to Senator Howard H. Baker US Senate, 1971—74, adminstrv. asst., 1977—80; fin. chmn. Tex. State Rep. Com., 1984—87; chmn. bd. Tex. Dept. Human Svcs., 1989—91; pres., CEO Mosbacher Energy Co., Houston, 1986—2005; vice chmn. Mosbacher Power Group, 1995—2003; pres., CEO Overseas Pvt. Investment Corp. (OPIC), 2005—09. Chmn. Tex. Welfare Reform Task Force, 1988. Author: Deep in the Heart: A Remedy for an Ailing Texas, 1993. Immediate past-chmn. Greater Houston Partnership, chmn. health care advisory com., mem. edn. and workforce advisory com.; founder, co-chmn. Rebuidling Together Houston; bd. dirs. South Tex. Coll. Law, Soc. Performing Arts. Recipient Pres. Volunteer Action award, 1988; named a Rising Star of Tex., Tex. Bus. mag., 1982. Republican. Episcopal.*

MOSBY, NORA JANE, music educator; b. El Paso, Tex., June 9, 1970; d. Knox Wesley and Bettie Mae Mosby. BS, U. Tex., Tyler, 1995, MA, 1997; MEd, No. Ariz. U., Flagstaff, 2005. Chair dept. fine arts Higley HS, Gilbert, Ariz., 2000—05; band dir. Florence Unified Sch. Dist., Ariz., 2005—07, Manor Intermediate Sch. Dist., 2007—. Recipient Reacher of Month, Higley Unified Sch. Dist., 2005. Mem.: Ariz. Music Educator's Assn., Soc. for Ethnomusicology, Internat. Clarinet Assn., Ariz. Band and Orch. Dirs. Assn., Phi Kappa Phi. Office: Florence Unified Sch Dist 250 S Main St Florence AZ 85232 Personal E-mail: muzik77@cox.net.

MOSCA-FOCHT, MARLENE, biology professor; d. John and Mary Ann Mosca; married, June 25, 1983. BS, Western Ct. State Coll., Danbury, 1968; MA, U. Conn., Storrs, 1971; EdD, Columbia U., NYC, 1978. Prin. Upper Dublin HS, Fort Washington, Pa., 1980—97; adj. prof. dept. biology Manate CC, Bradenton, Fla., 1997—. Co prodr. Sarasota Opera, Fla., 1997—. Fellowship, Franklin Marshall Coll., 1996. Avocations: sailing, reading, exercise. Office: Manatee CC 57th Bradenton FL 34210 Personal E-mail: marlefocht@aol.com.

MOSELEY, ANN, retired literature and language professor; b. Sulphur Springs, Tex., 1947; d. Paul Franklin Kernes and Ester Lue Kernes Vititow; m. Fred Moseley, 1969; children: Christie Moseley Welch, Davy. BA, East Tex. State U., Commerce, 1968, MA, 1969; PhD, U. Okla., Norman, 1974. Cert. tchr. Tex. State, 1968. Prof., lit., langs. Tex. A&M U., Commerce, 1982—2008, emeritus prof., 2009—. Plenary spkr. Eleventh Internat. Willa Cather Seminar, Paris, 2007, Avignon, France, 07; spkr. Willa Cather Spring Conf., Red Cloud, Nebr., 2009. Author: Willa Cather Newsletter & Review; co-author: (textbook) Interactions: A Thematic Reader, Strategies for College Writing, Contexts: Writing and Reading; contbr. articles to numerous profl. essays. Recipient William L. Mayo award, Tex. A&M U., 2000, H. M. Lafferty award, 2000; named Tchr. of Yr. award, 1992. Mem.: Am. Studies Assn. Tex., South Ctrl. MLA, South Ctrl. MLA (chair, devel. reading & writing programs 1983—90, chair, children's lit. sect. 1988), Western Lit. Assn., Willa Cather Pioneer Meml. Found. Presbyn. Office: Tex A&M Univ Hall Langs Commerce TX 75429 Business E-Mail: ann_moseley@tamu-commerce.edu.

MOSELEY, APRIL LOWE, artist; d. Irvin Thomas and Joyce Lowe; m. Spencer Moseley, Dec. 17, 1994. BBA in Fin., U. Ga., Athens, 1991. Painting, Snow Leopard, Elephant Family at Sunset on the African Savannah, Tiger, Lion, Licking His Paw, Koala, Stalking Tiger, Giant Panda, Southern Bobcat, California Cougar, Portrait of a Lion, Giant Panda #2, Eastern Gray Squirrel. Mem.: Juried Online Arts Festival, Nat. Oil & Acrylic Painter's Soc. Conservative. Baptist. Avocations: gourmet cooking, travel, photography, hiking. Personal E-mail: moseleysa@hotmail.com.

MOSELEY, JAMES FRANCIS, lawyer; b. Charleston, SC, Dec. 6, 1936; s. John Olin and Kathryn (Moran) M.; m. Anne McGehee, June 10, 1961; children: James Francis Jr., John McGehee. AB, The Citadel, 1958; JD, U. Fla., 1961. Bar: Fla. 1961, U.S. Supreme Ct. 1970. Pres. Moseley, Prichard, Parrish, Knight & Jones, Jacksonville, Fla., 1963—. Chmn. jud. nominating com. 4th Jud. Cir., 1978-80 Editor: American Maritime Cases; contbr. articles on admiralty, transp. and ins. law to legal jours. Pres. Jacksonville United Way, 1979; chmn. bd. dirs. United Way Fla., 1992-93, S.E. regional coun. United Way, 1992-96; trustee Jacksonville Cmty. Found.; chmn. bd. trustees Jacksonville Pub. Libr.; trustee Libr. Found., sec., 1987-91; trustee CMI Am. Found.; chmn. Jacksonville Human Svcs. Coun., 1989-91; chmn. bd. trustees United Way N.E. Fla., 1995-97; bd. govs. United Way Am., 1996-2002. Recipient Meritorious Pub. Svc. award/medal U.S. Dept. Transp./USCG, 1998. Fellow Am. Coll. Trial Lawyers, Am. Bar Found.; mem. ABA (house of del. 2002-08), Jacksonville Bar Assn. (pres. 1975), Fla. Coun. Bar Pres. (chmn. 1979), Maritime Law Assn. U.S. (exec. com. 1978-81, chmn. navigation com. 1981-88, v.p. 1992-96, pres. 1996-98), Comm. Maritime Internat. (titulary), Com. on Collision (Lisbon Rules), Fed. Ins. Corp. Counsel (chmn. maritime law sect.), Internat. Assn. Def. Counsel (chmn. maritime com. 1989-91), Am. Inns of Ct. (master of bench), Assn. of Citadel Men (bd. dir. 1989-93, exec. com. 1994, Man of Yr. award 1992, S.C. Palmetto medal and award 2001, Citadel Inn of Ct. sr. bencher), Deerwood Club, River Club, India House (NYC), Army Navy Club (Washington), St. John's Dinner Club (pres. 1988). Office: Moseley Prichard Parrish Knight & Jones 501 West Bay Bldg 1887 Jacksonville FL 32202 Office Phone: 904-356-1306. Office Fax: 904-354-0194.

MOSELEY, JOHN TRAVIS, academic administrator, physicist, researcher; b. New Orleans, Feb. 26, 1942; s. Fred Baker and Lily Gay (Lord) M.; m. Belva McCall Hudson, Aug. 11 1964 (div. June 1979); m. Susan Diane Callow, Aug. 6, 1979; children: Melanie Lord, John Mark, Stephanie Marie, Shannon Eleanor. BS in Physics, Ga. Inst. Tech., 1964, MS in Physics, 1966, PhD in Physics, 1969. Asst. prof. physics U. West Fla., Pensacola, 1968-69; sr. physicist SRI Internat., Menlo Park, Calif., 1969-75, program mgr., 1976-79; vis. prof. U. Paris, 1975-76; assoc. prof. U. Oreg., Eugene, 1979-81, dir. chem. physics inst., 1980-84, prof. physics, 1984—, head physics dept., 1984-85, v.p. rsch., 1985-94, v.p. acad. affairs, provost, 1994-2001, sr. v.p., provost, 2001—06, spl. asst. to pres. and provost, 2006—. Mem. exec. com., coun. on acad. affairs NASULGC, 1994-2000, chair, 1996-97; bd. dirs. Oreg. Resource and Tech., Portland; mem. com. on Atomic and Molecular Sci., 1983-85. Contbr. numerous articles to profl. jours. Mem. So. Willamette Rsch. Corridor, Eugene, 1985-00, Lane Econ. Devel. Com., Eugene, 1988-94; bd. dirs. Eugene/Springfield Metro Partnership, 1985-01, Oreg. Bach Festival, Eugene, 1987-94, Eugene Arts Found., 1995-97. Recipient Doctoral Thesis award Sigma Xi, 1969; Fulbright fellow, 1975; numerous rsch. grants, 1969—. Fellow AAAS, Am. Physical Soc.; mem. AAUP, Am. Chem. Soc. Avocations: skiing, backpacking. Home: 2140 Essex Ln Eugene OR 97403-1851 Office: U Oreg Office of Sr VP and Provost Eugene OR 97403-1258 Business E-Mail: jtm@uoregon.edu.

MOSELEY, JULIA W., music educator, preservationist; b. Tampa, Fla., Mar. 21, 1919; d. Hallock Preston and Ruby Winifred Moseley. BA, Agnes Scott Coll., Decatur, Ga., 1940. Nat. cert. music tchr. Asst. food and fashion editor Atlanta Constn., 1940-41; credit report typist, publicist, fund raiser Mchts. Assn. Tampa, 1942-43; teletype operator, writer/editor, commodities marketer USDA, Atlanta, 1943-47; self-employed music tchr. Atlanta, 1945-47; hist. rschr. New Orleans, 1947—48; self-employed music tchr. Fla., 1948—; also cattle raiser, citrus grower; preservationist Moseley Homestead, Brandon, Fla., 1948—. Author, editor: Come to My Sunland, 1997; co-author: Internet Lake Atlas, 1999, Recipes and Remembrances, 1999-2004; composer song Brandon, Brandon. Mem. Brandon Citizens Adv. Com.; established Timberly Trust, Inc., 1994; worked with Historic Tampa/Hillsborough Cunty Preservation Bd., 1983-92; spokesperson to Hillsborough County Bd. Commrs. on land use and preservation, 1966-99; mem. Brandon Task Force involved with county devel. issues; mem. hist. com. Brandon Centennial Celebration, 1990. Elizabeth Ordaway Dunn Found. grantee, 1998. Mem.: Fla. State Music Tchrs. Assn. (past officer), Limona Acad. Arts, Letters and Scis. (past officer and dir.), Art Publ. Soc. (Guild tchr.), Nat. Fedn. Music Clubs, Nat. Guild Piano Tchrs., Music Tchrs. Nat. Assn., Tampa Music Tchrs. Assn. (officer), Fla. Breeding Bird Atlas, Tampa Preservation, Inc., Nature Conservancy, Fla. Trust for Historic Preservation, Nat. Trust for Historic Preservation, Friday Morning Musicale Club. Avocations: bird watching, reading, walking, photography, star gazing. Personal E-mail: ttland@hotmail.com.

MOSELEY, LISA LENT, counseling administrator; b. Niskayuna, NY, Mar. 28, 1968; d. David and Marilyn Lent; m. Steve Moseley, Aug. 3, 1991; children: Samuel, Jacquelyn. BA, Stetson U., Deland, Fla., 1990; MA in Counseling, U. South Fla., Tampa, 1994. Cert. in counsleing State Fla., 1990. HS tchr. Santa Fe Cath. HS, Lakeland, Fla., 1992—96; dir. guidance All Saints' Acad., Winter Haven, 1996—2000; guidance counselor St. Paul Luth. Sch., Lakeland, 2004—. Sponser Kalideascope: Inclusive Playground, Lakeland, 2005—07. Christian Ch. Avocations: fishing, tennis. Home: 6408 Longwood Trace Ln N Lakeland FL 33811 Office: St Paul Lutheran Sch 4450 Harden Blvd Lakeland FL 33813 Personal E-mail: lisamoseley@tampabay.rr.com. Business E-Mail: lmoseley@stpaullakeland.org.

MOSELEY, PATRICIA ANN, lawyer; d. Percy and Virginia Elizabeth (Gregg) M.; m. Norman L. Williamson, Oct. 15, 1981; children: Norma Williamson Nash, W. Scott Williamson. BS in Secondary Edn., Tex. A&I, 1968; MA, U. Tex., 1972; JD, Tex. Tech U., 1978. Bar: Tex. 1978, U.S. Dist. Ct. (No. dist.) Tex. 1979, U.S. Ct. Appeals (5th cir.) 1981. Tchr. Galena Park Ind. Sch. Dist., Houston, 1968-70; teaching asst. journalism dept. U. Tex., Austin, 1970-71; tchr. Corsicana (Tex.) Ind. Sch. Dist., 1972-75; atty. West Tex. Legal Svcs., Lubbock, 1978-83; pvt. practice Lubbock, 1983-92. Apptd. IV-D Assoc. Judge 9th Region Tex., 1989. Mem. Tex. Bar Assn. (family law sect. 1989—), Lubbock County Bar Assn. (family law sect.), Lubbock Women Lawyers Assn., Lubbock LWV (bd. dirs. 1981-84, v.p. 1986-87, bd. 1988), WIN Club (Lubbock). Home: PO Box 466 Lubbock TX 79408-0466 Office: 904 Broadway Ste 421 Lubbock TX 79401-3421 Business E-Mail: pmoseley@co.lubbock.tx.us.

MOSELEY BRAUN, CAROL ELIZABETH, food products executive, former United States Senator from Illinois; b. Chgo., Aug. 16, 1947; d. Joseph J. and Edna A. (Davie) Moseley; m. Michael Braun, 1973 (div. 1986); 1 child, Matthew. BA, U. Ill., Chgo., 1969; JD, U. Chgo., 1972. Asst. US atty. (no. dist.) Ill. US Dept. Justice, 1973-77; mem. Ill. House of Reps. from Dist. 25, 1979-88, asst. majority leader; recorder of deeds Cook County, Ill., 1988-92; US Senator from Ill. Washington, 1993-99; US amb. to New Zealand and Samoa US Dept. State, 1999—2001; adj. prof., mgmt. DePaul U., 2002; founder, pres. Good Food Organics, Chgo., 2005—; founder Moseley Braun LLC; corp. bd. mem. MWH Engring., NC Mutual Life Ins. Co. Bd. dirs. Good Food Organics, 2005—, MWH, 2008—. Mem. advisory bd. Healthy Foods Campaign. Recipient Atty. General's Spl. Achievement award, US Dept. Justice, Woman of the Yr. award, 1992, Best Legislator award, Ind. Voters Ill., 1980, Outstanding Women Struggle award, Chgo. Alliance Against Racist & Polit. Oppression, 1981, Dist. Svc. award, Concerned Black Executives Social Svc. Org., 1983, Outstanding Legislator award, Ill. Pub. Action Coun., 1983, Leadership award, Assn. Human Svc. Providers, 1984, Legislative Leadership award, Chgo. Pub. Schools & Coalition to Save Our Schools, 1985, Beautiful People award, Urban League, 1985, Legislator of the Yr. award, Nurses Assn., 1986, Certificate of Appreciation, Chgo. Bar Assn., 1986, Svc. award, Ill. Pro Choice Alliance, 1986, Best Legislator award, Ind. Voters Ill. Ind. Precinct Org., 1986, Friends Edn. award, Ill. State Bd. Edn. award, 1988, "Day Breaker" award, Mayor Harold Washington, 1988, Martin Luther King Jr. Excellence award, Interdominational Ministerial Alliance Chgo., 1997; named Woman of the Yr., Minority Econ. Resources Corp., 1997. Mem.: Internat. Women's Assn., Chgo. Network, Delta Sigma Theta. Democrat. Episcopalian. Achievements include being the only African American woman to be elected to the United States Senate, 1992. Office: Good Food Organics 1634 E 53rd St 2nd Fl Chicago IL 60615 Office Phone: 773-288-3700. Office Fax: 773-288-3708. E-mail: cmbraun@pobox.com.

MOSEMANN, LLOYD KENNETH, II, retired research and development company executive; b. Lancaster, Pa., May 16, 1936; s. Lloyd Kreider and Beatrice Elizabeth (Frey) M.; m. Arlene K. White, Sept. 6, 1957; children— Gigi Renee Mosemann Falke, Lloyd Kenneth III, Douglas Lamar, Holly Joy AB in Social Sci., U. Chgo., 1957, AM in Internat. Rels., 1959. Gen. supply officer Navy Electronics Supply Office, Great Lakes, Ill., 1958-62; inventory mgmt. specialist Def. Electronics Supply Ctr., Dayton, Ohio, 1962-63; head integrated-retail supply and support br. Naval Supply Systems Command, Washington, 1963-69; dep. chief logistics support analysis office Def. Logistics Agy., Alexandria, Va., 1969-71; dep. for supply and maintenance Office Sec. of Air Force, Washington, 1971-74; dep. asst. sec. for logistics and communications Dept. Air Force, Washington, 1974-91, dep. asst. sec. for comm., computers and logistics, 1991-93, dep. asst. sec. for comm., computers and support systems, 1993-96; software and acquisition cons., 1996-97; sr. v.p. corp. devel. Sci. Applications Internat. Corp., McLean, Va., 1997—2007; ret., 2007. Mem. Air Force Exec. Resources Bd., 1981—95. Author: AntiChrist in the Midst, 2006. Decorated DSM; recipient Meritorious Svc. medal Sec. Air Force, 1977, Exceptional Civilian Svc. medal sec. Air Force, 1979, 81, 82, 87, 96, Meritorious Sr. Exec. award Pres. of US, 1982, 87, Def. Meritorious Civilian Svc. medal, 1985. Mem. Soc. Logistics Engrs. (bd. advisers 1983—90, Founders medal 1983, H. Mark Grove award for excellence in software mgmt. 1996, Govt. Computer News Hall of Fame 1996, Fed. Computer Week "100" award 1996), Am. Def. Preparedness Assn. (bd. dirs. 1974-83), Nat. Inst. for Urban Search and Rescue (exec. bd. dirs. 1990-2005).

MOSENA, DAVID R., museum administrator; BA in Bus. Adminstrn., U. Tenn., 1969, MA in City Planning, 1971. Dir. rsch. Am. Planning Assn., Chgo.; mem. staff City of Chgo., 1984-89, planning commr., 1989-91, chief of staff, 1991-92, aviation commr., 1991—96; pres. Chgo. Transit Authority, 1996—97; pres., CEO Mus. Sci. and Industry, Chgo., 1997—. Mem. vis. com., phys. scis. divsn. U. Chgo., 1998—. Chmn. bd. dirs. U. Chgo. Lab. Schs.; chmn. Commn. on Chicagoland Landmarks; bd. dirs. Exec. Coun. of Metropolis 2020, After Sch. Matters, Leadership Greater Chgo., South East Chgo. Commn. Mem.: Greater Chicagoland C. of C., Econ. Club Chgo., Comml. Club Chgo. Office: Mus Sci and Industry 5700 S Lake Shore Dr Chicago IL 60637 Office Phone: 773-684-1414.

MOSER, ANN BOODY, biochemist; b. Wakefield, Mass., Feb. 7, 1940; d. Philip Cutler and Esther (Hanson) Boody; m. Hugo Wolfgang Moser, Dec. 28, 1963; children: Karen Maria, Lauren Esther. BA, Radcliffe Coll., 1961. Rsch. technician McLean Hosp., Belmont, Mass., 1961-63, Mass. Gen. Hosp., Boston, 1963-68, Eunice Kennedy Shriver Ctr., Waltham, Mass., 1968-76; sr. technician Kennedy Inst., Balt., 1976—. Asst. in neurology Johns Hopkin's U./Kennedy Inst., Balt., 1982-91, rsch. assoc. neurology, 1991—. Author: (chpt.) The Metabolic Basis of Inherited Disease, Techniques in Diagnostic Human Biochemical Genetics, 1991; contbr. numerous articles to profl. jours. Mem. choir Univ. Bapt. Ch., Balt., 1984-90, music com., 1986-90. Mem. LWV, Am. Soc. Neurochemistry, Am. Soc. Human Genetics. Avocation: gardening. Home: 100 Beechdale Rd Baltimore MD 21210-2209 Office: Kennedy Krieger Inst 707 N Broadway Baltimore MD 21205-1888 Office Phone: 443-923-2761. Business E-Mail: mosera@kennedykrieger.org.

MOSER, BARRY, artist; b. Chattanooga, Oct. 15, 1940; Student, Auburn U., U. Tenn., Chattanooga; postgrad., U. Mass. Owner, pub. Pennyroyal Press, 1970—; faculty RI Sch. Design, 1991—98; prof. in residence, printer to the coll. Smith Coll., 2001—. Illustrator: The Divine Comedy, 1980, Alice in Wonderland, 1983 (Nat. Book award for Design and illustration), Scarlet Letter, 1984, A River Runs Through It, 1989, Appalachia, the Voices of Sleeping Birds, 1991 (Boston Globe-Horn Book award), And Still the Turtle Watched, 1991, Tales of Edgar Allan Poe, 1991, Ariadne, Awake!, 1994, Call of the Wild, 1994, Cloud Eyes, 1994, Farm Summer 1942, 1994, Pilgrim's Progress, 1994, What You Know First, 1995, When Birds Could Talk and Bats Could Sing, 1996, Pennyroyal-Caxton Bible, 1999, Earthquack!, 2002, Voices of Egypt, 2003; represented in permanent collections: Met. Mus., British Mus., Harvard U., Princeton U., Libr. of Congress, Victoria & Albert, Vatican Libr. Mem.: NAD (academician 1994—). Business E-Mail: cmoser@pennyroyal-caxton.com.

MOSER, ELEANOR T. PENDELL, federal administrative law judge; b. Great Bend, Kans., July 26, 1937; d. John J. and Ida Berniece (Littrell) Ashley; m. George M. Pendell Jr., June 25, 1960 (div. July 1977); children: George III, Wade A.; m. Cal K. Moser, Feb. 18, 1994. BA, U. Okla., 1960, MEd, 1965; JD, Oklahoma City Univ., 1967. Bar: Okla. 1967, U.S. Dist. Ct. (we. dist.) Okla. 1967, U.S. Dist. Ct. (no. dist.) Okla. 1972, U.S. Supreme Ct. 1980. Pvt. practice, Oklahoma City, 1966—67; ptnr. Pendell & Pendell Lawyers, Oklahoma City, 1967-73; assoc. Pritchett & Pendell, Oklahoma City, 1973-75; judge Oklahoma City Mcpl. Ct., Oklahoma City, 1975-90, Okla. Worker's Compensation Ct., State of Okla., Oklahoma City, 1990-96; ptnr. Pritchett, Snyder & Pendell, Oklahoma City, 1996—2001; law judge Office Hearings and Appeals, Oklahoma City, 2001—, chief admin. law judge, 2003—. Adj. law prof. Okla. City U., 1998; adminstrv. law judge, 2006—. Dir. Cmty. Coun. Ctrl. Okla., 1980-2002; chmn. to TB Task Force to the Homeless, Oklahoma City, 1997—. Recipient Spotlight award Okla. Bar Assn. Women in Law sect., 1999, Okla. Exec. Woman of the Yr. award High Noon, 2001. Mem.: Ruth Bader Ginsberg Inn of Ct. (officer 1995—), Nat. Assn. Women Judges (bd. dirs. 1982—84), Okla. City U. Law Alumni Assn. (bd. dirs. 1997—99, Outstanding Law Sch. Alumni award 1994), Gamma Phi Beta (Panhellenic Woman of the Yr. 2007), Zeta Phi Eta (nat. v.p., Outstanding Svc. award 1975—87), Iota Tau Tau (Supreme Dean). Office: Office Disability Adjudication and Review 301 N W 6th St Rm 300 Oklahoma City OK 73102 Office Phone: 866-201-8094 29755. Business E-Mail: eleanor.moser@ssa.gov.

MOSER, GLENDA FAYE, media specialist; b. Fairview, Okla., May 27, 1944; d. Leon Lyle Hunt and Faye Gladys Hunt (Gooch); m. James Calvin Moser; children: Bruce Wayne Brinson, Bret Orin Brinson, James Lee Huckaby, Darla Durree Brinson, Dianna Leigh Fisher. B in Edn., Brinson U., 1978; M in Libr. Edn. (hon.), SW Okla. State U., 1982. 3rd gr. tchr., libr. Verden (Okla.) Pub. Sch., 1990—91; humanities 8th gr. tchr., k-12 libr. media specialist Davenport (Okla.) Pub. Sch., 1992—98; libr. media specialist Tecumseh Humanities (Okla.) Mid. Sch., 1998—. Author (illustrator): (children's book) Mancestor (Writer's award at NWOSU, 1980). Writer marionette play Lincoln County Children's Mus., Chandler, Okla., 1994—2006. Recipient Overall Best Show for History Day, S.W. Okla. State U., 1982—84. Mem.: NEA, ALA (assoc. Pres. 1985). Independent. Achievements include research in teaching the 8 parts of speech for middle School, I called it NAPVAPIC' IT'S MAGIC!. Avocations: cake decorating, sewing, farm animals, reading, writing. Home: RR #1 Box 27 Sparks OK 74869 Office: Tecumseh Mid Sch 315 W Park St Tecumseh OK 74873 Office Fax: 405-598-1948. Personal E-mail: jgmosaic@yahoo.com. Business E-Mail: moserg@tecumseh.k12.ok.us.

MOSER, JAMES MICHAEL, medical educator; b. Cincinnati; s. James L. and Bettie Moser; m. Joanna M. Mack; 1 child. BS, U. Dayton, Ohio; MD, U. Ky., Lexington; MPH, U. NC, Chapel Hill. Diplomate in general preventive medicine and public health Am. Bd. Preventive Medicine, in internal medicine Am. Bd. Internal Medicine. Asst. prof. Ohio State U., Columbus, 1983—87; dir. epidemiology divsn. Ky. Dept. Health Svcs., Frankfort, 1987—89; epidemiologist NC HHS, Raleigh, 1995—97; assoc. prof. U. Kans., 1993—95; dir. health Kans. Dept. Health and Environment, Topeka, 1999—2003; dir. Akron Health Dist., 2003—; prof. Northeastern Ohio Univs. Coll. Medicine, Rootstown, 2003—. Adj. asst. prof. U. NC, 1981—83, adj. assoc. prof., 1995—99; res. dir. Ohio State U. Coll. Medicine, 1985—87; MPH dir. U. Kans., 1993—95; dir. Kans. Turning Point Project, 1999—2003, Office Pub. Health Practice, Northeastern Ohio Univs. Coll. Medicine, 2006—; asst. clin. prof. U. Ky., 1987—89; adj. prof. Consortium Eastern Ohio MPH Program, 2004—. Contbr. chapters to books, articles to profl. jours. Mem. Kans. Commn. Emergency Planning and Response, 1999—2003; chmn. Kans. Bioterrorism Coordinating Coun., 2002—03; bd. dirs. Planned Parenthood Summit, Portage, and Medina Counties, Akron, Ohio, 2003—07; bd. trustees Summit/Akron Solid Waste Mgmt. Authority, Ohio, 2003—; chmn. Emergency Med. Svcs. Bd., Akron, Ohio, 2003—; pres. Summit-Portage Area Health Edn. Ctr., Akron, Ohio, 2006—; vice chmn. Summit County Family and Children First Coun., 2007—08; co-chair Cmty. Health Adv. Com., Summa Health Sys., Akron, Ohio, 2007—; mem. Coun. Linkages Between Academia and Pub. Health Practice, 2003—04; co-chair, epidemiology core competencies panel Assn. Schs. Pub. Health, 2004—05, mem., applied epidemiology competencies task force, 2006—08. Fellow: Am. Coll. Preventive Medicine; mem.: APHA, Nat. Assn. City and County Health Officials, Assn. State and Territorial Health Officials (exec. com. 2001—03), Assn. Ohio Health Commrs. (bd. mem. 2006—). Office: Akron Health Dept 177 South Broadway Akron OH 44308

MOSER, JEFFERY RICHARD, not profit developer, director, grant writer; b. Miller, SD, Feb. 8, 1961; s. Richard and Ardessa Joan (Yost) M. Student, U. Minn., 1979—84, Duke U., 1995, Northwestern U., 1997, U. Denver, 2005—. BA in English, 2008, attending in Lit., 2008—. Cert. lay ministry; cert. in pub. policy and pub. fin.; cert. CPR, Am. Red Cross. Lab asst., intern U. Minn. Dept. Limnology, Mpls., 1980-81; exec. intern pub. affairs dept. Target Corp., Mpls., 1982, Nat. Farmers Union, Nat. Youth Adv. Coun., Denver, 1980-81; intern/asst. for legis. and policy Minn. Agri-Growth Coun., Bloomington, 1984-85; field office asst. US Congressman Thomas A. Daschle, Aberdeen, SD, 1986; pvt. cons. to non-profit orgns. Huron, SD, 1986—89; notary pub. State of SD, 1986-99; acting camp dir. SD Farmers Union Edn. Program, 1987-88; small bus. owner Wessington, SD, 1986—2002; exec. dir. SD Assn. Towns and Twps., 1990-95; dep. state treas. to treas. Richard D. Butler State of SD, Pierre, 1995-99; dir. econ. and coop. devel. Nat. Farmer's Union, Greenwood Village, Colo., 1999—2009, ind. contractor, 2009—. Participant 4-H/UN/USAID Presdl. young adult exch. program to Kenya and Botswana, Africa, summer 1985. Vol. U. Minn. Hosps., 1979-83, U. Minn. Dept. Minn. Unions, Mpls., 1983-84; gen. election poll watcher Hand County Rural precincts, 1988; past mem. Beadle County Dems., Hand County Dems., Brown County Dems., Hughes County Dems., v.p., 1997-98, Arapahoe County Dems., 1999—; del. State Dem. Conv., 1990, 92, 94; alt. del. Nat. Dem. Conv., Chgo., 1996, Clinton for Pres., 1992, Colo. State Dem. Conv., 2008, elect judge Apapa Co., 2008; nom. Dem. candidate State Auditor, 1994, US House, 1998; donor SD Dems., Dem. Nat. Com.; Dem. Nat. Senate Task Force; Dem. Congl. Campaign Com.; chair, del. Selection/Affirmative Action Com., 1996; Clinton-Gore, mem. State Adv. Com., 1996; at. del. Dem. Nat. Conv., 1996; mem. Hughes County Steering Com. to Re-Elect Senator Tom Daschle, 1997-98; dem. candidate SD at-large dist. US Ho. of Rep., 1998; vol. leader, advisor, and state fair judge SD 4-H Program, 1981-94; bd. dirs. SD Rural Devel. Coun., 1993-95, SD State Adv. Com. for Green Thumb, Inc., 1993-95; mem. task force Nat. Urban Comparative Risk Environ., 1994, Common Cause SD, 1991-94; dist. edn. dir. SD Farmers Union, 1988-93; dir. Minn. Union Coordinating Bd., U. Minn., 1982-84; bd. dirs. Golden Razor Hair Salon, Inc., Mpls., 1983-84, bd. dirs. Internat. Study & Travel Assn., Mpls., 1982-83; mem. Rose Hill Presbyn. Ch.-in Active, Clan Campbell Soc. (N.Am.), E. River Sierra Club, Rocky Mountains/Hi Plains Group Sierra Club, SD AG Heritage Mus., SD Com. for World Food Day, SD Bread for the World, Dakota Rural Action, SD Project Prosperity Coalition, SD Farmers Union, SD Horticulture Soc., Dakota Rural Action, South Dakotans For the Arts, Wilson Ctr., Am. Mus. Nat. Hist., Smithsonian Assocs., Lib. Congress, Oscar Howe Art Ctr., Siouxland chpt. Alzheimer's Assn., SD Health Care Reform Coalition, S.D. Artists Network, SD Hist. Soc., Colo. Pub. Radio/TV (donor), Comereta Singers of Montery, Nat. Farmers Union Found. (donor), Cmty. Shares of Colo. (donor), 9th Jud. Circuit Ct. Soc., Nat. Resource Defense Coun., Nat. Audubon Soc., Internat. 4-H Programs; host family Botswana Agr. Exch. Program, 1992; Presbytery of S.D., sec. Congl. Devel. Ministry, 1988-91, Advocacy Devel. Ministry unit, 1992-93, ch. camp dean, moderator Soc. Witness and Action Com., 1995-99, mem. com. representation, 1995-99, mem. com. Self-Devel. People, 1995-99; exec. Presbytery Search com., 1995-96; donar Presbyn. Peace Found., 2007-; active Am. Heart Assn. Pierre Area Heart Walk, 1995, 97; vol. coord. Bread for the World Hunger Awareness event, Huron, 1993; mem. planning com. 1993 Regional 4-H Leaders Forum, Sioux Falls; past del. rep. SD Nat. 4-H Congress, 1981; past del. rep. Nat. Farmers Union Nat. conf., Presbyn. Ch. USA Gen. Assembly, 1990, Presbyn. Ch. USA Consultation on Sustainable Devel., 1995, Nat. 4-H Coun. Master Communicators Conf., Albuquerque, Presbyn. Ch. USA Synod Lakes and Prairies Workshop on Representation and Nominations, Rochester, Minn., 1997, Common Cause Nat. Leadership conf., Washington, 1993, Sharing Global Harvests Nat. Tng., Nat. Assn. Towns and Twps. Am.'s Town Meeting, Washington, 1992, strategic leadership for state execs. course Duke U., 1995, Inst. Pub. Fin. Northwestern U., 1997; bd. co-chair Huron Postal Customer Adv. Bd., 1993-95; bd. dirs. SD Peace and Justice Ctr., sec.-treas., 1994, v.p., 1995, dir. 1994-97; copywriter Minn. Ag. Manual, 1985; with Farmers Union Fed. Credit Union, bd. dirs, 2007-09; vol.

comty. data reporter US Census Bur., 2000-2002; participant Future Coop Leaders program N.C.B.A., Washington, 2002; mem. Nat. Grants Rev. panel USDA, CSREES, 2001-03, 05; vol. Population, Employment and Labor Survey Reporting, US Census Bur., 2001-02; mem. Nat. Trust for Hist. Preservation; sec. Mich. Farmers Union Found., 1999—2009; mem. Colo. Criminal Justice Reform Coalition, Bread for the World, Cmty. Alliance with Family Farmers 2003-05. Mem. Nat. Audubon Soc., Nat. Co-op. Bus. Assn., Nat. Farmers Union, Phi Beta Kappa, Sigma Tau Delta, Omicron Delta Kappa, Mortar Bd., Golden Key, Modern Lang. Assn. Democrat. Avocations: piano, painting, poetry, writing, genealogy. Personal E-mail: jeff.moser@msn.com.

MOSER, JOHN EVAN, history professor; b. Pitts., Dec. 29, 1966; s. Frank H. and Judith L. Moser; m. Monica Lynn Henry, Aug. 13, 1994. AB in History, Ohio U., Athens, 1989; MA in History, U. Ill., Urbana, 1991, PhD in History, 1995. Program officer Inst. Humane Studies, Fairfax, Va., 1996—99; franklin tchg. fellow U. Ga., Athens, 1999—2001; asst. prof. history Ashland U., Ashland, 2001—05, assoc. prof. history, 2005—. Author: (book) Right Turn: John T. Flynn and the Transformation of American Liberalism, Presidents from Hoover through Truman, 1929-1953, Twisting the Lion's Tail: American Anglophobia between the World Wars. 2nd v.p. Mansfield Playhouse, Ohio, 2007—. Fellowship, Earhart Found., 2002. Roman Catholic. Avocation: theater. Home: 1003 Jackson Dr Ashland OH 44805 Office: Ashland Univ 401 College Ave Ashland OH 44805

MOSER, KENNETH ALLEN, lawyer; b. Rowan County, NC, Sept. 8, 1942; BA, Wake Forest U., 1965, JD cum laude, 1968. Bar: NC 1968. Former mng. mem. Winston-Salem office Womble Carlyle Sandridge & Rice PLLC. Former mem. faculty Grad. Sch. Banking of South, Baton Rouge, La., 1987-89; pres. Wake Forest Law Rev., 1967-68. Named one of The Best Lawyers in Am., in Banking Law and Real Estate Law, Chambers USA, Am.'s Bus. Lawyers. Mem.: ABA (chair loan practices and lender liability com. 1988—93, mem. books and media com. 1995—99, real estate, probate and trust law sect.), Wake Forest U. Sch. Law (Bd. Visitors 2008—), Wake Forest U. Law Alumni Coun. (pres. 1998), Am. Counsel Assn., Forsyth County Bar Assn., NC Bar Assn., Am. Coll. Mortgage Attorneys, Am. Coll. Real Estate Lawyers. Office: Womble Carlyle Sandridge & Rice PLLC One West Fourth St Winston Salem NC 27101 Home Phone: 336-761-0127; Office Phone: 336-721-3504. Business E-Mail: kmoser@wcsr.com.

MOSER, LARRY EDWARD, marketing professional; b. Chgo., Ill., Oct. 29, 1952; s. Paul Edward and Catherine Molly (Sittner) M.; children: Jennifer, Jacqueline; m. Ruth Ellen Hyland, July 6, 2003. BS in Mktg., No. Ill. U., 1974, MBA, 1976. CLU, CPCU. Statis. analyst Addressograph-Multigraph, Mt. Prospect, Ill., 1974-75; grad. asst., mktg. instr. No. Ill. U., DeKalb, 1975-76, 77; mktg. asst. Allstate Ins. Co., Northbrook, Ill., 1977-78, project coord., 1978-80, ins. agt. West Dundee, Ill., 1980, mktg. project mgr. to sales mgr. Northbrook, 1981—, prin. coord. Allstate WYO flood ins. program, 1994—2003, mem. nat. flood ins. program mktg. com., 1995—2003. V.p. Flood Ins. Svc. Cos. Am., 1997-2003; chmn. Allstate Share (United Way) Campaign, Northbrook, 1982-83, Allstate Helping Hands Com., Northbrook, 1985-86, Allstate Family Day Sports, Northbrook, 1991-94; mem. flood com. Inst. for Bus. and Home Safety, 1999-2003, vice chmn. flood com., 2002-03; dir. Chgo. Northwest Suburban CPCU Chpt., 2004-06, sec., 2006-07, v.p., 2007-08, pres., 2009-. Active Twinbrook YMCA parent/child prog., Schaumburg, Ill., 1983-90; commr. Schaumburg Athletic Assn. Girls Softball, 1990-92; pres. Allstate Men's Softball League, 1984—. Recipient Am. Mktg. Assn. Scholastic Achievement award No. Ill. Univ., DeKalb, 1974, James E. Bell Superior Promise & Scholarship in Mktg. Mgmt. No. Ill. Univ. Dept. Mktg., DeKalb, 1976, William J. Hendrickson award for Outstanding Contbn. From An Alumni, DeKalb, 1988., All-State Chmn. award, 2006 Mem. Am. Soc. CLU, CPCU Soc. (chpt. bd. dirs.), Pi Sigma Epsilon (pres. 1975-76), Phi Kappa Sigma, Beta Gamma Sigma, Omicron Delta Kappa. Roman Catholic. Avocations: travel, golf, tennis, skiing, snorkeling. Home: 611 W Burning Tree Ln Arlington Heights IL 60004-2034 Office: 2775 Sanders Rd Ste B2 Northbrook IL 60062-6110 Office Phone: 847-402-9773. Business E-Mail: larrymoser@comcast.net, lmaster@akstate.com.

MOSER, MARVIN, physician, educator, author; b. Newark, Jan. 24, 1924; s. Sol and Sophia (Markowitz) M.; m. Joy Diane Lipez, July 1, 1954; children: Jill, Stephen, John. AB, Cornell U., 1943; MD, Suny Downstate Coll. Medicine, NYC, 1947. Diplomate in internal medicine and cardiovasc. disease Am. Bd. Internal Medicine; cert. specialist in hypertension Am. Soc. Hypertension. Intern univ. div. Kings County Hosp., NYC, 1947-48, resident in medicine, 1948-49, Montefiore Hosp., NYC, 1949-50; Nat. Heart Assn. fellow Mt. Sinai Hosp., NYC, 1950-51; charge vascular service Walter Reed Army Hosp. Med. Centre, Washington, 1951-53; practice medicine specializing in cardiology White Plains, NY, 1953-95; assoc. physician cardiology Montefiore Hosp., 1953-75, in charge hypertension sect., 1960—74. Attending physician cardiology White Plains Hosp., 1968-95, chief cardiology, 1969-78; adj. physician in cardiology Grasslands Hosp., Valhalla, NY, 1953-60; attending physician in medicine in charge Hypertension Clinic, Westchester County Med. Center, Valhalla, 1974-84; asst. clin. prof. medicine Albert Einstein Coll. Medicine, 1965-75; clin. prof. medicine NY Med. Coll., 1974-84, Yale U. Sch. Medicine, 1984—; sr. med. cons. nat. high blood pressure program NIH, 1975-2002, mem. nat. high blood pressure coordinating com., 1976-2005; chmn. Joint Nat. Com. Hypertension, 1977, vice-chmn., 1979, mem., 1984-88, 92, 96, 2003; exec. com. Nat. Citizens for Treatment High Blood Pressure, 1976-78, vice-chmn., 1978-88; mem. NY State Adv. Com. on Hypertension, 1977-84; chmn. Nat. Conf. on High Blood Pressure Control, 1979; mem. select panel on hypertension in Am. Congl. Subcom. on Aging, 1978-79; cons. cardiology NY State Dept. Health, Gen. Hosp., Saranac Lake, NY, 1980-90; med. dir. Westchester County Hypertension Program, NY, 1979-88, editor-chief The Med. Roundtable, 2009- Author: (with A.M. Master, M. Moser. H. Jaffee) Cardiac Emergencies and Heart Failure, 2d edit., 1955; (with A. Goldman) Hypertensive Vascular Disease, 1967, Hypertension, A Practical Approach, 1975, Lower Your Blood Pressure and Live Longer, 1988; co-editor, contbr. Yale University School of Medicine Heart Book, 1992, Week by Week to a Strong Heart, 1992, Heart Healthy Cooking for all Seasons, 1996, Clinical Management of Hypertension, 1996, 7th edit., 2004, 8th edit., 2008, Myths, Misconceptions and Heroics, the Story of the Treatment of Hypertension, 1997, 2002, (with J. Sowers) Management of Cardiovascular Risk Factors in Diabetes, 2001, 2d edit., 2005, 3rd edit., 2007; mem. editl. bd. Preventive Cardiology, 1998—, Jour. Medicine and Sports, 1999-2004; assoc. editor Angiology, 1976-85; bd. editors Primary Cardiology, 1975-78, assoc. editor-in-chief, 1978-96; editor-in-chief Jour. Clin. Hypertension, 1999—2009, emeritus, 2009-; sr. editor Jour. of Cardio Metabolic Syndrome, 2006—; contbr. 500 scientific papers. Chmn. Narcotics Guidance Coun., Scarsdale, 1968-72; trustee Scarsdale Bd. Edn., 1970-73, Trudeau Inst., 1990-2004, Nat. Hypertension Found., 1992-2001, Nutrition 21, 1997-2001, Comprehensive Neuroscience; bd. dirs. Third Ave. Value and Small Cap Funds, 1994—; pres. Hypertension Edn. Found., 1977—. Served U.S. Army, 1941-46; capt. M.C. USAF, 1951-53. Recipient Achievement awards Nat. Heart lung and Blood Inst., 1985, 95, 97, award Internat. Soc. Hypertension, 2004, 06, award Am. Soc. Hypertension, 2006, award Suny Down State Coll. Medicine, 2007; grantee NIH, 1958-62. Fellow: ACP, Am. Soc. Hypertension, Am. Heart Assn. ((various offices: pres. coun. geriatric cardiology 1996-97, others)), Am. Coll. Cardiology, Royal Coll. Physicians and Surgeons (hon.); mem.: Century Country Club. Home and Office: 13 Murray Hill Rd Scarsdale NY 10583 Personal E-mail: moserbp@aol.com.

MOSER, MARY ANN, music educator, director; d. Jose Jaime Uribe and Maria Nunez; m. Jonathan Raymond Moser, Dec. 4, 1993; 1 child, David Ricardo. MusB, U. Pacific, Stockton, Calif., 1998; MusM, Ariz. State U., Tempe, 2004. Instr. Grove City Coll., Pa., 2004—, Pitts. Music Acad., 2006—. Dir. music intern tchg. program Westminster Coll., New Wilmington, Pa., 2007—. Mem.: Suzuki Assn. Americas. Office: Grove City Coll 100 Campus Dr Grove City PA 16127 Personal E-mail: mary@majormosermusic.com. Business E-Mail: moserma@gcc.edu.

MOSER, ROBERT HARLAN, internist, educator, writer; b. Trenton, NJ, June 16, 1923; s. Simon and Helena (Silvers) Moser; m. Linda Mae Salsinger, Mar. 18, 1989; children from previous marriage: Steven Michael, Jonathan Evan. BS, Loyola U., Balt., 1944; MD, Georgetown U., Washington, DC, 1948. Diplomate Am. Bd. Internal Medicine. Commd. 1st lt. U.S. Army, 1948, advanced through grades to col., 1966, intern D.C. Gen. Hosp., 1948—49, fellow pulmonary disease D.C. Gen. Hosp., 1949—50, bn. surgeon Republic of Korea, 1950—51; asst. resident Georgetown U. Hosp., 1951—52; chief resident Georgetown U. Hosp. U.S. Army, 1952—53, chief med. service U.S. Army Hosp. Salzburg, Austria, 1953—55, Wurzburg, Germany, 1955—56, resident in cardiology Brooke Gen. Hosp., 1956—57, asst. chief dept. medicine Brooke Gen. Hosp., 1957—59, chief Brooke Gen. Hosp., 1967—68, fellow hematology U. Utah Coll. Medicine, 1959—60, asst. chief U.S. Army Tripler Gen. Hosp., 1960—64, chief William Beaumont Gen. Hosp., 1965—67, chief Walter Reed Gen. Hosp., 1968—69, ret., 1969; chief of staff Maui (Hawaii) Meml. Hosp., 1969—73, chief dept. medicine, 1975—77; exec. v.p. Am. Coll. Physicians, Phila., 1976—86; v.p. med. affairs The NutraSweet Co., Deerfield, Ill., 1986—91. Assoc. prof. medicine Baylor U., 1958—59; clin. prof. medicine Hawaii U., 1969—77, Washington U., 1970—77, Abraham Lincoln Sch. Medicine, 1974—75; adj. prof. medicine U. Pa., 1977—86, Northwestern U., 1987—91; adj. prof. Uniformed Svcs. U. Health Scis., 1979—97; clin. prof. medicine U. N.Mex. Coll. Medicine, 1992—96, emeritus, 1996—; flight contr. Project Mercury, 1959—62; cons. mem. med. evaluation team Project Gemini, 1962—66; cons. Project Apollo, 1967—73, Tripler Gen. Hosp., 1970—77, Walter Reed Army Med. Ctr., 1974—86; sr. med. cons. Canyon Cons. Corp., 1991—2004; mem. cardiovascular and renal adv. com. FDA, 1978—82; chmn. life scis. adv. com. NASA, 1984—87, mem. adv. coun., 1983—88; chmn. gen. med. panel Hosp. Satellite Network, 1984—86; mem. adv. com. NASA Space Sta., 1988—93; mem. Dept. Def. Com. on Grad. Med. Edn., 1986—87, Life Scis. Strategic Planning Study Group, 1986—88; mem. space studies bd. NRC, 1988—93, space exploration initiation study, 1990; mem. NASA Space Sta. Commn., 1992—93, mem. com. adv. tech. human supp. space, 1996—97; mem. med. adv. bd. the patient channel GE Healthcare, 2001—. Editor, chief divsn. sci. publs. Jour. AMA, Chgo., 1973—75, contbg. editor Med. Opinion and Rev., 1966—75, chmn. editorial bd. Diagnosis mag., 1986—89, mem. editorial bd. Hawaii Med. Jour., Family Physicians, Archives of Internal Medicine, 1967—73, Western Jour. Medicine, 1975—87, Chest, 1975—80, Med. Times, 1977—84, Quality Rev. Bull., 1979—91, The Pharos, 1991—, book rev. editor, 2000—05, mem. editorial bd. Travel Medicine, 1994—96; contbr. over 200 articles to med. sci. jours. and med. books; author: Diseases of Medical Progress, 1955, 1969, House Officer Training, 1970, Decade of Decision, 1992, Past Imperfect A Personal History of Life In and Around Medicine, 2003; co-author Adventures in Medical Writing, 1970, editor chief divsn. sci. publs. Jour. AMA, Chgo., 1973—75, contbg. editor Med. Opinion and Rev., 1966—75, chmn. editl. bd. Diagnosis mag., 1986—89; contbr. articles to med. sci. jours. and med. books. Master: ACP (exec. v.p. 1977—86); fellow: Am. Clin. and Climatol. Assn., Am. Coll. Cardiology, Royal Coll. Physicians and Surgeons Can. (hon.); mem.: AMA (adv. panel registry of adverse drug reactions 1960—67, coun. on drugs 1967—73), Soc. Med. Cons. to Armed Forces, Coll. Physicians Phila., Chgo. Soc. Internal Medicine, Nat. Assn. Physician Broadcasters, Inst. Medicine-NAS, Am. Osler Soc., Am. Therapeutic Soc., Am. Med. Writers Assn., Alpha Omega Alpha, Alpha Sigma Nu. Democrat. Jewish. Avocations: hiking, travel, writing. Home and Office: 943 E Sawmill Canyon Pl Green Valley AZ 85614 Office Phone: 520-399-2526. Personal E-mail: rhmoser@earthlink.net.

MOSER, ROYCE, JR., preventive medicine physician, educator; b. Versailles, Mo., Aug. 21, 1935; s. Royce and Russie Frances (Stringer) M.; m. Lois Anne Hunter, June 14, 1958; children: Beth Anne Moser McLean, Donald Royce. BA, Harvard U., Cambridge, Mass., 1957, MD, 1961; MPH, Harvard Sch. Pub. Health, Boston, 1965. Diplomate Am. Bd. Preventive Medicine (trustee 1989-98). Commd. officer USAF, 1962, advanced through grades to col., 1974; resident in aerospace medicine USAF Sch. Aerospace Medicine, Brooks AFB, Tex., 1965-67; chief aerospace medicine Aerospace Def. Command, Colorado Springs, Colo., 1967-70; comdr. 35th USAF Dispensary Phan Rang, Vietnam, 1970-71; chief aerospace medicine br. USAF Sch. Aerospace Medicine, Brooks AFB, 1971-77; comdr. USAF Hosp., Tyndall AFB, Fla., 1977-79; chief clin. scis. divsn. USAF Sch. Aerospace Medicine, Brooks AFB, 1979-81, chief edn. divsn., 1981-83, sch. comdr., 1983-85, ret., 1985; prof. dept. family and preventive medicine U. Utah Sch. Medicine, Salt Lake City, 1985—, vice chmn. dept., 1985-95; dir. Rocky Mountain Ctr. for Occupl. and Environ. Health, Salt Lake City, 1987—2003. Cons. in occupl., environ. and aerospace medicine, Salt Lake City, 1985—; presenter in field. Author: Effective Management of Health and Safety Programs, 1992, 3d. edit. 2008; contbr. chpts. to books, articles to profl. jours. Past pres. 1st Bapt. Ch. Found., Salt Lake City, 1987-89, moderator, 2006; chmn. numerous univ. coms., Salt Lake City, 1985—; bd. dirs. Hanford Environ. Health Found., 1990-92; preventive medicine residency rev. com. Accreditation Coun. Grad. Med. Edn., 1991-97; ednl. adv. bd. USAF Human Sys. Ctr., 1991-96; chmn. long-range planning com. Am. Bd. Preventive Medicine, 1992-95; mem. alumni coun. Harvard Sch. Pub. Health, 2003-06, chair alumni award of merit com., 2005—, chair elect, 2007—; pres. elect Harvard Sch. Pub. Health Alumni Assn., 2007—. Decorated Legion of Merit (2); recipient Harriet Hardy award New Eng. Coll. Occupl. and Environ. Medicine, 1998, Rutherford T. Johnstone award Western Occupl. and Environ. Med. Assn., 2002. Fellow Aerospace Med. Assn. (pres. 1989-90, chair fellows group 1994-97, Harry G. Mosely award 1981, Theodore C. Lyster award 1988, Eric Liljencrantz award 2001, Pres.'s citation, 2006), Am. Coll. Preventive Medicine (regent 1981-82), Am. Coll. Occupl. and Environ. Medicine (v.p. med. affairs 1995-97, Robert A. Kehoe award 1996); mem. Internat. Acad. Aviation and Space Medicine (selector 1989-94, chancellor 1994-98), Soc. of USAF Flight Surgeons (pres. 1978-79, George E. Schafer award 1982), Phi Beta Kappa. Avocations: photography, fishing. Home: 664 Aloha Rd Salt Lake City UT 84103-3329 Office: Rocky Mountain Ctr Occupl & Environ Health 391 Chipeta Way Ste C Salt Lake City UT 84108 Office Phone: 801-581-4800. Business E-Mail: Royce.Moser@hsc.utah.edu.

MOSES, ALFRED HENRY, lawyer, writer, diplomat; b. Balt., July 24, 1929; s. Leslie William and Helene Amelia (Lobe) Moses; m. Carol Whitehill, Nov. 24, 1955 (dec.); children: Barbara, Jennifer, David, Amalie; m. Fern Magonet Schad, Aug. 28, 2005. BA, Dartmouth, 1951; postgrad., Woodrow Wilson Sch., Princeton U., 1951-52; JD, Georgetown U., 1956. Bar: D.C. 1956. Assoc. Covington & Burling, Washington, 1956-65, ptnr., 1965—94, 1997—99, sr. counsel, 1999—. Co-founder, sr. ptnr., COO Promontory Fin. Group LLC and affiliates, Washington, 2001—; legal advisor minority rights Dem. Nat. Com., Washington, DC Commn. Urban Renewal; commr. Pub. Housing Fairfax County, Va., 1971—72; spl. advisor, spl. counsel Pres. Jimmy Carter, Washington, 1980—81; amb. U.S. Dept. State, Romania, 1994—97; spl. Presdl. emissary Cyprus conflict Pres. William J. Clinton, 1999—2001; chmn. UN Watch, Geneva, 2001—; chmn. nat. bd. Hebrew Coll., Newton Ctr., Mass., 2002—09; bd. chair Project on Ethnic Rels., Inc., Princeton, NJ, 2006—; lectr. in field. Contbr. articles to profl. jours. Pres. Am. Jewish Com., 1991—94, chmn. centennial com., 2005—07, chmn. adv. coun., 1997—; bd. dirs. Paralysis Cure Rsch. Found., 1978—81; trustee Phelps Stokes Fund, NYC, 1978—84, Jewish Publ. Soc., 1989—94, Haifa U., 1988—90; co-chmn. legal divsn. United Givers Fund, Washington, 1975—76; active Coun. Fgn. Rels., NYC, 1977—; pres. Nat. Children's Island, Washington, 1975—76, Golda Meir Assn., 1986—88, nat. chmn., 1988—93; bd. regents Georgetown U., 1986—92. Recipient Frizis award, Nat. Coordinated Effort of Helenes, 1999, Pentru Merit award, Govt. of Romania, 2002. Mem.: ABA, D.C. Bar Assn., Econ. Club Washington, Met. Club. Democrat. Jewish. Home: 7710 Georgetown Pike Mc Lean VA 22102-1431 Office: 1201 Pennsylvania Ave NW Washington DC 20004-2401

MOSES, HAMILTON, III, neurologist, hospital administrator, consultant, author; s. Hamilton Jr. and Betty Anne Moses; m. Elizabeth Hormel, 1977 (dec. 1988); m. Alexandra McCullough Gibson, 1992. BA in Psychology, U. Pa., 1972; MD, Rush Med. Coll., Chgo., 1975. Clk. Nat. Hosp. for Nervous Diseases, London, 1974; intern in medicine Johns Hopkins Hosp., Balt., 1976-77, resident in neurology, 1977-79, chief resident, 1979-80, assoc. prof. neurology, 1986-94, vice chmn. neurology and neurosurgery, 1980-88, v.p., 1988-94, dir. Parkinson's Ctr., 1984-94; dir. neurol. inst., prof. neurology and neurosurgery and mgmt. U. Va., Charlottesville, 1994-97; sr. advisor Boston Cons. Group, 1995—; prof. Darden Sch. Bus. U. Va., Charlottesville, 1994-98; cons. neurologist Mass. Gen. Hosp., Boston, 1997—; vis. prof. neurology and psychiatry Harvard U. Sch. Medicine, Boston, 1997-99; chmn. The Alerion Inst., 2002—; hon. prof. neurology Johns Hopkins U. Sch. Medicine, 2009—. Sr. advisor Ptnrs. Healthcare, Boston; spl. advisor Nat. Health Svc., Eng., 1988-91; dir. various tech. companies. Co-editor, major author: Hopkins' Principles and Practice of Medicine, 1985-96; editor newsletter Johns Hopkins Health, 1988-94; contbr. articles to profl. jours. Com. on med. ministries Episcopal Diocese Md., Balt., 1987; bd. dirs. Valleys Planning Ct.; trustee McLean Hosp., Belmont, Mass., 1997—. Recipient Hon. col., Nat. Pk. Svc. Fellow Am. Acad. Neurology (sec. 1989-91), Royal Soc. Medicine (UK); mem. Am. Neurol. Assn., Md. Neurol. Soc. (pres. 1984-86), Movement Disorders Soc. Episcopalian. Avocations: photography, sailing. Office: PO Box 150 North Garden VA 22959-0150 Business E-Mail: hm3@alerion.us.

MOSES, JEFFREY WARREN, cardiologist, educator; b. Bklyn., May 12, 1948; s. Julian and Mildred Moses; m. Laurie Levinberg, Nov. 4, 1983 (div. 2008); children: Ariel, Jarret, Chandler, Harrison. BA, Yale U., New Haven, Conn., 1970; MD, U. Pa., Phila., 1974. Intern Presbyn.-U. Pa., Phila., 1974—75, resident in medicine, 1975—77, fellow in cardiology, 1978—80; asst. instr. U. Pa., Phila., 1975—77; med. adv. staff Blue Cross/Blue Shield Greater N.Y., 1977—78; asst. med. dir. Equitable Life Soc., NYC, 1977—78; asst. attending physician NY Hosp., NYC, 1980—87, asst. dir. Adult Cardiac Catheterization Lab., 1980—83, dir. clin. electrophysiology, 1981—87, assoc. dir. Adult Cardiac Catheterization Lab., 1983—87, assoc. attending physician, 1987; instr. medicine Cornell U. Med. Coll., NYC, 1980—81, asst. prof., 1981—87, assoc. prof. clin. medicine, 1987; chief interventional cardiology Lenox Hill Hosp., NYC, 1987—2004, assoc. attending physician, 1987—88, sr. attending physician, 1988—2004; clin. assoc. prof. medicine NYU Sch. Medicine, NYC, 1993—96, clin. prof. medicine, 1996—2004; prof. medicine, dir. Ctr. Interventional Vascular Therapy, dir. Cardiac Catheterization Lab. NY Presbyn. Hosp./Columbia U. Med. Ctr., NYC, 2004—, interventional cardiologist, 2005—. Fellow: ACP, Soc. Cardiac Angiography and Intervention, Am. Coll. Cardiology. Office: NY Presbyn Hosp Columbia U Med Ctr 161 Fort Washington Ave New York NY 10032 Office Phone: 212-305-7060. Office Fax: 212-305-4825, 212-342-3660. Business E-Mail: jm2456@columbia.edu.

MOSES, JOEL, computer scientist, educator; b. Petach Tikvah, Israel, Nov. 25, 1941; came to U.S., 1954, naturalized, 1960; s. Bernhard and Golda (Losner) M.; m. Margaret A. Garvey, Dec. 27, 1970; children: Jesse, David. BA, Columbia U., 1962, MA, 1963; PhD, MIT, 1967. Asst. prof. dept. elec. engring. and computer sci. MIT, Cambridge, 1967-71, assoc. prof., 1971-77, prof., 1977—, assoc. dir. Lab for Computer Sci., 1974-78, assoc. head computer sci. and engring., dept. elec. engring. and computer sci., 1978-81, head dept., 1981-89, D.C. Jackson prof., 1989-99, dean Sch. Engring., 1991-95, provost, 1995-98, prof. engring. sys. divsn., 1999—, Inst. prof., 1999—, acting dir. engring. sys. divsn., 2006—07, acting. dir. Ctr. Tech., Policy and Indsl. Devel., 2006—. Vis. prof. Harvard Grad. Sch. Bus. Adminstrn., 1989-90; vis. adj. sr. rsch. scientist Columbia U. FU Found. Sch. Engring. and Applied Sci., 1998. Editor: The Computer Age: A Twenty Year View, 1979; co-originator Knowledge Based System Concept; developer MACSYMA system for formula manipulation, complexity and flexibility of large scale systems. Recipient Achievement award MIT Lab. for Computer Sci., 1985. Fellow IEEE, AAAS, Am. Acad. Arts and Scis.; mem. NAE, Assn. for Computing Machinery, Am. Soc. Engring. Edn. (Centennial cert.). Office: MIT Computer Sci Artificial Intelligence Lab 32-249 Cambridge MA 02139 Office Phone: 617-253-8592. E-mail: moses@mit.edu.

MOSES, LOUIS J., psychology professor, department chairman; BA in Psychology, U. Western Australia, 1983; PhD in Psychology, Stanford U., Calif., 1991. Tutor, dept. psychology U. Western Australia, 1984—85; lectr., dept. psychology U. BC, Canada, 1991—92, Simon Fraser U., 1992; asst. prof., dept. psychology U. Oreg., Eugene, 1992—99, assoc. prof., dept. psychology, 1999—, prin. investigator, developing mind lab, associated faculty, inst. cognitive and decision sciences, chmn., dept. psychology. Co-editor (with B.F. Malle and D.A. Baldwin): Intentions and Intentionality: Foundations of Social Cognition, 2001; contbr. articles to profl. jours. Vis. scholar, Stanford U. Dept. Psychology, 1999—2000; Izaak Walton Killam Meml. Postdoctoral Rsch. fellow, U. BC, 1990—92. Mem.: Am. Psychol. Soc., Cognitive Devel. Soc., Soc. Rsch. in Child Devel. Office: Dept Psychology 1227 Univ Oreg Eugene OR 97403-1227 Office Phone: 541-346-4918. Office Fax: 541-346-4911. Business E-Mail: moses@uoregon.edu.*

MOSES, MARSHA ANNE, biochemist, researcher; b. New Bedford, Mass., July 21, 1953; d. George Francis and Matilda Theresa (Thomas) M. BS, Stonehill Coll., 1975; PhD, Boston U., 1986. Postdoctoral rsch.

assoc., rsch. fellow Children's Hosp. Med. Ctr., Boston, 1986—; rsch. fellow Harvard Med. Sch., Boston, 1986-90, instr. dept. surgery, 1991-92, asst. prof. surgery, assoc. prof. surgery, 1992—2006, prof. surgery, 2006—; interim dir. vascular biology prog. Children's Hosp. Boston. Author: (with others) Microcirculation and Cancer Metastasis, 1991, Clinical Applications of Cytokines, 1991; contbr. articles to various sci. jours. Recipient Cancer Rsch. Found. award, Am. Cancer Soc. Rsch. award, CaPCURE Rsch. award, A. Clifford Barger Mentoring award, Harvard Med. Sch., 2003; Gordon Conf. postdoctoral scholar, 1986; NIH postdoctoral rsch. fellow, 1987-89, Mary Ingraham Bunting Inst. Biomed. Rsch. fellow. Mem. AAAS, Am. Soc. Biochemistry and Molecular Biology (Young Investigator Travel award 1991), Am. Soc. Cell Biology, Am. Women in Sci., Assn. Rsch. in Vision and Ophthalmology, Inst. Medicine. Achievements include patents pending in field; rsch. in vascular growth control via endogenous inhibitors, the role of metalloproteinases and their inhibitors in the control of neovascularization. Office: Childrens Hosp Karp 12-214 300 Longwood Ave Boston MA 02115 Office Phone: 617-919-2207. Office Fax: 617-730-0231. E-mail: marsha.moses@childrens.harvard.edu.*

MOSES, RAPHAEL JACOB, lawyer; b. Girard, Ala., Nov. 6, 1913; s. William Moultrie and Anna (Green) M.; m. Marian Eva Beck, Aug. 22, 1938 (dec. Feb. 1976); 1 child, Marcia (Mrs. William S. Johnson); m. Fletcher Lee Westgaard, Jan. 20, 1979. AB, U. Colo., 1935, JD, 1937. Bar: Colo. 1938. Practiced in, Alamosa, 1938-62, Boulder, 1962—; pres. Moses, Wittemyer, Harrison & Woodruff (P.C.), from 1970, now of counsel. Spl. asst. atty. gen. Rio Grande Compact, 1957-58; mem. Colo. Water Conservation Bd., 1952-58, chmn., counsel, 1958-76, cons., 1976-77; research asso., faculty law U. Colo., 1962-66, vis. lectr., 1966-76, resident counsel, 1964-66, regent, 1973-74; grad. faculty Colo. State U., 1963-67; mem. Western States Water Council, 1965-77, chmn., 1966-70. Trustee Rocky Mountain Mineral Law Inst., 1964-66; bd. dirs. U. Colo. Found., 1977-97, chmn., 1977-79, mem. chancellor's adv. coun., 1981-97; bd. dirs. Colo. Open Lands, 1983-91, U. Colo. Improvement Corp., 1980-90, Colo. Endowment for Humanities, 1986-89; mem. adv. bd. Natural Resources Ctr., U. Colo. Sch. Law, 1983-92, chmn., 1986-88; mem. Sr. Citizens Adv. Bd., Boulder, Colo., 2003—. Served to lt. (s.g.) USNR, 1942-45. Decorated Purple Heart; recipient William E. Knous award U. Colo. Sch. Law, 1971, Norlin award U. Colo., 1972; Raphael J. Moses Disting. Natural Resources professorship established U. Colo., 1994. Fellow Am. Bar Found. (life), Colo. Bar Found. (trustee 1977-90), Am. Coll. Trial Lawyers; mem. ABA (chmn. water rights com. sect. natural resources 1959-60), Colo. Bar Assn. (pres. 1959-60, Award of Merit 1972), San Luis Valley Bar Assn. (pres. 1942), Am. Counsel Assn., Order of Coif (hon.). Presbyterian (elder) Home: 4913 Clubhouse Cir Boulder CO 80301-3715 E-mail: raymoise@aol.com.

MOSES, SAMUEL B., certified public accountant, consultant; s. Alfred J. and Alice R. Moses. BA, Calif. State U., Fullerton, 1985. CPA Calif., 1990. Auditor Arthur Andersen & Co., Costa Mesa, Calif., 1985—86; tax sr. cpa BDO Seidman, Orange, Calif., 1987—90; owner Samuel B. Moses, CPA, Santa Monica, Calif., 1991—. Western dir. Intertel (Top 1% IQs), LA, 2002—03. Recipient Peat Marwick award, Beta Alpha Psi Chpt., 1985. Mem.: Mensa (life mem., licentiate; chmn. Greater L.A. area Mensa chpt. 1996—2000). Office: Samuel B Moses CPA Ste 1800 100 Wilshire Blvd Santa Monica CA 90401 Business E-Mail: smosescpa@aol.com.

MOSESSO, VINCENT NICHOLAS, JR., emergency physician; b. Pitts., Pa., Sept. 28, 1957; s. Vincent Nicholas and Jean Lois Mosesso; m. Janet L. Mosesso, June 17, 1983; children: Jennifer Moss, Chadwick. BA, Duquesne U., Pitts., 1979; MD, U. of Pitts., 1988. Lic. emergency medicine Am. Bd. of Emergency Medicine. Assoc. prof. of emergency medicine U. of Pitts. Sch. of Medicine, 1991—. Asst. med. dir. dept. of pub. safety City of Pitts., 1993—; med. dir. prehospital care U. of Pitts. Med. Ctr., 1996—; mem. nat. BLS subcom. Am. Heart Assn., Emergency Cardiac Care Com., Dallas, 2001—08; med. dir. advanced med. life support Nat. Assn. of Emergency Med. Technicians, Clinton, Miss., 2002—. Mem. editl. bd.: med. jours. Prehospital Emergency Care, Reservation. Mem. Allegheny divsn. Am. Heart Assn., Pitts., 1998—2008; bd. dirs., med. dir. Sudden Cardiac Arrest Assn., Washington, 2005—. Named Emergency Physician of the Yr., Pa. Emergency Health Svcs. Coun., 1998; grantee, Medtrionic Found., 2000—02. Fellow: Am. Coll. of Emergency Medicine; mem.: Nat. Assn. of EMS Physicians (bd. dirs. 2003—05). Avocations: golf, travel, sports, exercise. Office: U Pitt Ste 911 230 McKee Pl Pittsburgh PA 15213 E-mail: mosessovn@upmc.edu.

MOSHER, JOYCE DEVLIN, literature and language professor; PhD in English Lit. and Criticism, Ind. U. Pa., 2007. Instr., lit. and composition Colo. Mountain Coll., Breckenridge, 1975—. Vol. Cmty. Theatre. Recipient Profl. Excellence award, Rotary. Home: PO Box 54 Breckenridge CO 80424 Office: Colo Mountain Coll Breckenridge CO 80424

MOSHER, SALLY EKENBERG, lawyer, musician; b. NYC, July 26, 1934; d. Leslie Joseph and Frances Josephine (McArdle) Ekenberg; m. James Kimberly Mosher, Aug. 13, 1960 (dec. Aug. 1982). MusB, Manhattanville Coll., 1956; postgrad., Hofstra U., 1958-60, U. So. Calif., 1971-73, JD, 1981. Bar: Calif., 1982. Musician, pianist, tchr., 1957-74; music critic Pasadena Star-News, 1967-72; mgr. Contrasts Concerts, Pasadena Art Mus., 1971-72; rep. Occidental Life Ins. Co., Pasadena, 1975-78; v.p. James K. Mosher Co., Pasadena, 1961-82, pres., 1982—, Oakhill Enterprises, Pasadena, 1984—; assoc. White-Howell, Inc., Pasadena, 1984-94; real estate broker, 1984-96. Harpsichordist, lectr., composer, 1994—; pub. Silver Wheels Pub., ASCAP. Musician (CD recs.) William Byrd: Songs, Dances, Battles, Games, 1995, From Now On: New Directions For Harpsichord, 1998, Sally Mosher Plays English Renaissance Harpsichord Music, Images and Moods, (with Patrick Lindley, Scott Frasier, Justin Weaver) Towards the Light; author: People and Their Contexts: A Chronology of the 16th Century World; contbr. articles to various publs. Bd. dirs. Jr. League Pasadena, 1966-67, Encounters Concerts, Pasadena, 1966-72, U. So. Calif. Friends of Music, L.A., 1973-76, Calif. Music Theatre, 1988-90, Pasadena Hist. Soc., 1989-91, I Cantori, 1989-91; bd. dirs. Pasadena Arts Coun., 1986-92, pres., 1989-92, chair adv. bd., 1992-93; v.p., bd. dirs. Pasadena Chamber Orch., 1986-88, pres., 1987-88; mem. Calif. 200 Coun. for Bicentennial of U.S. Constn., 1987-90; mem. Endowment Adv. Commn., Pasadena, 1988-90; bd. dirs. Foothill Area Cmty. Svcs., 1990-95, treas., 1991, vice chair, 1992-94, chair, 1994-95; sec., bd. dirs. Piano Spheres, 2001-02, pres., 2002—. Manhattanville Coll. hon. scholar, 1952-56. Mem. ABA, Calif. Bar Assn., Assocs. of Calif. Inst. Tech., So. Calif. Baroque Assn. (bd. dirs., 2004—), Athenaeum, Kappa Gamma Pi, Mu Phi Epsilon, Phi Alpha Delta. Home: 1260 Rancheros Rd Pasadena CA 91103-2759 Fax: 626-795-3146. E-mail: sally@cyberverse.com.

MOSHMAN, JACK, statistical consultant; b. Richmond Hill, N.Y., Aug. 12, 1924; s. Morris and Sadye (Posner) M.; m. Annette Gordon, Aug. 10, 1947; children: Gordon, Marc, Sherri, Ira. BA, NYU, 1946; MA, Columbia U., NYC, 1947; PhD, U. Tenn., Knoxville, 1953. Instr. Queens Coll., Flushing, NY, 1946-47, U. Tenn., Knoxville, 1947-53; statistician AEC, Oak Ridge, Tenn., 1948-50; sr. statistician Oak Ridge Nat. Labs., Tenn., 1950-54; mem. tech. staff Bell Tel. Labs., Murray Hill, NJ, 1954-57; v.p. C-E-I-R Inc., Washington, 1957-66; mng. dir. EBS Mgmt. Cons., Washington, 1966-68; sr. v.p. Leasco Systems & Rsch., Bethesda, Md., 1968-69; pres. Moshman Assocs. Inc., Bethesda, Md., 1970—. Adj. prof. Rutgers U., 1963-66; professorial lectr. George Washington U., 1959-62; chmn. Inst. for Safety Analysis, Rockville, Md., 1975-89, mem. office of mgmt. and budget adv. com. on statistical policy. Editor: Faith, Hope & Parity, 1967; author Ency. sect. Computers & Politics, 1985, 90, 93; contbr. articles to profl. jours. Trustee Babbage Found., St. Paul, 1983-87; pres. Moshman Charitable Found., Bethesda, 1996—; v.p. Eleanor & George Kokiko Sr. Found., Bethesda, 1997—. With U.S. Army, 1943-46, ETO. Fellow Am. Statis. Assn. (coun. 1956, 58); mem. Am. Fedn. Info. Processing Soc. Am. (bd. dirs., pres. 1986-87), Assn. for Computing Machinery (sec. 1956-64, v.p 1965), Inst. for Math. Stats., Inst. for Mgmt. Scis., Ops. Rsch. Soc. Am., Biometrics Soc. Avocation: psephology. Office: Moshman Assocs Inc 6000 Executive Blvd Ste 201 North Bethesda MD 20852-3803 Home Phone: 301-229-4040; Office Phone: 301-229-3000. Personal E-mail: jmoshman@aol.com.

MOSHOLDER, ANDREW DONALD, psychiatrist; b. Washington, Sept. 25, 1957; s. Donald and Mary Mosholder; m. Janet Marie Rauch, Aug. 5, 1989; 1 stepchild, Erik Harrison. BA, Haverford Coll., Pa., 1979; MD, U. Va., 1983; MPH, Johns Hopkins U., 2001. Diplomate Am. Bd. Psychiatry and Neurology, 1988, lic. in child and adolescent psychiatry Am. Bd. Psychiatry and Neurology, 1991, psychiatrist Va., 1985. Resident psychiatry Med. Coll. Va., Richmond, 1983—87; resident child and adolescent psychiatry U. Va., Charlottesville, 1987—89; psychiatrist Ctrl. Va. Cmty. Svcs., Lynchburg, Va., 1989—92; med. officer FDA, Rockville, Md., 1992—. Recipient Frances Kelsey Drug Safety Excellence award, FDA Ctr. for Drug Evaluation and Rsch., 2005. Mem.: APHA, Am. Acad. Child and Adolescent Psychiatry. Mem. Soc. Of Friends. Avocation: bass guitar. Office: FDA 10903 New Hampshire Ave Mail Stop 3411 Silver Spring MD 20993-0002 Business E-Mail: andrew.mosholder@fda.hhs.gov.

MOSIER, ARVIN RAY, chemist, researcher; b. Olney Springs, Colo., June 11, 1945; s. Isaac James Ellen Rena (Ross) M.; m. Susan Minnick, Dec. 30, 1965; children: Andrew, Katherine. BS, Colo. State U., 1967, MS, 1967-68, PhD, 1974. Chemist agr. rsch. svcs. USDA, Ft. Collins, 1967—2004, with global environ. change and food sys. program Gainesville, Fla., 2005—06, cons., 2006—. Contbr. papers and book chpt. to profl. publ. Mem. AAAS, Am. Soc. Agronomy, Soil Sci. Soc. Am., Internat. Soil Sci. Sco., Council Agrl. Sci. Tech., Phi Kappa Phi, Sigma XI, Gamma Sigma Delta. Republican. Methodist. Avocations: tennis, soccer. Home and Office: 1494 Oakhurst Dr Mount Pleasant SC 29466 Office Phone: 843-881-3129. E-mail: a.mosier12@comcast.net.

MOSIER, CHERYL ANGELINE, secondary school educator, consultant; b. Longmont, Colo., Mar. 31, 1968; d. Douglas and Evangeline Martfeld; m. Christopher R. Mosier, July 4, 1997; 1 child, Ryan Matthew. BA in Earth Sci. Edn., U. No. Colo., Greeley, 1992, BA in Phys. Sci. Edn., 1992; MEd, Grand Canyon U., Phoenix, 2003. Lic. Profl. Tchr. Colo., 2006. Sci. tchr. Columbine HS, Littleton, Colo., 1997—, instrnl. leader. Cons. It's About Time Pub., Herrf Jones Edn. Divsn., Armonk, NY, 2005—, Am. Geol. Inst., 2005—; presenter Colo. Sci. Conv., Denver, 2005—. Founding mem. Am. Geological Inst. Geosci. Tchrs. Acad. Recipient Math and Sci. medal of achievement, Colo. Sch. Mines, 1986, Departmental Scholar in Earth Sci., U. No. Colo., 1990, Excellence in Tchg. of Earth Scis. award, Rocky Mountain Assn. Geologists Found., 2005, Math. and Sci. Tchg. Excellence, Presdl. award, 2007; grantee Lockheed Martin Columbine Meml. scholarship, 2002. Mem.: NSTA, Colo. Assn. Sci. Tchrs., Nat. Earth Sci. Tchrs. Assn. Office: Columbine HS 6201 S Pierce St Littleton CO 80123 Business E-Mail: camosier@jeffco.k12.co.us.

MOSIER, VIRGINIA LOU, school system administrator; b. Clinton, Okla., Dec. 2, 1951; d. Bert Eugene and Martha Virginia (Fike) M. BE, Abilene Christian U., 1973; MS, East Tex. State U., 1980; PhD, U. North Tex., Denton, 1989. Cert. tchr. Bus. tchr. Christian Schs., Inc., Dallas, 1973-77; sec. Underwood, Neuhaus Co., Inc., Houston, 1977-78; bus. tchr. Magnet HS, Dallas, 1978-79; vocat. tchr. Mesquite HS, Tex., 1979-81; curriculum writer East Tex. State U., Commerce, 1980; vocat. tchr. J.J. Pearce HS, Richardson, Tex., 1981-89; office adminstrn. tchr. Richardson HS, 1989-92, chair vocat. edn. dept., 1990-92; asst. prof. occupl. tng. and devel. Tex. A&M U., Corpus Christi, 1992—98, dir. field experiences, 1999—2000; assoc. prof. edn., dir. field experiences Abilene Christian U., 2000—04; dir. career and tech. edn. Abilene Ind. Sch. Dist., 2004—07, exec. dir. career and tech. edn., 2007—. Presenter T & I Summer Workshop, Houston, 1983-87; mem. Coordinated Vocat. Acad. Edn. Co-op Organizing Com., 1983-88; adj. prof. rural schs., Tex. 1984-86, U. North Tex., Denton, 1984-85, East Tex. State U., San Marcos, 1990, 91; nat. rev. com. Addison-Wesley high sch. text, 1990-92; profl. com. state adv. com. Tex. State Bd. for Educator Certification, 1997-98; gen. adv. com. Weslaco Indp. Sch. Dist. Career and Tech. Edn. Dept., 1992-96; mem. Rio Grande Valley Workforce Consortium, 1992-96; mem. state validation com. ExCET Cert. examin Comprehensive Bus. Edn., 1987; bd. dirs. Jr. Achievement Abilene, 2005-; workforce devel. bd. West Ctrl. Tex., 2006-; adv. bd. West Ctrl. Tex. Prep., 2004-. Author: Coordinated Vocational Academic Education Curriculum Guide, 1980, Vocational Opportunities Clubs of Texas Competitive Guide, 1985, Vocational Opportunities Clubs of Texas Advisor's Tool Kit, 1986; contbr. articles to profl. jours. Sec. Christian Schs. PTA, Dallas, 1976-77. Recipient Outstanding Tchr. award Richardson Assn. for Children with Learning Disabilities, 1985, Spl. Recognition award Mercedes Ind. Sch. Dist. Career and Tech. Edn. Dept., 1994, 95, Spl. Appreciation awards Tuloso-Midway Alternative Career Ctr. chpt. Vocat. Indsl. Clubs of Am., 1997, 98, Outstanding Svc. award Am. Vocat. Assn., 1998, Outstanding Alumnus award Abilene Christian U., 2006; grantee Tex. Edn. Agy., Secondary T&I Tchr. Cert. Actitivies for South Tex., Rio Grade Valley, 1995-96, 96-97, 97-98. Mem. Tex. Bus. Edn. Assn. (pres., v.p., sec. 1982-85, state legis. com. 1986, Tchr. of Yr. award Dist. 10 1984), Assn. Tex. Profl. Educators, Assn. Career and Tech. Edn., Tex. Indsl. Vocat. Assn. (Outstanding Tchr. Educator award 1998), Tex. Vocat Tech. Assn., Assn. Supervision and Curriculum Devel., Tex. Career and Tech. Educators, Nat. Assn. Indsl. Tech. Tchr. Edn., Tex. Vocat. Tchr. Educators Assn. (pres.-elect 1993-94, pres. 1994-95), Vocat. Opportunities Clubs Tex. (state adv. com. 1992-93), Vocat. Indsl. Clubs Am. (mem. adv. com.), Tex. Assn. (chmn. 1994—), Career and Tech. Assn. Tex. (area pres. 2006-), Iota Lambda Sigma (state and area outstanding tchr. awards 1985), Kiwanis Club Abilene. Republican. Mem. Ch. of Christ. Avocations: travel, antiques, sports, cooking. Business E-Mail: virginia.mosier@abileneisd.org.

MOSIER, WILLIAM ARTHUR, psychiatrist, psychotherapist, director, medical educator, researcher; b. Richmond, Calif., Oct. 21, 1946; s. William Nathaniel and Violet Olga (Luzum) M.; m. Virginia Rondero (div. Apr. 1992); children: Robert Carlos, Cristina Dominique; m. Gloria Sifuentes (div. 1998); 1 child, William Nathaniel; m. Gabriela Pickett; children: Gabriela, Diana. BA, Webster U., 1971, MA in Tchg., 1973; MD, U. Ctrl. del Este, Dominican Republic, 1986; EdD, U. So. Calif., 1987; BS with distinction, U. Okla., 1991; MPAS in Psychiatry, U. Nebr., 1997. Diplomate Am. Bd. Forensic Medicine, Am. Bd. Med. Psychotherapists, Am. Bd. Psychol. Specialties, lic. physician asst. Tex., Fla., N.Y., Va.; marraige and family therapist, chem. dependency counselor Tex.; marraige and family therapist Ohio. Tchr. St. Louis Pub. Schs., 1971—74; tchr., ctr. dir. Project Head Start, Vallejo, Calif., 1975—77; dir. rsch. Ctr. for Study of Child Devel., Sacramento, 1977—95; physician asst. U.S. Army, Ft. Hood/Ft. Sam Houston, Tex., 1989—91; assoc. prof. U. Mary Hardin-Baylor, Belton, Tex., 1991—92; psychotherapist pvt. practice, Tex., 1993—95; mem. adj. faculty dept. psychiatry Barry U., Miami Shores, Fla., 1997—2000; med. dir. Fla. Inst. Neuro Devel., Vero Beach, Fla., 1995—2000; clin. assoc. prof. psychiatry Nova Southeastern U., Ft. Lauderdale, Fla., 1997—99; asst. prof. medicine, assoc. dir. acad. curriculum George Washington U., 2000—01; assoc. prof. psychiatry Kettering Coll. med. Arts Kettering (Ohio) Med. Ctr., 2001—02, dir. physicians asst. program; child devel. cons., marriage and family therapist, 2001—; asst. prof., child devel. Wright State U., Dayton, Ohio, 2002—. Mem. test writing com. Nat. Assn. Cert. Physicians Assts., 1995—, Nat. Bd. Med. Examiners; bd. dir. Ohio State Counselor, Social Worker and Marriage and Family Therapist Regulatory Bd. Newspaper columnist:, mem. editl. adv. bd.: Advance for PAs; contbr. articles to profl. jours., chapters to books. Lt. col. USAF, 1967-68, Vietnam, maj. USAFR, 1987—. Decorated Bronze Star, Air medal. Fellow: APA (mem. adv. bd. 1997—, editl. adv. bd. Annals of Am. Psychotherapy Assn.), Am. Assn. Surg. PAS, Am. Acad. Physician Assts., Assn. Mil. Surgeons U.S. (life), Aerospace Med. Assn. (life), Am. Coll. Forensic Examners (life); mem.: Ohio Assn. Marriage and Family Therapy (bd. dir.), Am. Assn. Marriage and Family Therapy (del. regulatory bd. Ohio), Assn. of Psychiat. PAs (founding mem., pres.), Soc. PAs in the Addiction Medicine (exec. bd., pres.). Democrat. Mem. Soc. Of Friends. Avocations: musical composition, piano, guitar, swimming, yoga. E-mail: drwillmosier@yahoo.com.

MOSIMAN, RITA ESTHER, music educator, performing artist; children: Theresa, Mark, Brian. B in Music (hon.), U. Ariz., 1963. Lic. secondary tchg. Ariz., 1963. Solo artist No. Ariz. Symphony, 1962; English, speech tchr. Dreux Am. HS, France, 1964—65; adminstrv. asst. US Dept. Def., Supt. Sch. Office, Orleans, France, 1965—66; choral dir. Los Lunas Consol. Sch., N.Mex., 1980; pvt. voice and piano tchr. Albuquerque, 1980—. Guest conductor, choral clinician Am. All Spain HS Music Festival, Zaragoza, Spain, 1979. Singer (soloist): Northern Ariz. Symphony, 1962, U. N.Mex., Albuquerque, 1982, N.Mex. Italian Film Festival Benefit, 2008, U. Ariz., 1985, Whitworth Coll., 1988; prodr.(vocalist, pianist): America's Best Kept Secret-Rita M., 2004; dir.(soloist): La Gran Via, 1988, Santa Fe Spirit, 1989. Vol. Concert for Humanity, Albuquerque, 1984; dir., pianist benefit concert Pennies for the Homeless, Albuquerque, 1998. Recipient Leadership award, Sigma Alpha Iota, we. dist., 1963; named Outstanding Ind. Woman, U. Ariz., 1963. Mem.: Nat. Assn. Tchrs. Singing. Avocations: hiking, photography, travel, birdwatching. Office Phone: 505-294-6018. Personal E-mail: ritaem@gmail.com.

MOSJIDIS, JORGE, agricultural studies educator, researcher; b. Santiago, Chile; arrived in U.S., 1976; d. Georgios and Aliky Mosjidis; m. Cecilia O'Hara Mosjidis, Mar. 23, 1986; children: Christina Zoe Wood, Alexis Georgios. B in Agronomy, U. Chile, Santiago, 1970; PhD, U. Calif., Riverside, 1981. Asst. prof. Auburn (Ala.) U., assoc. prof., 1986—96, prof., 1996—. Chair clover crop germplasm com. USDA, 2005—08, sec., 2002—05; assoc. editor Crop Sci., 1995—2000; editor Diversity, 2009—. Contbr. articles to profl. jours. Recipient Dir.'s Rsch. award, Ala. Agr. Exptl. Sta., 2005; grantee, USDA-CSREES-NRI, 2003—06, CSREES, Integrated Organic Program, 2005—, So. Region SARE, 2005—, 2005—. Mem.: Am. Forage and Grassland Coun., Am. Genetic Assn., Am. Soc. Agronomy, Crop Sci. Soc. Am. (assoc. editor 2000, chair G.O. Matt. mem. com.), Gamma Sigma Delta, Sigma Xi. Greek Orthodox. Achievements include patents pending for utilization of a plant to control gastrointestinal parasites in ruminants; obtained a certificate of plant variety protection for 18 years for a sericea lespedeza cultivar. Avocations: yoga, flower and vegetable gardening, tai chi, qi kung. Office: Auburn Univ 202 Funchess Hall Auburn University AL 36849-5412

MOSK, RICHARD MITCHELL, judge; b. LA, May 18, 1939; s. Stanley and Edna M.; m. Sandra Lee Budnitz, Mar. 21, 1964; children: Julie, Matthew. AB with great distinction, Stanford U., 1960; JD cum laude, Harvard U., 1963. Bar: Calif. 1964, US Supreme Ct. 1970, US Ct. Mil. Appeals 1970, US Dist. Ct. (no., so., ea., and cen. dists.) Calif 1964, US Ct. Appeals (9th dist.) 1964. Staff Pres.'s Commn. on Assassination Pres. Kennedy, 1964; rsch. clk. Calif. Supreme Ct., 1964-65; ptnr. Mitchell, Silberberg & Knupp, LA, 1965-87; prin. Sanders, Barnet, Goldman, Simons & Mosk, PC, LA, 1987-2000; justice Calif. Ct. Appeal, 2nd Dist., 2001—. Spl. dep. Fed. Pub. Defender, LA, 1975—76; instr. U. So. Calif. Law Sch., 1978; judge Iran-U.S. Claims Tribunal, 1981—84, 1997—2001, substitute arbitrator, 1984—97; mem. L.A. County Jud. Procedures Commn., 1973—82, chmn., 1978; chmn., co-chmn. Motion Picture Assn. Classification and Rating Adminstrn., 1994—2000; mem. panel Ct. Arbitration for Sport-Geneva, 1998—2001; lectr. internat. law Hague Acad., 2003. Contbr. articles to profl. jours. Mem. L.A. City-County Inquiry on Brush Fires, 1970; bd. dirs. Calif. Mus. Sci. and Industry, 1979-82, Vista Del Mar Child Ctr., 1979-82; trustee L.A. County Law Libr., 1985-86; bd. govs. Town Hall Calif., 1986-91; mem. Christopher Commn. on L.A. Police Dept., 1991; mem. Stanford U. Athletic Bd., 1991-95. With USNR, 1964-75. Hon. Woodrow Wilson fellow, 1960; recipient Roscoe Pound prize, 1961. Mem.: ABA (coun. internat. law sect. 1986—90), Am. Law Inst., L.A. County Bar Assn., Beverly Hills Bar Assn., Am. Bar Found., Phi Beta Kappa. Office: Ct Appeal 300 S Spring St Los Angeles CA 90013

MOSKAL, ROBERT M., bishop; b. Carnegie, Pa., Oct. 24, 1937; s. William and Jean (Popivchak) Moskal. BA, St. Basil Coll. Sem., Stamford, Conn., 1959; lic. in Sacred Theology, Cath. U. Am., 1963; student, Phila. Mus. Acad. and Conservatory of Mus., 1963—66. Ordained priest Archeparchy of Phila. (Ukrainian), 1963; founder, pastor St. Anne's Ukrainian Cath. Ch., Warrington, Pa., 1963—72; sec. Archbishop's Chancery, Phila., 1963—67; vice-chancellor Archeparchy of Phila. (Ukrainian), 1967—74; pastor Annunciation Ukrainian Cath. Ch., Melrose Park, Pa., 1972—74; chancellor Archeparchy of Phila. (Ukrainian), 1974—83; pastor Ukrainian Cath. Cathedral of the Immaculate Conception, Phila., 1974—83; ordained bishop, 1981; aux. bishop Archeparchy of Phila. (Ukrainian), 1981—83; bishop Diocese of St. Josaphat in Parma (Ukrainian), Parma, Ohio, 1983—2009, bishop emeritus, 2009—. Founder Ukrainian Cath. Hour, God is with Us, Sta. WIBF-FM, Phila., 1972—77, Christ Among Us, Sat. WTEL, 1975—; mem. Ukrainian Cath. Ch. Liturgical Subcommn., 1980—; host to His Holiness Pope John Paul II; Bd. dirs. Ascension Manor, Inc., Phila., 1964—84, sec.-treas., 1964—78, exec. v.p., 1977—84; pro-synodal judge Archdiocesan Tribunal, Phila., 1965—67. Roman Catholic. Office: PO Box 347180 5720 State Rd Parma OH 44134-2500*

MOSKIN, JOHN ROBERT, editor, writer; b. NYC, May 9, 1923; s. Morris and Irma (Rosenfeld) M.; m. Doris Marianne Bloch, Oct. 7, 1948 (div. 1978); children: Mark Douglas, David Scott, Nancy Irma; m. Lynn Carole Goldberg, Apr. 10, 1986. Grad., Horace Mann Sch., 1940; BS, Harvard U., 1944; MA, Columbia U., 1947. Reporter Boston Post, 1941-42, Newark News, 1947-48; asst. to gen. mgr. N.Y. Star, 1948-49; editor Westport (Conn.) Town Crier, 1949; med. editor Look mag., NYC, 1950-51, articles editor, 1951-53, sr. editor, 1956-66, fgn. editor, 1966-71; mng. editor Woman's Home Companion, 1953-56; sr. editor Collier's, 1956; editor at large Saturday Rev., 1972-75; sr. editor World Press Rev., 1976-87, contbg. editor, 1987-93; editl. dir. Aspen Inst., 1977-83. Editl. dir. Commonwealth Fund, 1984-87, sr. editl. advisor, 1987-93. Author: (with others) The Decline of the American Male, 1958, Morality in America, 1966, Turncoat, 1968, The U.S. Marine Corps Story, 1977, 82, 87, 92, Among Lions, 1982, (with Julia Vitullo-Martin) The Executive's Book of Quotations, 1994, Mr. Truman's War, 1996, 2002; editor: The Marines, 1998; mem. editl. adv. com. Dimensions mag. 1970-71, Present Tense, 1973-90. Trustee Scarsdale Adult Sch., 1965—72, chmn., 1969—70; mem. comm. screening com. Coun. Internat. Exch. Scholars, 1974—77, Pres.'s Coun. Heritage U., 1995—; bd. dirs. SIECUS, 1972—80, Jerusalem Found., 1977—2003, Marine Corps Hist. Found., 1979—82, 1989—95, Faculty for Continuing Med. Edn., 1983—86, Authors Guild Found., 2000—; bd. dirs., sec. Lotos Club Found., 2000—; mem. Dana Reed Prize com. Harvard U., 1947—2000, mem. com. Class of 1944, 1943—. With AUS, 1943—46. Recipient Benjamin Franklin Gold medal for pub. svc. Woman's Home Companion, 1955, Page One award Newspaper Guild N.Y., 1965, Sidney Hillman Found. award, 1965, National Headliners award, 1967, Overseas Press Club award, 1969, citation for excellence, 1971, Disting. Svc. award Marine Corps Combat Corrs. Assn., 1978, 99, Nat. Jewish Book award, 1983, Disting. Svc. award Marine Corps Hist. Found., 1996, Gen. O.P. Smith award Marine Corps Heritage Found., 1999. Mem.: PEN, Nat. Press Club (Washington), Fgn. Editors Group (chmn. 1970—71), Am. Hist. Assn., Soc. Mil. History, Authors Guild, Lotos Club (bd. dirs. 1988—90, pres. 1991—94, bd. dirs. 1994—2002, historian), Harvard Club (N.Y.C.), The Century Assn., Overseas Press Club (gov. 1975—79), Sigma Delta Chi (nat. freedom of info. com. 1964, 1971). Home: 945 5th Ave New York NY 10021-2666 also: 157 Jerusalem Rd Tyringham MA 01264 E-mail: jrmedit@att.net.

MOSKIN, MORTON, lawyer, director; b. NYC, Mar. 28, 1927; s. Barnett and Sonia (Burr) M.; m. Rita Lee Goldberg, June 15, 1952; children: Tina, Ilene, Jonathan. BA, Pa. State Coll., 1947; LLB, Cornell U., 1950. Assoc. White & Case, NYC, 1950—61, ptnr., 1962—94, cons., 1995—. Chmn. exec. com. Mallinckrodt, Inc. (formerly IMCERA, previously Internat. Minerals and Chem. Corp.), St. Louis, 1988-91, chmn. corp. governance com., 1993-97; sec. BT Mortgage Investors, Garden City, NY, 1975-82; bd. dirs. NY County Lawyers' Assn. Found., Inc., 2004, 05, 06. Author (with E. Carolan Berkley): Third Party Legal Opinions, 2005; editor (with Field): New York and Delaware Business Entities: Choice, Formation, Operation, Financing, Acquisitions, 1997, Transactional Lawyer's Deskbook: Advising Business Entities, 2001; editor: Commercial Contracts: Strategies for Drafting and Negotiating, 2002. Bd. dirs. Fedn. Employment and Guidance Svcs.; bd. dirs., pres. Henry M. Blackmer Found., N.Y.C.; bd. dirs. Achievement Found., Stamford, Conn., pres., 1988-94; bd. dirs. Jewish Cmty. Svcs. L.I., 1974-93, pres., 1984-87. Fellow Am. Bar Found.; mem. ABA, NY County Lawyers Assn. (bd. dirs. 1981-86, 99-02, 04, 05, 06), N.Y. County Lawyers Assn. Found. Inc. (bd. dirs. 2004-06), Norfolk (Conn.) Country Club, Cornell Club. Home: 1160 Park Ave Apt 15B New York NY 10128-1212 Office: White & Case 1155 Ave of Americas New York NY 10036-2711 Business E-Mail: mmoskin@whitecase.com.

MOSKOVITZ, DUSTIN AARON, Internet company executive, entrepreneur, application developer; b. May 22, 1984; s. Richard A. Moskovitz and Nancy Siegel. Econ. major, Harvard U., 2002—04. Co-founder & v.p. engring. Facebook, Inc., Palo Alto, Calif., 2004—08. Achievements include development of one of the most widely used networking websites among college and high school students with over 11 million users throughout the US, Canada and Europe; the ninth most highly trafficked website in US. Office: Facebook Inc 151 University Ave Ste 200 Palo Alto CA 94301-1675

MOSKOW, MICHAEL HAROLD, retired bank executive; b. Paterson, NJ, Jan. 7, 1938; s. Jacob and Sylvia (Edelstein) M.; m. Constance Bain, Dec. 18, 1966 (dec.); children: Robert Bain, Eliot Marc, Lisa Danielle; m. Suzanne Kopp Feb. 9, 2008. AB, Lafayette Coll., Easton, Pa., 1959; MA in Econs., U. Pa., 1962, PhD, 1965; degree (hon.), Depaul U., Dominican U., Lafayette Coll., Lewis U. Instr. econs. Lafayette Coll., 1964—65; asst. prof. mgmt. Drexel Inst. Tech., Phila., 1963-64, 65-67; assoc. prof. econs., dir. Bus. Econ. and Bus. Research, Temple U., Phila., 1967-69; sr. staff economist Coun. Econ. Advisers The White House, Washington, 1969-70; exec. dir. Constrn. Industry Collective Bargaining Commn., 1970-71; dep. under sec. US Dept. Labor, 1971-72, asst. sec. for policy, evaluation & research, 1972-73, under sec., 1976-77; asst. sec. for policy devel. and research US Dept. Housing & Urban Devel., 1973-75; dir. Council on Wage and Price Stability, 1975-76; cons. Com. for Econ. Devel., 1977; dir. corp. devel. and planning Esmark, Inc., 1977-78, v.p. corp. devel. and planning, 1978-80; exec. v.p. Estronics, Inc. div. Esmark, Inc., 1980-82; pres. Velsicol Chem. Corp. div. N.W. Industries, Inc., Chgo., 1982-84; v.p. corp. devel. Dart & Kraft, Inc., Northbrook, Ill., 1985-86; v.p. strategy and bus. devel. Premark Internat. Inc. (spinoff from Dart & Kraft), Deerfield, 1986-90; dep. US Trade Rep. Exec. Office of the Pres., Washington, 1991-93; prof. strategy & internat mgmt. Northwestern U. Kellogg Grad. Sch. Mgmt., Evanston, Ill., 1993-94; pres. Fed. Res. Bank Chgo., 1994—2007; vice chmn. sr. fellow Chgo. Coun. on Global Affairs, 2007—. Bd. mem. Discover Fin. Svcs. 2007-, Northern Funds 2007-, Diamond Mgmt. & Tech. Consultants Inc. 2008-; bd. dirs. Commonwealth Edison Co., 2008-, Taylor Capital Group, Inc., 2008-. Author: Teachers and Unions, 1966, Labor Relations in the Performing Arts: An Introductory Survey, 1970; co-author: Collective Negotiations for Teachers, 1966, Collective Bargaining in Public Employment, 1970, Strategic Planning in Business and Government, 1978; co-editor: Readings on Collective Negotiations in Public Education, 1967, Employment Relations in Higher Education, 1969, Women and Work, 1987; contbr. articles to profl. jours. Bd. trustees Lafayette Coll; mem. Coun. Foreign Location; bd. dirs. Chgo. Coun. Global Affairs, Northwestern Meml. Found., World Bus. Chgo., Chicagoland C. of C., Chgo. Metropolis 2020, Civic Consulting Alliance; deans adv. bd. Kellogg Grad. Sch. Mgmt.; chmn. Japan Am. Soc. Chgo.; mem. governing bd. Ill. Coun. Econ. Edn.; 1st lt. AUS, 1959-60. Fellow Nat. Acad. Pub. Adnminstrn.; mem. Indsl. Rels. Rsch. Assn. (pres. 1987), Nat. Bur. Econ. Rsch. (chmn. 2002-05), Comml. Club Chgo. (civic com.), Econs. Club Chgo. (chmn. 2001-03). Office Phone: 312-821-6851.

MOSKOWITZ, DAVID K., lawyer; b. Glen Burnie, Md., Apr. 24, 1958; m. Hallie A. Moskowitz. BA summa cum laude, Western Md. College, 1980; JD with honors, George Washington U., 1983. Corp. counsel MDC Holdings Inc., 1986—90; with Echostar Communications, Englewood, Colo., 1990, exec. v.p., gen. counsel, sec., dir. Mem.: Am. Corp. Counsel Assn., Denver Bar Assn., Colo. Bar Assn., ABA. Office: Echostar Communications 9601 S Meridan Blvd Englewood CO 80112 Home: 7 Waterside Ter Englewood CO 80113-4141 Office Phone: 303-723-1040. Office Fax: 303-723-1699. Business E-Mail: david.moskowitz@echostar.com.

MOSKOWITZ, ELLEN HOPE, lawyer; b. NYC, Apr. 15, 1958; AB, Princeton U., 1980; JD, Columbia U., 1986. Bar: N.Y. 1987, U.S. Supreme Ct. 1996. Assoc. Webster & Sheffield, NYC, 1986-90; counsel N.Y. State Task Force on Life and the Law, NYC, 1990-92; assoc. for law The Hastings Ctr., Briarcliff Manor, N.Y., 1992-97; assoc. Proskauer Rose, LLP, NYC, 1997—2000, sr. counsel, 2000—. Office: Proskauer Rose LLP 1585 Broadway Fl 27 New York NY 10036-8299 Office Phone: 212-969-3232. Personal E-mail: emoskowitz@proskauer.com.

MOSKOWITZ, EVA S., educational association administrator; b. Mar. 4, 1964; m. Eric Grannis; children: Culver, Dillon, Hannah. BA, U. Pa.; PhD in Am. History, Johns Hopkins U. Mem. NYC Coun. from Dist. 4, 1999—2005, chairwomen Coun. Edn. Com., 2002—05; CEO Success Charter Network, NYC, 2006—. Prof. history Vanderbilt U., U. Va., CUNY; exec. dir. ReadNet; dir. pub. affairs, civics tchr. Prep for Prep. Author: In Therapy We Trust: America's Obsession with Self-Fulfillment, 2001. Democrat. Office: Harlem Success Acad 34 W 118th St, 2nd Fl New York NY 10026 Office Phone: 646-277-7170. Office Fax: 212-457-5659.*

MOSKOWITZ, HERBERT, management educator; b. Paterson, NJ, May 26, 1935; s. David and Ruth (Abrams) Moskowitz; m. Heather Mary Lesgnier, Feb. 25, 1968; children: Tobias, Rebecca, Jonas. BS in Mech. Engring., Newark Coll. Engring., 1956; MBA, U.S. Internat. U., 1964; PhD, UCLA, 1970. Rsch. engr. GE, 1956-60; systems design engr. Gen. Dynamics Convair, San Diego, 1960-65; asst. prof. Purdue U., West Lafayette, Ind., 1970-75, assoc. prof., 1975-79, prof., 1979-85, Disting. prof. mfg. mgmt., 1985-87, James B. Henderson Disting. prof., 1987-91, dir. Dauch Ctr. Mgmt. Mfg. Enterprises, 1991—2005, Lewis B. Cullman Disting. prof. mfg. mgmt., 1991—. Cons. AT&T, Inland Steel Co.; adv. panelist NSF, 1990—. Author: Management Science and Statistics Texts, 1975—90; assoc. editor Decision Scis. Jour., 1984—90, Jour. Behavioral Decision Making, 1986—90; contbr. articles to jours. in field. Bd. dirs. Sons of Abraham Synagogue, Lafayette; mem. Lafayette Klezmorem, 1973—. Capt. USAF, 1956—60. Recipient Disting. Doctoral Student award, UCLA Alumni Assn., 1969—70; Fulbright Rsch. scholar, 1985—86. Fellow: Decision Scis. Inst. (sec. 1985—87, v.p. 1978—80); mem.: Ops. Rsch. Soc. Am./Inst. Mgmt. Sci. (liaison officer 1977—, panelist, advisor NSF and Fulbright Scholar program 1993—), Pi Tau Sigma, Tau Beta Pi. Jewish. Avocations: jewish music, tennis. Home: 1430 N Salisbury St West Lafayette IN 47906-2420 Office: Purdue Univ Krannert Sch Mgmt 100 S Grant St West Lafayette IN 47907-2076 Business E-Mail: herbm@purdue.edu.

MOSKOWITZ, JAY, health science association administrator, educator, dean; b. NYC, Jan. 9, 1943; s. Murray and Helene Moskowitz; m. Joanne Cathy Schindelheim, Dec. 27, 1970; children: Michael Bradley, Andrew Cory. BS, Queens Coll., 1964; postgrad., CUNY, 1965; PhD, Brown U., 1969. From research assoc. in pharmacology to dep. dir. NIH, Bethesda, Md., 1969—93, dep. dir. sci. policy and tech. transfer, prin. dep. dir., 1993; with Nat. Heart, Lung and Blood Inst., Bethesda, 1976—86; acting dir. Nat. Inst. Deafness and Other Comm. Disorders, Bethesda, 1988—90, dep. dir., 1993—95; sr. assoc. dean rsch. devel., prof. pub. health scis. Wake Forest U. Sch. Medicine, Winston-Salem, NC, 1995—2001, sr. assoc. dean, 1997—2001; assoc. v.p. health sci. rsch. Pa. State U., University Park, 2002—, vice dean rsch. coll. medicine, 2002—07, prof. medicine, 2002—07; chief sci. officer Milton Hershey Med. Ctr., Pa., 2004—07; pres., CEO Health Scis. SC, Columbia, 2007—; prof. medicine Med. U. SC, 2007—; prof. pub. health U. SC, 2007—; adj. prof. Clemson U. Contbr. articles to profl. jours. Served to lt. comdr. USPHS. Recipient Meritorious award William A. Jump Meml. Found., 1977, Dir.'s award NIH, 1978, Superior Svc. award USPHS, 1980, performance awards Sr. Exec. Svc., Presdl. Meritorious Exch. Rank award 1989, Disting. Svc. award HHS, 1991, Disting. Svc. award Nat. Inst. on Deafness and Other Comm. Disorders, 1994. Mem. AAAS, Soc. Exptl. Biology and Medicine, N.C. Inst. Medicine. Jewish. Home: 1760 Adeline Dr Mechanicsburg PA 17050 Office: 1320 Main St Ste 625 Columbia SC 29201 Home Phone: 717-732-1874; Office Phone: 803-576-5902. Business E-Mail: jmoskowitz@healthsciencesc.org.

MOSKOWITZ, JEDD I., legislative staff member; b. Bronx, NY, Apr. 13, 1951; m. Wendy Beckerman, May 21, 1983. BA, Queens Coll., CUNY, Flushing, 1973. Exec. asst. for Senator Gary L. Ackerman, NY State Senate, 1979—83; adminstrv. asst. for Rep. Gary L. Ackerman, US House of Reps., 1983—2000, chief of staff, 2000—. Mem.: House Chiefs of Staff Assn. (mem. region 10 reps.). Office: Office of Congressman Gary L Ackerman 2243 Rayburn House Office Bldg Washington DC 20515 Office Phone: 202-225-2601. Business E-Mail: jedd.moskowitz@mail.house.gov.*

MOSKOWITZ, JOEL M., psychologist, researcher; b. July 16, 1948; married. BA, Rutgers Coll., New Brunswick, 1970; MA, U. Calif., Santa Barbara, 1972, PhD, 1976. Assoc. rsch. scientist Sys. Devel. Corp., Santa Monica, Calif., 1977—88; dir. rsch. Pacific Inst. Rsch. and Evaluation, Napa, Calif., 1978—83; assoc. dir. rsch. Prevention Rsch. Ctr., Berkeley, Calif., 1983—86; assoc. rsch. psychologist Sch. Pub. Health, U. Calif., Berkeley, 1986—95, lectr., 1987—89, adj. assoc. prof., 1989—90, rsch. psychologist, 1995—; assoc. dir. Ctr. Family and Cmty. Health, U. Calif., Berkeley, 1993—98, dir., 1998—. Contbr. articles to numerous peer-review publn. Mem.: APHA, Am. Evaluation Assn., Pi Mu Epsilon. Office: Univ of California Berkeley 50 Univ Hall Berkeley CA 94720-7360

MOSKOWITZ, RANDI ZUCKER, nurse; b. NYC, Oct. 19, 1948; d. Seymour and Gertrude (Levy) Zucker; m. Marc N. Moskowitz, July 11, 1976. RN, Jewish Hosp. and Med. Ctr., 1969; BA, Marymount Manhattan Coll., 1975; MS, Hunter Coll., 1979; MBA, Columbia U., 1990. Gen. staff nurse neurosurgery unit N.Y. Hosp., NYC, 1969—71, sr. staff nurse recovery rm., 1971—76, nurse coord. utilization rev., 1976—79; health educator Office of Cancer Commn. Meml. Sloan-Kettering Cancer Ctr., NYC, 1979—81; adminstrv. nurse oncologist Bklyn. Cmty. Hosp. and Meth. Hosp., 1981—83, grants coord. radiotherapy dept., 1983—86; adminstr. Ambulatory Oncology Ctr. Columbia-Presbyn. Med. Ctr., NYC, 1986—89; adminstr. Surg. Day Hosp., 1990—98; mgr. Oncology Svcs., St. Vincent Cath. Med. Ctrs., Jamaica, NY, 1999—2006; adminstr. pediat. oncology Columbia U. Med. Ctr., NYC, 2006—. Masters prof. oncology Columbia U. Sch. Nursing. Co-editor Oncology Nursing: Advances, Treatments and Trends into the Twenty-first Century; contbr. articles to profl. jours. Mem. N.Y. Assn. Ambulatory Care, Oncology Nursing Soc. (sec. N.Y.C. chpt. 1983-87, pres. 1988-89). Home: 446 E 86th St Apt 5F New York NY 10028-6474 Office: Columbia Univ Med Ctr 161 Ft Washington Ave New York NY 10032 Office Phone: 212-342-3455. Personal E-mail: rm2505@columbia.edu.

MOSKOWITZ, ROBERT LAWRENCE, biology professor; b. Bklyn., Feb. 20, 1949; s. Leo Jacob Moskowitz and Ethel Sara Moskowitz-Sherman; m. Donna C. Axelrod, Aug. 23, 1992; children: Hannah S. Chornock, Danielle J. Chornock; m. Deborah A. Schwartz, June 29, 1973 (div. Feb. 20, 1988); children: Meir Y., Jillian Eve, Tamara T. BSc, SUNY, New Paltz, 1971; MSc, LI U. - Zeckendorf Campus, Bklyn., 1976; EdD, Rugers U., Grad. Sch. Edn., NB, NJ, 1984. Registered cardiovasc. technologist Nat. Bd. Cardiopulmonary & Cardiovasc. Tech., 1978, sonographer Am. Registry Diagnostic Med. Sonographers, 1978. Copy editor, dept. sci. jours. Academic Press, NYC, 1971; cardiovasc. technologist, dept. Cardiology Maimonides Med. Ctr., Bklyn., 1971—76; program dir., cardiovasc. tech. C.C. Phila., 1976—88, assoc. prof., dept biology, 1988—. Biol. writer Franklyn Inst. Rsch. Lab., Phila., 1977; coord. echocardiographic svcs. Cooper Med. Ctr., Amden, NJ, 1977—79; ultrasound tech. specialist, echocardiography Met. Hosp. Cardiology, Phila., 1979—81; instrnl. devel. specialist Wash. Sch. Nuc. Medicine Tech., Turnersville, NJ, 1980—81; ednl. cons. Diagnostic Sonics, Inc., 1983—84. Contbr. articles to profl. jours. Named Outstanding Young Men America, US Jacees, 1984. Office: CC Phila 1700 Spring Garden St Philadelphia PA 19130 Office Fax: 215-751-8937.

MOSKOWITZ, ROLAND WALLACE, internist; b. Shamokin, Pa., Nov. 3, 1929; MD, Temple U., 1953. Intern Temple U. Hosp., Phila., 1953-54; fellow in internal medicine Mayo Clinic, Rochester, Minn., 1954-55, 57-60; mem. staff U. Hosps. Cleve.; prof. medicine Case Western Res. U. Sch. Medicine, Cleve. Mem.: ACR, Alpha Omega Alpha. Office: Parkway Med Ctr 3609 Park East Dr STe 307N Beachwood OH 44122

MOSKOWITZ, STANLEY ADAM, finance company executive; b. NYC, June 8, 1956; s. Sol and Kate (Mermelstein) M.; m. Eve Kronenberger, Sept. 20, 1981 (div Apr. 2003); children: Alana, Kate. BA, Queens Coll., 1978; MBA in Fin., St. John's U., 1980. Sr. credit analyst Mfrs. Hanover Leasing Corp., NYC, 1979-81; gen. ptnr. Exec. Leasing Co., NYC, 1981-83; pres. Execulease Corp., Elmont, NY, 1983-97; pres., CEO QuesTech Fin. LLC, Danbury, Conn., 1998—2007, Petroleum & Franchise Capital LLC, Danbury, 2007—. Treas. UJA/Fedn. of Greenwich, Conn., 1997-2003. Named finalist, Ernst & Young Entrepreneur of Yr., 2001. Mem. Ea. Assn. Equipment Lessors (chmn. pub. rels. 1985-90, bd. dirs. 1988-92, Meretorious Svc. award 1986-87, chmn. ethics com. 1991-92), Omicron Delta Epsilon, ADL (regional bd. mem. 2008-). Republican. Jewish. Avocations: reading, bicycling. Office: Petroleum & Franchise Capital LLC 33 Mill Plain Rd Danbury CT 06811-6101 Office Phone: 203-778-1000. E-mail: sammy@qtfc.com.

MOSKUS, JERRY RAY, retired academic administrator; b. Springfield, Ill., Dec. 10, 1942; s. Raymond Charles and Jean (Riley) M.; children: Elizabeth, Jane. BS in English, Ill. State U., 1965, MS in English, 1968, PhD in Edn. Adminstrn., 1983. Tchr. English Saybrook (Ill.) Arrowsmith High Sch., 1966-69; instr. Lincoln Land CC, Springfield, 1969-71, asst. to pres., 1971-73, dir. rsch., 1973-75, dean, 1975-84, v.p. acad. svcs., 1984-85; exec. v.p. Des Moines Area CC, Ankeny, Iowa, 1985-90; pres. Lane CC, Eugene, Oreg., 1990—2001, Metro. CC, Omaha, 2001—05; ret. Mem. Am. Assn. C.C.s (bd. dir. 1999-2001), League for Innovation, Phi Delta Kappa, Sigma Tau Delta. Home: 1100 County Rd P15 Arlington NE 68002-5621 Business E-Mail: jmoskus@gmail.com.

MOSLER, BRUCE ELLIOT, real estate company executive; b. NYC, Oct. 16, 1957; s. John and Sheila Sanders Mosler; m. Wendy Beth Fass, Aug. 15, 1981. BA in History, Duke U., 1980. Salesman comml. leasing divsn. Newmark & Co.; exec. v.p. Cushman & Wakefield, Inc., NYC, pres. U.S. ops., 2000—05, pres., CEO, 2005—. Bd. mem. Modell Found., Urban Tech.; mem. bd. govs., exec. com. Real Estate Bd. N.Y.; mem. profl. svcs. adv. coun. Lower Manhattan Devel. Corp. Capital campaign com. Am. Cancer Soc.; vice chmn. Intrepid Sea, Air and Space Mus.; bd. mem. Fisher Ctr. Alzheimer's Rsch. Found., Fuqua Sch. Bus., Duke U., Bowery Residents Com., Intrepid Mus. Found., Achilles Track Club, Kingsbrook Hosp., Partnership for the City of NY. Recipient Humanitarian award, Jeffrey M. Modell Found., 1996, NY Ten award, Exec. Coun. NY, 2004; named Property Svcs. Exec. of Yr., Comml. Property News, 2002, Brokerage Exec. of Yr., 2004; named one of 40 Under 40, Crain's N.Y. Bus., 1994. Mem.: Real Estate Bd. NY (mem. exec. com., Deal of Yr. award 1998, 1999, Kenneth R. Gerrety Humanitarian award 2003, Louis Smadbeck Broker Recognition award 2008), NY Hist. Soc. (bd. mem.). Office: Cushman & Wakefield Inc 51 W 52nd St New York NY 10019-6178 Office Phone: 212-841-7500. Office Fax: 212-841-7767.

MOSLEY, GREGG ALLEN, microbiologist; b. Kalispell, Mont., Apr. 9, 1947; s. Shirley Joan Kennedy and Oliver Mosley; m. Joy Bennett Farrell, July 14, 2001; 1 child, Graham Whitney. BS in Microbiology, U. Mont., Missoula, 1969, MS, 1972. Bacteriologist Missoula City-County Health Dept., 1969—70; microbiologist Infectious Disease Ctr., Missoula, 1970—71; chemist U. Mont., 1972—78; dir. labs. Skyland Sci. Svcs. Inc., Belgrade, Mont., 1978—84, dir. quality assurance, 1984—86; cons. J.R. Gillis Assocs., Belgrade, 1986—88; pres. Biotest Labs. Inc., Mpls., 1988—. Lead instr., indsl. sterilization Assn. Advancement Med. Instrumentation, Arlington, Va., 2001—, co-chair biol. indicator com., 2002—, co-chair moist heat sterilization com., 2004—; expert, biol. indicators Internat. Stds. Orgn., Geneva, 2002—, expert, moist heat sterilization, 2004—. Author: (math. formulae) Equations of Mosley, Gillis and Whitborne. Mem.: Assn. Advancement Med. Instrumentation (bd. dirs. 2003—06). Avocations: fishing, hiking, canoeing, hunting. Office: Biotest Labs Inc 8990 Springbrook Dr NW Ste 100 Minneapolis MN 55433 Office Fax: 763-785-9054. Business E-Mail: gmosley@biotestlabs.com.

MOSLEY, MARY NELL H., retired elementary school educator; b. Bowdon, Ga., June 27, 1927; d. Lee Alexander and Lizzie Annie (Kight) Hunt; m. Loye Edmon Harrell (dec.); children: Dennis Calvin Harrell, Joel Vincent Harrell; m. John Wesley Mosley, July 14, 1967. BS, Rust Coll., Holly Springs, Miss., 1953, HHD (hon.), 2005; MEd, Miss. State U., Starkville, 1978. EdS Miss. State U., 1978. Tchr. Oktibbeha County Sch., Sturgis, Miss., 1950—52, Starkville, 1955—62, prin., 1952—55; tchr. Starkville Pub. Sch., 1962—70, 1975—84, Winona Pub. Sch., Miss., 1970—75; ret., 1984. Chairperson UNICEF, Starkville. Recipient Emma Elzy award, United Meth. Ch., 2001; named Honoree of the Yr., NAACP, Alumni of the Yr., Rust Coll., 1972, Tchr. of the Yr., Starkville Pub. Sch., 1984. Mem.: Min. Wives Oktibbeha County (sec. S.E. NC), Zeta Phi Beta. Methodist. Avocations: travel, reading, gardening, cooking. Home: 72 Chickasaw Dr Starkville MS 39759

MOSLEY, SHANE, boxer; b. Lynwood, Calif., Sept. 7, 1971; m. Jin Mosley (separated 2009); children: Shane Jr., Norman, Najee, Tai, Mee-Yon Jinae. Profl. boxer, 1993—. Winner internat. title vs. Philip Holiday by unanimous decision, lightweight divsn. Internat. Boxing Fedn., 1997, winner internat. title def. vs. Manuel Gomez by knockout, lightweight divsn., 97, winner internat. title def. vs. Demetrio Ceballos by tech. knockout, lightweight divsn., 98, winner internat. title def. vs. John John Molina by tech. knockout, lightweight divsn., 98, winner internat. title def. vs. Wilfredo Ruiz by knockout, lightweight divsn., 98, winner internat. title def. vs. Eduardo Bartolome Morales by tech. knockout, lightweight divsn., 98, winner internat. title def. vs. Jesse James Leija by tech. knockout, lightweight divsn., 98, winner internat. title def. vs. Golden Johnson by knockout, lightweight divsn., 99, winner internat. title def. vs. John Brown by tech. knockout, lightweight divsn., 99; winner internat. title vs. Oscar de la Hoya by split decision, welterweight divsn. Internat. Boxing Assn., 2000; winner world title vs. Oscar de la Hoya by split decision, welterweight divsn. World Boxing Coun., 2000, winner world title def. vs. Antonio Diaz by tech. knockout, welterweight divsn., 00, winner world title def. vs. Shannan Taylor by tech. knockout, welterweight divsn., 01, winner world title def. vs. Adrian Stone by knockout, welterweight divsn., 01, winner world title vs. Oscar de la Hoya by unanimous decision, light middleweight divsn., 03, World Boxing Assn., 2003; winner internat. title vs. Oscar de la Hoya by unanimous decision, light middleweight divsn. Internat. Boxing Assn., 2003; winner world title vs. Luis Collazo by unanimous decision, welterweight divsn. World Boxing Coun., 2007; winner inter-continental title vs. Ricardo Mayorga by knock out, light middleweight divsn. World Boxing Assn., 2008, winner world title vs. Antonio Margarito by tech. knock out, welterweight divsn., 09. Achievements include being the only boxer to beat Oscar de la Hoya twice. Mailing: c/o Sugar Shane Inc PO Box 8318 La Verne CA 91750*

MOSLEY, TIMOTHY Z. See TIMBALAND

MOSLEY, WALTER ELLIS, writer; b. LA, Jan. 12, 1952; s. LeRoy and Ella Mosley; m. Joy Kellman, 1987 (div.) Student, Goddard Coll., 1971; BA, Johnson State Coll., 1977; PhD (hon.), City Coll., CUNY. Artist in residence Africana Studies Inst., NYU, NYC, 1996—. Bd. dir. Full Frame Documentary Film Festival. Author: (fiction) Devil in a Blue Dress, 1990 (Shamus award Private Eye Writers America 1990, Edgar award nomination Mystery Writers Am. 1990), A Red Death, 1991, White Butterfly, 1992, Black Betty, 1994, RL's Dream, 1995, A Little Yellow Dog, 1996, Gone Fishin', 1997, Always Outnumbered, Always Outgunned: The Socrates Fortlow Stories, 1998, Blue Light, 1998, Walkin' the Dog, 1999, Fearless Jones: A Novel, 2001, Futureland: Nine Stories of an Imminent Future, 2001, Bad Boy Brawley Brown, 2002, Six Easy Pieces, 2003, Fear Itself: A Mystery, 2003, The Man in My Basement, 2004, Little Scarlet, 2004, Cinnamon Kiss, 2005, The Wave, 2005, Fortunate Son: A Novel, 2006, Fear of the Dark, 2006, Killing Johnny Fry: A Sexistential Novel, 2006, Blonde Faith, 2007 (NAACP Image award for Outstanding Literary Work-Fiction, 2008), Diablerie: A Novel, 2007, The Right Mistake: The Further Philosophical Investigations of Socrates Fortlow, 2008, The Tempest Tales, 2008, The Long Fall, 2009; (non-fiction) Workin' on the Chain Gang: Shaking Off the Dead Hand of History, 2000, What Next: An African American Initiative Toward World Peace, 2003, Life Out of Context: Which Includes a Proposal for the Non-violent Takeover of the House of Representatives, 2006, This Year You Write Your Novel, 2007; (children's books) 47, 2005; writer, prodr. (films) Devil in a Blue Dress, 1995. Recipient John Creasey Meml. award, Black Caucus of the Am. Library Assn. Literary award, O. Henry award, 1996, Anisfield-Wolf Book award, 1996, TransAfrican Internat. Literary prize, 1998, Risktaker award Sundance Inst., 2004, PEN America's Lifetime Achievement award, 2004, Carl Brandon Soc. Parallax award, 2006. Mem.: Mystery Writers Am. (past pres.), Manhattan Theater Club, Poetry Soc. Am. (bd. dir.), Nat. Book Found., TransAfrica (bd. dir.). Office: c/o Gloria Loomis Watkins Loomis Agy #1 133 East 35th St New York NY 10016*

MOSMAN, MICHAEL W., federal judge, former prosecutor; b. Eugene, Ore. BA, Utah State U., 1981; JD, Brigham Young U., 1984. Law clk. U.S. Ct. Appeals, 1984—85, U.S. Supreme Ct., 1985—86; assoc. Miller, Nash, Portland, Oreg., 1986—88; asst. U.S. atty. Dist. Oreg. U.S. Dept. Justice, 1988—2001, U.S. atty. Dist. Oreg., 2001—03; judge U.S. Dist. Ct., Oreg., 2003—. Office: 1000 SW 3rd Ave Portland OR 97204-2902

MOSORA-STAN, FLORENTINA IOANA, physics professor; b. Cluj, Romania, Jan. 7, 1940; arrived in Belgium, 1968; d. Oprea and Cornelia (Stanescu) M.; m. Stephan Stan, Jan. 22, 1977; 1 child, Guy Bart. B in Biol. Sci. with highest distinction, U. Bucharest, Romania, 1961, B in Phys. Sci. with highest distinction, 1967, PhD in Biophysics cum laude, 1971. Cert. biologist and physicist. Rsch. fellow U. Bucharest, 1967-71, U. Liege, Belgium, 1971-74, maitre de conferences, 1974-75; head rsch. fellow Inst. Physics, U. Liege, Belgium, 1975-79, lectr., 1979-88, prof., 1988—. Author: Elements of General Physics and Biophysics, vol. 1, 1974, vol. 2, 1975, Introduction to the Mechanics of Physiologic Fluids, 1984-85, Mechanics of Microcirculation, 1990: Editor: Biomechanical Transport Processes, 1991. Mem. European Med. Rsch. Coun. Devel. of Resch. in Nutrition and Stable Isotopes, 1991—. Decorated officer Ordre of Leopold II, (Belgium), 1981, comdr. Ordre de la Couronne (Belgium, 1992; recipient Agathon de Potter prize Royal Acad. Belgium, 1982. Mem. Stareso Oceanographic Rsch. Calvi (sci. coun. 1987—), Isotopes Stables (v.p. 1987—), Inst. Recherches Marines et Interactions Air-Mer (pres. 1989—), Hemo Liege (founder), Belgian Soc. Biophysics, Internat. Soc. Rsch. Circulation and Environ. Diseases, N.Y. Acad. Scis. Roman Catholic. Avocations: swimming, gymnastics. Home: Residence Verdi Av Blonden 7 4000 Liège Belgium Office: U Liege Inst Physics B5 4000 Liège Belgium

MOSQUEDA-PONCE, THERESE, counselor, professor; m. Rudy Ponce, July 1, 1989. PhD, US Internat. U., San Diego, 1994. Counselor NOCCCD- Cypress Coll., Calif., 1979—. Recipient Golden Apple Award, Hispanic Edn. Endowment Fund, 1999. Roman Catholic. Avocations: travel, swimming, dance, piano, walking. Office: Cypress Coll 9200 Valley View St Cypress CA 90630

MOSS, ADAM, editor-in-chief; b. Bklyn., May 6, 1957; s. Paul and Abigail (Wender) Moss. BA, Oberlin Coll., Ohio, 1979. Assoc. editor Rolling Stone Collected Papers, NYC, 1979-81; from asst. editor to dep. editor Esquire mag. Hearst Corp., NYC, 1981-87; editor-in-chief 7 Days mag. NY Media, 1987-90; cons. editor NY Times, 1991—93, assoc. mng. editor, 2002—03, asst. mng. editor, features, 2003—04; editl. dir. NY Times Mag., 1993—98, editor, 1998—2003; editor-in-chief New York mag., 2004—. Named Editor of Yr., Advt. Age mag., 2001, 2007. Mem.: Am. Soc. Mag. Editors (sec. 2007—08, 5 Nat. Mag. awards for Gen. Excellence, Profile Writing, Mag. Sect, Design, and Interactive Feature 2007, Nat. Mag. award for Leisure Interests 2008). Office: NY Media 75 Varick St New York NY 10013 Office Phone: 212-508-0700.*

MOSS, AMBLER HOLMES, JR., lawyer, educator, former ambassador; b. Balt., Sept. 1, 1937; s. Ambler Holmes and Dorothea Dandridge (Williams) M.; m. Serena Welles, May 6, 1972; children: Ambler H., Benjamin Sumner, Serena Montserrat, Nicholas George Oliver. BA, Yale U., 1960; JD, George Washington U., 1970. Bar: D.C., Fla. Joined Fgn. Svc., Dept. State, 1964; vice consul Barcelona, 1964—66; adviser U.S. del. to OAS, 1966—69; Spanish desk officer Dept. State, Washington, 1968—70; assoc. Coudert Bros., Washington, 1971—73, resident atty. Brussels, 1973—76; mem. U.S. Negotiating Team for Panama Canal treaties, 1977; dep. asst. Sec. of State, Washington, 1977—78; amb. to Panama Am. Embassy, Panama City, 1978—82; of counsel Greenberg, Traurig, LLP, Miami, 1982—87, 1995—; prof. U. Miami, Fla., 1984—, dean Grad. Sch. Internat. Studies, 1984—94. Bd. dirs. Espirito Santo Bank of Fla., Caucedo Investments Inc. Mem. Panama Canal Consultative Com., 1995-2000. With USN, 1960-64. Mem. ABA, Am. Soc. Internat. Law, Am. Fgn. Svc. Assn., Coun. Fgn. Rels., Am. Legion, Inter-Am. Dialogue (Washington), Navy League, Greater Miami C. of C. (gov. 1983-86), Royal Inst. Internat. Affairs (London), Internat. Inst. Strategic Studies (London), Army and Navy Club, Order of the Coif. Home: 5711 San Vicente St Coral Gables FL 33146-2724 Business E-Mail: ahmoss@miami.edu, mossa@gtlaw.com.

MOSS, ARTHUR HENSHEY, lawyer; b. Reading, Pa., July 26, 1930; s. John Arthur and Christine Bracken (Henshey) M.; m. E. Leslie Fritz, Feb. 1982; 1 child by previous marriage, John Arthur. AB, Williams Coll., 1952; JD, U. Pa., 1955. Bar: Pa. 1956. Assoc. Montgomery, McCracken, Walker & Rhoads, Phila., 1960-69, ptnr., 1969-2000, of counsel, 2000—. Editor U. Pa. Law Rev., 1953-55; contbr. articles to profl. jours. Pres. Wayne Civic Assn., 1964—65; commr. gen. assembly Presbyn. Ch. (U.S.A.), 1983; steward, deacon Wayne Presbyn. Ch., 1966—72, 1979—84, 1989—95, ruling elder, 1966—72, 1979—84, 1989—95, clk. of session, 1973—74, 1978—89, trustee, 1987—93, Presbytery of Phila., 1984, 1994—2001, treas., 1996—2001; chmn. Radnor-Haverford-Marple Sewer Authority, 1968—83; bd. dir. John Bartram Assn., 1987—2002, treas., 1989—2002, emeritus dir., 2002—; trustee Radnor Twp. Meml. Libr., 2001—. Lt. JAGC USN, 1956—60. Mem. Radnor Hist. Soc. (dir., sec. 1978-90), Broadacres Trouting Assn., Merion Golf Club. Home: 200 Walnut Ave Wayne PA 19087-3423 Office: Montgomery McCracken Walker & Rhoads 123 S Broad St Philadelphia PA 19109-1030 Home Phone: 610-688-0983; Office Phone: 215-772-1500.

MOSS, ARTHUR JAY, physician; b. White Plains, NY, June 21, 1931; s. Abraham Loeb and Ida (Bank) M.; m. Joy Folkman, June 23, 1957; children: Katherine, Deborah, David. BA, Yale U., 1953; MD, Harvard U., 1957. Resident Mass. Gen. Hosp., 1957-58, 60-61; fellow in cardiology med. ctr. U. Rochester, NY, 1961-65, from asst. to assoc. prof. sch. medicine and dentistry, 1966-71, clin. assoc. prof., 1971-82, clin. prof., 1982-91, prof. medicine, 1991—, dir. heart rsch. follow-up program med. ctr., 1971—. Mem. cardiology adv. com. Nat. Heart, Lung, and Blood Inst., NIH, 1980-82, chmn., 1982-84, mem. epidemiology and disease control study sect., 1998—. Author: Antiarrhythmic Agents, 1973; editor: Clinical Aspects of Life-threatening Arrhythmias, 1984, QT Prolongation and Ventricular Arrhythmias, 1992, Noninvasive Electrocardiology, 1995; editor-in-chief Ann. Noninvasive Electrocardiology, 1996—; mem. editl. bd. Am. Jour. Cardiology, 1988—, Jour. Am. Coll. Cardiology, 1997-2001, 2005— Lt. USNR, 1958—60. Mem.: Assn. Am. Physicians, Alpha Omega Alpha. Home: 581 Claybourne Rd Rochester NY 14618-1224 Office: Univ Rochester Med Ctr PO Box 653 Rochester NY 14642-8653 Home Phone: 585-244-3809; Office Phone: 585-275-5391. Business E-Mail: heartajm@heart.rochester.edu.

MOSS, BILL RALPH, lawyer; b. Amarillo, Tex., Sept. 27, 1950; s. Ralph Voniver and Virginia May (Atkins) M.; 1 child, Brandon Price. BS with honors, West Tex. A&M U., 1972, MA, 1974; JD, Baylor U., 1976; cert. regulatory studies program, Mich. State U., 1981. Bar: Tex. 1976, U.S. Dist. Ct. (no. dist.) Tex. 1976, U.S. Dist. Ct. (we. dist.) Tex. 2005, U.S. Tax Ct. 1979, U.S. Ct. Appeals (5th cir.) 1983. Briefing atty. Ct. Appeals 7th Supreme Jud. Dist. Tex., Amarillo, 1976-77; assoc. Culton, Morgan, Britain & White, Amarillo, 1977-80; hearings examiner Pub. Utility Commn. Tex., Austin, 1981-83; asst. gen. counsel State Bar Tex., Austin, 1983-87; founder, owner Price & Co. Publs., Austin, 1987-97; asst. gen. counsel Tex. Ethics Commn., Austin, 1997—2004; asst. atty. gen. antitrust and civil medicaid fraud div. Office Atty. Gen., Tex., 2004—. Instr., lectr. West Tex. State U., Canyon, Ea. N.Mex. U., Portales, 1977-80; spkr. in field. Active St. Matthew's Episcopal Ch.; election inspector State of Tex., 1998—. Mem. ABA (panel dir. & issues facing profession), Tex. Bar Assn., Nat. Orgn. Bar Counsel, Nat. Coun. Prescription Drug Programs, Internat. Platform Assn., Capitol of Tex. Rotary Club, Alpha Chi, Lambda Chi Alpha, Omicron Delta Epsilon, Phi Alpha Delta, Sigma Tau Delta, Pi Gamma Mu. Home: 506 Explorer St Lakeway TX 78734-3447 Office: Office of Atty Gen William P Clements Bldg 300 W 15th St 9th Fl Austin TX 78701 Business E-Mail: bill.moss@oag.state.tx.us.

MOSS, DOUGLAS G., professional sports team executive; children: Geoffrey, Brian, Kristen. Attended, Pace U. Gen. sales mgr. Cable Networks, NY, 1982—85; sr. v.p. sales Madison Square Garden Network (MSG), NYC, 1986—92, pres., 1992—94; pres., CEO Buffalo Sabres, 1994—96, Internat. Hockey League (IHL), 1998—2001; sr. v.p. bus. ops. Mighty Ducks of Anaheim; pres., COO, alt. gov. Phoenix Coyotes, 2002—. Gov. Arizona Sting. Pres., COO Coyotes Charities, 2002—. Office: Phoenix Coyotes Hockey Club 6751 N Sunset Blvd, #200 Glendale AZ 85305 Office Phone: 623-772-3200. E-mail: doug.moss@phoenixcoyotes.com.

MOSS, GARY CURTIS, lawyer; b. Taylorville, Ill., Feb. 17, 1944; s. William Clary and Sophronia Irene (McClellan) Moss; m. Judith K. Jones; children: Gary Curtis, Kristin Suzanne. BA, U. Ill., Champaign, 1966; JD, U. Iowa, 1969. Bar: Iowa 1969, Calif. 1970, US Dist. Ct. (ctrl. dist.) Calif. 1972, Nev. 1991, US Ct. Appeals (9th cir.) 1974, US Dist. Ct. (so. and no. dists.) Calif. 1981, US Dist. Ct. Nev. 1991. Assoc. O'Melveny & Myers, LA, 1969—75, Seyfarth, Shaw, Fairweather & Geraldson, 1975—78, ptnr., 1978—87; judge pro tem West LA Mcpl. Ct., 1981—83, Pasadena Mcpl. Ct., 1983—. Ptnr.-in-charge Las Vegas Office DLA Piper Rudnick Gary Cary. Mem.: ABA, LA County Bar Assn., State Bar Iowa, State Bar Calif. (hearing referee, arbitrator mandatory fee arbitrations), Athletic Club LA. Republican. Office: DLA Piper Rudnick Gray Cary Ste 400 3960 Howard Hughes Pkwy Las Vegas NV 89109-0993 Office Phone: 702-737-3433, 702-737-1612. Business E-Mail: gary.moss@piperrudnick.com.

MOSS, GERALD S., medical educator; b. Cleve., Mar. 4, 1935; s. Harry and Lillian (Alter) M.; m. Wilma Jabak, Sept. 1, 1957; children: William Alan, Robert Daniel, Sharon Lynn. BA, Ohio State U., 1956, MD cum laude, 1960. Diplomate Am. Bd. Surgery (apptd. assoc. examiner com. 1989); lic. Ill. Intern Mass. Gen. Hosp., Boston, 1960-61, resident, 1961-65; from asst. prof. to assoc. prof. dept. surgery Coll. Medicine U. Ill., Chgo., 1968-72, prof., 1973-77, 89—; prof. dept. surgery Pritzker Sch. Medicine U. Chgo., 1977-89; head dept. surgery U. Ill., Chgo., 1989; dean U. Ill. Coll. of Medicine, Chgo., 1989—2004. Tutor in surgery Manchester (Eng.) Royal Infirmary, 1964; asst. chief surgical svcs. VA West Side Hosp., Chgo., 1968-70; attending surgeon dept. surgery Cook County Hosp., Chgo. 1970-72, chmn. 1972-77; dir. surgical rsch. Hektoen Inst. for Med. Rsch., Cook County Hosp., 1972-77, Michael Reese Hosp. and Med. Ctr., Chgo., 1977-89, chmn. dept. surgery, 1977-89, chief svc. 1989, trustee, 1981, and numerous coms.; appointed to Nat. Rsch. Coun., NAS, 1966-68, Ad Hoc Subcom., NAE, 1970, Ad Hoc Study Sect., 1970, del. to Third Joint U.S-USSR Symposium, 1983, Blood Diseases and Resources Adv. Com., 1984-88, Planning Com. for discussing key blood problems, Nat. Heart and Lung Inst., 1987, chmn. Plasma and Plasma Products Com., 1979, bd. dirs., 1983, v.p., 1985, Ad Hoc Transition Com., Am. Blood Commn., 1989, Panel on Rsch. Opportunities, Office Naval Rsch. Program, 1987, exec. com., coord. com., Nat. Blood Edn. Program, 1988, Tech. Adv. Task Force Am. Hosp. Assn., 1988, chmn. review panel contract proposals, NIH, 1975, program project site visit, 1976, chmn. site-visit review group, 1977, adv. com. Blood Resources Work group, 1978, Planning Com. for Consensus, 1987, Small Bus. Innovation Rsch., 1988, Med. Rsch. Scv. Merit Review Bd. VA, 1978-81, Liaison Com. Graduate Med. Edn. AMA, 1979, and numerous other coms. for various med. organizations; cons. Nat. Heart and Lung Inst., Transfusion Medicine Acad. Awardees Program; vis. prof. Montefiore Med. Ctr. Bronx, N.Y., 1986, Ohio State U., 1988, U. N.Mex., Albuquerque, 1989, Seton Med. Ctr., Austin, Tex., 1990, U. Ill. Coll. Medicine, Peoria, 1991; guest lectr., participant numerous meetings, symposiums; cons. in field. Contbr. numerous articles to profl. jours., chpts. to books. With USN, 1965—68, Vietnam. Teaching fellow Harvard Med. Sch., 1962; recipient Stitt Lectr. award Assn. Mil. Surgeons U.S.A., 1981; grantee U.S. Navy, 1969-84, U.S. Army, 1971-74, 75-78, NIH, 1969, 83-84, Dept. Pub. Health, 1973, HEW, 1974-77, UpJohn, 1974, Northfield Labs. 1985-89. Fellow ACS (pre and postoperative care com. 1975-83, rep. Am. blood commn. 1977—, mem. various coms., speaker various symposiums), Am. Soc. Surgery Trauma; mem. Am. Surgical Assn. (rep. Nat. Soc. Med. Rsch. 1984-88), Am. Trauma Soc., Am. Physicians Fellowship (rep. Israel Med. Assn.), Assn. Acad. Surgery (chmn. membership selection com. 1973-75, pres. elect 1974-75, pres. 1975-76, exec. coun. 1977-79), Soc. Univ. Surgeons (rep. Nat. Soc. Med. Rsch. 1973-77, com. Surgical Edn. 1979-81), Ctrl. Surgical Soc. (rep. Nat. Soc. Med. Rsch. 1973-77), Shock Soc. (chmn. planning com. 1986, chmn. program com. 1986, pres. elect 1986-87, pres. 1987-88), Soc. for Surgery Alimentary Tract (mem. com. west north ctrl. region 1978-82), Internat. Soc. Blood Transfusion, Surgical Biology Club II, Nat. Soc. for Med. Rsch., Collegium Internationale Chirugiae Digestivae, Societe Internationale de Chirugie, Sigma XI, Alpha Omega Alpha (faculty advisor 1972-73). Office: U Ill Coll Medicine Chgo 1853 W Polk St # M/C 784 Chicago IL 60612-4316 Home Phone: 847-433-6106; Office Phone: 312-996-3500. E-mail: gmoss@uic.edu.

MOSS, HOLLYE K., finance educator; m. John W. Huffman. BA, Converse Coll., Spartanburg, SC, 1983; MBA, Wake Forest U., Winston Salem, NC, 1993; MS, Clemson U., SC, 1985, PhD, 2002. Cert. in production and inventory mgmt. APICS, 2006, in integrated resource mgmt. 2007. Assoc. prof. Western Carolina U., Cullowhee, NC, 2002—. Recipient Several Tchg. Awards, WCU Coll. of Busines. Mem.: APICS (chpt. pres. 2008—). Achievements include research in publications in the area of operations management. Office: Western Carolina Univ Coll Bus Cullowhee NC 28723 Business E-Mail: hmoss@wcu.edu.

MOSS, JEFFREY P., language educator; b. Greensboro, NC, Aug. 29, 1981; s. Alvin H. and Marlene Moss. BA in Bibl. Studies, Trinity Coll. of Bible, Newburgh, Ind., 2000; BA in Fgn. Langs., W.Va. U., Morgantown, 2002; MA in Tchg. ESL, U. Idaho, Moscow, 2007. Cert. in tchg. ESL Internat. Tng. Network, Bournemouth, Eng., Ministerial Tng. Greyfriars Hall, Moscow, Id. Instr. Wash. State U., Pullman, 2004—, U. Idaho, Moscow, 2005—07, New St Andrews Coll, Moscow, Id, 2007—09. Missionary Operation Moblzn., St. Petersburg, Russia, 2002—04. Mem.: WAESOL. Office: Wash State U PO Box 643251 Pullman WA 99164-3251 Office Phone: 509-335-7488. Business E-Mail: jmoss@wsu.edu.

MOSS, JEREMY ETHAN, dermatologist; b. New Hyde Pk., NY; s. Steven and Linda Moss; m. Susan Soskis. MD, NYU, PhD, 2001. Diplomate Am. Bd. Dermatology, 2005. Immunology rschr. Yale U., New Haven, 2005—06; dermatologist Kenneth J. Maiocco MD PC, Bridgeport, Conn., 2006—. Clin. faculty Bridgeport, St Vincent's. Yale U., & West Haven Veterans Hosp., Bridgeport, Conn., 2006—. Mem.: Am. Acad. Dermatology. Achievements include research in immunology of infectious and inflammatory diseases. Office: Kenneth J Maiocco MD PC 4639 Main St Bridgeport CT 06606

MOSS, KATE, model; b. Croydon, Eng., Jan. 16, 1974; 1 child, Lila Grace. With Storm Agy., England, Women Model Mgmt., NYC; model Calvin Klein Jeans, Yves Saint Laurent, Prada, Versace, Burberry, Celine, Gucci, Louis Vuitton, Chanel, Dior, Virgin Mobile, Rimmel, Nokion; clothing designer Topshop, 2007—; perfume designer Kate by Kate Moss. Actress (films) Unzipped, 1995, Catwalk, 1995, Beautopia, 1998, Blackadder Back and Forth, 1999, Original Copies, 1999, (TV films) Inferno, 1992, Naomi Conquers Africa, 1998, Astley's Way, 2001, We Know Where You Live, 2001, Terry & Liz, 2004, (TV series) French and Saunders, 1987, appearances in music videos include "Kowalski" by Primal Scream, "I Just Don't Know What to do with Myself" by the White Stripes, "Something About The Way You Look Tonight" by Elton John, "Sex with Strangers" by Marianne Faithfull, "God's Gonna Cut You Down" by Johnny Cash. Recipient Lifetime Achievement award, Coun. Fashion Designers of America, 2005; named Model of Yr., British Fashion Awards, 2006; named one of The World's Most Influential People, TIME mag., 2007, World's Richest Models, Forbes mag., 2007, The 100 Most Powerful Celebrities, Forbes.com, 2008. Achievements include being the second highest paid model in the world, 99th richest woman in Britain. Office: Storm Model Mgmt 5 Jubilee Pl 1st Fl London SW3 3TD England

MOSS, KEVIN, literature and language professor; b. Lake Charles, La., Nov. 3, 1955; s. Clement Murphy and Betty Moss; life ptnr. Ernest McLeod. BA, Amherst Coll., 1977; PhD, Cornell U., 1984. Prof. Russian Middlebury Coll., Vt., 1983—. Musician (choral dir.): Middlebury Russian Choir; editor (translator): (anthology) Out of the Blue: Russia's Hidden Gay Literature; contbr. articles to profl. jour. Postdoc. fellowship, Social Scis. Rsch. Coun., 1988—89, Transl. grant, NEH, 1996, Individual Advanced Rsch. grant, IREX, 2007. Mem.: AAASS, AATSEEL, Phi Beta Kappa. Office: Middlebury Coll Old Chapel Ln Middlebury VT 05753 Business E-Mail: moss@middlebury.edu.

MOSS, LESLIE OTHA, homeland security specialist; b. Detroit, Mar. 8, 1952; s. Lonnie and Emma (Robinson) M. BA, U. Mich., 1982, postgrad., 1990—. Cert. protection officer, security supr. Dept. Homeland Security, protection profl., security specialist 2005. Technician oper. rm. Sinai Hosp., Detroit, 1972-75; nurses' technician Detroit Osteo. Hosp., 1976-83; supr. Southfield Placement Ctr., Mich., 1983-85; rsch. asst. Wayne County Commr.'s Office, Detroit, 1985-86; fin. aid counselor Wayne State U., 1986-87; probation officer Dept. Corrections State of Mich., 1988—; exec. asst. Human Rights Dept., City of Detroit; rsch. asst. Law Dept. City of Detroit, 1990; asst. pers. mgr. Detroit Osteo. Hosp., 1991-93, Highland Pk. C.C., 1991-93; mental health worker Mich. Health Ctr.-Adult Mental Health and New Ctr. Hosp., Detroit, 1992-94; legal technician Ptnrs. Against Crime, Detroit, 1994; social work technician, 1994. Sgt. of arms Detroit Police Res., 1987—; intern, assoc. prodr. local TV sta., Detroit, 1993; mem. bd. advisors, mem. bd. govs. Am. Biog. Rsch. Inst., dep. gov., 1994; exec. cons. in field.,

1993—; asst. pers. mgr., 1993—. Mem. re-election com. Mayor Coleman A. Young, Detroit, 1989-93; patient care counselor; adv. various causes, including industrialized Am., higher edn., automotive quality. Recipient Twentieth Century Achievement award Biog. Centre, 1994, Spl. Recognition award Detroit Pub. Sch. Sys., 1992, Internat. Man of Yr. award, 1992-93; award for mass media svc. participation Barden Cable Vision, Detorit, 1991, Man of the Yr. award, 1996, Disting. Alumni Award Mumford H.S. Detroit, 1996, Most Outstanding Men of the Twentieth Century award, 1999; named Most Admired Man of Decade, 1994, Disting. Alumnus, Detroit Pub. Schs. Mich., 1995, Most Admired Man of the Yr., State of Mich., 1995; named to Internat. Honors Hall of Fame, 1998, Millenium Hall of Fame, 1998; inducted 500 Leaders of Influence Pub., 2000. Mem. NAFE, NAACP (advisor 1989), Internat. Order of Merit, Assn. Pre-Med Students (cons. 1988—), Assn. Psychologists, Am. Biog. Rsch. Inst. Assn. (mem. bd. govs. 1993, dep. gov.), Internat. Platform Assn., U. Mich. Alumni Assn., Golden Key Internat. Honor Soc. (life), Kappa Alpha Psi, Phi Theta Kappa. Home and Office: 1190 Seward St Apt 304 Detroit MI 48202-2336 Home Phone: 313-978-4445; Office Phone: 248-796-5991. Business E-Mail: patricemumsumba@yahoo.com.

MOSS, LINDA ELAINE, science educator; d. Howard Adkins and Reva Helen Barnes Tribble; m. Leonard Joe Moss, July 25, 1980; children: Gayle Lynne Nichols, Cheryl Diane Zeiss. BS Agr., U. of Mo., 1972; BS in Chemistry Edn., Ark. State U., 1991, MS in Chemistry Edn., 1991, Specialist in C.C. Tchg., Biology, 1993, D of Ednl. Leadership, 2000. Lic. tchr. Ark. Acctg. clk. Empire Gas, Lebanon, Mo., 1972—73; sci. and fgn. lang. tchr. Poughkeepsie H.S., Ark., 1987—89, Evening Shade H.S., Ark., 1987—95; sci. instr. Ozarka Tech. Coll., Melbourne, Ark., 1993—95, Black River Tech. Coll., Pocahontas, Ark., 1995—. Beta delta phi chpt. adv. Phi Theta Kappa Internat. Honor Soc., Pocahontas, Ark., 2000—; sci. club adv. Black River Tech. Coll., Pocahontas, Ark., 1995—, north ctrl. accreditation steering com., 1998—2003, north ctrl. accreditation instl. integrity com. chair, 1998—2003; pres. black river coll. edn. assn. Ark. Edn. Assn., 1995—; chair, hazards identification com. Black River Tech. Coll., Pocahontas, 2003—. Mem. Keep Randolph County Beautiful, Pocahontas, Ark., 1998—2006. Recipient Ark. Acad. of Sci. Best Grad. Student Presentation, Ark. Acad. of Sci., 1995, Student Body Choice Tchr., Black River Tech. Coll. Student Coun., 1997, Phi Theta Kappa Faculty Scholar, Phi Theta Kappa Internat. Honor Soc., 2002, Most Disting. Faculty Advisor, Okla./Ark. Region Phi Theta Kappa Internat. Honor Soc., 2006, Empire Who's Who Registry of Executives and Professionals, 2005, Appreciation of Outstanding Svc., Okla./Ark. Region Phi Theta Kappa Internat. Honor Soc., 2006. Mem.: NEA, Ark. Edn. Assn. (assoc.; pres. local chpt. 1995—2006), Okla./Ark. Region Assn. of Chpt. Advisors Phi Theta Kappa Internat. Honor Soc., Phi Theta Kappa Internat. Honor Soc., Kappa Delta Phi Internat. Edn. Honor Soc. Home: 314 Elmont Road Maynard AR 72444 Office: Black River Tech Coll Highway 304 East Pocahontas AR 72455 Office Fax: 870-248-4100. E-mail: lindam@blackrivertech.org.

MOSS, LOGAN VANSEN, lawyer; b. Atlanta, Apr. 17, 1957; s. Joseph Henry and Elsie Louise (McCown); m. Janet Moss; children: Logan Jr., Hannah, Abigail. BA, Bates Coll., Lewiston, Maine, 1979; JD, U. Tulsa, Okla., 1982; MTS, Ave Maria U., Orchard Lake, Mich., 2003; cert. of Advanced Study in Bioethics and Health Policy, Loyola U., 2006. Bar: Okla. 1982, US Dist. Ct. Okla. 1982, Maine 1984, US Dist. Ct. Maine 1984, US Supreme Ct. 1986, Tex. 1991, NY 2007. Law clk. to presiding justice Okla. Ct. Appeals, Tulsa, 1982—84; assoc. Strout, Payson et al, Rockland, Maine, 1984—87, Joseph M. Cloutier & Assocs., Camden, Maine, 1987—88, Armstrong & Assoc., Tulsa, 1988—91; asst. gen. counsel Temple-Inland Forest Products Corp., Diboll, Tex., 1991—2002; gen. counsel litig. Temple-Inland, Austin, 2003—. Pro bono legal assistance Caritas, Austin. Named Best Bus. Atty. Large Staff Dept., Austin Bus. Jour., 2007. Mem.: Order of Preachers of Roman Cath. Ch. Republican. Roman Catholic. Avocation: catholic studies. Office: Temple Inland Foundation 1300 S Mo Pac Expy Fl 3 Austin TX 78746-6933 Home Phone: 512-402-1688; Office Phone: 512-434-8050. Business E-Mail: loganmoss@templeinland.com.

MOSS, MADISON SCOTT, retired editor; b. Charlotte, NC, May 23, 1948; s. James Madison and Nellie Lee (Jenkins) M. BA in English, U. N.C., 1970. Editl. aide NASW, Inc., Washington, 1974, promotions specialist, 1974-79, assoc. editor, 1979-80, editor, 1980-90, mng. editor, 1990—2008. Campaign coord. Eugene McCarthy for Pres., Rutherford County, N.C., 1968. Recipient award for Pub. Excellence Comms. Concepts, 1993, 94, 95, 96, 97, 98, Bronze award newspaper gen. excellence Soc. Nat. Assn. Publs., 1996, Silver award, 1997, Bronze awards, 2005, 06. Mem. Am. Assn. Ret. Persons, U. N.C. Gen. Alumni Assn. Democrat.

MOSS, MARC, medical educator; s. Naomi Waxman; m. Heather Harris, Sept. 6, 1992; children: Parker Jaffe, Dylan Alexander. BA, Amherst Coll., Mass., 1983. Cert. U. Pa., 1987. Roger S. Mitchell prof. medicine U. Colo. Denver, 2006—.

MOSS, MARCIA LYNN, retired biochemist; d. Frank and Loretta Moss; m. Fred Harold Rasmussen; 1 child, Alden Rasmussen. PhD, U. Wis., 1989. Organic chemist U. Mich., Ann Arbor, 1980—84; postdoctoral U. Wis. Sch. Pharmacy, Madison, 1990—92; postdoctoral dept. physiology U. Wis., Madison, Wis., 1989—90; rsch. investigator I and II Glaxo, Research Triangle Park, NC, 1992—99, ret., 1999; sr. project leader Cognosci, Research Triangle Park, NC, 2001—02; dir. rsch. BioZyme Inc., Apex, NC, 2003—04. Author (primary investigator): (identification of novel metalloprotease) Cloning of a disintegrin metalloproteinase that processes precursor tumour-necrosis factor-alpha; author: (graduate student) (mechanism of enzyme) The role of S-adenosylmethionine in the lysine 2, 3-aminomutase reaction; author: (co-investigator) (mechanistic studies on finasteride) Mechanism of time-dependent inhibition of 5 alpha-reductases by delta 1-4-azasteroids: toward perfection of rates of time-dependent inhibition by using ligand-binding energies; author: (senior investigator) (phage display) Substrate specificity of human collagenase-3 assessed using a phage display library, (novel enzyme in tgf alpha processing) Multiple Metalloproteinases Process ProTransforming Growth Factor-(ProTGF-.; prin. author: rev. articles Shedding Membrane Proteins by ADAM Family Proteases, Therapeutic Benefits from Targeting of ADAM Family Members; contbr. articles to profl. jours. Ch. mem. New Horizons, Apex, NC. Grantee, NIH, 2001, 2002, 2002-2005, 2004—; Procter and Gamble fellowship, U. Wis., 1988, 1989, Fellowship grant, NIH, 1989, 1990. Mem.: ACS, Internat. Proteolysis Soc., Jour. Biol. Chemistry. Achievements include patents pending for Assays to measure matrix metalloproteinases. Home: 1513 Old White Oak Church Rd Apex NC 27523 Office: Duke Univ Research Dr 242 Nanaline Durham NC 27710 Personal E-mail: mmoss@biozyme-inc.com. E-mail: moss120@bellsouth.net.

MOSS, MYRA ELLEN (MYRA MOSS ROLLE), philosophy educator; b. LA, Mar. 22, 1937; m. Andrew Rolle, Nov. 5, 1983. BA, U. Rome, Italy, 1958; PhD, Johns Hopkins U., Balt., 1965. Asst. prof. Santa Clara (Calif.) U., 1968-74; prof. Claremont McKenna Coll., 1975—2007, emeritus prof., 2007—, chmn. dept. philosophy, 1992—95. Assoc. dir. Gould Ctr. for Humanities, Claremont, Calif., 1993-94; adv. coun. Milton S. Eisenhower Libr./Johns Hopkins U., 1994-96, 2001— Author: Benedetto Croce Reconsidered, 1987, Mussolini's Fascist Philosopher: Giovanni Gentile Reconsidered, 2004, Italian edit., Armando, 2007, rev. Mussolini's Brain Trust, 2006; translator: Benedetto Croce's Essays on Literature & Literary Criticism, 1990; co-author: Values and Education, 1998; assoc. editor Special Issues; Journal of Value Inquiry, 1990-95 (Honorable Mention, Phoenix award); cons. editor Jour. Social Philosophy, 1988—; assoc. editor: Value Enquiry Book Series, 1990-95; editor: The Philosophy of José Gaos, by Pio Colonnello, Value Inquiry Book Series, 1997. Bogliasco fellow, Liguria, Italy, 2000; vis. scholar Am. Acad. Rome, 2005. Mem. Am. Philos. Assn., Am. and Internat. Soc. for Value Inquiry, Soc. for Aesthetics, Internat. Ctr. for the Arts, Humanities and Value Inquiry (assoc.), Collingwood Soc. (life), Phi Beta Kappa (Plato Excellence Edn. award 2009). Avocations: gardening, horseback riding. Office: Claremont McKenna Coll 850 Columbia Ave Claremont CA 91711-3901 Business E-Mail: mmoss@cmc.edu.

MOSS, PATRICIA L., bank executive; m. Greg Moss; children: Jennifer, Jeffrey. BS in Bus. Adminstrn., Linfield Coll., Oreg.; grad. studies, Portland State U. Cert. U. Okla., ABA Comml. Banking Sch. Various banking positions Cascade Bancorp, Bend, Oreg., 1977—98, pres., CEO, 1998—; CEO Bank of the Cascades, Bend, 1998—. Bd. dirs. Cascade Bancorp, Bank of the Cascades, Aquilla Tax-Free Trust of Oreg., Ctrl. Oreg. Ind. Health Svcs., MDU Resources Group Inc., 2003—. Adv. bd. Oreg. State U. Cascade Campus. Named Disting. Citizen of Yr., Bend C. of C., Ctrl. Oreg. Bus. Woman of Yr.; named one of 25 Most Powerful Women in Banking, US Banker, 2006, 2007. Mem.: Ind. Cmty. Bankers Assn. Am., Oreg. Bankers Assn. (bd. dir.), Oreg. Women's Forum. Office: Cascade Bancorp 1100 NW Wall St Bend OR 97701

MOSS, PRINCESS RENAI, elementary school educator; b. Fredericksburg, Va., Apr. 26, 1961; d. Ernest and Hazel Jeanette Moss. BA, Mary Washington Coll., Fredericksburg, 1983; MEd, U. Va., Charlettesville, 1986. Tchr. Louisa (Va.) County Pub. Sch., 1983—. Apptd. mem. P-16 edn. coun., Richmond, Va., 2005—. Mem.: NEA (bd. dirs. 2006—), Va. Educators Assn. (pres. 2004—). Baptist. Home: 13001 Chimney Stone Ct Richmond VA 23233 Office: Va Edn Asn 116 S 3rd St Richmond VA 23219 Office Phone: 804-648-5801. Office Fax: 904-775-8399. Business E-Mail: pmoss@veanea.org.

MOSS, RANDY GENE, professional football player; b. Rand, W.Va., Feb. 13, 1977; s. Randy Pratt and Maxine Moss; children: Sidney, Senali, Thaddeus, Montigo. Attended, Fla. State U., 1996, Marshall U., 1996—98. Wide receiver Minn. Vikings, 1998—2005, Oakland Raiders, 2005—07, New England Patriots, 2007—. Owner Moss Motorsports LLC, 2008—. Recipient Fred Biletnikoff award, 1997, ESPY award, Breakthrough Athlete of Yr., ESPN, 1999; named NFL Offensive Rookie of Yr., AP, 1998, 1st Team All-Pro, NFL, 1998, 2000, 2002—03, 2007, NFL Pro Bowl MVP, 2000; named to Nat. Football Conf. Pro Bowl Team, 1998—2000, 2002—03, Am. Football Conf. Pro Bowl Team, 2007. Achievements include leading the NFL in: receiving touchdowns, 1998, 2000, 2003, 2007, total touchdowns, 2007; setting the NFL record for touchdowns receptions in a single season as a rookie (17), 1998; setting the NFL record for touchdown receptions in a season (23), 2007; setting the NFL record for fewest games to reach 5,000 career receiving yards (59 games). Office: New England Patriots One Patriot Pl Foxboro MA 02035-1388

MOSS, ROBERT ALLEN, chemistry professor; b. Bklyn., May 27, 1940; s. Benjamin and Frances Moss; m. Sandra Wolman, June 11, 1967; children: Kenneth Benjamin, Daniel David. BS, Bklyn. Coll., 1960; PhD, U. Chgo., 1963. NAS-NRC postdoc. fellow Columbia U., NYC, 1963—64; chemistry prof. Rutgers U., NB, NJ, 1964—, L.P. Hammett prof., chemistry, 1993—2006, rsch. prof., 2006—; vis. scientist MIT, Cambridge, 1971—72, U. Oxford, England, 1976—77; Michael vis. prof. Weizmann Inst., Rehovoth, Israel, 1984; Wynberg vis. prof. U. Groningen, Netherlands, 1992; Forchheimer vis. prof. Hebrew U., Jerusalem, 1999. Contbr. scientific papers to profl. jours. Rsch. grant, NSF, 1965—. Fellow: AAAS; mem.: Am. Chem. Soc., Baker St. Irregulars. Avocations: baseball, stamp collecting/philately. Office: Dept Chemistry Rutgers Univ New Brunswick NJ 08903

MOSS, ROGER WILLIAM, historian, writer, administrator; b. Zanesville, Ohio, Jan. 31, 1940; s. Roger William and Dorothy Elizabeth Moss; m. Gail Caskey Winkler, 1981; 1 child, Sweeney; children: Elizabeth Moss McQuiston, Victoria Stiles. BS in Edn., Ohio U., 1963, MA, 1964; postgrad., Attingham, Eng., 1966; PhD, U. Del., 1972. Staff Peace Corps, Cameroon, 1962-63; curator of rare books Ohio U., 1962-64; lectr., dept. history U. Del., 1966-68, U. Md., 1967-68; exec. dir. Athenaeum of Phila., 1968—2008; emeritus, 2008—; partner LCA Assoc., 1981—. Lectr. to adj. prof. architecture U. Pa., Phila., 1981—2004. Publs. include Master Builders, 1972, Century of Color, 1981, Biographical Dictionary of Philadelphia Architects, 1985, Victorian Interior Decoration, 1986, Victorian Exterior Decoration, 1987, Lighting for Historic Buildings, 1988 (Joel Polsky prize 1989), The American Country House, 1990, Philadelphia Victorian, 1998, Historic Houses of Philadelphia, 1998, Historic Sacred Places of Philadelphia, 2004, Historic Landmarks of Philadelphia, 2008; editor: Paint in America, 1994; contbr. articles to profl. jours. Assoc. mem. Nat. Preservation Inst., 1982—93; sec. Christopher Ludwick Found., 1969—, bd. dirs., 1969—; sec.-treas. Brit. Cathedrals and Hist. Chs. Found., 1996—2001, pres., 2002—04, bd. dirs.; sec. Victorian Soc. in Am., 1969—88, treas., 1969—88, bd. dirs., 1969—88; treas. Phila. Area Cultural Consortium, 1977—82, bd. dirs., 1977—82; sec. Hopkinson House Coun., 1982—93, Cliveden Coun., Nat. Trust Hist. Preservation, 1974—81, 1984—86; exec. com. Phila. Area Consortium Spl. Coll., 1988—93, Friends of Laurel Hill, 1978—83; bd. dirs. Conservation Ctr. for Art and Hist. Artifacts, 1984—96, chmn., 1993—95; sec. Harriton House, 1969—81, bd. dirs., 1969—81, Hist. House Assn. Am., 1978—83, Com. Preservation of Archtl. Records, 1978—80, Mus. Coun. Phila., 1976—78, Woodlands Cemetery Co., 1990—99, Rsch. Librs. Group, 1993—96, Abraham Lincoln Found., 1996—2005, Am. Friends Attingham Summer Schs., 2006—. NEH grantee, 1983-85; recipient Biddle award Preservation Alliance, 2004, Athenaeum Lit. award, 2005. Mem. Carpenters' Co. (hon.), PA Chpt. AIA Lifetime Contributions Architecture Non Architect, 2008, Hist. New Eng., Hist. Sec. Pa. Library Co. Phila., Castine Yacht Club. Office: 604 S Washington Sq Unit 102 Philadelphia PA 19106 Office Phone: 215-925-8367. Personal E-mail: moss@winklerandmoss.com.

MOSS, SANTANA TERRELL, professional football player; b. Miami, Fla., June 1, 1979; s. Lloyd, Natalie; married; children: Santana Jr., Saniya. BA in Liberal Arts, U. Miami, Fla., 2000. Wide receiver NY Jets, 2000—04, Wash. Redskins, 2005—. Recipient Offensive and Special Teams Player Yr. awards, Big East Conf., 2000; named to Nat. Football Conf. Pro Bowl Team, NFL, 2005. Office: Washington Redskins 21300 Redskin Park Dr Ashburn VA 20147*

MOSS, SARA E., lawyer, cosmetics executive; b. NYC, Nov. 13, 1946; 4 children. BA magna cum laude, U. Mass., 1968; JD, NYU, 1974. Bar: NY 1975, US Dist. Ct. (so. dist. NY) 1976, US Ct. Appeals (2nd cir.) 1975, US Tax Ct. 1983, US Supreme Ct. 1983. Law clk. to Hon. Constance Baker Motley US Dist. Ct. (so. dist. NY), 1974-75, asst. US atty., 1978-81; law clk. Davis, Polk & Wardell, 1975-78, 80-84; ptnr. Howard, Smith & Levin, 1984-96; v.p., gen. counsel Pitney Bowes, Inc., Stamford, Conn., 1996—2003; sr. v.p., gen. counsel, sec. Estée Lauder, NYC, 2003—. Instr. Nat. Inst. Trial Advocacy. Contbr. articles to profl. jours. Mem. ABA, Fed. Bar Coun. (trustee 1996—), Am. Arbitration Assn. (bd. dirs.), NY Coun. Def. Lawyers (bd. dirs. 1994-96), Assn. Bar City of NY (mem. fed. cts. com., mem. litig. com.), Phi Beta Kappa. Office: Estee Lauder 767 Fifth Ave New York NY 10153 Office Phone: 212-572-4200. E-mail: emoss@estee.com.

MOSS, SHAD GREGORY (BOW WOW, LIL' BOW WOW), rap artist; b. Columbus, Ohio, Mar. 9, 1987; s. Teresa and Alfonso Moss, Rodney Caldwell (Stepfather). Singer: (albums) Beware of Dog, 2000, Doggy Bag, 2001, Unleashed, 2003, Wanted, 2005, Signal Fire, 2006, The Price of Fame, 2006, New Jack City, Part II, 2009, (with Omarion) Face Off, 2007, (songs) Bounce With Me, 2000, Let Me Hold You, 2005, Fresh Azimiz, 2005, Like You, 2006, (featured on film soundtracks) Hardball, 2001, Like Mike, 2002; actor: (TV films) Carmen: A Hip Hopera, 2001; (films) All About the Benjamins, 2002, Like Mike, 2002, Johnson Family Vacation, 2004, Roll Bounce, 2005, The Fast & the Furious: Tokyo Drift, 2006. Achievements include youngest solo rapper to ever hit number one. Office: Bow Wow Found Ste 307 6555 Sugarloaf Pkwy PMB 223 Duluth GA 30097 also: c/o Jeff Frasco or Ken Stovitz Creative Artists Agy LCC 2000 Ave of the Stars Los Angeles CA 90067 Office Fax: 678-376-5911.

MOSS, SHAWNDA L., theater educator; d. Victor and Virginia Ludlow; m. Bradley D. Moss, May 28, 1999; children: Anton, Isaac, Isabel. MA, Brigham Young U., Provo, Utah, 2005. Cert. in pub. sch. tchg. Utah, 1996. Theatre tchr. Riverton HS, Utah, 1999—2005; theatre edn. instr. Brigham Young U., 2004—. Conf. adminstr. Utah Theatre Assn., Salt Lake City, 1997—2008. Mem.: Ednl. Theatre Assn., Am. Alliance Theatre and Edn. Office: Brigham Young Univ HFAC D-581 Provo UT 84602

MOSS, STEPHEN BRUCE, lawyer; b. Jacksonville, Fla., July 14, 1943; s. Rudy and Betty (Sobel) M.; m. Rhoda Goodman, Nov. 24, 1984; children: Kurt, Shannon. BA, Tulane U., 1964; JD, Cumberland Sch. Law, 1968. Bar: Fla. 1968, U.S. Dist. Ct. (So. Dist.) Fla., U.S. Tax Ct. 1971. From assoc. to ptnr. Heiman & Crary, Miami, Fla., 1971-74; pvt. practice law So. Miami, Fla., 1974-75; ptnr. Glass, Schultz, Weinstein & Moss P.A., Coral Gables, Fla., 1975-78, Ft. Lauderdale, Fla., 1978-80, Holland & Knight, LLP, Ft. Lauderdale, 1980—, mem. dir. com., 2004—06. Lectr. in the field. Mem. pro bono com. 17th Jud. Cir., 2000; co-founder, co-chair Broward County Child Welfare Initiative, 2001. Capt. U.S. Army, 1968-70, Vietnam. Named Outstanding Kiwanian, Miami, Fla., 1974, Child Advocate of the Yr., Broward County, Fla., 2003, Role Model, 2004, Legal Elite, Fla. Trend Mag., 2004; named an Olympic torchbearer, 1996; named one of Best Lawyers in Am., 2007, 2008, 2009. Fellow: Am. Bar Found., Fla. Bar Found.; mem.: Broward County Chpt. Fla. Resturant Lodging Assn. (bd. dir. 2007—09), Internat. Law Moot Ct., Broward County Bar Assn., Legal Aid Svc. of Broward County (bd. dirs. 2000), Fla. Bar Assn. (real property, probate and trust law sect.), Greater Ft. Lauderdale C. of C. (gen. counsel 1991—92, chmn. bd. dirs., bd. govs. 1995, past chair 1995, trustee rep. 2005—09, Ft. Lauderdale centinnial com., Chmn.'s award 1991, 2000, Sr. Exec. Alumni of Year 2003), Tower Forum (pres. 1993—94, bd. dirs. 1995—2005), Phi Alpha Delta. Democrat. Jewish. Avocations: baseball, child welfare, spinning. Office: Holland & Knight LLP 1 E Broward Blvd Ste 1300 Fort Lauderdale FL 33301-1845 Office Phone: 954-468-7857. Business E-Mail: stephen.moss@hklaw.com.

MOSS, THOMAS E., prosecutor; b. 1937; BA, U. Idaho; JD, U. Idaho Coll. Law, 1965. Prosecuting atty. Bingham County Dist. Ct., 1967—71, 1979—99; ptnr. Moss, Cannon and Romrell, Blackfoot, Idaho; mem. Idaho Ho. Reps., 2001; US atty. US Dept. Justice, Boise, Idaho, 2001—. Faculty mem. Nat. Advocacy Ctr., Columbia, SC; adv. coun. U. Idaho Coll. of Law; mem. Attn. Gen. Adv. Com., 2005—; Atty. Gen. Exec. Working Grp. Pres. Blackfoot Chamber of Commerce, Blackfoot Rotary Club; mem. Governor's Coordinating Coun. for Families and Children. Fellow: Am. Coll. Trial Lawyers; mem.: Idaho Prosecuting Attorneys' Assn. (pres.), Seventh Jud. Dist. Bar Assn. (pres.), Idaho State Bar Assn. (pres.), Idaho Ho. of Reps. Office: US Attys Office MK Plaza IV Ste 600 800 Park Blvd Boise ID 83712-9903

MOSS, THOMAS HENRY, science foundation director, physicist; b. Cleve., June 27, 1939; s. Joseph Harold and Elsa Margaret (Lemkau) M.; m. Kathleen Goddard, May 31, 1966; children: Ellen, Joseph, Cheryl, David. AB, Harvard U., 1961; PhD, Cornell U., 1965. Cons. analyst govtl. sci. policy U.S. Govt. Office Mgmt. and Budget, Washington, 1963-67; research physicist IBM Corp., Yorktown, NY, 1967-74, 75-76; staff dir., sci. advisor Office of Congressman George E. Brown, Washington, 1976-79; staff dir. subcom. sci., research and tech. Ho. of Reps., Washington, 1979-82; prof. physics, dean grad. studies and research Case Western Res. U., Cleve., 1982-96; exec. dir. Govt.-U.-Industry Roundtable, 1996—2001; with Nat. Acad. Scis, Washington; dir. U. relations Ohio Aerospace Inst., 2001—03. Adj. prof. physics Columbia U., NYC, 1966-76; mem. nat rev. com. Office of Nuclear Waste Isolation, Columbus, 1983-87; bd. dirs. U. Tech. Inc., Cleve., G. Mason U. Intellectual Properties, Inc., 2004—; bd. dirs. Ctr. Great Lakes, Chgo., 1985-89; v.p. Edison Poymer Innovation Corp., Independence, Ohio, 1986-90. Editor: The Three Mile Island Nuclear Accident-Lessons, 1981; asst. editor Environ. Profl. mag.; cons. editor Sci, Tech. and Human Values Environ. mag.; contbr. articles to profl. jours. Treas. Lake Bancroft Cmty. Assn., Falls Church, Va., 1980; mem. adv. bd. Small Bus. SBIR Program, Cleve., 1983-85; mem., v.p. Shaker Heights Bd. Edn., Ohio, 1989-96; chmn. NE Region Ohio Systemic Statewide Initiative in Sci. and Math. Edn., 1992-95. ASME fellow, 1995-96, NSF fellow Nobel Instn., 1966-67. Fellow Am. Phys. Soc. (chmn. forum on physics and soc. 1990-91), Nat. Coun. U. Rsch. Adminstrs. (Nat. Innovation Program award 1987), Scientists Inst. Pub. Info. (Disting. Svc. award Harlem Prep. Sch. 1971), AAAS (chmn. com. on sci., engring. and pub. policy 1989-91, chmn. sect. X 1998-99, exec. com. sect. P 2004—). Avocations: gardening, camping. Office Phone: 703-914-2854. Personal E-mail: tomhmoss@verizon.net.

MOSSAVAR-RAHMANI, SHARMIN, diversified financial services company executive; BA, Princeton U., 1980; MS, Stanford U., 1982. Various positions through chief investment officer Fidelity Mgmt. Trust Co.; joined as ptnr. Goldman, Sachs & Co., 1993, chief investment officer, mng. dir., Pvt. Wealth Mgmt. Group, Investment Mgmt. Divsn. Author 2 books; contbr. numerous articles on portfolio mgmt. issues. Mem. adv. coun. Bendheim Ctr. Fin., Princeton U.; mem. investment com. NY Presbyn. Hosp., bd. trustees; mem. nat. adv. bd. Merage Inst. for the Am. Dream.

MOSSBRUCKER, JOERG, engineering educator; Deng, U. Kaiserslautern, Germany, 1998. Mgr. electronic devel. United Parts, Dassel, Niedersachsen, Germany, 1998—2001; assoc. prof. MSOE, Milw., 2001—. Mem.: IEEE, ASEE. Office: MSOE 1025 N Broadway Milwaukee WI 53202 Office Fax: 414-277-7465. Business E-Mail: mossbruc@msoe.edu.

MOSSE, PETER JOHN CHARLES, financial services executive; b. Mtarfa, Malta, Sept. 8, 1947; arrived in US, 1977; s. John Herbert Charles and Barbara Haworth (Holden) M.; m. Christine Marielle St. Preux, Oct. 17, 1994. BA, Oxford U., Eng., 1969, MA, 1989; MBA, U. Pa., Phila., 1971. Bank officer N.M. Rothschild & Sons Ltd., London, 1971-76; spl. projects officer banking Bumiputra Mcht. Bankers Berhad, Kuala Lumpur, Malaysia, 1976-77; v.p., treas., sec. NMR Metals Incorp., NYC, 1977-79, exec. v.p., 1979-83; sr. v.p. Rothschild, Inc., NYC, 1983-90; v.p., CFO, The Arista Group Inc., NYC, 1991-93; U.S. rep. Travelex Fin. Svcs. Ltd., London, 1994-95; ptnr. Creelman Fine Arts, NYC, 1995—2003; chmn. 2nd Ave. Physician Practice, 2005—. Treas. Circumnavigators Found., 2004—05, dir., 2009—. Fellow Royal Soc. Arts.; mem. NY Acad. Scis., Pilgrims of the U.S. (life), St. George's Soc. NY (life, bd. dirs. 2006-09), Oxford U. Alumni Soc. (exec. com. 1994-96), Gold Inst. (co. rep., bd. dirs. 1985-90), Silver Inst. (co. rep., bd. dirs. 1989-90), NY Acad. Scis., Copper Club, Commodity Exch., Inc. (co. rep. 1979-90), Circumnavigators Club (bd. govs. 2006-), Travelers Century Club. Episcopalian. Avocations: travel, trains, railroad art. Home and Office: 353 E 72nd St Apt 33D New York NY 10021-4622

MOSSELMANS, CAREL MAURITS, investment banker; b. East Knoyle, Wiltshire, Eng., Mar. 9, 1929; s. Adriaan Willem and Nancy Henriette (Van der Wyck) M.; m. Prudence Fiona McCorquodale, Jan. 4, 1962; children: Michael Lodowick Stewart, Julian Frederick Willem. MA, Trinity Coll., Cambridge, Eng., 1952. With Sedgwick Collins & Co., 1952-63; dir. Sedgwick Collins & Co. Ltd., 1963-71; dir., mng. dir. Sedgwick Collins (Underwriting) Ltd., 1971, 72-73; chmn. Sedgwick Lloyd's Underwriting Agts., 1974-89, Sedgwick Forbes Marine Ltd., 1974-78, Sedgwick Forbes Svcs. Ltd., 1978-81, Sedgwick Ltd., 1981-84, Sedgwick Group Plc., 1984-89, The Sumitomo Marine & Fire Ins. Co. (Europe) Ltd., 1981-90; Coutts & Co., 1981-95; chmn. Rothschild Asset Mgmt. Ltd., 1989-99, Rothschild Int. Asset Mgmt., 1989-96. Chmn. Exco Plc, 1991-96, Janson Green Holdings Spl. Trust Ltd., 1993-96, Rothschild Fund Mgmt. Ltd., 1990-96; chmn. Janson Green Ltd., 1993-96, non-exec. dir., 1997-98. Avocations: shooting, fishing, music, golf. Home: 15 Chelsea Sq London SW3 6LF England

MOSS GREENBERG, JILL, special education administrator, civil rights activist; b. Bklyn., Jan. 4, 1943; d. Louis B. and Dorris T. Moss; m. James D. Greenberg; children: Joshua, Micah. Student, William Smith Coll., Geneva, NY, 1960-62; BS cum laude, Syracuse U., 1964; MA, U. Conn., 1967. Spl. educator Newington Children's Hosp., Conn., 1964-67; vocat. equity specialist, race equity specialist Md. State Dept. of Edn., Baltimore, 1981-85; project coord. Spl. Edn. Dept. U. Maryland, College Park, 1985-88; dir. multicultural programs Mid Atlantic Equity Ctr., 1988-95; homeless edn. coord. Balt. County Pub. Schs.; exec. dir. Nat. Assn. Multicultural Edn., Washington. Bd. dirs. Mid-Atlantic Equity, Md. Multicultural Coalition; v.p. Md. Com. for Children; co-founder Sch. for Students With Disabilities, Syracuse; founder, v.p. Md. Women's Heritage Ctr. and Mus., Inc.; founding exec. dir., Md. Women's Heritage Ctr. and Mus., 2005-. Author: (tng. manual) Gender and Disability; author, editor: (book) The Adolescent Directory: Alcohol and Drug Abuse Resources; editor: Building Bridges; coord. (curriculum guide) Black History at Your Doorstep. Apptd. mem. Md. Adv. Com. to U.S. Civil Rights Commn., Md. State Commn. for Women, gov.'s advisory bd. on homelessness; founding mem. Nat. Md. and Prince George's Women's Political Caucus; apptd. Md. coordinating com. Martin Luther King, Jr. Holiday; bd. mem. Nat. Conf. for Cmty. and Justice; founder/mem. Md. Women's History Project, Title IX Adv. Com., 1972—; cons. Civil Rights, Diversity, Aging, Intergroup Dialogue, Prejudice Reduction, Multicultural and Homeless Edn. Named to Md. Women's Hall of Fame, Md. Com. for Women and Women Legislators, 1995, Prince George's County Hall of Fame, Prince George's Commn. for Women and County Govt., 1993; recipient Brotherhood/Sisterhood Human Rels. award NCCJ, 1987. Jewish. Avocations: handcrafts, community service. Office Phone: 410-767-0675. Personal E-mail: mwhcjill@comcast.net.

MOSSINGHOFF, GERALD JOSEPH, lawyer, educator; b. St. Louis, Sept. 30, 1935; m. Jeanne Carole Jack, Dec. 29, 1958; children: Pamela Ann Jennings, Gregory Joseph, Melissa M. Ronayne. BSEE, St. Louis U., 1957; JD with honors, George Washington U., 1961. Bar: Mo. 1961, DC 1965, Va. 1981. Project engr. Sachs Electric Corp., 1954-57; dir. congl. liaison NASA, Washington, 1967-73, dep. gen. counsel, 1976-81; asst. Sec. Commerce, commr. patents and trademarks U.S. Patent Office, 1981-85; pres. Pharm. Rsch. and Mfrs. Am., Washington, 1985-96; Cifelli prof. intellectual property law George Washington U., Washington, 1996—; sr. counsel Oblon, Spivak, McClelland, Maier & Neustadt, Arlington, Va., 1997—. Amb. Paris Conv. Diplomatic Conf. Recipient Exceptional Svc. medal, NASA, 1971, DSM, 1980, Outstanding Leadership medal, 1981, Jefferson medal, 2000, Disting. Pub. Svc. award, Sec. of Commerce, 1983; named Disting. Alumnus, George Washington U., 1996, presdl. rank of meritorious exec., 1980. Fellow: Am. Acad. Pub. Adminstrn.; mem.: Reagan Alumni Assn. (bd. dirs.), Cosmos Club, Knights of Malta, Order of Coif, Pi Mu Epsilon, Eta Kappa Nu. Home: 1530 Key Blvd Penthouse 28 Arlington VA 22209-1532 Office: Oblon Spivak McClelland Maier and Neustadt 1940 Duke St Alexandria VA 22314

MOSSMAN, DOUGLAS, psychiatrist, educator; b. East Grand Rapids, Mich., Oct. 10, 1954; s. Sidney and Agnes (Daye) M.; m. Nancy Elizabeth Hoevenaar, Sept. 4, 1983 (div. Mar. 1989); 1 child, Rachel; m. Kathleen Joan Hart, Oct. 29, 1989; children: Sarah, Leah. BA, Oberlin Coll., 1976; MD, U. Mich., 1981. Instr. Med. U. S.C., Charleston, 1986—88; vol. asst. prof. U. Cin., 1988—90, assoc. prof. clin. psychiatry, 1990—93; assoc. clin. prof., dir. divsn. forensic psychiatry Wright State U. Sch. Medicine, Dayton, Ohio, 1993—97, prof., 1997—; adminstrv. dir. Glenn M. Weaver Inst. Law & Psychiatry, 2005—. Adminstrv. dir. Glenn M. Weaver Inst. Law and Psychiatry, U. Cin. Coll. Law, 2005—. Contbr. more than 80 articles to profl. jours. Recipient Levine Essay awards U. Cin., 1984, 85, 86, Mental Health Media award Cin. Mental Health Assn., 1990; Ohio Dept. Mental Health rsch. fellow, 1990-91. Fellow: Am. Psychiat. Assn. (Disting.); mem.: AMA, Soc. for Med. Decision Making, Am. Acad. Psychiatry and the Law, Ohio Psychiat. Assn., Group Advancement of Psychiatry, Phi Beta Kappa, Alpha Omega Alpha. Democrat. Jewish. Avocations: music, statistics, investing. Office: Wright State U Dept Psychiatry PO Box 927 Dayton OH 45401-0927 Office Phone: 937-223-8840. Business E-Mail: douglas.mossman@wright.edu.

MOSS-SALENTIJN, LETTY (ALEIDA), anatomist, educator; b. Amsterdam, The Netherlands, Apr. 14, 1943; arrived in U.S., 1968; d. Ewoud and Johanna Maria (Schoonhoven) Salentijn; m. Melvin Lionel Moss, Apr. 17, 1970. DDS, State U. Utrecht, Netherlands, 1967, PhD, 1976. Asst. prof. histology State U. Utrecht, 1967-68; asst. prof. Columbia U., NYC, 1968-74, assoc. prof., 1974-86, prof., 1986—, Edwin S. Robinson prof., 1999—, dir. dental radiology, 1980-86, dir. grad. program dental sci., 1986—, dir. postdoctoral affairs, 1987-90, asst. dean postdoctoral programs, 1990-94, assoc. dean acad. affairs, 1994—2005, sr. assoc. dean acad. affairs, 2005—. Author: Orofacial Histology & Embryology, 1972; Dental and Oral Tissues, 1980, 2d edit., 1984, 3d edit., 1990; contbr. chpts. to books, articles to profl. jours. Fellow Royal Microscopical Soc., Am. Coll. Dentists, NY Acad. Dentistry; mem. Am. Assn. Anatomists, Internat. Assn. Dental Rsch., Am. Soc. Biomechs., Sigma Xi (chpt. sec. 1980-87, pres. 1987-89, 98-99), Omicron Kappa Upsilon (pres. local chpt. 1987, 2009). Avocation: stained glass art. Home: 560 Riverside Dr Apt 20K New York NY 10027-3239 Office: Columbia Univ Coll Dental Medicine Sr Assoc Dean Acad Affairs 630 W 168th St New York NY 10032-3702 Office Phone: 212-305-8334. Business E-Mail: lm23@columbia.edu.

MOST, GLENN WARREN, classics professor; b. Miami, Fla., June 12, 1952; s. William and Sylvia (Nussbaum) M.; m. Angela Citernesi, Dec. 9, 1989; children: Corinna Angelica, Miranda Angelica. BA, Harvard U., 1972; MPhil, Yale U., 1978, PhD, 1980; DPhil, Tübingen U., 1980. Andrew W. Mellon asst. prof. classics Princeton U., 1980—85; prof. classics U. Siena, Italy, 1985—86; assoc. prof. classics U. Mich., Ann Arbor, 1986-87; prof. classics U. Innsbruck, Austria, 1987-91, U. Heidelberg, Germany, 1991—2001; prof. social thought U. Chgo., 1996—; prof. Ordinario di Filologia Greca Scuola Normale Superiore, Pisa, Italy, 2001—. Vis. fellow U. Mich. Inst. Humanities, 1993; vis. prof. Collège de France, 2003, Université Paris 4-Sorbonne, 2006; Lurcie vis. prof. U. Chgo., 1996. Author: The Measures of Praise, 1985, Doubting Thomas, 2005; co-editor: The Poetics of Murder, 1983, F.A. Wolf - Prolegomena to Homer, 1985, Theophraste, Metaphysique, 1993. Recipient Gottfried Wilhelm Leibniz prize, Deutsche Forschungsgemeinschaft, 1994-99; Mellon fellow, Am. Acad. in Rome, 1982, fellow Wissenschaftskolleg zu Berlin, 1988-98. Fellow Am. Acad. Arts and Sciences; mem. Am. Philol. Assn., Mommsen Gesellschaft, Phi Beta Kappa. Office: Scuola Normale Superiore di Pisa Piazza dei Cavalieri 7 I-56126 Pisa Italy also: U Chgo Com on Social Thought 1130 E 59th St Chicago IL 60637-1543 Business E-Mail: g.most@sns.it. E-mail: gmost@midway.uchicago.edu.

MOSTAFAVI ABDOLMALEKY, HAMID, psychiatrist, researcher; b. Behshahr, Mazandaran, Iran, Apr. 9, 1956; arrived in US, 2001, arrived in Canada, 2005; s. Hossein Mostafavi Abdolmaleky and Massomeh Motamedi Nassab; m. Batol Aleali, Sept. 14, 1984; children: Sahar, Saba, Siavash. MD, Iran Nat. U., Tehran, 1982; specialist in Psychiatry, Iran U. Med. Sci., Tehran, 1988. Asst. prof. psychiatry Kermanshah U. Med. Scis., Kermanshah, Bakhtaran, Iran, 1988—92, Iran U. Med. Scis., Tehran, 1992—; postdoctoral rsch. fellowship Harvard Med. Sch., Boston, 2001—07. Dir. Farabi Mental Hosp., Kermanshah, Bakhtaran, Iran, 1989—92; dir. edn. Esmaeli Mental Hosp., Tehran, 1994—2000. Contbr. articles to profl. jours. Fellow, Harvard U., 2001—07, Harvard Med. Sch., Boston, 2001—07. Mem.: Collegium Internationale Neuro-Psycho-Pharmacologicum, Epigenetics Soc., Internat. Soc. Psychiat. Genetics, Iranian Med. Coun. Achievements include patents pending for treatment of psychiatric disorders using entacapone, tolcapone and other COMT inhibitor drugs. Office: Harvard Med Sch Lab Nutrition 330 Brookline Ave BIDMC Dana Bldg Rm 838 Boston MA 02215 Personal E-mail: hamostafavi@yahoo.com, hamostafavi@gmail.com.

MOSTAGHEL, ELAHE A., medical educator; MD, Duke U., Durham, NC, PHD, 2000; BA, Harvard U., Cambridge, Mass., 2002. Diplomate in internal medicine Am. Bd. Internal Medicine, 2003, in med. oncology ABIM, 2006. Resident internal medicine UCSF, San Francisco, 2000—03; fellow hematology & oncology U. Wash., Seattle, 2003—06; asst. prof. FHCRC-UW, Seattle, 2008—. Recipient Career Devel. award, NIH, 2006—, Physician Rsch. Tng. award, Dept. Def., 2006—, Found. Young Investigator award, Am. Soc. Clin. Oncology, 2006, Donald S. Coffey Career Devel. award, Prostate Cancer Found., 2006, Clin. Investigator award, Damon Runyon Cancer Rsch. Found., 2008—. Mem.: Phi Beta Kappa. Office: Fred Hutchinson Cancer Rsch Ctr 1100 Fairview Ave N MS D4-100 Seattle WA 98109

MOSTAGHIMI, LADAN, psychiatrist; b. Mashhad, Iran, Jan. 29, 1959; 2 children. MD Summa Cum Laude, U. Tehran, Iran, 1986. Diplomate Am. Bd. Psychiatry & Neurology, 2003, psychosomatic medicine Am. Bd. Psychiatry & Neurology, 2005, registered Dr. Med. sci. in dermatology & venereology France Min. Nat. Edn., higher learning & rsch., 1994. UW dermatology & psychiatry faculty U. Wis. Madison, 2001—, dir. psychocutaneous medicine, 2001—; psychiatrist MPA, Madison, 2001—. Mem.: AMA. Office: Univ Wis 1 S Pk 7th fl dermatology Madison WI 53715

MOSTAGHIMI, MEHDI, economist, educator; arrived in U.S., 1975; s. Abolfazle Mostaghimi and Toba Rashidzadeh; m. Du D Cheng, Aug. 28, 1991; children: Darius, Alexander. BA in Econs., Nat. U. Iran, 1975; PhD in Info. and Sys. Engring., U. Va., 1987; MS in Ops. Rsch., We. Mich. U., 1999. Sr. mgr. portfolio and decision analysis group Pfizer Pharm., NYC, 1997—99; prof. economics and decision scis. Sch. of Bus. So. Conn. State U., New Haven, 1984—. Chmn. internat. chapts. subcom. Inst. of Ops. Rsch. and Mgmt. Scis., 2001—03; Grad. Rsch. Fellowship panel NSF, 2006. Co-author: Analysis of Bus. Cycles, 2004; contbr. articles to profl. jours. Fellow: Inst. of Ops. Rsch. and the Mgmt. Scis. (chmn. internat. chapts. subcommittee 2001—02); mem.: Am. Statis. Assn. (pres. Conn. chpt. 1994—97, com. on internat. rels. 1994—98). Achievements include research in modeling combining information and forecasts; predicting a turning point in economy; strategic and policy decision making. Home: PO Box 569 Madison CT 06443 Office: Southern Connecticut State Univ 501 Crescent Street New Haven CT 06515 Personal E-mail: mostaghimi@yahoo.com.

MOSTELLER, DARLA BROOKS, singer, educator; d. Thomas Jefferson and Sue Osborne Brooks; m. Paul W. Mosteller. MusB, Birmingham-Southern Coll., Ala., 1977. Young artist Lyric Opera Chgo., 1980—81; leading soprano Lucerne (Switzerland) Opera, 1984—85, Würzburg (Germany) Opera, 1985—86, Cologne (Germany) Opera, 1987—96; pvt. voice tchr. Birmingham, Ala., 2000—. Guest artist Dortmund (Germany) Opera, 1990—96; guest soloist Vienna (Austria) State Opera, 1991—96; artist Schwetzingen (Germany) Festival, 1993—95; soloist Trondheim (Norway) Symphony, 1993—95, Bergen (Norway) Symphony, 1995; guest artist Opera Bonn, Bonn, Germany, 1986—87, Mannheim (Germany) Opera, 1986—95, German Opera on the Rhine, Düsseldorf, Germany, 1989—96, Gran Teatre del Liceu, Barcelona, 1991—96, Mozart Festival, Prague, Czech Republic, 1991, Bavarian State Opera, Munich, 1993—94, Deutsche Oper, Berlin, 1993—95, Min-On Concert Assn., Tokyo, 1993, Salzburg (Austria) Festival, 1995—96; tchr. voice Birmingham Southern Coll., 1997—2000; pvt. voice tchr., 2000—. Singer (actor): (TV films) LIncoronazione di Poppea, 1991, (films) Falstaff (Salieri), 1993. Finalist, Met. Opera Nat. Coun., 1976, 1977, 1978, 1980, 1983, 1984; scholar, Am. Inst. Musical Studies, 1981; Singer's scholar, Norman Treigle Scholarship Fund, 1980. Mem.: Coll. Music Soc., Nat. Assn. Tchrs. Singing. Personal E-mail: pmosteller3476@charter.net.

MOSTELLER, SANDRA MARIE, music educator; d. Robert Eugene and Murielle Alma (Maureen) Garner; m. Paul Wayne Mosteller (div.). B of Music Edn., Truman State U., Kirksville, Mo., 1985, MA in Music Edn., 1987; MusM in Solo Performance, Ariz. State U., Tempe, 1997; DMA in Clarinet Performance, U. NC, Greensboro, 2001. Adj. instr. U. Ala., Birmingham, 1988—95, Radford U., Va., 1997—2000, U. NC, Charlotte, 2000—01; assoc. prof. music Wayland Bapt. U., Plainview, Tex., 2001—07, 2007—. Clinician, pvt. woodwind instr., various locations, 1981—; performer, clarinetist various solo, orch., and chamber performances, 1988—; rep. Plainview Arts Coun., Tex., 2006; presenter in field. Contbr. articles to profl. jours. Recipient Excellence Found. fellowship, U. NC, 1997, Regents Music scholarship, Ariz. State U., 1995—97; named Outstanding Tchr. Asst., U. NC, 2001. Mem.: Tex. Music Educator's Assn., Soc. for Ethnomusicology, Nat. Saxophone Alliance, Nat. Assn. Coll. Wind and Percussion Instrs., Internat. Clarinet Assn., Music Educators Nat. Conf., Coll. Music Soc. (lectr. 2005), Plainview Mus. Arts Club, Pi Kappa Lambda, Sigma Alpha Iota. Avocations: music, reading, exercise, drawing. Office: Wayland Bapt U 1900 W 7th St # 491 Plainview TX 79072

MOSTERT, PAUL STALLINGS, retired mathematician; b. Morrilton, Ark., Nov. 27, 1927; s. Johannes F. T. and Lucy (Stallings) Mostert; m. Barbara Bond; children: Paul Theodore, Richard Stallings, Kathleen, Kristina. AB, Rhodes Coll., 1950; MS, U. Chgo., 1951; PhD, Purdue U., 1953. Mem. faculty Tulane U., 1953-70, prof. math., 1962-70, chmn. dept., 1968-70; prof. U. Kans., 1970-91, prof. emeritus math., 1991—, chmn. dept., 1970-73. Vis. prof. U. Tubingen, Germany, 1962—63; mem. Inst. Advanced Study, Princeton, 1967—68; vis. prof. math. U. Ky., 1984—85; chmn. Rhodes Coll. Sci. Initiaitve Task Force, 1989—90; pres. Equix, Inc., 1984—85, Pennfield Biomechanics Corp., Inc., 1985—89, Equix Biomechanics, 1989—97, Equix Rsch. Corp., 1989—2005; proprietor Mostert Group, 1997—2003; dir. rsch. Mostert-Group LLC-Equix Biomechanics, 2004—06; mgr. MSRCO, LLC, 2004—; pi NSF, 2008—. Co-author: Splitting in Topological Groups, 1963, 3d edit., 1993, Elements of Compact Semigroups, 1966, The Cohomology Ring of Finite and Compact Abelian Groups, 1974; editor: Proc. Conf. Transformation Groups at New Orleans, 1969, Questiones Mathematicae, 1973—95; exec. editor Semigroup Forum, 1973—84, creator 11 software programs one of which selected matings that produced Kentucky derby winners Lil E.T. and Big Brown; mng. editor: Semigroup Forum, 1969. Mem. Ky. Statewide Exptl. Program Stimulate Competitive Rsch. Com., 1994—96. With USN, 1945—46. Recipient Rsch. awards, Small Bus. Innovative Rsch., 2000—05, NIHS, 2006—08; Sr. postdoctoral fellow, NSF, 1987—88, STTR grant. Mem.: AAAS, Assn. Computing Machinery, Assn. Mems. Inst. Advanced Studies, Am. Math. Soc. (mem. at large coun. 1972—75, chmn. com. acad. freedom, tenure and employment security 1973—76), Thoroughbred Owners and Breeders Assn. Achievements include patents for methods and computer-readable medium for tracking motion and for navigating between a plurality of discrete images. Office: 3298 Roxburg Dr Lexington KY 40503-3432 Office Phone: 859-223-1490. E-mail: pmostert@windstream.net.

MOSTILLO, RALPH, medical association administrator; s. Joseph and Antoinette Mostillo. BA in Chemistry magna cum laude, Rutgers U., Newark, 1972; MA in Biochemistry, Princeton U., NJ, 1974, PhD in Biochemistry, 1978. Rsch. fellow Princeton U., 1972-78; sr. scientist drug regulatory affairs Hoffmann-La Roche, Inc., Nutley, NJ, 1979-85; founder, chmn., CEO Am. Cancer Assn., Nutley, 1986—. With USN, 1962—66, Vietnam. Fellow, NIH, 1972—78. Mem.: NY Acad. Scis., Am. Mktg. Assn., Am. Mgmt. Assn., Am. Chem. Soc., Vietnam Vets. Am., Am. Legion, Phi Beta Kappa, Sigma Xi. Achievements include research in molecular transport systems in E. coli as general models for drug delivery into cells. Home: PO Box 505 Nutley NJ 07110-0505 Office: Am Cancer Assn PO Box 87 Nutley NJ 07110-0087

MOSTOFF, ALLAN SAMUEL, lawyer, consultant; b. NYC, Oct. 19, 1932; s. Morris and Ida (Goldman) M.; m. Alice Tamara Popelowsky, July 31, 1955; children: Peter Alexander, Nina Valerie. BS, Cornell U., 1953; MBA, NYU, 1954; LLB, NY Law Sch., 1957. Bar: NY 1958, DC 1964. Assoc. Olwine Connelly Chase O'Donnell & Weyher, NYC, 1958-61; atty. SEC, Washington, 1962-66, asst. dir., 1966-69, assoc. dir., 1969-72, dir. divsn. investment mgmt. regulation, 1972-76; ptnr. Dechert Price & Rhoads, Washington, 1976—2002, Dechert, Washington, 2000—03; ptnr. emeritus, sr. counsel Dechert LLP, Washington, 2002—03, of counsel, 2004—; pres. Mut. Fund Dirs. Forum, 2002—. Adj. prof. Georgetown U. Law Ctr., 1972-82; mem. Fin. Acctg. Standards Adv. Bd., 1982-86; mem. adv. bd. Investment Lawyer, 2000—, BNA Securities Regulation and Law Report, 1977-87. Recipient Lifetime Achievement award, Fund Directions, 2007. Mem. ABA, Assn. of Bar of City of NY, Fed. Bar Assn. (past chmn. exec. coun. securities regulation com. 1990-92), Am. Law Inst. Home: 6417 Waterway Dr Falls Church VA 22044-1325 also: 3469 Doubleton Dr SE Stuart FL 34997 Office: 1501 M St NW Ste 1150 Washington DC 20005 Office Phone: 202-507-4496. Business E-Mail: allan.mostoff@mfdf.com.

MOSTOV, KEITH ELLIOT, cell biologist, educator; b. NYC, Mar. 6, 1956; s. Philip M. and Frances (Landau) M.; m. Emily Leah Silverman, Apr. 9, 1989. BA, U. Chgo., 1976; postgrad., Oxford U., Eng., 1976-77; PhD, Rockefeller U., 1983; MD, Cornell U., 1984. Whitehead fellow Whitehead Inst. Biomed. Rsch., Cambridge, Mass., 1984-89; asst. prof. cell biology U. Calif., San Francisco, 1989-92, assoc. prof., 1992—. Editorial bd. Internat. Rev. Cytology, 1986—; guest editor Saunders Press series Seminars in Cell Biology, 1990—; contbr. numerous sci. papers to profl. publs. Rhodes scholar Rhodes Trust, 1976; recipient Investigator award Hood Found. Med. Rsch., Boston, 1985, Cancer Rsch. Investigator award Cancer Rsch. Inst., N.Y.C., 1990, Med. scholarship Charles Culpeper Found., 1992, Med. scholar Edward Mallnokrodt Found., 1992, Established Investigator award Am. Heart Assn., 1993; Searle scholar Searle Family Trust, Chgo., 1989. Mem. AAAS, Am. Soc. Cell Biology, Soc. Murosal Immunology. Democrat. Jewish. Office: U Calif San Francisco Sch Med 513 Parnassus Ave San Francisco CA 94122-2722

MOSTOW, GEORGE DANIEL, mathematics professor; b. Boston, July 4, 1923; s. Isaac J. and Ida (Rotman) M.; m. Evelyn Davidoff, Sept. 1, 1947 (dec. Sept. 16, 2005); children: Mark Alan, David Jechiel, Carol Held, Jonathan Carl; m. Srdnie Feit, June 15, 2007. Grad., Boston Pub. Latin Sch., 1940, Hebrew Coll., Boston, 1942; BA, Harvard U., 1943, MA, 1946, PhD, 1948; DSc (hon.), U. Ill., Chgo., 1989. Instr. math. Princeton U., 1947-48; mem. Inst. Advanced Study, 1947-49, 56-57, 75, mem. bd. of trustees, 1982-92; asst. prof. Syracuse U., 1949-52; asst. prof. math. Johns Hopkins U., 1952-53, assoc. prof., 1954-56, prof., 1957-61; prof. math. Yale U., 1961-66, James E. English prof. math., 1966-81, Henry Ford II prof. math., 1981-98, chmn., 1971-74, prof. emeritus, 1998—. Vis. prof. Conselho Nat. des Pesquisas, Inst. de

Matematica, Rio de Janiero, Brazil, 1953-54, 91, U. Paris, 1966-67, Hebrew U., Jerusalem, 1967, Tata Inst. Fundamental Rsch., Bombay, 1970, Inst. des Hautes Etudes Scientifiques, Bures-Sur-Yvette, 1966, 71, 75, Japan Soc. for Promotion of Sci., 1985, Eidgenossische Technische Hochschule, Switzerland, 1986; chmn. U.S. Nat. Com. for Math, 1971-73, 83-85, Office Math. Scis., NRC, 1975-78; mem. sci. adv. coun. Math. Scis. Rsch. Inst., Berkeley, Calif., 1988-91; mem. sci. adv. com., bd. govs. Weizmann Inst., Israel, 1987—2003; bd. govs. Tel Aviv U., 1990-2000; mem. Harvard Grad. Coun., 1988-91; mem. vis. com. dept. math. Harvard U., 1975-81, MIT, 1981-94; Ritt lectr. Columbia U., 1982, Bergman lectr. Stanford U., 1983, Sachar lectr. Tel Aviv U., 1985, Karcher lectr. U. Okla., 1986, Markert lectr. Pa. State U., 1993. Assoc. editor Annals of Math., 1957—64, Trans. Am. Math. Soc., 1958—65, Am. Scientist, 1970—82, Geometriae Dedicata, 1985—90, bd. cons. Jour. D'Analyse Mathématique, 1994—; editor: Am. Jour. Math., 1965—69; assoc. editor Am. Jour. Math., 1969—79; author rsch. articles:. Fulbright rsch. scholar, Utrecht U., The Netherlands; Guggenheim fellow, 1957-58 Mem. AAAS, NAS (chmn. sect. math. 1982-84), Am. Math. Soc. (pres. 1987-88, Steele prize for Paper of Lasting Importance 1993), Internat. Math. Union (chmn. U.S. del. to Gen. Assembly Warsaw 1982, exec. com. 1983-86), Phi Beta Kappa, Sigma Xi. Office: Yale Univ Dept Mathematics New Haven CT 06520 Business E-Mail: mostow@math.yale.edu.

MOSYCHUK, SUSAN, legislative staff member; b. Boston; BS in Govt., Suffolk U., Boston, 1992; MA in Polit. Sci., Am. U., Washington. Rsch. asst. to House Com. on Govt. Ops. Fla. House of Reps., Tallahassee, profl. staff mem. to House Com. on Govt. Reform, appropriations analyst; dir. govt. affairs Citizens Against Govt. Waste; legis. dir. for Rep. Bob Barr US House of Reps., Washington, legis. dir. for Rep. Tim Murphy, 2003—04, chief of staff for Rep. Tim Murphy, 2004—. Mem.: Pi Sigma Alpha. Avocation: languages. Office: Office of Congressman Tim Murphy 412 Cannon House Office Bldg Washington DC 20515 Office Phone: 202-225-2301. Business E-Mail: susan.mosychuk@mail.house.gov.*

MOTAGHIANNEZAM, REZA MOHAMMAD, engineering educator; s. Ali Motaghiannezam and Nahid Roohi; m. Farnaz Khameneh; 1 child, Ariana. BS, Sharif U. Tech., Tehran, 1995; MS, U. So. Calif., Los Angeles, 2002, PhD, 2004. Postdoc. rschr. Harvard Med. Sch., 2005—07; faculty Caltech, 2007—. Author: (book) Optical Performance Monitoring. Recipient APSIH Outstanding Achievement award, 2004, APSIH Young Scholar award, 2004, Outstanding Rschr. award, 2007; IEEE LEOS Grad. Student fellowship, 2003. Mem.: IEEE, Optical Soc. Am., Lasers and Electro-Optics Soc., Comm. Soc. Avocations: soccer, music, travel.

MOTAMED, THOMAS FIROUZ, insurance company executive; BA in Biology, Adelphi U., Garden City, NY, 1971; JD, Widener U., 1975. Sci. faculty Malvern Prep. Sch., Pa., 1975-76; field underwriter NY Life, Carle Place, NY, 1976-77; claims trainee The Chubb Corp., LI, 1977—78, claims unit mgr., 1978—80, NY br. office mgr., 1980—81, litig. mgr. claims dept. Short Hills, NJ, 1981—83, nat. claim audit mgr. Warren, NJ, 1983—84, nat. claim adminstr., 1984—86, claim mgr. NYC, 1986—88, adminstrv. mgr., 1988—89, LI mktg. mgr., 1989—90, br. mgr. Westchester, NY, 1990—93, midtown NY br. mgr., 1993—96, western zone officer, 1996—97, exec. v.p., COO Warren, NJ, 1997—2002, vice chmn., COO, 2002—08; pres., COO, mng. dir. Chubb & Son Inc. divsn. of Fed. Ins. Co., Warren, NJ.

MOTCH, MARJORIE MCCULLOUGH, service organization executive; b. Cin., July 12, 1923; d. Robert Stedman and Mildred (Rogers) McCullough; m. Homer E. Lunken, Apr. 15, 1944 (dec. 1970); children: Karen Lunken(dec.), Kathryn Lunken Summers, Margo Lunken Yesner; m. William McLeod Ittmann, Mar. 17, 1972 (dec. 1982); m. Harold Hiatt, Apr. 14, 1984 (dec. 1999); m. Graham E. Marx, Jan. 4, 2003 (dec. 2003); m. Arthur E. Motch Jr., Sept. 18, 2004 (dec. 2005). Student, U. Cin., 1941—43, DFA (hon.), 2003. Active Girl Scouts US, 1962—, chmn. conv. com., 1972, del. world convs., 1969, 72, 75, 78, 81, 84, 87, 93, chmn. pub. relations com., 1963-66, mem. nat. exec. com., 1963-75, mem. nat. bd., 1962—, 4th v.p., 1966-69, 1st v.p., 1969-72, nat. pres., 1972-75, chmn. nat. adv. coun., 1975-82, mem. birthplace adv. com., 1980-97. Vice chmn. world conf., Orleans, France, 1981; world com. World Assn. Girl Guides and Girl Scouts, 1978-87, vice chmn., 1984-87; trustee emeritus U. Cin. Found. Regional dir. Assn. Jr. Leagues Am., 1958—60, nat. pres., 1960—62; mem. br. Nat. Assembly for Social Policy and Devel., 1968—71; mem. exec. com. Coun. Nat. Orgns. for Children and Youth, 1960—62, 1968—72; mem. br. Jr. League Cin., 1944—58, Nat. Tng. Labs., 1963—66; mem. policy com. Ctr. Vol. Soc., 1971—72; mem. Ohio Citizens Coun., 1956—58; mem. bd. advisors U. Cin. Coll. Nursing, 2000—; bd. dirs. 7th Presbyn. Ch., 1967—74, 1985—, ruling elder, 1976—78, 2000—, chmn. bd. trustees, 1992—94; sr. warden St. Martin's in the Field, Biddeford Pool, Maine; bd. dirs. United Way Am., 1962—67, sec., 1965—66, v.p., 1966—67, 1989—; bd. dirs. Fine Arts Fund, 2002—, Coll. Prep. Sch., Cin., 1962—69, pres., 1964—69; bd. dirs. Cin. Speech and Hearing Ctr., 1955—66, v.p., 1958—62, pres., 1963—66, trustee emeritus, 1966—; mem. bd. Children's Theatre, Cin., 1948—58, pres., 1948—50; bd. dirs. Cmty. Health and Welfare Coun. Cin., 1957—63, Hamilton County Rsch. Found., Ohio, 1963—65, Cancer Family Care, Cin., 1971—72, Boys Clubs Greater Cin., Marjorie P. Lee Home for the Aged, Ctrl. Psychiat. Clinic, Music Hall Assn., Cin. Symphony Orch., Beechwood Home for Incurables, 1975—87, St. Margaret Hall, 1991—, Cin. Civic Garden Ctr., 1992—95, Greater Cin. Found., 1979—87, Ctrl. Clinic, 2000—, YWCA, 1998—, Fine Arts Fund, 2002—. Recipient Mary Herriman award, 2000, Mardee Wachs Vol. Svc. award, Hearing, Speech, and Deaf Ctrs., 2006. Mem. Olave Baden-Powell Soc. (v.p. 1991-93, pres. 1993-97), World Found. for Girl Guides and Girl Scouts (v.p. 1989—), Garden Club Am. (vice chmn. founder's fund 1991-92), Am. Psychiat. Assn. Aux. (bd. dirs., rec. sec. 1991-92). Home: 2353 Bedford Ave Cincinnati OH 45208-2656

MOTE, CLAYTON DANIEL, JR., academic administrator, mechanical engineer, educator; b. San Francisco, Feb. 5, 1937; s. Clayton Daniel and Eugenia (Isnardi) M.; m. Patricia Jane Lewis, Aug. 18, 1962; children: Melissa Michelle, Adam Jonathan. BSc, U. Calif., Berkeley, 1959, MS, 1960, PhD, 1963; Doctorate (hon.), Tashkent State Tech. U., 2001; DSc, Ohio State U., 2001; Dr Sci. and Tech. (hon.), Carnegie Mellon U., 2004. Registered profl. engr., Calif. Asst. specialist U. Calif. Forest Products Lab., 1961-62, asst. mech. engr., 1962-63; lectr. mech. engring. U. Calif., Berkeley, 1962-63, asst. prof., 1967-69, asst. research engr., 1968-69, assoc. prof., assoc. research engr., 1969-73, prof., 1973-98, vice chmn. mech. engring. dept., 1976-80, 83-86, chmn. mech. engring. dept., 1987-91, vice chancellor univ. rels., FANUC chair mech. systems, 1991-98; research fellow U. Birmingham, Eng., 1963-64; asst. prof. Carnegie Inst. Tech., 1964-67; Glen L. Martin Inst. prof. engring. U. Md., College Park, 1998—, pres., 1998—. Vis. prof. Norwegian Inst. Wood Tech., 1972—73, vis. sr. scientist, 1976, 78, 80, 84, 85; cons. in engring., design and analysis; cons. in engring. NAE, 1988, Nat. Acad. Arts and Sci., 2004; sr. scientist Alexander Von Humboldt Found., Germany, 1988, Japan Soc. for Promotion of Sci., Japan, 1991. Mem. editl. bd. Soma Jour. Sound and Vibration, Machine Vibration; contbr. articles to profl. jours.; patentee in field. NSF fellow, 1963-64, Sr. Scientist fellow Japan Soc. Promotion Sci., 1991, Berkeley fellow, 2001; recipient Disting. Tchg. award U. Calif., 1971, Pi Tau Sigma Excellence in Tchg. award U. Calif., 1975, Humboldt prize, Fed. Republic Germany, 1988, Disting. Engring. Alumnus award U. Calif., 2001, Frederick W. Taylor Rsch. medal. Soc. Mfg. Engrs., 1991, Hetenyi award Soc. Exptl. Mechanics, 1992, Eagle award Met. Washington chpt. ARCS, 2000, Excellence in Achievement award Calif. Alumni Assn., 2007. Fellow: Am. Acad. Arts and Sci. (coun. del. Sect M 2003—), NAE (councillor 2002—08, former program com., peer com., treas. 2009, Founder's award 2005), ASME (hon.; chmn. San Francisco sect. 1978—79, nat. chmn. noise control and acoustics 1980—84, v.p. environ. and transp. 1986—90, Blackall award 1975, Disting. Svc. award 1991, Charles Russ Richards award 1994, Rayleigh lectr. 1994, Applied Mechanics award 2001, Den Hertog award 2005), Acoustical Soc. Am., Internat. Acad. Wood Sci.; mem.: NRC (vice chair com. on dept. basic rsch. 2004, nat. acad. press 2005, com. on sci., engring. and pub. policy 2005, governing bd. 2007—, com. on prospering in global economy of the 21st century), AAAS, ASTM (com. on snow skiing F-27 1984—87), Orthopaedic Rsch. Soc., Am. Soc. Biomechanics, Am. Acad. Mechanics, Am. Soc. Engring. Edn. (Ralph Coast Roe award 1997), Internat. Soc. Skiing Safety (hon.; sec. 1977—85, bd.dirs. 1977—, chmn. sci. com. 1985—, v.p.), Tau Beta Pi, Sigma Xi, Nat. Soc. Collegiate Scholars, Golden Key Nat. Honor Soc., Phi Kappa Phi, Omicron Delta Kappa, Pi Tau Sigma. Office: Office of Pres U Md Main Adminstrn Bldg College Park MD 20742-5025 Office Phone: 301-405-5803. Business E-Mail: president@umd.edu.

MOTEN, DARLENE, elementary school educator; d. Spencer and Arlishie Moten; children: Nichole Antoinette, Ana Lisa, Candy Sue, Sandy Darlene, Micah Jeremiah, Ann Marie, Taheerah Janiece, Donald Vance, Ebonee Lashey, Aleizah Janae. BS in Bus. Edn., U. Ariz., Tucson, 1975; MEd, U. Ariz., 1981. Sec. U. Ariz., Tucson, 1972—76; tchr. bus. edn. Amphitheater Pub. Schs., Tucson, 1977—. Libr. rev. com. Amphitheater Pub. Schs., Tucson, 1995—99; poetry contest judge Amphitheater Mid. Sch., Tucson, 2004—. Dir. of children's ministry Mt. Olive Ch. Of God In Christ, Tucson, 1975; state children's dir. Ch. Of God In Christ, Phoenix, 1986. Recipient Cmty. Svc. award, Mayor City of Tucson, 2000, Pima County Supr. Dan Eckstrom, 2000. Mem.: NEA (assoc.), Amphitheater Edn. Assn. (assoc.). Penecostal. Avocations: reading, travel, writing, home remodeling. Office: Amphitheater Public Schools 315 E Prince Rd Tucson AZ 85705 E-mail: dmoten@amphi.com.

MOTEN, SEBRENA R., law educator; d. Oliver W. and Katherine M. Moten. AA in Pre-Law Studies, Alexander City State Jr. Coll., Ala., 1983; BA in Polit. Sci., U. Ala., Tuscaloosa, 1985, JD, 1989. Bar: Ala. State Bar Assn. 1992. Law clk. City Tuscaloosa Legal Dept., Ala., 1988—89; legal rsch. aide Ala. Atty. General's Office, Montgomery, Ala., 1989—90; instr. Tuskegee U., Ala., 1990—94; assoc. prof. Troy U., Ala., 1992—. Advisor Phi Gamma Nu Bus. Frat., Troy, Ala., 1991—2008. Recipient Dedication and Self-Sacrifice award, Combat Communication Squadron, 2001; named Prof. of Month, Troy U. SGA, 1997, Outstanding Young Women of America. Mem.: Ala. Black Faculty Assn., Ala. State Bar Assn., Phi Alpha Delta Internat. Legal Frat., Ala. Lawyers Assn., Sigma Gamma Rho (Outstanding U. Prof.). Methodist. Office: Trpy Univ Univ Ave Troy AL 36082 Office Fax: 334-670-3599. Business E-Mail: smoten@troy.edu.

MOTENKO, NEIL PHILIP, lawyer; b. Chgo., July 27, 1951; s. Max Narad Motenko and Carolyn (Friedman) Rose; children: Adam, Joshua, Micah. AB magna cum laude (hon.), Harvard U., 1973, JD, 1976. Bar: Mass. 1977, US Dist. Ct. Mass. 1978. Assoc. Nutter, McClennen & Fish, Boston, 1976-81, jr. ptnr., 1981-85, ptnr., 1985—2008; chambers and ptnr. Boston Mag., 2003—08; sr. conflicts counsel Ropes & Gray LLP, 2009—. Co-chmn. New Eng. Antitrust Conf., Boston, 1987-96, taught Harvard Sch. of Pub. Health, Boston U Sch. of Law, Tufts Sch of Medicine, spkr. in field. Contbr. articles to profl. jour. Named The Best Lawyers in Am., Leading US Antitrust Atty., Chambers and Ptnr., 2003—08, Mass. Super Lawyer, Boston mag., 2004—08, Am. Leading Bus. Lawyers, Chambers USA. Mem. ABA (antitrust sect.,litigation sect. chmn. health care com., co-chair ops. com.), Boston Bar Assn. (past chmn. antitrust com. coun.). Office: Ropes & Gray LLP 1 International Pl Boston MA 02110 Office Phone: 617-951-7463. Office Fax: 617-235-7328. Business E-Mail: neil.motenko@ropesgray.com.

MOTEVALLI, VAHID, engineering educator; s. Morteza Aliabadi Motevalli and Mahvash Baroutchian; m. Hosi Karzai; 3 children. PhD in Engring., U. Md., Coll. Pk., 1989. Asst. prof. Worcester Poly. Inst., Mass., 1988—94, assoc. prof., 1994—98; assoc. rsch. prof., sch. engring. George Wash. U., 1998—2004, 2004—, dir. aviation inst., 2002—08; prof. Dubai Aerospace Enterprise U., 2008, assoc. provost grad. studies and rsch., 2008. Pres. Sigma Xi Chpt., Worcester, 1992—94; chairperson ASME Worcester Sect., 1992—94. Recipient Prof. of Yr., Sch. Engring., George Wash. U., 2000—01, U. Rep. award, Transp. Rsch. Bd., Nat. Academies, 2005—08; Grad. Doc. Rsch. award, U. Md., 1985—98. Fellow: ASEE; mem.: ASME (Congl. fellow 1995—96), SAE Internat., Combustion Inst., Royal Aero. Soc. (Wash.), Internat. Aviation Club. Achievements include Congressional Fellow. Office: George Washington Univ 801 22nd St NW Rm 641 Washington DC 20052 Personal E-mail: vahid_2000@yahoo.com. Business E-Mail: vahidm@gwu.edu.

MOTHERAL, BRENDA R., health products executive; Grad., MBA, U. Ky.; PhD, U. SC. Dir. Ctr. Pharm. Policy; mem. faculty U. Ariz. Coll. Pharmacy; sr. dir. rsch. Express Scripts, Inc., Md. Heights, Mo., 2000—03, v.p. rsch., 2003, v.p. rsch. and trend mgmt., 2003—04, v.p. product devel., 2005—06, sr. v.p. product mgmt., 2006, sr. v.p. rsch. and product mgmt., 2006—. Contbr. articles to profl. jours.

MOTHERWAY, NICHOLAS J., lawyer; b. Chgo., Jan. 21, 1940; s. Daniel Lawrence and Margaret Ann Motherway; m. Kathleen Elizabeth Butler, Dec. 23, 1967; children: Daniel, Nicholas, Carolyn, Brian. BSc, Loyola U., 1961; JD, DePaul U., 1965. Bar: Ill. 1965, U.S. Dist. Ct. (no. dist.) Ill. 1965, U.S. Ct. Appeals (7th cir.) 1996. Asst. states atty. Cook County States Atty., Chgo., 1966—73; assoc. Philip H. Corboy, Chgo., 1973—82; prin. Motherway and Napleton, Chgo., 1982—. Mem. Ill. Supreme Ct. Rules Com., 2007—. Lt. USAR, 1961—67. Fellow: Am. Coll. Trial Lawyers; mem.: ATLA (bd. govs. 1990—95), Am. Bd. Trial Adv. (pres. Ill. chpt. 1995—96, nat. bd. dirs. 1996—). Office: Motherway and Napleton 100 W Monroe St Chicago IL 60603 Office Phone: 312-726-2699. Business E-Mail: nmotherway@mnlawoffice.com.

MOTIKA, LIDIA See BASTIANICH, LIDIA

MOTIN, SUSAN HUBBS, school librarian; d. Lewis Taylor and Dorothy Eloise Hubbs; m. Paul Stephen Motin, Nov. 11, 1989; children: Elizabeth, Emily. BA, Albion Coll., Mich., 1982; MLS, U. Mich., Ann Arbor, 1984. Libr. Saginaw Coop. Hosp., Inc., Mich., 1984—86, Loyola U. Chgo., 1986—90; libr., prof. St. Cloud State U., Minn., 1990—. Contbr. articles to numerous profl. jours. Grant, Libr. Am., 2004, ALA, 2006—08, Nat. Endowment Humanities, 2007, NY Hist. Soc., 2007. Mem.: ALA, Minnsota Libr. Assn., Assn. Coll. and Rsch. Librs. Office: St Cloud State Univ 720 Fourth Ave S Saint Cloud MN 56301-4498 Business E-Mail: smotin@stcloudstate.edu.

MOTLEY, TRAVIS, surgeon; s. Herman Michael and Donna Faye Motley; m. Tiffany Crockett; children: Madison, Makinley. BS, Tex. Christian U., Ft. Worth, 1993, MS, 1995; DPM, Des Moines U., Iowa, 2000. Cert. Am. Coll. Foot and Ankle Surgeons, 2005. Attending physician U. Orthop. Assocs., Ft. Worth, 2003—. Contbr. articles to med. jours. Named Young Practitioner of Yr., Tex. Pediat. Med. Assn., 2008; named one of Top Drs., Ft. Worth Mag., 2005—07. Fellow: Am. Coll. Foot and Ankle Surgeons. Conservative. Office: Univ Orthop Assocs 1500 S Main St Fort Worth TX 76104 Office Fax: 817-927-3955. Business E-Mail: tmotley@jpshealth.org.

MOTRONI, HECTOR JOHN, retired printing company executive; b. Havana, Cuba, Dec. 2, 1943; came to US, 1956; s. Marco Antonio and Lilia Ines (Suarez) M.; m. Myra Helene Egan, Aug. 9, 1969; children: Marcus Alan, Melissa Aimee. BA, Dartmouth Coll., 1966, BE, 1967, ME, 1968. Engr. USPHS, Bethesda, Md., 1969-71, Xerox Corp., 1971—2007, various positions Stamford, Conn., 1971-99, with Xerox Latin Am. Group, 1973, group v.p. quality, customer satisfaction and orgnl. effectiveness, 1991, v.p. human resources and quality, corp. sr. v.p., chief staff officer Stamford, 1999—2002, corp. sr. v.p., chief staff and ethics officer, 2003—07. Bd. dirs. Prep for Prep. Trustee Temple Israel, Westport, Conn., 1981-84; bd. adv. Outward Bound USA, 1998; bd. dirs. Nat. Action Coun. Minorities in Engring., Horizons at Green Farms Acad., 2005; chmn. bd. trustees Xerox Polit. Action Com., 2001-07. Recipient Eagle award, Nat. Eagle Inst., 1997; named Hispanic Achiever of Yr., Hispanic Corp. Achievers, 1997; named one of 50 Most Important Hispanics in Bus. and Tech., Hispanic Engrs. and Info. Tech. Mag., 2003, 2004, 2005, 2006, 25 Top Hispanic Execs., Hispanic Trends Mag., 2005, 100 Most Important Hispanics of 2005, Hispanic Bus. Mag. Mem. Nat. Policy Assn. (bd. dirs., chmn. com. new Am. realities 1996-2002), Dartmouth Soc. Engrs. (pres. 1977-85), Dartmouth Coll. Alumni Coun. (chmn. comm. 1983-88, Dartmouth Alumni award 2006), Coun. of the Ams. (adv. bd. 1983-89), Forum for World Affairs (bd. dirs. 1996-2001). Avocation: running.

MOTT, RANDY (RANDALL D. MOTT), computer company executive; b. 1956; BS in Math., U. Ark., Fayetteville, 1978. Various positions Wal-Mart Stores, Inc., 1978—94, sr. v.p., chief info. officer, 1994—97, mem. exec. com., 1997; sr. v.p., chief info. officer Dell, Inc., Round Rock, Tex., 2000—05; exec. v.p., chief info. officer Hewlett-Packard Co., Palo Alto, Calif., 2005—. Mem. Pres. Info. Tech. Adv. Com., 2003—. Named Chief Info. Officer of Yr., Info. Week mag., 1997, Disting. Alumni, Fulbright Coll. Alumni Acad., 2005. Office: Hewlett-Packard Co 3000 Hanover St Palo Alto CA 94304-1185 Office Phone: 650-857-1501. Office Fax: 650-857-5518.*

MOTT, RODNEY B., metal products executive; BS in Indsl. Engring., Northeastern U., 1974; MSc in Mgmt., Trenton State Coll., 1978. Various mgmt. positions US Steel, Fairless Hills, Pa., 1974—86; supt. ops. Lone Star Steel, 1986—88; v.p., gen. mgr. South Carolina plant, Arkansas plant, Crawfordsville plant Nucor Steel, 1988—2000; pres., CEO Pechiney Rolled Products, 2000—01, Internat. Steel Group, Richfield, Ohio, 2002—05; cons. Tricap Mgmt. Ltd.; pres, CEO Stelco Inc., Hamilton, Ont., 2006—. Named Mgr. of Yr., New Steel Mag., 1995. Mem.: Am. Iron and Steel Engrs. (pres. 1998).

MOTTE, WARREN F., JR., literature and language professor; b. Newton, Mass., Oct. 5, 1951; s. Warren F. and Lois T. Motte; m. Marie Molia Molia, July 7, 1977; children: Nicholas Warren Holmes Motte, Nathaniel Warren Seth Motte. AB, U. Pa., Phila., 1974, AM, 1978, PhD, 1981; MA, U. Bordeaux, France, 1977. Asst. prof. U. Nebr., Lincoln, 1982—86, assoc. prof., 1986—87, U. Colo., Boulder, 1987—91, prof., 1991—. Critic: to numerous books. Office: Dept French and Italian Univ Colo Boulder CO 80309-0238

MOTTELSON, BEN ROY, physicist; b. Chgo., July 9, 1926; naturalized Danish citizen, 1971. s. Goodman and Georgia (Blum) M.; m. Nancy Jane Reno, 1948 (dec. 1975); 3 children; m. Britta Marger Siegumfeldt, 1983. BSc, Purdue U., 1947; PhD, Harvard U., 1950; degree (hon.), Purdue U., U. Heidelberg, Fed. Republic Germany, Lund U., Sweden, Liverpool U., Eng. Sheldon traveling fellow Inst. Theoretical Physics, Copenhagen, 1950—51, U.S. AEC fellow, 1951—53; with theoretical study group CERN, Copenhagen, 1953—57; prof. Nordic Inst. for Theoretical Atomic Physics, Copenhagen, 1957—; dir. European ctr. Theoretical Studies in Nuc. Physics and Related Areas, Trento, Italy, 1980—97. Physicist Neils Bohr Inst., Copenhagen; bd. dir. Nordita; vis. prof. U. Calif., Berkeley, 1959, Berkeley, 84; adj. prof. Niels Bohr Inst., Copenhagen, 1994; Feshbach lectureship, 96. Author: Nuclear Structure, vol. 1, 1969, vol. 2 (with A. Bohr), 1975; numerous other publications in field. Recipient Wetherill award, Franklin Inst., 1974, Nobel prize for physics, 1975. Mem.: Norwegian Acad. of Sci. and Letters, Polish Acad. of Sci., Kroatian Acad. Sci. (fgn. assoc.), Finnish Soc. Sci. and Letters, European Acad. of Arts, Sci., and Letters, Kgl. Fys. Graf, Lund, Sweden, Am. Acad. Arts and Letters, Royal Dan. Acad. Sci. and Letters, Nat. Acad. Sci. (fgn. assoc.). Address: NORDITA and The Niels Bohr Inst Blegdamsvej 17 DK-2100 Copenhagen Denmark Business E-Mail: mottelson@nordita.dk.

MOTTO, JEROME ARTHUR, psychiatrist, educator; b. Kansas City, Mo., Oct. 16, 1921; MD, U. Calif., San Francisco, 1951. Diplomate Am. Bd. Neurology and Psychiatry. Intern San Francisco Gen. Hosp., 1951-52; resident Johns Hopkins Hosp., Balt., 1952-55; sr. resident U. Calif., San Francisco, 1955-56; from instr. to prof. U. Calif. Sch. Medicine, San Francisco, 1956—91, prof. emeritus, 1991—. Pres. Am. Assn. Suicidology, 1972—73; sec. gen. Internat. Assn. Suicide Prevention, 1973—77. Contbr. articles to profl. jours. With AUS, 1942-46, ETO. Recipient Outstanding Achievement award, Northern Calif. Psychiatric Soc., 2009, Marcia Linehan award, Am. Assn. Suicidology, 2009. Fellow: Am. Psychiatric Assn. (life; disting. fellow).

MOTTOLA, TOMMY (THOMAS DANIEL MOTTOLA), recording industry executive; b. Bronx, NY, July 14, 1949; m. Lisa Clark, 1971 (div. 1990); 2 children; m. Mariah Carey, June 5, 1993 (div. Mar. 5, 1998); m. Thalía Sodi, Dec. 2, 2000; 1 child, Sabrina Sakae. Attended, Hofstra U. Pres., CEO Sony Music Entertainment Inc, NYC, chmn., CEO, 1998—2003; pres. Casablanca Records, 2004—.

MOTTS, WARREN EARL, museum director; b. Brice, Ohio, Nov. 10, 1940; s. Wilbur Ernest and Mabel Marie Motts; m. Daisy Nell Blair, July 1, 1966; children: Wayne Earl, Lori Lynn. M in photography, Profl. Photographers of Am., 1977; MS in photography, Brooks Inst. Sch. of Profl. Photography, 1990; M, China, 1990, Mexico, 1990. Photo lab tech. Battelle Meml. Inst., Columbus, Ohio, 1960—62; med. photographer Ohio State Hosp., Columbus, 1962—64; photographer Columbus and Southern Electric, Columbus, 1964—67; commercial photographer Columbus Art, Columbus, 1967—69; v.p. Moor Photography, Columbus, 1969—72; pres., owner Motts Photographic Ctr., Columbus, 1972—97; founder, dir. Motts Mil. Mus., Groveport, Ohio, 1988—. Pres. Profl. Photo of Am., Atlanta, 1990—91, Mil. Vets Edn., Columbus, Ohio, 1999—2000; bd. dirs. Veterans Meml., Columbus, 2001—; lectr. Mathew Brady: Civil War Photographer, 1994. Creator: (films) American Freedom Train, 1976; Gettysburg: A Portrait in Red, Gray, and Blue; contbr. articles various profl. jours. Pres. Groveport Lions Club, Groveport, Ohio, 1999—2000, Columbus Civil War, Columbus, Ohio, 1967; chmn. of bd. Brice United Meth. Ch., Brice, Ohio, 1981—; 32nd Mason Masonic Order, Columbus, Ohio, 1981. With Ohio Nat. Guard, 1959—68. Recipient Patriotic, Daughters of Am. Revolution, 1982, Dist. Svc. award, PP of Am., 1991; named Communicator of Yr., Communicatings Arts, 1991. Mem.: Ohio Hist. Mus., Am. Mus. Assoc., Airforce Assn. (life). Republican. Meth. Avocation: antiques. Office: Motts Mil Mus 5075 S Hamilton Rd Groveport OH 43125 Office Phone: 614-836-1500. Office Fax: 614-836-5110.

MOTULSKY, ARNO GUNTHER, internist, geneticist, educator; b. Fischhausen, Germany, July 5, 1923; arrived in U.S., 1941; s. Herman and Rena (Sass) Molton; m. Gretel C. Stern, Mar. 22, 1945; children: Judy, Harvey, Arlene. Student, Cen. YMCA Coll., Chgo., 1941—43, Yale U., 1943—44; BS, U. Ill., 1945, MD, 1947, DSc (hon.), 1982, MD (hon.), 1991. Diplomate Am. Bd. Internal Medicine, Am. Bd. Med. Genetics. Intern, fellow, resident Michael Reese Hosp., Chgo., 1947—51; staff mem. charge clin. investigation dept. hematology Army Med. Service Grad. Sch., Walter Reed Army Med. Ctr., Washington, 1952—53; research assoc. internal medicine George Washington U. Sch. Medicine, 1952—53; from instr. to assoc. prof. dept. medicine U. Wash. Sch. Medicine, Seattle, 1953—61, prof. medicine, prof. genetics, 1961—; head div. med. genetics, dir. genetics clinic Univ. Hosp., Seattle, 1959—89; dir. Ctr. for Inherited Diseases, Seattle, 1972—90. Attending physician Univ. Hosp., Seattle; cons. Pres.'s Commn. for Study of Ethical Problems in Medicine and Biomed. and Behavioral Rsch., 1979—83; cons. various coms. NRC, NIH, WHO, and others. Editor: Am. Jour. Human Genetics, 1969—75, Human Genetics, 1969—97. Fellow Commonwealth Fund in human genetics, Univ. Coll., London, 1957—58, Ctr. Advanced Study in Behavorial Scis., Stanford U., 1976—77, Inst. Advanced Study, Berlin, 1984; scholar John and Mary Markle in med. sci., 1957—62. Fellow: AAAS, ACP; mem.: NAS, Am. Philos. Soc., Am. Acad. Arts and Scis., Inst. of Medicine, Am. Assn. Physicians, Am. Soc. Clin. Investigation, Am. Soc. Human Genetics, Western Soc. Clin. Rsch., Genetics Soc. Am., Am. Fedn. Clin. Rsch., Internat. Soc. Hematology. Home: 4347 53rd Ave NE Seattle WA 98105-4938 Office: Univ Wash Medicine and Genome Scis PO Box 355065 Seattle WA 98195-5065 Business E-Mail: agmot@u.washington.edu.

MOTYKIE, GARY, plastic surgeon; Attended night sch., Kellogg Grad. Sch. Mgmt., 1997—99; BS in Bio-Med. Engring. (summa cum laude), Univ. Ill., Chgo., 1993; MD, Northwestern Univ. Med. Sch., Chgo., 1999. Clin. rsch. fellow, dept. surgery Northwestern U. Med. Sch., 1997—99; resident, plastic surgery U. Tex. Med. Branch, Galveston, Tex., 1999—2004; externship, Aesthetic Surgery James M. Stuzin, Thomas & Tracy Baker, Miami, Fla., 2003; externship, Microsurgery & Cancer Reconstruction M.D. Anderson Cancer Ctr., Houston, 2003; fellow in advanced cosmetic surgery Beverly Hills, Calif., 2004; with Beverly Hills Body, Calif. Spkr. in field. Contbr. articles to profl. jours., chapters to books; featured in The Smart Surgeon, plasticsurgeryproductsonline.com, 2007. Mem.: ACS (cand. and assoc. soc. 2000—, mem.-elect, issues com. 2002—, mem. adv. coun. for plastic and maxillofacial surgery cand. 2002—, assoc. soc. respresentative 2002—), Am. Soc. Plastic Surgeons (mem., resident affiliate group 2000—, mem. com. edn., ASMS 2002—), Plastic Surgery Rsch. Coun., Tex. Med. Assn. (resident and fellow sect. 1999—2004, representative, com. continuing edn. 1999—2004), AMA (mem. polit. action com. 2002—), Tau Beta Pi. Office: Beverly Hills Body 9201 Sunset Blvd Ste 202 Los Angeles CA 90069 Office Phone: 310-276-3183.

MOTZ, DIANA GRIBBON, federal judge; b. Washington, July 15, 1943; d. Daniel McNamara and Jane (Retzler) Gribbon; m. John Frederick Motz, Sept. 20, 1968; children: Catherine Jane, Daniel Gribbon. BA, Vassar Coll., 1965; LLB, U. Va., 1968. Bar: US Dist. Ct. Md. 1969, US Ct. Appeals (4th cir.) 1969, US Supreme Ct. 1980. Assoc. Piper & Marbury, Balt., 1968—71; asst. atty. gen. State of Md., Balt., 1972—81, chief of litigation, 1981—86; ptnr. Frank, Bernstein, Conaway & Goldman, Balt., 1986—91; judge Md. Ct. of Special Appeals, 1991—94, US Ct. Appeals (4th cir.), 1994—. Mem.: ABA, Fed. Cts. Study Com., Lawyers Round Table, Md. Bar Found., Am. Bar Found., Am. Law Inst., Balt. City Bar Assn. (exec. com. 1988), Md. Bar Assn., Wranglers Law Club. Roman Catholic. Office: 920 US Courthouse 101 W Lombard St Ste 920 Baltimore MD 21201-2611*

MOTZ, JOHN FREDERICK, federal judge; b. Balt., Dec. 30, 1942; s. John Eldred and Catherine (Grauel) M.; m. Diana Jane Gribbon, Sept. 20, 1968; children: Catherine Jane, Daniel Gribbon AB, Wesleyan U., Conn., 1964; LLB, U. Va., 1967. Bar: Md. 1967, U.S. Ct. Appeals (4th cir.) 1968, U.S. Dist. Ct. Md. 1968. Law clk. to Hon. Harrison L. Winter US Ct. Appeals (4th cir.), 1967-68; assoc. Venable, Baetjer & Howard LLP, Balt., 1968-69; asst. U.S. atty. US Dept. Justice, Balt., 1969-71; assoc. Venable, Baetjer & Howard, Balt., 1971-75; ptnr. Venable, Baetjer & Howard LLP, Balt., 1976-81; US atty. US Dept. Justice, Balt., 1981-85; judge US Dist. Ct. Md., Balt., 1985—, chief judge, 1994—2001; chair Com. Intercircuit Assignment, 2008—. Mem. US Jud. Panel on Multidistrict Litig., 2001—09. Trustees Friends Sch., Balt., 1970-77, 1981-88, Sheppard Pratt Hosp., 1987-97, 99—. Mem.: ABA, Am. Coll. Trial Lawyers (mem. bd. editors. Manual of Complex Litigation (4th)), Am. Law Inst., Am. Bar Found., Md. State Bar Assn. Mem. Soc. Of Friends. Office: US Dist Ct 101 W Lombard St Rm 510 Baltimore MD 21201-2605

MOU, BO, philosopher, educator; BS in Math., PLA Inst. Tech., Luoyang, Zhengzhou, 1982; MA in Philosophy, Grad. Sch. Chinese Acad. Social Sci., Beijing, 1987; PhD, U. Rochester, NY, 1997. Asst. rsch. fellow Inst. Philosophy, Chinese Acad. Social Scis., Beijing, 1987—89; vis. asst. prof. Le Moyne Coll., Syracuse, NY, 1998—99; asst. prof. San Jose State U., Calif., 2000—05, assoc. prof., 2005—09, prof., 2009—. Author: (reference book) Chinese Philosophy A-Z; editor: History of Chinese Philosophy; contbr. monograph. Mem.: Internat. Soc. Comparative Studies Chinese and Western Philosophy (pres. 2002—05), Am. Philos. Assn. Office: San Jose State Univ Dept Philosophy San Jose CA 95192-0096 Business E-Mail: bo.mou@sjsu.edu.

MOUDON, ANNE VERNEZ, urban design educator; b. Yverdon, Vaud, Switzerland, Dec. 24, 1945; came to U.S., 1966; d. Ernest Edouard and Mauricette Lina (Duc) Moudon; children: Louisa Moudon Seferis, Constantine Thomas Seferis. BArch with honors, U. Calif., Berkeley, 1969; DSc, Ecole Poly. Fed., Lausanne, Switzerland, 1987. Fed. Register of Swiss Archs. Rsch. assoc. Bldg. Sys. Devel., Inc., San Francisco, 1969-70; sr. project planner J.C. Warnecke and Assocs., NYC, 1973-74; archtl. cons. McCue, Boone & Tomsick, San Francisco, 1974-76; asst. to assoc. prof. architecture MIT, Cambridge, Mass., 1975-81, Ford internat. career chair, 1977-79; sec. Assn. Collegiate Schs. Arch., 1978-80; assoc. prof. urban design U. Wash., Seattle, 1981-87, prof. architecture, landscape architecture, urban design and planning, 1987—, dir. urban design program, 1987-93, assoc. dean acad. affairs Coll. Arch. and Urban Planning, 1992-95; dir. Cascadia Cmty. and Environ. Inst., Seattle, 1993-98. Lectr. architecture U. Calif., Berkeley, 1973-75; sr. rschr. Kungl Tekniska Hogskolan, Sch. Architecture, Stockholm, 1989; faculty assoc. Lincoln Inst. Land Policy, 1997—2005; mem. adv. com. Robert Wood Johnson Found., 2002—. Author: Built for Change, 1986; editor: Public Streets for Public Use, 1987, 91, (monograph) Master-Planned Communities, 1990, Urban Design: Reshaping Our Cities, 1995, Land Supply Monitoring with Geographic Information Systems, 2000; contbr. articles to profl. jours. Recipient Applied Rsch. award, Progressive Architecture, 1983; grantee Nat. Endowment for the Arts, 1976—89, Wash. State Dept. Transp., 1991—, CDC, 2001—04; fellow Nat. Endowment for the Arts, 1986—87, Urban Land Inst., 1999—2006; grant, NIH, 1995—2000, 2007—, Robert Wood Johnson Found., 2007—08. Fellow: Inst. for Urban Design. Avocations: walking, gardening, skiing. Office: U Wash Box 355740 PO Box Jo-40 Goul Seattle WA 98195-5740 Home: 2125 First Ave #1006 Seattle WA 98121 Business E-Mail: moudon@uwashington.edu.

MOUILLET, ALAIN CHARLES, retired engineering educator, researcher; b. Saint Germain sur Meuse, Meuse, France, Sept. 11, 1944; s. Paul Maurice Mouillet and Yvonne Marguerite Labbe; m. Viviane Albert, Dec. 17, 1966; children: Dominique, Jean-Luc, Isabelle. PhD, U. of Tech., Compiègne, France, 1975. Asst. prof. U. Paris XI, Cachan, Val de Marne, France, 1968—73, U. of Tech., Compiègne, Oise, France, 1973—88; prof. U. of Burgundy - IUT Le Creusot, Le Creusot, Saône et Loire, France, 1988—93, U. Paul Cézanne - Aix-Marseille III, Marseille, Bouches du Rhône, France, 1993—2006. Dir. elec. engring. diploma U. of Tech., Compiègne, Oise, 1977—88; mem. French Coun. Univs., 1982—85; dir. Profl. U. Inst. of Elec. Engring., Marseille, Bouches du Rhône, 1999—2006, Laboratoire de Génie des Systèmes Electriques, Marseille, Bouches du Rhône, 2004—06. Contbr. articles to profl. jours. Mem.: Société des Electriciens et Electroniciens (reg. treas. 1998—2005, Sr. mem. 2000). Catholic. Achievements include patents in field. Avocations: opera, travel, riding, genealogy.

MOUL, WILLIAM CHARLES, lawyer; b. Columbus, Ohio, Jan. 12, 1940; s. Charles Emerson and Lillian Ann (Mackenbach) M.; m. Margine Ann Tessendorf, June 10, 1962; children: Gregory, Geoffrey. BA, Miami U., Oxford, Ohio, 1961; JD, Ohio State U., 1964. Bar: Ohio 1964, U.S. Dist. Ct. (so. dist.) Ohio 1965, U.S. Ct. Appeals (2d cir.) 1982, U.S. Ct. Appeals (6th cir.) 1984, U.S. Ct. Appeals (3d cir.) 1985. Assoc., ptnr. George, Greek, King, McMahon & McConnaughey, Columbus, 1964-79; ptnr. McConnaughey, Stradley, Mone & Moul, Columbus, 1979-81; ptnr.-in-charge Thompson, Hine & Flory, Columbus, 1981-89, exec. com., 1989-98. Chmn. Upper Arlington Civil Svc. Commn., Ohio, 1981-86. Mem. ABA, Ohio State Bar Assn. (labor sect. bd. dirs. 1983—), Columbus Bar Assn. (chmn. ethics com. 1980-82), Lawyers Club Columbus (pres. 1976-77), Athletic Club, Scioto Country Club, Wedgewood Country Club, Masons. Lutheran. Home: 2512 Danvers Ct Columbus OH 43220-2822 Office: Thompson Hine LLP 10 W Broad St Ste 700 Columbus OH 43215-3435 Office Phone: 614-469-3220. Business E-Mail: william.moul@thompsonhine.com.

MOULD, JEREMY RICHARD, astronomer; b. Bristol, Eng., July 31, 1949; s. Michael Thomas and Sheila Patricia (Pickering Clarke) Mould; m. Joan Mary Milesi, Dec. 11, 1971; children: Helen, Kate. BSc with honors, U. Melbourne, Australia, 1971; PhD, Australian Nat. U., 1975. Rsch. fellow Royal Greenwich Obs., England, 1976; postdoctoral fellow Kitt Peak Nat. Obs., Tucson, 1976—78, asst. astronomer, 1980—82; Carnegie fellow Hale Obs., 1978—79; prof. Calif. Inst. Tech., Pasadena, 1982—93, exec. officer for astronomy, 1987—90; prof. Australian Nat. U., Canberra, 1993—2001; dir. Mt. Stromlo & Siding Obs., Weston, Australia, 1993—2001, Nat. Optical Astronomy Obs., Tucson, 2001—. Mem. Anglo Australian Telescope Bd., 1993—2001, chair, 1999; mem. Australia Telescope Steering Com., 1995—2000; mem. space sci. adv. com. NASA. Mem.: Australian Acad. Sci., Assn. Univ. Rsch. Astronomy (bd. dirs. 1997—2001), Astron. Soc. Pacific, Astron. Soc. Australia, Am. Astron. Soc. Office: NOAO Mail Stop DODP 950 N Cherry Ave Tucson AZ 85726-6732 Business E-Mail: jmould@noao.edu.

MOULDER, PETER VINCENT, cardiovascular surgeon, educator; b. Jackson, Mich., Jan. 26, 1921; s. Peter Vincent and Marcella (McDonald) M.; m. Jane Eleanor Lyons, Feb. 9, 1946; children: Mary E. Moulder Jaeger, Peter Vincent III, James L., Jane A. Moulder Kauzlarich. BS magna cum laude, U. Notre Dame, 1942; MD with honors, U. Chgo., 1945; MA (hon.), U. Pa., 1971. Diplomate Am. Bd. Surgery, Am. Bd. Thoracic Surgery. Intern U. Chgo., 1945-46, resident in surgery, 1946-52, 52-53, chief resident in gen. surgery, 1953-54, chief resident thoracic surgery, 1954-55, from instr. to prof. dept. surgery, 1952-68; resident in surgery U. Ill. Rsch. and Ednl. Hosp., Chgo., 1952; prof. dept. surgery U. Pa., Phila., 1968-73, U. Fla., Gainesville, 1973-79, Sch. Medicine, Tulane U., New Orleans, 1980-92, adj. prof. dept. biomed. engring., 1984—; emeritus prof. Tulane U., New Orleans, 1992—; clin. prof. La. State U. Sch. Medicine, 1992—; med. dir. Biosouth Rsch. Labs., 1992—; thoracic surgeon New Orleans Vets. Administrn. Hosp., 1992—. Cons. cardiovascular surgery Naval Hosp., Great Lakes, Ill., 1955-68; cons. thoracic surgery Cook County Hosp., Chgo., 1966-68, Naval Hosp., Phila., 1969-73; dir. surgery Pa. Hosp., Phila., 1968-72; chief thoracic and cardiovascular surgery VA Hosp., Gainesville, 1973-79; med. investigator VA, 1973-80; mem. editorial bd. Annals of Thoracic Surgery, 1965-68, Chest, 1968-73. Mem. editorial bd. Annals Thoracic Surgery, 1965-68, Surg. Clinics N.Am. New Operations, 1966, Chest, 1968-73; contbr. some 275 articles to profl. publs. Lt. (j.g.) USNR, 1942-57, active duty, 1943-48. Recipient Alexander Vishnevsky medal USSR, 1966, Centennial Sci. Honor award U. Notre Dame, 1965, Gold medal Law Sci. Acad., 1968, George Bloch award for Excellence in Tchg. Surgery, U. Chgo., 2002, Outstanding Acheivement award, INPEX XVII Inventors, 2001; named to Mil and Hospitaller Order of St. Lazarus, 1990. Fellow Soc. for Vascular Surgery (disting.); mem. AMA, ACS, IEEE, IEEE Soc. Acoustics, Speech and Signal Processing, IEEE Computer Soc., Am. Physiol. Soc., Am. Assn. Thoracic Surgery, Am. Surg. Assn., Am. Soc. Clin. Surgery, Am. Soc. Artificial Internal Organs, Internat. Soc. Artificial Organs, Am. Math. Assn., Am. Coll. Chest Physicians, Am. Coll. Cardiology, Am. Heart Assn., Cen. Surg. Assn., Soc. Clin. Surgery, Soc. Univ. Surgeons, Soc. Thoracic Surgeons, Internat. Cardiovascular Soc., So. Thoracic Surg. Assn., Assn. for Computing Machinery and SigBio, Assn. for Advancement Med. Instrumentation, Soc. Critical Care Medicine, Orleans Parish Med. Soc., La. State Med. Soc., Alton Ochsner Surg. Soc., New Orleans Surg. Soc., Surg. Soc. La., Chgo. Surg. Soc., Tulane Surg. Soc. (founder), Midwest Chest Club, Cardiovascular Surgeons Club, Coll. Physicians Phila., Alpha Omega Alpha. Roman Catholic. Achievements include having 2 patents in field. Home: 2734 Saint Charles Ave New Orleans LA 70130-5930 also: La State Univ Sch Medicine Dept Surgery 533 Bolivar St New Orleans LA 70112-2825 Home Phone: 504-891-0200; Office Phone: 504-568-3090, 504-568-4750. Personal E-mail: pmouldermd@gmail.com. Business E-Mail: pmould@lsuhsc.edu.

MOULDS, ERIC SHANNON, professional football player; b. Lucedale, Miss., July 17, 1973; BS in Edn. Psychology, Miss. State U. Wide receiver, kickoff return Buffalo Bills, 1996—2005, Houston Texans, 2006, Tenn. Titans, 2007. Named to Pro-Bowl, 1998, 2000, 2002. Achievements include first round draft pick NFL, 1996.

MOULDS, JOHN F., judge; m. Elizabeth Fry, Aug. 29, 1964; children: Donald B., Gerald B. Student, Stanford U., 1955-58; BA with honors, Calif. State U., Sacramento, 1960; JD, U. Calif, Berkeley, 1963. Bar: U.S. Supreme Ct., U.S. Dist. Ct. (no. dist.) Calif., U.S. Dist. Ct. (ea. dist.) Calif. 1968, U.S. Ct. Claims 1982, U.S. Ct. Appeals (9th cir.) 1967, Calif. Rsch. analyst Calif. State Senate Fact-Finding Com. on Edn., 1960-61; adminstrv. asst. Senator Albert S. Rodda, Calif., 1961-63; staff atty. Calif. Rural Legal Assistance, Marysville, 1966-68, dir. atty. Marysville field office and Sacramento legis. adv. office, 1968-69; staff atty. Sacramento Legal Aid, 1968-69; ptnr. Blackmon, Isenberg & Moulds, 1969-85, Isenberg, Moulds & Hemmer, 1985; magistrate judge U.S. Dist. Ct. (ea. dist.) Calif., 1985—, chief magistrate jduge, 1988-97. Moot ct. and trial practice judge U. Calif. Davis Law Sch., 1975—, U. of Pacific McGeorge Coll. Law, 1985—; part-time U.S. magistrate judge U.S. Dist. Ct. (ea. dist.) Calif., 1983-85; mem. 9th Cir. Capital Case Com., 1992—, U.S. Jud. Conf. Com. on the Magistrate Judge Sys., 1992—, Adv. Com. to the Magistrate Judges' Divsn. Adminstv. Office of U.S. Jud. Conf., 1989—. Author: (with others) Review of California Code Legislation, 1965, Welfare Recipients' Handbook, 1967; editor: Ninth Circuit Capital Punishment Handbook, 1991. Atty. Sacramento Singlemen's Self-Help Ctr., 1969-74; active Sacramento Human Relations Commn., 1969-75, chair, 1974-75; active community support orgn. U. Calif. at Davis Law Sch., 1971—; mem., atty. Sacramento Community Coalition for Media Change, 1972-75; bd. dirs. Sacramento Country Day Sch., 1982-90, Sacramento Pub. Libr. Found., 1985-87; active various polit. orgns. and campaigns, 1960-82. Mem. ABA, Fed. Bar Assn., Nat. Coun. Magistrates (cir. dir. 1986-88, treas. 1988-89, 2d v.p. 1989-90, 1st v.p. 1990-91), Fed. Magistrate Judges Assn. (pres.-elect 1991, pres. 1992-93), Calif. State-Fed. Jud. Coun. Conf. (panelist capital habeas corpus litigation 1992), Fed. Jud. Ctr. Training Conf. for U.S. Magistrate Judges (panel leader 1993), Milton L. Schwartz Inns of Ct. Office: 16-400 US Courthouse 501 I St 16th Fl Ste 1640 Sacramento CA 95814-7300

MOULEDOUS, PIERRETTE MARIE, music educator; d. Roland Marie Robert Palasset and Marthe Germaine Normand; children: Alfred Eugene III, Laurie Michele Farris, Daniel Walter. Studied with Paul Kovalov, Russian Conservatory; studied with Isabelle Poncin and Reine Gianoli, Ecole Normale de Musique; MusM, So. Meth. U., Dallas, Tex., 1970. Head Dept. Piano El Centro Coll., Dallas, 1966—70, Eastfield Coll., Mesquite, Tex., 1970—. Staff pianist Am. Inst. Musical Studies, Graz, Austria, 1972—77; co-founder, co-dir. French Organ Seminar, Paris, 1985—91; founder Eastfield Metroplex East Piano Festival, Mesquite, 2004—. Musician (founder): Trio Accord, 1984—91, Elysee Piano Quartet, 1994—2006. Cons. Mesquite Symphony Orch. Bd., 2001—05. Recipient Excellence in Tchg. award, Nat. Inst. Staff and Orgnl. Devel., 1990. Business E-Mail: pxm4433@dcccd.edu.

MOUNASAMY, VARATHARAJ, orthopedist, educator; MD, Madras Med. Coll., Chennai, India, 1989; MBBS, U. Madras, 1990. Asst. prof. VCU Health Sys., Richmond, Va., 2007—. Assoc. editor European Jour. Orthop. Surgery & Traumatology, 2008—. Fellowship, Royal Coll. Physicians & Surgeons Glasgow, 1998, Musculoskeletal Oncology fellowship, U. Miami, 2003—04, Pediat. Orthop. Surgery fellowship, Orlando Regional Health Care, 2004—05, Adult Reconstruction Orthop. fellowship, U. Va., 2005—06, Orthop. Trauma fellowship, Va. Commonwealth U., 2006—07. Mem.: FRCS, Va. Orthop. Soc., Med. Soc. Va., AMA. Personal E-mail: vmounasa@yahoo.com.

MOUNT, MINDY (MELINDA J. MOUNT), computer software company executive; BBA, U. Wis.-Madison; MBA, Harvard U. V.p. mergers and acquisitions Morgan Stanley & Co.; v.p. corp. strategy and devel. Time Warner; exec. v.p., co-mng. dir. AOL UK, London; joined Microsoft Corp, 2006, corp. v.p. ops. and fin. group, CFO entertainment and devices divsn. Redmond, Wash., 2006. Bd. dirs. U. Wis. Found.; advisor to students Applied Corp. Fin. Program, U. Wis.-Madison Sch. Bus. Avocations: golf, hiking, bicycling. Office: Microsoft Corp One Microsoft Way Redmond WA 98052-6399*

MOUNT, WILLIE LANDRY, state legislator; b. Lake Charles, La., Aug. 25, 1949; BS, McNeese State U., 1971. Geophys. asst. La. Land and Exploration, Lake Charles, La., 1971-76; pharm. rep. Lederle, Lake Charles, 1976-80; realtor Mary Kay Hopkins, Lake Charles, 1976-87; co-owner Paper Place, Lake Charles, 1991-95; mayor City of Lake Charles, 1993—2000; mem. select com. on consumer protection La. State Senate, mem. jud. C, health and welfare, legis. audit adv. commn., bond commn., mem. state tech. adv. commn., joint juvenile justice commn., millennium port com., sch. fin. rev. commn., mem. edn. com., vice chair joint legis. com. on capital outlay, chmn. revenue and fiscal affairs com., mem. Dist. 27, 2000—. Gov. Violent Crime & Homicide Task Force, Baton Rouge, 1993—95; mem. steering com. La. conf. Mayors bd. pres. La. Asset Mgmt. Pool Bd., 1997. Guest condr. Lake Charles Symphony, 1992; active La. Mcpl. Assn., Baton Rouge, 1995-98; pres. Jr. League of Lake Charles; mem. state interag. coordinating coun. Dyslexia Study Com.; mem. adv. bd. S.W. La. Literacy Coalition; mem. adv. coun. Pet Overpopulation; active First United Meth. Ch., La. Meth. Conf., McNeese State U. Found., Prevent Child Abuse bd. Micro-Enterprise Devel. Alliance of La. Bd., McNeese State U. Found. Bd., St. Patrick Hosp. Bd. Councillors, Coastal Plain Conservancy Bd., United Way, Children's Miracle Network; exec. com. Coun. for a Better La. Recipient Spiritual Aims award Kiwanis Club, 1991, Cmty. Svc. award, 1995, Citizen of Yr. 1996-97, Dorthea Combre award NAACP, 1994, La. Mcpl. Assn. Cmty. Achievement award, 1995-97, Disting. Citizen award Boy Scouts Am., 1999, Patron Architecture, 2000, Disting. Alumni award McNeese State U., 2000, Golden Apple award Delta Kappa Gamma, 2002, Disting. Svc. award La. Restaurant Assn., 2002, Spl. Friend of La. Mcpl. Assn. award, 2003, Wilton Bellard Jr. award S.W. La. Ctr. for Health Svcs., Ron Schroeder award MEDAL; named Woman of Yr., Quota Club, 1991, Citizen of Yr., Women's com. S.W. La., 1992, Woman of Yr., Pub. Ofcl. of Yr. Msgr. Cramers KC, Pub. Ofcl. of Yr., NASW, 1997, Legislator of Yr., La. Orthopaedic Assn., Champion for Children, Prevent Child Abuse. Mem.: LWV, S.W. La. Mayor's Assn. (chmn. 1993—94). Democrat. Methodist. Home: 205 Shell Beach Dr Lake Charles LA 70601-5933 Office: PO Box 3004 Lake Charles LA 70602-3004 Business E-Mail: lasen27@legis.state.la.us.*

MOUNTAIN, JANET M., foundation administrator, former computer company executive; b. Oct. 19, 1967; BBA, U. Tex., Austin; MBA, Harvard Bus. Sch. Former sr. consultant Andersen Consulting, Houston; v.p., gen. mgr., US consumer divsn. Dell Inc., Round Rock, Tex.,

1993—2003; exec. dir. The Michael & Susan Dell Found., Austin, Tex., 2003—. Named a Young Global Leader, Forum of Young Global Leaders, 2006. Office: The Michael & Susan Dell Found PO Box 163867 Austin TX 78716

MOUNTCASTLE, VERNON BENJAMIN, retired neuroscientist; b. Shelbyville, Ky., July 15, 1918; s. Vernon and Anne-Francis Marguerite (Waugh) Mountcastle; m. Nancy Clayton Pierpont, Sept. 6, 1945; children: Vernon Benjamin III, Anne Clayton, George Earle Pierpont. BS in Chemistry, Roanoke Coll., Salem, Va., 1938, DSc (hon.), 1968; MD, Johns Hopkins U., 1942; DSc (hon.), U. Pa., 1976, Northwestern U., 1985, U. Minn., 1995; MD (hon.), U. Zurich, 1983, U. Siena, 1984, U. Santiago, Spain, 1990. House officer surgery Johns Hopkins Hosp., 1942—43; mem. faculty Johns Hopkins Sch. Medicine, 1946—, prof. physiology, 1959, dir. dept., 1964—80, prof. neurosci., 1980—92, prof. emeritus, 1992—; dir. Bard Labs. Neurophysiology Johns Hopkins U., Balt., 1981—91. Spl. rsch. physiology brain; chmn. physiology study sect., mem. physiology tng. com. NIH, 1958—61; adv. coun. Nat. Eye Inst., 1971—74; vis. prof. Coll. de France, Paris, 1980. Author: Perciptual Neuroscience: The Cerebrel Cortex, 1996, The Sensory Hand: Neural Mechanisms in Somatic Sensation, 2005; editor-in-chief: Jour. Neurophysiology, 1961—64, editor, contbr.: Med. Physiology, 12th edit., 1968, Med. Physiology, 13th edit., 1974, Med. Physiology, 14th edit., 1980; contbr. articles to profl. jours. Lt. (s.g.) M.C. USNR, 1943—46. Recipient Lashley prize, Am. Philos. Soc., 1974, F.O. Schmitt prize and medal, MIT, 1975, Sherrington prize and Gold medal, Royal Acad. Medicine, London, 1977, Horowitz prize, Columbia U., 1978, Helmholtz prize, 1982, Fyssen Internat. prize, Paris, 1983, Lasker award, 1983, Nat. Medal Sci., 1986, Zotterman prize and medal, Swedish Physiol. Soc., 1989, award in neurosci., Fidia Fedn., 1990, Australia prize, 1993. Mem.: AAAS (McGovern prize and medal 1990), NAS (chmn. sect. on physiology 1971—74, award in neurosci. 1998), Acad. Sci. (Finland, fgn.), Royal Soc. London (fgn.), Acad. Scis. (France, fgn.), Nat. Inst. Medicine, Am. Philos. Soc. (councillor 1979—82), Soc. Neurosci. (pres. 1970—72, Gerard prize 1980), Harvey Cushing Soc., Am. Acad. Arts and Scis., Am. Physiol. Soc., Physiol. Soc. London (hon.), Am. Neurol. Assn. (hon. Bennett lectr. 1978), Sigma Xi, Phi Chi, Alpha Omega Alpha, Phi Beta Kappa. Home: 6605 Walnutwood Cir Baltimore MD 21212 Business E-Mail: mountcastle@mbi.mb.jhu.edu.

MOUNTCASTLE, WILLIAM WALLACE, JR., retired philosophy and religion educator; b. Hanover, NH, July 10, 1925; s. William Wallace and Grace Elizabeth (Zottarelli) M.; m. Ila M. Warner (div.); children: Christine, Susan, Gregory, Eric; m. Barbara Kaye Teelin, Oct. 19, 1979; 1 child, Cathleena; stepdaughter, Dasha Teelin. BA, Whittier Coll., 1951; STB, Boston U., 1954, PhD, 1958. Ordained to ministry United Meth. Ch. Asst. prof. philosophy and religion High Point Coll., NC, 1958—60; mem. So. Calif. Ann. Conf. United Meth. Ch., 1954—60; assoc. prof., head dept. philosophy Nebr. Wesleyan U., Lincoln, 1960—63, prof., head dept. philosophy, 1963—67; mem. Nebr. Ann. Conf. United Meth. Ch., 1960—95; prof. philosophy Fla. So. Coll., Lakeland, 1967—68; assoc. prof. philosophy and religion U. West Fla., Pensacola, 1968—79, prof. philosophy and religion, 1979—, M.L. Tipton prof. philosophy and religion, 1980—2003, emeritus M.L. Tipton prof., 2003. Author: Religion in Planetary Perspective, 1979, Science Fantasy Voices and Visions of Cosmic Religion, 1996, The Secret Ministry of Jesus, 2007; contbr. articles to profl. jours. Fighter pilot USAAF, 1942-48, PTO. Mem. NEA/United Faculty Fla., Am. Assn. Religion, Am. Philos. Assn., Democrat. Office: U West Fla Dept Phil-Religious Studies Pensacola FL 32514 Office Phone: 850-474-2678.

MOUNTS, L. DAVID, food service executive; b. 1963; married; 3 children. BSBA in Fin. & Mgmt. Info., U. Nev.; MBA, U. Pa. Wharton Sch. Bus., 2004. Joined UPS Inc., 1983, v.p. mergers & acquisitions, 1999—2002, CFO Supply Chain Solutions Group, 2002—04, corp. contr. US ops., 2004—05; exec. v.p., CFO Domino's Pizza, Inc., Ann Arbor, Mich., 2005—07, exec. v.p. supply chain services, 2007—. Bd. dirs. Procuri Inc., 2006—. Bd. dirs. The Genesis Shelter. Office: Domino's Pizza Inc 30 Frank Lloyd Wright Dr Ann Arbor MI 48106

MOUNTZ, JAMES MICHAEL, radiologist, educator, biomedical researcher; b. Dayton, Ohio, Nov. 15, 1947; s. Taulbeel Preston and Mary (Sawyer) M.; m. Kathy Ann Mountz, Dec. 17, 1988; children: Jammie Michelle, Kristina Ann, Jennifer Mary, Victorial Natalie, Elizabeth Joan BS in Physics magna cum laude, Wright State U., 1969; MS in Physics, Mich. State U., 1971, PhD in Physics, 1974; MD, Case Western Res. U., 1981. Diplomate Am. Bd. Radiology, Am. Bd. Nuclear Medicine. Intern, resident and fellow U. Mich. Med. Ctr., Ann Arbor, 1981-86; asst. chief VA Med. Ctr., Ann Arbor, 1986-90; asst. prof. U. Mich. Med. Ctr., Ann Arbor, 1986-90; scientist U. Ala., Birmingham, 1994—, dir. molecular imaging devel. lab., 1994—, dir. neuro-nuclear medicine, 1990—, prof. radiology, 1990—; dir. neuro-nuclear medicine U. Pitts. Med. Ctr, 2003—, chief, divsn. nuclear medicine, med. dir. pet imaging, 2005—. Lectr., presenter in field. Patentee in field; contbr. articles to profl. jours. Mem. AMA, AAAS, Soc. Nuclear Medicine (bd. dirs. 1994-96, com. organizer brain imaging coun. 1996), Radiol. Soc. N.Am., Am. Coll. Radiology, Ala. Soc. Nuclear Medicine (pres. 1996-97), Sigma Pi Sigma, Phi Eta Tau. Avocations: flying, trumpet playing, amateur radio, photography, astronomy. Office: Univ Pitts Med Ctr 200 Lothrop St B-938 Pet Facility Pittsburgh PA 15215 Office Phone: 412-647-0104. Business E-Mail: mountzjm@upmc.edu.

MOUNTZ, WADE, retired healthcare executive; b. Winona, Ohio, Nov. 19, 1924; s. Lowell J. and Ethel M. (Coppock) M.; m. Betty G. Wilson, June 3, 1946; children: David John, Timothy Wilson. BA, Baldwin-Wallace Coll., Berea, Ohio, 1948; MHA, U. Minn., Mpls., 1951; LHD (hon.), Ky. Wesleyan Coll., Owensboro, 1991. With Norton Meml. Infirmary, Louisville, 1951-69, adminstr., 1969—81; pres. Norton-Children's Hosps., Inc., Louisville, 1981—87, NKC, Inc., Louisville, 1981-85, vice chmn., 1985-87; pres. emeritus Norton Healthcare, 1987—. Vice chmn. Comprehensive Health Planning Council Ky., 1968-73, chmn., 1973-79; bd. dirs. Louisville chpt. ARC, 1961-74; trustee Blue Cross Hosp. Plan, 1959-72; trustee Am. Hosp. Assn., 1971-76, chmn. bd., 1975. Served with A.C., USNR, 1943-45. Recipient Disting. Service award Ky. Hosp. Assn.; Disting. Layman award Ky. Med. Assn. Fellow Am. Coll. Hosp. Healthcare Execs. (life, gold medal), Modern Health Hall of Fame 2008, Masons. Home and Office: Betty & Wade Mountz 8021 Christian Ct # 401 Louisville KY 40222-9023 Home Phone: 502-426-5478; Office Phone: 502-412-9210. Personal E-mail: wmountz@insightbb.com.

MOURDOCK, RICHARD E., state treasurer; m. Marilyn Mourdock. BS, Defiance Coll.; MS in Geology, Ball State Univ. Lic. Profl. Geologist. Exec. Koester Companies, Inc.; former commr. Vanderburgh County; chief investment officer State of Ind., 2006—; chmn. Ind. Bond Bank. Actively involved in Christian mission services to Bolivia; county commr. Vanderburgh County, 1995—2002. Avocation: running. Office: State Treas 242 State House Indianapolis IN 46204 Office Phone: 317-232-6386. Office Fax: 317-233-1780.*

MOURNING, PAUL W., lawyer; b. Hattiesburg, Miss., Dec. 21, 1957; BA magna cum laude, Dartmouth Coll., 1980; JD, Univ. Va., 1983. Bar: N.Y. 1984. Ptnr. Health Corp. dept., recruiting ptnr. Cadwalader Wickersham & Taft, NYC. Editor (in chief): Va. Jour. Internat. Law. Mem.: ABA, N.Y. State Bar Assn., Phi Beta Kappa. Office: Cadwalader Wickersham & Taft LLP 1 World Fin Ctr New York NY 10281 Office Phone: 212-504-6216. Office Fax: 212-504-6666. Business E-Mail: paul.mourning@cwt.com.

MOURTZINOS, ARTHUR, urologist; b. Lowell, Mass., Apr. 4, 1974; s. Paraskevas and Mary Mourtzinos; m. Stephanie Athanasoulas, Aug. 31, 2003; children: Perry Michael, Stella Mary. MD, Boston U., 1999. Sr. staff physician Lahey Clinic Med. Ctr., Burlington, Mass., 2006—. Office: Lahey Clinic Med Ctr 41 Mall Rd Burlington MA 01805 Office Fax: 781-744-5429. Business E-Mail: arthur.mourtzinos@lahey.org.

MOUSTAFA LEONARD, KAREN, finance educator; d. Ray South; m. John D. Leonard, Jan. 6, 2007; children: Mark Kemp, Sara Leonard Harmon, Daniel Leonard. MPhil, MS, U. Auckland, New Zealand, 1989; PhD, U. Memphis, 2004. Asst. prof. mgmt. Ind. U. Purdue U., Ft. Wayne, 2004—. Recipient Bus. Edn. awards, AACSB East Mid Continent, 2007, Travel award, Ind. U., Bloomington, 2006; finalist, Acad. Mgmt. Critical Studies Divsn., 2007; Course Devel. grant, Divsn. Continuing Studies, IPFW, 2008. Mem.: North Am. Case Rsch. Assn., Internat. Acad. Intercultural Rsch., Am. Coll. Healthcare Execs., Acad. Internat. Bus., Acad. Mgmt. Office: Ind Univ-Purdue Univ Ft Wayne 2101 E Coliseum Blvd Fort Wayne IN 46805 Business E-Mail: moustafk@ipfw.edu.

MOUSTAKAS, THEODORE D., engineering educator, researcher; s. Demetrios T. and Elefteria Moustakas; m. Elena M. Palumbo, July 6, 1974; children: Demetri T., Christiana M. Ohara-Moustakas. BS, Aristotle U., Thessaloniki, Greece, 1964; PhD, Columbia U., NY, 1974. Rsch. fellow Harvard U., Cambridge, Mass., 1974—77; sr. rsch. scientist Exxon Rsch. Corp. Rsch. Labs., Clinton, NJ, 1977—87; prof. Boston U., 1987—, mem. Photonics Ctr., 1994—, assoc. head, materials sci. and engring. divsn., 2008—. Vis. prof. MIT, Cambridge, 2001—02. Editor: (books) Gallium Nitride I and Gallium Nitride II, (book) Wide Band Gap Semiconductors (Vol. 242), 1992, III-V Nitrides (Materials Rsch. Soc.), 1997, Diamond and Diamond Films (Electrochem. Soc.), 1989; contbr. articles to profl. jours., chapters to books. Adv. bd. N.Am. Molecular Beam Epitaxy, 2000—08; sci. bd. CNR-INFM MDM Nat. Lab., Milan, 2006—08; indsl. adv. bd. CUNY, NYC, 2003—08. Fellow: Electrochem. Soc. (honors and awards 1993—99), Am. Phys. Soc. Achievements include numerous patents related to amorphous silicon solar cells, diamond and cubic boron nitride; 16 US patents related to gallium nitride and light emitting devices. Home: 26 Rockybrook Rd Dover MA 02030 Office: Boston Univ 8 Saint Mary's St Boston MA 02215 Office Fax: 617-353-6440. Business E-Mail: moustakas@bu.edu.

MOUTAFAKIS, NICHOLAS JAMES, philosopher, educator; b. NYC; m. Elaine Marie Principe. PhD, NYU, 1968. Prof. philoasophy Cleve. State U., 1988—. Author: Rescher on Rationality, Values and Social Responsibility; author: (translator) Basil Tatakis'. Byzantine Philosophy; author: The Logics of Preference. Named Outstanding Educator, Outstanding Educators America, 1974—75; grantee, Nat. Endowment Humanities, 1979. Fellow: Am. Philos. Assn. Office: Cleve State Univ 1932 Rhodes Tower Cleveland OH 44115 Business E-Mail: n.moutafakis@csuohio.edu.

MOVAHEDZADEH, FARAHNAZ, medical researcher, educator; d. Hossein Movahedzadeh and Tala Nemati; m. Abour Cherif; 1 child, Seyed Reza Heydarian. BSc in Med. Tech., Med. Scis. U. Iran, Tehran, 1985, PhD (hon.) in Clin. Lab. Scis., 1993; PhD in Microbiology & Molecular Biology, U. Coll. London, 1997. Postdoc. rsch. fellow Nat. Inst. Med. Rsch., London, 1996—98, London Sch. Hygiene & Tropical Medicine, 1998—2001; rsch. fellow Royal Vet. Coll., London, 2001—06; rsch. asst. prof. U. Ill. Inst. Tb Rsch., Chgo., 2007—, prin. investigator, 2008—; faculty Harold Wash. Coll., Chgo., 2008—. Editor: (book) Microbiology and Chemistry: An Integrated Approach.; exec. prodr.: (book) Foundations of Modern Biology & Chemistry; contbr. to profl. publs. Grant, Am. Lung Assn., 2008—, Chgo. Biomed. Consortium, 2009—. Mem.: Assn. Coll. & U. Biology Educators, Nat. Assn. Biology Tchrs., Internat. Union Against Tb & Lung Disease (North America), Acid Fast Club. Achievements include development of safe strain of mycobacterium tuberculosis for protection of laboratory workers. Business E-Mail: movahed@uic.edu, fmovahedzadeh@ccc.edu.

MOVILEANU, LIVIU, physics professor; s. Ion and Silvia Movileanu; m. Iulia Movileanu; 1 child, Andrada-Lucia. PhD, U. Bucharest, Romania, 1997. Postdoc. Tex. A&M U., Coll. Station, 1999—2004. Contbr. scientific papers. Mem.: Biophysical Soc. Office: Syracuse Univ 201 Physics Bldg Syracuse NY 13244

MOVSHON, J. ANTHONY (JOSEPH ANTHONY MOVSHON), neuroscience educator; b. NYC, Dec. 10, 1950; s. George and Irene (Dann) M.; m. Margaret Elizabeth Beardsley, Aug. 30, 1975; children: Nicholas Anthony, Clare Elizabeth. BA, Cambridge U., 1972, PhD, 1975, MA, 1976. Asst. prof. psychology NYU, NYC, 1975-78, assoc. prof., 1978-84, prof. psychology, 1984—, prof. neural sci., 1987—, dir. Ctr. for Neural Sci., 1987-91, 1993—98, 2004—, Presdl. prof., 1999—2002, Silver prof., 2002—; investigator Howard Hughes Med. Inst., NYC, 1991—2003. Mem. visual scis. study sect. NIH, Bethesda, Md., 1982-87; adj. prof. physiology and neurosci. NYU Sch. Medicine, 1990-. Mem. editorial bd. Ann. Rev. Neurosci., 1983-87, Visual Neurosci., 1987-90, Jour. Cognitive Neurosci., 1988—; contbr. numerous articles to sci. jours., chpts. to books. Recipient rsch. career devel. award Nat. Eye Inst., 1980-85; NIH grantee, 1976—, NSF grantee, 1976—; Alfred P. Sloan Found. fellow, 1977-81. Fellow AAAS, Am. Psychol. Soc.; mem. NAS, Assn. Rsch. in Vision and Ophthalmology, Soc. Neurosci. (program com. 1987-91, chmn. 1991, Young Investigator award 1985), Am. Physiol. Soc., Cognitive Neurosci. Soc., Vision Sciences Soc. (bd. dirs. 2007-, pres. 2009-)Am. Acad. Arts & Sciences. Democrat. Avocations: music, opera. Office: NYU Ctr for Neural Sci 4 Washington Pl New York NY 10003-6621 Office Phone: 212-998-7880. Office Fax: 212-995-4183. Business E-Mail: movshon@nyu.edu.

MOW, ROBERT HENRY, JR., lawyer; b. Cape Girardeau, Mo., Dec. 10, 1938; s. Robert H. Sr. and Ann Elise (Beck) M.; m. Jody K. Boggs, Aug. 29, 1987; children: Robert M., Brynn A., W. Brett, Rebecca M., W. Kirk, Allison M. Student, Westminster Coll., 1956-57; AB with distinction, U. Mo., 1960; LLB magna cum laude, So. Meth. U., 1963. Bar: Tex. 1963, US Dist. Ct. (no. dist. Tex.) 1965, US Dist. Ct. (so. dist. Tex.) 1969, US Dist. Ct. (ea. and we. dists. Tex.) 1976, US Ct. Appeals (5th cir.) 1972, US Ct. Appeals (11th cir.) 1981, US Ct. Appeals (fed. cir.) 1994, US Supreme Ct. 1978. Assoc. Carrington, Johnson & Stephens, Dallas, 1963-69; ptnr. Carrington, Coleman, Sloman & Blumenthal, Dallas, 1970-85, Hughes & Luce, LLP, Dallas, 1985—, mng. ptnr., 2003—07. Editor-in-chief Southwestern Law Jour., 1962-63. Trustee First Bapt. Acad., chair, 1999-2002. Served to 1st lt. US Army, 1963-65. Recipient Disting. Alumni award, Pvt. Practice, SMU Sch. Law, 2008; named one of Best Lawyers in America, Comml. Litigation Legal Malpractice, 1984—, Best Lawyers in Dallas, 2005, 2008. Fellow: Am. Coll. Trial Lawyers; mem.: Dallas Bus. Jour. Defenders, Chambers & Ptnrs. Gen. Litig., Tex., Chambers USA, Dallas Bar Assn. (Dallas Bar Trial Lawyer of Yr. 2003), ABA (first chair intellectual property com. litig. sect.), State Bar Tex., Dallas Bar Fellows (chmn. com. qualified judiciary 2003—04), Am. Bd. Trial Advs. (pres. Dallas chpt. 1983—84), Tex. Assn. Def. Counsel (v.p. and dir. 1981—82), Dallas Assn. Def. Counsel. Republican. Baptist. Office: K & L Gates 1717 Main St Ste 2800 Dallas TX 75201 Office Phone: 214-939-5448. Office Fax: 214-939-5849. Business E-Mail: bob.mow@klgates.com.

MOW, VAN C., engineering educator, researcher; b. Chengdu, China, Jan. 10, 1939; B. Aero. Engring., Rensselaer Poly. Inst., 1962, PhD, 1966. Mem. tech. staff Bell Telephone Labs., Whippany, NJ, 1968-69; assoc. prof. mechanics Rensselaer Poly. Inst., Troy, NY, 1969-76, prof. mechanics and biomed. engring., 1976-82, John A. Clark and Edward T. Crossan prof. engring., 1982-86; prof. mech. engring. and orthopedic bioengring. Columbia U., NYC, 1986—98, chmn. dept. biomed. engring. Fu Found. Sch. Engring. and Applied Sci., 1998—; dir. Orthopedic Rsch. Lab., Columbia-Presbyn. Med. Ctr., NYC, 1986—, Stanley Dicker prof. biomed. engring., 1998—. Vis. mem. Courant Inst. Math. Sci., NYU, 1967-68; vis. prof. Harvard U., Boston, 1976-77; chmn. orthopaedics and musculoskeletal study sect. NIH, Bethesda, Md., 1982-84; hon. prof. Sichuan U., 1981, Shanghai Jiao Tong U., 1987, Shanghai U., 1983, Hong Kong Poly. U., 2003, Zhejiang U., 2004, Beihang U., 2004; chmn. grants rev. bd. Orthopaedic Rsch. Edn. Found., 1992-96; bd. dirs. Hoar Rsch. Found., 1993—; chmn. adv. com. divsn. Med. Engring. Rsch. Nat. Health Rsch. Inst., Taiwan, 1999—; cons. in field. Assoc. editor Jour. Biomechanics, 1981—, Jour. Biomech. Engring., 1979-86; chmn. editorial adv. bd. Jour. Orthopedic Rsch., 1983-90; adv. editor Clin. Orthopedic Rel. Rsch., 1993—; assoc./co-editor Osteo-arthritis & Cartilage; contbr. numerous articles to profl. jours. Founder Gordon Research Conf. on Bioengring. and Orthopedic Sci., 1980, chair, editl. adv. bd.Cellular and Molecular Biology. NATO sr. fellow, 1978; recipient William H. Wiley Disting. Faculty award Rensselaer Poly. Inst., 1981, ASME Van C. Mow medal for bioengring., 2004; Japan Soc. for Promotion Sci. Fellow, 1986, Fogarty Sr. Internat. fellow, 1987; Alza disting. lectr. Biomed. Engring. Soc., 1987; H.R. Lissner award ASME, 1987, Kappa Delta award AAOS, 1980, Giovani Borelli award, 1991, Outstanding Basuc Sci. award, OARSI, 2008. Fellow ASME (chmn. biomechanics divsn. 1984-85, Melville medal 1982, R.H. Thurston lectr.), Am. Inst. Med. Biol. Engring.; mem. Orthopaedic Rsch. Soc. (pres. 1982-83), Am. Soc. Biomechanics (founding), Internat. Soc. Biorheology, U.S. Nat. Com. on Biomechanics (sec.-treas. 1985-90, chmn. 1991-94), Nat. Acad. Engring., Inst. of Medicine, Nat. Acad. Sci., Academia Sinica, Acad. Sci. Developing World. Business E-Mail: vcm1@columbia.edu.

MOWATT-LARSSEN, ROLF, former federal agency administrator; Grad., US Mil. Acad., West Point, NY. Intelligence officer in various domestic and internat. posts CIA, dep. assoc. dir. Ctrl. Intelligence, mil. support, chief, WMD dept., chief, Europe divsn. in the Directorate of Ops.; dir., office intelligence and counterintelligence US Dept. Energy, Washington, 2005—08; sr. fellow, Belfer Ctr. Sci. and Internat. Affairs Harvard U. John F. Kennedy Sch. Govt., Cambridge, Mass., 2008—. Recipient Director's award, CIA, Disting. Career Intelligence medal, Commendation medal, Civilian Disting. Svc. medal, Sec. Def. Office: Belfer Ctr Sci and Internat Affairs John F Kennedy Sch Govt 79 JFK St Cambridge MA 02138 Business E-Mail: Rolf_mowatt-larssen@ksg.harvard.edu.

MOWBRAY, KEVIN D., publishing executive; b. 1962; m. Linda Mowbray; 4 children. BA, Western Ill. U. Advt. sales rep. Lee Enterprises, Inc., Kewanee, Ill., 1986, nat. sales mgr. corp. sales & mktg. Chgo.; advt. mgr. Lincoln Jour. Star, Nebr., 1995—98; gen. mgr. Missoulian, Missoula, Mont., 1998—2000; pub. Bismarck Tribune, ND, 2000—02, v.p. sales & mktg., 2002—04; v.p. pub., pub. Times of Northwest Ind., Munster, Ind., 2004—05; pres. & pub. St. Louis Post-Dispatch, 2006—. Office: St Louis Post-Dispatch 900 N Tucker Blvd Saint Louis MO 63101 Office Phone: 314-340-8970. E-mail: kmowbray@post-dispatch.com.*

MOWE, GREGORY ROBERT, lawyer; b. Aberdeen, Wash., Feb. 23, 1946; s. Robert Eden and Jeannette Effie (Deyoung) M.; m. Rebecca Louise Nobles, June 14, 1969; children: Emily, Tom. BA, U. Oreg., 1968, MA, 1969; JD magna cum laude, Harvard Law Sch., 1974. Bar: Oreg. 1974, U.S. Dist. Ct. Oreg. 1974, U.S. Ct. Appeals (9th cir.) 1974. Assoc. atty. Stoel Rives Boley Jones & Grey, Portland, Oreg., 1974-79, ptnr., 1979—. Pres. bd. dirs. Planned Parenthood of Columbia/Willamette, Portland, 1989-90. 1st lt. U.S. Army, 1969-71, Vietnam. Mem. ABA, Phi Beta Kappa. Office: Stoel Rives Boley Jones & Grey 900 SW 5th Ave Ste 2300 Portland OR 97204-1229 Home Phone: 503-294-9458; Office Phone: 503-294-9458. Business E-Mail: grmowe@stoel.com.

MOWER, MORTON MAIMON, cardiologist; b. Balt., Jan. 31, 1933; MD, U. Md. Sch. Medicine, 1959. Diplomate Am. Bd. Internal Medicine, Am. Bd. Cardiovac. Disease. Intern U. Md. Hosp., Balt., 1959-60; resident Sinai Hosp., Balt., 1960-63, fellow in cardiology, 1965-66; v.p. med. scis. Guidant Corp., St. Paul, 1989—96; assoc. prof. medicine Johns Hopkins U. Sch. Medicine, Balt.; prof. physiology and biophysics Howard U. Sch. Medicine; chmn., CEO Mower Rsch. Assocs., Balt., 1996—2006; chmn. MR3 Med., Balt., 2006—. Named to Nat. Inventors Hall of Fame, 2002. Fellow: ACP, Am. Coll. Chest Physicians, Am. Coll. Cardiology; mem.: Am. Soc. Internal Medicine, Am. Fedn. Clin. Rsch. E-mail: mmower@aol.com.

MOWERY, GERALD EUGENE, publishing executive, writer; b. Buena, Wash., Mar. 7, 1927; s. Jennings Bryan and Opal Mae Mowery; children: Colleen, Theresa, Rhonda, Laura, Victoria, Charles, Peggy. Degree in bus., Kinmen's U. Lic. pub. acct., Wash. Supr. Boeing Airplane Co., Seattle, 1968-78; owner Jerry's Coin, Book and Frame Shops, Puyallup, Wash., 1978-85, Rudolph Maurer Pub., Puyallup, Wash., Tampa, Fla., 1985—. Author and pub. more than 152 books including All Matter Originates from Electrons, Positrons and Neutrinos, 1981, E=GM Squared, 1994, The Revised Periodic Table of Elements, The Four Unacknowledged Elements, 1999; co-author with Gene Buck: The Entrepreneurs Favorite Short Stories, Favorite Poems, Favorite Facts and Stuff; author, publ. Adjusted Periodic Table of Elements, 1982, 93, 97, 98, 2001; author children's books The Adventures of Alexander Smiriotes series including Alexander Smiriotes Rides his Alligator Through Tampa, Alexander Visits Athens, Greece, Chelsea Thompson Visits Seattle. Achievements include defining the atomic mass make up of sub atomic particles and their relationship to carbon 12; prepared (atomic mass) sub atomic particle table from the equation atomic mass squared x 938.27231 equals measured MeV Values; illustrated that elements are periodic, paired functions of Electrons, Protons, Neutrinos and .000249089 atomic mass particles; developed periodic table of elements progression law of 1+2+2+2+2; confirming the existence of six additional elements within the table and predicting their measurements, configuration, composition, charge, isotopes, and other values; established that isotopes have a periodic progression and are not randomly added; established the theory and concept of compact neutrons as the basis for the periodic table; illustrated that the configuration and measurements of elements are paired with themselves, that all atoms are paired in a solid state, singular in a gas state, and both paired and unpaired in a liquid state; confirmed and illustrated how matter has a periodic atomic mass progression from the subatomic particles through the elements; put on a firm basis the theory that subatomic particles are the result of Proton Fractures at certain points in the 27 electron/proton chain and releasing energy (MeV) in the process; illustrated that the atomic number of an element should be two times its configuration plus one. Address: 1601 S Union Ave # 416 Tacoma WA 98405-1999 Personal E-mail: gemowery@msn.com.

MOWRIS, GERALD WILLIAM, lawyer; b. Grand Forks, ND, Oct. 2, 1948; s. Robert Earl and Lillian Vivian Mowris; m. Susan Leah Sachtjen; children: Danae E., Jeffrey W. Student, Mich. State U., East Lansing, 1966-67; JD, U. Wis., 1973. Bar: Wis. 1973, US Dist. Ct. (we. dist.) Wis. 1973, US Ct. Appeals (7th cir.) 1984, US Ct. Mil. Appeals 1984. Asst. dist. atty. Dane County Dist. Atty.'s Office, Madison, 1973-79; ptnr. Pellino, Rosen, Mowris & Kirkhuff, Madison, 1979—. Co-founder, mem. steering com. Wis. Criminal Justice Study Commn. Bd. dirs. YMCA of Met. Madison, 1991-94; mem. ARC Cmty. Svcs., Madison, 1980—, past pres., apptd. by gov. Wis. Sentencing Commn., 2003-07. Major JAG Corp, USAR, 1970—92. Mem. State Bar Wis. (co-chmn. com. for local bar leaders 1995-97, bd. govs. 1999-2003, pres. 2001-02), Dane County Bar Assn. (pres. 1994-95), Wis. Assn. Criminal Def. Lawyers (pres. 1995-96), Nat. Assn. Criminal Def. Lawyers, Wis. Acad. Trial Lawyers, Nat. Ski Patrol (patroller 1967—). Avocations: skiing, fishing, hiking, canoeing, golf. Office: Pellino Rosen Mowris & Kirkhuff SC 131 W Wilson St Ste 1201 Madison WI 53703-3243 Office Phone: 608-255-4501. Office Fax: 608-255-4345. Business E-Mail: gmowris@prmk.com.

MOWSHOWITZ, ABBE, computer scientist; b. Liberty, NY, Nov. 13, 1939; s. Jacob and Minnie Mowshowitz; m. Harriet Angell Hobson, Feb. 1, 1964; children: Jed Elijah, Seth Isaiah. BS, U. Chgo., 1961; MS, MA, PhD, U. Mich., 1967. Rsch. assoc. Human Scis. Rsch., McLean, Va., 1962—63; rsch. asst. U. Mich., Ann Arbor, 1963—67, lectr., 1967—68; asst. prof. U. Toronto, 1968—69, U. B.C., Vancouver, Canada, 1969—74, assoc. prof., 1974—80; prof. Grad. Sch. Mgmt., Delft, Netherlands, 1979—80, Rensselaer Poly. Inst., Troy, NY, 1982—84, CCNY, 1984—. Vis. fellow Ctr. for Study Dem. Instns., Santa Barbara, Calif., 1975; rsch. assoc. Cornell U., Ithaca, NY, 1975—76; dir. Croton Rsch. Group, Croton-on-Hudson, NY, 1980—82; pres. Tech. Impact Rsch., Inc., Larchmont, NY, 1983—94; prof. Erasmus U., Rotterdam, Netherlands, 1990—91, U. Amsterdam, 1991—93, 1994—95; Tinbergen chair Erasmus U., Rotterdam, 1990—91, prof., 2001—02; CeTim chair in tech. innovation Rotterdam Sch. Mgmt., 2001—02. Author: (book) The Conquest of Will: Information Processing in Human Affairs, 1976, Inside Information: Computers in Fiction, 1977, Human Choice and Computers, 2, 1988, Virtual Organization: Toward a Theory of Societal Transformation Stimulated by Information Technology, 2002. Recipient award, Internat. Tech. Alliance Project, 2006—. Mem.: IEEE (assoc.), Assn. for Computing Machinery (corr.; chmn., vice-chmn. 1983—87). Achievements include research in comprehensive analyses of the social effects of computers; structural complexity of combinatorial graphs; development of concept of virtual organization; design of method for measuring the bias of search engines. Office: CCNY Convent Ave at 138th St New York NY 10031 Office Fax: 212-650-6248. Personal E-mail: abbemow@earthlink.net. E-mail: abbe@cs.ccny.cuny.edu.

MOXLEY, JOHN HOWARD, III, internist; b. Elizabeth, NJ, Jan. 10, 1935; s. John Howard Jr. and Cleopatra (Mundy) Moxley; m. Doris Banchik; children: John Howard IV, Brook, Mark. BA, Williams Coll., 1957; MD, U. Colo., 1961; DSc (hon.), Sch. Medicine Hannemann U. Diplomate Am. Bd. Internal Medicine. Intern Peter Bent Brigham Hosp., Boston, 1961—62, resident in internal medicine, 1962—66; with Nat. Cancer Inst., USPHS, 1963—65; asst. to dean, instr. medicine Harvard Med. Sch., Boston, 1966—69; dean Sch. Medicine, U. Md., 1969—73; vice chancellor health scis., dean Med. Sch., U. Calif.-San Diego, 1973—79; asst. sec. for health affairs Dept. Def., Washington, 1979—81; sr. v.p. Am. Med. Internat., Beverly Hills, Calif., 1981—87; pres. MetaMed. Inc., Playa Del Rey, Calif., 1987—89; mgr. dir. Korn/Ferry Internat., LA, 1989—. Cons. FDA, NIH; dir. Nat. Fund for Med. Edn., 1986—94, chmn., 1993—94; dir. Henry M. Jackson Found. for Adv. Mil. Medicine. Contbr. articles to profl. jours. Dir. Polyclinic Health Svcs. Games of XXIII Olympiad. Recipient Gold and Silver award, U. Colo. Med. Sch., 1974, commr.'s citation for outstanding svc. to over-the-counter drug study, FDA, 1977, spl. achievement citation, Am. Hosp. Assn., 1983, Sec. of Def. medal for disting. pub. svc., 1981. Fellow: ACP, Am. Coll. Physician Execs. (disting.); mem.: AMA (chmn. coun. sci. affairs 1985), Am. Hosp. Assn. (trustee 1979—81), Soc. Med. Adminstrs., Calif. Med. Assn. (chmn. sci. bd. 1978—83, councilor), Inst. Medicine NAS, San Diego C. of C., Rotary, Alpha Omega Alpha. Office: Korn Ferry Internat 1900 Ave of the Stars Ste 2600 Los Angeles CA 90067-1512 Office Phone: 310-200-1296. E-mail: moxleyj@kornferry.com.

MOXON, KAREN ANNE, medical educator; b. Manhasset; d. William John and Nancy A. Flach; m. Robert W. Moxon, Aug. 17, 1996; 1 child, Benjamin Y. BSChemE, U. Mich., 1984; MS, U. Colo., Boulder, 1991, PhD, 1994. Postdoc. fellow U. Colo. Health Sci. Ctr., Denver, 1994—97, MCP Hahnemann U., Phila., 1997—98; asst. prof. Sch. Biomed. Engring., Phila., 2000—05, assoc. prof., 2005—. Rsch. asst. prof. Allegheny U. Health Scis., Phila., 1998—99. Contbr. scientific papers, chapters to books. Travel fellowship, Fields Inst. Rsch. Math. Sci., 1994, IEEE Engring. Medicine and Biology Soc., 2001. Mem.: IEEE, AAAS, Am. Inst. Chem. Engrs. (v.p. U. Mich. chpt. 1983—84), Soc. Women Engrs. (exec. sec. 1984—84), Soc. Neurosci. Achievements include patents for ceramic based multi-site electrode arrays and methods for their production; patents pending for method to quantitatively measure effect of psychotropic drugs on sensory discrimination; wireless multi-channel neural signal processing device and method for multiple, single neuron recording; real-time seizure detection and control system using our patented ceramic-base multi-site electrode; optoelectronic remotely powered silicon-based hybrid neural electrode. Office: Drexel Univ 3141 Chestnut St Philadelphia PA 19104 Office Fax: 215-895-0570. Business E-Mail: km57@drexel.edu.

MOY, EDMUND C., federal agency administrator; b. 1957; m. Karen Moy; 1 child, Nora. Grad., U. Wis., 1979. Sales and mktg. exec. Blue Cross Blue Shield United, Wis., 1979—89; polit. appointee Health Care Financing Adminstrn. US Dept. Health and Human Svcs., 1989—93; with Welsh, Carson, Anderson & Stowe; various positions with venture capital firms; spl. asst. to Pres. for presdl. personnel The White House, Washington; dir., US Mint US Dept. Treasury, Washington, 2006—. Bd. dirs. Christianity Today, Christianity Today Found. Office: US Mint 801 9th St NW Washington DC 20220*

MOY, RONALD LEONARD, dermasurgeon; b. Stuttgart, Germany, June 10, 1957; s. Howard Leonard Stephen and Jenny (Yee) M.; m. Lisa Wing Lan Lin, Aug. 10, 1986; children: Lauren, Erin. Grad., Rensselaer Poly. Inst., 1977, Albany Med. Coll., 1981. Dir. Mohs micrographic surgery div. dermatology UCLA, 1988-93, dir. dermatologic surgery div. dermatology, 1988-93, co-chief div. dermatology, 1992-93, clin. prof. David Geffen Sch. Medicine, 2005—; chief dermatologic surgery VA-West Los Angeles Med. Ctr., 1988—. Mem. Med. Bd. Calif., 2000-07, pres. divsn. med. quality, 2005—. Author: Atlas of Cutaneous Flaps and Grafts, 1990, Facial Rejuvenation, 1999; editor: Principle and Practice of Dermatologic Surgery, 1993, Facial Rejuenation, 2000, Advanced Facelift, 2006, Blepharoplasty, 2006; editor-in-chief: Dermatologic Surgery, 1997—2001; mem. editl. bd. Archives Facial Plastic Surgery, Archives of Dermatology, Jour. Am. Acad. Cosmetic Surgery; contbr. articles to profl. jours. Bd. dirs. L.A. Costal unit Am. Cancer Soc., 1988. Recipient J. Lewis Pipkin award in dermatology Nat. Student Rsch. Forum, 1981, Henry Christian award Am. Fedn. Clin. Rsch., T-cell and Cytokine Patterns in Skin Cancer award NIH, 1992. Fellow: Am. Acad. Cosmetic Surgery (bd. dirs. 2004—), Am. Acad. Dermatology (bd. dirs., pres. elect 2009—, Gold award 1986); mem.: Pacific Dermatol. Assn. (pres. 2006—07), Am. Acad. Facial Plastic Surgery, L.A. County Med. Assn. (pres. Bay dist. 1997—98), Assn. Acad. Dermatol. Surgeons (bd. dirs. 1992—95), Am. Coll. Mohs Micrographic Surgery and Cutaneous Oncology (bd. dirs. 1992—95), Am. Soc. Dermatol. Surgery (bd. dirs. 1993—96, v.p. 2001—02, pres. 2003—04). Presbyterian. Office: 100 UCLA Med Plz Ste 590 Los Angeles CA 90024-6992 Office Phone: 310-794-7422.

MOYA, CARLOS, professional tennis player; b. Palma de Mallorca, Spain, Aug. 27, 1976; s. Andres and Pilar Moya. Profl. tennis player ATP, 1995—. Owner cologne product line, 2000—. Actor: (films) Torrente II, 2001. Named Arthur Ashe Humanitarian of Yr., 2005. Achievements include winning 20 career singles titles, ATP; winning Buenos Aires, 1995, 2003, 2006, Umag, 1996, 2001-03, 2007, LI, 1997, Monte Carlo, 1998, Roland Garros, 1998, Estoril, 2000, Acapulco, 2002, 2004, Chennai, 2004-05; winning 18 European singles and doubles titles. Avocations: video games, music, soccer. Office: c/o ATP Tour Internat Hdqrs 201 Atp Tour Blvd Ponte Vedra Beach FL 32082

MOYA, EVA M., health services executive; b. El Paso Ciudad Juarez; BA, MS, U. Tex. Exec. dir. U.S.-Mex. Border Health Commn. Sr. program coord. U.S.-Mex. Border health collaborative outreach project U. Ariz., 1995—2001, assoc. dir. health career occupation program; project dir. Cmty. Health Worker's Evaluation Tool Kit Project, 1998—2001; co-dir. Cmty. Access Program for Ariz.; pres. U.S.-Mex. Border Health Assn., 1999—2000. Contbr. articles to profl. jours. Recipient Adelante Mujer Hispana: Cmty. Involvement award, Tex. Cmty. Health Program award, 1990, Award for Excellence, U.S. Dept. Health & Human Services, Human Svcs. Nat. Health Program award; named one of Top 10 Latinos in Healthcare, LatinoLeaders mag., 2004. Office: Us Mx Border Health Commission 211 N Florence St # 101 El Paso TX 79901-1424 E-mail: emoya@borderhealth.net.

MOYA, PATRICK ROBERT, lawyer; b. Belen, N.Mex., Nov. 7, 1944; s. Adelicio E. and Eva (Sanchez) Moya; m. Sara Dreier, May 30, 1966; children: Jeremy Brill, Joshua Dreier. AB, Princeton U., 1966; JD, Stanford U., 1969. Bar: Calif. 1970, Ariz. 1970, DC 1970, U.S. Dist. Ct. (no. dist.) Calif. 1970, U.S. Ct. Claims 1970, U.S. Tax Ct. 1970, U.S. Ct. Appeals (DC cir.) 1970, U.S. Supreme Ct. 1973. Assoc. Lewis and Roca, Phoenix, 1969—73, ptnr., 1973—83; sr. ptnr. Moya, Bailey, Bowers & Jones, P.C., Phoenix, 1983—84; ptnr., mem. nat. exec. com. Gaston & Snow, Phoenix, 1985—91; ptnr. Quarles & Brady LLP, Phoenix, 1991—2003, mem. nat. exec. com., 2000—02, of counsel, 2005—; exec. v.p. Insight Enterprises, Inc., Tempe, Ariz., 2002—05, chief adminstrv. officer, 2003—05, sec., 2002—05, gen. counsel, 2002—05; exec. v.p., gen. counsel and sec. Apollo Group, Inc., Phoenix, 2007—. Instr. Sch. of Law, Ariz. State U., 1972; bd. dirs. Plusnet, plc, 2003—07, InPlay Techs., Inc., 2005—. Mem. Paradise Valley Bd. Adjustment, 1976-80, chmn., 1978-80; mem. Paradise Valley Town Coun., 1980-82; bd. dirs. Phoenix Men's Arts Coun., 1973-81, pres., 1979-80; bd. dirs. The Silent Witness, Inc., 1979-84, pres., 1981-83; bd. dirs. Enterprise Network, Inc., 1989-94, pres., 1991-92; bd. dirs. Phoenix Little Theatre, 1973-75, Interfaith Counseling Svc., 1973-75; precinct committeeman Phoenix Rep. Com., 1975-77; dep. voter registrar Maricopa County, 1975-76; mem. exec. bd. dirs. Gov.'s Strategic Partnership for Econ. Devel.; pres. GSPED, Inc.; mem. of Steering Com. for Sonora-Ariz. Joint Econ. Plan; mem. Gov.'s Adv. Com., Ariz. and Mex., Ariz. Corp. Commn. Stock Exch. Adv. Coun., Ariz. Town Hall. Mem. ABA, Nat. Hispanic Bar Assn., Los Abogados Hispanic Lawyers Assn., Nat. Assn. Bond Lawyers, Ariz. Bar Assn., Maricopa County Bar Assn., Paradise Valley Country Club, Univ. Club. Office Phone: 602-230-5580.

MOYAL, MAURICE, lawyer, former accounting and business law educator; b. Mazagan, Morocco, Mar. 2, 1930; s. David and Mira Moyal; m. Lisette A. Keane Weber Moyal, July 4, 1951; children: Paulette, David, Colette, Maurice Jr., Yvette; m. Rohan R. Plischke Moyal, Sept. 27, 1974; children: Brigitte, Kenneth. AA, Diablo Valley Coll., 1954; BS, U. Calif., Berkeley, 1956; MBA, U. Calif., 1958; JD, John F. Kennedy U., 1970; PhD, Pacific Western U., 1979. Bar: Calif. 1972, US Dist. Ct. (ea. dist.) Calif. 1972, US Ct. Appeals (9th cir.) 1972, US Tax Ct. 1972, US Supreme Ct. 1980, US Ct. Mil. Appeals 1982, DC 1983. Prof. acctg. & bus. law, 1962—82; ret., 1982; pvt. practice Concord, Calif.; prin. PLC, Concord. Mem. Calif. Alumni Assn., Res. Officers Assn., Assn. Former Intelligence Officers, Assn. US Army. Served to col. USAR. Decorated Army Commendation medal with 2 oak leaf clusters, Legion of Merit, Meritorious Svc. medal. Mem.: ABA, AAJ, Calif. Trial Lawyers Assn., Nat. Assn. Accts., Contra Costa County Bar Assn., Shriners, Masons, Beta Alpha Psi, Beta Gamma Sigma. Address: 1899 Clayton Rd Concord CA 94520-2541 Office Phone: 925-686-0200. Personal E-mail: moyallaw@sbcglobal.net.

MOYANO, MARCELA, communications educator; d. Julio Alberto Moyano and Lydia Beatriz Bautista; m. Fernando Jose Rosero, Oct. 7, 2006. BA in Comm. Arts, St. Thomas U., Miami Gardens, Fla., 2002; EdD in Ednl. Leadership, St. Thomas U., Miami Gardens, 2007; MA in Comm. Arts, Barry U., Miami Gardens, 2005. Dir. UNILATINA UL Sch. Bus., Davie, Fla., 2001—06; instr. St. Thomas U., 2006—. Advisor St. Thomas U., 2006—; dir. St. Thomas U., Sch. Leadership Studies, 2007—. Cinematographer: (films, documentary film) Blooming Hope: Harvesting Smiles in Port-de-Paix. Trustee UNILATINA UL Sch. Bus., Colombia, 2003—08; mktg. coord. Haiti Relief Project St. Thomas U., 2007—08. Mem.: PDK Chpt. (comm. coord. 2007—08). Peace Party. Roman Catholic. Achievements include research in 21st century leadership qualitative study. Avocations: yoga, travel, writing, running.

MOYARS-JOHNSON, MARY ANNIS, retired academic administrator; b. Lafayette, Ind., July 19, 1938; d. Edward Raymond and Veronica Marie (Quigg) Moyars; m. Raymond Leon Molter, Aug. 1, 1959 (div. 1970); children: Marilyn Eileen Molter Davis, William Raymond Molter Johnson, Ann Marie Molter Guentert; m. Thomas Elmer Johnson, May 25, 1973 (div. 1989); children: Thomas Edward, John Alan, Barbara Suzanne, Johnson Camp BS, Purdue U., 1960; MA, Purdue U., West Lafayette, Ind., 1991, postgrad., 1985—. Grader great issues Purdue U., West Lafayette, 1960-63, writer ednl. films, 1962-65, publicity dir. convocations and lectures, 1969-74, devel. officer Sch. Humanities, 1979-88, asst. to dir. Optoelectronics Rsch. Ctr., 1989-90, mgr. indsl. rels. Sch. Elec. and Computer Engring., 1990—2002, assoc. v.p. for info. tech., for comm., 2002—04; tchr. English and math. Benton Cmty. Schs., Fowler, Ind., 1966-69; pub. rels. dir. Sycamore Girl Scout Coun., Lafayette, Ind., 1974-78; dir. pub. info. Ind. Senate, Majority Caucus, Indpls., 1977-78; sr. script writer Walters & Steinberg, Lafayette, 1988-89; ret., 2004. Adj. faculty Ivy Tech State Univ., 2005. Author: Colonial Potpourri, 1975, Ouiatanon--The French Post Among the Ouia, 2000; co-author: Historic Colonial French Dress, 1982, 2nd edit., 1998; contbr. articles to profl. jours. Bd. govs. Tippecanoe County Hist. Assn., Lafayette, 1981-97. Mem. Women in Comms., Inc. (Pres. award 1983, pres. Lafayette chpt. 2004-05), Ctr. for French Colonial Rsch. (dir. 1986-89, 2006-07, editor 1988-89), Palatines to Am., Ind. History Assn., Ind. Hist. Soc., French Colonial Hist. Soc. Roman Catholic. Avocations: history, genealogy, embroidery. Home: 924 Elm Dr West Lafayette IN 47906-2246 Personal E-mail: mamoyars@indy.net.

MOYER, ALAN DEAN, retired newspaper editor; b. Galva, Iowa, Sept. 4, 1928; s. Clifford Lee and Harriet (Jacques) M.; m. Patricia Helen Krecker, July 15, 1950; children: Virginia, Stanley, Glenn. BS in Journalism, U. Iowa, 1950. Reporter, copy editor Wis. State Jour., Madison, 1950-53; reporter, photographer Bartlesville (Okla.) Examiner-Enterprise, 1953; telegraph editor Abilene (Tex.) Reporter-News, 1954-55; makeup editor Cleve. Plain Dealer, 1955-63; mng. editor Wichita (Kans.) Eagle, 1963-70; exec. editor Wichita Eagle and Beacon, 1970-73; mng. editor Phoenix Gazette, 1973-82, Ariz. Republic, 1982-89; ret., 1989. Pres., dir. Wichita Profl. Baseball, Inc., 1969-75; mem. jury Pulitzer Prizes, 1973-74, 85, 86, 88. Mem. AP Mng. Editors Assn. (dir. 1973-78), Am. Soc. Newspaper Editors, Wichita Area C. of C. (dir. 1970-72), Sigma Delta Chi. Office: Phoenix Newspapers Inc 200 E Van Buren St Phoenix AZ 85004-2238 Personal E-mail: moyeralan@cox.net.

MOYER, F. STANTON, financial executive; b. Phila., June 7, 1929; s. Edward T. and Beatrice (Stanton) M.; m. Ann P. Stovell, May 16, 1953; 1 child, Alice E. BS in Econs., U. Pa., 1951. Registered rep. Smith, Barney & Co., Phila., 1951-54, Kidder, Peabody & Co., Phila., 1954-60; mgr. corp. dept. Blyth Eastman Dillon & Co., Inc. (formerly Eastman Dillon, Union Securities & Co.), Phila., 1960-65, instl. sales mgr., 1965-67, gen. partner, 1967-71, 1st v.p., 1971-74, sr. v.p., 1974-80; v.p., resident officer Kidder, Peabody & Co. Inc., Phila., 1980-86; chmn. Pa. Mcht. Group Ltd., Radnor, 1987-88; exec. v.p. Rorer Asset Mgmt., Phila., 1990-92; chmn. Mercer Capital Mgmt., 1992-93, Global Mgmt. Group, Inc., 1993-95; mng. dir. Avonwood Capital Corp., 1995-97; chmn. Main Line Capital Ptnrs. Inc., 1997—. Trustee U. Pa., 1978-83, Hosp. of U. Pa., 1978-87. Mem. Racquet Club (Phila.), St. Anthony Club (Phila.), Merion Cricket Club (Haverford, Pa.), Gulph Mills Golf Club (King of Prussia, Pa.), Delta Psi. Republican. Episcopalian. Home (Summer): 445 Caversham Rd Bryn Mawr PA 19010 Office Phone: 561-274-8378, 610-527-5015. E-mail: growthguy@aol.com.

MOYER, H. WAYNE, political science professor; b. Phila., Aug. 18, 1939; s. H. Wayne and Ruth Stevens Moyer; m. Helen Johnson, June 29, 1963. BA with honors, U. Va., 1961; MA in Internat. Rels., Yale U., 1969, MPhil in Polit. Sci., 1972, PhD in Polit. Sci., 1976. Instr. polit. sci. Grinnell (Iowa) Coll., 1972-76, asst. prof., 1976-79, assoc. prof., 1979-86, prof. polit. sci., 1986—, Rosenfield prof., 1985—. Author: Agricultural Policy Reform: Politics and Process in the USA and EC, 1990, Agricultural Policy Reform: Politics and Process in the EU and U.S. in the 1990s, 2002. Lt. USN, 1961-67. Mem. Am. Polit. Sci. Assn., Internat. Studies Assn., Iowa Conf. Polit. Sci., European Union Studies Assn. Democrat. Avocations: sailing, gardening. Home: 890 Juniper Ave Kellogg IA 50135 Office: Grinnell Coll 1131 Park St Grinnell IA 50112 Home Phone: 641-236-4377; Office Phone: 641-269-3176. Business E-Mail: moyer@grinnell.edu.

MOYER, JAMIE, professional baseball player; b. Sellersville, Pa., Nov. 18, 1962; m. Karen Moyer; 7 children. Attended, St. Joseph's U., Phila.; B in Gen. Studies, Ind. U., South Bend, 1996. Pitcher Chgo. Cubs, 1986—88, Tex. Rangers, 1989, St. Louis Cardinals, 1991, Balt. Orioles, 1993—95, Boston Red Sox, 1996, Seattle Mariners, 1996—2006, Phila. Phillies, 2006—. Founder The Moyer Found., 2000—. Recipient Nat. Sports Philanthropy award, Hutch award, 2003, Roberto Clemente award, 2003, Lou Gehrig Meml. award, 2003, Branch Rickey Humanitarian award, 2004; named to St. Joseph's U. Baseball Hall of Fame, Am. League All-Star Team, Maj. League Baseball, 2003. Achievements include member of the World Series Championship winning Philadelphia Phillies, 2008; recording his 250th career win against the Washington Nationals, May 31, 2009. Office: Phila Phillies Citizens Bank Pk One Citizens Bank Way Philadelphia PA 19148 also: The Moyer Found 2436 32d Ave Ste 200 Seattle WA 98199 Office Phone: 206-298-1217. Office Fax: 206-298-1207.*

MOYER, JEFFREY S., plastic surgeon, educator; married. MD, U. NC Sch. Medicine, Chapel Hill, 1997. Diplomate Am. Bd. Facial Plastic and Reconstructive Surgery, 2008, Am. Bd. Otolaryngology-Head and Neck Surgery, 2004. Lectr. U. Mich. Med. Sch., Ann Arbor, 2003—05, staff physician, 2003—, asst. prof., 2005—. Surg. cons. IRX Therapeutics, Inc., NYC, 2005—. Fellow: ACS, Am. Acad. Facial Plastics and Reconstructive Surgery; mem.: Soc. U. Otolaryngologists-Head and Neck Surgeons, Am. Head and Neck Soc., Am. Assn. Cancer Rsch., Am. Acad. Otolaryngology-Head and Neck Surgery, Alpha Omega Alpha (Award 1996). Office: Univ of Mich Dept of OTO 1904 TC 1500 E Medical Center Dr Ann Arbor MI 48109-0312 Office Fax: 734-936-9625. Business E-Mail: jmoyer@umich.edu.

MOYER, LINDA LEE, artist, educator, author; b. Niles, Mich, Feb. 11, 1942; d. Roy Delbert and Estelle Leona (Beaty) Moyer; m. Brock David Williams Dec. 3, 1994; 1 child from previous marriage, Metin Ata Gunsay. Student, Occidental Coll., 1959-61; BA, UCLA, 1964; MA, Calif. State U., Long Beach, 1977, MFA, 1980. Cert. tchr. secondary edn., cert. computer graphics, Calif. Instr. art. Huntington Beach Union HS, Calif., 1967-81, Calif. State U., Long Beach, 1981-85, Saddleback Coll., Mission Viejo, Calif., 1986-88, Fullerton Coll., Calif., 1990, 94, Goldenwest Coll., Huntington Beach, 1990. Artist-in-residence St. Margaret's Episc. Sch., San Juan Capistrano, 1993; lectr., workshop presenter Santa Barbara C.C., Calif., 1992, So. Watercolor Soc., 2008; series lectr. Rancho Santiago Coll., 1985, 90; lectr. Cypress Coll., 1986, Watercolor West, 1987, others; methods and materials show instr. Am. Artist Mag., 1996, 97, 98, 99, 99, 2000, 01, 03; juror fine art exhbns So. Watercolor Soc., 2008; presenter workshops in field; website co-founder watercolor-online.com. One-woman shows include Orange County Ctr. Contemporary Art, 1982, 1985, Laguna Beach Mus. Art, Calif., 1982, Orlando Gallery, Sherman Oaks, Calif., 1983, Orange County Ctr. Contemporary Art, 1985, Cerritos Coll., Norwalk, Calif., 1986, Louis Newman Galleries, Beverly Hills, 1986, 1988, 1990, Westmont Coll., Santa Barbara, 1992, Maturango Mus., Ridgecrest, Calif., 1996, exhibited in group shows at Owensboro, Mus. Fine Arts, Ky., 1979, Newport Harbor Art Mus., Newport Beach, Calif., 1981, Burpee Art Mus., Rockford, Ill., 1981, Nat. Acad. Galleries, NYC, 1982, Leslie Levy Gallery, Scottsdale, Ariz., 1983, Art Inst. So. Calif., 1984, Saddleback Coll., Mission Viejo, Calif., 1988, Ch. of Jesus Christ of LDS Mus. Art and History, Salt Lake City, 1988, Riverside (Calif.) Art Mus., 1989, Ch. of Jesus Christ of LDS Mus. Art and History, Salt Lake City, 1991, Mt. San Antonio Coll., Calif., 1996, Springville Art Mus., Utah, 1999, Kimball Art Ctr., Park City, Utah, 2003, Springville Art Mus., Utah, 2000, others, Represented in permanent collections Springville Mus. Art, Home Savs. Bank of Am., Nat. Bank of La Jolla, Greenburg Deposit Bank, Ashland, Ky., INMA Gallery, Saudi Arabia, pvt. collectors; author: Light Up Your Watercolors Layer by Layer, 2003; included in: The Watercolorists Answer Book, 2005; Mid So. Watercolorists, 2006, Southern Watercolor Soc. Recipient Gold Medal of Honor, Am. Watercolor Soc., 1982, Walser S. Greathouse medal, 1988, Gold Medal of Honor for Watercolor Allied Artists Am., 1982, cash merit award Ch. of Jesus Christ Latter Day Saints Mus. Art and History, 1991, Best of Show award Utah Watercolor Soc., 2000, 2d award, Religious and Spiritual Art of Utah Exhbn., 2d award, 1998, 3d award, 1999, Best of Show, Challenge of Champions, Watercolor Art Soc. Houston, 2003. Signature mem. Nat. Watercolor Soc., Watercolor West (1st award 1984, N.W.S. award 1999, pres. 1999-2001), Watercolor West (life), Utah Watercolor Soc. Mem. Lds Ch. Avocations: reading, playing piano, genealogy. Home and Office: 413 Lakeside Stansbury Park UT 84074 Office Phone: 435-843-1611. Business E-Mail: lindamoyer@watercolor-online.com.

MOYER, MARY A., media specialist; b. Norristown, Pa., Mar. 7, 1959; d. Harvey C. and Minerva M. Moyer; 1 child, Meagan M. BA, Millersville U., Pa., 1981; MA, Rowan U., 1996. Cert. Sch. Libr. Media Specialist NJ. Dept. Edn., 1983, Tchr.Social Studies 1983, Supervisor 1999. Sch. libr. media specialist Gateway Regional HS, Woodbury Heights, NJ, 1981—92, Woodland Mid. Sch., Barrington Sch. Dist., NJ, 1992—94, Logan Twp. Elem. Sch., NJ, 1994—2000, Delsea Regional H.S., Franklinville, NJ, 2000—. Mentoring com. chair NJ. Assn. Sch. Librs., 2002—04, njea liaison, 2007—; congl. contact chair NJ. Edn. Assn., Trenton, 2007—; profl. devel. com. Delsea Regional Sch. Dist., 2007—. Contbr. articles to profl. jours. Recipient Libr. Champion, NJ. Libr. Assn., 2008; named Sch. Libr. Media Specialist of Yr., NJ Assoc. Sch. Librs., 2003. Mem.: NJ. Assn. Sch. Librs. (assoc.; pres. 2006—07). Democrat. Avocations: cooking, reading, travel. Home: 2201 Lakeshore Dr Millville NJ 08332 Office: Delsea Regional High Sch Box 405 Fries Mill Rd Franklinville NJ 08322 Office Fax: 856-694-3146. Personal E-mail: mmoyerlib@gmail.com. Business E-Mail: mmoyer@delsearegional.us.

MOYER, R. CHARLES, finance company executive, educator, retired dean; b. Reading, Pa., July 11, 1945; s. Ralph Charles and Jane Anne (Huls) M.; m. Sally Louise Prizer, May 19, 1973; children: Laura Prizer, Craig Prizer. BA in Econs., Howard U., 1967; MBA, U. Pitts., 1968, PhD in Fin., 1971. Asst. prof. fin. U. Houston, 1971-76; fin. economist U.S. Maritime Adminstrn., Washington, 1973-74; assoc. prof. Lehigh U., Bethlehem, Pa., 1976-77; from assoc. prof. to prof. U. N.Mex., Albuquerque, 1977-80; prof., chmn. fin. dept. Tex. Tech U., Lubbock, 1980-87; GMAC ins. chair in fin., Babcock Grad. Sch. Wake Forest U., Winston-Salem, NC, 1988—2004, dean Babcock Grad. Sch. of Mgmt., 1996—2003, dean emeritus, 2003—; dir. King Pharm., Inc., Bristol, Tenn., 2000—; dean Coll. Bus. U. Louisville, 2005—. Pres., founder R.O.E. Cons. Group, Lubbock, 1978; cons. Pub. Svc. Co. N.Mex., 1978—, KN Energy, Denver, 1979—, Gas Co. N.Mex., 1985—, San Diego Gas Electric Co., 1986—, Source Gas LLC, 2007-; mem. adv. bd. Amarr Garage Door Co., Winston-Salem, 2001-05; bd. dirs. Seed Capital Fund, Capital South Ptnrs., LLC. Author: Financial Management with Lotus 1-2-3, 1986, Contemporary Financial Management, 11th edit., 2009, Contemporary Financial Management Fundamentals, 2d edit., 2007, Managerial Economics, 11th edit., 2008; contbr. numerous articles to profl. jours. Vice-chmn. Lubbock Gen. Hosp. Found., 1985-88; bd. Louisville Ballet and Louisville Small Bus. Devel. Corp. Capt. US Army, 1972-74. Fed. Res. Bank Cleve. fellow, 1970-71. Mem.: We. Fin. Assn., Ea. Fin. Assn., So. Fin. Assn. (v.p. 1990—93, pres. 1993), Am. Econs. Assn., Am. Fin. Assn., Fin. Mgmt. Assn. (bd. dir. ombudsman 1985—87, v.p. 1988—, sec.-treas. 1994—2002), Louisville Country Club, Louisville Boat Club, Beta Gamma Sigma, Phi Beta Kappa. Avocations: tennis, golf, bicycling. Office Phone: 502-852-6443. Business E-Mail: charlie.moyer@louisville.edu.

MOYER, THOMAS J., state supreme court chief justice; b. Sandusky, Ohio, Apr. 18, 1939; s. Clarence and Idamae (Hessler) Moyer; m. Mary Francis Moyer, Dec. 15, 1984; 1 child, Drew stepchildren: Anne, Jack, Alaine. BA, Ohio State U., 1961, JD, 1964. Asst. atty. gen. State of Ohio, Columbus, 1964-66; pvt. practice law Columbus, 1966-69; dep. asst. Office Gov. State of Ohio, Columbus, 1969-71, exec. asst., 1975-79; assoc. Crabbe, Brown, Jones, Potts & Schmidt, Columbus, 1972-75; judge U.S. Ct. Appeals (10th cir.), Columbus, 1979-86; chief justice Ohio Supreme Ct., Columbus, 1987—. Chair Conference of Chief Justices, 1995—96, Nat. Conf. on Ct. Security, 2005. Sec. bd. trustees Franklin U., Columbus, 1986-87; trustee Univ. Club, Columbus, 1986; mem. nat. coun. adv. com. Ohio State U. Coll. Law, Columbus. Recipient Award of Merit, Ohio Legal Ctr. Inst., Am. Judicature Soc. award, Disting. Svc. award, Nat. Ctr. State Cts., 1997, Innovative Program award, Assn. Family & Conciliation Cts., 1998, Better World award, Ohio Mediation Assn., 1999, Whitney North Seymour medal, Am. Arbitration Assn., 2000, James F. Henry award, 2003; named Outstanding Young Man of Columbus, Columbus Jaycees, 1969. Fellow: Ohio State Bar Found. (Ritter award 1996); mem.: Ohio State Bar Assn. (exec. com., council dels., Ohio Bar medal 1991), Columbus Bar Assn. (pres. 1980-81, Liberty Bell award), Critchon Club, Columbus Maennerchor Club Republican. Avocations: sailing, tennis. Office: Ohio Supreme Ct 65 S Front St Columbus OH 43215*

MOYER-HORNER, LUCAS, conservationist, educator; s. Jeff Horner and Laurie Moyer. BS in Genetics and Conservation Biology, U. Wis. Madison, 2001, attending in Zoology, 2004—. Alpine rschr. Glacier Nat. Pk., Mont., 2007—; tchg. asst. U. Wis. Madison, 2004—. Tchg. fellow Howard Hughes Med. Inst., Madison, Wis., 2007. Contbr. articles to profl. jours. Recipient Numerous awards, Glacier Nat. Pk. Fund, 2004. Achievements include research in effects of climate change on mountain species, especially the American Pika. Avocations: mountain climbing, travel. Home: 916 E Gorham St Apt E Madison WI 53703 Personal E-mail: lrmhorner@hotmail.com.

MOYERS, BILL, journalist, writer, former White House press secretary; b. Hugo, Okla., June 5, 1934; s. John Henry and Ruby (Johnson) M.; m. Judith Suzanne Davidson, Dec. 18, 1954; children: William Cope, Suzanne, John. BJ with honors, U. Tex., 1956; grad. student, U. Edinburgh, Scotland, 1956-57; MDiv with honors, Southwestern Baptist Theol. Sem., 1959; DFA (hon.), Am. Film Inst. Personal asst. to Senator Lyndon B. Johnson US Senate, 1960—61; assoc. dir. pub. affairs Peace Corps, 1961-62, dept. dir., 1963; spl. asst. to Pres. The White House, 1963-67, press sec., 1965-67; pub. Newsday, Garden City, NY, 1967-70; editor-in-chief Bill Moyers Jour. (weekly pub. affairs program on pub. TV), 1971-76, 78-81; chief corr. CBS Reports, CBS-TV, 1976-78; sr. news analyst CBS News, CBS-TV, 1981-86; founder Pub. Affairs Programming, Inc., 1986—; anchor, writer NOW with Bill Moyers, 2002—04, Bill Moyers Jour., 2006—. Author, editor: Listening to America, 1971, Report from Philadelphia, 1987, The Secret Government, 1988; editor: Joseph Campbell and the Power of Myth, 1988, A World of Ideas, 1989, 2d edit., 1990, Genesis, 1996, Fooling With Words, 1999, Moyers on America, 2004; prodr. (TV series) Creativity with Bill Moyers, 1982, Healing and the Mind, 1993, Bill Moyers on Faith and Reason, Moyers on America, Moyers on Democracy, 2008. Pres. The Florence and John Schumann Found., 1991—. Recipient over 30 Emmy awards, Ralph Lowell medal for contbn. to pub. TV, George Peabody award, 1976, 80, 85-86, 88-90, 99, 2000, 04, DuPont-Columbia U. Silver Baton, 1979, 86, 88, Gold baton award, 1991, 99, George Polk award, 1981, 86, career achievement award Internat. Documentary Assn., Eric Barnouw award Orgn. Am. Historians, medal of excellence N.Y. State Bd. Regents, James Madison award Nat. Broadcasting Editl. Assn., Communicator of Decade award Religious Comm. Congress, Elmer Holmes Bibst award NYU, Religious Liberty award Am. Jewish Com., 1995, Walter Cronkite award for excellence in journalism, 1995, The Fred Friendly First Amendment award, 1995, NEH Charles Frankel prize for outstanding contbns. to cultural life, 1997, Best News - Analysis, Feature or Commentary, Writers Guild America, 2009; elected to TV Hall of Fame, 1995; George Polk award for career achievement, 2005. Fellow AAAS; mem. Am. Philos. Soc., Org. Am. Historians. Independent. Protestant. Office: Pub Affairs TV Inc 450 W 33rd St New York NY 10001-2603

MOYERS, SYLVIA DEAN, retired medical librarian; b. Independence, W.Va., Oct. 22, 1936; d. Wilkie Russell and Ina Laura (Watkins) Collins; m. Paul Franklin Moyers, June 29, 1957; children: Tammy Jeanne, Thomas Paul, Tara Sue. Student, Am. Med. Record Assn., 1977—79. Sec. Teets Lumber Co., Terra Alta, W.Va., 1954-58, Preston County News, 1958-60; med. record clk. med. record dept. Hopemont (W.Va.) Hosp., W.Va., 1960-75, dir., 1975-88; sec. The Terra Alta Bank, 1990-95; ret., 1995. Charter mem., past mother advisor Order of Rainbow Girls (Terra Alta Assembly No. 26), past grand editor Mountain Echoes; vol. Preston Meml. Hosp., ARC, Salvation Army, Am. Cancer Soc., Boy Scouts Am.; active Kingwood Fire Dept. Aux. Mem.: Preston County Hist. Soc., Kingwood Red Hat Mamas (charter), Preston Meml. Hosp. Aux., Kingwood Women's Civic Club. Republican. Methodist. Home: 120 Miller Rd Kingwood WV 26537-1321

MOYES, JERRY C., transportation executive, professional sports team executive; b. Plain City, Utah; m. Vickie Moyes; 10 children. Grad., Weber State Coll. Co-founder Swift Transp. Co., Inc., 1966—, v.p., 1966—84, chmn., pres., CEO Phoenix, 1984—2005, 2007—; owner SME Steel. Limited ptnr. Ariz. Diamondbacks, Phoenix Suns; co-owner Phoenix Coyotes, 2001—. Mem.: Am. Trucking Assn. (v.p.), Ariz. Motor Transportation Assn. (pres. 1987—88). Office: Swift Transp Co 2200 S 75th Ave Phoenix AZ 85043-7410 also: PO Box 29243 Phoenix AZ 85038-9243 Fax: 623-907-7380.

MOYLAN, JAMES JOSEPH, lawyer; b. Forest Hills, NY, Feb. 3, 1948; s. James Gerard and Jessie Cora (Geary) M.; m. Barbara Chesrow, Aug. 29, 1970; children: James, C., Joseph O., Alicia G. BSBA, U. Denver, 1969, JD, 1971. Bar: Colo. 1972, DC 1972, Ill. 1975, US Dist. Ct. Colo. 1972, US Supreme Ct. 1975. Trial atty. SEC, Washington, 1972-75; assoc. gen. counsel Chgo. Bd. Options Exch., Ill., 1975-77; assoc. Abramson & Fox, Chgo., 1977-80; ptnr. Bowen, Knepper & Moylan Ltd., Chgo., 1980-82, Moylan & Early, Ltd., Chgo., 1983-84; prin. James J. Moylan and Assocs., Ltd., Chgo., 1984-95, 2003—; ptnr. Arnstein & Lehr, Chgo., 1995-2000, Tressler, Soderstrom, Maloney & Priess, Chgo., 2000—03, James J. Moylan and Assocs. PC, 2003—. Adj. prof. law IIT Chgo. Kent Coll. Law, 1976-2002, U. Denver Coll. Law, 2005—; former pub. dir. MidAm. Commodity Exch. divsn. Chgo. Bd. Trade, Chgo. Contbr. articles to profl. jours. Mem.: ABA (sect. corp., banking and bus. law, sect. litigation), Colo. Bar Assn., D.C. Bar Assn., Chgo. Bar Assn., Ill. State Bar Assn. (sect. coun. mem.), Theta Chi (grand chpt. 1993—2000, funds bd. 2000—03, found. chpt. 2003—). Republican. Roman Catholic. Office: PO Box 775965 31685 Inca Way Steamboat Springs CO 80477-5965 Office Phone: 970-870-0730. Business E-Mail: jjmoylanlaw@aol.com.

MOYLE, PETER BRIGGS, marine biologist, educator; b. May 29, 1942; s. John Briggs and Evelyn (Wood) M.; m. Marilyn Arneson, June 11, 1966; children: Petrea Ruth, John Noah. BA, U. Minn., 1964, PhD, 1969; MS, Cornell U., 1966. Asst. prof. Calif. State U., Fresno, 1969-72; from asst. prof. to prof. U. Calif., Davis, 1972—, chmn. dept. wildlife and fisheries, 1982-87, Pres.'s chair in undergrad. edn., 2003—06. Head, Delta Native Fishes Recovery Team, 1993-95. Author: Inland Fishes of California, 1976, 2d edit., 2002, Fishes: An Introduction to Ichthyology, 5th edit., 2003, Fish: An Enthusiast's Guide, 1993. Fellow Calif. Acad. Sci.; mem. Am. Fisheries Soc. (life, award of excellence West divsn. 1991, Outstanding Educator award 1995, award of excellence, 2007), Ecol. Soc. Am., Am. Soc. Ichthyologists and Herpetologists, Soc. Conservation Biology, Natural Heritage Inst. (v.p. 1994-2007). Home: 612 Eisenhower St Davis CA 95616-3031 Office: U Calif Dept Wildlife Fish & Conservation Biolog 1 Shields Ave Davis CA 95616 E-mail: pbmoyle@ucdavis.edu.

MOYNA, JOHN LAWRENCE, priest; b. NYC, Aug. 20, 1945; s. John Lawrence and Margaret Mary (Healy) Moyna. BA, St. Joseph's Sem. Coll., 1969; MDiv, Christ the King Sem., 1975. Ordained Roman Catholic Priest Diocese of Albany, 1973. Assoc. pastor St. Clare's Ch., Colonie, NY, 1973—75, St. Mary's Ch., Clinton Heights, NY, 1975—79, St. Pius X Ch., Londonville, NY, 1979—83, St. John the Evangelist Ch., Schenectady, NY, 1983—86; pastor St. Mary's Ch., Coxsackie, NY, 1986—; chaplain N.Y. State Dept. of Corrections, 1996—. Dean Suburban Albany, NY, 1982—83, dean Greene County, NY, 2006—. Mem. Ministerial Assoc., Coxsackie, 1986—, Presbyterial Coun., Albany, 1975—79, 1988—93, chmn., 1991—93; mem. strategic pastoral planning com. Diocese of Albany, 1990—91; mem. NY State Cath. Conf. Com. On Apostolate, 2006—. Mem.: Am. Correctional Assn., Acad. Correctional Health Profls. Roman Catholic. Achievements include development of hospice tng. for prison inmates. Home and Office: St Mary's Ch 80 Mansion St Coxsackie NY 12051 Office Phone: 518-731-8800.

MOYNAHAN, JOHN DANIEL, JR., retired insurance executive; b. Chgo., Dec. 10, 1935; s. John Daniel and Helen (Hurley) M.; m. Virginia Thomas, Oct. 10, 1959; children: Laura, Mark, Tricia, Kate. BA cum laude, U. Notre Dame, 1957. With Met. Life Ins. Co., NYC, 1957—, regional v.p., from 1971, with nat. div. group nat. accounts, 1979-80, sr. v.p. group life and health ops., 1980-86, exec. v.p., 1986-97; ret., 1997.

MOYNIHAN, BRIAN T., investment company executive, bank executive; b. 1959; m. Susan Berry; 3 children. BA, Brown U., 1981; JD, U. Notre Dame Law Sch. Assoc. Edwards & Angell LLP, 1984—91, ptnr., 1991—93; dep. gen. coun. FleetBoston Fin. Corp., 1993—94, mng. dir. corp. strategy and devel., 1994—2000, sr. v.p., 1998—99, exec. v.p., 1999—2000, exec. v.p. brokerage and wealth mgmt., 2000—04; pres. global wealth & investment mgmt. Bank of America Corp., 2004—07, exec. v.p., gen. counsel, 2008—09, pres. global corp. & investment banking, 2007—08, pres. global banking, global wealth & investment mgmt., 2009, chmn., global diversity & inclusion coun., pres., consumer & small bus. banking, 2004—, head consumer banking, 2009—; CEO Merrill Lynch (div. of Bank of America), 2009. Bd. dirs. YouthBuild Boston, Boys and Girls Clubs of Boston; chmn. Travelers Aid Soc., Rhode Island, Providence Haitian Project, Inc. Office: Bank of America Corp 100 N Tryon St Charlotte NC 28255 Office Phone: 704-386-5681. Office Fax: 704-386-6699.*

MOYNIHAN, GARY PETER, industrial engineering educator; b. Little Falls, NY, Mar. 5, 1956; s. Peter H. and Frances S. (Ferjanec) M.; m. Eleanor T. McCusker, Mar. 10, 1984; children: Andrew Ross, Keith Patrick. BS in Chemistry, Rensselaer Polytech. Inst., 1978, MBA in Opsl. Mgmt., 1980; PhD in Indsl. Engring., U. Ctrl. Fla., 1990. Prodn. supr. Am. Cyanamid, Bound Brook, N.J., 1978-79, Nat. Micronetics, Kingston, N.Y., 1980-81; assoc. mfg. engr. Martin Marietta Aerospace, Orlando, Fla., 1981-82, indsl. engr., 1982-85, sr. indsl. engr., 1985-87, group indsl. engr., 1987-90; asst. prof. indsl. engring. U. Ala., Tuscaloosa, 1990-96, assoc. prof., 1996—2001, prof., 2001—. Cons. in field. Contbr. articles to profl. jours. Regents scholar N.Y. State Bd. Regents, 1974-78; rsch. fellow NASA, 1992-93, 98-99; rsch. grant BellSouth Telecomm., 1994-96; recipient Outstanding Tchg. award AMOCO Found., 1993-94, Ralph R. Teetor Engring. Educator award Soc. Automotive Engrs, 2000. Mem.: IEEE (sr.), Aerospace and Def. Soc. (v.p. fin. and adminstrn. 1994—97), Inst. Indsl. Engrs. (sr.; chpt. dir. 1991—95, chpt. pres. 1996—97, regional v.p. 2004—06, Outstanding Faculty Adv. SE Region award 2004, 2006, Nat. Outstanding Faculty Adv. award 2006). Achievements include design and development of information systems applications for the aerospace and foundry industries; 4 software copyrights. Office: U Ala Dept Indsl Engring Tuscaloosa AL 35487-0001

MOYNIHAN, JAMES MICHAEL, bishop; b. Rochester, NY, July 16, 1932; s. Michael Joseph and Carolyn Elizabeth Horigan Moynihan. Attended, St. Bernard's Sem., Rochester, North American Coll., Rome, Gregorian U. Ordained priest Diocese of Rochester, NY, 1957; assoc. pastor Our Lady of Mount Carmel Parish, Rochester, 1961—63; chaplain Rochester Police Dept., 1962—73; sec. Most Rev. James E. Kearney, 1963—66; vice chancellor Diocese of Rochester, 1965—67, chancellor, 1967—74; chaplain Highland Hosp., Rochester, 1974—76; pastor St. Joseph Parish, Penfield, NY, 1976—91; ordained bishop, 1995; bishop Diocese of Syracuse, NY, 1995—2009, bishop emeritus, 2009—. Defender of bond and promoter of justice Diocesan Tribunal, Rochester, 1961—66; dir. Bishop's Ann. Cath. Thanksgiving Appeal, 1985—89; mem. bd. trustees Wadhams Hall Sem., Ogdensburg, NY, 1996—2001; mem. Com. on Relationship Between Eastern and Latin Cath. Churches, 1996; founding mem. Bishop Sheen Housing Found. Mem.: Cath. Near East Welfare Assn. (assoc. sec. gen. 1991—95). Roman Catholic. Office: 240 E Onondaga St Syracuse NY 13202-2608*

MOYNIHAN, JOHN BIGNELL, retired lawyer; b. NYC, July 25, 1933; s. Jerome J. and Stephanie (Bignell) M.; m. Odilia Marie Jacques, Nov. 13, 1965; children: Blair, Dana. BS, Fordham U., 1955; JD, St. John's U., NYC, 1958. Bar: Tex. 1961, U.S. Supreme Ct. 1965, U.S. Dist. Ct. (we. dist.) Tex. 1968, U.S. Ct. Appeals (5th cir.) 1973. Sole practice, Brownsville, Tex., 1961-62; asst. city atty. City of San Antonio, 1962-63; sole practice San Antonio, 1963-65; estate tax atty. IRS, San Antonio, 1965-73; dist. counsel EEOC, San Antonio, 1974-79; asst. U.S. atty. Office U.S. Atty., San Antonio, 1980-87, sr. litigation counsel, 1987-94; sole practice San Antonio, 1995-98; ret., 1998. Chmn. reform and renewal com., San Antonio Roman Cath. Archdiocese, 1968. Served with U.S. Army, 1958-60; lt. col. USAFR (ret.), 1986. Mem. San Antonio Bar Assn. (chmn. state and nat. legis. com. 1972-73, Meritorious Svc. award 1968), Fed. Bar Assn. (bd. dirs. San Antonio chpt. 1983—, pres. elect 1986, pres. 1987), KC (pres. 1967). Home: 11011 Whispering Wind St San Antonio TX 78230-3746 E-mail: jmoynihan@satx.rr.com.

MOYNIHAN, WILLIAM J., museum executive; b. Little Falls, NY, Apr. 8, 1942; s. Bernard J. and Mary A. (Flynn) M.; m. Irene A. Sheilds, July 2, 1966; children: Patricia, Erin, Sean. BA, SUNY, Binghamton, 1964; MA, Colgate U., 1966; PhD, Syracuse U., 1973. From asst. to assoc. prof. Colgate U., Hamilton, NY, 1973—77, from asst. to assoc. dean faculty, 1977—80, dean students, 1980—83, dean coll., 1983—88; v.p.m. dir. Am. Mus. Natural History, NYC, 1988—95; pres., CEO Milw. Pub. Mus., 1995—2002; ret., 2002. Bd. dirs. N.Y. State Mus.; adv. com. arts and culture Congressman J. Nadler, N.Y.C., 1993-95. Adv. editor Curator jour., 1991-95. Mem. Am. Mus. Assn., Am. Assn. Museums (mem. ethics com., bd. dirs.), Wis. Acad. of Scis., Arts and Letters (councillor-at-large 1995-02), Univ. Club. Home: 84 Eaton St Hamilton NY 13346

MOYNIHAN, WILLIAM TRUMBULL, educator; b. Haverhill, Mass., June 23, 1926; s. Richard Hull and Harriet (Trumbull) M.; m. Ruth MacKenzie Barnes, Mar. 26, 1953; children: Robert, Elaine, Edward, Neil, Susan, Richard, Benjamin. BA, St. Bonaventure U., 1952; MA, U. Conn., 1957; PhD (Kent fellow), Brown U., 1962. Newsman, 1952-55; faculty U. Conn., Storrs, 1956-59, 61-91, prof., 1966—, head English dept., 1966-86. Faculty Brown U., 1959-61 Author: The Craft and Art of Dylan Thomas, 1966; also numerous textbooks, articles, unpublished plays. Served with USMC, 1946-50. Lilly fellow, 1959-60 Home: 37 Farrell Rd Storrs Mansfield CT 06268-2216 Personal E-mail: billmoya@charter.net.

MOYO, DAMBISA, economist, writer; b. Lusaka, Zambia; BS in Chemistry, Am. U., Washington, MBA in Fin.; M, Harvard U., Cambridge, Mass.; PhD in Econs., Oxford U., Eng. Cons. World Bank, Washington, 1993—95; mem. capital markets, hedge fund coverage and global macroeconomics teams Goldman Sachs, 2001—08. Bd. dirs. Lundin Petroleum. Author: Dead Aid: Destroying the Biggest Global Myth of Our Time, 2008, Dead Aid: Why Aid Is Not Working and How There Is a Better Way for Africa, 2009 (NY Times bestseller). Patron Absolute Return for Kids; bd. mem. Lundin for Africa Found., Room to Read. Named one of The World's Most Influential People, TIME mag., 2009; named to Young Global Leaders, World Econ. Forum, 2009. Mem.: Royal Inst. Internat. Affairs, Cambridge U. Ctr. Internat. Bus. and Mgmt. Office: c/o Farrar Straus and Giroux 18 W 18th St New York NY 10011*

MOYO, DEBAYO R., communications executive; b. Accra, Ghana; m. Rashida Moyo; 1 child, Jamal Debayo. BSc, U. Lagos, Nigeria, 1986; MA, Howard U., Washington, PhD, 1996. Gen. mgr. WURC-FM, pub. radio Rust Coll., Holly Springs, Miss., assoc. prof., dept. chair, mass comm., 1997—. Recipient Journalism Educators award, Am. Press Inst., 2005; fellow, Cable Satellite Pub. Affairs Networks, 1998, Dow Jones Newspaper Fund, 2000, Nat. Endowment Humanities, U. Hawaii, 2000, Journalism Excellence Program fellow, Am. Soc. Newspaper Editors, 2002. Fellow: Nat. Acad. TV Arts & Sci.; mem.: Nat. Assn. Broadcasters, Nat. Assn. Black Journalists, Assn. Edn. Journalism and Mass Comm. Home: PO Box 5283 Holly Springs MS 38634 Office: Rust Coll 150 Rust Ave Holly Springs MS 38635 Office Fax: 662-252-8869. Personal E-mail: dmoyo@hotmail.com. Business E-Mail: dmoyo@rustcollege.edu.

MOYSE, HERMANN, III, banker; b. Baton Rouge, Dec. 28, 1948; s. Hermann Jr. and Marie Louise (Levy) M.; m. Janet Lee Doise; children: Allison Leze, David Hermann, Aaron Lewis. BA, Coll. of Emporia, 1970; MSW, La. State U., 1973. Asst. dir. Capital Area Health Planning Agy., 1973-74; research assoc. La. State U., Baton Rouge, 1974-78; trainee to v.p. City Nat. Bank, Baton Rouge, 1978—, sr. v.p., 1985-94, also bd. dirs., chmn., 1994-98; owner, pres. HM3 Corp., 1999—. Sec.-treas. Melrose Devel. Corp., Baton Rouge, 1986-87; bd. dirs. La. Cos., Charter Chambers, LLC, First NBC Bank, New Orleans, Bizzuka, Inc.; CEO Health Net One, 1999; adv. bd. Iberra Bank, 2004-05; pres. WRKF Radio, 2003-04. Active Capital Area United Way Agy. Svcs. Div., Baton Rouge, 1979-86, 88-91, vice chmn. 1981, bd. dirs., 1987—, chmn., 1989-90; v.p. Arts Coun. Greater Baton Rouge, 1990—; 1st v.p. La. Arts & Sci. Ctr., Baton Rouge, 1985—, pres., 1988; mem. Community Funds for Arts, 1989-90; mem. Arts & Humanities Coun., 1990—, v.p., 1991—, treas., 1992; mem. Cmty. Funds for the Arts, 1989—, vice-chmn., 1992; pres. Cath. Cmty. Life Office, Baton Rouge, 1981, Baton Rouge Speech and Hearing Found., 1986, pres. 1983, treas., 1981; v.p. St. Joseph's Acad. Adv. Bd., 1986-88, pres., 1987-88; bd. dirs. St. James Place; treas. Baton Rouge Crisis Intervention Ctr., 1984-85, v.p., 1987, pres., 1987; sec. St. Joseph's Children's Home, 1980; bd. dirs. Crime Stoppers, Inc., 1986—, v.p., 1989, pres. 1991—; pres. Mid City Devel. Alliance, 1991-93, 97—; adv. bd. Tau Ctr., 1990-93; trustee Episc. HS, 1990-92; treas. La. Delta Svc. Corps. Inc., 1995—; bd. trustees Gen. Health Sys., Inc, 1994-98, La. Nature Conservancy, 2001—, Our Lady of Lake Coll., 2001—, sec., 2003-05; chmn. fin. com. Baton Rouge Crimestoppers, 1997—; chmn. First Commerce Cmty. Devel. Corp., 1993-99, La. State U. Health Care Svcs. Found., 2002—. Mem. La. Bankers Assn. (fed. affairs com. 1990—), La. Coun. Econ. Edn. (trustee 1987, regional v.p. 1990—, Community Vol. Activist award 1988), NCCJ (chpt. bd. dirs. 1988, treas. 1995), City Club, Baton Rouge Country Club. Democrat. Jewish. Office Phone: 225-926-1600. Personal E-mail: hmoyse3@yahoo.com.

MOZELL, HERBERT LEE, mental health services professional; b. Miami, Fla., Feb. 16, 1963; s. Alfonzo and Ethel Mae Mozell. BA in Psychology, A&T State U., 1988, MS in Adult Edn., 1997; EdD, Nova Southeastern U., 2008. Habilitation tech, Greensboro, NC, 1990—96; exec. dir. Visions of N.C. Inc., Greensboro, 1997—. Mental health tech., Greensboro, 1988—97; tchr. Allen Jay Mid. Sch., Archdale, 1999—2001; cons., Greensboro, 2004—, Little Seedlings, Greensboro, 2004—, Faith House, Lexington, 2004—, Sensational Living, Raleigh, 2004—. Recipient Humanitarian award, Nova S.E. U., 2004. Mem.: Am. Mental Health Counselor Assn., Kappa Delta Pi. Democrat. Baptist. Avocations: Karate, weightlifting. Office: Visions of NC Inc 7607-A Alcorn Rd Greensboro NC 27409 Office Phone: 336-931-0432. E-mail: hmozell@hotmail.com.

MOZENA, DAN W., United States ambassador to Angola; b. Dubuque, Iowa, May 1, 1949; m. Grace Mozena; children: Anne, Mark. B in Polit. Sci. and Hist., Iowa State U.; M in Pub. Adminstrn. and Polit. Sci., U. Wis., Madison. Joined US Dept. State, 1982, various positions including dep. dir. So. African Affairs, officer-in-charge for South Africa, dep. chief of mission Lusaka, Zambia, then dir. Office So. African Affairs, 2004—07, US amb. to Angola, 2007—. Former vol. Peace Corps, Zaire. Office: DOS Amb 2550 Luanda Pl Washington DC 20521-2550*

MOZER, ATTILA JANOS, materials scientist, researcher; b. Kiskunmajsa, Bacs-Kiskun, Hungary, Jan. 20, 1977; s. Janos Ferenc Mozer and Piroska Sara Izbeki; m. Tomoko Murakami, Apr. 19, 2003. M in Chem. Engring., Budapest U. Tech. and Econs., 2001; D in Phys. Chemistry, Johannes Keppler U., Linz, Austria, 2004. Rschr. Konarka Austria, Linz, 2002—03, Linz Inst. Organic Solar Cells, 2002—04; rsch. fellow Osaka U., Japanese Soc. Promotion Sci., Suita, Japan, 2005—. Contbr. scientific papers. Scholar, Internat. Student Ctr. Osaka U., U. NH, BUTE Internat. Edn. Ctr. Mem.: Electrochem. Soc., Material Rsch. Soc. Achievements include development of Plastic Solar Cells, Novel Characterization Techniques. Office: Univ Wollongong Squires Way, Fairy Meadow New South Wales 2522 Australia Business E-Mail: attila@uow.edu.au.

MOZHAEV, VADIM, research scientist; PhD, Moscow State U. Sr. scientist AMRI, Albany, NY, 1999—. Office: AMRI 21 Corp Cir Albany NY 12212 Office Fax: 518-512-2078. Business E-Mail: dima.mozhaev@amriglobal.com.

MOZILO, ANGELO R., retired mortgage company executive; b. NYC, 1938; m. Phyllis Mozilo; 5 children. BS, Fordham U., 1960; LLD (hon.), Pepperdine U. Co-founder, vice chmn. Countrywide Fin. Corp., Calabasas, Calif., 1969—99, pres., 2000—03, CEO, 1998—99, chmn., CEO, 1999—2008. Bd. dirs. The Home Depot, Inc., 2006—07. Bd. mem. Nat. Housing Endowment, Joint Ctr. for Housing Studies, Harvard U., Homes for Working Families; trustee Gonzaga U. Recipient Boy Scouts of Am. James E. West Fellowship award, Ellis Island Medal of Honor, Albert Schweitzer award, Special Achiev. award, Nat. Italian Am. Found., Horatio Alger Assn. of Disting. Am. award, Lifetime Achievement award, Am. Banker mag, 2006; named one of The 30 Most Respected CEOs, Barron's mag., 2005; named to Nat. Assn. of Home Builders' Hall of Fame. Mem.: Mortgage Bankers Assn. of Am. (pres. 1991—92).

MOZZATO, LUCIANO, manufacturing company executive; Diploma in Elec. Engring., ITI U., Italy; BS in Mech. Engring., Hartford U., CT. Started his career as mechanic; product dir. United Technologies, v.p., global supply chain & logistics worldwide, 2000—04, v.p., gen. mgr. L.Am. bus.,otis elevator divsn., 2004—08; dir., engring. United Technologies (Italian subs.), mgr., field svc., v.p., gen. mgr., 2004—08; exec. v.p., product svcs. worldwide Dresser-Rand Group Inc., 2009—. Office: Dresser-Rand Group Inc 10205 Westheimer Rd Ste 1000 Houston TX 77042 Office Phone: 713-354-6100. Office Fax: 713-354-6110.

MRACHEK, LORIN LOUIS, lawyer; b. Fairmont, Minn., Jan. 5, 1946; s. Louis L. and Kathleen (Loring) M.; m. Elizabeth Moss, Aug. 31, 1968; children: Kathleen Elizabeth, Louis Moss. BA with honors, Fla. State U., 1968; MBA, JD, Columbia U., 1974. Bar: Fla. 1974, Va. 1977, U.S. Ct. Mil. Appeals 1977, U.S. Dist. Ct., U.S. Ct. Appeals (5th cir.), U.S. Ct. Appeals (7th cir.), U.S. Ct. (11th cir.), U.S. Supreme Ct. 1978, U.S. Bankruptcy Ct. (so. dist.) Fla., U.S. Bankruptcy Ct. (mid. dist.) Fla., U.S. Bankruptcy Ct. (no. dist.) Fla.; cert. in civil trial law, 1985, bus. litigation, 1997, Fla. Bar Bd. Certification; cert. in bus. bankruptcy law Am. Bd. Bankruptcy Certification, 1992; cert. in civil trial advocacy Nat. Bd. Trial Advocacy, 1995. Commd. 2d lt. USMC, 1969, advanced through grades to capt., 1974, chief def. counsel Marine Corps. Recruit Depoit, Paris Island, 1975-77, resigned, 1977; spl. asst. to gen. counsel U.S. Ry. Assn., Washington, 1977-78; shareholder Gunster, Yoakley, Valdes-Fauli & Stewart, P.A., West Palm Beach, Fla., 1978-2000; founding shareholder Page, Mrachek, Fitzgerald & Rose, West Palm Beach, Fla., 2000—. Editor-in-chief Columbia Jour. Law and Social Problems, 1973-74; contbr. articles to profl. jours. Named one of Best Lawyers in Am.; Harlan Fiske Stone scholar. Fellow Am. Coll. Trial Attys.; mem. ABA, Am. Bankruptcy Inst., So. Fla. Bankruptcy Bar Assn. Avocations: travel, golf. Office: 505 S Flagler Dr Ste 600 West Palm Beach FL 33401-5941 Office Phone: 561-655-2250. Business E-Mail: lmrachek@pm-law.com.

MRACKY, RONALD SYDNEY, marketing executive, tourism consultant, media specialist; b. Sydney, Oct. 22, 1932; came to US, 1947, naturalized, 1957; s. Joseph and Anna (Janousek) M.; m. Sylvia Frommer, Jan. 1, 1960; children: Enid Hillevi, Jason Adam. Student, English Inst., Prague, Czech Republic, 1943—47; grad., Parsons Sch. Design, NYC, 1953—2001; postgrad., NYU, 1953—54. Designer D. Deskey Assocs., NYC, 1952-53; art dir., designer ABC-TV, Hollywood, Calif., 1956-57; creative dir. Neal Advt. Assocs., LA, 1957-59; pres. Richter & Mracky Design Assocs., LA, 1959-68; pres., CEO Richter & Mracky-Bates divsn. Ted Bates & Co., LA, 1968-73, Regency Fin., Internat. Fin. Svcs., Beverly Hills, Calif., 1974-76; sr. ptnr. Sylron Internat., LA, 1973—, mgmt. dir. for N.Am. Standard Advt.-Tokyo, 1978-91. CEO, Std./Worldwide Cons. Group, LA, Tokyo, 1981-87; officer, bd. dirs. Theme Resorts, Inc., Denver, 1979—; prin., officer Prodn. Travel & Tours, Universal City, 1981—, Eques Ltd., LA, 1988-93; mng. ptnr. GO! Pubs., 1993—; cons. in field; exec. dir. Inst. for Internat. Studies and Devel. LA, 1976-77; mng. ptnr. Africa Consult Group, 1998—. Dir. MedicusTravel.com, 2003—; mem. editl. bd., mktg. dir. The African Times and Africa Quar., 1990—; contbr. articles to profl. jours With US Army, 1954-56. Recipient nat. and internat. awards design and mktg. Mem. Am. Mktg. Assn., Africa Travel Assn. (amb.-at-large, internat. secretariat, bd. dirs.), Pacific Asia Travel Assn., S.Am. Travel Assn., Am. Soc. Travel Agts.

MRAK, ROBERT EMIL, neuropathologist, educator; b. Oakland, Calif., Dec. 18, 1948; s. Emil Marcel and Vera Dudley (Greaves) M.; m. Paula Elizabeth North, Oct. 18, 1980; children: Lara North, Eric North, Ian North. BS in Math., U. Calif., Davis, 1970, MD, 1975, PhD in Zoology, 1976. Diplomate Am. Bd. Pathology, Am. Bd. Neuropathology. Resident in pathology Vanderbilt U. Hosp., Nashville, 1976-78, fellow in molecular biology, 1978-80; asst. prof. pathology Vanderbilt U., 1980-84; assoc. prof. U. Ark. for Med. Scis., Little Rock, 1984—87, prof., 1993—98, chief neuropathology, 1999—2007, dir. neuropathology core, Alzheimer Disease Core Ctr., 2001—07, prof. pathology, neurobiology and devel. scis., 1998—2007, chief autopsy, 2003—07; prof., chmn. of pathology U. Toledo Health Sci. Campus, 2007—. Chief electron microscopy VA Hosp., Little Rock, 1984-98; cons. in neuropathology Ark. Children's Hosp., Little Rock, 1984—. Editl. bd. mem. Jour. Neuropathy & Explt. Neurology, 1996-99, Human Pathology, 1996-2004; editor-in-chief Jour. Neurinflammation, 2003—; contbr. articles and abstracts to profl. jours Rsch. grantee VA, 1980-83, 86-89, Muscular Dystrophy Assn., 1981-85, NIH, 1986-90, 95—. Mem. Am. Assn. Neuropathologists, Soc. for Neurosci., U.S. and Can. Acad. Pathology. Avocations: running, skiing. Office: Dept Pathology Univ Toledo Health Sci Campus 3000 Arlington Ave Toledo OH 43614 Office Phone: 419-383-3469. Business E-Mail: cathie.harman@utdedo.edu.

MRAMOR, MARTI, engineer, linguist; b. Indpls., Apr. 17, 1971; d. Joseph Thomas Mramor and Nancy Ann Clark Mramor. BA in Biology and Chemistry, Spring Arbor U., Mich., 1994; Paralegal Cert. in Gen. Law with highest honors, Nat. Ctr. for Paralegal Tng., Ga., 1995; AA in Russian, Def. Lang. Inst., Calif., 1998; AAS in Comm. Tech., C.C. of the Air Force, Ala., 2001; MS in Geosciences, Miss. State U., 2005. Engr. L-3 Comm., Bellevue, Nebr., 2004—. Vol. Fontenelle Nature Assn., Bellevue, 2002—06, Katherine and Fred Buffett Forest Learning Ctr., Bellevue, 2002—06, Neale Woods Nature Ctr./Obs., Omaha, 2002—06, Creighton U. Med. Ctr., Omaha, 2006—06; vol. tutor and transl. Staff sgt. USAF, 1997—2001, Okinawa, Japan, master sgt. USAFR, 2001—. Decorated Good Conduct medal USAF, Longevity Svc. medal, Overseas Long Tour ribbon, Aerial Achievement medals, Achievement medals, Noncommissioned Officer Grad. ribbon, Armed Forces Expeditionary medal, Global War on Terrorism Expeditionary medal, Iraq Campaign medal, Afghanistan Campaign medal, Air Force Expeditionary Svc. medal, Air medals, Meritorious Unit award, Commendation medal; recipient Martin J. Kellogg award for Excellence, Def. Lang. Inst., 1998; named Airman of the Yr., USAF, 1999; Academic Athlete scholar, Spring Arbor U., 1990—94. Mem.: VFW (life), Air Force Sgts. Assn., Nat. Weather Assn., Am. Meteorol. Soc., Am. Math. Soc., Am. Phys. Soc., Am. Mensa Soc. Avocations: swimming, running, writing, art, astronomy.

MRAOVIC, BORIS, medical educator, researcher; s. Mladen and Katica Mraovic; 1 child, David Gassmayr. MD, U. Rijeka, Faculty Medicine, Croatia, 1987. Cert. anesthesiology & reanimatolgy specialist Ministry Health, Croatia, 1996, ECFMG, 2000, diplomate in anesthesiology Am. Bd. Anesthesiology, 2006. Anesthesiologist Gen. Hosp. Sibenik, Croatia, 1996—99; rsch. assoc. Rush-Presbyterian St. Luke's Med. Ctr., Chgo., 2000; postdoc. rsch. fellow Med. Coll. Wis., Milw., 2000—01, resident, 2001—05; dir. clin. trials artificial pancreas ctr. Thomas Jefferson U., Phila., 2007—08, asst. prof., 2005—. Recipient Acad. Excellence award, Dept. Anesthesiology, Med. Coll. Wis., 2001—05, First Prize, MARC, Mayo Clinic, Rochester, Minn., 2004; Internat. scholar, Cleve. Clinic, 1998, Postdoc. Rsch. fellow, Dept. Anesthesiology, Med. Coll. Wis., 2000, 2001. Mem.: Am. Soc. Anesthesiologist. Achievements include research in intraperitoneal bupivacaine for analgesia after laparoscopic cholecystectomy. Office: Thomas Jefferson Univ 111 South 11th Str Ste G8490 Philadelphia PA 19107 Office Fax: 1-215-955-0677. Business E-Mail: boris.mraovic@jefferson.edu.

MRAZEK, DAVID ALLEN, child and adolescent psychiatrist; b. Ft. Riley, Kans., Oct. 1, 1947; s. Rudolph George and Hazel Ruth (Schayes) M.; m. Patricia Jean, Sept. 2, 1978; children: Nicola, Matthew, Michael, Alissa. AB in Genetics, Cornell U., 1969; MD, Wake Forest U., 1973. Lic. psychiatrist, child psychiatrist, N.C., Ohio, Colo., D.C., Va., Md., Minn., Ariz., Fla. Lectr. child psychiatry Inst. of Psychiatry, London, 1977-79; dir. pediatric psychiatry Nat. Jewish Ctr. for Immunology and Respiratory Medicine, Denver, 1979-91; chmn. psychiatry Children's Nat. Med. Ctr., Washington, 1991-98; chair psychiatry and behavioral scis. George Washington U. Sch. Medicine, 1996-2000; dir. Children's Rsch. Inst. Neurosci., 1995-98; chair psychiatry and psychology Mayo Clinic, Rochester, Minn., 2000—; prof. psychiatry and pediatrics Mayo Sch. Medicine, Rochester, 2000—; dir. Mayo Clinic S.C. Johnson Genomics of Addictions Program, 2004—. Asst. prof. psychiatry U. Colo. Sch. Medicine, 1979-83, assoc. prof. psychiatry and pediatrics, 1984-89, prof., 1990-91; prof. psychiatry and pediatrics George Washington U. Sch. Medicine, 1991-2000, Leon Yochelson prof. psychiatry and behavioral scis.; dir. Am. Bd. Psychiatry and Neurology, 2003-. Contbr. chapters to books, articles to profl. jours. Recipient Rsch. Scientist Devel. awards NIMH, 1983-88, 88-91, Irving Phillips Meml. award for outstanding rsch. in prevention Acad. Child and Adolescent Psychiatry, 2000, Simon Wile award Am. Acad. Child and Adolescent Psychiatry, 2005, Agnes Purcell McGavin award for Lifetime Achievement in Child and Adolescent Psychiatry, Am. Psychiatric Assn., 2008, Pyschiat. Edn. award Am. Coll., 2005. Fellow Am. Acad. Child and Adolescent Psychiatry (Simon Wile award 2005), Am. Psychiat. Assn. (life, disting. fellow, 2009, chmn. coun. children, adolescents and families 2006-08, Blanche F. Ittleson award 1996, Agnes Purcell McGavin award 1999, 2008), Royal Coll. Psychiatrists, Am. Coll. Psychiatrists; mem. Group for the Advancement of Psychiatry, Colo. Child and Adolescent Psychiatry Soc. (pres. 1984), Benjamin Rush Soc., Am. Bd. Psychiatry Neurology (bd. dirs. 2003—). Office: Mayo Clinic Dept Psychiatry/Pschology 200 1st St SW Rochester MN 55905 Home Phone: 507-285-5656; Office Phone: 507-284-8891. Office Fax: 507-266-3319. Business E-Mail: mrazek.david@mayo.edu.

MROCZKA, VICTOR STANISLAW, lawyer; b. Buffalo, May 6, 1971; s. Stanislaw and Eva Mroczka; m. Fabienne Lemalle, May 10, 1994. HS, Canisius HS, Buffalo, 1989; BS in Fgn. Svc., Georgetown U. Sch. Fgn. Svc., Wash., 1993; JD, Am. U., Wash., 1999. Bar: DC 2001, Supreme Ct SC 2000, U.S. Ct. Internat. Trade 2000, U.S. Ct. of Appeals Fed. Circuit 2000, U.S. Dist. Ct. DC 2001, U.S. Tax Ct. 2001. Assoc. Dorsey & Whitney LLP, Wash., 2000—04, Willkie Farr & Gallagher LLP, Wash., 2004—06, Vinson & Elkins LLP, Wash., 2006—08; internat. trade counsel Hughes Hubbard & Reed LLP, Wash., 2008—. Chair ABA, Africa Law Com., Wash., 2008; bd. mem. Customs and Internat. Trade Bar Assn., NYC. Moderator (book) U.S. Trade and Investment Policy: Diversifying Africa's Exports Under AGOA (Am. Bar Assn.), Export Controls Post 9/11: The Changing Enforcement Landscape (Customs and Internat. Trade Bar Assn.). At large bd. mem. Fed. Triangles Soccer Club, Washington, 2005—06. Independent. Achievements include Attorney in first steel case to have order revoked under U.S. Avocations: travel, hiking. Office: Hughes Hubbard & Reed LLP 1775 I StNW Washington DC 20006 Office Fax: 202-721-4646. Business E-Mail: mroczka@hugheshubbard.com.

MROWKA, TOMASZ, mathematics professor; BS in Math., MIT, 1983; PhD, U. Calif., Berkeley, 1988. Faculty Stanford U., Calif. Inst. Tech., Harvard U.; prof., math. MIT, 1996—. Recipient Nat. Young Investigator award, 1993; co-recipient AMS Oswald Veblen Prize in Geometry, 2007; grantee Alfred P. Sloan Rsch. Fellowship, 1993. Fellow: Am. Acad. Arts & Scis. Office: Dept Math MIT Rm 2-367 77 Massachusetts Ave Cambridge MA 02139-4307

MROZ, ERIK SHANE, lawyer; b. South Bend, Ind., Jan. 9, 1978; s. Thomas Edward and Marian Kay Mroz; m. Ivana Jovanovic, Sept. 13, 2003. BS cum laude, Ball State U., Muncie, Ind., 1999; JD, Ind. U., Indpls., 2003. Bar: Calif. 2003, Ill. 2005, U.S. Dist. Ct. (no. dist.) Calif. 2004, U.S. Dist. Ct. (ctrl. dist.) Calif. 2004, U.S. Dist. Ct. (ea. dist.) Calif. 2004, U.S. Dist. Ct. (so. dist.) Calif. 2004, U.S. Ct. Appeals Armed Svcs. 2004, U.S. Ct. Appeals (9th cir.) 2004, U.S. Ct. Appeals (fed. cir.) 2004, US Supreme Ct. 2007, U.S. Dist. Ct. (East) Wis. Atty. Resolution Law Group, P.C., Woodland Hills, Calif., 2003—. Mem.: ABA, Golden Key, Pi Sigma Alpha, Phi Delta Phi. Avocations: travel, boating, cooking, hiking, camping. Office: Resolution Law Group PC 21800 Oxnard St Ste 780 Woodland Hills CA 91367 Office Fax: 818-598-8350.

MROZEK, LAWRENCE JAMES, educator; s. Mary Anna and Albin Bruno Mrozek. BS in Psychology, Mich. State U., 1984, MA in Phys. Exercise and Exercise Sci., 1989; Cert. - Alcohol and Other Drug Specialist, Calif. State Univeristy, LA, Los Angeles, CA, 1992—93; Cert. - Family Violence and Child Maltreatment, Calif. State U., LA, Los Angeles, CA, 1993—2003; PhD in Edn., Ohio State U., Columbus, 2003—. Cert. alcohol and other drug specialist Calif. State U., 1993, family violence and child maltreatment specialist Calif. State U., 2003. Area coord. Whittier Coll., Calif., 1986—87; resident dir. Calif. State U., LA, 1987—89; from asst. to dir. to asst. dir. for programs U. Student Union, LA, 1989—92, from asst. dir. for ops. to ops. mgr. Northridge, Calif., 1992—2002; rsch. asst., student affairs assessment Ohio State U., 2003—07, coord., Multicultural Ctr., 2006; asst. prof. Wright State U., 2007—; dir. Commn. Social Justice Educators, 2009—, ACDA, Coll. Student Educators Internat. Directorate - commn. for alcohol and other drug issues Am. Coll. Pers. Assn., Washington, 1990—92, directorate - commn. for assessment and evaluation, 2002—03, Washington, 2006—08; conf. planning com. Assn. of Coll. Unions Internat. - Region 15, LA, 1995—95, San Bernardino, Calif., 1997—97. Del. Coun. of Grad. Students, Columbus, Ohio, 2005. Recipient Employee of Yr. award, U. Student Union - Calif. State U., Northridge, 1994-1995, Aida C. Salazar award, 1995-1996; grantee, Ohio State U., 2007; fellow Dai Ho Chun, 2006—07. Mem.: NEA, Ohio Coll. Pers. Assn., Am. Ednl. Rsch. Assn., Assn. for Study of Higher Edn., Nat. Assn. of Student Pers. Administrs., Am. Coll. Pers. Assn., Phi Kappa Phi, Pi Lambda Theta. Office: Wright State Univ 442 Allyn Hall 3640 Col Glenn Hwy Dayton OH 45435-0001

MU, MINGQUAN, meteorologist; s. Wenzhong Mu and Suzhen Chen; m. Linying Zhang; 1 child, Carol. PhD in Meteorology, Inst. Atmospheric Physics, Chinese Acad. Sci., Beijing, 1997; BS in Meteorology, Chengdu Inst. Meteorology, China, 1992. Asst. rschr. Inst. Atmospheric Physics, Chinese Acad. Scis., 1997—2000; rsch. assoc. Rutgers U., New Brunswick, NJ, 2001—03; meteorologist Scripps Instn. Oceanography, La Jolla, Calif., 2003—07; project scientist U. Calif., Irvine, 2007—. Contbr. scientific papers to internat. jours. Grantee, Dept. Sci. and Tech. China, 1998—2002, NSF, 2001—03, 2003—05. Mem.: Am. Geophys. Union, Am. Meteorol. Soc. Achievements include studies on physical mechanism of Madden-Julian Oscillation and energy conversions in the process of Madden-Julian Oscillation development; discovery of limited role of Eurasian snow and soil moisture on Asian summer monsoon variations, new evidence of recent global warming. Avocations: swimming, basketball, movies. Home: 128 Veneto Irvine CA 92614 Office: Univ Calif Irvine Dept Earth Sys Sci 1101B Croul Hall Irvine CA 92697-3100 Office Fax: 858-825-3874. Personal E-mail: mmu@uci.edu.

MUBARAK, KAMAL K., pulmonologist, intensivist; arrived in US, 1989; s. Ali Khan and Azra Mubarak; m. Tabinda Khan Mubarak, Dec. 20, 1995; children: Eman Azra, Izan Ali. MD, Aga Khan U., Karachi, 1988. Cert. in pulmonary medicine and critical care medicine, diplomate Am. Bd. Internal Medicine. Asst. prof. internal medicine Wayne State U., Detroit, 2000—07; dir. Pulmonary Hypertension Clinic, Detroit, 2001—07; dir., Pulmonary Vascular Disease Program U. Fla., Gainesville, 2007—. Fellow: Am. Coll. Chest Physicians; mem.: Am. Thoracic Soc., Internat. Soc. Philos. Enquiry. Office: 1600 SW Archer Rd M452 Gainesville FL 32610 Office Fax: 352-239-0821. Business E-Mail: mubarak@ufl.edu.

MUCCI, GARY LOUIS, lawyer; b. Buffalo, Nov. 12, 1946; s. Guy Charles and Sally Rose (Battaglia) M.; m. Carolyn Belle Taylor, May 4, 1991. BA cum laude, St. John Fisher Coll., 1968; JD, Cath. U., 1972. Bar: N.Y. 1972. Law clk. to Hon. John T. Curtin U.S. Dist. Ct., Buffalo, 1972-74; assoc. atty. Donovan Leisure Newton & Irvine, NYC, 1974-75, Saperston & Day P.C., Buffalo, 1975-80, sr. ptnr., 1980—2001; ptnr. Hiscock Barclay, 2001—07, of counsel, 2007—. Chmn. bd. Buffalo Philharm. Orch., 1985-86; pres. Hospice Buffalo, 1986-87; mem. N.Y. State Coun. on the Arts, 1987-2000; chmn. Citizens Com. on Cultural Aid, Buffalo, 1992-98; trustee St. John Fisher Coll.; chmn. bd. trustees Nardin Acad., 2005—08; sec. Buffalo Olmsted Conservancy, 08-. Recipient Brotherhood award NCCJ, Buffalo, 1983; named Man of Yr. William Paca Soc., 1984. Mem. Erie County Bar Assn., N.Y. State Bar Assn. Home: 27 Tudor Pl Buffalo NY 14222-1615 Office: Hiscock Barclay 3 Fountain Plz Ste 1100 Buffalo NY 14203-1486 Home Phone: 716-885-5175; Office Phone: 716-566-1520. Business E-Mail: gmucci@hblaw.com.

MUCCI, PATRICK JOHN, financial consultant, realtor, commercial loan broker; b. Albany, NY, July 5, 1947; s. Philip and Angelina (Patrella) M.; m. Beverly Ann Scully, June 8, 1968; children: Philip Michael, Angelina Maria. AAS, Hudson Valley Community Coll., Troy, NY, 1967; BS, SUNY, Albany, 1977; MBA, Fairleigh Dickinson U., 1979. Cert. review appraiser, comml. investment mgr., real estate broker, internat. financier; registered mortgage underwriter; lic. ins. broker for life and accident ins. Adminstrv. asst. Nat. Savs. Bank, Albany, 1973-76; asst. v.p. Heritage Savs. Bank, Kingston, N.Y., 1976-78, Home Savs. Bank, Albany, 1978-81, v.p., 1981, Home & City Savs. Bank, Albany, 1981-83, sr. v.p. lending, 1983-90; pres., chmn. bd., founder Greenbush Assocs., Inc., East Greenbush, 1990—2003. Chmn. bd., founder, pres. Patrician Funding, Inc., 1997-2006, East Greenbush; bd. dirs. Vec Tech., Inc., Philangie Corp.; v.p., sr. comml. loan officer Provantage Funding Corp., 2000-02; v.p. govt. guaranteed lending, Key Bank, 2003-. Active Nat. Assn. Govt. Guarenteed Lenders; treas., bd. dirs. Theater Voices, 1990; bd. dirs. Albany League Arts, Discovery Ctr. Capital Region, 1990, N.Y. State Mus. Inst., Capital Affordable Housing Funding Com., Albany County Affordable Housing Corp., Grand St. Cmty. Arts; mem. Rensselaer County Com. Sewer & Water Authority, 1993-94. Staff sgt. USAF, 1969-72. Mem. NY Assn. Bus. Brokers (bd. dirs., treas., sec. 2006—), Internat. Bus. Brokers Assn., NY State Comml. Assn. Realtors (assoc.). Avocations: travel, reading, photography, computers. Home: 296 Luther Rd East Greenbush NY 12061-4312 Office Phone: 518-257-9405. Business E-Mail: patrick_mucci@keybank.com.

MUCCI, RICHARD L., insurance company executive; BS in Math., MS in Math., Boston Coll. Various positions including exec. v.p. and COO Paul Revere Ins. Co.; sr. v.p. disability income bus. Mass. Mutual life Ins. Co.; sr. v.p. Hartford Life group benefits divsn. Hartford Fin. Services Group, Inc., exec. v.p., dir.; exec. v.p., chmn., CEO NY Life Internat., LLC, 2007—. Exec. mgmt. com. NY Life Ins. Co. Office: c/o NY Life Ins Co 51 Madison Ave Rm 1016 New York NY 10010 Office Phone: 212-576-7260. Office Fax: 212-576-4291.*

MUCCIE, MARY ROSE, publishing executive; BA, U. Pa. Editl., prod. positions Phila. Bar Assn., 1986, J.B. Lippencott Co., 1986—93; mng. editor Soc. Indsl. & Applied Math., Phila., 1993—97, pub., 1997—2006; dir. project MUSE Johns Hopkins U. Press, Balt., 2006—. Mem.: No. Am. Serials Interest Group, Spl. Libraries Assn., Soc. Scholarly Publishing. Office: Project MUSE Johns Hopkins Univ Press 2715 N Charles St Baltimore MD 21218 Office Phone: 410-516-6900. Business E-Mail: mrm@press.jhu.edu.

MUCCIOLI, GIULIO G., science educator; b. Bruxelles, Belgium, Jan. 9, 1978; PharmD, U. Catholique Louvain, Bruxelles, Belgium, 2001; PharmM, U. Catholique Louvain, 2003, PhD in Pharm. Scis., 2005. Sr. fellow U. Wash., Seattle, 2005—07; asst. prof. U. Catholique Louvain, 2008—. Office: Univ Catholique Louvain Ave E Mounier 72 Brussels 1200 Belgium Business E-Mail: giulio.muccioli@uclouvain.be.

MUCHLINSKI, MAGDALENA NATALIA, anthropologist, educator; b. Martinez, Calif., Dec. 1, 1978; d. Henryk S. and Barbara Elizabeth Muchlinski; m. Gary Allen Dickerson, Dec. 20, 2008. BA, U. Calif., Santa Cruz, 1999; MA, U. Tex., Austin, 2002, PhD, 2008. Postdoc. fellow U. Tex., Austin, 2008—; lectr. Baylor U., Waco, Tex., 2009—. Grant, PEO, 2008, Hd Hutchinson fellowship, U. Tex. Austin, 2007—08. Mem.: Am. Soc. Primatology (ednl. com. 2005—), Soc. Vertebrate Paleontology, Am. Assn. Phys. Anthropology (Mildred Trotter award 2005). Office: Univ Tex Austin 1130 Eps C3200 Austin TX 78712 Business E-Mail: magdalena@mail.utexas.edu.

MUCHMORE, ROBERT BOYER, engineering executive, consultant; b. Augusta, Kans., July 8, 1917; s. Ray Boyer and Charlotte (McPherron) M.; m. Betty Vaughan, Jan. 29, 1944; children: Andrew Vaughan, Douglas Boyer. BS, U. Calif., Berkeley, 1939; degree in Elec. Engring., Stanford U., 1942. Project engr. Sperry Gyroscope Co., Garden City, NY, 1942-46; sr. mem. tech. staff Hughes Aircraft, Culver City, Calif., 1946-54; v.p., chief scientist TRW Systems, Redondo Beach, Calif., 1954-73, cons. Sonoma, Calif., 1973—. Lectr. in engring. UCLA, 1954-58. Author: Essentials of Microwaves, 1952. Fellow IEEE; mem. AAAS, Assn. Computing Machinery, Sierra Club. Home: 4311 Grove St Sonoma CA 95476-6046 E-mail: rbm@sonic.net.

MUCHNICK, RICHARD STUART, ophthalmologist, educator; b. Bklyn., June 21, 1942; s. Max and Rae (Kozinsky) Muchnick; m. Felice Dee Greenberg, Oct. 29, 1978; 1 child, Amanda Michelle. BA with honors, Cornell U., 1963, MD, 1967. Diplomate Am. Bd. Ophthalmology, Nat. Bd. Med. Examiners. Intern in medicine N.Y. Hosp., NYC, 1967—68, now assoc. attending ophthalmologist, chief Pediatric Ophthalmology Clinic, resident in ophthalmology, 1970—73, practice medicine, specializing in ophthalmology, notably strabismus and ophthalmic plastic surgery, 1974—. Attending surgeon, chief Ocular Motility Clinic Manhattan Eye, Ear and Throat Hosp., NYC; clin. assoc. prof. ophthalmology Cornell U., NYC, 1984—; clin. rschr. strabismus, ophthalmic plastic surgery, 1973—. With USPHS, 1968—70. Recipient Coryell Prize Surgery, Cornell U. Med. Coll., 1967, McLean Medal in Ophthalmology, Weill Med. Coll. of Cornell U., 2006. Fellow: ACS, Am. Acad. Ophthalmology; mem.: AMA, Manhattan Ophthal. Soc., Greater N.Y. Soc. Pediat. Ophthalmology and Strabismus (pres.), N.Y. Acad. Medicine, N.Y. Soc. Clin. Ophthalmology, Internat. Strabismological Assn., Am. Assn. Pediatric Ophthalmology and Strabismus, Am. Soc. Ophthalmic Plastic and Reconstructive Surgery, 7th Regt. Tennis, Lotos, Alpha Epsilon Delta, Alpha Omega Alpha. Office: 69 E 71st St New York NY 10021-4213 Office Phone: 212-744-1726.

MUCI KÜCHLER, KARIM HEINZ, mechanical engineering educator; b. Valencia, Carabobo, Venezuela, May 22, 1964; came to Mexico, 1981; s. Moussa and Luise Gertrud (Küchler) Muci Abraham; m. Alejandra Castañeda González, June 25, 1983; children: Karim Ibrahim, Moses Alejandro, Claudia María. BS, Inst. Tech. y Estudios Superiores Monterrey, Mexico, 1985; MS, Inst. Tech. y Estudios Superiores Monterrey, 1988; PhD, Iowa State U., 1992. Mech. maintenance Altos Hornos de Mexico, Monclova, 1986; teaching asst. Iowa State U., Ames, 1989, rsch. asst., 1989-92; prof. mech. engring. Inst. Tech. y Estudios Superiores Monterrey, 1993—. Mem. ASME (assoc.), Internat. Soc. Boundary Elements, Sigma Xi (assoc.), Tau Beta Pi, Phi Kappa Phi. Achievements include development of higher order boundary elements for three dimensional problems. Office: South Dakota Sch of Mines 501 E Saint Joseph St Rapid City SD 57701 Office Fax: 605-394-2405.

MUCKEL, ROBERT DALE, retired biology professor; b. Bloomington, Nebr., Sept. 10, 1933; s. Arthur Benjamin and Florence Miriam Muckel; m. Jean Marilyn Dainton, Aug. 20, 1958; children: Brett William, Jacqueline Sue Silva. PhD, U. Ersity Nebr., Lincoln, 1978. Cert. tchr. Nebr., 1960. Prof. emeritus biology Doane Coll., Crete, Nebr., 1968—2009. Dir. NEBIONET, Crete. Trustee Grace United Meth. Ch., Crete, 1999—2009. With USN, 1952—56, Calif. & Far East. Recipient award, Doane Coll., 1998—99. Mem.: UNMC (bd. counselors 1998—99). Methodist. Avocations: golf, photography, exercise, hunting, fishing. Home: 460 Eastridge Crete NE 68333 Office: Doane Coll 1014 Boswell Crete NE 68333

MUCKENFUSS, CANTWELL FAULKNER, III, lawyer; b. Montgomery, Ala., Apr. 25, 1945; s. Cantwell F. and Dorothy (Dauphine) M.; m. A. Angela Lancaster, June 25, 1978; children: Alice Paran Lancaster, Cantwell F. IV. BA, Vanderbilt U., 1967; JD, Yale U., 1971. Bar: N.Y. 1973, D.C. 1976. Law clk. to Hon. William E. Miller U.S. Ct. Appeals (6th Cir.), 1971-72; atty., project developer Bedford Stuyvesant D and S Corp., Bklyn., 1972-73; spl. asst. to the dir. FDIC, Washington, 1974-77, counsel to the chmn., 1977-78; sr. dep. comptroller for policy Office of the Comptroller of the Currency, Washington, 1978-81; ptnr. Gibson, Dunn & Crutcher LLP, Washington, 1981—. Mem. editorial adv. bd. Issues in Bank Regulation, Rolling Meadows, Ill., 1977-91, Electronic Banking Law and Commerce Report, 1996—; mem. bd. advisors Rev. Banking and Fin. Svcs., N.Y.C., 1985—; bd. dis. Fair Tax Edn. Fund, Washington, 1987-90. Served with USNG, 1968-70, USAR, 1970-74. Recipient Spl. Achievement award U.S. Dept. Treasury, 1979, Presdl. Rank award U.S. Govt., 1980. Mem. ABA, Fed. Bar Assn. Clubs: Kenwood Country (Bethesda, Md.); Yale (N.Y.C.). Democrat. Episcopalian. Office: Gibson Dunn & Crutcher LLP 1050 Connecticut Ave NW Ste 900 Washington DC 20036-5306

MUCKENHOUPT, BENJAMIN, retired mathematics professor; b. Newton, Mass., Dec. 22, 1933; s. Carl Frederick and Sarah Joanna (Boell) M.; m. Mary Kathryn Heath, Aug. 29, 1964; children: Margaret, Carl Edward. AB, Harvard U., 1954; MS, U. Chgo., 1955, PhD, 1958. Instr. DePaul U., Chgo., 1958-59, asst. prof. math., 1959-60; faculty Rutgers U., New Brunswick, NJ, 1960-91, prof. math., 1970-91. Vis. assoc. prof. Mt. Holyoke Coll., 1963-65; visitor Inst. Advanced Study, Princeton, N.J., 1968-69, 75-76; vis. prof. SUNY-Albany, 1970-71 Contbr. articles to profl. jours. NSF rsch. grantee, 1965-88; Rutgers Rsch. Coun. fellow, 1968-69. Mem. Am. Math. Soc., Math. Assn. Am., Phi Beta Kappa, Sigma Xi. Home: 196 Woodfern Rd Neshanic Station NJ 08853-4054 E-mail: muckenho@post.harvard.edu.

MUDANAI, SIVAKUMAR P., research scientist; m. Anjum Mukadam. PhD, U. Tex., Austin, 2001. Staff rsch. scientist Intel Corp., Hillsboro, Oreg., 2001—. Achievements include development of advanced transistors models. Home: 662 NE Valarie Ct Hillsboro OR 97124

MUDAVANHU, BLESSING, research scientist; b. Harare, Mashonaland, Zimbabwe, May 26, 1971; s. Jackson and Gladys Mudavanhu; m. Mutsa Tongoona, July 22, 1996; children: Mandisa, Thandeka, Baraka. BS in Gen. Math. and Stats., U. Zimbabwe, Harare, 1993, BS in Math., 1995; M in Fin. Engring., U. Calif., Berkeley, 2002; MS, U. Wash., Seattle, 1998, PhD, 2002. Rsch. asst. U. Wash., Seattle, 1996—2001; derivatives quantitative analyst Am. Internat. Group, NYC, 2002—05, v.p., 2002—05; v.p. corp. risk mgmt. Merrill Lynch & Co., NYC, 2005—, dir. corp. risk mgmt., 2007—. Book reviewer: Soc. Indsl. and Applied Math., 2003—; contbr. articles to profl. jours. Fellow U. of Zimbabwe Math. fellow, 1995; scholar Fulbright scholar, U.S. Govt., 1996—98. Mem.: Internat. Assn. for Fin. Engrs., Soc. for Indsl. and Applied Math., Am. Math. Soc., Fulbright Assn. (bd. dirs. Puget Sound chpt. 2000—02). Home Phone: 212-945-1271; Office Phone: 212-449-4464. Personal E-mail: blessingmudavanhu@yahoo.com.

MUDD, DANIEL H., investment company executive, former mortgage company executive; b. 1958; married; 4 children. BA in Am. Hist., U. Va., 1980; MPA in Economics & Internat. Affairs, Harvard U., 1986. V.p. bus. devel. GE Capital, 1991—93, mng. dir. internat. financing, 1993—95; pres., CEO GE European Fleet Services, Brussels, 1995—96; pres. GE Capital Asia-Pacific, 1996-99; pres., CEO GE Capital, Japan, 1999—2000; vice chmn., COO Fannie Mae (Fed. Nat. Mortgage Assn.), Washington, 2000—04, interim CEO, 2004—05, pres., CEO, 2005—08; CEO Fortress Investment Group LLC, NYC, 2009—. Bd. dirs. Fannie Mae (Fed. Nat. Mortgage Assn.), 2000—08, Ryder System, Inc., 2002—07, Fortress Investment Group LLC, 2007—, Oriental & Gen. Fund Ltd., Fannie Mae Found., Local Initiative Support Corp., Nat. Bldg. Museum, Hampton U., St. Patrick Sch. Bd. mem. Sidwell Friends Sch., Hampton U.; bd. managers U. Va. Alumni Assn. Officer USMC. Robert Bosch Found. fellow, 1989. Mem.: Coun. Fgn. Relations. Office: Fortress Investment Group LLC 1345 Ave of the Americas New York NY 10105*

MUDD, JOHN PHILIP, lawyer; b. Washington, Aug. 22, 1932; s. Thomas Paul and Frances Mary (Finotti) M.; m. Barbara Eve Sweeney, Aug. 10, 1957; children: Laura, Ellen, Philip, Clare, David. BSS, Georgetown U., 1954; JD, Georgetown Law Center, 1956. Bar: Md. 1956, D.C. 1963, Fla. 1964, Calif. 1973. Pvt. practice, Upper Marlboro, Md., 1956-66; v.p., sec., gen. counsel Deltona Corp., Miami, Fla., 1966-72; sec., gen. counsel Nat. Community Builders, San Diego, 1972-73; gen. counsel Continental Advisers (adviser to Continental Mortgage Investors), 1973-75, sr. v.p., gen. counsel, 1975-80, Am. Hosp. Mgmt. Corp., Miami, 1980-89; legal coord. Amerifirst Bank, Miami, 1989-92; v.p., legal counsel Cartaret Savs. Bank, Morristown, N.J., 1991-93, cons., 1991-92; gen. counsel Golden Glades Hosp., Miami, 1992-93, Bank of N.Am., Miami, 1994—. Gen. counsel Golden Glades Hosp., Miami, 1992-93; cons. FSLIC, 1988-89, J.E. Robert Cos., Alexandria, Va., 1988-89, Real Estate Recovery, Inc., Boca Raton, Fla., 1991-92, Bank N.Am., Ft. Lauderdale, Fla., 1992; dir. Unitower Mortgage Corp., Miami, Fla.; dir. Unitower Mortgage Corp., Miami; pres. Marquette Realty Corp., Miami. Former mem. Land Devel. Adv. Com. N.Y. State; chmn. student interview com. Georgetown U.; bd. dirs. Lasalle High Sch., Miami; corp. counsel Com. of Dade County, Fla.; trustee Golden Glades Gen. Hosp., Miami, Fla., 1992—, gen. counsel, 1991—, Bank of North Am., Miami, 1992—. Mem. Fla. Bar Assn., Calif. Bar Assn., Md. Bar Assn., D.C. Bar Assn., Fla. State Bar (exec. com. on corp. counsel com.). Democrat. Roman Catholic. Home: 607 Velarde Ave Coral Gables FL 33134-7044 Office: Bank of North Am Golden Glades Med Plz 8701 SW 137th Ave Ste 301 Miami FL 33183-4498

MUDD, MARY MICHAELS, historian; b. Oak Park, Ill., July 24, 1948; m. John Edward Mudd, Sept. 4, 1976 (dec.); 1 child, Andrew. BA in English cum laude, U. Houston, 1969, BS in Math., 1969; MA in History, Rutgers U., New Brunswick, NJ, 1974, PhD in History, 1984. Ind. scholar Roman and Byzantine History, Wall, NJ, 1984—; med. sec., 1997—; physician credentials coord., interpreter French Meridian Health, Wall, 2004—; cert. provider credentialing specialist, 2008. Freelance lectr. archaeology and Roman history, 1978—95. Author: I, Livia: The Counterfeit Criminal, 2005, Studies in Reign of Constantius II, 1989; contbr. articles to scholarly publs. Recording sec. Freedom Theatre Parents Group, Phila., 1993—95; environ. activist Clean Ocean Action, Highlands, NJ, 1984—. Mem.: Nat. Assn. Med. Staff Svcs., NJ State Assn. Med. Staff Svcs. (treas. ctrl. chpt.), NJ Environ. Fedn. Democrat. Avocations: bicycling, swimming, theater, ballet, cooking, classic rock, reggae. Home and Office: PO Box 1275 Wall NJ 07719 Office Phone: 732-299-8608.

MUDER, ROBERT RICHARD, physician, epidemiologist; b. Pitts., June 11, 1951; s. Richard Edward and Gemma (Lombardi) M.; m. Janet D. Vlha, June 4, 1977 (div. 1993); children: Jane Elizabeth, Michael Richard. BA, Oberlin Coll., Ohio, 1973; MD, U. Pitts. Sch. Medicine, 1977. Diplomate Am. Bd. Internal Medicine; subspecialty of infectious diseases. Intern then resident internal medicine Mercy Hosp., Pitts., 1977—80, chief med. resident, 1980—81, asst. coord. med. edn., 1983-84, coord. med. edn., 1984-86, assoc. program dir., 1986-89, fellow in infectious disease, 1981-83; asst. prof. medicine U. Pitts., 1989-94, assoc. prof., 1994—2001, prof. medicine, divsn. infectious diseases; chief infection control VA Pitts. Healthcare Sys., 1986—2006, chief infectious disease sect., 2007—. Sect. editor Infectious Disease Alert; contbr. articles to profl. jours. Mem. Infectious Diseases Soc. Am., Soc. for Healthcare Epidemiology Am. Office: VA Pitts Healthcare Sys 2A135 Veterans Affairs Med Ctr University Dr C ID Section Pittsburgh PA 15240 Office Phone: 412-360-6179. Office Fax: 412-360-6950. Business E-Mail: robert.muder@va.gov.

MUDGE, GILBERT H., JR., cardiologist; b. Cooperstown, NY; MD, Columbia U. Coll. Physicians & Surgeons, 1970. Cert. Internal Medicine, 1973, Cardiovasc. Disease, 1979. Intern Presbyn. Hosp., NYC, 1970—71, resident in internal medicine, 1971—73; fellow in cardiology Peter Bent Brigham Hosp., 1977; sr. cardiologist Brigham & Women's Hosp., Boston, dir. Brigham Cardiovasc. Cons.; assoc. prof. Harvard Med. Sch., Boston. Sr. med. advisor Partners Internat. Med. Services, Boston. Office: Brigham & Womens Hosp Cardiovasc Divsn 75 Francis St PBB-1 Boston MA 02115 Office Phone: 617-732-7140. Office Fax: 617-278-6931. E-mail: gmudge@partners.org.

MUDICK, STEPHANIE B., diversified financial services company executive, lawyer; m. David Mudick; children: Lily, Dahlia. BA, Smith Coll.; JD, Yeshiva U. Joined Salomon Smith Barney, 1993, gen. counsel investment banking divsn.; dep. gen. counsel Travelers Group; co-gen. counsel Citigroup, Inc., gen. counsel Global Consumer Group, chief adminstrv. officer Global Consumer Group, 2002; now head global retail strategy JP Morgan Chase & Co. Bd. dirs. Tchrs. Network. Office: JP Morgan Chase & Co 270 Park Ave New York NY 10017*

MUDIGONDA, ASHWIN, electrical engineer, researcher; b. Hyderabad, Andhra Pradesh, India, June 30, 1981; s. Veerabhadra Rao and Vijaya Mudigonda. BEng, Madras U., India, 2002; MS, Ohio U., Athens, 2006. Rsch. engr. Orbital Rsch. Inc., Cleve., 2005—. Vol. Save the Turtles, Madras, Tamil Nadu, India, 1998—2002. Mem.: IEEE, Mensa. Achievements include invention of all terrain walking/rolling wheelchair. Avocations: classical guitar, short story writing, poetry writing, photography, cooking.

MUDIPALLI, ANURADHA, biologist, researcher; b. SR Agraharam, Nagari, India, July 28, 1963; d. Soundara Rajan Srinivasa Mudipalli and Prameela Kidambi; m. Srikanth Srinivasa Nadadur, July 13, 1987; 1 child, Saikrishna Srikanth. BSc, Sri Venkateswara U., India, 1983; MSc, Sri Venkateswara U., 1985, PhD, 1990. Rsch. asst. dept. home sci. Sri Venkateswara U., Tirupati, India, 1985—86; rsch. asst., nutritionist Nat. Inst. Nutrition, Hyderabad, India, 1986—87. Rsch. affiliate Roswell Pk. Cancer Inst., Buffalo, 1991—94; rsch. assoc. Roswell Pk. Cancer Inst., Buffalo, 1994—98; postdoc. fellow Ctr. Lung Biology to biologist U.S. EPA, Chapel Hill, NC, 1998—99, biologist Nat. Health Effects Rsch. Lab., 2000—04, biologist Nat. Ctr. Environ. Affect, 2005—. Vol. Sri Sathya Sai Biologist Orgn. USA, Raleigh, NC, 1998—2005. Recipient Sci. Technol. Achievement award, Level 1, USEPA, 2006; Jr. Rsch. fellowship, Indian Coun. Of Med. Rsch., 1987-1988, Sr. Rsch. fellowship, 1988-1990. Mem.: Soc. Toxicology. Avocation: song writing. Office: Ncea Usepa 109 TW Alexander Dr Durham NC 27711 Office Fax: 919-541-2985. E-mail: mudipalli.anu@epa.gov.

MUDRY, MICHAEL, pension and benefit consultant; b. Lucina, Czechoslovakia, Dec. 5, 1926; (parents Am. citizens); s. John Zaleta and Helen (Molchan) M.; m. Kendall Archer, June 17, 1960; children: F. Goodrich Archer, Benjamin Kendall. BA, U. Conn., 1951. Sr. v.p. Hay/Huggins Co. Inc., Phila., 1956-93; self-employed pension and benefit cons. Wayne, Pa., 1994—. Former actuary Ch. Pensions Conf. Contbr. articles to profl. jours. Bd. dirs., actuary Am. Coun. on Gift Annuities, Indpls., 1978—; mem. exec. bd., treas. St. Davids Park Condominium Assn., 2005-. With US Army, 1945—46. Fellow: Conf. Cons. Actuaries, Soc. Actuaries; mem.: Internat. Assn. Cons. Actuaries, Internat. Actuarial Assn., Am. Acad. Actuaries, Tri-State Jazz Soc. (bd. dirs. 2001—, treas. 2001—).

MUECKENHEIM, ROBERT CARL, literature and language professor; b. Detroit, Feb. 2, 1943; s. Ralph Decker and Grace Lucille Mueckenheim; m. Mercedes Deanna Molina. BA, Wayne State U., Detroit, 1966, MA, 1974; JD, Detroit Coll. Law, 1975. Bar: Mich. Bar Assn. 1975. English prof. Wayne County CC, Detroit, 1970—; atty. Mueckenheim & Mueckenheim, P.C., Detroit, 1975—2004. Office: Wayne County CC 1001 W Fort St Detroit MI 48226 Business E-Mail: rmueckel@wcccd.edu.

MUEHLBAUER, ESTHER INDELMAN, biology professor; d. Elchanan and Leah Krechevsky Indelman; m. Eric Mark Muehlbauer, Jan. 30, 1982; children: Stefan Milton, Evan Ilan, Sarah Rachel, Mikael Blake. PhD, NY U., NYC, 1987. Biology instr. Barnard Coll., NYC, 1980—87; prof. biology Queens Coll. CUNY, Flushing, 1998—, sci. writer & editor biology, 2007—. Parents' assn. pres. William Sidney Mt. Sch., Rego Pk., NY, 1995—2004; organizer & grant writer, dept. cultural affairs Ctr. Arts Edn., NYC; founding mem. North Fork Opponents Nuc. Energy, Southold, NY, 1977—85. Grant-in-Aid, Sigma Xi, Sci. Rsch. Soc., 1979—87. Mem.: North Fork Environ. Coun. (cons. 1987—), Nature Conservancy (local chpt. 1980—). Achievements include research in tidal activity in the Turtle, Malaclemys terrapin. Home: 65-16 Cromwell Crescent Rego Park NY 11374 Office: Queens Coll CUNY 65-30 Kissena Blvd Flushing NY 11367 Home Phone: 718-896-9114; Office Phone: 718-997-3400. Business E-Mail: esther.muehlbauer@qc.cuny.edu.

MUEHLBAUER, JAMES HERMAN, manufacturing and distribution executive; b. Evansville, Ind., Nov. 13, 1940; s. Herman Joseph and Anna Louise (Overfield) M.; m. Mary Kay Koch, June 26, 1965; children: Stacey, Brad, Glen, Beth, Katy. BSME, Purdue U., West Lafayette, Ind., 1963, MS in Indsl. Adminstrn., 1964. Registered profl. engr., Ind., 1970. Engr. George Koch Sons, Inc., Evansville, 1966-67, chief estimator, 1968-72, chief engr., 1973-74, v.p., 1975-81, dir., 1978—98, exec. v.p., 1982-98; pres. George Koch Sons LLC, Evansville, 1999—2003, chmn., 2003—04; exec. v.p., bd. dirs. Koch Enterprises, Inc., 1999—; pres. Koch Air LLC, 2003—. V.p., bd. dirs. Brake Supply Co., Evansville, Gibbs Die Casting Corp., Henderson, Ky., Uniseal, Inc., Evansville, George Koch Sons LLC, Evansville, Southwestern Comm., Inc., Evansville, 2006-, Comfort Fin. Svcs. LLC, Evansville; bd. dirs. Fifth Third Bank Indiana, George Koch Sons Ltd., Lichfield, Eng., Anchor Industries Inc., Evansville, George Koch Sons de Mex., Monterrey, Koch Air LLC, Evansville. Co-author: Tool & Manufacturing Engineering Handbook, 1976; patentee in paint finishing equipment. Bd. dirs., past pres. Evansville Indsl. Found., 1980—; bd. dirs., past pres., past campaign chmn. United Way S.W. Ind., Evansville, 1983—; bd. dirs., past vice-chmn. Univ. So. Ind. Found., Evansville, 1988-2001; bd. dirs. Deaconess Hosp., Evansville, 1986-2007, treas., 1991-96, vice-chmn., 1999-2003, chmn., 2003-07; bd. dirs. Cath. Found. Southwestern Ind., 1998-2004; dir. bd. advisors U. So. Ind. Sch. Bus., 1997—, chmn., 2001-02; bd. dirs. Ind. Assn. United Ways, 2000-06, Alliance Indpls., 1993-2004, pres. 1999; mem. Brute Soc., Cath. Diocese Evansville, 1997; mem. fin. coun., 2008-, Equestrian Order of the Holy Sepulchre of Jerusalem, 1996—. Named Engr. of Yr. S.W. chpt. Ind. Soc. Profl. Engrs., 1983; recipient Tech. Achievement award Tri-State Coun. for Sci. and Engring., Evansville, 1984, Purdue U. Alumni Citizenship award, 1991. Mem. Soc. Mfg. Engrs. (past nat. chmn. finishing and coating tech. divsn.), ASME, NSPE, Evansville Country Club, Evansville Kennel Club (bd. dirs. 1997-2001). Republican. Roman Catholic. Home: 2300 E Gum St Evansville IN 47714-2338 Office: Koch Enterprises 14 S 11th Ave Evansville IN 47744-0001 Home Phone: 812-477-8495; Office Phone: 812-962-5260. Business E-Mail: jmuehlbauer@kochair.com.

MUEHLBAUER, JAMES L., retail executive; b. 1961; BS in Acctg., St. Cloud State U. CPA. Sr. mgr. audit and consulting practice Coopers & Lybrand LLP; v.p., worldwide controller The Pillsbury Co.; CFO Musicland Best Buy Co., Inc., Richfield, Minn., 2002, sr. v.p., CFO US bus., 2006—07, interim CFO, 2007—08, exec. v.p. fin., CFO, 2008—. Office: Best Buy Co, Inc 7601 Penn Ave S Richfield MN 55423*

MUEHLEISEN, RALPH T., architectural engineer, educator; BS, U. Wis., Madison, 1989; PhD, Pa. State U., Univ. Pk., 1996. Cert. profl. engr., Ill., 2007. Asst. prof. U. Colo., Boulder, 1998—2003, Ill. Inst. Tech., Chgo., 2003—. Contbr. articles to profl. jours. Mem.: Soc. Bldg. Sci. Educators, Am. Soc. Testing and Materials, Audio Engring. Soc., ASCE, Inst. Elec. and Electronic Engrs., Inst. Noise Control Engring., Acoustical Soc. America. Achievements include research in acoustic radiosity; acoustics of porous media; uncertainty in acoustic measurements. Office: Ill Inst Tech CAEE 3201 S Dearborn St Rm 228 Chicago IL 60616

MUELLER, ADA ROSE, elementary school educator; b. Grove City, Pa., Dec. 3, 1926; d. David Stanton and Mary Louella (Giebner) Peden; m. Bertram Arthur Mueller, Aug. 29, 1947; children: Janet Rose, Frederick Arthur, Margaret Eileen, Carl Edwin, Mary Annette, James David, Richard Keith, Robert Kevin, John Mark. BA in Music cum laude with high honors, Grove City Coll., Pa., 1976; postgrad., Slippery Rock U., Pa. Kindergarten tchr. Karns City Pub. Schs., Pa., 1979—86, tchr. 2d grade, 1986—87, kindergarten tchr., 1987—91. Piano, voice, organ tchr., 1946-2005. Dir. choir Tower Presbyn. Ch. (formerly First Presbyn. Ch.), Grove City, Pa., 1946-48, English Luth. Ch., Zelienople, Pa., 1956-58, Westminster United Presbyn. Ch., Evans City, Pa., 1960-62, Presbyn. Ch., Parker, Pa., 1970-72; dir. music Vacation Bible Sch., Martinsburg Presbyn. Ch., Bruin, Pa., 1964-74; organist, dir. choir Martinsburg Presbyn. Ch., Bruin, Pa., 1976-88. Recipient Quill and Scroll Lit. award, 1943, Arion Music award, Grove City H.S., 1944. Mem.: Evans City Music Club (past pres.), North Butler County Music Club (past pres.), PTA-PTO (past treas.). Personal E-mail: armueller2@zoominternet.net.

MUELLER, BERNDT, physics professor; b. Markneukirchen, Germany, Feb. 8, 1950; came to U.S., 1990; Dr.Phil.Nat., U. Frankfurt, Fed. Republic Germany, 1973. Prof. physics U. Frankfurt, 1976-89; prof. physics Duke U., Durham, N.C., 1990—. Author: Structured Vacuum, 1985, Quark-Gluon Plasma, 1985, Neural Networks, 1990; contbr. articles to profl. jours. Recipient Roentgen prize U. Giessen, 1975. Fellow AAAS, Am. Phys. Soc. Office Phone: 919-660-2570.

MUELLER, BETTY JEANNE, social work educator; b. Wichita, Kans., July 7, 1925; d. Bert C. and Clara A. (Pelton) Judkins; children—Michael J., Madelynn J. MSSW, U. Wis., Madison, 1964, PhD, 1969. Asst. prof. U. Wis., Madison, 1969-72; vis. asso. prof. Bryn Mawr (Pa.) Coll., 1971-72; asso. prof., dir. social work Cornell U., Ithaca, NY, 1972-78, prof. human svcs. studies, 1979-96, prof. policy and mgmt., 1996-98, prof. emeritus, 1998—, 1999—. Nat. cons. Head Start, Follow Through, Appalachian Regional Commn., N.Y. State Office Planning Svcs., N.Y. State Dept. Social Svcs., N.Y. State Divsn. Mental Hygiene, Nat. Congress PTA, ILO; mem. internat. adv. com. Family Resources Tng. Ctr., Singapore, 1999—. Author: (with H. Morgan) Social Services in Early Education, 1974, (with R. Reinoehl) Computers in Human Service Education, 1989, Determinants of Human Behavior, 1995; contbr. articles to profl. jours. Recipient Fulbright Rsch. award, 1990; grantee, HEW, 1974—76, 1979—80, State of N.Y., 1975—95, Israeli Jewish Agy., 1985—87. Mem. Leadership Am., Chi Omega. Democrat. Unitarian Universalist. Home: 412 Highland Rd Ithaca NY 14850-2216 Office: Cornell U Policy and Mgmt 108 MVR Hall Ithaca NY 14853 Office Phone: 607-342-4494. Personal E-mail: bjm5@cornell.edu.

MUELLER, CHARLES FREDERICK, radiologist, educator; b. Dayton, Ohio, May 26, 1936; s. Susan Elizabeth (Wine) W.; m. Kathe Louise Lutterbei, May 28, 1966; children: Charles Jeffrey, Theodore Martin, Kathryn Suzanne. BA in English, U. Cin., 1958, MD, 1962. Diplomate Am. Bd. Radiology, Am. Bd. Nuclear Medicine. Asst. prof. radiology U. N.Mex., Albuquerque, 1968-72, assoc. prof. radiology, 1972-74, Ohio State U., Columbus, 1974-79, acting chmn. dept. radiology, 1975, prof. radiology, 1979—2002, prof. radiology, dir. post grad. program radiology, 1980-2000, acting chmn. dept. radiology, 1990—93, prof. emeritus, 2002—. Bd. dirs. Univ. Radiologists, Inc., Columbus, v.p., 1980—86; pres., founder Ambulatory Imaging, Inc., Columbus, 1985—2002. Author: Emergency Radiology, 1982; contbr. numerous articles to profl. jours.; editl. bd. Emergency radiology, 1995-2002; editor Internat. Trauma, Am. Jour. Roentgenology, 1997-2004. Com. chmn. Boy Scouts Am., Columbus, 1980—84; vol. Columbus Free Clinic, 2003—, Franklin Park Conservatory, 2003—. Capt. USAF, 1966—68. Research grantee Ohio State U. 1975, Gen. Electric Co., 1986-88; Gold medalist ASER, 2001. Fellow Am. Coll. Radiologists; mem. AMA, Assn. Univ. Radiologists, Am. Roentgen Ray Soc., Am. Soc. Emergency Radiology (founder 1988, pres. 1993-94, Gold medal 2001), Radiol. Soc. N.Am., N.Mex. Soc. Radiologists (pres. 1973-74), Ohio State Radiol. Soc. (pres. 1986-87). Republican. Presbyterian. Avocations: fly fishing, hiking, model railroading. Office: Ohio State Univ Hosps Dept Radiology 410 W 10th Ave Columbus OH 43210-1240 E-mail: cmueller@columbus.rr.com.

MUELLER, CHRISTA, radiologist; b. Sonthofen, Germany, June 5, 1962; d. Joachim Friedrich and Waltraud Mueller. MD, Ludwig-Maximilians U., Munich, Germany, 1994; PhD, Ludwig-Maximilians U., 1995. Physician Technic U., Munich, 1992—93, Ludwig-Maximilians U., Munich, 1994—96, Katharinen Hosp., Stuttgart, Germany, 1996—98; physician, rschr. Georg-August U., Goettingen, Germany, 1998—2002, sr. radiologist, rschr., 2002—04; radiologist Paracelsus U., Salzburg, Austria, 2004—. Contbr. articles to profl. jours. Mem.: German Roentgen Soc. Office: Paracelsus Univ Hinterreit 478 A 5084 Grossgmain Austria Home Phone: 0043-6247-7369; Office Phone: 0043-662-4482-57769. Personal E-mail: christamueller@yahoo.de. Business E-Mail: ch.mueller@salk.at.

MUELLER, EDWARD A., telecommunications industry executive; b. St. Louis, Mo. BCE, U. Mo.; MBA, Wash. U. Pres., CEO Southwestern Bell Telephone, Pacific Bell, 1997—99; pres. SBC Internat. Ops., 1999—2000; pres., CEO SBC Ameritech, San Antonio, 2000—02; CEO Williams-Sonoma, Inc., 2003—06; chmn. VeriSign, Inc., 2007—; chmn., CEO Qwest Communications Internat. Inc., Denver, 2007—. Chmn. Nat. Security Telecommunications Advisory Com., 2008—; bd. dirs. VeriSign, Inc., 2005—, Clorox Co., McKesson Corp., 2008—. Office: Qwest Communications International Inc 1801 California St Denver CO 80202

MUELLER, EDWARD ALBERT, retired transportation engineer; b. Madison, Wis., May 12, 1923; s. Edward F. and Lulu (Wittl) M.; m. Margaret Wetzel, Sept. 12, 1953; children: Lynn, Karen. Student, U. Wis., 1941-43; BCE, Notre Dame U., 1947; cert. in traffic, Yale U., 1953, postgrad., 1952—53, Fla. State U., 1955-62; MCE, Catholic U. Am., 1967. Registered profl. engr., Fla. Project engr. Carl C. Crane, Inc., 1947-50; engr. Ammann & Whitney, Inc., Milw., 1950-52; rsch. asst. Yale U., 1953-55; asst. dir., dir. traffic and planning div. Fla. State Rd. Dept., Tallahassee, 1955-63; engr. traffic and ops. Transp. Rsch. Bd., Washington, 1963-70; sec. Fla. Dept. Transp., Tallahassee, 1970-72; exec. dir. Jacksonville (Fla.) Transp. Authority, 1972-80; mgr. transp. div. Reynolds, Smith & Hills, 1980-83; v.p. Morales and Shumer Engrs., Inc., 1983-95. Occasional lectr. U. Fla., 1971-76, U. N.Fla., 1974-76 Author: Steamboating on the St. Johns, 1979, Ocklawaha River Steamboats, 1983, St. Johns River Steamboats, 1986, Perilous Journeys, 1990, Upper Mississippi River Rasting Steamboats, 1995, Steamships of the Two Henrys, 1996, Images of St. Johns and Ocklawaha River Steamboats, 1999, Queen of Sea Routes, 2000, The Savannah Line, 2001, First Coast Steamboat Days, 2005, (DVD) St. Johns Steamboat Days, 2006, (DVD) Suwannee River Steamboats, 2007, (DVD) Ocklawaha River Steamboats, 2008, (DVD) The Suwannee River in Sang, (DVD) Henry Bradley Plant's Transportation Empire; contbr. engring. articles to profl. jours. Mem. Fla. Com. of 100, 1970-72; bd. dirs. Luth. Social Svcs., Jacksonville, 1982-94, v.p., 1981-91; regional v.p. Fla.-Ga. dist. Luth. Laymen's League, 1982-92; curator Jacksonville Maritime Mus., 1990-99, mem. exec. com., 1989-95, pres., 1993-95, exec. dir., 1995-99. Recipient Disting. Svc. award Coll. Engring., U. Fla., 1975, Samuel Ward Stanton award for life achievement Steamship Hist. Soc. Am., 2001; named one of top 10 pub. works ofcls. in U.S., 1978. Mem. Southeastern Assn. State Hwy. Ofcls. (pres., v.p. 1971-72), Engrs. in Govt. (chmn., vice-chmn. sec.), Fla. Engring. Soc. (pres. Northeast chpt. 1982-83, Engr. of Yr. Tallahassee chpt. 1972, Jacksonville chpt. 1974, award for outstanding tech. achievement 1976, outstanding svc. to engring. profession 1989, James Shivler award 1993), Inst. Transp. Engrs. (pres. 1977, disting. svc. award Fla. sect. 1976), Fla. Transit Assn. (pres. 1974-75), Fla. Engring. Found. (sec. 1986-95). Lutheran. Home: 4734 Empire Ave Jacksonville FL 32207-2136 Home Phone: 904-398-9687.

MUELLER, GARY ALFRED, software engineer; b. Denver, Oct. 6, 1950; s. Alfred Henry and Verna Mae (Ashmore) M. BS in Mineral Engring. Physics, Colo. Sch. Mines, 1972, BS in Mineral Engring. Math., 1973; BSEE and Computer Sci. with honors, U. Colo., Denver, 1975; MSEE, U. Colo., Boulder, 1995. Registered profl. engr., Colo. Computer programmer, mathematician U.S. Geol. Survey, Denver, 1977-81; mem. tech. staff AT&T Bell Labs., Denver, 1982-84; adv. software engr. Storage Tech. Corp., Louisville, Colo., 1985—2001, cons., 2002—07; staff software engr. Sun Microsystems, 2007—. Adj. prof. U. Phoenix, 2002—. Mem.: Assn. for Computing Machinery, IEEE (sr.), Tau Beta Pi, Kappa Mu Epsilon, Eta Kappa Nu.

MUELLER, GERHARD GOTTLOB, retired financial accounting standard setter, educator; b. Eineborn, Germany, Dec. 4, 1930; arrived in US, 1952, naturalized, 1957; s. Gottlob Karl and Elisabeth Charlotte (Hossack) M.; m. Coralie George, June 7, 1958; children: Kent, Elisabeth, Jeffrey. AA, Coll. of Sequoias, 1954; BS with honors, U. Calif.-Berkeley, 1956, MBA, 1957, PhD, 1962; D Econs. (hon.), Swedish Sch. Econs. and Bus. Adminstrn., 1994; D Laws (hon.), Kwansei Gakuin U., 2000. CPA (ret.), Wash. Staff acct. FMC Corp., San Jose, Calif., 1957-58; faculty dept. acctg. U. Wash., Seattle, 1960-96, assoc. prof., 1963-67, prof., 1967-96, chmn. dept., 1969-78, dir. grad. profl. acctg. program, 1979-90, sr. assoc. dean, 1990-95, acting dean, 1994, Hughes M. Blake prof. internat. bus. mgmt., 1992-95, Julius A. Roller prof. acctg., 1995-96, mem. fin. acctg. stds. bd., 1996—2001; ret., 2001. Dir. U. Wash. Acctg. Devel. Fund, Overlake Hosp. Med. Ctr., Bellevue, 1984-96, chmn. bd. trustees, 1991-93; cons. internat. tax matters U.S. Treasury Dept., 1963-68; cons. Internat. Acctg. Rsch., 1964-96; vis. prof. Cranfield Sch. Mgmt., Eng., 1973-74, U. Zurich, Switzerland, 1973-74; lectr. San Diego State U., 2006—; lectr. in field. Author: International Accounting, 1967; co-author: Introductory Financial Accounting, 3d edit., 1991, A Brief Introduction to Managerial and Social Uses of Accounting, 1975, International Accounting, 1978, 2nd edit., 1992, Accounting: An International Perspective, 1987, 4th edit., 1997; editor: Readings in International Accounting, 1969, Accounting-A Book of Readings, 2d edit., 1976, A New Introduction to Accounting, 1971, A Bibliography of Internat. Accounting, 3d edit., 1973, Essentials of Multinational Accounting— An Anthology, 1979, Frontiers of International Accounting, 1986, AACSB Curriculum Internationalization Resource Guide, 1988; contbr. chpts. to books, numerous articles to profl. jours. Recipient U. Wash. Disting. Tchg. award, 1983, Disting. Svc. award, U. Wash., 1984; Ford Found. fellow, 1958—59, Price Waterhouse Internat. Acctg. Rsch. fellow, 1962—64. Fellow Acad. Internat. Bus.; mem. AICPA (internat. practice exec. com. 1972-75, exec. coun. 1987-89, Disting. Achievement in Acctg. Edn. award 2000), Am. Acctg. Assn. (pres. 1988-89, acad. v.p. 1970-71, chmn. adv. bd. internat. acctg. sect. 1977-79, Wildman medal 1986, Nat. Outstanding Educator 1981, Disting. Internat. Lectr. in Black Africa 1987, Outstanding Internat. Acctg. Educator 1991), Wash. Soc. CPAs (pres. 1988-89, Outstanding Educator award 1985, Pub. Svc. award 1995), Acctg. Edn. Change Commn. (chmn. 1994-96), Beta Alpha Psi (Acad. Acct. of Yr. 1987), Beta Gamma Sigma (Disting. scholar 1978-79), Alpha Gamma Sigma. Home: 23200 Via Esplendor Villa 35 Cupertino CA 95014-6547 Home Phone: 650-965-4270. Business E-Mail: gmueller@u.washington.edu. *It has always been important to me to associate with people and tangible and intangible things of the highest quality. I make it a practice to set clear goals and then pursue them actively. A broad world view on all aspects of life engenders more success and happiness than special interest perspectives. I welcome change in professional matters, but seek constancy in personal and family affairs. Fate has played a role in my successes. I believe in God, Protestant ethics, and the merits of classical academic scholarship.*

MUELLER, JOHN ERNEST, political science professor, dance critic; b. St. Paul, June 21, 1937; s. Ernst A. and Elsie E. (Schleh) M.; m. Judy A. Reader, Sept. 6, 1960; children: Karl, Karen, Susan AB, U. Chgo., 1960; MA, UCLA, 1963, PhD, 1965. Asst. prof. polit. sci. U. Rochester, NY, 1965-69, assoc. prof., 1969-72, prof., 1972-2000, prof. film studies, 1983-2000, founder, dir. Dance Film Archive, 1973—; prof. polit. sci., Woody Hayes chair nat. security studies Ohio State U., 2000—. Lectr. on dance in U.S., Europe, Australia, 1973—; OP-ED columnist Wall St. Jour., 1984—, L.A. Times, 1988—, N.Y. Times, 1990—; mem. dance panel NEA, 1983-85; columnist Dance Mag., 1974-82; dance critic Rochester Dem. and Chronicle, 1974-82; mem. adv. bd. Dance in Am., PBS, 1975; mem. editl. bd. Ohio State U. Press, 2000—04. Author: War, Presidents and Public Opinion, 1973 (one of Fifty Books That Significantly Shaped Public Opinion Rsch. 1946-95 Am. Assn. Pub. Opinion Rsch. 1995, Mitofsky Award Roper Ctr., 2007), Dance Film Directory, 1979, Astaire Dancing: The Musical Films, 1985 (de la Torre Bueno prize 1983), Retreat From Doomsday: The Obsolescence of Major War, 1989, Policy and Opinion in the Gulf War, 1994, Quiet Cataclysm: Reflections on the Recent Transformation of World Politics, 1995, Capitalism, Democracy, and Ralph's Pretty Good Grocery, 1999, The Remnants of War, 2004 (Lepgold prize 2004), Overblown, 2006; co-author: Trends in Public Opinion: A Compendium of Survey Data, 1989; editor: Approaches to Measurement, 1969, Peace, Prosperity, and Politics, 2000; co-editor Jour. Policy Analysis and Mgmt., 1985-89; mem. editl. bd. Pub. Opinion Quar., 1988-91, Jour. Cold War Studies, 1999—, Internat. Polit. Sociology, 2005—; prodr. 12 dance films, 3 dance DVDs; commentator on 2nd soundtrack of laser disc edit. Swing Time, 1986, DVD edit., 2005; co-adapter (musical) A Foggy Day, 1998; prodr. Shaw Festival Niagara-on-the-Lake, Ont., 1998, 99. Recipient Susan Strange award, Internat. Studies Assn., 2009; grantee NSF, 1967-70, 74-75, NEH, 1972-73, 74-75, 77-78, 79-81; Guggenheim fellow, 1988. Mem. Am. Acad. Arts and Scis., Am. Polit. Sci. Assn., Dance Critics Assn. (bd. dirs. 1983-85). Home: 420 W 5th Ave Columbus OH 43201-3159 Office: Ohio State U Polit Sci Dept Columbus OH 43210-1373 Office Phone: 614-247-6007. Business E-Mail: bbbb@osu.edu.

MUELLER, LISEL, writer, poet; b. Hamburg, Germany, Feb. 8, 1924; BA in Sociology, U. Evansville; postgrad., Ind. U. Vis. faculty Goddard Coll., 1977-80, Warren Wilson Coll., 1983, 85-86; vis. lectr. U. Chgo., 1984; disting. writer-in-residence Wichita State U., 1981. Author: Dependencies, 1965, 2d edit. 1998, Life of a Queen, 1970, The Private Life, 1976, Voices from the Forest, 1977, The Need to Hold Still, 1980, Waving from Shore, 1989, Second Language, 1986, Learning to Play by Ear, 1990, Alive Together: New & Selected Poems, 1996 (Pulitzer prize). Recipient Pulitzer prize for poetry, Nat. Book award for poetry, Carl Sandburg award, Ruth Lilly Poetry prize, 2002, Jacob Glatstein Meml. prize, Eunice Tietjens Meml. prize; NEA fellow. Mem.: Poetry Ctr. Chgo. (founding mem.). Office: La State U Press PO Box 25053 Baton Rouge LA 10894-5053 Home: 5333 N Sheridans Apt 19C Chicago IL 60640

MUELLER, MARK CHRISTOPHER, lawyer; b. Dallas, June 19, 1945; s. Herman August and Hazel Deane (Hatzenbuehler) M.; m. Linda Jane Reed. BA in Econs., So. Meth. U., Dallas, 1967; MBA in Acctg., 1969, JD, 1971. Bar: Tex. 1971, US Dist. Ct. (no. dist.) Tex. 1974, US Tax Ct. 1974; CPA, Tex. Acct. Arthur Young & Co., Dallas, 1967-68, A.E. Krutilek, Dallas, 1968-71; pvt. practice law Dallas, 1971—; assoc. L. Vance Stanton, Dallas, 1971-72. Instr. legal writing and rsch. So. Meth. U., Dallas, 1970-71, instr. legal acctg., 1975; unauthorized practice of law com. Supreme Ct. Tex. Leading articles editor Southwestern Law Jour., 1970-71. Mem. NRA (benefactor mem.), Tex. Bar Assn., Tex. State Rifle Assn. (life), Dallas Arms Coll. (life), Tex. Soc. CPA's, Dallas Bar Assn., SAR, Sons Republic Tex., Sons of Union Vets. of Civil War, Sons Confederate Vets., Mil. Order Stars and Bars, Dallas Arms Coll., Order of Coif, Dallas Hist. Soc., Dallas County Pioneer Assn., Rock Creek Barbeque Club, Masons (Hillcrest Lodge #1318, Tannehill Lodge #52), Shriners, York Rite, Grotto, Scottish Rite (32 degree knight comdr. Ct. of Honor), Beta Alpha Psi, Phi Delta Phi, Sigma Chi (life). Home: 7310 Brennans Dr Dallas TX 75214-2804 Office: 6820 Walling Dallas TX 75231 Office Phone: 214-221-6888.

MUELLER, NANCY SCHNEIDER, retired biology professor; b. Wooster, Ohio, Mar. 8, 1933; d. Gilbert Daniel and Winifred (Porter) Schneider; m. Helmut Charles Mueller, Jan. 27, 1959; 1 child, Karl Gilbert. AB in Biology, Coll. of Wooster, Ohio, 1955; MS in Zoology, U. Wis., Madison, 1957, PhD in Zoology, 1962. Instr. zoology U. Wis., Madison, 1966; asst. prof. poultry sci. and zoology N.C. State U., Raleigh, 1968-71; vis. prof. biology N.C. Ctrl. U., Durham, 1971-73, assoc. prof., 1973-79, prof., 1979-93; ret., 1993. Vis. scientist U. Vienna, Austria, 1975. Contbr. articles, abstracts to profl. publs. Mem. Soc. for Integrative and Comparative Biology, Wis. Acad. Sci., Arts and Letters, N.C. Acad. Sci., Sigma Xi. Avocations: bird migration, conservation and environmental issues. Home: 409 Moonridge Rd Chapel Hill NC 27516-5576

MUELLER, PAUL HENRY, retired bank executive; b. NYC, June 24, 1917; s. Paul Herbert and Helen (Cantwell) M.; m. Jean Bonnel Vreeland, Sept. 10, 1949; 1 child, Donald Vreeland. BS, NYU, 1940; AB, Princeton U., 1941; LittD (hon.), Heriot-Watt U., Edinburgh, Scotland, 1981; LHD (hon.), Bloomfield Coll., 1991. From page to sr. v.p. Citibank N.A., 1934—65, sr. v.p., 1965—74, chmn. credit policy com., 1974—82; chmn. Saab-Scania Am. Inc., 1982—90; ret., 1990. Joined U.S. Fgn. Svc., served in Panama, Cairo, Washington, 1941-43; asst. adminstrv. sec. UN Montary and Fin. Conf., Bretton Woods, N.H., 1944; divisional asst. Dept. State, 1946; sec. West Indian Conf., 2d session, St. Thomas, V.I., 1946; vis. lectr. U. Va., 1980-2001; founding chmn., sr. fellow Ctr. Internat. Banking Studies, 1977-91. Author (contbg.): Offshore Lending by U.S. Commercial Banks, 1975, 2d edit., 1981, Bank Credit, 1981, Classics in Commercial Bank Lending, 1981, Vol. II, 1985, Loan Portfolio Management, 1988, Credit Culture, 1994, Credit Risk Management, 1995; author: (with Leif H. Olsen) Credit and the Business Cycle, 1979; author: Learning from Lending, 1979, Credit Doctrine for Lending Officers, 1976, 1981, 2d edit., 1997, Credit Endpapers, 1982, Perspective on Credit Risk, 1988, In a Nutshell, 2002; contbr. articles to profl. jours. Trustee Bloomfield Coll., N.J., 1983-91, vice chmn., 1987-88, chmn., 1988-91, trustee emeritus; treas. Marcus Wallenberg Found. (U.S.), 1984—. Served from 2d lt. to capt. USMCR, 1944-59. Decorated Order Polar Star, Sweden; recipient Alumni award Grad. Sch. Credit and Fin. Mgmt., Dartmouth Coll., 1958, Disting. Svc.

award Robert Morris Assocs., 1981. Mem. Bankers Assn. Fgn. Trade (hon., v.p. 1976), Pilgrims, SAR, Swedish-Am. C. of C. USA (chmn. 1989-90, hon. dir.), Royal Econ. Soc. (U.K.), Univ. Club (N.Y.C.), Beta Gamma Sigma. Republican. Presbyterian. Home: 75 Rotary Dr Summit NJ 07901-3131

MUELLER, PEGGY JEAN, dance educator, choreographer, rancher; b. Austin, Tex., June 14, 1952; d. Rudolph George Jr. and Margaret Jean (Locke) M.; m. John Yerby Tarlton, June 24, 1972 (div. June 1983). BS in Home Econs., Child Devel., U. Tex., Austin, 1974. Dance tchr. Shirley McPhail Sch. Dance, Austin, 1972-75, Jean Tarlton Sch. Dance, Alpine, Tex., 1975-77, College Station, Tex., 1977-80, Sul Ross State U., Alpine, 1975-77, Tex. A&M U., College Station, 1977-80, A&M Consol. Community Edn., Coll. Station, 1977-78, Jean Mueller Sch. Dance, Austin, 1980—, U. Tex., Austin, 1980—. Dancer, contest judge Gt. Tex. Dance-Off, Austin, 1985—86; mem. equestrian com. Austin Travis County Livestock Show and Rodeo, 1980—92, chmn. trail ride, 1986—, Star Tex. Fair and PRCA Rodeo, 2000—; trial boss, pres. Austin Founders Trail Ride, 1986—; trail boss Bandera Longhorn Cattle Dr. and Trail Ride, 1990, 91; choreographer, head cheerleader Austin Texans Pro Football Team, 1981; dance tchr. Austin Ballroom Dancers, 1988, the Austin Club, 1997, 98; dancer, agt. George Strait/Bud Light Comml. Auditions, 1990; head contest judge Am.'s Ultimate Dance Contest, Austin, 1994; contest judge Two-Stepping Across Am., Austin, 1994; hon. trial boss Dream Catcher Ranch Trail Ride, Franklin, Tex., 1995, 96, Grapevine/Housgon Country Donkey, Mule and Horse Trail Ride, 1997, 2000. Dancer Oklahoma, Austin, 1969, Kiss Me Kate, Austin, 1970; choreographer, lead role Cabaret, Alpine, 1976, (mini-series) True Women, 1997. Active Women's Symphony League Austin, 1972—, Settlement Club, Austin, 1987—; recreation chmn. St. Martin's Evang. Luth. Ch., Austin, 1972—; hon. trail boss St. Jude Children's Rsch. Hosp. Trail Ride, Austin and Kyle, Tex., 1991. Recipient Outstanding Trail Rider of Yr. award Wild Horse Trail Ride, Okla., 1984; named Tex. First Lady Trail Boss, Gov. Mark White, Mayor Frank Cooksey, Austin City Coun., 1986, Judge Bill Aleshire, Travis County Commrs., 1989, Outstanding Intramural Sports Team Mgr.-Player, Tex. A&M U., 1978-79. Mem. Tex Assn. Tchrs. of Dancing, Inc., U.S. Twirling and Gymnastics Assn., Univ. Tex. Ex-Students Assn., Tex. Execs. in Home Econs., Am. Vet. Med. Assn. Aux. (v.p. 1978-79, pres. 1979-80), Am. Horse Shows Assn., Internat. Arabian Horse Assn., Austin Women's Tennis Assn. (v.p. 1985-86, pres. 1986-90, spl. events chmn. 1990-92, advisor 1990—, winner 2d ann. Harriet Crosson Outstanding Player & Community Svc. award), Women's Team Tennis of Austin Assn. (pres.-elect 1992-93, pres. 1993-94), Capital Area Tennis Assn. (membership com. 1991, 92), Houston Salt Grass Trail Ride Assn., San Antonio Alamo Trail Ride Assn., Ft. Worth Chisholm Trail Ride Assn., U. Tex. Longhorn Alumni Band, Austin C. of C., Am. Bus. Women's Assn., Austin Alumnae Panhellenic Assn. (1st v.p. 1989-90, rush forum chmn. 1990, pres. 1990-91, parliamentarian 1991-92), Lone Grove Cmty. Club (treas. 199697, v.p. 1997-99, pres. 1999—, exec. trustee 1997-99, exec. dir. 1999-2000), Omicron Nu (v.p. 1973-74), Jr. Austin Woman's Club (historian 1990-91), Austin Country Club (team tennis captain 1994-95, player 1994—, dance tchr. 1993-96), Zeta Tau Alpha (Austin Alumnae Chpt., alumnae photographer, social advisor 1982-87, treas. 1987-89, publicity chmn. 1989, Easter Seals fundraiser, Honor Cup winner 1990, pres. 1991-92, internat. convention official del. 1988, 92, nominating chmn. 1992-93, mem. yearbook com. 1992-94, 2d v.p. 1993-94). Clubs: Cen. Tex. Arabian Horse, Capitol Area Quarter Horse Assn., Jr. Austin Woman's, Austin Country. Republican. Avocations: theater, piano, drums, sports, travel. Home and Office: PO Box 5868 Austin TX 78763-5868 E-mail: aftr@USATrailRides.com.

MUELLER, PETER STERLING, psychiatrist, educator; b. NYC, Dec. 28, 1930; s. Reginald Sterling and Edith Louise (Welleck) M.; m. Ruth Antonia Shipman, Aug. 9, 1958; children: Anne Louise, Peter Sterling, Paul Shipman, Elizabeth Ruth. AB, Princeton U., 1952; MD, U. Rochester, 1956. Am. Cancer Soc. student fellow Francis Delafield Hosp., NYC, summer 1955; intern Bellevue Hosp., Columbia U., NYC, 1956-57; asst. resident in psychiatry Henry Phipps Psychiat. Clinic, Johns Hopkins Hosp., Balt., 1963-66; asst. prof. psychiatry Sch. Medicine, Yale U., New Haven, 1966-72; asso. prof. psychiatry Coll. Medicine and Dentistry of N.J., Rutgers Med. Sch., Piscataway, 1972-76, clin. prof. psychiatry, 1976-82; cons. for Rehab. Unit and Center for Indsl. Human Resources, Community Mental Health Center, 1973—; mem. courtesy staff dept. psychiatry Princeton Med. Center, 1976—. Cons. in psychotherapy Conn. Valley Hosp., Middletown, 1966-72; cons. in psychiatry Carrier Clinic, Belle Mead, N.J., 1973-82, VA Hosp., Lyons, N.J., 1975-78 Contbr. writings in field to profl. publs. U.S. and Brit., papers to profl. confs. on the use patents in U.S. and fgn. countries for direct dopamine agonists in the treatment of tobacco addiction. Served with USPHS, 1957-63. Recipient Exemplary Psychiatrist award Nat. Alliance for the Mentally Ill, 1994. Mem. Am. Psychosomatic Soc., Am. Psychiat. Assn., AAAS, Amyotrophic Lateral Sclerosis Found. (adv. bd.), Sigma Xi. Episcopalian. Achievements include patents for treatment of disorders secondary to organic impairment with sibutramine; method of treatment of Irritable Bowel Syndrome with a fibric acid. Home: 182 Snowden Ln Princeton NJ 08540-3915 Office: 601 Ewing St Ste B-3 Princeton NJ 08540-2757 Office Phone: 609-924-4061. *For some, a hyperactive learning disorder is a curse that hobbles them throughout life; but for others, including myself, this disorder has become a somewhat uncomfortable and bewildering spur for lifelong compulsive puzzle-solving. This bittersweet mandate has produced the original, serendipitous, and occasionally disconcerting ideas which have marked my life.*

MUELLER, ROBERT LOUIS, manufacturing executive; b. Denver, Aug. 25, 1927; s. George Winchester and Ruth Mabel (Cole) M.; m. Sue McCoy, July 3, 1949; children: Robert, Richard, Edward, Mark; m. Susan Galbraith, June 23, 1985. BSMechE, Yale U., 1948. Chief computer Western Geophys. Co., Mont., Wyo., Colo., Tex., 1949-50; dist. mgr. Armco Steel Corp., Colo., Ohio, N.Y., 1950-63, L.B. Foster Co., NYC, 1963-66; v.p. Wheeling Pitts. Steel Co., W.Va. and Pa., 1966-75; chmn., pres., chief exec. officer Connors Steel Co., Ala., 1975-82; pres., chief exec. officer Judson Steel Co., Calif., 1982-87; pres., COO Proler Internat., Houston, 1987-94, also bd. dirs., 1987-94, cons., 1994—; dir. Employee Solutions, Inc., 1995—; pres. Mueller Resources, Inc., Sedona, Ariz., 1993—. Co-author: Handbook of Drainage and Construction Products, 1954. With USN, 1945-46. Mem. ASCE, Assn. Iron and Steel Engrs., Duquesne Club (Pitts.), Houston City Club, Sedona Racquet Club, The Sedona 30.

MUELLER, ROBERT SWAN, III, FBI director; b. NYC, Aug. 7, 1944; s. Robert Swan Jr. and Alice (Truesdale) Mueller; m. Ann Standish, Sept. 3, 1966; children: Cynthia, Melissa. BA, Princeton U., 1966; MA, NYU, 1967; JD, U. Va., 1973. Bar: Mass., US Dist. Ct. Mass., US Ct. Appeals (1st cir.), Calif., US Dist. Ct. (no. dist.) Calif., US Ct Appeals (9th cir.). Assoc. Pillsbury, Madison & Sutro, San Francisco, 1973-76; asst. US atty. (no. dist.) Calif. US Dept. Justice, San Francisco, 1976-80, chief unit spl. prosecutions, 1980-81, chief criminal divsn., 1981-82, chief criminal divsn. Mass. dist. Boston, 1982-85, 1st asst. US atty., 1985, US atty., 1986-87, dep. US atty., 1987-88; ptnr. Hill & Barlow, Boston, 1988-89; asst. to atty. gen. for criminal matters US Dept. Justice, Washington, 1989-90, asst. atty. gen. criminal divsn., 1990-93; lawyer Hale & Dorr, Washington, 1993—95; sr. litigator, homicide sect., DC US Atty's Office US Dept. Justice, Washington, 1995—98, US atty. (no. dist) Calif., 1998—2001, acting dep. atty. gen., 2001, dir. FBI, 2001—. Capt. USMC, 1967-70; Vietnam. Decorated Bronze Star, Purple Heart, Vietnamese Cross of Gallantry. Mem.: Calif. Bar Assn., Mass. Bar Assn. Office: FBI J Edgar Hoover Bldg 935 Pennsylvania Ave NW Washington DC 20535-3404

MUELLER, SHARON LEE (SHERRY MUELLER), educational organization executive; b. Chgo., Aug. 17, 1943; d. LeRoy Elmer Arthur and Lucille Viola (Armborst) M. BA, Am. U., DC, 1965; MA in Law and Diplomacy, Tufts U., Medford, Mass., 1966, PhD, 1977. Group leader Experiment in Internat. Living, 1969; cross-cultural trainer Nat. 4-H Found., 1970-71; cons. U.S. Dept. State, 1972, contract escort officer, 1970-77; cons. Fletcher Sch. Law and Diplomacy, 1976-81; lectr. dept. polit. sci. U. R.I., Kingston, 1975-77; adj. prof. Sch. Internat. Svc. Am. U., Washington, 1981—89; program officer Inst. Internat. Edn., Washington, 1978-82, dir. prof. exch. programs, 1982-96; exec. dir. Nat. Coun. for Internat. Visitors, Washington, 1996—2001, pres., 2001—. Mem. editl. adv. bd. Internat. Educator, 1991-2005; bd. dir. Nat. Coun. for Internat. Visitors, 1983-88; bd. dir., trustee World Learning, 1999-, bd. mem. Pub. Diplomacy Coun., 2005—. Co-Author:(with Mark Overmann) Working World: Careers in International Education, Exchange, and Development, 2008; contbr. chpts. to books; guest editor, contbr. Internat. Educator, 1992. Mem. exec. com. Internat. Student House, Washington, 1992-95; usher Foundry Meth. Ch., Washington, 1990-2004; mem. The Pres.'s Cir. Coun., Am. U., Washington, 1988-98, chair, 1996-98; mem. bd. Friendship Force Internat., 2007—, Bus. Diplomatic Action, 2009-. Recipient Alumni Recognition award Am. U., 1990, award of appreciation Nat. Coun. for Internat. Visitors, 1988, Disting. Alumni award Lake Park High Sch., 1995. Mem. Nat. Press Club (assoc.), Sch. Internat. Svc. Alumni Assn. The Am. U. (founding pres. 1981-83, Outstanding Svc. award, 1996 Alumna of Yr. 2007), Sigma Iota Rho (hon.), Cosmos Club. Home: 1317 N Lynnbrook Dr Arlington VA 22201-4918 Office: NCIV 1420 K St NW Ste 800 Washington DC 20005-2500 Office Phone: 202-842-1414.

MUELLER, THOMAS M., lawyer; b. Mulheim, Germany, Jan. 1, 1961; s. Friedrich W. and Christel E. Mueller; m. Pia Mueller, Sept. 2, 1989. BA magna cum laude in History and Internat. Rels., Lehigh U., Bethlehem, Pa., 1983; JD, U. Mich., Ann Arbor, 1986. Bar: NY 1987. Assoc. Olwine Connelly Chase O'Donnell & Weyhaw, NYC, 1986—90, Shearman & Sterling, NYC, 1990—97; counsel Mayer Brown & Platt, NYC, 1997—99; ptnr. Mayer Brown Rowe & Maw, NYC, 2000—06, Morrison & Foerster LLP, NYC, 2006—. Mem.: N.Y. State Bar Assn. (mem. exec. com. antitrust sect. 2004—06). Office: Morrison & Foerster LLP 1290 Ave of the Americas New York NY 10104 Office Phone: 212-468-8164. Business E-Mail: tmueller@mofo.com.

MUELLER, TIMOTHY I., psychiatrist; married. MD, Stanford U. Sch. Medicine, Palo Alto, CA, 1977. Diplomate Am. Bd. Internal Medicine, 1981, Am. Bd. Psychiatry and Neurology, 1992. Clin. dir. inpatient svcs. So. Ariz. VA Health Care Sys., Tucson, 2003—. Office: SAVAHCS 3601 S 6th Ave Oracle AZ 85623

MUELLER, WERNER HEINRICH, chemical company executive; b. Aldersbach, Germany, Apr. 7, 1939; came to U.S., 1984; s. August and Rosina (Schned) M.; m. Janice Williams, Aug. 14, 1968; children: Carolyn, Alexander. BS, Tech. U. Munich, 1963, MS in Organic Chemistry, 1965, PhD in Organic Chemistry, 1967; postgrad., Temple U., 1967-68. Rsch. specialist Monsanto Co., Pensacola, Fla., 1968-72; group leader spl. chemistry Hoechst AG, Frankfurt, Germany, 1972-80, asst. to mem. bd., 1980-83, rsch. specialist div. electronic products Wiesbaden, Germany, 1983-84, asst. ops. mgr. Knapsack Works, 1984-85; mgr. indsl. chemistry Am. Hoechst Corp., Coventry, R.I., 1985-88; assoc. dir. R&D adv. tech. group Hoechst Celanese, Corpus Christi, Tex., 1988-89, tech. dir. chems. group, 1989-93, dir. tech. devel. group engring., spl. chems. group Charlotte, N.C., 1993-97; pres. CHD Techs. Inc., Charlotte, N.C., 1997—. Mem. indsl. vis. com. dept. chemistry and biochem. U. Tex., Austin, 1990-93. Contbr. articles to profl. jours. Mem. Am. Chem. Soc. Achievements include 80 patents in field of specialty chemicals, polymers, nylon intermediates, pharmaceuticals and agricultural chemicals. Office: CHD Technologies Inc 4725 Wyndfield Ln Charlotte NC 28270-0460 Home Phone: 704-846-9239; Office Phone: 803-329-8096.

MUELLER, WILLARD FRITZ, economics professor; b. Ortonville, Minn., Jan. 23, 1925; s. Fritz and Adele C. (Thrmaehlen) Mueller; m. Shirley I. Liesch, June 26, 1948; children: Keith, Scott, Kay. BS, U. Wis., 1950, MS, 1951; PhD, Vanderbilt U., 1955. Asst. prof. U. Calif., Davis, 1954-57; prof. U. Wis., 1957-61, prof. agrl. and applied econs. dept. econ. Sch. Law Madison, 1969—; chief economist small bus. com. U.S. Ho. of Reps., 1961; chief economist, dir. bur. econs. FTC, 1961-68; exec. dir. Pres.'s Cabinet Com. Price Stability, 1968-69. Expert House and Senate Com., 1960—96; cons. in indsl. orgn. and pub. policy. Author: (book) Pioneers of Industrial Organization: How The Economics of Congeal of Monopoly Took Shape; past bd. editors Rev. Ind. Orgn., Antitrust Law and Econ. Rev., Antitrust Bull., Jour. Reprints for Antitrust Law and Econs. Mem. Econ. Policy Inst., 1987—90. With USN, 1943—46. Recipient Disting. Svc. award, FTC, 1978; named one of Maj. 20th Century Pioneers of Indsl. Org., 2007. Fellow: Am. Agrl. Econs. Assn. (profl. excellence awards in policy contbn. 1980, in comm. 1985, in rsch. discovery 1988); mem.: Argus Econ. Svcs. (pres. 1985—), Indsl. Orgn. Soc. (pres. 1989—90), Assn. Evolutionary Econs. (pres. 1974—75). Unitarian Universalist. Office: U Wis 427 Lorch St Madison WI 53706-1513 Home: 8625 Wood Violet Way Madison WI 53717 Personal E-mail: wfritzmueller@aol.com.

MUELLER-HEUBACH, EBERHARD, medical educator; b. Berlin, Feb. 24, 1942; came to U.S., 1968; s. Heinrich Gustav and Elisabeth (Heubach) M.; m. Cornelia Rosemarie Uffmann, Sept. 6, 1941; 1 child, Oliver Maximilian. MD, U. Koeln, 1966. Intern U. Koeln (Germany) Women's Hosp., 1967-68, Middlesex Gen. Hosp., New Brunswick, NJ, 1968-69; rsch. fellow Columbia U., 1969-71; resident Columbia-Presbyn. Med. Ctr., NYC, 1971-74, chief resident, 1974-75; asst. prof. Magee-Women's Hosp. U. Pitts., 1975-81, assoc. prof. Magee-Women's Hosp., 1981-89; prof., chmn. ob-gyn. Sch. Medicine Wake Forest U., Winston-Salem, 1989—2002, prof. ob-gyn., 2002—07, prof. emeritus, 2007—. Mem. editl. bd.: Ob-Gyn, 1999—2002. Mem. Am. Gyn.-Ob. Soc. (asst. sec. 1999-2001, sec. 2002-04, pres.-elect 2004-05, pres. 2005-06), Soc. Gynecol. Investigation, The Perinatal Rsch. Soc., Coun. Univ. Chairs Ob-Gyn. (pres. 1998-2000). Avocations: horses, travel, arts. E-mail: emueller@wfubmc.edu.

MUELLER-WESTERHOFF, ULRICH THEODOR, retired chemistry professor; m. Eda Easton, July 4, 1963. Dr. rer.nat, Tech. U., Darmstadt, 1967; BS, Philipps U., Marburg, Germany, 1961; MS, Maximilians U., Munich, 1965. Postdoc. rschr. U. Calif., Berkeley, 1967—68; staff mem. IBM Rsch. Lab., San Jose, Calif., 1968—82; chemistry prof. U. Conn., Storrs, 1982—2002, emeritus prof., 2002—. Recipient Sr. Scientist award, Alexander Von Humboldt Soc., 1988—89. Mem.: German Chem. Soc., Am. Chem. Soc. Office: Univ Conn 55 N Eagleville Rd Storrs CT 06269-3060

MUENCH, KARL HUGO, clinical geneticist; b. St. Louis, May 3, 1934; MD, Washington U., St. Louis, 1960. Diplomate Am. Bd. Med. Genetics. Intern Barnes Hosp., St. Louis, 1960-61; fellow in biological chemistry Stanford U. Sch. Medicine, 1961-65; staff mem. Jackson Meml. Hosp., Miami, Fla.; prof. medicine U. Miami Sch. Medicine. Mem. AMA, ACP, Am. Coll. Med. Genetics. Office: U Miami Sch Med Div Genetic Med PO Box 16960 Miami FL 33101-6960 Office Phone: 305-243-6653. Business E-Mail: kmuench@med.miami.edu.

MUENCH, ROBERT WILLIAM, bishop; b. Louisville, Dec. 28, 1942; s. William Anthony Muench and Mary Kathryn Allgeier. BA in Philosophy, Notre Dame Sem., New Orleans; MA in Edn., Cath. U. Am., Washington, 1968, grad. in Theol. Sem. Studies, 1968. Ordained priest Archdiocese of New Orleans, 1968, vicar, christian formation, 1977—81, archdiocesan vocations dir., 1981—83, dir., Pope John XXIII House for Vocation Discernment, 1983—90, aux. bishop, 1990—96; various positions through rector St. John Vianney Prep Sch., 1969—76; assoc. pastor to co-pastor St. Matthias Parish, New Orleans, 1976—82; bishop Diocese of Covington, Ky., 1996—2001, Diocese of Baton Rouge, 2001—. Faculty mem. St. John Vianney Prep Sch., 1969—77. Named a Prelate of Honor, 1985. Roman Catholic. Office: Diocese of Baton Rouge PO Box 2028 1800 S Acadian Thruway Baton Rouge LA 70821 Office Phone: 225-387-0561. Office Fax: 225-336-8789.

MUERTH, CHERIE ANNE, retired social worker; b. Atlanta, July 22, 1946; d. Albert Martin and Ruth (Wheeler) M. BS in Edn., U. Tenn., 1968; MSW, Va. Commonwealth U., 1973. Lic. clin. social worker Ga., Diplomate NASW, cert. social worker specialist 2004, Acad. Cert. Social Workers, 1975. Med. social cons. Team Evaluation Ctr., Chattanooga, 1973-78; caseworker Family and Children Svcs., Chattanooga, 1978-83; sch. social worker Walker County Dept. Edn., Lafayette, Ga., 1983—2007; ret. Mem.: Sch. Social Workers Ga., Profl. Assn. Ga. Educators. Democrat. Presbyterian. Home: 617 Debbie Ln Ringgold GA 30736-5560 Home Phone: 706-866-6298. Personal E-mail: cheranne@peoplepc.com, cmuerth@aol.com.

MUES, ROBERT LEIGHTON, lawyer; b. Summit, NJ, Apr. 14, 1954; s. Edward Frederick Jr. and Evelyn (Moulton) M.; m. Elizabeth Ann Beard, Aug. 26, 1978; children: Jeffrey Scott, Robert Colin. BA, Wittenberg U., Springfield, Ohio, 1975; JD, U. Dayton, 1978. Bar: Ohio 1978, U.S. Dist. Ct. (so. dist.) Ohio 1978, U.S. Ct. Appeals (6th cir.) 1995. With firm Meily & Mues Attys., Dayton, Ohio, 1981-91, Holzfaster, Cecil, McKnight & Mues, Dayton, 1991—. Impartial due process hearing officer Ohio Dept. Edn., 1981-96, State of Ohio hearing rev. officer, 1997. Author brochure: Divorce in Ohio, 1994. Bd. dirs. For Love of Children, Inc., Dayton, 1983-91, Montgomery County Children Svcs. Bd., Dayton, 1988-91; state legal rev. officer State of Ohio Dept. Edn., 1997-; treas. Dayton Children's Med. Ctr. Found. Bd., 2004-. Mem. ABA, Assn. Trial Lawyers Am., Ohio State Bar Assn., Ohio Acad. Trial Lawyers, Dayton Bar Assn. (com. on profl. ethics 1982—), Miami Valley Trial Lawyers Assn. Office: Holzfaster Cecil McKnight & Mues 1105 Wilmington Ave Ste 1 Dayton OH 45420-4108 Office Phone: 937-293-2141. Business E-Mail: mues@hcmmlaw.com.

MUESER, JOHN ALAN, elementary school educator; b. NYC, Jan. 29, 1951; s. Alfred Otto and Elaine Mueser; children: James Andrew, Catherine. BA, Columbia U., NYC, 1971, MA, 1975, MEd, 1986. Tchr. elem. sch. St. Hilda's and St. Hugh's Sch., NYC, 1971—80, Riverdale Country Sch., Bronx, 1980—. Counselor day camp Riverdale Country Sch., 1971—88, dir. day camp, 1993—. Vestry Christ Ch. Riverdale. Mem.: Nat. Coun. Tchrs. Math. Home: 107 Manhattan Ave Tuckahoe NY 10707 Office: Riverdale Country School 5250 Fieldston Rd Bronx NY 10471 Business E-Mail: jmueser@riverdale.edu.

MUETH, JOSEPH EDWARD, lawyer; b. St. Louis, Aug. 8, 1935; s. Joseph and Marie Clare (Reher) M.; m. Ellen Agnes O'Heron, Dec. 24, 1973; children: Erin R., Patricia A. B.Chem. Engring., U. Dayton, 1957; LL.B., Georgetown U., 1960, LL.M., 1961. Bar: Calif. 1964. Practice law, LA; ptnr. Wills, Green & Mueth, LA, 1974-83; pvt. practice law Calif., 1983-94; of counsel Sheldon & Mak, Pasadena, Calif., 1994—. Adj. prof. law U. Calif. Hastings Coll. Law, San Francisco, 1972-75; lectr. Claremont Grad. Sch., 1982—. Author: Copyrights Patents and Trademarks, 1974. Chmn. bd. Rio Hondo council Camp Fire Girls Inc., 1967-72. Mem. AAAS, Am., Los Angeles County bar assns., State Bar Calif., N.Y. Acad. Scis., L.A. Athletic Club. Home: PO Box 3369 1217 Seal Way Seal Beach CA 90740-6419 Office: 100 E Corson St Pasadena CA 91103

MUFFLY, TYLER, medical educator; married. MD, Jefferson Med. Coll., Phila., 2004. Asst. prof. U. Mo., Kans. City, 2008—. Office: Univ Mo 2301 Holmes St Kansas City MO 64108

MUFFOLETTO, MARY LU, retired educational association administrator, editor; b. Chgo., May 25, 1932; d. Anthony Joseph and Lucile (Di Giacomo) Muffoletto. PhB in Philosophy, De Paul U., Chgo., 1959; ME, U. Ill., 1967. Tchr. elem. edn. Cmty. Cons., Palatine, Ill., 1959-65; tchr. gifted children Sch. Dist. 15, Palatine, 1965-67, curriculum supr., 1967-75, dir. gifted edn. program, 1972-95, coord. state and fed. programs, 1975-95, asst. prin., 1975-95, retired, 1995; assoc. prof. Nat. Coll. Edn., Evanston, Ill., 1979-95; editor Tchg. Ink, Inc., 1995—. Chair State Bd. of Edn. Adv. Com. on Gifted Edn., Springfield, Ill., 1977-85; pres. No. Ill. Planning Commn. for Gifted, 1978-80. Editor: (tchr. activity books) Teaching Ink, 1995—. Mem. Nat. Coun. for Social Studies, Assn. for Curriculum and Supervision, Coun. for Exceptional Children, U. Ill. Alumni Assn. (pres. 1982-85, Loyalty award), Kiwanis, Phi Delta Kappa (sec. 1985-87). Home: 21302 W Brandon Rd Kildeer IL 60047-8618

MUFSON, MAURICE ALBERT, infectious diseases physician, educator; b. NYC, July 7, 1932; s. Max and Faye M.; m. Diane Cecile Weiss, Apr. 1, 1962; children: Michael Jeffrey, Karen Andrea, Pamela Beth. AB, Bucknell U., 1953; MD, NYU, 1957. Intern Bellevue Hosp., NYC, 1957-58, resident, 1958-59; chief resident Cook County Hosp., Chgo., 1965-66; sr. surgeon USPHS Lab. Infectious Diseases, NIH, 1961-65; from asst. prof. medicine to prof. U. Ill., 1965-76; prof. Marshall U., 1976—2002, prof. emeritus, 2002—, chmn. dept. medicine, 1976—2000, chmn. emeritus, 2000—. Vis. scientist Karolinska Inst., 1984-85. Contbr. articles to profl. jours. Served with U.S. Navy, 1959-61. WHO grantee, 1967; recipient Meet-the-Scholar award Marshall U., 1986, Rschr. of Yr. award Sigma Xi, Marshall U., 1989, Solomon A. Berson Alumni Achievement award in health sci. NYU Sch Medicine, 1997; co-recipient Louis Weinstein award Jour. Clin. Infectious Diseases, 1994; named to Greater Huntington Wall of Fame, 2002. Master ACP (traveling scholar 1987, Laureate award W.Va. chpt.), Infectious Diseases Soc. Am.; mem. AMA, Soc. Exptl. Biology and

Medicine, Ctrl. Soc. Clin. Rsch., So. Soc. Clin. Investigation, W.Va. State Med. Assn., Assn. Profs. Medicine (counselor 1992-95, pres.-elect 1995-96, pres. 1996-97, past pres. 1997-98), Marshall U. Joan C. Edwards Sch. Medicine Alumni Assn. (hon.), Alpha Omega Alpha. Office: Marshall U Sch Medicine 1249 15th St 2nd Fl Huntington WV 25701 Home Phone: 304-522-9357. Personal E-mail: maurymufson@comcast.net. Business E-Mail: mufson@marshall.edu.

MUFSON, ROBERT ALLAN, cell biologist; b. NYC, June 10, 1946; s. Morton and Anne T. (Stein) M.; m. Doris Ettlinger, May 14, 1973 (div. Dec. 30, 1980); m. Dolores V. Espinoza; children: Jeffrey, Laura. BA, CUNY, 1968; PhD, Brown U., 1974. Postdoctoral fellow Nat. Cancer Inst. U. Wis., Madison, 1974-77; staff fellow Inst. Cancer Rsch. Columbia U., NYC, 1977-80; asst. prof. Inst. Environ. Medicine NYU, 1980-83; sr. sci. Genetics Inst. Inc., Cambridge, Mass., 1983-88; sr. sci. dept. immunology Holland Lab./ARC, Rockville, Md., 1988-98; program dir. cancer immunology and hematology br. Nat. Cancer Inst., NIH, Bethesda, Md., 1998—, br. chief Cancer Immunology and Hematology br., 2000—. Adj. assoc. prof. dept. pharmacology George Washington U.; cons. Genetics INst., Cambridge, Mass., 1988-89, Otsuka Pharm., Rockville, 1989; ad hoc study sect. mem. NIH, Bethesda, 1989-95. NIH fellow, 1974; grantee NIH, 1981, 82, 91. Mem. Internat. Soc. for Exptl. Hematology, Am. Assn. Cancer Rsch., Am. Soc. Hematology, Am. Soc. for Biochemistry & Molecular Biology. Office: Nat Cancer Inst Cancer Immunol Hematology 9000 Rockville Pike Bethesda MD 20892-0001 Office Phone: 301-496-7815. Business E-Mail: rm401g@nih.gov.

MUFTI, AFTAB A., civil engineering educator; b. Sukkur, Sind, Pakistan, Apr. 24, 1940; arrived in Can., 1963; s. Abdul Wahid D. and Shah Jahan M.; children: Javed, Alex; m. Zehra Mehdi, Sept. 22, 2000. BCE, NED Engring. U., Karachi, 1962; MCE, McGill U., Montreal, 1965, PhD, 1969. Registered profl. engr., Man., B.C. Asst. prof. McGill U., 1969-72; assoc. prof., head dept. comp. sci. Acadia U., Wolfville, N.S., 1972-76, prof., dir. Sch. Comp. Sci., 1976-80; prof. civil engring. Dalhousie U., Halifax, 1980-2000; pres. Intelligent Sensing for Innovative Structures Can. Network of Ctrs. of Excellence U. Man., Winnipeg, Canada, 2000—, prof. structural engring., 2000—, pres. Internat. Soc. Structural Health Monitoring Intelligent Infrastructure, 2002—. Pres. Advanced Composite Materials in Bridges and Structures Network of Can., 1992-98; judge Can. Cons. Engring. Awards, 1987; earthquake cons. Lepereau Nuclear Power Plant and Confedn. Bridge. Author: Elementary Computer Graphics, 1982, Bridge Engineering, 1994; editor: Advanced Composite Materials in Bridges and Structures, 1972, Finite Element Method in Civil Engineering, 1993, Developments in Short and Medium Span Bridge Engineering, 1994, Bridge Superstructures New Developments, 1996, Advances in Bridge Engineering, 2008; contbr. numerous articles to refereed jours., also conf. papers. Vol. fireman Wolfville Fire Dept., 1976-77. Recipient award for Distinction in Engring., Assn. Profl. Engrs. of N.S., 1996, award of merit Consulting Engrs. Man., 2003, award of excellence Consulting Engrs. Man., 2003, award of recognition Natural Scis. and Engring. Rsch. Coun., 2004, award of appreciation ISIS Can. Rsch. Network, 2004, Mirko-Ros Gold medal outstanding life's work rsch. and edn. Swiss Fed. Labs. Materials, Testing and Rsch., Dubendorf, Switzerland, 2005, Merit award Assn. Profl. Engrs. and Geoscientists Man., 2005, Nat. Sci. and Rsch Found. Synergy award, 2005, Lifetime Achivement award, Internat. Inst. Files Reinforced Polymers Constrn., 2006. Fellow Can. Acad. Engring., Engring. Inst. Can. (Phelps Johnson prize 1969), Can. Soc. Civil Engring. (Whitman Wright award 1990, Pratley award 1993, 2008, A.B. Sanderson award 2006), ASCE (Lt. Govs. award Engring. Excellence in Nova Scotia 1996, IRF award 1997, ACI design award 1998, Nova award 2000). Achievements include patents for Bridge Deck and Steel Free Bridge Deck. Office: ISIS Can Admin Ctr U Man A250-96 Dafoe Rd Winnipeg MB Canada R3T 2N2 Office Phone: 204-474-7476. Office Fax: 204-474-7519. Business E-Mail: muftia@cc.umanitoba.ca.

MUGAMBI, HELEN NABASUTA, literature educator; b. Uganda, Jan. 29, 1941; d. John M. Kyebasuuta and Anne Teresa Nakafu; 1 child, Kendelina Nettie. BA, Makerere U., Uganada; PhD in Comparative Lit., Ind. U., Bloomington, 1989. Sr. rschr. Interdisciplinary Genocide Studies Ctr., Kigali, Rwanda. Edtl. bd. mem. JENDA; adv. bd. mem. STEP UP-Am. Assn. Rwanda Women. Adv. Am. Assn. Rwanda Women; active Ednl. Program African Children. Mem.: EPAC (governing bd. mem.), Assn. African Women Scholars. Business E-Mail: nmugambi@fullerton.edu.

MUGANE, JOHN MURATHA, literature and language professor; m. Judith M. Mmari. PhD, U. Ariz., Tucson, 1996. Asst. prof. Ohio U., Athens, Mass., 1999—2003; prof. Harvard U., Cambridge, Mass., 2003—. Office: Harvard Univ Barker Ctr 244 12 Quincy St Cambridge MA 02138

MUGAVERO, THOMAS COLLIER, lawyer; b. Greenwich, Conn., Nov. 1, 1962; s. Thomas Franklin and Ann Collier Mugavero; m. Patricia Lynn Scott, May 6, 1995. BA, Yale U., New Haven, Conn., 1985; M, JD, Georgetown U., Washington, 1989. Bar: Va. 1989, US Ct. Appeals (4th cir.) 1989, US Ct. Appeals (DC cir.) 1992, US Dist. Ct. (ea. dist.) Va. 1992, US Dist. Ct. DC 1993, US Dist. Ct. (we. dist.) Va. 1993, US Ct. Appeals (DC cir.) 1993, Md. 1995, US Dist. Ct. Md. 1997. Assoc. Tanaka Ritger Middleton, Washington, 1989—92; assoc., then ptnr. Montedonico, Hamilton & Altman, 1992—2002; staff counsel Hartford Ins. Co., Alexandria, Va., 2002—05; of counsel Whiteford, Taylor & Preston, LLP, Washington, 2005—. Mem. Masterchorale of Washington, 1988—. Mem.: ACLU, ABA, Fairfax Bar Assn., Fairfax C. of C., Fed. Bar Assn., Italian-Am. Bar Assn., Fairfax Bar Assn., Amnesty Internat. Liberal. Lutheran. Avocations: music, cooking. Office: Whiteford Taylor & Preston LLP 3190 Fairview Park Dr Ste 200 Falls Church VA 22042 Office Fax: 202-327-6171. Business E-Mail: tmugavero@wtplaw.com.

MUGGERIDGE, DEREK BRIAN, engineering executive, consultant; b. Godalming, Surrey, U.K., Oct. 10, 1943; arrived in Can., 1956; s. Donald William and Vera Elvina (Jackson) M.; m. Hanny Meta Buurman, Dec. 4, 1965; children: Karen Julie, Michael Brent. BS in Aero. Engring., Calif. State Polytech. U., 1965; MASc in Aerospace Engring., U. Toronto, 1966, PhD in Aerospace Engring., 1970. Grad. fellow U. Toronto, 1965—66, NRC, Canada, 1967—70, indsl. postdoctoral fellow, 1971—72, Fleet Mfg. Co., Fort Erie, Ont., 1970-72; spl. lectr. U. Toronto, Ont., Canada, 1971; from asst. prof. to prof. Meml. U. of Nfld., St. John's, 1972-93, univ. rsch. prof., 1990-93; dir. Ocean Engring. Rsch. Ctr., 1982-93; dean Okanagan U. Coll., Kelowna, B.C., Canada, 1993—2003, assoc. v.p. rsch., 1998—2003; pvt. practice Lake County, B.C., Canada, 2003—; prof. emeritus U. BC, 2007—. Pres. Offshore Design Assocs. Ltd., St. John's, Nfld., 1980—; sec., ptnr. Nfld. Ocean Cons., St. John's, 1981-93; ptnr. LNF Joint Venture Ltd., St. John's, 1984-90; vis. prof. Norwegian Inst. Tech., Trondheim, Norway, 1976, NRC, Ottawa, Can., 1976, U. Victoria, B.C., 1988-89. Co-author: Ice Interaction with Offshore Structures, 1988; contbr. articles to profl. jours.; contbr. conf. articles, reports. Mem. Assn. Profl. Engrs. and Geoscientists of Province of B.C. Marine and Naval. Avocations: windsurfing, sailing, rock collecting. Home and Office: 16438 Carr's Landing Rd Lake Country BC Canada V4V 1C3 Office Phone: 250-766-1023. Business E-Mail: dmuggeridge@shaw.ca.

MUGLIA, BOB (ROBERT L. MUGLIA), computer software company executive; BS in Computer Sci., U. Mich., 1981. Devel. mgr. ROLM Co.; with Microsoft Corp., Redmond, Wash., 1988—, v.p. enterprise storage svcs. group, 2001—03, sr. v.p. server and tools bus. Platforms & Svcs. Divsn., 2003—09, pres. server and tools bus., 2009—. Mem. Sr. Leadership Team, Bus. Leadship Team, Microsoft. Office: Microsoft One Microsoft Way Redmond WA 98052-6399*

MUHAMMAD, CLAUDETTE MARIE, religious organization administrator; d. Travis and Ernestine Johnson; 1 child, Anthony L. Pinkins. Student, U. Abidjan, 1978—79; BA, Am. U., 1982; postgrad., UN, Geneva, 1982, U. Geneva, 1982, Johns Hopkins Sch. Advanced Internat. Studies, 1982. Tech. libr. Gen. Dynamics Astronautics, 1960—62; sec. to Congressman Lionel Van Deerlin U.S. Congress, Washington, 1963—68; spl. asst. to commrs. Pres.'s Commn. on Civil Disorders, Washington, 1968—69; dir. cmty. affairs Fed. City Coll., Washington, 1973—75; dir. of mayor's call program Dep. Mayor Econ. Devel., Washington; dir. mktg. Manara Travel Agy., Washington, 1987—88; enrollment mgmt./recruitment counselor U. D.C., Washington, 1988; chief protocol to Hon. Min. Louis Farrakhan Nation of Islam, 1989—2009; commr. commn. discrimination and hate crimes Gov. Ill., 2005—. Author: (web site) claudettesmemories.com; contbr. articles to profl. jours.; author: Memories, 2007. Model Ebony Fashion Model, 1963; pres. Jimmy Carter's Inauguration Com. Protocol; mem. exec. bd. Millions More Movement, Inc., 2005; nat. dep. dir. Million Man March, Washington, 1995, Million Family March, Washington, 2000. Recipient Women in History award, Urban League, 2002, Jerusalem 2000 Unity Day Conf. award, 2000, Jr. Achievement award, 1961—62; finalist 3d runner-up Miss Bronze California, 1958. Office Phone: 773-324-6000.

MUHAMMAD, MIKE, advocate; Grad., Bloomsburg U., 1988. Polit. intern Hon. Max Weiner, 1987; salesman; elem. sch. tchr.; counselor; advt. & mktg. cons.; media analyst; motivational spkr.; spl. events coord.; cmty. & civic advocate. Author. Served with 103rd Inf. Bn. USAR, 1985—93. Republican. Mailing: 7134 Ogontz Ave Philadelphia PA 19138-7502 Office Phone: 215-620-7502.

MUHAMMAD, MUHSIN, II, professional football player; b. Lansing, Mich., May 5, 1973; s. Muhsin & Marian Muhammad; Christa Muhammad; children: Jordan Taylor, Chase Soen, Muhsin III, Kennedy Rain; 2 adopted children Grad, Mich. State U., 1996. Wide receiver Carolina Panthers, 1996—2004, 2008—, Chgo. Bears, 2005—08. Founder, pres., The M2 Found. for Kids, 1999-; spokesperson Men For Change. Named Man of Yr., Carolina Panthers, 1999, First Team All-Pro, NFL, 2004; named to Nat. Football Conf. Pro Bowl Team, 1999, 2004. Muslim. Achievements include leading the NFL in: receptions, 2000, receiving yards, 2004, receiving yards per game, 2004, receiving touchdowns, 2004. Office: Carolina Panthers 800 S Mint St Ste 2 Charlotte NC 28202-1502 also: The M2 Foundation for Kids 6420 A1 Rea Rd Ste 367 Charlotte NC 28277*

MUHAMMAD, NAJEE EMERSON, education educator; s. Emerson Clarence and Frazelia Amy Sherman; m. Robin D. Dearmon, Nov. 18, 2008; m. Benita Y. Kennedy, Apr. 20, 1966 (div. June 20, 1980); children: Sean Emerson Sherman, Julian Kennedy Sherman, Dawn Ean Sherman. EdD, U. Cin., 1999. Assoc. prof. Coll. Edn. Ohio U., Athens, 2002—, interim chair, dept. African Am. studies, 2007—08. Head start dir. Cath. Charities Archdiocese, Chgo., 1984—91. Contbr. articles to profl. jours. Mem.: Ohio Valley Philosophy Edn. Soc. (pres. 2007—08). Avocations: golf, jazz. Office: Ohio Univ Coll Edn 321B McCracken Hall Athens OH 45701-2979 Business E-Mail: muhammad@ohio.edu.

MÜHLANGER, ERICH, ski manufacturing company executive; b. Aug. 26, 1941; arrived in U.S., 1971, naturalized, 1975; s. Alois Mühlnager and Maria (Stückelschweiger) Mühlanger; m. Gilda V. Oliver, July 13, 1973; 1 child, Erich. A in Engring., Murau Berufsschule Spl. Trade, Austria, 1959; student, Inst. Tech. and Engring., Weiler Im Allgau, Germany, 1963—65. Salesman Olin Ski Co. (Olin-Authier), Switzerland, 1965—67, mem. mktg. dept., 1967—67, svc. and mfg., 1969—71, quality control insp. Middletown, Conn., 1971—77, supr., 1977—78, gen. foreman, 1978—83, process control mgr., 1983—88; dir. mfg. Entech Corp., 1988—89; prodn. mgr. metallizing divsn. Risden Corp., Thomaston, Conn., 1989—94, quality process engr., 1994—. Pres. Bus. Consolidating Svcs. Internat., Rocky Hill, Conn., 1989—, quality control technician, 1990—, quality process request divsn., fragrance divsn., 1993—; pres. Bus. Cons. Svcs. Internat., 2004—. Chartered mem. Presdl. Task Force, trustee; preferred mem. U.S. Senatorial Club. Served to cpl. Austrian Air Force, 1959—60. Mem.: Mgmt. Club, Am. Soc. Quality Control, Am. Mgmt. Assn., Screenprinting Assn. Am. Roman Catholic. Home: 13 Clemens Ct Rocky Hill CT 06067-3218 Office: 60 Electric Ave Thomaston CT 06787-1617 also: Bus Consolidating Svcs Internat Rocky Hill CT 06067 Office Phone: 860-416-5849. E-mail: erich.muhlanger@cox.net.

MUHLBACH, ROBERT ARTHUR, lawyer; b. LA, Apr. 13, 1946; s. Richard and Jeanette (Marcus) M.; m. Kerry Eldene Mahoney, July 26, 1986. BSME, U. Calif., Berkeley, 1967; JD, U. Calif., San Francisco, 1976; MME, Calif. State U., 1969; M in Pub. Adminstrn., U. So. Calif., 1978. Bar: Calif. 1976. Pub. defender County of Los Angeles, 1977-79; assoc. Kirtland & Packard LLP, Los Angeles, 1979—85, ptnr., 1986—2001, sr. ptnr., 2001—. Chmn. Santa Monica Airport Commn., Calif., 1984-87, chmn., bd. dirs. Hawthorne Airport Cmty. Assn. Inc. Served to capt. USAF, 1969-73. Mem. AIAA, Internat. Assn. Def. Counsel, Am. Bd. Trial Advs. Office: Kirtland & Packard LLP 2361 Rosecrans Ave 4th Fl El Segundo CA 90245 Office Phone: 310-536-1000. Business E-Mail: ram@kirtlandpackard.com.

MUHLENBRUCK-FLEISCHER, DEBORAH LYNN, music educator; b. Mason City, Iowa, Oct. 28, 1969; d. Robert Floyd and Jeannette Jeraldine Muhlenbruck; m. Eric Matthew Fleischer, May 22, 1999; 1 child, Julia Lynn Fleischer. MusB in Vocal Performance, No. Ariz. U., 1993; MusM in Vocal Performance, U. Nev., 1997. Pvt. voice prof. U. Nev., Las Vegas, 1997—2002, C.C. So. Nev., 1998—2001. Prodr.: (vocal instruction cd) Sing Like the Pros. Recipient Rave Rev. award, Clark County Sch. Dist., 2001—02. Mem.: Music Educators Nat. Conf., Am. Choral Dirs. Assn. (assoc.), Nat. Assn.Tchrs. Singing (life; Las Vegas chpt. v.p. 2000—01, Las Vegas chpt. pres. 2001—03), U. Nev. Alumni Assn. (life). Conservative. Presbyterian. Office: Schofield Mid Sch Choirs 8625 Spencer St Las Vegas NV 89123

MUHLENFELD, ELISABETH SHOWALTER, academic administrator, literature educator, writer; b. Washington, Nov. 12, 1944; d. Merle Roberts and Cornelia Elizabeth (Herring) Showalter; m. Edward F. Muhlenfeld, Sept. 10, 1966 (div. 1975); children: Allison Elisabeth Finch, David Edward; m. Laurin A. Wollan, Jr., June 5, 1982; stepchildren: Ann Louise Wollan Westberg, Laurin A. Wollan III. BA in Philosophy, Goucher Coll., 1966; MA in English, U. Tex., Arlington, 1973; PhD, U. S.C., 1978. With U. SC, Columbia, 1975-78; asst. prof. English Fla. State U., Tallahassee, 1978-82, assoc. prof., 1982-87, prof. English, 1987-96, dean undergrad. studies, 1984—96; pres. Sweet Briar Coll., Va., 1996—. Mem. ABA Commn. on Coll. and Univ. Legal Studies, 1991—94; mem. adv. com. US Com. UN Devel. Fund for Women; bd. dirs. United Way Ctrl. Va., chair, 2003. Author: Mary Boykin Chesnut: A Biography, 1981; editor: William Faulkner's Absolom, Absolom: A Critical Casebook, 1984, The Private Mary Chesnut: The Unpublished Civil War Diaries, 1984, Two Novels By Mary Chestnut, 2002; contbr. chpts. to books and articles to publs. Chair Coun. Ind. Colls. in Va., 2001—02; mem. exec. com. Va. Found. Ind. Colls.; mem. commn. on colls. So. Assn. Colls. and Schs., 2001—06, mem. exec. com., 2003—05, vice chair, 2005—06; bd. dirs. Am. Civil War Ctr. at Tredegar, Coun. Ind. Colls., 2005—, Women's Coll. Coalition, 2004—, chair, 2007—. NEH Dir.'s grantee, 1983-84. Mem. MLA, St. George Tucker Soc. (charter fellow), So. Assn. Women Historians, William Faulkner Soc. (charter mem; sec.-treas. 1991-94), Phi Kappa Phi (exec. bd., pres. 1992-93). Office: Sweet Briar Coll Pres's Office Box C Sweet Briar VA 24595 Home Phone: 434-381-6261; Office Phone: 434-381-6210. Business E-Mail: muhlenfeld@sbc.edu.

MUHLERT, JAN KEENE, art museum director; b. Oak Park, Ill., Oct. 4, 1942; d. William Henry and Isabel Janette (Cole) Keene; m. Christopher Layton Muhlert, Jan. 1, 1966; 1 son, Michael Keene. BA in Art and French, Albion Coll., Mich., 1964; MA in Art History, Oberlin Coll., Ohio, 1967; student, Neuchatel U., Switzerland, Inst. European Studies, Paris, Inst. de Phonetique, Acad. Grande Chaumiere. Asst. curator Allen Meml. Art Mus., Oberlin, 1967-68; asst. curator 20th Century painting and sculpture Nat. Collection Fine Arts, Smithsonian Instn., Washington, 1968-73, assoc. curator, 1974-75; dir. U. Iowa Mus. Art, 1975-79, Amon Carter Mus., Ft. Worth, 1980-95, Palmer Museum of Art, University Park, Pa., 1996—. Author museum brochures, catalogues. Mem. Nat. Mus. Act. Adv. Coun., 1980—83; vis. com. Allen Meml. Art Mus. Oberlin Coll., Ohio, 1992—2003; chair adv. com. North Tex. Inst. Educators on the Visual Arts, U. North Tex., 1992—95. Grantee Nat. Endowment Arts-Donner Found., 1979; recipient Friend of Art Edn. award Tex. Art Edn. Assn., 1994. Mem. Assn. Art Mus. Dirs. (trustee 1981-82, 84-86, 92-93, chmn. govt. and art com. 1982-84, chmn. profl. practices com. 1990-92), Western Assn. Art Mus. (regional rep. 1978-79), Am. Assn. Mus. (commn. for new century 1981-84, gen. co-chair 1993 ann. meeting), Am. Arts Alliance (dir. 1980-86, vice-chmn. 1982-84). Office: Palmer Museum of Art Pa State U Curtin Rd University Park PA 16802-2507 Office Phone: 814-865-7673.

MUHN, JUDY ANN, psychologist, genealogist, trainer; b. Detroit, Dec. 29, 1952; d. Wilbur William and Dolores Eleanor (Sutinen) Nimer; m. Dennis James Muhn, June 6, 1975. BS, Mich. State U., East Lansing, 1975; MEd, Boston U., Mass., 1992; MA in Counseling, U. San Francisco, Calif., 1997. Lic. psychologist Mich. Legis. aide pres sec. to Calif. state senator, 1982—84; dir. pub. rels. Tierra del Oro coun. Girl Scouts U.S., 1984—86, mgr. mem. devel. San Antonio area coun., 1986—90; adj. faculty U. Md. Germany, 1992—94; ind. cons. Capital Enquiry, Sacramento, 1994—96; counselor Yuba City Indian Health Ctr., 1997; intervention counselor Sutter-Yuba Mental Health, 1997—98; counselor, intern White Ho. Cmty. Counseling Ctr., 1998; pvt. practice Wixom, Mich., 1998—; dep. exec. dir. U. Santo Tomas Alumni Assn., 1998—2000; therapist Brighton Hosp., 2000—01, Advanced Counseling Svcs., Brighton, 2001—03; dir. adult devel. and vol. svcs. Girl Scouts Metro Detroit, 2002—08; Area Mngr. Oakland County United Way, Southeastern, Mich., 2008—. Adj. faculty Henry Ford CC, 1998—2001, Oakland CC, 1998—2001; spkr. in field. Columnist: Press-Republican, 1995—98. Bd. dirs., chmn. pub. affairs com. Planned Parenthood Clinton County, NY, 1980—81; bd. dirs. Family Planning Advs., Albany, 1981, Planned Parenthood San Antonio, 1987—89; founder Women's Roundtable, Plattsburgh, 1981; pres. Planned Parenthood Assn. Sacramento Valley, 1982—84; sec. San Antonio Coun. Native Ams., 1986—89; co-founder Womanspirit Rising, 1987—89; mem. Metis Cmty. Ea. Can. Recipient Human Rights award, Sacramento Fair Housing Commn., 1983, Woman of Yr. award-Nonprofit, YWCA, Sacramento, 1984, Diversity Champien award, Birmingham Race Rels. U. Task Force, 2009; named Bd. Mem. of Yr., Planned Parenthood Sacramento Valley, 1982. Mem.: ASTD, Nat. Geneal. Soc., Assn. Prof. Genealogists, Metis Cmty. Ea. Can., Assn. Vol. Adminstrs., Met. Detroit Vol. Adminstrs., Assn. Univ. Women, Amnesty Internat., Greenpeace, San Antonio Women's C. of C. (bd. dirs. 1989), Assn. Girl Scout Exec. Staff. Personal E-mail: jmuhn@aol.com. Business E-Mail: judy.muhn@uwsem.org.

MUHONEN, MICHAEL GORDON, neurological surgeon; b. Boise, Idaho, Dec. 7, 1960; MD, Oral Roberts U. Diplomate Am. Bd. Neurological Surgery. Intern U. Iowa Hosp., Iowa City, 1987-88, resident in neurol. surgery, 1988-93; dir. neurol. surgery Children's Hosp., Orange County, Calif., 1993—; pvt. practice pediat. neurol. surgery Orange, Calif., 1994—. Office: Children Hosp Orange County 455 S Main St Orange CA 92868-3835

MUILENBURG, JOHN POWELL, minister; b. Grand Rapids, Mich., Oct. 26, 1911; s. Teunis William and Sena Muilenburg; m. Virgina Louise Turpin, Apr. 2, 1944; children: Peter, Jonathan, Stephan, Bartholomew. BA, Hope Coll., Holland, Mich., 1933; ThM, Princeton Theology Sem., 1938; MDiv, New Brunswick Theology Sem., New Brunswick, NJ, 1936. Pastor Ref. Ch. in Am., Rocky Hill, NJ, 1938—40, asst. pastor Kingston, NY, 1940—41, missionary to China, 1942—50, missionary to Philippines, 1952—67, exec. staff nat. coun. of ch., 1967—76. Town coun. Town of Penney Farms, Fla., 1995—98, mayor Fla., 1999—2000. Recipient A.J. Muste award, New Brunswick Theology Sem., 1986. Democrat. Reformed Ch. In Am. Avocations: tennis, golf, music, sailing. Home: Pavillion 2A POB 646 Penney Farms FL 32079

MUIR, CHRISTOPHER BRYANT, financial analyst; b. Washington, Apr. 30, 1968; s. John Dapray and Louise Rutherford Muir; m. Elizabeth Charlotte Hathway, July 14, 2001; children: Julia Catherine, Peter Angus, Emily Pierrepont. BS in Bus. Adminstrn., U. Vt., Burlington, 1996. Asst. analyst Prudential Securities, NYC, 1996—97; assoc. analyst PaineWebber, NYC, 1997—2000, UBS Warburg, NYC, 2000—03; fixed income analyst ABN Amro, NYC, 2003—05; sr. industry analyst Std. & Poor's, NYC, 2005—. With USN, 1988—93, RTC/NTC Great Lakes, Ill., FF1089 Charleston, SC, CV67 Norfolk, Va. Conservative. Roman Catholic. Home: 33 W End Ave Summit NJ 07901-1213 Office: Standard & Poor's 55 Water St 44th Fl New York NY 10041

MUIR, J. DAPRAY, lawyer; b. Washington, Nov. 9, 1936; s. Brockett and Helen Cassin (Dapray) M.; m. Louise Rutherfurd Pierrepont, July 16, 1966. AB, Williams Coll., 1958; JD, U. Va., 1964. Bar: Md., Va., D.C. 1964, U.S. Supreme Ct. 1967. Asst. legal advisor for econ. and bus. affairs U.S. Dept. State, 1971-73; pvt. practice Washington, 1973—. Mem. U.S. del. to Joint U.S./USSR Comml. Commn., 1972; chmn. D.C. Securities Adv. Com., 1981-84, mem. 1985-88. Bd. editors Va. Law Rev, 1963-64; contbr. articles to profl. jours. Bd. dirs. Trust Mus. Exhbns.,

1997—2005, Internat. Fedn. Insts. Advanced Study, 1992—97. Lt. (j.g.) USNR, 1958—61. Mem. Am. Arbitration Assn. (panel of comml. arbitrators, 1997—2009), DC Bar (chmn. internat. law div. 1977-78, chmn. environ., energy and natural resources div. 1982-83), Met. Club, Washington, Chevy Chase Club, Md. Office Phone: 202-337-1724. Business E-Mail: jdmuir@muirlaw.net.

MUIR, MALCOLM, federal judge; b. Englewood, NJ, Oct. 20, 1914; s. John Merton and Sarah Elizabeth Muir; m. Alma M. Brohard, Sept. 6, 1940 (dec. 1985); children: Malcolm, Thomas, Ann Muir, Barbara (dec.), David Clay. BA, Lehigh U., 1935; LL.B., Harvard U., 1938. Sole practice, Williamsport, Pa., 1938-42, 45-49, 68-70; mem. firm, 1949-68; judge U.S. Dist. Ct. (mid. dist.) Pa., 1970—. Active charitable orgns., Williamsport, 1939-70. Mem. ABA, Pa. Bar Assn. (pres.-elect 1970) Avocation: reading. Office: US Dist Ct Ste 401 240 W 3rd St Williamsport PA 17701-6461 Office Phone: 570-322-0287.

MUIR, RUTH BROOKS, alcohol/drug abuse services professional, consultant; b. Washington, Nov. 27, 1924; d. Charles and Adelaide Chenery (Masters) B.; m. Robert Mathew Muir, Nov. 26, 1947 (dec. Feb. 20, 1996); children: Robert Brooks, Martha Louise, Heather Sue. BA in Art, Rollins Coll., Winter Park, Fla., 1947; MA in Rehab. Counseling, U. Iowa, 1979. Cert. substance abuse counselor, Iowa. Program advisor Iowa Meml. Union, Iowa City, 1959-66; counselor, coord. Mid Eastern Coun. on Chem. Abuse, Iowa City, 1976-81; patient rep. Univ. Hosp., Iowa City, 1982-85; rsch. project interviewer dept. psychiatry U. Iowa Coll. Medicine, 1985-88; pvt. practice family counselor, 1984—. Artist: exhibitions include Iowa City Sr. Ctr., 1987, 92, Iowa City Art Ctr., 1989, U. Iowa Hosp., 1991, Great Midwestern Ice Cream Co., 1991, Summit St. Gallery, 1995, Iowa City C. of C., 2001, Iowa City's First Art Walk March, 2003; creator, coord. therapeutic series Taking Control, Iowa City Sr. Ctr., 1986-87, Art Walk Lorenz Boot Shop, 2003; one woman shows include Pastels, Paintings and Prints Englert Theatre, Iowa City, 2006. Vol. coord. art exhibits Sr. Ctr., Iowa City, 1992-94, Iowa City Arts Exhbn. Com., 1996, Arrowmont Sch. Art, 1996—, Arrowmont Amb., 1996-98; treas. bd. dirs. Crisis Ctr., Iowa City, 1976-77; sec. coun. elders Sr. Citizens Ctr., Iowa City, 1976-78; pres. Unitarian-Universalist Iowa City Women's Fedn., 1985, mem. pastoral com., 2006; friend U. Iowa Mus. Art, docent, 1999-2006; active Opera Supers, Iowa City Unitarian U.N. Envoy; fgn. rels. coun., bd. dirs. annual changing family conf. U. Iowa, 1986-92; non-govtl. rep. Earth Summit Global Forum, 1992; care review bd. Mental Health Homes, 1997-99; bd. dirs., exhbn. chair Arts Iowa City, 2002—; coord. art exhbns. Melrose Meadows, 2004—; UU pastoral care com. 2005-07. Mem.: AAUW (state cultural rep. 1990—92, Iowa City chpt. co-chair for programs 1998—99), Health Care: Health Svcs., Nat. League Am. PEN Women (membership chair 2002—04, v.p. 2004—, 2007—, program chair 2008—), Iowa City Unitarian Soc. (adult program com. 1993—94, unitarian care com. 1993—, membership com.), Nat. Soc. Colonial Dames, U. Iowa Retirees Assn. (bd. mem. 2004—, chair membership 2005—), U. Iowa Print and Drawing Study Club (bd. dirs. 2003—04, pres. elect 2005), Pi Beta Phi (pres. alumnae club 1995—97). Home and Office: 6 Glendale Ct Iowa City IA 52245-4430 Office Phone: 319-337-7287. Business E-Mail: ruthmuir@q.com.

MUIR, TOM WILLIAM, chemistry professor; b. Stranraer, Scotland, June 21, 1967; s. George Alexander and Catherine Haxton Muir; m. Rosalind Young, Aug. 10, 1997; children: James Ian Young, Derek Thomas. BSc, Edinburgh U., 1989, PhD, 1992. Postdoc. fellow Scripps Rsch. Inst., San Diego, 1992—95; prof. Rockefeller U., NYC, 1996—. Achievements include research in protein chemistry. Office: Rockefeller Univ 1230 York Ave New York NY 10065 Business E-Mail: muirt@rockefeller.edu.

MUIR, WARREN ROGER, chemist, educator; b. NY, 1945; s. Ernest Roger and Phyllis (Stirn) M.; m. Jo-Ann McNally; children: Amy, Douglas, Michael, Gregory, Daniel. AB in Chemistry cum laude, Amherst Coll., 1967; MS in Chemistry, Northwestern U., Evanston, Ill., 1968, PhD in Chemistry, 1971; postgrad. in epidemiology, Johns Hopkins U., 1975-77. Sr. staff mem. environ. health Council on Environ. Quality, EPA, Washington, 1971-78; dir. Office of Toxic Substances, EPA, 1978-81; pres. Hampshire Rsch. Assocs., Inc., 1981-99, Hampshire Rsch. Inst., 1987-99; exec. dir. divsn. earth and life studies NRC/Nat. Acad. Scis., 1999—. Assoc. environ. health scis. Johns Hopkins U., 1981-99; rsch. prof. biology Am. U., 1985; sr. fellow INFORM, 1982-95; mem. Nat. Conf. Lawyers and Scientists, 1987-89; bd. environ. scis. and toxicology NRC, 1997-99. Contbr. articles on environ. quality to profl. jours. Mem., chair several Nat. Rsch. Coun. coms.; pres. Children's Friendship Project for No. Ireland, 1997-99, bd. dirs. 1995-2007, chair 1997-2002, bd. dirs. HasNa, Inc., 2003—, chair, 2007-, Cypress Friendship Program. Recpient NSF Acad. award, 1966, Howard Waters Doughty prize Amherst Coll., 1967, Forris Jewett Moore fellow, 1967; comdr., 1996, officer brother Most Venerable Order of St. John, 1992; co-recipient Adminstrs. award U.S. EPA, 1992, Cmty. Svc. award Nat. Acads., 2003. Mem.: AAAS, Am. Chem. Soc. Home: 9426 Forest Haven Dr Alexandria VA 22309-3151

MUIR, WILLIAM F., finance company executive; b. Freeport, NY; BS in Indsl. Engring., Ops. Rsch., Cornell U., Ithaca, NY, 1977; MBA, Harvard U., 1983. Treas. office Gen. Motors, NYC, 1983—86, dir. fgn. exch. and internat. cash mgmt., 1986—87, dir. overseas borrowings, 1987—89, dir. corp. fin. and investor rels., 1989—90, gen. dir. bus. devel., 1990—92; v.p. nat. accts. Gen. Motors Acceptance Corp., 1992—95, v.p. ea. US ops., 1995—96, exec. v.p., CFO, 1998—2004, chmn. ins. group, 1999—, pres., 2004—; exec.-in-charge of ops., exec. dir. planning Delphi Automotive Systems, 1996—98. Bd. dirs. Gen. Motors Acceptance Corp., Gen. Motors Acceptance Corp. Mortgage Group, Gen. Motors Acceptance Corp. Comml. Fin. Office: Gen Motors Acceptance Corp PO Box 200 Detroit MI 48265-0001 Office Phone: 313-556-5000.*

MUIR, WILLIAM KER, JR., political science professor; b. Detroit, Oct. 30, 1931; s. William Ker and Florence Taylor (Bodman) M.; m. Paulette Irene Wauters, Jan. 16, 1960; children: Kerry Macaire, Harriet Bodman. BA, Yale U., 1954, PhD, 1965; JD, U. Mich., 1958. Bar: N.Y. 1960, Conn. 1965. Instr. U. Mich. Law Sch., 1958-59; assoc. firm Davis Polk & Wardwell, NYC, 1959-60; lectr. in polit. sci. Yale U., 1960-64, 65-67; from assoc. to ptnr. Tyler Cooper Grant Bowerman & Keefe, New Haven, 1964-68; prof. emeritus polit. sci. U. Calif., Berkeley, 1968-98, dept. chmn., 1980-83; speechwriter v.p. U.S., 1983-85; columnist Oakland (Calif.) Tribune, 1992-93; writer Gov. of Calif., Sacramento, 1994. Sr. cons. Calif. State Assembly, Sacramento, 1975-76; cons. Oakland Police Dept., 1969-74; vis. prof. polit. sci. Harvard U., summers 1976, 79; vis. prof. Hawaii Pacific U., 2000, U. Ariz., 2002. Author: Prayer in the Public School, 1967, later republished as Law and Attitude Change, 1974, Police: Streetcorner Politicians, 1977, Legislature: California's School for Politics, 1982, The Bully Pulpit: The Presidential Leadership of Ronald Reagan, 1993, Memoirs, 2003. Mem. Berkeley Police Rev. Commn., 1981-83; chmn. New Haven Civil Liberties Coun., 1965-68; Rep. candidate Calif. State Assembly, 1996. Recipient Hadley B. Cantril Meml. award, 1979, Disting. Tchg. award U. Calif., Berkeley, 1974, Phi Beta Kappa No. Calif. Assoc. Excellence in Tchg. award, 1994. Mem. Am. Polit. Sci. Assn. (Edward S. Corwin award 1966). Republican. Presbyterian. Office: U Calif Dept Polit Sci Berkeley CA 94720-1950 Personal E-mail: sandymuir@aol.com.

MUIRHEAD, VINCENT URIEL, retired aerospace engineer; b. Dresden, Kans., Feb. 6, 1919; s. John Hadsell and Lily Irene (McKinney) M.; m. Bobby Jo Thompson, Nov. 5, 1943; children: Rosalind, Jean, Juleigh. BS, U.S. Naval Acad., 1941; BS in Aero. Engring, U.S. Naval Postgrad. Sch., 1948; Aero. Engr., Calif. Inst. Tech., 1949; postgrad., U. Ariz., 1962-64, Okla. State U., 1963. Midshipman U.S. Navy, 1937, commd. ensign, 1941, advanced through grades to comdr., 1951; nav. officer U.S.S. White Plains, 1945-46; comdr. Fleet Aircraft Service Squad, 1951-52; with Bur. Aeros., Ft. Worth, 1953-54; comdr. Helicopter Utility Squadron I, Pacific Fleet, 1955-56; chief staff officer Comdr. Fleet Air, Philippines, 1956-58; exec. officer Naval Air Tng. Center, Memphis, 1958-61; ret., 1961; asst. prof. U. Kans., Lawrence, 1961-63, assoc. prof. aerospace engring., 1964-76, prof., 1976-89, prof. emeritus, 1989—, chmn. dept., 1976-88. Cons. Black & Veatch (cons. engrs.), Kansas City, Mo., 1964— Author: Introduction to Aerospace, 1972, 6th edit., 2004, Thunderstorms, Tornadoes and Building Damage, 1975. Decorated Air medal. Fellow AIAA (assoc.); mem. Am. Acad. Mechanics, Am. Soc. Engring. Edn., Tau Beta Pi, Sigma Gamma Tau. Mem. Ch. of Christ (elder 1972-96). Achievements include research on aircraft, tornado vortices, shock tubes and waves. Home: 503 Park Hill Ter Lawrence KS 66046-4841 Office: Dept Aerospace Engring Univ Kans Lawrence KS 66045-0001 Personal E-mail: vmuirhead@sunflower.com.

MUIR-TAYLOR, DOUGLAS JAMES, ophthalmologist; b. Edinburgh, May 4, 1932; s. Thomas William and Jane Craig Muir-Taylor; m. Lesley Elizabeth Muir-Taylor; children: Victoria Grace, Elizabeth Laura. Grad., Heriot-Watt U., Edinburgh, 1954; MB BChir, U. London, 1960. House surgeon ophthalmology Kings Coll. Hosp., London, 1960—60, house physician medicine, 1960—61; sr. house surgeon A&E Lewisham Hosp., London, 1961—62; gen. practice prin. London Redbridge, 1962; clin. assoc. ophthalmology Moorfields Hosp., London, 1962—66, Royal London Hosp., 1978—85, assoc. specialist ophthalmology, 1978—85, clin. dir. contact lens and prosthetic dept., 1991—. Clin. dir. Telephone Cables GEC, London, 1963—90, Electric Windings Ltd., London, 1970—94, F.J. Cipa Panel Craft PT Ltd., London, 1996—. Fellow: Rpyal Soc. Medicine, Brit. Optical Assn., Brit. Coll. Optometry; mem.: Contact Lens Assn. Ophthalmologists, Royal Coll. Physicians (licentiate), Am. Soc. Cataract and Refractive Surgery, Royal Coll. Ophthalmologists, Royal Coll. Surgeons. Achievements include research in photorefractive keratectomy in high myopia; photorefractive keratectomy after corneal surgery; photorefractive keratectomy in pregnancy and menopause; correction of aphakia with extended wear gas permeable contact lenses, serum markers in germ cell tumours. Avocations: fishing, winter sports, shooting, fine wines, golf. Home: 63 Plover Way London SE16 7TS England Office: Blackheath Eyecare Ctr 16 Old Dover Rd London SE16 7TS England Office Fax: 020 8858 5627. E-mail: muirtaylor@aol.com.

MUJICA, BARBARA LOUISE, language educator, writer; d. Louis and Frieda (Kline) Kaminar; m. Mauro E. Mujica, Dec. 26, 1966; children: Lillian Louise, Mariana Ximena, Mauro Eduardo Ignacio. AB, UCLA, 1964; MA, Middlebury Coll., 1965; PhD, NYU, 1974. Instr. French UCLA, 1963-64; assoc. editor modern langs. Harcourt Brace Jovanovich, NYC, 1966-73; instr., asst. prof. Romance langs. CUNY, 1973-74; prof. Spanish Georgetown U., Washington, 1974—. Mem. faculty NEH Summer Inst., 1980. Author: (book) A-LM Spanish, Levels I-IV, 1969—74, Readings in Spanish Literature, 1975, Calderon's Characters: An Existential Point of View, 1980, Pasaporte, 1980, rev. edit., 1984, Aqui y ahora, 1979, Entrevista, 1982, Iberian Pastoral Characters, 1986, Texto y Espectáculo, 1987, Et in Arcadia Ego, 1990, Texto y Vida: Introduccion a la Literatura Española, 1990, Antología de la Literatura Española: La Edad Media, 1991, Renacimiento y Siglo de Oro, 1991, Siglos XVII y XIX, 1991, Texto y Vida: Introduccion a la Literatura Hispano-Americana, 1992, Looking at the Comedia in the Year of the Quincentennial, 1993, Premio Nobel, 1997, Books of the Americas, 1997, El Texto Puesto en Escena, 2000, (novels) Sanchez Across the Street, 1997, The Deaths of Don Bernardo, 1990, Far From My Mother's Home, 1999, Frida: A Novel, 2001, (book) Teresa de Jesus: Espiritualidad y feminismo, Milenio, 2002, Sister Teresa, 2007, Teresa de Avila: Lettered Woman, 2008; editor: Comedia Performance Jour.; editor, pub. Verbena: Bilingual Rev. of Arts, 1979—85, sr. assoc. editor, bd. dirs. Washington Rev., mem. editl. bd. Bull. of Comediantes Hispana; editor: (jour.) Comedia Performance, (book) Women Writers of Early Modern Spain: Sophia's Daughters, 2004. Recipient Pangolin prize best short story, 1998, Hoepner award for fiction, 2002, Trailblazers award, 2004; named winner, E.L. Doctorow Internat. Fiction Competition, 1992; named one of 50 Best Op Eds of Decade, N.Y. Times, 1990; grantee, Spanish Govt., 1987, Poets and Writers of N.Y., Georgetown U., 2005—06; Penfield fellow, 1971. Mem.: MLA (pres. Golden Age sect.), Assn. Hispanic Classical Theater (pres.). Office: Georgetown U Dept Spanish Washington DC 20057-1039 Home Phone: 301-365-7733; Office Phone: 202-687-5778. Business E-Mail: mujica@georgetown.edu.

MUJICA-PARODI, MAURO E., architect; b. Antofagasta, Chile, Apr. 20, 1941; came to U.S., 1965, naturalized, 1970; s. Mauro Raul and Graciela (Parodi-Blayfus) M.; m. Barbara Louise Kaminar, Dec. 26, 1966; children: Lillian Louise, Mariana Ximena, Mauro Eduardo Ignacio III. BArch, MArch, Columbia U., 1971. Head designer Columbia U. Office Archtl. Planning, NYC, 1966-71; project mgr. Walker, Sander, Ford & Kerr, Architects, Princeton, NJ, 1971-72; prin. Mauro E. Mujica, Architect, NYC, 1972-74; dir. internat. divsn. Greenhorne & O'Mara, Inc., Riverdale, Md., 1974-78; ptnr. Mujica & Reddy Architects, Washington, 1978-80; prin. Mauro E. Mujica, Architect, Washington, 1980-81; ptnr. Mujica & Berlin Investment Bankers, Washington, 1982-85, Mujica Keppie Henderson Internat., Washington and Glasgow, Scotland, 1981-83, Mujica-Seifert Architects, Washington and London, 1983-87; pres.,CDEO, The Pace Group, Washington, 1987-91; ptnr. Pace/Walsh Internat., London and Washington. Chmn. bd., CEO, U.S. English Found., Washington, 1993—; hon. mem. Emmanuel Coll. Cambridge (Eng.) U., 1995; mem. adv. bd. U.S.-U.K. Fulbright Commn., 1995-2000.

MUKAI, AI, physiatrist; b. Tokyo, Oct. 13, 1977; arrived in U.S., 1989; d. Kazuko Mukai. Studied piano, Manhattan Sch. of Music, 1993—95; BA in Psychology, Columbia U., NYC, 1999; MD, Pa. State U., 2004. Lic. Ill., 2005, cert. in advanced cardiac life support 2004, in pediat. advanced life support 2004; in advanced cardiac. life support & basic life support 2004, lic. Calif. State Med., 2008. Intern Pa. State U. Coll. Medicine, Hershey Med. Ctr., 2004—05; resident phys. medicine and rehab. Northwestern U., Rehab. Inst. Chgo., 2005—; with Tex. Orthop., Sports & Rehab., 2009—. Preceptor phys. diagnosis curriculum Pa. State Coll. Medicine, 2004—05; co-moderator Phys. Medicine and Rehab. Forum, Studentdoctor.net, 2005—; mem. various coms. Rehab. Inst. Chgo., 2005—, mem. ethics com., 2005—06, mem. continuous quality improvement, 2005—, mem. labs. and x-rays com., 2006—, super-user, Cerner Project Mercury, 2006—; presenter, lectr., rschr. in field. Contbg. editor, coord.: Rehab in Review, 2006—, book reviewer: Lippincott Williams and Wilkins, 2001—; contbr. articles to profl. jours., chapters to books; jour. reviewer: Archives of Phys. Medicine and Rehab., 2005—, Jour. Gen. Internal Medicine, 2005. Recipient 1st pl., NYC Dept. Health, Health Rsch. Tng. Program Competition, 1998, Med. Student Rsch. award, Pa. State Coll. Medicine, 2004, 2nd pl., Pa. Med. Soc. Poster Competition, 2004, Sarah Baskin award, 2008, Scholl Recognition award, 2008; named Intern of Yr., Hershey Med. Ctr., Dept. Gastroenterology and Hepatology, 2005, Hershey Med. Ctr., Dept. Hematology and Oncology, 2005; grantee, William Randolph Hearst Found., 2006—08; scholar, Internat. Starr Found., 1995, Japanese-Am. Assn., 1995; Roslyn S. Silver '27 scholar, 1999, Gen. Clin. Rsch. Ctr. scholar, Pa. State Coll. Medicine, 2000, Mohler scholar, 2000, Hammersla scholar, 2001, 2002, Hershey Foods scholar, 2003. Mem.: AMA, Asian and Pacific Islander Am. Health Forum, Student Nat. Med. Assn. (chpt. co-pres. Penn State Coll. Medicine 2000—01, nat. liaison to Am. Med. Student Assn. 2001—02), Asian and Pacific Am. Med. Student Assn., Am. Med. Student Assn. (chpt. co-pres. Penn State Coll. Medicine 2000—01, assoc. trustee region III 2001—02), Am. Acad. Phys. Medicine and Rehab. (chair bylaws/ops. and strategic planning com. resident physician coun. 2004—05, sec. 2005—06, mentor med. student mentoring program 2005—, pres. resident physician coun. 2006—07), Am. Congress Rehab. Medicine (mem. membership com. and info. tech. com. 2005—06, 2005—), Physiatric Assn. for Spine Sports and Occupl. Rehab., Assn. Acad. Physiatrists, Ill. State Phys. Medicine and Rehab. Soc. Avocations: piano, drawing, photography, languages. Office: Tex Orthop, Sports & Rehab 4700 Seton Ctr Pky Austin TX 78757 Home: 421 W 3RD ST APT 1008 Chicago IL 60611-3240

MUKAMAL, KENNETH J., internist; b. Oct. 20, 1966; MD, U. Calif., San Francisco, 1990. Cert. Internal Medicine, 1993. Intern and resident in internal medicine Yale-New Haven Hosp., 1993; fellow in internal medicine Beth Israel Deaconess Med. Ctr., Boston, 1998, physician; assoc. prof. medicine Harvard Med. Sch., Boston. Office: Healthcare Associates Beth Israel Deaconess Med Ctr E 330 Brookline Ave E/CC-6 Boston MA 02215 Office Phone: 617-667-9600. Office Fax: 617-667-8665.*

MUKASEY, MARC L., lawyer; b. 1967; s. Michael Bernard and Susan Mukasey; m. Nancy Eve Rothenberg, Mar. 19, 1994. BA, Dartmouth Coll., Hanover, NH, 1989; JD cum laude, Benjamin N. Cardozo Sch Law, NYC, 1993. Bar: NY, admitted: US Ct. Appeals 2nd Cir., US Dist. Ct. (So. Dist.) NY, US Dist. Ct. (Ea. Dist.) NY. Law clk. to Hon. I. Leo Glasser US Dist. Ct. (ea. dist.) NY; staff atty. Securities & Exch. Commn. (SEC), 1993—96; dep. chief appellate atty., chief narcotics unit US Attorney's Office US Dept. Justice, 1997—2005; ptnr. Bracewell & Giuliani LLP, NYC, 2005—. Recipient Award for Superior Performance by an Asst. US Atty., US Dept. Justice, 2003, 2005; named to NY Super Lawyers, 2007, 2008, Benchmark Litigation, 2008, Super Lawyers, Corp. Counsel Edition, 2009. Office: Bracewell & Giuliani LLP 1177 Ave of Americas 19th Fl New York NY 10036-2714 Office Phone: 212-508-6134. Office Fax: 212-938-3833. Business E-Mail: marc.mukasey@bgllp.com.*

MUKASEY, MICHAEL BERNARD, lawyer, former United States Attorney General; b. Bronx, NY, July 28, 1941; m. Susan Mukasey; children: Marc, Jessica. AB, Columbia U., 1963; LLB, Yale U., 1967; Degree (hon.), Bklyn. Law Sch., 2002. Bar: NY 1967. Assoc. Webster, Sheffield, Fleischmann, Hitchcock & Brookfield, 1967-72, Patterson Belknap Webb & Tyler, NYC, 1976-88; ptnr. Patterson Belknap Webb & Tyler LLP, 2006—07; asst. US atty. criminal divsn. (so. dist.) NY US Dept. Justice, 1972-76, chief corruption unit, 1975—76; judge US Dist. Ct. (so. dist.) NY, 1988—2006, chief judge, 2000—06, sr. judge, 2006; atty. gen. US Dept. Justice, 2007—09; ptnr. litigation dept. Debevoise & Plimpton LLP, NYC, 2009—. Lectr. Columbia Law Sch., 1993—. Mem. bd. editors: Yale Law Jour., 1966—67; contbr. articles to profl. jour. Recipient Learned Hand medal for Excellence in Fed. Jurisprudence, Fed. Bar Coun. Mem.: ABA, NY State Bar Assn. (mem., Fed. Courts Com. 1978—82, chmn., Com. on Pub. Access to Info. & Proceedings 1984—), Assn. Bar City of NY (mem., Fed. Courts Com. 1979—81, Com. on Communications 1983—86). Republican. Jewish. Office: Debevoise & Plimpton LLP 919 Third Ave New York NY 10022 Office Phone: 212-909-6589. E-mail: mmukasey@debevoise.com.*

MUKERJEE, PASUPATI, chemistry professor; b. Calcutta, India, Feb. 13, 1932; s. Nani Gopal and Probhabati (Ghosal) M.; m. Lalita Sarkar, Feb. 29, 1964 (dec.); m. Mina Maitra, Nov. 14, 1998. B.Sc., Calcutta U., 1949, M.Sc., 1951; PhD, U. So. Calif., 1957. Lectr., vis. asst. prof. U. So. Calif., 1956-57; rsch. assoc. Brookhaven Nat. Lab., LI, 1957-59; reader in phys. chemistry Indian Assn. Cultivation of Sci., Calcutta, 1959-64; guest scientist U. Utrecht, Holland, 1964; sr. scientist chemistry dept. U. So. Calif., 1964-66; vis. assoc. prof. U. Wis., Madison, 1966-67, prof. Sch. Pharmacy, 1967-94, emeritus prof., 1994—. Vis. prof. Indian Inst. Tech., Kharagpur, 1971-72; mem. commn. on colloid and surface chemistry Internat. Union Pure and Applied Chemistry Contbr. articles to profl. jours.; mem. editl. bd. Jour. Colloid and Interface Sci., 1978-80, Asian Jour. Pharm. Scis., 1978-85, Colloids and Surfaces, 1980-86. Grantee USPHS, NSF, Nat. Bur. Stds., Petroleum Rsch. Fund. Fellow AAAS, Acad. Pharm. Scis., Am. Inst. Chemistry; mem. Am. Chem. Soc. (editorial bd. Langmuir 1985-86), Am. Pharm. Assn., Acad. Pharm. Scis., Rho Chi. Home: 5526 Varsity Hl Madison WI 53705-4652 Office: 777 Highland Ave Madison WI 53705-2222 Office Phone: 608-262-7289. Personal E-mail: pmukherjee@aol.com.

MUKHERJEE, AMIYA K., metallurgy and materials science educator; PhD, Oxford U., Eng., 1962. Prof. U. Calif., Davis. Recipient Alexander von Humboldt award Fed. Republic Germany, 1988, Albert Easton White Disting. Tchr. award Am. Soc. Materials, 1992, Pfeil medal and prize Inst. Materials, 1993, U. Calif. prize and citation, 1993, Anatoly Bochvar medal U. Moscow, 1996, Inst. medal Max Planck Inst. for Metallforschung, 1997. Office: U Calif Davis Dept Chem Engring & Material Sci Davis CA 95616 E-mail: akmukherjee@ucdavis.edu.

MUKHERJEE, DEBABRATA, cardiologist, researcher; naturalized, USA; s. Prabodh Chandra Mukherjee. MD, Govt. Med. Coll., Nagpur, India, 1988; M in Clin. Rsch., U. Mich., Ann Arbor, 2003. Med. lic. Ohio, Mich., Ky., bd. cert. in internal medicine 1996, bd. cert. in cardiovascular diseases 1999, bd. cert. in interventional cardiology 2000. Fellow in molecular cardiology Cleveland Clinic Found., 1989—92, resident in internal medicine, 1993—96, fellow in clin. cardiology, 1996—99, fellow in interventional cardiology and peripheral vascular interventions, 1999—2000, chief interventional cardiology fellow, 2000—01; dir. peripheral vascular interventions for cardiology, asst. prof. divsn. cardiology U. Mich., 2001—04; Gill Foundation prof. interventional cardiology, dir. peripheral vascular interventions, dir. cardiac catheterization lab U. Ky., Ky., 2006—. Mem. spl. emphasis panel Nat. Heart Lung and Blood Inst., 2003; external reviewer Can. Inst. Health Rsch., 2003. Asst. editor ACC Current Jour. Review, 2002—, internat. editor The Reviews, 2004—, mem. editl. bd. Vascular Disease Prevention, 2003—, Internat. Jour. Angiology, 2005—, Am.

Heart Jour., 2005—;, author manual of vascular diseases; reviewer (various manuscripts); contbr. chapters to books. Recipient Recognition award, Indian Coun. Med. Rsch., 1986, LN Jaiswal Gold Medal, 1988, Sadiq Vali Gold Medal, 1988, DB Jaiswal Gold Medal, 1988, Robert C. Tarazi Fellowship award for Excellence in Cardiovascular Rsch., 1990, Joseph Cash Meml. award for excellence in health outcome rsch., 2001; finalist Astra-Zeneca Young Investigator, 1999, 2000; McKay Rsch. grant for peripheral arterial disease, U. Mich. Cardiovascular Ctr., 2003—04. Fellow: Am. Coll. Cardiology, Soc. Vascular Medicine and Biology; mem.: AAAS, AMA, ACP, Am. Heart Assn. (Rsch. fellowship 1990, 1991, Bristol-Myers Squibb Travel award 1997, Grant-in-Aid 1999—2001), Internat. Fedn. Advancement Genetic Engring. and Biotechnology, Am. Coll. Cardiology (mem. cardiac catheterization and intervention com. 2005—08, summit adv. work group 2006—09, Affiliate Travel award 1998, finalist Young Investigator award 1999, First prize for abstract 1999, Career Devel. Award 2002—03, First prize for abstract 2000, William F. Keating Career Devel. award for hypertension and peripheral vascular disease 2002—03). Achievements include research in Impact of combination evidence-based med. therapy on mortality in patients with acute coronary syndromes; Missed opportunities to treat atherosclerosis in patients undergoing peripheral vascular interventions; Risk of cardiovascular events associated with selective COX-2 inhibitors. Office: Univ Ky 326B Wethington Bldg 900 S Limestone St Lexington KY 40536-0200 Office Fax: 859-323-6475.

MUKHERJEE, DIPANKAR, surgeon; b. New Delhi, Feb. 9, 1953; arrived in US, 1976; BS, U. New Delhi, 1970; MD, All-India Inst. Med. Sci., New Delhi, 1975. Cert. Am. Bd. Surgery, Am. Registry Diagnostic Med. Sonographers. Sr. house officer surgery Auckland Hosp. Bd., New Zealand, 1976—77; intern gen. surgery St. Mary's Hosp., Rochester, NY, 1977—78; resident gen. surgery Genesee, Highland and Rochester Gen. Hosps., 1978—79, 1981—82, Genesee, Rochester Gen. and Strong Meml. Hosps., 1979—82, Rochester Gen. and Strong Meml. Hosps., 1980—81; fellow peripheral vascular surgery St. Vincent Hosp., Portland, Oreg., 1982—83; pvt. practice, 1983—87; chief divsn. vascular surgery Madigan Army Med. Ctr., Tacoma, 1988—90, surg. dir. ICU, 1988—90; active staff Inova Fairfax Hosp., Falls Church, Va., 1990—, apptd. chief sect. vascular surgery, 2008—; active staff Va. Hosp. Ctr., Arlington, 1990—, Columbia Reston Hosp., Va., 1990—, chief dept. surgery, 1998—99; clin. asst. prof. surgery Uniformed Svs. U. Health Scis., F. Edward Herbert Sch. Medicine, Bethesda, Md., 1990—, Georgetown U. Hosp., Washington, 1998—; pvt. practice Cardiac, Vascular and Thoracic Surgery Assocs., P.C., Annandale, Va., 2003—; clin. assoc. prof. surgery and neurol. surgery George Washington U. Sch. Medicine and Health Scis., 2006—. Clin. asst. prof. surgery divsn. vascular surgery Oreg. Health Scis. U. Sch. Medicine, Portland, 1983—88; program co-chmn. Pacific NW Vascular Soc., 1988; pres. India Physicians No. Va., 1995—96; spkr. in field. Contbr. articles to profl. jours. Decorated Army Commendation medal Dept. of the Army; named Outstanding Tchr. of Yr., Georgetown U. Med. Ctr., 1999; named one of Top Doctors, Washingtonian Mag., 1993, 1995, 1999, 2001, 2003, 2005, 2008, Area's Outstanding Physician Specialists, Washington Consumers Checkbook, 1996, 1998, 2000, 2002, 2004, 2006, Best Doctors in Am., 1998. Fellow: ACS, Soc. for Vascular Surgery (disting.); mem.: Faifax County Med. Soc., Portland Surg. Soc. (program chmn. 1986), Portland Vascular Soc. (program chmn. 1985), NW Vascular Soc., North Pacific Surg. Assn., Internat. Soc. for Endovascular Surgery, Internat. Soc. for Cardiovasc. Surgery, Chesapeake Vascular Soc. (pres.-elect 2004—05). Achievements include patents for catheter introducer for antegrade and retrograde medical procedures. Office: Cardiac Vascular and Thoracic Surgery Assocs 2921 Telestar Ct Ste 140 Falls Church VA 22042

MUKHERJEE, SUSHMITA, science educator; d. Sibdas and Banani Mukherjee; m. George C. Collins, Aug. 31, 2003; 1 child, Tara Nandita Collins. PhD, Ctr. Cellular and Molecular Biology, Hyderabad, India, 1995. Rsch. assoc. Weill Cornell Med. Coll., NYC, 2002—07, asst. prof., 2007—, dir., multiphoton microscopy facility, 2007—. Mem.: AAAS, SPIE. Office: Weill Cornell Med Coll 1300 York Ave Rm E0002 New York NY 10065 Business E-Mail: smukherj@med.cornell.edu.

MUKHOPADHYAY, SHARMILA MITRA, materials engineer, educator; d. Arun Kumar and Bani Mitra; m. Bhaskar Mukhopadhyay, June 29, 1985; 1 child, Amrita. BS, MS, Indian Inst. Tech.; PhD, Cornell U., 1989. Assoc./asst. prof. Wright Sate U., Dayton, Ohio, 1997—2003, prof. materials sci. and engring., 2003—, dir. Ctr. for Nanoscale Materials, 2007—. Reviewer NSF, 1994—. Editor: MPMD Fifth Global Innovations Procs: Surfaces and Interfacesin Nanostructured Materials; contbr. articles to profl. jours. Recipient cert. for nat. ranking (top 10), Indian Sch. Cert. Orgn., 1977, several scholarship awards, including Nat. Merit scholarship, Indian Inst. Tech. and W.B. Govt., 1981, rsch. awards, NSF, DOE, NASA, AFOSR, EPA, several rsch. grants, Procter & Gamble; Summer Faculty Rsch. fellow, Air Force Rsch. Lab., Propulsion Directorate. Fellow: Am. Ceramic Soc. (exec. com. electronics divsn. 2005—); mem.: Materials Rsch. Soc., Am. Soc. Engring. Edn., TMS (symposium organizer 2003—06), ASM Internat. (exec. com. Dayton chpt. 1998—). Achievements include development of thin film techniques, including fabrication of superconducting oxides from nanoparticles; research in modification of interfaces using plasma; surface activity measurements using XPS; modification of nanostructural materials. Avocations: travel, painting, poetry. Office: Wright State U Mech and Materials Engring Dept Dayton OH 45435 Business E-Mail: sharmila.mukhopadhyay@wright.edu.

MUKHTAR, MOHAMED HAJI, social sciences educator; b. Huddur, Bakool, Somalia, June 13, 1947; s. Keera Alyow Haydar and Malak Mukhtar Malak Hassan Mursal, Shamsa Sheikh Emet Moallim (Stepmother); children: Saida Mohamed, Salah Mohamed, Subeida Mohamed. MA, Al-Azhar U., Cairo, 1973, PhD, 1983. Cert. translator and interpreter English-Arabic and Arabic-English Polytecnic Ctrl. London, U.K., 1986. Prof. Somali, African and Mid. Ea. history Somali Nat. U., Lafoole Coll., Somalia, 1975—85; assoc. prof. U. Kebangsaan Malaysia, Kuala Lumpur, 1986—90; prof. African and Mid. Ea. history Savannah State U., Ga., 1991—. Chmn. Ergada, Harrisburg, Pa., 1996; pres. Ctr. for Peace Bldg. Initiative, Savannah, 2006; vis. prof. U. SC, Columbia, 1984—85. Author: Methodology of Writing History, 1978, Historical Dictionary of Somalia, 2003, English-Maay Dictionary, 2007; prodr.(and correspondent): BBC programs concerning African history and politics, 1986—; mem. editl. bd.: Islamiyyat, Annual Jour. for U. Kebangsaan Malaysia, 1987—90; editor (with others): Somalia World Bibliographical Series, 1989; mem. internat. adv. bd.: Bildhan, Internat. Quarterly Jour. for Somali Studies, 2001—; contbr. chapters to books, articles to profl. pubs. Advisor Guardians of the Culture, Savannah; mem. global adv. bd. Human Dignity and Humiliation Studies, 2003—; founding mem., mem. exec. bd. Somali Profl. Trust, London, 1997—; advisor Somalia Internat. Rehab. Ctr., Lund, Sweden; mem. internat. com. Red Cross, pres. Savannah chpt., 2004—. Grantee, Swedish Life and Peace Inst., 1993—94; fellow, Istituto Italiano per L'Africa, 1979—80, NEH, 2002; scholar, Arab League Edn. Culture and Sci. Orgn., 1980—82, Fulbright, 1983, 1984—85. Mem.: Royal Inst. Internat. Affairs, UK, Egyptian Hist. Soc., Assn. Muslim Social Scientists, Mid. Ea. Studies Assn., Somali Internat. Studies Assn. (founding mem.), Inter-riverine Studies Assn. (chmn. 1996—, Chief editor Demenedung 1996—2001), African Studies Assn. Muslim. Home: 1916 E 64th St Savannah GA 31404 Office: Savannah State Univ 3219 College St Savannah GA 31404 Office Fax: 912-692-4558. Personal E-mail: demenedung@comcast.net. Business E-Mail: mukhtarm@savstate.edu.

MUKKAMALA, SRINIVAS, research scientist; b. Vijayawada, Andhra Pradesh, India, Oct. 13, 1976; s. Sambasiva Rao and Subha Mukkamala; m. Jyotsna Paturi, May 17, 2006. PhD, N.Mex. Inst. Mining and Tech., Socorro, 2005. Rsch. asst. N.Mex. Tech., 2000—05, sr. rsch. scientist, 2006—. Contbr. articles to profl. jours. Assisted native Am. populations Santa Fe Indian Sch., 2001—08. Achievements include development of fragmented RFID malware. Home: 801 Leroy Pl Campus Box 3001 Socorro NM 87801 Home Fax: 505-835-5587.

MUKOYAMA, JAMES HIDEFUMI, JR., security firm executive; b. Chgo., Aug. 3, 1944; s. Hidefumi James and Miye (Maruyama) M.; m. Kyung Ja Woo, June 20, 1971; children: Sumi Martha, Jae Thomas. BA in English, U. Ill., 1965, MA in Social Studies, 1966; grad. (hon.), US Army Inf. Sch., 1966; grad., US Army Command Gen. Staff Coll., 1979, US Army War Coll., 1984. Registered prin., sr. registered options prin. Nat. Assn. Securities Dealers. Commd. 2d lt. U.S. Army, 1965; advanced through grades to maj. gen. USAR, 1990, ret., 2004; asst. dept. mgr. Mitsui & Co. (USA), Inc., Chgo., 1971-74; mem. Chgo. Bd. Options Exch., 1974—75; allied mem. N.Y. Stock Exch., 1982-84; v.p. Heartland Securities Inc. & Lefta Advt., Chgo., 1976-90, Fleet Brokerage, Chgo., 1990-95; exec. v.p., COO, Regal Securities, 1995—. Mem. exec. bd. Hillside Free Meth. Ch., Evanston, Ill., 1982-93, participating mem. Willow Creek Ch., 2003-; dir. Chgo. coun. Boy Scouts Am., 1993-95; bd. dirs. Nat. Japanese Am. Meml. Found., 1995-2004; patient vol. Rainbow Hospice, 2003-08; chair adv. com. minority vets. Dept. VA, 2003-09; pres. bd. dirs. Japanese Assn. Svc. Corr. Housing Corp., 1998-2008. Decorated Silver Star, Legion of Merit, Purple Heart, 3 Bronze Stars, Disting. Svc. medal; Vietnamese Army Cross of Gallantry; Japanese Army Parachutist badge; recipient cert. of merit Korean Army, others. Mem. VFW (life), U. Ill. Alumni Assn. (life), Assn. U.S. Army (life), U.S. Army War Coll. Alumni Assn. (life), Army Res. Assn. (pres., founder 1992—), Mil. Order Purple Heart (life), Am. Legion (life), Res. Officers Assn. (life), Sr. Army Res. Comdrs. Assn. (life), Nat. Infantryman's Assn. (life). Home: 4009 Tracey Ct Glenview IL 60025-2468 Office: Regal Securities 950 Milwaukee Ave Ste 101 Glenview IL 60025-3766 Personal E-mail: jhmukoyama@yahoo.com.

MULALLY, ALAN R., automotive company executive, former aerospace company executive; b. Oakland, Calif., Aug. 4, 1945; m. Nicki Mulally; 5 children. BS in Aerospace Engring., U. Kans., 1968, MS in Aerospace Engring., 1969; MA in Mgmt., MIT, 1982. With Boeing Def. and Space Group, Seattle, 1969—2006, v.p. 777 engring., v.p., gen. mgr. 777 divsn., sr. v.p. airplane devel., 1994—97, pres., 1997-99; exec. v.p Boeing Co., 1997—2006; pres. Boeing Comml. Air Group, 1998—2006; pres., CEO Ford Motor Co., Dearborn, Mich., 2006—. Mem. adv. bd. NASA, U. Wash., U. Kans.; mem. sci. adv. bd. USAF. Alfred P. Sloan fellow, 1982; recipient Leadership Tomorrow Program award, Seattle C. of C., 1984, One of 25 Bus. Leaders award, Puget Sound Bus. Jour., 1985, Disting. Engring. Svc. award, U. Kans. Engring. Sch., 1994, Laurels award, Aviation Week and Space Tech. mag., 1996, Engr. of Yr. award, Design News, 1996, Robert J. Collier Trophy (on behalf of 777 team), Nat. Aero. Assn., 1996; named one of The World's Most Influential People, 2009. Fellow Royal Aero. Soc. (Eng.), AIAA (Tech. Mgmt. award 1986, Reed Aeronautics award 1996); mem. NSPE (Industry Engr. of Yr. 1978), NAE. Avocations: private pilot, reading, tennis, golf. Office: Ford Motor Co 1 American Rd Dearborn MI 48126*

MULARZ, THEODORE LEONARD, architect; b. Chgo., Nov. 6, 1933; s. Stanley A. and Frances (Baycar) Mularz; m. Ruth L. Larson, Nov. 9, 1963; children: Anne Catherine, Mark Andrew. BArch, U. Ill., 1959. Registered arch., Colo., Oreg. Prin. Theodore L. Mularz, AIA Architects, Aspen, Colo., 1981-90; v.p. Benedict-Mularz Assocs., Inc., 1978-81; pvt. practice Ashland, Oreg., 1990—. Prin. works include numerous archtl. projects, including comml., indsl., religious, recreational, residential and hist. restoration. Vice-chmn. Pitkin County Bd. Appeals, 1972—90; mem. Colo. Bd. Examiners Archs., 1975—85, pres., 1976—80, v.p., 1978; vice-chmn. City of Aspen Bd. Appeals, 1985—90; mem. adv. com. City of Aspen Planning/Bldg. Dept., 1989; bd. dirs. Rogue Valley Symphony, Ashland, 1990—92, treas., 1991—92, chmn. fin. com., 1991—92; mem. Oreg. Bd. Examiners Archs., 1996—2000. With USCGR, 1953—55. Fellow: AIA; mem.: Colo. Soc. Archs. (Cmty. Svc. award 1975), Nat. Coun. Archtl. Registration Bds. (profl. conduct com. 1977—78, procedures/docs. com. 1978—82, chmn. edn. com. 1982—83, bd. dirs. 1982—87, chmn. 1983—84, mem. interprofessional coun. registration 1984—85, exec. com. 1984—87, internat. rels. com. 1984—89, interant. oral exam. com. 1984—89, v.p. 1985, pres. 1985, 1986, broadly experienced arch. interview com. 1987—2001), Aspen Hist. Soc. (com. chmn. 1963—64), Aspen C. of C. (past dir., pres., v.p.), Rotary (dir. Ashland Found. 2001—03, pres. 2001—02). Roman Catholic. Studio: 793 Elkader St Ashland OR 97520-3307

MULAWKA, DIANE L., mathematics educator; BS, Montclair State U., NJ, 2006, MS in Math., 2008. Math. tchr. Kearny HS, NJ, 2006—. Co-advisor Class 2009, Kearny, 2006—; internal coord. Mid. States Com., Kearny, 2006. Bd. mem. John F. Kennedy Meml. Libr., Wallington, NJ, 2007.

MULCAHY, ANNE MARIE, copier company executive; b. Rockville Centre, NY, Oct. 21, 1952; d. Thomas and Anne Dolan; m. Joe Mulcahy; 2 children. BA in English & Journalism, Marymount Coll., Tarrytown, NY, 1974. With Chase Manhattan Bank, 1974—76; various mgmt. positions Xerox Corp., 1976—88, v.p. regional gen. mgr., 1988—91, v.p. worldwide mktg. ops. planning, 1991, dir. corp. human resources, 1991—92, v.p. human resources, 1992-95, v.p., staff officer customer ops., 1996-97, chief staff officer, 1997, sr. v.p., 1998, pres. gen. markets ops. Stamford, Conn., 1999—2000, pres., COO, 2000—01, chmn., CEO, 2001—09, chmn., 2009—. Bd. dirs. Xerox Corp., 2000—, Fannie Mae (Fed. Nat. Mortgage Assn.), 2000—04, Target Corp., 2000—, Citigroup Inc., 2004—, The Washington Post Co., 2008—, Fuji-Xerox Co. Ltd., Catalyst. Named one of 100 Most Powerful Women, Forbes mag., 2005—09, World's Best CEO, Barron's Mag., 2006, The TIME 100-The People Who Shape Our World, 2006, 50 Most Powerful Women in Bus., Fortune mag., 2006—08, 50 Women to Watch, The Wall St. Jour., 2006, 2008, America's Best Leaders, US News & World Report, 2008. Mem.: Bus. Roundtable (chmn. corp. governance task force), Bus. Coun. Office: Xerox Corp 800 Long Ridge Rd Stamford CT 06904-1227 Office Phone: 203-968-3000. Office Fax: 203-968-3218.*

MULCAHY, DANIEL G., education educator; married. PhD, U. Ill., Urbana, 1970. Prof. edn. U. Coll., Cork, Ireland, 1978—92; prof., sch. edn. Ctrl. Conn. State U., New Britain, 1992—. Home: 59 Shepard Rd West Hartford CT 06107 Office: Ctrl Conn State Univ 1615 Stanley St New Britain CT 06050 Business E-Mail: mulcahy@ccsu.edu.

MULCAHY, GABRIEL M., pathologist; b. Jersey City, Feb. 16, 1929; s. Joseph Alphonsus and Anna Elizabeth Mulcahy; m. Vesna Maria Mulcahy, May 24, 1958; children: Mary, Michael, Robert, Richard, Thomas, John, Gabriel Jr. AB, St. Peter's Coll., Jersey City, 1950; MD, Georgetown U., 1954. Diplomate Nat. Bd. Med. Examiners, Am. Bd. Pathology. Intern St. Michaels Hosp., Newark, 1954-55; med. officer U.S. Pub. Health Svc., Crownpoint, N.Mex., 1955-57, resident in pathology Seattle, 1957-59, Staten Island, NY, 1959-61, chief pathology svc. Detroit, 1961-62; with pathology faculty Creighton U., Omaha, 1962-69; dir. pathology Jersey City Med. Ctr., 1969-78; mem. pathology faculty Univ. Medicine and Dentistry N.J., Newark, 1978-2001; chief lab. med. Univ. Hosp., Newark, 1978-2001. Mem. editl bd.: Annals of Clin. and Lab. Sci., 2000—; contbr. articles to profl. jours. Mem. adv. bd. St. Ann's Home for the Aged, Jersey City, 1973-89, sec., 1973-83; pres. bd. edn. St. Paul's Parish Sch., Jersey City, 1973-78. Mem. AAAS, Am. Soc. Human Genetics, Am. Assn. Blood Banks, Assn. Clin. Scientists (sci. coun. 1999—), Coll. Am. Pathologists, Soc. Med. Decision Making. Roman Catholic. Avocations: history, philosophy, philology, photography. Home Phone: 201-434-1897. Personal E-mail: mulcahy21@comcast.net.

MULCAHY, ROBERT EDWARD, management consultant; b. Cambridge, Mass., Mar. 2, 1932; s. George Frances and Hazel (Douglas) M.; m. Ethel Walworth, Nov. 14, 1953; children: Linda, Scott, Steven, Susan. BS, Lowell Textile Inst., 1953. With Allied Chem. Corp., Morristown, NJ, 1953—; from engr. to mktg. mgr. Nat. Aniline div. Allied Corp., 1953-63, from dir. indsl. mktg. to v.p.-mktg. Fibers div., 1963-69, asst. to group v.p., corporate office, 1969, v.p. and gen. mgr.-consumer group Fabricated Products div., 1969-71, pres. Fibers div., 1971-74, group v.p., 1974-75, pres., dir., 1975-79, asst. to chmn. and dir., 1979-80; sr. assoc. The Corp. Dir., Inc., NYC, 1981-83; pres. Counselors to Mgmt. Inc., 1984—.

MULCAHY, ROBERT WILLIAM, lawyer; b. Milw., Jan. 11, 1951; s. T. Larry and Mary Margaret (Chambers) M.; m. Mary M. Andrews, Aug. 3, 1974; children: Molly, Kathleen, Margaret, Michael. BS, Marquette U., 1973, JD, 1976. Staff atty. NLRB, Milw., 1976-79; ptnr. Mulcahy & Wherry, S.C., Milw., 1979-90, Michael, Best & Friedrich, Milw., 1990—. Co-author: Strike Prevention and Control Handbook, 1983, 2d edit., 2006, Comparable Worth: A Negotiator's Guide, 1985, Public Sector Labor Relations in Wisconsin, 1994. Bd. dirs. Milw. Repertory Theater, 1993-97, Gateway Tech. Coll. Found., 2004—; chmn. St. Monica Parish Coun., 1988-96, Charles Allis/Villa Terrace, 1991-, Whitefish Bay Police Commn.; divsn. chmn. United Performing Arts Fund, 1993-94; co-chmn. Villa Terrace Garden Renaissance Project, 2000-04, bd. mem. Am. Diabetes Assn. Mem. ABA(bd. mem.), State Bar Wis. (chair labor sect. 1986-87), Milw. Bar Assn. (co-chair labor sect. 1988-95), Nat. Assn. Counties, Nat. Pub. Employers Labor Rels. Assn., Nat. Assn. Coll. & Univ. Attys., Wis. Counties Assn., Indsl. Rels. Rsch. Assn., Mgmt. Resources Assn., Wis. Sch. Attys. Assn., Milw. Area Mcpl. Employers Assn., cmty leadership coun.(bd. mem. 2007) Office: Michael Best & Friedrich 100 E Wisconsin Ave Ste 3300 Milwaukee WI 53202-4108 E-mail: rwmulcahy@mbf-law.com, rwmulcahy@michaelbest.com.

MULCHINOCK, DAVID STEWARD, lawyer; b. Allentown, Pa., Feb. 10, 1945; s. Daniel F. and May E. (Heffner) M. BA, Georgetown U., 1967; JD, Cornell U., 1970. Bar: N.Y. 1971, N.J. 1974, U.S. Supreme Ct. 1978, Pa. 1994. Assoc. Hale, Grant, Meyerson, O'Brien & McCormick, NYC, 1970-72, ptnr., 1972-77; pvt. practice law Princeton, N.J., 1977—. Office: One Palmer Sq Princeton NJ 08542 Office Phone: 609-924-9622. Business E-Mail: ward210@aol.com.

MULDAUR, DIANA CHARLTON, actress; b. NYC, Aug. 19, 1938; d. Charles Edward Arrowsmith and Alice Patricia (Jones) M.; m. James Mitchell Vickery, July 26, 1969 (dec. 1979); m. Robert J. Dozier, Oct. 11, 1981. BA, Sweet Briar Coll., 1960. Actress appearing in: Off-Broadway theatrical prodns., summer stock, Broadway plays including A Very Rich Woman, 1963-68; guest appearances on TV in maj. dramatic shows; appeared on: TV series Survivors, 1970-71, McCloud, 1971-73, Tony Randall Show, 1976, Black Beauty, 1978; star: TV series Born Free, 1974, Hizzoner, 1979, Fitz & Bones, 1980, Star Trek: The Next Generation, 1988-89; NBC miniseries and TV series A Year in the Life, 1986; TV movie Murder in Three Acts, The Return of Sam McCloud, 1989; TV series L.A. Law, 1989-91; motion picture credits include McQ, The Lawyer, The Other, One More Train to Rob, Mati, etc. Bd. dirs. Los Angeles chpt. Asthma and Allergy Found. Am.; bd. advisors Nat. Ctr. Film and Video Preservation, John F. Kennedy Ctr. Performing Arts, 1986. Recipient 13th Ann. Commendation award Am. Women in Radio and TV, 1988, Disting. Alumnae award Sweet Briar Coll., 1988. Mem. Acad. Motion Picture Arts and Scis., Screen Actors Guild (dir. 1978), Acad. TV Arts and Scis. (exec. bd., dir., pres. 1983-85), Conservation Soc. Martha's Vineyard Island. Office: Bauman Bedanty & Shaul 5757 Wilshire Blvd Ste 473 Los Angeles CA 90036 Home Phone: 508-627-5070.

MULDER, DAVID S., cardiovascular surgeon; b. Eston, Sask., Can., July 28, 1938; s. Peter and Laura (Lovie) M.; m. Norma D. Johnston, Aug. 19, 1961; children— Scott D., Lizabeth J., John C. MD, U. Sask., 1962; M.Sc., McGill U., 1964. Intern, resident in surgery Montreal Gen. Hosp., McGill U., 1963-67; resident in cardiac surgery U. Iowa, 1967-69; surgeon-in-chief Montreal Gen. Hosp., 1977-98; prof. surgery McGill U., 1979—; chmn. dept. surgery, 1993-98. Contbr. articles to med. jours. Fellow: ACS, Royal Coll. Surgeons Can.; mem.: Soc. Thoracic Surgeons (named Order Can. 1997), Am. Assn Thoracic Surgery, Am. Assn. Trauma, Nat. Hockey League Team Physicians Assn., Soc. Univ. Surgeons. Conservative. Home: 76 Sunnyside Ave Westmount PQ Canada H34 1C2 Office: Montreal Gen Hosp Room L-512 Montreal PQ Canada H3G 1A4 Home Phone: 514-482-4620; Office Phone: 514-935-4888. Personal E-mail: dsmulder@sympatico.ca. Business E-Mail: david.mulder@muhc.mcgill.ca.

MULDOON, PAUL B., poet, educator; b. Portadown, No. Ireland, 1951; arrived in US, 1987; m. Jean Hanff Korelitz; 2 children. BA in English Lang. and Lit., Queen's U., Belfast, No. Ireland, 1973. Prodr. arts programs radio BBC No. Ireland, 1973-78, sr. prodr. arts programs radio, 1978-85, TV prodr., 1985-86; Judith E. Wilson vis. fellow Cambridge U., 1986-87; creative writing fellow U. East Anglia, 1987; Roberta Holloway lectr. U. Calif., Berkeley, 1989; dir. creative writing program Princeton U., 1993—2002, lectr. NJ, 1990—, Howard G.B. Clark '21 Univ. Prof. humanities and creative writing, 1998—; poetry editor New Yorker, 2007—. Part-time tchr. writing divsn. Columbia U. Sch. of Arts, 1987—88; part-time tchr. creative writing prog. Princeton U., 1987—88; vis. prof. U. Mass., Amherst, 1989—90; prof. poetry U. Oxford, 1999—2004; founding chair Lewis Ctr. for Arts, 2006—. Author (poetry): Knowing My Place, 1971, New Weather, 1973, Spirit of Dawn, 1975, Mules, 1977, Names and Addresses, 1978, Immram, 1980, Why Brownlee Left, 1980, Out of Siberia, 1982, Quoof, 1983, The Wishbone, 1984, Selected Poems 1968-1983, 1986, Meeting the British, 1987, Madoc: A Mystery, 1990 (Geoffrey Faber Meml. prize, 1992), The Annals of Chile, 1994 (T. S. Eliot prize, 1994), The Prince of the

Quotidian, 1994, Six Honest Serving Men, 1995, Kerry Slides, 1996, New Selected Poems: 1968-1994, 1996 (Irish Times Lit. Prize for poetry, 1997), Hopewell Haiku, 1997, Hay, 1998, Poems 1968-1998, 2001, Moy Sand and Gravel, 2002 (Internat. Griffin Poetry prize, Pulitzer Prize for poetry, 2003, Griffin Internat. Prize for excellence in poetry, 2003), Medley for Morin Khur, 2005, Sixty Instant Messages to Tom Moore, 2005, Horse Latitudes, 2006, General Admission, 2006, When the Pie Was Opened, 2008, Plan B, 2008; author: (children's books) The O-O's Party, New Year's Eve, 1980, The Noctuary of Narcissus Batt, 1997; author: (critical prose) To Ireland, I, 2000, The End of the Poem: Oxford Lectures in Poetry, 2006; translator (Irish to English): The Astrakhan Cloak, 1992; editor: The Scrake of Dawn: Poems by Young People from Northern Ireland, 1979, The Faber Book of Contemporary Irish Poetry, 1986, The Faber Book of Beasts, 1997, The Oxford and Cambridge May Anthologies 2000: Poetry, 2000, The Best American Poetry, 2005. Recipient Eric Gregory award, 1972, Acad. award in lit., Am. Acad. Arts and Letters, 1996, Shakespeare prize, 2004, Am. Ireland Fund Lit. award, 2004, Aspen prize for poetry, 2005; named a John Simon Guggenheim Meml. fellow, 1990. Fellow: Royal Soc. Lit.; mem.: AAAL, Am. Acad. Arts and Letters, Am. Acad. Arts and Scis. Office: Princeton U Rm 122 185 Nassau St Princeton NJ 08544-0001 Office Phone: 609-258-4708. E-mail: muldoon@princeton.edu.

MULDOON, ROBERT JOSEPH, JR., lawyer; b. Somerville, Mass., Nov. 16, 1936; s. Robert Joseph and Catherine Eileen (Hurley) M.; m. Barbara Joyce Mooney, Aug. 24, 1968; children: Andrew Robert, Catherine Lane, Timothy John. AB, Boston Coll., 1960, MA, 1961, LLB, 1965. Bar: Mass. 1965, U.S. Tax Ct. 1966, U.S. Supreme Ct. 1970. Law clk. Supreme Jud. Ct. Mass., 1965-66; assoc. Withington, Cross, Park & Groden, Boston, 1966-71, ptnr., 1972-82, Sherin and Lodgen, LLP, Boston, 1982—. Mem. Bd. Bar Examiners Mass., 1974-2006, chmn., 2005-06; chmn. Nat. Conf. Bar Examiners, 1985-86; pres. Mass. Continuing Legal Edn., Inc., 1992-94. Trustee Boston Coll. H.S., 1990-96, chmn. bd. trustees, 1995-96. Fellow Am. Coll. Trial Lawyers; mem. Am. Law Inst., Boston Bar Assn., Curtis Club, Nisi Prius Club, Tavern Club. Office: Sherin and Lodgen LLP 101 Federal St Boston MA 02110 Office Phone: 617-646-2225. Business E-Mail: rjmuldoon@sherin.com.

MULÉ, ANN C., oil industry executive; b. Phila., Oct. 22, 1956; BA magna cum laude, St. Joseph's U., 1978; JD cum laude, Villanova U., 1981. Bar: Pa. 1981, U.S. Supreme Ct. 1988. From atty. to chief governance officer Sunoco Inc., Phila., 1980—2002, chief governance officer, 2002—. Bd. dirs. Phila. Zoo; mem. adv. bd. Ctr. Corp. Governance, U. Del. Mem.: ABA, Am. Corp. Counsel Assn. (vice chmn. exec. counsel, mem. corp. and securities law com.), Phila. Bar Assn., Pa. Bar Assn. (chmn. bus. law sect., mem. bd. govs., chmn. com. securities regulation, mem. title 15 task force), Am. Soc. Corp. Secs. (bd. dir., mem. exec. steering com., mem. nat. conf. com., mem. corp. practices com.). Office: Sunoco Inc Mellon Bank Ctr 1735 Market St Ste LL Philadelphia PA 19103 Office Phone: 215-977-6430. E-mail: acmule@sunocoinc.com.

MULÉ, LISA NYSTROM, speech pathology/audiology services professional; d. John Frances and Carol Long Nystrom; m. Robert M. Mulé, Aug. 15, 1981; children: Amanda, Matthew. BA magna cum laude in Comm. Scis. and Disorders, U. Vt., Burlington, 1979; MS in Speech/Lang. Pathology, Boston U., 1981. Cert. clinical competence Am. Speech, Hearing & Lang. Assn., 1981, profl. educator Conn., 2006. Supervising speech/lang. pathologist Child Devel. Ctr., Conn. Children's Med. Ctr., Hartford, Conn., 1981—98; speech/lang. pathologist Orchard Hill Sch., S.Windsor, Conn., 1998—. Cons. autism spectrum disorders Ctr. Children Spl. Needs, Glastonbury, Conn., 1996—. Contbr. articles to profl. jours. Adult com. chair Simsbury Summer Theater Youth, Simsbury, Conn., 2005—. Recipient Disting. Svc. award, Conn. Speech, Hearing & Lang. Assn., 1988. Mem.: South Windsor Edn. Assn., Conn. Speech/Hearing Lang. Assn. (chair continuing edn. com. 1984—88, Disting. Svc. award 1988), Am. Speech, Hearing & Lang. Assn., U. Vt. Mortar Bd., Alpha Delta Pi (corr. sec., social chmn. 1977—79, 2d Honors Dorothy Shaw Leadership award 1979). Avocations: reading, sports, gardening, music. Office: Orchard Hill Sch 350 Foster St South Windsor CT 06074

MULFORD, CLAY (ROSS CLAYTON MULFORD), think-tank executive, lawyer; b. Bethesda, Md., Mar. 13, 1956; s. Ross Leonard and Diane (Clayton) M.; m. Nancy Elizabeth Perot, June 6, 1987; children: Ross Clayton, Price Perot, Benjamin Fell. BA cum laude, Amherst Coll., 1978; MBA, JD, U. Va., 1982. Bar: Tex. 1982. From assoc. to ptnr. Hughes and Luce, LLP, Dallas, 1982—2004; ptnr. Jones Day, Dallas, 2004—07; COO Nat. Math & Sci. Initiative (NMSI), Dallas, 2007. Fellow Inst. Politics, vis. lectr. John F. Kennedy Sch. Govt., Harvard U., 1995; trustee Citizens Rsch. Found., 1994—; gen. counsel, sr. advisor Perot '92 Presdl. Campaign, Dallas, 1992; mem. nat. adv. com. Money, Politics and the Pub. Voice project LWV, 1995—; fellow Brit.-Am. Project Johns Hopkins Sch. Advanced Internat. Studies and the Royal Inst. Internat. Affairs, 1995. Contbr. articles to profl. jours. Dir. Dallas Zoo, 1990—, Episcopal Sch., Dallas, 1991—, Ctr. for Human Nutrition S.W. Med. Sch., U. Tex., 1993—, Baylor Hosp. Found., 1997—; gen. counsel Perot 96, 1996. Mem. ABA (spl. select com. Coalition for Justice 1993-94, adv. commn. on election law 1994-95, 99-2001, standing com. on election law 1995-99), State Bar Tex. Episcopalian. Office: National Math & Science Initiative (NMSI) 325 N St Paul St Ste 2900 Dallas TX 75201 Office Phone: 214-665-2548.*

MULFORD, DAVID CAMPBELL, finance company executive, former ambassador; b. Rockford, Ill., June 27, 1937; s. Robert Lewis Mulford and Theodora Henie Countryman; m. Jeannie Louise Simmons, Oct. 19, 1985; children: Robert Ian, Edward Maitland. BA cum laude in Econs., Lawrence U., 1959; postgraduate student, U. Cape Town, South Africa, 1960; MA in Polit. Sci., Boston U., 1962; PhD, Oxford U., 1966; LLD (hon.), Lawrence U., 1984. White House fellow US Dept. Treasury, Washington, 1965-66, under asst. sec. internat. affairs, 1984-89; dir. White Weld & Co., NYC and London, 1966-74; sr. investment adv. Saudi Arabian Monetary Agy., Riyadh, 1974-84; asst. sec. internat. affairs US Dept. Treasury, 1984-89, under sec. treasury internat. affairs Washington, 1989-92; vice chmn. CS First Boston, NYC, 1992—93; chmn. Credit Suisse First Boston, London, 1993-98, internat. chmn., 1998—2003; US amb. to India US Dept. State, New Delhi, 2004—09; vice-chmn. internat. Credit Suisse Group, NYC, 2009—. Author: Northern Rhodesia General Election, 1962, Zambia: The Politics of Independence, 1967. Trustee Lawrence U., 1986—. Decorated Legion d'Honneur, 1990; recipient Order of May Merit Pres. Argentina, 1993, Officers Cross of the Medal of Merit Pres. Poland, 1995; Rotary Internat. fellow Oxford U., U. Cape Town, 1961-62, Woodrow Wilson fellow Boston U., Oxford U., 1962, Ford Found. fellow St. Anthony's Coll., Oxford, 1963-65; named Disting. Alumni Boston U., 1992; Disting. scholar Ctr. Strategic and Internat. Studies, Washington, 1993—. Mem. Coun. Fgn. Rels., White House Fellows Assn., Met. Club, Washington. Republican. Office: Credit Suisse Group 11 Madison Ave New York NY 10010-3629*

MULFORD, RICHARD ALBERT, mechanical engineer, professional society administrator; b. Phila., Dec. 13, 1930; s. William Abernathy and Jeanne Ann (Roy) Mulford. BSME, U. Pa., 1952, MS in Mech. Engring., 1957; Diploma in Bus., Dartmouth Coll., 1985. Registered profl. engr., Pa. Engr. Phila. Elec. Co., 1952-64, sr. engr., 1964-67, project mgr., 1967-85, staff engr., 1985-91. Vol. Paoli Meml. Hosp., Pa., 1991—; donor Phila. Orch. Assn., 1980—; treas., donor Phila. Engring. Found., 1991—. Recipient Disting. Svc. award, Pa. Soc. Profl. Engrs., 1991, 1998, D. Robert Yarnall award (Outstanding Engring. Alumnus), U. Pa., 1981, Alumni award of merit, 1993, Presdl. award, Phila. sect. ASCE, 2002, Outstanding Svc. award, Del. Valley Engrs. Week Coun., 2003. Fellow: Engrs. Club Phila. (treas. 1953—, exec. dir. 1991—2007, George Washington medal 1988, Lifetime Achievement award 2007); mem.: NSPE, Union League Phila. (scholarship trustee 1963—), Racquet Club Phila. Republican. Achievements include patents in field. Avocations: classical music, antique cars, home and lawn maintenance. Home: 1231 Wisteria Dr Malvern PA 19355-9736 Home Phone: 610-644-1983; Office Phone: 215-985-5701. Business E-Mail: info@engrclub.org.

MULHADIONO, YOGA PRATOMO, petroleum geologist, consultant; b. Pekalongan, Indonesia, Dec. 21, 1941; s. Mulyono and Mulyatri Pringgo Prawiro; m. Anur Erawati Sutaji; children: Dick, Aria, Donan, Saras. M in Geology, ITB, Bandung, Indonesia, 1968. Field and wellside geologist Pertamina, Jakarta, Indonesia, 1968-72, sr. geologist P. Brandar, North Sumatra, 1972-78, chief geologist, 1978-82, exploration new venture Jarkarta, 1982-89; exploration mgr. Japex, Jarkarta, 1989-94; specialist group Pertamina, Jarkarta, 1994-96; pres. dir. PT Mineralyasa Perdana, 1997—; sec. Koperan Ganesha Patramadani. Contbr. articles to profl. jours. Mem. IPA, SPWLA, Soc. Profl. Engrs. Avocations: golf, swimming, travel, reading, writing. Office: PT Mineralyasa Perdana Jalan Akasia Rayd Blok I/13 Bekasi Jakarta Indonesia

MULHERN, MARK F., electric power company executive; b. 1960; Grad., St. Bonaventure U., 1982; grad. nuclear exec. program, MIT. CPA, cert. Mgmt. Acct., Internal Auditor. Acctg. positions Price Waterhouse, Syracuse, NY; CFO Hydra Co. Enterprises (subs. Niagara Mohawk); v.p., contr. Progress Energy Inc., 1996—97, v.p., treas., 1997—2000, v.p., strategic planning, 2000—03; sr. v.p., competitive comml. ops. Progress Ventures (subs. Progress Energy), 2003—05, pres., 2005—08; sr. v.p., fin. Progress Energy Inc., 2007—08, sr. v.p., CFO, 2008—. Bd. dir. Microcell Corp.; mem. fin. adv. com. Edison Elec. Inst. Served in a number of vol. and leadership roles St. Michaels Elementary Sch., Leadership NC, Planning Inst. Ctrl. NY. Office: Progress Energy Inc 410 South Willington St Raleigh NC 27601 Office Phone: 919-508-5400.*

MULHOLLAND, JASON CHRISTOPHER, lawyer; b. Doylestown, Pa., Sept. 25, 1971; s. John Robert Mulholland and Linda Lee Fogel; m. Holly Springer Wright, May 2, 1992; children: Colton James, Elyse Julianna. BS, Excelsior Coll., Albany, NY, 1995; JD, U. Fla., Gainesville, 1999. Bar: Fla. 1999, US Dist. Ct. (mid. dist.) Fla. 2000, US Dist. Ct. (no. dist.) Fla. 2000, US Dist. Ct. (so. dist.) Fla. 2000. Paralegal, law clk. Peter A. Robertson and Assocs., Gainesville, 1996—98; law clk., assoc. Strickland and Molhem, Tampa, Fla., 1998—2002; assoc. Swope Law Group, Tampa, 2002—03; pres. Mulholland Law, Tampa, 2003—. Contbr., fundraiser Fla. Lawyers Action Group, Tallahassee, 2004—, Endowment for Acad. Giving to Law and Edn., Tallahassee, 2005—; contbr. Voices for Children, Tampa, 2005—. Served with USN, 1990—95. Mem.: ABA (tort and ins. practice sect.), ATLA, Tampa Bay Trial Lawyers Assn. (bd. dirs., membership com. 2005—), Acad. Fla. Trial Lawyers (mem. ins. com.). Office: Mulholland Law Profl Assn 13902 North Dale Mabry Hwy Ste 163 Tampa FL 33618 Office Fax: 813-935-8402. Business E-Mail: esquire@tampabay.rr.com.

MULHOLLAND, SEAN, economics professor; s. Gary and Kathleen Mulholland. PhD, Clemson U., 2004. Asst. prof. economics Moravian Coll., Bethlehem, Pa., 2005—07, Mercer U., Macon, Ga., 2007—. Office: Mercer Univ 1400 Coleman Ave Macon GA 31207

MULINDER, AUSTEN, computer software company executive; arrived in USA, 1994; m. Sally Mulinder; 4 children. Degree in law, U. Nottingham; attended, INSEAD Bus. Sch., France, Stanford U., Calif. Joined ICL plc, UK, 1984, various leadership positions in sales, mktg., profl. services, devel. and customer svc., sr. v.p. retail systems, joined exec. mgmt. team, 1999, exec. v.p., pres., CEO North Am. bus. Dallas, 2000—01; pres., CEO Fujitsu Transaction Solutions, Inc., 2001—07; v.p. worldwide enterprise sales Microsoft Corp., Redmond, Wash., 2007—09, corp. v.p. comm. sector, 2009—. Past chmn. StoreNext Retail Technologies, LLC; co-exec. sponsor Microsoft World-Class Selling Program. Bd. mem. Am. Heart Assn., Vietnam Veterans Meml. Fund Corp. Coun. Mem.: Young President's Orgn. Office: Microsoft Corp One Microsoft Way Redmond WA 98052-6399*

MULKERN-KOLOSEY, SANDY KATHLEEN, college counselor, educator, realtor; d. Thomas Joseph and Elizabeth (Bjornson) Mulkern; m. Michael George Kolosey, July 15, 1972; 1 child, Michael Thomas Kolosey. AA, Coll. Marin, Kentfield, Calif., 1989; AA in Humanities, SRJ U., 2007, AA in Social Behaviour Scarce, 2007; AS in Dental Assisting with honors, Coll. Marin, Kentfield, Calif., 1989; BA in Clin. Psychology summa cum laude, San Francisco State U., 1991; MA in Counseling, Psychology, Edn., U. San Francisco, 1993, EdD in Orgn., Leadership and Mgmt., 2006. Cert. in pupil pers. svcs., psychol. svcs. Acad. advisor, counselor Santa Rosa (Calif.) Jr. Coll., 1992—. Ednl. cons., San Francisco Bay area, 1994; career coach and workshop facilitator, Sonoma County. Named Deans Highest Honour. Mem. AAUW, APA, Alumni Assn. U. San Francisco and San Francisco State U., Golden Key Nat. Honor Soc., N. Bay Assn. Realtors and Bay Area Real Estate Info. Sys., Psi Chi, Alpha Gamma Sigma, Phi Delta Kappa. Avocations: bicycling, reading, computers, travel, real estate investing. Home: PO Box 543 Valley Ford CA 94972 Personal E-mail: sandy.kolosey@gmail.com.

MULKEY, DANIEL K., research scientist; b. Albiqurque, Mar. 13, 1970; s. Marion K. Allen; m. Xinnian Chen, May 26, 2007. PhD, Wright State U, Dayton, Ohio, 2002. Postdoc. fellow U. Va., Charlottesville, 2003—07. Contbr. articles to profl. jours. NRSA grants, NIH, 2005—07. Mem.: Soc. Neurosci. Liberal. Home: 147 Davis Rd Storrs Mansfield CT 06268 Office: Univ Conn 75 N Eagleville Rd Storrs Mansfield CT 06269 Business E-Mail: daniel.mulkey@uconn.edu.

MULKEY, JACK CLARENDON, retired library director; b. Shreveport, La., Oct. 31, 1939; s. Jack Youmans and Hilda Lillian (Beatty) Mulkey; m. Mary Lynn Shepherd, Jan. 30, 1971; 1 child, Mary Clarendon. BA, Centenary Coll., 1961; postgrad. (Rotary scholar), U. Dijon, France, 1961-62, Duke U. Law Sch., 1962-63; MS, La. State U., 1969. Jr. exec. Lykes Bros. S.S. Co., 1964-66; asst. dir. admissions Centenary Coll. of La., 1966-67; head reference services and acquisitions Shreveport Pub. Library, 1968-71; dir. Green Gold Library System of N.W. La., 1971-73; mgmt. cons. Miss. Library Commn., 1973-74, asst. dir., 1974-76, dir., 1976-78, Jackson Met. Library System, 1978-85; assoc. dir. Ark. State Library, 1986-2000; State Librarian of Ark., 2000—05; ret., 2005. Adj. prof. U. So. Miss. Grad. Sch. Libr. Sci., 1979—; treas., bd. dirs. Southeastern Library Network (SOLINET), 1985-86; cons. in field; mem. White House Conf. Taskforce on Libraries and Info. Services, 1980—. Chmn. Miss. Govs. Conf. on Libraries, 1979; chmn. Miss. delegation White House Conf. on Libraries, 1979; hon. del. White House Conf. on Librs., 1991. Served with USAF, 1963-64. Mem. ALA (chmn. state libr. agy. sect. 1995-97), Southeastern Libr. Assn. (bd. dirs. 1994—), Miss. Libr. Assn. (pres. 1981-82), Ark. Libr. Assn. (exec. bd. dirs. 1994—), Chief Officers of State Libr. Agys., Phi Alpha Delta, Beta Phi Mu, Omicron Delta Kappa, Phi Kappa Phi. Episcopalian. Home: 1805 Martha Dr Little Rock AR 72212-3840 Office: 1 Capitol Mall Little Rock AR 72201-1049 Personal E-mail: jmulkey@webtv.net.

MULKEY, KIM, women's college basketball coach; b. Santa Ana, Calif., May 17, 1962; children: Makenzie, Kramer. B, La. Tech U., 1984. Asst. coach La. Tech U. Lady Techsters, 1985—96, assoc. head coach, 1996—2000; head coach Baylor U. Lady Bears, 2000—. Mem. women's nat. team USA Basketball, 1982—84. Co-author (with P. May): (autobiography) Won't Back Down, 2007. Recipient Gold medal, Pan Am. Games, 1983, Summer Olympic Games, 1984, James Corbett award, La., 1984; named Naismith Small Player of Yr., 1984, Nat. Coach of Yr., Real Sport Mag., 2000, Big 12 Coach of Yr., Dallas Morning News, 2001, Waco Tribune-Herald, 2001, Sr. Coll. Coach of Yr., Tex. Assn. Basketball Coaches, 2002, Coach of Yr., Big 12 Conf., 2005; named to Nat. HS Hall of Fame, 1985, La. HS Hall of Fame, 1986, La. Sports Writers Hall of Fame, 1990, La. Tech Athletics Hall of Fame, 1992, Women's Basketball Hall of Fame, 2000, Academic Hall of Fame, Coll. Sports Info. Directors America, 2003, Baylor Athletic Hall of Fame, 2007. Achievements include head coach of the NCAA Women's Final Four national championship winning University of Baylor Lady Bears, 2005. Office: Baylor Univ Athletics 1500 S University Parks Dr Waco TX 76706 Office Phone: 254-710-3947. Business E-Mail: kim_mulkey@baylor.edu.*

MULL, ROBERT W., filmmaker, curator; b. Great Bend, Kans., Mar. 8, 1953; s. Charles Laverne and Mary Anne Mull; m. Donna Lee Howell, May 24, 1976 (div. Jan. 1980). B in Gen. Studies, U. Kans., 1976; MA, Ea. Wash. U., 1982. Curator Yakima (Wash.) Valley Mus., 1981—85, Pacific Sci. Ctr., Seattle, 1985—88; ind. documentary filmmaker Wash., 1981—93; ind. writer Seattle, 1993—. Cons. Wash. Commn. for Humanities, Olympia, 1982—85; founder, officer Wash. State Folklife Coun., Olympia, 1983—87; mem. planning com. Wash. 1989 Centennial, Seattle, 1988—89. Author: The Lupus Kid and Other Stories, 2002; prodr.: (documentaries) When Court Adjourned, 1982 (PBS award, 1983, Sepia award (State of Wash. award) 1988), Something To Win the War, 1985 (TLC award, 1987). Grants writer Harbor Assn. Vols., Westport, Wash., 1996—2000; publicist Seattle Housing Authority, 1999—2003; bd. dirs. Internat. Cmty. Health Svcs., 2008—. Named Alumnus of Yr., Ea. Wash. U., 1996; grantee, Wash. Commn. for Humanities, 1981, Wash. Centennial Commn., 1988. Mem.: Internat. Cmty. Health Svcs. (bd. dir. 2008—), Olive Ridge Cmty. Coun., Ea. Wash. U. Alumni Assn., N.W. chpt. Lupus Found. (event chmn. 2002, bd. dirs. 2003—, pres. 2005—). Congregationalist. Avocations: travel, reading, volunteer work. Home: 1700 17th Ave #608 Seattle WA 98122

MULLA, DAVID JAMIL, physicist; b. Riverside, Calif., June 18, 1956; s. Mir S. and Lelia L. (Patterson) M. BS in Earth Sci., U. Calif., Riverside, 1979; MS in Agronomy, Purdue U., 1981, PhD in Agronomy, 1983. Asst. prof. dept. crop and soil sci. Wash. State U., Pullman, 1983-88, assoc. prof. dept. crop and soil sci., 1988-93, prof. dept. crop and soil sci., 1993-95; W.E. Larson prof. soil and water resources U. Minn., St. Paul, 1995—. Panel mem. USDA-CSRS-NRI Water Resources Assessment Program, Washington, 1994; cons. Soil TEQ, Inc., Waconia, Minn., 1986-88. Author: (chpt.) Water, Fungi and Plants, 1986, Geochemical Processes at Mineral Surfaces, 1986, Irrigation of Agricultural Crops, 1989, Dryland Agriculture: Strategies for Sustainability, 1990, Field-Scale Solute & Water Transport, 1990, Automated Agriculture for 21st Century, 1991. NSF fellow, 1980; Regents scholar U. Calif., 1974; recipient Faculty Rsch. award Wash. State U., 1991. NSF fellow, 1980; Regents scholar U. Calif., 1974. Mem. Soil Sci. Soc. Am., Phi Beta Kappa, Gamma Sigma Delta, Sigma Xi. Achievements include development of computer program involving geostatistics and geographical information systems that allows tractors to spread fertilizers and pesticides at varying rates in farmers fields; research on computer modeling of water and solute movement in the vadose zone, spatial variability using stochastic and geostatistical methods. Office: U Minn Dept Soil Water and Climate 1991 Upper Buford Cir Saint Paul MN 55108-0010

MULLA, ZUBER, epidemiologist; b. Gujarat, India; BA, U. Ariz., Tucson, 1991; MSPH, U. South Fla., 1994, PhD, 2001. Epidemiologist Fla. Assn. of Pediatric Tumor Programs, Tampa, Fla., 1994—97; regional epidemiologist Fla. Dept. of Health, Orlando, Fla., 1998—2002; asst. prof. epidemiology U. Tex.-Houston Sch. Pub. Health, El Paso, Tex., 2002—. Dean's alumni adv. bd. U. South Fla. Coll. Pub. Health, Tampa, Fla., 1995—98. Contbr. articles to profl. jours., chpt. to book. Mem.: Am. Coll. Epidemiology, Delta Omega. Achievements include investigation of anthrax outbreak in Florida in 2001; research in treatment of invasive group A streptococcal infections. Office: U Tex Sch Pub Health 1100 N Stanton St Suite 110 El Paso TX 79902 E-mail: zmulla@sph.uth.tmc.edu.

MULLALLY, MEGAN, actress; b. LA, Nov. 12, 1958; d. Carter and Martha Mullally; m. Michael A. Katcher, 1992 (div. 1996); m. Nick Offerman, Sept. 20, 2003. Student, Northwestern U. Actor: (TV films) Rainbow Drive, 1990, Winchell, 1998, Everything Put Together, 2000, Lifetime, The Pact, 2002; (TV series) My Life and Times, 1991, Ellen Burstyn Show, 1986, Fish Police, 1992, Rachel Gunn, RN, 1992, Will and Grace, 1998—2006 (Emmy Award Supporting Actress in a Comedy, 2000, Outstanding Comedy Series award, 2000, Am. Comedy Award, 2001, Outstanding Female Actor Award, 2001, Screen Actors Guild award Oustanding Actress in a Comedy Series, 2001, 2002, 2003, Emmy award for Outstanding Supporting Actress in a Comedy Series, 2006), In the Motherhood, 2009; (Broadway plays) Grease, 1994, How to Succeed in Business Without Really Trying, 1995—96, Young Frankenstein, 2008; host (talk show) Megan Mullally Show, 2006—07; actor: (films) Once Bitten, 1985, Last Resort, 1986, About Last Night, 1986, Anywhere But Here, 1999, Best Man in Grass Creek, 1999, Everything Put Together, 2000, Monkey Bone, 2001, Stealing Harvard, 2002; actor, actor: (films) Speaking of Sex, 2001, (voice) Teacher's Pet, 2004, Rebound, 2005, (voice) Bee Movie, 2007, (guest appearance): (TV series) Murder, She Wrote, 1988, China Beach, 1989, Wings, 1990, Herman's Head, 1991, Seinfeld, 1993, Frasier, 1997, Mad About You, 1997, Caroline in the City, 1997, Just Shoot Me!, 1998, 3rd Rock from the Sun, 2000; (TV series, voice) King of the Hill, 2002. Office: The Gersh Agency PO Box 5617 Beverly Hills CA 90210*

MULLANE, JOHN FRANCIS, pharmaceutical executive; b. NYC, Mar. 10, 1937; s. John Gerald and Rita Ann (Hoben) Mullane; m. Ruth Ann Cecka, Nov. 17, 1962; children: Rosemarie, Michael, Kathleen, Therese, Thomas. MD, SUNY Med. Ctr., 1963; PhD, SUNY, 1968; JD, Fordham U., 1977. Bar: NY 1978, DC 1979. Assoc. med. dir. Ayerst Labs. div. Am. Home Products Corp., NYC, 1973-75, dir. clin. research, 1975-76, v.p. clin., 1977, v.p. sci., 1978-82, sr. v.p., 1982, exec. v.p., 1983-88; pres. Mullane Health Care Cons., NYC and Sarasota, Fla., 1989—; dir. drug devel. DuPont Med. Products, Wilmington, Del., 1990; sr. v.p. DuPont-Merck, Wilmington, 1991-94; exec. v.p. Amylin Pharms., 1994-96. Contbr. articles to profl. jours. Served to lt. col. US Army, 1970-73 Recipient Upjohn Achievement award, 1970; NY Heart Assn. Crawford-Maynard fellow, 1966-68 Fellow Am. Coll. Clin. Pharmacology; mem. ABA, Am. Soc. Clin. Pharmacology and Therapeutics, Am. Assn. Study of Liver Diseases, Misty Creek Country Club (pres. 2004-2005). Roman Catholic. Achievements include development of major drugs including Inderal, Premarin, Lodine, Coumadin, Cozaar. Avocation: golf. Home and Office: 9047 Misty Creek Dr Sarasota FL 34241-9542 E-mail: johnmullane9047@comcast.net.

MULLANEY, BETH JO, school librarian; d. Robert John and Miriam A. Mullaney. BA, Coll. Arts and Sci., U. Pittsburgh, 1979; MLS, Sch. Libr. and Info. Sci., U. Pittsburgh, 1980, PhD, 1995. Info. sys. libr. Cheyney U. Pa., 1997—; dir. Green Tree Pub. Libr., Pa., 1996—97. Mem. Friends Norristown Pub. Libr., Pa., 1998—2008. Fellow: Oxford Roundtable; mem.: Libr. and Info. Tech. Assn., Assn. Coll. and Rsch. Libraries, Am. Libr. Assn., Phi Eta Sigma, Beta Phi Mu. Office: Cheyney Univ PA 1837 Univ Cir Cheyney PA 19319-0200

MULLANEY, CRAIG MICHAEL, writer; b. RI, 1978; s. Ellen Mullaney; m. Meena Seshamani, May 7, 2005. Grad., US Mil. Acad., West Point, NY, 2000; MA in Economics & Social Hist., Oxford U., Eng. Commd. US Army, 2000, infantry rifle platoon leader 10th Mountain Divsn. Afghanistan, 2003—04, asst. ops. officer 3rd Inf. Rgt. Arlington, Va., exchange officer to history faculty, US Naval Acad. Annapolis, Md., ret.; nat. security adv. Barack Obama Presdl. Campaign, 2008; chief of staff Dept. Def. Review Team, 2008—09. Author: The Unforgiving Minute: A Soldier's Education, 2009. Decorated Bronze Star, Army Commendation medal with "V" Device, Combat Infantryman's Badge, Ranger Tab, Parachutist Badge; recipient Rhodes scholarship. Office: c/o Liz Calamari Penguin Group USA Inc 375 Hudson St New York NY 10014 Office Phone: 212-366-2857.*

MULLANEY, WILLIAM J., insurance company executive; BA, Univ. Pitts.; MBA, Pace Univ. CLU Am. Coll. Mgmt. positions Met Life Inc., 1982—90, v.p., 1990—2002, v.p. group nat. accounts. claim ops., 1992—94, v.p. nat. accounts, 1994—96, v.p. Gen. Motors account, 1996—98, v.p. voluntary benefits, 1998—2002, sr. v.p. claims & customer svc., auto & home, 2002—04, pres. auto & home, 2004—07, pres. inst. bus. segment, 2007—. Bd. dir. Hyatt Legal Plans, Ins. Info. Inst., Ins. Inst. Highway Safety. Bd. dir. Greater Providence C.of C. Office: Met Life Inc 200 Park Ave New York NY 10166*

MULLANY, KEVIN FERGUS, music educator, director; b. NYC, June 7, 1968; s. Fergus and Elaine (Sigle); 1 child, Meghan L. BA in English, Queens Coll., 1997; MA in Music Edn., CUNY, 2004. Cert. music, English tchr. N.Y. Tchr. Forest Hills (N.Y.) Montessori Sch., 1992-97, Harbor Conservatory, NYC, 1994-96; music dir. Garden Sch., Jackson Heights, NY, 1997—98; choral dir. Flushing HS, Queens, NY, 1999—. Author: (novel) Complete Literary Works, 2004, composer: Complete Musical Works, 2005, conductor Avery Fisher Hall Lincoln Ctr., 2008, condr. Avery Fisher Lincoln Centre. Choir dir., organist St. Lucy-St. Patrick Ch., Bklyn., 1995—2001; children's choir dir. St. John Evangelist Ch., Bklyn., 1996-98. Writing award Queens Coll., 1994, 96, Silver award level IV work with chorus NY State Sch. Music Assn., 2006; hon. mention Composers Guild's Music Composition Comp., 2005, Composers Guilds Annual Choral Composition Contest, First Place winner, Composer Guild's Annual Choral Composition Contest, 2008, Hon. mention, 2008, Choral Recital Avery Fisher Lincoln Ctr., NY, 2008. Mem. Tri-M Music Honor Soc., Music Educators Nat. Conf., Composers Guild, Am. Choral Dirs. Assn., Nat. Assn. Composers (life). Home: 210-50 41 Ave Apt 4H Bayside NY 11361 Home Phone: 718-423-2532; Office Phone: 718-888-7500 ext. 155. Personal E-mail: mullanykevin@aol.com. Business E-Mail: kmullan@schools.nyc.gov.

MULLARE, T(HOMAS) KENWOOD, JR., lawyer; b. Milton, Mass., Jan. 19, 1939; s. Thomas Kenwood and Catherine Marie (Leonard); m. Joan Marie O'Donnell, May 27, 1967; children: Jennifer M. Cedrone, Tracy K. Mullare, Jill M. Hegarty, Joyce M. Mullare AB, Holy Cross Coll., 1961; LLB, Boston Coll., 1964. Bar: Mass. 1964. Atty. New Eng. Electric Sys., 1964—69; v.p., gen. counsel, sec. AVX Corp., NYC, 1970—73; v.p., gen. counsel, clk. Tyco Labs., Inc., Exeter, NH, 1974—77; v.p., gen. counsel, sec. SCA Svcs., Inc., Boston, 1978—83; spl. counsel Houghton Mifflin Co., Boston, 1984—85, v.p., dir. bus. software divsn., 1985—92; pres. North River Capital Co., Inc., Norwell, Mass., 1990—; gen. counsel, sec. Aztec Tech. Partners, Inc., Braintree, Mass., 1999—2002; prin., owner Law Office T. Kenwood Mullare, Norwell, 2002—. Mem. regional adv. bd. Mass. Dept. Mental Retardation, 1994—97; pres. Ch. Hillers, Norwell, 1983—84; bd. dirs. Barque Hill Assn., Norwell, 1980—84, pres., 1981—83; bd. dirs. South Shore Assn. for Retarded Citizens, Weymouth, Mass., 1993—98, chmn., 1995—97; bd. dirs. Friendship Home, Inc., Norwell, 1997—, New Eng. Village, Inc., Pembroke, Mass., 2007—. Mem.: Assn. Corp. Counsel, Boston Bar Assn. Home: 31 Barque Hill Dr Norwell MA 02061-2815

MULLARKEY, MARY J., state supreme court chief justice; b. New London, Wis., Sept. 28, 1943; d. John Clifford and Isabelle A. (Steffes) M.; m. Thomas E. Korson, July 24, 1971; 1 child, Andrew Steffes Korson. BA, St. Norbert Coll., 1965, LLD (hon.), 1989; LLB, Harvard U., 1968. Bar: Wis. 1968, Colo. 1974. Atty.-advisor U.S. Dept. Interior, Washington, 1968-73; asst. regional atty. EEOC, Denver, 1973-75; 1st atty. gen. Colo. Dept. Law, Denver, 1975-79, solicitor gen., 1979-82; legal advisor to Gov. Lamm State of Colo., Denver, 1982-85; ptnr. Mullarkey & Seymour, Denver, 1985-87; justice Colo. Supreme Ct., Denver, 1987—, chief justice, 1998—. Fellow: Colo. Bar Found., ABA Found.; mem.: ABA, Denver Bar Assn. (Jud. Excellence award 2003), Colo. Women's Bar Assn. (Mary Lathrop award 2002), Colo. Bar Assn., Thompson G. Marsh Inn of Ct. (pres. 1993—94). Office: Supreme Ct Colo Jud Bldg 2 E 14th Ave Denver CO 80203-2115*

MULLEN, ANTHONY J., special education educator; b. Bronx, NY, May 1960; m. Susan Mullen; 3 children. B in Criminal Justice, LI U., 1990; MS in Elem. Edn. and Spl. Edn., Mercy Coll., 2002. Former narcotics detective NYC Police Dept.; spl. edn. tchr. No. Westchester Bd. Cooperative Ednl. Svcs., Yorktown Heights, NY, 2002, ARCH Sch., Greenwich, Conn., 2002—. Named Nat. Tchr. of Yr., Coun. Chief State Sch. Officers, 2009. Office: Greenwich HS ARCH Sch 10 Hillside Rd Greenwich CT 06830*

MULLEN, CHARLES FREDERICK, health educator; b. Washington, June 14, 1938; s. DeWitt Cliffton and Annabelle (Fischer) M.; m. Rita Mae Keintz, Oct. 23, 1996; children from a previous marriage: Henry John, Elizabeth Mary. BA, U. Va., 1962; BS, New England Coll. Optometry, 1969, OD, 1970; D of Ocular Sci., So. Coll. Optometry, 1994. Dir. clinics New Eng. Coll. Optometry, Boston, 1970-76; exec. dir. The Eye Inst., Pa. Coll. Optometry, Phila., 1976-90; dir. optometry svc. Dept. VA, Washington, 1990-96; pres. Ill. Coll. Optometry, Chgo., 1996—2002. Mem. Dept. VA Spl. Subcom. Eye Care, Washington, 1990-96; observer Eye Coun., Nat. Eye Inst., Bethesda, Md., 1990-96; bd. dirs. New Eng. Eye Inst. Contbr. articles to profl. jours. Host parent Overbrook Sch. Blind, Phila., 1985-86; vol. Big. Bros., West Chester, Pa., 1988-89; trustee New England Coll. Optometry; bd. dirs. Clavary, Washington, 1990-92. Lt. (j.g.) USNR. Mem. Am. Acad. Optometry, Am. Optometric Assn., Nat. Assn. VA Ops., Pa. Coll. Optometry (trustee 2003-2007). Episcopalian. Home: 401 Shady Ave Apt D307 Pittsburgh PA 15206 E-mail: cfmalex@aol.com.

MULLEN, DANIEL ROBERT, finance company executive; b. Swedesboro, NJ, Apr. 17, 1941; s. Harold Legrand and Gladys (DeVault) M.; m. Elizabeth A. Willers, Dec. 17, 1977; children: William H., Jonathan O. BS in Fin., Ariz. State U., 1966, postgrad., 1966-67. Appraiser Ariz. Dept. Revenue, 1966—68; financial analyst Amerco, 1968—70, treas., 1970—82; pres., dir. Continental Leasing Co., 1980—; v.p. Southwest Pipe and Supply Co., 1982; treas. Talley Industries, Inc., 1982—93, v.p., 1993—98; COO Friendship Publs., 1998—99. Bd. dirs. C. Myers Corp., 2000-09, Amerco Real Estate, U-Haul Internat. Oxford Life Ins. Co. Del. Ariz. Presdl. Dem. Conv., 1972; bd. dirs. Big Sisters of Ariz., 1975, Found. for Blind Children, 1984-90, Phoenix Little Theatre, 1985-91, Kachina Country Day Sch., 1988-94, New Way Sch., 1994-2000, Interfaith Coop. Ministries, 2003-09, Arz. State U. Alumni Assn., 2009-; With U.S. Army, 1959-62. Ariz. Soc. CPAs grantee, 1964-65 Mem. Fin. Execs. Internat. Home: 3627 E Medlock Dr Phoenix AZ 85018-1505 Office Phone: 602-263-6123.

MULLEN, DEBORAH W., elementary school educator; b. Muskogee, Okla., Aug. 9, 1955; d. William Hoile and Helen Lorene Withrow; m. Jon David Withrow, May 9, 1986; children: Alisa Suzanne, Jonny Buck. M, Northeastern State U., Tahlequah, Okla., 1985. Tchr. Inola Pub. Schs., Okla., 1983—; prof. Rogers State U., Claremore, 2003—06. Dept. head Pub. Edn., Inola, 1992—2006. Democrat. Baptist. Avocations: ranching, horseback riding, travel. Home: 8729 S 427 Inola OK 74036 Office: Inola Public School 801 E Commercial Inola OK 74036 Office Fax: 918-543-2345. Personal E-mail: dmullen@inola.k12.ok.us.

MULLEN, EDWARD JOHN, JR., Spanish language educator; b. Hackensack, NJ, July 12, 1942; s. Edward J. and Elsie (Powell) Mullen; m. Helen Cloe Braley, Apr. 2, 1971; children: Kathleen, Julie Ann. BA, W.Va. Wesleyan Coll., 1964; MA, Northwestern U., 1965, PhD, 1968. Asst. prof. modern langs. Purdue U., West Lafayette, Ind., 1967-71; assoc. prof. Spanish U. Mo., Columbia, 1971-78, prof. Spanish, 1978—. Author: La Revista Contemporaneos, 1972, Carlos Pellicer, 1977, Langston Hughes in the Hispanic World and Haiti, 1977, The Life and Poems of Cuban Slave: Juan Francisco Manzano 1797-1854, 1981, Critical Essays on Langston Hughes, 1986, Sendas Literarias: Hispanoamerica, 1988, El Cuento Hispanico, 1980, 2007, Afro-Cuban Literature: Critical Junctures, 1998; editor: The Harlem Group of Negro Writers (Melvin B. Tolson), 2001; co-editor: Afro-Hispanic Rev., 1987—2005. Recipient diploma de honor, Inst. de Cultura Hispanica, 1964; grantee, Am. Coun. Learned Socs., 1979; fellow, Northwestern U., 1965—67; Woodrow Wilson fellow, 1964—65, Rsch. grantee, U. Mo., 1972, 1976. Mem.: MLA, Assn. Depts. Fgn. Langs. (pres. 1989—91), Am. Tchrs. Spanish and Protuguese. Home: 207 Edgewood Ave Columbia MO 65203-3413 Office: U Mo Dept Romance Langs 143 Arts And Sci Bldg Columbia MO 65211-0001 Office Phone: 573-882-5041. Business E-Mail: mullene@missouri.edu.

MULLEN, EILEEN ANNE, human resources executive; b. Phila., Feb. 14, 1943; d. Joseph Gregory and Helen Rita (Kane) M.; m. William John Raschiatore (dec.). BS in English, St. Joseph's U., 1967; MA in English, Villanova U., 1978. Cert. tchr., Pa. Tchr. St. Anastasia Sch., Newtown Square, 1960-67, West Cath. Girls H.S., 1967-74; mgr. staff tng. and devel. ASTM, Phila., 1974-96, dir. human resources, 1996—. Instr. lit., speech and communications Widener U., Chester, Pa. and Wilmington, Del. Contbg. author articles on comms. tng. programs; contbr. articles to profl. jours. Mem. ASTD (pres. Phila./Del. Valley chpt. 1980-81, Outstanding Leadership as Pres. award 1981), Soc. for Human Resource Mgmt. Democrat. Roman Catholic. Office: ASTM 100 Barr Harbor Dr West Conshohocken PA 19428-0700 Home Phone: 610-240-9090; Office Phone: 610-832-9766. Business E-Mail: emullen@astm.org.

MULLEN, GRAHAM CALDER, federal judge; b. 1940; BA, Duke U., 1962, JD, 1969. Bar: NC 1969. Ptnr. Mullen, Holland, Cooper, Morrow, Wilder & Sumner, 1969-90; judge US Dist. Ct. (We. Dist.) NC, Charlotte, 1990—98, chief judge, 1998—2005, sr. judge, 2005—. Lt. USN, 1962—66. Mem.: Mecklenburg County Bar Assn., NC Bar Assn. (bd. gov. 1983—88). Office: US Courthouse 401 W Trade St Rm 230 Charlotte NC 28202-1619 Office Phone: 704-350-7450. Business E-Mail: graham_mullen@ncwd.uscourts.gov.

MULLEN, JAMES C., biotechnology company executive; b. 1959; m. Justine Mullen; 4 children. BS in Chem. Engring., Rensselaer Polytech. Inst., 1980; MBA, Villanova U., 1984. Various positions SmithKline Beckman Corp. (now GlaxoSmithKline plc), 1984—88; dir. facilities engring. Biogen, Inc., 1989—92, v.p. ops., 1992—96, v.p. internat., 1996—99, CEO, pres., 2000—03, chmn. bd., 2002—03; pres., CEO Biogen Idec Inc., 2003—. Bd. trustees Rensselaer Polytech. Inst.; bd. dirs. Biotech. Industry Orgn., Biomed. Scis. Careers Program, Pharmaceuticals Rsch. and Manufacturers Am., PerkinElmer, Inc., 2004—. Co-chair capital campaign steering com. Cambridge Family and Children's Svc. Responsible for the manufacturing and successful launch of AVONEX (Interferon beta-la), a world leading therapy for relapsing forms of multiple sclerosis. Office: Biogen Idec Inc 14 Cambridge Ctr Cambridge MA 02142*

MULLEN, MAUREEN ANN, social worker; b. Chgo., Mar. 22, 1949; d. Robert Vincent and Mary Geraldine M. BA, U. Ill., 1971; MEd, Coll. of William and Mary, 1974; MSW, Univ. Ill., 1990; postgrad., U. Chgo., 1985-86. Programmer Computer Task Group, NYC, 1980-81; analyst, programmer Guy Carpenter, NYC, 1981-82; analyst C.N.A. Ins., Chgo., 1982-84; analyst, programmer Lakeshore Nat. Bank, Chgo., 1984-85; sales support Sterling Software, Chgo., 1986; owner Mullen Designs, Chgo., 1987; dir. of social svcs. Vista Health, Fayetteville, Ark., 2002—03; employee assistance counselor Ark. Employee Assistance Program, Fayetteville, 2003—06. Prodr., host (TV show) Ozarks Live!, 2003—06. Vol. Samaritans Hotline, Chgo., 1986; adv. bd. Lakeview Mental Health Ctr., Chgo., 1986; active Chgo. Coun. on Fgn. Rels., 1986—87; chmn. fundraiser Habitat for Humanity, 1987; vol. Manic Depressive and Depressive Assn. and Nat. Alliance for Rsch. into Schizophrenia and Depression, 1988, Wilmette Sch. Bd. Caucus, 1997, endowment fund com., 1996—97; vol. Chgo. Bot. Garden, 1999; spkrs. chmn. Fayetteville Freedom Festival, 2003; nominating com. ACLU, 2005—06; vol. Thomas Hynes campaign, Chgo., 1987, New Trier Dem. Orgn., 2000; alderman candidate, 2004; bd. dirs. ACLU N.W. Ark., 2005—06, N.W. Ark. Mental Health Assn., 2002—04, chmn. sch. libr. book project, 2002, 2003; bd. dirs. Cmty. Access TV, Fayetteville, 2003—. Recipient Fat Cat award, Cmty. Access TV, Fayetteville, 2003—05; Ill. State scholar, 1971. Mem.: ACLU (bd. dirs. NW Ark. chpt. 2005—06), NOW, Nature Conservancy, Sierra Club, Dem. Nat. Com., So. Poverty Law Ctr. Avocations: painting, poetry, backpacking, photography, acting. Home: 11 Edinboro Ter Newtonville MA 02460-1303 Office Phone: 617-678-3773. Personal E-mail: momoses2002@yahoo.com.

MULLEN, MIKE (MICHAEL GLENN MULLEN), Chairman of the Joint Chiefs of Staff; b. L.A., Oct. 4, 1946; m. Deborah Morgan, 1969; children: John, Michael. Grad., US Naval Acad., 1968; MSc in Ops. Rsch., Naval Postgraduate Sch., 1985. Enlisted USN, 1968, advanced through grades to adm., 2003; stationed on USS Collett, USS Blandy; comdr. USS Noxubee, 1973-75; company officer, exec. asst. U.S. Naval Acad., 1975-78; chief engr. USS Fox, 1978-80; exec. officer USS Sterett, 1981-83; comdr. USS Goldsborough, 1985-87; dir. divsn. officer course Surface Warfare Officer's Sch., 1987-89; staff asst. for navy programs Office of the Sec. Defense, 1989-91; comdr. USS Yorktown, 1992-94; from dir. surface officer distribution divsn. to dep. dir. Bureau of Naval Personnel, 1994-96; comdr. Cruiser-Destroyer Group 2, 1996-98; dir. surface warfare divsn. Office of Chief of Naval Ops., 1998—2000; comdr. SECOND fleet/ Striking Fleet Atlantic, 2000—01; dep. chief naval ops., resources, requirements & assessments USN, 2001—03, vice chief naval ops., 2003—04, chief naval ops. Washington, 2005—07; chmn. Joint Chiefs of Staff, US Dept. Def., Washington, 2007—; comdr. US Naval Forces Europe, Naples, Italy, 2004—05, Regional Command South, Naples, Italy, 2004—05. Decorated Def. Superior Svc. medal, Legion of Merit (6), Def. Disting. Svc. medal, Navy & Marine Corps Commendation medal, Navy & Marine Corps Achievement medal, Navy Disting. Svc. medal, Meritorious Svc. medal, Navy Expeditionary medal, Nat. Def. Svc. medal (3), Armed Forces Expeditionary medal, Vietnam Svc. medal, Global War on Terrorism Svc. medal, Humanitarian Svc. medal (2), Republic of Vietnam Gallantry Cross Unit Citation medal, Joint Chiefs of Staff Identification Badge, Navy Surface Warfare Badge, Navy Unit Commendation Ribbon, Navy Meritorious Unit Commendation Ribbon, Navy "E" Ribbon, Navy Overseas Svc. Ribbon (4), Navy Sea Svc. Deployment Ribbon (2), Republic of Vietnam Civil Action Unit Citation Ribbon; recipient Vice Adm. James Bond Stockdale award for Leadership, USN, 1987, Gold medal, The Union League Phila., 2008. Office: Chmn Joint Chiefs US Dept Def Pentagon Rm 2E676 Washington DC 20318*

MULLEN, ROBERT W., construction executive; BS, MS, NJ Inst. Tech., Newark. Pres., CEO Sordoni Skanska Constrn. Co.; various positions including corp. exec. v.p., pres. Skanska Sci. and Tech. divsn. and COO NE, mid-Atlantic and PR ops. Skanska USA Bldg. (formerly Sordoni Skanska Constrn. Co.); CEO Structure Tone, NYC, 2005—. Office: Structure Tone 770 Broadway New York NY 10003 Office Phone: 212-481-6100. E-mail: NYInfo@structuretone.com.

MULLEN, ROD, nonprofit organization executive; b. Puyallup, Wash., Aug. 2, 1943; s. Charles Rodney and Grace Violet (Fritsch) M.; m. Lois Fern Tobiska, May 3, 1963 (div. Jan. 1977); children: Cristina, Charles, Moneka; m. Naya Arbiter, Oct. 17, 1977; 1 child: Angelo. Student, U. Idaho, Moscow, 1961—63; AB in Polit. Sci., U. Calif., Berkeley, 1966; postgrad., San Francisco Art Inst., 1968. Dir. Oakland (Calif.) facility Synanon Found., Inc., 1971-72, dir. San Francisco facility, 1972-73, dir. Tomales Bay (Calif.) facility, 1976-78, dir. Synanon edn. programs, 1973-76; treatment dir. nat. programs Vision Quest, Inc., Tucson, 1981-82; dir. resources and devel. Amity, Inc., Tucson, 1982-84, exec. dir., 1984-95; founder, pres., CEO, Amity Found., Porterville, Calif., 1995—. Mem. Nat. Adv. Com. Substance Abuse Prevention, 1990-96; adv. bd. Ctr. Therapeutic Cmty. Rsch., Nat. Devel. and Rsch. Insts., NYC, 1991-2002; cons. Calif. Office Criminal Justice Planning, Sacramento, 1993; prin. investigator program Nat. Inst. on Drug Abuse, 1990-93; pres. Calif. Therapeutic Com., 2004-06; editl. adv. bd. Offender Substance Abuse Report, 2000-2004; bd. dirs. Amity Found., Calif., 1995-, Amity Works Found., Ariz., 2006-. Dir.: (documentaries) Prodigal Daughters, 2002, TC Pioneers, 2003, Essential Elements of the Therapeutic Community, 2005, Improving TC Encounter Groups, 2006, History of Therapeutic Communities in Corrections, 2006, Tell Me About It, 2008; contbr. chapters to books, articles to profl. jours. Mem.: Calif. Therapetic C. (pes. 2004—06), Therapeutic Coms. of Am. (treas. 2006—08), Am. Correctional Assn. Achievements include development of in-prison therapeutic community programs for addicted offenders and violent offenders which demonstrated significant reductions in recidivism to drug abuse, violence and other criminal activities; co-development and implementation of a comprehensive holistic curriculum for therapeutic communities; research in holistic addiction treatment. Avocations: hiking, photography, videography. Office: Amity Found 120 S Houghton Rd Ste 138-321 Tucson AZ 85748-2155 Office Phone: 520-749-7178. Business E-Mail: rmullen@amityfdn.org.

MULLEN, TERRI ANN, retired special education educator; b. St. Louis, Apr. 01; d. William Earl and Sophia Kinniff; m. Thomas Patrick Mullen; children: David, Mark, Debi. BS in Edn., S.E. Mo. State U.; M in Sch. Adminstrn., Calif. State U., 1978, M in Spl. Edn., 1981; EdD in Institutional Mgmt., Pepperdine U., 1985. Cert. spl. edn., std. sec., std. elem., adminstrv. svc. K-12, cmty. coll. instr. Tchr. Irvine (Calif.) Unified Sch. Dist., 1972-84; lectr., spl. edn. Calif. State U., Fullerton, 1989-90; asst. prin. Moreno Valley (Calif.) Unified Sch. Dist., 1984-85; adminstr. of spl. svcs. Centralia Sch. Dist., Buena Park, Calif., 1984-89; elem. prin. Capistrano Unified Sch. Dist., San Juan Capistrano, 1989-93; spl. edn. tchr., dept. chair Moreno Valley (Calif.) Unified Sch. Dist., 1993—. Chair, cmty. staff ednl. planning com. Santiago Elem. Sch., Irvine Unified Sch. Dist., 1981; dir., staff devel. for spl. programs pers. Centralia Sch. Dist., Buena Park, 1984-89; workshop presenter Assn. of Calif. Sch. Adminstrs. Conf., San Francisco, 1983. Author: Resource Book of Classroom Interventions for the Collaborative Teaching Model, 1994, Tips of the Trade for the Classroom Aide, 1984; contbr. articles to profl. jours. Adv. bd. for sp. edn. Calif. State U. Fullerton, 1988-89. Recipient Cmty. Svc. award Disneyland, 1992, 93; named Outstanding Educator of Yr. Rotary Club, 1983. Mem. Coun. for Exceptional Children, Kappa Delta Pi, Phi Kappa Phi. Avocations: roller skating, fashion design, interior design, computer applications, writing. Personal E-mail: tmullen@pacbell.net.

MULLEN, WILLIAM JOSEPH, III, retired career army officer; b. Plattsburg, NY, Dec. 26, 1937; s. William Joseph Jr. and Georgia (Cook) M.; m. Norma Sturgeon, Aug. 6, 1962; 1 child, William Joseph IV. BS, U.S. Mil. Acad., West Point, NY, 1959; MS in Internat. Affairs, George Washington U., Washington, 1971. Commd. 2d lt. U.S. Army, 1959, advanced through grades to brig. gen., 1987; various assignments in U.S., Vietnam, Korea, Panama, Germany, Saudi Arabia, 1959-92; mem. staff, faculty U.S. Mil. Acad., West Point, 1967-70; comdr. 1st Brigade, 1st Inf. Div., Ft. Riley, Kans., 1983-86; asst. div. comdr. 5th Inf. Div., Ft.

Polk, La., 1986-87; comdg. gen. U.S. Army Combined Arms Tng. Activity, Ft. Leavenworth, Kans., 1987-89, 1st Inf. Div. (Forward), Germany, 1989-91; dep. dir. ops. J3 Forces Command, Ft. McPherson, Ga., 1991-92; sr. mgr. mil. tng. and analysis sys. BDM Fed., Inc., Monterey, Calif., 1992-98; sr. program mgr. tng. mgmt. sys. Northrop Grumman Mission Sys., Monterey, 1998—2004; ret., 2004; cons. Army Operations and Tng., 2004—08. Co-author: Changing an Army, An Oral History of Gen. W.E. DePuy, 1979; contbr. articles, book revs. to Mil. Rev. Decorated D.S.C., D.S.M. Mem. Assn. U.S. Army, Assn. Grads. U.S. Mil. Acad. (bd. dir. West Point Soc. of Monterey Peninsula 2005-08), Soc. 1st Div. (chpt. officer 1968, assoc. 1989-93, trustee found. 1989-93, bd. dir.), Legion of Valor (bd. dir. 2005-08), Nat. Infantry Assn. (Order of St. Maurice). Avocations: sports, reading, writing. *When in doubt, I have always found direction from the guidance explicit in the 1st Infantry Division's motto, "Duty First!".*

MULLENDORE, WALTER EDWARD, retired economist; b. Harrah, Okla., Apr. 22, 1940; s. Newton and Ida Minnie (Lohmann) M.; m. Edra Janell Havenstrite, July 4, 1963; children: Matthew Edward, Karen Kay, Mark Andrew. BS, Okla. State U., 1961, MS, 1963; PhD in Econs., Iowa State U., 1968. Grad. asst. Okla. State U., 1961-63; instr. Iowa State U., 1965-67; mem. faculty dept. econs. U. Tex., Arlington, 1968—2002, prof., 1975—2002, dean Coll. of Bus., 1980—93; ret., 2002. Contbr. articles to profl. jours. Served with U.S. Army, 1963-65. Mem. Mo. Valley Econ. Assn. (v.p. 1980-81, pres. 1982-83), Gt. S.W. Rotary (pres. 1989-90), Omicron Delta Epsilon. Methodist. Home: 8003 John T White Rd Fort Worth TX 76120-3611

MULLENIX, LINDA SUSAN, law educator; b. NYC, Oct. 16, 1950; d. Andrew Michael and Roslyn Marasco; children: Robert Bartholomew, John Theodore, William Joseph. BA, CCNY, 1971; M Philosophy, Columbia U., 1974; PhD Pres.'s fellow, 1977; JD, Georgetown U., 1980. Bar: D.C. 1981, U.S. Dist. Ct. D.C. 1981, U.S. Ct. Appeals (D.C. cir.) 1981, U.S. Supreme Ct. 1986, Tex. 1991, U.S. Ct. Appeals (5th cir.) 1995. U. Md. European divsn., Ramstein, Germany, 1974; adj. instr. Fordham U., NYC, 1975—76, adj. asst. prof., 1977; instr. N.Y. Inst. Tech., NYC, 1976; assoc. prof., lectr. George Washington U., Washington, 1977-80; asst. prof. Am. U., Washington, 1979; assoc. Pierson, Ball & Dowd, Washington, 1980-81; clin. prof. Loyola U. Law Sch., LA, 1981-82; asst. prof. Cath. U. Law Sch., Washington, 1983—86; assoc. prof., 1986-90; prof., 1990; Reuschlein disting. vis. chair Villanova Law Sch., 2000. Vis. asst. prof. CCNY, 1977, Cooper Union Advancement Sci., Art, N.Y.C., 1977, Loyola U. Law Sch., L.A., 1982-83; jud. fellow U.S. Supreme ct. and fed. Jud. Ctr., 1989-90; Bernard J. Ward Centennial prof. U. Tex., 1991-2001, Morris and Rita Atlas chair in advocacy, 2001—; vis. prof. Harvard Law Sch., 1994-95, Mich. Law Sch., 1996; resident scholar Rockefeller Found. Bellagio (Italy) Study Ctr., 2002; Fulbright scholar Disting. Chair in Law, Trento, Italy, 2007. Author: Mass Tort Litigation: Cases and Materials, 1996, 2d cd 2008, Civil Procedure Roadmap, 1997, 2d cd 2006, Casenotes: Federal Courts, 1997, ExamPro: Civil Procedure, 1998, 2d cd 2007, State Class Actions: Practice and Procedure, 2000, Civil Procedure, 2004; co-author: Understanding Federal Courts, 1998, Federal Courts in the Twenty-First Century, 1996, 3d edit., 2007; Moore's Federal Practice and Procedure, 1991, 97, and annual updates; editor bibliographies Polit. Theory, A. Jour. Polit. Philosophy, 1972-74, The Tax Lawyer Jour., 1978-80; columnist The National Law Jour., 1998—; contbr. editor preview of U.S. Supreme Ct. Cases; co-reporter Report and Plan of Civil Justice Reform Act Adv. Group, S.d., Tex., 1991; assoc. reporter ALI, Restatement of the Law Governing Lawyers; contbr. articles to profl. jours. Alt. del. Dem. State Conv., 1980. Fellow NDEA, 1971-74; N.Y. State Regents Scholar, 1967-71. Fellow Tex. Bar Found.; mem. ABA (reporter task force on class actions 1995-97), Internat. Assn. Procedural Law, Am. Law Inst., DC Bar Assn. (com. on ethics, CLE and the Model Rules 1987), Am. Assn. Law Schs. (exec. com. sect. on civil proc. 1987-88, exec. com. sec. on conflicts of law 1991-92, chair prof. devel. com. 1991-93), Jour. Legal Edn. (editl. bd. 1997-1999), Revista Processo, Phi Beta Kappa. Home: 722 Crystal Creek Dr Austin TX 78746-4730 Office: U Tex Sch Law 727 E Dean Keeton St Austin TX 78705-3224 Office Phone: 512-232-1375. Business E-Mail: lmullenix@law.utexas.edu.

MULLENWEG, MATT(HEW) (CHARLES), software developer, blogger; b. Houston, Jan. 11, 1984; s. Louis Charles Mullenweg, IV and Kathleen Anne (Hageney) Mullenweg. Founding developer WordPress, 2003, lead developer, head bug creation, 2003—; co-founder Global Multimedia Protocols Group, 2003; with CNET, 2004—05; founder Automattic, 2005. Advisor Sphere, WeGame; spkr. in field. Blog writer PhotoMatt, WordPress. Named one of Most Important People on the Web, PC World, 2007. Mailing: Automattic Inc 355 First St San Francisco CA 94105

MULLER, CHARLOTTE FELDMAN, economist, educator; b. NYC, Feb. 19, 1921; d. Louis and Lillian (Drogin) Feldman; m. Jonas N. Muller, 1942 (dec.); m. Carl Schoenberg, 1970; children: Jeremy Lewis Muller, Sara Linda Muller. AB, Vassar Coll., 1941; A.M., Columbia U., 1942, PhD in Econs., 1946. Instr. econs. Bklyn. Coll., 1943; lectr. Barnard Coll., 1943-46; asst. prof. Occidental Coll., 1947; asst. study dir. Survey Rsch. Ctr., U. Mich., 1948; rsch. assoc. U. Calif., Berkeley, 1948-50; lectr. Yale U. Sch. Pub. Health, 1952-53; asst. prof. Columbia U. Sch. Pub. Health, 1957-67; assoc. dir. Ctr. for Social Rsch. CUNY, 1967-86, prof. econs., 1978-91, prof. emerita, 1991—, prof. sociology, 1982-91, prof. urban studies Ctr. for Social Rsch., 1967-78; v.p. CUNY Acad. for Humanities and Scis., 1985-88; prof. health econs. Mt. Sinai Sch. Medicine, 1986-91, prof. emerita, 1991—, dir. div. health econs., 1988-91, prof. dept. geriatrics, 1990-91, assoc. dir. Internat. Longevity Ctr.-USA, Ltd., 1991-97, sr. economist Internat. Longevity Ctr.-USA, Ltd., 1998—, co-dir. rsch. program Internat. Longevity Ctr.-USA, Ltd., 1999—2004, dir. longevity rsch. Internat. Longevity Ctr.-USA, Ltd., 2005—; sr. investigator health indicators, productive engagement Alliance for Health and the Future, 2003—04. Cons. Health Care Financing Adminstrn., U.S. VA; disting. alumna speaker Vassar Centennial, 1971. Author: Health Care and Gender, 1990; mem. editorial bd. Am. Jour. Pub. Health, 1980-84, Women and Health, Rsch. on Aging; contbr. numerous articles on health econs. to profl. publs. Mem. N.Y.C. Mayor's Com. on Prescription Drug Abuse, 1970-73; bd. dirs. Alan Guttmacher Inst., 1972-81, CUNY Rsch. Found., 1985-91; vice chmn. Med. and Health Rsch. Assn., N.Y.C.; mem. health care tech. study sect. Nat. Ctr. Health Svcs. Rsch., 1976-79; mem. commn. on nat. policy Am. Jewish Congress, 1980-91. Grantee Ford/Rockefeller Founds., 1972-73, 75-76, Russell Sage Found., 1985-90. Mem.: APHA, Am. Econ. Assn. Jewish. Achievements include presenting report on Economic Status of Older Women to UN 2nd World Assembly on Aging., Madrid, 2002; sr. investigator Indicators of Health and Productive Engagement, Occupations of Older Workers. Office: Internat Longevity Ctr-USA Ltd 60 E 86th St New York NY 10028-1009 Business E-Mail: charlottem@ilcusa.org.

MULLER, EDWARD ROBERT, energy executive, lawyer; b. Phila., Mar. 26, 1952; s. Rudolph E. and Elizabeth (Steiner) M.; m. Patricia Eileen Bauer, Sept. 27, 1980; children: Margaret Anne, John Frederick. AB summa cum laude, Dartmouth Coll., 1973; JD, Yale U., 1976. Assoc. Leva, Hawes, Symington, Martin & Oppenheimer, Washington, 1977-83; dir. legal affairs Life Scis. group Whittaker Corp., Arlington, Va., 1983-84; v.p. Whittaker Health Svcs., Arlington, Va., 1984-85; v.p., gen. counsel, sec. Whittaker Corp., LA, 1985-93, chief adminstrv. officer, 1988-92, CFO, 1992-93, bd. dirs., 1993-99; v.p., gen. counsel, sec. BioWhittaker, Inc., Walkersville, Md., 1991-93; pres., CEO, bd. dirs. Edison Mission Energy, Irvine, Calif., 1993-2000; chmn., pres., CEO Mirant Corp., Atlanta, 2005—. Bd. dirs. Oasis Residential, Inc., Las Vegas, 1995—98, Global Marine, Inc., Houston, 1997—2001, GlobalSantaFe Corp., Houston, 2001—07, Interval, Inc., Marina del Rey, Calif., 2000—05, Strategic Data Corp., Santa Monica, Calif., 2001—05, The Keith Cos., Inc., Irvine, Calif., 2001—05, RigNet, Inc., Houston, 2002—05, RealEnergy, Inc., Woodland Hills, Calif., 2003—05, Ormat Tech., Inc., Sparks, Nev., 2004—05, Transocean Ltd., Zug, 2007—; mem. Brookings Task Force on Civil Justice Reform, 1988—89; chmn. U.S.-Philippines Bus. Com., 1998—2000; adv. bd. Tennenbaum Capital Ptnrs., LLC, LA, 1997—2003; mem. Coun. on Fgn. Rels., 1998—, Pacific Coun. on Internat. Policy, 1998—; dep. chmn. Contact Energy Ltd., Wellington, New Zealand, 1999—2000. Trustee Exceptional Children's Found., L.A., 1988-94, treas., 1988-93; co-chair Internat. Energy Devel. Coun., Washington, 1993-00; bd. govs. Jr. Achievement of Orange County and the Inland Empire, 1995-96; mem. Pres. Leadership Coun., Dartmouth Coll., 2003—; trustee Riverview Sch., East Sandwich, Mass, 2004—, chmn., 2008-; bd. advisors The Pathway Program UCLA Ext., LA, 2004—; bd. councilors Carter Ctr., Atlanta, 2008-. Office: Mirant Corp 1155 Perimeter Ctr W Atlanta GA 30338

MÜLLER, HANS-GEORG, statistician; b. Stuttgart, Germany; s. Siegfried Otto Paul and Frida (Mantel) M. MD, U. Heidelberg, 1982; PhD, U. Ulm, 1983. Asst. prof. U. Marburg, Germany, 1984-87; assoc. prof. U. Erlangen, Germany, 1987-88; from assoc. prof. to prof. U. Calif., Davis, 1988—. Author: Nonparametric Regression Analysis, 1988; co-editor: Change-Point Problems, 1993. Fellow AAAS, Inst. Math. Statistics, Am. Statis. Assn.; mem. Internat. Statis. Inst., World Innovation Found. Office: U Calif Dept Statistics Davis CA 95616

MULLER, HENRY JAMES, journalist, magazine editor; b. Garmisch-Partenkirchen, Germany, Feb. 10, 1947; came to U.S., 1953; s. Henri Jacques and Helga (Mensch) M.; m. Maggie McComas, June 19, 1968. BA, Stanford U., 1968. Tchr. U.S. Peace Corps, Ethiopia, 1968-70; chief Vancouver (B.C., Can.) bur. Time mag., 1971-73, European econ. corr. Brussels, 1973-77, chief Paris bur., 1977-81, world editor NYC, 1982-85, chief of corrs., 1986-87, mng. editor, 1987-93; editorial dir. Time Inc., 1993-2000, editor-at-large, 2000—. Faculty mem. profl. pub. course Stanford (Calif.) U., 1989—; bd. visitors Columbia Journalism Sch., 1998—. Trustee Stanford U., 1991-2001, Carnegie Corp., 1992-2000, Overseas Press Club, 1993-97; dir. Media Action Internat., 2000—. Recipient David Brower Environ. Journalism award Sierra Club, 1990, Gerald Loeb award for disting. bus. and fin. journalism, 1992. Mem. Am. Soc. Mag. Editors (bd. dirs. 1991-95), Coun. of Fgn. Rels. Avocations: hiking, reading, skiing.

MULLER, HENRY NICHOLAS, III, retired foundation administrator; b. Pitts., Nov. 18, 1938; s. Henry N., Jr. and Harriet (Kerschner) Muller; m. Nancy Clagett, June 20, 1959 (div. 1985); children: Charles T., Brook W.; m. Carol A. Cook, Jan. 4, 1986. BA, Dartmouth Coll., 1960; PhD, U. Rochester, 1968. Instr. Dartmouth Coll., Hanover, NH, 1964; lectr. Mt. Allison U., Sackville, Canada, 1964—66; asst. prof., prof. history U. Vt., Burlington, 1966—78, asst. dean Coll. Arts, Scis., 1969—70, assoc. dean Coll. Arts, Scis., 1970—73, dir. Living, Learning Ctr., 1973—78; pres. Colby-Sawyer Coll., New London, NH, 1978—85; dir. State Hist. Soc. Wis., Madison, 1985—96; pres., CEO Frank Lloyd Wright Found., Scotsdale, Ariz., 1996—2002; ret., 2002. Chair corp. governance and nom. com. Standex Internat. Corp., mem. retirement plans, pension plan investment and compensation com., also bd. dirs.; mem. Wis. State Hist. Records Adv. Bd., 1985—96, Gov. Coun. Tourism, 1987—96; chmn. Wis. Burial Sites Bd., 1988—96; trustee Nat. Trust Hist. Preservation, 1989—98; chair Wis. Submerged Cultural Resources, 1993—96; bd. dirs. Nat. Trust CDFI Corp., 2006—, Willsboro Devel. Corp., 2006—. Co-author: An Anxious Democracy, 1982; co-editor: Science, Technology and Culture, 1974, In a state of Nature, 1982, The Quotable Ethan Allen, 2005; sr. editor: Vt. Life mag., 1975—87; editor: Vt. History, 1977—85. Fin. chmn. Vt. Bicentennial Commn., 1970—77; trustee Vt. Hist. Soc., 1972—85, 2003—, v.p., 1975—82, treas., 2008—; chmn. Vt. Coun. Hist. Preservation, 1977—78, Bicentennial Com., Burlington, 1976; active NH Postsecondary Edn. Commn., 1983—85, Wis. Sesquicentennial Commn., 1995—99; trustee, pres. Taliesin Preservation, Inc., 1991—2001; trustee Frank Lloyd Wright Found., 1996—2004; v.p. Ind. Coll. Univ. Coun. Ariz., 1998—2000, bd. dirs., 1998—2002; interim chmn. Taliesin Archs., 2000—01; counselor Essex Cmty. Fund, NY, 2002—, sec.-treas., 2007—; counselor Adirondack Archtl. Heritage Ctr., 2005—; bd. dirs. Wis. Preservation Fund Inc., 1989—2006, USS Wis., 1989—93; trustee Ethan Allen Homestead Trust, 2002—, treas., 2003—05; v.p., 2005—; dir., vice chmn. Essex Cmty. Heritage Orgn., NY, 2003—04; bd. dirs., vice chmn., chmn. Smith House Health Care Ctr., Willsboro, NY, 2004—, chmn., 2006—; active Essex Bicentennial Com., 2004—05, Essex Planning Bd., 2005—; dir. Nat. Trust CDFI, Inc., 2006—. Fellow: Ctr. Rsch. Vt.; mem.: Ctr. Nythem Woodlands Edn. (bd. advisors 2009—), Am. Assn. State and Local History (councillor 1988—91), Vt. Archeol. Soc. (pres. 1971—74), Nat. Coun. Pub. History (bd. dirs. 1988—90), Madison Club.

MULLER, JANICE ELAINE, secondary school educator; b. Littlefield, Tex., Oct. 23, 1955; d. Calvin Roy and Hazel Louise Stevens; m. Mark C. Muller, Aug. 24, 1973; 1 child, Amanda Marie Thompson. BS, Tex. Tech U., Lubbock, 1977, MEd, 1995. Cert. tchr. Tex., 1977, mid mgmt./ednl. adminstrn. Tex., 1995. Tchr. Littlefield H.S., Tex., 1984—. Mem. reading com. ETS/TEA, Austin, 1996—99; mem. site based com. on edn. Littlefield H.S., 1998—, TAKS com. chmn., 2000—04; academic coord. U. Interscholastic League, Littlefield, 1999—. Founder Friends of the Libr., Littlefield, 1978—84; mem. adminstrv. bd. First United Meth. Ch., Littlefield, 2003—06; bd. dirs. Meals on Wheels, Littlefield, 1978—90. Named Outstanding Tex. H.S. Tchr., U. Tex., 1992, Tchr. of Yr., Tex. Assn. of Future Educators, 1997, 2005; fellow Caprock Area Writing Project, Tex. Tech. U., 1992. Mem.: Tex. Classroom Tchrs. Assn. (assoc.), Golden Key Nat. Honor Soc. (assoc.), Delta Kappa Gamma (assoc.; sec. 2000—02, Achievement award 2003). Democrat. Methodist. Avocations: golf, travel, writing. Home: 136 E 23rd St Littlefield TX 79339 Office: Littlefield HS 1100 Waylon Jennings Blvd Littlefield TX 79339 Personal E-mail: jmu1952672@aol.com.

MULLER, JENNIFER, choreographer, dancer; b. Yonkers, NY, Oct. 16, 1944; d. Don Medford and Lynette (Heldman) Muller. BS, Juilliard Sch. Music, 1967. Instr. in dance H.S. Performing Arts, 1967-72, Sarah Lawrence Coll., 1968-72, The Juilliard Sch., 1969-70, Nederlands Dans Theater, 1971-76, Utah rep., 1973-74, Centre Nat. de la Dance, Paris, 1998, Acad. Isola Danzo, Venice, 1999-2001, Atelier de Paris, 1999, Institut del Teatre de Barcelona, 2001, Centro Andaluz de Danza-Seville, 2003-05 Internat. de Danza Sarcewna, 2007-08; commns.: Alvin Ailey Am. Dance Theatre, N.Y.C., 1977, 85, 2005, Festival d'Avignon, France, 1980, Lyon Opera Ballet, France, 1984, Aterballetto, 1988, Ballet Stagium, 1991, Dansgroep Krisztina de Chatel, 1992, Tanz-Forum Staatsoper Koln, Sachsische Staatopera-Dresden, ARTSCAPE-Balt., 1991, 95, Aterballetto, Italy, 1993, Les Ballet Jazz de Montreal, 1994, Ballet du Nord, France, 1995, White Wave Rising, 1996, Bat Dor Dance Co., Israel, Nederlands Dans Theatre 3, Ballet Contemporaneo, Argentina, Ohio Ballet, 2000, Dance Inst. U. Akron, 2003, Gestores Dance Co., 2006, Wylliams Henry Dance Theatre, 2008; cons. Met. Mus. Art, 1971-72, Marymount Manhatton Coll., 2006. Mem. Pearl Lang Dance Co., NYC, 1959-63; prin. dancer: Jose Limon Dance Co., NYC, 1963-71; assoc. dir., choreographer, prin. dancer: Louis Falco Dance Co., NYC, 1968-74; founder, dir., choreographer: Jennifer Muller/The Works, NYC, 1974-; choreographic works include: Nostalgia, 1971, Rust, 1971, Cantata, 1972, Tub, 1973, An American Beauty Rose, 1974, Biography, 1974, Speeds, 1974, Winter Pieces, 1974, Clown, 1974, Four Chairs, 1974, Wyeth, 1974, White, 1975, Strangers, 1975, Beach, 1976, Crossword, 1977, Predicaments for Five, 1977, Mondriaan, 1977, Lovers, 1978, Solo, 1979, Conversations, 1979, Chant, 1980, Terrain, 1981, Shed, 1982, Kite, 1983, Souls, 1984, The Enigma, 1986, Fields, 1986, Couches, 1986, Life/Times, 1986, Darkness and Light, 1986, Interrupted River, 1987, Occasional Encounters, 1988, City, 1988, The Flight of a Predatory Bird, 1989, Refracted Light, 1990, RIGHTeous About Passing (on the LEFT), 1990, Woman with Visitors at 3am, 1991, Regards, 1991, arm in arm in arm..., 1991, Thesaurus, 1991, Glass Houses, 1991, Z+1=1/Attic, 1992, Momentary Gathering, 1992, The Waiting Room, 1993, The Politician/Peeling the Onion, 1993, Orbs, Spheres and Other Circular Bodies, 1993, HUMAN/NATURE-A Response to the Longhouse Gardens, 1993, Pierrot, 1993, Desire-That DNA Urge, 1994, Point of View (A Case of Persimmons and Picasso), 1994, The Spotted Owl, 1995, Some Days are Like That, 1995, Promontory, 1996, Fruit, 1996, The Dinner Party, 1996, A Broken Wing, 1996, Ricochet, 1997, Degas Revisited, 1998, Dialectics Part I, 1998, Spores, Solitude & Summer Humming, 1999, Beethoven-Not Four Naught, 2000, aSOlo, 2000, Hymn for Her, 2000, Time Treading, 2000, China Project: Sagone; Suk Road; Dancing Waves, 2001, The Door, 2001, Never in The Same Room, 2002, To Live Alone..., 2002, Moon, 2002, It's a c#!* City, 2002, Prayer, 2003, Bounce, 2003, Footprints, 2003, Flowers, 2004, Ecstatic Poems, 2004, A Candle at Both Ends, 2004, Island, 2005, Sunlight and Shadow, 2005, Momentum, 2005, Metamorphosis, 2006, Passion Fruit, 2006, Edge, 2007, Aria, 2008, Tangle 2009, Bench 2009, Walk it Off 2009; choreographer (theatre) Frimbo, 1980, The Death of von Richthofen..., 1982, Fame, The Musical, 1988, Up Against It, 1989, The Seven Deadly Sins, 1990, Signature, 1990, Esther, 1993, Once Around the City, 1998, 2001; dir.: Le Jongleur, 2000. Recipient Best Performance award Berlin Festival, 1977, Acad. award Juilliard Sch. Music, 1967, Carbonell award, 1989; grantee Nat. Endowment for Arts, 1971-77, 80-85, 86-87, 87-88, Creative Artists Pub. Svc., 1976-77, NY State Coun. on Arts, 1976-77, 78-79, 85-93, NYC Dept. Cultural Affairs, 1978-79, 94-2009, NYC Dept. Youth and Cmty. Devel., 2001-05. Mem. Am. Guild Mus. Artists, Soc. Stage Dirs. and Choreographers, World Arts Coun. (founding mem.). Home and Office: The Muller Works Found Inc 131 W 24th St New York NY 10011-1942 Office Phone: 212-691-3803. Business E-Mail: jmuller@jmtw.org, twinfo@jmtw.org.

MULLER, JENNY HELEN, physician, psychiatrist; b. Johannesburg, Dec. 21, 1953; d. Eric and Lily Muller; 1 child, Jonathan Meshekow. MD, U. Witwatersrand, South Africa, 1977. Diplomate Am. Bd. Psychiatry and Neurology. Intern in internal medicine, surgery, orthop., Johannesburg, 1978; intern in internal medicine and psychiatry Va. Med. Ctr., Sepulveda, Calif., 1986—87, resident in psychiatry, 1987—90, VA and Olive View Hosp. Child and Adolescent Rotation UCLA, 1987—90; pvt. practice LA, 1990—. Mem.: APA, So. Calif. Psychiat. Assn. Avocation: horseback riding. Office: 9808 Venice Blvd Ste 505 Culver City CA 90232-6818 Office Phone: 310-204-1057. Office Fax: 310-204-1006.

MULLER, JEROME KENNETH, photographer, art director, editor; b. Amityville, NY, July 18, 1934; s. Alphons and Helen (Haberl) M.; m. Nora Marie (Nestor), Dec. 21, 1974. BS, Marquette U., Milw., 1961; post grad., Calif. State U., Fullerton, 1985—86; MA, Nat. U., San Diego, 1988; post grad., Newport Psychoanalytic Inst., 1988—90. Comml. and editorial photographer, NYC, 1952-55; mng. editor Country Beautiful mag., Milw., 1961-62, Reproductions Rev. mag., NYC, 1967-68; editor, art dir. Orange County Illustrated, Newport Beach, Calif., 1962-67, art editor, 1970-79, exec. editor, art dir., 1968-69; owner, CEO Creative Svcs. Advt. Agy., Newport Beach, Calif., 1969-79. Founder, CEO, Mus. Graphics, Costa Mesa, Calif., 1978—; tchr. photography Lindenhurst H.S., NY, 1952-54, comic art U. Calif., Irvine, 1979, publ. design Orange Coast Coll., Costa Mesa, Calif., 1997-2002; guest curator Fiftieth Anniversary Exhbn. Mickey Mouse, 1928-78, The Bower's Mus., Santa Ana, Calif., 1978. One-man shows include Souk Gallery, Newport Beach, 1970, Gallery Two, Santa Ana, Calif., 1972, Cannery Gallery, Newport Beach, 1974, Mus. Graphics Gallery, 1993, White Gallery Portland State U., 1996, U. Calif., Irvine, 1997, Nat. Telephone and Comm., Irvine, Calif., 1998, Robert Mondavi Wine and Food Center, Costa Mesa, 2000, Reflective Image Gallery, Santa Ana, Calif., 2007; author: Rex Brandt, 1972, Publication Design and Production, 2000; contbr. photographs and articles to mag. Mem. Cultural Arts Com., City of Costa Mesa, CA., 2000-2002. With USAF, 1956-57. Recipient, two silver medals Twentieth Ann. Exhbn. Advt. and Editorial Art in West, 1965, Inkpot award, San Diego Comic Conv., 1980. Mem.: Laguna Beach Art Mus., Met. Mus. Art, Mus. Modern Art (NYC), Orange County Mus. Art, Alpha Sigma Nu. Office: PO Box 11155 Costa Mesa CA 92627 Office Phone: 949-644-0808.

MULLER, JOHN BARTLETT, academic administrator; b. Port Jefferson, NY, Nov. 8, 1940; s. Frederick Henry and Estelle May (Reeve) M.; m. Barbara Ann Schmidt, May 30, 1964 (dec. 1972); m. Lynn Anne Spongberg, Oct. 10, 1987. AB in Polit. Sci., U. Rochester, 1962; postgrad. in apologetics, Westminster Sem., Phila., 1962-63; MS in Psychology, Purdue U., 1968, PhD in Psychology, 1975. Asst. prof. psychology Roberts Wesleyan Coll., Rochester, NY, 1964-66, acting chmn. div. behavioral sci., dir. instl. research, 1967-70; vis. asst. prof. psychology Wabash Coll., Crawfordsville, Ind., 1970-71; research assoc. Ind. U.-Purdue U., Indpls., 1971-72; prof. psychology, v.p. for acad. affairs Hillsdale Coll., Mich., 1972-85; pres. BMW Assocs., Osseo, Mich., 1984-85, Bellevue U., Nebr., 1985—2009, chancellor Nebr., 2009—; CEO Bellevue U. Found., 2009—. Bd. dir. Nebr. Ind. Coll. Found., Omaha, Assn. Ind. Colls. Nebr., Lincoln. Contbr. articles to profl. jours. and textbooks. Bd. dir. Mid-American Coun. Boy Scouts Mental Health fellowship Purdue U., 1963, Nat. Tchg. fellowship Fed. Govt., 1967, Townsend fellowship U. Rochester, 1962. Mem. APA, Bellevue C. of C. (bd. dir. 1989-95), Phi Beta Kappa, Phi Kappa Phi. Republican. Home: 13303 Lochmoor Cir Bellevue NE 68123-3770 Office: Bellevue U Office of Chancellor 1000 Galvin Rd S Bellevue NE 68005-3098 Office Phone: 402-557-7001. Business E-Mail: jmuller@bellevue.edu.

MÜLLER, KARL ALEXANDER (K. ALEX MUELLER), physicist, researcher; b. Apr. 20, 1927; PhD in Physics, Swiss Fed. Inst. Tech., 1958; DSc (hon.), U. Geneva, 1987, Tech. U. Munich, 1987, U. Studi di Pavia, Italy, 1987; DSc (hon.) (hon.), U. Leuven, Belgium, 1988, Boston U., 1988, Tel Aviv U., 1988, Tech. U. Darmstadt, Germany, 1988, U. Nice, France, 1989, U. Politecnia, Madrid, 1989, U. Bochum, Germany, 1990, U. degli Studi di Rome, 1990, U. Trondheim, Norway, 1992, U. Metz, France, 1995, U. Salzburg, Austria, 1995, U. Regensburg, Germany, 1996, U. Cottbus, 1997, U. Leipzig, 2000. Project mgr. Battelle Inst., Geneva, 1958-63; lectr., titular prof., prof. U. Zurich, Switzerland, 1962-70, 1970-87, 1987—; researcher solid-state physics IBM Zurich Research Lab., Rüschlikon, Switzerland, 1963-73, mgr. dept. physics, 1973-82, fellow, 1982-85; prof. Physik-Inst., U. Zurich, Switzerland, 1985—. Contbr. over 400 articles to tech. publs. Recipient Marcel-Benoist Found. prize, 1986, Nobel prize in physics, 1987, Dannie Heineman prize, Acad. Scis. Göttingen, Fed. Republic of Germany, 1987, Robert Wichard Pohl prize, German Phys. Soc., 1987, Europhysics prize Hewlett-Packard Co., 1988, Minnie Rosen award, Ross U., N.Y., Spl. Tsukuba award, Japan, 1989, Internat. Aldo Villa prize for spl. contbn. to sci. and tech. of ceramic materials, Italian Ceramic Soc., 1991; co-recipient (with J. Georg Bednorz) Fritz London Meml. award, 1987. Fellow Am. Phys. Soc. (Internat. prize for new materials research 1988); mem. European Phys. Soc. (mem. ferroelectricity group), Swiss Phys. Soc., Zurich Phys. Soc. (pres. 1968-69), Groupement Ampère, Nat. Acad. Scis. (fgn. assoc.). Office: Univ Zürich-Irchel Physics Inst 36 H 50 Winterthurerstr 190 CH-8057 Zurich Switzerland

MULLER, KURT ALEXANDER, lawyer; b. Chgo., June 21, 1955; s. Jack and Janet (Kasten) M.; m. Sylvia Saltoon, Apr. 6, 1986; 1 child, Marissa Grace. BS, U. Wis., Parkside, 1977; JD, John Marshall Law Sch., 1986. Bar: Ill. 1986, U.S. Dist. Ct. (no. dist.) Ill. 1986, Ariz. 1987, U.S. Dist. Ct. (ea. dist.) Wis. 1989; approved child rep. Cook County Ct. Creative dir. Brand Advt., Chgo., 1977-80; dep. sheriff Cook County, Chgo., 1978-86; broker Gerstenberg Commodities, Chgo., 1980-83; assoc. Gordon & Glickson, P.C., Chgo., 1986-87, Michael Harry Minton, P.C., Chgo., 1987-90; pvt. practice Chgo., 1990-92; ptnr. Law Offices of Richter-Muller, P.C., Chgo., 1992-95; lawyer, CEO The Muller Firm, Ltd., Chgo., 1995—. Lectr. Nat. Bus. Inst. Author: In Consideration of Divorce: Giving Credit (and Debits) to Dissolution, 1991, 3d edit., 1998; host (Air Am. radio show) Kurt Muller's Uncommon Law; information source for FOX news.; contbr. The Jewish American Prince Handbook, 1986, articles to profl. jours. and newspapers. Mem. ABA, ACLU, Chgo. Bar Assn., Masons. Avocations: interior decorating, films, theater, writing. Office: The Muller Bldg 110 W Grand Ave Chicago IL 60610-4269 Office Phone: 312-467-6700. Business E-Mail: kmuller@mullaw.com.

MULLER, MERVIN EDGAR, computer scientist, consultant, statistician, educator; b. Hollywood, Calif., June 1, 1928; s. Emanuel and Bertha (Zimmerman) Muller; m. Barabara McAdam, July 13, 1963; children: Jeffrey McAdam, Stephen McAdam, Todd McAdam. AB, UCLA, 1949, MA, 1951, PhD, 1954. Instr. in math. Cornell U., 1954-56; rsch. assoc. in math. Princeton (NJ) U., 1956-59, sr. scientist statis. and elec. engring., 1968-69; sr. statistician, dept. mgr. IBM, NYC, White Plains, 1956-64; prof. computer sci. and stats. U. Wis., 1964-71; prof. computer sci. George Mason U., 1985; dept. dir. World Bank, Washington, 1971-81, sr. advisor, 1981-85; Robert M. Critchfield prof. computer info. sci. Ohio State U., 1985-98, prof. emeritus, 1994-98, dept. chair, 1985-94. Chair sci. and tech. info. bd. NRC, NAS; bd. dirs. Advanced Info. Tech. Ctr., Columbus, Ohio. Mem. editl. bd. Computation and Stats., 1990—2007, Jour. Computational and Graphical Stats., 1990—2007; contbr. articles to profl. jours. Trustee First Unitarian Ch., Bethesda, Md., 1975—79; bd. mem. Chamber Music Columbus, 2006. Rsch. grantee, AT&T, Columbus, 1987. Fellow: World Acad. Productivity Sci., Am. Statis. Assn.; mem.: Internat. Assn. Statis. Computing (sci. sec. 1979—83, pres. 1977—79), Internat. Statis. Inst. (mem. steering com. Internat. Rsch. Ctr. 1987—89). Avocations: reading, exercise, walking, bridge. Home: 4171 Clairmont Rd Upper Arlington OH 43220-4501 Office: Ohio State U Dept Computer Info Sci Rm 395 2015 Neil Ave Columbus OH 43210-1210 Office Phone: 614-292-4281. E-mail: mmuller@columbus.rr.com, muller.m@cse-ohio-state.edu.

MULLER, MICHAEL, land use planner, educator; married. BEd., BFA, Eastern Oreg. U., La Grande, 1976; BArch, U. Idaho, Moscow, 1983. Art instr. Helen McCune Jr. HS, Pendleton, Oreg., 1976—77, La Grande HS, 1977—79; civil engring. tech. instr. Blue Mountain CC, Pendleton, 1990—. Tchg. asst. U. Idaho Coll. Art & Architecture, Moscow, 1979—80; draftsman Clearwater Econ. Devel. Devel. Assoc., Moscow, 1980—81; primary draftsman City of Moscow, 1981—83; intern arch. Rick Sparks AIA, Ellensburg, Wash., 1983—84, Pence & Assocs., Pasco, Wash., 1984—86; job capt. and designer Lynch Fitzgerald & Assocs., Pendleton, 1986—88; land use planner Umatilla County, Pendleton, 1988—90, planning commr., 1993—2004; city planner City of Pendleton, 2004—08. Elder First Presbyn. Ch., Pendleton, 1987—2004. Mem.: AIA, ASCE. Office: Blue Mountain CC 2411 NW Carden Ave Pendleton OR 97801 Business E-Mail: mmuller@bluecc.edu.

MULLER, PATRICIA ANN, nursing administrator, educator; b. NYC, July 22, 1943; d. Joseph H. and Rosanne (Bautz) Felter; m. David G. Smith, Mar. 19, 1988; children: Frank M. Muller III, Kimberly M. Muller. BSN, Georgetown U., 1965; MA, U. Tulsa, 1978, EdD, 1983. RN. Coord. staff devel. St. Francis Hosp., Tulsa, 1978—79, asst. dir. for nursing svc., nursing edn., 1979—82, dir. dept. edn., 1982—98, St. Francis Health Sys., 1998—2002, cons., 2002—; CEO, Smith Assocs. LLC, 2002. Mem. faculty Okla. U., Northeastern U., Tulsa U.; presenter at confs. and convs. Contbg. editor JOPAN, 1992-2001; contbr. articles to profl. jours. Mem. Leadership Tulsa, 1991; bd. dirs. Am. Heart Assn., Ronald McDonald House. Mem. ANA, Nat. League for Nursing, Am. Soc. for Nursing Svc. Adminstrs., Am. Soc. for Health Manpower Edn. and Tng., Okla. Nurses Assn., Okla. Orgn. of Nurse Execs. (pres. 1992-93), Sigma Theta Tau. Home and Office: 6203 W Utica Ct Broken Arrow OK 74011 Office Phone: 918-671-7767. E-mail: mullsmi@aol.com.

MULLER, PETER, lawyer, film company and retail executive; b. Teplitz-Sanov, Czech Republic, Mar. 4, 1947; arrived in US, 1949, naturalized; s. Alexander and Elizabeth Rudolpha (Weingarten) M.; m. Irene Smolarski, Nov. 18, 1971 (div. 1973); children: Chloe, Aurisha; m. Esther Unterman Meisler, Jan. 4, 1987 (div. 1995). BA, NYU, 1968, JD cum laude. Entertainment editor Ambience mag., NYC, 1978-79, Women's Life mag., NYC, 1980-81; private practice NYC, 1984—; entertainment writer Jewish Press; CEO Producers Releasing Corp., NY, 1987-88, Nev., 1987—88, pres. entertainment div. NY, 1987-88, Nev., 1987—88; pres., founder Muller Entertainment Group, NYC, 1988—, Calif., 1988—; pres., chief oper. officer ACA Joe, Inc., San Francisco and NYC, also bd. dirs. Expert tech. adv. svc. for attys., Pa., 1987—; adj. prof. NYU, UCLA, LaGuardia CUNY, Zicklin Sch. Bus. Baruch Coll. CUNY; arbitrator ICC Internat. Ct. Arbitration, 2007; lectr. entertainment and comm. bus. to various orgns. Author: Show Business Law, 1991, The Music Business: A Legal Perspective, 1994. Bd. dirs. Coll. Arts and Sci. NYU, mem. alumni coun.; vol. Lawyers for the Arts, NYC, 1987—. Mem. ABA (forum on entertainment and sports industries, forum on copyright, trademark and patent law), NY State Bar Assn., NYU Alumni Assn. (bd. dirs. 1987—, v.p. bd. dirs., coun.), Assn. of Am. Mgmt. Assn. Avocations: sports, history, writing, travel, hiking. Home Phone: 212-358-3406; Office Phone: 212-358-3406.

MULLER, RALPH W., hospital administrator; b. Oct. 26, 1945; married. BA in economics, Syracuse U., NY, 1966; MA in govt., Harvard U., Cambridge, Mass., 1968. Asst. to commr. Nicholas Johnson FCC, Washington, 1967; assoc., health care consulting Orgn. for Social and Tech. Innovation, Cambridge, Mass., 1969-70; rsch. asst. to Prof. Samuel H. Beer Harvard U., 1967—68, teaching fellow, govt., and resident tutor, 1969—72; govt. instr. Suffolk U., Boston, 1972—74; budget dir., dept. of public welfare Commonwealth of Mass., Boston, 1975—78, dep. commr., dept. public welfare, 1978—80; dir. fin. planning and budget U. Chgo., 1980—83, assoc. v.p. budget, computing and info. sys., 1984, v.p., hospitals and clinics and dep. dean, divsn. biological sciences, 1985—86; pres., CEO U. Chgo. Hospitals and Health Sys., 1986—2003; CEO U. Pa. Health Sys., 2003—. Fellow: AAAS; mem.: Inst. Medicine, Coun. of Tchg. Hospitals (chmn. 1997—98), Am. Assoc. of Med. Colleges (AAMC) (chmn. 1999—2000). Office: U Pa Health Sys 3400 Spruce St Philadelphia PA 19104*

MULLER, RIANA RICCI, musician, educator; b. Orange, Calif., July 14, 1943; d. Ruggerio Ricci and Ruth (Ricci) (Rink) Mairs; m. William Paul Muller, Aug. 17, 1968; 1 child, Christine Rae. BM with distinction, Eastman Sch. Music, Rochester, NY, 1965, MM in Performance, Music Lit., 1969. Instr. Amarillo Coll, Tex., 1973—76; asst. prof. Coll. St. Benedict, St. Joseph, Minn., 1976—78; violinist Puerto Rico Symphony, San Juan, 1978—79; music tchr. (orch.) Hendrick Hudson Pub. Sch., Montrose, NY, 1984—2004; violinist freelance, Greater NY Area, 1984—2004, Pa., 2004—, Muller Duo, Lewisburg, Pa., 1979—; instr. Lycoming Coll., Williamsport, Pa., 2005—. Violin study with Carrol Glenn, Joseph Knitzer, Louis Persinger and Ruggerio Ricci (her father). Author (and violinist): (DVD) Classical Music in the Foreign Language Classes, 2005; author: Ear Training Exercises for Violin Students, 2006, 2008. Decorated with medal and Diplome d'Honneur Eugene Ysaÿe Found., Brussels; recipient Cert. of Commendation for Chamber Music Tchg., Chamber Music Am., 1993. Mem.: Sigma Alpha Iota. Achievements include world premiere performance of Ysaÿe Violin Concerto No.8 (1977). Home: 1119 W Market St Lewisburg PA 17837 Personal E-mail: wpmuller@ptd.net.

MULLER, RICHARD STEPHEN, electrical engineer, educator; b. Weehawken, NJ, May 5, 1933; s. Irving Ernest and Marie Victoria Muller; m. Joyce E. Regal, June 29, 1957; children: Paul Stephen, Thomas Richard. ME, Stevens Inst. Tech., Hoboken, NJ, 1955; MSEE, Calif. Inst. Tech., Pasadena, 1957, PhD in Elec. Engring. and Physics, 1962. Test engr. Wright Aero/Curtiss Wright, Woodridge, NJ, 1953-54; mem. tech. staff Hughes Aircraft Co., Culver City, Calif., 1955-61; instr. U. So. Calif., LA, 1960-61; asst. prof., then assoc. prof. U. Calif., Berkeley, 1962-72, prof., 1973—. Guest prof. Swiss Fed. Inst. Tech., 1993; founder, dir. Berkeley Sensor & Actuator Ctr., 1985—; chmn. sensors electron devices NRC Army Rsch. Lab., 2003-04, chmn. microtech. adv. com. Helmholtz Assn., Germany, 2003—; chmn. steering com. Internat. Sensor and Actuator Meeting. Co-author: Device Electronics for Integrated Circuits, 1977, 3d, rev. edit., 2002, Microsensors, 1990; editor-in-chief IEEE/ASME Jour. Microelectromech. Sys., 1998—; contbr. over 200 articles to profl. jours. Pres. Kensington Mcpl. Adv. Coun., Calif., 1992-98; trustee Stevens Inst. Tech., 1996-2005. Fellow NSF Grad. Res., 1959-62, NATO postdoctoral fellow, 1968-69, Fulbright fellow, 1982-83, Alexander von Humboldt Rsch. Prof., 1993, Tech. U. Berlin, 1994; Berkeley citation, 1994, Stevens Renaissance award, 1995, Career Achievement award Internat. Conf. on Sensors and Actuators, 1997. Fellow IEEE (life, Cledo Brunetti award 1998, Millennium prize 2000); mem. IEEE Press Bd., NAE, NRC (chmn. sensors adv. bd. U.S. Army Rsch. Lab. 2003-04, liaison between NAE and NRC 2003—), Nat. Acad. Engring., Nat. Materials (adv. bd. 1994-98), IEEE Electron Devices Soc. (adv. com. 1984-98, Disting. Svc. award 2007, Tech. Svc. award, 2008). Achievements include 23 patents in field; development of world's first operating micromotor and introduction of silicon surface micromachining; invention of polycrystalline. Office: U Calif Dept EECS # 1770 401 Cory Hall Berkeley CA 94720-1770 Office Phone: 510-642-0614. Business E-Mail: r.muller@ieee.org.

MULLER, SCOTT WILLIAM, lawyer; b. Stamford, Conn., Feb. 15, 1950; s. Robert Sielke and Patricia (Harris) M.; m. Caroline Severance Adams, June 24, 1972; children: Christopher Adams, Robin McPherson, Peter Severance. BA cum laude, Princeton U., 1971; JD, Georgetown U. Law Ctr., 1975. Bar: NY 1976, US Dist. Ct. (so. dist.) NY 1977, US Ct. Appeals (2d. cir.) 1978, US Supreme Ct. 1978, US Tax Ct. 1984, DC 1986. Law clk. to Hon. Frances L. Van Dusen US Ct. Appeals (3rd Cir.), Phila., 1975-76; asst. US atty. US Dept. Justice, NYC, 1978-82; assoc. Davis, Polk & Wardwell, Washington, 1976-78, 82-84, ptnr., 1985—2002, 2004—; gen. counsel CIA, Washington, 2002—04. Adj. prof. in fed. law enforcement Georgetown U. Law Ctr. Nat. trustee Boys and Girls Clubs of Am.; mem. governing bd. St. Albans Sch.; mem. audit com. Protestant Episcopal Cathedral Found. (the Nat. Cathedral); chmn. bd. Ctr. for the Community Interest, 1998—2002. Served N.G., 1971—72. Mem. ABA (vice-chmn, white collar crime com.), NY State Bar Assn., Fed. Bar Assn., Assn. of Bar of City of NY, Am. Law Inst. Republican. Episcopalian. Office: Davis Polk & Wardwell 450 Lexington Ave New York NY 10017 E-mail: scott.muller@dpw.com.

MULLER, STEVEN, international studies educator, academic administrator; b. Hamburg, Germany, Nov. 22, 1927; came to U.S., 1940, naturalized, 1949; 0. Werner Adolph and Marianne (Hartstein) M.; m. Margie Hellman, June 19, 1951 (dec. July 1999); children: Julie, Elizabeth; m. Jill E. McGovern, Feb. 5, 2000. BA, UCLA, 1948; BLitt (Rhodes scholar), Oxford U., Eng., 1951; PhD, Cornell U., 1958. Asst. prof. Haverford (Pa.) Coll., 1956-58; mem. faculty and adminstrn. Cornell U., 1958-71, dir. Ctr. Internat. Studies, 1961-66, v.p. pub. affairs, 1966-71; provost Johns Hopkins U., 1971-72, pres., 1972-90, pres. emeritus, 1990—, fellow Fgn. Policy Inst., disting. lectr., 1993—. Cons. Dept. Def., 1962-67, ACDA, 1967-77; bd. dirs. Orgn. Resources Counselors, Inc., Atlantic Coun. of the U.S. Author: Documents on European Government, 1963; co-editor: From Occupation to Cooperation, 1992, In Search of Germany, 1996; editor: Universities in the Twenty First Century, 1996. Trustee, chmn. St. Mary's Coll., 1991—2003; trustee German Marshall Fund of the US. Decorated comdr. Order of Merit (Fed. Republic of Germany), commendatore Republic of Italy. Mem. Am. Inst. Contemporary German Studies (co-chmn. emeritus), Coun. Fgn. Rels., Am. Polit. Sci. Assn., Internat. Inst. Strategic Studies, Am. Assn. Rhodes Scholars, Phi Beta Kappa, Cosmos Club (Washington). Office: Johns Hopkins U Sch Advanced Internat Studies 1619 Massachusetts Ave NW Washington DC 20036-2213 Office Phone: 202-663-5821. Business E-Mail: smuller1@jhu.edu.

MULLER-PARKER, GISÈLE THÈRÉSE, marine biologist, educator; b. NYC, July 4, 1953; d. Robert Georges Muller and Margarita (Gallo de) Chinchilla; m. Michael B. Parker; children: Henry, Curtis. BS in Biology, SUNY, Stony Brook, 1975; MS in Marine Studies, U. Del., 1978; PhD in Biology, UCLA, 1984. Rsch. asst. U. Nebr., Lincoln, 1984-86, U. Md., Solomons, 1986-89; asst. prof. Western Wash. U., Bellingham, 1990-94, assoc. prof., 1994-2000, prof., 2000—, interim chair, biology dept., 2003—04. Asst. dir. Shannon Point Mar Ctr.-Western Wash. U., Anacortes, 1997—2004; assoc. program dir. Ocean Edn., NSF, 2004—06, program dir. Grad. Rsch. Fellowship Divsn. Grad. Edn., 2008-; panelist NSF and NOAA funding agencies; sci. advisor to pub. ednl. films BBC, IMAX Contbr. articles to profl. jours.; assoc. editor: Coral Reefs, The Biol. Bull., mem. editl. bd. Grantee NSF, NOAA. Mem. AAAS, Am. Soc. Limnology and Oceanography, Internat. Soc. Coral Reef Studies, Phycological Soc. Am., Sigma Xi. Avocations: scuba, swimming. Office: Nat Sci Found Divsn Grad Edn Ste 875 4201 Wilson Blvd Arlington VA 22230 Office Phone: 703-292-7468. Business E-Mail: gmullerp@nsf.gov, gtmuller@nsf.gov, gisele.muller-parker@www.edu.

MULLIGAN, DONAL L., consumer products company executive; Fin. mgmt. positions PepsiCo Inc. & YUM! Brands, 1987—98, Pillsbury Co., 1998—2001; v.p. fin. ops. internat. div. Gen. Mills, Mpls., 2001—04, v.p. fin. ops., 2004—06, v.p., treas., 2006—07, sr. v.p. fin. ops., 2007, exec. v.p., CFO, 2007—. Office: General Mills 1 General Mills Blvd Minneapolis MN 55426

MULLIGAN, JAMES CHRISTOPHER, safety and environmental engineer and manager; m. Pamela Ann Brink, July 29, 2000. BSChemE, Cath. U. America, Washington, 1985; MBA, Villanova U., Pa., 1993. Chem. engr. Jacobs Engring. Group, Washington, 1986—87; ESOH regulatory mgr. Am. Chemistry Coun., Arlington, Va., 1987—90; sr. process safety engr. Chilworth Tech. Inc., Plainsboro, NJ, 1993—2004; sr. safety engr. Lockheed Martin Corp., Moorestown, NJ, 2004—. Mem.: ASTM, AIChE, Nat. Fire Protection Assn., Am. Soc. Safety Engrs. Office: Lockheed Martin Corp 199 Borton Landing Rd Moorestown NJ 08057 Office Fax: 856-359-3445. Business E-Mail: james.c.mulligan@lmco.com.

MULLIGAN, JEREMIAH T., lawyer; b. Rochester, NY, 1944; BA, St. Bernard's Seminary and Coll., 1966; JD, Fordham U., 1970. Mem. Curtis, Mallet-Prevost, Colt & Mosle, NYC. Office: Curtis Mallet-Prevost Colt & Mosle 101 Park Ave Fl 34 New York NY 10178-0061 Office Phone: 212-696-6040. Business E-Mail: jmulligan@curtis.com.

MULLIGAN, JOHN J., tobacco company executive; Student, Holy Cross Coll.; BA in Liberal Arts, St. John's U., NYC, 1976; M in Bus. and Acctg., Fordham U., NYC, 1981. With Mfrs. Hanover Leasing Corp., 1979—86; mgr. lease financing Philip Morris Capital Corp., 1986—87, dir. structured fin., 1987—94, v.p. lease/structured fin., 1994—2001, pres., CEO, 2001—. Office: Altria Group Inc 120 Park Ave New York NY 10017

MULLIGAN, MICHAEL DENNIS, lawyer; b. St. Louis, Mar. 9, 1947; s. Leo Virgil and Elizabeth (Leyse) M.; m. Theresa Baker, Aug. 7, 1971; children: Brennan, Colin. BA in Biology, Amherst Coll., 1968; JD, Columbia U., 1971. Bar: Mo. 1971, U.S. Dist. Ct. (ea. dist.) Mo. 1972, U.S. Ct. Appeals (8th cir.) 1982, U.S. Tax Ct. 1985. Law clk. to judge U.S. Dist. Ct. (ea. dist.) Mo., 1971-72; assoc. Lewis, Rice & Fingersh, L.C., St. Louis, 1972-80, ptnr., 1980—. Mem. editl. bd. Estate Planning Mag., 1985—, Jour. of Taxation, BNA Estates, Gifts and Trusts Jour. Served as cpl. USMC, 1968-70. Fellow Am. Coll. Trust and Estate Counsel; mem. ABA (mem. real property, probate and trust, and taxation sects.), Mo. Bar Assn. (mem. probate and trust, taxation sects.). Office: Lewis Rice & Fingersh LC 500 N Broadway Ste 2000 Saint Louis MO 63102-2147 Home Phone: 317-726-0139; Office Phone: 314-444-7757. Business E-Mail: mmulligan@lewisrice.com.

MULLIKIN, THOMAS WILSON, mathematics professor; b. Flintville, Tenn., Jan. 9, 1928; s. Houston Yost and Daisy (Copeland) M.; m. Mildred Virginia Sugg, June 14, 1952; children: Sarah Virginia, Thomas Wilson, James Copeland. Student, U. South, 1946-47; AB, U. Tenn., 1950; postgrad., Iowa State U., 1952-53; A.M., Harvard, 1954, PhD, 1958. Mathematician Rand Corp., Santa Monica, Calif., 1957-64; prof. math. Purdue U., 1964-93, interim v.p., dean grad. sch., 1991-93, dean grad. sch., prof. math emeritus, 1993—. Served with USNR, 1950-52. Mem.: AAAS, Am. Math. Soc. Home: 104 Club Ct Cape Carteret NC 28584-9736

MULLIN, BERNARD JAMES, media consultant; b. Liverpool, Eng., May 3, 1949; came to US, 1973; s. Bernard F. and Mary A. Mullin; m. Valerie Mullin; children: Julie, Lara, Steven 1 stepchild, Chad. BA in Bus. Studies, Coventry U., Eng., 1972; MS in Mktg., U. Kans., 1974, MBA, 1976, PhD in Bus., 1978. Mgr. mktg. rsch. Brit. Leyland Motor Corp., Oxford, England, 1970—73; mktg. devel. mgr. Serck Tubes Ltd., Birmingham, England, 1973; instr. U. Kans., Lawrence, 1974-77; prof. sport mgmt. U. Mass., Amherst, 1977-86; pres. NSM Mgmt. Cons., Amherst, 1979-86; sr. v.p. bus. Maj. League Baseball Pitts. Pirates, 1986—91; sr. v.p. bus. ops. Maj. League Baseball Colo. Rockies, 1991—93; pres., gen. mgr. Internat. Hockey League Denver Grizzlies, 1993; vice chancellor athletics U. Denver; sr. v.p. mktg. and team bus. ops. NBA, 2000—04; pres., CEO Atlanta Spirit, LLC (parent co. of NBA Atlanta Hawks, NHL Atlanta Thrashers and Philips Arena), 2004—08; founder, prin. The Aspire Group, Inc., Atlanta, 2008—. Author: Sport Marketing. Chmn. bd. mgmt. YMCA Pitts., 1988; bd. mem. Ctrl. Atlanta Progress, Atlanta Sports Coun., Metro Atlanta C. of C. Mem. Rotary Internat. (substance abuse com. 1988), Beta Gamma Sigma. Roman Catholic. Avocations: golf, tennis, soccer, reading. Office: The Aspire Group Inc 3340 Peachtree Rd NE Ste 1800 Atlanta GA 30326 Office Phone: 404-814-5250. Business E-Mail: bernie.mullin@theaspiregroupinc.com.

MULLIN, CHRISTOPHER PAUL, professional sports team executive, retired professional basketball player; b. NYC, July 30, 1963; m. Liz Mullin; children: Sean, Christopher, Liam. Student, St. John's U., 1981—85. Player Golden State Warriors, 1985—97, 2000—01, Ind. Pacers, 1997—2000; exec. v.p. basketball ops. Golden State Warriors, 2004—, gen. mgr., 2007—. Mem. US Men's Olympic Basketball Team, LA, 1984, Barcelona, 92. Recipient Olympic Gold medal, 1984, 1992, Wooden award, 1985; named to Sporting News All-Am. First Team, 1985, NBA All-Star Team, 1989-93, All-NBA First Team, 1992. Office: Golden State Warriors 1011 Broadway Oakland CA 94607*

MULLIN, HADLEY (MARY HADLEY MULLIN), private equity firm executive; b. 1974; BA in Govt., Dartmouth Coll., Hanover, NH, 1996; MBA, Stanford U. Grad. Sch. Bus., Calif., 2002. Various positions in consumer products, retail and healthcare Bain & Co.; joined TSG Consumer Ptnrs. (formerly Shansby Group), San Francisco, 2004, ptnr., mng. dir., 2006—. Bd. dirs. Radio Sys. Corp., 2006—. Named an Arjay

Miller Scholar, Stanford U. Grad. Sch. Bus., 2002. Office: TSG Consumer Ptnrs 600 Montgomery St Ste 2900 San Francisco CA 94111 Office Phone: 415-217-2336. Business E-Mail: hmullin@tsgconsumer.com.*

MULLIN, PATRICK ALLEN, lawyer; b. Newark, Jan. 13, 1950; s. Gerard Vincent and Frances Regina (Magnanti) M. BA, William Paterson U., 1972, MEd, 1974; JD with honors, NY Law Sch., 1979, LLM in Taxation, 1990; postgrad., Harvard Law Sch., 1979. Bar: NJ 1979, DC 1980, NY 1990; cert. criminal trial atty. NJ Supreme Ct. Law clk. to Hon. Dickinson R. DeBevoise, US Dist. Ct. NJ, Trenton, 1979-80; assoc. Charles Morgan Assocs., Washington, 1980-81; pvt. practice, Hackensack, NJ, 1988—; instr., 1985—; criminal trial practise, 1999—2009. Mem. Practitioners Adv. Group US Sentencing Commn., 1995—; lectr. Seton Hall Law Sch., 2001, 02, 04, 2006-, ATLA, 2003; instr. Gerry Spence's Trial Lawyers Coll., 2001-06; moderator ICLE program Upheaval in Fed. and State Sentencing, 2005, lectr. criminal trial practice, 1999-2009; lectr. criminal trial practice Seton Hall Law Sch., 2005. Contbr. articles to profl. jours. Named Super Lawyers, 2009, NJ, 2009; named one of Top 100 Trial Lawyers, Am. Trial Lawyers Assn., NY & NJ, 2007—08. Mem. ABA. Roman Catholic. Avocations: jogging, martial arts. Address: 25 Main St # 200 Hackensack NJ 07601-7015 also: 305 Madison Ave Ste 449 New York NY 10165-0006 Office Phone: 212-639-1600. Home Fax: 201-487-2840. E-mail: mullin@taxdefense.com.

MULLIN, THOMAS J., lawyer, food products executive; b. 1951; BA, NYU; JD, Albany Law Sch. Bar: NY 1977. Prtnr. Phillips, Lytle, Hitchcock, Blaine & Huber, 1982—85; vice chmn., sr. exec. v.p. First Federal Savings and Loan Assn., Rochester, 1985—97; exec. v.p. bus. devel. & corp. strategy C.T. Financial Services, Inc., 1997—2000; pres., CEO TD Waterhouse Bank, 2000; exec. v.p., gen. counsel Constellation Brands, Inc. (formerly Canandaigua Brands, Inc.), 2000—. Office: Constellation Brands Inc 207 High Point Dr # 100 Victor NY 14564-1061 Office Phone: 585-218-3600.

MULLINEAUX, DONAL RAY, geologist; b. Weed, Calif., Feb. 16, 1925; s. Lester Ray and Mary Lorene (Drew) M.; m. Diana Suzanne Charais, Nov. 21, 1951; children: Peter, Lauren, Keith. Student, U. Wash., 1942, BS in Math., 1947, BS in Geology, 1949, MS in Geology, 1950, PhD in Geology, 1961. Drilling insp. U.S. Army C.E., 1948; geologist U.S. Geol. Survey, 1950-86; contracting geologist, 1987-90; scientist emeritus U.S. Geol. Survey, 1990—2005. Author articles on volcanic activity and hazards, Mt. St. Helens, other Cascade Range volcanoes, stratigraphy and engring. geology of Puget Sound Lowland, Wash.; co-author: Forecast of a Mount Saint Helens Eruption, 1978. With USNR, 1943-54, active duty, 1943-46, 51-53. Rsch. fellow Engring. Expt. Sta. U. Wash., 1949-50. Fellow Geol. Soc. Am. (E.B. Burwell Jr. award 1983). Home: 14155 W 54th Ave Arvada CO 80002-1513 Home Phone: 303-278-7245. Personal E-mail: don@mullineaux.us.

MULLINS, CHARLES BROWN, physician, academic administrator; b. Rochester, Ind., July 29, 1934; s. Charles E. and Mary Ruth B. (Bamberger) M.; BA, N. Tex. State U., 1954; MD, U. Tex., 1958; m. Stella Churchill, Dec. 27, 1955; children: Holly, David. Diplomate Am. Bd. Internal Medicine. Intern, U. Colo. Med. Ctr., Denver, 1958-59; resident in internal medicine Parkland Meml. Hosp., Dallas, 1962-64; USPHS rsch. fellow U. Tex. Southwestern Med. Sch., Dallas, 1964-65; chief resident medicine Parkland Meml. Hosp., 1965-66; USPHS spl. rsch. fellow cardiology br. Nat. Heart Inst., Bethesda, Md., 1967-68; practice medicine specializing in cardiology, Dallas, 1966-81; sr. attending staff Parkland Meml. Hosp., dir. med. affairs, 1977-79; asst. prof. medicine U. Tex. Southwestern Med. Sch., Dallas, 1968-71, assoc. prof., 1971-75, dir. clin. cardiology, 1971-77, prof., 1975-79, clin. prof. medicine, 1979-81; prof. medicine U. Tex. Health Sci. Ctr., Dallas, 1981-; exec. vice-chancellor health affairs U. Tex. System, 1981-2001, spl. projects dir., 2001-02; CEO Dallas County Hosp. Dist., 1979-81. Contbr. articles to profl. jours. With M.C., USAF, 1959-62. Fellow ACP, Am. Coll. Cardiology (Tex. gov. 1974-77, chmn. bd. govs. 1976), Am. Heart Assn. Coun. on Clin. Cardiology; mem. AMA, Am. Fedn. Clin. Rsch., Assn. Acad. Health Ctrs., Assn. Univ. Cardiologists, Laennec Soc., Alpha Omega Alpha.

MULLINS, CHRISTOPHER M., physical education educator; b. Columbus, Ohio, July 9, 1970; s. A. Michael and Janet Mullins; m. Tracy Lee Amborn, June 20, 1999; children: Kaitlyn, Geoffrey, Graigory, Alyssa. BS, Excelsior Coll.; MS, Miss. State U. Cert. health education specialist Nat. Commn. Health Edn. Credentialing, Inc., 2004. Health & phys. edn. tchr. Father Duenas Meml. Sch., Hagatna, 2004—; adj. prof. U. Guam, Mangilao, 2005—. Head coach cross-country Father Duenas Meml. Sch., Hagatna, 2004—, head coach track & field, 2005—; health promotion activity program coord. U. Guam, Mangilao, 2005—; co-chair phys. fitness edn. com. Guam Pub. Sch. Sys., Hagatna, 2006. Hosp. corpsman USN, 1988—2001. Decorated Navy Achievement medal US Navy. Mem.: AAHPERD. Cath. Office: Father Duenas Meml Sch PO Box FD Hagatna GU 96932 Home: 415 Chalan San Antonio Ste 101 Barrigada GU 96913-3620 Personal E-mail: chrisatmet@yahoo.com.

MULLINS, JACK ALLEN, cardiologist, educator; b. Oklahoma City, 1952; MD, U. Okla., 1982. Diplomate in internal medicine, cardiovasc. disease, interventional cardiology Am. Bd. Internal Medicine. Intern U. Tex., Houston, 1982-83, resident in internal medicine, 1983-85; fellow in cardiology U. Okla., Oklahoma City, 1985-88; dir. cardiac cath. lab. Columbia Bayshore Med. Ctr., Pasadena, Tex.; clin. instr. cardiology Baylor Coll. Medicine, 1988—, U. Tex. Med. Sch., Houston, 1988—. Mem. ACP, Am. Coll. Cardiology, Am. Heart Assn. Office: Cardiovasc Ctr PA 3337 Plainview St Ste 8 Pasadena TX 77504-1924 Office Phone: 713-941-6083.

MULLINS, JOHN MADISON, educational consultant; b. NYC, May 2, 1919; s. George W. and Hazel (Provence) M.; m. Alice N. Drury, Aug. 15, 1942; children: John W., Ross H., David D. AB, Columbia U., 1941. Rsch. asst. Coll. Entrance Exam. Bd., Princeton, N.J., 1941; asst. registrar Columbia U., NYC, 1946-50, assoc. registrar, 1950-52, registrar, 1952-56, dir. budget, 1956-61; asst. treas. Coll. Entrance Exam. Bd., NYC, 1961, controller, 1962-63, treas., 1964, v.p., treas., 1964-80; sr. v.p., 1981; ednl. cons. Coll. Entrance Exam. Bd., NYC, 1982—87. Chmn. evaluation teams Middle States Assn. Colls. and Secondary Schs., 1949-90; chmn. spl. com. N.Y. State Dept. Edn., 1955-56; mem. No. Valley Regional High Sch. Dist., N.J. Bd. Edn., 1954-63, pres., 1957; cons. Ford Found., 1965-68 Trustee Am. U. in Paris, 1965-2001, vice-chmn., 1981-2001 trustee emeritus, 2001—; bd. dirs. Am. U. in Paris Found., 1985-2001, treas., sec.; trustee Demarest Libr. Assn., 1966-67; bd. dirs. Enriched Summer Forum No. Valley, N.J., 1966-69. Lt. comdr. USNR, 1941-45. Mem. Soc. Columbia Grads. (bd. dirs. 1980-86), Loomis Village Residents Assn. (v.p., 1996-1997, pres., 1997-1999), Phi Gamma Delta. Independent. Home: 20 Bayon Dr Apt 308 South Hadley MA 01075-3336

MULLINS, PATRICK, communications educator; MA in Comm., William Paterson U., Wayne, NJ, 1996; MA in Cinema Studies, NYU, 1999. Editor Motion Picture Editors Local 700, NYC, 1980—2002. Dir.: (documentaries, video documentary) Bracero Stories (Best Documentary, et al., 2008). Office: Univ Texas El Paso Comm Dept 500 W Univ Ave El Paso TX 79968-0556 Office Fax: 915-747-5236. Business E-Mail: pmullins@utep.edu.

MULLIS, KARY BANKS, biochemist; b. Lenoir, NC, Dec. 28, 1944; s. Cecil Banks Mullis and Bernice Alberta (Barker) Fredericks; m. Richards Mullis (div.); 1 child, Louise; m. Cynthia Mullis (div.); children: Christopher, Jeremy; m. Nancy Lier Cosgrove, 1998. BS in Chemistry, Ga. Inst. Tech, 1966; PhD in Biochemistry, U. Calif., Berkeley, 1973; DSc (hon.), U. S.C., 1994. Lectr. biochemistry U. Calif., Berkeley, 1972, postdoctoral fellow San Francisco, 1977—79, U. Kans. Med. Sch., Kansas City, 1973—76; scientist Cetus Corp., Emeryville, Calif., 1979—86; dir. molecular biology Xytronyx, Inc., San Diego, 1986—88; cons. Specialty Labs, Inc., Amersham, Inc., Chiron Inc. and various others, Calif., 1988—96; chmn. StarGene, Inc., San Rafael, Calif.; v.p. Histotec, Inc., Cedar Rapids, Iowa; v.p. molecular biology chemistry Vyrex Inc., La Jolla, Calif.; disting. rschr. Children's Hosp., Rsch. Inst., Oakland, Calif., 2003—; founder, chief scientific officer Altermune LLC, 2003—. Disting. vis. prof. U. S.C. Coll. of Sci. and Math. Author: (autobiography) Dancing Naked in the Mind Field, 1998; contbr. articles to profl. jours.; patentee in field. Bd. dir. Nat. Orgn. Reform of Marijuana Laws, 2000—. Recipient Preis Biochemische Analytik award, German Soc. Clin. Chem., 1990, Allan award, 1990, award, Gairdner Found. Internat., 1991, Nat. Biotech. award, 1991, Robert Koch award, 1992, Chiron Corp. Biotechnology Rsch. award, Am. Soc. Microbiology, 1992, Japan prize, Sci. and Tech. Found. Japan, 1993, Nobel Prize in Chemistry, Nobel Foundation, 1993; named Scientist of Yr., R&D Mag., 1991, Calif. Scientist of Yr., 1992; named to National Inventors Hall of Fame, 1998. Mem.: Inst. Further Study (dir. 1983—), Am. Acad. Achievement, Am. Chem. Soc. Achievements include invention of Polymerase Chain Reaction (PCR). Avocations: astrology, surfing.*

MULLIS, TONY RANDALL, military history educator; s. Don and Susan Mullis (Stepmother); m. Maureen Heller, Apr. 11, 1981; children: Sean, Seth, Scot. B, Auburn U., 1981; M, Va. Tech, 1982; PhD, U. Kans., 2002. Commd. 2d lt. USAF, 1982; acad. instr., advisor Air Command and Staff Coll., Montgomery, Ala., 2002—05; advanced through grades to lt. col USAF; assoc. prof. Command and Gen. Staff Coll., Ft. Leavenworth, Kans., 2005—. Adj. instr. Auburn U., Montgomery, 1997—2005. Author: (book) Peacekeeping on the Plains: Army Operations in Bleeding Kansas; contbr. book. Decorated Meritorious Svc. medal Air Force; Alf Landon Rsch. grant, Kans. State Hist. Soc., 2001. Mem.: Kans. State Hist. Soc., Soc. Mil. History. Avocations: tennis, golf. Office: Command and Gen Staff Coll 100 Simpson Ave Fort Leavenworth KS 66027

MULLOY, MARTIN J., automotive executive; Grad. magna cum laude, Purdue U., West Lafayette, Ind., 1979; M in Indsl. Rels., Wayne State U., Detroit, 1985. Indsl. rels. analyst climate control divsn. Ford Motor Co., 1979, various labor rels./personnel planning positions in Ford Credit, elec. fuel handling divsn. and truck ops., v.p. human resources Ford of Australia, 1996, exec. dir. North & South America labor affairs, then v.p. labor affairs, 2005—. Office: Ford Motor Co N Am Hdqs 1 American Rd Dearborn MI 48126 Office Phone: 313-322-3000. Business E-Mail: mmulloy@ford.com.*

MULLOY, PATRICK ALOYSIUS, lawyer; b. Wilkes-Barre, Pa., Sept. 14, 1941; s. Hugh Patrick and Ellen Mary (Meagher) M.; m. Marjorie Baumer; children: Maura Alice, Daniel Patrick, Claire Ellen. BA magna cum laude, King's Coll., 1963; MA, U. Notre Dame, 1965; JD with honors, George Washington U., 1971; LLM, Harvard U., 1978. Bar: D.C. 1972, Pa. 1972, U.S. Ct. Appeals (D.C., 2d, and 9th cirs.) 1975, U.S. Supreme Ct. 1975, U.S. Ct. Appeals (5th and 9th cirs.) 1976. Fgn. service officer U.S. Dept. State, Washington, 1965-72; trial lawyer Dept. Justice, Washington, 1973-77, sr. lawyer antitrust div., 1978-82; Congl. fellow U.S. Congress, 1983; minority gen. counsel U.S. Senate Banking Com., 1984-86, gen. counsel, 1987-89, sr. counsel, internat. affairs advisor, 1989-92, chief internat. counsel, 1993-94, chief internat. coun. (minority) Washington, 1995-98; asst. sec. market access and compliance Internat. Trade Adminstrn., U.S. Dept. Commerce, Washington, 1998-2001. Apptd. asst. sec., exec. br. commn. on security and coop. in Europe by Pres. Clinton, 1999-2001; apptd. commr. Joint House Senate U.S.-China Econ. and Security Rev. Commn., Washington, 2001—06, 2008-; adj. prof. internat. trade law Cath. U. Law Sch., Washington, 2002-, George Mason Law Sch., Arlington, Va., 2003—; cons. Alfred P. Sloan Found., Washington, 2006-08. Home: 304 W Masonic View Ave Alexandria VA 22301-2419 Office: Hall of States Ste 373 444 N Capitol St NW Washington DC 20001 Office Phone: 202-220-1327. Business E-Mail: pmulloy@sso.org, pmulloy@uscg.gov. E-mail: pamulloy@aol.com.

MULRONEY, BRIAN (MARTIN BRIAN MULRONEY), former Prime Minister of Canada; b. Baie Comeau, Que., Can., Mar. 20, 1939; s. Benedict and Irene (O'Shea) M.; m. Mila Pivnicki, 1973; children: Caroline, Benedict, Mark, Nicolas. BA, St. Francis Xavier U., LLD, 1979; LLL, U. Laval, Que.; LLD (hon.), Meml. U. Nfld., Nfld., 1980, U. W.I., 1993, Tel Aviv U., 1994, Ctrl. Conn. State U., 1994, Barry U., 1995. Ptnr. Ogilvy Renault, Montreal, Canada, 1965-76; exec. v.p. Iron Ore Co. Can., Montreal, 1977-83, 1976-77, pres., 1977-83; mem. Parliament Can. from Ctrl. N.S., Ottawa, Ont., 1983-84; mem. Parliament Can. from Manicouagan, 1984-88; mem. Parliament Can. from Charlevoix, 1988-93; leader of Her Majesty's Loyal Opposition, 1983-84; prime min., 1984-93; royal commr. Cliche Commn. investigating violence in Que. constrn. industry, 1974; sr. ptnr. Ogilvy Renault, Montreal, 1993—. Chmn. internat. adv. bd. Barrick Gold Corp.; mem. adv. bd. The China Internat. Trust and Investment Corp.; mem. Hicks Muse Capital Ptnrs. Ind. News and Media, PLC; mem. internat. adv. coun. Inst. Internat. Studies; bd. dirs. Archer Daniels Midland Co., Barrick Gold Corp., Quebecor World Inc.; capital ptnr. Holdings Corp.; chmn. Forbes, NYC. Author: Where I Stand, 1983, Memoirs, 1939-1993, 2007. Trustee Montreal Heart Inst.; mem. internat. adv. coun. Les Hautes Etudes Commerciales l'Université de Montréal. Recipient Companion of the Order of Can.; named Grand Officer, Ordre Nat. du Que. Office: Ogilvy Renault 1981 McGill College Ave Ste 1100 Montreal PQ Canada H3A 3C1 Business E-Mail: bmulroney@ogilvyrenault.com.

MULROONEY, MELISSA HUTCHENS, museum director; b. Newport, RI, Apr. 19, 1955; BA in Theatre/Performance, U. Delaware, 1977. Copywriter, acct. exec., designer Richard R. Evans Advt., Wilmington, Dela., 1978-80; creative writer, sr. writer Design Group, Wilmington, 1980-81; acct. exec. Assocs. Internat., Inc., Wilmington, 1981-83; dir. mktg. comm. Del. Art Mus., Wilmington, 1984-94, interim exec. dir., 2005; v.p., mus. dir. Internat. Tennis Hall of Fame, Newport, RI, 1994—2000, dir. mktg. comm., 1996—2000; dep. dir. external affairs Chess-In-Schools prog., NYC, 2001—02; cons. dir., capital campaign Mus. Arts & Design, NYC, 2002—03; founder Hitchens & Co. NYC, 2004—05; exec. dir. Stamford Mus. & Nature Ctr., Conn., 2005—. Self-employed promotional writer, radio and video voice-overs, 1978—. Creator Del. Art Mus. Quarterly Mag., 1984; lectr. and presenter in field. Mem. Am. Assn. Museums, Women's Sports Found., New Eng. Mus. Assn., Advt. Club of Del. (bd. dirs. 1978-81, 85-88, award 1980, 81, 84, 90), Del. Press Women. Office: Stamford Mus & Nature Ctr 39 Scofieldtown Rd Stamford CT 06903

MULROW, CYNTHIA DIANE, internist, editor; b. May 23, 1953; MD, Baylor U., 1978; MS. Cert. Internal Medicine, 1981. Dir. VA Cochrane Ctr., San Antonio; prof. medicine U. Tex. Health Sci. Ctr., San Antonio; dir. generalist physician faculty scholars prog. Robert Wood Johnson Found.; dep. editor Annals of Internal Medicine. Fellow: ACP, Coun. for High Blood Pressure Rsch., Am. Heart Assn.; mem.: Inst. Medicine. Mailing: 11711 Elmscourt San Antonio TX 78230*

MULROW, PATRICK JOSEPH, medical educator; s. Patrick J. and Delia M.; m. Jacquelyn Pinover, Aug. 8, 1953; children: Deborah, Nancy, Robert, Catherine. AB, Colgate U., 1947; MD, Cornell U., 1951; MSc (hon.), Yale U., 1969; DSc (hon.), Med. Coll. Ohio, 2005. Intern N.Y. Hosp., 1951-52, resident, 1952-54; instr. physiology Med. Coll. Cornell U., 1954-55; research fellow Stanford U., 1955-57; instr. medicine Yale U., 1957-60, asst. prof., 1960-66, assoc. prof., 1966-69, prof. medicine, 1969-75; chmn. dept. medicine Med. Coll. Ohio, Toledo, 1975—95, prof. medicine, 1975—97, prof. emeritus, 1997—. Chmn. ednl. com. Council for high blood pressure rsch. Am. Heart Assn., 1968-70, mem. exec. com., 1986-96, vice-chmn. of coun., 1990-92, chmn. 1992-94, past chmn., 1995-96; mem. study sect. NIH, 1970-74. Editorial bd. Jour. Clin. Endocrinology and Metabolism, 1966-70, 75-79, Endocrine Rsch., 1974—, Jour. Exptl. Biology and Medicine, Hypertension, 1994-98; contbr. articles to profl. jours. With USNR, 1944-46. Mem. ACP, Am. Soc. Clin. Investigation, Assn. Am. Physicians, Am. Physiol. Soc., Endocrine Soc., Am. Fedn. Clin. Rsch., Am. Clin. and Climatol. Assn., Am. Heart Assn. (nat. rsch. com., chmn. cardiovasc. regulation rsch. study com. 1986-91), Assn. Profs. Medicine, Assn. Program Dirs. in Internal Medicine, Cen. Soc. Clin. Rsch. (pres. 1988-89), Internat. Soc. Hypertension, World Hypertension League (sec.-gen. 1995-2005), Inter-Am. Soc. Hypertension, Sigma Xi (pres. Yale chpt. 1965-66), Alpha Omega Alpha. Home: 9526 Carnoustie Rd Perrysburg OH 43551-3501 Office: Univ Toledo Dept Medicine 3000 Arlington Ave Toledo OH 43614-5809 Office Phone: 419-383-6016.

MULRYAN, HENRY TRIST, mining executive, consultant; b. Palo Alto, Calif., Jan. 6, 1927; s. Henry and Marian Abigail (Trist) M.; m. Lenore Hoag, Aug. 25, 1948; children: James W., Carol. Student, Yale U., 1945-46; AB in Econs., Stanford U., 1948; postgrad., Am. Grad. Sch. Internat. Bus., 1949, Columbia U., 1983. V.p. mktg. Sierra Talc Co., South Pasadena, Calif., 1955-65, United Sierra, Trenton, NJ, 1965-67, v.p., gen. mgr., 1967-70, pres., 1970-77; v.p. Cyprus Mines Corp., Los Angeles, 1978-80; sr. v.p. ops. Cyprus indsl. minerals div. Amoco Minerals Co., Englewood, Colo., 1980-85; pres. Cyprus Indls. Minerals Co., Englewood, 1985-87; v.p. Cyprus Minerals Co., Englewood, 1985-87, sr. v.p. mktg., corp. adminstr., 1987-89; pres. Mineral Econs. Internat., 1989—. Vol. exec. Internat. Exec. Svc. Corps., Zimbabwe, 1998, Romania, 98, Jordan, 2000, Jordan, 01, Jordan, 02, Jordan, 04, Armenia, 03; dir. Jonathan Art Found., 1997—2005, pres., 2004—05. Served with U.S. Army, 1944-46. Mem.: Rotary (pres. South Pasadena club 1964—65, bd. dir. Princeton, N.J. club 1969—75), Jonathan Club. Office: 539 Muskingum Ave Pacific Palisades CA 90272-4252 E-mail: htmulryan@verizon.net.

MULUZI, ELSON BAKILI, former President of Malawi; b. Mar. 17, 1943; Diploma in Tech. Edn., Thirsted Tech. Coll., Denmark, Huddersfield Coll. Edn., England; LLD (hon.), Lincoln U., Mo., 1995, Glasgow U., 1997; D in Polit. Sci. (hon.), Nat. Chengchi U., Taipei, Taiwan, 1999; LittD (hon.), U. Strathclyde, Glasgow, 2000. Regional sec., then branch sec. Malawi Congress Party, 1959-60, sec. gen., adminstrv. sec.; elected M.P., 1975; parliamentary sec. Ministry of Youth and Culture, 1976; min. edn. Republic of Malawi, Lilongwe, 1976-77, min. without portfolio, 1977-82, min. transport and comm., 1982, pres., 1994—2004. Prin. Nasawa Tech. Coll., 1973-75; mem. Commonwealth Parliamentary Assn., 1975. Mem. United Dem. Front (pres. 1992—). Mem. United Democratic Front.

MULVA, JAMES JOSEPH, oil industry executive; b. Oshkosh, Wis., June 19, 1946; m. Miriam Mulva; 2 children. BBA in Fin., U. Tex., 1968, MBA in Fin., 1969. Mgmt. trainee, treas. Phillips Petroleum Co., Bartlesville, Okla., 1973, asst. treas. London, 1974, mgr. fgn. exch. and investment Bartlesville, Okla., 1976, v.p., treas. Europe/Africa div. London, 1980, mgr. corp. and planning Bartlesville, Okla., 1984, asst. treas., 1985, treas., 1986, v.p., treas., 1988—90, chief fin. officer, 1990—99, pres., COO, 1994—99, vice-chmn., pres. & CEO, 1999, chmn., CEO, 1999—2002; pres., CEO ConocoPhillips, Houston, 2002—04, chmn., pres., CEO, 2004—. Officer Navy, 1969—73. Roman Catholic. Office: ConocoPhillips PO Box 2197 Houston TX 77252-2197*

MULVA, PATRICK T., oil industry executive; b. Green Bay; BBA, Notre Dame U.; MBA, U. Tex. Fin. analyst Exxon Mobil Corp., Baton Rouge, 1976, exec. asst. to pres. U.S. affiliate, 1987, asst. contr. internat. affiliate, fin. dir. Malaysia, 1991, upstream to asst. contr., 1993, v.p. investor rels. and sec., 2002—04, v.p., contr., 2004—; contr. Imperial Oil Ltd., 1996, sr. v.p. fin. and adminstrn., 1998—2002, contr., 2000—02. With USAF, 1972—75. Office: Exxon Mobil Corp Hdqs 5959 Las Colinas Blvd Irving TX 75039-2298*

MULVANEY, MARY JEAN, retired physical education educator; b. Omaha, Jan. 6, 1927; d. Marion Fowler and Blanche Gibons (McKee) M. BS, U. Nebr., 1948; MS, Wellesley Coll., 1951; LHD (hon.), U. Nebr., 1986. Instr. Kans. State U., Manhattan, 1948-50, U. Nebr., Lincoln, 1951-57, asst. prof., 1957-62, U. Kans., Lawrence, 1962-66; assoc. prof. U. Chgo., 1966-76, prof., 1976-90, prof. emeritus, 1990—, chmn. women's divsn., 1966-76, chmn. dept. phys. edn. and athletics, 1976-90; mem. vis. com. on athletics MIT, 1978-81, Wellesley Coll., 1978-79. Dir. athletics U. Chgo., 1980—90; mem. selection com. U. Chgo. Athletic Hall of Fame, 2004—07. Recipient Honor award Nebr. Assn. Health, Phys. Edn. and Recreation, 1962, U. Nebr. Alumni Achievement award, 1998; named to U. Chgo. Athletic Hall of Fame, 2003; Office of Dir. Athletics, U. Chgo., named in honor, 2003. Mem.: AAHPERD, Univ. Athletic Assn. (chmn. athletic adminstrs. com. 1986—88, sec. 1986—90, exec. com. 1986—90, dels. com. 1986—90), Ill. Assn. Intercollegiate Athletics for Women (chmn. 1978—80), Nat. Assn. Collegiate Dirs. of Athletics (exec. com. 1976—80, Hall of Fame 1990), Midwest Assn. Intercollegiate Athletics for Women (chmn. 1979—81), Nat. Collegiate Assn. Women Athletic Adminstrs. (Lifetime Achievement award 2006), Nat. Collegiate Athletic Assn. (coun. 1983—87, com. mem.), Alpha Chi Omega, Mortar Bd. Home: 5821 Kennelley Ct Lincoln NE 68516-3799 Personal E-mail: maryjeanmulvany@aol.com.

MULVANEY, SEAN R., federal agency administrator; b. Jan. 6, 1968; married; 2 children. BA, Wash. U., St. Louis; MA in Internat. Mgmt., Thunderbird, Am. Grad. Sch. Internat. Mgmt. Budget analyst Com. on Budget US Ho. of Reps., Washington, legis. asst., fgn.-ops. and trade advisor to US Rep. Jim Kolbe, asst. to spkr. for policy, Office of Speaker of Ho. of Reps. J. Dennis Hastert, 1999—2006; asst. adminstr. for mgmt. US Agy. Internat. Devel., Washington, 2007—. Office: US Agy Internat Devel Ronald Regan Bldg Rm 609-038 1300 Pennsylvania Ave NW Washington DC 20523-1000 Office Phone: 202-712-1200. Office Fax: 202-216-3393. E-mail: smulvaney@usaid.gov.

MULVEE, ROBERT EDWARD, bishop emeritus; b. Boston, Feb. 15, 1930; s. John F. and Jennie T. Mulvee. BA, PhB, U. Sem. Ottawa, 1953; MRE, Am. Coll., Louvain, Belgium, 1957; D Canon Law, Lateran U., Rome, 1964; DD (hon.), Rivier Coll., Nashua, NH, 1979. Ordained priest Diocese of Manchester, NH, 1957, aux. bishop NH, 1977—85; asst. chancellor of diocese, 1964—72; named monsignor, 1966; elevated to domestic prelate, 1970; named chancellor, 1972; ordained bishop, 1977; bishop Diocese of Wilmington, Del., 1985—95; coadjutor bishop Diocese of Providence, RI, 1995—97, bishop RI, 1997—2005, bishop emeritus, 2005—. Trustee Nat. Shrine Immaculate Conception, Washington, 1987. Mem.: Nat. Conf. Cath. Bishops. Roman Catholic.

MULVEY, VICTORIA A., counselor; b. Jamaica, NY, Sept. 15, 1941; m. Francis E. Mulvey; children: Francis, James, Lisa. BA, MS, L.I. U. Nat. cert. counselor. Lic. mental health counselor pvt. practice, 1994. Mem. Am. Counseling Assn., Nat. Assn. Children Alcoholics, N.Y. State Mental Health Counselors. Office Phone: 631-728-5723. E-mail: vfmulvey@optonline.net.

MULVEY, WILLIAM J., lawyer; b. Euclid, Ohio, Aug. 22, 1948; s. William J. and Muriel (McMahon) Mulvey; m. Marsha Cassiere Mulvey, June 29, 1974; children: William Cassiere, M. Joseph, Timothy R. BA, Athenium of Ohio, Cin., 1970; JD, U. Cin., 1975. Bar: Ohio 1975, U.S. Dist. Ct. (so. dist.) Ohio 1975, cert.: Nat. Bd. Civil Trial Advocates (civil trial advocate). Atty. Lyons & Fries, Cin., 1975—2004; atty./ptnr. Mulvey & Muller LLC, Cin., 2004—. Mem.: Trucking Insurance Def. Assn., TDA, Ohio Assn. Civil Trial Attys., Def. Rsch. Inst., Cin. Bar Assn., Ohio State Bar Assn. Office: Mulvey and Muller LLC 35 E 7th St Ste 750 Cincinnati OH 45202-2411 Office Phone: 513-621-6674 ext 114.

MULVIHILL, JAMES EDWARD, periodontist, educator, health center administrator; b. Cleve., Sept. 24, 1940; s. John F. and Teresa J. (Carlos) M.; m. May Jane Forino, 1963; children— Karen, Kristen, Jason BA, Coll. of Holy Cross, 1962; DMD, Harvard U., 1966. Asst. dean for student affairs, coordinator Harvard-VA continuing edn. program Harvard Sch. Dental Medicine, Boston, 1970-71; dean clin. campus L.I. Jewish-Hillside Med. Ctr., Queens Hosp. Ctr. Affiliation, Jewish Inst. for Geriatric Care, Health Scis. Ctr. SUNY-Stony Brook, 1971-80; v.p. for edn. and research L.I. Jewish-Hillside Med. Ctr., New Hyde Park, NY, 1975-80; v.p., provost for health affairs, exec. dir. Health Ctr., prof. periodontics U. Conn., Farmington, 1980-92; attending periodontist John Dempsey Hosp., U. Conn. Health Ctr., Farmington, 1982-92; pres. John Dempsey Fin. Corp., Farmington, 1988-92; sr. v.p. for health policy The Travelers Corp., Hartford, Conn., 1992-94; chmn. bd. The Travelers Health Co., Hartford, 1992-93; sr. fellow in health policy Assn. of Acad. Health Ctrs., 1994; pres., CEO Managed Health, Inc., 1994, Comty. Health Plan of Queens/Nassau, New Hyde Park, NY, 1994-95, Forsyth Dental Ctr., Boston, 1995-96, Juvenile Diabetes Found. Internat., 1996-99; dir. instnl. advancement and corp. rels. Am. Dental Edn. Assn., 2000—08; asst. to pres. So. Maine Med. Ctr., 2000—01; chief dept. dentistry Harvard U. Health Svcs., 2003—07; resource devel. mgr. The First Tee. Adv. bd. mem. TBS Techs., Inc; cons. in field. Author: (with others) Guide to Foreign Medical Schools, 1975, Editorial Instructions for Dental Authors, 1979-80, 1979, Human Subjects Research: The Operational Handbook for IRB's, 1982, 2d edit., 1984, Japanese edit., 1987; also articles, chpt. in book Bd. dirs. Nat. Dentex Corp., Nat. Fund for Med. Edn.; overseer Joslin Diabetes Ctr. Recipient Disting. Alumnus award Harvard Sch. Dental Medicine, 1982, Disting. alumnus award Holy Cross Coll., 1991, Disting. Svc. award Am. Dental Edn. Assn., 2008. Fellow AAAS, Am. Coll. Dentistry, Internat. Coll. Dentistry; mem. ADA, Am. Acad. Periodontology, Conn. State Dental Assn. (Fones award 2004), Alpha Sigma Nu, Sigma Psi. Avocations: golf, gardening, photography. Address: 117 Kings Hwy Kennebunkport ME 04046-5606 Personal E-mail: mulvi@roadrunner.com.

MULVIHILL, MAUREEN ESTHER, writer, professor; b. Detroit; d. Charles James and Esther (Byrne) M.; m. Daniel R. Harris, June 18, 1983. PhD in English, U. Wis., 1982; postgrad., Columbia U., Met. Mus. Art, Yale U. Instr., faculty U. Detroit, 1968-70; instr. Wayne State U., Detroit, 1969-70, Penn Valley C.C., Kansas City, Mo., 1970-71; project writer Office of Gov., State of Wis., Madison, 1972-82; chief mktg. and sales writer Gruntal & Co., Inc. Wall St., NYC, 1983-85; writer Victorian Soc. America, 2008, Rapportage Lit. Mag., Lancaster, Pa., 2008—; vis. asst. prof. Hunter Coll. CUNY, 1984; assoc. fellow Inst. for Rsch. in History, NYC, 1984-89; vis. asst. prof. Touro Coll., NYC, 1985; elected mem. Princeton (N.J.) Rsch. Forum, 1991—, mem., 1991—; cons. writer-editor Securities Industry Automated Corp./NYSE, NYC, 1986-94; residence Park Slope, Brooklyn, NY, 1983—. Proposal evaluator NEH, Washington, 1989—; juror Clifford Com. Am. Soc. for 18th Century Studies, 1991; vis. faculty NYU, 1983-85, 93, 2007, Marymount Manhattan Coll., 1993-94, Nyack Coll., N.Y.C., 2004; vis. assoc. prof. Fordham U.-Lincoln Ctr., 1994-96; vis. prof. English, St. Joseph Coll., Bklyn., 1997, St. John's U., Manhattan, 2005-2007; guest spkr. Bklyn. Mus., Bklyn. Pub. Libr., NYU, Princeton U., Utah State U., Tex. State U., San Marcos, Am. Irish Hist. Soc., NYC, Sweeney Conf., Stony Brook-SUNY, Pollock-Krasner Found., 2008; corp. liaison Irish Art Exhbn., U.S., U.K.; writer mktg. com. Saatchi & Saatchi, N.Y.C., 1998-99; cons. book devel., book proposal evaluator MLA, N.Y.C., 1998—; cons. book devel., book proposal evaluator MLA, N.Y.C., 1998-; cons. submissions evaluator, rewriter, editor profl. jours. and U.S./UK pubs. Editor: Poems by Ephelia (ca. 1679), 1992, 1993, Ephelia, 2003; author: Thumbprints of Ephelia: An Online, Multimedia Archive, 2001—; adv. editor: ABC-CLIO Ireland and the Americas, 3 vols., 2008; editor: (poems) Mary Leadbeater, Irish Women Poets online textbase, 2008; contbr. articles to profl. jours. Recipient scholarships and awards Wayne State U., 1966, 67-68, U. Wis., 1971-81, Inst. Rsch. History, N.Y.C., 1984-89; NEH fellow, Johns Hopkins U., 1990, Princeton Rsch. Forum, N.J., 1992, 95, 97, Honors List of Scholars & Tchrs, Women's Caucus, Am. Soc. Eighteenth-Century Stds, 2001. Democrat. Roman Catholic. Avocation: rare book collecting.

MUMFORD, CHRISTOPHER GREENE, corporate financial executive; b. Washington, Oct. 21, 1945; s. Milton C. and Dorothea L. (Greene) Mumford. BA, Stanford U., 1968, MBA, 1975. Cons. Internat. Tech. Resources Inc., 1974; asst. v.p. Wells Fargo Bank, San Francisco, 1975-78; asst. treas. Arcata Corp., San Francisco, 1978-82, v.p. fin., 1982-87, exec. v.p. fin., 1987-94. Gen. ptnr. Scarff, Sears & Assocs., San Francisco, 1986—95; mng. dir. Questor Ptnrs. Fund, L.P., San Francisco, 1995—98; v.p. bd. dirs. Triangle Pacific Corp., Dallas, 1986—88, Norton Enterprises Inc., Salt Lake City, 1988—90, Crown Pacific Ptnrs., Portland, Oreg., 1991—2004, Ryder TRS, Inc., Miami, Fla., 1996—98, Ockham PLC, London, 1996—98, Impco Technologies, Inc., Cerritos, Calif., 1998—2000. Office: PO Box 1340 Mill Valley CA 94942-1340 Office Phone: 415-601-6800. Personal E-mail: cgmumford@aol.com.

MUMFORD, DAVID BRYANT, mathematics professor; b. Worth, Sussex, Eng., June 11, 1937; came to U.S., 1940; s. William Bryant and Grace (Schiott) M.; m. Erika Jentsch, June 27, 1959 (dec. July 30, 1988); children: Stephen, Peter, Jeremy, Suchitra; m. Jenifer Moore, Dec. 29, 1989. BA, Harvard U., 1957, PhD, 1961; DSc (hon.), U. Warwick, 1983, Norwegian U. Sci. Tech., 2000, Rockefeller U., 2001. Jr. fellow Harvard U., 1958-61, assoc. prof., 1962—67, prof. math., 1967—77, Higgins prof., 1977-97, chmn. dept. math, 1981-84, prof., divsn. applied math., 1995—96, Brown U., 1996—. V.p. Internat. Math. Union, 1991-94, pres., 1995-99. Author: Geometric Invariant Theory, 1965, Abelian Varieties, 1970, Introduction to Algebraic Geometry, 1976, 2 and 3 Dimensional Patterns of the Face, 1999, Indra's Pearls, 2002. Recipient Fields medal Internat. Congress Mathematicians, 1974, Longuet-Higgins prize, 2005, Shaw prize in Math. Sciences, Shaw Found., Hong Kong, 2006, Leroy P. Steele prize for Math. Exposition, Am. Math. Soc., 2007; co-recipient Wolf Found. prize in Math., Israel, 2008; MacArthur Found. fellow, 1987-92. Fellow Tata Inst. (hon.); mem. Acad. Nazionale dei Lincei, Nat. Acad. Scis., Am. Acad. Arts and Scis., Am. Philos. Soc., Norwegian Acad. Sci. and Letters, Royal Soc. London (fgn. mem.). Office: Brown U 182 George St Providence RI 02912-9056 Home: 15 Sleeper St Boston MA 02210 Office Phone: 401-863-3441. E-mail: david_mumford@brown.edu.

MUMFORD, LAWRENCE R., composer, educator; s. Richard W. and Mary Margaret Mumford; m. Donna L. Mumford, Mar. 9, 1996. BA in Music, George Washington U., 1975; MMus, Peabody Conservatory, Balt., 1976; DMus, U. So. Calif., LA, 1989. Cert. tchr. Ind. U., Bloomington, 1977. Music accompanist Glendale Coll., Calif., 1990—91; music prof. The Master's Coll., Santa Clarita, Calif., 1992—2004; adj. music prof. Calif. State U., Northridge, 1993—94, Concordia U., Irvine, Calif., 2001—04; prof. music Vanguard U., Costa Mesa, 2004—07, Biola U., La Mirada, Calif., 2008—. Compositions and arrangements published by 8 different cos. Recipient Composition Prize, Culver Chamber Soc., 1999. Mem.: Soc. for Music Theory, Soc. of Composers, Inc., Music Tchrs. Assn. of Calif. (branch pres. 1989—90, pres. emeritus), Pi Kappa Lambda, Phi Beta Kappa. Home: 15 Cortona Irvine CA 92614 Office: Conservatory Music 13800 Biola Ave La Mirada CA 90639

MUMFORD, ROBIN BRUCE, foundation administrator, director, lighting designer; b. London, June 20, 1931; s. Ivor Ross James and Hannah Mumford; life ptnr. Shirley Jenny Handisyde, Dec. 29, 1954; children: Roger Andrew, Richard. BSc in Chemistry, London, 1953. Fellow Plastics and Rubber Inst., London, 1953—54; exec. dir. Ctrl. Pk. Hist. Field Trips Inc., NYC, 1985—. V.p. Devel. Delay Resources, Pitts., 2004—, dir. Dir. Nat. Assn. for Visually Handicapped, NYC. Lt. Royal Signals, 1954—56, UK. Achievements include 12 patents in fields. Home: 330 Shore Dr C-5 Highlands NJ 07732 Office: Central Park Historical Field Trips Inc 598 Broadway New York NY 10012 Office Fax: 212-625-8020. Personal E-mail: mumford.robin@gmail.com. Business E-Mail: robin@theleadershipprogram.com.

MUMM, STEVEN ROBERT, geneticist, educator; s. Harry John and Louisa Elizabeth Mumm; m. Kimberly Allen Baker, May 27, 1978; children: Eric Anderson, Emily Baker. BS in BioChemistry, U. Mo., 1978, MS in Chemistry, 1983; PhD in Cellular and Molecular Biology, St. Louis U., 1992. Asst. prof. medicine Washington U. Sch. Medicine, St. Louis, 1999—. Mem. sci. staff Shriners Hosps. for Children, St. Louis. Contbr. articles to profl.jours. Predoctoral trainee, NIH, 1984—88, postdoctoral trainee, 1994—95, Markey postdoctoral fellow, Washington U. Sch. Medicine, 1992—94, postdoctoral fellow, Shriners Hosps. for Children, 1995—97. Mem.: Am. Soc. Bone and Mineral Rsch., Am. Soc. Human Genetics, Am. Soc. Microbiology. Office: Washington U Sch Medicine Saint Louis MO E-mail: smumm@wustl.edu.

MUMMA, ALBERT GIRARD, JR., architect; b. Long Beach, Calif., July 2, 1928; s. Albert Girard and Carmen (Braley) M.; m. Janeal Thomas Woolf, Dec. 24, 1973; children: Eugenia M. Villagra, Albert Girard III, Peter Brenaman. B.Arch., U. Va., 1951. Designer McLeod & Ferrara, Architects, Washington, 1951-56; assoc. Deigert & Yerkes, Architects, 1956-62; prin. Mumma & Assocs., Washington, 1962—. Archtl. designer hotel div. Marriott Corp., 1980-82 Prin. archtl. works include Nat. Arboretum Hdqrs. Bldg, 1961, Finnmark Sq., Silver Spring, Md., 1964, Inverness townhouses, Potomac, Md., 1971, Post Office and Fed. Bldg., Elkins, W.Va., 1971, U.S. Trade Fairs in Spain, Finland, Japan, El Salvador, Poland 1963-72, Fallswood housing project, Falls Church, Va., 1972, Bristow Village townhouses, Annandale, Va., 1972-73, Marriott Hotel, Dayton, Ohio, 1982, Plaza Venetia, Biscayne Bay, Miami, Fla., 1983, Houston Med. Ctr. Hotel, Newark Airport Hotel, 1984, pvt. residences, No. Neck, Rappahanock River, Lancaster County, Va., 1993-2004, subdivision and townhouse projects, Washington, Md., Va., Pa., 1962—. Served with USMC, 1945-47. Recipient Design award Washington Bd. Trade, 1964; winner Newark Airport Hotel Competition, 1981. Mem. AIA (medal 1951), Rappahannock River Yacht Club, Indian Creek Yacht and Country Club, Moran Creek Yacht Club.

MUMMA, MICHAEL JON, research scientist; b. Lancaster, Pa., Dec. 3, 1941; s. John Henry and Violet Lyndell (Baxter) M.; m. Sage Bailey Tower, Aug. 20, 1966; children: Peter Robb, Amy Elizabeth. AB in Physics with honors, Franklin and Marshall Coll., 1963; PhD in Physics, U. Pitts., 1970. Grad. research asst. U. Pitts., 1963-70; astrophysicist NASA Goddard Space Flight Center, Greenbelt, Md., 1970-76, head br. Infrared and Radio Astronomy, 1976-84, assoc. chief Lab. Extraterrestrial Physics, 1984-85, head Planetary Systems br., 1985-90, chief scientist Lab. Extraterrestrial Physics, 1990—, dir. Goddard Ctr. Astrobiology, 2003—; adj. rsch. assoc. in physics Pa. State U., 1978—81, prof. physics, 1981-88; sr. scientist Solar Sys. Exploration Divsn., 2005—. Mem. numerous working groups and adv. coms. NASA, Nat. Bur. Standards, NSF, Nat. Acad. Scis., 1973—; adj. prof. physics U. Toledo, 2002-05; lectr. in field. Contbr. numerous articles to profl. publs., 1970—; editor: The Study of Comets, Vols. 1, 2, 1976, Vibrational-Rotational Spectroscopy for Planetary Atmospheres, vols. 1, 2, 1982, Astrophysics from the Moon, 1990. Recipient NASA medal for Exceptional Sci. Achievement, 1988, 97; Kershner award for physics, 1962; Coll. Trustee's scholar, 1963; Alumni Citation Career Achievement, Franklin Marshall Coll., 2008; Asteroid 8340 named "Michael J. Mumma" by Internat. Astron. Union, 1999. Fellow Am. Phys. Soc., Washington Acad. Sci.; mem. AAAS, Am. Astron. Soc., Am. Geophys. Union, Internat. Astron. Union, Sigma Pi Sigma. Achievements include discovery of natural lasers in atmospheres of Mars, Venus, and Jupiter; first detection of water vapor in comets, discovery of formaldehyde, methanol, methane, and ethane in comets; discovery of x-rays in comets; first definitive measurements of deuterium and hydrogen on Mars and Venus; first absolute wind measurements on Venus and Mars; invention of tunable diode laser heterodyne spectrometer and other advanced instruments; development of Doppler-limited infrared spectroscopy for laboratory and astrophysical applications, of absolute calibration procedures in vacuum ultraviolet, of molecular branching ratio technique for intensity calibration in vacuum ultraviolet; measurement of many absolute cross sections in vacuum ultraviolet; research on atomic and molecular physics and chemistry, on comets, on planetary atmospheres, on infrared astronomy, on high-resolution spectroscopy, and in the field of dissociative excitation of molecules. Office: Code 690 3 Goddard Space Flight Ctr Greenbelt MD 20771-0001

MUMMANENI, PADMAJA, research scientist, educator; d. Ram Mohan Rao and Lakshmiswaramma Mummaneni. BSc in Life Scis., Delhi U., India, 1980, MSc, 1982, PhD, 1989. Postdoctoral rsch. fellow U. Ky., Lexington, 1989—96; staff fellow NIH, Bethesda, Md., 1996—2000; scientist Neuralstem Inc., Gaithersburg, Md., 2000—03; vol. consult dir. Neuronascent Inc., Md., 2004; contract RSR fellow CDER, FDA, Rockville, Md., 2004—05; adj. prof. microbiology Marymount U., Va., 2005. Guest lectr. Found. for Advanced Edn. in the Scis. NIH, Bethesda, Md., 1998—2000, juror, 1998—2000. Contbr. articles to profl./peer-reviewed jours. Fellow: AAAS, Am. Soc. of Cellular and Molecular Biology, N.Y. Acad. Scis.; mem.: Am. Women In Sci. Hindu. Avocations: painting, art. Home: 10513 Montrose Ave Bethesda MD 20814 Office: FDA 1451 Rockville Pike Rockville MD 20852 Personal E-mail: pmummaneni@aol.com.

MUMPHREY, J. WAYNE, lawyer; b. New Orleans, July 16, 1947; m. Victoria B. Brown, Dec. 27, 1969; children: Claude S. II, Wayne B., Sarah B. JD, Loyola U., 1971. Bar: La. 1971, U.S. Ct. Appeals (5th cir.) 1983, U.S. Claims Ct. 1990. Atty. pvt. practice, Chalmette, La., 1981—. Mem.: La. Trial Lawyers Assn., Am. Trial Lawyers Assn. Home: PO Box 90 Chalmette LA 70044 Office: Mumphrey Law Firm LLC 9061 West Judge Perez Dr Chalmette LA 70043 E-mail: jwmumphrey@mumphreylaw.com.

MUMPOWER, CARL, III, councilman; b. London, Dec. 4, 1952; m. Lisa Mumpower; children: Kristen, Matthew. AA in Gen. Studies, Okaloosa-Walton Jr. Coll., Fla., 1973; BA in Psychology, St. Leo Coll., Fla., 1974; MA in Counseling, Western Carolina U., Cullowhee, NC, 1975; MSW in Clin. Social Work, U. Ga., Athens, 1976; PhD in Clin. Psychology, Union Inst. & Univ., Cin., 1985. Lic. practicing psychologist NC, health care provider in psychology NC, practicing psychologist NC; LCSW NC. Chmn. United Services Credit Union; vice mayor City of Ashville, NC, councilman. Mem. NC Marriage and Family Therapy Lic. Bd.; chmn. NC Social Work Lic. Bd. Founder Top-A-Stop Bus Shelter Program; chair For Our Kids... Pub. Housing Initiative; chmn. Meml. Stadium Restoration Comm., Asheville-Buncombe Drug Commn., Asheville Civic Ctr. Commn.; mem. First Bapt. Ch.; bd. dirs. John Locke Found. Served with USAF, 1970—73, Vietnam. Republican. Office: c/o Asheville City Coun 70 Court Plz PO Box 7148 Asheville NC 28802 Office Phone: 828-251-1122.

MUNASINGHE, RANJITH ARACHCHIGE, mathematics professor, engineer; b. Galle, Sri Lanka, Jan. 16, 1957; arrived in U.S., 1985; s. Martin Silva and Roslin Munasinghe; m. Lakmalie Fernando Munasinghe, Jan. 1, 1991; children: Ranga, Malie. BS in Elec. and Electronic Engring., U. Peradeniya, Sri Lanka, 1982; MS in Math., U. Wyo., Laramie, 1987, PhD in Math., 1992. Engr. Dept. Telecomm., Colombo, Sri Lanka, 1982—83, Saudi Telecomm., Riyadh, 1983—85; tchg. asst. U. Wyo., Laramie, 1985—92; prof. math. W. Va. Inst. Tech., Montgomery, 1992—. Author: (articles) Houston Jour. Math., Coll. Jour. Math. Recipient Jathika Navodaya scholarship, Sri Lanka; nominee Golden Apple award for Tchg., U. Wyo.; grantee, Dept. Defense/Alton Sys., Montgomery, 2003—, SURE project, Dept. Energy, Montgomery, 2005—. Mem.: Am. Soc. Engring. Edn. Avocations: chess, camping, reading. Home: 101 Stratford Pl Charleston WV 25303 Office: W Va Inst Tech Dept Math Montgomery WV 25136 Business E-Mail: ranjith.munasinghe@mail.wvu.edu.

MUNCH, DAVID, retired chemistry professor; b. St. Louis, Nov. 20, 1942; s. Ralph Howard and Charlotte Erwin Munch; m. Helen Weist, July 3, 2004; m. Martha Kingsbury, Dec. 23, 1966 (div. Sept. 1990); 1 child, Margaret Kingsbury. BS, Portland State U., OR, 1966; PhD, U. Wash., Seattle, 1974. Harvard rsch. fellow U. Paris VII, 1974—75; asst. prof. Am. U. Paris, 1975—76; vis. asst. prof. U. Puget Sound, Tacoma, 1977—84; instr. U. Wash., Seattle, 1976—77; vis. scientist Hiroshima U., Japan, 1984—85; chemistry prof. Seattle Ctrl. CC, 1988—2006; treas. Puget Sound Sect. Am. Chem. Soc., Seattle, 1989—. Rsch. Grant, Centre Nat. de la Recherche Scientifique, 1974—75. Mem.: Phi Lambda Epsilon, Am. Chem. Soc. Avocations: travel, gardening, hiking, bicycling. Home: 7322 21st Ave NE Seattle WA 98115-5716 Business E-Mail: dmunch@sccd.ctc.edu.

MUNCH, JANET BUTLER, librarian; b. NYC, Dec. 1, 1950; d. William Leland Butler and Mary Teresa O'Leary; m. Vincent Arthur Munch, Mar. 18, 1978; children: Jennifer Antonia, Andrew Leland. BA, Mercy Coll., Dobbs Ferry, NY, 1972; MLS, Pratt Inst., Bklyn., 1974; DLS, Columbia U., 1992. Libr. The Bronx County Hist. Soc., NY, 1974—77; br. libr. Mercy Coll., Bronx, 1977—85; spl. collections libr. Lehman Coll., CUNY, NY, 1985—. Pres. The Bronx Libr. Assn., 1974—78. Faculty coun. CUNY Inst. Irish-Am. Studies, Bronx, NY, 2004—; libr. panel liaison U. Com. Rsch. Awards, CUNY, NYC, 2007—. Recipient Plaque award, Bronx Libr. Assn., 1979, PSC-CUNY Rsch. award, 1992, Plaque award, CUNY Inst. Irish-Am. Studies, 2008, Traveling Exhibits awards, Am. Libr. Assn.,Nat. Endowment Humanities, 2006, Retrospective Conversion Archive & Manuscript Records award, METRO, 2004, NYC Digitization Project award, 2006, 2008, Coordinated Collection Devel. Aid award, NYS Libr., 1992—2000; grantee Mini grant, NY Coun. Humanities, 2006; Shared-Cost Retrospective Newspaper Microfilming grant, NYS Libr., 1986, Maj. Instl. grant, CUNY, 2003, 2006, Profl. Reassignment Leave in Libr., Lehman Coll., CUNY, 1987—88, 1993, 1996, George N. Shuster fellowship, 1987, 1988, 1993, 1996, Conservation/Preservation Discretionary grant, NYS Edn. Dept., 1985, 1990, 1992, 1993, 2006. Mem.: Assn. Coll. & Rsch. Libraries (symposium planning comm. 1996—99), Archivists Roundtable Met. NY, Libr. Assn. CUNY (chair, profl. devel. com. 2005—07). Office: Lehman Coll Leonard Lief Library 250 Bedford Park Blvd W Bronx NY 10468-1589 Office Fax: 718-960-8952. Business E-Mail: janet.munch@lehman.cuny.edu.

MUNCK, ALLAN ULF, physiologist, educator; b. Buenos Aires, July 4, 1925; came to U.S., 1945, naturalized, 1959; s. Carl and Elisabeth (Schmidt) M.; m. Claire Brosi, Oct. 5, 1957; children: Alexander Charles, Ingrid Claire, Kirsten Tanya. BS in Chem. Engring, MIT, 1948, MS, 1949, PhD in Biophysics, 1956. Chem. engr., Ducilo, Buenos Aires, 1949-50; mem. staff Huntington Lab. Mass. Gen. Hosp., Boston, 1956-57, Worcester Found. Exptl. Biology, Shrewsbury, Mass., 1957-59; mem. med. sch. faculty Dartmouth Coll., 1959—; prof. physiology Dartmouth Med. Sch., 1967—2001, prof. physiology emeritus, 2001—. Marius Tausk prof. Leiden U., The Netherlands, 1998. Served with

Argentine Army, 1949. Office: Dartmouth Med Sch Dept Physiology Lebanon NH 03756 Home: 80 Lyme Rd Apt 422 Hanover NH 03755 Business E-Mail: allan.u.munck@dartmouth.edu.

MÜNCK, ECKARD, chemistry professor; PhD in Nuclear Physics, Technical Univ. Darmstadt, Germany, 1967. Rsch. assoc., dept. physics U. Ill., 1967—69, rsch. asst. prof., dept. physics, 1969—73; assoc. prof., biochemistry, Gray Freshwater Biol. Inst. U. Minn., 1974—78, prof. biochemistry, Gray Freshwater Biol. Inst., 1978—90; acting dir. Gray Freshwater Biol. Inst., 1979—81; prof. chemistry Carnegie Mellon U., 1990—. Recipient Alfred Bader award in Bioinorganic and Bioorganic Chemistry, Am. Chem. Soc., 2007. Fellow: AAAS. Office: Carnegie Mellon U Mellon Inst Rm 546 4400 Fifth Ave Pittsburgh PA 15213 Office Phone: 412-268-5058. Office Fax: 412-268-1061. Business E-Mail: emunck@cmu.edu.

MUND, GERALDINE, judge; b. LA, July 7, 1943; d. Charles J. and Pearl M. BA, Brandeis U., 1965; MS, Smith Coll., 1967; JD, Loyola U., 1977; MA, Calif. State U., Northridge, 2007. Bar: Calif. 1977. Bankruptcy judge U.S. Ctrl. Dist. Calif., 1984—, bankruptcy chief judge, 1997—2002. Past pres. Temple Israel, Hollywood, Calif.; past mem. Bd. Jewish Fedn. Coun. of Greater L.A. Mem.: Nat. Confs. Bankruptcy Judges, Am. Coll. Bankruptcy. Office: 21041 Burbank Blvd Woodland Hills CA 91367-6606 Office Phone: 818-587-2840.

MUNDAY, JOHN HENRY, chemist, physicist, educator; s. John Henry and Maude Irene (Perrott) Munday. AA, Hagerstown C.C., Md., 1973; BS, Shepherd Coll., 1975. Cert. secondary tchr. Md. Sci. tchr. St. Maria Goretti HS, Hagerstown, Md., 1976—. Genealogist, bd. dirs. Conococheague Inst., Greencastle, Pa., 1997—2004, 2007—. Treas. Wash. County Genealogy Soc., Hagerstown, 1979—; mem. Hagerstown Civil War Round Table, 2004—, bd. dirs., 2006—. Recipient Excellence in Edn. award, Md. C. of C., 1985; named Tchr. of Yr., St. Maria Goretti HS/Archdiocese of Balt., 2002. Mem.: Wash. County Geneaology Soc. (treas. 1979—2008), Nat. Assn. Sci. Tchrs. (assoc.), Hagerstown Civil War Roundtable (bd. dirs. 2006—). Republican. Methodist. Avocations: genealogy, history, collecting toy soldiers, collecting model trains, travel. Home: 848 Jefferson Blvd Hagerstown MD 21740 Office: St Maria Goretti High Sch 1535 Oak Hill Ave Hagerstown MD 21742 Personal E-mail: mundayjohn@hotmail.com.

MUNDELL, ROBERT ALEXANDER, economist, educator; b. Kingston, Ont., Can., Oct. 24, 1932; s. William C. and Lila (Knifton) Mundell; m. Barbara Sheff, Oct. 14, 1957 (div. 1972); children: Paul Alexander, William Andrew, Robyn Leslie; m. Valerie Sophia Natsios, Nov. 10, 1998; 1 child, Nicholas Robert. BA, U. B.C., Can., 1953; postgrad., U. Wash., 1953—54, London Sch. Econs. and Polit. Sci., 1955—56; PhD, MIT, 1956; postdoc., U. Chgo., 1956—57; PhD (hon.), Renmin U. China, 1985, U. Paris, 1992. Instr. econs. U. B.C., Vancouver, Canada, 1957—58; acting asst. prof. econs. Stanford U., Calif., 1958—59; vis. prof. econs. Sch. Advanced Internat. Studies, Johns Hopkins U. Ctr., Bologna, Italy, 1959—61; sr. economist research dept. IMF, Washington, 1961—63; vis. prof. econs. McGill U., Montreal, Que., Canada, 1963—64; Rockefeller vis. research prof. internat. econs. Brookings Instn., Washington, 1964—65; prof. Grad. Inst. Internat. Studies, Geneva, 1965—75; Ford Found. vis. research prof. econs. U. Chgo., 1965—66, prof., 1966—71; prof. econs., chmn. dept. U. Waterloo, Ont., Canada, 1972—74; prof. econs. Columbia U., NYC, 1974—. Marshall lectr. Cambridge U., 1974; economist Can. Royal Commnl on Price Spreads on Food Products, 1957; mem. joint fiscal mission to Peru OAS and Inter-am. Devel. Bank, 1964; cons. FRS, IBRD, 1966—, U.S. Treasury Dept., 1969—74, EEC, 1970—73, UN, Govt. Panama; organizer, participant internat. confs.; lectr. numerous univs. and profl. orgn. meetings; hon. prof. Renmin U. China, Beijing. Author: The Internat. Monetary System- Conflict and Reform, 1965, Man and Economics, 1968, International Economics, 1968, Monetary Theory-Interest, Inflation and Growth in the World Economy, 1971; contbr. articles to profl. jours.; co-editor: Monetary Problems of the International Economy, 1969, Trade Blaance of Payments and Growth, 1971, The International Monetary System, 1977; editor: Jour. Polit. Economy, 1966—70, Global Disequilibrium in the World Economy, 1989, 1992, Building the New Europe, 1991, Debt, Deficit and Economic Importance, 1990, Inflation and Growth in China, 1996. Recipient James Rueff medal, French Senate, 1983, Nobel prize in Econs., 1999; named Companion of Order of Can., 2003; grantee, NSF, 1967—70; fellow, Guggenheim, 1970—71. Fellow: AAAS, 1998; mem.: Am. Econ. Assn. (Disting. fellow 1997). Office: Dept Econs Columbia U 1031 Internat Affairs 420 W 118th St # Mc3308 New York NY 10027-7213*

MUNDHEIM, ROBERT HARRY, law educator; b. Hamburg, Germany, Feb. 24, 1933; m. Guna Smitchens; children: Susan, Peter. BA, Harvard U., 1954, LLB, 1957; MA (hon.), U. Pa., 1971. Bar: NY 1958, Pa. 1979. Assoc. Shearman & Sterling, NYC, 1958-61; spl. counsel to SEC Washington, 1962-63; vis. prof. Duke Law Sch., Durham, NC, 1964; prof. law U. Pa., Phila., 1965—. Univ. prof. law and fin., 1980-93, dean, 1982-89, Bernard G. Segal prof. law, 1987-89; gen. counsel U.S. Dept. Treasury, Washington, 1977-80; co-chmn. Fried, Frank, Harris, Shriver & Jacobson, NYC, 1990-92; exec. v.p., gen. counsel Salomon Inc., 1992-97; sr. exec. v.p., gen. counsel Salomon Smith Barney Holdings, Inc., 1997-98; of counsel Shearman & Sterling, 1999—; trustee, pres., 2000-06, Am. Acad. in Berlin; chmn. legal adv. bd. NASDAQ, chmn. legal adv. bd. NASD; dir. Appleseed Found., 1996-06; trustee New Sch. U.; coun., mem. exe. com. Am. Law Inst.; bd. dirs. eCollege, 2001-2007, Arnhold & S. Bleichroder, 2004-09, Quadra Real Estate Investment Trust, chair 2007-08; gen. counsel Chrysler Loan Guarantee Bd., 1980; mng. dir., mgmt. bd. Salomon Bros. Inc., NYC, 1992-97; trustee Curtis Inst., 2000—; mem. supervisory bd. Hypo Real Estate Holdings AG, 2004-07. Author: Outside Director of the Publicity Held Corporation, 1976; American Attitudes Toward Foreign Direct Investment in the United States, 1979; Conflict of Interest and the Former Government Employee: Re-thinking the Revolving Door, 1981; chmn. adv. bd. Jour. Internat. Econ. Law, 1996-97. With USAF, 1961-62. Recipient Alexander Hamilton award U.S. Dept. Treasury, 1980, Harold P. Seligson award Practicing Law Inst., 1988, Francis J. Rawle award, ABA-ALI, 1992, Anti-Defamation League Human Rels. award, 1999, Officer's Cross of Order Merit, Republic of Germany, 2007. Mem. ABA (task force on corp. responsibliity, chair, chmn. standing com. on ethics and professional responsibility), Am. Law Inst., San Diego Securities Regulation Inst. (exec. com.). Office: Shearman & Sterling 599 Lexington Ave Fl 16 New York NY 10022-6069 Office Phone: 212-848-7738.

MUNDIE, CRAIG JAMES, computer software company executive; b. 1949; BEE, Ga. Inst. Tech., M in Info. Theory and Computer Sci. Software developer Data Gen. Corp., 1972; co-founder, CEO Alliant Computer Systems Corp., 1982—92; with Microsoft Corp., Redmond, Wash., 1992—, gen. mgr., advanced consumer tech., 1992—93, v.p., advanced consumer tech. group, 1993—96, sr. v.p., consumer platforms divsn., 1996—2001, sr. v.p. advanced strategies and policy, 2001—02, chief tech. officer, advanced strategies & policy, 2001—06, sr. v.p., advanced strategies & policy, 2001—06, chief rsch. & strategy officer, 2006—. Presdl. appointee Nat. Security Telecom. Adv. Com., 2000; mem. Coun. on Fgn. Rels., 2002—, Task Force on Nat. Security in the Info. Age, 2002—; trustee Fred Hutchinson Cancer Rsch. Ctr., Seattle; adv. bd. mem. Coll. of Computing Ga. Inst. Tech., Atlanta; mem. adv. bd., Live Labs (Rsch. partnership between MSN and Microsoft Rsch.) Microsoft Corp., 2006—. Office: Microsoft Corp One Microsoft Way Redmond WA 98052-6399*

MUNDINGER, DONALD CHARLES, retired college president; b. Chgo., Sept. 2, 1929; s. George Edward and Bertha (Trelkenberg) M.; m. June Myrtle Grubbe, June 17, 1951; children: Debra Sue, Donald William, Mary Ruth (dec.). Student, U. Ill., 1947-48; BA, Concordia Coll., River Forest, Ill., 1951, LLD (hon.), 1982; MA, Northwestern U., 1952; PhD, Washington U., St. Louis, 1956; DH (hon.), MacMurray Coll., Jacksonville, Ill., 1984, Ritsumeikan U., Kyoto, Japan, 1992; LLD (hon.), Ill. Coll., Jacksonville, 1993; postdoctoral study, Cambridge U.Eng., 1967-68. Asst. prof. polit. sci., chmn. dept. Augustana Coll., Sioux Falls, S.D., 1956-58; asst. prof. govt. Valparaiso (Ind.) U., 1958-61, assoc. prof., 1961-65, prof., 1965-73; dean Valparaiso (Ind.) U. (Coll. Arts and Scis.), 1965-67; dir. Overseas Center, Cambridge, Eng., 1967-68, v.p. acad. affairs, 1968-73; pres. Ill. Coll., Jacksonville, 1973-93; chmn. Fedn. Ind. Ill. Colls. and Univs., 1975-78; chmn. non-public adv. com. Ill. Bd. Higher Edn., 1988-91. Postdoctoral fellow Center Study Higher Edn., U. Mich., 1964-65; chmn. bd. Council Ind. Colls., 1988-90. Contbr. articles to profl. jours. Mem. Ill. State Bar Assn. (com. on fed. judicial and related appointments 1983-89), Nat. Assn. Ind. Colls. and Univs. (commn. on new initiatives, 1988-90), Pi Sigma Alpha, Phi Eta Sigma. Home: 3803 Pheasant Walk Dr Valparaiso IN 46383-2205

MUNDT, ARNO J., oncologist, department chairman; MD, U. Mich., Ann Arbor, 1987. Prof. Dept Radiation Cellular Oncology, Chgo., 2004—06; prof. & chair UCSD Moores Cancer Ctr. Radiation Oncology Dept., La Jolla, Calif., 2004—. Mem. U. Calif. Bd. Govs., La Jolla, 2007—. Contbr. articles to profl. jours. Health care legislation adv. ASTRO, Washington, 2007—08. Named one of America's Top Doctors, Castle Connolly, 2008. Mem.: Am. Soc. Therapeutic Radiation Oncology. Achievements include research in radiation oncology, proton, particle & their treatment. Office: UCSD Moores Cancer Center 3855 Health Scis Dr La Jolla CA 92093-0843

MUNDT, BARRY MAYNARD, management consultant; b. San Francisco, June 28, 1936; s. Kenneth Francis and Janet (Doughty) M.; m. Sally Hanscom, June 13, 1960; children: Kevin Warren, Trevor Stevens, Stacey Corbin BS in Indsl. Engring., Stanford U., 1959; MBA, Santa Clara U., 1964. Registered indsl. engr., Calif. Statistician Aerojet-Gen., Sacramento, 1957-58; reliability engr. Lockheed Missiles, Sunnyvale, Calif., 1959-61; mgmt. engr. C-E-I-R, Inc., Los Altos, Calif., 1961-65; sr. cons. Peat, Marwick, Livingston & Co., Los Angeles, 1965-68; mgr., prin. Peat, Marwick, Mitchell & Co., Atlanta, 1968-84; ptnr.-in-charge, ops. mgmt. cons. KPMG Peat Marwick Main & Co., NYC, 1984-88; internat. mgmt. cons. ptnr. KPMG Internat., NYC and Amsterdam, The Netherlands, 1988-92; mgmt. cons., ptnr. KPMG Peat Marwick U.S., Montvale, NJ, 1992-95; prin. The Strategy Facilitation Group, Asheville, NC, 1995—. Bd. dirs. Adjusters Internat., Inc., 2005—, Mosaic Acctg., Inc., 2005—. Author-editor: Managing Public Resources, 1982; co-author Il Manager Pubblico (Italy), 1986; mem. editl. bd., contbg. author Handbook of Industrial Engineering, 3rd edit., 2001; contbr. articles to profl. jours. Mem. ann. campaign Atlanta Symphony Orch., 1974-82, Atlanta Arts Alliance, 1976-81; del. to assembly United Way of Met. Atlanta, 1974-84; bd. chmn., mem. Brandon Hall Sch., Atlanta, 1980—2002; chmn. steering coun., NC Ctr. Creative Retirement, 2008-Fellow Inst. Indsl. Engrs. (treas. 1976-81, pres. 1982-83, asst. treas. 1985-92); mem. Asheville Country Club. Episcopalian. Avocations: golf, boating. Home and Office: 175 Windsor Rd Asheville NC 28804 Office Phone: 828-254-2769. Personal E-mail: bmundt@charter.net.

MUNDT, MARVIN GLEN, retired mathematics professor; b. Ossian, Iowa, Apr. 5, 1933; s. Glen Charles and Edna Marie (Gipp) M.; m. Margaret Rose Fuchs, Mar. 20, 1958; children: Mark Osroe, Marlon Paul, Martin David, Marshall Jared, Marston Charles. BA magna cum laude, Luther Coll., 1955; MS, Iowa State U., 1958, PhD, 1961. Tchg. asst. Iowa State U., Ames, 1955—60; mathematician White Sands Missile Range, N.Mex., 1956—59; assoc. prof. math. Tex. Luth. Coll., Seguin, 1966—68; asst. prof. math. Valparaiso (Ind.) U., 1961—66, prof. math., 1964—95; ret., 1995. Tchr. NSF Inst., Valparaiso, 1962—69; tchg. chair in math. Tex. Luth.; faculty adviser Sigma Tau Gamma; chmn. math. dept. Valparaiso U., 1976—80. Contbr. articles to profl. jours. Vol. St. Agnes Ctr. for Srs., Valparaiso, 1999—, Meals on Wheels, Valparaiso, 1998—; communion asst., mem. choir Immanuel Luth. Ch., Valparaiso, 1982—; treas. Family House Bd., Valparaiso, 1986—. Mem.: Am. Math. Soc., Math. Assn. Am. (chmn. Ind. sect. 1982), Nat. Exch. Club (pres. No. Ind. dist. 1999), Pi Mu Epsilon. Avocations: golf, racquetball, softball, travel. Home: 555 Meadlow Ln Valparaiso IN 46385

MUNDY, PATRICIA WALL, lawyer; b. 1972; BA, Boston Coll., 1994, JD, 2000. Bar: Mass. 2001. Assoc. Corp. Dept. Sullivan & Worcester LLP, Boston. Mem.: Boston Bar Assn. Office: Sullivan & Worcester LLP One Post Office Square Boston MA 02109 Office Phone: 617-338-2882. E-mail: pmundy@sanw.com.

MUNERA, GERARD EMMANUEL, manufacturing executive; b. Algiers, Algeria, Dec. 2, 1935; s. Gabriel and Laure (Labrousse) M.; m. Paule A. Ramos, July 28, 1959; children: Catherine, Philippe, Emmanuelle, Jean-Marie. M Math., M Physics, M Chemistry, Ecole Poly., Paris, 1956; CE, Ecole Ponts et Chaussees, Paris, 1959. Chief county engr. Dept. Rds. and Bridges, South Algiers, 1959-62; cons. French Ministry Fgn. Affairs, Argentina, 1962-66; sr. v.p. fin. Camea Group Pechiney Ugine Kuhlmann, Buenos Aires, 1966-70, chmn. bd., chief exec. officer, 1976-77; exec. v.p. Howmet Aluminum Corp., Greenwich, Conn., 1976-77, pres., chief operating officer, 1977-79, pres., chief exec. officer, 1980-83; corporate v.p. nuclear fuels Pechiney, Brussels, 1983-85; vice chmn., chief exec. officer Union Minière, Brussels, 1985-89; head corp. planning and devel. RTZ, London, 1989-90; pres., CEO Minorco USA, Englewood, Colo., 1990-94, also bd. dirs.; chmn. and CEO Latin Am. Gold, Inc., NYC, 1994-96, Synergex Inc., 1996—. Bd. dirs. Nevsun Resources, Inc., Dynamic Materials Corp., Inc., Mag Industries; chmn., Arcadia Inc., mng. ptnr. Synergex Group LLC. Patentee low-income housing system. Served with French Air Force, 1956-57. Decorated officer Legion of Honor (France). Roman Catholic. Office: Arcadia 60 Bonner St Stamford CT 06902-6610 Home Phone: 203-869-7268; Office Phone: 203-316-8000.

MUNERA, PEDRO ANTONIO, child and adolescent psychiatrist; b. Granollers, Spain, May 16, 1970; s. Pedro Munera and Dolores Cordoba; m. Sherry Lynn Rowlett, Mar. 7, 2003. MD, U. Autonoma de Barcelona, Spain, 1994. Diplomate in psychiatry and in child and adolescent psychiatry Am. Bd. Psychiatry and Neurology. Child and adolescent psychiatrist Weems Cmty. Mental Health Ctr., Meridian, Miss., 2003—; clin. asst. prof. dept. psychiatry U. Miss., Jackson, 2003—; owner, operator Children's Clinic Meridian, 2009—. Author book reviews and case reports. Mem.: Miss. Psychiat. Assn. (assoc.; chair early career psychiatrist com., exec.coun. 2006—), Am. Acad. Child and Adolescent Psychiatry (assoc.; residents and early career psychiatrists com. 2002—03), Am. Psychiat. Assn. (assoc.). Roman Catholic. Avocations: travel, reading. Office: Univ Miss Med Ctr 2500 N State St Jackson MS 39216 Address: 1430 Highway 19 N Meridian MS 39307 Office Phone: 601-282-5346. Personal E-mail: pedromunera@comcast.net, ccom@comcast.net.

MUNGAN, CARL EDWARD, physics professor; b. Tulsa, Okla., Mar. 19, 1964; s. Necmettin and Gunilla Ersman Mungan; m. Peckbee Lim Mungan, Aug. 8, 1992; children: Evan Lim, Annabel Lim. BSc with honours, Queen's U., Kingston, Ontario, Canada, 1986; MS, Cornell U., Ithaca, 1989, PhD, 1994. Rsch. assoc. Los Alamos Nat. Lab., N.Mex., 1994—96; asst. prof. U. West Fla., Pensacola, 1996—2000, US Naval Acad., Annapolis, Md., 2000—06, assoc. prof., 2006—. Contbr. articles to profl. jours. Recipient Graduation medal, Queen's U., 1986, Cottrell Coll. Sci. award, Rsch. Corp., 1999—2005, Frank Haig prize. Mem.: Am. Assn. Physics Tchrs., Am. Phys. Soc. Achievements include discovery of experimental observation of laser cooling of a solid; ultrafast vibrational relaxation of hydrogen diatomics in salt crystals. Office: US Naval Acad 572C Holloway Rd Annapolis MD 21402-5002 Office Fax: 410-293-3729. Business E-Mail: mungan@usna.edu.

MUNGER, CHARLES T., diversified company executive; b. Omaha, Nebr., 1924; m. Nancy Munger; 8 children. Student, U. of Mich., 1941—42, Calif. Inst. Technol., 1943; JD, Harvard Law Sch., 1948. Joined Musick Peeler & Garrett, Los Angeles, Calif.; co-founder Munger, Tolles & Olson, 1962—, ptnr., 1962—65, Wheeler Munger & Co., LA, 1962—75; chmn., CEO, Blue Chip Stamps, 1976—; vice chmn. Berkshire Hathaway, Inc., Omaha, 1978—, also chmn., CEO Wesco Fin. subs., 1983—. Chmn. Daily Jour. Corp.; bd. dirs. Costco, 1997—. Meteorological officer USAF, World War II. Named one of Forbes' Richest Americans, 2006. Office: Berkshire Hathaway Inc 1440 Kiewit Plz Omaha NE 68131-3302 also: Munger Tolles and Olson 355 S Grand Ave Los Angeles CA 90071-1560*

MUNGER, MICHAEL CURTIS, public policy educator; b. Orlando, Fla., Sept. 23, 1958; s. Herbert Elmer and Marjorie (Guernsey) M.; m. Donna Marie Gingerella, July 5, 1986; 1 child, Kevin Michael. BA, Davidson Coll., 1980; MA, Washington U., St. Louis, 1982, PhD, 1984. Rsch. analyst Ctr. Study Am. Bus., St. Louis, 1982-83; rsch. economist FTC, Washington, 1984-86; prof. econs. Dartmouth Coll., Hanover, N.H., 1985-86; prof. polit. sci. U. Tex., Austin, 1986-90, U. N.C., Chapel Hill, 1990—. Coord. policy analysis concentration Masters in Pub. Adminstrn. Program U. N.C.; cons. in field. Co-author: lSpatial Theory of Ideology, 1992; contbr. articles to profl. jours. Mem. Am. Econ. Assn., So. Econ. Assn., Pub. Choice Soc., Midwest Polit. Sci. Assn. Office: Univ North Carolina Dept Polit Sci Chapel Hill NC 27599-0001

MUNICH, RICHARD LEE, psychiatrist; b. Lexington, Ky., Feb. 16, 1939; s. Edwin Herman and Dorothy Burdette (Cohen) M.; m. Adrienne Bryna Auslander, June 18, 1991; children: Edwin Seth, Matthew Aaron. AB, Yale U., 1961; MD, U. Ky., 1965; postgrad., Western New Eng. Inst. Psycho., New Haven, 1973-81. Diplomate in psychiatry Am. Bd. Psyhiatry and Neurology, Am. Psychoanalytic Assn.; lic. physician, Ky., N.Y. Med. intern Kings County-Downstate Med. Ctr., NYC, 1965-66; resident psychiatry Yale-West Haven (Conn.) VA Med. Ctr., 1966, Yale-New Haven Hosp., 1968, Yale Psychiat. Inst., New Haven, 1969-71; asst. prof. psychiatry Yale U. Sch. Medicine, 1971-75, asst. clin. prof., 1975-78, assoc. clin. prof., 1978-83; assoc. prof. clin. psychiatry Cornell U. Med. Coll., White Plains, N.Y., 1982-90, prof., 1990—. Asst. med. dir., chief resident, dir. admissions Yale Psychiat. Inst., 1971-72, assoc. med. dir., dir. grad. edn., dir. sociotherapy, 1972-74, clin. dir., 1974-75; ward chief West Haven VA Med. Ctr., 1975-79, dir. inpatient psychiat. svcs., 1979-81; attending psychiatrist N.Y. Hosp.-Cornell Med. Ctr., dir. divsn. extended treatment Westchester divsn.; lectr. psychiatry Yale U. Sch. Medicine; assoc. attending psychiatry Yale-New Haven Hosp. Mem. editorial bds. Psychiat. Hosp.,Bull. Menninger Clinic, Am. Jour. Psychotherapy; contbr. articles to profl. jours., chpts. to books. Fellow Am. Psychiat. Assn. (com. on practice of psychotherapy, coun. on psychiat. svcs. 1992—), Am. Coll. Psychoanalysts; mem. AMA, Am. Psychoanalytic Assn., Assn. Acad. Psychiatry, Assn. Psychoanalytic Medicine, Internat. Psychoanalytic Assn., Soc. Health and Human Values, Westchester Psychiat. Soc. (chairperson ethics com. 1988—), Westchester Psychoanalytic Soc., Western New Eng. Inst. Psychoanalysis, Nat. Assn. Psychiat. Health Systems (trustee 1993—). Office: 21 Bloomingdale Rd White Plains NY 10605-1504

MUNIR, MUHAMMAD, pain medicine physician, director; MB & Surgery, King Edward Med. Coll., Lahore, Pakistan, 1991—97. Diplomate Am. Bd. Anesthesiology, 2004. Fellow pain medicine Harvard Med. Sch., Brigham and Women's Hosp., Boston, 2003—04; clin. instr. Wash. U., St Louis, 2004—05; program dir. pain medicine, asst. prof. U. Cin., 2005—. Mem. exec. & edn. com. dept. anesthesiology U. Cin., 2005—06. Contbr. scientific papers. Recipient Chmns. Academic Achievement award, Dept. Anesthesiology, U. Ark. for Med. Scis., 2003; grantee Rsch. grant, Carl Koller Meml., 2002. Mem.: Am. Soc. Anesthesiology. Achievements include development of multiple new pain and anesthesia techniques. Office: Univ Cin 234 Goodman St PO Box 670764 Cincinnati OH 45267-0764

MUNISTERI, JOSEPH GEORGE, construction executive; b. Rome, Sept. 24, 1930; arrived in USA, 1934; s. Peter P. and Inez Gertrude (Ziniti) Munisteri; m. Theresa Grasso, June 7, 1952 (div. Dec. 2000); children: Joanne, Robert, Laura, Stephen, James, Richard; m. Barbra Coffman, Nov. 30, 2001. BE, Yale U., 1952. With Bechtel Corp., San Francisco, 1952-59; with The Lummus Co., NYC, London and Houston, 1959-67, gen. mgr., 1967—70; sr. v.p. sales Brown & Root, Inc., Houston, 1970—75, group v.p. power div., 1975-80, group v.p. corp. devel., 1980-81, also bd. dirs.; pres. Enserch Engrs. & Constructors, Inc., Houston, 1981-85; exec. v.p. Ford, Bacon & Davis, Inc., Dallas, 1985-87; chmn., pres., CEO Comstock Group, Inc., Danbury, Conn., 1987-88; pres. Joseph G. Munisteri Co., Houston, 1989—. Former chmn. bd. Pine-O-Pine. Former mem. Bd. dirs. Atomic Indsl. Forum; Bd. dirs. Am. Nuclear Energy Council. Mem. Atomic Indsl. Forum, Am. Inst. Chem. Engrs., Am. Nuclear Soc., Atomic Indsl. Forum, ASTM, Council Engring. Law, ASCE, Assn. Iron and Steel Engring., Assoc. Builders and Contractors (dir.), Yale Club of Houston, Yale Club of N.Y. Office: 4265 San Felipe St Ste 1100 Houston TX 77027-2998 Home Phone: 713-877-0240; Office Phone: 713-960-1272. Business E-Mail: jmunisteri@comcast.net.

MUNITZ, BARRY A., former foundation administrator; b. Bklyn., July 26, 1941; m. Anne Tomfohrde. BA, Bklyn. Coll., 1963; MA, Princeton U., 1965, PhD, 1968; cert., U. Leiden, Netherlands, 1962; doctorate (hon.), Claremont U., Calif. State Univ. Sys., Whittier Coll., U. Notre Dame. Asst. prof. lit. and drama U. Calif., Berkeley, 1966-68; staff assoc. Carnegie Commn. Higher Edn., 1968-70; acad. v.p. U. Ill. System, 1971—76; v.p., dean faculties Central Campus U. Houston, 1976-77, chancellor, 1977-82; pres., COO Federated Devel. Co., 1982-

91; vice chmn. Maxxam Inc., LA, 1982-91; chancellor Calif. State U. System, Long Beach, Calif., 1991-98; prof. English lit. Calif. State U., LA, 1991—98; pres., CEO, trustee J.Paul Getty Trust, LA, 1998—2006; chmn. P-16 Edn. Council Calif. Dept. Edn., Sacramento, 2004—; trustee prof. Calif. State U., LA, 2006—. Bd. dirs. KCET-TV, SLM Holdings, KB Home; trustee Princeton U. Author: The Assessment of Institutional Leadership, also articles, monographs. Mem. art mus. vis. com. Princeton and Harvard; former chair bd. dirs. ACE; former co-chair trustees planning com. Gardner Mus.; former chair Calif. Gov. Transition Team. Recipient Disting. Alumnus award Bklyn. Coll., 1979, U. Houston Alumni Pres.'s medal, 1981; Woodrow Wilson fellow. Fellow Am. Acad. Arts and Scis.; mem. Phi Beta Kappa.

MUNIZ, JORGE, composer, music educator; b. Fribourg, Switzerland, Aug. 5, 1974; s. Jose Florencio Muniz and Maria Ascension Salas; m. Jennifer Muniz, Jan. 26, 1976. MusM in Composition, Carnegie Mellon U., 2000; B in Music Composition, Royal Conservatory, Madrid, 1997; D of Musical Arts in Composition, Manhattan Sch. Music, 2004. Accompanist Conservatory of Asturias, Oviedo, Spain, 1990—95; asst. condr. Oviedo Opera Festival Chorus, Oviedo, Asturias, Spain, 1996—98; sound engr. Pitts. Digital, 1999—2000; theory faculty, coord. aural skills Manhattan Sch. Music, NYC, 2002—06; prof. music theory and composition Ind. U., South Bend, 2006—, dir. grad. studies, 2009—, coord. music. Artistic dir., composition faculty Magistralia Summer Music Festival, Gijon, Asturias, 2005—07; dir. New Music Festival Ind. U., South Bend, 2007—. Composer: (opera) Germinal, (symphonic) Arche (First Grand Prize European Young Composers Competition, 1998), Piano Concerto (Second Prize Spanish Soc. of Authors Composition Competition, 1999), Areiotolmos (Joaquin Turinal Prize, 1995), In Memoriam (H.G. Archer Prize of Symphonic Composition, 2000). Named Asturian of Month, Newspaper La Nueva Espana, 2005; grantee, Atlantic Ctr. for Arts, 2003; fellow Goodwill Amb., Rotary Internat., 2000—01, John Duffy Composers Inst., Va. Arts Festival, 2007—08; scholar Fulbright scholar, 1998—2000; New Frontiers Arts and Humanities grant, Ind. U., 2009. Mem.: Coll. Music Soc., Pi-Kappa-Lambda. Home: 908 Woodside St South Bend IN 46614 Office: Indiana Univ NS 0068L Ernestine Raclin Sch Arts 1700 Mishawaka Ave PO Box 7111 South Bend IN 46634 Business E-Mail: contact@jorgemuniz.com.

MUNK, PETER, mining executive; b. Budapest, Hungary, Nov. 8, 1927; arrived in Can., 1948; s. Louis L. and Katherine (Adler) M.; m. Linda Gutterson; children: Anthony, Nina; m. Melanie Jane Bosanquet, 1973; children: Natalie, Cheyne, Marc David. BASc in Elec. Engring., U. Toronto, Ont., Can., 1953, LLD, 1995, Upsala Coll., NJ, 1991, U. Toronto, Que., Can., 1995, Bishops Coll., 1995, Concordia U., Montreal, Que., 1999. Chmn., CEO So. Pacific Hotel Corp., Sydney, Australia, 1969-81; chmn. Barrick Resources, Toronto, 1981-83, Am. Barrick Resources Corp. (now Barrick Gold Corp.), Toronto, 1983—, The Horsham Corp., Toronto, 1987-96; CEO Trizec Hahn Corp., Toronto, 1996—2000, chmn., 2001—06; chmn., pres., CEO Trizec Can. Inc., Toronto, 2002—04, chmn., CEO, 2005—06. Decorated companion Order of Can. Office: Barrick Gold Corp 161 Bay St 3700 Toronto ON Canada M5J 2S1 Business E-Mail: sfennessy@barrick.com.

MUNK, ZEV MOSHE, physician, researcher; b. Stockholm, July 14, 1950; m. Susan Deitcher; 4 children. BS, McGill U., 1972; MD, C.M., 1974. Licentiate Med. Coun. Can.; diplomate Am. Bd. Internal Medicine, Am. Bd. Allergy and Clin. Immunology. Intern Royal Victoria Hosp., Montreal, 1974-75, resident, 1975-76; resident in clin. immunology and allergy Montreal Gen. Hosp., 1976-78; practice medicine specializing in allergy/clin. immunology Houston, 1978—2005; founder, CEO Pharm-Olam Internat. Contbr. articles to med. jours. Pres. Young Israel Synagogue of Houston, 1994-96; founder Allergy Ctr., P.A., Houston, Breco Rsch., Houston; founder, past pres. Torah and Outreach Resource Ctr. of Houston. McGill U. scholar, 1968-74. Fellow ACP, Am. Acad. Allergy Asthma and Immunology, Am. Coll. Allergy and Immunogy, Royal Coll. Physicians (Can.); mem. Tex. Med. Assn., Que. Med. Assn., Tex. Allergy Soc., Harris County Med. Soc., Houston Allergy Soc. Office: 450 N Sam Houston Pwky Ste 250 Houston TX 77060

MUNKARAH, ADNAN R, medical educator, department chairman; b. Tripoli, Lebanon, Apr. 12, 1962; MD, Am. U. Beirut, 1986. Diplomate in gynecologic oncology Am. Bd. Ob-Gyn., 1998. Prof., ob-gyn. Wayne State U., Detroit, 2005—; chmn., dept. women's health svcs. Henry Ford Health Sys., Detroit, 2008—. Recipient award, Alpha Omega Alpha, 1985. Office: Henry Ford Health Sys 3031 W Grand Blvd 7th floor Detroit MI 48202 Business E-Mail: amunkar1@hfhs.org.

MUNLEY, PATRICK H., psychologist, educator; b. Somerville, NJ, July 9, 1947; s. Edward Francis Munley and Elizabeth Mildred Toolan; m. Mary Anne Collins, June 5, 1971; children: Elizabeth Anne (Munley) Peot, Thomas Edward, John Patrick, Katherine Claire, Michael Patrick. BS in Math., Seton Hall U., South Orange, NJ, 1969; MA in Psychology, U. Md., Coll. Pk., 1972, PhD in Counseling Psychology, 1973. Lic. Nat. Register Health Svc. Providers Psychology, 1977, diplomate in counseling psychology Am. Bd. Profl. Psychology, 1984, lic. psychologist Mich., 1989, profl. counselor Mich., 2005. Psychologist VA Med. Ctr., Lyons, NJ, 1973—80, East Orange, NJ, 1980—84, chief, psychology svc. Battle Creek, Mich., 1984—99; adj. faculty Western Mich. U., Kalamazoo, 1987—98, assoc. prof. tng. dir. counseling psychology doctoral program, 1999—2005, prof., chair dept. counselor edn. counseling psychology, 2005—. Editl. bd. Jour. Counseling Psychology, 1981—87, Counseling Psychologist, 2003—05. Contbr. articles numerous prof. jours. (W.James Cosse Disting. Svc. award, 2006). Fellow: Am. Psychol. Assn., Am. Acad. Counseling Psychology (pres. 2004—05, past pres. 2006—07, sec. 2004—06). Office: Western Michigan Univ 1903 West Michigan Ave Kalamazoo MI 49008-5226 Office Fax: 269-387-5090. Business E-Mail: patrick.munley@wmich.edu.

MUNLEY, WILLIAM EDWARD, health services administrator; b. Scranton, Pa., Apr. 8, 1958; s. William Edward and Ann J. (McLaughlin) M.; m. Catherine Mary, Sept. 10, 1988; children: William E. III, Patrick S. BS in Gen. Sci., U. Rochester, 1981; M in Health Svcs. Adminstrn., George Washington U., 1984. cert. rehab. adminstr. Team leader-emergency Strong Meml. Hosp., Rochester, N.Y., 1979-81; adminstrv. resident Muhlenburg Med. Ctr., Bethlehem, Pa., 1983; from dir. ops. to outpatient mgr. Good Shepherd Rehab. Hosp., Allentown, Pa., 1983-86; from dir. vitality ctr. to adminstr. rehab. svcs. St. Francis Hosp., Greenville, S.C., 1988—. Home: 303 Clevington Way Simpsonville SC 29681-4641

MUNN, CECIL EDWIN, lawyer; b. Enid, Okla., Aug. 8, 1923; s. Cecil Edwin and Margaret (Kittrell) M.; m. Carolyn Taylor Culver, May 8, 1948; children: Franklin Culver, Charlotte Munn Forswall. BA, U. Okla., 1945; JD cum laude, Harvard U., 1947. Bar: Okla. 1948, Tex. 1956. Practice in, Enid, 1947-54, Ft. Worth, 1954—; partner firm Cantey & Hanger, Ft. Worth, 1960-91, of counsel, 1992—. With Champlin Petroleum Co., 1954-60, v.p., atty., 1958-60, dir., 1962-75. Fellow Am. Coll. Trial Lawyers, Am. Bar Found.; mem. ABA (chmn. natural resources law sect. 1970-71), Southwestern Legal Found. (past dir.), Tex. Bar Found., Phi Delta Theta, Phi Delta Phi. Presbyterian. Office: 2100 Burnett Plz 801 Cherry St Fort Worth TX 76102-6803 *Some things in life are better decided wrong than left undecided. It is amazing how much one can accomplish if unconcerned with who gets the credit.*

MUNN, JOHN, state banking agency administrator; BE, Nebr. Wesleyan U., 1970; grad., Colo. Grad. Sch. Banking, 1980. Corr. officer Nat. Bank Commerce, Lincoln, Nebr.; v.p., dir. Cattle Nat. Bank, Seward, Nebr.; sr. v.p., dir. Cornerstone Bank, N.A., York, Nebr., 1983—2001; CEO, pres., dir. First Nat. Bank & Trust, Syracuse, Nebr., 2001—05; dir. Nebr. Dept. Banking and Fin., 2005—. Bd. mem. Nebr. Ednl. Fin. Authority, Nebr. Bankers Assn., Nebr. diplomat, former chair govt. rels. com.; former instr., past pres. Schs. Banking, Inc.; founding bd. mem. Syracuse Area Econ. Devel. Corp. Office: Nebr Dept Banking & Fin PO Box 95006 Lincoln NE 68509-5006 Office Phone: 402-471-2171. Office Fax: 402-471-3062. E-mail: John.Munn@bkg.ne.gov.*

MUNNEKE, GARY ARTHUR, law educator, consultant; b. Cedar Rapids, Iowa, Dec. 29, 1947; s. Leslie Earl and Margaret Frances (Fortsch) M.; children: Richard Arthur, Matthew Frederick. BA in Psychology, U. Tex., 1970, JD, 1973. Bar: Tex. 1973, Pa. 1987. Asst. dean, dir. placement U. Tex., Austin, 1978-80; asst. prof., asst. dean Del. Law Sch. Widener U., Wilmington, 1980-84, assoc. prof., 1984-87; pres. Legal Info. Sys., 1987-92; prof. Sch. Law Pace U., 1988—. Contbr. articles to profl. jours. Fellow Am. Bar Found., Coll. Law Practice Mgmt.; mem. ABA (chmn. standing com. on profl. utilization and career devel. 1981-85, articles editor Legal Econs. mag. 1984-86, chmn. law practice mgmt. sect. pub. bd. 1992-95, chmn. law practice mgmt. sect. 1998-99, house dels. 2000-09, bd. gov. 2006-09), State Bar Tex. Office: Pace U Sch Law 78 N Broadway White Plains NY 10603-3710 Home Phone: 410-287-9083. Business E-Mail: gmunneke@law.pace.edu.

MUNNELL, ALICIA HAYDOCK, economist; b. NYC, Dec. 6, 1942; d. Walter Howe Haydock and Alicia (Wildman) Haydock Roux; m. Thomas Clark Munnell (div.); children: Thomas Clark Jr., Hamilton Haydock; m. Henry Scanlon Healy, Feb. 2, 1980. BA in Econs., Wellesley, 1964; MA in Econs., Boston U., 1966; PhD in Econs., Harvard U., 1973. Staff asst. bus. rsch. div. New Eng. Tel. Co., Boston, 1964-65; teaching fellow econs. dept. Boston U., 1965-66; rsch. asst. for dir. econ. studies program Brookings Instn., Washington, 1966-68; teaching fellow Harvard U., Cambridge, Mass., 1971-73; asst. prof. econs. Wellesley Coll., Mass., 1974; economist Fed. Res. Bank Boston, 1973-76, asst. v.p., economist, 1976-78, v.p., economist, 1979-84, sr. v.p., dir. rsch., 1984-93; asst. sec. for econ. policy Dept. Treasury, Washington, 1993-95; mem. Coun. of Econ. Advisors, 1995—97; prof. Carroll Sch. Mgmt., Boston Coll., 1997—; dir. Ctr. for Retirement Rsch., Boston Coll., 1998—. Mem. Gov.'s Task Force on Unemployment Compensation, Mass., 1975; mem. spl. funding adv. com. for Mass. pensions, 1976; mem. Mass. Retirement Law Commn., 1976-82; staff dir. joint com. on pub. pensions Nat. Planning Assn., 1978; mem. adv. com. for urban inst. HUD grant on state-local pensions, 1978-81; mem. pension rsch. council Wharton Sch. Fin. and Commerce, U. Pa., 1979—; mem. adv. group Nat. Commn. for Employment Policy, 1980-82; mem. adv. bd. Nat. Aging Policy Ctr. in Income Maintenance, Brandeis U., 1980-84; participant pvt. sector retirement security and U.S. tax policy roundtable discussions Govt. Rsch. Corp., 1984; mem. supervisory panel Forum Inst. of Villers Found., 1984; mem. Medicare working group, div. of health policy rsch. and edn. Harvard U., 1984-87; mem. Commn. on Coll. Retirement, 1984-86; mem. com. to plan major study of nat. long term care policies Inst. Medicine, Nat. Acad. Scis., 1984-87; mem. steering com. Am. Assn. Ret. Persons, 1987-89; mem. adv. coun. Am. Enterprise Inst., 1987-93; com. mem. Inst. Medicine, Nat. Acad. Scis., 1986—; co-founder, pres., mem. Nat. Acad. Social Ins., 1986—; bd. dirs. Pension Rights Ctr., 1984-93, 97; mem. program rev. com. Brigham and Women's Hosp., 1988-90; mem. Commn. to Rev. Mass. Anti-Takeover Laws, 1988-89; mem. econs. vis. com. MIT, 1989-92. Author: The Impact of Social Security on Personal Saving, 1974, Future of Social Security, 1977 (various awards), Pensions for Public Employees, 1979, The Economics of Private Pensions, 1982; co-author: Options for Fiscal Structure Reform in Massachusetts, 1975, Coming Up Short: The Challenge of 401(K) Plans, 2004, Social Security and the Stock Market: How the Pursuit of Market Magic Shapes the System, 2006, Social Security Fix-it Book, 2007, Working Longer: The Solution to the Retirement Income Challenge, 2008; editor: Lessons from the Income Maintenance Experiments, 1987, Is There a Shortfall in Public Capital Investment?, 1991, (conf. proc.) Retirement and Public Policy, 1991, Framing the Social Security Debate: Values, Politics and Economics: The Role of Gifts and Bequests in America, 2003, Death and Dollars: The Role of Gifts and Bequests in America, 2003, Oxford Handbook of Pensions and Retirement Income, 2006, others; co-editor: Pensions and the Economy: Sources, Uses, and Limitations of Data, 1992; contbr. articles to profl. jours., chpts. to books. Fellow AAAS; Mem. Inst. Medicine NAS., Century Found. (bd. mem., 1998-), Nat. Bureau Econ. Rsch. (bd. mem. 2001-). Office: c/o Boston College 140 Commonwealth Ave Chestnut Hill MA 02467 Office Phone: 617-552-1934. Business E-Mail: munnell@bc.edu.

MUNOFF, GERALD J., university librarian; BA in Art and Photography, Antioch Coll., Ohio; MLS, U. Ky. Past libr. Berea Coll., Ky.; U. Ky.; dir. adminstrv. svc. Ky. Dept. Libr. and Archives, dep. state libr. and dep. commr.; asst. dir. adminstrv. svc. U. Chgo. Libr., 1985—89, dept. dir., 1989—98; univ. libr. U. Calif. Irvine, 1998—. Office: U Calif Irvine 566 Main Libr PO Box 19557 Irvine CA 92623-9557 Office Phone: 949-824-5213. Office Fax: 949-824-2472. E-mail: gmunoff@uci.edu.

MUNOZ, ANDREA LEE, human resources specialist; b. Inglewood, Calif., May 21, 1968; d. Lou and Alma Lou Munoz. BS in psychology, Lamar U., Beaumont, Tex., 1996, MS in indsl. orgnl. psychology, 2003. Store mgr. Merry-Go-Round, Beaumont, 1989—93; tech. svcs. cons. Helena Lab., Beaumont, 1993—2000; workforce devel. specialist Tex. Workforce Ctr., Port Arthur, Tex., 2000—02; spl. populations and disability coord. Lamar State Coll., Port Arthur, 2002—. Mem. bd. Workforce Devel. Ctr., Port Arthur, 2002—03; adv. bd. Lamar State Coll. Port Arthur, 2002—03. Bd. mem. S.E. Tex. Hispanic Cultural and Ednl. Ctr., Inc., 2002—, bd. dirs., 2002—04, Jefferson County Coun. on Alcohol and Drug Abuse. Grantee, Lamar U., 1987, Dr. Harry Starr Pre-Med scholarship, 1989, Maime McFadden-Ward Health Sci. scholarship, 1997. Mem.: Assn. on Higher Edn. and Disability, Disability Consotrium of SE Tex., Psi Chi. Roman Catholic. Office: Lamar State Coll Port Arthur 1500 Procter St Port Arthur TX 77641 Office Phone: 409-984-6241.

MUÑOZ, CECILIA, federal official, civil rights advocate; b. Detroit, July 27, 1962; m. Amit Muñoz-Pandya; children: Cristina, Meera. B in English and L.Am. Studies, U. Mich., Ann Arbor, 1984; M, U. Calif., Berkeley. Former head legalization outreach prog. for Cath. charities Roman Cath. Archdiocese Chgo.; various positions from sr. immigration policy analyst to sr. v.p., Office Rsch., Advocacy & Legis. Nat. Coun. of La Raza, 1988—2009; dir. intergovernmental affairs The White House, Washington, 2009—. Mem. US progs. bd. Open Soc. Inst., NYC; bd. dirs. Atlantic Philanthropies Inc.; chmn. bd. dirs. Ctr. for Cmty. Change, Washington. Former vol. tutor state prison, Jackson, Mich. Fellow John D. & Catherine T. MacArthur Found., 2000. Democrat. Roman Catholic. Office: The White House Office Intergovtl Affairs 160 Pennsylvania Ave NW Washington DC 20500 Office Phone: 202-456-1414.*

MUNOZ, CELIA ALVAREZ, artist; b. El Paso, Tex., Aug. 15, 1937; d. Frank P. and Enriqueta (Limon) Alvarez; m. Andres Munoz, July 27, 1965; children: Anna Celia, Andres III. BA, U. Tex., 1964; MFA, U. North Tex., 1982. Fashion illustrator White House Dept. Store, El Paso, Tex., 1961; art instr. El Paso Pub. Schs., 1964-74, Bauder Fashion Coll., Arlington, Tex., 1984-88; lectr. U. Tex., Arlington, 1984-89. Adv. bd. Arlington Mus. Art, 1993—; design team Sky Harbor Internat. Airport, 1993, NY Percent for Art, P.S. 8, 1995—, Henry B. Gonzalez Convention Ctr. Expansion Project, 1995-98, Dallas Area Rapid Transit, 1998, Dallas Dept. Cultural Affairs Commn. Latino Cultural Ctr., 1999, Hist. Civic Ctr. River Link Project, San Antonio, 2001; lead artist Main Plz., San Antonio, 2007. Author: If Walls Could Speak, 1991, Biennial Whitney Mus. Am. Art.; one woman shows include El Paso Mus. Art, 2003; group shows include Mus. Am. History, Smithsonian Instn., 2004, Women's Mus., Dallas 2005, Sta. Mus., Houston, 2006, Mus. Contemporary Art, San Diego, 2006, Blanton Mus. Art, Austin, Tex., 2006, Art Mus. South Tex., Corpus Christi, 2007. NEA fellow, 1988, 91; recipient Outstanding Achievement in the Arts award Women's Caucus, Coll. Arts Assn., Com. on Women With Ann. Recognisation Awards. Avocations: bicycling, walking, cinema, music, photography. Home: 5815 Arbor Valley Dr Arlington TX 76016-1522

MUÑOZ, EDUARDO RAFAEL, elementary school educator; arrived in U.S., 1961; s. Luis Alberto and Clara Luz Muñoz; m. Maria Judith Amador Muñoz, Dec. 28, 1979; children: Cristina, Rebeca. BA, U. Calif., Davis, 1974, elem. tchg. credential, secondary tchg. credential, U. Calif., Davis, 1975; MA in Edn., Santa Clara U., Calif., 1981. Elem. sch,. tchr. New Haven Unified Sch. Dist., Union City, Calif., 1975—. Sch. site coord. Decoto Elem., Union City, 1975—98, summer sch. prin., 1981, Union City, 82; PTA pres. Maloney Elem., Fremont, Calif., 1991—93. Vol. Cmty. Emergency Response Team, Fremont, Calif., 1996—. Recipient Gold Leaf PTA Svc. award, Fremont, 1993; named Outstanding Individual, Union City, 1981; named one of Tchr. of the Yr., Kitayama Elem. Sch., 2009. Mem.: NEA, AARP, KC, Calif. Tchrs. Assn. (nominee Cesar Chavez award 2006). Democrat. Roman Catholic. Avocations: soccer, golf, baseball, hiking, audio-visual programs. Office: New Haven Unified Sch Dist 34200 Alvarado-Niles Blvd Union City CA 94587

MUÑOZ, GEORGE, investment company executive, former federal agency administrator; BBA with high honors, U. Tex., 1974; M in Pub. Policy, Harvard U., 1978, JD, 1978; LLM, DePaul U., 1984. CPA. Assoc. Gary, Thomasson, Hall & Marks, Corpus Christi, Tex., 1978-80; assoc., ptnr. Mayer, Brown & Platt, Chgo., 1980-89; mng. ptnr. GM&A Internat. Attys. & Bus. Counselors, P.C., Chgo., 1989-93; CFO, asst. sec. for mgmt. US Dept. Treasury, Washington, 1993-97; pres., CEO Overseas Pvt. Investment Corp., Washington, 1997—2001; co-founder, prin. Muñoz Group, Washington, 2001—. Mem. Coun. Fgn. Rels., 2002—. Pres. Chgo. Bd. Edn., 1984-86; trustee Chgo. Symphony Orch., Northwestern Meml. Hosp., DePaul U., Chgo. Coun. on Fgn. Rels., Ill. Internat. Port Authority, Chgo. Econ. Devel. Commn. Office: Muñoz Group 2111 Wilson Blvd Ste 850 Arlington VA 22201

MUÑOZ, LEO R., legislative staff member; BA in English, Govt., U. Tex., Austin, 1997. Policy assoc. Am. Assn. State Colleges and Universities, 2003—04; spl. asst., Rep. Gene Green US House of Reps., Washington, 2004, legis. asst., Rep. Gene Green, 2004—07, legis. dir., Rep. Charlie Gonzalez, 2007—09, chief of staff to Rep. Charlie Gonzalez, 2009—. Democrat. Office: 303 Cannon House Office Bldg Washington DC 20515 Office Phone: 202-225-3236. Office Fax: 202-225-1915.*

MUNOZ, MARIO ALEJANDRO, civil engineer, retired consultant; b. Havana, Cuba, Feb. 27, 1928; arrived in US, 1961, naturalized, 1968; s. Ramón and Concepción (Bermudo) M.; m. Julia Josephine Garrofe, Jan. 17, 1970. M.Arch., U. Havana, 1954; postgrad., City Colls., Chgo., 1974, U. Wis., 1974. Owner Muñoz Bermudo-Construcciones, Havana, 1954-61; designer various cos. Chgo., 1961-65; designer Chgo. Transit Authority, Mdse. Mart, 1965-69; civil engr. Dept. Water and Sewers, City of Chgo., 1969-79; supervising engr. Dept. of Sewers, 1979-85, coordinating engr., 1985-88, asst. chief engr., 1988-93. Mem. ctrl. area subway sys. utilities com. City of Chgo., 1974-93, mem. computer graphics com., 1977-78. Mem. Am. Pub. Works Assn., Western Soc. Engrs., Chgo. Architecture Found., Theodore Thomas Soc. Chgo. Symphony, Chgo. Coun. Fgn. Rels., Soc. of the shield of Loyola, The Overture soc. of the Lyric Opera, Ground Hog Club, Execs. Club (speaker's table com.), Oak Brook Bath and Tennis Club, Barrington Polo Club. Roman Catholic.

MUNOZ, OSCAR, corporate financial executive; BS, U. So. Calif., 1982; MBA, Pepperdine U., 1986. Fin. analyst, acctg. mgr., mgr. fin. control Pepsico Inc., L.A. and Purchase, NY, 1983—86; divsn. contr., dir. fin. ops., asst. corp. contr. Coca-Cola Enterprises, L.A. and Atlanta, 1986—91, CFO, region v.p. Hollywood, Calif., 1991—96; exec. dir. Coca-Cola Co., Atlanta, 1996—97; v.p. fin., contr. USWEST Comms. Inc., Denver, 1997—99; CFO, v.p. U.S. West Retail Markets, Denver, 1999—2000; sr. v.p. fin. and adminstrn. Qwest Comms. Internat. Inc., Denver, 2000; CFO, v.p. AT&T Consumer Svcs. AT&T Corp., Basking Ridge, NJ, 2001—03; exec. v.p., CFO CSX Corp., Jacksonville, Fla., 2003—. Mem.: Fin. Execs. Inst. Office: CSX Corp 500 Water St 15th Floor Jacksonville FL 32202

MUÑOZ, RICARDO, alderman; b. Monterrey, Mex. m. Betty Muñoz; children: Ricardo Alejandro, Angelica Maria. Grad., No. Ill. U., DeKalb. Legis. liaison Mayor's Office Intergovernmental Affairs, Chgo., 1988-89; adminstrv. asst., labor rels. dept. Dept. of Health, Chgo., 1989; chief of staff to Alderman Jesus Garcia, pub. svc. office Chgo. City Coun., 1990-93, alderman, 22d ward, 1993—. Independent. Office: 2500 S St Louis Ave Chicago IL 60623-3925 also: City Hall 121 N La Salle St Rm 300 Office 22 Chicago IL 60602 Office Phone: 773-762-1771, 312-744-9491. Office Fax: 773-762-1825. Business E-Mail: Ward22@cityofchicago.org.*

MUÑOZ, ROMEO SOLANO, audio visual curator; b. Daraga, Philippines, July 2, 1933; s. Maximo M. and Fe (Solano) M.; m. Soledad Roselada, Jan. 2, 1964; children: Francis Vincent, Theresa Lourdes, Romualdo Romeo, Maria Cecilia, Anafe, Stephen Ignatius. BA in Psychology, Letran Coll., Manila, 1965; MS, Ea. Ill. U., 1968; MA, Gov's. State U., 1989; EdD, No. Ill. U., 1995; PhD., So. Ill. U. Audio visual curator Ateneo U., Quezon City, Philippines, 1962-67; audio visual dir. Olive-Harvey Coll., Chgo., 1969—. Prof. City Coll. Chgo., 1969—, prof. emeritus; cons. adminstrv. svcs., fin. City Coll. Bd. Trustees, Chgo., 1988—; v.p. Gov.'s State U., University Park, Ill. Author: Filipino Americans: From Invisibility to Empowerment, 2002. Del. AFL/CIO, Chgo., 1989, 90; deacon Archdiocese Chgo. Roman

Cath. Ch., 1976—, Professed Secular Franciscan; trustee Calumet City Libr., 1993. Recipient fellowship Ea. Ill. U., Charleston, 1967-68, So. Ill. U., Carbondale, 1968-70, Gov.'s State U., Univ. Park, Ill., 1981-2000. Mem. ALA, Gov.'s State U. Alumni (bd. dirs.), Philippine Profls. Assn. (pres.), Nat. Fedn. of Filipino-Am. Orgns., Philippine Hist. Soc., Phi Delta Kappa (pres. 2000), Philippine Educators in Am. (pres.). Avocation: physical fitness. Home: 383 Hoxie Ave Calumet City IL 60409-2330 Office Phone: 708-231-8196. E-mail: rmunoz@ccc.edu, rs-munoz@yahoo.com.

MUÑOZ DONES DE CARRASCAL, ELOISA (ELOISE MUNOZ DONES), hospital administrator, pediatrician, educator; b. San Lorenzo, PR, Oct. 25, 1922; d. Pedro and Maria (Dones) Muñoz; m. José D. Carrascal, Dec. 7, 1962; children: Lilia, Maria. BA in Edn. cum laude, BS in Chemistry cum laude, U. P.R., Rio Piedras, 1943; MD, Tulane U., 1948. Diplomate Am. Bd. Pediatrics. Intern Arecibo Charity Dist. Hosp., 1948-49; resident in pediatrics San Juan (P.R.) City Hosp., 1949-51, chief newborn svc., attending pediatrician, 1951—, dir. neonatal-perinatal medicine, 1965—, dir. fellowship tng. program, 1972—; from instr. to assoc. prof. clin. pediatrics sch. medicine U. P.R., 1951-89, prof., 1989—. Courtesy pediatrician neonatologist Tchrs. Hosp., Hato Rey, P.R., 1951-76, Ashford Presbyn. Drs. Hosp., Santurce, P.R., 1951-76, San Jorge H. H. Pavia Fernandez, Santurce, 1951-76; cons. pediatrician neonatologist Tchrs. H. Auxilio Mutuo H., Hato Rey, 1976—, Drs. H. San Jorge H. Ashford, San Juan, 1976—; mem. exec. com. San Juan City Hosp., 1976—, pres. med. faculty, 1976-77, 87-89, mem. instl. rev. bd., mem. ednl. rev. bd., mem. various coms.; lectr. in field. Contbr. articles to profl. jours. U.S. del. Care Orgn. Latin Am., 1962-63. Recipient Bronze medal Brazilian Acad. Human Scis., 1975, Hon. Cert. Internat. Yr. Women, City Mayor Lodo Carlos Romero Barceló, 1975, Hon. Cert. Disting. Svc. to Cmty., Julio Sellés Solá Elem. Sch., 1976, Pioneer Pediatrician award P.R. Pediat. Sect. Convention, 1993, Pioneer in Neonatology award P.R. Pediat. Sect. Convention, 1995, Pioneer Pidiat. Critical Care award Pediat. Critical Care Assn., 1996; grantee NIH, 1962. Fellow Am. Acad. Pediatrics (neonatal perinatal sect., mem. com. fetus and newborn P.R. chpt. 1956—, sec.-treas. 1962-64, mem. com. history perinatal sect. 1992—, Plaque in Recognition Disting. Pediatrician and Tchr. 1985), Pan Am. Pediatrics; mem. Am. Med. Women Assn., P.R. Med. Assn. (pediat. sect., mem. chamber of dels. 1962-63, Bronze plaque 1967, 91, Gold Pin 1980), P.R. Med. Women Assn. (sec.-treas. 1957-60, pres. 1960-64), Pan Am. Med. Women Assn. (pres. P.R. chpt. 1960-64, P.R. del. VIII Congress Manizales Colombia 1962), Pan Am. Med. Women Alliance (vis. lectr. 1962), Tulane Med. Alumni, London Royal Soc. Health, Colegio de Químicos, Soc. Dominicana de Pediatría (hon., vis. lectr. 1971), Dominican Rep. Soc. (hon.). Avocation: poetry.

MUÑOZ-SOLÁ, HAYDEÉ SOCORRO, retired library administrator; b. Caguas, PR, Dec. 27, 1943; d. Gilberto Muñoz and Carmen Haydeé (Solá) de Muñoz; m. Juan M. Masini-Soler, Jan. 8, 1966 (div. 1979); children: Juan Martín Masini-Muñoz, Haydeé Milagros Masini-Muñoz. BA in Psychology, U. P.R., Río Piedras, 1965, MLS, 1970; D in Libr. Sci., Columbia U., 1985. Asst. libr. U. P.R., Río Piedras, 1964-67; dir. libr. Interam. U., Aguadilla, PR, 1974-75; head svcs. to pub. U. P.R., Aguadilla, 1975-76; cataloguer Cath. U., Ponce, PR, 1976-79, U. P.R., Río Piedras, 1982-84, head libr. and info. sci. libr., 1984-85, prof. grad. libr. sch., 1986, 99, dir. libr. sys., 1986-93, coord. external resources libr. sys., 1994-97, dir. of libr. Ponce, PR, 1997, collection devel. officer Rio Piedras, 1998, sabbatical leave, 2000-01; compiler, editor Puerto Rican Bibliography, 2001—07. Dir. P.R. Newspaper Project, Río Piedras, 1986-90; mem. Adv. Com. on Pub. Librs., San Juan, 1987-93; proposal reviewer NEH, 1990-2007; chmn. Puerto Rican Del. to Nat. White House Conf. on Libr. and Info. Svcs., 1991. Author: La Información y la Documentación Educativa/Informe Sobre la Situación Actual en Puerto Rico, 1991, Memorias: Sequnda Pre-Conferencia de Casa Blanca Sobre Bibliotecas y Servicios de Información en Puerto Rico, 1991, Lineamientos para Colecciones Bibliograficas Nacionales, 1997, Premio por Excelencia en Investigación Aplicada y Publicación, 1997; contbr. articles to profl. jours. Mem. Ponce Sport Club, 1976—83, ARC, Ponce, 1978. Recipient plaque White House Pre-Conf. on Libr. and Info. Sci., 1990, others, Leccion Magistral Josefina del Toro Fulladosa, 2002; French Alps Study Tour scholar Assn. Caribbean Univ. Rsch. and Instl. Libr., 1989, Germany Study Tour scholar Fgn. Rels. Office, Germany, 1991, coord. So. area 1974, Lauro award 1989, Leccion Magistral Josefina del Toro Fulladosa award, 2002. Mem. ALA, Am. Mgmt. Assn., Grad. Sch. Libr. and Info. Sci. Alumni Assn. (pres. 1988-90), Seminar for Acquisitions L.Am. Libr. Materials, Iberoamerican Nat. Libr. Assn. (pres. 1992-93), Puerto Rican Libr. Soc., Assn. Caribbean U. Rsch. and Instnl. Libr. (Parchment award 1988), Asoc. para las Comunicaciones y Tecnología Educativa, Mid. States Assn. Coll. and Sch. (collaborator), Am. Women Assn., Nat. Commn. P.R. Women, Phi Delta Kappa (chair P.R. com. 1988-90, Kappan of Yr. 1990), Eta Gamma Delta. Roman Catholic. Avocations: reading, crewel work, embroidery, knitting, movies. E-mail: hms@onelinkpr.net.

MUNRO, ALICE ANN, writer; b. Wingham, Ont., Can., July 10, 1931; d. Robert Eric and Anne Clarke (Chamney) Laidlaw; m. James Armstrong Munro, 1951 (div. 1976); children: Sheila, Andrea; m. Gerald Fremlin, 1976; 1 child, Jenny. BA, U. Western Ont., 1952, DLitt (hon.), 1976. Established Munro Books, Victoria, Brit. Columbia, 1963. Writer in residence U. BC & U. Queensland, 1980. Author: (short story collections) Dance of the Happy Shades, 1968 (Gov. Gen.'s award for fiction, Can., 1968), Lives of Girls and Women, 1971 (Can. Booksellers Assn. Internat. Book of Yr., 1972), Something I've Been Meaning to Tell You, 1974, Who Do You Think You Are?, 1978 (Gov. Gen.'s award for fiction, Can., 1978), The Moons of Jupiter, 1982, The Progress of Love, 1986 (Gov. Gen.'s award for fiction, Can., 1986), Friend of My Youth, 1990 (Trillium Book award, 1991, Commonwealth Writers' prize, 1991), Open Secrets, 1994 (WH Smith award, 1995), Selected Stories, 1996, The Love of a Good Woman, 1998 (Giller prize, 1998, Nat. Book Critics Circle award for fiction, 1998, Can. Booksellers Assn. Fiction Book of Yr., 1999), Hateship, Friendship, Courtship, Loveship, Marriage, 2001, No Love Lost, 2003, Vintage Munro, 2004, Runaway, 2004 (Giller prize, 2004), The View from Castle Rock, 2006, Too Much Happiness, 2009; contbr. short stories to numerous periodicals. Recipient Marian Engel award, Writers' Trust Canada, 1986, Lorne Pierce medal, Royal Soc. Can., 1993, PEN/Malamud award for excellence in short fiction, 1997, Rea Award for the short story, 2001, O. Henry award, 2004, 2008, Medal of Honor for lit., US Nat. Arts Club, 2005, Man Booker Internat. prize, 2009; named one of 100 Most Influential People, TIME mag., 2005. Mem.: AAAL (fgn. hon. mem.). Office: William Morris Agy 16th Fl 1325 Ave of Americas New York NY 10019 Office Phone: 212-903-1121.*

MUNRO, BARBARA HAZARD, retired nursing educator, dean, researcher; b. Wakefield, RI, Nov. 28, 1938; d. Robert J. and Honore (Egan) Hazard; children: Karen Aimee, Craig Michael, Stephanie Anne. BS, MS, U. RI, Kingston; PhD, U. Conn. RN, Conn. Asst. prof. U. RI Coll. Nursing, Kingston; assoc. prof., chmn. program in nursing rsch. Yale U., New Haven; assoc. prof., asst. dir. Ctr. for Nursing Rsch. U. Pa., Phila.; dean, prof. Boston Coll. Sch. Nursing, 1991—2008. Presenter and workshop leader various nursing confs. and seminars in U.S. Contbr. articles and rsch. to profl. pubs. Trustee St. Elizabeth's Med. Ctr. Boston, 1994—. Recipient Nat. Rsch. Svc. award. Fellow Am. Acad. Nursing; mem. ANA, Golden Key, Sigma Theta Tau, Pi Lambda Theta, Phi Kappa Phi. Personal E-mail: barbara.hazard.1@verizon.net. Business E-Mail: barbara.hazard.1@bc.edu.

MUNRO, DONALD JACQUES, philosopher, educator; b. New Brunswick, NJ, Mar. 5, 1931; s. Thomas B. and Lucile (Nadler) M.; m. Ann Maples Patterson, Mar. 3, 1956; 1 child, Sarah de la Roche. AB, Harvard U., 1953; PhD (Ford Found. fellow), Columbia U., 1964. Asst. prof. philosophy U. Mich., 1964-68, assoc. prof., 1968-73, prof. philosophy, 1973—90, prof. philosophy and Asian langs., 1990-96; prof. emeritus philosophy and Chinese, 1996—; chmn. dept. Asian langs. and cultures U. Mich., 1993-95, with Ctr. Chinese Studies, 1964—; vis. rsch. philosopher Ctr. Chinese Studies U. Calif., Berkeley, 1969-70; mem. Assn. for Asian studies China and Inner Asia Coun., 1970—72; chmn. com. on studies of Chinese civilization Am. Council Learned Socs., 1979-81. Mem. Com. on Scholarly Comm. with People's Republic China, NAS, 1978-82, China Coun. of Asia Soc., 1977-80, Com. on Advanced Study in China, 1978-82; Evans-Wentz lectr. Stanford U., 1970; Fritz lectr. U. Wash., 1980; Gilbert Ryle lectr. Trent U., Ont., 1983; John Dewey lectr. U. Vt., 1989; Ch'ien Mu lectr. Chinese U. Hong Kong, 2002-03; Tang Chun I vis. prof. Chinese U. Hong Kong, 2006. Author: The Concept of Man in Early China, 1969, the Concept of Man in Contemporary China, 1977; editor: Individualism and Holism, 1985, Images of Human Nature: A Sung Portrait, 1988, The Imperial Style of Inquiry in Twentieth Century China, 1996, A Chinese Ethics for the New Century, 2005, Ethics In Action: Workable Guidelines For Private And Public Choices, 2008. Exec. com. Coll. Literature, Sci. and The Arts U. Mich., 1986-89. Lt. (j.g.) USNR, 1953-57. Recipient letter of commendation Chief Naval Ops.; Disting. Svc. award U. Mich., 1968, Excellence in Edn. award, 1992; Rice Humanities award, 1993-94; Nat. Humanities faculty fellow, 1971-72; John Simon Guggenheim Found. fellow, 1978-79; grantee Social Sci. Rsch. Coun., 1965-66, Am. Coun. Learned Socs., 1982-83, China com. grantee NAS, 1990; vis. rsch. scholar Chinese Acad. Social Scis. Inst. Philosophy, Beijing, 1983, dept. philosophy Beijing U., 1990. Home: 14 Ridgeway St Ann Arbor MI 48104-1739 *I believe that much knowledge is interrelated and that academic disciplinary boundaries are transitory conveniences. The human significance of any research task I undertake should be obvious to those inside and outside my professional group (a goal I seek but do not always achieve).*

MUNRO, DONALD WILLIAM, JR., non-profit organization executive; b. Phila., Dec. 27, 1937; s. Donald William and Emily McCoy (Graham) M.; m. Joyce Eleanor Thomas, Sept. 9, 1961; children: Deborah Joy, Mark William. BS, Wheaton Coll., 1959; MS, Pa. State U., 1963, PhD, 1966. Prof. biology Houghton (N.Y.) Coll., 1966-94; exec. dir. Am. Sci. Affiliation, Ipswich, Mass., 1994—2005. Adj. prof. biology Gordon Coll., Wenham, Mass., 1995-2004; chmn. biology dept. Houghton Coll., 1972-94. Capt. U.S. Army, 1960-69. Predoctoral fellow NIH, 1964-66. Mem. Am. Philatelic Soc., Houghton Stamp Club (pres. 1988-90), Elizabeth City Rotary Club. Republican. Baptist. Avocations: stamps, piano, hiking, bioethics.

MUNRO, DOUG, musician, director; b. Yonkers, NY, July 9, 1953; s. Lydia Levy; m. Kathleen Marie Kraus, July 25, 1982; children: Eugene Paul, John Anthony. MFA in Jazz performance, Purchase Coll., NY, 1994. Founder and dir. jazz studies Purchase Coll., 1993—2003, dir. emeritus jazz studies, 2003—. Rec. artist Chase Music Group, Glendale, Calif., 1993—. Author: (guitar book) Swing To Bebop (Music And Sound Retailers Award, 2000). Home: 258 Madison St Mamaroneck NY 10543 Office: Purchase Coll 735 Anderson Hill Rd Purchase NY Office Fax: 914-251-6739. Personal E-mail: doug.munro@optonline.net. Business E-Mail: doug.munro@purchase.edu.

MUNRO, GEORGE E., history professor; s. John Ker Munro and Johanna Fredericke Voget; m. Natalia Illenzeer, July 21, 2002; 1 child, Emily Munro Scott. PhD, U. NC, Chapel Hill, 1973. Prof. history Va. Commonwealth U., Richmond, 1971—. Author: (book) The Most Intentional City: St Petersburg in the Reign of Catherine the Great; translator: The Rule of Catherine the Great: War, Diplomacy and Domestic Affairs, 1972, The Reign of Empress Elizabeth Petrovna: Academy of Sciences, Domestic Unrest, Catherine II's Charters of 1785 to the Nobility and the Towns. 1st lt. US Army, 1965—73. Fulbright, CIES, 1998, 2006. Office: Va Commonwealth Univ 813 Cathedral Pl S Richmond VA 23220

MUNROE, GEORGE BARBER, retired mining and manufacturing company executive; b. Joliet, Ill., Jan. 5, 1922; s. George Mueller and Ruth (Barber) Munroe; m. Elinor Bunin, May 30, 1968; children from previous marriage: George Taylor, Ralph W. Taylor. AB, Dartmouth Coll., 1943; LLB, Harvard U., 1949; BA (Rhodes scholar), Christ Church, Oxford U., Eng., 1951, MA, 1956; DHL (hon.), No. Ariz. U., 1981; LLD (hon.), Dartmouth Coll., 1993. Bar: N.Y. 1949. Assoc. Cravath, Swaine & Moore, NYC, 1949; atty. Office Gen. Counsel U.S. High Commn. Germany, Frankfurt and Bonn, 1951-53; justice U.S. Ct. Restitution Appeals Allied High Commn. Germany, Nuremberg, 1953-54; assoc. Debevoise, Plimpton & McLean, NYC, 1954-58; with Phelps Dodge Corp., 1958-87, v.p., 1962-66, pres., 1966-75, 80-82, chief exec. officer, 1969-87, chmn. bd., 1975-87, dir., 1966-94. Trustee emeritus Met. Mus. Art; chmn. emeritus bd. dirs. Acad. Polit. Sci. Served to lt. (j.g.) USNR, 1943—46. Mem. Mining and Metall. Soc. Am., Coun. Fgn. Rels., Century Assn., River Club, Univ. Club (N.Y.C.), Bridgehampton Club. Office: George B Munroe 870 United Nations Plz New York NY 10017-1826 Home Phone: 212-421-4016.

MUNROE, JENNIFER, literature and language professor; PhD in Lit., U. Ill., Urbana-Champaign, 2004. Prof. U. NC, Charlotte, 2004—. Sec. Shakespeare Action Ctr., UNC Charlotte. Author: (book) Making Gardens of Their Own: Gardening Manuals for Women, Gender and the Garden in Early Modern English Literature. Creator and dir. Shakespeare At Risk, Charlotte, 2008—09. Grantee Francis Lumsden Gwynn award, U. NC, Charlotte, 2007—08. Mem.: MLA, Group Early Modern Cultural Studies, Shakespeare Assn. Am., Soc. Study Early Modern Women, Renaissance Soc. America. Home: 333 W Trade St 2504 Charlotte NC 28202 Office: Univ NC Charlotte 9201 University City Blvd Charlotte NC 28202 Business E-Mail: munroe37@gmail.com.

MUNROE, STEPHEN H., biology professor; s. John Andrew and Dorothy Levis Munroe; m. Cordelia Swain Munroe; children: David Andrew, Margaret Parrish. BA, Haverford Coll., Pa., 1968; PhD, Ind. U., Bloomington, 1974. Rsch. fellow Children's Hosp. Med. Ctr., Boston, 1974—77; postdoc. fellow Worcester Found. Exptl. Biology, Shrewsbury, Mass., 1977—78; asst. & prof. Marquette U., Milw., 1978—; vis. scientist Cold Spring Harbor Lab., NY, 1987—88; vis. prof. genetics Harvard Med. Sch., Boston, 2002—03. Recipient Nat. Rsch. Svc. award, NIH, 1987—88. Mem.: RNA Soc. Achievements include research in RNA structure, processing and annealing proteins. Office: Marquette Univ 530 N 15th St Milwaukee WI 53233

MUNSELL, DEBRA S., physician assistant, educator; b. Pt. Arthur, Tex., June 13, 1957; d. Rosemond B. and Bettie Lawrence Schoenberg; m. Lloyd Allen Foreman III, Feb. 16, 1985 (dec. Mar. 1991); m. William Peter Munsell, July 18, 1998. BS in Biology, Stephen F. Austin State U., 1979; BS in Health, U. Tex., Galveston, 1981; MPhysician Asst. Studies in Otolaryng., U. Nebr., 2000. Cert. phys. asst. Physician asst. Angleton (Tex.) Clinic, 1981-83, Tex. Dept. Corrections, Huntsville, 1983-84; physician asst. med. br. Galveston U. Tex., 1985-90, clin. instr. med. br. Galveston, 1985—2004, physician asst. M.D. Anderson Cancer Ctr. Houston, 1990—2005, dir. physician asst. student edn. program M.D. Anderson Cancer Ctr., 1996—2005; clin. assoc. prof. physician asst. edn. We. U. Health Sci., Pomona, Calif., 1999—2004; asst. prof. U. Tex. Med. Br., Sch. Allied Health Sci., Galveston, 2005—. Clin. instr. Baylor Coll. Medicine, Houston, 1999-2004. Author: (with others) Primary Care Oncology, 1999, Primary Care: A Collaborative Approach, 1999, Primary Care, A Collaborative Practice, 2d edit., 2003, The Physician Assistant Medical Handbook, 2d edit., 2004. Life mem. Brazoria County Fair Assn., Angleton, Tex., 1992—. Glaxo/Wellcome Leadership fellow Am. Acad. Physician Assts./Physician Asst. Found., 1997-98. Fellow: Assn. Physician Assts. in Oncology, Soc. Physician Assts. in Otolaryngology, Head and Neck Surgery (charter mem. 1991, bd. dirs. 1992—94, chair continuing med. edn 1994—96, pres. 1996—2000), Am. Acad. Otolaryngology, Head and Neck Surgery, Am. Acad. Physician Assts. (chair nominating com. 1998—2002, external liaison 2001—); mem.: Tex. Acad. Physician Assts., Nat. Patient Advocate Found., Houston Yacht Club. Avocations: sailing, gardening. Home: 9807 Williams Bend Ct Missouri City TX 77459-6279 Office: U Tex Med Br-Galveston SAHS 301 University Blvd Galveston TX 77553-1028 Home Phone: 281-778-7494; Office Phone: 409-772-9559. Business E-Mail: dsmunsel@utmb.edu.

MUNSELL, ELSIE LOUISE, retired lawyer; b. NYC, Feb. 15, 1939; d. Elmer Stanley and Eleanor Harriet (Dickinson) M.; m. George P. Williams, July 14, 1979. AB, Marietta Coll., 1960; JD, Marshall-Wythe Coll. William and Mary, 1972. Bar: Va. 1972, U.S. Dist. Ct. (ea. dist.) Va. 1974, U.S. Ct. Appeals (4th cir.) 1976, U.S. Supreme Ct. 1980. Tchr. Norview High Sch., Norfolk, Va., 1964-69; asst. Commonwealth atty. Commonwealth Atty.'s Office, Alexandria, Va., 1972-73; asst. U.S. atty. Alexandria, 1974-79; U.S. magistrate U.S. Dist. Ct. (ea. dist.) Va., Alexandria, 1979-81; U.S. atty. Dept. Justice, Alexandria, 1981-86; sr. trial atty. Office of Gen. Counsel, Dept. Navy, Washington, 1986-89, asst. gen. counsel installations and environ. law, 1989-91; dep. asst. environ. and safety Sec. Navy, 1991-2001, ret., 2001. Mem. USEPA Clean Air Act Adv. Com., 1997—; bd. dirs. BMT Designers & Planners, 2007. Active Va. Commn. on Status of Women, 1966-74; bd. vistors Coll. William and Mary, 1972-76; active Atty. Gen.'s Adv. Com. U.S. Attys., 1981-83; bd. dirs. Carpenter's Shelter, Inc., 1990-93; vestry St. Alban's Ch., Annandale, Va., 1996-99, 2003; fed. preservation officer Dept. Navy, 1999. Presdl. Meritorious Exec., 1999; recipient Spl. Achievement award Nat. Mil. Fish and Wildlife Assn., 2001, Disting. Civilian Svc. award, 2001. Mem. Sr. Execs. Assn., Chi Omega.

MUNSELL, WILLIAM A., healthcare insurance company executive; With UnitedHealth Group, Mpls., 1997—, CFO, 1997—2000, COO, 2000—03, chief adminstrv. officer, 2003—04, CEO specialized care svc., 2004—, exec. v.p., 2006—07, exec. v.p., pres. enterprise services group, 2007—. Office: UnitedHealth Grp PO Box 1459 Minneapolis MN 55440-1459*

MUNSEY, VIRDELL EVERARD, JR., retired utilities executive; b. Washington, Sept. 25, 1933; s. Virdell Everard and Mildred Lovenia (Wood) M.; m. Bernice Ann Wilson, Sept. 20, 1956; children: Wanda Louise, Allan Coll, Andrew Everard, Carolyn Jane. BA magna cum laude, Yale U., 1955; M.P.A., Harvard U., 1967. Reporter Washington Post, 1957-63; legis. asst. Rep. Henry S. Reuss, Washington, 1963-68; info. dir. United Democrats for Humphrey, Washington, 1968; asst. dir. public affairs Dem. Nat. Com., 1968; with Nat. Planning Assn., Washington, 1969-77, exec. v.p., 1974-76; dep. asst. sec. for public affairs Dept. Treasury, Washington, 1977-81; cons. World Bank, 1981; with Va. Electric and Power Co., 1981-86, mgr. corp. communications, 1982-83, exec. dir. pub. policy, 1983-86, v.p. pub. policy, 1986, Dominion Resources Inc., 1986-96; cons., 1996—2002. Mem. Va. Coal and Energy Commn., 1983-95. Chmn. Arlington County Dem. Party, 1967-69; mem. Arlington County Bd., 1972-75, chmn., 1973; vice chmn. No. Va. Transp. Commn., 1973, chmn., 1974; bd. dirs. Washington Met. Area Transit Authority, 1975; mem. transp. planning bd. Met. Washington Coun. Govts., 1973-75; treas. Competitive Power Policy Forum, 1990-96. Served with U.S. Army, 1955-57, treas Pilgrim Henry Samson Kindred, 2005-, asst. Pilgrim Hopkins Heritage Soc., 2005-. Recipient Am. Political Sci. Assn. award Disting. Reporting of Public Affairs, 1962; Am. Polit. Sci Assn. Fellow, 1966—67. Mem. United Ch. Christ. Personal E-mail: everard1933@yahoo.com.

MUNSHI, SADAF, linguistics professor, researcher; b. Srinagar, Jammu & Kashmir, India, Oct. 24, 1974; d. Abul-Hassan Munshi and Syeda Bano; m. Tasaduq Hussain Mir, May 30, 2002; 1 child, Anoush Aymen Mir. BS, U. Kashmir, Srinagar, 1997; MA, U. Delhi, India, 1999; MPhil, U. Delhi, 2001; PhD, U. Tex., Austin, 2006. Asst. instr. U. Tex., 2003—05; assessment objects developer Nat. Fgn. Lang. Ctr., Coll. Pk., Md., 2005—06, content object selector, 2005—06; asst. prof. U. North Tex., Denton, 2006—. Author (playwright): (films) Taqdeer Aur Haadise; contbr. columns in newspapers to profl. jour. Recipient Profl. Devel. award, U. Tex., 2002, Shri Aggrasain Gold medal, U. Delhi, 1999; grantee Doc. Dissertation Improvement grant, NSF, 2004—06; Jr. Rsch. fellowship, U. Grants Commn. India, 1999—2001, U. fellowship, U. Tex., 2005—06. Achievements include research in documentation of endangered languages; development of Indo-Aryan languages. Home: 2216 Vanderbilt Ct Denton TX 76201 Office: Univ N TX 1155 Union Cir 305298 Denton TX 76203 Office Phone: 940-369-8944. Office Fax: 940-369-8976. Personal E-mail: smunshi2002@yahoo.com. Business E-Mail: sadafmunshi@unt.edu.

MUNSON, ALDEN V., JR., federal official; BS in Mech. Engring., San Jose State U., Calif.; MS in Mech. Engring., U. Calif., Berkeley; attended exec. program in competition and strategy, Harvard U., Mass.; attended exec. program in mgmt. high tech. enterprises, Stanford U., Calif. Sys. engring. support Aerospace Corp.; v.p., sys. integration group, space and electronics group, information systems group TRW; sr. v.p., group exec. pres. Litton Information Systems Group; affiliated cons., def., space, and intelligence Windsor Group; dep. dir. nat. intelligence for future capabilities Office the Dir. Nat. Security. Founding dir. Paracel Inc.; bd. mem. BD Systems, Armed Forces Comm. Electronics Assn. Advisor San Jose State U. Coll. Engring., Manhattan Beach Edn. Found. Named Disting. Grad., San Jose State U. Coll. Engring., 1997; named to Pioneers of Nat. Reconnaissance, Nat. Reconnaissance Office, 2000. Office: Office the Dir Nat Intelligence Washington DC 20511*

MUNSON, ALEXANDER LEE, management consultant; b. Hempstead, NY, Aug. 22, 1931; s. Alexander Lawrence and Bertha Louise (Geer) M.; m. Betty Sue Shideler, Dec. 14, 1957 (div. June 1978);

children: Eric Lawrence, Genevieve Sue, Anna Lee; m. Merla Zellerbach, Apr. 18, 1998. BA, Amherst Coll., 1953; MBA, Harvard, 1960. Mgmt. trainee, credit analyst Mellon Nat. Bank & Trust Co., Pitts., 1953-54; assoc. Cresap, McCormick & Paget, NYC, mgmt. cons., 1960-62; fin. adv. internat. fin. Mobil Oil Corp., NYC, 1962-64, Melbourne, Australia, 1964-65; mgr. spl. projects treas. dept. Mobil Internat., NYC, 1965-66, mgr. treasury reports and analysis, 1966-67; treas. Mobil Latin Am. Inc., NYC, 1968-70; v.p.-treas. Fairchild Camera & Instrument Co., Mountain View, Calif., 1971-72, Crown Zellerbach Corp., San Francisco, 1972-82; pres. A.L. Munson & Co., San Francisco, 1982—; CFO Consortium of Reading Excellence, Emeryville, Calif., 1998—2000; CFO, dir. ACTI, Inc., Petaluma, Calif., 2000—01; adj. prof. fin. Ageno Sch. Bus., Golden Gate U., San Francisco, 2002—06. Mem. Mayor's Fiscal Adv. Com., 1976—2007, mem. exec. com., 1982—2007; mem. San Francisco Civil Svc. Commn., 1984—2000, v.p. 1986, 89, pres. 1987, 90-91; mem. San Francisco Public Libr. Commn., 2006-,v.p., 2008-. Lt. res. USCG, 1954—64. Recipient SBA Advocate of Yr. award, 1976. Mem. Harvard Bus. Sch. Assn. of No. Calif., Phi Gamma Delta. Democrat. Home and Office: 24 Presidio Ter San Francisco CA 94118-1411 Office Phone: 415-752-5300. Personal E-mail: aleem@att.net. *In problem solving, I've found problems also contain interesting new opportunities if you reflect enough on the alternatives. In managing people and in working for others, I've found the greatest motivator is the opportunity for personal growth.*

MUNSON, DAVID C., computer engineer, educator, dean; BS in Elec. Engring. (with distinction), Univ. Del., 1975; MS in Elec. Engring., Princeton Univ., 1977, PhD in Elec. Engring., 1979. Prof. Dept. Computer and Elec. Engring. U. Ill., 1979—2003, rsch. prof., coord. studies lab., faculty mem. Beckman Inst. Advanced Sci. and Tech.; prof., dept. chair, Dept. Elec. Engring. and Computer Sci. U. Mich., Ann Arbor, 2003—, Robert J. Vlasic dean engring., 2006—. Recipient Outstanding Prof. award, Alpha Chap. Eta Kappa Nu, 1990, Robert C. MacClinchie Distinguished Professor of Elec. and Computer Engring., Univ. Ill., 2001; named Outstanding Teacher in Elec. Engring., 1999. Fellow: IEEE (past editor, past v.p., past bd. gov., past chmn., active mem. circuits and sys. soc., Meritorious Svc. award, named Processing Soc. Distinguished Lectr., Third Millenium Medal 2000, Soc. award 2003). Office: U Mich Coll Engring Robert H Lurie Engring Ctr 1221 Beal Ave Ann Arbor MI 48109-2102 Office Phone: 734-647-7010. Office Fax: 734-647-7009. E-mail: munson@umich.edu.

MUNSON, DAVID ROY, Mayor, Sioux Falls, South Dakota; b. Sioux Falls, SD, Apr. 16, 1942; s. Roy Elmer Munson and Theil Severson; m. Linda Marie Carlson, 1972; children: Steven David, Paul James, John Jeffrey. BA, Sioux Falls Coll.; Master's Degree, Augustana Coll. Mem. S.D. House of Reps., 1979-96, asst. majority whip, 1983-84, 89-90, mem. commerce and health and human svc. coms., vice chmn. state affairs com.; with Citibank S.D.; mem., Dist. 10 S.D. Senate, Pierre, 1996—2002, chair, commerce com., mem., edn. com., mem. com. state affairs; mayor City of Sioux Falls, SD, 2002—. Mem. commerce, labor and regulation coms., state-fed. assembly Nat. Conf. State Legislators. Past mem. Sioux Vocat. Bd.; mem. Multiple Sclerosis Bd., Luth. Social Svc. Consumers Credit Adv. Bd. and Cmty. Disabilities Svc. Bd.; mem. S.D. Devel. Corp.; mem. Sioux Empire Fire Bd.; vol. coach Boys' YMCA Tri-State Tournament. Fellow Augustana Coll.; recipient Dr. A. O. Larsen Disting. Alumni award, U. Sioux Falls. Mem. NEA. Office: Mayor's Office 224 W Ninth St (City Hall - First Floor) PO Box 7402 Sioux Falls SD 57117-7402 Office Fax: 605-367-8800, 605-367-8490.*

MUNSON, EDWARD HARRY, JR., medical investigator; b. Birmingham, Ala., Apr. 3, 1948; s. Edward H. Sr. and Elizabeth (W.) M.; married, Dec. 6, 1968 (div. Dec. 1985); children: Laura Davis, Kathleen DeLacy Munson, Matthew Edward; m. Patricia Beth Wool, July 29, 1989. BA in Biology, Huntingdon Coll., 1971; student, U. Mo. Law Enforcemnt Tng. Nat. cert. investigator. Investigator Montgomery (Ala.) Police Dept., 1970-81; instr. Ala. Advanced Criminal Justice Acad., 1974-80; med. investigator Ala. Bd. Med. Examiners, Montgomery, 1981—. Cons. State Bd. of Health-Controlled Substance Adv. Panel, Montgomery, 1989—, Stae Methadone Authority, Fedn. of State Med. Bds., Ft. Worth, 1990—; mem. Med. Investigator Tng. Com., chair, 1994, 97; mem. work com. prescription monitoring programs Nat. Alliance for Model State Drug Laws. Recipient Silver Star, Am. Fedn. Police, Miami, Fla., 1975, Ronald K. Williamson Meml. award Nat. Adminstrs. in Medicine, 2004; named Firearms Expert, NRA, 1978. Mem. Internat. Narcotic Officers Assn., Nat. Assn. Drug Diversion Investigators, Nat. Criminal Justice Assn., Nat. Assn. State Controlled Substance Authorities. Jewish. Avocations: travel, cooking, shooting. Office: Ala Bd Med Examiners PO Box 946 Montgomery AL 36101-0946

MUNSON, ETHAN VINCENT, engineering educator; b. Boston, Dec. 15, 1956; s. Paul Lewis Munson and Mary Ellen Jones; m. Marta Andrade Fernandes, July 19, 2007. BA, U. Calif., San Diego, 1978, BA, 1986; MS, U. Calif., Berkeley, 1989, PhD, 1994. Asst. prof. U. Wis., 1994—2000, assoc. prof., 2000—. Chair, steering com. ACM Symposium Document Engring., 2000—07; sec., treas. ACM Spl. Interest Group Hypertext, Hypermedia and Web, 2005—06, chair, 2006—. Mem.: SBC, ACM. Office: Univ Wis Milw PO Box 784 Milwaukee WI 53201 Office Fax: 414-229-2769. Business E-Mail: munson@uwm.edu.

MUNSON, HAROLD LEWIS, education educator; b. Windham, NY, Aug. 2, 1923; s. Esmond Lewis and Gladys (Disbrow) M.; m. Evelyn Claire Moore, Sept. 8, 1946; children: Michael Lewis, Jeffrey Charles. AB, Hobart Coll., 1947; MA, SUNY, Albany, 1948; Ed.D., NYU, 1961. Tchr. social studies, counselor Cairo Ctrl. Sch., NY, 1948-50; dir. guidance Williamson Central Sch., NY, 1950-54; supr. guidance NY State Edn. Dept., Albany, 1954-59; prof. edn., chmn. Ctr. for Counseling, Family and Worklife Studies, U. Rochester, NY, 1959-85, prof. emeritus, 1985—; prof. edn. Overseas Program, Boston U., 1985-87; pres. Munson Assocs., 1988—. Vocat. cons. Social Security Adminstrn., HEW, 1962-79 Author: (with H.W. Houghton) Organizing Orientation Activities, 1956, My Educational Plans, 1959, 70, Guidance Activities for Teachers of English, Social Studies, Science, Mathematics and Foreign Languages, 1965, (with Gilbert Gockley) Career Insights and Self Awareness Games, 1973; contbg. author: Ency. of Careers, 1967, Elementary School Guidance: Concepts, Dimensions and Practice, 1970, The Foundations of Developmental Guidance, 1971, Career Education for Deaf Students: An Inservice Leader's Guide, 1975, The Land In The Sky, 2004, South Street Story, 2008. Served with USNR, 1944-46. Mem. Am. Counseling Assn., Nat. Career Devel. Assn., Am. Sch. Counselor Assn., Phi Delta Kappa. Home: 9 Charleston Dr Mendon NY 14506 Office Phone: 585-582-3275. Personal E-mail: hmunson@rochester.rr.com. *Success is whatever you want it to be. By defining it in such personal terms, everyone should be able to experience some degree of success. For me, it has been being able to feel a measure of personal fulfillment through my accomplishments in helping others to define and examine their own existence.*

MUNSON, JOHN BACKUS, computer scientist, retired data processing executive; b. Chgo., May 1, 1933; s. Mark Frame and Catherine Louise (Cherry) M.; m. Anne Lorraine Cooper, July 6, 1957; children: David B., Sharon A. BA, Knox Coll., Galesburg, Ill., 1955. With Unisys Corp., McLean, Va., 1957-93, v.p. corp. software engring., 1977-81, v.p. tech. ops., 1981-84, v.p. gen. mgr. space transp. systems, 1984-89, 89-93, v.p., gen. mgr. Space Systems divsn., 1989-94, ret., 1994. Mem. sci. adv. bd. USAF, 1981-86, mem. USN panel on F14D issues, 1987-88. Mem. bd. advisors U. Houston, Clear Lake, 1988-93, chmn. 1990-92; bd. dirs. Bay Area YMCA, 1988-93, chmn. 1992, Clear Lake Am. Heart Assn., 1989-93; co-chmn. Bay Area United Way, 1988—, chmn., 1992; Disting. visitor IEEE Computing Soc., 1981-94. Capt. US Army, 1955-57. Recipient Exceptional Civilian Svc. award USAF, 1986, Superior Pub. Svc. award USN, 1988, cert. of appreciation NATO, 1984; named to Mgmt. Assn. Hall of Fame, 1994. Fellow IEEE (editor Trans. of Software Engring. 1982-84, bd. dirs. tech. com. software engring. 1982—); mem. AIA, Am. Astronautical Soc. (bd. dirs. S.W. sect. 1989-94), Aerospace Industries Assn. (space com. 1989-94), US Army Assn., Nat. Security Indsl. Assn., Armed Forces Comm. Electronics Assn. (pres. Houston chpt. 1987-90), S.W. Regional Coun. Corp. CEOs. Home and Office: 1018 Westcreek Ln Westlake Village CA 91362-5462 Personal E-mail: jaxg3@aol.com.

MUNSON, JOHN CHRISTIAN, acoustician; b. Clinton, Iowa, Oct. 9, 1926; s. Arthur J. and Frances (Christian) M.; m. Elaine Hendershot, Sept. 2, 1950; children: John Christian, Holly Elizabeth. BS, Iowa State Coll., 1949; MS, U. Md., 1952, PhD, 1962; Navy Dept. scholar, MIT, 1956. Electronic scientist Naval Ordnance Lab., Washington, 1949-66; tech. dir. navy portion Practice Nine, Naval Air Systems Command, 1967; supt. acoustics divsn. Naval Rsch. Lab., 1968-85; v.p. Engring. & Sci. Assocs., 1983-94; chmn. bd. dirs., 1994; ret. Asst. extension prof. elec. engring. U. Md., 1964-66; mem. Underwater Sound Adv. Group, 1969-75, U.S. Sonar Team, 1971-85, Mobile Sonar Tech. Com., 1972-85; cons., 1985-. Editor U.S. Navy Jour. Underwater Acoustics, 1983-91; patentee in field. Mem. exec. bd. DC Bapt. Conv., 1973—, chmn. fin. com., 1973, v.p., 1996-97, pres., 1997-98; trustee Midwestern Bapt. Theol. Sem., 1970-80; trustee Bapt. Sr. Adult Ministries Washington Met. Area, 1976-91, 92-04, pres., 1981-88, CEO, 1991-92; mem. Gen. Bd. Am. Bapt. Chs. USA, 1994-99; pres. Allied Silver Spring Interfaith Svcs. to Srs. Today, 1994-00, bd. dirs. 1994-03; bd. mgrs. Am. Bapt. Hist. Soc., 1996-03, sec., 1997-03; corp. mem. Am. Bapt. Homes of the West, 1999, dir., 2000-04. Fellow IEEE, Signal Processing Soc. (mem. adminstrv. com. 1974-76, chmn. underwater acoustics com. 1973-76), Acoustical Soc. Am.; mem. Sigma Xi. Home: 3118 Chartwell Crescent Ln Adamstown MD 21710-9643 E-mail: johncmunsonsr@edurostream.com. *I have a positive joy for life, and I am an incurable optimist: my basic attitude is that things will work out for the best— but only if we do our very best. Each of us has a responsibility to grow to our maximum capacity and to be of reasonable service to mankind. The proper balance among family, job, service to God, service to others, and attention to yourself is essential. Whatever you are doing, do it from the right motivation and with enthusiasm.*

MUNSON, LESTER, legislative staff member; AB in Polit. Sci., U. Chgo., 1989; MS, St. John's Coll., 1996. Comm. dir., internat. rels. com. US House of Reps., Washington, 1999—2001, chief of staff to Mark Kirk, 2007—; sr. profl. staff mem., fgn. rels. com. US Senate, Washington, 2001—03; dep. asst. adminstr. US Agency Internat. Devel., 2003—07. Republican. Office: 1030 Longworth House Office Bldg Washington DC 20515 Office Phone: 202-225-4835. Office Fax: 202-225-0837.*

MUNSON, RICHARD HOWARD, horticulturist; b. Toledo, Dec. 20, 1948; s. Stanley Warren and Margaret Rose (Winter) M. BS, Ohio State U., 1971; MS, Cornell U., 1973, PhD, 1981. Plant propagator The Holden Arboretum, Kirtland, Ohio, 1973-76; asst. prof. Agrl. Tech. Inst., Wooster, Ohio, 1976-78, Tex. Tech U., Lubbock, 1981-84; dir. botanic garden Smith Coll., Northampton, Mass., 1984-95; exec. dir. The Holden Arboretum, Kirtland, Ohio, 1995-2000; dir. botanic garden U. Mo., Columbia, Mo., 2001—04; mgr. The Conservatory, Miami U., Hamilton, Ohio, 2004—. Ret. lt. col. USAR, 1971-99. Recipient Disting. Alumnus award Ohio State U. Coll. Agr., 1998. Fellow Internat. Plant Propagator's Soc.; mem. Am. Pub. Garden Assn. (com. chmn. 1987-92, 01-03), Sigma Xi, Pi Alpha Xi, Gamma Sigma Delta. Avocations: fishing, fly-tying, golf, woodworking, gardening. Office: Miami U-Hamilton 1601 University Blvd Hamilton OH 45011 Home Phone: 513-523-5168; Office Phone: 513-785-3086. Business E-Mail: munsonrh@muohio.edu.

MUNSON, RONALD ALFRED, retired chemist; b. Lancaster, Pa., Aug. 12, 1933; s. Saron Erik and Millicent Edwards Munson; m. Sarah Elizabeth Robinson, June 24, 1967; children: Katherine, Elizabeth Pickens, Hilma, Erika Sliger. BS, Franklin and Marshall Coll., 1955; PhD, Northwestern U., 1958. Post-doctoral rsch. assoc. Max-Planck-Institut fuer Physikalische Chemie, Goettingen, Germany, 1958—60; rsch. chemist GE Rsch. Lab., Schenectady, NY, 1960—67; rsch. supr. US Bur. Of Mines, College Park, 1967—72; rsch. staff assistent US Bur. of Mines Hdqs., Washington, 1972—82; chief office of mineral institutes US Bur. of Mines, Washington, 1982—96. Contbr. articles to profl. jours. Pres. Arlington County Parent Tchr. Assn., Arlington, Va., 1980—81. Recipient predoctoral fellowship, NSF, 1955—58, postdoctoral fellowship, 1958—60, meritorious svc. award, Dept. of the Interior, 1991. Mem.: AIME (chmn. Washington sect. 1981—82), Am. Chem. Soc. Unitarian Universalist. Achievements include discovery of transition metal disulfides having the pyrite structure using ultra-high pressure synthesis techniques. Avocations: skiing, tennis. Personal E-mail: rmunson@gmu.edu.

MUNSON, WILLIAM LESLIE, insurance company executive; b. Chgo., Apr. 28, 1941; s. David Curtiss and Leona Ruth (Anderson) M.; m. Marian Lee Blanton, July 16, 1966; children: Katherine, Sandra, Deborah. Student, U. Md., 1959-62; BBA cum laude, Coll. of Ins., 1968. CPCU, 1967. Asst. mgr. N.Y. Fire Ins. Rating Orgn., NYC, 1959-69; br. mgr. CNA Ins. Co., NYC, 1969-75; pres., dir. Commerce & Industry Ins. Co., NYC, 1975-83; pres. Commerce & Industry of Can., 1980-83; sr. v.p., chief underwriting officer Am. Internat. Underwriters, 1983-87; exec. v.p. Home Ins. Co., 1987-93; pres., chief exec. officer Home Indemnity Ins. Co., 1987-93, also bd. dirs.; chmn. City Internat. Ins. Co. Ltd., 1991-93; pres., COO Merc. and Gen. Reins. Co. Am., 1993-97; chmn., pres., CEO Toa-Re-Ins. Co. Am. (now Toa Reins. Co. Am.), 1993—2003. Bd. dirs. USF Ins. Co., Victoria Ins. Co.; trustee Coll. of Ins., 1985—2001, Am. Inst. for Property Casualty Underwriters, 1996—2002; bd. overseers Sch. of Risk Mgmt., Ins. and Actuarial Sci. St. John's U., 2001—06; mem. bd. visitors Drew U., 2002—; mem. comml. lines. com. Ins. Svcs. Office, 1989—92. Pres. Wyckoff (NJ) Bd. Edn., 1979-82; chmn. bd. lay leaders Grace United Meth. Ch., Wyckoff, 1989-92, trustee, 1999—, pres. bd. trustees, 2005-. Past mem. Soc. CPCUs (bd. dirs. N.Y. chpt.); mem., Conf. Spl. Risk Underwriters, Reinsurance Assn. Am. (bd. dirs. 1993-2002). Clubs: John St. (N.Y.C.). Republican. Home: 762 Albemarle St Wyckoff NJ 07481-1005 Home Phone: 201-891-7834; Office Phone: 201-891-7834. Business E-Mail: wlmunson@verizon.net.

MUNT, JANET STAPLES, state senator; b. NYC, June 14, 1923; m. Plummer Coldwell Munt (dec.); 4 children. BA, Sweet Briar Coll., 1944; MS, Columbia U., 1948. Bd. cert. diplomate. Dir. maternal and child health divsn. Vis. Nurse Assn. Chittenden County, 1978—95; pvt. practice clin. social worker, 1995—. Trustee Burlington Coll., Columbia U. Sch. Social Work. Sgt. WAC, WWII. Fellow Am. Orthopsychiat. Assn., Inc.; mem. NASW, Acad. Cert. Social Workers. Democrat.

MUNTER, CAMERON, United States Ambassador to Serbia; b. Calif., 1954; Attended, Cornell U., Ithaca, NY, universities in Freiburg and Marburg, Germany; D in Modern English History, Johns Hopkins U., Balt., 1983. Lectr. in European history UCLA, 1982—84; dir. European studies Twentieth Century Fund, NY, 1984—85; fgn. svc. assignment US Dept. State, Warsaw, 1986—88, staff asst., Bur. European Affairs, 1988—89, country dir. Czechoslovakia, 1989—91, fgn. svc. assignment Prague, 1992—95, Bonn, Germany, 1995—97, chief of staff, NATO Enlargement Ratification Office, 1997—98, dir., Northern European Initiative, 1998, exec. asst. to the counselor, 1998—99; dir., Ctrl. Ea. and No. Europe Nat. Security Coun., 1999—2001; dep. chief of mission US Dept. State, Warsaw, 2002—05, Prague, 2005—07, head, Provincial Reconstrn. Team Mosul, Iraq, 2006, US amb. to Serbia Belgrade, 2007—. Dean Rusk fellow, Georgetown U. Inst. the Study of Diplomacy, 1991. Office: DOS Amb 5070 Belgrade Pl Washington DC 20521-5070*

MUNTZ, ERIC PHILLIP, aerospace and mechanical engineering educator, consultant; b. Hamilton, Ont., Can., May 18, 1934; came to U.S., 1961, naturalized, 1985; s. Eric Percival and Marjorie Louise (Weller) M.; m. Janice Margaret Furey, Oct. 21, 1964; children: Sabrina Weller, Eric Phillip. BASc., U. Toronto, 1956, MASc., 1957, PhD, 1961. Halfback Toronto Argonauts, 1957-60; group leader Gen. Electric, Valley Forge, Pa., 1961-69; assoc. prof. aerospace engring. and radiology U. So. Calif., Los Angeles, 1969-71, prof., 1971-87, chmn. aerospace engring., 1987-97, A.B. Freeman prof. engring., 1992—, chmn. aerospace and mech. engring., 2000—03. Cons. to aerospace and med. device cos., 1967—; mem. rev. of physics (plasma and fluids) panel NRC, Washington, 1983-85 Contbr. numerous articles in gas dynamics, micromech. sys., and med. diagnostics to profl. publs., 1961—; patentee med. imaging, isotope separation, nondestructive testing, net shape mfg., transient energy release micromachines, microscale vacuum sys., micropropulsion sys. Mem. Citizens Environ. Avc. Coun., Pasadena, Calif., 1972-76. Pilot RCAF, 1955-60. U.S. Air Force grantee, 1961-74, 82—; NSF grantee, 1970-76, 87-92; NASA grantee, 1990-94, 2001—; FDA grantee, 1980-86. Fellow AIAA (aerospace Contbn. to Soc. award 1987), Am. Phys. Soc.; mem. NAE. Episcopalian. Home: 1560 E California Blvd Pasadena CA 91106-4104 Office: U So Calif Univ Pk Los Angeles CA 90089-1191 Office Phone: 213-740-5366. Business E-Mail: muntz@usc.edu.

MUNVER, RAVI, urologist; b. NYC, Jan. 29, 1971; BA, Cornell U., 1992, MD, 1996. Resident in gen. surgery Duke U. Med. Ctr., 1996—98, resident in urology, 1998—2002; fellow in endourology and laparoscopy N.Y. Presbyn. Hosp./Cornell Med. Ctr., 2002—. Mem.: Am. Assn. Clin. Urologists, Endourol. Soc., Am. Urol. Assn., Phi Beta Kappa.

MUNYER, EDWARD ARNOLD, zoologist; b. Chgo., May 8, 1936; s. G. and M. Munyer; m. Marianna J. Munyer, Dec. 12, 1981; children: Robert, William, Richard, Laura, Cheryl. BS, Ill. State U., 1958, MS, 1962. Biology tchr. MDR High Sch., Minonk, Ill., 1961-63; instr. Ill. State U., Normal, 1963-64; curator zoology Ill. State Mus., Springfield, 1964-67, asst. dir., 1981-98, asst. dir. emeritus, 1998—; assoc. prof. Vincennes (Ind.) U., 1967-70; dir. Vincennes U. Mus., 1968-70; assoc. curator Fla. Mus. Natural History, Gainesville, 1970-81. Contbr. articles to profl. jours. Mem. Am. Assn. Mus. (bd. dirs. 1990-95), Assn. Midwest Mus. (pres. 1990-92, lifetime achievement award for disting. svc. 1998), Ill. Assn. Mus. (bd. dirs. 1981-86, lifetime profl. achievement award 1998), Wilson Ornithol. Soc. (life). Office: Ill State Mus Spring & Edward Sts Springfield IL 62706-0001

MUNZNER, ROBERT FREDERICK, biomedical engineer; s. Robert F. Munzner and Catherine E. (Appel) Gay; m. Jo Ann Goettee, Sept. 2, 1960 (div. 1980); children: Elizabeth Mae, Robert Victor, Ann Catherine; m. Karen E. Winstedt, Oct. 1, 1988. BS in Physics, Loyola Coll., Balt., 1963; PhD in Biomed. Engring., U. Va., 1976. Aerospace engr. Westinghouse Def. and Space, Balt., 1963-69; rsch. assoc. Johns Hopkins U., Balt., 1975-77; chief, neurol. devices br. U.S. FDA, Rockville, Md., 1977-97, expert sci. reviewer, 1998-99; regulatory affairs cons. Schuyler, Va., 1999—. Exec. sec. neurol. device adv. panel. U.S. FDA, Rockville, Md.; bd. standards IEEE, 1999-2001; mem. biomed. engring. adv. bd. N.U.C., Chapel Hill, 2004—08. Co-author: Cerebellar Stimulation for Spasticity, 1984, The Physicians Perspective on Medical Law, 1997, Wiley Encyclopedia of Biomedical Engineering, 2006; contbr. articles to profl. jours. Fellow Johns Hopkins U., Balt., 1975, U. Va. fellow, Charlottesville, 1972-73, Thornton fellow, 1971. Mem. IEEE (sr., Millennium medal 2000), Biomed. Engring. Soc., Engring. in Medicine and Biology Soc. (chmn. stds. com., ad com. 1999-2005), Sigma Xi. Achievements include research in atrial mechanical stimulation producing vasomotor reflex. Home Phone: 434-263-8862; Office Phone: 434-263-8862. Business E-Mail: robert@doctordevice.com.

MUOGHALU, MICHAEL I., finance educator; s. Okeke James and Theresa O. Muoghalu; m. Sandra N. Anumba, Aug. 8, 1991; children: Michael I., James C., Christine O. PhD, La. Tech U., Ruston, 1987. Fin. prof. Pittsburg State U., Kans., MBA program dir., 2001—. Fulbright Rsch. fellowship, US Dept. State, 2000. Office: Pittsburg State Univ 1701 S Broadway Pittsburg KS 66762

MURABITO, JOHN M., insurance company executive; BA in Econs., Augustana Coll., Ill., 1980; MA in Indsl. Rels., U. Iowa, 1983. With The Trane Co., Symbion, Inc.; with Frito-Lay divsn. PepsiCo; sr. v.p. human resources and corp. svcs. Monsanto; exec. v.p. human resources and svcs. CIGNA Corp., Phila., 2003—. Bd. dirs. Cornell U. Ctr. Advanced Human Resources Studies, U. SC Riegel & Emory Sch. Bus. Mem.: Human Resources Rsch. Group, Human Resources Policy Assn. Office: CIGNA Corp Two Liberty Pl 1601 Chestnut St Philadelphia PA 19192-1550 Office Phone: 215-761-1000.

MURAD, FERID, physician; b. Whiting, Ind., Sept. 14, 1936; s. John and Josephine Murad; m. Carol Ann Leopold, June 21, 1958; children: Christine, Marianne, Carrie, Julie, Joseph. BA, DePauw U., 1958; MD, PhD, Case Western Res. U., 1965; Degree (hon.), Tirana U., 1999, Thomas Jefferson U., 2000, Case Western REs. U., 2000, State U. Ceara, 2000, Chinese U., Hong Kong, 2002, DePauw U., 2004, Charles U., 2005, Southeastern U., 2006. Diplomate Nat. Bd. Med. Examiners.

Intern and resident Mass. Gen. Hosp., Boston, 1965—67; clin. assoc. NIH, Bethesda, Md., 1967—70; dir. clin. rsch. ctr. U. Va., Charlottesville, 1971—81, prof. internal medicine and pharmacology, 1975—81, Stanford U., Calif., 1981—88, acting chmn. dept. medicine, 1986—88; chief of medicine VA Med. Ctr., Palo Alto, Calif., 1981—88; v.p. pharm. divsn. Abbott Labs., 1988—92, CEO, pres. molecular geriatrics, 1993—95; prof. dept. medicine, chmn. dept. integrative biology and pharmacology U. Tex., Houston, 1997—, dir. Inst. Molecular Medicine, 1999—. Co-editor: The Pharmacological Basis of Therapeutics, 1985; contbr. articles to profl. jours. Recipient Ciba award, 1988, Albert Lasker award for Basic Med. Rsch., Lasker Found., 1996, Nobel Prize for Medicine, 1998, others. Mem.: NAS, Inst. of Medicine, Western Assn. Physicians, Assn. Am. Physicians, Am. Soc. Clin. Investigation, Am. Soc. Physiology, Am. Soc. Biol. Chemists, Am. Soc. for Pharmacology and Exptl. Therapeutics, Am. Acad. Arts and Scis., NAS Inst. Medicine. Achievements include patents in field. Avocations: golf, carpentry. Office: U Tex Med Sch Inst Molecular Medicine 1825 Pressler Ste 530 Houston TX 77225-0708 Office Phone: 713-500-2433. Business E-Mail: ferid.murad@uth.tmc.edu.

MURAI, KEVIN M., electronics executive; b. 1964; BSEE, U. Waterloo, Ontario. Former mgr. mgmt. info. svcs. Verifact, Inc., Ontario, Canada; joined Ingram Micro Inc., 1988; v.p., operations Ingram Micro Can., Canada, 1993—97, pres., 1997—2000; sr. v.p. Ingram Micro Inc., 1997—2002, exec. v.p. Santa Ana, Calif., 2000—05; pres. Ingram Micro US, 2000—01, COO, 2000—02; pres., COO Ingram Micro N. Am., 2002—05, Ingram Micro Inc., 2005—07; co-CEO Synnex Corp., Fremont, Calif., 2008, pres., CEO, 2008—. Office: Synnex Corp 44201 Nobel Dr Fremont CA 94538 Office Phone: 714-566-1000. Office Fax: 714-566-7900.*

MURAI, RENE VICENTE, lawyer; b. Havana, Cuba, Mar. 11, 1945; came to the U.S., 1960; s. Andres and Silvia (Muñiz) M.; m. Luisa Botifoll, June 12, 1970; 1 child, Elisa. BA, Brown U., 1966; JD cum laude, Columbia U., 1969. Bar: Fla. 1970, N.Y. 1972, U.S. Supreme Ct. 1977. Atty. Reginald Heber Smith Fellow Legal Svcs. Greater Miami, Fla., 1969-71; assoc. Willkie, Farr & Gallagher, NYC, 1971-73; ptnr. Paul, Landy & Beiley, Miami, 1973-79; shareholder Murai, Wald, Biondo & Moreno, Miami, 1979—. Vice-chmn. Premier Am. Bank, Miami; dir. Cuban Am. Bar Assn., 1982-96, pres., 1985; vice chmn., lectr. Internat. Conf. for Lawyers of the Ams., 1982, chmn. and lectr., 1984; mem. panel grievance com. Fla. Bar, 1983-86. Mng. editor Columbia Law Rev., 1967-69. Facts About Cuban Exiles, Inc., 1982—, pres., 1989, Legal Svcs. of Greater Miami, Inc., 1980-90, pres. 1986-88, ARC, 1984-90, exec. com., 1988-90, Mercy Hosp. Found., 1985-91, Dade Cmty. Found., 1988-93, chair grants com., 1991-93, United Way, 1989-95; chmn. adminstrn. of justice com. Fla. Bar Found., 1996-98, bd. dirs., 1991-00, chmn. audit and fin. com., 1993-98, sec., 1997-98, pres. 1999-2000; mem. task force leadership Dade County Ptnrs. for Safe Neighborhoods, 1994-95, Code Enforcement Bd. City of Coral Gables, 1982-86, Bd. Adjustment, 1987-89, city mgr. selection com., 1987, charter rev. commn., 1980; trustee U. Miami, 1994-96; bd. dirs. Miami Children's Hosp., 2000—07, chmn. 2004-07; com. mem. Orange Bowl, 2000-, bd. dir., 2005-; bd. dir. Riviera Country Club, 2005-07. Mem. Cuban-Am. Bar Assn., Dade County Bar Assn. (dir. 1987-88), Greater Miami C. of C., Miami City Club (bd. dirs. 1997—2001, pres. 2000—01). Democrat. Roman Catholic. Avocation: sports. Home: 3833 Alhambra Ct Coral Gables FL 33134-6229 Office: Murai Wald Biondo Moreno & Brochin PA 2 Alhambra Plz PH 1B Coral Gables FL 33134 Office Phone: 305-444-0101. Business E-Mail: rmurai@mwbm.com.

MURAKAMI, EISUKE, biochemist; b. Tokyo, Sept. 23, 1970; s. Tadashi and Aiko Murakami; m. Chiaki Murakami, May 28, 2007. PhD, U. Nebr. Lincoln, Lincoln, 2000. Assoc. rsch. scientist Yale U. Sch. Medicine, New Haven, 2000—04; sr. scientist Pharmasset Inc., Princeton, NJ, 2004—. Office: Pharmasset Inc 303A College Road East Princeton NJ 08540

MURALI, SUPRAJA, optical engineer, researcher; b. Chennai, Tamil Nadu, India, Feb. 19, 1982; d. Murali Srinivasagopalan and Lakshmi Murali. BS, Birla Inst. Tech. and Sci., Pilani, India, 2003; MS in Optics, U. Ctrl. Fla., Orlando, 2005; student in Optics, U. Cent., Orlando, 2009. Rsch. intern Bharat Electronics Ltd, Bangalore, Karnataka, India, 2002—02. Contbr. scientific papers to profl. publs. Vol. Nat. Gandhi Day Svc., Orlando, 2004; vol. svc. Hindu Temple, Orlando, 2004—08. Fellow Rsch. fellowship, CREOL and FPCE, Coll. of Optics and Photonics, U. of Ctrl. Fla., 2004;, U. Ctrl. Fla., 2006—07. Mem.: SPIE, Soc. Info. Display (sec. 2008), Optical Soc. America. Achievements include patents in field. Office: CREOL Univ Ctrl Florida 4000 Central Florida Blvd Orlando FL 32816 Business E-Mail: smurali@creol.ucf.edu.

MURANAKA, JAMI, biology educator; m. Garett Muranaka; children: Emi, Misa. BS in Biology, UCLA; MEd, U. Hawai'i-Manoa. Cert. Nat. Bd. Profl. Tchg. Standards. Sci. tchr. Kaimuki H.S., Honolulu, 1999—. Named Honolulu Dist. Tchr. of Yr., Hawaii Tchr. of Yr., 2007. Office: Kaimuki High Sch 2705 Kaimuki Ave Honolulu HI 96816 Business E-Mail: jami_muranaka@notes.k12.hi.us.

MURANE, WILLIAM EDWARD, lawyer; b. Denver, Mar. 4, 1933; s. Edward E. and Theodora (Wilson) M.; m. Rosemarie Palmerone, Mar. 26, 1960; children: Edward Wheelock, Peter Davenport, Alexander Phelps. AB, Dartmouth Coll., 1954; LLB, Stanford U., 1957. Bar: Colo. 1958, D.C. 1978, U.S. Supreme Ct. 1977. Assoc. then ptnr. Holland & Hart, Denver, 1961-69; dep. gen. counsel U.S. Dept. Commerce, Washington, 1969-71; gen. counsel FDIC, Washington, 1971-72; ptnr. Holland & Hart, Denver, 1972—2000. Pub. mem. Adminstrv. Conf. of the U.S., Washington, 1978-81. Bd. dirs. Ctr. for Law and Rsch., Denver, 1973-76, Colo. Bus. Com. for Arts, 2002—; trustee Colo. Symphony Orch., 1994-2000; mem. bd. visitors Stanford U. Law Sch.; mem. vestry St. John's Cathedral, Denver, 2007-. Capt. USAF, 1958-61. Fellow Am. Coll. Trial Lawyers; mem. ABA (ho of dels. 1991-96), U. Club, Cactus Club. Avocations: fishing, classical music. Office: Holland & Hart 555 17th St Ste 2700 Denver CO 80202-3950 Business E-Mail: wmurane@hollandhart.com.

MURANO, ELSA A., agricultural studies educator, former academic administrator; b. Havana, Cuba, Aug. 14, 1959; m. Peter S. Murano. BS in Biol. Sci., Fla. Internat. U., 1981; MS in Anaerobic Microbiology, Va. Polytechnic Inst., 1987, PhD in Food Sci. & Tech., 1990. Rsch. lab technician Fla. Internat. U., 1981—83; researcher, teaching asst. Va. Tech. U., Blacksburg, Va., 1984—90; asst. prof. dept. microbiology, immunology & preventive medicine Iowa State U., Ames, 1990—92, prof. in charge rsch. programs linear accelertor facility, 1992—95; various positions including dir. food safety Tex. A&M U., College Station, Tex., 1995—2001, assoc. prof. animal sci., 1995—2000, prof. dept. animal sci., 2000—01, vice chancellor, dean agrl. & life scis., 2005—08, pres., 2008—09, prof. animal sci., 2009—; dir. Tex. Agrl. Experiment Station, 2005; under sec. for food safety USDA, Washington, 2001—04. Chair food safety state initiative com. Tex. Agr. Ext. Sta., 1999—2001; nat. adv. com. meat and poultry inspection USDA, 2001; mem. Nat. Alliance for Food Safety Ops. Com., 1998—2001, chair, 2000—01; bd. dirs. Hormel Foods Corp., 2006—. Named one of The 100 Most Influential Hispanics, Hispanic Bus. mag., 2002; named to The Alumni Hall of Fame, Hispanic Scholarship Fund, 2005. Mem.: Intenat. Assn. Food Protection, Poultry Sci. Assn., Inst. Food Technologists, Assn. Meat Sci., Am. Soc. Microbiology. Avocations: astronomy, drums. Office: Tex A&M U Mailstop 2471 College Station TX 77843 Office Phone: 979-845-2217. Office Fax: 979-845-5027. E-mail: president@tamu.edu, emurano@tamu.edu.*

MURARKA, NARAYAN P., electronics engineer, engineering executive; s. Misri L. and Moni Bai Murarka; m. Usha; children: Monica, Naveen N. BS in Physics, U. Calcutta, India, 1959, B. Tech., 1961, M. Tech., 1962; PhD, U. Birmingham, Eng., 1968; MBA, U. Chgo., 1980. Rsch. engr. IIT Rsch. Inst., Chgo., 1969-73, sr. engr., 1973-77, mgr., 1977-84, dir., 1984-88, v.p., 1988-93, sr. sci. adv., 1993-95; pres. Mutronix, Inc., South Barrington, Ill., 1995—. Contbr. articles to profl. jours.; patentee for rugate optical filter sys. Mem. Village of South Barrington Planning and Zoning Commn., 2005—. Mem. IEEE (sr.; publicity chmn. Chgo. sect. 1995-97), Optical Soc. Am., Rotary Club (pres. Barrington Breakfast 2002-03), Rotary Dist. 6440 (asst. dist. gov. 2003-06), Barrington 4th of July Parade Com. (treas.). Avocation: travel. Home and Office: 19 Westlake Dr South Barrington IL 60010-5332 Office Phone: 847-836-0497. Personal E-mail: npmurarka@comcast.net.

MURARKA, SHYAM PRASAD, science and engineering educator, administrator; b. Jaynagar, Bihar, India, Mar. 13, 1940; came to U.S., 1966; s. Bihari L. and Suti Murarka; m. Saroj Murarka, May 21, 1962; children: Sumeet, Amal. BS in Chemistry with honors, Bihar U., Muzaffarpur, 1958, MS in Chemistry, 1960; PhD in Chemistry, Agra U., India, 1970; PhD in Materials Sci. and Metals, U. Minn., 1970. Lectr., rsch. assoc. Bihar U., 1960-61; trainee Atomic Energy Est., Trombay, Maharastra, 1961-62, sci. officer, 1962-66; rsch. asst. U. Minn., Mpls., 1966-70, rsch. assoc., 1970-72; mem. tech. staff, supr. Bell Labs., Murray Hill, NJ, 1972-84; prof. Rensselaer Poly. Inst., Troy, NY, 1984—2002, dir. Ctr. for Integrated Electronics and Electronics Mfg., 1994-96, dir. Ctr. for Advanced Interconnect Sci. and Tech., 1996-2000, dir. Sematech Ctr. of Excellence, 1989-96, Elaine S. & Jack S. Parker chair engrng., 1997—2002, prof. emeritus, 2002—. Cons. Bell Labs., Murray Hill, N.J., 1984-89, Applied Materials, Santa Clara, Calif., 1997-99; spkr. in field Author: Silicides for VLSI Applications, 1983, Metallization Theory and Practice for VLSI and ULSI, 1993; (with others) Electronic Materials Science and Technology, 1989, Chemical Mechanical Planarization of Microelectronic Materials, 1997, Copper Fundamental Mechanisms for Micorelectronic Applications, 2000, Interlayer Dielectrics for Semiconductor Technologies, 2003; co-editor: Advanced Metallizations in Microelectronics, 1990, Advanced Metallization and Processing for Semiconductor Devices and Circuits II, 1992, Interface Control of Electrical, Chemical, and Mechanical Properties, 1994, Advaned Metallization for Devices and Circuits, 1994, Microelectronics Technology and Process Integration, 1994, Low Dielectric Constant Materials Synthesis in Microelectronics, 1995, Interlayer Dielectrics for Semiconductor Technologies, 2003; contbr. book chpt. Transition Metal Silicides, 1983, Handbook of Semiconductor Technology, 2000, Diffusion Processes in Advanced Technological Materials, 2005; over 290 rsch. articles to profl. jours. and 280 talks Conf. & Seminars. Mem. Tri-City India Assn.'s Indian Comty. Support Group, Albany, 1996. Recipient Gold medal Bihar U., 1960; Univ. Grants Commn. scholar, 1961; Disting. Tech. Staff award, Bell Labs, 1982. Fellow IEEE, Am. Vacuum Soc., Am. Soc. Metals and Electrochem. Soc. (Thomas Callinan award 1987, Electronics Divsn. award 2001); mem. Materials Rsch Soc., Bihar U. Chem. Soc. (hon. life). Achievements include 20 patents in field.

MURASE, JIRO, lawyer; b. NYC, May 16, 1928; BBA, CCNY, 1955; JD, Georgetown U., 1958, LL.D. (hon.), 1982. Bar: D.C. 1958, N.Y. 1959. Sr. ptnr. Marks & Murase L.L.P., NYC, 1971-97, Bingham McCutchen Murase, NYC, 1997—. Legal counsel Consulate Gen. of Japan; mem. Pres.'s Adv. Com. Trade Negotiations, 1980-82; mem. Trilateral Commn., 1985—; apptd. mem. World Trade Coun., 1984-94; adv. com. internat. investment, tech. and devel. Dept. State, 1975. Editorial bd.: Law and Policy in Internat. Bus. Trustee Asia Found., 1979-83, Japanese Ednl. Inst. N.Y.; bd. dirs. Japan Soc., Japanese C. of C. in N.Y., Inc.; hon. bd. regents Georgetown U.; bd. visitors Georgetown Law Ctr.; adv. coun. Pace U., Internat. House Japan; pres. Japanese-Am. Assn. N.Y., Inc., 1996-98—, Japan Ctr. Internat. Exch., 2001—. Recipient N.Y. Gov.'s citation for contbns. to internat. trade, 1982; named to Second Order of Sacred Treasure (Japan), 1989. Mem. ABA, Assn. of Bar of City of N.Y., N.Y. State Bar Assn., N.Y. County Lawyers Assn., Maritime Law Assn., Consular Law Soc., Fed. Bar Coun., Am. Soc. Internat. Law, World Assn. Lawyers, Japanese-Am. Soc. Legal Studies, Am. Arbitration Assn., Lic. Execs. Soc., U.S. C. of C. Clubs: Nippon (dir.); Ardsley Country; N.Y. Athletic; Mid-Ocean (Bermuda). Office: Bingham McCutchen Murase 399 Park Ave New York NY 10022-4614 Office Phone: 212-705-7878. Business E-Mail: jiro.murase@bingham.com.

MURASHIMA, KUMIKO, artist, educator; arrived in US, 1967; d. Minoru and Michiko (Nagashima) M. BFA in Fiber Arts, Women's Coll. Fine Arts, Tokyo, 1962; MFA in Fiber Arts, Ind. U., 1970. Craftsman apprentice Serizawa Dyed Paper Inst., Tokyo, 1963-65; freelance textile designer Izumi Archtl. Design Co., Tokyo, 1965-67, Saphier, Lerner, Schindler Environetics, Inc., Chgo., 1970-71; asst. prof. art dept. Rowan U., 1971—, assoc. prof. art dept., 1974—. Artistic dir. Trio Creations, Sewell, 1987—. Author: Katazome in Contemporary Use, 1994. Recipient Malcolm Koch Mus. Purchase, Evansville (Ind.) Mus. Art, 1969, Wilber D. Peat Meml. award, 1970, Mr. and Mrs. Paul Arnold Merit award Herron Mus. Art, 1971; Craftsman's fellow N.J. State Coun. on Arts, 1985. Mem. Am. Crafts Coun., Artists Equity Assn. (Dorothy Grafly Meml. award 1981), Coll. Art Assn. Am., N.J. Designer and Craftsmen, Inc. (chairperson 1985-87), Am. Fedn. Tchrs. Avocations: reading, theater, classical music, gourmet foods, walking. Home: PO Box 515 Williamstown NJ 08094-0515 E-mail: murashima@rowan.edu.

MURASKI, SISTER ROSALYN, special education educator; d. Cyril Andrew and Eva Ann Muraski. MA, Cardinal Stritch U., Milw., 1986. Cert. in elem. edn. Wis. Dept. Pub. Instrn., 1975. Elem. tchr. St. Joseph Sch., Oneida, Wis., 1976—82, St. Francis Sch., Manistique, Wis., 1982—85; prof., spl. edn. Silver Lake Coll., Manitowoc, Wis., 1986—. Advisor & dir. Student Coun. Exceptional Children, Manitowoc, 1990—2007. Mem.: Coun. Exceptional Children. Liberal. Roman Catholic. Avocations: gardening, flower arranging. Home and Office: Silver Lake Coll 2406 S Alverno Rd Manitowoc WI 54220 Business E-Mail: rosalyn@silver.sl.edu.

MURAT, WILLIAM M., legislative staff member; b. Stevens Point, Wis., Dec. 4, 1957; s. James L. and Rose Murat. BS, U. Wis., Stevens Point, 1980; JD, U. Wis., Madison, 1983; MBA, Columbia U., 1992. Dist. atty. Portage County, Wis., 1987—91; assemblyman Wis. State Assembly. from Dist. 71, 1995—99; dist. dir. for Rep. Tammy Baldwin, US House of Reps., 1999—2001, chief of staff Washington, 2001—. Vice chmn. Portage County Dem. Com., 1976-80, chmn., 1985-86; exec. dir. Wis. Young Dems., 1978-79, pres., 1982-83; mem. exec. com. Seventh Dist. Dems., Wis., 1978-80, 82-90; adminstrv. com. Wis. Dem. Com., 1982-99; mem. Dem. Nat. Com., 1997-99; 1st vice chair Dem. Wis., 1997-99. Bd. dirs. Wis. Children's Mus., 1996—97. Mem. Phi Delta Phi, Pi Kappa Delta. Office: 2446 Rayburn Bldg Washington DC 20515 also: 10 E Doty St, Ste 405 Madison WI 53703*

MURAT, YUSEF J., plastic surgeon; b. Oaxaca, Mex., Sept. 2, 1964; arrived in U.S., 2003; s. Mateo Jiménez and Zandra Luz Murat; m. Ireri Salazar Urquiza, Nov. 29, 1997; children: Valentina, Miranda. MD, UNAM, Mexico City, 1989. Cert. plastic surgeon UNAM, 1996, Bd., 1997. Fellowship hand surgeon UNAM, Mexico City, 1997; fellowship microsurgery Hosp. Gen. Manuel Gea Gonzalez, UNAM, Mexico City, 1998, prof. plastic surgery, hand surgery, microsurgery, 1997—. Contbr. scientific papers in plastic surgery, hand surgery and microsurgery. Mem.: Assn. Dr. Ortiz-Monasterio. Avocations: tennis, golf. Office Phone: 956-544-7197. E-mail: yusmd@prodigy.net.mx.

MURATA, TADAO, engineering and computer science educator; b. Takayama, Gifu, Japan, June 26, 1938; arrived in U.S., 1962; s. Yonosuke and Ryu (Aomame) M.; m. Nellie Kit-Ha Shin, 1964; children: Patricia Emi, Theresa Terumi. BSE.E., Tokai U., 1962; MSE.E., U. Ill., 1964, PhD in Elec. Engring., 1966. Rsch. asst. U. Ill., Urbana, 1962-66; asst. prof. U. Ill. at Chgo., 1966-68, assoc. prof., 1970-76, prof., 1977—, UIC disting. prof., 2002—; assoc. prof. Tokai U., Tokyo, 1968-70. Vis. prof. U. Calif., Berkeley, 1976-77; cons. Nat. Bur. Stds., Gaithersburg, Md., 1984-85; panel mem. NAS, Washington, 1981-82, 83-85; vis. scientist Nat. Ctr. For Sci. Rsch., France, 1981; guest rschr. Gesellschaft für Mathematik und Datenverbeitung, Germany, 1979; Hitachi-Endowed prof. Osaka (Japan) U., 1993-94. Editor IEEE Trans. on Software Engring., 1986-92; assoc. editor Jour. of Cirs., Sysems and Computers, 1990—; contbr. articles to sci. and engring. jours. Recipient C.A. Petri Disting. Tech. Achievement award Soc. Design and Process Scis., 2000; Sr. univ. scholar award U. Ill., 1990; NSF grantee, 1978—, U.S.-Spain coop. rsch. grantee, 1985-87. Fellow IEEE (life; golden core charter mem. IEEE Computer Soc., Donald G. Fink Prize award 1991), Inst. Electronics, Info. and Comm. Engrs., European Assn. Theoretical Computer Sci., Upsilon Pi Epsilon. Avocations: golf, travel. Office: U Ill Dept Computer Sci m/c 152 851 S Morgan St Chicago IL 60607-7042

MURAVCHICK, STANLEY, anesthesiologist, educator; b. Miami Beach, Fla., Oct. 23, 1945; s. Harry Muravchick and Rebecca Gold; m. Arlene Olson, Dec. 24, 1979; 1 child, Rose Evelyn. BA with honors, Johns Hopkins U., Balt., 1967; MD, NY U., NYC, PhD, 1973. Diplomate Am. Bd. Anesthesiology, 1974. Fellow, med. scientist tng. program US Pub. Health Svc., 1967—73; prof. anesthesiology, critical care U. Pa., Sch. Medicine, Phila., 1991—, interim chair, dept. anesthesiology, 2002—03. Sr. assoc. examiner Am. Bd. Anesthesiology. Author: (med. textbooks) The Anesthetic Plan, Geroanesthesia. Dir. Coun. Relationships, Phila. Office: Hosp Univ Pa 3400 Spruce St Philadelphia PA 19104-4283

MURAYAMA, MAKIO, biochemist; b. San Francisco, Aug. 10, 1912; s. Hakuyo and Namiye (Miyasaka) M.; children: Gibbs Soga, Alice Myra. BA, U. Calif., Berkeley, 1938, MA, 1940; PhD (NIH fellow), U. Mich., 1953; ScD honoris causa, Open Internat. U., Sri Lanka, 1994. Rsch. biochemist Children's Hosp. Mich., Detroit, 1943, 1945—48, Bellevue Hosp., NYC, 1943—45, Harper Hosp., Detroit, 1949—54; rsch. fellow chemistry Calif. Inst. Tech., Pasadena, 1954—56; rsch. assoc. biochemistry Grad. Sch. Medicine U. Pa., Phila., 1956—58; spl. rsch. fellow Cavendish Lab. Nat. Cancer Inst., Cambridge, England, 1958; sr. rsch. biochemist NIH, Bethesda, Md., 1958—93. Author: (with Robert M. Nalbandian) Sickle Cell Hemoglobin, 1973; discovered DIPA (decompression-inducible platelet aggregation), 1975; discovered DIPA causes vascular occlusion in both acute mountain sickness and diver's syndrome, 1984. Fellow Am. Inst. Chemists; mem. AAAS, Am. Chem. Soc., Am. Soc. Biol. Chemists, Assn. Clin. Scientists, Undersea and Hyperbaric Med. Soc., Aerospace Med. Assn., Internat. Platform Assn., West African Soc. Pharmacology (hon.), N.Y. Acad. Sci., Sigma Xi. Achievements include patent for automatic amperometric titration apparatus, 1958; development of molecular mechanism of human red cell sickling and prevention of sickle cell crisis by oral prophylactic carbamide, 1972; discovery of decompression inducible platelet aggregation by means of simulation of decompression-inducible platelet aggregation of diving in frogs and mice that diver's disease and acute mountain sickness could be alleviated by piracetam and thymol, antiplatelet agents, 1986. Home: 5010 Benton Ave Bethesda MD 20814-2804 Personal E-mail: mmurayama@aol.com.

MURAYAMA, YUJI, geographer, science professor; BSc in Geography, 1977, MA in Area Studies, 1979, DSc in Geography, 1987. Rsch. assoc. divsn. human geography U. Tsukuba Inst. Geoscience, 1983—85, asst. prof., 1988—99, assoc. prof., 1999—2001, prof., 2001—04; prof. grad. sch. life and environ. scis. U. Tsukuba, 2004—; adj. prof. U. Tokyo, 2005—; lectr. dept. geography Mie U., 1985—87, assoc. prof., 1987—88. Sec. Internat. Geog. Union Commn. on Monitoring Cities of Tomorrow, 2000—; organizer Geog. Info. Systems Forum for Edn., Japan, 2002—; v.p. Geog. Info. Systems Rsch. Inst., Ibaraki, 2003—. Mem. editl. bd.: Jour. Transport Geography, 2001—, GeoJournal, 2001—, Urban Geography, 2002—, Geog. Rev. Japan, 2002—08, Theory and Applications of Geog. Info. Systems, 2008—, Jour. Geography, 2005—. Decorated Order of Sci. and Tech. Merit Am. Biog. Inst.; recipient Abe Fellow award, Social Sci. Rsch. Coun., 1991, Best Book award, Japan Sect. Regional Sci. Assn., 2002, Outstanding Scientists award, IBC, Eng., 2008—09; named Intaernat. Scientist of Yr., 2007. Mem.: Sci. Coun. Japan, Assn. Japanese Geographers (mem. bd. drs. 2004—, Assn. prize 2003), Geog. Info. Systems Assn. (v.p. 2004—). Office: Grad Sch Life and Environ Scis U Tsukuba 1-1-1 Tennodai Tsukuba 305-8572 Japan Office Phone: 81298 534211. Business E-Mail: mura1@sakura.cc.tsukuba.ac.jp.

MURBURG, THELMA D., retired elementary school educator; b. Illon, NY, Jan. 24, 1924; d. Horace L. and Margaret (Kruger) White; children: Michele, Michael, John(dec.). BEd, SUNY, Oneonta, 1945; MA, William Paterson Coll., NJ, 1974, MA, 1976. Cert. tchr., adminstr. NJ. Tchr. Seaford (NY) Sch., 1945—47, Franklin Sch., Englewood, NJ, 1947—52, Bryan Sch., Cresskill, NJ, 1962, Roberge Sch., Rivervale, NJ, 1962—95, Woodside Sch., Rivervale, 1962—95; ret., 1995. Author curriculum materials in social studies and lang. arts. Negotiator Rivervale Tchrs. Union, 1990—95; vol. Hospice Pascack Valley Hospice Hosp., Emerson, 1998—, chaplain asst., 2003—06; facilitator Hernando-Pasco Hospice, Bereavement Groups, Emerson, 2005—06; vol. Hernando-Pasco Hospice, 2009—; founder choral group, 2005; asst. pastor nursing home svcs. Named Vol. of Yr., P.U. Hospice, 2005. Avocations: music, painting, writing poetry, gardening, reading. Home (Summer): 300 Piermont Rd Norwood NJ 07648 Home (Winter): 4414 Northampton Dr New Port Richey FL 34653 Home Phone: 201-768-1419.

MURCHISON, DAVID CLAUDIUS, lawyer; b. NYC, Aug. 19, 1923; s. Claudius Temple and Constance (Waterman) M.; m. June Margaret Guilfoyle, Dec. 19, 1946 (dec. June 2001); children: David Roderick, Brian, Courtney, Bradley, Stacy. AA, George Washington U., 1947, BA, 1949, JD with honors, 1949. Bar: DC 1949, Supreme Ct. 1955. Assoc. Dorr, Hand & Dawson, NYC, 1949-50; founding ptnr. Howrey & Simon, Washington, 1956-90, counsel, 1990—. Legal asst. under sec. army, 1949-51; counsel motor vehicle, textile, aircraft, ordinance and shipbldg. divsns. Nat. Prodn. Authority, 1951-52; assoc. gen. counsel Small Def. Plants Adminstrn., 1952-53; legal adv. and asst. to chmn. FTC, 1953-55 Chmn. So. Africa Wildlife Trust. With AUS, 1943-45, ETO. Mem. ABA (chmn. com. internat. restrictive bus. practices sect. antitrust law 1954-55, sect. adminstrv. law, sect. litigation), FBA, DC Bar Assn., Order of Coif, Met. Club, Chevy Chase Club, Talbot Country Club. Republican.

MURCHISON, GAYLE MINETTA, music educator; b. Fayetteville, NC, Sept. 29, 1962; d. Theodore Washington and Beulah Amanda (McQueen) M. BA, Yale U., 1984, MPhil, 1989, postgrad., U. Hartford. Asst. prof. U. Ark., Fayetteville, 1992—. Composer: JB's Traité sur la Midi, 1992. Mem. AAUP, Soc. for Ethnomusicology, Am. Musicological Soc., Sonneck Soc. for Am. Music. Office: U Arkansas MB 201 Fayetteville AR 72701

MURCKO, MARY, publishing executive; Advt. sales positions Self mag., Condé Nast Publs.; gen. mgr., group pub. Hachette Filipacchi Post Co., Bangkok, 1994—2001; assoc. pub. W mag., Fairchild Publs. Inc., 2001—03, pub. Elegant Bride, 2003—04, pub. W Jewelry, 2004; founding pub. Best Life mag., Rodale Mags. Inc., 2004—06, v.p., pub. Women's Health, 2006—09, sr. v.p., pub. Prevention, 2009—. Named Sales Team Leader of Yr., MinOnline mag., 2008; named a Woman to Watch, Advt. Age, 2009. Office: Rodale Inc 33 E Minor St Emmaus PA 18098 also: Rodale Inc 733 Third Ave 15th Fl New York NY 10017 Business E-Mail: mary.murcko@rodale.com.*

MURDEN, ROBERT A., medical administrator, physician; b. Radford, Va., May 5, 1951; s. William P. and Mabel S. Murden; m. Linda L. Murden; children: Rob, Nick, Chelsea. BS, U. Mich., 1972; MD, U. Mo., Columbia, 1977. Diplomate Am. Bd. Internal Medicine; cert. added qualifications in geriatrics. Resident in internal medicine U. Tex., Galveston, 1977-80; fellow in geriatrics Mt. Sinai Sch. Medicine, NYC, 1983-85; faculty medicine and geriatrics SUNY, Stony Brook, 1985-86, Bklyn., 1986-89, U. Kans. Med. Ctr., Kansas City, 1990-91; faculty medicine Ohio State U., Columbus, 1991—, divsn. dir. gen. medicine, 1994—2006, fellowship dir. geriatrics, 2006—. Co-dir. Alzheimer's Disease Assistance Ctr., SUNY, Bklyn., 1988-89. Contbr. articles to profl. jours. Fellow ACP; mem. Soc. Gen. Internal Medicine, Am. Geriatrics Soc. Office: Ohio State Univ 2050 Kenny Rd Ste 2400 Columbus OH 43221 Office Phone: 614-293-4953. Business E-Mail: robert.murden@osumc.edu.

MURDOCH, AMELIA CLARA, educational association administrator; d. Thomas Jerome and Viola Scanlan Murdoch. AB with honors, U. Pa., 1945, PhD, 1952. Instr. Juniata Coll., Huntingdon, Pa., 1950—51; linguist Nat. Security Agy., Ft. George Meade, Md., 1951—82, 1985—94; pres. and founder Nat. Mus. Lang., College Park, Md., 1998—. Mem. Tree and Landscape Bd., College Park, 1991—; chair Com. for a Better Environment, College Park, 1983—97, Vets. Meml. Improvement Com., College Park, 1991—2003. Am. Coun. Learned Socs. and Jusserand study and travel fellow, U. Pa., 1948—49. Mem.: MLA, Medieval Acad. Am., Internat. Arthurian Soc., Phi Beta Kappa (Mary Isabel Sibley fellow 1947—48). Avocations: reading, gardening. Office: Nat Museum of Language 7100 Baltimore Ave Ste 202 College Park MD 20740 Home Phone: 301-864-4999; Office Phone: 301-864-7071. Business E-Mail: acmurdoch@languagemuseum.org.

MURDOCH, DAVID ARMOR, lawyer; b. Pitts., May 30, 1942; s. Armor M. and N. Edna (Jones) M.; m. Joan Wilkie, Mar. 9, 1974; children: Christina, Timothy, Deborah. AB magna cum laude, Harvard U., 1964, LLB, 1967. Bar: Pa. 1967, U.S. Dist. Ct. (we. dist.) Pa. 1967, U.S. Ct. Mil. Appeals 1968, U.S. Supreme Ct. 1990, U.S. Ct. Appeals (3d cir.) 1991. Assoc. K & L Gates LLP, Pitts., 1971—78, ptnr., 1978—. Co-author: Business Workouts Manual. V.p., bd. dirs. Avonworth Sch. Dist., 1977-83; bd. dirs. Pitts. Expt., 1988-93, chmn., 1989-90; mem. Pa. Housing Fin. Agy., 1981-88, vice-chmn., 1983-87; alt. del. Rep. Nat. Conv., 1980; elder Presbyn. Ch. Sewickley, 1986-92, 2006-; past pres. Harvard Law Sch. Assn. W. Pa.; bd. adv. Geneva Coll., 1993-94, trustee, 1994-97; trustee Sewickley Pub. Libr., 1994-2002, vice-chmn., 1997-2002; trustee World Learning, Inc., 1995-04, vice chmn., 1998-2000, chmn., 2000-04, chmn. emeritus, 2004—; bd. dirs. Allegheny County Libr. Assn., 1994-96; chair Czech Working Group, Presbyn. Ch. USA, 1995-2000; bd. vis. U. Ctr. Internat. Studies, U. Pitts., 1996—; bd. advisors Ctr. for Bus., Religion, and Pub. Life, Pitts. Theol. Sem., 1997—; adv. bd. Ctr. for Internat. Legal Edn., U. Pitts. Sch. Law, 1997—; mem. Global Focus Adv. Bd., Chatham Coll., 2005—, Holocaust Ctr. Commn., Pitts., 2007—, Adv. Bd., Expt. e.v.; bd. dirs., exec. com., vice-chmn. World Affairs Coun. Pitts., 1997-2007, chmn., 2008-; bd. dirs. Am. Coun. Germany, 1998-2007; hon. consul Fed. Rep. Germany in Pitts., 2002—. Capt. US Army, 1968—71. Recipient Disting. Svc. award Allegheny County Libr. Assn., 2001. Fellow Am. Coll. Bankruptcy, Am. Bar Found.; mem. ABA (bus. bankruptcy com., chmn. subcom. on bankruptcy coms., trust indentures and claims trading 1991-97), Am. Law Inst., Internat. Insolvency Inst. Office: K & L Gates LLP Henry W Oliver Bldg 535 Smithfield St Pittsburgh PA 15222-2312 Office Phone: 412-355-6472. Business E-Mail: david.murdoch@klgates.com.

MURDOCH, JOHN, museum director; Asst. dir. collections Victoria and Albert Mus., London; dir. Gallery Courtauld, U. London, 1993—2002, Huntington Art Collections, San Marino, Calif., 2002—. Office: Huntington Art Collections 1151 Oxford Rd San Marino CA 91108

MURDOCH, ROBERT WHITTEN, lawyer; b. Pitts., Mar. 21, 1937; s. Thomas and Julia (Whitten) Murdoch; m. Eleanore L. Uram, Sept. 26, 1967; 1 child, Robert John. BA, U. Pitts., 1960; pvt. law study, 1963-67. Bar: Pa. 1967, US Dist. Ct. (we. dist.) Pa. 1968, US Ct. Appeals (3d cir.) 1978, US Supreme Ct. 1978, US Ct. Appeals (8th cir.) 1983, US Ct. Appeals (11th cir.) 1986. Ptnr. Jones, Gregg, Creehan & Gerace, Pitts., 1967-85, Grogan, Graffam, McGinley & Lucchino, P.C., Pitts., 1985-98, Zimmer Kunz P.C., 1998—2004, Rawle & Henderson LLP, 2004—. Chmn. Scottish Nat. Rm., U. Pitts. Author: Pfeifer: The Supreme Court on the Longshoremen's and Harbor Workers compensation Act and Inflation, 1983, 1984; CD, Ae Fond Kis from the Tartan Tenor. Nat. chmn. Tartan Day; bd. dirs. Scotland-Pa. Bus. Links; bd. trustees Caledonian Found. USA, Inc.; adv. bd. Scottish Coalition USA. With US Army, 1960—61, 2nd lt. intelligence USAR, 1961—68. Recipient Nat. Tartan Day award, 2007, Disting. Svc. medal, Clan Donald, 2004; Personal Coat Arms grant, Ct. Lord Lyon, Scotland, 2009. Fellow: Soc. Antiquities Scotland; mem.: SAR, ABA, Am. Soc. Law and Medicine, Am. Coll. Legal Medicine, Acad. Trial Lawyers Allegheny County, Maritime Law Assn. US, Allegheny County Bar Assn., Pa. Bar Assn., Pitt Varsity Letter Club, An Ceud Fear, Clan Donald, Descs. Colonial Clergy, Sons Union Vets. Civil War, Nat. Soc. Sons Colonial New Eng., Hon. Order Blue Goose Internat., Pitt. Golden Panthers, Scottish Coalition, Plymouth Herditary Soc., St. Andrews Soc. Pitts., Continental Soc. Sons Indian Wars, Caledonian Found., Phi Alpha Delta. Republican. Presbyterian. Avocations: genealogy, golf, tenor soloist. Office: Rawle & Henderson LLP Ste 1000 535 Smithfield St Pittsburgh PA 15222 Home Phone: 412-885-1703; Office Phone: 412-261-5709. Personal E-mail: tartantenor66@yahoo.com. Business E-Mail: rmurdoch@rawle.com.

MURDOCH, RUPERT (KEITH RUPERT MURDOCH), multi media company executive; b. Melbourne, Australia, Mar. 11, 1931; arrived in US, 1974, naturalized, 1985; s. Sir Keith and Dame Elisabeth Joy (Greene) Murdoch; m. Patricia Booker, 1956 (div. 1960); 1 child, Prudence; m. Anna Maria Torv, Apr. 28, 1967 (div. June 8, 1999); children: Elisabeth, Lachlan, James; m. Wendi Deng, June 25, 1999; children: Grace Helen, Chloe. BA, BS, Oxford U.; MA, Worcester Coll., Oxford, Eng., 1953. Pub. NY Post, 1976—86, 2005; CEO News Corp., 1979—, chmn., 1991—, Brit. Sky Broadcasting Group PLC (BSkyB), 1999—2007, DirecTV Group, 2003—07. Chmn. STAR Group Ltd., 1993—98; bd. dirs. Philip Morris Cos. Inc., 1989—2002, China Netcom Group Corp. Ltd., 2001—05, Brit. Sky Broadcasting Group PLC (BSkyB), 1990—2007; owner, pub. numerous newspapers, mags., TV ops. in USA, Australia, UK, Asia. Named Companion of the Order of Australia, 1984, Knight Order of St. Gregory the Great, 1998; named one of The World's 100 Most Influential People, TIME mag., 2005, 2008, Forbes Richest Americans, 1999—, The 50 Who Matter Now, CNNMoney.com Bus. 2.0, 2006, 2007, The 25 Most Powerful People in Bus., Fortune mag., 2007, The Most Influential People in the World of Sports, Bus. Week, 2007, 2008, The Global Elite, Newsweek mag., 2008, The Top 25 Market Movers, US News & World Report, 2009. Avocation: sailing. Office: News Corp 8th Fl 1211 Ave of Americas New York NY 10036*

MURDOCK, CHARLES WILLIAM, lawyer, educator; b. Chgo., Feb. 10, 1935; s. Charles C. and Lucille Marie (Tracy) Murdock; m. Mary Margaret Hennessy, May 25, 1963; children: Kathleen, Michael, Kevin, Sean. BSChemE, Ill. Inst. Tech., 1956; JD cum laude, Loyola U., Chgo., 1963. Bar: Ill. 1963, Ind. 1971. Asst. prof. law DePaul U., 1968-69; assoc. prof. law U. Notre Dame, 1969-75; prof., dean Law Sch. Loyola U., Chgo., 1975-83, 86—; dep. atty. gen. State of Ill., Chgo., 1983-86; of counsel Chadwell & Kayser, Ltd., 1986-89. Vis. prof. U. Calif., 1974; cons. Pay Bd., summer 1972, SEC, summer 1973; co-founder Loyola U. Family Bus. Program; arbitrator Chgo. Bd. Options Exch., Nat. Assn. Securities Dealers, N.Y. Stock Exch., Am. Arbitration Assn.; co-founder, mem. exec. com. Loyola Family Bus. Ctr., 1990—; bd. dirs. Plymouth Tube Co., 1993—. Author: Business Organizations, 2 vols., 1996; editor: Illinois Business Corporation Act Annotated, 2 vols., 1975; tech. editor The Business Lawyer, 1989-90. Chmn. St. Joseph County (Ind.) Air Pollution Control Bd., 1971; bd. dirs. Nat. Center for Law and the Handicapped, 1973-75, Minority Venture Capital Inc., 1973-75. Capt. USMCR. Mem. ABA, Ill. Bar Assn. (cert. of award for continuing legal edn.), Chgo. Bar Assn. (cert. of award for continuing legal edn., bd. mgrs. 1976-78), Ill. Inst. Continuing Legal Edn. (adv. com) Roman Catholic. Home: 2126 Thornwood Ave Wilmette IL 60091-1452 Office: Loyola U Sch Law 1 E Pearson St Chicago IL 60611-2055 Office Phone: 312-915-7142. Business E-Mail: cmurdoc@luc.edu.

MURDOCK, DAVID H., food products executive; b. Kansas City, Mo., Apr. 10, 1923; m. Gabriele Bryant Murdock (dec. 1985); children: Gene, David H. Jr., Justin M.; m. Tracy Vakzad. LLD (hon.), Pepperdine U., 1978; LHD (hon.), U. Nebr., 1984, Hawaii Loa Coll., 1989. Sole proprietor, chmn., CEO Murdock Holding Co. (formerly Pacific Holding Co.), LA, 1995—; chmn., CEO Dole Food Co., LA, 1985—2007, chmn., 2007—; owner, chmn. Castle & Cooke, Inc., 1985—. CEO Huntington Tile, Yankie Hill Brick, Murdock Devel. Corp., Wiscassett Mills, Flexi-Van Leasing, Goettel, Stair Co., Ventura Farms. Trustee Asia Soc., NYC, LA; founder, bd. dirs. Found. for Advanced Brain Studies, LA; bd. visitors UCLA Grad. Sch. Mgmt.;bd. govs. Performing Arts Coun. of Music Ctr., LA; bd. govs. East-West Ctr., LA; patron Met. Opera, NYC. With USAAC, 1943-45. Served US Army. Named one of Forbes' Richest Americans, 1999—, Forbes' Exec. Pay, 1999—, World's Richest People, Forbes mag., 2001—, 25 Most Influential Republicans, Newsmax Mag., 2008. Mem. Regency Club (founder, pres.) Bel-Air Bay Country Club, Sherwood Country Club (founder, pres.), Met. Club (N.Y.C.). Office: Murdock Holding Co 10900 Wilshire Blvd Ste 1600 Los Angeles CA 90024-6530*

MURDOCK, DORIS DEAN, special education educator, program developer; b. Pacific Junction, Iowa, Feb. 7, 1913; m. Myron J. Murdock, June 28, 1933; 1 child, John Timothy. BS in Elem. Edn., So. Oreg. U., 1964; MS in Remedial Edn., U. Oreg., 1968. Primary tchr. Days Creek Elem. Sch., Oreg., 1962—66, Grants Pass Dist., 1966—67, Riddle Elem., Riddle, Oreg., 1968—71; founder, dir. Plowshare Sch., Rogue River, Oreg., 1972—78, Child Life Sanctuary, Rogue River, 1978—88; founder, dir., special education program developer Ctr. for Habilitation Living, Grants Pass, 1989—. Author: No Thank You! No Ritalin for Me Today!, 2003. Vol. Peace Corp., 1978—80. Mem.: Coun. for Exceptional Children (life). Republican. Seventh Day Adventist. Office: Ctr for Habilitative Living Inc 4493 Jerome Prairie Grants Pass OR 97527

MURDOCK, GLENN, state supreme court justice; b. Enterprise, Ala., June 25, 1956; s. Billy A. and Marita H. Murdock; m. Margaret Gilchrist; children: Emily, Bailey, John Taylor. BA summa cum laude, U. Ala., 1978; JD, U. Va. Law Sch., 1981. Law clk. United Dist. Judge (No. Ala. dist.) Clarence W. Allgood; atty. Wallace, Jordan, Ratliff & Brandt, Birmingham/Montgomery, Ala., 1992—; judge Ala. Ct. Civil Appeals, 2001—07; assoc. justice Ala. Supreme Ct., 2007—. Mem.: Ala. Bar Assn., Birmingham Bar. Assn., Birmingham Rotary Club, Phi Beta Kappa. Office: Ala Supreme Ct 300 Dexter Ave Montgomery AL 36104*

MURDOCK, JOHN CAREY, economics professor, investor; b. Blackwell, Okla., Dec. 10, 1922; s. Frank Elbert and Nannine (Watt) M.; m. Jean Boardman, Oct. 15, 1949 (dec.); children: John B., Robert C.; m. Betty Lassiter, Nov. 14, 2000. BS, U. Okla., 1947; MS, U. Wis., 1951, PhD, 1955. Faculty U. Mo., Columbia, 1951—, prof. econs., 1958—, chmn. dept., 1962-64; dean U. Mo. (Grad. Sch.), dir. research adminstrn., 1967-71. Project dir. NASA study location of research, 1964-67; cons. to industry, 1962—; vis. prof. Massey U., New Zealand, 1972-73. Author: (with J. Graves) Regions and Research, 1966; contbr. articles to profl. jours. Chmn. Mid-Am. State Univs. Assn. Grad. Schs., 1970-71; active Wyo. Coun. for the Humanities, 1981-84, vice chmn., 1984; bd. dirs. Wyo. Centennial Cmty. Found., 1990—. Gulf Refining Co. fellow, 1957; U. Mo. fellow, 1958; Community Studies fellow, 1960-61 Mem. Am. Econs. Assn., Econ. History Assn., Royal Econs. Soc. Home: 1028 Fearrington Post Pittsboro NC 27312 Office Phone: 919-542-3680. Business E-Mail: jmurdock@nc.rr.com.

MURDOCK, JOHN GUSTAF, physics professor; s. John Wilson and Sandra Sandstrom Murdock; m. Kimberly Ann Donoghue, Nov. 7, 1998; children: Faith Helen, John Patrick. BS in Mech. Engring., Johns Hopkins U., Balt., Md., 1992; MA, Stanford U., Calif., 1993; EdD, George Washington U., 2006. Physics tchr. Howard County Pub. Schs., Columbia, Md., 2000—06; asst. clin. prof. U. Md., Balt. County, 2006—. Contbr. articles to profl. jour. Mem.: NSTA, Am. Ednl. Rsch. Assn., Nat. Assn. Rsch. Sci. Tchg. Democrat. Avocations: running, skiing, hiking/climbing, sudoku/crosswords.

MURDOCK, LARRY PAUL, religious studies educator, director; b. Lawrenceburg, Tenn., Mar. 10, 1946; s. Walker Woodson and Ada Belle Murdock; m. Iva Nell Lee, June 11, 1967; children: Holly Denise Kinslow, Jamison Paul. MA in Religion, Harding U., Memphis, 1981. Ctr. dir. Faulkner U., Montgomery, Ala., 1990—95; dir., instl. rsch. Heritage Christian U., Florence, Ala., 1996—. Ministry Ctrl. Heights Ch. Christ, Florence, 1986—. Contbr. articles. Preacher Chs. Christ, Florance, 1968—2008. Recipient B.C. Goodpasture Bible award, David Lipscomb U., 1968. Avocations: travel, reading, writing, keyboards. Business E-Mail: lmurdock@hcu.edu.

MURDOCK, REBECCA THERESE, management consultant, director; m. Douglas William Murdock, Sept. 19, 1987; children: Thomas William, Steven Allen. BA, Wayne State Coll., NE, 1981; MBA, U. Sioux Falls, SD, 2001. Dir. U. Sioux Falls, 2005—. Fin. com. mem. Sioux Falls Cath. Sch., 2003—08. Recipient Faculty tchng award. Mem.: ASTD, Acad. Mgmt., Orgn. Devel. Network, Soc. Human Resource Mgmt. Office: Univ Sioux Falls 1101 W 22nd St Sioux Falls SD 57105

MURDOCK, ROBERT MEAD, curator; b. NYC, Dec. 18, 1941; s. Robert Davidson and Elizabeth Brundage (Mead) M.; m. Ellen Rebecca Olson, Apr. 22, 1967 (div.); children: Alison Mead, Anne Davidson; m. Deborah C. Ryan, Apr. 28, 1995. BA, Trinity Coll., Conn., 1963; MA, Yale U., 1965; student, Mus. Mgmt. Inst., U. Calif., Berkeley, 1980. Ford Found. intern Walker Art Center, Mpls., 1965-67; curator Albright-Knox Art Gallery, Buffalo, 1967-70; curator contemporary art Dallas Mus. Fine Arts, 1970-78; dir. Grand Rapids (Mich.) Art Mus., 1978-83; chief curator Walker Art Ctr., Mpls., 1983-85; program dir. IBM Gallery of Sci. and Art, NYC, 1985-87, 90-93; dir. exhbns. Am. Fedn. Arts, NYC, 1987-88. Panelist, cons. Nat. Endowment for Arts, 1974-90. Author: (with others) Tyler Graphics: The Extended Image, 1987, A Gallery of Modern Art, 1994, Paris Modern, The Swedish Ballet 1920-1925, 1995, Works by Leland Bell, 1950's-1991, 2001, Constellation, Pavel Zoubok Gallery, NYC, 2006; contbr. articles on David Novros, William Conlon, 1985, Bill Freeland, 1989, Nassos Daphnis, 1990, Cai Guo-Qiang, 1998, John Evans, 2004; exhbn. catalogues Early 20th Century Art from Midwestern Museums, 1981, Berlin/Hanover: The 1920's, 1977, Richard Tuttle: Books and Prints, 1996, Lesley Dill, 1998, Jim Torok, 1999, Debra Bermingham, 2002. Nat. Endowment for Arts fellow, 1973 Home and Office: 8 W 13th St 10F New York NY 10011

MURDOCK, STEVEN H., former federal agency administrator; b. 1948; BA, ND State U., 1970; MA, U. Ky., 1972, PhD, 1975. Asst. prof. dept. sociology ND State U., 1975—77; asst. prof. dept. rural sociology and sociology Tex. A&M U., Coll. Sta., 1977—80, assoc. prof., 1980—84, prof., 1984—2004, regents prof., 1997—2004, asst. dir. Ctr. Energy and Mineral Resources, 1979—83, head dept. rural sociology and sociology, 1980—2004, assoc. dir. Ctr. Energy and Mineral Resources, 1983—86, dir. Ctr. Demographic & Socioeconomic Rsch. & Edn., 1994—2004, dir. Strategic Policies Rsch. Group, 1997—2000; dir. Census Bur. US Dept. Commerce, Washington, 2007—09. Recipient Disting. Achievement award for Rsch., Assn. Former Students, 1994, Excellence in Rsch. award, Rural Sociological Soc. Office Phone: 301-763-2135.*

MURDOCK, WENDY JEAN, finance company executive; b. Montreal, Que., Can., Aug. 28, 1952; came to U.S., 1983; d. James David and Bernice Evelyn (Dean) M. BA, McGill U., 1973; MBA, U. Western Ont., 1982. Assoc. McKinsey & Co. Inc., NYC, 1982-87, ptnr., fin. inst. practice, 1988—93; dir. strategic planning Salomon Smith Barney, NYC, 1993—98; COO, high net worth group Citicorp Asset Mgmt., NYC, 1998—2002; cons., merchant banking practice Putnam Lowell NBF, 2004—05; chief product officer MasterCard Worldwide, Purchase, NY, 2005—. Bd. dirs. Syniverse Technologies, 2009—. Office: MasterCard Worldwide 2000 Purchase St Purchase NY 10577*

MUREN, DENNIS E., special effects expert; b. Glendale, Calif., Nov. 1, 1946; s. Elmer Ernest and Charline Louise (Clayton) M.; m. Zara Pinfold, Aug. 29, 1981; children: Gregory, Gwendolen. AA, Pasadena City Coll., Calif., 1966; student, Calif. State U., LA. Freelance spl. effects expert, 1968-75; camera operator Cascade of Calif., Hollywood, 1975-76; visual effects dir. photography Indsl. Light & Magic, San Rafael, Calif., 1976-80, visual effects dir., 1980—. Guest speaker Berlin Film Festival, UCLA, Film Dept., U. Calif. Berkeley Film Series, Liverpool (Eng.) U. Film Program, Mill Valley Film Festival Program, Siggraph '86, Siggraph '87, Am. Film Inst., Portland Creative Conf. '89. Cameraman, photographer various films including Star Wars, 1977, Close Encounters of the Third Kind, 1977, Battlestar Galactica, 1978, The Empire Strikes Back, 1980 (Oscar award); visual effects supr. films include Dragonslayer, 1981 (Oscar nomination), ET: The Extraterrestrial, 1982 (Oscar award), Return of the Jedi, 1983 (Oscar award, Brit. Acad. of Film and TV award), Indiana Jones and the Temple of Doom, 1984 (Oscar award, Brit. Acad. of Film and TV award), Young Sherlock Holmes, 1985 (Oscar nomination), Captain Eo, 1986, Star Tours, 1986, Innerspace, 1987 (Oscar award), Empire of the Sun, 1987, Willow, 1988 (Oscar nomination), Ghostbusters II, 1989, The Abyss, 1989 (Oscar award), Terminator 2, 1991 (Oscar award, Brit. Film and TV award), Jurassic Park, 1993 (Oscar award, Brit. Film and TV award), Casper, 1995; visual effects supr. (TV program) Caravan of Courage (Emmy award); creative advisor Twister, 1995, Mission Impossible, 1995, Jurassic Park: The Lost World, 1997 (Academy award nomination), Star Wars: The Phantom Menace, 1999, (Acad. award nomination, Saturn award for best visual effects, Best Action Sequence award MTV), A.I., 2001 (acad. award nomination), Star Wars: The Attack of the Clones, 2002, The Hulk, 2003, The Day After Toorrow, 2004, War of the Worlds 2005 (Acad. award nomination, Hollywood Film Festival award for Best Visual Effects, Visual Cons. Wall E, 2008); prodr., dir. The Equinox, 1967. Recipient Acad. Sci./Tech. Award for the devel. of a Motion Picture Figure Mover for animation photography, 1981, Edit/VES Honors award, 2003; star on Hollywood Walk of Fame, 1999, Nikola Tesla award, 2007. Mem.: Visual Effects Soc. (Lifetime Achievement award 2007), Acad. Motion Picture Arts and Scis., Am. Soc. Cinematographers. Office: Indsl Light & Magic Box 29909 San Francisco CA 94129-0909

MURFF, ELIZABETH JANE TIPTON, mathematician, statistician, educator; b. Wilmington, Del., Nov. 20, 1963; d. Lawrence Wilfred and Yvonne (Ward) Tipton; m. Darrel L. Murff III, Dec. 14, 1985; children: James, Catherine. BS in Math., BS in Physics, U. Tex. Dallas, Richardson, 1987; postgrad., U. Tex., Austin, 1987-88, 93. Tchg. asst. U. Tex.,

Austin, 1987-88, 93-97; evaluator Tex. Future Problems Solvers, Austin, 1989-93; instr. Collegiate Test Prep, Austin, 1990-93; adj. instr. Austin C.C., 1992-97, asst. prof. math. and stats. Cedar Park, 1997—. Math. tutor, Georgetown, Tex., 1991—; stats. cons., Austin, 1993—. Mem. Am. Stats. Assn., Internat. Stats. Assn. Lutheran. Avocation: Tae Kwon Do.

MURGIA, CHARLES E., retired classicist; b. Boston, Mass., Feb. 18, 1935; s. John and Antonietta Murgia. PhD, Harvard U., Cambridge, MA, 1956; AB with Honors, Boston Coll., Chestnut Hill, Mass., 1966; MA, Harvard U., Cambridge, Mass., 1960. Vis. instr. Franklin and Marshall Coll., Lancaster, Pa., 1960—61; vis. prof. Harvard U., Cambridge, Mass., 1996; instr. Dartmouth Coll., Hanover, NH, 1964—65; asst. prof. U. Calif., Berkeley, 1966—72, assoc. prof., 1972—78, prof., 1978—94, chair dept. classics, 1980—83, prof. emeritus, 1994—, prof. grad. sch., 1995—2000. Exec. mem. Ctr. Hermeneutic Studies, Berkeley, 1978—83; mem. editl. bd. Classical Philology, Chgo., 1984—. Contbr. chapters to books, articles to jours. Fellow fellowship, Nat. Endowmnet for the Humanities, 1979; Travel grant, ACLS, 1967, fellowship, 1974—75, Humanities Rsch. fellowship, U. Calif., 1970, President's Summer fellowship, 1971, Humanities Rsch. Summer Travel grant, 1973, fellowship, Guggenheim, 1983—84. Mem.: Am. Philol. Assn., Humanities Club (chair 2008). Home: 240 Modoc Ave Oakland CA 94618-2535 Office: Univ Calif Dept Classics #2520 Berkeley CA 94720-2520 Business E-Mail: cem@berkeley.edu.

MURGUIA, JANET, non-profit organization administrator; b. 1960; BS in Journalism, Kans. U., 1982, BA in Spanish, 1982, JD, 1985. Legis. coun. to Rep. Jim Slattery US Congress, Washington, 1987—94; various positions including dep. asst. to Pres. Clinton, dep. dir. legis. affairs, sr. liaison to Congress The White House, Washington, 1994—2000; exec. vice. chancellor univ. rels. U. Kans., 2001—04; exec. dir., COO Nat. Coun. La Raza, Washington, 2004, pres., CEO, 2005—. Bd. trustees YouthFriends; bd. mem. Ind. Sector, Hispanic Assn. on Corp. Responsibility, Nat. Hispanic Leadership Agenda; mem. Merrill Lynch Diversity & Inclusion Coun. Recipient Kans. U. Law Alumni Assn. Disting. Alumnus award, 2005; named one of The 80 Elite Hispanic Women, Hispanic Bus. mag., 2003, The 100 Most Influential Hispanics, 2004, The 100 Most Powerful Women in Washington, The Washingtonian mag., 2006, The 100 Top Latinos, Hispanic mag., 2007. Office: Nat Coun La Raza 1111 19th St NW Ste 1000 Washington DC 20036 Office Phone: 202-785-1670.

MURIEL, AMADOR CRUZ, physicist; b. Marikina, Philippines, Nov. 24, 1939; came to the U.S., 1963; s. Amado and Lucena (Cruz) M.; children: Anna Christina, Rosemarie. MA, SUNY, Stony Brook, 1965, PhD, 1968. Assoc. prof. Hostos Community Coll., Bronx, N.Y., 1972-79, acting dean, 1979-80; v.p. Burlington County (N.J.) Coll., 1980-81; project mgr. Citibank, NYC, 1981-82; assoc. prof. CUNY-Baruch Coll., NYC, 1982-85; pres. Data Transport Systems, NYC, 1985—. Cons. UN, N.Y.C., Geneva, Austria, 1985—. Editor: Stellar Dynamics I, II, 1980, Stellar Evolution, 1980; contbr. articles to Phys. Rev., Physica, Physics Letters. Rockefeller Found. scholar, 1965-68, All Nations Women's Group scholar, 1957, Fulbright scholar, 1963. Mem. Am. Phys. Soc., AAAS. Achievements include discovery of occurrence of traveling depressions in density evolution of one-dimensional gravitational system; development of Prigogine results without diagrams in non-equilibrium statistical mechanics; research in molecular theory of turbulence; co founder of new field of physic-quantum turbulence. Home: 347 E 62nd St New York NY 10021-7755 Office: Data Transport Systems 347 E 62nd St New York NY 10021-7755 Office Phone: 347-782-1215. Personal E-mail: amador_muriel@msn.com.

MURIN, JOSEPH J., former mortgage company executive; b. 1949; m. Angela Murin; 2 children. BA in Bus., Nat. Louis U., Chgo., 1990. Loan officer Pitts. Nat. Bank (now PNC), 1972—78; pres. Murin Brothers, Inc., 1979—82; divsn. mgr. CitiFed Mortgage, 1983—84; sr. v.p. Standard Fed. Savings, 1984—89; regional pres. American Pioneer Fed., 1989—2001; pres., CEO Lender's Svc., Inc., 1996—2000; sr. v.p. Prudential Home Mortgage, 2001—02; pres., COO Basis100, Toronto, Canada, 2001—02, CEO, 2002—04; mng. ptnr. Mortgage Settlement Network, LLC, Pitts., 2004—07; pres. Govt. Nat. Mortgage Assn. (Ginnie Mae), Washington, 2008—09. Bd. dirs. Point Park U., Pitts.*

MURKOWSKI, FRANK HUGHES, former Governor of Alaska; b. Seattle, Mar. 28, 1933; s. Frank Michael and Helen (Hughes) M.; m. Nancy Rena Gore, Aug. 28, 1954; children: Carol Victoria Murkowski Sturgulewski, Lisa Ann Murkowski Martell, Frank Michael, Eileen Marie Murkowski Van Wyhe, Mary Catherine Murkowski Judson, Brian Patrick. Student, Santa Clara U., Calif., 1952—53; BA in Econs., Seattle U., 1955. With Pacific Nat. Bank of Seattle, 1957-58, Nat. Bank of Alaska, Anchorage, 1959-67; asst. v.p., mgr. Nat. Bank of Alaska (Wrangell br.), 1963-66; v.p. charge bus. devel. Nat. Bank of Alaska, Anchorage, 1966-67; commr. dept. econ. devel. State of Alaska, Juneau, 1967-70; pres. Alaska Nat. Bank, Fairbanks, 1971-80; US Senator from Alaska, 1981—2002; ranking mem. Com. on Energy and Natural Resources; mem. Com. on Fin., Vets Affairs Com., Indian Affairs Com., Japan-US Friendship Com.; mem. intelligence com. fgn. affairs; gov. State of Alaska, Juneau, 2002—06. Rep. nominee for U.S. Congress from Alaska, 1970; chmn. Can.-U.S. Interparliamentary Group. Former v.p. B.C. and Alaska Bd. Trade; mem. U.S. Holocaust Mus. Coun. Served with U.S. Coast Guard, 1955-57. Mem. AAA, AMVETS, NRA, Am. Legion, Ducks Unlimited, Res. Officer's Assn., Alaska World Affairs Coun., Coalition Am. Vets., Alaska Native Brotherhood, Am. Bankers Assn., Alaska Bankers Assn. (pres. 1973), Young Pres.'s Orgn., Alaska C. of C. (pres. 1977), Anchorage C. of C. (bd. dirs. 1966), Fairbanks C. of C. (bd. dirs. 1973-78), Pioneers of Alaska, Internat. Alaska Nippon Kai, Capital Hill Club, Washington Athletic Club, Elks, Lions. Republican. Catholic. Mailing: PO Box 70049 Fairbanks AK 99707 Personal E-mail: nrgdc@earthlink.net.

MURKOWSKI, LISA ANN, United States Senator from Alaska; b. Ketchikan, Alaska, May 22, 1957; d. Frank Hughes Murkowski & Nancy (Gore); m. Verne Martell, Aug. 22, 1987; children: Nicholas, Matthew. BA in Economics, Georgetown U., 1980; JD, Willamette Coll., 1985. Dist. coun. atty., Anchorage, 1987-89; comml. atty. Hoge and Lekisch, 1989-96; pvt. law practice, 1989—96; mem. Alaska House of Reps., Anchorage, 1999—2002, majority leader, 2002; US Senator from Alaska, 2002—; mem. US Senate Energy & Nat. Resources Com., US Senate Indian Affairs Com., US Senate Health, Edn., & Labor Com., US Senate Appropriations Com., 2009—; vice chmn. US Senate Republican Conf., 2009—. Dir. First Bank; mem. Mayor's Task Force Homeless, 1990-91; state ctrl. com. Dist. 14 Rep. chair, 1993-98; commr. Anchorage Equal Rights Commn., 1997-2002; citizens adv. bd. Joint Com. Mil. Bases in Alaska, 1998—. Trustee Cath. Svcs.; pres. Govt. Hill Elem. PTA; dir. Alaskan Drug Free Youth; mem. YWCA, Arctic Power. Recipient Comunity Leadership award, FBI Dir., 1993, Outstanding Volunteer award, Alaska Sch. Dist., 1998, 2000, Food Safety award, Nat. Food Processors Assn., 2003. Mem. Alaska Bar Assn., Anchorage Bar Assn., Alaska Fedn. Rep. Women (bd. dirs.), Anchorage Rep. Womens Club, Midnight Sun Rep. Women. Republican. Roman Catholic. Office: US Senate 709 Hart Senate Office Bldg Washington DC 20510 also: 510 L St # 550 Anchorage AK 99501 Office Phone: 202-224-6665.*

MURNION, WILLIAM EDWARD, philosopher, theologian; b. NYC, Jan. 27, 1933; s. William Edward and Frances Annie (Canavan) M.; m. Deborah Warren Cary, June 14, 1969; children: William Cary, Gregory Thomas. BA, St. Joseph's Coll., 1954; STL, Gregorian U., Rome, 1958, PhD, 1969. Ordained priest Roman Cath. Ch., 1957. Parish priest Roman Cath. Archdiocese of N.Y., 1958—68; lectr. St. John's Sem., Little Rock, 1966-67; asst. prof. Duquesne U., Pitts., 1967-68; faculty fellow Boston Coll., Chestnut Hill, Mass., 1968-69; asst. prof. Newton (Mass.) Coll., 1969-72; prof. Ramapo Coll., Mahwah, NJ, 1972-2000; writer, lectr., counselor PhilosophyWorks, Bellvale, NY, 2000—. Dir. NEH summer seminar, 1992, 95. Author: St. Thomas's Theory of Understanding, 1969; contbr. articles to profl. jours., chpts. to books. Mem. Am. Philos. Assn., Am. Cath. Philos. Assn. Avocations: painting, gardening, sports. Home and Office: PO Box 23 Bellvale NY 10912-0023 Office Phone: 845-986-5406. Business E-Mail: philosophyworks@optonline.net.

MURO, STEVE L., federal agency administrator; b. 1949; AA, Mt. San Antonio Jr. Coll. Automotive mechanic LA Nat. Cemetery, maintenance foreman, asst. to dir.; dir. Baton Rouge Cemetery, Port Hudson Nat. Cemetery; asst. to dir. LI Nat. Cemetery; asst. dir. Riverside Nat. Cemetery; dir. Fort Snelling Nat. Cemetery; acting dir. Golden Gate and San Francisco Nat. Cemeteries; dir. Meml. Svc. Network V, 2001—02; dir. Office Field Programs US Dept. Veterans Affairs, 2003—08, acting dep. under sec. for meml. affairs, 2005, dep. under sec. for meml. affairs, 2008—. Served in USN, 1968—72. Office: US Dept Veterans Affairs 810 Vermont Ave NW Washington DC 20420*

MUROFF, LAWRENCE ROSS, nuclear medicine physician, educator; b. Phila., Dec. 26, 1942; s. John M. and Carolyn (Kramer) M.; m. Carol R. Savoy, July 12, 1969; children: Michael Bruce, Julie Anne. AB cum laude, Dartmouth Coll., Hanover, NH, 1964, B of Med. Sci., 1965; MD cum laude, Harvard U., Cambridge, Mass., 1967. Diplomate Am. Bd. Radiology, Am. Bd. Nuclear Medicine. Intern Boston City Hosp., Harvard, 1968; resident in radiology Columbia-Presbyn. Med. Ctr., NYC, 1970-73, chief resident, 1973; instr. dept. radiology, asst. radiologist Columbia U. Med. Ctr., NYC, 1973-74; dir. dept. nuc. medicine, computed tomography and MRI Univ. Cmty. Hosp., Tampa, Fla., 1974-94, H. Lee Moffitt Cancer Hosp., Tampa, 1994—; pres. Edn. Symposia Inc., Tampa, 1975-2001; pres., CEO Imaging Cons. Inc., Tampa, 1994—; chmn. bd. Am. Phys. Ptnrs. Inc. (Radiologix), Dallas, 1996—98. Clin. asst. prof. radiology U. South Fla., 1974-78, clin. assoc. prof., 1978-82, clin. prof., 1982—; clin. prof. U. Fla., 1988—. Contbr. articles to profl. jours. Lt. comdr. USPHS, 1968-70. Fellow Am. Coll. Nuclear Medicine (disting. fellow., Fla. del.), Am. Coll. Nuclear Physicians (regents 1976-78, pres.-elect 1978, pres. 1979), Am. Coll. Radiology (councilor 1979-80, 91-96, 2001-06, 08-, chancellor 1981-87, chmn. commn. on nuclear medicine 1981-87); mem. Am. Assn. Acad. Chief Residents Radiology (chmn. 1973), AMA, Boylston Soc., Fla. Assn. Nuclear Physician (pres. 1976), Fla. Med. Assn., Hillsborough County Med. Assn., Radiol. Soc. N.Am., Soc. Nuclear Medicine (coun. 1975-90, trustee 1980-84, 86-89, pres. Southeastern chpt. 1983, vice chmn. correlative imaging coun. 1983), Fla. Radiol. Soc. (exec. com. 1976-91, treas. 1984, sec. 1985, v.p. 1986, pres. elect 1987, pres. 1988, gold medal 1995), West Coast Radiol. Soc., Soc. Magnetic Resonance Imaging (bd. dirs. 1988-91, chmn. ednl. program 1989, chmn. membership com. 1989-93), Clin. Magnetic Resonance Soc. (pres.-elect 1995-98, pres. 1998-2000, bd. dirs. 1995—). Office: 16804 Avila Blvd Tampa FL 33613-5220 Personal E-mail: lrmuroff@hotmail.com.

MURPHEY, ARTHUR GAGE, JR., law educator; b. Macon, Miss., June 16, 1927; s. Arthur Gage and Elizabeth (Crutcher) Murphey; m. Linda Chaney, May 17, 1975 (dec. June 2007); 1 stepchild, Leslie Jo Pafford;children from previous marriage: Mason Alexander, Arthur Nesbit. Student, Vanderbilt U., 1947—48; AB, U. N.C., 1951; JD, U. Miss., 1953; postgrad., London Sch. Econs., U. London, 1953—54; LLM, Yale U., 1962. Assoc. Satterfield, Ewing, Williams and Shell, Jackson, Miss., 1953; asst. prof. U. Ga., Athens, 1956-58, Emory U., Atlanta, 1958-61, U. Akron (Ohio), 1962-63, assoc. prof., 1963-67; prof. U. Ark., Little Rock, 1967-96, asst. dean Sch. Law, 1970-73, Ark. Bar Found. prof., 1996-97, Ark. Bar Found. prof. emeritus, 1997—. Vis. lectr. Case Western Res. U., Cleve., 1966; vis. prof. U. Miss., 1977. Faculty editor: Jour. Pub. Law, 1958—61; faculty advisor Ga. Bar Jour., 1958—61; contbr. articles to profl. jours. With USAAF, 1945—47. Fulbright scholar, 1953—54, Ford Found. grantee, 1964. Mem.: ABA, Phi Beta Kappa, Beta Theta Pi, Phi Delta Phi. Anglican. Home: 1918 Old Forge Dr Little Rock AR 72227-5515 Office: U Ark Sch Law 1201 McMath Ave Little Rock AR 72202-5142

MURPHEY, MURRAY GRIFFIN, history professor; b. Colorado Springs, Colo., Feb. 22, 1928; s. Bradford James and Margaret Winifred (Griffin) M.; children— Kathleen Rachel, Christopher Bradford, Jessica Lenoir. AB, Harvard U., 1949; PhD, Yale U., 1954. Asst. prof. U. Pa., Phila., 1956-61, assoc. prof., 1961-66, prof., 1966-2000, chmn. dept. Am. civilization, 1969-81, 87-94. Author: Development of Peirce's Philosophy, 1961, Our Knowledge of the Historical Past, 1973, (with E. Flower) A History of Philosophy in America, 1977, Philosophical Foundations of Historical Knowledge, 1994, C.I Lewis: The Last Great Pragmatist, 2005, Truth and History, Albany, 2008. Democrat. Home: 200 Rhyle Ln Bala Cynwyd PA 19004-2324

MURPHEY, SHEILA ANN, infectious diseases physician, educator, researcher; b. Phila., July 10, 1943; d. William Joseph and Sara Esther (Mallon) M. AB, Chestnut Hill Coll., 1965; MD, Women's Med. Coll. of Pa., 1969. Diplomate Am. Bd. Internal Medicine, Am. Bd. Infectious Diseases. Intern in internal medicine Mt. Sinai Hosp. of NY, 1969—70, resident in internal medicine, 1970—72, instr. internal medicine, 1971—72; fellow infectious diseases U. Pa. Sch. Medicine, Phila., 1972—74, instr. dept. medicine, 1974—75, asst. prof. dept. medicine, 1975—77; chief infectious diseases sect. Phila. Gen. Hosp., 1974—77; attending physician Hosp. U. Pa., Phila. Gen. Hosp., 1974—77; dir. divsn. infectious diseases, asst. prof. medicine Jefferson Med. Coll., Phila., 1977—80, clin. assoc. prof. medicine, 1980—2003; dir. divsn. infectious diseases Thomas Jefferson U., Phila., 1977—88; infection control officer, attending physician Thomas Jefferson U. Hosp., Phila., 1977—2003; br. chief infection control devices br., Office Device Evaluation Ctr. for Devices and Radiologic Health, FDA, Rockville, Md., 2005—. Contbr. articles to profl. jours. Fellow Coll. Physicians Phila.; mem. ACP, Am. Soc. Microbiology, Soc. Healthcare Epidemiology of Am., Infectious Diseases Soc. Am., Alpha Omega Alpha. Democrat. Roman Catholic.

MURPHREY, ELIZABETH HOBGOOD, history professor, librarian; b. Rocky Mount, NC, Mar. 22, 1947; d. Isaac Green and Ernestine Ragsdale (Hobgood) Murphrey. BA, U. N.C., Greensboro, 1969; MA, Duke U., 1971, PhD, 1976; postgrad., U. Fla., 1984; MLS, U. N.C., Chapel Hill, 1993. Vis. instr. history Wake Forest U., Winston-Salem, NC, 1976; asst. prof. history N.C. A&T State U., Greensboro, 1977—81; intelligence rsch. specialist U.S. Army, Fayetteville, NC, 1982—89; adj. prof. history Fayetteville State U., 1989—90; adj. instr. history Everest U. South Campus, Orlando, 2000—03, co-dir. libr., 2004—, adj. history, instr. Columbia Coll. Orlando divsn., 2005, rsch. libr., 1998—; lib. Everest U., South Orlando, 1998—, co-dir, 2004—. Vis. asst. prof. of history Elizabeth City State U., NC, 1993—96. Editor (guidebook): Socialist Party of America Papers, microfilm edit., 2 vols., 1973—77. Apptd. Seminole County Disiability Adv. Coun., 2005, vice chair, 2008. Recipient award, NEH, 1994, 1996, 2000. Mem.: LWV (bd. dirs. Seminole County chpt. 2001—, bd. dirs. Guilford County chpt. 1978—82), ALA, Fla. Libr. Assn., Am. Hist. Assn. Home: 424 Windmeadows St Altamonte Springs FL 32701 Office: Everest Univ South Orlando Campus 9200 Southpark Center Loop Orlando FL 32819 Office Phone: 407-851-2525 ext 179. Personal E-mail: emurphrey@hotmail.com.

MURPHY, ARTHUR WILLIAM, lawyer, educator; b. Boston, Jan. 25, 1922; s. Arthur W. and Rose (Spillane) M.; m. Jane Marks, Dec. 21, 1948 (dec. Sept. 1951); 1 dau., Lois; m. Jean C. Marks, Sept. 30, 1954; children: Rachel, Paul. AB cum laude, Harvard, 1943; LL.B., Columbia, 1948. Bar: N.Y. State bar 1949. Asso. in law Columbia Sch. Law, NYC, 1948-49; asso. dir. Legislative Drafting Research Fund, 1956, prof. law, 1963—; trial atty. U.S. Dept. Justice, 1950-52; asso. firm Hughes, Hubbard, Blair & Reed, NYC, 1953-56, 57-58; partner firm Baer, Marks, Friedman & Berliner, NYC, 1959-63. Mem. safety and licensing panel AEC, 1962-73; mem. spl. commn. on weather modification NSF, 1964-66; mem. Presdl. Commn. on Catastrophic Nuclear Accidents, 1988-90 Author: Financial Protection against Atomic Hazards, 1957, (with others) Cases on Gratuitous Transfers, 1968, 3d edit., 1985, The Nuclear Power Controversy, 1976. Served with AUS, 1943-46. Decorated Purple Heart. Mem. ABA, Assn. of Bar of City of N.Y. (spl. com. on sci. and law) Office: Columbia Sch of Law 435 W 116th St New York NY 10027-7297

MURPHY, BETTY SOUTHARD, lawyer; b. East Orange, NJ; d. Floyd Theodore and Thelma (Casto) Southard; m. Cornelius F. Murphy, May 1, 1965; children: Cornelius Francis Jr., Ann Southard Murphy; m. H. Leland Hernly, Apr. 26, 2003; 1 child: Samuel Southard Hernly. AB, Ohio State U.; student, Alliance Française and U. Sorbonne, Paris; JD, Am. U. Washington Coll. Law, Washington, DC; LLD (hon.), Ea. Mich. U., Ypsilanti, 1975, Capital U., Columbus, Ohio, 1976, Seattle U., 1986; LHD (hon.), Tusculum Coll., Greenville, Tenn., 1987. Bar: D.C. Corr., free lance journalist, Europe and Asia, UPI, Washington; mem. firm McInnis, Wilson, Munson & Woods (and predecessor firm Roberts & McInnis); dep. asst. sec., adminstr. Wage and Hour Divsn. Dept. Labor, 1974-75; chmn. and mem. NLRB, 1975-79; ptnr. firm Baker & Hostetler, LLP, 1980—. Adj. prof. law Am. U., 1972-80, 99—; mem. adv. com. on rights and responsibilities of women to Sec. HHS; mem. panel conciliators Internat. Ctr. Settlement Investment Disputes, 1974-85; mem. Adminstrv. Conf. U.S., 1976-80, Pub. Svc. Adv. Bd., 1976-79; mem. human resouces com. Nat. Ctr. for Productivity and Quality of Working Life, 1976-80; mem. Presdl. Commn. on Exec. Exch., 1981-85, Ctr. for Study of the Presidency, 1998—02. Trustee Mary Baldwin Coll., Staunton, Va., 1977—85, Am. U., Washington, 1980—99, George Mason U. Found., Inc., Fairfax, Va., 1993—2000, 2001—, Friends of Dept. of Labor, 1984—2007, Friends of Congl. Law Libr., 1992—2008; US Constn. mem. exec com. Commn. on Bicentennial, 1985—92; chmn. internat. adv. com. Commn. on Bicentennial of US Constn., 1985—92; vice chmn. James Madison Meml. Fellowship Found., 1990—96; mediator World Intellectual Property Orgn., 1996—; nat. bd. dirs. Med. Coll. Pa., Phila., bd. corporators, 1976—85; bd. dirs. Ctr. for Women in Medicine, Phila., 1980—86, Meridian Internat. Ctr., 1992—98; bd. mem. Summer Opera Theatre, 2006—08; bd. govs. St. Agnes Sch., Alexandria, Va., 1981—87. Recipient Ohio Gov.'s award, 1980, fellow award, 1981, Outstanding Pub. Service award, U.S. Info. Service, 1987; named Disting. fellow, John Sherman Myers Soc., 1986, 1996; named one of 24 Legends of Law, DC Bar Assn., 2006, Top 20 Lawyers, Washingtonian Mag., 2008; fellow, Nat. Acad. Human Resources, 1998. Mem.: Internat. Law Sect., Task Force on Legal Outsourcing & Paralegal Outsourcing, US-Mexico Bar Assn. (US chair labor and law com. 2006—07, bd. dirs. 2007—), Am. Inns Ct. (Professionalism award 2006), Nat. Acad. Human Resources, Nat. Assn. Women Lawyers, Women's Bar Assn., Internat Bar Assn., Am. U. Alumni Assn. (Women's Leadership Award 2004), Supreme Ct. Hist. Soc., Union Internat. des Advocats (gov. bd. 1997—2000, 2003—), Rep. Nat. Lawyers Assn. (nat. v.p. 1990—95, nat. vice chmn. 1996—2000, 2001—03, co-chmn. 2003—08, mem. exec. bd. 2003—, Rep. Lawyer of Yr. 2005), Am. Arbitration Assn. (bd. dirs. 1985—2000, mem. editl. bd. 1992, mem. exec. com. 1995—2000, mem. internat. arbitration com. 1997—, steering com. lawyers for Bush 2000, bd. dirs. 2001—04, mem. Lawyers for McCain 2007—08), Bar Assn. D.C., Inter-Am. Bar Assn. (co-chmn. labor law com. 1975—83, editor newsletter, Silver medal 1967), FBA, ABA (chmn. labor law com. 1980—83, chmn. internat. and comparative law adminstrv. law sect. 1983—88, chmn. customs, tariff and trade com. 1988—90, employment law sect. 1990—2004, chmn. internat. com. dispute resolution sect. 1995—, co-chair, task force internat. outsourcing, sect. internat. law 2008—, Sec. Dispute Resolution Spl. Achievement award 1995—2009), World Peace Through Law Ctr., Mortar Bd., Kappa Beta Pi. Republican. Office: Baker & Hostetler LLP Ste 1100 1050 Connecticut Ave NW Washington DC 20036-5304 Office Phone: 202-861-1500, 202-861-1586. Office Fax: 202-861-1783. Business E-Mail: bsmurphy@bakerlaw.com.

MURPHY, BRITTANY, actress; b. Atlanta, Nov. 10, 1977; d. Angelo Bertolotti and Sharon Murphy; m. Simon Monjack, Apr. 2007. Actor: (films) Clueless, 1995, Freeway, 1996, Drive, 1997, The Prophecy II, 1998, Bongwater, 1998, Phoenix, 1998, Zack and Reba, 1998, Falling Sky, 1998, Drop Dead Gorgeous, 1999, Girl, Interrupted, 1999, Trixie, 2000, Angels!, 2000, Cherry Falls, 2000, The Audition, 2000, Sidewalks of NY, 2001, Summer Catch, 2001, Don't Say a Word, 2001, Riding in Cars with Boys, 2001, Spun, 2002, 8 Mile, 2002, Just Married, 2003, Uptown Girls, 2003, (voice only) Good Boy!, 2003, Little Black Book, 2004, Sin City, 2005, Neverwas, 2005, The Groomsmen, 2006, Love and Other Disasters, 2006, (voice only) Happy Feet, 2006,: (TV films) Double Jeopardy, 1996, David and Lisa, 1998, The Devil's Arithmetic, 1999, Common Ground, 2000, (TV appearances) Drexell's Class, 1991, Murphy Brown, 1991, Kids Incorporated, 1992, Parker Lewis Can't Lose, 1992, Almost Home, 1993, Blossom, 1993, Frasier, 1994, Party of Five, 1994, Sister, Sister, 1994, Boy Meets World, 1995, Murder One, 1995, The Marshal, 1995, SeaQuest DSV, 1995, Nash Bridges, 1996, Clueless, 1996, (voice only) Pepper Ann, 1997; (TV series) King of the Hill, 1997—2006. Office: Endeavor Talent Agy 9601 Wilshire Blvd Beverly Hills CA 90212

MURPHY, BRUCE ALLEN, government and law educator, writer; b. Abington, Mass., Sept. 30, 1951; m. Carol Lynn Wright, June 14, 1975; children: Emily, Geoffrey. BA, U. Mass., Amherst, 1973; PhD, U. Va., Charlottesville, 1978. Fred Morgan Kirby prof. civil rights Lafayette Coll., Easton, Pa. Author: The Brandeis/Frankfurter Connection: The Secret Political Activities of Two Supreme Court Justices, 1982, Fortas:

The Rise and Ruin of a Supreme Court Justice, 1988, (with Larry Berman) Approaching Democracy, 1996, 6th edit., 2008, Wild Bill: The Legend and Life of William O. Douglas, 2003. Avocations: fishing, reading, sports. Office: Lafayette Coll Dept Govt and Law 200 Kirby Hall Civil Rights Easton PA 18042 Office Phone: 610-330-5395. Business E-Mail: murphyb@lafayette.edu.

MURPHY, CHRISTOPHER S., United States Representative from Connecticut, former state senator; b. White Plains, NY, Aug. 3, 1973; s. Scott and Catherine Murphy; m. Cathy Holahan, Aug. 2007. Student, Exeter Coll., Oxford U., Eng.; BA in Hist. & Polit. Sci., with honors, Williams Coll., Mass., 1996; JD, U. Conn. Sch. Law, 2002. Mem. dist. 81 Conn. Ho. of Reps., 1998—2002, mem. environ., judiciary & pub. health com., mem. Prescription Drug Task Force; atty. Ruben, Johnson, and Morgan, PC, Hartford, Conn., 2002—06; mem. dist. 16 Conn. State Senate, 2003—06, chair pub. health com., caucus whip; mem. US Congress from 5th Conn. dist., 2007—, mem. fin. svcs. com., oversight & govt. reform com. Staff mem. Conn. State Senate Majority Caucus, 1996—98; mem. Southington Planning & Zoning Commn., 1997—99. Democrat. Office: 1 Grove St New Britain CT 06053 also: US House of Reps 412 Cannon House Office Bldg Washington DC 20515 Office Phone: 860-240-0567. E-mail: murphy@senatedems.ct.gov.*

MURPHY, CORNELIUS B., JR., (NEIL MURPHY), academic administrator; b. July 17, 1944; m. Joanne Murphy; children: Tracy, Megan, Maureen, Michael. B in Chemistry magna cum laude, St. Michael's Coll., 1966; PhD in Chemistry, Syracuse U., 1970; DSc (hon.), Clarkson U., 1997. Joined as a lab technician O'Brien & Gere Cos., East Syracuse, NY, 1970; sr. v.p. O'Brien & Gere Engrs., Inc., East Syracuse, 1982—92, pres., 1992, chmn., chief scientist, 1998; pres. O'Brien & Gere Ltd., East Syracuse, 1996, chmn., 1999; pres. SUNY Coll. Environ. Sci. and Forestry, East Syracuse, 2000—. Mem.: AAAS, Am. Chem. Soc. Office: SUNY Coll Environ Sci and Forestry 1 Forestry Dr Syracuse NY 13210 E-mail: cbmurphy@esf.edu.*

MURPHY, DANIEL J., JR., aerospace and defense manufacturing company executive, military officer; b. Newport, RI, May 30, 1948; m. Pam Murphy; children: Dan, Kate. BS, U.S. Naval Acad., 1970; M in Law and Diplomacy, Tufts U., 1981. Exec. asst. to chief of naval ops. USN; exec. asst. to Supreme Allied Comdr. Atlantic; adminstrv. aide to Sec. of Navy; plans officer Plans and Ops. Directorate; mil. analyst Bur. Intelligence and Rsch. Dept. of State; rear adm., dir. surface warfare USN, 1996-98, vice adm., comdr. Sixth Fleet, and NATO striking & support forces So. Europe, 1998—2000; pres. ATK Tactical Sys., 2001—02; group v.p., precision systems and pres. tactical systems Alliant Techsystems (ATK), Edina, Minn., 2000—03; group v.p., ATK Precision Sys. Group Alliant Techsystems Inc., 2002—03; CEO Alliant Techsystems (ATK), 2003—, chmn. Edina, Minn., 2005—. Comdr. Eisenhower Battle Group and Cruiser-Destroyer Group 8, comdr. Destroyer Squadron 14, commdg. officer USS Kidd, sea tours with USS Goldsborough, USS Richard L. Page, USS Edson, USN. Vice admiral USN, 2000. Office: Alliant Techsystems Inc 7480 Flying Cloud Dr Eden Prairie MN 55344 Office Phone: 952-351-3000.*

MURPHY, DIANA E., federal judge; b. Faribault, Minn., Jan. 4, 1934; d. Albert W. and Adleyne (Heiker) Kuske; m. Joseph Murphy, July 24, 1958; children: Michael, John E. BA magna cum laude, U. Minn., 1954, JD magna cum laude, 1974; postgrad., Johannes Gutenberg U., 1954—55, U. Minn., 1955—58; LLD, St. Johns U., 2000, U. St. Thomas, 2003. Bar: Minn. 1974, US Supreme Ct. 1980. Assoc. Lindquist & Vennum, 1974—76; mcpl. judge Hennepin County, 1976—78, Minn. State dist. judge, 1978—80; judge US Dist. Ct. for Minn., Mpls., 1980—94, chief judge, 1992—94; judge US Ct. Appeals (8th cir.), Mpls., 1994—. Chair US Sentencing Commn., 1999—2004. Bd. editors: Minn. Law Rev., Georgetown U. Jour. on Cts., Health Scis. and the Law, 1989—92. Bd. dirs. Nat. Assn. Pub. Interest Law Fellowships for Equal Justice, 1992—95, Mpls. United Way, 1985—2001, treas., 1990—94, vice-chmn., 1996—97, chmn. bd. dirs., 1997—98; bd. dirs. Bush Found., 1982—2006, chmn. bd. dirs., 1986—91; organizer, 1st chmn. adv. coun. Amicus, bd. dirs., 1976—80; chair Mpls. Charter Commn., 1973—76; bd. dirs. Ops. De Novo, 1971—76, chmn. bd. dirs., 1974—75; mem., chmn. bill of rights com. Minn. Constl. Study Commn., 1971—73; regent St. Johns U., 1978—87, 1988—98, chmn. bd., 1995—98, bd. overseers sch. theology, 1998—2001; mem. Minn. Bicentennial Commn., 1987—88; trustee Twin Cities Pub. TV, 1985—94, chmn. bd., 1990—92; trustee U. Minn. Found., 1990—, chmn. of bd., 2003—05; bd. dirs. Sci. Mus. Minn., 1988—94, vice-chmn., 1991—94; trustee U. St. Thomas, 1991—, chair exec. com., 2006—; vice chair bd. govs. U. St. Thomas Law Sch., 2001—04, chair, 2004—06; bd. dirs. Spring Hill Conf. Ctr., 1978—84; bd. govs. Hill Mus. and Manuscript Libr., 2005—; bd. dirs. Minn. Opera, 1998—2004, 2005—. Recipient Amicus Founders' award, 1980, Outstanding Achievement award, U. Minn., 1983, YWCA, 1981, Disting. Citizen award, Alpha Gamma Delta, 1985, Devitt Disting. Svc. to Justice award, 2001, Disting. Alumnus award, U. Minn. Law Sch., 2002, Woman Who Makes a Difference award, Internat. Women's Forum, 2003, Iustitia et Lex award, 2006; scholar Fulbright. Fellow: Am. Bar Found.; mem.: ABA (ethics and profl. responsibility judges adv. com. 1981—88, standing com. on jud. selection, tenure and compensation 1991—94, standing com. on fed. jud. improvements 1994—97, Appellate Judges conf. exec. com. 1996—99, chmn. ethics and profl. responsibility judges adv. com. 1997—2000), Fed. Jud. Ctr. (bd. dirs. 1990—94, 8th cir. jud. coun. 1992—94, 1992—94, convener gender fairness task force 1993, U.S. jud. conf. com. on ct. adminstrn. and case mgmt. 1994—99, chair gender fairness implementation com. 1997—98), Hist. Soc. for 8th Cir. (bd. dirs. 1988—91), Fed. Judges Assn. (bd. dirs. 1982—2003, v.p. 1984—89, pres. 1989—91), U. Minn. Alumni Assn. (bd. dirs. 1975—83, nat. pres. 1981—82), Minn. Women Lawyers (Myra Bradwell award 1996), Nat. Assn. Women Judges (Leadership Judges Jud. Adminstrn. award 1998, Honoree of Yr. 2002), Nat. Assn. Governing Bds. Univs. Colls. (dir. 1998—, vice chair 2006—), Am. Judicature Soc. (bd. dirs. 1982—93, v.p. 1985—88, treas. 1988—89, chmn. bd. 1989—91), Am. Law Inst., Hennepin County Bar Assn. (gov. coun. 1976—81), Minn. Bar Assn. (bd. govs. 1977—81), Order of Coif, Phi Beta Kappa. Office: 11 E US Courthouse 300 S 4th St Minneapolis MN 55415-1320*

MURPHY, DONNA, actress; b. Corona, NY, Mar. 7, 1959; m. Shawn Elliott, 1990; 1 adopted child, Darmia. Student, NYU Sch. of the Arts. Actor: (Broadway plays) They're Playing Our Song, The Human Comedy, The Mystery of Edwin Drood, Passion, 1994—95 (Tony award best actress in a musical, 1994, Drama Desk award, Drama League award), 2004, The King and I, 1996 (Tony award best actress in a musical, 1996, Drama League award), Wonderful Town, 2003—04 (Tony nom. best actress in a musical, 2004, Drama Desk award best actress in a musical, 2004, Drama League award, 2004), Children & Art, 2005, LoveMusik, 2007 (Outer Critics Cir. award outstanding actress in a musical, 2007, Drama Desk award outstanding actress in a musical, 2007); (plays) Song of Singapore, Privates on Parade, Showing Off, Birds of Paradise, Little Shop of Horrors, A...My Name Is Alice, Twelve Dreams, 1995, Hello Again, 1994, Follies, 2007; (TV series) Murder One, 1995—96, Law & Order, 1993, 1997, 2000, The Practice, 1998, Ally McBeal, 1998, What About Joan, 2001, Hack, 2002—03; (TV miniseries) LIBERTY! The American Revolution, 1997; (TV films) Tales from the Hollywood Hills: A Table at Ciro's, 1987, Power, Passion and Murder, 1987, Passion, 1996, Someone Had to Be Benny, 1996 (Cable ACE award, 1996, Daytime Emmy, 1996), The Day Lincoln Was Shot, 1998, The Last Debate, 2000; (films) Jade, 1995, October 22, 1998, Star Trek: Insurrection, 1998, The Astronaut's Wife, 1999, Center Stage, 2001, The Door in the Floor, 2004, Spiderman 2, 2004, Ira and Abby, 2006, World Trade Center, 2006, The Fountain, 2006, The Nanny Diaries, 2007. Office: Innovative Artists 235 Park Ave S New York NY 10003

MURPHY, DOUGLAS A., cardiothoracic surgeon; b. Mpls., Minn., Oct. 14, 1949; BS, Middlebury Coll., Middlebury. Vt., 1971; MD, U. Pa., 1975. Cert. Am. Bd. Thoracic Surgeons, Am. Bd. Surgery. Intern, internal medicine Mass. Gen. Hosp., Boston, 1975—76, resident, internal medicine, 1976—77, intern, gen. surgery, 1977—78, resident, gen. surgery, 1978—81; resident, cardiothoracic surgery Emory U. Affliated Hosps., Atlanta, 1981—83; with Peachtree Cardiothoracic and Thoracic Surgeons, PA, Atlanta, 1983—; chief, cardiothoracic surgery St. Joseph's Hosp., Atlanta; chair St. Joseph's Heart and Vascular Inst., Ga., 2007—. Hosp. appointment St. Joseph's Hosp., Atlanta, 1987—, Piedmont Hosp., Atlanta. Office: 5669 Peachtree Rd NE Ste 390 Atlanta GA 30342 Address: Peachtree Cardiovascular and Thoracic Surgeons PA 5665 Peachtree Dunwoody Rd Ste 150 Atlanta GA 30342 Office Phone: 404-847-9683, 404-252-6104. Office Fax: 404-257-1808. E-mail: dmurphy407@aol.com.

MURPHY, EDDIE, actor, comedian; b. Bklyn., Apr. 3, 1961; s. Vernon and Lillian Murphy Lynch; m. Nicole Mitchell, March 18, 1993 (div. Apr. 17, 2006); children: Bria, Myles Mitchell, Shayne Audra, Zola Ivy, Bella Zehra; 1 child with Melanie Brown, Angel Iris; m. Tracey Edmonds, Jan. 1, 2008 (separated 2008). Student pub. schs., Bklyn. Began performing Richard M. Dixon's White House, LI, N.Y.; performed at various N.Y.C. clubs, including The Comic Strip; with Saturday Night Live, NYC, 1980-84; host 35th Ann. Emmy Awards, 1983. Actor: (films) 48 Hrs., 1982, Trading Places, 1983, Best Defense, 1984, Beverly Hills Cop, 1984, The Distinguished Gentleman, 1992, Beverly Hills Cop III, 1994, The Nutty Professor, 1996, Metro, 1997, Mulan (voice only), 1998, Dr. Dolittle, 1998, Holy Man, 1998, Bowfinger, 1999, Shrek (voice only), 2001, Dr. Dolittle 2, 2001, Showtime, 2002, The Adventures of Pluto Nash, 2002, I Spy, 2002, Daddy Day Care, 2003, The Haunted Mansion, 2003, Shrek 2 (voice only), 2004, Dreamgirls, 2006 (Best Supporting Actor, African-American Film Critics Assn., 2006, 2006 Best Supporting Actor, Critics Choice award, Broadcast Film Critics Assn., 2007, Best Performance by an Actor in a Supporting Role in a Motion Picture, Golden Globe award, Hollywood Fgn. Press Assn., 2007, Outstanding Performance by a Male Actor in a Supporting Role, SAG, 2007), Shrek the Third (voice only), 2007, Meet Dave, 2008, Imagine That, 2009; actor, exec. prodr.: The Golden Child, 1986; The Nutty Professor II: The Klumps, 2000; Harlem Nights, 1989; actor(actor, prodr.): Vampire in Brooklyn, 1995; actor, prodr.: Life, 1999; actor, writer, prodr. Norbit, 2007; actor, writer Beverly Hills Cop II, 1987; Coming to America, 1988; Another 48 Hrs., 1990; actor, writer: films Boomerang, 1992; actor: (TV films) Eddie Murphy Delirious, 1983, Eddie Murphy Raw, 1987; actor (voice only), exec. prodr. (TV series) The PJ's, 1999—2001. Office: c/o Rogers & Cowan Pacific Design Ctr 8687 Melrose Avenue 7th fl Los Angeles CA 90069*

MURPHY, EDWARD FRANCIS, sales executive; b. Chgo., July 30, 1947; s. Edward F. and Marjorie (Mooney) M.; m. Kay A. Worcester, Apr. 17, 1970; 1 child, Dean D. BA in Mktg., No. Ill. U., 1976. Dist. mgr. Midas Internat. Corp., Chgo., 1977-85; sales mgr. Raybestos, McHenry, Ill., 1985-89, Wagner Brakes, St. Louis, 1989-99; owner Displays of Distinction, Mesa, Ariz., 1998—. V.p. Associated Roof Structures, Mesa, 1999-2007; sales mgr. Stellar Structure, 2008-. Author: Vietnam Medal of Honor Heroes, 1987, Heroes of World War II, 1990, Korea's Heroes, 1990, Dak To, 1993, Semper Fi-Vietnam, 1996, Khe Sahn-The Hill Fights, 2000; hist. cons. (book) Above and Beyond, 1985. Sgt. U.S. Army, 1965-68. Recipient Dist. Svc. award Congl. Medal of Honor Soc., 1989. Mem. Medal of Honor Hist. Soc. (founder, pres. 1975—). Republican. Avocations: writing, flying. Home: 2659 E Kael St Mesa AZ 85213-2363 Office: 1237 S Val Vista Dr Mesa AZ 85204 Office Phone: 480-279-6296.

MURPHY, EDWARD JOSEPH, government agency administrator; b. Washington, Aug. 17, 1948; s. Edward Conley Murphy and Pauline Anne Ehlers. BA, So. Ill. U., Carbondale, 1970; JD, Georgetown U., Washington, 1973. Bar: Washington 1973. Policy analyst US EPA, Washington, 1980—86, chief contracts policy, 1987—97, mgr. superfund contract ctr., 1997—2003, mgr. lab. analysis svc. ctr., 2003—06, dir. competitive sourcing staff, 2006—. Rep. US Civilian Agy. Acquisition Coun., Washington, 1986—92. Recipient Silver medal for Superior Svc., US EPA, 1995. Mem.: ABA (pub. contract law divsn.), Nat. Contract Mgmt. Assn., Phi Kappa Phi, Pi Sigma Alpha. Democrat. Avocations: piano, swimming, history, films, travel. Office: US EPA 1200 Penn Ave NW Washington DC 20460

MURPHY, EILEEN BRIDGET, retired mathematics and computer science professor; b. Newport, RI, Dec. 28, 1940; d. Henry Timothy and Mary Anne (Lyne) M. BA in Teaching Math., Elms Coll., 1969; MAT in Math., Purdue U., 1971; MSA in Adminstrn., U. Notre Dame, 1981; postgrad., Nova Southeastern U., 1992—96. Cert. secondary edn., math. and adminstrn. Mass. Tchr. math. Cathedral H.S., Springfield, Mass., 1961-71; tchr. Holyoke Cath. H.S., Mass., 1971-84, dept. chair, 1975-84; asst. prof., lectr. Elms Coll., Chicopee, 1984—2006, dept. chair math. scis., 1985-90, div. chair math. and sci., 1987-89; ret., 1989. Steering com. Accreditations New Eng. Assn. Secondary Schs. and Colls., Chicopee, 1991-92. Mem. Sisters of St. Joseph of Springfield, Sisters of St. Joseph Fin. Team; co-treas. Sisters of St. Joseph Festival, 1984-86; bd. dirs. Mont Marie Health Care Ctr., 1999-2005; vol. computer tchr. Hampden County Dept. Corrections; vol. tchr. math. and computer applications Elms Coll., 2006—. Recipient Econs. of Pvt. Enterprise grant Strathmore Paper Co., Springfield Coll., Mass., 1978. Mem. Assn. Computing Machinery (Western Mass. chpt. pub. rels. com. 1985-86, sec. 1986-91). Democrat. Roman Catholic. Achievements include the introduction of computers into the curriculum at Holyoke Catholic High School in 1980. Avocations: peer support for multiple sclerosis groups, knitting, puzzle solving. Home: 32 Lower Westfield Rd Apt 316 Holyoke MA 01040 Home Phone: 413-533-4030. Personal E-mail: murp1228@verizon.net. Business E-Mail: murphye@elms.edu.

MURPHY, (FRANCES) ELAINE, musician, harpist, flutist; b. Chattanooga, July 15; MusB, Boston U., 1982; postgrad., Aspen Sch. Music, 1988; MM, Rice U., 1990; DMA, U. So. Calif., 1997, MMEd, 2002. Flutist Brookline (Mass.) Symphony Orch., 1982-84; piccolo player North Shore Symphony Orch., Marblehead, Mass., 1982-83, Cape Ann Symphony Orch., Gloucester, Mass., 1983-84; prin. flutist Orch. Sinfonica Del Valle, Cali, Colombia, 1984-87; flutist Pro Musica Chamber Orch., El Paso, Tex., 1987-88; prin. flutist Internat. Orchestra and Internat. Chamber Players, San Diego, 1990-91; harpist Lake Ave. Orch., 2005—. Solo harpist Beverly Hills Hotel, Harp Palace Hotel, Tokyo; music instr. LAUSD, 2001-. Musician Scotia Festival of Music, 1988; participant in Festival de Hispanidad, Houston, 1990, Schladming Wind Festival, Austria, 2007; albums Thou Shalt Play Upon the Harp, 2001; CD An Angel's Harp for the Holidays. Scholar Boston U., 1978-82, Crescendo Club Boston, 1982, Aspen Music Sch., 1988-89, Rice U., 1988-90; recipient Shepherd Soc. Award. U. S. C., D.M.A.,1991-97 Office: Murphy's Music PMB 449 3175 South Hoover St Los Angeles CA 90007 E-mail: murphsnews@aol.com.

MURPHY, EVELYN FRANCES, economist; b. Panama Canal Zone, May 14, 1940; d. Clement Bernard and Dorothy Eloise (Jackson) M. AB, Duke U., 1961, PhD, 1965; MA, Columbia U., 1963; degree (hon.), Regis Coll., 1978, Curry Coll., Northeastern U., Simmons Coll., Wheaton Coll., Anna Maria Coll., Bridgewater State Coll., Salem State Coll., Emmanuel Coll., Suffolk U.; degree, Lasell Coll. Pres. Ancon Assocs., Boston, 1971-72; ptnr. Llewelyn-Davies, Weeks, Forrester-Walker & Bor, London, 1973-74; sec. environ. affairs Commonwealth of Mass., Boston, 1975-79, sec. econ. affairs, 1983-86, lt. gov., 1987-91; mng. dir. Brown Rudnick Freed and Gesmer, Boston, 1991-93; exec. v.p. Blue Cross/Blue Shield of Mass., Boston, 1994-98; also bd. dirs. Blue Cross Blue Shield Mass., Boston; bd. dirs. Showmet Nat. Bank, Fleet Nat. Bank; resident scholar Brandeis U. Women's Studies Rsch. Ctr., 1999—; founder, pres. The Wage Project, Inc., 2003—. Vice-chmn., chmn. Nat. Adv. Com. on Oceans and Atmosphere, 1979-80; bd. dirs. Citizens Energy Corp., The Commonwealth Inst., Nat. Ctr. on Women and Aging, chair, 1998-2002, chmn. emeritus, 2002, Polaris Project, 2007; pres. Health Care and Policy Inst., 1997-98; resident scholar Brandeis U., 1998—; bd. trustees Regis Coll., 2003-08; vice chair SBLI USA Mut. Life Ins. Author: (books) Getting Even: Why Women Don't Get Paid Like Men & What to Do About It, 2005. Recipient Dist. Svc. award New Eng. Coun., 1996, Nat. Sierra Club, 1978, Nat. Bd. Govs. Assn., 1978, Outstanding Citizen award Mass. Audobon Soc., 1978; Harvard U. fellow, 1979-80. Mem. Women Execs. in State Govt. (chair 1987), Internat. Women's Forum, 1993—. Democrat. Avocation: jogging. Personal E-mail: evmurphy1@aol.com.

MURPHY, EWELL EDWARD, JR., lawyer; b. Washington, Feb. 21, 1928; s. Ewell Edward and Lou (Phillips) M.; m. Patricia Bredell Purnell, June 26, 1954 (dec. 1964); children: Michaela, Megan Patricia, Harlan Ewell. BA, U. Tex., 1946, LLB, 1948; DPhil, Oxford U., Eng., 1951. Bar: Tex. 1948. Assoc. Baker & Botts, Houston, 1954-63, ptnr., 1964-93, head internat. dept., 1972-89. Pres. Houston World Trade Assn., 1972-74; trustee Southwestern Legal Found., 1978—2003; chmn. Houston Com. on Fgn. Rels., 1984-85, Inst. Transnat. Arbitration, 1985-89, Internat. and Comparative Law Ctr., 1986-87; mem. J. William Fulbright Fgn. Scholarship Bd., 1991-96, vice chmn., 1992-93, chmn., 1993-95; vis. prof. U. Tex. Law Sch., 1993-97; disting. lectr., U. Houston Law Ctr., 1996-2006, adj. prof., 2007-. Contbr. articles to profl. jours. Served to lt. USAF, 1952—54. Recipient Carl H. Fulda award U. Tex. Internat. Law Jour., 1980; Rhodes scholar, 1948-51 Mem.: ABA (chmn. sect. internat. law 1970—71), Internat. Law Inst. (bd. dirs. 1994—2008), Houston Bar Assn. (chmn. internat. law com. 1963—64, 1970—71), Coun. on Fgn. Rels., Philos. Soc. Tex., Houston C. of C. (chmn. internat. bus. com. 1964—65), Fulbright Assn. (bd. dirs. 1999—2004, v.p. 2002—04). Home and Office: 17 W Oak Dr Houston TX 77056-2117 Home Phone: 713-622-3840; Office Phone: 713-622-3840. E-mail: ewellmurphyjr@sbcglobal.net.

MURPHY, FRANCES M., federal agency administrator; MD with honors, Georgetown U., Washington, 1979; MPH, Uniformed Svcs. U. of the Health Scis., 1993. Diplomate Am. Coll. Psychiatry and Neurology. Resident in neurology Georgetown U., Washington; staff neurologist Andrews AFB, Md., 1983—87; chief cons. occupl. and environ. medicine US Dept. Veterans Affairs, Washington, dep. under sec. for health, 1999—2002, acting under sec. for health, 2002, dep. under sec. for health policy coordination, 2002—. Adj. assoc. prof. neurology Uniformed Svcs. U. of the Health Scis. Contbr. articles to profl. jours. With USAF. Office: US Dept Veterans Affairs 810 Vermont Ave NW Washington DC 20420*

MURPHY, FRANCIS, language educator; b. Springfield, Mass., Mar. 13, 1932; s. Frank Edward and Sarah (O'Connor) M. BA, Am. Internat. Coll., 1953; MA, U. Conn., 1955; PhD, Harvard U., 1960; LittD (hon.), Am. Internat. Coll., 1986. Mem. faculty English lang. and lit. Smith Coll., 1959-99, assoc. prof., 1966-69, prof., 1970-99, prof. emeritus, 1999—. Vis. curator Springfield Mus. Fine Arts, 1975-76, Hudson River Mus., 1983-84. Editor: The Diary of Edward Taylor, 1964, Major Am. Poets, 1967, Form and Structure in Poetry, 1964, Edwin Arlington Robinson, 1970, Walt Whitman, 1969, The Uncollected Essays of Yvor Winters, 1973, The Complete Poems of Walt Whitman, 1975, Of Plymouth Plantation (William Bradford), 1981; author: Willard Leroy Metcalf, 1976, (with Dean Flower) A Catalogue of American Paintings, Water Colors and Drawings (to 1923) in the G.W.V. Smith Museum, 1976, The Landscape Within: J. Francis Murphy, 1982, The Book of Nature: American Painters and the Natural Sublime, 1983; co-editor: Norton Anthology of American Literature, 1979—, Mass. Rev., 1966-67.

MURPHY, FREDERICK AUGUSTUS, virologist, researcher; b. NYC, June 14, 1934; s. Frederick A. and Louise A. (Knizak) Murphy; m. Irene M. Warwas, July 2, 1960 (dec.); children: Frederick A., W. Timothy, John G., Terence D. BS in Microbiology, Cornell U., 1956, DVM, 1959; PhD in Comparative Pathology, U. Calif., Davis, 1964; MD (hon.), U. Turku, Finland, 1987; DSc (hon.), U. Guelph, Can., 2000. Chief viral pathology br. Ctrs. for Disease Control, Atlanta, 1964-78; assoc. dean Coll. Vet. Medicine Colo. State U., Ft. Collins, 1978-83; dir. divsn. viral & rickettsial diseases Ctrs. for Disease Control, Atlanta, 1983-87, dir. Nat. Ctr. for Infectious Diseases, 1987-91; dean Sch. Vet. Medicine U. Calif., Davis, 1991-96, disting. prof. Sch. Vet. Medicine, 1996—2005, disting. prof and dean emeritus, 2006—; prof. dept. pathology U. Tex. Med. Br., Galveston, 2006—. Program chair virology divsn. Internat. Union Microbiology Socs., 1978—87, chair virology divsn., 1981—84; adv. bds. Lawrence Livermore Nat. Lab., 1996—; v.p. Found. Human Rabies Edn. & Eradication, 1999—; com. mem. on Future Contributions to Public Health, Agr., Basic Rsch. Counterterrorism, Non-Proliferation Activities in Russia US Nat. Acad. Scis., 2001—03, co-chair Comm. on Occupational Health and Safety in Care of Non-Human primates, 2001—03, com. mem. on Food Safety and Nutrition, 2001—02; com. mem. on Emerging Microbial Threats to Health in 21st Century Inst. Medicine and US Nat. Acad. Scis., 2001—03, com. mem. on Transmissible Spongiform Encephalopathies, 2002—04. Editor: (book series) Advances in Virus Research, 1983—, (book) Virus Taxonomy, 1995; editor in chief: jour. Archives of Virology, 1984—2000, sr. author: book Veterinary Virology III, 1999; contbr. over 450 articles to profl. jours., reports, reviews, monographs, books, and chapters to books. Mem. Pew Trusts Nat. Vet. Edn. Program: Future Directions in Vet. Medicine, 1986—89; mem. Internat. Advisory Group Royal Vet. Coll., London, 2004—; mem. Secretary's Coun. Public Health Preparedness US Dept HHS, 2002—. Capt. US Army, 1959—62, cmdr. USPHS, 1964—68. Recipient K.F. Meyers Gold

Headed Cane, Am. Vet. Epidemiology Soc., 1986, Davis medal, U. Calif., 1998, Pres. Rank award, US Govt., 1992, Richard Moreland Taylor award, Am. Com. Arthropod-Borne Viruses, Am. Soc. Tropical Medicine & Hygeine, 2003; named elected mem., German Acad. Nat. Scis., 1985, Inst. Medicine, US Nat. Acad. Scis., 1999, Acad. Medicine Engring. Sci. Tex., 2006. Fellow: Infectious Diseases Soc. Am., John Curtin Sch. Med. Rsch., Australian Nat. U. (hon.); mem.: Am. Soc. Virology (founding coun. mem.), Internat. Com. on Taxonomy of Viruses (life; pres. 1990—96), Am. Soc. Microbiology (com. public health 2006—, public and scientific affairs bd.). Democrat. Roman Catholic. Office: U Tex Med Br Dept Pathology 3 145 A Keiller Bldg 301 Univ Blvd Galveston TX 77555-0609 Office Phone: 409-747-2430. Business E-Mail: famurphy@utmb.edu.

MURPHY, GEORGE FRANCIS, dermatopathologist, educator; b. Natick, Mass., Feb. 12, 1950; s. George Francis and Barbara Elizabeth Murphy; m. Sharon Elizabeth Walters, Aug. 26, 1972; children: Erin Elizabeth, Emily Elise. BA, U. Pa., 1972; MD, U. Vt., 1976. Diplomate Nat. Bd. Med. Examiners, Am. Bd. Pathology, Am. Bd. Pathology and Dermatology. Resident, fellow Harvard Med. Sch., Mass. Gen. Hosp., Boston, 1977-81; assoc. prof. pathology Harvard Med. Sch., Boston, 1982-87; prof. dermatology and pathology U. Pa. Sch. Medicine, Phila., 1987-97, Herman Beerman endowed chair dermatology, 1991-97; prof. pathology Thomas Jefferson Med. Coll., Phila., 1997—2004, Harvard Med. Sch., Boston, 2004—. Vis. prof. pathology, dermatology and oncology Johns Hopkins U. Sch. Medicine, Balt., 2000—; pres., chmn. bd. dirs. Am. Soc. for Dermatopathology, 1997-98. Author: Fasicles in Skin Pathology, 1991, Dermatopathology, 1995; contbr. numerous articles to profl. jours. Mem. Am. Soc. for Clin. Investigation. Office: Brigham and Women's Hosp Dept Pathology 75 Francis St Boston MA 02115 Business E-Mail: gmurphy@rics.bwh.harvard.edu.

MURPHY, GERALD, retired federal official; b. Washington, Aug. 25, 1938; s. Jeremiah T. and Jean (Curley) M.; m. Kathryn Beckman, Sept. 24, 1988; children by previous marriage: William Michael, Janet Marie, Kathleen Anne B.C.S. with honors, Benjamin Franklin U., Washington, 1960, M.C.S., 1963. C.P.A., D.C. Dep. div. dir. Dept. Treasury, Washington, 1970-71, div. dir., 1971-74, asst. commr., 1974-75, dep. commr., 1975-79, dep. fiscal asst. sec., 1979-86, fiscal asst. sec., 1986-98; sr. prin. Keane Pub. Enterprise Consulting, Washington, 1998-2000; ind. cons., 2000—. Lectr. in acctg. Southeastern U., Washington, 1965-70, Dept. Agr. Grad. Sch., Washington, 1970-76; mem. Govt. Acctg. Standards Adv. Council, 1984-89; mem. Fed. Acctg. Standards Adv. Bd., 1991-98. Served with U.S. Army, 1956 Recipient Disting. Alumni award Benjamin Franklin U., Washington, 1976. Mem. Am. Inst. C.P.A.s, Assn. Govt. Accts. (nat. pres. 1977-78, Robert W. King award 1983, Meritorious Exec. Rsch. award 1992), Sr. Execs. Assn., Fed. Exec. Inst. Alumni Assn. Roman Catholic. Personal E-mail: gmurph825@aol.com.

MURPHY, GERARD NORRIS, trade association executive; b. Washington, July 10, 1950; s. Maurice J. and Marguerite (Norris) M.; m. Jacqueline Franz, May 26, 1973; children: Anne Marie, Michael Jonathan, Kathleen Elizabeth. BA, U. Md., 1972, MA, 1975; JD, George Mason U., 1980. Mgmt. trainee Washington Area New Automobile Dealers Assn., 1972-74, asst. CEO, 1974-82, pres., CEO, 1982—; prodr. Washington Auto Show, 2003—. Bd. dirs. Met. Washington BBB, chmn., 1992—97; bd. dirs. Small Bus. Legis. Coun., 2000—; mem. exec. com. Washington Workforce Investment Coun., 2000—, vice-chmn., 2007—08, chmn., 2008—, Nat. Capital Area Transp. Fedn., Washington, 1990—2000. Co-founder, past chmn. Washington Regional Alcohol Program, Vienna, Va., 1983-86; trustee Nat. Automobile Dealers Assn. Sales Rep. Cert. Commn., 1995-99; sec. Boys and Girls Clubs Greater Washington, Silver Spring, 1987-02, v.p. 2002-05, bd. dirs., 2006—; trustee Greater Washington Bd. Trade PACs, Va., 2000—, Md. treas., 2003—; co-founder Montgomery Students Automotive Trades Found., Montgomery Pub. Schs., 1978, sec., 1990—. Paul Harris fellow Rotary, 1990; recipient Govs. citation (Md.)Gov. William Donald Schaefer, 1990, Gov. Martin O'Malley, Md., 2008, Silver medal Boys and Girls Clubs Am., 1997, Mattie Stepanek Heartsongs award, Muscular Dystrophy Assn., 2009; named Automotive Trade Exec. of Yr., Northwood U., 1997. Fellow Am. Soc. Assn. Execs. (cert., com. chmn. 1989-90, 96-97, 2005-06); mem. ABA, Assn. Healthcare Coalition (sec. 1995, v.p. 1996-97, pres. 1998-00), Automotive Trade Assn. Execs. (bd. dirs. 1987-88, sec., treas. 1996, v.p. 1997, pres. 1998), D.C. Bar Assn., Greater Washington Soc. Assn. Execs. (com. chmn. 1993-94, trustee Found. 1997-00, chmn. award 1994), Leadership Washington (8th class 1993-94), Rotary (sec. 1998-00, v.p. 2001-02, dist. conf. chmn. 2001, pres. 2002-03, 06, v.p. found. 2005, pres. found. 2006-07), Delta Theta Phi, Delta Tau Delta. Democrat. Roman Catholic. Office: Washington Area New Auto Dealers Assn Ste 210 5301 Wisconsin Ave NW Washington DC 20015-2015 Office Phone: 202-237-7200. Business E-Mail: gm@wanada.org.

MURPHY, GLENN T., retail executive; BA, Univ. We. Ontario. Mgmt. positions A.C. Nielsen, Loblaw Companies Ltd., Canada; pres., CEO Chapters, Canada; chmn., CEO Shoppers Drug Mart, Canada, 2001—07, The Gap Inc., San Francisco, 2007—. Office: The Gap Inc 2 Folsom St San Francisco CA 94105

MURPHY, GORDON JOHN, electrical engineer, educator; b. Milw., Feb. 16, 1927; s. Gordon M. and Cecelia A. (Knerr) M.; m. Dorothy F. Brautigam, June 26, 1948; children: Lynne, Craig. BS, Milw. Sch. Engring., 1949; MS, U. Wis., 1952; PhD, U. Minn., 1956. Asst. prof. elec. engring. Milw. Sch. Engring., 1949-51; systems engr. A C Spark Plug divsn. GM, 1951-52, cons., 1959-62; instr. U. Minn., 1952-56, asst. prof. elec. engring., 1956-57; assoc. prof. elec. engring. Northwestern U., Evanston, Ill., 1957-60, prof., 1960-97, head dept. elec. engring., 1960-69; pres. IPC Systems, Inc., 1975—2004; dir. Lab. for Design of Electronic Systems Northwestern U., Evanston, Ill., 1987-97, prof. emeritus, 1997—. Cons. numerous corps., 1959—; founder, 1st chmn. Mpls. chpt. Inst. Radio Engrs. Profl. Group on Automatic Control, 1956-57, Chgo. chpt., 1959-61; expert witness in numerous patent suits, 1997-2004. Author: Basic Automatic Control Theory, 1957, 2d edit., 1966, Control Engineering, 1959; contbr. numerous articles, papers to profl. jours.; patentee TV, electronic timers, periodontal instruments and motion control systems. Mem. indsl. adv. com. Milw. Sch. Engring., 1971-2001. Served with USN, 1945-46. Recipient ECE Centennial medal U. Wis., 1991, Outstanding Alumnus award Milw. Sch. Engring. Alumni Assn., 1974; named One of Chgo.'s Ten Outstanding Young Men Chgo. Jaycees, 1961. Fellow IEEE (for edn. and rsch. in automatic control 1967); mem. feedback control systems com. 1960-68, discrete systems com. 1962-68, adminstrv. com. profl. group on automatic control 1966-69, chmn. membership and nominating coms. 1966-67); mem. Am. Automatic Control Coun. (edn. com. 1967-69), Engr.'s Coun. for Profl. Devel. (guidance com. 1967-69), Nat. Electronic Conf. (bd. dirs. 1983-85), Am. Electronics Assn. (exec. com. M.W. coun. 1990-93), Sigma Xi, Eta Kappa Nu, Tau Beta Pi. Home: 638 Garden Ct Glenview IL 60025-4105 Office: Northwestern U Elec Engring & Computer Sci Dept Evanston IL 60208 Office Phone: 847-491-7258.

MURPHY, GREGORY E., insurance company executive; Grad., Boston Coll.; grad. Advanced Mgmt. Program, Harvard Univ.; grad., MIT Sloan Sch. Mgmt. CPA Harvard Advanced Mgmt. Program, MIT Solan Sch. Mgmt. Joined Selective Ins. Group Inc., 1980, sr. v.p. fin., 1994—95, sr. v.p., CFO, 1995—97, COO, 1997—99, pres., 1997—, CEO, 1999—, chmn., 2000—. Bd. trustees Newton Meml. Hosp. Found. Mem.: Newton Meml. Hosp. Found. (bd. trustees), Property Casualty Insurers Assn. America (bd. gov.'s), Ins. Info. Inst. (Ill.) (bd. dirs.), Am. Inst. for Chartered Property Casualty Underwriters (bd. trustees), Ins. Inst. of Am. (bd. trustees). Office: Selective Ins Group 40 Wantage Ave Branchville NJ 07890 Office Phone: 973-948-3000.

MURPHY, HAROLD LOYD, federal judge; b. Haralson County, Ga., Mar. 31, 1927; s. James Loyd and Georgia Gladys (McBrayer) M.; m. Jacqueline Marie Ferri, Dec. 20, 1958; children: Mark Harold, Paul Bailey. Student, West Ga. Coll., 1944-45, U. Miss., 1945-46; LL.B., U. Ga., 1949. Bar: Ga. 1949. Pvt. practice, Buchanan, Ga., from 1949; ptnr. Howe & Murphy, Buchanan and Tallapoosa, Ga., 1958-71; judge Superior Cts., Tallapoosa Circuit, 1971-77; U.S. dist. judge No. Dist. of Ga., Rome, 1977—. Rep. Gen. Assembly of Ga., 1951-61; asst. solicitor gen. Tallapoosa Jud. Circuit, 1956; mem. Jud. Qualifications Commn., State of Ga., 1977 With USNR, 1945-46. Fellow Am. Bar Found.; mem. ABA, Ga. Bar Assn., Dist. Judges Assn. for 11th Cir. Bar Assn., Am. Judicature Soc., Tallapoosa Cir. Bar Assn., Old War Horse Lawyers Club, Am. Inns Ct. (past pres. Joseph Henry Lumpkin sect.), Fed. Judges Assn. Methodist. Home: 3 Haley Dr SE Rome GA 30161 also: 600 E 1st St Rm 311 Rome GA 30161-3187

MURPHY, HELEN, recording industry executive; b. Glasgow, Scotland, Oct. 2, 1962; came to U.S., 1990; d. Francis and Kathleen (Gallagher) M.; m. Michael Christopher Luksha, Apr. 1, 1989. BA in Econs. with honors, U. Guelph, Can., 1982; MBA, U. Western Ontario, Can., 1984. CFA. Asst. mgr. securities rsch. Confederation Life, Toronto, Can., 1984-86; sr. analyst entertainment & merchandising Prudential Bache Securities, Toronto, Can., 1986-89; v.p. rsch. Richardson Greenshields Can., Toronto, 1989-90; v.p. investor rels. Polygram Holding, Inc., NYC, 1990-91; v.p., treas. Polygram Records Inc., NYC, 1991-92, sr. v.p. corp. fin., treas., 1992-95; sr. v.p. investor rels. PolyGram Internat. Ltd., NYC, 1995-97; sr. v.p. mergers and acquisitions PolyGram Holding, Inc., NYC, 1995-97, CFO, 1997-99, Westvaco Corp., 1999; CFO & chief adminstrv. office Martha Stewart Living Omnimedia, Inc., NYC, 1999—2001; exec. v.p., CFO Warner Music Group, 2001—. Lectr. U. Guelph, 1982-90. Fellow Nat. Investor Rels. Inst., N.Y. Soc. Security Analysts, N.Y. Treas. Group. Office: Warner Music Group 75 Rockefeller Plz New York NY 10019

MURPHY, J. ANDREW (DREW MURPHY), energy executive, lawyer; b. Stanford, Calif., Jan. 21, 1961; Student, Univ. Munich, Germany; BA cum laude, Harvard Univ., 1983; JD high honors, George Washington Univ., 1987. Ptnr., head, Project Devel., Fin., Leasing Team Hunton & Williams LLP, Washington & NYC, and mem. exec. com.; exec. v.p., gen. counsel NRG Energy, Inc., Princeton, NJ, 2006—09, exec. v.p., regional pres. N.E., 2009—. Mem.: ABA, Am. Coll. Investment Counsel. Office: NRG Energy, Inc 211 Carnegie Ctr Princeton NJ 08540 Office Phone: 609-524-4500.*

MURPHY, JAMES EDWARD, public relations and marketing executive; Degree in Journalism, U. Ill. Sr. corp. comms. officer Owens-Corning Fiberglas, Beatrice, Merrill Lynch; exec. v.p. Burson-Marsteller, vice chmn., 1990, chmn., CEO Ams., 1991-93; chmn., CEO Murphy & Co., 1993—; chief mktg. and comm. officer Accenture (formerly known as Andersen Cons.), 1993—. Mem. bd. advisors Medill Sch. Journalism, Northwestern U.; mem. devel. bd. Coll. Comm., U. Ill.; past pres., bd. dirs. Arthur Page Soc.; chmn. PR Coalition. Mem. Inst. Pub. Rels. Rsch. (trustee), Union League Club, Belle Haven Club, Woodway Country Club, Palmetto Golf Club, Preston Mountain Club. Office: Accenture 6th Fl 1345 Avenue of the Americas New York NY 10105 E-mail: james.e.murphy@accenture.com.

MURPHY, JANE HOLT, history professor; b. Denver, July 18, 1972; d. John Leo and Isabel Holt Murphy; m. Safwan A. Almomani, June 2, 1998; children: Sophia Momani, Zaid Momani. BA magna cum laude, Yale U., New Haven, Conn., 1995; PhD, Princeton U., NJ, 2006. Lectr. Princeton U., 2006—07; asst. prof. Colo. Coll., 2007—. Contbr. articles to profl. jours. Rsch. fellowship, Am. Rsch. Ctr. Egypt, 2003. Mem.: History Sci. Soc., Mid. East Studies Assn., Phi Beta Kappa (Yale U. Chpt.). Office: Colo Coll 14 E Cache La Poudre Colorado Springs CO 80903 Office Fax: 719-389-6524. Business E-Mail: jane.murphy@coloradocollege.edu.

MURPHY, JENNIFER H. (BUFFY MURPHY), elementary school educator; b. Columbia, SC; BA in Recreational Therapy, Clemson (SC) Univ.; MA in Edn., Univ. SC; grad. student, Coll. Charleston. Cert. Nat. Bd. Tchg. Standards, Assisting, Developing, and Evaluating Profl. Tchg. (ADEPT) evaluator. Tchr. Irmo (SC) Elem. Sch. Tchr.-in-residence and adv. bd. mem. Ctr. for Educator Recruitment, Retention and Advancement (CERRA) Inst. Higher Edn., SC; clin. adj. Univ. SC Profl. Devel. Sch. Program. Named SC Tchr. of Yr., 2007. Office: Irmo Elem Sch 7401 Gibbes St Irmo SC 29063 Business E-Mail: bmurphy@lex5.k12.sc.us.

MURPHY, JEREMIAH T., professional sports team, construction executive; b. NYC, July 21, 1944; m. Sandra Murphy; children: Lisa, Tara, Gregory. BA, Bernard Baruch Coll. CPA Calif. Sr. ptnr. Bowman and Co., Stockton, Calif., 1971-82; CFO A.G. Spanos Companies, Stockton, Calif., 1982—; v.p. San Diego Chargers. Mem.: Calif. Soc. of CPAs, Am. Inst. of CPAs. Office: AG Spanos Companies 10100 Trinity Pky Stockton CA 95219 also: San Diego Chargers 4020 Murphy Canyon Rd San Diego CA 92123

MURPHY, JOHN B., portfolio manager; b. Pitts., May 30, 1947; s. John Bernard and Knolle Cordelia (Bonham) M.; m. Lauren Osa Brown, Mar. 20, 1994; children: Kira Mei Li, Anya Cai Li. BA, U. New Orleans, 1970; MBA, Columbia U., 1984. CFA 1987. Dir. La. Heritage Fair, New Orleans, 1974-75, 78-80; assoc. dir. New Orleans Jazz and Heritage Festival, 1978-80; exec. dir. New Orleans Jazz and Heritage Found. Inc., 1980; assoc. editor, analyst Value Line Pubs., NYC, 1984-86; equity analyst, v.p. Drexel, Burnham, Lambert, NYC, 1986-90; portfolio mgr., mng. dir., head convertible investments Guardian, NYC, 1990—. Mng. dir. Family Svc. Life and other Guardian subs., 1998—; mem. alumni counseling bd. Sch. Bus. Columbia U., NYC, 1986—; prodn. cons. Newport Jazz Festival, Capitol Radio Jazz Festival, Memphis Heritage Festival, 1978-80. Recipient Mayoralty Merit award City of New Orleans, 1978. Mem. Assn. Investment Mgmt. and Rsch., N.Y. Soc. Security Analysts, Beta Gamma Sigma (scholarship award 1983). Avocations: poetry, photography, golf. Office: Guardian 7 Hanover Sq New York NY 10004-2616 Home: PO Box 72 Ardsley On Hudson NY 10503-0072

MURPHY, JOHN CONDRON, JR., lawyer; b. Mpls., May 26, 1945; s. John Condron and Elaine Anne (Wentink) M.; m. Marie Antoinette Calcara, Aug. 17, 1968; children: Justin Peter, Jonathan Patrick. AB cum laude, Georgetown U., Washington, 1967; JD cum laude, U. Pa., 1972. Bar: Calif. 1972, D.C. 1978. Assoc. O'Melveny & Myers, LA, 1972-75; spl. counsel U.S Securities & Exch. Commn., Washington, 1975-77; assoc. Cleary Gottlieb Steen & Hamilton LLP, Washington, 1977—81, ptnr., 1982-84, 87—; gen. counsel Fed. Deposit Ins. Corp., Washington, 1984-87. Mem. bd. editors Banking Policy Report, 1988—; contbr. articles to profl. jours. Lt. (j.g.) USNR, 1968-69. Mem. ABA (subcom. chmn. banking law com., chmn. acquisitions and dispositions subcom. 1992-95), Fed. Bar Assn. (chmn. banking law com. 1992-94), Columbia Country Club (Chevy Chase, Md.). Roman Catholic. Home: 6 Newlands St Chevy Chase MD 20815-4202 Office Phone: 202-974-1580.

MURPHY, JOHN F., lawyer; b. Jersey City, May 24, 1954; s. John Francis and Helen Joan (Makowski) M.; m. Bridget Fagan, Aug. 4, 1984; children: Helen Mary, John William. BA, U. Conn., 1976; JD, Washington & Lee U., 1979. Bar: Mo. 1979, US Dist. Ct. (we. dist.) Mo. 1979, US Ct. Appeals (8th cir.) 1982, US Supreme Ct. 1991. Assoc. Shook, Hardy & Bacon LLP, Kansas City, Mo., 1979-85, ptnr., 1985—, chmn., 2003—. Bd. dirs. Lakemary Ctr. Endowment Assn., Paola, Kans., Friends of Spl. People, Starlight Theatre, Cath. Edn. Found.; pres. Waterford Homes Assn., 1994. Mem. Fedn. Defense and Corp. Counsel, Mo. Bar Assn., Kansas City Met. Bar Assn., Greater Kansas City C. of C. (bd. dirs.), Kansas City Econ. Devel. Corp.(bd. dirs.), Civic Coun. Greater Kans. City, Phi Beta Kappa, Phi Kappa Phi, Omicron Delta Kappa. Republican. Roman Catholic. Avocations: running, spectator sports. Office: Shook Hardy & Bacon LLP 2555 Grand Blvd Kansas City MO 64108 Office Phone: 816-474-6550. Office Fax: 816-421-5547. Business E-Mail: jmurphy@shb.com.

MURPHY, JOHN FRANCIS, law educator, consultant; b. Portchester, NY, Apr. 25, 1937; s. Francis John and Emilie (Tourtellot) M.; m. Laura S. Murphy; children: Andrew, Robert; stepchildren: Dan, Jessie, Gabriel. BA, Cornell U., 1959, LLB in Internat. Affairs, 1962. Bar: D.C. 1963, Kans. 1970, Pa. 1987. Afro-Asia Pub. Svc. fellow, India, 1962-63; assoc. Winthrop, Stimson, Putnam & Roberts, NYC, 1963-64; atty. Office Legal Adv., Dept. State, Washington, 1964-67; assoc. Kirkland, Ellis, Hodson, Chaffetz & Masters, Washington, 1967-69; assoc. prof. law U. Kans., Lawrence, 1969-72, prof. law, 1972-84, assoc. dean Sch. Law, 1975-77; vis. prof. law Villanova U., Pa., 1983-84, prof. law sch. law, 1984—. Vis. prof. law Cornell U., Ithaca, N.Y., fall 1979, Georgetown U., summer 1982, San Diego U., summer Paris, 1986, 95, Mexico City, 1988, London, 1989, La. State U. summer, Aix-en-Provence, 1990, Haifa (Israel) U., 1997; Charles H. Stockton Prof. Internat. Law, Naval War Coll., 1980-81. Author: Legal Aspects of International Terrorism: Summary Report of an International Conference, 1980, The United Nations and the Control of International Violence, 1982, Punishing International Terrorists, 1985, State Support of International Terrorism: Legal, Political and Economic Dimensions, 1989, (with Alan Swan) The Regulation of International Business and Economic Relations, 1991, Supplements, 1994, 95, 2d edit., 1999 (cert. of merit Am. Soc. Internat. Law 1992), (with James D. Dinnage) The Constitutional Law of the European Union, 1996, Supplement, 1999, 2d edit., 2008, The United States and The Rule of Law in International Affairs, 2004; contbr. articles, comments, book revs. to profl., popular jours.; editor (with Alona E. Evans), contbg. author: Legal Aspects of International Terrorism, 1978; bd. editors Cornell Law Quar., 1961, 62; mem. bd. editors Terrorism: An Internat. Jour., 1981-92, Terrorism and Polit. Violence, 1993-2003, The Internat. Lawyer, 1998—, Transnat. Publishers, 1999-2006; mem. editl. bd. Internat. Law Studies, Naval War Coll., 2003—. Mem.: ABA (alt. rep. to US Mission to UN 2006—), Internat. Law Assn. (hon. v.p., Am. Br. 2005—), Am. Soc. Internat. Law. Episcopalian. Office: Villanova U Sch Law 299 N Spring Mill Rd Villanova PA 19085 Home Phone: 610-431-1984; Office Phone: 610-519-7065. Business E-Mail: murphy@law.villanova.edu.

MURPHY, JOHN JOSEPH, manufacturing executive; b. Olean, NY, Nov. 24, 1931; s. John Joseph and Mary M.; m. Louise John; children: Kathleen A. Murphy Bell, Karen L. Murphy Rochelli, Patricia L. Murphy Smith, Michael J. AAS in Mech. Engring., Rochester Inst. Tech., 1952; MBA, So. Meth. U., 1981. Engr. Clark div. Dresser Industries, Olean, 1952-67, gen. mgr. roots blower div. Connersville, Ind., 1967-69, pres. crane, hoist and tower div. Muskegon, Mich., 1969-70, pres. machinery group Houston, 1970-75, sr. v.p. ops. Dallas, 1980, exec. v.p., 1982, pres., 1982-92, CEO, 1983—95, chmn. bd., 1983-96; mng. dir. SMG Mgmt. L.L.C., Dallas, 1997-2000. Bd. dirs. W.R. Grace & Co.,emeritus mem. Bus. Coun. With US Army, 1954—56. Office: 3838 Oak Lawn Ave Ste 777 Dallas TX 75219

MURPHY, JOHN VINCENT, investment company executive; b. Boston, July 12, 1949; s. James Gerald and Mary Lee (Dolan) Murphy; m. Kathleen Ryan, Nov. 17, 1973; children: Elizabeth Ryan, Christopher John, Carolyn Holmes. BS, Boston Coll., 1971. CPA Mass. Acct. Arthur Andersen & Co., CPAs, Boston, 1972—77; contr. Continental Investment Corp., Boston, 1977—81; v.p., contr. Torchmark Fin. Svcs. Co., Boston, 1981—85; sr. v.p. fin., CFO Liberty Fin. Svcs., Inc., Boston, 1985; exec. v.p. Mass. Mut. Life Ins. Co.; with OppenheimerFunds, Inc., 2000—, pres., 2001—07, COO, chmn., CEO, 2001—. Treas. Liberty Real Estate Corp., 1981, Torchmark Leasing Programs, Inc., Boston, 1981—85, Copley Venture Capital Inc., 1984, Liberty Asset Mgmt. Co., 1985; bd. dirs. Fiduciary Trust Co. NH, Chatham Fin. Assocs., 1983—85; bd. dirs., pres. MassMutual Instl. Funds., MML Series Funds; bd. govs. Investment Co. Inst.; del. Fin. Svcs. Roundtable; pres., bd. mem. Oppenheimer Acquisition Corp. Chmn. Alumni Capital Campaign Boston Coll. HS, 1986—87, mem. devel. adv. com. to bd. trustees; mem. Wall St. Coun. exec. com. Boston Coll.; bd. dirs. Project Rebirth, Inc., 2004—. Served in US Army, 1971—72. Recipient Man of Yr. award, NY Gov.'s Com. on Scholastic Achievement; named one of 30 Most Influential People in Investing, SmartMoney mag., 2001. Mem.: AICPA, Greater Boston C. of C. Execs. Club, Fin. Execs. Inst., Mass. Soc. CPAs, Shriver, Charitable Irish Soc., Algonquin, Blue Chips, Boston Racquet, Boston Coll Varsity (pres. 1980—82). Office: OppenheimerFunds Inc Two World Fin Ctr 225 Liberty St New York NY 10281-1008

MURPHY, JOSEPH ALBERT, JR., lawyer; b. Grosse Pointe, Mich., May 29, 1934; s. Joseph Albert and Isabel C. (Callahan) M.; m. Joanne Becker, June 24, 1961; children: Michael, Joseph III. BS, Georgetown U., 1956; JD, Detroit Coll. Law, Mich. State U., 1962. Bar: Mich. 1962, D.C. 1996. House counsel Blue Cross Mich., Detroit, 1964-69, gen. counsel, corp. sec., 1969-75; v.p., gen. counsel Blue Cross & Blue Shield Mich., Detroit, 1975—88; chief Washington counsel Blue Cross and Blue Shield Assn., Washington, 1989—2001; cons. eLawForum, Washington, 2002—. Chmn. Health Care Network, Southfield, Mich., 1981-85, Blue Care Inc., Southfield, 1986-88;. Editl. adv. bd. Thompson Pub., 2005—. Allocations panel United Found., Detroit, 1985-88; treas. Grosse Pointe Dem. Club, 1972-73; chmn. Health and People's Polit. Action Commn., Detroit, 1978-84; fundraiser United Way of Nat. Capital Area, 2005—. With U.S. Army, 1957-59. Mem. ABA, Mich. Bar

Assn., Detroit Bar Assn., DC Bar Assn., Am. Health Lawyers Assn. (pres. 1981-82), Am. Corp. Counsel Assn., Am. Arbitrators Assn. (panel of arbitrators). Roman Catholic. Home: 2717 O St NW Washington DC 20007-3128

MURPHY, JOSEPH EDWARD, JR., broadcast executive; b. Mpls., Mar. 13, 1930; s. Joseph Edward Murphy and Ann Hynes; m. Diana Kuske, July 24, 1958; children: Michael, John. BA, Princeton U., 1952; postgrad., U. Minn., 1956-60. Chartered fin. analyst. Dir. investment rsch. Woodward-Elwood & Co., Mpls., 1961-67; v.p. Northwestern Nat. Bank, Mpls., 1967-83; chmn. Midwest Communications, Inc., Mpls., 1990-92; ret. Dir. Midwest Comm., Inc., 1956-89, vice chmn., 1985-89. Author: Adventure Beyond the Clouds: How We Climbed China's Highest Mountain and Survived, 1986 (Friends Am. Writers award 1986), With Interest: How to Profit From Interest Rate Fluctuations, 1987, Stock Market Probability, 1988, revised edit., 1994, South to the Pole by Ski, 1990, The Random Character of Interest Rates, 1990, To the Poles by Ski and Dogsled, 1996, Bond Tables of Probable Future Yields, 1996, The Random Character of Corporate Earnings, 1997, Why the Stock Market Rises, 1998. Vice chmn. Minn. Coun. on Quality Edn., 1971-77; trustee Macalester Coll., St. Paul, 1973-87, Mpls. Soc. Fine Arts, 1977-78, Voyageur Outward Bound, 1985-92; bd. dirs. Minn. Opera Co., 1971-80, Childrens Theater Co., 1975-80, Minn. Ctr. for Book Arts, 1987-93, Greater Mpls. coun. Girl Scouts U.S.A., 1987-93, Fund for Peace, 1988-92, Minn. Nature Conservancy, 1991-96. 2d lt. U.S. Army, 1952-55. Mem. Am. Alpine Club (life, v.p. and bd. dirs. 1975-81), Himalayan Club (life), Mpls. Club. Avocations: mountain climbing, exploration. Home: 2116 W Lake Isle Minneapolis MN 55405-2425

MURPHY, JOSEPH F., Judge, Maryland Court of Appeals; b. Fitchburg, Mass., Jan. 9, 1944; AB, Boston Coll., 1965; JD, U. Md. Sch. Law, 1969. Bar: Md. 1969. Asst. state's atty. Baltimore City, 1970—75, dep. state's atty., 1975—76; instr., evidence U. Balt. Sch. Law, 1974; instr., trial practice U. Md. Sch. Law, 1981—; assoc. judge, 3rd jud. cir. Balt. County Cir. Ct., 1984—93; judge Md. Ct. Spl. Appeals, 1993—96, chief judge at-large, 1996—2007; judge Md. Ct. of Appeals, 2007—. Mem. Code Revision Com., 1991—2004; chair Article 27 (crimes & punishments) Revision Com., 1991—; mem. Task Force to Examine Crime Victims' Rights Law in Md., 1995—2003; chair Court of Appeals Standing Com. on Rules of Practice and Procedure, 1996—; mem. libr. com. State Law Libr., 1997—2007; mem. Md. Alternative Dispute Resolution Commn., 1998—2001, Tech. Oversight Bd., 1999—2007, Jud. Cabinet, 2000—07; jud. coun. Md. Jud. Conf., 2000—07; adv. bd. Md. Mediation and Conflict Resolution Office, 2001—. Contbr. articles to legal jours. Officer, trustee Md. Inst. the Continuing Profl. Edn. of Lawyers, 1984—88; bd. dirs. Md. Jud. Inst., 1985—93, 1995—2000; pres. J. Dudley Digges Inn of Court, 1989—90. Recipient Outstanding Part-Time Instr. award, U. Balt., 1976—77, 1996, Profl. Excellence in the Advancement of Legal Competence award, Maryland Bar Found., 1994, Md. Champion for Victims award, Md. Crime Victims' Resource Ctr., 2003, Md. Top Leadership in Law award, Daily Record, 2003, Man of All Seasons award, St. Thomas More Soc. Md., 2004; fellow, Md. Bar Found. Inc., 1984—. Mem.: Md. Criminal Def. Attorneys Assn. (pres. 1984), Md. State's Attorneys' Assn., Balt. County Bar Assn., Md. State Bar Assn. (criminal pattern jury instructions com. 1980—, com. on laws 1988—, chair, criminal law sect. coun. 1987—88, Robert C. Heeney Meml. award, criminal law sect. coun. 1990). Office: County Cts Bldg 401 Bosley Ave Towson MD 21204 Office Phone: 410-887-3206.*

MURPHY, JOSEPH JAMES, chiropractic physician; b. Newark, July 30, 1956; s. Joseph P. and Roberta (Nittolo) Murphy; children: Joseph Raymond, Alexandra Renee; m. Maria Elena Sileo, Feb. 17, 2002; children: Sean Alfred, Mia Carmen. BA in Biology, Rider Coll., Lawrenceville, NJ, 1978; D in Chiropractic Medicine, Palmer Coll., Davenport, Iowa, 1984. Diplomate Nat. Bd. Chiropractic Examiners; cert. NJ State Bd. Med. Examiners. Rsch. chemist Mallinkrodt, Inc., Englewood, NJ, 1979-81; staff physician Mid-Island Chiropractic, Levittown, NY, 1984; dir., chief exec. officer Suburban Chiropractic Ctr., Chatham, NJ, 1984—. Apptd. mem. NJ Bd. Chiropractic Examiners, 2000—, sec., 2003, pres., 2006. Mem. editl. bd. Am. Chiropractor Mag., 2000—; editor-in-chief newsletter The Column. Advisor Chatham High Sch. Key Club, 1986-87; chmn. Bd. Trustees, 2008; trustee Early Childhood Learning Ctr., Chatham, 1999—, sec. 2002, chmn. bd., 2008-; mem. spkrs. bur. Am. Heart Assn. D. D. Palmer scholar, 1981, 82, 83. Mem.: AAAS, APHA, Morris County Chiropractic Soc. (pres. 1987—, bd. pres. 2006), Bd. Chiropractic Examiners (apptd. mem. State of N.J.), Internat. Soc. Food Technologists, NY Acad. Sci., NJ Chiropractic Soc. (editor-in-chief Jersey Jour. 1986—, bd. dirs. 1987—, chmn. inter profl. rels. com. 1989—, 1st v.p. 1992—95, pres. 1995—, Meritorious Svc. award 1986, Disting. Svc. award 1987—97), Am. Chiropractic Assn., Am. Assn. Cereal Chemists, Chatham C. of C. (chmn. profl. rels. com. 1988—92, pres. 1989—92, Dist. Mem. Svc. award 1996), Chatham Hist. Preservation Commn. (mayor apptd. mem.), Kiwanis (bd. dirs. Chatham club 1986—89, Disting. Svc. award 1995), Tri Beta. Republican. Presbyn. Avocations: skiing, photography, model building, automobiles, bicycling. Home: 20 Squire Ct Basking Ridge NJ 07920 Office: Suburban Chiropractic Ctr 301 Main St Chatham NJ 07928-2410 Office Phone: 973-635-0036. Business E-Mail: drmurphy@drmurphy.com.

MURPHY, JUDITH CHISHOLM, trust company executive; b. Chippewa Falls, Wis., Jan. 26, 1942; d. John David and Bernice A. (Hartman) Chisholm. BA, Manhattanville Coll., 1964; postgrad., New Sch. for Social Research, 1965-68, Nat. Grad. Trust Sch., 1975. Asst. portfolio mgr. Chase Manhattan Bank, N.A., NYC, 1964-68; trust investment officer Marshall & Ilsley Bank, Milw., 1968-72, asst. v.p., 1972-74, v.p., 1974-75; v.p., treas. Marshall & Ilsley Invesmtent Mgmt. Corp., Milw., 1975-94; v.p. Marshall & Ilsley Trust Co., Phoenix, 1982—, Marshall & Ilsley Trust Co. Fla., Naples, 1985—; v.p., dir. instnl. sales Marshall & Ilsley Trust Co., Milw., 1994-97, sr. v.p., 1997-98, M&I Investment Mgmt. Corp., 1998—. Coun. mem. Am. Bankers Assn., Washington, 1984-86; govt. relations com. Wis. Bankers Assn., Madison, 1982-88. Contbr. articles to profl. jours. Chmn. Milw. City Plan Commn., 1986—97; commr. Milw. County Commn. on Handicapped, 1988—90; bd. dirs. Cardinal Stritch Coll., Milw., 1980—89, Children's Hosp. Wis., Milw., 1989—98, Milw. Ballet Co., 1996—2001, Milw. Ctr. for Independence, 1999—2004, Girl Scouts Milw. Area, 2002—06, Milw. Symphony Orch., 2002—, Alzheimers Assn., 2007—. Recipient Outstanding Achievement award YWCA Greater Milw., 1985, Sacajawea award Profl. Dimensions, Milw., 1988, Pro Urbe award Mt. Mary Coll., 1988, Vol. award Milw. Found., 1992; named Disting. Woman in Banking, Comml. West Mag., 1988. Mem. Milw. Analysts Soc. (sec. 1974-77, bd. dirs. 1977-80), Fin. Women Internat. (bd. dirs., v.p. 1976-80), Am. Inst. Banking (instr. 1975-78), TEMPO (charter), Profl. Dimensions (hon.), University Club, Woman's Club Wis., Rotary. Democrat. Roman Catholic. Home: 3622 N Lake Dr Milwaukee WI 53211-2644 Office: M&I Investment Mgmt Corp 111 E Kilbourn Ave Milwaukee WI 53202-3197 Office Phone: 414-287-8768. Business E-Mail: judith.murphy@micorp.com.

MURPHY, KATHLEEN A., diversified financial services company executive; m. George Hornyak; 1 child, Jack. BA in Econs. & Polit. Sci., summa cum laude, Fairfield U., Conn., 1984; JD with highest honors, U. Conn., 1987. Various leadership positions including gen. counsel and chief compliance officer Aetna Fin. Services, 1985—2000; with ING US Fin. Services, 2000—08, gen. counsel, chief adminstrv. officer, group pres., worksite and instl. fin. services, 2003—06, CEO, wealth mgmt., 2006—08; pres. personal investing Fidelity Investments, 2009—. Sec., treas. bd. dirs. America's Promise; vice chair, bd. dirs. Conn. Bus. and Industry Assn.; mem. leader's coun. ING; bd. dirs. ING Can. Nat. trustee Boys & Girls Club America; adv. bd. U. Dublin Smurfit Sch. Bus.; bd. dirs. U. Conn. Found. Named one of The 50 Most Powerful Women in Bus., Fortune mag., 2007, 2008, The 25 Most Powerful Women in Banking, US Banker mag., 2008; named to Bus. 100 List, Irish Am. Mag., Wall St. 50. Office: Fidelity Investments 82 Devonshire St Boston MA 02109-3605 Office Phone: 617-392-2100. Office Fax: 617-476-6150.*

MURPHY, KATHLEEN S., science educator; b. Cleve., July 16, 1956; d. Janice Lee and Raymond L Maher; children: James L. Globokar, Leo F., Kristine E. BS, Cleve. State U., 1978; MEd, Ashland U., Ohio, 1995. Lic. sci., health and phys. edn. tchr. Ohio, 1978, class I umpire Ohio HS Athletic Assn., 1978. Sci. tchr. Twinsburg Sch. Dist., Ohio, 1993—. Umpire Regional and State Tournament, 1997—2000, 2003—08, NCAA Divsn. II Nat. Tournament, 1999, 2000, Ohio Athletic Conf., 2004, 05, 06, 07; bd. dirs. Suburban Umpires Assn., Berea, Ohio, 2002—; regional umpire NAIA, 2007, 08. Recipient Exemplary Tchr. award, Summit County Ednl. Assn., 1998—99. Mem.: NEA (union rep.), Ohio Edn. Assn., Ohio HS Assn., World Wildlife Fedn. Roman Catholic. Avocations: golf, travel. Office: Twinsburg High Sch 10084 Ravenna Rd Twinsburg OH 44087 Home: 7100 W Cross Creek Trail Brecksville OH 44141

MURPHY, KENNY R., finance educator; b. Weikegan, Ill., Apr. 21, 1969; s. Kenneth R. and Peggy J. Murphy; m. Dawn M. Bonnell. BS, Ga. Southern U., Statesboro, 1994. Bus. edn. instr. Valdosta HS, Ga., 1995—2000, Bacon County Sch. Dist., Alma, Ga., 2000—05, alternative sch. dir., 2005—. Bd. mem. Tax Equalization Bd., Alma, Ga., 2008. Mem.: PAGE. Methodist. Home: 103 New Hope Ch Rd Alma GA 31510 Office: Bacon County Sch Dist 102 W 4th St Alma GA 31510 Business E-Mail: kmurphy@bcraiders.com.

MURPHY, KEVIN M., economics professor; AB, U. Calif., 1981; PhD, U. Chgo., 1986. Asst. prof. bus. economics and indsl. rels. U. Chgo., 1986—88, assoc. prof., 1988—89, prof., 1989—93, George Pratt Schultz prof., 1993—2002, George J. Stigler prof. economics, 2002—, George J. Stigler disting. svc. prof. economics, dept. economics and grad. sch. bus., 2005—. Faculty rsch. assoc. Nat. Bur. Econ. Rsch. Co-author: Social Economics: Market Behavior in a Social Environment, 2000; co-editor: Measuring the Gains from Medical Research: An Economic Approach, 2003; contbr. articles to profl. jours. Recipient John Bates Clark Medal, Am. Econ. Assn., 1998; named MacArthur fellow, John D. and Catherin T. MacArthur Found., 2005; fellow, Earhart Found., 1980—81, 1983—84, Friedman Fund, 1981—83, Sloan Found., 1989—91. Fellow: Econometric Soc.; mem.: Am. Acad. Arts and Scis., Phi Beta Kappa. Office: Univ Chgo Grad Sch Bus 5807 S Woodlawn Ave Chicago IL 60637 Office Phone: 773-702-7280. Office Fax: 773-702-2699. E-mail: murphy@chicagogsb.edu.*

MURPHY, KEVIN M., state banking agency administrator; Grad., Northeastern U., Boston, Rutgers U. Stonier Grad. Sch. Banking. Positions including bank examiner in MW and New Eng. FDIC, asst. regional dir. Mpls. regional office Washington, 1982—96; pvt. sector banking cons.; dep. commr. Minn. Dept. Commerce Fin. Instn. Divsn., 1998—. Office: Minn Dept Commerce Fin Instn Divsn 85 7th Place E Ste 500 Saint Paul MN 55101-2198 Office Phone: 651-296-2715. Office Fax: 651-296-8591. E-mail: kevin.murphy@state.mn.us.*

MURPHY, KEVIN R., psychology professor; BA in Psychology, Siena Coll., Loudonville, NY, 1974; MS in Indsl./Orgnl. Psychology, Rensselaer Poly. Inst., 1976; PhD in Indsl./Orgnl. Psychology, Pa. State U., 1979. Asst. prof. psychology Rice U., Tex., 1979—81, NYU, NYC, 1981—84, Colo. State U., 1984—86, assoc. prof. psychology, 1986—88, prof. psychology, 1988—2000, Pa. State U., 2000—06, head dept. psychology, 2003—06, dir., Internat. Ctr. the Study Terrorism, 2006—, prof. psychology and info. sciences and tech., 2006—. Editor: Jour. Applied Psychology; editl. bd. Human Performance, Human Resource Mgmt. Rev., Jour. Indsl. Psychology, Internat. Jour. Mgmt. Rev., Internat. Jour. Selection and Assessment. Fellow: APA (coun. editors 1996—, mem. conf. rev. com., sci. directorate 2004—06, mem. com. on sci. awards 2006—08), Assn. Psychol. Sci., Soc. Indsl. and Orgnl. Psychology (pres. 1997, Disting. Sci. Contbn. award 2004); mem.: Internat. Assn. Applied Psychology. Office: Dept Psychology Pa State Univ 415 Moore Bldg & 431 Beam Bldg University Park PA 16802-3106 Office Phone: 814-863-3373, 814-865-4818. Office Fax: 814-863-7002. E-mail: krmurphy@psu.edu.*

MURPHY, KIMBERLY ANN, biology professor; b. Mexico, Mo. d. James William and Carol Ruth Murphy. BS in Cell & Molecular Biology, Winona State U., Minn.; PhD in Genetics and Cell Biology, Wash. State U., Pullman. Postdoc. fellow Syracuse U., NY, 2005—07; asst. prof. biology Waldorf Coll., Forest City, Iowa, 2007—. Jr. high judging chair State Sci. and Tech. Fair Iowa. Mem.: Iowa Acad. Sci., Am. Soc. Microbiology. Achievements include research in myxococcus xanthus fruiting body development.

MURPHY, LESLEY RYANN, geneticist; d. Lea Ann Ekman; 1 child, William. BS in Marine Biology, U. NC, Wilmington, 1996, MS in Biology, 2000; PhD in Botany, Wash. State U., Pullman, 2007. Grad. tchg. asst. Wash. State U., 2000—05, USDA Biol. Sci. Tech., 2005—08; geneticist USDA, Pullman, 2008—. Contbr. articles to profl. jours. Recipient Aace award, Wash. State U., 2000—01.

MURPHY, SISTER LILLIAN, sister, not-for-profit organization executive; BS in Social Sci., U. San Francisco; MS in Pub. Health, U. Calif., Berkeley; LHD (hon.), U. San Francisco, 1998. Mem. Religious Order Sisters of Mercy, Burlingame, Calif., 1959—; pres., CEO Mercy Housing, Inc., Denver, 1987—. Bd. dirs. Nat. Housing Trust, Fannie Mae Nat. Housing Adv. Coun., Washington Mutual Nat. Cmty. Coun.; mem. editl. adv. bd. Affordable Housing Fin. mag.; past adv. com. mem. Fed. Home Loan Bank, Bank of America Cmty. Devel. Bank. Bd. dirs. Alegent Health Sys., Omaha; past bd. dirs. Cath. Health Corp., Cath. Healthcare West, Low Income Investment Fund, Colo. Trust; former pub. interest dir. Fed. Home Loan Bank, Topeka. Recipient Affordable Housing Leadership award for Lifetime Achievement, Non-Profit Housing Assn. No. Calif., 1999, Woman of Distinction award, Girl Scouts of America, 2002, 25th Ann. Housing Leadership award, Nat. Low Income Housing Coalition, 2006. Roman Catholic. Office: Mercy House 1999 Broadway Ste 1000 Denver CO 80202 Office Phone: 303-830-3300. Office Fax: 303-830-3301.*

MURPHY, MARILYN JANE, library director; b. Des Moines, Feb. 9, 1952; d. Leonard James and Susan Genevieve Condon; m. Stephen Charles Murphy, May 24, 1974; 1 child, Michael James. BA, U. Northern Iowa, Cedar Falls, 1974, MA in Ednl. Tech., 2001; MA in Libr. Sci., U. Iowa, Iowa City, 1979. Plant and soil sci. libr. Mont. State U., Bozeman, 1974—75; pub. svcs. libr. Mt. Mercy Coll., Cedar Rapids, Iowa, 1979—82, dir. libr. svcs., 1982—. Com. mem. St. Joseph Sch., Marion, Iowa, 1997—98. Recipient Women Achievement award, Waypoint Svcs. Women, Children & Families, 2003. Mem.: Linn County Libr. Consortium (pres.), Iowa Pvt. Academic Librs. (pres. 1994—94), Iowa Libr. Assn. (exec. bd. mem. 1997—2008).

MURPHY, MARION COLUCCI, writer, poet; b. Queens, NY, Mar. 6, 1940; s. Frank and Ida (Giotta) Colucci; children: Carrie, Maureen, Raygen, Erin. Free-lance profl. painter, N.Y., 1950's-80's; freelance costume mask designer, N.Y., 1969-78. Writer numerous poems; lyric recs. for syndicated radio shows, also, Petunia Revival, D.O.A. Dog, 1998, Fun Baby, Up Shoes, 1999; host radio poetry broadcastings Sta. WNYG-AM, 2003-. Mem.: Internat. Soc. Poets, Internat. Poetry Hall Fame. Avocations: solitude, music, innovating, walking and loving god's creations.

MURPHY, MARK HODGE, professional football team executive, retired professional football player; b. Fulton, NY, July 13, 1955; m. Laurie Murphy; children: Kate, Emily, Brian, Anna. Grad., Colgate U., 1977; MBA, Am. U., 1983; JD, Georgetown U. Safety Wash. Redskins, 1977—85; asst. exec. dir. Nat. Football League Players Assn.; trial atty. US Dept. Justice; commentator Nat. Pub. Radio; athletic dir. Colgate U., 1992—2003; dir. intercollegiate athletics and recreation Northwestern U., 2003—07; pres., CEO Green Bay Packers, 2008—. Recipient AstroTurf Football Bowl Subdivsn. Ctrl. Region Athletic Dir. of Yr. award, Nat. Assn. Collegiate Dirs. Athletics, 2006—07; named one of Most Influential Sports Educators in Am., Inst. Internat. Sport, 2007; named to Nat. Football Conf. Pro Bowl Team, 1983, Greater Buffalo Sports Hall of Fame, 2002. Achievements include leading the NFL with 9 interceptions in 1983; being a member of the Super Bowl XVIII Champion Washington Redskins, 1984. Office: Green Bay Packers Lambeau Field Atrium 1265 Lombardi Ave Green Bay WI 54304

MURPHY, MARK KENNETH, physicist, researcher; s. Kenneth George Murphy and Dorothy Alice Murphy-Cearns; m. Kalleen Ann Reeder, Oct. 20, 1990; children: Brian Thomas, Evan Patrick Goldsmith. BS in Physics, We. Wash. U., Bellingham, 1986; MS in Environ. and Radiol. Sci., Wash. State U., Pullman, 1999. Sr. rsch. scientist Pacific NW Nat. Lab., Richland, Wash., 1986—. Cons. Sunna Sys. Corp., Richland, Wash., 2000—04, v.p., 2006—. Contbr. articles to profl. jours. Recipient Entrepreneurial award, Battelle, 1999, R&D100 award, R&D Mag., 2000, 2006, Fed. Lab. Consortium award, U.S. Dept. Energy, 2006. Mem.: ASTM. Achievements include being part of a team that discovered compound that can prevent female infertility after radiation therapy; original scientific evaluations on the new IsoRay cesium-131 medical implant seed for cancer therapy. Avocations: genealogy, writing, camping. Office: Pacific NW Nat Lab PO Box 999 Richland WA 99354

MURPHY, MARY, retired librarian; b. Hibbing, Minn., Aug. 14, 1917; d. John Philip and Ethel Robinson Murphy. BA, St. Lawrence U., Canton, NY, 1940; BSLS, U. Ill., Urbana, 1941. Map cataloger Army Map Svc. Libr., Washington, 1943—45, acquisition specialist, 1945—46, book cataloger, reviser, 1946—52, chief reference unit, asst. chief book and periodical br., 1956—65, chief document br., 1965—68; chief info. sect. Army Topographic Command, Washington, 1968—70; chief analysis br. Def. Mapping Agy. Info. Ctr., Washington, 1970—80; ret., 1980. Spkr. in field. Contbr. articles to profl. jours. Mem.: Spl. Librs. Assn. (editor Geography and Map Divsn. Bull.), Zonta Club, Phi Beta Kappa. Democrat. Episcopalian. Avocations: reading, dance, travel, photography. Home: 8102 Birnam Wood Dr Mc Lean VA 22102-2713

MURPHY, MARY LEIGH, artist; d. Terence John and Mary Stuart Murphy. BFA in Graphic Design, U. Fla., Gainesville, 1988. Artist-in-residence Duval County Pub. Schs., Jacksonville, Fla., 1999—2000. Watercolor paintings, oil paintings, stone and bronze sculpture, mosaics, acrylic, mixed medica paintings; contbr. articles to profl. jours. and mags. Recipient Grumbacher Silver medal winner, Best of Show award, Cummer Mus. Art, Julington Creek Plantation Art Exhbn., 1999, Fabulous Fla. Exhbn., 2002, Jacksonville Watercolor Soc., 2004, FCCJ Wilson Ctr. for Arts, 2005, Ponte Vedra Cultural Ctr., 2005, Karpeles Mus., 2006, First Pl. Watercolor award, Coconut Grove Arts Fest, 2000, Meml. award, Appleton Mus. Art, Fla. Watercolor Soc. Exhbn., 2000, 1st Pl. award, Jacksonville Coalition Visual Arts, 2003, Region 1 winner, Nat. Parks Acad. Arts, 2003, Mus. Dirs. award, Cornell Museum Arts, 2003; Individual Artist fellow, Cultural Coun. of Jacksonville, 2001, 2004. Mem.: St. Augustine Art Assn. (corr.), Jacksonvile Coalition Visual Arts (assoc.), Fla. Watercolor Soc. (life Am. Artist Mags. Honor award 2002, Meml. award 2006), Jacksonville Watercolor Soc. (corr.; pres. 1999—2001, Artist Yr. award 1998), Jacksonville Shell Club (assoc.). Personal E-mail: leighmurphyart@yahoo.com.

MURPHY, MAX RAY, lawyer; b. July 18, 1934; s. Loren A. and Lois (Mink) M.; children: Michael Lee, Chad Woodrow. BA, DePauw U., 1956; JD, Yale U., 1959; postgrad., Mich. State U., 1960. Bar: Mich. 1960. Assoc. Glassen, Parr, Rhead & McLean, Lansing, Mich., 1960—67, Lokker, Boter & Dalman, Holland, Mich., 1967—69; ptnr. Dalman, Murphy, Bidol, & Bouwens, P.C., Holland, 1969—91, Cunningham Dalman, P.C., Holland, 1991—. Instr. Lansing Bus. U., 1963-67; asst. pros. atty. Ottawa County, Mich., 1967-69. Dem. candidate for Ingham County (Mich.) Pros. Atty., 1962, 1964. Mem. ABA, Ottawa County Bar Assn. (sec. 1970-71), Mich. Bar Assn. (mem. family law sect.). Home: 3169 E Crystal Waters 3 Holland MI 49424-8091 Office: 321 Settlers Rd Holland MI 49423-3778 Office Phone: 616-392-1821. Business E-Mail: maxmurphy01@charter.net.

MURPHY, MEISSA BLEU, music educator, behaviorist; d. Raymond Edward and Delcia Lucille Spry; m. Hershel Ring Murphy, Sept. 22, 1990; m. Harry Angevin Rider (dec.); children: William Cary Rider, Sheri Kay Rider, B. Ann Rider, Tiffany Ann Rider. Student, Ind. Music Sch., 1954, U. of L, 1956—60, La Salle Interior Design, 1972—78; BA in Art History and Fine Arts, Herron Art Sch., Indpls., 1987; BA in Psychology, Purdue U., 1990. Tchr. music, Indpls., pub. schs., Indpls.; behaviorist St. Vincent Hosp., New Hope-Indpls. Vocal coach, piano tchr., Indpls.; mem. faculty Am. Coll. Music, Austin, Tex.; profl. musician, guitarist and vocalist for internat. performances; chairperson Am. Coll. Musicians Nat. Auditions Piano Performance, Indpls., 2006—07. Composer: Is It Raining, 1971, Small House for Sale; composer: (music score) Christmas Mouse, 1972; composer: TV comml. Mem. Wildlife Fedn., Hist. Soc., Indpls. Zoo, Heart Drive, First Monday Symphony, Harmony Club, Symphony Womans Group. Recipient Arion award for music, 1976, Boston Mensa award, 1980, Chgo. Mensa award, 1981, Rosa Parks Tolerance award, 2002. Mem.: Am. Coll. Music, Indpls. Matinee Musicales, Indpls. Piano Tchrs. Assn., Musician's Union (Local 3), Indpls. Zool. Soc., Am. Mensa, Indpls. Art Mus., Hiking Club Indpls., First Monday Symphony Club, Harmony

Club, Psi Chi (pres. 1987—89). Methodist. Avocations: flying, music, antiques, art, art history. Office: Mrs Murphy's Westside Piano Studio 7988 Fishback Rd Indianapolis IN 46278 Office Phone: 317-297-1139. Personal E-mail: meissableu@aol.com.

MURPHY, MICHAEL EMMETT, retired food company executive; b. Winchester, Mass., Oct. 16, 1936; s. Michael Cornelius and Bridie (Curran) M.; m. Adele Anne Kasupski, Sept. 12, 1959; children: Leslie Maura, Glenn Stephen, Christopher McNeil. BS in Bus. Adminstrn, Boston Coll., 1958; MBA, Harvard, 1962. Financial analyst Maxwell House div. Gen. Foods Corp., White Plains, NY, 1962-64, cost mgr. San Leandro, Calif., 1964-65, controller Jacksonville, Fla., 1965-67, Hoboken, NJ, 1967-68, mgr. fin. planning and analysis, 1968-69; mgr. planning Hanes Corp., Winston-Salem, NC, 1969-70, corp. controller, 1970-72; v.p. adminstrn. Hanes Corp. (Hanes Knitwear), Winston-Salem, NC, 1972-74; v.p. fin. Ryder System Inc., Miami, Fla., 1974-75, exec. v.p., 1975-79; exec. v.p., dir. Sara Lee Corp., Chgo., 1979-93, vice chmn., 1993-97. Bd. dirs. GATX Corp., Payless Shoe Source, Inc., CNH Global N.V., Coach Inc., Bassett Furniture Industries, Inc., No. Funds. Mgmt. adviser Jr. Achievement, 1965-66; mem. exec. com. Hudson County Tax Rsch. Coun., 1967-68; trustee Boston Coll., 1980-88; chmn. Civic Fedn. Chgo., 1984-86; bd. dirs. Jobs for Youth, Chgo., 1983-86, Lyric Opera, 1986-2002; bd. dirs. Northwestern Meml. Hosp., Chgo., 1989-2000, Big Shoulders Fund, Chgo. Ctrl. Area Com., 1995—, Chgo. Cultural Ctr. Found., 1995—, Met. Pier and Exposition Authority, 2004—, Joffrey Ballet, 2006—; prin. Chgo. United, 1995-98. Mem. Nat. Assn. Mfrs. (bd. dirs. 1989-96, dir. Big Shoulders Fund 1995—), Cath. Theol. Union (bd. trustee 2009-), Fin. Execs. Inst., Hoboken C. of C., Winson-Salem C. of C., Miami C. of C., Internat. Platform Assn., UN Assn., Ouimet Scholar Alumni Group, Beta Gamma Sigma. Roman Catholic. Home: 1242 N Lake Shore Dr Chicago IL 60610-2361 Office: Sara Lee Corp 3 First National Plz Chicago IL 60602 Personal E-mail: mebmurphy@aol.com.

MURPHY, MICHAEL JOSEPH, former state treasurer; b. Seattle, May 24, 1947; s. John Anthony and Helen Elizabeth (Domick) M.; m. Theresa Ann Smith. BA in History, Seattle U., 1969; MBA, Pacific Luth. U., 1978. Chief adjudicator vet.'s program Office of the State Treas., Olympia, Wash., 1972-75, adminstr. pub. deposit protection commn., 1975-81, internal auditor to state treas., 1981-87; treas. Thurston County, Olympia, 1987-96, State of Wash., Olympia, 1997—2007. Mem. adv. bd. asset/liability com. Twin County Credit Union, Olympia, 1987-96; instr. profl. orgns., govt. Treas. Thurston County Dems., 1973-77. Mem. Wash. Assn. County Treasurers (bd. dirs., officer 1987-96, legis. coord. 1989-96, Pres. award 1994), Wash. Assn. County Ofcls. (bd. dirs. 1989-90), Wash. Mcpl. Treasurers Assn. (bd. dirs. 1990—, Cert. Excellence for investment policy 1992), Wash. Fin. Officers Assn. (profl. fin. officer 1988—, bd. dirs. 1997—), Nat. Assn. State Treasurers, Olympia Yacht Club, Olympia Country and Golf Club, Valley Athletic Club. Roman Catholic. Avocations: sailing, golf, travel.

MURPHY, MICHAEL R., federal judge; b. Denver, Aug. 1947; s. Roland and Mary Cecilia (Maloney) M.; m. Maureen Elizabeth Donnelly, Aug. 22, 1970; children: Amy Christina, Michael Donnelly. BA in History, Creighton U., 1969; JD, U. Wyo., 1972. Bar: Wyo. 1972, US Ct. Appeals (10th cir.) 1972, UT 1973, US Dist. Ct. UT 1974, US Dist. Ct. Wyo. 1976, US Ct. Appeals (5th cir.) 1976, US Tax Ct. 1980, US Ct. Appeals (9th cir.) 1981, US Ct. Appeals (fed. cir.) 1984. Law clk. to chief judge US Ct. Appeals (10th cir.), Salt Lake City, 1972-73; with Jones, Waldo, Holbrook & McDonough, Salt Lake City, 1973-86; judge 3rd Dist. Ct., Salt Lake City, 1986-95, presiding judge, 1990-95; judge US Ct. Appeals (10th cir.), Salt Lake City, 1995—. Mem. adv. com. on rules of civil procedure UT Supreme Ct., 1985—95, mem. bd. dist. ct. judges, 1989—90; mem. UT State Sentencing Commn., 1993—95, UT Adv. Com. on Child Support Guidelines, 1989—95, UT Child Sexual Abuse Task Force, 1989—93; mem. com. on fed.-state jurisdiction Jud. Conf. of US, 2001—07. Recipient Freedom of Info. award, Soc. Profl. Journalists, 1989, UT Minority Bar Assn. award, 1995, Alumni Achievement citation, Creighton U., 1997, Disting. Svc. award, Fed. Bar Assn. Utah Chapter, 2008; named Judge of Yr., UT State Bar, 1992. Fellow Am. Bar Found.; mem. ABA (editl. bd. Judges' Jour. 1997-99), UT Bar Assn. (chmn. alternative dispute resolution com. 1985-88), Sutherland Inn of Ct. II (past pres.). Office: 5438 Federal Bldg 125 S State St Salt Lake City UT 84138-1102 Office Phone: 801-524-5955.*

MURPHY, PAMELA ANN, musician, educator, actress; b. Cooperstown, NY, June 8, 1962; d. William John and Mary Kathryn Barrett; m. Michael Francis Murphy, II, July 11, 1987; children: Michael Francis III, Sean Patrick, Timothy Andrew. MusB, SUNY, Potsdam, 1984; MS, Western Conn. State U., 1990. Permanent tchg. lic. N.Y., cert. adjudicator NYSSMA. Music tchr. Valley Ctrl. Mid. Sch., Montgomery, NY, 1984—89, Valley Ctr. Mid. Sch., Montgomery, 1999—, Valley Ctrl. H.S., Montgomery, 1991—94, Kinry Rd. Elem. Sch., Poughkeepsie, NY, 1994—97. Guest condr. for all-county chorus Dutchess County (N.Y.) Music Educators Assn., 1994; owner, music dir. Hudson Valley Conservatory Fine Arts, Walden, NY, 1995—; profl. vocalist and keyboard player for various radio commls., weddings and bands; adjudicator state and local vocal competitions. Composer: (songs) My Love, 2002; actor: New Rose Theatre, 1996—. Facilitator fundraising activities Am. Heart Assn., Otego, NY, 1995; artistic dir. Hudson Valley Parents Performing Students, Walden, 1997—; fundraiser Muscular Dystrophy Assn., Newburgh, NY, 2003. Mem.: Orange County Music Educators Assn. (guest condr. for all-county chorus 1986, 1989, 2002, govt. rels. officer), N.Y. State Sch. Assn., Music Educators Nat. Conf., Nat. Write Your Congressman. Roman Catholic. Avocations: singing, dance, acting, flute, painting. Home: 30 Browns Rd Walden NY 12586 Office: Hudson Valley Conservatory Fine Arts PO Box 704 35 E Main St Walden NY 12586 Home Phone: 845-778-0491; Office Phone: 845-778-2478. Personal E-mail: murphhvc@yahoo.com.

MURPHY, PATRICIA M., art gallery director; AA, Elgin Coll., Ill., 1973; BS in Art Edn. magnum cum laude, Northern Ill. U., 1976; MFA, Sch. of Art Inst., Chgo.; MA in Interdisciplinary Art, Columbia Coll., Chgo., 1982. Founder, dir. Beacon St. Gallery, 1983—. Artist over 55 exhbns., 1982—, (mosaics) Lily, Birth, Rebirth, Clarendon Pk., 1999, Prairie Whispers, Black Eyed Susans, Walter Payton HS, 2003, The Scent of Roses, Mary, Anderson Pk., 2004, One Red Wing, Lakeview HS, 2005, The Promise of Summer, Madden and Seward Pks., 2005, A Time of Trumpets, Berger Pk., 2006, Chicago Voices Flower-A Lily A Day, Millennium Pk., 2007. Office: Beacon Street Gallery 410 S Michigan Ave Ste 732 Chicago IL 60605 Office Phone: 312-212-1323. Personal E-mail: patricia@patriciamurphyart.com. Business E-Mail: beaconstreet@sbcglobal.net.

MURPHY, PATRICK, oceanographer; MS in Oceanography, Old Dominion U., Norfolk, Va., 2003. Corps. officer NOAA Ship Albatross IV, Woods Hole, Mass., 2004—06; staff scientist NOAA Nat. Marine Fisheries Svc., Panama City, Fla., 2006—. V.p. Sterling Cove Homeowners Assn., Panama City, 2007—. Lt. NOAA Corps. Recipient Sci. award, Assn. Commissioned Officers, 2008. Office: Nat Marine Fisheries Svc 3500 Delwood Beach Rd Panama City FL 32408

MURPHY, PATRICK JOSEPH, United States Representative from Pennsylvania; b. Phila., Oct. 19, 1973; s. Jack Murphy; m. Jennifer Safford, June 17, 2006. Ed., Bucks County Cmty. coll., 1991; BS, King's Coll., Wilkes-Barre, 1996; JD, Widener U.; grad., Judge Adv. General's Sch., Charlottesville, Va., 2000. Bar: Minn. 1999, Pa. 2003, US Ct. Appeals (Armed Svc.), US Dist. Ct. (Ea. Dist. Pa.), US Supreme Ct. Intern Office of Phila. Dist. Atty.; leader Harrisburg Civil Law Clinic; legis. aide to Rep. Thomas Tangretti Pa. Ho. of Reps; assoc. Murphy & O'Connor, Phila.; judge adv. US Army Judge Adv. General's Corps; assoc. Cozen O'Connor, Pa., 2005—; mem. US Congress from 8th Pa. dist., 2007—, mem. armed svcs. com., 2007—, mem. permanent select com. on intelligence, 2007—. Asst. prof. constitutional law, values edn. officer US Mil. Acad., 2001—03; adj. prof. Am. govt. Mt. St. Mary Coll., 2000—03; lectr. US Air Force Acad., Internat. Inst. Humanitarian Rights, San Remo, Italy, Judge Adv. General's Sch.; instr. Intensive Trial Advocacy Program Widener U. Sch. Law, 2004—05. Cadet in ROTC US Army, 2nd lt. US Army, served with US Army, 2002, Bosnia, served as paratrooper 82nd Airborne Divsn. US Army, 2003—04, Baghdad, Iraq, capt. US Army, 2005—. Decorated Bronze Star; named a Rising Star, Law & Politics, 2005. Mem.: ABA, Pa. Bar Assn., Phila. Bar Assn., Bucks County Bar Assn. Democrat. Office: 414 Mill St Bristol PA 19007 Office Phone: 215-826-1963. Office Fax: 215-826-1997.*

MURPHY, PAUL REGIS, JR., business educator; b. DC, Aug. 12, 1954; m. Sheryl Anne Booher, July 4, 1995. AB, U. Notre Dame, Ind., 1972—76; MBA, U. Md., College Park, 1976—79, PhD, 1980—85. Prof. bus. logistics John Carroll U., Univ. Heights, Ohio, 1995—. Author: (textbook) Contemporary Logistics, 8th edit., 2004. Recipient Disting. Doctoral Alumnus award, Smith Sch. Bus., U. Md., 1998, Disting. Faculty award, John Carroll U., 2002. Mem.: Am. Soc. Transp. & Logistics (bd. mem. 2002—05). Office: John Carroll Univ 20700 N Park Blvd University Heights OH 44118 Business E-Mail: drmurphy@jcu.edu.

MURPHY, PETER E., corporate financial executive; BA, Dartmouth Coll.; MBA, Wharton Sch. Bus. With The Walt Disney Co., Burbank, Calif., 1988—; sr. v.p., CFO ABC, Inc., Burbank, Calif., 1997-98; exec. v.p., chief strategic officer The Walt Disney Co., Burbank, Calif., 1998-99, sr. exec. v.p., chief strategic officer, 1999—. Office: The Walt Disney Co 500 S Buena Vista St Burbank CA 91521

MURPHY, PHILIP D., investment company executive, professional sports team executive; b. 1957; m. Tammy Murphy; children: Emma, Josh, Charlie, Sam. AB in Econs., Harvard U., Cambridge, Mass., 1979; MBA, U. Pa. Wharton Sch. Bus., Phila., 1983. Summer assoc. to numerous positions of increasing responsibility in the US, Europe and Asia Goldman Sachs Group, Inc., 1982—2006, head, German region, pres., Goldman Sachs Asia, co-head, investment mgmt. divsn., sr. dir.; nat. fin. chair Dem. Nat. Com., Washington, 2006—09; principal Murphy Endeavors, LLC, Red Bank, NJ; principal owner Sky Blue Soccer, Somerset, NJ, 2009—. Sponsor, women's network Goldman Sachs, mem. mgmt. com. Former mem. grad. exec. bd., Asian adv. bd. Wharton Sch. Bus.; former trustee Prosperity NJ, The Goldman Sachs Found.; former chair, benefits rev. task force State of NJ; former co-chair Renewing Our Schools, Securing Our Future: A Task Force on Public Education for the 21st Century; pres./CEO search com. NAACP, bd. trustees, spl. contbn. fund; chmn., exec. com. Local Initiatives Support Corp.; bd. trustees Ctr. Am. Progress; bd. pres. 180 Turning Lives Around; bd. dirs. US Soccer Found.; Huntsman program adv. bd. U. Pa.; mem. bid. com. USA Soccer. Named Bus. Leader of Yr., Am. Woman's Econ. Devel. Corp., 2003. Democrat. Office: Murphy Endeavors LLC 21 E Front St Red Bank NJ 07701-1874 also: Sky Blue Soccer 80 Cottontail Ln Ste 400 Somerset NJ 08873 Office Phone: 732-933-9988, 732-271-7700.*

MURPHY, PHILIP M., biomedical researcher; b. S.I., NY, July 16, 1953; s. James Joseph and Clare Marie (Meehan) M.; m. Nancy Carolyn Smith, Jan. 3, 1982; children: Carolyn Anne, Clare Elizabeth. AB, Princeton U., 1975; MD, Cornell U., 1981. Resident in internal medicine NYU-Bellevue Hosp., NYC, 1981-85; infectious diseases fellow Nat. Inst. Allergy & Infectious Diseases/NIH, Bethesda, Md., 1985-90, sr. staff fellow, 1990-93, sr. investigator with tenure, 1993—, head molecular signaling sect. Lab. Host Defs. & Lab. Molecular Immunology, 1998—, chief, 2003—. Assoc. editor Cellular Immunology, 1992—; sect. editor Jour. Leukocyte Biology, 1994—; editor Jour. Biol. Chemistry, 1996-2007; contbr. articles, revs. to profl. jours. Mem. AAAS, Am. Soc. Biochemistry and Molecular Biology, Soc. Leukocyte Biology, Am. Soc. Clin. Investigation, Assn. Am. Physicians. Achievements include patent for cloning cDNA for human interleukin-8 receptor; discovery of viral chemokine receptors, a family of leukocyte chemoattractant receptors, HIV coreceptor CCR5. Office: NIH Rm 11n113 Bldg 10 Bethesda MD 20892-0001 Office Phone: 301-496-8616. Business E-Mail: pmm@nih.gov.

MURPHY, R. BLAIR, management consulting company executive; b. Phila., Jan. 19, 1931; s. William Beverly and Helen Marie (Brennan) M.; children: Stephen, Emily, Julia, David, Catherine. BS, Yale, 1953. Indsl. engr. DuPont Corp., Aiken, SC, 1953-55; mgr. sales can divsn. Reynolds Metals Co., Richmond, Va., 1955-69; gen. mgr. corrugated divsn. Continental Can Co., NYC, 1969-73; v.p. and gen. mgr. beverage divsn. Am. Can Co., Greenwich, Conn., 1973-75; assoc. Heidrick & Struggles, Inc., NYC, 1976-78, v.p., 1978; v.p., mng. dir. Stamford office Spencer Stuart & Assocs., 1978-84, ptnr., 1982-84; co-founder and CEO Sullivan-Murphy Assocs., 1984—. Mem. Riverside Yacht Club (Greenwich), Yale Club (N.Y.C.), Merion Cricket Club (Haverford, Pa.). Home: 11 Indian Mill Rd Cos Cob CT 06807-1315

MURPHY, RAMON J.C. (RAMON JEREMIAH CASTROVIEJO MURPHY), pediatrician, physician, educator; b. NYC, Feb. 12, 1944; s. William J. and Angelines (Castroviejo) M.; m. Lila, Sept. 12, 1971; children: Jessica, David. BA, U. Notre Dame, 1965; MD, Northwestern U., 1969; MPH, Columbia U., 1974. Diplomate Am. Bd. Pediats. Intern medicine Cook County Hosp., Chgo., 1969—70; resident in pediats. Children's Meml. Hosp., Chgo., 1970—71, Babies Hosp.-Columbia-Presbyn. Med. Ctr., NYC, 1971—73; resident in cmty. medicine Mt. Sinai Hosp., NYC, 1973—74, clin. asst. pediatrician, 1974—75, asst. attending pediatrician, 1975—83, assoc. attending pediatrician, 1983—, assoc. instr. cmty. medicine, 1974—75, asst. prof. clin. pediats., asst. prof. cmty. medicine, 1975—83, assoc. prof. clin. pediats., 1983—2006, clin. prof. pediat., clin. prof. preventive and cmty. medicine, 2006—07; pediatrician Uptown Pediat., P.C., NYC, 1976—, pres., 1990—. Co-dir. Mt. Sinai Children's Cmty. Health, 1999—, Mt. Sinai Global Health Ctr., 2005-; dir. Mt. Sinai Off-Site Pediat. Residency Tng. Program, 1999—, Mt. Sinai Pediat. Global Health Tng. Program, 2004—; vis. clin. fellow pediat. Columbia U., Coll. Physicians and Surgeons, NYC, 1971-73; pediat. cons. Oxford Health Plan, 1990-94, Children's Aid Soc., 2000—, Commonwealth Fund, 1995—. Contbr. articles to profl. jours. Co-med. dir. Benito Juarez People's Health Ctr., Chgo., 1970-71; dep. co-dir. Wagner Child Health Project, NYC, 1973-75; sch. physician The Day Sch., 1984—, The Trinity Sch., 1992—, trustee, 1993-99. Named one of Top Doctors in NY, NY Mag. Fellow Am. Acad. Pediat.; mem. NY Pediat. Soc. (program chmn. 1986-89, pres. 1989-90), Soc. for Adolescent Medicine, Mt. Sinai Alumni Assn. Avocations: golf, fishing. Office: 1245 Park Ave New York NY 10128-1211 Office Phone: 212-427-0540. Office Fax: 212-534-1086. E-mail: ramon.murphy@mssm.edu.

MURPHY, RANDALL KENT, writer, educator, consultant; b. Laramie, Wyo., Nov. 8, 1943; s. Robert Joseph and Sally (McConnell) M.; m. Cynthia Laura Hillhouse, Dec. 29, 1978; children: Caroline, Scott, Emily. Student, U. Wyo., 1961—65; MBA, So. Meth. U., 1983. Dir. mktg. Wycoa, Inc., Denver, 1967—70; dir. Comm. Resource Inst., Dallas, 1971—72; account exec. Xerox Learning Sys., Dallas, 1973—74; regional mgr. Systema Corp., Dallas, 1975; pres. Performance Assocs.; pres., dir. Acclivus Corp., Dallas, 1976—; founder, chmn. Acclivus Inst., 1982—. Author: Performance Management, Coaching and Counseling and Performance, 1980, Managing Development and Performance, 1982, Acclivus Performance Planning System, 1983, (with others) BASE For Performance, 1983, Acclivus Coaching, 1984, Acclivus Negotiation, 1985, R3 Service, 1997, BASE for Effective Presentations, 1987, BASE for Strategic Presentations, 1988, The New BASE for Excellence, 1988, Major Account Planning and Strategy, 1989, Strategic Management, 1989, Building on the BASE, 1992, Negotiation Mastery, 1995, R3 Service, 1997, Co-creating R3 Value, 2002, Getting the Meeting, 2004, R3 Interaction, 2005, R3 Negotiation, 2009; co-inventor The Randy-Band multi-purpose apparel accessory, 1968. Vice chmn. bd. trustees The Winston Sch., 1994-96, chmn. bd. trustees, 1997-2000; mem. adv. bd. The Women's Ctr. of Dallas, 1995-98. With AUS, 1966. Mem. ASTD, Inst. Mgmt. Scis., Soc. Applied Learning Tech., Nat. Soc. Performance and Instrn., Assn. Mgmt. Cons., Am. Assn. Higher Edn., World Future Soc., Soc. for Intercultural Edn., Tng. and Rsch., Internat. Fedn. Tng. and Devel. Orgns., Inst. Noetic Scis., Nat. Peace Inst., Amnesty Internat., Acad. Polit. Sci., The Nature Conservancy, Theosophical Soc. Am., Children's Arts and Ideas Found., So. Meth. U. Alumni Assn., U. Wyo. Alumni Assn, Assn. Humanistic Psychology. Office Phone: 972-385-1277. Business E-Mail: randall.murphy@acclivus.com.

MURPHY, REMINGTON MORRIS, clerk; b. Phila., Jan. 18, 1958; s. Remington Morris Murphy and Edith Anna Hyer; m. Valerie Brian Anderson, Sept. 26, 1999. BA magna cum laude, Temple U., Phila., 1980, MA, 1983. Instr. Temple U., 1980—84, Camden County CC, Blackwood, 1985; clerk US Postal Svc., Abington, 1986—. Editor Magic Bullet Sci. Fiction Anthology, Phila., 1988. Contbr. columns in newspapers to poetry mags. Avocations: travel, reading, baseball. Personal E-mail: rmurphy483@aol.com.

MURPHY, RICHARD WILLIAM, retired diplomat; b. Boston, July 29, 1929; s. John Deneen Murphy and Jane (Diehl) Bonner; m. Anne Herrick Cook, Aug. 25, 1955; children: Katherine Anne, Elizabeth Drew, Richard McGill. Grad., Phillips Exeter Acad., 1947; AB, Harvard U., 1951, Cambridge U., Eng., 1953; postgrad. Arabic studies, U.S. Fgn. Service Inst., Beirut, 1959-60; LLD (hon.), New Eng. Coll., 1989, Balt. Hebrew U., 1992. Vice consul U.S. Consulate Gen., Salisbury, So. Rhodesia, 1955-58; consul Aleppo, Syria, 1960-63; polit. officer Am. Embassy, Jedda, Saudi Arabia, 1963-66, Amman, Jordan, 1966-68; pers. officer U.S. State Dept., Washington, 1968-69, dir. Office Arabian Peninsula Affairs, 1969-71, asst. sec. state for Near Ea. and South Asian affairs, 1983-89; U.S. amb. to Mauritania, 1971-74, to Syria, 1974-78, to the Philippines, 1978-81, to Saudi Arabia, 1981-83; amb., 1987; sr. fellow for Middle East Coun. Fgn. Rels., NYC, 1989—2004; cons. Richard Murphy Assocs., NYC, 1993—. Chmn. Fgn. Students Svc. Coun., Washington, 1989—93, Mid. East Inst., Washington, 1993—2001, Chatham House Found., 1993—2004; mem. bd. advisors Naval War Coll., 1991—94; dir. Music in NC, 2009—. Trustee Am. U. of Beirut, 1995-2007; mem. vis. com. Harvard Mid. East Ctr., 1999-2002, Near East Found., 2000-2003; dir. Found. Mid. East Peace, 2000—; chmn. Friends of UN Relief and Works Agy. Assn., 2005-09, dir., 2009-. Served with US Army, 1953-55. Recipient Superior Honor award, U.S. Dept. State, 1969, Pres.'s Disting. Svc. award, 1986, 88, 89. Mem. Coun. Fgn. Rels., Fgn. Svc. Assn., Century Club. Republican. Episcopalian. Avocations: tennis, scuba diving. Home: 16 Sutton Pl 9A New York NY 10022-3057 Office Phone: 212-319-6541. Home Fax: 212-421-7067. Business E-Mail: richard@rwmurphyassociates.com.

MURPHY, ROBERT, executive recruiter, consultant; b. Davenport, Iowa; s. James and Patricia. BS, U. Ill., Chgo., 1963. Registered pharmacist, Ill. With Walgreen Co., Chgo., 1963—73; corp. mgr. Coll. Rels. & Recruiting; mgr. Human Resource Planning; Corp. dir. Orgn. and Human Resource Planning & Devel.; US ptnr.-in-charge exec. search PricewaterhouseCoopers, Chgo., 1974—93; founder, chmn. Murphy Ptnrs. Internat., global exec. search firm, 1993—. Contbr. articles to profl. jours. including Wall St. Jour., Newsweek. Mem. Internat. Human Resource Assn., Soc. Human Resource Mgrs., Internat. Cons. Assn., Am. Soc. Pers. Adminstrs., Soc. Human Resource Profls., Kappa Psi. Office: 956 Shoreline Rd Barrington IL 60010-3815

MURPHY, ROBERT JAMES, language educator, consultant, pianist, pipe organ performer; b. Decatur, Ind., Aug. 31, 1941; s. James William and Catherine Agnes (Schumacker) Murphy; m. Linda L. Nolan, June 28, 1975; 1 child, Christina Lyn. BS in Edn., Ball State U., Muncie, Ind., 1963, postgrad., 1972; MS in Edn., St. Francis U., Ft. Wayne, Ind., 1967; postgrad., U. Denver, 1986. Cert. English, speech, drama and journalism tchr. Ind. Speech and drama tchr. Rochester H.S., Ind., 1976—78; chair dept. English Lawrenceburg H.S., Ind., 1978—81, Holy Family H.S., Denver, 1981—86; prin. Randall-Moore Sch., Denver, 1986—87; dir. edn. Mansfield Bus. Sch., Denver, 1987—89; prin. St. John the Bapt. Cath. Sch., Ft. Wayne, Ind., 1989—94; pres., founder Murphy Ednl. Consulting, Ft. Wayne, Ind., 1995—, D/B/A Alternative Edn. Curriculum and The Learning Kaleidoscope, Pensacola, Fla., 1995—2006. Cons. Am. Printing House for Blind, Louisville, 1999—2002; cons., writer, spkr. homeschooling groups, 1995—; exec. dir., co-founder The Kaleidoscope Edn. Ctr., Ft. Wayne, Ind., 2003, co-founder, dir., 03; tchr., supr. Aurora Evening H.S., Colo., 1986—87; tchr. U. St. Francis, Ft. Wayne, 2003—08, IVY Tech. CC, Ft. Wayne, 2008—09; edn. coord., tchr. M.A.Y.A. Unity Ctr., Ft. Wayne, 2003; dir. edn. Phoenix Youth Ctr., 2003—06; musician Colo., Ind., Ill., 1961—; dir. edn. Med Tech. Coll. Author: All in One Big Book, 1998, The Pump Man, 1998; co-author: Teaching the Student with a Visual Impairment, 2000, author reading and writing curriculum; dir.: Firehouse Theater, 2006—07. Bd. dirs. Ft. Wayne Pub. Transp. Co., 2000—09, League for Blind and Disabled, Ft. Wayne, 2000—07; chmn. bd. dirs. United Voice Coalition, Ft. Wayne, 2002—05; chmn. bd. dirs. State Ind. Alliance Cmty. Inclusion, 2003—; site visitor U.S. Dept. Edn. Blue Ribbon Sch., 1991; devel. dir. Fifth Freedom Network for People with Disabilities, Ft. Wayne, 2006—07; founding bd. dirs., exec. asst. dir. Phoenix Youth Ctr.-Club Unified, Ft. Wayne, 2003—06. Recipient Disting. Graduate award, Decatur (Ind.) Cath. Elem. and HS, 2003; named Advocate of Yr., League for the Blind and Disabled, 2002. Mem.: Arvada Festival Playhouse (dir. musical dir. 1974—79), Knights Columbus 451, Deputy Grand Knight, Am. Guild

Organists. Avocations: gardening, hiking, swimming, piano, organ. Home and Office: Robert Murphy Cons 1601 N Coll Ave 96 Fort Collins CO 80524 Home Phone: 970-221-8541. Personal E-mail: murphymuse@yahoo.com.

MURPHY, ROSEMARY, actress; b. Munich, Jan. 13, 1927; came to U.S., 1939; d. Robert D. and Mildred (Taylor) M. Student, Paris, France and Kansas City, Mo. Broadway appearances include Look Homeward Angel, 1958, Night of the Iguana, World premier at Spoleto (Italy) Festival of Two Worlds, 1959, Period of Adjustment, 1961, King Lear, 1963, Any Wednesday, 1964-66, Delicate Balance, 1966, Weekend, 1968, Butterflies are Free, 1970, Lady Macbeth, Stratford, Conn., 1973, Ladies of the Alamo, 1977, John Gabriel Borkman, 1980, Learned Ladies, 1982, Coastal Disturbances, 1987, The Devil's Disciple, 1988, A Delicate Balance, 1996, Waiting in the Wings, 1999; motion picture appearances include To Kill a Mockingbird, 1962, Any Wednesday, 1966, Ben, 1972, Walking Tall, 1972, You'll Like My Mother, 1972, Forty Carats, 1973, Julia, 1976, September, 1987, For the Boys, 1991, And The Band Played On, 1993, The Tuskegee Airmen, 1995, Message in a Bottle, 1998, Dust, 2001, The Savages, 2006, Synecdoche New York, 2007; TV appearance Eleanor and Franklin, 1975 (Emmy award for best supporting actress 1976), George Washington, 1983 (Tony award nominations 1961, 64, 67, award Motion Picture Arts Club 1966), E-Z Streets, 1996, The Unicorn's Secret, 1998, Frasier, 1997, 99, Life After Wealth, 2008. Recipient Variety Poll award, 1961, 67. Address: 220 E 73rd St New York NY 10021-4319 Office Phone: 212-713-5299.

MURPHY, RYAN, legislative staff member; B, Wash. and Lee U., Lexington, Va., 2003. Staff asst., Rep. Tom Price US House of Reps., Washington, 2005, legis. correspondent, Rep. Tom Price, 2006—07, dep. press sec., constituent services rep., Rep. Tom Price, 2007, comm. dir. to Rep. Joe Wilson, 2009—. Republican. Office: 212 Cannon House Office Bldg Washington DC 20515 Office Phone: 202-225-2452. Office Fax: 202-225-2455.*

MURPHY, SCOTT (MATTHEW SCOTT MURPHY), United States Representative from New York; b. Mo., Jan. 26, 1970; s. Alan and Marcia Murphy; m. Jen Hogan, Mar. 11, 2000; children: Simone, Lux, Duke. AB magna cum laude, Harvard Coll., 1992. Chartered Fin. Analyst. Founder Small World Software (purchased by iXL, 1998), 1994; sr. v.p. iXL, 1998—2000; mng. dir. Advantage Capital Partners, Glens Falls, NY, 2001—09; mem. US Congress from 20th NY Dist., 2009—, US House Agrl. Com., 2009—, US House Armed Services Com., 2009—. Aide to Gov. Mel Carhahan State of Mo., Mo., dep. chief of staff to Gov. Roger Wilson, Mo. Recipient 20 Under 40 award, Glens Falls Post-Star, 2008. Mem.: Upstate Venture Assn. NY (pres. 2008—09). Democrat. Office: US Congress 120 Cannon House Office Bldg Washington DC 20515*

MURPHY, STACIA, former health service association executive; BA, Talladega Coll., aLA. With Cmty. Service Soc., N.Y. City Mission Soc., NY State Divsn. Youth, Alcoholism Coun. of N.Y.; exec. dir. NYC affiliate Nat. Coun. on Alcoholism and Drug Dependence, Inc., 1990-99, pres. NYC, 1999—2005.

MURPHY, STEPHEN JOSEPH, III, federal judge, former prosecutor; b. St. Louis, Sept. 23, 1962; s. Stephen Joseph and Mary Elizabeth Murphy; m. Amy Elizabeth Uhl, June 8, 1996. BS, Marquette U., 1984; JD, St. Louis U., 1987. Bar: Mo. 1987, Mich. 1998. Trial atty. US Dept. Justice, Washington, 1987-92, asst. US atty. (ea. dist.) Mich. Detroit, 1992-2000, US atty. (ea. dist.) Mich., 2005—08; asst. gen. counsel Gen. Motors Corp., Detroit, 2000—05; judge US Dist. Ct. (ea. dist.) Mich., 2008—. Adj. prof. trial practice, bus. crime U. Detroit Mercy, 1993-2000; adj. prof. evidence Ave. Maria, 2002; master of the bench Am. Inn of Ct., Detroit, 1996-99. Contbr. articles to profl. jours. Big brother Big Bros./Big Sisters of S.E. Mich., Southfield, 1993-96; co-chmn. Combined Fed. Campaign, Detroit, 1993. Recipient Commendation, Bur. ATF, 1993, Letter of Thanks from Dir. of FBI, 1996, Commendation, U.S. Secret Svc., 1998, Commendation, Detroit FBI, 1999, Commendation, Motion Picture Assn. Am., 1999. Mem. State Bar Mich. (bd. commrs. 2002-05, com. rules criminal procedure 2001-05), Fed. Bar Assn., Nat. Lawyers Assn., Pros. Attys. Assn. Mich. Roman Catholic. Office: US Dist Ct Theodore Levin US Courthouse 231 W Lafayette Blvd Detroit MI 48226

MURPHY, SUZANNE, publishing executive; Various positions including edn., libr. pub. and trade mktg. Doubleday, Dell Books for Young Readers, Bantam Doubleday Dell, Random House Children's Pub.; v.p., mktg. Simon & Schuster Children's Pub.; v.p., trade mktg. Scholastic, 2005—07, v.p. & pub., trade pub. and mktg., 2008—. Office: Scholastic 557 Broadway New York NY 10012 Office Phone: 212-343-6100.

MURPHY, TERENCE MARTIN, biology professor; b. Seattle, July 1, 1942; s. Norman Walter and Dorothy Louise (Smith) M.; m Judith Baron, July 12, 1969; 1 child, Shannon Elaine Knotts. BS, Calif. Inst. Tech., 1964; PhD, U. Calif. San Diego, La Jolla, 1968. Sr. fellow dept. biochemistry U. Wash., Seattle, 1969-70; asst. prof. botany U. Calif., Davis, 1971-76, assoc. prof., 1976-82, prof. plant biology, 1982—, chmn. dept. botany, 1986-90. Author: Plant Molecular Development, 1988; co-author: Plant Biology, 1998, 2nd edit. 2006; N.Am. exec. editor, N.Am. office, Physiologia Plantarum, 1988-98; contbr. articles to profl. jours. Mem. AAAS, Am. Soc. Plant Biologists, Am. Soc. Photobiology, Scandinavian Soc. Plant Physiology. Home: 725 N Campus Way Davis CA 95616-3518 Office: U Calif Plant Biology Davis CA 95616 Home Phone: 530-753-3783; Office Phone: 530-752-2413. E-mail: tmmurphy@ucdavis.edu.

MURPHY, TERENCE ROCHE, lawyer, international trade executive; b. Oct. 20, 1937; s. M. Leonard and Alice Lenore (Roche) Murphy; m. Suzanne Kathryn Dupré, Oct. 14, 1967 (div. Apr. 1980); children: Braden Mathias, Fiona Elizabeth Dupré; m. Patricia Ann Sherman, May 21, 1983. AB, Harvard Coll., 1959; JD with distinction, U. Mich., 1966. Bar: D.C. 1967, U.S. Supreme Ct. 1971. Trial atty. Dept. Justice, Washington, 1966-68; assoc. Wald, Harkrader & Ross, Washington, 1968-72, ptnr., 1972-83, McDermott, Will & Emery, Washington, 1983-84, Adams, Duque & Hazeltine, Washington, 1984-86; founding ptnr. Murphy Ellis Weber and predecessors, Washington, 1986—2003; sr. assoc. Ctr. Strat. and Internat. Studies, 2004—; chmn. MK Tech., Washington, 2003—, CEO, 2003—08; fgn. trade advisor Belgian Embassy, Wash., 2003—. Bd. dirs. Am. Assn. Exporters and Importers; founding chmn. Brit.-Am. Bus. Coun., 1989-90, legal counsel, 1993-96; officer, bd. dirs. Industry Coalition of Tech. Transfer; lectr. North and South Am., Asia, Europe and Mediterranean on internat. and bus. law and on strategic issues, Harvard Coll., U. Mich. Law Sch., 2004; chmn. and lectr. ann. Globalization of Export Controls Conf., London, 1997-2008; bd. advisors European Inst., 1993-2002; advisor on munitions export policy, Ctr. for Strategic and Internat. Studies, 2000—, US Dept. Def., 2003; advisor on export regulation, US Dept. Commerce, 2001-05. Author, lectr. on internat. trade, antitrust and administrv. law; co-editor: Coping With US Export Controls, ann. edits., 1986, 87, 88; contbr. articles to European and Am. legal and policy publs. Mem. com. visitors U. Mich. Law Sch., 1975—2007; trustee Lawyer's Com. for Civil Rights Under Law, 1975-89; councilor RSC Am., 2003—05. Lt. USN, 1959-63. Decorated hon. officer Order Brit. Empire, 1993, knight officer Order Leopold (Belgium), 2007; recipient US Navy commendation Cuban Missile Crisis, 1962. Mem. ABA (coun. adminstrv. law sect. 1980-83, co-chmn. com. on internat. and comparative adminstrv. law 1994-97, Am. Law Inst., Internat. Bar Assn. (sec. antitrust and monopolies com. 1981-83), Am. Soc. Internat. law, Brit.-Am. Bus. Assn. (Washington, founding dir. 1987—, chmn., CEO, 1989-92, legal adv. 1992-95), Royal Inst. Internat. Affairs (London), Atlantic Coun. of US, Met. Club (Washington), Harvard Club (NYC), Miscowaubik Club (Calumet, Mich.), Harvard Faculty Club (Cambridge, sr. adv.), Export Controls and Economic Sanctions (internat. law sec., 2008-). Home: 4425 Boxwood Rd Bethesda MD 20816-1817 Office: MK Tech 1823 Jefferson Pl Washington DC 20036 Office Phone: 202-463-0904. E-mail: tmurphy@mktechnology.com.

MURPHY, THOMAS MILES, pediatrician, educator; m. Priscilla Rollin Coit. AB in Math., Harvard Coll., 1969; MD, U. Rochester, 1973. Diplomate Am. Bd. Med. Examiners, Am. Bd. Internal Medicine, Am. Bd. Pediatrics, subbd. pulmonology; lic. physician, N.C. Intern Georgetown U. Med. Divsn., D.C. Gen. Hosp., Washington, 1973-74; resident in internal medicine Georgetown U. Med. Ctr., Washington, 1974-76, fellow pediat. pulmonary medicine, 1976-78; asst. prof. pediat. Georgetown U. Sch. Medicine, Washington, 1979-80, asst. prof. clin. pediat., 1980-85, U. Chgo., 1985-87, asst. prof. pediat. and medicine, 1990-93; asst. prof. pediat. U. Chgo. Pritzker Sch. Medicine, 1987-90, chief sect. pulmonary medicine dept. pediat., 1992-93; assoc. prof., chief divsn. pediat. pulmonary diseases Duke U., Durham, NC, 1993—. Assoc. dir. Pediatric Pulmonary and Cystic Fibrosis Ctr., Georgetown U., 1978-80; asst. prof. child health and devel. George Washington U. Sch. Medicine and Health Scis., Washington, 1980-85; assoc. chmn. dept. pulmonary medicine, co-dir. Cystic Fibrosis Ctr. for Care, Teaching and Rsch., Children's Hosp. Nat. Med. Ctr., Washington, 1980-85; dir. pediatric pulmonary fellowship tng. program U. Chgo., 1990-93, dir. Cystic Fibrosis Ctr., 1991-93, assoc. chief sect. allergy, immunology and pulmonology, dept. pediatrics, 1991-92; editor ATS Pediat. Assembly Website, 2000—; ad hoc mem. lung biology and pathology study sect. NIH, 2002. Contbr. articles to profl. jours., chpts. to books; cons. referee editor New Eng. Jour. Medicine, 1989, Am. Rev. Respiratory Disease, 1989—, Am. Jour. Physiology: Lung Cellular and Molecular Physiology, 1990—, Pediatric Rsch., 1991—, Jour. Applied Physiology, 1991—, Pediat. Pulmonology, 1993—, mem. editl. bd., 1996—; contbg. editor The Hudson Monitor. Mem. ctr. com. Cystic Fibrosis Found., 1992-97, 2000-2002; chmn. childhood lung disease com. D.C. Lung Assn., 1980-83, lung disease com., 1984; mem. adv. coun. D.C. Sudden Infant Death Syndrome, 1981-83, chmn. med. adv. com., 1982-83. Recipient Cmty. Svc. award So. Md. Lung Assn., 1980, Media award Am. Acad. Pediatrics, 1980, Svc. award homicide br. Met. Police Dept. D.C., 1983, Svc. award Met. D.C. chpt. Cystic Fibrosis Foun., Washington, 1985, Nat. Cystic Fibrosis Found., 1997; Rsch. grantee Am. Lung Assn., N.Y.C., 1992, NIH, Bethesda, Md., 1993, 98. Mem.: AAAS, European Respiratory Soc., Am. Thoracic Soc. (program com. assembly on respiratory structure and function 1993—96, chair long range planning com. 2000—02, chair subcom. on physician scientists, pediat. assembly 1997—, liaison officer pediat. assembly 2000—), N.Y. Acad. Scis., Am. Physiol. Soc., Soc. Pediatric Rsch. Avocations: refereeing soccer, jazz. Office: Duke U Med Ctr PO Box 2994 Durham NC 27710-2994

MURPHY, THOMAS PATRICK, science educator, researcher; b. San Francisco, Nov. 1, 1951; m. Elaine Marie Murphy. BS in Math., U. Calif., Santa Cruz, 1973; MS in Math., U. Calif., Berkeley, 1974, U. Calif., 1982, MS in Computer Sci. Programmer EDS Nuc., San Francisco, 1968—78, engr.; pre-sales analyst Control Data Corp., Bloomington, Minn., 1978—89, Multiflow Computer, Branford, Conn., 1989—90; mem. tech. staff Silicon Graphics, Mountain View, Calif., 1990—2001; prof. computer sci. Contra Costa Coll., San Pablo, Calif., 2001—08. Mem. parallel and distributed working group Nat. Computational Sci. Inst., Durham, NC, 2002—; cons. to internet to the hogon and dine grid Navajo Nation, Crownpoint, N.Mex., 2005—08; steering com. supercomputing edn. SuperComputing, Washington, 2007—, 3d internet chair, 2007—09. Actor: (ind. film) Oregon, Ashes to Ashes; contbr. articles to profl. jours. Presenting couple marriage encounter Cath. Engaged Encounter, Wahington, 1981—2001, western region coordinators engaged encounter; presenting couple Worldwide Marriage Encounter, San Bernardino, Calif., 1976—81. Office: Contra Costa Coll 2600 Mission Bell Dr San Pablo CA 94806 Business E-Mail: tmurphy@contracosta.edu.

MURPHY, TIMOTHY E., lawyer; b. Niagara Falls, NY, Feb. 27, 1970; s. James E. Murphy and Janet Bierbower; m. Lisa M. Droge, July 12, 1997; children: Dustin Jr., Joshua P., Elizabeth B. BSEE, Boise State U., Idaho, 2002; MSEE, U. Mich., Ann Arbor, 2005, JD, 2008. Power plant operator Idaho Power, Hagerman, 1994—95; engr. Micron Tech., Inc., Boise, Idaho, 1995—2002; atty. Marger, Johnson & McCollom, PC, Portland, Oreg., 2006—. Contbr. articles to rsch. jours. Petty officer 2nd class, reactor plant mechanic USN, 1988—94, SC, Norfolk, Va. Decorated SW Asia Svc. medal USN. Mem.: IEEE. Libertarian. Achievements include patents pending for. Home: 3698 E Fort Boise Ln Boise ID 83716 Office: Marger Johnson & McCollom PC 210 SW Morrison St Ste 400 Portland OR 97204 Business E-Mail: tim.murphy@techlaw.com.

MURPHY, TIMOTHY F., United States Representative from Pennsylvania; b. Cleve., Sept. 11, 1952; s. John and Florence Murphy; m. Nanette Missign, Aug. 23, 1975; 1 child, Bevin. BS, Wheeling Jesuit U., 1974; MA, Cleve. State U., 1976; PhD in Psych., U. Pitts., 1979. Mem. Pa. State Senate from Dist. 37, Harrisburg, 1997—2002, US Congress from 18th Pa. dist., 2003—, mem. energy and commerce com., co-chair Congl. Mental Health Caucus, mem. 21st Century Healthcare Caucus. Chmn. aging and youth com. Pa. State Senate, chmn. pub. health and welfare com., comm. and high tech. com., cmty. and econ. devel. com., edn. com., health care task force; asst. prof. U. Pitts. Sch. Medicine. Author: The Angry Child, Overcoming Passive-Aggression. Bd. dirs. Head Start, Alliance for Infants, Parents Helping Parents, Korean War Vets. Western Pa. Meml. Fund; founding dir. Sr. Aides Employment Svc.; mem. St. Thomas More Ch., Bethel Park, Pa.; mem. adv. bd. Allegheny Co. Ct. of Common Pleas Family Ct. Divsn., steering com. on children's issues roundtable; mem. US Mil. Acad. Rev. Bd. Mem. Pa. Perinatal Assn. (bd. dirs.), Bethel Park C. of C., South Park C. of C., Brentwood-Baldwin-Whitehall C. of C., Greater Bridgeville C. of C., Sons of Am. Legion Republican. Roman Catholic. Office: US House Reps 322 Cannon House Office Bldg Washington DC 20515 Office Phone: 202-225-2301. Office Fax: 202-225-1844.*

MURPHY, TIMOTHY JAMES, lawyer; b. Topeka, Sept. 30, 1946; s. Miles J. and Norine D. Murphy; m. Patricia MacKinnon, Apr. 7, 1990. BA, U. Ga., 1968; JD with honors, Washington & Lee U., 1970; LLM, Harvard U., 1976. Bar: Va. 1970, Fla. 1972. Atty. Anderson, Mori & Rabinowitz, Tokyo, 1970—71, Shutts & Bowen, Miami, Fla., 1976—. Contbr. articles to profl. jours. Mem. Fla. Ho. of Reps., 1982-84; bd. dirs. Cath. Charities, Inc., 1982-97, Cath. Charities Legal Svcs., Inc., Miami, 2000—; pres., 2008-, The Barnacle soc., 1991-2002, pres. 2000-02; mem. adv. bd. Miami-Dade County Pub. Libr., 1988-2002. Col. JAG Corps USAFR, 1971-95. Mem.: Biscayne Bay Yacht Club, Army and Navy Club (Washington). Democrat. Roman Catholic. Avocation: sailing. Office: Shutts & Bowen 201 S Biscayne Blvd Ste 1500 Miami FL 33131-4308 Office Phone: 305-379-9137.

MURPHY, TIMOTHY P., federal agency administrator; married; 2 children. BS in Criminal Justice, Ferris State U., 1983. Police officer, Mich.; spl. agent. FBI, 1988, asst. spl. agent in charge Washington, DC Field Office, mem. Dir.'s SAC Adv. Com., spl. asst. to dir., spl. agent in charge (SAC) Cin. Divsn., 2006—07, asst. dir., CFO Washington, asst. dir. Fin. Divsn., 2007, assoc. dep. dir., 2008—. Office: FBI J Edgar Hoover Bldg 935 Pennsylvania Ave NW Washington DC 20535*

MURPHY, WILLIAM ALEXANDER, JR., diagnostic radiologist, educator; b. Pitts., Apr. 26, 1945; s. William Alexander and LaRue (Eshbaugh); m. Judy Marie Lang, June 18, 1977; children: Abigail Norris, William Lawrence, Joseph Ryan. BS, U. Pitts., 1967; MD, Pa. State U., 1971. Diplomate Am. Bd. Radiology. Intern Barnes Hosp., St. Louis, 1971-72, staff radiologist, 1975-93; radiology resident Washington U., St. Louis, 1972-75, prof. radiology, 1983-93; sec. chief Mallinckrodt Inst. Radiology, St. Louis, 1975-93; cons. Office Med. Examiner City and County St. Louis, 1993—. Radiologist, prof. radiology, John S. Dunn Sr. prof., disting. chair MD Anderson Cancer Ctr. U. Tex., 1993—, v.p. hosp. and clinics, 1996-97, COO, 1997; chmn. bd. dirs. MD Anderson Physicians Network Corp., 2001—. Fellow Am. Acad. Forensic Scis., Am. Coll. Radiology; mem. Radiol. Soc. N.Am. (1st. v.p. 1997-98), Am. Roentgen Ray Soc., Am. Soc. Bone and Mineral Rsch., Internat. Skeletal Soc., Assn. Univ. Radiologists. Methodist. Home: 4808 Bellview St Bellaire TX 77401-5306 Office: U Texas Anderson Cancer Ctr Div Dx Imaging 057 1515 Holcombe Blvd Houston TX 77030-4009 Office Phone: 713-792-4916. Business E-Mail: wmurphy@di.mdacc.tmc.edu.

MURPHY, WILLIAM FRANCIS, bishop; b. Boston, May 14, 1940; s. Cornelius John and Norma (Duggan) M. AB, St. John Sem., Brighton, Mass., 1961; S.T. Lic., Pontifical Gregorian U., Rome, 1965, S.T.D., 1974. Ordained priest Archdiocese of Boston, 1964, asst. pastor, 1965-70, sec. for community rels. Brighton, 1987—, aux. bishop, 1995—2001; asst. prof. theology Emmanuel Coll., Boston, 1968-74, Pope John XXIII Sem., Weston, Mass., 1974; under-sec. Pontifical Coun., Justice and Peace, Rome, 1974-87; lectr. social ethics St. John Sem., Brighton, 1987—; bishop Diocese of Rockville Centre, NY, 2001—. Author: Social Ethics, 1978, 80, International Politics, 1983, Theology, 1985. Mem. Tavern Club (Boston). Roman Catholic. Office: Diocese of Rockville Centre 50 N Park Ave Rockville Centre NY 11570

MURPHY-O'CONNOR, CORMAC CARDINAL, cardinal, archbishop; b. Aug. 24, 1932; s. George Patrick and Ellen Theresa (Cuddigan) M.-O'C. PhL, STL, Gregorian U., Rome, 1956; DD, Archbishop of Canterbury, 1999. Ordained priest Diocese of Portsmouth, England, 1956; asst. pastor Corpus Christi Parish, Portsmouth, 1956-63, Sacred Heart Parish, Fareham, 1963-66; pvt. sec., chaplain to bishop Diocese of Portsmouth, 1966-70; pastor Parish of the Immaculate Conception, Southampton, England, 1970-71; rector sem. Venerable English Coll., 1971-77; ordained bishop, 1977; bishop Diocese of Arundel and Brighton, West Sussex, England, 1977-2000; archbishop Archdiocese of Westminster, England, 2000—09, archbishop emeritus, 2009—; elevated to cardinal, 2001; cardinal-priest S. Maria sopra Minerva, 2001—. 1st chmn. Bishops' Com. for Europe, 1978-83; chmn. Com. for Christian Unity, 1983-2000; co-chmn. 2d Anglican-Roman Cath. Internat. Commn., 1983-2000; chmn. Bishops' Dept. for Mission and Unity, 1993-2000; pres. Cath. Bishops' Conf. of Eng. and Wales, 2000—; v.p. Coun. of Episcopal Confs. of Europe, 2001—; mem. Pontifical Congregation for Divine Worship and the Discipline of the Sacraments, 2001—; adminstr. Patrimony of the Holy See, 2001—; mem. Coun. for the Study of Orgnl. and Econ. Problems of the Holy See, 2001—; mem. presdl. com. Pontifical Coun. for the Family, 2001—, Pontifical Coun. for Culture, 2002—; mem. Pontifical Coun. for Promoting Christian Unity, 2002—; mem. Pontifical Commn. for Cultural Heritage of the Ch., 2002—. Author: The Family of the Church, 1984, At the Heart of the World, 2004. Freeman City of London, 2001; prior Brit. and Irish Del. of Constantinian Order, 2002; hon. bencher Inner Temple, 2001; Bailiff Grand Cross of Sovereign Mil. Order of Malta, 2002. Roman Catholic. Home and Office: Archbishop's House Ambrosden Ave Westminster London SW1P 1QJ England Office Phone: 0207 798 9033. Business E-Mail: archbiship@rcdow.org.uk.

MURRAY, ALAN STEWART, publishing executive; b. Akron, Ohio, Nov. 16, 1954; s. John and Catherine Case Murray; m. Lori Esposito, Sept. 8, 1984; children: Amanda, Lucy Ann. BA in English Lit., U. NC; MS in Econs., London Sch. Econs. Editor bus. and econs. Chattanooga Times, 1977-79; reporter Congl. Quarterly, Washington, 1980-81, 82-83, Japan Econ. Jour., Tokyo, 1981-82; reporter econs. Wall Street Jour., Washington, 1983-92, dep. bur. chief, 1992-93, bur. chief, 1993—2002, Sta. CNBC, Washington, 2002—05; asst. mng. editor to online exec. editor Wall Street Jour., 2005—08, dep. mng. editor, 2008—. Co-author: Showdown At Gucci Gulch: Lawmakers, Lobbyists, and the Unlikely Triumph of Tax Reform, 1987 (Carey McWilliams award, Am. Polit. Sci. Assn., 1998); commentary News at Sunrise, Sta. NBC, Washington in Rev., Sta. PBS, co-host Capital Report with Alan Murray and Gloria Borger, Sta. CNBC; author: The Wealth of Choices: How the New Economy Puts Power in Your Hands and Money in Your Pocket, 1991, Revolt in the Board Room: The New Rules of Power in Corporate America, 2007. Gov. coun. Miller Ctr. Pub. Affairs U. Va.; bd. dirs., exec. com. Small Enterprise Assistance Fund, Washington; bd. trustees St. Patrick's Episcopal Sch. Recipient Gerald Loeb award, 1992, John Hancock award for Excellence in bus./fin. journalism, 1992, Overseas Press Club award, 1991, 1997; named a John Motley Morehaed scholar, Luce fellow, Tokyo, 1981. Mem.: Coun. Fgn. Rels., U. NC Gen. Alumnus Assn. (bd. visitors, Disting. Young Alumnus award), Gridiron Club, Phi Beta Kappa. Office: Wall St Jour 1025 Connecticut Ave NW Washington DC 20036-5405

MURRAY, ANDY, professional hockey coach; b. Gladstone, MB, Can., 1951; m. Ruth Murray; children: Braden, Jordan, Sarah. BA in Polit. Sci./Sociology, Brandon U., 1972, BA in Edn., 1974; MS in Sports Mgmt., St. Thomas U., 1986. Asst. coach Brandon U., 1974—76, head coach, 1978—81; asst. coach Hershey Bears, 1987—88; head coach Brandon Travelers, Manitoba Jr. A Hockey League, 1976—78; asst. coach Phila. Flyers, 1988-90, Minn. North Stars, 1990-92, Winnipeg Jets, 1993-95; head coach Can. Nat. Team, 1996-98, LA Kings, 1999—2006, St. Louis Blues, 2006—. Office: St Louis Blues Hockey Club Savvis Ctr 1401 Clark Ave Saint Louis MO 63103

MURRAY, ANTHONY, lawyer; b. LA, Apr. 25, 1937; s. Bernard Anthony and Frances Louise (Simpson) M.; children— Matthew Anthony, Thomas Andrew. JD, Loyola U., LA, 1964. Bar: Calif. 1965. Ptnr. Loeb & Loeb LLP, LA, 1995—. Fellow Am. Coll. Trial Lawyers (bd. regents 1995-99, mem. ABA, Chancery Club, LA County Bar Assn., Long Beach Bar Assn., State Bar Calif. (bd. govs. 1980-83, pres. 1982-83, numerous other positions). Democrat. Office: Loeb & Loeb LLP 10100 Santa Monica Blvd Ste 2200 Los Angeles CA 90067-4120 Office Phone: 310-282-2000. E-mail: amurray@loeb.com.

MURRAY, BILL, actor, writer; b. Wilmette, Ill., Sept. 21, 1950; s. Edward and Lucille Murray; m. Margaret Kelly, 1980 (div. 1994); children: Homer, Luke; m. Jennifer Butler, July 4, 1997 (div. June 2008); children: Jackson, Cal, Cooper, Lincoln. Student, Regis Coll., Denver, Second City Workshop, Chgo. Owner minor league baseball team the Riverdogs, Charleston, SC; co-owner Caddyshack Restaurant, Jacksonville, Fla.; team psychologist St. Paul Saints baseball club. Performer, Second City Comedy Troupe, 1973-75; voice, Nat. Lampoon Radio Hour, 1975; actor, writer, Saturday Night Live, 1977-80; actor: (films) Next Stop, Greenwich Village, 1976, Meatballs, 1979, Mr. Mike's Mondo Video, 1979, Where the Buffalo Roam, 1980, Caddyshack, 1980, Loose Shoes, 1980, Stripes, 1981, Tootsie, 1982, Ghostbusters, 1984, The Razor's Edge, 1984, Nothing Lasts Forever, 1984, Little Shop of Horrors, 1986, Scrooged, 1988, Ghostbusters II, 1989, What About Bob?, 1991, Groundhog Day, 1993, Mad Dog and Glory, 1993, Ed Wood, 1994, Kingpin, 1996, Larger Than Life, 1996, Space Jam, 1996, The Man Who Knew Too Little, 1997, With Friends Like These, 1998, Veeck As In Wreck, 1998, Rushmore, 1998, Wild Things, 1998, The Cradle Will Rock, 1999, Scout's Honor, 1999, Hamlet, 1999, Company Man, 1999, Charlie's Angels, 2000, Speaking of Sex, 2001, The Royal Tenenbaums, 2001, Osmosis Jones, 2001, Coffee and Cigarettes, 2003, Lost in Translation, 2003 (Golden Globe for best actor in a musical or comedy, 2004, Acad. Award nomination for best actor, 2004, Screen Actors Guild Award nomination for best actor, 2004), Garfield: The Movie (voice), 2004, The Life Acquatic with Steve Zissou, 2004, Broken Flowers, 2005, The Lost City, 2005, Garfield: A Tail of Two Kitties (voice), 2006, The Darjeeling Limited, 2007, Get Smart, 2008, City of Ember, 2008, The Limits of Control, 2009; actor, dir., prodr. Quick Change, 1990; (TV movies) The Rutles: All you Need Is Cash, 1978; (TV series) Stories from My Childhood (voice only), 1998, The Sweet Spot, 2002 Recipient Emmy award for best writing for comedy series, 1977, Sons of the Desert Comedy Performer award, 1997. Office: c/o The St Paul Saints Midway Stadium 1771 Energy Park Dr Saint Paul MN 55108*

MURRAY, BOB (ROBERT FREDERICK MURRAY), professional sports team executive, former professional hockey player; b. Kingston, Ont., Can., Nov. 26, 1954; m. Betsy Murray; children: Kevin, Andrew, Amanda, Katie. Defenseman Chgo Blackhawks, 1975—90; dir. player personnel Chgo. Blackhawks, 1991—97, gen. mgr., 1997—99; scouting cons. Anaheim Ducks (formerly Mighty Ducks of Anaheim), 1999, sr. v.p. hockey ops., 2005—08, gen. mgr., 2008—; profl. scout Vancouver Canucks, 1999—2005; gen. mgr. Iowa Chops (Am. Hockey League), 2008—. Named to NHL All-Star Game, 1981, 1983. Office: Anaheim Ducks Honda Ctr 2695 E Katella Ave Anaheim CA 92806*

MURRAY, BRIAN, publishing executive; With new media grp. Hearst Corp.; cons. media practice Booz Allen & Hamilton; dir. finance and analysis, adult book trade HarperCollins Publishers, 1997—98, v.p., finance and publishing operations, 1998—99, sr. v.p., mng. dir. gen. books group, 1999—2001, group pres., 2004—08; CEO HarperCollins Australia/New Zealand, 2001—04; pres., CEO HarperCollins Publishers Worldwide, 2008—. Office: HarperCollins 10 E 53rd St New York NY 10022

MURRAY, BRYAN CLARENCE, professional sports team executive, former professional hockey coach; b. Shawville, Que., Can., Dec. 5, 1942; s. Clarence Herbert and Rhoda (Schwartz) Murray; m. Geraldine Frances Sutton, July 8, 1967; children: Heide Alicia, Brittany. Grad., McGill U., 1964. Former athletic dir., hockey coach McGill U.; athletic dir. MacDonald Coll., Ste. Anne de Bellevue, Que., 1968-72; coach, tchr. Rockland Nat.-Pontiac HS, Rockland, Ont., 1974-76; coach Pembroke-Kings, Pembroke, Ont., 1976-79, Regina Pats, Sask., 1979-80, Hershey Bears, Pa., 1980-81; former coach Washington Capitals, Landover, Md., 1981; coach, gen. mgr. Detroit Red Wings, 1990-94; gen. manager Florida Panthers, 1994—2001; head coach Mighty Ducks Anaheim, 2001—02, sr. v.p., gen. mgr., 2002—04; head coach Ottawa Senators, 2004—07, 2008, gen. mgr., 2007—, exec. v.p., 2009—. Recipient Jack Adams award, 1984; named NHL Coach of Yr., Sporting News, 1984, NHL Exec. of Yr., 1996. Office: Ottawa Senators Scotiabank Place 1000 Palladium Dr Kanata ON K2V 1A5 Canada*

MURRAY, CARLA MARY, sound effects artist; b. North Bay, Ont., Can., Apr. 3, 1957; d. Thomas Joseph and Laura Catherine Murray; life ptnr. Paula Kathleen Fairfield. BFA, N.S. Coll. Art and Design, Halifax, Can., 1982; MFA, York U., Toronto, Ont., 1996. Cofounder, adminstrv. dir. Women's Art Resource Ctr., Toronto, 1984—91; contract art adminstr., writer, rschr. various clients Toronto, 1992—94; sound designer, sound effects editor MHz Sound Design Inc., LA, 1997—. Ways and means com., adminstr. Trinity Sq. Video, Toronto, 1987; author, exhbn. co-coord. Graphic Feminism: Graphic Art of the Ont. Women's Movement 1970-1986, (catalogue) Women's Movement Archives, Toronto, 1986; founding mem. Power Up, LA, 2000, vol. sound designer, sound effects editor, 2001—03. One-woman shows include Gallery 940, Toronto, Stride Gallery, Calgary, IDA Gallery, Toronto, exhibitions include Out of the Frame, Advocate Gallery, LA; sound designer, sound effects editor (films) A Rumour of Angels; sound designer, sound effects editor: (films) Spy Kids 3D: Game Over; Terminator 3: Rise of the Machines; The Adventures of Shark Boy and Lava Girl in 3D; Assault on Precinct 13; Sin City; Lucky Number Slevin; The Black Dahlia; sound designer: films The Reaping, 2006; sound designer, sound effects editor: (TV series) Lost, 2006—09; founding mem. editl. bd.: Matriart: A Can. Feminist Art Jour., 1990—91. Bd. dirs. A Space Gallery, Toronto, 1984; jury mem. Ont. Arts Coun., Toronto, 1994. Recipient Golden Reel award, Motion Picture Sound Editors USA, 2007; grantee, Ont. Arts Coun., 1984—91; Explorations grant, Can. Coun., 1984, Photography grant, 1992. Mem.: Motion Picture Sound Editors USA (Golden Reel award 2007—08, nominee Emmy award 2007), Am. Film Inst., Nat. Mus. Women in Arts, Internat. Alliance Theatrical Stage Employees, Moving Picture Technicians, Artists and Allied Crafts of the US, Its Territories and Can., Motion Picture Editor's Guild.

MURRAY, CHAD MICHAEL, actor; b. Buffalo, Aug. 24, 1981; m. Sophia Bush, Apr. 16, 2005 (div. Dec. 29, 2006). Actor(guest appearances): (TV series) Diagnosis Murder, 2000, CSI: Crime Scene Investigation, 2002,: (TV films) Murphy's Dozen, 2001, Aftermath, 2001, The Lone Ranger, 2003; (films) Megiddo: The Omega Code 2, 2001, Freaky Friday, 2003, A Cinderella Story, 2004 (Choice Movie Breakout Male, Teen Choice Awards, 2004), House of Wax, 2005 (Choice Movie Actor: Action/Adventure/Thriller, Teen Choice Awards, 2005), Home of the Brave, 2006; (TV series) Gilmore Girls, 2000—01, Dawson's Creek, 2001—02, One Tree Hill, 2003— (Choice TV Breakout Star Male, Teen Choice Awards, 2004, Choice TV Actor: Drama, Teen Choice Awards, 2008). Office: Simmons And Scott Entertainment 7942 Mulholland Dr Los Angeles CA 90046-1225

MURRAY, CHERRY ANN, physicist, researcher, dean; b. Ft. Riley, Kans., Feb. 6, 1952; d. John Lewis and Cherry Mary (Roberts) M.; m. Dirk Joachim Muehlner, Feb. 18, 1977; children: James Joachim, Sara Hester. BS in Physics, MIT, 1973, PhD in Physics, 1978. Rsch. asst. physics dept. MIT, Cambridge, Mass., 1969-78; rsch. assoc. Bell Labs., Murray Hill, NJ, 1976-77; mem. tech. staff AT&T Bell Labs., Murray Hill, NJ, 1978-85, disting. mem. tech. staff, 1985-87, dept. head low-temperature and solid-state physics rsch., 1987-90, dept. head condensed matter physics rsch., 1990-93, dept. head semicond. physics rsch., 1993-97, dir. phys. rsch. lab., 1997—2000, sr. v.p. physical sciences, 2000—01, sr. v.p. for rsch. strategy, physical sci. & wireless rsch., 2001—04; prin. assoc. dir. for sci. & tech. Lawrence Livermore Nat. Laboratory, Livermore, Calif., 2004—09; dean Harvard U. Sch. Engrng. & Applied Sciences (SEAS), Cambridge, 2009—, John A. & Elizabeth S. Armstrong Prof. Engineering & Applied Sciences, 2009—. Co-chair Gordon Rsch., Wolfeboro, N.H., 1982, chair, 1984; mem. vis. com. Harvard U. Dept. Physics, 1993-2004 Contbr. numerous articles to profl. jours. and chpts. to books. NSF fellow, 1969; IBM fellow MIT, 1974-76; recipient Maria Goeppert-Mayer award, American Physical Soc. (APS), 1989, George E. Pake Prize, 2005; named one of The 50 Most Important Women in Sci., Discover mag., 2002 Fellow AAAS, Nat. Acad. Engrng., Am. Phys. Soc. (Maria Goeppert-Mayer award 1989), Nat. Acad. Sciences, American Physical Soc. (v.p., 2007-08, pres., 2008-09) Sigma Xi. Office: Harvard Sch Engineering & Applied Sciences (SEAS) Pierce Hall 217A Cambridge MA 02138 Office Phone: 617-495-5829. Office Fax: 617-496-5264. Business E-Mail: mfreeman@seas.harvard.edu.*

MURRAY, CHRISTOPHER CHARLES, III, architect; b. Bklyn., July 6, 1950; s. Christopher Charles and Gertrude Rose (Marr) M.; m. Ann Herring, Nov. 16, 1974. BArch, U. Notre Dame, 1973; MSc in Real Estate, Johns Hopkins U., 2005. Registered arch., N.Y., Md., D.C., Va., Ga., Fla., W.V., Pa., Ky. Project arch. Hibner Archs., Garden City, NY, 1973-76; project mgr. BBM Archs., NYC, 1976-79; project dir. Gensler & Assocs., NYC, 1979-84; office dir., v.p., mem. nat. mgmt. com. Gensler, Washington, 1984-96, internat. practice leader profl. svc. firms, 1996—. Prin. works include interior design Sidley & Austin Worldwide, McDermott, Will & Emery, Latham & Watkins, Baker McKenzie, Covington & Burling. Asst. v.p., bd. dirs. Nat. Capital Area Coun.; active Greater Washington Bd. Trade, 1986; bd. dirs. Archdiocese Washington. Mem. AIA, Md. Soc. Archs., Notre Dame Club, Club at Franklin Sq. Roman Catholic. Home: 12517 Knightsbridge Ct Rockville MD 20850-3732 Office: Gensler 2020 K St NW Washington DC 20006-1806 Office Phone: 202-721-5300. Business E-Mail: christopher_murray@gensler.com.

MURRAY, CHRISTOPHER J.L., medical educator; BA in biology, summa cum laude, Harvard U., 1984; DPhil in internat. health economics, Oxford U., 1987; MD magna cum laude, Harvard Med. Sch., 1991. Asst. prof. internat. health economics Harvard Sch. Pub. Health, 1991—94, assoc. prof. internat. health economics, 1994—98, prof. internat. health economics, 1998—2001, adj. prof. internat. health economics, 2001—03, Richard Saltonsall prof. pub. policy, 2003—07; dir. burden of disease unit Harvard Ctr. Pop. and Devel. Studies, 1994—2007, dir., 2005—07, Harvard Initiative for Global Health, 2003—07; prof. social medicine Harvard Med. Sch., 2003—07; dir. global prog. on evidence of health policy, evidence and info. for policy cluster WHO, 1998—2000, exec. dir. evidence and info. for policy cluster, 2001—03; dir. Inst. Health Metrics and Evaluation U. Wash. Sch. Medicine, Seattle, 2007—, prof. global health, 2007—. Editor-in-chief Pop. Health Metrics. Recipient Elias Bengtsson medal, 2000; MacArthur fellow, Ctr. Pop. and Devel. Studies, 1990—92. Mem.: Inst. Medicine. Office: Inst Health Metrics and Evaluation Ste 600 2301 5th Ave Seattle WA 98121 E-mail: cjlm@u.washington.edu.*

MURRAY, CINDY, bank executive; 2 children. BEd, Ill. State U.; M in Indsl. Rels., Loyola U., Chgo. Human resources tng. and devel. dept. Exch. Nat. Bank; head, svc. products group LaSalle Bank, exec. v.p., head transaction banking divsn.; head, product innovation and devel. global product solutions in global corp. and investment banking Bank of America, 2007—. N.Am. regional mgmt. com. ABN AMRO Holding NV, tech. steering com.; exec. mgmt. com. LaSalle Bank; bd. dirs. Nat. Automated Clearing House Assn.; mng. bd. Clearing House Payments Co. Active Am. Cancer Soc. Named one of 25 Women to Watch, US Banker, 2007. Office: Bank of America Corp Ctr 100 N Tryon St Charlotte NC 28255

MURRAY, DANIEL RICHARD, lawyer; b. Mar. 23, 1946; s. Alfred W. and Gloria D. Murray. AB, U. Notre Dame, 1967; JD, Harvard U., 1970. Bar: Ill. 1970, U.S. Dist. Ct. (no. dist.) Ill. 1970, U.S. Ct. Appeals (7th cir.) 1971, U.S. Supreme Ct. 1974. Ptnr. Jenner & Block, Chgo., 1970—. Trustee Chgo. Mo. and Western Rlwy. Co., 1988-97; adj. prof. U. Notre Dame, 1997—. Co-author: Secured Transactions, 1978, Illinois Practice: Uniform Commercial Code Forms, 2006, Uniform Laws Annotated-Uniform Commercial Code Forms, 2007, Illinois Practice: Uniform Commercial Code with Illinois Code Comments, 2007. Bd. regents Big Shoulders Fund, Archdiocese of Chgo., Bernardin Ctr., Cath. Theol. Union. Mem.: Assn. Transp. Practitioners, Transp. Lawyers Assn., Am. Coll. Comml. Fin. Lawyers, Am. Bankruptcy Coll., Am. Law Inst., Am. Bankruptcy Inst., Cath. Lawyers Guild (bd. dirs.), Lawyers' Club Chgo. Roman Catholic. Home: 1307 N Sutton Pl Chicago IL 60610-2007 Office: Jenner & Block LLP 330 N Wabash Ave Ste 3800 Chicago IL 60611-3605 Office Phone: 312-923-2953. Business E-Mail: dmurray@jenner.com.

MURRAY, DAVID GEORGE, architect; b. Tulsa, Nov. 9, 1919; s. Lee Cloyd and Marion (Bennett) M.; m. Margaret Elizabeth Oldham, Sept. 23, 1944; children: Michael Allen, Lucy Margaret (Mrs. Norman Scheer), Patrick David. BArch, Okla. State U., Stillwater, 1942. Registered architect, Okla. Ptnr. Atkinson & Murray, Tulsa, 1949-52; prin. David G. Murray & Assocs., Tulsa, 1952-56; pres. Murray, Jones, Murray, Inc., Tulsa, 1957-85, chmn., 1986-89. Chmn., bd. govs. Licensed Architects, Oklahoma City, 1964-74. Prin. works include Cities Service Technology Ctr., Broken Arrow, Okla., Terminal Bldg. Tulsa Internat. Airport, St. Patrick's Ch., Oklahoma City, Coll. of Osteopathic Medicine and Surgery, Tulsa, First Nat. Tower, Tulsa, Hillcrest Med. Ctr., Tulsa, Thomas Gilcrease Mus., Tulsa, Tulsa Civic Ctr. Bldgs. Chmn., dir. Goodwill Industries of Tulsa, 1966-87; chmn., exec. com. Downtown Tulsa Unltd., 1975-87; v.p., exec. com., dir. Met. Tulsa C. of C., 1979-85. Served to 1st lt. USAF, 1942-45. Named to Hall of Fame Coll. Engrng. Okla. State U., 1969. Fellow AIA (pres. Tulsa chpt. 1964, mem. com. office practice 1983-87). Republican. Methodist. Avocations: travel, golf.

MURRAY, DIANE ELIZABETH, librarian; b. Detroit, Oct. 15, 1942; d. Gordon Lisle and Dorothy Anne (Steketee) LaBoueff; m. Donald Edgar Murray, Apr. 22, 1968. AB, Hope Coll., 1964; postgrad., Mich. State U., East Lansing, 1964-66; MLS, Western Mich. U., 1968; MM, Aquinas Coll., 1982. Catalog libr., asst. head acquisitions sect. Mich. State U. Librs., East Lansing, 1968-77; libr. tech. and automated svcs. Hope Coll., Holland, Mich., 1977-88; dir. librs. DePauw U., Greencastle, Ind., 1988-91; acquisitions libr. Grand Valley State U., Allendale, Mich., 1991—2008. Sec., vice chair, chairperson bd. trustees Mich. Libr. Consortium, Lansing, 1981—85. V.p. Humane Soc. Putnam County, Greencastle, 1990—91; bd. dirs. Loutit Dist. Libr., 1999—2008. Mem.: ALA. Methodist. Avocations: dog breeding and showing, handbell ringing. Office: Grand Valley State U Zumberge Libr Allendale MI 49401 Business E-Mail: murrayd@gvsu.edu.

MURRAY, DWAYNE M., fraternity organization administrator, lawyer; B, M, U. La., Lafayette; JD, Southern U. Sr. ptnr. Murray & Murray Personal Injury and Bankruptcy Attys. Mem. chpt. 7 panel trustees US Mid. Dist. Bankruptcy Ct.; founder Kappa Camp. Recipient Outstanding Citizen, Govt. La.; named to Power 150, Ebony mag., 2008. Mem.: Nat. Assn. Bankruptcy Trustees (bd. mem. 2006—), Kappa Alpha Psi, Frat., Inc. (life; grand polemarch 2007—, sr. grand polemarch, charter mem. Lafayette Alumni, state bd. mem. Province Alumni, sr. vice province polemarch Southwestern province, mem. Baton Rouge Alumni Chpt.). Office: Kappa Alpha Psi Frat Inc 2322-24 N Broad St Philadelphia PA 19132-4590

MURRAY, EILEEN K., investment company executive; b. NYC; BS in Acctg., Manhattan Coll., NY, 1980. Formerly with Peat Marwick; with Morgan Stanley, 1984—2002; v.p. Morgan Stanley Group Inc., 1988—91, prin., 1991—94, mng. dir., 1994, controller and treas.; chief adminstrv. officer, instl. securities group Morgan Stanley Dean Witter & Co., 1999—2002; head of global tech, ops. & product control Credit Suisse First Boston, NYC, 2002—05; head global ops. & tech., mem. mgmt. com. Morgan Stanley, NYC, 2005—07; pres., co-CEO, ptnr. Duff Capital Advisors; CEO Investment Risk Mgmt., LLC. Bd. mem. Am. Women's Econ. Devel. Corp.; bd. advisors Hewlett Packard Fin. Services; bd. dirs. OMGEO, LLC, 2001—. Mem. Argonne Nat. Lab. bd. governors UChicago Argonne, LLC, 2007—. Recipient Merit Achievement award, Women's Bond Club, 2003, Humanitarian award, Urban Stages, 2005; named one of Top 20 Nonbank Women in Fin., US Banker, 2007, 2008. Office: c/o UChicago Argonne LLC Argonne Dr Woodridge IL 60517*

MURRAY, HAYDN HERBERT, geology educator; b. Kewanee, Ill., Aug. 31, 1924; s. Herbert A. and Ardis M. (Adams) M.; m. Juanita A. Appenheimer, Dec. 16, 1944; children: Steven, Marilyn, Lisa. BS, U. Ill., Urbana-Champaign, 1948, MS, 1950, PhD, 1951; D (hon.), Universidad del Sol Blanca, Argentina, 2001, Ind. U., 2004. Asst. prof. geology Ind. U., 1951-53, assoc. prof., 1953-57, prof., chmn. dept. geology, 1973-84, prof. geology, 1984-94, prof. emeritus, 1994—; dir. research Georgia Kaolin Co., Elizabeth, N.J., 1957-60, mgr. ops., 1960-62, v.p. ops., 1962-64, exec. v.p., 1964-73; ret., 1994; cons. clay mineralogy, 1994—. Bd. dirs. Sabia Corp. Contbr. numerous articles to profl. jours.; patentee in field. Trustee Union Found., E.J. Grassmann Trust. Served with AUS, 1943-46. Recipient Disting. Svc. award Ind. U., 1993, Scholarship Achievement award, Ind. Acad., 2005, Lifetime Achievement award Ind. Profl. Geologists. Fellow Geol. Soc. Am., Mineral Soc. Am., Am. Ceramic Soc. (v.p. 1974-75), Tech. Assn. Pulp and Paper Industry; mem. Clay Minerals Soc. (pres. 1965-66, Disting. mem. 1980), Soc. Mining Metallurgy and Exploration (dist. mem., pres. elect 1987, pres. 1988, Hal Williams Hardinge award 1976, found. bd. trustees 1993-96), Internat. Clay Minerals Soc. (pres. 1993-97), Am. Assn. Petroleum Geologists, Am. Inst. Profl. Geologists (pres.-elect 1990, pres. 1991), Am. Geol. Inst. Found. (dir. 1990-96), Geol. Soc. Am. Fdn. (trustee 1992-97), Nat. Acad. Engring. Home: 901 South Fieldcrest Ct Bloomington IN 47401 Office Phone: 812-855-5583. Business E-Mail: murrayh@indiana.edu.

MURRAY, HEATHER M., history professor; Instr., history North Ga. Coll. and State U., Dahlonega, 2007—, Gainesville State Coll., Ga., 2007—. Grantee Rsch. grant, Colonial Dames America, 2004; T. Harry Williams fellowship, La. State U., 2005—06. Mem.: Southern Assn. Women Historians, Soc. Mil. History, Phi Kappa Phi, Phi Beta Kappa. Office: North Ga Coll and State Univ Young Hall Dahlonega GA 30597

MURRAY, JAMES A., bishop; b. Jackson, Mich., July 5, 1932; s. James Albert and Marcella Clare (Harris) Murray. BA, Sacred Heart Sem., Detroit; STB, St. John Sem., Plymouth, Mich.; JCL, Cath. U. Am., Washington. DC. Ordained priest Diocese of Lansing, Mich., 1958—, chancellor, moderator of curia, judge of tribunal; pastor St. Joseph Parish, St. Joseph, Mich., 1958—61, St. Mary Cathedral, 1962—73, rector, 1973—97; pastor St. Therese Parish, St. Gerard Parish, Lansing; monsignor, 1993; ordained bishop, 1998; bishop Diocese of Kalamazoo, Mich., 1997—2009, bishop emeritus Mich., 2009—. Roman Catholic. Office: Kalamazoo Diocese 215 N Westnedge Ave Kalamazoo MI 49007-3718

MURRAY, JAMES E., managed health care company executive; Ptnr. Coopers & Lybrand, Louisville; joined Humana Inc., Louisville, 1989, interim CFO, until 1997, CFO, 1997-2000, COO Health Plan Div., 2000—01, COO svc. ops., 2001—02, COO Market and Bus. Segments Ops., 2002—06, COO, 2006—. Office: Humana Inc 500 West Main St Louisville KY 40202*

MURRAY, JAMES MICHAEL, librarian, lawyer; b. Seattle, Nov. 8, 1944; s. Clarence Nicholas and Della May (Snyder) M.; m. Linda Monthy Murray. MLaw Librarianship, U. Wash., 1978; JD, Gonzaga U., 1971. Bar: Wash. 1974, U.S. Dist. Ct. (we. dist.) Wash. 1975, U.S. Dist. Ct. (ea. dist.) Wash. 1985. Reference/res. libr. U. Tex. Law Libr., Austin, 1978-81; assoc. law libr. Washington U. Law Libr., St. Louis, 1981-84; law libr., asst. prof. Gonzaga U. Sch. Law, Spokane, 1984-91; libr. East Bonner County Libr., 1991-97, U.S. Cts. Libr., Spokane, 1997—. Mem. state adv. bd. Nat. Reporter on Legal Ethics and Profl. Responsibility, 1982-91; cons. in field. Author: (with Reams and McDermott) American Legal Literature: Bibliography of Selected Legal Resources, 1985, (with Gasaway and Johnson) Law Library Administration During Fiscal Austerity, 1992; editor Tex. Bar Jour. (Books Appraisals Column), 1979-82; contbr. numerous articles and revs. to profl. jours., acknowledgements and bibliographies in field. Bd. dirs. ACLU, Spokane chpt., 1987-91, Wash. Vol. Lawyers for the Arts, 1976-78. Mem. ABA, Idaho Libr. Assn., Wash. State Bar Assn. (law sch. liaison com. 1986-88). Home: 921 W 29th Ave Spokane WA 99203-1318 Office Phone: 509-353-3293. Business E-Mail: James_Murray@lb9.uscourts.gov.

MURRAY, JAMES WILLIAM, III, manufacturing executive, lawyer; s. James William and Betty Murray; m. Susan Todd Murray; children: James William IV, Alyssa Ashley. BS, Okla. State U., Stillwater, Okla., 1977; JD, U. Okla., Norman, Okla., 1981. Bar: Okla. 1981. Atty. Linn, Helms, Kirk and Burket, Okla. City, Okla., 1981—82, Kirk and Chaney,

Okla. City, 1982—87, Cliff Wright and Assocs., Okla. City, Okla., 1987—90; v.p. LSB Industries, Inc., Okla. City, 1990—, sr. assoc. gen. counsel, 1990—. Coach youth soccer Frontier Country Soccer Assn., Okla. City, 2000—06, Mustang Youth Soccer Assn., Okla., 1989—2003. Avocations: soccer, boating. Office: LSB Industries Inc 16 S Pennsylvania Ave Oklahoma City OK 73107

MURRAY, JANET HOROWITZ, humanities educator, multimedia designer; b. NYC, June 8, 1946; d. Harry and Lillian (Lowlicht) H.; m. Thomas Murray, June 9, 1971; 2 children. BA, SUNY, Binghamton, 1967; MA, Harvard U., 1968, PhD, 1974. Systems programmer IBN, 1967; teaching fellow in English Harvard U., Cambridge, Mass., 1969-71; sr. rsch. sci. dept. humanities, dir. lab. advanced tech. in humanities MIT, Cambridge, 1971—. Presenter and speaker at profl. confs. and seminars, 1977—. Co-author: (with Anna Clark) An Index to the Englishwoman's Review, 1984; co-editor: The Englishwoman's Review of Social and Industrial Questions, 1866-1910 (with Myra Stark), 1980-84; author: Courtship and the English Novel: Feminist Readings in the Fiction of George Meredith, 1987, Strong-Minded Women and Other Lost Voices from Ninteenth Century England, 1982, 1984 (Am.), (Notable Book 1982 N.Y. Times Book Rev.), Miss Miles: A Tale of Yorkshire Life 60 Years Ago (1890) by Mary Taylor, 1991; co-author: (multimedia software) A la rencontre de Philippe, 1993 (Cindy Gold medal 1989, 1st Place Ivie award Internat. Interactive Comm. Soc. 1989, Nebr. Videodisc Merit award 1989, Spl. Recognition award Educom 1991, 1st prize Expolangues 1993), Dans le quartier St. Gervais, 1994; contbr. chapters to books, articles to profl. jours. Grantee: Annenberg/CPB Project, 1985-92, Consortium for Lang. Teaching and Learning, 1987-90, 91, 992-93, NEH, 1991, 1992-94 (3), Florence Gould Found., 1992-93, U.S. Dept. Edn., 1992-93. Mem. MLA (com. on computers and emerging techs. in teaching and rsch., nominee Dana award of Am. Assn. Colls.), Fgn. Lang.-Humanities Adv. Group Inst. for Acad. Tech. U. N.C. Office: Georgia Inst of Technology 686 Cherry St - Skiles 340 Atlanta GA 30309

MURRAY, JOHN EDWARD, JR., academic administrator, law educator; b. Phila., Dec. 20, 1932; s. John Edward and Mary Catherine (Small) M.; m. Isabelle A. Bogusevich, Apr. 11, 1955; children: Bruce, Susan, Timothy, Jacqueline. BS, LaSalle U., 1955; JD scholar, Cath. U., 1958; SJD fellow, U. Wis., 1959. Bar: Wis. 1959, Pa. 1986. Assoc. prof. Duquesne U. Sch. Law, Pitts., 1963-64, prof., 1965-67, Villanova U. Sch. Law, 1964-65, U. Pitts. Sch. Law, 1967-84, dean, 1977-84; dean Sch. Law Villanova U., 1984-86; disting. svc. prof. U. Pitts., 1986-88; pres. Duquesne U., Pitts., 1988—2001, chancellor, prof. law, 2001—. Cons. to law firms; chmn. Pa. Chief Justice's com. on comprehensive jud. and lawyer edn. Author: Murray on Contracts, 1974, 90, Murray, Commercial Transactions, 1975, Murray, Cases & Materials on Contracts, 1969, 76, 83, 91, Purchasing and the Law, 1978, Problems & Materials on Sales, 1982, Murray, Problems & Materials on Secured Transactions, 1987, Sales & Leases: Problems and Materials in National/International Transactions, 1993. Mayor Borough of Pleasant Hills, Pa., 1970-74. Mem. Assn. Am. Law Schs. (life, editor Jour. Legal Edn.), mem. Am. Law Inst. Democrat. Roman Catholic. Office: Duquesne U Office of Chancellor 600 Forbes Ave Pittsburgh PA 15282 Office Phone: 412-396-1750. Office Fax: 412-396-1754. E-mail: murray@duq.edu.*

MURRAY, JOHN FRANCIS, psychologist; b. Ft. Lauderdale, Fla., Nov. 30, 1961; s. John Richard and Joan Pfluger Murray; m. Charlotte Greenman, June 14, 1997; 1 child, Caroline. BA, Loyola U., La., 1983; M of Exercise/Sport Scis., U. Fla., 1992, MS, 1995, PhD, 1998. Lic. Psychologist Fla., 2000. Pvt. practice clin. and sport performance psychologist John F. Murray, PhD, Palm Beach, Fla., 1999—. Author: Smart Tennis: How to Play and Win the Mental Game; creator (performance index for football teams) Mental Performance Index (MPI); prodr.(radio talk show host): (sport psychology radio program) Mental Equipment Radio; author: (performance checklist for tennis players) Tennis Mind-Body Checklist. Post-Doctoral fellow, Fla. Internat. U., 1998—99. Mem.: APA (assoc.), Fla. Psychol. Assn. Palm Beach County Chpt. (assoc.; pres. 2002—02), Alpha Delta Gamma Epsilon Chpt. (life; treas. 1981—81, Most Valuable Athlete Epsilon Chpt. 1982). Avocations: travel, tennis, reading, writing, pub. speaking. Office: 139 N County Rd Ste 18C Palm Beach FL 33480 Office Fax: 561-805-8662; Home Fax: 561-805-8662. Personal E-mail: johnfmurray@mindspring.com.

MURRAY, JOHN LOYOLA, judge; b. Limerick, Ireland, June 27, 1943; s. John Cecil and Catherine Mary (Casey) M.; m. Gabrielle Mary Walsh, May 25, 1969; children: Catriona Joanne, Brian Conor. Barrister-at-law, King's Inns, Dublin, 1967, sr. counsel, 1981; LLD (hon.), U. Limerick, Ireland, 1992, New Eng. Sch. Law, 2006. Pvt. practice, Ireland, 1967-81, 83-87; atty. Gen. of Ireland, Dublin, 1982, 87-91; mem. Coun. of State, Ireland, 1987-91, 2004—; judge Ct. of Justice, EEC, Luxembourg, 1991—99, Supreme Ct. Ireland, Dublin, 1999—2004, chief justice, 2004—. Vis. prof. law U. Catholique de Louvain, 1997-2000. Recipient Order of Merit, Grand Cross Luxembourg. Mem. King's Inns (bencher), Fitzwilliam Lawn Tennis Club, Royal Irish Yacht Club, Stephen's Green Club. Avocations: yachting, swimming, art, travel. Office: Supreme Ct Ireland Four Cts Dublin 7 Ireland Office Phone: 01 888 6540.

MURRAY, JOHN PATRICK, psychologist, educator, researcher; b. Cleve., Sept. 14, 1943; s. John Augustine and Helen Marie (Lynch) M.; m. Ann Coke Dennison, Apr. 17, 1971; children: Jonathan Coke, Ian Patrick. PhD, Cath. U. Am., 1970. Rsch. dir. Office U.S. Surgeon Gen. NIMH, Bethesda, Md., 1969-72; asst. to assoc. prof. psychology Macquarie U., Sydney, 1973-79; vis. assoc. prof. U. Mich., Ann Arbor, 1979-80; dir. youth and family policy Boys Town Ctr., Boys Town, Nebr., 1980-85; prof., dir. Sch. Family Studies and Human Svcs. Kans. State U., Manhattan, 1985-98, interim assoc. vice provost rsch., 1998—2000; Scholar-in-residence Mind Sci. Found., San Antonio, 1996—97; mem. children's TV com. CBS, 1996—99; emeritus prof. devel. psychology Kans. State U., 2008—; vis. scholar Ctr. on Media and Child Health Harvard U. Med. Sch., 2004—; rsch. fellow dept. psychology Wash. Coll., 2009—. Author: Television and Youth: 25 Years of Research and Controversy, 1980, The Future of Children's TV, 1984, (with H.T. Rubin) Status Offenders: A Sourcebook, 1983, (with E.A. Rubenstein, G.A. Comstock) Television and Social Behavior, 3 vols., 1972, (with A. Huston and others) Big World, Small Screen: The Role of Television in American Society, 1992, (with C. Fisher and others) Applied Developmental Science, 1996, Children and Television: Fifty Years of Research (with N. Pecora and E. Wartella), 2006; contbr. numerous articles to profl. jours. Mem. Nebr. Foster Care Rev. Bd., 1982-84; mem. Advocacy Office for Children and Youth, 1980-85; mem. Nat. Coun. Children and TV, 1982-87; trustee The Villages Children's Homes, 1986—, Menninger Found., 1996—; mem. children's TV adv. bd. CBS-TV, 1996-99. Fellow Am. Psychol. Assn. (pres. div. child youth and family svcs. 1990); mem. Internat. Comm. Assn., Soc. Rsch. in Child Devel., Royal Commonwealth Soc. (London), Chester River Yachland Country Club. Office: Kans State U 303 Justin Hall Manhattan KS 66506-1304 Home: 312 Landing Ln Chestertown MD 21620 Home Phone: 443-282-0593. Personal E-mail: johnpatrickmurray@hotmail.com. E-mail: jpm@ksu.edu.

MURRAY, JOHN PATRICK, education educator; b. Watertown, NY, Mar. 7, 1947; s. Patrick and Madeline Irene (Palmer) M.; m. Judy Irene Farr, Aug. 31, 1968; children: Todd Michael, Tyson Patrick. BA, SUNY, 1969; MA, Ariz. State U., 1971; EdS, Wright State U., 1987; PhD, Ohio State U., 1990. Prof., adminstr. Clark State CC, Springfield, Ohio, 1971-92; assoc. dean curriculum., instrn. Genesee CC, Batavia, NY, 1992-96; asst. prof. SUNY, Brockport, NY, 1996-98; prof. higher edn. adminstrn. Tex. Tech. U., Lubbock, 1998—2007, Calif. St. U., LB, 2007—. Cons., presenter in field. Contbr. articles to profl. jours. NEH grantee, 1978, 78-81, 79, 94, NSF grantee, 1982, Ohio Program Humanities grantee, 1988, Ohio Bd. Regents REACH grantee, 1990; Ohio Humanities scholar, 1987-92, scholar Am. Assn. C.C. Study Coun., 1998, Fulbright-Hays scholar, 2004; recipient Disting. Svc. award Ohio Youth Commn., 1974, Disting. Rsch. award Tex. Tech. U., 2000. Mem. Assn. for the Study of Higher Edn., Am. Ednl. Rsch. Assn., Lions. Avocations: scuba, photography. Office: Calif State U Coll Edn 1250 Bellflower Blvd Long Beach CA 90840 Office Phone: 562-985-2458. Personal E-mail: 030747@msn.com. Business E-Mail: jmurray@csulb.edu.

MURRAY, JOSEPH EDWARD, retired plastic surgeon; b. Milford, Mass., Apr. 1, 1919; s. William Andrew and Mary (DePasquale) Murray; m. Virginia Link, June 2, 1945; children: Virginia, Margaret, Joseph Link, Katharine, Thomas, Richard. AB, Holy Cross Coll., 1940, DSc, 1965; MD, Harvard, 1943; DSc, Rockford Coll., Ill., 1966, Roger Williams Coll., 1986; PhD (hon.), Anna Marie Coll., 1993, SUNY, Albany, 1993, U. Suffolk, 1993, Magill U., Montreal, 1996; degree (hon.), Jefferson Med. Sch., 2006. Diplomate Am. Bd. Surgery, Am. Bd. Plastic Surgery. Chief plastic surgeon Peter Bent Brigham Hosp., Boston, 1951—86; chief plastic surgeon Children's Hosp. Med. Center, Boston, 1972—85; prof. surgery Harvard Med. Sch., 1970—86; ret., 1986. Chmn. Am. Bd. Plastic Surgery, 1969. Maj. M.C. US Army, 1944—47. Recipient Gold medal, Internat. Soc. Surgeons, 1963, Nobel prize for medicine or physiology, 1990, Sabin award, 1994, Lifetime Achievement award, Mass. Med. Soc., 1988, Laetare medal, Notre Dame, 2005. Fellow: AMA, AAAS (hon.), Royal Coll. Surgeons Edinburgh, Royal Coll. Surgeons Ireland, Royal Coll. Surgeons of Eng., Royal Australasian Coll. Surgeons; mem.: NAS, ACS (regent 1970—79, v.p. 1983), Am. Acad. Arts and Scis. (Hon. award 1962), Am. Assn. Plastic Surgeons (pres. 1964—65, Hon. award 1969), Soc. U. Surgeons, Boston Surg. Soc. (pres. 1975), New Eng. Surg. Assn. (pres. 1986—87), Am. Surg. Assn. (v.p. 1979), Harvard Med. Sch. Alumni Coun. (pres. 1984), Tavern Club, Badminton and Tennis Club, Wellesley Country Club, Alpha Omega Alpha. Home: 108 Abbott Rd Wellesley MA 02481-6104*

MURRAY, JULIA KAORU (MRS. JOSEPH E. MURRAY), occupational therapist; b. Wahiawa, Oahu, Hawaii, 1934; d. Gijun and Edna Tsuruko (Taba) Funakoshi; m. Joseph Edward Murray, 1961; children: Michael, Susan, Leslie. BA, U. Hawaii, 1956; cert. occupl. therapy, U. Puget Sound, 1958. Therapist Inst. Logopedics, Wichita, Kans., 1958; sr. therapist Hawaii State Hosp., Kaneohe, 1959; part-time therapist Centre County Ctr. for Crippled Children and Adults, State College, Pa., 1963; vice chmn. adv. bd. Hosp. Improvement Program East Oreg. State Hosp., Pendleton, 1974; v.p. Ind. Living, Inc., 1976—79; instr. job search; mem. adv. com. Oreg. Ednl. Coordinating Commn., 1979—82; mem. Oreg. Bd. Engring. Examiners, 1979—87; supr., occupl. therapist Fairview Tng. Ctr., Salem, Oreg., 1984—94; occupl. therapist U.S. Naval Hosp., Okinawa, Japan, 1994—99, occupl. therapist, Yokota A B divsn. Yokosuka, Japan, 1999—2005, occupl. therapist Misawa AB divsn., 2005—. Rep. from Umatilla County Commrs. to Blue Mountain Econ. Devel. Council, 1976-78; mem. Ashland Park and Recreation Bd., 1972-73; vice chmn. adv. bd. LINC, 1978; mem. exec. bd. Liberty-Boone Neighborhood Assn., 1979-83. Decorated Meritorious Civilian Svc. medal USN. Mem. Am. Occupational Therapy Assn., Oreg. Occupational Therapy Assn., Hawaii Occupational Therapy Assn. (sec. 1960, LWV (bd. dirs. Pendleton 1974, 77-78, pres. 1975-77; bd. dirs. Oreg. 1979-81, Ashland, Wis., 1967-71, Wis. v.p. 1970). Home Phone: 503-363-6558. Personal E-mail: jkfmurray@hotmail.com.

MURRAY, KATHLEEN ANNE, lawyer; b. LA, Feb. 14, 1946; d. Francis Albert and Dorothy (Thompson) M.; 1 child, Anne Murray Ladd; m. Arthur T. Perkins Jr., June 29, 1991. BA, U. Mich., 1967; JD, Hastings Coll. Law, 1973. Bar: Calif. 1973, U.S. Dist. Ct. (no. dist.) Calif. 1973, U.S. Ct. Appeals (9th cir.) 1973. Sr. staff atty Child Care Law Ctr., San Francisco, 1979—84, cons. child day care law and regulation, 1984—86; atty Epstein & Harris, San Francisco, 1985—86; gen. counsel Fisher Friedman Assocs., San Francisco, 1986—89; assoc. gen. counsel Calif. State Automobile Assn., San Francisco, 1989—98; sr. counsel Firemen's Fund Ins. Co., San Francisco, 1998—2002; prin. Mercer, 2003—. Exec. dir., editl. adv. bd. Parenting Mag., 1985-87; chair Labor and Employment Law Com. Assn. Corp. Coun. Am., 2001-03 Editor: Child Care Center Legal Handbook; Tax Guide for California Child Care Providers; contbr. articles to profl. jours. Mem. adv. coun. Humanities West, Inc., 1986-96; vestry Episcopal Ch. of St. Mary the Virgin, 1990-92; pres. Parents' Assn., Lick-Wilmerding H.S., 1993-94; Pers. Practices Com. Episcopal Diocese of Calif., 1998-2003. Mem.: Assn. Corp. Counsel (chair labor and employment law com. 2001—03). Democrat. Episcopalian. Office: Mercer Four Embarcadeo Ctr Ste 400 San Francisco CA 94111-4156 Business E-Mail: kathleen.murray@mercer.com.

MURRAY, KEITH, educational association administrator; b. Mpls., June 26, 1958; s. Donald and Joyce Murray; m. Dagmar Clever, Oct. 18, 1980; children: Aubryn Cooperman, Tavia, Kyle. BS in Mech. Engring., Purdue U., West Lafayette, Ind., 1979, MS in Indsl. Adminstrn., 1980, MME, 1982. Dir., space mgmt. and academic scheduling Purdue U., 1998—; founding ptnr. UniTime LLC, West Lafayette, 2008—. Bd. dirs. Higher Edn. Facilities Mgmt. Assn., Chgo., 1995—2002; with, facilities acad. Soc. Coll. and U. Planning, Ann Arbor, Mich., 2006—. Contbr. articles to profl. jours. Com. mem. City West Lafayette Recycling Adv. Com., 1988—2004; cmty. rep. City West Lafayette Strategic Planning Forum, 1996—2008. Scholar, Nat. Merit Scholarship Corp., 1976—80. Avocation: mountain climbing. Office: Purdue Univ 400 Centennial Mall Dr West Lafayette IN 47906-2016 Business E-Mail: kmurray@purdue.edu.

MURRAY, KEVIN DENNIS, surgeon; b. Paterson, NJ, June 22, 1953; s. Robert Emmet and Florence Sophie (Nordman) M. BS in Chemistry, Mt. St. Mary's Coll., 1974; MD, U. Md., 1978. Cert. Am. Bd. of Surgery, 1995, Am. Bd. of Thoracic Surgery, 1997. Intern U. Chgo.-Pritzker Med. Sch., 1978-79; resident in surgery U. Chgo.-Pritzker Med. Sch. Hosps. and Clinics, 1979-82; Cardiothor resident Yale-New Haven (Conn.) Hosp.-Yale U. Sch. Medicine, 1984-86; fellow in bioengring. U. Utah, 1982-84; asst. prof. Ohio State U., 1986-93; staff Arthur James Cancer Inst., Columbus, Ohio, 1990-93; staff cardiothoracic surgery Barnes-Jewish Hosp., St. Louis, 1996-97; faculty cardiothoracic surgery Washington U., St. Louis, 1996-97; assoc. prof., chief cardiothoracic surgery U. Nev. Sch. of Medicine, Las Vegas, 1997—2002; chief thoracic surgery So. Nev. VA Sys., 1998—2002; cardiothoracic surgeon Kaiser Permanenti Moanalua Hosp., Honolulu, 2003—06. Med. dir. dept. circulation tech. Sch. Allied Health, Ohio State U., 1988-93; cons. Inst. Bioengring., Salt Lake City, 1995—; dir. The Heart and Lung Inst., U. Nev. Sch. Medicine, 1999-2002. Fellow Am. Coll. Surgery, Am. Coll. Cardiology, Am. Coll. Chest Physicians, Internat. Soc. Heart and Lung Transplantation, Soc. Thoracic Surgeons; mem. Am. Soc. Artificial Internal Organs, Assn. Thoracic Surgeons, Alpha Omega Alpha. Home: 309 S 48th St Richmond IN 47374-6071 Personal E-mail: kdmurray622@aol.com.

MURRAY, LAWRENCE, management consultant; b. NYC, May 10, 1939; s. Gilbert and Edna (Blatt) M.; m. Jun Liu Murray; children: Robert, Stacy, David, Daniel, Abigail, Adam. BA, Cornell U., 1961; MBA, U. Okla., 1966; PhD, Pacific Western U., 1993. Cert. Pa. Food Mgmt. Account exec. Merrill Lynch, Paramus, NJ, 1965-69; chmn., pres. Murray, Lind & Co., Inc., Jersey City, 1969-72; dir. investor rels. IU Internat. Corp., Phila., 1972-73, dir. spl. projects, 1974-75; dir. fin. comm., mem. exec. staff of chmn. bd. ARA Svcs., Inc., Phila., 1975—78; chmn., chief exec. officer Century Mgmt. and affiliated cos., West Chester, Pa., 1976-82; chmn. bd., CEO Creative Mgmt. Corp., Bala Cynwyd and West Chester, Pa., 1982-87, Fin. Mgmt. Profl. Corp., West Chester, 1983-89; chmn. bd. dirs. Venture Frontiers Co., Denver, 1984-89; chmn. bd., CEO Fin. Intelligence Corp., West Chester, 1989-95; CEO, chmn. bd. dirs. Healthy Living Ctrs., West Chester, 1993—. Lectr. bus. orgn. and mgmt. Bergen C.C., 1971-72; chmn. bd. dirs. Med. Intelligence Corp., West Chester, 1993-95; CEO, chmn. bd. dirs. Miramax Corp., 1996-; chmn. bd. dirs., CEO, Tax Doctor Corp., West Chester, 2002-08; cons. US Mgmt. Corp., West Chester, 2008-. Author: The Organized Stockbroker, 1970; A New Era in Mergers and Acquisitions, 1974; Communications: Management's Newest Marketing Skill, 1976, Powerful Tax-Saving Strategies for Honest People, 1992, Teach Your Children How to Eat Properly and Add 20 Years to Their Lives, 1999; contbr. articles to profl. jours. Pres., Congregation Beth Israel, Media, Pa., 1977-78, Parents Without Ptnrs., Valley Forge, Pa., 1982-83, PTO West Chester East HS, Pa., 2007-09; v.p. Cornell U. Class of 1961, 1981-86; mem. White House Conf. on Bus. Ethics in Am., 1986; active Beth Chaim Reform Synagogue. Served to 1st lt. arty./intelligence US Army, 1963—64. Decorated U.S. Army Commendation medal. Mem. Nat. Investor Rels. Inst. (pres. Phila. chpt. 1976-78), Internat. Coun. Shopping Ctrs., Am. Health Info. Mgmt. Assn., C. of C. Greater West Chester. Home: 625 Beaumont Cir West Chester PA 19380 Personal E-mail: lmurray761@aol.com.

MURRAY, LIZ, legislative staff member; b. Rochester, NY; BA, Yale U., New Haven; MPP, Harvard U. Kennedy Sch. Govt. Sr. policy advisor, Rep. Steny Hoyer US House of Reps., Washington. Democrat. Office: 1705 Longworth House Office Bldg Washington DC 20515 Office Phone: 202-225-4131. Office Fax: 202-225-4300.*

MURRAY, MICHAEL, gynecologist, department chairman; b. Stanford, Calif., May 19, 1967; s. James and Gail Murray; m. Gayle Murray, May 1, 1993. BA, UC Santa Barbara, Calif., 1989; MD, Tulane U. Sch. Medicine, New Orleans, 1993; Internship & Residency, Oreg. Health Scis. U., Portland, 1997; fellow, U. NC, Chapel Hill, 1999. Lic. State Calif., 1999, cert. in ob-gyn. 2000, in reproductive endocrinology,infertility Am. Coll. Ob-Gyn., 2002. Asst. prof. UC Davis Med. Sch., Sacramento, 1999—2000; dir. reproductive endocrinology & infertility Kaiser Permanente, Sacramento, 2000—04; owner Northern Calif. Fertility Med. Ctr., Roseville, 2004—. Contbr. scientific papers (ACOG Rsch. award, 1998). Recipient Spl. Excellence in Endoscopic Procedures, Am. Assn. Gynecologic Laparoscopists, 1997; grant, Protein Techs. Internat., 1999—2001, USDA, 2002—06. Fellow: Soc. Reproductive Endocrinolgy & Infertility; mem.: Northern Calif. Ob-Gyn. Soc. (bd. mem. 2008—), Am. Soc. Reproductive Medicine. Office: Ncfmc 1130 Conroy Land Roseville CA 95661 Office Fax: 916-773-8391. Business E-Mail: mmurray@ncfmc.com.

MURRAY, MICHAEL PATRICK, lawyer; b. Milw., Jan. 31, 1930; s. Michael James and Florence Mary M.; m. Allene Vereen, May 8, 1976; children: Bryan Patrick, Laura Renee. BA, Milton Coll., Wis., 1953; JD, Marquette U., 1958; LLM, John Marshall Law Sch., 1960; D of Juridicial Sci., George Washington U., DC, 1973; M of Liberal Arts, Johns Hopkins U., 1996. Bar: Wis. 1958, Calif. 1966, U.S. Supreme Ct. 1967, U.S. Ct. Appeals (9th cir.) 1982, D.C. 1989, Va. 1989, U.S. Ct. Appeals (D.C. cir.) 1989, U.S. Ct. Appeals (4th cir.) 1990. Commd. 2d lt. USMC, 1953, advanced through grades to col., 1975, prosecutor and def. counsel, 1960—66, trial judge and SJA, 1966—69, dir. policy and research Washington, 1969—72, dir. Law Ctr. Iwakuni, Japan, 1973—74; dep. legal advisor, chmn. Joint Chiefs of Staff, Washington, 1974—75; ret. USMC, 1978; trial atty. Anderson & Murphy, Milw., 1958—60; apellate judge USN Ct. of Rev., Washington, 1975—78; pvt. practice, San Diego, 1982—89; atty., counsel Clary, Lawrence, Lickstein & Moore, Falls Church, Va., 1989—91; ptnr. Michael Patrick Murray & Assocs., South Riding, Va., 1991—; asst. gen. counsel NRA, Washington, 1992—95. Assoc. prof. law Pepperdine U., Malibu, Calif., 1978-80, Marquette U., Milw., 1980-81; adj. prof. law Western State U., San Diego, 1983-88, Nat. U. Coll. Law, 1988-89; pro bono vol. atty. for indigents, San Diego, 1982-89. Author: Quarter: the Warrior's Dilemma, 1967, (law study) Eichman and Major German War Criminal Trials, 1973, O'Ryans Law, 1992, Murder By Class, 1997, Law Is a Jealous Mistress, 1999, People Needing People, 2000, Love's Mirror, 2003, Judgment in NAM, 2005, Passion, Prose and Poetry, 2005. Mem. Calif. Bar Assn., Wis. Bar Assn., D.C. Bar Assn., Va. Bar Assn., Am. Legion, First and Third Marine Div. Assn., Marine Corps Assn., Marine Mustang Assn., Phi Delta Phi. Roman Catholic. Avocations: poetry, creative writing. Office: Michael Patrick Murray & Assocs 26083 Glasgow Dr South Riding VA 20152 Office Phone: 703-327-1350. E-mail: michael.p.murray@att.net.

MURRAY, NIAL PATRICK, retired anesthesiologist educator; b. Dec. 9, 1927; came to U.S. MD, Nat. U. Ireland, 1954. Diplomate Am. Bd. Anesthesiology. Resident in anesthesiology Liverpool (Eng.) Hosps., 1959-64; asst. prof. anesthesiology Wake Forest U.; retired. Fellow Royal Coll. Anaesthetists (diplomate); mem. Am. Soc. Anesthesiologists. Home: 3252 Merion Ct Winston Salem NC 27104-3947

MURRAY, PATTY (PATRICIA LYNN MURRAY), United States Senator from Washington; b. Seattle, Wash., Oct. 11, 1950; d. David L. and Beverly A. (McLaughlin) Johns; m. Robert R. Murray, June 2, 1972; children: Randy P., Sara A. BA, Wash. State U., 1972. Sec. various companies, Seattle, 1972-76; citizen lobbyist various ednl. groups, Seattle, 1983-88; legis. lobbyist Orgn. for Parent Edn., Seattle, 1977-84; instr. Shoreline Community Coll., Seattle, 1984-88; mem. Wash. State Senate, Seattle, 1989-92; US Senator from Wash., 1993—; mem. US Senate Appropriations Com., US Senate Veterans Affairs Com., US Senate Health, Edn., Labor, & Pensions Com., US Senate Budget Com., US Senate Rules & Adminstrn. Com., Joint Congressional Com. on Printing. Chairwoman Democratic Senatorial Campaign Com. (DSCC),

2001—03; sec. US Senate Democratic Conf., 2007—. Co-author (with Catherine Whitney): Nine and Counting: The Women of the Senate, 2000. Mem. bd. Shoreline Sch., Seattle, 1985-89; mem. steering com. Demonstration for Edn., Seattle, 1987; founder, chmn. Orgn. for Parent Edn., Wash., 1981-85; 1st Congl. rep. Wash. Women United, 1983-85. Recipient Outstanding award Washing. Women United, 1986, Recognition of Svc. to Children award Shoreline PTA Coun., 1986, Golden Acorn Svc. award, 1989; Outstanding Svc. award Wash. Women United, 1986, Outstanding Svc. to Pub. Edn. award Citizens Ednl. Ctr. NW, Seattle, 1987, Wash. State Legis. of Yr., 1990, George Falcon Spike award Nat. Assn. Railroad Passengers, 2003, Person of Yr. award Wash. State VFW, 2004. Democrat. Roman Catholic. Office: US Senate 173 Russell Senate Office Bldg Washington DC 20510-0001 also: Henry M Jackson Federal Bldg Ste 2988 915 Second Ave Seattle WA 98174-4067 Office Phone: 202-224-2621, 206-553-5545. Office Fax: 202-224-0238, 206-553-0891. E-mail: senator_murray@murray.senate.gov.*

MURRAY, R. SCOTT, computer software company executive; Grad., U. We. Ont. Chartered acct. Arthur Andersen, Canada; exec. v.p., CFO The Learning Co., 1994—99; pres., COO Stream Internat., 2000—01; CEO Modus Media Internat., 2002—05; pres., CEO 3Com Corp., Marlborough, Mass., 2006—. Office: 3Com Corp 350 Campus Dr Marlborough MA 01752-3064

MURRAY, RAYMOND LE ROY, nuclear engineering educator; b. Lincoln, Nebr., Feb. 14, 1920; s. Ray Annis and Bertha (Mann) M.; m. Ilah Mae Rengler, June 16, 1941; children: Stephen, Maureen, Marshall; m. Quin Meyer, June 3, 1967; 1 stepdau., Tucker; m. Elizabeth Reid, May 12, 1979; stepchildren: Michael, Nancy, James. BS, U. Nebr., 1940, MS, 1941; PhD, U. Tenn., 1950; postgrad., U. Calif., Berkeley, 1941-43. Physicist U. Calif. Radiation Lab., Berkeley, 1942-43; asst. dept. supt. Tenn. Eastman Corp., Oak Ridge, 1943-47; research physicist Carbide & Carbon Chem. Co., Oak Ridge, 1947-50; prof. physics N.C. State U., 1950-57, Burlington prof. physics, 1957-80, prof. emeritus, 1980—, head dept. physics, 1960-63, head dept. nuclear engring., 1963-74. Acting dir. Nuclear Reactor Project, 1956-57; cons. Oak Ridge Nat. Lab., 1950-68, Los Alamos Nat. Lab., 1988-92, also to industry and govt. Author: Introduction to Nuclear Engineering, 1954, 2d edit., 1961, Nuclear Reactor Physics, 1957, Physics: Concepts and Consequences, 1970, Nuclear Energy, 1975, 6th edit., 2009, Understanding Radioactive Waste, 1982, 5th edit., 2003; mem. edit. adv. bd., U.S. exec. editor Jour. Nuclear Energy, 1963-73; adv. editor Annals Nuclear Energy, 1973—; contbr. numerous articles to profl. jours. and encys. Mem. adv. com. on radiation N.C. Bd. Health, 1958-59; mem. Gov.'s Tech. Adv. Com. on Low Level Radioactive Waste, 1980-87; mem. N.C. Radiation Protection Commn., 1979-87, chmn., 1980-82; mem., vice chmn., chmn. N.C. Low Level Radioactive Waste Mgm. Authority, 1987-93. Recipient O. Max Gardner award U. N.C., 1965; Arthur H. Compton award, 1970, Donald G. Fink award IEEE, 1988, Eugene P. Wigner Reactor Physicist award, 1994. Fellow Am. Phys. Soc., Am. Nuclear Soc. (chmn. edn. div. 1966-67, chmn. Eastern Carolinas sect. 1976-77, mem. nominating com. 1989); mem. Am. Soc. Engring. Edn. (chmn. com. on relationships with AEC 1967-68, chmn. nuclear engring. div. 1970-71, Glenn Murphy award 1976), N.C. Soc. Engrs. (Outstanding Engring. Achievement award 1975), Atomic Indsl. Forum (edn. coun. 1970-73), Inst. Nuclear Power Ops. (adv. coun. 1985-87, 89-94), Phi Beta Kappa, Sigma Xi, Pi Mu Epsilon, Phi Kappa Phi. Home: 235 Springmoor Dr Raleigh NC 27615 Business E-Mail: murray@eos.ncsu.edu.

MURRAY, RICHARD BENNETT, retired physics professor; b. Marietta, Ga., Dec. 5, 1928; s. William Moore and Ruth (Mozley) M.; m. Clella Bay, Apr. 1, 1956; children: Ada, Annette. BA, Emory U., 1947; MS, Ohio State U., 1950; PhD, U. Tenn., 1955. Rsch. asst. Gaseous Diffusion Plant, Oak Ridge, Tenn., 1947-48; rsch. physicist Oak Ridge Nat. Lab., 1955-66; vis. assoc. prof. physics U. Del, Newark, 1962-63, assoc. prof., 1966-69, prof., 1969-98, prof. emeritus, 1999—, acting chmn. dept. physics, 1975-76, univ. coord. for grad. studies, 1979-85, assoc. provost grad. studies, 1986-88, acting provost, v.p. acad. affairs, 1988-91, provost, 1993-94, ret., 1998. Lectr. physics U. Tenn., Knoxville, 1963-66; vis. rsch. physicist U.S. Naval Rsch. Lab., 1991-92; vis. scientist Clarendon Lab., Oxford U., 1992; cons. to industry, 1957-93; councillor Oak Ridge Associated Univs., 1979-88, bd. dirs., 1983-94, vice chmn. coun., 1983-85, chmn. coun., 1985-88; sec.-treas. NE Assn. Grad. Schs., 1982-84; dir. U. Del. Press, 1979-82. Contbr. numerous articles on exptl. nuclear and solid state physics to profl. publs., 1948-85. Trustee Sanford Sch., Hockessin, Del., 1981-85; chmn. bd. dirs. Oak Ridge Associated Univs. Found., 1989-94; bd. dirs. Del. Inst. for Med. Edn. and Rsch., 1989-91. Predoctoral fellow Oak Ridge Inst. Nuclear Studies, 1953-55; grantee AEC, NSF, Dept. Energy, 1967-84. Fellow AAAS, Am. Phys. Soc.; mem. Southeastern Univs. Rsch. Assn. (bd. dirs. 1989-97), Phi Beta Kappa, Sigma Xi, Sigma Pi Sigma, Phi Kappa Phi, Cosmos Club. Home: 4 Bridlebrook Ln Newark DE 19711-2058 Office: U Del Dept Physics & Astronomy Newark DE 19716 Office Phone: 302-731-4520. Business E-Mail: rmurray@udel.edu.

MURRAY, RICHARD M., engineering educator; BS with honors in elec. engring., Calif. Inst. Tech., 1985; MS in elec. engring. and computer sciences, U. Calif., Berkeley, 1989, PhD, 1991. Asst. prof. mech. engring. Calif. Inst. Tech., 1991—97, assoc. prof. mech. engring., 1997—2000, prof. mech. engring., 2000—05, chair Divsn. Engring. and Applied Sci., 2000, prof. Control and Dynamical Sys., 2005—; dir. mechatronic systems United Technologies Rsch. Ctr., 1998—2000. Mem. info. sci. and tech. study group Def. Advanced Rsch. Projects Agy., Dept. Def., 2000—; mem. R&D strategy adv. com. Rockwell Sci. Co., 2001—; mem. Jet Propulsion Lab. adv. coun. NASA, 2001—; mem. vis. com. Dept. Mech. Engring., MIT, 2001—; chair exec. bd. Collaborative Ctr. on Control Sci., 2002—; mem. sci. adv. bd. USAF, 2002—; cons. Alphatech, Raytheon, United Technologies Rsch. Ctr., Northrop Corp. Recipient Eliahu Jury Award, U. Calif. Berkeley, 1991, Early Faculty Career Devel. Award, NSF, 1995, Young Investigator Award, Office Naval Rsch., 1995, Donald P. Eckman Award, Am. Automatic Control Coun., 1997; Richard P. Feynman-Hughes Faculty Fellowship, Calif. Inst. Tech., 1993. Achievements include patents for Actuator Bandwidth and Rate Limit Reduction for Control of Compressor Rotating Stall (with Simon Yeung), US Patent 5,984,625, Nov. 1999. Office: Control and Dynamical Systems 107-81 Calif Inst Tech MC 107-81 Pasadena CA 91125

MURRAY, RICHARD MAXIMILIAN, insurance company executive; b. Vienna, Nov. 21, 1922; came to U.S., 1955, naturalized, 1961; s. and Elizabeth Helen Peiker. Grad. in world commerce studies, U. Vienna; postgrad., Columbia U. Asst. sec. Sterling Offices Ltd. (reins. intermediaries), London, Toronto, NYC, 1951—59; v.p. Guy Carpenter, Inc. (reins. intermediaries), NYC, 1959—68, Travelers Ins. Cos., 1968—87, ret., 1987. Mng. dir. La Metropole Ins. Co., Brussels, ret., 1987; chmn. bd. Nippon Mgmt. Corp., N.Y.C., ret., 1991; chmn. bd. Travelers Marine Corp., ret., 1987; pres. Travelers Reins Co. Bermuda Ltd., ret., 1987; pres. Travelers of Asia Ltd., Hong Kong, ret., 1987; vice-chmn. bd. La Prov Corp., N.Y.C.; bd. electors Ins. Hall of Fame; bd. dirs. United Am. Inst. Co., United Am. Holdings Co., Inc.; mem. adv. bd. Firemark Global Ins. Fund, L.P.; dir. emeritus Davis Internat. Total Return Fund.; guest prof. Donau U., Krems, Austria. Contbr. articles to profl. publs. Decorated for promotion of pvt. ins. (Peru); Knight Order of St. John, Knights of Malta (ambassador at large). Mem. Internat. Ins. Coun. (chmn. 1979-81, award 1990). Home: 60 Remsen St Apt 10C Brooklyn NY 11201-3453 Office: 5 Penn Plz Ste 1916 New York NY 10001 Personal E-mail: richardmurray@usa.net. Business E-Mail: nyork@gnp.com.mx.

MURRAY, ROBERT FULTON, JR., physician; b. Newburgh, NY, Oct. 19, 1931; s. Robert Fulton and Henrietta Frances (Judd) Murray; m. Isobel Ann Parks, Aug. 26, 1956; children: Colin Charles(dec.), Robert Fulton III, Suzanne Frances, Dianne Akwe. BS, Union Coll., Schenectady, 1953; MD, U. Rochester, NYC, 1958; MS, U. Wash., Seattle, 1968. Diplomate Am. Bd. Internal Medicine, Am. Bd. Med. Genetics. Intern Denver Gen. Hosp., 1958—59; resident in internal medicine U. Colo. Med. Ctr., 1959—62; staff investigator (service with USPHS) Nat. Inst. Arthritis and Metabolic Diseases, NIH, Bethesda, Md., 1962—65; NIH spl. fellow med. genetics U. Wash., 1965—67; faculty Howard U. Coll. Medicine, Washington, 1967—74, prof. pediatrics and medicine, 1974—, grad. prof., 1976, prof. oncology, 1976, chief divsn. med. genetics, 1968—; chmn. dept. genetics and human genetics Howard U. Coll. Medicine Grad. Sch., 1976—. Nat. adv. gen. med. scis. coun. NIH, 1971—75, recombinant DNA adv. com., 1988—92; ethics adv. bd. to sec. HEW, 1978—80; chmn. Washington Mayor's Adv. Com. on Metabolic Disorders, 1980—89; mem. Med. Com. Human Rights. Co-author: Genetic Variation and Disorders in Peoples of African Origin, 1990; co-editor: Genetic, Metabolic and Developmental Aspects of Mental Retardation, 1972, Genetic Counseling: Facts, Values and Norms, 1979, The Human Genome Project and the Future of Health Care, 1996; mem. editl. bd.: Am. Jour. Clin. Genetics, 1977—93, Ency. Bioethics, 1975—77, 1993—95, Jour. Clin. Ethics, 1990. Sci. adv. bd. Nat. Sickle Cell Anemia Found.; trustee Union Coll., 1972—80. Grantee Rsch. grantee, NIH, 1969—75; fellow Rotary Found. fellow, 1955—56. Fellow: AAAS, ACP, Am. Coll. Med. Genetics, Inst. Soc., Ethics and Life Scis., Inst. Medicine; mem.: Acad. Medicine Washington, Genetics Soc. Am., Am. Soc. Human Genetics, Assn. Acad. Minority Physicians, AAUP, Neighbors Inc. D.C., Alpha Omega Alpha, Sigma Xi. Unitarian Universalist. Home: 510 Aspen St NW Washington DC 20012-2740 Office: Howard U Coll Medicine PO Box 75 Washington DC 20059-0001 Office Phone: 202-806-6382. Personal E-mail: murrayjrf31@rcn.com.

MURRAY, ROBERT GRAY, sculptor; b. Vancouver, BC, Can., Mar. 2, 1936; U.S. citizen; s. John Gray and Vera (Meakin) M.; m. Cintra Wetherill Lofting, Jan. 23, 1971; children: Rebecca and Megan (twins), Claire, Hillary. Student, U. Sask., Can., 1956-58. One man shows Betty Parsons Gallery, N.Y.C., 1965, 66, 68, David Mirvish Gallery, Toronto, 1967, 68, 72, 73, 74, 75, Jewish Mus., N.Y.C., 1967, Hammarskjold Plaza, N.Y.C., 1971, Paula Cooper Gallery, N.Y.C., 1974, Janie Lee Gallery, Houston, 1977, Hamilton Gallery, N.Y.C., 1977, 79, 80, Klonaridis Inc., Toronto, 1979, 81, 82, Rice U., 1978, Dayton Mus., 1979, Columbus Mus., 1979, Lamont Gallery, Phillips Acad., Exeter, N.H., 1983, Art Gallery Greater Victoria, 1983, Gallery One, Toronto, 1985, Culturale Canadese Roma, 1985, Gallery 291, Atlanta, 1986, Richard Greene Gallery, N.Y.C.,1986, L.A., 1987, Del. Art Mus., Wilmington, 1990, Muhlenberg Coll., Allentown, Pa., 1992, Mira Godard Gallery, Toronto, Reading (Pa.) Pub. Mus., 1994, 96, Andre Zarre Gallery, N.Y.C., 1994, 04, 05, spl. showing Hillary Ground for Sculpture, Trenton N.J., 1997, retrospective, 1997, Moore Gallery, Toronto, 1999, 2001, 03, Ericson Gallery, Phila., 1999, McLaren Gallery, Barrie, 2001, Nat. Gallery of Can., Ottawa, 1999, Winchester Galleries, Victoria, 2004, Freedman Gallery, Reading, 2004; exhibited in group shows at Whitney Mus. 1996— Am., Art, N.Y.C., 1964-66, Tibor de Nagy Gallery, N.Y.C., 1965, Musée cantonal des Beaux Arts, Lausanne, Switzerland, 1966, World House Gallery, N.Y.C., 1966, Betty Parsons Gallery, 1966, Sch. Visual Arts, N.Y.C., 1967, Los Angeles County Mus., 1967, Nat. Gallery Can., Toronto, 1967, Inst. Contemporary Art, Boston, 1967, U. Toronto, 1967, Guggenheim Mus., N.Y.C., 1967, Inst. Torcuato Di Tella, Buenos Aires, 1967, Musée d'Art Moderne, Paris, 1968, Whitney Mus., 1967, Walker Art Gallery, 1969, X Sao Paulo Biennial, Brazil, 1969, Boston City Hall, 1971, Artist and Fabricator, Amherst, Mass., 1975, Met. Mus., N.Y.C., 1983, Del. Art Mus., 1990, GrandRapids (Mich.) Mus., 1994; represented in permanent collections, Montreal Mus. Fine Arts, Nat. Gallery Can., Joseph Hirshhorn Collection, Art Gallery Ont., Larry Aldrich Mus., Ridgefield, Conn., New Brunswick Mus., Whitney Mus. Am. Art, Met. Mus., N.Y.C., Columbus Mus., Dayton Art Inst., Storm King Art Center, Del. Art. Mus., Wilmington, Muhlenberg Coll., Allentown, Pa., others; major commns. include, Everson Mus., Syracuse, N.Y., Fredonia (N.Y.) State Coll., Canadian Dept. External Affairs, Ottawa, Ont., U. Mass., U. Toronto, Ont., State Mus., Juneau, Alaska, Honeywell Corp., Mpls., CNIB, One King West, Toronto, also others. Decorated Order of Can. Home Phone: 610-869-8696. E-mail: rob_murray@earthlink.net.

MURRAY, ROBERT PATRICK, musician, educator; b. Emporia, Kans., Dec. 26, 1958; s. Robert Patrick and Gloria Jacqueline Murray; m. Lauren Baker Murray, June 26, 2001. MusB, Portland State U., 1994, MusM, 1996; Mus D, U. North Tex., 2002. Asst. dir. bands U. Wash., Seattle, 1983—87; regional tng. dir. Kay-Bee Toys, Portland, Oreg., 1988—93; prof. trumpet Murray State U., Ky., 1999—2003, U. North Colo., Greeley, Colo., 2003—. Prin. trumpet Portland Musical Theater Co., Portland, Oreg., 1990—98; trumpet Dallas Brass, Dallas, 1997—2000; prin. trumpet Portland Opera, Portland, Oreg., 1998—99, Owensboro Symphony Orch., Owensboro, Ky., 1999—2003, Orquesta Sinfonica de Mineria, Mexico City, 2000—03; trumpet Harmonie del Sur, Evans, Colo., 1999—; first trumpet Rocky Mountain Brass Quintet, Greeley, Colo., 2003—. Musician: (trumpet soloist and clinician) World Association of Symphonic Bands and Ensembles, British Association of Symphonic Bands and Ensembles, (trumpet soloist and performer) International Trumpet Guild, (trumpet soloist) Owensboro Symphony Orchestra; author (lecture recital): (college music society) Synthesis and Integration: World and Electro-Acoustic Music in the Applied Studio, (nat. symposium on music instruction tech) A Global View: Applying World and Electro-Acoustic Music to the Intrumental Studio; author: (dissertation) A Performance Guide to Tomas Svoboda's Duo Concerto for Trumpet and Organ. V.p. prodn. programming Murray Civic Music Assn., Murray, Ky., 1999—2003. Recipient Spl. Commendation, Colo. House of Reps. Mem.: Hist. Brass Soc., Coll. Music Soc., Music Educators Nat. Conf., Internat. Trumpet Guild. Achievements include research in The introduction of world music and electro-acoustic music into the Applied Music Studio. Office: U Northern Colorado School Music Campus Box 28 Greeley CO 80639 Business E-Mail: robert.murray@unco.edu.

MURRAY, ROBERT WALLACE, chemistry professor; b. Brockton, Mass., June 20, 1928; s. Wallace James and Rose Elizabeth (Harper) M.; m. Claire K. Murphy, June 10, 1951; children: Kathleen A., Lynn E., Robert Wallace, Elizabeth A., Daniel J., William M., Padraic O'D. AB, Brown U., 1951; MA, Wesleyan U., Middletown, Conn., 1956; PhD, Yale U., 1960. Mem. tech. staff Bell Labs., Murray Hill, NJ, 1959-68; prof. chemistry U. Mo., St. Louis, 1968-81, chmn. dept., 1975-80, Curators' prof., 1981-2000, Curators' prof. emeritus, 2001—. Vis. prof. Engler-Bunte Inst. U. Karlsruhe, Fed. Republic Germany, 1982, dept. chemistry Univ. Coll., Cork, Ireland, 1989; cons. to govt. and industry. Co-editor: Singlet Oxygen, 1979; contbr. articles to profl. jours. Mem. Warren (N.J.) Twp. Com., 1962-63, mayor, 1963; mem. Planning Com. and Bd. Health, 1962-64, Bd. Edn., 1966-68. Served with USN, 1951-54; Lt. comdr. USNR. Grantee EPA, NSF, NIH, Office of Naval Research. Fellow AAAS, Am. Inst. Chemists, N.Y. Acad. Scis.; mem. Am. Soc. Photobiology, Am. Chem. Soc., The Oxygen Soc., Sigma Xi. Home: 1810 Walnutway Dr Saint Louis MO 63146-3659 Personal E-mail: kinsale63@aol.com.

MURRAY, STEPHEN JAMES, lawyer; b. Phila., Jan. 27, 1943; s. Paul Martin and Hannah (Smith) M.; m. Linda Sanders, June 20, 1970; children: Gordon Joshua, Cara Sanders. AB cum laude, Brown U., 1963; JD, Harvard U., 1966; LLM, George Washington U., 1967. Bar: N.Y. 1968, U.S. Ct. Appeals (2nd cir.) 1971, U.S. Ct. Appeals (fed. cir.) 1998, U.S. Dist. Ct. (so. and ea. dists.) N.Y. 1972, U.S. Ct. Claims 1974, U.S. Supreme Ct. 1975, Conn. 1988, U.S. Dist. Ct. Conn. 1988, U.S. Ct. Internat. Trade 1998. Spl. asst. SEC, Washington, 1966-67, Maritime Adminstrn., Washington, 1967-68; assoc. Hill, Betts & Nash, NYC, 1970-76; transp. atty. Union Carbide Corp., NYC, 1976-78, sr. transp. atty., 1978-85, chief transp. counsel Danbury, Conn., 1985—2001, group counsel, 1986—2001, chief real estate counsel, 1992—2001, comml. counsel, 1993—2001, customs and internat. trade counsel, 1997—2001; of counsel Mahoney & Keane, New York City, 2001—. Spkr. in field. Contbr. articles to profl. jours. Lt. JAGC, USN, 1968-70. Mem. ABA, Conn. State Bar Assn., U.S. Naval Inst., Navy League of U.S., Maritime Law Assn., U.S. Transp. Lawyers Assn., N.Y. State Bar Assn., Am. Corp. Counsel Assn. (co-chair real estate com. Westchester-So. Conn. chpt.), Conn. Maritime Assn., Harvard Club, Brown Club (co-pres.), Brown Faculty Club, Brown Alumni Schs. Commn. (chmn. Fairfield County), Brown Alumni Assn. (bd. govs.), Am. Chem. Soc. Office: Mahoney & Keane 14 Pilgrim Ln Weston CT 06883 Office Phone: 203-222-1019. Personal E-mail: murraysj@optonline.net.

MURRAY, SUSAN LYONS, library director; b. Barksdale Air Force Base, La., Feb. 23, 1948; BA, Trinity Coll., Washington, 1971; MSLS, Fla. State U., 1976; MBA, Rosary Coll., 1989. Pub. svcs. libr. St. Mary's Coll., Moraga, Calif., 1976-79; head pub. svcs. Hood Coll., Frederick, Md., 1979-85, Dominican U. (formerly Rosary Coll.), River Forest, Ill., 1985-87; dir. libr. Aurora (Ill.) U., 1987-97; dir. libr. and acad. info. svcs. Trinity Coll. Libr. (now Trinity U.), Washington, 1997—2005; dir. libr. Valencia Cmty. Coll., Winter Park, Fla., 2005—. Adj. assoc. prof Rosary Coll. Grad. Sch. Libr. and Info. Sci., 1990-97. Mem. ALA, Assn. Coll. and Rsch. Librs. (nat. adv. com., rep. Ill. chpt. 1991-95), Pvt. Acad. Librs. of Ill. (pres. 1994-96), Ill. Libr. Assn. (del. pre-White House Conf., Chgo., 1989-90), Beta Phi Mu, Phi Eta Sigma (hon.). Office: Winter Park Campus Valencia Cmty Coll 850 W Morse Blvd Winter Park FL 32789 Office Phone: 407-582-6815. Personal E-mail: susanmurray238@yahoo.com. Business E-Mail: smurray27@valenciacc.edu.

MURRAY, TERRY (TERENCE RODNEY MURRAY), professional hockey coach; b. Shawville, Que., Can., July 20, 1950; m. Linda Murray; children: Megan, Lindsey. Defenseman Calif. Golden Seals, 1972—75, Phila. Flyers, 1975—77, 1979—81, Detroit Red Wings, 1977, Washington Capitals, 1981—82, asst. coach, 1982—88, head coach, 1990—94, Balt. Skipjacks, 1988—90, Phila. Flyers, 1994—97, Fla. Panthers, 1998—2000; pro scout Phila. Flyers, 2000—01, 2002—03, asst. coach, 2003—08; head coach LA Kings, 2008—. Recipient Eddie Shore Award, 1978, 1979. Office: LA Kings Hockey Club 1111 S Figueroa St, Ste 3100 Los Angeles CA 90015

MURRAY, THOMAS HENRY, bioethics educator, writer; b. Phila., July 30, 1946; s. Thomas Henry and Colombia Rita (Lucci) M.; m. Sharon Marie Engelkraut, Jan. 1968 (div. Sept. 1975); children: Kathleen Elizabeth, Dominique Maria, Peter Albert; m. Cynthia Sarah Aberle, Apr. 1, 1978; 1 child, Emily Sarah Aberle. BA in Psychology, Temple U., 1968; PhD in Social Psychology, Princeton U., 1976; MD (hon.), Uppsala U., 2003. Instr. New Coll., Sarasota, Fla., 1971-75; asst. prof. Interdisciplinary Studies Miami U., Oxford, Ohio, 1975-80, assoc. prof., 1980; assoc. social behavioral studies The Hastings Ctr., Hastings-on Hudson, NY, 1980-84, pres. Garrison, NY, 1999—; assoc. prof. Inst. Med. Humanities U. Tex. Med. Br., Galveston, 1984-86, prof., 1986-87; prof., dir. Ctr. Biomed. Ethics Case Western Res. U., Cleve., 1987-99, Susan E. Watson prof. bioethics, 1998—99. Mem. Nat. Bioethics Adv. Commn., 1996-2001; mem. ethical, legal and social issues working group Human Genome Project NIH/Dept. Energy, 1989-95. Author: The Worth of a Child, 1996; founder, editor Med. Humanities Rev.; mem. editl. bd. Human Gene Therapy, Cloning, Politics and the Life Scis., Hastings Ctr. Report, Jour. of Law, Medicine and Ethics; editor: Encyclopedia of Ethical, Legal, and Policy Issues in Biotechnology, (with K.W.M. Fulford and D.L. Dickenson) Healthcare Ethics and Human Values: An Introductory Text with Readings and Case Studies, 2002, (with Carol Levine) The Cultures of Caregiving: Conflict and Common Ground Among Families, Health Professionals and Policy Makers, 2004, (with M. Rothstein, G.E Kaebkick and M.A. Majunder) Genetic Ties and the Family: The Impact of Paternity Testing on Parents and Children, 2005. Fellow NEH, 1977-78, 1979-80, Aspen Inst., 1989. Fellow Hastings Ctr.; mem. APHA, Assn. Practical and Profl. Ethics, Am. Soc. Law Medicine and Ethics (bd. dirs. 1993-97), Assn. Integrative Studies (bd. dirs. 1980-87, pres. 1983), Soc. Health and Human Values (chair program dirs. sect. 1989-90, faculty assn. 1989-90, SHHV program com. 1990, pres.-elect 1992-93, pres. 1993-94), Am. Soc. Human Genetics (chair social issues com. 1998-99), Am. Coll. Ob-Gyn. (com. on ethics 1996-2001), Am. Soc. Bioethics and Humanities (pres.-elect 1998-99, pres. 1999-2000), Human Genome Org. (ethics com.), World Anti-Doping Agy. (chair ethical issues rev. panel 2004—), Charity Navigator (bd. dir.), Internat. Panel Experts, Singapore Bioethics (adv. bd.), Oxford Uehiro Ctr. Practical Ethics (internat. adv. bd.). Office: The Hastings Ctr 21 Malcolm Gordon Rd Garrison NY 10524-5555 Office Phone: 845-424-4040.

MURRAY, THOMAS J., advertising executive; b. Bridgeport, Conn., Mar. 12, 1924; s. Thomas and Mary (Diskin) M.; m. Mary Elizabeth Cull, Feb. 22, 1945; children: Joshua Francis, Mary Elizabeth, Katherine Diskin. AB, Dartmouth Coll., 1947. Instr., Dartmouth Coll., 1947-48; with Warwick & Legler, NYC, 1948-68, sr. v.p., mgmt. account supr., 1964-68; sr. v.p. group supr. Gaynor & Ducas, Inc., 1968-74, exec. v.p., 1974—, chief fin. officer and gen. mgr., 1978-87; pres. TJM & Assn., 1987—. Pres., trustee Hillcrest Gen. Hosp., N.Y.C.; Westchester Inst. for tng. in Psychoanalysis and Psychotherapy, Mt. Kisco, N.Y. Served as 1st lt. USAAF, 1942-45. Decorated D.F.C., Air medal with 4 oak leaf clusters. Mem. Nat. Wholesale Druggists Assn., Propriety Assn., Nat. Assn. Chain Drug Stores, Am. Mktg. Assn. Home and Office: 65 Norfield Rd Weston CT 06883-2213 Office Phone: 800-749-4254. E-mail: tjma@optonline.net.

MURRAY, THOMAS JOHN (JOCK MURRAY), physician, neurologist, educator; b. Halifax, NS, Can., May 30, 1938; m. Janet Kathleen Pottie; children: Shannon, Bruce, Suellen, Brian. Grad. pre-med, St. Francis Xavier U., 1958, LLD (hon.), 1989; MD, Dalhousie U., 1963; DSc (hon.), Acadia U., 1991; DLitt (hon.), St. Thomas U., 2004. Family physician, Nashwaaksis, N.S., 1963-65; chief medicine Camp Hill Hosp., Halifax, N.S., 1974-79; chief neurology Dalhousie U., Halifax, 1979-85, dir. multiple sclerosis rsch. unit, 1980—2003, dean medicine, 1985-92, prof. med. humanities, 1992—2003, prof. emeritus, 2003—. Mem. working group on Diability in U.S. Pres., 1994—96. Co-author: (textbook) Essential Neurology, Quotable Osler, Medicine in Quotations, Treatment and Management of MS, History of MS; author over 200 pub. works, including 7 books and contbns. to 24 textbooks. Bd. dirs. St. Francis Xavier U., Pictou Acad. Found., Robert Pope Found., Nat. Coun. on Bioethics and Health Rsch., Mus. Healthcare. Decorated officer Order Can., order of Nova Scotia; recipient Neilson award Hannah Inst. for Med. History, Disting. Profl. award Discovery Ctr., 2005; named Dalhousie Alumnus of Yr., Dalhousie U., 2003; grantee 91 rsch. grants. Fellow Royal Coll. Physicians (Can. and London, Mentor of Yr. award 2002), ACP (master; gov. 1985-90, chmn. bd. govs. 1990-91, chair bd. regents 1995-97, emeritus chair, Dr. Nicholas Davies award, Laureate award, Stengel award); mem. Can. Neurol. Soc. (pres. 1982-84), Am. Acad. Neurology (v.p. 1981-83, Dr. A.B. Baker award, Lawrence McHenry award), Am. Osler Soc. (pres. 2006-07), London Osler Club (hon. mem.), Royal Soc. Med., Can. Med. Assn., N.S. Med. Soc., Assn. Can. Med. Colls. (pres. 1991-92), Can. Med. Forum (chmn. 1992-95), Multiple Sclerosis Soc. Can. (chmn. med. adv. bd., Perkins award), Consortium of Multiple Sclerosis Ctrs. (pres. 1997-99), Can. Soc. for History of Medicine (pres. 1997-99, Scheinberg award), Canadian Acad Hlth. Scis. (fellow), FRCP (London), Rotary Internat. (Paul Harris fellow). Avocations: medical history, piano, windsurfing. Home: 16 Bobolink St Halifax NS Canada B3M 1W3 Office: Dalhousie Med Sch Clin Rsch Ctr Halifax NS Canada B3H 4H7 Home Phone: 902-443-1074; Office Phone: 902-494-1533. Business E-Mail: jock.murray@dal.ca.

MURRAY, THOMAS VEATCH, lawyer; b. Phoenix, July 17, 1947; s. Robert Morrison Jr. and Jane Veatch (Murray) Barber and Richard A. Barber; m. Cynthia Ann Burnett, June 2, 1971; children: Anne Caroline, Thomas Veatch Jr. BA, U. Kans., 1969; JD, U. Mich., 1972. Bar: Kans. 1972, U.S. Dist. Ct. Kans. 1972, U.S. Ct. Appeals (10th cir.) 1983, U.S. Supreme Ct. 1976. Assoc. Barber, Emerson, Six, Springer & Zinn, Lawrence, Kans., 1972-76; mem. Barber, Emerson, Springer, Zinn & Murray, L.C., Lawrence, Kans., 1976—2003; of counsel Lathrop & Gage L.C., Overland Park, Kans., 2004—. Adj. prof. western civilization U. Kans., 1975-77, Sch. Law., 1990-91, instr. bar rev. course, 1975-82; dir. The First Nat. Bank of Lawrence, Kans., 1980-91, The Reuter Organ Co., 1991-, Hall Ctr. for the Humanities, Lawrence, Kans., 1988-. Contbr. articles to profl. jours. Mem. adv. bd. Lawrence Consumer Affairs Assn., 1974—77, Sta. KANU, Lawrence, 1975—80; mem. Bd. Edn. Unified Sch. Dist. 497, Lawrence, 1991—95; mem. Kans. Bd. Law Examiners, 1995—, chmn., 2006—; mem. Lawrence Emergency Svcs. Coun., 1998—2002; dir. Lawrence C. of C., 1993—95; treas. Louie Holcom Baseball Assn., 1972—73; trustee First Presbyn. Ch., 1975—76. Fellow Am. Bar Found.; mem. ABA, Fedn. Def. and Corp. Counsel (regional v.p. 1994-97, dir. 1997-99), Kans. Assn. Def. Counsel (dir. 1993-97), Def. Rsch. Inst., Kans. Bar Assn. (pres. corporation, banking and bus. law sect. 1983), Kans. Bar Found. (trustee 1999-2005), Johnson County Bar Assn., Judge Hugh Means Inn Ct., Douglas County Bar Assn., Coaches' Corner (Lawrence), Lawrence Lions Alumni Assn., Supreme Ct. Hist. Soc., Nelson Gallery Advs., The River Club, Lawrence Country Club, Fortnightly Club (Lawrence). Republican. Presbyterian. Avocation: classical and operatic music. Office: Lathrop & Gage LC 10851 Mastin Blvd Bldg 82 Ste 1000 Overland Park KS 66210-1669 Home Phone: 785-843-2629; Office Phone: 913-451-5100. Business E-Mail: tmurray@lathropgage.com.

MURRAY, TIMOTHY PATRICK, Lieutenant Governor of Massachusetts, former mayor; b. Worcester, Mass., June 7, 1968; m. Tammy L. Sullivan; children: Helen, Katerine. BA in Am. Studies, Fordham U., 1990; JD, We. New England Sch. Law, 1994. Ptnr. Tattan, Leonard and Murray, Worcester, Mass.; councillor-at-large City of Worcester, mayor, 2002—06; lt. gov. State of Mass., Boston, 2007—. Democrat. Roman Catholic. Office Phone: 617-725-4000. Business E-Mail: ltgovoffice@state.ma.us.

MURRAY-GALELLA, SUZANNE, special education educator, consultant; d. Robert Joseph and Carol Ann Murray; m. Robert William Galella, Aug. 6, 2004; 1 child, Olivia Murray Galella. MS, Marywood U., Scranton, Pa., 1997. Cert. in tchg. students with special needs Pa. Dept. Edn., 1997. Spl. edn. tchr. Abington Heights Sch. Dist., Clarks Summit, Pa., 1997—2004; prof. Wilkes U., Wilkes-Barre, Pa., 2004—. Office: Wilkes Univ 84 W South St Wilkes Barre PA 18766

MURRAY-NSEULA, MARLENE, educator; d. Caldwell and Dorcas Murray; m. Dalitso Nseula, July 27, 2008. PhD, Wayne State U., Detroit, 1999. Postdoc. fellow U. Ill., Chgo., 1999—2001; asst. prof. Andrews U., Berrien Springs, Mich., 2001—. Office: Andrews Univ Hwy 31 Berrien Springs MI 49104 Business E-Mail: mmurray@andrews.edu.

MURRAY SHAW, JULEEN, actress; d. Marianne Polly Eileen Arnold; m. Mathew Scott Shaw, May 8, 1988; 1 child, Sophie Fay Jiaoxin Shaw. BA, Moorhead State U., Minn., 1979. Co-founder Nursery Tap, LLC, Gig Harbor, Wash., 2004—. Prodr., dir., actor, writer (performing arts dvd's for children) Nursery Tap Hip to Toe, Vol. I (George Foster Peabody award, 2005, Parents Choice Recommended award, 2005, iParenting Media award, 2005, KIDS FIRST! Endorsement, 2005, Dr. Toy's Best Products award, 2005, Creative Child Mag. Preferred award, 2005, Dove Found. Seal of Approval Highest Rating, 2004), Vol. II (Parents Choice Silver Honor award, 2006, Creative Child Mag. DVD of Yr. award, 2006, Dove Found. Seal of Approval Highest Rating, 2006). Recipient Award of Excellence, reviewcorner.com, 2005. Mem.: Screen Actor's Guild. D-Liberal. Personal E-mail: info@nurserytap.com.

MURRELL, JILL PONGRACZ, music educator, director; b. Lorain, Ohio, Mar. 10, 1956; d. Julius Albert and Donna Jean Pongracz; m. Richard Albert Murrell, Aug. 12, 1978 (div. Oct. 31, 1989); children: Rebekka Anne, Zachary Albert. MusB, Miami U., Oxford, Ohio, 1977; M in the Art of Tchg., Marygrove Coll., Mich., 1998. Choir dir. Lorain (Ohio) Hungarian Ref. Ch., 1978—; music tchr. Keystone Local Schs., LaGrange, Ohio, 1979—89; vocal music tchr., vocal music coord. Lorain City Schs., 1989—2001; choral dir. Southview HS, Lorain, 2002—; artistic musical dir. Ashland (Ohio) Symphonic Youth Chorus, 2004—. Music mentor Cleve. Opera on Tour. Musician (flutist): Patriots Symphonic Band. Com. chair Boy Scouts of Am., Sheffield Lake, Ohio, 1999—2003; trustee Lorain Internat. Assn., 1998—2006; officer Sheffield-Sheffield Lake (Ohio) Band Boosters, 1994—2003; music com. chair Lorain Hungarian Ref. Ch., 1978—2006. Mem.: Lorain Edn. Assn. (bldg. rep. 2001—06), Ohio Choral Dirs. Assn., Ohio Music Edn. Assn. (state curriculum com. 2004—06, gen. music rep. 2002—). Democrat. United Church Of Christ. Home: 219 Gayle Dr Sheffield Lake OH 44054 Office: Southview High Sch 2270 E 42nd St Lorain OH Personal E-mail: jponmurr@hotmail.com. Business E-Mail: jmurre@lorainschools.org.

MURRELL, KENNETH DARWIN, microbiologist, parasitologist; b. Burley, Idaho, Jan. 19, 1940; s. Kenneth Leland and Margaret (Manning) M.; m. Joyce Voyce, July 10, 1965; children: Duncan, Amy. BA, Chico State U., Calif, 1957; MSPH, U. N.C., 1963, PhD, 1969. Rsch. assoc. U. Chgo., 1967-71; rsch. scientist Naval Med. Rsch. Inst., Bethesda, Md., 1971-78, USDA Agrl. Rsch. Svc., Beltsville, Md., 1978-87; assoc. area dir. Agrl. Rsch. Svc., Beltsville, Md., 1987-89; area dir. midwest area USDA Agrl. Rsch. Svc., Beltsville, 1989-92, dir. Beltsville area, 1992-97; dep. adminstr. USDA-Agrl. Rsch. Svc., Beltsville, 1997—. Bd. dirs. Internat. Trichinell Comm., 1994—. Fulbright fellow Royal Vet. Agrl. U., Copenhagen, 1996, Presdl. Disting. Presdl. Rank award, 1997. Mem. AAAS, Am. Soc. Parasitologists (pres. 1993), Am. Assn. Vet. parasitology (pres. 1986-87, Disting. Parasitologist 1987), Internat. Trichinosis Commn. (pres. 1998—, Disting. Presdl. Exec. award 1998). Office: BARC-West Bldg 005 Agrl Rsch Svc NPS Beltsville MD 20705

MURREN, JAMES JOSEPH, hotel corporation executive; b. 1961; s. John and Jean-Marie Murren; m. Heather Hay. BA in Art History & Urban Studies, Trinity Coll., 1983. Chartered Fin. Analyst. Various positions Deutsche Morgan Grenfell, 1984—94; mng. dir., dir. rsch. Deutsche Bank, 1994—98; exec. v.p., CFO MGM Mirage, Las Vegas, 1998—99, pres., CFO, 1999—2007, treas., 2001—07, pres., COO, 2007—08, chmn., CEO, 2008—. Bd. dirs. MGM Mirage, 2000—, Delta Petroleum Corp., 2008—. Co-founder, bd. dirs. Nevada Cancer Inst., 2005—; trustee U. Nev. Las Vegas Found., U. Nevada Reno Found. Office: MGM Mirage 3600 Las Vegas Blvd South Las Vegas NV 89109*

MURRETT, ROBERT B., federal agency administrator, career military officer; b. Oct. 8, 1952; BA, U. Buffalo; M in Govt. and Strategic Intelligence, Georgetown U.; M, Def. Intelligence Coll. Advanced through ranks to vice admiral USN, 2006, watch stander and briefing officer, chief naval ops. intelligence plot, 1980—83, asst. intelligence officer, 1983—85; asst. naval attache U.S. Embassy, Oslo, 1986—89; ops. intelligence officer U.S. Pacific Fleet USN, 1989—92, asst. chief of staff intelligence for comdr, carrier group eight, 1992—95, asst. chief of staff intelligence for comdr, second fleet, 1995—97, exec. asst. to dir. naval intelligence, 1997—98, dir., intelligence directorate Office of Naval Intelligence Washington, 1998; comdr. Atlantic Intelligence Command, 1999; dir. intelligence U.S. Joint Forces Command, 2000—02; vice dir. intelligence Joint Staff USN, 2002—05, dir. naval intelligence Washington, 2005—06; dir. Nat. Geospatial-Intelligence Agy. US Dept. Def., Bethesda, Md., 2006—. Office: Nat Geospatial-Intelligence Agy 4600 Sangamore Rd Bethesda MD 20816*

MURRI, LUELLA DAVIS, personnel and language professional; b. Boston, July 28, 1920; d. Arthur DeForest and Gertrude Davis; m. Albert Thomas Murri, Sept. 15, 1951 (dec. Nov. 1973); children: Thomas Allen, Daniel Glenn. Diploma Univ. Studies, U. Paris, 1939; BA in French summa cum laude, Wheaton Coll., Norton, Mass., 1940; MA in French, Radcliffe Coll., 1941. Position classifier Navy Dept., NYC, 1944—45, VA, Boston, 1946, Navy Dept., Phila., 1946—51; chief classification sect. Office of Price Stblzn., Phila., 1951—53; survey leader, then tech. asst. to chief classification divsn. U.S. Civil Svc. Commn., Phila., 1953—55; pvt. tchr. French Springfield, Va., 1975—81. Co-chmn. fgn. lang. subcom. citizens' curriculum adv. com. Sch. Bd., Fairfax County, Va., 1965-69; rep. Compagnons de la Parole Française, Vienna, Va. to Ceret, France, 1975, 76, mem. host com. bi-centennial visit of Ceretans to Vienna, Va., 1976. Editor: Magnetic Field Therapy Handbook, 1993; moderator (TV program) America's Best Kept Medical Secrets, 1994, photographer (exhibitions) in India Thru Your Lens, Smithsonian Inst., 2001, host (TV series) Photographers of Northern Virginia, 2001—06. Parent rep. self-study com. North Springfield Elem. Sch., Springfield, Va., 1965-66, vol. tchr. French, 1967-68; vol. tutor Lit. Coun. No. Va., Fairfax County, Va., 1987-88. Recipient French and German prizes, Wheaton Coll., 1940, 1st Pl. wildlife category, Hon. Mention humor category photography competition Soc. Expeditions, 1990; grant to AAUW Ednl. Found. named in her honor by Springfield-Annandale (Va.) br., 1969. Mem. AAUW (pres. Springfield-Annandale br. 1964-66), No. Va. Photog. Soc. (Comml. Print Photographer of Yr. 1999, Nature's Best mag. award 2003, numerous awards), Antarctican Soc., Circumnavigators Club, Phi Beta Kappa. Democrat. Mem. Unitarian Ch. Avocations: photography, swimming, walking, dance, exotic travel. Home: 5426 Lehigh Ln Springfield VA 22151-3423

MURRIAN, ROBERT PHILLIP, retired federal judge, educator; b. Knoxville, Tenn., Apr. 1, 1945; s. Albert Kinzel and Mary Gilbert (Eppes) M.; m. Jerrilyn Sue Boone, Oct. 29, 1983; children: Kimberley Ann, Jennifer Rebecca, Albert Boone, Samuel Robert. BS, U.S. Naval Acad., 1967; JD, U. Tenn., 1974. Bar: Tenn. 1974, U.S. Dist. Ct. (ea. dist.) Tenn. 1975, U.S. Dist. Ct. (mid. dist.) Tenn. 2005, U.S. Ct. Appeals (6th cir.) 1982. Law clk. to judge US Dist. Ct. (ea. dist.) Tenn., Knoxville, 1974-76, magistrate judge, 1978—2002; assoc. Butler, Vines, Babb & Threadgill, Knoxville, 1976-78; ptnr. Kramer Rayson LLP, Knoxville, 2002—08, Reeves, Herbert & Murrian, P. A., Tenn., 2008—. Adj. prof. U. Tenn. Coll. Law, 1990-93, 95-96, 2002; trial lawyer, arbitrator, mediator, spl. master litigation. Lt. USN, 1967-71. Green scholar, 1973-74, Nat. Moot Ct. scholar, 1974; named one of Best Lawyers in Am., 2005-09. Fellow Tenn. Bar Found.; mem. ABA, Tenn. Bar Assn., Knoxville Bar Assn. (bd. govs. 1994, 2002—), Sixth Cir. Jud. Conf. (life), Order of Coif, Am. Inn of Ct. (master of the bench, pres. 1997-98), Phi Kappa Phi. Presbyterian (Elder). Office: Reeves Herbert & Murrian PA Tyson Pl 2607 Kingston Pike Ste 130 Knoxville TN 37919 Office Phone: 865-540-1977. Business E-Mail: rmurrian@arclaw.net.

MURRIN, LEONARD CHARLES, II, pharmacology educator, researcher; b. Iowa City, Oct. 9, 1943; s. Leonard Charles and Huberta Frances (Jones) M.; m. Kathryn Grace McDermott, Aug. 17, 1968; children: Leonard Charles, Rose Colleen, Clare Rita. B.A., St. John's Coll., 1965; student Kearney State Coll., 1967-69; Ph.D., Yale U., 1975. Postdoc. assoc. Yale U. Med. Sch., New Haven, 1975; postdoctoral fellow Johns Hopkins U. Med. Sch., Balt., 1975-78; asst. prof. U. Nebr. Med. Sch., Omaha, 1978-83, assoc. prof., 1983-88; prof., 1988—, vice-chmn., 1988-2004. Contbr. articles to profl. jours. and chpts. to books. Adv. med. bd. Southeast Nebr. March of Dimes, Omaha, 1979-85; treas. Boyd Sch. PTA, Omaha, 1979; pres. Keystone Community Task Force, Omaha, 1982; bd. dirs. 1980-86. Fellow NIH, 1975-78; grantee Nat. Sci. Found., 1980-84, March of Dimes Found., 1982-85, NIH, 1986—; recipient Basil O'Connor award March of Dimes Found., 1979. Mem. Am. Soc. Pharmacology Exptl. Therapeutics, Am. Soc. Neurochemistry, Soc. for Neurosci., Internat. Soc. Neurochemistry, Internat. Soc. Devel. Neurosci. Avocations: golf, cooking, wine, reading. Home: 1670 N 53rd St Omaha NE 68104-4948 Office: Univ Nebr Med Sch Dept Pharmacology & Exptl Neurosci 985800 Nebr Med Ctr Omaha NE 68198-5800 Office Phone: 402-559-4552. Business E-Mail: cmurrin@unmc.edu.

MURRIN, REGIS DOUBET, retired lawyer; b. Erie, Pa., July 2, 1930; s. John III and Gabrielle (Doubet) M.; m. Evelyn L. Alessio, Aug. 22, 1959; children: Catherine Shaw Murrin Hargenrader, Mary Murrin, Elizabeth Murrin Talotta, Rebecca Fielding Lamanna. BA, U. Notre Dame, 1952; JD, Harvard U., 1959; LLM, Temple U., 1968. Bar: Pa. 1959, U.S. Supreme Ct. 1971. Assoc. Murrin & Murrin, Butler, Pa., 1959-62; atty. Housing & Home Fin. Agy., Phila., 1962-64; ptnr. Baskin & Sears, Pitts., 1964-84, Reed Smith Shaw & McClay, Pitts., 1985-95, of counsel, 1995-99, counsel, 1999—2006. Trustee Pitts. Oratory, 1976—97; chmn. Zoning Bd. Adjustment, City of Pitts., 1994—2006; bd. dirs. Ellis Sch., 1991—99. Lt. USNR, 1952—55, Korea, Vietnam. Mem. and fellow Allegheny County Bar Assn., Founders Circles, Edwin Sorin Soc. Democrat. Roman Catholic. Office: Reed Smith Shaw & McClay 435 6th Ave Ste 2 Pittsburgh PA 15219-1886 Office Phone: 412-288-3352.

MURRISH, CHARLES HOWARD, oil and gas exploration compant executive; b. Rochester, Mich., Dec. 27, 1940; s. Richard John and Emily Louise (Marsh) M.; m. Brigitte Marie Furlotte, Oct. 23, 1965; children: Stephanie, Stephen, Brian. Student, Mexico City Coll., 1962; BS, Mich. State U., 1963, MS, 1966. Exploration geologist and geophysicist Chevron, New Orleans, 1966-71; mgr. exploration Odeco, New Orleans, 1971-77; v.p. McMoRan Offshore Exploration Co., Metairie, La., 1977-79, sr. v.p., 1979-81; pres. McMoRan-Freeport Oil Co., Metairie, 1981-83, McMoRan Exploration Co., Metairie, 1983-86; exec. v.p. McMoRan Oil & Gas Co., 1986, sr. exec. v.p., 1986-90, Freeport-McMoRan Oil & Gas Co., 1990-92; ptnr. CLK Co., 1992-94; pres., COO McMoRan Oil & Gas Co., New Orleans, 1994—2001, McMoRan Oil & Gas LLC, New Orleans, 1998-2001; exec. v.p. McMoRan Exploration Co., New Orleans, 1998—, vice-chmn., 2001—. Chmn. bd. Hysell Ballet Arts, Inc., New Orleans, 1982-83; chmn. petroleum majors campaign United Way, 1996, 98; bd. dirs. Lenpac, Metairie, 1983; chmn. citizenship com. McMoRan Exploration Co., 2000—. Mem. New Orleans Geol. Soc., Geol. Soc. Am., Am. Assn. Petroleum Geologists, Petroleum Club of New Orleans (bd. dirs. 1988, 89, 90), Houston Geol. Soc., La. Assn. Ind. Producers, Mid-Continent Oil and Gas Assn. also: PO Box 60004 New Orleans LA 70160-0004 Office: McMoran Exploration Co 1615 Poydras St New Orleans LA 70112-1254

MURROW, WAYNE LEE, retired communications educator, dean; b. Alva, Okla., Jan. 23, 1935; s. Everett Emmet Murrow and Stella Jean McGlothlin; m. Marti L. Rogers, Aug. 19, 1956 (dec. Sept. 1966); children: Sherri, Randal, Cynthia, Jeffrey; m. Nila Arlene West, Jan. 19, 1968. BA, Bethany Nazarene Coll., 1956; M of Tchg., Ctrl. State U., 1968; PhD, U. Okla., 1972. Min. Ch. of the Nazarene, Tex., Okla.; prof. So. Nazarene U., Bethany, Okla., 1968-80, dean, prof., 1980—2002; ret. emeritus prof., 2002—. Evaluation team mem. Okla. State Dept. Edn., Oklahoma City, 1980-94. Mem. Nat. Comm. Assn, Ctrl. States Comm. Assn. (adv. coun. 1977-90), Okla. Theatre Speech Comm. Assn. (pres. 1976-77, Outstanding Tchr. award 1980), Christian Adult Higher Edn. Assn. (coun. mem. 1994-2000, pres. 1997-98), North Ctrl. Assn. (evaluation team mem. 1968-80, cons.-evaluator for colls. and univs. 1994—). Avocation: family history. Home: 8105 Bridgeport Ln Bethany OK 73008 Personal E-mail: murrow@cox.net.

MURRY, CHARLES EMERSON, lawyer, federal official; b. Hope, ND, June 23, 1924; s. Raymond Henry and Estelle Margarete (Skeim) M.; m. Donna Deane Kleve, June 20, 1948; children: Barbara, Karla, Susan, Bruce, Charles. BS, U. ND, Grand Forks, 1948, JD, 1950. Bar: ND 1950. Mem. firm Nelson and Heringer, Rugby, ND, 1950-51; dir. ND Legis. Council, 1951-75; adj. gen. with rank of maj. gen. State of ND, Bismarck, 1975-84; mgr. Garrison Diversion Conservancy Dist., 1985-93. Cons. Council State Govts.; mem. res. forces policy bd. Sec. of Def. Vice-pres. Mo. Slope Luth. Home of Bismarck, 1965-66. Served with AUS, 1942-45. Decorated D.S.M., Legion of Merit, Meritorious Service medal, Bronze Star, Army Commendation medal; Fourragere Belgium; Orange Lanyard Netherlands; recipient Sioux award U. ND, 1970; Gov.'s award of excellence, 1971; Nat. Leadership award Bismarck C. of C., 1971 Mem. Adjs. Gen. Assn. (exec. com., sec. 1983-84), Nat. Legis. Conf. (past chmn.), N.G. Assn., Am. Bar Assn., ND Bar Assn., Commrs. Uniform State Laws. Lodges: Elks, Masons. Lutheran. Office: 5505 Ponderosa Ave Bismarck ND 58503-9159

MURRY, DONALD ARVIL, economics professor; s. Richard Bland Murry and Frieda Hoerle; m. Lari Leaver, June 15, 1963; children: Karen Christie Flynn, Alison Anne. BSBA, U. Mo., Columbia, 1959—59, MA in Economics, 1961, PhD, 1966. V.p. C.H. Guernsey & Co., Okla., 1998—; prof. emeritus U. Okla., Norman, Okla., 1998—. Contbr. articles to profl.jours. 1st lt. Army Artillary US Army, 1959—60, Fort Sill, Okla. Recipient Meritorious Svc. award, FPC, 1972. Mem.: Beta Gama Sigma (award 1975). Office: C H Guernsey & Company 5555 N Grand Boulevard Oklahoma City OK 73112

MURRY, GEORGE VANCE, bishop; b. Camden, NJ, Dec. 28, 1948; BA, St. Mary's Sem., Balt., 1972; MDiv, Jesuit Sch. Theology, Berkeley, Calif.; MPhil in Am. Cultural History, PhD in Am. Cultural History, George Washington U., Washington. Ordained priest Soc. of Jesus, 1979; ordained bishop, 1995; aux. bishop Archdiocese of Chgo., 1995—98; coadjutor bishop Diocese of Saint Thomas, USVI, 1998—99, bishop, 1999—2007, Diocese of Youngstown, Ohio, 2007—. Nat. chaplain Knights and Ladies of Peter Claver, 1998—. Bd. trustees Loyola U., Chgo. Mem.: Bishops' Cath. Legal Immigration Network (treas., chmn. bishops com.). Roman Catholic. Office: Diocese of Youngstown 144 W Wood St Youngstown OH 44503 Office Phone: 330-744-8451. Office Fax: 330-742-6448.

MURRY, HAROLD DAVID, JR., lawyer; b. Holdenville, Okla., June 30, 1943; s. Harold David Sr. and Willie Elizabeth (Dees) M.; m. Ann Moore Earnhardt, Nov. 1, 1975; children: Elizabeth Ann, Sarah Bryant. BA, Okla. U., 1965, JD, 1968. Bar: Okla. 1968, D.C. 1974. Asst. to v.p. U. Okla., Norman, 1968-71, legal counsel Research Inst., 1969-71; atty. U.S. Dept. Justice, Washington, 1971-74; spl. asst. U.S. Atty., Washington, 1972; assoc. Clifford & Warnke, Washington, 1974-78, ptnr., 1978-91, Howrey & Simon, Washington, 1991-98, Baker Botts LLP, Washington, 1998—. Mem. ABA, Okla. Bar Assn., D.C. Bar Assn., Fed. Bar Assn., Met. Club (Washington), Chevy Chase Club (Md.), Phi Alpha Delta. Democrat. Office: Baker Botts LLP Ste 1300 1299 Pennsylvania Ave NW Washington DC 20004-2408 Home: 3711 Village Park Dr Chevy Chase MD 20815-5745

MURRY, J. WARREN, surgeon, educator; b. Kansas City, Mo., Mar. 28, 1925; BS in Medicine, U. Ark., 1946; MD, U. Ark., Little Rock, 1947. Diplomate Am. Bd. Surgery. Intern Charity Hosp., New Orleans, 1947-48; resident in surgery Univ. Hosp., Little Rock, 1948-53; instr. family medicine dept. U. Ark. for Med. Sci., Little Rock, 1993—2002, instr. N.W. Ark. A.H.E.C. Family Med. Ctr. Fayetteville; pvt. practice Fayetteville, Ark., 1957—89, Heber Springs, Ark., 1989—92; ret., 2002. Fellow ACS; mem. AMA, So. Med. Assn. Personal E-mail: jwmurry@cox.net.

MURTHA, JOHN PATRICK, JR., United States Representative from Pennsylvania; b. New Martinsville, W.Va., June 17, 1932; s. John Patrick and Mary Edna (Ray) Murtha; m. Joyce Bell, June 10, 1955; children: Donna Sue, John, Patrick. BA in Econs., U. Pitts., 1961; postgraduate student, Ind. U. Pa., 1962-65. Mem. Pa. State Ho. Reps., 1969-73, US Congress from 12th Pa. dist., 1974—, mem. appropriations com., chmn. def. appropriations subcommittee. Author (with John Plashall): From Vietnam to 9/11: On the Front Lines of National Security, 2003. Served in USMC, as lt. 1952-55, as maj. 1966-67, USMC Res., 1955-66, 1967-90 Decorated Bronze Star, 2 Purple Hearts, Cross of Gallantry Vietnam; Recipient Pa. Disting. Svc. medal, 1978, Pa. Meritorious Svc. medal, numerous service awards for work during Johnstown flood, 1977, Iron Mike award Marine Corps League, 1988, Disting. Am. award (Nation's Capital chpt.) Air Force Assn., 1989, Outstanding Vet. award Vets. Caucus of Am. Acad. Physician Assts., 1989, Man of Steel award Cold Finished Steel Bar Inst., 1989, Pa. Disting. Svc. medal & Pa. Meritorious Svc. medal, 2000, Spirit of Hope award United Svc. Orgns., Inc., 2000, Funding Hero award Breast Cancer Rsch. Found., 2002, Profile in Courage award John F. Kennedy Libr. Found., 2006; named Man of Yr. Johnstown Jaycees, 1978 Mem.: VFW, Salvation Army, Am. Legion. Democrat. Roman Catholic. Office: US House Reps 2423 Rayburn House Office Bldg Washington DC 20515-0001 also: 647 Main St Ste 401 Johnstown PA 15901 Office Phone: 202-225-2065, 814-535-2642. Office Fax: 814-539-6229.*

MURTHA, JOSEPH PATRICK, civil engineer, educator; b. South Connellsville, Pa., July 18, 1931; s. Joseph Paul and Dorothy Frances (Maxwell) M.; m. Rita Jean O'Hara, Aug. 7, 1955; children: Michael Joseph, Patricia Ellen Stoffregen, Kathleen Mary Yost, Eileen Dorothy Jonikas, Timothy O'Hara. BS, Carnegie Mellon U., 1953, MS, 1955; PhD, U. Ill., 1961. Registered civil engr., Calif. Dir. Water Resource Ctr. U. Ill., 1962-66, prof. civil engring. Urbana, 1969-94, prof. emeritus, 1994—; dir. Harbor Divsn. U.S. Naval Civil Engr. Lab., Port Hueneme, Calif., 1966-67; sr. rsch. engr. Western Offshore Drilling and Export Co., Santa Fe Springs, Calif., 1967-68; rsch. dir. Deep Oil Tech., Long Beach, Calif., 1968-69; prin. J.P. Murtha, Urbana, 1958. Vis. prof. Herriot-Watt U., Edinburgh, Scotland, 1976-77; rsch. engr. ocean engring. divsn. NOAA, Washington, 1977-78; chmn. rsch. need form Civil Engr. Rsch. Found., Washinton, 1989-92; dir. U. Ill. Advanced Constrn. Tech. Ctr., 1986-93. Bd. trustees Serra Internat., Chgo., 1982-85, v.p. 1984-85. Lt. (j.g.) USN, 1955-58. Recipient Swedish Rsch. Tour award Sweden-Am. Found., 1965; Fellow Fulbright-Hays Sr. Rsch. fellowship, 1976-77; Grantee U.S. Army U. Rsch. Invitation grant. Fellow ASCE. Roman Catholic. Home: 71 Lakeview Dr Terra Alta WV 26764 Office: U Ill Newmark Civil Engr Lab 205 N Mathews Ave Urbana IL 61801-2350 Office Phone: 304-789-2897. Personal E-mail: joemurtha@juno.com, joemurtha@verizon.net.

MURTHA, ROGER GERRY, music educator; MusB, U. Hartford, 1960, BS in Music Edn., 1961, MusM, 1963. Asst. prin. trumpet, orch. and negotiating coms. mem. Hartford Symphony Orch., 1960—, union steward, 1979—, bd. dirs., mem., 1991—95, exec. com., mem., 1991—95; dir. music grad. Dartmouth Coll., 1962—; prof., acting asst. dean U. Harford, Hartt Coll. Music, 1963—, dir. student fin. aid, 1969—94, dir. admissions, 1971—72, chmn., African Am. Music, 1983—94, chmn. performing orgns., 1992—. Vis. tchr. trumpt Wesleyan U., 1986—96; bd. dirs., v.p. Native Sun Symphony Orch., 1997—2003; com. mem. Mohegan Tribe Constn., 2003—08. Mem.: Omega Phi Epsilon (Delta chpt.). Address: 102 Beelzebub Rd South Windsor CT 06074 Business E-Mail: murtha@mail.hartford.edu.

MURTHY, N. SANJEEVA, physicist; b. Mysore, Karnataka, India, May 12, 1949; came to U.S., 1972; s. M.U. and Mahadevamma Narasimhaiah; m. Meena S. Kumari, Feb. 19, 1979; children: Sandeep N., Praveen G. BE, U. Mysore, 1969; M Tech., Indian Inst. Sci., Bangalore, 1971; MS, U. Conn., 1974, PhD, 1976. Lectr. U. Mysore, Tumkur, India, 1971-72; rsch. asst. U. Conn., Storrs, 1972-75; postdoctoral fellow Carnegie-Mellon U., Pitts., 1976-77, N.Y. State Dept. Health, Albany, 1977-79, MIT, Cambridge, 1979-81; rsch. scientist AlliedSignal Inc., Morristown, N.J., 1981—. Contbr. articles to profl. jours. including Jour. Applied Polymer Sci., Polymer, Jour. Polymer Sci. Polymer Physics, Jour. Polymer Sci. and Engring., Macromolecules, Chemistry of Materials, Phys. Rev., Polymer Comms., Biopolymers, Jour. Macromolecular Sci.-Physics, others. Fellow Am. Phys. Soc.; mem. Am. Chem. Soc., Sigma Xi. Hindu. Achievements include research on structures in conducting polymers; study of the noncrystalline phase in polymers. Office: AlliedSignal 101 Columbia Rd Morristown NJ 07960-4640

MURTHY, NARASIMHA S., pharmaceutical scientist, researcher; b. Bangalore, Karnataka, India, Apr. 29, 1971; s. Sathyanarayana K. and Vijayalakshmi Murthy; m. Reena N. Murthy, Nov. 18, 1999; 1 child, Srujana N. B in Pharmacy, Bangalore U., 1992, M in Pharmacy, 1994, PhD, 2003. Lectr. M.S.Ramaiah coll. of Pharmacy, Bangalore, Karnataka, India, 1994—97, asst. prof., 1997—2002; rsch. affiliate Roswell Pk. Cancer Inst., Buffalo, 2002—05; asst. prof. pharm. scis. Ohio Northern Univ., Ada, Ohio, 2005—. Tchg. M.S.Ramaiah coll. of Pharmacy, Bangalore, Karnataka, India, 1994—2002; rsch. affiliate Roswell Pk. Cancer Inst., Buffalo, 2002—. Mem.: Am. Assn. of Pharm. Scientists (life). Achievements include invention of Magnetophoresis: a Novel technique for enhancement of Transdermal delivery of drugs. Home: 805 College Hill Rd Apt 8 Oxford MS 38655 Office Fax: 662-915-1177.

MURTHY, SUDISH C., thoracic surgeon; MD, Columbia U., Coll. Physicians and Surgeons, NYC, 1992; PhD, U. BC, Vancouver, Canada, 1988. Profl. staff Cleve. Clinic, 1999—. Office: Cleveland Clinic 9500 Euclid Ave / J4-1 Cleveland OH 44195 Office Fax: 216-636-1267.

MURTHY, VADIRAJA VENKATESA, retired biochemist, researcher, educator; b. Bombay, Mar. 27, 1940; came to U.S., 1961; s. Ramanathpur Venkatesa and Saroja (Bai) M.; m. Jayashree Deshpande, Sept. 21, 1969; children: Deepti, Seema. BSc with honors, U. Bombay, 1959, MSc first rank valedectorian, 1961; PhD in Biochemistry, U. Md., 1968. Clin. chemist Nat. Registry of Clin. Chemists; lic. dir. clin. chemistry, N.Y.C. and N.Y. state. Sr. rsch. biochemist, asst. group leader USV Pharms., Yonkers, N.Y., 1970-71; rsch. assoc. Toxicology Ctr., U. Iowa, Iowa City, 1971-72; vis. scientist NIH-Environ., Research Triangle Park, N.C., 1972-74; sr. rsch. assoc. Emory U. Sch. Medicine, Atlanta, 1974-75; adj. asst. prof. Atlanta (Ga.) Univ., 1975-76; prof., co-dir. Talladega (Ala.) Coll., 1976-83; clin. assoc. prof. Albert Einstein Coll. Medicine, Bronx, NY, 1983—2008, co-dir., 1983-95; dir. spl. chem. lab., coord. mgr. labs. Jacobi Med. Ctr., Bronx, NY, 1995—2008, assoc. prof. pathology, 1996—2008. Chmn. sci. rev. San Diego (Calif.) Conf. on Nucleic Acids, 1992; chmn. sci. symposium on molecular diagnostics Am. Assn. Clin. Chemistry Nat. Meetings, N.Y., 1993. Contbr. chpt. to book and articles to profl. jours. Hon. sec. Vishwa Kalyana Trust, Washington, 1989—2003. Named Fogarty Internat. Vis. Scientist Nat. Inst. Environ. Health Scis., NIH, 1972-74; rsch. grantee NIH, 1976-83, Resource Ctr. grantee NSF, 1981-83. Mem. Am. Assn. for Clin. Chemistry (chmn.-elect molecular pathology divsn. 1992-93, chair 1993-94), Am. Assn. Cancer Rsch., Am. Chem. Soc., Assn. Clin. Lab. Physicians and Scientists, Am. Soc. Biochem. and Molecular Biology. Hindu. Achievements include patents in field. Avocations: painting, writing popular science articles. Home: 100 Lindbergh Blvd Teaneck NJ 07666-5347 Personal E-mail: vadimurphy@hotmail.com.

MUSA, SAMUEL ALBERT, university executive; m. Judith Friedman; children: Gregory, Jeffrey. BA, BSEE, Rutgers U., 1961; MS in Applied Physics, Harvard U., 1962, PhD in Applied Physics, 1965. Rsch. scientist Gen. Precision Inc., Little Falls, NJ, 1965-66; asst. prof. elec. engring. U. Pa., Phila., 1966-71; project leader Inst. for Def. Analyses, Arlington, Va., 1971-78; dep. dir. Office of Under Sec. Def., Washington, 1978-83; dir. rsch. and advanced tech. E-Systems, Inc., Dallas, 1983-86, v.p. rsch. and advanced tech., 1986-95; exec. dir. Ctr. Display Tech. and Mfg. U. Mich., 1995-99; assoc. v.p. for strategic initiative, prof. elec. and computer engring. Northwestern U., Evanston, Ill., 1999—2007; sr. rsch. fellow ctr. tech. and nat. security Nat. Def. U., chmn., Homeland Security Sci. Tech., 2005—. Mem. sci. adv. bd. USAF; mem. sci. bd. Def. Intelligence Agy., Army Sci. Bd. Contbr. articles to profl. jours. Recipient Exceptional Civilian Svc. award, Sec. of Air Force, cert. of appreciation, Sec. Def. Fellow IEEE; mem. AIA (tech. and ops. coun. 1986-95, vice chmn. 1993, chmn. 1994), Sigma Xi, Tau Beta Pi, Pi Mu Epsilon.

MUSACCHIO, MARILYN JEAN, nurse midwife, educator; b. Louisville, Dec. 7, 1938; d. Robert William and Loretta C. (Liebert) Poulter; m. David Edward Musacchio, May 13, 1961; children: Richard Peter, Michelle Marie. BSN cum laude, Spalding Coll., 1968; MSN, U. Ky., 1972, cert. in nurse-midwifery, 1976; PhD, Case Western Res U., 1993. RN; cert. nurse-midwife; advanced registered nurse practitioner; registered nurse-midwife. Staff nurse gynecol. unit St. Joseph Infirmary, Louisville, 1959-60, staff nurse male gen. surgery unit, 1960; instr. St. Joseph Infirmary Sch. Nursing, Louisville, 1960-71; from asst. prof. to assoc. prof., dir. dept. nursing edn. Ky. State U., Frankfort, 1972-75; asst. prof. U. Ky. Coll. Nursing, Lexington, 1976-79, assoc. prof., coord., 1979-92, acting coordinator nurse-midwifery, 1982-84, coordinator for nurse-midwifery, 1987-92; assoc. prof., dir. nurse-midwifery U. Ala., Birmingham, 1992-96, assoc. prof., 1997-98; dean, prof. Tenn. Technol. U., Cookeville, 1998—2005; prof. Spalding U., Louisville, 2005—09, chmn.; dir. RN to BSN Program Aquinas Coll., Nashville, 2008—09; dean nursing edn. Sullivan U. Spencerian Coll., Louisville, 2009—. Cons. in field, dean nursing edn. Sullvian U. Mem. editorial bd. Jour. Obstet., Gynecol. and Neonatal Nursing, 1976-82; author pamphlet; contbr. articles to profl. jours. Mem.Louisville Safety Coun., 1973-80. Brig. Gen. Army Nurse Corps, USAR, 1992-95. Recipient Disting. Citizen award City of Louisville, 1977, Jefferson Cup award Jefferson County, Ky., 1991; named Outstanding Alumna, Mercy Acad., 1993; named to Hall of Disting. Alumni, U. Ky., 1995; recipient scholarships and fellowships, other awards. Fellow Am. Acad. Nursing; mem. AWHONN, NAFE, ANA, Nurse Assn. Am. Coll. Ob-Gyn. (charter; nat. sec. 1970-72, chmn. dist. V 1969), Am. Coll. Nurse-Midwives, Res. Officers Assn., Assn. Mil. Surgeons U.S., Sr. Army Res. Comdr. Assn., Assn. U.S. Army, Army Nurse Corps. Assn., Army War Coll. Alumni Assn. (life). Roman Catholic. Avocations: reading, candy making, cake decorating, cooking, sewing. Home: PO Box 4907 Louisville KY 40204-4907 Office Fax: 502-588-7175. Personal E-mail: mjmusacchio@gmail.com.

MUSANTE, TONY (ANTHONY PETER MUSANTE JR.), actor; s. Anthony Peter and Natalie Anne (Salerno) M.; m. Jane Ashley Sparkes, June 2, 1962. BA (Baker scholar), Oberlin Coll., 1958; postgrad., Northwestern U., 1957; student, HB Studios, NYC, 1961-65. Appearances include: (off Broadway prodns.) Borak, 1960, Zoo Story, Night of the Dunce, The Collection, Match-Play, Kiss Mama, L'Histoire du Soldat, A Gun Play, Falling Man, Cassatt, Grand Magic, The Big Knife, The Taming of the Shrew, Two Brothers, The Archbishop's Ceiling, Souvenir, A Streetcar Named Desire, Double Play, Dancing in the End Zone, Snow Orchid, Wait until Dark, Widows, Anthony Rose, Mount Allegro, Frankie and Johnny in the Clair de Lune, Breaking Legs, The Flip Side, Love Letters, The Sisters, Italian Funerals and Other Festive Occasions (Broadway prodns.) PS Your Cat is Dead, 1975 (N.Y. Drama Desk nomination), Memory of Two Mondays, 27 Wagons Full of Cotton, The Lady from Dubuque; films: Once a Thief, 1964, The Incident (Best Actor award Mar del Plata Internat. Film Festival), 1967, The Detective, 1968, The Mercenary, 1968, One Night at Dinner, 1969, Bird with the Crystal Plumage, 1970, Anonymous Venetian, 1970, Grissom Gang, 1971, The Last Run, 1971, Pisciotta Case, 1972, Goodbye and Amen, 1977, Break-Up, 1978, Collector's Item, 1985, The Repenter, 1985, Devil's Hill, Appointment in Trieste, 1987, Nocturne, The Pope of Greenwich Village, The Deep End of the Ocean, The Yards, Life As It Comes, Love's Promise, We Own The Night, 2007; TV appearances include Ride with Terror, 1963, star series Toma, 1973-74 (Photoplay Gold medal award 1974), scriptwriter several episodes; star HBO series Oz, A&E series 100 Centre Street; also starred in TV miniseries and movies: Pompeii, Traffic, Exiled, The Seventh Scroll, Deep Family Secrets, A Kiss In the Dark, High Ice, Breaking Up is Hard to Do, The Baron, Legend of the Black Hand, The Story of Esther, My Husband is Missing, Nowhere to Hide, The Quality of Mercy (Emmy nominee 1975), Court Martial of Lt. William Calley, Night Heat, Rearview Mirror, Nutcracker: Money, Madness and Murder, Acapulco HEAT, Nothing Sacred, American Playhouse: Weekend, Last Waltz on a Tightrope; daytime TV (guest star): Loving, ABC, 1993, As The World Turns, CBS, 2000. Mem. SAG, AFTRA, ATAS, Actors Equity Assn., Writers Guild Am. West, Acad. Motion Picture Arts and Scis.

MUSAT, KATHERINE GADUS, retired music educator; b. Cleve., Feb. 6, 1944; d. William Robert Gadus and Catherine Ruth Salmon; m. John George Musat, July 5, 1969; children: John William, Mary Katherine Smith, Danielle Eleanor. MusB in Edn., Baldwin-Wallace Coll., Berea, Ohio, 1966; MSc in Edn., Coll. Mt. St. Joseph, Cin., Ohio, 1988. Cert. tchr. Ohio, 1966. Dir. instrumental music Parma (Ohio) City Schs., 1967—2004; ret., 2004. Mem. jazz ensemble Baldwin-Wallace Coll., 1984—, studio brass tchr., 1985—; prin. trumpet Parma Symphony Orch., 1967—, Hermit Club Orch., 1985—. Vol. church musician various chs., 1964—. Mem.: Baldwin-Wallace Coll. Alumni Jazz Ensembles. Home: 2141 Jacqueline Dr Parma OH 44134-6858 Personal E-mail: kagy@cox.net.

MUSCAT, JOSHUA ETHAN, epidemiologist; b. Bangkok, Jan. 18, 1961; s. Robert Jaffe and Juliette Lee (Comparte) M.; m. Jill Davies Ottenberg, Apr. 6, 1991; children: Neil, Timothy. AB, Vassar Coll., 1982; M Pub. Health, Yale U., 1985. came to U.S., 1966. Mgmt. analyst D.C. Dept. Transp., Washington, 1982-83; epidemiol. investigator Ohio Dept. Health, Columbus, 1985-87; rsch. analyst Meml. Sloan-Kettering Cancer Ctr., NYC, 1987-88; staff epidemiologist Am. Health Found., NYC, 1988-97; asst. dir. IPRD Inc., Lake Success, N.Y., 1997—. Staff assoc. Cornell U. Med. Coll., N.Y.C., 1988-93. Referee biomedical jours.; contbr. articles to profl. jours. Mem. Am. Pub. Health Assn., N.Y. Acad. Scis. Office: IPRD 1979 Marcus Ave New Hyde Park NY 11042-1002

MUSCATO, ANDREW, lawyer; b. Newark, Aug. 28, 1953; s. Salvatore and Bertha (Kubilus) M.; m. Ann Marie Hughes, Aug. 19, 1978; children: Amy, Andrew Joseph, Amanda. AB magna cum laude, Brown U., 1975; JD, Seton Hall U., 1978. Bar: NJ 1978, NY 1984, U.S. Dist. Ct. NJ 1978, U.S. Dist. Ct. (so. and ea. dists.) NY 1984, U.S. Dist. Ct. (no. dist.) NY 1998, U.S. Ct. Appeals (3d cir.) 1981, U.S. Ct. Appeals (2d cir.) 2005. Law clk. to presiding judge, appellate div. N.J. Superior Ct., Somerville, 1978-79; staff atty. Adminstrv. Office of Cts., Trenton, NJ, 1979-80; assoc. Simon & Allen, Newark, 1980-86; ptnr. Kirsten & Simon, Newark, 1987-89, Whitman & Ransom, Newark, 1989-93, Whitman Breed Abbott & Morgan, LLP, Newark, 1993-99; counsel Skadden, Arps, Slate, Meagher & Flom LLP, Newark, 1999—2004, NYC, 2004—; commr. N.J. Pub. Employee Rels. Commn., 1999—2002; mem. N.J. Banking Adv. Bd., 2002—07. Atty. Irvington (N.J.) Rent Leveling Bd., 1980—. Author: The Parliminary Injunction in Bus. Litigation NYU Jour. of Law & Bus., Sparing, 2007, Executing on a Debtor's Interest in a Tenancy by the Entirety, 1986, Conbtr. to profl. jours. Mem. ABA, Essex County Bar Assn., Trial Attys. N.J., N.J. Inst. Mcpl. Attys., Def. Rsch. Inst. Republican. Roman Catholic. Home: 66 Addison Dr Basking Ridge NJ 07920-2202 Office: Skadden Arps Slate Meagher & Flom LLP 4 Times Sq New York NY 10036 Office Phone: 212-735-2217. Business E-Mail: amuscato@skadden.com, andrew.muscato@skadden.com.

MUSCHINSKI, ANDREAS, atmospheric physicist, educator; b. Salzgitter, Germany, Feb. 15, 1964; m. Andrea Muschinski; children: Thomas, Jana. Physics diploma, Tech. U. Braunschweig, Germany, 1990; D Natural Scis., U. Hannover, Germany, 1992. Scientist Inst. for Meteorology and Climatology, U. Hannover, 1990—. Privat-dozent U. Hannover, 1998. Contbr. articles on theory, measurement and simulation of atmospheric turbulence, on theoretical, observational and tech. aspects of clear-air radars to sci. jours., including Beitr. Phys. Atmospherics, Jour. Applied Mechanics, Jour. Fluid Mechanics, Meteorol. Zeitschrift, Radio Sci., Jour. Atmospheric Sci. German Rsch. Soc. Habilitation scholar Nat. Ctr. for Atmospheric Rsch., Boulder, Colo., 1996-97; Habilitation Meteorlogy scholar U. Hannover, Germany, 1998. Mem. German Meteorol. Soc. (Young Scientist award 1993), German Phys. Soc. Office: Univ of Massachusetts 151 Holdsworth Way Amherst MA 01003-9284

MUSE, JOHN R., investment company executive; b. Ft. Worth, Feb. 24, 1951; s. Arthur C. and Betty L. (Smith) M.; m. Lyn A. Reynolds, Aug. 10, 1975; children: Michael J., J. Tyler, Whitney J. BS, USAF Acad., 1973; MBA, UCLA, 1974. Commd. 2d lt. USAF, 1973, advanced through grades to capt., resigned, 1978; sr. v.p., corp. fin. dir. Schneider, Bernet & Hickman, Dallas, 1980-84; mng. dir. Prudential Bache Capital Funding, Dallas, 1984—89; co-founder, ptnr., mem. mgmt. com. HM Capital Partners (formerly Hicks, Muse, Tate & Furst Inc.), Dallas, 1989—, chmn., 2005—. Bd. dirs. Dean Foods Co., 1997—, Swift & Co., 2002—. Bd. visitors UCLA Anderson Sch. Mgmt. Presbyterian. Office: HM Captial Ste 1600 200 Crescent Ct Dallas TX 75201 Office Phone: 214-740-7300. Office Fax: 214-720-7888. E-mail: jmuse@hmcapital.com.*

MUSEL, DONNA SUE, academic administrator; b. Spencer, Iowa, Nov. 27, 1965; d. William Robert Salton and Darlene Marie Salton-Embry; m. Tom P. Salton, June 14, 1997; children: Nathan A. Robey, Logan T., Katrin A. BA, Buena Vista U., Storm Lake, Iowa, 1988, MS, 2001. English tchr. Emmetsburg HS, Iowa, 1991—97, Hartley-Melvin-Sanborn HS, Iowa, 1997—2001; dir. Ctr. Academic Excellence Buena Vista U., 2001—. Mem. Summit E-Free Ch., Alta, Iowa, 2005—08; sch. bd. mem. Concordia Luth. Sch., Storm Lake, 2008; vol. ILCC Jazz Camp, Estherville, Iowa, 2000—08. Mem.: AHEAD. Conservative. Evangelical. Avocations: photography, reading, music. Office: Buena Vista Univ 610 W 4th St Storm Lake IA 50588 Office Fax: 712-749-2038. Business E-Mail: museld@bvu.edu.

MUSETH, KEN, application developer, educator; b. Hjorring, Denmark, Sept. 7, 1967; s. Hanne Bruus and Hanne Museth; m. Katrine Happe; 1 child, Anders Peter. BS in Chemistry, Aarhus U., Denmark, 1990; MS in Phys. Chemistry, U. Copenhagen, 1994, PhD in Qunatum Dynamics, 1997. Vis. faculty mem. and sr. rsch. scientist Calif. Inst. Tech., Pasadena, 1998—2003; sr. rsch. scientist NASA's Jet Propulsion Lab., Pasadena, 2000—01; prof. Linkoping U., Sweden, 2003—07, adj. prof., 2008—, Aarhus U., Denmark, 2005—; sr. software engr. Digital Domain, Venice, Calif., 2007—. Conf. chair EuroVis, 2007; conferencetutorial chair Eurographics, Munich, 2008; bd. mem. Media Tech. U., Linköping, 2003—07, Ctr. Med. Image Sci. and Visualization, Linkoping, 2005—07, Jour. Graphics Tools, 2008—. Contbr. articles to profl. sci. jours. (NASA's NOVA award, 2000), chapters to books. Recipient VR Rsch. award, Swedish Sci. Coun., 2004; Skou fellowship, Danish Sci. Coun., 2003, Rsch. grant, Wallenbergs Found., 2005. Mem.: ACM. Achievements include research in computer graphics; patents pending for system and method for improved grid processing; fitting curves from one model to another. Office: Digital Domain 300 Rose Ave Venice CA 90291

MUSGRAVE, MARILYN NEOMA, former United States Representative from Colorado; b. Greeley, Colo., Jan. 27, 1949; m. Steven Musgrave; children: Chad, Becky, Amy, John. BA in Social Studies, Colo. State U., 1972. Co-owner Musgrave Bale Stacking; former tchr.; mem. RE-3 School Dist. Bd. Edn., 1990—94, Colo. House of Reps. from Dist. 65, 1994—98, Colo. State Senate from Dist. 1, Denver, 1998—2002, chmn. transp. com., mem. health, environment, welfare & institutions com., state, vets. & mil. affairs com.; mem. US Congress from 4th Colo. dist., 2003—09, mem. agriculture com., edn. & workforce com., resources com., small bus. com., ranking minority mem. fgn. agriculture com.; project dir. Votes Have Consequences The Susan B. Anthony List, Arlington, Va., 2009—. Mem. Immigration Reform Caucus, Liberty Caucus, NAVY/Marine Corps Caucus, Rep. Steering Com., Rep. Study Com., Spl. Forces Ops. Caucus, Values Action Team, Wash. Waste Watchers; policy chair Western Caucus; founder Congl. Second Amendment Caucus. Past pres. Morgan County Rep. Women; mem. First Assembly of God Ch., Fort Morgan. Recipient Disting. Christian Statesman award, D. James Kennedy Ctr. for Christian Statesmanship, 2005; named Gun Rights Legislator of the Yr., Gun Rights Policy Conf., 2004. Republican. Assemblies Of God. Office: The Susan B Anthony List 1800 N Kent St Ste 1070 Arlington VA 22209*

MUSGRAVE, R. KENTON, federal judge; b. Clearwater, Fla., Sept. 7, 1927; Student, Ga. Inst. Tech., 1945-46, U. Fla., 1946-47; BA, U. Wash., 1948; JD with distinction, Emory U., 1953. Asst. gen. counsel Lockheed Internat., 1953-62; v.p., gen. counsel Mattel, Inc., 1963-71; mem. firm Musgrave, Welbourn and Fertman, 1972-75; asst. gen. counsel Pacific Enterprises, 1975-81; v.p., gen. counsel Vivitar Corp, 1981-85; v.p., dir. Santa Barbara Applied Rsch., 1982-87; judge US Ct. Internat. Trade, NYC, 1987—97, sr. judge, 1997—. Trustee The Dian Fossey Gorilla Fund, Dolphins of Sharks Bay (Australia); hon. trustee Pet Protection Soc.; mem. United Way, Save the Redwoods League; active Palos Verdes Community Assn. Mem. Internat. Bar Assn., Pan American Bar

Assn., State Bar Calif. (chmn. corporate law sect. 1965-66, del. 1966-67), L.A. County Bar Assn., Fgn. Trade Assn. So. Calif. (bd. dirs.). Office: US Ct Internat Trade 1 Federal Plz New York NY 10278-0001*

MUSGRAVE MOOSBRUGGER, MEGAN, literature and language professor; b. Grand Rapids, Mich., Mar. 8, 1972; d. John Michael and Portia Elaine Musgrave; m. Eric Moosbrugger, Aug. 5, 2001; children: Oscar John Moosbrugger, Daniel Jude Moosbrugger. BA in English, Coll. William and Mary, Williamsburg, VA, 1994; MA in English, Loyola U. Chgo., 1999, PhD in English, 2007. Lectr. English Ind. U. - Purdue U. Indpls., 2004—. Office: IUPUI - Dept English 425 University Blvd Indianapolis IN 46202 Business E-Mail: memusgra@iupui.edu.

MUSHER, DANIEL MICHAEL, medical educator, researcher, epidemiologist, director; b. NYC, Feb. 27, 1938; s. Sidney and Hadassah Musher; m. Karol Sue Katz; children: Rebecca Gross, Benjamin, Deborah. AB magna cum laude, Harvard Coll., 1959; MD, Columbia U. Coll. Physicians and Surgeons, 1963; postgrad., MIT, 1969-70. Cert. Am. Bd. Internal Medicine, 1970, diplomate infectious diseases specialist Am. Bd. Internal Medicine, 1974. Intern, jr. med. resident first med. divsn. Bellevue Hosp., NYC, 1963—65; chief internal medicine 3640 USAF Hosp., Laredo AFB, Tex., 1965—67; instr. medicine Tufts U., Boston, 1970—71; chief infectious diseases Michael E. DeBakey Veterans Hosp., Houston, 1971—; asst. to assoc. prof. mmicrobiology and immunology Baylor Coll. Medicine, 1972—78, prof. medicine, 1979—, prof. microbiology and immunology, 1979—, prof. microbiology and molecular virology, 2000—. Chief infectious diseases Michael E. DeBakey Veterans Hosp., Houston, 1971—; mem. editl. bd. Sexually Trasmitted Diseases, 1979—83, Infection and Immunity, 1996—2000; assoc. editor Jour. Infectious Diseases, 1983—88; head infectious diseases Baylor Coll. Medicine, 1992—99, mem. curriculum com., 1999—; mem. adv. bd. treatment of STD's Centers for Disease Control, 1995—, mem. working group on drug resistant pneumococci, 1996—. Contbr. more than 450 chpts. to books, articles to profl. jours. Bd. mem., v.p. and pres. Houston Friends of Music, 1975—; mem. Tex. State Commn. on Judicious Use of Antibiotics, 1997—; bd. mem. Congregation Beth Yshurun; mem. Hillel, Jewish Fedn. Gtr. Houston; chmn. edn. William Malev Schs. of Congregation Beth Yeshurun, 1993—; bd. mem. and past pres. I. Weiner Jewish Secondary Sch., 1979—. With USAF, 1965—67. Recipient Outstanding Faculty Member award, Baylor Coll. Medicine Grad. Class, 1988, 2003, Dir.'s Profl. Leadership award, Michael E. DeBaket Veterans Hosp., 1991, Physician's Recognition award, AMA, 1991—, Nakano citation Outstanding Paper Epidemiology, Ctrs. Disease Control, 1993, Excellence in Tchg. award, Baylor Coll. Medicine, 1997—2002, Outstanding Tchr. award, Baylor Dept. Medicine, 1999, DeBakey medal excellence in Rsch., Baylor Coll. Medicine, 1990—99, Outstanding Tchr. Basic Scis., Baylor Coll. Medicine 2d Yr. Students, 1995, 1999, 2001—07, Outstanding Faculty Member award, Baylor Coll. Medicine Grad. Class, 1994, 2000, 2002, 2004—06, Most Outstanding Tchr., VA Med. Ctr. Med. Residents, 1992, 1998, 1999, 2002, 2008—09, Barbara and Corbin J. Robertson Pres. award, Baylor Coll. Medicine, 2003, John P. McGovern Outstanding Tchg. award, 2003; named to Baylor Hall of Fame Excellence in Tchg., 2003, Baylor Tchg. Hall of Fame, 2006; nominee Outstanding Contbn. Pub. Health, Centers for Disease Control, 2001. Fellow: ACP; mem.: AAAS, Am. Fedn. Clin. Rsch., Infectious Diseases Soc. Am. (Louis Weinstein prize Best Clin. article 1994, Clin. Tchr. award 2007, De Bakey medal 1999), Am. Soc. Microbiology, Am. Soc. Clin. Investigation, Am. Assn. Immunologists. Avocations: string quartet player, reading, music. Office: Michael E DeBakey VA Hosp 2002 Holcombe Blvd Houston TX 77030-4211 Office Fax: 713-794-7045. E-mail: Daniel.Musher@med.va.gov.

MUSHINSKY, HENRY R., biology professor; b. Passaic, NJ, Oct. 3, 1945; m. Patricia E. Yarnot; children: Erich R., Brad H. BS, Tusculum Coll., Greeneville, Tenn., 1967; MS, East Tenn. State U., Johnson City, 1969; PhD in Zoology, Clemson U., SC, 1973. Prof. & grad. dir. U. South Fla., Tampa, 1979—. Mem.: Am. Soc. Ichthyologists & Herpetologists (pres. 2008). Office: Univ South Fla 4202 Fowler Ave SCA 110 Tampa FL 33620 Business E-Mail: mushinsk@cas.usf.edu.

MUSHNICK, ASHLEY, legislative staff member; BA in Polit. Sci., Philosophy, Am. U., Washington, 2007. Constituency press sec. Senator Barack Obama's Presdl. Campaign, Fla.; press asst., Rep. Robert Wexler US House of Reps., Washington, 2007—08, dep. press sec., Rep. Robert Wexler, 2008—. Democrat. Office: 2241 Rayburn House Office Bldg Washington DC 20515 Office Phone: 202-225-3001. Office Fax: 202-225-5974.*

MUSICK, GERALD JOE, retired entomology educator; b. Ponca City, Okla., May 24, 1940; s. Arlie A. and Leona (Beier) M.; m. Florene Ione Thompson, May 11, 1962; children: Linda Kaye, Mary Louise. BS, Okla. State U., 1962; MS, Iowa State U., 1964; PhD, U. Mo., 1969. Grad. asst. Iowa State U., 1962-64; instr. U. Mo., 1964-69; asst. prof. Ohio State U., Wooster, 1969—76, assoc. prof., 1971-76; dept. head U. Ga., Tifton, 1976-79; prof., dept. head U. Ark., Fayetteville, 1979-86, interium dir. agrl. exptl. sta., 1986-87, dean, assoc. v.p. agrl. rsch., 1987-93, univ. prof. entomology, 1993—2002, chmn.-elect faculty coun. Dale Bumpers Coll. Agrl., Food and Life Scis., 1997, chmn., 1998, prof. emeritus, 2002—, ret., 2002—; chmn. faculty coun. Dale Bumpers Coll. of Agrl. Food and Life Scis., 1998; gen. mgr. Razerback Pk. Golf Course, Fayetteville, Ark., 2003—. Author and co-author numerous publs. Vice-chairperson com. Coop. States Rsch. Svc., 1993, So. Expt. Sta.; chairperson steering com. Midwest Food Safety Consortium, 1991-93; mem. U. Ark. Faculty Senate, 1994-2002, chair campus faculty, 1998-99, chair faculty sentate 1999-2000, faculty exec. com., 1999-2001; coord. Pest Mgmt. Programs, 1998—. Mem. Entomol. Soc. Am. (pres. S.E. br. 1983-84), Ark. Acad. Sci., Ctrl. States Entomol. Soc. (v.p. 1995-96, pres. 1996-97), Sigma Xi, Gamma Sigma Delta. Lutheran. Avocation: golf. Office: Razorback Park Golf Course Fayetteville AR 72704 Personal E-mail: gjmfim@cox.net.

MUSICK, KATHERINE M., research scientist; b. Indpls., Apr. 2, 1982; d. John Allen and Victoria Allen Musick; m. Christopher M. Long, July 20, 2007; 1 child, William Christopher Long. BSEE, Valparaiso U., Ind., 2003; PhD, U. Ill., Urbana-Champaign, 2008. Grad. rschr. U. Ill., 2003—. Lector St. Mary's Cath. Ch., Champaign, 2007—08. Grad. Rsch. fellowship, NSF, 2003—06. Conservative. Achievements include research in three dimensional microelectrode array for recording dissociated neuronal cultures. Personal E-mail: katmusick@juno.com.

MUSIHIN, KONSTANTIN K., electrical engineer; b. Harbin, China, June 17, 1927; came to US, 1967, naturalized, 1973; s. Konstantin N. and Alexandra A. (Lapitsky) M.; m. Natalia Krilova, Oct. 18, 1964; 1 child, Nicholas. Student, YMCA Inst., 1942, North Manchurian U., 1945, Harbin Poly. Inst., 1948. Registered profl. engr., Calif., NY, Pa., Wash. Asst. prof. Harbin Poly. Inst., 1950-53; elec. engr. Moinho Santista, Sao Paulo, Brazil, 1955-60; constrn. project mgr. Caterpillar-Brazil, Santo Amaro, 1960-61; mech. engr. Matarazzo Industries, Sao Paulo, 1961-62; chief of works Vidrobras, St. Gobain, Brazil, 1962-64; project engr. Brown Boveri, Sao Paulo, 1965-67; sr. engr. Kaiser Engrs., Oakland, Calif., 1967-73, Bechtel Power Corp., San Francisco, 1973-75; supr. power and control San Francisco Bay Area Rapid Transit, Oakland, 1976-78; chief elec. engr. L.K. Comstock Engring. Co., San Francisco, 1978-79; prin. engr. Morrison Knudsen Co., San Francisco, 1979-84, Brown & Caldwell, Cons. Engrs., Pleasant Hill, Calif., 1984-85; cons. engr. Pacific Gas and Electric Co., San Francisco, 1986-89; sr. engr. Bechtel Corp., San Francisco, 1989. Mem. IEEE (life, sr.), NSPE, Calif. Soc. Profl. Engrs. Mem. Christian Orthodox Ch.

MUSIL, ROBERT KIRKLAND, global environmental politics professor; b. NYC, Oct. 27, 1943; s. Ralph A. and Margaret Hooker (Kirkland) M.; m. Caryn Lynne McTighe, June 15, 1968; children: Rebecca M. Unruh, Emily Kirkland. BA, Yale U., 1964; MA, Northwestern U., 1966, PhD, 1970; MPH, Johns Hopkins U., 2001; LHD, Mitchell Coll., 2009. Instr. Def. Info. Sch., Ft. Benjamin Harrison, Ind., 1969-71; co-dir. CCCO/An Agy. for Mil. and Draft Counseling, Phila., 1971-74; dir. mil. affairs project Ctr. for Nat. Security Studies, Washington, 1974-75; asst. prof. English and Am. studies Temple U., Phila., 1976-78; prodr., host Consider the Alternatives Radio, Phila., 1978-92; exec. dir. SANE Edn. Fund, Phila. and Washington, 1984-88, Profls. Coalition for Nuclear Arms Control, Washington, 1988-92; dir. policy and programs Physicians for Social Responsibility, Washington, 1992-95, exec. dir., CEO, 1995—2006; sr. fellow Ctr. Congl. and Presdl. Studies, Sch. Pub. Affairs, Am. U., 2009—. Adj. prof. Sch. Internat. Svc., Am. U., 1997—; vis. scholar Churches' Ctr. Theology Pub. Policy, Wesley Theol. Sem., 2007—. Prodr.: (documentary series) Shadows of the Nuclear Age: American Culture and the Bomb, 1980 (NEH grantee); Author: Hope for a Heated Planet: How Americans are Fighting Global Warming and Building a Better Future, 2009. Bd. dirs. SANE, 1978-84, Scoville Fellowships, Washington, 1989-92, 95—, pres., 2007—; bd. dirs. Environ. Alliance, 2006—, chmn., 2007—; chmn. bd. dirs. 20/20 Vision, 2006-09, Coun. for a Livable World, 2006—, Population Connection, 2006—, treas. 2009-. Capt. U.S. Army, 1969-71. Recipient Maj. Armstrong award for radio Armstrong Found., Columbia U., N.Y.C., 1988, 89. Mem. United Ch. of Christ. Home and Office: 8600 Irvington Ave Bethesda MD 20817-3604 Office Phone: 301-493-4571. Personal E-mail: bmusil1@yahoo.com.

MUSK, ELON, aerospace transportation executive; b. South Africa, June 28, 1971; m. Justine Musk; 5 children. Student, Queen's U., Kingston, Ont.; BS in Economics, U. Pa., 1994, BS in Physics, 1994; postgraduates studies, Stanford U. With Pinnacle Rsch.; software devel. Rocket Sci., Microsoft; co-founder, chmn., CEO, chief tech. officer Zip2 Corp. (acquired by Compaq), 1995—99; co-founder, chmn., CEO X.com (changed legal name to PayPal in 2001, acquired by eBay in 2002), 1999—2002; founder, CEO, chief tech. officer Space Exploration Tech. Corp. (SpaceX), 2002—; product architect, chmn. Tesla Motors, Inc., San Carlos, 2003—. Prin. owner, chmn. bd. Tesla Motors; primary investor, chmn. bd. Solar City; bd. dirs. The Planetary Society, 2003—. Chmn. Musk Found.; bd. trustee X-Prize Found. Named one of 50 Who Matter Now, Business 2.0, 2007. Fellow: World Tech. Network; mem.: US NAS (bd. dir, Aeronautics and Space Engring.). Office: Space Exploration Tech Corp 1310 E Grand Ave El Segundo CA 90245 also: Tesla Motors Inc 1050 Bing St San Carlos CA 94070

MUSKAL, TAMAR, composer; b. Jerusalem, 1965; arrived in US, 1994; BA, Rubin Acad. Music and Dance, Jerusalem, 1991; MA, Yale U.; continued studies, CUNY. Edn. composer-in-residence Westchester Philharm., 2001—04. Composer: The Yellow Wind (Theodore Front prize, Internat. Alliance for Women in Music, 2007, Pulitzer nominee). Grantee Meet the Composer, 2006, Am. Composers Forum/Jerome Found., 2007, Fromm Music Found., Harvard U., 2007, Am. Music Ctr., 2008; fellow John Simon Guggenheim Meml. Found., 2009; Charles Ives scholar, AAAL, 2004. Mem.: Am. Composers Forum. Mailing: 33 Riverside Dr New York NY 10023*

MUSLINER, THOMAS ALLEN, cardiologist, director; b. NYC, May 5, 1945; s. Stephen and Thea Rhein Musliner; children: Katherine Louise, Robert Weston, Angela Grace. BS summa cum laude, Harvard Coll., Cambridge, Mass., 1967; MD magna cum laude, Harvard Med. Sch., 1972. Cert. in internal medicine Bd. Med. Examiners, 1977, in endocrinology & metabolism 1978. Staff med. scientist, Donner Lab. U. Calif., Berkeley, 1981—91; exec. dir., cardiovasc. disease Merck Rsch. Labs., Merck & Co., Inc., North Wales, Pa., 1991—. Intern, internal medicine Peter Bent Brigham Hosp., Boston, 1972—73, resident, internal medicine, 1973—74; clin. assoc. NIH, Bethesda, Md., 1974—77, fellow endocrinology and metabolism, 1975—77; asst. prof. medicine Brown U. Sch. Medicine, Providence, 1978—81; staff endocrinologist, dir. lipoprotein rsch., asst. dir. Clin. Investigation Ctr., Oakland Naval Hosp., Calif., 1982—85; staff endocrinologist Alta Bates Hosp., Berkeley, 1985—91. Lt. comdr. USN, 1982—85, Oakland. Named to Jr. Eight, Phi Beta Kappa Soc., 1966; Fulbright scholarship, US Fulbright Scholarship Program, 1967—68. Fellow: Am. Heart Assn., Coun. Arteriosclerosis; mem.: Endocrine Soc. Achievements include research in lipoprotein metabolism and atherosclerosis; atherosclerosis prevention. Office: Merck Rsch Labs 351 N Sumneytown Pike North Wales PA 19454 Home: 98 Woodview Ln North Wales PA 19454 Office Fax: 267-305-6476. Personal E-mail: thomas_musliner@comcast.net. Business E-Mail: thomas_musliner@merck.com.

MUSOLF, LLOYD DARYL, political science professor, educational association administrator; b. Yale, SD, Oct. 14, 1919; s. William Ferdinand and Emma Marie (Pautz) M.; m. Berdyne Peet, June 30, 1944; children: Stephanie, Michael, Laura. BA, Huron Coll., 1941; MA, U. SD, 1946; PhD, Johns Hopkins U., 1950. Mem. faculty Vassar Coll., Poughkeepsie, NY, 1949-59, assoc. prof. polit. sci., 1955-59; chief of party adv. group Mich. State U., East Lansing, 1959-61, prof. polit. sci., 1961-63, U. Calif.-Davis, 1963-87, prof. emeritus, 1988—, dir. Inst. Govtl. Affairs, 1963-84. Vis. prof. Johns Hopkins U., Balt., 1953, U. Del.; 1954, U. Mich., 1955-56; US Nat. rapporteur for Internat. Congress Adminstrv. Scis., Berlin, 1983; cons., lectr. in field. Author: Federal Examiners and the Conflict of Law and Administration, 1953, Public Ownership and Accountability: The Canadian Experience, 1959, Promoting the General Welfare, Government and the Economy, 1965, (with others) American National Government-Policies and Politics, 1971, Mixed Enterprise-A Developmental Perspective, 1972, (with Springer) Malaysia's Parliamentary System-Representative Politics and Policy-making in a Divided Society, 1979, Uncle Sam's Private Profitseeking Corporations-Comsat, Fannie Mae, Amtrak and Conrail, 1983; editor: (with Krislov) The Politics of Regulation, 1964, Communications Satellites in Political Orbit, 1968, (with Kornberg) Legislatures in Developmental Perspective, 1970, (with Joel Smith) Legislatures in Development-Dynamics of Change in New and Old States, 1979; contbr. monographs, chpts. to books, articles to profl. jours. Served to lt. USNR, 1942-45. Johnston scholar Johns Hopkins U., 1946-48; Faculty fellow Vassar Coll., 1954-55; sr. assoc. East-West Ctr., Honolulu, 1968-69; vis. scholar Brookings Instn., Washington, 1980. Mem. ASPA (exec. coun. 1967-70), Nat. Assn. Schs. Pub. Affairs and Adminstrn. (exec. coun. 1972-75), Western Govtl. Rsch. Assn. (exec. bd. 1966-68), Am. Polit. Sci. Assn., Nat. Assn. State Univs. and Land Grant Colls. (rsch. com. divsn. urban affairs 1980-81). Office: U Calif Dept Polit Sci Davis CA 95616 Home Phone: 530-747-6536; Office Phone: 530-752-0946.

MUSON, HOWARD HENRY, writer, consultant; b. Mt. Vernon, NY, Mar. 19, 1935; s. Joseph Ernest and Beatrice (Hakmaier) Muson; m. Dorothy Regina Tyor, May 21, 1967; children: Eve, Stephanie, Nickolas, Alice. AB magna cum laude, Harvard U., Cambridge, Mass., 1956; cert., Johns Hopkins Sch. Advanced Internat. Studies, Bologna, Italy, 1956-57; postgrad., U. Calif., Berkeley, 1957-58. Dir. program research CARE Inc., NYC, 1960-62; bur. chief Hartford Courant, Conn., 1962; newsman, columnist AP, Boston, 1963-66; contbg. editor Time mag., NYC, 1966-70; articles editor N.Y. Times mag., NYC, 1970-77; exec. editor Psychology Today mag., NYC, 1977-82; editor Across The Board, NYC, 1983-89; editor, pub. Family Bus. mag., Phila., 1992-2000; rsch. assoc. Lansberg Gersick & Assocs., New Haven, 1998—. Vis. lectr. in residential colls. Yale U., New Haven, 1982-83; instr. in sci. and environ. reporting program NYU, 1992; lead writer, exec. action reports, Mid-Market Series, The Conf. Bd., 2002-. Author: Triumph of the American Spirit: Johnstown, Pennsylvania, 1989, Managing Growth: Smart Strategies for Smaller and Midsize Companies, 2000, Valuing Experience: How to Motivate and Retain Mature Workers, 2002, The Family Business Growth Handbook, 2002; co-author: Generations of Giving: Leadership and Continuity in Family Foundations, 2004; contbr. articles to profl. jours., popular mags. Dir. Project Concern/No. Westchester Walk for Mankind, Mt. Kisco, NY, 1986-90; media rels. Westchester Walk for Diabetes, 2002-03. Home Phone: 914-941-1616; Office Phone: 914-941-1881. Personal E-mail: h_muson@yahoo.com.

MUSONERA, ETIENNE, finance educator, consultant; b. Nyanza, Rwanda, Sept. 25, 1961; s. Amiel Munyangeyo and Marita Nyirabakiga; m. Agnes Mukabera Musonera, Sept. 25, 1992; children: Grace, Blyss, Bercy-Dylan. BBA, Davenport U., Kalamazoo, 1990; MSc in Engring. Mgmt., We. Mich. U., Kalamazoo, 1995; PhD in Indsl. Engring. and Internat. Mktg., Wayne State U., Detroit, 2005, MSc in Indsl. Engring., 2005. Rsch. asst. Wayne State U., 1998—2005; asst. prof. mktg. Ea. N.Mex U., Portales, N.Mex., 2006—. Mfg. quality sys. engr. Gen. Motors Co., Warren, Mich., 1999—2002, HRU, Inc., Warren, 1999—2002. Author: (book) A Theoretical Model To Optimize Fdi Inflows: Wcm Best Practices And Spillovers Effect In Value Added Activities; contbr. scientific papers to profl. jours. Mem.: Phi Beta Delta (hon.). Office: Eastern New Mexico Univ 1500 S Ave K Portales NM 88130 Home: 3247 Flowers Rd S Apt O Atlanta GA 30341-5682 Personal E-mail: musonera@yahoo.com. Business E-Mail: etienne.musonera@enmu.edu.

MUSS, HYMAN BERNARD, oncologist, educator; b. Bklyn., Apr. 18, 1943; m. Loretta Anne Lassam; children: Sarah, Jonathan, Daniel. BA in Chemistry cum laude, Lafayette Coll., 1964; MD summa cum laude, SUNY, 1968. Diplomate Am. Bd. Internal Medicine, sub-splty. med. oncology, Am. Bd. Hematology, Am. Bd. Oncology. Intern Peter Bent Brigham Hosp., Boston, 1968-69, jr. asst. resident, 1969-70, rsch. fellow in medicine, 1972-73, rsch. fellow in hematology, 1973-74, Children's Hosp. Med. Ctr., Boston, 1972-73; fellow in oncology Dana Farber Cancer Inst., Boston, 1973-74; asst. prof. medicine, hematology/oncology Wake Forest U., Winston-Salem, N.C., 1974-78, assoc. prof., 1978-85, assoc. dir. clin. rsch. Comprehensive Cancer Ctr., 1979-96, prof. medicine, 1985-96, U. Vt., 1996—2009; assoc. dir. U. Vt. Cancer Ctr., 1996—2009; prof. medicine, breast cancer & geriatric oncology Lineberger Comprehensive Cancer Ctr., U. NC. Sch. Medicine, Chapel Hill, 2009—. Peer review com. Health Scis. Consortium, Inc., 1978-80; sci. adv. com. black/white survival study, 1985-96; com.consulting staff Forsyth Meml. Hosp., Winston-Salem, N.C., N.C. Bapt. Hosp., Winston Salem. Mem. editl. bd. Am. Jour. Med. Sci., 1986—, Jour. Clin. Oncology, 1994, Nat. Cancer Insts. Computerized, 1986-91, Contemporary Oncology, 1990—; reviewer New Eng. Jour. Medicine, Jour. Clin. Oncology, Archives of Internal Medicine, Breast Cancer Rsch. & Treatment, Cancer, Gynecologic Oncology, Surg. Neurology, Jour. Nat. Cancer Inst., Jour. Immunotherapy, Clin. Chemistry; contbr. articles, abstracts to profl. jours., chpts. to books. Active Am. Cancer Soc., 1978—, bd. dirs., 1985-87; trustee Blumenthal Jewish Home, 1992-93, chair med. ethics com., chair HIV/infectious disease com. Maj. U.S. Army, 1970-72, Vietnam. Decorated Bronze Star U.S. Army; recipient Cooper Meml. award Wake County, 1979; Jr. Faculty fellow Am. Cancer Soc., 1975-79. Fellow ACP; mem. AMA, Am. Coll. Obstetricians and Gynecologists (com. human rsch.), Internal Soc. Geriatric Oncology, Vt. State Med. Soc., New England Cancer Soc., Am. Bd. Internal Medicine, Internat. Soc. Breast Disease, Am. Soc. Hematology, Am. Fedn. Clin. Rsch., Am. Soc. Clin. Oncology, Am. Assn. Cancer Rsch., Internat. Gynecologic Cancer Soc., Internat. Assn. Breast Cancer Rsch., So. Assn. Oncology (edn. com. 1988—), So. Med. Assn., So. Soc. Clin. Rsch., N.C. Med. Soc. (cancer com.), Forsyth County Med. Soc. (chmn. cancer com. 1977-80, med. adv. com. 1977-79), Cancer and Acute Leukemia Group B, Gynecologic Oncology Group (sarcoma com. 1977-79, endometrial com. 1978-90, quality control com. 1978-90, chemotherapy com. 1977—, chmn., 1980—, protocol com. 1980-90, new drug liaison com. 1980—, exec. comb. 1991—, quality of life com. 1993—, cervix com. 1993—), Piedmont Oncology Assn. (chmn. 1991—), Phi Beta Kappa, Alpha Omega Alpha. Office: UNC Lineberger Comprehensive Cancer Ctr Sch Medicine CB #7295 450 West Dr Chapel Hill NC 27599-7259 Office Phone: 919-966-3856. E-mail: muss@email.unc.edu.

MUSSA, MICHAEL L., economist, educator; b. LA, Apr. 15, 1944; AB, UCLA, 1966; MA, U. Chgo., 1970, PhD, 1974. Asst. prof. econs. U. Rochester, 1971—75, assoc. prof., 1975—76; assoc. prof. econs. U. Chgo., 1976—80, prof. internat. bus., 1980—91; mem. US Coun. of Econ. Advisers, 1986—88; econ. counselor, dir. Dept. Rsch. IMF, 1991—2001; sr. fellow Inst. Internat. Econs., Washington, 2001—. Rsch. fellow London Sch. Econs., 1975—76, Grad. Sch. Internat. Studies, Geneva, 1976—81; vis. prof. Asian Dept. IMF, 1980; vis. faculty mem. CUNY Grad. Ctr. Author: Argentina and the Fund: From Triumph to Tragedy, 2002; contbr. articles to profl. jours. Office: Inst Internat Econs 1750 Massachusetts Ave, NW Washington DC 20036-1903 Office Phone: 202-328-9000. Office Fax: 202-659-3225. E-mail: mmussa@iie.com.

MUSSEHL, ROBERT CLARENCE, lawyer; b. Washington, May 1, 1936; s. Chester Carl and Clara Cecelia (Greenwalt) Mussehl; m. Misook Chung, Mar. 22, 1987; 1 child, Omar;children from previous marriage: Debra Lee(dec.), David Lee. BA, Am. U., 1964, JD, 1966. Bar: Wash. 1967, U.S. Dist. Ct. (we. dist.) Wash. 1967, U.S. Ct. Appeals (9th cir.) 1968, U.S. Supreme Ct. 1971. Sr. ptnr. Thom, Mussehl, Navoni, Hoff, Pierson & Ryder, Seattle, 1967-78, Neubauer & Mussehl, Seattle, 1978-80, Mussehl & Rosenberg, Seattle, 1980—2001, Mussehl & Khan, 2004—09. Spkr. law convs. and other profl. orgns.; chmn. bd. dirs., CEO Seattle Smashers, 1976—80; moot ct. judge Nat. Appellate Adv. Competition, San Francisco, 1987; panel mem. ABA Symposium Compulsory Jurisdiction World Ct., San Francisco, 1987. Contbr. articles to profl. jours. Mem. Wash. Vol. Lawyers Arts, 1976—80; bd. dirs. Wash. State Pub. Interest Law Ctr., 1976—81; founder, past chair

Lawyers Helping Hungry Children, bd. dirs., 1991—2009; founder, past chair Wash. State Lawyers Campaign Hunger Relief, 1991—; statewide chair Lawyers for Duming for Gov., 1976; mem. task force single adult and ch. Ch. Coun. Greater Seattle, 1976—78. Recipient Jefferson award for Cmty. and Pub. Svc., State of Wash., Am. Inst. Pub. Svc., 1997. Fellow: Am. Acad. Matrimonial Lawyers, Am. Bar Found. (life); mem.: ABA (ho. dels. 1979—91, mem. assembly resolutions com. 1979—91, chair marriage and family counseling and concilliation com. 1981—83, mem. world order under law standing com. 1983—89, chair 1986—89, chair ad hoc com. assembly 1986—89, mem. blue ribbon com. world ct. 1987—88, mem. spl. adv. com. internat. activities 1989—91, mem. standing com. dispute resolution 1992—93, mem. exec. coun. sect. dispute resolution 1993—95, asst. budget officer 1995—97, budget officer 1997—99, chair 2001—02, sect. liaison commn. racial and ethnic diversity 2002—04, ho. dels. 2003—, commn. racial and ethnic diversity 2004—06, editor Goal IX newsletter 2004—), World Assn. Lawyers World Peace through Law Ctr. (founding mem.), Am. Arbitration Assn. (panel arbitrators), Seattle-King County Bar Assn. (mem. other coms. 1970—, chmn. young lawyers sect. 1971—72, mem. family law sect. 1971—90, sec. 1972—73, trustee), Wash. State Trial Lawyers Assn., Wash. State Bar Assn. (mem. exec. com. family law sect. 1973—75, chmn. internat. law com. 1974—76, sec.-treas., mem. exec. com. world peace through law sect. 1980—, chair 1981—82, mem. editl. bd. Family Law Deskbook 1987—89), UN Assn. USA (bd. dirs. Seattle chpt. 1989—91), Heritage Club YMCA Greater Seattle (charter 1977—). Avocations: squash, bicycling, tennis, weightlifting, painting. Office: 520 Pike St Ste 2210 Seattle WA 98101 Home: 2415 34th Ave W Seattle WA 98199 Office Phone: 206-386-7200. Personal E-mail: bobmussehl@earthlink.net.

MUSSELMAN, CECELIA ANNE, linguist, educator; b. Port Hueneme, Calif., Apr. 25, 1965; d. John F. and Michele G. Musselman. BA, U. RI, Kingston, 1987; PhD, Columbia U., NY, 1997. Project mgmt., page layout Argosy Pub., Newton, Mass., 1997—2007; adj. faculty Northeastern U., Boston, 2002—07, faculty mentor, 2006—, postdoc. fellow, 2007—. Grant, Finlandia Found., 1989, Fulbright fellowship, US Dept. State, 1990—91. Mem.: Phi Beta Kappa. Avocations: ceramics, travel. Office: Northeastern Univ English Dept 360 Huntington Ave Boston MA 02115 Business E-Mail: c.musselman@neu.edu.

MUSSELMAN, LARRY L., retired chemical engineer; b. Erie, Pa., Aug. 16, 1947; s. Lloyd H. and Lyda Musselman; m. Susan E., Nov. 25, 1966; children: Cheri A., Jason L., Lucy A., Gavin A., Lauren A. BSChemE magna cum laude, Akron U., 1971, MS in Engring., 1972. Rsch. engr. Timken Co., 1971-77; sr. rsch. engr. Alcoa Co., Alcoa Center, Pa., 1977-79, sr. scientist, 1979-81, staff engr., 1981-83, tech. svc. mgr., 1983-86, tech. mgr., 1986-89; dir. tech. and ops. Polymer Additives Group, Apollo, Pa., 1989-93, v.p. tech. and ops. polymer additives group, 1993—2008; ret., 2008. Mem. tech. adv. com. Ohio Legislature. Author: Handbooks of Science and Technology of Alumna Chemicals, Plastics Additives; contbr. over 50 articles on polymers and fire retardants to profl. jours.; numerous patents in field. Akron U. scholar. Mem. ASME (sect. dir.), ASTM (fire testing coms.), Am. Soc. Lubrication Engrs., Soc. Plastics Engrs., Fire Retardant Chems. Assn., Soc. Plastics Industry Coms., Sigma Xi, Sigma Tau, Alpha Chi Sigma. Office Phone: 724-727-3846.

MUSSENDEN, GEORG ANTONIO, electronics engineer; b. San Juan, Aug. 25, 1959; s. Gustavo Adolfo and Christa-Maria (Gotsch) M. Student, U. P.R.-Rio Piedras, 1977-79; BS in E.E. with honors, U. Fla., Gainesville, 1982; postgrad. in elec. engring., U. Fla. Electronics technician Radiotelephone Communicators of P.R. (Motorola), 1976; computer sys. programmer and operator U. P.R., Rio Piedras, 1978-79, rsch. asst. dept. physics, 1978-79; computer programmer Regional Electrocardiogram Analysis Ctr. J. Hillis Miller Health Ctr., U. Fla., Gainesville, 1981; pre-profl. engr. IBM Corp. Devel. Lab., Endicott, N.Y., 1981; sr. assoc. engr./scientist entry sys. tech. SPD, CPD and ESD design and devel. labs., Boca Raton, Fla., 1982-93; elec. hardware devel. engr. sci. Core Internat. Rsch. and Devel. Corp., Boca Raton, 1993—. Contbr. articles to profl. jours. Scholar San Jose Alumni, 1973-77, Fonalledas Found., 1977-79, Procter and Gamble, 1980; U.F. Sr. Honors scholar, 1980; scholar Nat. Fund Minority Engring., 1980, Du Pont, 1981; Nat. Consortium for Grad. Degrees for Minorities in Engring. fellow, 1981. Mem. IEEE, SMPTE, AES, N.Y. Acad. Scis., Audio-Visual Club, Amateur Radio Club, Golden Key, Eta Kappa Nu, Tau Beta Pi, Phi Kappa Phi. Roman Catholic. Achievements include 12 technological invention disclosures. Home: 3815 NW 4th Ave Boca Raton FL 33431 Office Phone: 954-723-3461. E-mail: gmussen@bellsouth.net.

MUSSER, CHERRI M., information technology executive; m. Jack Musser. BA in Math., Miss. State Univ., 1973; MBA, Southern Methodist Univ. Various positions from programmer to dir. bus. sys. Texas Instruments, 1973—94, v.p. R&D, TI software, 1994—96; process information officer, supply chain GM, 1996; group v.p., CIO GMAC, Detroit, 2003—08; v.p., CIO Electronic Data Systems, Plano, Tex., 2008—. Recipient Coll. of Arts & Scis. Alumnus of Yr., Miss. State Univ., 1999. Mem.: Mich. Coun. Women in Tech. (pres. 2005—08). Office: EDS 5400 Legacy Dr Plano TX 75024 Office Phone: 313-665-5906, 972-605-1959. Business E-Mail: cherri.musser@gm.com, cherri.musser@eds.com.

MUSSETT, RICHARD EARL, city official; b. Erie, Pa., June 24, 1948; s. Clarence Harold and Elva (Brueckner) M.; m. Alaine Kathleen Rau, Aug. 14, 1971; children: Matthew, Mark. BPA, U. N.D., 1974; M of Urban Planning, U. Mich., 1975. Chief planner City of Largo, Fla., 1976-77; chief long-range planning Pinellas County Planning Dept., Clearwater, Fla., 1977-80; planning dir. City of St. Petersburg, Fla., 1980-85, dep. city mgr., adminstr. Fla., 1987—; adminstr. cmty. devel. City of Bloomington, Minn., 1985-87. Chmn. Pinellas County Planners Adv. Com., 1982. Alternate del. N.D. Dem. Conv., 1972; mem. Tampa Bay Study Commn., 1984-85; mem. environ. quality com. Fla. League of Cities, 1984-85, devel. strategies legis. policy com., 1986; bd. dirs. Mahaffey Theater, 1994-2007, Tampa Bay Partnership, 1997-2007. Rackham grantee, 1975. Mem. Am. Inst. Cert. Planners (charter), Am. Planning Assn. (chmn. Suncoast sect. 1984, mem. legis. policy com. Fla. chpt. 1984-85, editor Suncoast sect. newsletter 1985). Lutheran. Avocations: reading, sports, politics. Office: City of St Petersburg 175 5th St N Saint Petersburg FL 33701-3708 Office Phone: 727-892-5400. E-mail: rick.mussett@stpete.org.

MUSSEY, JOSEPH ARTHUR, health and medical product executive; b. Cleve., July 17, 1948; s. Arthur Glenn and Mary Jane (Silvaroli) M.; m. Mary Elizabeth Stone, July 11, 1975; 1 child, Joanna Lee. BS in Indsl. Engring. with distinction, Cornell U., 1970; MBA, Harvard U., 1976. Engring. mgmt. officer U.S. Navy Pub. Works Ctr., Pearl Harbor, Hawaii, 1971-75; mktg. exec. B.F. Goodrich, Akron, Ohio, 1976-80, fin. exec., 1980-84; v.p. fin. Combustion Engring., Stamford, Conn., 1984-85, v.p. ops., 1985-86; exec. v.p. Process Automation Bus. Combustion Engring., Columbus, Ohio, 1987-90; pres., CEO Danninger Med. Tech., Inc., Columbus, 1990—98; pres., CEO, dir. Interpore Cross Internat., Irvine, Calif., 1998—. Served as lt. U.S. Navy, 1971-75. Decorated Disting. Naval Grad. (USN), 1971, Disting. Grad. U.S. Navy Civil Engring. Corps., 1971. Mem. Alpha Pi Mu, Tau Beta Pi, Phi Eta Sigma. Clubs: Skull & Daggar. Republican. Roman Catholic. Office: Interpore Cross International 181 Technology Dr Irvine CA 92618 Home: 812 NE Bay Isle Dr Boca Raton FL 33487-1731

MUSSINA, MICHAEL COLE (MIKE MUSSINA), retired professional baseball player; b. Williamsport, Pa., Dec. 8, 1968; BA in Econs., Stanford U., Calif., 1990. Pitcher Balt. Orioles, 1990-2000, N.Y. Yankees, 2001—08; ret., 2008. Recipient Am. League Gold Glove award, MLB, 1996—99, 2001, 2003, 2008, Casey Stengel You Could Look It Up award, Baseball Writers' Assn. America, NY Chpt., 2009; named to Am. League All-Star Team, MLB, 1992—94, 1997, 1999. Achievements include leading the American League in: wins (19), shutouts (4), 1995; starts, 1996, 2008; innings, 2000; becoming the oldest first time 20-game winner in MLB history, 2008. Office: c/o Wasserman Media Group Llc 12100 W Olympic Blvd Ste 400 Los Angeles CA 90064

MUSSOMELI, JOSEPH ADAMO, ambassador; b. NYC, May 26, 1952; s. Mariano Mussomeli; m. Sharon Flack; children: Isaac, Alexis, Thomas. BA in Polit. Sci., Trenton State Coll., 1975; JD, Rutgers Sch. Law, 1978. Law clk. NJ Appellate Ct., 1978—79; dep. atty. gen. NJ Divsn. Gaming Enforcement, 1979—80; gen. svc. officer US Embassy, Cairo, 1980; staff asst. to under sec. for security assistance US Dept. State; consular officer US Embassy, Manilla, Philippines, 1984—86, desk officer Republic of Korea, 1986—88, sr. watch officer, 1989—90, econ. counselor Colombo, Sri Lanka, 1990—92, polit, counselor Rabat, Morocco, 1995—98, dep. chief of mission Manama, Bahrain, 1998—2001; mem. sr. seimnar US Dept. State, 2001—02; insp., Office Insp. Gen. US Dept State, Washington, 1992—94; dep. chief of mission US Dept. State, Manila, Philippines, 2002—05, US amb. to Cambodia Phnom Penh, 2005—08, asst. amb. to Afghanistan Kabul, 2009—. Office: US Embassy 6180 Kabul Pl Dulles VA 20189*

MUSTACCHI, PIERO, preventive medicine physician, educator; b. Cairo, May 29, 1920; came to U.S., 1947; naturalized, 1962; s. Gino and Gilda (Rieti) M.; m. Dora Lisa Ancona, Sept. 26, 1948; children: Roberto, Michael. BS in Humanities, U. Florence, Italy, 1938; postgrad. in anatomy, U. Lausanne, Switzerland, 1938-39; MB, ChB, Fouad I U., Cairo, Egypt, 1944, grad. in Arabic lang. and lit., 1946; D Medicine and Surgery, U. Pisa, 1986; Degree (hon.), U. Aix-Marseille, France, 1988, U. Alexandria, Egypt, 1985. Qualified med. examiner, Calif. Indsl. Accident Commn., 1994. House officer English Hosp., Ch. Missionary Soc., Cairo, 1945-47; clin. affiliate U. Calif., San Francisco, 1947-48; intern Franklin Hosp., San Francisco, 1948-49; resident in pathology U. Calif., San Francisco, 1949-51; resident in medicine Meml. Ctr. Cancer and Allied Diseases, NYC, 1951-53; rsch. epidemiologist Dept. HEW, Nat. Cancer Inst., Bethesda, Md., 1955-57; cons. allergy clinic U. Calif., San Francisco, 1957-70, clin. prof. medicine and preventive medicine, 1970-90, clin. prof. medicine and epidemiology, 1990-96, head occupl. epidemiology, 1975-90, head divsn. internat. health edn. dept. epidemiology and internat. health, 1985-90; médecin agréé, official physician Consulate Gen. of France, San Francisco, 1995—2007; sr. cons. internat. health care U. Calif., San Francisco. Med. cons., vis. prof. numerous ednl. & profl. instns., U. Marseilles, 1981—82, U. Pisa, Italy, 1983, U. Gabon, 1984, U. Siena, Italy, 1985; cons. U. Calif., 1975—, U. El Azhar, 1986; sr. cons. internat. med. care U. Calif., San Francisco, 2000—. Contbr. chpts. to books, articles to profl. jours. Editorial bd. Medecine d'Afrique Noire, Ospedali d'Italia. With USPHS USN, 1955—57. Decorated comdr. Order of Merit (Italy), officer Ordre de la Legion d'Honneur (France), Medal of St. John of Jerusalem, Sovereign Order of Malta, Order of the Republic (Egypt); Scroll, Leonardo da Vinci Soc., San Francisco, 1965; award Internat. Inst. Oakland, 1964; Hon. Vice Consul. Italy, 1971-90. Fellow ACP, Am. Soc. Environ. and Occupational Health; mem. AAAS, Am. Assn. Cancer Rsch., Calif. Soc. Allergy and Immunology, Calif. Med. Assn., San Francisco Med. Soc., West Coast Allergy Soc. (founding), Mex. Congress on Hypertension (corr.), Internat. Assn. Med. Rsch. and Continuing Edn. (U.S. rep.), Acad. Italiana della Cucina, Acta Medico Historica Adriatica, 2007. Democrat. Avocations: music, math, languages. also: 3838 California St San Francisco CA 94118-1522 Office Phone: 415-668-2626.

MUSTAFA, MOHAMAD, engineering educator; b. Palestine; PhD, Wayne State U., Detroit, 1994. Prof. Savannah State U., Ga., 1994—. Mem.: Golden Key Nat. Honor Soc., ASCE, Chi Epsilon, Tau Peta Pi. Office: Savannah State Univ 3219 College St Savannah GA 31404 Business E-Mail: mustafam@savannahstate.edu.

MUSTAIN, DOUGLAS DEE, lawyer; b. Shreveport, La., Nov. 2, 1945; s. Reginald K. and Dorothy J. (Green) Mustain; m. Sharon L. Tegarden, Aug. 19, 1967; children: Kristi Kaye, Kari Dee, Kenton Douglas, Kyle Robert, Kirk Stephen, Kali Elizabeth. Student, Knox Coll., 1963—64, Murray State U., 1964—66; BS, U. Ill., 1971; JD, U. Iowa, 1974. Bar: Iowa 1974, Ill. 1974, US Dist. Ct. (cen. dist.) Ill. 1974, US Ct. Appeals (7th cir.) 1980, US Supreme Ct. 1986. Law clk. Shulman, Phelan, Tucker, Boyle & Mullin, Iowa City, 1972—74; assoc. Stuart, Neagle & West, Galesburg, Ill., 1974—76; ptnr. West, Neagle & Williamson, Galesburg, 1977—89, Mustain & Lindstrom, Galesburg, 1989—2008, Mustain Law Office, 2009—; instr. real estate law Carl Sandburg Coll., Galesburg, 1977—81. Trustee 1st Presbyn. Ch., Galesburg, 1984; bd. dirs. YMCA, Galesburg, 1983—88, Cottage Hosp. Care Corp., Galesburg, 1984—90; chmn. Citizens Referendum Com., Galesburg, 1983, 1987—88; commr. Galesburg Pub. Transp. Commn., 1985—; pres., founder Galesburg Pub. Sch. Found., 1987—. With SP5 US Army, 1966—69, Vietnam. Decorated Army Commendation with oak leaf cluster. Mem.: AAJ, ABA (comml. litigation com. 1981—), Ill. Trial Lawyers Assn., Knox County Bar Assn. (pres. 1980—82). Republican. Home: 1234 N Prairie St Galesburg IL 61401-1852 Office: Mustain Law Office 1865 N Henderson St Ste 11B Galesburg IL 61401-1377

MUSTAIN, MEGAN RUST, philosopher, educator; d. Ronald F. and Kerri R. Mustain; m. Stephen Barnes. BS, Tex. A&M U., Coll. Sta., 1999; MA, Southern Ill. U., Carbondale, 2002, PhD, 2006. Asst. prof. philosophy St. Mary's U., San Antonio, 2005—. Office: Philosophy Dept St Mary's Univ 1 Camino Santa Maria San Antonio TX 78228

MUSTARD, LEWIS WILLIAMS, management consultant, educator; b. Durham, NC, Sept. 4, 1942; s. Harry S. and Elizabeth (Williams) M.; divorced; children: Juliana Janice, Lewis Williams Jr. AB in English, U. NC, Chapel Hill, 1966; cert. in hosp. adminstrn., Duke U., 1970; LLB, La Salle U., Chgo., 1974; D Bus. Adminstrn., Western Coll. U., 1976; PhD in Health Adminstrn., Union Grad. Sch., Cin., 1992; MA in Humanities, Calif. State U., Dominguez Hills, 1995. Hosp. adminstr. Woodruff (S.C.) Hosp., 1968-70; exec. dir. AID, Inc., Bryn Mawr, Pa., 1970-73; sr. hosp. cons. Summerour & Assocs., Atlanta, 1975-76; regional v.p. Qualicare, Inc., New Orleans, 1976-78; regional adminstr., v.p. Triage Corp., Clearwater, Fla., 1978-80; pres. Healthcare Mgmt. Cons., Atlanta, 1980-88; CEO Healthcare Negligence Control, Inc., Chapel Hill, NC, 1993—. Legal cons., sole practitioner, 1992-; adj. prof. Ctrl. Mich. U., Mt. Pleasant, 1993-, So. Ill. U., Carbondale, 1993-, Webster U., St. Louis, 1994-, MBA program, NY Inst. Tech., 2004-, Bellevue U., Nebr., 2005-, Strayer U., 2005-, MPH program, A.T. Still U.; prof. North Ctrl. U., Prescott, Ariz., 2004-; adj. charter Oak State Coll., 2002-, New Britain, Conn., 2003-. Served with USNR Res., 1959-68. Episcopalian. Personal E-mail: executivehealthcare@yahoo.com.

MUSTARD, MARY CAROLYN, financial executive; b. North Bend, Nebr., Sept. 21, 1948; d. Joseph Louis and Rosalie Margaret (Emanuel) Smaus; m. Ronald L. Mustard, Apr. 19, 1969 (div. 1988); children: Joel Jonathan, Dana Marie. Student, Creighton U., 1966—67, C.E. Sch. Commerce, 1967—68, Coll. of St. Mary, 1983—84, Met. C.C., Omaha, 1988—90, Bellevue U., 1991—92. With Platte County Dept. Pub. Welfare, Columbus, Nebr., 1968-69; sec. to plant mgr. B.L. Montague Steel Co., Sumter, SC, 1969-70; property disposal technician Property Disposal Office, Shaw AFB, SC, 1970-71; libr. technician Hdqs. Strategic Air Command Libr., Offutt AFB, Nebr., 1971-76; sec.-steno Hdqs. Strategic Air Command Comm./Frequency Mgmt., Offutt AFB, 1976-79; security specialist/program analyst Hdqs. Strategic Air Command Security Police, Offutt AFB, 1979-88; budget analyst Hdqs. Strategic Air Command Fin. Mgmt., Offutt AFB, 1988-92; funds control analyst Hdqs. Air Mobility Command, Scott AFB, Ill., 1992-93, chief hdqs. and comm. account, 1993-94, chief hdqs. relocation, transition assistance/comm. programs, 1994-95; chief base realignment and closure program Air Mobility Command, Scott AFB, 1995-96; sys. adminstr. Def. Fin. and Acctg. Svc., Kansas City, Mo., 1996-2000, fin. sys. mgmt., 2000—02, fin. ops. analyst, bus. mgmt. office, 2002—08, acting dir. site support office, 2008. Mem. Am. Soc. Mil. Comptrs. (SAC Budget Analyst of Yr. 1990). Democrat. Roman Catholic. Avocations: walking, reading, biking. Home: 7137 Aminda St Shawnee KS 66227-2117

MUSTION, ALAN LEE, pharmacist; b. Oklahoma City, Feb. 6, 1947; s. Granville E. and Iris E. (Graham) Mustion; m. Mary Jane Bozek, Dec. 4, 1982; children from previous marriage: Jeffrey Alan, Jennifer Chere. BS in Pharmacy, Southwestern Okla. State U., 1970. Staff pharmacist VA Med. Ctr., Oklahoma City, 1970—74, dir. pharmacy Richmond, Va., 1976—77, Iowa City, 1977—90; dir. pharmacy svcs. VA Hosp., Houston, 1990—2002; pharmacy mgr. Integris Bapt. Med. Ctr., Oklahoma City, 2002—. Clin. instr. clin./hosp. divsn. U. Iowa, 1977—90; adj. asst. prof. pharmacy practice U. Houston, 1990—2002. Contbr. articles to profl. jours. Served to lt. col. USAR. Grantee Rsch., Travenol Labs., 1980—87, VA HSR&D, 1984, 1988. Mem.: Okla. Soc. Health Sys. Pharmacists, Am. Soc. Health Sys. Pharmacists, Kappa Psi. Methodist. Office: 3300 NW Expressway Oklahoma City OK 73112 Home: 513 Winding Creek Rd Yukon OK 73099-4471 E-mail: alan.mustion@integris-health.com.

MUSTO, DAVID FRANKLIN, medical researcher, educator, historian, consultant; b. Tacoma, Jan. 8, 1936; s. Charles Hiram and Hilda Marie (Hanson) Mustoe; m. Emma Jean Baudendistel, June 2, 1961; children: Jeanne Marie, David Kyle, John Baird, Christopher Edward. BA, U. Wash., 1956, MD, 1963; MA, Yale U., 1961. Lic. physician, Conn., Pa. Clerk Nat. Hosp. for Nervous Disease, London, 1961; intern Pa. Hosp., Phila., 1963-64; resident Yale U. Med. Ctr., New Haven, 1964-67; spl. asst. to dir. NIMH, Bethesda, Md., 1967-69; vis. asst. prof. Johns Hopkins U., 1968-69; asst. prof. Yale U., 1969-73, assoc. prof., 1973-78, sr. rsch. scientist, 1978-81, prof., 1981—, exec. fellow Davenport Coll., 1983-88; mem. adv. editorial com. Yale Edits. Private Papers James Boswell, 1975—; cons. Exec. Office of Pres., 1973-75; mem. White House Strategy Coun., 1978-81; mem. panel on alcohol policy NAS, Washington, 1978-82; cons. White House Conf. on Families, 1979-80. Vis. fellow Clare Coll., Cambridge U., 1994; mem. alcohol adv. com. Nat. Assn. Broadcasters, 1994—; DuMez lectr. U. Md.; Walter Reed meml. lectr. Richmond Acad. Medicine; Galdston lectr. N.Y. Acad. Medicine; Sirridge lectr. U. Mo. Med. Sch.; Clendening lectr. U. Kans. Med. Sch. Author: The American Disease: Origins of Narcotic Control, 1973, expanded edit., 1987, 3rd edit., 1999; co-author: (with P. Korsmeyer) The Quest for Drug Control: Politics and Federal Policy in a Period of Increasing Drug Use, 1963-1981, 2002; editor: One Hundred Years of Heroin, 2002, Drugs in America: A Documentary History, 2002. Historian Pres.'s Commn. on Mental Health, 1977-78; adv. U.S. Del. to UN Commn. Narcotic Drugs, Geneva, 1978-79; mem. nat. coun. Smithsonian Instn., Washington, 1981-90, hon. mem., 1991—; hist. cons. Presdl. Commn. Human Immuno-deficiency Virus Epidemic, 1988; mem. nat. adv. com. on anti-drug program Robert Wood Johnson Found., 1989-2002; mem. nat. adv. com. on internat. narcotic policy UN Assn. of U.S.A., 1991; mem. adv. com. causes drug abuse Office Tech. Assessment, Congress U.S., 1992-94; commr. Conn. Alcohol and Drug Abuse Commn., 1992-93; bd. dirs. Coll. on Problems of Drug Dependence, 1990-94; trustee Assocs. of Cushing-Whitney Med. Libr., 1994—. With USPHS, 1967-69. Fellow: Coll. Problems of Drug Dependence, Am. Psychiat. Assn. (disting.); mem.: Soc. of Cin. in the State of Conn. (pres. 1998—2001), English-Speaking Union (pres. New Haven br. 1995—98), Am. Assn. History of Medicine (William Osler medal 1961), Am. Hist. Assn., Am. Inst. History of Pharmacy (Kraemers award 1974), New Haven County Med. Assn. (chmn. bicentennial com. 1983), Century Assn., Athenaeum Club (London), Cosmos Club. Office: Yale U PO Box 207900 New Haven CT 06520-7900 Office Phone: 203-785-4258. E-mail: david.musto@yale.edu.

MUSTOE, THOMAS ANTHONY, physician, plastic surgeon; b. Columbia, Mo., June 29, 1951; s. Robert Moore and Carolyn (Swett) M.; m. Kathryn Claire Stallcup, Aug. 13, 1977; children: Anthony, Lisa. BA cum laude in biology, Harvard Coll., 1973, MD cum laude, 1978. Diplomate Am. Bd. Otolaryngology, Am. Bd. Plastic Surgery; licensed Miss. 1985, Ill. 1991. Rsch. assoc. dept. microbiology Harvard Med. Sch., Cambridge, Mass., 1976-77; intern in medicine Mass. Gen. Hosp., Boston, 1978-79; resident in surgery Peter Bent Brigham Hosp., Boston, 1979-80; resident in otolaryngology Mass. Eye and Ear Infirmary, Boston, 1980-82, chief resident, 1982-83; resident in plastic surgery Brigham and Women;s Hosp., Children's Hosp., Boston, 1983-84, chief resident, 1984-85; asst. prof. in surgery Wash. U. Sch. Medicine, St. Louis, 1985-89, assoc. prof., 1989-91; prof., chief divsn. plastic surgery Northwestern U. Med. Sch., Chgo., 1991—; plastic surgeon Northwestern Meml. Hosp., 1991—, Evanston Hosp., 1991—, Children's Meml. Hosp., 1992—, Shriner's Hosp. Chgo., 1994—. Co-chmn. Gorden Rsch. Conf., 1995; spl. cons. FDA, 1994—98; mem. sci. adv. panel Biologies, 1997, NCI, 1998; lectr. seminars, 2001. Editl. bd. Archives of Surgery, 1992-2004, Plastic and Reconstructive Surgery, 1993-2001, Wound Repair and Regeneration, 1992—, Jour. Surg. Rsch., 1997-2006; contbr. articles to profl. jours., more than 200 publs., book chpts.; book reviewer. Named one of Top Chgo. Doctors, Chgo. Mag., 1998, 2001, 2004, 2006-08, America's Top Physicians, Consumers Rsch. Coun. America, 2003-07; Harvard Nat. scholar, 1969-73; Rhodes scholar candidate, Harvard Coll., 1973. Fellow: ACS (adv. coun. plastic surgery 1999—2002, surg. forum com. 1999—2002, editl. bd. jour. 2003—, surg. biology club III); mem.: AMA, Am. Soc. Plastic Surgery (sci. program chair 2005—), Am. Bd. Plastic Surgery (bd. dirs. 2006—12), Coun. Plastic Surger Org., Double Boarded Soc. (pres. 1995—98),

Chgo. Surg. Soc., Chgo. Plastic Surg. Soc. (sec. 1996—97), Wound Healing Soc. (program com. 1990, audit com. 1992, program com. 1992, bd. dir. 1993—96, program com. 1994, fin. com. 1994—96, program com. 1997, pres. 1997—99, v.p. 1999—2001, bd. mem. 2000—05, bd. dirs. 2006—09, Lifetime Achievement award 2004), Assn. Acad. Chmn. Plastic Surgery (matching program and ctrl. application svc. com. 1994), Soc. U. Surgeons, Soc. Head and Neck Surgeons (membership com. 1993—95), Plastic Surgery Rsch. Coun. (rep. coun. acad. surgeons 1991—94, com. indsl. rels. 1992, program com. 1992—94, 1995, Judge Snyder & Crikelair awards 1991), Midwest Assn. Plastic Surgeons, Lipoplasty Soc. N.Am. (lipoplasty ednl. rsch. found. 1998—2000), Am. Assn. Plastic Surgery (rsch. and edn. com. 1994—96, chmn. 1996, mem. com. 1998—, co-chmn.ASPRS-ASAPS task force on emerging trends 1999—2000, chmn. instl. coun. com. 1999—), Am. Soc. Plastic and Reconstructive Surgery (rsch. fund proposal com. 1987—92, plastic surgery device com. 1989—93, resource book for plastic surgery residents com. 1991—93, socioecon. 1992—94, sci. program com. 1993—95, chmn. device and tecyhnique assessment com. 1994—96, co-chmn. gen. reconstruction subcom. 1995, ultrasonic lipectomy task force 1995—96, task force for outcomes and guidelines 1995—98, devices and tech. com. 1995—98, chmn. instrnl. com. 1999—2002, chmn. edn. com. 1999—, chmn. resource book com.), Aesculapian Club, Sigma Xi. Avocations: reading, golf, gardening, sports. Home: 144 Greenwood St Evanston IL 60201-4712 E-mail: tmustoe@nmh.org.

MUSTOKOFF, MICHAEL MARK, lawyer; b. Phila., Oct. 19, 1947; s. Harry and Ethel (Sobel) Mustokoff; m. Rae Janet Vogel, June 7, 1970; children: Matthew Leo, Jessica Beth. BA, Albright Coll., Peading, Pa., 1969; JD, U. Pa. Law Sch., 1972. Bar: Pa. 1972, US Dist. Ct. (ea. dist.) Pa. 1980, US Ct. Appeals (3d cir.) 1981, Supreme Ct. Pa., US Supreme Ct. 1983. Asst. dist. atty. Phila. Dist. Atty.'s Office, 1972—79, chief econ. crime unit, 1975-79; assoc. Duane Morris LLP, Phila., 1980-84, ptnr., 1984—, mem. ptnrs. bd., 1996—. Author various ednl. law manuals; contbr. articles to profl. jours. Candidate for U.S. Congress, 4th Congl. Dist. Phila., 1980; bd. dirs. Citizens Crime Commn., Jewish Community Relations Council, Am. Jewish Com., Cub Scout Pack Com. 338. Named a Star of the Bar, Phila. Mag., 1980, SuperLawyer, 2004—08. Fellow: Am. Bar Found.; mem.: ABA, Health Care Fin. Mgmt. Assn., Def. Rsch. Inst., Nat. Assn. Criminal Def. Counsel, Am. Health Lawyers Assn., Am. Trial Lawyers Assn., Phila. Bar Assn., Pa. Bar Assn. Democrat. Jewish. Office: Duane Morris LLP 30 S 17th St Philadelphia PA 19103-7301 Office Phone: 215-979-1810. Office Fax: 215-689-3607. Business E-Mail: MMustokoff@duanemorris.com.*

MUSZYNSKA, AGNIESZKA (AGNES), mechanical engineering researcher, consultant; b. Warsaw, Oct. 10, 1935; came to U.S., 1980; d. Zdzislaw E. and Wida-Wanda (Jellinek) Galinowski; m. Jerzy Muszynski, Dec. 2, 1954 (div. July 1974); 1 child, Roman. MSME, Warsaw Tech. U., Poland, 1960; PhD Tech. Scis., Polish Acad. Scis., Warsaw, 1966, habilitation, 1977. Designer Machine Tool Design Co., Warsaw, 1960—61; asst. prof. Inst. Fundamental Tech. Rsch., Polish Acad. Scis., 1961—78, assoc. prof., 1978—82; sr. rsch. scientist Bently Nev. Corp., Minden, 1981—82; rsch. mgr. Bently Rotor Dynamics Rsch. Corp., Minden, 1982—99; cons. A.M. Cons., Minden, 1999—. Vis. prof. Inst. Nat. Scis., Lyon, France, 1975—77; vis. rsch. scientist U. Dayton, Ohio, 1980—81; mem. faculty U. Nev., Reno, 1984—89; vis. prof. Swiss Fed. Inst. Tech., Zurich, 2000—01, U. Franche Comte, Besancon, France, 2001; co-sponsor Bently-Muszynska Found. Rotordynamics Cleve. U., 2003; co-sponsor Bently Muszynska Found. Energy Korean Advanced Inst. Sci. Tech., 2004; co-sponsor Bently-Muszynska Found. Life Scis. Korea U., Seoul, 2004. Author: Rotordynamics, 2005; editor: Nonlinear Vibration Problems, 1967-99; sci. editor: Dynamics of Machines (in Polish), 1974, Dynamics of Machines: Vibration Control in Machines (in Polish and English), 1978, (with D. E. Bently, R.C. Hendricks) Instability of Rotating Machinery, 1985, (with J.C. Simonis) Rotating Machinery Dynamics, 1987, Trans. ASME, 1988-94, Internat. Jour. Rotating Machines, 1994-, Don Bently Through the Eyes of Others, 1995, Procs. of 7th Internat. Symposium on Transport Phenomena and Dynamics of Rotating Machinery, 1998, Internat. Symposium Stability Control Rotating Machinery, 2003, 05, 07; contbr. over 250 articles to profl. jours. Recipient Gold Cross Merit Polish Acad. Scis., 1975, Innovation award NASA, 1990, Outstanding Rsch. award Pacific Ctr. Thermal Fluids Engrng., 1996; titled Prof. Tech. Scis., Polish Acad. Scis., Pres. Poland, 1998, Paul Harris fellow. Fellow ASME (assoc. editor Trans. 1988-94); mem. Am. Acad. Scis., Rotary Internat. Achievements include rsch. in mechanical engineering, vibrational diagnostics of rotating machines. Personal E-mail: agnesm@charter.net.

MUTALE, CHRISTIAN THALES, research scientist; s. Seraphin Mutale; m. Denise Chargois; 1 child, Christian Thales Jr. MSc in Engrng., U. Lubumbashi, D.R. Congo, 1992; PhD, Tech. U. Clausthal, Germany, 2000. Doctor of Engineering, Tech. U. Clausthal, 2000. Jr. lectr. Universite de Lubumbashi, D.R. Congo, 1993—94; rsch. engr. Gecamines, Likasi, D.R. Congo, 1994—95; rsch. scientist Tech. U. Clausthal, Calusthal-Zellerfeld, Niedersachsen, Germany, 1996—2001; post doctoral fellow U. Pretoria, Pretoria, Gauteng, South Africa, 2001—03; rsch. assoc. CISR - MSE - Carnegie Mellon, Pitts., 2003—05; sr. scientist Alcoa Tech., Alcoa Tech. Ctr., Pa., 2005—. Mem.: Assn. Iron and Steel Tech., Electrochem. Soc., German Soc. Mining, Metallurgy, Resource and Environ. Tech., South African Inst. Mining and Metallurgy, Assn. Iron and Steel Tech., Sigma Xi. Achievements include research in research and publications in extractive ferrous & non-ferrous metallurgy, materials science and recycling of metals and alloys.

MUTCHLER, J.C., history professor; s. James and Joy Owen; m. Lissa Howe, Mar. 16, 2006. PhD, Yale U., New Haven, 2002. Lectr. Princeton U., 2002—03; asst. prof. U. Ariz. South, Sierra Vista, 2003—. Pres., faculty forum U. Ariz. South, Sierra Vista, 2005—06; chair, Ariz. Faculties Coun. Ariz. Bd. Regents, Phoenix, 2008—; sec., faculty senate U. Ariz., Tucson, 2008—. Pres. & founder Camp Naco Ariz. Preservation Com., Ariz., 2003—08. Recipient Deans award for Tchg. Excellence, U. Ariz. South, 2006. Mem.: Western HIstory Assn. Achievements include research in environmental history of SW New Mexico; preservation & restoration of buffalo soldier Fort in Naco, Ariz. Avocations: horseback riding, farming. Office: Univ Ariz S 1140 Colombo Sierra Vista AZ 85635 Business E-Mail: mutchler@email.arizona.edu.

MUTH, ERIC PETER, optician, consultant; b. Munich, July 25, 1940; came to US, 1948, naturalized 1955; s. Erich Walter and Anna Lisa (Pentenrieder) M.; m. Rachel Hubbard, Apr. 4, 1971; children: Karl George, Ellen Anna. BS, Charter Oak Coll., 1978; degree (hon.), Anoka-Hennipen Tech. Coll., 1995. Lic. Skip Barber, Sch. Racing, 2009. Lic. optician, past owner Park Lane Opticians, Milford, 1967—2002. Sr. rsch. fellow Internat. Soc. for Philosophical Inquiry, 1991—96, pers. cons., 1996; cons. Nat. Acad. Opthamology Found. Mus., San Francisco, 1982—88, Nat. Mus. Hist. Smithsonian Inst., 1983—94, Gesell Inst. Human Devel., 1984—89; mem. adv. com. South. Cen. Cmty. Coll., Seattle, 1984—89; mem. adv. bd. internat. Scientific Inst., PR, 1989; adv. bd. Middlesex C.C. (vice chmn.)., 1989; vol. VA, West Haven, Conn., 2001—. Mem. editl. bd. Dispensing Opticians, Butterworths Heinmann, 1998, co-author 2nd edit., 1998; contbr. the Social History of Eyeglasses in Japan, 1991, die Brille, Leipzig, 1989, Thinking on the Edge Agamennon, 1993; contbr. over 250 articles to profl. jours.; contbg. editor Optical Mgmt., 1979-80, OpticScan Canada, 1981-82, Indian Optician, 1982, Prism Mag., Can., 1988, 92; tech. editor Optical Index, 1980-82; book reviewer in field. Presdl. appointment US Selective Svc. Sys., 1991-92; scoutmaster Boy Scouts Am., 1960-62; bd. dirs. ARC Conn. chpt., 1988; advisor Tri Hi-Y YMCA, 1964; founder, chmn. Korea-Vietnam Meml. com., Milford, 1985-86; organizer WWII Monument Com. 1991; trustee Conn. Visual Health Ctr., 1982-84; commr. Nat. Commn. on Opticianry Edn., 1989-93; life mem. Soc. 3d. US Inf. Div., 1987; hon. Capt. 25th Bn. Royal Fusiliers, 1999; trooper Ct. State Militia, 2d co. gov.'s horse guard, 2002-04. Served with US Army, 1957-59, Selected Reserves, 1965-69; Conn. Army N.G., 1960-64. Decorated Roman Cath. Knight Malta, Equestrian Knight of The Order of the Holy Sepulchre, Knight Comdr., Army Commendation medal; recipient Eng. Nelson/Wingate prize, 1983, Service Above Self award, Rotary, 1986, Optician of the Yr., Guild of Prescription Opticians Am., 1993, Senate Citation, State of Conn., 1993, German-Am. Friendship award, Germany, 1995, State of Conn. Justice of the Peace, 1995, cert. of appreciation, Nat. Libr. Medicine, Bethesda, Md., 1995, Med. Scis. Divsn. Nat. Mus. History, 1995, Mayoral Proclamation, Milford, Conn., 1998, Bronze medal of merit, Austrian Albert Schweitzer Soc., 1998, Chemical Corps Regimental Assn. Order of the Dragon, 1999, Oeuvre Humanitaire Croix d'Honneur, 1999, medal of merit, El Salvador Red Cross, 1999, Award of Merit, Army and Navy Union of USA, 2000, Vol. award, VA, 2003; named DOD Amb., Combat Related Spl. Compensation Program, 2008. Fellow: Conn. Opticians Assn. (pres. 1974, amb., chmn. membership and ethics coms., Optician of Yr. 1975), Opticians Assn. Am. (historian citation 1993, advancing opticinary award 1994, diploma in refractometry 1995, disting. svc. award 2000, honored fellow), Nat. Acad. Opticianry (regional membership chmn., faculty speakers bur., citation 1988), Internat. Acad. Opticianry; mem.: Nat. Contact Lens Examiners (cert.), Guild Prescription Opticians Am. (councilor 2001—02), Royal Lifesaving Soc. Can. (hon. assoc. 1998), Soc. Am. Mil. Engrs., Calif. Soc. Dispensing Opticians (hon.), Ari. Soc. Dispensing Opticians (hon.), Am. Bd. of Opticianry (master of ophthalmic optics 1972), Internat. Platform Assn., Contact Lens Soc. Am., Contact Lens Soc. Conn., Internat. Found. in Ophthalmics Optics, Conn. Guild Dispensing Opticians (pres. 1980, Optician of Yr. 1981), Charter Oak Coll. Alumni Assn. (bd. dirs. 1987, alumni citation 1995), Milford C. of C. (chmn. law and safety com. 1975, Cmty. Svc. award 1986), Disabled Am. Vets. (life; chpt. svc. officer, judge advocate, DAV-NSF commendation 2004), Am. Legion Post 196 (life; parade marshal 1998, citation 1986). Avocations: skydiving, parasailing, ballooning, motorcycling, Tae Kwon Do. Home: 25 Parkland Pl Milford CT 06460-7723 Home Phone: 203-874-4595. Personal E-mail: eepmuth@nyc.com.

MUTH, RICHARD FERRIS, economics professor; b. Chgo., May 14, 1927; s. Merlin Arthur and Margaret Ferris Muth; m. Helene Louise Martin, Dec. 23, 1955; children: Lisa Helene, Laurianne Love Doster. Student, USCG Acad., 1945-47; AB, Washington U., St. Louis, 1949, MA, 1950; PhD, U. Chgo., 1958; M of Theol. Studies, Emory U., 1995. Lectr. polit. economy Johns Hopkins U., Balt., 1955-56; economist Resources for Future, Washington, 1956-58; assoc. prof. urban econs. U. Chgo., 1959-64; economist Inst. Def. Analyses, Arlington, Va., 1964-66, cons., 1966-69; prof. econs. Washington U., St. Louis, 1966-70, Stanford U., Calif., 1970-83; Callaway prof. econs. Emory U., Atlanta, 1983—2001, chmn. dept., 1983-90, prof. emeritus, 2001—. Vis. assoc. prof. econs. Vanderbilt U., 1958—59; vis. sr. fellow Urban Inst., Washington, 1976—77; vis. prof. Sch. Bus. U. Calif., Berkeley, 1991. Author (with others): Regions, Resources and Economic Growth, 1960, Cities and Housing, 1969, Public Housing, 1974, Urban Economic Problems, 1975; co-author (with Allen C. Goodman): The Economics of Housing Markets, 1989. Mem. Presdl. Task Force on Urban Renewal, 1969, Presdl. Task Forces on Urban Affairs and Housing, 1980—81, Presdl. Commn. on Housing, 1981—82. With USCG, 1951—52. Libertarian. Methodist. Office: Emory U Dept Econs Atlanta GA 30322-2240 Office Phone: 404-727-8643. Business E-Mail: rmuth@emory.edu.

MUTHAIYAH, SARAVANAN, dean; s. Muthaiyah Arunaslam and Lailitha Muthiah; m. Manimala Subramanian, Mar. 1, 2003; 1 child, Shibhani Saravanan. PhD, George Mason U., 2008. Auditor Arthur Anderson, Kuala Lumpur, Wilayah Persekutuan, Malaysia, 1997—99; fin. analyst IBM World Trade Corp., Kuala Lumpur, 1998—2001; lectr. Multimedia U., CYberjaya, Selangor, Malaysia, 2001—04, sr. lectr., 2004—08, dep. dean postgrad. studies, 2008—. Contbr. articles to profl. jours. Recipient Best Paper award, Internat. Applied Bus. Rsch. Conf., 2002, 2004, Presdl. Tchg. award, MMU, 2001—03, award, George Mason U., 2001—03; Fulbright scholar, US Dept. State. Office: Multimedia Univ Jalan Multimedia Cyberjaya Selangor 63100 Malaysia Business E-Mail: smuthaiy@gmu.edu.

MUTHUKRISHNAN, SWARNA, research scientist; BS in Chemistry, U. Madras, India, 1993; MS in Environ. Chemistry, U. Madras Guindy Campus, India, 1995; PhD, Jawaharlal Nehru U., New Delhi, 2001. Postdoc. rsch. fellow ORISE EPA-Office R & D, Edison, NJ, 2003—07; rsch. analyst Am. Water, Delran, NJ, 2008—. Internat. DAAD summer fellow Fed. Inst. Materials & Testing, Adlershof, Berlin, Germany, 1999. Mem.: Am. Chem. Soc.

MUTI, RICCARDO, conductor, music director; b. Naples, Italy, July 28, 1941; m. Cristina Mazzavillani; 3 children. Studied piano, Conservatory San Pietro a Majella, Naples; diploma in Composition and Conducting, Milan Conservatory; MusD (hon.), U. Pa., Curtis Inst. Music, U. Bologna, Mt. Holyoke Coll.; LLD (hon.), Warwick U., Eng.; Doctor (hon.), Westminster Choir Coll., Princeton, NJ. Prin. condr., music dir. Maggio Musicale Fiorentino, Florence, Italy, 1968—80; prin. condr. Philharmonia Orch., London, 1972—82; music dir. Phila. Orch., 1980—92, Teatro alla Scala, Milan, 1986—2005; founder, condr. Luigi Cherubini Youth Orch., Italy, 2004—; music dir. designate Chgo. Symphony Orch., 2009—. Condr. Salzburg Festival, Austria, 1971—; artistic dir. Pentecost Festival, Salzburg, 2007—; guest condr. Berlin Philharm., Bayerischer Rundfunk, NY Philharm., Orchestre National de France, Vienna Philharm. Decorated Cavaliere di Gran Croce, Italy, Order of Merit, Fed. Republic of Germaly, Knight of Brit. Empire, Queen Elizabeth II, Order of Friendship, Russia; recipient Wolf prize in arts (music), Wolf Found., Israel, 2000. Mem.: Am. Acad. Arts & Scis. (fgn.), Royal Acad. Music (hon.). Office: c/o Chgo Symphony Orch 220 S Michigan Ave Chicago IL 60604*

MUTISYA, ELIZABETH M., pharmaceutical executive; B in Neurobiology, Cornell U., Ithaca, NY; med. degree, Harvar Med. Sch.; MBA, U. Pa. Intern gen. surgery U. Calif. San Francisco, resident neurological surgery; with Pfizer, Inc.; sr. dir., clinical leader Johnson & Johnson; v.p. US med. affairs, chief med. officer Solvay Pharmaceuticals, Inc., 2008—. Office: Solvay Pharmaceuticals Inc 901 Sawyer Rd Marietta GA 30062*

MUTLU, ONUR, research scientist; BSEE, U. Mich., Ann Arbor, 2000; MSEE, U. Tex., Austin, 2002, PhD, 2006. Rsch. and tchg. asst. U. Tex., 2000—06; grad. tech. intern Intel Corp., Hillsboro, Oreg., 2001—03; coop. engr. Advanced Micro Devices, Sunnyvale, Calif., 2004—05; rschr. Microsoft Rsch., Redmond, Wash., 2006—. Contbr. scientific papers and articles. Recipient Gold Star award, Microsoft Corp., 2008. Mem.: IEEE, ACM, Eta Kappa Nu, Tau Beta Pi. Achievements include research in computer architecture, focusing on high performance, energy efficient reliable system; patents in field; patents pending in field. Office: Carnegie Mellon Univ Dept ECE 5000 Forbes Ave Pittsburgh PA 15213

MUTO, TAKASUKE, sociologist, educator; b. Kawagoe, Japan, Feb. 18, 1930; s. Saburo and Kimi (Ishii) M.; m. Masako Nagashima, June 23, 1958; children: Mayumi (Mrs. Akihiro Saito), Toshiya. M Edn., Tokyo U. Edn., 1955. Rschr. Rsch. Inst. Edn., Shinano Ednl. Assn., 1958-66; lectr., faculty edn. Shinshu U., Nagano, Japan, 1966-67, assoc. prof., 1967-78, prof., 1978-94, hon. prof., 1994—; prof. Tokyo Denki U., Saitama-ken, Japan, 1994-2000. Vis. prof. Univ. of the Air, Chiba, Japan, 1990-99. Author: The Development of Pupils' Value-Judgements and Valuation Process in the Classroom, 1969, Group Guidance in the Classroom, 1976, Moral Education in the Life-World (with Kihara), 1978; editor: Theory of School Guidance, 1991, Theory and Practice of Guidance and Extra-Curricular Activities, 1994, Moral Education (with Kihara), 1995; editor: The new development of the character and values education--Japan, the US and the UK, 2002, The Devel. of Personal and Social Edn.Citizenship in European Schs., 2007, The Situation in France, Germany and Britain, 2007. Mem. Japan Soc. Ednl. Sociology (counselor), Japanese Assn. for Study of Extraclass Activities (ex-pres.). Home: 2 8 4 Kashiwaza Ageo-shi Saitama 362-0075 Japan Business E-Mail: muto@mxt.mesh.ne.jp.

MUTOMBO, DIKEMBE (DIKEMBE MUTOMBO MPOLONDO MUKAMBA JEAN JACQUE WAMUTOMBO), retired professional basketball player; b. Kinshasa, Zaire, June 25, 1966; m. Rose Mutombo; children: Carrie Biamba Wamutumbo, Jean Jacques Dikembe Mutumbo Mplombo Jr.; 4 adopted children. BA in Linguistics and Diplomacy, Georgetown U., 1991; LHD, SUNY, Cortland, 2004. Ctr. Denver Nuggets, 1991—96, Atlanta Hawks, 1996—2001, Phila. 76ers, 2001—02, NJ Nets, 2002—03, NY Knicks, 2003—04, Chgo. Bulls, 2004, Houston Rockets, 2004—09; ret., 2009. Founder Dikembe Mutombo Found., Inc., 1997—; youth emissary UN Devel. Program, 1999; founder Biamba Marie Mutombo Hosp. and Rsch. Ctr., Kinshasa, Democratic Republic of Congo, 2001; adv. bd. mem. NIH Fogarty Internat. Ctr., 2003. Recipient Most Caring Athlete award, USA Weekend, 1999, President's Svc. award, Points of Light Found., 1999, Henry P. Iba Citizen Athlete award, 1999, J. Walter Kennedy Citizenship award, NBA, 2001, Trailblazer award, Constituency for Africa, 2001, Internat. Health Sect. award, Am. Pub. Health Assn., 2002, Samuel J. Halsey award, Georgetown U., 2002, European Hero award, TIME mag., 2003, Helen Hayes MacArthur award, Helen Hayes Hosp. Found., NY, 2003, African-Am. Legacy Coun. Creed medal, Cmty. Found. Greater New Haven, 2005, Jackie Robinson Humanitarian award, US Sports Acad., 2007, Order of the Eagle Exemplar, 2007; named NBA Defensive Player of Yr., 1995, 1997, 1998, 2001; named to We. Conf. All-Star Team, NBA, 1992, 1995, 1996, Ea. Conf. All-Star Team, 1997, 1998, 2000—02, All-Rookie Team, 1992. Achievements include leading the NBA in: total rebounds, 1995, 1997, 1999, 2000; defensive rebounds, 1999, 2000; offensive rebounds, 2001; blocked shots, 1994-1998; ranking second all-time in blocked shots (3,289); fluent in English, French, Spanish, Portuguese and five African dialects. Office: Dikembe Mutumbo Found Inc PO Box 250225 Atlanta GA 30325-1225 Office Phone: 404-262-2109. Office Fax: 404-262-2168.*

MUTTER, JENNIE, secondary school educator, artist; b. Pikeville, Ky., May 20, 1956; d. Ruey and Delois Jean Mutter; children: Ruey Thomas Bentley, Kelley Michelle Faster. BS in Secondary Edn., Pikeville Coll., 1991; MS, Morehead State U., Ky., 1996, AP cert. U.S. history, 2002; Army cert. marksmanship tng., Fort Campbell, Ky., 2005. Headstart tchr. Lookout Grade Sch., Ky., 1977—78; subsitute tchr. Pike County Bd. Edn., Ky., 1979—96; history/art educator Feds Creek H.S., Ky., 1996—2002, East Ridge H.S., Lick Creek, Ky., 2002—. Mem. Coalfield Edn. Endeavor, Grundy, Va., 2000—, pres., 2000—03, v.p., 2003—. Coord. Goals 2000, 1996—99; capt. Civil Air Patrol, Grundy, 2002—; marksmanship coach Warrior Battalion JROTC, Lick Creek, 2004—; camp photographer Sons of Confederate Vets.-Camp 1863, Grundy, Va., 1999—2003; conductress Order Ea. Star Pine Mountain Chpt. #247, Jenkins, Ky., 1990, 1994, assoc. matron, 1991, 1995, worthy matron, 1992, 1996. Cedar grantee, Cedar Coal Group, 1996—2002. Mem.: Pike County Edn. Assn. (sec. 1996—97, rep. 1996—2003), Ea. Ky. Edn. Assn., Ky. Edn. Assn. Avocations: drawing, painting, photography, motorcycling, dance. Home: 380 Upper Chloe Creek Pikeville KY 41501

MUTTER, JOHN J., JR., writer, researcher; s. John J. Mutter, Sr. and Burnette V. Mutter; m. Karen L. Boerst, Aug. 21, 1982. Grad., Shawano Sr. H.S., Wis., 1961. Power plant operator State of Wis., Madison, Winnebago, Green Bay, Wis., 1982—2001, ret., 2001. Author: To Slay a Giant, 2000, Out in the Country, 2005; ghostwriter: I Will Sing My Songs Again, the biography of Ronnie Fuller, 2004; co-editor Shawano County Sesquicentennial 1853-2003. With USN, 1961—64, with U.S. Mcht. Marine, 1969—70, with U.S. Mcht. Marine, 1973—77, West Coast. Decorated The Vietnam Svc. Bar; recipient Outdoor Writing award, Coun. for Wis. Writers, 1990, Buzzard Buster award, Wolf Watershed Ednl. Project, 2000, 50th Bo Carter Meml. award, Waukesha Writers Group, 2002, 2d Pl. award, Al P. Nelson Feature Writing Contest, 2004. Mem.: Coun. for Wis. Writers, Wis. Regional Writers Assoc., Shawno County Hist. Soc. (life), Shawano Area Writers (pres. 2002—08). Avocations: writing, fishing, hunting, reading. Office: Burstone LLC N2787 McDonald Rd Shawano WI 54166-6956

MUTTERPERL, WILLIAM CHARLES, lawyer, corporate financial executive; b. NYC, July 15, 1946; s. Martin and Muriel (Wurtzel) M.; m. Nancy Fay Borson, July 2, 1968; children: Matthew, Adam. BA, Dartmouth Coll., 1968; JD, Columbia U., NYC, 1971. Bar: N.Y. 1972, R.I. 1978, U.S. Dist. Ct. (so. and ea. dists.) N.Y. 1973, U.S. Dist. Ct. R.I. 1979. Assoc. atty. Cleary, Gottleib, Steen and Hamilton, NYC, 1971-77; asst. gen. counsel Fleet Nat. Bank, Providence, 1977-79, gen. counsel, 1979-85; v.p., gen. counsel, sec. Fleet Fin. Group, Inc. (now Fleet Boston Fin Inc.), Providence, 1985-89, sr. v.p., gen. counsel, sec., 1989—2001; exec. dir. ind. oversight bd. Arthur Andersen LLP, 2002; ptnr. bus. law divsn. Brown, Rudnick, Berlack, Israels, LLP, 2002; vice chmn. PNC Fin. Svcs. Group, Pitts., 2002—. Bd. mem. Black Rock, Inc., NY, Beth Israel Deaconess Hosp., Boston; former pres. Boston Bar Found. Mem. Phi Beta Kappa. Democrat. Jewish. Office: PNC Fin Svcs Group One PNC Plaza 249 Fifth Ave Pittsburgh PA 15222-2707

MUTU, WANGECHI, collage artist, painter; b. Nairobi, Kenya, 1972; Grad., United World Coll. of the Atlantic, Wales, 1991; BFA, Cooper Union for the Advancement Sci. and Art, 1996; MFA, Yale U., 2000. One-woman shows include Jamaica Ctr. Arts and Learning, Queens, NY, 2003, Susanne Vielmetter LA Projects, 2003, 2005, 2008, Miami Art

Mus., 2005, San Francisco Mus. Modern Art, 2006, Sikkema Jenkins & Co., NYC, 2006, SITE Santa Fe, 2006—07, exhibited in group shows at Out of the Box, Queens Mus., NY, 2001, Africaine, Studio Mus. Harlem, NYC, 2002, Figuratively, 2004, African Queen, Black President, traveling, 2003, Open House, Bklyn. Mus. Art, 2003, 2004, Only Skin Deep, Internat. Ctr. Photography, NYC, 2003, New, Susanne Vielmetter LA Projects, 2004, Cut, 2005, Pin-Up: Contemporary Collage and Drawing, Tate Modern, London, 2004, Greater NY, P.S.1 Contemporary Art Ctr., 2005, Drawing from the Modern, Mus. Modern Art, NYC, 2005, Matisse and Beyond, San Francisco Mus. Modern Art, 2005, After Cezanne, Mus. Contemporary Art LA, 2005, Triumph of Painting, Saatchi Gallery, London, 2006, USA Today, Royal Acad. Arts, London, 2006, Collage: The Unmonumental Picture, New Mus., NYC, 2008. Recipient Richard Leakey merit award, 1994; grantee Joan Mitchell Found., 2007, Louis Comfort Tiffany Found., 2008; fellow Fannie B. Pardee Found., 2000, Jamaica Ctr. Arts, 2001. Studio: 849 Lafayette Ave Brooklyn NY 11221-1901 Office: c/o Sikkema Jenkins & Co 530 W 22nd St New York NY 10011 also: c/o Susanne Vielmetter LA Projects 5795 W Washington Blvd Culver City CA 90232*

MUTUA, MAKAU WA, dean, law educator; b. Kitui, Kenya, Mar. 14, 1958; came to U.S., 1984; s. Joseph and Rose Nduni (Mbiti) M.; m. Athena Diane Harris, Aug. 16, 1986; children: Lumumba Theodus Maxwell, Amani Dlop Dioko, Mwalimu, Eugene. LLB, U. Dar-es-Salaam, Tanzania, 1983, LLM, 1984, Harvard U., 1985, JD, 1987. Bar: N.Y. 1988. Lectr. law U. Dar-es-Salaam, 1983-84; assoc. White & Case, NYC, 1987-88; dir. Africa Project Lawyers Com. for Human Rights, NYC, 1989-91; assoc. dir. human rights program Harvard Law Sch., Cambridge, Mass., 1991-96; assoc. prof. U. Buffalo Law Sch., SUNY, 1996—99, prof., 1999—, Floyd H. & Hilda L. Hurst faculty scholar, 2006—, SUNY disting. prof., 2007—, interim dean, 2007—08, dean, 2008—. Vis. prof. U. Puerto Rico Sch. Law, San Juan, 1995, 2001, Harvard Law Sch., 1999, U. Iowa Coll. Law, Iowa City, 2000, UN Univ. for Peace, Costa Rica, 2005—07, U. Deusto, Bilbao, Spain, 2009; dir. Human Rights Ctr. U. at Buffalo, SUNY, 1996—, co-dir. Baldy Ctr. Law & Social Policy, 1998—2004; co-chair Am. Soc. Internat. Law, 2000; faculty mem., Law & Soc. Assn. U. Witwatersrand, Johannesburg, 2006; bd. mem. for various internat. orgns. and acad. jours.; spkr. in fields. Mem. editl bd. Internat. Third World Legal Studies Assn., 1996-98; guest editor Jour. Law and Policy, 1996; author: Zaire: Depression as Policy 1990, Political and Cultural Critique 2002, contbr. articles to profl. journs. Chmn. Kenya Human Rights Commn., Nairobi, 1992—; mem. adv. bd. Robert F. Kennedy Meml. Human Rights Award, Washington, 1995—. Mem. ABA, N.Y. State Bar Assn., African Studies Assn., African Assn. Polti. Sci. Avocations: reading, travel, cooking. Office: Univ at Buffalo Law Sch SUNY 319 John Lord O'Brien Hall Buffalo NY 14260 Office Phone: 716-645-2052.*

MUTURI, EPHANTUS J., entomologist, researcher; s. Hudson Muturi Kibuthu and Rosemary Wangui Muturi. PhD in Entomology, U. Ill., Urban-Champaign, 2007. Grad. rsch. asst. U. Ill., 2005—07; postdoc. fellow U. Ala., Birmingham, 2007—. Rsch. asst. Internat. Ctr. Insect Physiology and Ecology, Nairobi, Kenya, 2003—05. Contbr. articles to profl. jours. Francis M. and Harlie M. Clark Rsch. Support grant, Sch. Integrative Biology, U. Ill., 2006, Postdoc. fellowship, NIH, 2007—. Mem.: Sigma XI (full mem.), Soc. Vector Ecology, Am. Soc. Tropical Medicine and Hygiene. Office: Univ Ala Birmingham 845 19th St S 206C BBRB Birmingham AL 35294 Personal E-mail: ephajumu@yahoo.com.

MUTZ, DIANA C., political science professor; m. Robin Pemantle; children: Walden Pemantle, Maria, Simone. BS with highest distinction, Northwestern U., 1984; AM, Stanford U., 1985, PhD, 1988. Asst. prof., dept. polit. sci. and sch. journalism and mass comm. U. Wis.-Madison, 1988—94, assoc. prof., dept. political sch., 1994—99, assoc. chair, dept. polit. sci., 1996—99; prof., polit. sci. and journalism and mass comm. Ohio State U., 1999—2003; Samuel A. Stouffer Prof. Polit. Sci. and Comm. U. Pa., 2003—; dir., Inst. for the Study of Citizens and Politics Annenberg Pub. Policy Ctr., Pa., 2003—. Mem. steering com. U. Wis. Survey Ctr., 1989—; regional US rep. World Assn. for Pub. Opinion Rsch., 1993—94; conf. planning com. Am. Assn. for Pub. Opinion Rsch., 1994—95; co-private investigator Time-Sharing Experiments for the Social Scis., Ctr. for Human Resources Rsch., Ohio State U., 2001—06. Co-editor: Political Persuasion and Attitude Change, 1996; author: Impersonal Influence: How Perceptions of Mass Collectives Affect Polit. Attitudes, 1998 (Robert Lane prize for the best book in polit. psychology, Am. Polit. Sci. Assn., 1999, Doris Graber prize for most influential book on political comm. published in the last 10 years, 2004), Hearing the Other Side: Deliberative Versus Participatory Democracy, 2006 (Goldsmith prize, Harvard U., 2007); refereed several jour. articles, manuscript reviewer for several profl. jours., editl. bd. mem. Journal of Communication, 1991—96, Political Communication, 1992—98, 2001—, Ohio State U. Press, 2002—03, Journal of Politics, 2004—, editor-in-chief Political Behavior, 1998—2003, editl. bd. mem. Public Opinion Quarterly, 1991—2000, mem. adv. bd., 1996—98. Mem. pilot com. Am. Nat. Election Studies, 1998—99, bd. overseers, 2003—. Recipient Winner of Paper Competition, Am. Assn. for Pub. Opinion Rsch., 1989; named one of 50 Top Educators at U. Wis.-Madison, Interfraternity Coun. and Panhellenic Assn.; Romnes Rsch. Fellowship, 1998, Fellowship, Ctr. for Advanced Study in the Behavioral Scis., Stanford, Calif., 1999—2000, Sr. Fellow, Brookings Institution. Fellow: Am. Acad. Arts & Scis.; mem.: Midwest Polit. Sci. Assn. (chair, breckinridge award com. 1990—91, program com., sect. head for polit. psychology and pub. opinion 1996—97, mem. nominations com. 1998, chair, nominations com. 1999, program co-chair 2000, coun. mem. 2001—, chair, Pi Sigma Alpha award com. 2003—04), Am. Polit. Sci. Assn. (chair, Murray Edelman Career Achievement award com. 1991—92, exec. bd. mem., polit. comm. divsn. 1992—93, vice-chair, polit. comm. divsn. 1994—95, chair, polit. comm. divsn. 1995—96, exec. bd., elections and voting behavior divsn. 1997—98, polit. psychology book award com. 2000, v.p. elections, pub. opinion, polit. behavior sect. 2002—04, chair, Warren Miller award com. 2005, Graber award com. mem., polit. comm. sect., Ithiel de sola Pool award for best paper dealing with polit. comm. 1991), Internat. Soc. for Polit. Psychology, Internat. Comm. Assn. (sec., polit. comm. divsn. 1993—94, Top Three paper in Polit. Comm. Divsn. 1986, 1989, award for best paper on polit. comm. published in 1997 1998, award for top paper in polit. comm. divsn. 2003). Office: U Pa 248 Stiteler Hall/235 Stiteler Hall 208 S 37th St Philadelphia PA 19104-6215 also: Inst for the Study of Citizens and Politics Annenberg Public Policy Ctr 3620 Walnut St Philadelphia PA 19104-6220 Office Phone: 610-896-2484, 215-573-1974. Business E-Mail: mutz@sas.upenn.edu.

MUTZ, OSCAR ULYSSES, manufacturing and distribution executive; b. Edinburg, Ind., Feb. 12, 1928; s. Harold Winterberg and Laura Belle (Sawin) M.; m. Jean Greiling, Aug. 22, 1948; children: Marcia, H. William. BS, Ind. U., 1949. Vice pres. Peerless Corp., Indpls., 1954-63; v.p., gen. mgr. Space Conditioning, Inc., Harrisonburg, Va., 1964-66; v.p., treas. Cosco, Inc., Columbus, Ind., 1966-67; exec. v.p., 1967-69; pres., 1969-71; chmn. bd. Court Manor Corp., Columbus, 1971-73; pres. Jenn Air Corp., Indpls., 1973-75; pres., CEO Mutz Corp., 1975-81; pres., dir. Haag Drug Co., 1977-78; pres. Forum Group, Inc. (merger Mutz Corp. and Excepticon, Inc.), Indpls., 1981-91; chmn., CEO, bd. dirs. Capital Industries, Inc., Indpls., 1991-96; chmn. Lakeland Auto Mall, 1996—. Pres. Ct. Manor Corp., co-chmn. bd. dirs. Sargent & Greenleaf, Safemasters; pres. Security Group, Inc., 1991-2004, also bd. dirs. Nat. trustee Fellowship Christian Athletes, 1985-91, chmn. nat. conf. ctr., 1994-96; mem. pres. coun. and dean's adv. coun. Ind. U., elder Presbyn. Ch. Mem. Ind. Mfrs. Assn. (chmn. 1980), Acad. Alumnae Fellows Ind. U. Sch. Bus., Lakeland Yacht Club, Grasslands Country Club, Lone Palm Country Club. Republican. Presbyterian. Office: Mutz Corporation 5119 Lake in the Woods Blvd Lakeland FL 33813-2942 Office Phone: 863-644-4485.

MUTZ, STEVEN, astronomer, educator; BS in Astronomy, U. Calif., Berkeley, 1985, BS in Applied Math., 1985; MS in Astronomy, San Diego State U., 1991. Prof. astronomy & physics Scottsdale CC, Ariz., 1994—, planetarium dir., 2001—. Office: Scottsdale CC 9000 E Chaparral Rd Scottsdale AZ 85256-2626 Office Fax: 480-423-6101. Business E-Mail: steven.mutz@sccmail.maricopa.edu.

MUUSS, ROLF EDUARD, retired psychologist, author; b. Tating, Germany, Sept. 26, 1924; came to U.S., 1953, naturalized, 1992. s. Rudolf A. and Else M.; m. Gertrude Louise Kremser, Dec. 22, 1953 (dec. April 1999); children: Michael John (dec.), Gretchen Elise. Diploma, Tchr. Coll., Flensburg, Germany, 1951; student, U. Hamburg, Germany, 1951, Ctrl. Mo. State Coll., 1951—52, Columbia Tchrs. Coll., 1952; MEd, Western Md. Coll., 1954; PhD, U. Ill., 1957; Masters Degree (hon.), U. Ambrosiana, Milan, 2004. Tchr. pub. sch., Germany, 1945-46, 51, 52-53; substitute prin., 1952-53; tchr. trainee U.S. Office Edn., 1951-52; houseparent Child Study Ctr., Balt., 1953; grad. asst. U. Ill., 1954-57; rsch. assoc. prof. Iowa Child Welfare Rsch. Sta., State U. Iowa, 1957-59; rsch. cons., 1960, 61; mem. faculty Goucher Coll., 1959-95, prof. edn., 1964-95, chmn. dept., 1972-75, dir. spl. edn., 1977-92, Elizabeth C. Todd disting. prof., 1980-85, chmn. dept. sociology and anthropology, 1983-85, prof. emeritus, 1995—. Rsch. assoc. edn. Johns Hopkins, 1962-63; tchr. U. B.C., 1962, Johns Hopkins U., 1962, 65, U. Del., 1965, Towson U., 1967, U. Ill., 1967; tchg. assoc. Sheppard and Enoch Pratt Hosp., 1969-80; guest lectr. Tchrs. Coll., Kiel, Fed. Republic Germany, 1977-78; hearing officer spl. edn. cases State of Md., 1980-96. Author: First-Aid for Classroom Discipline Problems, 1962, Theories of Adolescence, 1962, 6th edit., 1996, Grundlagen der Jugendpsychologie, 1982; editor: Adolescent Behavior and Society: A Book of Readings, 1971, 5th edit., 1998; contbr. articles to profl. jours. Served with German Air Force, 1942-45. Recipient award for disting. scholarship Goucher Coll., 1979; grantee Andrew W. Mellon Found., 1976-77. Fellow Am. Psychol. Soc., Am. Psychol. Assn., Md. Psychol. Assn. (treas. 1971-73); mem. Balt. Psychol. Assn. (chmn. membership com. 1966, v.p. 1970-71), Soc. Rsch. Child Devel., Soc. Rsch. on Adolescence, Kappa Delta Pi (v.p. Alpha chpt. 1956-57), Phi Delta Kappa. Home: Edenwald # 304 800 Southerly Rd Towson MD 21286-8403

MUY-RIVERA, MARTIN, biochemist, researcher; b. Mexico, Jan. 30, 1963; s. Raul Muy and Blanca Rivera; m. Irina Pavlova, Jan. 21, 2001. PhD, 1989. Rsch. scientist InBios, Seattle, 2001—02, Swedish Med. Ctr., Seattle, 2002—. Cons. in field. Contbr. articles to profl. jours. Recipient Dr. Jorge Rosenkranz Med. Rsch. award, 1989. Mem.: AAAS, AAMI. Home: 1717 E Jefferson St Apt 107 Seattle WA 98122-5751 Personal E-mail: martinmuy@earthlink.net.

MUZA, JAY PHILLIP, oceanographer, educator, paleontologist; b. Oshkosh, Wis., June 18, 1956; s. Jerrold J. Muza and Sharon F. Ehlinger; m. Sharon K. Grossman-Muza, Oct. 19, 2007. PhD in Geol. Oceanography, Fla. State U., Tallahassee, 1996. Prof. oceanography and geology Broward Coll., Ft. Lauderdale, Fla., 1997—. Ship bd. paleontologist, joides resolution, equatorial pacific ocean. Bd. mem. Urban Wilderness Adv. Bd., Broward County, Fla. Achievements include research in micropaleontology and paleoceanography. Office: Broward Coll Dept Phys Sci 3501 SW Davie Rd Fort Lauderdale FL 33314 Business E-Mail: jmuza@broward.edu.

MUZINGA, LAURENT, finance educator; b. Kinshasa, Dem. Republic of Congo, Mar. 20, 1959; s. Theodore Muzinga and Marie-Josee Mbuku; m. Annie Kinwa, June 2, 1990; children: Ted Al, Tisia Felicia, Tina Marie Esther. PhD, U. Ill., Champaign-Urbana, 2004. Bank mgr. BCZ, Democratic Republic of Congo, 1986—91; grad. tchg. asst. U. Ill., Champaign-Urbana, 1994—2002; assoc. prof. U. Dubuque, Iowa, 2009—. Named Top Grad. Tchg. Asst. Office: Univ Dubuque 2000 Univ Ave Dubuque IA 52001 Business E-Mail: lmuzinga@dbq.edu.

MUZNY, CHRISTINA A., infectious diseases physician; b. Freeport, Tex., Oct. 13, 1976; d. Robert Thomas and Sharon Ann Muzny. BA in Biology, U. Tex., Austin, 1998; MD with honors, Tex. A&M Coll. Medicine, Coll. Sta., 2003. Diplomate in internal medicine Am. Bd. Internal Medicine, 2006, in infectious disease Am. Bd. Internal Medicine, 2008. Internal medicine resident U. Miss. Med. Ctr., Jackson, 2003—06, infectious diseases fellow, 2006—09, mem., grad. med. edn. com., 2007—. Contbr. scientific papers to med. publs. (1st Pl., 2007). Spkr. Sistas Jackson, Inc., Miss., 2008; physician, med. mission trip Projectos Amazonas, Iquitos, Loreto, Peru, 2006—08. Named to Natural Scis. Dean's List, U. Tex., 1995—98. Mem.: ACP, Infectious Diseases Soc. America. Independent. Roman Catholic. Achievements include research in study to determine prevalence rates of sexually transmitted infections, sexual risk behaviors and sexual practices in African-American women who have sex with women. Avocations: travel, reading, writing. Office: Univ Miss Med Ctr 2500 N State St Jackson MS 39216 Office Fax: 601-984-5565. Business E-Mail: cmuzny@medicine.umsmed.edu.

MWAKABUTA, NDAGA STANSLAUS, electrical engineer; b. Kyela, Mbeya, Tanzania, Aug. 14, 1971; s. Mayrick Ambwene Mwakalobo and Rehema Kyusa Mwakabuta; m. Veronica Gasper Sheikbaha; children: Mayrick Ambwene, Rehema Kyusa, Joel Ndaga. BS in Engring., U. Dar es Salaam, Dar es Salaam, Tanzania, 1999, MS in Engring., 2002; PhD in Engring., Tenn. Technol. U., Cookeville, 2008. Energy engr. Tanzania Traditional Energy Devel. Orgn., Dar es Salaam, 2002—04; lectr. U. Dar es salaam, 2004—06; rsch. asst. Tenn. Technol. U., 2006—08; sr. elec. engr. Cummins Inc., Mpls., 2008—. Contbr. scientific papers. Mem.: Nat. Soc. Black Engrs. (senator 2006—08), IEEE. Home: 3209 Diamond Eight Ter Apt 102 Minneapolis MN 55421 Office: Cummins Inc 1400 73rd Ave Minneapolis MN 55432 Personal E-mail: ndagam@yahoo.com.

MWENDA, KENNETH KAOMA, legal association administrator, consultant; LLB, U. Zambia, 1990; Gr.Dip, LCCI, UK, 1991; DMS, IoC, UK, 1992; BCL, U. Oxford, UK, 1994; MBA, U. Hull, Eng., 1995; DBA, Pacific Western U., LA, 1996, PhD in Publs., 1999; PhD, U. Warwick, UK, 2000; LLD, Rhodes U., South Africa, 2008. Cert. Bar, Zambia, 1991; cert. cumpolsory edn., devels. in comml. securities, intellectual property law. With trust funds and co-financing dept. Vice-Presidency of World Bank, Washington, 1998—99, with poverty reduction, mgmt. and pub. sector reform unit, 1999; counsel legal dept. World Bank, Washington, 1999—2000, projects officer, 2000—03, sr. projects officer, 2003—04, sr. counsel, 2004—. Vis. prof. U. Pretoria Sch. Law, South Africa, 2007, extraordinary prof., South Africa, 2009—; vis. prof. U. Wester Cape Sch. Law, South Africa, 2008, U. Miskolc Sch. Law, Hungary, 1996; lectr. U. Zambia Law Sch., 1991—95, vis. prof., 2001; lectr. Warwick U. Law Sch., 1995—98; spkr. and presenter in field. Author: Legal Aspects of Corporate Capital and Finance, 1999, Contemporary Issues In Corporate Finance and Investment Law, 2000, Banking Supervision and Systemic Bank Restructuring, 2000, Zambia's Stock Exchange and Privatization Programme, 2001, The Dynamics of Market Integration: African Stock Exchange's in the New Millennium, 2000, Banking Supervision and Microfinance Regulation: Lessons from Zambia, 2002, Principles of Arbitration Law, 2003, Frontiers of Legal Knowledge: Business and Economic Law in Context, 2003, Anti-Money Laundering Law and Practice, 2005, Legal Aspects of Financial Services Regulation and the Concept of a Unified Regulator, 2006, The Legal Administration of Financial Services in Common Law Jurisdictions: with special attention to the dual regulation system in Zambia, 2006, Combating Financial Crime: Legal, Regulatory and Institutional Frameworks, 2006, Contemporary Issues in International Economic Law, 2006, Economic Integration and Development in Africa, 2006, Comparing American and British Legal Education Systems, 2007, Made in Australia, 2007, Legal Aspects of Combating Corruption: The Case of Zambia, 2007. Tutor U. Zambia Law Sch., 1991—95. Staff Devel. fellow in law U. Zambia, 1991, U. Yale Law Faculty fellow, 1998; Rhodes scholar U. Zambia, 1992, U. Oxford, 1992-94, U. Hull, 1994-95. Fellow Royal Soc. Arts. of England, Inst. Commerce of England; mem. Internat. Bar Assn., Law Assn. of Zambia, Brit. Assn. Lawyers for Def. of Unborn. Office: The World Bank 1818 H St NW Washington DC 20433-0001 Office Phone: 202-458-0295. Personal E-mail: kmwenda@yahoo.com.

MWINYELLE, JEROME BANAYA, language educator; PhD, U. Tex., Austin. Spanish lectr. Clemson U., SC, 2003—04; asst. prof. Spanish East Tenn. State U., Johnson City, 2004—. Dir., summer program Migrant Edn. Program, ETSU, Johnson. Mem.: The Am. Assn. Teachers Spanish and Portuguese, The Am. Coun. Tchg. Fgn. Languages, Am. Assn. Applied Linguistics, Modern Languages Assn. Office: E Tenn State Univ 213 Gilbreath Hall Johnson City TN 37614 Office Fax: 423-439-4448. Business E-Mail: mwinyell@etsu.edu.

MYATT, WILLIAM HOWARD, theater educator, director, actor; b. Maquoketa, Iowa, Mar. 1, 1961; s. Robert Bruce and Adabelle Marie Myatt; m. Christina Marie Schnock, Aug. 10, 2002; children: Anna Marie, Alexander Ashton, Zachary Leonard. BA, U. No. Iowa, Cedar Falls, 1979—84, MA, 1985—90. Cert. 7 - 12 Libr./Media Specialist Dept. of Edn., Iowa, 2001, k - 12 Talented and Gifted Educator Dept. of Edn., Iowa, 1995. Dir., actor Meml. Union Summer Resident Theatre, Ames, Iowa, 1982—83; drama dir., tchr. Burlington HS, Wis., 1984—85, No. U. HS, Cedar Falls, Iowa, 1985—87, Clinton HS, Iowa, 1987—90, Pleasant Valley Cmty. HS, Pleasant Valley, Iowa, 1990—. Workshop presenter Tenn. Thespian Conf., Nashville, 1991, Va. Thespian Conf., 1991—94, Ednl. Theatre Assn., Regional Conf., Minneapolis, Minn., 1991, Kans. Thespian Conf., 1992; workshop presenter, adjudicator Fla. Thespian Conf., Tampa Bay, 1992; workshop presenter Iowa HS Speech Assn., Des Moines, 1997—; mainstage adjudicator Ednl. Theatre Assn., Cincinnati, Ohio, 1994—, trustee, 1996—99. Contbr. articles. Aids quilt display com. Scholar Hazel B. Strayer award, U. No. Iowa Theatre Dept., 1982. Mem.: Iowa Ednl. Theatre Assn. (Hall of Fame 2005), Ednl. Theatre Assn. (pres., v.p. 2001—05, bd. dirs. local chpt. 2005, Hall of Fame 2005). Avocations: theater, reading, science fiction. Office: Pleasant Valley Comm HS 604 Belmont Rd Bettendorf IA 52722 Business E-Mail: myattw@pleasval.k12.ia.us.

MYCIELSKI, JAN, retired mathematics professor; b. Wisniowa, Poland, Feb. 7, 1932; s. Jan and Helena (Bal) M.; m. Emilia Przezdziecka, Apr. 25, 1959. MS, U. Wroclaw, Poland, 1955, PhD, 1957. With Inst. Math., Polish Acad. Scis., Wroclaw, 1956-68; prof. math. U. Colo., Boulder, 1969—2002, prof. emeritus, 2002—. Vis. prof. Case Western Res. U., Cleve., 1967, U. Colo., 1967, Inst. des Hautes Etudes Scientifiques, Bures-sur-Yvette, 1978-79, dept. math. U. Hawaii, 1987; attache de recherche Centre National de la Recherche Scientifique, Paris, 1957-58; asst. prof. U. Calif., Berkeley, 1961-62, 70; long-term vis. staff mem. Los Alamos Nat. Lab., 1989-90. Author over 150 rsch. papers. Recipient Stefan Banach prize, 1965, Alfred Jurzykowski award, 1977, Waclaw Sierpinski medal, 1990. Mem. Am. Math. Soc., Math. Assn. Am., Polish Math. Soc., Assn. for Symbolic Logic. Office: U Colo Dept Math Boulder CO 80309-0395

MYDLACK, DANIEL JAMES, filmmaker, educator; b. Elmhurst, Ill., Aug. 3, 1959; s. Louis J. and Darleen A. Mydlack; m. Caroline Burwell Landis Chavasse; children: Louis James Chavasse, Frances Letha Chavasse. MFA, U. Calif. San Diego, 1999. Assoc. prof. Towson U., Md., 2003—; mem. San Diego Zen Ctr. Dir.: (documentary film) Voices from the New American Schoolhouse. Founder & dir. Arts & Ideas Sudbury Sch., Balt., 2008—. Democrat. Home: 3611 Parkside Dr Baltimore MD 21214 Office: Towson Univ 8000 York Rd Baltimore MD 21252 Business E-Mail: dmydlack@towson.edu.

MYER, DONALD BEEKMAN, architect; b. Cleve., Aug. 25, 1937; s. Beekman Walter and Jennie Helen (Gimpel) M.; m. Ellen Jane Schwartz, June 10, 1970; 1 child, Jamie Beekman. BArch, U. Ill., 1961, MArch, 1962. Registered architect Va., D.C. Supervisory architect Nat. Park Svc., Phila., Washington, Cape, Mass., 1962-65; asst. sec. Commn. Fine Arts, Washington, 1965-97; adminstrn., budget and grants cons. Keyes, Lethbridge & Condon, Architects, Washington, 1968-70; clk. of works Washington Nat. Cathedral, 1998-2001; curator bldg. and grounds Tudor Place, Georgetown, 2001—02; strategic counsel cons., 2002—. Cons. Preservation Galveston (Tex.) History Found., 1968-69, Joint Com. on Landmarks, Washington, 1969; faculty cons. Sch. of Architecture, Cath. U. Am., 1990—2008; mem. bldgs. and grounds com. Protestant Episcopal Cathedral, 2003—; mem. U.S. Capital Vis. Ctr. Arts Panel, 2004-05; bd., dirs., chair design adv. com. Adams Meml. Found., 2006—, dir., Dist. Columbia Preservation Leaque, 2008—; chair Preservation League Project Review Com., 2009-. Author: Bridges and the City of Washington, 1974, Building Potomac Aqueduct, 1975; editor: Centennial History of Washington AIA, 1987; artist: Lewis & Clark Show, Corcoran Gallery, 2006. Mem. faculty Smithsonian Resident Assocs., Washington, 1973-81; pres. Washington Archtl. Found., 1998-2000; trustee Com. of 100 on the Fed. City, 1997-2000; mem. bldgs. and grounds com., Protestant Episc. Cathedral, 2003—. Named Arch. of Yr., DC Coun. Engring. and Archtl. Socs., 2005; named one of 77 People to Watch award, Washingtonian Mag., 1987; grantee Europa-Nostra Seminar Smithsonian Fgn. Currency Program, Poland, 1974. Fellow AIA (chair hist. resources 1976, v.p. found. 1980, chpt. pres. 1987, fellows selection jury 1998-2000, awarded Centennial Medal, Washington chpt. 2004); mem. Woodley Park Men's Club (pres. 1979-82), Lambda Alpha (hon.). Avocations: history, travel, photography, painting. Personal E-mail: aspire2@earthlink.net.

MYER, KEATS, museum director; 3 children. BS in Econs., U. NH; MPA, Robert F. Wagner Sch. Pub. Svc., NYU. With internat. mktg. and fin. dept. AT&T; mgr., design and constrn. Nat. Track & Field Hall of Fame, 2000—2004; exec. dir. Children's Mus. of Arts, 2004—. Office: Childrens Mus of Arts 182 Lafayette St New York NY 10013 Office Phone: 212-274-0986 ext. 110. Office Fax: 212-274-1776. Business E-Mail: kmyer@cmany.org.

MYERBERG, MARCIA, investment banker; b. Boston, Mar. 25, 1945; d. George and Evelyn (Lewis) Katz; m. Jonathan Gene Myerberg, June 4, 1967 (div. Mar. 1994); 1 child, Gillian Michelle. BS, U. Wis., 1966. Corp. trust adminstr. Chase Manhattan Bank, NYC, 1966-67; asst. cashier Glore Forgan, Wm. R. Staats, Phoenix, 1967-68; bond portfolio analyst Trust Co. of Ga., Atlanta, 1969-72; asst. v.p. 1st Union Nat. Bank, Charlotte, NC, 1973-78; dir. cash mgmt. Carolina Power & Light Co., Raleigh, NC, 1978-79; sr. v.p., treas. Fed Home Loan Mortgage Corp., Washington, 1979-85; dir. Salomon Bros. Inc., NYC, 1985-89; sr. mng. dir. Bear, Stearns & Co. Inc., NYC, 1989-93; mng. dir. Bear, Stearns Home Loans, London, 1989-93; chief exec. Myerberg & Co., L.P., NYC, 1994—. Home: 37 W 12th St Apt 6K New York NY 10011-3205 Office: 39 Broadway Ste 1601 New York NY 10006

MYEROWITZ, P(AUL) DAVID, cardiac surgeon, educator, writer; b. Balt., Jan. 18, 1947; s. Joseph Robert and Merry (Brown) M.; m. Susan Karen Macks, June 28, 1967 (div.); children: Morris Brown, Elissa Suzanne, Ian Matthew; m. Kathleen Mary Murphy, Aug. 10, 2001. BS, U. Md., 1966; MD, 1970; MS, U. Minn., 1977. Intern in surgery U. Minn., Mpls., 1970-71, resident in surgery, 1971-72, 74-77; resident in cardiothoracic surgery U. Chgo., 1977-79; practice medicine specializing in cardiovascular surgery Madison, Wis., 1979—; asst. prof. thoracic and cardiovascular surgery U. Wis., Madison, 1979-85; assoc. prof., 1985; chief sect. cardiac transplantation, 1984-85; Karl P. Klassen prof., 1985-97; chief thoracic and cardiovascular surgery Ohio State U. and Hosps., Columbus, 1985-97. Author: (book) Heart Transplantation, 1987, Heartland for Profit, 2004; contbr. articles to profl. jours. Served with USPHS, 1972-74. Mem.: ACS, Am. Assn. Thoracic Surgeons, Am. Coll. Cardiology. Jewish. Business E-Mail: hrttx1@aol.com.

MYERS, A. MAURICE, waste management executive; b. Long Beach, Calif., May 20, 1940; s. Walter Ray and H. Priscilla (Larsen) M.; m. Elizabeth Jean Ashburn, July 16, 1960; children: Michele, Tracy, Leanne. BA, Calif. State U., Fullerton, 1964; MBA, Calif. State U., Long Beach, 1972. Fin. mgr. Ford Motor Co., Newport Beach, Calif., 1964-72; fin. cons. Merrill Lynch, Newport Beach, 1972-75; mktg. dir. Continental Airlines, LA, 1975-82; v.p. ops. On TV, LA, 1982-83; pres., CEO Aloha Airgroup, Honolulu, 1983-93; pres. Am. West Airlines, Phoenix, 1993-95; chmn., pres., CEO, bd. dirs. Yellow Corp., Overland Park, Kans., 1996-99; pres., CEO Waste Mgmt., Inc., Houston, 1999—2004; chmn. Waste Mgmt. Inc., Houston, 1999—. Bd. dirs. Hawaiian Elec. Industries, Honolulu, Tesoro Petroleum Inc., San Antonio, Pleasant Holidays, West Lake Village, Calif. Bd. dirs. Greater Houston Partnership, Keep Am. Beautiful. Mem. Nat. Assn. Mfrs., Waialae Country Club (Honolulu). Avocations: reading, golf, travel. Office: Waste Management 1001 Fannin St Ste 4000 Houston TX 77002-6711

MYERS, ALLEN RICHARD, rheumatologist; b. Balt., Jan. 14, 1935; s. Ellis Benjamin and Rosina (Blumberg) M.; m. Ellen Patz, Nov. 26, 1960; children: David Joseph, Robert Todd, Scott Patz. BA, U. Pa., Phila., 1956; MD, U. Md., 1960. Diplomate Am. Bd. Internal Medicine, Am. Bd. Rheumatology. Intern Univ. Hosp., Balt., 1960-61, resident in medicine Ann Arbor, Mich., 1961-64; fellow in rheumatology Mass. Gen. Hosp. and Harvard Med. Sch., Boston, 1966-69; dir. clin. tng. rheumatology U. Pa. Sch. Medicine, Phila., 1969-72, chief rheumatology sect., 1972-78; dep. chair medicine Temple U. Sch. Medicine, Phila., 1978-84, acting chmn. medicine, 1984-86, dean, 1991-95, prof. medicine, 1978—, assoc. v.p. Health Scis. Ctr., 1988-95. Vis. prof. Cardiothoracic Inst., U. London, 1988; mem. med. adv. bd. Scleroderma Rsch. Found., Santa Barbara, Calif., 1986. Mem. editl. bd. Arthritis & Rheumatism, 1985—90, Brit. Jour. Rheumatology, 1989—94; editor: Systemic Sclerosis, 1985, Medicine, 1986, 1993, 1996, 2000, 2004. Pres. Phila. Health Care Congress, 1994—; adv. com. Pa. Lupus Found., 1976—; bd. dirs. Phila. Conv. and Visitors Bur., 1994—. With USPHS, 1964-66. Recipient Margaret Whitaker prize U. Md. Sch. Medicine, 1960, Lindback Found. award Temple, 1981; named Physician of Yr. Temple U. Hosp., 1986. Master: Am. Coll. Rheumatology; fellow: ACP, Phila. Coll. Physicians (pres. 2000); mem.: Am. Fedn. Clin. Rsch. Avocations: walking, classical music, reading. Office Phone: 215-707-5127.

MYERS, ANGELA MICHELLE, music educator, department chairman; b. Kokomo, Ind., Nov. 29, 1978; d. Ronald Wayne Myers and Sandra Jane Myers Gaiser. BS in Instrumental Music Edn., Ball State U., Muncie, Ind., 2001. Band dir. Prince William County Sch., Stonewall Jackson HS, Manassas, Va., 2002; band dir., dept. chair Prince William County Sch., Bull Run Mid. Sch., Gainesville, Va., 2002—, presenter, 2004—, mem. music literacy com., 2006—, mem. music syllabus com., 2006—. Fine arts rep. Bull Run Mid. Sch. Adv. Council, Gainesville, Va., 2004—; curriculum cons. Prince William County Sch., Manassas, Va., 2004—, camp dir., instr., 2004—; presenter in field. Band pres. Ball State U., Sch. of Music, Muncie, Ind., 2000—01; presenter Prince William County Schs., 2004—, music literacy com. mem., 2006—, music syllabus com. mem., 2006—. Recipient Richard L. Dunham Band award, Ball State U. Marching Band, 2000, John R. Emens Leadership award, Ball State U. Sch. Music. Mem.: Sigma Alpha Iota, Va. Music Educators Assn., Music Educators Nat. Conf. Achievements include founding staff mem. Bull Run Mid. Sch., 2002.

MYERS, BETTY J., retired music specialist; b. Kansas City, Mo., Feb. 24, 1935; d. Marion O. and Jennie Lillian (Dickinson) Williams; m. Alfred M. Myers, June 6, 1958; children: Sherylyn, Douglas, Carol. BS in Edn., Cen. Mo. State U., 1956; MS in Edn. Adminstrn., CMSU, 1976. Elem. tchr. Kansas City Pub. Schs., 1956—58, elem. classrm. tchr., 1962—80, elem. music tchr., 1980—94; elem. tchr. R5 Schs., Parkville, Mo., 1958—60. Leader adult Sunday sch., 1972-. Mem. Am. Bus. Women's Assn., 1972-2000 (v.p., sec., treas., chair com. 1980-2000, pres. 1984-85, Woman of Yr. 1985), Internat. Order of The King's, Daus. and Sons (pres. Perry Crosby Cir. 1976-80 Kans. City Union 1983-85, v.p. Mo. br. 1987-90, pres. 1998-2002, Mo. br. bd. dirs., 1996-1998, 2002-, Mo. br. treas. 2004-07, Mo. Br. endowment chair 2007-09, Internat. Chautauqua scholarship dir. 1994-98, Chautauqua program com. chair 2006-), Delta Kappa Gamma Soc. Internat.(pres. Alpha chpt. 1984-86, pres. Kansas City area coun. 1985-87, pres. chpt. 2002-04). Baptist. Avocation: church pianist. Home: 13407 E 51st St Kansas City MO 64133-2631

MYERS, BRADLEY KEVIN, lawyer, educator; b. Detroit, July 23, 1960; s. Jane Arden Hardy and William James Myers, David John Hardy (Stepfather); m. Yee Han Chu; children: Annika Ying, Thomas Chu. BS, U. Calif., LA, 1983, MS, 1986; JD, U. Oreg., Eugene, 1994; LLM in Taxation, NY U., 1995. Cert.: Calif. (bar mem.) 1995, Oreg. 1995, Nev. 1995, ND 2004. Assoc. atty. Lentz, Evans and King, Denver, 2000—01; assoc. prof. and Randy H. Lee prof. U. ND Sch. Law, Grand Forks, ND, 2001—. Commr. Nat. Conf. Commrs. Uniform States Laws, Chgo., 2008—. Contbr. articles to profl. jours. Mem.: Phi Sigma Biol. Sci. Honor Soc., Order Coif. Avocation: swimming. Office: Univ ND Sch Law Centennial Dr Stop 9003 Grand Forks ND 58202 Business E-Mail: myers@law.und.edu.

MYERS, CAITLIN KNOWLES, economics professor; d. Allen and Iris Knowles; m. Adam Myers; 1 child, Finnegan James. BA, Tulane U., New Orleans, 1999; PhD, U. Tex., Austin, 2005. Asst. prof. economics Middlebury Coll., Vt., 2005—.

MYERS, CHRISTOPHER D., bank executive; b. Calif. BA, Harvard U.; MBA, U. Calif. Various positions including v.p., mgr. First Interstate Bank; comml. bank ctr. mgr. Bank of the West (Sanwa Bank of Calif.); chmn., CEO Mellon First Bus. Bank, LA, 1996—2006; pres., CEO, chmn. CVB Fin. Corp., Citizens Bus. Bank, 2006—. Office: CVB Fin Corp 701 North Haven Ave Ste 350 Ontario CA 91764 Office Phone: 909-980-4030. Office Fax: 909-481-2130.

MYERS, CHRISTOPHER D., defense company executive; b. Riverside, NJ, Dec. 2, 1965; m. Tiffany Myers; 2 children. Grad., U. Colo.; grad. in pub. adminstrn., Cornell U., Ithaca, NY. Comm. officer, anti-air warfare officer, ops. officer, Persian Gulf War USS Bunker Hill, US Navy; joint air def. officer US-NATO Staff of Comdr., Second Fleet; comdr., Striking Fleet Atlantic USS Mt. Whitney, US Navy; v.p. sea-based missile def. Lockheed Martin, v.p. maritime systems & sensors bus. devel.; mem. Medford Township Coun., NJ, 2001—. Decorated Meritorious Svc. Medal, Joint Svc. Commendation Medal, Joint Svc. Achievement Medal, Navy Commendation Medal (Combat V), Navy Achievement medals, Combat Action Ribbon, Liberation of Kuwait Medal. Republican. Office: Lockheed Martin Maritime Systems & Sensors 199 Borton Landing Rd Moorestown NJ 08057

MYERS, DANIEL WILLIAM, II, lawyer; b. Camden, NJ, Mar. 21, 1931; s. Charles Rudolph II and Myrtle Henrietta (Kress) M.; m. Eileen Ethel Kohn, Nov. 22, 1959 (dec.); children: Susan Leigh, Meredith Ann Myers Winner, Kathryn Kress Gilbert. BS in Commerce, U. Va., 1952, LLB, 1957. Bar: Va. 1957, N.J. 1958, U.S. Dist. Ct. N.J. 1958, U.S. Supreme Ct. 1980. Assoc. Lewis & Hutchinson, Camden, 1958-60; ptnr. Myers, Matteo, Rabii, Norcross & Landgraf and predecessors, Camden, Cherry Hill, NJ, 1960-89, Montgomery, McCracken, Walker & Rhoads, 1989-94, of counsel, 1994-98, Steven J. Jozwiak, Cherry Hill, NJ, 1998—. 1st lt. U.S. Army, 1952-54. Mem. N.J. Bar Assn., Va. State Bar, Camden County Bar Assn., Am. Arbitration Assn., Exch. Club (pres. Cherry Hill chpt. 1969). Republican. Lutheran. Home: 1 E Atlantic Ave Harvey Cedars NJ 08008 Office: 532 Hollywood Ave at Rte 38 Cherry Hill NJ 08002 Office Phone: 856-661-1822.

MYERS, DEBBIE, graphics designer, educator; b. Aug. 19, 1954; BEd in Art, U. Miami, Coral Gables, Fla., 1976, MFA in Graphic Arts, 1997; MS in Mass Comm., Fla. State U., Tallahassee, 1977; Edn. Specialist in Computer Applications, Nova Southeastern U., Ft. Lauderdale, Fla., 1994. Cert. tchr. Fla. Instr. Art Inst. Ft. Lauderdale, 1978—95; adj. instr. graphic design Broward CC, Hollywood, Fla., 1987, 1996—2000; curriculum coord., graphic design instr. Art Inst. Ft. Lauderdale, 1997—; instr. graphic design Fla. Atlantic U., Ft. Lauderdale, 1994—97; coord. electronic media Art Inst. Ft. Lauderdale, 1988—94; acting coord. Fla. Atlantic U., Ft. Lauderdale, 1996; adj. instr. humanities Nova Southeastern U., 1997—. Presenter in field; judge in-house art event Am. Express, 2000. Two-woman show, Savitch Cultural Art Gallery, 1997, exhibited in group shows at Fla. Atlantic U., 1995—2006, PrePress Virtual Internet Art Show, 1996, Ft. Lauderdale Mus. Art, 1996, 1997 (Best in 3-D Mixed Media award), 2002, 2006, Boca Mus. Art, 1999, AIFL Art Gallery, 2006; author: Against the Clock-Non-linear Editing, 2001, The Graphic Designer's Guide to Portfolio Designs, 2005. Recipient Best in Show, U. Miami Grad. Art Show, 1997, EMC Graphic Design Competition, 2001, 2d pl. for art direction in nat. student contest, QuarkXPress Inc. Mem.: NATAS, Am. Film Inst., Women's Caucus Arts, Nat. Desktop Pubs. Assn., Nat. Art Edn. Assn. Home: 2804 E Abiaca Cir Davie FL 33328 Office Phone: 954-308-2339. Personal E-mail: dg_myers@bellsouth.net.

MYERS, DEE DEE (MARGARET JANE MYERS), television personality, former White House press secretary; b. Quonset Pt., RI, Sept. 1, 1961; d. Stephen George and Judith Ann (Burleigh) M.; m. Todd Stanley Purdum, 1997; children: Katherine, Stephen BS, U. Santa Clara, 1983. Press asst. Mondale for Pres., LA, 1984; deputy Senator Art Torres, LA, 1985; dep. press sec. to press sec. Mayor Tom Bradley, LA, 1985-87; deputy press sec. Tom Bradley For Gov., LA, 1986; Calif. press sec. Dukakis for Pres., LA, 1988; press sec. Feinstein for Gov., L.A. and San Francisco, 1989-90; campaign dir. Jordan for Mayor, San Francisco, 1991; comm. cons. DeeDee Myers Assocs., Valencia, Calif., 1991—; press sec. Clinton for Pres., Little Rock, 1991-92, The White House, Washington, 1993-94; co-host Equal Time, CNBC, Washington, 1995-97; contbg. editor Vanity Fair, Washington, 1995—. Mem. bd. of trustees, Calif. State U.,1999— Author: Why Women Should Rule the World: A Memoir, 2008. Recipient Robert F. Kennedy award Emerson Coll., Boston, 1993. Democrat. Roman Catholic. Achievements include being the first woman to serve as White House press secretary. Avocations: running, bicycling, music, major league baseball.

MYERS, DENSEL LEE, economics professor; b. Altus, Okla., Aug. 8, 1953; s. James Donald and Hattie Lois Myers; m. Darla Lyman, Aug. 16, 1985; children: James Robert, Briley Norris. MEd, U. Ctrl. Okla., Edmond, 1977. Cert. forensics examiner SE Cybercrime Inst., 2004. Radio announcer KWHP Radio, Edmond, 1973—77; prof., economics Okla. City CC, 1977—96. Vice-mayor City Yukon, Okla., 1994—2000. Home: 1148 Dawn Yukon OK 73099 Office: Okla City CC 7777 S May Ave Oklahoma City OK 73159

MYERS, DONALD ALAN, transportation executive; b. Denver, Nov. 6, 1959; s. Charles Myers and Donna Lorraine Billis. Cert. MTA Truck Driving Sch., 1999. Painter Decorative and Coatings Sys., Denver, 1989—99; truck driver Carlson Sys., LLC, Denver, 1999—. Photographer Prime Focus Studios, Deer Trail, Colo., 2008. Achievements include invention of waffle pro white balance filter. Avocation: photography.

MYERS, DOROTHY ROATZ, artist; b. Detroit, Mar. 24, 1921; d. Harry Agustus and Lola May (Kelly) Roatz; children: Bruce, Leslie Ann, Douglas. Student, Antioch Coll., 1941, Corcoran Gallery Art Sch., 1943, Art Students League, 1965—. Asst. to design dir. Harper & Row Pub., NYC, 1981-87. Lectr. and writer on art-related affairs. Contbr. revs. to profl. publs.; ongoing exhibited in numerous shows including N.Y. ArtExpo, 1992, Art Miami, 1992, Cornell Med. Libr. Ann., 1992, Hellenic Art Inst. Exhbn., 1991, Vt. Inst. Natural Sci., 1983, Montserrat Gallery Internat. Exhbn. (hon. mention 1993); represented in permanent collection Ward-Nasse Gallery, N.Y.C. Recipient 1st place award for drawing Brookdale Coll., 1994, 2d place award for sculpture, 1993, Bronze medal for animal art, 1986, 20th Century award for Achievement Internat. Biog. Ctr.; apptd. Acad. Ofcl. Knight Acad. Internazionale Dept. Arts, Italy. Mem.: Academia del Verbano, Italy, N.Y. Artists Equity, Garrison Art Ctr., Hellenic Art Inst., League Sci. et Edn. Sociale, Arts, Scis., Lettres: Soc. Academique de Edn. et Encouragement, Art Students League (life), Acad. Am. Poets.

MYERS, DOUGLAS GEORGE, zoological society administrator; b. LA, Aug. 30, 1949; s. George Walter and Daydeen (Schroeder) Myers; m. Barbara Firestone Myers, Nov. 30, 1980; children: Amy, Andrew. BA, Christopher Newport Coll., 1981. Tour and show supr. Annheuser-Busch (Bird Sanctuary), Van Nuys, Calif., 1970-74, mgr. zool. ops., 1974-75, asst. mgr. ops., 1975-77, mgr. ops., 1977-78; gen. services mgr. Annheuser-Busch (Old Country), Williamsburg, Va., 1978-80, park ops. dir., 1980-81; gen. mgr. San Diego Wild Animal Park, 1981-83, dep. dir. ops., 1983-85; CEO, Exec. Dir. Zool. Soc. San Diego, 1985—. Mem. Balboa Park Cultural Partnership, Steering Com. Conservation Breeding Specialists Group, Ctrl. Balboa Park Assn. Bd. dirs. Nat. Mus. Libr. Svcs., 2007—. Mem.: Calif. Assn. Zoos and Aquariums, World Assn. Zoos and Aquariums, Am. Zoo and Aquarium Assn., Am. Assn. Museums (bd. dir.), Rotary Club San Diego. Office: Zool Soc San Diego PO Box 120551 San Diego CA 92112-0551

MYERS, ELISSA MATULIS, publishing executive, professional society administrator; b. Munich, Aug. 4, 1950; (parents Am. citizens); d. Raymond George and Anne Constance (Moley) Matulis; m. John Wake Myers, Sept. 13, 1967 (div. 1972); 1 child, Jennifer Anne Myers Bick. BA in English Lit., George Mason U., 1972, MA in English Lit., 1982. Dir. rsch. and info. Am. Soc. Assn. Execs., Washington, 1972-80, dir. mem. svcs., 1980-88, v.p., pub. Assn. Mgmt. mag., 1988-97; pres., CEO Nat. Informercial Mktg. Assn., Washington, 1997—2004, Electronic Retailing Assn., Washington, 1998—2003; chmn. Assn. Internet Radio Network. Chmn. Assn. Internet Radio Network, 2004; pres. Advice & Consensus, 2007—; host weekly radio show Assn. Nation, Assn. Power and Politics; advisor Mcpl. Fin. Officers Assn., Republic of Georgia. Pub. Principles of Association Management, 1976, 3d edit., 1996; columnist Footnotes, 1988-97. Bd. dirs. Ethics Resource Ctr., Washington, 1982-86; mem. Universal Postal Union Adv. Group 2000-; mem. Fed. Adv. Commn. on e-commerce; appointee DofC 1fac-4 Ecommerce, 2001-. Mem. Am. Soc. Assn. Execs. (cert.), Assn. Conv. Mktg. Execs., Greater Washington Soc. Assn. Execs. (bd. dirs. 2000—), Nat. Assn. Hispanic Mktg. Profls. (adv. bd.), Soc. Nat. Assn. Publs., Com. of 100 U.S. C. of C., Soc. Scholarly Pubs. Roman Catholic. Avocations: running, scuba diving. Home: 5315 Moultrie Rd Springfield VA 22151-1915 Office: AIR 5673 Ravnel Ln Springfield VA 22151 Office Phone: 703-626-9087. E-mail: elissa@elissamyers.com.

MYERS, ELLEN HOWELL, historian, educator; b. Bryan, Tex., Feb. 16, 1941; d. Douglas Wister and Ann Olive (Emory) Howell; m. William Allen Myers, Dec. 23, 1967; 1 child, William Webb. Student, Mt. Vernon Jr. Coll., 1959—61, U. Madrid, 1961—62; BA, Sophie Newcomb Coll. of Tulane U., 1963; MA, U. Va., 1965, PhD, 1970. Lectr. U. Houston, 1966—67; instr. Okla. State U., Stillwater, 1967—70; asst. prof. San Antonio Coll., 1970—73, assoc. prof., 1973—77, prof. history, 1977—. Author: (student's rev. manuals, instrs. manuals) The American Nation, 1975, 1977, 1979, 1983, 1987, Test Bank for the West Transformed, 2000; contbr. articles to profl. jours. Mem. S.W. Conf. Commn. on Higher Edn. and Campus Ministry Meth. Ch., 1978—81; bd. dirs. Family Svc. Assn., 1978—85, pres., 1983—84; bd. dirs. San Antonio Area Red Cross, 1979—85, Laurel Heights Weekday Sch., 1980—83, chmn., 1982—83. Mem.: AAUP (exec. com. San Antonio Coll. 1973—74), Conf. on L.Am. History, S.W. Conf. on L.Am. Studies (exec. com. 1974—75), Tex. C.C. Tchrs. Assn., Tues. Musical Club, Jr. League of San Antonio (bd. dirs. 1977—79), Kappa Alpha Theta, Phi Alpha Theta. Democrat. Methodist. Home: 307 Arcadia Pl San Antonio TX 78209-5950 Office: 1300 San Pedro Ave San Antonio TX 78212-4201

MYERS, EUGENE NICHOLAS, otolaryngologist, educator; b. Phila., Nov. 27, 1933; s. David and Rosalind (Nicholas) Myers; m. Barbara Labov, June 10, 1956; children: Marjorie Rose Fulbright, Jeffrey N. BS in Econs., U. Pa., 1954; MD, Temple U., 1960. Diplomate Am. Bd. Otolaryngology. Intern Mt. Sinai Hosp., NYC, 1960—61; resident Mass. Eye and Ear Infirmary, Boston, 1963—65; asst. prof. clin. otolaryngology U. Pa., 1968—72; prof. clin. oncology dept. oral pathology U. Pitts. Sch. Dental Medicine, 1975—82, prof. dept. diagnostic svcs., 1982—2000, prof. dept. oral and maxillofacial surgery, 2000—; prof., chmn., chief dept. otolaryngology U. Pitts. Med. Ctr., 1972—2007, emeritus chmn., 2005—, disting. prof. otolaryngology, 2006—. Cons. VA Med. Ctr., Pitts., 1972—, Children's Hosp., Pitts., 1972—2007. Editor: Cancer of the Head and Neck, 1981, 4th edit., 2003, Tracheotomy, 1985, 2d edit., 1998, 4th edit., 2007, Operative Otolaryngology: Head and Neck Surgery, 1997, Disorder of the Salivary Glands, 2007; mem. editl. bd. Laryngoscope, 1973—95, exec. editl. bd., 1995—2004, mem. editl. bd. Head and Neck Surgery, 1978—92, 1998—, AMA Archives of Otolaryngology, 1981—, Annals of Otology Rhinology and Laryngology, 1984—2005, Oncology, 1986—2007, European Archives of Oto-Rhino-Laryngology, 1990—97, Auris Nasus Larynx, 1996—, editor-in-chief (book) Advances in Otolaryngology, 1985—2001; co-editor: Butterworth's Intern Med. Revs., 1981—82; internat. editor Otolaryngology-Head and Neck Surgery, 1996—2005. Mem. adv. bd. Pa. Lion Hearing Rsch. Found., Pitts., 1983—99. Capt. M.C. US Army, 1965—67. Recipient Cert. of Merit Com. Rsch., Am. Acad. Otolaryngology-Salicylate Otoxicity, 1965, Award of Merit, Am. Acad. Otolaryngology-Head and Neck Surgery Inc., 1978, Robert E. Shoemaker Rsch. award, Pa. Acad. Ophthalmology and Otolaryngology, 1979, Disting. Svc. award, Am. Acad. Oto-HNS, 2001. Fellow: Am. Acad. Otolaryngology (chmn. com. on head and neck surgery 1981—83, bd. dirs. 1985—88, 1990—2003, pres. 1994—95, internat. coord. 1996—2003), Am. Laryngol. Assn. (sec. 1982—88, pres. 1989—90, mem. coun. 1990—93, James Newcomb award 1993, DeRoaldes award 2001, ALA award 2001), ACS (bd. govs. 1981—87, mem. adv. coun. 1985—87); mem.: Triological Soc. (mem. coun. 1989—92, v.p. Ea. sect. 1994—95), Am. Soc. Head and Neck Surgery (mem. coun. 1977—93, pres. 1988—90), Nat. Cancer Inst. (chmn. upper aerodigestive tract working group 1986—89), Assn. Acad. Depts. Otolaryngology (mem. coun. 1978—80), Am. Bd. Otolaryngology (bd. dirs. 1981—99, pres.-elect 1994—96, pres. 1996—98), Pitts. Athletic Assn. Republican. Jewish. Office: U Pitts Sch Med Eye and Ear Inst Ste 519 200 Lothrop St Pittsburgh PA 15213-2546 Office Phone: 412-647-2111. Business E-Mail: myersen@upmc.edu.

MYERS, FRANKLIN, oil industry executive; b. Pensacola, Fla., Nov. 2, 1952; m. Elizabeth A. Berner; children: Amanda C., Adam F., Anne Marie M., Mary Lauren Miller, Zachary J., Thomas J. BS, Miss. State U., 1974; JD, U. Miss., 1977. Bar: Miss. 1977, Tex. 1978. Ptnr. Fulbright and Jaworski, Houston, 1978-88; sr. v.p., gen. counsel Baker Hughes Inc., Houston, 1988-95; sr. v.p. Cooper Cameron Corp., Houston,

1995—2008, CFO, 2002—08. Adj. prof. U. Tex. Sch. Law, 1990—2003; bd. dirs. InPut Output Inc., Comfort Sys., Inc. Fellow: Houston Bar Assn., Miss. Bar Assn., Tex. Bar Assn., Houston Bar Found.; mem.: Tex. Bar Found.

MYERS, HARDY, former state attorney general; b. Electric Mills, Miss., Oct. 25, 1939; m. Mary Ann Thalhofer, 1962; children: Hardy III, Christopher, Jonathan. AB with distinction, U. Miss., 1961; LLB, U. Oreg., 1964. Bar: Oreg., U.S. Ct. of Appeals (9th cir.), U.S. Dist. Ct. (Dist. of Oreg.). Law clk. to US Dist. Judge William G. East, 1964—65; pvt. practice Stoel Rives LLP and predecessor firms, 1965—96; atty. gen. State of Oreg., 1997—2009. Mem. Oreg Ho. Reps., 1975—85, spkr. of the ho., 1979—83; chair Com. on Judiciary, 1977—78, 1983—84; councilor Met. Svc. Dist. (now Metro), 1985—86. Bd. editors Oregon Law Rev. Pres. Portland City Planning Commn., 1973—74; chair Oreg. Jail Project, 1984—86, Citizens' Task Force on Mass Transit Policy, 1985—86, Oreg. Criminal Justice Coun., 1987—91, Portland Future Focus, 1990—91, Metro Charter com., 1991—92, task force on state employee benefits, 1994; co-chair gov. task force on state employee compensation, 1995; mem. Commn. on Jud. Br., 1983—85. Mem.: Multnomah County Bar Assn., Oreg. State Bar, Omicron Delta Kappa, Phi Kappa Phi, Phi Eta Sigma. Democrat. Office: PO Box 9236 Portland OR 97207 Office Phone: 503-378-6002, 503-378-4732.*

MYERS, HECTOR, psychology professor, department chairman; AA in Behavioral Sci., Canal Zone Coll., Panama, 1966; BA in Psychology cum laude, Claremont Men's Coll., 1969; MA in Psychology, UCLA, 1971, PhD in Clin. Psychology, 1974. Dir. children's early identification program Ctrl. City Cmty. Mental Health Ctr., 1973—76; asst. prof. psychology UCLA, 1974—81, assoc. prof. psychology, 1981—92, dir. minority health tng. program, 1983—93, prof. psychology, 1993—, chmn. clin. psychology; dir. rsch. & scholar-in-residence, Fanon R&D Ctr. Charles R. Drew Postgraduate Med. Sch., 1975—85; dir. behavioral lab., dept. psychology Charles R. Drew U. Medicine and Sci., 1985—93, prof. psychiatry, 1993—, dir. rsch., ctr. on ethnicity, health and behavior, 1993—. Contbr. articles to profl. jours. Grantee, NIH Nat. Inst. Mental Health. Fellow: APA. Office: UCLA Dept Psychology 1285 Franz Hall Box 951563 Los Angeles CA 90095-1563 Office Phone: 310-825-1813. Business E-Mail: myers@psych.ucla.edu.*

MYERS, IONA RAYMER, retired real estate property manager; b. Guymon, Okla., Sept. 18, 1931; m. Harold Rudolph Myers, Mar. 28, 1953 (dec. Apr. 13, 2003); children: Richard Galen, Sandra Dawn, Paula Colleen. BS magna cum laude, So. Nazarene U., 1952; MEd, U. Okla., 1959; postgrad., McNeese State U., 1970. Tchr. home econs. Can. County Pub. Schs., Mustang, Okla., 1952-53; tchr. elem. Oklahoma City Pub. Schs., 1955-61, Transylvania County Pub. Schs., Brevard, NC, 1961—67; elem. tchr., student tchr. supr. Allen Parish Pub. Schs., Oakdale, La., 1967-71; mgr. DeRidder Tracts and Comml. Property, Metairie, 1968-94; tchr. elem. and jr. high history Lafourche Parish Pub. Schs., Raceland and Lockport, La., 1974-76; tchr. elem. sci. Jefferson Parish Pub. Schs., Metairie, 1976-80; treas. Harold R. Myers Engring. (divsn. Harold R. Myers, Inc.), Metairie, 1993—2003; mgr. Harion Properties, LLC, Metairie, 1980—2007; ret. Vol. founding bd. dirs. Jefferson Performing Arts Soc., Metairie, 1977-83; vol. founding mem. cmty. adv. coun. East Jefferson Gen. Hosp., Metairie, 1980-87. Vol. scout leader SE La. Girl Scouts US coun., Metairie, 1977-89, fund raising com., 1992-93, spl. contbr., 2001-05; vol. tchr. music Harold Keller Elem. Sch., Metairie, 1981-83; life mem. Rep. Nat. Com., Washington, 1980-91, mem. fin. com., 1988; jubilee chmn., fundraiser Jefferson Performing Arts Soc., Metairie, 1987; candidate La. House of Reps. Dist. 88, Baton Rouge, 1991; com. YWCA New Orleans Role Model Luncheon, 1994-95; financier Bus. and Profl. Women USA Found., 1990-95, Golden Circle donor, 1996-2005; sec. East Jefferson Rep. Parish Coun., 1998-99; parlimentarian Nat. Women's Polit. Caucus Greater New Orleans Region, 1998-99, pres., 1999-2000, v.p. polit. activity, 2000-01. New Orleans Mus. of Art fellow, 1984-94, So. Nazarene U. fellow, 1985-94; recipient Rice in the Ear award SE La. Girl Scouts U.S., 1982, Great Lady/Great Gentleman award Ladies Aux. East Jefferson Gen. Hosp., 1987, Commendation award Jefferson Performing Arts Soc., 1988, Women as Winners award YWCA New Orleans, 1993; honoree City Business Woman of the Year, 2001. Mem.: AAUW (del. 5 nat. and 5 regional convs. 1987—94, pres. 1988—90, corr. sec. La. chpt. 1989—91, vol. coord. Metairie chpt. 1990—91, Magnolia editor 1991—96, chair nominating com. 1992—93, Magnolia co-editor 1996—97, program v.p. Metairie br. 1997—99, del. 5 nat. and 5 regional convs. 1998, chair nominating com. 1998—99, sec. 1998—2000, del. 5 nat. and 5 regional convs. 1999, Parliamentarian br. 1999—2000, state parliamentarian 2000—01, chmn. fin. 2000—01, state pres. 2002—04, pres. Metairie chpt. 2002—06, state sec. 2004—06, scholar and grantee 1989, grant honoree 1994), Jefferson Twenty-Five Bd. (sec. 2003—04, pres. 2005, Patty Strong award 1997), Nat. Women's Polit. Caucus (del. nat. conv. 1997, 1999, New Orleans region pres. 1999—2000, v.p. polit. activity 2000—01, del. nat. conv. 2001, br. pres. 2002—, del. nat. conv. 2003), E. Jefferson Parish Rep. Coun., La. Assn. Parliamentarians (2d v.p., edn. chair 1997—2001, state 1st v.p. 2001—05), La. Landmarks Soc. (life), Jefferson Hist. Soc. (life), Nat. Assn. Parliamentarians (pres. Metairie unit 1996—97, del. nat. conv. 1997—99, pres. Metairie unit 1998—99, v.p. program chair 1999—2000, parliamentarian 2000—01, pres. 2002—03, sec. 2003—04, treas. 2004—05, parliamentarian 2005—09, parl 2005—09, sec. 2008—09, 2008—09), New Orleans Mus. Art (fellow 1984—94), Metairie Woman's Club (corr. sec. 1994—96, parliamentarian 2002—03, pres.-elect 2008—09, state fin. chmn. 2008—09, pres. elect 2008—09, pres. 2009—, 2009—), La. Fedn. Bus. Profl. Women's Clubs, Inc. (pres. Jefferson Parish chpt. 1980—82, auditor, legis. chmn. 1990—91, rec. sec. 1991—92, membership v.p. 1992—93, 1st v.p. 1993—94, program v.p. 1993—94, Vision editor 1993—96, Jefferson Parish Voice editor 1993—2004, pres.-elect 1994—95, state pres. 1995—96, state newsletter Pelican editor 1995—2000, sec. 1998—99, parliamentarian 1999—2001, pres. 2001—02, state historian 2001—05, state treas. 2006—08, state fin. chmn. 2008—09, Outstanding Dist. Dir. award 1985, Nike award 1991, Higher Mem. honor 1992—93, Best Membership Recruiter 1993—94). Methodist. Avocations: plate collector, gardening, lobbyist. Home: 4701 Chastant St Metairie LA 70006-2059

MYERS, JAMES CLARK, advertising and public relations executive; b. Chgo., Aug. 26, 1941; s. Herbert George Myers and Lenore (Goldberg) Levi; m. Judy Anne Schnitzer, Feb. 9, 1964; children: Jeffrey Stephan, Jeremy H. BA, Washington U., St. Louis, 1964. Acct. exec. Nahas, Blumberg, Zelikow, Houston, 1967-69; mgr. spl. events Houston Post, 1969-73; pres., creative dir. Motivators, Inc., Houston, 1973—2006; dir. cmty. svcs. Brays Oaks Mgmt. Dist., Houston, 2006—. Employment vice-chmn. Internat. Sci. and Engring. Fair Coun., Washington, 1972-73; bd. dirs. Sci. Engring. Fair of Houston, 1969-73; spl. corrs. Navy Times Newspaper; pres. SW Houston 2000, Inc., 1999-05; chmn. US Cong AGreen TX-9 Mil. Acad. Selection Bd. Contbr. articles to newspapers. Chmn. Houston chpt. Boy Scouts Am.; mem. City of Houston Bldgs. and Stds. Commn., 2005-. Served to capt. USNR, 1964-96. Recipient Wood Badge award, Boy Scouts Am., 1979, Shofar award, 1981; named Fondren SW Citizen of Yr., 2002. Mem. Pub. Relations Soc. Am. (accredited, Silver Anvil award 1983, 87, Excalibur 2001), Bus. Adv. Fedn. (cert.) Jewish. Avocations: model railroading, square dancing, photography. Home: 8006 Duffield Ln Houston TX 77071-2017 Office Phone: 713-995-9116, 713-595-1221. Personal E-mail: jcjamyers@juno.com, braysoaksmd@hhcllp.com.

MYERS, JAMES R., lawyer; b. Valdosta, Ga., Aug. 29, 1952; s. J. Walter Jr. and Mary M.; m. Monica Faeth Myers, Sept. 19, 1992. BA cum laude, Harvard U., 1972, JD, 1975. Bar: Mass. 1975, US Dist. Ct. (DC dist.) 1976, DC 1977, US Ct. Appeals (DC cir.) 1977, US Supreme Ct. 1983, US Ct. Appeals (fed. cir.) 1991, Va. 1992, US Ct. Appeals (4th cir.) 1992. Assoc. Wald, Harkrader & Ross, Wash., 1976-77; assoc. solicitor US Dept. Energy, Wash., 1977-79; assoc. Andrews & Kurth, Wash., 1980-85; ptnr. Steele, Simmons & Fornaciari, Wash., 1985-86, Robbins & Laramie, Wash., 1986-89, Venable, Baetjer, Howard & Civiletti, Wash., 1990-97, Kilpatrick Stockton LLP, 1997—2004, Ropes & Gray LLP, 2004—. Master Giles S. Rich Am. Inn Court for intellectual property litigators, 1989—2007; mem. editl. bd. Practical Lawyer; spkr. in field. Contbr. articles to jour. Mem.: ABA (bd. mem. 2005—07, mem. ALI-ABA bd. dirs. 2002—07). Office: Ropes & Gray LLP 700 12th St NW Ste 900 Washington DC 20005 Home Phone: 301-897-9672; Office Phone: 202-508-4647. Personal E-mail: jmyers@ropesgray.com.

MYERS, JEANETTE MOORE, music educator, director; b. Asheville, NC, Mar. 18, 1957; d. Calvin Hardin and Edith Haynes Moore; m. Roger Harrison Myers; children: David Anderson, Seth Andrew. BME, Mars Hill Coll., NC, 1979. Cert. tchg. NC, 1970. Band dir. Gaston County Schs., NC, 1979—; musician Luth. Chapel Ch., Gastonia, 1984—. Guest dir. Lutheridge Summer Camps, Arden, NC, 1995—; chmn. gaston county band dirs. GCBDA, Gastonia, NC, 1998—2000. Founding bd. dirs. Gaston Symphonic Band, NC, 1990—95. Recipient Award Excellence, NC Band Masters; named Dir. of Yr., Gaston County Schs., 1997—98, Tchr. of Yr., Holbrook Mid. Sch., 1998. Mem.: NCAE, Nat. Music Educators Assn., Gaston Music Edn. Found., Luth. Area Musician Planners. Lutheran. Avocations: cooking, travel, reading, seashell collecting. Home: 4200 Queensberry Rd Gastonia NC 28056 Office: Holbrook Middle Sch 418 South Church St Lowell NC 28098 Personal E-mail: holbrookband@yahoo.com. Business E-Mail: jmyers@gaston.k12.nc.us.

MYERS, JEFF L., surgeon; b. Lawton, Okla., Nov. 11, 1964; s. Lawrence Joseph and Rita Joyce Myers; m. Dahri Anna Zenker, Sept. 3, 1989; children: Connor Joseph, Cameron Marie, Tyler Gustave. MD with distinction, U. Okla., Okla. City, 1991; PhD, Georgetown U., DC, 2006. Diplomate Am. Bd. Surgery, 2002, Am. Bd. Thoracic Surgery, 2003. Chief pediatric cardiac surgery Tulane U., New Orleans, 2003—05, Lebonheur Children's Med. Ctr., Memphis, 2005—07, Mass. Gen. Hosp., 2007—; assoc. prof. surgery Harvard Med. Sch., 2007—; assoc. residency dir., cardiac surgery Mass. Gen. Hosp. Dir. cardiac surg. rsch. Tulane U., 2003—05; vis. prof. surgery UCLA, 2006. Editor: (web-based textbook) E-medicine, Textbook of Pediatrics, 2005; author: articles, book chpts. Bd. govs. Operation Mend-a-Heart, New Orleans, 2004—05; mem. Children's Heartlink, Rochester, Minn., 2005. Recipient Pfizer Prize, Wash. Soc. History of Medicine, 1999. Fellow: ACS (Zehner Travelling fellowship 1999); mem.: Am. Physiol. Soc., Am. Coll. Cardiology, Internat. Soc. for Heart and Lung Transplantation, Soc. Thoracic Surgeons, Kappa Sigma (chpt. pres. 1986). Office: Mass Gen Hosp 55 Fruit St Cox 662 Boston MA 02114 Personal E-mail: myersjeff@yahoo.com.

MYERS, JEFFREY DANIEL, concert pianist, music educator; b. Erie, Pa., June 7, 1970; s. Neal Anthony and Beryl Diane Myers; m. Molly R. Knapp, July 3, 2004; 1 child, Sophia Roberta. MusB, Mercyhurst Coll., Erie, Pa., 1993; MusM, Manhattan Sch. Music, NYC, 1999; student, Chautauqua Sch. Performing Arts. Dir. Erie Piano Acad., Pa., 1999—2006; chmn. Neal A. Myers Found. Music Edn., 2004; mem. faculty Montessori Regional Charter Sch., Erie, 2006, Veritas Prep. Acad., Phoenix, 2006—; mem. faculty, chair dept. piano, coll. counselor Ariz. Sch. for the Arts, Phoenix, 2007—. Soloist: piano recital Hubbard Hall, 1999, Cancer Benefit St. Andrews Roman Cath. Ch., 2006, performer: chamber music recital Lincoln Heights Christian Ch., 2007, piano soloist: Erie Chamber Orch., 2000, debut piano and violin concert: Classical Concert Series, Kent State U., 2002; Classical Concert Series, Kent State U., Ashtabula, Ohio, 2003. Avocations: painting, art history, travel, world history. Business E-Mail: jeff@myers-usa.com.

MYERS, JESSE JEROME, lawyer; b. Anthony, Kans., Sept. 30, 1940; s. Claud Lewis and Lucille S. (Robertson) M.; m. Claire H. Conni, Nov., 1966; children: Timothy Todd, Jessica Joy. BS, McPherson Coll., Kans., 1963; JD, Washburn U., Kans., 1970. Bar: Kans. 1970, Mo.1996, US Dist. Ct. Kans. 1970. Law clk. U.S. Dist. Ct. Judge Frank Theis, Wichita, Kans., 1970—72; individual practice law Wichita, Kans., 1972—74, 1995—; lawyer Cessna Aircraft Co., Wichita, Kans., 1974—75; v.p., dir., gen. counsel Martin K. Eby Constrn. Co., Wichita, Kans., 1975—95. Served with USN, 1963-67.

MYERS, JOHN, research scientist, consultant; b. Portland, Oreg., June 8, 1935; s. Louis McCorry Myers and Cornelia Bowden Pipes; m. Merloyd Ludington, May 18, 1985; children: Christopher P., Anne Myers Brandt, Samuel Skipworth. BS, Calif. Tech., 1956; PhD, Harvard U., 1963. Sr. rsch. scientist Raytheon Co., Waltham, Mass., 1962—65, prin. rsch. scientist, 1965—67; analyst Office Sec. of Def., Washington, 1967—68; asst. adminstr. Boston Model City Adminstrn., 1968—73; pvt. practice cons. scientist Boston, 1973—85; project scientist Harvard U., Cambridge, Mass., 1985—. IBM vis. prof. Brown U., Providence, 1998. Achievements include patents for positive-operator-valued-measure receiver for quantum cryptography. Office: Cruft Lab 19 Oxford St Cambridge MA 02138 Business E-Mail: myers@seas.harvard.edu.

MYERS, JOHN JOSEPH, archbishop; b. Ottawa, Ill., July 26, 1941; s. M.W. and Margaret Louise (Donahue) M. BA maxima cum laude, Loras Coll., 1963; Licentiate in Sacred Theology, Gregorian U., Rome, 1967; Doctor of Canon Law, Cath. U. Am., 1977; DD (hon.), Apostolic See, Vatican City, 1987. Ordained priest Diocese of Peoria, Ill., 1966; asst. pastor Holy Family Parish, Peoria, Ill., 1967-70; asst. dept. internat. affairs US Cath. Conf., Washington, 1970-71; assoc. pastor St. Matthew Parish, Champaign, Ill., 1971-74; adminstr. St. Mary's Cathedral, Peoria, Ill., 1977—78, 1984; vice chancellor Diocese of Peoria, 1977-78, vocation dir., 1977-87, chancellor, 1978-87, vicar gen., 1982-90, mem. Presbyteral Coun., 1968—70, 1984—90, bd. Consultors, 1978—90; ordained bishop, 1987; coadjutor bishop Diocese of Peoria, 1987-90, bishop, 1990—2001; Superior Mission of Turks & Caicos, Turks and Caicos Islands, 2001—; archbishop Archdiocese of Newark, NJ, 2001—. Bd. govs. Canon Law Soc. Am., Washington, 1985-87; bd. dirs. Nat. Cath. Bio Ethics Ctr., Boston, 1999—, bd. gov.; mem. sem. com. Mt. St. Mary's Sem., Md., 1989-94; bd. trustees Cath. U. Am., Washington, 1999-2005; seminary com., fin. com., Ad Hoc Com. for By-Laws., Cat. U. Am., Washington; seminary bd. Kenrick-Glennon of the Archdiocese of St. Louis. Author: (commentary) Book V of the Code of Canon Law, 1983; contbr. numerous articles to religious publs. Mem. Canon Law Soc. America, Nat. Conf. Cath. Bishops. (canonical affairs com. 1988-2002, com. shrines and pilgrimages 1990-2007, vocations com. 1995-1998, aid to Eastern Europe com. 1999-, ad hoc com. on sexual abuse 2002, Hispanic affairs com. 2002-), Pontifical Coun. Legislative Tips, USCCB Com. Canonical Affair (chair 2005-08) Roman Catholic. Office: Archdiocese of Newark 171 Clifton Ave Newark NJ 07104-0500 Office Phone: 973-497-4004.

MYERS, JOHN T., physical therapist, educator; s. Robert and Helen Myers. BS in Gen. Sci. summa cum laude, Cleve. State U., Ohio, 1984; MBA, Heriot-Watt U., Edinburgh, Scotland, 1998. Lic. phys. therapist Ohio OTPTAT Bd., 1984. From staff phys. therapist to sr. phys. therapist, supr. phys. therapy Cleve. Clinic Found., 1984—97; program dir., assoc. prof. Lorain County C.C., Elyria, Ohio, 1997—. Team leader. on-site reviewer for phys. therapist asst. programs Commn. on Accreditation in Phys. Therapy Edn., Dept. of Accreditation, Am. Phys. Therapy Assn., Alexandria, Va., 2005—; spkr. continuing med. edn., Cleve., 1984—; cons. to musicians and orchestras regarding injury prevention and treatment, Cleve., 1988—. Author: (chpt.) Treatment Approaches in the Performer with Cervico-brachial Pain, 1992; co-reviewer (textbook) Measurement of Joint Motion: A Guide to Goniometry; contbr. articles to profl. jours. Mem. Lorain County Tech. Prep. Consortium, Ohio, 1999—2003; chair Loraine County C.C. PTA Program Cmty. Adv. Cmty., Elyria, Ohio, 1997—2006; mem. Coll. Found. Adv. Bd., Lorain, Ohio, 2000—03. Recipient Outstanding Faculty award, Lorain County C.C., 1998-1999, Faculty Excellence award, Lorain County C.C. Found., 2001; Gait and Motion Analysis Sys. for Tchg. grant, 2001. Mem.: Ohio Phys. Therapy Assn. (faculty liaison com.), Am. Phys. Therapy Assn. Achievements include design and development of structure and curriculum for the Physical Therapist Assistant Program at Lorain County Community College. Office: Lorain County CC 1005 Abbe Rd N HS 223 Elyria OH 44035

MYERS, LARRY LEONARD, otolaryngologist, educator; b. NY, June 10, 1966; s. Leonard and Retie Elizabeth Myers; m. Nancy Carthan, July 2, 2005; children: Sky I. children: Chancellor A., Elle Sanaa. BA, Northwestern U., Evanston, Ill., 1988; MD, U. Chgo., 1992. Cert. in head & neck surgery Am. Bd. Otolaryngology, 1999. Academic faculty Dept. Otolaryngology-Head & Neck Surgery, Dallas, 2000—. Fellow: ACS; mem.: AMA, Nat. Med. Assn. Office: Univ Texas Southwestern Med Ctr 5323 Harry Hines Blvd Dallas TX 75390-9035 Office Fax: 214-648-9122. Business E-Mail: larry.myers@utsouthwestern.edu.

MYERS, LAWRENCE STANLEY, JR., retired radiation biologist; b. Memphis, Apr. 29, 1919; s. Lawrence Stanley and Jane Myers; m. Janet Vanderwalker, June 13, 1942; children: David Lee, Frederick Lawrence, Lee Scott. BS, U. Chgo., 1941, PhD, 1949. Jr. chemist Metall. Lab. of Manhattan Engring. Dist. U. Chgo., 1942—44; asst. chemist Clinton Labs. Manhattan Engring. Dist., Oak Ridge, Tenn., 1944—46; chemist Inst. Nuc. Studies U. Chgo., 1947—48; assoc. chemist Argonne Nat. Lab., Lemont, Ill., 1948—52; assoc. rsch. phys. chemist Atomic Energy project UCLA, 1952—59, asst. prof. radiology, 1953—70, lectr. in radiol. scis., 1970—76, adj. prof. radiol. scis., 1976—82; rsch. radiobiologist, chief radiobiology div. UCLA Lab. Nuclear Medicine and Radiation Biology, 1959—76; prof. radiology and nuclear medicine Uniformed Svcs. U. Health Scis., Bethesda, Md., 1982—88; sci. advisor Armed Forces Radiobiology Rsch. Inst., Bethesda, 1982—87; cons. Oak Ridge Assoc. Univs., 1987—94; adj. biophysicist radiation biology br. Nat. Cancer Inst. NIH, Bethesda, 1993—2007; ret., 2007. Vis. scientist AFRRI, 1987-93; co-organizer UCLA Internat. Conf. on Radiation Biology, 1957, 59; participant in three major Fed. Govt. planning exercises related to energy rsch. and devel. in U.S., 1973-74; mem. adv. com. Ctr. Fast Kinetic Rsch. U. Tex., Austin, 1975-81, chmn., 1977-81; mem. adv. bd. Radiation Chemistry Data Ctr., U. Notre Dame, 1976-84, sec. 1979-81, chmn. 1981-83; chmn. Long Range Planning Com., Radiation Rsch. Soc., 1976-78; dir. Issues and Requirements Workshop Analysis of 1976 Inventory of Fed. Energy Related Environ. and Safety Rsch., 1977. Contbr. more than 100 sci. articles and abstracts to profl. jours. Com. mem. Boy Scouts of Am., Pacific Palisades and Malibu, Calif., 1956-67. Fellow AAAS; mem. Radiation Rsch. Soc., N.Y. Acad, Sci., Soc. for Free Radical Biology and Medicine, Sigma Xi. Home: 11810 Coldstream Dr Potomac MD 20854-3612 E-mail: larrymyers@earthlink.net.

MYERS, LONN WILLIAM, lawyer; b. Rockford, Ill., Nov. 14, 1946; s. William H. and Leona V. (Janvrin) M.; m. Janet L. Forbes, May 14, 1968; children: Andrew, Hillary, Corwin. BA, Mich. State U., 1968; MBA, Ind. U., 1973; JD, Harvard U., 1976. Bar: Ill. 1976, U.S. Ct. of Fed. Claims 1977, U.S. Tax Ct. 1977, U.S. Ct. Appeals (7th cir.) 1977. Ptnr. McDermott Will & Emery LLP, Chgo., 1976—2005, counsel, 2006—. Served to maj. USAR, 1968—80. Mem. ABA (capital recovery and leasing com. tax sect., tax exempt fin. com. tax sect.). Episcopalian. Office: McDermott Will & Emery LLP 227 W Monroe St Chicago IL 60606-5096 Home: 1623 Glenview Rd Unit 316 Glenview IL 60025-2982 Office Phone: 312-984-7537. Business E-Mail: lmyers@mwe.com.

MYERS, MARILYN GLADYS, pediatric hematologist, oncologist; b. Lyons, Nebr., July 17, 1930; d. Leonard Clarence and Marian N. (Manning) M.; m. Paul Frederick Motzkus, July 24, 1957 (dec. Aug. 1982). BA cum laude, U. Omaha, 1954; MD, U. Nebr., 1959. Diplomate Am. Bd. Pediat. Intern Orange County Gen. Hosp., Orange, Calif., 1959-60, resident, 1960-62; fellow in hematology/oncology Orange County Gen. Hosp./Children's Hosp. L.A., 1962-64; assoc. in rsch., chief dept. hematology/oncology Children's Hosp., Orange, 1964-80, dir. outpatient dept., 1964-73, assoc. dir. leukapheresis unit, 1971-80; clin. practice hematology, oncology, rheumatology Orange, 1964-80; instr. Coll. Medicine U. Calif., Irvine, 1968-71, asst. clin. prof. pediatrics, 1971—; pvt. practice hematology, oncology, rheumatology Santa Ana, Calif., 1980—. Clin. rschr. exptl. drugs. Contbr. articles to med. jours. Med. adv. com. Orange County Blood Bank Hemophiliac Found. Grantee Am. Leukemia Soc., 1963, Am. Heart Assn., 1964. Fellow Am. Acad. Pediat.; mem. AMA, Calif. Med. Assn., LA County Med. Assn., Orange County Med. Assn., Orange County Pediat. Soc., Southwestern Pediat. Soc., LA Pediat. Soc., Internat. Coll. Pediat., Orange County Oncologic Soc., Am. Heart Assn. (Cardiopulmonary Coun.). Republican. Methodist. Avocation: reading. Office: 2220 E Fruit St Ste 217 Santa Ana CA 92701-4459 Office Phone: 714-541-3393, 714-541-3343.

MYERS, MARK D., geologist, former federal official; b. Monroe, Wis., Apr. 24, 1955; s. Rhea Bowman and Ardelle Ione (Van Matre) M.; m. Alice Reding Myers, April 30, 1983; children: Justine Alice, Nathan Mark. BS in Geology and Geophysics with honors, U. Wis., 1977, MS in Geology, 1981; PhD in Geology, U. Alaska, 1994. Petroleum geologist ARCO Oil & Gas, Lafayette, La., 1981-83, ARCO Alaska, Inc., Anchorage, 1983-87; geologist, dir. Divsn. Oil & Gas, State of Alaska, Anchorage, 1988—2005; dir. US Geological Survey, US Dept. Interior, Reston, Va., 2006—09. Contbr. articles to scientific jours. Lt. USAF Reserve, 1977-2003 Mem. Am. Assn. Petroleum Geologists (del.

1992—), Alaska Geological Soc. (v.p. 1993, mem. bd. dirs. 1993-95), Soc. Sedimentary Geology, Eagle River Presbyn. Ch. (pres. bd. trustees 1993—). Avocations: commercial multiengine instrument pilot ratings, skiing, fishing, sailing.*

MYERS, MARY KATHLEEN, publishing executive; b. Cedar Rapids, Iowa, Aug. 19, 1945; d. Joseph Bernard and Marjorie Helen (Huntsman) Weaver; m. David F. Myers, Dec. 30, 1967; children: Mindy, James. BA in English and Psychology, U. Iowa, 1967. Tchr. Lincoln HS, Des Moines, 1967-80; editor Perfection Learning Corp., Des Moines, 1980-87, v.p., editor-in-chief, 1987-93; pres., founding ptnr. orgn. to promote Edward de Bono Advanced Practical Thinking Tng., Des Moines, 1992—2008; founder Myers House LLC, 2002. Pres. Innova Tng. & Cons., Inc., 2000-05. Editor: Six Thinking Hats, 1991, Lateral Thinking, 1993, Direct Attention Thinking Tools, 1997, Total Creativity, 1997 Focus on Facilitation, 2004, Simplicity, 2005 (Six Value Medals, 2007); pub. A Disgrace to the Profession, 2002, Igniting Innovation, 2008; Pirateson the Prairie, 2008. Adv. bd. Sch. Bus., Econs. and Acctg., Simpson Coll., 1998—. Mem. ASTD, Am. Creativity Assn. (bd. dirs. 1997-2000, pres. 1999), Instrnl. Systems Assn. (mem. bd. dirs. 2002-04). Home and Office: 813 56th St West Des Moines IA 50266-6314 Home Phone: 515-225-7866; Office Phone: 515-205-7208. Personal E-mail: myershousebooks@gmail.com.

MYERS, MICHELE TOLELA, former academic administrator; b. Rabat, Morocco, Sept. 25, 1941; arrived in US, 1964; d. Albert and Lillie (Abecassis) Tolela; m. Pierre Vajda, Sept. 12, 1962 (div. Jan. 1965); m. Gail E. Myers, Dec. 20, 1968 (div. Oct. 2003); children: Erika, David. Diploma, Inst. Polit. Studies, U. Paris, 1962; MA, U. Denver, 1966, PhD, 1967; MA, Trinity U., 1977; LHD, Wittenberg U., 1994, Denison U., 1998, U. Denver, 1999. Asst. prof. speech Manchester Coll., North Manchester, Ind., 1967—68; asst. prof. speech and sociology Monticello Coll., Godfrey, Ill., 1968—71; asst. prof. comm. Trinity U., San Antonio, 1975—80, assoc. prof., 1980—86, asst. v.p. for academic affairs, 1982—85, assoc. v.p., 1985—86; assoc. prof. sociology, dean Undergrad. Coll. Bryn Mawr Coll., Pa., 1986—89; pres. Denison U., Granville, Ohio, 1989—98, Sarah Lawrence Coll., Bronxville, NY, 1998—2007, pres. emerita, 2007—. Comm. analyst Psychology and Commn., San Antonio, 1974—83; bd. dirs. Sherman Fairchild Found., 1992—; mem. Fed. Res. Bank Cleve., 1995—98; pres.'s commn. Nat. Collegiate Athletic Assn., 1993—97, JSTOR, 1999—, ARTSTOR, 2003—. Co-author (with Gail Myers): The Dynamics of Human Communication, 1973, The Dynamics of Human Communication, 6th and internat. edits., 1992, The Dynamics of Human Communication, French transl., 1984, Communicating When We Speak, 1975, Communicating When We Speak, 2d edit., 1978, Communication for the Urban Professional, 1977, Managing by Communicaton: An Organizational Approach, 1982, Managing by Communicaton: An Organizational Approach, Spanish transl., 1983, Managing by Communicaton: An Organizational Approach, internat. edit., 1982. Trustee Phila. Child Guidance Clinic, 1988—89; trustee assoc. The Bryn Mawr Sch., Balt., 1987—89; v.p., bd. dirs. San Antonio Cmty. Guidance Ctr., 1979—83, Bank One, Columbus, 1990—94. Recipient Chevalier de la Legion d'Honneur, 2007; fellow in academic adminstrn., Am. Coun. Edn., 1981—82. Mem.: Am. Coun. Edn. (commn. on women in higher edn. 1990—92, bd. dirs. 1993—99, chmn. 1997—98).

MYERS, MICHELLE, publishing executive; married; 4 children. BA, Marymount U. Group advt. mgr. Mode mag., Girl mag.; advt. dir. Shape mag. Weider Publs., 1999—2000, v.p., assoc. pub., 2000—01; v.p., assoc. pub. Allure mag. Condé Nast Publs., 2001—04; v.p., pub. Star mag. American Media, Inc., 2004—07; pub. People StyleWatch Time Inc, 2007—. Mem.: Fragrance Found. (bd. dirs. 2008—). Office: Time Inc 1271 Ave of Americas New York NY 10020 Office Phone: 212-522-1212.*

MYERS, MIKE, actor, scriptwriter, film producer; b. Toronto, Ont., Can., May 25, 1963; s. Eric and Bunny (Hind) M.; m. Robin Ruzan, 1993 (separated). Stage appearences: The Second City, Toronto, 1986-88, Chgo., 1988-89; actor, writer: Mullarkey & Myers, Can., 1984-86, (TV show) Saturday Night Live, 1989-94 (Emmy award for outstanding writing in a comedy or variety series 1989), (film) Wayne's World, 1992, So I Married an Axe Murderer, 1993, Wayne's World II (also screenwriter, prodr.), 1993, Austin Powers: International Man Of Mystery (also screenwriter, prodr.), 1997, Pete's Meteor, 1998, It's a Dog's Life, 1998, 54, 1998, Austin Powers: The Spy Who Shagged Me (also screenwriter, prodr.), 1999, Austin Powers: The Animated Series, 1999, Shrek (voice), 2001, Austin Powers Goldmember (also writer, prodr.), 2002, View from the Top, 2003, Shrek 4-D (voice), 2003, The Cat in the Hat, 2003, Shrek 2 (voice), 2004, Shrek the Third (voice), 2007, The Love Guru (also writer, prodr.), 2008; actor: (TV movie) John and Yoko, 1985, Elvis Stories, 1989, Saturday Night Live: The Best of Phil Hartman, 1998, Saturday Night Live: the Best of Mike Myers, 1998, Saturday Night Live: 25th Anniversary, 1999, Madonna: The Video Collection 93.99, 1999; screenwriter: (tv movie) Murderers Among Us: The Simon Wiesenthal Story, 1989, Saturday Night Live: The Best of Mike Myers, 1998; (video) Far Far Away Idol (voice), 2004; (video game voice) Shrek: Smash n' Crash Racing, 2006; TV appearances The Littlest Hobo, 1979, Russell Gilbert Show, 1998, Night of Too Many Stars: An Overbooked Event for Autism Edn., 2006; dir. (film) The Bacchae, 1999. Recipient Can. comedy award, 2000, MTV Generation award, 2007. Office: c/o David O'Connor Creative Artists Agy 9830 Wilshire Blvd Beverly Hills CA 90212-1804

MYERS, MILES ALVIN, educational association administrator, researcher; b. Newton, Kans., Feb. 4, 1931; s. Alvin F. and Katheryn P. (Miles) M.; m. Celeste Myers; children: Royce, Brant, Roslyn. BA in Rhetoric, U. Calif., Berkeley, 1953, MAT in English, 1979, MA in English, 1982, PhD in Lang. and Literacy, 1982. Cert. secondary tchr. English. Tchr. English Washington Union High Sch., Fremont, Calif., 1957-59, Oakland (Calif.) High Sch., 1959-67, 69-74, Concord High Sch., Mt. Diablo, Calif., 1967-69; chmn. bd. dirs. Alpha Plus Corp. Preschs., Piedmont, Calif., 1968—2002; dir. All City High, 1973-74; tchr. English Castlemont High Sch., Oakland, 1974-75; mem. faculty U. Calif., Berkeley, 1975-85, adminstrv. dir. Bay Area writing project Sch. Edn., 1976-85, adminstrv. dir. nat. writing project Sch. Edn., 1979-85; pres., CEO Calif. Fedn. Tchrs., 1985-90; exec. dir. Edschool.com of Edvantage/Riverdeep, 1999—2001; dir. Inst. Rsch. on Learning and Tchg., Berkeley, Calif., 1998—; sr. rschr. Inst. for Stds. Curricula and Assessment, United Tchrs. LA, 2000—. Co-dir. Nat. Standards Project for English Language Arts, 1992-96; adj. prof. English U. Ill., Champaign-Urbana, 1991-94; vis. lectr. at numerous colleges and Univs.; rschr. in field. Author: The Meaning of Literature, 1973; co-author: Writing: Unit Lessons in Composition, Book III, 1965, The English Book-Composition Skills, 1980; author: A Procedure for Holistic Scoring, 1980, Changing our Minds, 1996; co-author: Exemplars of Standards for English Language Arts, 3 vols., 1997, Asilomar Testing Report, 2001, CSC Professional Code for English/ELA Teachers, 2005; editor Calif. Tchr., 1966-81; contbr. articles to profl. jours. Sgt. US Army, 1953—55. Recipient cert. of Merit, Ctrl. Calif. Coun. Tchrs. of English, 1969, Commendation award Oakland Fedn. Tchrs., 1970, First Place award Internat. Labor Assn., 1971, Disting. Svc. award Calif. Coun. Classified Employees, 1991, Svc. award Nat. Writing Project, 1996. Fellow Nat. Conf. Rsch. in English; mem. Nat. Coun. Tchrs. English (exec. dir. 1990-97), Nat. Conf. on Rsch. in English, Am. Fedn. Tchrs. (legis. dir. Calif. Fedn. Tchrs. 1971-72, Union Tchr. Press awards 1969-75, 86-89, 91, Ben Rust award Calif. Fedn. Tchrs. 1994), Am. Edn. Rsch. Assn., Calif. Assn. Tchrs. English (Disting. Svc. award 86), U. Calif. Berkeley Alumni Assn. Home: 5823 Scarborough Dr Oakland CA 94611-2721 Office: Dir Inst Rsch on Learning & Tchg Berkeley CA 94704 Home Fax: 510-531-0409. Business E-Mail: milesmye@pacbell.net.

MYERS, MINDY, legislative staff member; d. Jay and Annette Myers. BA magna cum laude, Am. U., 1998. With Office of Legis. Affairs The White House, Washington, 1998—2000; dep. dir. cmty. outreach Al Gore presdl. campaign, 2000; sr. advisor, polit. dir. Senator Tom Daschle, 2000—04; mgr. Sheldon Whitehouse senatorial campaign, 2005—06; chief of staff Senator Sheldon Whitehouse, Washington, 2007—; NH state dir. Barack Obama presdl. campaign, 2008. Mem.: Phi Beta Kappa. Office: Office of Senator Sheldon Whitehouse 502 Senate Hart Office Bldg Washington DC 20510-3905 Office Phone: 202-224-2921. E-mail: mindy_myers@whitehouse.senate.gov.*

MYERS, PERRY W., language educator; s. Perry and Carlyn Myers; m. Susanne C. Abel, July 22, 1988; children: Larissa S., Marina C. PhD, U. Tex., Austin, 2003. Investment banker J. P. Morgan, Frankfurt, Germany, 1991—94; assoc. prof. Albion Coll., Mich., 2004—. Author: (academic book) The Double-Edged Sword. Rsch. grant, SCMLA, 2004. Mem.: MLA, German Studies Assn. Avocation: bicycling. Office: Albion Coll 611 East Porter St Albion MI 49224

MYERS, PHILLIP FENTON, corporate financial, technology executive; b. Cleve., June 24, 1935; s. Max I. and Rebecca (Rosenblum) M.; m. Hope Gail Strum, Aug. 13, 1961 B in Indsl. Engring., Ohio State U., 1958, MBA, 1960; D in Bus. Adminstrn., Harvard U., 1966. Staff indsl. engr. Procter & Gamble Co., Cin., 1958; sr. cons. Cresap, McCormack & Paget, NYC, 1960—61; staff assoc. Mitre Corp., Bedford, Mass., 1961; cons. Sys. Devel. Corp., Santa Monica, Calif., 1963—64; dir. long range planning Electronic Splty. Co., LA, 1966—68; chmn. Atek Industries, 1968—72; pres. Myers Fin. Corp., 1973—82; chmn. Amvid Comm. Svcs., Inc., 1975—79, Omni Resources Devel. Corp., 1979—83; chmn., pres. Am. Internat. Mining Co., Inc., 1979—83; pres. Advent Internat. Mgmt. Co., Inc., 1982—; chmn. Global Bond Mktg. Svcs., Inc., 1987—90; pres., CEO Whitehall Container Mfg. Corp., 1988—91; pres. Whitehall Motors Co., 1989—97, Allied Metamatter Tech. Corp., 1994—96; chmn. U.S. Water Resources, Inc., 1994—96; pres. Am. Tech. Venture Fund Mgmt., Inc., Advent Internat. Realty Corp., 1996—98, First Internat. Capital Corp., 1996—2000. Pres. Advent Internat. Mgmt. Co., 1982—, Turbogen, Inc., 1995-98, Blue Star Material Techs. Inc., 1997-2000, Advent Power Systems, 2006—; founding dir. Warner Ctr. Bank, 1980-83; bd. dirs., pres. Cyber Security Systems, Inc., 2000—03; lectr. bus. adminstrn. U. So. Calif., L.A., 1967-74; prof. Grad. Sch. Bus. Adminstrn. Pepperdine U., 1974-81. Trustee, treas. Chamber Symphony Soc. Calif., 1971-78; mem. campaign issues com. Reagan for Pres., 1976, 80; pub. safety commr. City of Hidden Hills, Calif., 1976-83, chmn., 1982-83; co-chmn. budget adv. com. Las Virgenes Sch. Dist., 1983-86; mem. Mayor's Blue Ribbon Fin. Com., 1981-82; mem. dean's select adv. com. Coll. Engring., Ohio State U., 1984-94; mem. state exec. com. Calif. Libertarian Party, chmn. region 61, 1989-90, chmn. strategic planning com.; dep. chmn. Los Angeles County Libertarian Party, 1991-92; chairperson campaign issues com. Marrou for Pres., 1991-92; chmn. bd. trustees WWII Hist. Soc., 1992—; first v.p. Armed Forces Cmty. Rels. Coun. Ctrl. Ohio, 2001-04. Capt. USAF, 1958-60. Ford Found. fellow, 1961-64 Mem. Soc. Automotive Engrs., Harvard Bus. Sch. Assn., Ohio State Alumni Assn., Harvard Bus. Club Columbus (bd. dirs. 1998-2005, pres. 1996-98), Ohio State Alumni Club (pres. 1998-99), Harvard Club Ctrl. Ohio (bd. dirs.). *Personal philosophy: All out all the time. I stand for the creation of a new system of global governance which stresses individual liberty, freedom and responsibility, and which leads to a world that works for everyone with no one left out. In business, I stand for exceptional vision, creativity, innovation, and contribution.*

MYERS, PHILLIP WARD, retired otolaryngologist; b. Evanston, Ill., Nov. 11, 1939; s. R. Maurice and Vivian (Ward) M.; m. Lynetta Sargent, Dec. 22, 1963; children: Andrea, Ward, Alycia, Amanda, Andrew. BS, Western Ill. U., 1961; MD, U. Ill., 1965. Diplomate: Am. Bd. Otolaryngology. Intern St. Paul-Ramsey Hosp., 1965-66; resident in otolaryngology U. Louisville, 1966-68; resident Northwestern U., 1968-70, fellow, 1970-71; practice medicine specializing in otolaryngology Springfield, Ill., 1973—; clin. prof. otolaryngology So. Ill. U., Springfield, 1973—2002. Served to maj. M.C. AUS, 1971-73. Fellow Am. Soc. for Head and Neck Surgery, Am. Acad. Facial Plastic and Reconstructive Surgery; ACS, Am. Acad. Otolaryngology-Head and Neck Surgery. Achievements include research in perilymphatic fistulas. Home: 3423 N Oak Hill Rd Rochester IL 62563-9273

MYERS, R(ALPH) CHANDLER, lawyer; b. LA, Jan. 9, 1933; s. Ralph Cather and Winifred (Chandler) M.; m. Rebecca Blythe Borkgren, Jan. 11, 1963. BA, Stanford U., 1954, JD, 1958; LLD (hon.), Whittier Coll., 1988. Bar: Calif. 1959, U.S. Dist. Ct. (ctrl. dist.) Calif. 1959, U.S. Supreme Ct. 1971. Law clk., then assoc. Parker, Stanbury, Reese & McGee, LA, 1958-63; assoc. Nicholas, Kolliner & Van Tassel, LA, 1963-65; ptnr. Myers & D'Angelo and predecessors, L.A. and Pasadena, Calif., 1965—. Nat. panelist Am. Arbitration Assn., LA, 1964-2000; bd. visitors Stanford U. Law Sch., Calif., 1970-73; judge pro tem panel LA Mcpl. Ct., 1971-81; mem. LA County Dist. Atty.'s Adv. Coun., 1976-83. Nat. vice chmn. Keystone Gifts, Stanford Centennial Campaign, 1987—92; trustee Whittier Coll., Calif., 1973—2001, chmn. bd. trustees Calif., 1981—87, trustee emeritus Calif., 2001—; trustee Flintridge Prep. Sch., LaCanada-Flintridge, Calif., 1981—88, chmn. bd. trustees, 1985—88; co-founder Whittier Law Sch., 1975, trustee, 1975—2001, chmn. bd. trustees, 1981—87, trustee emeritus, 2001—; bd. dirs. Opera Guild So. Calif., LA, 1971—83, pres., 1980—82; bd. dirs. Guild Opera Co. L.A., 1974—83, pres., 1975—77; bd. dirs. Western Justice Ctr. Found., 1993—2008, pres., 2003—05, adv. coun., 2008—; bd. dirs. L.A. Child Guidance Clinic, 1972—83, pres., 1977—79; bd. dirs. Opera Assocs. of the Music Ctr., LA, 1976—78. Recipient Stanford Assocs. award, 1984, Centennial Medallion award, 1991, Gold Spike award Stanford U., 1989, Disting. Svc. award Whittier Law Sch., 1993, Outstanding Achievement award Stanford Assocs., 1998; named R. Chandler Myers Dean's Suite in his honor Whittier Law Sch., 1997; Master's Cir. honoree Flintridge Prep. Sch., 1989. Mem. Wilshire Bar Assn. (bd. govs. 1972-81, pres. 1979-80), LA County Bar Assn. (trustee 1979-81), Stanford Law Soc. So. Calif. (bd. dirs. 1967-72, pres. 1970-71), Stanford Assocs. (bd. govs. 1992-97, treas. 1995-97), Jonathan Club, Univ. Club (Pasadena), Stanford Club LA (bd. dirs. 1963-70, pres. 1968-69). Home: La Canada 5623 Burning Tree Dr La Canada Flintridge CA 91011-2861 Office: Myers & D'Angelo 301 N Lake Ave Ste 800 Pasadena CA 91101-4108 Home Phone: 818-790-0888; Office Phone: 626-792-0007.

MYERS, R(ALPH) THOMAS, chemist, educator; b. Maidsville, W.Va., Mar. 28, 1921; s. Harrison Lonzo and Martha Jane (Nuce) M.; m. Dorothy Kraus (div.); m. Evelyn Lightfoot (div.); children: Paul, Alice, Mary; m. Dorothy Van Wert, Mar. 22, 1986. AB in Chemistry, W.Va. U., 1941, PhD in Chemistry, 1949. Rsch. assoc. Manhattan Project Columbia U., NYC, 1944-45; assoc. prof. Waynesburg Coll., Waynesburg, Pa., 1948-51; asst. prof. chemistry Colo. Sch. Mines, Golden, 1951-56; prof. chemistry Kent (Ohio) State U., 1956-87, prof. emeritus, 1987—. Co-author: Holt Chemistry, 2006. Bd. edn., Kent, 1990-93, pres., 1993. Mem. AAAS, Am. Chem. Soc., Sigma Xi. Democrat. Unitarian-Universalist. Avocations: environment, skiing. Home: 4285 Kent Rd Apt 431 Stow OH 44224 Office: Kent State U Dept Chemistry Kent OH 44242-0001

MYERS, REX CHARLES, historian, educator, retired dean; b. Cleve., July 1, 1945; s. Charles F. and Merial W. (Jones) M.; m. Susan L. Richards, Jan. 10, 1987; children: Gary W., Laura M. BA, Western State Coll., 1967; MA, U. Mont., 1970, PhD, 1972; postgrad., U. Wash., 1983, Harvard U., 1990. Instr. Palo Verde Coll., Blythe, Calif., 1972-75; reference librarian Mont. Hist. Soc., Helena, 1975-78; prof., divsn. chmn., dean Western Mont. Coll., Dillon, 1979-86; dean S.D. State U., Brookings, 1986-91; acad. dean Lyndon State Coll., Lyndonville, Vt., 1991-95; lectr. Western State Coll., Gunnison, Colo., 1995-98, Mesa State Coll., 1998-99, Lawrence U., 1999—2005, Northwest Coll., Powell, Wyo., 2005—. Author: Montana Symbols, 1976, Montana Trolleys, 1970, Lizzie, 1989; co-author: Marble Colorado, 1970, Montana: Our Land and People, 1978, Montana and the West, 1984; contbr. articles to profl. jours. Bd. dirs. Ctr. for Western Studies, Sioux Falls, SD, 1990—, Gunnison Arts Ctr., Gunnison County Libr., Fox Valley Arts Alliance, Meml. Park Arboretum and Gardens, Park County Arts Coun. Summer stipend NEH, 1973; fellow James J. Hill Library, 1985. Mem.: AAUW, Mont. Oral History Assn. (chmn. 1980—83), Am. Conf. Acad. Deans, Western History Assn. (chmn. membership com. 1980—83), N.E. Kingdom C. of C. (bd. dirs.), Westerners (sheriff, Cody 2007), Kiwanis (pres. Dillon 1983, lt. gov. 1984, 1997, pres. Gunnison 1997, lt. gov. 2003, pres. Powell 2007), Masons (master 1984), Phi Alpha Theta, Phi Kappa Phi. Unitarian Universalist. Office: Nortwest Coll 231 W Sixth St Powell WY 82435 Home: PO Box 503 Powell WY 82435 Office Phone: 307-754-6172.

MYERS, RICHARD BOWMAN, former Chairman of the Joint Chiefs of Staff; b. Kansas City, Mo., Mar. 1, 1942; m. Mary Jo Rupp; 3 children. BSME, Kans. State U., 1965; MBA, Auburn U., 1977; Diploma, Air Command/Staff Coll., Maxwell AFB, Ala., 1977, U.S. Army War Coll., 1981; postgrad., Harvard U., 1991. Commd. 2d lt. USAF, 1965, advanced through ranks to gen., 1997, ret., 2005, dir. tactical weapons & command & control acquisition programs, 1991—93, comdr. U.S. Forces Japan & 5th Air Force Yokota AFB, Japan, 1993-96; asst. to the chmn. of the Joint Chiefs of Staff US Dept. Def., Washington, 1996-97; comdr. Pacific Air Forces, Hickam AFB, Hawaii, 1997-98; comdr.-in-chief N.Am. Aerospace Def. Comm./U.S. Space Command, Peterson AFB, Colo., 1998—2000; vice chmn. Joint Chiefs of Staff, US Dept. Def., Washington, 2000—01, chmn., 2001—05; prof. mil. history & leadership Kans. State. U., Manhattan, Kans., 2006—, Colin Powell Chair of Character, Leadership and Ethics at Nat. Defense U. Bd. dirs. Northrop Grumman Corp., 2006—, Deere & Co., 2006—, United Technologies Corp., 2006—, Aon Corp., 2006—, Air Force Assn., Folcon Found. Trustee, Excutive Com. Kans. State U. Found.; USO bd. dirs. Fisuer House Bd. of Trustees. Decorated Def. Disting. Svc. medal with three bronze oak leaf cluster, Disting. Svc. medal, Legion of Merit, Disting. Flying Cross with oak leaf cluster, Air Force, Army, Navy, Coast Guard, Meritorious Svc. medal with three oak leaf clusters, Air medal with 18 oak leaf clusters, Air Force Commendation medal, others; recipient: Presdl. Medal of Freedom, The White House, 2005, Harry S. Truman Good Neighbor award, The Harry S. Truman Good Neighbor Award Found., 2006 Office: Kans State U Dept History 208 Eisenhower Hall Manhattan KS 66506 Home Phone: 703-979-0154.*

MYERS, ROBERT, museum director; Exec. dir. Sangre de Cristo Arts and Conf. Ctr., Colo.; dir. Shanghai Theatre, 1988—93; mgr. Norris Theatre for Performing Arts, Rolling Hills Estates; cultural services dir. Torrance Cultural Arts Ctr.; pres. Mus. Latin Am. Art, Long Beach, Calif. Office: Mus Latin Am Art 628 Alamitos Ave Long Beach CA 90802 Business E-Mail: rmyers@molaa.org.

MYERS, ROBERT DAVID, judge; b. Springfield, Mass., Nov. 20, 1937; s. William and Pearl (Weiss) M.; m. Judith G. Dickenman, July 1, 1962; children: Mandy Susan, Jay Brandt, Seth William. AB, U. Mass., 1959; JD, Boston U., 1962. Bar: Ariz. 1963. Pvt. practice, Phoenix, 1963—89; judge Ariz. Superior Ct., 1989—2002; presiding judge civil dept. Superior Ct. Ariz. Maricopa County, Phoenix, 1991—92, presiding judge probate and mental health dept., 1992—95, presiding judge, 1995—2000; pro tem judge Ariz. Ct. Appeals, Phoenix; chief dep. Ariz. Atty. Gen., 2003—04; gen. counsel Ariz. Dept. Corrections, Phoenix, 2004—06; pvt. practice Law Firm Adelman German PLC, 2009—. Adj. prof. Ariz. State U. Sch. Law, 1997—, Phoenix Sch. Law, 2007-; chmn. com. on exams and admissions Ariz. Supreme Ct., 1974-75, chmn. com. on character and fitness, 1975-76, mem. multi-state bar exam. com., 1976-85; bd. dirs. Nat. Conf. Met. Judges, 1997—, pres., 1998-99. Pres. Valley of Sun chpt. City of Hope, 1965-66, Cmty. Orgn. for Drug Abuse Control, 1972-73, Valley Big Bros., 1975; chmn. Mayors Ad Hoc Com. on Drug Abuse, 1974-75; bd. dirs. Maricopa County Legal Aid Soc., 1978. Recipient award for outstanding svc. and dedication to improving the legal profession and professionalism of the bar and bench Maricopa County Bar Assn., 1999, Superior Svc. award Ariz. chpt. ASPA, 2000, Justice Tom C. Clark award Nat. Conf. Metro. Cts., 2000. Mem. ATLA (nat. chmn. gov.), Ariz. Bar Assn. (gov., com. chmn., sect. pres., Top 50 Pro Bono Atty's of Yr., 2008), Maricopa County Bar Assn. (dir., pres. 1979-80, Judge of yr., 1999, Henry S. Steven award 2000, Pro Bono Advocate of Yr., 2008), Ariz. Trial Lawyers Assn. (pres., dir., co-editor newsletter), Phoenix Trial Lawyers Assn. (pres., dir.), Western Trial Lawyers Assn. (pres. 1977), Am. Judicature Soc. (spl. merit citation outstanding svc. improvement of adminstrn. justice 1986), Am. Bd. Trial Advocates (Phoenix chpt. Judicial Officer of Yr. award 2001), Sandra Day O'Connor Inn of Ct. (pres. 1991-92), Thurgood Marshall Inn Ct, Ariz. Assn. Justice(Lifetime Advocate Civil Justice award, 2009). Office Phone: 602-980-0848. Personal E-mail: bojudy62@cox.net.

MYERS, ROBERT EUGENE, writer, educator; b. LA, Jan. 15, 1924; s. Harold Eugene and Margaret (Anawalt) M.; m. Joyce E. Daily, 1946 (div. 1949); 1 child, Kathleen; m. Patricia A. Tazer, Aug. 17, 1956; children: Edward E., Margaret A., Hal R., Karen I. AB, U. Calif., Berkeley, 1955; MA (Crown-Zellerbach fellow), Reed Coll., 1960; EdD, U. Ga., 1968. Employed in phonograph record bus., 1946-54; tchr. elem. sch. Calif., Oreg., Minn., 1954-61; rsch. asst. U. Minn., 1961-62; asst. prof. Augsburg Coll., 1962-63, U. Oreg., 1963-66; elem. tchr. Eugene, Oreg., 1966-67; assoc. prof. U. Victoria, 1968-70; assoc. rsch. prof. Oreg. System of Higher Edn., 1970-73; film maker, producer ednl. films, filmstrips, books, recs., 1973-77; learning resources specialist Oreg. Dept. Edn., Salem, 1977-81; with Linn-Benton Edn. Svc. Dist., Albany, Oreg., 1982-87; ret., 1987. Author: (with E. Paul Torrance) Creative

Learning and Teaching (Pi Lambda Theta award 1971), 1970, La Ensenanza Creativa, 1970, Can You Imagine?, 1965, Invitations to Thinking and Doing, 1964, Invitations to Speaking and Writing Creatively, 1965, Plots, Puzzles, and Ploys, 1966, For Those Who Wonder, 1966, Stretch, 1968, Timberwood Tales, Vol. II, 1977, Wondering, 1984, Imagining, 1985, What Next?, 1994, Facing the Issues, 1995, Cognitive Connections, 1996, Mind Sparklers, 1997, Multiple Ways of Thinking with Social Studies, 1997, Character Matters, 1999, It's Your Attitude That Counts, 2000, Mind Stretchers, 2001, Stories That Build Character, 2001, Think and Write, 2002, Now What, 2002, Spurs to Creative Thinking, 2002, Word Play, 2002, Developing Creative Thinking Skills, 2003, Learning from Nature, 2005, Exploring Character, 2005, Respect Matters, 2005 (Tchr's. Choice award 2006), Language FUNdamentals Books 1 and 2, 2005, Lively Language 1 and 2, 2005, Motivational Writing Lessons, 2005, Lessons in Writing, 2006, Writing a Persuasive Essay, 2006, Time to Write, 2006, Writing a Personal Essay, 2008, Figures of Speech, 2008; films: Feather (CINE Golden Eagle award), 1972, The Magic Net, 1972, Elephants, 1973, (book) Golden Quills, 2008. Exec. bd. Nat. Assn. Gifted Children, 1974-77. With U.S. Mcht. Marine, 1944-45. Recipient CINE Golden Eagle award Coun. Internat. Non-theatrical Events, 1973. Democrat. Home: 1357 Meadow Ct Healdsburg CA 95448-3347

MYERS, ROBERT J., retail executive; Sr. v.p. Casey's General Stores, Ankeny, Iowa, 1998—2002, pres., COO, 2002—06, pres., CEO, 2006—. Office: Casey's General Stores 1 Convenience Blvd Ankeny IA 50021

MYERS, ROBERT JAY, retired aerospace executive; b. Bklyn., Oct. 15, 1934; s. John J. and Clara S. (Martinsen) M.; m. Carolyn Erland, Aug. 10, 1963; children: Susan, Kenneth. BCE, NYU, 1955, postgrad., 1957-65; P.MD, Harvard U., 1972. With Grumman Corp., Bethpage, NY, 1964-94, v.p. resources, 1980-83, sr. v.p. bus. and resource mgmt., 1983-85, sr. v.p. corp. svcs., 1985-86; pres. Grumman Data Systems Corp., Bethpage, 1986-90; pres., chief operating officer, bd. dirs. Grumman Corp., 1991-94, ret., 1994. Sci. adv. coun. Ala. Space and Rocket Ctr., 1986-91. Adv. panel on econ. devel. N.Y. State Project 2000, 1985-86; mem. L.I. Project 2000; adv. bd. L.I. Youth Guidance, 1986-91; bd. dirs. Poly. U., 1991-98, North Shore Health System, 1994—, L.I. Mus. of Sci. and Tech., 1994-96; chmn. Huntington Hosp., 1996—2000. 1st lt. U.S. Army, 1955-57. Fellow Poly. U., 1987, Disting. Alumni award, 1989. Mem. Am. Def. Preparedness Assn. (dir. 1992-94), Navy League, Industry Exec. Bd., Nat. Space Club (bd. govs. 1986-89), Huntington Country Club (N.Y.), Audubon Country Club (Naples, Fla.). Presbyterian. Home: 200 Cheshire Way Naples FL 34110 Personal E-mail: rjm34@aol.com.

MYERS, ROBERT K., III, director, musician, composer; b. Fredericksburg, Va., Aug. 20, 1941; s. Robert K. Jr. and Ruby King Myers; m. Barbara Jo Bishop, May 18, 1977; children: Stephanie Conway, Amy Grammer. MusB, Eastman Sch. of Music, Rochester, NY, 1963; MusM, Eastman Sch. of Music, 1964; MusD, Northwestern U., 1985. Chmn. music dept. Saginaw Valley State Coll., University Center, Mich., 1967—74; head music program Grant MacEwan Coll., Edmonton, Alta., Canada, 1974—83; assoc. v.p. instl. assessment Berklee Coll. Music, Boston, 1985—. Composer-in-residence Midland (Mich.) Pub. Schs., 1967—69; vis. composer Northwestern U., Evanston, Ill., 1986; accreditation visitor/evaluator New Eng. Assn. Schs. and Colls., Bedford, Mass., 1987—2003. Composer: Enigma Virginia (1st prize Percussive Arts Soc., 1985). Fulbright Study grantee, US Govt./French Govt., 1965—67, Composer-in-Residence grantee, Ford Found., 1967—69. Mem.: Internat. Assn. Jazz Educators (nat. curriculum facilitator), New Eng. Ednl. Assessment Network (v.p. 2000—04). Office: Berklee Coll Music 1140 Boylston St MS-899 OP Boston MA 02215

MYERS, ROBERT MANSON, language educator, writer; b. Charlottesville, Va., May 29, 1921; s. Horwood Prettyman and Matilda Manson (Wynn) M. BA summa cum laude, Vanderbilt U., 1941; MA, Columbia, 1942, Harvard, 1943; PhD, Columbia, 1948. Instr. English Yale, 1945-47; asst. prof. Coll. William and Mary, 1947-48, Tulane U., 1948-54; tchr. English Brearley Sch., NYC, 1954-56; chmn. dept. English Osbourn High Sch., Manassas, Va., 1956-59; mem. faculty U. Md., College Park, 1959—, prof. English, 1968-86, prof. emeritus, 1986—. Author: Handel's Messiah, 1948, From Beowulf to Virginia Woolf, 1952, rev., 1984, Handel, Dryden, and Milton, 1956, Restoration Comedy, 1961, The Children of Pride, 1972, abridged edit., 1984 (Carey-Thomas award 1972, Nat. Book award 1973), A Georgian at Princeton, 1976, Quintet: Five Plays, 1991, Sixes and Sevens: Three Plays, 2004, The Bostonians: A Play, 2005, Poynton Park: A Play, 2005, Ars Amatoria: An Anthology, 2009. Mem. bd. visitors Winthrop U. Fulbright Postdoctoral Research fellow U. London, 1953-54; Fulbright lectr. Rotterdam, Netherlands, 1958-59; recipient Medal of Honor in Arts Winthrop U., 2003. Mem. Modern Lang. Assn. Am., Am. Soc. 18th Century Studies, Jane Austen Soc. N.Am., Phi Beta Kappa. Home: 3804 Deckford Pl Charlotte NC 28211-3408

MYERS, ROBERTA A. (ROBBIE MYERS), editor-in-chief; b. Oct. 11, 1959; m. Frank Michielli; children: Francesca, Michael. BA, Colo. State U., 1982. Editl. asst. Rolling Stone Wenner Media LLC, 1982; mng. editor Seventeen mag. Hearst Corp.; sr. editor In Style Time Inc.; editor-in-chief Tell mag. Hachette Filipacchi Media Inc., 1993—95, sr. articles editor ELLE mag., 1995—97, editor-in-chief Mirabella mag. NYC, 1997—2000, editor-in-chief ELLE, 2000—. Mem.: Am. Soc. Mag. Editors (v.p. 2007—). Office: Elle 1633 Broadway 44th Fl New York NY 10019 Office Phone: 212-767-5800.*

MYERS, ROLLAND GRAHAM, investment counselor; Diploma, St. Louis Country Day Sch., 1963; AB cum laude in History and Lit., Harvard U., 1966; postgrad. Faculties of Social Scis. and Law, U. Edinburgh, Scotland, 1966-67; postgrad. Fondation Nationale des Sciences Politiques and Faculte de Lettres et des Sciences Humaines, U. Paris, 1967-68. Trainee global credit dept. Case Manhattan Bank, NYC, 1968—69; mem. 32nd spl. devel. program J.P. Morgan Chase & Co., 1969, strategic planner internat. dept., 1969—70, securities analyst, mktg. rep., fiduciary investment dept., 1970; assoc. Smith, Barney & Co., Inc., NYC, 1971, account exec. N.Y. sales dept., 1971-72, instl. account exec. N.Y. internat. sales dept., 1972-74, 2nd v.p., stockholder, 1975-76; v.p., stockholder Smith Barney, Harris Upham & Co., Inc. (subs. SBHU Holdings, Inc.), NYC, 1976-78; prin. W.H. Graham & Sons, family investment office, 1977-82, investment counsel, 1982—. Ltd. ptnr. Croke Patterson Campbell, Ltd., Denver, 1975—; pres., chmn. exec. com., bd. dirs. Fifty-Five Residents Corp., N.Y.C., 1980-84; bd. dirs. Fifty-Six Danbury Rd. Assn., Inc., New Milford, Conn. Trustee, mem. corp. Bishop Rhinelander Found. (Episcopal Chaplaincy at Harvard and Radcliffe Colls.), Cambridge, 1973-75; v.p., treas., bd. dirs. The Whitehill Graham Found., St. Louis, 1976—; bd. dirs., fin. com., bylaws com., mem. corp. Eliot Pratt Edn. Ctr., Inc. (The Pratt Ctr.: Your Connection with the Natural World), New Milford, 1987-94; mem. corp. Kent (Conn.) Land Trust, Inc., 1989—, treas., 1989-93, bd. dirs., 1989-2003, adv. bd., 2003-; project financier Restoration of 1851 Samuel Curtiss Hosford House, Nat. Register Historic Dist., Falls Village, Conn., 1984-86; commr. Housatonic River Commn., Warren, Conn., 1985-93, vice chmn., 1986-87, chmn., 1988-92; commr. Conservation, Inland Wetlands and Watercourses Commn., Kent, 1988-93, vice chmn., 1988-92; mem. schs. and scholarships com., Office of Admissions and Fin. Aid, Harvard and Radcliffe Colls., 1991—. Mem. Cum Laude Soc., Mary Inst. and St. Louis Country Day Sch. Alumni Assn., Harvard Alumni Assn., Capitol Hill Club (Washington), Harvard Club (N.Y.C.), Hasty Pudding-Inst. of 1770 (Cambridge), Wyo. Bus. Alliance, Wyo. Heritage Found., St. Andrew's Soc., New Eng. Soc. in City N.Y., St. George's Soc. N.Y. Republican. Episcopalian. Office: W H Graham & Sons Investment Counsel 1818 Evans Ave Ste 207 Cheyenne WY 82001-4664

MYERS, SOPHIA M., writer, researcher, artist, cartographer, translator; b. Coffeyville, Kans., Oct. 25, 1928; d. Anastasios M. and Georgia A. Mardikes; m. Ralph E. Myers, Dec. 24, 1980 (dec. Oct. 5, 2006); children: George A. Vedros, Nicholas M. Vedros. Degree, Mt. St. Scholastica, 1948. Cert. tchg. Avila Coll., 1949. Tchr. elem art several Grade Schs., 1949—54; advt. mgr., artist, writer Cavanaugh Cattle Co., 1955—59, Weldwheels, 1960—64; advt. mgr. Oppenheimer Industries, 1965—71; advt. mgr., ops. mgr. The Nat. Secs. Assn., Internat., Kansas City, Mo., 1972—80; pvt. practice, 1980—. Red Herring, Potpourri; poems featured Sunday Kansas City Star; contbr. poetry, short stories, essays and articles publ. in numerous mags., anthologies and newspapers. Recipient 1st Pl. free verse award, Springfield Writers Guild, 2002, The Vicki Millikin Bright award best poem, 2003, 2004, Winner two nat. contests; named to Women's Found. Greater Kansas City, 2005. Mem.: Ptnrs. in Crime, Sisters in Crime, Okla. Writers' Fedn., Inc., The Writers' Cir., Warrensburg Writers Cir., Kans. City Press Club, Soc. Profl. Journalists, Kans. City Writers' Group, Okla. Writer's Federation, Inc., Mo. Poetry Soc., Mo. Writers Guild (1st Pl. free verse, 1st Pl. Best Lit. Poem award), Nat. League Am. Pen Women: Arts and Letters (pres. Kansas City br., 1st Pl. best poem Best Free Verse award). Avocations: painting, sculpting. Personal E-mail: smyers@kc.rr.com.

MYERS, STEPHEN, preventive medicine physician; b. Sept. 18, 1947; BS, Tulane U., 1969; DO, Phila. Coll. Osteo. Medicine, 1973. Attending physician Michael Reese Hosp., Chgo., 1981—85; dir. maternal fetal medicine Mt. Sinai Hosp., Chgo., Idaho, 1985—96, asst. chmn., 1990—97; dir. maternal fetal medicine Ill. Regional Perinatal Group, St. Joseph Hosp., Elgin, 1997—2000; assoc. prof. U. Kans. Med. Ctr., 2000—06, med. dir. obstetrics, 2001—03, clerkship dir., 2002—05; attending physican to dir. fetal diagnostic ctr. MetroHealth Med. Ctr., Cleve., 2006—. Recipient Disting. Svc. award, Mt. Sinai Med. Ctr., 1993, Nat. Faculty award, Coun. Resident Edn. Ob-gyn., 1995, 2003, 2006. Mem.: Soc. Maternal Fetal Medicine. Office: MetroHealth Med Ctr 2500 MetroHealth Dr Cleveland OH 44109

MYERS, VIRGINIA ANNE, art educator; b. Greencastle, Ind., May 8, 1927; d. Everett Clark Myers and Hurst (McKann) Bessie. BA in Fine Arts, George Washington U., Corcoran Sch. Art, 1949; MFA in Drawing and Painting, Calif. Coll. of Arts & Crafts, Oakland, 1951; postgrad. in print making, U. Ill., 1953—55, U. Iowa, Iowa City, 1955—61; studied with Stanley William Hayter, Paris, 1961—62. Rsch. asst. Sch. Art and Art History U. Iowa, Iowa City, 1958-61; instr. arts and crafts, phys. edn. Tucson Indian Tng. Sch., 1949-50; teaching asst. dept. art and architecture U. Ill., Champaign-Urbana, 1954-55; instr. printmaking U. Iowa, Iowa City, 1962-69, asst. prof. printmaking, 1969-74, assoc. prof., 1974-82, prof., 1982—. Bd. dirs. Elizabeth Found. for Arts, NY, 1994-2008, treas. 1994-2005; pres. Iowa Foil Printer Corp., 1986-2009. Author: (manual) Creating Original Prints with Hot-Stamped foil, 1993, (hardbound) Foil Imaging...A New Art Form, 2001, Foil Imaging: The Original Editioned Prints, 2006, (limited edit.), 2006; A Time of Malfeasance (21 engravings and drypoints), 1976, The Views from Tenacre: The Seasons (66 paintings and drawings), 1979, Landscape in Iowa (36 paintings, prints and drawings), 1986, The Ghost Elm and Other Views from Tenacre, 2006, one-woman shows include 36 prints and drawings State St. Gallery, Chgo., 2009; contbr. articles to profl. jours. Fulbright fellow, Paris, 1961-62; grantee U. Iowa, 1973, 78, 84, 89, 93, 98-99, Iowa Arts Coun., 1974-77, 80, 85, Stanley Found., 1984-88, Thorson Found., 1984, 86, Arts and Humanities Initiative, 2005, 06; elected to Iowa Women's Archives, U. Iowa, 1999; The Virginia A. Myers Print Study Room at U. Iowa Mus. Art named in her honor, 2006; recipient Excellence in Tchg. Printmaking award, Southern Graphics Coun., 2009. Mem. Foil Stamping and Embossing Assn. (charter), Nat. Mus. of Women in Arts (charter). Achievements include patents for iowa foil printer, 1992, 2009; underwriters laboratories listing, 1997. Avocations: gardening, reading, swimming. Home: Tenacre Print 4244 210th St NE Solon IA 52333-9657 Office: Univ Iowa Sch Arts & Art History Iowa City IA 52242 Office Phone: 319-644-2763. Business E-Mail: virginia-myers@uiowa.edu.

MYERSON, JACOB MYER, retired diplomat; b. Rock Hill, SC, June 11, 1926; s. Solomon and Lena (Clein) Myerson; m. Nicole Neuray, June 10, 1965 (dec. Oct. 1968); 1 child, Sylvie Anne; m. Helen Hayashi, Mar. 9, 1974 (dec. Jan. 1995). Student, Pa. State Coll., 1944; BA with distinction, George Washington U., 1949, MA, 1950; grad., Fgn. Service Inst., 1953. Joined U.S. Fgn. Svc., 1950; 3d sec. Office U.S. High Commr. Germany, Berlin, 1950-52; 2d sec. U.S. Mission to NATO and European Regional Orgn., Paris, 1953-55; also mem. U.S. permanent del. to coordinating com. InterGovtl. Consultative Group on EastWest Trade; internat. economist, internat. rels. officer State Dept., 1956-60, spl. asst. to under sec. state, 1965-66; adviser U.S. del. GATT session, Geneva, 1958; ministerial session OEEC, Paris, 1958; 1st sec., chief polit. sect. U.S. Mission to European Communities, Brussels, 1960-65; officer-in-charge NATO Polit. Affairs, Dept. State, 1966-68; adviser U.S. delegation ministerial sessions North Atlantic Council, 1966-67; dep. polit. adviser, counselor U.S. Mission to NATO, Brussels, 1968-70; counselor econ. affairs U.S. Mission to European Communities, Brussels, 1970-74, minister counselor, from 1974; U.S. rep. to UN Econ. and Social Council with rank of ambassador, 1975-77; alt. U.S. del. UN Gen. Assembly, 1975—76; alt. U.S. rep. UN Conf. on Trade and Devel., 1976; minister-counselor econ. and comml. affairs Am. Embassy, Paris, 1977-80; ret., 1980; dep. sec. gen. OECD, Paris, 1980-88. With US Army, 1944—46, ETO. Decorated Bronze Star, Order of the Sacred treasure Gold and Silver medal Japan; recipient Meritorious Svc. award, State Dept., 1960. Mem.: Am. Fgn. Svc. Assn. (Rivkin award 1969), Artus, Phi Beta Kappa, Phi Eta Sigma, Pi Gamma Mu. Address: 2 rue Lucien Gaulard 75018 Paris France

MYERSON, JAY BARRY, lawyer; b. NYC; s. Martin and Sylvia Waldner Myerson; m. Barbara J. Myerson, June 17, 1973; children: Joshua, Jennifer M.R. Hurwitz, Matthew. BA cum laude, Georgetown U., Washington, 1973, JD, 1976. Bar: US Ct. Appeals (DC cir.) 1977, US Dist. Ct. DC 1977, DC 1977, US Ct. Appeals (fed. cir.) 1983, US Supreme Ct. 1985, Va. 1986, US Dist. Ct. Va. (ea. dist.) 1986, US Ct. Appeals (4th cir.) 1987, US Ct. Appeals (1st cir.) 1990. Assoc. Gerald M. Feder Law Offices, Washington, 1976—78; litigation, enforcement atty. Fed. Election Commn., Washington, 1978—80; assoc. mem. Israel and Raley, Chartered, Washington, 1980—86; pvt. practice Reston, Va., 1986—. Treas. Com. for Progressive Congress, 1994—; mem. Fairfax County Environ. Quality Adv. Coun., Va., 1987—92, vice chmn. Va., 1988—89, chmn. Va., 1989—91; coach, mgr. youth baseball, 1987—96; alumni interviewer alumni admissions program Georgetown U., 1989—2004; counsel to treas. Dem. Nat. Com., 1982—86, asst. gen. counsel, 1985—86, mem. nat. lawyers coun., 1998—; gen. counsel Dem. Party Va., 1997—99, 2004—; mem. youth orgn. adult bd. B'nai B'rith, 1992—2002, chmn. No. Va. coun. adult bd., 1999—2002; bd. dirs. Congregation Beth Emeth, 1985—94, v.p., 1986—88, pres., 1988—90, trustee, 1998—2000. Master: George Mason Inn of Ct. (treas. 2002—06, pres.-elect 2006—08, pres. 2007—08); mem.: ABA (vice chmn. Com. on Election Law Sect. Adminstrv. Law and Regulatory Pr 1994—95, liaison Standing Com. on Election Law 1997—2000, co-chmn. Com. on Election Law 1997—2000), Nat. Lawyers Assn., Va. Assn. Dem. Campaign Counsel, Va. Trial Lawyers Assn., Va. Bar Assn., Fairfax Bar Assn. (mem. Gen. Dist. Ct. Com. 1990—97, mem. lawyer referral svc. com. 1993—97, co-chmn. Conciliation Program Fairfax County Cts. 2001—02, chmn. Conciliation Task Force Fairfax County Cts. 2002—07, bd. dirs. 2004—, Pres.' award 2005). Jewish. Avocations: baseball, politics, community service, gardening. Office: 11860 Sunrise Valley Dr Reston VA 20191

MYERSON, ROBERT J., radiologist, educator; b. Boston, May 12, 1947; s. Richard Louis and Rosemarie M.; m. Carla Wheatley, Aug. 8, 1970; 1 child, Jacob Wheatley. BA, Princeton U., 1969; PhD, U. Calif., Berkeley, 1974; MD, U. Miami, 1980. Diplomate Am. Bd. Radiology. Asst. prof. dept. physics Pa. State U., State Coll., 1974-76; fellow Inst. Advanced Studies, Princeton, NJ, 1976-78; resident U. Pa. Hosp., Phila., 1981-84; assoc. prof. radiology Washington U. Sch. Medicine, St. Louis, 1984-97; prof. radiation oncology Wash. U. Sch. Medicine, St. Louis, 1997—. Contbr. articles to profl. jours. Recipient Career Devel. award Am. Cancer Soc., 1985. Fellow Am. Coll. Radiology; mem. Am. Coll. Radiation, Am. Soc. Therapeutic Radiologists, Am. Phys. Soc. Democrat. Jewish. Avocation: bicycling. Office: Washington U Radiation Oncology Ctr Box 8224 4921 Parkview Pl Saint Louis MO 63110-1001 Office Phone: 314-362-8516. Business E-Mail: myerson@radonc.wustl.edu.

MYERSON, ROGER BRUCE, economist, educator; b. Boston, Mar. 29, 1951; s. Richard L. and Rosemarie (Farkas) M.; m. Regina M. Weber, Aug. 29, 1982; children: Daniel, Rebecca. AB summa cum laude, Harvard U., 1973, SM in Applied Math., 1973, PhD in Applied Math., 1976; D (hon.), U. Basel, Switzerland, 2002. Asst. prof. managerial econs. and decision scis. Northwestern U., Evanston, Ill., 1976-78, assoc. prof., 1979-82, prof., 1982-2001, Harold Stuart prof. decision scis., 1986-2001, prof. econs., 1987-2001; W.C. Norby prof. economics U. Chgo., 2001—, Glen A. Lloyd Disting. Svc. Prof., 2007—. Guest researcher U. Bielefeld, Federal Republic of Germany, 1978-79; vis. prof. econs. U. Chgo., 1985-86, 2000-01. Author: Game Theory: Analysis of Conflict, 1991, Probability Models for Economic Decisions, 2005; creater: (software) Formlist.xla, Simtools.xla; mem. editorial bd. Internat. Jour. Game Theory, 1982-92, Games and Econ. Behavior, 1989-97; assoc. editor Jour. Econ. Theory, 1983-93; also articles. Guggenheim fellow, 1983-84; Sloan rsch. fellow, 1984-86; co-recipient Nobel Memorial Prize in Econ. Scis., 2007. Fellow Econometric Soc. (coun. mem. 1996-2002, 2005-, v.p. 2007-08, pres. 2009), Am. Acad. Arts and Scis. (Midwest Coun. mem. 1995-2002, dir. Midwest Ctr. and v.p. 1999-2002). Office: U Chgo Dept Econs 1126 E 59th St Chicago IL 60637 Business E-Mail: myerson@uchicago.edu.

MYERSON, TERRY, computer software company executive; BS in Mech. Engring., Duke U., Durham, NC, 1991. Founder, pres., CEO Intersé Corp. (acquired by Microsoft Corp.), 1994—97; joined Microsoft Corp., Redmond, Wash., 1997, corp. v.p. Exch. team, 2001—09, corp. v.p. Windows Mobile, 2009—. Office: Microsoft Corp One Microsoft Way Redmond WA 98052-6399*

MYERSON, TOBY SALTER, lawyer; b. Chgo., July 20, 1949; s. Raymond King and Natalie Anita (Salter) M. BA, Yale U., 1971; JD, Harvard U., 1975. Bar: N.Y. 1977, Calif. 1977. Assoc. Coudert Bros., NYC, 1975-77, 81, San Francisco, 1977-81, Paul, Weiss, Rifkind, Wharton & Garrison, NYC, 1981-83, ptnr., 1983-89; mng. dir. Wasserstein Perella & Co., Inc., NYC, 1989-90; ptnr. Paul, Weiss, Rifkind, Wharton & Garrison, NYC, 1990—, co-chair, Corp. Dept. Lectr. U. Calif. Berkeley, 1979-81, Harvard U., Cambridge, Mass., 1982-83; visiting lectr. Yale U., New Haven, 1983-84; bd. dirs. Myerson, Van Den Berg & Co., Santa Barbara, Calif. Contbg. editor: Doing Business in Japan, 1983, Council on Foreign Rels., 1993—, Foreign Policy Assn., 1995—. Sec. Japan Soc., Inc., N.Y.C., 1985-89; bd. dirs. 1056 Fifth Ave. Corp., N.Y.C., 1985-88; mem. univ. resources com. Harvard U., 1997—. Mem. ABA (subcom. internat. banking, corp. and bus. law sect.), Internat. Bar Assn., N.Y. State Bar Assn., Assn. Bar City N.Y. (com. on fgn. and comparative law, chmn. 1988-89), Calif. Bar Assn. Avocations: art, music, literature, tennis, golf. Home: 1056 5th Ave New York NY 10028-0112 Office: Paul Weiss Rifkind Wharton & Garrison 1285 Ave of the Americas New York NY 10019-6065 Fax: 212-373-2753. E-mail: tmyerson@paulweiss.com.

MYHAND, CHERYL, minister, educator; d. Jack and Ora Williams; children: Anjela, Patrick, Bernadette, Nikita, Kenyana. DD (hon.), Solomon's Temple U. World, LA, 1980; BA in Theology, New Life Theological Sem., Orangeburg, SC, 2006, MA in Theology, 2007. Lic. pastor United Meth. Ch., Mich., 1990; cert. prevention specialist Detroit Pub. Schs., 2000. Pres. Myhand and Assocs. Pub. Rels. Co., Detroit, 1977—89; site coord. Detroit Coun. Arts, 1987—89; pastor N. Detroit United Meth. Ch., 1990—94; adminstr., non-profit sector Inner City Sub. Ctr., Detroit, 1989—2001; prevention specialist Detroit Pub. Schs., 2000—; pastor John Wesley United Meth. Ch., River Rouge, Mich., 2000—06; founder Wish Ministries, Inc., sr. pastor. Youth commr. Detroit City Coun., 1987—90; mem. bioethics com. Aurora Youth and Adolescent Hosp., Detroit, 1994—99; interim pastor St. James United Meth. Ch., Westland, Mich., 1999—2000; mem. exec. team Faith Base Initiative, Wayne County, Detroit, 2000—02; mem. bd. global ministries United Meth. Detroit Ann. Conf., 2000—. Prodr.: (plays) What You Believe You Can Achieve - The Ron Milner; prodn. asst. (films) One In A Million - The Ron LeFleur Story, 1980, assoc. prodr. (albums) Lord We Need A Miracle, 1983, prodn. asst. (TV films) United Negro College Fund - Lou Rawls Telethon, mng. editor Detroit Life Magazine, assoc. editor-writer (newspaper) For My People; contbg. editor: Tribe Mag. Goodwill amb. Sarvodaya Shramadana Movement Sri Lanka, 2004; planning com. Gov. Jennifer Granholm Inaugural, Detroit, 2002—03, Mayor Dennis Archer Inaugural, Detroit, 1994, 1998; transition team Mayor Kilpartick, Detroit, 2000; apptd. bishop-elect World Pentecostal Fellowship Ministers, Inc.; chmn., bd. dirs. Hunger Action Coalition, Detroit, 1994—; bd. dirs. Detroit Empowerment Zone Devel. Corp., 1998—; cmty. adv. panel Pub. TV-56, Detroit, 1999; chmn., bd. dirs. In The Light, 2005—. Recipient Disting. Citizen award, Detroit City Clerk's Office, 1981, Cmty. Leader award, Wayne County C.C., 1992, Outstanding Cmty. Leadership and Spirit of Detroit award, Mayor City of Detroit, 1994, Outstanding Clergy Leadership, Wayne County Commn., 1997, Crescent award - Outstanding Spiritual Leadership, Nation of Islam, 1998, Proclamation for Outstanding Leadership, United

State Congl., 2000, Outstanding Leadership award, Detroit 300 Com., 2001, Outstanding Svc. award, Wayne County Commn. and NAACP, 2002, Peace award, Denby H.S., Detroit, 2003; fellow, Eureka Communities, 1994, Golden Inst. for Internat. Partnership and Peace, 2002. Mem.: NAACP (life Human Svc. award 2002), Inkster Ministerial Alliance (polit. action chairperson 1999). Democrat. Methodist. Avocations: travel, writing, reading, collecting dolls. Home: 19685 Eastland Village Dr Apt 4 Harper Woods MI 48225-1570 Personal E-mail: bishopcmyhand@yahoo.com.

MYHRE, JANET, statistician, educator, consultant; b. Tacoma, Wash., Sept. 24, 1932; d. Leif Christian Klippen, Thelma Gladys Klippen; m. Philip Cushman Myhre, June 12, 1954 (div. Dec. 1984); 1 child, Karin Elizabeth; m. Leon Hollerman, May 29, 1988; 1 child, Jeremy Hollerman. BA summa cum laude, Pacific Luth. U., 1954; MA, U. Wash., 1956; PhD in Math. Stats, U. Stockholm, 1968. Prof. math. Claremont McKenna Coll., Claremont, Calif., 1962—2008. Vis. prof. U. Stockholm, 1971—72, Swiss Fed. Inst. Tech., Zurich, 1971—72, Wash. State U., Pullman, 1978; prof. math. Claremont Grad. U., 1968—; founder, pres. Math. Analysis Rsch. Corp., Claremont, 1973—; dir. Reed Inst. for Decision Sci. Claremont McKenna Coll., Claremont, 1975—2008; cons. Strategic Sys. Programs USN, Washington, 1968—; cons. EPA, Washington, 1976—77. Contbr. chpts. in books, articles to profl. jours. Bd. trustees mem. The Webb Schs., Claremont, 1984—88; officer Padua Hills Homeowners Assn., Claremont, 1988—94; mem. numerous blue ribbon com. USN involving reliability, nuclear safety and risk assessment, 1972—. Recipient Austin Bonis award, Am. Soc. Quality Control, 1984, hon. alumna, Claremont McKenna Coll., 1996; Rsch. grant, Office Naval Rsch., 1973—83. Fellow: Am. Statis. Assn. (assoc. editor Technometrics 1969—75, coun. rep. 2001—03, pres. So. Calif. chpt. 2003—05); mem.: Claremont Mus. Art (bd. trustees 2007—), Padua Hills Mus. Com., Phi Beta Kappa (pres. CMC chpt. 2004—07). Achievements include development of models/statistical theory used since 1972 by USN Ballistic Missile Program for reliability assessments; software/theory used by Fleet Ballistic Missile Program since 1990 for safety and risk assessment. Avocations: gardening, cooking, hiking, weaving. Office: Math Analysis Rsch Corp 4239 Via Padova Claremont CA 91711 Office Phone: 909-624-5298. Personal E-mail: MARCmath@aol.com.

MYHREN, TRYGVE EDWARD, communications company executive; b. Palmerton, Pa., Jan. 3, 1937; s. Arne Johannes and Anita (Blatz) M.; m. Carol Jane Enman, Aug. 8, 1964; children: Erik, Kirsten, Tor; m. 2d Victoria Hamilton, Nov. 14, 1981; 1 stepchild, Paige. BA in Philosophy and Polit. Sci., Dartmouth Coll., 1958, MBA, 1959. Sales mgr., unit mgr. Procter and Gamble, Cin., 1963-65; sr. cons. Glendinning Cos., Westport, Conn., 1965-69; pres. Auberge Vintners, 1970-73; exec. v.p. Mktg. Continental, Westport, 1969-73; v.p., gen. mgr. CRM, Inc., Del Mar, Calif., 1973-75; from v.p. mktg. to pres. Am. TV and Comm. Corp., Englewood, Colo., 1975-80, chmn. bd., CEO, 1981-88; pres. Myhren Media Inc., Denver, 1989—. V.p., then exec. v.p. Time Inc., N.Y.C., 1981-88; mem. exec. com., treas., vice chmn., then chmn. bd. dirs. Nat. Cable TV Assn., Washington, 1982-91; mem. adv. com. on HDTV, FCC, 1987-89, pres. Providence Jour. Co.; bd. dirs. Advanced Mktg. Svcs., Inc., La Jolla, Calif.; Dreyfus Founders Funds, Inc., J. D. Edwards, Inc., Verio, Inc., Nat. Cable TV Ctr., Denver, Cable Labs, Inc., Boulder, Colo., Peapod, Inc., Skokie, Ill.; pres. Myhren Media, 1989—; pres., CEO King Broadcast Co., 1991-96. Mem. Colo. Forum, 1984—, chmn. higher edn. com., 1986; bd. dirs., co-founder Colo. Bus. Com. for the Arts, 1985-91; mem. exec. coun. Found. for Commemoration U.S. Constn., 1987-90; mem. Nat. GED Task Force, 1987-90, Colo. Baseball Commn., 1989-91, Colo. Film Commn., 1989-91; trustee Nat. Jewish Hosp., 1989— (Humanitarian award 1996), R.I. Hosp., 1991-95, Lifespan Health Sys., 1994-97, U.S. Ski and Snowboard Team Found., 1998—; chmn. Local Organizing Commn. 1995 NCAA Hockey Championship; trustee, exec. com., chmn. fin. com. U. Denver, 1997—. Lt. (j.g.) USNR, 1959-63. Recipient Disting. Leader award Nat. Cable TV Assn., 1988. Mem. Cable TV Adminstrn. and Mktg. Soc. (pres. 1978-79, Grand Tam award 1985, One of A Kind award 1994), Cable Adv. Bur. (co-founder 1978), Cable TV Pioneers. Episcopalian. Address: Myhren Media Inc 280 Detroit St # 200 Denver CO 80206-4807 E-mail: trygm@earthlink.net.

MYHRVOLD, NATHAN P., technology executive; b. Seattle, Aug. 3, 1959; BS in Math., UCLA, 1979, MS in Geophysics and Space Physics, 1979; M in Math. Econs., Princeton U., 1981; D in Theoretical and Math. Physics, 1983. Fellow dept. applied math. and theoretical physics Cambridge U., 1981-83; founder, pres., CEO Dynamical Sys., 1984-86; dir. spl. projects Microsoft Corp., Redmond, Wash., 1986, v.p. applications and content; chief tech. officer Advanced Tech. and Rsch., Redmond, Wash., Microsoft Corp., Redmond, Wash., 1996—99; founder, mgr. Microsoft Rsch.; CEO Intellectual Ventures, Bellevue, Wash., 2000—. Bd. trustees Inst. Advanced Study, Princeton, N.J.; mem. Nat. Info. Infrastructure Adv. Coun.; adv. bd. Princeton U. dept. physics. Photographer America 24/7, Washington 24/7; contbr. scientific papers articles to Science, Nature, Paleobiology, Physical Review, Fortune, Time, National Geographic Traveler and online mag. Slate; provided forward Juice: The Creative Fuel that Drives World Class Inventors. Mem. United Way Million Dollar Roundtable; co-contbr. with Paul Allen SETI Found. for Allen Telescope Array, 2000. Recipient 1st and 2nd Place title, World Championship of Barbecue, Memphis, James Madison medal, Princeton U., 2005. Achievements include patents in field; patents pending in field. Avocations: mountain climbing, photography, French Cooking, Formula Car Racing. Office: Intellectual Ventures 1756 114th Ave SE Ste 110 Bellevue WA 98004

MYINT, SOE WIN, geographer, educator; s. Pe Than Tun and Khin Nu Nu; m. Susie Tin Maung Aye, Dec. 26, 1987; 1 child, Su Thinzar. BS in Forestry, Rangoon U., 1983; postgrad., Internat. Inst.Aerospace Survey and Earth Sciences, 1988—89; MS in Natural Resources, Asian Inst. Tech., 1994; PhD in Geography, La. State U., 2001. Asst. plantation officer Forest Dept., Rangoon, Rangoon Division, Burma, 1983—85; dep. mgr. Timber Corp., 1985—92; rsch. assoc. UNEP/Environment Assessment Program for Asia and the Pacific, Bangkok, 1994—96, rsch. specialist, 1996—98; asst. prof. dept. geography U. Okla., Norman, 2001—05, Ariz. State U., Tempe, 2005—. Geog. info. sci. cons. WHO, Geneva, 1999. Recipient Best Poster Presentation award, 18th Asian Conf. on Remote Sensing, 1998, Robert C. West Field Rsch. award, La. State U. Dept. Geography and Anthropology, 2000, US Geog. Sci. Scholar award, First Internat. Conf. GISci., 2000, Best Student Paper award, Am. Soc. for Photogrammetry and Remote Sensing-Mid-South Region Meeting, 2000, William G. Haag award, La. State U., 2001, Best Student Paper award, U. Consortium Geog. Info. Scis. Assembly, 2000, Remote Sensing Speciality Group, Assn. Am. Geographers, 2001, Otis Paul Starkey award, Assn. Am. Geographers, 2001, Intergraph Young Scholar award, U. Consortium Geog. Info. Sci., 2002, Runner-up Early Career award, Remote Sensing Specialty Group, Assn. Am. Geographers, 2004; grantee, NASA EPSCoR, 2001, 2002, U. Okla., 2002, Inst. Advanced Edn. Geospatial Scis., NASA, 2003—04, U. Calif., Santa Barbara, 2003, NSF, 2004—; fellow, Netherlands Govt., 1988—89; scholar, French Govt., 1993—94, La. State U., 1999—2001; CPGIS scholar, 2005, CSISS scholar, 2003. Office: Ariz State U Dept Geography PO Box 870104 Tempe AZ 85287-0104 Home: 4175 W Shannon St Chandler AZ 85226 Office Fax: 405-325-6090, 480-965-8313. Business E-Mail: soe.myint@asu.edu.

MYLARI, BANAVARA L., retired chemist; b. Bangalore, India, Jan. 29, 1937; arrived in U.S., 1962; s. Lakshman S. and Kaveramma Mylari; m. Aparna Pandit Mylari, Sept. 10, 1967; 1 child, Ravi. BSc with honors, Central Coll., Bangalore, India, 1960, MSc in Organic Chemistry, 1961; PhD in Organic Chemistry, Ind. U., 1966. Project leader Pfizer Inc., Groton, Conn., 1974—78, mgr., 1989, rsch. advisor, 1989—97, sr. rsch. fellow, 1997—. Pvt. medicinal chemistry cons., East Lyme, Conn., 2001—; presenter in field. Contbr. articles to profl. jours. Exec. com. mem. Conn. Valley Hindu Temple, Middletown, Conn. Mem.: Am. Chem. Soc. (fundraiser heterocyclic chemistry 1986—96, Fundraiser Extraordinary award 1992). Hindu. Achievements include patents for therapeutic agents for diabetic complications; research in diabetes aldose reductase inhibitors; patents in field. Avocations: travel, sanskrit literature, vedic literature, invited speaker on hindu religion. Home: Harvest Glen East Lyme CT 06333 Personal E-mail: blmylari@aol.com.

MYLES, MARIANNE MATUZIC, United States ambassador to Cape Verde; BA in Econs., SUNY, Oswego; M in Pub. Adminstrn., Harvard U.; MS in Nat. Security Strategy, Nat. Def. U. Joined Fgn. Svc. US Dept. State, 1975, econ. officer Bogota, Colombia, 1976—78, asst. comml. attaché Rome, 1978—81, export control officer, Office East-West Trade, 1982—84, internat. economist, Office Bus. Practices, 1985—88, prin. officer, Consulate Porto Alegre, Brazil, 1988—90, dep. prin. officer, econ. sect. chief Consulate Rio de Janeiro, 1991—92, sr. pers. officer, US Embassy Brasilia, 1992—94, dir. policy coord. for Fgn. Svc. dir. gen. Washington, dir. Office Aviation Negotiations, dir. Office Recruitment, Examination & Employment, consul gen. Naples, Italy, 1997—2000, charge d'affaires Uruguay, 2001, dep. chief of mission US Embassy Montevideo, Uruguay, then US amb. to Republic of Cape Verde, 2008—. Recipient Superior and Meritorious Honor awards, US Dept. State. Address: DOS Amb 2460 Praia Pl Washington DC 20521-2460 Office Phone: 238-260-8929.

MYLONAKIS, STAMATIOS GREGORY, artist, research scientist, retired lawyer; b. Athens, Aug. 18, 1937; s. Gregory S. and Vassiliki (Charalambopoulos) Mylonakis; m. Pamela H. Morton, May 5, 1965 (dec. Mar. 1978); 1 child, Gregory (dec.). BS, Nat. U. of Athens, 1961; MS, Ill. Inst. of Tech., 1964; PhD, Mich. State U., 1970. Rsch. assoc. Ill. Inst. of Tech., Chgo., 1964—65; rsch. scientist Brookhaven Nat. Lab., Upton, NY, 1965—68; instr. U. Calif., Berkeley, 1971—73; group leader Rohm and Haas Co., Springhouse, Pa., 1973—76; supr. DeSoto, Inc., Des Plaines, Ill., 1976—79; staff scientist Borg-Warner Corp., Des Plaines, 1979—82, mgr., 1982—87; dept. head Enichem Am., Monmouth Junction, NJ, 1988—94; tech. advisor, registered patent agt. law firm Oblon, Spivak, Arlington, Va., 1994—2000; cons., patent law practitioner, 2000—08; sci. fellow Nuc. Rsch. Ctr. Democritos, Athens, 1960—62. Tech. adv. bd. Ctr. Applied Polymer Rsch. Case Western Res. U., Cleve.; adv. bd. NSF Ctr. Polymer Interfaces Lehigh U. Assoc. editor: Jour. Applied Polymer Sci.; contbr. more than thirty peer reviewd articles to profl. jours. Lt. Greek Army. Fellow Sci., Nuc. Rsch. Ctr. Democritos, Athens, Greece, 1960—62, NSF, Mich. State U., 1968—70, U. Calif., 1971—73. Mem.: AAAS, Strathmore Art Ctr, Bethesda, Md., Am. Chem. Soc., N.Y. Acad. Scis., Sigma Xi. Greek Orthodox. Achievements include patents in polymer science technology. Avocations: photography, painting, travel. Home and Office: 7009 Cashell Manor Ct Derwood MD 20855-1201 Personal E-mail: sgmylonakis@yahoo.com.

MYLOTTE, JOHN ARNOLD, writer, educator; b. Phila., Aug. 26, 1942; s. Thomas Joseph and Pauline Ellen (Arnold) Mylotte; m. Eva Benda, Sept. 20, 1997; 1 stepchild, Ilya; m. Florence Ellen Noonan, Aug. 14, 1977 (div. Nov. 1992). BA in english, Villanova U., 1964; MA in english, Lehigh U., 1967; JD, Suffolk U. Law Sch., 1980; post grad, MIT, 1981. Bar: Mass. 1981. Tech. editor Naval Air Engring. Ctr., Phila., 1967—68; sr. tech. editor Navy Clothing & Textile Rsch. Lab., 1968—72, dir. tech. publ., 1973—91, dir. pub. rels., 1974—91; pres. TechWrite Assoc., 1987—. Adj. prof.,sr. lectr. Northeastern U., Boston, 1981—. Author: (book) Guide to Writing the Formal Technical Report, 1985, The Art of Technical Writing, 1987; contbr. articles to jours.; numerous appearances on TV, 2006—09. Elected mem. Framingham Town Mtg., 1975—78; Relay for Life Vol. Am. Cancer Society, 1995—; bd. mem. Big Brother-Big Sister Assn., Framingham, Mass., 1975—78, bd. pres., 1977—78. Recipient Command Hist. award, U.S. Navy Hist., 1981, Outstanding Performance award, U.S. Navy Dept., 1980—85. Mem.: Worcester County Poetry Soc., Longfellow Soc. (treas. 2005—), Soc. for Tech. Commn. (5 competitive tech. writing awards 1984—86). Independent. Unitarian Universalist. Avocation: writing. Office: TechWrite Assoc 11 Clemmons St Southborough MA 01772

MYMIT, CHUCK W., music educator, musician; b. NYC, Dec. 15, 1948; s. Jack Mymit, Gloria Epstein; BMus in Composition, Berklee Coll. of Music, Boston, 1971; MA in Composition, NYU, 1982; postgrad., Five Towne Coll., NY, 2004—. Asst. prof. Five Towns Coll., Seaford, NY, 1973—87, prof. jazz studies Dix Hills, NY, 1973—87, 2000—; tchr. music N.Y.C. Bd. Edn., 1987—97; coord. music Peninsula Counceling Ctr., LI, NY, 1997—2000; house pianist Nordstroms Dept. Store, LI, 1997—2000. Jazz comml. pianist AF of M, Local 802, NYC, 1973—; freelance arranger/composer, NYC, 1973—; editor FTC Press Five Towns Coll., 2000—; guest condr. NMEA All State Jazz Ensemble, NY, 2002. Author: (book) A Beginner's Approach to Jazz Improvisation, 1973, Contemporary Harmony I and Workbook, 1977, Contemporary Harmony II and Workbook, 1979, Arranging for Small Band, 1980, Club Date Pianist, 1981, Voicing Techniques for the Arranger, 1997, Contemporary Concepts in Jazz Harmony, 2001; composer, pianist, arranger: CD's Tú Eras Mi Corazon, 1995; composer (pianist, arranger): The Romantic Pianist, 1995 (X-Tisch Sch. of Arts award for film composition, 95), Reflections, 1998, Ambience, 2001, music score, music performed at Carnegie Hall and Tilles Ctr., (commd.) Deer Park Sch., 2005, Lincoln Ctr., 2005. Named Most Valuable Player, Nordstroms Dept. Store, N.Y., 1997. Mem.: ASCAP, Manhatten Assn. Cabaret Artists, Internat. Assn. Jazz Educators. Avocation: sports. Office: Five Towns College 305 N Service Rd Dix Hills NY 11746

MYREN, RICHARD ALBERT, criminologist, consultant; b. Madison, Wis., Aug. 9, 1924; s. Andrew Olaus and Olyanna (Olson) M.; m. Patricia Ross Hubin, June 12, 1948; children: Nina Ross Schroepfer, Tania Ellis Myren Zobel, Kristina Albee Myren Sheldon, Andrew James. BS, U. Wis., 1948; LLB, Harvard U., 1952; LLD (hon.), U. New Haven, 1976. Bar: N.C. 1954. Rsch. chemist U.S. Dept. Agr., No. Regional Rsch. Lab., Peoria, Ill., 1948-49; asst. to assoc. rsch. prof. pub. law and govt. Inst. Govt., Chapel Hill, NC, 1952-56; asst. to assoc. prof. Ind. U., 1956-66; dean, prof. Sch. Criminal Justice, State U. N.Y., Albany, 1966-76, Sch. Justice, Am. U., Washington, 1976-86, prof. emeritus, 1986—; cons. Washington, 1987—. Vis. prof. Inst. Criminology, Cambridge (Eng.) U., 1973-74, East China Inst. for Politics and Law, Shanghai, People's Republic of China, 1988; cons. law enforcement programs for children and youth Children's Bur., HEW, Washington, 1960-62; cons. Pres.'s. Com. on Juvenile Delinquency and Youth Crime, 1962-64, Pres.'s Commn. on Law Enforcement and Adminstrn. Criminal Justice, 1966, U.S. Law Enforcement Assistance Adminstrn., 1968-82, N.Y. State Temp. Commn. on Constl. Conv., 1967, N.Y. State Dept. Edn., 1967, 69, Calif. Coordinating Coun. for Higher Edn., 1969-70, Nat. Adv. Commn. on Criminal Justice Standards and Goals, 1971-72, Tenn. Higher Edn. Commn., 1976, Ky. Dept. Justice, 1977-78, NSF, 1978—, U.S. Civil Rights Commn., 1978, others. Author: Coroners in North Carolina: A Discussion of Their Problems, 1953, Indiana Sheriffs' Manual of Law and Practice, rev. edit, 1959, Indiana Conservation Officers' Manual of Law and Practice, 1961; (with Lynn D. Swanson) Police Work With Children, 1962; (with Carroll L. Christenson) The Walsh-Healey Public Contracts Act: A Critical Review of Prevailing Minimum Wage Determinations, 1966, Education in Criminal Justice, 1970, Law and Justice: An Introduction, 1988, Investigation for Determination of Fact: A Primer on Proof, 1989; contbr. to: Bases for Justice Systems: Law and the Social Sciences (Gordon E. Misner), 1980, Five Year Outlook: Problems, Opportunities and Constraints in Science and Technology, 1980; assoc. editor: Jour. Criminal Justice; contbr. articles to profl. jours. Bd. dirs. Sex Info. and Edn. Coun. U.S., 1972-75. Served with inf. AUS, 1943-46, ETO; with USNR, 1954-68. Fulbright rsch. scholar to Argentina Cordoba, 1964-65 Mem. N.C. Bar Assn., Sociedad Argentina de Sociología Home Phone: 570-271-1086. Personal E-mail: mrpmyren@aol.com.

MYRICK, BISMARCK, diplomat, history professor; b. Portsmouth, Va., Dec. 23, 1940; m. Marie Pierre Mbaye; children: Bismarck Jr., Wesley Todd, Allison Elizabeth. BA, U. Tampa, 1972; MA, Syracuse U., 1973, postgrad., 1979-80; LHD (hon.), Spelman Coll., 2002. Enlisted U.S. Army, 1959; desk officer for Somalia, U.S. Dept. State, Washington, 1980-82; advanced through grades to maj., 1975; ret., 1979; polit. officer Am. Embassy, Monrovia, Liberia, 1982-84; action officer office strategic nuclear policy bur. politico-milit. affairs U.S. Dept. State, 1985-87, dep. dir. policy plans and coordination bur. inter-Am. affairs, 1987-89, Una Chapman Cox fellow US-African Policy, 1988-90; consul gen. Am. Consulate Gen., Durban, South Africa, 1990-93, Capetown, South Africa, 1993-95; amb. to Lesotho, Am. Embassy, Maseru, 1995-98; diplomat-in-residence Atlanta U. Ctr. at Spelman Coll., 1998-99; U.S. amb. to Liberia Dept. of State, Monrovia, Liberia, 1999—2002; univ. lectr. internat. affairs Old Dominion U., 2002—; sr. fellow Joint Forces Staff Coll., Norfolk, Va., 2002—. Adj. prof. history and polit. sci. Old Dominion U., 2002—03, amb.-in-residence. Author: Three Aspects of Crisis in Colonial Kenya, 1975; contbr. chpt. to book. Goodwill amb. for West Africa, Graceland, Senegal, 2008. Decorated Silver Star, Purple Heart, 4 Bronze Stars; named to U.S. Army Hall of Fame, 1996; named Ambassador Bismarck Myrick Days, City of Portsmouth, Va., 2000; named one of Portsmouth Notable, 2006; Bismarck Myrick St. and Bismarck Myrick Crescent St. named in his honor, 2002. Mem.: World Affairs Coun. Hampton Rds. (bd. dirs. 2004—). Address: 1200 Mill Run Chesapeake VA 23322 Personal E-mail: myrickbx@hotmail.com.

MYRICK, GARY, legislative staff member; b. 1967; married; 1 child. BA, U. Maine; JD, Am. U. Bar: 1996. Staff Senator George Mitchell, Senator Tom Daschle, Senator Harry M. Reid, Washington, 2003—04, dep. chief of staff, 2004—06, chief of staff, 2006—. Office: Office of Senator Harry Reid 528 Senate Hart Office Bldg Washington DC 20510-2803 E-mail: gary_myrick@reid.senate.gov.*

MYRICK, SUE WILKINS, United States Representative from North Carolina, former mayor; b. Tiffin, Ohio, Aug. 1, 1941; d. William Henry and Margaret Ellen (Roby) Wilkins; m. Jim Forest (div.); children: Greg, Dan; m. Wilbur Edward Myrick Jr., Sept. 11, 1977. Student, Heidelberg Coll., 1959-60, LLD (hon.), 1995. Exec. sec. to mayor and city mgr., Alliance, Ohio, 1962-63; dir. br. office Stark County Ct. of Juvenile and Domestic Rels., Alliance, Ohio, 1963-65; pres. Myrick Advt. and Pub. Rels., Charlotte, NC, 1971-95; at-large mem. City Coun., Charlotte, NC, 1983—85; mayor Charlotte, NC, 1987-91; pres. Myrick Enterprises, 1992—94; mem. US Congress from 9th NC dist., 1995—. Candidate for US Senate, NC, 1992; mem. energy and commerce com. US Congress, mem. corrections day com., dep. whip, 2003—, co-chair cancer caucus. Active Heart Fund, Multiple Sclerosis, March of Dimes, Arts and Scis. Fund Dr.; bd. dirs. NC Inst. Politics; v.p. Sister Cities Internat.; mem. Pres. Bush's Affordable Housing Commn.; founder, coord. Charlotte vol. tornado relief effort; lay leader, Sunday sch. tchr. 1st United Meth. Ch.; treas. Mecklenburg Ministries. Recipient Woman of Yr. award Harrisonburg, Va., 1968; named one of Outstanding Young Women of Am., 1968, Pub. Svc. Leadership award, 2002, Small Bus. Survival Com. award, 2004, Oncology Medal of Honor award, 2005. Mem. Women's Polit. Caucus, Beta Sigma Phi. Republican. Methodist. also: US House Reps 230 Cannon House Office Bldg Washington DC 20515-0001 Home and Office: 8437 Olde Troon Dr Charlotte NC 28277 Office Phone: 202-225-1976. Office Fax: 202-225-3389. E-mail: myrick@mail.house.gov.*

MYRRDIN, TERRY A., state agency administrator; b. San Diego, Aug. 31, 1950; d. Bernard O. Wallen, Jr. and Mary Ann Snyder; children: Sherilyn Ann Pillsbury, Gina Marie Legalle. AA, Am. River Coll., Sacramento, CA, 1970. Cert. clinical hypnotherapist Am. Coun. Hypnotists Examiners. Asst. govtl. program analyst Dept. Indsl. Rels., Sacramento, 1994—2000; spl. asst. Gov. Gray Davis, Sacramento, 2000—03; chief facilities oversight, security Sec. of State, Sacramento, 2003—; leadership team CA State Employees Charitable Campaign, 2004—. Chair Constl. Divsn. Recipient Outstanding Leadership award, 2006, Gov.'s Campaign Leadership award, 2007, Outstanding Leadership Support award, 2008. Avocations: travel, gardening, reading. Office: Sec of State 1500 11th St 6th Fl Sacramento CA 95814 Personal E-mail: terrymyrrdin@comcast.net.

MYRSIADES, KOSTAS YANNIS, literature educator; b. Vourliotes, Samos, Greece, May 21, 1940; came to U.S., 1948; s. John and Mary (Lagos) M.; m. Linda Suny, June 6, 1965; children: Yani, Leni. BA in English, Iowa U., 1963; MA in Comparative Lit., Ind. U., 1965, PhD in Comparative Lit., 1972; cert. in modern and classical Greek, U. Athens, Greece, 1966. Instr. English Greek-Am. Cultural Inst., Athens, 1965-66, 69; asst. prof. modern Greek, dir. Ctr. for Hellenic Studies Deree Coll., Athens, 1973-74; asst. prof. English West Chester (Pa.) U., 1969-73, assoc. prof., 1974-77, prof., 1977—, chair dept. English, 1985-90. Coord. grad. English studies West Chester U., 1983-85, coord. comparative lit. studies, 1983-2000, assoc. dean. faculty of arts and scis., 1982-83, active numerous coms., 1972—; conf. organizer Balch Inst. Ethnic Studies, Phila., 1985; participant Delaware Valley Faculty Exch. at U. Pa., 1984; editorial cons. Centrum Phila. Pub. Co., 1981-83, G.K. Hall, Boston, 1974-81, N.J. Dept. Higher Edn.; Greek examiner Temple U., Phila., 1977—, U. Md., 1978—, Albright Coll., Reading, Pa., 1980-83; presenter numerous profl. confs., 1969—. Author: Takis Paptsonis, 1974, Approaches to Teaching Homer's Iliad and Odyssey, 1987, (with Kimon Friar) Yannis Ritsos: Scripture of the Blind, 1979, Yannis Ritsos: Monovasis and the Women of Monemvasia, 1987, Takis Papatsonis, Ursa Minor and Other Poems, 1988, Cultural Representation in Historical Resistance, 1999, (with Linda S. Myrsiades) The Karagiozis Heroic Performance in Greek Shadow Theater, 1988, Karagiozis: Culture and Comedy in Greek Puppet Theater, 1992, (with Kimon Friar) Yannis Ritsos: Selected Poems, 1938-88, 1989, Others Must Dance for the Lord Dionysus Now, 1993, Margins in the Classroom: Teaching Literature, 1994; editor: (with Jerry McGuire) Order and Partialities; Theory, Pedagogy, and the "Postcolonial," 1995, Racing Representation, 1998, Un-Disciplining Literature, 1999, (with Henry Giroux) Beyond the Corporate University, 2001, The Beat Generation, 2002; editor Coll. Lit., 1990—, Jour. Hellenic Diaspora, 1991—; contbr. book revs. to World Lit. Today, Coll. Lit. Planning grantee Phila. Coun. Humanities, 1983; dissertation grantee Ind. U., 1967; Lily fellow U. Pa., 1981; honorarium recipient G.K. Hall, 1976-81, Temple U. Press, 1979—, Ohio State U. Press, 1982—, Holt, Reinhart and Winston, 1982—, Centrum Phila., 1983—. Mem. Am. Lit. Translators Assn., Am. Comparative Lit. Assn., Assn. of Depts. of English, Assn. for Computers and the Humanities, Modern Lang. Assn. (honorarium 1982—), Nat. Assn. Self-Instructional Programs, Modern Greek Studies Assn., Assn. Pa. State Coll. and Univ. Faculty (chmn. com. of departmental chairs 1986—), English Assn. of Pa. State Univs., Greek-Turkish Univ. Alliance (co-dir. 1984—), Hellenic-Am. League of Phila., Hellenic Univ. Club of Phila. Home: 370 Malin Rd Newtown Square PA 19073-4271 Office: West Chester U Dept English 210 E Rosedale Ave West Chester PA 19380 Office Phone: 610-436-2901. Business E-Mail: kmyrsiades@wcupa.edu.

MYRTH, JUDY G., retired editor; d. James Douglas and Ruth Evelyn Sheeran; children: Susanne, Evelyn. BA, SUNY Albany and U. Würzburg, Germany, 1968; MA, SUNY, Albany, 1969; postgrad., Ind. U., Bloomington, 1969—70, Free U., Berlin, 1970—71; MLS, SUNY, Albany, 1988. Cert. pub. libr. N.Y., permanent tchg. cert. in German N.Y. Tchr. English Gymnasium Landau a.d. Isar, Germany, 1971—73, Realschule Niederviehbach, 1973—76; editor Bibliography of the History of Art J. Paul Getty Trust, Williamstown, Mass., 1989—2000, LA, 2001—07. Mem.: Coll. Art Assn. Avocations: travel, reading.

MYSAK, LAWRENCE ALEXANDER, oceanographer, climatologist and mathematics educator; b. Saskatoon, Sask., Can., Jan. 1940; s. Stephen and Nettie Mysak; m. Diane Mary Eeles, Aug. 15, 1974; children: Paul Alexander, Claire Anastasia. BSc, U. Alta., Can., 1961; MSc, U. Adelaide, Australia, 1963; AM, Harvard U., 1964, PhD, 1967. Rsch. fellow Harvard U., 1966-67; mem. faculty U. B.C., Vancouver, 1967-86, prof. math. and oceanography, 1976-86; Atmospheric Environ. Svc./Natural Scis. Engring. Rsch. Coun.; sr. indsl. rsch. prof. climatology McGill U., Montreal, Que., Canada, 1986-96, dir. Climate Rsch Group, 1986-90, Can. Steamship Lines prof. meteorology, 1989—, founding dir. Ctr. for Climate and Global Change Rsch., 1990-96. Vis. rsch. assoc. Oreg. State U., summer 1968; sr. visitor Cambridge U., England, 1971-72; vis. scientist Inst. Ocean Sci., Sidney, B.C., fall 1976, Nat. Ctr. Atmospheric Rsch., Boulder, Colo., 1977; vis. prof. US Naval Postgrad. Sch., Monterey, Calif., summer 1981, Swiss Fed. Inst., Tech., Zurich, 1982-83, 2000-2001, 2007, Italian Nat. Inst. Geophysics and Volcanology, Bologna, 2001; George's Lemaître vis. prof. Cath. U. Louvain, Belgium, 1995, Stockholm U., 2008; invitation fellowship for rsch. in Japan, Japan Soc. for Promotion of Scis., 1997; supr. 75 grad. and postdoctoral students, 1967—; vis. prof. exch. lectr. Royal Soc. Can. Nat. Acad. Scis. of Ukraine, 2002, presenter & lectr. in fields Co-author: Waves in the Ocean, 1978;assoc. editor Jour. Phys. Oceanography, 1977-92, Atmospheric-Ocean, 1988-91, Climatol. Bull., 1992-93; contbg. editor: Am. Geophys. Union books on coastal and esturaine studies, 1987-2000; mem. edit. bd. Geophys. and Astrophys. Fluid Dynamics, 1983-96; series editor: Springer Atmospheric and Oceanographic Scis. Libr., 2001-; contbr. over 160 articles in profl. jours. Decorated Order of Can.; recipient Patterson Disting. Svc. medal Environ. Can. Atmospheric Environment Svc., 1997, prix Michel-Jurdant, ACFAS, 2005, Marie-Victorin, prix, Que., 2006, Disting. Alumni award, U. Alberta, 2009 Fellow Acad. of Sci. of Royal Soc. Can. (v.p. Acad. of Sci. 1991-93, pres. 1993-96), Am. Meteorol. Soc., Am. Geophys. Union (Sverdrup lectr. 2004); mem. Can. Meteorol. and Oceanog. Soc. (co-recipient Pres.'s prize 1980, J.P. Tully medal Oceanography 1997, inaugural fellow 1999), Royal Soc. Can. (life), European Geosciences Union (hon.; Alfred Wegener medal 2006), Academia Europaea (fgn.), Internat. Assn. for Phys. Scis. of Ocean (v.p. 2003-07, pres. 2007-). Office: McGill U 805 Sherbrooke St W Montreal PQ Canada H3A 2K6 Office Phone: 514-398-3768. Business E-Mail: lawrence.mysak@mcgill.ca.

MYSKINA, ANASTASIA, professional tennis player; b. Moscow, July 8, 1981; d. Andrey and Galina Myskina. Profl. tennis player WTA Tour, 1998—. Recipient Commitment to Cmty Award, Fla. Times-Union, 2005. Achievements include Winner 10 WTA Tour singles titles; Winner 5 WTA Tour doubles title; Winner 3 ITF Women's Circuit singles titles; Winner 3 ITF Women's Circuit doubles titles; Member Russian Olympic Team 2000, 2004. Office: c/o WTA Tour Corp Hdqs One Progress Plz Ste 1500 Saint Petersburg FL 33701

MYSKOWSKI, PATRICIA LOIS, dermatologist; b. Washington, Aug. 30, 1950; d. Walter Joseph and Mary Ruth (Funderburk) M.; m. Alexander Julian Swistel, July 31, 1976; children: Emily Lois, Gregory Daniel. AB in Biology, Brown U., 1972, ScM in Biology, 1974, MD, 1975. Diplomate Am. Bd. Dermatology, Am. Bd. Dermatologic Immunology/Lab. and Diagnostic Immunology. Intern in internal medicine Rochester (N.Y.) Gen. Hosp., 1975-76, VA Hosp., Bronx, 1976-77; resident in dermatology N.Y. Hosp., Cornell U. Med. Ctr., 1977-80; fellow in dermatology Meml. Sloan-Kettering Cancer Ctr., NYC, 1980-81; asst. attending physician, dermatology Meml. Hosp. for Cancer and Allied Diseases, NYC, 1981-88, assoc. attending physician, dermatology, 1988—2005, attending physician dermatology, 2005—; asst. prof. medicine Cornell U. Med. Coll., NYC, 1981-88, assoc. prof. clin. medicine, 1989-95, assoc. prof. dermatology, 1995—2005, prof., dermatology, 2007—. Contbr. articles to profl. jours. Jr. Faculty Clin. fellowship Am. Cancer Soc., 1981-84. Fellow Am. Acad. Dermatology; mem. AMA, Soc. Investigative Dermatology, Manhattan Met. Dermatologic Soc. Roman Catholic. Office: Meml Sloan Kettering Cancer 1275 York Ave New York NY 10021-6094 Office Phone: 212-610-0768.

MYSORE, SHASHIDHAR C., computer scientist; b. Bangalore, Karnataka, India; s. Chandrasekharamurthy S. and Ahalya C. Mysore; m. Shalini Kakar. BE in Computer Sci., BMS Coll. Engring., Bangalore, 2002; MS in Computer Sci., U. Calif., Santa Barbara, 2007, PhD candidate, 2003—. Rsch. asst. Indian Inst. Sci., Bangalore, 2002—03; rschr. U. Calif., 2004—, mem. grad. admissions com. computer sci., 2008; summer rsch. intern Google Inc., Mountain View, Calif., 2005—06. Reviewer Micro, ISCA, TACO, ANCS, IISWC; pres. Sanskrit Assn. BMS, Bangalore, 1999—2002. Recipient Silver medal, Sura Saraswathi Sabha, 1995, award, Visveswaraya Technol. U., 2002. Mem.: IEEE, Assn. Computing Machinery (pres. student chpt. 2005—07, reviewer). Achievements include invention of range adaptive profiling.

MYTELKA, ARNOLD KRIEGER, lawyer; b. Jersey City, July 24, 1937; s. Herman Donald and Jeannette (Krieger) M.; m. Rosalind Marcia Kaplan, Dec. 17, 1961; children: Andrew Charles, Daniel Sommer. AB, Princeton U., 1958; LLB cum laude, Harvard U., 1961; postgrad., London Sch. Econs., 1961—62. Bar: N.J. 1961, U.S. Dist. Ct. N.J. 1963, U.S. Supreme Ct. 1970, U.S. Ct. Appeals (3d cir.) 1978, U.S. Dist. Ct. (so. and ea. dist.) N.Y. 1983. Law sec. Chief Justice N.J. Supreme Ct., Newark, 1962-63; assoc. Clapp & Eisenberg, Newark, 1963-68, ptnr., 1968-94; prin. Kraemer, Burns, Mytelka, Lovell & Kulka, Springfield, N.J., 1994—. Lectr. Rutgers Law Sch., Newark, 1973; mem. Am. Law Inst., Phila., 1989—; mem. cons. group The Law Governing Lawyers, 1990-99, Restatement of Restitution and Unjust Enrichments; founding trustee Newark Legal Svcs. Project, 1965-68; trustee Edn. Law Ctr., 1974-75; chmn. dist. V ethics com. Supreme Ct. N.J., 1983-84, mem. 1981-84; trustee Legal Svcs. Found. Essex County, 1982—, pres., 1990-92; lectr. in land use law. Mem. editorial bd. N.J. Law Jour., 1991—; contbr. legal articles to profl. jours. Chmn. bd. trustees Ramapo Coll. NJ, 1979-80; mediator chancery divsn. NJ Superior Ct., 1990—, trustee, 1998-2000, 03-06, spl. fiscal agt., 1997, 2003, 2005, 2009, spl. master, 1999-00. Frank Knox Meml. fellow Harvard U., London Sch. Econs. and Polit. Sci., 1961-62. Mem.: ABA (mem. litigation sect.), N.J. State Bar Assn. (chmn. appellate practices study com. 1977—79, chmn. land use law sect. 1984—85). Home: 56 Hall Rd Chatham NJ 07928-1723 Office: Kraemer Burns Mytelka Lovell & Kulka 675 Morris Ave Springfield NJ 07081-1523 Office Phone: 973-912-8700. E-mail: amytelka@kraemerburns.com.

NA, KWAN-SIK, management information systems professor; b. Sancheong, Kyungnam, Republic of Korea, Nov. 7, 1961; s. Jun-Tae Na and Ok-Seon Jung; m. Eun-Ji Chun, May 20, 1992; children: Kyung-Eun (Rachel), Kyung-Ho (Ryan). BA in Bus. Adminstrn., Kwangwoon U., Seoul, Republic of Korea, 1985, MA in Bus. Adminstrn., 1987, PhD in Mgmt. Info. Sys. and Mgmt. Sys., 1992. Affiliated faculty mem., vis. scholar U. Ala., Huntsville, 2001—, thesis com. mem. Grad. Sch., 2005—06. Nat. bd. mem. Iso/Iec, 1994—2000; advisor Small and Medium Bus. Adminstrn., Daejeon, 1997—; external auditor Bd. Audit and Inspection Korea, Seoul, 1997—98; advisor Seoul Bus. Agy., Seoul, Republic Of Korea, 2000—01. First lt. Republic of Korea Airforce, 1988—91, Taegu. Recipient Best Paper award, Korea Soc. IT Svc., 2003, Best Suggestion award, Seowon U., 1997; named Best Prof., 2006; grantee, Ministry Def., 1996, Korea Agy. for Digital Opportunity and Promotion, 1997, LG, 1997, Nat. Info. Soc. Agy., 1997, Inst. for Info. Tech. Advancement, 1998, 1999, Ministry Info. and Comm., 2001, 2002, Korea Edn. Frontier Assn., 2003, Korea Youth Counseling Inst., 2005, Korea Rsch. Found., 2006, 2008, Nat. Emergency Mgmt. Agy., 2007, Small Bus. Devel. Ctr., 2007. Fellow: Korea Corp. Mgmt. Assn. (mem. exec. bd. 2007—); mem.: Korea Soc. Info. Tech. Applications, Korea Soc. MIS, Korean Academic Soc. Bus. Adminstrn. Achievements include development of software risk model, software project performance measurement method, and performance measurement model of supply chain management systems. Avocations: tennis, golf. Office: Seowon U 241 Musimseoro Heungduk-ku Chungbuk Cheongju 361-742 Republic of Korea Office Fax: 82-43-283-8822. Business E-Mail: ksna@seowon.ac.kr.

NA, TSUNG SHUN (TERRY NA), Chinese studies educator, writer; b. Beijing, Nov. 3, 1932; came to U.S., 1964; s. Chi-L and Hui (Hu) N.; m. Yen Yen Chao, 1964. BA, Taiwan Normal U., 1956; MA, U. B.C., 1970; PhD, U. Minn., 1978. Assoc. prof. Taipei Normal Coll., Taiwan, Republic of China, 1956-64; vis. lectr. Ind. U., Bloomington, 1964-66; asst. prof. U. Minn., Mpls., 1970-80; vis. prof. Sun Yat-sen U., Taiwan, 1981-84; prof., dir. Am. Inst. Chinese Studies, Charles Town, W.Va., 1985—. Author: (English books) A Linguistic Study of P'i-pa Chi, 1969, Studies on Dream of the Red Chamber: A Selected and Classified Bibliography, 1979, Supplement, 1981, Taiwan Studies on Dream of the Red Chamber: A Selected and Classified Bibliography, 1983, Chinese Studies in English: A Selected Bibliography, 1991, (Chinese) Mandarin Pronunciation, 1966, Teaching Chinese in the U.S.A., 1983, Studies on Chinese Classical Novels, 1985, A Collection of Short Stories, 1987, Phonological Study of Yun Lue Yi Tong, 2008; contbr. numerous articles, short stories, and research essays to jours. and newspapers in U.S., Taiwan, ROC, and China. Mem. MLA, Assn. Asian Studies. Office: Am Inst Chinese Studies PO Box 453 Charles Town WV 25414-0453

NAADIMUTHU, GOVINDASAMI, finance educator; b. Sirkali, Tamilnadu, India, Aug. 9, 1947; came to the U.S., 1969; s. Ganapathi and Saraswathi (Balamudaliar) Govindasami; m. Amirtha Doraiswamy, Aug. 17, 1975; children: Revathi, Sathish. BS, U. Madras, India, 1968; diploma, Indian Inst. Tech., Madras, 1969; MS, Kans. State U., 1971, PhD, 1974. Grad. rsch. asst. Kans. State U., Manhattan, 1969-73; asst. prof. Calif. Poly. State U., San Luis Obispo, 1973-74, Fairleigh Dickinson U., Teaneck, N.J., 1974-78, assoc. prof., 1978-83, prof., 1983—, chmn., 1982-95, assoc. dean, 1995—2006. Lectr. indsl. engring. continuing edn. program Bendix Corp., N.J., spring 1975; lectr. indsl. engring. tng. program GAF Corp., N.J., spring 1976; program coord. Pumps in Desalination and Chem. Plants, St. Croix, V.I., 1978; faculty advisor Fairleigh Dickinson U. Inst. of Indsl. Engrs. Student Chpt., Teaneck, 1981-86, 89-90; mem. organizing com. Math. and Computer Modelling Conf., 1991, 93, 97, 99. Co-author: Operations Research, 2nd edit., 1997; reviewer various books and jours.; contbr. articles to profl. jours. Chmn. bd. govs. Metro N.J. Inst. of Indsl. Engrs. chpt., 1990-91, 93-94, pres., 1991-92. Mem. Prodn. and Ops. Mgmt. Soc., Soc. for Info. Mgmt., Inst. Indsl. Engrs., Inst. for Ops. Rsch. and the Mgmt. Scis., Decision Scis. Inst., Sigma Xi, Tau Beta Pi, Phi Kappa Phi, Alpha Pi Mu. Avocations: reading, photography, bicycling, jogging. Office: Fairleigh Dickinson Univ ISDS/SCB M-MS2-04 Madison NJ 07940 Office Phone: 973-443-8850. Business E-Mail: naadi@fdu.edu.

NAAKE, JOAN MURRAY, English professor; m. Larry E. Naake; 2 children. B in English, Emmanuel Coll., Boston; M in English Lit., Boston Coll.; grad. student in English Lit., U. Oxford, Eng. Tchr. Prince George's CC, No. Va. CC, Marymount U.; prof. English Cosumnes River Coll., Sacramento; faculty mem. to prof., chair English dept. Montgomery Coll., Germantown, Md., 1992. Recipient Nat. Inst. Staff and Orgn. Devel. award, Faculty Outstanding Svc. award, Montgomery Coll., 2002, US Prof. of Yr. award, Carnegie Found. for Advancement of Tchg. and Coun. for Advancement and Support of Edn., 2006. Office: Humanities Social Scis and Edn Montgomery Coll 20200 Observation Dr Germantown MD 20876 Office Phone: 301-353-1951. Office Fax: 301-353-7752. E-mail: joan.naake@montgomerycollege.edu.

NABEL, ELIZABETH GUENTHNER, federal agency administrator, cardiologist, researcher; b. 1952; BA summa cum laude, St. Olaf Coll., Northfield, Minn., 1974; student, Union Theol. Sem., NYC, Columbia U.; MD, Cornell U., Ithaca, NY, 1981; DSc (hon.), U. Leuven, Belgium, 2001, Mt. Sinai Sch. Medicine, NY, 2006, U. Glasgow, Scotland, 2008. Diplomate Am. Bd. Internal Medicine & Cardiovasc. Diseases. Intern/resident internal medicine Brigham & Women's Hosp.-Harvard Med. Sch., Boston, 1981—84, clin. rsch. fellow cardiovasc. divsn., 1984-87; asst. prof. internal medicine U. Mich., Ann Arbor, 1987-91, assoc. prof. internal medicine, 1991-94, dir. Cardiovasc. Rsch. Ctr., 1992—99, prof. internal medicine & physiology, 1994—99, dir. divsn. cardiology, 1997-99; sci. dir. clin. rsch. Nat. Heart, Lung & Blood Inst. (NHLBI), NIH, Bethesda, Md., 1999—2005, dir. NHLBI, 2005—. Mem. sci. adv. bd. Vical Inc., San Diego, 1992—96, Keystone Symposia, Silverthorne, Colo.; pres. N.Am. Vascular Biology Orgn., 1996—97; disting. vis. prof. Molecular Cardiology Rsch. Inst., Tufts-New Eng. Med. Ctr., 2004; physician-in-chief pro tempore, dept. internal medicine Brigham & Women's Hosp., 2006; Sampson vis. prof. U. Calif., LA, 2007; Bulfinch vis. prof. Mass. Gen. Hosp., Boston, 2008. Assoc. editor Jour. Clin. Investigation, 1997—2002, mem. editl. bd., 2002—05, New Eng. Jour. Medicine, 2001—, mem. bd. reviewing editors Science, 1998—2005; editor: Trends in Cardiovasc. Medicine, 2001; cons. editor Circulation, Circulation Rsch., Atherial Thrombosis & Vascular Biology, 2000—05; contbr. articles to profl. jours. Recipient Leadership award, Personalized Medicine Coalition, 2006, Vision & Advocacy award, Nat. Alliance Hispanic Health, 2007, Spl. Recognition award, Nat. Human Genome Rsch. Inst., 2008, WomenHeart's Wenger award for disting. leadership, 2008, Sci. Leadership award, Nat. Marfan Found., 2008. Fellow: Am. Coll. Cardiology, Am. Heart Assn. (bd. dirs. 1996—97, Russell Ross Meml. Lectureship in vascular biology 2005, Disting. Achievement award 2005, Eugene Braunwald Academic Mentorship award 2008); mem.: ACP, AAAS, Inst. Medicine (coun. mem.), Am. Acad. Arts & Sciences, Am. Soc. Gene Therapy (bd. dirs. 1996), Am. Soc. Investigative Pathology, Am. Fedn. Clin. Rsch., Am. Soc. Biochemistry & Molecular Biology (Amgen-Sci. Achievement award 1996), Assn. Am. Physicians, Am. Soc. Clin. Investigation, Alpha Omega Alpha, Phi Beta Kappa. Office: NHLBI Bldg 31 Rm 5A52 31 Ctr Dr MSC 2486 Bethesda MD 20892 Office Phone: 301-592-8573. Office Fax: 240-629-3246. Business E-Mail: elizabeth.nabel@nih.hhs.gov.

NABEL, GARY JAN, virologist; b. July 2, 1953; BA in Biochemistry magna cum laude, Harvard Coll., 1975; PhD in Cell and Devel. Biology, Harvard U., 1980, MD, 1982. Instr. biology Harvard U., Boston, 1980-81, resident tutor in biology, 1980-83, clin. fellow medicine, 1983-85; intern and resident in internal medicine Brigham and Women's Hosp., Boston, 1983-85; instr. Harvard Med. Sch., Boston, 1984-87; assoc. Howard Hughes Med. Inst., Whitehead Inst., MIT, Lab. David Baltimore, 1985-87; assoc. physician Brigham and Women's Hosp., 1985-87; asst. prof. internal medicine and biol. chemistry U. Mich., Ann Arbor, 1987-90, asst. investigator Howard Hughes Med. Inst., 1987-91, assoc. prof. internal medicine and biol. chemistry, 1990-93, assoc. investigator Howard Hughes Med. Inst., 1991-94, prof. internal medicine and biol. chemistry, 1993—, investigator Howard Hughes Med. Inst., 1994—, Henry Sewall prof., 1995—99; dir. Vaccine Rsch. Ctr. NIH, 1999—. Mem. AIDS rsch. adv. com. Nat. Inst. Allergy and Infectious Diseases, NIH. Contbr. articles to profl. jours. Fellow Dana-Farber Cancer Inst., Harvard U., 1980-84; Harvard Nat. scholar, 1971-75, Harvard Grad. Nat. scholar, 1976-82; recipient Mallinkrodt Book prize, 1975, James Tolbert Shipley prize for rsch. Harvard Med. Sch., 1982, Ofcl. citation Conn. State Gen. Assembly for Contbns. to Human Gene Therapy, 1992, Young Investigator award Midwest Am. Fedn. for Clin. Rsch., 1992, Amgen award Am. Soc. Biochemistry and Molecular Biology, 1996. Mem. Am. Soc. Clin. Investigation, Assn. Am. Physicians. Office: Vaccine Rsch Ctr 40 Convent Dr Bldg 40 Rm 4502 Bethesda MD 20892 E-mail: gnabel@nih.gov.

NABERGOJ, ANDREJ, entrepreneur; b. Koper, Slovenia, Aug. 3, 1976; m. Anja Nabergoj; 1 child, Jun. Corr. for a scientific econ. and social jour.; co-founder Parsek Systems Ltd., 1999—2006; co-founder, chmn. Httpool Ltd. (www.httpool.com), 2001—; co-founder, CEO Noovo (www. noovo.com), 2007—. Co-founder, chmn. Ctr. for Entrepreneurship and Exec. Develop. (CEED), 2006—08; bd. dirs. RSG Fund, 2006—07; spkr. in field. Host (weblog) andrej.nabergoj.com. Named one of Young Global Leaders, World Econ. Forum, 2009. Mem.: Young Exec. Soc. (YES) (pres. 2004—, co-founder 2003), Young Entrepreneurs of Europe (v.p. 2005—09). Avocations: music, guitar, juggling, japanese, blogging, astronomy, chess, Karate. Office: Noovo Cesta v Gorice 8 1000 Ljubljana Slovenia Office Phone: 386 01 479 04 80. E-mail: nabergoj@noovo.com.*

NABI, STANLEY ANDREW, brokerage house executive; b. Baghdad, Iraq, Sept. 17, 1930; arrived in U.S., 1947; s. Moshi S. and Victoria T. (Mukamal) N.; m. Bette E. Miller, Mar. 31, 1968; children: Deborah Susan, Lisa Meryl. BA, Columbia U., 1952; postgrad., NYU, 1954—58. Gen. ptnr. Schweickart & Co., NYC, 1954-72; gen. ptnr., chief investment officer Lazard Freres & Co., NYC, 1973-84; exec. v.p. Bessemer Trust Co., N.A., 1985-95; pres., CEO Bessemer Investors Svcs., 1985-95; vice chmn., chmn. investment policy com. Wood, Struthers & Winthrop, NYC, 1995-2000; chief investment officer DLJ Asset Mgmt. Corp., NYC, 1996-2000; mng. dir., sr. advisor Credit Suisse Asset Mgmt., 2000—03; vice chmn. Silvercrest Asset Mgmt. Group, 2004—. Lectr. New Sch. Social Rsch., N.Y.C., 1963-68; investment cons. U.S. Steel and Carnegie Pension Fund, N.Y.C., 1979—; dir. Bargain Town U.S.A., N.Y.C., 1962-69; mem. pres.'s coun. New Sch. U., N.Y.C., 1989—; adj. prof. fin. Grad. Sch. Bus., Fordham U., N.Y.C., 1992-97. Editor: weekly jour. The Analyst, 1957-72; assoc. editor: jour. The Fin. Analysts Jour., 1971-83. Trustee NABI Found., 1964—. Served with U.S. Army, 1952-54. Mem. N.Y. Soc. Security Analysts (pres. 1971-72), Inst. Chartered Fin. Analysts, Assn. for Investment Mgmt. and Rsch. Office: 1330 Ave of the Americas New York NY 10019 Home: 1 Kensington Gate (PH-1) Great Neck NY 11021-1202 Home Phone: 516-487-3175; Office Phone: 212-649-0702. Business E-Mail: snabi@silvercrestgroup.com.

NABOKOV, EVGENI, professional hockey player; b. Ust-Kamenogorsk, Kazakhstan, July 25, 1975; m. Tabitha Nabokov; 1 child, Emily. Goaltender San Jose Sharks, 2000—. Mem. Team Russia, Olympic Games, Torino, Italy, 2006. Recipient Calder Meml. Trophy, 2001; named NHL Rookie of Yr., Sporting News, 2001; named to All-Rookie Team, NHL, 2001, NHL All-Star Game, 2008, First All-Star Team, NHL, 2008. Avocations: golf, tennis. Office: San Jose Sharks 525 W Santa Clara St San Jose CA 95113

NABORS, GARY SCOTT, medical products executive; s. Charles William and Cecily Sparks Nabors; m. Susan Casey Nabors. BA, Wake Forest U., Winston-Salem, NC, 1985; PhD, U. Ga., Athens, 1991. Postdoc. assoc. U. Pa., Phila., 1991—95; mgr., immunology Sanofi Aventis, Swiftwater, Pa., 1995—2001; dir., product devel. Emergent BioSolutions, Gaithersburg, Md., 2004—07, v.p., product devel. and site ops., 2007—. Numerous grants, NIH, 2003—. Mem.: Am. Assn. Immunologists, Infectious Disease Soc. Am. Office: Emergent BioSolutions 300 Professional Dr Gaithersburg MD 20879

NABORS, MARION CARROLL, retired English educator; b. Marshall, Tex., Mar. 12, 1948; d. Aldon Edgar and Iola Hall; 1 child, Inetha Iola Sheffield. MS, U. Dallas, Irving, Tex., 1993; PhD, U. North Tex., Denton, 2006. Cert. supt. Tex. Edn. Agy., 2001, prin.-EC-12 Tex. Edn. Agy., 2000, tchr. English, French Tex. Edn. Agy., 1976. English tchr. Lincoln Humanities and Comm. Magnet, Dallas, 1983—98; adminstr. Yvonne Ewell Townview Ctr., Dallas, 1998—2005; adj. prof. ElCentro CC, Dallas, 1993—98, Cedar Valley C.C., Lancaster, Tex., 2002—04; coll. prof. adj. Eastfield Coll., Mesquite, Tex., 2005—; adj. prof. Paul Quinn Coll., Dallas, 2006—; co-owner Izanhour and Nabors Tutoring

Co., Dallas, 2006—. Cons. Paul Quinn Coll., Dallas, 2006—. Tutor Dallas Ind. Sch. Dist., 1986—2004. Named Tchr. of the Yr., Lincoln H.S. and Acad. Evening Sch., 1987, 1988, 1990, 1995, 1996. Mem.: Nat. Alliance of Black Sch. Educators (life). Independent. Roman Catholic. Avocations: reading, baking, cooking, chess. Home and Office: Izanhova and Nabors Tutoring Co 1438 Mirage Canyon Dr Dallas TX 75232

NABORS, ROBERT LEE, SR., military officer; b. Boston, 1946; married; children: Robert, Richard, Jonathan. BS in Systems Engring., U. Ariz.; MS in Systems Mgmt., U. So. Calif.; grad. Sr. Officials in Nat. Security, Harvard U.; grad., Armed Forces Staff Coll. Commd. 2d lt. U.S. Army, advanced through grades to maj. gen., with 67th Signal Battalion Ft. Riley, Kans., overseas tours in Vietnam and Worms, Germany, also active duty tours Ft. Dix, NJ, Aberdeen Proving Grounds, Md., aide-de-Camp for Comdg. Gen., VII Corps, 1979-81; with Office of Dir. of Plans, Programs and Policy U.S. Army Readiness Command, 1983; then comdr. 509th signal Battalion U.S. Army, Italy; spl. asst. to U.S. Army's Dir. of Info. Sys. for Command Control. Comm. and Computers; chief Integration div. Architecture Directorate U.S. Army, dep. comdr. White House Comm. Agy., comdr. 2d Signal Brigade, 1990, comdr. 5th Signal Command, 1995-98, comdr. Comm.-Electronics Command and comdr. Ft. Monmouth NJ, 1998-2001. Decorated DSM, Def. Superior Svc. medal, Legion of Merit with 4 oak leaf clusters, Bronze Star, Meritorious Svc. medal with 4 oak leaf clusters, others; recipient Roy Wilkins award of Reknown, NAACP, 2000, Fed. Asian-Pacific Am. Coun. award, 2000, others. Mem. Mensa.

NABORS, ROBERT LEE, II, federal official; b. Fort Dix, NJ, 1971; m. Theresa Nabors; children: Georgia, Jude. BS, U. Notre Dame, 1993; MA, U. NC, Chapel Hill, 1996. Program examiner Office Mgmt. & Budget (OMB), Exec. Office of the Pres., Washington, 1996—98, sr. adviser to dir., 1998—2000, asst. dir. for adminstrn., exec. sec., 2000—01, dep. dir., 2009—; minority staff mem. US House Appropriations Com., Washington, 2001—04, minority staff dir., 2004—06, majority staff dir., 2006—08. Office: Office of Mgmt and Budget 725 17th St, NW Washington DC 20503*

NABORS, STEVEN THOMAS, theater educator; b. Kittery, Maine, Sept. 11, 1954; s. William Allen and Janet Anne Nabors; m. Laura Munson Reinstatler, Sept. 9, 2006; 1 child, Colin Reinstatler. MA in Theatre Arts, Ctrl. Wash. U., Ellensburg, 2004. Theatre arts instr. Olympic Coll., Bremerton, Wash., 2000—01, Ctrl. Wash. U., 2005—, Meridian CC, Miss., 2007—. Mem.: AFTRA, SAG, Soc. Am. Fight Dirs. Home: 4640 Psd # C-14 Meridian MS 39305 Office: Meridian CC 910 Hwy 19 N Meridian MS 39307 Personal E-mail: naborss2001@yahoo.com. Business E-Mail: snabors@meridiancc.edu.

NABOZNY, HEATHER, professional sports team groundskeeper; b. Milford, Mich., 1970; Grad. Turf Mgmt. Prog., Mich. State U., 1993. Groundskeeper Toronto Blue Jays spring tng. camp, Dunedin, Fla.; head groundskeeper Class A West Mich. Whitecaps, 1994, Detroit Tigers, 1999—. Named one of 40 Under 40, Crain's Detroit Bus., 2006. Achievements include becoming first female goundskeeper in Major League Baseball and World Series game. Office: c/o Detroit Tigers Comerica Park 2100 Woodward Ave Detroit MI 48201

NACE, DORU, mathematics professor; s. Nicholas and Sevasta Nace; m. Manuela Mihu, Mar. 16, 1968. MS, Tech. U., Bucharest, Romania, 1969; PhD, Petroleum Inst., Ploiesti, Romania, 1982. Pres., founder Dynamic Sys., NYC, 1990—99; design engr. L-3 Comm., Muskegon, Mich., 1998—; math. coll. prof. Baker Coll., Muskegon, 2000—. Achievements include research in college mathematics. Office: Baker Coll 1903 Marquette Ave Muskegon MI 49442 Office Phone: 231-777-5371. Business E-Mail: doru.nace@baker.edu.

NACHAMIE, MARK SPENCER, cardiologist, educator; b. NYC, Dec. 11, 1955; s. David and Evelyn Nachamie. BA in Biology, summa cum laude, Columbia Coll., NYC, 1976; MD, NYU Med. Sch., 1980. Diplomate Am. Bd. Internal Medicine, 1983, cariovascular diseases, 1987. Instr. clin. medicine NYU Med. Sch., 1986—; attending physician Tisch Hosp., NYC, 1986—, Bellevue Hosp. Ctr., NYC, 1986—; dir. cardiology Gouvenrneur Diagnostic and Treatment Ctr., NYC, 1986—. Fellow Am. Coll. Cardiology; mem. Am. Heart Assn., Am. Soc. Echocardiology, Phi Beta Kappa, Alpha Omega Alpha. Office: 345 East 37th St Ste 308 New York NY 10016-3256 Office Phone: 212-599-7005. Business E-Mail: mark.nachamie@nyumc.org.

NACHEF, JOANNA MEDAWAR, performing company executive; b. Beirut, Jan. 15, 1959; d. Michel Shakeeb and Yolla Akl Medawar; m. Hani Elias Nachef, June 27, 1987; children: Hannah Marie, Timothy Elias. PhD in Musical Arts, U. Southern Calif., LA, 1988. Artistic dir. Los Cancioneros Master Chorale, Torrance, Calif., 1991—; dir., choral activities El Camino Coll., Torrance, 1996—. Music dir. Calif. Acad. Math. and Sci., Carson, 1991—, Peninsula Cmty. Ch., Rancho Palos Verdes, Calif., 1980—97, choir dir., 2003—; adj. faculty Calif. State U. Dominguez Hills, Carson, 1990—. Dir.(guest conductor): (debut) Carnegie Hall, NY, 2005 (Excellence in Arts award in Music, City of Torrance, 2005), (choral multicultural music) Ambassadors of Harmony, 2007. Cultural chair LA, Beirut Sister City Orgn., 2006; lectr. US Dept. State, 2004—05, citizen diplomat, 2004—05. Recipient Dir. award, Daily Breeze, 2008, Alumnus, US Inst. Peace, 2008; named 1st Woman Condr., Mid. East. Mem.: Torrance Performing Arts Consortium (directors' rep. 2003). Avocation: travel. Office: El Camino CC 16007 Crenshaw Blvd Torrance CA 90506 Business E-Mail: jnachef@elcamino.edu.

NACHEMAN, ELINOR LAURIE, librarian; b. Bklyn., Jan. 19, 1949; d. Leo and Helen Nacheman. BA in English, Adelphi U., Garden City, NY, 1971; MLS, SUNY, Albany, 1974. Libr. Sarah Lawrence Coll., Bronxville, NY, 1975—79; cataloger, reference libr. Fleet Libr., RISD, Providence, 1980—. Author: (book) Unveiled: a directory and guide to 19th century born artists active in Rhode Island, and where to find their work in publicly accessible Rhode Island Collections. Faculty Devel. grant, RISD, 2007. Mem.: ARLIS-NE (New Eng. chpt.) (treas. 1987—88, 1991—93), ARLIS-NA (N.Am.) (Worldwide Books award 2008). Avocations: ceramics, walking, travel, theater, art. Office: RI Sch Design 2 College St Providence RI 02903 Office Fax: 401-709-5932.

NACHMAN, DAVID HOWARD, lawyer; b. NYC, Feb. 14, 1963; s. Gerald and Harriet Nachman; m. Laura Joy Nachman, Sept. 2, 2001; children: Michael, Marc, Daniel. BS, Georgetown U., Washington, 1985; JD, Case Western Res. U., Cleve., 1988, MBA, 1989; LLM, NYU, NYC. Bar: NJ 1990, US Ct. Appeals (3d cir.), US Ct. Internat. Trade 1991, US Dist. Ct. NJ 1990. Asst. corrs. sec. Office of US Senator Bill Bradley, Washington, 1982—83; legal asst. Law Offices of Goldberg, Guggenheimer, Gelman & Dubroff, NYC, 1983; asst. probation officer DC Office of Probation, Family Svcs. divsn., Washington, 1984—85; law clk. US Atty.'s Office, No. Dist. Ohio, Cleve., 1986; summer assoc. Gibbons, Del Deo, Dolan, Griffinger & Vecchione, Newark, 1987—88, atty., 1988—92, Giordano, Halleran & Ciesla, P.C., Middletown, NJ, 1992—93; immigration dept. chair Grotta, Glassman & Hoffman, P.A., Roseland, NJ, 2000—03; mng. atty. Nachman & Assocs., PC, Paramus, NJ, 1993—2000, Upper Saddle River, NJ, 1993—. Lectr. in field; coord. jud. affairs Office of Dean of Student Affairs Case Western Res. U., Cleve., 1988—89; adj. prof. paralegal studies Fairleigh Dickinson U., 1995—; adj. prof. paralegal studies, mem. adv. bd. Bergen CC, Paramus, 2003—; ptnr. Bistro En, Lounge Zen, Teaneck, NJ, 2003—. Contbr. articles to profl. jours. Mem. Affiliated Bus. Cons., N.J. Tech. Coun., Greater Mahwah C. of C. Mem.: Am. Immigration Lawyers Assn. (mentor 1995—, state dept. liaison NJ chpt. 2003—), Soc. Human Resource Mgmt. of North Jersey/Rockland County, Bergen County Bar Assn., NJ State Bar Assn., Psi Chi, Delta Phi Epsilon. Achievements include having restaurants featured in The Record and the NY Times. Avocations: sailing, golf. Office: Nachman & Associates PC The Visaserve Bldg 487 Goffle Rd Ridgewood NJ 07450

NACHMAN, GERALD WEIL, columnist, critic, writer; b. Oakland, Calif., Jan. 13, 1938; s. Leonard Calvert and Isabel (Weil) N.; m. Mary Campbell McGeachy, Sept. 3, 1966 (div. 1979). Student, Merritt Coll., 1955-57; BA in Journalism, San Jose State U., 1960. TV and humor columnist San Jose (Calif.) Mercury, 1960-63; feature writer N.Y. Post, NYC, 1963-66; drama critic Oakland (Calif.) Tribune, 1966-71; syndicated humor columnist N.Y. Daily News, 1973-79; critic and columnist San Francisco Chronicle, 1979-93. Juror Pulitzer Prize Com. to choose best play, 1991. Author: The Portable Nachman, 1960, Playing House, 1978, Out on a Whim, 1983, The Fragile Bachelor, 1989; contbr. to (book) Snooze, 1986, Raised on Radio, 1998, Seriously Funny: The Rebel Comedians of the 1950's and 1960's, 2003, Right Here on Our Stage Tonight! Ed Sullivan's America, 2009; contbr. articles to newspapers, mag.; author, co-lyricist (revues) Quirks, 1979, Aftershocks, 1992, New Wrinkles, 1999, 2005, 2009. Recipient Page One award N.Y. Newspaper Guild, 1965, Deems Taylor award ASCAP, 1989. E-mail: nachnach@comcast.net.

NACHMAN, JAMES BURT, pediatric hematologist-oncologist; b. Chgo., 1948; MD, Johns Hopkins U., Balt., 1974. Cert. in pediat. 1979, in pediatric hematology-oncology 1980. Internship in pediat. Children's Meml. Hosp., Chgo., 1974—75, residency in pediat., 1975—77, fellowship, 1977—79; residency in pediatric hematol. oncology Wylers Children's Hosp., Chgo., 1979—80, hosp. appointment; prof. pediat., dir. clin. programs, hematology/oncology U. Chgo. Comer Children's Hosp. Contbr. articles to profl. jours. including the New Eng. Jour. Medicine. Mem.: Am. Soc. Hematology, Am. Soc. Pediatric Hematology Oncology, Children's Oncology Group (mem. acute lymphoblastic leukemia and Hodgkin's disease study com.), Internat. Ponte de Legno (co-founder internat. acute lymphoblastic leukemia study com.), Nat. Cancer Inst. (mem. PDQ bd. pediatric cancer). Office: Univ Chgo Comer Children's Hosp 5841 S Maryland Ave MC 4060 Chicago IL 60637 Office Phone: 773-702-6808. Office Fax: 773-702-9881. Business E-Mail: jnachman@peds.bsd.uchicago.edu.

NACHMAN, RONALD JAMES, chemist, researcher; b. Takoma Park, Md., Feb. 1, 1954; s. Joseph Frank and Rosemary (Anderson) N.; m. Lita Rose Wilson, Dec. 18, 1976 (div. 1987); m. Isidora Austria Panis, May 6, 1989. BS in Chemistry, U. Calif., San Diego, 1976; PhD in Organic Chemistry, Stanford U., 1981. Rsch. asst. Scripps Inst. Oceanography, La Jolla, Calif., 1974-76; chemist Western Regional Rsch. Ctr., USDA, Berkeley, Calif., 1981-89, Vet. Toxicology and Entomology Rsch. Lab., College Station, Tex., 1989—. Vis. scientist dept. molecular biology Salk Inst., La Jolla, 1985, Scripps Rsch. Inst., La Jolla, 1988-89. Mem. editl. adv. bd. Pesticides, The Jour. Peptides, guest editor, 2001-07; mem. organizing com. Ann. Invertebrate Neuropeptide Conf.; contbr. sci. articles to profl. jours. Recipient USDA Cert. of Merit, 1988, 1991, 1994—2007, Arthur S. Flemming award for sci. achievement, 1994. Fellow Internat. Neoropeptide Soc. (bd. dirs. 2000—); mem. AAAS, Internat. Neuropeptide Soc., Am. Chem. Soc., N.Y. Acad. Scis., Sigma Xi. Avocations: travel, photography, jogging, racquetball. Home: 14891 Pollux Dr Willis TX 77318-5079 Office: USDA Southern Plains Agrl Rsch Ctr 2881 F And B Rd College Station TX 77845-4988

NACHMANOVITCH, STEPHEN, violinist, composer, author and educator; BA, Harvard U., 1971; PhD in History of Consciousness, U. Calif., Santa Cruz, 1975. Improvisational violinist performing internationally, numerous appearances on radio, TV and at music and theater festivals. Author: Free Play: Improvisation in Life and Art, 1990, Improvisation as Teching as Learning, as Evolution, 2006, Improvisation as a Tool for Investigating Reality, 2006, Beateson and the Arts, 2007, Improvisation and the Pattern Which Connects, 2007, It Don'y Mean a Thing if it Ain't got that Swing: Bateson's Epistemology and the Rhythms of Life, 2008, This is Play, 2009; musical and media works: The Four Zoas, 1978, Doors of Perception, 1979, Music From Before the Beginning, 1980, Minding the Earth, 1981, Blake's Vision, 1982, Earth's Answer, 1982, Training the Mind Ox, 1984, Path of Light, 1986, First Life, 1986, Music for Rachel's Brain, 1987, Ain Soph, 1991, Wheel of Time, 1991, Merging at Merging Ore, 1992; 5 artsworks fron the Vishvamati series, 1998, 9 artsworks fron the Visual Music Tone Painter series, 1999, Unstoppable, 2000, Visible Music, 2000, Job Returns, 2002, Electric and Acoustic Improvisations, Vol. 1, 2005, Traming the Mind-Ox, 2006, Theater Games, 2006, Ludi Fecundus, 2008, Saraswati steps up to bat, 2008, Impermanence, 2009; computer music softwware: The World Music Menu, Visual Music Music Tone Painter. Office: PO Box 667 Ivy VA 22945-0667

NACHSHIN, ROBERT JAY, lawyer; b. NYC, June 3, 1950; s. Edward and Eleanor (Ciporin) N.; m. Monica Jane Lipkin, May 22, 1976. BA cum laude, Bucknell U., 1972; M in Internat. Affairs, JD, Columbia U., 1976. Bar: Calif. 1977, U.S. Dist. Ct. (cen. dist.) Calif. 1977. Assoc. Loeb & Loeb, LA, 1976-80, Greenberg & Gluster, LA, 1980-82, ptnr., 1982-87; ptnr., head family law dept. Jeffer, Mangels, Butler & Marmaro, LA, 1987—89; founding ptnr. Nachshin & Weston, LLP, LA, 1989—. Mediator family law L.A. Superior Ct., 1982—. Co-author (with Scott N. Weston): Do, You Do... But Sign Here: A Quick and Easy Guide to Cohabitation, Prenuptial and Postnuptial Agreements, 2004. Bd. dirs. Juvenile Diabetes Found., 1983-87. Named one of So. Calif. Super Lawyers, L.A. Magazine, 2005. Mem. ABA, L.A. County Bar Assn. (exec. com. family law sect., 1983-89), Beverly Hills Bar Assn., Calif. Bd. Legal Specialization (cert. specialist 1982—), Columbia U. Alumni Assn. (v.p. 1981—), Pi Sigma Alpha, Omicron Delta Kappa. Democrat. Avocations: hiking, running, scuba diving, skiing, travel. Office: Nachshin & Weston LLP 11601 Wilshire Blvd Ste 1500 Los Angeles CA 90025

NACHT, MICHAEL LEONARD, federal agency administrator, political science educator; b. NYC, Sept. 1, 1942; s. Jack and Ann Bertha N.; m. Marjorie Jo, Jan. 25, 1964; children: David Allen, Alexander Carey. BS in Aeronautics and Astronautics, NYU, 1963, MS in Ops. Rsch., 1969; MS in Stats., Case Western Res., 1966; MA in Polit. Sci., New Sch. U., 1970; PhD in Polit. Sci., Columbia U., 1973. Aero. engr. NASA Lewis Rsch. Ctr., Cleve., 1963-66; sr. scientist Dunlap & Associates, Inc., Darien, Conn., 1966-70; assoc. prof. pub. policy Harvard U., Cambridge, Mass., 1973-84; dean, prof. U. Md., College Park, 1984-94, 97-98; asst. dir. US Arms Control & Disarmament Agy., Washington, 1994-97; dean, prof. pub. policy U. Calif., Berkeley, 1998—2009; asst. sec. for global strategic affairs US Dept. Def., 2009—. Author: The Age of Vulnerability, 1985; co-author: Missing the Boat, 1991, Beyond Government, 1995. Fgn. policy advisor Gore for Pres., 1999-2000; mem. Threat Reduction Advisory Com. US Dept. Def., 2001-04. Pres.'s fellow Columbia U., 1972, Traveling fellow Internat. Rsch. Edn. Exchange Bd., 1983. Mem. Internat. Inst. Strategic Studies, Coun. Fgn. Rels., Cosmos Club. Democrat. Jewish. Avocations: racquetball, basketball, tennis, backgammon, chess. Office: US Dept Def 2900 Def Pentagon Washington DC 20301*

NACHTIGAL, MAURICE, pathology professor; b. Bucharest, Romania, May 17, 1933; s. Alphonse Nachtigal and Adina Bercovici; m. Sidonia Aurelia Ciugudean, June 27, 1964; children: Noel Maurice, Alina Nachtigal Kale. MD, Faculty Medicine, Bucharest, 1957; PhD, Romanian Acad. Med. Scis., Bucharest, 1973. Diplomate Ednl. Commn. Fgn. Med. Grads., 1984. Sci. investigator Inst. Oncology, Bucharest, 1964—66; prin. sci. investigator Stefan Nicolau Inst. Virology, Bucharest, 1966—71; assoc. prof. of biology and genetics U. Craiova Faculty Medicine, Romania, 1971—77; microbiologist Cantacuzino Inst. Sera and Vaccines, Bucharest, 1977—80; adj. prof. pediat. U. SC. Sch. Medicine, Columbia, 1984—86, adj. prof. microbiology & immunology, 1985—86; mentor U. SC., 1984—2005, prof. pathology Columbia, 1981—2006, disting. prof. emeritus pathology and microbiology, 2005—09. Pathology cons. Dorn Veterans Adminstrn. Med. Ctr., Columbia, 1996—2002; clin. pathology cons. Craiova Gen. Hosp., Craiova, Romania. Author: (book) Cytogenetics, Principles and Methods., The role of Herpesviruses in Atherogenesis, Cardiovascular Disease, Molecular and Cellular Mechanisms, Prevention and Treatment., Textbook of Biology and Genetics; contbr. articles to profl. jours. (Intelectual Property award, 2000). Mem. Am. Soc. Investigative Pathology Membership Com., 1996—2000; sci. advisor Oncology Inst., Cluj-Napoca, Romania, 2001—02; voting mem. U. SC. Faculty Senate, 1993—96; full mem. VA Med. Ctr. Human Studies Com., Columbia, 1996—2004. Recipient Stefan Nicolau medal, Romanian Acad. Med. Scis., 2001; Exch. Vis. Scientist fellowship, Acad. Med. Scis. USSR, 1968, Cancer rsch. fellowship, Internat. Agy. Rsch. Cancer, 1969—70, grant, McNeil Consumer & Splty. Pharms., 2003—04. Mem.: Am. Soc. Investigative Pathology (membership com. 1996—2000). Achievements include patents for method of diagnosing cancer in human cells using a reverse transcriptase-polymerase chain reaction; discovery of isolation and cloning of a new human chromosome 4 repetitive centromeric DNA and amplification of stromelysin-3. Avocations: hiking, gardening, music, history. Home: 111 Westlake Ridge Dr Blythewood SC 29016-7861 Office: Univ SC Sch Medicine Columbia SC 29209 Personal E-mail: maur.nac@gmail.com. Business E-Mail: maurice.nachtigal@uscmed.sc.edu.

NACHTIGAL, PATRICIA, lawyer; b. 1946; BA, Montclair State U.; JD, Rutgers U.; LLM, NYU. Corporate atty. Ingersoll-Rand Plc, Dublin, 1979—83, dir. taxes and legal, 1983—88, sec., mng. atty., 1988—91, v.p., gen. counsel, 1991—2000, sr. v.p., gen. counsel, 2000—, bd. dirs., 2002—. Gov., trustee Rutgers, State U. N.J., 1996—, chair, 2003—04. Office: Ingersoll-Rand Plc 1 Centennial Ave Piscataway NJ 08855 Office Phone: 732-652-6734. Business E-Mail: patricia_nachtigal@irco.com.

NACHTWEY, JAMES ALAN, photojournalist; b. Syracuse, NY, Mar. 14, 1948; s. James Vincent and Jean (Stockton) N. BA cum laude, Dartmouth Coll., 1970; DFA (hon.), Mass. Coll. Art, 1997. Contract photographer Time mag., NYC, 1984—; mem. Magnum Photos, NYC, 1986—. Tchr. Internat. Ctr. Photography, N.Y.C., 1993, 94, 95, 96, Santa Fe Workshop, 1994, Photography at the Summit, Jackson Hole, Wyo., 1994, 96. Author, photographer: Deeds of War, 1989 (Leica award 1989), The Inferno, 1995 (catalog), Ground Level (catalog), 1998; contbg. photographer (books) War Torn, El Salvador, In Our Time-40 Years of Magnum, The Indelible Image, Odyssey-Photography at the National Geographic, National Geographic, The Photographs, (mags.) Time, Life, Nat. Geographic, N.Y. Times mag., GEO, L'Express, Stern LeFigaro; one-man shows Internat. Ctr. Photography, 1989, Hasselblad Ctr., Goteborg, Sweden, 1992, Canon Gallery, Amsterdam, The Netherlands, 1992, Carolinum, Prague, Czech Republic, 1994, Nieuwe Kerk, Amsterdam, 1995, Hood Mus., Dartmouth Coll., 1995, Internat. Forum, Tokyo, 1997, Fleethof, Hamburg, Germany, 1997, Japanese Palace, Dresden, Germany, 1997, Mass. Coll. Art, Boston, 1997. Recipient Robert Capa gold medal Overseas Press Club, 1983, 84, 86, 94, Olivier Rebbot award, 1992, 93; photography award World Press Photo Found., 1992, 94, Mag. Photographer of Yr. award Nat. Press Photographers Assn., 1983, 86, 88, 90, 92, 94, Canon Photog. essayist award, 1992; Infinity award Internat. Ctr. Photography, 1991, 93, Leica award New Sch. for Social Rsch., 1989, 90, award Budapest Photgraphic Festival, 1985, Nikon award Maine Workshop, 1985, Nikon World Image award New Sch.-Parsons Sch. Design, 1991, Bayeaux award for war correspondents, 1995, Heinz Found. Achievement award, 2006, Common Wealth award, Martin Luther King award, Dr. Jean Mayer Global Citizenship award, Henry Luce award, Alfred Eisenstaedt award; Eugene Smith Meml. grantee, 1994; co-recipient, Tech. Entertainment Design (TED) award, 2007. Fellow Royal Photographic Soc. Avocations: fly fishing, skiing. Office: Magnum Photos 151 W 25th St New York NY 10001-7204

NACHWALTER, MICHAEL, lawyer; b. NYC, Aug. 31, 1940; s. Samuel J. Nachwalter; m. Irene, Aug. 15, 1965; children: Helynn, Robert. BS, Bucknell U., 1962; MS, LI U., 1967; JD cum laude, U. Miami, 1967; LLM, Yale U., 1968. Bar: Fla. 1967, DC 1979, US Dist. Ct. (so. dist.) Fla. 1967, US Dist. Ct. (mid. dist.) Fla. 1982, US Ct. Appeals (5th and 11th cirs.) 1967, US Supreme Ct. 1975. Law clk. to judge US Dist. Ct. (so. dist.) Fla.; shareholder Kelly, Black, Black & Kenny; now shareholder Kenny Nachwalter, P.A., Miami. Lectr. Law Sch. U. Miami. Editor-in-chief U. Miami Law Rev., 1966-67. Fellow Am. Coll. Trial Lawyers; mem. ABA, FBA, Am. Bd. Trial Advs., Fla. Bar Assn. (bd. govs. 1982-90), Internat. Soc. Barristers (dir.), Dade County Bar Assn., Iron Arrow, Soc. Wig and Robe, Omicron Delta Kappa, Phi Kappa Phi, Phi Delta Phi. Office: Kenny Nachwalter PA 201 S Biscayne Blvd Ste 1100 Miami FL 33131-4327

NACKEL, JOHN GEORGE, health venture capital executive; b. Medford, Mass., Nov. 4, 1951; s. Michael and Josephine (Maria) N.; m. Gail Helen Becker, Oct. 30, 1976; children: Melissa Anne, Allison Elizabeth. BS, Tufts U., 1973; MS in Pub. Health and Indsl. Engring., U. Mo., 1975, PhD, 1977. Sr. mgr. Ernst & Young, Chgo., 1977—83; nat. dir. health care cons. Cleve., 1983—87; regional dir. health industry svcs., 1987—91; mng. dir. health care Ernst & Young, Cleve., 1991—93; mng. dir. Health Consulting, LA, 1993—99, New Ventures, 1999—2000; CEO, Sogeti USA, LLC, 2000—01; chmn., CEO, Sértan Corp., Santa Fe Springs, Calif., 2002—03; exec. v.p. US Tech., Beverly Hills, Calif., 2003—05; pres., COO Salick Cardiovascular Ctrs., 2006—07; CEO Three Sixty Group, 2007—. Author: Cost Management for Hospitals, 1987 (Am. Hosp. Assn. book award 1988); mem. editl bd. Jour. Med. Systems, 1983-; contbr. articles to profl. jours Grantee Dept. Health Edn. Welfare, Washington, 1973-76. Fellow Am. Coll. Healthcare Execs., Healthcare Info. and Mgmt. Systems Soc. (articles award); mem. Inst. Indsl. Engrs. (sr.), U. Mo. Health Svcs. Mgmt. Alumni Assn. (pres.), L.A. Country Club, Annandale Golf Club. Republican. Avocations: golf, tennis, squash, paddle, photography. Home: 666 Linda Vista Ave Pasadena CA 91105-1145 Office Phone: 310-674-9360. Personal E-mail: jnackel@360ag.com.

NACKMAN, LEE, computer software company executive; m. Ava Nackman; 3 children. BS in Computer Sci., Brown U., Providence; PhD in Computer Sci., U. NC, Chapel Hill, 1982. Rschr. IBM Thomas J. Watson Rsch. Ctr.; v.p. application devel. tools IBM, CTO rational divsn., v.p. product devel. and customer support, rational software divsn.; v.p. identity and security divsn. Microsoft Corp., Redmond, Wash., 2009—. Bd. dirs. med. image processing start-up. Author more than 50 technical papers. Named to IBM Acad. Tech. Achievements include patents in field. Office: Microsoft Corp One Microsoft Way Redmond WA 98052-6399*

NADAL, ANITA, language educator; d. Jose A. and Althea C. Nadal. MA, U. Richmond, 2006. Prof. Va. Commonwealth U., Richmond, 2005—. Vol. MCV, Richmond, 2006—08. Mem.: ATA. Office: Va Commonwealth Univ 312 N Shafer St Richmond VA 23284

NADAL, KEVIN L., psychology professor, director; s. Leo and Charity Nadal. BA in Psychology & Polit. Sci., U. Calif., Irvine, 2000; MA in Counseling, Mich. State U., East Lansing, 2002; PhD, Columbia U., NY, 2008. Cons. Kevin Nadal Consulting, NYC, 2005—; asst. prof. John Jay Coll. Criminal Justice, NYC, 2006—, dep. dir., forensic mental health counseling program, 2008—. Cons. NY Police Dept., NYC, 2008—. Comedy, poetry, Kevin Nadal's One Man Show. Recipient Svc. award, Philippine Econ. & Cultural Endowment, Inc., 2008; Minority fellowship, Tchrs. Coll. Columbia U., 2002—04. Mem.: Filipino Am. Nat. Hist. Soc., Asian Am. Psychol. Assn. Liberal. Achievements include research in microaggressions and LGBT issues. Office: John Jay Coll Criminal Justice 445 W 59th St New York NY 10019 Business E-Mail: knadal@jjay.cuny.edu.

NADAS, JOHN ADALBERT, psychiatrist, educator; b. Innsbruck, Austria, Mar. 14, 1949; arrived in U.S., 1950; s. Julius Zoltan and Ibolya Erzsebet (Szöllösy) Nadas; m. Gabriella Ilona Ormay, Apr. 11, 1981; children: János, Miklós, István. BA, Case We. Res. U., 1970; MD, Duke U., 1974. Resident in psychiatry U. Chgo., 1974—77; pvt. practice Munster, Ind., 1977—84, Canton, Ohio, 1984—; instr. psychiatry Northeastern Ohio U. Coll. Medicine, Rootstown, 1985—86, asst. prof., 1986; coord. psychiat. edn. Mercy Med. Ctr., Canton, 1985—87, clin. dir. psychiat. svcs., 1990-91. Cons. Crisis Ctr., Canton, 1985—92. Author: Philosophical Basis of Depth Psychotherapy, 1983, Journey Toward Energy, 1995, Transformation, 1999, (book) Sweet Nonexistence, 2006. Trustee Sisters of Charity Found., Canton, 1996—2003. Named NCAA nat. collegiate epee champion, 1970; named to All-Am. Fencing Team, 1969, 1970. Mem.: AMA, Am. Psychiat. Assn., Hungarian Assn. (pres. 2000—03). Roman Catholic. Avocations: basketball, computer programming. Office: 1330 Mercy Dr NW Ste 320 Canton OH 44708-2624 Office Phone: 330-489-1495.

NADEAU, ROBERT BERTRAND, JR., lawyer; b. Miami Beach, Fla., July 15, 1950; s. Robert B. and Ernestine Inez (Nicholson) N. BBA magna cum laude, U. Notre Dame, 1972; JD with honors, U. Fla., 1975. Bar: Fla. 1975, U.S. Dist. Ct. (mid. dist.) Fla. 1976, U.S. Dist. Ct. (so. dist.) Fla. 1982, U.S. Ct. Appeals (11th cir.) 1982. Asst. to pres. The Fla. Bar, Tampa, 1975-76; ptnr. Akerman, Senterfitt & Eidson, P.A., Orlando, Fla., 1976—. Arbitrator Am. Arbitration Assn., Orlando, 1987—. Mem. ABA, The Fla. Bar (chmn. student edn. and admission to bar com., vice chmn. 9th cir. grievance com.), Notre Dame Club Greater Orlando (pres. 1979-80). Avocations: golf, running. Office: Akerman Senterfitt PO Box 231 Orlando FL 32802 Home Phone: 407-834-5059; Office Phone: 407-423-4000. Business E-Mail: robert.nadeau@akerman.com.

NADEAU, ROBERT M., geophysicist; PhD, U. Calif., Berkeley, 1995. Assoc. rsch. geophysicist UC Berkeley Seismol. Lab., 1998—. Contbr. articles to profl. jours. Grant, US Geol. Survey, 2008—. Mem.: Am. Geophys. Union, Seismol. Soc. Am.

NADEEM, TAMER M., research scientist; b. Alexandria, Egypt, Apr. 8, 1972; married. PhD, U. Md., Coll. Pk. Grad. rsch. asst. Md. Info. and Network Dynamics lab., Coll. Pk., 2001—05; rsch. internship Fujitsu Labs. Am., Inc., Coll. Pk., 2004—05; rsch. scientist Siemens Corp. Rsch., Princeton, NJ, 2005—. Recipient 1st prize, Assn. Computing Machinery, 2006; Travel grants, NSF, 2004—05. Mem.: IEEE, Assn. Computing Machinery, Phi Kappa Phi, Sigma Xi. Achievements include patents for transparent digital rights management for extendible content viewers; vehicular information transfer protocol; patents pending for improved utilization of wireless network using interference estimation; data rate adjustment in 802.15.4 networks for harsh industrial environments; scalable traffic monitoring system. Avocation: travel, reading, squash, music. Home: 6003 Ravens Crest Dr Plainsboro NJ 08536 Office: Siemens Corp Rsch 755 College Rd E Princeton NJ 08540 Personal E-mail: tamernadeem@hotmail.com. Business E-Mail: tamer.nadeem@siemens.com.

NADEL, ELLIOTT, investment company executive; b. NYC, Nov. 23, 1945; s. Archie and Faye (Braverman) N.; children: Lindsey, Amanda. BBA, Baruch Coll., 1969, MBA, 1971. Portfolio mgr. SwissRe Advisors, NYC, 1973-74; v.p., stockbroker E. F. Hutton, NYC, 1975-84, Shearson Lehman Bros., NYC, 1984-85, Oppenheimer & Co., NYC, 1985, Rooney Pace Inc., NYC, 1986-87, Philips Appel & Walden, NYC, 1987-88; sr. v.p. investments Moore, Schley & Cameron, NYC, 1988-90, Prudential-Securities, NYC, 1990-94; sr. v.p. Gilford Securities, NYC, 1994—96, SFY Investments, 1996—97, Westrock Advisor, 1997—99, Tarpon Scurry Investments, 1999—2000, Chgo. Investments Group, 2001, EN Investments, 2001—; prin. Hedge Fund. With US Army, 1969-74. Jewish. Avocations: jogging, reading, cars, golf, travel. Home Phone: 917-301-7600. E-mail: mrch1123@aol.com.

NADEL, NORMAN ALLEN, civil engineer; b. NYC, Apr. 10, 1927; s. Louis and Bertha (Julius) N.; m. Cynthia Esther Jereski, July 6, 1952; children: Nancy Sarah Frank, Lawrence Bruce. B.C.E., CCNY, 1949; postgrad., Columbia U., 1949-50. Registered profl. engr., N.Y., Conn. Engr. Arthur A. Johnson Corp., NYC, 1950-53; engr. Slattery Contracting Corp., NYC, 1953-56; mgr., estimator Hartsdale Constrn. Corp., Hartsdale, NY, 1956-59; engr. MacLean Grove & Co., Inc., Greenwich, Conn., 1959-63, project mgr., 1963-66, v.p., 1966-70, pres., 1970-94; chmn. Nadel Assocs., Inc., Brewster, NY, 1988—. Cons. tunnel and underground constrn.; mem. com. on tunneling Transp. Rsch. Bd., Washington, 1974-75; mem. U.S. Nat. Com. on Tunneling Tech., Washington, 1976-82, chmn., 1980-81; chmn. adv. com. Superconducting Super Collider Underground Tech., 1992-94. Trustee Tunnel Workers Welfare Fund, N.Y.C., 1976-88; mem. adv bd. CCNY Engring. Sch., 1992—. With USNR, 1945-46 Named Heavy Constrn. Man of Yr., United Jewish Appeal, 1984; Benjamin Wright award Conn. Soc. Civil Engrs., 1984, Townsend Harris medal City Coll. of N.Y. Alumni Assn., 1987. Fellow ASCE (Constrn. Mgmt. award 1986); mem. NAE, Conn. Acad. Sci. and Engring., The Moles (pres. 1982-83, Outstanding Achievement in Constrn. award 1985), Am. Arbitration Assn., Tau Beta Pi, Chi Epsilon. Office: Nadel Assocs Inc 420 Clock Tower Commons Brewster NY 10509-4060 Office Phone: 845-279-5516.

NADELLA, SATYA, computer software company executive; b. 1967; MS in Computer Sci., U. Wis.; MBA, U. Chgo. Software devel. engr. Sun Microsystems Inc.; joined Microsoft Corp., 1992, program mgr. Windows developer rels. group, founder bCentral small bus. online svc., leader bCentral mktg. & bus. devel., 1999—2002, gen. mgr. commerce platforms group, corp. v.p. Microsoft bus. solutions, 2002—08, sr. v.p. search, portal & advt. platform group, 2008—09, sr. v.p. rsch. and devel., online services divsn., 2009—. Office: Microsoft Corp One Microsoft Way Redmond WA 98052-6399*

NADELSON, SANDRA G., nursing educator; m. Louis Nadelson. MSN, MEd, Calif. State U., LA, 1990; PhD, U. Nev., Las Vegas, 2007. RN Calif., 1984. Faculty mem. CC of S. Nev., Las Vegas, 2002—04, U. Nev. Las Vegas, 2005—07, Boise State U., 2008—. Mem.: MENSA, Sigma Theta Tau (assoc.; sec. 2005—06). Office: 1910 University Dr Boise ID 83725 Office Phone: 208-426-4679. Business E-Mail: sandranadelson@boisestate.edu.

NADER, LAURA, anthropologist, educator; b. Winsted, Conn., Sept. 30, 1930; m. Norman Milleron, Sept. 1, 1962; 3 children BA, Wells Coll., Aurora, NY, 1952; PhD, Radcliffe Coll., Cambridge, Mass., 1961. Faculty mem. U. Calif., Berkeley, 1960—, prof. anthropology; vis. prof. Yale Law Sch., New Haven, fall 1971; Henry R. Luce prof. Sch. Law Harvard Wellesley Coll., Mass., 1983-84; vis. prof. Stanford U. Law Sch., 1987-89. Field work in Mex., Lebanon, Morocco and US; mem. adv. com. NSF, 1971-75; mem. cultural anthropology com. NIMH, 1968—, chmn. to 1971, chmn. social scis. rsch. tng. rev. com., 1976-78; mem. NAS-NRC assembly behavioral and social scis., 1969-71, 73-75, 75—; mem. com. Nuclear and Alternative Energy Forms, NAS, 1976-80. Editor: Law in Culture and Society, 1969, The Disputing Process, 1978, No Access to Law-Alternatives to the American Judicial System, 1980, Harmony Ideology, 1990, Naked Science, 1996, The Life of the Law, 2000; co-author (with U. Mattei): Plunder: When the Rule of Law is Illegal, 2008; contbr. articles to profl. jours.; author edni. films, mem. editl. com. Law and Soc. Rev., 1967—. Mem. Calif. Coun. for the Humanities, 1975—79, Carnegie Coun. on Children, 1972—77; active Coun. Librs. at Libr. of Congress, Washington, 1988—. Radcliffe Coll. grantee, 1954-59; Thaw fellow Harvard U., 1955-56, 58-59; Peabody Mus. grantee, 1954-59; Am. Philos. Assn. grantee, 1955; Mexican Govt. grantee, 1957-58; Milton Fund grantee, 1959-60, Wellness Found. grantee, 1993-96; fellow Ctr. Advanced Study in Behavioral Scis., Stanford, Calif., 1963-64; NSF grantee, 1966-68; Wenner Gren Found. grantee, 1964, 66, 73; Carnegie Corp. grantee, 1975; Woodrow Wilson fellow, 1979-80; Wells Coll. Alumnae award, 1980; Radcliffe Coll. Alumnae award, 1984. Mem.: AAAS, Soc. Women Geographers (Outstanding Achievement award 1990), Am. Acad. Arts and Scis., Ctr. for Study of Responsive Law (trustee 1968—), Law and Soc. Assn. (trustee 1967—72, Harry Kalven prize 1995), Social Sci. Rsch. Coun., Am. Anthrop. Assn. (planning and devel. com. 1968—71, 1975—76), Am. Acad. Arts and Scis. Office: U Calif Dept Anthropology 313 Kroeber Hl Berkeley CA 94720-0001 Office Phone: 510-642-1218. Office Fax: 510-643-8557.

NADER, RALPH, advocate, lawyer, writer; b. Winsted, Conn., Feb. 27, 1934; s. Nadra and Rose (Bouziane) Nader. AB magna cum laude, Princeton U., 1955; LLB with distinction, Harvard U., 1958. Bar: Conn. 1958, Mass. 1959, US Supreme Ct 1959. Former atty., Hartford, Conn.; prof. hist. & govt. U. Hartford, 1961-63; staff mem. to asst. sec. of labor US Senate, Washington, 1964; founder, dir. Pub. Citizen, Washington, 1971—80; founder of numerous non-profit orgn.'s, 1969—, including Ctr. for Study of Responsive Law, 1969, Ctr. Women's Policy Studies, 1972, Ctr. Ins. Rsch., 1995, Ctr. Justice & Democracy, 1998, others. Author: Crashing the Party, 2002, Unsafe at Any Speed, 1965, Working on the System: A Manual for Citizen's Access to Federal Agencies, 1972, Action for a Change, 1972, You and Your Pension, 1973, Taming the Giant Corporation, 1976, The Lemon Book, 1980, The Big Boys, 1986, Winning The Insurance Game, 1990, No Contest: Corporate Lawyers and the Perversion of Justice in America, 1996, The Ralph Nader Reader, 2000, Crashing the Party: Taking on the Corporate Government in an Age of Surrender, 2002, In Pursuit of Justice: Collected Writing, 2004, The Good Fight: Declare Your Independence and Close the Democracy Gap, 2004, Civic Arousal, 2004, The Seventeen Traditions, 2007; co-author: (with John Abbots) Menace of Atomic Energy, 1979, (with Wesley J. Smith) Collision Course:The Truth About Airline Safety, 1993; editor: Whistle Blowing: The Report on the Conference on Professional Responsibility, 1972, The Consumer and Corporate Accountability, 1973; co-editor: Corporate Power in America, 1973, Verdicts on Lawyers, 1976, Who's Poisoning America, 1981. US presdl. candidate Green Party, 1996, 2000, Ind. Party, 2004, 2008. Served with US Army, 1959. Recipient Nieman Fellows award, 1965—66; named one of 10 Outstanding Young Men of Yr., US Jr. C. of C., 1967. Mem.: AAAS, ABA, Phi Beta Kappa. Independent. Address: Ctr for Study of Responsive Law PO Box 19367 Washington DC 20036-9367*

NADER, ROBERT ALEXANDER, retired judge, lawyer; b. Warren, Ohio, Mar. 31, 1928; s. Nassef J. and Emily (Nader) N.; m. Nancy M. Veauthier. BA, Western Res. U., 1950, LL.B., 1953. Bar: Ohio 1953. Ptnr. Paul G. Nader, Warren, 1953-83. Pres. Warren City Police and Fire Pension Bds., 1960-66; trustee Office Econ. Opportunity, 1970-72; mem. Warren City Coun., 1960-66, pres. pro tem, 1964-66; mem. Ohio Ho. of Reps., 1971-83, chmn. reference com., 1977-81, chmn. judiciary com., 1981-83; presiding judge Trumbull County Ct. Common Pleas, 1983-91; judge Ohio 11th Dist. Ct. of Appeals, 1991-03; trustee Family Svc. Assn., 1959-65. With AUS, 1946-48. Recipient Outstanding Young Man of Yr. award, 1964, award Am. Arbitration Assn., 1965, Community Action award Warren Area Bd. Realtors, 1967, Outstanding Svc. award Kent State U., Trumbull campus. 1978, Outstanding Svc. award Children's Rehab. Ctr., 1980; named to Warren H.S. Disting. Alumni Hall of Fame, 1993, Sports Hall of Fame, 2003. Mem. Ohio State Bar Assn., Trumbull County Bar Assn. (past pres., Pres.'s award for disting. svc. 2003), Ct. Appeals Judges Assn. (chmn. legis. com. 1995-98), Trumbull County Law Libr. Assn. (trustee 1958-72), Trumbull New Theatre (past pres.), KC, Elks, Lambda Chi Alpha. Roman Catholic. Home: 798 Wildwood Dr NE Warren OH 44483-4458 *My parents provided me with a strong moral background and the inspiration to improve. I will never feel that I have achieved success and thus may continue to improve.*

NADIG, GERALD GEORGE, retired manufacturing executive; b. Astoria, NY, May 9, 1945; s. Charles Edwin and Louise (Hahn) N.; m. Nancy Hanford Stewart, June 20, 1970; children: Sara Hanford, Jennifer Stewart. AB cum laude, Harvard Coll., 1967, MBA, 1974. Various manfacturing positions, 1974—85; dir. mfg. Toyoda Machinery USA, Arlington Heights, Ill., 1985-87, v.p., gen. mgr., 1987-88; v.p., gen. mgr. Littell div. Allied Products Corp., Chgo., 1988-89; exec. v.p. pre finish metals Material Scis. Corp., 1989-90; pres. Pre Finish Metals Materials Scis. Corp., 1990-91; pres., chief oper. officer Material Scis. Corp., Chgo., 1991-96, pres., CEO, 1997—2003, chmn. bd. dirs., 1998—2003; bd. dirs. Tokheim Corp., 2000—03; ret. Mem. adv. bd. Masters in Mgmt. Program Northwestern U. Trustee Village of Lake Barrington, 1989-91. With U.S. Army, 1966-70. Mem. Soc. Mfg. Engrs. (sr.), Nat. Assn. Corp. Dirs. (bd. dirs. Chgo. chpt. 2002—), Barrington Area Cmty. Found. (bd. dirs.) Avocations: golf, tennis, game theory. Home: 24354 N Grandview Dr Barrington IL 60010-6218 Office Phone: 847-381-3464. Personal E-mail: gerrynadig@aol.com.

NADLER, DAVID A., professional services executive; Founder, chmn., CEO Delta Consulting Grp., Inc., 1980—2000; chmn., CEO Mercer Delta Consulting (following acquisition by Marsh & McLennan Cos.), 2000—05; vice chmn., mem. internat. adv. bd. Marsh & McLennan Cos.; sr. ptnr. Delta orgn. and Leadership unit Oliver Wyman (merger of Mercer Delta Consulting, Mercer Oliver Wyman and Mercer Mgmt. Consulting), 2007—. Office: Marsh & McLennan Cos 1166 Avenue of the Americas New York NY 10036 Office Phone: 212-345-5000.

NADLER, GERALD, management consultant, educator; b. Cin., Mar. 12, 1924; s. Samuel and Minnie (Krumbein) N.; m. Elaine Muriel Dubin, June 22, 1947; children: Burton Alan, Janice Susan, Robert Daniel. Student, U. Cin., 1942-43; BSME, Purdue U., 1945, MS in Indsl. Engring, 1946, PhD, 1949. Instr. Purdue U., 1948-49; asst. prof. indsl. engring. Washington U., St. Louis, 1949-52, assoc. prof., 1952-55, prof., head dept. indsl. engring., 1955-64; prof. U. Wis., Madison, 1964-83, chmn. dept. indsl. engring., 1964-67, 71-75; prof., chmn. dept. indsl. and sys. engring. U. So. Calif., LA, 1983-93, IBM chair engring. mgmt., 1986-93, IBM chair emeritus, prof. emeritus, 1993—; v.p. Artcraft Mfg. Co., St. Louis, 1956-57; dir. Intertherm Inc., St. Louis, 1969-85. Pres. Ctr. for Breakthrough Thinking Inc., L.A., 1989—; vis. prof. U. Birmingham, Eng., 1959, Waseda U., Tokyo, 1963-64, Ind. U., 1964, U. Louvain, Belgium, 1975, Technion-Israel Inst. Tech., Haifa, 1975-76; spkr. in field. Author: The Planning and Design Approach, 1981; (with S. Hibino) Breakthrough Thinking, 1990, 2d edit., 1994, Creative Solution Finding, 1995; (with G. Hoffherr, J. Moran) Breakthrough Thinking in Total Quality Management, 1994, (with W. Chandon) Ask the Right Questions, 2003, Smart Questions, 2004; contbr. articles to profl. jours.; reviewer books, papers, proposals. Mem. Ladue Bd. Edn., St. Louis County, 1960-63, L.A. County Quality and Productivity Commn., 1997—; chmn. planning com. Wis. Regional Med. Program, 1966-69; bd. dirs. USC Credit Union, 1994—. Served with USN, 1943-45. Gilbreth medal Soc. Advancement Mgmt., 1961, Editl. award Hosp. Mgmt. Mag., 1966, Disting. Engring. Alumnus award Purdue U., 1975, Outstanding Indsl. Engr. award, 1997; Book of Yr. award Inst. Indsl. Engrs., 1983, Frank and Lillian Gilbreth award, 1992; Phi Kappa Phi Faculty Recognition award U. So. Calif., 1990, Engring. Disting. Svc. award U. Wis. Madison, 2000. Fellow AAAS, Inst. Indsl. Engrs. (pres. 1989-90), Inst. Operations Rsch. and Mgmt. Scis., Inst. for Advancement Engrs., Am. Soc. Engring. Edn.; mem. NAE, Japan Work Design Soc. (hon. adv. 1968—), World Future Soc., Acad. Mgmt., Engring. Mgmt. Soc., Sigma Xi, Alpha Pi Mu (nat. officer), Pi Tau Sigma, Omega Rho, Tau Beta Pi. Office: Univ Park GER 240 Dept Of I&se Los Angeles CA 90089-0193 Office Phone: 213-740-6415. Personal E-mail: gnadler@breakthroughthinking.com. Business E-Mail: nadler@usc.edu.

NADLER, HENRY LOUIS, pediatrician, educator, geneticist; b. NYC, Apr. 15, 1936; s. Herbert and Mary (Kartiganer) N.; m. Benita Weinhard, June 16, 1957; children: Karen, Gary, Debra, Amy. AB, Colgate U., 1957; MD, Northwestern U., 1961; MS, U. Wis., 1965. Diplomate Am. Bd. Pediatrics, Am. Bd. Med. Genetics. Intern NYU Med. Ctr., 1961-62, sr. resident pediatrics, 1962-63, chief resident, 1963-64; teaching asst. NYU Sch. Medicine, 1962-63, clin. instr., 1963-64, U. Wis. Sch. Medicine, 1964-65; practice medicine specializing in pediatrics Chgo., 1965—; fellow Children's Meml. Hosp. dept. pediatrics Northwestern U., 1964-65; assoc. in pediatrics Northwestern U. Med. Sch., 1965-66, asst. prof., 1967-68, assoc. prof., 1968-70, prof., 1970-81, chmn. dept. pediatrics, 1970-81; prof. Northwestern U. Med. Sch. (Grad. Sch.), 1971-80; mem. staff Children's Meml. Hosp., 1965-81, head div. genetics, 1969-81, chief of staff, 1970-81; dean, prof. pediatrics, ob-gyn Wayne State U. Med. Sch., Detroit, 1981-88; prof. U. Chgo., 1988-89, U. Ill., 1989—; pres. Michael Reese Hosp. and Med. Ctr., Chgo., 1988-91; market med. dir. Aetna Health Plans, Phoenix, 1993-94, mktg. v.p., CEO, 1994-95; v.p. managed care/physician integration, med. dir. Am. Healthcare Sys., San Diego, 1995. Mem. vis. staff, div. medicine Northwestern Meml. Hosp., 1972-81; staff Children's Hosp. of Mich., 1981-88. Mem. editl. bd. Comprehensive Therapy, 1973-84, Am. Jour. Human Genetics, 1979-83, Pediatrics in Rev., 1980-83, Am. Jour. Diseases of Children, 1983-91; contbr. articles to profl. jours. Recipient E. Mead Johnson award for pediatric rsch., 1973, Meyer O. Cantor award for Disting. Svc. Internat. Coll. Surgeons, 1987; Irene Heinz Given and John La Porte Given rsch. prof. pediatrics, 1970-81. Fellow Am. Acad. Pediatrics; mem. Am. Soc. for Clin. Investigation, Am. Soc. Human Genetics, Am. Pediatric Soc., Soc. for Pediatric Rsch., Midwest Soc. for Pediatric Rsch., Pan Am. Med. Assn., Alpha Omega Alpha. Home and Office: 17720 Camino de La Mitra PO Box 3665 Rancho Santa Fe CA 92067-3665 Personal E-mail: hlnadler@aol.com.

NADLER, JERROLD LEWIS, United States Representative from New York, lawyer; b. Bklyn., June 13, 1947; m. Joyce L. Miller, 1976; 1 child, Michael. AB in Govt., Columbia U., 1969; JD, Fordham U. Sch. Law, 1978. Mem. Cmty. Planning Bd. Number 7, Manhattan, 1967-71; dem. leader 67th Assembly Dist. Part C, 1969-71; exec. dir. Cmty. Free Dem., 1972; dem. dist. leader 69th Assembly Dist. Part A, 1973-77; law clk. Morgan, Finnegan, Pine, Foley and Lee, 1976; mem. NY State Assembly from 69th dist., 1977-82, NY State Assembly from 67th dist., 1983-92, US Congress from 8th NY Dist., 1993—, mem. subcommittees on surface transp., water resources, environment, 1993—94, ranking minority mem. subcom. on comml./adminstrv. law, 1997—2000, mem. subcom. on constrn., 1997—2006, mem. judiciary com., chmn. constn., civil rights and civil liberties subcom., mem. transp. and infrastructure com., asst. whip, 2003—. Chmn. Assembly Com. on Corps, Authorities and Commn., 1991-92, Assembly Consumer Affairs and Protection Com., 1987-90, Assembly Com. on Ethics and Guidance, 1985-86, Assembly Subcom. on Mass Transit and Rail Freight, 1979-86, mem. Assembly Com. on Judiciary, Gov. Ops., Legis. Tax Study Commn.; mem. Assembly Com. Ways and Means, Housing, Real Property Tax, Health, Election Law, Ins. Founder, chmn. West Side Peace Com., 1969-71; pres. Zionist Orgn. Am. dist. 7A; active Common Cause, Met. Coun. on Housing, West Side Tenants Union; mem. nat. governing coun. Am. Jewish Congress. Recipient hon. recognition award NY State Nurses Assn., 1982, Disting. Svc. award Coalition on Domestic Violence, 1989, Legislator of Yr. award Internat. Assn. Firefighters, 2003; Pulitzer scholar Columbia U. Mem. NOW (Assembly Mem. of Yr. from NY chpt, 1980), NAACP, NY Bar Assn., NY Civil Liberties Union (honor roll), Citizens Union, League Conservation Voters, New Dem.

Coalition, Ams. for Dem. Action (bd. dirs., nat. v.p.). Democrat. Office: US House Reps 2334 Rayburn House Office Bldgb Washington DC 20515-3208 Office Phone: 202-225-5635. E-mail: jerrold.nadler@mail.house.gov.*

NADLER, JUDITH, library director; b. Romania; BA in English and Romance Studies, U. Jerusalem; MLS, Israel Grad. Sch. With U. Chgo. Libr., 1966—, cataloger fgn. language materials, dir., 2004—. Office: Joseph Regenstein Libr U Chgo 1100 E 57 St 180 Chicago IL 60637 Office Phone: 773-702-8743. Office Fax: 773-702-6623. E-mail: judi@uchicago.edu.

NADLER-HURVICH, HEDDA CAROL, public relations executive; b. Bronx, NY, June 15, 1944; d. Julius Louis and Julia Cohen; m. David George Nadler, Oct. 3, 1965 (div. 1979); 1 child, Laura Lee Nadler; m. Burton Earl Hurvich, Dec. 8, 1984. BBA, Baruch Coll., 1965. V.p., sec. Irving L. Straus Assocs., Inc., NYC, 1965-80; pres. Mount & Nadler Inc., NYC, 1999—. Avocations: aerobics, yoga. Office: Mount & Nadler 425 Madison Ave New York NY 10017-1110 Home Phone: 914-631-8834; Office Phone: 212-759-4440. E-mail: Hedda615@aol.com.

NADOLSKI, DORA J., social sciences educator, researcher; d. Harold V. and Dora H. Glidewell; m. Thomas P. Nadolski (div.); 1 child, Christopher A. MA in Social Sci., Antioch U., Yellow Springs, OH, 1965; PhD in polit. social sci., U. Mo., Kansas City, 2000. Assoc. prof. polit. sci. Northwest Nazarene Coll., Nampa, Idaho, 1966—68; lectr. Rockhurst U., Kansas City, 1995—97; prof., lectr. Park U., Kansas City, 1997—. Instr. Bedai U., Kanazawa, Japan, Kanazawa U., Peace Corps, Turkey. Co-author: Survey of U.S. Econometric Modeling Organizations; author: Special Curriculum Methods for Teaching Foreign Students; editor: Social Science Consortium Newsletter; author: The Etatist Turkish Republic and Its Political and SocioEconomic Performance from 1980-1999: A Developing State Impacted by International Organizations and Interdependence, Ottoman and Secular Civil Law International Journal of Middle East Studies, 1977. Chair Cub Scouts Am., Reston, Va., 1982—88; donor, supporter Disabled Am. Vets., Washington, 1995—. Grantee, NEH; fellow, NDEA, Soc. Sci. Rsch. Coun., U.Erfurt; scholar Fulbright, Sophia U.; Chancellor's Interdisciplinary Fellowship, U. Mo. Mem.: Am. Polit. Sci. Assn., Soc. Advancement Socio-Economics, Pi Sigma Alpha. Roman Catholic. Avocations: cross country skiing, swimming, church choir. Personal E-mail: dora.nadolski@sbcglobal.net.

NAEEM, RIZWAN C., geneticist, educator, lab administrator, director; s. Chawdhry M. and Anwar Naeem; m. Rubina A. Heptulla, Nov. 5, 1992; children: Sameer, Nadia. MBBS, U. Karachi, Pakistan, 1985. Diplomate in clin. cytogenetics Am. Bd. Med. Genetics, 1993, in clin. molecular genetics 1996. Asst. prof., dir. divsn. molecular pathology and genetics Baystate Med. Ctr., Tuft U. Sch. Medicine, Boston, 1993—2001; assoc. prof. dept. pediat., dir. cytogenetics and molecular labs. Baylor Coll. Medicine, Tex. Children's Hosp., Houston, 2001—. Contbr. scientific papers. Fellow: Am. Coll. Med. Genetics (Travel grant 1996); mem.: Assn. Physicians Pakistani Descent N.Am. (Chgo.) (mem. nomination com. 2007—08, treas. 2006—07). Independent. Achievements include research in cancer genetics. Office: Baylor Coll Medicine One Baylor Plz Houston TX 77030

NAEGELE, JANICE RAE, science educator; d. Eugene and Irene Naegele; m. Paul Lombroso, May 25, 1985; children: Christopher Lombroso, Adam Lombroso, Sonia Lombroso. BA, Mt. Holyoke Coll., South Hadley,Mass., 1978; PhD, Mass. Inst. Tech., Cambridge, 1984. Prof. Wesleyan U., Middletown, Conn., 1991—. Recipient Am. Epilepsy Award, Am. Epilepsy Found., 2008; grant, NIH, 1992—97, NSF, 1996—2001, McKnight Found., 2007—. Mem.: Assn. for the Advancement of Women in Sci. Achievements include research in Functional Integration Of Embryonic Stem Cell Derived Neuronal Precursors In Mouse Models Of Epilepsy. Office: Wesleyan Univ 52 Lawn Ave Middletown CT 06459

NAEGELE, PHILIPP OTTO, musician, educator; b. Stuttgart, Germany, Jan. 22, 1928; came to US, 1940; s. Reinhold and Alice (Nordlinger) N.; m. Susanne Rusin (div. 1980); 1 child, Matthias Dominic; m. Barbara Wright, Mar. 1992; 1 adopted child, Olivia Kaihua. BA, Queens Coll., Flushing, NY, 1949; MFA, Princeton U., NJ, 1950, PhD, 1955. Violinist, violist Marlboro (Vt.) Music Festival, 1950—; violinist Cleve. Orch., 1956-64; from asst. prof. to William R. Kenan Jr. prof. Dept. Music Smith Coll., Northampton, Mass., 1964—2000, William R. Kenan Jr. prof. music emeritus Dept. Music, 2000—; violist Cantilena Piano Quartet, 1980-96; mem. Boccherini Ensemble, 1980-84; adj. prof. violin Amherst Coll., 2000—. Resident string quartet Kent (Ohio) State U., 1960-64; violin faculty Cleve. Inst. Music, 1961-64, Vegh String Quartet, 1977-79; rec. artist Columbia, Mus. Heritage Soc., Pro Arte, Nonesuch Records, Bis Records, Marlboro Rec. Soc., Arabesque Records, Da Camera, Spectrum Records, Bayer Records, Sony Classical, Philomusica, Qualitone Records. Author: Gustav Mahler and Johann Sebastian Bach, 1983, Marlboro Music/German Vocal Texts in Translation, An Anthology, 2006; contbr: articles to profl. jours. With US Army, 1955-56. Fellow Am. Council Learned Socs., 1949-50, Proctor fellow, 1952-53, Fulbright fellow, 1953-54. Mem. Phi Beta Kappa. Home: 57 Prospect St Northampton MA 01060-2130 Business E-Mail: pnaegele@smith.edu.

NAEGLE, SUE E. (SUZANNE), broadcast executive; b. NJ, 1969; m. Dana Gould; 2 children. BA in Comm. and Comparative Lit., Ind. U., Bloomington, 1991. Mailroom staff United Talent Agy., LA, 1992—94, ptnr., 1994—2008, co-head TV dept., 1999—2008; pres. HBO Entertainment, NYC, 2008—. Mem. bd. govs. Hollygrove. Named one of The 100 Most Powerful Women in Entertainment, Hollywood Reporter, 2003, 2007. Office: HBO Entertainment 1100 Ave of Americas New York NY 10036 Office Phone: 212-512-7467. Office Fax: 212-512-8700.*

NAES, JENNIFER LE, medical technologist; d. Jackie Mare. BS in Clin. Lab. Sci., SUNY, Stonybrook, 2002; M in Forensic Scis., Nat. U., San Diego, 2004. Cert. med. technologist Am. Soc. Clin. Pathology, 2003, lic. Fla., 2005. Med. technologist Boca Raton Cmty. Hosp., Fla., 2006—, point of care coord., 2006—. Mem.: Pi Delta Chi (assoc.).

NAESER, NANCY DEARIEN, geologist, researcher; b. Morgantown, W.Va., Apr. 15, 1944; d. William Harold and Katherine Elizabeth (Dearien) Cozad; m. Charles Wilbur Naeser, Feb. 6, 1982. BS, U. Ariz., 1966; PhD, Victoria U., Wellington, New Zealand, 1973. Geol. field asst. U.S. Geol. Survey, Flagstaff, Ariz., 1966; sci. editor New Zealand Jour. Geology and Geophysics, New Zealand Dept. Sci. and Indsl. Rsch., Wellington, 1974-76; postdoctoral rsch. assoc. U. Toronto, 1976-79, U.S. Geol. Survey, Denver, 1979-81, geologist, 1981—2006, scientist emeritus, 2006—. Adj. prof. Dartmouth Coll., Hanover, NH, 1985—97, U. Wyo., Laramie, 1984—91. Editor: Thermal History of Sedimentary Basins--Methods and Case Histories, 1989, Debris-Flow Hazards - Mechanics, Prediction and Assessment, 2000; contbr. articles on fission-track analysis to profl. jours. Docent, Denver Zoo, 1991-99. Fulbright fellow, New Zealand, 1967-68. Fellow Geol. Soc. Am.; mem. Geol. Soc. New Zealand, Mortar Board, Phi Kappa Phi. Methodist. Office: US Geol Survey Mail Stop 926 A 12201 Sunrise Valley Dr Reston VA 20192-0002 Office Phone: 703-648-5328. Business E-Mail: nnaeser@usgs.gov.

NAEVE, DENISE R., music educator; b. Story City, Iowa, Nov. 29, 1959; d. Russell LeRoy Staples and Donna Mae Essing; m. Brent Loren Naeve, May 30, 1981; children: Nashay Lynn, Brennon Royce. MusB, Iowa State U., Ames, 1982; MusM, So. Ill. U., Carbondale, 2004. Cert. music tchr. Music Teachers Nat. Assn., 2003, lic. Iowa, 2007. Music instr. Rolfe Cmty. Sch., Iowa; music tchr. Holy Rosary Sch., Ft. Dodge, Iowa; choral dir. Congl. United Ch. Christ, Humboldt, Iowa, 1984—90; music tchr. St. Mary's Sch., Humboldt, 1990—93; pianist First Bapt. Ch., Eagle Grove, Iowa, 1998—2001; prof. piano voice Iowa Ctrl. C.C., Ft. Dodge, 1998—. Adv. bd. music Iowa State U., 1999—2000; clinician McClosky Inst. Voice, Boston, 2000—, instr. summer certification program, 2006; v.p. Auditions Iowa Music Tendors Assn., 2007—; pres. McClosky tech. choirs Am. choral dirs. Nat. Convention, 2009—. Musician: (pianist) Beethoven Symphonies. Recipient Hall of Fame, Nat. Piano Guild, 1999. Mem.: Am. Coll. Musicians Piano Guild (adjudicator 1993—), Solfeggietto Music Tchrs., Music Educators Nat. Conf., Am. Choral Directors Assn., Nat. Assn. Teachers Singing, Iowa Music Teachers Assn. (festival chairperson 1990—94), McClosky Inst. Voice (pres. 2006—07, v.p. 2004—06). Home: 114 Hall St Humboldt IA 50548 Office: Iowa Ctrl Cmty Coll 330 Avenue M Fort Dodge IA 50501 Office Phone: 515-576-0099 ext. 2075, 515-576-0099 2075. Personal E-mail: drsnstudio@aol.com. Business E-Mail: naeve@iowacentral.com.

NAEYE, RICHARD L., pathologist, educator; b. Rochester, NY, Nov. 27, 1929; s. Peter John and Gertrude Ellen (Lookup) N.; m. Patricia Ann Dahl, June 4, 1955; children: Nancy Ellen, Susan Amy, Robert Peter. AB, Colgate U., 1951; MD, Columbia U., 1955. Diplomate: Am. Bd. Pathology. Intern N.Y. Hosp., NYC, 1955-56; resident Columbia-Presbyn. Med. Ctr., 1956-58, Mary Fletcher Hosp., Burlington, Vt., 1958-60; practice medicine, specializing in pathology Burlington, 1960-67, Hershey, Pa., 1967—2008; asst. attending pathologist Mary Fletcher Hosp., 1960-63; assoc. prof. U. Vt., 1963-67, prof. pathology, 1967; prof. dept. pathology M.S. Hershey Med. Ctr., Pa. State U. Coll. Medicine, 1967—2008, chmn. dept. pathology, 1967-97. Mem. NIH study sect. USPHS, 1968-72. Mem. editl. bd. Human Pathology, 1982-96, Pediatric Pathology, 1983-96, Pediatric and Perinatal Epidemiology, 1987-94, Modern Pathology, 1993-96, Fetal and Pediatric Pathology, 2004-09; contbr. articles to med. jours. Markle scholar in acad. medicine, 1960-65. Mem. Am. Soc. Exptl. Pathology, U.S. Can. Acad. Pathology, Am. Soc. Pathologists, Am. Soc. Clin. Pathologists, Coll. Am. Pathologists, Pediatric Pathology Soc., Pa. Soc. Clin. Pathologists, Investigative Pathology. Home: 50 Laurel Ridge Rd Hershey PA 17033-2513 Office: Pa State U Coll Medicine Dept Pathology 500 University Dr Hershey PA 17033 Home Phone: 717-533-3014. Personal E-mail: richardnaeye@aol.com.

NAFTALI, TIMOTHY J., library director, historian, educator, writer; BA magna cum laude, Yale U., 1983; MA in Internat. Econs., Johns Hopkins U., 1987; MA in History, PhD in History, Harvard U., 1993. Asst. prof. dept. history U. Hawaii, 1993—97; assoc. prof. U. Va., 1998—2006, dir. Presdl. recordings program, Kremlin decision-making project, 1999—2006; dir. Richard Nixon Presdl. Libr. & Mus., Yorba Linda, Calif., 2006—. Vis. prof. Dept. History Yale U., 1996—98; hist. cons. Nazi War Crimes and Imperial Japanese Govt. Records Interagency Working Group, Nat. Archives, US Dept. Justice, Nat. Commn. Terrorist Attacks upon US (9/11 Commn.), 2003—04; instr. Centre Counterintelligence and Security Studies, 2003—. Co-author: US-Canadian Softwood Lumber: Trade Dispute Negotiations, 1987, One Hell of a Gamble: Khrushchev, Castro and Kennedy, 1958-1964, 1997, The Presidential Recordings: John F. Kennedy, 2001, US Intelligence and the Nazis, 2004, 2005, Blindspot: The Secret History of American Counterterrorism, 2005; gen. editor Presdl. Recordings Series, 2003—; contbr. articles to profl. jours. Co-recipient Akira Iriye Prize for Internat. Hist., 1997—98; named prin. investigator, Nat. Hist. Publs. and Records Commn., 2002—; grantee MacArthur Fellowship in Internat. Security, 1990—91, Rsch. Fellowship, Kennan Inst. for Advance Russian Studies, Woodrow Wilson Internat. Ctr. for Scholars, 1996, Olin Fellowship in Nat. Security, 1996—98. Office: Richard Nixon Presdl Libr 18001 Yorba Linda Blvd Yorba Linda CA 92886 Office Phone: 714-983-9120. Office Fax: 714-983-9111. Business E-Mail: timothy.naftali@nara.gov.

NAFTALIS, GARY PHILIP, lawyer, educator; b. Newark, Nov. 23, 1941; s. Gilbert and Bertha Beatrice Naftalis; m. Donna Arditi, June 30, 1974; children: Benjamin, Joshua, Daniel, Sarah. AB, Rutgers U., 1963; AM, Brown U., 1965; LLB, Columbia U., 1967. Bar: N.Y. 1967, U.S. Dist. Ct. (so. dist.) N.Y. 1969, U.S. Ct. Appeals (2d cir.) 1968, U.S. Ct. Appeals (3d cir.) 1973, U.S. Ct. Appeals (D.C. cir.) 1993, U.S. Supreme Ct. 1974. Law clk. to judge U.S. Dist. Ct. So. Dist. N.Y., 1967—68; asst. U.S. atty. So. Dist. N.Y., 1968—74, asst. chief criminal divsn., 1972—74; spl. asst. U.S. atty. for V.I., 1972—73; spl. counsel U.S. Senate Subcom. on Long Term Care, 1975, N.Y. State Temp. Commn. on Living Costs and Economy, 1975; ptnr. Orans, Elsen, Polstein & Naftalis, NYC, 1974—81, Kramer, Levin, Naftalis & Frankel, NYC, 1981—. Lectr. Law Sch. Columbia U., 1976-88; vis. lectr. Law Sch. Harvard U., 1979; mem. deptl. disciplinary com. Appellate div. 1st Dept., 1980-86. Author: (with Marvin E. Frankel) The Grand Jury: An Institution on Trial, 1977, Considerations in Representing Attorneys in Civil and Criminal Enforcement Proceedings, 1981, Sentencing: Helping Judges Do Their Jobs, 1986, SEC Actions Seeking to Bar Securities Professionals, 1995, SEC Cease and Desist Powers Limited, 1997, The Foreign Corrupt Practices Act, 1997, Prosecuting Lawyers Who Defend Clients in SEC Actions, 1998, Obtaining Reports from a Credit Bureau for Litigation May be a Crime, 1999, Encouraging Cooperation by Individual Respondents in SEC Enforcement Investigations, 2002, Navigating the Foreign Corrupt Practices Act, 2002, Fugitive Disentitlement in Civil Forfeiture Proceedings, 2002; editor: White Collar Crimes, 1980. Trustee Boys Brotherhood Rep., 1978—, Blueberry Treatment Ctr., 1981-91, Joseph Haggerty Children's Fund, 1991—; bd. dirs. The Legal Aid Soc., 2000—. Named one of 100 Most Influential Lawyers, Nat. Law Jour., 2006. Fellow: Am. Coll. Trial Lawyers; mem.: ABA (white collar crime com. criminal justice sect. 1985—, coun. criminal justice sect. 2002—05), N.Y. Coun. Def. Lawyers (bd. dirs. 2000—01), Internat. Bar Assn. (bus. crimes com. 1988—), N.Y. Bar Assn. (com. state legis. 1974—76, exec. com. comml. and fed. litigation sect.), Fed. Bar. Coun. (com. cts. 2d cir. 1974—77), Assn. of Bar of City of N.Y. (com. criminal cts. 1980—83, com. judiciary 1984—87, coun. criminal justice 1985—88, com. on criminal law 1987—90, 1997—2001), Phi Beta Kappa. Home: 1125 Park Ave Apt 7B New York NY 10128-1243 Office: Kramer Levin Naftalis & Frankel 1177 Ave of The Americas New York NY 10036 Office Phone: 212-715-9253. E-mail: gnaftalis@kramerlevin.com.

NAFTOLIN, FREDERICK, gynecologist, educator; b. Bronx, NY, Apr. 7, 1936; s. Nathan and Jean (Pesacov) N.; children: Michael Eugene, Joshua Joseph; m. Marcie Myerson, Nov. 1, 1987. AA, UCLA, 1957; BA with honors, U. Calif., Berkeley, 1958; MD with honors, U. Calif., San Francisco, 1961; DPhil, U. Oxford, 1970. Intern King County Hosp., Seattle, 1961-62; resident in ob-gyn UCLA, 1962-66; asst. chief gynecology, reproductive endocrine fellow USPHS, Seattle, 1966-68; NIH fellow Oxford U., England, 1968-70; asst. prof. ob-gyn U. Calif., San Diego Sch. Medicine, 1970-73; assoc. prof. ob-gyn Harvard Med. Sch., 1973-75; prof., chmn. dept. ob-gyn McGill Faculty Medicine, Montreal, 1975-78, Yale Med. Sch., New Haven, 1978-2000, prof. debt. ob-gyn., 1978—2005, prof. dept. biology, 1983—2005; dir. Yale U. Ctr. for Rsch. in Reproductive Biology, 1986—2005, head reproductive neurosci. unit, 2000—03; prof. dept. ob-gyn. NYU, 2006—, dir. rsch. in reproductive biology, 2006—. Co-dir., Inter-disciplinary Prog., Menopausal Medicine, 2007; vis. prof. U. Geneva, 1982-83, Weizmann Inst., 1991-92; vis. prof. Complutense U., Spain, 1999, prof extraordinaire, 1999. Author: 15 books including: Subcellular Mechanisms in Reproductive Neuroendocrinology, 1976, Abnormal Fetal Growth, 1978, Clinical Neuroendocrinology, 1979, Dilation of the Uterine Cervix, 1980, 2-vol. series Basic Reproductive Medicine, Vol. I, Basis of Normal Reproduction, Vol. II, 1981, Male Reproduction, Vol. III, Metabolism of Steroids by Neuroendocrine Tissues, Follicle Stimulation and Ovulation Induction, 1986; mem. editl. bd.: Jour. Soc. Gynecologic Investigation, Menopause, Gynecol. Endocrinology, African Jour. Reproductive Medicine, sect. editor: Reproductive Biology, jour. Exptl. Zoology, 2002—; editor: Reproductive Divsn. Am. Jour. Zoology; contbr. more than 600 articles to med. jours. Recipient Arnaldo Bruno prize, Acad. Di Lincei, Italy, 2002; named Fogarty Internat. fellow, 1982, John Simon Guggenheim fellow, 1983, Berlex Internat. scholar, 1991; fellow ad enundem, Royal Coll. Ob-Gyn. Mem. Am. Gynecol. and Obstet. Soc., Soc. Gynecol. Investigation (pres. 1991-92, Disting. Scientist award 2003), Endocrine Soc., Internat. Soc. Neuroendocrinology, New Haven Ob-Gyn. Soc., Can. Fertility Soc., Soc. for Neurosci., N.Am. Menopause Soc. (pres. 1998-99), Internat. Menopause Soc. (exec. com. 2000-08), Soc. Exptl. Biology and Medicine (coun. 2000-06), Pan Am. Health and Edn. Found. (bd. trustees 2005-). Office: NYU Dept Ob-Gyn 550 1st Ave Tish 528 New York NY 10016 Business E-Mail: frederick.naptolin@med.nyu.edu.

NAFZIGER, ESTEL WAYNE, economics professor; b. Bloomington, Ill., Aug. 14, 1938; s. Orrin and Beatrice Mae (Slabaugh) N.; m. Elfrieda Nettie Toews, Aug. 20, 1966 (dec. 2007); children: Brian Wayne, Kevin Jon. BA, Goshen Coll., 1960; MA, U. Mich., 1962; PhD, U. Ill., 1967. Rsch. assoc. Econ. Devel. Inst., Enugu, Nigeria, 1964-65; asst. prof. Kans. State U., Manhattan, 1966-73, assoc. prof., 1973-78, prof., 1978-99, univ. disting. prof., 1999—; Fulbright prof. Andhra U., Waltair, India, 1970-71; fellow East West Ctr., Honolulu, 1972-73. Vis. scholar Cambridge U., 1976; vis. prof. Internat. U. Japan, Yamato-machi, 1983; external rsch. fellow World Acad. Devel. and Coop., College Park, Md., 1984-85; Indo-Am. Found. scholar Andura U., Waltair, India, 1993; World Inst. for Devel. Econ. Rsch., UN Univ., Helsinki, Finland, 1996-98, Inst. Social & Econ. Rsch., Bangalore, India, 2007; Higuchi fellow, 2005-. Author: African Capitalism, 1977, Class, Caste and Entrepreneurship, 1978; author: (with others) Development Theory, 1979; author: Economics of Political Instability, 1983, Economics of Developing Countries, 1984, 2nd edit., 1990, 3rd edit., 1997, Entrepreneurship Equity and Economic Development, 1986, Inequality in Africa, 1988 (one of Outstanding Acad. Books, Choice, 1989-90), The Debt Crisis in Africa, 1993, Poverty and Wealth, 1994, Learning From the Japanese, 1995, Fathers, Sons, and Daughters: Industrial Entrepreneurs under India's Liberalization, 1998; co-editor: War, Hunger, and Displacement, 2 vols., 2000, Prevention of Humanitarian Emergencies, 2002, Economic Development, Inequality, and War, 2003, Economic Development, 2006. Sec. bd. overseers Hesston Coll., Kans., 1980-85; chmn. Lou Douglas Lecture Series, 1984-91, 92-93; pres. faculty senate Kans. State U., 1990-92. Recipient Honor Lectr. award Mid Am. State U.'s Assn., 1984-85; grantee Social Sci. Found., 1969 Mem. Am. Econ. Assn., AAUP (pres. chpt. 1981-82), African Studies Assn., Assn. Comparative Econ. Studies, Omicron Delta Epsilon (hon.), Phi Kappa Phi (hon.) Democrat. Avocations: reading, running. Home: 1919 Bluestem Ter # 785 Manhattan KS 66502-4508 Office: Kans State U Dept Econs Waters Hall Manhattan KS 66506-4001 Office Phone: 785-532-4579.

NAFZIGER, JAMES ALBERT RICHMOND, law educator; b. Mpls., Sept. 24, 1940; s. Ralph Otto and Charlotte Monona (Hamilton) N. BA, U. Wis., 1962, MA, 1969; JD, Harvard U., Cambridge, Mass., 1967. Bar: Wis. 1967. Law clk. to chief judge U.S. Dist. Ct. (ea. dist.) Wis., 1967-69; fellow Am. Soc. Internat. Law, Washington, 1969-70, adminstrv. dir., 1970-74; exec. sec. Assn. Student Internat. Law Socs., 1969-70; lectr. Sch. Law Cath. U. Am., Washington, 1970-74; assoc. prof. law Coll. Law Willamette U., Salem, Oreg., 1977-80, prof., 1980-95, Thomas B. Stoel prof., 1995—, assoc. dean, 1985-86, dir. internat. programs, 1984—. Vis. assoc. prof. Sch. Law, U. Oreg. 1974-77; vis. prof. Nat. Autonomous U. Mex., 1978; lectr. tutor Inst. Pub. Internat. Law and Internat. Rels., Thessaloniki, Greece, 1982; scholar-in-residence Rockefeller Found. Ctr., Bellagio, Italy, 1985; cons. Adminstrv. Conf. US, 1988-90, Internat. Com. Migration, 1997—; hon. prof. East China U. of Politics and Law, 1999—; dir. rsch. ctr., Hague Acad. Internat. Law, 2005. Author: Conflict of Laws: A Northwest Perspective, 1985, Internat. Sports Law, 1988, 2d edit., 2004; editor: Procs. of Am. Soc. Internat. Law, 1977; co-editor: Law and Justice in a Multistate World, 2002; bd. dirs.: Am. Jour. Comparative Law, 1985—, mem. bd. advisors: Denver Jour. Internat. Law and Policy; contbr. articles to profl. jours. Dir. Rsch. Ctr., Hague Acad. Internat. Law, 2005; adv. com. on internat. law U.S. Dept. of State, 2001—; bd. dirs. N.W. Regional China Coun., 1987—89. 1st lt. US Army, 1962—64. Recipient Burlington No. Faculty Achievement award, 1988, Willamette U. Pres.'s award for excellence in scholarship, 2000. Mem.: UNA-USA (pres., Oreg. divsn. 1987—90, v.p. 1990—94, bd. dirs. 1990—2004, nat. coun. 2004—, chpt., divsn. pres.'s exec. com.), ACLU (pres. chpt. 1980—81, mem. state bd. 1982—88, sec. 1983—87), ABA (legal spl. ctrl. and east European law initiative 1992—), Internat. Law Assn. Am. Br. (human rights com. chmn. 1983—88, co-dir. studies 1991—95, v.p. 1994—2000, pres. 2000—04, chmn. exec. com. 2004—08, hon. v.p. 2008—), Internat. Law Assn. (rapporteur and chmn. cultural heritage law com. 1988—, mem. exec. coun. 2000—), Nat. Sports Law Inst. (bd. advisors 2002—), Internat. Sports Law Assn. (v.p. 1992, pres. 2004—), Oreg. Internat. Coun. (pres. 1990—92), Am. Law Inst., Assn. Am. Law Schs. (chmn. law and arts sect. 1981—83, chmn. internat. law sect. 1984—85, chmn. law and arts sect. 1989—91, chmn. immigration law sect. 1990—91, chmn. internat. law workshop 1995, com. on sects. and ann. meeting 1995—98, chmn. internat. exchs. sect. 1999—2000, chmn. conflict of laws sect. 2003—04, US Dept. of State adv. com.), Am. Coun. Learned Socs. (exec. com. 2002—, conf. adminstrv. officers), Internat. Studies Assn. (exec. bd. 1974—77, exec. coun. 2000—, internat. law sect.), Washington Fgn. Law Soc. (v.p. 1973—74), Internat. Acad. Comparative Law, Am. Soc. Comparative Law (bd. dirs. 1985—, treas. 1997—2005, chief adminstrv. officer 2005—), Am. Soc. Internat. Law (exec. coun. 1983—86, chmn. ann. meeting 1988, chmn. nominating com. 1989, exec. coun. 1992—95, exec. com. 1994—95), Phi Kappa Phi, Phi Beta Kappa. Home: 3775 Saxon Dr S Salem OR 97302-6041 Office: Willamette U Coll Law Salem OR 97301

NAGAE, YOSHIO, English educator; b. Tokushima, Japan, May 20, 1928; m. Fumiko Yamane, Jan. 10, 1960; children: Miyako, Shiro. B in Pharmacology, Kyoto Pharm. Coll., 1948; BA, Kyoto U., 1953, MA, 1957. Cert. pharmacist. Import clk. Internat. Engrs. Inc., Tokyo, 1957-59, Dodwell & Co. Ltd., Tokyo, 1959-61; translator Pfizer-Taito Co. Ltd., Tokyo, 1961-63; English lectr. to prof. emeritus Kinki U., Higashi, Osaka, Japan, 1963—. Lectr. English Kwansei Gakuin U., Nishinomiya, 1967-03, Osaka U. Fgn. Studies, 1970-77, Tezukayama Gakuin U., Osaka, 1977-91. Author, editor: Writing Current English, 1987; author: How to Express Current Topics in English, 1991, rev. edit., 1997, How to Express Japan's Current Topics in English, 2002; editor and annotator: Profiles of American Presidents, 1974, Impressive Speech of Our Own Day, 1972; co-author: Strategy of Export Marketing, 1964. Mem. Japan Assn. Current English (bd. dirs. 1980-90, head Kansai br. 1986-90, councilor 1990-), Japan Soc. Translators (bd. dirs. 1981-97), Japanese Assn. Studies in English Communication (v.p., bd. dirs. 1991-03, adviser 2003-). Home: Nishiyamadai 2-22-9 Osaka 589 Japan Personal E-mail: ffafc103@jcmo.zaq.ne.jp.

NAGAI, CHIKAKO, social sciences educator; MSW, U. Washinton, Seattle; PhD, Smith Coll., Northampton, Mass., 2007. Lic. social worker Wash., 2002. Clin. supr., trainer & cons. Asian Counseling & Referral Svc., Seattle, 1997—2007; asst. prof. Calif. State U., Long Beach, 2007—. Contbr. articles to jours. Founder, co-chair Southern Calif. Soc. Spirituality & Social Work, LA, 2007—. Office: Calif State Univ Long Beach 1250 Bellflower Blvd Long Beach CA 90840 Business E-Mail: cnagai@csulb.edu.

NAGAI, NELSON KEI, economics professor, history professor; b. Stockton, Calif., Sept. 11, 1950; s. Katsuto Kenneth and Grace Rayko Nagai; m. Beverly J. Kordziel, June 2, 1976; children: Tyrone K., Tyree Ranko Anderson. BA in Polit. Sci., Stanford U., Calif., 1972; MS in Internat. Agr. Devel., U. Calif., Davis, 1979. Cert. in tchg. State of Calif., 1982. Tofu maker Azumaya, Inc., San Francisco, 1972—75; gen. coord. Internat. Farmers Edn., Berkeley, Calif., 1975—77; asst. prodn. mgr. Tri-Valley Growers, Modesto, Calif., 1979—81; supr. Carnation Co., Stockton, Calif., 1981—82; instr., HEP U. Pacific, Stockton, 1982—86; instr. economics and history San Joaquin Delta Coll., Stockton, 1986—. Cons. U. Calif. EOP, 1984—89. Author: (book) I Come from a Yellow Seed. Pres. Assn. Asian Am. Educators, Stockton, 1983—85, Japanese Am. Citizens League, Stockton, 1997—2002; chairperson Bay Area Asian Coalition Against War, San Francisco, 1972—75; constn. com. Yellow Seed, Stockton, 1969—74; auditor Internat. Hotel Tenants Assn., San Francisco, 1973—75; chairperson Stockton-Shizuoka Sister City Assn., 2007. Named to Hall of Fame, Edison Sr. HS, 2006. Mem.: Nihonmachi Little Friends (founding mem.), Filipino Am. Nat. Hist. Soc., Nat. Japanese Am. Hist. Soc., Phi Delta Kappa. Buddhist. Avocations: golf, travel. Home: 1246 Greeley Way Stockton CA 95207 Office: San Joaquin Delta Coll 5151 Pacific Ave Stockton CA 95207 Business E-Mail: nnagai@deltacollege.edu.

NAGANO, KENT GEORGE, conductor, music director; b. Berkeley, Calif., Nov. 22, 1951; m. Mari Kodama; 1 child. BA in Sociology & Music, U. Calif., Santa Cruz, 1974; MA in Composition, San Francisco State U., 1976. Asst. condr. Opera Co. Boston; former prin. guest condr. Ensemble InterContemporain, Dutch Radio Orch.; mus. dir., condr. Berkeley Symphony, 1978—2009; mus. dir. Opéra de Lyon, France, 1988—98; prin. condr. Hallé Orch., Manchester, England, 1992—99; artistic dir., prin. condr. Deutsches Symphonie-Orchester Berlin, 2000—06; prin. condr. LA Opera, 2001—02, mus. dir., 2003—06, Bavarian State Opera, Munich, 2006—, Montréal Symphony Orch., 2006—. Has performed with numerous orchestras around the world; recordings include: Songs of the Auvergne, Peter and the Wolf, Turandot and Arlecchino (Grammy nom.), La Boheme, Dialogues of the Carelites, The Death of Klinghoffer (Grammy nom.), Love for Three Oranges (Grammy nom.), Susannah (Grammy award), La damnation de Faust, The Rite of Spring, Rodrgue et chimene. Decorated Order of Rising Sun, Japan, 2008; recipient Conductors award, Seaver Inst./NEA, 1985. Mailing: Van Walsum Mgmt Ltd 4 Addison Bridge Place London W14 8XP England Office: Montreal Symphony Orch 260 de Maisonneuve Blvd W, 2nd Fl Montreal PQ H2X 1Y9 Canada*

NAGAO, MAKOTO, academic administrator, engineering educator; b. Ise City, Japan, Oct. 4, 1936; s. Kaoru and Yukie Nagao; m. Mikiko Nagao, Dec. 5, 1964; children: Noriko, Fumiko, Takashi. BS in Engring., Kyoto U., Japan, 1959, MS in Engring., 1961, PhD in Engring., 1966; DSc (hon.), Nottingham U., Eng., 1999. Asst. prof. engring. Kyoto U., 1961-68, lecture engring., 1967, assoc. prof. engring., 1968-73, prof. elec. engring., 1973-97, dir., data processing ctr., 1986—90, dir. libr., 1995-97, dean faculty engring., 1997, v.p., 1996-97, pres., 1997—2003, Nat. Inst. Info. and Comms. Tech., Japan, 2004—07, Nat. Diet Libr., 2007—. Vis. assoc. prof., dept. informatics, Grenoble U., 1969-70; prof. Nat. Mus. Ethnology, Osaka, Japan, 1976-94; hon. prof. Beijing U. Posts and Telecomms., 2006. Author: Knowledge and Inference, 1988, English transl., 1990, Machine Translation, How Far Can It Go?, 1986, English transl., 1989, (Japanese Books) Engineering for Pattern Recognition and Language Understanding, 1989, Artificial Intelligence and Human, 1992, Digital Library, 1994, (co-author) Natural Language Processing, 1996, What is Understanding, 2001; editor Ency. Computer Sci., 1990, Multimedia Digital Libr., 1994, Natural Language Processing, 1996, Basis of Multimedia Information Processing, 1999. Recipient Culture prize, Bunka-shou, honored by Kyoto Shimbun, 1994, Medal with Purple Ribbon, Japan Govt., 1997, Achievement award, Japanese Soc. Agrl. Informatics, 1998, Broadcast Cultural award, NHK, 1998, C&C prize, 1999, Memorial award, Takayanagi Kinen-shou, 2000, Lifetime Achievement award Assn. Computational Linguistics, 2003, Chevalier dans l'Ordre Nat. de la Légion d'honneur, 2004, Japan prize: Information and Media Technology, Sci. and Tech. Found. Japan, 2005. Fellow: IEEE (Emanuel R. Piore award 1993); mem.: Asia-Pacific Assn. for Machine Translation (pres. 1992—96), Japan Libr. Assn. (pres. 2002—07), IEEE Japan Coun. (chair 2005—07), Japan Assn. Nat. Univs. (pres. 2001—03), Assn. Natural Lang. Processing (pres. 1994—96), Info. Processing Soc. Japan (pres. 1999—2001, Contributions award 1997), Internat. Assn. Pattern Recognition (v.p. 1986—88), Cognitive Sci. Soc. Japan (pres. 1988—90), Internat. Assn. Machine Translation (pres. 1991—93, Medal of Honor 1997), Inst. Elect. Info. Comm. Engring. Japan (v.p. 1993—98, pres. 1998—99, Disting. Achievement and Contributions award 1997), Japan Sci. Coun. of Japan. Avocations: reading, golf, Chinese calligraphy, classical music, walking. Home: 39-1 Kitaikedacho Iwakura Sakyo Kyoto 606-0004 Japan Office: Nat Diet Libr 1-10 Nagata-cho Chiyoda Tokyo 100-8924 Japan Office Phone: 810335812331. E-mail: maknag@fmu2.seikyou.ne.jp.

NAGARAJ, VENGALATTORE THATTAI, aerospace engineer; s. Vengalattore and Ramalakshmi Srinivasan; m. Brindha Muthu, Jan. 21, 1971; children: Srikar Thattai Vengallatore, Mukund Thattai Vengalattore. BE, U. Mysore, 1959; MEng, Indian Inst. Sci., Bangalore, 1961; PhD, Loughborough U. Tech., Eng., 1968. Aero. engr. Hindustan Aeronautics Ltd., Bangalore, Karnataka, India, 1961—64; sr. rearch scientist U. Md., Coll. Pk.; asst. prof. Indian Inst. Tech., Bombay, Maharashtra, 1969—70; project engr., design engr. Hindustan Aeronautics Ltd., Karnataka, 1970—79, sr. design engr., additional gen. mgr., 1979—97. Mem. aircraft design tech. com. Am. Helicopter Soc. Internat., Alexandria, Va., 2001—; lectr. in field. Assoc. editor: Jour. Am. Helicoptor Soc. Internat., 2007—; contbr. articles to profl. pubs. Recipient Disting. Alumnus, Indian Inst. Sci., 1992, Nat. Aero. prize, Aero. Soc. India, 2004, Svc. award, Alfred Gessow Rotorcraft Ctr., 2007. Fellow: Aero. Soc. India; mem.: AIAA, Am. Helicopter Soc. Internat. (mem., tech. com. on design 2000). Achievements include design of advanced light helicopters; research in structural dynamics of aircraft and helicopters, composite structures.

NAGARKATTI, JAI PRAKASH, chemical company executive; b. Hyderabad, India, Feb. 18, 1947; came to U.S., 1970; s. Surendranath and Shakuntala (Bai) N.; m. Linda Susan Slaughter, Mar. 14, 1975; 1 child, Shanti. BS, Osmania U., 1966, MS, 1968, Texas A&M Univ., 1973, PhD, 1976. Group leader Aldrich Chem. Co. Inc., Milw., 1977-78, supr. prodn., 1978-79, mgr. prodn., 1979-84, dir. prodn., 1985, v.p., 1985-87, pres., 1987—99; pres. fine chemicals Sigma Aldrich Corp., St. Louis, 1999—2002, pres. sci. rsch., 2002—04, pres., COO, 2004—05, pres., CEO, 2005—, bd. dir., 2005—. Lectr. chemistry V.V. Coll., Hyderabad, 1969-70. Contbr. articles to profl. jours. Robert A. Welch fellow East Tex. State U., Commerce, 1974-76. Fellow Indian Chem. Soc.; mem. Am. Chem. Soc. (chmn. membership Milw. chpt. 1981). Avocations: stamp collecting/philately, tennis. Office: Sigma Aldrich Corp 3050 Spruce St Saint Louis MO 63103

NAGASHIMA, MASAYUKI, chemical and mechanical engineer, researcher; s. Mitsuo and Sachiko Nagashima; m. Kinuko Chiken; 1 child, Naoka. BS in Chem. Engring., Kyoto U., Japan, 1991, PhD, 2006. Asst. mgr. Integrated Mfg. Tech. Lab. Dai Nippon Printing Co., Ltd., Tsukuba-Shi, Japan, 1996—2001, mgr. Integrated Mfg. Tech. Lab., 2001—07, sr. expert, mgr. Integrated Mfg. Tech. Lab., 2007—08, sr. expert, gen. mgr. Integrated Mfg. Tech. Lab., 2008—. Achievements include patents in field.

NAGATA, MINORU, retired electronics engineer; b. Shinjuku-ku, Tokyo, Japan, June 4, 1933; s. Kikushiro and Sigeko Nagata; m. Yasuko Fukukita, Mar. 31, 1963; children: Haruko, Noboru, Mitsuru. BS, U. Tokyo, 1952, PhD, 1966. Rsch. assoc. Stanford (Calif.) Electronics Lab., Stanford U., 1964; head VLSI dept. Ctrl. Rsch. Lab., Hitachi Ltd., Kokubunji, Tokyo, 1972-75, dir., sr. chief scientist, 1985-98, dir., sr. chief engr. corp. tech., 1998, advisor emeritus, 1998—. Recipient Gov.'s award, Metropolis of Tokyo, 1979, Nat. Medal Honor with purple ribbon, 1993, Frederik Philips award, Inst. Elec. and Electronic Engrs., 1994. Fellow: IEEE (Third Millenium medal 2000); mem.: Engring. Acad. Japan. Avocations: swimming, golf, amateur radio. Home: 4-5-3 Josuihon-cho kodaira-shi Tokyo 187-0022 Japan Home Phone: 81-42-322-3157. E-mail: HQL02621@nifty.ne.jp.

NAGATHIHALLI, NAGARAJ, biochemist, researcher; b. Nagathihalli, Karnataka, India, May 18, 1974; arrived in US, 2001, permanent resident, 2008; s. Nagathihalli Srinivasan and Narihalli Kempamma; m. Deepa Chandrashekar, Feb. 8, 2004. BS in Chemistry, Botany and Zoology, U. Mysore Yuvaraja Coll., 1994; MS in Biochemistry, U. Mysore, 1996; PhD in Biochemistry, U. Mysore, India, 2001. Rsch. assoc. U. Louisville, 2001—07; rsch. instr. Vanderbilt U., Nashville, 2007—. Mng. editor Nutrition Jour., 2006—; assoc. editor Am. Jour. Biochemistry Biotech., Annual Rev. Biomed. Scis., Internet Jour. Oncology; editl. bd. mem. Internat. Jour. Cancer Rsch. Therapeutics, Internat. Jour. Toxicology, Rsch. Jour. Biol. Sci., Rsch. Jour. Pharmacology, Internet Jour. Head Neck Surgery, Rsch. Jour. Animal Sci., Internat. Jour. Cancer Rsch.; sci. adv. bd. Austral-Asian Jour. Cancer; editl. bd. mem. Internat. Jour. Biol. Sci., Internat. Jour. Tourism and Travel Health; reviewer sci. jours. Contbr. articles to profl. jours., chapters to books. Cadet Nat. Cadet Corps., Channarayapatna, India, 1986—88, Mysore, India, 1989—91, sgt., 1991—92, under officer, 1992—93. Recipient Ed Nelson Rsch. award, 2004, Best Poster award, India, 2000, 2003, US, 2004; named Internat. Scientist of Yr., Gt. Britain, 2008; fellow, Def. Rsch. and Devel. Orgn., Mysore, 1997—2001, James Graham Brown Cancer Ctr., 2004; scholar, Am. Inst. Cancer Rsch., 2006. Mem.: AAAS (assoc.), Am. Soc. Nutrition, Am. Assn. Cancer Rsch. (assoc.), Am. Soc. Biochemistry and Molecular Biology (assoc.), Sigma Xi. Achievements include discovery of cathepsin and calpain enzyme system in goat musles and postmortem aging effect on this enzyme system; antioxidant properties of E. Officinalis (amla) and coriander seeds (spice); tumor progression and therapeutic intervention for smokers with lung cancer by E-cadherin regulation; development of novel cell death mechanism where lysosomal cathepsins act as pro-apoptotic factors; identified molecular factors which contribute to the increased risk of smokers for oral cancer; elucidated the mechanism of apoptotic cell death induced by hypoxia in oral cancer cells; investigated e-cadherin regulation in smokers; studied TGF-beta signaling in colon cancer in vivo; EGFR and Src signaling in pancreatic cancer. Office: Vanderbilt Univ 7131 Sonya Dr Nashville TN 37209 Personal E-mail: nagahalli@gmail.com.

NAGEL, ALEXANDER, mathematics professor; b. NYC, Sept. 13, 1945; s. Ernest and Edith Nagel; m. Yvonne Yuen, May 27, 1973; children: Katherine Irene, Rebecca Elizabeth. PhD, Columbia U., NY, 1971. Instr. Dept. Math., U. Wis., Madison, 1970—72; asst. prof. U. Wis.-Madison, 1972—74, assoc. prof, 1974—77, prof., 1977—, lipman bers prof., 2001—, steenbock prof. math. scis., 2004—. Fellowship, John Simon Guggenheim Found., 1987—88, AAAS, 2009. Office: Dept Math Univ Wis 480 Lincoln Dr Madison WI 53706 Office Fax: 608-263-8891. Business E-Mail: nagel@math.wisc.edu.

NAGEL, JEFFREY A., energy executive; BS in Mech. Engring., Carnegie Mellon U., 1987, MBA. Mgr. bus. devel. GE Lighting, 1997—98; pres. GE Home Electric Products, 1998—2000; gen. mgr., bus. devel. GE Aviation, 2001—03; pres. GE Inspection Technologies, 2003—06; v.p., global services GE Oil & Gas, 2006—. Office: GE Energy 4200 Wildwood Pkwy Atlanta GA 30339 Office Phone: 678-844-6000. Office Fax: 678-844-6690.*

NAGEL, THOMAS, philosopher, lawyer, educator; b. Belgrade, Yugoslavia, July 4, 1937; came to U.S., 1939, naturalized, 1944; s. Walter and Carolyn (Baer) N.; m. Doris Blum, June 18, 1958 (div. 1973); m. Anne Hollander, June 26, 1979. BA, Cornell U., 1958; B.Phil., Oxford U., Eng., 1960, DLitt (hon.), 2008; PhD, Harvard, 1963. Asst. prof. philosophy U. Calif., Berkeley, 1963-66; asst. prof. Princeton U., 1966-69, assoc., 1969-72, prof., 1972-80, NYU, 1980—, prof. philosophy and law, 1986—, Fiorello LaGuardia prof. law, 2001—03, Univ. prof., 2002—. Vis. prof. Rockefeller U., 1973, U. Mex., 1977, U. Witwatersrand, 1982, UCLA, 1986, U. Calif., Berkeley, 2004. Author: The Possibility of Altruism, 1970, Mortal Questions, 1979, The View from Nowhere, 1986, What Does It All Mean?, 1987, Equality and Partiality, 1991, Other Minds, 1995, The Last Word, 1997; author: (with Liam Murphy) The Myth of Ownership, 2002; author: Concealment and Exposure, 2002; assoc. editor: Philosophy and Public Affairs, 1970—82. Guggenheim fellow, 1966, NSF fellow, 1967-69, NEH fellow, 1978, 84-85, vis. fellow All Souls Coll., Oxford, Eng., 1990; recipient Mellon Disting. Achievement award, Andrew Mellon Found., 2006, Rolf Shock prize, Royal Swedish Acad. Sci., 2008. Mem.: Am. Philos. Soc., Brit. Acad., Am. Acad. Arts and Scis., Am. Philos. Assn.

NAGEL, VERNON J., chemicals and electronics executive; BBA, U. Mich. V.p. fin., CFO, treas., sec. Stericycle Inc.; exec. v.p., CFO, treas. Kuhlman Corp., 1993—99; prin. Jepson Assocs., Inc., 1999—2001; CFO Acuity Brands, Inc., Atlanta, 2001—04, vice chmn., 2004, chmn., pres., CEO, 2004—. Office: Acuity Brands Inc 1170 Peachtree St NE Atlanta GA 30309

NAGERA, HUMBERTO, psychiatrist, psychoanalyst, educator, writer; b. Havana, Cuba, May 23, 1927; m. Gloria Maria Hernandez, Sept. 8, 1952; children: Lisette Maria, Humberto Felipe, Daniel. B.Sc., U. Havana, 1945; MD, Havana Med. Sch., 1952. Intern, resident in psychiatry Havana U. Hosp., 1950-55; sr. staff, chmn. research Anna Freud's Clinic, London, 1958-68; prof. psychiatry U. Mich., Ann Arbor, 1968-87, chief youth services, 1973-79, prof. emeritus, 1987; prof. psychiatry U. South Fla., 1987—, dir. adolescent inpatient unit and children's inpatient unit, 1987-97, dir. Carter Jenkin Ctr., 2002—. Lectr. in field. Author: Early Childhood Disturbances, Problems of Developmental Psychoanalytic Psychology, 1966, Vincent Van Gogh, 1966, Basic Psychoanalytic Concepts on the Libido Theory, 1969, Basic Psychoanalytic Concepts on the Theory of Instincts, 1970, Basic Psychoanalytic Concepts of Metapsychology Conflicts, Anxiety, and Other Subjects, 1970, Female Sexuality and the Oedipus Complex, 1975, Obsessional Neurosis: Developmental Psychopathology, 1977, 2nd edit., 1993, The Developmental Approach in Child Psychopathology, 1981; Contbr. articles to profl. jours. Mem. Am. Psychiat. Assn., Internat. Psychoanalytic Assn., Mich. Psychoanalytic Inst. (pres. 1975-77), Am. Assn. Child Psychoanalysis, Cuba Med. Assn. in Exile, South Fla. Tampa Bay Psychoanalytic Soc. (pres. 1992-93). Home: 5202 Dwire Ct Tampa FL 33647-1016 Office: U South Fla Dept Psychiatry 3515 E Fletcher Ave Tampa FL 33613-4706 Office Phone: 813-974-8900, 813-908-8686.

NAGESWARA RAO, MADHUGIRI, research scientist; b. Madhugiri, Karnataka, India, Jan. 18, 1973; s. Mukunda and Rangubai Rao; m. Jaya Ramesh Soneji, Oct. 21, 2003; 1 child, Yasheeta Nageswara Rao. BS, Govt. Sci. Coll., Bangalore U., Tumkur, Karnataka, 1993; MS, Ctrl. Coll., Bangalore U., Karnataka, 1996; PhD, Forest Rsch. Inst., Dehra Dun, Uttaranchal, India, 2004. Chemist Karnataka Breweries and Distilleries Pvt. Ltd, Bangalore, 1993—94; rsch. asst. U. Agrl. Sci., GKVK, Bangalore, 1996—98, sr. rsch. fellow, 1998—2001, rsch. assoc., 2001—04; postdoc. rsch. assoc. U. Fla., IFAS, Citrus Rsch. and Edn. Ctr., Lake Alfred, 2004—. Editl. bd. mem. internat. sci. jours. Contbr. articles to profl. jours., chapters to books. Bd. trustees life mem. Samatva Trust, Bangalore, 2007; mem. Biodiversity Conservation and Rsch. Trust, Hassan, Karnataka, 2007; invited judge Jewett Sci. Fair, Winter Haven, Fla., 2007—08, State Sci. and Engring. Fair, Lakeland, Fla., 2008—09, Polk Region Sci. and Engring. Fair, Bartow, Fla., 2008—09. Recipient Secured Silver award, BP Conservation Programme, 2003, Excellence and Outstanding Performance award, Sri Bhavasara Kshatriya Trust, 2008; named one of Rising Young Investigators, Genome Tech., 2008; fellow Rsch. assistantship, Ctr. Internat. Forest Rsch., 1996—98, Rsch. associateship, Dept. Biotech., 2001—04; Sr. Rsch. fellowship, 1998—2001. Mem.: BioinfoIndia (young advisor 2008—), Sci. Adv. Bd. (Named to Mem. Spotlight 2007), Am. Soc. Plant Biologists (mem. corner 2008), Internat. Soc. Hort. Scis., Bioclues: Clues for Innovation (Young-Scientist 2007), Genome India Internat. (joint sec. 2009, Named to Com. and Mem. Spotlight 2006), Soc. Conservation Biology, Ashoka Trust Rsch. in Ecology and Environment, Evol Dir: Internat. Sci. Network, BioTechniques® Molecular Biology Forums, Forestgen: Internat. Sci. Network. Office: Univ Fla IFAS Citrus Rsch and Edn Ctr 700 Experiment Station Rd Lake Alfred FL 33850 Personal E-mail: mnrbhav@yahoo.com.

NAGIN, RAY C. (CLARENCE RAY NAGIN JR.), Mayor, New Orleans; b. New Orleans, June 11, 1956; m. Seletha Smith, 1982; children: Jeremy, Jarin, Tianna. BSc in Acctg., Tuskegee U., 1978; MBA, Tulane U., 1994. With GM, 1978—81, Associates Corp., Dallas, 1981—85; contr. Cox Comm. S.E. La. cable sys., 1985—89, v.p., gen. mgr., 1989—2002; mayor City of New Orleans, La., 2002—. Mem. bd. dirs. United Way, Convenant Ho.; chmn. United Negro Coll. Fund Walkathon fundraising campaign; pres. 100 Black Men Metro New Orleans. Recipient Excellent Customer Svc. award, Better Bus. Bur., 1993, Disting. Bus. Ptnr. award, La. State Bd. Edn., 1994, Diversity and Role Model award, Young Leadership Coun., 1995, New Orleanian of Yr. award, Gambit weekly, 1998, Nat. Telly award, 2001, Most Influential Black Americans, Ebony mag., 2006; named to Power 150, 2008. Achievements include development of Bring New Orleans Back Commn; mandated largest mass evacuation; development of multi million dollar housing plan. Office: Office of the Mayor New Orleans City Hall 1300 Perdido St Rm 2E04 New Orleans LA 70112 Office Phone: 504-565-7793. Office Fax: 504-565-6423.*

NAGLE, EUGENIA SUSAN KARABACZ, retired sociologist, psychologist; b. Detroit, 1936; d. Peter and Hedy (Grusczynski) Karabacz; m. Robert D. Nagle, Nov. 20, 1956; children: Carl A., Sonya L., Paula E. BS in Sociology, Wayne State U., 1956; postgrad., U. Chgo., 1953-55; MA, N.Mex. Highlands U., 1960; PhD, Union Grad. Sch., 1977; postgrad., Bryn Mawr. Inst., 1981. Diagnostic technician Vocat. Counseling Inst., Detroit, 1952; rsch. technician United Auto Workers-CIO, Detroit, 1958; clin. psychology intern N.Mex. State Hosp., Las Vegas, 1962-63; clin. psychology trainee VA Hosp., Omah and Lincoln, Nebr., 1963-64; instr. sociology N.W. Mo. State U., Maryville, 1965-70, prof. sociology and psychology, 1971-92, ret., 1992. Bd. dirs. Inst. Discourse. Grantee N.W. Mo. State U., 1981, 82. Mem. APA, Am. Sociol. Assn., Am. Psychol. Soc., Midwest Sociol. Soc., Psychology/Sociology Club, Mo. Psychol. Assn., World Federalists, Psi Chi, Pi Gamma Mu.

NAGLE, THOMAS W., legislative staff member; Chief of staff to Rep. Tom Udall US House of Reps., Washington, staff mem., appropriations com., 2007—08; chief of staff to Senator Tom Udall US Senate, Washington, 2008—. Office: B40D Dirksen Senate Office Bldg Washington DC 20510 Office Phone: 202-224-6621.*

NAGLER, LORNA E., apparel executive; b. Oct. 5, 1956; Divisional merchandise mgr. Lane Bryant, Inc., Columbus, Ohio; v.p., divisional merchandise mgr. Kids 'R Us; sr. v.p., gen. merchandise mgr., apparel Kmart Corp., Hoffman Estates, Ill.; pres. Catherine Stores Corp., 2002—04, Lane Bryant, Inc., 2004—07; pres., CEO Christopher & Banks Corp., Plymouth, Minn., 2007—. Bd. dirs. Christopher & Banks Corp., 2007—, Ulta Salon, Cosmetics & Fragrance, Inc., 2009—. Office: Christopher and Banks Corp 2400 Xenium Ln N Plymouth MN 55441-3626 Office Phone: 763-551-5000. Office Fax: 763-551-5198.*

NAGLER, STEWART GORDON, retired insurance company executive; b. Bklyn., Jan. 30, 1943; s. Henry and Mary Nagler; m. Bonnie Lawrence, Aug. 9, 1964 (dec.); children: David, Ellen; m. Ronnie Hendler, Jan. 9, 2000. BS summa cum laude, Poly. U., 1963. With Met. Life Ins. Co., NYC, 1963—2004, exec. v.p., 1983-85, sr. exec. v.p., 1985-93, sr. exec. v.p., CFO, 1993-98, vice chmn. bd., 1998—2004, CFO, 1998—2004. Fellow Soc. Actuaries, Acad. Actuaries. E-mail: stunagler@optonline.net.

NAGOSKI, MARCELLE, music educator; children: Ian, Emily, Amelia. MusB, U. Del., Newark, 1995; MusM, Westminster Choir Coll., Princeton, NJ, 1997. Music faculty U. Del. Cmty. Music Sch., Newark; vocal coach First Unitarian Ch., Wilmington, Del., 1994—, accompanist, 1994—; music tchr. Wilmington Friends Sch., 1998—99, Springer Mid. Sch., Wilmington, 1999—2000; faculty Marple Newtown HS, Pa., 2000—02, Owen J. Roberts HS, Pottstown, Pa., 2002—03, Del. County CC, Media, Pa., 2004—06; music dept. chair Pa. Leadership Charter Sch. Ctr. Performing and Fine Art, West Chester, 2006—08; faculty U. Md. Eastern Shore, Princess Anne, 2007—. Adjudicator Ann Arundle County Arts Festival, Annapolis, Md., 1997; guest clinician Somerset County Sch. Dist., Md., 2007—08; guest condr. Worchester HS Honors Choir, Md., 2008. Musician: (recital) Songs of Love and Loss. Recipient award, Golden Key Nat. Honors Soc., 1994, Quigley Award, U. Del., 1994—95. Mem.: Am. Choral Dir.'s Assn., Nat. Assn. Tchrs. Singing, Phi Kappa Lambda (award 1995). Avocation: cooking. Office: Univ Md Eastern Shore Backbone Rd Princess Anne MD 21853 Personal E-mail: musicdma@gmail.com. Business E-Mail: msnagoski@umes.edu.

NAGRA, PARMINDER, actress; b. Leicester, England, Oct. 5, 1975; m. James Stenson, Jan. 17, 2009; 1 child, Kai David Singh. DLitt (hon.), Leicester U., 2007. Actor: (films) Bend It Like Beckham, 2002, Ella Enchanted, 2004, (voice only) Maya, the Indian Princess, 2005, In Your Dreams, 2006; (TV series) Turning World, 1996, Always and Everyone, 1999, ER, 2003—09; (TV films) King Girl, 1996, Donovan Quick, 1999, Twelfth Night, 2003, Second Generation, 2003, Compulsion, 2008. Office: c/o ARG 4 Great Portland St London W1W 8PA England*

NAGY, CHRISTA FIEDLER, biochemist; b. Marienbad, Czech Republic, July 8, 1943; d. Herbert A. Fiedler and Anna C. (Gluth) Rathmann; m. Bela Imre Nagy, Aug. 22, 1969; 1 child, Byron. BS in Biology, Fairleigh Dickinson U., Teaneck, NJ, 1967, MS in Biochemistry, 1974; PhD in Biochemistry, Rutgers U., 1981. Sr. scientist Hoffmann-La Roche Inc., Nutley, NJ, 1981-88, assoc. rsch. investigator, 1988-95; asst. dir. preclin. rsch. Eisai Inc., Teaneck, 1997-98; assoc. dir. clin. pharmacology Eisai Med. Rsch., Inc., Ridgefield Park, NJ, 1998—2005, dir. clin. pharmacology, 2005—. Mem.: Am. Soc. Clin. Pharmacology and Therapeutics, Drug Info. Assn., Am. Soc. Biol. Chemists. Roman Catholic. Avocations: travel, skiing, tennis, hiking. Office: Eisai Med Rsch Inc 55 Challenger Rd Ridgefield Park NJ 07660 Office Phone: 201-287-2174. Business E-Mail: christa_nagy@eisai.com.

NAGY, ELIZABETH GARVER, artist; b. Martinsville, Ill., Jan. 14, 1928; d. Ralph Tibbs and Evelyn Fasig Garver; m. William Roger Achleman (dec.); children: Shelly Marth, Todd Jeffrey; m. Stephen Michael Nagy (dec.); children: Stephanie Nagy-Agren, Patricia Nagy Adelman. Degree in art, Studio Sch. Advt. Art, Cin., 1948. Illustrator Wolf & Dessauer, Ft. Wayne, Ind., 1949—51; freelance illustrator Ft. Wayne, 1951—; art instr. Springfield (Ohio) Art Ctr., 1968—77, Fine Line Creative Arts Ctr., St. Charles, Ill., 1986—92. Presenter in field. One-woman shows include Mountainlair Gallery, W.Va. U., Morgantown, W.Va., 1974, Clay N Caboodle Cadence, Geneva, Ill., 1993, Transylvania County Arts Ctr., Brevard, N.C., 1999, many others, exhibited in group shows at Schumacher Gallery, Columbus, Ohio, 1975, Old State Capitol Galleries, Baton Rouge, La., 1976, 1978, 1979, Greenhill, Woodmere Gallery, 1976—90, Phila. Civic Ctr., 1976—90, Port History Mus., Phila., 1976—90, Tweed Mus., Duluth, Minn., 1978, Rahr-West Mus., Manitowoc, Wis., 1979, Springfield Art Assn., Ill., 1981, 1991, 1992, Davenport Art Mus., Iowa, 1983, LA Artcore Gallery, 1988, Maurice Spertus Mus., Chgo., 1990, The Fine Line Creative Arts Ctr., St. Charles, 1993, Transylvania County Arts Coun. Gallery 7, Brevard, 1996, 1997, Transylvania County Arts Ctr., Brevard, 1999—2005, many others, Represented in permanent collections Time Temporary, Ft. Wayne, Kane County Jud. Ctr., Geneva, Bankers Club Worldwide Ho., Taipei, Taiwan, Springfield (Ohio) Art Mus., many others. Sec., bd. dirs. Springfield Art Ctr., 1969—76; mem. visual arts com. Dellora A. Norris Cultural Arts Ctr., St. Charles, 1980—88. Recipient award of excellence, Midwest Watercolor Soc., 1983, 3d award, 41st Ann. Artists Guild of Chgo., 1983, award of merit, The Anderson (Ind.) Fine Arts Ctr., 1988. Mem.: Phila. Water Color Soc. (hon. life), Transparent Watercolor Soc. Am. (signature), Watercolor West (signature), Western Ohio Watercolor Soc. (founder, 1st pres.). Avocations: creating wearable art, knitting, weaving, sewing, embroidery.

NAGY, GEORGE, education educator; b. Budapest, Hungary, July 7, 1937; s. Stephen and Helen Nagy; m. Jill Beckoff Nagy, July 20, 1963; children: Naomi, Edwin. B in Engring. Physics, McGill U., Montreal, 1959, M in Engring., 1960; PhD, Cornell U., 1962. Tech. staff IBM T.J. Watson Rsch. Ctr., Yorktown, NY, 1963—73; dept. chair computer sci. U. Nebr., Lincoln, 1972—81, prof. computer sci., 1981—85; prof. computer engring. Rensselaer Polytech. Inst., Troy, NY, 1985—. Co-author: (book) Optical Character Recognition, 1989; contbr. articles to profl. jours. Recipient Lifetime Rsch. award, Internat. Conf. Document Analysis and Recognition, 2001. Fellow: IEEE (life), Internat. Assn. Pattern Recognition. Avocations: skiing, hiking, sailing. Office: Rensselaer Polytech Inst 110 8th St Troy NY 12180 Office Phone: 518-276-6078.

NAGY, REBECCA MARTIN, museum director; b. Statesboro, Ga., Jan. 16, 1953; d. John Staten and Kate Purvis Martin; m. Paul Davis Nagy, Dec. 9, 1989. BA, Ga. So. U., 1975; PhD, U. NC, 1983. Instr. Cleve. Mus. Art, Dept. Art Hist. Edn., 1982—85; sr. program coord. NC Mus. Art, Raleigh, NC, 1985—94, curator African art, 1997—2002, assoc. dir. edn., 1994—2002; dir. Harn Mus. Art, U. Fla., Gainesville, 2002—. Pres., bd. dirs. Gallery Art and Design, NC So. U., Raleigh, NC, 1999—2000; bd. mem. Arts Coun. African Studies Assn., 2003—05, Art in Public Places Trust, Gainesville, Fla., 2004—; curator various exhibitions NC Mus. Art, 1996—2003. Editor (author): North Carolina Museum of Art Handbook of the Collections, 1998, Sepphoris in Galitees Crosscurrents of Culture, 1998; author: Textiles in Daily Life in The Middle Ages, 1988. Recipient Dist. Alumna award, Ga. So. U., 2004; fellow, Internat. Partnership Among Mus. Programs, Am. Assn. Mus., 1994, Fulbright-Hays grant, U.S. Dept. Edn., 2000. Mem.: S.E. Art Mus. Dirs. Consortium, Fla. Art Mus. Dirs. Assn., Assn. Art Mus. Dirs., Gainesville Women's Forum, Rotary Club Gainesville. Office: Samuel P Harn Mus Art PO Box 112700 Gainesville FL 32611 Office Phone: 352-392-9826. Office Fax: 352-392-3892. Business E-Mail: rnagy@harn.ufl.edu.

NAGY, STEPHEN MEARS, JR., physician, allergist; b. Yonkers, NY, Apr. 1, 1939; s. Stephen Mears and Olga (Zahoruiko) N.; m. Brenda Yu Nagy, 1966; children: Catherine, Stephen III. BA, Princeton U., 1960; MD, Tufts U., 1964. Diplomate Am. Bd. Internal Medicine, Am. Bd. Allergy and Immunology. Pvt. practice, Sacramento, Calif., 1971-2000; prof. Sch. Medicine U. Calif., Davis, 1974—. Author, editor Evaluation & Management of Allergic and Asthmatic Diseases, 1981; mem. editl. bd. Clinical Reviews in Allergy; creator Famous Teachings in Modern Medicine-Allergy Series slide collection. Capt. U.S. Army, 1966-68, Vietnam. Fellow Am. Acad. Allergy, Am. Coll. Allergy; mem. CMA, Sacramento-El Dorado Med. Soc. (bd. dirs. 1971-95, 1989-95). Avocations: bicycling, book collecting, opera, fencing. Office: 4801 J St Ste A Sacramento CA 95819-3746 Office Phone: 916-456-4782.

NAHAB, FATTA B., neurologist, educator; m. Farah M. Mahir, Aug. 7, 2002. Degree in Biology with Honors, La Sierra U., Riverside, Calif., 1996. Registered MD Calif., 2000. Clin. neurology fellow Nat. Insts. Health-NINDS, Bethesda, Md., 2004—07, asst. clin. investigator, 2007—08; asst. prof. neurology, rsch. dir., divsn. movement disorders U. Miami Miller Sch. Medicine, Fla., 2008—. Fellow, Am. Soc. Exptl. NeuroTherapeutics, 2008. Mem.: Movement Disorder Soc., Am. Acad. Neurology, Alpha Omega Alpha. Achievements include first to delineating the brain networks involved in the sense of volition. Office: Univ Miami Miller Sch Med 1120 NW 14th St Ste 1347 Miami FL 33136

NAHABEDIAN, MAURICE Y., plastic surgeon; MD, U. Calif., Irvine, 1983—87. Diplomate Am. Bd. Plastic Surgery, 1997. Intern in surgery U. Calif., Irvine, 1987—88, resident in plastic surgery, 1988—92; resident in surgery John Hopkins U., Balt., 1992—95, attending in plastic surgery, 1996; assoc. prof. plastic surgery Johns Hopkins U., Balt., 1996—. Achievements include research in breast reconstruction with autologous tissue. Office: Johns Hopkins Med Instns 601 N Caroline St 8152C Baltimore MD 21287 E-mail: mnahabed@jhmi.edu.

NAHAI, FOAD, plastic surgeon, educator; b. Teheran, Iran, Sept. 23, 1943; came to U.S., 1970; m. Shahnaz Mossanen, Aug. 4, 1969; children: Farzad, Fariba BSc with honors, U. Bristol, Eng., 1966, MB ChB, 1969. Diplomate Am. Bd. Surgery, Am. Bd. Plastic Surgery (dir. 2001-2007); lic. Eng., Ga. Med. and surg. intern United Bristol Hosps., Bristol, England, 1969-70; intern in surgery Balt. City Hosps., 1970-71; resident in surgery Johns Hopkins Hosp., Balt., 1971-72; resident in gen. surgery Emory U. Affiliated Hosps., Atlanta, 1972-74, chief resident, gen. surgery, 1974-75, fellow in hand surgery and microsurgery, 1975-76, resident in plastic surgery, 1976-77; instr. in surgery Emory U., Atlanta, 1975—76, 1978, asst. prof. surgery (plastic surgery), 1978—83, assoc. prof. surgery (plastic surgery), 1983—91, prof. plastic surgery, 1991—97; pvt. practice Paces Plastic Surgery, Atlanta, 1998—. Invited spkr. in field; vis. prof. at various universities, colleges and institutions, domestically and internationally. Co-author (with S.J. Mathes) Clinical Atlas of Muscle and Musculocutaneous Flaps, 1979, Clinical Applications for Muscle and Musculocutaneous Flaps, 1982, Reconstructive Surgery: Principles Anatomy and Technique, 1996, (with others) Microvascular Surgery in Reconstruction of the Head and Neck, 1989, Plastic and Reconstructive Breast Surgery, 1990, Grabb's Encyclopedia of Flaps, 1990, Chirurgie Due Cancer Due Sein Diagnostique, 1997, (with Bostwick and Eaves) Endoscopic Plastic Surgery, 1995; mem. editl. bd. Annals Plastic Surgery, 1984-88, Outlook Plastic Surgery, 1988-97, Perspectives in Plastic Surgery 1994-97, Plastic and Reconstructive Surgery 1998, Aesthetic Plastic Surgery, 1999, Aesthetic Surgery Jour., 2000, Roundtables in Plastic Surgery, 2003; author Art of Aesthetic Surgery Principles and Techniques, 2005; co-editor Vertical Scar Mammoplasty, 2005; contbr. articles to profl. jours.; co-prodr. (movies) Breast Reconstruction After a Radical Mastectomy with Latissimus Dorsi Musculocutaneous Flap, 1978, The Tensor Fascia Lata Free Flap, 1979; prodr. (videotapes) TFL Neurosensory Flap for Coverage of Greater Trochanteric and Ischium, Rectus Abdominis Flap for Sternal Coverage, Gastrocnemius Muscle Flap for Coverage of Tibia, others; contbr. chpts. to books. Recipient Russell Cooper prize, U. Bristol, Eng., 1968, Gold Medal Paper Presentation Southeastern Surg. Conf., 1976, Best Paper award Atlanta Clin. Soc., 1980, award Am. Med. Writers Assn., 1983; named one of Best Doctors in Am., Best Doctors in the US, Top Plastic Surgeon Good Housekeeping, More Mag., Atlanta Mag., Top Plastic Surgeon in the World, W Mag. Fellow ACS (3d Ann. Residents Competition award Ga. chpt. 1977); mem. Am. Soc. Plastic Surgeons (President's award, 2005), Am. Assn. Plastic Surgeons (James Barrett Brown award 1982), Am. Soc. for Aesthetic Plastic Surgery (jud. coun. 1997, bd. dirs. 1999-, tchg. course subcommittee chmn., 1999-2002, sec. 2002-04, edn. commn. co-chair, 2002-05 chair 2005, v.p. 2005, pres.elect 2006, pres. 2007-2008), Am. Soc. Plastic and Reconstructive Surgeons (rsch. grantee ednl. found.), Ga. Soc. Plastic Surgeons, Med. Assn. Ga., Ga. Surg. Soc., Med. Assn. Atlanta, Southeastern Soc. Plastic and Reconstructive Surgeons (Outstanding Resident award 1977), Internat. Assn. Univ. Plastic Surgeons, Plastic Surgery Rsch. Coun. (program chmn. 1988, chmn. 1989), Soc. Residents and Ex Residents of Inst. Reconstructive Surgery (hon.), Sociedad Jaime Planas de Cirurgia Plastica (hon.), Internat. Soc. Aesthetic Plastic Surgery (1st term course dir. 1999, sec. gen. 2000-2004, 2d v.p. 2004-06, 1st v.p. 2006-07, pres.-elect 2007, pres. 2008), Am. Soc. for Laser Medicine and Surgery, Plastic Surgery Ednl. Found. (bd. dirs. 2003-05), Internat. Plastic & Reconstructive Surgery Found. (v.p. 1999), Am. Soc. for Reconstructive Microsurgery (sec. 1986-89); corr. mem. Brazilian Coll. Surgeons, Brazilian Soc. Plastic Surgeons, Italian Soc. Plastic, Reconstructive and Aesthetic Surgery, Fla. Soc. Plastic and Reconstructive Surgeons, Israeli Assn. Plastic and Cosmetic Surgeons, Japanese Soc. Plastic and Reconstructive Surgery, Assn. Plastic and Reconstructive Surgeons So. Africa (also hon.), Lebanese Soc. Plastic, Reconstructive, and Aesthetic Surgery (hon.), New Eng. Soc. Plastic Surgeons (hon.). Office: Paces Plastic Surgery 3200 Downwood Cir NW Ste 640 Atlanta GA 30327-1624 Office Phone: 404-351-0051. Office Fax: 404-351-0632. Business E-Mail: nahaimd@aol.com. E-mail: pacesplasticsurgery@aol.com.

NAHARIN, OHAD, choreographer, performing company executive; b. Mazra, Israel; naturalized, US, 1991; m. Mari Kajiwara, 1978 (dec. 2001). Student, Juilliard Sch., Sch. Am. Ballet. Dancer Batsheva Dance Co., Tel Aviv, Martha Graham Dance Co., NYC; choreographic debut NYC, 1980; artistic dir. Batsheva Dance Co., Tel Aviv, 1990—2003, house choreographer, 2003—. Recipient Chevalier de l'Ordre des Arts et des Lettres, France, 1998, Israel prize, 2005, Samuel H. Scripps/Am. Dance Festival award for Lifetime Achievement, 2009. Mailing: 241 W 108th St #4A New York NY 10025 Office: Batsheva Dance Co POB 50280 61500 Tel Aviv Israel*

NAHAS, GABRIEL GEORGES, pharmacologist, educator, writer; b. Alexandria, Egypt, Mar. 4, 1920; came to U.S., 1947, naturalized, 1962; s. Bishara and Gabrielle (Wolff) N.; m. Marilyn Cashman, Feb. 13, 1954; children: Michele, Anthony, Christiane. BA, U. Toulouse, France, 1937, MD, 1944; MS, U. Rochester, 1949; PhD, U. Minn., 1953; DSc (hon.), U. Uppsala, 1988. Rockefeller Found. fellow U. Rochester, 1947-48; Mayo Found. fellow Mayo Clinic, 1949-50; rsch. fellow U. Minn., 1950-53, mem. faculty, 1955-57; mem. staff Walter Reed Army Inst. Rsch., 1957-59; faculty George Washington U. Med. Sch., 1957-59; mem. faculty Columbia U. Coll. Physicians and Surgeons, NYC, 1959-92, prof. anesthesiology, 1962-92; prof. emeritus, 1992; rsch. prof. anesthesiology NYU Med. Sch., NYC, 1992—. Disting. vis. scientist Addiction Rsch. Ctr., NIDA, 1987; adj. rsch. prof. anesthesiology U. Paris, 1968-71; fellow Coun. Circulation and Basic Sci., Am. Heart Assn., 1961—; mem. com. on trauma NRC, 1964-66; mem. adv. bd. Cousteau Soc.; cons. commn. on narcotics, drug control program UN. Author 700 sci. publs. and 40 books and monographs in English and French. Decorated Presdl. Medal of Freedom with gold palm Govt. of U.S.; comdr. Legion of Honor, Croix de Guerre with 3 palms (France), Order Brit. Empire, Order Orange Nassau Netherlands, Silver medal City of Paris; recipient Medal of Honor, Statue of Liberty Centennial, 1986; Fulbright scholar, 1966. Fellow AAAS, N.Y. Acad. Sci.; mem. Am. Physiol. Soc., Harvey Soc., Am. Soc. Pharmacology and Exptl. Therapeutics, Soc. Physiol. Langue Française, French Acad. Medicine (laureate 1995, 96), Brit. Pharm. Soc., Sigma Xi. Achievements include research on med. instrumentation, pharmacology Tham, acid-base regulation, pharmacology of cannabis and cocaine, drug dependence, consciousness, college problem on drug dependence. Home: 40 E 74th St New York NY 10021-2732 *Courage is to stand by one's own conviction unheeding the trends of fashion or pressure groups. It is to suffer alone and be scorned for a lifetime. But, in the end, one will hear "he was right!".*

NAHAT, DENNIS F., performing company executive, choreographer; b. Detroit, Feb. 20, 1946; s. Fred H. and Linda M. (Haddad) N. Hon. degree, Juilliard Sch. Music, 1965. Prin. dancer Joffrey Ballet, NYC, 1965-66; prin. dancer Am. Ballet Theatre, NYC, 1968-79; co-founder Cleve. Ballet, 1976, Sch. of Cleve. Ballet, 1972; founder, artistic dir. Sch. Cleve. San Jose Ballet, 1996; founder New Sch. of Cleve. San Jose Ballet, 1996—; founder, artistic dir. San Jose Cleve. Ballet (now Ballet San Jose), San Jose, 1985—. Co-chair Artists Round Table Dance USA, 1991; trustee Cecchetti Coun. Am., 1991; mem. adv. bd. Ohio Dance Regional Dance Am.; dir. dance USDAN Ctr. for the Creative Performing Arts, NY, 1999—. Prin. performer Broadway show Sweet Charity, 1966-67; choreographer Two Gentlemen of Verona (Tony award 1972), 1969-70; (ballet) Celebrations and Ode (resolution award 1985), 1985, Green Table, Three Virgins and a Devil (Isadora Duncan award 1985); conceived, directed, choreographed Blue Suede Shoes, PBS, 1997-98. Grantee Nat. Endowment Arts, 1978, Andrew Mellow Found., 1985; recipient Outstanding Achievement award Am. Dance Guild, 1995, 96, 2000—. Avocation: cooking. also: Ballet San Jose PO Box 1666 40 N 1st St San Jose CA 95109-1666 Office Phone: 408-288-2820 Ext.225. Business E-Mail: dnahat@balletsanjose.org.*

NAHATA, BABU L., economics professor, researcher; b. Sardarshahr, Rajasthan, India, June 2, 1944; s. Bhikam Chand and Manohari Nahata; m. Kusum Lodha, Aug. 8, 1949; children: Ritu Nahata Rowland, Rohit. BS, Birla Inst. Tech., Ranchi, India, 1967; MS, Ill. Inst. Tech., Chgo., 1970, Poly. U., Bklyn., 1974; PHD, No. Ill. U., Dekalb, 1977. Prof., co-dir., ctr. emerging market economies U. Louisville, 1978—. Vis. exch. prof. Hiroshima Shudo U., Japan, 1986—87. Fellow, Fukuoka U., Japan, 1992, Japan Soc. Promotion Sci., Tokyo, 1996—97; scholar, Indian Inst. Mgmt., Calcutta, 1989, Fukuoka U., 2000. Mem.: Am. Econ. Assn., Sigma Xi. Office: U Louisville Dept Econs COB Louisville KY 40292 Office Fax: 502-852-7672. Business E-Mail: nahata@louisville.edu.

NAHATA, MILAP CHAND, pharmacy educator; b. Sardar Shahr, Rajasthan, India, Oct. 20, 1950; came to U.S., 1974; s. Bachh Rajji and Ratani Devi (Anchalia) N.; m. Suchitra Kothari, June 22, 1978; 1 child, Leena. BS, U. Jodhpur, India, 1970; BS in Pharmacy, U. Bombay, India, 1973; MS in Pharmaceutics, Duquesne U., 1975, PharmD, 1977. Asst. prof. pharmacy Ohio State U., Columbus, 1977-83, asst. prof. pediatrics, 1979-83, assoc. prof. pharmacy, pediatrics, 1983-88, prof. pharmacy, pediatrics, 1988—. Dir. infectious disease rsch. lab. Children's Hosp., Columbus, 1980—; cons. Hoechst Roussel Pharms., N.J., 1989—, Adria Labs., Columbus, 1990; presenter in field. Author: Pediatric Drug Formulations, 1990, 92; sr. editor: Annals of Pharmacotherapy; column editor; Jour. Clin. Pharmacy and Therapeutics; guest editor: Jour. Pharmacy Practice, 1990; mem. editl. bd. pharmacy-related jours., 1980—; referee 20 pharmacy and med. jours., 1980—; contbr. over 300 articles to profl. publs. Named Pharmacist of Yr., Ohio Soc. Hosp. Pharmacists, 1987, Outstanding Tchr. of Yr., Student Nat. Pharm. Assn., 1993; recipient Award for Sustained Contbns. to Lit., Am. Soc. Hosp. Pharmacists, 1987, R.G. Leonard award U. Tex., 1989, Edn. Award for Sustained and Outstanding Contbns. to Clin. Pharmacy Edn., Am. Coll. Clin. Pharmacy, 1990, Alumni award for disting. teaching Ohio State U., 1991, Disting. Pharmacy Educator award Am. Assn. Coll. Pharmacy, 1993. Fellow AAAS, Am. Coll. Clin. Pharmacy (pres. 1990-93, regent 1986-89, Edn. award 1990), Am. Acad. Microbiology; mem. Inst. Medicine. Avocation: golf. Office: Childrens Hosp 700 Childrens Dr Columbus OH 43205-2696 also: Ohio State U A206 Parks Hall 500 W 12th Ave Columbus OH 43210-1291 E-mail: nahata.1@osu.edu.*

NAHAVANDI, AMIR NEZAMEDDIN, retired engineering firm executive; b. Tehran, Iran, Apr. 6, 1924; arrived in U.S., 1956, naturalized, 1970; s. Ahmad and Fatima Razaghi Nahavandi. Electromech. Engring. degree, Tehran U., 1947; MS in Mech. Engring, Carnegie Inst. Tech., 1957, PhD, 1960. Registered profl. engr., Pa. Engr. Tehran U., 1948-50; head design group Nat. Iranian Oil Co., Tehran, 1950-56; adv. engr. Westinghouse Electric Corp., Pitts., 1957-66; prof., chmn. dept. mech. engring. U. Vt., 1967-68; rsch. prof. N.J. Inst. Tech., 1969-77; prof. engring. and applied sci. Columbia U., NYC, 1977-81; chief scientist Electronic Assocs., Inc., West Long Branch, NJ, 1981-82; pres. Mazen, Inc., Long Branch, NJ, 1982-92. Decorated Sci. medal Govt. Iran. Fellow ASME; mem. N.Y. Acad. Scis., Phi Kappa Phi, Sigma Xi, Tau Beta Pi. Achievements include development of analytical models for stock market forecasting; research and development in dynamics of steam generators and boiling systems; research in thermal pollution of lakes and rivers; vibration of reactor structures; dynamic and accident analysis of conventional and nuclear power plants; solid-fluid interaction. Home: 7635 Eads Ave Unit 202 La Jolla CA 92037-4832 Personal E-mail: anahav@aol.com.

NAHM, WALTER K., dermatologist, researcher; s. James J. and Hyun S. Nahm; m. Lauren Y. Nahm; 1 child, William J. BA, U. Tex., Austin, 1993; PhD, Baylor Coll., 1996; MD, Baylor Med. Sch., 1998. Diplomate Am. Bd. Dermatology. Intern St. Joseph Hosp., Houston, 1999; chief resident Boston U. Sch. Medicine, 2002; Mohs Micrographic Surgery fellow Conn U. Calif., LA Sch. Medicine, 2003, cosmetic surgery fellow, 2003; staff physician Scripps Mercy Hosp., San Diego, 2003—, VA San Diego Healtcare Sys., 2003—, West LA VA Med. Ctr., 2003—04, Kindred Hosp., San Diego, 2004—05; dir. Mohs Micrographic Surgery U. Calif., San Diego, 2005—. Asst. clin. prof. U. Calif., 2003—. Editor: PCI Jour. Recipient Excellence in Scholarly Activities award, Boston U. Sch. Medicine, 2002, Citizen's award, 2002; named Young Investigator of Yr., Tex. Neurol. Soc. Tex. Med., 1997; grantee, Soc. Investigative Dermatology, 2002; fellow Albert M. Kligman fellow, Soc. for Investigative Dermatology, 2002. Fellow: AMA (Physician's Recognition award 2005), Am. Soc. Dermatologic Surgery (Young Investigator's Writing Competition award 2003), Am. Acad. Cosmetic Surgery (membership com. 2005—, Excellence award 2005), Am. Acad. Dermatology (Continuing Med. Edn. award 2005), Am. Coll. Mohs Micrographic Surgery and Cutaneous Oncology, Am. Soc. for Laser Medicine and Surgery; mem.: San Diego Dermatology Soc. (pres. 2008), Internat. Hyperhidrosis Soc., San Diego County Med. Soc., Calif. Med. Assn., Am. Soc. for Lipo-Suction Surgery, San Diego Soc. Dermatologic Surgery (pres. 2007), Soc. for Investigative Dermatology, Am. Soc. Cosmetic Dermatology and Aesthetic Surgery, Phi Beta Kappa. Office: 7695 Cardinal Ct Ste 200 San Diego CA 92123 Office Phone: 858-278-8835. Office Fax: 858-386-4776. Personal E-mail: tire99@yahoo.com.

NAHMAD, ALBERT H., manufacturing executive; b. Oct. 15, 1940; m. Jane Davis; 2 children. BS in Mech. Engring., U. N. Mex., 1962; MS in Indsl. Adminstrn., Purdue U., 1963. Mgmt. cons. Arthur Young, NYC; group v.p. W.R. Grace & Co.; chmn. pres., CEO Watsco, Inc., Coconut Grove, Fla., 1973—. Bd. dirs. Am. Bankers Ins. Group, Mayor's Jewelers. Mem. Fla. Coun. 100; chmn. bd. of trustees Miami Children's Hosp.; past chmn. Fla. chpt Young Presidents' Org.; bd. dir. Cmty. Partnership for the Homeless Inc. Mem. Chief Executives Org., World Presidents' Org. Office: Watsco Inc 2665 S Bayshore Dr Ste 901 Miami FL 33133

NAHMAD, MICHEL HENRY, thoracic surgeon; b. Nov. 7, 1938; married; 4 children. BSc in Biology, U. NM, Albuquerque, 1960; MD, Tulane U. Med. Sch., New Orleans, 1964. Diplomate Am. Bd. Surgery, 1971, Am. Bd. Thoracic and Cardiac Surgery, 1971, cert. spl. competence pediatric surgery 2005. Internship in mixed medicine Charity Hosp. La., Tulane Svc., New Orleans, 1964—65, residency in gen. surgery, 1965—66; residency in gen. surgery, assoc. resident in surgery Bronx Mcpl. Hosp., the Albert Einstein Coll. Medicine, NY, 1966—67, clin. instr., surgery, 1966—70, surg. rsch. fellow, 1967—68, residency in surgery, 1968—69, chief resident in surgery, 1969—70; clin. instr., surgery Ohio State U. Coll. Medicine, Columbus, 1967—70, thoracic surgery specialist, U. Hosp., 1970—71, instr. surgery, 1970—72, pediatric surgery specialist, gen., thoracic and urologic surg. tng., Children's Hosp., 1971—72; attending pediatric surgeon, chief thoracic surgery Miami Children's Hosp. Pediatric and Thoracic Surgery, Fla., 1972—; pvt. practice in pediatric and thoracic surgery Dade and Broward Counties, Fla. Active Bapt. Hosp., Miami, 1972—; cons. Mt. Sinai Hosp., Miami, 1972—. Contbr. articles to profl. jours. Former med. bd. mem., treas. Miami Children's Hosp., vice chmn. bd. trustees; mem. Soc. Hosp. Founders. Grantee Gen. Rsch. Support, CHRF NIH, 1972. Fellow: ACS, Am. Acad. Pediat.; mem.: AMA, Greater Miami Pediatric Soc., Fla. Assn. Pediatric Surgeons, Dade County Med. Assn., Fla. Med. Assn. Office: Miami Children's Hosp 3200 SW 60th Ct Ste 201 Miami FL 33155 Office Phone: 305-662-8320. Office Fax: 305-665-2467.

NAHMAN, NORRIS STANLEY, electrical engineer; b. San Francisco, Nov. 9, 1925; s. Hyman Cohen and Rae (Levin) Nahman; m. Shirley D. Maxwell, July 20, 1968; children: Norris Stanley, Vicki L., Vance W., Scott T. BS in Electronics Engring, Calif. Poly. State U., 1951; MSE.E., Stanford U., 1952; PhD in Elec. Engring, U. Kans., 1961. Registered profl. engr., Colo. Electronic scientist Nat. Security Agy., Washington, 1952-55; prof. elec. engring., dir. electronics rsch. lab. U. Kans., Lawrence, 1955-66; sci. cons., chief pulse and time domain sect. Nat. Bur. Stds., Boulder, Colo., 1966-73, chief time domain metrology, sr. scientist, 1975-83, group leader field characterization group, 1984-85; v.p. Picosecond Pulse Labs, Inc., Boulder, 1986-90, scientific advisor, co-chair tech. adv. bd., 1990—; cons. elec. engr., 1990—; prof., chmn. dept. elec. engring. U. Toledo, 1973—75; prof. elec. engring. U. Colo., Boulder, 1966—; affiliate staff Los Alamos Nat. Lab., N.Mex., 1990—2006. Disting. lectr., prin. prof. Ctr. Nat. d'Etudes des Telcom. Summer Sch., Lanion, France, 1978; disting. lectr. Harbin Inst. Tech., China, 1982; mem. faculty NATO Advanced Study Inst., Castelvecchio, Italy, 1983, Internat. Radio Sci. Union/NRC; chmn. Internat. Intercomm. Group Waveform Measurements, 1981—90, Commn. A, 1985—86. Contbr. articles to profl. jours. Asst. scoutmaster Longs Peak coun. Boy Scouts Am., 1970—73, 1975—89. With US Mcht. Marine, 1943—46, with US Army, 1952—55. Recipient Disting. Alumnus award, Calif. Poly. State U., 1972, Order of Arrow, Boy Scouts Am., 1976; Ford Found. Faculty fellow, MIT, 1962, Nat. Bur. Stds. Sr. Staff fellow, 1978—79. Fellow: IEEE (life), Internat. Sci. Radio Union; mem.: Electromagnetic Acad., Am. Assn. Engring. Edn. (life), Instrumentation and Measurement Soc. of IEEE (mem. admnstrv. com. 1982—84, editl. bd. Trans. 1982—86, Andrew H. Chi Best Tech. Paper award 1984, Tech. Leadership and Achievement award 1987), Am. Mcht. Marine Vets., Stanford U. (life), U. Kans. (life), Calif. Poly. State U. Alumni Assn. (life), US Mcht. Marine Vets. World War II (life), Am. Radio Relay League Club (life), Am. Legion, Sigma Xi, Sigma Tau, Eta Kappa Nu, Tau Beta Pi, Sigma Pi Sigma. Achievements include patents in field.

NAHMIAS, DAVID E., prosecutor; b. Atlanta, 1964; BA summa cum laude, Duke Univ.; JD magna cum laude, Harvard Univ. Bar: Ga. 1991. Law clerk to Hon. Laurence H. Silberman US Ct. Appeals (DC cir.), 1991—92; law clerk to Justice Antonin Scalia US Supreme Ct., 1992—93; assoc. Hogan & Hartson LLP, Washington, 1993—95; asst. US atty. (no. dist.) Ga. US Dept. Justice, Atlanta, 1995—2001, counsel for the asst. atty. gen. criminal divsn. Washington, 2001—03, dep. asst. atty. gen. criminal divsn., 2003—04, US atty. (no. dist.) Ga., 2004—. Editor: Harvard Law Review. Office: US Attys Office 600 US Courthouse 75 Spring St SW Atlanta GA 30303-3309*

NAHMIAS, YAAKOV, biomedical engineer; b. Tel Aviv, Apr. 2, 1974; married. BSc, Technion, Haifa, Israel, 1999; PhD, U. Minn., Mpls., 2004; Postdoc., Harvard Med. Sch., Boston, Mass., 2006. Instr. surgery & bioengring. Harvard Med. Sch., Boston, 2006—. Recipient Mentored Rsch. Scientist Career award, Nat. Inst. Health, 2008. Jewish. Achievements include discovery of grapefruit flavonoid for HCV treatment. Office: MA Gen Hosp 114 16th St Room 2450 Charlestown MA 02129 Office Fax: 617-371-4950. Business E-Mail: ynahmias@partners.org.

NAHRA, LYNDA J., bank executive; b. 1951; Gard., Calf. Western U., Pacific Coast Banking School. Various positions Bank of America; management Community West Bancshares, Goleta, Calif., 1997—, pres., CEO, 2000—. Dir. Women's Economic Ventures; mem., Loan Com. Community West Bancshares, mem., Asset/Liability Com., mem., Compliance Com., mem., Mgmt. Succession Com. Mem. United Way, Santa Barbara; mem., Fin. Com. Goleta Montessori Ctr. Sch. Named one of 25 Women to Watch, US Banker, 2006. Mem.: Montecito Rotary Club. Office: c/o Community West Bank 5827 Hollister Avenue Goleta CA 93117

NAHRWOLD, DAVID LANGE, surgeon, educator; b. St. Louis, Dec. 21, 1935; s. Elmer William and Magdalen Louise (Lange) Nahrwold; m. Carolyn Louise Hoffman, June 14, 1958; children: Stephen Michael, Susan Alane, Thomas James, Anne Elizabeth. AB, Ind. U., Bloomington, 1957; MD, Ind. U., Indpls., 1960. Diplomate Am. Bd. Surgery, Am. Bd. Thoracic Surgery. Postdoctoral scholar in gastrointestinal physiology VA Ctr., UCLA, 1965; asst. prof. surgery Ind. U. Med. Sch., 1968-70; assoc. prof. Coll. Medicine Pa. State U., 1970-73; vice-chmn. dept. surgery Pa. State U., 1971-82, assoc. provost, dean health affairs, 1981-82, prof., chief divsn. gen. surgery, 1974-82; Loyal and Edith Davis prof., chmn. dept. surgery Northwestern U. Med. Sch., Chgo., 1982-97; surgeon-in-chief Northwestern Meml. Hosp., Chgo., 1982-97; intern, then resident in surgery Ind. U. Med. Ctr., Indpls., 1960-65; pres., CEO Northwestern Med. Faculty Found., Inc., 1996-99; prof. surgery, exec. assoc. dean clin. affairs Northwestern U. Med. Sch., 1997-99, prof. emeritus, 1999—. Mem. Nat. Digestive Disease Adv. Bd., 1985—89; bd. dirs. Am. Bd. Surgery, vice chmn., 1994—95, chmn., 1995—96; bd. dirs. Am. Bd. Med. Specialties, 1997—2005, pres., 2002—04; bd. dirs. Northwestern Healthcare Network; mem. exec. com. Accreditation Coun. for Grad. Med. Edn., 1999—2000; bd. commrs. Joint Commn. Accreditation Healthcare Orgns., 2002—08, vice chmn. bd. commrs., 2005—06, chmn. bd. commrs., 2007—08; bd. dirs. Joint Commn. Resources, 2004—08, vice chmn. bd. dirs., 2005—06; bd. dirs. Luth. Social Svcs., Ill., 2008—, Holy Family Ministries, 2006—. Editor emeritus Jour. Laparoendoscopic Surgery, 1997-2004; mem. editl. bd. Surgery, 1981-94, Archives of Surgery, 1983-93, Digestive Surgery, 1986-99, Am. Jour. Surgery, 1994-2000, Jour. Gastrointestinal Surgery, 1996-2000, Current Opinion in Gen. Surgery, Jour. Lithotripsy and Stone Disease, 1988-92; contbr. articles to profl. jours. With MC US Army, 1966—68. Recipient John P. Hubbard award, Nat. Bd. Med. Examiners, 2003, Derrick Vail award, Am. Bd. Med. Specialties, 2007. Fellow: ACS (bd. govs. 1992—98, vice chmn. 1994—96, chmn. bd. govs. exec. com. 1996—98, interim dir. 1999—2000, 1st v.p. elect 2005—06, 1st v.p. 2006—07, bd. regents, Disting. Svc. award 2001), Philippine Coll. Surgeons (hon.); mem.: AMA, Chgo. Surg. Soc. (pres. 1993—94), Chgo. Med. Soc., We. Surg. Assn., Soc. Univ. Surgeons, Soc. Surgery Alimentary Tract (pres. 1989—90, trustee), Soc. Clin. Surgery (sec. 1984—88), Internat. Biliary Assn., Ill. Surg. Soc., Ill. State Med. Soc., Internat. Fedn. Surg. Colls. (hon.; treas. 1999—2002), Gastroenterology Rsch. Group, Collegium Internat. Chirurgiae Digestive (pres. U.S. chpt. 1988—90), Ctrl. Surg. Assn. (sec. 1994—97, pres.-elect 1997—98, pres. 1998—99, pres. Found. 2002—03), Assn. Surg. Edn., Assn. Acad. Surgery, Am. Surg. Assn. (2d v.p. 1993—94), Am. Phys. Soc., Alpha Omega Alpha, Sigma Xi. Office: Dept Surgery 676 N St Clair St Chicago IL 60611 Home Phone: 847-714-1143; Office Phone: 312-695-1414. Business E-Mail: dnahrwold@northwestern.edu.

NAIDICH, THOMAS PAUL, neuroradiologist, educator; b. Bklyn., Apr. 8, 1944; s. James and Rose (Bitko) N.; m. Rochele Miriam Pudlowksi, Feb. 2, 1975 (div. Nov. 1981); children: 1 child, Sandra Rebecca; m. Michele W. Levin, Dec. 29, 1990. BA, Cornell U., 1965; MD, NYU, NY, 1969. Diplomate in radiology and in neuroradiology Am. Bd. Radiology. Intern Bronx Mcpl. Hosp. Ctr., NY, 1969-70; resident in radiology Montefiore Hosp., Bronx, NY, 1970-73; fellow in neuroradiology NYU Sch. Medicine, NY, 1973-75; prof. radiology and neurosurgery Mt. Sinai Med. Ctr. NYU, NY, 1998—, dir. neuroradiology NY, 1998—, vice chmn. radiology for acad. affairs, 2001—, Irving and Dorothy Regenstreif Rsch. prof. of neurosci., 2002—; asst. prof. Albert Einstein Coll. Medicine, Bronx, NY, 1975-77; from asst. prof. to assoc. prof. Mallinckrodt Inst. Radiology, St. Louis, 1978-80; from assoc. prof. to prof. Northwestern U. Sch. Medicine, Chgo., 1980-88; clin. prof. neuroradiology U. Miami Sch. Med., Fla., 1988-98; dir. neuroradiology Bapt. Hosp. Miami, Fla., 1988-98; dir Clin. Imaging Rsch. Core, Mt. Sinai Med. Ctr., Mt. Sinai, NY, 2001—05. Author: (with R. M. Quencer) Clinical Neurosonography, 1987; (with Valavanis, Schubiger) Clinical Imaging of the Cerebello-Pontine Angle, 1987; (with Daniels, Haughton) Cranial and Spinal Magnetic Ressonance Imaging, 1987, (with Duvernoy, Cattin, Fatterpeker, Raybaud, Risold, Salvolini, Scarabino) The Human Hippocampus, Anatomy, Vascularization and Serial Sections with MRAI, 3d edit., 2005; editor-in-chief Neuroradiology, 1980-91, chmn. editl. bd., 1991-93; assoc. editor Surg. and Radiol. Anatomy, 1991-97; founding editor Internat. Jour. Neuroradiology, 1994-00; contbr. articles to profl. jours. Recipient John Caffey award Soc. Pediatric Radiology, 1983. Mem. Am. Soc. Neuroradiology (treas. 1991-93, Cornelius Dyke award 1975), Am. Soc. Pediatric Neuroradiology (pres. 1994-95, Gold medal), Sociedad Ibero-latino Americana de Neurorradiologia (SILAN, Gold medal), European Soc. Neuroradiology (hon.), Brit. Soc. Neuroradiologists (hon.), Swiss Soc. Neuroradiology (hon.). Avocation: antique furniture. Office: Mt Sinai Med Ctr Dept Radiology Box 1234 1 Gustave Levy Pl New York NY 10029 Business E-Mail: thomas.naidich@mountsinai.org.

NAIDOO, LOREN JAY, psychology professor; BSc, McGill U., Montreal, 1998; PhD, U. Akron, Ohio, 2005. Asst. prof. Baruch Coll., NYC, 2005—. Mem.: Soc. Human Resource Mgmt., Assn. Psychol. Sci., Acad. Mgmt., Soc. Indsl. & Orgnl. Psychology. Office: Baruch Coll PO Box B8-215 55 Lexington Ave New York NY 10010

NAIDOO, ROBIN, biologist, researcher; b. Montreal, Que., Can., Apr. 23, 1973; s. Bala and Pauline Naidoo. BSc, McGill U., Montreal, 1995, MSc, 1997; PhD, U. Alta., Edmonton, Can., 2003. Conservation scientist WWF-US, Washington, 2003—. Contbr. articles to numerous profl. jours., chapters to books. Mem.: Soc. Conservation Biology.

NAIDORF, LOUIS MURRAY, architect; b. LA, Aug. 15, 1928; s. Jack and Meriam (Abbott) N.; m. Dorise D. Roberts, June 1948 (div.); children: Victoria Beth Naidorf; m. Patricia Ann Shea, June 1, 1968 (div.); m. Patricia Ruth Allen, Dec. 6, 1992 (dec.); m. Sandra Chronis, Apr. 20, 2004. BA, U. Calif., Berkeley, 1949, MA, 1950; Doctorate (hon.), Woodbury U., 2000. Registered architect, Calif. Designer Welton Becket Assocs., LA, 1950-51, Pereira and Luckman, LA, 1951-52; project designer Welton Becket Assocs., LA, 1952-55, sr. project designer, 1955-59, v.p. asst., dir. design, 1959-70, sr. v.p., dir. rsch., 1970-73; sr. v.p., design prin. Ellerbe Becket Assocs., LA, 1973-95; dean Sch. Architecture and Design Woodbury U., LA, 1990-2000; prin. Allen/Naidorf Design Cons., 1995—. Mem. peer rev. panel Nat. Endowment Arts, 1995—; vis. lectr. Calif. Poly. Sch. Architecture, San Luis Obispo, 1975-82; instr. UCLA Sch. Architecture, 1985, UCLA Landscape Archtl. Program, 1980-85, Otis-Parsons, L.A., 1986-92. Prin. works include Capitol Records Bldg., Century City, Los Angeles, Hyatt Regency, Dallas, Restoration Calif. State Capitol Bldg. Bd. dir. Inst. for Garden Studies, L.A., 1986—, ARC, 2000; trustee Woodbury U., 2000. Recipient Honor award Nat. Trust for Hist. Preservation, 1985. Fellow AIA (bd. dir. L.A. chpt. 1977-79, Silver Medal 1950, Nat. Honor award 1985, Educator of Yr. 1997, Legacy award 2005, Lifetime Achievement award 2009). Personal E-mail: naidorf@msn.com. *Leadership often requires decisions based on limited information. Course corrections can be made but only after action is taken because you can't steer a car that isn't moving.*

NAIDU, D. SUBBARAM, electrical engineer, educator; arrived in U.S., 1985; m. Sita Desineni Chalasani. BSEE, Sri Venkateswara U. India, 1964; MTech in Control Sys. Engring., Indian Inst. Tech., Kharagpur, 1967; PhD in Elec. Engring., Indian Inst. Tech., Kharagpur, India, 1977. Engr., Nat. Council Examiners Engring. and Surveying, 1994. Sr. nat. rsch. coun. assoc. NASA Langley Rsch. Ctr., Hampton, Va., 1985—90; assoc. dean Idaho State U., Pocatello, 1998—, prof. elec. engring., 1990—. Dir. measurement control engring. rsch. ctr. Idaho State U.; sr. associateship NRC, 1985—87, 1998—99; vis. prof. Nantong U., China, 2007; sabbatical U. Southern Australia, 2008, U. Western Australia, Perth, 2008. Author: Five Books; contbr. articles to profl. jours. Fellow, Norwegian Rsch. Coun., 2004. Fellow: IEEE, AIAA (assoc.). Office: Idaho State Univ 921 S 8th Ave Stop 8060 Pocatello ID 83209-8060 Business E-Mail: naiduds@isu.edu.

NAIK, DAYANAND N., statistician, educator; s. Narayana C. and Beeramma N. Naik; m. Sujatha D. Naik; children: Navin D., Rishi D. PhD, U. Pitts., 1985. Asst. prof. & assoc. prof. Old Dominion U., Norfolk, Va., 1985—2001, prof., 2001—. Author: (textbook) Applied Multivariate Analysis using SAS Software, Second Edition, Multivariate Data Reduction and Discrimination with SAS Software. Fellowship, Internat. Statis. Inst., 2006. Mem.: Internat. Indian Statis. Assn. (treas. 1999—2001), Inst. Math. Stats., Am. Statis. Assn. (chair membership com. 2005—08). Office: Old Dominion Univ Dept Math & Stats Norfolk VA 23529 Office Fax: 757-683-3885. Business E-Mail: dnaik@odu.edu.

NAIK, RUPALI K., researcher; d. Krishnakumar and Asha Naik; m. Anoop Menon. BSc in Pharmacy with Distinction, U. Pune, Maharashtra, India, 2000, MBA with Distinction, 2002; MS in Pharmacoeconomics and Outcomes Rsch. with Distinction, U. N.Mex, Albuquerque, 2006, PhD student in Pharmacoeconomics and Outcomes Rsch., 2006—. Registered pharmacist Maharashtra State Pharmacy Coun., 2000. Intern Emcure Pharms. Ltd., Pune, 2001; tchg. asst. U. N.Mex, 2002—; pharmacoeconomics intern Vets. Affairs Coop. Studies Program, Albuquerque, 2006. Reviewer Jour. Am. Pharmacists Assn., Washington, 2005, Rsch. Social and Adminstrv. Pharmacy, St. Louis, 2006, Am. Jour. Managed Care, Plainsboro, NJ, 2006, Expert Rev. Pharmacoeconomics and Outcomes Rsch., London, 2006, Annals Pharmacotherapy, Cin., 2006. Contbr. numerous sci. papers to profl. jours. Mem. Assn. India's Devel., Albuquerque, 2003—04. Mem.: Am. Assn. Colls. Pharmacy, Internat. Soc. Pharmacoeconomics and Outcomes Rsch. (pres. 2007—08, 2003—04, Best Student Podium Presentation 2004, Disting. Svc. award 2004). Personal E-mail: rupalimenon@gmail.com.

NAIK, SAMEER VIJAYKUMAR, mechanical engineer, educator; arrived in U.S., 1998; s. Vijaykumar and Vijaya Naik. BSME, U. Bombay, India, 1997; MSME, Purdue U., West Lafayette, Ind., 2000; PhD, Purdue U., 2004. Grad. rsch. asst. Purdue U., West Lafayette, Ind., 1998—2004, vis. asst. prof., 2004—, sr. rsch. assoc., 2007. Recipient Top Grad. Gold medal, U. Bombay, 1997; finalist Chorafas award, Dmitris A. Chorafas Found., 2004. Mem.: AAAS, ASME, AIAA (sr.), Am. Phys. Soc., Am. Soc. Engring. Edn., Am. Chem. Soc., The Combustion Inst., Optical Soc. Am. Office: Purdue Univ Mech Engring 585 Purdue Mall West Lafayette IN 47907-2088 Business E-Mail: naiks@ecn.purdue.edu.

NAIK, VINAYAK SHASHIKANT, research scientist; b. Mumbai, Maharashtra, India, Apr. 11, 1978; s. Shashikant Narayan and Pushpa Shashikant Naik; 1 child, Ram Vinayak. BEng, VJTI, Mumbai, 2000; PhD, Ohio State U., Columbus, 2006. Asst. sys. engr. Tata Consultancy Svcs., Mumbai, 1999—2000; rsch. asst. Ohio State U., 2002—06; rsch. staff CENS-UCLA, 2006—. Contbr. articles to profl. jours. Pres. Sankalpa, Columbus, 2004—06. Mem.: ACM, IEEE. Achievements include discovery of vivo characterization of a wide area 802.11b wireless seismic array; research in bonsai of wireless networks; development of an extreme scale wireless sensor network and a wireless sensor network for target detection, classification and tracking; design of Whisper: Local Secret Maintenance in Sensor Networks, Structural Monitoring and Performance-Based Assessment and Kansei: A Testbed for Sensing at Scale. Office: CENS-UCLA 420 Westwood Plaza Los Angeles CA 90024-1596 Office Fax: 310-206-3053. Business E-Mail: naik@cens.ucla.edu.

NAILON, REGINA EILEEN, nurse; m. James Allen Nailon; 1 child, Jordan A. AAS, Lower Columbia Coll. Nursing Program, Longview, Wash., 1988; BSN, Wash. State U., Vancouver, 1994; MS, U. Portland, Oreg., 1997; PhD, Oreg. Health & Sci. U., Portland, 2004. RN. Asst. prof. U. Nebr. Med. Ctr. Coll. Nursing, Omaha, 2006—07; advanced nurse rsch. specialist Alegent Health, Omaha, 2007—. Postdoc. rsch. fellow Ctr. Health Outcomes & Policy Rsch. U. Pa. Sch. Nursing, Phila., 2005—06. Post katrina health svcs. relief worker ARC, Baton Rouge, 2005; pastoral coun. mem. St. Thomas More Ch., Omaha, 2008; bd. mem. Ethnic Support Coun., Longview, 1999—2002, Habitat Humanity, Greeley, Colo., 2004; coord., health room Cmty. House Broadway, Longview, Wash., 1995—98. Predoc. Rsch. fellow, Oreg. Health & Sci. U., 1999, Postdoc. fellowship, U. Pa., 2005—06. Mem.: ANA, Nebr. Nurses Assn., Midwest Nursing Rsch. Soc., Acad. Health, Gamma PI-At-Large Chpt. (sec. 1995—97), Sigma Theta Tau Internat. Honor Soc. Nursing. Office: Alegent Health 12809 W Dodge Rd Omaha NE 68154 Office Fax: 402-343-4636. Business E-Mail: regina.nailon@alegent.org.

NAÍM, MOISÉS, editor-in-chief; b. Venezuela, 1952; MSc, PhD, MIT. Prof., dean Inst. Higher Adminstrn. Studies (IESA), Caracas, Venezuela; min. of trade & industry Venezuela, 1989—90; exec. dir., sr. adv. then pres. World Bank; editor-in-chief Foreign Policy mag., 1996—. Dir. projects/econ. reforms Carnegie Endowment Internat. Peace, Washington; bd. dirs. Internat. Crisis Group, Nat. Endowment for Democracy, Population Action Internat., World Econ. Forum Internat. Media Coun. Author: Paper Tigers & Minotaurs: The Politics of Venezuela's Economic Reforms, 1993, Illicit: How Smugglers, Traffickers, and Copycats are Hijacking the Global Economy, 2005 (named one of Washington Post's best nonfiction books, 2005); co-author: Altered States: Globalization, Sovereignty, and Governance, 2000; co-editor: Lessons of the Venezuelan Experience, 1995, Mexico 1994: Anatomy of an Emerging-Market Crash, 1998, Competition Policy, Deregulation, and Modernization in Latin America, 1999; contbr. articles on fgn. policy to Washington Post, LA Times, NY Times, Newsweek, TIME. Recipient Nat. Mag. award for Gen. excellence, Am. Soc. Mag. Editors, 2003, 2007, 2009. Office: Fgn Policy 1899 L St NW Ste 550 Washington DC 20036 Office Phone: 202-728-7300. Office Fax: 202-728-7342. E-mail: mnaim@CarnegieEndowment.org.*

NAIMA, HASAN A., academic administrator, department chairman; married. PhD, U. Idaho, 1986. Cert. in engring., IR, 1985. Educator Kans. City Kans. CC, 2003—08, dean engring., math. and scis., 2008—. Recipient Hennery Louis award in Excellence Tchg., Kans. City Kans. CC, 2007. Mem.: Allied Med. and Tech. Careers. Home: 6650 Lowell Dr Merriam KS 66202-3721 Office: Kans City Kans CC 7250 State Ave Kansas City KS 66112 Office Fax: 913-288-7677. Business E-Mail: hnaima@kckcc.edu.

NAIMARK, GEORGE MODELL, marketing and management consultant; b. NYC, Feb. 5, 1925; s. Myron S. and Mary (Modell) N.; m. Helen Anne Wythes, June 24, 1946; children: Ann, Richard, Jane. BS, Bucknell U., 1947, MS, 1948; PhD, U. Del., 1951. Rsch. biochemist Brush Devel. Co., Cleve., 1951; dir. quality control Strong, Cobb & Co.,

Inc., Cleve., 1951-54; dir. sci. svcs. White Labs., Inc., Kenilworth, NJ, 1954-60; v.p. Burdick Assocs., Inc., NYC, 1960-66; pres. Rajah Press, Summit, NJ, 1963—, Naimark and Barba, Inc., Florham Park, NJ, 1966—, Naimark & Assocs., Inc., Florham Park, NJ, 1994—; dir. Alteon, Inc., 2000—06. Author: A Patent Manual for Scientists and Engineers, 1961, Communications on Communication, 1971, 3d edit., 1987, A Man Called Skeeter, 1996, How To Be a Truly Rotten Boss, 2006, Cleaning Out My Attic, 2006, Adamant Eve Alias Myrtle Reed, 2006, How to be a Truly Rotten Driver, 2007; patentee in field; contbr. articles in profl. jours. With USNR, 1944-46. Fellow AAAS, Am. Inst. Chemists; mem. Am. Chem. Soc., N.Y. Acad. Scis., Am. Mktg. Assn. Home: 87 Canoe Brook Pky Summit NJ 07901-1404 Office: Naimark & Barba Inc 248 Columbia Tpke Ste 1 Florham Park NJ 07932-1210 Home Phone: 908-273-8725.

NAIMOLI, VINCENT JOSEPH, diversified financial services company executive; b. Paterson, NJ, Sept. 16, 1937; s. Ralph A. and Margaret R. (Calabrese) N.; children— Christine, Tory Ann, Alyson, Lindsey. BSM.E., U. Notre Dame, 1959; MSM.E., N.J. Inst. Tech., 1962; MBA, Fairleigh Dickinson U., 1964; grad. Advanced Mgmt. Program, Harvard Bus. Sch., 1974. With Continental Group, 1965-77, v.p., gen. mgr. ops., 1975-77; pres., chief oper. officer Allegheny Beverage Corp., Balt., 1977-78; sr. v.p., group exec. Jim Walter Corp., Tampa, Fla., 1978-81; group v.p. packaging Anchor Hocking Corp., Lancaster, Ohio, 1981-83; chmn. bd., pres., chief exec. officer Anchor Glass Container Corp., Lancaster, 1983-89; chmn., pres., CEO Anchor Industries Internat., Tampa, Fla., 1990—; chmn., chief exec. officer Electrolux Corp., Atlanta, 1990-91; chmn., CEO Doehler Jarvis Corp., Toledo, 1991-95; CEO Ladish, Inc., Milw., 1992-95; chmn., pres., CEO Harvard Industries, 1993-97; mng. gen. ptnr., CEO Tampa Bay Devil Rays, 1992—2005, chmn., 2006—. Bd. dirs. Strategic Materials, Inc. Roman Catholic. Office: Anchor Industries Internat 1 Tropicana Dr Saint Petersburg FL 33705-1703

NAINA, HARRIS V.K., hematologist; b. Cochin, India, May 1, 1975; s. Kunjali Naina and Haleema Naina; m. Samar Haris, Feb. 14, 2003; 1 child, Adam Harris. MD, Christian Med. Coll., Vellore, Tamil Nadu, India, 1997. Cert. physician Am. Bd. Internal Medicine, 2007. Resident clin. hematology Christian Med. Coll., 1997—98, resident clin. pathology, 1998—2002; sr. house office Nat. Health Sys., Kent, England, 2002—04; fellow hematology and oncology Mayo Clinic, Coll. Medicine, Rochester, 2004—. Contbr. articles to profl. jour. Mem.: Am. Soc. Hematology, Am. Soc. Clin. Oncology, Am. Med. Assn. Office: Mayo Clinic Coll Medicine 200 1st St SW Rochester MN 55905 Personal E-mail: harrisvk2002@yahoo.com.

NAIR, LAURA, retired music educator; d. John Henry and Elizabeth Richards Nair. MusB, Ohio Wesleyan U., Delaware, 1973. Music tchr. Saratoga Springs City Schs., NY, 1973—2007; coord. music ministries Shenendehowa United Meth. Ch., Clifton Park, NY, 1979—. Music camp dir. Skye Farm Camps, Warrensburg, NY, 1976—. Nominating com. mem. Troy Ann. Conf., United Meth. Ch., Saratoga Springs. Mem.: NY State United Tchrs., Choristers' Guild, Fellowship of United Methodists in Music and Worship Arts, Am. Choral Dirs.' Assn., Music Educators' Nat. Conf., Chi Omega (rush chairperson 1972—73). Methodist. Avocations: travel, golf, swimming. Home: 42 Chatsworth Way Clifton Park NY 12065 Office: Shenendehowa United Meth Ch 971 Rte 146 Clifton Park NY 12065 Office Fax: 518-373-9601. Business E-Mail: lauri@shenmeth.org.

NAIR, RAJEEV, engineering educator, researcher; s. Madhavan Nair and Ratnakutty Amma; m. Shyama Geetha Somanathan Nair, Dec. 23, 2007. PhD, Iowa State U., Ames, 2006. Cert. preparing future facility assoc., Grad. Coll. Iowa State U., 2004. Project engr. Photon Energy Tech. Inc., Ames, v.p.; quality control engr. Holmarc Slides & Controls Pvt. Ltd., Cochin, Kerala, India, 1998—99; grad. rsch. asst., mech. engring. dept. Wichita State U., Kans., 1999—2001, tchg. asst., 2000—01; mem., SANKALP Iowa State U., 2002—05, tchg. asst., mech. engring. dept., 2002—06, vol., PERMAR, 2002—06, communication sec., cricket club, 2004—05, rsch. asst., mech. engring. dept., 2005—06, postdoc. rsch. assoc., mech. engring. dept., 2007—, faculty, mech. engring. dept., 2007—. Internship Cochin Shipyard Ltd., 1996. Rsch. grant, NSF, 2007—08. Mem.: ASME, Soc. Mfg. Engrs., Sigma Xi. Home: 2810 Grand Ave Apt 1 Ames IA 50010-4642 Office: Iowa State Univ 2025 Black Engring Bldg Ames IA 50011-2161 Office Phone: 515-294-4850. Personal E-mail: c_tallboy@yahoo.com. Business E-Mail: rxmadhav@iastate.edu.

NAIR, RAMACHANDRAN P.K., agroforestry educator, researcher; b. Trivandrum, Kerala, India, Mar. 12, 1942; came to U.S., 1987. s. Krishna Kittu Pillai and Parukutty Amma; m. Vimala Devi Pillai, Aug. 29, 1973; children: Bindu, Deepa, Rekha. BS in Agr., Kerala Agrl. U., 1961, MS in Agr., 1968; PhD, Pantnagar U., India, 1971; DSc in Agr., U. Goettingen, W. Germany, 1978; DSc (hon.), Kyoto U., 2002, U. Sci. and Tech., Kumasi, Ghana, 2005, U. Guelph, Ont., Can., 2006, U. Santiago de Compostela, Spain, 2008. Research asst. Kerala Agrl. U., 1961-66, lectr. in agronomy, 1966; post-doctoral fellow Rothamsted Experimental Sta., Harpenden, Eng., 1971-72; agronomist ICAR (CPCRI), Kasaragod, Kerala, 1972-76; Humboldt fellow U. Goettingen, 1976-78; prin. sci. Internat. Centre for Rsch. in Agroforestry, Nairobi, Kenya, 1978-87; prof. agroforestry U. Fla., Gainesville, 1987-2001, Disting. prof., 2001—. Cons., rschr. numerous orgns. Author: Intensive Multiple Cropping with Coconuts in India, 1979, Agroforestry Species: A Crop Sheets Manual, 1980, Soil Productivity Aspects of Agroforestry, 1984, An Introduction to Agroforestry, 1993; co-editor: Agroforestry: A Decade of Developments, 1987, Directions in Tropical Agroforestry Research, 1998, New Vistas in Agroforestry, 2004, Tropical Homegardens, 2006; editor: Agroforestry Systems in the Tropics, 1989, Agroforestry Systems, 1982—, chief editor, 1994. Recipient Internat. Soil Sci. award, 2001, Internat. Agronomy award, 2000, Internat. Crop Sci. award, 2004, Disting. Internat. Educator, U. Fla., 2004, Sci. Achievement award, Internat. Union of Forest Rsch. Orgns., 2005, Advisor/Mentoring award, U. Fla., 2006, Humboldt prize, Germany, 2006. Fellow AAAS, Am. Soc. Agronomy (chair divsn. A-6 internat. agronomy 1995-96), Crop Sci. Soc. Am., Nat. Acad. Agrl. Scis. India, Soil Sci. Soc. Am.; mem. Internat. Soil Sci. Soc., Internat. Soc. Tropical Foresters, Soc. Am. Foresters (Barington-Moore award, 2004). Office: U Fla 118 Newins Ziegler Hall Gainesville FL 32611-0410 Office Phone: 352-846-0880. E-mail: pknair@ufl.edu.

NAIR, SARASWATHY, molecular biologist, educator; PhD, SUNY, Buffalo, 1992. Asst. prof. U. Tex. at Brownsville, 2006—. Grant, Borderplex, 2006—09. Mem.: Obesity Soc., Am. Diabetes Assn. Office: Univ Texas at Brownsville 80 Ft Brown Brownsville TX 78520

NAIR, VELAYUDHAN, pharmacologist, educator, academic administrator; arrived in U.S., 1956, naturalized, 1963; m. Jo Ann Burke, Nov. 30, 1957; children: David, Larry, Sharon. PhD in Medicine, U. London, 1956, DSc, 1976, LHD (hon.) h.c., 2003. Rsch. assoc. U. Ill. Coll. Medicine, 1956-58; asst. prof. U. Chgo. Sch. Medicine, 1958-63; dir. lab. neuropharmacology and biochemistry Michael Reese Hosp. and Med. Ctr., Chgo., 1963-68, dir. therapeutic rsch., 1968-71; prof. pharmacology FUHS/Chgo. Med. Sch., 1971—, disting. prof., 2001, vice chmn. dept. pharmacology and therapeutics, 1971—76, dean Sch. Grad. and Postdoctoral Studies, 1976—2003, v.p. rsch., 1999—2003, v.p., dean emeritus, 2003—, disting. prof., 2001. Vis. assoc. prof. pharmacology FUHS/Chgo. Med. Sch., 1963—68, vis. prof., 1968—71, Harvard U., 1994, Johns Hopkins Sch. Medicine, 1995. Contbr. articles to profl. jours. Recipient Morris Parker award, U. Health Scis./Chgo. Med. Sch., 1972. Fellow: AAAS, Am. Coll. Clin. Pharmacology, NY Acad. Scis.; mem.: AAUP, Internat. Soc. Devel. Neurosci., Am. Coll. Toxicology, Internat. Soc. Chronobiology, Soc. Neurosci., Soc. Exptl. Biology & Medicine, Pan Am. Med. Assn. (coun. on toxicology), Royal Inst. Chemistry (London), Brit. Chem. Soc., Am. Chem. Soc., Soc. Toxicology, Radiation Rsch. Soc., Am. Soc. Clin. Pharmacology & Therapeutics, Am. Soc. Pharmacology & Exptl. Therapeutics, Internat. Soc. Biochem. Pharmacology, Internat. Brain Rsch. Orgn., Cosmos Club (Washington), Alpha Omega Alpha, Sigma Xi. Office: Rosalind Franklin Univ Medicine and Sci 3333 Green Bay Rd North Chicago IL 60064-3037 Personal E-mail: velnair@comcast.net. *Success like happiness is relative and can only be gauged by one's own standards and ideals. There is probably no universal formula for either of them, but I have been guided by the following tenets: Dedication and committment to one's responsibilities and in the conduct of everyday life, honesty and sincerity in personal relations. One must have tolerance for those in less fortunate situations. As one grows older, one recognizes that no one makes it alone. As for me, I have received help from many; some of whom I can never repay except by passing on the gift which I was privileged to share. Above all, a faith that looks beyond the immediate helps to bear the inevitable ups and downs in life.*

NAITHANI, RAJESH, oncologist; b. Pauri, Uttarakhand, India, Mar. 15, 1971; s. Ansuya Prasad and Anandi Naithani; m. Pratibha Maindola, Feb. 3, 2001; 1 child, Shatakshi. PhD, Kurukshetra U., India, 2000. Rsch. asst. prof. UIC, Chgo., 2004—07; rsch. scientist IITRI, Chgo., 2007—. Pub. relation Aadi Shakti Bhuvneshwari Trust, Pauri, 2009. Mem.: Am. Chem. Soc. Achievements include research in cancer chemoprevention. Home: 1926 W Harrison 307 Chicago IL 60612 Personal E-mail: rajesh.naithani@gmail.com.

NAJAFI, MAHMOUD, mathematics professor; b. Esfahan, Idaho, Iran; Assoc. prof. applied math. Kent State U., Ashtabula, Ohio, 1995—. Office: Kent State Univ Ashtabula 3325 W 13th St Ashtabula OH 44004

NAJARIAN, JOHN SARKIS, surgeon, educator; b. Oakland, Calif., Dec. 22, 1927; s. Garabed L. and Siranoush T. (Demirjian) N.; m. Arlys Viola Mignette Anderson, Apr. 27, 1952; children: Jon, David, Paul, Peter. AB with honors, U. Calif., Berkeley, 1948; MD, U. Calif., San Francisco, 1952; LHD (hon.), U. Athens, 1980; DSc (hon.), Gustavus Adolphus Coll., 1981; LHD (hon.), Calif. Luth. Coll., 1983. Diplomate Am. Bd. Surgery. Surg. intern U. Calif., San Francisco, 1952-53, surg. resident, 1955-60, asst. prof. surgery, dir. surg. research labs., chief transplant service dept. surgery, 1963-66, prof., vice chmn., 1966-67; spl. research fellow in immunopathology U. Pitts. Med. Sch., 1960-61; NIH sr. fellow and assoc. in tissue transplantation immunology Scripps Clinic and Research Found., La Jolla, Calif., 1961-63; Markle scholar Acad. Medicine, 1964-69; prof., chmn. dept. surgery U. Minn. Hosp., Mpls., 1967-93; med. dir. Transplant Ctr., clin. chief surgery Univ. Hosp., 1967-94; chief hosp. staff U. Minn. Hosp., Mpls., 1970-71, Regents' prof., 1985-95, Jay Phillips Disting. Chair in Surgery, 1986-95, prof. emeritus, prof. surgery, 1995—. Spl. cons. USPHS, NIH Clin. Rsch. Tng. Com., Inst. Gen. Med. Scis., 1965-69; cons. U.S. Bur. Budget, 1966-68; mem. sci. adv. bd. Nat. Kidney Found., 1968; mem. surg. study sect. A div. rsch. grants NIH, 1970; chmn. renal transplant adv. group VA Hosps., 1971; mem. bd. sci. cons. Sloan-Kettering Inst. Cancer Rsch., 1971-78; mem. screening com. Dernham Postdoctoral Fellowships in Oncology, Calif. div. Am. Cancer Soc. Editor: (with Richard L. Simmons) Transplantation, 1972; co-editor: Manual of Vascular Access, Organ Donation, and Transplantation, 1984; mem. editorial bd. Jour. Surg. Rsch., 1968—, Minn. Medicine, 1968—, Jour. Surg. Oncology, 1968—, Am. Jour. Surgery, 1967—, assoc. editor, 1982—; mem. editorial bd. Year Book of Surgery, 1970-85, Transplantation, 1970—, Transplantation Procs, 1970—, Bd. Clin. Editors, 1981-84, Annals of Surgery, 1972—, World Jour. Surgery, 1976—, Hippocrates, 1986—, Jour. Transplant Coordination, 1990—; assoc. editor: Surgery, 1971; editor-in-chief: Clin. Transplantation, 1986—. Bd. dirs., v.p. Variety Club Heart Hosp., U. Minn.; trustee, v.p. Minn. Med. Found. Served with USAF, 1953-55. Hon. fellow Royal Coll. Surgeons of Eng., 1987; hon. prof. U. Madrid, 1990; named Alumnus of Yr., U. Calif. Med. Sch., San Francisco, 1977; recipient award Calif. Trudeau Soc., 1962, Ann. Brotherhood award NCCJ, 1978, Disting. Achievement award Modern Medicine, 1978, Internat. Gt. Am. award B'nai B'rith Found., 1982, Uncommon Citizen award, 1985, Sir James Carreras award Variety Clubs Internat., 1987, Silver medal IXth Centenary, U. Bologna, 1988, Humanitarian of Yr. award, U. Minn., 1992, Najarian Festschrift award Am. Jour. Surgery, 1993, Jubilee medal Swedish Soc. Medicine, 1994. Fellow ACS; mem. AAAS, AMA, Internat. Pediat. Transplantation Assn. (pres. 1998-2000), Soc. Univ. Surgeons, Soc. Exptl. Biology and Medicine, Am. Soc. Exptl. Pathology, Am. Surg. Assn. (pres. 1988-89), Am. Assn. Immunologists, Transplantation Soc. (v.p. western hemisphere 1984-86, pres. 1994-96, Medawar prize 2004, Ellis Island medal of Hon, 2005), Am. Soc. Nephrology, Internat. Soc. Nephrology, Am. Assn. Lab. Animal Sci., Assn. Acad. Surgery (pres. 1969), Internat Soc. Surgery, Soc. Surg. Chairmen, Soc. Clin. Surgery, Ctrl. Surg. Assn., Minn. Med. Soc., Hennepin County Med. Socs., Minn. Surg. Soc., Mpls. Surg Soc., St. Paul Surg. Soc. Howard C. Nafziger Surg. Soc., Portland Surg Soc., Halsted Surg. Soc., Am. Heart Assn., Am. Soc. Transplant Surgeons (pres. 1977-78), Coun on Kidney in Cardiovasc. Disease, Hagfish Soc., Italian Rsch. Soc., Minn. Acad. Medicine, Minn. Med. Assn., Minn. Med. Found., Surg. Biology Club, Sigma Xi, Alpha Omega Alpha, others. Office: U Minn Surgery Dept Mayo Mail Code 195 420 Delaware St SE Minneapolis MN 55455-0374 Home Phone: 612-823-0051; Office Phone: 612-625-8444. Business E-Mail: najar001@umn.edu.

NAJIB, JADWIGA S., pharmacist, educator; m. Jamal Najib; children: Daniel, Nicole. BS in Pharmacy, St. John's U., 1987; PharmD, U. Minn., 1989. Lic. pharmacist State Edn. Dept., NY, 1989. Asst. prof. pharmacy practice LI U., Arnold & Marie Schwartz Coll. of Pharmacy, Bklyn., 1989—98; assoc. prof. pharmacy practice LI U. Coll. Pharmacy, Bklyn., 1998—. Clin. pharmacist St. Luke's Roosevelt Hosp. Ctr., NCY, 1989—. Contbr. articles to profl. jours. Mem. leadership coun. in local schs., NY, 2004—06. Recipient David Newton Excellence Tchg. award, LI U., 1993. Mem.: Pharmacists Soc. State NY, NY State Coun. Health Sys. Pharmacists, Am. Assn. Colls. Pharmacy, Am. Soc. Health System Pharmacists. Achievements include research in pscyhopharmacotherapeutics. Office: Arnold & Marie Schwartz Coll Pharmacy 75 DeKalb Ave Brooklyn NY 11201 Business E-Mail: jadwiga.najib@liu.edu.

NAJJAR, DIANA, elementary school educator; d. Carl and Mary Snider; children: David, Mark. BS in Elem. Edn., Ball State U., 1970; MS in Edn. with concentration in Spl. Edn., Ind. U.-Purdue U., Indpls., 1977; postgrad. in gifted edn., Purdue U., 1981—83. Cert. elem. edn. tchr. Ind. Dept. Edn. Tchr. Indpls. Pub. Schs., 1970—72, The Orchard Sch., Indpls., 1984—. Gov.'s sch. task group State Dept. of Ind., 1984—86; creator dance curriculum; dance instr., choreographer sch. musicals, plays, operettas; screenwriter math. video, 1999. Author: (book and math. kit) Namagram, 1997, (video) Factor Blocks, 1999. Catechism coach St. George Ch., Indpls., 1989—95, 2005—06. Mem.: Ind. Assn. for the Gifted (legis. team 2005—05, legis. chmn. 1979—88, Svc. award 1985). Achievements include discovery of 4 set Venn diagram; created test to measure conceptual understanding of mathematical concepts through constructions; copyright Namagram book and design. Office: The Orchard Sch 615 W 64th St Indianapolis IN 46260

NAJJAR, SAMER S., internist, educator; s. Samir S. and Amal T. Najjar; m. Reem Sayegh, Dec. 28, 2000; children: Rami S., Karim S., Lara M. AB, Harvard U., Cambridge, Mass., 1989; MD, Yale U., New Haven, 1993. Head, human cardiovasc. studies unit Nat. Inst. Aging, NIH, Balt., 2000—; asst. prof. medicine Johns Hopkins U., Balt., 2000—. Achievements include research in cardiovascular aging.

NAJM, WADIE I., geriatrician, educator; m. Lizbeth Scott, June 1993. MD, U. Libre Bruxelles, Brusseles, 1984. Diplomate Calif., 1988. Staff geriatrician VA Med. Ctr., Long Beach, Calif., 1993—94; clin. prof. U. Calif., Irvine, 1994—. Med. dir. Susan Samueli Integrative Medicine Clinic, Irvine, 2008—; course dir., nutrition and dietary supplement, Orange County Med. Assn., editl. bd. mem., med. acupuncture. Founding mem. and pres. Calif. Acad. Med. Acupuncture, LA, 2005. Recipient Physician Excellence award, Orange County Med. Assn., 2004, 2005, 2007, 2008, Excellence Tchg. award, U. Calif., 2004—05, Best Dr. America award, 2007. Fellow: Am. Acad. Family Physicians; mem.: Am. Acad. Med. Acupuncture (editl. bd. 2006—08), Soc. Teachers Family Medicine. Office: Univ Calif Irvine 101 The City Dr Bldg 200 # 512 Orange CA 92868 Office Fax: 714-456-7984.

NAKAJIMA, FUMIHITO ANDY, priest, educator; s. Hiroaki and Yoko Nakajima; m. Emma Nakajima; children: Leia, Noelle. MDiv, Western Theol. Sem., Holland, Mich., 1995; MA, Columbia U., NY, 2000. Cert. tchr. Hokkaido Ministry Edn., 1990. Pastor Japanese Worship Svc., RCA, Holland, Mich., 1992—; assoc. prof. japanese Hope Coll., Holland, 1995—. Recipient Janet Anderson award, 2009; Willard C. Wichers Faculty Devel. grant, Hope Coll., 2004. Office: Hope Coll 257 Columbia Ave Holland MI 49423 Office Fax: 616-395-7559. Business E-Mail: nakajima@hope.edu.

NAKAJIMA, HIROSHI, education educator; b. Hiroshima, Japan, June 12, 1923; s. Iwao and Tamae (Takenaka) N.; m. Sei Sakao, May 2, 1966; children: Akihiko, Takehiko. Student, Nishogakusha Coll., 1942-44; BA, Waseda U., 1950; MA, 1954, EdD (hon.), 1989. Asst. prof. Japan women's Coll. Econs., 1954-59; lectr. Waseda U., 1954-63; asst. prof., 1963-68; prof. comparative and internat. edn., 1968-94; prof. emeritus, 1994—. Vis. prof. U. Helsinki, 1962-63; advisor Japanese Inst. Social Studies on Sweden, 1989—; vice-chmn. youth com. Higashikurumeshi, 1978-83; mem. bd. edn. Higashikurumeshi, 1983-91. Served with Japanese Army, 1943-46. Recipient Acad. Hon. Medal U. Helsinki, 1963; decorated Nat. 3rd Order, 2000. Mem.: Comparative and Internat. Edn. Soc. (mem. 1963), Finnish Acad. Sci. and Letters (fgn. 1984). Home: 1-4-37 Minamisawa Higashikurume-shi Tokyo 203-0023 Japan Office Phone: 81-3-5606-4311. Business E-Mail: nakajima@textbook-rc.or.jp.

NAKAMOTO, TOKUMASA, science educator; b. Kohala, Hawaii, July 8, 1928; m. Lilian Yuriko Mayeda, Mar. 23, 1950; children: Daniel Shoji, Katherine Yaeko Biala, Kenneth Nobuo. PhD, U. Chgo., 1959. Asst.-assoc. prof. U. Chgo., 1965—89, emeritus assoc. prof., 1989—. Sgt. first class M.I. Servuce, 1949—52, Various continental U.S, Japan. Achievements include research in mechanism of the initiation of protein synthesis. Home: 6532 N Hazel Ave Fresno CA 93711 Personal E-mail: tokumasa@sbcglobal.net.

NAKAMURA, HIROSHI, urology educator; b. Tokyo, Mar. 22, 1933; s. Yataroh and Hideko (Tanaka) N.; m. Miyoko Kodachi, Aug. 13, 1966. MD, Keio U., Tokyo, 1960, PhD, 1966. Med. diplomate. Asst. resident Mt. Sinai Hosp., NYC, 1962—63; rsch. fellow Cornell U. Med. Coll., NYC, 1966—68; asst. Sch. Medicine Keio U., Tokyo, 1968—70; chmn. urology dept. Tokyo Elec. Power Hosp., Tokyo, 1970—73; vis. asst. prof. surgery Cornell U. Med. Coll., NYC, 1973; chmn. urology Kitasato Inst. Hosp., Tokyo, 1973—77; chmn. dept., prof. urology Nat. Def. Med. Coll., Tokorozawa, Saitama, Japan, 1977—98, dir. dept. acad. affairs, 1994—96, prof. emeritus, 1999—; emeritus dir. Tokorozawa Ishikawa Clinic, 1998—. Author: Bedside Urology, 1983, Modern Clinical Point-Urology, 1993; editor: Up-to-Date Urology, 1983, Caveats & Pitfalls in Clinical Urology, 1999, Medical Ethics Q&A, 2002. Recipient Tamura award, Keio U. Sch. Medicine, 1967, All-around Med. award, Igaku-Shoin, Ltd., Tokyo, 1967, The Order of the Sacred Treasure, Emperor of Japan, 2003, Proclamation of Thanks, New Orleans City Coun., 2008. Buddhist. Avocations: jazz, audiophile, travel. Home: 11-1-1204 Higashicho Tokorozawa Saitama 359-1116 Japan Office: Tokorozawa Ishikawa Clin Iseki Bldg 4F 9-22 Hiyoshicho Tokorozawa 359-1123 Japan Office Phone: 81 4 2925 7355.

NAKAMURA, LAWRENCE T., microbiologist, educator; PhD, UCLA. Prof. microbiology LA Valley Coll., Valley Glen, Calif., 1996—. Office: LA Valley Coll 5800 Fulton Ave Van Nuys CA 91401-4096 Business E-Mail: nakamult@lavc.edu.

NAKAMURA, ROBERT MOTOHARU, pathologist; b. Montebello, Calif., June 10, 1927; s. Mosaburo and Haru (Suematsu) N.; m. Shigeyo Jane Hayashi, July 29, 1957; children: Mary, Nancy. AB, Whittier Coll., 1949; MD, Temple U., 1954. Cert. of spl. qualification in pathologic anatomy, clin pathology, immunopathology, Am. Bd. Pathology. Prof. pathology U. Calif., Irvine, 1971-74, adj. prof. pathology, 1974-75; chmn. dept. pathology Scripps Clinic and Rsch. Found., La Jolla, Calif., 1974-92; sr. cons., 1992—; pres. Scripps Clinic Med. Group, La Jolla, 1981-91; prof. dept. immunology and exptl. and molecular medicine Scripps Rsch. Inst., 1997—; chmn. pathology Scripps Clinic, 1998-99, chmn. emeritus pathology, 1999—. Adj. prof. pathology U. Calif., San Diego, 1975-93. Co-editor: Jr. Clin. Lab. Analysis, 1989—; contbr. articles to profl. jours. Fellow: Coll. Am. Pathologists, Am. Soc. Clin. Pathologists, Assn. Clin. Scientists, Am. Coll. Nutrition; mem. Internat. Acad. Pathology. Avocation: reading. Home: 8841 Nottingham Pl La Jolla CA 92037-2131 Office Phone: 858-554-8166, 858-410-2804.

NAKANISHI, KIYOSHI, retired automotive executive; b. Hyogo, Japan, 1945; m. Kumiko Nakanishi; 2 children. Degree in Mech. Engring., Kyoto U., 1970. Joined Toyota Motor Corp., 1970, mgr. engine design team, 1995, mgr., 1996, gen. mgr. engine engring. divsn., 1997, dir., 2000, mng. officer, 2003—04. Avocations: bicycling, walking. Office: Genesis Rsch Inst Inc 4-1-35 Noritake Shinmachi Nishi-ku Nagoya 451-0051 Japan Office Phone: 81-52-551-6330. E-mail: kiyonaka@tcp-ip.or.jp.

NAKARAI, CHARLES FREDERICK TOYOZO, music educator; b. Indpls., Apr. 25, 1936; s. Toyozo Wada and Frances Aileen N. BA cum laude, Butler U., 1958, Mus.M., 1967; postgrad., U. N.C., 1967-70. Organist, dir. choirs Northwood Christian Ch., Indpls., 1954-57; min. music Broad Ripple Christian Ch., Indpls., 1957-58; asst. prof. music Milligan Coll., Tenn., 1970-72; pvt. instr. organ, piano Durham, NC, 1972—. Mem. faculty piano camp U. N.C.-Greensboro, 1996, 97, 2000, 01; adjudicator N.C. Music Tchrs. Assn., N.C. Fedn. Music Clubs, Raleigh Music Tchrs. Assn., Charlotte Piano Tchrs. Forum, Chapel Hill Music Tchrs. Assn. Composer: Three Movements for Chorus, 1971, Bluesy, 1979. With USAF, 1958—64. Mem. Am. Musicol. Soc., Coll. Music Soc., Am. Guild Organists, Music Tchrs. Nat. Assn., N.C. Music Tchrs. Assn., Durham Music Tchrs. Assn. Address: 2312 Anthony Drive Durham NC 27705

NAKASHIMA, TADAYOSHI, retired biochemist, researcher; b. Yokkaichi, Mie-ken, Japan, Dec. 1, 1922; s. Chunosuke and Hina Nakashima; m. Fukuko Kondo, Nov. 15, 1947; 1 child, Rieko. BP, Nagoya Pharm. Coll., Aichi-ken, 1941—43; BS, Taihoku Imperial U., Taihoku, 1943—46; PhD, Kyushu U., Fukuoka, 1960—61. Rsch. Scientist U. of Miami, 1964. Acting chief, rsch. lab. Sanyo Penicillin Co., Nagoya, 1946—50; assoc. prof. Kwassui Coll., Nagasaki, 1951—62; post doctoral U. of Hawaii, 1962—64; vis. rsch. scientist U. of Bonn, Germany, 1966—69; rsch. prof. Inst. for Molecular and Cellular Evolution, U. of Miami, 1964—89. Author: (molecular evolution) Journals, (protoribosomes) In Molecular Evolution and Protobiology, 1984, (genetic code) Proc. Nat. Acad. Sci., 1972, (amino acid sequence) J. Biol. Chem.1966. Mem.: ISSOL, Am. Chem. Soc. Home: 7400 SW 159th Ter Palmetto Bay FL 33157-2452

NAKATA, AKINORI, epidemiologist, psychologist, researcher; b. Kawasaki, Kanagawa, Japan, Feb. 23, 1967; s. Kenzo and Yoshiko Nakata; m. Sonoko Shiibashi, May 26, 2004. PhD, U. Tokyo, 1997. Domestic rsch. fellow Japan Soc. for Promotion of Sci., Kawaguchi, 1997—2000; rsch. fellow Nat. Inst. Indsl. Health, Kawasaki, 2000—, Nat. Inst. Occup. Safety Health, Cin, 2004—. Guest editor Nat. Inst. Indsl. Health, Kawasaki, 2005—; vis. rschr. U. Tokyo, 1997—2005. Contbr. articles to med. jours. Avocations: tennis, fishing, baseball. Office: Nat Inst Occup Safety Health CDC 4676 Columbia Pky Cincinnati OH 45226 Office Fax: 513-533-8596. Personal E-mail: nakata-tky@umin.ac.jp.

NAKATA, CHERYL, finance educator; PhD, U. Ill., Chgo., 1997. Assoc. prof. mktg. & internat. bus. U. Ill., 1997—. Contbr. articles. Mem.: Am. Mktg. Assn. (Acad. & Mktg. Sci. Paper award). Office: Univ IL Chgo 601 S Morgan (MC 243) Chicago IL 60607

NAKATA, GARY KENJI, lawyer; b. Okinawa, Japan, Nov. 13, 1964; arrived in U.S., 1971; s. Hiroshi Nakata and Miwako Kin; m. Jo Ann Akiko Tengan, Aug. 22, 1998. BBA in Fin., U. Hawaii, 1988; JD with distinction, U. of the Pacific, 1995. Bar: Hawaii 1996, Calif. 1996, US Dist. Ct. Hawaii, 1996; cert. mgmt. acct.; cert. fin. mgr.; cert. grad. Am. Banker's Assn. Nat. Sch. Regulatory Compliance. Credit analyst Bank of Hawaii, Honolulu, 1988-90, sr. credit analyst, 1990-92; law clk. Hawaii Atty. Gen. Tax Divsn., Honolulu, 1994; sr. assoc. Kobayashi, Sugita & Goda, Honolulu, 1995—2003; dep. corp. counsel City and County of Honolulu, 2003—04; CFO Honolulu City & County Employees Fed. Credit Union, 2004—. Mem. new product devel. adv. bd. Warren Gorham & Lamont, NYC, 1997-98. Editor-in-chief: The Transnational Lawyer, 1994, 95. Pres., enlisted adv. coun. Hawaii Air Nat. Guard, Honolulu, 1986-92; mem. ex officio alumni coun., mem. membership com., mem. membership benefits subcom. U. Hawaii Alumni Assn., Honolulu, 1990-91; mem. fin. com. and bylaws subcom. Soc. Coll. Bus. Alumni and Friends, U. Hawaii Coll. Bus. Adminstrn. Alumni Affairs, Honolulu, 1990-91, founding mem., treas., 1990-91, mem. steering com. to form alumni orgn., 1997-98, pres., 1998-2000; at-large rep., treas., legis. liaison Neighborhood Bd., Kaneohe, Hawaii, 1991-92. Mem.: ABA (bus. law sect., comml. fin. svcs. com., consumer fin. svcs. com.), Hawaii Fin. Regulatory Compliance Assn. (bd. dirs. 1997—2003, chairperson fair credit reporting act regulatory update com. 1998—2003), Inst. Cert. Mgmt. Accts. (bd. dirs. 1998—2000, dir. mem. acquisition 1998—2000), Calif. State Bar Assn., Hawaii State Bar Assn. (mem. real property and fin. svcs. sect. 1997—), Hawaii Jaycees (legal counsel 2000—01, exec. v.p. 2002, pres. 2003), Hawaii Bus. Jaycees (charter pres. 1991—92, chmn. bd. 1992—93, charter mem.). Office: Honolulu City & County Employees Fed Credit Union 2200 Kamehameha Hwy Ste 208 Honolulu HI 96819-2356 E-mail: gary@kalanet.com.

NAKAYAMA, GRANTA YONEO, lawyer, former federal agency administrator; b. 1958; BS, MS, MIT, 1981; JD, George Mason U., 1994. Bar: Va. 1994, DC 1995, US Ct. Appeals (4th cir.). Chief engr. Nuclear Core Mfg., Naval Nuclear Propulsion Program, USN, chief quality control Welding and Nondestructive Testing Branch; ptnr. environ. law/product safety Kirkland & Ellis LLP, Washington, 1994—2005, 2009—; asst. adminstr. for enforcement & compliance assurance EPA, Washington, 2005—09. Writing instr. George Mason U. Sch. Law, 1993—94, adj. prof., 1998—. Contbr. articles to profl. jours. Lt. USN, 1981—86. Mem.: Soc. Automotive Engrs., Am. Welding Soc. Office: Kirkland & Ellis LLP 655 Fifteenth St NW Washington DC 20005-5793 Office Phone: 202-879-5074. Office Fax: 202-879-5200. E-mail: gnakayama@kirkland.com.*

NAKAYAMA, PAULA AIKO, state supreme court justice; b. Honolulu, Oct. 19, 1953; m. Charles W. Totto; children: Elizabeth Murakami, Alexander Totto. BS, U. Calif., Davis, 1975; JD, U. Calif., 1979. Bar: Hawaii 1979. Dep. pros. atty. City and County of Honolulu, 1979-82; ptnr. Shim, Tam & Kirimitsu, Honolulu, 1982-92; judge 1st Cir. Ct. State of Hawaii, Oahu, 1992-93; assoc. justice Hawaii Supreme Ct., Honolulu, 1993—. Mem. Am. Judicature Soc., Hawaii Bar Assn., Sons and Daughters of 442. Office: Hawaii Supreme Ct Ali'iolani Hale 417 S King St Honolulu HI 96813-2902*

NAKONECZNY, MICHAEL MARTIN, artist; b. Detroit, Oct. 30, 1952; s. Michael and Edithe (Pheil) N.; 1 child, Alysha. Student, Kent State U., 1972-74; BA, Cleve. State U., 1979; MFA, Univ. Cin., 1981. Artist in residence Pub. Sch. 1, Long Island City, NY, 1986; instr. Cuyahoga C.C., Cleve., 1987, Cleve. Inst. of Art, 1988; vis. artist Herron Sch. of Art Ind. U., Indpls., 1990, Kansas City (Mo.) Art Inst., 1991; artist in residence Bemis Found., Omaha, 1992; vis. artist Tamarind Inst., Albuquerque, 1995, Ill. State U., 1997; assoc. prof. U. Alaska, Fairbanks, 2000—. Vis. artist Mont. State U., 1998. One-man shows include Grover Thurston Gallery, Seattle, Graham Modern Gallery, NYC, 1988, Cleve. Ctr. Contemporary Art, 1993, Zolla Liberman Gallery, Chgo., 1991—93, 1996—2003, 2008, Rena Sterberg, Chgo., Horwitch LewAllen Gallery, Santa Fe, 1995, Purdue U., West Lafayette, Ind., 1995, Clark Gallery, Boston, 1999, Anchorage Mus. History and Art, South Bend Regional Mus. Art, 2003, Kat Kho Kong Gallery, Cambodia, 2006, U. Alaska, Fairbanks, 2007, Rockford Art Mus., Ill., 2008, exhibited in group shows at Corcoran Gallery Art, Washington, 1985, Alternative Mus., NY, 1986, LA County Mus. Art, 1987, Graham Modern Gallery, NYC, 1989, Machida City Mus. Graphic Arts, Tokyo, 1993, Galleria Art, Sao Paulo, Brazil, 1994, Weatherspoon Art Gallery, U. NC, 1995, Chgo. Ctr. Book & Paper Arts, Columbia Coll., 1996, Banco Ctrl., Cuenca, Ecuador, 1996, Calif. Mus. Art, Santa Rosa, 1997, U. Alaska Mus., Fairbanks. Fellow, U. Cin., 1979—81, Ohio Arts Coun., 1990, Arts Midwest NEA Regional fellow, 1994—95, Ill. Arts Coun., 1995, Visual Arts 7, 1987; Individual Artist grantee, Rasmuson Found. Address: 660 Rebecca St Apt 16 Fairbanks AK 99709-3563 Office Phone: 907-474-6545. Business E-Mail: ffmmn@uaf.edu.

NALBANDIAN, DAVID, professional tennis player; b. Cordoba, Argentina, Jan. 1, 1982; s. Norbeto and Alda. Jr. champion Jrs.-US Open, 1998; finalist Wimbledon, 2002; semi-finalist US Open, 2003, French Open, 2004; mem. Argentina Davis Cup team, 2002—04; winner Estoril Open, 2006, Mutua Madrilena Masters Madrid, 2007, BNP Paribas Masters, Paris, 2007, Copa Telmex, Buenos Aires, 2008, If Stockholm Open, 2008, Medibank Internat., 2009. Named World Newcomer Yr.; nominee, Laureus World Sports Awards, 2003. Achievements include highest world ranking #4, 2004. Avocations: fishing, soccer. Office: c/o Assn Tennis Profl 201 ATP Blvd Ponte Vedra Beach FL 32082

NALBANDIAN, RUBEN, engineering company executive; b. Tehran, Iran, Aug. 22, 1948; s. Ashot and Anooshik Nalbandian; m. Doris Stepanian, Dec. 30, 1978; children: Gregory, Christina, Eric. MS, UMIST, Manchester, 1977. Registered Profl. Engr., Consumer Affairs/Calif., 1985. Chief engr. Pettibone Corp., Fairfield, NJ, 1979—82; engrng. sect. head Airesearch Garret Co., Torrance, Calif., 1982—85; engrng. mgr. Teledyne Sys. Co., Northridge, Calif., 1985—89, Moog Inc., Chatsworth, Calif., 1989—. Cons. Parametrics, Chatsworth, 1985—2005. Mem.: Am. Inst. Aeronautics & Astronautics. Independent-Republican. Achievements include first to to specialize spacecraft mechanisms. Avocations: travel, music, painting, cooking, exercise. Office: Moog Inc 21339 Nordhoff St Chatsworth CA 91311 Office Fax: 818-341-3884. E-mail: rnalbandian@moog.com.

NALDER, ERIC CHRISTOPHER, investigative reporter; b. Coulee Dam, Wash., Mar. 2, 1946; s. Philip Richard and Mibs Dorothy (Aurdal) Nalder; m. Jan Christiansen, Dec. 20, 1968; 1 child, Britt Hillary. BA in Comm., U. Wash., 1968. News editor Whidbey News-Times, Oak Harbor, Wash., 1971; reporter Lynnwood Enterprise, Wash., 1972, Everett Herald, Lynnwood, 1972—75; gen. assignment reporter Seattle Post-Intelligencer, 1975—78, edn. writer, 1977—78, investigative reporter, 1978—83, chief investigative reporter, 2004—09, Seattle Times, 1983—2001; investigative reporter San Jose Mercury News, 2001—04; sr. enterprise reporter Hearst Newspapers, NYC, 2009—. Author: (book) Tankers Full of Trouble, 1994 (Investigative Reporters & Editors Book award, 1994). Recipient Edn. Writers Assn. award, Charles Stewart Mott Found., 1978, Hearst Cmty. Svc. award, 1978, Pub. Svc. in Journalism award, Sigma Delta Chi, 1987, Edward J. Meeman award, Scripps Howard Found., 1987, 1999, Thomas Stokes award, Washington Journalism Ctr., 1990, Pulitzer Prize for Nat. Reporting, 1990, Nat. Headline award, 1991, AP Sports Editors Investigative Reporting award, 1992, Pub. Svc. award, AP Mag. Editors Assn., 1992, Goldsmith prize for Investigative Reporting, 1992, Worth Bingham prize for investigative reporting, 1992, Headliner award, 1992, Silver Gavel award, ABA, 1995, Pulitzer prize for Investigative Reporting, 1997, John B. Oakes award for Disting. Environ. Journalism, 1998, Robert L. Kozik award, Nat. Press Club, 1999, Excellence in Journalism Investigative Reporting award, Soc. Profl. Journalism, 2001, Clarion award for Investigative Reporting, 2001, George Polk award for Mil. Reporting, 2008, Outstanding Govt. Reporting award, Seattle Mcpl. League; co-recipient John Jay award for Criminal Justice Reporting, 2008. Mem.: Pacific NW Newspaper Guild, Investigative Reporters & Editors Assn. Avocation: downhill skiing. Office: Hearst Newspapers 959 8th Ave New York NY 10019*

NALDRETT, ANTHONY JAMES, geology educator; b. London, June 23, 1933; emigrated to Can., 1957; s. Anthony George and Violet Ethel (Latham) N.; m. Sylvia Robb Clark, Apr. 23, 1960 (div.); children: Anne, Jennifer, Penelope; m. Galina Stanislavovna Rylkova, July 6, 1991. BA, U. Cambridge, 1956, MA, 1962; MS, Queens U., Can., 1961, PhD, 1964; DS (hon.), Laurentian U., Sudbury, Can., 2000, U. Pretoria, South Africa, 2001. Geologist Falconbridge Nickel Mines, Ltd., Sudbury, 1957-59; fellow Carnegie Inst. Washington, Geophys. Lab., 1964-67; asst. prof. U. Toronto, Ont., 1967-68, assoc. prof., 1968-72, prof. mineral deposits geology, 1972-84, univ. prof., 1984-98, univ. prof. emeritus, 1998—. Mine geologist Falconbridge Nickel, 1957-59, exploration geologist, summers 1959-63, sr. prin. rsch. officer CSIRO, Australia, 1972-73; vis. prof. U. Pretoria, South Africa, 1979-80; chercheur associé CNRS, Orleans, France, 1986-87; stagiére BRGM, Orleans, France, 1993-94; hon. prof. U. Witwatersrand, South Africa, 2005-. Contbr. articles to profl. jours.; editor: Jour. Petrology, 1974-82. Served with Royal Air Force, 1951-53. Recipient Barlow medal Can. Inst. Mining/Metallurgy, 1974, Duncan Derry medal Geol. Assn. Can., 1980, Logan medal Geol. Assn. Can., 1994, Bownocker gold medal Ohio State U., 1986; mineral Naldrettite named in his honor. Fellow: Internat. Mineral. Assn. (1st v.p. 1994—98, pres. 1998—), Societé de Mineralogie et Crystallagrphie (v.p. 1987), Russian Mineral. Soc. (hon. fellow 1999), Mineral. Assn. Can. (pres. 1982, 1983, Past-Presidents medal 1991), Soc. Econ. Geologists (v.p. 1982, pres. 1991—92, Soc. medal 1982, Disting. lectr. 1996, Penrose medal 2002), Geol. Assn. Can., Geol. Soc. Am. (v.p. 2000, pres. 2001—02), Royal Soc. Can., European Union Geoscientists (hon.; fgn.), Mineral. Soc. (hon.). Avocations: sailing, skiing, carpentry. Office: 15 Apers Av Woking Surrey GU22 9NB England Personal E-mail: ajnaldrett@yahoo.com.

NALEN, CRAIG ANTHONY, federal agency administrator; b. Montclair, NJ, Apr. 17, 1930; s. Paul Anthony and Mildred A. (Tucker) N.; m. Katherine Andrews, Dec. 30, 1953; children: Katherine M., David A., Peter H. BA, Princeton U., 1952; MBA, Stanford U., 1957. Mktg. exec. Procter & Gamble, Cin., 1957-62, Foremost-McKesson, San Francisco, 1962-64; divisional gen. mgr., corp. v.p. Gen. Mills Inc., Mpls., 1964-72; pres., also bd. dirs. Am. Photograph Corp., Great Neck, NY, 1972-75; pres., chmn. bd. dirs. STP Corp., Ft. Lauderdale, Fla., 1975-80; pres., chief exec. officer Overseas Pvt. Investment Corp. (govt. agy.), Washington, 1981-89, also bd. dirs.; chmn. AES Transpower, Washington, 1989-92. Bd. dirs. Glendale Internat. Corp., Ont., Canada, Sonex Corp. Bd. dirs., founder Children's World, Denver. Lt. USNR, 1952-55. Mem. Chevy Chase (Md.) Club, Gulf Stream Golf Club (Fla.), Gulf Stream Bath & Tennis Club (Delray Beach, Fla.), Valley Golf Club (Sun Valley, Idaho). Republican. also: PO Box 2439 Ketchum ID 83340-2439 Home: 532 Banyon Rd Gulf Stream FL 33483

NALLY, DENNIS MATHEW, finance company executive; b. Washington, Oct. 11, 1952; s. Thomas J. and Margaret (Allen) N.; m. Karen L. Kidder, June 18, 1977; children: Brian, Lindsay, Kathryn, Lauren. BBA, Western Mich. U., 1974; completed, Columbia U. Exec. Program, Penn State U. Exec. Program. CPA, Mich., Ohio. Staff acct. Price Waterhouse, Detroit, 1974-77, audit sr., 1977-78, audit mgr., 1978-85, audit ptnr., 1985, NYC, 1985-88, ptnr.-in-charge Dayton, Ohio, 1988—92, nat. dir. strategic planning, 1992—95, vice chmn fin. and key client svc. support, 1995—97, also mem. US firm policy com., US mgmt. com., and gen. coun. worldwide orgn., 1995—97; (Price Waterhouse merged with Coopers Lybrand in 1998); assurance and bus. adv. services leader for Americas theatre PricewaterhouseCoopers LLP, 1996—2000, mng. ptnr. US Firm, 2000—01, chmn., sr. ptnr., 2002—09; chmn. PricewaterhouseCoopers Internat. Network, 2009—. Mem. US bd. partners and principals PricewaterhouseCoopers, mem. US mgmt. com. Bd. dirs. US C. of C., US-Japan Bus. Coun.; bd. trustees St. Michael's Coll., Colchester, VT, NY POPs; mem. fin. com. Diocese of Bridgeport, Conn. Mem. AICPA, NY State Soc. CPAs. Avocations: golf, sailing, jogging, computers. Office: PricewaterhouseCoopers 300 Madison Ave New York NY 10017-6204 Office Phone: 646-471-4000.*

NAM, CHARLES BENJAMIN, demographer, sociologist, educator, writer; b. Lynbrook, NY, Mar. 25, 1926; s. Samuel and Yetta (Huff) N.; m. Marjorie Lee Tallant, Jan. 1, 1956; children: David Wallace, Rebecca Jane. BA, NYU, 1950; MA, U. N.C., 1957, PhD, 1959. Statistician U.S. Bur. Census, Washington, 1950-53, chief edn. and social stratification br., 1957-64; statistician USAF, Montgomery, Ala., 1953-54; rsch. asst. U. N.C., Chapel Hill, 1954-57; prof. sociology Fla. State U., Tallahassee, 1964—96, chmn. dept. sociology, 1968—71, disting. rsch. prof., 1994—96, disting. rsch. prof. emeritus, 1996—; rsch. assoc. Ctr. for Demography and Population Health, 1967—, dir., 1967—82; mem. population adv. com. U.S. Bur. Census, 1978-81. Cons. population divsn. Orgn. for Econ. Coop. and Devel., 1968-70, UNESCO, 1978-83, Indonesian Ministry of Population and Environment, Jakarta, 1988-90; Social Sci. Rsch. Coun., 1981-88. Author: (with John K. Folger) Education of the American Population, 1967, Population and Society, 1968, (with Susan Gustavus) Population: The Dynamics of Demographic Change, 1976, Nationality Groups and Social Stratification, 1981; (with Susan Philliber) Population: A Basic Orientation, 1983; (with Mary Powers) The Socioeconomic Approach to Status Measurement, 1983, Our Population: The Face of America, 1988, Understanding Population Change, 1994; (with Richard Rogers and Robert Hummer) Living and Dying in the USA, 2000; (with Janusz Balicki and Ewa Fratczak) Mechanisms of Population Changes and Population Policy (in Polish), 2003, The Golden Door, 2006; editor: Demography, 1972-75; co-editor: (with David Sly, William Serow) International Handbook of Internal Migration, 1990, Handbook of International Migration, 1990; mem. editl. bd. Population Research and Policy Review, 1993-94. Fellow AAAS (rep. sect. K 1999-2004); mem. Am. Sociol. Assn. (chmn. sect. on population 1976-78), Population Assn. Am. (pres. 1979), Internat. Union for Sci. Study Population, Am. Statis. Assn. (chmn. social statistics sect. 1974, fellow 1980), So. Sociol. Soc. (pres. 1981-82), So. Demographic Assn. (vice chmn. 1974-75; fellow 2001; hon. pres. 2007), Soc. Study Social Biology (bd. dirs. 1996-2006, exec. com. 1998-99). Home: 820 Live Oak Plantation Rd Tallahassee FL 32312-2413 Personal E-mail: charlesnam2@embarqmail.com.

NAM, ELLIS K., orthopedist; b. Evanston, Ill., Dec. 31, 1970; MD, Northwestern Med. Sch., Chgo., 1997. Diplomate Am. Bd. Orthop. Surgeons, Chgo. Orthop. surgeon Chgo. Orthops. & Sports Medicine, 2003—. Office: Chgo Orthops & Sports Medicine 3000 N Halsted St Ste 525 Chicago IL 60657 Home Phone: 312-371-1924; Office Phone: 773-433-3130.

NAM, HA HAI, computer science educator, researcher; b. Namdinh, Vietnam, Feb. 10, 1975; s. Ha Quoc Thuy and Nguyen Thi Vinh; m. Nguyen Thi Thanh Dung, Jan. 11, 2006. BSc in Telecomm. Engrng., Hanoi U. Comm. and Transport, Vietnam, 2000; MS in Signal Processing and Comm., Hanoi U. Tech., Vietnam, 2003; PhD in Computer Sci., Newcastle U., England, 2005. Lectr. Posts & Telecom. Inst. Tech., Hanoi, 2000—05; rschr. Sch. Computing Sci., Newcastle U., 2005—. Achievements include research in perception based and wavelets-based lighting-by-example; explorations in declarative lighting design; perception-based lighting design; a scientific document management system for neuroscience; immersive video as a rapid prototyping and evaluation tool for mobile and ambient applications; evaluating future traveller information systems. Avocations: games programming, interior decorating. Home: No 3 345/91/27 Khuong Trung Rd 345 91 27 Hanoi Vietnam Personal E-mail: h.n.ha@ncl.ac.uk. Business E-Mail: namhh@dnx.vn.

NAM, KI-BONG, mathematics professor; b. Masan, Korea, 1955; arrived in US, 1983; s. Moon-Woo and Eul-Yeon (Koo) Nam; m. Young Hee Esther Joo, May 9, 1982; children: Grace Hye-Eun, Tae-Young. BS Math., Hanyang U., Seoul, 1981; MA Math., Hanyang U., 1983; MS Math., U. Wis., Madison, 1996; PhD, U. Wis., 1998. Tchg. asst. Hanyang U., Seoul, 1981—83, Iowa State U., Ames, 1983—84; lectr. U. Wis., Whitewater, 1999—2002, asst. prof., 2003—06, assoc. prof., 2006—; vis. prof. Hanyang U., Republic of Korea, 2009. Organizer Internat. Math. Conf., Jeonju City, Republic of Korea, 2004, 06; mem. organizing com. Internat. Conf. Grp. Theory and Related Topics, Xouzhou, China, 2008; presenter, lectr. in field. Editor: Jour. Computational Math. and Optimization, 2005—, Jour. Applied Algebra and Discrete Structures, 2005—, Internat. Jour. Applied Math. and Stats., 2005—07, 2008—; assoc. editor: Internat. Jour. Rsch. in Edn.; contbr. articles to profl. jours. Recipient Rsch. awards, Coll. Letters and Scis., U. Wis., Whitewater, 2006, Rsch. award, U. Wis., Whitewater, 2007. Mem.: Korean-Am. U. Prof. Assn., Am. Math. Soc. (reviewer). Avocations: Go, chess. Home: 468 Presidential Ln Madison WI 53711 Office: Univ Wis Dept Math 800 W Main St Whitewater WI 53190 Home Phone: 608-231-2320; Office Phone: 262-472-5164. Business E-Mail: namk@uww.edu.

NAM, MIN-YOUNG, computer scientist; s. Kil-Hyun Nam and Bonghack Kim; m. Na Yun Joo; 1 child, Grace Yuri. MS, Ohio State U., Columbus, 2006. Rsch. assoc. Ohio State U., Columbus, 2003—06, U. Ill., Urbana, 2007—. Sgt. G3 CofS, 1998—2001, Seoul. Decorated Army Commendation medal US Army; Nat. scholarship, Info. and Telecom., 2002—03. Mem.: Phi Kappa Phi. Office: Univ Ill Dept Computer Sci 201 N Goodwin Ave Urbana IL 61801 Business E-Mail: mnam@illinois.edu.

NAM, SANG SEOK, special education educator; b. Jungkyo ree, Kyong Nam, Republic Of Korea, Sept. 25, 1954; m. Kyong Ok Lee. PhD, Ariz. State U., Tempe, 1996. Cert. in spl. edn. tchg. credential Bd. Edn., Pusan, 1986. Asst. prof. Albany State U., Georgia, 2002—06; assoc. prof. Calif. State U., San Bernardino, 2006—. Tchr. Improvement grant, Dept. Edn., 2005. Mem.: Coun. Exceptional Children. Office: Calif State Univ SB COE 5500 Univ Pky San Bernardino CA 92407

NAM, SEUNG YEOB, network technician, researcher; b. Deagu, Republic of Korea, Aug. 21, 1975; s. Sang Jik Nam and Ok-Nam Hwang. BSEE, Korea Advanced Inst. Sci. and Tech., 1997, MSEE, 1999; PhD, Korea Advanced Inst.Sci. and Tech., 2004. Postdoctoral Carnegie Mellon U., Pitts., 2004—06, Korea Advanced Inst. Sci. and Tech., Daejeon, Republic of Korea, 2006—07; prof. dept. info and comm. engring. Yeungnam U., Republic of Korea, 2007—. Contbr. articles to profl. jours., confs. Recipient 4th prize, Korea Math. Competition for Undergrads., 1995, Best Paper award, Asia-Pacific Conf. on Comm., 2000, Bronze Prize, Samsung Humantech Paper Contest, 2004;

postdoctoral fellow, Korea Sci. Engring. Found., 2004. Mem.: IEEE, Korea Info. and Comm. Soc. Achievements include patents for a fast convolution approximation scheme for estimating end-to-end delay performance; partitioned crossbar switch with multiple input/output buffers; patents pending for quasi-shaped output buffer type switching apparatus; method and apparatus for two-dimensional-scalable crossbar matrix switch. Avocation: skiing. Office Fax: 8253 810 4742. Personal E-mail: nsyeob@gmail.com.

NAMA, ADILIFU, educator; b. Cleve., Mar. 21, 1969; m. Tamu Usher-Nama, May 16, 1998; children: Nia Z., Nizam J. PhD, U. Southern Calif., LA, 2002. Assoc. prof. Calif. State U. Northridge, 2002—. Author: (book) Black Space: Imagining Race in Science Fiction Film; contbr. articles to profl. jours. Achievements include research in first book-length examination of African American representation in science fiction film. Office: Calif State Univ Northridge 18111 Nordhoff St Northridge CA 91330 Office Fax: 818-677-3619. Business E-Mail: docnama@csun.edu.

NAMBU, YOICHIRO, physics professor; b. Toyko, Jan. 18, 1921; arrived in U.S., 1952; m. Chieko Hida Nambu, Nov. 3, 1945; 1 child, Jun-ichi. BS, U. Tokyo, 1942, DSc, 1952; DSc (hon.), Northwestern U., Evanston, Ill., 1987; degree (hon.), Osaka U., 1996. Research asst. U. Tokyo, 1945—49; prof. physics Osaka City U., Japan, 1950—56; mem. Inst. Advanced Study, Princeton, 1952—54; research assoc. U. Chgo., 1954—56, mem. faculty, 1956—, prof. physics, 1958, Henry Pratt Judson Disting. Svc. Prof., 1978—91; Henry Pratt Judson Disting. Svc. Prof. Emeritus, dept. physics U. Chgo., Enrico Fermi Inst., 1991—. Contbr. articles to profl. jours. Recipient J. Robert Oppenheimer prize, 1976, Order of Culture, Japan Govt., 1978, US Nat. Medal Sci., 1982, Max Planck medal, German Physical Soc., 1985, Dirac medal, Internat. Centre for Theoretical Physics, 1986, Wolf prize in physics, Wolf Found., Israel, 1994, Gian Carlo Wick Commemorative medal, World Fedn. Scientists, 1995, Bogoliubov prize, Joint Inst. for Nuclear Rsch., 2003, Benjamin Franklin medal in Physics, Franklin Inst., 2005, I. Ya. Pomeranchuk prize, Inst. Theoretical and Exptl. Physics, Moscow, 2007; co-recipient Nobel Prize in Physics, 2008; named one of The World's Most Influential People, TIME mag., 2009. Mem.: NAS, Georgian Acad. Sciences (fgn. fellow 1996), Am. Phys. Soc. (Sakurai prize 1994, Dannie Heineman prize for Math. Physics 1970), Am. Acad. Arts and Scis., Japan Acad. (hon.). Office: Univ of Chicago Enrico Fermi Inst 5640 S Ellis Ave EFI Box 29 RI 267 Chicago IL 60637 Office Phone: 773-702-7286. Business E-Mail: nambu@theory.uchicago.edu.

NAMDARI, BAHRAM, surgeon; b. Oct. 26, 1939; s. Rostam and Sarvar Namdari; m. Kathleen Wilmore, Jan. 5, 1976; children: Mondona, Mietra, Ariana. MD, 1966. Diplomate Am. Bd. Surgery. Resident in gen. surgery St. John's Mercy Med. Ctr., St. Louis, 1969-73; practice medicine specializing in gen. and vascular surgery Milw., 1976—. Mem. staff St. Mary's Hosp., Milw., St. Luke's Hosp., Milw.; founder, pres. Famous Mealwaukee Foods Enterprises. Contbr. articles to med. jours.; patentee med. instruments and other devices. Cardiovascular Surgery fellow with Michael DeBakey, Baylor Coll. Medicine, Houston, 1974-75. Fellow ACS, Internat. Surgeons; mem. AMA, Med. Soc. Milwaukee County, Milw. Acad. Surgery, Wis. Med. Soc., Wis. Surg. Soc., Royal Soc. Medicine Eng. (affiliate), Am. Soc. Bariatric Surgery, World Med. Assn., Internat. Acad. Bariatric Medicine (founding mem.), Am. Acad. Cosmetic Surgery, Michael DeBakey Internat. Cardiovascular Soc. Office: Great Lakes Med and Surg Ctr 6000 S 27th St Milwaukee WI 53221-4805

NAMEROW, DAVID MARK, pediatrician; b. NYC, Dec. 12, 1947; s. Nathan and Claire (Goodstein) N.; m. Pearila Brickner, June 14, 1981; children: Jordan Ilana, Evan Gabrielle, Zoe Alexandra. BS, CCNY, 1968; MD, U. Louisville, 1972. Pediatric intern Children's Hosp. Med. Ctr., Cin., 1972-73, resident in pediatrics, 1973-75; fellow in adolescent medicine U. Md. Hosps., Balt., 1975-77; pediatrician Plaza Med. Assocs., Flanders, NJ, 1977-79; dir. adolescent medicine St. Joseph's Hosp. Med. Ctr., Paterson, NJ, 1977-81; founder, pediatrician PediatriCare Assocs., Fair Lawn, NJ, 1979—. Attending pediatrician, assoc. dir. dept. pediatrics Valley Hosp., Ridgewood, N.J., 1979—; adj. asst. clin. prof. pediatrics N.Y. Hosp.-Cornell Med. Ctr., N.Y.C., 1979—; dir. dept. pediatrics Valley Hosp., 2001-05. Fellow Am. Acad. Pediatrics; mem. Soc. for Adolescent Medicine, Ambulatory Pediatric Assn. Office: PediatriCare Assocs 20-20 Fair Lawn Ave Fair Lawn NJ 07410-2319 also: 400 Franklin Tpke Mahwah NJ 07430-3516 also: 901 Rte 23 S Pompton Plains NJ 07444 Office Phone: 201-791-4545. Personal E-mail: dnamerow@optonline.net.

NAMNOUM, ANNE BRAWNER, obstetrician, gynecologist; b. Balt., Apr. 26, 1960; m. James Daniel Namnoum; children: Timothy Spencer, Anne Addison, Reed Daniel, Hannah Paine, Eliza Stewart, Isabelle Austin. MD, Johns Hopkins U., Balt., 1987. Diplomate Am. Bd. Ob-Gyn., cert. in Reproductive Endocrinology/Infertility. Ob-gyn. intern Johns Hopkins U., 1987-88, resident in ob-gyn., 1988-91, fellow in reproductive endocrinology, 1991-93, asst. prof., 1993-95, Emory U. Sch. Medicine, Atlanta, 1995—. Contbr. articles to profl. jours. Mem.: Am. Coll. Ob-Gyn. Office: Emory Ctr Reproductive Medicine & Infertility 20 Linden Ave NW Atlanta GA 30308-2107 also: 2001 Peachtree Rd NE Ste 545 Savannah GA 30309*

NAMNOUM, JAMES DANIEL, plastic surgeon; b. Hartford, Conn. m. Anne Brawner Namnoum; 6 children. MD, John Hopkins Sch. Medicine, 1987. Cert. Am. Bd. Plastic Surgery. Resident, surgery John Hopkins Hosp., Baltimore, Md., 1987—93, resident, plastic surgery, 1993—95; fellow, plastic surgery Reconstructive Surgery Found., Atlanta, 1996; co-dir. Atlanta Breast Symposium; chief, plastic surgery St. Joseph's Hosp.; med. dir. AYA Med. Spa; private practice Atlanta Plastic Surgery. Lectr. in field; cons. to companies specializing in products for cosmetic surgery. Mem.: Med. Assn. Ga., Med. Assn. Atlanta, Ga. Soc. Plastic Surgery, Southeastern Soc. Plastic Surgery, Am. Soc. Aesthetic Plastic Surgery, Am. Soc. Plastic Surgeons. Avocations: cooking, reading, fitness tng., wine enthusiast. Office: Atlanta Plastyic Surgery PC STE 100 975 Johnson Ferry RD NE Atlanta GA 30342-1618 Office Phone: 404-256-1311. Office Fax: 404-256-5487. Business E-Mail: aps@atlplastic.com.

NAMPET, WAJIRA, psychology professor; b. Ayutthaya, Thailand, Jan. 22, 1955; s. Panya and Amporn Nampet. PhD, Ateneo de Naga U., Quezon City, Philippines. Vis. prof. Boston Coll., Chestnut Hill, 2001—02; prof. Loyola Marymount U., LA, 2005—07; prof. & rschr. Ateneo de Manila U., 2007—. Priest SJ, Quezon City, 1997—2009. Mem.: Kappa Delta Pi. Roman Catholic.

NAN, FEI, application developer; s. Chaozheng Nan and Xingzhi Liu. Degree, McGill U., Montreal, Quebec, Canada; B in Engring. (hon.), Northeastern U., Shenyang, Liaoning, China, 2002; MS, W.Va. U., Morgantown, PhD, 2008. Cert. advance programmer credential SAS Inst. Inc., 2006. Grad. rsch. asst. W.Va. U., Morgantown, 2003—08; intern biomed. algorithm Applied Biosys., Foster City, Calif., 2007; software engr. Microsoft Corp., Redmond, Wash., 2008—. Mem.: IEEE, Assn. Computing Machinery, Upsilon Pi Epsilon, Sigma Xi. Achievements include research in direct suffix sorting and its applications. Avocations: swimming, travel. Office: Microsoft Corp One Microsoft Way Redmond WA 98052

NANA, GEORGES, language educator; s. Emmanuel Nkombou and Cécile Tcoumba; m. Ide Chantale T. Nana, Sept. 4, 1999; children: Ruth Sophonie Chiegang, Manuela Nono, Claleb-Wesley Siyapze. PhD, U. Bordeaux, France, 2007. Cert. tchr. Ga. Profl. Std. Com., 2008. Instr. Spanish Clark Atlanta U., 2004—08; lectr. Spanish Spelman Coll., Atlanta, 2006—. Soldier Salvation Army, Doraville, Ga., 2004—08. Mem.: MLA. Home: 8645 Regent St Jonesboro GA 30238 Office: Spelman Coll 350 Spelman Ln Atlanta GA 30314 Office Fax: 404-270-5532. Business E-Mail: gnana@spelman.edu.

NANCE, ALLAN TAYLOR, retired lawyer; b. Dallas, Jan. 31, 1933; s. A.Q. and Lois Rebecca (Taylor) N. BA, So. Meth. U., 1954, LLB, 1957; LLM, NYU, 1978. Bar: Tex. 1957, N.Y. 1961. With Simpson Thacher & Bartlett, NYC, 1960-65; asst. counsel J.P. Stevens & Co., Inc., NYC, 1965-70, sec., 1970-78, asst. gen. counsel, 1970-89; counsel J.P. Stevens & Co. Inc. and WestPoint-Pepperell Inc., 1989-93; asst. gen. counsel WestPoint Stevens Inc., NYC, 1993-98, ret., 1998. With USNR, 1957-59. Woodrow Wilson fellow Columbia U., 1959-60. Mem. Phi Beta Kappa. Home: 201 E 66th St New York NY 10021-6451

NANCE, CYNTHIA ELEANOR (CYNDI NANCE), dean, law educator; b. Chgo., Sept. 3, 1958; d. Eual Dean and Fern Elizabeth Nance. BS in Econs., Chgo. State U., 1986; JD with distinction, U. Iowa, 1990, MA in Fin., 1991, ABD in Indsl. Rels., 1993. Lic.: Iowa Supreme Ct. 1990. Law clk. Glasson, Grove, Sole & McMannus, Cedar Rapids, Iowa, 1989; program coord. U. Iowa Labor Ctr., 1989—91; tchg. asst. U. Iowa Coll. Bus., 1991—93; faculty fellow U. Iowa Coll. Law, 1993—94; asst. prof. to prof. law U. Ark. Sch. Law, Fayetteville, 1994—, dean, 2006—. Mem. audit com. Law Sch. Admissions Coun., Newtown, Pa., 1994—98, fin. and legal affairs com., 1998—, chair fin. and legal affairs com., 2003—, CEO search com.; mem. sect. on minorities in the law Am. Assn. Law Schools, Washington, 1994—, chair labor and employment law sect., 2000—01, chair employment discrimination sect., 2001—02. Co-chair Greensboro Massacre Truth and Reconciliation Commn. Adv. Com., NC, 2001—; pres. Ozark Mountain Masters Swim Team, Springdale, Ark., 1999—2001; women of the ELCA anti-racism trainer Evang. Luth. Ch. America, Chgo., 1996—2002, mem. adv. com. on corp. social responsibility, 1999—; mem. ch. coun. Good Shepherd Luth. Ch., Fayetteville, 2002—03; bd. dirs. Sources for Ind. Living, Ark., 1994—99, ACLU, Little Rock, 1998—99, Nat. Interfaith Com. Worker Justice, Chgo., 1999. Recipient Martin Luther King Jr. Individual Achievement award, 2004, Woman of Distinction award, Girl Scouts N.W. Ark., Heritage award for profl. achievement, NIA, 2006; fellow Grad. Opportunities for Advanced Level Studies Found., U. of Iowa Coll. of Bus., 1990—92; Tchg. Fellow, U. of Iowa, Coll. of Law, 1993—94. Mem.: ABA (co-chair labor and employmentlaw sect. ethics and professionalism com. 2001—, mem. pro bono com. labor and employment law sect. 2003—, Outstanding Lawyer), Indsl. Rels. Rsch. Assn., Ark. Bar Assn. (jurisprudence and law reform com. 1995—, lawyer assistance program com. 1999—, com. on diversity 2000—, labor law sect.), W. B. Putman Am. Inn of Ct., Nat. Bar Assn., Alpha Kappa Alpha (chpt. pres. 1999—2002, faculty advisor 2001—, Outstanding Svc. award 2000), Beta Gamma Sigma, Phi Delta Phi. Liberal. Evangelical Lutheran. Avocations: swimming, travel, cooking. Office: Univ Ark Sch Law 128 Waterman Hall Fayetteville AR 72701 Personal E-mail: cnance@uark.edu.*

NANCE, HELEN STRAYHORN, pre-school administrator, educator; b. Dec. 23, 1942; Degree in Early Childhood Edn., Dyersburg State CC, Tenn., 2002. Prin., owner Strayhorn Day Care, Gates, Tenn., 1993—. Mem.: West Tenn. Assn. Childhood Edn., Tenn. Family Childcare Alliance (Amb. award 2006), Nat. Assn. Edn. Young (Childcare award 2003). Home and Office: Strayhorn Day Care LLC 328 Huntington St Gates TN 38037 Office Phone: 731-836-7333. E-mail: sdaycare@bellsouth.net.

NANCE, MARIONE E., biology educator; b. Tuscaloosa, Ala., May 27, 1951; d. Francis Elmond and Ella Lucinda (Dunning) Evans; m. Thomas Stanley Nance; children: Gwen Lucinda, Frances Marione. MS in Biology, Samford U., Homewood, Ala., 1977. Instr. biology dept. Samford U., 1973—2007, Asst. Prof., 2007—. Senate chmn., faculty pres., com. mem. numerous univ., coll. and departmental coms. Samford U. Vol. spokesman, asst. to veterinarian Birmingham (Ala.) Zoo, 1980—82; vol. tchr. microbiology and dissection local elem. and high schs., Homewood, Mountain Brook, Bessemer, Ala., 1991—95; club pres., dist. sgt.-at-arms Toastmaster's Internat., Birmingham, 1981—82. Mem.: Ala. Acad. Sci., Am. Bryological and Lichenological Soc., Am. Soc. Microbiology, Beta Beta Beta. Achievements include first biodisaster drill resulting in written protocols for first responders; developed a course for elementary school teachers to teach microbiology; developed the first dual credit course at Samford U. Avocations: reading, travel, singing, speaking. Office: Samford Univ Biology Dept 800 Lakeshore Dr Birmingham AL 35229-2234 Home Phone: 205-942-1508. E-mail: menance@samford.edu.

NANCE, MARY JOE, retired secondary school educator; b. Carthage, Tex., Aug. 7, 1921; d. F.F. and Mary Elizabeth (Knight) Born; m. Earl C. Nance, July 12, 1946; 1 child, David Earl. BBA, U. North Tex., Denton, 1953; postgrad., Northwestern State U. La., Shreveport, 1974; ME, Antioch U., Seattle, 1978. Cert. bus. educator. Tchr. Port Isabel (Tex.) Ind. Sch. Dist., 1953-79; tchr. English Tex., 1965, Splendora (Tex.) H.S., 1979-80, McLeod, Tex., 1980-81, Bremond, Tex., 1981-84; ret., 1985. Vol. tchr. for Indian students, 1964—65; vol. tutor, tchr. ESL; active WAAC, 1942—43, WAC, 1945. Recipient Image Maker award Carthage C. of C., 1984; named on Meml. for Women, Washington. Mem. NEA, Tex. Tchrs. Assn., Tex. Bus. Tchrs. Assn. (Cert. of Appreciation 1978), Nat. Women's Army Corps Vets. Assn., Air Force Assn. (life), Gwinnett Hist. Soc., Hist. Soc. Panola County, Panola County Hist. & Geneal. Assn., Nat. Hist. Soc. Baptist.

NANCE, RICHARD DAMIAN, geologist, consultant; b. St. Ives, UK, Oct. 25, 1951; s. Richard William Morton and Edith Eleanor (Leach) N.; children: André Bernard Carpenter, Sarah Marie Eleanor, Christopher Louis Morton. BS in Geology with honors, Leicester U., Eng., 1972; PhD in Geology, Cambridge U., Eng., 1978. Asst. prof. St. Francis Xavier U., Antigonish, Nova Scotia, 1976-80, Ohio U., Athens, 1980-82; sr. rsch. geologist Exxon Prodn. Rsch. Co., Houston, 1982-83; assoc. prof. Ohio U., Athens, 1983-90, dept. chmn., 1995—2000, prof., 1991—2009, disting. prof., 2009—. Rsch. cons. Inst. for Environ. Studies, La. State U., Baton Rouge, 1977-81, Cominco Am. Inc., Spokane, Wash., 1984-85, Argonne Nat. Labs., Chgo., 1984-88. Author, editor: 30 chpts. in books; contbr. over 100 articles to profl. jours. Grantee Geol. Survey Can., 1987-88, NSF, 90-94, 2003-06, Earthwatch, 1991-94, Nat. Geographic, 1993-95, Ohio U., 1981-92, 2001-09, US Dept. Edn., 1996-2000, Unesco, 2004-08. Fellow Geol. Assn. Can.; mem. Geol. Soc. Am., Am. Geophys. Union, Am. Assn. Petroleum Geologists, Royal Geol. Soc. Cornwall, Ussher Soc., Trevithick Soc., Soc. for Indsl. Archeology, Sigma Xi. Avocations: cornish mining history, stationary steam engines, jogging. Office: Ohio U Dept Geol Scis 316 Clippinger Labs Athens OH 45701 Office Phone: 740-593-1107. Business E-Mail: nance@ohio.edu.

NANCE, TONY MAX-PERRY, designer, illustrator; b. Montclair, NJ, Feb. 25, 1955; s. Perry Hedgeman and Ida Delea (King) N.; m. June Anne Percival, Oct. 31, 1986 (div. May 1994); children: Jack Anthony, Jacqlene Angela, Jihad Conan. Student, U. Denver, 1978; BA, NY Sch. Visual Arts, 1976, postgrad., 1980-81, NJ Inst. Tech., 1977-78, Rutgers U., 1980-82; AS, Gibbs Coll., 2004; M in Fine Art & Graphics Design, NY Sch. Visual Arts, 2007. Design engr. Automation Controls, Montclair, 1975-77; artist, designer Greg Copeland, Inc., Fairfield, NJ, 1976-79; owner, designer Stalhaus, Inc., Montclair, 1976-80; editor contemporary ads Graphis Mag., NYC, 1977-79; illustrator, artist L.C. Graphics, Inc., Clifton, NJ, 1979-80; illustrator, printer Graphics III, Clifton, 1974—75; carrier supr. Montclair Post Office, 1980-93; freelance illustrator Exec. Imports Group, NYC, 1981—2004; freelance illustrator & designer A. Schram & Sons, 1985—2004; owner, design engr. Decotech Alternations (became Decotech/NANCEtech), Montclair, NJ, 1984—98, Decotech/NANCEtech, 1998—, Electronics Tech-Atlas Soundolier, 1992-95, Machine Tech-Atlas Soudolier, 1995-98; illustrator, designer, artist Magic Circle Printing, NY, NJ, 1998—2000; owner NANCEart/ NANCEtech, Montclair, 1998—2005; advt. & media designer Advansia Corp., 2003—04. Adj. instr. computer graphics, fine art, media arts Gibbs Coll. Editor Graphis mag.; artist, art dir. (album covers) Bhang, 1984 Ron Smyth I, 1986, Bhang II, When Music Becomes a Tool, 1978-2003; artist, illustrator (album cover, tour and advt. promotion) Passport Greatest Hits/Doldinger, 1977 (album cover, internat. poster) Zap and the Wires, 1979, The Saga of the Black Silk Jetmen; producer, illustrator (album cover) The Little Things by Dogs, 1988, Eating Glass with Loren Tindall; one man shows include Discovery Galleries, Montclair, 1978, The Gallery, Fairfield, 1979, Broghton Galleries, Bloomfield, NJ, 1983, Scotland Galleries, Laurinburg, NC, 1993; contbr. artist mags. Verotika, 1996, Hard Core, 1996; various musical and graphic copyrights; mem. Southern Ambition band, 1993-97, Southern Fried Dogs band, 1996-98; creator comic strip Appliances, 1995-97, Just Buggin', 1998; head guitarist, writer, keyboardist, vocalist Walsh-Nance Band, 2006-08; illustrator, (Children's Book, Akadu's Tears, 2005. Art dir. Montclair Coalition for Performing Arts, Montclair, 1982, patron, 1998—. Mem. Soc. for Creative Anachronism (founding assoc.), Local Musicians Union, Nat. Rifle Assn., Mensa, Porsche Club Am., Arts Coun.Montclair. Avocations: music, prop and special effect design, collecting plastic toys, computer software design, collecting guitars.

NAND, SUCHA, medical educator; b. Thiriewal, Punjab, India, Feb. 3, 1948; d. Narsingh Dass and Swaran Devi; m. Surinder S. Nand, June 15, 1973; children: Ranveer, Rahul. Pre-med. student, Dayanand Ayur Vedic Coll., Amritsar, India, 1966; MB, BS, Med. Coll., Amritsar, India, 1971. Diplomate Am. Bd. Internal Medicine, Am. Bd. Hemotology, Am. Bd. Med. Oncology. Asst. prof. Stritch Sch. Medicine Loyola U., Maywood, Ill., 1981-88, assoc. prof. Stritch Sch. Medicine, 1989-95; prof. medicine, 1996—. Editor Jour. of Med. Coll., 1969-71; contbr. articles to profl. jours. Clin. fellow Am. Cancer Soc., 1981; Brilliant Student scholarships, 1962-71. Mem. Am. Soc. Hematology, Am. Soc. Clin. Oncology, S.W. Oncology Group (mem. leukemia com. 1988—). Avocations: chess, reading, running. Office: Loyola Univ Med Ctr 2160 S 1st Ave Maywood IL 60153-3304 Office Phone: 708-327-3182.

NANDA, NAVIN CHANDAR, cardiologist, educator; b. Kabarnet, Kenya, July 6, 1937; came to U.S., 1971; s. Balwantrai and Maya (Vati) N.; m. Kanta Kumari Markan, Sept. 13, 1967; children: Nitin, Anil, Anita. Inter Sci. cert., Bombay U., 1956, MD, 1962. Resident house officer King George IV Hosp., Nairobi, Kenya, 1962; med. registrar King Edward Meml. Hosp., Bombay, 1963-64, sr. med. registrar, 1964-67; fellow Inst. Cardiology and Nat. Heart Hosp., London, 1967-68; sr. house physician, registrar Rotherham (Eng.) Hosp., 1968-71; instr., trainee in cardiology U. Rochester (N.Y.) Sch. Medicine, 1971-73; asst. prof. medicine and radiology, assoc. physician U. Rochester Sch. Medicine and Strong Meml. Hosp., Rochester, 1971-73, assoc. prof. medicine, dir. noninvasive cardiology labs.; cons. cardiology Genesee Hosp., Rochester Gen. Hosp., 1979—84; prof. of medicine div. cardiovascular disease U. Ala., Birmingham, 1984—. Dir. heart sta. and echocardiography labs. U. Ala.-Birmingham Hosp., 1984—, past pres. soc. geriat. cardiology, 2008-09; hon. vis. dean Dr. Navin C. Nanda Nat. Inst. Echocardiography and Cardiac Rsch., Mool Chand K.R. Hosp., New Delhi, 1988—; hon. vis. cons. dept. cardiology Bombay Hosp. Inst. of Med. Scis., 1988—; overseas vis. coms. P.D. Hinduja Hosp. and Med. Rsch. Ctr., Bombay, 1989—. Author: (with R. Gramiak) Clinical Echocardiography, 1978; editor: Doppler Echocardiography, 1985, 2d edit., 1993, Atlas of Color Doppler Echocardiography, 1989, Textbook of Color Doppler Echocardiography, 1989; (videotapes) Videotextbook of Two-Dimensional and Doppler Echocardiography, 1982-88; Case Studies in Doppler Echocardiography, 1985, Case Studies in Color Doppler Echocardiography; mem. editorial bd. numerous jours.; contbr. numerous articles, abstracts, revs. to profl. publs. Recipient Ellis Island medal of honor, Nat. Ethnic Coalition of Orgns., 2006. Fellow Am. Coll. Angiology, Am. Coll. Cardiology (mem. com.), Am. Heart Assn. (coun. on clin. cardiology, coun. on geriat. cardiology), Internat. Coll. Angiology, Soc. Geriatric Cardiology, Rochester Acad. Medicine, N.Y. Cardiol. Soc., Soc. Geriat. Cardiology (past pres.); mem. AAAS, AMA, Am. Inst. Ultrasound Medicine, Am. Soc. Echocardiography (bd. dirs. 1978-80), Assn. Acad. Minority Physicians, Inc., Ala. Acad. Sci., Internat. Soc. Cardiovasc. Ultrasound (pres.), Am. Assn. Cardiologists Indian Origin (founding pres.), Am. Assn. Physicians Indian Origin (past pres.), numerous others. Achievements include pioneering use of new innovative technique of color Doppler flow mapping. Office: U Ala Birmingham Heart Sta Swb S 102 Birmingham AL 35249 Business E-Mail: nanda@uab.edu. E-mail: navinnanda@bellsouth.net.

NANDA, VED PRAKASH, law educator, director, academic administrator; b. Gujranwala, India, Nov. 20, 1934; arrived in U.S., 1960; s. Jagan Nath and Attar (Kaur) N.; m. Katharine Kunz, Dec. 19, 1982; 1 child, Anjali Devi. MA, Punjab U., 1952; LLB, U. Delhi, 1955, LLM, 1958, Northwestern U., 1962; postgrad., Yale U., 1962-65; LLD, Soka U., Tokyo, 1997, Bundelkhand U., Jhansi, India, 2000, doctorate (hon.), 2000, Soka U., Tokyo, 1997. Asst. prof. law U. Denver, 1965—68, assoc. prof. law, 1968—70, prof. law, dir. Internat. Legal Studies Program, 1970—, Thompson G. Marsh prof. law, 1987—, Evans U. prof., 1992—, asst. provost, 1993—94, vice provost, 1994—. Vis. prof. Coll. Law U. Iowa, Iowa City, 1974—75; vis. prof. Fla. State U., 1973, U. San Diego, 1979, U. Colo., 1992; disting. vis. prof. internat. law Kent Coll. Law, 1981, Calif. We. Sch. Law, San Diego, 1983—84; disting. vis. scholar Sch. Law U. Hawaii, Honolulu, 1986—87; cons. Solar Energy Rsch. Inst., 1978—81, Dept. Energy, 1980—81; vis. prof. numerous summer programs. Co-author (with David Pansius): Litigation of International Disputes in U.S. Courts, 1987; editor: Law in the War Against International Terrorism, 2005; co-editor (with M. Cherif Bassiouni): A

Treatise on International Criminal Law, 1973, Water Needs for the Future, 1977; co-editor: (with George Shepherd) Human Rights and Third World Development, 1985; co-editor: (with others) Global Human Rights, 1981, The Law of Transnational Business Transactions, 1981, World Climate Change, 1983, Breach and Adaption of International Contracts, 1992, World Debt and Human Conditions, 1993, Europe Community Law After 1992, 1993, International Environmental Law and Policy, 1995, European Union Law After Maastricht, 1996; co-editor: (with William M. Evan) Nuclear Proliferation and the Legality of Nuclear Weapons, 1995; co-editor: (with S.P. Sinha) Hindu Law and Legal Theory, 1996; co-editor: (with D. Krieger) Nuclear Weapons and the World Court, 1998; co-editor: (with George Pring) International Environmental Law and Policy for the 21st Century, 2003; co-editor: Law in the War Against International Terrorism, 2004; editor, contbr. Refugee Law and Policy, 1989, mem. editl. bd. Jour. Am. Comparative Law, Indian Jour. Internat. Law, Transnational Pubs.; columnist: Denver Post. O-chmn. Colo. Pub. Broadcasting Fedn., 1977—78; mem. Gov.'s Commn. on Pub. Telecomm., 1980—82; UN day chair State of Colo., 2000—; vice chair exec. coun. World Fedn. UN Assn., Geneva; bd. dir. various nat. and state civic orgns. Recipient Univ. Gold Medal, Delhi U. Faculty of Law, Internat. Excellence award, Colo. Coun. Internat. Orgns., 1985, Burlington Northern Found. Scholar award, U. Denver, 1990, World Legal Scholar award, World Peace Through Law Ctr., Beijing, 1990, Highest honor award, Soka U., Tokyo, 1994, Alumni Faculty award, U. Denver Coll. Law, 1994, India Devel. Assn. award, 1996, Civil Right's award, Anti-Defamation League, 1996, Pioneer award, U. Denver, 1997, Medal of Honor, World Congress of Ukranian Lawyers, 1999, Rotary fellowship established in his honor, Denver Rotary, 2000, Gold Medal established in his honor, Bundelkhand U., 2000, Spl. Achievement award, Indo-Am. Assn., 2002, Cmty. Peace Bldg. award, Gandhi King Ikeda, 2004, Highest Order of Justice award, World Jurist Assn., 2005, Human Rights award, India-Can. Assn., 2006; co-recipient Hyde Prize in Internat. Law, Northwestern U. Law Sch.; named Thompson G. Marsh Prof. of Law, 1987—, John Evans U. Prof., 1994—, Amb. for Peace, Interreligious and Internat. Fedn. for World Peace, 2001; graduate fellow, U. Delhi Faculty of Law, Yale Law Sch., Northwestern U. Law Sch. Mem. World Jurist Assn. (v.p. 1991—, pres. 1998-2000, hon. pres. 2000—), World Assn. Law Profs. (pres. 1987-93), UN Assn. (v.p. Colo. divsn. 1973-76, pres. 1986-88, 93-96, nat. coun. UNA-USA 1990—, mem. governing bd. UNA-USA 1995-2005, Arthur Goodman Leadership award 1995, Human Rights award 1997), World Fedn. UN Assns. (vice-chmn. 1995-2001), Am. Assn. Comparative Study Law (bd. dirs.), Am. Soc. Internat. Law (v.p. 1987-88, exec. coun. 1969-72, 81-84, bd. rev. and devel. 1988-91, hon. v.p. 1995-96, counselor 2000—), Assn. Am. Law Schs., U.S. Inst. Human Rights, Internat. Law Assn. (exec. com. 1986—, hon. pres. 2001—), Colo. Coun. Internat. Orgns. (pres. 1988-90), Assn. U.S. Mems. Internat. Inst. Space Law (bd. dirs., exec. com. 1980-88), Internat. Acad. Comparative Law (assoc.), Acad. Internat. Commercial and Consumer Law, Order St. Ives (pres.), Rotary, Cactus Club, Univ. Club, Colo. Athletic Club. Office Phone: 303-871-6276. Business E-Mail: vnanda@law.du.edu.

NANDIKOLLA, VIDYA K., engineering educator, researcher; married. Doctorate, Idaho State U., 2005. Rsch. asst. Idaho State U., 2004—06; faculty Boise State U., Idaho, 2006—. Pres. Syna Intelligence LLP, Boise, 2007—. Recipient Hon. Materials Scientist award, Boise State U., 2008—09; Faculty fellow, NAE, 2008. Mem.: ASME, Soc. Women Engrs. (scholarship co-chair, mentor 2008—).

NANE, ERKAN, mathematics professor; s. Abdurrahman and Naciye Nane; m. Melek Nane; children: Yagmur, Asim. BS in Math, Bogazici U., Istanbul, Turkey, 1998, MS in Math, 2000; PhD in Math, Purdue U., West Lafayette, Ind., US, 2006. Vis. asst. prof. Mich. State U., East Lansing, 2006—08; asst. prof. Auburn U., Ala., 2009—. Contbr. scientific papers. Office: Auburn Univ 221 Parker Hall Auburn AL 36849

NANFITO, JACQUELINE, literature and language professor; d. Charles Anthony Nanfito and Ethelyn Nora Major; m. Enrique Luengo, Sept. 14, 1985; 1 child, Nathaniel Nicolás Luengo. PhD, UCLA, 1985. Assoc. prof. Case Western Res. U., Cleve., 1996—. Office: Case Western Res Univ 10900 Euclid Ave Cleveland OH 44106-7118

NANKO, RAYMOND S., physician; b. Inglewood, Calif., Feb. 13, 1962; s. John and Veronica Marie (Thunder) N. DC, Cleve. Chiropractic Coll., 1985; MD, Ross U., 1994. Diplomate Am. Bd. Disability Analysts, Am. Bd. Family Practice, Am. Bd. Chiropractic Orthopedics, Am. Bd. Pain Mgmt. With ActiveCare Med. Spine & Pain Ctr., Muncie, Ind. Fellow Am. Back Soc., Am. Bd. Chiropractic Orthopedics; mem. AMA, Am. Acad. Spine Physicians, Ind. State Med. Assn., Ind. State Chiropractic Assn., Am. Chiropractic Assn., Am. Acad. Orthop. Medicine, Nat. Found., Ind. State Med. Assn., Ind. State Chiropractic Assn., Coun. Orthop., Acad. Chiropractic Orthopedics, Arthritis Found., Internat. Spinal Injection Soc., Am. Assn. Orthopedic Medicine. Office: Active Care Med Spine & Pain Ctr 919 W Jackson St Muncie IN 47305-1554

NANNES, MICHAEL EDWARD, lawyer; b. Detroit, Mar. 21, 1953; s. Charles and Maxine Nannes; m. Nancy E. Everett, Apr. 7, 1979; children: Caleb, Marshall, Helena. BBA with high distinction, U. Mich., 1974; JD, Georgetown U., 1977. Bar: DC 1977, Fla. 1978, registered: US Dist. Ct. Md. 1987, US Ct. Appeals (4th cir.) 1981, US Supreme Ct. 1982. Law clk. to Hon. John H. Pratt US Dist. Ct. DC, Washington, 1977-78; ptnr. Dickstein Shapiro & Morin LLP, Washington, 1978—94, firmwide dep. mng. ptnr., 1994—2004, firmwide mng. ptnr., 2004—06; chmn. Dickstein Shapiro LLP (formerly Dickstein Shapiro & Morin LLP), Washington, 2006—. Topics editor The Georgetown Law Jour., 1976—77; co-author (with Richard J. Leveridge): Using Smart Contracting to Assure Efficiency in Resolving Complex Construction Cases, 1993; author: First of Its Kind Wastewater Privatization - A Lesson in Teamwork., 1997, Dickstein's Quest for Family Values, 1999, Leaving No One Behind, 2002. Office: Dickstein Shapiro LLP 1825 Eye St NW Washington DC 20006 E-mail: nannesm@dicksteinshapiro.com.

NANNEY, DAVID LEDBETTER, geneticist, educator; b. Abingdon, Va., Oct. 10, 1925; s. Thomas Grady and Pearl (Ledbetter) Nanney; m. Jean Kelley, June 15, 1951; children: Douglas Paul, Ruth Elizabeth Beshears. AB, Okla. Bapt. U., 1946; PhD, Ind. U., 1951; Laurea honoris causa, U. Pisa, Italy, 1994. Asst. prof. zoology U. Mich., Ann Arbor, 1951-56, assoc. prof., 1956-58; prof. U. Ill., Urbana-Champaign, 1959-76, prof. genetics and devel., 1976-86, prof. ecology, ethology and evolution, 1987-91, prof. emeritus, 1991—. NIH sr. postdoctoral fellow Ind. U., 1949—51. Author (with Herbert Stern): The Biology of Cells, 1965, Experimental Ciliatology, 1980. Recipient Disting. Alumnus award, Okla. Bapt. U., 1972, Preisträger, Alexander von Humboldt Stiftung, Germany, 1984; named Disting. Lectr., Sch. Life Scis., U. Ill., 1981. Fellow: AAAS, Am. Acad. Arts and Scis.; mem.: Soc. Protozoologists, Am. Genetic Assn. (pres. 1982), Genetics Soc. Am. Home: 703 W Indiana Ave Urbana IL 61801-4835 Office: U Ill Dept Animal Biology 505 S Gregory St Urbana IL 61801 Business E-Mail: d-nanney@life.uiuc.edu.

NANOS, GEORGE PETER, JR., former science administrator, military officer, physicist; b. Torrington, Conn., Apr. 11, 1945; s. George N.; m. Joanne Louise Knowles, July 5, 1969; 1 child, George. Grad., U.S. Naval Acad., 1967; PhD in Physics, Princeton U., 1974; attended, U.S. Naval Destroyer Sch., Newport, RI, 1974, Def. Sys. Mgmt. Coll., Ft. Belvoir, Va., 1991. Joined US Navy, 1967; commd. ensign USN; advanced through grades to vice admiral; antisub warfare gunnery officer USS Glennon (DD-840), 1967-69; engr. officer USS Forrest Sherman (DD-931), 1974-76; material officer mem. staff destroyer squadron 10, 1976-78; mgr. tech. devel. high energy laser program offie (NAVSEA PMS-405), 1978-82; engring. duty officer, 1980; combat sys. officer Norfolk Naval Shipyard, 1982-84; engr. officer USS America (CV-66); dep. dir. warfare sys. engring. space and naval warfare sys. cmd., 1984-86; head navigation br., 1988-90; head missile br. devel., prodn., operational support missile subsys., 1990-92; dir. tech. divsn. strategic syss. program, 1992-94; dir. strategic sys. program, 1994-98; commr. naval sea sys. command, 1998—2002, retired, 2002; prin. dep. assoc. dir. Threat Reduction Directorate Los Alamos Nat. Lab., N.Mex., 2002—03, interim dir. N.Mex., 2003, dir. N.Mex., 2003—05. Decorated Legion of Merit, Disting. Svc. medal, Meritorious Svc. medal, Navy Achievement medal.

NANTON, LISA SEEMAN, music educator; b. Perth Amboy, NJ, Oct. 25, 1950; d. Elizabeth Ann and William Anthony Seeman; m. Morris Patrick Nanton, Oct. 10, 1982; children: Seth Morris, Jesse Josef; m. Michael John Caruso, May 6, 1973 (dec. Nov. 11, 1977). BA in Music Edn., Glassboro State Coll., 1972; MA in Counselor Edn., Kean U., 1989. Cert. music tchr. NJ Dept. Edn., 1972; in student personnel svcs. NJ Dept. Edn., 1989. Elem. music tchr. Madison Pk. Sch., Old Bridge, NJ, 1972—98; choral dir., music tchr. Carl Sandburg Mid. Sch., Old Bridge, NJ, 1998—. Musical, choral dir. Madison Pk. Sch., Old Bridge, NJ, 1972—83, musical, concert dir., 1991—98; jr. choir dir. St. Peter's Episcopal Ch., Perth Amboy, 1991—98, Sunday sch. tchr., 1991—98; organizer, dir. Music in Our Schools Month, Old Bridge, 1991—97; staff devel. presenter music dept. Old Bridge Twp. Bd. Edn., 1997—98; profl. day organizer Music Dept., Old Bridge, 1997; musical dir. Carl Sandburg Mid. Sch., Old Bridge, NJ, 1998—2001. Mem. Proprietary Ho. Assn., Perth Amboy, 1986—98, Olde Amboy Civic Assn., Perth Amboy, 1989—98, Local Assistance Bd., Perth Amboy, 1989—96, Concerts by the Bay, Perth Amboy, 1992—98, Royal Garden Club by the Bay, Perth Amboy, NJ, 1993—2008, pres., 1997—99, chmn. home and garden tours, 1998—2003; mem. Mayors Transition Team economic cmty. devel. Perth Amboy, NJ, 2008; dem. committeewoman Perth Amboy Dem. Assn., 1989—2008; chmn. curriculum com. Perth Amboy Bd. Edn., 2000—03, mem., 2000—03; com. mem. Office Economic Cmty. Devel., 2009; pres. Thomas Mundy Peterson PTO, Perth Amboy, NJ, 1990—92; assn. rep. Old Bridge Edn. Assn., NJ, 2004—08. Recipient Membership award, Garden Club NJ, 1997, Cert. of Merit, 1997, Silver Trophy, Gold Seal cert., 1997. Mem.: NEA, Music Educator's Nat. Conf., NJ Edn. Assn., Am. Choral Directors Assn., Raritan Yacht Club, Kappa Delta Pi. Office: Carl Sandburg Middle Sch County Rte 516 Old Bridge NJ 08857 Business E-Mail: lnanton@obps.org.

NANTZ, JIM (JAMES WILLIAM NANTZ), sportscaster; b. Charlotte, NC, May 17, 1959; s. James William Jr. and Doris (Trull) N.; m. Ann-Lorraine Carlsen, Apr. 16, 1983; 1 child, Caroline Mackenzie. BA in Radio and TV, U. Houston, 1981. Radio announcer Sta. KTRH, Houston; sports announcer Sta. KHOU-TV, Houston; sports announcer, anchor Sta. KSL-TV, Salt Lake City; announcer CBS Sports, NYC, 1985—. Actor: (films) Tin Cup, 1996; co-author (with Eli Spielman): Always By My Side: A Father's Grace and a Sports Journey Unlike Any Other, 2008. Named one of Top 50 Sportscasters, Am. Sportscaster Assn., 2009. Achievements include being the CBS announcer for major Sporting events including NCAA Men's Basketball Final Four, PGA Master's Tournament. Office: CBS Sports 51 W 52nd St New York NY 10019-6119*

NAOR, DANIEL, food products executive; b. Paris, July 1, 1960; s. Shlomo and Sarah (Puderbeutel) N.; 1 child, Nathalie. BS in Elec. Engring., MIT, 1981, MS in Elec. Engring. and Computer Sci., 1981; MBA, INSEAD, 1990. Cert. engr. Project mgr. ELOP, Rehovot, Israel, 1985-87, mktg. mgr., 1988—89; assoc. McKinsey & Co., Paris, 1990—95, prin., 1995—98, Dallas, 1998—2002; group v.p. strategy, planning and bus. devel. Frito Lay N.Am., Plano, 2002—05, sr. v.p. bus. innovation, chief strategist, 2005—09; sr. v.p. bus. innovation PepsiCo Americas Foods, 2009—, Frito Lay N. Am. Contbr. articles to profl. jours. Mem. bd. dirs. Dallas Theater Ctr. Bd., 1999-2002, Variety, 1997—. Capt. Israeli Air Force, 1981-85. Mem. IEEE, Tau Beta Pi, Sigma Xi (assoc.). Jewish. Avocations: films, theater, ballroom and Latin dancing. Office: Frito Lay N Am 7701 Legacy Dr 3A-254 Plano TX 75024 Business E-Mail: Daniel.Naor@FritoLay.com.

NAOUMOV, VIATCHESLAV I., mechanical and aerospace engineer, educator; b. Kazan, Russia, Mar. 2, 1953; s. Igor P. Naoumov and Ludmila I. Naoumova; m. Irina Y. Guskova; 1 child, Anton V. Grad., Kazan Aviation Inst., Russia, 1976, PhD in AE Engring., 1981, DS in AE and ME Engring., 1994. Asst. prof. Kazan Aviation Inst., Russia, 1982—89, assoc. prof., 1993—96; dean coll. Kazan State Tech. U., Russia, 1995—99, prof., dept. head, 1996—2004. Vis. prof. U. Tenn., Knoxville, 2001—07; assoc. prof. Ctrl. Conn. State U., 2007—. Recipient Outstanding Rsch. award, USSR, 1998; named Soros Assoc. Prof., 1995, Disting. Scientist, Russia, 1999. Office: Ctrl Conn State Univ 1615 Stanley St Copernicus Hall 23512 New Britain CT 06050 Office Phone: 860-832-1820. Business E-Mail: naoumovvii@ccsu.edu.

NAOUMOVA, IRINA YEVGENIEVNA, business educator, consultant; 1 child, Anton V. Naoumov. Grad., Kazan State U., Russia, 1982, PhD in Econs. and Mgmt., 1989. Asst. prof. Kazan State Tech. U., 1982—93, assoc. prof., 1993—95; assoc. prof., head mgmt. dept. Kazan State U., 1995—2003; vis. prof. U. Tenn., Knoxville, 2001—08; prof. dir. inst. entrepreneuship U. Hartford, 2008—. Pres. bd. Alliance Univs. Democracy, 2000—. Grantee, Jr. Fellowship Devel. Program, 1996—97, Fulbright Prof., 2000—01. Mem.: Acad. Int. Bus., Am. Acad. Mgmt., Internat. Acad. Edn. Office Phone: 860-768-4760. Business E-Mail: naoumova@hartford.edu.

NAPIER, CAMERON MAYSON FREEMAN, historic preservationist; b. Shanghai, Dec. 5, 1931; d. Hamner Garland and Cameron Middleton (Brame) Freeman; m. John Hawkins Napier III, Sept. 11, 1964. Student, L'Ecole des Artes Municipale, Paris, 1950-51, Westhampton Coll./U. Richmond, 1951—53; BA, U. Ala., 1955. Photographer's asst. Scott, Demott & Perry, Montgomery, Ala., 1951; art dir. WCOV-TV, Montgomery, 1955; self-employed graphic designer Dallas, 1956-64; self-employed designer Alexandria, Va., 1965-71; restoration chmn. White House Assn. Ala., Montgomery, 1973-76, 1st vice regent, 1976-80, regent, 1980—2009. Co-founder Friends of Stratford Hall for No. Va., Alexandria, late 1960s; docent chmn. Lee's Boyhood Home, late 1960s; bd. dirs. Landmarks Found., Montgomery, 1971-75; advisor Conde Charlotte House, Mobile, Ala., 1994-95. Author, designer booklet: The First White House of the Confederacy, 1978 (nat. printers award 1979), The Struggle to Preserve the First White House of the Confederacy, 1982; contbr. to Ency. of So. Culture, 1989, Ency. of Ala.-online, 2006. Bd. dirs. English Speaking Union, Montgomery, 1980—83. Recipient Award of Excellence, Advt. Artists Assn., Dallas, 1960—62, disting. svc. award, Ala. Hist. Commn., Montgomery, 1977, Cert. of Commendation, Gov. Ala., 1986, Gov. Bob Riley, 2009, So. Patriot award, 1997, Lifetime Achievement award, Ala. Preservation Alliance, 2001, Jefferson Davis award, 1984, Winnie Davis award, United Daus. of Confederacy, 1985; named Hon. First Lady, by the Gov.'s wife, Montgomery, Ala., 1985. Mem.: Antiquarian Soc. (pres. 1981—82), Sojourners Lit. Club (pres.), Order of Merovingian Dynasty, Militi Templi Scotia, Daus. of Barons Runnymede, Nat. Soc. Colonial Dames in Am. (hist. properties com. 1994—95, state bd. mgrs. 1998—2000, ctr. vice chmn. 1998—2000), Am. Soc. Most Venerable Order of the Hosp. St. John of Jerusalem (assoc. officer sister 1995, named Comdr. Sister 2002), Soc. Descs. of Colonial Clergy, Order of the Crown in Am., Kappa Delta. Episcopalian. Avocations: jumbles, cryptoquotes, crossword puzzles, afternoon tea.

NAPIER, JOHN HAWKINS, III, historian; b. Berkeley, Calif., Feb. 6, 1925; s. John Hawkins and Lena Mae (Tate) Napier; m. Harriet Elizabeth McGehee, Aug. 30, 1950 (dec.); m. Cameron Mayson Freeman, Sept. 11, 1964. BA, U. Miss., 1949; MA, Auburn U., 1967; postgrad., Georgetown U., 1971; D (hon.), Napier U., Edinburgh, 2000. Journalist, tchr. Picayune (Miss.) H.S., 1946; commd. 2d lt. U.S. Air Force, 1949, advanced through grades to lt. col., 1966; ret., 1977. Staff dir. Congressional Com. on S.E. Asia, 1970; faculty Air War Coll., 1971-74; Air U. Command historian, 1974-77; asst. to exec. dir. Ala. Commn. on Higher Edn., Montgomery, 1977-78; adj. history faculty Auburn U., Montgomery, 1980-85; columnist Montgomery Advertiser, 1980-87; lectr. in field. Author: Lower Pearl River's Piney Woods: Its Land and People, 1985; The Air Force Officers Guide, 30th edit., 1995, Dr. Patrick Napier: His Ancestors and Some Descendants, 1991; contbr. articles to profl. jours. With USMC, 1943-46, col. Ala. State Defense Force, 1991-97, brig. gen., dep. comdr., 1997-99. Decorated Legion of Merit; Order of St. John of Jerusalem, Milit. and Hospitaller Order of St. Lazarus of Jerusalem, Sovereign Mil. Order of Temple of Jerusalem; recipient award of merit Ala. Hist. Commn., 1976, Ala. Disting. Svc. medal, 1999, merit award English-Speaking Union U.S., 1983; Taylor medal and grad. fellow U. Miss., 1949; Storrs scholar Pomona Coll., 1942-43. Fellow: Soc. Antiquaries Scotland; mem.: S.R. SAR (pres. 1974—75), SCV (vice comdr. Ala. 1979—80), Ala. Hist. Assn. (pres. 1979—80), Royal Order Scotland, English-Speaking Union (pres. 1978—87, nat. dir. 1980—86, 1987—90, 1991—94), Scabbard and Blade, Royal Scots (Edinburgh), Mil. Order Carabao, Soc. Colonial Wars, Soc. War of 1812 (pres. Ala. 1980—82), St. Andrews Soc., Clan Napier in N.Am. (lt. to chief 1985—), Order 1st Families Va., Jamestowne Soc., Soc. Cincinnati, Ala. Assn. (pres. 1998—2001), Aztec 1847, Soc. Pioneers Montgomery (pres. 1979—80), Montgomery Country Club, Masons (32d degree), Pi Sigma Alpha, Phi Alpha Theta, Omicron Delta Kappa, Phi Kappa Phi, Sigma Chi. Democrat. Episcopalian. Home: Kilmahew 158 Mt Zion Rd Ramer AL 36069-6505 Home Phone: 334-281-0505.

NAPLES, RONALD JAMES, manufacturing executive; b. Passaic, NJ, Sept. 10, 1945; s. James V. and Lee A. Naples; m. Suzanne Lorraine Shoudy, June 17, 1967; children: Regen Jeffrey, Marcus Jamison, Tiffany Marie. BS, U.S. Mil. Acad., 1967; MA, Fletcher Sch. Law, 1972; MBA with distinction, Harvard U., 1974. Assoc. in corp. fin. Loeb Rhoades Co., 1973; fellow, spl. asst. to counselor to Pres. The White House, 1974; spl. asst. to adminstr. Fed. Energy Adminstrn., 1975; exec. dir. Presdl. Task Force on Energy, Washington, 1975-76; v.p. internat. Hunt Mfg. Co., Phila., 1976, exec. v.p., 1980-81, vice chmn., pres., CEO, 1981-86, chmn., CEO, 1987-95; pres. Hunt Internat. Co., 1977-82, Quaker Chem. Corp., 1995—98, CEO, 1995—2008, chmn., 1997—. Bd. dirs. Quaker Chem. Corp., 1995—, Glatfelter Paper Co.; chmn. Fed. Res. Bank, Phila., U. of Arts. Bd. dirs. Rock Sch. Pa. Ballet, ARC, Fgn. Policy Rsch. Inst., Phila., Phila. Mus. Art, Franklin Inst. With US Army, 1967—71. Decorated Bronze star with oak leaf cluster, Army Commindation medal with oak leaf cluster, Air medal, Cross of Gallantry Vietnam; recipient Mil. Order Wars medal, U.S. Mil. Acad., 1967, Phila. Inc. Cmty. Leadership award, 1990, Human Rels. Civic Achievement award, Am. Jewish Coun., 1989, Semper Fidelis award, Marine Corps Scholarship Fedn., 1991, Stephen Girard award, Phila. Fin. Assn., 1992, Touching a Life award, Boys and Girls Club Am., 1994, Torch of Liberty award, Anti-Defamation League, 2002; named Outstanding Young Man Am., U.S. Jaycees, 1977, CEO of Decade Bus. Equipment, Fin. World Mag., 1989; Walter Heller fellow, Harvard U., 1974, White Ho. fellow, 1974—75. Mem.: Assn. Grad. U.S. Mil. Acad., Chief Execs. Orgn., World Pres.' Orgn., White Ho. Fellows Assn., Harvard Bus. Sch. Alumni Assn., Phila. Country Club, Harvard Bus. Sch. Club Phila., Pyramid Club, Racquet Club. Office: Quaker Chem Corp One Quaker Park 901 Hector St Conshohocken PA 19428

NAPOLITANO, ANDREW P., lawyer, former judge; b. Newark, June 6, 1950; s. Andrew A. and Rita N. (Caruso). AB, Princeton U., 1972; JD, U. Notre Dame, 1975. Bar: NJ 1975, U.S. Supreme Ct. 1985, U.S. Ct. Appeals (3rd cir.) 1997, U.S. Dist. Ct. NY (So. Dist.) 2000, U.S. Dist. Ct. NY (Ea. Dist.) 2001, U.S. Ct. Appeals (2nd Cir.) 2001. Atty. Riker, Danzig, Scherer & Debevoise, Newark, Winne, Banta & Rizzi, Hackensack, NJ, 1975—87; judge Superior Ct. NJ, 1987-95; news analyst Fox News Channel, NYC, 1998-2000, judge, Power of Atty., 2000—01, sr. jud. analyst, 2001—. V.p., gen. counsel Hackensack U. Med. Ctr., 1986-1987; asst. prof. law, constl. law, criminal law and procedure, and profl. ethics, Del. Law Sch. of Widener U., Wilmington, Del., 1980-81; adj. prof. law, basic and advanced constl. law, Seton Hall U., Newark, 1989-2001; faculty mem., NJ Civil Practice and Procedure, NJ Jud. Coll., Teaneck, NJ, 1989-97; lectr., NJ Civil Practice and Procedure, Constl. Law, Profl. Responsibility, Inst. for Continuing Legal Edn., New Brunswick, NJ, 1996, NJ Law Jour. Lecture Series, Newark, NJ, 1995-; legal/polit. commentator, Courtroom TV Network, NYC, 1996-97, MSNBC, Secaucus, NJ, 1997-98, Fox News Channel, NYC, 1998-2000; at-large trustee Am. Inns of Ct. Fedn.; founding pres., master, Justice Morris Pashman Am. Inn Ct., Hackensack, NJ, 1989-98; mem. NJ Supreme Ct. Com. on Civil Practice, 1982-85, 1989-94, 1996-98. Author: Constitutional Chaos: What Happens When the Government Breaks Its Own Laws, 2004, A Nation of Sheep, 2007; contbr. articles to profl. jours. Bd. governor Hackensack U. Med. Ctr., 1994—2002. With USAR, 1971—72. Fellow: Am. Bar Found.; mem.: Assn. Criminal Defense Lawyers NJ, Trial Attys. NJ, Assn. Trial Lawyers Am., NJ State Bar Assn., Essex County Bar Assn., Bergen County Bar Assn. Office: Fischbein Badillo Wagner Harding 909 Third Ave New York NY 10022 Address: Fox News Network LLC 1211 Ave of the Americas New York NY 10036 Office Phone: 212-453-3717. Business E-Mail: anapolitano@fbwhlaw.com.*

NAPOLITANO, GRACE FLORES, United States Representative from California; b. Brownsville, Tex., Dec. 4, 1936; d. Miguel and Maria Alicia (Ledezma) Flores; m. Frank Napolitano, 1982; children: Yolando, Fred, Edward, Michael, Cynthia. Student, Cerritos Coll., LA Trade-Tech. Coll., Tec Southwest Coll. Councilwoman City of Norwalk, Calif.,

1986—92, mayor, 1989—90; mem. Calif. Assembly, 1993-98, US Congress from 38th Calif. dist., Washington, 1999—, mem. resources com., transp. & infrastructure com., chair water & power subcom. Dir. LA County Sanitation Dist.; mem. Am. Legion Auxiliary, Norwalk Internat. Friendship Commn., Health Task Force, Mfg. Task Force, Women's Caucus, New Dem. Coalition; founder Southeast Coalition Safe Drinking Water; founder, co-chair Congl. Mental Health Caucus; chair Southeast LA County Pvt. Industry Coun.; former chair Congl. Hispanic Caucus. Active Cerritos Coll. Found. Mem.: US/Mex. Sister Cities Assn., Vets. of Foreign Wars, Lions Club. Democrat. Roman Catholic. Office: US House Reps 1610 Longworth House Office Bldg Washington DC 20515-0538 Office Phone: 202-225-5256.*

NAPOLITANO, JANET ANN, Secretary of Homeland Security, former Governor of Arizona; b. NYC, Nov. 29, 1957; d. Leonard Michael and Jane Marie (Winer) Napolitano. BS summa cum laude, U. Santa Clara, Calif., 1979; JD, U. Va., 1983. Bar: Ariz. 1984, U.S. Dist. Ct. Ariz. 1984, U.S. Ct. Appeals (9th cir.) 1984, U.S. Ct. Appeals (10th cir.) 1988, U.S. Ct. Appeals (5th cir.), U.S. Ct. Appeals, U.S. Ct. Appeals (7th cir.), U.S. Ct. Appeals (8th cir.). Law clk. to Hon. Mary Schroeder U.S Ct. Appeals (9th Cir.), 1983—84; assoc. Lewis & Roca, Phoenix, 1984—89, ptnr., 1989—93, 1997—98; US atty. Dist. Ariz. US Dept. Justice, Phoenix, 1993—97; atty. gen. State of Ariz., Phoenix, 1999—2002, gov., 2003—09; sec. US Dept. Homeland Security, Washington, 2009—. Mem. Atty. Gen.'s Adv. Com., 1983—, chair, 1995—96; chair victims rights subcom. Ariz. Criminal Justice Commn.; chair Ariz. High Intensity Drug Traficking Area; mem. Ariz. Peace Officer Stds. and Tng. Bd., Ariz. Pros. Attys.' Adv. Coun.; past com. to study civil litigation abuse, cost and delay Ariz. Supreme Ct.; past pres. Ariz. Cmty. Legal Svcs. Corp.; past judge pro tem Ariz. Ct. Appeals. Contbr. articles to profl. jours. Chmn. Nucleus, 1989—91; active Phoenix Design Stds. Rev. Com., 1989—91, Ariz. Women's Forum, Charter 100; hon. chmn. Camp Fire Boys and Girls, 1999; 1st vice-chmn. Ariz. Dem. Com., 1990—92; active Dem. Nat. Com., 1990—92; chmn. Ariz. del. Dem. Nat. Conv., 1992, chmn., 2000; active Ariz. Bd. Tech. Registration, 1989—92; bd. dirs. Ariz. Fire Fighters and Emergency Paramedics Meml., Phoenix Children's Hosp., Actors' Lab Ariz., Inc., Ariz. Peace Officers Meml.; bd. regents Santa Clara U., 1992—. Recipient Leader of Distinction award, Anti-Defamation League, Human Betterment award, Roots and Wings, Golden Apple award, West Valley NOW, Nat. Network To End Domestic Violence award, Woman of Distinction award, Crohns and Colitis Disease Found., Women Making History award, Nat. Mus. Women's History, Tribute to Women award, YWCA, Disting. Alumna award, U. Va. Women's Ctr., 2004; named Ariz. Dem. of Yr., 1989; named one of The 5 Best Governors in the US, TIME mag., 2005, 100 Most Powerful Women, Forbes mag., 2009; scholar, Truman Scholarship Found., 1977; Hardy Cross Dillard fellow, U. Va. Sch. Law. Fellow: Ariz. Bar Found.; mem.: ABA, Raven Soc., Sandra Day O'Connor Inn of Ct. (barrister), Ariz. Women Lawyers Assn., Ariz. State Bar (chmn. civil practice and procedure com. 1991—92), Am. Judicature Soc., Maricopa County Bar Assn. (past long range planning com.), Ariz. Bar Assn. (past com. on minorities in law, past chmn. civil practice and procedure com.), Nat. Assn. Attys. Gen. (exec. com., tobacco bankruptcy working group, health care fraud group, co-chmn. civil rights com., stop underage smoking com., exec. working group on prosecutorial rels.), Am. Law Inst., Alpha Sigma Nu, Phi Beta Kappa. Democrat. Avocations: hiking, walking, travel, reading, films. Office: US Dept Homeland Security 3801 Nebraska Ave NW Washington DC 20528 Office Phone: 202-282-8203. Office Fax: 202-282-9188.*

NAPOLITANO, LENA MARIE, surgeon, educator; b. Waterbury, Conn., Oct. 31, 1957; d. Carmine and Mary (Dell'Anno) N. BA, Boston U., 1979; MD, George Washington U., 1984. Diplomate Nat. Bd. Med. Examiners, Am. Bd. Surgery. Rsch. asst. dept. surgery Yale U. Med. Ctr., New Haven, 1979-80; resident in gen. surgery George Washington U. Med. Ctr., Washington, 1984-87, sr. resident in gen. surgery, asst. in surgery, 1988-89, chief resident in gen. surgery, clin. instr. in surgery, 1989-90; clin. and rsch. fellow dept. anesthesia and surgery Mass. Gen. Hosp./Harvard Med. Sch., Boston, 1987-88; instr., fellow in surg. critical care and trauma U. NC Hosp., Chapel Hill, 1990-91; trauma rsch. fellow dept. surgery U. NC, Chapel Hill, 1991-92, attending in surgery, trauma and critical care, 1991-92; asst. prof. surgery and anesthesia U. Mass. Med. Ctr., Boston, 1992-95, dir. surg. critical care, co-dir. surg. ICU, trauma svcs., 1992-95; asst. prof. surgery U. Md. Med. Ctr. and Balt. VA Med. Ctr., 1995-97, assoc. prof., 1997—2000, prof. surgery, 2000—05, dir. surg. critical care, nutrition support svcs., 1995—2005; divsn. chief surg. critical care U. Md. Med. Systems; prof. surgery, chief surgical critical care, assoc. chair surgery U. Mich., Ann Arbor, Mich., 2005—. Program dir., surg. critical care fellow U. Md. Med. Sys.; mem. disaster med. assistance team Internat. Inst. for Disaster and Emergency Medicine, U. Mass. Med. Ctr., 1993—; rschr., lectr. in field. Contbr. chpts. to books and articles to profl. publs.; reviewer Critical Care Medicine, Jour. Intensive Care Medicine, Chest. Conn. State scholar, 1975-79, Davis & Geck scholar, 1991; recipient Outstanding Resident award Holy Cross Hosp., 1988, Surg. Resident award Alpha Omega Alpha, 1989; grantee U. Mass. Med. Ctr., 1993, Burroughs Wellcome, Sterling Winthrop Inc., Soc. Critical Care Medicine, Cetus Corp., Alpha-Beta Tech., Inc., Healthcare Innovation. Fellow ACS (Harry Zehner Jr. Meml. Travelling Fellowship award Wash. chpt. 1989), Am. Coll. Chest Physicians; mem. AMA, Assn. for Acad. Surgery (mem. exec. coun. 1993—, mem. nominations com. 1994—), Surg. Infection Soc. (mem. edn. and fellowship com. 1995—), Assn. Women Surgeons (specialty rep. for trauma and critical care), Nathan Womack Surg. Soc., Soc. Critical Care Medicine, Worcester Med. Soc., Am. Med. Women's Assn., Ea. Assn. for Surgery of Trauma, Am. Soc. Parenteral and Enteral Nutrition, Am. Burn Assn., Shock Soc., Assn. VA Surgeons, Phi Beta Kappa. Office: Univ Mich Sch Medicine 1C421 UH SPC 5033 1500 East Medical Center Dr Room IC421 Ann Arbor MI 48109-0033 Business E-Mail: lenan@umich.edu.*

NAPORA, ROBERT ALAN, physics professor; b. Elgin, Ill., Nov. 29, 1971; s. Robert Allen Napora and Rose Marie Brown; m. Kristin Marie Moore. BS, ND State U., Fargo, 1998; PhD, Johns Hopkins U., Balt., 2004. Contbr. scientific papers. Sgt. USMC, 1989—94. Decorated Navy Achievement medal US Dept. Navy, Navy Commendatin medal; recipient Eivind Horvik Meml. award, ND State U., 1994, Ralph L. Pitman award, NDSU Coll. Sci. and Math., 1994. Office: Purdue Univ Calumet 2200 169th St Hammond IN 46323

NAPPIER, DENISE L., state treasurer; BA, Va. State U., 1973; MA in Cmty. Planning, U. Cin., 1975. Analyst Office Hartford (Conn.) City Mgr.; cons. Conn. Office of Policy and Mgmt.; dir. instnl. rels. U. Conn. Health Ctr.; city treas. City of Hartford, 1989—98; treas. State of Conn., Hartford, 1999—. Exec. dir. Riverfront Recapture, Inc. Achievements include being the first African American woman elected state treasurer. Office: Office of State Treas 55 Elm St Hartford CT 06106-1746 Office Phone: 860-702-3001. Business E-Mail: state.treasurer@ct.gov.*

NAQVI, NASIR HASNAIN, psychiatrist, neuroscientist; BS, NYU, NYC, 1994; MD, PhD, U. Iowa, Iowa City, 2007. Lic. NY State, 2008. Grad. rsch. asst., dept. neurology U. Iowa, 2000—06; resident, dept. psychiatry Columbia U., NYC, 2007—. Mem.: Soc. Neurosci., Am. Psychiat. Assn. Achievements include discovery of damage to the insula disrupts addiction to cigarette smoking. Office: Columbia Univ Dept Psychiatry 1051 Riverside Dr New York NY 10032

NAQVI, SHAHID ABBAS, physicist, educator; b. Karachi, Pakistan, June 19, 1969; s. Hasan Mohammad and Khurshid Fatima Naqvi; m. Sumaira Rizvi, Jan. 29, 2005. BSEE, San Diego State U., 1991; PhD, Cornell U., 1996. Cert. therapeutic physicist Am. Bd. Radiology. Asst. prof. U. Md., Balt., 2001—. Mem.: Am. Assn. Physicists Medicine. Home: 4503 Rebekka Cir Owings Mills MD 21117 Office: Univ Md 22 S Greene St Baltimore MD 21117 E-mail: snaqvi@umm.edu.

NARAHASHI, TOSHIO, pharmacology educator; b. Fukuoka, Japan, Jan. 30, 1927; arrived in U.S., 1961; s. Asahachi and Itoko (Yamasaki) Ishii; m. Kyoko Narahashi, Apr. 21, 1956; children: Keiko, Taro. BS, U. Tokyo, 1948, PhD, 1960. Instr. U. Tokyo, 1951-65; research assoc. U. Chgo., 1961, asst. prof., 1962, Duke U., Durham, NC, 1962-63, 65-67, assoc. prof., 1967-69, prof., 1969-77, head pharmacology div., 1970-73, vice chmn. dept. physiology and pharmacology, 1973-75; prof., chmn. dept. pharmacology Northwestern U. Med. Sch., Chgo., 1977-94, Alfred Newton Richards prof., 1982—2005; John Evans prof. Northwestern U., Evanston, Ill., 1986—. Mem. pharmacology study sect. NIH, 1976-80; rsch. rev. com. Chgo. Heart Assn., 1977-82, vice chmn. rsch. coun., 1986-87, chmn., 1988-90; mem. Nat. Environ. Health Scis. Coun., 1982-86; rev. com. Nat. Inst. Environ. Health Scis., 1991-95. Editor: Cellular Pharmacology of Insecticides and Pheromones, 1979, Cellular and Molecular Neurotoxicology, 1984, Insecticide Action: From Molecule to Organism, 1989, Ion Channels, 1988—; specific field editor Jour. Pharmacology and Exptl. Therapeutics, 1972-97; assoc. editor Neurotoxicology, 1994—; contbr. articles to profl. jours. Recipient Javits Neurosci. Investigator award, NIH, 1986. Fellow AAAS, Acad. Toxicol. Scis.; mem. Am. Soc. for Pharmacology and Exptl. Therapeutics (Otto Krayer award 2000), Am. Physiol. Soc., Soc. for Neurosci., Biophys. Soc. (Cole award 1981), Soc. Toxicology (DuBois award 1988, Merit award 1991, Disting. Investigator Lifetime Achievement award 2001, Disting. Lifetime Toxicology Scholar award 2008), Agrochem. Divsn. Am. Chem. Soc. (Burdick L. Jackson Internat. award 1989). Home: 175 E Delaware Pl Apt 7911 Chicago IL 60611-7745 Office: Northwestern U Med Sch Dept Mol Pharmaco Biol Chem 303 E Chicago Ave Chicago IL 60611-3008 Office Phone: 312-503-8284. Business E-Mail: narahashi@northwestern.edu.

NARAIN, RALPH B., biologist; b. Wakenaam, Guyana, Feb. 22, 1968; s. Aaron and Rose Narain. AS, Suffolk County CC, Riverhead, NY, 2001; BS, SUNY, Oneonta, 2003; MS in entomology, U. Nebr., Lincoln, 2006—. Lab. tech. Aroaima Mining Co., Berbice, Guyana, 1992—96; machine operator NY Twist Drills Inc., Bohemia, NY, 1997—2000; biologist Suffolk County Dept. Health Services, Arthropod-Borne Diseases Lab., Yaphank, 2003—07; grad. asst. U. Nebr., Lincoln, 2006—. Field evaluator dept. entomology U. Nebr., Lincoln, Nebr. Contbr. articles to profl. jours. Vol. Shiv Uma Ganesh Temple, Central Islip, NY, 2000—06. Scholar, Proctor & Gamble, 2002—03; John J. New scholar, SUNY Coll., Oneonta, 2002—03. Mem.: Entomology Soc. Am, Nat. Scholar Honor Soc., Phi Theta Kappa. Avocations: travel, coin collecting/numismatics, photography. Home: 745 S 45 St Lincoln NE 68510 Office: U Nebr Lincoln 201A Entomology Hall Lincoln NE 68583-0816 Business E-Mail: ralph@huskers.unl.edu.

NARAINE, CHAMELI, bank executive; B in Econs., Wilfred Laurier U, Waterloo, Ont.; B in Ops. Mgmt., Conestoga Coll., Kitchener, Ont. Various sr. mgmt. positions including gen. mgr. outsourcing bus., dir. bus. devel. Asia and dir. mfg. ops. Supply Chain and Indsl. Engring. NCR Corp.; sr. v.p. acquisition and strategic sourcing Nat. City Corp., Cleve., 2002—03, dir. corp. ops. and strategic outsourcing, 2003—, sr. v.p., 2004—. Office: Nat City Corp Nat City Ctr 1900 E Ninth St Cleveland OH 44114-3484 Office Phone: 216-222-2000.

NARASIMHAN, PRIYA, engineering educator; b. Madras, India, Dec. 28, 1970; d. Kala and Nallan Chakravarty Narasimhan; m. Rajeev Gandhi, Aug. 23, 2001; 1 child, Nikhil Narasimhan Gandhi. PhD, U. Calif., Santa Barbara, 1999. V.p. engring. CTO Eternal Sys., Inc., Santa Barbara, 1999—2001; asst. prof. Carnegie Mellon U., Pitts., 2001—06, assoc. prof., 2006—. Contbr. articles to profl. jours. Recipient Faculty Partnership award, IBM Rsch., 2002—05, CAREER award, NSF, 2003—, Excellence in Tchg. award, Eta Kappa Nu Sigma Chpt., 2008; fellowship, Alfred Sloan Found., 2006—. Mem.: IEEE, ACM. Office: Carnegie Mellon Univ ECE Dept 5000 Forbes Ave Pittsburgh PA 15213 Business E-Mail: priya@cs.cmu.edu.

NARAYAN, AMARENDRA, telecommunications executive; b. Matukpur, India, Nov. 21, 1945; s. Binod and Tara Devi Narayan; m. Asha Narayan, July 10, 1970; 1 child, Ashish. BS in Engring., Bihar Coll. Engring., 1966. Asst. prof. elect. engring. Govt. Poly. U., Bihar, 1966-75; asst. divisional engr. dept. telecomms. Govt. of India, 1975-79, divisional engr., 1979-82, dir. telecomms. Nagpur, 1985-87, dep. gen. mgr. Jabalpur, 1987-90; mgr. Telecom Cons. India Ltd., New Delhi, 1982-85; project engr. Asia Pacific Telecommunity, Bangkok, 1990, dir. project devel., 1991—98, deputy exec. dir., 1998—2001, exec. dir., 2001—. Editor: Telecomms., 1987-90, APT Jour., 1990—, APT Yearbook, 1994. Fellow Instn. Telecom Engrs. India, Instn. Engrs. India; commnr. Global Info. Infrastructure Commn. Home: 299/207 Pongpet Chaengwatta Bangkok 10210 Thailand Office: Asia Pacific Telecommunity 12/49 501 5 Chaengwattana Bangkok 10210 Thailand

NARAYAN, JAGDISH, materials science educator; b. Kanpur, India, Oct. 15; came to U.S., 1969; s. Shri Sheo Nath and Radha Prasad; m. Ratna (Katyar) Narayan, Nov. 27, 1973; 1 child, Roger. BS in Materials Sci. with highest honors, Indian Inst. Tech., Kanpur, 1969; MS, U. Calif., Berkeley, 1970, PhD, 1971. Group leader solid state dvsn. Oak Ridge (Tenn.) Nat. Lab., 1971-84; dir. div. materials rsch. NSF, Washington, 1990-92, maj. facilities reviewer; disting. univ. prof. materials sci. and engring. N.C. State U., Raleigh, 1984—. Dir. Microelectronic Ctr. N.C., Raleigh, 1984-86; tech. adv. bd. Kopin Corp., Taunton, Mass., 1988—; mem. exec. coun. electronic, magnetic and photonic materials dvsn. TMS, awards chair. Editor: Defects in Semiconductors, 1981, Laser-Solid Interactions and Transient Thermal Processing of Metals, 1984, High-Temperature Superconductors, 1990, others; contbr. numerous sci. papers to profl. jours. Pres. bd. trustees Hindi Vikas Mandal, Raleigh, 1990. Recipient Outstanding Sustained Rsch. award, Dept. Energy, Disting. Svc. award, NSF. Fellow AAAS, TMS (life), Am. Phys. Soc. (life), Nat. Acad. Scis. India (life), Am. Soc. Metals Internat. (Internat. Gold medal 1999); mem. Materials Rsch. Soc. (fall meeting co-chair 1984, councillor 1984-87, long-range planning com. 1987-89), Böhmische Physikalische Gesellschaft. Achievements include 35 patents in fields of laser processing of materials, high performance ceramics, novel methods for materials synthesis and processing, laser processing and patterning of diamond films. Office: NC State Univ Dept Materials Sci Eng Raleigh NC 27695-0001 Office Phone: 919-515-7874.

NARAYAN, RAMESH, astronomy educator; b. Bombay, Sept. 25, 1950; came to U.S., 1983; s. G.N. and Rajalakshmi (Sankaran) Ramachandran; m. G.V. Vani, June 6, 1977. BS in Physics, Madras U., 1971; MS in Physics, Bangalore U., 1973, PhD in Physics, 1979. Rsch. scientist Raman Rsch. Inst., Bangalore, India, 1978-83; postdoctoral fellow Calif. Inst. Tech., 1983-84, sr. rsch. fellow, 1984-85; assoc. prof. astronomy U. Ariz., Tucson, 1985-90, prof., 1990-91; prof. astronomy Harvard U., Cambridge, Mass., 1991—2003, chmn. dept., 1997-2001, Thomas Dudley Cabot prof. natural scis., 2003—. Sr. astronomer Harvard-Smithsonian Ctr. for Astrophysics, 1991—, assoc. dir., 1996-97; adv. bd. Inst. Theoretical Physics U. Calif., Santa Barbara, 1994-98, chmn., 1996-97; com. gravitational physics NRC, 1997-99; chmn. adv. bd. Ctr. for Gravitational Wave Physics, Pa. State U., 2001—; mem. adv. bd. Max Planck Inst. for Astrophysics, 2002-05, chmn., 2003-05. Contbr. articles to profl. jours. Named NSF Presdl. Young Investigator, 1989, George Darwin lectr. Royal Astron. Soc., 2002. Fellow: Royal Soc. London; mem.: AAAS, Internat. Astron. Union (mem. U.S. nat. com. 2000—03), Am. Astron. Soc. (mem. exec. com. High Energy Astrophys. Divsn. 2002—04). Achievements include research in the general area of theoretical astrophysics, specializing in accretion disks, black holes, gravitational lenses, gamma-ray bursts, radio pulsars, image processing and scintillation. Office: Harvard-Smithsonian Ctr Astrophysics 60 Garden St # 51 Cambridge MA 02138-1516

NARAYAN, SUMIT, research assistant; b. Patna, Bihar, India, May 3, 1981; s. Sunil and Reena Narayan. BS in Engring., U. Madras, Chennai, India, 2002; MS, U.Conn., Storrs, 2004. Bar: Exploit Technologies (A-STAR), Singapore (commercial law & intellectual property management) 2005. Engr. (r&d services) MindTree Consulting Pvt. Ltd., Bangalore, India, 2004—05; rsch. officer Data Storage Inst. (A-STAR), Singapore, 2005—06; rsch. aide Argonne Nat. Lab., Chgo., 2008; grad. rsch. asst. U. Conn., Storrs, 2003—04, 2006—. Contbr. to profl. jours. Exec. com. mem. Tarang - South Asian Grad. Students, Storrs, 2003—04. Summer Fellowship, U. Conn., 2008. Mem.: IEEE Computer Soc., Assn. Computing Machinery (assoc. editor crossroads), Inst. Elec. & Electronics Engineers. Office: Univ Conn Unit 2157 Dept EE 371 Fairfield Way Storrs Mansfield CT 06269 Office Fax: +1-860-486-2447. Business E-Mail: sumit.narayan@uconn.edu.

NARAYANAMURTI, VENKATESH, engineering professor, former dean; b. Bangalore, Karnataka, India, Sept. 9, 1939; came to U.S., 1961; s. Duraiswami and Janaki (Subramaniam) N.; m. Jayalakshmi Krishnayya, Aug. 23, 1961; children: Arjun, Ranjini, Krishna. BSc, MSc, St. Stephen's Coll., Delhi, India, 1958; PhD, Cornell U., 1965. Instr., rsch. assoc. Cornell U., Ithaca, NY, 1965-68; mem. tech. staff AT&T Bell Labs., Murray Hill, NJ, 1968-76, dept.head, 1976-81, dir., 1981-87; v.p. rsch. Sandia Nat. Labs., Albuquerque, 1987-92; dean U. Calif. Sch. Engring., Santa Barbara, Calif., 1992-98, Harvard U. Sch. Engring & Applied Sciences, Cambridge, Mass., 1998—2008; dir. Belfer Ctr. Sci., Tech. & Pub. Policy program John F. Kennedy Sch. Govt., Harvard U., Cambridge, Mass., 2009—, Benjamin Pierce prof. tech. & pub. policy, 2009—. Chmn. condensed matter and materials phys. panel NRC, 1996-99; mem. U. Calif. Pres.' Coun. for Nat. Labs., 1995-98; mem. NAE Pub. Info. Adv. Bd., 1993-94, NSF Dir.'s Strategic Planning Bd., 1994-98; mem. adv. bd. Miller Inst. for Basic Sci., U. Calif. Berkeley, 1999-2006. Author more than 190 publs.; patentee in field. Fellow IEEE, AAAS, Am. Phys. Soc., Indian Acad. Scis.; mem. NAE, Royal Swedish Acad. Engring. Scis. (fgn.). Avocations: long distance running, squash. Office: Harvard U Littauer 370 79 John F Kennedy St Mailbox 53 Cambridge MA 02138 Office Phone: 617-495-1464. Office Fax: 617-495-8963. E-mail: venky@seas.harvard.edu.*

NARAYANAMURTI, VENKATESH, engineering educator, physics professor; BSc, Univ. Delhi, 1958, MSc in Physics, 1960; PhD in Physics, Cornell Univ., 1960. With AT&T Bell Labs., 1968, dir., Solid State Electronics Rsch. Lab., 1981—87; v.p. rsch., exploratory tech. Sandia Nat. Lab., 1987—92; dean, coll. engring. Univ. Calif., Santa Barbara, 1992—98; dean, engring., applied sci. Harvard Univ., 1998—2006, dean, phys. sci., 2003—06, John A. and Elizabeth S. Armstrong prof., engring., applied sci., 2006—. Fellow: AAAS, Royal Swedish Acad. Engring Sci., IEEE, Am. Physical Soc., Am. Acad. Arts & Scis.; mem.: NAE. Office: Engring & Applied Sci Harvard -Pierce 217A 29 Oxford St Cambridge MA 02138 Office Phone: 617-495-5829. Business E-Mail: venky@deas.harvard.edu.

NARAYANAN, KUMARAN, medical educator; PhD, U. Melbourne, Australia, 1999. Asst. prof. Mt. Sinai Sch. Medicine, NYC, 2003—. Office: Mt Sinai Sch Medicine 1425 Madison Ave New York NY 10029

NARAYANAN, NARAYANAN NARAYANAN, biologist, researcher; b. Trichy, India, July 22, 1975; s. Umayal Narayenan; m. Vijaya Pasupatham, Aug. 21, 2002. PhD, U. Madras, India, 2001. Rsch. assoc. Iowa State U., Ames, 2001—04, Baylor Coll. Medicine, Houston, 2004—, Ohio State U., 2007—08; rsch. scientist Donald Banform Plan Sci. Ctr., St. Louis, 2008—. Contbr. scientific papers. Recipient Cert. Merit and Gold medal Proficiency Botany, Loyola Coll., U. Madras, India, 1993—94; fellow, Rockefeller Found., Ctr. Advanced Studies Botany, U. Madras, 1998—99, Rockefeller Found., 1999—2001; scholar, All India Sr. Secondary Censor Exam Bd., 1992—95. Mem.: Am. Soc. Plant Biologists (assoc.). Achievements include research in improving the productivity of two popular high-yielding indica rice varieties, IR50 and CO39, which is severely, affected by these two major rice diseases; having multiple resistances for blast and blight in these cultivars, these blast-resistant pyramids (Pi-1+ Piz-5) were transformed with the cloned bacterial blight resistance gene Xa21, which is kn; improving soybean against the drastic disease root and stem rot caused by Phytophthora sojae, this pathogencauses over 0.12 million dollars damage annually; the gene structure of Rps1-k; isolating soybean genes those are transcriptionally regulated immediately following infection with the pathogen; the expression profiling of various metal homeostasis genes and to perform functional characterization of selected genes to improve mineral nutritional quality of rice grains; integrating new methods in genomics, genetics, and molecular biology to identify and understand plant genes of nutritional importance, specifically those related to iron and zinc; the role of metals related genes in metal transport in rice by the heterologous expression in yeast; characterizing temporal and tissue-specific expression of metal homeostasis genes in rice and to study the diverse rice genotypes exhibiting high and low concentrations of these metals because thes. Home: 11062 Oak Spur CT Apt B Saint Louis MO 63146-1974 Office: Donald Danforth plant Sci Ctr 975 N Warson Rd Saint Louis MO 63132 Personal E-mail: narayanan752000@yahoo.com.

NARAYANASAMY, PRABAGARAN, research scientist; PhD, IIT, Chennai, Tamilnadu, India, 2002. Cert. tchg. grad. CSU, 2008. Postdoc. Harvard U., Boston, 2004—06; rsch. scientist Colo. State U., Fort Collins, 2006—, advisor, 2007—08. Cons. Polymercompany, 1999—2002. Contbr. articles to profl. jours. (Kothari award, 1995). Recipient Best Sec. award, IIT, 2000, Most Depended Person award, Internat. Office, NDSU, 2004; CSIR-JRF and UGC grant, Coun. Sci. and Indsl. Rsch., 1997—2002. Mem.: ACS. Achievements include patents for enantioselective synthesis of A, B, disubstituted B-amino acids; discovery of men inhibitor for gram positive bacteria TB, malaria, etc; development of synthesis of MEP, CDPME, CDPME2P; discovery of new ligand and polymer for active catalyst; imprinted glucose polymer to check glucose level. Office: Colorado State Univ 1682 Campus Delivery Fort Collins CO 80523

NARAYEN, SHANTANU, computer software company executive; BS in Elec. Engring., Osmania U., India; MS in Computer Sci., Bowling Green U.; MBA, U. Calif. Berkeley, Haas Sch. Bus., 1993. Sr. mgr. Apple Computer, Inc.; dir. desktop & collaboration products Silicon Graphics, Inc.; co-founder Pictra, Inc.; v.p., gen. mgr. engring. tech. group Adobe Systems, Inc., San Jose, Calif., 1998—99, sr. v.p. worldwide products, 1999—2001, exec. v.p. worldwide product mktg. & devel., 2001—05, pres., COO, 2005—07, pres., CEO, 2007—. Bd. dirs. Adobe Systems, Inc., 2007—; spkr. in field. Adv. bd. Haas Sch. Bus., U. Calif., Berkeley. Achievements include patents in field. Office: Adobe Sys Inc 345 Park Ave San Jose CA 95110-2704 Office Phone: 408-536-6000.

NARBON, LILIAN, writer; b. Marroco, Nov. 9, 1957; children: Roi, Reut, Anat, Kineret. Author: Avodat Habirurim-The Vital Connection Between Psychology and Spirituality, 2002, (children's book) Lily Pily, 2005; composer: (songs) The Face of America; lyricist:, 2005; author: (children's book) The Agama Sisters. Jewish. Achievements include patents for safe ear clean button and protection with attachment device. Personal E-mail: Liliannarboni@aol.com.

NARCISO, CARMEN VERONICA, elementary school educator; b. Caracas, Venezuela, Nov. 19, 1967; d. Jose DelValle Narciso and Lourdes Isabel Farias-Narciso. B in Biology Edn., U. Oriente, Cumana-Sucre-Venezuela, 1984—92; MEd, Hamline U., St. Paul, 1999—2001. Cert. cert. life sci. 7-12 Minn. Dept. Edn., 2004, reading tchr. K-12 Minn. Dept. Edn., 2005, elem. tchr. Minn. Dept. Edn., 2006, Spanish tchr. K-8 Minn. Dept. Edn., 2006. Prof. asst. U. Oriente, Cumana, Sucre, Venezuela, 1990—92; HS tchr. UE Jose Francisco Bermudez, Carupano, 1992—94; mid. sch. tchr. UE Rafael Osio Perez, Carupano, 1992—93; adult edn. tchr. UE Fermin Toro, Carupano, 1992—93; elem. tchr. UE J.A. Rodriguez Abreu, Carupano, 1993—94; HS tchr. UE Virgen del Carmen, Barcelona, Anzoategui, Venezuela, 1994—96; mid. sch. tchr. UE P.R. Herrera, Puerto Piritu, Anzoategui, Venezuela, 1994—98, UE La Consolacion, Barcelona, 1996—97, UE Dr. Jose Antonio Ramos Sucre, Barcelona, 1997—98, Cumana, 1998—99; early childhood tchr. St. Paul Childhood Ctr., 2000—02; elem. tchr. Aurora Charter Sch., Mpls., 2001—. Mem., tchr. Aurora Charter Sch., Mpls., 2002—04. Recipient Cert. Recognition award, Aurora Charter Sch., 2006. Office: Aurora Charter Sch 2520 Minnehaha Av Minneapolis MN 55404

NARDI RIDDLE, CLARINE, chief staff, lawyer; b. Clinton, Ind., Apr. 23, 1949; d. Frank Jr. and Alice (Mattioda) Nardi; children: Carl Nardi, Julia Nardi. AB in Math with honors, Ind. U., 1971, JD, 1974; LHD (hon.), St. Joseph Coll., 1991. Bar: Ind. 1974, U.S. Dist. Ct. (so. dist.) Ind. 1974, Conn. 1979, Fed. Dist. Ct. Conn. 1980, U.S. Supreme Ct. 1980, U.S. Ct. Appeals (2d cir.) 1986, U.S. Ct. Appeals (D.C. cir.) 1994. Staff atty. Ind. Legis. Svc. Agy., Indpls., 1974-78, legal counsel, 1978-79; dep. corp. counsel City of New Haven, 1980-83; counsel to atty. gen. State of Conn., Hartford, 1983-86, dep. atty. gen., 1986-89, acting atty. gen., 1989, atty. gen., 1989-91, judge Superior Ct., 1991-93; assn. exec., sr. v.p., gen. counsel Nat. Multi-Housing Coun., Nat. Apartment Assn., 1995—2003; chief of staff to Senator Joseph I. Lieberman US Senate, Washington, 2003—. Asst. counsel state majority Conn. Gen. Assembly, Hartford, 1979, legal rsch. asst. to prof. Yale U., New Haven, 1979; legal counsel com. on law revision Indpls. State Bar Assn., 1979; mem. Chief Justice's Task Force on Gender Bias, Hartford, 1988-90; mem. ethics and values com. Ind. Sector, Washington, 1988-90; co-organizer Ind. Continuing Legal Edn. Forum Inst. Legal Drafting Legislature and Pvt. Practice; Internat. Women's Yr. panelist Credit Laws and Their Enforcement; mem. Atty. Gen.'s Blue Ribbon Commn., Chief Justice's Com. Study Publs. Policy Conn. Law. Jour., Law Revision Commn. Adminstrv. Law Study, Chief Justice's Task Force Gender, Justice and Cts., Gov.'s Task Force Fed. Revenue Enhancements; mem. exec. com. Jud. Dept.; mem. panel arbitrators Am. Arbitration Assn., 1994; gen. counsel Nat. Multi Housing Coun.; lectr. in field. Author: (with F.R. Rembusch) Drafting Manual for the Indiana General Assembly, 1976; sr. editor Ind. U. Law Sch. Interdisciplinary Law Jour.; contbr. articles to profl. jours. Bd. visitors Ind. U., Bloomington, 1974-92; mem. Gov.'s Missing Children Com., Hartford, Conn. Child Support Guidelines Com., Gov.'s Task Force on Justice for Abused Children, Hartford, 1988-90; mem. Mayor's City of New Haven Task Force Reorganization Corp. Counsel's Office, Gov.'s Child Support Commn., Mayor of New Haven's Blue Ribbon Commn.; former bd. dirs. New Haven Neighborhood Music Sch.; bd. dirs., mem. youth adv. com. Gov.'s Partnership Prevent Substance Abuse Workforce-Drugs Don't Work; mem. Blue Ribbon Com. Army War Coll., 2006. Recipient Women in Leadership Recognition award Hartford Region YWCA, 1986, Award of Merit, Women & Law Sect. Conn. Bar Assn., 1989, Fellowship award South End Ladies Dem. Club, 1989, Woman of Yr. award Greater Hartford Fedn. of Bus. & Profl. Women's Clubs, 1990, Conn. Original award Somers-Mabelle B. Avery Sch., 1990, Cert. of Recognition, Consortium Law-Related Edn., 1990, Citizen award Conn. Task Force Children's Constl. Rights, 1991, Ann. award Hartford Assn. Women Attys., 1993; named Conn. History Maker, U.S. Dept. Labor, Women's Bur. & Permanent Commn. Status Women, 1989, Impact Player, The Conn. Law Tribune, 1992; inductee Ind. U. Sch. Law Alumni Acad. Fellow, 1999. Mem. ABA, Conn. Bar Assn. (chair com. on gender bias, Citation of Merit women and law sect. 1989), Nat. Assn. Attys. Gen. (chair charitable trusts and solicitation 1988-90), New Haven Neighborhood Music Sch. (bd. dirs.), Am. Arbitration Assn. (arbitration panel 1994), Ind. Bar Assn., Conn. Bar Assn. (chair com. gender bias legal profession), Indpls. Bar Assn., Ind. Civil Liberties Union (bd. dirs., mem. exec. com., chair long range planning com., mem. women's rights project, membership v.p., Disting. Svc. award), Conn. Consortium Law and Citizenship Edn., Inc. (bd. dirs.), Conn. Judges Assn. (mem. legislation com.), Ind. U. Law Sch. Alumni Assn. (bd. dirs.), Enomene Hon. Soc., Pleiades Hon. Soc., Mortar Bd. (nat. fellow), Alpha Lambda Delta. Democrat. Presbyterian. Office: 706 Hart Senate Office Bldg Washington DC 20510-0703 Office Phone: 202-224-4041. Business E-Mail: clarine_nardi_riddle@lieberman.senate.gov.

NARE, OTSEBELE E., engineering educator, researcher; s. Koketso Samson Nare and Joyce Thabo Nyathi; m. Sihawusenkosi Tankwa, May 25, 2007; 1 child, Unkarabile Lerato. BS in Elec. Engring., Morgan State U., Balt., 1998, Deng in Elec. Engring., 2005. Rsch. engr. Morgan State U., 2005—07; asst. prof. Hampton U., Va., 2007—. Recipient Dept. Chair award, Sch. Engring., Morgan State U., 1999. Mem.: IEEE, ASEE, Tau Beta Pi. Office: Hampton Univ 168 Marshall Ave Hampton VA 23668 Business E-Mail: otsebele.nare@hamptonu.edu.

NARENDRA, KUMPATI SUBRAHMANYA, electrical engineer, educator; b. Madras, India, Apr. 14, 1933; came to U.S., 1954, naturalized, 1974; s. Subrahmanya and Sarada (Alladi) Kumpati; m. Barbara Lamb, Nov. 3, 1961. BEE with honors, U. Madras, India, 1954; MS, Harvard U., Cambridge, Mass., 1955, PhD, 1959; MA (hon.), Yale U., New Haven, 1968; DSc (hon.), Anna U., Madras, 1995, Nat. U. Ireland, Dublin, 2007. Lectr., postdoctoral asst. Harvard U., Cambridge, Mass., 1959-61, asst. prof., 1961-65; assoc. prof. Yale U., New Haven, 1965-68, prof. elec. engring., 1968—, Harold W. Cheel prof. elec. engring., 2003—, chmn. dept. elec. engring., 1984-87, dir. Neuroengring. and Neurosci. Ctr., 1995-96. Cons. to comml. firms, 1961—; dir. Ctr. for Systems Sci., 1981—; disting. lectr. Tex. A&M Coll., 1997; disting. vis. scientist Jet Propulsion Lab., 1994—95; hon. vis. prof. Anna U., Madras, India, 1993—; mem. adv. bd. Inst. Advanced Engring., Republic of Korea; disting. lectr. U. N.Mex., 1999, U. Va., 2001; plenary spkr. Am. Control Conf., 2000; keynote spkr. Conf. on Intelligent Control, U. Va., 2001, Internat. Conf. of Soc. of Indsl. and Control Engring., Osaka, Japan, 2002; Hamilton lectr. Hamilton Inst., Ireland, 2003. Author: Frequency Domain Criteria for Absolute Stability, 1973, Stable Adaptive Systems, 1989, Learning Automata-An Introduction, 1989; editor: Applications of Adaptive Control, 1980, Adaptive and Learning Systems: Theory and Applications, 1987, Advances in Adaptive Control, 1991; editor issue on learning automata Jour. Cybernetics and Info. Sci., vol. I, 1977. Recipient John R. Ragazzini Edn. award Am. Automatic Control Coun., 1990, Leadership award Neural Network Soc., 1994, Hendrik W. Bode prize/Lectr. award Control Sys. Soc., 1995, Richard E. Bellman Control Heritage award 2003, Walton Visitor award Sci. Found. Ireland, 2007. Fellow AAAS, IEEE (life, Franklin V. Taylor award 1973, George S. Axelby award 1988, Outstanding Paper of neural network coun. 1991, Pioneer award Internat. Computation Soc., 2008), Inst. Elec. Engrs. (U.K.); mem. Conn. Acad. Sci. and Engring., Sigma Xi. Home: 35 Old Mill Rd Woodbridge CT 06525-1523 Office: Yale U Ctr Systems Sci PO Box 2157 New Haven CT 06520-2157 Business E-Mail: kumpati.narendra@yale.edu.

NARENDRANATH, NEELAKANTAM V., microbiologist, researcher; b. Chennai, TamilNadu, India, Aug. 28, 1971; s. Neelakantam V. Varadarajulu and NagamaDevi Cherukuri; m. Srividya Adusumilli, Mar. 1, 2002; 1 child, Vishnu. BS in Agr., Tamil Nadu Agrl. U., Coimbatore, India, 1992, MS in Agrl. Microbiology, 1995; PhD, U. Sask., Saskatoon, Can., 2000. Postdoctoral rschr. Alltech, Inc., Nicholasville, Ky., 2001—02, coord. alcohol rsch., 2002—04, coord. alcohol rsch., grad. student affairs, 2003—04, coord. yeast physiology rsch., grad. student affairs, 2004—05; fermentation rsch. dir. POET Rsch., Inc., Sioux Falls, SD, 2005—. Author: Bacterial Contamination and Control in Ethanol Production; contbr. articles to profl. jours. Scholar, U. Sask., 1995—99; Merit scholar, Tamil Nadu Agrl. U., 1988—92, Jr. Rsch. fellow, 1993—95. Mem.: Soc. Indsl. Microbiology, Am. Soc. Microbiology. Home: 3909 W 84th St Sioux Falls SD 57108

NARINS, RHODA S., dermatologist, educator; d. Lou and Sydelle Scharf; m. David J. Narins, June 30, 1962; children: Jonathan, Valerie Malsch. MD, NY U. Sch. Medicine, NYC, 1965. Pres. Am. Soc. Dermatologic Surgery; clin. prof. dermatology NY U. Sch. Medicine, 1995—. Med. adv. bd. and clin. investigator Medicis, Allergan, Merz, Stiefel, Genzyme, Colbar, Orthoneutrogena, Mentor, Artes, Bioform, Revance. Author text books; contbr. articles to med. jours. Pres. adv. bd. Barnard Coll., Columbia U., NYC. Mem.: WDS, ASMLS, ISDS, ADA, ASDS, AAD. Achievements include first to bring liposuction to the US in 1982 and development of tumescent liposuction with local anesthesia. Office: Dermatology Surgery and Laser Ctr 222 Westchester Ave White Plains NY 10604 Office Fax: 914-682-9006.

NARISETTI, RAJU, editor; b. Hyderabad, India, June 26, 1966; m. Kim Barrington; children: Leila, Zola. BS in Economics & Sociology, Osmania U., Hyderabad, India, 1985; post grad. diploma in Rural Mgmt., Inst. Rural Mgmt., Anand, 1987; post grad. diploma, Times of India Sch. Journalism, 1989; MA in Journalism, Indiana U., Bloomington, 1991. Regional sales mgr. A.P. Dairy Fedn., 1987—88; bus. writer Economic Times, India, 1989—90, Dayton Daily News, Ohio, 1992—94, Wall St. Jour., Pitts., 1994, NYC, 1997, asst. news ed. nat. news desk, 1999, news ed. media, retail, advt. and consumer prod. coverage, 1999—2001, news ed. technology-news coverage, 2000—01, dep. nat. ed., 2002; mng. ed. Wall St. Jour. Europe The Wall St. Jour., Brussels, 2003, ed. Wall St. Jour. Europe, 2005—06; editor Mint, 2007—09; mng. editor The Washington Post., 2009—. Office: The Washington Post 1150 15th St NW Washington DC 20071*

NARITA, HIRO, cinematographer; b. Seoul, Republic of Korea, June 26, 1941; arrived in Japan, 1945, arrived in U.S., 1957; s. Masao and Masako (Kojima) Morikawa; m. Barbara Parker, Sept. 8, 1971. BFA in Design, San Francisco Art Inst., 1964. Lectr. Mill Valley Film Festival, 1984, Hawaii Internat. Film Festival, 1984, San Jose State U., 2006, 07, SF Art Inst., 2008. Dir. photography: (films) Farewell to Manzanar, 1976 (Emmy nomination, 1976); Never Cry Wolf, 1983 (Best Cinematography award Nat. Soc. Film Critics, 1983); Solomon Northrup's Odyssey, 1984; Go Tell It on the Mountain, 1985; Amerika, 1987; Honey, I Shrunk the Kids, 1989; The Rocketeer, 1991; Star Trek VI, 1992; Hocus Pocus, 1993; White Fang II, 1994; James & The Giant Peach, 1995; The Arrival, 1995; Stones & Paper, 1997; Conceiving Ada, 1998; Shadrach, 1998; I'll Be Home for Christmas, 1998; Dirty Pictures, 1999 (Emmy nomination, 2000); Half Past Autumn, 2001 (Emmy nomination, 2001); Technolust, 2002; The Darwin Awards, 2005; The Valley of the Heats' Delight, 2006 (Best Cinematography award Boston Internat. Film Festival); Strange Culture, 2007; La Mission, 2009. With US Army, 1964—66. Mem.: Acad. Motion Picture Arts and Scis., Am. Soc. Cinematographers, Internat. Photographers Guild. Personal E-mail: hnarita@comcast.net.

NARITA, NORIKO, social studies educator; d. Shoji and Misao Ishigami; married, June 22, 1968; children: Masashi, Joe. MA, Bucknell U., Lewisburg, Pa., 1994. Instr. U. Va., Charlottesvill, 1986—90, Bucknell U., 1990—95, Wash. Coll., Chestertown, Md., 1998—. Author: (textbook) Elementary Japanese, Intermediate Japanese. Mem.: Assn. Asian Studies. Office: Washington Coll 300 Washington Ave Chestertown MD 21620

NARRON, JERRY AUSTIN, former professional baseball manager; b. Goldboro, NC, Jan. 15, 1956; 1 child, Connor. Catcher NY Yankees, 1979, Seattle Mariners, 1980—81, 1987, Calif. Angels, 1983—86; mgr. Orioles' sys., 1989—92; mgr. minor league Double-A Hagerstown, 1990—91; mgr. minor league Triple-A Rochester, 1992; 3nd base coach Tex. Rangers, 1994, interim mgr., 2001, mgr., 2001—02, Cin. Reds, 2005—07.

NARULA, CHAITANYA KUMAR, research scientist; b. Etawah, India, Apr. 9, 1955; came to U.S., 1981; s. Suraj Parkash and Kanta Rani (Sudarshana) N. BS, Kanpur U., India, 1973; MS, U. Roorkee, India, 1975; PG diploma, Panjab U., India, 1976; PhD, Rajasthan U., Jaipur, India, 1981. Postdoctoral fellow U. Del., Newark, 1982; Alexander von Humboldt fellow U. Munich, 1983-84; rsch. assoc. U. N.Mex., Albuquerque, 1985-88; sr. rsch. sci. Ford Motor Co., Dearborn, Mich., 1988-92, prin. rsch. sci., 1992-96, staff tech. specialist, 1996—. Vis. sci. MIT, Cambridge, Mass., 1993-94; vis. assoc. Calif. Inst. Tech., Pasadena, summer 1996. Author Ceramic Precursor Technology and Its Applications, 1995; contbr. articles to sci. publs.; patentee in field. Mem. Am. Chem. Soc., Am. Ceramic Soc., Materials Rsch. Soc., Sigma Xi. Avocations: bicycling, tennis. Office: PO Box 2053 Dearborn MI 48123-2087

NARUM, DAVID L., parasitologist; s. Harvey L. Narum and Maxine A. McWilliams; m. Julie L. Eggart; children: Rebekah L., Lydia A. BS, Wash. State U., Pullman; MS, Tulane U., New Orleans; PhD, U. Md., Balt. Assoc. dir. malaria program EntreMed. Inc., Rockville, Md., 2000—02; head, process devel. sect. MVDB, NIAID, NIH, Rockville, Md., 2003—. Contbr. scientific papers. Achievements include patents for development of a malaria vaccine. Office: MVDB NIAID NIH 5640 Fishers Ln Montgomery Village MD 20886 Business E-Mail: dnarum@niaid.nih.gov.

NARUMANCHI, SREEKANT VENKAT JAGANNATH, energy executive; b. Vijayawada, Andhra Pradesh, India, Mar. 22, 1975; s. Rajeswara Rao and Rama Devi Narumanchi; m. Srilakshmi Venkata Naga Jonnalagadda, June 26, 2005. BTech, Indian Inst Tech., Kanpur, 1997; MS, Wash. State U., Pullman, 1999; PhD, Carnegie Mellon U., Pitts., 2003. Tchg. asst. Wash. State U., 1997—99; rsch. asst. Carnegie Mellon U., Pitts., 1999—2003, rsch. assoc., 2003—04; sr. engr. Nat. Renewable Energy Lab., Golden, Colo., 2004—. Contbr. chapters to books. Recipient R & D award, Nat. Renewable Energy Lab., Best Paper award, ASME, 2003—04. Mem.: IEEE, ASME, Soc. Automotive Engrs., Sigma Xi. Personal E-mail: sreekant_narumanchi@yahoo.com.

NASGAARD, ROALD, museum curator; b. Denmark, Oct. 14, 1941; s. Jens Larsen and Petra (Guldbaek) N.; m. Lori J. Walters (June 15, 2007). BA, U. B.C., 1965, MA, 1967; PhD, Inst. Fine Arts, N.Y. U., 1973. Lectr., asst. prof. U. Guelph, 1971-75; curator contemporary art Art Gallery of Ont., Toronto, 1975-78, chief curator, 1978-89, deputy dir., chief curator, 1989-93, sr. curator rsch., 1993; chair dept. art Fla. State U., Tallahassee, 1995—2006, prof. art history, 2006—; co-dir. programming Inst. of Modern and Contemporary Art, Calgary, Alta., Canada. Vis. lectr. U. Guelph, York U.; vis. lectr., adj. prof. U. Toronto; rsch. fellow Nat. Gallery Phila. Libr. and Archives (summer), 2002. Author, curator: Ron Martin: World Paintings, 1976, Structures for Behavior, 1977, Garry Neill Kennedy: Recent Work, 1978, Ten Canadian Artists in the 1970's, 1980, Yves Gaucher: A Fifteen Year Perspective, 1978, The Mystic North: Symbolist Landscape Painting in Northern Europe and North America, 1890-1940, 1984, Gerhard Richter: Paintings, 1988, Individualites: 14 Contemporary Artists from France, 1991, Free Worlds: Metaphors and Realities in Contemporary Hungarian Art, 1991, Concealing/Revealing: Voices from the Canadian Foothills, 1997, Pleasures of Sight and States of Being: Radical Abstract Painting, 2001, Abstract Painting in Canada, 2007; actor:, co-organizer: The European Iceberg: Creativity in Germany and Italy Today, 1985, The Automatistic Revolution:Montreal 1941-1960, 2009. Mem. Toronto Pub. Art Commn., Gershon Iskowitz Found. Can. Council fellow, 1967-68, 70-71 Mem. Coll. Art Assn., Univ. Art Assn. Can. Business E-Mail: rnasgaard@fsu.edu.

NASH, ALICIA LARDÉ, application developer, physicist; b. San Salvador, Jan. 1, 1933; came to U.S., 1944; d. Carlos Roberto and Alicia (Lopez-Harrison) Larde; m. John Forbes Nash, Jr., Feb. 16, 1957; children: John Charles Martin Nash. BS in Physics, MIT, 1955, postgrad., 1959. Physicist Nuclear Devel. Corp. of Am., White Plains, NY, 1956-57, Tech. Ops., Burlington, Mass., 1957-58; rsch. assoc. MIT Computation Ctr., Cambridge, Mass., 1958-59; physicist, aerospace engr. R.C.A. Astro Divsn., Hightstown, NJ, 1960-66; programmer, analyst Mgmt. Data Processing, NYC, 1972-74, Con Edison, NYC, 1974-80, Blue Cross Blue Shield of N.Y., NYC, 1980-82; systems/analyst programmer specialist N.J. Transit, Newark, 1983—. Mem. AAUW, MIT Club of Princeton (past pres., bd. dirs.), Soc. of Women Engring. Achievements include being the subject for the role of Alicia Nash in the movie "A Beautiful Mind". Home: 932 Alexander Rd Princeton Junction NJ 08550-1002 Office: NJ Transit One Penn Plaza East Newark NJ 07105 E-mail: alroad932@hotmail.com.

NASH, ANTHONY J., military analyst; b. Edina, Minn., Apr. 9, 1974; s. James Allen Nash and Maureen G. Mendelsohn; m. Bethany Lynn Clough, Aug. 1, 1998. BS in Liberal Studies cum laude, Excelsior Coll., Albany, NY, 2002; AAS in Comm. Applications Tech., CC of Air Force, Denver, 2006. Prodn. mgr. Northstar Home Improvement, St. Louis Park, Minn., 1995—96; lead intelligence and ops. support Logos Techs., Arlington, Va., 2006—. Varsity football coach Meade HS, Ft. Meade, Md., 2005—07. Sgt. USAF, 1997—2006. Decorated Air Force Good Conduct medal USAF, Air Force Achievement medal, Armed Forces Expeditionary medal, Air Force Expeditionary medal, Global War on Terrorism Svc. medal, Global War on Terrorism Expeditionary medal, Air and Space Campaign medal, Combat Readiness medal, Air Force Commendation medal, Joint Svc. Achievement medal; recipient John Levitow award, 2000. Office: Logos Techs 3811 N Fairfax Dr Ste 100 Arlington VA 22203

NASH, BOB J., political organization worker; b. Texarkana, Ark., 1947; m. Janis F. Kearney, 1994; 2 children. ABA Sociology, U. Ark., 1969; MA Urban Studies, Howard U., 1972. Asst. to dep. mayor, Washington, 1970-71; asst. to city mgr. Fairfax, Va., 1971-72; adminstrv. officer Nat. Tng. and Devel. Svc., Washington, 1972-74; dir. cmty. and regional affairs Ark. Dept. Planning, 1974-75; v.p. Winthrop Rockefeller Found., Little Rock, 1975-83; sr. exec. asst. econ. devel. Office Ark. gov., 1983-89; pres. Ark. Devel. Fin. Authority, Little Rock, 1989-92; under sec. agr. for small cmty. and rural devel. USDA, Washington, 1993-1995; asst. to Pres., dir. presdl. pers. White House, Washington, 1995—2001; vice chmn. ShoreBank Corp., Chgo., 2001—07; deputy campaign mgr. for 2008 presidential race Hillary Clinton, 2007—. Office: Hillary Clinton for Pres 4420 N Fairfax Dr Arlington VA 22203

NASH, DAVID REINTHAL, pediatrician; b. Dec. 25, 1960; MD, U. Cin. Coll. Medicine, 1989. Cert. Am. Bd. Pediat., 2007, Am. Bd. Allergy and Immunology, 2005. Residency Northwestern U. Sch. Medicine, Chgo.; fellowship Duke U. Med. Ctr., Durham, NC; chief and clin. services dir., allergy and immunology sect., asthma ctr. U. Pitts. Sch. Medicine, asst. prof. pediat., divsn. allergy, immunology, and infectious diseases. Contbr. articles to profl. jours. Mem.: Am. Acad. Allergy and Immunology, Am. Bd. Pediat. Office: Divsn Pediatric Allergy and Immunology Children's Hosp Pitts UPMC 3705 Fifth Ave Ste 32 Pittsburgh PA 15213 Office Phone: 412-692-7885. Office Fax: 412-692-8499. Business E-Mail: david.nash@chp.edu.

NASH, DONALD GENE, retired federal investigator, economist; b. Paris, Ill., July 20, 1945; s. Lelan and Mildred (Washburn) N.; m. Jo Ann Bellew, Aug. 29, 1964; children: Stacey Alan, Ryan Christopher, Shaun Christian BS, So. Ill. U., 1967, MS, 1969; postgrad., DePaul U., Chgo., 1970-71. Farm mgr., test farms So. Ill. U., Carbondale, 1968-69; economist Commodity Futures Trading Commn., Chgo., 1969-77; v.p.-ops. Mid. Am. Commodity Exch., Chgo., 1977-86; sr. futures trading investigator Commodity Futures Trading Commn., Chgo., 1986—2008. Pres. Friends of Danada, Wheaton, Ill., 2007—. With N.G. US Army, 1968—74. Recipient Outstanding Mktg. award Wall St. Jour., 1966, award of merit Am. Farm Econ. Assn., 1967, cert. of merit Commodity Exch. Authority, merit award Naperville Art League, 1994, Honorable Mention award Danada Nature Show, 1995, 2002. Methodist. Avocations: photography, woodworking, sketching. Home: 923 Bainbridge Dr Naperville IL 60563-2002

NASH, EDWARD L., advertising executive; b. NYC, Nov. 8, 1936; s. Irving and Mina (Koppel) N.; m. Diana R. Kithcart, June 2, 1968; 1 child, Amelia. BA, CCNY, 1953. Dir. advt. Crowell, Collier, Macmillan, Inc., NYC, 1961-62; v.p. mktg. LaSalle Extension U., Chgo., 1962-64; pres. Capitol Record Club, Inc., Los Angeles, 1964-69; founder, pres. Nash Pub., Los Angeles, 1969-74; exec. v.p. Rapp & Collins, NYC, 1975-82; pres., chief exec. officer BBDO Direct, NYC, 1982-86; owner, pres. Nash Direct Inc., NYC, 1986-91; chmn. Nash, Wakeman & de Forrest, Inc., 1991-92; exec. v.p. Bozell, Jacobs, Kenyon & Eckhardt, NYC, 1992-95; CEO, mng. ptnr. Team Nash, Inc., NYC, 1996—. Lectr. in field; chmn. Direct Mktg. Day, N.Y.C., 1985, Internat. Direct Mktg. Conf., 1996; instr. NYU, 1998—, Va. Commonwealth U., 1998—. Author: Direct Marketing: Strategy/Planning/Execution, 1982, 2d edit., 1986, 3d edit., 1995, 4th edit., 2000; editor: The Direct Marketing Handbook, 1984, 2d edit., 1991, Database Marketing, 1993. Mem. Direct Mktg. Assn. (chmn. mktg. coun. 1980-82), NY Direct Mktg. Club (Silver Apple award 1999). Office: Team Nash Inc 4 Jonathan Dr East Hampton NY 11937-2110 Office Phone: 646-497-0297. Business E-Mail: ednash@teamnash.com.

NASH, ELIZABETH HAMILTON, music and theater educator, vocalist, writer; b. New Rochelle, NY, July 13, 1934; d. Allan Benjamin and Renee N. BFA, Columbia U., 1957, AM, 1971; PhD, Ind. U., 1975. Assoc. instr. Sch. Music, Ind. U., 1971-74; assoc. prof. U. Minn., Theater Arts, Mpls., 1975—. Vis. prof. U. Tex., Austin, 1991-92; Theater Hochschule Hans Otto, Leipzig, 1989, 92; voice prodn. coach, presentation stylist to Christian Sci. Monitor, 1975-90, Herold World Radio, 1975—; lectr., presenter, panelist in field. Leading coloratura soprano Pfalz Theater, Kaiserslautern, 1961—62, Theater am Domhof, Osnabrück, 1962—63, Landes Theater, Detmold, 1963—64, Hessisches Staats Theater, Kassel, 1964—67; singer (guest artist): Mozart's Magic Flute, Amiens, Nancy, Strasbourg, Bruges, Ghent, Luxembourg, Lugano, 1968—70; singer: (soloist) Vt. Philharm. Orch., 1963; soloist Vt. Philharm. Orch., Montpelier, 1965, 1982; leading singer, actress: Children's Theater Co., 1979—80; author: Always First Class, The Career of Geraldine Farrar, 1981, The Luminous Ones, A History of the Gt. Actresses, 1991, Pieces of Rainbow, 1994, The Memoirs of Sylvia Olden Lee, Premier African Am. Classical Vocal Coach, 2001, Autobiographical Reminiscences of African-American Classical Singers, 1853—, Introducing Their Spiritual Heritage into the Concert Repertoire, 2007; contbr. articles to profl. jours., TV and radio interviews, commercials and essay readings. Nat. Honor Soc. grantee, 1952; Fulbright grant, Staatliche Hochschule für Musik und Darstellende Kunst, Stuttgart, Germany, 1959-61; Bush Found. sabbatical grant, Guildhall Sch. Music and Drama, London, 1982-83; Bush Found. fellow, Inst. Arts Adminstrn., Harvard U., 1978. Mem. Nat. Assn. Tchr. of Singing, Voice and Speech Trainers Assn., German Equity. Mem. Christian Scientist. Home: 4504 Oak Dr Edina MN 55424-1531 Office: U Minn Dept Theater Arts and Dance Minneapolis MN 55455 E-mail: nashx001@tc.umn.edu.

NASH, HENRY WARREN, marketing educator; b. Tampa, Fla., Sept. 19, 1927; s. Leslie Dikeman and Mildred (Johnson) N.; m. Frances Lora Venters, Aug. 20, 1950; children: Warren Leslie, Richard Dale. BS in Bus. Adminstrn, U. Fla., 1950, MBA, 1951; postgrad., Ind. U., 1951-53; PhD, U. Ala., 1965. Student asst. U. Fla., 1948-50, grad. asst., 1950-51, Ind. U., 1951-53; salesman Field Enterprises, Inc., Chgo., 1953; assoc. prof. bus. and econs. Miss. Coll., 1953-57; assoc. prof. marketing Miss. State U., 1957-66, prof., head dept., 1966-96; emeritus prof. mktg.; emeritus head dept. mktg., quantitative analysis, bus. law; dir. Coll. Bus. and Industry Acad. Advising Ctr., 1995-2000; ptnr. Southland Cons. Assos., 1968-84; bd. dirs. Govt. Employees Credit Union, 1969-92, v.p., 1969-73, pres., 1973-78; ret., 2000. Author: (with others) Principles of Marketing, 1961 Served with USNR, 1945-46. Loveman's Merchandising fellow U. Ala., 1961-62 Mem. Am. Mktg. Assn., Am. Acad. Advt., Acad. Internat. Bus., So. Econ. Assn., So. Mktg. Assn. (sec. 1974-75, pres. 1976-77), Sales and Mktg. Execs. (internat. chmn. educators com. 1967-70), Miss. Retail Mchts. Assn. (bd. dirs.), Pi Sigma Epsilon (nat. educator, v.p. 1967-69, nat. pres. 1969-71), Kiwanis (treas. Starkville club 1969-70, v.p. 1973-74, pres. 1974-75, lt. gov. 1977-78, gov. 1982-83), Blue Key, Beta Gamma Sigma, Omicron Delta Kappa, Mu Kappa Tau (nat. v.p. 1977-79, 86-88, pres. 1979-81, 88-90), Alpha Kappa Psi, Phi Kappa Phi (v.p. Miss. State U. 1990-91, pres. 1991-92). Baptist (tchr., deacon). Home: 2800 W Main St Cottage 302B Tupelo MS 38801-3027

NASH, HORACE LYONS, lawyer; b. San Jose, Calif., Dec. 19, 1955; BA with honors, U. Chgo., 1975; PhD, Stanford U., 1982; JD cum laude, Harvard U., 1985. Bar: Calif. 1985. Ptnr. Fenwick & West LLP, Mountain View, Calif., chair securities group. Named a Dealmaker of the Yr., Am. Lawyer mag., 2006. Mem.: State Bar Calif. Office: Fenwick & West LLP Silcon Valley Ctr 801 California St Mountain View CA 94041 Office Phone: 650-988-8500, 650-335-7934. Office Fax: 650-938-5200. E-mail: hnash@fenwick.com.

NASH, JAMES LEE, poet, security official; b. Lynchburg, Va., Oct. 1, 1957; s. James Belvy and Marjorie Lea Glden (Campbell) N. Grad., Brookville H.S., Lynchburg, 1977. VIP info. aide de camp Greater Ft. Lauderdale Broward County Conv. Ctr. Author: (poetry) Casus Belli, 1993, Enduring Significance, 1996; contbg. author: T.P.O.A., 1994, Treasure the Moment, 1996, A Shadow in the Light, 1999, Love and Other Observations, 1999, Melodies and Madness, 1999, Explanations, 2000, Other Planets are Places Too, 2000, The Erotic Adventures of a White Trash Southern Boy, 2002, Faces and Places on Capitol Hill, 2004, I Try Not to Cuss, 2006. Mem. at large Dem. Exec. Com., Broward County, Fla., 1997-2000; mem. Croissant Park Civic Assn., Ft. Lauderdale, Fla., 1997-2000. Mem. Titanic Hist. Soc., Soc. Am. Magicians. Home: 1114 F St NE #402 Washington DC 20002 Office: Zack's Taverna: The Greek Islands 305 Pennsylvania Ave SE Washington DC 20003 E-mail: chg4600@aol.com.

NASH, JESSIE MADELEINE, journalist, science writer; b. Elizabeth City, NC, Sept. 11, 1943; d. John V. and Jessie B.; m. E. Thomas Nash, June 9, 1970. AB in History magna cum laude, Bryn Mawr Coll., 1965. Clip girl to sec. Time Mag., NYC, 1965-66, reporter rschr., 1966-70, stringer Bonn, Germany and Chgo., 1970-74, staff corr. Chgo., 1974-87, sr. sci. corr., 1987—. Mem. adv. com. on pub. infor. Am. Inst. of Physics, 1993-95. Author: El Niño: Unlocking the Secrets of the Master Weather-Maker, 2002. Recipient Page One award Newspaper Guild of N.Y., 1981, award Leukemia Soc. Am., 1994, Popular Sci. Writing award, Am. Astronomical Soc., 1997. David Perlman award, 2004. Mem. AAAS (Westinghouse award 1987, 90, Sci. Journalism award 1987, 91, 96,), Nat. Assn. Sci. Writers, Author's Guild, Sigma Xi (hon. mem). Avocation: travel. Office: Time Mag 303 E Ohio St Chicago IL 60611-3373

NASH, JILL, communications executive; BA in Journalism, San Diego State U. Head corp. comm. Transamerica Life Companies; with KPMG; v.p. corp. comm. Charles Schwab Corp.; v.p. employee comm. Gap, Inc., 2003—05, v.p. corp. comm., 2005—07; sr. v.p., chief comm. officer Yahoo! Inc., 2007—09; chief comm. officer, v.p. corp. affairs Levi Strauss & Co., San Francisco, 2009—. Past pres. Orgn. of Women Executives. Recipient multiple Gold Quill awards. Office: Levi Strauss & Co 155 Battery St San Francisco CA 94111*

NASH, JOHN DAVIDSON, JR., economist; b. Houston, Apr. 12, 1953; s. John Davidson and Virginia (Bryant) Nash; m. Sarah Hendrickson, June 26, 1962; children: Scott, Rachel. BS, Tex. A&M U., College Station, 1975; MA, U. Chgo., 1978, PhD, 1982. Asst. prof. econ. Tex. A&M U., College Station, 1980—83; economist Bur. Econ. FTC, Washington, 1982—83; dep. asst. dir. consumer protection FTC, 1983—84, asst. dir. trade regulation rules, 1984—86, advisor to chmn., 1986; from agrl. sector economist agrl. products divsn. to lead economist L.Am. and Caribbean The World Bank, 1986—2007, lead economist sustainable devel. dept. L.Am. and Caribbean, 2007—. Author (with others): Strategic Minerals for Defense Needs, 1979, Colombia: External Sector and Agriculture Policies for Adjustment and Growth, 1985, Best Practices in Trade Policy Reform, 1991, Trade Policy and Exchange Rate Reform in Sub-Saharan Africa, 1997, Trade Policy Reform: Lessons and Implications, 1998, Food and Agricultural Policy in Russia: Progress to Date and The Road Forward, 2002, Agriculture and the WTO: Creating a Trading System for Development, Liberalizing Agricultural Trade: Issues and Options for Sub-Saharan Africa in the WTO, 2003, Agricutura, Comercio y Desarcello: Multilateralism vs Proteccionism, 2005, Reforming Agricultural Trade for Developing Countries, 2 vols., 2007; author: Low Carbon High Growth: Latin American Responses to Climate Change, 2009; contbr. articles to profl. jours. Mem.: So. Econ. Assn., We. Econ. Assn., Am. Econ. Assn., Omicron Delta Epsilon, Phi Kappa Phi, Phi Eta Sigma. Libertarian. Avocations: scuba diving, tennis, running. Home: 3307 Brandy Ct Falls Church VA 22042-3705 Office: The World Bank 18th And H Sts NW Washington DC 20433-0001 E-mail: jnash1@worldbank.org.

NASH, JOHN FORBES, JR., mathematician, researcher; b. Bluefield, W.Va., 1928; BS in Math., MS in Math., Carnegie-Mellon U., Pitts., 1948, ScD (hon.), 1999; PhD, Princeton U., New Brunswick, NJ, 1950; PhD (hon.), U. Athens, Greece, 2000, U. Naples, Italy, 2003, U. Charleston, W.Va., 2003; DSc (hon.), W.Va. U., Morgantown, 2006; PhD in Applied Econ. (hon.), U. Antwerp, Belgium, 2007; DSc (hon.), U. Medicine Dentistry NJ, 2008. Rsch. asst., instr. Princeton (N.J.) U., 1950—51; Moore instr. MIT, 1951—53, asst. prof., 1953—57, assoc. prof., 1957—59; sr. rsch. mathematician Princeton U. Cons. RAND Corp., 1950, 52, 54; vis. mem. Inst. Advanced Study Princeton U., 1956—57, 1961—62, 1963—64; rsch. assoc. math. MIT, 1966—67. Recipient von Neumann Theory prize, Ops. Rsch. Soc. Am., Pres.'s award, Nat. Alliance for the Mentally Ill, 1999, Herbert Simon award, New Eng. Complex Sys. Inst., 2006; co-recipient Nobel Prize in Econ. Scis., 1994, Bus. Week award, Erasmus U., Rotterdam, 1998, Leroy P. Steele prize in math., 1999; Sloan fellow, NSF fellow, Westinghouse scholar. Fellow: Am. Acad. Arts and Scis., Econometric Soc.; mem.: NAS. Office: Princeton U Fine Hall Math Dept Princeton NJ 08544-0001*

NASH, JUDITH KLUCK, mathematics professor; b. Manchester, Conn., Dec. 26, 1946; d. Erwin John and Eleanor May (Starke) Kluck; m. Stephen T. Nash, Apr. 7, 1990. BS, So. Conn. State U., 1969, MS, 1976. Math. tchr. Cheshire (Conn.) Pub. Schs., 1969-93; instr. math. Tunxis CC, Farmington, Conn., 1994—. Home: 72 Tunxis Path Plantsville CT 06479-1348 Office: Tunxis CC 271 Scott Swamp Rd Farmington CT 06032-3324

NASH, KATHLEEN, nursing educator; d. James William and Carmela Galvin; m. Bert Nash, Aug. 3, 1989; children: David, Elissa. AAS, County Coll. Morris, Randolf, NJ, 1982; BSN, Georgetown U., Washington, 1984; MSN, U. Tex. Med. Br., Galveston, 1991, PhD, 2003. Nurse practitioner, faculty U. Tex. Med. Br., 1989—. Office: Univ Texas Med Br 301 University Blvd Galveston TX 77555-1173 Business E-Mail: kanash@utmb.edu.

NASH, LEONARD KOLLENDER, retired chemistry professor; b. NYC, Oct. 27, 1918; s. Adolph and Carol (Kollender) N.; m. Ava Byer, Mar. 3, 1945; children: Vivian C., David B. BS, Harvard, 1939, MA, 1941, PhD, 1944. Rsch. asst. Harvard U., Cambridge, Mass., 1943-44, instr., 1946-48, asst. prof., 1948-53, assoc. prof., 1953-59, prof. chemistry, 1959-86, chmn. dept., 1971-74; rsch. assoc. Columbia, 1944-45; instr. U. Ill., 1945-46; ret. Staff Manhattan Project, 1944-45 Author: Elements of Chemical Thermodynamics, 1962, The Nature of the Natural Sciences, 1963, Stoichiometry, 1966, Elements of Statistical Thermodynamics, 1968, ChemThermo, 1972. Recipient Mfg. Chemists' award, 1966; James Flack Norris award, 1975 Home: 1443 Beacon St Apt 614 Brookline MA 02446-4712

NASH, LINDA KAY, music educator; b. Fort Worth, Tex., Feb. 23, 1946; d. Charles Edwin and Mary Ella Webb; m. Hollis Westbrook Nash, Aug. 26, 1965; children: Stephen Hollis, Sean Michael. BMusEd magna cum laude, Tex. Christian U., Ft. Worth, 1968, MMusEd, 1974. Cert. elem. tchr. Tex., 1969, vocal music tchr. Tex., 1969, music tchr. K-12 Fla., 1995, early, mid. music tchr. Nat. Bd. of Profl. Tchg. Standards, 2002, Level III Orff Am. Orff Schulwerk Assn., 1999. Grad. tchg. asst. Tex. Christian U., Fort Worth, 1968—69; elem. tchr., grade 5 and music Ft. Worth Ind. Sch. Dist., 1969—71; first grade tchr. Spaulding/Griffin Co. Schs., Griffin, Ga., 1973—74; dir. music Winterfield United Meth. Ch., Longview, Tex., 1974—77; adj. voice instr. East Tex. Bapt. Coll., Marshall, 1975—76; elem. music tchr. Immaculate Conception Cath. Sch., Laurel, Miss., 1977—87, Va. Beach City Pub. Schs., Va., 1991—95, Sch. Dist. of Lee County, Ft. Myers, Fla., 1995—. Bd. dirs. Windamere Sch., Longview, Tex., 1976—77; mem. unified arts coun. Sch. Dist. of Lee County, Ft. Myers, Fla., 2005—, coord. of all county elem. chorus, 2003—05; mem., pre-sch. insvc. tng. cadre Sch. Bd. of Lee County, Ft. Myers, Fla., 2006—. Named Elem. Music Tchr. of the Yr., Sch. Dist. of Lee County, 1998, Subject Area Tchr. of the Yr., 1998; grantee World Music Resources, Found. for Lee County Schs., 2001; scholar Tchg. Assistantship, Tex. Christian U., 1968—69. Mem.: Lee County Network of Nat. Bd. Cert. Tchrs. (bd. mem. 2005—06), S.W.Fla. Orff (pres. 2006—), Am. Orff Schulwerk Assn., NEA, Fla. Elem. Music Edn. Assn., Fla. Music Edn. Assn., Music Educators Nat. Conf. Avocations: swimming, boating, fishing, collecting owl art.

NASH, MELVIN SAMUEL, lawyer; b. Atlanta, Aug. 26, 1949; s. Ralph Samuel and Mary Pauline (Quarles) Nash; m. Cynthia Joanna Hamrick, Aug. 21, 1980 (dec.); m. Kristine Marie Clark, Nov. 22, 1997. AB, Ga. State U., 1974; JD, U. Fla., 1976. Bar: Ga. 1977, US Ct. Claims 1983, US Ct. Internat. Trade 1983, US Tax Ct. 1982, US Ct. Appeals (5th cir.) 1978, US Ct. Appeals (11th cir.) 1981, US Supreme Ct. 1985. Asst. solicitor State Ct., Cobb County, Marietta, Ga., 1977—78; assoc. Milam & Smith, Austell, 1978; ptnr. Milam, Smith & Nash, Austell, 1978—79; sole practice Marietta, 1979—; spl. master Cobb Superior Ct., 1982—; dir. Nash Trucking Co., Inc., Marietta, Security Fidelity Mortgage, Nash Properties. Magistrate Prohac Vice State Ct. Cobb County, Marietta, 1980—82; candidate state rep. Dist. 21, Ga., 1982. With USAF, 1967—71. Mem.: ABA, Atlanta Track (Marathon finisher), State Bar Ga. (fee arbitrator 1982—), Cobb Criminal Def. Bar Assn. (sec., Seminar award 1984), Cobb County Bar Assn. (com. 1983—84), Ga. Assn. Criminal Def. Lawyers, Nat. Assn. Criminal Def. Lawyers, Assn. Trial Lawyers Am., Acad. Fla. Trial Lawyers, Atlanta Lawyers Club, Atlanta Ski Club. Democrat. Presbyn. Office Phone: 770-422-0878. E-mail: melvinsnash@msn.com.

NASH, MIKE, computer software company executive; married; 3 children. B in Computer Sci. with honors, Cornell U. Coll. Engring.; MBA with Distinction, Wharton Sch. Bus., U. Pa. Project leader, software developer Gen. Data Corp.; joined Microsoft Corp., Redmond, Wash., 1991, various positions in Windows mktg., 1991, gen. mgr. bus. Windows product mgmt., corp. v.p. content devel. and delivery group, corp. v.p. security tech. unit, 2002—06, corp. v.p. Windows product mgmt., 2007—. Palmer Scholar, Wharton Sch., U. Pa. Office: Microsoft Corp One Microsoft Way Redmond WA 98052-6399 Office Phone: 425-882-8080.*

NASH, NICHOLAS DAVID, retail executive; b. Mpls., June 11, 1939; s. Edgar Vanderhoef and Nancy (Van Slyke) N. AB, Harvard U., 1962; MEd, Bowling Green State U., 1970; PhD, U. Minn., 1975. Head lower sch. Maumee Valley (Ohio) Country Day Sch., 1965-71; assoc. dir. Univ. Council for Ednl. Adminstrn.; adj. asst. prof. Ohio State U., 1975-78; v.p. programming Minn. Public Radio, St. Paul, 1978-82, Am. Pub. Radio, St. Paul, 1982-85; pres. The Nash Co., 1985—. Bd. dirs. Artspace Projects, Inc. Contbr. articles to profl. jours. Bd. dirs. Nash Found., 1975-04, Humane Soc. Companion Animals, 2002—06. Mem. Univ. Club St. Paul. Episcopalian. Home: 1340 N Birch Lake Blvd Saint Paul MN 55110-6716 Office: 2129 2nd St Saint Paul MN 55110-3457 Business E-Mail: nicholasnash@post.harvard.edu.

NASH, RICK, professional hockey player; b. Brampton, Ont., Can., July 16, 1984; Left wing Columbus Blue Jackets, 2002—, capt., 2008—; left wing HC Davos, Switzerland, 2004—05. Mem. Team Can., IIHF World Championship, Vienna, 2005, Moscow, 07. Recipient All-Rookie Team, 2003, NHL Found. Player Award, 2009; co-recipient Maurice Richard Trophy, 2004; named to NHL YoungStars Game, 2003, NHL All-Star Game, 2004, 2007, 2008, 2009. Achievements include being the first overall draft pick in NHL entry draft, 2002. Avocation: golf. Office: Columbus Blue Jackets Nationwide Arena 200 W Nationwide Blvd, Ste Level Columbus OH 43215*

NASH, RUTH S., foundation administrator; b. Westfield, Mass., May 7, 1916; d. George Whitney and Marguerite (Mueller) Searle; m. Clayton Richmond Nash, Sept. 7, 1940 (dec. 1990); children: Roberta Marie, Marguerite Louise, Gail Winifred; m. Charles Williams, Mar. 13, 2002 (dec. 2004) Student, Simmons Coll., 1935-37; Diploma, Sch. Handicraft and Occupl. Therapy, 1937-39; B in Liberal Studies, Fla. So. Coll., 1996. Leader Girl Scouts, Winthrop, Mass., 1934-40, field dir., exec. dir. Greater Lynn (Mass.), 1940-43; leader, bd. mem. Reading, Mass., 1940-60; field dir., exec. dir. Naumkeag Area Girl Scouts, Salem, Mass., 1949-56, field dir., tng. dir. Greater Lawrence (Mass.), 1958-63; leader Mystick Side Medford, Mass., 1960-63; field dir., pub. rels., tng. dir., camping svcs. dir. Merrimack River Coun., Andover, Mass., 1978, Stroke, 2000; leader Tropic Sr. GS Mex. Svc. US. Author: High Seas to High Stakes, 2002, Tales & Tails From Stagecoach Lodge, 2007, Monah: Adventures By Stagecoach in New Hampshire Mid 1800's, 2006, Scouting Has Changed The World, 2007; editor: Monthly Civic Newspaper Beacon, 1984-99; contbr. articles to profl. jours. Vol. Meals on Wheels, 1991-96, Cmty. Svc., 1978-98; sec., mem. choir, handbell ringer Harbour Heights (Fla.) United Meth. Ch., 1991-2004; mem., founder H.H. Kitchen Band, 1991-2004; trail guide Charotte Harbor Environ. Ctr., Punta Gorda, Fla., 1990-2004; leader disadvantaged girls Girl Scouts USA, 1998-2000, study ptnr. for disadvantaged children, 1998-2000 Decorated Thanks Badge II G.S.U.S.A.; recipient Crystal Heart award, Gulf Coast Coun. Girl Scouts, 1997, 80 Yr. award, Girl Scouts USA, 2006, Grad. Golden Eaglect, 1932. Mem. AAUW (sec. 1998-2003), Learning in Retirement (sec. bd.), Alzheimers Assn. (support leader, bd. dirs. 1992-97, garden club 2004—), Friends Camp Runels Republican. Methodist. Avocations: writing, watercolors, canoeing, golf, camping. Home: 3524 Peace River Dr Harbour Heights FL 33983-3523 also: 99 Stage Coach Rd Alton NH 03809-9719

NASH, STEVE, professional basketball player; b. Feb. 7, 1974; Degree, Santa Clara Coll., 1996. Player Phoenix Suns, 1996, Dallas Mavericks, 1998—2004, Phoenix Suns, 2004—. Named Best NBA Player, ESPY awards, 2005, MVP, NBA, 2005—06, Man of Yr., GQ mag., 2005; named one of 100 Most Influential People, Time Mag., 2006; named to Western Conf. All-Star Team, NBA, 2002, 2003, 2005, 2007, 2008, All-NBA Third Team, 2002, 2003, All-NBA First Team, 2005—07. Office: c/o Phoenix Suns 201 E Jefferson St Phoenix AZ 85004

NASH, STEVEN ALAN, museum director, curator, art historian; b. Wadsworth, Ohio, Apr. 8, 1944; s. Frank W. N. and LaDema (Siffert) N.; m. Carol Ostrowski, June 14, 1969; children: Colin H., Jessica K. BA, Dartmouth Coll., 1966; PhD, Stanford U., 1973. Curator Albright-Knox Art Gallery, Buffalo, 1973-80; dep. dir., chief curator Dallas Mus. Art, 1980-88; assoc. dir., chief curator, European Arts Fine Arts Mus. of San Francisco, 1988; dir. Nasher Sculpture Ctr., Dallas, 2001—07; exec. dir. Palm Springs Desert Mus., Calif., 2007—. Panelist Nat. Endowment for the Arts, Washington, 1986—, Inst. Mus. Svcs., Washington, 1979—; bd. dirs. Oberlin (Ohio) Intermus. Conservation Labs., 1976-80. Author: Catalogue: Albright-Knox Art Gallery, 1976, Ben Nicholson, 1977, Naum Gabo: Constructivism, 1986, Century of Modern Sculpture, 1987. Bd. dirs. Lakehill Prep. Sch., Dallas, 1987-88, Buffalo Archtl. Guidebook, 1979-80. Mus. Profl. fellow Nat. Endowment for Arts, 1980; fellow Mabelle McLeod Lewis Found., 1970-71. Mem. Coll. Art Assn., Am. Assn. Mus., Dartmouth Alumni Club. Office: Palm Springs Desert Mus 101 N Museum Dr Palm Springs CA 92262 Business E-Mail: kcarr@psmuseum.org.

NASH, WILLIAM RHODES, retired psychology professor; b. Cin., Aug. 25, 1943; s. William Roscoe and Edna Harrison Nash; m. Diane Woods Nash, Jan. 16, 1970; children: Mary Stuart Russell, Brinson Nash Lundegard. BA, Ga. Southern Coll., Statesboro, 1965, MEd, 1967; EdD, U. Ga., Athens, 1971. Prof. Tex. A&M U., Coll. Sta., 1972—2008, prof. emeritus, 2008—, dir., inst. for the gifted & talented, 1980—2007; vis. prof. U. Ga., Athens, 1985. Mem. Nat. Assn. Gifted Children, Washington; mem. and adv. bd. mem. Am. Creativity Assn., Phila. Home: 428 E Intendencia St Pensacola FL 32502-6140 Office: Tex A&M Univ Dept Ednl Psychology College Station TX 77843-4225

NASHAT, GUITY, historian, education educator, researcher; b. Bagdad, Iraq, July 28, 1937; arrived in U.S., 1956; d. Muhammad Sadegh Nashat-Mirdamad and Qamar Afshar; m. Gary S. Becker, Oct. 31, 1979; children: Michael, Cryus Claffey stepchildren: Judy, Catherine. BA, Barnard Coll., NYC, 1958; MS journalism, Columbia Univ., NYC, 1959; PhD hist., Univ. Chgo., Chgo., 1974. Vis. asst. prof. Loyola U., Chgo., 1974—75; asst. prof. U. Ill., Chgo., 1975—83, assoc. prof., 1983—2005, prof., 2005—08, prof. emeritus, 2008—. Rsch. fellow Hoover Inst., Stanford Univ., 1995—. Author: The Origins of Modern Reform in Iran 1870-1880, 1982, Middle Eastern History Selected Reading Lists and Course Outlines from American Colleges and Universities, 1988; editor: Women and Revolution in Iran, 1984; co-author: Women in the Middle East and North Africa, 1999; co-editor: The Economics of Life, 1996, Women in Iran From the Rise of Islam to 1800, 2003, Women in Iran from 1800 to the Islamic Republic, 2003. Grantee Ford Found. Grant, Univ. Chgo., 1968—69, Soc. Sci. Rsch. Coun. summer grant, 1978, Soc. Sci. Rsch. Coun. grant, 1976—77; Ford Found. fellowship, Columbia Sch. of Journalism, 1958—59. Mem.: Mont Pelerin Soc., Qajar Studies Assn., Iranian Studies (exec. bd. mem. 1986—89), Middle Eastern Studies Assn.

NASHED, M. ZUHAIR, mathematics professor, editor; b. Aleppo, Syria, May 14, 1936; s. Zaki Nashed and Nabiha Mosalati; m. Ragda Yagan, Dec. 23, 1959; children: Ziad, Zaki, Zane, Nadia. SB in Elec. Engring., MIT, 1957, SM in Elec. Engring., 1958; MS in Math., PhD in Math., U. Mich., 1963. Asst. prof. Ga. Inst. Tech., Atlanta, 1963—65, assoc. prof., 1965—69, prof., 1969—76; prof. math. and elec. engring. U. Del.; prof., chair U. Ctrl. Fla., Orlando, 2002—. Assoc. prof. Am. U. Beirut, Lebanon, 1967—69; vis. prof. U. Mich., U. Wis., European and Middle Eastern univs. Editor: Jour. Numerical Functional Analysis & Optimization, 1979—, Jour. Integral Equations, 1987—; mem. editl. bd.: 15 jours., exec. editor: 2 book series; author: over 120 papers in math. and engring. jours.; editor: 7 books; contbr.: numerous books. Recipient Sigma Xi Rsch. award, Ga. Tech., 1966, 1974, Lester Ford award, Math. Assn. Am., 1969; grantee rsch. and conf. grants, U.S. Army Rsch. Office and USAF Rsch. Mem.: Am. Math. Soc. (chair, VLP program 2000—), Soc. Indsl. & Applied Math. (education com. 2000—). Office: Univ Central Florida 209 MAP Bldg Orlando FL 32816 Business E-Mail: znashed@mail.ucf.edu.

NASIRI, ADEL, retired engineering educator; married. PhD, Ill. Inst. Tech., Chgo., 2004. Elec. engr. Baxter Healthcare Corp., Round Lake; sr. elec. engr. Moshanir Power Engring., Tehran, Iran, 1997—2001, ForHealth Techs., Daytona Beach, Fla., 2004—05; asst. prof. U. Wis., Milw., 2005—. Cons. in field, Milw. Contbr. articles to profl. jours. Rsch. grant, UWM Rsch. Found., 2007, We Energies, 2008—. Mem.: IEEE (chair, Milw. IES, IAS chpt. 2007—08). Achievements include patents for reconstituting a drug vial and medication dose underfill detection system in an automated syringe preparing system; automated use of a vision system to detect foreign matter in reconstituted drugs before transfer to a syringe; patents pending for reliable in vivo power generation system for implanted electronic devices; research in energy storage for renewable energy. Office: Univ Wis Milw 3200 N Cramer St EMS W236 Milwaukee WI 53211 Business E-Mail: nasiri@uwm.edu.

NASKY, H(AROLD) GREGORY, lawyer; b. Titusville, Pa., June 9, 1942; s. Harold G. and Majella Marie (Beck) N.; m. Rosanne Guson, July 22, 1967. AB, St. Bonaventure U., 1964; JD, U. Notre Dame, 1967. Bar: Pa. 1967, Nev. 1972, Hawaii, 2003. Assoc. Eaton & Hill, Warren, Pa., 1967-68, Vargas, Bartlett & Dixon, Reno, 1972-73; ptnr. Vargas & Bartlett, Las Vegas, Nev., 1974-94, mng. ptnr., 1981-91; of counsel Kummer, Kaempfer, Bonner & Renshaw, 1994—2006; prin. Resort Devel. Cons., 1998—2008; ptnr. Goodsill Anderson, Quinn & Stifel, Honolulu, 2006—. Corp. sec. Showboat, Inc. (NYSE-SBO), Las Vegas, 1978-98, bd. dirs., 1983-98, exec. v.p., 1995-98; bd. dirs. U. Notre Dame Law Assn., 1990-2000; mem. adv. bd. U. Nev. Sch. Medicine.; chmn. 1993, bd. dirs. Author: Inter Alia Jour. of State Bar of Nevada, A Glimpse of China, 1986; Nev. contbg. author: Real Property, Probate & Trust Law Jour., Disposition of Rents, 1981. Legal advisor Nev. Dance Theatre, Las Vegas, 1977-94, bd. dirs. 1988-2000; legal com. Nev. Resort Assn., Las Vegas, gaming regulations com. 1990-93; bd. dirs. Boulder Dam coun. Boy Scouts Am., Las Vegas, 1986-93; del. People to People Citizen Ambassador Program, People's Republic China, 1985, New Zealand/Australia, 1987, Hungary, Czechoslovakia and Poland, 1990, Russia and Estonia, 1992. Served to capt. JAGC, U.S. Army, 1968-72, Vietnam. Decorated Bronze Star, 1970. Mem. ABA (bus. sect. task force conflicts interest com. 1993-95), Inter-Pacific Bar Assn., Hawaii State Bar Assn., State Bar Nev. (chmn. fee dispute com. 1983-89, exec. com. mem. Gaming Law Sect. 1985-93), Am. Soc. Corp. Secs., Internat. Assn. Gaming Attys., Notre Dame Club Las Vegas (past pres. 1978-79), U. Nev. Las Vegas Found. (president's assocs. 1993, chmn.). Office: Goodsill Anderson Quinn and Stifel 1099 Alakea St Ste 1800 Honolulu HI 96813 Home: 4340 Pahoa Ave 8A Honolulu HI 96816 Office Phone: 808-547-5600. Business E-Mail: gnasky@goodsill.com.

NASLUND, HOWARD RICHARD, geological science educator; b. Green Hills, Ohio, Nov. 25, 1950; married, 1979; 5 children. BS, U. Ill., 1972; MS, U. Oreg., 1977, PhD, 1980. Leader East Greenland Expeditions, 1985, 1986, 1988, 1989; igneous petrologist Ocean Drilling Program, 1991, 97; asst. prof. Dartmouth Coll., 1979-87; assoc. prof. dept. geol. scis. and environ. studies SUNY, Binghamton, 1987-95, assoc. chmn. geol. scis. and environ. studies, 1987-88, dir. grad. studies geol. scis., 1988-92, prof. dept. geol. scis. and environ. studies, 1995—, chmn. geol. scis. and environ. studies, 1992-95,97-2000. Vis. prof. Departamento de Geologia, U. Chile, 1995-96, vis. prof. Departamento de Ingenieriá en Minas, U. de Santiago, Chile, 2001-02; sponsored programs adv. coun., 1994-97, grad. coun., 1994-97, chair adv. com. on scholarship and rsch., 1994-97, material rsch. inst., 1991—, faculty senate, 1988-90, 96-98, 2005—, chair faculty senate, 2007—; trustee Glenn G. Bartle Meml. Fund, 1988-90, 96-98, 2004-06; exec. com. of faculty Dartmouth Coll., 1982-85, com. on stds., 1981-86. Contbr. articles to profl. jours. J. William Fulbright scholar, 1995-96; rsch. grant USSAC, 1991, 92, 97, 98, 2005, NSF, 1982, 88, 90, 99, 2004, equipment grant NSF, 1990, 91. Mem. Geol. Soc. of Am. (Penrose Rsch. award 1974, 76), Mineralogical Soc. Am., Am. Geophys. Union, Sociedad Geologica de Chile, NY State Geol. Assn. (pres. 1997-98), Internat. Assn. Volcanology Chemistry Earth Interior. Office: Geol Scis SUNY Binghamton NY 13902-6000 Home Phone: 607-786-0430; Office Phone: 607-777-4313. Business E-Mail: Naslund@Binghamton.edu.

NASLUND, MARKUS, retired professional hockey player; b. Ornskoldsvik, Sweden, July 30, 1973; m. Lotta Naslund; children: Rebecca, Isabella, Alex. Left wing Pitts. Penguins, 1993—96, Vancouver Canucks, 1996—2008, capt., 2000—08; left wing NY Rangers, 2008—09; ret., 2009. Player NHL All-Star Game, 1999, 2001—04; mem. Team Sweden, Olympic Games, Salt Lake City, 2002. Recipient Lester B. Person Award, NHL, 2003; named one of First All-Star Team, 2002—04. Avocations: tennis, boating, water sports.

NASMYTH, KIM, science association director; b. London, 1952; PhD in Zoology, U. Edinburgh, 1977. Postdoctoral rsch., Seattle, 1978—80; Robertson rsch. fellow at Cold Spring, molecular biology Cambridge U., 1982—87; sr. scientist Rsch. Inst. Molecular Pathology, Vienna, 1988—97, dir., 1997—2006; Whitley Chair, Biochemistry, Dept. Biochemistry, head, dept. biochemistry U. Oxford, 2006—. Invited lectr. in field. Recipient FEBS Silver medal, 1995, Max Perutz prize, Unilever Sci. prize, 1996, Louis Jeantet prize for medicine, 1997, Austrian Wittgenstein prize, 1999, Boveri award for Molecular Cancer Genetics, 2003, Gairdner Found. Internat. award, 2007. Fellow: Royal Soc. (Croonian lecture/medal 2002); mem.: European Molecular Biology Orgn., Am. Acad. Arts and Scis. (fgn.) (hon.), Austrian Acad. Scis. Achievements include being the co-discover of cohesin, a protein complex crucial for faithful chromosome segregation during cell division. Office: Dept Biochemistry U Oxford South Parks Road Oxford OX1 3QU England

NASON, DAVID GEORGE, financial consulting firm executive, former federal agency administrator; b. 1970; m. Nicole R. Nason; children: Alexandra, Abigail. BS in Fin., Am. U., 1992; JD, Washington Coll. Law, 1995. Law clk. to Hon. Marvin J. Garbis US Dist. Ct. Md., 1995—96; assoc. Covington & Burling LLP, Washington, 1996—2002; counsel to commr. Paul Atkins US Securities & Exchange Commn. (SEC), 2002—05; under sec. for domestic fin. US Dept. Treasury, 2005—07; asst. sec. for fin. institutions US Dept Treasury, 2007—09; mng. dir. Promontory Financial Group, LLC, Washington, 2009—. Bd. dirs. Nat. Consumer Cooperative Bank, 2007—. Office: Promontory Financial Group LLC 1201 Pennsylvania Ave NW Ste 617 Washington DC 20004 Office Phone: 202-384-1200. Office Fax: 202-783-2924.*

NASON, DOLORES IRENE, computer company executive, social services administrator, minister; b. Seattle; d. William Joseph and Ruby Irene Lockinger; m. George Malcolm Nason, Jr.; children: George Malcolm III, Scott James, Lance William, Natalie Joan. Student, Long Beach City Coll., Calif.; cert. in Religious Edn. for elem tchrs., Immaculate Heart Coll., cert. teaching, cert. secondary teaching; attended, Salesian Sem. Buyer J. C. Penney Co., Barstow, Calif.; prin. St. Cyprian Confraternity of Christian Doctrine Elem. Sch., Long Beach; prin. summer sch. St. Cyprian Confraternity of Christian Doctrine Elem. Sch., Long Beach; pres. St. Cyprian Confraternity Orgn., Long Beach; dist. co-chmn. L.A. Diocese; v.p. Nason & Assocs., Inc., Long Beach, 1978—; pres. L.A. County Commn. on Obscenity & Pornography, 1984—; eucharistic minister St. Cyprian Ch., Long Beach, 1985—; bd. dirs. L.A. County Children's Svcs., 1988—; exec. dir. social svcs. Disabled Resources Ctr., Inc., Long Beach, 1992—. Scholarship com. Long Beach City Coll., 1984—90, Calif. State U., Long Beach, 1984—90; chmn. bd. dirs. LA County Access Para Transit Svcs. Inc., 2004—; chairman Long Beach Transit Paratransit Coms., 2007—. Mem. Nat. Com. Am. Disabilities Act; active Long Beach Civic Light Opera, 1973—96, Assistance League Long Beach, 1976—; vol. Meml. Children's Hosp., Long Beach, 1977—92; founding mem. Theater West Footlighters; pres. St. Cyprian's Parish Coun., 1962—; adv. com. mem. Long beach City Coll. DSPS, 2007—. Mem.: KC (Family of Month award 1988). Roman Catholic. Avocations: physical fitness, theater, choir, travel.

NASON, NICOLE R., National Highway Traffic Safety Administrator, United States Department of Transportation; b. LI, NY, Aug. 12, 1970; m. David G. Nason; children: Alexandra, Abigail. Grad., Am. U., Washington, 1992; JD, Case Western Res. U., Cleve., 1995. Counsel to Rep. Henry Hyde House Judiciary Subcom. on Crime, Washington, 1995—99; govt. affairs counsel Met. Life Ins. Co., 1999—2000; comm. dir., counsel to US Rep. Porter J. Goss House Intelligence Com., 2000—02; asst. commr. Office of Congl. Affairs, U.S. Customs Svc., Washington, 2002—03; asst. sec. for govtl. affairs US Dept. Transp., Washington, 2003—06, adminstr., Nat. Hwy. Traffic Safety Adminstrn., 2006—. Office: Nat Hwy Traffic Safety Adminstrn US Dept Transp 400 7th St Washington DC 20590

NASR, SAMYA Z., pediatric pulmonologist; b. June 15, 1952; MB BCh, Ain Shams U., Cairo, 1977; postgrad., Cin. Med. Ctr., 1979. Diplomate Am. Bd. Pediats. Intern Aim Shams U. Hosps., Cairo, 1977-78; rotating tng. in pvt. pediats. Ob/Gyn and Allergy Offices, Midland, Mich., 1983-84; clk. in pediats. and psychiatry Mich. State U., Lansing, 1984-85; intern in pediats. Children's Hosp. Mich., Detroit, 1985-86, resident in pediats., 1986-88, fellow in pediat. pulmonary medicine, 1988-89, U. Mich., Ann Arbor, 1989-91, lectr. in pediat. divsn. pulmonary medicine, 1991-93, asst. prof. pediats., 1993—, dir. Cystic Fibrosis Ctr., 1993—, dir. pediat. pulmonology fellowship tng. program, 1994—, interim dir. pediat. pulmonology, 1999—. Mem. staff U. Mich. Med. Ctr., 1991—; cons. mem. staff Genesys Regional Med. Ctr., Grand Blanc, Mich., 1996, St. Luke's Hosp., Saginaw, Mich., 1997; reviewer jour. Adolescent Health, Jour. Human Molecular Genetics, Human Mutation, Chest; organizer Cystic Fibrosis Speakers Bur., Genentech, Inc., 1997—, PathoGenesis, Inc., 1999—; mem. cystic fibrosis leadership adv. panel Solvay Pharm., 1998—; cons., spkr., presenter in field; organizer ednl. spkrs.' program ICE Coun. Editor: CFC Reporter, 1989—; contbr. numerous articles to sci. jours. Participant Grest Strides, A Walk to Cure Cystic Fibrosis, 1988—; physician vol. 10K Asthma Run, Am. Lung Assn., 1989-98. Grantee U. Mich., 1989-90, Genentech, Inc., 1992—, Cystic Fibrosis Found., 1992—, Glaxo, Inc., 1993-94, PathoGenesis Co., 1995—, Gen. Clin. Rsch. Ctr., U. Mich., 1994— U. N.C.-Chapel Hill, 1994-98. Mem. AMA, AAAS, Am. Acad. Pediats., Am. Thoracic Soc., Mich. Assn. Apnea Profls., Cystic Fibrosis Genetic Analysis Consortium, Ain Shams Med. Sch. Alumni. Address: 973 Mcdonald Dr Northville MI 48167-1072

NASR, VALI REZA, international politics professor; b. Tehran, Iran, 1960; s. Seyyed Hossein Nasr; m. Darya Nasr; children: Amir, Hossein, Donia. BA, Tufts U., Medford, Mass.; MA, Tufts U. Fletcher Sch. Law & Diplomacy; PhD in Polit. Sci., MIT, 1991. Vis. asst. prof. Tufts U., 1991—92; asst. prof. U. San Diego, 1992—96, assoc. prof., 1996—2002; prof., chair rsch. Dept. Nat. Security Affairs, Naval Postgrad. Sch., Monterey, Calif., 2003—07; prof. internat. politics Tufts U. Fletcher Sch. Law & Diplomacy, 2007—. Faculty assoc. Harvard U., 1991—93; assoc. UCLA Gustav E. von Grunebaum Ctr. Near East Studies, 1994—2004; vis. assoc. prof. U. Calif., San Diego, 1998—2001; mem. adv. com. Tufts U. Faris Ctr. Eastern Mediterranean Studies, 2001—; bd. trustees Found. Iranian Studies, 2003—; dir. Islamic Ednl. Reform in South Asia Project, Nat. Bur. Asian Rsch., 2005—07; vis. prof. Stanford U., 2006; sr. fellow The Dubai Initiative, Harvard U. John F. Kennedy Sch. Govt., 2006; co-dir. Iran Policy Forum, US Inst. Peace, 2006—07; mem. academic coun. Georgetown U. Prince Alwaleed Bin Talal Ctr. Muslim-Christian Understanding, 2006—; sr. fellow Harvard U. Belfer Ctr., 2006—; adv. US-Iran rels. Exec. Office of Pres., 2009—. Author: Mawdudi and the Making of Islamic Revivalism, 1996, The Islamic Leviathan: Islam and the Making of State Power, 2001, The Shia Revival: How Conflicts Within Islam will Shape the Future, 2006; co-author: Democracy in Iran: History and the Quest for Liberty, 2006; editor: Oxford Dictionary of Islam, 2003; co-editor: Expectation of the Millennium: Shi'ism in History, 1989; contbr. articles to profl. jours. Grantee Harry Frank Guggenheim Found., 1996, John D. and Catherine T. MacArthur Found., 2000; scholar, Carnegie Corp. NY, 2006. Mem.: Coun. Fgn. Rels. (life; adj. sr. fellow 2006—07). Office: Tufts U The Fletcher Sch 160 Packard Ave Medford MA 02155 Office Phone: 617-339-9192. Business E-Mail: vali.nasr@tufts.edu.*

NASRALLAH, HENRY ATA, psychiatry researcher, educator; b. Apr. 30, 1947; came to U.S., 1972; s. Ata George and Rose G. (Yameen) N.; m. Amelia C. Tebsherani, June 9, 1972; children: Ramzy George, Rima Alice. BS in Biology, Am. U. of Beirut, 1967; MD, Am. U. Coll Medicine, Beirut-Lebanon, 1971. Intern Am. U. Med. Ctr., Beirut, 1972; resident in psychiatry U. Rochester, N.Y., 1972-75; rsch. assoc. NIMH, Washington, 1975-77; asst. prof. psychiatry U. Calif., San Diego, 1977-79; from assoc. prof. to prof. psychiatry U. Iowa, Iowa City, 1979-85; prof., chair psychiatry Ohio State U., Columbus, 1985-98; prof. psychiatry U. Miss. Med. Ctr., Jackson, 1998—2002; assoc. dean U. Cin. Coll. Medicine, 2003—. Staff psychiatrist VA Med. Ctr., La Jolla, Calif., 1977—79, chief psychiatry svc., Iowa City, 1979—85. Editor: (5 vol. book series) Handbook of Schizophrenia, 1986-90; co-editor: NMR Spectroscopy in Psychiatric Brain Disorders, 1995; editor-in-chief Schizophrenia Rsch., 1987—, Jour. Psychiatry Disorders, 1996—; author and co-author over 200 published articles, 1976—. Pres. Psychiat. Rsch. Found. of Columbus, 1985—; mem. Alliance for the Mentally Ill, Columbus, 1987—. Recipient VA grants, 1979-84, NIMH, 1983—. Fellow Am. Psychiat. Assn. (coun. on rsch.), Am. Coll. Neuropsychopharmacology (chmn. pubs. com. 1992-95), Am. Coll. Psychiatrists (Deans Award com. 1996—), Am. Acad. Clin. Psychiatrists (pres. 1989-90), Soc. Biol. Psychiatry (awards com. 1988-90). Avocations: photography, tennis, poetry. Office: U Cin Med Ctr Dept Psychiatry 231 Albert Sabin Way Cincinnati OH 45267-0559

NASRAOUI, OLFA, computer scientist, educator, electrical engineer; b. Tunis, Tunisia, July 6, 1968; d. Ezzeddine Zidane Nasraoui and Fatma Braiek; m. Hichem Frigui, Apr. 3, 1993; children: Yasmine Frigui, Sara Frigui. BS in Computer Engring. with honors, U. Mo., Columbia, 1990, BSEE with honors, 1990, MSEE, 1992, PhD in Computer Engring. and Computer Sci., 1999. Asst. prof. dept. elec. and computer engring. U. Memphis, 2000—04; endowed chmn. e-commerce dept. computer sci. and computer engring. U. Louisville, 2004—, founder, dir. Knowledge Discovery and Web Mining Rsch. Lab., 2004—. Panel organizer internat. confs., outreach/sci. fair activities; reviewer rsch. proposals NASA; mem. program com., organizing com. various internat. confs.; reviewer internat. jours. in field. Editor conf. procs. Faculty advisor local chpt. Soc. Women Engrs., Memphis, 2000—04. Recipient Best Paper award for Theoretical Developments in Computational Intelligence, Procs. Artificial Neural Networks in Engring., 2001, Career award, NSF, 2002; grantee, 2002—, So. Consortium for Elec. Engring. Edn., 2002—03, NASA, 2004—, Innovative Productivity Inc., 2006. Mem.: IEEE, IEEE Women in Engring., Internal Adv. Bd. Logistics and Distbn. Inst., MentorNet, Assn. Computing Machinery. Office: U Louisville Sch Engring CECS Dept Speed Louisville KY 40292

NASS, CONNIE KAY, state auditor; m. Alan Nass; 3 children. V.p. Nass & Son, Inc., 1974—; auditor State of Ind., 1999—. Bd. Senator Richard Lugar's Excellence in Pub. Svc. Program. Bd. mem. Huntingburg Utility Bd., 1975—; city coun. mem., Huntingburg, 1979-88, mayor, 1988-96; mgr. municipally owned utility cos., Huntingburg, 1988-96; candidate for lt. gov. State of Ind., 1995-96; mem. GOP Platform Com., 1992; del. Rep. Nat. Conv., 1996; bd. dirs. Welborn Found. Evansville, S.W. Ind. Regional Health Care Ctr., Inc.; adv. bd. AAA, Evansville, 1990—; mem. fin. com. and emergency svcs. com. ARC Greater Indpls., 1999—; nat. gen. synod del. Ind.-Ky. Conf. United Ch. of Christ, 1981, com. on planning and evaluation, 1990—, bd. dirs., 1996—; Sunday sch. tchr., music dir. Salem United Ch. of Christ. Recipient Protect Our Woods Environtl. award, 1995; named Outstanding Rep. Woman Ind. Reps Mayor's Assn., 1995. Mem. Nat. Automated Clearing House Assn. (internet coun., electronic benefits coun., strategic expansion bd.), Nat. Assn. State Auditors, Comptrs. and Treas., Network Women in Bus., Women Execs. in State Govt., Ind. State Auditor Adv. Coun., Ind. Farm Bur., Ind. Assn. of Cities and Towns (bd. dirs.), Dubois County GOP Women's Club (pres. 1996-98), Marion County GOP Women's Club, Huntingburg C. of C. Republican. Office: State House Rm 240 200 W Washington St Indianapolis IN 46204-2728

NASS, MARTIN LEO, psychology professor, psychologist; s. Nathan and Esther Nass; m. Marilyn Lipkin, Oct. 29, 1950; children: Eric Walter, Marjorie Ann. BA, LIU, 1948; MA, NYU, NYC, 1949, PhD in Clin. Psychology, 1954. Lic. psychologist NY State Dept. Edn., 1959, cert. in psychoanalysis and psychotherapy NYU, 1965. From asst. prof. to prof. CUNY, NYC, 1955—71; rschr. Nat. Inst. Mental Health, 1962—63; clin. prof. psychology NYU, 1966—; post doctoral program in psychology & psychoanalysis. Contbr. chapters to books, articles to profl. jours. Trustee Composers Conf., Wellesley, Mass., 1993—. With USN, 1944—46. Mem.: APA, NY Freudian Soc., Am. Psychoanalytic Assn., Psychoanalytic Soc. (pres. 1968—72). Avocation: violin. Office: Martin L Nass PhD 19 W 9th St New York NY 10011 Home Fax: 212-533-9440.

NASS, SHARYL JEANNE, medical educator; d. Wiliam Nass and Jeanne Goeglein; m. Eric John Costello, May 13, 2000; children: Elisa Costello, Kenna Costello, Mia Costello. BS, U. Wis.-Madison, 1989, MS, 1991; PhD, Georgetown U., Washington, 1996. Health sci. policy study dir. Nat. Acads. Inst. Medicine, Washington. Guest lectr. U. Md. Sch. Nursing, Balt., 2001—. Contbr. scientific papers. Recipient Cecil award, 2007; Fullbright fellow, 1992, Heinrich-Hertz-Stiftung fellowship, 1992—93. Mem.: AAAS, Am. Assn. Cancer Rsch. Office: Nat Acads Inst Medicine 500 5th St NW Washington DC 20001

NASS, THOMAS P., religious studies educator; s. Paul W. and Lorraine Nass; m. Janice A. Dale, Aug. 9, 1980; children: Allison R., Timothy E., Nathan C., David C. MDiv, Wis. Luth. Sem., Mequon, 1982; MA, U. Wis., Madison, 1999. Registered ordained clergy Wis. Evang. Luth. Synod, 1982. Pastor St. Paul's Luth. Ch., North Mankato, 1984—92, St. Lucas Luth. Ch., Milw., 1992—94; instr. Northwestern Coll., Watertown, 1982—84, prof., 1994—95, Martin Luther Coll., New Ulm, 1995—. Sec. WELS Commn. Inter-Church Rels., 1993—2003, chmn., 2007—; sec. Confessional Evang. Luth. Conf., 2008—. Author: (hebrew textbook) Biblical Hebrew for Beginners, Let's Study Hebrew. Mem.: Nat. Assn. Prof. Hebrew, Soc. Bibl. Lit. Evangelical.

NASSAR, RAJA, statistics educator, researcher, consultant; b. Lebanon, 1936; came to U.S., 1958; naturalized, 1971; m. Ita G. Schaeffer, 1965; 1 child, Mark. BS, Am. U., Beirut, Lebanon, 1958; MS, U. Idaho, 1960; PhD, U. Calif., Davis, 1963. Rsch. fellow U. Idaho, Moscow, 1958—60; rsch. asst. U. Calif., Davis, 1960—63, rsch. assoc., 1963—64; mem. vis. faculty U. Minn., St. Paul, 1964—66; asst. prof. Kans. State U., Manhattan, 1966—68, assoc. prof., 1968—74, prof. stats., 1974—; prof. emeritus La. Tech. U., 2007—. Maxfield prof. math. and stats. La. Tech. U., 1995-2007; vis. prof. Govt. Research Inst., Hamburg, Germany, 1969-70, Nat. Research Inst., Toulouse, France,

1974-75, U. Kiel, Germany, 1982-83, U. Giessen, Germany, 1992-93 Contbr. numerous articles to sci. jours.; editor sci. jours. Alexander von Humboldt fellow, 1969, 82, French Govt. fellow, 1974; rsch. grantee. Greek Orthodox. Avocations: tennis, travel, piano, reading. Office: La Tech U Math and Stats 305 Wisteria St Ruston LA 71270-4235 Business E-Mail: nassar@coes.latech.edu.

NASSAU, MICHAEL JAY, lawyer; b. NYC, June 3, 1935; s. Benjamin and Belle (Nassau) N.; m. Roberta Bluma Herzlich, June 26, 1971; children: Stephanie Ellen, William Michael. BA summa cum laude, Yale U., 1956, LLB cum laude, 1960. Bar: NY 1960, US Ct. Appeals (2d cir.) 1963, US Tax Ct. 1963, US Supreme Ct. 1965, US Dist. Ct. (so. dist.) NY 1978. Asst. instr. in constl. law Yale U., 1959-60; law clk. judge US Ct. Appeals 2d Cir., 1960-61; assoc. tax dept. Paul, Weiss, Rifkind, Wharton & Garrison, NYC, 1961-73; fomer ptnr, counsel Kramer Levin Naftails & Frankel LLP, NYC, 1974—2009; mem. adv. bd. Jour. Retirement Planning, 2009—. Mem. adv. bd. Matthew Bender Fed. Pension Law Service, 1975-76; mem. adv. com. NYU Ann. Inst. Employee Plans Exec. Compensation, 1976-79; mem. steering com. Am. Pension Conf., 1981-83; lectr. field; chair PLI Seminars, Deferred Compensation after Treasury Guidance, 2005, 2007; panelist various seminars employee benefits; mem. NE Region Pension Liaison Group IRS, EPTA Pension Liaison Group Nat. Office. Mem. editl. bd. Bank Corp. Governance Law Reporter, 1989—; contbr. chpts. to books and articles to profl. jours. Recipient Excellence in Benefits award lifetime achievement benefits svc., Worldwide Employee Benefits Network, 2003. Charter fellow Am. Coll. Employee Benefits Counsel; mem. ABA (sect. taxation, employee benefits com. 1993—), NY State Bar Assn. (co-chmn. employee benefits sect. taxation 1976-78, mem. exec. com. sect. taxation 1976-79), Assn. Bar City NY (chmn. subcom. pension legis. of com. taxation 1975-76, employee benefits com. 1987-92), WEB (NY chpt. bd. dirs. 1990—, pres. 1993-94), Phi Beta Kappa. Office: Kramer Levin Naftalis & Frankel LLP 1177 Sixth Ave New York NY 10036 Office Phone: 212-715-9416. Business E-Mail: mnassau@kramerlevin.com.

NASSER, JACQUES, private equity firm executive, former automotive company executive; b. Beirut, Dec. 12, 1947; Degree in Bus. studies, Royal Melbourne Inst. Tech., Doctorate in Tech. (hon.). With Ford of Australia, 1968-73; mem. fin. staff N. Am. truck ops. Ford Motor Co., 1973, mgr. profit analysis, product programming, 1973-75, with Asia-Pacific and Latin-Am. ops., 1970—80, dir., v.p. fin. and adminstrn., Autolatina joint venture, 1987-90, chmn. Ford Europe, 1993—99, exec. v.p., pres. Ford automotive ops., 1996—99, v.p., 1993-96, pres., CEO, 1999—2001, Ford of Australia, 1990-93; sr. ptnr. One Equity Partners LLC (OEP), NYC, 2002—; non-exec. chmn. Polaroid Corp., Waltham, Mass., 2002—. Bd. dirs. Ford Motor Co., 1999—2001, British Sky Broadcasting PLC, 2002—, BHP Billiton Ltd., 2006—; mem. internat. advisory bd. Allianz AG. Recipient Centenary medal, Order of the Cedar, Lebanese Govt., Ellis I. Medal of Honor. Office: One Equity Partners LLC 320 Park Ave 18th Fl New York NY 10022*

NASSER, JENNIFER ANN, nutritionist, researcher, healthcare educator; d. Joseph J. Nasser and Eleanor M. Gilmartin. BA, Elmira Coll., NYC, 1974; MS, Lehigh U., Bethlehem, Pa., 1978; PhD, Rutgers U., New Brunswick, NJ, 1998. Registered dietitian Commn. Dietetics Registration, 2004, clin. chemistry techonologist Nat. Registry Clin. Chemists, 1981, cert. dietitian-nutritionist N.Y. State Dept Edn., 2003. Rsch. scientist, Bridgewater, NJ, 1979—91; rsch. assoc. N.Y. Obesity Rsch. Ctr., NYC, 1998—. Reviewer Appetite, Obesity Rsch. Jour. Am. Dietetic Assn., 2000—; adj. asst. prof. nutrition Hunter Coll., NYC, 2002—; cons. CURA Hospitality, Allentown, Pa., 2004—. Contbr. articles to profl. jours. Bd. mem. Am. Singers Opera Project, NYC, 1998—2000. Grantee, Van Slyke Rsch. Soc., 1991, NIH, 2000—, Internat. Life Scis. Inst., 2004—; fellow, NIH, 1999—2002. Mem.: NAASO, The Obesity Soc., Am. Soc. Clin. Nutrition, Am. Dietetics Assn. Achievements include patents for immunopharmaceuticals. Avocation: professional musician. Office: St Lukes Roosevelt Hosp Ctr WH1020 NY Obesity Rsch Ctr 1111 Amsterdam Ave New York NY 10025 Office Fax: 212-523-4830. Business E-Mail: jnasser@chpnet.org.

NASSER, JOSEPH YOUSEF, public safety administrator, consultant; b. Welch, W.Va., Mar. 19, 1943; s. Joseph H. and Betty Anne (Caldwell) N.; m: Janis Halligan Nasser; children: Robert, Eric, Melanie, Matthew, Michelle. BS, Pacific Western U., 1989, PhD, 1991. Patrolman, firefighter, emergency med. technician Mich. Dept. Pub. Safety, Oak Park, 1962-75; patrolman Daytona Beach (Fla.) Police Dept., 1975-76; lt., capt., dir. Volusia County (Fla.) Sheriff's Dept., 1976-90; pres., founder, owner Ctr. for Pub. Safety Studies, Ormond Beach, Fla., 1990—97; sr. v.p. RCC Cons., Inc, 1997—. Pres. Associated Pub. Safety Comm. Officer, Inc., 1987-88, Land Mobile Comm. Coun., Washington, 1988-89; chmn. Nat. Pub. Safety Planning Com./F.C.C., 1987-88; life mem. APCO, Inc. Past chmn. Fla. State Standards and Telecommunicator Cert. Com., Fla. State Emergency Mgmt. 9-1-1 Com.; past mem. exec. coun. Volusia County Emergency Med. Found.; past chmn. Volusia County Emergency Med. Svcs. Trust Fund Adv. Bd. Recipient Dayton Beach Cooper-Taylor Pub. Safety Achievement award, 1985, Nat. Achievement award Pub. Safety Comm. Coun., 1987, FCC Recognition award, 1987, APCO Life Mem. award, 1988, Emergency Mgmt. Recognition award State of Fla., 1989, Appreciation award Emergency Med. Found., 1990, Disting. Svc. award Volusia County Sheriff's Dept., 1990. Fellow Radio Club of Am.; mem. Associated Pub. Safety Comms. Ofcls. Internat. (life, Outstanding Achievement in Pub. Safety, 2001), Internat. Mcpl. Signal Assn. (sustaining, Journalistic Excellence award 1991). Republican. Methodist. Avocations: fishing, boating. Home: 4507 Rangewood Dr Tallahassee FL 32309-8965 Office Phone: 850-224-4451. Personal E-mail: jynasser@comcast.net, jnasser@rcc.com.

NASSERIPOUR, MOHAMMAD MICHEL, artist, architect; b. Teheran, Iran, Sept. 9, 1942; arrived in U.S., 1982; s. Moussa and Zari Nasseripour; m. Nooshazar Mary Sanei, Nov. 7, 1974; children: Melanie, Pearl. M in Art and Arch., Teheran U., 1971. Exhibitions include France, Paris, 1981, Art Gallery, NYC, 1988, Am. U., Washington, 1988, George Washington U., 1988, Beaux Art Mus., Teheran, 1996, Silk Road Festival, Smithsonian Instn., 2002, Opening Minds, Washington, 2003, NY Art Expo, 2006; author: The Life and Work of Behzad, 1999; co-author: Splendors of Iran: Lacquer Work Section, 2002, Guide to Iran: Persian Miniatures and Artists, 2003. Recipient Agha Khan award, Agha Khan Found., 2001, Silk Road Festival award, Smithsonian Inst., 2002, Opening Mind award, Iranian Am. Tech. Coun., 2003. Mem.: Internat. Coun. Mus., Am. Inst. for Conservation. Home: 5225 Popoks Hill Rd Bethesda MD 20814-6704 Office Phone: 202-489-4050.

NASSETTA, CHRISTOPHER J., hotel executive; b. 1962; m. Paige Nassetta; 6 children. BS in Fin., McIntire Sch. Commerce, U. Va., 1984. Various positions Oliver Carr Co., 1984-91, chief devel. officer; pres. Bailey Realty Corp., 1991-95; exec. v.p. Host Hotels and Resorts Inc., 1995—97, COO, 1997—2000, pres., CEO Bethesda, Md., 2000—07, Hilton Hotels Corp., Beverly Hills, Calif., 2007—. Bd. dirs. CoStar Group Inc.; trustee Prime Group Realty Trust. Adv. bd. McIntire Sch. Commerce, U. Va. Office: Hilton Hotels 9336 Civic Ctr Dr Beverly Hills CA 90210

NASSIF, BRADLEY LOUIS, research scholar; b. Cedar Rapids, Iowa, July 25, 1954; s. Louis Rustom and Lydia (Ferris) N.; m. Barbara Anne Strait, June 11, 1988. BA, Friends U., 1977; MA in New Testament, Denver Sem., 1981; MA in European Hist., Wichita State U., 1984; MDiv, St. Vladimir's Othodox Sem., Scarsdale, NY, 1985; PhD in Patristics and Ea. Christianity, Fordham U., 1991. Mentor SUNY, Nanuet, 1985; owner, operator Gt. Plains Smokemaster, Wichita, Kans., 1980—. Adj. prof. Friends U., Wichita, Kans., 1986, St. Francis Coll., Bklyn., 1988; cons. editor Christianity Today mag., Carol Stream, Ill., 1981; guest preacher for joint ann. meeting Am. Missiology Soc., and Am. Assn. Mission Profs., 1989; speaker in field. Contbr. articles to religious mags. Paraprofl. Wichita Pub. Schs., 1982-84. Recipient Antiochian scholarship, Antiochian Orthodox Archdiocese N. Am., 1983-85, Presidential scholarship, Grad. Sch. Arts & Scis. Fordham U., 1987-88, Grad. Asst. Fellowship, Fordham U. Theology dept., 1987-88. Mem. Internat. Patristic Soc., N. Am. Patristic Soc., Orthodox Theol. Soc Am., Evang. Theol. Soc., Soc. Bibl. Lit., Am. Acad. Religion, Am. Soc. Ch. History, Soc. for Study Ea. Orthodoxy and Evangelicalism (founder, pres.). Republican. Home: 225 N Gow St Wichita KS 67203-5433 *The most valuable perspectives on the present are those which have carefully digested the past.*

NASSIF, CARRIE, psychologist, educator; 1 child, Emily. PhD, U. SD, Vermillion. Lic. psychologist Kans. BSRB, 2008. Assoc. prof. dept. psychology Ft. Hays State U., Kans., 2001—, psychologist counseling ctr. Office: Ft Hays State Univ 600 Park St Hays KS 67601 Business E-Mail: cnassif@fhsu.edu.

NASSIF, NABIL, engineering executive, director; s. Ibrahim Nassif and Najia Daod; m. Oula Ahmad, Apr. 20, 1974; 1 child, Adam Ibrahim. PhD, Ecole de technologie superiere, Montreal, Can., 2005. Postdoc. fellow, mech. engring. U. Nev. Las Vegas, 2006—07; dir. engring. Bldg. Energy Solutions & Tech., San Jose, Calif., 2007—. Mem.: ASHRAE. Home: 1901 Halford Ave #14 Santa Clara CA 95051 Personal E-mail: nassif_nabil@hotmail.com.

NASSIF, PAUL S., facial plastic and reconstructive surgeon; b. LA, Calif., June 6, 1962; m. Adrienne Nassif; 1 child, Galvin Paul. BS in Bus., U. So. Calif., LA, 1984; attended, U. Health Sciences Chgo. Med. Sch., 1988—89; MD, U. So. Calif. Sch. Medicine, 1992. Diplomate Am. Bd. Otolaryngology-Head and Neck Surgery, 1998, Am. Bd. Facial Plastic and Reconstructive Surgery, 2000, lic. Calif., Nevada. Intern, general surgery U. N.Mex. Health Sciences Ctr., 1992—93, resident, otolaryngology-head and neck surgery, 1993—96, chief resident, otolaryngology-head and neck surgery, 1996—97; fellowship, facial plastic and reconstructive surgery Am. Acad. Facial & Plastic & Reconstructive Surgery, J. Regan Thomas, MD, Preceptor St. Louis U. Sch. Medicine, Dept. Otolaryngology-Head and Neck Surgery, Mo., 1997—98; instructor, Dept. Otolaryngology-Head and Neck Surgery St. Louis U. Sch. Medicine, 1997; attending, Divsn. Facial Plastic & Reconstructive Surgery, Dept. Otolaryngology-Head and Neck Surgery VA Med. Ctr., West LA, Calif., 1998; clin. asst. prof., Divsn. Facial Plastic & Reconstructive Surgery, Dept. Otolaryngology-Head and Neck Surgery U. So. Calif. Sch. Medicine, LA, 1998, UCLA Sch. Medicine, 1998; rhinoplasty specialist, co-owner Spaulding Drive Cosmetic Surgery & Dermatology, Beverly Hills, Calif., 1999—. Presenter in field; hospital affiliations include Cedars-Sinai Med. Ctr., LA County, U. So. Calif. Med. Ctr., West LA VA, UCLA Med. Ctr. Contbr. articles to peer-reviewed jours.; featured on Dr. 90210, mem. editl. adv. bd. Plastic Surgery Products Mag., 2002—05, guest appearances NBC Nightly News, Inside Edition, CBS Healthbeat, Entertainment Tonight, EXTRA, Good Morning America, Tom Brokaw, Peter Jennings and other members of the media, interviewed by People Mag., USA Today, LA Times, Wall Street Journal and AP, Anti-Gravity Facelift featured on Good Morning America and Entertainment Tonight. Participates Face to Face, Lymphoma Rsch. Found. Am., Race to Erase MS, Coach for Kids, Arthritis Found., Portraits of Hope; mem., Salerni Collegium U. So. Calif. Sch. Medicine. Fellow: ACS, Am. Acad. Facial Plastic & Reconstructive Surgery (mem. Face-to-Face (anti-domestic violence) com. 2000—, mem. new technologies and devices com., chmn. young physicians com. 2002—05, mem. strategic develop. com., mem. ethics com.), Am. Acad. Otolaryngology-Head and Neck Surgery; mem.: Calif. Soc. Facial Plastic Surgery (membership chmn. 1999—2004), LA Soc. Otolaryngologists, AMA, Calif. Soc. Facial Plastic Surgery, Alpha Omega Alpha (sec. 1991—92). Achievements include development of the Anti-Gravity Facelift, leaves no visible scars and achieves natural-looking results with a short recovery time. Avocations: golf, tennis, water-skiing, boating, snow sking, scuba diving, fishing. Office: Spalding Drive Cosmetic Surgery & Dermatology 120 S Spalding Dr Ste 315 Beverly Hills CA 90212 Office Phone: 310-275-2467. Office Fax: 310-275-6651.

NASSIF, SHAKEEB JOSEPH, performing arts educator; b. Cedar Rapids, Iowa, Aug. 30, 1938; s. Samuel Joseph and Mary Nassif; children: Jonathan James, Alexandra Marie Magargee. BA, Grinnell Coll., Iowa, 1960; MFA, Yale U., New Haven, 1963; PhD, U. Denver, 1973. Cert. Nat. Theatre Conf. NYC. Prof. English St. Bonaventure U., 1963, U. Mont., 1965—66, U. Southern Calif., 1966—67; exec. dir. Point Pk. Coll., Pitts., 1969—75, prof. performing arts, 1969—75, Rollins Coll., 1981—2004, producing dir., 1981—2004, exec. dir., bach festival, 2004—06, prof. emeritus performing arts, 2004—. Gen. mgr. Pitts. Ballet Theatre, 1972—76; visiting prof. U. Mich., 1974, Ohio State U., 1981—83. Author: (book) History of the Pittsburgh Playhouse, An Approach to Acting. Trustee Piscator Found. NYC, 1974—80; adjudicator Am. Theatre Festival, Wash., 1983—2003; mem. Fla. Theatre Panel Arts, Tallahassee, 1986—95; chmn. St. George Orthodox Ch., Cedar Rapids, Iowa, 2005—08. Recipient Alumni award, Yale U., 2000, Excellence Merit award, Antiochian Archdiocese North America, 1980, Arthur Vining Davis award, Rollins Coll., 1992. Mem.: U. Iowa Mus. Art, Cedar Rapids Opera Assn., United Arts Fla. Avocations: tennis, travel. Home: 2202 Upland Dr Cedar Rapids IA 52403 Personal E-mail: sjnassif@msn.com.

NASSOUR, JENNIFER A., political organization administrator; b. Flushing, NY, Oct. 20, 1971; m. C.J. Brucato, III; children: Georgia, Grace. BA in polit. sci., SUNY, Stony Brook, 1995; MA in polit. sci., LI U., C.W. Post, 1995; JD, St. John's U., 2000. Bar: Mass. 2002, US Dist. Ct. (Mass.) 2003. Dir. personnel for Gov. Jane M. Swift State of Mass., 2001—02; of counsel Consigli & Brucato, PC, Milford, Mass.; chmn. Mass. Republican Party, Boston, 2009—. Active in Jr. League of Boston, Charlestown Mother's Assn., Hill House Coun.; mem. devel. bd. Park St. Sch.; bd. trustees Bridgewater State Coll. Mem.: Women's Bar Assn., Mass. Bar Assn., Boston Bar Assn. Republican. Office: Consigli & Brucato PC 189 Main St PO Box 170 Milford MA 01757-0170 also: Mass Republican Party 85 Merrimac St Ste 400 Boston MA 02114 Office Phone: 508-478-2054, 617-523-5005, 617-523-6311. Office Fax: 508-479-7394. E-mail: jennifer@consigliandbrucato.com, jennifer@massgop.com.*

NASSTROM, ROY RICHARD, educational consultant; b. Oakland, Calif., Oct. 28, 1930; s. Roy Richard and Edith Dolores (Spilman) N.; m. Sally Louise Shaw, Aug. 29, 1964; children: Karen, Eric. AA, U. Calif., Berkeley, 1955, BA, 1956, MA, 1964, PhD, 1971. Asst. to supt. Ravenswood Sch. Dist., East Palo Alto, Calif., 1964-65; acting instr. edn. U. Calif., Berkeley, 1965-68; asst. prof. ednl. adminstrn. U. Ky., Lexington, 1969-70; asst. prof. edn. Purdue U., West Lafayette, Ind., 1971-76; mediator, fact finder Ind. Edn. Employment Rels. Bd., 1974-76; asst. grad. dean Winona (Minn.) State U., 1976-77, chmn. ednl. adminstrn. dept., 1976-88, prof., 1976-01, prof. emeritus, 2001—, chmn. ednl. leadership dept., 1998-01; ednl. polit. cons. R. Nasstrom, 2002—. Cons., spkr. various orgns. and schs., 1969—; mem. bd. abstractors Ednl. Adminstrn. Abstracts, 1976-83; dir. post-masters studies, Winona State U., 1992-99. Editor Ravenswood Report, 1964-65, U. Calif.-Berkeley Sch. Edn. Newsletter, 1965-68; bd of editors AASA Prof., 1979-82; manuscript reviewer various jours. and pubs, 1983-87; contbr. articles and revs. to profl. jours., chpts. to books. List mgr. Winona On-line Democracy, 2005—08, mem. steering com., 2003—. With US Army, 1952—54. Recipient numerous grants, 1969-98. Mem.Am. Ednl. Rsch. Assn. (paper reviewer 1983-2000), Calif. Alumni Assn., Am. Assn. Colls. for Tchr. Edn. (instnl. rep., paper reviewer), Nat. Assn. Scholars, Pi Sigma Alpha Avocations: reading, history, politics. Home: 1702 Edgewood Rd Winona MN 55987-2149 Personal E-mail: nasstrom@cal.berkeley.edu.

NAST, DIANNE MARTHA, lawyer; b. Mount Holly, NJ, Jan. 30, 1948; d. Henry Daniel and Anastasia (Lovenduski) N.; m. Joseph Francis Roda, Aug. 23, 1980; children: Michael, Daniel, Joseph, Joshua, Anastasia. BA, Pa. State U.; JD, Rutgers U., 1976. Bar: Pa. 1976, U.S. Dist. Ct. Pa. 1976, N.J. 1976, U.S. Dist. Ct. N.J. 1976, U.S. Ct. Appeals (3d, 5th, 6th, 7th, 8th and 11th cirs.) 1976, U.S. Supreme Ct. 1982, U.S. Dist. Ct. Ariz. 1985. Dir., v.p. Kohn, Nast & Graf, P.C., Phila., 1976-95, Roda & Nast, P.C., Lancaster, Pa., 1995—. Mem. lawyers adv. com. U.S. Ct. Appeals (3d cir.), 1982-84, chmn., 1983-84, mem. com. on revision jud. conf. conduct rules, 1982-84; mem. Third Cir. Task Force on Selection of Class Clunsel, 2001-02mem. U.S. Ct. Appeals for the 3d Cir. Jud. Conf. Permanent Planning Com., 1983-90; bd. dirs. 3d Cir. Hist. Soc., Phila. Pub. Def., 1980-89, Fed. Jud. Ctr. Found., 1992-2002, chmn. 1997-2002; chmn. lawyers adv. com. U.S. Dist. Ct. (ea. dist.) Pa., 1982-90. Pres. Hist. Soc., 1988-91. Fellow ABA (coun. litigation sect. 1986-89, co-chmn. anti-trust com. litigation sect. 1984-86, div. dir. 1990-91, practical litigation editl. bd. 1989—, ho. of dels. 1992-94, mem. task force state justice initiatives, mem. task force state of justice system, 1993, mem. task force long range planning com. 1994), Am. Law Inst. (chair internat. professionalism com. 1991-94, civil justice task force 1993-95), Am. Arbitration Assn. (bd. dirs., mem. alt. dispute resolution and mass torts task force), Am. Judicature Soc., Pa. Bar Assn. (bd. of dels. 1983-95), N.J. Bar Assn., Pa. Trial Lawyers Assn., Phila. Bar Assn. (bd. govs. 1985-87, chmn., bicentennial com. 1986-87, chmn. bench bar conf. 1988-89), Lancaster Bar Assn. (co-chair civil litigation and rules com. trial law sect.), Rutgers Law Sch. Alumni Assn. Home: 1059 Sylvan Rd Lancaster PA 17601-1923 Office: Roda & Nast PC 801 Estelle Dr Lancaster PA 17601-2130 Home Phone: 717-397-3059; Office Phone: 717-892-3000. Business E-Mail: dnast@rodanast.com.

NASTASE, FLORIN, physicist, research scientist; b. Bals, Romania, May 1, 1974; s. Gheorghe and Paulina Nastase; m. Claudia Nastase, Aug. 21, 1999. BS in Physics, U. Bucharest, Romania, 2001, MS in Polymer Physics with honors, 2003, PhD in Solid State Physics summa cum laude, 2007. Sci. rschr., dept. polymer sci. U. Bucharest, 2002—07, rsch. scientist, polymer sci. group, 2007—. Mem.: European Phys. Soc., European Materials Rsch. Soc. (assoc.), Inst. Nanotechnology (assoc.), French Phys. Soc. (assoc.). Achievements include research in plasma polymerization field; polymer physics domain; organic semiconductor domain. Avocations: history, classical music, painting. Office: Univ Bucharest Polymer Sci Group PSG PO Box MG 40 Magurele 077125 Bucharest Romania Home: 5 Apt 28 Str Fizicieni nr 8 Ilfov 077125 Magurele Romania Office Fax: 40-21-457-44-18. Personal E-mail: nastasef@gmail.com. Business E-Mail: nastasef@psg.unibuc.ro.

NATALE, PATRICK J., professional society administrator; m. Sheila Natale; 2 children. BS in Civil Engring., Newark Coll.of Engring.; MS in Engring. Mgmt., NJ Inst. of Tech.; grad., exec. mgmt. program, Yale U. Lic. profl. engr., NJ; cert. Assn. Exec. (CAE). Various mgmt. positions PSE&G, NJ; v.p., northeast region Nat. Soc. Profl. Engr., exec. dir., 1999—2002; exec. dir., chief staff officer, sec. Am. Soc. Civil Engr., Reston, Va., 2002—. Pres. Am. Soc. Civil Engr. Found., 2003—. Chmn. Goodwill Ind. of NJ; bd. dir. C. of C., Am. Red Cross; asst. dist. commr. Boy Scouts of Am. Office: Exec Dir Am Soc Civil Engr 1801 Alexander Bell Dr Reston VA 20191-4400

NATALICIO, DIANA SIEDHOFF, academic administrator; b. St. Louis, Aug. 25, 1939; d. William and Eleanor J. (Biermann) Siedhoff. BS in Spanish summa cum laude, St. Louis U., 1961; MA in Portuguese lang., U. Tex., 1964, PhD in Linguistics, 1969; PhD (hon.), Smith Coll., Universidad Autonoma de Nuevo Leon. Chmn. dept. modern langs. U. Tex., El Paso, 1973-77, assoc. dean liberal arts, 1977-79, acting dean liberal arts, 1979-80, dean Coll. Liberal Arts, 1980-84, v.p. acad. affairs, 1984-88, pres., 1988—. Bd. dirs. El Paso br. Fed. Res. Bd. Dallas, chmn., 1989; mem. Presdl. Adv. Commn. on Ednl. Excellence for Hispanic Ams., 1991; bd. dirs. Sandia Corp., Trinity Industries; bd. dirs. Nat. Action Coun. for Minorities in Engring., 1993—; mem. Nat. Sci. Bd. 1994-2006; mem. NASA Adv. Coun., 1994-96; bd. mem. Fund for Improvement of Post-Secondary Edn., 1993-97; bd. dirs. Fogarty Internat. Ctr. of NIH, 1993-96; bd. chair Am. Assn. Higher Edn., 1995-96; bd. dirs. U.S.-Mexico Commn. for Ednl. and Cultural Exch., 1994—. Co-author: Sounds of Children, 1977; contbr. articles to profl. jours. Bd. dirs. United Way El Paso, 1990-93, chmn. needs survey com., 1990-91, chmn. edn. divsn., 1989; chmn. Quality Edn. for Minorities Network in Math. Sci. and Engring., 1991-92; chairperson Leadership El Paso, Class 12, 1989-90, mem. adv. coun., 1987-90, participant, 1980-81; mem. Historically Black Colls. and Univs./Minority Instns. Consortium on Environ. Tech. chairperson, 1991-93; trustee Rockefeller Found. Recipient Harold W. McGraw. Jr. prize in edn., 1997, Torch of Liberty award Anti-Defamation League B'nai B'rith, 1991, Conquistador award City of El Paso, 1990, Humanitarian award El Paso chpt. NCCJ, 1990, Disting. Alumnus Award, U. Tex. Austin, 2006; named to El Paso Women's Hall of Fame, 1990, Tex. Women's Hall of Fame, 1998. Mem. Philos. Soc. Tex. Avocations: hiking, bicycling, skiing, skating. Office: U Tex at El Paso Office of the Pres 500 W University Ave El Paso TX 79968-0001

NATANI, KIRMACH, forensic psychologist; b. Milw., June 5, 1935; s. Whit Baer Naabane and Natasha Rucoss Nabona. MSc in Clin. Psychology, Okla. U., 1970; PhD in Biopsychology, Okla. U. Health Sci. Ctr., 1977; postgrad., USAF Sch. Aerospace Medicine, San Antonio,

1977—79. Lic. clin. psychologist, health svc. provider, cert. forensic neuropsychologist, sr. disability analyst, divorce mediator. Physics tech./profl. Lawrence Berkeley Lab., Berkeley, Calif., 1958—63; vol. Peace Corps, Thailand, 1963—65; clin. rschr. Okla. City VA Hosp., 1966—77; human factors engr. McDonnell-Douglas, St. Louis, 1980—92; postodoctoral resident/cons. St. Mary's Hosp., East St. Louis, Ill., 1992—97; pvt. practice clin. neuropsychologist, cons. Bi-State Neurometric Svcs., various cities, 1998—. Clin. mgr. Mo. Dept. Corrections, Farmington, Mo., 1999—2001; sr. care mgr. Magellan Behavior Health, St. Louis, 2001—02; ad hoc peer reviewer profl. psychology, rsch., practice, 2001—; mem. adv. com. NRC, 1978—83; assoc. Social Security Disability Attorney, Clayton. Contbr. numerous articles to profl. jours., chpts. to books. With USAF, 1955—63. Recipient, Roche Labs. awards, 1973; grantee, Divsn. Polar Programs, NSF, 1966—75, Nature Publishing Group, 2006. Fellow: Am. Coll. Forensic Examiners; mem.: APA, Mo. Am. Psychol. Assn., Am. Bd. Disability Analysts, Am. Bd. Psychol. Specialities, Internat. Soc. Neurofeedback and Rsch. Avocations: computer graphics, digital photographic restoration. Office Phone: 314-426-1875. Personal E-mail: knat3@juno.com.

NATARAJAN, ARUTSELVAN, chemistry professor, researcher; s. Natarajan Arumugam and Padmavathy Natarajan; m. Bhuvaneswari Ponnuswamy, Dec. 10, 2000. PhD, Algappa U., Karaikudi, 2000. Rschr. UC Davis, Sacramento, 2002—05, asst. prof., 2005—. Scientist Ctrl. Leather Rsch. Inst., Madras, TamilNadu, 1998—2001. Contbr. scientific papers. Mem.: Soc. Nuc. Medicine (Young Profl. award 2006). Home: 3014 O St Sacramento CA 95816 Office: Univ Calif Davis 1508 Alhmbara Blvd Sacramento CA 95816 Office Fax: 916-703-5014. Personal E-mail: arutselvan@gmail.com. Business E-Mail: arutselvan.natarajan@ucdmc.ucdavis.edu.

NATARAJAN, GITHA, elementary school educator; b. Toronto; m. Arun Natarajan. Tchr. Prince George's County, 1998—99, John Eaton Elem. Sch., Washington, 1999—. Named DC Tchr. of Yr., 2007. Office: John Eaton Elem Sch 3301 Lowell St NW Washington DC 20008 E-mail: githadn@aol.com.

NATARAJAN, RAMESH, medical educator; m. Seema Gupta, Feb. 3, 1995; children: Pallavi, Mallavika. PhD, Va. Commonwealth U., Richmond, 1997. Asst. prof. Va. Commonwealth U., 2003—. Contbr. scientific papers to profl. jours. Achievements include discovery of prolyl hydroxylase inhibition in ischemia-reperfusion injury. Office: Va Commonwealth Univ 1101 E Marshall St Richmond VA 23298 Office Phone: 804-827-1013.

NATARAJAN, SRIRAAM, research scientist; s. Natarajan Sundaram and Kalavathi Natarajan; 1 child, Ramya. PhD, Oreg. State U., Corvallis, 2007. Rsch. asst. Oreg. State U., 2003—07; rsch. assoc. U. Wis., Madison, 2008—. Achievements include research in over 20 publications machine learning, statistical relational learning, graphical models and reinforcement learning.

NATARUS, BURTON F., lawyer, former city alderman; b. Wausau, Wis., Nov. 7, 1933; BS in Polit. Sci., U. Wis., 1956, JD, 1960; student, Harvard U. John F. Kennedy Sch. Govt. Former commr. Cook County Justice Commn.; alderman 42nd ward City of Chgo., 1971—2007, chair traffic & safety com., elected Dem. committeeman, mem. fin., zoning, rules & ethics, lic. & consumer protection, budget & govt. ops., and housing & real estate coms. Man of Year, Jewish Nat Fund, B'nai B'rith, 75; Recognition Award, Deborah's Pl; Jerusalem Award, Shaarc Zedek Hosp; Serv Award State Street Coun; Appreciation Award, Landmark Preservation Coun of Ill. Founding member Sandburg Village Coun (president, formerly); founding member Near N Model Cities Advisor Coun; Greater N Michigan Ave Association; Streeterville Chamber of Commerce; River North Association; North Dearborn Association; North State, Astor, Lake Shore Dr Association; Cen Michigan Ave Association; River North Association. Jewish. Office: 121 N La Salle St Rm 306 Chicago IL 60602 Office Phone: 312-744-3062. Business E-Mail: bnatarus@cityofchicago.org.

NATCHER, STEPHEN DARLINGTON, retired lawyer, electronics executive; b. San Francisco, Nov. 19, 1940; m. Carolyn Anne Bowman, Aug. 23, 1969; children: Tanya Michelle, Stephanie Elizabeth. AB in Polit. Sci., Stanford U., 1962; JD, U. Calif., San Francisco, 1965. Bar: Calif. 1966. Assoc. firm Pillsbury, Madison & Sutro, San Francisco, 1966-68; counsel Douglas Aircraft div. McDonnell Douglas Corp., Long Beach, Calif., 1968-70; v.p., sec. Security Pacific Nat. Bank, 1971-79; asst. gen. counsel Security Pacific Corp., 1979-80; v.p., sec., gen. counsel Lear Siegler, Inc., Santa Monica, Calif., 1980-87; v.p., gen. counsel Computer Sci. Corp., El Segundo, Calif., 1987-88; exec. v.p., gen. counsel, sec. CalFed Inc., 1989-90; sr. v.p. adminstrn., gen. counsel, sec. Wyle Electronics, Irvine, Calif., 1991-98; gen. counsel VEBA Electronics LLC, Santa Clara, Calif., 1998—2002, ret., 2002. With USCG, 1965-71. Mem.: St. Francis Yacht Club (San Francisco). Republican. E-mail: snatcher@starstream.net.

NATH, LOPITA, history professor; b. Guwahati, Assam, India, July 20, 1965; d. Tarun Kumar and Reba Nath; m. Jagadish Kakoti, Jan. 24, 1992; 1 child, Avinash Kakoti. BA, Gauhati U., India, 1985, MA in History, 1987, PhD in History, 2000. Asst. prof. Cotton Coll., Guwahati, 1989—2005, U. Virginia's Coll., Wise, Va., 2006—07, U. Incarnate Word, San Antonio, 2007—. Vis. prof. U. Incarnate Word, San Antonio, 2004—05, Coll. William and Mary, Williamsburg, Va., 2005—06. Contbr. scientific papers. Recipient Gold medal, Gauhati U., India, 1989; Minor Rsch. fellowship, U. Grants Commn., India, 1993, NE India Devel. fellowship, Maulana Abul Kalam Azad Inst. Asian Studies, 2001—02, South Asia Rsch. fellowship, Social Sci. Rsch. Coun., 2004—05, Fulbright scholar, 2004—05. Mem.: NE India History Assoc., Indian History Congress, Assn. Asian Studies, Phi Alpha Theta. Hindu. Avocation: travel. Office: Univ Incarnate Word 4301 Broadway San Antonio TX 78209

NATH, NIHARIKA, biology professor; d. Chittaranjan and Arati Nath; m. Pradip Kumar Nath; 1 child, Uma Nandini. PhD, Indian Inst. Tech.-Delhi, New Delhi, 1996. Asst. prof. NY Inst. Tech., 2005—. Contbr. articles to profl. med. jour. Vol. Mar. Dimes, Trenton, NJ. Mem.: Am. Assn. Cancer Rsch. Achievements include research in mechanism of novel compounds with potential for cancer prevention, interaction of cell cycle regulators and signaling pathways relevant to carcinogenesis. Home: 4 Ann St Bergenfield NJ 07621 Office: NY Inst Tech 1855 Broadway New York NY 10023 Home Phone: 201-384-7459; Office Phone: 212-261-1623. Business E-Mail: nnath@nyit.edu.

NATHAN, DUSTY, journalist, shop owner; B, Temple U., Phila., M, 2009. Cert. tchr. Pa., 2009. Journalist, analyst, columnist Gannett, Phila., 1987—2001; owner Dust In The Wind Productions, Southampton, Pa., 1994—. Contbr. columns in newspapers. Fundraiser, voter registration. Office: Dust In The Wind Productions PO Box 1655 Southampton PA 18966 Personal E-mail: misterwriter111@hotmail.com.

NATHAN, FREDERIC SOLIS, lawyer; b. NYC, June 24, 1922; s. Edgar Joshua and Mabel (Unterberg) N.; m. Frances E., Oct. 28, 1956; children: Jean E., Frederic S. Jr., William E. BA, Williams Coll., Williamstown, Mass., 1943; LLD, Yale U., 1948. Bar: N.Y. 1948, U.S. Dist. Ct. (so. and ea. dists) N.Y. 1948, U.S. Ct. Appeals (2d cir.) 1953, U.S. Supreme Ct. 1968. Instr. Williams Coll., Williamstown, 1948; assoc. Rathbone Perry Kelley & Drye, NYC, 1948-53; asst. U.S. atty. U.S. Atty. (so. dist.) N.Y., NYC, 1953-56; assoc. Greenbaum, Wolff & Ernst, NYC, 1956-58, ptnr., 1959-65, 70-82; 1st asst. corp. counsel N.Y.C. Law Dept., NYC, 1966-69; ptnr. Kelley, Drye & Warren, NYC, 1982—. Mem. N.Y. Rep. County Com., N.Y.C., 1948-65; trustee Mt. Sinai Hosp., N.Y.C., 1970—; chmn. bd. FOJP Svc. Corp., N.Y.C., 1977-85, bd. dirs., 1979—; bd. dirs. Am. Jewish Soc. for Svc., N.Y.C., 1950—; bd. dirs. Everybody Wins Found., Inc., 1992—. With U.S. Army, 1943-45, ETO. Fellow Am. Coll. Trial Lawyers; mem. ABA, Assn. of Bar of City of N.Y. (exec. com. 1979-81), Fed. Bar Council (pres. 1975-76), Clubs: Century Assn., Yale of N.Y.C.; Sunningdale Country. Republican. Jewish. Home: 180 East End Ave New York NY 10128-7763 Office: Kelley Drye & Warren 101 Park Ave New York NY 10178-0062 Office Phone: 212-808-7840. Business E-Mail: fnathan@kelleydrye.com.

NATHAN, GERALD DALE, retired psychologist, researcher, writer; b. Norfolk, Nebr., Oct. 1, 1938; s. Raymond John and Esther Marie (Neuwerk) N.; m. Jo Anne Williams, Aug. 19, 1993; 1 child, Jerald John; stepchildren: Rodney Wade, Erica Wren. Student, Wayne State Coll., Nebr., 1956—57, Yale U., 1959—60; BA, U. Nebr., 1966, MA, 1968, PhD (NDEA fellow), 1970. Diplomate Am. Bd. Sexology; lic. marriage counselor, Calif., lic. marital therapist, Oreg.; cert. sex educator, sex therapist; lic. psychologist, Oreg. Cons. psychologist Calavaras County Edn. Dept., San Andreas, Calif., 1970—72; pvt. practice sex and marital therapy, lifestyle stress mgmt. Salem, Oreg., 1972—2000; ret., 2000. Cons. psychologist Cmty. Counseling Center, Salem, 1972-73, William Temple House, Portland, Oreg., 1974-77; sex educator Oreg. Dept. Continuing Edn., Salem, 1972-74; vis. prof. Willamette U., Salem, 1981; bd. dirs. Morrison Charter H.S., Dallas, Oreg.; adj. instr. Chemeketa C.C., Salem, 2001-04 Active Salem Cmty. Chorus, 1978-84, pres., 1980-81; active Festival Chorale Oreg., 1986, 96, 2001-05; adv. bd. Friends Oreg. Area, 1997-98. With USAF, 1959-63 Fellow Am. Bd. Sexology; mem. APA, Am. Assn. Marriage and Family Therapy, Am. Assn. Sex Educators, Counselors and Therapists, Oreg. Assn. Marriage and Family Therapists (dir. 1976-77), Soc. Sci. Study Sex, Salem Psychol. Soc. (co-chmn. 1981-82), Nature Conservancy, Union Concerned Scientists, Am. Farmland Trust, Am. Minor Breeds Conservancy, World Wildlife Fund Personal E-mail: j_nathan1977@hotmail.com.

NATHAN, JOSEPH MICHAEL (JOE NATHAN), professional baseball player; b. Houston, Nov. 22, 1974; m. Lisa Lemoncelli; 1 child, Cole. Grad. in bus. mgmt., SUNY, Stony Brook, 1997. Pitcher San Francisco Giants, 1999—2003, Minn. Twins, 2003—. Mem. US nat. team World Baseball Classic, 2006. Recipient Univ. medal, SUNY Stony Brook; named to Am. League All-Star Team, Maj. League Baseball, 2004, 2005, 2008, 2009. Mem.: Golden Key Internat. Honor Soc. Office: Minn Twins 34 Kirby Puckett Pl Minneapolis MN 55415*

NATHAN, MATTHEW LINCOLN, career military officer, physician; b. Feb. 10, 1955; Grad., Ga. Inst. Tech., Atlanta, 1977; MD, Med. Coll. Ga., 1981; M, Indsl. Coll. Armed Forces, Washington, 1999. Intern, spl. residency internal medicine U. South Fla. Affiliated Hosps., 1981—84; internal medicine specialist Naval Hosp., Guantanamo Bay, Cuba, 1984; practicing internist, leader Med. Mobilization Amphibious Readiness Team, Naval Hosp., Groton, Conn., 1985—87; head divsn. internal medicine Naval Med. Ctr., San Diego, 1987—90; acting dept. head Naval Hosp., Beaufort, SC; various positions Naval Clinics Command, London; med. specialist assignment officer Bur. Naval Pers.; fleet surgeon to comdr. US 7th Fleet, USS Blue Ridge, Yokosuka, Japan, 1999—2001; dep. comdr. Naval Med. Ctr., Portsmouth, Va.; command tour Naval Hosp., Pensacola, Fla.; fleet surgeon to comdr. US Fleet Forces Command, 2006—07; comdr. Navy Medicine East & Naval Med. Ctr., Portsmouth, 2007—08, Navy Medicine Nat. Capitol Area & Nat. Naval Med. Ctr., Bethesda, Md., 2008—. Decorated Legion of Merit (5), Meritorious Svc. Medal (2), Navy Achievement Medal (2), Navy Commendation Medal; recipient Excellence in Leadership award, Am. Hosp. Assn., 2005. Office: Nat Naval Med Ctr 8901 Rockville Pike Bethesda MD 20889 Office Phone: 301-295-4611.*

NATHAN, RICHARD P(ERLE), political science professor; b. Schenectady, NY, Nov. 24, 1935; s. Sidney Robert and Betty (Green) N.; m. Mary McNamara, June 5, 1957; children: Robert Joseph, Carol Hewit. AB, Brown U., 1957; M in Pub. Adminstrn., Harvard U., 1959, PhD, 1966. Legis. asst. U.S. Senator Kenneth B. Keating, Washington, 1959-62; dir. domestic policy rsch. Nelson A. Rockefeller, 1963-64; rsch. assoc. The Brookings Instn., Washington, 1966-69, sr. fellow, project dir. monitoring studies gen. revenue sharing, community devel. block grant and pub. svc. employment programs, 1972-79; associated staff The Brookings Inst., Washington, 1980-85; asst. dir. U.S. Office of Mgmt. and Budget, Washington, 1969-71; dep. undersec. U.S Dept. Health, Edn. and Welfare, Washington, 1971-72; prof. pub. and internat. affairs Woodrow Wilson Sch. Pub. and Internat. Affairs Princeton (N.J.) U., 1979-89, also dir. Princeton Urban and Regional Rsch. Ctr., 1979-89; Disting. prof. polit. sci. and pub. policy SUNY, Albany, 1989-97; provost Rockefeller Coll. Pub. Affairs and Policy, Albany, 1989-98. Dir. Rockefeller Inst., 1989-2004, co-dir., 2005—; assoc. dir. Nat. Adv. Commn. on Civil Disorders, 1967-68; vis. prof. govt. and fgn. affairs U. Va., 1972-77; chmn. Nixon Adminstrn. Transition Task Forces on Poverty and Intergovtl. Fiscal Rels., 1968, Domestic Coun. Com. on Welfare Reform Planning, 1969-70; mem. Commn. on Orgn. Govt. of D.C., 1970-72; bd. overseers New Sch. for Social Rsch., 1982-88; mem. working seminar on family and welfare Marquette U., 1986-87; selection com. Rockefeller Pub. Svc. Awards Program, 1976-78; income maintenance task force Nat. Urban Coalition, 1975-78; treas. Manpower Demonstration Rsch. Corp., 1974-81, chmn., 1981-98; mem. coun. scholars U.S. Libr. of Congress, 1989—; mem. N.Y. State Temp. Commn. Constl. Revision, 1993-94; mem. U.S. Adv. Commn. on Intergovtl. Rels., 1995-96; vis. fellow GAO, 1998-2000; cons. U.S. Gen. Acctg. Office, 1994-96. Author: Jobs and Civil Rights, The Role of the Federal Government in Promoting Equal Opportunity in Employment and Training, 1969, The Plot That Failed: Nixon and the Administrative Presidency, 1975, Monitoring Revenue Sharing, 1975, Revenue Sharing, The Second Round., 1977, Monitoring the Public Service Employment Program, 1978, America's Government: A Fact Book of Census Data on the Organization, Finances, and Employment of Federal, State, and Local Governments, 1979, Public Service Employment: A Field Evaluation, 1981, The Administrative Presidency, 1983, Reagan and the States, 1987, Social Science in Government Uses and Abuses, 1988, A New Agenda for Cities, 1992, Turning Promises into Performance: The Management Challenge of Implementing Workfare, 1993; co-author: (with Thomas L. Gais) Implementing the Personal Responsibility Act: A First Look, 1999, Social Science in Government, 2000; (with Gerald Benjamin) Regionalism and Realism, A Study of Governments in the New York Metropolitan Area, 2001; contbr. chpts. to books; editor: (with Harvey S. Perloff) Revenue Sharing and the City, 1968; (with John D. DiJulio, Jr.) The View From the States, Making Health Reform Work, Brookings Instn., 1994; mem. editl. bd. Urban Affairs Quar., 1978-85. Eisenhower fellow European Econ. Commn., 1977. Mem. ASPA (Intergovtl. Mgmt. award 1985), Nat. Acad. Social Inst., Nat. Acad. Pub. Adminstrn. (James E. Webb award 1986), Am. Pub. Human Svcs. Assn. (bd. dirs. 2000-02), Am. Polit. Sci. Assn. (Charles E. Merriam award 1987), Assn. for Pub. Policy Analysis and Mgmt.(pres.-elect 2000—pres. 2003-04), Phi Beta Kappa, Theta Delta Chi. Republican. Jewish. Avocations: reading, travel, movies. Office: SUNY Rockefeller Inst Office of Co-Dir 411 State St Albany NY 12203-1003 Office Phone: 518-443-5831. Business E-Mail: nathanr@rockinst.org.

NATHANIELSZ, PETER WILLIAM, physiologist; b. Colombo, Sri Lanka, Jan. 31, 1941; came to the U.S., 1976; s. Arthur Holman and Constance Ethel (Mouncy) N.; m. Diana Joyce Crawford-Smith, Mar. 19, 1966 (div.); children: Helen Julie, David William. PhD, Cambridge U., 1969, MD, 1977, ScD, 1993, FRCOG, 1998. Physician Brit. Med. Assn., London, 1964-76; intern Univ. Coll. Hosp., London; resident Cambridge (Eng.) U., 1980—2002; dir. lab. for pregnancy and newborn rsch. Coll. Vet. Medicine, Cornell U., Ithaca, N.Y.; dir. ctr. women's health rsch. NYU Med. Sch. Chairperson maternal-child health rsch. com. Nat. Inst. of Child Health and Human Devel., Washington, 1992—. Author: Life Before Birth and a Time To Be Born, 1992, Life in the Womb: The Orgin of Health and Disease, 1999. Achievements include discovery of signal giving ability of fetal brain to start the birth process. Office: NYU Sch Medicine 550 First Ave 9E2 NBV New York NY 10016

NATHANS, LARRY ALLEN, lawyer; b. Washington; s. Murray Alan Nathans and Paula Nita Ginsberg; m. Kathleen Ann Harris, Dec. 31, 2006; children: Marc, Andrew. BA, U. Fla., Gainesville, 1978; JD, Northeastern U., Boston, Mass., 1982. Shareholder Nathans & Biddle, Balt., 2004—, Bennett & Nathans, 1998—2003, Law Office Larry Natham, 1995—97; chief asst. Fed. Pub. Defender, 1986—94; adj. prof. Cath. Law Sch., Washington, 1989—96; asst. pub. defender Office Pub. Defender, Jacksonville, Fla., 1982—85. Named one of Best Lawyers, 2008—. Fellow: Md. Bar Found. Avocations: bicycling, reading. Office: Nathans & Biddle LLP 120 E Balt St Ste 1800 Baltimore MD 21202

NATHANSON, HARVEY CHARLES, electrical engineer; b. Pitts., Oct. 22, 1936; s. David Benjamin and Ella (Sachs) N.; m. Esther Janet Mishelevich, Oct. 13, 1963; children: Marc Elliot, Elinor Sharon. BSEE, Carnegie Inst. Tech., 1958, MSEE, 1959, PhD, 1962. Sr. engr. Junction Device Physics, Westinghouse, Research/Devel. Center, Pitts., 1962-67, fellow engr., 1968-72, mgr. silicon junction physics, 1972-77, mgr. microelectronics dept., 1978-90, chief scientist electronic div., 1990-95; chief scientist Northrop Grumman Sci. Tech. Ctr., 1996—2001; cons. Northrop Grumman, 2002—. Instr. Carnegie Inst. Tech., Pitts., 1959-60; chmn. Westinghouse Sat. Sci. Honors Inst. for High Sch. Students, 1970-76; mem. adv. group on electron devices U.S. Dept. Def., 1976-86; adviser to Nat. Materials Bd., 1986-87. Contbr. articles to profl. jours.; mem. editorial bd. Solid State Electronics, 1985—; patentee in field. Bd. dirs. Temple Sinai, 1981-83, 95-97; pres. Brotherhood, 1993-95. Recipient IR100 award, 1965, hon. mention Outstanding Young Engr. award Eta Kappa Nu, 1967, Best Display Paper award Soc. Info. Display, 1972, Carnegie-Mellon Alumni award, 1982, Westinghouse Top Corp. Patent award, 1990; named to Westinghouse Order of Merit, Westinghouse Electric Corp., 1987, named Pitts. Inventor Yr., 2002. Fellow IEEE (editl. bd. Spectrum mag. 1989-91, 3e Millennium medal 2000); mem. IEEE Electron Device Soc. (pres. 1978-80), Fedn. Materials Socs. (bd. dirs. 1987-90), Sigma Xi, Eta Kappa Nu. Democrat. Jewish. Home: 5635 Marlborough Rd Pittsburgh PA 15217-1404 Office: Northrop Grumman Sci-Tech Ctr Advanced Tech Lab PO Box 1521-MS 3B10 Baltimore MD 21203 Business E-Mail: harvey.c.nathanson@ngc.com.

NATHANSON, IAN THOMAS, pediatric pulmonologist; b. NYC, Nov. 22, 1948; BA, SUNY Buffalo, MD, 1974. Cert. Am. Bd. Pediat., 1979, in pediatric pulmonology Am. Bd. Pediat., 2003, in sleep medicine Am. Bd. Pediat., 2007. Internship in pediat. Buffalo Gen. Hosp., 1974; residency in pediatric pulmonology Children's Hosp., Buffalo, 1976—77, fellowship in pediatric pulmonology, 1977—79; rsch. fellowship U. Calif. Med. Sch., San Farancisco; pediat. staff Arnold Palmer Hosp. Women & Children, Jacksonville, Fla.; assoc. prof. Mayo Med. Sch., Fla.; med. dir. Nemours Children's Clinic, Orlando, Fla. Contbr. articles to profl. jours. Office: Nemours Childrens Clinic 496 Delaney Ave Ste 408 Orlando FL 32801-3851 Office Phone: 407-650-7000. Office Fax: 407-650-7124.

NATHANSON, KATHERINE L., medical geneticist, educator; BA in Biology, Haverford Coll., 1987; MD, U. Pa. Sch. Medicine, 1993. Diplomate Am. Bd. Internal Medicine, Am. Bd. Med. Genetics. Resident Beth Israel Hosp.; chief resident West Roxbury VA Hosp.; fellow in med. genetics Phila. Children's Hosp.; asst. prof. divsn. med. genetics U. Pa. Sch. Medicine. Office: University of Pennsylvania Division of Medical Genetics 421 Curie Blvd 513 BRB2/3 Philadelphia PA 19104 Office Phone: 215-573-9840. Office Fax: 215-573-2486.*

NATHANSON, LARRY, medical educator; b. Boston, Dec. 23, 1928; s. Robert Bernard and Leah (Rabin) N.; m. Anna Bloch, May 27, 1962; children: Andrew, Aran, Nicholas. AB, Harvard Coll., 1950; MD, U. Chgo., 1955. Diplomate Am. Bd. Internal Medicine, Am. Bd. Med. Oncology. Instr. medicine Harvard Med. Sch., Boston, 1966-68; from asst. to prof. Tufts U. Sch. Medicine, Boston, 1968-79; prof. medicine SUNY Stony Brook Sch. of Medicine, 1980-96, prof. emeritus, 1996—. Pres., CEO Oncology Cons., Cambridge, Mass., 1996—; cons. John Wayne Cancer Inst., Santa Monica, Calif., 1996—; councilor Cambridge Hist. Soc.; bd. dirs. Mass. Soc. for Med. Rsch. Editl. bd. Cancer, 1977—, Jour. Clin. Oncology, 1995-98, Seminars in Oncology, 1979-83, Med. & Pediat. Oncology, 1977-96, Jour. Cancer Edn., 1986-92; editor 6 books; contbr. articles to profl. jours. Trustee Cold Spring Harbor Lab., 1990-94, Soc. Preservation L.I. Antiquities, Setauket, N.Y., 1982-92, Cambridge Sch. of Weston, 1997—, Mass. Soc. Med. Rsch., 2002—; active Herreshoff Marine Mus., Bristol, R.I., 2000—, Reliance Soc. Capt. U.S. Army Med. Corps., 1956-58, mem. Harvard Inst. For Learning in Retirement, 2006-. Recipient Disting Svc. award Cancer Rsch., Vet. Affairs Rev. Bd., 1974—78, Disting Svc. award, Winthrop U. Hosp., 1993, Disting Alumni award, Cambridge Sch. Weston, 2006; grantee, Nat. Cancer Inst., 1964—80. Fellow ACP; mem. Mass. Soc. Med. Rsch. (trustee 2002—), Harvard Club (N.Y.), Seawanhaka Corinthian Yacht Club (race com. 1990-96), Harvard Faculty Club (chair 60th reunion com., Harvard Coll. Class of 1950), Sigma Xi. Achievements include advances in biology and chemoprevention of melanoma, combination chemotherapy and immunotherapy of cancer, clinical trials design. Avocations: sailing, squash, tennis, history. Office: Oncology Cons 3 Gray Gdns E Cambridge MA 02138-1401 Personal E-mail: larrymd1@comcast.net.

NATHANSON, LINDA SUE, publishing executive, writer; b. Washington, Aug. 11, 1946; d. Nat and Edith (Weinstein) N.; m. James F. Barrett. BS, U. Md., 1969; MA, UCLA, 1970, PhD, 1975. Tng. dir.

Rockland Rsch. Inst., Orangeburg, NY, 1975—77; asst. prof. psychology SUNY, 1978—79; pres. Cabri Prodns., Inc., Ft. Lee, NJ, 1979—81; rsch. supr. Darcy, McManus & Masius, St. Louis, 1981—83; mgr. software tng., documentation On-Line Software Internat., Ft. Lee, 1983—85; pvt. practice Ft. Lee, 1985—87; founder, exec. dir. Edin. Group, Inc., Gillette, NJ, 1987—98; founder, pres. Edin Books, Inc., Gillette, 1994—. Sr. tech. trainer Schering-Plough, 2002—. Author: (with others) Psychological Testing: An Introduction to Tests and Measurements, 1988; (with S.J. Thayer) Interview with an Angel, 1997, The Heart of Interview with an Angel, 1998; publ. A Funny Thing Happened at the Interview (G.F. Farrell), 1996, Angel Talk (R. Crystal), 1996; (audiobook with W. Barnes) I Built the Titanic: Past-Life Memories of a Master Shipbuilder, 1999, Thomas Andrews, Voyage into History, 2000; (audio book on CD with W. Barnes and F. Baranowski) My Life and Death: A Past-Life Interview with Titanic's Designer, 2005. Recipient Rsch. Svc. award 1978; Rsch. fellow Albert Einstein Coll. Medicine, 1978-79. Jewish. Home and Office: 102 Sunrise Dr Gillette NJ 07933-1944 Home Phone: 908-647-3346. Business E-Mail: edinbooks@comcast.net.

NATHANSON, NEAL, virologist, epidemiologist, educator; b. Boston, Sept. 1, 1927; s. Robert B. and Leah (Rabinowitch) N.; m. Constance Allen, June 8, 1954; children: Katherine L., John A., Daniel R.; m. Phoebe Starfield, Oct. 7, 1984. BA, Harvard U., 1949, MD, 1953. Chief polio surveillance unit USPHS, 1955-57; rsch. assoc., asst. prof. anatomy Johns Hopkins U., Balt., 1957-63, assoc. prof. epidemiology, 1963-68, prof., 1968-79; chmn. dept. microbiology U. Pa., Phila., 1979-93, vice dean rsch., 1993-95, dir. Office of AIDS Rsch., 1998-2000, vice provost rsch., 2000—03; assoc. dean Global Health Programs, 2003—. Editor-in-chief: Am. Jour. Epidemiology, 1964-79, Microbial Pathogenesis, 1985-88. Achievements include research in pathogenesis, immunology, and epidemiology of viral infections. Home: 1600 Hagys Ford Rd Apt 9W Narberth PA 19072-1049 Office Phone: 215-898-0848. E-mail: nathansn@mail.med.upenn.edu.

NATHANSON, REBECCA, education educator, law educator; PhD, U. Calif., Santa Barbara. Prof. Tex. Tech U., Lubbock, 1995—2000; Rogers prof. edn. & law U. Nev., Las Vegas, 2000—. Office: Univ Nev Las Vegas 4505 Maryland Pky Las Vegas NV 89154 Office Fax: 702-895-2081. Business E-Mail: rebecca.nathanson@unlv.edu.

NATHANSON, SAUL DAVID, oncologist, surgeon, educator; b. Johannesburg, Dec. 12, 1943; came to U.S., 1975; s. Hymie Barnett and Freda Charlotte (Weinberg) N.; m. Maxine Elaine Zacks, Nov. 29, 1966 (div. Sept. 1978); children: Laurence Cecil, Joshua Russel; m. Jerrilyn Marie Burke, Feb. 18, 1979; children: Abigail Mary, Alison Megan. MD, U. Witwatersrand, Johannesburg, 1966. Diplomate Am. Bd. Surgery. Resident in surgery U. Witwatersrand, 1967-74; fellow in immunology UCLA, 1975-77, fellow in surg. oncology, 1977-80; chief resident in surgery U. Calif.-Davis, Sacramento, 1980-82; surg. oncologist Henry Ford Health Sys., Detroit, 1982—, dir. breast cancer ctr., 1995—; prof. surgery Case Western Res. U., Cleve., 1993—2005, Wayne State U. Sch. Medicine, 2008—; dir. Breast Ctr. Henry Ford Hosp., West Bloomfield, Mich. Assoc. clin. prof. surgery U. Mich., Ann Arbor, 1985—2000; adj. assoc. prof. med. physics Oakland U., Rochester, Mich., 1993—; cancer liaison physician, Commn. on Cancer; prin. investigator for HFHS, ACS Oncology Group; endowed chair Breast Cancer Rsch., 2001. Author: Ordinary Miracles, 2006; contbr. over 200 articles and abstracts to sci. jours., chpts. to books. Recipient Outstanding Tchr. awards U. Mich., 1982-2000, Humanitarian Cancer award, 2006; named Resident Tchr. of Yr., Henry Ford Health Sys. Dept. Surgery, 2006; NIH grantee Nat. Cancer Inst., 1989. Fellow ACS, Soc. Surg. Oncology, Royal Coll. Surgeons; mem. Am. Soc. Clin. Oncology, Western Surg. Assn., Am. Assn. Cancer Rsch., Wayne County Med. Soc. (alt. del. 1994—96). Office: Henry Ford Health Sys 2799 W Grand Blvd Detroit MI 48202-2608 Office Phone: 248-661-6592, 313-916-2917. Business E-Mail: dnathan1@hfhs.org.

NATHANSON, THEODORE HERZL, aeronautical engineer, architect; b. Montreal, Que., Can., Apr. 20, 1923; came to U.S., 1949, naturalized, 1983; s. Henry and Minnie (Goldberg) N. Student, McGill U., 1940-42; SB in Aero. Engring., MIT, 1944; MArch, Harvard U., 1955. Rsch. engr. Noorduyn Aviation Ltd., Montreal, 1944-45; stress engr. Canadair Ltd., Montreal, 1945-46; structural engr. A.V. Roe (Can.) Ltd., Malton, Ont., 1946-47; with Mies van der Rohe, Chgo., summer 1949, Buckminster Fuller, Forest Hills, N.Y., summer 1951; cons. engr., arch. Montreal, Boston, L.A., 1955—. Mem. tech. staff Rockwell Internat., 1979-92, structural analysis and advanced design Space Transp. Systems divsn., Downey, Calif., 1979-86, mission ops. and advanced concepts Space Sta. Systems divsn., 1986-87, space sta. elec. power system Rocketdyne div., Canoga Park, Calif., 1987-92; cons. Aerospace Engr., L.A., 1992—; lectr. arch. McGill U., 1967-68. Projects and models included in group shows: Mus. Fine Arts, Springfield, Mass., 1961, N.Y. World's Fair, 1965, Winterfest, Boston, 1966, Boston Artists' Project '70. Fellow Brit. Interplanetary Soc.; mem. Order Engrs. Que., Order Archs. Que., Soc. Am. Registered Archs., Nat. Soc. Profl. Engrs., AIAA, AIA (assoc.), Royal Archtl. Inst. Can., Nat. Mgmt. Assn., Copley Soc. Boston, MIT Club So. Calif. (bd. govs.), Can. Soc. (L.A.). Jewish. Home: 225 S Olive St Apt 1502 Los Angeles CA 90012-4906 Office Phone: 213-620-0456. Personal E-mail: thanso@hotmail.com.

NATHWANI, BHARAT N., pathologist, educator; b. Bombay, Jan. 20, 1945; came to US, 1972; MBBS, Grant Med. Coll., Bombay, 1969, MD in Pathology, 1972. Intern Grant Med. Coll., Bombay U., 1968-69; asst. prof. pathology Grant Med. Coll., 1972; fellow in hematology Cook County Hosp., Chgo., 1972-73; resident in pathology Rush U., Chgo., 1973-74; fellow in hematopathology City of Hope Med. Ctr., Duarte, Calif., 1975-76, pathologist, 1977-84; prof. pathology, chief hematopathology U. So. Calif., LA, 1984—. Contbr. 135 articles to profl. jours. Recipient Grant awards Nat. Libr. Medicine, Bethesda, Md., Nat. Cancer Inst., 1991. Mem. Internat. Acad. Pathology, Am. Soc. Clin. Pathology, Am. Soc. Hematology, Am. Soc. Oncology. Office: Hmr 209 2011 Zonal Ave Los Angeles CA 90033 Office Phone: 323-226-7064. Business E-Mail: nathwani@usc.edu.

NATINSKY, RON, city councilman, entrepreneur; m. Nancy Natinsky; 2 children. Student, North Tex. State U. Owner various mfg., automotive, tech. and cons. small businesses, Tex., 1967—2004; councilman, Dist. 12 Dallas City Coun., 2005—, chair econ. devel. com., mem. pub. safety com., transp. & environ. com., audit & fin. com. Bd, dirs. North Dallas Neighborhood Alliance; mem. Greater Dallas Planning Coun., Sign & Billboard Task Force, Lic. Appeal Bd., Urban Design Task Force, Planning Policy Papers Com., Mayor's Neighborhood Adv. Com.; vice-chair Citizens Police Review Bd. Mem.: Promotional Products Assn. Internat., Homeowners Assn. (pres.), North Dallas C. of C., Internat. Big Train Operators Club (chmn. fin. com.), North Tex. Garden Train Club (treas.). Mailing: Dallas City Coun 1500 Marilla St Ste 5FN Dallas TX 75201-6390 Business E-Mail: rnatinsky@mail.ci.dallas.tx.us.*

NATION, DAVID ARTHUR, retired computer scientist, sculptor; s. Harold Stanley and Martha Elizabeth (Loonan) N.; m. Jean Lea Bielefeldt, Aug. 9, 1969 (div. May 1979); 1 child, Justin David; m. Rebecca L. Johnson, Oct. 27, 1979. BS in Computer Sci., Iowa State U., 1970; MS, Johns Hopkins U., 1979. Computer scientist U.S. Govt., Washington, 1975—2001; ret., 2001. Author mapping software, pattern classification software, Web software, information visualization software; sculptor;solo shows: Dave Nation's Art Gallery, 1995—; Bay Country Art Guild Member Show, 2000, 08. Treas., Emmanuel United Meth. Ch., Dorsey, md., 1987-2006. Sgt. USAF, 1970—73. Mem. SAG. Democrat. Unitarian Universalist. Achievements include 5 patents in field. Avocations: sculpting, birdwatching, genealogy, photography, community theater. Home Phone: 301-875-3639. Personal E-mail: dave@davenation.com.

NATIONS, HOWARD LYNN, lawyer; b. Dalton, Ga., Jan. 9, 1938; s. Howard Lynn and Eva Earline (Armstrong) Lamb; m. Ella Lois Johnson, June 4, 1960 (div. Nov. 1976); children: Cynthia Lynn Nations Garcia, Angela Jean Gordon Hernandez. BA, Fla. State U., 1963, JD, 1966. Bar: Tex. 1966; cert. trial atty. Tex. Bd. Legal Specialization. Assoc. Butler, Rice Cook & Knapp, Houston, 1966-71; pres. Nations & Cross, Houston, 1971—; v.p., dir., co-founder Ins. Corp. Am., Houston, 1972—; pres. Caplinger & Nations Galleries, Houston, 1973—, Nations Investment Corp., Houston, 1975—, NCM Trade Corp., Houston, 1975; v.p. Delher Am. Inc., Houston, 1975—; pres. Howard L. Nations, PC, Houston, 1971—, Trial Focus, Inc., 1995—. Founder Nations Found.; adj. prof. So. Tex. Coll. Law, Houston, 1967—; speaker in field. Author: Structuring Settlements, 1987; co-author: Texas Workers' Compensation, 1988, (with others) The Anatomy of a Personal Injury Lawsuit, 3rd rev. edit. 1991; editor: Maximizing Damages in Wrongful Death and Personal Injury Litigation, 1985; contbr. articles to profl. jours. Chmn., trustee Nat. Coll. Advocacy, Washington, 1985-92. With M.I. Corps, U.S. Army, 1957-60. Recipient Gene Cavin Excellence award State Bar Tex., 2000, STLA War House award, 2009. Fellow Tex. Bar Found., Houston Bar Found. (life); mem. ATLA (exec. com. 1991-95), Nat. Bd. Trial Advocacy (diplomate civil trial advocacy), Southern Trial Lawyers Assn. (pres. 1994-95, Warhorse award 2009), Tex. Trial Lawyers Assn. (pres. 1992-93), Melven Belli Soc. (pres. 2007-08). Office: The Sterling Mansion 4515 Yoakum Blvd Houston TX 77006-5821 Office Phone: 713-807-8400.

NATIVIDAD, IRENE, women's rights advocate; b. Manila, Philippines, Sept. 14, 1948; m. Andrea Cortese; 1 child, Carlo Natividad Cortese. BA, LI Univ., 1971; MA, Columbus U., 1973, MPhil, 1978; LHD (hon.), LI Univ., 1989, Marymount Coll., 1994. Pres. Globe Women, Inc., Washington, Nat. Women's Political Caucus, 1985—89; chmn. Nat. Commn. on Working Women, 1989—98. Dep. vice chair Dem. Party Asian Caucus, 1982—84; pres. Global Summit of Women; co-chair Corp. Women Dir. Internat.; exec. dir. Philippine Am. Found.; bd. dir. Nat. Mus. Women in Arts, Nat. Assn. Corp. Dir., Sallie Mae; adv. bd. Cigna, Wyndham Internat. Exec. editor Asian American Almanac, 1995, frequent commentator, panelist on TV news shows; contbr. columns in newspapers. Recipient Women Making History award, Women's Congl. Caucus, 1985, Magnificent 7 award, Bus. & Profl. Women/USA, 1995, Women of Genius award, Trinity Coll., Washington, DC, 2001; named one of 100 Most Power Women in Am., Ladies Home Jour., 1988, 74 Women Changing Am. Politics, Campaigns & Elections Mag., 1993, 25 Most Influential Working Mothers, Working Mother Mag., 1997, 21 Leaders for the 21st Century, Women's eNews, 2004, Top 25 Influental Asian Americans, A. Mag. Office: Natividad Associates 1100 G St NW Ste 700 Washington DC 20005-7412 Business E-Mail: president@globewomen.com.

NATOLI, JOSEPH, language educator; b. Bklyn., Aug. 24, 1943; m. Elaine Tuminelli, June 6, 1970; children: Amelia, Brenda. BA, Bklyn. Coll., 1965, MA, 1968; PhD, SUNY, Albany, 1973. Asst. prof. English New Eng. Coll., Henniker, NH, 1971-73, 1973-75; acting dir. libr., adj. lectr. English Bluefield State Coll., W.Va., 1975-77; head reference and bibliography libr. Wake Forest U., Winston Salem, NC, 1977-81; bibliographer, adj. lectr. humanities U. Calif., Irvine, 1981-83, Mich. State U., East Lansing, 1983—, dir. study abroad program Europe, 1996—. Series editor SUNY Press Postmodern Culture, Albany, 1990—. Author: Mots D'Ordre, 1992, Hauntings, 1994, Primer to Postmodernity, 1997, Speeding to the Millenium, 1998, Postmodern Journeys, 2000, Memory's Orbit, 2003, This is a Picture and Not the World, 2007; editor: Twentieth Century Blake Criticism, 1982, Psychological Perspectives on Literature, 1984, Psychocriticism, 1984, Tracing Literary Theory, 1987, Literary Theory's Future(s), 1989, A Postmodern Reader, 1993, Postmodernism: The Key Figures, 2002. Office: Mich State Univ Writing Rhetoric Am Culture Dept 241 Bessey Hall East Lansing MI 48824 Business E-Mail: natoli@msu.edu.

NATONSKI, DAVE, legislative staff member; B, U. Conn., Storrs, 2002. Constituent services rep., Rep. Christopher Shays US House of Reps., Washington, 2002—04, systems adminstr., Rep. Christopher Shays, 2004—05, legis. asst., Rep. Christopher Shays, 2005—08, press sec., Rep. Christopher Shays, 2007—08, comm. dir. to Rep. Aaron Schock, 2009—. Republican. Office: 509 Cannon House Office Bldg Washington DC 20515 Office Phone: 202-225-6201. Office Fax: 202-225-9249.*

NATORI, JOSIE CRUZ (JOSEFINA ALMEDA CRUZ NATORI), apparel designer; b. Manila, Philippines, May 9, 1947; arrived in US, 1964; d. Felipe F. and Angelita A. (Almeda) Cruz; m. Kenneth R. Natori, May 20, 1972; 1 child, Kenneth E.F. BA in Econs., Manhattanville Coll., 1968; Degree (hon.), Acad. Art Coll., San Francisco, 2003. With Bache Securities, NYC; joined Merrill-Lynch Co. as an investment banker, 1971; v.p., 1976—77; owner, CEO The Natori Co., NYC, 1977—. Bd. dirs. The Alltel Corp., 1995—. Bd. dirs. Philippine Am. Found., Jr. Achievement, Inc., 1992, Ednl. Found. for Fashion Industries; trustee Manhattanville Coll., Asian Cultural Coun.; commr. White House Conf. on Small Bus., 1993. Recipient Human Relations award Am. Jewish Com., NYC., 1986, Harriet Alger award Working Woman, NY, 1987, Castle award Manhattanville Coll., Purchase, 1988, Galleon award Pres. Philippines, 1988, NYC Asian-Am. award, Friendship award Philippine-Am. Found., Hall of Fame award Mega Mags., Salute to Am. Fashion Designers award Dept. of Commerce, Ellis Island medal of Honor, 1994, Presdl. Awards for Filipino Individuals and Orgns. Overseas, Pamana ng Pilipino award Philippine Consulate Gen., 2002; named Bus. Woman of Yr. NYC Partnership and C. of C., 1998. Mem. CFDA, Young Pres.'s Orgn., Fashion Group, Com. of 200. Avocations: pianist, tennis player. Home: 45 E 62nd St New York NY 10021-8025 Office: The Natori Company 180 Madison Ave # 19 New York NY 10016-5267

NATOUR, NAHILLE I., obstetrician, gynecologist; b. Midland, Tex., Oct. 18, 1974; d. I. J. and Janet I. Natour. MD, Tex. A&M U. Health Sci. Ctr., College Station, 2001. Cert. 2008. Intern and resident Baylor U. Med. Ctr., Dallas, 2001—05; physician Women's Health Ptnrs., Health Tex. Provider Network, Irving, 2005—. Mem.: AMA, Tex. Assn. Ob-gyn., Dallas County Med. Soc., Tex. Med. Assn., Am. Coll. Ob-gyn. Office: Women's Health Partners 2021 N MacArthur Blvd Suite 500 Irving TX 75061

NATSIOS, ANDREW STEPHEN, diplomat, former federal agency administrator; b. Phila., Pa., Sept. 22, 1949; s. Basil Andrew and Eta (Lappas) Natsios; m. Elizabeth E. Macdonald; children: Emily, Alexander, Phillip. BA, Georgetown U., 1971; MPA, Harvard U., 1979. Treas. Holliston Indsl. Devel. Commn., 1973—75; chmn. Holliston Rep. Town Com., 1974—75; mem. Mass. Ho. Reps. from Dist. 8, 1975—87; exec. dir. Northeast Pub. Power Assn., Milford, Mass., 1987—89; dir. Office Fgn. Disaster Assistance US Agy. Internat. Devel. (USAID), 1989—91, asst. adminstr. Bur. Food & Humanitarian Assistance, 1991—93, adminstr. Washington, 2001—05; v.p. World Vision US, 1993—98; sec. adminstrn. & fin. Commonwealth Mass., 1999—2000; chmn. Mass. Turnpike Authority, 2000—01; Disting. Prof in the Practice of Diplomacy and Advisor on Internat. Devel., Edmund A. Walsh Sch. Fgn. Svc. Georgetown U., 2006—. Spl. coord. for Internat. Disaster Assistance & Spl. Humanitarian Coord. for Sudan The White House, 2004; spl. envoy to pursue ending the violence in the Darfur region of Sudan US Dept. State, 2006—. Author: U.S. Foreign Policy and the Four Horsemen of the Apocalypse, 1997, The Great North Korean Famine, 2001. With USAR, 1972—95. Named Legis. of Yr., Mass. Mcpl. Assn., 1978, Mass. Assn. Sch. Committees, 1986, Citizens for Limited Taxation, 1986; fellow Jennings Randolph Fellowship, US Inst. Peace, 1998—99. Office: Edmund A Walsh Sch Fgn Svc 301 Intercultural Ctr 37th & O St NW Washington DC 20057 E-mail: asn8@georgetown.edu.

NATTEL, STANLEY, cardiologist, research scientist; b. Haifa, Israel, Jan. 28, 1951; arrived in Can., 1952; s. William and Julie (Zwirek) N.; m. Celia Anne Reich, Sept. 25, 1973; children: Jonathan, Ilana, Daniel, Sarah. BSc magna cum laude, McGill U., 1972, MD, 1974. Diplomate Am. Bd. Internal Medicine, Am. Bd. Cardiology. Intern in medicine Royal Victoria Hosp., 1974-75, resident in internal medicine, 1975-76; resident in clin. pharmacology Montreal Gen. Hosp., Que., Canada, 1976-78, cardiologist, clin. pharmacologist, 1981-87, dir. coronary care unit, 1983-87; fellow in cardiology Ind. U., 1978-80; fellow in physiology U. Pa., 1980-81; asst. prof. pharmacology, medicine McGill U., Montreal, 1981-87, assoc. prof., 1987—; cardiologist Montreal Heart Inst., 1987—, dir. rsch. ctr., 1990—2004; prof. dept. medicine U. Montreal, 1995—, Paul-David chair in cardiovasc. electrophysiology, 2003—. External reviewer Med. Rsch. Coun., 1981—, Ont. Health Ministry, 1983-84, NSF, 1992, others; chmn. libr. com. dept. pharmacology McGill U., 1982-86, mem. grad. com., 1984-89, chmn. grad. tng. com., 1986-89, departmental rep. grad. faculty coun., 1989-91, coord. grad. tchg. pharmacology, 1989-91; mem. oper. grants com. Can. Heart Found., 1983-86; chmn. clin. trials com. Montreal Gen. Hosp., 1983-87, chmn. pharmacy and therapeutics com., 1984-87, sec. clin. chemistry rev. com., 1984, course dir. drug therapy, 1984-87, acting dir. divsn. clin. pharmacology, 1984-85, mem. various coms., 1985-87; mem. fellowship awards com. FRSQ, 1988-90, mem. ctr. grants pharmacology/pharmacy com., 1989-90; chmn. pharmacology com. Montreal Heart Inst., 1988-90, mem. search com. pharmacist-in-chief, 1989-90, mem. ethics com., 1991-2004, chmn. internal rsch. com., 1991-2004, mem. consultative com. exec. dir., 1991-2004, chmn. consultative com. rsch. ctr., 1991-2004; cons. coun. pharmacology Province of Quebec, 1989-90; mem. safety monitoring com. CAMIAT Study, 1990-95; assoc. prof. medicine U. Montreal, 1991-95, prof. 1995—, chmn. search com. dir. rsch. Sacré-Coeur Hosp., 1991, mem. rsch. com. Cormes faculty medicine, 1991—2002, mem. rsch. com. dept. medicine, 1991-2004; chmn. search com., dir. rsch. Maisonneuve Rosemont Hosp., 1996; mem. site visit team program project grant NIH, 1991, cons. program project grant, 1993, spl. reviewer cardiovascular study sect., 1993, 95, 97, 98; mem. oper. grants com. Med. Rsch. Coun. Can., 1988-93, chmn., 2002-05; mem. sr. pers. awards com. Can. Heart Found., 1994-96; lectr. in field. Assoc. editor Can. Jour. Physiology and Pharmacology, 1990-95, Br. Jour. Pharmacology, 2000-2005; mem. editl. bd. Jour. Cardiovasc. Electrophysiology, 1991—, Drugs, 1993—, Cardiovasc. Drugs and Therapy, 1993-2001, Circulation Rsch., 1995—, JACC, 1995-2000, Cardiovascular Rsch., 1999-2002, J Physiol, 2007, JMCC, 2007, others; manuscript reviewer Am. Jour. Cardiology, Nature, Nature Medicine, Nature Genetics, New Eng. Jour. Medicine, PNAS, Science, others; contbr. chpts. to books and articles to profl. jours. Chmn. edn. com. Hebrew Acad. Sch., Montreal, 1991-92. Grantee Que. Heart Found., 1981—, Nordic Pharms., 1985-87, Knoll Pharms., 1991-93, others; fellow Med. Rsch. Coun. Can., 1979-81; McGill U. scholar, 1967-74, Sir Edward Beatty scholar McGill U., 1967-70, Rsch. scholar Med. Rsch. Coun., 1982-87, Sr. Rsch. scholar Fonds de la Recherche en Santé du Quebec, 1990-93; recipient Career Rsch. Achievement award Can. Cardiovasc. Soc., 2001. Fellow Am. Coll. Cardiology, Royal Coll. Physicians Can. (cert. medicine, cardiology), Acad. Scis. Royal Soc. Can.; mem. Am. Heart Assn. (coun. basic sci., leadership com. 2003-05), Royal Soc. Can., Heart Rhythm Soc., Am. Soc. Pharmacology and Exptl. Therapeutics, Can. Cardiovasc. Soc. (councilor 1992-95), Can. Soc. Clin. Pharmacology (Kenneth M. Piafsky Young Investigator award 1985), Pharm. Soc. Can. Biophys. Soc., Am. Heart Assn. (leadership com.). Avocations: studying jewish religious works, sports. Home: 5609 Alpine Ave Côte Saint Luc PQ Canada H4V 2X6 Office: Montreal Heart Inst 5000 Belanger St E Montreal PQ Canada H1T 1C8 Home Phone: 514-482-0715; Office Phone: 514-376-3330. Personal E-mail: stanleynattel@aol.com. Business E-Mail: stanley.nattel@icm-mhi.org.

NATTINGER, ANN B., internist, researcher, medical educator; b. Chgo., Oct. 9, 1957; d. John Joseph and Evelyn Elizabeth Butler; m. Bruce Edward Nattinger, June 9, 1979; children: Kevin, Kinsey, Michael. BS, U. Ill., 1979, MD, 1983; MPH, U. Rochester, 1988. Diplomate Am. Bd. Internal Medicine. Resident, fellow Strong Meml. Hosp., U. Rochester, NY, 1983—88; from asst. prof. to assoc. prof. Med. Coll. Wis., Milw., 1988—2000, prof. medicine and health svcs. rsch., 2000—, chief gen. internal medicine, 1999—, dir. Ctr. Patient Care and Outcomes Rsch., 2000—; endowed chair Lady Riders Prof. Breast Cancer Rsch., 2005—. Cons. NIH, Bethesda, Md., 2000—; reviewer Inst. Medicine, Washington, 2000. Mem. editl. bd.: Jour. Gen. Internal Medicine, 1996—99; contbr. articles to profl. jours.; assoc. editor: Arch Internal Medicine, 2004—08. Grantee RO-1, NIH/NCI, 1993—97, 2000—, Dept. Def., 1994—99, 1996—2001, 2004—. Fellow: ACP; mem.: Ctrl. Soc. Clin. Rsch. (coun. mem. 1995—98), Soc. Gen. Internal Medicine (coun. mem. 1994—97, sec. 2000—03). Office: Med Coll Wis 8701 Watertown Plank Rd Milwaukee WI 53226 Office Phone: 414-805-0840. Business E-Mail: anatting@mcw.edu.

NAUERT, RICK, healthcare educator, consultant; b. Austin, Tex., Oct. 13, 1955; PhD, U. Tex., Austin, 2002. Sr. health news editor PsychCentral.com; assoc. prof. sch. health adminstrn. Tex. State U., San Marcos, 2007—. Cons.-physical therapist Austin Home Health Agy. Office: Texas State Univ 601 University Dr San Marcos TX 78666 Office Phone: 512-245-3949. Business E-Mail: rn14@txstate.edu.

NAUGHTON, JAMES MARTIN, journalist; b. Pitts., Aug. 13, 1938; s. Francis Patrick and Martha Ann (Clear) N.; m. Diana Marie Thomas, Sept. 5, 1964; children: Jenifer Mary Naughton Genovesi, Lara Marie, Michael Thomas, Kerry Marie. BA cum laude, U. Notre Dame, 1960. Reporter, photographer Painesville (Ohio) Telegraph, summer, 1955-60; reporter Cleve. Plain Dealer, 1962-69; Washington corr. N.Y. Times, 1969-77; nat. editor Phila. Inquirer, 1977-79, met. editor, 1979-83, assoc. mng. editor, 1980-86, dep. mng. editor, 1986-90, mng. editor, 1990-91, exec. editor, 1991-96; pres. The Poynter Inst. for Media Studies, St. Petersburg, Fla., 1996—2003, pres. emeritus, 2003—. Marsh prof. U. Mich., Ann Arbor, 1997; Pulitzer prize juror, 1998—99; Heinz award juror, 2005—07. With USMC, 1960—62. Recipient Disting. Svc. award Sigma Delta Chi, 1973. Roman Catholic. Home: 2500 Coffee Pot Blvd NE Saint Petersburg FL 33704-3466 E-mail: swamijim@mac.com.

NAUGHTON, JOHN PATRICK, cardiologist, educator; b. West Nanticoke, Pa., May 20, 1933; s. John Patrick and Anne Frances (McCormick) N.; children: Bruce, Marcia, Lisa, George, Michael, Thomas. AA, Cameron State U., Lawton, Okla., 1952; BS, St. Louis U., 1954; MD, Okla. U., 1958; MD (hon.), Kosin U., 1995. Intern George Washington U. Hosp., Washington, 1958-59; resident U. Okla. Med. Center, 1959-64; asst. prof. medicine U. Okla., 1966-68; assoc. prof. medicine U. Ill., 1968-70; prof. medicine George Washington U., 1970-75, dean acad. affairs, 1973-75, dir. div. rehab. medicine and Regional Rehab. Research and Tng. Center, 1970-75; dean Sch. Medicine SUNY, Buffalo, 1975-96, prof. medicine, physiology, social, preventive and rehab. medicine Sch. Medicine, 1975—, acting v.p. for health scis., 1983-84, v.p. clin. affairs, 1984-96, interim chmn. rehab. medicine, 2003—. Dir. Nat. Exercise and Heart Disease Project, 1972-83; chmn. policy adv. bd. Beta-blocker Heart Attack Trial Nat. Heart, Lung and Blood Inst., 1977-82; pres. Western N.Y. chpt. Am. Heart Assn., 1983-85, v.p. N.Y. State affiliate, 1985, pres. N.Y. State affiliate, 1988-90; chmn. clin. applications and preventions adv. com. Nat. Heart, Lung and Blood Inst., 1984; mem. Fed. COGME working group on consortia, 1996-97, N.Y. Gov.'s Commn. on Grad. Med. Edn., 1985, N.Y. State Coun. on Grad. Med. Edn., 1988-90, chmn. 1996—; pres. Assoc. Med. Schs. N.Y., 1982-84, mem. adminstrv. com. Coun. of Deans, 1983-89; mem. N.Y. State Dept. of Health Adv. Com. on Physician Recredentialing; mem. exec. coun. Nat. Inst. on Disability and Rehab. Rsch. 1991-92; v.p. James H. Cummings Found. Author: Exercise Testing and Exercise Training in Coronary Heart Disease, 1973, Exercise Testing: Physiological, Biomechanical, and Clinical Principles, 1988 Career devel. awardee Nat. Heart Inst., 1966-71; recipient Brotherhood-Sisterhood award in medicine NCCJ, N.E. Minority Educators award, 1990, Acad. Alumnus of Yr. award Okla. U., 1990, award for svc. to minorities in med. edn., 1991, Frank Sindelar award N.Y. State Am. Heart Assn., 1995, James Platt White Soc. award, 1995, Outstanding Contbns. in the field of Health Care award Sheehan Meml. Hosp., 1995, Chancellor Charles P. Norton medal, SUNY, Buffalo, 1997, AMS Disting. Svc. award, 2001. Fellow ACP, Am. Coll. Cardiology, Am. Coll. Sports Medicine (pres. 1970-71, Citation award 2000), Am. Coll. Chest Physicians; Am. Coll. Preventive Medicine, Am. Heart Assn. (epidemiology coun. 2000—, coun. on nutrition, phys. activity and metabolism), Acad. Health Profls. Ins. Assn. (hon.). Office: SUNY Buffalo 128 Farber Hall 3435 Main St Buffalo NY 14214-3099 Home Phone: 716-668-3753. Business E-Mail: jpn@buffalo.edu.

NAULT, WILLIAM HENRY, publishing executive; b. Ishpeming, Mich., June 9, 1926; s. Henry J. and Eva (Perrault) N.; m. Helen E. Matthews, Nov. 28, 1946; children: William Henry, Rebecca Nault Marks, Ronald, George, Peter, Julia Nault Doyle, Robert, David. AB, No. Mich. U., 1948, LittD (hon.), 1988; MA, U. Mich., 1949; EdD, Columbia U., 1953, LHD (hon.), 1980, LLD (hon.), 1986, LittD (hon.), 1988. Dir. adult edn., Battle Creek, Mich., 1948—49; guidance counselor, 1949-50; prin. W.K. Kellogg High Sch., Battle Creek, 1950-53; research assoc. Columbia U., 1953-54; asst. supt. Ridgewood, NJ, 1954-55; adj. prof. William Patterson U. N.J., 1954—55; dir. research World Book, Inc. (formerly Field Enterprises Edn. Corp.), Chgo., 1955-63, v.p., 1963-66, sr. v.p., editorial dir., 1966-68, exec. v.p. and editorial dir., 1968-83; pres., pub., chief operating officer World Book, Inc., 1983-84, gen. chmn. editorial adv. bds., 1968-99, pub., 1983-95, pub. emeritus, 1995—. Past vice chmn. Govt. Adv. Com. on Internat. Library and Book Programs, U.S. Dept. State; past mem. nat. adv. bd. Ctr. on Ednl. Media and Materials for Handicapped; past mem. exec. bd. Commn. Instns. Higher Edn., North Central Assn. Colls. and Secondary Schs.; mem. dean's adv. council Coll. Bus. and Pub. Adminstrn., U. Mo., Columbia; mem. nat. council Inst. Internat. Edn. Author material on courses of study. Mem. alumni com. Columbia Tchrs. Coll. Capital Campaign; mem. White House Conf. on Youth, White House Conf. on Librs., White House Conf. on Edn.; pres. Oak Park (Ill.) Bd. Edn., 1960-63; v.p. LaGrange (Ill.) Libr. Bd.; bd. regents Lincoln Acad., Ill.; past trustee Adler Planetarium, De Paul U., Chgo. Geol. Soc.; bd. dirs. H.V. Phalin Found. Grad. Study, World Book, Inc., A.J. Nystrom Co., Field Edn. Co., Libr. Movens, Inc.; mem. adv. bd. Rosary Coll.; mem. liberal arts and scis. adv. council De Paul U. Served with F.A., AUS, 1944-45. Recipient Columbia U. Tchrs. Coll. medal for disting. svc. in edn.; named Disting. Alumnus No. Mich. U., U. Mich., Columbia U. Fellow AAAS; mem. ALA, Chgo. Planetarium Soc. (trustee), Chgo. Geog. Soc. (dir.), Am. Acad. Polit. and Social Sci., Am. Edn. Rsch. Assn., Am. Assn. Sch. Adminstrs., ASCD, Chgo. Pubs. Assn. (past pres.), Ill. Assn. Sch. Adminstrs., Ill. Acad. Sci., NSTA, Nat. Council Tchrs. English, Assn. Am. Geographers, Assn. Childhood Edn. Internat., NAESP, Nat. Assn. Secondary Sch. Prins., Council for Advancement Sci. Writing, Internat. Platform Assn., Nat. Council Social Studies, Nat. Soc. Study Edn. Clubs: Mid-Am, Mchts. and Mfrs. Roman Catholic. Office: World Book Inc 525 W Monroe St Chicago IL 60661-3629 Personal E-mail: naultwh@aol.com, naultwh@comcast.net.

NAUM, CHRISTOPHER JOHN, fire protection, emergengy management, training consultant, educator, firefighter safety advocate; b. Syracuse, NY, Feb. 8, 1957; s. John and Florence (Karafile) N.; m. Ann M. McCabe, July 21, 1984 (div.); children: Lauren K., Ashley C.; m. Lori A. Drosi, Sept. 13, 1997; 1 child, Emily N. BA, Syracuse U., 1981; student, SUNY-Onondaga C.C., 1980-86, Nat. Fire Acad., Emmitsburg, Md., 1982-92, 99-01, U. Md., 1982-84. Cet. fire instr., hazardous materials technician, fire prevention and bldg. code enforcement officer and instr., fire protection engr.; cert. fire officer; safety specialist; cert. emergency mgmt. profl. devel. Fed. Emergency Mgmt. Agy./Emergency Mgmt. Inst., 2004. From fire explorer to fire lt. Moyers Corners Fire Dept., Town of Clay, NY, 1975-81; fire capt. Moyers Corners Fire Dept., Onondaga County Fire System, Town of Clay, NY, 1981—93, tng. instr., 1991-99, FD tng. officer, 1999—2000; battalion capt. Moyers Corners Fire Dept., Onondaga County Fire Sys., Town of Clay, NY, 2002—06; project architect Maniktala Assocs., P.C., Syracuse, NY, 1981-91; pres., exec. cons. Americana Fire Cons., Inc., Syracuse, 1988-91; fire protection engr. Entergy Nuc. N.E., James A. FitzPatrick Nuclear Power Plant, Lycoming, 1992-93, fire protection specialist, 1993-98, fire and safety specialist, 1998-99, fire and safety specialist II, 2000—02, dep. fire chief, 1995—2002, fire chief, fire protection and indsl. safety mgr., 2002—07; acting fire protection supr. N.Y. Power Authority, James A. Fitzpatrick Nuc. Power Plant, Lycoming, 1999-2000; pres. EMAC Internat. LLC, 2005—, Columbia Southern U. BA Arc, 2007—; chief tng. command inst. Washington, 2008—. Coord. dept. fire protection tech. Onondaga C.C., SUNY, Syracuse, 1984-89; co-dir. Onondaga County Fire Rescue Inst., 1987-89, Town of Clay Fire Tng. Tower, 2000-02; pres. L.A. Emergency Mgmt. and Tng. Cons., Syracuse, 1992-2004; adj. faculty instr. U.S. Fire Adminstrn., Nat. Fire Acad., Md., 2000—; mem. adj. faculty Command Sch., Inc., 2002-04; apptd. mem. Onondaga County Fire Adv. Bd., 2005—. Contbg. editor Firehouse Mag., 1988—, On-Call Mag., 1995-96, Nat. Fire Protection Assn. Handbook, 18th edit., 1997, Firehouse.com, 2002—; contbr. articles to profl. jours. Mem. FEMA US&R Task Force Working Group, 1989-92. Recipient Kodak/KINSA internat. medallion for excellence in photography, 1977, FEMA cert. of appreciation, 1991; others. Mem. AIA, Internat. Soc. Fire Svc. Instrs. (bd. dirs., dir.-at-large 2005—08, del. U.S./U.K. Fire Svc. Rsch. Symposium 2005, 2nd v.p. 2008), George D. Post award 1987, Nat. Fire Instr. of Yr. award 1987), World Safety Orgn., Internat. Assn. Fire Chiefs (nat. com. on urban rescue and structural collapse 1988-98, Cert. of Appreciation 1993), Internat. Fire Photographers Assn., Nat. Fire Protection Assn. (nat. com. 1988—, chair tech. rescue com., trench rescue working group), Nat. Assn. for Search and Rescue, Soc. Fire Protection Engrs., N.Y. State Assn. Fire Chiefs, Alliance for Fire and Emergency Mgmt. (steering com. for Nat. Search and Rescue Assn. 1996-97, Internat. Fire Instr. Exch. fellow 1996), Soc. Fire Protection Engrs., Open Fire Acad. Internat. (bd. dirs. 2006-), Firefighter Nation (com. mem.), Firefighter Safety Advocate, Fire Rescue 1.com (contbg. biogger 2009-), Internat. Assn. Fire Chiefs (appt.bd. dirs. safety, health survival sect. 2008-). Greek Orthodox. Avocations: downhill skiing, drawing and painting, photography. Home: 4286 Ironwood Cir Liverpool NY 13090-2402 E-mail: cnaum@twcny.rr.com.

NAUMAN, BRUCE, artist; b. Ft. Wayne, Ind., Dec. 6, 1941; m. Judy Nauman, 1964 (div.); 2 children; m. Susan Rothenberg, 1989. BFA, U. Wis.-Madison, 1964; MFA, U. Calif., Davis, 1966; studied with, Italo Scango, William Wiley, Robert Arneson, Frank Owen, Stephen Kaltenbach.; DFA (hon.), San Francisco Art Inst., 1989; ArtsD (hon.), Calif. Inst. Arts, 2000. Tchr. asst. to Wayne Thiebaud, 1964; instr. San Francisco Art Inst., 1966-68; instr. sculpture U. Calif., Irvine, 1970 Author: Pictures of Sculptures in a Room, 1966, Clear Sky, 1968, Burning Small Fires, 1968; one man shows include Nicholas Wilder Gallery, L.A., Sacramento State Coll., 1968, Galerie Konrad Fischer Dusseldorff, 1968, Los Angeles County Mus. Art (retrospective), 1972, U. Calif., Irvine, 1973, Stadtische Kunsthalle (retrospective), Dusseldorf, W. Ger., Art/Voir, Centre Beaubourg, Paris, 1974, Sculpture Am. Directions 1945-1975, Nat. Collection of Fine Arts, Smithsonian Inst., 1975, Body Works, Mus. Contemporary Art, Chgo., 1975, Drawing Now, Mus. Modern Art, N.Y.C., 1975, 200 Years Am. Sculpture, Whitney Mus., NYC, 1976, The Artist and the Photograph, Israel Mus., 1976, Sculpture, Munster, W. Ger., 1977, A View of a Decade, Mus. Contemporary Art, Chgo., 1977, Made by Sculptors, Stedelijk Mus., Amsterdam, 1978, Words Words, Mus. Bochum, W. Ger., 1979, The Broadening of the Concept of Reality in the Art of the 60s and 70s, Mus. Haus Lange Krefeld, W. Ger., 1979, Albright-Knox Art Gallery, Buffalo, 1975, U. Nev., 1976, Mpls. Inst. Arts, 1978, Portland Center for Visual Arts, 1979, Leo Castelli Gallery, NYC, 1982, Sperone Westwater Fischer, NYC, 1982, Sperone Westwater, NYC, 1990, 1996, 2001, 2002, 2008, Dia Ctr. for Arts, NYC, 2002, Corcoran Gallery Art, Washington, 2002-03, Ludwig Mus. Cologne, Germany, 2003, Deutsche Guggenheim, Berlin, 2003-04, Tate Modern, London, 2004-05, Tate Liverpool, 2006, Milw. Art Mus., 2006, U. Calif. Berkeley Art Mus. and Pacific Film Archive, 2007, others; group exhbns. include Fischbach Gallery, William Geis, Bruce Nauman, San Francisco Art Inst., 1966, Am. Sculpture of the Sixties, Los Angeles County Mus. Art, 1967, Documenta IV, Kassel, W. Ger., 1968, When Attitudes Become Form, Kunsthalle, Berne, Switzerland, toured, Europe, 1969, Kompass IV, Van Abbermuseum, Eindohoven, Netherlands, 1969, Corcoran Gallery Art, Washington, 1969, Anti-Illusion: Procedures-Materials, Whitney Mus. Am. Art, NYC, 1969, Whitney Biennial, 1987, Soloman R. Guggenheim Mus., NYC, 1969, Holograms and Lasers, Mus. Contemporary Art, Chgo., 1970, Conceptual Art and Conceptual Aspects, NY Cultural Center, 1970, Am. Art Since 1960, Princeton U., 1970, Info, Mus. Modern Art, NYC, 1971, Diagrams and Drawing, Rijksmuseum Kroller-Mueller, 1972, USA West Coast, Kunstverein, Hamburg, W. Ger., 1972, Documenta V, Kassel, W. Ger., 1972, Gilder, Objedte, Filme, Konzepte, Stadische Galerie, Munich, 1973, Art and Image in Recent Art, Art Inst., Chgo., 1974, Carol Taylor Art, Dallas, 1983, Kunsthalle, Basel, Switzerland, 1986, Carnegie Mus. Art, 1991-92, La. Mus. Art, 1997-98, Henry Art Gallery, Seattle, 2000, Art Gallery NSW, 2001, Donald Young Gallery, Chgo., 2002, Austin Mus. Art, Austin, Tex., 2003, Cleve. Mus. Art, 2003, SITE Santa Fe Internat. Biennail, 2004, Wexner Ctr. Arts, Ohio, 2005, Mus. Modern Art, NYC, 2006, Venice Biennale, 2007, others; represented in permanent collections: Whitney Mus. Am. Art, Los Angeles County Mus. Art; prodr. numerous video works. Nat. Endowment Arts grantee, 1968; Aspen Inst. Humanistic Studies, grantee, 1970; recipient Wolf Prize in arts (xculpture) Wolf Found., Israel, 1993, Praemium Imperiale award, Japan, 2004; named Best Internat. Artist, Beaux-Arts Mag., Paris, 2004. Fellow: Am. Acad. Arts and Scis.; mem.: Am. Acad. Arts and Letters. Avocation: horseback riding. Office: Sperone Westwater 415 W 13 St New York NY 10014

NAUMANN, JOSEPH FRED, archbishop; b. St. Louis, June 4, 1949; s. Fred and Louise (Lukens) Naumann. BA, Cardinal Glennon Coll., St. Louis, 1971; degree in theology, Kenrick Sem., St. Louis, 1975. Deacon St. Christopher's Parish, Florissant, Mo., 1974-75; ordained priest Archdiocese of St. Louis, 1975; assoc. pastor St. Dominic Savio Parish, Affton, Mo., 1975-79, Our Lady of Sorrows Parish, St. Louis, 1979-84; part-time assoc. pastor Most Blessed Sacrament Parish, St. Louis, 1984-89; pastor Ascension Parish, Normandy, Mo., 1989-94; vicar gen. Archdiocese of St. Louis, 1994—97, aux. bishop, 1997—2004, apostolic adminstr., 2003—04; coadjutor archbishop Archdiocese of Kansas City in Kans., 2004, archbishop, 2005—. Chmn. Kans. Cath. Conf.; trustee Kenrick-Glennon Sem. Roman Catholic. Office: Archdiocese of Kansas City 12615 Parallel Pkwy Kansas City KS 66109

NAUMANN, WILLIAM CARL, consumer products company executive; b. Peoria, Ill., Mar. 25, 1938; s. William Louis and Emma (Bottin) N.; m. Polly Roby, May 20, 1962 (div. 1980); children: Jeff, Heather, Derek; m. Patricia Gallagher, Sept. 9, 1993 BSCE, Purdue U., 1960; MBA, U. Chgo., 1975. With Inland Steel Products Co., Chgo., 1960—68, N.Y. dist. mgr., 1968—70, divsn. gen. mgr., 1971—74; group v.p., bd. dirs. Inryco, Melrose Park, Ill., 1974—81; asst. chief engr. Inland Steel Co., Chgo., 1981—82, asst. gen. mgr. corp. planning, 1982—83, asst. gen. mgr. sales, 1983—85, gen. mgr. sales and mktg., 1985—87; exec. v.p. internat. ops. Hussmann Corp., Bridgeton, Mo., 1987, exec. v.p. sales and mktg., 1987; pres. Hussmann Food Svc. Co., Bridgeton, 1987—89; corp. v.p., chief quality officer Whitman Corp., Chgo., 1990—91; CEO Ranger Industries, 1992; sr. v.p., COO Pexco Holdings, Inc., Tulsa, 1993—96; chmn. bd. dirs., CEO Sports Holdings Corp., Montreal, Canada, 1996—97; pres., CEO Hatteras Collection, Inc., New Bern, NC, 1997—2005; chmn. Hatteras Collection, 2008—, Hatteras Yachts and Cabo Yachts, 2008—. Past chmn., bd. dir. New Bern C. of C.; trustee Cravers CC; chmn. C. of C. NC Eastern Region, bd. dirs., Swiss Bear, New Bern Mil. Alliance. Mem. New Bern 300th Celebration, U. Chgo. Exec. Program Club (past pres.), U. Chgo. Alumni Assn. (past pres., bd. govs. 1986-95), Ea. Carolina Yacht Club, Ocean Reef Club, New Bern Golf and Country Club, Beta Gamma Sigma Avocations: boating, travel, cooking. Home: 41 Gables Rd New Bern NC 28562-7079 Office: Hatteras Yachts Inc 110 N Glenburnie Rd New Bern NC 28560-2703 Office Phone: 252-634-4868. Personal E-mail: wcnaumann@embargmail.com.

NAUMER, CAROLA, art historian, educator; d. Helmuth and Tomee Naumer. BA, San Francisco State U., 1983, MA, 1987; PhD, Fla. State U., 1998. Instr. Fla. A&M U., Tallahassee, 1989—95, Bainbridge Coll., Ga., 1995—96, Tallahssee C.C., 1995—98; grad. tchg. asst. Fla. State U., Tallahassee, 1998—98; prof. Truckee Meadows C.C., Reno, 1999—. Participant NEH Summer Seminar, Naples, Italy, 2000. Contbr. articles to profl. jours. Mem.: Coll. Art Assn., Archaeol. Inst. Am. Office Fax: 775-674-4853. Business E-Mail: cnaumer@tmcc.edu.

NAUMER, JANET NOLL, retired dean; b. Phila., May 26, 1933; d. Ray Clifford and Julia Barton (Coffey) Noll; m. Carlos Naumer, Sept. 30, 1960 (div. 1972); 1 child, Mark. BA in Journalism, Pa. State U., 1955; MA, U. Denver, 1968; PhD in Edn., U. Colo., 1978. Media specialist Santa Fe Sr. High Sch., 1968-69; edn. specialist Inst. Am. Indian Arts, Santa Fe, 1969-73; instr. U. N.Mex., Albuquerque, 1973-74; media specialist Kubasaki High Sch., Zukeran, Okinawa, Japan, 1974-75; asst. prof. grad. sch. libr. and info. mgmt. U. Denver, 1977-83; dir. libr. and media ctr. Porterville (Calif.) Coll., 1983-92; assoc. dean, libr. and media svcs. Glendale (Calif.) Coll., 1992-96, dean libr. and learning resources, 1996-98; ret. Author: Media Center Management with an Apple II, 1984; editor LRACCC Intercom, 1989-98; co-author: The Works for Library and Media Center Management, 1998, Electronic Learning Resource Centers: Guidelines, Planning, Examples, 1997; contbr. articles to profl. jours. No. Calif. Community Colls. rsch. grantee, 1985-86; named Kern Dist. Innovator of Yr., League for Innovation, 1988; Libr. Achievement award Coun. of Chief Librarians, Calif. Cmty. Colls., 1997-98. Democrat. Avocation: photography. E-mail: jnaumer@npgcable.com.

NAURATH, DAVID ALLISON, engineering psychologist, researcher; b. Houston, Mar. 11, 1927; s. Walter Arthur and Joy Frances (Bradbury) N.; m. Barbara Ellen Coverdell; children: Kathleen Ann, David Allen, Cynthia Ellyn, Randall Austin. BA, Simpson Coll., Indianola, Iowa, 1948; MA, Southern Meth. U., 1949; postgrad., U. Denver, 1955-57. Job analyst U.S. Air Force, San Antonio and Denver, 1951-55, rsch. psychologist Lowry AFB, Colo., 1955-60, Navy, Life Scis. & Systems div., Point Mugu, Calif., 1960-76; engring. psychologist Navy Systems Engring., Point Mugu, 1976-83; ret. Presenter at profl. socs. and orgns. in field. Contbr. articles to Jour. Engring. Psychology, jour. Soc. for Info. Display, jour. Soc. Photo-optical Instrument Engrs. With USAAF, 1944-46; svc. counsel LA Police Commn. Rampart Independent Review Panel. Mem. AAAS (life), IEEE (sr.), Am. Psychol. Assn., N.Y. Acad. Sci. (emeritus), Human Factors Soc. (panel mem. Certification of Human Factors Engrs. 1976), Soc. Engring. Psychologists, Soc. for Info. Display (life), Defense Rsch. Inst. Methodist. Home: 5633 Pembroke St Ventura CA 93003-2200

NAVA, ELIZABETH M., history professor; d. Juana Pedraza, Nava and Martin Nava; m. Thomas G. Russell, Nov. 20, 1974; children: Elena J. Russell - Nava, Maya A.A. Russell - Nava, Cecilia E. Russell - Nava. MA, U. Calif., Santa Cruz, 1989. History instr. Evergreen Valley Coll., San Jose, Calif., 1995—. Office: Evergreen Valley Coll 3095 Yerba Buena Rd San Jose CA 95135-1598

NAVAB, MOHAMAD, cardiologist, educator; b. Shiraz, Espahan, Iran, Feb. 8, 1945; came to U.S., 1969; s. Noor and Fakhr Taj (Nazem) N.; m. Neda Navab, Jan. 1, 1982; children: Kaveh Danial, Anahita Donya. BSc, Nat. Coll. Nutrition, Tehran, Iran, 1967; MSc, Columbia U., NYC, 1971, PhD, 1976. Dep. dir. rsch. Nat. Inst. Nutrition, Tehran, 1979-80; head clin. lab. Talegh Med. Ctr. Nat. Univ., Tehran, 1980-82; postdoctoral fellow cardiology ctr. UCLA, 1982-84, asst. rsch. cardiologist, 1984-88, asst. prof., 1988-92, assoc. prof., 1992-96, prof. cardiology, 1996—. Assoc. editor Aterioscleorsis and Thrombosis, 1994-98, mem. editl. bd. 1999-2005; contbr. articles to profl. jours.; patentee in field. Active Democratic campaigns, 1970-71, 82—. Lt. Iranian Health Corps, 1967-69. Fellow NIH, 1983-86. Fellow Am. Heart Assn. (arteriosclerosis coun. 1990—, credentials com. 1994-96), Iranians for Internat. Coop. (sec. bd. dirs. 1999—), Anti Discrimination Orgn. (bd. advisors 2000—). Avocations: tennis, skiing. Office: UCLA Box 951679 Los Angeles CA 90095-1679 Home: 1135 N Bundy Dr Los Angeles CA 90049-1512

NAVAL, NEERAJ, medical educator; married. MD, Johns Hopkins U., Balt. Cert. asst. prof. Neurocritical Care, UCNS. Asst. prof, neurocritical care Johns Hopkins U. Sch. Med., 2004—. NCRR grant, Nat. Ctr. Rsch. Resources, NIH, 2008. Business E-Mail: nnaval1@jhmi.edu.

NAVALTA, JAMES W., physical education educator; b. Riverside, Calif. s. S. Wilfred and Tauna Navalta; m. Bess Flora; children: Kalei W., Koa J., Kawelo M. BS, Brigham Young U., Laie, Hawaii, 1996; MS, U. Nev., Las Vegas, 1998; PhD, Purdue U., West Lafayette, Ind., 2003. Cert. health fitness instr. Am. Coll. Sports Medicine. Asst. prof. exercise sci. Southern Ark. U., Magnolia, 2003—06, Western Ky. U., Bowling Green, 2006—. Editor-in-chief Internat. Jour. Exercise Sci., 2008—. Mem.: Am. Coll.Sports Medicine. Office: Western Ky Univ 1906 College Heights Blvd #11089 Bowling Green KY 42101-1089 Office Fax: 270-745-6043. Business E-Mail: james.navalta@wku.edu.

NAVAR, LUIS GABRIEL, physiology educator, director, researcher; b. El Paso, Tex., Mar. 24, 1941; s. Luis and Concepcion (Najera) N.; m. Randa Ann Bumgarner, Oct. 15, 1965; children: Tonia, Tess, Gabriel, Daniel. BS, Tex. A&M U., 1962; PhD, U. Miss., 1966, postdoctoral study, 1966-69. Instr. dept. physiology/biophysics U. Miss., Jackson, 1966-67, asst. prof., 1967-71, assoc. prof., 1971-74, U. Ala., Birmingham, 1974-76, prof., 1976-88, assoc. prof. Nephrology Rsch. and Tng. Ctr., 1979-83, prof., 1983-88; prof., chmn. dept. physiology Tulane U. Med. Sch., New Orleans, 1988—, co-dir. Hypertension and Renal Ctr. of Excellence, 2001—. Vis. scientist Duke U. Med. Ctr., Durham, N.C., 1972-73; adv. bd. NIH Ctr. Sci. Rev., 1998-99; bd. dirs. Fedn. Am. Socs. Exptl. Biology, 1997-01. Assoc. editor News in Physiol. Scis., 1994-2000, Am. Jour. Physiology, 1983-89, mem. editl. bd., 1982-83, 97—; mem. editl. bd. Kidney Internat., 1976-87, Kidney, 1992—, Clin. Sci., 1994-99, Jour. Am. Soc. Nephrology, 1996-2001, Jour. Am. Soc. Nephrology, 1996-2001, Am. Jour. Kidney Disease, 1997-2001, Am. Jour. Hypertension, 1999—, Hypertension, 1980-83, 2002-04, assoc. editor, 1993-2000, cons. editor, 2006—; contbr. chpts. to books, articles to profl. jours. Cardiovascular and renal study sects. NIH, 1998—2000, chmn., 2000—02; bd. dirs. Consortium for Southeastern Hypertension Control, 1998—2000. Recipient Rsch. Career Devel. award, Nat. Heart, Lung and Blood Inst., 1974—79, Merit award, 1988—97, Bodil M.

Schmidt Nielson Disting. Mentor and Scientist award, 2006, Lifetime Achievement award, COSEHC, 2006, Robert W. Berliner award for excellence in renal physiology, 2007, Daggs award, 2008; vis. scholar Pfizer/ACCF, 2002. Fellow: AAAS; mem.: High Blood Pressure Rsch. Am. Heart Assn., Assn. of Am. Med. Coll. (administrv. bd. of coun. of academic soc. 2004—), Assn. Chmn. Depts. Physiology (councillor 1993—95, pres.-elect 1995—96, pres. 1996—97, Disting. Svc. award 2003), Interam. Soc. Hypertension (chair awards com. 2003—), Am. Soc. Hypertension (coun. 1992—94, chmn. basic. sci. com. 1997, treas. 1997—2001, Richard Bright award 2001), Internat. Soc. Nephrology, Am. Soc. Nephrology, Am. Heart Assn. (chmn. cardiorenal rsch. study com. 1994—95, nat. rsch. com. 1994—99, Lewis K. Dahl Lectr. 1997, profl. and pub. edn. com. 1999—, chmn. coun. high blood pressure rsch. 2006—, kidney, high blood pressure couns., vice chmn. leadership com. coun. high blood pressure rsch., Sci. Coun. Disting. Achievement award 1999, Corcoran Lectr. award 2001), Am. Physiol. Soc. (coun. 1991—94, Gottschalk Disting. Lectr. Renal Physiology 1997, pres.-elect 1997—98, pres. 1998—99, Bodil M. Schmidt-Nielson Disting. Mentor and Sci. award 2006, Robert W. Berliner award 2007, Ray G. Daggs award 2008). Democrat. Roman Catholic. Home: 10020 Hyde Pl New Orleans LA 70123-1522 Office: Tulane U Med Sch Dept Physiology 1430 Tulane Ave New Orleans LA 70112-2699 Home Phone: 504-738-5547; Office Phone: 504-988-5251. Business E-Mail: navar@tulane.edu.

NAVARRA, TOVA, writer, artist; b. Newark, July 10, 1948; d. Joe and Rose Leslie Treihart; m. John G. Navarra Jr., Aug. 26, 1967 (div. 1998); children: Yolanda, John G. III; m. Robert B. Kern, July 10, 2004. BA magna cum laude, Seton Hall Univ., 1974; AAS, Brookdale C.C., Lincroft, NJ, 1984; postgrad., Fairleigh Dickinson U. Elem. sch. tchr., Jersey City, 1967-69; corr. Village Times, Long Island, NY, 1974-75; tchr. music, humanities, German, art, art history Seton Hall Prep. Sch., South Orange, NJ, 1975-78; entertainment, feature writer, press corr. Asbury Park Press, Neptune, NJ, 1978-85, feature writer, art critic, family writer, 1985-92; feature writer, art columnist Two River Times, Red Bank, NJ, 1993-94. Psychiatric charge nurse, 1985; supr. grant rsch. Vis. Nurse Assn. Ctrl. Jersey, Red Bank, NJ, 1993-94; art coord. Monmouth Players, Navesink, NJ; lectr. at writing confs; instr. Bayshore fitness and Wellness Ctr., Hazlet, NJ, 2005. Author: The New Jersey Shore: A Vanishing Splendor, 1985, Jim Gary: His Life and Art, 1987, Your Body: Highlights of Human Anatomy, 1990, Playing It Smart: What to Do When You're on Your Own, 1989, also, pub. On My Own: Helping Kids Help Themselves, (translated into Italian, Portuguese and Hebrew) 1994, 2d edit., 2003, An Insider's Guide to Home Health Care: An Interdisciplinary Approach (with Margaret Lundrigan), 1995, Wisdom for Caregivers, 1995; (staged readings) Through the Kunai Grass with Dad, 1988, Don't Cry, Pandora, 1989; (with Myron A. Lipkowitz and John G. Navarra) Therapeutic Communication: A Guide to Effective Interpersonal Skills for Health Care Professionals, 1990, Encyclopedia of Vitamins, Minerals, and Supplements, 1995, 2d edit., 2004; (with Lipkowitz), Allergies A-Z, 1994; Images of America: Howell and Farmingdale 1996; (with Lundrigan) Image of America: Levittown: The First Fifty Years, 1997, Staten Island, 1997, Staten Island II, 1998, Levittown II, 1998; Toward Painless Writing, 1998; The American Century: Staten Island (with Lundrigan), 1999; Seton Hall University: A Photographic History, 1999, Monmouth University, 2001, A Kids Guidebook: Great Advice to Help Kids Cope, 2002, Encyclopedia of Asthma and Respiratory Disorders, 2003, Young People/Tough Problems, 2003, Encyclopedia of Allergies 2d edit., 2004, Encyclopedia of Complementary and Alternative Medicine, 2004; illustrator Drugs and Man, 1973; editor in chief Shore Affinity, 1979-81; contbg. editor Am. Jour. Nursing, 1990-94, "d." Mag., Red Bank, NJ, 2007; staff writer, illustrator, photographer NJ Music and Arts, 1978-81; editor Associated Univ. Presses, 1981-82; copywriter, photographer Jersey Shore Med. Ctr., 1985; feature writer, columnist Copley News Svc., 1988-93; health trend columnist Personal Fitness, 1989-90; assoc. editor The Courier, Middletown, NJ, May-Dec. 1998; assoc. contbg. editor M.A.R. Mag., Red Bank, 2005; lifestyle editor The Two River Times, Red Bank, May 1999-2000; contr. to Nursing Spectrum Mag.; photography exhbns. in NY, NJ, Pa. Mid-Atlantic Riviera Magazine, 2005; guest various radio and TV programs; contbr. photographs to books, articles and photogs. to mags., newspapers; solo exhibits include Atlantic City Art Ctr., 1982, O.K. Harris Works of Art, NYC, 1990, Gallery Axiom, Phila., 1991, Monmouth U., 1991, M. Thomson Kravetz Gallery, Bay Head, NJ, Oceanic Pub. Libr., 2000, Navesink Libr. Theater, 2004, 05; two-person exhbn. Tova Navarra and Santo Pezzutti: Two Visions at 800 Gallery, Monmouth U., 2007, AAA World's Photo Contest award, 2006; group shows at Art Forms, Red Bank, 1991, Moravian Coll., Bethlehem, Pa., 1992. Mem. Gov.'s Coun. on Alcoholism and Drug Abuse Prevention, co-chair Later Childhood subcom., 1992 Mem. NJ Playwrights Workshop (charter), NJ State Nurses Assn. Avocations: singing, guitar, piano, dance, crafts. Office: Sanford J Greenburger Assocs care Faith H Hamlin 55 5th Ave New York NY 10003-4301

NAVARRE, RICHARD A., energy executive; Dir. fin. planning Peabody Energy Corp., St. Louis, 1993, v.p., CFO, exec. v.p., CFO, 2001—08, exec. v.p. corp. develop., 2006—08, pres., chief comml. officer, 2008—. Pres., v.p. fin., controller Peabody COALSALES; bd. advisors Coll. Bus. and Adminstrn. and Sch. Acct. So. Ill. U., Carbondale; chmn. Bituminous Coal Operators' Assn.; mem. Fin. Execs. Internat.; exec. comm. Civic Entrepeneurs Organization; advisor New York Mercantile Exchange. Bd. advsr. So. Ill. Univ. - Carbondale Coll. Bus. Admin. Office: Peabody Energy Corp 701 Market St Saint Louis MO 63101

NAVARRO, JOSEPH ANTHONY, retired statistician, consultant; b. New Britain, Conn., July 6, 1927; s. Charles C. and Josephine V. (Bianco) N.; m. Dorothy G. Gnazzo; children: Kenneth M., Bruce C., Joseph S. BS, Cen. Conn. State U., 1950; MS, Purdue U., 1952, PhD, 1955. Rsch. staff, cons. GE, 1955-59; rsch. staff, mgmt. IBM, 1962-64; sr. staff mem., asst. dir. Inst. Def. Analyses, Alexandria, Va., 1964-72; pres., chief oper. officer System Planning Corp., Arlington, Va., 1972-86; dep. undersec. test and evaluation Dept. Defense, Washington, 1986-87; now pvt. practice cons., 1987—2005; pres. Wackenhut Applied Technologies Ctr., Fairfax, Va., 1989-90; ret., 2005. Contbr. articles to profl. jours. Mem. Bd. Trade, Washington, 1983-85. Mem. Internat. Test and Evaluation Assn. Clubs: COSMOS (Washington). Republican. Roman Catholic. Home: 8010 Grand Teton Dr Potomac MD 20854-4074 Personal E-mail: jadgnav@verizon.net.

NAVARRO, MONICA, lawyer; b. 1967; arrived in US, 1984; m. Mark Crane. BA in Polit. Sci. and Internat. Rels., Fla. Internat. U., 1990; JD, U. Mich. Law Sch., 1993. Bar: Ill., Mich., US Supreme Ct., US Ct. of Appeals Sixth Cir., US Dist. Ct. Eastern Dist. Mich., US Dist. Ct. Western Dist. Mich. Judicial clerk Hon. Julian Abele Cook, Jr., US Dist. Ct., Eastern Dist. Mich.; atty. Frank, Haron; prin. mem., ptnr. Frank, Haron, Weiner and Navarro, 2004—; vis. prof. Thomas M Cooley Law Sch. Civil Procedure & Health Law. Mem., HIPAA Compliance Com. Troy Chamber of Commerce; trustee Mich. Psychoanalytic Found., Southwest Solutions; chair tech. subcom. Health Law Sect. Mich. Bar. Guest Hospitals and Physicians: Friends and Foes, Bloomfield Cmty. TV, 2006. Recipient Am. Jurisprudence award in Adminstrv. Law, Best Oralist award; named a Mich. Super Lawyer, 2007; named one of Top 10 Qui Tam Lawyers in Country, Corp. Crime Reporter, 40 Under 40, Crain's Detroit Bus., 2006. Fellow: Oakland County Bar Found.; mem.: State of Mich. Bd. Psych. (mem. disciplinary subcom.), Mich. Trial Lawyers Assn., Assn. Trial Lawyers Am., Oakland County Women's Bar Assn. (Work Life balance award 2006), Oakland County Bar Assn. (Med./Legal Com.), Mich. Assn. Health Lawyers (mem. Tech. Subcommittee), Hispanic Bar Assn. Mich., Am. Health Lawyers Assn. Office: Frank, Haron, Weiner and Navarro 5435 Corporate Dr Ste 225 Troy MI 48098 Office Phone: 248-952-0400. Office Fax: 248-952-0890. Business E-Mail: mnavarro@fhwnlaw.com.

NAVAS, WILLIAM ANTONIO, JR., former civilian military employee, retired military officer; b. Mayaguez, PR, Dec. 15, 1942; s. William Antonio Sr. and Ethel Ines (Marin) N.; m. Wilda Margarita Cordova Navas, Aug. 7, 1965; children: William Antonio III, Gretchen Maria. BSCE, U. P.R., 1965; MS in Engring. Mgmt., U. Bridgeport, 1979. Registered profl. engr., P.R. Commd. 2d. lt. U.S. Army, 1966, advanced through grades to maj. gen., 1990, ret., 1998; served in U.S. Army Corps of Engrs., 1966-70; project engr. Empresas Navas, Inc., Mayaguez, P.R., 1970-72; ptnr., prin. W.A. Navas Jr. & Assocs., Mayaguez, 1972-80; dir. Navas & Moreda, Inc., Mayaguez, 1973-81; with Interamerican Def. Coll., Washington, 1981-82; dir. ops. P.R. Army Nat. Guard, San Juan, 1982-84, 84-87; comdr. Engr. Task Force, Panama, 1984; dep. dir. Army Nat. Guard, Washington, 1987-97; vice chief Nat. Guard Bur., 1990; mil. exec. reserve. forces policy bd. US Dept. Def., 1992-94, dep. asst. sec., 1994-95, asst. sec. for manpower & reserve affairs, Dept. of Navy, 2001—07; dir. Army Nat. Guard, 1995—98. Chmn. Dept. of Army Hispanic Employment Commn., Washington, 1988. Decorated Knight Eq. Order of Holy Sepulchre. Mem. Nat. Guard Assn. of the U.S. (del. 1980-86), Nat. Guard Assn. of P.R., Soc. of Am. Mil. Engrs. Roman Catholic. Avocations: militaria collection, reading, running, travel, tennis. E-mail: bnavas@aol.com.

NAVASKY, VICTOR SAUL, journalism professor, director, publisher emeritus; b. NYC, July 5, 1932; s. Macy and Esther Blanche (Goldberg) N.; m. Anne Landey Strongin, Mar. 27, 1966; children: Bruno, Miri, Jenny. AB with highest honors, Swarthmore Coll., 1954; LLB, Yale U., 1959. Spl. asst. to Gov. G. Mennen Williams, Mich., 1959-60; editor, pub. Monocle Mag., 1961-65; editor NY Times mag., 1970-72, The Nation Mag., NYC, 1978-94, pub., gen. ptnr., 1995—2005, pub. emeritus, 2005—; Delacorte prof. mag. journalism Columbia U., NYC, 1999—, dir., George T. Delacorte Ctr. Mag. Journalism. Vis. scholar Russell Sage Found., 1975—76; Ferris prof. journalism Princeton U., 1976—77; chmn. Columbia Journalism Rev. Author: Kennedy Justice, 1971 (Nat. Book award nominee), Naming Names, 1980 (Nat. Book award 1981), rev. edit., 2003, A Matter of Opinion, 2005 (George S. Polk Book award, 2006); co-author (with Christopher Cerf): Mission Accomplished!, 2008; co-playwright (with Richard R. Lingeman): Starr's Last Tape, 1999; co-editor (with C. Cerf): The Experts Speak, 1984, rev. edit., 1998; commentator (pub. radio program) Marketplace; contbr. numerous article and revs. to profl. pubs. Mem. bd. mgrs. Swarthmore Coll., 1991-94; bd. trustees The New Sch. Served with U.S. Army, 1954-56. Guggenheim fellow, 1974-75; fellow Inst. Politics, Harvard U., 1994; Sr. fellow Freedom Forum, 1994. Fellow Am. Acad. Arts & Scis.; mem. PEN (bd. mem.), Author's Guild (bd. mem.), Com. To Protect Journalists (exec. com.), Phi Beta Kappa. Democrat. Jewish. Office Phone: 212-209-5411. Business E-Mail: vic@thenation.com.

NAVETTA, CHRISTOPHER J., metal products executive; BBA, Mich. State U., East Lansing, 1969. Cert. mgmt. acct. Acctg. trainee Gary Works US Steel, Ind., 1969—72, various fin. positions Chems. Divsn. Pitts., 1972—75, mgr. acctg. Molded Plastic Products Ind., 1975—76, mgr. acctg. West Coast Products Divsn. Alameda, Calif., 1976—79, staff asst. Ctrl. Steel Divsn. Chgo., 1979—81, staff supr. comml. analysis Pitts., 1981, various managerial acctg. positions, 1981—85, mgr. acctg. Fairless Works Pa., 1985—87, dir. analysis and gen. acctg. Pitts., 1987—89, gen. mgr. adminstrn., group comptr. Diversified Group, 1989—92, comptr. raw materials Diversified Bus. and Joint Ventures, 1992—94, gen. mgr. plate products Gary Works, 1994—2001, pres. USX Engineers & Consultants, 2001—02, exec. v.p. US Steel Kosice, 2002—03, pres. US Steel Kosice, 2003—05, sr. v.p. procurement, logistics & diversified businesses, 2005—08, sr. v.p. procurement, real estate, raw materials & integration, 2008—. Mem.: Inst. Mgmt. Accts. Office Phone: 412-433-1121.

NAVIAUX, LAREE DEVEE, psychologist; b. Lewellen, Nebr., Aug. 18, 1937; d. Prosper Leo and Dorothy DeVee (Walters) N.; m. Frank Anthony D'Abreo, June 16, 1973. B.S., U. Nebr., 1959; M.S., Iowa State U., 1963; Ph.D., Duquesne U., 1973. Instr. Iowa State U., Ames, 1963-65; asst. prof. Kans. State U., Manhattan, 1965-66; grad. faculty part-time assoc. Margaret Morrison Coll. Carnegie-Mellon U., Pitts., 1966-69; asst. prof. West Ga. Coll., Carrollton, 1969-72; regional dir. Children's Mental Health, Charleston, W.Va., 1973-80; therapist, educator Cmty. Mental Health Ctr., Charleston, 1980-82; pvt. practice, 1982—04, ret., 2004; assoc. spiritual dir. W.Va. Inst. Spirituality, 2004—; asst. clin. prof. W.Va. U., 1977-87. bd. dirs. Creative Arts Clinic, 1981-83, Parents Anonymous of W.Va., 1979-82, YWCA, 1991-97, Charleston Chamber Music Bd., 2004-, W.Va. Pub. Broadcasting Friends, 2004-. Grantee Humanities Found. W.Va., 1978, 79, 81, 82, 05. Mem. U. Nebr. Alumni (life), Iowa State U. Alumni (life), Am. Psychol. Assn. (life), Mental Health Assn. (life). Democrat. Clubs: Gourmet, Indian Assn., Collectors Club Clay Ctr. (bd. dirs. 2009-), Contbr. articles to profl. jours. and books. Home Phone: 304-344-9091. Personal E-mail: naviauxld@aol.com.

NAVON, IONEL MICHAEL, mathematics professor; b. Bucharest, Romania, Apr. 28, 1940; s. David and Sarah (Schwartzman) N.; m. Lily Marcu, May 11, 1967; children: Daria, Livia. BSc in Math., Hebrew U. Jerusalem, 1967, MSc in Atmospheric Scis., 1971; PhD in Applied Math., U. Witwatersrand, Johannesburg, South Africa, 1979. Sr. rsch. meteorologist Israel Meteorol. Office, Tel Aviv, 1973-74; head applied math. sect. Tamam/Israel Aircraft Industry, Tel Aviv, 1974-76; sr. rsch. officer Counc. Sci. and Indsl. Rsch., Pretoria, South Africa, 1976-78, chief rsch. officer, 1979-80, sr. chief rsch. officer, 1981-83; sr. vis. scientist NASA/Goddard Space Flight Ctr., Greenbelt, Md., 1983-84; cons. NASA/Goddarad Space Flight Ctr., Greenbelt, Md., 1984-85; sr. specialist researcher Coun. Sci. and Indsl. Rsch., Pretoria, 1984-85; assoc. rsch. scientist Supercomputer Rsch. Inst., Tallahassee, Fla., 1985-87; assoc. prof. math. Fla. State U., Tallahassee, 1987-1990, prof., 1991—, program dir. optimization and optimal control, 1993—, hon. prof. dept. meteorology Supercomputer Rsch. Inst., 1987—, faculty assoc. Supercomputer Computation Rsch. Inst., 1988—, faculty assoc. Geophys. Fluid Dynamics Inst., 1989—, dir. applied math dept. math, 1998—. Dir. applied math. Fla. State U., 1998—; cons. Ctr. Analysis Prediction of Storms, Norman, Okla., 1989, French Navy, 1995; leader Argonne Nat. Lab.; co-organizer Internat. Conf. Element Methods in Geophysics, Tallahassee, 1991; summer lecture series scientist NASA, 1991—; mem. panel nat. experts to rev. and conduct site visiting Okla. Sci. and Tech. Ctr.; keynote spkr. Internat. Conf. on Finite Element Methods, South Africa, 1992, Internat. Conf. on Optimization Techniques and Applications, Singapore, 1992, Assimilation of Meteorological and Oceanographic Observations, France, 1993. Editor spl. issues Computer and Math. with Applications, editor Monthly Weather Rev., 1991-94, Jour. Numerical Linear Algebra with Applications, editor Monthly Weather Rev., 2001, 2008- Editor Internat. Jour. Numerical Methods in Fluids. 1991, Computational Fluid Dynamics Jour., 1992; chief editor spl. issue Dynamics of Atmospheres and Oceans, 1998; spl. editor Internat. Jour. on Computational Fluid Dynamics, 2003; contbr. over 95 refereed articles to sci. jours. Lt. Israel Civil Def., 1960-63. Grantee NSF, 1988, 91, 94—, 98-2001, 2002, 2003-06, NASA, 1991, 94, 97-99, 2006-; rsch. grantee Air Force Office Sci., 1989, 91, 94. Fellow Am. Meteorol. Soc.; Nat. Rsch. Coun. NASA/GSFC Delta Assimilation Office, 2000 (sr.); mem. Am. Math. Soc., Am. Geophys. Union, Soc. Indsl. and Applied Math. (organizer symposiums 2004-05), Israel Assn. Profl. Engrs., Am. Computing Machinery Assn. Avocations: ping-pong, photography, books. Home: 3138 Ferns Glen Dr Tallahassee FL 32309-2304 Office: Fla State U Ditac Sci Library Bldg Rm 483 Tallahassee FL 32306 Business E-Mail: navon@ses.fsu.edu.

NAVROTSKY, ALEXANDRA, geophysics educator; BS, U. Chgo., 1963, MS, 1964, PhD, 1967. Rsch. assoc. Technische Hochschule, Clausthal, Germany, 1967-68, Pa. State U., State College, 1968-69; mem. geology and chemistry faculty Ariz. State U., 1969-85, dir. Ctr. Solid State Sci., 1984-85; prof. dept. geol. & geophys. sci. Princeton (N.J.) U., 1985—, Albert G. Blanke Jr. prof. geol. and geophys. scis., 1992—, chair geol. and geophys. scis., 1988-91. Albert G. Blanke, Jr. chmn., 1992—. Editor: Physics and Chemistry of Minerals, 1986-91; contbr. articles to profl. jours. Alfred P. Sloan fellow, 1973. Fellow Am. Geophys. Union; mem. NAS, Am. Ceramic Soc., Mineral. Soc. Am. (pres. 1992-93, v.p. 1991-92, award 1981), Princeton Materials Inst., Nat. Acad. Scis., Sigma Xi. Office: U California - Davis Peter A Rock Thermochem Lab Davis CA 95616 Office Fax: 530-752-9307. Business E-Mail: anavrotsky@ucdavis.edu.

NAVY, ERNEST JUDE, educator, writer; b. New Orleans, Nov. 3, 1969; M, Lamar U., Beaumont, Tex., 1994. Pub. sch. tchr. Houston Ind. Sch. Dist., 1993—2001; prof. Coll. Mainland, Texas City, Tex., 2001—. Author: (novel) Loved One and Savior Mary. Organizer Dem. Party, Clear Lake, Tex., 2001—08. Progressive. Avocations: writing, travel. Home: 4735 Widerop Ln Friendswood TX 77546 Office: Coll Mainland 1200Amburn Rd Texas City TX 77591 Personal E-mail: judenavy@hotmail.com.

NAWAB, SYED HAMID, engineering educator; b. Swindon, Wiltshire, Eng., Jan. 13, 1955; s. Syed Ali and Razia Ali Nawab; m. Ghazala Alam, Nov. 27, 1998; 1 child, Faiz. BS, MS, MIT, Cambridge, PhD, 1982. Staff mem. MIT Lincoln Lab., Lexington, 1982—85; prof. elec. and computer engring., joint prof. biomedical engring. Boston U., Boston, 1985—. Vis. prof., computer sci. U. Mass., Amherst, 1989—90; vis. prof., elec. engring. MIT, 1994—95; rsch. prof. NeuroMuscular Rsch. Ctr. Boston U., 2004—. Author: (engineering textbook) Signals and Systems; editor: (book) Symbolic and Knowledge Based Signal Processing. Recipient Paper award, IEEE Signal Processing Soc., 1987, Metcalf Excellence Tchg. award, Boston U., 1993; Rsch. grant, NSF and NIH. Fellow: Am. Inst. Med. and Biol. Engring.; mem.: IEEE, Tau Beta Pi. Achievements include patents for low power digital filtering.

NAWALKHA, SANJAY K., finance educator; s. Moti C. and Shanta Devi Nawalkha. BSc, St Xavier's Coll., Mumbai U., 1984; PhD, U. Mass., Amherst, 1990. Assoc. prof. fin. U. Mass., 1998—. Editor: (books) Interest Rate Risk Measurement and Management; author: Interest Rate Risk Modeling: The Fixed Income Valuation Course, Dynamic Term Structure Modeling: The Fixed Income Valuation Course. Independent. Achievements include invention of single-plus term structure models. Business E-Mail: nawalkha@som.umass.edu.

NAWASH, JALAL MOHAMMAD, physics professor; PhD, Wash. State U., Pullman, 2006. Cert. in optoelectronics, Wash. State U., 2004. Rsch. assoc. Wash. State U., 2003—07. Spkr. Democrat. Office: Gonzaga Univ 502 E Boone Ave Spokane WA 99258 Personal E-mail: jalalnawash@hotmail.com. Business E-Mail: nawashj@gonzaga.edu.

NAWROCKI, MICHAEL ALEXANDER, veterinarian; b. Elm Grove, Wis., Nov. 26, 1975; s. Lawrence Joseph and Elizabeth Eileen Nevers; m. Jill Dianna Murphy. DVM, Kans. State U., Manhattan, 2000. Registered small animal surgeon Am. Coll. Vet. Surgeons, 2006. Head surgery Vet. Emergency and Splty. Hosp., Wichita, Kans., 2005—. Mem.: Am. Coll. Vet. Surgeons. Office: VESHW 727 S Washington Wichita KS 67211 Office Fax: 316-262-8305. Personal E-mail: m_nawrocki@hotmail.com.

NAYAR, RITU, pathologist, educator; married. MBBS, Maulana Azad Med. Sch., Delhi, 1988. Diplomate anatomic and clin. pathology Am. Bd. Pathology, 1997, cytopathology 1997. Prof., pathology Northwestern U. Feinberg Sch. Medicine, Chgo., 1997—; dir., cytopathology Northwestern Meml. Hosp., Chgo., 2001—. Resident, surg. pathology fellow George Wash. U., 1991—96; cytopathology fellow U. Rochester, NY, 1996—97. Contbg. editor. Fellow: Coll. Am. Pathologists (mem. cytopathology resource com. 2008), Am. Soc. Clin. Pathology (chair resident physician sect., chair gynecologic PT com.); mem.: Internat. Acad. Cytology (mem. ASC-IAC liaison com. 2004—08), Am. Soc. Cytopathology (mem. exec. bd., chair sci. program com. 2007—08, Pres. award 2004). Office: Northwestern Univ 251 E Huron St Chicago IL 60611

NAYEEM, AKBAR, chemist; s. Ghulam and Ayesha Nayeem; m. Zakira Amanullah, June 8, 1981; children: Omar, Aamir, Sarah. BSc with honors, St. Xavier's Coll., Calcutta U., India, 1977; MSc, Indian Inst. Tech., Kanpur, 1979; PhD, Cornell U., Ithaca, NY, 1985. Sr. scientist Tripos Inc., St. Louis, 1993—2001; sr. rsch. investigator Bristol-Myers Squibb, Hopewell, NJ, 2001—. Bd. trustees Faith Unity, Inc., Bensalem, Pa., 2006—. Peter Debye fellow, Cornell U., 1979. Mem.: Am. Chem. Soc. Achievements include development of a humanized-mouse for in-vivo drug testing. Office: Bristol-Myers Squibb 311 Pennington & Rocky Hill Rd Pennington NJ 08534 Business E-Mail: akbar.nayeem@bms.com.

NAYLOR, C. DAVID, academic administrator; b. Woodstock, Ont., Canada, 1954; s. Thomas and Edna Naylor; m. Ilse Naylor; 4 children. MD (hon.), U. Toronto, 1978; Rhodes Scholar, Oxford U., 1979; DPhil, 1983. Fellow Royal Coll. Physicians & Surgeons, 1986; trainee in gen. internal medicine U. Western Ontario, 1983—86; fellow in clin. epidemiology Med. Rsch. Coun. Can., Toronto, 1986—87; asst. prof. dept. medicine U. Toronto, 1988—92, assoc. prof., 1992—96, prof., 1996—, dean of medicine, 1999—2005, vice provost, Relations with Health Care Institutions, 1999—2005, pres., 2005—. Head rsch. program Sunnybrook Health Sci. Ctr., Toronto, 1990—96; CEO Inst. Clin. Evaluative Sciences, 1991—98; sr. scientist Med. Rsch. Coun. Can., 1999; editorial bd. Jour. Am. Med. Assn., Brit. Med. Jour., 1996—98, Can. Med. Assn. Jour., 1996—2000. Co-author approximately 300 scholarly publications.

Chair Nat. Adv. Com. on SARS & Pub. Health, Canada, 2003. Decorated officer Order of Can.; recipient John Dinham Cottrell medal, Royal Australasian Coll. Physicians, 1996, Malcolm Brown award, Royal Coll. Physicians & Surgeons, 1996, Michael Smith award, Med. Rsch. Coun., 1999, Rsch. Achievement award, Can. Cardiovascular Soc., 2002, Defries award, Can. Pub. Health Assn., 2005. Fellow: Royal Soc. Can.; mem.: Inst. Medicine (fgn. assoc.). Office: UToronto Office of the President 27 King's College Circle Toronto ON Canada M5S 1A1 Home Phone: 416-929-3800. Business E-Mail: president@utoronto.ca.

NAYLOR, JAMES CHARLES, psychologist, educator; b. Chgo., Feb. 8, 1932; s. Joseph Sewell and Berniece (Berg) N.; m. Georgia Lou Mason, Feb. 14, 1953; children— Mary Denise, Diana Darice, Shari Dalice. BS, Purdue U., 1957, MS, 1958, PhD, 1960. Asst. prof. Ohio State U., 1960-63, asso. prof., 1963-67, prof. vice chmn. dept. psychology, 1967-68; prof. Purdue U., Lafayette, Ind., 1968-86, head dept. psychol. scis., 1968-79; prof., chmn. dept. psychology Ohio State U., Columbus, 1986-98, prof. emeritus, 1999—. Fulbright rsch. scholar, Umea, Sweden, 1976; Disting. scholar, vis. scientist Flinders U., South Australia, 1982-83, UNESCO ednl. cons. to Hangzhou U., Peoples Republic of China, 1984; chmn. Coun. Grad. Depts. Psychology, 1993-94; lead reviewer Psychology Program Rev., State U. Sys. Fla., 1996. Author: Industrial Psychology, 1968, A Theory of Behavior in Organizations, 1980; founder, editor: Organizational Behavior and Human Decision Processes; mem. editorial bd.: Prof. Psychology; Contbr. articles to profl. jours. Served with USN, 1950-54. Fellow AAAS, Am. Psychol. Soc., Am. Psychol. Assn.; mem. Psychonomic Soc., Psychmetric Soc., Internat. Assn. Applied Psychology, Soc. Organizational Behavior (founder), Midwestern Psychol. Assn. (coun. 1994-97), Phi Beta Kappa, Sigma Xi. Home: 176 Tucker Dr Columbus OH 43085-3064 Office: Ohio State U Dept Psychology Columbus OH 43210 E-mail: naylor.2@osu.edu.

NAYLOR, JEFFREY GORDON, retail executive; b. Montreal, Que., Can., Nov. 15, 1958; s. Gordon Charles and Patricia Grace (Pryde) N.; m. Shawn Elizabeth Baker, Oct. 6, 1984; 1 child, Madeleine Baker Naylor. BA in Econs., Northwestern U., 1980, MBA, 1982. CPA, Ill. Pub. acct. Deloitte, Haskins & Sells, Chgo., 1982-86; assoc. N.Am. Venture Capital, Chgo., 1986-88; mgr. mergers and acquisitions A.C. Nielsen, Northbrook, Ill., 1988-90, dir. fin. analysis, 1990-91; dir. fin. Kraft Foods Sales, Northfield, Ill., 1991-93, Kraft Foods Corp., Northfield, 1993-95; v.p. credit divsn. Sears Roebuck & Co., Hoffman Estates, Ill., 1995; v.p., contr The LimitedInc; CFO, sr. v.p. fin. Dade Behring, Dearfield, Ill., 2000—01; sr. v.p., CFO Big Lots Inc., 2001—04; sr. exec. v.p. TJX Companies Inc., Framingham, Mass., 2004—, CFO, 2004—07, 2009—, chief adminstrv. officer, bus. develop. officer, 2007—. Prof. acctg. Keller Grad. Sch. Mgmt., Chgo., 1987-91. Treas. Episcopal Ch. of Northwestern U., Evanston, 1996; mem. Brookfield Zoo, 1995, Northwestern U. "N" Club, 1980. Mem. AICPA, Ill. CPA Soc. Episcopalian. Avocations: swimming, gourmet cooking, reading, ice skating. Office: TJX Cos 770 Cochituate Rd Framingham MA 01701

NAYLOR, MAGDALENA RACZKOWSKA, psychiatrist, educator; b. Warsaw, Aug. 4, 1950; arrived in U.S., 1981; d. Wlodzimierz Raczkowski and Urszula Raczkowska-Cieslik; m. Thomas Herbert Naylor, Dec. 14, 1985; 1 child, Alexander Watkins. MD, Warsaw Med. U., Poland, 1976, PhD, 1987. Diplomate psychiatry and neurology Nat. Bd. Certification in Psychiatry and Neurology, 1994. Asst. prof. Warsaw Med. U., 1977—83; rsch. assoc. Med. Coll. Va., Richmond, 1981—82; resident psychiatry Duke U., Durham, NC, 1984—88; pvt. practice psychiatry Richmond, Va., 1988—93; attending physician psychiatry Fletcher Allen Health Care, Burlington, Vt.; asst. prof. U. Vt., Burlington, 1993—99, assoc. prof., 1999—2008, prof. psychiatry, 2008—. Rsch. assoc. Med. Coll. Va., Richmond, Va., 1981—82; med. dir. women's program Psychiat. Inst. Richmond, Va., 1991—92; med. dir. partial hospitalization program Charter Westbrook Hosp., 1992—93; med. dir. psychiat. unit Flecher Allen Health Care, Burlington, Vt., 1994—97; dir. mindbody medicine clinic U. Vt. Med./Flecher Allen Health Care, 1998—; assoc. dir. clin. neuroscience rsch. unit U. Vt. Med.; spkr. on search for meaning and integration of mind, body and spirit into med. practice. Author (with Thomas Naylor and William Willimon): The Search for Meaning, 1994, The Search for Meaning Workbook, 1994; contbr. articles to profl. jours. Com. mem. Vt. Pain & Symptom Mgmt. Com.; mem. Gailer Sch., Shelburn, Vt., 2001—03. Recipient Best Tchr. of Yr. Dept. of Psychiatry, U. Vt. Med. Sch., 1996, 1998; grantee, NIH, 2002, 2004—05, 2008, U. Vt. Med. Sch., 2004. Mem.: Am. Pain Soc., Vt. Med. Assn. Achievements include research in coping skills training for patients in chronic pain, neuroimaging. Home: 202 Stockbridge Rd Charlotte VT 05445 Office: U Vt UHC 1 S Prospect St Burlington VT 05401 Business E-Mail: magdalena.naylor@uvm.edu.

NAYLOR, PAUL DONALD, retired lawyer; b. St. Bernard, Ohio, May 28, 1925; s. David Frederick and Erna Helen (Miller) N.; m. Geraldine L. Lacy, Jan. 20, 1945; children: Linda S., Paul Scott, Todd L. JD, U. Cin., 1948. Bar: Ohio 198. Ptnr. Pulse & Naylor, Cin., 1949-65; pvt. practice Cin., 1965—2003; ret., 2003. Mem. Nat. Rep. Com. Lt. (j.g.) USN, 1943-46. Recipient Svc. to Mankind award Sertoma Internat. Mem. Cin. Bar Assn. (real property com. 1966-86), Ohio Bar Assn., Cin. Lawyers Club (pres. 1955), Order of the Coif. Home: 304 Amherst Ave Terrace Park OH 45174-1104

NAYLOR, PHYLLIS REYNOLDS, writer; b. Anderson, Ind., Jan. 4, 1933; d. Eugene Spencer and Lura Mae (Schield) Reynolds; m. Thomas A. Tedesco, Jr., Sept. 9, 1951 (div. 1960); m. Rex V. Naylor, May 26, 1960; children: Jeffrey, Michael. Diploma, Joliet Jr. Coll., 1953; BA, Am. U., 1963. Author: Crazy Love: An Autobiographical Account of Marriage and Madness, 1977, Revelations, 1979, A String of Chances, 1982 (ALA notable book), The Agony of Alice, 1985 (ALA notable book), The Keeper, 1986 (ALA notable book), Unexpected Pleasures, 1986, Send No Blessings, 1990 (YASD best book for young adults), Shiloh, 1991 (ALA notable book, John Newbery medal, 1992), The Fear Place, 1994, Sang Spell, 1998, Walker's Crossing, 1999, Blizzard's Wake, 2002, After, 2003, Cricket Man, 2008, Faith, Hope, and Ivy, 2009. Recipient Golden Kite award, Soc. Children's Book Writers Am., 1985, Child Study award, Bank St. Coll., 1983, Edgar Allan Poe award, Mystery Writers Am., 1985, 2004, Internat. Book award, Soc. Sch. Librs., 1988, Christopher award, 1989, Md. Author award, 2009; Nat. Endowments Arts Creative Writing fellow, 1987. Mem.: ACLU, PEN, Authors Guild, Soc. Children's Book Writers, Children's Book Guild Washington (pres. 1974—75, 1983—84), Amnesty Internat., Nat. Coalition Against Censorship. Unitarian Universalist. Avocations: theater, swimming. Home and Office: 401 Russell Ave Apt 713 Gaithersburg MD 20877

NAYLOR, REBEKAH ANN, surgeon, educator; b. Arkadelphia, Ark., Jan. 3, 1944; d. Robert Naylor. BA, Baylor U., Waco, Tex., 1964; MD, Vanderbilt U., Nashville, Tenn., 1968. Diplomate Am. Bd. Surgery, 1974. Missionary Internat. Mission Bd., SBC, Richmond, Va., 1973—2009; surgeon Bangalore Bapt. Hosp., India, 1974—2002; clin. asst. prof. surgery U. Tex. Southwestern Med. Ctr., Dallas, 2002—07, clin. assoc. prof. surgery, 2007—. Recipient Disting. Alumnus award, Southwestern Bapt. Theol. Sem., 1994, Disting. Clin. Sci. Educator award, UT Southwestern Med. Ctr., 2007, Disting. Alumnus Lectr. award, Parkland Surg. Soc., 2008; named Missionary of Yr., Christian Med. and Dental Assn., 2003. Fellow: ACS. Baptist. Home: 41 Brenton Rd Fort Worth TX 76134 Office: Univ Tex Southwestern Med Ctr 5323 Harry Hines Blvd Dallas TX 75390-9156 Business E-Mail: rebekah.naylor@utsouthwestern.edu.

NAYLOR, RHONDA, mathematics instructor; b. Bklyn., Sept. 27, 1950; d. Joseph and Elaine Blossom Primack; children: Jaci Layne Smith, Travis Colin Wanger. BS, U. Colo., Boulder, 1971, MA, 1976. Cert. in early adolescence math. Nat. Bd. Profl. Tchg. Stds., Washington, 1999. 6th grade tchr. Jefferson County Sch., Lakewood, Colo., 1971—75; math. tchr. Cherry Creek Sch., Englewood, Colo., 1984—2006, Met. State Coll., Denver, 2006—; lead mentor Denver Pub. Sch., 2008—. Trainer assessors Nat. Bd. Profl. Tchg. Stds., 2000—08; tchr. tng. corps. US Dept. Edn., Washington, 2004—08. Pres. Colo. Coun. Tchrs. Math., Englewood, 2001—03. Personal E-mail: rhondanaylor@comcast.net.

NAYLOR, SUSAN EMBRY, music educator; b. Huntington Park, Calif., Feb. 21, 1951; d. Hollie J. and Sara Mozelle (Maddox) E. MusB in piano performance, Converse Coll., Spartanburg, SC, 1973; MusM, Ga. State U., Atlanta, 1975. Cert. music tchr. Ga. Prof. piano and music theory Reinhardt Coll., Waleska, Ga., 1975—, music program coord., 1995-2000, program coord. undergrad. studies music, 2009—. Pvt. piano tchr. Waleska, Marietta, and Kennesaw, Ga., 1973—. Performer solo piano and ensemble recitals colls., chs. and profl. orgns., 1973—; pianist Spartanburg (S.C.) Symphony Orch., 1970-73, featured soloist, 1972; guest pianist Nat. Pub. Radio, 1988. Ch. pianist Bapt., Meth. Churches in Marietta, Dallas, and Kennesaw, 1973—. Recipient Cobb County Young Artist Award; Cobb County Arts Coun. Parks and Recreation and Jr. League, 1983, 86. Mem. Ga. Music Tchr. Assn. (adjudicator 1976—, coll. faculty chair 1996-98, cert. credentials chair 1997-99, pres.-elect 1998-2000, pres. 2000-2002, fin. advisory com., 2000—), Ga. Fedn. Music Clubs (adjudicator 1976—), Cherokee Music Tchr. Assn. (pres. 1988-91, 2006-07, 2007-09, 1st v.p. program 1997-99), Cherokee County Arts Coun. (exec. bd., v.p. 1993-95), Music Tchr. Nat. Assn. (nat. coll. faculty cert., nat. cert. evaluation team 1993-96, ho. dels. 2000-2002). Baptist. Avocations: antiques, reading. Home: 109 Myrtle Ct Waleska GA 30183-4202 Office: Reinhardt Coll 7300 Reinhardt Coll Cir Waleska GA 30183-2981 Business E-Mail: sen@reinhardt.edu.

NAYLOR, THOMAS HERBERT, economist, educator, consultant; b. Jackson, Miss., May 30, 1936; s. Thomas Hector and Martha (Watkins) N.; m. Magdalena Raczkowska, Dec. 14, 1985; children: Susanne, Alexander. BS in Math., Millsaps Coll., 1958; BS in Indsl. Engring., Columbia U., 1959; MBA in Quantitative Bus. Analysis, Ind. U., 1961; PhD in Econs., Tulane U., 1964. Instr. Sch. Bus. Adminstrn. Tulane U., 1961-63; asst. prof. econs. Duke U., 1964-66, assoc. prof. econs., 1966-68, prof. econs., 1968-93, prof. emeritus econs., 1994—. Vis. prof. U. Wis., 1969-70, Middlebury Coll., 1993-94, U. Vt., 1994-96; pres. Social Systems, Inc., 1971-80; mng. dir. Naylor Group, 1980; cons., lectr. in over 30 countries. Co-author: (with Eugene Byrne) Linear Programming, 1963, (with Joseph L. Balintfy, Donald S. Burdick and Kong Chu) Computer Simulation Techniques, 1966, translated into Japanese, Portuguese and Spanish, (with John Vernon) Microeconomics and Decision Models of the Firm, 1969, translated into Spanish, (with James Clotfelter) Strategies for Change in the South, 1975, (with John M. Vernon and Kenneth Wertz) Managerial Economics: Corporate Economics and Strategy, 1983, (with William H. Willimon) The Abandoned Generation: Rethinking Higher Education, 1995, Downsizing the U.S.A., 1997, (with Rolf Österberg and William H. Willimon) The Search for Meaning in the Workplace, 1996, others; author or co-author of 30 books including: Computer Simulation Experiments with Models of Economic Systems, 1971, translated into Spanish, Polish, and Russian, Corporate Planning Models, 1979, Strategic Planning Management, 1980, The Corporate Strategy Matrix, 1986, translated into Hungarian, The Gorbachev Strategy, 1988, The Cold War Legacy, 1991, (with William H. Willimon and Magdalena R. Naylor), The Search for Meaning, 1994; editor: The Impact of the Computer on Society, 1967, The Design of Computer Simulation Experiments, 1969, The Politics of Corporate Planning and Modeling, 1978, Simulation Models in Corporate Planning, 1979, Simulation in Business Planning and Decision Making, 1981, others; co-editor: (with H. Brandt Ayers) You Can't Eat Magnolias, 1972, (with Michele H. Mann) Portfolio Planning and Corporate Strategy, 1983, (with Celia Thomas) Optimization Models for Strategic Planning, 1984, (with John DeGraff and David Wann), Affluenza, 2001, translated into French, German, Japanese and other langs., The Vermont Manifesto, 2003, Secession, 2008, others; contbr. numerous articles to profl. publs.; mem. editl. bd. jours. Exec. dir., founder. L.Q.C. Lamar Soc., Washington, 1969-73; founder Second Vt. Republic, 2003. Named to Lambda Chi Alpha Alumni Hall of Fame, 1996. Mem.: Beta Gamma Sigma, Omicron Delta Kappa. Home: 202 Stockbridge Rd Charlotte VT 05445-9358 Office Phone: 802-425-4133.

NAZAIRE, MICHEL HARRY, physician; b. Jérémie, Haiti, Sept. 29, 1939; s. Joseph and Hermance Nazaire; m. Nicole Lamarque, Dec. 28, 1968 (div.); children: Hanick, Carline. BS, DOE, Port-Au-Prince, Haiti, 1959; MD Faculty of Medicine and Pharmacology, State U. Haiti, 1966. Intern State U. Hosp., Port-Au-Prince, Haiti, 1965-66; resident physician Sanitarium, Port-Au-Prince, Haiti, 1966-68; physician pneumology, 1966-68; physician pneumo-phtisiology Port-Au-Prince, 1966—; fellow Klinik Havelhohe and Heckeshorn, Berlin, 1969-70, 89-91; attending physician Sanitarium, Port-Au-Prince, 1976-91. Dep. mem. Internat. Parliament for Safety and Peace, envoy-at-large Internat. State Parliament, mem. global environ. technol. network WHO. Contbr. articles to profl. jours. Recipient Physician's Recognition award, Am. Med. Assn., 2002, AMA, 2002, 2005. Fellow Internat. Soc. for Respiratory Protection, Am. Coll. Chest Physicians (recognition award, 2006); mem. AMA (Physician's Recognition award 2002, 2005), APHA, Am. Conf. Govtl. Indsl. Hygienists, Internat. Union Against Tb, Internat. Platform Assn., Physicians for Social Responsibility, European Respiratory Soc. Home: 386 Rugby Road Brooklyn NY 11226 Home Fax: 253-333-6520. Personal E-mail: michelharrynazaire@live.com.

NAZARETH, ANNETTE LAPORTE, lawyer, former commissioner; b. Providence, Jan. 27, 1956; d. George Robert and Dolores (LaPorte) Nazareth; m. Roger Walton Fergunson, May 3, 1986; 2 children. AB magna cum laude, Brown U., 1978; JD, Columbia U., 1981. Bar: NY. Assoc. Davis Polk & Wardwell, NYC, 1981-86; gen. ptnr., gen. counsel Mabon, Nugent & Co., NYC, 1986-91; mng. dir., gen. counsel Mabon Securities Corp., NYC, 1991—94; sr. v.p. Lehman Brothers, Inc., NYC, 1994—97; mng. dir., dep. head Salomon Smith Barney, NYC, 1997—98; sr. counsel to chmn. US Securities & Exchange Commn. (SEC), Washington, 1998—99, acting dir., Divsn. Investment Mgmt., dir., Divsn. Mkt. Regulation, 1999—2005, commr., 2005—07; ptnr. Davis Polk & Wardwell, Washington, 2008—. Mem.: Securities Industry Assn., Phi Beta Kappa. Democrat. Office: Davis Polk & Wardwell 1300 I St NW 10th Fl E Washington DC 20005 Office Phone: 202-962-7075. Office Fax: 202-450-3804. E-mail: annette.nazareth@dpw.com.*

NAZAREWICZ, WITOLD, nuclear scientist, educator; b. Warsaw, Dec. 26, 1954; s. Ryszard and Hanna Nazarewicz; m. Krystyna Kustosik, Apr. 11, 1977; children: Pawel, Natalia. MS in Engring., Warsaw U. Tech., 1977, PhD, 1981. Cert. habilitation Warsaw U., 1986, tchr. Poland, 1994. Prof. Warsaw U. Tech., 1977—90, assoc. dean faculty tech. physics & applied math., 1987—90, prof. physics, 1991—, U. Tenn., Knoxville, 1995—; Holifield radioactive ion beam facility sci. dir. Oak Ridge Nat. Lab., Tenn., 1995—. Mem. program adv. com. EUROGAM, Strasbourg, France, 1990—94; mem. nuc. physics bd. European Phys. Soc., 1992—95; mem. spl. emphasis panel on evaluation of sflow-energy nuc. physics accelerator labs. NSF, 1993; mem. hribf program adv. com. physics divsn., ORNL, Oak Ridge, Tenn., 1994—96; mem. vivitron pac CNRS, Strasbourg, 1994—96; mem. nat. adv. com. Inst. Nuc. Theory, Seattle, 1995—98; mem. nscl pac Nscl, Msu, E.Lansing, Mich., 1995—98; mem. com. nuc. physics Bd. Physics and Astronomy, US NRC, DC, 1996—99; mem. atlas pac Argonne Nat. Lab., Ill., 1996—99; mem. 1988 cyclotron pac Lawrence Berkeley Nat. Lab., Calif., 1996—2000; mem. rev. com. for physics divsn. of anl U. Chgo., 1996—2004; mem. steering com. for nat. nuc. physics summer sch. divsn. nuc. physics, APS, 1998, aps divsn. of nuc. physics nominating com., 1999—2000, vice-chair, 2000, mem. dissertation award com., 2000—01, mem. dnp program com., 2007—, mem. dnp fellowship com., 2008—; mem. jihir directorate Joint Inst. Heavy Ion Rsch., Oak Ridge, Tenn., 1999—; mem. nuc. sci. adv. com. DOE/NSF, DC, 2000—03; chair RIA Working Grp. Steering Com., 2000—04; mem. program adv. com. NSCL, Mich. State U., E.Lansing, 2001—02; mem. acot com. NRC, Canada, 2001—05; dir., co-dir. RIA Summer Sch., 2002—05; chmn. Warsaw U., 2002—; chair, mem. exec. com. RIA Users Orgn., 2004—; mem. rare isotope sci. assessment com. US NRC, DC, 2005—07; mem. internat. adv. panel EURISOL Design Study Grp., France, 2005—; mem. of the steering com. of justipen Japan U.S. Theory Inst. for Physics with Exotic Nuclei, Tokyo, 2006—; mem. program adv. com. Jefferson Lab., Newport News, Va., 2006—; sci. expert, sci. adv. bd. for Finnish Ctr. Excellence in Nuc. and Accelerator Based Physics Acad. Finland, Jyvaskyla, Finland, 2006—. Co-editor, editl. bd. mem. European Phys. Jour., 2006—; contbr. articles to profl. jours. Recipient Individual Sci. award, Polish Phys. Soc., 1986, Rsch. and Creative achievement award, U. Tenn., 2004; named one of Most Highly-cited Physicists, ISI; grantee Rsch. and travel grants, NSF, 1992—, Rsch. grants, Dept. Energy, 1993—; fellowship, Inst. Physics, 2004. Fellow: Inst. Physics (mem. editl. bd. 2001—06), Am. Phys. Soc. (mem. editl. bd. 1994—96, nuc. physics assoc. editor 2006—); mem.: European Phys. Soc., Wash. Map Soc., Internat. Map Collector's Soc. Achievements include research in nuclear structure. Avocations: collecting ancient maps, history. Office: Univ Ten 401 Nielsen Physics Bldg Knoxville TN 37996 Business E-Mail: witek@utk.edu.

NAZARIAN, LAWRENCE FRED, pediatrician; b. NYC, May 17, 1940; s. Samuel George and Winifred Lucia (Zotian) N.; m. Sharon Louise Carlson, June 22, 1963; children: Douglas, Stephen, Sarah. BA, Yale U., 1960; MD, U. Rochester, 1964. Cert. Am. Bd. Pediatrics 1970. Pediatrician Panorama Pediatric Group, Rochester, NY, 1969—2004; clin. prof. pediatrics U. Rochester Sch. Medicine and Dentistry, 1969—. Bd. dirs. James P. Wilmot Found., Rochester. Assoc. editor Pediatrics in Rev. Jour., 1990-2004, editor-in-chief, 2005-; contbr. articles to profl. jours. Mem. troop com. Boy Scouts Am., Penfield, N.Y., 1978-88; mem. coun. com. Luth. Ch. of Reformation, Rochester, 1969—. Maj. USAR, 1967-69. Recipient Nat. Pediatric Tchg. award, Ambulatory Pediatric Assn., 2002. Fellow Am. Acad. Pediatrics; mem. Med. Soc. State of N.Y., Ctrl. N.Y. Pediatric Club, Monroe County Med. Soc., Rochester Acad. Medicine, Rochester Pediatric Soc. Avocations: hiking, camping, canoeing, gardening, cross country skiing. Office: U Rochester Med Ctr 601 Elmwood Ave Box 777 Rochester NY 14642 Office Phone: 585-275-0225.

NAZARIAN, SAM, hotel executive, film producer; b. Tehran, Iran, 1975; s. Younes Nazarian. Founder, CEO SBE Entertainment Group, LLC, 2002—. Owner Area, Hyde and Privilige. Exec. prodr.: (films) Home of Phobia, 2004, The Beautiful Country, 2004, Trespassing, 2004, Waiting..., 2005, Down in the Valley, 2005, Five Fingers, 2006, The Last Time, 2006, Pride, 2007, Mr. Brooks, 2007, College, 2008. Named one of The Top 100 Most Powerful People in So. Calif., West mag., 2006. Office: SBE Entertainment Group LLC 8000 Beverly Blvd Los Angeles CA 90048

NAZARYAN, HOVAKIM, mathematician, researcher, atmospheric scientist; b. Yerevan, Armenia, Apr. 20, 1974; arrived in U.S., 2000; s. Roland and Eli Nazaryan. MS in Math., Yerevan State U., 1994; PhD in Math., Byurakan Astrophysical Observatory, Yerevan State U., 1998. Rsch. assoc. Byurakan Astrophysical Observatory, Armenia, 1998—99; postdoctoral position U. Padua, Italy, 1999—2001; postdoctoral rsch. fellow Hampton U., 2003—08, rsch. asst. prof., 2008—. Contbr. articles to profl. jours. Mem.: Am. Geophys. Union. Avocation: painting. Office: Hampton U Ctr Atmospheric Scis 23 Tyler St Hampton VA 23668 Office Phone: 757-728-6368. Business E-Mail: hovakim.nazaryan@hamptonu.edu.

NAZARYAN, VAHAGN, physicist, medical researcher; arrived in US, 2000, permanent resident, 2010; s. Roland and Eli Nazaryan. MS, Yerevan State U., 1999; PhD, Coll. William and Mary, Williamsburg, Va., 2004. Postdoctoral rsch. assoc. Coll. William and Mary, Williamsburg, 2004—05, Hampton U., Va., 2005—07, supr. Med. Physics Rsch., 2007—08; med. physicist Hampton U. Proton Therapy Inst., 2008—. Contbr. articles to profl. jours. Recipient Rolf G. Winter award for Excellence in Tchg., Coll. William and Mary, Va., 2003; grantee Biologically Optimized Treatment Planning for Hadron Radiotherapy, Varian Med. Systems, Inc., 2007—09, Va. Commonwealth Tech. Rsch. Fund, 2008—, devel. of a Hampton U. program for novel breast cancer imaging and therapy rsch., US Dept. Defence, 2009—; Alikhanov — Alikhanian Bros. fellow for Academic Excellence, Yerevan Physics Inst., Armenia, 1997—99. Mem.: Am. Phys. Soc., Am. Assn. Physicists in Medicine (assoc.), Nat. Soc. Collegiate Scholars (life). Achievements include patents for proton beam treatment planning with adequate biological weighting; accelerated partial breast irradiation with shielded MammoSite applicator and method of use. Avocations: travel, tennis, music. Office: Hampton University Physics Department OLIN 102 Hampton VA 23668 Business E-Mail: vahagn.nazaryan@hamptonu.edu.

NAZEM, FEREYDOUN F., venture capitalist, entrepreneur; b. Tehran, Iran, Dec. 29, 1940; came to US, 1960; naturalized, 1976; s. Hassan and Afsar N.; m. Susie Gharib, Jan. 20, 1973; children: Alexander, Taraneh. BS, Ohio State U., 1964; MSc, U. Cin., 1967; MBA, Columbia U., 1971. Sr. rsch. chemist Matheson Coleman & Bell, Norwood, Ohio, 1967-68; asst. v.p., investment analyst Irving Trust Co., NYC, 1969-74; v.p., venture capital officer Charter NY, NYC, 1974-75; mng. dir. Collier Enterprises, NYC, 1976-81; mng. ptnr. Nazem & Co. I, II, III and IV, NYC, 1981—, Explorer Fund, NYC, 1997—, Transatlantic Venture

Fund, 1998—, Hedgeworth, L.L.C., NYC, 2003—; founder Flagship Global Health, NYC, 2004—. Author: The Chemical Industry and Energy Shortage, Hedgeworth Market Letter. Recipient Ellis Island Medal of Honor, 2007. Avocations: fine arts, sports, music, building trend-setting technology and healthcare companies. Office: 570 Lexington Ave New York NY 10022 Office Phone: 212-371-7900. Business E-Mail: ffn@nazem.com. *You can have success and serenity at the same time. Become a possibilitarian- spend time solving problems, not worrying about them.*

NAZEMETZ, PATRICIA M., printing company executive; b. Dec. 22, 1949; BA in Mathematics, Fordham U., 1971, MA in Philosophy, 1980. Benefits analyst W.R. Grace and Co.; various positions in human resources including benefits ops. mgr. Xerox Corp., Stamford, Conn., 1979—99, v.p. human resources, 1999—, chief human resources, ethics officer, 2007. Bd. dirs., chair human resources com. Nat. Bus. Group Health and Human Svcs., Long Island; bd. dirs. WMS Industries Inc., 2007—, Energy East Corp., 2007—. Trustee Fordham U. Office: Xerox Corp 800 Long Ridge Rd Stamford CT 06904 Office Phone: 203-968-3000. Office Fax: 203-968-3218.

NAZIRUDDIN, BASHOO, lab administrator, director; m. Syedah Durriya, Mar. 1, 1990; children: Omar Salman, Zahra Tahseen. PhD, U. Madras, India, 1987. Scientist Indian Inst. Sci., Bangalore, Karnataka, India, 1987; postdoc. assoc. U. Okla. Health Scis. Ctr., Okla. City, 1987—91; rsch. assoc. Wash. U. Sch. Medicine, St. Louis, 1991—95, rsch. instr., 1995—2000; scientist Nextran Inc., Baxter Healthcare Corp., Princeton, NJ, 2000—03. Dir. Baylor U. Med. Ctr., 2003—. Contbr. scientific papers to rsch. publs. (Am. Soc. Histocompatibility and Immunogenetics Scholar award, 1997). Study sect. mem. Juvenile Diabetes Rsch. Found., NYC, 2007—. Recipient Rsch. award, Seeger Found., 2004—06; grantee, Baylor Healthcare Sys., 2007—08; Scientist Devel. grant, Am. Heart Assn., 2000—03. Mem.: Am. Soc. Transplantation, Transplant Soc. Office: Baylor Regional Transplant Inst 3500 Gaston Ave Dallas TX 75246 Business E-Mail: bashoon@baylorhealth.edu.

NDEUMENI, CHARLES DECHATEAU, medical educator; b. Baboutcha, West, Cameroon, Jan. 1, 1958; s. Mathias Noubevam and Marceline Ngankam; m. Mary Combs Inoussa, Nov. 4, 2005. MD, Kiev Rsch. Inst. Oncology, Ukraine, PhD, 1991. Adj. faculty Montgomery Coll., Takoma Park, Md., 2005—. Home: 1126 W Nolcrest Dr Silver Spring MD 20903 Office: Montgomery Coll 7600 Takoma Ave Takoma Park MD 20912 Home Fax: 301-681-6043. Personal E-mail: cndeumeni@aol.com.

NDIBONGO-TRAUB, LULAMA, economist, educator; d. Virginia Lundstrom-Ndibongo and Manelisi Ndibongo; m. Jason Traub, Sept. 0, 2000. BA, Randolph-Macon Woman's Coll., Lynchburg, Va., 1996; MS, Mich. State U., East Lansing, 2003. Rsch. specialist Bur. Food and Agrl. Policy, Pretoria, Gauteng, South Africa, 2006—; adj. faculty Lansing CC, 2006—. Cons. FAO, Rome, 2007. Contbr. articles to profl. jour. Mem.: Internat. Assn. Agrl. Economists. Non-Partisan. Avocations: travel, reading, running, swimming.

NDUBISI, FORSTER O., landscape architect, educator; BSc with honors, U. Waterloo, Ont., Can., 1987, MS in Land Arch., 1987, PhD, 1987. Assoc. prof. Sch. Environ. Design, U. Ga., Athens, 1987—2007; dir. and prof. Interdisciplinary Design Inst., Wash. State U., Spokane, Wash., 1997—2004; prof. and dept. head Tex. A&M U., Coll. Sta., 2004—. Author: (book) Ecological Planning; contbr. scientific papers. Mem. Landscape Architecture Found., Washington, 1988—2001; pres. Coun. Educators Landscape Architecture, 1997—99. Recipient Merit award, Am. Soc. Landscape Architects, 1988, President's award, Coun. Educators Landscape Architecture, 1993; fellow, 2007. Office: Tex A&M Univ A310 Langford Architecture Ctr College Station TX 77843

NEACE, WILLIAM PHILLIP, psychology professor, consultant; b. Pitts., Nov. 14, 1962; s. William and Isabella Angelina Neace; married. PhD, U. Louisville, 2002. Sr. rsch. analyst Pacific Inst. Rsch. & Evaluation, Louisville, 2000—02, assoc. rsch. scientist, 2002—04; asst. prof. U. Hartford, Conn., vis. asst. prof., 2004—06. With US Army, 1985—89. Office: Univ Hartford 200 Bloomfield Ave West Hartford CT 06117 Office Fax: 860-768-5292. Business E-Mail: neace@hartford.edu.

NEAL, CAROLYN V., librarian; b. Jan. 19, 1964; MLIS, Clark Atlanta U., 1999. US Customs Svc. Inspector; libr. Cleve. Pub. Libr. Recipient Diversity Fair Best of Show award, ALA, 2004; named one of the Movers & Shakers, Libr. Jour., 2007. Office: Cleveland Public Library 325 Superior Ave NE Cleveland OH 44114 Office Phone: 216-623-2800, 216-623-2902. Office Fax: 216-623-7015. E-mail: cneal@cpl.org.

NEAL, DARWINA LEE, retired federal agency administrator; b. Mansfield, Pa., Mar. 31, 1942; d. Darwin Leonard and Ina Belle (Cooke) N. BS, Pa. State U., 1965; postgrad., Cath. U, 1968-70. Registered landscape architect. Landscape architect nat. capital region Nat. Pk. Svc., 1965-69, office of White House liaison, 1969-71, office of profl. services, 1971-74, div. design svcs., 1974-89, chief design svcs., 1989-95, chief landscape arch. office of stewardship and partnership Washington, 1996-98, chief cultural resource preservation svcs. nat. capital reg., 1998—2009. Judge numerous award juries. Contbr. articles to profl. jours.; co-author sects. of profl. bull., mag.; author introduction to book Women, Design and the Cambridge School; columnist: Land monthly, 1975-79. Recipient Merit award Landscape Contractors Met. Washington; recipient hon. mention Les Floralies Internat. Montreal, 1980 Alumni Achievement award Pa. State U. Arts and Architecture Alumni Soc., 1981 Fellow Am. Soc. Landscape Architects (v.p. 1979-81, pres. elect 1982-83, pres. 1983-84, trustee 1976-77, nat. treas. 1977-79, legis. coord. 1975-79, sec. Coun. Fellows 1988-90, del. to Internat. Fedn. Landscape Architects 1989-92, 00-03, ex-officio rep. to U.S./internat. coun. on monuments and sites 1985-98, liaison to historically black coll. and univ. program Dept. Interior, chair internat. task force 1999-2000, Pres.' medal 1987), U.S. Internat. Coun. on Monuments and Sites (treas. 1998-2004, trustee 2004-07, fellow, 2007), Internat. Fed. Landscape Architects (sec. West Region, 2003-06, v.p. Am.'s Region 2006—); mem. Landscape Archtl. Accreditation Bd. (roster vis. evaluators), Nat. Recreation and Parks Assn., Nat. Soc. Park Resources (bd. dirs. 1978-80), Nat. Trust Hist. Preservation, Pa. State U. Alumni Assn. (Washington met. chpt. trustee 1972-74), Am. Arbitration Assn. (nat. panel arbitrators), Com. 100 for the Fed. City, Preservation Action, Nat. Assn. Olmsted Parks, Beekman Pl. Condominium Assn. (bd. dirs. 1985-91, archtl. control com. 1977-00, landscape com. 2000-02), Alliance for Historic Preservation, Garden Conservancy, Scenic Am., Preservation Action, Preservation Roundtable, Hist. Soc. Washington

NEAL, GAIL FALLON, physical therapist, educator; b. New Haven, May 6, 1938; d. Edward Francis and Ruth Alexina (Hutchinson) Fallon; m. Marcus Pinson Neal Jr.; children: Sandra Neal Dawson, Marcus Pinson III, Ruth-Catherine Neal Perkins. Student, Mary Washington Coll., 1955-57; BS in Phys. Therapy, Med. Coll. Va., 1959. Lic. phys. therapist. Staff phys. therpist Univ. Hosps., U. Wis., Madison, 1959-61; chief phys. therapy Stoughton (Wis.) Cmty. Hosp., 1961-63; vol. phys. therapy Cerebral Palsy Ctr., Richmond, Va., 1963-64; pvt. practice Richmond, 1965—68; interim dir. Stuart Cir. Hosp., Richmond, 1968-69; phys. therpist on call St. Mary's Hosp., Richmond, 1968-74; pres., owner Capital Phys. Therapy Assocs., Richmond, 1989—. Phys. therapist St. Mary's Hosp., Richmond, 1975-88; lectr. Med. Coll. Va., Richmond, 1992-93, John Tyler C.C., Richmond, 1992-94; adv. bd. phys. therapy Va. State Bd. Medicine, 1990-96, vice chmn., 1992-93, chmn. 1995-96. Adv. bd. Va. Opera, 1979—; bd. visitors Mary Washington Coll., Fredericksburg, Va., 1980-82, rector bd. visitors, 1982-84; pres. Richmond Symphony Orch. League, 1986-88. Named Clubwoman of Yr., Richmond Newsleader, 1972. Mem. Am. Phys. Therapy Assn., Richmond Acad. Medicine Aux. (pres. 1967-68), Med. Soc. Va. Alliance (pres. 1980-81), Med. Coll. Va. Hosps. Aux. (pres. 1973-75), Va. Cultural Laureate Soc. Avocations: reading, music, skiing, indian folklore. Home: Pony Bluffs 7301 Riverside Dr Richmond VA 23225-1066 Office: Capital Phys Therapy Assocs Pony Bluffs Richmond VA 23225 Office Phone: 804-330-2440.

NEAL, JAMES G., university librarian; BA in Russian Studies, Rutgers U., 1965—69; MA in History, Columbia U., 1969—71, MS in Libr. Sci., 1972—73. Cert. in advanced Librarianship Columbia U., 1978. Social sciences libr. Queensborough Cmty. Coll., CUNY, 1973—76; head collection develop. dept. U. Notre Dame, 1977—79, head collection mgmt. dept., 1979—82, asst. dir. pub. services, 1982—83; asst dean & head reference Pa. State U. Libraries, 1983—89; dean univ. libraries Ind. U., 1989—95; Sheridan Dir. Milton S. Eisenhower Libr. Johns Hopkins U., 1995—2001, dean libraries, 1998—2001; v.p. info. services & univ. libr. Columbia U., NYC, 2001—. Bd. dirs. Nat. Info. Standards Orgn.; chair bd. dirs. Rsch. Libraries Group; chair steering com. Scholarly Pub. and Academic Resources Coalition; editl. bd. Coll. and Rsch. Libraries, 1990—96, Jour. Libr. Adminstrn., 1995—2003, portal: Libraries and the Academy, 2000—; editl. adv. bd. The Bottom Line: Mng. Libr. Finances, 1993—98. Bd. trustees Freedom to Read Found., 2007—. Recipient Hugh C. Atkinson Meml. award, ALA, 2007; named Outstanding Librarian of Yr., Indiana Libr. Fedn., 1993, Academic/Rsch. Libr. of Year, Assn. Coll. and Rsch. Libraries, ALA, 1997. Mem.: Baltimore Bibliophiles, Grolier Club. Office: Columbia U 517 Butler Libr 535 W 114th St New York NY 10027 Office Phone: 212-854-2247. Office Fax: 212-854-4972. Business E-Mail: jneal@columbia.edu.

NEAL, JAMES PRESTON, state senator, project engineer; b. Cin., July 1, 1935; s. James Preston and Desha Frank (Thompson) N.; m. Nancy Joan Tyner, June 11, 1961; children: Leslie Neal Driscoll, Karen Desha, James P. BSME, U. Ill., 1960. Registered profl. engr., Del. Project engr. DuPont Co., 1960-92; dir. Tetra Tech Inc., Christiana, Del., 1992-95; pres. Tech. Mgmt., 1994—2001. Mem. Del. Ho. of Reps., 1978-80; mem. Del. Senate, 1980-94; trustee U. Del., 2002-08. Patentee in field. Councilman City of Newark, 1973-78; elder Presbyn. Ch.; bd. dirs. Christina Conservancy, 2004—; mem. Gov.'s Task Force on Sch. Librs., 2003—. With U.S. Army, 1954-56. Recipient Disting. Svc. award Forum to Advance Minorities in Engring., 1989, Disting. Svc. citation Del. Libr. Assn., 1994, Appreciation award Del. Autistic Program, 1999. Mem. Am. Legis. Exch. Coun. (sr. fellow, nat. officer 1991-94, Outstanding Leader 1989, Outstanding Legis. mem. 1994), Del. Engring. Soc. (Engr. of Yr. 1989), Del. Acad. Scis. (bd. dirs. 1996—), Torch Club of Del., Lincoln Club (bd. dirs. 2006—). Republican. Presbyterian. Avocations: photography, reading. Home and Office: 50 Bridlebrook Ln Newark DE 19711-2061 Personal E-mail: jnealdelware@yahoo.com.

NEAL, JOAN BURKES, retired librarian; b. Phenix City, Ala., Feb. 27, 1928; d. George Ashby and Maybelle Ethel (Barnes) Burkes; m. Charles A. Land, May 25, 1944 (dec. Sept. 1947); 1 child, Jo Sandra Land; m. Ray Verlin Neal, Dec. 25, 1952 (dec. May 8, 1996); children: Jo Griffeth, J. Kim, Roger Verlin, Kathy Brown. BS in Edn., U. Ga., Athens, 1951, postgrad., 1966. Dir. kindergarten Fayetteville First Bapt. Ch., Ga., 1958-63; tchr. 3d grade Fayetteville Elem. Sch., 1964-67, libr., 1967—91; ret., 1991. Bd. dirs. Ga. PTA, 1977-80; spkr. Silver Haired Legis. Mem. Ga. State Dem. Party, Atlanta, 1977—; sec. ARC, Fayetteville, 1979-83; pres. Band and Athletic Boosters, Fayetteville, 1968-70; hosp. vol., Fayette Sr. Svcs. Mem. Fayette County Assn. Educators (pres., v.p., sec. 1963—), Ga. Assn. Educators (governing bd. Ga. chpt. 1976-79, legis. chair 1981, 83), Fayette County Bus. and Profl. Women (pres. 1976-78, treas., sec.), Kappa Kappa Iota (pres. Fayetteville chpt. 1970-72). Avocations: reading, golf, politics, walking. Home: 432 Forrest Ave Fayetteville GA 30214-1327 Personal E-mail: joann2271@bellsouth.net.

NEAL, JOSEPH M., anesthesiologist, educator; married. BS cum laude, Wake Forest U., Winston-Salem, NC, 1973; MD, W.Va. U., Morgantown, 1978. Diplomate Am. Bd. Anesthesiology, 1988. Anesthesiology faculty Va. Mason Med. Ctr., Seattle, 1989—. Chief editor Regional Anesthesia and Pain Medicine, 2002—. Bd. visitors Wake Forest U., Winston-Salem, 2004—. Mem.: Am. Soc. Regional Anesthesia and Pain Medicine (dir.). Office: Va Mason Med Ctr 1100 Ninth Ave B2-AN Seattle WA 98111

NEAL, LEORA LOUISE HASKETT, social services administrator; b. NYC, Feb. 23, 1943; d. Melvin Elias and Miriam Emily (Johnson) Haskett; m. Robert A. Neal, Apr. 23, 1966; children: Marla Patrice, Johnathan Robert. BA in Psychology and Sociology, City Coll. N.Y., 1965; MS in Social Work, Columbia U., 1970, cert. adoption specialist, 1977; IBM cert. community exec. tng. program, NYC, 1982. Cert. social worker NY, 1970; lic. master social worker, NY, 2004, clin. social worker, NY, 2005. Caseworker N.Y.C. Dept. Social Service, 1965-67, Windham Child Care, NYC, 1967-73; exec. dir., founder Assn. Black Social Workers Child Adoption Counseling and Referral Service, NYC, 1975-96; adoption tng. specialist Ctr. for Devel. Human Svcs., SUNY-N.Y. State Office Children and Family Svcs., Yonkers, 1996—. Cons. in field; founder Haskett-Neal Publs., Bronx, N.Y., 1993. Co-author: Transracial Adoptive Parenting: A Black/White Community Issue, 1993; contbr. articles to profl. jours. Pres. bd. dirs., founder Fountain Ave. Cmty. Devel. Corp.; bd. dirs. Grandparents Advocacy Project, 2000—. Child Welfare League Am. fellow, 1976; recipient No Time to Lose cert. NY State Dept. Social Svcs., 1989. Mem. NAFE, Nat. Assn. Black Social Workers (co-chair task force on foster care and adoption 1994-08, Outstanding Cmty. Svc. award 1994, Pyramid award 2005, 08), Columbia U. Alumni Assn., CCNY Alumni Assn., Missionary Com. Revival Team (outreach chair 1982-88). Democrat. Avocations: writing, religious studies, travel, cultural activities, history. Office: NY State Office of Children and Family Svcs SUNY 11 Perlman Dr Spring Valley NY 10977 Office Phone: 845-708-2493.

NEAL, MELINDA K., science educator; d. James David and Judith Kay McCall; m. Melvin D. Young (div.); children: Clayton Young, Kristopher Young; m. Marcus L. Neal, July 1, 2000. BA, Southwestern Coll., Winfield, Kans., 1981, MEd, 1990. Tchr. sci. Dexter (Kans.) H.S., 1986—2002; instr. natural sci. Cowley Coll., Arkansas City, Kans., 2002—. Adviser Phi Theta Kappa, Arkansas City, 2006. Mem.: Cowley Coll. Edn. Assn. (sec. 2004—06), Delta Chi (sec. 2006). Office: Cowley Coll 125 S 2d Arkansas City KS 67005

NEAL, MICHAEL A., diversified technology and services company executive; b. May 9, 1953; BS, Ga. Inst. Tech., 1975. With Gen. Electric Co., 1979—; v.p. & gen. mgr., vendor fin. svcs. GE Capital, 1987—90, gen. mgr., comml. equip. financing, 1990—94, exec. v.p., 1994—99, pres., COO, 2000—02; pres., CEO comml. fin. GE, 2002—05, vice chmn., CEO comm. fin., 2005—08, vice-chmn. GE Capital, 2008—. Trustee Fairfield Univ., Ga. Tech. Found.; bd. mem. Soundwaters, Stamford, Conn.; mem. U.S. adv. bd. European Inst. Bus. Adminstrn. Office: General Electric Co 3135 Easton Tpke Fairfield CT 06828*

NEAL, PATRICIA, actress; b. Packard, Ky., Jan. 20, 1926; d. William Burdette and Eura Mildred (Petrey) N.; m. Roald Dahl, July 2, 1953 (div.; dec. 1990); children: Olivia Twenty (dec. 1962), Tessa Sophia, Theo Mathew Roald, Ophelia Magdalene, Lucy Neal. Student, Northwestern U., 1943-45; LHD (hon.), Simmons Coll., Rockford Coll., U. Mass., Northwestern U. Appeared in Broadway prodns.: Another Part of the Forest, 1946 (N.Y. Critics, Antoinette Perry, other awards 1946), Children's Hour, 1952, Roomful of Roses, 1955, Suddenly Last Summer, 1958, The Miracle Worker, 1960; films include: The Fountainhead, 1948, The Hasty Heart, 1948, The Breaking Point, 1949, Three Secrets, 1949, Bright Leaf, 1950, Raton Pass, 1951, Operation Pacific, 1951, The Day the Earth Stood Still, 1951, Weekend with Father, 1951, Diplomatic Courier, 1952, Washington Story, 1952, Something for the Birds, 1952, Face in the Crowd, 1956, Hud, 1963 (N.Y. Film Critics award 1964, Acad. Motion Picture Arts and Scis. award 1964, Best Fgn. Actress award Brit. Acad. 1964), Psych 59, 1964, In Harm's Way, 1965, The Subject Was Roses, 1968 (Oscar nomination), The Night Digger, 1970, Baxter, 1973, Happy Mother's Day, Love, George, 1973, Widows Nest, 1976, The Passage, 1978, Ghost Story, 1981, An Unremarkable Life, 1989, Cookies Fortune, 1999, For the Love of May, 2000; TV appearances, 1952—, including mini-series The Bastard, 1978, TV movies include The Homecoming, 1972, All Quiet on the Western Front, 1979, Caroline?, 1989, Heidi, 1993; also TV commls.; lectr.; author: (autobiography) As I Am, 1988. Com. mem. Internat. Help for Children, Eng.; hon. bd. dirs. Nat. Found. Encephalitis Research; mem. Washington Speakers Bur., 1978—. Named Most Outstanding Woman from Tenn. under 40, 1963; recipient Gold medal Nat. Inst. Social Scis., 1983; Patricia Neal Rehabilitation Hosp. named in her honor, Knoxville, Tenn. Mem. Actors Studio, Pi Beta Phi, Phi Beta. Mem. Ch. of England. Office: 45 E End Ave New York NY 10028-7953*

NEAL, PHIL HUDSON, JR., retired manufacturing executive; b. Birmingham, Ala., Nov. 17, 1926; s. Phil Hudson and Amy (Gross) N.; m. Sarah Swift Britton, Sept. 19, 1959; children: Amy Neal Ager, Phil Hudson, III, Samuel Abney Britton. AB, Duke U., 1950; MBA, Harvard U., 1952. Investment analyst First Nat. Bank, Birmingham, 1952-55; procedures analyst Gen. Electric Co., Hendersonville, NC, 1955-58; with Ala. By-Products Corp., Birmingham, 1958-79, asst. treas., 1964-68, treas., 1968-79; dir., v.p. Utility Tool Co., Birmingham, 1979-86; dir., pres. Nutec Metal Finishing Inc., Birmingham, 1986-92, chmn., 1992—2005; ret., 2005. Trustee Advent Episcopal Sch., 1967—, pres., 1968-89, trustee charitable endowment trust, 1981—; treas. Cathedral Ch. of Advent, 1981-82, mem. chpt., 1983-85, 86-89; bd. dirs. Greater Birmingham Ministries, 1975-77, Advent Episcopal Assn. for Edn., 1968-89, Jefferson County chpt. Ala. Soc. Crippled Children and Adults, Inc., 1977-79; trustee Ala. Found. for Hearing and Speech, 1967-74, v.p., 1968-69, pres., 1969-71. Served with USNR, 1945-46. Mem. Newcomen Soc. N.Am., Birmingham Country Club, The Club, The Summit Club, Phi Beta Kappa, Sigma Nu, Phi Eta Sigma. Episcopalian (vestryman, sr. warden). Home: 3336 Hermitage Rd Birmingham AL 35223-2004 also: 81 Old Duck Hole Rd East Orleans MA 02643

NEAL, RICHARD EDMUND, United States Representative from Massachusetts, former mayor; b. Worcester, Mass., Feb. 14, 1949; s. Edmund J. and Mary H. (Garvey) N.; m. Maureen Conway, Dec. 20, 1975; children: Rory, Brendan, Maura, Sean BS, Am. Internat. Coll., Springfield, Mass., 1972; M.P.A., U. Hartford, Conn., 1976; postgrad., U. Mass., Amherst, 1982. Adminstrv. aide to Mayor City of Springfield, Mass., 1973-78, mem. city council Mass., 1978-83, mayor Mass., 1984-88; mem. U.S. Congress from 2nd. Mass. dist., 1989—, mem. ways & means com., budget com., social security subcommittee. Lectr. history and politics Springfield Tech. Community Coll., Mass., 1973-83; lectr. bus. and govt. Western New Eng. Coll., Springfield, 1979-82; project dir. Springfield Tech. Community Coll., 1979-82 Trustee ARC, YMCA, Springfield Named to Outstanding Young Men in Am., U.S. Jr. C. of C., Springfield; recipient John F. Kennedy award & Amb.'s award, Holyoke, Mass. St. Patrick's Day Com., Internat. Leadership award, Am. Ireland Fund, 2002. Mem. Am. Internat. Coll. Alumni Assn. (pres. 1980, Alumni Achievement award 1985). Springfield Library and Mus. Assn. (trustee) Clubs: Valley Press. John Boyle O'Reilly (Springfield). Democrat. Roman Catholic. Office: US House Reps 2208 Rayburn House Office Bldg Washington DC 20515-2102*

NEAL, STEPHEN CASSIDY, lawyer; b. San Francisco, Mar. 26, 1949; AB, Harvard U., 1970; JD, Stanford U., 1973. Bar: Ill 1973, Calif. 1993. Ptnr. Kirkland & Ellis, Chgo.; ptnr., bus. litigation Cooley Godward Kronish LLP (formerly Cooley Godward LLP), Palo Alto, Calif., 1995—, CEO, 2001—08, chmn., 2001—. Named one of 100 Most Influential Lawyers, Nat. Law Jour., 2006. Fellow: Am. Coll. Trial Lawyers. Office: Cooley Godward Kronish LLP 5 Palo Alto Square #400 3000 El Camino Real Palo Alto CA 94306-2155 Office Phone: 650-843-5182. Office Fax: 650-857-0663. Business E-Mail: nealsc@cooley.com.

NEAL, TERESA SCHREIBEIS, secondary school educator; b. Wheatland, Wyo., Mar. 19, 1956; d. Gene L. and Bonnie Marie (Reed) Schreibeis; m. Michael R. Neal, Apr. 7, 1990; 1 child, Rianna Michele. BA in Am. Studies and English Edn., U. Wyo., 1978; MA in History, U. So. Calif., 1989, PhD, 1994, Cert. Studies of Women/Men in Soc., 1995. Tchr. lang. arts and social studies, asst. coach Carbon County Sch. Dist. 1, Rawlins, Wyo., 1978-86; asst. lectr. freshmen writing program U. So. Calif., LA, 1986-90; adj. prof. history Palomar (Calif.) C.C., San Diego, 1991; software support specialist Dynamic Data Systems, Westminster, Colo., 1992-93; tchr. humanities gifted and talented classes Arvada (Colo.) West H.S., 1993-98; tchr., program developer New Montessori Mid. Sch., 1998-00, Mountain Shadows Mid. Sch., Boulder, Colo., 1998-2000; adj. prof. history, humanities and English composition Red Rocks C.C., Lakewood and Arvada, Colo., 2002—04; tchr. English and Internat. Baccalaureate Program, Lakewood (Colo.) HS, 2004—, Ap History, 2009—. Secondary edn. tchr., Wyo., Colo., 1978-; participant critical thinking and humanities secondary edn. project NEH, Wyo., 1985-86; adj. prof. English Composition, Front Range C.C., Westminster, Colo., 2000-03; presenter Nat. Women's Hist. Project Fall Conf., 2005-06. Author: Evolution Toward Equality: Equality for Woman of the American West, 2006. Mem., chmn. Reading Is Fundamental Program, Rawlins, 1983-85, Women of the West Mus., 2001—; tchr., sponsor Denver-Metro YMCA Youth and Govt., 1994-97, Close Up, Washington, 1984-86, 97; tchr., advisor Nat. History Day Contest, 1995—2001, asst. examiner Internat. Baccalaureate, 2008-; tchr., sponsor World Affairs Challenge, Denver U., 1998; vol. math. tutor Foothills Acad., Wheat Ridge, Colo., 2001-02, sponsor, Lakewood HS, Knitters, 2004-. Mem. AAUW (Project Renew fellow 1987-88), Western Assn. Women Historians, G. Autrey Mus. Western Art, Denver Art Mus., Buffalo Bill Western Heritage Ctr. Avocations: travel, fine arts, reading, crafts. E-mail: tneal@jeffio.k12.co.us.

NEAL-BARNETT, ANGELA MARIE, psychology professor; b. Youngstown, Ohio, Feb. 13, 1960; d. Andrew Lee and Doris Lucille Neal; m. Edgar J. Barnett Jr., July 17, 1995; 1 child, Reece. BA, Mt. Union Coll., 1982; MA, DePaul U., 1985, PhD, 1988. Lic. psychologist, Ohio. Clin. therapist ECHO Community Health Orgn., Chgo., 1985-87; post-doctoral fellow U. Pitts. (Pa.), Western Psychiat. Inst., 1988-89; asst. prof. Kent (Ohio) State U., 1989—, 1989-95, assoc. prof., 1995—. Pres., founder Rise Sally Rise Prodn.; founder, CEO Rise, Sally, Rise, Inc.; bd. dirs. King-Kennedy Ctr., Ravenna, Ohio, 1989—95; rsch. fellow Inst. African Am. Affairs, Kent, 1991—; co-chair Allied Health Edn. Com., 1994—; mem. NIMH Child Psychopathology and Treatment Rev. Panel, 1996—99; spkr. in field. Author: Forging Limits: African American Children Clinical Developmental Perspectives; contbr. articles to profl. jours.; author: Soothe Your Nerves: The Black Women's Guide to Understanding and Overcoming Anxiety, Panic and Fear; author, prodr.: CD Believe and Succeed. Mem. alumni coun. Mt. Union Coll.; mem. governing bd. Ida B. Wells Cmty. Acad., 1998-2000. Urban Rsch. grantee Ohio Bd. Regents, 1990, biomed. support grantee NIH, 1991, small grantee NIMH, 1994-96; recipient Minority Career Advancement award NSF. Mem. APA (, mem. adv. com. minority fellowship program, Kenneth & Marie Clark award), Ohio Psychol. Assn., Assn. Advancement Behavior Therapy, Assn. Black Psychologists, African Am. Lit. Guild Kent. Methodist. Avocations: tennis, reading. Office: Kent State U Dept Psychology 118 Kent Hl Kent OH 44242-0001 also: Rise Sally Rise Inc 361 Starr Line Dr Tallmadge OH 44278 E-mail: aneal@kent.edu.

NEALEN, PAUL, science educator; PhD, U. Pa., 2000. Asst. prof. Ind. U. Pa., 2005—. Office: Ind Univ Pa 975 Oakland Ave Indiana PA 15705-1001

NEAL-PARKER, SHIRLEY ANITA, obstetrician, gynecologist; b. Washington, Aug. 28, 1949; d. Leon Walker and Pearl Anita (Shelton) Neal; m. Andre Cowan Dasent, June 21, 1971 (div. Feb. 1978); 1 child, Erika Michelle Dasent; m. James Carl Parker, Feb. 11, 1979; 1 child, Amirah Nabeehah. BS in Biology, Am. U., 1971; MD, Hahnemann U., 1979. Lic. Md., Calif., Wash., Oreg. Intern Howard U. Hosp., 1979-80, resident, 1980-84; physician Nat. Health Svc. Corp., Charleston, W. Va., 1984-86; clin. instr. W.Va. U., Charleston, 1985-86; pvt. practice ob./gyn. Sacramento, 1986-95; pvt. practice Chehalis, Wash., 1995—2004; chair dept. perinatology Providence Centralia Hosp., 1999-2000; group practice Tulare County Health and Human Svcs., 2004—05, Grand Med. Group, 2005—06; with St. Rita Med. Clinic, Montclair, Calif., 2006—07, Michael Women's Med. Group, 2008—. Bd. dirs. Ruth Rosenberg Dance Ensemble, Sacramento, 1992-95, Human Response Network, Chehalis, 1995-97. Mem.: Calif. Med. Assn., Wash. State Obstet. Assn., Tulare County Med. Soc., Lewis County Med. Soc., Wash. State Med. Assn., Am. Med. Women's Assn. (comty. svc. award Mother Hale br. 1994), Nat. Med. Assn., Am. Reproductive Health Profls., Am. Assn. Gynecologic Laparoscopists. Avocations: travel, reading, crocheting, collecting ethnic dolls, magnets. Home: 1949 Santa Maria Ave Porterville CA 93257-8863 Office: 575 W Putnam Ave Porterville CA 93257 Office Phone: 559-784-6878. Home Fax: 559-791-1897. Personal E-mail: drsanp@earthlink.net.

NEAMAN, ELLIOT YALE, history professor; b. San Francisco, Jan. 28, 1957; PhD, U. Calif., Berkeley, 1992. Prof. U. San Francisco, 1992—. Pres. USFFA, San Francisco, 1998—2008. Home: 2130 Fulton St San Francisco CA 94117 Office: Univ San Francisco 2130 Fulton St San Francisco CA 94117 Office Fax: 415-422-6784. Personal E-mail: elliotyale@yahoo.com.

NEAME, RONALD, director, producer; b. Hendon, Middlesex, Eng., Apr. 23, 1911; s. Stuart Elwin and Ivy Lillian (Close) N.; m. Beryl Yolanda Heanly, Oct. 15, 1933; 1 son, Christopher Elwyn; m. Dona Friedberg, Sept. 12, 1993. Student pvt. schs., London and Sussex, Eng. Asst. cameraman Brit. Internat. Pictures, Estree, Eng., 1928-35, chief cameraman, 1935-45. Dir.: photography, prodn. supr. various films, including In Which We Serve, 1942, This Happy Breed, 1943, Blithe Spirit, 1944; co-writer, producer: films Brief Encounter, 1945, Great Expectations, 1946; producer: film Oliver Twist, 1947; dir.: films Take My Life, 1948, Golden Salamander, 1949, The Promoter, 1952, Man with a Million, 1953, The Man Who Never Was, 1954, Windom's Way, 1957, The Horse's Mouth, 1958, Tunes of Glory, 1960, I Could Go On Singing, 1962, The Chalk Garden, 1963, Mr. Moses, 1964, Gambit, 1966, The Prime of Miss Jean Brodie, 1968, Scrooge, 1970, The Poseidon Adventure, 1972, The Odessa File, 1974, Meteor, 1978, Hopscotch, 1979, First Monday in October, 1980-81, Foreign Body, 1985, The Magic Baloon, 1989; co-founder film co. Cineguild Co., Denham, Eng., 1943-44. Decorated Comdr. of the Order of the Brit. Empire, 1996. Mem. Dirs. Guild Am., Am. Film Inst., Acad. Motion Picture Arts and Scis. (gov. 1977-79), Brit. Acad. Film and TV Arts (London and Los Angeles), Savile Club (London). *When I am asked which film I consider to be my best, I reply, "I haven't made it yet. Perhaps next time.".*

NEAR, DELIA MARY, librarian; b. Orange, Calif., Sept. 26, 1953; d. Benjamin Alfred and Carolyn Elizabeth Johnson; m. Guy David Near, Oct. 21, 1978; children: Hilary Robin, Carrie Wells. BA in History, U. Calif., Riverside, 1975; MLS, U. Calif., Berkeley, 1976. Libr. Yorba Linda Dist. Libr., Calif., 1976—78; tech. svcs. libr. Merced County Libr., Calif., 1978—93; reference libr. Merced Coll., 1994—. Troop leader Muir Trail Girl Scout Coun., Merced, 1991—2002; chair CROP Walk Merced, 2005—08; exec. com. mem. Catch, United Meth. Ch. Merced, 2001—08; mem. former sec. Wesley Found., Merced, 2003—08. Named Vol. of Yr., Merced County Bd. Supr., 2005. Mem.: AAUW (pres. 1985—86). Democrat. Methodist. Avocations: travel, reading. Home: 1004 Half Dome Ct Merced CA 95340 Office: Merced Coll 3600 M St Merced CA 95348

NEAR, TIMOTHY, theater director; Grad., San Francisco State U., Acad. Music and Dramatic Art, London. Artistic dir. San Jose Repertory Theatre, 1987—. Past actress, dir. with numerous prestigious theaters including The Guthrie Theatre, Berkeley (Calif.) Repertory Theater, La Jolla (Calif.) Playhouse, The Alliance Theatre, Atlanta, The Mark Taper Forum, L.A., Ford's Theatre, Washington, Repertory Theatre of St. Louis, N.Y. Shakespeare Festival, Stage West, Mass., A.C.T., Seattle. Dir. Ghosts on Fire, La Jolla Playhouse (Drama League award), Singer in the Storm, Mark Taper Forum (Drama League award), Thunder Knocking on the Door (Drama League award). Recipient 1997 Woman of Achievement in the Arts, San Jose Mercury News and The Woman's Fund. Office: San Jose Repertory Theatre 101 Paseo De San Antonio San Jose CA 95113-2603

NEARINE, ROBERT JAMES, educational psychologist; b. Fitchburg, Mass., May 15, 1930; s. Raymond Johns and Beatrice Aileen (Strickland) N.; children: Luke, Martha, Amy. BS, Fitchburg State Coll., 1951; EdM, Tufts Coll., 1952; MA, U. Conn., 1965, profl. diploma, 1996; EdD, Boston U., 1973. Cert. advanced grad. specialization Boston U. Tchr. pub. schs., Holbrook, Mass., 1952-54, Groton, Mass., 1954-55, Winchester, Mass., 1955-59, supr. Inverness, Mont., 1959-60, guidance counselor Manchester, Conn., 1961-66, supr. of evaluation, 1966-73, adminstr. for funding and evaluation, 1973-76, spl. asst. for funding Hartford, Conn., 1976-78; spl. asst. for evaluation rsch. and testing Bd. Edn., Hartford, 1978-93; ednl. cons. Glastonbury, Conn., 1993—. Mem. requirements adv. com., 1991-92. Contbr. articles to profl. jours. Col. ret. US Army. NDEA fellow Boston U., 1960-61, GE fellow Syracuse U., 1971, Ednl. Policy Inst. fellow George Washington U., 1979-80; Inducted into CT Veterans Hall of Fame, 2007. Mem. APA, Res. Officers Assn. (nat. councilman 1994-2007), Amvets, Civitan (pres. 1998-99), Conn. state com. employee support of Guard and Res.), Am. Legion (post comdr. 2006-08), Victory Svcs. Club U.K., Assn. of U.S. Army, NG Assn. U.S., Gov.'s Foot Guard, Freemasons, Scottish Rite, York Rite, Shriners, Jesters, Phi Delta Kappa. Avocations: military history, travel. E-mail: rjnear@sbcglobal.net.

NEARY, DANIEL GEORGE, soil scientist; b. Chippewa Falls, Wis., Oct. 1, 1946; s. Harry George and Emma Pauline Neary; m. Veronica Lou Oien, Aug. 29, 1970; children: Collin Daniel, Andrea Pauline Dutoit, David Andrew, Erika Lucylle Simon. BS, Mich. State U., East Lansing, 1969, MS, 1972, PhD, 1974. Cert. Soil Sci. Soc. Am., 1978. Postdoc. rsch. fellow Forest Rsch. Inst., Rotorua, New Zealand, 1974—78; rsch. soil scientist US Forest Svc., Otto, NC, 1978—81, Gainesville, Fla., 1981—87, project leader, 1987—93, Flagstaff, Ariz., 1993—2007, sci. team leader and rsch. soil scientist, 2007—. Country rep. Internat. Energy Agy. Bioenergy Task 31, Paris, 2000—. Author: (textbook) Fire's Effects on Ecosystems; contbr. articles to profl. jour. Emergency med. technician St John Ambulance, Rotorua, New Zealand, 1975—78, Macon County Ambulance, Franklin, NC, 1978—81, Alachua County Fire-Rescue, Gainesville, 1981—93, Northern Ariz. Incident Mgmt. Team, Flagstaff, 1993—2008. With USN, 1969—70, Pensacola, Fla. Fellow: Am. Soc. Agronomy, Soil Sci. Soc. Am. (bd. mem. 2005—), Northern Ariz. Celtic Heritage Soc.; mem.: Assn. Fire Ecology, Internat. Erosion Control Assn., Internat. Assn. Wildland Fire, Am. Water Resources Assn. Roman Catholic. Avocations: travel, hiking, swimming, genealogy. Office: US Forest Svc 2500 S Pine Knoll Dr Flagstaff AZ 86001 Office Fax: 928-556-2130. Personal E-mail: dgnvln@npgcable.com. Business E-Mail: dneary@fs.fed.us.

NEARY, DANIEL P., insurance company executive; b. Carroll, Iowa, 1952; m. Shirley Neary; 4 children. Degree, U. Iowa, 1974. With Mut. of Omaha, 1975—, exec. v.p. group benefit svcs., 1999—2003; pres., bd. dirs. Mut. of Omaha and United of Omaha, 2003—05, CEO, chmn., 2005—. Bd. dir. Comml. Fed. Bank, Comml. Fed. Corp., America's Health Ins. Plans, Creighton U. Bd. dirs. United Way, Midlands and Am. Red Cross; mem. Boy Scouts Am. Mid-Am. Coun.; chmn. Walk to Cure Diabetes Juvenile Diabetes Rsch. Found., 2004; bd. trustees Strategic Air & Space Mus. Mem.: Soc. Actuaries. Office: Mut of Omaha Mutual of Omaha Plz Omaha NE 68175

NEARY, PATRICIA ELINOR, ballet director; b. Miami, Fla. d. James Elliott and Elinor (Mitsitz) N. Corps de ballet Nat. Ballet of Can., Toronto, Ont., 1957-60; prin. dancer N.Y.C. Ballet, 1960-68; ballerina Geneva Ballet, Switzerland, 1968-70, ballet dir., 1973-78; guest artist Stuttgart Ballet, Germany, 1968-70; asst. ballet dir., ballerina West Berlin Ballet, 1970-73; ballet dir. Zurich Ballet, Switzerland, 1978-86, La Scala di Milano ballet co., Italy, 1986-88; tchr. Balanchine ballets, Balanchine Trust, 1987—.

NEAS, JOHN THEODORE, investment company executive; b. Tulsa, May 1, 1940; s. George and Lillian J. (Kaspar) N.; m. Sally Jane McPherson, June 10, 1966; children: Stephen, Gregory, Matthew. BS, Okla. State U., 1967, MS, 1968. With acctg. dept. Rockwell Internat., 1965; with contr.'s dept. Amoco Prodn. Co., 1966—67; audit and tax staff Deloitte, Haskins & Sells, 1968—75; pres. Nat. Petroleum Sales, Inc., Tulsa, 1975—; prin. Neas Investments Ltd. Partnership, 1997—, Sebring Investments Ltd. Partnership, 1997—. Mem. Coun. Oak Bldg. Mgmt., LLC, 1997—, Vet. Properties, LLC, 1994—; asst. instr. U. Tulsa, 1974; bd. dirs. Summit Bank. Mem. AICPA, Inst. Mgmt. Accts., Okla. Soc. CPAs, McClellan-Kerr Arkansas River Nav. Sys. Hist. Soc., Okla. Heritage Assn., Okla. State U. Pres.'s Club, Okla. State U. Coll. Bus. Adminstrn. Assocs. (v.p. memberships 1989-91, Hall of Fame 1991, Acctg. Dept. Hall of Fame 1993), Southern Hills Country Club, Gol Club Okla. Republican. Lutheran. Office: Nat Petroleum Sales Inc 5401 S Harvard Ave Ste 200 Tulsa OK 74135-3861

NEASMAN, ANNIE RUTH, health facility administrator; b. Moore Haven, Fla., Oct. 24, 1947; d. Nathan and Daisy Mae Miles; children: Beatrice Daizine, Barry Anthony. BSN, Fla. A&M U., 1969; MS, Fla. Internat. U., 1976. Registered Nurse, Fla. Dept. Health, Bd. Nursing. Staff nurse Jackson Meml. Hosp., Miami, 1969—71, adminstr., nursing R&D, 1976—84; adminstr. Jackson Meml. Health Sys., North Dade Health Ctr., Miami, 1984—90; adminstr., dept. health Fla. Dept. Health, Rehabilitative Svcs., Miami, 1990—92, dep. dist. adminstr., 1992—96; adminstr. Fla. Dept. Health, Miami, 1996—99, divsn. dir., family health svc. Tallahassee, 1999—2001, dep. sec., state nursing dir., 2001—04; pres., CEO Econ. Opportunity Health Ctr., Miami, 2004—. Bd. mem. Fla. Am. Lung Assn., Jacksonville, 2004—06; mem. Mt. Hermon AME Ch., Miami Gardens, Fla., 2004—06; bd. mem. Fla. Ctr. for Nursing, Orlando, 2002—04; mem. Fla. Nurses Assn., Orlando, 1976—2006, Black Nurses Assn., Miami, 2004—06. Recipient Woman of Yr., Pub. Health, 1994, Sr. Mgmt. Svc. award, Health and Rehab. Svcs., 1996; named to Nursing Hall of Fame, Fla. A&M, 1996. Mem.: Black Nurses Assn., Fla. Nurses Assn., Chi Eta Phi Nursing Sorority (Humanitarian award 1994), Delta Sigma Theta Sorority. Democrat-Npl. Ame. Avocations: travel, walking, reading. Home: 6799 Brookline Dr Miami FL 33015 Office: Econ Opportortunity Family Health Ctr Inc 700 S Royal Poinciana Blvd Ste 300 Miami Springs FL 33166 Office Fax: 305-805-1715. Personal E-mail: aruthmg47@aol.com. Business E-Mail: aneasman@hcnetwork.org.

NEAVEL, CELIA BETH, medical association administrator; b. Blommington, Ind., Aug. 30, 1959; d. Richard Charles and Nancy Trager Neavel; m. Jose Carlos Cortez; children: Elizabeth, Elena, Geordi. BA with honors in liberal arts, U. Tex., 1981; MD, Baylor Coll. of Medicine, 1985. Diplomate Am. Bd. of Family Medicine, cert. Added Qualification, Adolescent Medicine. Asst. prof. Dept. of Family Medicine, Cin., 1989—91; contract physician Austin Regional Clin., Austin, Tex., 1991—92; clin. asst., prof. of Pediat. Scott and White, Temple, Tex., 1991—95; physician adv. Easter Seals Ctrl. Tex., Austin, Tex., 1995—; faculty Austin Med. Edn. Program, Austin, Tex., 1995—2006; dir., adolescent medicine Ctr. for Adolescent Health at People's Cmty Clin., Austin, Tex., 1994—. Med. dir. Lifeworks St. Outreach Clin., Austin, Tex., 1996—, RGK Downtown Ctr. for Health Clin., Austin, Tex., 1996—, Phoenix Acad. Off-Site Clin., Austin, Tex., 2003—; dir. Devel. Behavioral Primary Care Program, People's Cmty. Clin., Austin, Tex., 2004—; clin. asst. prof. pediat. UTMB, Austin, 2006—. Co-author: (monograph) Integrating Child and Adolescent Mental Health Into Primary Care, 2002. Vol. lectr. Camp Disabled Children, Center Point, Tex., 1990—2005, physician, 1990—2005. Recipient Amb. award, St. Lukes Episcopal Health Charities, 2007; named Tex. Super Doctor, Tex. Monthly Mag., 2004; fellow, Soc. Adolescent Medicine, 2007; grant, Healthy Tomorrows from HRSA, 2005. Mem.: AMA, Physicians for Social Responsibility, Soc. of Adolescent Medicine, Tex. Med. Assn., Travis County Managed Care Regional Adv. Com. Office: Ctr for Adolescent Health Peoples Cmty Clin 2909 NIH 35 Austin TX 78722 Office Phone: 512-478-4939. Office Fax: 512-320-0702. E-mail: ibappmd@aol.com.

NEAVES, WILLIAM BARLOW, cell biologist, educator; b. Spur, Tex., Dec. 25, 1943; s. William Fred and Revvie Lee (Hefner) N.; m. Priscilla Wood, Jan. 28, 1965; children: William Barlow, Clarissa D'laine. AB magna cum laude, Harvard U., 1966; postgrad., Med. Sch., 1966-67, PhD, 1969. Lectr. vet. anatomy U. Nairobi, 1970-71, vis. prof., 1978; lectr. anatomy Harvard U., 1972; asst. prof. cell biology U. Tex. Health Sci. Ctr., Dallas, 1972-74, assoc. prof., 1974-77, prof., 1977—, Doris and Brian Wildenthal Prof. of Biomed. Sci., 1993—, dean Grad. Sch. Biomed. Scis., 1980-88, interim dean Southwestern Med. Sch., 1986-88, dean Southwestern Med. Sch., 1989-98, exec. v.p. acad. affairs, 1998—2000; prof. medicine U. Mo., Kans. City, 1998—2000; pres., CEO, bd. dirs. Stowers Inst. Med. Rsch., Kans. City, 2000—. Dir. Cerner Corp., Midwest Rsch. Inst., Kans. City Area Life Scis. Inst.; trustee Wash. U.; mem. nat. coun. Wash. U. Sch. Medicine; rsch. assoc. herpetology Los Angeles County Mus., 1970-73; vis. lectr. U. Chgo., 1976-77. Assoc. editor Anat. Record, 1975-87; mem. editl. bd. Biology of Reprodn., 1983-86, Jour. Andrology, 1987-89; contbr. chpts. to books, articles to profl. jours. Bd. dirs. Dallas Zool. Soc., 1989-94, Dallas Mus. Natural History, 1993-95, Damon Runyan-Walter Winchell Cancer Fund, 1986-92, v.p., 1990-92, Sarnoff Endowment, 1998—. Rockefeller Found. fellow, 1970-71; Milton Fund grantee, 1970-71; Population Council grantee, 1973-75; NIH grantee, 1973-89; Ford. Found. grantee, 1976-78. Fellow AAAS; mem. Am. Assn. Anatomists, Am. Soc. Andrology (Young Andrologist award 1983), Dallas Assembly, N.Y. Acad. Scis., Soc. Study of Reprodn., Liaison Com. on Med. Edn. (joint com. of AMA and Assn. Am. Med. Colls.), Sigma Xi, Alpha Omega Alpha. Methodist. Office: Stowers Inst Med Rsch 1000 East 50th St Kansas City MO 64110 Office Phone: 816-926-4040. Business E-Mail: wbn@stowers-institute.org.*

NEAVOLL, GEORGE FRANKLIN, writer; b. Lebanon, Oreg., Aug. 20, 1938; s. Jesse Hunter and Mazie Maude (Meyer) N.; m. Laney Lila Hunter Hough, June 21, 1969 (dec. Nov. 2000); m. Joanne Darlen MacRoberts, May 4, 2002. BS, U. Oreg., 1965. Reporter, photographer Lebanon (Oreg.) Express, 1969-70; state editor Idaho State Jour., Pocatello, 1970-72; editorial writer The Jour.-Gazette, Ft. Wayne, Ind., 1972-75, Detroit Free Press, 1975-78; editorial page editor The Wichita (Kans.) Eagle, 1978-91, Portland (Maine) Press Herald, Maine Sunday Telegram, 1991-99. Vol. Peace Corps, India, 1967-69; bd. councilors Save-the-Redwoods League, 1980—; bd. dirs. Population Inst., 2002-2008; Oreg. corr. Reporters Without Borders, 2009-. Recipient Edward J. Meeman award Scripps-Howard Found., 1973, Honor Roll award Izaak Walton League Am., 1974, Jamaica Daily Gleaner award Inter Am. Press Assn., 1985, Disting. Citizen award Bethany Coll., 1985, Servant Leadership award Southwestern Coll., 1987, Global Media award Population Inst., 1996, Henri A. Benoit award Greater Portland (Maine) C. of C., 1999, Restoration Leadership award Restore the North Woods, 2005; named Hon. Park Ranger, Nat. Park Svc., 1988. Mem.: Nat. Press Club, NAACP. Home: 1000 SW Vista Ave No 801 Portland OR 97205-1163 Personal E-mail: gneavoll@comcast.net.

NEBEKER, FRANK QUILL, Senior Judge, DC Court of Appeals; b. Salt Lake City, Apr. 23, 1930; s. J. Quill and Minnie (Holmgren) N.; m. Louana M. Visintainer, July 11, 1953; children: Caramaria, Melia, William Mark. Student, Weber Coll., 1948-50; BS in Polit. Sci, U. Utah, 1953; JD, Am. U., 1955. Bar: D.C. 1956. Corr. sec. The White House, 1953-56; trial atty. Internal Security div. Justice Dept., Washington, 1956-58; asst. U.S. atty. US Dept. Justice, 1958-69; judge DC Ct. Appeals, Washington, 1969-87, sr. judge, 2000—; dir. Office Govt. Ethics, Washington, 1987-89; chief judge US Ct. Appeals Vets. Claims, Washington, 1989-2000, recalled judge. Cons. Nat. Commn. on Reform of Fed. Criminal Laws, 1967-68; adj. prof. Am. U. Washington Coll. Law, 1967-85. Mem. Am., D.C. Bar Assn., Am. Law Inst. Office: DC Ct Appeals 500 Indiana Ave NW Washington DC 20001-2131*

NEBENZAHL, KENNETH, rare book and map dealer, author; b. Far Rockaway, NY, Sept. 16, 1927; s. Meyer and Ethel (Levin) N.; m. Jocelyn Hart Spitz, Feb. 7, 1953; children: Kenneth (dec.), Patricia Nebenzahl, Margaret Nebenzahl, Soozie Nichol. Student, Columbia U., 1947-48; L.H.D. (hon.), Coll. William and Mary, 1983. Solicitor new bus. United Factors Corp., NYC, 1947-50; sales rep. Fromm & Sichel, Inc., NYC, 1950-52; v.p. Cricketeer, Inc., Chgo., 1953-58; pres. Kenneth Nebenzahl, Inc., Chgo., 1957—. Bd. dirs. Imago Mundi, Ltd., London; cons. Rand McNally and Co., 1966-97. Author: Atlas of the American Revolution, 1974, Bibliography of Printed Battle Plans of the American Revolution, 1975, Maps of the Holy Land, 1986 (German edit. 1995), Atlas of Columbus and the Great Discoveries, 1990, also edits. in Spanish, German, Italian, Portugese and French langs., Mapping The Silk Road and Beyond, 2,000 Years of Exploring the East, 2004, also edits. in French and Japanese langs.; contbr. articles to profl. jours. Trustee Glencoe Pub. Libr., 1963-69, pres., 1966-69; bd. dirs. North Suburban Libr. System, 1966-69, Beverly Farm Found., Godfrey, Ill., 1961-67, Nature Conservancy of Ill., 1980-88; trustee Adler Planetarium, 1969—, chmn., 1977-81; mem. exec. com. Northwestern U. Libr. Coun., 1973-75; sponsor Kenneth Nebenzahl Jr. lectures history cartography Newberry Libr., Chgo., 1965—; trustee John Crear Libr., Chgo., 1976-84; trustee U. Chgo., 1982—, mem. vis. com. to libr., 1978-96, chmn., 1987-95; co-chair Phillips Soc.-Libr. of Congress, Washington, 1995-98; bd. dirs. Evanston Hosp. Corp., 1978-85, Am. Himalayan Found., 1994—; mem. U.S. nat. coun. World Wildlife Fund, 1993-; founding pres. Ill. Ctr. for Book, 1986-88. With USMCR, 1945-46. Recipient IMCoS-Tooley award (London), 1984. Fellow Royal Geog. Soc., Royal Soc. for Asian Affairs; mem. Manuscript Soc. (dir. 1965-71), Am. Library Trustees Assn. (nat. chmn. com. intellectual freedom 1967-68), Bibliog. Soc. Am., Newberry Library Assocs. (bd. govs. 1965-78, chmn. 1976-78), Newberry Library (trustee 1978-2003, vice chmn. 1994-2003, life trustee 2003—), Antiquarian Booksellers Assn. Am. (bd. govs. 1965-67, v.p. 1975-77), Am. Antiquarian Soc. (gov. 1981-85), Soc. History Discoveries (dir. 1974-76), Chgo. Map Soc. (dir. 1976-86), Caxton Club (Chgo.) (bd. govs. 1961-68, 74-80, pres. 1964-66), Wayfarers Club (Chgo.) (pres. 1979-80), Lake Shore Country Club, Century Assn. (NYC), Grolier Club (NYC) (bd. govs. 1998-99). Office: PO Box 370 Glencoe IL 60022-0370

NEBERT, DANIEL WALTER, molecular geneticist, research administrator; b. Portland, Oreg., Sept. 26, 1938; s. Walter Francis Nebert and Marie Sophie (Schick) Kirk; m. Myrna Sisk, Mar. 12, 1960 (div. 1975);

children: Douglas Daniel, Dietrich Andrew; m. Kathleen Dixon, Aug. 15, 1981 (div. 1997); children: Rosemarie Dixon, Rebecca Frances, David Porter, Lucas Daniel; m. Lucia Fung Jorge, Mar. 6, 2000. BA, Wesleyan U., 1959; BS and MS in Biochemistry, U. Oreg., 1964, MD, 1964. Lic. physician, Ohio; bd. qualified in pediats. and human genetics; Am. Bd. Pediat. and Human Genetics. Pediat. intern UCLA Hosps., 1964—65, resident pediat., 1965—66; postdoctoral fellow Nat. Cancer Inst., NIH, Bethesda, Md., 1966—68; sr. investigator Nat. Inst. Child Health and Human Devel., Bethesda, 1968—71, sect. head, 1971—74, lab. chief, 1974—89; prof. dept. environ. health U. Cin. Med. Ctr., 1989—, prof. dept. pediat. and molecular devel. biology, 1991—, Cin. Children's Hosp. Faculty bd. cert. in human genetics NIH, 1981-89; coord. med. genetics program US-China Coop. Med. Health Protocol, 1982-89; Pfizer lectr. U. Vt., Burlington, 1978, Stanford U., 1979; Wellcome vis. prof. biochemistry and molecular biology U. SD, Vermillion, 1991; assoc. dir. physician scientist tng. program MD/PhD, U. Cin. Med. Ctr., 1994-98; nat. adv. Environ. Health Scis. Coun., 2000-04; external adv. bd. Howard U. Cancer Ctr., Wash., 1998-2002, U. Lisbon, 1998-2002, Inst. DNA and Human Genomics U. Panama, 1999-2004; dir. Ctr. Environ. Genetics, 1992-97 Mem. editl. bd. Molecular Pharmacology, 1972-1984, Biochem. Pharmacology, 1972-2008, Archives of Biochemistry and Biophysics, 1973-76, Archieves Internationales de Pharmacodynamie et de Therapie, 1975-81, Jour. Environ. Scis. and Health, 1976-81, Chemico-Biol. Interactions, 1977-83, Teratogenesis, Carcinogenesis and Mutagenesis, 1978-82, Devel. Pharmacology and Therapeutics, 1980-86, Anticancer Rsch., 1981-83, DNA and Cell Biology, 1986—2003, Jour. Exptl. Pathology, 1986-1994, Molecular Endocrinology, 1988-1992, Endocrinology, 1989-2002, Molecular Toxicology, 1990-92, Pharmacogenetics Genomics, 1991—, Mutation Rsch., 1996-2001, European Jour. Pharmacology, 2002-, Human Genomics, 2003—; assoc. editor DNA and Cell Biology, 1987-2003, commn. edit. Biochem. Pharmacology (N.Am.), 1994-2001, Environ. Health Perspectives, 1997—; commn. edit. Human Mutation, 2005-; contbr. more than 590 articles to profl. jours. Capt. USPHS, 1966-89 Recipient Meritorious Svc. medal USPHS, 1978, Frank Ayrey fellow award in clin. pharmacology, U.K., 1984, Bernard B. Brodie award, 1986, Ernst A. Sommer Meml. award, 1988; GM scholar, 1956-59, Lawrence Selling scholar, 1961, 63, Disting. Rsch. Professorship award, U. Cin., 1998, George Rieveschl Jr. award for disting. sci. rsch., U. Cin., 1999 Fellow: AAAS; mem. Am. Soc. Human Genetics, Am. Soc. Pharmacology and Exptl. Therapeutics, Am. Soc. Biochemistry and Molecular Biology, Am. Soc. Clin. Investigation (emeritus 1984-), Soc. Toxicology (Disting. Lifetime Toxicology Scholar award, 2005), Human Genome Variation Soc. (founder), Sigma Xi. Republican. Avocations: gardening, golf, piano, skiing, art. Home: 20 Oliver Rd Cincinnati OH 45215-2631 Office: Univ Cin Med Ctr Dept Environ Health PO Box 670056 Cincinnati OH 45267-0056 Office Phone: 513-821-4664.

NEBGEN, DENISE R., physician, researcher; b. San Antonio, Feb. 23, 1964; d. Marvin Carl and Marlene Marie Nebgen; m. Jason Edward Johnson, Mar. 11, 2000; children: Christopher, Sean. DDS, U. Tex. Health Sci. Ctr., San Antonio, 1988; PhD, Northwestern U., Chgo., 1995, MD, 1997. Resident ob-gyn. Baylor Coll. Medicine, Houston, 2001; physician ob-gyn. U. Ob-Gyn. Tex., Houston, 2001—; physician minimally invasive surgery Sightline of Houston, 2005—. Mem. Meth. Ctr. Performing Arts Medicine, Houston, 2003—, Meth. Ctr. Pelvic Medicine, 2005—. Chmn. membership care Shepperd Heart United Meth. Ch., Pearland, 2007. Fellow: ACOG; mem.: AMA, Houston Gynecol. Obstet. Soc. Methodist. Avocations: running, camping. Office: U Ob-Gyn Tex 6550 Fannin Smith Tower Ste 2201 Houston TX 77030 Office Phone: 713-797-9498. Office Fax: 713-797-0661.

NEBLETT, CAROL, soprano; b. Modesto, Calif., Feb. 1, 1946; m. Philip R. Akre; 3 children. Studies with, William Vennard, Roger Wagner, Esther Andreas, Ernest St. John Metz, Lotte Lehmann, Pierre Bernac, Rosa Ponselle, George London, Jascha Heifetz, Norman Treigle, Sol Hurek, Dorothy Kirsten, Maestros Julius Rudel, Claudio Abbado, Daniel Barenboin, Erich Leinsdorf, James Levine, others. Soloist with Roger Wagner Chorale; performed in U.S. and abroad with various symphonies; debut with Carnegie Hall, 1966, N.Y.C. Opera, 1969, Met. Opera, 1979; sung with maj. opera cos. including Met. Opera, N.Y.C., Lyric Opera Chgo., Balt. Opera, Pitts. Opera, Houston Grand Opera, San Francisco Opera, Boston Opera Co., Milw. Florentine Opera, Washington Opera Soc., Covent Garden, Cologne. Opera, Vienna (Austria) Staatsoper, Paris Opera, Teatro Regio, Turin, Italy, Teatro San Carlo, Naples, Italy, Teatro Massimo, Palermo, Italy, Gran Teatro del Liceo, Barcelona, Spain, Kirov Opera Theatre, Leningrad, USSR, Dubrovnik (Yugoslavia) Summer Festival, Salzberg Festival, others; rec. artist RCA, DGG, EMI; appearances with symphony orchs., also solo recitals, (film) La Clemenza di Tito; filmed and recorded live performance with Placido Domingo, La Fancuilla del West; numerous TV appearances, artist, Residence Chapman U, assoc. dir., Opera Program; tchr, master Voice & Opera Acting.

NECHEMIAS, STEPHEN MURRAY, lawyer; b. St. Louis, July 27, 1944; s. Herbert Bernard and Toby Helen (Wax) N.; m. Marcia Rosenstein, June 19, 1966 (div. Dec. 1981); children: Daniel Jay, Scott Michael; m. Linda Adams, Aug. 20, 1983. BS, Ohio State U., 1966; JD, U. Cin., 1969. Bar: Ohio 1969. Ptnr. Taft, Stettinius & Hollister, Cin., 1969—. Adj. prof. law No. Ky. U., Chase Coll. Law. Tax comment author: Couse's Ohio Form Book, 6th edit., 1984. Mem. Ohio State Bar Assn. (former chmn. taxation com.), Cin. Bar Assn. (former chmn. taxation sect. 1985), Legal Aid Soc. Cin. (former pres., trustee), Am. Bar Assn. (taxation sect.) Democrat. Jewish. Home: 2490 Royalview Ct Cincinnati OH 45244 Office: 1800 US Bank Tower 425 Walnut St Cincinnati OH 45202-3923 Office Phone: 513-357-9392.

NECHIN, HERBERT BENJAMIN, lawyer; b. Chgo., Oct. 25, 1935; s. Abraham and Zelda (Benjamin) Nechin; m. Susan Zimmerman (div.); 1 child, Jill Rebecca; m. Roberta Fishman, Oct. 24, 1976; 1 child, Stefan. BA with distinction and with honors in History, Northwestern U., Evanston, Ill., 1956; JD, Harvard U. Law Sch., Cambridge, Mass., 1959. Bar: Ill. 1960. From assoc. to ptnr. Brown Fox & Blumberg, Chgo., 1960-75; ptnr. Taussig Wexler & Shaw, Chgo., 1975-79, Fink Coff Stern, Chgo., 1979-81, Holleb & Coff, Chgo., 1981-2000; of counsel Levin & Schreder, Ltd., Chgo., 2000—04; assoc. dir. gift planning Northwestern U., Evanston, Ill., 2004—. Contbr. articles to profl. jours. Pres. Emanuel Congregation, Chgo., 1994—97. Staff sgt. USAR, 1960—66. Mem.: ABA, Am. Coll. Trust and Estate Counsel, Chgo. Bar Assn. (chmn. trust law com. 1990—91), Ill. Bar Assn., Cliff Dwellers Club, Phi Beta Kappa, Assn. Chgo. Area (vice pres., bd. dirs.). Office: Northwestern U Office Alumini Rels and Devel 2020 Ridge Ave 3rd Fl Evanston IL 60208-4307 Home Phone: 773-929-5889; Office Phone: 847-491-7394. Business E-Mail: h-nechin@northwestern.edu.

NECIPOGLU, GÜLRU, art history and architecture professor; BA summa cum laude and honors, Wesleyan U., 1979; MA, Harvard U., 1982, PhD, 1986. Tchg. fellow Harvard U., 1981—84, asst. prof. fine arts, 1987—89, John L. Loeb assoc. prof. humanities, dept. fine arts, 1989—93, Aga Khan prof. Islamic art, dept. history of art and architecture, 1993—, dir. grad. studies, dept. fine arts, 1994—96, head undergraduate tutor, dept. history of art and architecture, 1999—2002; rsch. asst. Aga Khan Prog., Harvard U., 1984—85, rsch. assoc., 1985—86, exec. com., 1991—, dir., 1993—; lectr. art history and archaeology Columbia U., 1986—87. Exec. com. Ctr. Middle Eastern Studies, 1990—93, standing com., 1991—; bd. mem. Inst. Turkish Studies, Washington, 1996; exec. bd. Centro Internazionale di Studi di Archittettura Andrea Palladio, Italy, 2003—; adv. bd. Sabanci Mus., Istanbul, 2006—; bd. trustees Sabanci U., Istanbul, 2006—. Author: Architecture, Ceremonial and Power: The Topkapi Palace in the 15th and 16th Centuries, 1991, The Topkapi Scroll: Geometry and Ornament in Islamic Architecture, 1995 (Best New Book on Architecture and Urban Planning, Assn. Am. Publishers, 1996, Spiro Kostof book award, Soc. Archtl. Historians, 1996, Albert Hourani book award, Middle East Studies Assn., 1996), The Age of Sinan: Architectural Culture in the Ottoman Empire, 2005 (Fuat Köprülü book prize, Turkish Studies Assn., 2006); editor: Muqarnas: An Annual on the Visual Culture of the Islamic World, 1993—, Supplements to Muqarnas, 1993—. Recipient King Fahd Grand prize for Excellence of Rsch. in Islamic Architecture, 1986; grantee Aga Khan Prog., 1992; fellow NEH, 1993—94; Beinecke fellowship, 1978—81, Mellon Post-Doctoral fellowship, 1986—87, Samuel H. Kress publication fellowship, Archtl. History Found., 1989. Fellow: Am. Acad. Arts and Sciences; mem.: Am. Philos. Soc., Coll. Art Assn. (Millard Meiss Fund publication grant 1991), Soc. Archtl. Historians (bd. dirs. 1991—94, Founder's award 1987), Middle East Studies Assn., Iranian Studies Assn., Turkish Studies Assn. (Best Article award 1991), Am. Rsch. Inst. Turkey, Econ. and Social History Found. Turkey, Phi Beta Kappa. Office: History of Art & Architecture Harvard U Cambridge MA 02138 Office Phone: 617-495-2355.

NEDERLANDER, JAMES LAURENCE, theater producer; b. Detroit, Jan. 23, 1960; s. James Morton and Barbara (Smith) N. Student, Cranbrook Prep., Boston U. Asst. mgr. Pineknob, Clarkston, Mich., producer NYC; v.p. Nederlander, NYC, pres. Trustee Comprehensive Cancer Ctr. Wake Forest U.; bd. dirs. Comprehensive Cancer Ctr. Wake Forest U. Bapt. Med. Ctr. Assoc. prodr.: (plays) The Tragedy of Carmen, 1984 (Tony award, 1984); Starlight Express, 1989; Cafe Crown, 1989; A Midsummer Night's Dream, 1996; The Capeman, 1997, Private Lives, 2002 (Tony award); (with Kathleen Turner) Who's Afraid of Virginia Woolf?, 2005, Ivena's Vow, 2009, Mary Stuart, 2009; prodr.: (shows) Mort Sahl, 1988, (musicals) On Your Toes, 1987, Billy Joel and Twyla Tharp's Movin' Out, 2002 (Touring Broadway award, Best New Musical, Leaugue Am. Theaters & Prodn., 2005), Thoroughly Modern Millie, 2002 (Tony award), (with Alfred Molina) Fiddler on the Roof, 2004, La Cage Aux Folles, 2004, The 25th Annual Putnam County Spelling Bee 2005, Twyla Tharp and Bob Dylan's The Times They Are A-Changin', 2006, Legally Blonde, 2007, A Moon for the Misbegotten, 2007 Cyrano de Bergerac, West Side Story, 2009, Next to Normal, 2009, 9 to 5, 2009; co-prodr.: (concerts) Kenny Loggins, 1988, Barry Manilow, 1989, Billy Joel, Yankee Stadium, 1990, Harry Connick Jr., 1990, Yanni, 1993, Pink Floyd, Yankee Stadium, 1994, U2, Yankee Stadium, 1994, Basia, 1994, Shari Lewis and Lambchop, 1994, Laurie Anderson, 1995, Ray Davies-20th Century Man, 1996. Mem. Com. Am. Candlelite Vigil, 1990, Robin Williams Broadway, 2009; bd. trustees Intrepid Mus., 1990, Fizher Ctr. for Alzheimer's Rsch. Found.; bd. trustee, NYCACO; bd. dirs. ASPCA. Mem. Exec. League N.Y. Theatres.

NEDERLANDER, JAMES MORTON, theater executive; b. Detroit, Mar. 31, 1922; s. David T. and Sarah L. (Applebaum) N.; m. Charlene Saunders, Feb. 12, 1969; children: James Laurence, Sharon, Kristina. Student, Detroit Inst. Tech. Chmn. Nederlander Orgn., Inc. (formerly Nederlander Producing Co. Am., Inc., NYC, 1966—. Owner and operator of numerous theaters including Palace Theatre, Lunt-Fontanne Theatre, Nederlander Theatre, Brooks Atkinson Theatre, Gershwin Theatre, Neil Simon Theatre, Marquis Theatre, Minskoff Theatre, Richard Rodgers Theatre, N.Y.C., Greek Theatre, Pantages Theatre, Henry Fonda Theatre, L.A., Shubert Theatre, Chgo., Fisher Theatre, Masonic Temple, Detroit, Aldwych Theatre, Adelphi Theatre, Dominion Theatre, London; producer numerous shows for Broadway including She Loves Me, Will Rogers Follies, Me and My Girl, Orpheus Descending, Les Liaisons Dangereuses, Nicholas Nickleby, Annie, La Cage aux Folles, Nine, Applause, Not Now Darling, See Saw, Oliver, Abelard and Heloise, Sherlock Holmes, Treemonisha, Habeus Corpus, Otherwise Engaged, Whose Life is it Anyway?, Betrayal, Woman of the Year, Lena Horne: The Lady and Her Music, The Dresser, Noises Off, Merlin, Night and Day, My Fat Friend, Shirley MacLaine on Broadway, Sweet Charity, Benefactors, Breaking the Code; numerous road show prodns.; revivals: Peter Pan, She Loves Me, Hello Dolly, Porgy and Bess, The Music Man, I Do! I Do!, Oklahoma, On a Clear Day You Can See Forever, Fiddler on the Roof. Office: Nederlander Orgn Inc 1450 Broadway Fl 6 New York NY 10018-2201

NEDOM, H. ARTHUR, petroleum consultant; b. Lincoln, Nebr., Aug. 19, 1925; s. Henry Arthur and Pearle Bertrick (Swan) N.; m. Patricia Margaret Rankin, July 4, 1974; children: Richard A., Robert L., Nicole C. BS, U. Tulsa, 1949, MS, 1950; postgrad. in bus. adminstrn., Northwestern U., Evanston, Ill., 1968. Chief engr. Amerada Petroleum Corp., Tulsa, 1961-65, v.p., 1965—, Natomas Co., San Francisco, 1971-74; v.p, dir. pres. Norwegian Oil Co., Houston, 1974-75; pres., mng. dir. Weeks Petroleum Ltd., Westport, Conn., 1975-82; chmn. bd. arbitration Prudhoe Bay Unit. Chmn. Offshore Tech. Conf., 1971; bd. dirs. Engrs. Joint Council, 1978 Served with inf. U.S. Army, 1943-45, ETO. Decorated Bronze Star; named Disting. Alumnus U. Tulsa, 1972 Mem. Soc. Petroleum Engrs. (dir. 1965-68, pres. 1967, Disting. Lectr. 1973, Disting Svc. award 1978, DeGolyer Disting. Svc. medal 1981, Disting. mem. 1983, Disting. lectr. emeritus 1989, Legion of Honor 1998, v.p. SPE Found. 1988-89), AIME (dir. 1966-69, 76-79, pres. 1977, hon. mem. 1982, Disting. Svc. award 1993), Am. Assn. Engring. Soc. (dir. 1980-82, chmn. 1981, Spl. award 1979, Engring. Svc. award 1980). Home: 9924 S Sandusky Ave Tulsa OK 74137-5311 Personal E-mail: artnedom@aol.com.

NEDZBALA, MICHAEL, lawyer; b. Washington, Feb. 2, 1962; BA in Econ., Govt., Univ. Va., 1984; JD, UNC, 1987. Ptnr. Hunton & Williams LLP, Charlotte, NC, 1995—, co-head, asset securitization group, mem. global capital mkts. team. Mem.: Va. State Bar Assn., NC State Bar Assn., Mecklenburg Co. Bar Assn., UNC Banking Inst. (bd. adv.). Office: Hunton & Williams LLP Bank of Am Plz Ste 3500 101 S Tryon St Charlotte NC 28280 Office Phone: 704-378-4703. Office Fax: 704-378-4890. Business E-Mail: mnedzbala@hunton.com.

NEDZELNITSKY, VICTOR, electrical engineer, researcher; m. Marguerite Klein, Jan. 12, 1980. SB, MIT, Cambridge, 1966, SM, EE, MIT, Cambridge, 1969, ScD, 1974. Postdoc. rschr. MIT Rsch. Lab. Electronics and Eaton-Peabody Lab. Auditory Physiology, 1974—76; rsch. engr. (elec.) and acoustic metrology project leader Nat. Inst. Stds. Tech. (Nat. Bur. Stds.), Gaithersburg, Md., 1976—. Tech. advisor USNC, IEC, NYC, 1984—; NIST rep., Internat. Consultative Com. Acoustics, Ultrasound and Vibration BIPM, Internat. Bur. Weights and Measures, Sevres, France, 2000—. Contbr. scientific papers, chapters to books. Recipient Commendation for Outstanding Contbn., Dept. Vets. Affairs Audiology & Speech Pathology Program, 1995, Edward Bennett Rosa Award, Nat. Inst. Stds. Tech., US Dept. Commerce, 2007; Postdoc. fellowship, Am. Otol. Soc., 1974—75. Fellow: Acoustical Soc. America (pres., Washington chpt. 1988). Achievements include research in acoustical metrology, electroacoustical instrumentation, measurements, and applications, bioacoustics, physiological acoustics. Office: Natl Inst Stds and Tech 100 Bureau Dr Stop 8220 Gaithersburg MD 20899-8220

NEECE, OLIVIA HELENE ERNST, investment company executive, consultant; b. LA, Jan. 3, 1948; d. Robert and Beatrice Pearl Ernst; m. Huntley Lee Bluestein, 1967 (div. 1974); children: Melissa Dawn, Brendon Wade; m. Anthony Ray Neece, Mar. 20, 1976. BSBA, U. So. Calif., 1990; MBA, UCLA, 1993; postgrad., Peter F Drucker Inst. Mgmt., Claremont Grad. U., 1998—2004. Cert. interior designer Calif. Coun. for Interior Design, UCLA, 1975; lic. gen. contractor, real estate broker, Calif. Staff designer Frances Lux Designs, LA, 1974; project designer Yates Silverman Inc., LA, 1974-77; owner Olivia Neece Planning & Design, Tarzana, Calif., 1977-86; v.p. project devel. Design Svc. /Aircoa, Englewood, Colo., 1986-87; v.p. project adminstrn. Hirsch-Bedner Assoc., Santa Monica, Calif., 1987—89; treas.-sec. EON Corp., LA, 1980—; owner Olivia Neece Planning & Design, Tarzana, 1989—90; dir. ops. The Ernst Group, LA, 1989—2005, bd. dirs., 2005—; pres. Neece Assocs., 2003—. Instr. ext. program UCLA, 1981—83; assoc. prof. Calif. State U., Northridge, 1994—99; acad. rschr. Jet Propulsion Lab., 2000—02; univ. asst. prof. Peter F Drucker Sch. Mgmt., Claremont Academic Rsch., 2000—09; spkr. in field. Co-author: A Step by Step Approach to Hotel Devel., 1988; contbr. chapters to books, articles to profl. jours. Co-chair LA Master Chorale Gala, 1993—97; mem. Hollywood Bowl Soc.; vol. restoration San Diego R.R. Mus., 1985—92; patron LA Philharm., LA Opera Coun., LA County Mus. Art, 2002—; founder LA Music Ctr., 2002—; patron, inner cir. Ctr. Theatre Group; donor LA County Mus. Art, 2007—, mem. choir; deacon First Presbyn. Ch., Encino, Calif.; bd. dir., historian Master Choral Assoc., 1995—2005; bd. mem. Music Ctr. Club 100, 2000—. Recipient Holiday Inn Devel. award, Foster City, Calif., 1986, Warwick, R.I., 1988, 1st and 2d pl. awards, Lodging Hospitality Designers Cir., 1987, Gold Key award, Russell St. Inn, 1986, Best Paper award, Am. Conf. on Info. Systems, 2002. Mem. Am. Soc. Interior Designers (1st pl. portfolio competition 1974), Acad. Mgmt. (Best Paper award 2002), Fin. Mgmt. Assn., Internat. Inst. Designers & Arch. (profl., v.p., bd. dir.), Assn. Info. Sys., Inst. Ops. Rsch. and Mgmt. Sci, Beta Gamma Sigma. Personal E-mail: oneece@yahoo.com, olivianeece@earthlink.com.

NEEDHAM, GEORGE AUSTIN, investment banker; b. Beverly, Mass., Jan. 27, 1943; s. Everett Austin and Edith Strode (Walton) N.; m. Ellen Ann Levin, July 9, 1978; children: Michael Austin, Sarah Elisabeth, Paul Everett. BS in Bus. Adminstrn., Bucknell U., 1965; MBA, Stanford U., 1971. Portfolio mgr. Bankers Trust Co., NYC, 1967-69; mng. dir. First Boston Corp., NYC, 1971-84; chmn., CEO Needham & Co. Inc., NYC, 1985—. Trustee Stanford Bus. Sch. Trust, Palo Alto, Calif., 1983-89. Served to 1st lt. U.S. Army, 1965-67. Mem. Fin. Analysts Fedn., Bond Club N.Y., The Links, Univ. Club, Sleepy Hollow Country Club, Coral Beach Club. Republican. Home: 79 E 79th St New York NY 10075-0202 Office: Needham & Co Inc 445 Park Ave New York NY 10022-2606 Home Phone: 212-472-9167; Office Phone: 212-705-0307. Business E-Mail: gneedham@needhamco.com.

NEEDHAM, GEORGE MICHAEL, library consultant; b. Buffalo, July 3, 1955; s. Paul James and Dolores Ann (Duffy) N.; m. Joyce Elaine Leahy, Nov. 28, 1992; 1 stepchild, Katherine Callison. BA in English, SUNY, Buffalo, 1976, MLS, 1977. Various profl. positions Charleston (S.C.) County Libr., 1977-84; dir. Fairfield County Dist. Libr., Lancaster, Ohio, 1984-89; mem. svcs. dir. Ohio Libr. Assn., Columbus, 1990-92; exec. dir. Pub. Libr. Assn., Chgo., 1993-96; state librarian State of Mich., Lansing, 1996-99; v.p. OCLC Online Computer Libr. Ctr., Dublin, Ohio, 1999—. Trustee Learning Point Assocs., 2004-. Co-author: A Director's Checklist for Connecting Public Libraries to the Internet, 1995; author (book revs.) Booklist, 1994-2002 (video revs.), Libr. Jours., 1979-94. Bd. dirs. Fairfield County chpt. ARC, Lancaster, 1984-88, Mt. Prospect Theatre Soc., Mt. Prospect, Ill., 1993-96, Lib. Media Project, 1997-2007. Mem. ALA, Pub. Libr. Assn., Ohio Libr. Assn. Achievements include 2 time Jeopardy champion. Avocations: acting, traditional folk music, writing. Office: OCLC Online Computer Libr Ctr 6565 Kilgour Pl Dublin OH 43017-3395 Home Phone: 614-761-0372; Office Phone: 614-783-7973.

NEEDHAM, GLEN RAY, entomology and acarology educator, researcher; b. Lamar, Colo., Dec. 25, 1951; s. Robert Lee and Evor Elaine (Kern) N.; m. Karla Marie Lohr, May 28, 1983; children: Kathleen Marie, John Harrison, Elizabeth Anne. BS, S.W. Okla. State U., 1973; MS, Okla. State U., 1975, PhD, 1978. Grad. rsch. asst. Okla. State U., Stillwater, 1974-78; asst. prof. Ohio State U., Columbus, 1978-84, assoc. prof., 1984—, co-organizer and coord. acarology summer program. Co-editor: Africanized Honey Bees and Bee Mites, 1988, Acarology IX: Proceedings and Symposia. Donor ARC, Columbus. Recipient Dist. Alumnus award Okla. State U., 1992; Faculty Christian fellowship Ohio State U. Mem. Acarology Soc. Am. (pres. 1994), Ohio Asthma Coalition (chair 2009-), Ctrl. Ohio Asthma Coalition, Gamma Sigma Delta. Methodist. Achievements include research in tick dust mite flea bedbug biology and control. Office: Ohio State U 318 W 12th Ave Columbus OH 43210 Office Phone: 614-688-3026. Business E-Mail: needham.1@osu.edu.

NEEDHAM, KEITH ALAN, language educator; b. Bay City, Tex., Jan. 5, 1967; s. Douglas Earl and Melba Louise Needham. BA, Tex. State U., 1991, MA, 1993. Cert. secondary English Tex. State U., 1991. Tchg. asst. Tex. State U., San Marcos, 1991—93; tchr. Austin Ind. Sch. Dist., Tex., 1993—94; instr. English Lamar U., Beaumont, Tex., 1994—. Dir. TALHent On Wheels, Beaumont, Tex., 2001—04, Adopt-A-Grandchild, Beaumont, 2004—, P.A.L.S. Unite!, Beaumont, 2006—. Recipient Julie and Ben Rogers Outstanding Cmty. Svc. award, 2004. Office: Lamar Univ PO Box 10023 Beaumont TX 77710 E-mail: KNForest34@aol.com.

NEEDHAM, RICHARD LEE, magazine editor; b. Cleve., Jan. 16, 1939; s. Lester Hayes and Helen (Bender) N.; m. Irene Juechter, Aug. 7, 1965; children: Margaret, Richard, Trevor. BA, Denison U., 1961; MA, U. Mo., 1967. Copy editor Sat. Rev., NYC, 1967-68; editor-in-chief Preview Internat., NYC, 1968-69; financial and N.Y. editor Instns. mag.; also editor Service World Internat., NYC, 1969-70; copy dir. American Home mag., NYC, 1970-71; exec. editor Ski Mag., NYC, 1971-74, editor, 1974-92, editor-in-chief, 1992-94, sr. contbg. editor, 1994—; contbg. editor Yachting Mag., NYC, 1996; editor Ency. of Skiing, 1978, Ski Fever, 1995; editl. dir. Times Mirror Mags. Conservation Coun., 1994-96; editor-in-chief Inside Tracks, 1996—2002; automotive writer Gannett Suburban Newspapers, 1995—; editor Arthritis Advisor, 2002—, Skiing Heritage, 2002—. Broadcaster: Ski Spot, CBS Radio, N.Y.C., 1978-83, On the Slopes, Audio Features Syndicate, 1984-87; author: Ski--50 Years in North America, 1992, Ski Fever!, 1995. Served to lt. USNR, 1961-65. Recipient Lowell Thomas award, 1985 Mem.

N.Am. Ski Journalists Assn., Ea. Ski Writers Assn., Internat. Assn. Ski Journalists, Internat. Skiing History Assn. (Lifetime Achievement award). Home and Office: 481 Sandy Point Ave Portsmouth RI 02871-3515

NEEDHAM, TRISTAN, mathematics professor; b. Oxford, Eng., May 4, 1958; s. Rodney and Claudia Needham; m. Mary Needham. PhD, Oxford U., 1987. Prof. math. U. San Francisco. Author: (book) Visual Complex Analysis. Recipient Carl B. Allendoerfer award, Math. Assn. Am., 1995, Nat. SJ Book award, Alpha Sigma Nu and the Assn. SJ Coll. and U., 1997. Mem.: Am. Math. Soc., Math. Assn. Am. Office: Univ San Francisco 2130 Fulton St San Francisco CA 94117

NEEDLEMAN, ALAN, mechanical engineering educator; b. Phila., Sept. 2, 1944; s. Herman and Hannah (Goodman) N.; m. Wanda Sapolsky, Apr. 12, 1970; children: Deborah, Daniel BS, U. Pa., 1966; MS, Harvard U., 1967, PhD, 1970. Instr. applied math. MIT, Cambridge, 1970-72, asst. prof., 1972-75; asst. prof. engring. Brown U., Providence, 1975-78, assoc. prof., 1978-81, prof., 1981—2009, dean engring., 1988-91, Florence Pirce Grant Univ. prof., 1996—2009, Florence Pirce Grant Univ. prof. emeritus, 2009—; prof. U. North Tex., 2009—. Vis. asst. prof. Tech. U. Denmark, Lyngby, 1973; vis. fellow Clare Hall, U. Cambridge, Eng., 1978; vis. prof. MIT, Cambridge, 1991. Contbr. articles to profl. jours. Guggenheim fellow, 1977. Fellow ASME, Am. Acad. Mechanics, Danish Ctr. for Applied Math. and Mechanics (fgn.), Groupe Francais de Macanique des Matèriaux (hon.), Am. Acad. Arts & Scis.; mem. NAE. Office: Univ North Tex 1155 Union Circle # 305310 Denton TX 76203-5017 Business E-Mail: needle@unt.edu.

NEEDLEMAN, JACK, education educator, researcher; b. NYC, May 12, 1948; s. Charles and Bella Needleman; m. Barbara Berney, May 30, 1981; children: Rachel Berney Needleman, David Berney Needleman. BS, CCNY, 1969; MA, Syracuse U., NY, 1973; PhD, Harvard U., Cambridge, Mass., 1995. V.p. Lewin/ICF, Washington, 1973—90; asst. prof. Harvard U. Sch. Pub. Health, Boston, 1995—2003; assoc. prof. UCLA Sch. Pub. Health, 2003—. Mem. nursing adv. coun. Joint Commn., Oakbrook Terrace, Ill., 2003—. Recipient Health Svcs. Rsch. Impact award, Acad. Health, 2006; numerous grants, NIH, US Agy. Healthcare Rsch. and Quality and Robert Wood Johnson Found. Fellow: Acad. Nursing; mem.: Phi Beta Kappa. Jewish. Achievements include conducted widely-cited landmark studies on the association of hospital nurse staffing and quality of care. Office: UCLA Sch Pub Health PO Box 951772 Los Angeles CA 90095-1772 Business E-Mail: needlema@ucla.edu.

NEEDLEMAN, JACOB, philosophy educator, writer; b. Phila., Oct. 6, 1934; s. Benjamin and Ida (Seltzer) Needleman; m. Carla Satzman, Aug. 30, 1959 (div. 1989); children: Raphael, Eve; m. Gail Anderson, Dec. 1989. BA, Harvard U., 1956; grad., U. Freiburg, 1957-58; PhD, Yale U., 1961. Clin. psychology trainee West Haven (Conn.) Veterans Hosp. Adminstrn., 1960-61; rsch. assoc. Rockefeller Inst., NY, 1961-62; from asst. prof. to assoc. prof. philosophy San Francisco State U., 1962-66, prof philosophy, 1967—, chair dept. philosophy, 1968-69. Vis. scholar Union Theol. Seminary, 1967-68; dir. Ctr. Study New Religions, 1977-83; lectr. psychiatry, cons. med. ethics U. Calif., 1981-84. Author: Being-in-the-World, 1963, The New Religions, 1970, Religion for a New Generation, 1973, A Sense of the Cosmos, 1975, On the Way to Self-Knowledge: Sacred Tradition and Psychotherapy, 1976, Lost Christianity, 1980, Consciousness and Tradition, 1982, The Heart of Philosophy, 1982, Sorcerers, 1986, Sin and Scientism, 1986, Lost Christianity: A Journey of Rediscovery to the Centre of Christian Experience, 1990, Money and the Meaning of Life, 1991, Modern Esoteric Spirituality, 1992, The Way of the Physician, 1993, The Indestructible Question, 1994, A Little Book on Love, 1996, Time and the Soul, 1998; The American Soul, 2002, The Wisdom of Love, 2005, Why Can't We Be Good?, 2007, What Is God?, 2009; (trans.) The Essential Marcus Aurelius, 2008, The Primary World of Senses, 1963, Essays on Ego Psychology, 1964; editor Care of Patients with Fatal Illness, 1969, The Sword of Gnosis, 1973, Sacred Tradition and Present Need, 1974, Understanding the New Religions, 1978, Speaking of My Life: The Art of Living in the Cultural Revolution, 1979, Real Philosophy: An Anthology of the Universal Search for Meaning, 1991, The American Soul, 2002; contbr. Death and Bereavement, 1969, To Live Within, 1971, My Life with a Brahmin Family, 1972, The New Man, 1972, The Universal Meaning of the Kabbalah, 1973, The Phenomenon of Death. Grantee Religion in Higher Edn., Marsden Found., 1967—68, Ella Lymna Cabot Trust, 1969, Far West Inst., 1975. Office: San Francisco State U Dept Philosophy 1600 Holloway Ave San Francisco CA 94132-1722 Office Phone: 415-338-2216, 415-338-1596. Personal E-mail: jacob.needleman@qmail.com. Business E-Mail: jneedle@sfsu.edu.

NEEDLEMAN, RUTH ANN, social sciences educator; b. Phila., Jan. 30, 1945; d. Leon and Florence Needleman. PhD, Harvard U., Cambridge, Mass, 1968. Asst. prof. U. Calif., Santa Cruz, 1969—73; editor United Farm Workers America, Delano, 1973—74; prof. labor studies Ind. U., Gary, 1981—; edn. dir. Svc. Employees Internat. Union, Washington, 1990—92. Vis. faculty U. Fed. Ceara, Fortaleza, Brazil, 2008. Author: (book) Black Freedom Fighters Steel: struggle dem. unionism (IU Excellence Rsch., 2004); contbr. articles to profl. jours. Recipient IRRA award Tchg. Excellence, Indsl. Rels. Rsch. Assn., 2003, Mesa Refuge Writer Residency award; fellow Nat. Endowment, 1996—98, Am. Assn. State and Local History, 1988. Mem.: Labor And Working Class History Assn. (exec. bd. and com. 2004—08), Phi Beta Kappa. Office: Labor Studies Ind Univ 3400 Broadway Gary IN 46408 Home Fax: 219-980-6834. Business E-Mail: rneedle@iun.edu.

NEEDLES, BELVERD EARL, JR., accountant, educator; b. Lubbock, Tex., Sept. 16, 1942; s. Belverd Earl and Billie (Anderson) N.; m. Marian Powers, May 23, 1976; children: Jennifer Helen, Jeffrey Scott, Annabelle Marian, Abigail Marian. BBA, Tex. Tech. U., 1964, MBA, 1965; PhD, U. Ill., 1969. CPA, Ill.; cert mgmt. acct. Asst. prof., assoc. prof. acctg. Tex. Tech. U., Lubbock, 1968—72; dean Coll. Bus. and Adminstrn. Chgo. State U., 1972—76; prof. acctg. U. Ill., Urbana, 1976—78; dir. Sch. Accountancy DePaul U., Chgo., 1976—86, prof. acctg., 1976—88, Arthur Andersen & Co. alumni disting. prof. acctg., 1988—2002, Ernst & Young dist. prof. acctg., 2003—. Author: Accounting and Organizational Control, 1973, Modern Business, 2d edit., 1977, Principles of Accounting, 1980, 10 edit., 2008 (McGuffey Longevity award 2008), Financial Accounting, 1982, The CPA Examination: A Complete Review, 7th edit., 1986, Comparative International Auditing Standards, 1985, Financial and Managerial Accounting, 8th edit., 2008; editor Accounting Instructor's Report, 1981—, The Accounting Profession and the Middle Market, 1986, Creating and Enhancing The Value of Post-Baccalareate Accounting Education, 1988, A Profession in Transition: The Ethical and Responsibilities of Accountants, 1989, Comparative International Accounting Educational Standards, 1990, Accounting Education for the 21st Century: The Global Challenges, 1994, Financial Accounting: A Global Approach, 1999, (in Russian), 2006. Treas., bd. dirs. CPAs for Pub. Interest, 1978-86. Gen. Electric fellow, 1965-66, Deloitte Haskins and Sells fellow, 1966-68; named Disting. Alumnus Tex. Tech. U., 1986; recipient Award of Merit DePaul U., 1986, Faculty Award of Merit Fedn. of Schs. of Accountancy, 1990, Excellence in Tchg. Award DePaul U., 1998; named among 100 most influential accts. Acctg. Today, 2001. Fellow Am. Acctg. Assn. (sec. internat. sect. 1984-86, vice chmn. 1986-87, chmn. 1987-88, v.p. edn. 2008-, named outstanding internat. acctg. educator 1996); mem. AICPA (mem. coun. 2003-05, named Outstanding Educator 1992), Fedn. Schs. Accountancy (bd. dirs. 1980-87, pres. 1986), Acad. Internat. Bus., Ill. CPA Soc. (bd. dirs. 1994-96, vice chair 2001-02, sr. vice chair 2002-2003, chmn., 2003-04, Outstanding Acctg. Educator 1990, Lifetime Achievement award, 2008), European Acctg. Assn. (exec. com. 1986-89), Intenrat. Assn. for Edn. & Rsch. in Acctg. (v.p. 1989-92, sec.-treas. 1992-97, pres. 1997-2002), Phi Delta Kappa, Phi Kappa Phi, Beta Alpha Psi (named Acct. of Yr. for Edn. 1992), Beta Gamma Sigma. Business E-Mail: bneedles@depaul.edu.

NEEL, HARRY BRYAN, III, surgeon, scientist, educator; b. Rochester, Minn., Oct. 28, 1939; s. Harry Bryan and May Birgitta (Bjornsson) N.; m. Ingrid Helene Vaga, Aug. 29, 1964; children: Carlton Bryan, Harry Bryan IV, Roger Clifton. BS, Cornell U., 1962; MD, SUNY-Bklyn., 1966; PhD, U. Minn., 1976. Diplomate Am. Bd. Otolaryngology. Intern Kings County Hosp., Bklyn., 1966-67; resident in gen. surgery U. Minn. Hosps., Mpls., 1967-68; clin. assoc. NCI/NIH, 1968—70; resident in otolaryngology Mayo Grad. Sch. Medicine Mayo Clinic, Rochester, Minn., 1970-74, cons. in otorhinolaryngology, 1974—2005, cons. in cell biology, 1981—2005, assoc. prof. otolaryngology and microbiology Med. Sch., 1979-84, prof., 1984—, also chmn. dept. otolaryngology. Mem. sci. adv. com. Pitts. Eye and Ear Found.; lifetime vis. prof. Hunan U., China, 2003—. Author: Cryosurgery for Cancer, 1976; contbr. chpts. to books, articles to profl. jours. V.p. bd. dirs. Minn. Orch. in Rochester, Inc., 1982, pres., chmn., 1983—84; mem. devel. com. Minn. Orchestral Assn., 1983, Mayo Found., 1983—86, mem. acad. appointments and promotion com., 2005—07; bd. dirs. Mayo Health Plan, 1986—92, chmn., 1990—92; mem. bd. Mayo Mgmt. Svcs., Inc., 1992—94; mem. bd. regents U. Minn., 1991—2003, chair faculty staff, student affairs com., 1993—95, 1999, vice chmn. bd., 1995—97, chmn. fin. and ops. com., 1999, mem. audit com., 1995—2000, chair litigation review com., 2001—03, chair facilities com., 2001—03, chmn. investment adv. com., 1999—2003, mem. conflict interest com., 2006—, founder Neel Scholarship Endowment Fund Health Scis. Rochester, 2003; bd. dirs. Greater Rochester Area Univ. Ctr., 1993—2003; trustee U. Minn. Found., 1996—2005, mem. fin. com., 1999—2005; mem. State Commn. on U. Minn. Excellence, 2002. With USPHS, 1968—70. Recipient travel award Soc. Acad. Chmn. Otolaryngology, 1974, Ira J. Tresley rsch. award Am. Acad. Facial and Reconstructive Surgery, 1982, Master Tchr. award in surgery Alumni Assn. Coll. Medicine, SUNY, Health Sci. Ctr., Bklyn., 1991, Notable award Nat. Assn. Collegiate Women Athletic Admisntrs., 1992; name one of Best Drs. in Am., Good Housekeeping, 1991, Best Drs. in Am., Woodward/White, 1992—, Best Drs. in Minn., Minn. Monthly, 2003, Cmty. Leaders of World, Am.'s Top Physicians, Consumers' Rsch. Coun., Neel lectrship Otolaryn. Head Neck Surgery Mayo Found. Endowment Fund Mem. AMA, ACS (bd. govs. 1985-90, devel. bd. 1988-04, treas. 1990-98, sec.-treas. Minn. chpt. 1983-85, pres. 1988-89), Am. Acad. Otolaryngology-Head and Neck Surgery (prize for basic rsch. in otolaryngology 1972, bd. dirs. 1988-91, established Neel Disting. Rsch. Lectureship Endowment Fund 1994, audit com. 1998-2000, chair investment adv. com. 1995—, chmn. audit com. 1999-2000), Minn. Med. Assn. (com. on adminstrn. and fin. 2003—05, Cmty. Svc. award for outstanding cmty. svc. 2003, Pub. Svc. Achievement award 2003), Zumbro Valley Med. Soc., Am. Broncho-Esophagological Assn. (pres. 1989-90), Am. Laryngological, Rhinological and Oto. Soc. (Mosher award 1980, pres.-elect 1995-96, centennial pres. 1996-97, investment com. 1994—, historian, 2001—), Am. Laryngological Assn. (Casselberry award 1985, sec. 1988-93, v.p. 1994, pres. 1994—, Newcomb award 1996, Baker lectr. 1998, presdl. citation 2009), Assn. for Rsch. in Otolaryngology, Assn. Acad. Depts. in Otolaryngology (sec.-treas. 1984-86, pres.-elect 1986, pres. 1988-9), Alumni Assn. Cornell U. (Outstanding Alumni award 1985), Collegium ORL Amicitiae Sacrum (bd. dirs., 2d sec. 2000-08, Svc. medal, 2008), Am. Bd. Otolaryngology (bd. dirs. 1986-2005, treas. 1998-2004), Am Laryngol. Voice Rsch. and Edn. Found. (charter bd. dirs. 1996-2003), Rochester Golf and Country Club. Republican. Presbyterian. Home: 828 8th St SW Rochester MN 55902-6310 Office: Mayo Clinic 200 1st St SW Rochester MN 55905-0002 Home Phone: 507-282-0035. Office Fax: 507-284-5036. Personal E-mail: ivyneel@aol.com.

NEEL, JOHN DODD, cemetery executive; b. McKeesport, Pa., Aug. 7, 1923; s. Harry Campbell and Anna (Dodd) N.; m. Daisy Jean Wyatt, Feb. 11, 1948; children: Harry C., John Dodd II, W. Wyatt (dec.), Jeffrey J BA, Pa. State U., 1946. From salesman to pres. Jefferson Meml. Park, Pitts., 1946-88, chmn. bd. dirs., 1988—; chmn. Jefferson Meml. Funeral Home. Former mem., and chmn now alt. Zoning Hearing Bd., Pleasant Hills, Pa., 1970—. Mem. emeritus adv. bd. Pa. State U., Greater Allegheny; former mem. Pa. State Real Estate Commn. 1st lt. USAAF, 1943-45 Decorated Air medal with 4 clusters, D.F.C.; recipient George Washington cert. Freedom Found., 1974 Mem. Pa. Cemetery Cremation Funeral Assn. (pres. 1963-65), Internat. Cemetery Cremation and Funeral Assn. (pres. 1973-74), West Jefferson Hills C. of C. (pres. 1984), VFW, Am. Legion 57th Bomb Wing Assn., South Hills Country Club, Indian Lake Golf Club, Aero Club, OX-5CLUB, Kiwanis (pres. 1959), Masons, Shriner, Tau Kappa Epsilon, Delta Sigma Pi Presbyterian. Office: 401 Curry Hollow Rd Pittsburgh PA 15236-4636

NEEL, JUDY MURPHY, management consultant; b. Rhome, Tex. d. James W. and Linna B. (Vess) Neel; m. Ellis F. Murphy, Jr., Dec. 30, 1975; children from previous marriage: Mary B. Schmidt, Janet E. Hollingsworth, Susan E. Salinas. BS, Northwestern U., 1977; MBA, Roosevelt U., 1983. V.p. Murphy, Tashjian & Assocs., Chgo., 1960-73; exec. dir. Automotive Affiliated Rep. Assn., Chgo., 1973-78; mgr. Automotive Svc. Ind. Assn., Chgo., 1978-80; exec. dir. Am. Soc. Safety Engrs., Des Plaines, Ill., 1980-98, Am. Assn. Diabetes Educators, 1999—2003; dir. Borgess-Lee Meml. Hosp. Found., 1997—; mgmt. cons., 2003—. Recipient Assn. Leadership Award Bus. Women's Network/Assn. Trends Mag., 1998. Mem. Chgo. Soc. Assn. Execs. (bd. dirs. 1979—, pres. 1985—, Shapiro award 1991), Am. Soc. Assn. Execs. (sec.-treas. 1994, found. dir. 1986-90, bd. dirs. 1990-95, Key award 1986). Republican. Personal E-mail: jneelcae@aol.com.

NEEL, RICHARD EUGENE, economist, educator; b. Bluefield, Va., Jan. 7, 1932; s. Charles Richard and Zell LaVerne (Bowling) Neel; m. Binnie Jo LeFever, June 10, 1961; children: Jeffrey Richard, Cynthia Jo. BS, U. Tenn., 1954, MS, 1955; PhD, Ohio State U., 1960. Instr. econs. Ohio State U., 1958-60; asst. prof. econs. Coll. William and Mary, 1960-61; asst. prof. U. South Fla., 1961-63, assoc. prof., 1963-66, chmn. econs. and fin. programs, 1964-66, acting chmn. grad. program Coll. Bus Adminstrn., 1965-66; dir. instl. planning Fla. Tech. U., 1966-68, chmn. dept. econs., prof. econs., 1968-69; assoc. dean Sch. Bus. Adminstrn. Ga. State U., 1969-77, dean grad. studies Sch. Bus. Adminstrn., 1973-77, prof. econs. Sch. Bus. Adminstrn., 1969-78; dean Coll. Bus. Adminstrn. U. NC, Charlotte, 1978-93, prof. econs., 1978-97, dean emeritus Belk Coll. Bus., 1997—, prof. econs. emeritus, 1997—. Editor: (book) Readings in Price Theory, 1973; contbr. chapters to books, articles and monographs to profl. publs. Mem.: Beta Gamma Sigma, Phi Kappa Phi. Presbyterian. Office: U NC at Charlotte Dept Economics Charlotte NC 28223 Office Phone: 704-687-7634. Business E-Mail: reneel@uncc.edu.

NEEL, SANDRA KING, conductor; d. Charles Edward and Frances Elizabeth King. AA with honors, St. Petersburg Jr. Coll., 1982; MusB in Edn. with honors, U. of S.Fla., Tampa, 1984. Cert. tchr. Nat. Bd. Profl. Tchg. Standards, Fla., 2003. Condr. Patel Conservatory Youth Orch., Tampa, 1984—. Musician: Rosewood String Quartet; condr.: Brevard County Secondary All County Music Festival, 2004. Recipient Music Demonstration Specialist award, Fla. Edn. Dept., 1986, Dedicated Svc. award, Tampa Bay Youth Orch., 1995, Silver Orch. Condr. Clinician award, Broward County All County Honors Orch., 2006; named Tchr. of Yr., Sch. Dist. Hillsborough County, 2003—04. Mem.: Fla. Orch. Assn. (assoc.; cert. adjudicator 2006—, orch. clinician, condr.), Fla. Music Educator's Assn. (assoc. Enrollment award 1987—88, 2001—02, 2004—05, 2007—08, Excellence in Musical Performance award 2008). Avocation: Tae Kwon Do. Home: 4710 Summerall Rd Plant City FL 33567 Office Phone: 813-744-8383. Business E-Mail: sandy.neel@sdhc.k12.fl.us.

NEELD, ELIZABETH HARPER, writer, educational business company owner; b. Brooks, Ga., Dec. 25, 1940; d. Tommie Frank and Rachel (Leach) Harper; m. Gregory Cowan, Feb. 24, 1975 (dec. 1979); m. Jerele Don Neeld, 1983. BS, U. Chattanooga, 1962, MEd, 1966; PhD, U. Tenn., Knoxville, 1973. Dir. English programs MLA, NYC, 1973-76; prof. English Tex. A&M U., College Station, 1976-83; exec. prof. U. Houston Sch. Bus., 1992—98; internat. cons. on change, 1990—2000; pres., owner Centerpoint MBI Ednl. Svcs., 2000—. Author: Sister Bernadette: Cowboy Nun From Texas, 1991, A Sacred Primer: The Essential Guide to Quiet Time and Prayer, 2005, Seven Choices: Finding Daylight After Loss Shatters Your World, 2003, Tough Transitions: Navigating Your Way Through Difficult Times, 2005; author: (audiocassette) Yes! You Can Write; anchor and subject (pub. t.v. documentaries) The Challenge of Grief, 1991, Seven Choices for Healing Your Grief, 2005 Democrat. Episcopalian. Avocations: cooking, opera, art collaging. Home: 6706 Beauford Dr Austin TX 78750-8124 Personal E-mail: ehn@elizabethharperneeld.com. Business E-Mail: pondlodgefinds@earthlink.net.

NEELEY, BEVERLY EVON, sociologist, consultant; b. Oakland, Calif., June 14, 1947; d. Chester Arthur Neeley Jr. and Thalia Evon Neeley-Littlefield; m. Niles Bruce, Sept. 13, 1970 (div. Aug. 1977); 1 child, Autumn Yvonne Curd BA, U. Calif., Berkeley, 1970, MPH, 1972; PhD, U. Calif., San Diego, 1983. Eligibility supr. W. Oakland Health Ctr., 1970-72; health edn. supr. San Diego County Drug Edn., 1972-74; proposal writer, cons. Cmty. Crisis Ctr., San Diego, 1974-77; sociologist, dir., sec., treas. Image Mind, Inc., Oakland, 1993—. Instr. Calif. State U., San Diego, 1976; health planner Health Sys. Agy., San Diego, 1978; mem. adv. bd. Help Other People Evole Inst., Oakland, 2000—; sr. acad. cons. Hercules NAACP Saturday Sch., 2002; tchrs., rschr. Oakland Pub. Schs., 1983—. Author: The Ethiopian Grail: On the Origin of Cultural Excellence, 1994, Ancient Ethiopian Egyptian Cultural Excellence, 2003. Founder S.E. Drug Coalition, San Diego, 1974, Nu-Way Youth Svc. Ctr., San Diego, 1976. Mem. NAACP, Sojourner Truth Tenants Assn., Nat. Assn. Negro Bus. and Profl. Women's Clubs Inc. Avocations: reading, walking, cooking. Home: 2999 S Hampton Rd Apt 6212 Dallas TX 75224-3068 Office Phone: 510-653-7561, 214-337-8283. Business E-Mail: drneeley@live.com. E-mail: drbneeley3@hotmail.com.

NEELEY, HENRIETTA NANCE, music school administrator; d. Henry Vernon Nance and Annie Jeanette Mitchell; m. Richard Ray Neeley, June 25, 1994; m. Roger Martin Janssen, Mar. 5, 1971 (div. Nov. 22, 1983). MusB, U. NC, Greensboro, 1965; MusM, Cin. Coll. Conservatory Music, Ohio, 1969. Violist Various Orchestras And Other Performing Groups, Chgo., 1970—; coord., cmty. music ctr. Harper Coll., Palatine, Ill., 2002—. Mem.: Am. String Tchrs. Assn., Chgo. Musicians Club Women, Coll. Music Soc. Office: Harper CC Music Ctr 1200 WAlgonquin Rd Palatine IL 60067

NEELY, CAM (CAMERON MICHAEL), professional sports team executive, retired professional hockey player; b. Comox, BC, Can., June 6, 1965; Right wing Vancouver Canucks, 1983-86, Boston Bruins, 1986-96, v.p., 2007—. Player NHL All-Star Game, 1988-91. Actor: (films) Dumb & Dumber, 1994, Me, Myself & Irene, 2000, Stuck on You, 2003; guest appearance (TV series) Rescue Me, 2004, 2005. Co-founder Cam Neely Found. for Cancer Care, Boston, 1995. Recipient Bill Masterton Meml. Trophy, 1993-94; named to Sporting News All-Star Team, 1987-88, 93-94; elected to the Hockey Hall of Fame, 2005 Office: Boston Profl Hockey Assn TD Banknorth Garden 100 Legends Way Boston MA 02114 also: Cam Neely Found Neely House 30 Winter St, 2nd Fl Boston MA 02108-4720

NEELY, JOHN GAIL, otolaryngologist; b. Oklahoma City, Dec. 10, 1939; MD, U. Okla., 1965. Intern U. Oreg. Med. Ctr., Portland, 1965-66; resident in surgery Baylor Hosp., Houston, 1968-69, resident in otolaryngology, 1969-72; fellow Otologic Med. Group, LA, 1972-73; staff Barnes Hosp., St. Louis, 1992—, Jewish Hosp., St. Louis, 1992—; prof., dir. rsch. Washington U., St. Louis, 1992—. Mem. ACS, Am. Neurotology Soc., Am. Otol. Soc., Am. Acad. Otolaryngology, Head and Neck Surgery, Soc. Univ. Otolaryngologists, Triologic Soc. Office: Washington U Sch Medicine Dept Oto Head-Neck Surgery 660 S Euclid Ave Box 8115 Saint Louis MO 63110-1010 Office Phone: 314-362-7344. Business E-Mail: neelyg@ent.wustl.edu.

NEELY, PEGGY, councilwoman; m. Brian Neely; children: Gloria, Mackenzie. Lic. real estate broker. Former owner Ariz. Home Team; councilwoman, Dist. 2 Phoenix City Coun., 2001—. Chmn. Transp. & Infrastructure Com.; mem. Downtown & Aviation, Seniors, Families & Youth, Census coms. Chmn. Paradise Village Planning Com., Phoenix Water & Sewer Rate Adv. Com.; vice chmn. Maricopa Assn. Govts. Regional Coun. Exec. Com.; bd. mem. Phoenix Women's Sports Assn., Greater Phoenix Conv. Ctr. & Visitors Bur.; former pres. Paradise Valley Sch. Dist. United Parent Coun.; mem. Paradise Valley Cmty. Coll. Pres. Roundtable. Mem.: Women's Coun. Realtors Phoenix Chpt. (former pres.), Phoenix Assn. Realtors (bd. dirs.), Ariz. Assn. Realtors (bd. dirs.). Office: 200 W Washington 11th Fl Phoenix AZ 85003 Office Phone: 602-262-7445. Office Fax: 602-495-0527. Business E-Mail: council.district.2@phoenix.gov.*

NEELY, RICHARD, lawyer; b. Aug. 2, 1941; s. John Champ and Elinore (Forlani) N.; m. Carolyn Elaine Elmore, 1979; children: John Champ, Charles Whittaker. AB, Dartmouth Coll., 1964; LLB, Yale U., 1967. Bar: W.Va. 1967. Practiced in, Fairmont, W.Va., 1969-73; chmn. Marion County Bd. Pub. Health, 1971-72; mem. W.Va. Ho. of Dels., 1971-73; justice, chief justice W.Va. Supreme Ct. of Appeals, Charleston, 1973-95; ptnr. Neely & Hunter, Charleston, 1995—2007, Neely & Callaghan, Charleston, 2007—. Chmn. bd. Kane & Keyser Co., Belington, W.Va., 1970-88. Author: How Courts Govern America, 1980, Why Courts Don't Work, 1983, The Divorce Decision, 1984, Judicial Jeopardy: When Business Collides with the Courts, 1986, The Product Liability Mess: How Business Can Be Rescued from State Court Politics, 1988, Take Back Your Neighborhood: A Case for Modern-Day Vigilantism, 1990, Tragedies of our Own Making: How Private Choices have Created Public Bankruptcy, 1994; contbr. articles to nat. mags. Mem. bd. advisors BNA Class Action Litigation Report. Capt. US Army, 1967-69. Decorated Bronze Star, Vietnam Honor medal 1st Class. Mem.: Am. Legion, VFW, Internat. Brotherhood Elec. Workers, W.Va. Bar Assn., Fourth Cir. Jud. Conf. (life), Moose, Phi Sigma Kappa, Phi Delta Phi. Episcopalian. Office: Neely & Callaghan 159 Summers St Charleston WV 25301-2134 Office Phone: 304-343-6500. Business E-Mail: rneely@neelycallaghan.com.

NEELY, STEPHANIE, librarian; 4 children. M in Libr. and Info. Sci., U. Tex., Austin, 1989. Tel. reference rschr. Austin Pub. Libr., Tex., 1985, mng. dir. Little Walnut Creek br., 1997, mng. libr. Daniel E. Ruiz br. Recipient NY Times Libr. award, 2006. Mem.: Tex. Libr. Assn. Office: Daniel E Ruiz Br Austin Pub Libr 1600 Grove Blvd Austin TX 78741 Office Phone: 512-836-8975. E-mail: Stephanie.Neely@ci.austin.tx.us.

NEFF, ALICE ELAINE, costume designer; d. George Neff and Ann Baker; m. Gregory Williams, Aug. 16, 2008. BFA, U. Tex., Austin, 1991. Freelance costume shop supr., draper various theaters and univs., 1991—2001; costume studio supr. Appalachian State U., Boone, NC, 2001—. Mem.: US Inst. Theatre Tech. Avocations: gardening, cooking. Home: PO Box 55 Boone NC 28607 Office: Appalachian State Univ Theatre & Dance Dept PO Box 32123 Boone NC 28608 Office Fax: 828-265-8694. Personal E-mail: aliceneff2@yahoo.com. Business E-Mail: neffae@appstate.edu.

NEFF, DANIEL A., lawyer; b. Phila., Jan. 7, 1953; AB magna cum laude, Brown U., 1974; JD, Columbia U., 1977. Bar: N.Y. 1978, D.C. 1980. Ptnr., corp. dept. Wachtell, Lipton, Rosen & Katz, NYC, co-chmn. exec. com. Notes and comments editor: Columbia Law Rev., 1976-77. Named in Dealmaker of the Year article, Am. Lawyer mag., 2001. Mem. ABA, Phi Beta Kappa. Office: Wachtell Lipton Rosen & Katz c/o Gail Edelman 51 W 52nd St Fl 29 New York NY 10019-6150 Office Phone: 212-403-1218. Office Fax: 212-403-2218. Business E-Mail: daneff@wlrk.com.

NEFF, DAVID M., lawyer; b. Allentown, Pa., Nov. 18, 1960; BSJ, Northwestern Univ., 1982; JD, DePaul U., 1985. Bar: Ill. 1985, US Dist. Ct. (no. Ill., ea. & we. Wis., we. Mich. dist.). Law clk. Judge Robert E. Ginsberg, US Bankruptcy Ct., no. dist. Ill., 1985—86; ptnr., co-chmn. Lodging & Timeshare practice group DLA Piper US LLP, Chgo. Contbr. articles to profl. jours. Mem.: Internat. Soc. Hospitality Consultants (chmn.), ABA (co-chmn. publications, Bankruptcy & Insolvency subcommittee.), Am. Bankruptcy Inst., 7th Cir. Bar Assn. (Ill. bankruptcy liason), Chgo. Bar Assn. (chmn. bankruptcy & reorganization com. 1998—99). Office: Perkins Coie LLP 131 S Dearborn St Ste 1700 Chicago IL 60603-5559 Office Phone: 312-324-8689. Business E-Mail: dneff@perkinscoie.com.

NEFF, DONALD LLOYD, news correspondent, writer; b. York, Pa., Oct. 15, 1930; s. Harry William and Gertrude Marie N.; m. Abigail Trafford; 1 son, Gregory Harry. Student, Trinity Coll., San Antonio, 1949, York Coll., 1950-52, N.Y. U., 1953. Reporter York Dispatch, 1954-56, L.A. Mirror-News, 1956-57, UPI, LA, 1957-61; with L.A. Times, 1961-64, bur. chief Tokyo, 1964; with Time mag., 1965-81, corr. Vietnam, 1965-66, writer NYC, 1966-68, bur. chief Houston, 1968-70, LA, 1970-73, Jerusalem, 1975-78, NYC, 1978-79, sr. editor, 1973-75; news svcs. editor Washington Star, 1979-80; Wash. correspondant Mid. East Internat., London, 1991—2001. Author: Warriors at Suez: Eisenhower Takes America into the Middle East, 1981, Warriors for Jerusalem, The Six Days That Changed the Middle East, 1984; Warriors Against Israel, 1988, Fallen Pillars; U.S. Policy Toward Palestine and Israel since 1945, 1995, 2d edit., 2002, Fifty Years of Israel, 1998. Served with AUS, 1948-50. Recipient Theta Sigma Phi Matrix award, 1962, Calif.-Nev. AP Writing Contest best met. spot news story award, 1962, Overseas Press Club award for best fgn. article in a mag., 1979; finalist Am. Book Award History category, 1982. Mem. Fgn. Press Assn. (Israel pres. 1977, v.p. 1978)

NEFF, FRED LEONARD, lawyer; b. St. Paul, Nov. 1, 1948; s. Elliott Ira and Mollie (Poboisk) N.; m. Christa Ruth Powell, Sept. 10, 1989; 1 child, Lena. BS with high distinction, U. Minn., 1970; JD, William Mitchell Coll. Law, 1976. Bar: Minn. 1976, ND 1994, US Dist. Ct. Minn. 1977, US Ct. Appeals (8th cir.) 1985, US Supreme Ct. 1985, Wis. 1986, US Dist. Ct. (ea. and we. dists.) Wis. 1992. Tchr. Hopkins Pub. Schs., Minn., 1970-72; instr. U. Minn., Mpls., 1974-76; pvt. practice Mpls., 1976-79; asst. county atty. Sibley County, Gaylord, Minn., 1979-80; mng. atty. Hyatt Legal Svcs., St. Paul, 1981-83, regional ptnr., 1983-85, profl. devel. ptnr., 1985-86; pres. Neff Law Firm, PA, Mpls., 1986—; CEO Profl. Devel. Inst. Inc., Edina, Minn., 1994—, also bd. dirs. Instr. Inver Hills Coll., 1973-77; counsel Am. Tool Supply Co., St. Paul, 1976-78; cons. Nat. Detective Agy., Inc., St. Paul, 1980-83; CEO A Basic Legal Svc., Bloomington, 1990—; CEO, bd. dirs. Profl. Devel. Inst., Inc., Edina, Minn., 1994—; lectr., guest instr. U. Wis., River Falls, 1976-77; spl. instr. Hamline U., St. Paul, 1977; vis. lectr. Coll. St. Scholastica, Duluth, Minn., 1977; program. faculty, cons. Employment Law Seminar for Colo., Fla., La., Oreg., Employment and Labor Law Seminar for Ala., Alaska, Calif., Conn., Ind., NC, Ohio, Va., NC Safety and Health at the Workplace, SC Labor Law, Ohio Safety at the Workplace; bd. dirs. Acceptance Ins. Holdings, Inc., Omaha; active Internat. Confederation Jurists, 1993; mem. faculty sem. Ariz. Safety at Workplace, Hawaii Employment & Labor, Miss. Employment & Labor Law, Del. Employment & Labor, Alaska Employment and Labor Law, Ga. Employment & Labor Law, NJ Employment & Labor, Wash. Employment Law, Mass. Employment & Labor Law, 1995—, Ark. Employment and Labor Law, Mo. Employment and Labor Law, Iowa Employment and Labor Law, Utah Employment and Labor Law; pres. Martial Arts Bookstore Internat., Inc., 1998; pres. Endless Fist Soc., Inc., 1998. Author: Fred Neff's Self-Defense Library, 1976, Everybody's Self-Defense Book, 1978, Karate Is for Me, 1980, Running Is for Me, 1980, Lessons from the Samurai, 1986, Lessons from the Art of Kempo, 1986, Lessons from the Western Warriors, 1986, Lessons from the Fighting Commandos, 1990, Lessons from the Ancient Japanese Masters of Self-Defense, 1990, Lessons from the Eastern Warriors, 1990, Mysterious Persons of the Past, 1991, Great Mysteries of Crime, 1991; host TV series Great Puzzles In History; co-host TV series Great Unsolved Crimes, Minn.; asst. editor: Hennepic County Lawyer, 1992—. Advisor to bd. Sibley County Commrs., 1979-80; speaker civic groups, 1976-82; mem. Hennepin County Juvenile Justice Panel, 1980-82, Hennepin County (Minn.) Pub. Def. Conflict Panel, 1980-82, 86—, Hennepin County Bar Assn. Advice Panel Law Day, 1987, mem. dist. ethics com., 1990-2004; mem. Panel Union Privilege Legal Svcs. div. AFL-CIO, 1986—, Signature Legal Svcs., 2003—, Montgomery Wards Legal Svcs. Panel, 1986—, Edina Hist. Soc., Decathlon Athletic Club; charter mem. Commn. for the Battle of Normandy Mus.; founding sponsor Civil Justice Found., 1986—; mem. com. for publ. Hennepin County Lawyer, 1992; pres. Endless Fist Soc., Inc., 1998—, martial arts website, 2007. Recipient Outstanding Tchr. award Inver Hills Coll. Student Body, 1973, St. Paul Citizen of Month award Citizens Group, 1975, Kempo Club award U. Minn., 1975, U. Minn. Student Appreciation award Kempo Club, 1978, Sibley County Atty. Commendation award, 1980, Good Neighbor award WCCO Radio, 1985, Lamp of Knowledge award Twin Cities Lawyers Guild, 1986, NW Cmty. TV Commendation award, 1989-91, Presdl. Merit medal Pres. George Bush, 1990, NW Cmty. TV award, 1991, HLS Leadership award, 1984, Mng. Attys. Guidance award, 1985, Creative Thinker award Regional Staff, 1986, HLS Justice award, 1986, Honors cert. for Authors, Childrens Reading Round Table of Chgo., 1988, Wisdom Soc. Wisdom award, 1998; numerous martial arts awards. Fellow Roscoe Pound Found., Nat. Dist. Attys. Assn.; mem. ABA, ATLA, Minn. Bar Assn. (com. on ethics 1994-2004, com. on alternative dispute resolution 1994—), Minn. Trial Lawyers Assn., Hennepin County Bar Assn. (dist. ethics com. 1990—2004, Wis. Bar Assn., Ramsey County Bar Assn., Am. Judicature Soc., Internat. Platform Assn., Am. Arbitration Assn. (panel of arbitrators 1992), Minn. Martial Arts Assn. (pres. 1974-78, Outstanding Instr. award 1973), Nippon Kobudo Rengokai (bd. dirs. North Ctrl. States 1972-76, regional dir. 1972-76), Endless Fist Soc. (pres. 1998), Internat. Confedn. Jurists, Edina C. of C., Southview Country Club, Masons, Kiwanis, Scottish Rite, Sigma Alpha Mu. Avocations: reading, far eastern and oriental studies, civic activities, physical conditioning. also: 1711 County Road B W Ste 340N Roseville MN 55113-4077 Office: 7400 Metro Blvd Ste 390 Edina MN 55439 Home: 4908 Poppy Ln Minneapolis MN 55435-4013 Office Phone: 952-831-6555. Business E-Mail: nefflawfirm@yahoo.com, info@neff.law-firm.com.

NEFF, GREGORY PALL, mechanical engineer, educator; b. Detroit, Nov. 23, 1942; s. Jacob John and Bonnie Alice (Pall) Neff; m. Bonita Jean Dostal, Apr. 27, 1974; 1 child, Kristiana Dostal. BS in Physics, U. Mich., 1964, MA in Math., 1966, MS in Physics, 1967; MSME, Mich. State U., 1982. Registered profl. engr., Ind., cert. mfg. engr., mfg. technologist. Rsch. asst. cyclotron lab U. Mich., Ann Arbor, 1968—72, tchg. fellow physics dept., 1973; instr. sci. dept. Lansing (Mich.) CC, 1976-82; guest lectr. Purdue U. Calumet, Hammond, Ind., 1982-83, from asst. prof. to assoc. prof., 1984—2003, prof., 2003—. Cons. Inland Steel Co., East Chicago, Ind., 1984—86; program evaluator tech. accreditation commn. Accreditation Bd. Engrng. and Tech., 1996—2003; mem., team chair Tech. Accreditation Commn., 2003—06, alternate mem., 2005—06. Contbr. chapters to books, articles to profl. jours. Mem. Tri-County Regional Planning Commn., Lansing, 1978—80; chair non-motorized adv. coun. Mich. Dept. Transp., Lansing, 1982—83; commr. Ingham County Bd. Commrs., Mason, Mich., 1977—80. Mem.: ASME (sec. MET dept. heads com. 1999, webmaster 1999—2004, vice chair 2000, chair 2001, bd. engring. edn. 2001—03, mem. com. tech. accreditation 2002—06), ASHRAE, Order Engrs., Am. Soc. Engring. Edn. (Merl K. Miller award 1994), Soc. Mfg. Engrs. (chpt. 112 bd. dirs. 1986—, webmaster 1999—2004, Appreciation award 1990, 1992, Outstanding Faculty Advisor award 1991), Tau Alpha Pi, Sigma Alpha Epsilon. Democrat. Roman Catholic. Office: Purdue U Calumet 2200 169th St Hammond IN 46323-2068 Business E-Mail: gneff@purdue.edu.

NEFF, JANET T., federal judge; b. Wilkinsburg, Pa., 1945; BA, U. Pitts., 1967; JD, Wayne State U., 1970. Bar: Mich. 1971. Asst. city atty. City of Grand Rapids, Mich., 1971—73; atty. VanderVeen, Freihofer & Cook, 1973—78, William G. Reamon, PC, 1980—88; commr. Mich. State Supreme Ct., 1978—80; asst. US atty. (we. dist.) Mich. US Dept. Justice, 1980; judge Mich. Ct. Appeals, 1989—2007, US Dist. Ct. (we. dist.) Mich., 2007—. Office: 401 Federal Bldg 110 Michigan St NW Grand Rapids MI 49503 Office Phone: 616-456-6774. Business E-Mail: janet_neff@wdmi.uscourts.gov.

NEFF, KATHY S., swimming and water safety educator; b. Rochester, Ind., Apr. 24, 1959; Cert. pool operator. Head coach girls swimming, diving Rochester Cmty. Sch. Corp., 1988-97, aquatic dir., swimming and water safety instr. grades K-12, 1991—, asst. men's swim coach, 1994-97, dir. substitute svcs., 1998—2001; farmer Neff Farms, 1998—; coach Swim Analysis Camp Ind. U., summers 93-97; v.p. Ptnrs. in Edn., 1996-98, pres., 1998-2000. Bd. dirs. Rochester Royals Swim Team, 1992-94; asst. men's swim coach Culver Mil. Acad., 1993-94; aquatic supr. Culver (Ind.) Mil. Summer Camps, 1992, 93, 98, waterfront dir., 1999-2000; swimming and diving ofcl. Ind. H.S. Athletic Assn., 1991—. Mem. Nat. Fedn. Interscholastic Ofcls. Assn., North Ctrl. Ind. Athletic Ofcls. Assn. Avocations: sailing, horseback riding, reading. Office: Rochester Comty Schs Po Box 108 Rochester IN 46975

NEFF, MARIE TAYLOR, museum director, artist; d. James Arthur Taylor and Pearl Jackson; m. Edward Lewis Neff, June 24, 1946 (dec. July 1, 1994); children: James Edward, Charles Lewis(dec.). Degree in art and photography, Western Tex. Coll., 1985. Studio artist, Post, 1943—; art instr. Neff Art Sch., Post, 1963—78; co-owner retail bus. Post, 1963—88; art instr. Post Art Guild, Kids n Art, Post, 1975—85; dir. OS Ranch Found. Mus., Post, 1991—. Permanent art collections, pvt. collections. Pres., bd. dirs. Post Area C. of C., 1994—2002, dir., 2008; adv. bd. mem. Mental Health and Mental Retardation, Lubbock br., 1998—2007; dir., coord. Tex. Plains Trail Region, 2002—04, treas., 2004—. Named Queen Panhandle South Plains, Mrs. Tex. Sr. Pageant, 1999. Mem.: North Tex. Mus. Assn. (pres. 2001—04), Tex. Assn. Mus. (planning bd. state conv. 1997—2001, trustee-sec. 2000—05), Post C. of C. (designer commemorative coin 1976, pres., founding mem. women's divsn. 1969—, Woman of Yr. 1972), Post Art Guild (pres., founding mem. 1974—), Rotary. Avocations: archaeology, photography, reading, travel. Office: OS Ranch Found Mus Ste 3 201 E Main St Post TX 79356 E-mail: mtneff@caprock-spur.com.

NEFF, MARY ELLEN ANDRE, retired elementary school educator; b. Indiana, Pa., July 6, 1943; d. Frank Vincent and Marie Isabel (Elrick) Andre; children: Gary V. Jr., Traci Dawn. BS, Indiana U. Pa., 1965, MEd, 1971. Elem. sch. tchr. Blairsville (Pa.)-Saltsburg Sch. Dist., Derry (Pa.) Area Sch. Dist.; ret., 2002. Zone chmn. Lions Dist. 14E; bd. mem. Ind. County Tourist Bur., Derry Hist. Soc., Ind. County Tourist Bur. Mem.: PTA, NEA, Pa. State Edn. Assn., Derry Area Hist. Soc. (bd. dirs.), Saltsburg Hist. Soc. (pres.), Nat. Soc. DAR (vice regent), Westmoreland County Hist. Soc. (bd. dirs., sec.), Latrobe Lions Club (pres., dist. zone chmn.), Delta Kappa Gamma (pres. 1986—90, treas. 1992—2000). Home: 17 Carriage Rd Greensburg PA 15601-9014 Personal E-mail: mneff@infionline.net.

NEFF, ROBERT MATTHEW, lawyer, finance company executive; b. Huntington, Ind., Mar. 26, 1955; s. Robert Eugene and Ann (Bash) N.; m. Lee Ann Loving, Aug. 23, 1980; children: Alexandra, Graydon, Philip. BA in English, DePauw U., 1977; JD, Ind. U., Indpls., 1980. Bar: Ind. 1980, U.S. Dist. Ct. (so. dist.) Ind. 1980, U.S. Supreme Ct., 1993. Assoc. Krieg, DeVault, Alexander & Capehart, Indpls., 1980-85, ptnr., 1986-88, Baker & Daniels, Indpls., 1988-92; of counsel, 1993-96; dept. to chmn. Fed. Housing Fin. Bd., Washington, 1992-93; pres., CEO Circle Investors, Inc., Indpls., 1993-97, also bd. dirs.; chmn., CEO Senex Fin. Corp., Indpls., 1998—2007; pres., CEO Clarian Health Ventures, Inc., Indpls., 2007—. Mem. faculty Grad. Sch. of Banking of South, 1988—1990; chmn. Liberty Bankers Life Ins. Co., 1995—1998, Am. Founders Life Ins. Co., Laurel Life Ins. Co., Aztek Life Assurance Co., 1996—1997; bd. dirs. Quanta Specialty Lines Ins. Co., CH Assurance Ltd., Clarian Health RRG, Unified Fin. Svcs., Inc., Conseco Strategic Income Fund. Exec. editor Ind. Law Rev., 1979-80. Participant Lacy Exec. Leadership Conf., Indpls., 1985-86; trustee DePauw U., 1977-80; bd. govs. Riley Children's Found., 1999-; del. White House Conf. on Aging, 2005. Mem. ABA (chmn. bus. law com. young lawyers divsn. 1988-90, banking law com. 1990-92), Ind. Bar Assn. (chmn. corps. banking and bus. law sect. 1987-88), DePauw Alumni Assn. (bd. dirs. 1982-88), Phi Kappa Psi, Phi Beta Kappa. Avocations: golf, fishing. Home: 7202 Merriam Rd Indianapolis IN 46240 Office Phone: 317-963-7802. Business E-Mail: rmneff@clarian.org.

NEFF, ROBERT WILBUR, academic administrator, educator, minister; b. Lancaster, Pa., June 16, 1936; s. Wilbur Hildebr and Hazel Margaret (Martin) N.; m. Dorothy Rosewarne, Aug. 16, 1959; children: Charles Scott, Heather Lynn. BS, Pa. State U., 1958; BD, Yale Div. Sch., 1961, MA, 1963, PhD, 1969; DD, Juniata Coll., 1978, Manchester Coll., 1979; DHL, Bridgewater Coll., 1979, Mt. Aloysius Coll., 2009. Asst. prof. Bridgewater Coll., 1964-65; mem. faculty dept. Bibl. studies Bethany Theol. Sem., 1965-77, prof., 1973-77; gen. sec. Ch. of the Brethren, Elgin, Ill., 1978-86; pres. Juniata Coll., 1986-98, pres. emeritus, 1998—. Vis. prof. Pa. State U., 1998-2003; assoc. for resource devel. The Village at Morrison's Cove, 1999-, coord. chaplaincy svc., 2006-; mem. faculty North Park Sem., No. Bapt. Sem., Theol. Coll. No. Nigeria; bd. dirs. Mellon Bank (Ctrl.) Nat. Assn., exec. com., 1989, chair exec. com., 1993, chair CRA com., 1994-2001; mem. pres.'s com. NCAA, 1996-99; bd. dirs. Susquehanna Valley Ministry Ctr., 2002-07, chair, 2004-07; adj. faculty Bethany Theol. Sem., 1999—; cons. Archdiocese (Altoona/Johnstown), 2003—; lectr. Young Ctr. at Elizabethtown Coll., 2002; mem. USDA Del. to Baltic States, 2000. Mem. governing bd. Nat. Coun. Chs. of Christ, 1976-86, mem. exec. com., 1979-86; mem. Mid-East panel, 1980, 2d v.p., 1985-86; mem. ctrl. com. World Coun. Chs., 1983-92; rep. Assembly of World Coun. Chs., 1983, mem. exec. com. on interch. rels., 1980-84, mem. del. to China, 1981, chmn. presdl. panel, 1982-84; bd. dirs. Bethany Theol. Sem., 1978-86, So. Alleghenies chpt. ARC, 2004-07; campaign chmn. United Way, Huntington County, 1989; chair higher edn. com. Ch. of Brethren, 1993-98. Danforth fellow, 1958-69. Mem. Soc. Bibl. Lit., Soc. Old Testament Study, Chgo. Soc. Bibl. Rsch., Soc. Values in Higher Edn., Coun. Ind. Colls. (nat. bd. dirs. 1991-94, treas. 1995-98), Pa. Coun. Ind. Colls. and Univs. (exec. com. 1988-90, 92-96, chair ann. conf. nominating com. 1993-94), Mid Atlantic Athletic Conf. (sec., mem. exec. com. 1994-97). Democrat. Office: Village at Morrisons Cove 429 Market St Martinsburg PA 16662 Home: 3221 Shellers Bend Rd Unit 827 State College PA 16801 Home Phone: 814-235-1656; Office Phone: 814-793-5207.

NEFF, SEVERINE, music educator; b. Waterbury, Conn., Dec. 17, 1949; d. Victor and Evangeline Josephine Neff; m. Joel Stanley Feigin, June 7, 1986. AB, Barnard Coll., 1971; MA, Yale U., 1972; MFA, Princeton U., NJ, PhD, 1979. Asst. prof. Bates Coll., Lewiston, Maine, 1979—80, U. Hawaii, Honolulu, 1980—81, Barnard Coll., NYC, 1983—91; fellow Cornell U., Ithaca, NY, 1981—83; assoc. prof. Cin. Coll.-Conservatory, 1991—92, prof., 1993—95; prof. music U. NC, Chapel Hill, 1995—2003, Eugene Falk disting. prof., 2004—. Author: Coherence, Counterpoint, Instrumentation, Instruction in Form, 1994, The Musical Idea, 1995, Chinese edit., 2009, Norton Critical Score, Second String Quartet, Op. 10 by Arnold Schoenberg, 2006; editor: Theory and Practice, 1991—93, Music Theory Spectrum rev. edit., 1999—2002; editor chief: Music Theory Spectrum, 2009—; editor chief Schoenberg Words, Oxford U. Press, 2009. Grantee, NEH, 1993, Arnold Schoenberg Ctr., 2004, 2009, Korea Found., 2005; fellow, Mellon Found., 1981; scholar, Fulbright Found., 1998—99; Tchg. fellowship, Mannes Inst., 2005—07, Acad. Arnold Schoenberg Ctr., 2009. Mem.: Soc. Music Theory (sec. 1991—94, bd. dirs.), Coll. Music Soc. (theory rep. 2001—04, bd. dirs.). Achievements include discovery of two unknown works of Arnold Schoenberg. Avocation: antiques. Office: U NC CB 3320 Chapel Hill NC 27599 Office Phone: 919-962-1039.

NEFF, THOMAS JOSEPH, search firm executive; b. Easton, Pa., Oct. 2, 1937; s. John Wallace and Elizabeth Ann (Dougherty) N.; m. Susan Culver Paull, Nov. 26, 1971 (dec.); children: David Andrew, Mark Gregory, Scott Dougherty; m. Sarah Brown Hallingby, Jan. 20, 1989; stepchildren: Brooke, Bailey BS in Indsl. Engring., Lafayette Coll., 1959; MBA, Lehigh U., 1961. Assoc. McKinsey & Co., Inc., NYC and Australia, 1963-66; dir. mktg. planning Trans-World Airlines, NYC, 1966-69; pres. Hosp. Data Scis., Inc., NYC, 1969-74; prin. Booz, Allen & Hamilton, Inc., NYC, 1974-76; regional ptnr. Spencer Stuart, Inc., NYC, 1976-79; bd. dirs. Spencer Stuart & Assocs., NYC, 1976-79, pres., 1979-96, also bd. dirs., chmn. U.S., 1996—. Bd. dirs. Lord Abbett Mut. Funds, Ace Ltd., Hewitt Assocs., Inc.; chmn. Brunswick Sch., 1991-95. Co-author: Lessons From the Top, 1999, You're in Charge--Now What: The 8-Point Plan, 2005. Trustee, emeritus Lafayette Coll., 2004—. 1st lt. US Army, 1961-63. Mem. Links Club, Blind Brook Club, Quogue (NY) Beach Club, Quogue Field Club, Round Hill Club, Coral Beach Club, Quantuck Beach Club, Nat. Golf Links, Lost Tree Club, McArthur Golf Club. Republican. Roman Catholic. Office: Spencer Stuart & Assocs 277 Park Ave Fl 32 New York NY 10172-2999 Business E-Mail: tneff@spencerstuart.com.

NEFF, WILLIAM, educator; b. Amarillo, Tex., Oct. 12, 1959; s. Wa Neff and Juanita Potts; m. Cristy Aragoncillio, Sept. 9, 2006; children: Joshua, Bradley. BA, Calif. State U., Fresno, 1995, MA, 1997. Instr. Odessa Coll., Tex., 1999—2006, Coll. Southern Nev., North Las Vegas, 2007—. Sgt. USAF. Republican. Office: Coll Southern Nev 3200 E Cheyenne Ave North Las Vegas NV 89030-4228 Business E-Mail: william.neff@csn.edu.

NEFSKE, DONALD JOSEPH, engineer; b. Detroit, Dec. 18, 1938; s. Frank J. and Esther M. N.; m. Susan Sung, Dec. 10, 1983. BS magna cum laude, U. Detroit, 1962; MS, U. Mich., 1964, PhD, 1969. Engr. Ford Motor Co., Dearborn, Mich., 1960—61; rsch. engr. GM, Warren, Mich., 1969—70, sr. rsch. engr., 1970—85, sr. staff engr., 1985—93, prin. engr., 1993—2003, tech. fellow, 2003—05; dir. Engring. Mechanics Group, Troy, Mich., 2005—, SHS Cons., Troy, Mich., 2008—. Contbr. articles profl. jour., chapters to books. Fellow ASME; mem. AIAA, Acoustical Soc. Am., Soc. Automotive Engr., Sigma Xi. Roman Catholic. Achievements include research in CAE methods for automotive vehicle noise and vibration, airbag safety systems. Office: Engring Mechanics Group 4178 Drexel Dr Troy MI 48098

NEGELE, JOHN WILLIAM, physics professor, consultant; b. Cleve., Apr. 18, 1944; s. Charles Frederick and Virgil Lea (Wettich) N.; m. Rose Anne Meeks, June 18, 1967; Janette Andrea, Julia Elizabeth. BS, Purdue U., 1965; PhD, Cornell U., 1969. Research fellow Niels Bohr Inst., Copenhagen, 1969-70; vis. asst. prof. MIT, Cambridge, 1970-71, faculty mem., 1971—, prof. physics, 1979—, William A. Coolidge prof.,

1991—, head nuclear and particle theory divsn., 1988-89, dir. Ctr. for Theoretical Physics, 1989-98. Cons. Los Alamos Sci. Lab., Brookhaven Nat. Lab., Lawrence Livermore Nat. Lab., Oak Ridge Nat. Lab.; mem. physics div. rev. com. Argonne Nat. Lab., (Ill.), 1977-83; mem. nuclear sci. div. rev. com. Lawrence Berkeley Lab., (Calif.), 1982—; mem. adv. bd., steering com. Inst. for Theoretical Physics, U. Calif.-Santa Barbara, 1982-86; mem. adv. bd. inst. for Nuclear Theory U. Washington, 1990—, chair 1992-94; program adv. com. Tandem Van de Graaff Accelerator, Brookhaven Nat. Lab., 1977-78, Bates Linear Accelerator, 1977-80, Los Alamos Meson Prodn. Facility, 1986-89, Brookhaven Alternating Gradient Synchraton, 1987-90, mem. exec. com. on computational resources lattice QCD, Dept. Energy, 1999—. Author: Quantum Many Particle Systems, 1987; contbr. articles to profl. jours.; editor: Advances in Nuclear Physics, 1977—. Grantee NSF, 1965-69; grantee Danforth Found., 1965-69, Woodrow Wilson Found., 1965, Alfred P. Sloan Found., 1979, Japan Soc. for Promotion Sci., 1981, John Simon Guggenheim Found., 1982; Alexander von Humboldt Found. fellow, 1998. Fellow Am. Phys. Soc. (program com. 1980-82, editorial bd. Phys. Rev. 1980-82, exec. com. 1982-84, Bonner prize com. 1984-85, exec. com. topical group on computational physics 1992-93, chair divsn. of computational physics 1992-93, exec. com. 1992-94, fellowship com. 2007—, Bethe prize com., 2007—), AAAS (nominating com. 1987-91, mem. physics sect. com. 1991—), Fedn. Am. Scientists. Home: 70 Buckman Dr Lexington MA 02421-6000 Office: MIT Dept Physics 6-315 77 Massachusetts Ave Dept 6-308 Cambridge MA 02139-4307

NEGISHI, EI-ICHI, chemistry professor; arrived in U.S., 1960; BS in Organic Chemistry, U. Tokyo, 1958; PhD in Organic Chemistry, U. Pa., 1963. Rsch. chemist Teijin Ltd., 1958-65; postdoctoral assoc. Purdue U., 1966-68, asst. to H.C. Brown, 1968-72; asst. prof. Syracuse (N.Y.) U., 1972-76, assoc. prof., 1976-79; prof. Purdue U., West Lafayette, Ind., 1979-99, Herbert C. Brown disting. prof., 1999—. Lectr. in field. Recipient A. von Humboldt Rschr. award 1998—; Fulbright scholar, 1960-63. Mem.: Royal Soc. Chemistry (Sir E. Frankland Prize lectureship 2000), Japan Chem. Soc. (award 1997), Am. Chem. Soc. (Organometallic Chemistry award 1998), Sigma Xi, Phi Lambda Epsilon. Office: Purdue U Chem Dept 560 Oval Dr West Lafayette IN 47907-2084 Home Phone: 765-463-4439; Office Phone: 765-494-5301. Business E-Mail: negishi@purdue.edu.

NEGRIN, ROBERT S, medical educator; b. Plainfield, Nj, Mar. 6, 1955; s. David and Shirely Negrin; m. Bonnie Goodman, June 25, 1985; children: Emily, Danielle. MD, Harvard Med. Sch., Boston, 1984. Prof. Stanford U., Calif., 1990—. Pres. Am. Soc. Blood & Marrow Transplantation, 2005—06. Recipient Disting. Scientist award, Doris Duke Found., 2004—. Fellow: Am. Assn. Physicians. D-Liberal. Jewish. Achievements include research in bone marrow transplantation. Office: Stanford Univ CCSR Rm 2205 269 W Campus Dr Stanford CA 94305 Office Phone: 650-723-0836. Office Fax: 650-724-6182. Business E-Mail: negrs@stanford.edu.

NEGRO, MARY JOAN, art educator; d. Dante and Ardemia Negro; m. Norman Otto Snow, July 18, 1982; children: Daniel Benjamin Snow, John Claude Snow. BA, U. Mich., Ann Arbor, 1970. Cert. in acting Juilliard Sch., 1972. Part time faculty Calif. Inst. Arts, Valencia, 1999—2003; full time faculty U. Southern Calif., LA, 2005—. Founder, dir. Classics Alive, LA, 1995—2008. Actor: (broadway, film, TV, regional theatre) (nominee Tony award, 1979). Office: Univ Southern Calif 1029 Childs Way Los Angeles CA 90089 Personal E-mail: classicsalive@sbcglobal.net.

NEGRON-GARCIA, ANTONIO S., law educator, former commonwealth of Puerto Rico supreme court justice; b. Rio Piedras, P.R., Dec. 31, 1940; s. Luis Negron-Fernandez and Rosa M. Garcia-Saldana; m. Gloria Villardefrancos-Vergara, May 26, 1962; 1 son, Antonio Rogelio. BA, U. P.R., 1962, LL.B., 1964. Bar: P.R. bar 1964. Law aide and lawyer legal div. Water Resources Authority, 1962-64; judge Dist. Ct., 1964-69, Superior Ct., 1969-74; justice P.R. Supreme Ct., San Juan, 1974—2001; administrating judge, 1969-71; exec. officer Constl. Bd. for Revision Senatorial and Rep. Dists., 1971-72; mem. Jud. Conf., 1974—2000; first exec. sec. Council for Reform of System of Justice in P.R., 1973-74; prof. InterAmerican U. Puerto Rico, 2001—. Chmn. Gov.'s Advisory Com. for Jud. Appointments, 1973-74; lectr. U. P.R. Law Sch., 1973-74; columnist El Nuevo Dia newspaper, 2000. Mem. P.R. Bar Assn. Roman Catholic. Office: Univ InterAmericana de Puerto Rico Apartado 70351 San Juan PR 00936-8351

NEGRON-SOTO, LIZZIE, psychologist; MS, Caribbean Ctr. Advanced Studies, San Juan, PR, 1985. Cert. in sch. psychology NYS Edn. Dept., 1996. Sch. psychologist NYC Dept. Edn., 1996—.

NEGROPONTE, JOHN DIMITRI, former federal agency administrator, former Director of National Intelligence; b. London, July 21, 1939; s. Dimitri John and Catherine (Coumantaros) Negroponte; m. Diana Mary Villiers, Dec. 14, 1976; children: Marina, Alexandra, John, George, Sophia. BA, Yale U., 1960. Commd. fgn. svc. officer U.S. Dept. State, 1960; vice consul Hong Kong, 1961—63; 2nd sec. Saigon, 1964—68; mem. U.S. Del. to Paris Peace Talks on Vietnam, 1968—69; mem. staff NSC, 1970—73; polit. counselor Am. Embassy, Quito, Ecuador, 1973—75, consul gen. Thessaloniki, Greece, 1975—77; dep. asst. sec. for oceans & fisheries affairs US Dept. State, Washington, 1977—79, dep. asst. sec. for East Asian and Pacific affairs, 1980—81, U.S. amb. to Honduras Tegucigalpa, 1981—85, asst. sec. for oceans and internat. environ. and sci. affairs Washington, 1985—87; dep. asst. to Pres. for nat. security affairs NSC, Washington, 1987—89; US amb. to Mexico US Dept. State, Mexico City, 1989—93, US amb. to The Philippines Manilla, 1993—96, spl. coord. for post-1999 U.S. presence in Panama, 1996—97; exec. v.p. global markets McGraw-Hill Cos., NYC, 1997—2001; permanent U.S. rep. to UN US Dept. State, NYC, 2001—04, US amb. to Iraq Baghdad, 2004—05; dir. Office Nat. Intelligence, Washington, 2005—07; dep. sec. US Dept. State, Washington, 2007—09. Co-pres. U.S./Mex. Commn. for Ednl. and Cultural Exch., 1997—2001; chmn. The French-Am. Found., 1998—2001; mem. exec. com. U.S. Coun. for Internat. Bus., 1998—2001. Recipient Golden Plate award, Acad. Achievement, 2006. Mem.: Fgn. Policy Assn., Am. Acad. Diplomacy, Coun. on Fgn. Rels., Am. Fgn. Svc. Assn. Greek Orthodox.*

NEGUERUELA-AZAROLA, EDUARDO, linguist, educator; s. Dionisio Pablo Negueruela Fernandez de Velasco and Dora Elizabeth Azarola Samonati; m. Yvonne Gavela-Ramos. PhD, Pa. State U., 2003. Prof. U. Mass., Amherst, 2003—06, Coral Gables, Fla., 2006—. Author: (poetry) Tropologia (award, 2008). Office: Univ Miami Merrick Bldg Rm 212-14 Coral Gables FL 33134 Business E-Mail: enegueruela@miami.edu.

NEHAMAS, ALEXANDER, philosophy educator; b. Athens, Greece, Mar. 22, 1946; came to U.S., 1964; s. Albert and Christine (Yannuli) N.; m. Susan Glimcher, June 22, 1983; 1 child, Nicholas Albert Glimcher. BA, Swarthmore Coll., 1967; PhD, Princeton U., 1971; D in Philosophy (hon.), Athens, 1993. Asst. then assoc. prof. philosophy U. Pitts., 1971-81, prof., 1981-86; prof. philosophy U. Pa., 1986-90; vis. prof. Princeton (N.J.) U., 1978-79, 89, Edmund Carpenter prof. humanities, 1990—, prof. philosophy and comparative lit., 1990—, chair humanities coun., 1994—2002, chmn. program in Hellenic studies, 1994—2002. Dir. Princeton Soc. Fellow in Liberal Arts, 1999-2002; Mills vis. prof. U. Calif., Berkeley, 1983; Sather vis. prof., 1993; vis. prof. U. Calif., Santa Cruz, 1988; bd. dirs. Princeton U. Press; trustee Nat. Humanities Ctr., 1996-99, Athens Coll., 1996—; Tanner lectr., 2001.; Gilford Lectr., 2008 Author: Nietzche: Life as Literature, 1985, The Art of Living: Socratic Reflectionsfrom Plato to Foucault, 1998, Virtues of Authenticity: Essays on Plato and Socrates, 1999, Only a Promise of Happiness, 2007; translator Plato's Symposium, 1989, Plato's Phaedrus, 1995; co-editor: Aristotle's Rhetoric: Philosophical Essays, 1994; contbr. articles to profl. jours.; mem. editl. bd. Am. Philos. Quar., 1981-86, History of Philosophy Quar., 1983-88, Ancient Philosophy, 1984—, Jour. Modern Greek Studies, 1986—, Arion, 1989—, Philosophy and Lit., 1989—, Philosophy and Phenomenological Rsch., 1990—. Recipient Lindback Found. Tchg. award, U. Pa., 1989, Behrman award in humanities, Princeton U., 1999, Ann. prize in Hellenic Studies Acad., Athens, 2000, Internat. Nietsche prize, 2001, Mellon Disting. Achievement award, 2001; grantee Guggenheim fellow, 1983, NEH, 1978. Mem.: MLA, N.Am. Nietzsche Soc. (exec. com. 1988—91), Am. Soc. Aesthetics, Modern Greek Studies Assn. (exec. com. 1983—89), Am. Philos. Assn. (chmn. program 1982—83, exec. com. 1990—92, v.p. 2002, pres. 2003), Phi Beta Kappa (vis. prof. 1989, vis. scholar 1995). Office: Princeton U Dept Philosophy Princeton NJ 08544-0001

NEHER, ANDREW W., psychologist, educator; b. Pasadena, Calif., Nov. 29, 1937; s. H. Victor and Sarah E. Neher; m. Linda C. Carlson; children: Anya B., Kevin A., Melissa A. BA, Pomona Coll., Claremont, Calif., 1959; MA, U. Kans., Lawrence, 1960. Prof. psychology Cabrillo Coll., Aptos, Calif., 1969—2001; pvt. practice Santa Cruz, Calif., 1969—. Author: (book) The Psychology of Transcendence; contbr. scientific papers. Personal E-mail: andyneher@yahoo.com.

NEHLS, RICHARD CHARLES, lawyer; b. Detroit, Oct. 26, 1951; s. Edward J. and Helen (Hecker) N.; m. Sharon Kay Scudder, Mar. 29, 1975; children: Christopher, Jeffrey. BA, Miami U., Oxford, Ohio, 1973; JD, U. Chgo., 1976. Bar: Colo. 1976. Ptnr. Lirtzman & Nehls, Boulder, Colo., 1976—2006, Packard Dierking, LLC, Boulder, Colo., 2006—. Trustee Legal Aid Found., 1995-2003. Mem. Colo. Bar Assn. (trustee 1996-2002), Boulder County Bar Assn. (trustee 1990-95, pres. 1994-95). Democrat. Avocations: skiing, bicycling. Home: 385 Overlook Dr Boulder CO 80305-5258 Office: Packard Dierking 2595 Canyon Blvd Ste 200 Boulder CO 80302 Office Phone: 303-447-0450. Business E-Mail: rich@packarddierking.com.

NEHMÉ, PAUL J., beverage company executive; b. Lebanon, May 15, 1960; s. Joseph Nehmé and Rose Loutfi; m. Carole V. Combastet, June 25, 1994; children: Laetitia, Elliott. MSEE, U. Pierre at Marie Curie, Paris, 1983; MBA, INSEAD, Fontainebleau, France, 1989. Engr. GE, Paris, 1984-87; sales and mktg. mgr. Tex. Instruments, Paris, 1987-89; strategy cons. Arthur D. Little, Paris, 1990-91; fin. mgr. EuroDisney, Paris, 1991-93; founder, CEO NEMECO, Paris, 1993—. Avocations: golf, skiing, scuba diving, tennis, horseback riding. Office: NEMECO 49 Avenue d'Iéna 75116 Paris France Office Phone: 0156621515. Fax: 0156621516. E-mail: pnehme@nemeco.fr.

NEHRA, GERALD PETER, lawyer; b. Detroit, Mar. 25, 1940; s. Joseph P. and Jeanette M. (Bauer) N.; m. children: Teresa, Patricia; m. Peggy Jensen, Sept. 12, 1987. BIE, Gen. Motors Inst., Flint, Mich., 1962; JD, Detroit Coll. Law, 1970. Bar: Mich. 1970, N.Y. 1972, Colo. 1992, U.S. Dist. Ct. (ea. dist.) Mich. 1970, U.S. Dist. Ct. (so. dist.) N.Y. 1972, U.S. Dist. Ct. (no. dist.) N.Y. 1976, U.S. Ct. Appeals (6th cir.) 1978. Successively engr., supr., gen. supr. Gen. Motors Corp., 1958-67; mktg. rep. to regional counsel IBM Corp., 1967-79; v.p. gen. counsel Church & Dwight Co., Inc., 1979-82; dep. chief atty. Amway Corp., 1982-83; dep. gen. counsel, 1983-92; dir. legal div., 1989-91; sec., dir. corp. law, 1991-92; v.p. gen. cousnel Fuller Brush, Boulder, Colo., 1991-92; pvt. practice, 1992—. Adj. instr. Dale Carnegie Courses, 1983-91. Recipient Outstanding Contbn. award Am. Cancer Soc., 1976. Mem. ABA, Mich. Bar Assn., Colo. Bar Assn., N.Y. State Bar Assn. Home and Office: 1710 Beach St Muskegon MI 49441-1008 Home Phone: 231-755-3800; Office Phone: 231-755-3800. Business E-Mail: gnehra@mlmatty.com.

NEHRBASS, SETH MARTIN, lawyer; b. Lafayette, La., Nov. 10, 1960; s. Neil Martin and Janet (Himbert) N.; m. Mary Elizabeth Dennis, Aug. 12, 2000; children: Gabriel, Fabian. Student, U. Catholique de l'Ouest, Angers, France, 1980, U. Paul Valéry, Montpellier, France, 1981; BS in Physics summa cum laude, U. Southwestern La., 1982; JD cum laude, Loyola U., 1990. Bar: U.S. Patent & Trademark Office 1984, La. 1990, U.S. Dist. Ct. (ea., mid., and we. dists.) La. 1990, U.S. Ct. Appeals (5th and fed. cirs.) 1990, U.S. Supreme Ct. 2006; cert. notary public, La. Patent examiner U.S. Patent & Trademark Office, 1982-84; patent agt. with law firm New Orleans, 1986-87; assoc. Pravel, Hewitt, Kimball & Krieger, New Orleans, 1987-97, shareholder, 1997-98, Garvey, Smith, Nehrbass & North, L.L.C., Metairie, La., 1998—. Adj. law faculty Tulane Law Sch., 1997—; judge practice round moot ct. teams Loyola Law Sch., 1992—; preparer questions patent bar exam PTO Q & A Bd., 1992-93; presenter in field. Contbr. articles to profl. jours. Den leader 2d grade Cub Scouts, Boy Scouts Am., Lusher Sch., Audubon Dist., 1991-92, 3d grade, 1994-95, asst. den leader 3d grade, 1992-93, 4th grade, 1993-94; soccer coach Carrollton Booster Club, New Orleans, 1993-95, Lakeview Soccer Club, New Orleans, 1995-96; adv. mem. La. Ctr. for Law and Civic Edn., 1996-98; mem. New Orleans Citizen Diplomacy Coun., 2000—. Recipient Hornbook award West Pub. Co., 1986-87, 87-88, Corpus Juris Secundum award, 1986-87, Am. Jurisprudence awards (2), 1986; scholar La. State U. Alumni Fedn., 1978, Coun. Devel. French La./French Govt., 1980-81, Loyola Law Sch., 1986. Mem. ABA (sect. law, sci., tech. 1988-91, law student divsn. liaison patent trademark and copyright law 1988-90, intellectual property law sect. 1988—, chmn. law student com. 1996-98, chmn. spl. com. drug crisis 1990-93, co-chmn. ann. meeting arrangements com. 1993-94, internat. treaties and laws com. 1994—, co-chmn. young lawyers com. 1998-99), Am. Intellectual Property Law Assn. (ADR com., internat. and fgn. law com., patent law com. 1994-2000), La. Bar Assn. (internat. law sect. 1992—, intellectual property law sect. 1996—, vice chmn. 1997-98, chair-elect 1998-99, chair 1999-2000), New Orleans Bar Assn. (interim chmn. ad hoc com. drug crisis 1991-92, chmn. intellectual property law com. 1991-95, chmn. law related edn. com. 1995-97), Round Table Club, Plimsoll Club, Loyola Law Sch. Moot Ct. Alumni Assn., Sigma Pi Sigma, Pi Delta Phi, Alpha Sigma Nu. Democrat. Roman Catholic. Avocations: gardening, photography, travel, hunting, fishing. Home: 453 Audubon Blvd New Orleans LA 70125-3503 Office: 3838 N Causeway Blvd Ste 3290 Metairie LA 70002 Office Phone: 504-835-2000. Business E-Mail: nehrbass@gsnn.us. E-mail: Nehrbass@aol.com.

NEHRING, RON, political organization administrator; b. Islip, NY, May 22, 1970; BS in Polit. Sci., SUNY Stony Brook, 1988—92. Sr. cons. American's for Tax Reform; founder Nehring Strategies; chmn. Rep. Party San Diego County, 2001—07; vice chmn. Calif. Rep. Party, 2005—07, chmn., 2007—. Mem, Internat. Rep. Inst., Leadership Inst., Project for California's Future. Mem. Calif. Bd. Forestry and Fire Protection, 2005—06; trustee Grossmont Union High Sch. Dist., 2004—06. Mem.: Calif. Rep. County Chairmen's Assn. (pres. 2003). Republican. Office: Calif Rep Party 1201 K St #740 Sacramento CA 95814*

NEHRING, RONALD E., state supreme court justice; b. Wis., 1947; BA in History, Cornell U., 1976; JD, U. Utah, 1978. Bar: Utah 1978. Atty. Utah Legal Svcs.; shareholder Prince, Yeates and Geldzahler, Salt Lake City, 1982—94; judge U.S. Dist. Ct. (3d dist.) Utah, 1995—2003; justice Utah Supreme Ct., Salt Lake City, 2003—. Chmn. Bd. Dist. Ct. Judges; mem. adv. com. rules profl. conduct Utah Supreme Ct. Fellow: ABA. Office: Utah Supreme Ct PO Box 140210 Salt Lake City UT 84114-0210*

NEHRT, LEE CHARLES, management educator; b. Baldwin, Ill., Sept. 12, 1926; s. Martin William and Amanda Fredarika (Tillock) N.; m. Ardith Ann Saltzman, Mar. 26, 1952; children: Chadwick Charles, Philip Lee, Dana Ann. BS, USCG Acad., 1949; cert. d'etudes politiques, U. Paris, 1955; MBA, Columbia U., 1956, PhD, 1962. Fgn. ops. supr. Atomics Internat., Canoga Park, Calif., 1956-60; prof. internat. bus. Ind. U., 1962-65, 67-69, 71-74; Ford Found. adv. to minister planning, economy and industry Tunisia, 1965-67; chief adv. group U. Dacca, E. Pakistan, 1969-71; R.P. Clinton prof. internat. mgmt. Wichita (Kans.) State U., 1974-78; pres. World Trade Inst., NYC, 1978-81; Owens-Ill. prof. internat. mgmt. Ohio State U., Columbus, 1981-86. Cons. UN, World Bank, advisor Ministry Planning Govt. Indonesia, 1987-89; dir., curator The Blacksmith Mus., 1991-92. Author: Education in International Business, 1963, Foreign Marketing of Nuclear Power Plants, 1965, Financing Capital Equipment Exports, 1966, International Finance for Multinational Business, 1967, 2d rev. edit. 1972, International Business Research: Past, Present and Future, 1969, The Political Climate for Private Investment in North Africa, 1970, Managerial Policy and Strategy for Developing Countries, 1973, Managerial Policy, Strategy and Planning for South-East Asia, 1974, Managerial Policy and Strategy for the Philippines, 1976, 3d rev. edit. 1989, Business and International Education, 1977, The Internationalization of the Business School Curriculum, 1979, Case Studies in the Internationalization of the Business School Curriculum, 1981, The Politico-Economic Analysis of Countries, 1981; contbr. articles to profl. jours. Chmn. bd. dirs. Monroe County ARC, 1996-98. Lt. (j.g.) USCG, 1949-53. Mem. Acad. Internat. Bus. (pres. 1972-74, dean fellows 1978-81), Soc. Internat. Devel. (gov. 1968-71)

NEHS, (WILLIAM) SCOTT, lawyer; b. Janesville, Wis., Mar. 7, 1966; m. Jacqueline Nehs. BA, Northwestern U., 1988; JD, U. Wis., Madison, 1991. Bar: Ill. 1991, Wis. 1991, US Dist. Ct. No. Dist. Ill. 1991, US Dist. Ct. We. Dist. Wis. 1991, US Dist. Ct. Ea. Dist. Wis. 1993. Assoc. Wildman, Harrold, Allen & Dixon, Chgo., 1991—99; dep. gen. counsel Pepsi-Cola Gen. Bottlers Inc., Rolling Meadows, Ill., 2000—01; asst. gen. counsel PepsiAmericas Inc. (formerly Whitman Corp.), Rolling Meadows, Ill., 2000—01, v.p. legal, 2001—, chief compliance officer. Pro bono work Legal Clinic for the Disabled, 1992—, Les Turner ALS Found., 1995—. Named one of The Top 40 Lawyers Under 40 in Ill., Chgo. Daily Law Bulletin, 2004. Mem.: Assn. of Corp. Counsel, Wis. State Bar, Chgo. Bar Assn. Office: Pepsiamericas Caribbean Inc 1475 E Woodfield Rd Ste 1300 Schaumburg IL 60173-5482

NEI, MASATOSHI, biology professor; b. Miyazaki, Japan, Jan. 2, 1931; came to U.S., 1969; s. Tadashi and Masae (Kawasaki) N.; m. Nobuko Hara, April 25, 1963; children; Keitaro, Maromi. BS in Genetics, Miyazaki U., Japan, 1953; MS in Quantitative Genetics, Kyoto U., Japan, 1955, PhD in Quantitative Genetics, 1959; PhD (hon.), Miyazaki U., 2002. Postdoctoral in population genetics U. Calif. Davis and NC State U., 1960—61; asst. prof. Kyoto U., Japan, 1958—62; geneticist Nat. Inst. Radio. Scis., Japan, 1962-65, head population genetics lab., 1965-69; assoc. prof. biology Brown U., Providence, 1969-71, prof. biology, 1971-72; prof. population genetics U. Tex., Houston, 1972-80, acting dir. population genetics, 1978-80, 86-87; disting. prof. biology, dept. biology Pa. State U., University Park, 1990-94, dir. Inst. Molecular Evolutionary Genetics, 1990—, Evan Pugh prof. biology, dept. biology, 1994—. Staff population genetics dept. Univ. Calif., Davis, 1960, NC State Univ., Raleigh, 1961; mem. overseers com. Harvard Univ., Cambridge, Mass., 1988-94; mem. working group FAO, Rome, 1994; mem. DNA Forensic Sci., NRC, NAS, 1994-95; vis. prof. biology, Tokyo Inst. Tech., Japan, 2001; mem. adv. bd. Gene Geography, Rome, Italy, 1985-87, Gene: Evolutionary Genomics, 2004-. Author: Molecular Evolution and Phylogenetics, 2000, Molecular Population Genetics & Evolution, 1975, Molecular Evolutionary Genetics, 1987; assoc. editor Theoretical Population Biology, 1973-84; Genetics, 1977-85; mem. editl. bd. Evolutionary Theory, 1973-76, Jour. Molecular Evolution, 1979-2001; mng. editor Molecular Biology & Evolution, 1983-93; assoc. editor, Jour. Heredity, 1995-; cons. editor, Jour. Molecular Evolution, 2002-2004. Recipient Internat. prize for Biology, Japan Soc. for the Promotion Sci., Tokyo, 2002, Barbara Bowman award, Tex. Genetics Soc., Austin, Tex., 2003. Fellow AAAS, Am. Acad. Arts. and Sci. (Internat. prize 2002); mem. NAS (mem. editl. bd. Proceedings of NAS, 2003-), Genetics Soc. Am. (editl. bd., Kihara prize, 1990, Thomas Hunt Morgan medal, San Diego, Calif., 2006), Soc. Molecular Biology and Evolution (pres. 1994), Internat. Soc. Molecular Evolution, Am. Genetic Assoc. (pres. 1999), Soc. for Molecular Biology and Evolution (coun. mem. 1992-1995), Japan Soc. Human Genetics (hon. mem., award, 1977). Office: Penn State Univ 327 Mueller Lab University Park PA 16802-5303 E-mail: nxm2@psu.edu.

NEIBERGER, RICHARD EUGENE, pediatrician, nephrologist, educator; b. Onaga, Kans., Nov. 16, 1947; s. Earl Edward and Margaret Bell (Grim) N.; m. Mary June Chamberlin, Oct. 31, 1971; children: Ami, Eric, Chris, Robert. BS in Physics, U. Ctrl. Fla., 1971; PhD, U. Louisville, 1979, MD, 1982. Diplomate Am. Bd. Pediat., Nat. Bd. Med. Examiners. Intern, then resident in pediat. Albert Einstein Coll. Med., Bronx, N.Y., 1982-85, fellow in pediat. nephrology, 1985-88; asst. prof. U. Fla. Coll. Med., Gainesville, 1988-93, assoc. prof., 1993—; med. dir. pediatrics Renal Stone Disease Clinic, 1996—. Assoc. med. dir. Children's Kidney Ctr., Gainesville, 1989—; co-investigator on 4 rsch. studies, dir. Pediatric Rsch. Stone Disease Clin. U. Fla., rsch. peer rev. com. Am. Heart Assn., 1997-99; physician advisor Fla. Med. Quality Assurance, Tampa, 1994-2002; pres. Coll. Medicine Faculty Coun., 2008-. Contbr. articles to profl. jours. Pres. U. Fla. Coll. Med. Faculty Council; mem. Organ Transplant Adv. Com., Fla.; active Children's Home Soc., Gainesville, 1994—2002, Ronald McDonald House, 1996—2007. Named one of Best Drs. in Am., Best Drs. in Fla., Best Pediatricians in Am.; grantee, CoInvest, Bethesda, Md., 1995—2004. Mem. AMA, Fla. Med. Assn., So. Med. Assn., Am. Soc. Nephrology, Internat. Pediat. Nephrology Assn., Am. Soc. Pediat. Nephrology, Fla. Soc. Pediat. Nephrology (pres. 1998). Republican. Methodist. Avocations: camping, skiing, travel. Office: HD 216 Univ Fla Coll Med Pediats 1300 Archer Rd Gainesville FL 32610-0296 Office Phone: 352-392-4434. Personal E-mail: rienne@aol.com. Business E-Mail: neibere@peds.ufl.edu.

NEIDELL, MARTIN H., lawyer; b. Bklyn., Apr. 5, 1946; s. Sidney B. and Sophie (Goldstein) N.; m. Suzan C. Rucker, June 23, 1968; children: Michael, Sari. BA magna cum laude, Lehigh U., 1968; JD cum laude, NYU, 1971. Bar: N.Y. 1972, U.S. Dist. Ct. (ea. and so. dists.) N.Y. 1973, U.S. Ct. Appeals (2d cir.) 1973. Law clk. to presiding justice U.S. Dist. Ct. (ea. dist.) N.Y., Bklyn., 1971-73; assoc. Stroock & Stroock & Lavan LLP, NYC, 1973-79, ptnr., corp., securities law, 1980—, mem., operating exec. com. Editor NYU Law Rev., 1971. Trustee North Shore Synagogue, Syosset, N.Y., 1984-90. Office: Stroock & Stroock & Lavan LLP 180 Maiden Ln New York NY 10038-4925 Home Phone: 516-624-8006; Office Phone: 212-806-5836. Office Fax: 212-806-7836. Business E-Mail: mneidell@stroock.com.

NEIDICH, GEORGE, lawyer; b. NYC, Feb. 22, 1950; s. Hyman and Rosalyn N.; m. Alene Wendrow, Jan. 10, 1982; 1 child, Hannah Lauren. BA, SUNY, Binghamton, 1971; JD magna cum laude, SUNY, Buffalo, 1974; MLT, Georgetown U., 1981. Bar: N.Y. 1975, D.C. 1979, Va. 1996, Conn. 1990. Assoc. Runfola & Birzon, Buffalo, 1973-75, Duke, Holzman, Yaeger & Radlin, Buffalo, 1975-77; gen. counsel subcom. on capital, investments and bus. opportunity, com. on small bus. U.S. Ho. of Reps., Washington, 1977-79, subcom. on gen. oversight, 1979-80; sr. legal advisor Task Force Product Liability and Accident Compensation Office of Gen. Counsel, Dept. Commerce, Washington, 1980-81; assoc. Steptoe & Johnson, Washington, 1981-86, of counsel, 1986-89; gen. counsel, sr. v.p. Preferred Health Care, Ltd., Wilton, Conn., 1989-93; COO Value Behavioral Health, Inc., Falls Church, Va., 1993-95; counsellor at law, 1995—; gen. counsel CareAdvantage, Inc., Iselin, NJ, 1999—. Adj. prof. Georgetown U. Law Ctr., 1985—87. Office: 9301 Morison Ln Great Falls VA 22066-4153 Office Phone: 703-757-2820. Personal E-mail: gneidich@aol.com.

NEIDORFF, MICHAEL F., health care executive; b. Phila., Nov. 19, 1942; s. A. Harvey and Shirley R. (Rubin) N.; m. Noemi Karpati. BS, Trinity U., 1965; MA, St. Francis Coll., 1966. Mgr. Miles Labs., Ltd., 1969-75, dir., 1967-85; pres., CEO Physician Health Plan, 1985-95, Group Health Plan, Inc., St. Louis, 1995—96; treas. Centene Corp., St. Louis, 1996—2001, pres., CEO, 1996—2004, chmn., pres., CEO, 2004—. Bd. dirs. Mark Twain Bank, St. Louis. Bd. trustees St. Louis Symphony Orch., St. Louis; bd. dirs. St. Louis Area coun. Boy Scouts Am., Grand Ctr., St. Louis. Mem. Mo. Managed Healthcare Assn. Office: Centene Corp 7711 Carondelet Ave Saint Louis MO 63105*

NEIER, ARYEH, author, human rights organization administrator; b. Berlin, Apr. 22, 1937; came to U.S., 1947, naturalized, 1955; s. Wolf and Gitla (Bendzinska) N.; m. Yvette Celton, June 22, 1958; 1 son, David. BS, Cornell U., 1958; LL.D. (hon.), Hofstra U., 1975, Hamilton Coll., 1979, SUNY, Binghamton, 1988. Exec. dir. League Indsl. Democracy, NYC, 1958-60; assoc. editor Current mag., NYC, 1960-63; exec. dir. N.Y. Civil Liberties Union, NYC, 1965-70; field devel. officer ACLU, NYC, 1963-64, exec. dir., 1970-78; adj. prof. law NYU, NYC, 1978—; dir. 20th Century Fund Project on Litigation and Social Policy, 1978-81; exec. dir. Human Rights Watch, NYC, 1981-93; pres. Open Soc. Fund and Inst., NYC, 1993—. Lectr. Police Acad., NY, 1969-70. Author: Dossier, 1975, Crime and Punishment: A Radical Solution, 1976, Defending My Enemy, 1979, Only Judgment, 1982; co-editor series of handbooks on rights of Americans, 1972-78; mem. editorial bd. The Nation, 1978-86, columnist, 1990—. Commr. juvenile justice standards project Am. Bar Assn.— Inst. for Judicial Adminstrn. Recipient Gavel award Am. Bar Assn., 1974 Fellow Am. Acad. Arts & Scis. Address: Open Society Institute 400 W 59th St Fl 4 New York NY 10019-1105

NEIKIRK, WILLIAM ROBERT, retired journalist; b. Irvine, Ky., Jan. 6, 1938; s. Lewis Byron and Nancy Elizabeth (Green) N.; m. Ruth Ann Clary, Sept. 10, 1960; children: Paul Gregory, John Stuart, Christa Lynn. BA in Journalism, U. Ky., 1960. Reporter Lexington (Ky.) Herald, 1959-60; state capital corr. AP, Frankfort, Ky., 1961-66, Baton Rouge, 1966-69; econ. corr. AP (Washington Bur.), 1970-74; nat. econ. writer Chgo. Tribune, Washington, 1974-83, White House corr., 1977, 94-98—, econ. columnist, 1980—94, news editor Washington bur., 1983, fin. editor, 1988-91, sr. writer, 1991—2008, chief Washington corr., 1998—2008. Author: The Work Revolution, 1983, Volcker: The Money Man, 1987. Recipient Beck award Chgo. Tribune, 1975, Bus. Writing award U. Mo., 1978, 80, Bus. Writing award Amos Tuck Grad. Sch. Bus., Dartmouth Coll., 1980, John Hancock Bus. Writing award Wharton Sch. Fin., U. Pa., 1979, finalist, 1990, 91, John Hancock Bus. Writing award U. Houston, 1980, Loeb Bus. Writing award UCLA Grad. Sch. Mgmt., 1979, Chgo. Headliner Club award, 1979, 84, Raymond Clapper Meml. award, 1981, Barnet Nover award, 1994, Merriman Smith award, 1995, White House Correspondents Assn.; named to Ky. Journalism Hall of Fame, 1998, One of Top 100 Bus. News Luminaries of the Century, TJFR mag., 2000; co-recipient Pulitzer Prize, 2001. Mem.: Gridiron Club (pres. 2007). Mem. Christian Ch. (Disciples Of Christ). Home: 5121 38th St N Arlington VA 22207-1827 Personal E-mail: buineil638@gmail.com, billnei@ail.com.

NEIL, ROBERT F., broadcast executive; Program dir. WYYY-FM, WSYR-AM, 1983, ops. mgr., 1983—84, WYAY-FM, Gainesville, Ga., 1984—86; station mgr. WSB-AM/FM, 1986—88, v.p. & gen. mgr., 1989—92; joined Cox Broadcasting, 1986, v.p. east, 1989—92, exec. v.p. radio, 1992—96; pres. CEO Cox Radio, 1996—. Named Radio Exec. of Yr., Radio Ink, 2003. Office: Cox Radio Inc 6205 Peachtree Dunwoody Rd Atlanta GA 30328

NEIL, SANDRA EILLEEN SILVERBERG, psychologist; b. NYC, Sept. 30, 1945; d. Marcus and Pearl (Bloom) Glickfeld; m. Robert Silverberg; children: Gerard David, Simonne Elizabeth, Julien Richard, Shari Beth Silverberg. BA, LaTrobe U., Melbourne, Australia, 1974, BEd in Counseling, 1976; MA in Clin. Psychology, U. Melbourne, 1986, PhD in Medicine, 1993. Registered clin. and forensic psychologist 1979, cert. family therapist The Virginia Satir Global Network (formerly AVANTA), 1987. Rsch. asst. dept. ednl. psychology U. Melbourne, 1965—68; clin. psychologist Janefield Hosp., Melbourne, 1975—77, Prince Henry Hosp., Melbourne, 1977—79, Cairnmillar Inst., Melbourne, 1979—83; pvt. practice Melbourne, 1983—; clin. psychologist St. Vincent's Hosp., Melbourne, 1986—93; clin. psychologist and family therapist, founding dir. Satir Centre Australia, Armadale, Victoria, Australia, 1993—. Forensic psychologist Supreme Ct., Melbourne, 1976—87; media psychologist, 1977—; sworn marriage counsellor Atty. Gen.'s Dept., Melbourne, 1978—. Author: The Persistence of Obesity, 1986, The Psychodynamics of Obesity, 1993, The Family Chessboard, 1995; editor: A Matter Of Life: Psychological Theory, Research And Practice, 1999; author: A Journey Through Three Continents And Four Generations: A Family Reconstruction, 2001. Active Pres.'s Club Arts Australia. Fellow: Australian Psychol. Soc. (chmn. pub. and media rels. Victorian br. 1983—2004); mem.: APA, Internat. Coun. Psychologists (chair internat. rels. and human rights interest group 1990—, pres. 1997—2000, World Area chair coord. 2009—), Internat. Acad. Family Psychology (Australian nat. rep. 1997—), Patron Opera Australia. Office: Satir Centre of Australia Suite 2 1051-A/B High St Armadale VIC 3143 Australia Office Phone: 61398247755. Office Fax: 61398247865. Personal E-mail: drneil@satiraustralia.com.

NEILAN, AIDAN JOSEPH, radiologist; b. Galway, Ireland, Sept. 30, 1923; arrived in U.S., 1950; s. John and Honoria Killeen Neilan; m. Nuala Mary McCarthy, June 1, 1959; children: Katherine Rosemary, Rosemary Collette, David Aidan. MD, Nat. U. Ireland, 1948. Diplomate Am. Bd. Radiology. Intern New Rochelle Gen. Hosp., 1950—51; resident Wadsworth VA Hosp., 1970—74; chief orthop. radiology Wadsworth Hosp., LA; prof. radiology UCLA, LA, 1979, prof. emeritus. Pres., CEO AJNCO, Inc., LA, 1958. Capt. US Army, 1953—55, France. Mem.: AMA, Irish Med. Assn., Brit. Med. Assn. Republican. Roman Cath. Avocations: piano, swimming, reading. Home: 30639 Rue Langlois Rancho Palos Verdes CA 90275 Personal E-mail: neilan@cox.net.

NEILL, DEBRA R., history professor; d. Thomas H. Neill and Sharon Turner. BA, Ariz. State U., Tempe, 1995, MA, 2001, PhD, 2007. Adj. faculty Mesa CC, Ariz., 2001—03; faculty assoc. Ariz. State U., Tempe, 2004—07, Ariz. State U. Poly, Mesa, 2007—. Pres., students taking action Ariz. State U., 2006—07. Recipient Wallace A. Adams Meml. award, Dept. History at Ariz. State U., 2006. Avocation: dance.

NEILL, DENIS MICHAEL, management consultant; b. Grand Rapids, Mich., Apr. 27, 1943; s. Thomas Patrick and Agnes Josephine (Weber) N.; m. Mary Kathleen Golden, June 11, 1966; children: Mark, Erin. AB cum laude, St. Louis U., 1964, JD cum laude, 1967. Bar: Mo. 1967, D.C. 1969. Gen. atty. Office of Asst. Regional Counsel IRS, Newark, 1967-68; assoc. Arent, Fox, Kintner, Plotkin & Kahn, Washington, 1969-71, Morgan, Lewis & Bockius, Washington, 1971-72; atty. advisor office gen. counsel AID, Washington, 1972-73, asst. gen. counsel legis. and policy coordination, 1973-75, asst. adminstr. legis. affairs, 1975-77; sr. v.p., gen. counsel Aeromaritime Internat. Corp., Washington, 1977-80; counsel Surrey & Morse, Washington, 1980-81; sr. ptnr. Neill & Shaw, Washington, 1981-92; sr. law ptnr. Dalley, Neill, Assevero, Carroll & Nealer, Washington, 1992-93; pres. Neill & Co., Inc., Washington, 1981—; counsel Fin. Markets Internat., Inc., 1998—. Bd. dirs. Barker Found., 1981-86, Fed. City Nat. Bank, Washington, 1987. Lt. USCG, 1968-71. Recipient Superior Unit Citation AID, 1976, Disting. Honor award, 1977. Mem. ABA, FBA, D.C. Bar Assn., Mo. Bar Assn., Nat. Security Indsl. Assn. (bd. dirs. 1982-90), Capitol Hill Club, Columbia Country Club (Chevy Chase, Md.), Jefferson Islands Club. Democrat. Home: 5945 Searl Ter Bethesda MD 20816-2022 Office: Neill & Co 5945 Searl Ter Bethesda MD 20816-2022 E-mail: denisneill@aol.com.

NEILL, LISA, literature and language professor; b. Knoxville, Tenn. BA, Tex. A&M U., Coll. Station, 1990, MEd, 1996. English prof. Blinn Coll., Brenham, Tex., 1999—. Recipient Tchg. award, NISOD, 2005. Office: Blinn Coll 902 Coll Ave Brenham TX 77833 Business E-Mail: lneill@blinn.edu.

NEILL, REBECCA ANNE, middle school educator; b. Bryan, Tex., Jan. 6, 1960; d. Walter and Marilyn Goff; m. Travis L. Neill, June 11, 1994; children: Shannon, Darby. BS, Tex. A&M U., 1982, Master of Edn. Curriculum and Instrn., 1992. Cert. mid. sch. tchr., Tex. Tchr. sci. Klein Ind. Sch. Dist., Houston, 1989—2004; ESST collaborative TX-BESS; tchr. sci. Aldine Ind. Sch. Dist., Spring Ind. Sch. Dist. Mem. Nat. Coalition Coun., 1990—96; computer workshop facilitator, 2000—; presenter in field, 2000—. Contbr. rsch. to profl. jours. Recipient award, Honors Inst. Elem. Tchrs., 1987, Thanks to Tchrs. award, 1990; grantee technology grants. Mem. NSTA, Coun. Elem. Sci. Internat., Tex. Coun. Elem. Sci., Sci. Tchrs. Assn. Tex., Met. Area Tchrs. Sci. Home: 4719 Marywood Dr Spring TX 77388-4977

NEILL, RICHARD ROBERT, retired publishing executive; b. NYC, June 20, 1925; s. Robert Irving and Mildred Mary (Hall) N.; m. Patricia Mae Robinson, Dec. 27, 1952; 1 son, Robert Kenneth. AB summa cum laude, Princeton U., 1948; MA, N.Y. U., 1953. With Prentice-Hall, Inc., NYC and Englewood Cliffs, NJ, 1948-85, advt. mgr., 1953-58, v.p. advt., 1958-62; pres. Executive Reports Corporation, 1962-85, ret., 1985. Regional chmn. Princeton Alumni Giving, Yonkers, N.Y., 1960-63, Tarrytown-Irvington, N.Y., 1977-80 Pres. Tarrytown (N.Y.) Jr. High Sch. PTA, 1971-72; bd. dirs. Martling Owners, Tarrytown, 1980-84, 89-93. Lt. (j.g.) USNR, 1943-46, PTO. Mem. USN Meml. Found., Princeton Terrace Club (bd. govs. 1986-92), Phi Beta Kappa. Republican. Mem. Reform Ch. Home: 3306 Kendal Way Sleepy Hollow NY 10591-1066 *A thought acquired from one of my first bosses: "Everything happens for the best - or can be made to do so." This has been a lifelong help.*

NEILSON, BENJAMIN REATH, lawyer; b. Phila., July 11, 1938; s. Harry Rosengarten and Alberta (Reath) N.; m. Judith Rawle, June 20, 1959 (div. May 1983); children: Benjamin R. Jr., Theodora C., Johanna K., Alberta R., Marshall R.; m. Meta B. Grace, Dec. 26, 1983. AB magna cum laude, Harvard U., 1960, LLB, 1963. Bar: Pa. 1964. Law clk. to chief justice Pa. Supreme Ct., Phila., 1963-64; assoc. Ballard, Spahr, Andrews & Ingersoll, Phila., 1964-71, ptnr., 1971—2008, sr. counselor, 2009—. Sec.-treas. Chanticleer Found., Wayne, Pa. Mem. ABA, Pa. Bar Assn., Phila. Bar Assn., Am. Coll. Estate & Trust Counsel,Phi Beta Kappa. Episcopalian. Business E-Mail: neilson@ballardspahr.com.

NEILSON, ERIC GRANT, physician, educator, health facility administrator; b. Bklyn., Sept. 14, 1949; s. Jack Drew and Lynette Elsie (Lundquist) N.; m. Linda Rae Apolzon, May 27, 1972; children: Tinsley, Sigrid. BS magna cum laude, Denison U., 1971; MD magna cum laude, U. Ala., 1975; MA (hon.), U. Pa., 1987. Asst. prof. U. Pa., Phila., 1980-87, assoc. prof., 1987-91, prof., 1991-98, C. Mahlon Kline prof., 1993-98, chief renal-electrolyte & hypertension divsn. dept. medicine, 1988-98; Hugh Jackson Morgan prof., chmn. dept. medicine Vanderbilt U. Med. Ctr., Nashville, 1998—. Attending physician Hosp. of U. Pa., 1980-98; physician-in-chief Vanderbilt U. Hosp., 1998—; cons. in field. Med. editl. bds. on sci. jours.; assoc. editor Kidney Internat., 1997-2006; editor-in-chief Jour. Am. Soc. Nephrology, 2007-; contbr. numerous articles to profl. jours. Chmn. med. adv. bd. Lupus Found. of Phila., 1985-95; chmn. pathology A study sect. NIH, Bethesda, Md., 1990-92; chmn. grant rev. com. Nat. Kidney Found. of Delaware Valley; mem. adv. coun. NIDDK, NIH; mem. bd. sci. advisors Polycystic Kidney Found., 1997-2000; mem. postdoctoral fellowship com. Howard Hughes Med. Inst., 1997-2000. Recipient Clin. Scientist award Am. Heart Assn., 1980, Young Investigator award Am. Soc. Nephrology/Am. Heart Assn., 1985, Established Investigator award Am. Heart Assn., 1985-90, President's medal Am. Soc. Nephrology, 1994, AN Richard Disting. Achievement award U. Pa., 1998, John P. Peters award, Am. Soc. Nephrology, 2005; named Disting. Alumnus, U. Ala., Birmingham, 2006. Fellow: ACP; mem.: Internat. Soc. Nephrology (treas. 2003—), Assn. Prof. Medicine (chmn. rsch. com. 2000—), Assn. Subsplty. Profs. (pres. 1994—96, Disting. Prof. award 2003), Am. Assn. Immunologists, Am. Clin. Climatol. Assn., Am. Soc. Nephrology (John P. Peters award 2005), Assn. Am. Physicians, Am. Soc. Clin. investigation. Mem. Soc. Of Friends. Office: Vanderbilt U Med Ctr Dept Medicine D3100 Med Ctr N Nashville TN 37232-0001 Office Phone: 615-322-3146. Business E-Mail: eric.neilson@vanderbilt.edu.

NEILSON, WINTHROP CUNNINGHAM, III, retired communications executive, financial consultant, photographer; b. NYC, Jan. 7, 1934; s. Winthrop Cunningham, Jr. and Frances Fullerton (Jones) N.; m. Ilse Rossenbeck, Jan. 4, 1957; children: Luise R., Victoria F.; m. Demaris King Hetrick, July 5, 1985; 1 child, Whitney C. C.; stepchildren: Norman P. Hetrick Jr., D. Page Hetrick. BA, Harvard U., 1956; grad. in security analysis, N.Y. Inst. Finance, 1963. Asst. prodr., asst. dir. Rangley Lakes Theater, 1955; gen. assignment reporter Albany (N.Y.) Times-Union, 1959—60; pub. info. writer, spkr. Consol. Edison, 1960—61; asst. dir. pub. rels. Union Svc. Corp., 1962; with Georgeson & Co., NYC, 1962—81, prin., 1969—81; sr. v.p. D.F. King & Co. Inc., NYC, 1982—86; founder, mng. dir. Krone Comm., Harrisburg, Pa., 1986—87; pres. Krone Group Inc., Harrisburg, 1987—89; mng. dir. Neilson/Hetrick Group, Montclair, NJ, 1990—93, Harrisburg, Pa., 1993—97, chmn. Chambersburg, Pa., 1987—2006; guest lectr. NYU, 1991; profl. nature photographer, 2001—. Author: series Aunt Jane, 1971, 73, The Reluctant Marriage, 1978, Investorism, 1981, Annual Reports, The Agony and the Ecstasy, 1985, Individual Investors, a Counterbalance to Institutional Investors, 1986; writer, assoc. editor: Trends, 1965-81; contbr. articles to profl. jours. Mem. Mountain Lakes (N.J.) Econ. Devel. Council, 1974-79, chmn., 1977-79; pres. Robert A. Taft Republican Club, Queens, N.Y., 1964-65, chmn., 1966-67; treas. 23d Assembly Dist. Rep. Party, 1966-67; county committeeman, 1964-67; del. N.Y. State Nominating Conv., 1966; campaign mgr. for 2 assemblymen and state senator; mem. exec. com. Chambersburg Cmty. Theater, Inc., 2002-03. Served with AUS, 1956-59. With US Army, 1956—59. Decorated Cert. Achievement, US Army, 1956; recipient Investor Edn. Disting. Service award Nat. Assn. Investors Clubs, 1986. Mem. Nat. Investor Rels. Inst. (dir. 1980-84, v.p. manpower 1980-81, v.p. long-range planning 1981-84, charter mem.), Pub. Rels. Soc. Am. (charter, exec. com. investor rels. 1982-90, chmn. 1987, Pres. award 1987, charter inductee into Hall of Fame for Investor Rels.), Corp. Rels. Soc. Ctrl. Pa. (v.p. 1986-89, pres. 1994-95), Ctrl. Pa. Entrepreneurial Assn. (bd. dirs. 1988-89, adv. bd. tech. coun. Ctrl. Pa. 1994-96), DU Club, Hershey Mills Golf Club, Hasty Pudding Club, Ausable Club. Lutheran. Home (Summer): Ausable Club 14 Neilson Way Saint Huberts NY 12943

NEIMAN, JOSEPH BRUCE, dermatologist; b. NYC, July 28, 1947; s. Nathan and Sarah N.; BA, NYU, 1968; MD, U. Tenn., 1972; m. Karen Marcia Simon, Aug. 31, 1975. Intern, Brown U., Providence, 1973-74; resident SUNY, Buffalo, 1974-75, 76-78, chief resident, 1977; dir. adult health services, head cmty. health screening Erie County Health Dept., Buffalo, NY, 1975-76; practice medicine specializing in dermatology and dermatologic surgery Boston, 1978-79, Williamsville, NY, 1980—; mem. staffs Buffalo Gen. Hosp., Millard Fillmore Hosp., Buffalo, Sisters of Charity Hosp., Buffalo; clin. asst. prof. dept. dermatology SUNY, Buffalo, 1980—; cons. USPHS, Buffalo, 1979-81. Fellow Am. Acad. Dermatology; mem. AMA, Internat. Soc. Dermatologic Surgery, Internat. Soc. Hair Restoration Surgery, Am. Soc. Dermatologic Surgery, N.AM. Soc. Phlebology, NY State Soc. Dermatology, Buffalo-Rochester Dermatol. Soc., Erie County Med. Soc., NY State Med. Soc. Office: Neiman Ctr for Dermatology & Hair Transplantation 1140 Youngs Rd Williamsville NY 14221-3625 Home: 134 Capes Hatteras Walk East Amherst NY 14051 Office Phone: 716-688-0011. Personal E-mail: jneimanmd@aol.com.

NEIMAN, KENNETH PAUL, judge; b. NYC, July 4, 1945; s. Julius and Gertrude (Fox) N.; m. Jan Dumond, May 24, 1987; children: Jennifer Gottlieb, Anna L. Neiman, J. Matthew Gowdy, Kerri Escudero. BA, Tufts U., 1967; JD, Harvard Law Sch., 1971. Bar: N.Y. 1972, Mass. 1974, U.S. Dist. Ct. Mass. 1974, U.S. Ct. Appeals (1st cir.) 1981, U.S. Supreme Ct. 1978. Staff atty. Mental Health Info. Svcs., NYC, 1971, Ctr. Social Welfare, Policy & Law, NYC, 1971-73; rsch. fellow Legal Svcs. Corp. Rsch. Inst., Washington, 1978; mng. atty. Western Mass. Legal Svcs., Holyoke, 1973-81; ptnr. Fierst & Neiman, Northampton, Mass., 1981-94; U.S. magistrate judge Dist. Mass., Springfield, 1995—. Mem. ABA, Mass. Bar Assn., Mass. Bar Found., Hampshire County Bar Assn. Office: United States District Court 300 State St Ste 120 Springfield MA 01105-1711

NEIMAN, LEROY, artist; b. St. Paul, June 8, 1921; s. Charles and Lydia (Serline) Runquist; m. Janet Byrne, June 22, 1957. Student, Sch. Art Inst., Chgo., 1946-50, U. Ill., 1951, DePaul U., 1951; LittD (hon.), Franklin Pierce Coll., 1976; D (hon.), St. John's U., 1980, Iona Coll., 1985, Hofstra U., 1997, St. Francis Coll., 1998, St. Bonaventure U., 1999, Sch. Art Inst., Chgo., 2006. Instr. Sch. Art Inst. Chgo., 1950-60, LeRoy Neiman master classes, 2006—07; instr. Saugatuck Summer Sch. Painting, Mich., 1957-58, 63, Sch. Arts and Crafts, Winston-Salem, NC, 1963; instr. painting Atlanta Youth Coun., 1968-69; printmaker-graphics, 1971—; artist Olympics, ABC-TV, Munich, 1972, ofcl. artist Montreal, 1976, US Olympics, 1980, 84; computer artist CBS-TV (Superbowl), New Orleans, 1978; ofcl. artist Goodwill Games CNN-TV, Moscow, 1986; 1st ofcl. artist Ky. Derby, Louisville, 1997; ofcl. artist Mardi Gras, New Orleans, 2002. Mem. adv. com. LeRoy Neiman Ctr. Print Studies Sch. of the Arts Columbia U., 1995; mem. adv. com. for NYC Commn. Cultural Affairs, 1995, UCLA LeRoy Neiman Ctr. Study of Am. Soc. and Culture, 1998; established LeRoy Neiman Art Ctr. for Youth, San Francisco, 2000, 05, Watsonville, Calif., 2002; founder Arts Horizons LeRoy Neiman Art Ctr., Harlem, NY, 2008. One-man shows include Oehlschlaeger Gallery, Chgo., 1959, 61, O'Hana Gallery, London, Gallerie O. Bosc, Paris, 1962, Hammer Gallery, NYC, 1963, 65, 67, 70, 72, 76, 78-79, 81-83, 85-87, 89, 92, 94, 97, 2000, 03, Huntington-Hartford Gallery Modern Art, NYC, 1967, Heath Gallery, Atlanta, 1969, Abbey Theatre, Dublin, Ireland, 1970, Museo de Bellas Artes, Caracas, Indpls. Inst. Arts, 1972, Hermitage Mus., Leningrad, Tobu Gallery, Tokyo, 1974, Springfield Mus. Fine Arts, Mass., 1974, 84, Knoedler Gallery, London, 1976, Casa gratica, Helsinki, 1977, Renée Victor, Stockholm, 1977, Okla. Art Ctr., Oklahoma City, 1981, Harrod's, London, 1982, Arts Horizons LeRoy, Neiman Art Ctr., 2008; retrospective show, Minn. Mus. Art, St. Paul, 1975, Meredith Long Galleries, Houston, 1978, Hanae Mori Gallery, Tokyo, 1988, New State Tretyakov Mus., Moscow, 1988, Butler Inst., Youngstown, Ohio, 1990, Galerie Marcel Bernheim, Paris, 1993, Ky. Derby Mus., Louisville, 1995, 1997, Marlborough Gallery, NYC, 2000, The Fairfield, Sturgeon Bay, Wis., 2001, Nat. Art Mus. Sport, Ind. U.-Purdue U., 2001, Wildlife Experience, Parker, Colo., 2003; two-man show, Neiman-Warhol, LA Inst. Contemporary Art, 1981; exhibited in group shows at Art Inst. Chgo., 1954-60, Carnegie Internat., 1956, Corcoran Gallery Am., Washington, Walker Art Center, Mpls., 1957, Ringling Mus., Sarasota, Fla., 1959, Salon d'Art Mus., Paris, 1961, Nat. Gallery Portraiture, Smithsonian Instn., Washington, Minn. Mus. Art, 1969, Rotunda Della Basana, Milan, Italy, 1971, Royal Coll. Art, London, 1971, Minn. Mus. Art Nat. Tour, 1976-77, Whitney Mus., 1985; Master Prints of 19th and 20th Centuries, Hammer Gallery, NY, 1987, Salon d'Automne, Paris, 1992-

93, Newport Art Mus., 2004; represented in permanent collections Mpls. Inst. Arts, Ill. State Mus., Springfield, Joslyn Mus., Omaha, Wodham Coll., Oxford, Eng., Nat. Art Mus. Sport, NYC, Museo De Ballas Artes Caracas, Hermitage Mus., Indpls. Inst. Arts, U. Ill., Balt. Mus. Fine Art, The Armand Hammer Collection, LA, Edwin & Ruth Kennedy Mus. Am. Art at Ohio U., Midwest Mus. Am. Art, Elkhart, Ind., Nat. Art Mus. Sport, Indpls.; executed murals at Merc. Nat. Bank, Hammond, Ind., Continental Hotel, Chgo., Swedish Lloyd Ship S.S. Patricia, Stockholm, ceramic tile mural, Sportsmans Park, Chgo., The Muhammad Ali Ctr., Louisville, 2005, Polo Mural, Southampton, NY, 2005; author: LeRoy Neiman—Art and Life Style, 1974, Horses, 1979, LeRoy Neiman. Posters, 1980, LeRoy Neiman. Catalogue Raisonné, 1980, Carnaval, 1981, LeRoy Neiman: Winners, 1983, Japanese translation, 1985, LeRoy Neiman, Monte Carlo Chase, 1988, The Prints of LeRoy Neiman, 1980-90, Big Time Golf, 1992, LeRoy Neiman, An Am. in Paris, 1994, LeRoy Neiman on Safari, 1997, The Prints of LeRoy Neiman 1991-2000, LeRoy Neiman, Five Decades, 2003, deluxe ltd. edit. The LeRoy Neiman Sketchbook, 2004, Playboy Femlin, LeRoyn Neiman, 2007, Ltd. ed. Femlin, LeRoy Neiman, 2008; illustrator: 12 paintings deluxe edit. Moby Dick, 1975, 35 charcoal drawings deluxe edit. Casey at the Bat, 2000, trade edit., 2002. Served with AUS, 1942-46. Recipient 1st prize Twin City Show, 1953, 2nd prize Minn. State Show, 1954, Clark Meml. prize Chgo. Show, 1957, Hamilton-Graham prize Ball State Coll., 1958, Mcpl. prize Chgo. Show, 1958, Purchase prize Miss. Valley Show, 1959, Gold medal Salon d'Art Modern Paris, 1961; award of merit as nation's outstanding sports artist AAU, 1976; Olympic Artist of Century award, 1979, Gold Medal award St. John's U., 1985; named to Internat. Boxing Hall of Fame, 2007. Address: 1 W 67th St New York NY 10023-6200

NEIMAN, RICHARD H., state banking agency administrator; BA, Am. U., Washington; JD, Emory U. Spl. asst. to chief counsel Comptr. Currency; v.p., counsel including gen. counsel global equities group Citicorp, 1979—89; dir. regulatory adv. svcs. Price Waterhouse, LLP, 1990—94; exec. v.p., gen. counsel TD Waterhouse Group, 1994—2006; chmn., pres., CEO TD Bank USA, N.A., 2006—07; supt. banks NY State Banking Dept., 2007—. Office: Supt Banks NY State Banking Dept One State St New York NY 10004-1417 Office Phone: 212-709-3501. Office Fax: 212-709-3520. E-mail: richard.neiman@banking.state.ny.us.*

NEIMAN, SHIRAH, prosecutor; b. 1943; BA cum laude, Barnard Coll., 1965; JD magna cum laude, Columbia Univ., NYC, 1968. Bar: NY 1968. Law clk. to Hon. William B. Herlands US Dist. Ct. (So. dist.) NY, law clk. to Milton Pollack; asst. US atty. (So. dist.) NY US Dept Justice, 1970—, dep. chief criminal divsn., chief major crimes unit, dep. US atty., 1993—2002, chief counsel, 2002; instr. Columbia Law Sch., 1976—79. Asst. spl. prosecutor Watergate Spl. Prosecution Force; mem. Atty Gen. Advisors Com., 1996—97; guest faculty mem. Harvard Law Sch., NYU, Fordham Law, Cardozo Law. Mem.: Fed. Bar Coun., NYC Bar Assn. Office: US Attys Office SDNY Rm 829 One St Andrews Plz New York NY 10007 Office Phone: 212-637-2574.

NEIMARK, SHERIDAN, lawyer; b. Youngstown, Ohio, Apr. 7, 1935; s. David and Anne (Kamisar) N.; m. Dana Ellen Perlzweig, Jan. 5, 1963; children: David, Rebecca, Matthew. BS in Chem. Engring, Carnegie-Mellon U., 1957; JD, George Washington U., 1961. Bar: Va. 1962, D.C. 1962, U.S. Ct. of Customs and Patent Appeals 1963, U.S. Ct. Appeals (Fed. cir.) 1982, U.S. Supreme Ct. 1973. Patent examiner U.S. Patent Office, Washington, 1957-62; practiced in Washington, 1962—; patent atty. firms K. Flocks and A. Browdy, Washington, 1962-68; mem. firm Browdy and Neimark, Washington, 1969—, sr. ptnr., 1989—. Contbr. articles, papers to profl. jours. Charter mem. Gov.'s Planning and Adv. Coun. on Devel. Disabilities, State of Md., 1971-86, vice chmn., 1975-77; mem. Legal and Human Rights Task Force, Montgomery County (Md.) Com. for Employment of Handicapped, 1972-73; bd. dirs., co-founder Cmty. Svcs. for Autistic Adults and Children; past bd. dirs. Tifereth Israel Congregation. Recipient Gov.'s citation State of Md., 1986. Mem. Am. Bar Assn. (mem. adv. bd. developmental disabilities model legis. project 1977-81, mem. adv. bd. mental and phys. disabilities law reporter 1979—), D.C. Bar, Va. State Bar, Am. Intellectual Property Law Assn. (mem. com. patent law 1965-69, chem. practice 1970—), Md. Patent Law Assn., Internat. Assn. Jewish Lawyers and Jurists, Patent Office Soc., Autism Soc. Am. (nat. dir. 1973-77, dir. Montgomery County chpt. 1970-72, nat. Plaque awards 1972, 77), Md. State Soc. for Autistic Children (founder, dir. 1971-73), Am. Jewish Com., Am. Jewish Congress, B'nai Brith. Home: 12908 Ruxton Rd Silver Spring MD 20904-5278 Office: 624 9th St NW Washington DC 20001-5303

NEIMS, ALLEN HOWARD, pediatrician, educator, dean, researcher; b. Chgo., Oct. 24, 1938; s. Irving Morris and Ruth (Geller) N.; m. Myrna Gay Robins, June 18, 1961; children: Daniel Mark, Susan Roberta, Nancy Elizabeth. BA, BS, U. Chgo., 1957; MD, Johns Hopkins U., 1961, PhD, 1966. Intern, resident in pediatrics Johns Hopkins Hosp., 1961-62, 66-68; research asso. Lab. Neurochemistry, NIH, 1968-70; asst. prof. physiol. chemistry and pediatrics Johns Hopkins Med. Sch., 70-72; assoc. prof. McGill U., 1972-77, prof. pharmacology and pediatrics, 1977-78; dir. Roche developmental pharmacology unit, 1972-78; prof., chmn. dept. pharmacology and therapeutics, prof. pediatrics U. Fla., Gainesville, 1978-89, dean Coll. Medicine, 1989-96, prof. pharmcology, pediat., 1996—2007; dir. Ctr. for Spirituality and Health, 2002—07, prof. emeritus, 2007—. Dir. Ctr. Spirituality and Health; Fulton Bequest prof. U. Melbourne, Australia, 1974; mem. human embryology and devel. study sect. NIH, 1979-83; sci. cons. Can. Found. for Study of Sudden Infant Death, 1974-77, Nat. Soft Drink Assn., 1976-78, Internat. Life Scis. Inst., 1978-89; bd. sci. counsellors Nat. Inst. Child Health and Human Devel., 1984-89. Contbr. chpts. to books, articles to med. jours. Served to comdr. USPHS, 1968-70. NIH, Can. Med. Research Council grantee. Mem. Can. Assn. Research in Toxicology (pres. 1976-78), Am. Soc. Pharmacology and Exptl. Therapeutics (past mem. exec. coms. clin. pharmacology and drug metabolism), Am. Pediatric Soc., Am. Acad. Pediatrs. Democrat. Jewish. Office: U Fla Coll Medicine PO Box 100267 Gainesville FL 32610-0267 Office Phone: 352-392-0687. Personal E-mail: ahneims@aol.com. Business E-Mail: ahneims@ufl.edu.

NEIS, ARNOLD HAYWARD, pharmaceutical company executive; b. NYC, Feb. 13, 1940; s. Harry H. and Mary Ruth (Bishop) N.; children: Nancy R., Robert C. BS cum laude, Columbia U., 1960; MBA, NYU, 1967. With Scott Chem. Co., 1960—64; v.p. Odell, Inc., NYC, 1964—71, pres. Thayer Knomark divsn., 1969—71; pres., chief exec. officer E.T. Browne Drug Co., Inc., Englewood Cliffs, NJ, 1971—, chmn., 2000—. Dir. Esquire A.B. Stockholm, Knomark Can. Ltd., E.T. Browne Internat. Fellow Royal Soc. Chemists, Royal Geog. Soc., Am. Inst. Chemists, NY Acad. Scis.; mem. AAAS, Am. Chem. Soc., Am. Pharm. Assn., New Eng. Soc. (pres., bd. dirs., J.P. Morgan medal 2008), Explorers Club (v.p., bd. dirs., Sweeney medal 1997), Chemists Club, Lotos Club, Soldiers, Sailors and Airmans Club (bd. dirs.), St. Georges Soc. (bd. dirs.), Ch. Club (pres., bd. dirs.), Pilgrims of the US, Order St. John. Episcopalian. Home: 898 Park Ave New York NY 10021-0234 Office: PO Box 1613 440 Sylvan Ave Englewood Cliffs NJ 07632-2700 Personal E-mail: aneis@etbrowne.com.

NEIS, ARTHUR VERAL, healthcare and development company executive; b. Lawrence, Kans., May 30, 1940; s. Veral Herbert and Louise (Schlegel) N.; m. Fleeta Weigel, Apr. 12, 1969 (dec. 1999); children: Frederich Arthur, Benjamin Jason, Sarah Louise. BS in Bus., U. Kans., 1962, MS in Acctg., 1963. CPA, Kans., Iowa. Mgmt. cons. Arthur Andersen & Co., Kansas City, Mo. and Mpls., 1963-74; chief corp. acctg. Carlson Co., Mpls., 1974-76; contr. The Fullerton Cos., Mpls., 1976-78; asst. treas. Fru-Con Corp., St. Louis, 1978-80, asst. contr., 1981, contr., 1982-86; corp. contr. LCS Holdings, Inc. (Weitz Corp. and Subs.), Des Moines, 1986-87, v.p., treas., CFO, 1987—2007, v.p., treas., CFO, mem. exec. com., 1995—2007, also bd. dirs., trustee retirement plan; treas., CFO Weitz Co., Des Moines, 1987-93, Life Care Svcs. LLC, Des Moines, 1987—2007; pres. Alliance Minerals N.Am., LLC, 2007—. Adv. group Nat. Assn. Ins. Com., 1990—93; treas., exec. com. bd. Villa de Maria Montessori Sch., St. Louis, 1984—86; trustee Fin. Execs. Rsch. Found., 1994—2000, chair audit com., 1997—98, vice chair rsch., 1998—2000, chmn., 2000—01; mem. internat. acctg. stads. bd. working group Internat. Fin. Reporting Stads., 2005—08; mem., working group SME Reporting, 2005—08; trustee Plymouth Congl. Ch., 1997—97, found. trustee, 1998—2001, chair, 2000—01; active Des Moines Poetry Festival, 2000—04, treas. bd. dirs., 2003—04; bd. dirs. Inst. Humane Studies, George Mason U., Fairfax, Va., 1971—2006, exec. com., 1975—83, chmn., 1978—83; bd. dirs. Lake Country Sch., Mpls., 1973—78, Alliance for Arts and Understanding, co-chair, 1993—96, bd. trustees, 1993—2002, chair, 1996—2002. Recipient Amb. award, Iowa Asian Alliance, 2004; named to Bus. and Industry Hall Fame, AICPA, 2007. Mem. AICPA (pvt. co. fin. pvt. task force 2004, mem. task force pvt. co. reporting generally accepted acctg. practices 2004, mem. nominating com. 2006—07), Kans. Soc. CPAs, Iowa Soc. CPAs, Fin. Execs. Inst. (bd. dirs. Iowa chpt. 1986, 88-94, sec. 1988-90, v.p. 1990-91, pres. 1991-92, com. on pvt. cos. stds. subcom. 2005—), Internat. Acctg. Std. Bd., Pvt. Co. Working Group, 2005-. Avocations: history, Asian art. Office: 1575 NW 106th St Clive IA 50325 E-mail: veral01@att.net.

NEISER, BRENT ALLEN, foundation executive, public affairs and personal finance speaker, consultant; b. Cin., 1954; m. Marion, Apr. 1, 1978; children: Christy Jean, Steven José, April Reneé. BA in Pub. Affairs, George Washington U., 1976; MA in Urban Studies, Occidental Coll., 1978; MBA, U. Louisville, 1979; M in Global Studies Internat. Security, U. Denver, 2005. Cert. fin. planner, 1985; cert. assn. exec., 1994; cert. in Homeland Security U. Denver, 2005; chartered mut. fund counselor, 1996; accredited asset mgmt. specialist, 1998. Project mgr., analyst Legis. Research Com., Frankfort, Ky., 1978-84; pres. Moneyminder, Denver and Frankfort, 1983-91; dir. edn., govt. affairs Inst. Cert. Fin. Planners, Denver, 1985-91, exec. dir., 1991-94; pub. affairs, govt. rels. bus. strategies cons. The Brent Neiser Co., Englewood, Colo., 1994—97; dir. collaborative program Nat. Endowment for Fin. Edn., 1995—97, 1997—2007, dir. pub. edn. ctr., 1995—97, dir. strategic programs and alliances, 2007—. Mng. dir. Fin. Products Stds. Bd., Denver, 1985-91; co-creator Personal Econ. Summit '93, Washington; spkr. in field. Author: EPCOT/World Showcase External Directions, Walt Disney Imagineering, 1977, Personal Management, 1996, 2000, 03, Ignoring the Obvious: Public Diplomacy U.S. Foreign and Defense Policy, 2005; mem. editl. adv. bd. Jour. Fin. Planning, 2007. Vol., v.p. Big Bros./Big Sisters, Frankfort, 1982; del. Colo. Model Constn. Conv., 1987; mem. citizens budget rev. com. Greenwood Village; mem. long range planning com. Adoption Exch., Denver, 1992-93, bd. dirs., 1993-99; polit. action dir. Frankfort NAACP, 1983, legis. chmn. state conf., 1984; troop com. mem., asst. scoutmaster Boy Scouts Am., Englewood, 1993-99; bd. dirs. Young Ams. Bank Edn. Found., 1993-99, chair edn. coun.; mem. Leadership Denver, 1994; vol. host com. Denver Summit of the Eight, 1997; nat. spokesperson Protect our Children Campaign, 1996; active Annie E. Casey Found.: Nat. Foster Care Awareness Project, 1999-02; citizen's panelist News Hour with Jim Lehrer (PBS), 1998—; founding ptnr. Social Venture Ptnrs., Denver, 2000-04, Colo. Coun. of Advisors on Consumer Credit, 2000-07, chmn., 2005-07; mem. CFP bd. Consumer Adv. Coun. on Fin. Planning, 2001-03, 05-08; bd. advisors Coll. Visual and Performing Arts, Winthrop U., 2002-05; mem. cmty. rels. bd. Daniels Coll. Bus., 2006-, U. Denver; mem. Leadership Program of Rockies, 2007. Lt. (j.g.) USNR, 1985-92. Recipient award of Excellence, Assn. Advance Am., 1996, 98, Summit award, Am. Soc. Assn. Exec., 2004; Pub. Affairs fellow Coro Found., 1976-77; fellow Ctr. for Social Innovation Stanford U., 2003, exec. seminar Aspen Inst., 2006, exec. edn. performance measurement Harvard Bus. Sch., 2006, Kellogg S. Mgmt. Strategic Partnerships, 2006, Brookings Instn., 2007, Columbia U. Leadership Devel., 2008, U. Wis. Dirs. Summit, 2009. Mem. Global Philanthropy Forum, Denver World Affairs Coun., Denver Coun. on Fgn. Rels., Investors Edn. Assn. Colo. (bd. dirs. 1995-01), Nat. Assns. in Colo., Denver C. of C. (pub. affairs coun.), N.Am. Securities Adminstrs. Assn. (investment adviser and fin. planner adv. com.), Nat. Soc. Compliance Profls. (bd. dirs. 1987-89), Am. Film Inst. (writers workshop), Am. Polit. Items Collectors, Fin. Planning Assn. (academic groups, Foresight Group, chair awards task force, judge Fin. Frontier Awards), Alliance for Investor Edn., Nat. Eagle Scout Assn., Snowboard Outreach Soc. Achievements include co-inventor Trivia Express Game, Denver, 1986; developer over 100 projects for disaster victims, low income families and children. Avocations: snowboarding, drums (jazz) and latin percussion music, golf, swimming, modern design. Office: 5860 Big Canyon Dr Greenwood Village CO 80111-3516 Office Phone: 303-224-3501. E-mail: ban@nefe.org.

NEISSER, HENTIKE, editor, writer; b. Nuernberg, Germany, July 30, 1943; s. Heinrich and Eleonore (Mergner) Neisser. Student, U. Frankfurt, Germany, 1965-68; DPhil, U. Tuebingen, Germany, 1973. Subject specialist EKZ, Reutlingen, Germany, 1973-76; dir. City Libr. Saarbrücken, Germany, 1976-86, City Libr. Cologne, Germany, 1986—2007. Lectr Fochhochschule für Sozialwesen, Esslingen, Germany, 1973—76, Fachhochschule für Bibliotheken, Cologne, Germany, 1987—2001; adv. in field. Author: (book) Die Jugendzeitschrift, 1975, Diskotheken in Deutschland, 1979, Traumzeiten, 1984, Der Gott der Ameise, 1993, Centratur, 1996, Centratur II, 1997. Mem.: Verband Deutscher Schriftsteller. Avocations: painting, music. Office: Circel-Verlag Voderady 98 98 SK-91942 Voderady Slovakia Business E-Mail: neisser@circel.de.

NEITER, GERALD IRVING, lawyer; b. LA, Nov. 11, 1933; s. Harry and Ida Florence (Alperin) N.; m. Margaret P. Rowe, Mar. 5, 1961; children: David, Karen, Michael. BSL, JD, U. So. Calif., 1957. Bar: Calif. 1958. Judge pro tem Mcpl. Cts., L.A. and Beverly Hills, 1970-94, Calif. Superior Ct., L.A. County, 1974-94, family law mediator, 1976—; prin. Gerald I. Neiter, P.C., LA, 1981—. Lectr. State Bar of Calif., 1968, 76, 79, 81; former referee State Bar Ct.; arbitrator Am. Arbitration Assn.; mediator L.A. Superior Ct. Mem. ABA, Los Angeles County Bar Assn. (arbitrator), Beverly Hills Bar Assn., State Bar Calif. Office: 1925 Century Park E Ste 2000 Los Angeles CA 90067-2701 Office Phone: 310-277-2236. E-mail: Neitlaw@aol.com.

NEITHERCUT, DAVID J., real estate company officer; BA, St. Lawrence U.; MBA, Columbia U. With real estate dept. Continental Bank; with comml. mortgage banking div. Draper & Kramer, Inc.; sr. v.p. fin. Equity Group Investments; joined Equity Residential, 1993, CFO, 1995—2004, exec. v.p. corp. strategy, 2004—05, pres., 2005—, CEO, 2006—. Office: Equity Residential Properties Trust 2 N Riverside Plz Ste 450 Chicago IL 60606-2600

NEITZKE, ERIC KARL, lawyer; b. Mobile, Ala., Dec. 10, 1955; s. Howard and Otti S. Neitzke; m. Kathryn Sloan; children: Kyle, Blake, Blaire. BA, U. Fla., 1979, JD, 1982. Bar: Fla. 1982, U.S. Dist. Ct. (mid. dist.) Fla. 1987. Asst. state atty. 7th Jud. Cir., State Atty., Daytona Beach, Fla., 1982; assoc. Dunn, Smith & Withers, Daytona Beach, 1982—88, Monaco, Smith, Hood and Perkins, Daytona Beach, 1988—2003; sole practice Daytona Beach, 2003—. Adj. faculty family law and criminal law Daytona C.C.; chmn. adv. com. Juvenile Detention Ctr. Contbr. articles to profl. jours. Mem. ATLA, Fla. Acad. Trial Lawyers, Volusia Bar Assn., Fla. Assn. Criminal Def. Lawyers, Phi Beta Kappa. Avocations: water sports, shooting, travel. Home: 19 Lost Creek Ln Ormond Beach FL 32174-4840 Office: Eric K Neitzke PA 412 N Wild Olive Ave Daytona Beach FL 32118 Office Phone: 386-323-1900.

NEIWEEM, DAVID, music educator; b. Evanston, Ill., Oct. 13, 1953; life ptnr. Alan Parshley, Nov. 24, 2001. MusB, Oberlin Coll., Ohio, 1976; MusM, DMA, U. Wis., Madison, 1982. Prof. music U. Vt., Burlington, 1982—; music dir., artistic dir. Internat. Music Festival, Pitten, Austria, 1992—; music dir. Burlington Choral Soc., 1995—, First Congl. Ch., Burlington, 1999—. Musician performances throughout the US, Europe, and Can. Mem. Nat. Assn. Execs. Schs. Music, 1999—2007. Recipient Citation, Pitten, Austria Bd. of Aldermen, 2006; fellow, Deutscher Akademischer Austausch Dienst, 1979. Mem.: Am. Choral Directors Assn. (pres., Vt. region 1983—86), Am. Guild Organists, Nat. Assn. Tchrs. of Singing (gov., Vt. chpt. 1984—88). Office: Univ Vt 348 S Prospect St Burlington VT 05405 Personal E-mail: david.neiweem@uvm.edu.

NEKOVEI, REZA, engineering educator, researcher; BSEE, U. Maine, Orono, 1986, MS, 1988; PhD, U. RI, Kingston. Software engr. U. RI, Narragansett, 1990—2004; prof. Tex. A&M U., Kingsville, Tex., 1997—; fulbright sr. scholar Bucharest Poly. U., Romania, 2008—. Recipient Disting. Tchg. award, Javelina Alumni Assn., 2008. Mem.: IEEE. Achievements include development of Distributed Data Access Protocols (OPeNDAP, DODS); research in real-time remote sensing hardware; development of Intelligent System Integration (RoboChess, MacNeuron); research in teaching by design. Office: Texas A&M Univ EECS Dept MSC 192 Kingsville TX 78363 Office Fax: 361-593-4026. Personal E-mail: rnekovei@ieee.org. Business E-Mail: rnekovei@tamu.edu.

NEKRITZ, EDWARD STEVEN, lawyer; b. Chgo., Nov. 11, 1965; s. Barry Benjamin and Susan Ellen (Moss) N.; m. Wendy Nekritz, children: Jessica, Matthew AB, Harvard U., 1987; JD, U. Chgo. Law Sch., 1990. Bar: Ill. 1990. Assoc. Mayer, Brown & Platt (formerly Mayer, Brown, Rowe & Maw), Chgo., 1990-95; v.p. asset mgmt. Security Capital Indsl. Trust, Aurora, Colo., 1995-98; sr. v.p., gen. counsel, sec. ProLogis, Aurora, Colo., 1998—. Mem. Harvard Club of Chgo. (dir. 1989—).

NELIGAN, PETER C., plastic surgeon, educator; b. July 20, 1952; married; 2 children. BA, U. Dublin, Trinity Coll., 1973, MBBCh, 1975. Cert. Ont., 1985. Clin. fellow, plastic surgery The Hosp. for Sick Children, Toronto, Canada, 1983—84, rsch. fellow, plastic surgery, 1984—85, assoc. staff surgeon, 1995, rsch. project dir., rsch. inst., 1995; clin. fellow, microvascular surgery Toronto Gen. Hosp., Canada, 1985; clin. burn fellow The Ross Tilley Burn Ctr., Wellesley Hosp., Toronto, Canada, 1986; dir. The Ross Tilley Burn Ctr., The Wellesley Hosp., Toronto, Canada, 1992—93; attending plastic surgeon Laurentian Hosp., Sudbury, Canada, 1987—91, Sudbury Gen. Hosp., Canada, 1987—91, Sudbury Meml. Hosp., Canada, 1987—91, The Wellesley Hosp., Toronto, Canada, 1991—93, assoc. staff, 1993—2000; asst. prof., dept. surgery U. Toronto, Canada, 1991—97, chair, divsn. plastic surgery, 1996, assoc. prof., dept. surgery, 1997—2002, prof., dept. surgery, 2002—07; attending plastic surgeon The Toronto Hosp., Canada, 1993—2007, dep. head, divsn. plastic surgery, 1994—96; assoc. staff surgeon Mt. Sinai Hosp., Toronto, Canada, 1993; cons., dept. surg. oncology Princess Margaret Hosp., Toronto, Canada, 1995, Wharton chair in reconstructive plastic surgery, 1999; prof. surgery U. Wash., 2007—. Mem. editl. bd. Can. Jour. of Plastic Surgery, 1996—, Annals of Plastic Surgery, 2002—, Jour. of Reconstructive Microsurgery, 2002—, Brit. Jour. of Plastic Surgery, 2003—, editor-in-chief Jour. of Reconstructive Microsurgery, —. Fellow: Royal Coll. Physicians and Surgeons of Can., Am. Coll. Surgeons (mem., adv. com. on plastic and maxillofacial surgery 2000—03), Royal Coll. Surgeons Ireland; mem.: Plastic Surgery Ednl. Found. (nominating com. mem. 2002—, joint outcomes com. mem. 2002—, pres.), Ontario Soc. Plastic Surgery, Am. Burn Assn., Can. Med. Protective Assn., Irish Assn. Plastic Surgeons, Internat. Soc. for Burn Injuries, Can. Med. Assn., World Soc. Reconstructive Microsurgery (adv. coun. mem. 2001—), Plastic Surgery Rsch. Coun. (Snyder Award 1998, Hardesty Award 2000), Internat. Confederation for Plastic Reconstructive and Aesthetic Surgery, Internat. Microsurg. Soc., Ontario Med. Assn., N.Am. Skull Base Soc. (program com. mem. 2003—, v.p. 2007—08, pres.-elect), Can. Soc. Plastic Surgeons, Am. Soc. Plastic and Reconstructive Surgeons (mktg. com. mem. 1999—2002, scientific program com. mem. 1999—, bd. dirs. 2001—, ethics com. mem. 2003—, Certificate of Merit, Investigator award 1984), Am. Soc. for Reconstructive Microsurgery (nominating com. mem. 1999—2001, membership com. mem. 1999—, program com. mem. 2001—, pres.-elect), Am. Assn. Plastic Surgeons (comm. com. mem. 1999—), Inst. Med. Sci. Office: U Wash Med Ctr / Dept Surgery 1959 NE Pacific St Box 356410 Seattle WA 98195-6410 Office Phone: 206-543-5516. Office Fax: 206-543-8136. E-mail: pneligan@u.washington.edu.

NELKIN, BARRY DAVID, oncology researcher and educator; b. New Orleans, Dec. 12, 1951; s. Joseph William and Bertha (Washastrom) N.; m. Deborah Ann Medetsky, June 4, 1975; children: Moshe, Aryeh, Yehuda, Esther, Yisroel, Rivka, Bina, Yaakov, Miriam, Shira. BS, Johns Hopkins U., 1972; PhD, George Washington U., 1979. Postdoctoral fellow Johns Hopkins U. Sch. Medicine, Balt., 1979—82, instr. oncology, 1982—84, asst. prof., 1984—90, assoc. prof., 1990—2004, prof., 2004—. Mem. ad hoc study sect. U.S. Nat. Cancer Inst., Bethesda, 1989-; grant reviewer Dutch Cancer Soc., 1990, VA, 1990; co-founder Internat. Thyroid Oncology Group. Author: (with others) Tumor Cell Heterogeneity, vol. 4, 1982, Progress in Nonhistone Protein Research, 1985; editor: Genetic Mechanisms in Multiple Endocrine Neoplasia Type 2, 1996; mem. editl. bd. oncology rep., 1997-98; contbr. articles to profl. jours. Nat. Cancer Inst. grantee, 1988-. Mem. Am. Assn. Cancer Rsch., Am. Soc. Microbiology. Achievements include the cloning of human calcitonin gene; demonstration of oncogene mediated differentiation of medullary thyroid carcinoma cells; isolation of ras oncogene responsive transcriptional element in human calcitonin gene; cloning of human BARX2 and RREB transcription factor genes. Home: 3831 Labyrinth Rd Baltimore MD 21215-1505 Office: Johns Hopkins Sch Medicine 1650 Orleans St Baltimore MD 21231 Home Phone: 410-358-4975; Office Phone: 410-955-8506. Business E-Mail: bnelkin@jhmi.edu.

NELL, GAY, pre-school educator; b. Kiowa, Kans., May 9, 1970; d. Francis Marion, Jr. and Anita Joyce Erikson; 1 child, Candice Christel. First Aid and CPR for adult/child/infant Am. Heart Assn., AED Am. Heart Assn.; Child Devel. Assoc. Tulsa CC, 2005, Early Care and Edn. level II U. Okla., 2005. Pre-sch. lead tchr. Tulsa Pub. Schs., 1998—99; asst. tchr. Child Devel. Learning Ctr. of Tulsa, 1999—2000; pre-sch. lead tchr. Tulsa Co. Headstart, 2000—05; lead tchr. Blossom Child Care Ctr., Owasso, 2005—; pre-sch. lead tchr. Owasso Pub. Schs., 2006—. Composer songs. Mem.: Assn. Childhood Edn. Internat. Republican. Baptist. Avocations: music, writing. Home: PO Box 54812 Tulsa OK 74155-0812

NELLIGAN, WILLIAM DAVID, III, professional association executive; b. Halstead, Kans., Aug. 10, 1926; s. William D. and Katherine (Roberts) N.; m. Dorothy Meyer, Aug. 17, 1952; children: Richard, Arthur, Mark. Student, U. Wichita, 1944-46; BS, U. Kans., 1949. Display advt. salesman Kansas City Star and Times, Mo., 1949-51; mgr. SW Kans. Extension Ctr. U. Kans., Garden City, 1951-55, exec. dir. dept. postgrad. med. edn. Sch. Medicine Kansas City, Kans., 1955-64; asst. to pres. Med. Coll. Ga., Augusta, 1964-65; exec. v.p. Am. Coll. Cardiology, Bethesda, Md., 1965-92; v.p. Marion Merrell DOW, Inc., Kansas City, Mo., 1992-94; exec. dir. Am. Soc. Nuc. Cardiology, Bethesda, 1994-2001, Cert. Bd. Nuclear Cardiology, Damascus, Md., 1996—2004, Soc. Cardiovasc. CT, Damascus, Md., 2005—06. Mem. Nat. Commn. Diabetes, 1975-76, adv. coun. Nat. Diabetes and Digestive and Kidney Diseases, 1987-88; bd. dirs. Arthur E. Hertzler Research Found., Halstead, Kans., 1961—. Recipient Man with a Heart award NY Cardiol. Soc., 1970, Presdl. citation Am. Coll. Cardiology, 1975, Disting. Svc. award Am. Coll. Cardiology, 1986, CLC Hall of Leaders award, 1986. Fellow Am. Coll. Cardiology; mem. AMA (citation of layman for disting. svc. 1993), Profl. Conv. Mgmt. Assn. (pres. 1974-75, Disting. Svc. award 1990), Am. Med. Writers Assn. (dir., exec. com., treas. 1970-78, Harold Swanberg Disting. Svc. award), Am. Soc. Assn. Execs. (cert., dir. 1975-78, sec.-treas. 1987-88, Key award 1984), Am. Assn. Med. Soc. Execs. (pres. 1986-87), Brit. Cardiac Soc. (hon.), Alliance for Continuing Med. Edn. (Pres.'s award 1994), Masons.

NELLIS, WILLIAM J., physicist; b. Chgo. BS in Physics, Loyola U. Chgo., 1963; MS in Physics, Iowa State U., 1965, PhD in Physics, 1968. Postdoctoral rsch. assoc. materials sci. divsn. Argonne Nat. Lab., 1968-70; asst. prof. physics Monmouth Coll., Ill., 1970-73; computational physicist Lawrence Livermore Nat. Lab., 1973-76, high-dynamic-pressure exptl. group, 1976—, group leader, 1978-81, assoc. H divsn. leader for experiments, 1981-93, head Ctr. High Pressure Scis. U. Calif. Inst. Geophysics and Planetary Physics, 1984-94. Vis. prof. physics U. Calif., San Diego, 1989; spkr. in field. Contbr. over 150 articles to profl. jours.; patentee in field. Fellow Am. Phys. Soc. (chmn. topical group on shock compression of condensed matter 1987, tutorial lectr. shock compression of solids 1990, Shock Compression Sci. award 1997); mem. AAAS, AIRAPT Internat. High Pressure Assn. (exec. com. 1987-90), Materials Rsch. Soc., Am. Geophysical Union, Hypervelocity Impact Soc. Office: Lawrence Livermore Nat Lab PO Box 808 Livermore CA 94551-0808

NELMS, DAVID W., finance company executive; b. 1961; m. Daryl Nelms; 3 children. BS in Mech. Engring., U. Fla.; MBA, Harvard Univ., 1987. Mgmt. positions through exec. v.p & vice-chmn. MBNA Am. Bank, 1991—98; pres., COO Discover Fin. Services div., Morgan Stanley, Riverwoods, Ill., 1998—2004; CEO Discover Fin. Services, Riverwoods, Ill., 2004—09, chmn., CEO, 2009—. Bd. dirs. Discover Fin. Services, 2004—. Mem. Chgo. Bd. Juvenile Diabetes Rsch. Found. Avocations: boating, fishing, water-skiing. Office: Discover Financial Services 2500 Lake Cook Rd Riverwoods IL 60015*

NELMS, MICHELLE, pre-school educator; d. Hobert Dillard Ogle; m. James Larry Nelms; 1 child, Rylee Michaela. MEd, State U., Dalton, 2001. Presch. tchr. First Presbyn. Ch., Dalton, 1998—2000; pre-k tchr. Murray County Schs., Chatsworth, Ga., 2000—. Choir mem. Carolyn Bapt. Ch., Dalton, 1992—. Mem.: NEA. Conservative. Baptist. Avocations: travel, scrapbooks.

NELON, ROBERT DALE, lawyer; b. Shawnee, Okla., Aug. 8, 1946; s. Cecil Eugene and Neata Madelyn (Fox) N.; m. Freddie Anne Tipton, Aug. 2, 1975; children: Lindsay Anne, Gregory Tipton. BA, Northwestern U., 1968; JD, U. Okla., 1971. Bar: Okla. 1971, U.S. Dist. Ct. (we., no. and ea. dists) Okla. 1971, U.S. Ct. Appeals (10th cir.) 1971, (8th cir.) 1992, (2d cir.) 1993, U.S. Ct. Appeals for the Armed Forces 1972, U.S. Supreme Ct. 1989. Law clk. Okla. Atty. Gen., Oklahoma City, 1966-70; mem. Andrews, Davis, Legg, Bixler, Milsten & Price, Oklahoma City, 1971-95, Hall Estill Hardwick Gable Golden & Nelson, Oklahoma City, 1995—. Served to capt. USMCR, 1972-74. Mem. ABA, Okla. Bar Assn., Am. Judicature Soc. Democrat. Methodist. Office: Hall Estill Hardwick Gable Golden & Nelson Chase Tower Suite 2900 100 N Broadway Ave Oklahoma City OK 73102-8865 Home Phone: 405-721-8501; Office Phone: 405-553-2828. Business E-Mail: bnelon@hallestill.com.

NELSEN, HART MICHAEL, sociologist, educator; b. Pipestone, Minn., 1938; s. Noah I. and Nova Nelsen; m. Anne Kusener, June 13, 1964; 1 dau., Jennifer. BA, U. No. Iowa, 1959, MA, 1963; M.Div., Princeton Theol. Sem., 1963; PhD (NSF faculty fellow), Vanderbilt U., 1972. Asst. prof. sociology Western Ky. U., Bowling Green, 1965-70, assoc. prof., 1970-73, Catholic U. Am., 1973-74, prof., 1974-81, chmn. dept. sociology, 1974-77, mem. Boys Town Ctr. for Study Youth Devel., 1974-81; prof. sociology La. State U., Baton Rouge, 1981-84, chmn. dept. sociology, head dept. rural sociology, 1981-84, coordinator rural sociology research, 1981-84; dean Coll. Liberal Arts Pa. State U., 1984-90, prof. sociology, 1984—2004, prof. emeritus, 2004—. Author: (with Anne K. Nelsen) Black Church in the Sixties, 1975; co-author: The Religion of Children, 1977, Religion and American Youth, 1976; editor: (with others) The Black Church in America, 1971; adv. editor: Sociol. Quar, 1976-82; assoc. editor: Sociol. Analysis, 1977-80, Rev. Religious Research, 1977-80, 84—, editor, 1980-84; mem. editorial bd.: Social Forces, 1983-86. Co-rec. sec. Capitol Hill Restoration Soc., 1979-80, v.p., 1980-81; mem. exec. bd. Lafitte Hills Assn., 1983-84; pres. Midtown Sq. Condo. Assn., 1996-99, treas., 1999-2001; v.p. Market Sq. West Condominium Assn., 2006-. Presbyterian Chs. grantee, 1966-69; NIMH co-grantee, 1969-72; Russell Sage Found. co-grantee, 1972-73; La. Gov.'s Commn. on Alcoholism and Drug Abuse grantee, 1982 Mem. Assn. Sociology Religion (exec. coun. 1974-76, 78-82, v.p. 1978-79, pres. 1980-81), Religious Rsch. Assn. (dir. 1977-80, pres.-elect 1985-86, pres. 1987-88), Soc. Sci. Study Religion (coun. 1981-83, exec. sec. 1984-87), Am. Sociol. Assn., So. Sociol. Soc. (chmn. membership com. 1983-85), AAAS (rep. 1984-2000). Mem. United Ch. Of Christ. Home: 106 Copano Bay Cove Georgetown TX 78635-5358 Personal E-mail: hmnelsen@mindspring.com.

NELSON, ALICE CARLSTEDT, retired nursing educator; b. Strandquist, Minn., May 25, 1921; d. Peter Gustaf and Florence Olivia (Berg) Carlstedt; m. Armour Halstead Nelson June 5, 1954 (dec. Dec. 1993). RN, Bethesda Hosp., St. Paul, Minn., 1944; BS, Augustana Coll., Rock Island, Ill., 1948; MA, U. Chgo., 1954. RN, Minn., Ill., N.D., Iowa, Calif.; cert. lactation educator, cert. lifetime cmty. coll. tchr. Ob nurse Moline Luth. Hosp., Ill., 1943—44; asst. night supr. Bethesda Hosp., St. Paul, 1944—45; with Army Nurse Corps, 1945—46; ob nurse Miller Hosp., St. Paul, 1947; nurse intermediate grade Wadsworth VA Hosp., LA, 1947—48; head nurse Crippled Children's Sch., Jamestown, ND, 1948—50; head nurse Sch. Handicapped Children U. Iowa, Iowa City, 1950—51; clin. instr. Chgo. Lying-In Hosp., 1951—54, St. Luke's Hosp., Fargo, ND, 1954—60; tchr., supr. lab. pre-sch. N.D. State U., Fargo, 1962—64; coll. health svc. Calif. Luth. U., Thousand Oaks, 1968—74, faculty dept. nursing, 1982—85; pvt. duty nurse Thousand Oaks, 1976—81; ret., 1990. State sec. League for Nursing, N.D., 1956-64; team mem. preparation Nat. Achievement Test in Nursing of Children, NY, 1959 Author: Post-War Europe Through The Eyes of Youth, 2002; editor: The Conquest of Chicago, 2004; contbr. articles to profl. jours. Various offices including Ch. Coun. Holy Trinity Luth. Ch., Thousand Oaks, Calif., 1964-90; founding bd. dirs. Honey Tree Pre-Sch., Thousand Oaks, Calif., 1972; mem. task force on aging S.W. Pacific Luth. Synod Office, LA, 1979; parent-aide, hotline, etc. Child Abuse & Neglect, Ventura County, Calif., 1979-82; bd. dirs. La Serena Retirement Ctr., Thousand Oaks, Calif., 1985-88; mem. ch. choir Salemsborg Luth. Ch., Smolan, Kans., 1990-2000, mem. ch. coun., 1996-2000, tchr. adult classes, 1996-99 Recipient award writing contests Am. Jour. Nursing, 1969, Calif. Nurse, 1987, Outstanding Vol. award Ventura County Child Abuse & Neglect, 1982. Mem. Bethany Bibliophiles Book Club, Writer's Cramp Group Democrat. Avocations: travel, reading, writing.

NELSON, ALISON R., lawyer; BS in Criminal Justice, Mich. State U., 1987, JD, 1990. Atty., environ. Ford Motor Co., Dearborn, Mich., mng. counsel, consumer litig., 1994—. Former asst. gen. counsel Mich. State Coun. NAACP. Mem.: State Bar Mich., Nat. Bar Inst. (bd. dir., Presdl. award), Wolverine Bar Assn. (pres. 2000—01, Trailblazer award), ABA (bd. govs. 2005—08, Gavel Awards Com.), Legal Aid and Defenders Assn. Mich. Office: Consumer Litig Ford Motor Co American Rd Dearborn MI 48121-1899 Office Phone: 313-322-3000.

NELSON, ALLEN F., proxy solicitation company executive; b. Portland, Oreg., Oct. 17, 1943; s. Roy August and Mildred Mary (Jensen) N.; m. Johanna Molenaar, Dec. 8, 1973. BS, U. Iowa, 1965, MA, 1968. V.p. Shareholder Comm. Corp., NYC, 1970-72; v.p. Trafalgar Capital Corp., NYC, 1973; pres. Nelson, Lasky & Co., Inc., NYC, 1974-76; account exec. Corp. Comm., Inc., Seattle, 1976-77; pres. Allen Nelson & Co., Inc., Seattle, 1977—. Mem. CFA Inst., Nat. Investor Rels. Inst., Nat. Security Traders Assn., Practicing Law Inst. (U.S. Presdl. rank rev. bd.), Pub. Rels. Soc. Am., Soc. Corp. Secs. & Governance Profls., Can. Corp. Secs., Rainier Club, Montana Club, Vancouver Club. Home: 4400 Beach Dr SW Seattle WA 98116-3937 Office: Allen Nelson & Co Inc PO Box 16157 Seattle WA 98116-0157 Office Phone: 206-938-5783.

NELSON, ALLYSON LYN, lawyer; b. Honolulu, June 16, 1976; d. Craig E. and Pamela K. Nelson. BA in Polit. Sci. and Russian, U. Ala., 1998; JD, U. Miss. Sch. Law, 2002. Bar: U.S. Ct. Appeals (5th cir.) 2002, U.S. Dist. Ct. (no. and so. dists.) Miss. 2002, Miss. Supreme Ct. 2002. Legislative intern U.S. Senator Richard Shelby, Washington, 1996—96; law clk. U.S. Dept. of Justice, Hon. Charles E. Pazar, Memphis, 2001—01; atty. and com. counsel Miss. Ho. of Representatives, Jackson, Miss., 2002—03; assoc. atty. Rushing & Guice, PLLC, Biloxi, Miss., 2003—04; asst. dist. atty. Office of the Hinds County Dist. Atty., Jackson, 2004—07; profl. fellow Alfa Fellowship Program, Moscow, 2007—08; cons., advisor Kurdistan Regional Govt., Iraq, 2008—. Mem. Sexual Assault Response Team, Jackson, Miss., 2004—07, Hinds County Multi-Disciplinary Child Abuse Rev. Team, Jackson, Miss., 2004—07. Recipient Outstanding Student award, Oil and Gas Law, 2001, Energy Law, 2001; scholar Heidelberg & Woodliff Excellence award, 2001, Study in Prague, Czech Republic scholar, The Fund for Am. Studies, 1997, Scholarship for study in Russia, U.S. Dept. of State, 1999, Jeffery P. Reynolds, P.A. Environ. Law scholar, 2001, Miss. Bar Found., 2000; Strong scholarship for Outstanding Freshman in Russian, 1995. Mem.: ABA, Jour. of Nat. Security Law, Miss. Bar Assn., Hinds County Bar Assn., Miss. Prosecutors Assn., Nat. Dist. Attorneys Assn., Dobro Slovo, Phi Delta Phi, Gamma Beta Phi. Avocation: travel, politics, history, government, foreign languages. Personal E-mail: allyson.nelson@gmail.com.

NELSON, ALONDRA R., social sciences educator; b. Bethesda, Md., Apr. 22, 1968; d. Robert Samuel and Delores Yvonne Nelson; BA magna cum laude, U. Calif., San Diego, 1994; PhD, NYU, 2003. Trustee dissertation fellow Skidmore Coll., Saratoga Springs, NY, 2000—01; Ann E. Plato fellow Trinity Coll., Hartford, Conn., 2001—02; lectr. Yale U., New Haven, 2002—03, asst. prof. sociology and African Am. studies, 2003—. Co-editor: Technicolor: Race, Technology and Everyday Life, 2001. Fellow W.E.B. DuBois Inst., Harvard U., 2006; Career Enhancement fellow, Woodrow Wilson Nat. Fellowship Found., Andrew S. Mellon Found., 2006—07, Postdoc. fellowship, Ford Found., 2007. Mem.: Soc. for the Social Studies of Sci., Am. Studies Assn., Am. Sociol. Assn., Phi Beta Kappa. Office: Yale Univ Dept African Am Studies PO Box 203388 New Haven CT 06520-3388 Home Phone: 212-939-9330; Office Phone: 203-432-1170. Business E-Mail: alondra.nelson@yale.edu.

NELSON, ANNE, media consultant, educator, writer; b. Fort Sill, Okla., Nov. 26, 1954; married; 2 children. BA, Yale U. Reporter Central Am., 1980—83; dir. Com. to Protect Journalists, 1988—92; dir. Internat. Programs, Graduate Sch. Journalism Columbia U., 1995—2003; adj. assoc. prof., Internat. Media Sch. Internat. and Public Affairs, 2005—. Editor (and co-author): Twenty Years and Forty Days, 1985; author: (book) Murder Under Two Flags, 1989, (screenplays) The Guys, 2002, (plays), 2001, Paprika, 2005, Dependence Day, 2006, Savages, 2006, Petra, 2007, Red Orchestra: The Story of the Berlin Underground and the Circle of Friends Who Resisted Hittler, 2009, numerous essays, articles, and reports. Mem. editl. bd. Episcopal New Yorker, 2004—; bd. dir. Bridging the Gap Arab-American Dialogue, 2006. Recipient Audie award for Best Recorded Play, 2003, Livingston award for Internat. Reporting, 1989, Thomas More Storke award, 1989; Guggenheim fellow, 2005—06, New Harmony Dramatists fellow, 2004, 2005. Mem.: Coun. Fgn. Relation. Independent. Protestant. Mailing: 202 Riverside Dr 5A New York NY 10025-7265 Home Phone: 212-666-9909. Personal E-mail: anne.nelson@gmail.com. Business E-Mail: an115@columbia.edu.

NELSON, ARDINE, photographer; BS in Art Edn., Northern Ill. U., DeKalb, MA in Sculpture/Photography; MFA in Photography, U. Iowa City. Assoc. prof. art Ohio State U. Fellow Ohio Arts Coun., Greater Columbus Arts Coun., 1990, John Simon Guggenheim Meml. Found., 2008. Office: Ohio State U Dept Art Haskett Hall 303C 128 N Oval Mall Columbus OH 43210 Office Phone: 614-292-9683. Office Fax: 614-292-1674. E-mail: nelson.13@osu.edu.*

NELSON, ARLEEN BRUCE, social worker; b. Loma Linda, Calif., Oct. 25, 1926; d. Delbert Francis and Sarah Enns Bruce; m. A. Gordon Nelson, Oct. 29, 1948 (div. Sept. 1976); children: Gregory Bruce, Mark Andrew, Heidi, Scott Bradford. BA, UCLA, 1948; MSW, U. Wash., 1975. Cert. ACSW 1979, BCSW 1987, MSW Wash., 1989, LCSW Wash., 2001. Case worker L.A. County DPSS, LA, 1949—50, 1958—61, child protective Svc. Supr., 1966—69; dir. Manson Migrant Daycare Ctr., Manson, Wash., 1970—72; I and A coord. Sr. Svc., Seattle, 1975—78; co-dir., psychotherapist Soc. Workers N. W., Seattle, 1979—95; coord., HIV-AIDS Seattle Counseling Svc. for Sexual Minorities, 1986—94, psychotherapist, supr., 1994—2000, intern supr., 1993—96; aux. faculty U. Wash., 1995—2001; clin. cons. Seattle Counseling Svcs., 2000—; intern supr. Seattle Counseling Svc. for Sexual Minorities, 2002—. Edn. com. Wash. Soc. of Clin. Soc. Work, Seattle, 1986. Co-founder Nat. Parents and Friends of Gays and Lesbians; dir. PNW-Mountain Region Nat. PFLAG, multi states, 1981—83, v.p., 1983—89; gay and lesbian advocate multiple T.V. appearances, 1978—85; task force for gays and lesbians Ch. Coun. of Greater Seattle, 1977—80; bd. mem. The Dorian Group, Seattle, 1980; co-founder Seattle Chap. Parents and Friends of Lesbians and Gays, Seattle, 1979; pres. Seattle Chap. PFLAG, 1993—94; Bd. Ch. and soc. PNW Conf. United Meth. Ch., Wash., 1970—82, commn. of race and religion Wash., 1982—88. Recipient The Dorian Award, Dorian Group, 1982, 1998 Cmty. Leadership Award, Greater Seattle Bus. Assn., 1999, Founders Award, Seattle PFLAG, 1989, Nat. PFLAG, 1991, Award for Dedication and Svc., Seattle Gay Clinic, 1994, Award of Merit for Long Svc. to the Trans-gendered Cmty., Ingersol Gender Ctr., 2000. Mem.: Nat Assn. of Soc. Workers, Wash. Chap. NASW. Democrat. Avocations: travel, reading. Office: Seattle Counseling Svc 1216 Pine St Seattle WA 98101 Office Phone: 206-323-1768. Business E-Mail: arleenn@seattlecounsel.org.

NELSON, ARTHUR HUNT, real estate company executive; b. Kansas City, Mo., May 21, 1923; s. Carl Ferdinand and Hearty (Brown) N.; m. Eleanor Thomas, Dec. 27, 1954; children: Carl F., Frances, Pamela. AB, U. Kans., 1943; JD, Harvard U., 1949. Bar: Mass. 1949. Staff radiation lab. MIT, 1943-44; sr. engr., cons. Raytheon Mfg. Co., Boston, 1948-52; pvt. practice Boston, 1949; v.p., treas., dir. Gen. Electronic Labs., Inc., Cambridge, Mass., 1951-64, chmn. bd., 1959-63; treas., dir. Sci. Electronics, Inc., Cambridge, 1955-64, Assocs. for Internat. Rsch., Inc., Cambridge, 1954—2007, pres., 1968—2007; treas., dir. Victor Realty Devel., Inc., Cambridge, 1959-76, pres., 1972-76, gen. ptnr., 1976—, Prospect Hill Exec. Office Park, Waltham, Mass., 1977—; chmn. Nelson Cos., 1990—, Cambridge Devel. Lab., Cambridge, 1994—2001. Bd. dirs. Internat. Data Group, Inc., Sterling Bank. Pres., trustee Tech. Edn. Rsch. Ctrs., Inc., 1965—; trustee Winsor Sch., Boston, 1978-88, treas., 1978-82; bd. dirs. Charles River Mus. Industry, Waltham, 1986—, pres. 1994—, pres., dir. 128 Bus. Coun. Inc., 1987—, Hist. Waltham Inc., 1996—, Am. Computer Fedn. Inc., 1996—, Charles River Pub. Internet Ctr. Inc., 1996—. Ensign USNR, 1944-46. Recipient Ernst & Young New Eng. Master Entrepreneur of Yr. award, 1999. Mem. ABA, Mass. Bar Assn., Boston Bar Assn., Boston Computer Soc. (bd. dirs. 1985-97, chmn. 1994-97), Greater Boston C. of C., Harvard Club Boston, Beta Theta Pi, Phi Beta Kappa, Sigma Xi. Home: 75 Robin Rd Weston MA 02493-2436 Office: 75 3rd Ave Waltham MA 02451-7528

NELSON, BARBARA J., public policy professor, former dean; b. Ohio; d. Bernard James and Betty-Jane (James) N. BA, Ohio State U., 1971, MA in Polit. Sci., 1975, PhD in Polit. Sci., 1976. Policy rsch. assoc. Mershon Ctr. Pub. Policy, Columbus, Ohio, 1974-76; asst. prof. Princeton U., NJ, 1976-83; assoc. prof. Hubert H. Humphrey Inst. U. Minn., Mpls., 1983-89, program dir. MA program, 1987-90, dir. ctr. women & pub. policy, 1984-94, prof. Hubert H.Humphrey Inst., 1983-94; v.p., disting. prof. pub. policy Radcliffe Coll., Cambridge, Mass., 1994-96; founder, prin. investigator The Concord Project UCLA Sch. Pub. Affairs (formerly Sch. Pub. Policy & Social Rsch.), LA, 1993—, dean, prof. pub. policy, 1996—2008, prof. pub. policy, 2008—. Bd. trustees Ctr. Women in Pub., Mpls., 1984-98. Author: Making an Issue of Child Abuse, 1984, American Women in Politics, 1984; co-editor: Wage Justice, 1989, Women and Politics Worldwide, 1995. Bd. trustees Radcliffe Coll., 1994-96; mem. Minn. Supreme Ct.'s Commn., 1987-88; advisor Govt. of Sweden Parliamentary Commn. Women & Democracy. W.K. Kellogg Found. grantee, 1994-97, Ford Found. grantee, 1993-97, Hewlett Ctr. Conflict Resolution grantee, 1988, 93. Mem. Am. Polit. Sci. Assn. (bd. trustees 1988-98), Assn. Pub. Policy Analysis & Mgmt. Office: UCLA Sch Pub Affairs 3250 Public Affairs Bldg 337 Charles E Young Dr, E Los Angeles CA 90095-1656 Office Phone: 310-206-7979. Fax: 310-206-5773. E-mail: nelson@spa.ucla.edu.

NELSON, (EARL) BEN(JAMIN), United States Senator from Nebraska, former governor, lawyer; b. McCook, Nebr., May 17, 1941; s. Benjamin Earl and Birdella Ruby (Henderson) N.; m. Diane C. Gleason, Feb. 22, 1980; children from a previous marriage: Sarah Jane, Patrick James; stepchildren: Kevin Michael Gleason, Christine Marie Gleason. BA in Philosophy, U. Nebr., 1963, MA in Philosophy, 1966, JD, 1970; LLD (hon.), Creighton U., 1992, Peru State Coll., 1993. Bar: Nebr. 1970. Instr. dept. philosophy U. Nebr., Lincoln, 1963-65; supr. Dept. Ins. State of Nebr., Lincoln, 1965-72; dir. ins., 1975-76; asst. gen. counsel, gen. counsel, sec., v.p. The Ctrl. Nat. Ins. Group Omaha, 1972-75, exec. v.p., 1976-77, pres., 1978-81, CEO, 1980-81; of counsel Kennedy, Holland, DeLacy & Svoboda, Omaha, 1985-90, Lumson, Dugan and Murray, Omaha, 1999—2001; gov. State of Nebr., Lincoln, 1991—99; US Senator from Nebr., 2000—. Com. rules and adminstrn. US Senate, com. commerce, sci. and transp., com. armed services, com. agr., nutrition and forestry. Co-chmn. Carter/Mondale re-election campaign, Nebr., 1980; chair Nat. Edn. Goals Panel, 1992-94; co-founder Gov.'s Ethanol Coalition, chair, 1991, 94; pres. Coun. of State Govs., 1994; bd. trustee Wesley House Found., Omaha, 1970-76. Recipient Friends of Nebr. Broadcasters award Nebr. Broadcasters Assn., 1993, Disting. Eagle award Nat. Eagle Scout Assn., 1994; named Amb. Plenipotentiary, 1993. Mem. ABA, Nat. Assn. Independent Insurers, Nat. Assn. Ins. Commrs. (exec. v.p. 1982-85), Nebr. Bar Assn., Consumer Credit Ins. Assn., Midwestern Govs. Assn. (chair 1994), Western Govs. Assn. (vice chair 1994, chair 1995), Happy Hollow Club, Omaha Club, Hillcrest Country Club. Democrat. Methodist. Avocations: reading, hunting, fishing. Office: US Senate 720 Hart Office Bldg Washington DC 20510 also: District Office Ste 205 7602n Pacific St Omaha NE 68114 Office Phone: 202-224-6551, 402-391-3411. Office Fax: 202-224-0012, 402-391-4725.*

NELSON, BETTE STURR, secondary school educator; b. Bethesda, Md., Nov. 19, 1947; d. Henry Dixon and Mildred Rogers Sturr; children: Sarah Elizabeth Turner, Elissa Marie Noble. BA in History and English, U. Calif., Santa Barbara, 1969; MA in Counseling, Ohio State U., Columbus, 1973. Cert. tchr. Edn. Dept., Calif., 1970. Tchr., counselor Kalamazoo Juvenile Home, 1972—75; tchr. Thomas Jefferson H.S., Fairfax, Va., 1976—84; reading tchr. Bloomfield Schs., NJ, 1987—88; tchr. Mt. Diablo Unified Schs., Concord, Calif., 1989—. Gate chmn. Mt. Diablo Schs., 2004—. Mem. vestry term concluded Episc. Ch., Martinez, Calif., 2005—07, Calif. League Mid. Schs. Outstanding Tchr., 2007—. Recipient Nat. Honor Roll Outstanding Educator award, Nat. Coun. Tchrs. English, 2006; named Tchr. of Year, Calif. League Mid. Sch., 2007—08. Mem.: NEA (assoc.), Calif. Tchrs. Assn. (corr.), NCTE (life; v.p. 1980—81, named Tchr. of Yr. 1984), Kappa Delta Pi (life). Democrat. Episcopalian. Avocations: travel, swimming, acting, theater. Office: Sequoia Middle School 265 Boyd Road Pleasant Hill CA 94523 Office Fax: 925-946-9063. Personal E-mail: bettnel@comcast.net. Business E-Mail: nelsonb@mdusd.k-12.ca.us.

NELSON, BILL (CLARENCE WILLIAM NELSON), United States Senator from Florida; b. Miami, Fla., Sept. 29, 1942; s. C.W. and Nannie (Merle) N.; m. Grace H. Cavert, Feb. 19, 1972; children: C. William, Nan Ellen. BA, Yale U., 1965; JD, U. Va., 1968. Bar: Fla. 1968. Atty. Nelson, Normile and Dettmer, Melbourne, Fla., 1970-79, Maguire, Vorrhis and Wells, Pa., 1991—94; mem. Fla. Ho. of Reps., 1972-78, US Congress, 1979-91; payload specialist 1 Space Shuttle Columbia seventh orbital mission, 1986; treas. State of Fla., Tallahassee, 1995—2000; US Senator from Fla., 2001—; vice chmn. Dem. Senatorial Campaign com., 2000—. Mem. com. armed services US Senate, com. budget, com. commerce, sci., transp., com. fgn. relations, spl. com. aging. Author: Mission: An American Congressman's Voyage to Space, 1988. Bd. dirs. Am. Astronautical Soc.; mem. Fla. Space Bus. Roundtable. Served to capt. USAR, 1965—75, served with US Army, 1968—70. Recipient Public Svc. award, Nat. Crystallography Assn., 1988, Debus award, Nat. Space Club, Fla. Com., 1993, President's award, Fla. State Conf. NAACP, 2001. Mem.: Fla. Bar Assn., Brevard County Bar Assn., Assn. Space Explorers. Democrat. Episcopalian. Office: US Senate 716 Hart Sen Office Bldg Rm 716 Washington DC 20510 Address: Landmark Ctr Two Ste 410 225 E Robinson St Orlando FL 32801 Office Phone: 202-224-5274, 407-872-7161. Office Fax: 202-228-2183, 407-872-7165.*

NELSON, BILL, broadcast executive; b. 1949; CPA. Audit supr. Ernst & Young, NYC, 1975—79; dir. external reporting & risk mgmt. Time Inc., 1979—84; v.p., asst. contr. HBO, 1984—85, v.p., contr., 1985—91, sr. v.p., CFO, 1991—94, exec. v.p. fin., info., ops. tech. & bus. affairs, 1994—2002, COO, 2002—07, chmn., CEO, 2007—. Served in US Army. Mem.: NY State Soc. Certified Pub. Accountants, Am. Inst. Certified Pub. Accountants. Office: HBO 100 Ave of the Americas New York NY 10036 Office Phone: 212-484-8000.*

NELSON, BRUCE (MURRAY BRUCE NELSON), former consumer products company executive; m. LaVaun Nelson; children: Suzanne, Connor. Grad., ID State U., 1968. Sr. mgmt. positions Boise Cascade, 1968-90; pres., CEO BT Office Products USA, 1991-94, Viking, 1995—98; pres. Office Depot Inc., Delray Beach, Fla., 1998—2000, CEO, 2000—04, chmn., 2001—04. Home: 750 Ocean Royal Way Apt 605 Juno Beach FL 33408-1312

NELSON, CALEB EDWARD, law educator; b. Cleve., Sept. 20, 1966; s. David Aldrich and Mary Dickson Nelson; m. Elizabeth Kristol, Aug. 11, 1991; children: Maxwell David, Katherine Ellen. AB, Harvard U., 1988; JD, Yale U., 1993. Bar: Ohio 1993. Mng. editor and other editl. positions The Pub. Interest, Washington, 1988—90; law clk. to judge Stephen F. Williams U.S. Ct. of Appeals for the D.C. Circuit, Washington, 1993—94; law clk. to justice Clarence Thomas U.S. Supreme Ct., Washington, 1994—95; assoc. litig. dept. Taft, Stettinius & Hollister, Cin., 1995—98; prof. U. Va. Sch. Law, Charlottesville, 1998—. Vis. prof. Harvard Law Sch., 2006. Contbr. articles to profl. jours. Recipient Paul M. Bator award, Federalist Soc., 2006; named Winner Scholarly Papers Competition, Assn. Am. Law Schs., 2000. Mem.: Phi Beta Kappa. Republican. Office: Univ Virginia School Law 580 Massie Rd Charlottesville VA 22903-1789

NELSON, CALEB P., urologist, educator; BA, Dartmouth Coll., Hanover, NH, 1992; MD, Duke U., Durham, NC, 1997; MPH, U. Mich., Ann Arbor, 2003. Cert. urologist Am. Bd. Urology, 2008. Instr. surgery Harvard Med. Sch., Boston, 2006—; asst. urology Children's Hosp., Boston, 2006—. Contbr. scientific papers. Mem.: Am. Urol. Assn. Office: Children's Hosp Boston 300 Longwood Ave Boston MA 02115 Business E-Mail: caleb.nelson@childrens.harvard.edu.

NELSON, CARL ALFRED, author, international business educator, Former Captain USN; b. Pitts., Oct. 11, 1930; s. Alfred Helge Nelson and Isabel Alice (Younger) Newbauer; m. Barbara Long, June 2, 1956 (dec.); children: Jennifer, Allison, Monica; m. Dolores Hansen, Apr. 8, 2006. BS, U.S. Naval Acad., 1956; MS, U.S. Naval Post Grad., 1967; student, US Naval War Coll., 1970; DBA, U.S. Internat. U. Alliance, 1984. Enlisted USN, 1949, advanced through grades to capt., 1956-82; comdg. officer USS Worden CG-18, 4 others, Four Tours Duty VN War; v.p., dir. AMMEX Cons., Chula Vista, Calif., 1985-86; pres. Global Bus. & Trade, San Diego, 1982—2004. Prof. Calif. Internat. Bus. U.; lectr. in field. Author: Your Own Import-Export Business: Winning the Trade Game, 1988, Global Success, 1990, Managing Globally; A Complete Guide to Competing Worldwide, 1993, Protocol for Profit, 1998, International Business, 1998, The Advisor (Co-van), 1998, Exporting, 1999, Secret Players, 2003, Madam President And The Admiral, 2008, Import-Export: How To Take Your Business Across Borders, 4th edit., 2009; contbr. articles to profl. jours.; contbr. short stories to popular mags. Co-founder, Chula Vista Boys and Girls Club; pres. Chula Vista Boys Club, 1988; exec. bd. dirs. Calif. Dem. Party, 1992-97, pres. S.D. Writers/Editors Guild, 1998-2000; bd. dir. Vietnam Vets. America; Econ. Devel. Commr., Chula Vista, 2000-06. Decorated Legion of Merit, Bronze Star (V), Air medals, combat commendations; named Outstanding Alumni of Yr., U.S. Internat. U., 1989, Disting. Grad. Carrick HS, Pltts., 2006; recipient Disting. Global Educator award Calif. Sch. Internat. Mgmt., 2003. Mem. Authors's Guild of Am., Chula Vista C. of C. (dir. 1984-90, Internat. Focus award 1988), Optimist Club, 50+ Yr. Mason (32 deg.). Home: 1385 Don Carlos Ct Chula Vista CA 91910-7130 Office Phone: 619-421-9094. E-mail: canelson56@cox.net.

NELSON, CARL ROGER, retired lawyer; b. Gowrie, Iowa, Dec. 26, 1915; s. Carl Helge and Inez Olivia (West) N.; m. Elizabeth Boswell Campbell, Apr. 27, 1946; children: Thomas C., Nancy L. AB, Grinnell Coll., 1937; MA, Columbia, 1938, LLB, 1941. Bar: N.Y. 1941, D.C. 1947, U.S. Supreme Ct. 1947. Law clk. to Chief Justice Stone, 1941-42; Washington asso. firm Root, Ballantine, Harlan, Bushby & Palmer, 1946-51; mem. firm Purcell & Nelson, Washington, 1951-80, Reavis & McGrath, 1980-83, Nelson Thurston Jones & Blouch, 1984-86. Mem. Adminstrv. Conf. U.S., 1967—73. Served to capt. AUS, 1942-46. Fellow Am. Bar Found.; mem. ABA (mem. ho. dels. 1964-66, mem. coun. 1960-66, chmn. sect. adminstrv. law 1963-64), Chevy Chase (Md.) Club, Lawyers Club (Washington), Met. Club (Washington), Phi Beta Kappa. Mem. United Ch. of Christ. Personal E-mail: nelsoncrn@comcast.net.

NELSON, CAROL KOBUKE, bank executive; m. Ken Nelson; 2 children. BA in fin. magna cum laude, Seattle U., Wash., 1978, MBA, 1984; attended grad. sch. Credit & Fin. Mgmt., Santa Clara U., Calif. With SeaFirst Bank (now Bank of Am.); sr. v.p., northern regional consumer exec. Bank of America; pres., CEO Cascade Bank, Everett, Wash., 2001—; pres., COO Cascade Fin. Corp., Everett, Wash., 2001—02, pres., CEO, 2002—. Exec. adv. bd. Albers Sch. Bus. and Economics Seattle U. Chair bd. dirs. United Way, Snohomish County; bd. dirs. Boys and Girls Club, Snohomish County, Econ. Devel. Coun., Snohomish County; adv. bd. Leadership Snohomish County; bd. pub. facilities dist. Washington States Baseball Stadium. Named one of 25 Women to Watch, US Banker Mag., 2003, 2008, 25 Most Powerful Women in Banking, 2004, 2005, 2007. Mem.: Wash. Bankers Assn. (bd. dirs.), Wash. Fin. League (bd. dirs.). Office: Cascade Financial Corp 2828 Colby Ave Everett WA 98201*

NELSON, CAROLYN, state legislator; b. Madison, Wis., Oct. 8, 1937; m. Gilbert Nelson; 3 children. BS in Math & Music, ND State U., 1958, MS in Edn., 1960. Lectr. ND State U., 1968—2002, sr. lectr. emeritus, 2002—; mem. Dist. 45 ND House of Reps., 1986—88, mem. Dist. 21, 1992—94, ND State Senate, 1994—. Mem. N.D. State Investment Bd., 1989-92. Mem. Bd. Edn., Fargo, N.D., 1985-91, pres., 1989-90; trustee N.D. Tchrs. Fund for Retirement, 1985-92, pres., 1990-92; mem. N.D. PTA, pres., 1978-81, N.D. Women's and Children's Caucus. Recipient Merit Svc. award Gamma Phi Beta, 1978, 90, Legis. Voices award Children's Caucus, 1995; named Legislator of Yr., N.D. Bar Assn., 2000, N.D. Student Assn., 2001. Mem. LWV, Am. Guild English Handbell Ringers (area chmn. 1982-84, nat. bd. dirs. 1982-90), Nat. Fedn. Music Clubs (bd. dirs. 2003—, legis. chair 2003-07, regional v.p. 2005—07, 1st v.p. 2007-), N.D. Fedn. Music Clubs (life, pres. 1997-2001, nat. bd. mem. 2005—, legis. chair, Rose Fay Thomas fellow 2001), Gamma Phi Beta, Phi Kappa Phi, Sigma Alpha Iota. Democrat. Methodist. Office: State Capitol 600 E Blvd Bismarck ND 58505 also: One 2d St S 5-402 Fargo ND 58103-1959 Office Phone: 701-328-3373, 701-235-5161. Business E-Mail: cnelson@nd.gov.*

NELSON, CAROLYN, auditor; d. Milan and Betty Miller Wiley; m. Dareld Nelson; children: Jennifer, Natalie. MBA, Pitts. State U., Kans., 1982. CPA State Bd. Accountancy, Minn., 1992. Internal auditor Phillips Petroleum Co., Bartlesville, Okla., 1982—89; sr. internal auditor Minnegasco, Mpls., 1989—94. Cmty. leader Labette County 4-H, Altamont, Kans., 2002—08; treas. United Meth. Ch., Altamont, 2001—. Recipient Golden Apple award, Phi Theta Kappa-Eta Gamma Chpt. Mem.: AICPA, Midwest Economics Assn. Office: Coffeyville CC 400 West 11th Coffeyville KS 67337 Business E-Mail: carolynn@coffeyville.edu.

NELSON, CHARLES J., academic administrator, diplomat, consultant; b. Mich., Mar. 5, 1920; m. Maureen Tinsley (dec.). AB, Lincoln U., 1942; MPA, NYU, 1948; postgrad., Boston U., 1960, Oxford U., Eng., 1960. Research assoc. state govt., 1949-52; program asst. MSA Manila, 1952-53; pub. adminstrn. analyst FOA, 1953-54, pub. adminstrn. specialist, 1954-55; dep. spl. asst. for community devel. ICA, 1955-57; chief community devel. adviser Tehran, 1958; community devel. adviser Dept. State, 1960, chief Africa-Latin Am. br., 1960-61, detailed African br., 1960; assoc. dir. Office Program Devel. and Coordination PC, Washington, 1961-63; dir. Office Devel. Resources, AID, 1963-64, dir. North African affairs, 1964-66; dep. mission dir. Addis Ababa, 1966-68; mission dir. Dar es Salaam, 1968-71; ambassador to Botswana, Lesotho and Swaziland, 1971-74; mission dir. counsellor internat. devel. AID, Nairobi, Kenya, 1974-78; adminstr. program in internat. studies Sch. Human Ecology, Howard U., 1978-81. Mem. Overseas Devel. Coun.; chair Mayor's Internat. Adv. Council; bd. dirs. Nations Capital council Girl Scouts U.S.A., 1981-87, also mem. retention extension outreach com.; bd. dirs. D.C. Council Internat. Programs, 1981-87; v.p. nat. bd. dirs. Sister Cities Internat.; mem. U.S. D.C.-Beijing Friendship Council; mem. Thai-Am. Assn. Coun. Am. Ambassadors, U.S.-Dakar Capital Cities Friendship Council; former co-chmn. Soc. for Internat. Devel., Africa Roundtable. Served to capt. AUS, 1942-47. Mem. Georgetown Citizens Assn., Voice of Informed Cmty. Expression, Smithsonian Instn., Overseas Devel. Coun., The Atlantic Coun., Am. Polit. Sci. Assn., UN Assn., Diplomatic and Counselor Officers Ret., Friends of Ethiopia, Univ. Club (Washington). Address: 2853 Ontario Rd NW Apt 111 Washington DC 20009-2232

NELSON, CHARLOTTE BOWERS, retired public administrator; b. Bristol, Va., June 28, 1931; d. Thaddeus Ray and Ruth Nelson (Moore) Bowers; m. Gustav Carl Nelson, June 1, 1957; children: Ruth Elizabeth, David Carl, Thomas Gustav. BA summa cum laude, Duke U., 1954; MA, Columbia U., 1961; MPA, Drake U., 1983. Instr. Beaver Coll., 1957-58, Drake U., Des Moines, 1975-82; office mgr. LWV of Iowa, Des Moines, 1975-82; exec. asst. Iowa Dept. Human Svcs., Des Moines, 1983-85; exec. dir. Iowa Commn. on Status of Women Dept. Human Rights, Des Moines, 1985—2007; pub. adminstr. State of Iowa, 1983—2007. Bd. dirs., pres. LWV, Beloit, Wis., 1960-74; bd. dirs. LWV, Des Moines, 1974-82, Westminster House, Des Moines, 1988-97, pres. 1996-97. Recipient Gov.'s Golden Dome award as Leader of the Yr., 2002, Essential Support award Iowa Coalition Against Sexual Assault, 2007, Time To Educate award Iowa Coalition Against Domestic Violence, 2009; named Visionary Woman, Young Women's Resource Ctr., 1994. Mem. Am. Soc. Pub. Adminstrn. (mem. exec. coun. 1984-92, 98-99, past pres., Mem. of Yr. 1993), Phi Beta Kappa, Pi Alpha Alpha. Home: 1141 Cummins Cir Des Moines IA 50311-2113 E-mail: nelson514@mchsi.com.

NELSON, CHRIS A., Secretary of State, South Dakota; b. Mitchell, SD, Aug. 18, 1964; m. Penny Pfeifle; 1 child, Rebekah; 1 stepchild. BS in Animal Sci., SD State U., 1987. Self-employed farmer/rancher, 1981—; UCC supr. State of SD, Pierre, 1987—89, state election supr., 1989—2002, asst. sec. state, 2002—03, sec. state, 2003—. Nat. Govs. Assn. rep. US Election Assistance Commn. Bd. Advs., 2005. Recipient Excellence in SD Mcpl. Govt. award, SD Mcpl. League, 2003, Hazeltine/Taylor award, SD Kids Voting, 2004. Republican. Office: Office Sec State 500 E Capitol Ave Ste 204 Pierre SD 57501 Office Phone: 605-773-3537. Fax: 605-773-6580.

NELSON, CHRISTOPHER GRANT, dermatologist; b. Peoria, Ill., Feb. 11, 1946; s. Grant Leonard and Shirlee Ann (Brunnenmeyer) N.; m. Mary Jo Donnelly, June 30, 1972; children: Christopher Jr., Andrew Anthony. BS, U. Iowa, 1968, MD, 1971. Diplomate Am. Bd. Dermatology; cert. clin. trial investigator. Intern Ball Meml. Hosp., Muncie, Ind., 1971-72; resident in dermatology U. Tex. Med. Br., Galveston, 1974-77; staff Bayfront Med. Ctr., St. Petersburg, 1977—, St. Anthony's Hosp., St. Petersburg, 1977—; tchr. Bayfront Med. Ctr., 1977—; affiliate assoc. prof. U. South Fla. Coll. Medicine, 1977—; staff Tampa Gen. Hosp., 2001—. Contbr. articles to profl. jours. Vol. Am. Cancer Soc. Mem. ACP, So. Med. Assn., Fla. Med. Assn., Am. Acad. Dermatology (fellow), Am. Soc. Dermatologic Surgery, Soc. Investigative Dermatology, Pinellas County Med. Soc., Fla. West Coast Soc. Dermatology (sec.-treas. 1982-84, pres. 1984-87), Fla. Soc. Dermatologic Surgery, St. Petersburg Yacht Club (bd. dirs. 1989-95, entertainment chmn. 1989-92, house and grounds com. 1987-95), Dragon Club, Masons, Royal Order of Jesters. Presbyterian. Avocations: sailing, scuba diving, photography, amateur ham radio. Office Phone: 727-895-8131.

NELSON, CLARA SINGLETON, human resources consultant; b. Union Ridge, Tenn., Apr. 10, 1935; d. Ernest Caldwell and Willie Emma (Hord) Singleton; m. Joe Edward Nelson, July 26, 1953; children: Drexel Edward, Dorissia Lynett. Student, Tenn. State U., 1961-62, Middle Tenn. State U., 1984; AS, Motlow Coll., 1978; BS in Edn. with highest honors, U. Tenn., Knoxville, 1991. Sec., adminstrv. asst. Bedford County Sch., Shelbyville, Tenn., 1957-64; sec., personnel asst. Aro, Inc., Arnold Air Force Sta., Tenn., 1964-71; mem. pub. rels. staff, job interviewer Employment Security, Shelbyville, 1971-81; mgr. employment EEO Calspan Corp., Arnold Air Force Sta., 1981-94; with Micro Craft Tech., 1994-95; employment and recruiting mgr. Sverdrup Tech., 1995-97; pvt. practice human resource cons., 1998—. Cons. dir. Career Devel. Workshops, Shelbyville. Mem. adv. bd. Tenn. Area Vocat. Sch., Shelbyville, 1979-2001; chmn. adv. commn. Equal Employment Opportunity, 1983—, chmn. employer com. Tullahoma Job Svc., Tenn., 1985—; former mem. Patrons Coun. Argie Cooper Libr., Shelbyville; trustee Motlow Coll. Found.; former mem. Shelbyville Regional Planning Commn.; mem. Shelbyville Power, Water and Sewerage Bd. Recipient cert. of appreciation ARC, 1985. Mem.: Soc. of Human Resource Mgmt. (state diversity chair 2000—04, cert.), Nat. Assn. Bus. and Profl. Women's Clubs, Inc. (chair membership 1991—93, charter mem.), Nat. Mgmt. Assn., Nat. Assn. Female Execs. (network dir. 1985, charter mem.), Highland Rim Human Resources Mgmt. Assn. (treas. 1983—84, 1987, sec. 1988, chair program com. 1989, sec. 1994, SHRM affiliate), Am. Mgmt. Assn. (chair program com. 1994—, pres. 1998—2000), Am. Assn. Affirmative Action Tenn. State U. Cluster (chmn. 1984—2000), Better Homes and Gardens Shelbyville Club. Methodist. Avocations: reading, gardening, writing. Home and Office: 105 Sun Cir Shelbyville TN 37160-2519 Office Phone: 931-684-4184.

NELSON, CRAIG T., actor; b. Spokane, Wash., Apr. 4, 1944; m. Robin Nelson (div. 1978); m. Doria Cook-Nelson, 1987. Attended, U. Ariz., Ctrl. Washington U. Appeared in (feature films) And Justice for All, 1979, The Formula, 1980, Where the Buffalo Roam, 1980, Private Benjamin, 1980, Stir Crazy, 1981, Poltergeist, 1982, Man, Woman, and Child, 1983, The Osterman Weekend, 1983, All the Right Moves, 1983, The Killing Fields, 1984, Silkwood, 1984, Poltergeist II: The Other Side, 1986, Red Riding Hood, 1987, Action Jackson, 1988, Me and Him, 1988, Troup Beverly Hills, 1989, Rachel River, 1989, Turner & Hooch, 1989, I'm Not Rappaport, 1996, Ghosts of Mississippi, 1996, Devil's Advocate, 1997, Wag the Dog, 1997, The Skulls, 2000, All Over Again, 2001, The Incredibles (voice), 2004, The Family Stone, 2005, Blades of Glory, 2007, The Proposal, 2009; (stage prodns.) Friends, 1983-84, Ah, Wilderness!, 1998, (TV films) How the West Was Won, 1978, Diary of a Teenage Hitchiker, 1979, Rage, 1980, Inmates: A Love Story, 1981, Murder in Texas, 1981, Paper Dolls, 1983, Alex: The Life of a Child, 1986, The Ted Kennedy, Jr. Story, 1986, Murderers Among Us: The Simon Wiesenthal Story, 1989, Extreme Close-Up, 1990, Drug Wars: The Camarena Story, 1990, The Josephine Baker Story, 1991, The Fire Next Time, 1993, Probable Cause, 1994, Top of the World, 1997, The Fifty, 1998, Creature, 1998, To Serve and Protect, 1999, Family Shield, 1999, Dirty Pictures, 2000; (TV series) Heroes: Made in the U.S.A. (host), 1986, Coach, 1989-97 (Emmy award, Leading actor in a comedy series, 1992), The District, 2000—04; producer (film documentaries) American Still; screenwriter (TV shows) The Lohman and Barkley Show, The Tim Conway Show, The Alan King Special, (miniseries) Creature, 1998, To Serve and Protect, 1999; prodr., writer (TV) Ride With the Wind, 1994; TV appearances include WKRP in Cincinnati, 1978, The Mary Tyler Moore Show, 1970, The White Shadow, 1978, 4 episode Guest Star, My Name Is Earl, 2007.*

NELSON, D. MICHAEL, gynecologist, educator; b. Galesburg, Ill., Sept. 29, 1949; s. Leslie and Wilma Nelson; m. Peggy J. Naslund, June 6, 1971; children: Shane, Nathan, Jennie. MD, PhD, Wash. U., St. Louis, 1977. Diplomate Am. Bd. Ob-Gyn., Washington, 1984, maternal fetal medicine sub-specialist 1985. Va. S. Lang prof. ob-gyn. Wash. U. Sch. Medicine, St. Louis, 1997—, vice-chmn. dept. ob-gyn. Contbr. articles to sci. rsch. publs. Fellow: Am. Coll. Ob-Gyn.; mem.: Internat. Fedn. Placenta Assns. (mem. exec. coun. 2003—08, editor 2004—08), Am. Gynecol. and Obstet. Soc., Soc. Maternal Fetal Medicine (found. bd. mem. 2003—07), Soc. Gynecologic Investigation (mem. coun. 2003—06, Pres.'s Sr. Scientist award 2007). Office: Wash Univ Sch Medicine 4566 Scott Ave Saint Louis MO 63110 Office Fax: 314-362-8580.

NELSON, DAVID ALDRICH, retired federal judge; b. Watertown, NY, 1932; s. Carlton Low and Irene Demetria (Aldrich) Nelson; m. Mary Dickson, 1956; 3 children. AB, Hamilton Coll., 1954; postgrad., Cambridge U., Eng., 1954—55; LLB, Harvard U., 1958. Bar: Ohio 1958, NY 1982. Atty.-advisor Office of the Gen. Counsel, Dept. of the Air Force, 1959—62; assoc. Squire, Sanders & Dempsey, Cleve., 1958—67, ptnr., 1967—69, 1972—85; judge US Ct. Appeals (6th cir.), Cin., 1985—99, sr. judge, 1999—. Gen. counsel US Post Office Dept., Washington, 1969—71; sr. asst. postmaster gen., gen. counsel US Postal Svc., Washington, 1971; nat. coun. Ohio State U. Coll. Law, 1988—98. Trustee Hamilton Coll., 1984—88; dir. Alexander Hamilton Inst., 2007—. Served to maj. USAFR, 1959—73. Recipient Benjamin Franklin award, US Post Office Dept., 1969; Fulbright scholar, 1954—55. Fellow: Am. Coll. Trial Lawyers; mem.: Ohio Bar Assn., Fed. Bar Assn., Emerson Lit. Soc., Ct. of Nisi Prius (sgt. emeritus), Phi Beta Kappa.

NELSON, DAVID LEONARD, business executive; b. Omaha, May 8, 1930; s. Leonard A. and Cecelia (Steinert) N.; m. Jacqueline J. Zerbe, Dec. 26, 1952; 1 child, Nancy Jo. BS, Iowa State U., 1952. Mktg. adminstr. Ingersoll Rand, Chgo., 1954-56; with Accuray Corp., Columbus, Ohio, 1956-87, exec. v.p., gen. mgr., 1967, pres., 1967-87, chief exec. officer, 1970-87; pres. process automation bus. unit Combustion Engring., Inc., Columbus, 1987-90; pres. bus. area process automation Asea Brown Boveri, Stamford, Conn., 1990-91, v.p. customer satisfaction Ams. region, 1991-93, v.p. customer support Ams. region, 1994-95; chmn. bd. dirs. Herman Miller Inc., Zeeland, Mich., 1995-2000, counsel, 2000—04. Served to capt. USMCR, 1952-54. Mem. IEEE, Instrument Soc. Am., Newcomen Soc. N.Am., Tau Beta Pi, Phi Kappa Phi, Phi Eta Sigma, Delta Upsilon. Achievements include patents in field. Home: 1113 Roundhouse Ln Alexandria VA 22314-5935 Office Phone: 703-299-4588.

NELSON, DAVID LOREN, geneticist, educator; b. Washington, June 25, 1956; s. Erling Walter and Marlys Joan (Jorgenson) N.; m. Claudia Jane Hackbarth, July 31, 1982; children: Jorgen William, Erik Alexander. BA, U. Va., 1978; PhD, MIT, 1984. Staff fellow NIH, Bethesda, Md., 1985-86; sr. assoc. Baylor Coll. Medicine, Houston, 1986-89, instr., 1989-90, asst. prof., 1990-94, assoc. prof., 1994-99, prof., 1999—.

Dir. Human Genome Ctr., 1995-96. Editor: Genome Data Base, 1992-2000; assoc. editor Genomics, 1994-2002. Mem.: Am. Soc. Human Genetics (sec. 2002—). Achievements include development of Alu PCR; discovery of fragile X syndrome gene (FMR-1), new form of genetic mutation (simple repeat expansion); identification of gene defects in Lowe Syndrome and Incontinentia Pigmenti. Office: Baylor Coll Dept Medicine Molecular & Human Genetics 1 Baylor Plz Houston TX 77030-3411 Personal E-mail: nelson@bcm.edu.

NELSON, DEAN B., media company executive; Process ctrl. engr. Shell Oil Co., 1981—83; with Boston Consulting Group, 1985—98, sr. v.p., 1998—2000; founder Capstone Consulting LLC, 2000, CEO, 2000—; chmn. PRIMEDIA Inc., NYC, 2003—, pres., CEO, 2005—. Bd. dirs. PRIMEDIA Inc., 2003—.

NELSON, DELORES PRIVETTE, nurse; d. Reuben Privette; m. Wallace Franklin Nelson, Dec. 10, 1989; 1 child, Robert I. Briggs. Degree in Nursing, Tulsa Jr. Coll., Okla., 1976; BSN, Okla. Wesylean U., Bartlesville, 2002. Registered nurse, Okla. Bd. Nursing, 1976. Psychiat. nurse Laureate Psychiat. Hosp., Tulsa, 1997—2002; RN data analyst St. John Med. Ctr., Tulsa, 2002—. RN psychiat. cons. vol. D.O.D. Dugway Army Base, Utah, 1990—91. Contbr. scientific papers to profl. jours.

NELSON, DONALD ARVID (NELLIE NELSON), professional basketball coach; b. Muskegon, Mich., May 15, 1940; m. Joy Wolfgram, June 19, 1991; children: Julie, Donn, Christie, Katie, Lee. Student, U. Iowa. Player Chgo. Zephyrs, 1962-63, LA Lakers, 1963-65, Boston Celtics, 1965-76; asst. to head coach Milw. Bucks, 1976-87, dir. player pers.; exec. v.p., part owner, gen. mgr. Golden State Warriors, Oakland, Calif., 1987-95, head coach, 1988-95, 2006—, NY Knicks, 1995-96; head coach, gen. mgr. Dallas Mavericks, 1997—2005. Head coach NBA Western Conf. All-Star Team, 1992; head coach US Nat. Team World Championships (gold medal), Toronto, 1994. Named NBA Coach of Yr. 1983, 85, 92; named one of Top 10 Coaches in NBA Hist., 1997. Achievements include winning NBA Championships as a member of the Boston Celtics, 1966, 68, 69, 74, 76. Mailing: Golden State Warriors 1011 Broadway Oakland CA 94607*

NELSON, DONNA GAYLE, state legislator; b. Paducah, Tex., June 13, 1943; d. Jack Harold Williams and Hazel Louise (Cooper Moss) Stephens; m. Douglas Caldwell Nelson, June 24, 1966 (div. 1976); children: Kellye Lou Fetters, Robert Kreg Nelson, J. Graigory. AB, South Plains Coll., Levelland, Tex., 1963; BBA, West Tex. A&M U., Canyon, 1965, MBA, 1967. Founder Evergreen Mut., McMinnville, Oreg., 1975; co-founder Evergreen Life Line, McMinnville, 1978—; founder, corp. dir. AAA Profl. Promotions, McMinnville, 1977—; pres. Evergreen Bus. Mgmt. Co., McMinnville, 1978—; sr. v.p. Evergreen Helicopters, Inc., McMinnville, 1978—, Evergreen Internat. Aviation, Inc., McMinnville, 1978—; mem. Oreg. State Ho. of Reps., 2000—, chair veterans commn., vice chair edn. bus. com., vice chair govt. com., vice chair agr. com. Bd. dirs. Evergreen Air Ctr., Inc., Marana, Ariz., Evergreen Aircraft Sales & Leasing Co., Evergreen Aviation Ground Logistics Enterprises, Inc.; sr. v.p., bd. dirs. Evergreen Internat. Aviation, Inc., McMinnville; speaker Nat. Speakers' Assn., Phoenix, 1986—; mem. adv. bd. Chemeketa Community Coll., McMinnville, 1984-85; owner 3N & Assocs. Inc., Donna G. Nelson Auctions, LLC; founder Yamhill Co. Market; teacher Tex., Calif., and Oregon; author, journalist. Poet World's Most Beloved Poetry, 1985 (Silver poet); writer Aviation/Space Writers' Assn., 1989-90; columnist It Takes Grit. Mem. Team 100 Rep. party, Washington, 1989; co-founder Poyama Land Treatment Ctr., Independence, Oreg., 1973; den mother, sustained membership chmn. Boy Scouts Am., McMinnville, 1977-79; dr. mem. March of Dimes, Heart Fund, McMinnville, 1973-75; sr. mem. transportation, budget and parks com., Yamhill Co. Budget Parks, Elks Lions, Red Cross, NRA, N7IB Farm Bur.; founder Newcomers Club, Fund for Hope, Free Enterprise Fund for Kids; bd. dirs. Humane Soc., Linfield Chamber Orch., WOU Found., Salvation Army. Named Woman of Excellence, Portland, Oreg., 1985. Mem. DAR, C. of C., McMinnville Duplicate Bridge Assn. (founder), Soroptimists Club, Elks, Lions, Beta Sigma Phi (pres. 1974-75, Woman of Yr. 1990). Republican. Baptist. Avocations: music, sports, bridge, writing, fishing, speaking, travel, fishing, charity auctioneer. Home and Office: 2150 St Andrews Dr Mcminnville OR 97128-2436 Home Phone: 503-472-7446; Office Phone: 503-472-8015. Business E-Mail: donnanelson@state.or.us.

NELSON, DONNIE, professional sports team executive; b. Sept. 10, 1962; s. Don Nelson; m. Lotta Nelson; children: Christie, D.J. Grad., Wheaton Coll., Ill., 1986. Regional scout Milw. Bucks, 1984—86; asst. coach Golden State Warriors, 1986—94, Phoenix Suns, 1994—97; asst. coach, dir. player pers. Dallas Mavericks, 1998—2002, acting head coach, 2001, 2002, pres. basketball ops., 2002—, gen. mgr., 2005—. Asst. coach Lithuanian Nat. Team, 1990—; scout at World Championships USA Basketball, Toronto, Canada, 1994; founder Global Games, Dallas; hon. amb. League of Industries; chief advisor Chinese Nat. Basketball Team. Founder Assist Youth Found. (now combined with Heroes), 2002. Recipient Grand Cross of the Comdr., Pres. of Lithuania, 2004; named to Wheaton Coll. Hall of Honor, 1997. Office: Dallas Mavericks The Pavilion 2909 Taylor St Dallas TX 75226 E-mail: dcn@dallasmavs.com.*

NELSON, DOROTHY WRIGHT, federal judge; b. San Pedro, Calif., Sept. 30, 1928; d. Harry Earl and Lorna Amy Wright; m. James Frank Nelson, Dec. 27, 1950; children: Franklin Wright, Lorna Jean. BA, UCLA, 1950, JD, 1953; LLM, U. So. Calif., 1956; LLD (hon.), Western State U. Coll. Law, 1980, U. So. Calif., 1983, Georgetown U., 1988, Whittier U., 1989, U. Santa Clara, 1990, U. San Diego, 1997, Pepperdine U. Sch. of Law, 2003. Bar: Calif. 1954. Rsch. assoc. fellow U. So. Calif., 1953—56, instr., 1957, asst. prof., 1958—61, assoc. prof., 1961—67, prof., 1967—, assoc. dean., 1965—67, dean., 1967—80; judge US Ct. Appeals (9th cir.), 1979—95, sr. judge, 1995—. Com. to consider stds. for admission to practice in fed. cts. Jud. Conf. US, 1976—79; cons. project STAR Law Enforcement Assistance Adminstrn.; select com. on internal procedures Calif. Supreme Ct., 1987—; co-chair Sino-Am. Seminar on Mediation and Arbitration, Beijing, 1992. Contbr. articles to profl. jours.; author: Judicial Adminstration and The Administration of Justice, 1973; author: (with Christopher Goelz and Meredith Watts) Federal Ninth Circuit Civil Appellate Practice, 1995. Co-chair Confronting Myths in Edn. for Pres. Nixon's White House Conf. on Children, Pres. Carter's Commn. for Pension Policy, 1974—80; pres. Reagon's Madison Trust; mem. Nat. Spiritual Assembly Bahais US, 1967—2009; bd. dirs. Dialogue on Transition to a Global Soc., Weinacht, Switzerland, 1992; bd. vis. US Air Force Acad., 1978; bd. dirs. Coun. on Legal Edn. for Profl. Responsibility, 1971—80, Constl. Right Found., Am. Nat. Inst. for Social Advancement; adv. bd. Nat. Ctr. for State Cts., 1971—76; adv. com. to promote equality for woman and men in cts. Nat. Jud. Edn. Program; bd. dirs. Pacific Oaks Coll., Childrens Sch. & Rsch. Ctr., 1996—98; adv. bd. World Law Inst., 1997—, Tahirih Justice Inst., Washington, 1998—; chmn. bd. Western Justice Ctr., 1986—; chair 9th Cir. Standing Com. on Alternative Dispute Resolution, 1998—. Recipient Profl. Achievement award, 1969, AWARE Internat. award, 1970, Ernestine Stalhut Outstanding Woman Lawyer award, 1972, Humanitarian award, U. Judaism, 1973, Pax Orbis ex Jure medal, World Peace thru Law Ctr., 1975, Pub. Svc. award, Coro Found., 1978, Hollzer Human Rights award, Jewish Fedn. Coun., 1988, Medal of Honor, UCLA, 1993, Emil Gumpert Jud. ADR Recognition award, LA County Bar Assn., 1996, Julia Morgan award, YWCA, 1997, Samuel E. Gates Litigation award, Am. Coll. Trial Lawyers, 1999, Bernard E. Witkin award, State Bar Assn. Calif., 2000, Judge of Yr. award, Pasadena Bar Assn., 2002, Thurgood Marshall Career Achievement award, 2005, Harry Sheldon award, Pasadena Human Relations Comm., 2006, Meritorious Svc. award, U. Oreg. Sch. Law, 2007, Project Peace Lifetime Achievement award, 2009, Outstanding Jurist award, LA County Bar Assn., 2009, Humanitarian award, Inner City Law Ctr., 2009; named Law Alumnus of Yr., UCLA, 1967, Woman of Yr., Times, 1968, Disting. Jurist, Ind. U. Law, 1994; fellow, Davenport Coll.; Lustman fellow, Yale U., 1977. Fellow: Davenport Coll., Am. Bar Found.; mem.: ABA (sect. on jud. adminstrn., chmn. com. on edn. in jud. adminstrn. 1973—89, D'Alemberte/Raven award 2000), Assn. Am. Law Schs. (chmn. com. edn. in jud. adminstrn.), Am. Judicature Soc. (bd. dirs., Justice award 1985), Bar Calif. (bd. dirs. continuing edn. bar commn. 1967—74), Order of Coif (nat. v.p. 1974—76), Phi Beta Kappa. Office: US Ct Appeals Cir 125 S Grand Ave Ste 303 Pasadena CA 91105-1621 Office Phone: 626-229-7400. Business E-Mail: dorothy-nelson@ca9.uscourt.gov.

NELSON, DOUGLAS J., mathematician; b. Mpls., Nov. 5, 1945; s. Leonard E. and Frances G. Nelson; m. Ruth A. Benjamin, Aug. 29, 1970; children: Aaron D., Rachel M. BA in Math., U. Minn., Mpls., 1967; PhD in Math., Stanford U., Calif., 1972. Asst. prof. math. Carnegie-Mellon U., Pitts., 1972—75; mathematician, signals analyst US Dept. Def., Fort George G. Meade, Md., 1975—. Contbr. scientific papers. Mem.: SPIE, IEEE, Wash. Scottish Pipe Band (pipe sgt., instr.,q.m. 1995—), Balt. Scottish Country Dance Soc. (pres. 2004—09). Dfl. Avocations: bagpipes, scottish country dancing, woodworking, old house restoration. Office: US Dept Def 9800 Savage Rd Fort George G Meade MD 20755-6513 Personal E-mail: waveland@erols.com. Business E-Mail: djnleso@tycho.ncsc.mil.

NELSON, DOUGLAS SWEDE RAYMOND, sheriff; b. Oakland, Calif., May 6, 1945; s. Nels Raymond and Verna Miltidla Nelson; m. Jewel Lynn Smith, May 6, 1969 (div. Jan. 15, 1989); children: Brenda Lynn, Lynda Ann, Kathlene Goken. MBA (hon.), U. Phoenix, 2008. EIT Welder, Mig- Tig- Sticik, IAPMO, 1959, MIT, 1989, CALIF, 2000; cert. private pilot FAA, 1960. Dep. sheriff, search & rescue Humboldt County Sheriff, Homneydew, Calif., 1966—. Achievements include development of shale oil, recovery. Home: Post Office Box 23117 Pleasant Hill CA 94523 Office: BUREAU of CORRUPTION INVESTIGATORS 2242 Ste A MORELLO Mail POBX 23117 Pleasant Hill CA 94523 Office Fax: 530-386-5934. Personal E-mail: atte4nelson@yahoo.com. Business E-Mail: wildcat4nelson@aol.com.

NELSON, DOUGLAS THOMAS, lawyer; b. New Brunswick, NJ, Mar. 9, 1946; s. Lloyd Alfred and Vivian Cathryn (Eden) N. AB in History summa cum laude, Rutgers U., 1968; MA in History, Columbia U., 1969, PhD in History, 1976, JD, 1980. Bar: N.J. 1980, N.Y. 1981, Conn. 1988. Asst. prof. history N.C. State U., Raleigh, 1974-77; project officer NEH, Washington, 1977; asst. to chmn. FTC, Washington, 1978; assoc. Coudert Brothers, NYC, 1980-82, Paul, Weiss, Rifkind, Wharton & Garrison, NYC, 1982-85; counsel acquisitions and divestitures Union Carbide Corp., Danbury, Conn., 1985-90; asst. gen. counsel Unilever U.S., Inc., NYC, 1990—95; exec. v.p., gen. counsel, sec. Croplife America Inc., 1995—; lectr. Johns Hopkins U. American U. Sch. Law. Lectr. law New Sch. for Social Research, N.Y.C., 1983-84. Woodrow Wilson Dissertation fellow Columbia U., 1971, Stone scholar Columbia U. Law Sch., 1979. Mem. ABA, Phi Beta Kappa. Avocations: travel, singing, jogging, whitewater rafting, photography. Office: Croplife America Inc 1156 15th St NW Washington DC 20005 Office Phone: 202-872-3880. Business E-Mail: dnelson@croplifeamerica.org.

NELSON, DOUGLAS W., foundation administrator; b. 1946; BA, U. Ill., 1968; MA in Hist., U. Wyoming. Asst. sec. Wis. Dept. Health & Social Svcs., Madison, 1967-85; dep. dir. Ctr. Study of Policy, Washington, 1985-90; pres., CEO, mem. bd. trustees Annie E. Casey Found., Balt., 1990—. Bd. trustees Balt. Cmty. Found.; co-chair bd. trustees Jim Casey Youth Opportunities Initiative; chmn. Safe & Sound-Balt. Campaign Children & Youth; bd. dirs. East Balt. Develop. Initiative, Inc., Living Cities, Inc.; chair NYC Spl. Adv. Panel on Child Welfare; vice chair bd. trustees Foundation Ctr., NYC. Author: Heart Mountain: The History of an American Concentration Camp, 1976. Recipient Jane Addams Disting. Leadership award. Office: The Annie E Casey Found 701 St Paul St Baltimore MD 21202-2311 Office Phone: 410-547-6600. Office Fax: 410-547-6624.*

NELSON, EDITH ELLEN, dietician; b. Vicksburg, Mich., Sept. 26, 1940; d. Edward Kenneth and Anna (McManus) Rolffs; m. Douglas Keith Nelson; children: Daniel Lee, Jennifer Lynn. BS, Mich. State U., 1962; MEd in Applied Nutrition, U. Cin., 1979. Lic. dietitian, Fla. Clin. dietitian Macon (Ga.) Gen. Hosp., Blodgett Meml. Hosp., Grand Rapids, Mich.; grad. teaching asst. U. Cin., 1978-79; dir. nutrition svcs. Dialysis Clinic, Inc., Cin., 1979-88; cons. dietitian Panama City Devel. Ctr., Ft. Walton Beach Devel. Ctr., Fla., 1988-94; renal dietitian Dialysis Svcs. Fla., Ft. Walton Beach, 1989-92; cons. dietitian N.W. Fla. Community Hosp., Chipley, Fla., 1993-94, Beverly Enterprises, Panama City Beach, 1994-96, pvt. practice, Panama City, Fla., 1996—. Mich. Edn. Assn. scholar, 1958; Nat. Kidney Found. grantee, 1986. Mem. Am. Dietetic Assn., Fla. Dietetic Assn., Panhandle Dist. Dietetic Assn., Nat. Kidney Found. (coun. on renal nutrition, Fla. coun. on renal nutrition), Omicron Nu. Home and Office: 3522 Fox Run Blvd Panama City Beach FL 32408-7151 Office Phone: 850-258-8460. Personal E-mail: ediepcb@aol.com.

NELSON, EDWARD GAGE, brokerage house and bank executive, consultant; b. Nashville, May 17, 1931; s. Charles and Polly (Prentiss) N.; m. Carole Olivia Frances Minton, Sept. 17, 1960; children: Carole Gervais, Emily Minton, Ellen Prentiss BA in Polit. Sci., U. of South, Sewanee, Tenn., 1952. Exec. v.p. Clark, Landstreet & Kirkpatrick, Inc., Nashville, 1955-64, Commerce Union Bank, Nashville, 1968-72, pres., 1972-82, cons., 1985—, chmn., CEO, 1982-84; chmn., pres. Nelson Capital Corp., Nashville, 1985—. Hon. consul gen. Japan; bd. dirs. Werthan Packaging, Consumers Ins., Franklin Industries, Trans Arabian Investment Bank, Ctrl. Parking Sys., Ohio Star Forge, Bucyrus Internat., Inc.; mem. 1st adv. coun. Japan/Tenn. Soc. Trustee Vanderbilt U., Nashville, 1979—, chmn. med. ctr. bd., 1984-2003. Spl. agt. U.S. Army, 1955, Japan. Mem. Belle Meade Country Club, River Club (N.Y.C.). Republican. Episcopalian. Home: 1305 Chickering Rd Nashville TN 37215-4521 Office: 4525 Harding Pike STE 200 Nashville TN 37205-2154

NELSON, EDWARD HUMPHREY, architect; b. Winchester, Mass., Sept. 2, 1918; s. Richard MacDonald and Evelyn Miller (Humphrey) N.; m. Lois Whitaker Renouf, Sept. 24, 1948 (dec.); children: Susan, David, Sarah; m. Miriam P. Ketcham, Jan. 2, 1988 (dec.) Grad., Lenox Sch., 1936; B.Arch., Yale, 1950. Pvt. archtl. practice, Tucson, 1953-61; sr. v.p. CNWC Architects, Tucson, 1961-88, pres., 1989-94; ret., 1994. Mem. adv. com. U. Ariz. Coll. Architecture, 1984-93. Works include: design for Tucson Community Ctr. Pres. Tucson Cmty. Coun., 1969-71, Tucson Art Ctr., 1960; bd. dirs. Tucson Housing Found., 1969-06, Tucson Symphony, 1977-84, Tucson United Way, 1980, Tucson Art Mus., 1960-74, dir. Planned Parenthood, South Ariz., 1981-82, Tucson Trade Bur., 1976-91, pres., 1984; trustee Green Fields Sch., 1960-74; vestry St. Philips Episc. Ch., 1967-69, sr. warden, 1987-90, parish warden, 1993-94; convenor Episcopal Interparish Coun., 1990-92; 1st Phila. City Troop, 1940—, horse cavalry, 1940-42. Served to capt. AUS, 1940-41, WWII, ETO. Decorated Bronze Star with oak leaf cluster, Purple Heart; recipient Disting. Citizen award U. Ariz., 1981, St. Philips medal St. Philips Episc. Ch., 2000. Fellow: AIA (pres. So. Ariz. chpt. 1962, chmn. Ariz. Fellows 1986—94, emeritus 1994); mem.: Ariz. Soc. Archs. (pres. 1963), U. Ariz. Pres.'s Club, Yale Club (pres. Tucson chpt. 1962, dir. 1979—2006, pres. Tucson chpt. 1983).: 7500 N Calle Sin Envidia Apt 12107 Tucson AZ 85718-7359 E-mail: miriamned@msn.com.

NELSON, EDWARD LEE, biomedical researcher, educator; s. Gaile W. and Iona M. Nelson; m. Carla A. Nelson, June 10, 1995; children: Andrew Kristopher, Kira Celine. MD, Oreg. Health Sci. U., Portland, 1986. Lic. NY Med. Bd., 1987, Med. Bd. Calif., 1989, Md. Med. Bd., 1995, cert. in internal medicine ABIM, 1989, oncologist 1993. Peace corp. vol. US Govt., Cawaci, Fiji, 1977—80; pathology med. student program mem. OHSU, Portland, 1981—86; internal medicine resident Strong Meml. Hosp., U. Rochester, NY, 1986—89; med. oncology fellow Stanford U., Sch. Medicine, Palo Alto, Calif., 1989—92, pfizer immunology rsch. fellow, 1992—95; sr. scientist NIH, NCI-FCRDC, SAIC, Frederick, Md., 1995—2000, head immunotherapy lab., 1995—2000; asst. prof. medicine, molecular biology & biochemistry U. Calif., Irvine, 2000—08, mem., NCI designated chao family comprehensive cancer ctr., 2000—, mem., ctr. immunology, 2002—, faculty mem., 2006—, co-investigator, NSF lifechips igert program, 2006—, assoc. prof. medicine, molecular biology & biochemistry, 2008—. Contbr. articles to profl. jours., chapters to books. Advisor Cmty. Outreach Cancer Rsch., Irvine, 2002—08; coach Protect Our Nat. Youth Baseball, Irvine, 2004—08. Recipient Merck award, OHSU, 1986, Sneeden award, 1986; named one of Excellence Physician, OCMA, 2007—, Top Oncologists, Consumers' Rsch. Coun. America, 2008; fellowship, Tartar Student Rsch., 1982, grant, Berlex Inc., 2004—08, NIH-NCI, 2007—, Susan G. Komen Found., 2007—, DOD-CDMRP, 2008—, NIH, 2008—. Mem.: ACP, Clin. Immunology Soc., Am. Assn. Immunologists, Internat. Soc. Biol. Therapy Cancer, Am. Soc. Clin. Oncology (Merit award 1994), Am. Assn. Cancer Rsch., Alpha Omega Alpha. Office: Univ Calif Irvine Health Sci Rd Hewitt Hall Rm 3032 Irvine CA 92697-4120 Office Fax: 949-824-2305. Business E-Mail: enelson@uci.edu.

NELSON, EDWARD SHEFFIELD, lawyer, retired utilities executive; b. Keevil, Ark., Feb. 23, 1941; s. Robert Ford and Thelma Jo (Mayberry) N.; m. Mary Lynn McCastlain, Oct. 12, 1962; children: Cynthia, Lynn (dec.), Laura. BS, U. Cen. Ark., 1963; LLB, Ark. Law Sch., 1968; JD, U. Ark., 1969. Mgmt. trainee Ark. La. Gas Co., Little Rock, 1963-64, sales engr., 1964-67, sales coordinator, 1967-69, gen. sales mgr., 1969-71, v.p., gen. sales mgr., 1971-73, pres., dir., 1973-79, pres., chmn., chief exec. officer, 1979-85; ptnr., chmn. bd., chief exec. officer House, Wallace, Nelson & Jewel, Little Rock, 1985-86; pvt. practice law Little Rock, 1986—; of counsel Jack, Lyon & Jones, P.A., 1991—; ptnr. Jack, Nelson & Jones, Pa., 2008—. Bd. dirs. Fed. Res. Mem. N.G., 1957-63, Fellowship Bible Ch.; bd. dirs. U. Ark., Little Rock, vice chmn. bd. visitors, 1981; bd. dirs. Philander Smith Coll., 1981; chmn. Ark. Indsl. Devel. Commn., 1987, 88; past chmn. Little Rock br. Fed. Res. Bd. St. Louis; chmn. Econ. Expansion Study Commn., 1987—; bd. dirs. Ark. Ednl. TV Found., Ark. Game and Fish Commn. Found.; founder, 1st pres. Jr. Achievement Ark., 1987-88; Rep. nominee for Gov. of Ark., 1990, 94; co-state chmn. Ark. Reps., 1991-92, nat. committeeman Ark. GOP, 1993-2000; mem. Ark. Higher Edn. Coord. Bd., 1997-99; apptd. commr. Ark. Game and Fish Commn., 2000-07, chmn., 2007-. Named Ark.'s Outstanding Young Man Ark. J. C. of C., 1973; One of Am.'s Ten Outstanding Young Men U.S. Jr. C. of C., 1974; Citizen of Yr. Ark. chpt. March of Dimes, 1983; Humanitarian of Yr. NCCJ, 1983; Best Chief Exec. Officer in Natural Gas Industry Wall Street Transcript, 1983; recipient 1st Disting. Alumnus award U. Cen. Ark., 1987, Outstanding Svcs. award Dukes Internat., 2007, First Legacy award Jr. Achievement, Ark., 2008. Mem. Am., Ark., Pulaski County Bar Assns., Ark. C. of C. (dir.), Little Rock C. of C. (dir., pres. 1981), Sales and Mktg. Execs. Assn. (pres. 1975, Top Mgmt. award 1977), U. Ark. Law Sch. Alumni Assn. (pres. 1980), Sigma Tau Gamma (Ben T. Laney Leadership award for leadership and achievement 2000), Ark. Wildlife Fedn. (Conservationist of Yr. 2002), Am. Lung Assn. (chmn., Philanthropist of Yr. 2003, Jerry Jones Sportman's award 2007, Ducks Unlimited, Arks. Mpcl. League(Mpcl. Law award, 2008, Easter Seals Fellowship Bible Ch. Office: 6th and Broadway 3400 TCBY Bldg Little Rock AR 72201 Office Phone: 501-375-1122. Personal E-mail: esn@jlj.com.

NELSON, ELMER KINGSHOLM, JR., (KIM NELSON), political scientist, educator, writer, mediator, consultant; b. Laramie, Wyo., Sept. 14, 1922; s. Elmer Kingsholm and Alice (Downey) N.; m. Jane Beckwith Oliver, Aug. 4, 1945; 1 son, Elmer Kingsholm III (Kirk). BA, U. Wyo., 1943, JD, 1948, MA, 1949; Dr. Pub. Adminstrn., U. So. Calif., 1959. Instr. psychology U. Wyo., 1947-49; psychologist, staff psychologist dept. probation Contra Costa County, Calif., 1949-51; sr. psychologist Cal. State Dept. Corrections, San Quentin and Chino Prisons, 1951-52; asst. prof. criminology U. B.C., Can., 1952-54, assoc. prof., 1954-56, head criminology div., 1953-56; warden Haney Correctional Instn., B.C., 1956-58; assoc. dir. Youth Studies Ctr. U. So. Calif., 1958-59, dir. Youth Studies Ctr., 1959-64, assoc. prof. pub. adminstrn., 1958-61, prof., 1961—, dean Sch. Pub. Adminstrn., 1971-76, prof., co-dir. Sacramento Pub. Affairs Ctr.; head Bay Area Research Center, Berkeley, 1979—; prof. emeritus U. So. Calif. Dep. adminstr. Youth and Adult Corrections Agy., State of Calif., Sacramento, 1964-65; interim exec. dir. Office Criminal Justice Planning, spring 1975; dir. Nat. Study Probation and Parole, 1976-77; chmn. task force on corrections, asso. dir. Pres.'s Commn. on Law Enforcement and Adminstrn. of Justice, Washington, 1966-67; dir. nat. study of correctional adminstrn. U. So. Calif. for Joint Commn. on Correctional Manpower and Tng., 1967-69 Co-author: Corrections in America, 1975; contbr. articles, monographs, research reports to profl. jours. Advisor on mgmt. Boys Republic, Chino, Calif., 1967—; bd. dirs., v.p. Am. Justice Inst., Sacramento; bd. dirs. Human Interaction Rsch. Inst., L.A. Recipient Disting. Alumnus award U. Wyo., 1975, Exemplary Alumni award U. Wyo. Coll. Arts and Scis., 1994; Ford Found. Travel Study grantee, 1970-71; E. Kim Nelson endowed doctoral fellowship established at U. So. Calif., 1987. Sr. fellow Nat. Acad. Pub. Adminstrn.; mem. Wyo. Bar Assn., Alpha Tau Omega, Phi Beta Kappa, Phi Kappa Phi, Psi Chi. Home: 355 St Augustine Ct Benicia CA 94510-2866 Personal E-mail: eknscarq@aol.com.

NELSON, EMILY JANE, conservationist; d. Alan Edward and Linda Suzanne Nelson. BS, Northern Ariz. U., Flagstaff, 2004. Grad. tchg., rsch. asst. Northern Ariz. U., 2007—; edn. & outreach coord. Grand Canyon Wolf Recovery Project, 2008—. Mem. bd. dirs. Habitat Harmony, Inc., Flagstaff, 2006—. Rsch., comment writing Habitat Harmony, Inc., Flagstaff, 2006—. Mem.: Ariz. Chpt. Wildlife Soc., Soc. Conservation Biology, Sigma Xi (rsch. grant 2008), Phi Kappa Phi. Avocations: birdwatching, art. Office: Grand Canyon Wolf Recovery Project PO Box 1594 Flagstaff AZ 86002 Office Fax: 928-779-3567. Personal E-mail: emily.nelson@nau.edu. Business E-Mail: emily@gcwolfrecovery.org.

NELSON, ERIC DOLAINE, literature educator, consultant; s. Dolaine R. and Betty L. Nelson; m. Susan K. Allard, July 7, 2000; children: Jody R. Johnson, Erika C., Nils C-B. PhD, U. Wash., Seattle, 1992. Lectr. and vis. prof. Pacific Luth. U., Tacoma, 1988—98, asst. prof., 1998—2008, assoc. prof., 2008—; instr. U. Puget Sound, Tacoma, 1990—93; instr. Summer Myth Inst. U. Wash. Ext., 1994—98. Dir. Faculty Devel. Pacific Luth. U., 1998—2001. Author: (popular non-fiction) The Complete Idiot's Guide to Ancient Greece (2005), The Complete Idiot's Guide to the Roman Empire; contbr. to academic publ. Recipient Regency Advancement award, Pacific Luth. U., 2002, 2008; scholar Borsa di Studio, Internat. Sch. Written Records, Ericè, Italy., 1989; Rotary Internat. Found. Grad. fellowship, Rotary Internat., 1986—87, William W. Stout fellowship, Dissertation grant-in-Aid, U. Wash., 1988, Innovative Tchg. grant, Pacific Luth. U., 2002, Kelmer-Roe fellowship, 2005—06, Info. Resources Small grant, 2005—06. Office: Pacific Lutheran Univ Harstad 112C Tacoma WA 98447 Business E-Mail: nelsoned@plu.edu.

NELSON, ERIN MULLIGAN, computer company executive, marketing professional; BBA in Internat. Bus. and Mktg., U. Tex., Austin. Asst. brand mgr. Procter & Gamble Co., 1991—93; mgmt. cons. A.T. Kearney, 1994—98; mem. corp. strategy team Frito-Lay N.Am., Inc. (now PepsiCo, Inc.), 1998—99; sr. mktg. mgr. Dell Inc. (formerly Dell Computer Corp.), 1999—2001, dir. mktg., 2001—03, dir. sales, 2003—05, dir. eBusiness, EMEA (Europe, Middle East, Africa) home/small bus., 2006—07, dir. mktg., EMEA small/medium bus., 2007, v.p. mktg. EMEA, 2008—09, v.p. mktg., chief mktg. officer, 2009—. Office: Dell Inc Hdqs 1 Dell Way Round Rock TX 78682 Office Phone: 512-338-4400. Office Fax: 512-728-3653.*

NELSON, ETHELYN BARNETT, civic worker; b. Bessemer, Ala., Jan. 16, 1925; d. Laurence McBride and Ethel Victoria Fortesque (King) Barnett; m. Stuart David Nelson, May 6, 1949; children: Terryl Lynn, Cynthia Dianne, Jacqueline Margo. Student, Huntingdon Coll., 1943, U. Ala., 1948, George Washington U., 1948—49, student, 1974. Sec. U.S. Air Force, Montgomery, Ala. and Panama Canal Zone, 1944—49; sec. to dep. undersec. U.S. Dept. State, Washington, 1951—53, U.S. Ho. of Reps. and U.S. Senate, 1959—60; adminstrv. asst. editl. divsn. Nat. Geog. Soc., Washington, 1962—65; rec. sec. Dist. IV Nat. Capital Area Fedn. Garden Clubs, Inc., Washington, 1981—83. Mem. Women's Com. Nat. Symphony Orch. Mem.: Nat. Trust for Historic Preservation, Salvation Army Aux., Am. Scandinavian Assn., Landon Woods Garden Club (pres. 1978—80), Congl. Country Club. Republican. Methodist. Achievements include patentee. Home: 6410 Maiden Ln Bethesda MD 20817-5612

NELSON, FLAVIA, neurologist, professor, researcher, consultant; d. Jose Carlos Marrero and Maria Teresa Chapa; m. John Eric Nelson, Dec. 17, 1988 (div. Feb. 1, 2005); 1 child, Christopher Eric. MD, UACH, Mex., 1991. Cert. internist Am. Bd. Internal Medicine, 2001, in neurology U. Tex. Med. Sch. Houston, 2004, multiple sclerosis specialist UTHSC Houston, 2005, neurologist Am. Bd. Psychiatry, Neurology, 2008. Sci. dept. chair Radford Sch., El Paso, Tex., 1993—96; chief resident Neurology Residency Program, UT Med. Sch., Houston, 2003—04; bd. mem. Sun Country Sci. Fair, El Paso, 2004—06; asst. prof. neurology U. Tex. Health Sci. Ctr., 2005—; asst. dir. MRI Analysis Ctr. Multiple Sclerosis Rsch. Group, Houston, 2006—; clin. adv. com. mem. Multiple Sclerosis Soc., Lone Star Chpt., Houston, 2006—. Cons. Teva Neurosci., Biogen Idec, EMD Serono, Bayer, Houston, 2005—. Contbr. articles to profl. jour. Mem. Female Faculty Assn., Houston, 2005—. Recipient Excellency in Patient Care award, Thomason Hosp., El Paso, 1999—2000, Excellence in Tchg. award, U. Tex. Med. Sch., 2004. Mem.: Am. Acad. Neurology. Achievements include research in magnetic resonance imaging sequences which can detect brain lesions in the cortical gray matter of patients with multiple sclerosis. Avocations: yoga, meditation, travel. Office: Univ Texas Health Science Ctr 6431 Fannin St MSB 7044 Houston TX 77030

NELSON, FREDA NELL HEIN, librarian; b. Trenton, Mo., Dec. 16, 1929; d. Fred Albert and Mable Carman (Doan) Hein; m. Robert John Nelson, Nov. 1, 1957 (div. Apr. 1984); children: Thor, Hope. Nursing diploma, Trinity Luth. Hosp., Kansas City, Mo., 1950; B. Philosophy, Northwestern U., 1961; MS in Info. and Libr. Sci., U. Ill., 1986. RN. Operating rm. nurse Trinity Luth. Hosp., Kansas City, Mo., 1950-52, Johns Hopkins Hosp., Balt., 1952, Wesley Meml. Hosp., Chgo., 1952-58, Tacoma Gen. Hosp., 1958-59, Chgo. Wesley Hosp., 1959-61; libr. asst. Maple Woods Campus Met. Community Colls., Kansas City, 1987-89, libr., libr. mgr. Blue Springs Campus, 1989-96; ret., 1996. Co-founder Coll. for Kids, Knox Coll., Galesburg, Ill., 1982. Nurses scholar Edgar Bergen Found., 1947; recipient Award of Merit, Chgo. Bd. Health, 1952. Avocations: swimming, walking, cross-word puzzles. Home: 5708 N Polk Dr Kansas City MO 64151

NELSON, GLEN DAVID, health products executive, physician; b. Mpls., Mar. 28, 1937; s. Ralph and Edna S. Nelson; m. Marilyn Carlson, June 30, 1961; children: Diana, Curtis, Wendy. BA, Harvard U., Cambridge, Mass., 1959; MD, U. Minn., 1963. Diplomate Am. Bd. Surgery, also sub-bd. bariatric and peripheral vascular surgery; cert. Am. Bd. Surgery, 1970. Intern Hennepin County Gen. Hosp., Mpls., 1963—64, resident in gen. surgery, 1964—69; staff surgeon Park Nicollet Med. Ctr. (formerly St. Louis Park Med. Ctr.), Mpls.; practiced surgery, 1969—86; chmn., pres. and CEO Park Nicollet Med. Ctr., 1975—86; chmn. and CEO Am. MedCenters, Inc., 1984—86; dir. Medtronic, Inc., 1980—2002, exec. v.p., 1986—88, vice chmn., 1988—2002; chmn., prin. owner GDN Holdings, LLC, Minnetonka, Minn., 2002—. Bd. dirs. Arstasis, Inc., Harvard Bus. Sch. Healthcare Initiative Adv. Bd., Harvard U. Com. on U. Resources, Cardiovascular Systems, Inc., Carlson Holdings, Inc., Carlson Cos., Inc., Evera Med., Inc., Guided Delivery Sys., Inc., Harvard U. Com. on Sci. and Engring., Johns Hopkins Medicine Bd. of Advisors, Inspire Med. Sys., LLC, chmn.; bd. dirs., trustee and chmn. Am. Pub. Media/Minn. Pub. Radio; RedBrick Health, RF Dynamics., Stemedica Cell Technologies, Inc.; emeritus clin. prof. surgery, U. Minn.

NELSON, GORDON LEIGH, chemist, educator; b. Palo Alto, Calif., May 27, 1943; s. Nels Folke and Alice Virginia (Fredrickson) N. BS in Chemistry, U. Nev., 1965; MS, Yale U., 1967, PhD, 1970; DSc (hon.), William Carey Coll., 1988. Staff research chemist corp. research and devel. Gen. Electric Co., Schenectady, NY, 1970-74, mgr. combustibility tech. plastics div. Pittsfield, Mass., 1974-79, mgr. environ. protection plastics div., 1979-82; v.p. materials sci. and tech. Springborn Labs. Inc., Enfield, Conn., 1982-83; prof., chmn. dept. polymer sci. U. So. Miss., Hattiesburg, 1983-89; dean Coll. Sci. and Liberal Arts, prof. chemistry Fla. Inst. Tech., Melbourne, 1989—, mem. coun. sci., soc. pres., sec., 1989-90, chair-elect, 1991, chair, 1992. Cons. in field. Author: Carbon-13 Nuclear Magnetic Resonance for Organic Chemists, 1972, Carbon-13 Nuclear Magnetic Resonance for Organic Chemists, 2d edit., 1980; co-author: Polymeric Materials-Chemistry for the Future, 1989, Carbon Monoxide and Human Lethality, 1993; editor: Fire and Polymers-Materials and Tests for Hazard Prevention, 1990, 1995; co-editor: Fire and Polymers-Materials and Solutions for Hazard Prevention, 2001, Fire and Polymer IVs-Materials and Solutions for Hazard Prevention, 2005, editor books on coating sci. tech.; contbr. articles to profl. jours. Mem.: ASTM (E5 cert. of appreciation 1985, D1 1997), Soc. Advancement of Scandinavian Study, Coun. Colls Arts and Scis., Soc. Plastics Industry (structural plastics divsn., Man of Yr. 1979), Internat. Electrotech. Commn. (U.S. tech. adv. group on info. processing equipment), So. Soc. for Coatings Tech., Ctr. Sci. Tech. and the Media (bd. dir. 1991—94), Info. Tech. Industry Coun. (chmn. plastics task group), Am. Chem. Soc. (bd. dirs. 1977—85, 1987—89, pres. 1988, bd. dirs. 1992—94, 1st Nelson award Orlando sect. 1996, Charles Holmes Herty medal Ga. sect. 1998), Am. Inst. Chemists, Nev. Hist. Soc., Yale Chemists Assn. (pres. 1981—), Sigma Xi. Republican. Presbyterian. Avocations: travel, western U.S. history. Office: Fla Inst Tech Coll Sci & Liberal Arts 150 W University Blvd Melbourne FL 32901-6975 Office Phone: 321-674-7260.

NELSON, GRANT STEEL, law educator; b. Mitchell, SD, Apr. 18, 1939; s. Howard Steel and Clara Marie (Winandy) N.; m. Judith Ann Haugen, Sept. 22, 1962; children: Mary Elizabeth, Rebekah Anne, John Adam. BA magna cum laude, U. Minn., 1960; JD cum laude, 1963. Bar: Minn. 1963, Mo. 1971. Assoc. Faegre & Benson, Mpls., 1963-67; mem. law faculty U. Mo., Columbia, 1967-91, assoc. prof., 1970-72, prof., 1972-91, Enoch H. Crowder prof. law, 1974-91; prof. UCLA, 1991—2007; William H. Rehnquist prof. law Pepperdine U., Malibu, Calif., 2007—. Bd. legal advisors Gt. Plains Legal Found., 1978-85; vis. asst. prof. U. Mich., Ann Arbor, 1969-70, Brigham Young U., Provo, Utah, 1976; vis. prof. U. Minn., Mpls., 1981-82, UCLA, 1989-90; disting. vis. prof. Pepperdine U., 1987-88, 2006; vis. endowed Campbell prof. U. Mo., Columbia, 1996-98; commr. Nat. Conf. Commrs. Uniform State Laws, 1983-91; adv. bd. West Pub. Law Sch Author: (with Van Hecke and Leavell) Cases and Materials on Equitable Remedies and Restitution, 1973; (with Whitman) Cases and Materials on Real Estate Finance and Development, 1976, Cases and Materials on Real Estate Transfer, Finance and Development, 1981, (with Osborne and Whitman) Real Estate Finance Law, 1979, (with Leavell and Love) Cases and Materials on Equitable Remedies and Restitution, 1980; (with Whitman) Land Transactions and Finance, 1983, 4th edit., 2004, Real Estate Finance Law, 1985, 5th edit., 2007, Cases and Materials on Real Estate Transfer, Finance and Development, 1987, 8th edit., 2009; (with Leavell, Love and Kovacic-Fleischer) Cases and Materials on Equitable Remedies, Restitution and Damages, 1986, 7th edit., 2005; (with Browder, Cunningham, Stoebuck and Whitman) Basic Property Law, 1989; (with Stoebuck and Whitman) Contemporary Property, 1996, 3rd edit., 2008; co-reporter ALI Restatement of Property-Mortgages; contbr. articles to profl. jours. 1st lt. AUS, 1964-65. Recipient award for meritorious service and achievement U. Mo. Law Sch. Found., 1974, Disting. Faculty Svc. award U. Mo.-Columbia Alumni Assn., 1978, Disting. Faculty award, 1986, Disting. Non-Alumnus award, 1991, Rutter award UCLA Law Sch., 2000, Disting. Tchg. award UCLA Alumni Assn., 2002. Mem. Am. Law Inst., Assn. Am. Law Schs. (sect. chmn. 1976-77), Am. Coll. Real Estate Lawyers, Am. Coll. Mortgage Attys., Mo. Bar Assn. (vice chmn. property law com. 1974-75, chmn. 1975-77), Order of Coif, Phi Beta Kappa, Phi Delta Phi. Office: Pepperdine Sch Law 24255 Pacific Coast Hwy Malibu CA 90263 Office Phone: 310-506-4605. Business E-Mail: grant.nelson@pepperdine.edu.

NELSON, H. WAYNE, gerontologist, advocate; s. Hubert Wayne Nelson and Sandra Lynn Scott; m. Ela A. Alivio, Aug. 8, 2005; children: Cameron W., Sarah E. MA in History, Portland State U., 1980; MA in Humanities, Calif. State U., Dominguez Hills, 1982; MBA, City Coll., Bellevue, Wash., 1984; PhD, Oreg. State U., 1993. Asst. to Gov. Victor Atiyeh Gov.'s Office, Salem, Oreg., 1983—85; dep. state long-term care ombudsman Oreg. Office Long-Term Care Ombudsman, Salem, 1985—87, acting state ombudsman, 1987—89, dep. dir., 1987—98; assoc. prof. dept. health sci. Towson (Md.) U., 1998—. Cons. Nat. Citizen's Coalition Nursing Home Reform, Nat. Long-Term Care Ombudsman Resource Ctr., Washington, 1998—; cons, commd. report author Natonal Assn. State Ombudsman Programs, Washington, 2002—; cons., trainer numerous state aging programs; spkr. in field. Author: (book) Elder Advocacy: Essential Practice and Skills Across Settings, 2007; contbr. entries to encys., articles to profl. jours. Dep. comdr. 10th med. regiment Mil. Dept. Md., Pikesville Military Reservation, 2001—06; founder Balt. County Med. Emergency Volunteers, 2003—06. Decorated Oreg. N.G. Commendation medal Gov., Oreg. N.G. Meritorious Svc. medal, Oreg. N.G. Exceptional Svc. medal, Wash. Army N.G. Commendation medal Mil. Dept. Wash., Md. State Active Duty medal Mil. Dept. Md., Md. N.G. Meritorioius Svc. medal with Oak Leaf Cluster Gov.; recipient Iris award, Ky. Cabinet Human Resources; fellow, Nat. Inst. Aging, 1996. Fellow: Gerontol. Soc. Am. (life; chair elect fellowship com., social rsch. and pub. policy sect. 2002—06). Avocation: emergency public health service. Office: Towson U 8000 York Rd Towson MD 21252 Personal E-mail: wnelson@towson.edu.

NELSON, HARRY DONALD, telecommunications executive; b. Chgo., Nov. 23, 1933; s. Harry E. and Elsie I. (Liljedahl) N.; m. Carol J. Stewart, Mar. 31, 1957; children: Donald S., David S., Sharon J. Arnold. BS, Northwestern U., Evanston, Ill., 1955, MBA, 1959. Sales rep., sales trainer Procter & Gamble, Chgo., 1955-58; sales adminstr. internat. products GE, N.Y., Ky., 1959-70, Md., Ohio, 1959-72, product mgr. Louisville, Ky., 1978-81; mgr. mktg. Tex. Instruments, Dallas, 1972-74; v.p. mktg. Rockwell Internat., Anaheim, Calif., 1975, HMW-Pulsar, Lancaster, Pa., 1976-78, Genesco, Nashville, 1981-83; v.p. cellular ops. Tel. and Data Systems, Chgo., 1983-85; pres., CEO U.S. Cellular, Chgo., 1985—. Mem. Dean's Adv. Bd. Kellogg Sch. Mgmt. Northwestern U., Evanston, 1994—, Alumni Adv. Bd., 1991—. With U.S. Army, 1956-57. Recipient Dean's Alumni award Kellogg Sch. Mgmt., 1996. Mem. Cellular Telecomm. Industry Assn. (treas., bd. dirs., exec. com. 1986—, Pres.'s award 1996). Republican. Baptist. Avocations: paperweight collecting, antique sales, stamp and coin collecting. Office: US Cellular 8410 W Bryn Mawr Ave Ste 700 Chicago IL 60631-3486

NELSON, HOWARD JOSEPH, geographer, educator; b. Gowrie, Iowa, Jan. 12, 1919; s. Joseph A. and Hannah (Swanson) N.; m. Betty Marie Garlick, June 18, 1944; children: Linda Ann, James Allan. BA with high honors, Iowa State Tchrs. Coll., 1942; MA, U. Chgo., 1947, PhD, 1949. Mem. faculty UCLA, 1949—, prof. geography, 1963-86, prof. emeritus, 1986—, chmn. dept., 1966-71. Author: (with W.A.V. Clark) Los Angeles, The Metropolitan Experience, 1976, The Los Angeles Metropolis, 1983. Served with AUS, 1943-46. Mem. Assn. Am. Geographers (regional councillor 1968-71), Sigma Xi. Home: 3939 Walnut Ave #162 Carmichael CA 95608 Office: Univ Calif Dept Geography Los Angeles CA 90024

NELSON, IVORY VANCE, academic administrator; b. Curtis, La., June 11, 1934; s. Elijah H. and Mattie (White) N.; m. Patricia Robbins, Dec. 27, 1985; children: Cherlyn, Karyn, Eric Beatty, Kim Beatty. BS with distinction, Grambling U., La., 1959; PhD with distinction, U. Kans., Lawrence, 1963. Assoc. prof. chemistry So. U., Baton Rouge, 1963-67, head div. sci., 1966-68; prof. chemistry Prairie View A&M U., Tex., 1968-83, asst. acad. dean Tex., 1968-72, v.p. rsch. Tex., 1972-82, acting pres. Tex., 1982-83; exec. asst. Tex. A&M U. System, College Station, 1983-86; chancellor Alamo C.C. Dist., San Antonio, 1986-92; pres. Ctrl. Wash. U., Ellensburg, 1992-99, Lincoln U., Pa., 1999—. DuPont teaching fellow U. Kans., 1959; rsch. chemist Am. Oil Co., 1962; sr. rsch. chemist Union Carbide Co., 1969; vis. prof. U. Autonomous Guadalajara, Mex., 1966, Loyola U., 1967; Fulbright lectr., 1966; cons. evaluation coms. Oak Ridge Assoc. Univs., Tenn., NSF, Nat. Coun. for Accreditation Tchr. Edn., So. Assn. Colls. and Schs.; mem. regional policy coms. on minorities Western Interstate Com. on Higher Edn., 1986-88; mem. exec. com. Nat. Assn. State Univs. and Land Grant Colls., 1980-82. Contbr. articles to profl. jours. Bd. dirs. Target 90, Goals San Antonio, 1987-89, coun. of pres.NAIDA,(1993-96) Commn. on Student Learning, Wash., 1992—, United Way San Antonio, 1987-89, Alamo Area coun. Boy Scouts Am., 1987-89, San Antonio Symphony Soc., 1987-91, Key Bank of Wash.; mem. bd. dirs. assn. Western U., (1995—) mem. com. for jud. reform State of Tex., 1991; mem. edn. adv. bd. Tex. Rsch. Park, 1987-89; bd. givs. Am. Inst. for character Edn., Inc., 1988-91; mem. pres.'s bd. advisors on HBCUs, 2006-; mem. adv. com. Tex. Ho. of Reps., 1978; chmn. United Way Campaign Tex. A&M U. System, 1984, others. Staff sgt. USAF, 1951-55, Korea. T.H. Harris scholar Grambling State U., 1959; fellow Nat. Urban League, 1969; finalist Pulitzer for general non-fiction, 1992. Mem. AAAS, Am. Chem. Soc., Tex. Acad. Sci., NAACP, Phi Beta Kappa, Sigma Xi, Phi Lambda Upsilon, Beta Kappa Chi, Alpha Mu Gamma, Kappa Delta Pi, Sigma Pi Sigma, Omega Psi Phi, Sigma Pi Phi, Phi Kappa Phi. Avocations: fishing, photography, sports. Office: Lincoln U Office of Pres PO Box 179 Lincoln University PA 19352-0999 Office Phone: 484-365-8000. Business E-Mail: inelson@lincoln.edu.

NELSON, JACK LEE, education educator; b. Cheyenne, Wyo., Nov. 2, 1932; s. Myron Alfred and Mary Elizabeth (Baker) N.; m. Gwen Margret Names, Mar. 13, 1953; children: Barbara Louise Nelson Vollmer, Steven Lee. BA, U. Denver, 1954; MA, Calif. State U.-Los Angeles, 1958; Ed.D., U. So. Calif., 1961. Tchr. pub. schs., Riverside, Calif., 1956-58; instr. Calif. State U., Los Angeles, 1958-59, asst. prof., 1959-63; instr. Citrus Community Coll., Glendora, Calif., 1959-63; assoc. prof. SUNY, Buffalo, 1963-68, chmn. dept., 1966-68; prof. edn. Rutgers U., New Brunswick, NJ, 1968—, Disting. prof., 1975; dean, prof. Sch. Edn. San Jose (Calif.) State U., 1986-87. Chmn. dept. sci. and humanities edn. Rutgers U., 1972-75; vis. prof. Cambridge U., Eng., 1974, 75, 79, 80, 83, 84, 85; vis. scholar U. Calif., Berkeley, 1975-76, Stanford U., 1982-83, Western Australia Inst. Tech., 1985, U. Colo., 1989, U. Wash., 1993, U. Sydney, Australia, 1994-95, 2003, Edith Cowan U., Australia, 1997; cons. editor Random House Inc., McGraw-Hill Inc., Primis Pubs.; cons. author Scott, Foresman Publs.; mem. adv. coun. New World Dictionary; mem. San Diego County Supt. Com. on Tchr. Quality, 2000—. Author: (with J. Michaelis) Secondary Social Studies, 1980, (with V. Green) International Human Rights, 1980, (with Frank Besag) Foundations of Education, 1984, (with S. Palonsky and M. McCarthy) Critical Issues in Education, 1990, 7th edit., 2009; contbr. numerous articles to profl. jours.; editor: Social Sci. Rsch., 1964-68, Theory and Rsch. in Social Edn., 1982-85. Mem. exec. bd. ACLU, Middlesex County, NJ, 1968-83; mem. Erie County Dem. Com., 1967-68, NJ Gov.'s Task Force on Rehab. Edn. for Prisoners, 1970-74, Highland Park Bd. Edn., NJ, 1972-75, pres., 1974-75; mem. Highland Park Hist. Commn., 1980-86, NJ Rural Adv. Commn., 1992—, Carlsbad Sister Cities Commn., 2002-05, Carlsbad Sr. Citizen Commn., 2005—, vice chair 2006-07, chair, 2007-; mem. nat. panel Project Censored, 1976—. Commissioned 2d lt. US Army, 1954—55, Ft. Lee, Va., commissioned 2d lt. US Army, 1955—56, Ft. Hood, Tex., 1st lt. US Army, 1956, with Civil Affairs USAR, 1956—63, capt. USAR, 1959. Robert Taft Found. grantee Inst. in Govt., 1970, 86; Inst. for World Order grantee Rutgers U., 1973; Rutgers U. grantee; SUNY-Buffalo grantee, 1967-68; ACLU of N.J. grantee, 1972-73; U.S. Office Edn. grantee, 1967-68; N.J. Dept. Higher Edn. grantee, 1985-86 Mem. Am. Acad. Polit. and Social Sci., AAUP (editorial bd. 1977-80, rep. nat. council 1982-85, com. on acad. freedom and tenure 1983-86, com. on legis. affairs 1992-95, 96-99, exec. bd., state confs. 1996-98), Am. Ednl. Research Assn., Internat. Studies Assn., Nat. Council for Social Studies, Social Sci. Edn. Consortium (bd. dirs. 1983-85), Phi Delta Kappa Democrat. Home: 1360 Las Flores Dr Carlsbad CA 92008-1031 Office: Rutgers U Grad Sch Edn Rutgers U Grad Sch Edn New Brunswick NJ 08903 Business E-Mail: junelson@rci.rutgers.edu.

NELSON, JAMEER, professional basketball player; b. Chester, Pa., Feb. 9, 1982; s. Pete Nelson and Linda Billings; 1 child, Jameer Jr. B in Sociology, St. Joseph's U., Phila., 2004. Point guard Orlando Magic, 2004—. Recipient Adolph Rupp award, 2004, Oscar Robertson award, 2004, Francis Pomeroy Naismith award, 2004, Naismith Men's College Player of Yr. award, 2004, John R. Wooden award, 2004; co-recipient Player of Yr. award, Nat. Assn. Basketball Coaches, 2004; named Player of Yr., Atlantic 10 Conf., 2004, AP, 2004, 1st Team All-Am., 2004; named to Ea. Conf. All-Star Team, NBA, 2009. Office: Orlando Magic 8701 Maitland Summit Blvd Orlando FL 32810*

NELSON, JAMES ALONZO, radiologist, educator; b. Cherokee, Iowa, Oct. 20, 1938; s. Joe George and Ruth Geraldine (Jones) N.; m. Katherine Metcalf, July 16, 1966; children: John Metcalf, Julie Heaps. AB, Harvard U., 1961, MD, 1965. Asst. prof. radiology U. Calif., San Francisco, 1972-74; assoc. prof. U. Utah, Salt Lake City, 1974-79, prof., 1979-86, U. Wash., Seattle, 1986-2000, prof. emeritus, 2000—04; ptnr. Integra Ventures, Seattle, 2004. Dir. radiol. rsch. U. Calif./Ft. Miley VA Hosp., 1973—74, U. Utah, 1974—85, U. Wash., 1986—98; mem. bd. sci. advisors NeoVision, 1995—96, Oreg. Life Scis., 1995—; co-founder Circulation, Inc., 1996; mem. adv. panel on non-radioactive diagnostic agts. USP, 1984—96; mem. NIH RSN study sect., 1998—; RSN study sect., 1998—2004. Contbr. chpts. to books, articles to Am. Jour. Roentgenology, Radiology, Investigative Radiology, others. Capt. USAF, 1967-69. John Harvard scholar, 1957-61, James Picker Found. scholar, 1973-77; recipient Mallinkrodt prize Soc. Body Computerized Tomography, 1990, Roscoe Miller award Soc. Gastrointestinal Radiology, 1991. Fellow Am. Coll. Radiology (diplomate); mem. Radiol. Soc. N.Am., Assn. Univ. Radiology. Achievements include patents (with others) for Non-Surgical Peritoneal Lavage, Recursive Band-Pass Filter for Digital Angiography, for Unsharp Masking for Chest Films, Oral Hepatobiliary MRI Contrast Agent, non-surgical myocardial revascularization, magnetic gut motility monitor, k-edge brachy therapy enhancement, self-debriding catheter. Office: Integra Ventures 300 E Pine Seattle WA 98122 Home Phone: 206-523-4546; Office Phone: 206-832-1995. Business E-Mail: jalonzonel@comcast.net, nelson@integraventures.net.

NELSON, JAMES C, state supreme court justice; b. Moscow, Idaho, Feb. 20, 1944; m. Chari Werner; 2 children. BS, U. Idaho, 1966; JD cum laude, George Washington U., 1974. Fin. analyst SEC, Washington, 1970—73; pvt. practice Werner, Nelson and Epstein, Cut Bank, Mont., 1974—93; county atty. Glacier County, 1980—93; assoc. justice Mont. Supreme Ct., 1993—. Former mem. State Bd. Oil and Gas Conservation, also chmn.; former mem. State Gaming Adv. Counsel, Gov. Adv. Coun. on Corrections and Criminal Justice Policy; liaison to Commn. of Cts. of Ltd. Jurisdiction, mem. adv. com. Ct. Assessment Program. Former pres. Cut Bank Chamber of Commerce. First lieutenant US Army, 1966—69. Office: Supreme Ct PO Box 203004 Helena MT 59620*

NELSON, JAMES HAROLD, health sciences administrator; b. Gosnell, Ark., Apr. 26, 1936; s. J.D. and Louise (Gann) N.; m. Betty Sue Leonard, Sept. 21, 1974; children: Amelia Rebecca, Rachel Louise. BS, Ark. State U., 1961, MS, 1969; PhD, Okla. State U., 1972. Br. chief US Army Environ. Hygiene Agy., Edgewood, Md., 1972-76; from rsch. area mgr. to div. chief US Army Biomed. R & D Lab., Ft. Detrick, Md., 1976-92; project mgr. applied med. systems US Army Med. Materiel Devel. Activity, Ft. Detrick, Md., 1992-96, dir. & program mgr., combat med. sys., 1996—2000; chief liaison office US Army Med. Rsch. & Materiel Command US Army Med. Dept. Ctr. and Sch., Ft. Sam Houston, Tex., 2000—06, sr. med. cons., dir. combat and doctrine devel., 2006—07; sr. rsch. scientist Battelle Meml. Inst. San Antonio Battelle Ops., 2007—09. Mem. Fed. Work Group Pest Mgmt., Washington, 1977-81; chmn. equipment com. Armed Forces Pest Mgmt. Bd., Washington, 1979-83; cons. dir. engrs. Ft. Detrick, 1976-2000; guest lectr. Acad. Health Scis., U.S. Army, Ft. Sam Houston, Tex., 1986-88. Contbr. articles to profl. jours.; assoc. editor: Jour. Am. Mosquito Control Assn., 1982-88; chmn. editorial bd.: Equipment & Insecticides-Mosquito Control, 1989. With USN, 1954-58. Recipient numerous commendations U.S. Army, Ft. Detrick, 1981-2000, R&D Achievement award Asst. Sec. of the Army, 1988, Order of Mil. Med. Merit, 1992. Mem. AAAS, AMVETS, Am. Pub. Health Assn., Assn. Mil. Surgeons U.S., Am. Legion, N.Y. Acad. Scis., Sigma Xi (pres. 1987-88). Achievements include patent for far-forward surgical table. Home: 1315 Brook Bluff San Antonio TX 78248-2632 Home Phone: 210-408-0990. Personal E-mail: nelsonjh@sbcglobal.net. Business E-Mail: nelsonjh@batelle.org.

NELSON, JANIE RISH, health facility administrator; b. Mar. 1, 1941; d. William Hubert and Essie Dell (Davis) Rish; m. John Preston Nelson, Aug. 19, 1984. Student, S.W. Miss. Jr. Coll., 1959—61, Stephens Coll., 1981—. Accredited record tech. Admissions clk. Field Hosp., Centreville, Miss., 1963—68, asst. dir. med. records, 1968—73; dir. med. records West Feliciana Parish Hosp., St. Francisville, La., 1976—2000; ret., 2000. Med. records cons. Beverly Enterprises & Centreville Health Care, 1983—84. Mem. U.S. Congl. Adv. Bd. for La., 1985; fund raiser Rep. Com., 1984; mem. nat. adv. bd. Am. Security Coun., 1984—85. Mem.: NAFE, Tumor Registration Assn. La., La. Med. Records Assn., Am. Med. Records Assn., Miss. Sheriffs Assn. (hon.), Civic Club. Republican. Presbyterian. Avocations: reading, public speaking, gardening. Home: PO Box 374 Centreville MS 39631-0374

NELSON, JIM, editor-in-chief; b. Greenbelt, Md., Mar. 8, 1963; BA in Am. Studies, U. Notre Dame, Ind. Former writer/prodr. CNN, Washington; editor Harper's mag., 1994—97; sr. editor GQ mag. Condé Nast Publs., 1997—2002, co-exec. editor, 2002—03, editor-in-chief, 2003—. Former writer, producer CNN. Contbr. Recipient Feature Writing award, Nat. Mag. awards, Am. Soc. Mag. Editors, 2007, Nat. Mag. award for Gen. Excellence, Am. Soc. Mag. Editors, 2008, Nat. Mag. award for Photography, 2009; nominee Am. Soc. Mag. Editors, 2003. Office: GQ Mag 17th Fl 4 Times Square New York NY 10036 Office Phone: 212-286-5960.*

NELSON, JOELLE GRACE KENNEY, lawyer; b. Augusta, Maine, Dec. 4, 1973; d. Meylon Grant and Lois Marie Kenney; m. Christopher Caldwell Nelson, May 6, 2006; 1 child, Jocelyn Grace. BS, U. So. Maine, Portland, 1996; JD, South Tex. Coll. Law, Houston, 2000. Bar: Tex. 2001. Law clk. Justice Eric Andell First Dist. Ct. Appeals, State of Tex., Houston, 1999—2000; briefing atty. for Justice John S. Anderson 14th Dist. Ct. Appeals, State of Tex., Houston, 2000—01; med. malpractice assoc. McGehee & Pianelli, LLP, Houston, 2001—03; comml. litig. assoc. Johnson DeLuca Kennedy & Kurisky, P.C., Houston, 2003—. Author law seminar South Tex. Coll. Law, 2003, U. Houston Law Ctr., 2003; spkr. in field. Vol. Spl. Olympics, Houston, 1999—2006; participant bike tour Nat. Multiple Sclerosis Soc., Houston, 2005—06. Student advocacy scholar, South Tex. Coll. Law, 1998—2000. Mem.: Houston Young Lawyers Assn., Houston Bar Assn., Tex. Trial Lawyers Assn. (adv. 2001—06). Democrat. Rman Catholic. Avocations: marathon running, cycling, camping, travel. Office: Johnson DeLuca Kennedy & Kurisky PC 1221 Lamar St Ste 1000 Houston TX 77010 Office Fax: 713-652-5130. Business E-Mail: jnelson@jdkklaw.com.

NELSON, JOHN HARRISON, mathematics educator; b. Lubbock, Tex., Apr. 3, 1954; s. Orval Earl and Nancy Ann Nelson. BS, U. Montevallo, Ala., 1983—85. Cert. tchr. Tex. State Bd., 1999. Chemistry tchr. Russellville HS, Ala., 1985—86; sci. tchr. Brandon Hall Sch., Atlanta, 1987—93; math./sci. tchr. Iola HS, Tex., 1994—. Sgt. US Army, 1972—75, Neu-Ulm, Germany. Recipient Sr. Elite, U. Montevallo, 1985. Avocations: tennis, coin collecting/numismatics, puzzles. Home: 502 Southwest Pky #902 College Station TX 77840 Office: Iola HS 7237 Fort Worth St Iola TX 77861 Personal E-mail: jnelson3454@hotmail.com. Business E-Mail: jnelson@iolaisd.net.

NELSON, JOHN HOWARD (JACK HOWARD NELSON), journalist; b. Talladega, Ala., Oct. 11, 1929; s. Howard Alonzo and Barbara Lena (O'Donnell) N.; m. Virginia Dare Dickinson, Aug. 4, 1951 (div. Nov. 1974); children: Karen Dare, John Michael, Steven Howard; m. Barbara Joan Matusow, Dec. 7, 1974. Student, Ga. State Coll., 1953—57. Reporter Biloxi (Miss.) Daily Herald, 1947-51, Atlanta Constitution, 1952-65; so. bur. chief L.A. Times, Atlanta, 1965-70, with Washington bur., 1970—, Washington bur. chief, 1975-96, chief Washington corr., 1996—2002. Author: (with Gene Roberts, Jr.) The Censors and the Schools, 1963, (with Jack Bass) The Orangeburg Massacre, 1970, (with R.J. Ostrow) The FBI and the Berrigans, 1972, Captive Voices, Shocken Books, 1974, Terror in the Night, 1993. With AUS, 1951-52. Recipient Pulitzer prize for local reporting under deadline pressure, 1960; Drew Pearson award for gen. excellence in investigative reporting, 1974; Nieman fellow Harvard U., 1961-62, Shorenstein fellow Harvard U., 2002. Mem. The Gridiron Club. Home: 4 Wynkoop Ct Bethesda MD 20817-5936

NELSON, JOHN ROBERT, JR., manufacturing company executive; b. N.Y.C., Feb. 20, 1952; s. John Robert and Helen Ann (Michaelowski) N.; m. Doris Mae Mansi, Aug. 3, 1974; children— Alexandra, Kathryn. B.A. in Polit. Sci. with honors, Bucknell U., 1974; Ph.D. in Econ. History, No. Ill. U., 1979. Research assoc. Nat. Acad. Sci., Washington, 1978-79; assoc. study dir. U. Chgo., Nat. Opinion Ctr., 1980-82; mgr. pub. issues planning Philip Morris U.S.A., N.Y.C., 1982, sr. v.p. ops, Philip Morris USA; pres. Philip Morris Internat.; pres. Philip Morris USA; pres. ops. & tech. Philip Morris USA; exec. v.p., chief tech. officer Altria Group Inc.; Author: Black Lung: Program Study, 1985. Contbr. articles to profl. jours. Recipient Louis Pelzer award Orgn. Am. Historians; Phi Alpha Theta fellow, 1977. Mem. Nat. Assn. Bus. Economists; Am. Econ. Assn. Republican. Roman Catholic. Avocation: remodeling. Office: ALtria Group Inc 6601 W Broad St Richmond VA 23230*

NELSON, JOHN WOOLARD, neurology educator, physician; b. Hagerstown, Ind., Mar. 9, 1928; s. John Hans and Marvel May (Woolard) N.; m. Nancy Louise Elam, July 21, 1966; 1 son, John Hancock. AB, Earlham Coll., 1950; MD, Ind. U., 1953. Diplomate Am. Bd. Psychiatry and Neurology. Instr. neurology U. Tenn. Coll. Medicine, 1959-61; asst. prof. neurology W. Va. U. Sch. Medicine, 1961-63; assoc. prof. neurology U. Tenn., 1963-66; assoc. prof. to prof. Med. Coll. Wis., Milw., 1966-72; clin. prof. neurology U. Minn., Duluth, 1972-73; prof., head dept. neurology U. Okla. Coll. of Medicine, Oklahoma City, 1973-88, prof. emeritus neurology, 1989—. Served with M.C. U.S. Army, 1955-56. Mem. Okla. County Med. Soc., Okla. Med. Soc., AMA, Am. Acad. Neurology, Am. Electroencephalographic Soc., Am. Med. Electroencephalographic Soc.

NELSON, JONATHAN M., private equity firm executive; b. Providence, May 18, 1956; s. Eugene M. and Jane S. N.; m. Britt Anette Ansnars; m. Alexandra, Rebecca, Katja. AB, Brown U., 1977; MBA, Harvard U., 1983. Export mgr. Wellman, Inc., Boston, 1977-79; pres. Longlife Co., Stockholm, 1979-83; v.p. Narragansett Capital, Inc., Providence, 1983-88, co-chmn., 1988—91; founder, CEO Providence Equity Partners, 1991—. Co-chmn., pres. Narragansett TV, Inc., Providence; co-chmn. bd. dirs. Born In Pub., Inc., Numerous Companion; bd. dirs. Metro-Goldwyn-Mayer Inc., Warner Music Group Corp., 2004-, Yankees Entertainment & Sports Network, LLC, Trinity Repertory Co. Bd. govs. Gordon Sch., East Providence, R.I., 1984; bd. trustees Brown U., 2000-2006; pres., Jonathan M. Nelson Family Found. Avocation: skiing. Office: Providence Equity Partners Inc 18th Floor 50 Kennedy Plaza Providence RI 02903*

NELSON, K. BONITA, literary agent; b. Austin, Minn., July 5, 1945; d. Wallace Arthur and Margaret Rebecca (Lastine) N. BA, Hunter Coll., 1969; B in laws, LaSalle U., 1982. Lit. agt. Am. Play Co., Inc., NYC, 1970-75; legal sec., reviewer Eastman & DaSilva, Esqs., NYC, 1975-79; founder, pres. BK Nelson Literary Agy., NYC, 1983—, BK Nelson Lect. Bureau, NYC, 1994—; pres., publ. Internat. Media Comm., Inc., 1998. Bd. dirs. Dynaray, N.Y.; founder BK Nelson, Inc., 1995; founder Literacy Inst. for Edn. (Life) Inc., 1996. Collaborator: Looking for Canterbury, 1994; author: My Literary Agent, 1998; co-prodr. (movies) Dancing Dan's Christmas, 2006, (musical) Packed Full of Miracles, 2006, Mem. Authors Guild (assoc.), NAFE (assoc.), Nat. Assn. Campus Activities (assoc.), AAUW, (assoc.), Dramatists Guild (assoc.), Minority and Woman Owned Businesses. Avocations: yoga, stamp collecting/philately, automobiles. Office: Bk Nelson Lecture Bureau 1565 Paseo Vida Palm Springs CA 92264-9508 Address: 84 Woodland Rd Pleasantville NY 10570 Home Phone: 760-902-1868; Office Phone: 760-778-8800. Office Fax: 760-778-0034. E-mail: bknelson4@cs.com.

NELSON, KADIR, illustrator, artist; b. Washington; BFA with honors, Pratt Inst., Bklyn. Prin. works include Life of Marvin Gaye, Swizz Beatz: Ghetto Stories, Angel, Represented in permanent collections Debbie Allen, Denzel Washington, Will and Jada Pinckett Smith, Spike Lee, others, exhibitions include Simon Weisenthal Ctr., Acad. Motion Pictures and Sciences, LA, Mus. African Am. History, Detroit, Smithsonian Anacostia Mus., Washington, Soc. of Illustrators and Studio Mus., Harlem, Bristol Mus., Eng., Citizens Gallery, Yokohama, Japan, Ctr. for Culture, Tijuana, Mex., commissions, Dreamworks Studio, Sports Illustrated, Coca-Cola, NY Times, Major League Baseball, illustrator: (children's picture books), Brothers of the Knight, 1999, Big Jabe, 2000, Dancing in the Wings, 2000, Salt in His Shoes, 2000, Just the Two of Us, 2001 (NAACP Image Award), The Village that Vanished, 2002, Under the Christmas Tree, 2002, Please, Baby, Please, 2002, Thunder Rose, 2003, Ellington Was Not a Street, 2004 (Coretta Scott King Illustrator award, 2005), Tales from Shakespeare, 2004, Please, Puppy, Please, 2005, Hewitt Anderson's Great Big Life, 2005, The Real Slam Dunk, 2005, Moses: When Harriet Tubman Led her People to Freedom, 2006, Michael's Golden Rules, 2007, Henry's Freedom Box, 2007; author, illustrator: He's Got the Whole World in his Hands, 2005, We Are the Ship:The Story of Negro League Baseball, 2008 (Coretta Scott King Book award, 2009, Robert F. Sibert Informational Book medal, 2009). Recipient Silver Medal, Soc. of Illustrators. Achievements include being conceptual artist for feature film "Amistad" and animated feature "Spirit: Stallion of the Cimarron.". Office: Ste 124 6977 Navaho Rd San Diego CA 92119 Office Phone: 888-310-3222.*

NELSON, KAREN, legislative staff member; b. Elgin, Ill. BA, Cornell U., Ithaca, NY; grad. student, Harvard U., Cambridge, Mass. Staff mem. US Commn. on Civil Rights, Fed. Programs Divsn., 1965-66, Office Mgmt. and Budget, 1966-70; chief of office, program planning and evaluation Dept. Health, Edn. and Welfare, 1970-74; profl. staff mem., interstate and fgn. commerce com. US House of Reps., Washington, 1974-75, staff dir., energy & commerce com. subcom. on health & the environment, 1980—, spl. asst., Rep. Henry Waxman, health policy dir., govt. reform com. Democrat. Office: 2204 Rayburn House Office Bldg Washington DC 20515*

NELSON, KATHY, broadcast executive; Sr. v.p., gen. mgr. MCA Records Inc.; pres. film music The Walt Disney Motion Picture Group, 1996—2001, Universal Music Group & Universal Pictures, 2001—. Bd. dir. Women in Film. Named one of The 100 Most Powerful Women in Entertainment, Hollywood Reporter, 2006, 2007. Office: Universal Music Group 1755 Broadway New York NY 10019

NELSON, KAY LEROI, chemist, educator; b. Richmond, Utah, Apr. 4, 1926; s. Parley LeRoi and Margaret (Peterson) N.; m. Ina Shepherd, Sept. 4, 1947; children— Marlene, Alan LeRoi, Ronald Leslie, Harold Lynn, Karalee, David LeRoi. BS, Utah State U., 1948; PhD, Purdue U., 1952. AEC thesis research fellow Purdue U., 1950-52, instr., 1953-54; postdoctoral research Office Naval Research fellow UCLA, 1952-53; asst. prof. Wayne State U., 1954-56; asso. prof. Brigham Young U., Provo, Utah, 1956-61, prof., 1961-90, prof. emeritus, 1990—, dept. chmn., 1968-71. Vis. prof. Oreg. State U., 1971-72; vis. scientist Tex. A&M U., 1985 Author: Laboratory Projects in Organic Chemistry, 1966, Laboratory Excursions in Organic Chemistry, 1969, Correlated Organic Laboratory Experiences, 1972, rev. edit., 1975, Guided Organic Laboratory Experiences, 1983, 3d edit., 1986, ABC Nomograph, 1983; poem My Prayer, 1972. V.p. Deseret Villages Assn., Spanish Fork, Utah, 1980-89, exec. dir. 1990-93, treas., 1993-2004; pres. Mulberry Court Homeowners Assn., 1994-2001, Shadowbrook Homeowners Assn., 2007-. With AUS, 1944-45. Mem. AAAS, Am. Chem. Soc., Deseret Villages Assn., Kiwanis, Sigma Xi, Phi Kappa Phi, Phi Lambda Upsilon, Pi Kappa Alpha. *Willingness to work when there was no obvious reward, dissatisfaction with less than the best and an urge to try one more time have brought many satisfactions to me that I otherwise would have missed. I have sought for the long view and found it in books, in the laboratory, and in nature. I enjoy reading, thinking, and just looking. I believe in myself, am optimistic of the future, and have a firm faith in God.*

NELSON, KELLY, anthropologist, educator; b. Morristown, NJ, Dec. 31, 1963; d. Clinton David and Donna Tolkinen Nelson. BA in Advt., Mich. State U., East Lansing, 1986; MS in Adult Edn., U. Southern Maine, Gorham, 1991; PhD in Anthropology, Brandeis U., Waltham, Ma., 1999. Sr. lectr. Ariz. State U., Tempe, 1999—. Office: Ariz State Univ PO Box 871901 Tempe AZ 85287-1901 Business E-Mail: kelly.nelson@asu.edu.

NELSON, KENNETH D., bank executive; BA in Bus. Adminstrn., Econs., Mankato State U., Minn.; MBA, U. St. Thomas, VI. V.p. US Bancorp, Mpls., 2007—08, exec. v.p., corp treas., 2008—. Mem. disclosure com. US Bancorp. Office: US Bancorp 800 Nicollet Mall Minneapolis MN 55402 Office Phone: 651-466-3000.

NELSON, KEVIN, statistician; b. NYC, Dec. 29, 1964; s. Phillip Jacob and Lucie Anne Nelson. BA, U. Chgo., 1987; MA, Wesleyan U., Middletown, Conn., 1991; MPH, U. Ala., Birmingham, 1993; PhD, Med. U. SC., Charleston, 1998. Maternal and child health epidemio Mich. Dept. Pub. Health, Lansing, 2005—06; pub. health analyst US Health Resources and Svcs. Adminstrn., Rockville, Md., 2006—. Functional analyst Lockhead-Martin, Alexandria, Va., 2003. Fellow, Nat. Heart, Lung, and Blood Inst., 1998—2000, Nat. Cancer Inst., 2000—01. Mem.: Am. Statis. Assn. (assoc.), Mu Sigma Rho (assoc.). Office: Health Resources and Services Administra 5600 Fishers Ln Rockville MD Home: 404 Front St Owego NY 13827-1606 Personal E-mail: knelson@hrsa.gov.

NELSON, KIMBERLY TERESE, computer software company executive, former federal agency administrator; b. Phila., 1956; m. Kevin Cadden; children: Kelsey, Mackenzie. B, Shippensburg U., 1978; MPA, U. Pa., 1987. Spl. asst. to sec., spl. asst. to deputy sec. adminstrn., spl. asst. deputy sec. field ops. Pa. Dept. Environ. Resources, 1987—95; dir. program integration and effectiveness then chief info. officer Pa. Dept. Environ. Protection, 1999—2001; asst. adminstr. for environ. info. EPA, Washington, 2001—05; exec. dir. e-govt. Microsoft Corp., Redmond, Wash., 2006—. Office: Microsoft Corp 1 Microsoft Way Redmond WA 98052 also: Microsoft 5335 Wisconsin Ave NW Ste 600 Washington DC 20015

NELSON, KRISTIN SCHAD, otolaryngology, facial plastic surgeon; b. Ashland, Wis., Jan. 3, 1968; d. John Edward Schad and Lynda Jean Zeise; m. Brent David Nelson, June 23, 2002; 1 child, Lake Mattias. BS in Engring. Mechanics, U. Wis., 1990; MS in Engring., U. Ala., 1992; DO, Kirksville Coll. Osteo. Medicine, 1999. Alumni diplomate Kirksville Coll. Osteo. Medicine, 1999. Resident Northeast Regional Med. Ctr., Kirksville, Mo., 1999—2004; clin. asst. prof., divsn. clin. edn. Midwestern U., Ariz. Coll. Osteopathic Medicine, 2008—; otolaryngologist Phoenix, 2007—; cosmetic surgeon Scottsdale, Ariz., 2005—06; cosmetic surgeon, pres. Zen Surgical Aesthetics, Boise, 2006—07. Supv. physician free health clinic Golden Gate Cmty. Ctr., Phoenix, 2004—05; vol. physician Kirksville Coll. Osteo. Medicine, Belize, 2000—03. Fellow, The Body Sculpting Ctr., Scottsdale, 2004—05. Mem.: Ariz. Soc. Otolaryngology, Am. Osteo. Assn., Am. Acad. Otolaryngology, Am. Osteo. Coll. Ophthalmology and Otolaryngology, Ariz. Osteopathic Med. Assn. Avocations: travel, yoga, hiking, bicycling, running.

NELSON, KRYSIA CARMEL, lawyer; d. William L. and Anna K. Carmel; m. Robert L. S. Nelson, Jan. 16, 1999; 1 child. AB, Dartmouth Coll., Hanover, NH, 1992; JD, Villanova U., Pa., 1995. Bar: Va. 95, US Ct. App.(4th Cir.) 1996, U.S. Supreme Ct. 1999. Assoc. Barrick & McKay, Charlottesville, Va., 1995—96; ptnr. Jenkins & Carmel PLC, Charlottesville, 1996—98, Carmel Nelson & Dugger PLC, Charlottesville, 1999—2000, Nelson & Korth PLC, Charlottesville, 2000—06, Nelson & Tucker PLC, Charlottesville, 2006—. Adj. prof. Washington & Lee U. Sch. Law, Lexington, Va., 2005—; spl. projects counsel Va. Dept. Edn., Richmond, 2006—; criminal justice act panel atty. US Dist. Ct. (4th cir.). Editor: Equine Law and Bus. Letter, 1993—; exec. prodr.: (newsletter) The Champion, 1999—2002; contbr. articles to profl. jours.; dir.:. Dist. enrollment dir. Dartmouth Coll., 1999—2008; vol., fundraiser Svc. Dogs of Va., Charlottesville, 2006. Mem.: Charlottesville-Albemarle Bar Assn., Keswick Club, Farmington Hunt Club, Dartmouth Club Ctrl. Va. Avocation: horseback riding. Office: Nelson & Tucker PLC 600 Peter Jefferson Pkwy Ste 100 Charlottesville VA 22911

NELSON, LARRY A., statistics educator, consultant; b. Omaha, Oct. 28, 1932; s. Rudolph Lawrence and Elizabeth Coleman (Lewis) N. BS in Agronomy, Iowa State U., 1954; MS in Soil Sci., Tex. A&M U., 1958; PhD in Soil Sci.-Stats., N.C. State U., 1961. Soil scientist Iowa Agrl. Exptl. Sta., Ames, 1954-55; soils instr. Tex. A&I Coll., Kingsville, 1955; rsch. soil scientist Tex. A&M Rsch. Found., College Station, 1956; soils lab. instr. Tex. A&M U., College Station, 1956-58; rsch. asst. N.C. State U., Raleigh, 1959-61; asst. specialist in land classification Land Study Bur., U. Hawaii, Honolulu, 1961-64; asst. prof. exptl. stats. N.C. State U., Raleigh, 1964-66, assoc. prof. exptl. stats., 1966-71, prof. stats., 1971-89, prof. emeritus stats., 1989—, coord. Concade Project (Bolivia), 1999—2003, interim coord. internat. programs Coll. Agr. and Life Scis., 2002—03, asst. dean for internat. programs Coll. Agr. and Life Scis., 2003—07. Spl. advisor head dep. stats. Kasetsart U., Bangkok, Thailand, 1973; evaluator quantitative skills IADS, Bangladesh, 1984; mem. rev. team Ctr. for Agrl. Econs. and Ctr. for Data Processing, Winrock Internat., Indonesia, 1985; statis. cons. PROCAFE, El Salvador, 1993-96, ICRAF, Nairobi, Kenya, 1991-95; cons. Potash and Phosphate Inst. Can., China and India, 1990, 94, 96; ptnr. Statis. Rsch. Assocs., Honolulu, 1962-63; bd. dirs. Meadowlands Environ. Rsch. Inst., NJ, 2005-; lectr., tchr., cons. in field Assoc. editor Geoderma, 1976-84, Agronomy Jour., 1981-87; contbr. numerous articles to profl. publs. Mem. bd. NC-Bolivia Ptnrs. of Ams., 2007—, GDC Corp., 2007—. NATO fellow Data Analysis Lab., Lyngby, Denmark, 1978. Fellow AAAS, Am. Statis. Assn. (mem. biometrics sect. com. 1989-90, mem. com. on internat. rels. in stats. 1996-98), Am. Soc. Agronomy, Soil Sci. Soc. Am.; mem. Statis. Assn. Thailand (life), Internat. Biometric Soc. (bus. mgr. and treas. 1969-79, awards com. 1987-94, chmn. 1990-93, com. on edn. 1997-99), Internat. Statis. Inst., Sigma Xi, Gamma Sigma Delta (internat. pres. 1984-86, award of merit 1973-74, rep. to AAAS 1978-86), Phi Kappa Phi, Sigma Iota Rho. Baptist. Avocations: music, genealogy, diving, bicycling, travel. Home: 2816 Wycliff Rd Raleigh NC

27607-3035 Office: NC State U Coll of Agrl and Life Sci Office Internat Programs PO Box 7608 Raleigh NC 27695-7608 Office Phone: 919-515-2818. Personal E-mail: lnelson44@nc.rr.com. Business E-Mail: larry_nelson@ncsu.edu.

NELSON, LEON, retired data processing professional; b. Arkadelphia, Ark., Aug. 17, 1947; s. Freeman and Jewellene Nelson. BA in Fine Arts, Henderson State U., Arkadelphia, 1969; BFA in Fine Art and Design, Sch. of the Art Inst., Chgo., 1994. Adminstrv. asst. to dir. rsch. Ency. Britannica, 1972—73; CRT operator, svc. order processor Ill. Bell Tel., 1973—77; data entry specialist Stivers Temporary Pers., 1979—80; supr. computerized TWX and data processsing rm. Katz Comm., 1980—83; data entry specialist Norrel Employment, 1983—86, Chgo. Housing Authority, 1987—96. Author: (autobiography) My Soul is Untouchable, 2009. Bd. dirs. Alumni Assn. of Sch. of Art Inst., 1994—98. Served with US Army, 1967. Mem.: ACLU, Nat. Space Soc., Am. Chem. Soc., Internat. Planetary Soc. Baptist. Avocations: music, painting, drawing, desktop publishing, computer graphics and animation. Home: 354 Jones St Arkadelphia AR 71923 Home Phone: 870-230-1822.

NELSON, LIONEL M., otolaryngologist; BA Physics, CUNY Queens, 1965; MD, Yale U., 1969. Diplomate Am. Bd. Otolaryngology, 1974. Pvt. practice, otolaryngology-head and neck surgery Lionel M. Nelson, MD, San Jose, Calif., 1974—; clin. faculty Stanford U. Sch. Medicine, Calif., 1986—; co-founder and med. officer Apneon, Inc., Cupertino, Calif., 2003—08; med. advisor Gyrus ENT, Bartlett, Tenn., 2001—05; med. dir. Somnus Med. Technologies, Inc, Sunnyvale, Calif., 1998—2001. Guest lectr. sleep apnea treatments, surg. instrumentation, airway implants. Contbr. articles to profl. jours. Capt. USAFR, 1971—77, col. USAR, 1984—2002. Recipient Outstanding Tchr. Recognition Award, Am. Acad. Family Practice, 1987—91; Jonas Salk Med. Rsch. Scholar, City of NY, 1965. Fellow: ACS, Am. Acad. Otolaryngology-Head and Neck Surgery; mem.: Soc. U.S. Flight Surgeons, Am. Acad. Sleep Medicine, Alpha Omega Alpha, Phi Beta Kappa. Achievements include patents for Airway Implants for Sleep Apnea Treatment; Radiofrequency surgical instrumentation; invention of Airway implants for sleep apnea; development of Surgical and radiofrequency devices. Office: 2505 Samaritan Dr Ste 510 San Jose CA 95124

NELSON, MARILYN CARLSON, hotel and travel company executive; b. Mpls. m. Glen Nelson; children: Diana, Curtis C., Wendy. Student, U. Sorbonne, Paris, Inst. Hautes Etudes Econ., Geneva; degree in internat. econs. with honors, Smith Coll., 1961; DBA (hon.), Johnson & Wales U.; DHL (hon.), Coll. St. Catherine, Gustavus Adolphus Coll. Securities analyst Paine Webber, Mpls.; pres., COO Carlson Companies, Inc., Minnetonka, 1998—2003, chmn., CEO, 1998—2008, chmn., 2008—. Co-chair Carlson Holdings, Inc., 2000—; co-chair Carlson Wagonlit Travel, 1994-2003; disting. vis. prof. Johnson & Wales U.; bd. dirs. Exxonmobil Corp., Mayo Clinic Found., Com. to Encourage Corp. Philanthropy; chmn. Nat. Women's Bus. Coun., 2002-05; vice chair U.S. Travel and Tourism Adv. Bd.; bd. mem. Singapore Tourism Bur. Author: How We Lead Matters Reflections on A Life of Leadership, 2008. Pres. United Way Mpls., campaign chair, 1984; bd. dirs. United Way Am., 1984-90, U.S. Nat. Tourism Orgn., 1996-98, Ctr. for Internat. Leadership, 1989-2003; mem. disting. adv. coun. Coll. of St. Catherine, 1991-94; hon. bd. dirs. Svenska Inst., Stockholm, 1993—; mem. adv. bd. Hubert H. Humphrey Inst. Pub. Affairs, 1992-96; co-founder Minn. Women's Econ. Roundtable, 1974—; chair Minn. Super Bowl Task Force, 1984-92; chair, founder Midsummer Internat. Festival of Music, 1992; co-chair New Sweden '88; past bd. dirs. Guthrie Theatre, Greater Mpls. Girl Scout Coun., Jr. Achievement, Jr. League Mpls., KTCA Pub. TV, Minn. Econ. Assn., Minn. Congl. Award, Minn. Opera Co., Women's' Assn. Minn. Symphony Orch.; trustee Smith Coll., Northampton, Mass., 1980-85, Macalester Coll., St. Paul, 1974-80; mem. adv. bd. Minn. Women's Yearbook; trustee Curtis L. Carlson Family Found. Recipient Minn. Congl. award for initiative and svc. to cmty., Commendation cert., State of Minn., Cmty. Svc. award, YWCA, Independence award, Vinland Nat. Ctr., Cmty. Svc. award, Park-Nicollet Med. Ctr., Outstanding Mktg. Exec. of Yr. award, Minn. Distributive Edn. Club Am., Career Achievement award, Sales and Mktg. Execs. Mpls., Outstanding Achievement award, United Way Mpls., Extraordinary Leadership award, Greater Mpls. C. of C., Disting. Svc. award, United Way of Am., 1984—90, Nat. Caring award, Caring Inst., 1995, Outstanding Bus. Leader award, Northwood U., 1995, Disting. Svc. award (highest vol. honor), United Way Minn., 1998, Good Neighbor award, WCCO Radio, 1999, Caring Heart award, Larry King Cardiac Found., 1999, Svc. Above Self award, Rotary Club Downtown, Minn., 1999, Northwest Airlines Disting. World Traveler award, Hospitality Sales and Mktg. Assn. Internat., 2000, Responsible Capitalism award, FIRST mag., 2001, Glass Ceiling award, Minn. Women's Consortium, 2001, Great Swedish Heritage award, Swedish Coun. Am., 2002, Lifetime Achievement award, Internat. Investment Forum, 2002, Athena award, Athena Found., 2004, Lifetime Achievement award, Hospitality Sales and Mktg. Assn. Internat., 2004, 18th Ann. Lucia Travel award, 2005, Chevalier knight, French Legion Honor, 2006, Icon award, Nat. Bus. Travel Assn., 2006, Leadership award, Multicultural Devel. Ctr., 2006, Lifetime Achievement award, 2007; named Sales Exec. of Yr., Sales and Mktg. Exec. Mpls., Woman of Yr., Minn. Exec. Women in Tourism, 1991—92, Outstanding Individual in Tourism, Minn. Office Tourism, 1992, Woman of Yr., Roundtable Women in Food Svc., 1995, #1 Most Powerful Women in Travel, Travel Agent Mag., 1997—2003, Businesswoman of World, Bus. Women's Network, 2001, Swedish Am. of Yr., King and Queen of Sweden, 2003, Minnesotan of Yr., Minn. Monthly mag., 2003, Businesswoman of Yr., US Commerce Dept. Small Bus. Adminstrn., 2005, Life Dir., Minn. Orchestra, 2006, Hall of Fame, Am. Soc. Travel Agents, 2007, Entrepreneur of Decade, Women Pres. Orgn., 2007, 100 Most Influential People in Bus. Ethics, Ethisphere Mag., 2007, Bus. Hall of Fame Layreate, 2008; named one of Exec. Yr. Corp. Report Minn., 1999, Forbes Richest Americans, 2006, Am.'s Best Leaders, US News and World Report, 2006, 100 Most Powerful Women, Forbes mag., 2007; named to Hall of Fame, Sales and Mktg. Execs. Mpls., 2003. Mem. World Econ. Forum, World Travel and Tourism Coun., Travel Industry Assn. Am. (bd. dirs.), Hennepin County Med. Soc. Aux., Bus. Roundtable, Smith Coll. Alumni Assn., Smith Club Mpls., Woodhill Country Club, Mpls. Club, N.W. Tennis Club, Nat. Ctr. Social Entrepreneurs, Com. of 200, Hospitality Sales and Mktg. Assn. Internat. (Lifetime Achievement award 2004), Minn. Orchestral Assn., Orphei Dranger, Alpha Kappa Psi. Office: Carlson Companies Inc 701 Carlson Pkwy Minnetonka MN 55305

NELSON, MARK D., music educator, arts education administrator; b. NYC, June 4, 1954; s. Harry D. and Sylvia Allen Nelson. BA, Yale U., 1976; MusM, U. Ill., 1980; PhD, Princeton U., 1995. Asst. prof. music Lake Forest (Ill.) Coll., 1986—93; asst. prof., chmn. music dept. Wabash Coll., Crawfordsville, Ind., 1993—95; performing arts chmn., tchr. music, cultural history Hawken Upper Sch., Gates Mills, Ohio, 1998—2001, Ross Sch., East Hampton, NY, 2004—06, Webb Sch., Claremont, Calif., 2006—. Composer: Arboreal, 1985 (NJ Arts Coun. grant, 1985), Song Lines, 1998, 2d edit., 2006. Recipient William L. Dunn award for Outstanding Tchg. and Scholarly Promise., Lake Forest Coll., 1990, Excellence in Tchg. award, Thompson and Vivian Webb, 2007, Demetriades prize, 2008. Mem.: Phi Kappa Phi, Phi Beta Kappa. Independent. Avocations: backpacking, photography, music of India and Java. Home and Office: 2171 N Towne Ave Claremont CA 91711 Business E-Mail: mdnelson@wesleyan.edu.

NELSON, MARTHA JANE, editor; b. Pierre, SD, Aug. 13, 1952; d. Bernard Anton and Pauline Isabel (Noren) Nelson. BA, Barnard Coll., NYC, 1976. Mng. editor Signs: Jour. of Women in Culture, NYC, 1976—80; staff editor Ms. Mag., NYC, 1980—85; editor-in-chief Women's Sports and Fitness Mag., San Francisco, 1985—87; exec. editor Savvy, NYC, 1988—89, editor-in-chief, 1989—91, Who Weekly, Sydney, 1992; founding editor In Style Mag., NYC, 1993—2002; asst. mng. editor People Mag. Time Inc., NYC, 1993, mng. editor, 2002—06, editor People Grp. publs., 2006—, editor style & entertainment group, 2008—. Editor: Women in the American City, 1980; exec. prodr.: (TV series) Celebrity Weddings, 1997—2002, Celebrity Moms, Celebrity Homes; contbr. articles to profl. jours. Adv. bd. NYU Grad. Sch., 2000—07; bd. dirs. Drama Dept., NYC Theatre Co., Painting Space 122, NYC, 1982—85, 1995—96, Urban Athletic Assn., 1986, AIDS Comm. Rsch. Inst. America, Accessories Coun., 1999—2001, Athletic and Swim Club, 2000—07, Actor's Fund, 2006—. Recipient Child Victimization in the News award, Nat. Ctr. for Missing and Exploited Children, 2003, Achiever award, Cosmetic Exec. Women, 2000, Inspiration award, Women's Step Up Network, 2004; named one of Top 25 Most Influential People in Media, Brill's Content, 1999, 100 Most Powerful Women, Forbes Mag., 2004—06. Mem.: NY Women in Comm. (Matrix award 2004), Women in Film, Am. Soc. Mag. Editors (bd. dirs.). Office: People Grp Rockefeller Ctr 1271 Ave of the Americas New York NY 10020 Office Phone: 212-522-8671. E-mail: martha-nelson@peoplemag.com.*

NELSON, MARVIN RAY, retired life insurance company executive; b. Thornton, Iowa, Aug. 29, 1926; s. Clarence Anton and Rose Bessie (Nicolet) N.; m. Juanita Mae Brown, May 26, 1951; children: Nancy, Kenneth. BS, Drake U, 1951. Actuary Security Mut. Life Ins. Co., Lincoln, Nebr., 1951-58; assoc. actuary Life Ins. Co. N.Am., Phila., 1958-59; group actuary Bankers Life of Nebr., Lincoln, 1959-66; actuary Mut. Service Life Ins. Co., St. Paul, 1966-68; sr. v.p. Horace Mann Educators Corp., Springfield, Ill., 1968-77, Security Life of Denver, 1977-83, exec. v.p., 1988-91; pres., chief oper. officer, dir., mem. investment com. Midwestern United Life Ins. Co., Ft. Wayne, Ind., 1983-89; ret., 1991. Bd. dirs., treas. Ft. Wayne Urban League, 1983-87; bd. dirs. Taxpayers Research Assn., Ft. Wayne, 1984-88; pres. Shalom Pk. Men's Group, 2006-. With US Army, 1946—47. Fellow Soc. Actuaries; mem. Am. Acad. Actuaries, Pi Kappa Phi. Home: 5224 S Shalom Pk Cir Aurora CO 80015-2263

NELSON, MARY CARROLL, artist, writer; b. Bryan, Tex., Apr. 24, 1929; d. James Vincent and Mary Elizabeth (Langton) Carroll; m. Edwin Blakeley Nelson, June 27, 1950; children: Patricia Ann, Edwin Blakely. BA in Fine Arts, Barnard Coll., NYC, 1950; MA, U. N.Mex., Albuquerque, 1963. Juror Am. Artist Golden Anniversary Competition, 1987. Guest instr. continuing edn. U. N.Mex., 1991; conf. co-organizer Affirming Wholeness, The Art and Healing Experience, San Antonio, 1992, Artists of the Spirit Symposium, 1994. Exhibited in group shows at N.Mex. Mus., 1987, Art is for Healing, The Universal Link, San Antonio, 1992, Fuller Lodge Art Ctr. Los Alamos, N.Mex., 1993, Layering, Albuquerque, 1993, Crossings, Bradford, Mass., 1994, The Layered Perspective, Fayetteville, Ark., 1994, Tree of Life, San Miguel de Allende, Mex., 1996, (honoree Magnifico, Albuquerque, 1997, Bravos award Excellence in Arts 2004, Achievement award Masterworks, 2005), Guardian Spirits, Marlborough, Eng., 1997, Memories in Multi-Media, Columbus, Ohio, 1998, Agora Gallery, NYC, 1998, Celtic Connections, Mass., 1998, Bridging Time and Space, Calif., 1999, Musings on the Millennium, Ohio, 2000, Layerists in Multi-Media/Affirming Wholeness, Albuquerque, 2000, The Birth of Wisdom, N.M.and Gordes, France, 2000, Tides of Change, Tex., 2001, Earth-Spirit, Ohio, 2001, Shadow & Light, Albuquerque, 2001, Landscape and Memory, Sedona, Ariz., 2002, dsg Gallery, Albuquerque, 2002, Albuquerque Mus., 2003, 07, Fire in the Heart, Ashland, Oreg., 2003, Layered Images, Albuquerque, 2003, Masterworks Miniatures, Albuquerque, 2004 (1st award Mixed Media, Juror Masterworks award 2005), 2nd Pl. Mixed Media, 2008, (Miniatures Masterworks Bardean award, 2009); Get the Lead Out, Los Alamos U., 2005, Weynich Gallery, Alburquerque, 2006, N.Mex. State U., Las Cruces, 2006, Soul Shrines, Las Cruces, 2006, Mus. Fine Arts, Las Cruces, 2006, Rock, Paper, Scissors, Los Alamos, N.Mex., 2006, Connections: We Are All One, Lexington, Ky., 2006, Art of Space, Las Cruces, 2006, Exploring Multiple Dimensions, Albuquerque, 2007, Illumination, Ft. Myers, Fla., 2008, Beyond the I.Albuquerque, 2009; represented in pvt. collections; author: American Indian Biography Series, 1971-76, (with Robert E. Wood) Watercolor Workshop, 1974; (with Ramon Kelley) Ramon Kelley Paints Portraits and Figures, 1977, The Legendary Artists of Taos, 1980, (catalog) American Art in Peking, 1981, Masters of Western Art, 1982, Connecting, The Art of Beth Ames Swartz, 1984, Artists of the Spirit, 1994, Doris Steider, A Vision of Silence, 1997, Beyond Fear, A Toltec's Guide to Freedom and Joy, 1997, Layering, An Art of Time and Space, 1985, (catalog) Layering/Connecting, 1987; contbg. editor Am. Artist, 1976-91, Southwest Art, 1987-91; editor (video) Layering, 1990; arts corr. Albuquerque Jour., 1991-93; contbr. One Source Sacred Journeys, 1997, Lightstream, 2003; co-author: Bridging Time and Space, Essays on Layered Art, 1998, Toltec Prophecies of Don Miguel Ruiz, 2003; co-editor The Art of Layering: Making Connections, 2004, Crop Circles, An Art of Our Time, 2007. Mem. Albuquerque Arts Bd., 1984—88. Mem. Soc. Layerists in Multi-Media (founder 1982, coord. symposium 2007). Home: 1408 Georgia St NE Albuquerque NM 87110-6861 Personal E-mail: mcn50@comcast.net.

NELSON, MARY ELLEN GENEVIEVE, retired adult education educator; b. Milw., Sept. 13, 1948; d. William Paul and Evelyn Marie (Saduske) Naber; m. Kenneth Arthur Nelson, July 22, 1972; children: William Norris, Victoria Marie. BS in Edn., Mt. Mary Coll., 1970; MEd, Carroll Coll., 1994. Cert. tchr., Wis.; cert. in math., computers, careers Wis. Tech. Coll. Sys., ABE/GOAL basic edn.; lic. math computer careers, reading and writing. Clk. Oldline Life Ins., Milw., 1967-70; math. tchr. Menomonee Falls East HS, Wis., 1970-76; math. and adult basic edn. tchr. Waukesha County Tech. Coll., Pewaukee, Wis., 1978-82, math. tchr., goal instr., 1982-88, lead adult basic edn. tchr. and goal instr. Menomonee Falls, 1988—2005; ret., 2004. Co-chair Tech. Acad. Edn., 1995; initiator adult ESL pilot program Wis. Tech. Coll., 2001; mgr. adult ESL pilot program Menomonee Falls Sch. Dist., 2003—04, mgr. study program, 2003—04; established Tech. Coll. NABER Carpentry Classes, Dominican Republic, 2005—; presenter in field; cons. in field; founder Million NABER Blue & Gold Marquette, 2005, Friend of Butler Libr. Meml. Fund Evelyn NABER, 2008, Harwood Pl. Libr. Meml. Fund Evelyn NEBER, 2009. Contbr. papers to prof. jour. Dir. presch. program St. Agnes Cath. Ch., Butler, Wis., 1979-82, presch. tchr., 1977-79; den mother cub scout Pack 72, Boy Scouts Am., Butler, 1983-84, candy fundraiser chmn., 1985, 86; mem. Menomonee Falls Edn. Com., 1987-97; initiator and chair yearly student advancement fundraiser, Waukesha County. Tech. Coll., 1993-2004; mem. Leadership Menomonee Falls, 1995-96, mem. bd. govs., 1997-2000; initiator Families Learning Together, 2001-02, 02-03; mem. Com. Expansion Menomonee Falls Cmty. Ctr., 2001-02. Recipient Outstanding Svc. pin, Menomonee Falls Cmty. Sch. Dist., 1994, recognition mktg. efforts to improve ednl. opportunities in cmty., 2004, 35 Yr. Svc. Friend of Edn. award, 2006, 25th Yr. award, Wis. Math. Coun., 1995, award, YWCA, 1996, cert., U. Wis. Coop. Ext. Program, 2002, Mentor award, Leadership Menomonee Falls Orgn., 2004, Harwood Place Lit. Meml. award, 2009; nominee Gold Alumnus, Carroll Coll., 2004. Mem. Wis. Math. Coun., Wis. Adult and Continuing Edn. Assn., Menonomee Falls C. of C. (Waukesha County Tech. Coll. rep. 1993-2004, edn. com. 1986-2004), Rotary (partnership), St. Vincent de Paul Soc.(contbr., 2001-) Roman Catholic. Achievements include development of Luncheon Symposium format for Wis. Tech. Coll. Sys. Avocations: crafts, golf, travel, reading, stained glass art. Home: N54W15485 Northway Dr Menomonee Falls WI 53051-6716 Personal E-mail: menelson72@sbcglobal.net.

NELSON, MARY KATHRYN, bilingual counselor, small business owner, real estate and insurance agent, artist; b. Chgo., May 28, 1954; d. James C. Nelson and Leila R. Cooke. BS in Social Work, So. Ill. U., 1978; MS in Rehab. Counseling, U. Ariz., 1982. Cert. rehab. counselor, Ariz.; nat. cert. counselor; lic. real estate agt., Ariz., lic. ins. agent, 2006. Bilingual counselor Ill. Migrant Council, 1975-76; social worker Child Protective Svcs., 1980-85; bilingual clinician pvt. nonprofit agys., 1985-96; bilingual counselor contractor, counselor Suprme Ct. Ariz., Phoenix, 1995—; owner, mgr. Bilingual Svcs., LLC, Phoenix, 1985—, owner Peoria, Ariz., 1994—, ins. cons. Peoria C. of C., 2008—; real estate agt. Liberty Properties, Inc., Ariz., 2003—05, Ken Meade Realty, Sun City, Ariz., 2005—06; bilingual agent Am. Farmer's Ins., Peoria, Ariz., 2006—, Weinstein-Fehris Realty, Scottsdale, Ariz., 2006—; agt. Assurant Ins. Co., 2006—; ins. agt. Mutual of Omaha, Ariz., 2007—; realtor Liberty Properties, Inc., 2007—; vocat. rehab. counselor State Ariz., Phoenix, 2007; bilingual rehab. specialist Magellan Health Co., Phoenix, 2008—. Exhibited in group shows at Franciscan Renewal Ctr., Scottsdale, 2001, exhibitions include Artareas.com, 2001—, Fountain Hills Ariz. Art Exhibit, 1995, Channel 22 Phoenix Cable Amateur Hr., Spanish Songs, 1996, Iberoamericana Internat. Art Exhibit, Miami, Fla., 1997, Phoenix K Lite Radio TV Commn., 1997, Peoria Sportscomplex Art Fair, Ariz., 1998, Franciscan Renewal Ctr. Art Fair, Scottsdale, Ariz., 1999, 2001, ArtAreas.com, portrait artist, Sen. Kyl Ariz., 2007, Sen. McCain Ariz., 2007, Sen. Collins Ariz., 2007, US Senator Susan Collins, Maine, 2007; performer: Talent Show at Crossroads, 1999—2001; singer: Franciscan Renewal Ctr., 2000—01. Vol. Big Bros.-Big Sisters, Tucson, 1999; family advocate Cesar Chavez Farmworkers Union Labor Movement; art donor Ariz. Foster Care Assn., Paradise Valley, Ariz., 2001, donor original oil painting with World Trade Ctr. motif, 2001; founder Morris Dee's Ctr. for Justice/Civil Rights Mtml. Ctr.; mem. So. Poverty Law Ctr.; vol. campaign worker Jon Kyle for Senator, Phoenix, 1996—2007; fundraiser John Shadeg for Congressman, Ariz., 2002, Women Reps. for Kyl, 1996—2006; choir mem. Franciscan Renewal Ctr., Paradise Valley, Ariz., 1999—2002. Recipient humanitarian award Inst. Arts Plastiques, 1997; named to Martin Luther King Meml. Wall of Tolerance, 2003. Mem. Drama Beat Acting Club. Republican. Avocations: singing, comedy, acting. Home: 12667 W Maya Way Peoria AZ 85383-2829 Home Phone: 623-478-9149. Personal E-mail: marynelsonsc@aol.com.

NELSON, MATT, psychology professor; BA, Vanguard U., Costa Mesa, Calif., 1982; MA, Pepperdine U., Irvine, Calif., 1985; PhD, U. Southern Calif., LA, 1995. Sr. cons. McDonnell Douglas Corp., Long Beach, Calif., 1986—97, Huntington Beach, Calif., 1986—97; prof. Northwest U., Kirkland, Wash., 1997—. Office: Northwest Univ 5520 108th Ave NE Kirkland WA 98033 Business E-Mail: matt.nelson@northwestu.edu.

NELSON, MICHAEL ARNOLD, economics professor, department chairman; s. Arnold Raymond and Edna Mae Nelson; m. Particia Lou DiSanti, Aug. 10, 1991; children: Rachel Antionette, Stephanie Lucia. PhD, Purdue U., West Lafayette, Ind., 1980. Prof. Ill. State U., Normal, 1981—2000; prof., chair U. Akron, Ohio, 2000—. Home: 5911 Laurawood Ln Hudson OH 44236 Office: Univ Akron Dept Economics Akron OH 44325 Office Fax: 330-972-5356; Home Fax: 330-972-5356. Business E-Mail: nelson2@uakron.edu.

NELSON, MICHAEL CHAIM, city councilman; b. Nov. 23, 1945; m. Sheila Nelson. BS, Univ. Memphis. Dir. cmty. rels. for US Rep. Charles Schumer; chief of staff to NY State Senator Carl Krueger; city councilman Dist. 48 NY City Coun., 1999—. Chmn. Waterfronts com. NY City Coun. Served USAF. Recipient Schiller Member Award for Americanism & Patriotism, Jewish War Veterans of America; named Educator of Year, United Fedn. Teachers. Mem. Vietnam Veterans of America, KP, Friends of Hospice, Jewish War Veterans. Democrat. Mailing: 3810-A Nostrand Ave Brooklyn NY 11235 Office Phone: 212-788-7360, 718-368-9176. Office Fax: 718-368-9160. Business E-Mail: nelson@council.nyc.ny.us.*

NELSON, NANCY ELEANOR, retired pediatrician, educator; b. El Paso, Apr. 4, 1933; d. Harry Hamilton and Helen Maude (Murphy) Nelson. BA magna cum laude, U. Colo., 1955; MD, 1959. Intern. Case Western Res. U. Hosp., 1959—60, resident, 1960—63; pvt. practice Denver, 1963—70; assoc. dean student affairs U. Colo. Sch. Medicine, Denver, 1988—2002, clin. prof. emerita, 2002—. Mem.: AMA (sect. med. schs. governing coun. 1994—96), Denver Mus. Nature and Sci. (vol. 2007—), Colo. Med. Soc. (bd. dirs. 1985—88), Denver Med. Soc. (pres. 1983—84), Am. Acad. Pediats.

NELSON, NORMAN DANIEL, government official; married; 2 children. BSBA, U. Fla., 1991; MBA, U. Miami, 1997; MA, Georgetown U., 2000. Intern corp. fin. divsn. mergers and acquisitions Commerzbank AG, Frankfurt, 1992; intern corp. fin. divsn. internat. leasing and new stock issues Deutsche Bank AG, Frankfurt, 1992; commd. 2d lt. disting. mil. grad. USAR, 1991, advanced through grades to LTC, C.E. and Civil Affairs, 2008; econ. plans and program officer US Dept. State, 1997—2001, fgn. svc. officer, 2001—. Decorated Army Commendation medal (3); recipient Meritorious Honor award U.S. Dept. State, 2003; Fed. Chancellor scholar Alexander-von-Humboldt Found., 1991-92. Mem. Sigma Chi. Personal E-mail: texas_florida@hotmail.com.

NELSON, PAUL D., podiatrist; Attended, Scholl Coll. Podiatric Medicine. Cert. Am. Bd. Podiatric Surgery Examiners. Resident Genesys Regional Med. Ctr., Grand Blanc, Mich.; podiatrist Sacred Heart Hosp., Hosp. Plz. Foot and Ankle Inst. Mem.: Am. Podiatric Med. Assn. Office: Hosp Plz Foot and Ankle Inst Ste 102 3800 Highland Ave Downers Grove IL 60515*

NELSON, PAUL DOUGLAS, lawyer; b. Silverton, Oreg., Dec. 22, 1948; s. Robert Thorsen and Elene Nelson; m. Mary Linda Hilligoss, Feb. 28, 1981; children: Christopher R., Matthew D., Patrick D. BA cum laude, Lewis & Clark Coll., Portland, Oreg., 1971; JD, U. Oreg. Sch. Law, 1974. Bar: Calif. 1974, Oreg. 1975. Law clk. US atty.'s office US

Dist. Ct. Oreg., Portland, 1973; assoc. Hoge, Fenton, Jones & Appel, San Jose, 1974-75, Hancock, Rothert & Bunshoft LLP, San Francisco and London, 1975—81, ptnr., 1981—2005, Duane Morris LLP, San Francisco, 2006—. Contbr. articles to profl. jours. Mem.: ABA, Assn. Ski Def. Attorneys (founding mem.), Am. Law Firm Assn. (former officer and dir.), Bar Assn. San Francisco. Avocation: skiing. Office: Duane Morris LLP One Market Spear Tower Ste 2000 San Francisco CA 94105 Office Phone: 415-957-3138. Office Fax: 415-358-5593. Business E-Mail: PDNelson@duanemorris.com.*

NELSON, PAULA MORRISON BRONSON, retired reading specialist; b. Memphis, Mar. 26, 1944; d. Fred Ford and Julia (Morrison) Bronson: m. Jack Marvin Nelson, July 13, 1968; children: Eric Allen, Kelly Susan BS, U. N.Mex., 1967; MA, U. Colo., Denver, 1985. Tchr. phys. edn. Grant Union Sch. Dist., Sacramento, 1967—68, Denver Pub. Schs., 1968—74, with program for pupil assistance, 1974—80; tchr. ESL Douglas County Pub. Schs., Parker, Colo., 1982—83; Chpt. 1 reading specialist Denver Pub. Schs., 1983—96, computer/reading specialist, 1996—98, reading specialist, tchr. gifted and talented, 1998—99, lead tchr. in charge instrn., 1999—2001, edn. cons., 2001—02; ret. Demonstration tchr. Colo. Edn. Assn., 1970-72; mem. curriculum com. Denver Pub. Schs., 1970-72; mem. Douglas County Accountability Com., Castle Rock, Colo., 1986-92; mem. educators rev. panel Edn. for Freedom; computer trainer Denver Pub. Schs. Tech. Team, 1992-02; bd. dirs. Obie Harrington-Howes Found., 2005-08. Co-author: Gymnastics Teacher's Guide Elementary Physical Education, 1973, Applauding Our Constitution, 1989; editl. reviewer G is for Geography, Children's Literature and the Five Themes, 1993; prodr. slide shows Brotherhood, 1986, We the People...Our Dream Lives On, 1987, Celebration of Cultures, 1988 Named Pub. Edn. Coalition grantee, Denver, 1987, 88, 89, 90, grantee Rocky Mountain Global Edn. Project, 1987, Wake Forest Law Sch., Winston-Salem, N.C., 1988, 89, 90, 92, Read to Achieve grantee Colo. State Dept. Edn., 2000, Chpt. II grant, 1991, Tech. grant, 1993, Title VI Reading grant, 1999, 2000; recipient Three R's of Freedom award State Dept. Edn., 1987, Nat. Recognition award Commn. on Bicentennial of Constn., 1987, Disting. Tchr. award City of Denver, 1994 Mem.: Tech. in Edn. Independent. Methodist. Avocations: snow and water skiing, tennis, sailing. Home: 18 Covewood Dr Norwalk CT 06853

NELSON, PHILIP CHARLES, physics professor; b. Kansas City, Mo., Nov. 22, 1957; s. Oliver and Marion Nelson; m. Nily R. Dan; children: Rachel, Daniel. PhD, Harvard U., Cambridge, Mass., 1984. Prof. physics U. Pennsylvania, Phila., 1998—. Author: (textbook) Biological Physics (Emily Gray Prize of Biophysical Soc., 2009). Fellow: Am. Phys. Soc. Office: Physics and Astronomy Univ Penn 209 S 33d St Philadelphia PA 19104

NELSON, PHILIP EDWIN, food scientist, educator; b. Shelbyville, Ind., Nov. 12, 1934; s. Brainard R. and Alta E. (Pitts) N.; m. Sue Bayless, Dec. 27, 1955; children: Jennifer, Andrew, Bradley. BS, Purdue U., 1956, PhD, 1976. Plant mgr. Blue River Packing Co., Morristown, Ind., 1956-60; instr. Purdue U., West Lafayette, Ind., 1961-76, head dept. food sci., 1983—2003, Scholle chair prof., 2004—. Cons. PEN Cons., West Lafayette, 1974; chair Food Processors Inst., Washington, 1990-93; mem. adv. bd. USDA, 2002-06. Editor: Fruit Vegetable Juice Technology, 1980, Principles of Aseptic Processing and Packaging, 1992. Recipient Pers. Achievement award USDA, 1997, World Food Prize Laureate, 2007. Fellow Inst. Food Techs. (pres. 2001-02, Indsl. Achievement award 1976, Nicholas Appert award 1995, 49'er Svc. award 1995, Tanner lectr. 1999), Internat. Acad. Food Sci. and Tech. (USDA specialty crops com. 2005-07); mem. AAAS, Sigma Xi, Phi Tau Sigma (pres. 1976-77). Achievements include 11 U.S. and foreign patents. Office: Purdue U Dept Food Sci 745 Ag Mall Drive West Lafayette IN 47907-2009 E-mail: pen@purdue.edu.

NELSON, PHILIP FRANCIS, musicologist, consultant, conductor; b. Waseca, Minn., Feb. 17, 1928; s. Elmer Philip and Frances (Bretzke) Nelson; m. Georgia Ann Yelland, June 5, 1950; children: Curtis Ann, Philip Francis Jr. AB, Grinnell Coll., 1950; AM, U. N.C., 1956, PhD, 1958; Diplome (Fulbright scholar), U. Paris, 1957; student, Conservatoire Nat. de Paris, 1956-57; MA (hon.), Yale U., 1971; LHD (hon.), Grinnell Coll., 1981. Asst. prof. Ariz. State U., 1958-62, assoc. prof., 1962-63; prof., chmn. dept. music SUNY, Binghamton, 1963-70; prof., dean Sch. Music, Yale U., 1970-81; prof., provost, dean U. Calif., Santa Cruz, 1981-83; chmn. trustee com. Curtis Inst., 1982-83; sr. v.p. AED, NYC, 1984-87; v.p. Aspen Inst. Humanistic Studies, 1987-89; interim chancellor Sch. Arts U. N.C., 1989-90, interim vice chancellor Chapel Hill, 1991, chmn. grad. sch. adv. coun., 1993-96, cons. arts and humanities, 1996—; assoc. fellow Nat. Humanities Ctr., 1990-91; cons. edn., arts, 1992-93; interim dir. N.C. Sch. Sci. and Math., 1999-2000; sr. cons. U. N.C. and Nat. Humanities Ctr., 2000—; cons. Park Found., 2003—; trustee N.C. Sch. Arts, 2005—. Music critic Phoenix Gazette, 1959—62; music cons. Tallesin West, 1959—63; chmn. Nat. Screening Com. Fulbright Awards in Musicology, 1965—68; cons. Nat. Endowment Arts, 1984—90; vis. lectr. Duke U., 1992—. Contbg. editor: College and Adult Reading List, 1962, Nicolas Bernier, Principles of Composition, 1964, Recherches sur la musique Française classique, 1979, 1980; co-author: Groves Dictionary of Music, 6th edit.; editor: Aspen Inst. Humanities, 1987—89. Bd. dirs. various symphonies, chamber music socs., arts groups; trustee Curtis Inst. Music, Phila., 1980—83; bd. dirs. Conn. Hospice, 1983—87, Nat. Soc. Prevent Blindness, 1987—93, bd. dirs., v.p., 1987—93; mem. Chapel Hill Arts Ctr., 1992—, Triangle J. Coun. Govt., 1992—95; trustee N.C. Sch. Arts, 2005; mem. exec. com. Conn. State Golf Assn., 1975—81; founder Seven Springs Soc., 1975. Lt. comdr. USCGR, 1952—72. Found. grantee. Mem.: Soc. Ethnomusicology, Société Française de Musicologie, Coll. Music Soc. (nat. coun., editor jour. 1966—69), Internat. Musicol. Soc., Am. Musicol. Soc., U.S. Srs. Golf Assn., Chapel Hill Country Club, Finley Golf Club, Yale Golf Club, Carolina Club, Elizabethan Grads. Club, Yale Club (N.Y.C.), Mory's Club (New Haven). Home: 621 Greenwood Rd Chapel Hill NC 27514-5921 Office Phone: 919-968-6486. *Keep casting bread on the waters-it may come back as French toast.*

NELSON, PRINCE ROGERS See PRINCE

NELSON, RICHARD DAVID, lawyer; b. Chgo., Jan. 29, 1940; s. Irving E. and Dorothy (Apolsky) N.; m. Davida Distenfield, Dec. 17, 1960; children: Cheryl, Laurel. BS in Acctg., U. Ill., 1961, LLB, 1964. Bar: Ill. 1964. Ptnr. Defrees & Fiske Law Offices, Chgo., 1964-81; ptnr., counsel Heidrick & Struggles, Inc., Chgo., 1981—2001, chief fin. officer, 1981—97, chief adminstrv. officer, 1981—2001; pres. Galrk Sheridan, Inc., Highland Park, Ill., 2001—. Bd. dirs., exec. com. Heidrick & Struggles, Inc., Chgo., 1981-99. Pres. Jewish Cmty. Ctrs. of Chgo., 1987-89; chmn. Sign Graphics Task Force, Highland Park, Ill., 1986-88; mem. bus. and econ. devel. commn., Highland Park, 1993-96, 2000-08, chmn. 2004-06, Ft. Sheridan Joint Plan Commn., 1997-2000. Mem. Ill. State Bar Assn., Chgo. Bar Assn., Standard Club, Northmoor Country Club. Office: Galrk Sheridan Inc 1896 Sheridan Rd Ste 200 Highland Park IL 60035-4635

NELSON, ROBERT EDDINGER, retired management consultant; b. Mentone, Ind., Mar. 2, 1928; s. Arthur Irven and Tural Cecile (Eddinger) N.; m. Carol J., Nov. 24, 1951; children: Janet K., Eric P. BA, Northwestern U., 1949; LHD, Iowa Wesleyan Coll., 1969, North Ctrl. Coll., 1987. Asst. dir. alumni rels. Northwestern U., Evanston, Ill., 1950-51; v.p., dir. pub. rels. Iowa Wesleyan Coll., Mt. Pleasant, 1955-58; vice chancellor for devel. U. Kansas City, 1959—61; v.p. instl. devel. Ill. Inst. Tech., Chgo., 1961-68; pres. Robert Johnston Corp., Oak Brook, Ill., 1968-69, Robert E. Nelson Assocs., Inc., Oak Brook, 1969—2004; ret., 2004. Bd. dirs. Chautauqua Workshop in Fund Raising and Instl. Relations, Continental Bank Oak Brook Terr., Sun Cos.; nat. conf. chmn. and program dir. Am. Coll. Pub. Relations Assn., 1961; trustee Iowa Wesleyan Coll., 1962-68, Have a Heart Found.; faculty mem. Ind. U. Workshops on Coll. and Univ. Devel., 1963-65, Lorretto Heights Summer Inst. for Fund Raising and Pub. Rels., 1964-68; pub. rev. panel for grants programs Lilly Endowment, Inc., 1975. Contbr. chpt. to Handbook of College and University Administration, 1970. With U.S. Army, 1951-54. Mem.: Chgo. Soc. Fundraising Execs., Nat. Small Bus. Assn., Nat. Soc. Fundraisers, Pub. Rels. Soc. Am., Coun. Fin. Aid to Edn. (bd. dirs. 1957—63), Union League, Internat. Club (Chgo.), Blue Key, Execs. Club, Club Internat., DuPage Club, Econ. Club, Masons, Delta Tau Delta. Methodist. Home: 5 Oakbrook Club Dr N101 Oak Brook IL 60523-1348

NELSON, ROBERT LOUIS, lawyer; b. Dover, NH, Aug. 10, 1931; s. Albert Louis and Alice (Rogers) N.; m. Rita Jean Hutchins, June 11, 1955; children: Karen, Robin Andrea. BA, Bates Coll., Lewiston, Maine, 1956; LLB, Georgetown U., 1959. Bar: D.C. 1960. With U.S. Commn. Civil Rights, 1958-63, AID, 1963-66; program sec. U.S. Mission to Brazil, 1965-66; exec. dir. Lawyers Com. Civil Rights Under Law, 1966-70; dep. campaign mgr. Muskie for Pres., 1970-72; v.p. Perpetual Corp., Houston, 1972-74; sr. v.p., gen. counsel Washington Star, 1974-76; pres. broadcast div. Washington Star Communications, Inc., 1976-77; asst. sec. of army U.S. Dept. Def., 1977-79; spl. advisor to chief N.G. Bur., Dept. Def., 1980-85; pres., dir. Mid-Md. Communications Corp., 1981-85; ptnr. Verner, Liipfert, Bernhard, McPherson and Hand, 1979-87; gen. counsel Paralyzed Vets. Am., 1988-99, sr. counsel, 2000—04; prin. Non-Profit Advisors, 2005—. Vice chmn. D.C. Redevel. Land Agy., 1976-77; bd. dirs. Friends of Nat. Zoo, 1975—89, pres., 1982-84; bd. dirs. Downtown Progress, 1976-77, Fed. City Coun., 1976-77, 83-87, Pennsylvania Ave. Devel. Corp., 1976-77, Cmty. Found. Greater Washington, 1977-78, Pep Direct, 2003-04, Friends of Perry's Eagle Island. Served with AUS, 1953-54. Mem. Army Navy Club, Washington. Democrat. Episcopalian. Home (Summer): Robins Nest Orrs Island ME 04066 Home (Winter): 11 Zeitler Farm Rd Brunswick ME 04011 Office Fax: 207-725-8482.

NELSON, ROBERT LOUIS, education educator, consultant; b. Manitowoc, Wis., Sept. 14, 1927; s. Louis Robert and Germaine Emily (Moser) N.; m. Catherine Mary Wojtanowska, Oct. 2, 1948; children: Karen Marie, Christine Mary, Robert Stephen. B of Edn., U. Wis., Whitewater, 1959; MS, U. Wis., Madison, 1968; MA, Ohio State U., 1969; PhD, Mich. State U., 1974. Tchr., prin., adminstr. Bark River Elem. Sch., Nashotah, Wis., 1952-68; tchr. Ctrl. High Sch., West Allis, Wis., 1969-71, Hale High Sch., West Allis, Wis., 1972-77; lectr. Cardinal Stritch Coll., Milw., 1975-77, Milw. Area Tech. Coll., 1972-74; lectr., counselor U. Wis., LaCrosse, 1977-89; freelance speaker, cons. Manitowoc, Wis., 1990—. Cons., lectr. Luth. Hosp., LaCrosse, 1987-89. Author: Downhill to Uphill, 1980, Teaching Vocabulary in Sensible Ways, 1984; contbr. articles to profl. jours. Vol. guide Pinecrest Hist. Village, Manitowoc, 1990—; libr. asst. Manitowoc Pub. Libr., 1990—. With U.S. Army, 1945-46. Mich. State U. scholar, 1966, Calif. State U. scholar, 1967; Ohio State U. fellow, 1968-69. Mem. Internat. Reading Assn., Nat. Coun. Tchrs. English, Wis. Hist. Soc., Manitowoc County Hist. Soc., Retired Tchrs. Assn., Phi Delta Kappa. Avocations: travel, photography, model trains, walking, biking. Home: 1129 S 12th St Manitowoc WI 54220-5221

NELSON, ROGER HUGH, corporate financial executive, educator, consultant; b. Spring City, Utah, Mar. 7, 1931; s. Hugh Devere and Maudella Sarah (Larsen) N.; m. DeEtte Munk, Aug. 26, 1955 (dec. Sept. 1998); children: Steven R., Deanne, Mark L. BS, MS, U. Utah, 1953; Ed.D., Columbia U., 1958. Mem. faculty U. Utah Coll. Bus., 1953-97; mem. faculty Utah Mgmt. Inst., 1968-75; asst. dean U. Utah Coll. Bus., 1969-74, prof. mgmt., 1970-97, chmn. mgmt. dept., 1976-82, dir. programs in emerging bus., 1989-97, dir. MBA integrative field studies, 1993-96, prof. emeritus, 1997—; v.p. Computer Logic Corp., 1970-73; pres. Oil Resources, Inc., 1980-88, Puma Energy Corp., 1981-88, The Ultimate Choice Catalog Co., 1986—, David Eccles Sch. of Bus. Faculty, 1995-96; chmn. bd. Am. Recreation & Sports, 1996—. Fin. and mgmt. cons., 1965—; founder Utah Small Bus. Devel. Ctr., U. Utah, 1979; trustee Utah Tech. Fin. Corp., 1998-2003. Author: Personal Money Management, 1973, The Utah Entrepreneur's Guide, 1995, also articles, reports, manuals. Active local Am. Heart Assn., Am. Cancer Soc. campaigns; mem. exec. bd. Utah Opera Co., 1981-85, gen. bd., 1985-89. Danforth Teaching fellow, 1957 Mem. Acad. Mgmt., Adminstrv. Mgmt. Soc., NEA, AAUP, Phi Kappa Phi, Beta Gamma Sigma, Phi Delta Kappa, Delta Phi Epsilon. Inventor comml. color separation camera and related dye-transfer processes. Home: 2662 Skyline Dr Salt Lake City UT 84108-2855

NELSON, RON, composer, educator, conductor; b. Joliet, Ill., Dec. 14, 1929; s. Walter E. and Lois (Fulton) N.; m. Helen Mitchell, 1954 (dec. 1967); children: Marc W., Kristen R.; m. Michele Miller, 2004. Mus.B., Eastman Sch. Music, 1952, MusM, 1953, MusD, 1956; postgrad., L'École Normale, Normale, Paris, 1954-55; MA, Brown U., 1959; MusD (hon.), Oklahoma City U., 2006. Prof. Brown U., Providence, chmn. dept. music, 1963-73, Acuff chair of excellence in creative arts, 1991, prof. emeritus, 1993—. Film composer: HEW, Eastman Kodak, ARC, Columbia Pictures, commns. from, Cin. Symphony, Lima Symphony, Rochester Philharm., R.I. Philharm., Am. Bapt. Soc., U. Minn., Dartmouth Coll., Brown U., New Music Ensemble, LaSalle Coll., Western Mich. U., Classic Chorale, U.S. Air Force Band, Nat. Symphony Orch.; composer (for orch.) Savannah River Holiday, 1954, Sarabande: For Katherine in April, 1954, (opera) The Birthday of the Infanta, 1956; (cantata) The Christmas Story, 1958: (for orch.) Tocatta for Orchestra, 1963; (oratorio) What is Man?, 1964; (orch./wind ensemble) Rocky Point Holiday, 1968-69; This is the Orchestra; (orch. and tape trilogy) Trilogy: JFK-MLK-RFK, 1969; (choral) Prayer of Emperor of China, 1973; (choral) Thy Truth is Great, 1973; (choral) Psalm 95, 1974; (orch.) Five Pieces for Orchestra after Paintings by Andrew Wyeth, 1975; (choral) Prayer of St. Francis of Assisi, 1976; (orch.) Meditation and Dance for Orch., 1976; (choral) Six Pieces for Chamber Ensemble, 1977, Four Choral Pieces After the Seasons, 1978, Three Autumnal Sketches, 1979, Here We Come As in The Beginning, 1979, Mass in Honor of St. LaSalle, 1981, Three Nocturnal Pieces, 1982, Three Seasonal Reflections, 1982; composer: Fanfare for a Celebration, 1982; (choral) On Christmas Night, 1982; Medieval Suite, 1983; (choral) Dreams, 1982; (band) Fanfare for a Celebration, 1983; (cello-piano) And the Moon Rose Golden, 1983; (band) Medieval Suite, 1983; composer: Aspen Jubilee, 1984; (organ-brass) Pebble Beach Sojourn, 1984; (chorus-band) Te Deum Laudamus, 1985; (choral) Lost and Found, 1985, Light Years, 1985, Three Settings of the Moon, 1985, (strings-trumpet) Elegy, 1986, (brass) Brevard Fanfare, 1986, (chorus/band) Prime: The Hour of Sunrise, 1987, (choral) White, 1987, (choral) Another Spring, 1987, (choral) Miniatures from a Bestiary Parts I and II, 1988, (saxophone-band) Danza Capriccio, 1988, (choral) Three Pieces after Tennyson (1988), (choral) Three Mountain Ballads, 1989, (brass-winds-percussion) Fanfare for the Hour of Sunrise, 1989, (band) Morning Alleluias for the Winter Solstice, 1989, (band) Resonances, 1990; (chorus) And This Shall Be for Music, 1990, Invoking the Powers, 1991, Songs of Praise and Reconciliation, 1991, (band) Lauds: Praise High Day, 1992, To the Airborne, 1991, Passacaglia (Homage on B-A-C-H), 1992, Chaconne (In Memoriam), 1994, Sonoran Desert Holiday, 1994, (band), Epiphanies (Fanfares and Chorales bands), 1995, Courtly Airs and Dances, 1995, (orch.) Resonances II, 1996, (orch., band) Resonances III, 1996,(orch.) Panels (Epiphanies II), 1996, The Music of Ron Nelson, 1996, (euphonium and winds) Night Song, 1998, (band) Fanfare for the New Millennium, 1999, Proclaim This Day for Music, 2002, (choral) Let Us Find a Meadow, 2006, (band) Pastorale: Autumn Rune, 2006, (brass & perc.) Fanfare Kennedy Ctr., 2008. Recipient ASCAP awards, 1962-20047, Found. award for World tour, 1965-66, Nat. Band Assn. award, 1992, John Philip Sousa medal of merit, 1994; Fulbright fellow, 1954; Ford Found. commn., 1962, NEA grantee, 1973, 76, 79; awarded Acuff Chair of Excellence on the Creative Arts, 1991; winner Am. Bandmasters Assn. Ostwald Contest, 1993, Am. Band Assn. contest, 1992, Sudler Internat. Wind Band Competition, 1993.

NELSON, RONALD L., travel services company executive, former film company executive; MBA, UCLA; B, U. Calif., Berkeley. Exec. v.p., CFO Paramount Comm. Inc. (formerly Gulf & Western Inc), 1987-94, bd. dirs., 1992; CFO, founding mem. DreamWorks SKG, Univeral City, Calif., 1994—2003; sr. exec. v.p. fin. Cendant Corp., NYC, 2003, CFO, 2003—06, pres., 2004—06; chmn., CEO Avis Budget Group, Parsippany, NJ, 2006—. Bd. dir. Advanced Tissue Scis., Inc., 1997, PHH Corp., Hanesbrands Inc., 2008—. Office: Avis Budget Group 6 Sylvan Way Parsippany NJ 07054

NELSON, ROY JAY, retired French educator; b. Pitts., July 27, 1929; s. Roy J. and Ruth Brown (Bainbridge) N.; m. Anita Lee Chandler, Aug. 16, 1954; children: Wendy Nelson Wilson, Barbara Nelson Videira. BA, U. Pitts., 1951; MA, Middlebury Coll., 1952; PhD, U. Ill., 1958. Instr. French, U. Mich., Ann Arbor, 1957-60, asst. prof., 1960-65, assoc. prof., 1965-72, prof., 1972-94, prof. emeritus, 1994—. Author: Péguy poète du sacré, 1960, Causality and Narrative in French Fiction from Zola to Robbe-Grillet, 1989; editor: 20e siècle: La Problématique du discours, 1986; contbr. articles to French Rev. Recipient Ruth Sinclair counseling award U. Mich., 1982, cert. for outstanding tchg., 1986; faculty tchg. award Amoco Found., 1992. Mem. MLA, Am. Assn. Tchrs. French Avocation: writing fiction. Office: U Mich Dept Romance Langs and Lits Ann Arbor MI 48109-1275 Personal E-mail: rnelson01@comcast.net.

NELSON, RUSSELL MARION, surgeon, educator; b. Salt Lake City, Sept. 9, 1924; s. Marion C. and Edna (Anderson) N.; m. Dantzel White, Aug. 31, 1945 (dec.); children: Marsha Nelson McKellar, Wendy Nelson Maxfield, Gloria Nelson Irion, Brenda Nelson Miles, Sylvia Nelson Webster, Emily Nelson Wittwer (dec.), Laurie Nelson Marsh, Rosalie Nelson Ringwood, Marjorie Nelson Helsten, Russell Marion Jr.; m. Wendy Lee Watson, April 6, 2006. BA, U. Utah, 1945, MD, 1947; PhD in Surgery, U. Minn., 1954; ScD (hon.), Brigham Young U., 1970; DMS (hon.), Utah State U., 1989; LHD (hon.), Snow Coll., 1994. Diplomate: Am. Bd. Surgery, Am. Bd. Thoracic Surgery (dir. 1972-78). Intern U. Minn. Hosps., Mpls., 1947, asst. resident surgery, 1948-51; first asst. resident surgery Mass. Gen. Hosp., Boston, 1953-54; sr. resident surgery U. Minn. Hosps., Mpls., 1954-55; practice medicine (specializing in cardiovascular and thoracic surgery), Salt Lake City, 1959-84; staff surgeon LDS Hosp., Salt Lake City, 1959-84, dir. surg. research lab., 1959-72, chief cardiovascular-thoracic surg. div., 1967-72, also bd. govs., 1970-90, vice chmn., 1979-89; staff surgeon Primary Children's Hosp., Salt Lake City, 1960; attending in surgery VA Hosp., Salt Lake City, 1955-84, Univ. Hosp., Salt Lake City, 1955-84; asst. prof. surgery Med. Sch. U. Utah, Salt Lake City, 1955-59, asst. clin. prof. surgery, 1959-66, asso. clin. prof. surgery, clin. prof., 1966-69, research prof. surgery, 1970-84, clin. prof. emeritus, 1984—; staff services Utah Biomed. Test Lab., 1970-84. Dir. tng. program cardiovascular and thoracic surgery at Univ. Utah affiliated hosps., 1967-84; mem. policyholders adv. com. New Eng. Mut. Life Ins. Co., Boston, 1976-80 Contbr. articles to profl. jours. Mem. White House Conf. on Youth and Children, 1960; bd. dirs. Internat. Cardiol. Found.; bd. govs. LDS Hosp., 1970-90, Deseret Gymnasium, 1971-75, Promised Valley Playhouse, 1970-79; mem. adv. com. U.S. Sec. of State on Religious Freedom Abroad, 1996-99. lst lt. to capt. M.C., AUS, 1951-53. Markle scholar in med. scis., 1957-59; Fellowship of Medici Publici U. Utah Coll., 1967; Gold Medal of Merit, Argentina, 1974; named Hon. Prof. Shandong Med. U., Jinan, People's Republic of China, 1985; Old People's U., Jinan, 1986; Xi-an (People's Republic of China) Med. Coll., 1986, Legacy of Life award, 1993. Fellow A.C.S. (chmn. adv. council on thoracic surgery 1973-75), Am. Coll. Cardiology, Am. Coll. Chest Physicians; mem. Am. Assn. Thoracic Surgery, Am. Soc. Artificial Internal Organs, AMA, Dirs. Thoracic Residencies (pres. 1971-72), Utah Med. Assn. (pres. 1970-71), Salt Lake County Med. Soc., Am. Heart Assn. (exec. com. cardiovascular surgery 1972, dir. 1976-78, chmn. council cardiovascular surgery 1976-78), Utah Heart Assn. (pres. 1964-65), Soc. Thoracic Surgeons, Soc. Vascular Surgery (sec. 1968-72, pres. 1974), Utah Thoracic Soc., Salt Lake Surg. Soc., Samson Thoracic Surg. Soc., Western Soc. for Clin. Research, Soc. U. Surgeons, Am., Western, Pan-Pacific surg. assns., Inter. Am. Soc. Cardiology (bd. mgrs.), Phi Beta Kappa, Sigma Xi, Alpha Omega Alpha, Phi Kappa Phi, Sigma Chi. Mem. Ch. of Jesus Christ of Latter-day Saints (pres. Bonneville Stake 1964-71, gen. pres. Sunday sch. 1971-79, regional rep. 1979-84, Quorum of the Twelve Apostles 1984—). Office: 47 E South Temple Salt Lake City UT 84150-1200

NELSON, SARAH MILLEDGE, archaeology educator; b. Miami, Fla., Nov. 29, 1931; d. Stanley and Sarah Woodman (Franklin) M.; m. Harold Stanley Nelson, July 25, 1953; children: Erik Harold, Mark Milledge, Stanley Franklin. BA, Wellesley Coll., 1953; MA, U. Mich., 1969, PhD, 1973. Instr. archaeology U. Md. extension, Seoul, Republic Korea, 1970-71; asst. prof. U. Denver, 1974-79, assoc. prof., 1979-85, prof. archaeology, 1985—2004, rsch. prof., 2004—, chair dept. anthropology, 1985-95, dir. women's studies program, 1985-87, John Evans prof., dir. Asian studies, 1996, vice provost for rsch., 1998—2002, interim vice provost grad. studies and rsch., 2001—02. Vis. asst. prof. U. Colo., Boulder, 1974; resident Rockefeller Ctr. in Bellagio, Italy, 1996. Author: Archaeology of Korea, 1993, Gender in Archaeology: Analyzing Power and Prestige, 1997, 2d rev. edit., 2004, Shamanism in East Asian Archaeology, 2007; (novel) Spirit Bird Journey, 1999, Ancient Queens: Archaelogical Perspectives, 2003, Jade Dragon, 2004; co-author: Denver: An Archaeological History, 2001, new edit., 2008; editor: The Archaeology of Northeast China, 1995, Ancestors for the Pigs: Pigs in Prehistory, 1998, Handbook of Gender in Archeology,

2006, Women in Antiquity: Theoretical Approaches to Gender and Archaeology, 2007, Worlds of Gender, The Archaeology of Women's Lives Around the Globe, 2007; co-editor: Powers of Observation, 1990, Equity Issues for Women in Archaeology, 1994, Archaeology of the Russian Far East, 2005, In Pursuit of Gender: Worldwide Archaeological Perspectives, 2001, Korean Social Archaeology, 2005, Archeology of the Russian Far East, 2006, Integrating the Diversity of the 21st Century Anthropology, 2006. Active Earthwatch, 1989. Recipient Outstanding Scholar award U. Denver, 1989; grantee S.W. Inst. Rsch. on Women, 1981, Acad. Korean Studies, Seoul, 1983, Internat. Cultural Soc. Korea, 1986, Colo. Hist. Fund, 1995-97, Rockefeller Found. Residency, Bellagio, Italy, Wenner-Gren Found., 2000-02, Nat. Geographic Soc., 2000—. Fellow Am. Anthrop. Assn.; mem. Soc. Am. Archaeology, Assn. Asian Studies, Royal Asiatic Soc., Sigma Xi (sec.-treas. 1978-79), Phi Beta Kappa. Democrat. Avocations: travel, gardening. Home: 5878 S Dry Creek Ct Littleton CO 80121-1709 Office: U Denver Dept Anthropology Denver CO 80208-0001 Business E-Mail: snelson@du.edu.

NELSON, SCOTT BRUCE, psychologist; b. Ann Arbor, Mich., May 5, 1952; s. Bruce Kern and Frances Stakel Nelson; m. Sarah Howland Clark, Nov. 10, 1984; children: Margaret Frances, Elizabeth Jeanne. BS in Psychology, Ariz. State U., Tempe, 1974, PhD, 1987, MS in Counseling, 1976. Cert. physician Ariz. Bd. Psychologists Examiners, 1989, sch. psychologist Ariz. Dept. Edn., 1977. Asst. psychologist Tempe Elem. Sch. Dist. 3, 1976—80; psychologist Mesa Unified Sch. Dist. 4, Ariz., 1984—. Psychologist Ariz. Drug Abuse Program, Mesa, 1985—89, Ariz. Addiction Treatment Program, Mesa, 1994—99. Named Outstanding Educator, Mesa Unified Sch. Dist. 4, 1987, City Mesa, 1988, Outstanding Rehabilitator, 1988. Avocation: photography. Office: Mesa Unified Sch Dist 4 855 W 8th Ave Mesa AZ 85210 Business E-Mail: sbnelson@mpsaz.org.

NELSON, STEPHEN D., music educator; b. Clearwater, Fla., Apr. 5, 1957; adopted s. Brasher Parker and Catherine Land (Kit) Nelson. BA, U. Cen. Fla., 1982. Dir. music 1st Presbyn. Ch. Apopka; performer, co-founder Ars Antiqua - an Early Music Ensemble, Orlando, 1986—; dir. music 1st Presbyn. Ch. Apopka, 1983—; creative music cons. Nelson Music Svcs., Apopka, 1976—. Musician orch. arrangement of ednl. mus. materials, composer 2 For The Road; contbr. Arrangements for Harcourt Texts, 1995; musician: (ednl. video) Ars Antiqua - Music from a Distant Tyme, 1996. Mem.: Bears of Cen. Fla. (pres. 2001—02). Office: Park Maitland Sch 1450 S Orlando Ave Maitland FL 32751 Personal E-mail: nelsonmusic@cfl.rr.com.

NELSON, STEVEN CRAIG, lawyer; b. Oakland, Calif., May 11, 1944; s. Eskil Manfred and Florence Lucille (Boatman) N.; m. Kathryn Cassel Stoltz, Nov. 30, 1974 (div. Apr. 1997); children: Carleton Philip, Whitney Cassel. BA in Econs. with exceptional distinction, Yale U., 1966, LLB, 1969. Bar: DC 1969, Minn. Supreme Ct. 1975, U.S. Supreme Ct. 1973, Hong Kong 2000. From atty. adviser to asst. legal adviser U.S. Dept. State, Washington, 1969-74; from assoc. to ptnr. Oppenheimer, Wolff, Foster, Shepard & Donnelly, St. Paul and Mpls., 1975-85; ptnr., internat. practice group Dorsey & Whitney LLP, Mpls., 1985—, co-chmn., Asia practice Hong Kong & Mpls. Mem. bd. appeals NATO, Brussels. 1977-2003; adj. prof. law U. Minn, 1980-86; spkr. in field. Contbr. articles to profl. jours. Mem. ABA (chmn. internat. law and practice 1988-89), Minn. Bar Assn., Internat. Bar Assn. (mem. coun. 1996-2000, mem. WTO Working Group, 2000-present), Inter-Pacific Bar Assn., Minikahda Club. Avocations: golf, tennis, skiing, sailing. Office: Dorsey & Whitney 3008 One Pacific Pl 88 Queensway Hong Kong SAR China Office Phone: 852 2105 0211. Business E-Mail: nelson.steve@dorsey.com.

NELSON, STUART OWEN, agricultural engineer, researcher, educator; b. Pilger, Nebr., Jan. 23, 1927; s. Irvin Andrew and Agnes Emilie (Nissen) N.; m. Carolyn Joye Fricke, Dec. 27, 1953 (dec. Nov. 1975); children: Richard Lynn, Jana Sue; m. Martha Ellen White Fuller, Apr. 8, 1979. BS in Agrl. Engring., U. Nebr., 1950; MS in Agrl. Engring., 1952; MA in Physics, U. Nebr., 1954; PhD in Engring., Iowa State U., 1972; DSc (hon.), U. Nebr., 1989. Grad. asst. U. Nebr., Lincoln, 1952-54, rsch. assoc., 1954-60, assoc. prof., 1960-72, prof., 1972-76. Project leader Farm Electrification Rsch., Agrl. Rsch. Svc., USDA, Lincoln, 1954-59, rsch. investigations leader, 1959-72, rsch. leader 1972-76, rsch. agrl. engr. Russell Rsch. Ctr., Athens, Ga., 1976—; adj. prof. U. Ga., 1976-2007, collaborator 2007-; sci. adv. coun. Am. Seed Rsch. Found.; mem. CAST Task Force on Irradiation for Food Preservation and Pest Control; adv. com. grain moisture measurement Nat. Coun. Weights and Measures; mem. sci. bd. 4th Internat. Conf. on Phys. Properties Agrl. Materials, Prague, 1985. Assoc. editor Jour. Microwave Power 1975-76, 95-2000; contbr. more than 600 articles to sci. and tech. jours. With USN, 1946-48. Recipient HM Crops and Soils award Am. Soc. Agronomy, 1966, Founders Gold medal Fed. Engr. of Yr. NSPE, 1985, Superior Svc. award USDA, 1986, Profl. Achievement Citation Engring. award Iowa State U., 1987, Ga. Engring. Found. medal of honor, 1999; named to U. Nebr. Biol. Systems Engring. Hall of Fame, 1999, USDA-ARS Sci. Hall of Fame, 2002. Fellow IEEE, Am. Soc. Agrl. Engrs. (Tech. Paper award 1965, 94, 2005, 07, Engr. of Yr. award Ga. sect. 1988, chmn. Ga. sect. 1988-89, Cyrus Hall McCormick-Jerome Increase Case Gold Medal award 2000), Internat. Microwave Power Inst. (Decade award 1981), AAAS; mem. The Electromagnetics Acad., Internat. Soc. Agromaterials Sci. and Engring., Internat. Dielectric Soc., Ga. Soc. Profl. Engrs. (Engr. of Yr. in Govt. award 1991, Engr. of Yr. 1998), Nat. Acad. Engring., Nat. Soc. Profl. Engrs., Orgn. Profl. Employees of Dept. of Agrl. (pres. Athens area chpt. 1984-86, nat. coun. rep. 1988-95, Profl. of Yr. award 1987), Athens Optimist (pres. 1980-81, 2000-2001, lt. gov. Ga. dist. 1983-84, Optimist of Yr. award 1982, disting. and outstanding lt. gov. Ga. dist. 1985), Assn. for Microwave Power in Europe for Rsch. and Edn., Sigma Xi, Sigma Tau, Gamma Sigma Delta, Tau Beta Pi. Methodist. Home: 270 Idylwood Dr Athens GA 30605-4635 Office: USDA Agrl Rsch Svc Russell Rsch Ctr PO Box 5677 Athens GA 30604-5677

NELSON, SUE GRODSKY, humanities educator, consultant; b. Bklyn., Apr. 1, 1943; d. Juliette Dorfman and Louis Grodsky; m. Michael R. Nelson, Nov. 23, 1968; children: Andrew Robert, John Samuel. BA, Allegheny Coll., Meadville, Pa., 1964; EdM, John Carroll U., University Heights, Ohio, 1995. Cert. tchr. Ohio, 1988. Asst. prodn. mgr. CBS, NYC, 1964—65; tchr./dept. chair of English, honors English, reading, journalism, French Cleve. Bd. of Edn., 1965—71; group home foster parent Jewish Children's Bur., Shaker Heights, Ohio, 1971—75; tchr. of English, inclusion English/learning cmty., career edn., journalism East Cleve. Bd. of Edn., 1972—98; adj. instr., reading cons. Cuyahoga CC, Cleve. Mem. tchr. rev. panel McDougal, Littell & Co., Evanston, Ill., 1990—92; presenter Cons. - Multiple Intelligences Workshops, Ohio, 1994—99; mem. adv. com. John Carroll U., University Heights, Ohio, 1995—97; mem. Newbury Bd. of Edn., Ohio, 2000—04, past pres. Author: (instruction manual) Getting Elected to Public Office; contbr. anthology Humanities Programs Today; co-author/editor (instruction manual) Multiple Intelligences at Work!; editor: (inspirational lessons) Zen Shin Talks. Chairperson Social Action Coun., 2005—, People for Polensek, Cleve., 1977—90; vice chairperson and sec. Cuyahoga County Dem. Party, Cuyahoga County, Ohio, 1982—89; vol. coord. Boyle for Senate, Cleveland, Ohio, 1997—98; trustee Suburban Temple-Kol Ami, 2005—. Recipient Ashland Achievement award, Ashland Oil, Inc., 1992; Coach of State Champion - Oratorical Interpretation, Ohio H.S. Speech League, 1986. Mem.: NEA (life), East Cleve. Edn. Assn. (pres. 1982—83), Ohio Sch. Bd. Assn., Ohio Edn. Assn. (life; chairperson svc. coun. 1980—81). Democrat. Jewish. Avocations: reading, exercising, interior decorating, political activism, travel. Home: 10450 Bell St Newbury OH 44065 Office: Cuyahoga CC 2900 Community College Avenue Cleveland OH 44114 E-mail: m.s.nelson@juno.com.

NELSON, SUSAN RHODES, media specialist, educator; b. Birmingham, Ala., June 27, 1948; d. Horace and Evelyn Vines Rhodes; m. Roger Hudson Nelson, Dec. 19, 1970; children: Jay Matthew, Jon Bradley. BS, Auburn U., 1970; MA, U. Ala., Birmingham, 1973, EdS, 1985; MLIS, U. Ala., Tuscaloosa, 1997, EdD, 2001. Cert. tchr. Ala. Tchr. Jefferson County Bd. of Edn., Birmingham, 1970—94, media specialist, 1994—; adj. prof. U. Ala., Tuscaloosa, 2001—. Adv. bd. Jefferson County Librarians, Birmingham, 2001—; chmn. Jefferson County Elem. Librarians, Birmingham, 2003—; mem. bldg. leadership team Hueytown (Ala.) Elem. Sch., 1994—, tech. coord., 1994—; cons., rschr. Learning Through Sports, Birmingham, 2003—; leader People to People Ambassador Program, Birmingham, 2004—; online facilitator Ala. State Dept. Edn. Bd. dirs. Daycare, Bessemer, Ala., 2000—05. Recipient Exemplary Libr. Program award, Libr. and Media Professionals, 1999, 2003, Most Exemplary Elem. Libr. award, Jefferson County Libr. Links for Success, 2004; named Leader of the Yr., Jefferson County 4-H, 1975, Tchr. of Yr., Hueytown Elem. Sch., 2003. Mem.: ALA (assoc.), NEA (assoc.), Ala. Libr. Assn. (assoc.), Alpha Delta Kappa (treas. 2002—), Kappa Delta Pi (assoc.), Kappa Delta Epsilon (assoc.). Republican. Avocations: travel, music, reading, sports. Home: 11227 Apple Valley Rd Mc Calla AL 35111-2448 Office: Hueytown Elem Sch 112 Forest Rd Hueytown AL 35023 Personal E-mail: nelsonsr2@bellsouth.net. Business E-Mail: snelson@jefcoed.com.

NELSON, TERRY A., public relations executive; b. Marshaltown, Iowa; m. Marci Nelson; 3 children. BS in Polit. Sci., U. Iowa, Iowa City, 1994. Campaign mgr. Rep. Jim Nussle, 1992—95; field rep. Nat. Rep. Congl. Com., 1995—96, nat. field dir., 1997—99, polit. dir., 2000; majority staff dir. Iowa Senate, 1997; ptnr., co-founder Dawson, McCarthy, Nelson Media, Washington, 2001; dep. chief of staff, exec. dir. polit. ops. Rep. Nat. Com., 2002—03; nat. polit. dir. Bush/Cheney Re-Election campaign, 2003—04; founder, prin. Crosslink Strategy Group, Washington, 2005—; sr. advisor John McCain's presdl. campaign, 2006; ptnr. Mercury Pub. Affairs, Washington; cons., mem. Akerman Senterfitt's Policy practice group. Named one of Politics Fabulous Fifty. Republican. Office: Crosslink Strategy Group 1775 I St NW Ste 700 Washington DC 20006 Office Phone: 202-338-0022. Office Fax: 202-551-9966.*

NELSON, THOMAS ADAMS, electrical engineer, consultant; b. Berkeley, Calif., Aug. 26, 1921; s. Thomas Fleming and Mabel Margaretta (Adams) N.; m. Mary Anne Mares, July 12, 1958. AA, LA City Coll., 1942; BS, U. So. Calif., 1949, MS, 1953; postgrad. cert. bus. mgmt., UCLA, 1970. Registered profl. elec. and quality engr., Calif. Design engr. LA Dept. Water and Power, 1950—53, quality assurance engr., resident engr. factories in U.S., Europe and Japan, 1953—65, asst. chief quality assurance engr., 1965—68, chief quality assurance engr., 1968—72, sr. engr. in charge oper. engring., 1972—77, prin. engr., mgr. comm., transmission lines, sta. maintenance and distbn. trouble, 1977—80, rail transp. cons. on coal delivery to elec. generating stas. Ariz. and Nev., 1973-79, rep. to Calif. Power Pool, 1975-77; cons. engr., transp. cons. LA, 1980—. Reviewer rail transit plans So. Calif. Rapid Transit Dist., LA County Transp. Commn., LA County Met. Transp. Authority, Orange County Transit Dist., Caltrans, San Diego Met. Transit Devel. Bd., 1978—. Editor, maj. author Railroad Chronology Compendium, 1976, 50 Years of Railroading in Southern California, 2001; editor Jour. Pacific R.R. Soc., 1980-84, 87-94, cons. editor, 1994-2005; contbr. articles to profl. jours., academic publs. and newspapers, 1970—. Mem. Citizens Adv. Commn. for Met. Rail, Hollywood, Calif., 1982-84, Metro Rail CORE Forum, 1987; advisor Beijing ofcl. regarding rail transit, 2002, Spokane Transit Authority, 2003, 2006. Served to capt. USAAF, 1942-45, ETO. Mem. IEEE (sr.), Vehicular Tech. Soc., Pacific R.R. Soc. (bd. dirs. 1977-80, 82-85, v.p. 1986, pres. 1987-89, publs. mgr. 1981-94), Eta Kappa Nu, Tau Beta Pi, Phi Kappa Phi.

NELSON, THOMAS G., federal judge; b. Idaho Falls, Idaho, 1936; Student, U. Idaho, 1955—59, LLB, 1962. Ptnr. Parry, Robertson, and Daly, Twin Falls, Idaho, 1965—79, Nelson, Rosholt, Robertson, Tolman and Tucker, Twin Falls, 1979; judge US Ct. Appeals (9th cir.), Boise, Idaho, 1990—2003, sr. judge, 2003—. With Idaho Air N.G., 1962—65, with USAR, 1965—68. Mem.: ABA, Idaho Law Found., Am. Bd. Trial Advocates (pres. Idaho chpt.), Idaho Assn. Def. Counsel, Idaho State Bar (pres., bd. commrs.), Am. Coll. Trial Lawyers, Am. Bar Found., Phi Alpha Delta. Office: US Ct Appeals 9th Circuit 304 N Eighth St Boise ID 83702*

NELSON, TROY ALAN, music educator, church musician, assistant principal; b. Iowa City, Apr. 9, 1969; s. Verne Franklyn and Johanna Pearl Nelson; m. Kari Marie Urevig, Feb. 18, 1971; children: Haley Marie, Hannah Elizabeth, Ryan Laurence. BA, Luther Coll., 1991; MEd, Oakland U., 1998. Music educator grades 6-12 Eagle Grove Schs., Eagle Grove, Iowa, 1991—93, Clarenceville Schs., Livonia, Mich., 1993—2007; dir. music and worship St. John Luth. Ch., Farmington, 1993—; HS asst. prin. Clarence Sch., 2007—. Scheduling chair Clarenceville H.S. Block Scheduling Com., Livonia, Mich., 2000—02; participant Oakland Leadership Acad. Aspiring Principals, Waterford, 2001—01; adj. faculty Marygrove Coll., Detroit, 2001—05. Dir.: (musicals) Oliver, L'il Abner, All-American, Oklahoma, The Music Man, Pirates of Penzance, Guys and Dolls, Anything Goes, Once Upon A Mattress, Meet Me in St. Louis, Annie Get Your Gun, My Fair Lady, Damn Yankees; actor: (video) NCA Transitions Informational Video; choral director (song) (Overall Mixed Choir Trophy, St. Louis Festivals of Music, 1992), 1 high sch. choral dir. (songs) (Overall Divsn. One Rating, 2001, 2005, 2006, 2007). Recipient cert. appreciation, Clarenceville Schools Bd. Edn., 1999, 2002. Mem.: NEA, ASCD, Nat. Assn. of Secondary Sch. Prin., Assn. Luth. Ch. Musicians, Mich. Sch. Vocal Music Assn., Am. Choral Dirs. Assn. Lutheran. Avocations: running, reading, skiing, home improvement. Home: 36694 Saxony Rd Farmington MI 48335 Office: Clarenceville Schs 20155 Middlebelt Rd Livonia MI 48152 Personal E-mail: luthergrads@aol.com. E-mail: tnelson@clarenceville.k12.mi.us.

NELSON, VITA JOY, editor, publisher; b. NYC, Dec. 9, 1937; d. Leon Abraham and Bertha (Sher) Reiner; m. Lester Nelson, Aug. 27, 1961; children: Lee Reiner, Clifford Samuel, Cara Ritchie. BA, Boston U., 1959. Promotion copywriter Street & Smith, NYC, 1958-59; asst. to mng. editor Mademoiselle Mag., NYC, 1959-60; mcpl. bond trader Granger & Co., NYC, 1960-63; founder, editor, pub. Westchester Mag., Mamaroneck, NY, 1968-80, L.I. Mag., 1973-78; founder, editor, pub., pres. Moneypaper, 1981—. Pub. The Guide to Dividend Reinvestment Plans, Direct Investing; founder MP63 Fund; pres. Moneypaper Advisor Inc., 1999—. Author: (with Donald Korn) Create and Manage Your Own Mutual Fund, 1994. Bd. dirs. United Way of Westchester/Putnam County, 1998—2002; bd. govs., v.p. Am. Jewish Com., Westchester, 1979—89. Recipient citation Coun. Arts, 1972, Media award Pub. Rels. Soc. Am., 1974. Mem. Women in Comms. (Outstanding Communicator award 1983). Democrat. Home: Pleasant Ridge Rd Harrison NY 10528-1004 Office: The Moneypaper Inc 555 Theodore Frend Ave Rye NY 10580 Office Phone: 914-925-0022 100. Business E-Mail: vnelson@moneypaper.com. E-mail: vitajoy@aol.com.

NELSON, W. JAMES, biology professor, researcher; Prof. biology Stanford U., Calif., prof. molecular & cellular physiology; prin. investigator, Nelson Lab Molecular and Cellular Physiology Stanford U. Sch. Medicine. Contbr. articles to profl. jours. Mem.: Am. Acad. Arts & Sciences. Office: c/o Dept Biology Gilbert Hall Stanford Univ Stanford CA 94305-5020 Business E-Mail: wjnelson@stanford.edu.*

NELSON, WALTER GERALD, retired insurance company executive; b. Peoria, Ill., Jan. 2, 1930; s. Walter Dennis and Hazel Marie (Tucker) Nelson; m. Mary Ann Olberding, Jan. 28, 1952 (dec. Nov. 1989); children: Ann Larkin, Michael, Susan Boor, Patrick, Thomas, Timothy, Molly Edwards; m. Mary Jo Sunderland, Apr. 6, 1991. Student, St. Benedict's Coll., Atchison, Kans., 1947-49, Bradley U., Peoria, Ill., 1949; JD, Creighton U., Omaha, 1952. Bar: Nebr 1952, Ill 1955. Practice in, Peoria, 1955-56; with State Farm Life Ins. Co., Bloomington, Ill., 1956—, counsel, 1968—, v.p., 1970-96. Past dir Ill Life Ins Coun; past chmn legal sect Am Coun Life Ins; spkr in field. Contbr. articles to profl jours. Mem.: ABA, Nat. Orgn. Life and Health Ins. Guaranty Assn. (past pres.), Assn. Life Ins. Counsel (past pres.), Nebr. Bar Assn., Ill. Bar Assn., Bloomington Country Club, KofC. Republican. Roman Catholic. Personal E-mail: WGN1930@aol.com.

NELSON, WILLIAM EUGENE, lawyer; b. Roland, Iowa, Sept. 23, 1927; s. Sam J. and Katherine A. (Coffey) N.; m. Sherlee M. Stanford, July 11, 1959; children: Anne, Kristin, William. BA, U. Iowa, 1950; JD, Drake U., 1957. Bar: Iowa 1957, D.C. 1965, Md. 1976, W.Va. 2004. Trial atty. civil divsn. U.S. Dept. Justice, 1957—65, asst. chief tort sect., 1966—70, chief r.r. reorgn. unit, 1970—71; gen. counsel Cost of Living Coun. Phase I, 1971, chief econ. stblzn. sect., 1971—74; ptnr. Nelson and Nelson, LLP, Washington, Bethesda, Md., 1975—. Gen. counsel the Communicators, Inc., Myersville, Md. Assoc. editor Drake Law Rev., 1955-57. With USN, 1945—46. Recipient Atty. Gen.'s Disting. Svc. award, 1972. Mem.: Order of Coif. Home: 511 Colston Dr Falling Waters WV 25419 Office: Nelson & Nelson LLP 3 Bethesda Metro Ctr Ste 700 Bethesda MD 20814-6300 Office Phone: 301-961-1958. Personal E-mail: reg1927@aol.com, sswen@aol.com.

NELSON, WILLIE HUGH, musician, lyricist; b. Abbott, Tex., Apr. 30, 1933; children: Jacob, Lukas, Paula Carlene, Amy, Lana, Susie, Billy. Student, Baylor U. Salesman; announcer, host country music shows local Tex. stas.; bass player Ray Price's band; formed own band; personal appearances at Grand Ole Opry, Nashville, throughout U.S., 1964—; rec. artist Atlantic, Columbia and RCA records; founder Pedernales Studios, Spicewood, Tex., Pedernales Records, Austin, Tex., 2007; owner Pedernales Golf Club/Willie Nelson's Cut-N-Putt. Cofounder Willie Nelson's Biodiesel. Musician: (albums) Love & Pain, 1961, And Then I Wrote, 1962, Here's Willie Nelson, 1963, Country Willie: His Own Songs, 1965, Country Favorites: Willie Nelson Style, 1966, Live Country Music Concert, 1966, Make Way for Willie Nelson, 1967, Texas in My Soul, 1968, Good Times, 1968, My Own Peculiar Way, 1969, Both Sides Now, 1970, Laying My Burdens Down, Yesterday's Wine, 1971, Willie Nelson & Family, 1971, The Willie Way, 1972, The Words Don't Fit the Picture, 1972, Shotgun Willie, 1973, Phases and Stages, 1974, Red Headed Stranger, 1975 (Grammy award Best Country Vocal Performance for song "Blue Eyes Crying In The Rain", 1975), Willie Nelson Live, 1976, The Sound in Your Mind, 1976, The Troublemaker, 1976, To Lefty from Willie, 1977, Stardust, 1978 (Grammy award Best Country Vocal Performance for song "Georgia on My Mind", 1978), Waylon & Willie, 1978 (Grammy award Best Country Vocal Performance By A Duo Or Group for song "Mammas Don't Let Your Babies Grow Up to Be Cowboys", 1978), Willie and Family Live, 1978, The Electric Horseman, 1979, Sings Kris Kristofferson, 1979, One for the Road, 1979, Pretty Paper, 1979, San Antonio Rose, 1980, Honeysuckle Rose, 1980 (Grammy award Best Country Song for "On The Road Again", 1980), Blue Skies, 1981, Somewhere over the Rainbow, 1981, Pancho & Lefty, 1983 (Vocal Duo Yr. (with Merle Haggard) Country Music Assn. Awards, 1983), Old Friends, 1982, Always on My Mind, 1982 (Grammy award Best Country Vocal Performance for song "Always On My Mind", 1982, Country Music Assn. awards: Album Yr., 1982, Single Yr. for "Always On My Mind", 1982), Tougher Than Leather, 1983, Without a Song, 1983, Take It to the Limit, 1983, Music from Songwriter, 1984, Portrait in Music, 1984, Angel Eyes, 1984, City of New Orleans, 1984, Me and Paul, 1985, Half Nelson, 1985 (Vocal Duo Yr. (with Julio Iglesias) Country Music Assn. Awards, 1984), Brand on My Heart, 1985, Funny How Time Slips Away, 1985, Partners, 1986, The Promiseland, 1986, Island in the Sea, 1987, Seashores of Old Mexico, 1987, What a Wonderful World, 1988, Horse Called Music, 1989, Born for Trouble, 1990, The IRS Tapes: Who'll Buy My Memories?, Willie Nelson, 1993, Across the Borderline, 1993, Moonlight Becomes You, 1994, Healing Hands of Time, 1994, Pancho, Lefty and Rudolph, 1995, Six Hours at Pedernales, 1995, Just One Love, 1996, Spirit, 1996, How Great Thou Art, 1996, Christmas with Willie Nelson, 1997, Hill Country Christmas, 1997, Teatro, 1998, Life's Railway to Heaven, 1998, Back to Back: Willie Nelson and Patsy Cline, 1998, Night and Day, 1999, Clean Shirt, 2000, Outlaws, 2000, Memories of Hank Williams, Sr., 2000, Me and the Drummer, 2000, Milk Cow Blues, 2000, Good Ol' Country Singin', 2000, Rainbow Connection, 2001, Tales Out of Luck, 2001, The Great Divide, 2002, Home is Where You're Happy, 2002, All of Me Live...in Concert, 2002, Stars & Guitars, 2002 (Grammy award (with Lee Ann Womack) Best Country Collaboration With Vocals for song "Mendocino County Line", 2002), Night Life, 2002, Country Willie, 2002, Is There Something on Your Mind, 2002, On the Road Again, 2002, Honky Tonk Heroes, 2003, Broken Promises, 2003, Reunion - Can't Get the Hell Out of Texas, 2003, Willie Nelson and Friends: Live and Kickin', 2003, Standard Time, 2003, Keepsake, 2003, Run That By Me One More Time, 2003, I Just Don't Understand, 2003, Live in Amsterdam, 2004, Music Legends: The Best of Willie Live, 2004, Live at Billy Bob's Texas, 2004, It Always Will Be, 2004, Songs for Tsunami Relief, 2005, Countryman, 2005, You Don't Know Me, 2006, Just a Couple of Outlaws, 2006, All American Country, 2006, Last of the Breed, 2007 (Grammy award Best Country Vocal Collaboration, 2008), Willie Nelson Christmas, 2007, Gravedigger, 2007, Moment of Forever, 2008, Naked Willie, 2009; appeared on (album by Waylon Jennings) Good Hearted Woman, 1972 (Single Yr. (with Waylon Jennings) Country Music Assn. Awards, 1976), appeared with various artists (albums) Wanted: The Outlaws, 1976 (Vocal Duo Yr. (with Waylon Jennings) Country Music Assn. (CMA) Awards, 1976, Album Yr. (with Waylon Jennings, Tompall Glaser, Jessi Colter) Country Music Assn. Awards, 1976); actor: (films) The Electric Horseman, 1979, Honeysuckle Rose, 1980, Thief, 1981, Barbarosa, 1982,

Songwriter, 1984, Red-Headed Stranger, 1986, Starlight, 1996, Gone Fishin', 1997, Wag the Dog, 1997, Stardust, 2000, The Journeyman, 2001, The Big Bounce, 2004, The Dukes of Hazzard, 2005; appearances include (films) Anthem, 1997, Dill Scallion, 1999, Austin Powers: The Spy Who Shagged Me, 1999, Swing Vote, 2008; actor, co-writer musical score: (TV films) Stagecoach, 1986; performer: (theme song for film) Welcome Home, 1989, (songs) Cowboys Are Frequently, Secretly (Fond of Each Other), 2006, (movie soundtrack, Brokeback Mountain) He Was a Friend of Mine, 2005; (TV films appearances include) Where the Hell's That Gold, 1988, Once Upon a Texas Train, 1989, A Pair of Aces, 1990, Born for Trouble, 1990, Another Pair of Aces: Three of a Kind, 1991, Big Country, 1994, Big Dreams and Broken Hearts: The Dottie West Story, 1995, The Beach Boys: Nashville Sounds, 1996, Starlight, 1996, Farm Aid '96, 1996, Outlaw Justice, 1998; author: (autobiography) I Didn't Come Here (and I Ain't Leavin'), 1988; co-author (with Turk Pipkin): (memoir) The Tao of Willie, 2006. Served in USAF. Recipient citation for Top Album Artist, Billboard mag., 1976, Special Humanitarian award, Nat. Farmers Orgn., 1986, Grammy Lifetime Achievement award, 1989; named Entertainer Yr., Country Music Assn. (CMA), 1979; named to, Nashville Songwriters Assn. Hall Fame, 1973, Country Music Hall Fame, 1993. Achievements include performing Cowboys Are Frequently, Secretly (Fond of Each Other), which may be the first gay cowboy song by a major recording artist. Office: care Mark Rothbaum & Assocs Inc PO Box 2689 Danbury CT 06813-2689 Address: William Morris Agency 150 El Camino Beverly Hills CA 90212 Home: Austin TX

NELSON-KAUFFMAN, WENDY, history educator; b. Evanston, Ill., Mar. 7, 1961; d. Wayne Keith Nelson and Jane Van Dellen; m. Matthew William Kauffman, Oct. 5, 1961; children: David Alexander Nelson Kauffman, Sam VanDellen Nelson Kauffman. BS, Dartmouth Coll., Hanover, NH, 1983; MS, Northwestern U., Evanston, IL, 1984; MS in History, So. Conn. State U., New Haven, 1990. Cert. tchr. Conn., 1990. Tv news anchor, reporter WAOW-TV, Wausau, Wis., 1984—86; tv reporter WTNH-TV, New Haven, 1986—88; adult educator New Haven and Hartford Adult Edn., 1990—96; tchr., chair dept. Bloomfield H.S., 1996—2004; history educator Met. Learning Ctr., 2004—. Mem. closing achievement gap task force Conn. Dept. Edn., Hartford, 2003—04; advisor Student Abolitionists Stopping Slavery, Bloomfield, 2004—06; mem. conn. task force revise state social studies stds. Conn. Dept. Edn., 2005—06; tchr. adv. bd. Unitarian Universalist Ch., West Hartford, 2005—06. Recipient Conn. Tchr. of Yr. award, 2003, All-Star Tchg. Team awaqrd, USA Today, 2004, Kidger award for outstanding history tchr. in New Eng., 2004, Conn. History Tchr. of Yr., 2005. Mem.: Nat. Coun. History Edn., Nat. Coun. Social Studies, Conn. Coun. Social Studies (assoc.; bd. mem. 2004—06). Unitarian Universalist. Avocations: travel, reading, gardening, physical fitness. Home: 101 Four Mile Rd West Hartford CT 06107 Office: Metropolitan Learning Center 1551 Blue Hills Ave Bloomfield CT 06002 Personal E-mail: wnkauffman@yahoo.com. E-mail: wnelson-kauffman@crec.org.

NEMAZEE, HASSAN, investment banker; b. Washington, Jan. 27, 1950; AB, Harvard U., 1972. Chmn., CEO Nemazee Holdings, 1972—79, HN Properties, 1979—87, Nemazee Capital Corp., Washington, 1987—. Chmn. Iran Found., Shiraz Waterworks; mem., vis. com. U. Resources Harvard U., 1986—2002, mem., Mid. East Ctr. Adv. Coun., 1990—94, mem., Internat. Affairs Planning Com., 1990—95, mem., vis. com. Ctr. Internat. Affairs, 1998—2005; vice chmn. Encyclopedia Iranica, Columbia U., 1990—98; mem. Am. Iranian Coun., 2001; mem., policy adv. bd. Asia Soc., mem., bd. trustees, 2003; mem. Coun. Fgn. Rels., 2004; mem., adv. bd. Fgn. Policy Leadership Coun., 2004, RAND Ctr. Mid. East Pub. Policy, 2006; co-chair Carret Asset Mgmt. Grp. LLC, Brean Murray Carret & Co.; mem., bd. dirs. Iranian Am. Polit. Action Com., NYC. Chmn. Nemazee Hosp., Nemazee Sch. Nursing; bd. trustee Shiraz U., Spence Sch., 1993—97, Brain Trauma Found., 1996—. Office: 770 Park Ave New York NY 10021

NEMAZIE, SIAMACK, nephrologist, consultant; s. Farrokh and Fazileh Nemazie; m. Ammu Joyce James Gopalan, Nov. 3, 2000. MBBS, Kasturba Med. Coll., Manipal, India, 1998. Diplomate Am. Bd. Internal Medicine, 2004. House officer Rainy Hosp., Madras, 1998—99; resident house officer Apollo Specialty Hosp., Madras, 1999—2000, Harvey Heart Hosp., Madras, 2000—01, 2000—01; resident Brookdale Hosp. and Med. Ctr., Bklyn., 2001—04, chief resident internal medicine, 2003—04, nephrology fellow, 2004—. Hosp. del. Com. Interns and Residents, Bklyn., 2004—05. Named Best First Yr. Resident, Alumni Assn., 2002. Mem.: AMA, ACP, Am. Soc. Hypertension (cert. specialist in clin. hypertension 2005), Am. Soc. Nephrology (assoc.). Achievements include research in platelet dysfunction in hemodialysis patients. Avocation: travel. Office: Brookdale Hosp and Med Ctr Divsn Nephrology 1 Brookdale Plz Brooklyn NY 11236 E-mail: snemazie@hotmail.com.

NEMEC, CHRISTOPHER E., music educator; b. Park Ridge, Ill., July 31, 1962; s. Emil F. Nemec and Barbara A. Hamilton. MusB in Edn., U. Memphis, 1985, postgrad., 1998. Children's choir leadership cert. progra, Choristers Guild. Organist-music adminstr., dir. children's and youth music Lindenwood Christian Ch., Memphis, 1983—. With Lindenwood Concerts, Memphis, 1982—; accompanist, assoc. condr. Gary Beard Chorale, Memphis, 1987—; intern Am. Boychoir, Princeton, NJ, 1996; singer Carnegie Hall, NYC, 1997—2004; music dir. Gold Strike Casino, Tunica, Miss., 2003—04. Composer: (choral-orchetsral composition) Be Strong; prodr.: (musical productions) Producer of Lindenwood Concerts; performer: (CDs) Do You Remember? The Piano Stylings of Chris Nemec, Simply Delicious, As Time Goes By, The Very Best Time of Year, You Must Remember This as Time Goes By. Meal deliverer Memphis Interfaith Assn., Memphis, 2003—05; tutor Hollywood Elem. Sch., Memphis, 2003—04; vol. St. Jude's Children's Rsch. Hosp., 2007. Mem.: Chorus USA, Am. Choral Dirs. Assn., Choristers Guild (Five Exceptional Children's Choir Leaders 2007), Am. Guild Organists. Democrat. Mem. Christian Ch. (Disciples Of Christ). Avocations: travel, yoga. Home: 2263 Tunis Cove Memphis TN 38104 Office: Lindenwood Christian Ch 2400 Union Ave Memphis TN 38112 Office Fax: 901-458-0145; Home Fax: 901-458-0145. Personal E-mail: chrisnemec@bellsouth.net. Business E-Mail: chris.nemec@lindenwood.net.

NEMEC, JOSEF, retired organic chemist, researcher; b. Ostresany, Czechoslovakia, Sept. 7, 1929; came to U.S., 1969; s. Josef Nemec and Marie (Joskova) Nemcova; m. Anna Pastush, Aug. 29, 1975; 1 child, Marketa. MS, Inst. Chem. Tech., Prague, Czechoslovakia, 1954; PhD, Czechoslovak Acad. Scis., Prague, 1958. Organic chemist Inst. Chem. Tech., Prague, 1954-61; sr. rsch. chemist Czechoslovak Acad. Scis., Prague, 1961-69; rsch. fellow in organic chemistry Wayne State U., Detroit, 1969-70; sr. rsch. scientist Squibb Inst. Med. Rsch., New Brunswick, NJ, 1970-75; staff mem. St. Jude Children's Rsch. Hosp., Memphis, 1975-84; sr. scientist Nat. Cancer Inst.-Program Resources, Inc. Cancer R&D Ctr., Frederick, Md., 1984-95; ret., 1995. Adj. prof. med. chemistry U. Tenn., Memphis, 1979-91; external examiner U. Zimbabwe, Harare, 1994—; cons. in field. Contbr. articles to scholarly and profl. jours. Grantee Nat. Cancer Inst., 1975-85. Mem. AAAS, Am. Chem. Soc., Royal Soc. Chemistry, Czechoslovak Soc. Arts and Scis. Achievements include patents in fields of anticancer agents, organic chemicals, semimicroequipment in organic chemistry; research in natural products, synthetic anticancer agents, monosaccharides, experimental semimicrotechniques in organic chemistry.

NEMECEK, ALBERT DUNCAN, JR., retail executive, investment banker, management consultant; b. Helena, Mont., Mar. 10, 1936; s. Albert Duncan and Geneva (Reindle) N.; m. Marilyn Ann Shaughnessy, Sept. 7, 1963 (div.); children: Maureen Ann, Steven Mathew; m. Judith Eileen Swift, Sept. 18, 1981 (div.); 1 child, Jennifer Eileen. BS, U. Md., 1960, postgrad. in econs., 1961. Agt. IRS, Washington, 1961-65; tax dir. Macke Co., Washington, 1965-69; tax dir., then sec. Garfinckle, Brooks Bros., Miller & Rhoads, Inc., Washington, 1969-76, treas., 1976—, v.p., 1979—; mng. ptnr. Nemecek & Falleroni, 1987, Nemecek & Jacknis, investment bankers, mgmt. cons., Falls Church, Va., 1989; founder Nemecek & Co., Inc., Falls Church, 1990. Founder Entreprenurial Growth Fund, Falls Church, 1990. Founder The Leadership Group, 1996. Home: PO Box 21 Occoquan VA 22125-0021 Personal E-mail: fixit00001@aol.com. *A man's success is measured by the respect he has gained from his peers, his understanding and compassion, respect for the feelings of others, appreciation of the world's beauty, and his attempts to leave the world better than he found it.*

NEMEROFF, CHARLES BARNET, neurobiology and psychiatry educator; b. Bronx, NY, Sept. 7, 1949; s. Philip Peace and Sarah (Greenberg) N.; m. Melissa Ann Pilkington, May 24, 1980 (div.); children: Matthew P. (dec. 1997), Amanda P., Sarah-Frances P.; m. Gayle Applegate, June 11, 2001. BS, CCNY, 1970; MS, Northeastern U., 1973; PhD, U. N.C., 1976, MD, 1981. Diplomate Am. Bd. Psychiatry and Neurology; lic. physician, N.C., Ga. Rsch. asst. ichthyology Am. Mus. Natural History, NYC, 1968-71; neurochemistry lab. McLean Hosp., Belmont, Mass., 1971-72; rsch. assoc. surgery Beth Israel Hosp., Boston, 1972-73; tchg. asst. biology Northeastern U., 1972-73; postdoctoral fellow Biol. Scis. Rsch. Ctr., U. N.C., Chapell Hill, 1976-77, rsch. fellow, 1977-83, clin. instr. psychiatry, 1983; resident psychiatry N.C. Meml. Hosp., Chapel Hill, 1981-83; asst. prof. dept. psychiatry and pharmacology Duke U., Durham, NC, 1983-85, assoc. prof. psychiatry, 1985-89, assoc. prof. pharmacology, 1986-89, prof. depts. psychiatry and pharmacology, 1989-91, chief divsn. biol. psychiatry, 1988-91; prof., chmn. dept. psychiatry and behavioral scis. Emory U. Sch. Medicine, Atlanta, 1991—2008, Reunette W. Harris prof. psychiatry and behavioral scis., 1994—. Vis. prof. physiology Cath. U., Santiago, Chile, 1978; sci. coun. Nat. Alliance for Rsch. Schizophrenia and Depression, 1997—; mem. coun. NIMH, 1999-2002; mem. biomed. rsch. coun. NASA, 2000-03; bd. dirs. George West Mental Health Found., 1999—, Cypress Bioscis. Inc., 2001—05, NovaDel Pharma, 2005—. Editor: (with A.J. Prange Jr.) Neurotensin, a Brain and Gastrointestinal Peptide, 1982, (with A.J. Dunn) Peptides, Hormones and Behavior, 1984, (with P.T. Loosen) Handbook of Clinical Psychoneuroendocrinology, Neuropeptides in Psychiatric and Neurological Disorders, 1987, Neuropeptides in Psychiatric Disorders, 1991, Neuroendocrinology, 1992, (with P. Kitabgi) The Neurobiology of Neurotensin, 1992, (with A.F. Schatzberg) Textbook of Psychopharmacology, 1995, 4th edit., 2009, (with A. F. Schatzberg) Recognition and Treatment of Psychiatric Disorders, 1999, The Corsini Encyclopedia of Psychology and Behavioral Science, 3d edit., vols. 1-4, 2001, (with W.E. Craighead) concise edit. 2004, (with Dennis S. Charney) The Peace of Mind Prescription, 2004 (Ken award Nat. Alliance of The Mentally Ill), (with David Purselle and Arthur Jongsmia) The Psychopharmacology Treatment Planner, 2003, (with Jeffrey Kelsey and D. Jeffrey Newport) Principles of Psychopharmacology for Mental Health Professionals 2006; editor-in-chief: Depression, 1993-00, Psychopharmacology Bull., 2001-02, Neuropsychopharmacology, 2001-06; co-editor-in-chief: Critical Revs. in Neurobiology, 1992-01; contbr. chpts. to books and articles and abstracts to profl. jours. Recipient Michiko Kuno award U. N.C., 1978, 79, Merck award for acad. excellence, 1981, Merck award for young investigators Am. Geriatrics Soc., 1985, 2nd prize Anna Monica Found. for Rsch. in Endogenous Depression, 1987, Merit award NIMH, 1987, rsch. prize World Fedn. Socs. Biol. Psychiatry, 1991, Edward J. Sachar award Columbia U., 1993, Edward A. Strecker prize Instnl. Pa. Hosp., 1993, Outstanding Alumni award in health scis. Northeastern U., 1995, Disting. Alumni award U. NC Sch. Medicine, 1999, George Ham Alumni award dept. psychiatry U. NC, 2000, Charles Burlingame prize Inst. Living, 2002, Alumni award U. NC, 2006; grantee Nat. Inst. Aging, 1982-83, NIMH, 1983—, NIDA, 1996-98; predoctoral fellow Schizophrenia Rsch. Found., Soc. Scottish Rite, Lexington, Mass., 1975-76, postdoctoral fellow Nat. Inst. Neurol., Communicative Disorders and Stroke, 1977, Nanaline Duke fellow Duke U. Med. Ctr., 1985-87. Fellow Am. Coll. Neuropsychopharmacology (Mead Johnson Travel award 1982, Efron award 1987, coun. 1993—99, pres. 1997), Am. Coll. Psychiatrists (chmn. contbns. com. 1991-93, 95—, edn. com. 1993-96, 96—, bd. regents 1994-97, 1st v.p. 1999, pres.-elect 2000, pres. 2001, chair sci. program com. 2005-07, 2009, Mood Disorders Rsch. award 1998, Bowis award 1999, Dean award 2004); mem. AAAS, AMA, Soc. Neurosci. (program com. 1993-95), Internat. Soc. Psychoneuroendocrinology (pres. 1993-96, Curt P. Richter award 1985), Internat. Soc. Neuroendocrinology, Internat. Soc. Neurochemistry, Am. Soc. Neurochemistry (Jordi-Folch-Pi award 1987), Endocrine Soc., Soc. Neuroendocrinology, Soc. Biol. Psychiatry (A.E. Bennett award 1979, Gold medal award 1996), Am. Fedn. Clin. Rsch., Am. Pain Soc., Am. Psychiat. Assn. (coun. rsch. 1993-98, 02-04, chmn. 1994-95, bd. dirs. rsch. inst. 1999—2007, chair coun. rsch. subcom. on psychiat. treatments 1999-2003, chair, subcom. rsch. tng. 2006-, Kempf award 1989, Samuel Hibbs award 1991, Rsch. prize 1996, Rsch. Mentoring award 2006, Judson Marmor award, 2008, Vestermark award 2006, Disting. Psychiatrist lectr. Ann. Meeting 1999, 2003, Marmor prize 2008, Rsch. Mentoring award 2008), Am. Coll. Physicians (William C. Menninger award 2000), Argentine Assn. Psychoneuroendocrinology (sci. coun.), Nat. Depressive and Manic Depressive Disorders Assn. (vice chair 1996-98, bd. dirs. 1999—2002, chair 1999-2000, Gerald L. Klerman Lifetime Achievement award 1997), Anxiety Disorder Assn. Am. (chmn. sci. adv. bd. 2001-2003), NY Acad. Scis., Am. Found. for Suicide Prevention (sci. adv. bd. 1997—, bd. dirs. 1998—, v.p. 2006, pres. Sci. Coun. 2007—, pres. 2008-,Rsch. prize 2001), Inst. Medicine, Sigma Xi, Alpha Omega Alpha. Democrat. Jewish. Office: Emory U Sch Medicine Dept Psychiatry 101 Woodruff Cir Atlanta GA 30322-0001 Home Phone: 404-236-0372; Office Phone: 404-727-8254. Business E-Mail: cnemero@emory.edu.

NEMEROFF, MICHAEL ALAN, lawyer; b. Feb. 16, 1946; s. Bernard Gregor and Frances (Gotleib) N.; m. Sharon Lynn Leininger, Sept. 22, 1974; children: Theodore, Patrick, James. BA, U. Chgo., 1968; JD, Columbia U., 1971. Asst. counsel Subcom. on Juvenile Delinquency of Senate Jud. Com., Washington, 1971-73; assoc. Sidley Austin LLP, Washington, 1973-78, ptnr., 1978—. Treas. Friends of Jim Sasser, 1978-96, Andy Ireland Campaign Com., 1984-92. Office: Sidley Austin LLP 1501 K St NW Washington DC 20005 Office Phone: 202-736-8000.

NEMESKAL, NATALIE ANN, massage therapist; b. Boston, Jan. 28, 1975; d. Frederic Nemeskal; 1 child, Taylor Ashley Nemeskal-Ferrara. Attended, North Shore CC, Danvers, 2009; attending in Nursing, Regis Coll. Cert. IT specialist Mass., 1997; massage therapist Mass., 2005. Telecom. specialist Avid Tech., Andover, Mass., 1996—2002, IT specialist, 2002—03; massage therapist Therapeutic Sensation, S.Hamilton, 2004—; lab asst. North Shore CC, Danvers, 2008—. Ordained min. Regis Coll. Vol. Urban Salt & Light, Boxford, Mass., 2004—08; chair ways & means Asbury Grove, S. Hamilton, 2004—07. Recipient Red Carpet award, Endicott Coll., 1993. Mem.: Phi Theta Kappa. Independent. Office: Therapeutic Sensation Oak Ave South Hamilton MA 01982

NEMETH, CHARLAN JEANNE, psychology educator; b. St. Louis, Dec. 29, 1941; d. Joseph Frank and Loretto Julia (Linkul) N.; children: Brendan Gibbs Nemeth-Brown, Lauren Loretto Nemeth-Brown. BA, Washington U., 1963; MA, U. Wis., 1965; postgrad., Oxford U., Eng., 1965-66; PhD, Cornell U., 1968. Fellow in law and psychology Battelle Seattle Rsch. Ctr., 1974-75; asst. prof. dept. psychology U. Chgo., 1968-73, U. Va., Charlottesville, 1973-75, U. B.C., Can., 1975-77, U. Calif., Berkeley, 1977—. Vis. prof. U. Bristol, Eng., 1969-70, Ecole des Hautes Etudes, Paris, 1969-70, U. Mannheim, Fed. Republic of Germany, summer, 1977, Ecole des Hautes Etudes en Sciences Sociale, 1984, 89; cons. in psychology and law. Author: Social Psychology: Classic and Contemporary Integrations, 1974, Differential Contributions of Majority and Minority Influence, 1986; contbr. chpts. to books, articles to profl. jours. Grantee NIMH, 1970-81, NSF, 1986-89; Hon. Woodrow Wilson fellow, 1963. Fellow Am. Psychol. Assn., Am. Psychol. Soc.; mem. Soc. for Exptl. Social Psychology, European Assn. Soc. Psychology (affiliate), Phi Beta Kappa. Democrat. Roman Catholic. Office: U Calif Dept Psychology Berkeley CA 94720-0001 *Maintain respect both for yourself and your profession by never compromising excellence or ethical conduct.*

NEMETZ, PETER NEWMAN, economist, researcher, policy analysis educator; b. Vancouver, BC, Can., Feb. 19, 1944; s. Nathan Theodore and Bel Nemetz; m. Roma E.S. Kellock, July 16, 1994; 1 stepchild, Fiona Susan. BA in Econs. and Polit. Sci., U. BC, Can., 1966; AM in Econs., Harvard U., Cambridge, Mass., 1969, PhD in Econs., 1973. Tchg. fellow, tutor Harvard U., Cambridge, Mass., 1971-73; lectr. Sch. Planning U. BC, Vancouver, 1973-75, asst. prof. to assoc. prof. policy analysis, 1975-96, prof., 1996—, chmn., 1984-90. Non-resident faculty Green Coll., 1993-94, 95-97, St. John's Coll., 1997-2002; vis. scientist, rschr., collaborator Dept. Health Scis. Rsch. Mayo Clinic, 1986—; cons. consumer and corp. affairs, Can., 1977-80, BC Hydro, 2000-02; program chmn. The Vancouver Inst., 1987—; mem. bd. advisors evidence-based practice ctr. rsch. project U. Calif., San Francisco, 2000-01; mem. sr. faculty Ctr. Health Svcs. and Policy Rsch., U. BC, 1990-, dept. resource mgmt. and environ. studies, 1979—, Ctr. Japanese Studies, 1992—; mem. Inst. for Resources and Environment, U. BC, 1997—, selection com. Rhodes Scholarship, 1991-99, mem. senate, 1998-2002, mgmt. com. Ctr. Southeast Asia Rsch., 1992-99, assoc. mem. Faculty Medicine dept. health care and epidemiology faculty medicine, 1995—; bd. dirs. U. BC Press, 1993-2002; assoc. Ctr. Pacific Basin Monetary and Econ. Studies, Econ. Rsch. Dept., Fed. Reserve Bank of San Francisco, 1991—. Editor Jour. Bus. Adminstrn., 1978-04, Sustainable Resource Management: Reality or Illusion?, 2007; mem. editl. bd. Jour. Internat. Bus. Edn., 2001—; contbr. articles to sci. jours. Life mem. BC-Yukon divsn. Can Nat. Inst. for Blind. Recipient Tchg. Excellence award Commerce Undergrad. Soc., 2006-07; grantee Natural Scis. and Engring. Rsch. Coun. Can., 1976-92, Consumer and Corp. Affairs Can., 1978-80, Econ. Coun. Can., 1979-80, Max Bell Found., 1982-84; postdoctoral fellow Westwater Rsch. Ctr., Vancouver, 1973-75. Mem. Am. Econ. Assn., Internat. Epidemiol. Assn., Harvard Club of BC (pres. 1986-94), Vancouver Club. Jewish. Avocations: swimming, photography. Office: Univ BC Sauder Sch Bus Vancouver BC Canada V6T 1Z2 Home Phone: 604-224-5383; Office Phone: 604-822-8443. Business E-Mail: peter.nemetz@sauder.ubc.ca.

NEMFAKOS, CHARLES PANAGIOTIS, defense industry executive, strategic consultant; b. Athens, Greece, Oct. 21, 1942; s. Panagiotis Soterios and Mirka (Kyriakakis) N.; m. Suzenne Ertel Oct. 1965 (div.);children: Mirka Leigh, Charles Jr.; m. Pamela Durrant Aug., 1997; 1 child, Alexandra. BA, Pan Am. U., 1964; MA, Georgetown U., 1982. Cert. in nat. security. Health advisor USPHS, Washington, 1965-66; fed. mgmt. intern Dept. Navy, Washington, 1966-67; budget analyst Naval Ordnance Systems Command, Washington, 1967-71; supervisory budget analyst Naval Ship Systems Command, Washington, 1971-73; sr. budget analyst Office of Sec. of Def., Washington, 1973-75; divsn. dir. Office Budget and Reports Dept. Navy, Washington, 1975-76, assoc. dir., 1976-93, dep. asst. sec., 1994-95, dep. undersec., 1995—2001, sr. civilian ofcl. for fin. mgmt., comptr., 1998—2001; dir. internal programs devel. Lockheed Martin Corp., Manassas, Va., 2001—03; organizing mem. Nemfakos Ptnrs., LLC, Arlington, Va., 2003—07; sr. fellow Rand Corp., Santa Monica, Calif., 2007—. Bd. dirs. First Command Ednl. Found., Am. Automar and Atlantic Marine, Armed Forces Found.; mem. adv. bd. Advanced Tech. Inst., Global Maritek, Internat. Soc. Logistics; adj. Rand Corp., Logistics Mgmt. Inst., Ctr. Nval Analysis; lectr. fin. & resource allocation mgmt. Naval Postgrad. Sch., Monterey, Calif., Georgetown U., Washington, Ind. U. Grad. Sch., Def. Acquisition U.; mem. base structure com. Dept. Navy, Washington, 1990-91, mem. sr. advisors group, 1991-92, vice-chmn. base structure com., 1992-95; gen. adminstrn. bd. USDA Grad. Sch., 2000—08; bd. advisors, chmn. disaster relief and humanitarian assistance com. SOLE Internat., 2007. Contbr. articles to profl. jours.,author. Dept. of The Navy BRAC Processes, 1988-2005, Observations & Lessons learned, 2006, Effective Engagement of the Private sector in Stability operations, 2006, Logistics Management, Athens, Greece, 2006, National Security through Logistics, L & M Athens, 2007, NGA Financial Mgmt Sys., 2007, Transportation Security Through Logistics Transformation, 2008, Integrating Instruments of Power & Influence: Lessons Learned and Best Practice RAND Report of A Panel of Senior Practitioners, 2008, Building the capacity to Address the nations Drug Problems report on a panel NAPA fellows, 2008, Improoving Acquisition Outcomes: Organizational & management Issues, 2009, The perfect sterm: the Goldwater Nichols Act and its Effect on navy acquisition, 2009. Coach McLean (Va.) Youth Soccer, 1978-93, chmn., 1982-85; bd. dirs. McLean Youth, Inc., 1980-84; registrar Va. Youth Soccer Assn., 1984-86. Recipient Dept. Navy Superior Civilian Svc. award Asst. Sec. of Navy, 1980, Dept. Navy Disting. Civilian Svc. award Sec. of Navy, 1985, 87, 93, 2000, 01, Dept. Def. Disting. Civilian Svc. award Sec. of Def., 1990, 2000, 01, Dept. Navy Disting. Pub. Svc. award Sec. of Navy, 1995, Roger W. Jones award exec. leadership Am. U., 2000, Meritorious Svc. award, Pres. SOLE, 2007; named Career Civilian Exemplar Sec. of Def., 2004; named to Rank of Disting. Exec. Pres. of US, 1986, 95, to Rank of Meritorious Exec., 1981, 91. Fellow: Nat. Acad. Pub. Adminstrn.; Mem. Am. Assn. Budget and Program Analysis (dir.-at-large 1980-83), Am. Soc. Mil. Comptrs. (v.p. 1988-90), Fed. Execs. Inst. Alumni Assn., Tau Kappa Epsilon (chpt. pres. 1964-65). Greek Orthodox. Avocations: golf, tennis, soccer. Office Phone: 703-413-1100 ext. 5660. Personal E-mail: charles_nemfakos@rand.org.

NEMIR, DONALD PHILIP, lawyer; b. Oakland, Calif., Oct. 31, 1931; s. Philip F. and Mary (Shavor) N. AB, U. Calif., Berkeley, 1957, JD, 1960. Bar: Calif. 1961, U.S. Dist. Ct. (no. dist.) Calif. 1961, U.S. Ct. Appeals (9th cir.) 1961, U.S. Dist. Ct. (ctrl. dist.) Calif. 1975, U.S. Supreme Ct. 1980. Pvt. practice, San Francisco, 1961—. Home: PO Box 1089 Mill Valley CA 94942-1089 Office Phone: 415-421-0400. Personal E-mail: dnemir@earthlink.net.

NEMIRO, BEVERLY MIRIUM ANDERSON, author, educator; b. St. Paul, May 29, 1925; d. Martin and Anna Mae Anderson; m. Jerome Morton Nemiro, Feb. 10, 1951-75; children: Guy Samuel, Lee Anna, Dee Martin. Student, Reed Coll., 1943-44; BA, U. Colo., 1947; postgrad., U. Denver. Tchr. Seattle Pub. Sch., 1945-46; fashion coord., dir. Denver Dry Goods Co., 1948-51; fashion dir. Denver Market Week Assn., 1952-53; free-lance writer Denver, 1958—. Moderator TV program Your Presch. Child, Denver, 1955-56; instr. writing and comm. U. Colo. Denver Ctr., 1970—, U. Calif., San Diego, 1976-78, Met. State Coll., 1985; dir. pub. rels. Fairmont Hotel, Denver, 1979-80; freelance fashion and TV model. Author, co-author: The Complete Book of High Altitude Baking, 1961, Colorado a la Carte, 1963, Colorado a la Carte, Series II, 1966, (with Donna Hamilton) The High Altitude Cookbook, 1969, The Busy People's Cookbook, 1971 (Better Homes and Gardens Book Club selection 1971), Where to Eat in Colorado, 1967, Lunch Box Cookbook, 1965, Complete Book of High Altitude Baking, 1961, (under name Beverly Anderson) Single After 50, 1978, The New High Altitude Cookbook, 1980. Co-founder, pres. Jr. Symphony Guild, Denver, 1959-60; active Friends of Denver Libr., Opera Colo.; mem. Friends of Painting and Sculpture, Denver Art Mus. Recipient Top Hand award Colo. Authors' League, 1969, 72, 79-82, 100 Best Books of Yr. award NY Times, 1969, 71; named one of Colo. Women of Yr., Denver Post, 1964. Mem. Am. Soc. Journalists and Authors, Colo. Authors League (dir. 1969-79), Authors Guild, Friends Denver Libr., Denver Women's Press Club, Kappa Alpha Theta. Address: Park Towers 1299 Gilpin St Apt 15W Denver CO 80218-2556

NEMIROFF, MAXINE CELIA, small business owner, art historian; b. Chgo., Feb. 11, 1935; d. Oscar Bernard and Martha (Mann) Kessler; m. Paul Rubenstein, June 26, 1955 (div. 1974); children: Daniel, Peter, Anthony; m. Allan Nemiroff, Dec. 24, 1979. BA, U. So. Calif., 1955; MA, UCLA, 1974. Sr. instr. UCLA, 1974-92; dir., curator art gallery Doolittle Theater, Los Angeles, 1985-86; owner Nemiroff Deutsch Fine Art, Santa Monica, Calif. Leader of worldwide art tours; cons. L'Ermitage Hotel Group, Beverly Hills, Calif., 1982—, Broadway Dept. Stores, So. Calif., 1979—, Security Pacific Bank, Calif., 1978—, Am. Airlines, Calif. Pizza Kitchen Restaurants; art chmn. UCLA Thieves Market, Century City, 1960—, L.A. Music Ctr. Mercado, 1982—; art cons. Blackstone Group; lectr. in field. Apptd. bd. dirs. Dublin (Calif.) Fine Arts Found., 1989; mem. Calif. Govs. Adv. Coun. for Women, 1992; mem. art selection com. Calif. State Office Bldgs., 1997—. Named Woman of Yr. UCLA Panhellenic Council, 1982, Instr. of Yr. UCLA Dept. Arts, 1984; recipient Woman of Achievement award Friends of Sheba Med. Ctr., 2003; elected to Fashion Circle of the Costume Coun., L.A. County Mus. Art, 1997—; honoree L.A. Art Core 15th Ann. Awards Benefit, 2003. Mem. L.A. County Mus. Art Coun., UCLA Art Coun., UCLA Art Coun. Docents, Alpha Epsilon Phi (alumnus of yr. 1983). Avocations: tennis, horseback riding, skiing, piano and guitar. Personal E-mail: mumseyart@aol.com.

NEMIROW, ARNOLD MYLES, paper company executive; b. Hartford, Conn., Mar. 25, 1943; s. Benjamin and Elsie (Nozik) N.; m. Barbro Sandberg, Dec. 22, 1967 (dec. Aug. 1983); children: Matthew, Adam; m. Sharon Green, April 23, 1988; children: Kathryn, Robert. AB cum laude, Harvard U., 1966; JD, U. Mich., 1969. Bar: N.Y. Atty. Carter, Ledyard & Milburn, NYC, 1969-73; asst. gen. counsel Coleco Industries Inc., Hartford, 1973-74; atty., asst. gen. counsel Gt. No. Nekoosa Corp., Stamford, Conn., 1974-80, dir. indsl. rels., 1981-83, v.p., 1984-90; pres. Gt. Southern Paper Co., Cedar Springs, Ga., 1984-87, Nekoosa Papers Inc., Port Edwards, Wis., 1988-90; pres., CEO Wausau Papers, Wausau, Wis., 1990-94, Bowater Inc., Greenville, SC, 1995—2006, chmn., 1996—2006, non-exec. chmn., 2006.

NEMMERS, JOSEPH M., JR., pharmaceutical executive; b. Dec. 22, 1954; B in History, Ariz. State U. Numerous positions in comml. ops., mfg. and materials mgmt. Abbott Labs., Abbott Park, Ill., 1980—99, v.p., exec. dir. Clara Abbott Found., 1999—2000, divisional v.p. Acquisition Integration Mgmt., 2001—02, corp. v.p., 2001—02, v.p. hosp. products bus. sector, 2002, v.p. global comml. ops., 2002—03, sr. v.p. diagnostic ops., 2003—06, exec. v.p. diagnostics & animal health, 2006—. Mem. supervisory bd. Abbott Mgmt. GmbH and Abbott Holding GmbH. Chmn. bd. dirs. United Way Lake County, Carmel H.S.; bd. dirs. Ct. Appointed Spl. Advs., Boys and Girls Club Waukegan. With USAR. Office: Abbott Labs 100 Abbott Park Rd Abbott Park IL 60064-6400

NEMPHOS, GEORGE J., lawyer; BS, Boston U., 1991; JD magna cum laude, U. Balt. Sch. Law, 1994; LLM, Georgetown U. Law Ctr., 1996. Bar: Md. 1994. Assoc. gen. counsel ThermoChem, Inc., 1995—97; assoc. DLA Piper US LLP, 1997—2007, ptnr., 2002—06, Duane Morris LLP, 2006—, mng. ptnr. Balt. office. Contbr. articles to profl. jours. Bd. dirs. Emerging Tech. Ctr., Balt.; bd. dirs., of counsel Greater Balt. Tech. Coun.; bd. dirs., vice chmn. Early Stage East, Inc.; com. mem. Bryn Mawr Sch. Annual Fund, Balt. Named a Md. SuperLawyer, 2009; named one of 40 Under 40, Balt. Bus. Jour., 2001, 10 Rising Stars of Private Equity and M&A Law, Institutional Investor News, 2008. Mem.: ABA, Md. Bar Assn. Office: Duane Morris LLP 111 S Calvert St Ste 1000 Baltimore MD 21202 Office Phone: 410-949-2910. Office Fax: 410-949-2953. Business E-Mail: gjnemphos@duanemorris.com.*

NEMSER, EARL HAROLD, lawyer; b. NYC, Jan. 17, 1947; s. Harold Summers and Eleanor Patricia (Beckerman) N.; m. Randy Lynn Lehrer, June 17, 1974 (div.); children: Eliza Sarah, Maggie Lehrer. BA, NYU, 1967; JD magna cum laude, Boston U., 1970. Bar: N.Y. 1970, U.S. Supreme Ct. 1975, U.S. Claims Ct. 1979, U.S. Tax Ct. 1985. Law clk. Hon. Collins J. Seitz chief judge U.S. Ct. Appeals 3rd Cir., 1970-71; ptnr. Cadwalader, Wickersham & Taft, NYC, 1971-95, Swidler Berlin Shereff Friedman, LLP, NYC, 1996—2001, sr. of counsel, 2002—04; pres. Park and 76th Street Co., Inc., NYC, 1998—2007; spl. counsel Dechert LLC, NYC, 2005—. Vice chmn. Interactive Brokers Group, Inc., Greenwich, Conn., 1995—; dir. Timber Hill, LLC, Greenwich, Caribbean Cellular Telephone Ltd., Tortola, BVI, 1997-02; solicitor gen. H.C., Guana Island, BVI. Spl. town atty. Town of Southampton, NY, 2002—; mem. bd. advisors Lenox Hill Hosp., Greenwich Land Trust. Mem. Assn. Bar City NY; dir. The Quiogue Assn., Greenwich Riding Trails Assn. (dir. 2005-). Office: Interactive Brokers Group Inc One Pickwick Plz Greenwich CT 06830

NENÊ, (MAYBYNER RODNEY HILARIO), professional basketball player; b. Sao Carlos, Brazil, Sept. 13, 1982; Profl. basketball player Vasco da Gama, Brazil, 2000—02; draft pick NY Knicks, 2002; forward-ctr. Denver Nuggets, 2002—. Mem. Brazilian Nat. Team Goodwill Games, Australia, 2001. Named to All-Rookie First Team, NBA, 2003. Office: Denver Nuggets 1000 Chopper Cir Denver CO 80204*

NENOV, IVO P., mathematical and software researcher; b. Nikolaevo, Bulgaria, May 5, 1964; arrived in U.S., 1995; s. Panayot Nenov Ivanov and Maria Todorova Ivanova; m. Albena Dragomirova Stoilova-Nenova, Aug. 16, 1987 (div. Apr. 7, 1994); 1 child, Lubomir Ivov. MS, Tech. U. Sofia, Bulgaria, 1990, PhD (hon.), 2003; cert. in internat. bus. mgmt., U. Del., 1992. Rschr. Microprocessor Control Lab., Sofia, Bulgaria, 1986—86; rschr., developer CAD R&D Ctr. Ltd., Sofia, 1990—92; developer, technologist DataMap- Europe Ltd., Sofia, 1993—94; self-employed rschr., developer, cons. Calif., 1995—. Participated, set up European br. Frontline Sys., Inc., Incline Village, Nev., 2003; presenter in field. Contbr. articles to profl. jours. Capt. arty. Bulgarian armed forces, 1982—84. Recipient prize, Nat. Olympiad of Math., 1985, prize for tech., Nat. Competition for Tech., Sofia, 1989, award for extraordinaty ability in sci., INS, 2000. Mem.: Am. Owners and Pilots Assn., Soc. Indsl. and Applied Math. Bulgarian Orthodox. Avocation: flying. Home and Office: 3337 Saxonville Way Antelope CA 95843 Office Phone: 916-334-3465. Personal E-mail: inenov@sbcglobal.net.

NEOGI, NATASHA ANITA, astronaut, educator; d. Prabir Kumar and Joyottoma Neogi. BS in Engring. with honours, McGill U., Montreal, Que., Can., 1996; MA in Philosophy, Cambridge U., Eng., 1997; PhD, Mass. Inst. Tech., Cambridge, 2002. Asst. prof. U. Ill., Urbana-Champaign, 2002—. Astronaut candidate Can. Space Agy., Montreal, 2009—. Recipient Gen. Academic medal, Govt. Can., 1992; scholarship, 1992—96, Ameila Earhart fellowship, Zontas Found., 1997—99. Mem.: AIAA. Office: Univ Ill Urbana-Champaign 1308 W Main St Urbana IL 61801 Office Fax: 217-244-7171. Business E-Mail: neogi@uiuc.edu.

NEOPHYTOU, NEOPHYTOS, research scientist; b. Nicosia, Cyprus, June 11, 1978; s. Christodoulos and Dimitra Neophytou; m. Stella Papastylianou. BS, Purdue U., West Lafayette, Ind., 2001, MS, 2004, PhD, 2008. Postdoc. rschr. TU Wien, Vienna, 2008—. Tech. intern Intel Corp., Hillsboro, Oreg., 2006—07. Contbr. articles to sci. jours. Lt. Mil. Forces, 1996—98, Cyprus. Christian Orthodox. Avocations: travel, photography.

NEPAL, NEERAJ, physicist, researcher; s. Shiva Narayan and Khim Kumari Nepal; m. Kabita Ghimire, June 5, 2002. PhD, Kans. State U., Manhattan, 2006. Grad. rsch. asst. Kans. State U., 2001—06, rsch. assoc., 2006—07; NRC postdoc. fellow NC State U., Raleigh, 2007—. Contbr. articles to profl. jours. Postdoc. fellowship, NRC, 2006. Mem.: Am. Phys. Soc. Home: 3950 Jackson St Raleigh NC 27607

NEPHEW, EDMUND A., physicist, retired mayor; b. Kinsman, Ohio, Apr. 26, 1928; s. Seward Ralph Nephew and Carrie Alice Bascom; m. Maria Theresia Goebhardt, Sept. 1, 1956; children: Thomas, Robert. BS, Youngstown State U., Ohio; MS, Ohio State U.; grad. studies, U. Gottingen, Germany, U. Tenn. With Oak Ridge (Tenn.) Nat. Lab., 1959—89, City of Oak Ridge (Tenn.), 1984—89. Physicist Oak Ridge (Tenn.) Nat. Lab., 1959—89; councilman Oak Ridge (Tenn.) City Council, 1989—97, mayor, 1991—95. Mem., officer Sister Cities Orgn., Oak Ridge, Tenn., 1990—; chmn. ACLU (local chpt.), Oak Ridge, Tenn., 1998; commr. Oak Ridge (Tenn.) Regional Planning Assn., Oak Ridge, Tenn., 1984—88. Pvt. US Army, 1950—52. Democrat. Unitarian Universalist. Avocations: gardening, travel, reading, languages. Home: 119 Netherlands Rd Oak Ridge TN 37830

NEPPE, VERNON MICHAEL, neuropsychiatrist, behavioral neurologist, psychopharmacologist, writer, phenomenologist, conciousness researcher, forensic specialist, philosopher; b. Johannesburg, Transvaal, Rep. South Africa, Apr. 16, 1951; came to U.S., 1986; s. Solly Louis and Molly (Hesselson) N.; m. Elisabeth Selima Schachter, May 29, 1977; children: Jonathan, Shari. BA, U. South Africa, 1976; MB, BCh, U. Witwatersrand, Johannesburg, 1973, diploma in psychol. medicine, 1976, M in Medicine, 1979, PhD in Medicine, 1981; MD, U.S., 1982. Diplomate Am. Bd. Psychiatry and Neurology, 1994, specialties in psychiatry 1988, geriatric psychiatry 1991, 2001, forensic psychiatry 1994, Am. Bd. Psychol. Specialties in Psychopharmacology, 1991; registered psychiatry specialist U.S., Republic of South Africa, Can.; bd. cert. behavioral neurologist/neuropsychiatrist, 2006. Specialist in tng. dept. psychiatry U. Witwatersrand, Johannesburg, 1974-80; sr. cons. U. Witwatersrand Med. Sch., Johannesburg, 1980-82, 83-85; neuropsychiatry, behavioral neurology, psychopharmacology fellow Cornell U., NYC, 1982—83; divsn. dir. U. Wash. Med. Sch., Seattle, 1986-92; dir. Pacific Neuropsychiat. Inst., Seattle, 1992—; neuropsychiatrist, behavioral neurologist N.W. Hosp., 1992—. Adj. prof. psychiatry St. Louis U. Sch. of Medicine, dept. psychiatry and human behavior, 1994—; attending physician Overlake Hosp., 1993—; mem. clin. faculty dept. psychiatry and behavioral scis. U. Wash. Med. Sch., 1992-2001; neuropsychiatry cons. South African Brain Rsch. Inst., Johannesburg, 1985—; chief rsch. cons. Epilepsy Inst., N.Y.C., 1989; mem. faculty lectr. Epilepsy: Refining Med. Treatment, 1993-94. Author: The Psychology of Déjà Vu: Have I Been Here Before?, 1983, Innovative Psychopharmacotherapy, 1990, Cry the Beloved Mind: A Voyage of Hope, 1999, How Attorneys Can Best Utilize Their Medical Expert Consultant: A Medical Expert's Perspective, 2006, 2nd edit., 2009, BROCAS SCAN, 1992; (plays) Quakes, 2002, Tomorrow the Earthquake, 2001; Deja Vu: A Second Look, 2006, Deja Vu Revisited, 2006, Deja Vu: Glossary and Library, 2006; contbr. (with others) 64 book chpts.; editor 14 jours. issues; 200 other contbn., contbr. articles to profl. jours. Recipient Rupert Sheldrake prize for rsch. design award New Scientist, 1983, Marius Valkhoff medal South African Soc. for Psychical Rsch., 1982, George Elkin Bequest for Med. Rsch., U. Witwatersrand, 1980; named Overseas Travelling fellow, 1982-83. Fellow Am. Psychiat. Assn. (disting. fellow 2008, US transcultural collaborator diagnostic and statis. manual 1985-86, cons. organic brain disorders 1988-92), Psychiatry Coll. South Africa (faculty), Royal Soc. South Africa, Royal Coll. Physicians of Can., North Pacific Soc. for Neurology, Neurosurgery and Psychiatry, Coll. Internat. Neuropharmacologicum, Am. Coll. Forensic Examiners; mem. AMA, Parapsychologic Assn., Am. Epilepsy Soc., Soc. Biol. Psychiatry, Can. Psychiat. Assn., Soc. Sci. Exploration, Am. Soc. Clin. Psychopharmacology, Am. Neuropsychiat. Assn. (People to People del. leader for U.S. plus internat. del. in psychopharmacology and neuropsychiatry to China 2006), Internat. Soc. Philos. Enquiry (diplomat sr. rsch. fellow 2008). Jewish. Avocations: chess, tennis, computers, Scrabble. Office: Pacific Neuropsychiat Inst 6300 Ninth Ave NE Ste 353 Seattle WA 98115 Office Phone: 206-527-6289.

NEPPLE, JAMES ANTHONY, lawyer; b. Carroll, Iowa, Jan. 5, 1945; s. Herbert J. and Cecilia T. (Irlmeier) N.; m. Jeannine Ann Jennings, Sept. 9, 1967; children: Jeffrey B., Scott G., Carin J., Andrew J. BA, Creighton U., 1967; JD, U. Iowa, 1970; postgrad. in bus., Tex. Christian U., 1971; LLM in Taxation, NYU, 1982. Bar: Iowa 1970, Ill. 1973, U.S. Dist. Ct. (so. dist.) Iowa 1972, U.S. Dist. Ct. (cen. dist.) Ill. 1972, U.S. Dist. Ct.(no. dist.) Iowa 1975, U.S. Ct. Appeals (7th and 8th cirs.) 1975, U.S. Supreme Ct. 1975, U.S. Ct. Claims 1976, U.S. Tax Ct. 1976. Tax acct. Arthur Young & Co., Chgo., 1970; v.p., treas., bd. dirs. Stanley, Rehling, Lande & VanDerKamp, Muscatine, Iowa, 1972-92; pres. Nepple, VanDerKamp & Flynn, P.C., Rock Island, Ill., 1992-98, Nepple Law P.L.C., 1999—. Scoutmaster Boy Scouts Am., Muscatine, 1982—85, dist. chmn., 2005—; trustee State His. Soc. Iowa, 1986—92, vice-chmn., 1991—92; bd. dirs. Iowa Hist. Found., 1988—95, pres., 1991—93; trustee Musser Pub. Libr., 2000—04; pres. Muscatine Hist. Preservation Commn., 2001—07, chmn., 2001—04. Recipient Gov.'s Vol. award State of Iowa, 1988, 90, Jr. Achievement of the Quad Cities Bronze award, 1996, Silver award, 2000. Fellow: Ill. Bar Found., Iowa Bar Found., Am. Bar Found., Am. Coll. Trust and Estate Counsel; mem.: ABA (tax sect. 1972—, chair bus. coop. & agrl. tax com. 2001—03), Iowa Bar Assn. (mem. tax sect. 1978—91, chmn. tax sect. 1988—91), Quad City Estate Planning Coun. (pres. 1987), Iowa Assn. Bus. and Industry (tax com. 1978—, chmn. 1986—88), Rock Island County Bar Assn., Scott County Bar Assn., Muscatine Bar Assn. (pres. 1982—83), Ill. Bar Assn. (fed. tax. sect. coun. 1993—99, chair 1997—98, bus. advice and fin. planning sect. coun. 2000—09, chair 2007—08), Fed Bar Assn., Muscatine C. of C. (pres. 1985), Rotary Club, Geneva Golf and Country Club (pres. 1990—91), Elks, Kiwanis (pres. Muscatine chpt. 1978). Republican. Roman Catholic. Home: 2704 Mulberry Ave Muscatine IA 52761-2746 Office Phone: 563-264-6840. Office Fax: 563-264-6844. Personal E-mail: nepple@machlink.com. Business E-Mail: jim@nepplelaw.com.

NERBONNE, JULIA FROST, environmentalist, educator; b. Washington, Jan. 16, 1971; d. Edmund Bowen and Molly Spitzer Frost; m. Brian Frost Nerbonne, June 23, 2001; children: Lucas Frost, Clara Luette Frost. MS in Conservation Biology, U. Minn., St. Paul, 2000, PhD in Conservation Biology, 2003. Environ. sustainability program dir. Higher Edn. Consortium Urban Affairs, St. Paul, 2003—; adj. asst. prof. U. Minn., Dept. Fisheries & Wildlife, 2004—. Campaign mgr. Patricia Torres Ray Senate, Mpls., 2006; chair vol. com. Dispute Resolution Ctr., St. Paul, 2002—08; dir. Senate Dist. 62, Mpls., 2006—09. Rsch. grant, Miss. Watershed Mgmt. Orgn., 2004—05. Mem.: Soc. Conservation Biology (pres. minn. chpt. 2008—). Dfl. Office: Higher Edn Consortium Urban Affairs 2233 University Ave W Saint Paul MN 55114

NEREM, ROBERT MICHAEL, engineering educator, consultant; b. Chgo., July 20, 1937; s. Robert and Borghild Guneva (Bakken) Nerem; m. Jill Ann Thomson, Dec. 21, 1958 (div. 1977); children: Robert Steven, Nancy Ann; m. Marilyn Reed, Oct. 7, 1978; stepchildren: Christina Lynn Maser, Carol Marie Maser. BS, U. Okla., 1959; MS, Ohio State U., 1961, PhD in Aero. and Astronautical Engring., 1964; D (hon.), U. Paris, 1990. Asst. prof. Ohio State U., Columbus, 1964-68, assoc. prof., 1968-72, prof., 1972-79, assoc. dean Grad. Sch., 1975-79; prof. mech. engring., chmn. dept. U. Houston, 1979-86; Parker H. Petit prof. Ga. Inst. Tech., Atlanta, 1987—, Inst. prof., 1991—, dir. Parker H. Petit Inst. for Bioengring. and Biosci., 1995—; dir. Ga. Tech/Emory Ctr. for the Engring. of Living Tissues NSF Engring. Rsch. Ctr., Atlanta, 1998—. Mem. Ga. Gov.'s Adv. Coun. on Sci. and Tech. Devel., Atlanta, 1992—95; Alza disting. lectr. Biomed. Engring. Soc., 1991; ASME Thurston lectr., 94; mem. sci. bd. FDA, 2000—03; sr. adv. for bioengring. Nat. Inst. Biomed. Imaging and Bioengring., 2003—06. Contbr. articles to profl. jours. Fellow: AAAS, ASME, Instn. Mech. Engrs. UK (hon.), Am. Inst. Med. and Biol. Engring. (founding pres. 1992—94); mem.: NAE (Founders award 2008), Royal Swedish Acad. Engring. Scis., Polish Acad. Scis., US Nat. Com. on Biomechanics (chmn. 1988—91), Japanese Soc. for Med. & Biol. Engring. (hon.), Internat. Fedn. for Med. and Biol. Engring. (pres. 1988—91), Internat. Union for Phys. and Engring. Scis. in Medicine (pres. 1991—94), Inst. Medicine, Biomed. Engring. Soc., Am. Acad. Arts and Scis. Home: Park Springs 9435 Creekside Trail Stone Mountain GA 30087 Office Phone: 404-894-2768. Business E-Mail: robert.nerem@ibb.gatech.edu.

NERLOVE, MARC LEON, economics professor; b. Chgo., Oct. 12, 1933; s. Samuel Henry and Evelyn (Andelman) N.; children: Susan, Miriam. BA, U. Chgo., 1952; MA, Johns Hopkins U., 1955, PhD, 1956. Analytical statistician USDA, Washington, 1956-57; assoc. prof. U. Minn., Mpls., 1959-60; prof. Stanford (Calif.) U., 1960-65, Yale U., 1965-69; prof. econs. U. Chgo., 1969-74; F.W. Taussig rsch. prof. Harvard Coll., Cambridge, Mass., 1967-68; vis. Cook prof. Northwestern U., Evanston, Ill., 1973-74, Cook prof., 1974-82; prof. econs. U. Pa., Phila., 1982-86, Univ. prof., 1986-93; prof. agr. and resource econs. U. Md., College Park, 1993—. Author: Dynamics of Supply, 1958, Distributed Lags and Demand Analysis, 1958, Estimation and Identification of Cobb-Douglas Production Functions, 1965, Analysis of Economic Time Series: A Synthesis, 1979, Household and Economy: Welfare Economics of Endogenous Fertility, 1987, Essays on Panel Data Econometrics, 2002; contbr. numerous articles to profl. jours. 1st lt. AUS, 1957-59. Recipient award Am. Farm Econ. Assn., 1956, 58, 61, 79, P.S. Mahalanobis medal Indian Econ. Soc., 1975. Fellow Am. Statis. Assn., Econometric Soc. (v.p. 1980, pres. 1981), Am. Acad. Arts and Scis., Am. Agrl. Econ. Assn.; mem. NAS, Am. Econ. Assn. (mem. exec. com. 1977-79, John Bates Clark medal 1969), Royal Econ. Soc., Phi Beta Kappa, others. Achievements include research on economics of agriculture with particular reference to developing countries, population and economic growth; analysis of categorical data, particularly business and household surveys. Office: U Md Dept Agr and Resource Econs College Park MD 20742-0001 E-mail: mnerlove@arec.umd.edu.

NERODE, ANIL, mathematician, educator; b. LA, June 4, 1932; s. Nirad Ranjan and Agnes (Spencer) N.; m. Sondra Raines, Feb. 12, 1955 (div. 1968); children: Christopher Curtis, Gregory Daniel; m. Sally Riedel Sievers, May 16, 1970; 1 child, Nathanael Caldwell. BA, U. Chgo., 1949, BS, 1952, MS, 1953, PhD, 1956. Group leader automata and weapons systems Lab. Applied Sci., U. Chgo., 1954-57; mem. Inst. for Advanced Study, Princeton, 1957-58, 62-63; vis. asst. prof. math. U. Calif. at Berkeley, 1958-59; mem. faculty Cornell U., 1959—, prof. math., 1965—, Goldwin Smith prof. math., 1990—, chmn. dept. math., 1982-87, dir. Math. Sci. Inst., 1986-97; acting dir. Center for Applied Math., 1965-66; vis. prof. Monash U., Melbourne, Australia, 1970, 74, 78, 79, U. Chgo., 1976, M.I.T., 1980, U. Calif., San Diego, 1981; disting. vis. scientist EPA, 1985-87; dir. Ctr. for Found. of Intelligent Sys. Cornell U., 1997—2001. Prin. investigator numerous grants; mem. sci. adv. bd. EPA, 1988-93, chair tech. adv. panel Global Change, 1990-92; mem. sci. adv. bd. Ctr. for Intelligent Control, Harvard-MIT-Brown U., 1988-94; cons. to govt. and industry; co-founder Clearsight Corp., 1995. Author: (with John Crossley) Combinatorial Functors, 1974, (with Richard Shore) Logic for Applications, 2d edit., 1996, (with G.A. Metakides) Principles of Logic and Logic Programming, 1996, (with B. Khoussainov) Automata Theory and its Applications, 2001; editor Advances in Mathematics, 1967-70, Jour. Symbolic Logic, 1967-82, Annals of Pure and Applied Logic, 1983-96, Future Generation Computing Systems, 1983-97, Jour. Pure & Applied Algebra, 1988-2005, Annals of Math. and Artificial Intelligence, 1989—, Logical Methods in Computer Sci., 1991-94, Computer Modelling and Simulation, 1991—, Constraints, 1995-2001, Grammers, 1997-2001, (with J. Remmel, S. Goncharov, Y. Ershov) Handbook of Recursive Algebra, 1998. Mem. AIII, IEEE, Assn. Computing Machinery, Am. Math. Soc. (assoc. editor procs. 1962-65, v.p. 1991-94), Soc. Indsl. and Applied Math., Math.

Assn. Am., Assn. Symbolic Logic, European Assn. for Theoretical Computer Sci. Home: 406 Cayuga Heights Rd Ithaca NY 14850-1402 Office: Cornell U 545 Mallott Hall Dept Math Ithaca NY 14853-4201 Business E-Mail: anil@math.cornell.edu.

NERURKAR, SHAILESH B., research scientist; b. Mumbai, Feb. 27, 1978; s. Balwant G. and Uma B. Nerurkar; m. Priyanka D. Roy-chowdhury, Dec. 12, 2007. D, U. Dayton, Ohio, 2006. Gradaute rsch. asst. U. Dayton, 2003—06; prin. rschr. ASIC Advantage Inc., Sunnyvale, Calif., 2006—, design engr., 2006—. Grad. rsch. Wright State U., Dayton, 2001—03, tchg. asst, 2001—03. Contbr. scientific papers to publs. Tuition waiver grant, Wright State U., 2002—04. Mem.: IEEE (sec. 2009, voluntary award 2009). Achievements include design of very low power, hardware efficient circuits and systems. Office: ASIC Advantage Inc 1290 B Reamwood Ave Sunnyvale CA 94089 Home Phone: 408-598-6283. Personal E-mail: shailesh@ieee.org. E-mail: shailesh.nerurkar@asicadvantage.com.

NESANOVICH, STELLA ANN, literature educator, poet; d. Joseph Michael Nesanovich, Sr. and Etta Stella Nesanovich. PhD, La. State U., Baton Rouge, 1979. Instr. Winthrop U., Rock Hill, SC, 1979—82; English prof. McNeese State U., Lake Charles, La., 1982—2009. Author: (poetry) Vespers at Mount Angel: Poems. Artist fellowship, La. Divsn. Arts, 1999—2000. Mem.: Christianity and Lit. Roman Catholic.

NESBIT, ROBERT RAYMOND, JR., surgeon; b. New Haven, Apr. 1, 1939; BA, Harvard U., 1961; MD, U. Rochester, 1965. Diplomate Am. Bd. Surgery. Intern Strong Meml. Hosp., Rochester, 1965-66, resident in surgery, 1966-67, 69-74; chief vascular surgery Med. Coll. Ga. Hosps., Augusta, 1994-2000; prof. surgery Med. Coll. Ga., 1994-2000, prof. surgery emeritus, 2000—, dir. med. student edn. dept. surgery, 2002—. Fellow ACS; mem. Am. Assn. for Vascular Surgery, So. Surg. Assn., Assn. VA Surgeons, So. Assn. Vascular Surgery, Augusta-Richmond County Hist. Soc. (pres. 2003-05), Am. Osler Soc., Atlanta Vascular Soc., (pres. 2004-06), So. Assn. History Medicine and Sci. (pres. 2006-08), Assn. Surg. Edn. (chair surgery clerkship dirs. com. 2006-08), Phi Beta Kappa, Alpha Omega Alpha. Office: Med Coll Ga Dept Surgery Augusta GA 30912 Home Phone: 706-733-8861; Office Phone: 706-721-1967. Business E-Mail: rnesbit@mail.mcg.edu.

NESBIT, SANDI MICHELLE, corporate financial executive; b. Marietta, Ga., Aug. 30, 1963; d. Walter DeForest (Stepfather) and Linda S. Van Fleet, William E. Ray; m. Eric James E Nesbit, Oct. 11, 1998; 1 child, Cora Helene. Title Insurance Agent Tenn., 2002; Notary Public at Large Tenn., 2000. Ceo/founder NNBS, Inc., Anytime Services.com, Rockford, Tenn., 1999—; mgr. Nationwide Homes, Alcoa, Tenn., 1998—2000. Author: (educational workbook) The Title Searchers Handbook. Hon. chmn. Nat. Rep. Congl. Com., 2003. Pentacostal. Avocations: travel, reading, music, animals. Office: NNBS Inc 3532 Calvert St Rockford TN 37853-3926

NESBIT, WILLIAM TERRY, small business owner, consultant; b. Pitts., Jan. 30, 1945; s. William Frank and Glenna (Cleeton) N.; divorced. Owner, CEO Narrow Gauge Car Shop, Evergreen Outdoor Ctr., Shiremanstown, Pa., 1972—; mem. faculty Millersville (Pa.) U., 1976-81, Temple U., Phila., 1979, Nat. Aquatic and Small Craft Sch., Bemis Point, NY, 1980, Harrisburg (Pa.) Area C. C., 1981-82, 91, Dickinson Coll., Carlisle, Pa., 1982-83. Judge 32d Capital Area Sci., Engring. Fair, Dickinson Coll., Carlisle, Pa., 1989; mem. tech. briefs reader adv. panel NASA, 2000—. Co-developer ARC basic and whitewater canoeing programs for instrn., 1977-79; inventor, developer The Z Drag for Boat Rescues, 1980; developer, mfr. first HOn3 ready-to-run plastic rolling stock having NMRA warrant; contbg. author: The Brown Book, 2d edit., 1982. Vol. ARC, 1961—; contbr. A.C. Kalmbach Meml. Libr., Chattanooga; benefactor Carlyton Sch. Dist. Libr., Carnegie, Pa. Recipient award for Humanity ARC, 1967, award for 30 Yrs. Vol. Svc., 1991; named Class I Radiol. Protection Officer, U.S. Dept. Def. and NRC, 1993. Mem. Math. Assn. Am., Nat. Assn. Canoe Liveries and Outfitters (founding), Nat. Model Railroad Assn. (life, mid-eastern region bd. dirs. 1997-2001, supt. Susquehanna divsn. 1996-2000, edn. chair 2002-), Nat. Railroad Assn., Conewago Canoe Club (canoe tng. officer 1999—), Canoe Club of Greater Harrisburg (founding mem.), Ctrl. Pa. Rock and Mineral Club (bd. mem. and field trip coord., 2008-). Episcopalian. Avocation: ferroequinology. Office: Evergreen Outdoor Ctr PO Box 3081 Shiremanstown PA 17011-3081 Business E-Mail: william.nesbit@dla.mil.

NESBITT, DAVID JOHN, physics and chemistry professor; b. Westport, Conn., Oct. 1953; BA in Chemistry and Physics, Harvard U., Cambridge, Mass., 1975; PhD in Chem. Physics, U. Colo., 1981. Tchr. math., physics and chemistry Colo. Acad., Denver, 1975-77; rsch. asst. chem. physics program U. Colo., Boulder, 1977-81, NRC fellow Joint Inst. for Lab. Astrophysics, 1981-82, asst. prof. adjoint chemistry dept., 1984—87, fellow Joint Inst. for Lab. Astrophysics, 1985—, assoc. prof. adjoint, 1988—91, full prof. adjoint, 1992—, chair Joint Inst. for Lab. Astrophysics, 2007—; Miller postdoctoral fellow U. Calif., Berkeley, 1982-84; physicist Nat. Inst. Stds. and Tech., 1984—. Contbr. articles to sci. jours.; mem. editl. bd.: Jour. Chem. Physics, Jour. Phys. Chemistry. Recipient Camille and Henry Dreyfus Found. award, 1984, Wilson Prize Harvard U., 1989, Arthur S. Flemming award, 1991, Silver medal Dept. Commerce, 1992, Edward Uhler Condon award Nat. Inst. Stds. and Tech., 1995, William F. Meggers award Optical Soc. Am., 1999; Harvard Club scholar Harvard U., 1971-73; Univ. fellow U. Colo., 1977-80, Alfred P. Sloan rsch. fellow, 1987, Alexander von Humboldt fellow, 1999. Fellow Am. Phys. Soc. (Earle K. Plyler prize for Molecular Spectroscopy 1997), Royal Soc. Chemists; mem. Am. Chem. Soc. (Nobel Laureate Signature award for grad. edn. in chemistry 1983), Sigma Xi. Office: Joint Inst Lab Astrophysics U Colo 440 UCB Boulder CO 80309-0440 Office Phone: 303-492-8857. E-mail: djn@jila.colorado.edu.

NESBITT, DEETTE DUPREE, small business owner, investor; b. Houston, May 5, 1941; d. Raymond Benjamin DuPree and Alice Lula (Cade) Foster; children: Alice L., Charles S. Massey Nesbitt; m. Ernest V. Nesbitt, Aug. 20, 1971 (dec.). Student, Sam Houston State U., 1960-61, U. Houston, 1961-62, 81-83. Contbr. articles to various publs. Former trustee Pace Soc. Am., Inc., 1992-95, Inc.; bd. dirs. Evergreen Friends, Inc., 1991-92; dir., sec. competitive swim team Dad's Club YMCA, Houston, 1981-83; vol. adminstrv. asst. numerous orgns., Houston; patron Houston Jr. League, River Oaks Chamber Orchestra, Daus. of Republic Tex., San Jacinto Chpt., Life Mem., Daus. of Cin., NY, Life Mem. Recipient Varina Howell Davis medal Mil. Order Stars and Bars, 1992, Silver Good Citizenship medal SAR, 1992, Honor award Tex. SCV, 1992; featured on Eyes of Texas, NBC, 1992, Nat. Honor award Hereditary Soc. Cmty., 2003; Ky. Col. Mem.: Order of Crown Charlemagne USA (hon.), 100 Living Descs. Blood Royal (hon.), HSC Adv. Coun. (life; cons. 2007—09), Hereditary Soc. (cmty. cons. 2006—), Nat. Soc. Colonial Dames Am. in Commonwealth of Va., Nat. Soc. Sons and Daus. Antebellum Planters 1607-1861, Sons and Daus. of Pilgrims (nat. com. 1993—97), Colonial Dames Am. (pres. chpt. VIII 1995—97), Dames of Colonial Cavaliers 1640-1660 (organizing dep. gov. gen. 2001—03, gov. gen. 2003—05, life hon. gov. gen. emerita), Nat. Soc. DAR, Huguenot Soc. Am., S.C. Soc. Descs. of Colonial Clergy, Nat. Soc. Magna Charta Dames (Houston colony historian 1992—95), Plantagenet Soc., Am. Royal Descent, Nat. Jamestown Soc. (mem. coun. 1993—95, auditor gen. 1995—97, lt. gov. gen. 1997—98, gov. gen. 1998—2000, Resolution of Appreciation, Outstanding Leadership 2000), First Tex. Co. Jamestowne Soc. (lt. gov., gov. 1985—93, hon. gov. emerita), Nat. Gavel Soc., Soc. First Families of S.C. 1670-1700 (life; sec. 2003—05, 3rd v.p. 2005—07, pres. gen. 2007—09), Order of First Families of Va. 1607-1624 (life; mem. coun. 2001—, rec. sec. 2005—), Order of First Families of Miss. 1699-1817 (life), Daus. Rep. Tex. (Appreciation award 1996), United Daus. Confederacy (Confederate Ball com. 1985—95, co-chmn. ball 1988, adv. to chmn. 1989, 1990, hon. chmn. Houston's confederate ball 1995, So. Heritage Ball com. 2005—, Charleston chpt. #4, Jefferson Davis Hist. award, Winnie Davis medal, Spl. Recognition award), Freedoms Found. Valley Forge (George Washington Honor medal 1994), Harris County Hist. Commn., Galveston Yacht Club, Petroleum Club Houston, Order Descendants Colonial Cavaliers (life; organizing gov. gen. and hon. gov. gen. 2007). Republican. Episcopalian. Home: 15411 Old Stone Trail Houston TX 77079-4206

NESBITT, JOHN DUNVILLE, literature and language professor, writer; b. Lompoc, Calif., Dec. 14, 1948; s. Alexander Dunville and Elizabeth Margaret Nesbitt; m. Rocio Perez, June 21, 1995; m. Laura Margaret Stokes, Sept. 17, 1977 (div.); m. Liesa Ann Jensen, Jan. 4, 1988 (div.); 1 child, Dimitri Andres. BA, U. Calif., LA, 1971; MA, U. Calif., Davis, 1974, PhD, 1980. Diploma in Spanish philology Inst. Filología Hispánica, Saltillo, Coahuila, Mex., 1994. Instr. Eastern Wyo. Coll., Torrington, 1981—. Contbr. to numerous poems and short stories (Lit. fellowship, Wyo. Coun. Arts., 1988, Creative Writing fellowship, Wyo. Arts Coun., 2008). Bd. mem. Wyo. Ctr. Book, Cheyenne, 2006—. Recipient Fiction award, Wyo. Hist. Soc., 1999, 2001. Master: Phi Beta Kappa; mem.: Western Lit. Assn., Western Writers America (Albuquerque) (bd. mem. 2008—, Finalist Spur award 2008), Wyo. Writers (Arizola Magnenat award 1999, Emmie Mygatt award 2000). Home: PO Box 973 Torrington WY 82240 Office: Eastern Wyo Coll 3200 West C St Torrington WY 82240 Business E-Mail: john.nesbitt@ewc.wy.edu.

NESBITT, MITZI EVALEE, voice educator, director; d. Sylvan Julian and Mildred Evelyn (Moe) Nylander; divorced; 1 child, Travis Orlo. AA in Music, N.W. Coll., Kirkland, Wash., 1970; BA in Music, Calif State U., Hayward, 1975; MA in Music, Dance, Drama, Calif State U., Fullerton, 1994. Cert. tchr. Calif. Music tchr. Christian Ctr. Sch., Dublin, Calif., 1972—76; vocal music tchr. Phoenix Elem. Schs., 1976—79, Placentia (Calif.) Unified Sch. Dist., 1979—85, Corona/Norco (Calif.) Unified Sch. Dist., 1988—92, 1997—, 4th grade tchr., 1992—97. Pvt. practice, Norco, Calif., 1985—; adv. bd. Nat. Orff Schulwerk, Redlands, Calif., 1994. Author, composer: Oh California, 1994, Lion, Witch, and the Wardrobe, 1994. Music dir. Children's Theatre Experience, Chatsworth, Calif., 1996—; pianist Calvary Christian Ctr., Corona, 1987—97. Recipient Mentor Tchr. award, Corona Norco Unified Sch. Dist., 1994—96; named Tchr. of Yr., Stallings Elem. Sch., 2004, Bravo award finalist, 1995. Mem.: Am. Orff Schulwerk (sec. 1993—2006). Avocations: jogging, photography, sewing, yoga, tennis.

NESBITT, RICHARD, bank executive, former stock exchange executive; b. Oct. 7, 1955; BA in Bus. Adminstrn., U. Western Ontario; MBA, U. Toronto, 1985; MSc in Acctg. and Fin., London Sch. Econs. Position at Mobil Oil Can. Ltd., CIBC Wood Gundy; pres. and CEO HSBC Securities Can.; pres. and COO BayStreetDirect Inc.; gov. Toronto Stock Exch., 1996—99, pres. TSX Markets, 2001—04, CEO TSX Group Inc., 2004—08; chmn., CEO CIBC World Markets, 2008—. Former lectr. Univ. Western Ontario Sch. Bus.; bd. dirs. World Fedn. of Exchanges, Market Regulation Services, CanDeal, Frontier Coll., Prostate Cancer Rsch. Found. of Canada. Office: CIBC World Markets 161 Bay St, Brookfield Pl PO Box 500 Toronto ON M5J 2S8 Canada Office Phone: 416-947-4670. Office Fax: 416-947-4662.

NESBITT, ROBERT EDWARD LEE, JR., physician, educator, research scientist, writer, poet; b. Albany, Ga., Aug. 21, 1924; s. Robert E.L. and Anne Louise (Hill) N.; m. Ellen Therese Morrissey. BA, Vanderbilt U., 1944, MD, 1947. Diplomate Am. Bd. Ob-Gyn (assoc. examiner). Asst. prof. Johns Hopkins U., Balt., 1954—56, chief obstetric pathology lab., acting chief obstetrics, 1955—56; prof., chmn. dept. ob-gyn Albany Med. Coll., Union U., NY, 1956—61, SUNY Health Sci. Ctr., Syracuse, 1961—81, dir. gen. gynecology svc., 1982—84, prof., chmn. emeritus dept. ob-gyn; obstetrician-gynecologist-in-chief Albany Hosp., 1956—61, Syracuse Meml. Hosp., 1961—65, Crouse-Irving Hosp., 1963—70, attending staff, 1970—84; prof. surgery U. South Fla., Tampa, 1988—92, prof. ob-gyn, 1988—92. Chief ob-gyn State U. Hosp., 1964-81, chmn. med. staff and med. bd., 1964-66; attending staff St. Joseph's Hosp.; cons., chief gynecology sect. surg. svc. Syracuse VA Hosp., 1984-88; chief gynecology sect., asst. chief surgery, dir. urogynecology VA Med. Ctr., Bay Pines, Fla., 1988-92, acting chief staff, 1990, interim chief surgery, 1991-92, chmn. O.R. com. surg. svc., 1988-92, chmn. patient care evaluation com., 1989-90, chmn. clin. exec. bd., 1990, chmn. drug usage evaluation com., 1990-91, chmn. profl. stds. bd., 1990; cons. Syracuse Psychiat. Inst.; mem. cancer tng. grants and edn. com. Nat. Cancer Insts.; mem. adv. com. Bur. Maternal and Child Health, NY State Dept. Health, 1957-61; nat. adviser to Children, publ. of Children's Bur., HEW, 1959-63; cons. Children's Bur., 1959-62; mem. prenatal care guide subcom. APHA, 1962-64; cons. to regional adviser in maternal and child health Pan Am. San. Bur., WHO, 1963-65; numerous guest professorships including univs. in Mex., Chile, Uruguay, Colombia, St. Vincent (W.I.), Venezuela, People's Republic of China, We. Europe, Panama, Australia, Canada. Author: Perinatal Loss in Modern Obstetrics, 1957, Last Twig on the Bush?, 1999, In the Fullness of Time, 1999, Hearts of Flesh, 2001, Modern Towers Of Babel, 2006, (poetry collections) Chorales for Arid Souls, 1999, The Fullness Search, 2000, Visions Shared, 2000, Daily Relevance, 2000, Glimpses, 2002, Marked Off from Pagans, 2000, Puppet or Saint, 2001, Latent Harvest, 2002, Dry River Beds, 2003, Language of the Soul, 2003, Souls in Touch, 2004, Daybreak of Hope, 2004, Omen in the Sand, 2005, Pilgrims on Stage, 2005, Unitive Ways of Grace, 2005, Horizons Perceived, 2006, Timely Sparks, 2008, Muse Skitterings, 2008, Temple Light, 2009, Morsels of Enduring Taste, 2009, Crowned Jewels, 2009, more than 1381 poems, over 950 nuggets spiritual discernment and commentaries, sect. on ob-gyn in Rypin's Med. Licensure Exams; co-author: Infant, Perinatal, Maternal and Childhood Mortality in U.S, 1968; editor: (sect. on ob-gyn.) Stedman's Medical Dictionary, 1958—64, (sect. on fetus) Funk and Wagnalls Universal Std. Ency., 1959; first guest editor: sect. on fetus Clinics in Perinatology, 1974; first guest editor (sect. on fetus) Clinical Diagnosis Quiz for Obstetrics and Gynecology, 1976, Clini-Pearls in Obstetrics and Gynecology, 1977; contbr.: sect. on fetus Attorneys' Textbook of Medicine; contbr. poetry to 76 anthologies, 57 CD/audios and over 60 nat. poetry jours. and mags. (15 Editor's Choice awards, Best Poems and Poets, 2000-07). Capt. M.C., U.S. Army, 1952-54. Named One of Ten Outstanding Young Men in Am., US Jr. C. of C., 1957; Robert E.L. Nesbitt Jr. scholarship, Sr. Resident in Ob-Gyn, and Robert E.L. Nesbitt Jr. student scholarship established in his honor, SUNY Health Sci. Ctr. at Syracuse, 1987; recipient Wisdom award, 2001, named to Hall of Fame, Wisdom Soc., 2001, Winston Churchill medal of wisdom, 2002. Fellow: A.C.S. (com. forum fundamental surg. problems 1962—67), N.Y. Acad. Scis., Am. Coll. Obstetricians and Gynecologists (chmn. com. mental retardation and perinatal health 1966), Venezuelan Ob-Gyn Soc. (hon.), Am. Assn. Maternal and Child Health; mem.: AMA (residency accreditation com., site visit team), Internat. Soc. Poets (founding laureate mem.), Pub. Health Coun. N.Y. State, Am. Soc. Cytology, Southwest Ob-Gyn Soc. (hon.), Fla. Ob-Gyn Soc. (hon.), Onondaga County Med. Soc., Med. Soc. N.Y. State (regional obstetrics chmn., subcom. Maternal and Child Welfare), Pan Am. Med. Assn. (med. ambassador goodwill, life mem. sect. on cancer), Soc. Gynecol. Investigation (coun.), Alpha Omega Alpha. Achievements include research and 248 publications on cytologic, cytochemical and histochemical study of early cervical cancer, perinatal and placental pathology, cytologic and hormonal studies in normal and high-risk obstetrics patients, experimental production of abruptio placentae, reproductive endocrinology, animal experimentation, vitamin B12 studies, induced endocrine insults upon pregnant and nonpregnant ewes and hormonal influence on placentation, invitro placenta perfusion, fetal growth and development, female urology, surgical techniques for restoration of female pelvic floor integrity; human spirituality; inspirational poetry and essays. Home: 3743 Roscommon North Martinez GA 30907

NESBITT, WANDA L., United States Ambassador to Cote d'Ivoire; b. Phila., Dec. 7, 1956; m. James Stejskal. BA in Internat. Rels. & French, U. Pa., 1978; postgrad., Nat. War Coll., 1996—97. Vice-consul US Dept. State, Port-au-Prince, Haiti, 1982—83, Paris, 1983—85, with Bur. L.Am., 1986—88, regional consular officer Kinshasa, Zaire, 1990—92, with consular affairs, 1992—93, with legis. affairs, 1995—96, dep. chief of mission Kigali, Rwanda, 1997—99, Dar es Salaam, Tanzania, 1999—2001, US amb. to Madagascar, 2002—04, US amb. to Cote D'Ivoire Abdijan, 2007—. Avocations: gardening, tennis, music. Office: Am Embassy 2010 Abidjan Pl Washington DC 20521 E-mail: nesbittwl@state.gov.*

NESIN, JEFFREY DAVID, academic administrator; b. NYC; m. Diane Garvey, 1968; children: Kate Dillon, Sarah Grace. BA in Eng. Lit., Hobart Coll., 1966; MA in Eng. Lit, SUNY, Buffalo, 1971, MA in Am. Studies, 1973. Faculty dept. humanities & scis. Sch. Visual Arts, NYC, 1974-91; pres. Memphis Coll. Art, 1991—. Asst. to pres. Sch. Visual Arts, 1982-91; cons. Smithsonian Instn., IBM, 1st Tenn. Bank; panelist, speaker in field. Contbg. editor: High Fidelity, Creem; contbr. reviews, interviews, essays to mags.; adv. editor Jour. Popular Music and Society. Recipient Thomas W. Briggs Found. Cmty. Svc. award, 1998. Mem. Am. Studies Assn., Met. Am. Studies Assn. (past pres.), Assn. Ind. Colls. Art & Design (bd. dirs. 1991—), Nat. Assn. Schs. Art & Design (chair commn. on accreditation, exec. com. and bd. 1999—), Ctr. for So. Folklore (bd. and exec. com. 2000—), Memphis Rotary. Avocations: mystery novels, baseball, music. Office: Memphis Coll Art Office of President 1930 Poplar Ave Memphis TN 38104-2756 Office Phone: 901-272-5101. E-mail: jnesin@mca.edu.

NESLUND, SCOTT, former marketing and communications company executive; B, Ind. U., Bloomington, 1988; MBA in Internat. Bus. and Mktg., Northwestern U. Kellogg Sch. Mgmt., Evanston, Ill., 1994. Various mgmt. positions Starcom MediaVest Grp., Milan, Tokyo, Toronto, then sr. v.p., mng. dir. Canada, pres. StarLink Worldwide; mng. dir. MindShare N.Am., Chgo., 2005—07, CEO NYC, 2007—09. Jury mem. Cannes Internat. Advt. Film Festival, France, 2007. Named a Media Maven, Advt. Age, 2008.*

NESMITH, RICHARD A., education educator, consultant; b. Lakeland, Fla., Jan. 13, 1959; s. Wendell B. and Patricia A. NeSmith; m. Melissa M. NeSmith; children: Ricky A., Wendell C. BS, Hyles-Anderson Coll., 1983, MRE, 1984; D in Ministry, Bethany Theol. Sem., 1986; BS, USC, 1991, MEd, 1993; specialists in edn., Augusta State U., 1997; PhD, Curtin U. Tech., 2003. Tchg. cert. biology SC. State Dept. Edn., 1991, educator cert. biology, ednl. leadership, mid. grade Ga. State Dept. Edn., 1995, curriculum validator Western Australia Curriculum Coun., 2000, cert. prin., supt. Ill. Dept. Edn., 1981. Secondary sci. tchr. SC. Dept. Edn., Lexingington, 1992—93; sch. prin. Winfield Heights Christian Sch., Williston, SC, 1994—95; secondary sci. tchr. Ga. Pub. Schs., Ga., 1995—98; head sci. and math dept. Maranatha Christian Coll., Perth, Australia, 1999—2001; asst. prof. edn. Ea. Ill. U., Charleston, 2003—06; asst. prof. of edn. Lake Erie Coll., Painesville, Ohio, 2002—03; dean edn. North Greenville U., Tigerville, SC, 2006—. Bd. examiners Ohio State Dept. Edn., Columbus, 2002—03, SC Dept. Edn.; textbook reviewer Alyn-Bacon Pub. Sci. author, cons.: BioSci. Edn., 1996—, mid-level editor: Ill. Sci. Tchrs. Assn. Jour. (Spectrum). Mem.: Assn. Childhood Edn. Internat. (assoc.; v.p. Ill. chpt.), Am. Rsch. Ednl. Assn. (assoc.), NSTA (assoc.; reviewer), Nat. Mid. Sch. Assn. (assoc.), Phi Delta Kappa (assoc.). Baptist. Achievements include research in middle school students perception of effective teaching and learning; various approaches to improving the curriculum and teaching of science in secondary schools; professional development using multimedia DVD technology. Avocations: hiking, travel, computers, writing. Office: North Greenville U 7801 N Tigerville SC 29688

NESS, ANDREW DAVID, lawyer; b. San Francisco, Oct. 29, 1952; s. Orville Arne and Muriel Ruth (Trendt) N.; m. Rita M. Kobylenski, May 25, 1980; children: Katherine, Austin, Emily. BS, Stanford U., 1974; JD, Harvard U., 1977. Bar: Calif. 1977, D.C. 1979, Va. 1986, U.S. Dist. Ct. (No. Dist.) Calif. 1977, U.S. Dist. Ct. D.C. 1983, U.S. Dist. Ct. (Ea. Dist.) Va. 1988, U.S. Ct. Appeals (4th Cir.) 1989. Law clk. U.S. Dist. Ct., San Francisco, 1977-78; assoc. Lewis, Mitchell & Moore, Vienna, Va., 1979-82, ptnr., 1982-87, Morgan, Lewis & Bockius LLP, Washington, 1987-2000, Thelen Reid Brown Raysman & Steiner LLP, Washington, 2000—; mng. ptnr. D.C. office Thelen Reid & Priest LLP, Washington, 2001—, mem. partnership coun. and exec. com., 2003—. Instr. U. Md., College Park, 1987-90; mem. faculty constrn. exec. program Stanford (Calif.) U., 1984-87. Co-editor Fed. Govt. Construction Contracts, 2003; contbr. chpts. to books, articles to profl. jours. Mem. ABA (forum on constrn. industry, pub. contract law sect.). Avocations: hiking, bicycling. Office: Thelen Reid Brown Raysman & Steiner LLP 701 Eighth St NW Washington DC 20001 Office Phone: 202-508-4368. Business E-Mail: adness@thelen.com.

NESS, BERNICE HAGIE, retired music educator; b. Mpls., Sept. 4, 1926; d. John Leonard and Mathilda Caroline Hagie; m. Elmo Vernon Ness, Aug. 3, 1974. BS, U. Minn., Mpls., 1948, MEd, 1950. Elem. music supr. Lake Co. Schs., Two Harbors, Minn., 1950—51, Mounds View Dist. #621, New Brighton, Minn., 1951—54; tchr., choral music & music theory Mounds View H.S., New Brighton, Minn., 1954—81, tchr., choral music & French, 1981—83; ret., 1983. Mem. adv. bd. U. Minn. Alumni Band, Mpls., 1949—51, coun. mem., 1996—98; dir., arranger Mounds View Alumni Choir, New Brighton, Minn., 1996—2007. Interview Sta. KARE 11, 2007. Chair, music com. Abiding Savior Ch.,

Mounds View, Minn., 1985—94; mem., music com. Christ the King Ch., New Brighton, Minn., 1995—97. Recipient Pillar award, Mounds View H.S., 2005. Home Phone: 763-574-1886. Personal E-mail: enbns@msn.com.

NESS, NORMAN FREDERICK, retired astrophysicist, educator, administrator; b. Springfield, Mass., Apr. 15, 1933; s. Herman and Eva N.; children: Elizabeth Ann, Stephen Andrew. BS, Mass. Inst. Tech., 1955, PhD, 1959. Space physicist, asst. prof. geophysics UCLA, 1959-61; NAS-NRC postdoctoral rsch. assoc. NASA, 1960-61; rsch. physicist in space scis. Goddard Space Flight Center, Greenbelt, Md., 1961-86, head extraterrestrial physics br., 1968-69, chief Lab. for Extraterrestrial Physics, 1969-86; pres. Bartol Rsch. Inst. U. Del., Newark, 1987—2000, prof. Bartol Rsch. Inst., 1987—2005, prof. emeritus, 2005—; dir. NASA Space Grant Coll. Consortium, Del., 1991—2005. Lectr. math. U. Md., 1962-64, assoc. rsch. prof., 1965-67; vis. prof. U. Rome, 1968-69; liasion scientist US Office Naval Rsch., London, 1984-85. Contbr. articles profl. jours. Recipient Exceptional Sci. Achievement award NASA, 1966, 81, 86, Arthur S. Flemming award, 1968, Space Sci. award AIAA, 1971, Disting. Svc. medal NASA, 1986, Nat. Space Club Sci. award, 1993, Emil Wiechert medal German Geophys. Soc., 1993, Space Sci. award COSPAR, 1996. Fellow Am. Geophys. Union (John Adam Fleming award 1965); mem. US-NAS, Acad. Nat. dei Lincei. Achievements include research in publications reporting on experimental studies of interplanetary and planetary magnetic fields by satellites and space probes. Personal E-mail: nfnudel@yahoo.com.

NESS, TIMOTHY JOHN, anesthesiologist, researcher; b. Fort Dodge, Iowa, Apr. 25, 1960; s. John Melling and Marion Victoria Ness; m. Jayne Marie Theis; children: Emily, John, Madeline. MD, PhD, U. Iowa, 1988. Diplomate in anesthesiology and pain mgmt. Am. Bd. Anesthesiology. Assoc. prof. U. Ala., Birmingham, 1999—2003, Simon Gelman endowed prof. anesthesiology, 2003—. Contbr. over 100 articles to profl. jours. Office: U Ala at Birmingham BMR II 901 19th St S Birmingham AL 35233 Personal E-mail: tiness@uab.edu.

NESSEL, EDWARD HARRY, swimming coach; b. Roselle, NJ, 1945; s. Irving Meyer Nessel and Ruth Elliott; m. Eileen Robin Berstein, 1973; children: Lee Allyson, Jason Eric(dec.), Matthew Scott(dec.). BS in Chemistry, Rutgers U., 1967, degree in Pharmacy Chemistry, 1968; post grad., Jersey City State, 1970, Rutgers U., 1971; MS in Bacteriology, Wagner Coll., 1978, MPH, 1978. Registered pharmacist Calif., NJ, Fla.; cert. US swimming coach. Rschr., product developer Mennen Co., Morris Plains, NJ, 1967; pharmacist supr. Pathmark Pharmacies, NJ, 1968—79; pharmacist, mgr. Roxy Drug Co., Inc., Irvington, NJ, 1979—90. Diet and nutrition cons. Fanwood Scotch Plaines YMCA, 1985—91, masters swim coach, 1984—91, swimming and racing cons., head age group coach, asst. sr. coach, 1989—91; head swim coach Jewish Cmty. Ctr. Metrowest, West Orange, 1991—2001; head masters swim coach Rutgers U., New Brunswick, 2000—04; head swim coach Maccabi, 1990—91, 1992, 93, 94; head coach swimming USA Nat. Team World Maccabi Games, Israel, 1997; coach NJ Masters Swimming, 1981—2004; physiology and sports medicine cons. Nat. Health and Fitness; health and fitness chmn. NJ Masters Swimming; nat. masters swimming coaches com. Nat. Com. Sports Medicine; nat. libr. US Masters Swimming; chair NJ Masters Swimming Com.; pres. Jersey Masters Swimming Inc.; sports chair age group and masters swimming Garden State Games; summer coord. long-course 50 meter swim season Rayway YMCA, 1987—2004. Contbr. articles to profl. jours.; patents adjustable hand-swim paddle; author: (book) Swim to Win: Train Like a Champion, 2008. Athletic and swimming cons. NJ Spl. Olympics, 1986; cons. Essex County Narcotic Strike Force; ofcl. Garden State Games, chair gov. coun. phys. fitness swimming events, 1989—96. Recipient Presdl. Series award, 1986, Nat. Svc. award, US Masters Swimming, 1999; named winner, NJ State Pentathlon champion Masters Swimming, 1986—87, YMCA Masters Nat. Swim champion, 1988, 1991, 1995, 1998, 2000—04, Masters All Am. Relay, 1998—99, 2002—03, head swim coach, US Jr. Nat. Swim Team, 1997, Coach of the Yr., US Masters Swimming, Inc., 1998, mentor coach, 2000, 2003, USMS Nat. champion 100 meter breast stroke, 2003. Mem.: NRA (disting. expert rating pistol shotting), NJ Masters Swimming Inc (chmn. 1999—2003), Masters Aquatic Coaches Assn. Am. (pres.), Master Swim Coaches Assn. Am., US Swimming Coaches Assn. (masters swimming coaches and sports medicine coms., cert. level five), Am. Masters Aquatic Coaches Assn. (pres. 1999—2003), Internat. Practical Shooters Confedn. (NJ State champion 1982, 1983), NJ Guild Pharmacists, NJ Pharm. Assn., Am. Assn. Microbiologists, Am. Med. Athletic Assn. (life; clin. cons., contbg. editor quar. 1993—, clin. advisor 1996—), Am. Swimming Coaches Assn. (life master level cert. level five coach, cert. level four YMCA), Rutgers Coll. Pharmacy Alumni Assn., South River Pistol Club, Willow Grove Swim Club (bd. dirs. 1986—90). Avocations: clarinet, saxophone, flute, mus. quality ship builder. Home: 1950 Crane Creek Blvd Viera FL 32940-6831 Personal E-mail: Ednessel@aol.com.

NESTEROVIC, RASHO, professional basketball player; b. Ljubljana, Slovenia, May 30, 1976; Ctr. Olimpija Ljunljana, Slovenia, 1995—97, Virtus Bologna, Italy, Minn. Timberwolves, 1998—2003, San Antonio Spurs, 2003—06, Toronto Raptors, 2006—08, 2009—, Ind. Pacers, 2008—09. Mem., capt. Slovenian Nat. Basketball Team. Achievements include member of NBA Finals championship winning San Antonio Spurs, 2005. Office: Toronto Raptors Air Can Ctr 40 Bay St Toronto ON M5J 2X2 Canada*

NESTI, LEON J., orthopedist, educator; b. Burlington, Vt. s. Richard P. and Frances R. Nesti; m. Heather A. Maust; children: Richard G., Heidi A. BS, US Mil. Acad., West Point, NY, 1995; MD, Jefferson Med. Coll., Phila., 2002; PhD, Thomas Jefferson U., Phila., 2002. Fellow, hand, upper extremity re-constructive surgery, maj. Walter Reed Army Med. Ctr., Washington, 2002—; asst. prof., surgery Uniformed Svcs. U. Health Scis., Bethesda, Md.; spl. vol. NIAMS, Bethesda, Md., CBOB, Bethesda. Mem.: NIH (Bethesda) (spl. vol.). Office: Walter Reed Army Med Ctr 6900 Ga Ave NW Bldg 2 Ste 5B28 Washington DC 20307

NESTLER, JOHN EDWIN, endocrinology educator; b. Passaic, NJ, Sept. 24, 1952; m. Michelle Dumont, Dec. 29, 1990. BA in Chemistry (with honors) and German, Haverford Coll., Pa., 1975; MD, U. Pa., Phila., 1979. Diplomate Am. Bd. Internal Medicine, Am. Bd. Endocrinology and Metabolism; cert. Nat. Bd. Med. Examiners. Intern Med. Coll. Va., Richmond, 1979-80, resident, 1980-82, chief med. resident, instr. in medicine, 1982-83, fellow in endocrinology, 1985-86, asst. prof. medicine, 1986-91, assoc. prof. medicine, 1991—, dir. med. affairs, BioClin, 1991-95, prof. medicine, 1995—, chmn. divsn. endocrinology and metabolism, 1997—, vice chmn. dept. internal medicine, 2003—; fellow in endocrinology U. Pa., Phila., 1983-85. Reviewer various profl. jours.; vis. prof. Dalhousie U., Halifax, N.S., 1991; invited speaker several major confs. including NIH/NICHD Conf. on Polycystic Ovary Syndrome, Bethesda, Md., 1990. Author numerous original publs., book chpts., abstracts. Recipient Sandra Tate Russell Meml. Rsch. award Am. Diabetes Assn. Va. affiliate, 1986, Clin. Assoc. Physician award NIH, 1985-87, rsch. trainee awards Phila. Endocrine Soc., 1984, 85. Fellow Am. Coll. Physicians; mem. AAAS, Internat. Diabetes Found., European Assn. for Study of Diabetes, Cen Va. Assn. Diabetes Educators, Am. Assn. Diabetes Educators, Am. Diabetes Assn. (pres. 1990—), Am. Fedn. Clin. Rsch., Internat. Soc. for Androgenic Disorders, The Endocrine Soc., So. Soc. for Clin. Investigation. Achievements include research on diabetes, polycystic ovary syndrome, steroids, and insulin. Home: 5800 Three Chopt Rd Richmond VA 23226-2337 Office: Med Coll Va Div Endocrinology PO Box 980111 Richmond VA 23298-0111 Office Phone: 804-828-9696. Business E-Mail: jnestler@mcvh-vcu.edu.

NESTLER, PATRICIA C., English professor; BA, Gettysburg Coll., 1972; MA, U. NC, Chapel Hill, 1973. Faculty mem. to assoc. prof. English Montgomery County CC, Pa., 1977—. Recipient US Prof. of Yr. award, Carnegie Found. for Advancement of Tchg. and Coun. for Advancement and Support of Edn., 2006. Office: English Dept Montgomery County CC 101 College Dr Pottstown PA 19464 Office Phone: 215-641-6369. E-mail: pnestler@mc3.edu.

NETHERCOTT, MARK A., physics educator; Secondary tchg. cert. Named Wy. Tchr. of Yr., 2007. Mem.: Am. Assn. Physics Tchrs., Geology Soc. Am., Nat. Sci. Tchr.'s Assn. Office: Star Valley High Sch 455 West Swift Creek Ln PO Box 8000 Afton WY 83110 Business E-Mail: mnethercott@lcsd2.org.

NETHERCUTT, GEORGE RECTOR, JR., lawyer, consultant, former congressman; b. Spokane, Wash., Oct. 7, 1944; s. George Rector and Nancy N.; m. Mary Beth Socha Nethercutt, Apr. 2., 1977; children: Meredith, Elliott. BA in English, Wash. State U., 1967; JD, Gonzaga U., 1971. Bar: D.C. 1972. Law clk. to Hon. Raymond Plummer U.S. Dist. Ct. Alaska, Anchorage, 1971; staff counsel to U.S. Senator Ted Stevens Washington, 1972; chief of staff to U.S. Senator Ted Stevens, 1972-76; pvt. practice Spokane, Wash., 1977-94; mem. 104th-108th Congresses from 5th Wash. dist., Washington, 1995—2005; ptnr. Lundquist, Nethercutt & Griles, LLC, Washington, 2005—. Mem. house appropriations and sci. coms.; mem. bd. Hecla Mining Co., Arcadis Co., Washington Policy Ctr., Juvenile Diabetes Rsch. Found. Internat., 2005—; chmn. Netherea IT Consulting LLC, 2000, U.S. sect. Permanent Joint Bd. Def., U.S., Can., 2005—; of counsel Paine Hamblen LLP, 2005- Chmn. Spokane County Rep. Party, 1990-94, George Netherea IT Found., 2007-, co-founder Vanessa Behan Crisis Nursery, pres. Spokane Juvenile Diabetes Found., 1993-94. Mem. Masons (lodge #34), Lions Club (Spokane Ctrl.), Sigma Nu. Republican. Presbyterian. Avocations: running, handball, squash. Office: Nethercutt Consulting LLC 400 N Capital St Ste 475 Washington DC 20001 Home Phone: 703-827-2203; Office Phone: 202-589-0015. Business E-Mail: gnethercutt@bwstrategies.com.

NETHERLAND, LOUIS VICTOR, military officer, educator; b. Coral Gables, Fla., July 28, 1974; s. Carl Ray and Janet Christine Netherland-Brown; m. Jamie Melinda Barton, Dec. 22, 1995; children: Emily Catherine, Jack Louis. BA in History, Carson-Newman Coll., Jefferson City, Tenn., 1996; MS in Internat. Rels., Troy U., Ala., 2004. Platoon leader 1st Squadron, 4th US Cav., Schweinfurt, Germany, 2000—02, troop exec. officer, 2002—03; troop comdr. 5th Squadron, 15th US Cav., Ft. Knox, Ky., 2004—06; fgn. police advisor Afghan Nat. Police, Mehtar Lam, Laghman, Afghanistan, 2007—08; asst. prof. mil. sci. U. Tenn., Chattanooga, 2008—; capt. US Army, Germany, Turkey, Afghanistan, 1999—. Decorated Bronze Star. Office Fax: 423-425-5593. Personal E-mail: ljnetherland@hotmail.com. Business E-Mail: louis-netherland@utc.edu.

NETHERY, JOHN JAY, government official, military officer; b. Mpls., June 4, 1941; s. Ronald Jay and Mary Vesta (McVeety) N.; m. Sonya Elisabeth Magin, July 27, 1968; children: William Jay, Mary Elisabeth (dec.), Sarah Ann. BA, U. Denver, 1963, MPA, 1968. Mgmt. intern USAF Logistics Command, San Antonio, 1969-71, budget analyst Dayton, Ohio, 1971-72; chief, fiscal analysis USAF Hdqrs., Washington, 1973-80, chief, investment div., 1980-81, chief budget mgmt., 1981-85; dep. asst. sec. programs and budget Dept. of USAF, Washington, 1986-88, asst. to undersecretary, 1988-89, dep. asst. sec. fin. ops., 1989—. Mem. Air Force bd. for the correction of mil. records, Washington, 1980—. Recipient Gov.'s Scholastic award Gov. of Colo., 1968, Presdl. Rank award, 1988. Mem. Sr. Execs. Assn., Air Force Assn. Presbyterian. Avocations: history, military minatures. Office: Dept USAF SAF/FM The Pentagon Washington DC 20330-1130 E-mail: Jnethery@aol.com.

NETI, SUDHAKAR, mechanical engineering educator; b. Bapatla, India, Sept. 27, 1947; came to U.S., 1968; naturalized, 1977. s. Chiranjeeva Rao and Meenakshi Neti; m. Kathy Gibson, Jan. 11, 1974. BME, Osmania U., 1968; MS, U. Ky., 1970, PhD, 1977. Research asst. U. Ky., 1968-77; asst. prof. mech. engring. Lehigh U., Bethlehem, Pa., 1978-83, assoc. prof., 1983-92, prof., 1992—. Vis. fellow Wolfson Coll., Oxford U., Eng.; vis. rsch. assoc. U.K. Atomic Energy Rsch. Establishment, Harwell, Eng.; fallout shelter analyst Fed. Emergency Mgmt. Adminstrn.; chair Mech. Engring. Thermal-Fluids Divsn., 1996—, dir. Lehigh U. Indsl. Assessment Ctr., 2000—, mem. Asian studies program, 2001-, Global Citizenship Program, 2004-; bd. mem. Lehigh U. Press, 2006-, co-chair Lehigh Environ. Adv. Grp. 2008-; Lehigh Valley Planning Commn., 1996, 97; bd. dirs. ANS, PANE; cons. to industry. Contbr. articles to profl. jours. Summer faculty fellow NASA-Am. Soc. Engring. Edn., 1978; grantee electric Power Research Inst., Dept. Energy, NSF, NRC. Mem. ASME, AAAS, Sigma Xi (chpt. treas. 1997-2002), Phi Beta Delta. Office: Lehigh U Mech Engring Dept 19 Memorial Dr W Bethlehem PA 18015-3085 Business E-Mail: sn01@lehigh.edu.

NETSIRI, CHAIYAPOJ, research scientist, consultant; b. Bangkok, May 29, 1964; arrived in US, 2001, permanent resident, 2005; s. Chote and Patcharin Netsiri. BSEE, King Mongkut's Inst. Tech., Bangkok, Thailand, 1986; MS in Computer Sci., Chiba U., Japan, 1996; PhD in Elec. Engring., U. Tokyo, 1999. Prodn. engr. Kang Yang Electric MFG Co., Ltd., Samutprakarn, Thailand, 1987—89; elec. engr. Tom Tech Co., Ltd., Bangkok, 1990—92; R&D engr. Yamada Kikai Kogyo Co., Ltd., Chiba, Japan, 1992—94; rsch. assoc. U. Cambridge, England, 1999—2001, Albert Einstein Coll. Medicine, Bronx, NY, 2001—03; sr. staff assoc. Columbia U., NYC, 2003—04; rsch. scientist Rice U., Houston, 2004—05; sr. applications engr. MicroMRI, Inc., Phila., 2005—06; rsch. scientist NexTech Solutions Inc., Austin, Tex., 2006—07, Bench Tree Group LLC, Georgetown, Tex., 2007—08, DacQuest LLC, Wash., Mo., 2008—09, Nitto Denko Technical Corp., Oceanside, Calif., 2009—. Grantee, Royal Soc., 2000—01; fellow, U. Cambridge, 1999—2001; scholar, Nagai Found., 1994—95, Japanese Govt., 1995—99. Mem.: Soc. Neurosci. (assoc.), IEEE (assoc.). Buddhist. Avocation: tennis. Office: Nitto Denko Technical 501 Via Del Monte Oceanside CA 92058

NETTA-TURNER, DENISE, nurse; b. New Castle, Del., May 28, 1959; d. Anthony and Rita Netta; m. Timothy Turner, May 27, 1989. BSN, Wilmington Coll., New Castle, 2000. Registered Wound, Ostomy and Continence Certification Bd., 2004. Nurse Christiana Care Health System, 2009—. Contbr. chapters to books to profl. jours. Mem.: Wound Ostomy and Continence Nurse Soc., Del. Nurses Assn., Del. Valley Enterostomal Therapist Soc. Office: Christiana Care Health System 3506 Kennett Pike Wilmington DE 19807

NETTELS, ELSA, English language educator; b. Madison, Wis., May 25, 1931; d. Curtis Putnam and Elsie (Patterson) Nettels. BA, Cornell U., 1953; MA, U. Wis., 1955, PhD, 1960. From instr. to asst. prof. English Mt. Holyoke Coll., South Hadley, Mass., 1959—67; from asst. prof. to prof. English Coll. William and Mary, Williamsburg, Va., 1967—97, prof. emeritus, 1997—. Author: James and Conrad, 1977 (South Atlantic MLA award, 1975), Language, Race and Social Class in Howells' America, 1988, Language and Gender in American Fiction: Howells, James, Wharton, and Cather, 1997; contbr. articles to profl. jours. Fellow, NEH, 1984—85. Mem.: MLA, South Atlantic MLA (mem. editl. bdl. 1977—83), Henry James Soc. (mem. editl. bd. 1983—). Office: Coll William and Mary Dept English Williamsburg VA 23187 Office Phone: 757-221-3905. Business E-Mail: exnett@wm.edu.

NETTELS, GEORGE EDWARD, JR., retired mining executive; b. Pittsburg, Kans., Oct. 20, 1927; s. George Edward and Mathilde A. (Wulke) N.; m. Mary Joanne Myers, July 19, 1952; children: Christopher Bryan, Margaret Anne, Katherine Anne, Rebecca Jane. BSCE, U. Kans., Lawrence, 1950. With Black & Veatch Engrs., Kansas City, Mo., 1950-51, Spencer Chem. Co., Kansas City, Mo., 1951-55, Freeto Constrn. Co., Pittsburg, 1955-57; pres. Midwest Minerals, Inc., Pittsburg, 1957—; chmn. bd. McNally Pittsburg Mfg. Corp., 1970-76, pres., CEO, 1976-87, ret., 1987. Past chmn. bd. Nat. Limestone Inst.; bd. dirs. Pitts. Indsl. Devel. Com. Mem. bd. advisors U. Kans. Endowment Assn.; mem. Kans. U. Chancellor's Club, Kans., Inc.; past pres. Bd. Edn. 250, Pittsburg; past chmn. bd. trustees Mt. Carmel Hosp.; past mem. Kans. Commn. Civil Rights; chmn. Kans. Republican Com., 1966-68; Kans. del. Rep. Nat. Conv., 1968, Kans. Bus. and Industry Com. for Reelection of Pres., 1972. With AUS, 1946-47. Recipient Disting. Svc. citation U. Kans., 1980, Disting. Engring. citation U. Kans., 1985; named Kansan of Yr. Natives Sons and Daus. Kans., 1986. Mem. ASCE, NAM (past. dir.), Kans. C. of C. and Industry (dir., chmn. 1983-84), Kans. Right to Work (dir.), Pittsburg C. of C. (past dir.), Kans. U. Alumni Assn. (pres. 1977), Kans. Leadership Com., Crestwood Country Club, Wolf Creek Golf Club (Olathe), Tau Beta Pi, Omicron Delta Kappa, Beta Theta Pi. Office: Midwest Minerals Inc 509 W Quincy St Pittsburg KS 66762-5689

NETTL, BRUNO, anthropologist, musicologist, educator; b. Prague, Czechoslovakia, Mar. 14, 1930; s. Paul and Gertrud (Hutter) N.; m. Wanda Maria White, Sept. 15, 1952; children: Rebecca Nettl-Fiol, Gloria Roubal. AB, Ind. U., 1950, PhD, 1953; MA in L.S, U. Mich., 1960; LHD (hon.), U. Chgo., 1993; LHD (hon.), U. Ill., 1996, Carleton Coll., 2000, Kenyon Coll., 2002. Mem. faculty Wayne State U., Detroit, 1953-64, asst. prof., 1954-64, music librarian, 1958-64; mem. faculty U. Ill., Urbana, 1964—, prof. music and anthropology, 1967—, chmn. div. musicology, 1967-72, 75-77, 82-85. Vis. lectr., Fulbright grantee U. Kiel, Fed. Republic of Germany, 1956-58; cons. Ency. Brit., 1969—; cons. on ethnomusicology to various univs.; vis. prof. Williams Coll., 1971, Washington U., 1978, U. Louisville, 1983, U. Wash., 1985, 88, 89, 93, 95, 98, 2000, Fla. State U., 1988, Harvard U., 1989, U. Alta., 1991, Colo. Coll., 1992, Northwestern U., 1993, U. Minn., 1994, U. Chgo., 1996, 2006, Carleton Coll., 1996, U. So. Calif., 2002, U. Denver, 2005. Author: Theory and Method in Ethnomusicology, 1964, Music in Primitive Culture, 1956, Folk and Traditional Music of the Western Continents, 1965, 2nd edit., 1973, Eight Urban Musical Cultures, 1978, The Study of Ethnomusicology, 1983, new edit., 2005, The Western Impact on World Music, 1985, The Radif of Persian Music, 1987, rev. edit., 1992, Blackfoot Musical Thought, 1989, Comparative Musicology and Anthropology of Music, 1991, Heartland Excursions, 1995, In the course of Performance, 1998, Encounters in Ethnomusicology, a Memoir, 2002; co-author Excursions in World Music, 1992, 3rd edit., 2000, 5th edit., 2007; editor Ethnomusicology, 1961-65, 98-2002, Yearbook of the International Folk Music Council, 1975-77; sr. adv. editor Garland Ency. of World Music; co-editor: Musical Improvisation, 2009; contbr. articles to profl. jours. Recipient Koizumi prize in ethnomusicology, Tokyo, 1994, Patocka Meml. medal Acad. Scis. Czech Republic, 2008; named hon. prof. Ctrl. Conservatory Music, Beijing, 2007. Fellow Am. Acad. of Arts and Scis.; mem. Soc. Ethnomusicology (pres. 1969-71), Am., Internat. musicol. socs., Internat. Coun. for Traditional Music, Coll. Music Soc, Am. Musicological Soc. (hon.), Soc. for Ethnomusicology (hon.) Office: U Ill Sch Music Urbana IL 61801 Home: 1423 Cambridge Dr Champaign IL 61821-4958 Office Phone: 217-333-9613. Business E-Mail: b-nettl@uiuc.edu.

NETTLES, JENNIFER, singer; b. Atlanta, Ga., Sept. 12, 1974; BA, Agnes Scott Coll., Decatur, Ga. Lead singer Soul Miner's Daughter, 1996, Jennifer Nettles band, Sugarland, 2002—. Signed to Mercury Records. Singer: (albums) (solo albums) Story of Your Bones, 2000, (with Sugarland) Twice the Speed of Life, 2004, Enjoy the Ride, 2006, Love on the Inside, 2008, (songs) Want To, 2006 (Duo Video of Yr., Country Music TV, 2007), Stay, 2006 (Duo Video of Yr., Country Music TV, 2008, Single of Yr., Song of Yr., Acad. Country Music, 2008, Song of Yr., Country Music Assn., 2008, Best Country Song, Best Country Performance by a Duo or Group with Vocals, Grammy Awards, 2009), (with Bon Jovi) Who Says You Can't Go Home, 2005 (Collaborative Video of Yr., Country Music TV, 2006, Grammy award, Best Country Collaboration with Vocals, 2007). Recipient Independent Musician of Yr. award, 2001, New Duo/Group award, Acad. Country Music, 2006, Top Vocal Duo award, 2009, Crystal Milestone award, 2009, Vocal Duo of Yr. award, Country Music Assn., 2007, 2008. Office: Gail Gellman Mgmt 23852 PCH 920 Malibu CA 90265 Office Phone: 310-456-2620. Office Fax: 310-456-1415. E-mail: gellmanmgmt@aol.com, sugarlandmail@aol.com.*

NETTLES, JOHN BARNWELL, obstetrics and gynecology educator; b. Dover, NC, May 19, 1922; s. Stephen A. and Estelle (Hendrix) N.; m. Eunice Anita Saugstad, Apr. 28, 1956; children: Eric, Robert, John Barnwell; m. 2d, Sandra Williams, Sept. 14, 1991; stepchildren: Steven Williams, Clayton Williams. BS, U. S.C., 1941; MD, Med. Coll. S.C., 1944. Diplomate: Am. Bd. Obstetrics and Gynecology. Intern Garfield Meml. Hosp., Washington, 1944-45; research fellow in pathology Med. Coll. Ga., Augusta, 1946-47; resident in ob-gyn. U. Ill. Rsch. and Ednl. Hosps., Chgo., 1947-51; instr. to asst. prof. ob-gyn. U. Ill. Coll. Medicine, Chgo., 1951-57; asst. prof., assoc. prof., prof. ob-gyn. U. Ark. Med. Ctr., Little Rock, 1957-69; dir. grad. edn. Hillcrest Med. Ctr., Tulsa, 1969-73; prof. ob-gyn Coll. Medicine, U. Okla., Oklahoma City, 1969-78; chmn. dept. ob-gyn. U. Okla.-Tulsa Med. Coll., 1975-80, prof., 1980—, mem. coun. on residency edn. in ob-gyn., 1974-79. Dir. Tulsa Obstet. and Gynecol. Edn. Found., 1969-80; Coordinator med. edn. Nat. Def., Ark., 1961-69; mem. S.W. regional med. adv. com. Planned Parenthood Fedn. Am., 1974-78; mem. adv. com. Health Policy Agenda Am. People, 1982-85, rev. com. Accrediation Coun. for Continuing Med. Edn., 1987-92. Contbr. articles on uterine malignancy, kidney biopsy in pregnancy, perinatal morbidity and mortality, human sexuality sch. age pregnancy to profl. jours. Served as lt. (j.g.) M.C. USNR,

1945-46; as lt. 1953-54. Recipient Nat. Faculty award. Fellow Am. Coll. Ob-Gyn. (dist. sec.-treas. 1964-70, dist. chmn. exec. bd. 1970-73, v.p. 1977-78, Disting. Svc. award 1998, Dist. VII Outstanding Clin. Prof. award 1989, Nat. Tchr. award 1992), ACS (bd. govs. 1969-71, program com. 1970-71, Surg. forum 1977-84, adv. com. gyn/ob 1985-92), Royal Soc. Health, Royal Soc. Medicine; mem. Ark. Obstet. and Gynecol. Soc. (exec. sec. 1959-69), Ctrl. Assn. Obstetrics and Gynecology (exec. com. 1966-69, pres. 1978-79), Internat. Soc. Advancement Humanistic Studies in Gynecology, Assn. Mil. Surgeons U.S., AMA (sect. coun. on obstetrics and gynecology 1975-96, chmn. 1982-96, del. from Am. Coll. Obstetricians and Gynecologists 1987-96, governing coun. sr. physicians group 2003—, Young at Heart award Young Physicians sect. 1994), Nurses Assn. So. Med. Assn. (chmn. obstetrics 1973-74), Okla. Med. Soc. (Ed L. Calhoun Leadership in Organized Medicine award, 2004), Tulsa County Med. Soc., Chgo. Med. Soc., Am. Assn. for Maternal and Infant Health, Assn. Am. Med. Colls., APHA, Am. Assn. Sex Edn. Counselors and Therapists (S.W. regional bd. 1976-79), Soc. for Gynecol. Investigation, AAAS, Am. Soc. for Study Fertility and Sterility, Internat. Soc. Gen. Semantics, So. Gynecol. and Obstet. Soc. (pres. 1981-82), Am. Cancer Soc. (pres. Okla. div. 1979-83, St. George's medal 1991), Com. on In-Tng. Exam. in Ob-Gyn, Am. Coll. Nurse Midwives (governing bd. examiners 1979-83), Sigma Xi (pres. Tulsa chpt. 1992-93), Phi Rho Sigma. Lutheran. Office: 4502 E 41ST ST Tulsa OK 74104-4070 Office Phone: 918-582-0955. Business E-Mail: John-Nettles@ouhsc.edu. *To live life fully, with faith and trust in God and his people, working with others to make our world a little better, and willing to fill the gaps wherever they are.*

NETTO, AMBA CECILE, military officer; b. Lafayette, La., Aug. 3, 1980; d. Michael R. Netto and DeciAmba C. Morgan; m. Terry J. Meadows, June 25, 2003 (div.); children: Kailly M. Paulson, Kayne M. Paulson. Commd. lt. USAF, 1999, advanced through grades to staff sgt., 2003, security forces Albuquerque, 1999—2004, info. mgr. Columbus, Miss., 2004—06. Tng. assessor police reform directorate USAF, Kabul, Afghanistan, 2005—. Named Non-Commisioned Officer of Qua., 14th Comm. Squadron Comdr., USAF, 2005.

NETTO, PAUL V., critical care nurse; b. Santa Cruz, Calif., Oct. 1, 1951; s. Joseph and Mary C. Netto; m. Patricia L. Jaynes-Netto (dec.); children: Paul V. Jr., Joseph P., Matthew R.; m. Cathy J. Montgomery-Netto, Aug. 12, 1984. ASN, Sierra Coll., Rocklin, Calif., 1985, AA in Art, 1993; BA in Studio Art cum laude, Calif. State U., 2000. RN Calif., critical care RN. RN supr. Carmichael (Calif.) Convalescent, 1986—87; supr., dir. Mt. Olivette Care Ctr., Carmichael, 1988—89; RN, clin. mgr. Roseville (Calif.) Cmty. Hosp., 1989—95; asst. dir. Hilltop Manor, Auburn, Calif., 1993—95; RNII CICU/MSICU Sutter Roseville Med. Ctr., 1995—; libertarian candidate 4th US Congressional Dist., Calif., 2008. Nurse rep. Calif. Nurses Assn., Sacramento, 1998—. Author: Brothers and Friends, 2001; author, illustrator: The Birds In The Hand, 2005; composer, performer (audio album) Pearls and Swine, 1991. Mem.: NRA (life), Jews for Preservation of Firearms Ownership, Golden Key Nat. Honor Soc. Libertarian. Avocations: travel, scuba diving, fishing, target shooting, writing. Home: PO Box 756 Meadow Vista CA 95722 Office: Sutter Roseville Med Ctr 1 Medical Ctr Plz Roseville CA 95561 Office Phone: 916-781-1522.

NETZEL, PAUL ARTHUR, fundraising management executive, consultant; b. Tacoma, Sept. 11, 1941; s. Marden Arthur and Audrey Rose (Jones) Netzel; m. Diane Viscount, Mar. 21, 1963; children: Paul M., Shari Ann. BS in Group Work Edn., George Williams Coll., 1963. Program dir. S. Pasadena-San Marino YMCA, 1963—66; exec. dir. camp and youth programs Wenatchee YMCA, 1966—67; exec. dir. Culver-Palms Family YMCA, Culver City, Calif., 1967—73; v.p. met. fin. devel. YMCA Met. LA, 1978—78, exec. v.p. devel., 1979—85; pres. bd. dirs. YMCA Employees Credit Union, 1977—80; founding chmn. N. Am. Fellowship of YMCA Devel. Orricers, 1980—83; chmn., CEO Netzel Assocs., Inc., 1985—; pvt. practice cons., fund raiser. Adj. faculty U. So. Calif. Coll. Continuing Edn., 1983—86, Loyola Marymount U., 1986—90, Calif. State U., 1991—92, UCLA Extension, 1991—2002. Bd. mgrs. Culver-Palms YMCA, Culver City, 1985—2002, chmn., 1989—91, 1991—93; mem. Culver City Bd. Edn., 1975—79, pres., 1977—78; mem. Culver City Edn. Found., 1982—91, Culver City Redevel. Agy., 1980—88, chmn., 1983—84, 1987—88, vice chmn., 1985—86; chmn. bd. dirs. Calif. Youth Model Legislature, 1987—92; mem. World Affairs Coun., 1989—92; mem. adv. bd. Automobile Club So. Calif., 1996—2002; mem. Culver City City Coun., 1980—88, vice mayor, 1980—82, 1984—85, mayor, 1983—84, 1986—87; bd. dirs. L.A. Psychiat. Svc., 1971—74, Goodwill Industries of So. Calif., 1993—97, L.A. County Sanitation Dists., 1982—83, 1985—87, Western Region United Way, 1986—93, vice chmn., 1991—92. Recipient Man of Yr. award, Culver City C. of C., 1972. Mem.: Cmte RI Biuro (chairman exec. 2008—), Assn. Fundraising Profls. (v.p. bd. dirs. Greater L.A. chpt. 1986—88, pres. bd. dirs. 1989—90, nat. bd. dirs. 1989—91, vice chmn. 1994, Profl. of Yr. 1983), Mountain Gate Country Club, Rotary Internat. (L.A. # 5 pres. 1992—93, treas. L.A. found. 1995—96, gov. dist. 5280 1997—98, worldwide bd. dirs. 2007—, chmn. L.A. conv., founding chmn. internat. convention 2008 host orgn. com., chmn. exec. com., RI bd. dirs. 2008—09, named to Dist. 5280 Hall Fame 2005), Calif. Club. Office: Netzel Grigsby Assocs Inc 9696 Culver Blvd Ste 105 Culver City CA 90232-2753 Home: 12336 Ridge Cir Los Angeles CA 90049-1151

NEU, ALICIA MALLARE, pediatric nephrologist; married. MD, U. of Va., Charlottesville, 1988. Diplomate Am. Bd. Pediatric Nephrology. Intern in pediat. Johns Hopkins Hosp., Balt., 1988—89, resident in pediat., 1989—91, clin. and rsch. fellow pediat. nephrology, 1991—94; instr. pediat. nephrology Johns Hopkins U. Sch. Medicine, Balt., 1991—95; pediatric nephrologist Johns Hopkins Sch. of Medicine, Balt., 1994—; assoc. prof. pediat. nephrology Johns Hopkins U. Sch. Medicine, Balt., 2002—, clin. dir., med. dir. pediat. dialysis and renal transplantation, 2002—. Office: Johns Hopkins Hosp 200 N Wolfe St Rm 3065 Baltimore MD 21287*

NEU, CHARLES ERIC, historian, educator; b. Carroll, Iowa, Apr. 10, 1936; s. Arthur Nicholas and Martha Margaret (Frandsen) N.; m. Deborah Dunning, Sept. 2, 1961 (div. 1978); children: Hilary Adams, Douglas Bancroft.; m. Sabina deWerth Tuck, Mar. 27, 1999. BA, Northwestern U., 1958; PhD, Harvard U., 1964. Instr. history Rice U., 1963-64, asst. prof., 1964-67, asso. prof., 1968-70; asso. prof. history Brown U., Providence, 1970-76, prof., 1976—2003, prof. emeritus, 2003—, chmn. dept. history, 1995—98, 1999—2002. Dir. summer seminar NEH, 1979, 1986—87, 1989, 92, 2005; adj. prof. history U. Miami, 2004—. Author: An Uncertain Friendship: Theodore Roosevelt and Japan, 1906-1909, 1967, The Troubled Encounter: The United States and Japan, 1975, America's Lost War: Vietnam, 1945-1975, 2005; co-editor: The Wilson Era: Essays in Honor of Arthur S. Link, 1991, Artists of Power: Theodore Roosevelt, Woodrow Wilson, and Their Enduring Impact on U.S. Foreign Policy, 2006; editor: After Vietnam: Legacies of a Lost War, 2000. Adv. coun. Vietnam Ctr. Tex. Tech. U.; adv. bd. mem. Thesdole Roosevelt Assn., 2008—. Recipient, Woodrow Wilson Found. fellowship, 1958—59, Am. Coun. Learned Socs. fellowship, 1975—76, Charles Warren Ctr. fellowship, 1971—72, Howard Found. fellowship, 1976—77, Guggenheim fellowship, 1981—82, Barrett Hazeltine citation for disting. undergrad. tchg., 1998; fellow, NEH, 1968—69; guest scholar, Woodrow Wilson Ctr., 1988, Pub. Policy scholar, 2007. Mem. Am. Hist. Assn., Orgn. Am. Historians, Soc. Historians of Am. Fgn. Policy, Phi Beta Kappa. Democrat. Home: 4929 SW 71st Place Miami FL 33155 Home Phone: 305-668-7978. Personal E-mail: cneu@bellsouth.net.

NEUBAUER, DEAN VERAL, statistician; b. Battle Creek, Iowa, Oct. 8, 1955; s. Virgil Albert and Fanchon Kay Neubauer; m. Kimberly Jean Rennie, May 15, 1982; children: Jason Dean, Bryan Andrew, Laura Jean. BS in Stats., Iowa State U., 1981; MS in Applied and Math. Stats., Rochester Inst. Tech., 1988. Math. statistician U.S. Bur. of Census, Washington, 1979-80; statis. engr. II Corning Glass Works, NY, 1981-83, sr. statis. engr. I, 1983-86, sr. statis. engr. II, 1986-89; project engr. Corning Incorp., 1989-91, sr. project engr., 1991-95, engring. assoc., 1995—2003, sr. engring. assoc., 2003—. Adj. prof. stats. Rochester Inst. Tech., Rochester, NY, 1992—; mem. tech. adv. group com. on statis. methods ISO.TC-69, 1993—2001. Co-author: Process Quality Control, 3d and 4th edit., Acceptance Sampling in Quality Control, 2nd edit. Fellow Am. Soc. Quality, Royal Statis. Soc. (chartered statistician, cert. quality engr., program chmn. 1983-84, sect. chmn. 1985-86, examining chmn. 1994-2001, treas. chem. and proc. indsl. divsn. 2001-2002, sec. chem. and proc. indsl. divsn. 2002-2003, chmn.-elect chem. and proc. indsl. divsn. 2003-04, chmn. chem. and process indsl. divsn. 2004-05); mem. ASTM (mem. E-11 com. quality and stats. com. 1993—, mem.-at-large, chmn. E11.10 on sampling and data analysis 1999-2003, sec. e-11 com 2001-2003), Am. Statis. Assn. Achievements include research in applications of statistical mixture designs to exploring and discovering new glass and ceramic compositions, exact critical factors for simplified analysis of means; patents for liquid crystal display glass, mill board and refractory isopipe compositions. Office: Corning Incorp SP-PR-02-17 Corning NY 14831-0001 Office Phone: 607-974-6777. E-mail: neubauerdv@corning.com, dneubaue@stny.rr.com.

NEUBAUER, JOSEPH, food services company executive; b. Oct. 19, 1941; s. Max and Herta (Kahn) Neubauer; children: Lawrence, Melissa. BS in Chem. Engring, Tufts U., 1963; MBA in Fin, U. Chgo., 1965. Asst. treas. Chase Manhattan Bank, 1965—68, asst. v.p., 1968—70, v.p., 1970—71; asst. treas. Pepsico Inc., Purchase, NY, 1971—72, treas., 1972—73, v.p., 1973—76; v.p. fin. and control Wilson Sporting Goods Co., River Grove, Ill., 1976—77, sr. v.p., gen. mgr. team sports divsn., 1977—79; exec. v.p. fin. and devel., CFO, dir. ARA Svcs., Inc., Phila., 1979—81; pres., COO, dir. ARA Services, Inc., Phila., 1981—83, pres., CEO, 1983—84; chmn., CEO ARA Svcs., Inc. (in 1994, name changed to ARAMARK Corp.), Phila., 1984—. Bd. dirs. Wachovia Corp., Verizon Corp., Federated Dept. Stores; trustee Penn Mut. Life Ins. Co. Chmn., CEO Phila. Orch. Assn., Mann Music Ctr., Inroads/Phila., Inc.; trustee Hahnemann U., Tufts U., Mus. Am. Jewish History, Greater Phila. First Corp., Com. Econ. Devel., U. Chgo.; bd. govs. Joseph H. Lauder Inst. Mgmt. and Internat. Studies, U. Pa.; dir. The Barnes Found. Mem.: Bus. Roundtable, Bus. Coun., Phila. C. of C., Locust Club, Union League Club. Office: ARAMARK Corp 1101 Market St Philadelphia PA 19107

NEUBAUER, RICHARD A., library science educator, consultant; b. Meadville, Pa., Oct. 9, 1933; s. Carl Gustave and Velma Winston (Watson) N.; m. Janice Ernest; children: David, Lynda, Karl, Jennifer; m. Carol Barton. BS, Clarion U., Pa., 1955; MLS, SUNY, Geneseo, 1966; attended, Kent State U., Ohio, 1966-68, Simmons Coll., Boston, 1970-72. Cert. profl. libr., sch. libr., tchr. Tchr. geography Franklin Sch. Dept., Pa., 1957-58, N. Bedford County Schs., Woodbury, Mass., 1958-60; tchr. history Hornell Jr. H.S., NY, 1960-62, sch. libr. NY, 1962-65; prof. libr. sci. Edinboro U., Pa., 1965-68, assoc. libr. Hamilton Libr. Pa., 1965-68; dir. sch. librs. Duxbury Sch. Dept., Mass., 1968-69; dir., cons. Pub. Libr., Lincoln, Mass., 1969-70; prof. libr. sci. Bridgewater State Coll., Mass., 1969-78, chair dept. libr. sci. Mass., 1978-80, prof. libr. sci. Mass., 1980-91, coord. libr. media program Mass., 1991-95; prof. emeritus libr. sci., 1996—. Adj. prof. libr. sci. U. R.I., Kingston, 1975-88; cons. Tabor Acad., Marion, Mass., 1970-71, Abington (Mass.) Pub. Libr. Trustees, 1973-76, Duxbury Free Libr., 1968-72. Author: Planning the Elementary School Library, 1968; author, editor Exploring the U.S.-Northeast, 1994. Chmn. Mass. Dept. Edn. Cert., Quincy, 1989-90; resource cons. Project Contemporary Competitiveness, Bridgewater, Mass., 1973-83. 1st lt. USMC, 1955-57. Inst. grantee HEA of 1965 Edinboro U., 1968. Mem. NEA, Am. Libr. Assn., Intellectual Freedom Found., Mass. Assn. of Edn. Media, Mass. Sch. Libr. Media Assn., Mass. Tchrs. Assn. Democrat. Avocations: gardening, woodworking, reading. Home: 22 Pleasant St Carver MA 02330-1013

NEUERBURG, KENT M., mathematics professor; b. Calif. s. Merl M. and B. Jean Neuerburg; m. Donna J. Williams; children: Kent M., Elizabeth M. Neuerburg-Addison, Sean R. BS, U. Calif., Davis, 1983, MA in Tchg., 1985; PhD, MS, U. Mo., Columbia, 1998. Math. tchr. Luther Burbank HS, Sacramento, 1985—89; math. instr. Cosumnes River Coll., Sacramento, 1989—94; asst. prof. math. Southeastern La. U., Hammond, 1998—2004, interim dept. head, 2004—05, assoc. prof. math., 2004—, dir., honors program, 2006—. Organizer Cool Cities Campaign, Hammond, La., 2008—09, Sierra Club, Honey Island Group, Hammond, 2009. Mem.: Math. Assn. Am., Am. Math. Soc. Roman Catholic. Avocations: running, gardening. Office: Southeastern La Univ SLU Box 10687 Hammond LA 70402 Business E-Mail: kneuerburg@selu.edu.

NEUFELD, ELIZABETH FONDAL, biochemist, educator; b. Paris, Sept. 27, 1928; BSc, Queens Coll., NYC, 1948; PhD, U. Calif., Berkeley, 1956; DSc (hon.), U. Rene Descartes, Paris, 1978, Russell Sage Coll., Troy, NY, 1981, Hahnemann U. Sch. Medicine, Phila., 1984, Queens Coll., 1996. Rsch. asst. Jackson Lab., Bar Harbor, Maine; asst. rsch. biochemist U. Calif., Berkeley, 1957—63; rsch. biochemist Nat. Inst. Arthritis, Metabolism & Digestive Diseases, NIH, Bethesda, Md., 1963—73, chief sect. human biochem. genetics, 1973—79, chief genetics and biochem. br., 1979—84; prof. dept. biol. chemistry UCLA Sch. Medicine, 1984—, chmn. dept. biol. chemistry, 1984—2004. Contbr. articles to profl. jours. Recipient Dickson prize, U. Pitts., 1974, Hillenbrand award, 1975, Gairdner Found. Internat. award, 1981, Albert Lasker award for clin. med. rsch., 1982, William Allan award, 1982, Elliott Cresson medal, 1984, Wolf Found. prize in medicine, Israel, 1988, Christopher Columbus Discovery award for biomed. rsch., 1992, Nat. Medal of Sci., 1994; named Passano Found. sr. laureate, 1982, Calif. Scientist of Yr., 1990. Fellow: AAAS; mem.: NAS, Am. Soc. Gene Therapy, Am. Soc. Clin. Investigation, Am. Soc. Cell Biology, Am. Soc. Biochemistry & Molecular Biology (pres. 1992—93), Am. Chem. Soc., Am. Soc. Human Genetics, Am. Philos. Soc., Am. Acad. Arts & Scis, Inst. Medicine. Office: UCLA David Geffen Sch Medicine Dept Biol Chemistry BSRB 350B 615 Charles E Young Dr Los Angeles CA 90095-1737 Business E-Mail: eneufeld@mednet.ucla.edu.

NEUFELD, MACE, film company executive; b. NYC, July 13, 1928; s. Philip M. and Margaret Ruth (Braun) N.; Feb. 28, 1954; children: Bradley David, Glenn Jeremy, Nancy Ann. BA, Yale U., 1948; postgrad., NYU, 1958-60. Photographer various N.Y. pubs., 1943-45; prodn. asst. Raymond E. Nelson, 1949-50; founder, owner Ray Bloch Assos., Inc., NYC, 1951-59; ptnr. BNB Prodns., NYC, 1959-70, Neufeld-Davis Prodns., Inc., Beverly Hills, Calif., 1981—. Trustee Am. Film Inst., 1978—; chmn. life achievement award nominating com. and scholarship fund. Producer in assn. with Harvey Bernhard The Omen, 1976, Damien - Omen II, 1977, Omen III - The Final Conflict, 1980; producer: The Frisco Kid, 1979, Angel on My Shoulder, 1980, The American Dream, 1980; ABC-TV mini-series East of Eden, 1981; CBS-TV series Cagney and Lacey, 1984; MGM film The Aviator, 1984, ABC-TV A Death in California, 1985; producer films Transylvania 6-5000, 1985, No Way Out, 1987, The Hunt for Red October, 1989, Flight of the Intruder, 1990, Necessary Roughness, 1991, Patriot Games, 1992, Clear and Present Danger, 1994, Gettysburg, 1994, Beverly Hills Cop 3, 1994, The Saint, 1996, The General's Daughter, 1998. Photograph entitled Sammy's Home voted Picture of Yr. N.Y. World Telegram-Sun, 1955; recipient Grand prize Eastman Kodak's First Nat. Salon of Photography, 1945; named N.A.T.O./Showest Producer of the Yr., 1993. Mem. Acad. TV Arts and Scis., Acad. Motion Picture Arts and Scis., ASCAP, Am. Film Inst. Clubs: Friars, Yale of N.Y. Democrat. Office Phone: 310-401-6868.

NEUFELD, PETER J., lawyer; b. Bklyn., July 17, 1950; m. Adele Bernhard; children: Shane, Lena. BA, U. Wis., 1972; JD, NYU, 1975; LLD (hon.), Gonzaga U. Ptnr. Cochran, Neufeld & Scheck LLP, NYC. Co-founder, dir. The Innocence Project, Benjamin Cardoza Sch. Law, Yeshiva U., NYC, 1992—; mem. N.Y. State's Commn. Forensic Sci. Co-author (with Barry Scheck and Jim Dwyer): Actual Innocence: Five Days to Execution and Other Dispatches from the Wrongly Convicted, 2000. Named one of The Top 100 Influential Lawyers in America, Nat. Law Jour., 2000. Office: Cochran Neufeld & Scheck LLP 99 Hudson St 8th Fl New York NY 10013 also: Innocence Project 100 Fifth Ave 3rd Fl New York NY 10011 also: Benjamin N Cardozo Sch Law Yeshiva U Brookdale Ctr 55 Fifth Ave (at 12th St) New York NY 10003 Office Phone: 212-364-5340. E-mail: info@innocenceproject.org.*

NEUFELD, RONALD DAVID, environmental engineer, educator; b. NYC, Feb. 10, 1947; s. Milton and Norma Neufeld; m. Toby Heringer, Aug. 31, 1968; children: Steven, Todd, Jennifer. B Engring. in Chem. Engring., Copper Union, 1967; MS in Chem. Engring., Northwestern U., 1969, PhD in Civil & Environ. Health Engring., 1973. Registered profl. engr., Pa.; diplomate Am. Acad. Environ. Engrs. Asst. prof. U. Pitts., 1973-77, assoc. prof., 1977-82, prof. civil engring., 1982. Chmn. environ. sci. com. Fulbright Coun. Internat. Exch. Scholars; former mem. Effluent Guidelines Task Force EPA, 1992—; mem. indsl. waste com. WEF, 1992—, program com.; mem. edn. com. Am. Acad. Environ. Engring, 1992; program evaluator ABET Environ.; apptd. Pa. Cleanup Sci. Adv. Bd., 1995—; vice chair CSSAB, 2008-; former dir. Green Constrn. and Sustainable Devel. Program; expert witness in field; cons. in field. Contbr. articles to profl. jours. Fulbright sr. scholar, 1983-84. Mem. ASCE (bd. dirs. Pits. sect. 1984-87, chmn. energy divsn., mem. exec. bd. energy divsn. specialty conf. 1991, mem. nat. energy policy com. 1995—), Am. Inst. Chem. Engrs., Internat. Assn. Water Pollution Rsch., Assn. Environ. Engring. Profs., Assn. Engring. Educators, Water Environ. Fedn., Sigma Xi (pres. Pitts. chpt. 1997-99), Chi Epsilon. Achievements include research in biotechnology for remediation of liquid and solid wastes and soils containing fuel hydrocarbons, electrochemical sludge dewatering, heavy metals, and PCBs; environmental process engineering, environmental engineering for energy development, environmental implication of high fly ash content cellular concrete; stabilization of hazardous wastes with high lime content fly ash, ceramic membrane microfiltration for combined sewer overflows; aluminum containing acid rock discharge, high rate oxidation of acid mine drainage. Office Phone: 412-624-9874. Business E-Mail: neufeld@pitt.edu.

NEUGEBAUER, DALE, legislative staff member; Student, Orange Coast Coll., Costa Mesa, Calif. Calif. press sec. Dole/Kemp Congl. campaign, 1996; press sec. to congressman Dana Rohrabacher US House of Reps., Washington, 1993—97, chief of staff to congressman Darrell Issa, 2001—. Republican. Mailing: US House Reps 2347 Rayburn House Office Bldg Washington DC 20515 Office Phone: 202-225-3906. Office Fax: 202-225-3303. Business E-Mail: dale.neugebauer@mail.house.gov.*

NEUGEBAUER, MARCIA, physicist, researcher; b. NYC, Sept. 27, 1932; d. Howard Graeme MacDonald and Frances (Townsend) Marshall; m. Gerry Neugebauer, Aug. 25, 1956; children: Carol, Lee. BS, Cornell U., 1954; MS, U. Ill., 1956; D of Physics (hon.), U. New Hampshire, 1998. Grad. asst. U. Ill., Urbana, 1954-56; vis. fellow Clare Hall Coll., Cambridge, Eng., 1975; sr. research scientist Jet Propulsion Lab. Calif. Inst. Tech., Pasadena, 1956-96, disting. vis. scientist, 1996—2003; vis. prof. planetary sci. Calif. Inst. Tech., Pasadena, 1986-87. Mem. com. NASA, Washington, 1960-96, NAS, Washington, 1981-94; Regents lectr. UCLA, 1990-91; adj. sr. rsch. sci. Lunar & Planetary Lab., U. Ariz., 2002-; bd. dirs. Ariz. Sr. Acad., pres., 2004—. Contbr. numerous articles on physics to profl. jours. Named Calif. Woman Scientist of Yr. Calif., Mus. Sci. and Industry, 1967, to Women in Tech. Internat. Hall of Fame, 1997; recipient Exceptional Sci. Achievement medal NASA, 1970, Outstanding Leadership medal NASA, 1993, Disting. Svc. medal NASA, 1997, COSPAR award for space sci., 1998. Fellow Am. Geophys. Union (sec., pres. solar planetary relationships sect. 1979-84, editor-in-chief Rev. Geophysics 1988-92, pres.-elect 1992-94, pres. 1994-96) mem. governing bd. Amer. Inst. Physics, 1995-97. Democrat. Home: 7519 S Eliot Ln Tucson AZ 85747-9627 Office: U Ariz Lunar & Planetary Lab 1629 E Univ Blvd Tucson AZ 85721 Business E-Mail: nmeugeb@lpl.arizona.edu.

NEUGEBAUER, RANDY (ROBERT R. NEUGEBAUER), United States Representative from Texas; b. St. Louis, Dec. 24, 1949; m. Dana Collins; 2 children. BBA in Acctg., Tex. Tech U., Lubbock, 1972. Mgr. Sentry Property Mgmt., Lubbock, Tex., 1972—75; instr. South Plains Coll., Lubbock, 1975—78; v.p. First Nat. Bank, Lubbock, 1975—82; pres. Prestige Homes, Lubbock, 1983—87; pres., CEO Lubbock Land Co., 1987—2003; mem. US Congress from 19th Tex. dist., 2003—, mem. agr. com., 2006—, mem. fin. svcs. com. Chair Ports-to-Plains Trade Coalition, 1996—2003. Mem. City Coun., 1992—98; mayor pro tempore, 1994—96. Mem.: West Tex. Home Builders Assn. (pres. 1990). Republican. Baptist. Office: US Ho Reps 429 Cannon Ho Office Bldg Washington DC 20515 Office Phone: 202-225-4005.*

NEUGER, WIN JAY, insurance company executive; b. 1950; m. Christie Cozad Neuger. AB, Dartmouth Coll., 1973, MBA. With Northwestern Nat. Bank Mpls., 1973—82; chief investment officer Western Asset Mgmt. Co., LA, 1982—84; mng. dir. global investment mgmt.-equity Bankers Trust Co., NYC, 1984—95; sr. v.p., chief investment officer Am. Internat. Group, Inc. (AIG), 1995—2002, exec. v.p., chief investment officer, 2002—09, chmn., CEO, AIG Investments.

Bd. dirs. Wisdom Tree Investments, Inc., 2007—. Mem.: Am. Investment Mgmt. and Rsch., N.Y. Soc. Security Analysts. Office: Am Internat Group (AIG) 175 Water St 24th Fl New York NY 10038 also: 70 Pine St New York NY 10270*

NEUHAUS, PHILIP ROSS, investment banker; b. Houston, Dec. 25, 1919; s. Hugo Victor and Kate Padgitt (Rice) N.; m. Elizabeth Lacey Thompson, Oct. 31, 1942 (div. 1967); children: Philip Ross (dec.), Lacey Neuhaus Dorn, Elizabeth Neuhaus Armstrong, Joan Neuhaus Schaan; m. Barbara R. Haden, Aug. 14, 1968(dec. Feb 14, 2008); 5 stepchildren. Grad., St. Mark's Sch., Southborough, Mass., 1938; BA, Yale, 1942. With Nat. City Bank of Cleve., 1946-47, McDonald & Co., Cleve., 1947; with Neuhaus & Co., 1947; chmn. Underwood, Neuhaus & Co., Inc., Houston, 1948-89; hon. chmn. Lovett Underwood Neuhaus & Webb, Houston, 1989-92; sr. v.p. Kemper Securities Inc., Houston, 1992-95, Everen Securities, Inc., Houston, 1995-99, Wells Fargo Advisors (formerly Wachovia Securities Inc.), Houston, 1999—. Chmn. bd. Voss-Woodway, Inc., 1994-2007. Mem. adv. bd. Tex. Children's Hosp., 1973-; assoc. Rice U.; advisory bd. Salvation Army, Houston, 1969-91. Served to capt., cav. AUS, 1942-45. Mem. Securities Industry Assn. Am. (bd. govs., chmn. Tex. dist. 1973, exec. com. 1975), Houston Soc. Financial Analysts (pres. 1959), Stock and Bond Club Houston (past pres.), Nat. Fedn. Financial Analysts (v.p. 1963, dir.) Clubs: Bayou, Houston Country, Houston, Eagle Lake Rod and Gun. Home: 407 Thamer Ln Houston TX 77024-6939 Office: Wells Fargo Advisors Ste 1100 909 Fannin Houston TX 77010-1001 Office Phone: 713-853-2221.

NEUHAUSER, DUNCAN VONBRIESEN, medical educator; b. Phila., June 20, 1939; s. Edward Blaine Duncan and Gernda (vonBriesen) Neuhauser; m. Elinor Toaz, Mar. 6, 1965; children: Steven, Ann. BA, Harvard U., 1961; MHA, U. Mich., 1963; MBA, U. Chgo., 1966, PhD, 1971. Rsch. assoc. U. Chgo., 1965—70; asst. prof. Sch. Pub. Health, Harvard U., Boston, 1970—74, assoc. prof., 1974—79; cons. in medicine Mass. Gen. Hosp., Boston, 1975—80; assoc. dir. Health Systems Mgmt. Ctr. Case Western Res. U., Cleve., 1979—85, prof. epidemiology, biostats., orgnl. behavior, 1979—, prof. medicine, 1981—, prof. family medicine, 1990—, Charles Elton Blanchard prof. health mgmt., 1995—, co-dir. Health Systems Mgmt. Ctr., 1985—. Mem. biomed. staff Metrohealth Med. Ctr., 1981—; adj. mem. med. staff Cleve. Clinic Found., 1984—99; vis. prof. Vanderbilt U. Sch. Nursing, 1998—, Karolinska Med. Sch., Stockholm, 2002—. Author: numerous books, sci. papers; editor (jours.): Health Matrix, 1982—90, Med. Care, 1983—97. Vice chmn. bd. dirs. Vis. Nurse Assn. Greater Cleve., 1983—84, chmn., 1984—85; bd. dirs. New Eng. Grenfell Assn., Boston, 1972—, Braintree Hosp., Mass., 1975—86; trustee Internat. Grenfell Assn., St. Anthony, Nfld., Canada, 1975—83, Blue Hill Hosp., Maine, 1983—94, Hough Norwood Health Ctr., 1983—94, chmn., 1993—94; mem. vis. com. Columbia U. Sch. Nursing, 2000—; founding bd. dirs. Acad. for Healthcare Improvement, 2004—. Recipient E.F. Meyers Trustee award, Cleve. Hosp. Assn., 1987, Hope award, Nat. Multiple Sclerosis Soc., 1992, Neuhauser lectr., Soc. Pediatric Radiology, 1982, Freedlander lectr., Ohio Permanente Med. Group, 1986, Univ. medal, Tohoku Med. U., Sendai, Japan, 2001, Arthur Shapiro Best Book of Yr. Hypnosis award, 2003, McAuley lectr., Georgetown U., 2007; scholar Keck Found., 1982—; Duncan Neuhauser Endowed chair in cmty. health improvement at Case Western Res. U. and MetroHealth Med. Ctr., 2003, Kellogg fellow, U. Chgo., 1963—65. Mem.: Soc. for Clin. Decision Making, Inst. Medicine NAS, Cleve. Skating Club, Kollegewidgwok Yacht Club (Blue Hill) (commodore 1991—93), St. Botolph Club (Boston), Beta Gamma Sigma. Home (Summer): PO Box 932 Blue Hill ME 04614-0932 Office: Case Western Reserve U Med Sch 10900 Euclid Ave Cleveland OH 44106-4945 Home (Winter): 2641 Idlewood Rd 1st Fl Cleveland Heights OH 44118-4249 Office Phone: 216-368-3726. Office Fax: 216-368-3970. Business E-Mail: dvn@cwru.edu.

NEUHEISEL, RICK (RICHARD GERALD NEUHEISEL, JR.), college football coach; b. Madison, Wis., Feb. 7, 1961; s. Richard and Jane (Jackson) N.; m. Susan Wilkinson; children: Jerry, Jack, Joe. BA in Polit. Sci., UCLA, 1984; JD, U. Southern Calif., 1990. Bar: Ariz. 1991, DC 1993. Quarterback San Diego Chargers, 1987; asst. coach UCLA Bruins, 1988-93, U. Colo. Buffaloes, Boulder, 1994—95, head coach, 1995—98, U. Wash. Huskies, 1999—2002; vol. coach Rainier Beach HS, Seattle, 2003—04; quarterbacks coach Balt. Ravens, 2005—06, offensive coord., 2006—07; head coach UCLA Bruins, 2008—. Spkr. in field. Active Celebrity Golf Assn. Tour. Named to Rose Bowl Hall of Fame, 1998. Achievements include holding the San Diego Chargers' franchise record for completion percentage (81.8) in 1987; being the last player in the NFL to rush for a one-point conversion; becoming the first University of Colorado and University of Washington coach to lead the teams to a bowl game in his inaugural seasons. Office: c/o UCLA Bruins Intercollegiate Athletic Dept PO Box 24044 Los Angeles CA 90024

NEUHOFER, MARY DOROTHY, archivist, librarian; d. Joseph Peter and Helen Frances Neuhofer. BS, Barry Coll., Miami, 1964; MALS, Rosary Coll., River Forest, Ill., 1965; MChA in Canon Law, Cath. U. Am., Washington, DC, 1977; PhD in Libr. Studies, Fla. State U., Tallahassee, 1998. Elem. sch. tchr. Fla. Cath. Sch., 1950—64; elem. sch. prin. Epiphany Cath. Sch., Venice, Fla., 1959—63; ref. libr. St. Leo U., St. Leo, 1965—75, 1990—98, dir. libr. svc., 1975—88, 1999—2006, archivist, 1990—, archivist, spl. collections libr., 2007—; prioress Holy Name Monastery, St. Leo, 1972—75. Author: (book) In the Benedictine Tradition, 1999. Mem. Order St. Benedict. Fellow: Am. Benedictine Acad. (exec. bd. 1972—86, pres. 1982—84, awards com. 2006—); mem.: Fla. Libr. Assn., Soc. Fla. Archivists, Tampa Bay Libr. Consortium (sec. 1980—81, mem. exec. bd. 1980—89, pres. 1987—88), Pasco County Hist. Preservation Com., Canon Law Soc. Am., Soc. Am. Archivists, Cath. Libr. Assn. (exec. bd. 1999—2007, pres. 2003—05, mem. strategic planning com. 2007—09, mem. constitution and bylaws com. 2007—09, chair, nominations com. 2007—09), Assn. Coll. and Rsch. Libr., Am. Libr. Assn. Avocation: gardening. Home: Holy Name Monastery 33201 State Rd 52 Saint Leo FL 33574 Office: St Leo U 33701 State Rd 52 Saint Leo FL 33574 Business E-Mail: dorothy.neuhofer@saintleo.edu.

NEUHOUSER, MARIAN L., nutritionist, researcher; BS in Nutrition, U. Calif., Davis, 1980; PhD in Nutritional Sciences, U. Wash., 1996. Nutritionist Fred Hutchinson Cancer Rsch. Ctr. Recipient JACN Best Scientific Paper award, Am. Coll. Nutrition, Folate & Neural Tube Defects, 1999. Mem.: Am. Soc. Preventive Oncology, Am. Soc. Nutrition, Am. Dietetic Assn., Am. Assn. Cancer Rsch. Office: Fred Hutchinson Cancer Research Center 1100 Fairview Ave N PO Box 19024 Seattle WA 98109 Office Phone: 206-667-4797. Office Fax: 206-667-7850. E-mail: mneuhous@fhcrc.org.*

NEUKOM, WILLIAM H., professional sports team executive, lawyer; b. Chgo., Nov. 7, 1941; s. John Goudey and Ruth (Horlick) N.; m. Diane McMakin, Dec. 28, 1963 (div. Jun. 1977); children: Josselyn, Samantha, Gillian, John. BA, Dartmouth Coll., 1964; LLB, Stanford U., 1967. Bar: Calif., Wash., U.S. Dist. Ct. (we. dist.) Wash., U.S. Dist. Ct. (no. dist.) Calif., U.S. Ct. Appeals (9th cir.) 1968, U.S. Supreme Court 1974. Atty. MacDonald, Hoague & Bayless, Seattle, 1968—77; ptnr. Preston, Gates & Lucas (formerly Shidler, McBroom, Gates & Lucas), Seattle, 1978—85; v.p., law, corp. affairs Microsoft Corp., Redmond, Wash., 1985—93, exec. v.p. law & corp. affairs, sec., 1994—2002; ptnr. Bus. Practice Group Preston Gates & Ellis LLP, Seattle, 2002, mem. exec. com.; chair Preston Gates & Ellis LLP (now Kilpatrick & Lockhart Preston Gates Ellis), Seattle, 2004; mng. gen. ptnr., CEO San Francisco Baseball Assocs., 2008—. Wash. State Delegate House of Delegates, 1999—2005; chair Decennial Governance Commn.; mem. Pacific Coun. Internat. Policy, 2002—, Policy Consensus Ctr., 2004—; founder World Justice Project, 2006. Co-founder Neukom Family Found., 1995; mem. Dean's coun. Stanford Law Sch., 1999—; chair Gates Challenge Endowment Campaign United Way King County, 2002—07; mem. bd. trustees Greater Seattle C. of C., 1987—, chair bd. trustees, 2001—02; bd. dirs. YMCA Greater Seattle, 1988—2007, Corp. Coun. for the Arts, 1988, Oreg. Shakespeare Festival, 1993—99, U. Wash. Found.; trustee Seattle Art Mus., 1993—99; chmn., bd. dirs. Bus. Software Alliance, 1995—96, bd. dirs.; mem. bd. trustees U. Puget Sound, 1995—2006, Dartmouth Coll., 1996—2007, chair bd. trustees, 2004—07. Fellow: ABA (chmn. young lawyers divsn. 1977—78, ho. of dels. 1978—80, sec. 1983—87, ho. of dels. 1983—98, pres.-elect 2006—07, pres. 2007—08); mem.: Wash. State Trial Lawyers Assn., Wash. State Bar Assn., Seattle-King County Bar Assn. (chmn. young lawyers divsn. 1972—73). Avocations: fly fishing, skiing, running, golf, jazz. Office: San Francisco Giants AT&T Park 24 Willie Mays Plz San Francisco CA 94107*

NEUL, JEFFREY LORENZ, medical educator, researcher; married. BS, U. Ill., Champaign, Urbana, 1991; MD, PhD, U. Chgo., 2000. Cert. in child neurology Am. Bd. Psychiatry and Neurology, 2006. Asst. prof. Baylor Coll. Medicine, Houston, 2005—. Asst. med. dir. Blue Bird Cir. Rett Ctr., Houston, 2008—. Office: Baylor Coll Medicine One Baylor Plaza Houston TX 77030 Office Phone: 832-822-7388.

NEUMAIER, GERHARD JOHN, environmental services administrator, consultant; b. Covington, Ky., July 27, 1937; s. John Edward and Elli Anna (Raudies) N.; m. Ellen Elaine Klepper, Oct. 24, 1959; children: Kevin Scott, Kirsten Lynn. BME, Gen. Motors Inst., 1960; MA in Biophysics, U. Buffalo, 1963. Research ecologist, project mgr. Cornell Aero. Lab., Buffalo, 1963-70; pres., chief exec. Ecology and Environment Inc., Buffalo, 1970—2008, chmn. bd., 1970—. Recipient Theodore Roosevelt Citizen of Yr. award City of Buffalo, 1990, Paul McClennan Environ. Citizen of Yr. award Erie County, 2000. Mem. APHA, Air Pollution Control Assn., Internat. Assn. Gt. Lakes Research, Inst. Environ. Scis., Ecol. Soc. Am., Am. Inst. Biol. Scis., Urban Land Inst., Arctic Inst. N.Am., Nat. Parks and Conservation Assn., Defenders of Wildlife, Nat. Wildlife Fedn., Wilderness Soc., Am. Hort. Soc., Smithsonian Assocs., Nat. Audubon Soc. Home: 284 Mill Rd East Aurora NY 14052-2805 Office: Ecology & Environment Inc 368 Pleasant View Dr Lancaster NY 14086-1316 Office Phone: 716-684-8060.

NEUMAN, CHARLES P., electrical and computer engineering educator; b. Pitts., July 26, 1940; s. Daniel and Frances G. Neuman; m. Susan G. Neuman, Sept. 4, 1967 BSEE honors, Carnegie Inst. Tech., 1962; SM, Harvard U., 1963, PhD in Applied Math., 1968. Tchg. fellow Harvard U., Cambridge, Mass., 1962—64, rsch. asst., 1964—67; mem. tech. staff Bell Tel. Labs., Whippany, NJ, 1967—69; asst. prof. elec. engring. Carnegie-Mellon U., Pitts., 1969—71, assoc. prof., 1971—78, prof. elec. engring., 1978—83, prof. elec. and computer engring., 1983—, undergrad. advisor, 1994—. Mem. editl. bd. Internat. Jour. Modelling and Simulation, Control and Computers; contbr. numerous articles to profl. jours Mem. IEEE (sr., assoc. editor Trans. on Systems, Man and Cybernetics), AAAS, Inst. Mgmt. Scis., Instrument Soc. Am. (sr.), Soc. Harvard Engrs. and Scientists, Soc. Indsl. and Applied Math., Sigma Xi, Phi Kappa Phi, Tau Beta Pi, Eta Kappa Nu Office: Carnegie-Mellon U Dept Elec & Computer Engring Pittsburgh PA 15213 Office Phone: 412-268-2460. Business E-Mail: cpn@ece.cmu.edu.

NEUMAN, CLIFFORD, computer scientist, educator; s. Peter H-X. Neuman and Barbara Diane (Allen) Gordon; m. Grace Ruth (Kwok) Neuman. BS Computer Sci. and Engring., MIT, 1985; MS Computer Sci., U. Wash., 1988, PhD Computer Sci., 1992. With MIT Project Athena, Cambridge, 1985—86; sr. rsch. scientist U. So. Calif., Info. Scis. Inst., Marina del Rey, 1991—; rsch. assoc. prof. U. So. Calif., Dept. Computer Sci., LA, 1992—; chief scientist CyberSafe Corp., Issaquah, 1992—2001; dir. U. So. Calif., Ctr. Computer Sys. Security, Marina del Rey, 2002—. Participant Internet Rsch. Task Force, 1991—, Internet Engring. Task Force, 1991— Co-designer Kerberos computer security sys., designer Prospero distributed computer sys., NetCheque elec. payment sys.; contbr. articles to profl. jours Mem. King County (Wash.) Search and Rescue, 1987-91; bd. dirs. Beth Shir Sholom, 2006—, Ladera Heights Civic Assn., 2006—. Named Top Ten Tech. Innovators, InfoWorld Mag., 2002. Mem.: IEEE, Usenix Assn., Internet Soc., Assn. Computer Machinery. Achievements include development of Kerberos authentication sys; NetCheque electronic payment sys; Prospero Directory Svc. Avocations: flying, hiking, skiing, photography, cooking, amateur radio. Office: U So Calif Information Scis Inst 4676 Admiralty Way Marina Del Rey CA 90292 E-mail: ww09@clifford.neuman.name.

NEUMAN, DEBORAH, language educator; married. MA in Spanish Lit., U. Northern Iowa. Adj. Spanish instr. Wingate U., NC, 2001—04, Queens Coll., 2001—04, Ctrl. Piedmont CC, 2001—04; Spanish instr. Gaston Coll., Dallas, NC, 2004—. ESL instr. Iglesia Bautista Hickory Grove, Charlotte, NC, 2005—. Office: Gaston Coll 201 Hwy 321 S PO Box 140 Dallas NC 28034

NEUMAN, EDWARD GEORGE, mathematician, educator; b. Rydultowy, Katowice, Poland, Sept. 19, 1943; arrived in U.S., 1984; s. Emanuel and Matylda Neuman; children: Emanuel Karol, Magdalena Natalia. Diploma, U. Wroclaw, Poland, 1967, PhD in Math., 1972. Asst. prof. U. Wroclaw, 1976—84; assoc. prof. So. Ill. U., Carbondale, 1986—89, prof. math., 1989—. Chmn. numerical analysis dept. U. Wroclaw, 1981—84. Mem. editl. bd.: Australian Jour. Mathematical Analysis and Applications, 2005—, Internat. Jour. Applied Math. and Statis., 2005—; mem. editl. bd. Jour. Math. Inequalities, 2007—, Jour. Inequalities Pure and Applied Math., 2007—; contbr. articles to profl. jours. Grantee, Polish Acad. Scis., 1974—84; fellow Summer Undergrad. Tchg. fellow, So. Ill. U., Carbondale, 1999. Mem.: Polish Math. Soc. (assoc.), Rsch. Group in Math. Inequalities and Applications (assoc.), Soc. for Indsl. and Applied Math. (assoc.). Achievements include research in spline theory, special functions and mathematical inequalities. Office: So Ill Univ Carbondale Dept Math Neckers 385 Carbondale IL 62901-4408 Business E-Mail: edneuman@math.siu.edu.

NEUMAN, NANCY ADAMS MOSSHAMMER, civic leader; b. Greenwich, Conn., July 24, 1936; d. Alden Smith and Margaret (Mevis) Mosshammer; m. Mark Donald Neuman, Dec. 23, 1958; children: Deborah Adams, Jennifer Fuller, Jeffrey Abbott. BA, Pomona Coll., 1957; LLD, 1983; MA, U. Calif., Berkeley, 1961; LHD, Westminster Coll., 1987. Disting. lectr. Am. govt. Pomona Coll., 1990; disting. vis. prof. Washington and Jefferson Coll., 1991, 94, Bucknell U., 1992. Editor: A Voice of Our Own: Leading American Women Celebrate the Right to Vote, 1996, True to Ourselves: A Celebration of Women Making a Difference, 1998. Pres. Lewisburg (Pa.) LWV, 1967-70; bd. dirs. LWV Pa., 1970-77, pres., 1975-77; bd. dirs. LWV U.S., 1977-90, 2nd v.p., 1978-80, 1st v.p., 1982-84, pres., 1986-90; mem. Pa. Gov.'s Commn. on Mortgage and Interest Rates, 1973, Pa. Commonwealth Child Devel. com., 1974-75, Nat. Commn. on Pub. Svc., 1987-90; bd. dirs. Housing Assistance Coun., Inc., Washington, 1974—2003, pres., 1978-80; bd. dirs. Nat. Coun. Agrl. Life and Labor, 1974-79, Nat. Rural Housing Coalition, 1975-95, Pa. Housing Fin. Agy., 1975-80, Jud. Inquiry and Rev. Bd. Pa., 1989-93; disciplinary bd. Supreme Ct. Pa., 1980-85; mem. Pa. Gov.'s Task Force on Voter Registration, 1975-76, Nat. Task Force for Implementation Equal Rights Amendment, 1975-77; mem. adv. com. Pa. Gov.'s Interdepartmental Coun. on Seasonal Farmworkers, 1975-77; mem. Appellate Ct. Nominating Commn. Pa., 1976-79; mem. Fed. Jud. Nominating Commn. Pa., 1977-85, chmn., 1978-81, 82-83; mem. Pa. Gov.'s Study Commn. on Pub. Employee rels., 1976-78; del. Internat. Women's Yr. Conf., 1977; bd. dirs. ERAmerica, Inc., 1st v.p., 1977-79, Nat. Low Income Housing Coalition, 1979-82; Rural Am., 1979-81, Fed. Home Loan Bank Pitts., 1979-82; mem. Nat. adv. Com. Women, 1978-79; mem. nat. adv. com. Pa. Neighborhood Preservation Support Sys., 1976-77; bd. dirs. Pa. Women's Campaign fund, 1984-86, 92-2002, pres., 1992-96, 2001-02, Rural coalition, Washington, 1984-90, Com. on the Constitutional Sys., 1988-90, Am. Judicature Soc., 1989-93; exec. com. Leadership Conf. Civil Rights, 1986-90; bd. dirs. Pennsylvanians for Modern Cts., 1986—; trustee Citizen's Rsch. Found., 1989-99; mem. mid. dist. Pa. adv. com. judicial and U.S. atty. nominations, 1993-94; bd. dirs. Pathmakers, 1993-97, pres. 1993-95; bd. dirs. Capital Concerts, 1997—. Virginia Travis lectureship Bucknell U., 1982; Woodrow Wilson vis. fellow, 1993-2000; recipient Disting. Alumna Award MacDuffle Sch. Girls, 1979, Liberty Bell award Pa. Bar Assn., 1983, Barrows Alumni Award Pomona Coll., 1987, Disting. Daus. of Pa. award, 1987, Thomas P. O'Neill Jr. award for Exemplary Pub. Svc., 1989. Mem. ABA (com. election law and voter participation 1986-90, accreditation com. 1990-96, coun. sect. legal edn. 1997-03), Disting. Daughters Pa. (pres. 2005-07), Cosmos Club. Home: 190 Verna Rd Lewisburg PA 17837-8747 Business E-Mail: neuman@bucknell.edu.

NEUMAN, ROBERT STERLING, artist, educator; b. Kellogg, Idaho, Sept. 9, 1926; s. Oscar C. and Katherine (Samuelson) N.; m. Helen Patricia Feddersen, Apr. 6, 1947 (div. 1971); children— Ingrid Alexandra, Elizabeth Catherine; m. Sunne Savage, June 3, 1979; 1 dau., Christina Mary. Student, U. Idaho, 1944-46; BAA., M.F.A., Calif. Coll. Arts and Crafts, 1947-51; student, San Francisco Sch. Fine Arts, 1950-51, Mills Coll., 1951. Assoc. prof. art Brown U., 1962-63; lectr. drawing Carpenter Center for Visual Arts, Harvard, 1963-72; prof. art, chmn. dept. Keene (N.H.) State Coll., 1972-90. Exhbns. include, Mus. Modern Art, Whitney Mus. Am. Art, Carnegie Internat., American Painting Fogg Mus. Art, Harvard U., 2003, San Francisco Mus. Art, Boston Mus. Fine Arts, Worcester (Mass.) Art Mus., Sunne Savage Gallery, Selected Works Wheaton Coll., Norton Mass., 1954-2007, Allan Stone Gallery, NYC, 1956-, 50 Yrs., 2006, also Japan and Europe. Served with AUS and USAAF, 1945-46. Recipient Howard Found. award for painting, 1967; Fulbright grantee, 1953-54; Guggenheim fellow, 1956-57; Bender grantee San Francisco Art Assn., 1952. Home: 135 Cambridge St Winchester MA 01890-2411 Home Phone: 781-721-2410.

NEUMAN, SUSAN CATHERINE, public relations and marketing consultant; b. Detroit, Jan. 29, 1942; d. Paul Edmund and Elsie (Goetz) N. AB, U. Miami, Fla., 1964; MBA, Barry U., Miami Shores, Fla., 1985. Journalist, writer The Miami Herald, 1962-65; editor Miamian Mag., 1965-69; pres. Susan Neuman Inc., Miami, 1969—; ptnr. Neuman Enterprises Unltd., 1994—. Mem. Fla. Gov.'s Pub. Rels. Adv. Coun., 1978-86. Mem. Pub. Rels. Soc. Am. (accredited, past officer, bd. dirs.), Miami C. of C., Counselors Acad., Miami City Club (founder, bd. govs.), Miami Internat. Press Club (charter, founder, pres. 1985-86), Com. of One Hundred (bd. dirs., sec.). Democrat. Roman Catholic. Home: 13540 NE Miami Ct Miami FL 33161-2739 Office: Susan Neuman Inc Venetia 25th Fl 555 NE 15th St Ste 25K Miami FL 33132-1404 Office Phone: 305-372-9966. E-mail: susan@miamipr.net.

NEUMANN, DAVID, theater educator; b. Paris, May 29, 1965; s. Frederick and Honora Neumann. BFA in Acting, SUNY, Purchase, 1988. Prof. theater Sarah Lawrence Coll., Bronxville, NY, 2006—; guest lectr. acting Yale Sch. Drama, New Haven, 2006—. Choreographer (multi-disciplinary dance piece) Feed Forward. Recipient NY Dance & Performance award, Bessie Com., 1969, 1998. Avocations: photography, films. Business E-Mail: dneumann@slc.edu.

NEUMANN, DAVID A., city councilman, small business owner; m. Frances Neumann; children: Ivy, Corbin. BS in Bus., Ind. U., 1982. Co-founder, pres., CEO Ivy Jane (women's apparel mfr.), Dallas, 1989—; councilman, Dist. 3 Dallas City Coun., 2007—, chmn. fin., audit & accountability com., legis. com., pub. safety com., quality of life & govt. svcs. com. Chmn. Dallas Zoning Ordinance Adv. Com., Stemmons Corridor Bus. Assn., Dallas, North Oak Cliff Weed & Seed Initiative; v.p. bd. gov.'s Dallas Apparel Mart. Treas. Kessler Neighbors United; active Kessler Park United Meth. Ch.; bd. dirs. Trinity Commons Found., Dallas, Greater Dallas Planning Coun., Dallas Friday Group. Mem.: Dallas Apparel Mfr.'s Assn. (past treas.), Oak Cliff C. of C. (bd. dirs.), Oak Cliff Lions Club. Office: Dallas City Hall 1500 Marilla St Rm 5FS Dallas TX 75201 Office Phone: 214-670-0776. Office Fax: 214-670-5115.*

NEUMANN, EDWARD SCHREIBER, transportation engineering educator; b. Harvey, Ill., Mar. 6, 1942; s. Arthur Edward Schreiber and Adeline Ruth (Spenks) N.; m. Carole Ann Dunkelberger, Apr. 19, 1969; children: Edward Schreiber, Jonathan David. BSCE, Mich. Technol. U., 1964; MS, Northwestern U., 1967, PhD, 1969, Cert. in Prosthetics, 2000. Registered profl. engr., W.Va., Nev.; cert. prosthetist Am. Bd. Certification. Mem. faculty W.Va. U., Morgantown, 1970-90, prof. transp. engring., 1980-90, interim dir. Harley O. Staggers Nat. Transp. Ctr., 1982-95, dir., 1985-90, 2009—; prof. U. Nev., Las Vegas, 1991—, chmn. dept., 1991-99, 2009—, dir. Transp. Rsch. Ctr., 1991-98, dir. Ctr. Disability and Applied Biomechanics, 2003—. Founder Human Kinetics Engring., LLC; chair rsch. coun. Am. Acad. Orthotists and Prosthetists. Editor numerous conf. procs.; contbr. articles and rsch. reports to profl. lit. Bd. dirs. Mason Dixon Hist. Park Assn., 1978-90; chmn. new transp. systems and tech. com. transp. rsch. bd. mem, 1998-2004, emeritus, 2004. Capt., C.E., AUS, 1969-70. Resources for Future fellow, 1969. Fellow Inst. Transp. Engrs.; mem. ASCE (chmn. com. on automated people movers, chmn. exec. com. urban planning and devel. divsn., chmn. exec. com. urban transp. divsn., James Laurie prize 1996), Nat. Soc. Profl. Engrs., Am. Soc. Engring. Edn., OITAF-NACS, Advanced Transit Assn. (bd. dirs., pres. 1988-90), Sigma Xi, Tau Beta Pi, Phi Kappa Phi, Phi Eta Sigma, Chi Epsilon. Presbyterian. Home: 935 E Eldorado Ln Las Vegas NV 89123-0515 Office: UNLV Dept Civil Environ Engring Las Vegas NV 89154-4015 Office Phone: 702-895-1072. Business E-Mail: edward.neumann@unlv.edu.

NEUMANN, FORREST KARL, retired health facility administrator; b. St. Louis, Oct. 7, 1930; s. Metz Earl and Ruth (McGhee) N.; m. Erika Stefanie Turkl, Feb. 11, 1955; children: Tracey Neumann Liberson, Karen Neumann Kruger, Scott, Lisa. BS, Roosevelt U., 1953; MS in Hosp. Adminstrn., Northwestern U., 1955. Adminstrv. resident Louis A. Weiss Hosp., Chgo., 1954-55; mem. staff Sparrow Hosp., Lansing, Mich., 1958-90; CEO, pres., dir. Edward W. Sparrow Hosp., Lansing, 1962-90; pres., chief exec. officer, dir. Mason Gen. Hosp., Mich., 1973-85; chmn. bd. Caymich Ins. Co. Ltd., Cayman Islands, 1979-91, emeritus dir. Cayman Islands, 1991—; chmn. bd. Caymich Ins. Co. (Barbados) Ltd., 1986-91; pres., CEO, Mich. Hosp. Assn. Ins. Co., 1990-96; dir. Mich. Hosp. Assocs. Ins. Co., 1976-98; pres., CEO, Sparrow, Inc., 1984-90. Chmn. bd. Mich. Hosp. Assn. Ins. Co., 1979-90; dir. First of Am. Bank Corp., 1980-95, Auto Owners Ins. Co., 1980-90. Chmn. hosp. div. United Community Chest, 1965-68, chmn. budget steering com., 1970-71, bd. dirs., mem. exec. com., 1969-75; mem. adv. com. Capitol Area Comprehensive Health Planning Assn., 1969, bd. dirs., 1971-75, treas., 1974-75; mem., vice chmn. Mich. Arbitration Adv. Com., 1975-80; bd. dirs. Grad. Med. Edn., Inc., 1971-80, pres., 1972-73, treas. 1973. 1st lt. Med. Svcs. Corps USAF, 1955—58. Fellow Am. Coll. Hosp. Adminstrs. (life); mem. Southwestern Mich. Hosp. Council (trustee 1968-73, pres. 1970-71), Am. Hosp. Assn. (del. 1979-87), Mich. Hosp. Assn. (1st v.p. 1972-73, bd. dirs., exec. com., treas. 1974-75, chmn. 1976-77, Meritorious Key award 1979), Rotary. Personal E-mail: forrest.neumann@gmail.com.

NEUMANN, HARRY, philosophy educator; b. Dormoschel, Germany, Oct. 10, 1930; came to U.S., 1937, naturalized, 1948; s. Siegfried and Frieda (Lion) N.; m. Christina Sopher, Sept. 25, 1959. BA, St. John's Coll., 1952; MA, U. Chgo., 1954; PhD, Johns Hopkins U., 1962; postgrad., U. Heidelberg, Germany, 1956-58. Mem. faculty Mich. State U., 1962-63, Lake Forest Coll., 1963-65; prof. philosophy, and govt. Claremont Grad. U. Scripps Coll., Claremont (Calif.) Grad. Univ., 1966—. Research assoc. Rockefeller Inst., N.Y.C., 1963 Author: Liberalism, 1991; contbr. articles profl. jours. With AUS, 1954-56. Classical Philosophy fellow Ctr. Hellenic Studies, Dumbarton Oaks, Washington, 1965-66, rsch. fellow Salvatori Ctr. for Study of Individual Freedom in the Modern World, 1970; rsch. fellow Earhart Found., 1973-74, 78, 82, 86, 90, 94, 98. Office: Claremont Grad U Dept Politics & Policy Claremont CA 91711 Office Phone: 909-621-8171.

NEUMANN, HENRY W., JR., energy executive; B in Acctg. and Bus. Adminstrn., Ill. State U., Normal. With Kinder Morgan, Houston, 1976—, various positions in acctg. and info. tech., v.p. sys. devel., v.p., chief info. officer. Office: Kinder Morgan 500 Dallas St Ste 1000 Houston TX 77002 Office Phone: 713-369-9000.

NEUMANN, PETER GABRIEL, computer scientist; b. NYC, Sept. 21, 1932; s. J.B. and Elsa (Schmid) N.; m. Elizabeth Susan Neumann; 1 child, Helen K. AB, Harvard U., 1954, SM, 1955; Dr rerum naturarum, Technische Hochschule, Darmstadt, Fed. Republic Germany, 1960; PhD, Harvard U., 1961. Mem. tech. staff Bell Labs, Murray Hill, NJ, 1960-70; Mackay lectr. Stanford U., 1964, U. Calif., Berkeley, 1970-71; prin. scientist SRI Internat., Menlo Park, Calif., 1971—. Adj. prof. U. Md., 1999. Author: Computer-Related Risks, 1995. Recipient Nat. Computer Sys. Security award, 2002; Fulbright grantee, 1958—60. Fellow AAAS, IEEE, Assn. for Computing Machinery (editor jour. 1976-93, chmn. com. on computers and pub. policy 1985—). Avocations: music, tai chi. Office: SRI Internat EL-243 333 Ravenswood Ave Menlo Park CA 94025-3493 Business E-Mail: pneumann@acm.org.

NEUMANN, ROY COVERT, architect; b. Columbus, Nebr., Mar. 1, 1921; s. LeRoy Franklin and Clara Louise (Covert) N.; children: Tali, Scott; m. Donna Corwin, Oct. 11, 2003. Student, Midland Coll., 1939-40, U. Calif.-Berkeley Armed Forces Inst., overseas, 1942-43; AB, U. Nebr., 1948, BArch, 1949; MA, Harvard U., 1952; postgrad., U. Wis., Iowa State U. Registered profl. architect, Iowa, Nebr., Kans., Minn., SD, NY, Mass., Ohio, Pa., Tenn., Ky., Va., W.Va., Ga., Mich., Mo., Ill., Wis., Tex., Colo. Ptnr., architect R. Neumann Assocs., Lincoln, Nebr., 1952-55; officer mgr. Sargent, Webster, Crenshaw & Folley, Schenectady, NY, 1955-59; dir. architecture, ptnr. A.M. Kinney Assocs., Cin., 1959-65; officer mgr. Hunter, Campbell & Rea, Johnstown, Pa., 1965-66; dir. architecture, ptnr. Stanley Cons., Muscatine, Iowa, 1966-76; pres., chmn. bd. emeritus Neumann Monson P.C., Iowa City, 1976—. Ptnr. Clinton St. Ptnrs., Iowa City, 1983—, Iris City Devel. Co. Mt. Pleasant, Iowa, 1986, Linn Mar Elem./Mid. Sch., Marion, Iowa. Prin. works include Harbour Facilities, Antigua, W.I., SC Johnson Office Bldg., Racine, Wis., Iowa City Transit Facility Bldg., addition to Davenport Ctrl. High Sch., V.A. Adminstrv. Office Bldg., Iowa City, Johnson County Office Bldg., Iowa City Mercer Park Aquatic Ctr., Iowa City, Coll. Bus. U. Iowa, Iowa City, renovation Lawrence County Courthouse, Deadwood, SD, HS and Elem. Schs., Mt. Pleasant, Iowa, Riverview Ctr., Muscatine, Iowa, Muscatine County Adminstv. Bldg., Iowa. Mem. bd. edn. Muscatine Cmty. Sch. Dist., 1974-76. Served with USN, 1942—46, PTO. Recipient Honor award Portland Cement Assn., 1949, Lorraine D. Wright award for outstanding constrn. Camanche HS, Iowa, 1998-99. Mem. AIA (Honor award 1975), Constrn. Specifications Inst. (pres. 1974-76, Honor award 1983, 84, 85, 86), Soc. Archtl. Historians, Archtl. Assn. London, U. Nebr. Alumni Assn., Harvard U. Alumni Assn., Iowa City C. of C., Phi Kappa Psi, Univ. Athletic Club (Iowa City), Masons, Ea. Star, Elks Republican. Presbyterian. Avocations: golf, fishing, medieval history, big band music. Home: 312 Locust St Muscatine IA 52761-3510 Office: Neumann Monson Architects 221 E College St Iowa City IA 52240-4012 Home Phone: 563-236-7813; Office Phone: 319-338-7878. E-mail: roy@neumannmonson.com.

NEUMANN, SERINA ANN LOUISE, psychologist, researcher; b. Fitchburg, Mass., Dec. 29, 1970; d. James Martin Neumann and Annette Marie Rooney; m. Mark Cardiff, Feb. 19, 1973. BS in Psychology and Bus. cum laude, U. Pitts., 1992; MA in Clin. Psychology and Behavioral Medicine, U. Md., Balt., 1999, PhD in Clin. Psychology and Behavioral Medicine, 2001. Lic. psychologist Bur. Profl. Occupl. Affairs, Pa., 2003, Va., 2006. Postdoctoral scholar, cardiovasc. behavioral medicine rsch. tng. program U. Pitts., 2001—04, rsch. asst. prof., 2004—05; assoc. prof. psychiatry and behavioral scis. Eastern Va. Med. Sch., 2006—. Author articles and papers in field. Fellow Ruth L. Kirschstein Nat. Rsch. Svc. award, NIH, Nat. Heart, Lung, and Blood Inst., 2001-2004; Loan Repayment Program grant, NIH, 2002—, Grant (NIMH) Kiosk award, 2005—. Mem.: APA (mem. Health Psychology Divsn. 38), Internat. Soc. Behavioral Medicine, Soc. Behavioral Medicine, Am. Psychosomatic Soc. (program com. student mem. 2000—01, Citation award 2005), Phi Kappa Phi. Achievements include discovery of preliminary evidence of an association between genetic variation in the choline transporter gene and parasympathetic-cardiac function, depressive symptomatology; corticolimbic reactivity and subclinical measures of atherosclerosis. Office: Eastern Va Med Sch Dept Psychiatry 825 Fairfax Ave Norfolk VA 23501 Business E-Mail: neumansa@evms.edu.

NEUMANN, THOMAS WILLIAM, archaeologist; b. Cin., Aug. 30, 1951; s. William Henry and Virginia Marie Neumann; m. Mary Louise Spink, Sept. 3, 1988. BA in Anthropology, U. Ky., 1973; PhD in Anthropology, U. Minn., 1979. Instr. U. Minn., Mpls., 1977-79; asst. prof. Syracuse U., 1979-86, dir. archaeology field program, 1979-86; sr. ptnr. Neumann & Sanford Cultural Resource Assessments, Syracuse, 1985-87; sr. scientist R. Christopher Goodwin & Assocs., Inc., Frederick, Md., 1987-92. Rsch. assoc. Terrestrial Environ. Specialists, Phoenix, N.Y., 1980-83, SUNY Rsch. Found., Potsdam, 1985-87; external reviewer NSF, Washington, 1982-85; dir. Ctr. for Archaeol. Rsch. and Edn., Houston, Minn., 1982-84; vis. assoc. prof. Emory U., 1991-93, 96-2000, 2002-06, U. Ga., 1997; ind. cons., 1991—; mgr. Diachronics divsn. Pocket Park-Wentworth Analytical Facility, 1993-, prin. anthropologist and flight instr., Aviation Atlanta. Author, co-author more than 80 books and monographs including 2 winners of the Anne Arundell County Hist. Preservation award as well as Practicing Archaeology; asst. editor Amanuensis, 1972-73; contbr. more than 40 articles to profl. jours. Nat. Trust Historic Preservation honor award. Recipient Oswald award U. Ky., 1973; co-recipient Vt. Gov.'s medal for Stonewalls and Cellarholes; grantee Am. Philos. Soc., 1981, Appleby-Mosher Found., 1983, Landmarks Assn. Ctrl. N.Y., 1984. Mem. AAAS, N.Y. Acad. Sci., Soc. for Am. Archaeology, Ea. States Archaeol. Fedn., Mid. Atlantic Archaeol. Conf., Ga. Coun. Profl. Archaeologists, Register of Profl. Archaeologists, Phi Beta Kappa. Roman Catholic. Achievements include development of use of vegetation successional stages for cultural resource assessments; identification of cause of passenger pigeon extinctions, microlithic compound tool industry in the eastern prehistoric U.S., contingency planning budget system for Archdiocese of Atlanta. Home and Office: Ind Archeol Cons 3859 Wentworth Ln SW Lilburn GA 30047-2260

NEUMARK, LIZ, entrepreneur; b. NY, 1956; Degree in Urban Studies and Polit. Sci., Barnard Coll., NYC. Founder, pres., CEO Great Performances, NYC, 1979—. Owner, founder organic food line Katchkie Farm, Kinderhook, NY, 2006—; founder Sylvia Ctr., Kinderhook. Named one of The 100 Most Influential Women in NYC Bus., Crain's NY Bus., 2007. Mem.: N.E. Organic Farming Assn. NY, Food & Beverage Assn. America (Industry Profl. of Yr. 2008). Office: Great Performances 304 Hudson St New York NY 10013 Office Phone: 212-727-2424. Office Fax: 212-727-2820.

NEUMEIER, JOHN, choreographer, ballet company director; b. Milw., Feb. 24, 1942; s. Albert and Lucille N. BA, Marquette U., 1961, DFA (hon.), 1987; student, Stone-Camryn Ballet Sch., Chgo., 1957-62, Royal Ballet Sch., London, 1962-63; student of Vera Volkova, Copenhagen, 1962-63. Dancer Sybil Shearer Co., Chgo., 1960-62, Stuttgart Ballet, Germany, 1963-69; artistic dir. Frankfurt Opera Ballet, Germany, 1969-73, Hamburg State Opera Ballet, Germany, 1973—; prof. City of Hamburg, 1987; dir. Hamburg Ballet, 1996, ballettintendant, 1997—. Found. ballet sch. Hamburg State Opera, 1978; found. ballet ctr. John Neumeier, ballet sch., Hamburg State Opera co. tng. under one roof., 1989. Guest choreographer for various cos. including Am. Ballet Theatre, Royal Ballet London, Royal Danish Ballet, Nat. Ballet Can., Royal Winnipeg Ballet, Stuttgart Ballet, Munich Opera, Vienna Opera, Ballet du XX siecle, Brussels, Opera de Paris, Opera of Stockholm, Mariinsky Theatre, St. Petersburg; guest opera dir. Otello, Munich Opera, Hamburg State Opera; ballet dir. (films) Rondo, 1971 (Prix Italia 1972), Third Symphony of Gustav Mahler, Legend of Joseph, Wendungen (String Quintet in C major by Schubert), 1979, Scenes of Childhood, The Lady of the Camelias, 1986, St. Mathew Passion, 1981, Othello, 1987, Illusions - Like Swan Lake, 2002, Death in Venice, 2004, St. Matthew Passion and Sylvia, 2005; choreographer Romeo and Juliet, The Nutcracker, 1971, Daphnis and Chloé, 1972, Third Symphony of Gustav Mahler, 1975, Illusions-Like Swan Lake, 1976, A Midsummer Night's Dream, 1977, Sleeping Beauty, The Lady of the Camelias, 1978, Matthaeus-Passion, 1981, Giselle, 1983, Sixth Symphony of G. Mahler, 1984, Peer Gynt, 1989, Fifth Symphony of G. Mahler, 1989, Requiem, 1991, A Cinderella Story, 1992, Odyssee, 1995, Vivaldi Or What You Will, 1996, Sylvia, 1997, Images from Bartók, 1998, Messias, 1999 (Danza Danza award 2001), Nijinsky, 2000, Giselle, 2000, Sounds of Empty Pages, Winterreise, 2001, The Seagull, 2002, Death in Venice, 2003, Preludes CV, 2003, The Little Mermaid, a homage to Hans Christian Andersen for his 200th birthday celebrations, 2005, Songs of the Night, 2005, Parzival Episodes and Echo, 2006, Christmas Oratorio, 2007, Verklungene Feste, 2008, Le Pavillon d'Armide 2009. Founder John Neumeier Found., 2006—. Goldene Kamera award for TV series Ballet Workshops, 1977, Decorated knight's cross Danebrog Order (Denmark); recipient Dance mag. award, 1983, Fed. German Cross of Merit, German Dance prize, 1988; title of Prof. conferred by City of Hamburg, 1987, Deutscher Tanzpreis, Fed. Republic of Germany, 1988; recipient Prix Diaghilev award, France, 1988, Order Des Arts et des Lettres award French Minister Culture, 1991, Carina Ari award, Stockholm, 1994, Nijinsky medal Polish Minister Culture, 1996, Danebrog Order in Gold, Denmark, 2000, Bayerischer Theaterpreis, 2001, First prize for best contemporary choreography, Vasva 2002, Wilhelm Hansen prize, 2002, Medal for Art and Science, 2003; named Hon. Mem. Semper Opera, 2002, Knight of the Region of Knox French President Jacques Chirac, 2003, Porselli prize, Italy, 2004, Hans Christian Andersen Embassador, 2004, 05, Saeculum prize for his lifework, Dresden, 2005, Steffen Kempe prize, 2005; Golden Mask Moscow's Best Contemporary Dance Prodn., 2005, Portugaleser in Silver, Hamburg, 2006, Nijinsky award for lifetime achievement, 2006, Citizen of Yr. Hamburg, 2006, Honorary Citizen of Hamburg, 2007, German Critic prize for life achievement, 2007, Herbert von Karajan Music prize, 2007, German Anniversary Dance prize 2008. Mem. Acad. der Kuenste Hamburg, Acad. der Kuenste Berlin, Golden Mask, 2002 (Medal for Sci, 2003). Roman Catholic. Office: Ballettzentrum Hamburg Caspar-Voght-Strasse 54 D-20535 Hamburg Germany Business E-Mail: presse@hamburgballett.de.

NEUMEIER, MATTHEW MICHAEL, lawyer, educator; b. Racine, Wis., Sept. 13, 1954; s. Frank Edward and Ruth Irene (Effenberger) N.; m. Annmarie Prine, Jan. 31, 1987; children: Ruthann Marie, Emilie Irene, Matthew Charles. B in Gen. Studies with distinction, U. Mich., 1981; JD magna cum laude, Harvard U., 1984. Bar: NY 1987, Mich. 1988, Ill. 1991, US Dist. Ct. (ea. dist.) Mich. 1988, US Dist. Ct. (ea., no. dists. and trial bar) Ill. 1991, US Ct. Appeals (7th cir.) 1992, US Ct. Appeals (fed. cir.) 1998, US Supreme Ct. 1991. Sec.-treas. Ind. Roofing & Siding Co., Escanaba, Mich., 1973-78; mng. ptnr. Ind. Roofing Co., Menominee, Mich., 1977-78; law clk. to presiding justice US Ct. Appeals (9th cir.), San Diego, 1984-85; law clk. to chief justice Warren E. Burger US Supreme Ct., Washington, 1985-86; spl. asst. to chmn. US Constn. Bicentennial Commn., Washington, 1986; assoc. Cravath, Swaine & Moore, NYC, 1986-88; spl. counsel Burnham & Ritchie, Ann Arbor, Mich., 1988; assoc. Schlussel, Lifton, Simon, Rands, Galvin & Jackier, P.C., Ann Arbor, Mich., 1988-90, Skadden, Arps, Slate, Meagher & Flom, Chgo., 1990-96; ptnr. Jenner & Block, Chgo., 1996—2007, Howrey LLP, Chgo., 2007—. Adj. prof. computer law and high tech. litig. John Marshall Law Sch., Chgo., 1999—2008. Editor: Harvard Law Rev., 1982—84. Pres., bd. dirs. Univ. Cellar Inc., Ann Arbor, 1979-81; bd. dirs. Econ. Devel. Corp., Menominee, 1978-79, Midwestern divsn. Am. Suicide Found., sec., 1992-97, Commonwealth Plaza Condominium Assn., dir., 1999-2009, pres., 2000-07; dir. Harvard Law Soc. Ill., 2003-, sec., 2005-07, treas., 2007-08, 2nd v.p., 2008-; mem. vestry Ch. Our Savior, 1997-2000; bd. dirs. Chgo. Children's Mus., 1999-, sec., 2003-; chmn. Harvard Law Sch. 15 Yr. Reunion Gift Fund, 1999; vice chair Harvard Law Sch. 20 Yr. Reunion Gift Fund, 2003-04. Mem. ABA, State Bar Mich., Assn. of Bar City of NY, Chgo. Bar Assn., Ill. State Bar Assn., Def. Rsch. Inst., Econ. Club Chgo., City Club Chgo. Republican. Avocations: classic automobiles, piano, choir. Office: Howrey LLP 321 N Clark St Ste 3400 Chicago IL 60654 Office Phone: 312-846-5640. Business E-Mail: neumeierm@howrey.com.

NEUMEYER, JOHN LEOPOLD, chemistry professor; b. Munich, July 19, 1930; came to U.S., 1945, naturalized, 1950; s. Albert and Martha (Stern) N.; m. Evelyn Friedman, June 24, 1956; children: Ann Martha, David Alexander, Elizabeth Jean. BS, Columbia U., 1952; PhD, U. Wis., 1961. Rsch. chemist Ethicon Inc., New Brunswick, NJ, 1952-57, FMC Corp., Princeton, NJ, 1961-63; sr. staff chemist Arthur D. Little, Inc., Cambridge, Mass., 1963-69; prof. medicinal chemistry, chemistry Northeastern U., Boston, 1969-91, dir. grad. sch., 1978-85, univ. disting. prof., 1982—92, univ. disting. prof. emeritus, 1992—; chmn. bd., chief sci. officer, co-founder Rsch. Biochem. Internat., Natick, 1981-97; pres., co-founder Brain Rsch. Labs., Inc., 1999—2002. Mem. com. of revision U.S. Pharmacopeia, 1970-85; lectr. in psychiatry dept. psychiatry Harvard Med. Sch., 1996—; Boudewijn Tieboel vis. prof., Groningen-Utrecht Inst. for Drug Exploration, Holland, 1997, dir. medicinal chemistry program Alcohol and Drug Abuse Rsch. Ctr. McLean Hosp., Belmont, Mass., 1996—; vis. prof. chemistry U. Konstanz, Germany, 1975-77cons. in field. Contbr. articles to profl. jours., chapters to books; patentee in field. Mem. Bd. Health, Wayland, Mass., 1968-75, Pesticide Bd., Mass., 1972-75; mem. panel to sec. HEW Commn. on Pesticides and their Relationship to Environ. Health, 1969; mem. Mass. Tech. Collaborative, 1996-2002. Served to cpl. U.S. Army, 1953-55. Recipient Lunsford Richardson award, 1961, Marie Curie award in Nuclear Medicine, 1992; sr. Hayes Fulbright fellow, 1975-76, Henry A. Hill award for Outstanding Contbns. to the Northeastern Sect., Am. Chem. Soc., 1998. Fellow: AAAS (mem. at large 1983—87, chmn. pharm. sci. sec. 1992—93), Am. Assn. Pharm. Scis. (Rsch. Achievement award in medicinal chemistry 1982); mem.: Am. Chem. Soc. (bd. editors Jour. Medicinal Chemistry 1974—88, chmn. divsn. med. chem. 1982, councilor 1985—, trustee 1989—93, N.E. sect. chmn.-elect 2002, chmn. 2003, named to Divsn. Medicinal Chemistry Hall of Fame 2008), Am. Soc. Exptl. Pharm. and Exptl. Therapeutics, Am. Soc. Neurosci., Acad. Pharm. Scis. Office: Harvard Med Sch/McLean Hosp ADARC 115 Mill St Belmont MA 02478-1041 E-mail: jneumeyer@mclean.harvard.edu.

NEUNER, FRANK X., JR., lawyer; b. Baton Rouge, May 23, 1951; s. Frank X. and Mary Frances (Ellis) N.; m. Tracy Owens, May 27, 1972; children: Gretchen, Hearin, Trip, Mary Frances. BS in Mgmt., La. State U., 1972, JD, 1976. Bar: La. 1976, Tex. 1993; U.S. Dist. Ct. (Ea. Dist. La.) U.S. Dist. Ct. (We. Dist. La.), U.S. Ct. Appeals (5th cir.). Assoc. Franklin, Moore & Walsh, Baton Rouge, 1976-77; ptnr. Onebane, Donohoe, et al, Lafayette, La., 1977-87, Laborde & Neuner, Lafayette, 1987—. Pres. United Way Acadiana, campaign chmn.; chmn. bd. dirs. Our Lady of Lourdes Regional Med. Ctr., Lafayette; Lafayette adv. bd. Iberia Bank Corp.; founding mem. bd. dirs. Cmty. Found. Acadiana; co-chmn. Lafayette Outreach for Civil Justice. Bd. dirs. United Way, Lafayette, chmn. leadership campaign, 1992; pres. Cathedral Carmel Found., Lafayette, 1987-91; bd. dirs. Nike La. Open, Lafayette, 1992-93. Mem. ABA (mem. House of Delegates), Lafayette Parish Bar Assn. (pres. 1988), La. State Bar Assn. (mem. House of Delegates 1980-96, past chmn. professionalism and quality of life com., bd. gov. 1997-99, treas. 2002-04, pres. 2005-06; David A. Hamilton Lifetime Achievement award 2004, Professionalism award 2006, Pres. award 2006), Lafayette Parish Bar Assn. (past pres.), Maritime Law Assn., Def. Rsch. Inst., La. Assn. Def. Counsel, Internat. Assn. Def. Counsel, Southeastern Admiralty Law Inst., Fedn. Def. and Corp. Counsel, Acadiana Inns of Ct. (past pres., team leader). Republican. Roman Catholic. Office: Laborde & Neuner Ste 200 1001 W Pinhook Rd Lafayette LA 70505-2828 Office Phone: 337-237-7000. Office Fax: 337-233-9450. Business E-Mail: fxnjr@ln-law.com.

NEUNER, JOAN MARIE, medical educator; d. James Francis and Rita Cecilia Neuner; m. Paul Eric Koch, May 28, 1994; children: Stephen Neuner Koch, Anneliese Neuner Koch. BA, U. Notre Dame, Ind., 1990; MD, U. Wis., Madison, 1994; MPH, Harvard U., 2000. Diplomate Am. Bd. Internal Medicine, 1997. Asst. prof. Med. Coll. Wis., Milw., 2000—. Contbr. to profl. jours. Career Devel. grant, NIH, 2003—. Mem.: Am. Soc. Bone & Mineral Rsch., Soc. Gen. Internal Medicine (midwest regional coun. officer 2004—05). Achievements include research in investigation of osteoporosis care, fractures and their risk factors among cancer patients. Office: Med Coll WI 8701 Watertown Plank Rd Milwaukee WI 53211

NEUNHOFFER, STEVEN CHARLES, protective services official; b. Amuway, Venezuela, Aug. 21, 1953; s. Jack Albert Neunhoffer and Elizabeth Ann Stevens; m. Margaret Ann Neunhoffer, Nov. 3, 1990; children: Jacob Scot, John Anthony Frome. MA, U. Phoenix, 2008. Registered nurse, Calif., 1982. Firefighter paramedic LA County Fire Dept., 1988—2002; instr. Coll. Canyons, Santa Clarita, Calif., 2002—08. Mem. Calif. Fire Tech Dirs. Assn., 2007—08. Dir.: (fire tech. program) Proposal Of Fire Law Class. Vol. YMCA, Canyon Country, Calif., 1991—2000. With USN, 1971—75, Jacksonville, Fla. Recipient Paramedic of Yr., BPOE, 2001. Mem.: NFPA. Conservative. Baptist. Achievements include research in firefighter standardized training. Avocations: sports, skiing, fishing, swimming. Home: 27401 Fairport Ave Canyon Country CA 91351 Office: Coll Canyons 26455 Rockwell Canyon Rd Santa Clarita CA 91355 Personal E-mail: countyfireman@yahoo.com. Business E-Mail: steven.neunhoffer@canyons.edu.

NEUPERT, PETER, computer software company executive; BA, Colo. Coll.; MBA, Dartmouth Coll. With Microsoft Corp., Redmond, Wash., 1987—98, dir. oper. sys., v.p. news and pub., interactive media group, corp. v.p. health solutions group, 2005—; pres., CEO Drugstore.com Inc., 1998—2001, chmn. bd. dirs., 1999—2004. Mem. Inf. Tech. Adv. Com. (PITAC), 2003—05, co-chaired Health Info. Tech. subcommittee; mem. Inst. Medicine's Roundtable on Evidence-Based Medicine, Pacific Health Summit Adv. Bd.; bd. mem. infiLearn.com, Cranium, Inc.; spkr. in field. Recipient Ernst & Young Entrepreneur of Yr. award, 2004. Office: Microsoft Corp One Microsoft Way Redmond WA 98052-6399*

NEURAUTER, ELIZABETH STRAIN, secondary school educator; b. Indpls., Mar. 7, 1959; d. Edward Richard Strain and Elizabeth Meyer (Strain) Gunn; m. Ronald Otto Neurauter, July 7, 1984; children: Stacy Marie, Ronald Paul, Beatrice Grace, Clara Helen. BA, Elmhurst Coll., Ill., 1981; EdM, Nat. Louis U., Wheeling, Ill., 2004; cert. advanced studies ednl. leadership, Nat. Louis U., 2005. Cert. tchr. English, ESL and psychology Ill. Staff asst. for vol. affairs ESL/ABE dept. Coll. DuPage, Glen Ellyn, Ill., 1991—94, ESL tchr. H.S. summer credit program, 2002—06; tutor English lang. learners Glenbard South HS, Glen Ellyn, 1994—2008; English lang. learner, program coord. Proviso East High Sch., Maywood, Ill., 2008—09. Presenter in field; adj. faculty adult and family svcs. Joliet Jr. Coll., Ill., 2006—08. Legis. apptd. mem.

Ill. Literacy Coun., 1998. Named Person of Character, Glen Ellyn Character Counts Coalition, 2004; nominee Golden Apple award, 2000. Mem.: ASCD, Ill. Assn. Supervision Curriculum Devel., AFT-IFT, Ill. Assn. Tchrs. English, Nat. Coun. Tchrs. English, Archaeol. Conservancy. Republican. Avocations: archaeology, antiques, travel. Home: PO Box 2712 Glen Ellyn IL 60138

NEUREITER, NORMAN P., science association director; b. Jan. 24, 1932; m. Georgine Reid; 4 children. BS in Chemistry, U. Rochester, 1952; PhD in Organic Chemistry, Northwestern U., 1957. With Humble Oil & Refining Co., 1957—63, NSF Internat. Affairs Office, 1963—65; dep. sci. attache U.S. Dept. State, Bonn, 1965—67, sci. attache Warsaw, 1967—69; with White House Office Sci. and Tech. Policy, 1969—73, Tex. Instruments, 1973—96, v.p. corp. staff, 1980—89, dir. Japan, v.p. Asia, 1989—96; sci. and tech. adv. to U.S. Sec. of State, 2000—03; dir. ctr. sci., tech., and security policy AAAS, 2004—. Disting. presdl. fellow NAS Internat. Affairs, 2003—; space studies bd. NAS/Nat. Rsch. Coun., 2004—; mem. US Nat. Academies' delegation that traveled to Iran to expand a program of scientific cooperation with Iranian researchers and edn. centers, 2007; co-chair Indo-US Sci. and Tech., 2001—. Recipient Pub. Welfare medal, NAS, 2008. Fellow: Am. Acad. Arts & Scis. Office: AAAS 1200 New York Ave NW Washington DC 20005 Home Phone: 703-351-9655; Office Phone: 202-326-6493. Business E-Mail: neureit@aaas.org.

NEUROHR, SHIRLEY ANN, retired special education educator; b. Chgo., Nov. 18, 1936; d. Anton and Anna (Ludvik) Sedlak; m. Joseph Henry Neurohr, Apr. 7, 1956 (dec. 1995); children: Debora Neurohr-Wearne, Kathleen Neurohr Rodenhauser, Jacqueline Neurohr; m. James Brennan, 2001 (dec. 2007). AA in Edn., Morton Coll., 1955; BA Psychology/Sociology summa cum laude, Mundelein Coll., 1977; MS in Edn. Adminstrn. with dept. honors, Winona State U., 1983. Cert. elem. edn. tchr., learning disabilities edn., behavioral disorders edn., elem. adminstrn. Elem. tchr. St. Mary's Cath. Sch., Tomah, Wis., 1978-80, elem. prin., 1980-85; secondary tchr. behaviorally disordered Sparta (Wis.) Sr. H.S., 1985-86, 86—; elem. tchr. behaviorally disordered Tomah Area Sch. Dist., 1986-87, secondary tchr. behaviorally disordered, 1987-90, secondary tchr. learning disabled, 1990—2001; ret., 2001. Mem. Edn. for Employment Coun., Tomah, 1990-95, Spl. Edn. Transition Task Force, Tomah, 1988-93, Sch. to Work Task Force, Tomah, 1990-95. Troop leader, program cons., v.p. coun. Girl Scouts DuPage County Coun., DuPage, Ill., 1963-77; lay min. Diocese of LaCrosse, Wis., 1985; mem. St. Mary's Coun. Cath. Women, 1977—. Recipient Thanks Badge, DuPage County coun. Girl Scouts U.S., 1976; named Woman of Yr., St. Joseph's Coun. of Cath. Women, 1977. Mem. AAUW (Tomah br. 1977-2008, -treas.), ASCD, Nat. Coun. Tchrs. English, Midwest Reading Coun., Tomah Edn. Assn. (bldg. rep. 1986, asst. v.p., pres. 2000), Sierra Club Nat. Wildlife Found., Crane Found., Monroe County Ret. Tchrs. Assn (pres. 2008—), Master Gardeners Assn., Delta Kappa Gamma (past sec. Alpha Upsilon chpt., past pres.). Democrat. Roman Catholic. Avocations: travel, gardening, birding. Home: 23584 Emblem Ave Tomah WI 54660-9731 Personal E-mail: shirlgym@charter.net.

NEUSTADT, ARTHUR I., lawyer; BSEE, U. Md., College Park, 1964; JD, Georgetown U., Washington, 1968. Sr. ptnr. Oblon, Spivak, McClelland, Maier & Neustadt, Alexandria, Va., 1974—. Office: Oblon Spivak McClelland Maier & Neustadt 1940 Duke St Alexandria VA 22314

NEUSTADT, BERNARD RAY, chemist; b. Washington, May 7, 1943; s. Morris and Jeanne Neustadt; m. Helen Levine, Nov. 26, 1964; children: Charles, Nancy Jacobovits, Judith Shapiro, Rebecca Sinowitz, Barry, Tova Schachter, Esther. AB, Columbia Coll., NY, 1964; PhD, Brandeis U., Waltham, Mass., 1965—69. Rsch. fellow Schering Plough Corp., Kenilworth, NJ, 1969—. Recipient Thomas Edison award, NJ Rsch. Coun., 2004. Mem.: Am. Chem. Soc. Home: 24 Brook Pl West Orange NJ 07052 Office: Schering-Plough Rsch Inst 2015 Galloping Hill Rd Kenilworth NJ 07033 Business E-Mail: bernard.neustadt@spcorp.com.

NEUSTADT, DAVID HAROLD, physician; b. Evansville, Ind., Dec. 2, 1925; s. Mose and Leah (Epstein) N.; m. Carolyn Jacobson, June 15, 1952; children: Susan Miriam, Jeffrey Bruce, Robert Alan. Student, DePauw U., 1943-44, 46-47; MD, U. Louisville, 1950. Intern Morrisania City Hosp., NYC, 1950-51; resident in internal medicine Lenox Hill Hosp., NYC, 1951-52, NIH trainee in rheumatic diseases, 1952-53, resident in gastroenterology, 1953-54; practice medicine specializing in rheumatic diseases Louisville, 1954—; chief arthritis clinic Louisville Gen. Hosp., 1960-76; asst. prof. medicine Sch. Medicine, U. Louisville, 1963-67, asso. prof. clin. medicine, 1967-75, clin. prof. medicine, 1974—, head sect. rheumatic diseases, 1960-76; chief dept. medicine Jewish Hosp., Louisville, 1965-67, pres. med. staff, 1967-69; cons. in rheumatology VA, 1970—. Advisor Network for Continuing Med. Edn., 1983—. Author: The Chemistry and Therapy of Collagen Diseases, 1963, (with other) Aspiration and Injection Therapy in Arthritis and Musculoskeletal Disorders, 1972; editor: (with other) Arthritis Abstracts, References Indexes, 1970-75; contbr. articles to profl. jours. Former pres., chmn. bd. med. sci. com. Ky. chpt. Arthritis Found. Served with AUS, 1944-46. Master Am. Coll. Rheumatology (formerly Am. Rheumatism Assn.; mem. editl. bd. 1989-94, exec. com., pres. ctrl. region 1982-84, Disting. Rheumatologist award 1997); fellow Am. Med. Writers Assn., ACP; mem. AMA, N.Y. Acad. Sci., N.Y. Rheumatism Soc., Ky. Rheumatism Assn. (pres. 1956-57), Internat. Soc. Internal Medicine, So. Med. Assn. (edn. com., sect. rheumatology), Am. Physicians Fellowship (nat. trustee 1984—), Spondylitis Assn. (adv. bd. 1986—, contbg. editor 1989—, mem. editl. bd. Arthritis Care and Rsch. Newsletter 1989—), Mason, Shriner. Jewish. Home: 216 Smithfields Rd Louisville KY 40207-1267 Office: Med Towers Louisville KY 40202 Office Phone: 502-585-4163. E-mail: MD@DavidHNeustadt.com. *I believe the qualities necessary to achieve success include a combination of ability, commitment to hard work, enthusiasm or enjoyment of your work, plus a liberal chunk of optimism, faith, luck, and a supporting family and co-workers.*

NEUTEL, JOEL, medical educator, director; Dir. rsch. Orange County Rsch. Ctr., Tustin, Calif., 1993—; assoc. prof. medicine U. Calif. Irvine, 2003. Office: Orange County Rsch Ctr 14351 Myford Rd Tustin CA 92780

NEUWIRTH, BEBE (BEATRICE NEUWIRTH), dancer, actress; b. Newark, Dec. 31, 1958; d. Lee Paul and Sydney Anne Neuwirth; m. Paul Dorman, 1984 (div.); m. Michael Danek. Student, Juilliard Sch., 1976-77. Performer: (on Broadway) A Chorus Line (as Sheila), 1975-90, Dancin', 1978-82, Little Me, 1982, Sweet Charity, 1986-87 (Tony award for best featured actress in a musical, 1986), Damn Yankees, 1994-95, Chicago, 1996 (Tony award for best actress in a musical, 1997, Outer Critics Circle award for best actress in a musical, 1997, Drama League Award for disting. performance, 1997, Drama Desk Award for outstanding actress in a musical, 1997, Astaire Award for best female dancer, 1997), Fosse, 1999-2001, Funny Girl, 2002, Here Lies Jenny, 2004, Chicago, 2007; (off Broadway) West Side Story, 1981, Upstairs at O'Neal's, 1982-83, The Road to Hollywood, 1984, Just So, 1985, Waiting in the Wings: The Night the Understudies Take the Stage, 1986, Showing Off, 1989, Kiss of the Spider Woman (London), 1993, Pal Joey, 1995, Here Lies Jenny, 2004. Prin. dancer on Broadway Dancin', 1982; leading dance role Kicks, 1984. Actor: (TV series) The Edge of Night, 1981, Cheers, 1986-93 (Emmy award for Best Supporting Actress in a Comedy Series 1990, 91), (voice) Aladdin, 1994, (voice) All Dogs Go to Heaven: The Series, 1996, Deadline, 2000-01, Law & Order: Trial by Jury, 2005-06; (TV series guest appearances) Frasier, 1994-2003; (TV miniseries) Wild Palms, 1993; (TV films) Without Her Consent, 1990, Unspeakable Acts, 1990, Dash and Lilly, 1999, Cupid & Cate, 2000, Sounds From a Town I Love, 2001; (films) Say Anything, 1989, Green Card, 1990, Bugsy, 1991, The Paint Job, 1992, Malice, 1993, Jumanji, 1995, (voice) All Dogs Go to Heaven 2, 1996, The Adventures of Pinocchio, 1996, The Associate, 1996, Dear Diary, 1996, Celebrity, 1998, The Faculty, 1998, (voice) An All Dogs Christmas Carol, 1998, Summer of Sam, 1999, Liberty Heights, 1999, Getting to Know You, 1999, Tadpole, 2002, How to Lose a Guy in 10 Days, 2003, Le Divorce, 2003, The Big Bounce, 2004, Game 6, 2005, Adopt a Sailor, 2007. Vol. performances for March of Dimes Telethon, 1986, Cystic Fibrosis Benefit Children's Ball, 1986, Ensemble Studio Theater Benefit, 1986, Circle Repertory Co. Benefit, 1986, all in N.Y.C. Recipient Dance Mag. award, 2007. Democrat. Office: c/o Brian Mann Internat Creative Mgmt 10250 Constellation Blvd Los Angeles CA 90067

NEUWIRTH, GLORIA S., lawyer; b. NYC, Aug. 16, 1934; d. Nathan and Jennie (Leff) Salob; m. Robert S. Neuwirth, June 9, 1957; children: Susan Madeleine Guerra, Jessica Anne, Laura Helaine, Michael Jonathan. BA, Hunter Coll., NYC, 1955; JD, Yale U., New Haven, Conn., 1958. Bar: NY 1959, Fla. 1979, US Supreme Ct. 1976, US Dist. Ct. (so. and ea. dists.) NY 1976. Assoc. dir. Joint Rsch. Project on Ct. Calendar Congestion Columbia U., NYC, 1958—61; assoc. Kridel & Friou, NYC, 1974—76; ptnr. Kridel, Slater and Neuwirth, NYC, 1976—82, 1987—94; assoc. Kaye, Scholer, Fierman, Hays and Handler, NYC, 1982—84, Graubard Moskovitz McGoldrick Dannett & Horowitz, NYC, 1984—86; ptnr. Davidson, Dawson & Clark, NYC, 1995—. Vol. arbitrator Better Bus. Bur. Author: (with R.B. Hunting) Who Sues in New York City: A Study of Automobile Accident Claims, 1962; contbr. articles to profl. jours. Trustee Blueberry Inc., 1962-70, Riverdale Country Sch., 1981-86; trustee, v.p., sec. Nat. Kidney Found., Inc., NY/NJ; dir. Estate Planning Coun. NYC, Riverdale Mental Health Assn., Bronx Opera Co., The Ruth Turner Fund, The Associated Blind, Riverdale Sr. Svcs.; sec. Kidney & Urology Found. Am., 2002-. Recipient C. LaRue Munson prize, Yale Law Sch., 1958. Fellow Am. Coll. Trust and Estate Counsel; mem. ABA, NY State Bar Assn. (vice chmn. com. on law of the elderly), Assn. Bar City NY, Fin. Women's Assn., Estate Planning Coun. NY, Nat. Elder Law Attys., Appalachian Mtn. Club. Office: Davidson Dawson & Clark LLP Lincoln Bldg 60 E 42d St Fl 38 New York NY 10165-3897 Home Phone: 212-265-7214; Office Phone: 212-557-7720. Office Fax: 212-286-8513. Business E-Mail: gsneuwirth@davidsondawson.com.

NEUWIRTH, ROBERT SAMUEL, obstetrician, gynecologist, educator; b. NYC, July 11, 1933; s. Abraham Alexander and Phyllis Neuwirth; children from previous marriage: Susan, Jessica, Laura, Michael, Alexander. BS, Yale U., 1955, MD, 1958. Intern Presbyn. Hosp., NYC, 1958-59, resident, 1959-64; asst. prof. ob-gyn. Columbia U., NYC, 1964-68, assoc. prof., 1968-71, prof., 1972-2001, Babcock prof., 1977-2001, Babcock prof. emeritus, 2001—. Dir. ob-gyn. Bronx Lebanon Hosp., NYC, 1967-72, Woman's Hosp., NYC, St. Luke's Hosp. Ctr., 1974—, St. Luke's Roosevelt Hosp., 1981-91; prof. Albert Einstein Coll. Medicine, 1971-72; cons. WHO, NIH, AID, FDA; interim dir. St. Luke's Roosevelt Hosp., 1998-2000. Author: Hysteroscopy, 1975; contbr. articles to profl. jours. Mem.: ACOG, Assn. Vol. Sterilization (chmn. biomed. com. 1971—), Am. Assn. Profs. Ob-Gyn., NY Obstet. Soc., Soc. Gynecol. Investigation, Am. Gynecol. and Obstet. Soc. Office: St Lukes Roosevelt Hosp 1000 10th Ave Dept Ob New York NY 10019-1147 Office Phone: 212-523-8368.

NEUZIL, PETR, cardiologist, researcher; b. Prague, Feb. 1, 1962; s. Josef Neuzil and Marie Neuzilova; m. Ivana Boturova, Apr. 14, 1989; children: Ondra, Kamila Neuzilova. MD, Charles U., Prague, 1987, PhD, 2001. Residency in internal medicine Gen. Hosp. Charles U., Prague, Czech Republic, 1989—91; fellowship in cardiology Heart Centrum, Bad Krozingen, 1991—93; with Beth Israel Deaconnes Med. Ctr., 1997, 1998, Mass. Gen. Hosp., 1998—2000; dir. cardiac arrhythmia svc. Na Homolce Hosp., Prague, 2004—, head cardiology, 2009; dir. animal lab. Charles U., Prague, 2006—, assoc. prof., 2007. Dir. Cardiac Arrhythmias Found., Prague, 2005—07; cons. Tech. Sch., Prague, 2005—. Editor: (jour.) Practicioner. Grantee, NIH, 2003, 2006. Fellow: European Soc. Cardiology (assoc.); mem.: European Heart Rhythm Assn., Heart Rhythm Soc. Achievements include development of Esophageal temperature probe; research in robotic cardiac catheterization; electromechanical robotic catheterization system Sensei and electromagnetic navigation Niobe; balloon technology in catheter ablation technology, mainly laser energy. Office: Na Homolce Hosp Roentgenova 2 150 30 Prague Czech Republic Office Phone: 011420257272301. Personal E-mail: petr.neuzil@gmail.com. Business E-Mail: pneuzil@seznam.cz.

NEVELOFF, JAY A., lawyer; b. Bklyn., Oct. 11, 1950; m. Arlene Sillman, Aug. 26, 1972; children: David, Kevin. BA, Bklyn. Coll., 1971; JD, NYU, 1974. Bar: N.Y. 1975, D.C. 1992, U.S. Dist. Ct. (so. and ea. dists.) N.Y. 1975, U.S. Ct. Appeals (2d cir.) 1975, U.S. Supreme Ct. 1982. Assoc. Marshall, Bratter, Greene, Allison & Tucker, NYC, 1974-82, Rosenman, Colin, Freund, Lewis & Cohen, NYC, 1982-83, ptnr., 1983-88, Kramer, Levin, Naftalis, Nessen, Kamin & Frankel, NYC, 1988—. Editor N.Y. Real Property Service. Mem. planning bd. Briarcliff Manor, 1995—. Mem. ABA (vice chmn. com. partnerships, joint ventures and other investment vehicles 1988-95), Am. Law Inst., Am. Coll. Real Estate Attys., Am. Coll. Mortgage Attys., NY State Bar Assn. (financing com.), Practising Law Inst. (lectr. 1988—, mem. adv. bd. 1991—), Assn. Bar City NY (real property law com., lectr. 1984-88), Strategic Resources Inst. (lectr. 1994-98), Internat. Health Network Soc. (vice chmn. 1995-2000), Inst. Internat. Rsch. (lectr. 1994—), Info. Mgmt. Network (lectr. 2004-), Am. Conf. Inst. (lectr. 2006-). Home: 134 Alder Dr Briarcliff Manor NY 10510-2218 Office: Kramer Levin Naftalis & Frankel LLP 1177 Ave of the Americas New York NY 10036 Office Phone: 212-715-9290. Business E-Mail: jneveloff@kramerlevin.com.

NEVELS, JAMES EDWIN, investment company executive; m. Lourene Dellinger. AB cum laude, Bucknell Univ., 1974; MBA, JD, Univ. Pa., 1978. Fin. law practice & investment banking positions, 1974—91; founder, chmn. The Swarthmore Group Inc., Phila., 1991—; non-exec. chmn. The Hershey Co., Phila., 2009—. Bd. dir. The Hershey Co., 2007—, Tasty Baking Co. Chmn. Phila. Sch. Reform Commn., 2001—07; chmn. adv. com. Pension Benefit Guaranty Corp.; bd. dir. The Hershey Trust, Pro Football Hall of Fame, Canton, Ohio, The Phila. Orch. Assn.; bd. mem. Berea Coll., Assn. Governing Boards of Colleges & Universities; mem. bd. vis. Fox Sch. Bus. & Mgmt. Temple Univ.; mem. bd. overseers Univ. Pa. Law Sch.; mem. adv. bd. Drexel Univ.; past trustee, mem. exec. com. Bucknell Univ. Recipient Svc. to Humanity award, Bucknell Univ., 2009. Mailing: Hershey Co Bd Directors 1717 Arch St Philadelphia PA 19103*

NEVES, AEXANDRA MOREIRA, language educator; b. Curitiba, Brazil, July 15, 1969; arrived in US, 2003; d. José Onildo Moreira and Maria Luiza Moreira Neves; m. Ney Robson A. Koch (div.); children: Hannah Moreira Koch, Wilson A. Keanu; m. JJ Amaworo Wilson, Aug. 1, 2006. BA, U. do Sol, Tubarao, Brazil, 1994, MA, 2002; postgrad., N.Mex. State U., Las Cruces, 2003—. Tchr. Inst. Minsky, Laguna, Brazil, 1986—95; pvt. tchr. Laguna, 1995—98; prof. U. do Sol, Tubarao, 1999—2003; tchg. asst. N.Mex. State U., Las Cruces, 2003—. Mem. Grad. Students Union, Las Cruces, 2005; pres. Grad. Students Orgn., Las Cruces, 2005—06. Mem.: TESOL. Avocations: sports, travel. Office: NMex State Univ Las Cruces NM 88001 Home: 104 W Rhoda Rd Silver City NM 88061-3929 Office Phone: 575-538-6011.

NEVES, DAVID, musician, educator; b. Central Falls, RI, Aug. 7, 1955; s. Joaquim Almeida and Maria Rosa N.; m. Janice Poulin, Aug. 6, 1977; children: Kristin Marie, Jennifer Anne, Amanda Michaela. B in Music Edn., Berklee Coll. Music, 1976; MAT in Saxophone, R.I. Coll., 1981. Cert. music tchr., music supr., RI. Choral dir. Scituate (R.I.) High Sch., 1976-79, band dir., supr. music, 1979—. Prin. saxophone Am. Band, 1978—. Mem. Gov.'s Arts Task Force State of RI., 1999-00. Recipient Milken Edn. award Milken Family Found., 1991; named RI Tchr. of Yr., 2002. Mem. Nat. Band Assn., Nat. Edn. Assn., RI. Music Educators Assn. (mem. band, pres. 1985-87, treas. 1996-98, editor 1989-91, Meritorious Svc. award 1994, guest condr. concert band 1994, guest condr. jazz 1997). Avocation: computers. Home: 260 Phenix Ave Cranston RI 02920-4018 Office: Scituate High Sch 94 Trimtown Rd Scituate RI 02857-1947

NEVES, KERRY LANE, lawyer; b. San Angelo, Tex., Dec. 19, 1950; s. Herman Walter and Geraldine (Ball) N.; m. Sharon Lynn Briggs, July 28, 1973; 1 child, Erin Lesli. BBA, U. Tex., 1975, JD, 1978. Bar: Tex. 1978, U.S. Dist. Ct. (so. and ea. dists.) Tex. 1979, U.S. Ct. Appeals (5th cir.) 1979, U.S. Dist. Ct. (we. dist.) 1980; cert. personal injury trial law, Tex. Bd. Legal Specialization, 1994. Ptnr. Mills, Shirley, Eckel & Bassett, Galveston, Tex., 1978—93, Neves & Crowther, Galveston, Tex., 1993—2002; pvt. practice Law Offices of Kerry L. Neves, Galveston, 2002—06, Dickinson, Tex., 2007—. Vice-chmn. Bldg. Stds. Commn., Dickinson, Tex., 1991—98; mem. City Coun., Dickinson, 1998—; chmn. Galveston County Rep. Party, 2007—08; bd. dirs. Houston-Galveston Area Coun., 2002—, vice chmn., 2008—09, chmn. elect, 2009—. Sgt. USMC, 1969—72. Fellow Tex. Bar Found. (life); mem. ABA, State Bar Tex. (grievance com. 1989-92, disciplinary rules profl. conduct com. 1990-92, dir. dist. 5 1997-2000), Galveston County Bar Assn. (pres. 1989-90), U. Tex. Law Alumni Assn. (pres. 1991-92). Avocations: gardening, wine, reading. Home: 4025 Lovers Ln Dickinson TX 77539-9204 Home Phone: 281-337-4006; Office Phone: 281-337-5414. Personal E-mail: bkwds@aol.com.

NEVILL, WILLIAM ALBERT, chemistry professor; b. Indpls., Jan. 1, 1929; s. Irwin Lowell and Mary Marie (Barker) N.; m. Nancy Neiman (Roll), May 19, 1979; children: Paul David, John Michael, Steven Joseph, Anne Marie, Deborah Ruth. BS, Butler U., 1951; PhD, Calif. Inst. of Tech., 1954. Rsch. chemist Procter and Gamble, Cin., 1954; chemistry prof., chmn. dept. Grinnell Coll., 1956-67; prof. chemistry Ind. U., Purdue, Indpls., 1967-83, chmn. dept., 1967-72, dean sch. sci., 1972-79, dir. grad. studies, 1979-83; pres. B and N Cons. Co., 1972-93; vice chancellor acad. affairs La. State U., Shreveport, La., 1983-85, prof., 1983-94; pres. Catoctin Assoc., 1993—. Arbitrator, mediator, Ind. Employment Rels. Bd., 1975-83. Author: Gen. Chemistry, 1967, Expt. in Gen. Chemistry, 1968. Bd. dir. Indpls. Sci. and Engring. Found., 1972-75, 79-82, Westminster Found., Lafayette, Ind., 1972-74, Am. Chem. Soc., 1986-92. With U.S. Army, 1954-56; col., USAR, 1956-84. Grantee NSF, 1959-74; Grantee NIH, 1963-70; Grantee Office Naval Rsch., 1953 Mem. Ind. Acad. Sci., Am. Chem. Soc., chmn. sect. 1972, counselor 1973-92. Presbyterian.

NEVILLE, ELIZABETH EGAN, artist, educator; b. Albany, NY, May 16, 1937; d. Philip Sidney and Harriet Rust Egan; m. Robert Cummings Neville, June 8, 1963; children: Naomi Louise, Leonora Alice. BA, Smith Coll., 1959; MA in Tchg., Harvard U., 1961. Dir. Neville Art Enterprises, Milton, Mass., 1969—. Art instr. Town of Huntington, NY, 1982—88, Adelphi U., Garden City, NY, 1983—85; dir. Milton Art Mus., 1993—97, art instr., 1998—2008; lectr. in field, 1998—2006. Art critic: Art N.Eng., 1998—2008; Represented in permanent collections Heckscher Mus., Huntington, L.I., Fine Arts Mus. L.I., Hempstead, N.Y., Maritime Mus., State U. N.Y., Throgs Neck, Katonah Gallery, N.Y., Hudson-Athens Lighthouse Preservation Soc.; cover designer Ritual and Deference, 2008; Symbols of Jesus, 2001, Boston Confucianism, 2000, The God Who Beckons, 1999, The Cosmology of Freedom, 1995, Creativity and God, 1995, God the Creator, 1992, Eternity and Times Flow, 1993, A Theology Primer, 1991, Behind the Masks of God, 1991, Recovery of the Measure, 1989, The Butterfly as Companion, 1989, The Puritan Smile, 1987, solo exhbns., Neville Gallery, 2004, 2009, Visions Gallery, Brandford, Conn., 2008, 664 Thames St., Newport, RI, 2008, Boston U. Sch. Theology, 1998, Claremont Sch. Theology, Calif., 1997, 1995, 1991, Sturdy Meml. Hosp. Gallery, Attleboro, Mass., 1997, Weston Theol. Inst., Mass., 1995, U. Mass. Med. Ctr. Gallery, Worcester, 1994, Kaaterskill Gallery, Columbia-Greene C.C., Hudson, N.Y., 1992, Milton Art Mus, Mass., 1990, NoHo Gallery, NYC, 1981, 1983. Mem. Newport Art Mus., RI, 2002—, Capt. Robert Forbes Mus., Milton, 1989—2009; pres. bd. trustees Milton Art Mus., 2001—06, 2003. Grantee, Henry Luce Found., 1990, Milton Cultural Arts Coun., 1995, 1996, 1997, 2006. Mem.: Nat. Mus. Women in Art (charter mem.), Women's Caucus for Art, Harvard Club Boston (adv. bd. fine arts com. 1998—2009), Smith Coll. Club Boston, Milton Garden Club (chair Smithsonian garden history 2001—09), Alpha Kappa XI. Democrat. Avocations: landscape architecture, photography, history, citrus horticulture. Office Phone: 617-698-6112. Business E-Mail: eeneville@comcast.net.

NEVILLE, HELEN J., psychology professor, neuroscientist; BA in Psychology, Univ. BC; MA, Simon Fraser Univ.; PhD in Neuropsychology, Cornell Univ. Dir., brain devel. lab. Univ. Oreg., 1995—, prof., psychology, neuroscience, 1995—, assoc. dir., Inst. Neuroscience, 1998—2005, dir., Ctr. Cognitive Neuroscience, 1998—. Recipient Justine and Yves Sergent award, Montreal, 2000, Claude Pepper award, 1993—97. Fellow: Am. Psychological Soc., Am. Acad. Arts & Scis.; mem.: Soc. Exptl. Psychologists. Office: Brain Devel Lab 1227 Univ Oregon Eugene OR 97403-1227 Office Phone: 541-346-4248. Business E-Mail: neville@uoregon.edu.

NEVILLE, HOLLY LEIGH, pediatrician, surgeon; b. Morristown, NJ, Oct. 29, 1970; d. Stephen and Susan Neville; m. David William Schechter, July 18, 1992; children: David Zachary Schechter, Camille Susan Schechter, Chloe Viola Schechter. MD, U. Fla., Gainesville, 1996. Cert. Am. Bd. Surgery, 2004. Asst. prof. surgery U. Miami Miller Sch.

Medicine, Fla., 2006—. Fellow: ACS. Office: Univ Miami 1611 NW 12th Ave Holtz East tower -3019 Miami FL 33136 Office Fax: 305-326-0224. Business E-Mail: hneville@med.miami.edu.

NEVILLE, J. GABRIEL, legislative staff member; Grad., Franklin & Marshall Coll., Lancaster, Pa., 1990. Press sec., Rep. Joseph Pitts US House of Reps., Washington, chief of staff to Rep. Joseph Pitts, 2003—. Republican. Office: 420 Cannon House Office Bldg Washington DC 20515 Office Phone: 202-225-2411. Office Fax: 202-225-2013.*

NEVILLE, JAMES MORTON, retired lawyer, consumer products company executive; b. Mpls., May 28, 1939; s. Philip and Maurene (Morton) N.; m. Judie Martha Proctor, Sept. 9, 1961; children: Stephen Warren, Martha Maurene Hereford. BA, U. Minn., JD magna cum laude, 1964. Bar: Minn. 1964, Mo. 1984. Assoc. Neville, Johnson & Thompson, Mpls., 1964-69, ptnr., 1969-70; assoc. counsel Gen. Mills, Inc., Mpls., 1970-77, sr. assoc. counsel, 1977-83, corp. sec., 1976-83; v.p., sec., asst. gen. counsel Ralston Purina Co., St. Louis, 1983-84, v.p., gen. counsel, sec., 1984-96, v.p., gen. counsel, 1996-2000, v.p., sr. counsel, 2000-01; ret., 2001. Lectr. bus. law. U. Minn., 1967-71; chmn. The Thompson Ctr., 2002. Bd. mem. Haven of Grace, 1997—2000. Named Man of Yr., Edina Jaycees, 1967. Mem. ABA, Mo. Bar Assn., U.S. Supreme Ct. Bar Assn., St. Louis Bar Assn., U. Minn. Law Sch. Alumni Assn., Old Warson Country Club, Ladue Racquet Club, Order of Coif, Phi Delta Phi, Psi Upsilon. Episcopalian. Avocation: bridge. Home: 9810 Log Cabin Ct Saint Louis MO 63124-1133 Home Phone: 314-993-6607. Personal E-mail: jnev57@aol.com.

NEVILLE, LEONORA ALICE, history professor; m. Stephen Rhody, Apr. 27, 2002. PhD, Princeton U., NJ, 1998. Asst. prof. Cath. U. America, Washington, 1998—. Author: (book) Authority in Byzantine Provincial Society, 950-1100. Office: Cath Univ America History Dept Washington DC 20064

NEVILLE, PHOEBE, choreographer, dancer, educator; b. Swarthmore, Pa., Sept. 28, 1941; d. Kennith R. and Marion (Eberbach) Balsley; m. Philip E. Hipwell, June 21, 1969 (dissolved Sept. 1978); m. Philip Corner, Nov. 3, 1996. Student, Wilson Coll., 1959-61. Cert. practitioner body mind centering, registered somatic movement therapist. Instr. Bennington (Vt.) Coll., 1981-84, 87-88; vis. lectr. UCLA, 1984-86. Dancer, choreographer Judson Meml. Ch., N.Y.C., 1966—70, Dance Uptown Series, 1969, Cubiculo Theatre, 1972—75, Delacorte Dance Festival, 1976, Dance Umbrella Series, 1977, Riverside Dance Festival, 1976, 1978, N.Y. Seasons, 1979—, dancer, artistic dir. Phoebe Neville Dance Co., N.Y.C., 1975—, Jacob's Pillow Splash! Festival, 1988—, Dance Theater Workshop Winter Events, 1988—, Mersdith Wonk Benefit, 1994, performances with Philip Corner: Venice, Genoa, San Michele al' Adige, 1996—, BBB Festival, Thailand, Genoa, Salso Maggiore, Terme, 1997—, Seoul NY Max Festival, N.Y.C., 1998, Malpartida de Caseres, Spain, Caserano, Italy, 1998, Besancon, France, 1998, Paris, Lyon, 1999, Saluggia, Italy, 1999, Performance Festival, Odense, Denmark, 1999, 2001, Bassano del Grappa, Genoa, Italy, 2000, 2001, 2002, Novarra, Italy, 2002—; performances with, Ghent, Belgium, 2002—; performances with: Castelvetro di Modena, 2003; Argos Festival, 2003; performances with Roncolo, Rome Zamora Spain, Genoa Italy, 2008—09. Recipient Creative Artist Public Svc. award, 1975; Nat. Endowment for Arts fellow, 1975, 79, 80, 85-87, 92-94, Choreographic fellow N.Y. Found. for Arts, 1989. Mem.: Internat. Assn. Healthcare Practitioners, Internat. Somatic Movement Edn. and Therapy Assn. (registered), Body-Mind Centering Assn. (cert. practitioner and tchr.). Buddhist.

NEVILLE, THOMAS LEE, food service company executive; b. Columbus, Ind., Jan. 1, 1947; s. Frank Thomas and Esquline Coons (Davis) N.; m. Shavona Rose Lagneau, Aug. 10, 1966; children: Timothy David, Sherry Lynn. AAS, Austin Peay State U., Clarksville, Tenn., 1994. Cert. exec. chef; cert. food exec. Enlisted U.S. Army, 1966, apptd. WO1, 1976, commd. CW3, 1986; food advisor Army Food Rsch., Devel. and Engring. Ctr., Natick, Mass.; ret. U.S. Army, 1990; gen. mgr. KCA Corp., Hopkinsville, Ky., 1990—. Mem. Warrant Officers Assn., 1976-90. Mem. Ret. Officers Assn., Am. Soc. Quality Control, Am. Culinary Fedn., Am. Mgmt. Assn., Internat. Food Svc. Execs. Assn., Masons. Home: 1728 Clara Ct Clarksville TN 37040-7823 Office: KCA Corp PO Box 641 Hopkinsville KY 42241-0641 Business E-Mail: tneville@kcacorp.com.

NEVIN, CROCKER, investment banker; b. Tulsa, Mar. 14, 1923; s. Ethelbert Paul and Jennie Crocker (Fassett) N.; m. Mary Elizabeth Sherwin, Apr. 24, 1952 (div. 1984); children: Anne, Paul, Elizabeth, Crocker; m. Marilyn Elizabeth English, Nov. 3, 1984; 1 child, Jennie Fassett. Grad. with high honors, St. Paul's Sch., 1942; AB with high honors, Princeton U., 1946. With Vick Chem. Co., 1949-50, John Roberts Powers Cosmetic Co., 1950-52; with Marine Midland Grace Trust Co. of N.Y., 1952—, exec. v.p., 1964-66, pres., 1966-70, chmn. bd., chief exec. officer, 1968-73; also dir.; vice chmn. bd. Evans Products Co., NYC, 1974-76, Drexel Burnam Lambert Co., investment bankers, NYC, 1976-88; chmn. bd., chief exec. officer CF & I Steel Corp., Pueblo, Colo., 1985-93. Dir. Magnatck, Inc. Chmn. exec. com. ACCION Internat. Lt. (j.g.) AC USN, 1942-46. Mem. Riverside Yacht Club, N.Y. Yacht Club (N.Y.C.), Blind Brook Club. Home: 20 Hope Farm Rd Greenwich CT 06830 Home Phone: 203-869-3787.

NEVIN, PHILLIP, retired professional baseball player; b. Fullerton, Calif., Jan. 19, 1971; First baseman San Diego Padres, 1999—2005, Anaheim Angles, 1998—99, Detroit Tigers, 1995—97, Houston Astros, 1995—95, Tex. Rangers, 2005—06, Chgo. Cubs, 2006, Minn. Twins, 2006; ret., 2007.

NEVINS, ARTHUR GERARD, JR., lawyer; b. Bklyn., Dec. 23, 1948; s. Arthur Gerard Sr. and Gertrude Anna May (Schlueter) N.; m. Reine T. Hughes, June 26, 1982; m. Amanda Mitchell, May 16, 1989. BS, Cornell U., 1971; JD, Fordham U., 1974. Bar: N.Y. 1975, N.J. 1976. Assoc. Lester, Schwab, Katz & Dwer, NYC, 1975-77, Law Offices of Peter De Blasio, NYC, 1977-80, Law Offices of Robert Ginsberg, NYC, 1980-82; pvt. practice NYC, 1982—. Mem. ABA, N.Y. State Bar Assn., N.J. Bar Assn., N.Y. County Bar Assn., Hudson County Bar Assn., Phi Gamma Delta. Roman Catholic. Home: 41 Charlestown Rd Hampton NJ 08827-2781 Office: Plz 78 56 State Rt 173 W Hampton NJ 08827 also: 225 Broadway Ste 3111 New York NY 10007-3001 Home Phone: 908-730-6984; Office Phone: 212-406-2062, 908-713-6666.

NEVINS, JOHN JOSEPH, bishop emeritus; b. New Rochelle, NY, Jan. 19, 1932; Student, Iona Coll., NYC, Cath. U. Washington; MA, Tulane U., 1969. Ordained priest Archdiocese of Miami, Fla., 1959, aux. bishop, 1979—84; ordained bishop, 1979; first bishop Diocese of Venice, 1984—2007, bishop emeritus, 2007—. Roman Catholic. Office: 1000 Pinebrook Rd PO Box 2006 Venice FL 34292 Office Phone: 941-484-9543. Office Fax: 941-486-4761. E-mail: mcgrath@dioceseofvenice.org.

NEVINS, MARYBETH ELEANOR, anthropologist, educator; PhD, U. Va., Charlottesville, 2005. Asst. prof. San Diego State U., 2005—07, Anthropology, U. Nev. Rebi, Reno, 2007—. Contbr. articles to profl. jours. Office: Anthropology Dept UNR 1664 N Va MS0096 Reno NV 89557-0096

NEVINS, SHEILA, television producer; b. NYC; d. Benjamin and Stella Nevins; m. Sidney Koch, 1972; 1 child, David Andrew. BA, Barnard Coll.; MFA, Yale U. TV prodr. Great Am. Dream Machine, NET, 1971-73, The Reasoner Report, ABC, 1973, Feeling Good, Children's TV Workshop, 1975-76, Who's Who, CBS, 1977-78; dir. documentary & family programming HBO, NYC, 1978-82, v.p. documentary programming, 1986-95, sr. v.p. original programming, 1998-99, exec. v.p. original programming, 1999—2003, pres. documentary & family programming, 2004—. Bd. dirs. Film Forum, Creative Capital, Ind. Feature Project. Prodr.: Gang War: Bangin' in Little Rock, 1994, Taxicab Confessions, 1995, The Celluloid Closet, 1995, Going, Going, Almost Gone! Animals in Danger, 1995, One Survivor Remembers, 1995, 5 American Kids - 5 American Handguns, 1995, How Do You Spell God?, 1996, Without Pity: A Film About Abilities, 1996, Smoke Alarm, 1996, Paradise Lost, 1996, Kids of Survival, 1996, Heart of a Child, 1997, Wonderland, 1997, Mumia Abu-Jamal: A Case for Reasonable Doubt?, 1997, Little Dieter Needs to Fly, 1997, 4 Little Girls, 1997, Talked to Death, 1997, Thug Life in DC, 1998, Kids are Punny, 1998, Lenny Bruce: Swear to Tell the Truth, 1998, Dead Blue: Surviving Depression, 1998, King Gimp, 1999, Goodnight Moon & Other Sleepytime Tales, 1999, American Hollow, 1999, Cancer: Evolution to Revolution, 1999, Punitive Damage, 1999, Through a Blue Lens, 1999, Half Past Autumn: The Life & Works of Gordon Parks, 2000, Children in War, 2000, Paradise Lost 2, 2000, Bach in Auschwitz, 2000, Legacy, 2000, Dwarfs: Not a Fairy Tale, 2001, Living Dolls: The Making of a Child Beauty Queen, 2001, Through a Child's Eyes: September 11, 2001, Journeys with George, 2002, In Memoriam: New York City, 2002, Amandla!, 2002, Sister Helen, 2002, Secret Lives: Hidden Children & Their Rescuers During WWII, 2002, Telling Nicholas, 2002, Born Rich, 2003, Unchained Memories: Readings from the Slave Narratives, 2003, America Undercover, 2003, Death in Gaza, 2004, Last Letters Home, 2004, Happy to be Nappy & Other Stories of Me, 2004, Elaine Stritch at Liberty, 2004, I Have Tourrette's But Tourette's Doesn't Have Me, 2005, Classical Baby, 2005, Baghdad ER, 2006, All Aboard! Rosie's Family Cruise, 2006, When the Levees Broke: A Requiem in Four Acts, 2006, Friends of God, 2007. Bd. dirs. Women's Action Alliance. Recipient Peabody award, 1986, 1992, 1995, 1996, 1997, 1999, 2000, 2003, 2004, Glaad Media award, 1989, Acad. Award for Documentary, 1993, 1996, 1998, 1999, 2000, 2001, 2003, Emmy award, 1994, 3 Emmy awards, 1995, Emmy award, 1996, 1998, 1999, 2003, 2002, 2 Emmy awards, 1997, 2000, 2004, 2005, 2006, Media award, Mental Health Assn. NYC, 1996, Personal Peabody award, 1999, NATAS Silver Cir., 2000, Wellness Cmty. award, 2001, Humanitarian award, Nat. Bd. Rev., 2002, Lucy award, Women in Film, 2003, Three Arts award, Lifetime Achievement award, News & Documentary Emmy Awards, 2005, Alfred I. DuPont-Columbia U. award, 2007; named Woman of Achievement, YMCA, 1991; named one of The Top 25 Women in TV, Emmy mag., 1996, The Top 25 Smartest Women Am., Mirabella Mag., 1999, The Top 50 Women in TV, Hollywood Reporter Mag., 2005, The 100 Most Powerful Women in Entertainment, Hollywood Reporter, 2006, 2007, The 50 Most Powerful Women in NYC, NY Post, 2008; named to Broadcasting & Cable Hall of Fame, 2000. Mem.: Internt. Documentary Assn. (Vision award 1998), NY Women in Film (Muse award 1998), Writers Guild Am.*

NEVINS, TRACY ANNE, elementary school educator; d. Janet V. Sinusas; m. John J. Nevins, Sept. 7, 1991; children: Emily R., Laura R. BA cum laude, CUNY, NYC, 1992, MS magna cum laude in Edn., 1995. Cert. tchr. N.Y., 1994, perminent 6-8 English extention N.Y., 1995, profl. educator Conn., 2003, lic. tchr. highly qualified K-5 elem. Conn., 2006, tchr. highly qualified 6-12 sci. Conn., 2006. Tchr. mid. sch. St. Anselm's Sch., Bronx, NY, 1992—94; tchr. Elizabeth Blackwell Mid. Sch., South Ozone Park, NY, 1993—96, Schaghticoke Mid. Sch., New Milford, Conn., 1996—. Mem. bldg. com. H.S. New Milford (Conn.) Pub. Schs., 1997—98; team leader Schaghticoke Mid. Sch., 1999—2000, head tchr. summer sch., 1998—99. Contbr. chapters to books. Vol. Rep. Party, New Milford, 2004. Scholar, Local 721 Unionf Licensed Practical Nurses, 1987, Regents Com. N.Y. State, 1987. Master: Kappa Delta Pi (life; pres. 1990—91); mem.: Conn. Educator Assn. (licentiate), Conn. Sci. Educator Assn. (assoc.), Elem. Sci. Assn. (life), Golden Key Honor Soc. (life). Republican. Roman Catholic. Achievements include Nomination for Teacher of the Year 2004. Avocations: reading, gardening, crafts, bargain hunting, flying. Business E-Mail: nevinst@new-milford.k12.ct.us.

NEVLING, HARRY REED, human resources consultant; b. Rochester, Minn., Sept. 15, 1946; s. Edwin Reid and Ruth Margaret (Mulvihill) N.; m. Joanne Carol Meyer, Nov. 26, 1976; 1 son, Terry John. AA, Rochester C.C., 1973; BA cum laude, U. Winona, 1974; MBA, U. Colo., 1990. Cert. sr. profl. life designation Human Resources Cert. Inst., lic. real estate broker. Pers. rep. Rochester Meth. Hosp., 1974-75; dist. mgr. Internat. Dairy Queen Corp., 1975-76; with David Realty Corp., Littleton, Colo., 1976, v.p., 1979-83, gen. mgr., 1981-83, Longmont United Hosp., Colo., 1977-99, pers. dir., 1977-87, dir. human resources, 1988-95, v.p. human resources, 1995-99; prin. HR Cons., Rochester, Minn., 2000—. Cons. Front Range C.C. Denver, 1983-85; prin. Harry R. Nevling-Broker, 1983-85, 95-97; v.p. Realty Mart Internat., Inc., 1985-93, Dist. chmn. Am. party, 1973-74, St. Vrain Valley Sch. Dist., Health Occupations Adv. Com. 1977-99, chmn. 1979-85, Vocat. Edn. Adv. Coun. 1986-91, pres. 1986-91; with Citizen Amb. People to People Program, Hungary, Czech Republic, Germany, 1991; exec. com. Nat. Health Care Skills Stds. Project, 1993-95; spkr., presenter in field. Co-author: Healthcare Reform: The Human Resources Cornerstone to Successful Reform, 1992. Capt. US Army, 1965—72, Vietnam. Decorated D.F.C., 1969, Bronze Star with oakleaf cluster, 1969, Air medal (22, valor device), 1969; recipient Rescue citation for lifesaving Boeing Co., 1969, Helping Hand award United Way, 1974, Outstanding Svc. award, 1979, cert. of appreciation, 1982, Disting. Young Alumni award Winona State U., 1989. Mem. VFW (past post comdr.), Longmont Area Human Resources Assn., 1980-89, Boulder Area Human Resource Assn., 1978-00, Mountain States VHA (pers. com. 1989-96, chmn. 1989-93), Colo. Healthcare Assn. Human Resources Mgmt. (hon. life, sec. 1980, pres. elect 1981, pres. 1981-82, exec. com. 1986-00), Am. Soc. for Healthcare Human Resources Adminstrn. (hon. life, ann. meeting chmn. 1985-86, regional dir. 1986-90, legis. and labor liaison 1988-90, chpt. rels. com. 1990-91, pres. elect 1991-92, exec. com. 1991-95, pres. 1992-93, bylaws com. 1992-93, 96-99, chmn. nominating com. 1994-95, chmn. conflict of interest com., 1994-95, immediate past pres. 1994-95, nat. nominating com. 1996, Disting. Svc. award 1996), Soc. Human Resource Mgmt., Human Resource Cert. Inst. (life, sr. profl. in human resources), Vietnam Helicopter Pilots Assn., Bus. Dependent Care Assn. (pres. 1996, chmn. 1997-98), Region 10 Stakeholders (leader brain injury com. 2003—06, mem. steering com. 2005-, Rochester area brain injury cmty. com. 2002—, co-chair 2005-06, chair, 2006—07), Region 10 Quality Assurance Commn.(VOICE rev. quality assurance team mem. 2003—, mentor 2004—, adv. coun. 2004-, treas. 2006—07, chair pers. com. 2006-08, vice chair 2008-, abilities unltd. program com. 2003—), Olmsted County Social Svcs. Adv. Bd., 2007-(co chair 2009). Avocations: woodworking, furniture refinishing, ceramics. Home and Office: 1916 Century Hills Dr NE Rochester MN 55906-7623

NEVOLA, ROGER, lawyer; b. NYC, Apr. 30, 1947; m. Molly Cagle; children: Adrienne L., Jake F. Student, U. Notre Dame, 1964-66; BSME, Stanford U., 1968; JD, U. Tex., 1974. Bar: Tex. 1974. Assoc. Vinson & Elkins, Houston, 1974-79, Austin, 1979-81, ptnr., 1981-95; pvt. practice Austin, 1995—. Fellow Tex. Bar Found. (life). Home: 4304 Bennedict Ln Austin TX 78746-1940 Office: 1723 Palma Plz PO Box 2103 Austin TX 78768-2103 Office Phone: 512-499-0500. E-mail: roger@nevola.com.

NEW, ANTONIA S., psychiatrist, educator; b. NYC, Feb. 3, 1961; d. Bertrand Latimer and Maria Iandolo New; m. Benjamin C. Zipursky, Aug. 14, 1983; children: Emma Rose New Zipursky, Rebecca Latimer New Zipursky, Gillian Dorie New Zipursky. BA, Swarthmore Coll., Pa., 1982; MD, Cornell U., NYC, 1989. Cert. Am. Bd. Psychiatry and Neurology, 1994. Assoc. prof. psychiatry Mt. Sinai Sch. Medicine, NYC, 1995—. Achievements include research in neurobiology of borderline personality disorder. Office: James J Peters VA Med Ctr 130 West Kingsbridge Rd Bronx NY 10468 Business E-Mail: antonia.new@mssm.edu.

NEW, MARIA IANDOLO, pediatrician, educator; b. NYC; d. Loris J. and Esther B. (Giglio) Iandolo; m. Bertrand L. New, 1949 (dec. 1990); children: Erica, Daniel, Antonia. BA, Cornell U., 1950; MD, U. Pa., 1954; degree in medicine (hon.), U. degli Studi di Roma, Rome, 1999, U. di Parma, Italy, 2000. Diplomate Am. Bd. Pediat. Med. intern Bellevue Hosp., NYC, 1954-55; resident in pediat. N.Y. Hosp., 1955-57; fellow NIH, 1957-58, 61-64; practice medicine specializing in pediat. NYC, 1955—; mem. staff N.Y. Hosp., dir. Pediatric Endocrine and Metabolism Clinic, 1964—2004, attending pediatrician, 1971-80; pediatrician-in-chief N.Y.-Presbyn. Hosp., 1980—2002, dir. pediatric endocrinology, 1964—2004; prof. pediat. and human genetics Mt. Sinai Sch. Medicine, NYC. Asst. prof. dept. pediat. Joan and Sanford Weill Med. Coll. of Cornell U., N.Y.C., 1963-68, assoc. prof., 1968-71, prof., 1971-2004, Harold and Percy Uris prof. pediatric endocrinology, 1978-2004, prof., 1980-2004, chmn. dept. pediat., 1980-2002; program dir. Childrens Clin. Rsch. Ctr., 1996-2002; assoc. dir. Pediatric Clin. Rsch. Ctr., 1980-88; adj. faculty prof. Rockefeller U., 1981—; career scientist N.Y.C. Health Rsch. Coun., 1966-75; adj. attending pedatrician dept. pediat. Meml. Sloan-Kettering Cancer Ctr., 1979-93; cons. United Hosp., Port Chester, N.Y., 1977—, North Shore Univ. Hosp., 1982-97, dept. pediat. Cath. Med. Ctr. Bklyn. and Queens, N.Y., 1987—; vis. physician Rockefeller U. Hosp., N.Y.C., 1973-87; mem. endocrine study sect. NIH, 1977-80, Gen. Clin. Rsch. Ctrs. Adv. Com.; chmn. Divsn. Rsch. Resources Gen. Clin. Rsch. Ctrs. Com. NIH, 1987-88; bd. dirs. Robert Wood Johnson Clin. Scholars Program; mem. N.Y. State Gov.'s Task Force on Life and Law, 1985-2008; mem. NIH Reviewers Res.; mem. FDA endocrinology and metabolism drug adv. com., 1994—; panelist ACGME bd. appeals, 1994—; cons. Meml. Sloan-Kettering Cancer Ctr., 1993-2007, Meml. Hosp. for the Cancer and Allied Diseases, 1993—; hon. mem. pediat. dept. Blythedale Children's Hosp., Valhalla, N.Y., 1992—; mem. rsch. adv. com. Population Coun. Ctr. for Biomed. Rsch., 1991-97. Editor-in-chief Jour. Clin. Endocrinology and Metabolism, 1994-99; mem. editl. adv. coun. Jour. Endocrinological Investigation, 1995—; mem. editl. bd. Jour. Women's Health, 1993, Endotext; corr. editor Jour. Steroid Biochemistry, 1985; mem. adv. bd. pediatric anns., assoc. editor Metabolism. Trustee Irma T. Hirschl Trust. Recipient Mary Jane Kugel award Juvenile Diabetes Found., 1977, Katharine D. McCormick Disting. Lectureship, 1981, Robert H. Williams Disting. Leadership award, 1988, Albion O. Bernstein award Med. Soc. State N.Y., 1988, medal N.Y. Acad. Medicine, 1991, Disting. Grad. award U. Pa. Sch. Medicine, 1991, Optimate Recognition award Assn. Student-Profl. Italian-Ams., 1991, Outstanding Woman Scientist award N.Y. chpt. Am. Women in Sci., 1986, Maurice R. Greenberg Disting. Svc. award, 1994, Humanitarian award Juvenile Diabetes Found., 1994, Rhône Poulenc Rorer Clin. Investigator Lecture award, 1994, Dale medal Brit. Endocrine Soc., 1996, MERIT award USPHS, NIHCHD, 1998, 11th Ann. award for excellence in clin. rsch. USPHS, NIH, 1998; grantee; named to Hall of Honor, NICHD, 2003. Fellow AAAS, Italian Soc. Endocrinology (hon.); mem. NAS (sr. mem. Inst. Medicine), AAAS, APHA, Am. Soc. Human Genetics, Am. Acad. Pediat., Soc. for Pediatric Rsch., Harvey Soc., Endocrine Soc. (mem. coun. 1981-84, pres. 1991-92, Fred Conrad Koch award 2003), Lawson Wilkins Pediatric Endocrine Soc. (pres. 1985-86), Am. Soc. Nephrology, Am. Soc. Pediatric Nephrology, Am. Pediatric Soc., Am. Fedn. Clin. Rsch., Am. Diabetes Assn., European Soc. Pediatric Endocrinology, Soc. for the Advancement of Women's Health Rsch. (basic sci. award 1996), Am. Coll. Clin. Pharmacology, Am. Clin. and Climatol. Assn., N.Y. Acad. Scis., Pan Am. Med. Assn., Assn. Am. Physicians, Am. Fertility Soc., U.S. Pharmacopeial Conv. (elected), Am. Acad. of Arts and Scis. (elected 1992), Alpha Omega Alpha. Office: Mt Sinai Sch Medicine Box 1198 1 Gustave L Levy Pl New York NY 10029 Office Phone: 212-241-7847. E-mail: maria.new@mssm.edu.

NEW, MELVYN, retired literature and language professor; b. NYC, Oct. 8, 1938; s. Leonard and Evelyn New; m. Edith Joan Cockrell, June 19, 1959; children: David Matthew, Carl Samuel. PhD, Vanderbilt U., Nashville, 1966. Prof. English U.Fla., Gainesville, 1966—2008. Editor: The Florida Edition of the Works of Laurence Sterne. Lt. USN, 1959—61, Norfolk, Va. Rsch. fellowship, NEH, 1973—74, 1980—81, 1995—96. Home: 5400 Nw 14th Avenue Gainesville FL 32605 Business E-Mail: mnew@ufl.edu.

NEW, ROSETTA HOLBROCK, retired secondary school educator, retired department chairman, retired nutrition consultant; b. Aug. 26, 1921; d. Edward F. and Mabel (Kohler) Holbrock; m. John Lorton New, Sept. 3, 1943; 1 child, John Lorton Jr. BS, Miami U., Oxford, Ohio, 1943; MA, U. No. Colo., 1971; PhD, Ohio State U., 1974; student, Kantcentrum, Brugge, Belgium, 1992, Lesage Sch. Embroidery, Paris, 1995, Kent State U., 1998. Cert. tchr. Colo. Tchr. English and sci. Monahans (Tex.) H.S., 1943—44; emergency war food asst. USDA, College Station, Tex., 1945—46; dept. chmn. home econs., adult edn. Hamilton (Ohio) Pub. Schs., 1946—47; tchr., dept. chmn. home econs. East H.S., Denver, 1948—59, Thomas Jefferson H.S., Denver, 1959—83; ret., 1983. Exec. bd. Denver Pub. Schs.; lectr. in field; exec. dir. Ctr. Nutrition Info. U.S. Office Edn. Grantee, Ohio State U., 1971—73. Mem.: Internat. Platform Assn., Fairfield (Ohio) Hist. Soc., Ohio State Home Econs. Alumni Assn., Ohio State U. Assn., Hamilton Hist. Soc., Am. Vocat. Assn., Am. Home Econs. Assn., Nat. Trust for Hist. Preservation, Cin. Art Mus., Internat. Old Lacers, Embroiders Guild Am., Rep. Club Denver, Order White Shrine of Jerusalem, Daus. of the Nile, Masons, Order of Ea. Star, Phi Upsilon Omicron. Presbyterian.

NEWBERG, JOSEPH H., lawyer; b. Middletown, Conn., 1947; s. Mendel and Annette N.; m. Alice V. Melnikoff, 1973; children: Mark, Emily. BA, U. Mich., 1969; JD, Harvard U., 1972; LLM in Taxation,

Boston U., 1976. Bar: Mass. 1972, US Tax Ct. 1975. Assoc. Sullivan & Worcester, Boston, 1972-80, ptnr., 1980; stockholder Hutchins, Wheeler & Dittmar, Boston, 1997—2002; ptnr. Weil, Gotshal & Manges LLP, Boston, 2002—. Lectr. grad. tax prog. Boston U, 1982-84, adj. asst. prof. Bentley Grad. Tax Prog., Waltham, Mass., 1985-86, spkr. in field. Contbr. articles to profl. jour. Chmn. Planning Bd. of Town of Belmont. Mem. ABA, Boston Bar Assn. (past co-chmn. internat. tax com.). Office: Weil Gotshal & Manges LLP 100 Federal St Fl 34 Boston MA 02110 Office Phone: 617-772-8350, 617-772-8333. Business E-Mail: joseph.newberg@weil.com.

NEWBERN, WILLIAM DAVID, retired state supreme court justice; b. Oklahoma City, May 28, 1937; s. Charles Banks and Mary Frances (Harding) N.; m. Barbara Lee Rigsby, Aug. 19, 1961 (div. 1968); 1 child, Laura Harding; m. Carolyn Lewis, July 30, 1970; 1 child, Alistair Elizabeth. BA, U. Ark., 1959, JD, 1961; LL.M., George Washington U., 1963; MA, Tufts U., 1967. Bar: Ark. 1961, U.S. Dist. Ct. (we. dist.) Ark. 1961, U.S. Supreme Ct. 1968, U.S. Ct. Appeals (8th cir.) 1983, diplomat Fletcher Sch. Law. Commd. 1st lt. advanced to maj. U.S. Army JAGC, 1961-70; Prof. law U. Ark., Fayetteville, 1970-84; adminstr. Ozark Folk Ctr., Mountain View, Ark., 1973; judge Ark. Ct. Appeals, Little Rock, 1979-80; assoc. justice Ark. Supreme Ct., Little Rock, 1985-99; commr. Ark. Pub. Svc. Commn., 2008. Mem. faculty sr. appellate judges seminar NYU, 1987-91; panel chmn. com. on profl. conduct Ark. Supreme Ct., 2001—05. Editor Ark. Law Rev., 1961; author: Arkansas Civil Practice and Procedure, 1985, (with John J. Watkins) 4th edit., 2006. Mem. Fayetteville Bd. Adjustment, 1972-79; bd. dirs. Decision Point, Inc., Springdale, Ark., 1980-85, Hot Springs Music Festival, 2000—03, Little Rock Wind Symphony, 1993-2001, pres. 1993-95. Named a Disting. Alumnus, Fulbright Coll. Arts and Scis., U. Ark., 2004. Fellow Ark. Bar Found.; mem. Ark. Bar Assn., Am. Judicature Soc. (bd. dirs. 1985-89), Inst. Jud. Adminstrn., Ark. IOLTA Found. (bd. dirs. 1985-87). Democrat. Avocations: string band-guitar, mandolin, banjo and brass quintet-tuba. Personal E-mail: wdnewben@sbcglobal.net.

NEWBERRY, EDWARD J., lawyer; b. Schenectady, NY, Sept. 25, 1962; BA, BS, George Mason U., 1984; JD, Georgetown U., 1989. Staff mem. to Rep. Frank Wolf US House Reps., Washington; staff mem. US House Appropriations Com., Washington, 1984—91; ptnr., Public Policy, Mcpl. Representation, dep. mng. ptnr., mem. exec. and mgmt. com. Patton Boggs LLP, Washington, 1991—, acting COO, 2009—. Office: Patton Boggs LLP 2550 M St NW Washington DC 20037-1350 Office Phone: 202-457-5285. Office Fax: 202-457-6315. Business E-Mail: enewberry@pattonboggs.com.*

NEWBERRY, ELIZABETH CARTER, greenhouse and floral company owner; b. Blackwell, Tex., Nov. 25, 1921; m. Weldon Omar Newberry, Sept. 24, 1950 (dec. Nov. 1984); 1 child. Student Hardin Simmons U., 1938-39. Office mgr. F. W. Woolworth, Abilene, Tex., 1939-50; acct. Western Devel. & Investment Corp., Englewood, Colo., 1968-72; owner, operator Newberry Bros. Greenhouse and Florist, Denver, 1972—; bd. dirs. Western Devel. and Investment Corp. Englewood, Colo., 1979-87. Pres. Ellsworth Elem. Sch. PTA, Denver, 1961-62; v.p. Hill Jr. High Sch. PTA, Denver. Home: 201 Monroe St Denver CO 80206-5505 Office Phone: 303-322-0443.

NEWBERRY, JIM, Mayor, Lexington, Kentucky; m. Cheryl Ann Newberry, 1979; children: Drew, Will. Co-founder, atty. Newberry, Hargrove and Rambicure, 1990; former ptnr. Wyatt, Tarrant and Combs; former v.p., gen. mgr. Airdrie Stud, Ky.; former exec. officer agr., econ. develop., health care Office Lt. Gov., Ky.; acting sec. Natural Resources and Environ. Protection Cabinet, Ky.; mayor City of Lexington, Ky., 2007—. Former v.p. Health Ky., Bluegrass Cmty. Found.; former chmn. Bus. Com. for Character Coun. of Ctrl. Ky. Named Lexington's Outstanding Young Leader, 1992. Democrat. Baptist. Office: 200 E Main St 12th Fl Lexington KY 40507 Office Phone: 859-258-3100. Fax: 859-258-3194. E-mail: mayor@lfucg.com.

NEWBERRY, STEPHEN G., semiconductor equipment company executive; BS, USNA, Annapolis, 1975; MBA, Harvard Univ. Mgmt. positions through group v.p. global ops. & planning Applied Materials Inc., 1980—97; exec. v.p., COO Lam Rsch. Corp., Fremont, Calif., 1997—98, pres., COO, 1998—2005, pres., CEO, 2005—. Bd. dir. Nextest Systems Corp., Semiconductor Equip. & Materials Internat. Office: Lam Rsch Corp 4650 Cushing Pkwy Fremont CA 94538

NEWBORG, GERALD GORDON, retired state archives administrator; b. Ada, Minn., Dec. 13, 1942; s. George Harold and Olea (Halstad) N.; m. Jean Annette Gruhl, Aug. 14, 1964; children: Erica, Annette. BA, Concordia Coll., Moorhead, Minn., 1964; MA, U. N.D., 1969; MBA, Ohio State U., 1978. Cert. archivist. Tutor, preceptor Parsons Coll., Fairfield, Iowa, 1964-67; state archivist Ohio Hist. Soc., Columbus, 1968-76; v.p. Archival Systems Inc., Columbus, 1978-81; state archivist State Hist. Soc. of N.D., Bismarck, 1981—2007, archivist emeritus, 2007—. Instr. Franklin U., Columbus, 1974; adj. prof. Bismarck State Coll., 1985-86. Co-author: North Dakota: A Pictorial History, 1988. Recipient Resolution of Commendation Ohio Ho. of Reps., Columbus, 1976; Governor's award. Mem. Acad. Cert. Archivists Home: 1327 N 18th St Bismarck ND 58501-2827 Office: State Hist Soc 612 E Boulevard Ave Bismarck ND 58505-0660

NEWBORN, JUD, anthropologist, writer, curator, educator, historian; b. NYC, Nov. 8, 1952; s. Solomon and Rita Newborn. BA magna cum laude in Anthropology and English, NYU, 1974; postgrad., Clare Hall, Cambridge U., 1974-75; MA in Anthropology, U. Chgo., 1977, PhD with distinction, 1994. Free-lance writer, NYC, Munich, Chgo., 1974—; publicist Oxford U. Press, NYC, 1975-76; founding historian, co-creator Mus. Jewish Heritage (N.Y. Holocaust Meml. Commn.), NYC, 1986-92, 96-00. Spl. cons. Cinema Arts Ctr., 1986—2005; cons., spkr., lectr. in field; cons. Holocaust Resource Ctr. CUNY, Queensborough; consulting curator Cinema Arts Centre, LI, 2005—, fundraiser, 2005. Author: Shattering the German Night: The Story of the White Rose Anti-Nazi Resistance, 1986, Herder Verlag, 2002, Sophie Scholl and the White Rose, 2006; contbg. editor Diplomatic World Obs., UN, 1999-00; freelance writer, lyricist. Fulbright fellow, 1980-82; Newcombe fellow, 1984-85. Mem. ASCAP, Am. Anthrop. Assn., Am. Hist. Assn., Authors Guild, Assn. Holocaust Orgns., N.Y. Old Growth Forest Assn. (bd. mem.), Nat. Arts Club (hon. mem.), Phi Beta Kappa.

NEWBROUGH, WARREN WADE, farmer; b. Smithville, Mo., Nov. 5, 1962; s. Carl Louis and Opaldene Newbrough; m. Melody JoAnne Reed, Nov. 21, 1982; children: Zakkarya David, Gwynivere Luthien. BAE, Miss. U., Columbia, 1998; MA student in Ancient and Classical History, APU, West Va., 2007—. Cert. in mid. and secondary edn. Mo. Cook Audrain Med. Ctr., Mex. City, Mo., 1986—93; family farmer Labor Omnia Vincet, Newbrough Farms, Mo., 1972—. Contbr. articles to profl. jours. Inf. USMC, 1981—85, Camp Pendleton. Home: 1861 Cr 1270 Huntsville MO 65259

NEWBRUN, ERNEST, oral biology and periodontology educator; b. Vienna, Dec. 1, 1932; came to U.S., 1955; s. Victor and Elizabeth (Reichl) N; m. Eva Miriam, June 17, 1956; children: Deborah Anne, Daniel Eric, Karen Ruth. BDS, Sydney U., Australia, 1954; MS, U. Rochester, 1957; DMD, U. Ala., 1959; PhD, U. Calif., San Francisco, 1965; Odont. Dr. (hon.), U. Lund, Sweden, 1988; DDSc (hon.), U. Sydney, 1997. Cert. periodontology, 1983; hon. diplomate, Am. Bd. Dental Pub. Health, 2009. Rsch. assoc. Eastman Dental Ctr., Rochester, NY, 1955-57, U. Ala. Med. Ctr., Birmingham, 1957-59; rsch. fellow Inst. Dental Rsch., Sydney, 1960-61; rsch. tchr. trainee U. Calif., San Francisco, 1961-63, postdoctoral fellow, 1963-65, assoc. prof., 1965-70, prof. oral biology, 1970-83, prof. oral biology and periodontology, 1983-94, prof. emeritus, 1994—; prof. Fromm Inst. Lifelong Learning U. San Francisco, 2000—. Cons. FDA, 1983—. Author: Cariology, 1989, Pharmacology and Therapeutics for Dentistry, 2004, (with others) Pediatrics, 1991; editor: Fluorides and Dental Caries, 1986; mem. editl. bd. Jour. Periodontal Rsch., 1985-90, Jour. Periodontology, 1990-2005. Bd. dirs. Raoul Wallenberg Dem. Club, San Francisco, 1987-92. Fellow AAAS (chmn. dental section, 1988-89), Internat. Assn. Dental Rsch. (pres. 1989-90) Jewish. Avocations: gardening, hiking, skiing, opera, theater. Office Phone: 415-476-1004. Personal E-mail: enewbrun@gmail.com.

NEWBURG, DAVID STEPHEN, biochemist; b. Boston, Apr. 2, 1948; s. Harry I. and Miriam (Freeman) N.; m. Kathryn J. Woolley, June 2, 1972; children: Seth O., Adrianne R., Deborah S. BS in Chemistry, U. Mass., 1970; PhD in Biochemistry, Boston U., 1976. Rsch. asst. Boston U., 1971-73, rsch. assoc., 1973-76; asst. prof. U. Ky., Lexington, 1976-82, assoc. prof., 1982-86; rsch. fellow Harvard Med. Sch., Boston, 1988-91, instr., 1991—; asst. biochemist Mass. Gen. Hosp., Boston, 1988—; assoc. biochemist Shriver Ctr. for Mental Retardation, Waltham, Mass., 1986-92, sr. biochemist, 1992—. Contbr. articles to profl. jours. Grantee Nat. Inst. Child Health, 1987—, U.S.-Israel Bi-National Sci. Found., 1990—. Mem. AAAS, Am. Chem. Soc., Am. Inst. Nutrition, Internat. Soc. for Rsch. Human Milk and Lactation, Soc. for Complex Carbohydrates, Am. Soc. for Neurochemistry, N.Y. Acad. Scis. Avocations: running, rowing, caving, reading. Home: 15 Harrington St Newtonville MA 02460-1525 Office: Shriver Ctr for Mental Reta 200 Trapelo Rd Waltham MA 02452-6332

NEWBURGER, BETH WEINSTEIN, communications executive; b. Schenectady, July 8, 1937; d. H. Edward and Shirley (Diamond) Weinstein; m. Alan C. Newburger, Jan. 23, 1963 (dec. Oct. 1980); children: Mark, Lori, Eric, Jill; m. Richard Schwartz, May 26, 1989. BA, Cornell U., 1959. Dir. advt. New Republic, Washington, 1974-77; mktg. mgr. Washington Post, 1977-84; pres., Owlcat/Digital Rsch., Inc., Monterey, Calif., 1984-86; pres., CEO Corabi Internat. Telemetrics, Inc., Alexandria, Va., 1986-95; assoc. adminstr. Gen. Svcs. Adminstrn., Washington, 1996—2001; dir. comm. Nat. Trust for Hist. Preservation, 2001—04; pres., CEO Epoch Comm. LLC, 2004—. Chmn. bd. Health Street, Inc., Bethesda, Md., 1985—95; mem. NASA adv. coun. Tech. Commercialization Adv. Com., 1995—98; co-chmn. President's Comm. on Celebration of Women in Am. History, 1998—2000; commr., exec. dir. Women's Progress Commemorative Commn., 2000—01; bd. dirs. Nat. Women's History Project, 2000—02; adv. bd. Eleanor Roosevelt Papers, 2000—; bd. dirs. Nat. Women's Hall of Fame, 2001—04; trustee Jewish Women's Archives, 2002—. Chmn. bd. Capital Children's Mus., Washington, 1994—98, trustee, 1984—2005; trustee, exec. com. Nat. Childrens Mus., 2005—; bd. dirs. Arena Stage, Washington, 1993—, BOAT/U.S., 1990—, Tysons Nat. Bank, 1989—94. Named Woman of Yr., Svc. Guild, Washington, 1972, 73. Mem. Women in Advt. and Mktg. (bd. dirs. 1986-89). Home: 1401 N Oak St Arlington VA 22209-3648 Business E-Mail: beth@epoch1.net.

NEWBURGER, HOWARD MARTIN, psychoanalyst; b. NYC, May 16, 1924; s. Bernhard and Bertha (Travers) N.; m. Doris Schekter, July 3, 1949; children: Amy, Barry, Cary. BA, NYU, 1948, MA, 1950, PhD, 1952; tng. in Jungian, Neo-Freudian and Horneyian psychoanalysis. Cert. in group psychotherapy and psychodrama. Rotating intern N.J. Dept. Instns. and Agys., 1948-49; chief psychologist N.J. State Instn., Annandale, 1949-52; dir. psychoanalysis Div. Social Def. UN, 1952; pvt. practice in psychoanalysis and group psychotherapy, 1952—; dir. rsch. HEW, 1958; rsch. assoc. Beth Israel Hosp., 1958-69. Staff mem. St. Agnes Hosp., White Plains, 1991-93; lectr., adj. assoc. prof. NYU, 1951-60, chmn. dept. exceptional child and youth, 1954-62; chmn. faculty and supr. treatment Inst. Applied Human Dynamics, 1960-99; prelect prof. psychology John Jay Coll. Criminal Justice, 1969-72; chmn. bd. dirs. Inst. Applied Human Dynamics, N.Y.C. and Westchester, N.Y., 1960-81, exec. v.p., 1983-85; dean faculty IAHD, 1999-2002; forensic examiner N.Y.S. Supreme Ct., 2005-06; lectr., cons. in field. Co-author: Winners and Losers. Assoc. editor: Excerpta Medica, 1951-62. Contbr. articles and papers to tech. jours. Trustee Acad. Jewish Religion, 1991-96. Served with AUS, World War II, ETO; with AUS, MTO. Recipient Outstanding Service to Humanity award Inst. Applied Human Dynamics for Handicapped, 1970 Mem. Am. Psychol. Assn., Am. Soc. Group Psychotherapy and Psychodrama (sec.-treas. 1954-55). Office: 4 Timber Trl Rye NY 10580-1935 Office Phone: 914-967-4011. Business E-Mail: howardornew@optonline.net. *Our country affords tremendous opportunity. Through the development of our inner resources, and their assertion, we can all have happy and effective lives.*

NEWBURGER, JANE WIMPFHEIMER, pediatric cardiologist; b. NYC, 1949; AB summa cum laude, Bryn Mawr Coll., Pa., 1971; MD, Harvard U. Med. Sch., Boston, 1974; MPH, Harvard U. Sch. Pub. Health, 1980. Cert. Nat. Bd. Med. Examiners, 1975, Am. Bd. Pediat., 1979, in pediatric cardiology 1983, lic. Mass., 1979, registered in controlled substance US, 2002, Mass., 2003. Internship in medicine Children's Hosp. Med. Ctr., Boston, 1974—75, jr. asst. residency in medicine, 1975—76, fellowship in cardiology, 1976—79, attending physician, cardiology svc., 1979—, asst. in cardiology, 1979—80, assoc. in cardiology, 1980—90, sr. assoc. cardiology, 1990—, assoc. cardiologist-in-chief, dept. cardiology, 1995—2006, assoc. chief academic affairs, dept. cardiology, 2006—; clin. fellowship in pediat. Harvard U. Med. Sch., 1974—79, instr. pediat., 1979—84, asst. prof. pediat., assoc. prof. pediat., 1989—98, prof. pediat., 1998—. Dir. Friday cardiology clinic Children's Hosp. Med. Ctr., 1979—88, dir. preventive cardiology clinic, 1987—, dir. outpatient cardiology, 1990—94, assoc. dir. tng. program in pediatric cardiology and cardiovascular rsch., 1990—, dir. clin. rsch. svc., dept. cardiology, 1993—, mem. numerous adminstrv. and academic committees and boards, 1985—, Harvard U. Med. Sch., 1997—. Co-editor: Brain Injury and Pediatric Cardiac Surgery, 1995; ad hoc reviewer: New Eng. Jour. Medicine, Jour. Pediat., Pediat., Am. Jour. Cardiology, Jour. Thoracic and Cardiovascular Surgery, assoc. editor, ad hoc reviewer: Circulation, 2004—, mem. editl. bd.: Harvard Heart Letter, 1992—, theheart.org, 2000—, Cardiology in the Young, 2006—; contbr. articles to numerous profl. med. jours., chapters to books. Active on various committees Nat. Heart, Lung and Blood Inst. Recipient Scholastic Achievement award, Am. Women's Med. Assn., 1974, Nat. Rsch. Svc. award, Nat. Heart, Lung and Blood Inst., 1978—80, New Investigator award, 1982—85, Spirit award, Children's Hosp., 1991; named to Best Doctor's in America, 1992—, Best Doctor's in Boston, Boston Mag., 1997, 2003, Best Doctor's in Women's Health, 2001, America's Top Doctor's, Castle Connolly, 2002—, Boston Area's Top Doctors, Boston Consumer Checkbook, 2004—; grantee, NIH. Fellow: Am. Coll. Cardiology (program com., pediatric chair 1997—, pediatric cardiology fellowship subcom. 1997—, writing com., Bethesda conf. 2004—05, Disting. Scientist award, clin. 2007), Am. Heart Assn. (com. on tng. in pediatric cardiology 1993—95, membership com., Coun. on Cardiovascular Disease in the Young 1993—95, exec. com., Coun. on Cardiovascular Disease in the Young 1993—, rheumatic fever, endocarditis, Kawasaki disease com. 1994—97, assoc. chair, com. on RF, endocarditis, KD 1999, chair, com. on RF, ednocarditis, KD 2000—04, mem. writing group 2004—05, chair, comm. com., Quality of Care and Outcomes IWG 2004—), Am. Acad. Pediat. (exec. com., cardiology sect. 1999—, chair nominations com., pediatric cardiology sect. 2005—); mem.: Mass. Med. Soc., Soc. Pediatric Rsch. Office: Children's Hosp Boston Dept Cardiology 300 Longwood Ave Boston MA 02115 Office Phone: 617-355-5427. Office Fax: 617-739-3784. Business E-Mail: jane.newburger@cardio.chboston.org.

NEWBURGER, PETER E., hematologist, oncologist; b. NYC, May 10, 1949; s. Robert Anton and Rhoda Newburger; m. Jane Wimpfheimer, May 31, 1970; children: Margot, Daniel. BA, Haverford Coll., Pa., 1970; MD, Harvard Med. Sch., Boston, 1974. Intern, resident Children's Hosp., Boston, 1974—76; fellow, pediat. hematology, oncology Children's Hosp. & Sidney Farber Cancer Inst., Boston, 1976—79; dir., pediat. hematology-oncology U. Mass. Meml. Med. Ctr., Worcester, 1981—; instr. asst. prof. Harvard Med. Sch., Children's Hosp., Farber Cancer Inst.; asst. prof. to prof. U. Mass. Med. Sch., 1981—2003, Ali and John Pierce prof. pediat. hematology-oncology, 2003—. Med. dir. Caitlin Raymond Internat. Registry, Worcester, 1986—; editl. bd. Blood, 1988—92; sect. editor, hematology-oncology Current Opinion in Pediat., 1995—2006, editl. bd., 2006—; assoc. editor Pediat. Blood and Cancer, 2004—; editl. bd. Am. Jour. Hematology, 2006—; co-dir. Severe Chronic Neutropenia Internat. Registry, 2008—. Contbr. scientific papers. Recipient Established Investigator award, Am. Heart Assn., 1983—88; grants, NIH, 1981—. Mem.: Am. Bd. Pediat., Am. Soc. Hematology, Am. Soc. Pediat. Hematology Oncology, Soc. Pediat. Rsch., Am. Soc. Clin. Investigation, Am. Pediat. Soc. Achievements include research in biochemistry and molecular biology of phagocytes; genetics and treatment of chronic granulomatous disease; molecular biology of selenium incorporation into proteins. Office: Univ Mass Med Sch 55 Lake Ave N Worcester MA 01655 Office Phone: 508-856-4225. Business E-Mail: peter.newburger@umassmed.edu.

NEWBY, EARL FERNANDO, education educator; b. Louisville, Apr. 14, 1948; BS, Tenn. State U., 1970; MA, U. Louisville, 1972; EdD, Spalding U., 1998; MA, Vanderbilt U., 2002. Cons., tchr. edn. Ky. Dept. Edn., Frankfort, 1970; tchr., prin. Jefferson County Schs., Louisville, 1971-75, Greater Clark County Schs., Jeffersonville, Ind., 1975-98; cons., computer tech. Newby & Assocs., Louisville, 1996—; asst. prof. Morehead (Ky.) State U., 1998—. Adj. prof. Western Ky. U., Bowling Green, 1998; prof. Eastern Ky. U., 1999-2004; assoc. prof. Austin Peay State U., Clarksville, Tenn., 2004-2006; apptd. to serve on many scholastic audit sch. rev. teams, 2002—; presenter So. Regional Coun. Ednl. Adminstrs., 2004, NCPEA, Lexington, Ky., Washington, 2006, Chgo., 2007, SRCEA, Atlanta, 2005, Jacksonville, Fla., 2006, Kans., Md., 2007, NAESP, Washington, 2005, SanAntonio, Tex., 2006, AASA, Dallas, 2005, Arlington, Va., 2006, New Orleans, La., 2007, Internat. Conf. Profs. of Black Sch. Educators, 2004, Am. Assn. Sch. Adminstrs. Nat. Conf. (presentation and session convener), 2005, Nat. Conf., Nat. Coun. Profs. Ednl. Adminstrn., 2004, assoc. editor, 2009; asst. editor Internation Jour. Orgnl. Innovation, 2009. Author: Leadership Perspectives, 2004; contbr. articles to profl. publs. Named to Order Ky. Cols. Mem. Am. Assn. Sch. Adminstrs. (presenter confs.), NAESP (presenter ann. internat. conf. San Diego, Calif. 2001), So. Regional Coun. Ednl. Adminstrs., Nat. Coun. Profs. Ednl. Adminstrn. (presenter nat. conf. Houston 2001, Sedona, Ariz. 2003), Nat. Assn. Black Sch. Educators, Ky. Assn. Sch. Adminstrs., Ky. Assn. Black Sch. Educators, Lexington Assn. Black Sch. Educators, Kappa Alpha Psi, Phi Delta Kappa, Pi Lambda Theta (presenter profl. assn. in edn. ann. conf. Mpls. 2001), Sigma Rho Sigma. Democrat. Methodist. Avocations: tennis, basketball, reading, bowling, golf. Home: PO Box 211 Harrods Creek KY 40027-0211 Office: Austin Peay State U Educational Leadership programs Coll Liberal Arts and Education Petersburg VA 23806 also: Va State Univ Coll Liberal Arts and Edn Petersburg VA Fax: 804-524-5757. Personal E-mail: newbyez@gmail.com.

NEWBY, JOHN ROBERT, retired metallurgical engineer; b. Kansas City, Mo., Nov. 17, 1923; s. Merritt Owen and Gladys Mary (McCleery) N.; m. Audry Marie Loniker, Sept. 21, 1963 (div. 1980); children: Deborah A., Walter J., William F., Matthew O., Robert J. BA, U. Mo., Kansas City, 1947; BS in Metall. Engring., Colo. Sch. Mines, 1949; MS, U. Cin., 1963. Cert. profl. engr. Chemist Bar Rusto Plating Corp., Kansas City, 1949; supr. United Chromium, Ferndale, Mich., 1949-52; prin. rsch. metallurgist Armco Inc., Middletown, Ohio, 1952-85; prin. John Newby Cons., Middletown, 1985—2009; mem. The Edison Materials Tech. Ctr., Dayton, Ohio, 2001—. Cons. Phoenix Cons., Inc., Cin., 1988—. Author, editor: Formability 2000, 1982, Metallic Materials, 1978, Sheet Metal Forming, 1976; editor: Mechanical Testing, Vol. 8, 9th edit., 1985. Scoutmaster Boy Scouts Am., Middletown, 1952-86, now asst. dist. commr.; chmn. Safety Coun., Middletown, 1978-80. Staff sgt. USAF, 1943-46, PTO. Fellow ASTM (chmn. 1963—, chmn. E-28 com. on mech. testing 1998-2002, Award of Merit 1984), ASM (sustaining mem., chpt. chmn. 1970, Award of Merit 1980); mem. SAE (sect. chmn. 1984). Democrat. Achievements include patent for high strength formable steel sheet; development of interstitial free steel, strain analysis process for metallic sheet formability. Home and Office: 100 Marymont Ct Middletown OH 45042-3735

NEWBY, MICHAEL R., lawyer; b. Richmond, Va. BA, Randolph-Macon Coll., Ashland, Va., 1993; JD, U. Richmond, Va., 2002. CPCU Am. Inst. Property Casualty Underwriters, 1997, assoc. in risk mgmt. Ins. Inst. Am., 1997; bar: Va. 2002, DC 2006. Assoc. Hancock, Daniel, Johnson & Nagle, P.C., Glen Allen, Va., 2003—. Dir. West Jaycees Found., Glen Allen, Va., 2006. Mem.: Va. Bar Assn., Soc. Chartered Property Casualty Underwriters, Am. Health Lawyers Assn. Office: Hancock Daniel Johnson & Nagle PC 4701 Cox Rd Ste 400 Glen Allen VA 23060 Business E-Mail: mnewby@hdjn.com.

NEWBY, PAUL MARTIN, state supreme court justice; b. Asheboro, NC, May 5, 1955; s. Samuel O. and Ruth (Parks) Newby; m. Macon Tucker, Apr. 16, 1983. BA in Pub. Policy studies, magna cum laude, Duke U., Durham, NC, 1977; JD, U. NC, Chapel Hill, 1980. Bar: NC 1980, US Dist. Ct. (we. dist.) NC 1981, US Dist. Ct. (mid. dist.) NC 1983, US Dist. Ct. (ea. dist.) NC 1985, US Ct. Appeals (4th cir.) 1986. Rsch. & tchr. asst. U. NC Sch. Law, 1979—80; assoc. Van Winkle, Buck, Wall, Starnes & Davis, Asheville, NC, 1980-84; v.p., gen. counsel Cannon Mills Realty & Devel. Corp., Kannapolis, NC, 1984-85; asst. atty. (ea. dist.) N.C. US Dept. Justice, Raleigh, 1985—2004, chief fin. litigation (ea. dist.) N.C., 1994—99; assoc. justice Supreme Ct. NC,

Raleigh, 2004—. Chmn. bd. dirs. Pregnancy Life Care Ctr., Raleigh, 1986. Mem.: NC Bar Assn., Christian Legal Soc. Avocation: tennis. Office: NC Supreme Ct PO Box 1841 Raleigh NC 27602*

NEWCOM, JENNINGS JAY, lawyer, director; b. St. Joseph, Mo., Oct. 18, 1941; s. Arden Henderson and Loyal Beatrice (Winans) N.; m. Cherry Ann Phelps, Apr. 4, 1964; children: Shandra Karine, J. Derek Arden. BA, Graceland U., Lamoni, Iowa, 1964; JD, Harvard U., 1968; LLD (hon.), Graceland U., 1999. Bar: Ill. 1968, Calif. 1973, Mo. 1979, Kans. 1981, Colo. 1999. Atty. McDermott, Will & Emery, Chgo., 1968-73; ptnr. Rifkind, Sterling & Lockwood, Beverly Hills, Calif., 1973-79, Shook, Hardy & Bacon L.L.P., Kansas City, Mo., 1979-99, Davis, Graham & Stubbs, LLP, Denver, 1999—; gen. counsel Lovell Minnick Ptnrs. LLC, LA, 1999—; dir. Skillpath Seminars, Overland Park, Kans.; bd. dirs. Atlantic Asset Mgmt. LLC, Berkeley Capital Mgmt., LLC, ClariVest Asset Mgmt. LLC, Mercer Advisors Inc. Trustee Hubbard Found., Linde Found., Graceland U. Mem. Denver Bar Assn., State Bar Assn. Calif. Office: Davis Graham & Stubbs LLP 1550 17th St Ste 500 Denver CO 80202-1500 Office Phone: 303-892-7318. Business E-Mail: j.newcom@dgslaw.com.

NEWCOMB, ELDON HENRY, retired botany educator; b. Columbia, Mo., Jan. 19, 1919; s. Ernest Henry and Ruby Josephine (Anderson) N.; m. Joyce Bright Rieling, June 21, 1949; children: Norman Robert, Barbara Pauline, Cynthia Irma. Student, U. Kansas City, 1936-38; AB, U. Mo., 1940, A.M., 1942; PhD, U. Wis., 1949; DS honoris causa, U. Mo., Columbia, 1993. Asst. prof. botany U. Wis.-Madison, 1949-54, assoc. prof., 1954-58, prof., 1958-90, prof. emeritus, 1990—; dir. Inst. Plant Devel., 1979-88; chmn. dept. botany U. Wis.-Madison, 1982-88, Folke Skoog prof. botany, 1987—90; ret., 1990. Cons. Shell Devel. Co., 1954-59; mem. expdn. to Great Barrier Reef, 1973. Sr. author: Plants in Perspective, 1963; mng. editor Protoplasma, 1969-73; mem. editorial bd. Ann. Rev. Plant Physiology, 1965-69, Protoplasma, 1973-99, Planta, 1981-90; contbr. articles to profl. jours. Served with AUS, 1942-45. NRC predoctoral fellow U. Wis., 1946-49; Guggenheim Found. fellow U. Calif. at Berkeley, 1951-52; Sci. Faculty fellow Harvard, 1963-64; Fulbright Sr. Research scholar Australian Nat. U., Canberra, 1976 Mem. NAS, Am. Soc. Cell Biologists, Am. Acad. Arts and Scis., Bot. Soc. Am., Am. Soc. Plant Physiologists, Soc. Devel. Biology, Phi Beta Kappa (pres. Wis. Alpha chpt. 1978-79), Sigma Xi. Home: 52 Oak Creek Trl Madison WI 53717-1510 Home Phone: 608-833-9526. Personal E-mail: enewcomb@wisc.edu.

NEWCOMB, HELENE E., retired research scientist; b. NYC; d. Otto Wilhelm Post and Hella (Drexler) Walburga; m. Frederick J Newcomb, Aug. 15, 1953; children: J Mark, Paula Marie. Author: (books of poetry) Echoes in the Wind, 2002, On the Wings of Thought, 2002, (best poems and poets) Internat. Libr. Poetry, 2003. Mil. case worker ARC Mountain Valley Chpt., Provo, Utah, 1978—; Telecare ARC Mountain Valley Chpt., 1980—. With US Army, 1951—53. Recipient Vol. of Yr. award, ARC, 1981, Roberta Drissler Disting. Svc. award, 1986, Mil. Social Svc. Caseworker award, Clara Barton award, 1999, Portrait of Character award, Farm Bur. Mut. Ins. Co., Editors Choice awards, 2000, Merit Silver award Bowl, Internat. Soc. of Poets, 2002, Editors Choice awards, 2003, Silver cup, Internat. Soc. Poets, 2003, Silver Bowl and Medalian award, 2004, Editors Choice award, 2006, Pres.'s Vol. Svc. award, 2007, Vol. Svc. award, Utah Lt. Gov. Gary R. Herbert, 2008. Mem. Lds Ch. Avocations: stamp collecting/philately, crocheting. Home: 942 N 800 E Genola UT 84655

NEWCOMB, ROBERT WAYNE, electrical engineer educator; b. Glendale, Calif., June 27, 1933; s. Robert Dobson and Dorothy Opal (Bissinger) Newcomb; m. Sarah Eleanor Fritz, May 22, 1954; children: Gail E., Robert W. BSEE, Purdue U., 1955; MS, Stanford U., 1957; PhD, U. Calif., Berkeley, 1960. Registered profl. engr., Calif. Rsch. intern Stanford Rsch. Inst., Menlo Park, Calif., 1957-60; tchg. assoc. U. Calif., Berkeley, 1957-60; asst. and tenured assoc. prof. Stanford U., 1960—70; prof. elec. engring. U. Md., College Park, 1970—. Bd. dirs. PARCOR Rsch. program, Universidad Politecnica de Madrid, Spain. Author: Linear Multisport Synthesis, 1966, Active Integrated Circuit Synthesis, 1968, Concepts of Linear Systems and Control, 1968, Network Theory, 1967; editor: Neurocomputing Letters, 2002—06. Recipient IEEE CAS Edn. award, 2001; Fulbright fellow, 1963; Fulbright-Hays fellow, 1976; Robert Wayne Newcomb Lab. opened at U. Politecnica Madrid, 1995. Fellow IEEE (life, golden jubilee medal 1999), Am. Inst. Med. and Biol. Engrs.; mem. Soc. Indsl. and Applied Math., Math. Assn. Am., Acad. Am. Poets. Avocations: films, literature, poetry, guitar. Home: 13120 Two Farm Dr Silver Spring MD 20904-3418 Office: U Md Microsystems Lab Elec/Computer Engring College Park MD 20742-0001 Office Phone: 301-405-3662. Business E-Mail: newcomb@eng.umd.edu.

NEWCOMER, JOHN WHITNEY, psychiatrist, researcher, educator; b. Subic Bay Naval Base, Philippines; s. John L. and Barbara L. Newcomer; children: Leah Eliza, Adam Samuel. AB, Brown U., 1981; postgrad., U. Calif., San Francisco, 1984, Yale U., 1984; MD, Wayne State U., 1985. Diplomate Nat. Bd. Med. Examiners, Am. Bd. Psychiatry and Neurology. Intern in internal medicine Sinai Hosp., Detroit, 1985—86; resident in psychiatry Stanford U. Sch. Medicine, Calif., 1986—89, rsch. fellow in psychiatry Dept. Vets. Affairs Med. Ctr. Palo Alto, Calif., 1988—90; instr. dept. psychiatry Washington U. Sch. Medicine, St. Louis, 1990—92, asst. prof. psychiatry, 1992—2000, adj. asst. prof. psychology, 1997—2001, assoc. prof. psychiatry, 2000—, med. dir. Ctr. for Clin. Studies, 2006—; assoc. prof. psychology rsch. Malcolm Bliss Mental Health Ctr., St. Louis, 1990—95, prof. psychology rsch., 2005—08, Gregory B. Couch prof., 2008—; co-dir. Regulatory Support Ctr., Washington U., 2007, dir. clin. trials unit, 2007—. Chmn. drug utilization rev. bd. Mo. Dept. Social Svcs., Divsn. Med. Svc., 1997—; mem. study sect., spl. emphasis panels, ad hoc mem. treatment assessment sect. NIMH, 1998—; rsch. med. safety officer Gen. Clin. Rsch. Ctr., 2001—04; lectr. in field.; mem. med. staff Barnes Hosp., St. Louis, 1990—94, Jewish Hosp., St. Louis, 1990—94, Barnes/Jewish Hosps., St. Louis, 1994—; cons. in field; adhoc reviewer for numerous jours., 1990—; editl. bd. mem. neuropsychopharmacology, 2002—07; editl. bd. mem. Jour. Psychotic Disorders, 2003—, Clin. Schizophrenia & Related Psychoses, 2006—, Current Psychiatry, 2007—09, Obesity Jour., 2007—, Neuropsychiatry Reviews, 2008—, Schizophrenia Bulletin, 2009—. Contbr. numerous articles, abstracts to profl. publs. Recipient Scientist Devel. award, NIMH, 1992—97, Ind. Scientist award, 1997—2002. Mem.: AMA, AAAS, NIMH IRC, IIVA Commn., Am. Diabetes Assn., Am. Coll. Psychiatrists, Internat. Soc. Psychoneuroendocrinology, Soc. for Neurosci., Am. Pschopathol. Assn., Ea. Mo. Psychiat. Soc., Am. Psychiat. Assn., Am. Coll. Neuropsychopharmacology, Alpha Omega Alpha, Sigma Xi, Phi Beta Kappa. Office: Washington U Sch Medicine Dept Psychiatry 660 S Euclid Ave Campus Box 8134 Saint Louis MO 63110 Office Phone: 314-362-5939. E-mail: newcomerj@wustl.edu.

NEWELL, BARBARA ANN, coatings company executive; b. Portland, Oreg., Mar. 20, 1945; d. John Wesley and Marion Josephine (Hill) Clausen; children: Shamaz, Hukam (dec.), Mardana. BA, Lindenwood Coll. for Women, 1968; MA, Portland State U., 1972; PhD, Summit U., 2000. Owner Shamaz Trading Co., Ukiah, Calif., 1974-77; mgr. small bus. dept. Ernst & Ernst, Portland, 1977-78; CFO All Heart Lumber Co., Ukiah, 1978-83; CFO, CEO Performance Coatings Inc., Ukiah, 1983—, chmn. bd. dirs., 1992—. Chmn. bd. dirs. Rural Visions Found.; treas. chmn. fin. com. Mendocino County Health Clinic, chmn. bd. dirs., 2001-03; CEO, chmn. bd. dirs. Dusky Rose & Assoc., Botanics of Calif.; founder Potter Valley Cafe, 2000; owner Hukam Maj Arabian Horse Ranch, 1998—. Founder, chair Penofin Jazz Festival; chmn. bd. dirs. Mendocino Ballet Co.; bd. dirs. Potter Valley Youth and Cmty. Ctr. Mem. Nat. Paint and Coatings Assn., Golden State Paint and Coatings Assn., Ukiah C. of C. (mem. econ. devel. com. 1993-94), Women in Coatings (Leadership award 1994), Leadership Mendocino. Avocations: showing Arabian horses, reading, children, organic gardening, dance. Office: Penofin-Performance Coatings Inc PO Box 1569 Ukiah CA 95482-1569 Home Phone: 707-489-0241; Office Phone: 707-462-3023. Business E-Mail: ceo@penofin.com.

NEWELL, CHARLDEAN, public administration educator; b. Ft. Worth, Oct. 14, 1939; d. Charles Thurlow and Mildred Dean (Looney) Newell. BA, U. North Tex., Denton, 1960, MA, 1962; PhD, U. Tex., 1968; cert., Harvard U., Cambridge, Mass., 1988. Instr. U. North Tex., Denton, 1965-68, asst. prof., 1968-72; assoc. prof., dir. Fedn. North Tex. Area Univs., Denton, Dallas, 1972-74; assoc. prof., assoc. v.p. acad. affairs U. North Tex., Denton, 1974-76, assoc. prof., chair dept. polit. sci., 1976-80, prof. polit. sci., 1980-92, assoc. v.p., spl. asst. to chancellor, 1982-92, regents prof. pub. adminstrn., 1992—2002, prof. emerita, 2002—. Cons. Miss. Bd. Trustees State Instns. Higher Learning, Jackson, 1983—84, Ednl. Testing Svc., Princeton, NJ, 1980, Princeton, 82, Princeton, 85, Spear Down & Judin, Dallas, 1994—95, North Tex. Inst. Edn. Visual Arts, Denton, 1993—94; bd. regents Internat. City/County Mgmt. Assn., Washington, 1994—98, vol. credentialing adv. bd., 2002—; trainer Emerging Leaders Program, 2005—. Author: Essentials of Texas Politics, 2007; co-author (with others): City Executives: Leadership Roles, Work Characteristics and Time Management, 1989, The Effective Local Government Manager, 2004, Texas Politics, 2009; editor: Effective Local Government Management: Cases in Decision Making, 2008; contbr. articles to profl. jours. Chmn. Denton Charter Rev. Com., 1978—79; mem. Denton CSC, 1989—97, chmn., 1992—97; active Denton Blue Ribbon Capital Improvements Com., 1995—96; mem. Denton Devel. Plan Com., 1996—97, Denton Pub. Utilities Bd., 1997—2009, chmn., 2002—09; v.p. Denton Christian Pre-Sch. Bd., 2001—02, pres., 2002—05, mem., 2005—07, City Coun. Ethics Com., 2004; v.p. Our Daily Bread, 2005—08, vice-chair, 2005—06; mem. exec. coun. Episcopal Diocese Dallas, 1985—88. Recipient Elmer Staats Career Pub. Svc. award, Nat. Assn. Sch. Pub. Affairs Adminstrn., 1993. Fellow: Nat. Acad. Pub. Adminstrn.; mem.: Am. Soc. for Pub. Adminstrn. (sect. chmn. 1982—83, mem. editl. bd. 1985—88, Donald C. Stone award 2004), Internat. City/County Mgmt. Assn. (hon.), Pi Alpha Alpha (exec. coun. 1995—99), Pi Sigma Alpha (exec. coun. 1988—92). Democrat. Episcopalian. Avocations: spectator sports, reading. Home: 2008 Tremont Cir Denton TX 76205-7408 Business E-Mail: newellc@verizon.net.

NEWELL, ELIZABETH CAROLYN, retired secondary school educator; b. Georgetown, Ky., Mar. 26, 1940; d. George M. Newell, Sr. and Pearl Carlton Newell. BA in Speech and Drama, Georgetown Coll., 1961; student in Speech, Hist. and Theater, U. Ky., 1963—64; MA magna cum laude in Secondary Guidance and Counseling, Georgetown Coll., 1971. Tchr. Jefferson County Pub. Sch. Sys., 1961—97, ret., 1997, substitute tchr., 1997—; mutuel clk. Keeneland Downs, 2005—; clk. Churchill Downs, 2005—. Coach championship debate club Butler HS, dir. championship drama club, coach championship future problem-solving club. Editor: History of Butler Traditional High School: 50 Years of Excellence, 2004. Co-coord. crisis team JCTA, 1976. Recipient Tchr. Recognition award, Butler H.S., 1968; named Tchr. of Yr., Ky. H.S. Speech League, 1965, Elizabeth C. Newell Day, JC Judge Exec. David Armstrong, 1997; grantee, Capitol Holding, WAVE TV, 1992. Mem.: Svc. Employees Internat. Union, Jefferson County Tchrs. Assn. Retired, Ky. Edn. Assn. Avocations: horses, cats, U.K. ballgames, travel, genealogy. Home: 12001 Running Creek Rd Louisville KY 40243-1932

NEWELL, ERIC JAMES, financial planner, retired insurance company executive; b. Toronto, Ont., Can., Sept. 24, 1930; came to U.S., 1959, naturalized, 1970; s. James and Anne (Brown) N.; m. Essie Miskelly, Sept. 30, 1950; 1 son, Eric Wayne. Student, U. Toronto, 1951-53. Pub. acct. W.J. Wilcox & Co., Toronto, 1949-53; chief acct. Toronto Mut. Life Ins. Co., 1953-57; asst. sec. Holland Life Ins. Co., Toronto, 1957-59; with Penn Mut. Life Ins. Co., Phila., 1959-86, assoc. controller, 1965-70, 2d v.p., controller, 1970-84, v.p., controller, 1984-86, ret., 1986; fin., tax cons., 1986—; dir. Hotel Brunswick, Lancaster, Pa., 1982-85. Mem. Traffic and Transp. Bd., Cherry Hill, N.J., 1971-73, Zoning Bd., 1975-78; vice chmn. Cherry Hill Econ. Devel. Bd., 1973-75; pres. Greater Kingston Civic Assn., Cherry Hill, 1970-76; Democratic committeeman, Camden County, 1976-79; vice chmn. Dem. Party, Cherry Hill, 1976. Fellow Life Mgmt. Inst., Royal Commonwealth Soc.; mem. Fin. Execs. Inst., Am. Inst. Corp. Contrs., N.Y. Ins. Accts. Club (chmn. 1984), Nat. Soc. Tax Profls., Royal Black Knights of Ireland, Loyal Orange Assn. (past master), Scotch-Irish Soc. of U.S. (mem. coun., pres. 1999), Am. Legion, Masons. Presbyterian (deacon 1969-72). Home and Office: 20 Wordsworth Street Galloway NJ 08205

NEWELL, MICHAEL STEPHEN, finance company executive, protective services consultant; b. Denver, Dec. 22, 1949; s. Henry Michael and Marlene (McRae) N.; m. Linda Margaret Wolfe, Sept. 19, 1987 (div.); children: Katherine Margaret, Brittany Nicole; children from previous marriage: Troy, Angela, Michael, Jennifer. Grad., Denver Police Acad., 1972; CO Real Estate Lic., Real Estate Prep., 1977; HHD (hon.), Am. Acad. Inst. Pub. Theology, 1997. Cert. peace officer, Colo. Police officer Denver Police Dept., 1972-79; prin. Michael Newell & Assocs., Denver, 1979-82; sr. account exec. Am. Protection Industries, Los Angeles, 1982-84; chief exec. officer Newco Fin., Huntington Beach, Calif., 1984—; pres., CEO Am. Dream Devel., LLC, 2004. Chmn. The Newco Internat. Group/Newco Fin., Huntington Beach; with VALUES Self Improvement Program, Fountain Valley; bd. dirs. Lifesong Self-Esteem workshops, Huntington Beach.; expert witness stalking crimes and preador control techniques; condr. seminars on stalker suppression, stalking survival, threat mgmt. in the workplace. Author: The Security Manual, 1995, Stalker Suppression, 1996, (novel and screenplay) Balanger, TMC, Stalking Rescue, The Book of F.A.T.E. (From Abuse to Empowerment), (video prodns.) The Personal Protection Technique, 1995, Stalking Survival, 1995; author, facilitator: Your Paradigm Shift, Anger Management, 2000. Founder, bd. dirs. Law Enforcement Support Assn., Denver, 1981; bd. dirs. Axis Intervention and Tng. Inst./Stalking Rescue. With U.S. Army, 1968-71, Viet Nam. Decorated Bronze Star, Viet Svc. medal with clusters; recipient Pres.'s Nat. Patriotism medal Am. Police Hall of Fame, Nat. Assn. Chiefs Police, 1996, Knight Chevalier The Venerable Order of Michael the Archangel, others; named "The Real Life Equalizer", CBS News/48 Hours. Republican. Mem. Religious Sci. Ch. Avocations: music, photography, travel. Office: Internat Risk Cons PO Box 558 Littleton CO 80160-0558 Office Phone: 303-797-2635. Business E-Mail: newcofinancial@msn.com. E-mail: stalkthestalker@msn.com.

NEWELL, MIKE, film director; b. St. Albans, England, Mar. 28, 1942; m. Bernice Stegers; 3 children. Attended, Cambridge U. Films include: The Awakening, 1980, Bad Blood, 1983, Dance With a Stranger, 1985, The Good Father, 1986, Amazing Grace and Chuck, 1987, Soursweet, 1988, Enchanted April, 1991, Into the West, 1992, Four Weddings and a Funeral, 1994, An Awfully Big Adventure, 1995, Donnie Brasco, 1997, Pushing Tin, 1999, Mona Lisa Smile, 2003, Harry Potter and the Goblet of Fire, 2005, Love in the Time of Cholera, 2007; exec. prodr. (films) Photographing Fairies, 1997, 200 Cigarettes, 1999, Best Laid Plans, 1999, High Fidelity, 2000, Traffic, 2000; TV films include: Big Soft Nellie, Mrs. Mouse, Baa Baa Blacksheep, The Melancholy Hussar, Ready When You Are Mr. McGill, Destiny, The Man in the Iron Mask, 1977, The Gift of Friendship, Blood Feud, 1983, Common Ground, 1990; exec. prodr., dir. (TV series) The Branch, 2003, dir. (TV movie) Jo, 2002. Office: Dogstar UK 5 Sherwood St London W1V 7RA England

NEWELL, PAUL HAYNES, JR., engineering educator; b. Nashville, July 1, 1933; s. Paul Haynes Newell; m. Martha A. Newell; children: Paul Haynes III, Mike, Nan. B.M.E., U. Tenn., 1958, M.M.E., 1961; Mech.E., Mass. Inst. Tech., 1964, PhD, 1966. Registered profl. engr., Ala., Tenn., Tex., N.J. Student asst. mech. engring. U. Tenn., 1957, instr. mech. engring., 1958-62; NSF sci. faculty fellow MIT, 1962-65; asso. prof. U. Ala. Coll. Engring., 1966-69; prof. mech. Tex. A&M U., 1969-72, asso. dean engring., 1972, prof., head indsl. engring. dept., 1972-74, prof., head combined programs of behavioral engring., bioengring., cybernetic engring., hygiene and safety engring., indsl. engring., 1972-74; prof. biomed. engring., dept. phys. medicine Baylor Coll. Medicine, 1969-74, prof. biomed. engring., dept. physiology, 1970-74, prof. biomed. engring., dept community medicine, 1972-74, prof. biomed. engring., dept. rehab., 1972—, mem. grad. faculty, 1970-74, prof. Houston, from 1971; pres., prof. Newark Coll. Engring., NJ Inst. Tech., 1974-78; prof. Adminstrn. Prosthetics Ctr., NY, 1973-75, VA Hosp., Houston, 1972-75; pres. Newell Engring., Greenbrier, Tenn., 1979—. Bd. dirs. NJ Bell Tel. Co., Mid Atlantic Nat. Bank, Thomas-Betts Corp. Contbr. articles to profl. jours., chapters to books. Mem. liaison com. NSF, Newark Transp. Coun., N.J. Safety Coun.; sec. exec. com. coun. Boy Scouts Am., Birmingham, Ala., 1966—68; bd. dirs. N.J. State Opera, United Hosps. Newark. With USMCR, Korea. NSF Sci. Faculty fellow. Mem.: NSPE, ASME, AAAS, N.J. Soc. Engrs., Am. Fluid Power Soc., Pres.'s Assn., Soc. Engring. Sci., Soc. Advanced Med. Sys., Internat. Soc. Prosthetics and Orthotics, Inst. Engring. Deans, Biomedical Engring. Soc., Am. Soc. Engring. Edn., Am. Soc. Artificial Internal Organs, Am. Inst. Indsl. Engrs., Am. Heart Assn., Am. Congress Rehab. Medicine, Ala. Acad. Scis., N.Y. Acad. Scis., Am. Soc. Tool and Mfg. Engrs., Rotary, Sigma Xi, Pi Tau Sigma, Phi Kappa Phi, Tau Beta Pi. Home and Office: Newell Engring 1855 Lake Rd Greenbrier TN 37073-4619 Office Phone: 615-859-5873.

NEWELL, RACHEL PIERCE, music educator; b. Salisbury, Md., Nov. 22, 1949; d. Hersie Beale and Ann Howell Pierce; m. Wayne Linwood Newell, June 6, 1992; children: Margaret Davis Sullivan, Mary Darden Lentine. MusB, Westhampton Coll., 1972; MME, Shenandoah U., 1990. Music tchr. Louisa County Pub. Sch., Mineral, Va., 1972—74, Loudoun County Pub. Sch., Leesburg, Va., 1974—76, 1977—79, 1984—; tchr. Dales Sch. Lang., Cambridge, England, 1976—77; choir dir. St. James Episcopal Ch., Leesburg, Va., 1981—84. Mem. adv. coun. Shenandoah U., Leesburg, Va.; Summer in the Arts coord. Loudoun County Pub. Schs. Named Tchr. of Year, Shenandoah U., 1999, Agnes Meyer Tchr. of Year, Washington Post, 2003; Fulbright fellow, Japan, 2003. Mem.: NEA, Va. Edn. Assn., Music Educators Nat. Conf., Va. Music Educators Assn. Episcopalian. Avocations: reading, water sports, music, travel. Home: 101 Liberty St NW Leesburg VA 20176 Office: Loudoun County Pub Sch Hillside Elem Sch 43000 Ellzey Dr Ashburn VA 20148 Office Phone: 571-252-1622. Personal E-mail: rachnewell@aol.com.

NEWELL, SHIRLEY ANN CECIL, retired art dealer, artist; d. Francis M. and Ora A. Cherry, Sr.; m. Richard A. Cecil (div.); children: David B., Valerie A., Vicki E.; m. David B. Newell (div.). Student, U. Tenn., 1958—61, Calif. Luth. Coll., 1970, U. Calif., 1971, Ga. State U., 1977. Pvt. practice art instr., Atlanta, 1970; prin., owner Collectors Art, Atlanta, 1979—85, Cecil B. Day Investment Co., Ga., 1986—95, adminstrv. asst. Ga.; admistrv. asst. Siemens Energy and Automation, 1998—2006. Exhibitions include Oxnard Art Club Festival of Art, Hilton Head Art League, Garden Club of Ga., Habitat Atlanta. Mem. Nat. Mus. Women of the Arts, Washington, Roswell Cultural Arts, Americans for the Arts Action Fund, Washington; charter mem. High Mus. Art, Atlanta; bd. dirs. DeKalb Coun. Arts, 2005—; bd. dirs. Peachtree Arts Atlanta (Ga.) High Mus. Art, 1998—99, sec. suburban art com., 1982—83; mem. individual arts com. coalition Olympics '96, Atlanta, 1996. Recipient award, WSB Radio, Civic Svc. award, Boys Club Am., 1971. Mem.: Barrow County History Mus. (artist 2009—), Roswell Cultured Arts, Nat. Women Arts. Methodist. Avocations: reading, dance, art.

NEWELL, STEPHEN, finance educator, department chairman; BS, Mich. State U., East Lansing, 1985; MBA, Ind. U., Bloomington, 1990; PhD, Fla. State U., Tallahassee, 1993. Sales rep. Lever Bros, Ft. Wayne, Ind., 1985—86; sales rep. sales mgr. Terra Environ., Kalamazoo, 1986—88; asst. to assoc. prof. Bowling Green State U., 1993—2002; assoc. to prof. Western Mich. U., Kalamazoo, 2002—07, prof. and chair, mktg. dept., 2007—. Co-author: (text book) Professional Selling and Sales Management; contbr. articles to profl. jours.

NEWEY, WHITNEY K., economist, educator; b. July 17, 1954; married; 5 children. BA in Econs., Brigham Young Univ., 1978; PhD, MIT, 1983. Asst. prof., econs. Princeton Univ., 1983—88, assoc. prof., 1988—90; tech. staff Bell Comm. Rsch., 1988—90; prof., econs. MIT, 1990—2004, Jane Berkowitz Carlton and Dennis William Carlton prof., 2004—; internat. fellow Univ. Coll. London, 2004—. Grantee Alfred P. Sloan Rsch. Fellowship, 1987—91. Fellow: Am. Acad. Arts & Scis. Office: MIT Dept Economics E52-262D 50 Memorial Dr Cambridge MA 02142-1347 Office Phone: 617-253-6420. Business E-Mail: wnewey@mit.edu.

NEWGARD, CHRISTOPHER B., medical educator; B in Botany and Zoology, Duke U.; PhD, U. Tex., 1984. Prof. dept. biochemistry, dept. internal medicine U. Tex. Southwestern Med. Ctr., Dallas, Gifford O. Touchstone and Randolph G. Touchstone Disting. chair, prof., 1994—2002, co-dir., Touchstone Ctr. for Diabetes Rsch.; dir., Sarah W. Stedman Nutrition and Metabolism Ctr. Duke U. Sch. Medicine, 2002—, W. David and Sarah W. Stedman Disting. Prof., 2002—, prof. pharmacology and cancer biology, 2002—, prof. medicine, 2002—. Contbr. several articles to profl. jours. Trustee Insulin-Free World Fund. Mem.: NIH (mem. metabolism study sect.), Am. Diabetes Assn. (mem. grant rev. bd., Outstanding Sci. Achievement award 2001). Office: Duke

U Med Ctr Duke Independence Park Facility 4321 Medical Park Dr Durham NC 27704 Office Phone: 919-668-6059. Business E-Mail: christopher.newgard@utsouthwestern.edu, newga002@mc.duke.edu.*

NEWHALL, DAVID, III, retired federal official; b. Phila., Dec. 6, 1937; s. David, Jr. and Jane Martyn (Dunn) Newhall. AB in Politics, Princeton U., 1961. Mgr. Bell Tel. Co. of Pa., Norristown, 1961-63; adminstrv. asst. U.S. Rep. R.S. Schweiker, Washington, 1963-69; chief of staff U.S. Senator R.S. Schweiker, Washington, 1969-81, HHS, Washington, 1981-83; pres. Marmion Plantation Co., King George, Va., 1983—85; prin. dep. asst. sec. def.(health affairs) U.S. Dept. Def., Washington, 1985-90, acting asst. sec. def. (health affairs), 1989-90; gen. ptnr. Marmion Partnership Restorations, 1990—. Bd. dirs. Western Healthcare Alliance, Phoenix, 1995—97; chmn. compliance com., lead dir. TrailBlazer Health Enterprises, LLC, Dallas, 1997—2007; outside dir. First Coast Svc. Options, Inc., Jacksonville, 2007—. Mem.: Princeton Tower Club. Republican. Episcopalian. Home and Office: 7382M Marmion Ln King George VA 22485-7300

NEWHALL, JOHN HARRISON, retired business executive, management consultant; b. Phila., Sept. 29, 1933; s. Blackwell and Mary Large (Harrison); m. Jane Carol Ward, July 15, 1961 (dec. Apr. 22, 2008); children: Carol Newhall Neilson, Thomas Blackwell, Daniel Ward. BA, Williams Coll., 1955; MBA, Harvard U., 1960. Product mktg. mgr. Campbell Soup Co., Camden, NJ, 1960—67; product group mgr. Gen. Foods Corp. (now Kraft Corp.), White Plains, NY, 1967—70; dir. corp. planning, gen. mgr. Europe H.J. Heinz Co., Pitts., 1970—77; v.p. mktg. Sunoco Corp., Phila., 1977—81; chmn., CEO Aitkin-Kynett Co. (subs. Foote Cone & Belding), Phila., 1981—84; mng. dir., exec. v.p. Campbell-Ewald Co., NYC, 1984—86; prin. mgmt. cons. SRI Internat., Menlo Park, Calif., 1987—90; mng. dir. Strategic Directions, Narberth, Pa., 1990—99; pres. Advanced Promotion Techs., Deerfield Beach, Fla., 1992—93; CEO The Newcomen Soc. of the U.S., Exton, Pa., 1999—2003; ret., 2003. Mem. devel. coun. Williams Coll., Williamstown, Mass., 1977-87, regional vice chmn. capital campaign, 1991-93; mem. Com. of 70, Phila., 1981-84; bd. dirs. Bryn Mawr (Pa.) Hosp., 1982-88, The Haverford (Pa.) Sch., 1980-86, mem. headmaster selection com., 1992, mem. strategic planning com., 1994; bd. dirs. World Affairs Coun., Phila., 1982-86, Found. for Vascular Hypertension Rsch., Phila., 1982-2001, chmn., 1987; bd. dirs. Jr. Achievement, Phila., 1977-81, vice chmn., 1981; bd. dirs. SE chpt. ARC, Phila., 1981-84; bd. dirs. Pa. Economy League, 1981-84; vestryman, lay reader Episcopal Ch., 1964-70, chmn. ann. campaign, 1992, vice chmn. capital campaign, 1994; mem. bd. overseers Hospitality Hall of Honor, 2000-2003; bd. dirs. M.D.I. Drug and Alcohol Abuse Found., 2005—08. Lt. USN, 1955—58. Recipient Cert. of Merit Chapel of Four Chaplains, 1983, 85, Alumni Svc. award Haverford Sch., 2006. Mem. Assn. Nat. Advertisers (exec. com. 1977-81), Harvard Bus. Sch. Club Phila. (pres. 1994-96, chmn. 1996-98), Merion Cricket Club (Haverford), Gulph Mills (Pa.) Golf Club, Harbor Club (Seal Harbor, Maine), Union League Club Phila. Republican. Episcopalian. Avocations: skiing, gardening, sailing, swimming. Home: 414 Righters Mill Rd Narberth PA 19072-1423 Personal E-mail: jnewhall@verizon.net.

NEWHALL, MARY ANNE, dancer, educator; d. William Ervon and Isabel Santos Newhall; m. James Dale Danneskiold, Oct. 1, 1988; 1 child, Jesse John Bland. BA, U. N.Mex, Albuquerque, 2000, MA, 2002, PhD, 2008. Fellow Corp. Yaddo, 2005; asst. prof. U. N.Mex, Albuquerque, 2006—. Rsch. dir. Am. Dance Legacy Inst., Providence. Author: (book) Mary Wigman; dance performance, Tenant of the Street, Hexentanz; contbr. articles to profl. jours. Recipient Lectr. of Yr., U. N.Mex, 2005, Faculty Acknowledgment award, U. Librs., 2008; grantee, Nat. Endowment Arts, 2007. Home: 1 Jornada Loop Santa Fe NM 87508 Office: Univ NMex I Univ NMex Santa Fe NM 87508 Business E-Mail: marianew@unm.edu.

NEWHARD, JAMES MICHAEL LLOYD, medical educator; b. Pittsfield, Ill., Aug. 17, 1971; s. James Arthur and Amy Lucille Newhard; m. Kate Kenney, June 4, 1994; children: Christopher Dale, Sarah Michelle. BA, U. Mo., Columbia, 1994; MA, U. Cin., 1996, PhD, 2003. Archaeologist Gray & Pape, Inc., Cin., 2001—02; core faculty instr. Loyola Coll., Balt., 2002—03; asst. prof. Coll. Charleston, SC, 2003—, dir., interdisciplinary program in archaeology, 2005—08, chair, dept. classics, 2008—. Author: (book) Midea: The Megaron Complex and Shrine Area; contbr. articles to profl. jours. Geo-Archaeology fellow, Wiener Lab. Archaeological Sci., Am. Sch. Classical Studies, Fulbright-Hayes Rsch. fellowship. Mem.: Archaeological Inst. America (pres., Charleston soc. 2004—06, sec. 2006—08). Office: Coll Charleston 66 George St Charleston SC 29424 Business E-Mail: newhardj@cofc.edu.

NEWHART, BOB (GEORGE ROBERT NEWHART), entertainer; b. Oak Park, Ill., Sept. 5, 1929; m. Virginia Quinn, Jan. 12, 1963; 4 children. BS, Loyola U., Chgo., 1952. Acct. U.S. Gypsum Co.; copywriter Fred Niles Film Co.; star TV variety show Bob Newhart Show, 1961; star TV series The Bob Newhart Show, 1972—78, Newhart, 1982-90, Bob, 1992, George & Leo, 1997. Rec. artist (album) The Button Down Mind of Bob Newhart, 1960, The Button Down Mind Strikes Back, 1961, Behind the Button Down Mind, 1961, The Button Down Mind on TV, 1962, Bob Newhart Faces Bob Newhart, 1964, Windmille Are Weakening, 1965, This Is it, 1967, The Best of Bob Newhart, 1971, Very Funny Bob Newhart, 1973; royal command performance, London, 1964; appeared in films Hell is for Heroes, 1962, Hot Millions, 1968, Catch 22, 1970, On a Clear Day You Can See Forever, 1970, Cold Turkey, 1971, First Family, 1980, Little Miss Marker, 1980, In and Out, 1997, Rudolph the Red-Nosed Reindeer: The Movie (voice), 1998, Legally Blonde 2: Red, White & Blonde, 2003, Elf, 2003; TV films include Thursday's Game, 1974, Marathon, 1980, The Librarian: Quest for the Spear, 2004; TV appearances (1960-) include The Ed Sullivan Show (a.k.a. Toast of the Town, (8 Times), Jack Parr Show, 1960, The Andy Williams Show, 1962, 1964, & 1966, The Dean Martin Show (24 Times), Rowan & Martin's Laugh-In, 1968 & 1969, The Tonight Show Starring Johnny Carson (also guest host), It's Garry Shandling's Show, 1990, Late Night with David Letterman, 1993, Murphy Brown, 1994, The Simpsons (voice), 1996, Mad TV, 2001, ER, 2003, Saturday Night Live (host 1980, 1995), Desperate Housewives, 2005, (PBS) Bob Newhart: Unbuttoned (Honored Am. Master 2005), 2005, and numerous others. Grand marshall Tournament Roses Parade, 1991. With U.S. Army, 1952-54. Recipient Emmy award, 1961, Peabody award, 1961, Sword of Loyola award, 1976, Legend to Legend award, 1993, three Grammy awards 1960, Kennedy Ctr. Mark Twain award, 2002, Icon award, TVLand, 2005; named to TV Acad. of Arts & Sci. Hall of Fame, 1993, Broadcasting Hall of Fame, Nat. Assn. Broadcasters, 2009; honored as an American Master (Bob Newhart: Unbuttoned), PBS, 2005. Best Known Trademarks: Stammering delivery while talking; Telephone monologues as part of act; One-sided conversations. Office: c/o Capell Rudolph 11601 Wilshire Blvd Ste 1840 Los Angeles CA 90025-1759

NEWHAUSER, RICHARD GORDAN, Medieval philology educator; b. Cin., Nov. 24, 1947; s. Irwin Edward and Natalie Claire (Friedman) N.; m. Andrea Ilona Nemeth, July 24, 1975; children: Daniel Jonathan, Simon Samuel. BA, U. Cin., 1970; MA, U. Chgo., 1972; PhD, U. Pa., 1986. Instr. U. Cin., 1971, Rutgers U., Camden, N.J., 1977-79, U. Augsburg (Fed. Republic Germany), 1979-80; teaching fellow U. Pa., Phila., 1976-79; tutor U. Tuebingen (Fed. Republic Germany), 1975-76; faculty assoc. U. Tuebingen, San Antonio, 1980-86; asst. prof. Medieval philology U. Tuebingen (Fed. Republic Germany), 1986-90; assoc. prof. Medieval lit. Trinity U., San Antonio, 1990—. Contbr. essays, articles and revs. to profl. jours.; librettist The Tinderbox (Hans Christian Andersen), 1980. Recipient 3d prize H.C. Andersen Music Competition, 1980; Fulbright fellow, 1973; NEH Summer stipend, 1992. Mem. MLA, Medieval Acad. Am., New Chaucer Soc., Soc. Arthurienne, Wolfram von Eschenbach Gesellschaft. Jewish. Office: Trinity U Dept English 715 Stadium Dr San Antonio TX 78212-3104

NEWHOUSE, ALAN RUSSELL, retired federal official; b. NYC, Feb. 27, 1938; s. Russell Conwell and Clara Lucille (Scovell) N.; m. Margo Stiles Hicks, Feb. 3, 1960; children: Daryl, Jeffrey, William. BEE, Cornell U., 1960. Engr. Bur. of Ships, Washington, 1964-66; nuc. power engr., chief West Milton field office AEC, Schenectady, NY, 1966-69; sr. exec. AEC, ERDA, U.S. Dept. Energy, Washington, 1969-92; dep. asst. sec. Space and Def. Power Systems Office Nuc. Energy, Washington, 1992-93; dir. Office Space and Def. Power Systems, 1993-95; dir. Project Prometheus Office of Exploration, NASA, 2003—04; ind. cons., 1995—. Composer numerous musical works. Mem. Cmty. Orchestra So. Md. in Concert. Lt. USN, 1960-64. Mem.: AIAA, IEEE, Am. Nuc. Soc. Unitarian Universalist. Home and Office: 24670 Greenview Dr Hollywood MD 20636-4823 Business E-Mail: arn6@cornell.edu. E-mail: consultant@arnewhouse.com.

NEWHOUSE, DONALD E., newspaper publishing executive; b. 1930; s. Samuel Irving Newhouse Sr. and Mitzi Epstein; married; 3 children. Student, Syracuse U. With Advance Publs. Inc., Staten Island, NY, 1951—, pres., 1979—; chmn. The Associated Press, NYC, 1997—2002. Treas. Herald Am., Syracuse, 1960—, The Post Standard, Syracuse, 1960—, The Syracuse Herald Jour., 1960—, The Herald Co. Inc., 1960—; co-founder Metro-Suburbia, Inc., NYC, 1963; prin. The Trenton (N.J.) Times, Times of Trenton Pub. Corp.; pres. The Star Ledger, Newark. Named one of Forbes Richest Americans, 1999—, World's Richest People, Forbes Mag., 1999—. Office: Advance Publications Inc 950 Fingerboard Rd Staten Island NY 10305-1453

NEWHOUSE, JEFFREY H., radiologist, educator; b. NY, Dec. 10, 1942; s. Edward and Dorothy DeLay Newhouse; m. Nancy Hargadon, June 4, 1983; children: Amy Lee, Edward Walter. AB, Princeton U., NJ, 1963; MD, Harvard U., Boston, 1967. Diplomate Am. Bd. Radiology, 1972. Intern gen. surgery Roosevelt Hosp., NYC, 1967—68; resident diagnostic radiology Mass. Gen. Hosp., Boston, 1968—72; instr. radiology Med. Sch. Harvard U., Boston, 1974—78, asst. prof. radiology Med. Sch., 1978—83; assoc. prof. radiology Columbia-Presbyn. Med. Ctr. Columbia Coll. Physicians and Surgeons, NYC, 1983—88, chief divsn. abdominal radiology, 1983—; prof. radiology and urology Columbia Coll. Physicians and Surgeons/NY Presbyn. Hosp., 1988—; vice chmn. dept. radiology N.Y. Presbyn. Hosp., 1998—. Disting. scientist Armed Forces Inst. Pathology, Washington, 1996. Co-author: Understanding MRI, Essentials of Uroradiology, Textbook of Uroradiology; editor: Urologic Radiology and General Abdomen, MRI of the Urinary Tract, Clinical MRI, Gamuts in Radiology; contbr. 172 scientific papers. Maj. med. corps. US Army, 1972—74. Recipient Best Sci. Paper award, Soc. Uroradiology, 1981, Gold medal, 2009, Best Sci. Paper award, online jour., 2002, Tchr. of Yr. award, Dept. Urology, Columbia U. Med. Ctr., 2000, Dept. Radiology, Columbia U. Med. Ctr., 2004; scholar, Gen. Motors, 1959—63, James Picker Found., 1969—72. Fellow: Am. Coll. Radiology (chmn. com. appropriateness criteria 2002—05); mem.: Bronxville Field Club, Union Boat Club. Avocations: skiing, tennis, sailing, sculling. Home: 10 Hilltop Road Bronxville NY 10708 Office: Columbia University Medical Center 177 Fort Washington Avenue New York NY 10032 Business E-Mail: jhn2@columbia.edu.

NEWHOUSE, MARK WILLIAM, publishing executive; b. NYC, Oct. 14, 1948; s. Norman Nathan and Alice (Gross) Newhouse; m. Lorry A. Whitehead, June 1, 1974; children: Jesse Louis, Charlotte Ann. BA, Yale U., 1969. V.p., gen. mgr. The Star-Ledger, Newark, 1980—. Bd. dirs. Newspaper Assn. Am., 2005—. Bd. dirs. N.Y.C. Opera, 1992—, pres., 1993—; bd. dirs. Audit Bur. Circulations, 1995—2004, Glimmerglass Opera, 1997—, N.Y.C. Outward Bound Ctr., 2004—. Office: Newark Morning Star Ledger Co One Star Ledger Plz Newark NJ 07102-1200

NEWHOUSE, SAMUEL IRVING, JR., (SI NEWHOUSE JR.), publishing executive; b. NYC, Nov. 8, 1927; s. Samuel Irving Newhouse Sr. and Mitzi Epstein; m. Jane Franke (div.); children: Samuel Irving III, Wynn, Pamela; m. Victoria Carrington Benedict de Ramel. Pub. Vogue mag., 1964; chmn. Condé Nast Publications Inc., NYC, 1975—; chmn., CEO Advance Publications Inc., Staten Island, NY, 1979—. Recipient Henry J. Fisher award, Mag. Pubs. Assn., 1985; named one of Top 200 Collectors, ARTnews Mag., 2004—08, Forbes Richest Americans, 1999—, World's Richest People, Forbes Mag., 1999—. Jewish. Avocation: Collector of Modern and contemporary art. Office: Advance Pubs Inc 950 Fingerboard Rd Staten Island NY 10305-1453

NEWICK, CRAIG DAVID, architect; b. Orange, NJ, Feb. 14, 1960; s. Russel Forester and Helen (Welch) N.; m. Linda Hammer Lindroth, June 6, 1987; 1 child, Zachary Eran. BA in Architecture, Lehigh U., 1982; MArch, Yale U., 1987. Registered architect, Conn. Designer, draftsman The Archtl. Studio, Easton, Pa., 1983-84; job capt., project designer Svigals & Assocs., New Haven, 1985; designer, draftsman Centerbrook (Conn.) Architects, 1986; job capt., project designer Allan Dehar Assocs., Architects & Planners, New Haven, 1988-90; ptnr. Lindroth & Newick, New Haven, 1991—; designer Cesar Pelli & Assocs., Inc., New Haven, 1992; project arch. Tai Soo Kim Ptnrs., Hartford, Conn., 1995—2001; prin. Newick Archs., New Haven, 2001—. Vis. faculty Vis. Critics Studio, Lehigh U., 1993; vis. critic Wesleyan U., 1990-2005, R.I. Sch. Design, 1988, Yale U., 2000-05; faculty Creative Arts Workshop, New Haven, 1991, 92; co-dir. Eyebeam Competition, N.Y.C. Exhibitions include Out Of Bounds; author: Simultaneous Space (first prize artists books, 1994). Recipient 1st place award Am. Visionary Set Design Competition, 1989, 3d place award Astronauts Meml. Design Competition, 1988, ID Mag. Ann. Design Rev. award, 1990, 2d prize African Burial Ground Competition Mcpl. Arts Soc. N.Y., 1994, 1st place drawing award Conn. Soc. Architects, 1997, AIA Conn. honor award, 2000. AIA Conn. Design award, 2005, 07, Nat. AIA Design citation, 2006, AIA Coun. award, 2007; grantee New Eng. Found. for Arts, 1992, NEA Interarts grantee Rockefeller Found., 1989-90, Found. for Contemporary Performance Art, 1989, 90, Humanities Coun. of Fairfield U., 1995; AIA Conn. Designer award, 2006; New Eng. Found. for Arts Regional fellow, 1993, Conn. Commn. on the Arts fellow, 1998, others. Mem. Architecture League N.Y. (young architects forum 1991, emerging voices, 1996). Office: Newick Archs 85 Willow St New Haven CT 06511

NEWKIRK, INGRID, animal rights organization administrator; b. Surrey, Eng., July 11, 1949; m. Steve Newkirk, 1967 (div. 1980). Former animal protection officer and dep. sheriff, Md.; poundmaster Washington, 1978; former chief of animal disease control Commn. on Public Health, Washington; dir. cruelty investigations Washington Humane Soc., Washington, 1978-80; pres., co-founder (with Alex Pacheco) People for the Ethical Treatment of Animals (PETA), Washington, 1980—. Author: Kids Can Save the Animals! 101 Easy Things You Can Do, 1991, The Compassionate Cook: Please Don't Eat the Animals, 1993, 250 Things You Can Do To Make Your Cat Adore You, 1998, You Can Save the Animals: 251 Simple Ways to Stop Thoughtless Cruelty, 1999, Free the Animals: The Amazing True Story of the Animal Liberation Front, 2000, Making Kind Choices: Everyday Ways to Enhance Your Life Through Earth and Animal-Friendly Living, 2005, Let's Have a Dog Party!: 20 Tail-wagging Celebrations to Share With Your Best Friend, 2007, One Can Make a Difference: How Simple Actions Can Change the World, 2008; appeared in (documentaries) I Am an Animal: The Story of Ingrid Newkirk and PETA, 2007 Office: People for the Ethical Treatment of Animals (PETA) 501 Front St Norfolk VA 23510*

NEWKIRK, JOHN BURT, retired metallurgical research administrator; b. Mpls., Mar. 24, 1920; s. Burt Leroy and Mary Louise (Leavenworth) N.; m. Carolyn Mae Jordan, Aug. 4, 1951; children: Jeffrey Burt (dec.), John Jordan, Victoria Louise Lierheimer, Christina Newkirk Seldomridge. B in Metall. Engring., Rensselaer Poly. Inst., 1941; MS, Carnegie Inst. Tech., 1947, ScD, 1950. Metall. investigator Bethlehem Steel Co., Pa., 1941-42; Fulbright postdoctoral fellow Cambridge (Eng.) U., 1950-51; research metallurgist research lab. Gen. Electric Co., Schenectady, 1951-59; prof. Cornell U., 1959-65; Phillipson prof. U. Denver, 1965-74, prof. phys. chemistry, 1975-84, Phillipson prof. emeritus, 1984—; pres. Denver Biomaterials, Inc., 1969-86, Colo. Biomed., Inc., 1987-2000; ret., 2000. Editor Rews. on High Temperature Materials, 1973-78; co-editor: 16 ann. volumes Advances in X-Ray Analysis; contbr. articles profl. jours. Lt. USNR, 1942-46. Fellow Am. Soc. Metals (life); mem. NY Acad. Sci., Kiwanis, Sigma Xi, Tau Beta Pi, Phi Kappa Phi, Alpha Sigma Mu (internat. pres. 1950), Alpha Tau Omega. Republican. Baptist. Personal E-mail: jack@snowvalley.org.

NEWKIRK, THOMAS CHARLES, lawyer; b. NYC, June 6, 1942; s. Rudolph H. and Ruth H. (Wilson) N.; m. Nancy W., Dec. 23, 1965; children: Jennifer L., Christopher T. BA, Cornell U., 1964, LLB with distinction, 1966. Bar: NY 1966, DC 1976, DC Ct. Appeals, 1976, US Ct. Appeals (2d cir.) 1968, US Ct. Appeals (DC cir.) 2008. Assoc. Donovan Leisure Newton & Irvine, NY, 1966-72; asst. chief counsel Securities Industry Study, U.S. Senate, Washington, 1972; assoc. Donovan Leisure Newton & Irvine, Washington, 1973-75; sr. atty. Office of Legal Counsel, Dept. Justice, Washington, 1975-78; asst. gen. counsel US Dept. Energy, Washington, 1978-79, dep. gen. counsel, 1979-85, chief counsel for jud. litigation, 1985; chief litig. counsel SEC, Washington, 1986-93, assoc. dir. div. of enforcement, 1993—2004; ptnr. Jenner & Block LLP, Washington, 2004—. Lectr. in field. Contbr. articles to profl. jours. Recipient Presdl. Meritorious Exec. award Pres. of U.S., 1980, 92, Exceptional Svc. award Sec. of Energy, 1985, Outstanding Svc. medal Sec. of Energy, 1981. Mem. ABA, Assn. Bar City of N.Y. Avocations: skiing, sailing, tennis, opera. Office: Jenner & Block LLP 1099 NY Ave NW Ste 900 Washington DC 20001 Home Phone: 301-320-5007; Office Phone: 202-639-6099. Business E-Mail: tnewkirk@jenner.com.

NEWLAND, CHESTER ALBERT, public administration educator; b. Kansas City, Kans., June 18, 1930; s. Guy Wesley and Mary Virginia (Yoakum) N. BA, U. N. Tex., Denton, 1954; MA, U. Kans., 1955, PhD, 1958. Social Sci. Rsch. Coun. fellow U. Wis. and U.S. Supreme Ct., 1958-59; instr. polit. sci. Idaho State U., Pocatello, 1959-60; mem. faculty U. North Tex., Denton, 1960-66, prof. govt., 1963-66, dir. dept. govt., 1963-66; prof. polit. sci. U. Houston, 1967-68; dir. Lyndon Baines Johnson Libr., Austin, Tex., 1968-70; prof. pub. adminstrn. U. So. Calif., 1966-67, 68-71, 76-82, 84-92, Duggan disting. prof. pub. adminstrn., 1992—; prof. George Mason U., Fairfax, Va., 1982-84. Faculty Fed. Exec. Inst., 1971-76, dir. 1973-76, 80-81; mgr. task force on fed. labor-mgmt. rels. US Pers. Mgmt. Project, Pres.'s Reorgn., Washington, 1977-78. Editor in chief Pub. Adminstrn. Rev., 1984-90; contbr. articles to profl. jours. Chmn. Mcpl. Rsch. Coun., Denton, 1963-64; city councilman, Denton, 1964-66; mem. Pub. Sector Commn. on Productivity and Work Quality, 1974-78; trustee Sacramento (Calif.) Mus. History, Sci. and Tech., 1993-95; mem. UN Devel. Program Kazakhstan, 1997-2000, strategy review program, 2002, Moldova, 1994, Kuwait, 1991, 95-96; cons. Poland, 1990-91, Hungary, 1991, Czech and Slovak Republics, 1992, Bank of Greece, 1999-2002, 04, Taiwan, 2001. Fellow Nat. Acad. Pub. Adminstrn., (trustee 1979-82, nominating com. 2006—07); mem. Southwestern Social Sci. Assn. (chmn. govt. sect. 1964-65), Am. Soc. Pub. Adminstrn. (pres. Dallas-Ft. Worth chpt. 1964-65, nat. coun. 1976, 78-81, editl. bd. jour. 1972-76, chmn. publ. com. 1975-79, program chmn. 1977, nat. pres. 1981-82, Dimock award 1984, Van Riper award 2002, Waldo Lifetime Scholarly Pubs. award 2007), Am. Polit. Sci. Assn., Internat. Pers. Mgmt. Assn. (program chmn. 1978, Stockberger award 1979), Am. Acad. Polit. and Social Sci., Internat. City Mgmt. Assn. (hon., Calif. bd. 2003—, credentialing adv. bd. 2006—), Nat. Assn. Schs Pub. Affairs and Adminstrn. (Staats Pub. Svc. award 1989), Sacramento Charter Review Com. Office: Univ Southern California 1800 I St Sacramento CA 95811-3004

NEWLAND, PAMELA KAY, nursing educator; d. Beverly Kay Garner; m. John Newland. PhD, U. Mo., Columbia, 2006. Cert. MSRN, 2008. Asst. prof. SIUE, Edwardsville, Ill., 2006—. Office: Southern Ill Univ PO Box 1066 Edwardsville IL 62025 Business E-Mail: pnewlan@siue.edu.

NEWLIN, CHARLES FREMONT, lawyer; b. Palestine, Ill., Nov. 18, 1953; s. Charles Norris and Regina Helen (Correll) N.; m. Jean Bolt, Jan. 6, 1975; children: Christian N., Charles W., Ethan A. BA in Polit. Sci. summa cum laude, Ill. Wesleyan U., 1975; JD cum laude, Harvard U., 1978. Bar: Ill. 1978, US Dist. Ct. (no. dist.) Ill. 1978, US Tax Ct. 1980. Law clk. Sugarman, Rogers, Barshak & Cohen, Boston, 1976-78; assoc. Mayer, Brown & Platt, Chgo., 1978-84, ptnr., 1985-94, Sonnenschein, Nath & Rosenthal, 1994—2002, McGuire Woods LLP, 2002—03, Harrison & Held LLP, Chgo. Research asst., Harvard Law Sch., Mass., 1976, adj. prof. law DePaul U., Chgo., 1986-90, adminstr. Wealth Mgmt.(trusts, estates and found. practice area), 1989-1994. Contbg. author: Am. Law of Property, 1975, Trust Adminstrn. Ill., 1983, 87, 92, 99, Bogert on Trusts, 1986-91, The Lawyer's Guide to Retirement, 1991, 94; contbr. articles to profl. jours. Scouting coord. DuPage area coun. Boy Scouts Am., Woodridge, Ill., 1984-86; bishop's counselor Mormon Ch., Woodridge, 1984-86; mem. planned giving com. Ill. divsn. Am. Cancer Soc., 1988—, chair, 1997—; active Boys and Girls Clubs of Chgo., 1993—; mem. bd. dirs. Suburban Chgo. Planned Giving Coun., 1997, Ill. Inst. for Continuing Legal Edn., 1999—, vol. legal cons. The Tower Chorale, Westner Springs, Ill., 1989-91. Listed in Who's Who in Am., Who's Who in Am. Law, Who's Who of Emerging Leaders in Am., Who's Who in Practicing Atty., Internat. Who's Who Profl., named

Leading Ill. Atty., Am. Research Corp., 1997. Fellow Am. Coll. Trust and Estate Counsel; mem. Chgo. Bar Assn., 1982-, Chgo. Estate Planning Coun., Tech. Practice Com., 1991-2000, Elder Law Com., 1995-, Probate Practice Com., U Club Chgo., 1986-1992, Met. Club Chgo., 1994-2000. Democrat. Mem. Lds Ch. Office: Harrison & Held LLP 333 W Wacker Dr Ste 1700 Chicago IL 60606 Office Phone: 312-322-3940. Office Fax: 312-753-6191. Business E-Mail: mnewlin@harrisonheld.com.

NEWLIN, STEPHEN DORE, chemicals executive; b. Pierre, SD, Feb. 8, 1953; s. Douglas M. and Mary Newlin; m. Terry Ochsner, Aug. 17, 1975; children: Grant, Scott. BSCE, S.D. Sch. Mines & Tech., 1975; Advanced Mgmt. Program, Harvard U., 1990. Dist. rep. Nalco Chem. Co., Naperville, Ill., 1976-80, sales rep., 1980-82, dist. mgr. Watergy group, 1982-84, sales mgr. Watergy group, 1984-87, gen. mgr. Watergy group, 1987-90, gen. mgr. Unisolv group, 1990-92, gen. mgr. pulp & paper group, 1992-93, v.p.-pres. Nalco Pacific, 1993-94, pres. Nalco Europe, 1994, pres. specialty divsn., 1996, pres., 1998, COO, vice chmn., 2000; chmn. Nalco Exxon Energy Chemicals, 2000—01; private investor and bus. advisor, 2001—03; pres. indsl. ctr. Ecolab Inc., 2003—06; chmn., pres., CEO PolyOne Corp., Avon Lake, Ohio, 2006—. Bd. dirs. Black Hills Corp., 2004—. With USPHS. Mem. Paper Industry Mgrs., Triangle Alumni Assn. Avocation: sports. Office: PolyOne Corp 33587 Walker Rd Avon Lake OH 44012

NEWMAN, ANDREA FISCHER, air transportation executive; AB, U. Mich., Ann Arbor, 1979; JD, George Washington U., 1983. With Patton, Boggs, Washington; dept. asst. to V.P. George Bush The White House; spl. counsel to asst. sec. def. for acquisitions and logistics Dept. Def.; sr. ptnr Miller, Canfield, Paddock and Stone, Detroit; v.p. state and local affairs NW Airlines Corp., sr. v.p. govt. affairs Detroit, 2001—. Bd. regents U. Mich., Ann Arbor, 1994—; vice chmn. George W. Bush for Pres. Campaign, co-chmn. fin. com. Mich., 2000; bd. dirs. Mich. Econ. Devel. Corp. Found., Mich. Thanskgiving Day Parade Found., Isiah Thomas Found. Mem.: Detroit Econ. Club (v.p.). Office: NW Airlines Detroit Met Airport 2601 WorldGateway Pl Detroit MI 48242 E-mail: afnewman@umich.edu.

NEWMAN, BARBARA MILLER, psychologist, educator; b. Chgo., Sept. 6, 1944; d. Irving George and Florence (Levy) Miller; m. Philip R. Newman, June 12, 1966; children: Samuel Asher, Abraham Levy, Rachel Florence. Student, Bryn Mawr Coll.; AB with honors in Psychology, U. Mich., 1966, PhD in Devel. Psychology, 1971. Undergrad. research asst. in psychology U. Mich., 1963-64, research asst. in psychology, 1964-69, teaching fellow, 1965-71, asst. project dir. Inst. for Social Research, 1971-72, univ. lectr. in psychology and research assoc., 1971-72; asst. prof. psychology Russell Sage Coll., 1972-76, assoc. prof., 1977-78; assoc. prof. and chair dept. family rels. and human devel. Ohio State U., 1978-83, prof. and chair, 1983-86, assoc. provost for faculty recruitment and devel., 1987-92, prof., 1992-2000; prof., chair dept. human devel. and family studies U. R.I., 2000—06, prof., 2006—. Author (with P. Newman): Living: The Process of Adjustment, 1981; author: Development Through Life, 1975, 10th edit., 2009—, Adolescent Development, 1986, When Kids Go to College, 1992, Childhood and Adolescence, 1997; author: (with P. Newman) Understanding Adulthood, 1983; author: (with P. Newman, L. Landry-Meyer and B. Lohman) Life Span Development: A Case Book, 2003; author: (with P. Newman) Theories of Human Development, 2007; contbr. articles to profl. jours. Vis. scholar, UCLA, 2006—07. Mem.: AAAS, APA, Soc. Rsch. in Child Devel., Am. Psychol. Soc., Groves Conf. on Marriage and Family, Soc. for Rsch. on Adolescence. Office: U RI Human Devel and Family Studies Transition Ctr Kingston RI 02881 Home Phone: 401-559-1243; Office Phone: 401-874-7135. Business E-Mail: bnewman@uri.edu.

NEWMAN, BARRY INGALLS, retired bank executive; b. NYC, Mar. 19, 1932; s. M.A. and T.C. (Weitman) N.; m. Jean Short, Mar. 6, 1965; children: Suzanne, Cathy, David. BA, Alfred U., 1952; JD, NYU, 1955. Bar: N.Y. 1957, Ohio 1958, U.S. Supreme Ct. 1967, Calif. 1990; practice in N.Y.C., 1957. Assoc., then ptnr. firm Shapiro Persky Marken & Newman, Cleve., 1957-63; asst. v.p. Meinhard & Co. (now Meinhard Comml. Corp.), NYC, 1963-65; v.p. Amsterdam Overseas Corp., NYC, 1966-68; pres. No. Fin. Corp., LA, 1968-72; sr. v.p. Aetna Bus. Credit, Inc., Hartford, Conn., 1972-78; exec. v.p. Security Pacific Fin. Group, San Diego, 1978-81, chmn., pres., CEO, 1981-82; sr. exec. v.p. Gt. Am. Bank, 1982—88, ret., 1988. Vice chair, San Diego County Capital Asset Leasing Corp., 1984-, chmn. bd. dirs., 1984-2000. Chmn. San Diego County Treasury Oversight com., 1995—; bd. dirs., bd. govs. San Diego Found., 1999—; pres. San Diego County Civil Svc. Commn., 2000—; vice chmn. planning commn. City of Escondido, 2003—; judge pro tem Superior Ct., 2001—; vice chair Ind. Rates Oversight Com., San Diego, 2007—; dep. foreman County Grand Jury, 1999—2000; treas. The Episcopal Diocese of San Diego, 1993—2001; v.p., bd. dirs. Episcopal Diocese San Diego, 2006—, San Diego County Audit Com., 2001—, Justice of Peace State Conn., Conn., 1977—81. Recipient Disting. Svc. award Cleve. Jr. C. of C., 1961; named: Outstanding Young Man of Yr. Mem.: ABA, N.Y. State Bar Assn., Calif. Bar Assn., San Diego Bar Assn., San Diego County Taxpayers Assn. (past pres.), U. Club San Diego (past pres.), Masons, Calif. Ctr. Arts Escondido (bd. past chmn.). Republican. Home: 3308 Avenida Sierra Escondido CA 92029-7937 Home Phone: 760-743-2982; Office Phone: 760-743-5005. Personal E-mail: BNewmanlaw@aol.com.

NEWMAN, BERNIE SUE, social worker, educator; b. East Liverpool, Ohio, Apr. 6, 1953; d. Maurice Jerome and Esther Solomon Newman; life ptnr. Katherine Bezak, May 7, 1982; 1 child, Eric Garvey. BS, U. Pa., Phila., 1974; MSW, Fla. State U., Tallahassee, 1982; PhD, U. Pitts., 1985. Lic. clin. social worker Assn. Bd. Social Workers, 2001. Asst. prof. Temple U., Phila., 1989—92, assoc. prof., 1993—. Asst. prof. Southern Ill. U. Sch. Social Work, Carbondale, Ill., 1986—89; program evaluator Congreso de Latinos Unidos, Phila.; therapist sexual abuse counseling and family edn. treatment program Cath. Social Svcs., Phila., 2000—05; mental health therapist Congreso de Latinos Unidos, Phila., 2009—. Co-chair commn. Lesbian women and gay men Coun. Social Work Edn., Alexandria, Va., 1990—95. Mem.: NASW, Coun. Social Work Edn. Office: Temple Univ Sch Social Work 1301 Cecil B Moore Ave 5th floor Ritter Philadelphia PA 19122 Office Fax: 215-204-9606. Business E-Mail: bnewman@temple.edu.

NEWMAN, BRUCE IRA, marketing professional; b. Chgo., Feb. 12, 1953; s. Samuel and Tillie (Levin) N.; m. Judith Ann Volkman, Aug. 12, 1984. BS, U. Ill., Champaign, 1975; MBA, U. Ill., 1978, PhD, 1981. Teaching asst. U. Ill., Champaign, 1976-80; instr. U. Wis., Milw., 1980-81, asst. prof., 1981-86; assoc. prof. Baruch Coll. CUNY, NYC, 1986-87; vis. prof. Trinity Coll., Dublin, 1987; vis. scholar F.M.D. Research Inst., 1987; assoc. prof. DePaul U., Chgo., 1987—. Cons. C.I.M.A., Milw., 1983-85, Allstate Ins., 1991; guest lectr. Vienna Sch. of Bus., 1986. Author: Do It Yourself Marketing Research, 1985, A Theory of Political Theory, 1987, Consumption Values and Market Choices: Theory and Applications, 1991; editor: Political Marketing: Readings and Annotated Bibliography, 1985; contbr. articles to profl. jours. Am. Mktg. Assn., Am. Psychol. Assn., Am. Assn. for Pub. Opinion Research, Acad. of Mktg. Sci., Decision Sci. Inst., Iota Sigma Epsilon. Avocations: stamp collecting, news watching, camping, internat. travel. Home: 100 Pinyon Ct N Buffalo Grove IL 60089-6323 Office: DePaul U 243 S Wabash Ave Chicago IL 60604-2302

NEWMAN, BRUCE MURRAY, retired antiques gallery owner; b. NYC, Jan. 27, 1930; s. Meyer and Evelyn (Kantor) Newman; m. Judith S Brandus, June 26, 1965; 1 child, Emily Rachel. BA, Pratt Inst., 1953, D (hon.), BFA (hon.), 1998, degree (hon.) in fine arts, 1997. Pres. Newel Art Galleries Inc., NYC, 1975—2001. Lectr mus and univs; mem regional adv bd Chase Manhattan Bank; mem regional adv bd J P Morgan Chase Bank. Author: Fantasy Furniture, 1989, Don't Come Back Until You Find It, 2006; featured numerous TV & radio programs, mags, and other publs, guest CBS Morning Show, 1988; guest: Lifestyles of the Rich and Famous. Assoc mem Mt Sinia Med Ctr, 1988—; founder Kravis Ctr.; bd dirs New York City Ctr, 1988—90; trustee Pratt Inst, Brooklyn, NY, 1983—. Recipient Designer Award, Art Dirs. Club, 1984; named Man of the Yr., Pratt Inst., 1993. Mem.: Victorian Soc Am, Am Soc Interior Designers (bd dirs 1989—). Avocations: golf, reading, jogging, travel.

NEWMAN, CARLA RUTH, science educator; d. Robert Carl and Norma Dee Newman. BA, U. Tex., El Paso, 1992, MA, 2002, MFA, 2008. Archeologist aide Directorate Environment, Fort Bliss, Tex., 1996—99; archeologist rsch. scientist U. Tex., El Paso, 1999, tchg. asst., 1999—2001, rsch. asst., 2001—02, rsch. scientist, 2002; adj. instr. El Paso CC, Tex., 2003—. Author: (literary magazine) Chrysalis. Commr. Hist. Landmark Commn., El Paso, Tex., 2003—07. Mem.: Delta Kappa Gamma (v.p. 2008—). Office: El Paso CC PO Box 20500 El Paso TX 79998-0500 Business E-Mail: cnewman2@epcc.edu.

NEWMAN, CAROL L., lawyer; b. Yonkers, NY, Aug. 7, 1949; d. Richard J. and Pauline Frances (Stoll) N. AB/MA summa cum laude, Brown U., 1971; postgrad., Harvard U. Law Sch., 1972-73; JD cum laude, George Washington U., 1977. Bar: D.C. 1977, Calif. 1979. With antitrust divsn. U.S. Dept. Justice, Washington and L.A., 1977-80; assoc. Alschuler, Grossman & Pines, LA, 1980-82, Costello & Walcher, LA, 1982-85, Rosen, Wachtell & Gilbert, LA, 1985-88, ptnr., 1988-90, Keck, Mahin & Cate, LA, 1990-94; pvt. practice LA, 1994—. Adj. prof. Sch. Bus., Golden Gate U., spring 1982. Commr. L.A. Bd. Transp. Commrs., 1993—98, v.p., 1995—96; pres. Bd. Taxicab Commrs., 1999—2001; candidate for State Atty. Gen., 1986; bd. dirs. Women's Progress Alliance, 1996—98. Mem. State Bar Calif., L.A. County Bar Assn., LGLA (co. pres. 1991-92, bd. mem. 2008-), Log Cabin (bd. dirs. 1992-97, 2003-06, pres. 1996-97), Calif. Women Lawyers (bd. govs. 1991-94), Order of Coif, Phi Beta Kappa. Office Phone: 818-225-0056. E-mail: cnewman540@aol.com.

NEWMAN, CHARLES, lawyer; b. LA, Mar. 18, 1949; s. Arthur and Gladys Newman; m. Elizabeth F.; children: Anne R., Elyse S. BA magna cum laude, U. Calif., 1970; JD, Washington U., 1973. Bar: Mo. 1973, DC 1981, NY 2006, US Dist. Ct. (ea. dist.) Mo. 1973, US Dist. Ct. (so. dist.) Ill. 2001, US Dist. Ct. (ctrl. dist.) Ill. 1996, US Dist. Ct. (ea. dist.) Mich. 2002, US Ct. Appeals (8th cir.) 1975, US Supreme Ct. 1976, US Tax Ct. 1981, US Claims Ct. 1981, US Ct. Appeals (11th cir.) 1994, US Ct. Appeals (9th cir.) 1995, US Ct. Appeals (3d, 5th, 7th and 10th cirs.) 1996, US Ct. Appeals (6th cir.) 1997, US Dist. Ct. (so. dist.) Ill. 2001, US Dist. Ct. (ea. dist.) Wis. 2003, US Ct. Appeals (1st & 4th cirs.) 2006, US Ct. Appeals (2d cir.) 2006, US Ct. Appeals (DC cir.) 2006. From assoc. to ptnr. Thompson & Mitchell, St. Louis, 1973-96; ptnr. Thompson Coburn, St. Louis, 1996-97, Bryan Cave LLP, St. Louis, 1997—2009, Sonnenschan Nath & Rosenthal LLP, St. Louis, 2009—. Lectr. law Washington U., St. Louis, 1976-78. Bd. dirs. Hawthorn Found., 1997-2000; trustee Mo. Bar Found., 1990-96, mem. Mo. Bar Bd. Govs, 1980-84; bd. dirs. United Israel Appeal, N.Y.C., 1990-93, Coun. Jewish Fedns., N.Y.C., 1992-95, United Jewish Appeal Young Leadership Cabinet, N.Y.C., 1985-88, Ctr. for Study of Dispute Resolution, 1985-88, Legal Svcs. Ea. Mo., 1985-94, St. Louis Community Found., 1992-2001, vice-chmn. 1997-99, St. Louis chpt. Young Audiences 1993-95, Planned Parenthood St. Louis, 1986-89, Jewish Fedn., St. Louis, 1986-98, asst. treas., 1989-90, v.p. fin. planning, 1990-93, asst. sec., 1994-95; v.p. Repertory Theatre, St. Louis, 1986-89, sr. v.p., 1990-91; pres. St. Louis Opportunity Clearinghouse, 1974-78. Recipient Lon O. Hocker Meml. Trial award Mo. Bar Found., 1984, What's Right with the Region award, FOCUS St. Louis, 2005. Mem. Bar Assn. Met. St. Louis (Merit award 1976). Democrat. Avocations: golf, reading, music, sailing. Office: Sonnenschein Nath Rosenthal LLP One Metropolitan Square 30th Fl Saint Louis MO 63102-2741 Home Phone: 314-725-4199; Office Phone: 314-259-5399. Business E-Mail: canewman@bryancave.com, cnewsman@sonnenschein.com.

NEWMAN, CHARLES FORREST, lawyer; b. Grenada, Miss., Jan. 15, 1937; s. Wiley Clifford and Lurene (Westbrook) N.; m. Jeannette Kay Bailey, May 26, 1973. BA magna cum laude, Yale Coll., 1959, JD, Yale Law Sch. 1963; postgrad., U. Bonn, Fed. Republic Germany, 1959-60. Bar: Tenn. 1964, US Supreme Ct. 1981. Law clk. US Dist. Judge Bailey Brown, Western Dist. Tenn., 1963-64; mem. firm Burch Porter & Johnson, Attys., Memphis, 1965—, ptnr., 1966—; mem. exec. com. Yale U. Law Sch. Assn., 1984-88; chair Pres.'s Coun. Rhodes Coll., 1994-95; commr. Memphis Landmarks commn., 1983-87; mem. class coun. Class of '59, Yale Coll., 1980-90, Memphis Bar Assn., Environ. Law Inst.; former bd. dirs./trustees Lemoyne-Owen Coll., Memphis Coll. Art, Tenn. Nature Conservancy, Nat. Civil Rights Mus., Memphis Pub. Lib. Found.; recipient 1990 Disting. Svc. medal Rhodes Coll.; named to Best Lawyers in Am.; Fellow Am. Bar Found., Tenn. Bar Found.; Adenauer fellow U. Bonn, 1959-60; mem. ABA, Tenn. Bar Assn., Memphis Bar Assn. (bd. dirs. 1990-96, pres. 1996), Am. Inns Ct. (master of bench), Memphis Downtown Rotary Club, Yale Club of Memphis (past pres.), Yale Club NY, Phi Beta Kappa. Home: 3880 Poplar Ave Memphis TN 38111-7614 Office: Burch Porter & Johnson 130 N Court Ave Memphis TN 38103-2288 Office Phone: 901-524-5103.

NEWMAN, CHARLES MICHAEL, mathematician, physicist, educator; b. Chgo., Mar. 1, 1946; s. Harry M. and Dorothy Thelma (Pollack) N.; m. Arlene Milgram, July 5, 1970; children: Jennifer, Serena. BS in Physics, BS in Math., MIT, Cambridge, Mass., 1966; MA, Princeton U., NJ, 1968, PhD in Physics, 1971. Asst. prof. NYU, NYC, 1971-73, prof., 1989—, dir. grad. studies, 1996—98, dept. chair, 1998—2001, dir. Courant Inst. Math. Scis., 2002—06; asst. prof. Ind. U., Bloomington, 1973-75, assoc. prof., 1975-79; prof. U. Ariz., Tucson, 1979-90, regents prof., 1990-91. Editor book series on probability and applications, 1988—; assoc. editor: Annals of Probability, 1985-90, Annals of Applied Probability, 2006-08; author: Random Matrices and Their Applications, 1986, Topics in Disordered Systems, 1997; contbr. articles to Nature, Comm. Math. Physics, Physical Rev. Letters and others. J.S. Guggenheim fellow, 1984-85, A.P. Sloan fellow, 1978-81, NATO fellow, 1975-76; NSF grantee, 1974—, U.S.-Israel Binational grantee, 1978-81. Fellow Inst. Math. Stats., Am. Acad. Arts Scis.; mem. NAS, Internat. Assn. Math. Physicists, Am. Math. Soc., Brazilian Acad. Sci. Achievements include co-invention of cascade model of community food web structure, of model for three dimensional wetting phase transition; mathematical demonstration of consistency of neo-Darwinian evolution with fossil record patterns of punctuated equilibria; research concerning discontinuity of certain phase transitions; nature of spin glass models; full scaling limit of two-dimensional percolation. Office: Dept Math Warren Weaver Hall 1117 251 Mercer St New York NY 10012 Business E-Mail: newman@cims.nyu.edu.

NEWMAN, DAVA JEAN, aerospace engineering educator, director; b. Helena, Mont., Aug. 11, 1964; d. Daniel L. Newman and Deanna A. (Mack) Elliott. BS in Aerospace Engring., U. Notre Dame, 1986; MS in Tech. and Policy, MIT, 1989, MS in Aeronautics and Astronautics, 1989, PhD in Aerospace Biomed. Engring., 1992. Engr. Boeing Co., Seattle, 1986; cons., lectr. Internat. Space U., Strasbourg, France, 1987—; rsch. fellow NASA Ames Rsch. Ctr., Mountain View, Calif., 1989-92; asst. prof. U. Houston, 1992-93; C.S. Draper asst. prof. aerospace engring. MIT, Cambridge, Mass., 1993-95, prof. aeronautics, astronautics and engring. sys., 1998—2004, full prof. aeronautics, astronautics and engring. sys., 2004—, dir. Tech. and Policy Program, 2003—. Bd. dirs. Aeronautics and Space Engring. Nat. Acad.; cons. NASA Hdqs., Washington, 1995-96, Trotti and Assocs., Inc., Boston, 1996—, Nascent Technologies, Inc., 1999; affiliate faculty Health, Scis. and Tech. Harvard/MIT. Author: Interactive Aerospace Engineering and Design, 2002; contbr. author: Fundamentals of Space Life Sciences, 1997; contbr. over 100 articles to profl. jours.; author, prodr. U.S./Russian Astronaut Training Video, 1996. Bd. dirs. OMNISport 2001, 1990-2004; advisor KEYS To Empowring Youth, Cambridge, 1995—. Named Prof. of Yr., U. Houston, Soc. Automotive Engrs., 1993; recipient Manned Space Flight award NASA, 1995, Nat. Aerospace Educator award Women in Aerospace, 2001; numerous rsch. grants NASA, 1993—. Fellow AIAA (assoc.); mem. Am. Soc. for Engring. Edn., Internat. Soc. Biomechanics, Union Concerned Scientists, NY Acad. Scis., Soc. Women Engrs. Democrat. Achievements include rsch. in astronaut biomechanics and energetics for space flight and on the moon and Mars; world record holder of women's human-powered hydrofoil speed record; working with team to develop better design for astronaut suit. Office: MIT Rm 33-307 77 Massachusetts Ave Cambridge MA 02139-4307 Office Phone: 617-258-8799. Office Fax: 617-253-4196. Business E-Mail: dnewman@mit.edu.

NEWMAN, DAVID, environmental services administrator, educator; b. Santa Rosa, Calif., Jan. 12, 1954; PhD, Duke U., Durham, NC, 1986. Prof. U. Ga., Athens, 1988—2007, assoc. dean academic affairs, 2005—07; prof., chair SUNY ESF, Syracuse, 2007—. Office: SUNY ESF 1 Foresry Dr Syracuse NY 13210

NEWMAN, DAVID JOHN, chemist; b. Grays, Essex, Eng., May 2, 1939; s. Alfred Harrold and Clara Alma (King) N.; m. Peggy Lee Barnish, Aug. 2, 1969; 1 child, Alexander. PhD, U. Sussex, Falmer, Eng., 1968; MSLS, Drexel U., 1977. Chartered chemist, biologist, Eng. Rsch. assoc. U. Ga., Athens, 1968-70; sr. investigator Smith Kline & French Labs., Phila., 1970-85; lead biochemist Air products, Allentown, Pa., 1985-86; microbiology group leader SeaPharm Inc., Princeton, N.J., 1986-88; prin. microbiologist Lederle Labs., Pearl River, N.Y., 1988-90; sr. med. writer BioPharm Clin. Svc., BlueBell, Pa., 1990-91; chemist Nat. Products Br., Nat. Cancer Inst., Frederick, Md., 1991—2005; chief NPB, 2006—. Contbr. articles to profl. jours. Fellow Royal Soc. Chemistry; mem. Inst. Biology, Am. Chem. Soc., Am. Soc. for Microbiology. Republican. Episcopalian. Home: 664 Crestwood Rd Wayne PA 19087-2315 Office Phone: 301-846-5387.

NEWMAN, DAVID STEFAN, chemistry professor, consultant; b. NYC, Sept. 18, 1936; s. Bernard Newman and Bella Goodstein; m. Judith F. Fabrizio, June 22, 1959; children: Lisa Ann, Andrea Eve, Timothy David, Matthew Lester. PhD, U. Pa., Phila., 1964. Assoc. prof. Bowling Green State U., Ohio, 1969—74, prof., 1974—2006, prof. emeritus, 2006—. Author: (text book) An Invitation to Chemistry; contbr. articles to profl. sci. jours. Sr. Fulbright fellowship, USAID, 1974—75, 1984—85. Achievements include patents for salt splitter. Office: Bowling Green State Univ 138 Overman Hall Bowling Green OH 43403 Office Fax: 419-372-9809. Business E-Mail: dnewman@bgsu.edu.

NEWMAN, DEAN GORDON, community volunteer; b. North Branch, Iowa, Mar. 17, 1929; s. Floyd William and Hazel Jane (Covault) N.; m. Maggie Newman; children: Gary Dean, Craig William. BA, Simpson Coll., 1950; MBA, Stanford U., 1952. From trainee to mgr. GE, Syracuse, NY, Chgo., Milw., 1952—67, mgr. employee and cmty. rels. DeKalb, 1967—69; v.p. employee and pub. rels. United Nuclear Corp., Elmsford, NY, 1969—71; v.p. employee rels. Apache Corp., Mpls., 1971—84, v.p. human resources and comm., 1984—87; v.p. mktg. Nelson Cons. Group, Mpls., 1989-92; chmn., CFO Linear Fitness Systems, Inc., Allenspark, Colo., 1998—2004. Pres. Apache Found., 1973—87; v.p., bd. dirs. Boys Clubs, Mpls., 1978—85; chmn. Boys and Girls Club Mpls., 1985—88, exec. com., 1988—89; v.p. fin., bd. Boys and Girls Club Larimer County, 1993—96; vice chmn. Bus. Econs. Edn. Found., 1986—88, chmn. fin. com., 1988—89; com. mem., treas. Allenspark Sr. Adv. Com., 1999—2003; treas. Allenspark Fire Protection Dist., 2000—05, bd. dirs., 2000—05, Aging Svcs. Found., 2006—, pres., 2007—. With USNR, 1952—55, Korea. Nat. Meth. scholar, 1946—50, Hicks fellow, 1952. Mem.: Nat. Assn. Mfrs. (dir. 1981—87), Allenspark Area Club (bd. dirs., treas. 2000—03, Founder's award 2002, Boulder County Honoring Our Elders award 2003), Pi Gamma Mu, Sigma Tau Delta, Epsilon Sigma, Alpha Tau Omega. Republican. Methodist. Home and Office: 2930 Bryn Mawr Pl Longmont CO 80503 Personal E-mail: mdnewman85@msn.com.

NEWMAN, DIANA S., foundation administrator, consultant, writer; d. Fred Andrew and Thelma Elizabeth (Hewitt) Smith; m. Dennis Ryan Newman, Feb. 15, 1964; children: Barbara Lynn Newman LaBine, John Ryan, Elizabeth Anne. Student, Oberlin Coll., Ohio, 1961—64. Cert. fund raising exec. Asst. treas. Marble Cliff Quarries Co., 1964-68; cmty. vol., 1968-83; dir. Ohio Hist. Found., Columbus, 1983-90; v.p. advancement The Columbus (Ohio) Found., 1990-95; pres. Philanthropic Resource Group, Columbus, 1995—2009; exec. v.p. Benefactor Group, 2009—. Author: Opening Doors: Pathways to Diverse Donors, 2002 (AFP/Skystone Ryan prize for rsch., 2003), Nonprofit Essentials: Endowment Building, 2005. Bd. dirs. Leader Inst., Inc., 2001-04; mem. governing bd. First Cmty. Ch., 1983-88, chair, 1987-88; bd. dirs. LWV Ctrl. Ohio, 1968-72, Ohio Mus. Assn., 1985-90, Crittenton Family Svcs., Columbus, 1992-95; founder Franklin County Com. on Criminal Justice, Columbus, 1972; pres. Jr. League Columbus, 1980-81. Mem. Assn. Fundraising Profls. (bd. dirs. Ctrl. Ohio chpt. 1985-88, 2004-, nat. rsch. coun. 2003—, Outstanding Profl. Fundraiser Ctrl. Ohio chpt., 2004), Ctrl. Ohio Planned Giving Coun. (bd. dirs. 1990-2001, pres. 1998), Columbus Female Benevolent Soc. (bd. dirs. 1984—). Home: 926 Augusta Glen Dr Columbus OH 43235 Office: Benefactor Group 1488 Grandview Ave Columbus OH 43212 Office Phone: 614-437-3000. Business E-Mail: diana@dianaenewman.com.

NEWMAN, DIANE, publishing executive; 3 children. Grad., NYU, 1982. Sr. level advt. mgmt. positions Scholastic mag.; Prevention mag. Rodale Inc.; YM Gruner & Jahr; assoc. pub. Redbook Hearst Corp.; assoc. pub. Family Circle mag. Meredith Corp., pub. Fitness; sr. v.p., group pub. active lifestyle grp. Am. Media Internat.; v.p., pub. Parents mag. Meredith Corp., NYC, 2007—. Office: Parents 375 Lexington Ave 10th Fl New York NY 10017 Office Phone: 212-499-2000.*

NEWMAN, DONALD LYNN, psychologist, consultant; b. Jeffersonville, Ind., Jan. 5, 1951; s. Mason Lynn and Rita Scott Newman; m. Kathy Jean Hopkins, July 28, 1993; children: Higgens McPheaters, Isabella Catalina, Fannie Jean. BA in Sociology, U. Ariz., 1974; MSW, Ariz. State U., 1976; M in Sch. Psychology, No. Ariz. U., 1996. LCSW Ariz.; cert. sch. psychologist Ariz. Dept. Edn. Founder, CEO Family Preservationists: Counseling Assocs., Phoenix, 1991—94, AmeriPsych, Inc., Phoenix, 1994—2005; exec. dir. Gen. Health Corp. ResCare Inc. (formerly AmeriPsych, Inc.), Phoenix, 2005—07. Author: PREP-R: Parenting and Resource Education Program-Revised. Exec. dir. Cmtys. in Need, Phoenix, 1991—2005; pres. Children with Challenges, Phoenix, 1995—2005. Grantee State of Ariz., 1995—2005. Mem.: Nat. Assn. Sch. Psychologists (life). Democrat. Buddhist. Avocations: running, travel, fly fishing, gardening, food preserving. Office: D&K Diversified Investments Inc 3101 N Manor Dr E Phoenix AZ 85014 Personal E-mail: campladybug@msn.com.

NEWMAN, EARL E., transportation engineer, consultant; BS in Civil Engring., U. Mo., Columbia, 1967; M in Civil Engring., Bur. Hwy. Traffic, Pa. State U., 1972. Registered profl. engr., Mo., Ark., cert. accident reconstruction, Ctrl. Mo. State U., profl. traffic ops. engr. With George Butler Assocs., HNTB; city traffic engr. City of Springfield, Mo., 1974, asst. dir. pub. works for traffic engring. Mo. Named to Civil Engring. Acad. Disting. Alumni, U. Mo. Mem.: Inst. Transp. Engrs. (internat. pres. 2007, Mo. Valley Sect. Transp. Engr. of Yr. award 1995, Mo. Valley Sect. Disting. Mem. award 2003). Office: City of Springfield Pub Works 840 Boonville Ave PO Box 8368 Springfield MO 65801-8368 Office Phone: 417-864-1980.

NEWMAN, EDWIN HAROLD, news commentator; b. NYC, Jan. 25, 1919; s. Myron and Rose (Parker) N.; m. Rigel Grell, Aug. 14, 1944; 1 child, Nancy (Mrs. Henry Drucker). BA, U. Wis., 1940; postgrad. (fellow), La. State U., 1940. With Washington bur. Internat. News Svc., 1941, U.P., 1941-42, 45-46, N.Y. Daily PM, 1946-47; ind. Washington news bur., 1947; asst to Eric Sevareid at Washington bur. CBS, 1947-49; freelance writer, broadcaster London, 1949-52; with European Recovery Program, 1951-52, NBC, 1952—, chief news bur. London, 1956-57, Rome, 1957-58, Paris, 1958-61, news commentator NYC, 1961-83; columnist King Features Syndicate, 1984-89. Moderator 1st Ford-Carter Debate, 1976, 2d Reagan-Mondale debate, 1984; moderator ann. conf. former secs. of state, 1983—, former secs. of def., 1987—. Narrator: TV spls. including Japan: East is West, 1961, Orient Express, 1964, Who Shall Live?, 1965, Pensions-The Broken Promise, 1972, Violence in America, 1977, I Want It All Now, 1978, Spying for Uncle Sam, 1978, Oil and American Power, 1979, The Billionaire Hunts, 1981, Congress: We the People, 1983-84, On Television, 1985-86, Freud, 1987, The Borgias, 1988; host Saturday Night Live, 1984; drama critic WNB C-TV, 1965-71 (Emmy awards 1966, 68, 70, 72, 73, 74, 82, Peabody award 1966); author: Strictly Speaking: Will America Be The Death of English?, 1974, A Civil Tongue, 1976, Sunday Punch, 1979, I Must Say, 1988; contbr. articles and revs. to various periodicals, U.S., Can. and Eng.; chmn. usage panel Am. Heritage Dictionary, 1975-80. Served from ensign to lt. USNR, 1942-45. Decorated chevalier Legion of Honor France; recipient awards Overseas Press Club, 1961, awards U. Wis. Sch. Journalism, 1967, awards U. Mo. Sch. Journalism, 1975 Mem. AFTRA, Authors Guild, Screen Actors Guild.

NEWMAN, EILEEN, not-for-profit organization executive; 1 child. Exec. dir. Film/Video Arts, NYC, 1998—. Program officer New Visions for Pub. Schs. Mem.: The N.Y. Film/Video Coun. (bd. dirs.), N.Y. Women in Film and TV (bd. dirs., past v.p.), Educators for Social Responsibility (v.p.).

NEWMAN, JEANNE, lawyer; BA, Conn. Coll., New London, 1977; JD, U. So. Calif. Law Ctr., LA, 1980. Ptnr. Hansen, Jacobson, Teller, Hoberman, Newman, Warren & Richman, LLP, Beverly Hills. Named one of 100 Power Lawyers, Hollywood Reporter, 2007, The 100 Most Powerful Women in Entertainment, 2007; named to Southern Calif. Super Lawyers, 2007, 2008. Office: Hansen Jacobson Teller Hoberman Newman Warren & Richman LLP 450 N Roxbury Dr 8th Fl Beverly Hills CA 90210-4222 Office Phone: 310-271-8777. Office Fax: 310-276-8310. Business E-Mail: jn@hjth.com.

NEWMAN, JOAN MESKIEL, lawyer; b. Youngstown, Ohio, Dec. 12, 1947; d. John F. and Rosemary (Scarmuzzi) Meskiel; children: Anne R., Elyse S. BA in Polit. Sci., Case-Western Reserve U., 1969; JD, Washington U., St. Louis, 1972, LLM in Taxation, 1973. Bar: Mo. 1972. Assoc. Lewis & Rice, St. Louis, 1973-80, ptnr., 1981-90, Thompson Coburn, St. Louis, 1990—2005. Adj. prof. law Washington U. Sch. Law, St. Louis, 1975-92; past pres. St. Louis chpt., mem. Midwest Pension Conf. Mem. nat. coun. Washington U., Sch. Law, 1988—91; chmn. bd. dir. Great St. Louis Coun. Girl Scouts USA, 1975—92, officer, 1978—92; mem. cmty. wide youth svcs. panel United Way Greater St. Louis, 1992—96; fin. futures task force Kiwanis Camp Wyman, 1992—93; chmn. staff blue ribbon fin. com. Sch. Dist., Clayton, 1986—87; vol. Women's Self Help Ctr.; bd. dirs. Parents as Teachers, 2001—04; bd. dir., exec. com. Girl Scouts USA, 1993—99, nat. treas., 1996—99; bd. dirs. Met. Employment and Rehab. Svcs., 1980—2001, chmn. bd. dir., 1994—96, Women of Achievement, 1993—96; bd. dirs. Jewish Ctr. Aged, 1990—92, bd. dir., 1999—2001, Jewish Fedn. St. Louis, 1991—96, City Mus., 1998—2001, United Way Greater St. Louis, 2000—09, Oasis, 1999—2001; chair bd. dirs. MERS/Goodwill Industries, 2007—, chmn. bd. dirs., 2007—09; bd. dirs. Walker Scottish Rite Ctr., 2002—. Named Woman of Achievement St. Louis, 1991. Mem. Mo. Bar Assn. (staff pension and benefits com. 1991—), Bar Met. St. Louis (past chmn. taxation sect.), St. Louis Forum, Order of Coif (hon.). Home Phone: 314-781-3002; Office Phone: 314-645-5001. Business E-Mail: joan@joannewmanassociates.com.

NEWMAN, JOHN M., JR., lawyer; b. Youngstown, Ohio, Aug. 15, 1944; BA, Georgetown U., 1966; JD, Harvard U., 1969. BAr: Ill. 1970, Calif. 1972, Ohio 1976. Law clerk ctrl. dist. U.S. Dist. Ct., Calif., 1969-70, asst. U.S. Atty. ctrl. dist. Calif., 1970-75; ptnr. Jones, Day, Cleve. Fellow Am. Coll. Trial Lawyers; mem. Phi Beta Kappa. Office: Jones Day North Point 901 Lakeside Ave E Cleveland OH 44114-1190 Office Phone: 216-586-7207. Business E-Mail: jmnewman@jonesday.com.

NEWMAN, JOHN NICHOLAS, naval architect educator; b. New Haven, Mar. 10, 1935; s. Richard and Daisy (Neumann) N.; m. Kathleen Smedley Kirk, June 16, 1956; children— James Bartram, Nancy Kirk, Carol Ann. BS Mass. Inst. Tech, 1956, MS, 1957, Sc.D., 1960; postgrad., Cambridge U., Eng., 1958-59; D Technicae honoris causa, U. Trondheim, Norway, 1992. Research naval architect David Taylor Model Basin, Navy Dept., Washington, 1959-67; assoc. prof. naval architecture MIT, Cambridge, 1967-70, prof., 1970—, prof. emeritus. Vis. prof. U. New South Wales, Australia, 1973, U. Adelaide, Australia, 1974, Tech. U. Norway, 1981-82; cons. Navy Dept., Dept. Justice, pvt. firms. Author: Marine Hydrodynamics, 1977; Contbr.: articles to profl. jours., including Sci. Am. Recipient prize Am. Bur. Shipping, 1956; Walter Atkinson prize Royal Instn. Naval Architects, 1973, also Bronze medal, 1976; Guggenheim fellow, 1973-74; research grantee Office Naval Research; NSF. Mem. AAAS, NAE, Soc. Naval Architects and Marine Engrs. (Davidson medal 1988), Norwegian Acad. Sci. Home: 1 Bowditch Rd Woods Hole MA 02543-1201 Business E-Mail: jnn@mit.edu.

NEWMAN, JON O., federal judge; b. NYC, May 2, 1932; s. Harold W. Jr. and Estelle L. (Ormond) Newman; m. Martha G. Silberman, June 19, 1953 (dec. Feb. 8, 2005); children: Leigh, Scott, David; m. Ann Z. Leventhal, Jan. 1, 2007. Grad., Hotchkiss Sch., 1949; AB magna cum laude, Princeton U., 1953; LLB, Yale U., 1956; LLD (hon.), U. Hartford, 1975, U. Bridgeport, 1980, Bklyn. Law Sch., 1995, NY Law Sch., 1996. Bar: Conn. 1956, DC 1956. Law clk. to Hon. George T. Washington US Ct. Appeals, 1956—57; sr. law clk. to Hon. Earl Warren US Supreme Ct., 1957—58; ptnr. Ritter, Satter & Newman, Hartford, Conn., 1958—60; counsel to majority Conn. Gen. Assembly, 1959; spl. counsel to gov. Conn., 1959—61; asst. to sec. HEW, 1961—62; adminstrv. asst. to U.S. senator, 1963—64; U.S. atty. Dist. of Conn., 1964—69, U.S. dist. judge, 1972—79; pvt. practice, 1969—71; U.S. cir. judge US Ct. Appeals (2d cir.), 1979—93, chief judge, 1993—97, sr. judge, 1997—. Co-author: Politics: The American Way, 1964, A Genealogical Chart of Greek Mythology, 2003. With USAR, 1954—62. Recipient Learned Hand medal, Fed. Bar Coun., 1987. Fellow: Am. Bar Found.; mem.: ABA, Am. Judicature Soc., Conn. Bar Assn., Am. Law Inst. Democrat. Office: US Ct Appeals 2d Cir 450 Main St Hartford CT 06103-3022*

NEWMAN, JOSEPH HERZL, advertising executive, consultant; b. NYC, Dec. 1, 1928; s. Max A. and Tillie C. (Weitzman) N.; m. Ruth Zita Marcus, Dec. 19, 1954 (div. Feb. 1987); children: Deborah Lynn, David Alan, Mark Jonathan; m. Nancy Rose Kramer Deutschman, Aug. 19, 1990 (dec. Feb. 2005); stepchildren: Pamela Sue Deutschman, Douglas Hayes Deutschman, Cindi Elaine Deutschman-Ruiz. AB, Bethany Coll., W.Va., 1949; MS Grad. Sch. Bus., Columbia U., NYC, 1956. With 20th Century Fox Film Corp., NYC, 1949—53; media supr. Fred Wittner Advt. Agy., NYC, 1953—56; media dir. O.S. Tyson & Co., NYC, 1956—64; v.p., media dir. Marsteller Inc., NYC, 1965—85; v.p., assoc. media dir. HBM/Creamer, NYC, 1985—87, Della Femina, McNamee, Inc., NYC, 1987—89; pres. Newman And Assocs., Cleve., 1989—. Mem. faculty Advt. Age Media Workshop, 1972; past chmn. media mgrs. adv. com. Bus. Publs. Audit of Circulation Inc., NYC; condr. profl. media planning seminars, 1989-99. Contbr. articles to profl. jours. Past chmn. bus.-to-bus. media com. Am. Assn. Advt. Agys.; vice chmn. tax incentive rev. coun. City of Mayfield Heights, Ohio, 1994-97, chmn., 1997-2005, co-vice chmn., 2005-06; mem. master plan adv. com. City of Mayfield Heights, 2003-04, mem. mayor's cmty. coun., 2006-; rep. Mayfield Heights to Euclid Creek Watershed Coun., 2003-. With US Army, 1950-52. Mem. Bus. Mktg. Assn. (past mem. media comparability coun., media data form com. and rsch. resource com., Agy. Exec. of Yr., NY chpt. 1960, 66, 71, 73, cert. bus. communicator). Home and Office: 6338 Woodhawk Dr Mayfield Heights OH 44124-4153 Office Phone: 440-449-1804. E-mail: nknewmansion@aol.com.

NEWMAN, KENNETH E., lawyer; b. NYC, Sept. 28, 1946; s. Stanley and Muriel (Orenstein) N.; m. Michele M. Jette; children: Douglas C., Jason B., Gregory R. BA, Queens Coll., NYC, 1967; JD, St. John's U., NYC, 1971. Bar: N.Y. 1972, U.S. Supreme Ct. 1976, U.S. Ct. Appeals (2nd cir.) 1974, U.S. Ct. Appeals (D.C. cir.) 1974, U.S. Ct. Appeals (3d cir.) 1980, U.S. Ct. Appeals (10th cir.) 1982, (4th cir.) 1988, U.S. Dist. Ct. (so. dist.) N.Y. 1974, (ea. dist.) N.Y.) 1979. Trial atty. U.S. Dept. Justice, Washington, 1971-73, atty. gen. honors program appointee; assoc. Donovan Leisure Newton & Irvine, NYC, 1973-80, ptnr., 1980-95; sr. v.p., ea. regional counsel Walt Disney Co., NYC, 1995—. Trial faculty Practicing Law Inst., N.Y.C., 1983-94. Dir. Jr. Achievement NY. Mem. ABA, Fed. Bar Coun., Assn. Bar City of N.Y. Office: The Walt Disney Co 77 W 66th St New York NY 10023

NEWMAN, KIMBERLY EILEEN, adult education educator; d. James Benjamin and Eileen Wages Newman. BEE, Ga. Inst. Tech., Atlanta, 1992, PhD, 1999. Asst. prof. microprocessor systems, HDL, sensor networks Rochester Inst. Tech., NY, 2000—01, U. Denver, 2001—. Judge Computer Soc. Internat. Design Competition IEEE Computer Soc., Washington, 2001—06. Recipient Best Transactions Paper award, IEEE Edn. Soc., 2003. Mem.: IEEE (sr.). Achievements include patents for inspection system and method for bond detection and validation of surface mount devices. Office: University of Denver 2390 S York St Denver CO 80208 Office Fax: 303-871-4450. Business E-Mail: kinewman@du.edu.

NEWMAN, LANCE B., literature and language professor; b. Deland, Fla., Sept. 19, 1964; s. Hal Newman and Sarah Stinson; m. Willow Emilie Sellin; 1 child, Freya Elisabeth. PhD in English, Brown U., Providence, 1998. Asst. prof. State U. West Ga., Carrollton, 2000—02; assoc. prof. Calif. State U., San Marcos, 2002—08, Westminster Coll., Salt Lake City, 2008—. Office: Westminster Coll 1840 S 1300 E Salt Lake City UT 84105 Business E-Mail: lnewman@westminstercollege.edu.

NEWMAN, LAWRENCE WALKER, lawyer; b. Boston, July 1, 1935; s. Leon Bettoney and Hazel W. (Walker) N.; children: Timothy D., Isabel B., Thomas H. AB, Harvard U., 1957, LL.B., 1960. Bar: DC 1961, NY 1965. Atty. US Dept. Justice, 1960-61, Spl. Study of Securities Markets and Office Spl. Counsel on Investment Co. Act Matters, U.S. SEC, 1961-64; asst. US atty. So. Dist. NY, 1964-69; assoc. Baker & McKenzie, NYC, 1969-71, ptnr., 1971—. Mem. internat. adv. coun. World Arbitration Inst., 1984-87; adv. bd. Inst. for Transnat. Arbitration, 1988—; chmn. U.S. Iranian Claimants Com., 1982—1990; adv. bd. World Arbitration and Mediation Report, 1993-2008, co-chmn., 2002-08; bd. adv. to Corporate Counsel's Internat. Adviser, 1995—. Co-author: The Practice of Internat. Litigation, 2nd edit. 1998, Litigating Internat. Commercial Disputes, 1996; columnist NY Law Jour., 1982—; contbr. articles to profl. jours., chpts. to books; editor: Enforcement of Money Judgments, Attachment of Assets; co-editor: Internat. Arbitration Checklists, The Leading Arbitrators' Guide to International Arbitration, 2nd edit., 2009; co-editor Revolutionary Days: The Iran Hostage Crisis and the Hague Claims Tribunal, A Look Back, 1999, Take the Witness: The Experts Speak on Cross-examination, 2006. Fellow Coll. Comml. Arbitrators; mem. Am. Law Inst., Inter-Am. Bar Assn., Fed. Bar Coun., Am. Fgn. Law Assn., NY City Bar Assn. (com. on arbitration and alternative dispute resolution 1991-94, com. internat. comml. disputes, 2000—, chmn. 2003-07), Am. Arbitration Assn. (corp. counsel com. 1987—1995, panel internat. arbitrators), US Coun. Internat. Bus., Am. Law Inst., Internat. Inst. Prevention and Resolution Disputes (chmn. arbitration com. 2008-). Office: Baker & McKenzie 1114 Avenue of the Americas New York NY 10036 Office Phone: 212-891-3970. E-mail: lwn@bakernet.com.

NEWMAN, LAWRENCE WILLIAM, financial executive; b. Chgo., Jan. 14, 1939; s. Eskil William and Adele Diane (Lawnicki) N.; m. Christine Harriet Jaronski, Sept. 22, 1962; children: Paul, Scott, Ron. BBS, U. Ill., 1965; MBA, Northwestern U., 1970. CPA, Ill. Auditor Price Waterhouse, Chgo., 1965-66; controller ECM Corp., Schaumburg, Ill., 1966-70, Nachman Corp., Des Plaines, Ill., 1970-76, v.p., treas., controller, 1976-79; v.p. fin. P & S Mgmt. Inc., Schiller Park, Ill., 1979-83; controller Underwriters Labs., Northbrook, Ill., 1983-86, asst. treas., 1986-89, v.p., 1990-98, treas., 1990-97; CFO, 1997—; sr. v.p. Underwriters Labs., Northbrook, 1998—. Mem. Fin. Execs. Inst., Am. Inst. CPA's. Clubs: Exec. of Chgo. Office: Underwriters Labs 333 Pfingsten Rd Northbrook IL 60062-2002

NEWMAN, LESLÉA, writer; m. Mary Vazquez. BS in Edn., U. Vt., 1977; cert. in poetics, Naropa Inst., Boulder, Colo., 1980. Poet laureate, Northampton, Mass., 2008—. Author: A Letter to Harvey Milk, 1988, Heather Has Two Mommies, 1989, In Every Laugh a Tear, 1992, Fat Chance, 1994, Too Far Away to Touch, 1995, Remember That, 1996, Still Life with Buddy, 1997, Out of the Closet and Nothing to Wear, 1997, Matzo Ball Moon, 1998, Girls Will Be Girls, 2000, Signs of Love, 2001, Cats, Cats, Cats!, 2001, Dogs, Dogs, Dogs!, 2002, Runaway Dreidel, 2002;: She Loves Me, She Loves Me Not, 2002, Felicia's Favorite Story, 2002, Pigs, Pigs, Pigs!, 2003, Best Short Stories of Leslea Newman, 2003, The Best Cat in the World, 2004 (Muse Medallion Best Children's Book award Cat Writers Assn., awards), The Boy Who Cried Fabulous, 2004, A Fire Engine for Ruthie, 2004, Where is Bear?, 2004, Hachiko Waits, 2004 (Henry Bergh Children's Book Honor award), Jailbait, 2005, The Eight Nights of Chanukah, 2005, Skunk's Spring Surprise, 2007, Daddy's Song, 2007, Nobody's Mother, 2008, Mama, Mommy and Me, 2009, Daddy, Papa and Me, 2009, The Reluctant Daughter, 2009. Recipient fiction award Highlights for Children, 1992; fellow Mass. Artists Fellowship, 1989, NEA, 1997. Mem. Author's Guild, Poets and Writers, Soc. Children's Book Writers and Illustrators, Pub. Triangle. Jewish. Avocations: crossword puzzles, bowling, collage-making. Address: PO Box 815 Northampton MA 01061-0815

NEWMAN, LIBBY, painter, printmaker, curator; b. Rockland Del., Nov. 17, 1925; d. Hyman and Dora (Horowitz) Goldberg; children: Don, Andrea Newman Orsher. BFA U. Arts; Postgrad. U. Pa., Villanova U, U. Arts, U. Pa. Mem. visual arts panel Pa. Council on Arts, 1971-76; artist-in-residence/curator exhbns. University City Sci. Ctr., Phila., 1975—; co-curator sculpture Gov.'s Mansion, Harrisburg, Pa., 1979—88; one-woman shows Phila. Art Alliance, 1971, 2003, Mangel Gallery, Phila., 1972, 75, 78, 84, 88, 92, 95, 99, 2004-05, University City Sci. Ctr. Gallery, Phila., Tianjin Fine Arts Coll., China, 1988-89, Biblioteca Alexandrina, Egypt, 2006, Paper Mus., Tokyo, 2007; group shows include Mangel Gallery, 1972-2000, Pa. Acad. Fine Arts, Phila., Peale Galleries of Pa. Acad. Fine Arts, Woodmere Art Mus., Chestnut Hill, Pa., Moore Coll. Art, Phila., Fritz Miller Gallery, NYC, William Penn State Mus., Harrisburg, Pa., Fountain Gallery, Portland, Oreg., Del. Art Mus., Wilmington, Phila. Mus. Art, Circle Gallery, NYC, Chgo., So. Alleghenies Mus. Art, Loretto, Pa., Mus. Phila. Civic Ctr., Moore Coll. Art, Phila., 1982, Sichuan Fine Arts Inst., Changging, People's Republic China, 1985, Tianjin Fine Arts Coll., People's Republic China, 1986, Art in City Hall, Phila., 1986, King St. Mus., Szekesherva, Hungary; represented in permanent collections Phila. Mus. Art, Nat. Mus. Belgrade (Yugoslavia), Mus. Modern Art, Buenos Aires, Argentina, U. Pa. Law Sch., Mus. Phila. Civic Ctr., Temple U. Law Sch., Phila., Glassboro State Coll., NJ, Free Libr. Phila., University City Sci. Ctr., Phila., St. Joseph's Coll., Phila., St. Charles Borromeo Sem., Overbrook, Pa., Temple U. Health and Sci. Ctr., Phila., Nationalities Svc. Ctr., Phila., Phila. Assn. Clin. Trials., Mus. Andropologico, Guayagui, Equador, Indus Valley Sch. Arts and Architecture, Karachi, Pakistan; Editor: R. Buckminster Fuller Sketchbook, 1981; A City Sketched: A Guide to the Art and History of Philadelphia, 1976. Mem. Mayor's Com. for Sci. and Tech., 1979-82. Recipient Fleischer Art Meml. award; Cheltenham Nat. Graphic award; Best Pictures of the Yr. award Phila. Art Alliance; Carl Zigrosser Nat. Meml. award Am. Color Print Exhbn., Disting. Daus. Pa. award, 1992; chosen for vis. artist project Brandywine Graphics, 1984; Nat. Endowment grantee, 1973; Pa. Acad. of Fine Arts fellow, Perry Owens award, Mayor's citation City of Phila., 1995. Mem. Artists Equity Assn. (pres. Phila. chpt. 1969-71), Am. Color Print Assn., Phila. Art Alliance, Villanova U. Art Gallery Retrospective Exhbn. Home: 2401 Pennsylvania Ave Apt 7b34 Philadelphia PA 19130-3029 Office Phone: 215-765-4555. Personal E-mail: libby2401@aol.com.

NEWMAN, LISA ANN, surgical oncologist; b. May 24, 1959; BA, Harvard U., 1981; MD, SUNY Downstate Med. Ctr. Coll. Medicine, 1985; MPH, Harvard Sch. Pub. Health, 2001. Cert. Am. Bd. Surgery, Added Qualifications in Surgical Critical Care, lic. Tex., NY. Asst. clin. instr., gen. surgery resident SUNY Downstate Med. Ctr., Bklyn., 1985—89, surgical chief resident, 1989—90, asst. prof. surgery, 1990—97; surgical oncology fellow U. Tex., MD Anderson Cancer Ctr., Houston, 1997—99, asst. prof. surgery, 1999—2000; assoc. prof. surgery Wayne State U., 2000—02, U. Mich., 2002—08, prof. surgery, 2008—, dir., Breast Care Ctr., 2002—. Surgical rep., Telemedicine Breast Conference U. Tex. M.D. Anderson Cancer Ctr., Houston, 1998—, surgical rep., Breast Surgery Clin. Pathway Team, 1999—, surgical rep., Practice Outcomes Program Team, 1999—; invited lectr. in field; researcher in field. Guest commentaries and reviews for Breast Disease Quarterly, Annals of Surgical Oncology, International Journal of Radiation Oncology, Biology, and Physics, and Journal of Surgical Oncology; contbr. chapters to books, several articles to profl. jours.; reviewer, clinical trials website Susan G. Komen Found., 2000. Chairperson, first nat. conf. Sisters Network, Inc., Houston, 1999, co-chairperson, second nat. conference Atlanta, 2000; co-chairperson, Summit Conference on Breast Cancer Rsch. in African American Women Washington, 2000. Recipient Thomas W. Pollack award, 1990, Spirited Digest Magapaper Cmty. Svc., 1999, Pink Ribbons Project award for Breast Cancer Awareness Ednl. Activities, 2000, Minority Enterprise TV Prodn. award, 2000. Mem.: AMA, Am. Cancer Soc. (bd. dir. Greater Lakes Divsn.), Am. Soc. Breast Disease (bd. dir.), Intercultural Cancer Coun., Bklyn. Surgical Soc., Med. Soc. NY, Nat. Med. Assn., Assn. for Women Surgeons, Am. Assn. for Cancer Rsch., Am. Soc. Clin. Oncology, Soc. Critical Care Medicine, Am. Soc. Breast Surgeons, Soc. Surgical Oncology, ACS (mem. oncology group 1999—). Achievements include travels to Ghana to research an aggressive and rare form of breast cancer called triple negative breast cancer; focuses on ethnicity-related variation in breast cancer risk and outcome, evaluation and management of high risk patients and applications for induction chemotherapy. Office: University Michigan Health Services 1500 E Medical Center Dr 3308 CGC SPC 5932 Ann Arbor MI 48109-5932 Business E-Mail: lanewman@umich.edu.*

NEWMAN, MALANE L., computer graphics designer, cartoonist, illustrator, computer graphics designer, educator; b. San Diego, Aug. 6, 1955; d. Charles L. and Marlene A. (Walker) Newman. Cert., Art Instrn. Schs., Mpls., 1972; BA, U.S. Internat. U., San Diego, 1975. Graphic artist La Jolla (Calif.) Advt., 1972; lead illustrator PS Mag., Perspective Corp., San Diego, 1983; art dir. CBT Courseware, Inc., San Diego, 1986; owner, creator animated cards Imagination Enterprises, San Diego, 1986; creative dir., lead designer websites, WBT, electronic design Accenture Corp., 1989; owner Malane Newman Designs, Ramona, Calif., 2001; tchr. computer applications, computer art and design, multimedia Ramona H.S., 2004. Guest lectr. cartooning, self pub., copyright, mail order; cons. corp. graphics, bus. presentations. Mem.: So. Calif. Cartoonist Soc., Nat. Computer Graphics Assn., Nat. Cartoon Soc. Home: 16765 Daza Dr Ramona CA 92065-4613 Home Phone: 760-789-4583; Office Phone: 760-789-4583. Personal E-mail: malanenewman@cox.net.

NEWMAN, MALCOLM, mechanical and civil engineering consultant; b. NYC, June 29, 1931; m. Estelle Ruth Glotzer, June 11, 1955. BSCE, CCNY, 1952; MSCE, Columbia U., 1957; D in Engring. Sci., NYU, 1962. Registered profl. engr., N.Y. Chief structural mechanics Republic-Fairchild Hiller Corp., Farmingdale, N.Y., 1962-65, staff cons., 1970-71; dir. structural mechanics Harry Belock Assocs. Inc., Great Neck, N.Y., 1965-69; dir. structural mechanics and design Analytical Mechanics Assn., Jericho, N.Y., 1969-70; prof. mech. engring. Tel Aviv U., 1972-75; pres., tech. dir. Inter-City Testing and Cons., Mineola, NY, 1976—2004. Past pres. Athletic Safety Products Inc., Mineola, 1985—; adj. prof. engring. Cooper Union. Contbr. over 80 articles to profl. jours.; patentee in field. Bd. dirs. Cinema Arts Ctr., Huntington, N.Y., 1989—. Mem. NSPE, Am. Soc. Safety Engrs., Nat. Assn. Profl. Accident Reconstruction Specialists, Soc. Automotive Engrs., System Safety Soc. (pres. 1983-85). Office: Inter-City Testing & Cons 167 Willis Ave Ste 2 Mineola NY 11501-2680 E-mail: expt1@aol.com.

NEWMAN, MARI ALICE, artist, architect, art designer; d. David Gale Newman and Gloria Ann King. Student, Mpls. Tech. Coll., U. Minn. Art designer Jambalaya Mag., Mpls., 1995—96, Bruegger Bagels, Mpls., 1997—98; card designer Courage Ctr., Golden Valley, Minn., 1998—2002; art designer Hazelton Found., Center City, Minn., 1999—2000; art coord. and designer Allina/Abbott Northwestern Hosp., Mpls., 2000—02; art designer Dunn Bros. Coffee Inc, Mpls., 2003—. Pub. art project Lava Loinge Stores, Mpls., 2001—03. Represented in permanent collections Collection L'Art, Brut, Switzerland, Mus. Site de al Creation, France, Mus. L'Aracee, Mus. De Stadshof, Holland, JohnMcQuirk, England, Nek Chand Found., Columbus Mus. Art, New Orleans Mus. Art, Pensacola Mus. Art, Menello Mus. Art, Milw. Mus. Art, Minn. Mus. Am. Art, Metamorphase One, Permanent Collection Gallery, St. Paul, Moss Rehab. Hosp. Art, corp. collections, Alliance Corp., Mpls., Dunn Bros. Coffee, Brueggens Bagels, Fairview Hosps., exhibitions include Foot in the Door Show, Minn. Art Exhibit Program, Mpls. Inst. Arts, 1980, West '81 Art and The Law, Minn. Mus. Art West Pub. Co., St. Paul, 1981, The Art of Democracy Tools of Persuasion, Minn. Art Exhibit Program, Mpls. Inst. Arts, 2004, Real Artists and Landscapes, ND Mus. Art, 2006, Hackneyed Portraits from our Collection Works by Mary Newman the Cotty Lowry Craffiti Series, MOBA Mus., Deadham, Mass., 2006, Sister Kenny Juried Show (First Pl., 2002, 2004, 2007), Sister Kenny 44th Ann. lnternat. Juried Show (First Pl., 2007); contbr. articles to profl. jours. and mags. Advisor Folk Art Soc. Of Am., Richmond, Va., 2001—05. Recipient Courage Card award, 1998, Dunn Bros. Coffee award, 2004, Dunn Brothers Coffee award, 2004, Sister Kenny Juried Show 1st Pl., 2007; finalist VSA Internat. Festival Winner, 2003; grantee Puffin grantee, Puffin Found., 2002; Artist Recognition grant, Jerome Found., 1998. Mem.: Very Spl. Arts (assoc.; contbr. and internat. rep. 1997—2004, grant 1998). Avocations: stone carver, furniture maker, boat builder, vintage cars. Home: 5117 Penn Ave S Minneapolis MN 55419 Office: House At End Of Rainbow 5117 Penn Ave S Minneapolis MN 55419 Personal E-mail: marin7779@hotmail.com, marinewman@hotmail.com.

NEWMAN, MARK S., electronics company executive; BA, SUNY, Binghampton; MBA, Pace Univ. CPA. Mgmt. positions through CFO DRS Technologies Inc., Parsippany, NJ, 1974—94, pres., CEO, 1994—95, chmn., pres., CEO, 1995—2008, chmn., CEO, 2008—. Bd. dir. Congoleum Corp., Refac Optical Group, EFJ Inc., NJ Tech. Council; bd. gov. Aerospace Ind. Assn.; past chmn. Am. Electronics Assn. Mem.: Surface Navy Assn., Assn. U.S. Army, Nat. Defense Indsl. Assn., Navy League U.S., Bus. Executives for Nat. Security (bd. dir.). Office: DRS Technologies Inc Five Sylvan Way Parsippany NJ 07054*

NEWMAN, MICHAEL D., retail executive; b. 1957; Degree, Amherst Coll., Mass. With Gen. Electric, 1978—96; v.p., CFO Hussmann Internat., Inc., 1996—2000, Intimate Brands, Inc., 2000; sr. v.p., CFO RadioShack Corp., Ft. Worth, 2001—04; CFO Blackstone Crystal Holdings Capital Partners, 2004; sr. v.p., CFO Platinum Research Org., Dallas, 2007—08; exec. v.p., CFO Office Depot Inc., Delray Beach, Fla., 2008—. Office: Office Depot Inc 6600 N Military Trl Boca Raton FL 33496-2434

NEWMAN, MICHAEL RODNEY, lawyer; b. NYC, Oct. 2, 1945; s. Morris and Helen Gloria (Hendler) Newman; m. Cheryl Jeanne Anker, June 11, 1967; children: Hillary Abra, Nicole Brooke. Student NASA Inst. Space Physics, Columbia U., 1964; BA, U. Denver, 1967; JD, U. Chgo., 1970. Bar: Calif. 1971, U.S. Dist. Ct. (cen. dist.) Calif. 1972, U.S. Ct. Appeals (9th cir.) 1974, U.S. Dist. Ct. (no. dist.) Calif. 1975, U.S. Supreme Ct. 1978, U.S. Dist. Ct. (so. dist.) Calif. 1979, U.S. Tax Ct. 1979, U.S. Dist. Ct. (ea. dist.) Calif. 1983. Assoc. David Daar, 1971-76; ptnr. Daar & Newman, 1976-78, Miller & Daar, 1978-88, Miller, Daar & Newman, 1988-89, Daar & Newman, 1989—; judge pro-tem L.A. Mcpl. Ct., 1982—, L.A. Superior Ct., 1988—. Vice chmn., bd. dirs. German-Am. C. of C., 2001—02; bd. govs., fin. and phys. devel. com. U. Haifa, Israel; bd. dirs., mem. adv. bd., chmn. bus. generation com. Consulegis EEIG, 1995—; founder, facilitator 1st, 2d and 3d Ann. German-Am. Strategic Partnership Confs., 1992—2000; guest lectr., internat. law Calif. State U., Fullerton, 2006, 07, 09. Mem. L.A. Citizens Organizing Com. for Olympic Summer Games, 1984, mem. govtl. liaison adv. commn., 1984; mem. So. Calif. Com. for Olympic Summer Games, 1984; cert. ofcl. Athletics Congress of U.S., co-chmn. legal com. S.P.A.-T.A.C., chief finish judge; trustee Massada lodge B'nai Brith; bd. dirs. Ctr. for the Study of Emerging Markets, Calif. State U. Fullerton Grad. Sch. Bus. and Econs., 1997—. Recipient NYU medal, 1962, Maths. award, USN Sci., 1963. Mem.: TAC (bd. dirs., Disting. Svc. award 1988), ABA (multi-dist. litigation subcom., com. on class actions), German Am. Lawyers Assn. So. Calif. (mem. bd.), Lawyers Profl. Liability Bar Assn., Conf. Ins. Counsel, Los Angeles County Bar Assn. (chmn. attys. errors and omissions prevention com. 1995—2005, mem. cts. com., state cts. coord. com. litigation sect., exec. com., mem. internat. law sect. exec. com.), Rotary Club (internat. com.), City Club on Bunker Hill, Breakfast Club, Porter Valley Country Club. Office: Daar & Newman 865 S Figueroa St Ste 2300 Los Angeles CA 90017-2567 Office Phone: 213-892-0999. Business E-Mail: mnewman@daarnewman.com.

NEWMAN, NORMAN RICHARD, lawyer; b. Indpls., Dec. 10, 1934; s. Irving and Anne Newman; m. Pauline Nelson, Dec. 28, 1958; children: Anne Leslie Smeltzer, Mark Alan, Eric Daniel. AB, Ind. U., 1956, LLB, 1960. Bar: Ind. 1960. Ptnr. Dann, Pecar, Newman&Kleiman, P.C., Indpls., 1965—. Mem. Am. Coll. of Real Estate Lawyers, Washington, 1983—; spkr. in field; counsel to major nat. and regional real estate developers Projects Mall of Am. and Circle Ctr. Mall. Author: (legal commentary) Indiana Continuing Legal Education Forum, ALI/ABA - The Practical Lawyer. Recipient Listed in Best Lawyers in Am., 1983—, Named an Ind. Super Lawyer, 2004—. Avocation: golf. Office: Dann Pecar Newman&Kleiman PC One American Sq Ste 2300 Indianapolis IN 46282 E-mail: nnewman@dannpecar.com.

NEWMAN, PAUL, linguistics educator; b. Jacksonville, Fla., Mar. 7, 1937. B.A., U. Pa., 1958, M.A., 1961; Ph.D., UCLA, 1967; JD Ind. U., 2003; Asst. prof., then assoc. prof. Yale U., New Haven, 1966-73; prof. Bayero U., Kano, Nigeria, 1972-75, U. Leiden, Netherlands, 1975-82, Ind. U., Bloomington, 1983—2005; copyright specialist U. Mich., 2006-2008. Author: A Grammar of Tera: Transformational Syntax and Texts, 1970, Nominala nd Verbal Plurality in Chadic, 1990; On Being Right: Greenberg's African Linguistic Classification and the Methodological Principles which Underlie It, 1995; The Hausa Language: An Encyclopedic Reference Grammar, 2000, Klingenheben's Law in Hausa, 2004, A Hausa-English Dictionary, 2007, (with Anthony Kirk-Greene) West African Travels and Adventures: Two Autobiographical Narratives from Northern Nigeria, 1971, The Kanakuru Language, 1974, (with Roxana Ma Newman) Modern Hausa-English Dictionary, 1977, The Classification of Chadic within Afroasiatic, 1980. Co-editor (with Martha Ratliff) Linguistic Fieldwork, 2001, (with Larry M. Hyman) West African Linguistics: Papers in Honor of Russell G. Schuh, 2006. Contbr. articles to profl. publs. Named to Personal chair in African Linguistics, Juliana, Queen of the Netherlands, 1979, Disting. Prof., Ind U., 2002. Office: Ind U Dept Linguistics Bloomington IN 47405

NEWMAN, PAUL RICHARD, physicist; b. NYC, June 8, 1947; s. Bernard and Edna Ethel (Albert) N.; m. Sharan Elizabeth Hill, June 21, 1971; 1 child, Allison Catherine. BS, Antioch Coll., Yellow Springs, Ohio, 1970; PhD, Mich. State U., 1975. Post-doctoral rschr. U. Pa., Lab. for Rsch. on the Structure of Matter, Phila., 1975-77; mem. tech. staff Rockwell Internat. Sci. Ctr., Thousand Oaks, Calif., 1977-83, mgr., 1983-88, prin. scientist, 1988—. Vis. prof. Technion-Israel Inst. Tech., Haifa, 1982. Contbr. articles to profl. jours. Recipient Bauch & Lomb award Bauch & Lomb Co., 1965. Mem. Nat. Assn. for the Advancement Sci., Am. Phys. Soc., Am. Optical Soc., Materials Rsch. Soc. Achievements include patents for Process for Producing Electrically Conducting Composites and Composites Produced Therein, Method of Stabilizing Conductive Polymers, Laser Generated Electricity Conducting Pattern, others. Office: Rockwell Internat Sci Ctr 1049 Camino Dos Rios Thousand Oaks CA 91360-2362

NEWMAN, PAULINE, federal judge; b. NYC, June 20, 1927; d. Maxwell Henry and Rosella Newman. BA, Vassar Coll., 1947; MA, Columbia U., 1948; PhD, Yale U., 1952; LLB, NYU, 1958. Bar: NY 1958, US Supreme Ct. 1972, US Ct. Customs and Patent Appeals 1978, Pa. 1979, US Ct. Appeals (3d cir.) 1981, US Ct. Appeals (fed. cir.) 1982. Research chemist Am. Cyanamid Co., Bound Brook, NJ, 1951—54; mem. patent staff FMC Corp., NYC, 1954—75, Phila., 1975—84, dir. dept. patent and licensing, 1969—84; judge US Ct. Appeals (fed. cir.), Washington, 1984—; disting. prof. George Mason Law Sch., 1995—. Program specialist Dept. Natural Scis. UNESCO, Paris, 1961—62; mem. State Dept. Adv. Com. on Internat. Indsl. Property, 1974—84; lectr. in field. Contbr. articles to profl. jours. Trustee Phila. Coll. Pharmacy and Sci., 1983—84; bd. dirs. Med. Coll. Pa., 1975—84, Midgard Found., 1973—84. Mem.: ABA (coun. sect. patent trademark and copyright 1983—84), Coun. Fgn. Rels., U.S. Trademark Assn. (bd. dirs. 1975—79, v.p. 1978—79), Pacific Indsl. Property Assn. (pres. 1979—80), Am. Inst. Chemists (bd. dirs. 1960—66, 1970—76), Am. Chem. Soc. (bd. dirs. 1972—81), Am. Patent Law Assn. (bd. dirs. 1981—84), Yale Club, Vassar Club, Cosmos Club. Office: US Ct Appeals Nat Cts Bldg 717 Madison Pl Washington DC 20439-0002*

NEWMAN, PHILIP ROBERT, psychologist; b. Dec. 17, 1942; s. Samuel M. and Sara Rose (Dumain) N.; m. Barbara Miller, June 12, 1966; children: Samuel Asher, Abraham Levy, Rachel Florence. AB with high distinction, U. Mich., 1964, PhD, 1971. Asst. prof. psychology U. Mich., Ann Arbor, 1971-72, Union Coll., Schenectady, NY, 1972-76; dir. human behavior curriculum project APA, Washington, 1977-81; pvt. practice psychology Columbus, Ohio, 1978-2000, South Kingston, RI, 2000—. Adj. prof., sr. rschr. young scholars program Ohio State U., 1990-98; adj. prof. human devel. and family studies U. R.I., 2000—; cons. Agy. Instrnl. TV, 1979; vis. scholar psychology, UCLA, 2006-07. Author: (with B. Newman) Development through Life: A Psychosocial Approach, 1975, 10th edit., 2009; Infancy and Childhood Development and Its Context, 1978, An Introduction to the Psychology of Adolescence, 1979, Personality Development through the Life Span, 1980, Living: The Process of Adjustment, 1981, Understanding Adulthood, 1983, Principles of Psychology, 1983, Adolescent Development, 1986, When Kids Go to College: A Parents Guide to Changing Relationships, 1992, Childhood and Adolescence, 1997, Theories of Human Development, 2007, (with B. Newman, L. Landry-Meyer, B. Lohman) Life Span Development: A Case Book, 2003; editor: (with B. Newman) Development Through Life: A Case Study Approach, 1976. Woodrow Wilson fellow U. Mich., 1964, Univ. fellow, 1964-66, Horace H. Rackham Rsch. scholar, 1969-71. Mem. APA, APHA, Internat. Assn. Applied Psychology, Internat. Sociol. Assn., Soc. Psychol. Study Social Issues, Am. Sociol. Assn., Nat. Coun. Family Rels., Groves Conf. Marriage and Family, Ea. Psychol. Assn., N.Y. Acad. Sci., Gerontol. Soc. Am., Am. Orthopsychiat. Assn., Am. Statis. Assn., Soc. for Rsch. on Child Devel., Soc. for Rsch. on Adolescence, Soc. Study Human Devel., Phi Beta Kappa, Sigma Xi, Phi Kappa Phi. Personal E-mail: prn10@yahoo.com.

NEWMAN, PHYLLIS, counselor, therapist, hypnotist; b. NYC, Aug. 20, 1933; d. Max and Frieda Yetta (Pechter) Hershkowitz; BS, Mercy Coll., 1977; MS, LIU, 1979; m. Milton Newman, Dec. 28, 1952; children: Renee Holly, Eileen Sharon, Jeffrey Mark. Pvt. practice hypnosis and therapy, Peekskill, NY, 1977—89; lectr. Pepsico Fitness Ctr., Purchase, NY, 1984, Purdue U., 1986, 88, Girl Scouts' Coun., local radio; dir. counseling Hypnosis Group, 1979—89; featured local TV, 2004, 60 Minutes 2, 2004, Ivanhoe Broadcasting Co., 2005, Purdue Alumnus Mag., 2005. Mem. parents exec. bd. Purdue U., 1978-83, mem. pres.' council, 1982—89; bd. dirs. Hand to Mouth Players, Garrison, NY, Yorktown Cmty. Players, NY, 1988-89; v.p., prodr. Tempe Little Theatre, 1990-95; pres. Tempe Welcome Wagon Social Club, 1990-91; v.p. bd. dirs. Temple Emanuel Tempe, Ariz., 1996-2008; chair Beit Am. (Ho. of People), 2003-08, healing svc. 2005-08; active for Normal Pressure Hydrocephalus Support Group, Barrows Neurol. Inst., Phoenix, 2005-09, Hydrocephalus Assn., San Francisco, 2005—; lectr. Ahwautukee Cancer Assn., 2002; leader meditation JCC, 1994-2001; liaison Union of Reform Judaism, SW Coun. Jewish Family Concerns, 2006—. Mem. Am. Assn. Counseling and Devel., Am. Mental Health Counselors Assn., NY Soc. Ericksonian Hypnosis, Am. Assn. Profl. Hypnotherapists. Contbr. articles to profl. jours. Address: 2214 longmore Cir Velrico FL 33596 Home Phone: 813-651-3903. Personal E-mail: phylnew820@cox.net, phylnew@verizon.net.

NEWMAN, PHYLLIS, actress; b. Jersey City, Mar. 19, 1933; m. Adolph Green, 1960 (dec. 2002); children: Amanda Green, Adam Green. Founder Phyllis Newman Women's Health Initiative, Actor's Fund of America, 1995—. Performer: (Broadway plays) Wish You Were Here, 1952, Bells Are Ringing, 1956, First Impressions, 1959, Moonbirds, 1959, Subways Are for Sleeping, 1961 (Tony award for Best Featured Actress in a Musical, 1962), The Apple Tree, 1966, On the Town, 1971, The Prisoner of Second Avenue, 1971, Awake and Sing!, 1984, Broadway Bound, 1986; author, performer: Broadway plays The Madwoman of Central Park West, 1979; actor: (films) The Naked Witch, 1967, Bye Bye Braverman, 1968, To Find a Man, 1972, A Secret Space, 1977, Mannequin, 1987, Saying Kaddish, 1991, Only You, 1994, The Beautician and the Beast, 1997, A Price Above Rubies, 1998, A Fish in the Bathtub, 1999, It Had to Be You, 2000, The Human Stain, 2003, Everyone's Depressed, 2005; (TV series) One Life to Live, 1987, Thirtysomething, 1989—90, 100 Centre Street, 2001—02; author: Just in Time: Notes from My Life, 1984. Recipient Isabelle Stevenson award, Tony Awards, 2009.*

NEWMAN, R. DONALD, retired paper company executive; V.p., resident mgr. Bowater, Inc., Calhoun, Tenn., 1987; v.p. Bowater, Inc., Canadian Newsprint Oper., 1998—2001; v.p., strategic planning Bowater, Inc., 2001—02, exec. v.p., COO Greenville, SC, 2002—06; ret., 2006.

NEWMAN, RACHEL, editor; b. Malden, Mass., May 1, 1938; d. Maurice and Edythe Brenda (Tichell) Newman; m. Herbert Bleiweiss, Apr. 6, 1973 (div. Apr. 1989); m. Michael Lucas, Feb. 24, 2004. BA, Pa. State U., University Park, 1960; cert., NY Sch. Interior Design, NYC, 1963. Accessories editor Women's Wear Daily, NYC, 1964—65; designer, publicist Grandoe Glove Corp., NYC, 1965—67; assoc. editor McCall's Sportswear and Dress Merchandiser mag., NYC, 1967; mng. editor McCall's You-Do-It Home Decorating, 1968—70, Ladies Home Jour. Needle and Craft mag., NYC, 1970—72; editor-in-chief Am. Home Crafts mag., NYC, 1972—77; fashion dir. Good Housekeeping mag., NYC, 1977—78, home bldg. and decorating dir., 1978—82; editor-in-chief Country Living mag., NYC, 1978—98; founding editor Country Cooking mag., 1985—90, Dream Homes mag., 1989—2000, Country Kitchens mag., 1990—93, Country Living Gardener Mag., 1993—2000, Healthy Living mag., 1996—2000. Bd. dirs. Mothers and Others for a Livable Planet. Recipient Cir. of Excellence award, Internat. Furnishings and Design Assn., 1992, YMCA Hall of Fame, 1992; named Disting. Alumna, Pa. State U., 1988; Pa. State U. Alumni fellow, 1986. Mem.: Am. Soc. Mag. Editors, Am. Soc. Interior Designers, Nat. Home Fashions League, N.Y. Fashion Group. E-mail: Rachelsfree@earthlink.net.

NEWMAN, RANDY, singer, songwriter, musician; b. LA, Nov. 28, 1943; s. Irving and Adele N.; m. Gretchen Newman; children: Amos, Eric, John, Patrick, Alice. Degree, U. Calif. Arranger, singer, songwriter, musician various record firms; singer-composer: (albums) including Randy Newman, 1968, Twelve Songs, 1969, Live, 1971, Sail Away, 1972, Good Old Boys, 1974, Little Criminals, 1977, Born Again, 1979, Trouble In Paradise, 1983, Land of Dreams, 1988, Bad Love, 1999; (with others) Randy Newman's Faust, 1995; appeared in film: Ragtime, 1981; also TV and concert engagements; music composer for films: Performance, 1970, Pursuit of Happiness, 1971, Cold Turkey, 1971, Ragtime, 1981, The Natural, 1984 (Grammy award for Best Instrumental Composition, 1984), Three Amigos (also co-wrote screenplay), 1986, Parenthood, 1989, Avalon, 1990, Awakenings, 1990, Toy Story, 1995 (Annie award for Individual Achievement in Music, 1995), Michael, 1996, James and the Giant Peach, 1996, Cats Don't Dance, 1997 (Annie award for Feature Video Prodn. Music, 1997), A Bug's Life, 1998 (Grammy award for Best Instrumental Composition for Motion Picture, 2000), Pleasantville, 1998, Toy Story 2, 1999 (Grammy award for Best Song Written for Motion Picture, 2001, Annie award for Outstanding Individual Achievement for Music in an Animated Feature Prodn., 2000), Meet the Parents, 2000, Monsters, Inc., 2001 (ASCAP award for Top Box Office Film, 2001, Acad award for Best Original Song, 2002, Grammy award for Best Song Written for Motion Picture, 2003), Mike's New Car, 2002, Seabiscuit, 2003 (ASCAP award for Top Box Office Film), Mr. 3000, 2004, Meet the Fockers, 2004 (ASCAP award for Top Box Office Film, 2005), Cars, 2006 (Grammy award for Best Song Written for Motion Picture, 2007, ASCAP award, 2007); composer for TV Series: Monk, 2002 (Emmy award for Outstanding Main Title Theme Music, 2004, ASCAP award for Top TV Series, 2005); recorded 30 Years of Randy Newman (4 CD set), 1998. Named to Songwriters' Hall of Fame, 2002. Office: c/o Sacks & Co 427 W 14th St New York NY 10014 also: c/o Gorfaine/Schwartz Agy Inc Ste 509 4111 W Alameda Ave Burbank CA 91505

NEWMAN, RICHARD, history professor; b. Santa Monia, Calif., Mar. 6, 1967; s. Robert and Milda Newman; m. Lisa Hermsen, Oct. 29, 2007. PhD, SUNY, Buffalo, 1997. Vis. asst. prof. Clarion U., Pa., 1997; assoc. prof. Rochester Inst. Tech., NY, 1998—. Author: (book) Freedom's Prophet: Bishop Richard Allen, The AME Church, and the Black Founding Fathers, The Transformation of American Abolitionism: Fighting Slavery in the Early Republic (finalist, Avery Craven Prize, OAH, 2002); co-editor: Pamphlets of Protest, The Palgrave Environmental Reader. Adv. bd. mem. Gilder Lehrman Ctr., New Haven, 2004—08. Recipient Nat. Endowment for the Humanities We The People seminar awards, NEH, 2005, 2006, 2008. Business E-Mail: rsngsm@rit.edu.

NEWMAN, RICHARD G., engineering company executive; BSCE, Bucknell U.; MSCE, Columbia U.; grad. Exec. Mgmt. Program, UCLA. V.p. Daniel, Mann, Johnson & Mendenhall, 1977—85, pres., COO, 1985—88; pres. Ashland Tech., 1988—90, AECOM Tech. Corp., LA, 1990—93, chmn., pres., CEO, 1993—2000, chmn., CEO, 2000—05, chmn., 2005—. Bd. dirs. Southwest Water Co., 13 mutual funds under Capital Rsch. and Mgmt. Co., Sempra Energy, San Diego, 2002—. Fellow: Inst. for Advancement of Engring.; mem.: NSPE, Am. Soc. Civil Engrs., Chief Executives Orgn. Office: AECOM Tech Corp 555 S Flower St Ste 3700 Los Angeles CA 90071-2300 Office Phone: 215-593-8000. Office Fax: 213-593-8729.*

NEWMAN, RUTH GALLERT, psychologist; b. NYC, June 16, 1914; d. Ernest Ezra and Belle (Cohen) Gallert; m. James R. Newman (July 27, 1940 (dec.); children: Jeffrey Frederick, Brooke Anne. BA, Rtugers U., 1937; MA, George Washington U., 1942; PhD, U. Md., 1950. Tchr. Emerson Sch., NYC, 1938-40; remedial tutor Remedial Edn. Ctr., Washington, 1942-45; remedial tchr. Geroge Wahsington Day Sch., Washington, 1948-51; clin. tchr., supr. Children's Hosp., Washington, 1955-60; pvt. practice group therapy Washington Sch. Psychiatry, 1960—. Mem. AKPice Group Rels.; speaker in field; cons. in field. NIMH grantee. Democrat. Address: c/o Brooke Newman 273 Roaring Fork Dr Aspen CO 81611-2238 Personal E-mail: thelittletern@hotmail.com.

NEWMAN, RYAN JOSEPH, race car driver; b. South Bend, Ind., Dec. 8, 1977; m. Krissie Boyle. BS in Vehicle Structure Engring., Purdue U., 2001. Race car driver NASCAR Penske Racing South, 2001—08, Stewart-Haas Racing, 2009—. 1st pl. NH 300 NH Internat. Speedway, 2002, 1st pl. Sylvania 300, 05; 1st pl. Samsung/Radio Shack 500 Tex. Motor Speedway, 2003; 1st pl. MBNA Armed Forces Family 400 Dover Internat. Speedway, 2003, 1st pl. Dover 400, 03, 1st pl. MBNA Am. 400, 04; 1st pl. Tropicana 400 Chicagoland Speedway, 2003; 1st pl. Pa. 500 Pocono Raceway, 2003; 1st pl. GFS Marketplace 400 Mich. Internat. Speedway, 2003, 1st pl. DHL 400, 04; 1st pl. Chevy Rock and Roll 400 Richmond Internat. Raceway, 2003; 1st pl. Banquet 400 Kans. Speedway, 2003; 1st pl. Daytona 500 Daytona Internat. Speedway, 2008. Co-founder Ryan Newman Found. Named NASCAR Rookie of Yr., 2002, NASCAR Driver of Yr., 2003, Am. Driver of Yr., SPEED Channel, 2003. Office: Stewart-Haas Racing 6001 Haas Way Kannapolis NC 28081 Office Phone: 704-652-4227.

NEWMAN, SAMUEL, retired trust company executive; b. NYC, Mar. 12, 1938; s. Aaron and Rachel (Hershkowitz) Newman; m. Carolyn Gropper, Oct. 27, 1963; children: Marci Ann, Jodi Robin, Michael David. BBA, CUNY, 1971; grad. Advanced Mgmt. Program, Harvard U., 1982. Methods analyst Bankers Trust Co., NYC, 1960-67; project leader Clark O'Neill SVC Corp., Fairview, NJ, 1967-68; sr. v.p. Irving Trust Co., NYC, 1968-85; sr. v.p., gen. mgr. trade svcs. and GEOSERVE legal and regulatory support Mfrs. Hanover Trust (merger with Chem. Bank 1992), NYC, 1985-92; sr. v.p., gen. mgr. funds transfer and trade svcs. Chem. Bank, NYC, 1992-93; sr. v.p. and bus. head payment products First Fidelity Bank NA, Newark, 1993-95; head dept. project support Fleet Pa. Svcs. Inc., Scranton, Pa., 1995-98; dir. new bus. devel., mgr. customer svc., internat. fin. instns. Fleet Bank, NYC, 1998—2001; dir. float mgmt. Fleet Nat. Bank, Melville, NY, 2001—03. Past chmn. bd. dirs. SWIFT Terminal Svcs.; past chmn. NY Clearing House funds transfer com.; speaker industry confs. Contbr. articles to profl. jours. Advisor Nat. Conf. of Commrs. on Uniform State Laws; former mem. US coun. Internat. Banking Exec. Com., US del. to Uncitral Working Group on Internat. Payments; former chief US del. to tech. com. 168 Internat. Standards Orgn. Mem. Soc. Worldwide Fin. Telecom. (bd. dirs. 1978-92, dep. chmn 1989-92), Internat. Fin. Svcs. Assn. (bd. dirs. 2001—03). Avocation: foreign currency note collection. Office: 39 Wyandanch Ave Wyandanch NY 11798 Personal E-mail: wallstrbkr@aol.com.

NEWMAN, SANDRA SCHULTZ, lawyer, former state supreme court justice; b. Nov. 4, 1938; BS, Drexel U., 1959; MA, Temple U., 1969; JD, Villanova U., 1972; D (hon.), Gannon U., 1996, Widener U., 1996, Clarion U., 2000, Drexel U., 2001. Bar: Pa., U.S. Dist. Ct. (ea. dist.) Pa., U.S. Ct. Appeals (3d cir.), U.S. Supreme Ct. Asst. dist. atty. Montgomery County, Pa., 1972—74; pvt. practice, 1974—93; judge Commonwealth Ct. of Pa., 1993—95; justice Pa. Supreme Ct., 1995—2006; ptnr., head appellate practice Cozen O'Connor, Phila., 2007—. Past chair bd. consultors Villanova U. Law Sch.; mem. jud. coun. Supreme Ct. of Pa., liaison to the 3rd cir. task force on mgmt. of death penalty litigation, liaison to Pa. lawyers fund for client security bd., liaison to domestic rels. procedural rules com.; liaison Pa. Bar Inst.; jud. work group HHS; mem. adv. com. Nat. Ctr. for State Cts., Am. Law Inst.; mem. Drexel U. Coll. Bus. and Adminstrn.; lectr. and spkr. in field. Author: Alimony, Child Support and Counsel Fees, 1988; contbr. articles to profl. jours. Recipient Phila. award for Super Achiever, Pediatric Juvenile Colitis Found. Jefferson Med. Coll. and Hosp, 1979, award for Dedicated Leadership and Outstanding Contbns. to the Cmty. and Law Employment, Drexel 100 award, Police Chiefs Assn. of Southeastern Pa., 1993, Medallion of Achievement award, Villanova U., 1993, Susan B. Anthony award, Women's Bar Assn. Western Pa., 1996, award, Justinian Soc., 1996, Tau Epsilon Law Soc., 1996, Legion of Honor Gold Medallion award, Chapel of Four Chaplain, 1997, honored by, Women of Greater Phila., 1996, Person of Yr. award, Shomrim of Phila., 1998, Women of Distinction award, Greater Phila. Council of Jewish Women Internat., 2005, Person of Yr. award, Pa. State Constables Assoc., 2005; named named Disting. Daughter of Pa. Fellow: Pa. Bar Found., Am. Bar Found.; mem.: Montgomery Bar Assn., Nat. Assn. Women Judges, Am. Law Inst. Office: Cozen O'Connor 1900 Market St Philadelphia PA 19103

NEWMAN, SHERRYL HOBBS, former district secretary; BA in Chemistry, Rutgers U., 1986, BA in Economics, 1986; MBA in Management, Lubin Graduate Sch. of Bus. Pace Univ., White Plains, NY, 1992. Acting dep. dir.-Taxpayer Assistance Divsn. NYC-Dept. of Finance, 1992—93, city collector-Property Bureau, 1993—96; dir. Customer Svc. Adminstrn.-Office of Tax and Revenue, Washington, 1997—99, Citywide Customer Svc. Adminstrn.-Office of the City Adminstr., Washington, 1999, Dept. of Motor Vehicles, Washington, 1999—2003; sec. dist. DC Govt., 2003—05, dep. CFO, Office Tax & Revenue, 2005—. Democrat. Office: DC Office of Tax & Revenue 941 N Capitol St NE Ste 800 Washington DC 20002 Business E-Mail: shnewman@dc.gov.

NEWMAN, SLATER EDMUND, psychologist, educator; b. Boston, Sept. 8, 1924; s. Max and Gertrude (Raphael) N.; m. Corrine Lois Silfen, June 18, 1950 (div. 1968); children: Kurt Douglas, Jonathan Mark, Eric Bruce; m. Patricia Ellen Christopher Thomas, July 2, 1969; 1 stepchild, Arthur C. Thomas III. BS, U. Pa., 1947; MA, Boston U., 1948; PhD, Northwestern U., 1951. Research psychologist U.S. Air Force, 1951-57; mem. faculty N.C. State U., Raleigh, 1957—2003, prof. emeritus psychology, 2003—. Vis. fgn. mem. Exptl. Psychology Soc. U.K., 1973-74, 82-83, 90. Contbr. chpts. to books, articles to profl. publs. Bd. dirs. ACLU, 1992—97, mem. biennial conf. com., 1994—97, mem. task force internat. human rights, 1994—2005, mem. spl. nominating com., 1996, mem. constn. com., 1996—97, mem. youth affairs com., 1997, mem. nat. adv. coun., 1998—; organizing com. NC Civil Liberties Union, 1965, pres., 1980—82, exec. com., 1986—87, bd. dirs., 1969—73, 1976—82, 1984—90, 1992—97; chair Com. on Internat. Human Rights, 1988—; chair founding com. Wake County chpt. ACLU, 1969, pres., 1969—72, 1984—86, bd. dirs., 1969—73, 1976—82, 1984—90, life mem., 2002—; founding mem. North Carolinians Against the Death Penalty, 1967, bd. govs., 1967—73; mem. Mayor's Com. UN Week, Raleigh, 1986—95; active Amnesty Internat.; co-founder, coord. Com. to Reverse Arms Race, 1982—; co-founder, mem. steering com. North Carolinians Against Apartheid, 1985—87; mem. Wake County Com. Bicentennial US Constn., 1987—89; co-founder, co-chair NC Com. for Celebration of Human Rights, 1989—97; mem. Human Rights Week Com., NC State U., 1993—99, founder, 1993, chair, 1993—96; co-founder Human Rights Coalition NC, 1997—, co-chair, 1997—; co-founder North Carolinians for Ratification, Com. on Elimination of All Forms of Discrimination Against Women, 1997, chair, 1998—2009; mem. civil rights adv. bd. NC Mus. History, 2001—05. Served with USAAC, 1943—46, 2d lt. USAF, 1952—53. USPHS spl. rsch. fellow U. Calif.-Berkeley, 1965-66; U. London hon. rsch. fellow, 1973-74, 82-83, 90; recipient W.W. Finlator award ACLU of Wake County, 1997, Norman Smith award ACLU of NC, 1998; recipient Frank Porter Graham Award, ACLU of NC, 2004, Human Rights award, Wake County and West Triangle Chpts., UN Assn., 2007; Slater Newman annual debate established by Wake County ACLU, 2006. Fellow: APA, AAAS, Assn. for Psychol. Sci.; mem.: AAUP (pres. N.C. State U. chpt. 1968—69), Carolinas Conf. for Undergrad. Rsch. in Psychology (co-founder 1976, co-advisor), Ea. Psychol. Assn., N.C. Cognition Group (founder 1972), S.E. Psychol. Assn. (exec. com. 2001—07, sec.-treas. 2004—07), S.E. Workers in Memory (founder 1969), So. Soc. Philosophy and Psychology, Psychonomic Soc., UN Assn. (bd. dirs. Wake County chpt. 1991—95), Psi Chi (v.p. southea. region 1990—94, nat. coun. 1990—94, nat. pres.-elect 1996—97, nat. coun. 1996—99, nat. pres. 1997—98, nat. past pres. 1998—99), Sigma Xi. Home: 315 Shepherd St Raleigh NC 27607-4031 Office: NC State U Dept Psychology Raleigh NC 27695-7650 E-mail: slaterpat@mindspring.com.

NEWMAN, STACEY CLARFIELD, artist, curator; b. NYC, July 21, 1956; d. Wallace J. Clarfield and Elinor (Kandel) Clarfield-Toberoff; m. Fredric Alan Newman, Nov. 27, 1983; children: Benjamin Clarfield, Marissa Paige, Alexandra Brooke Degree, Franklin & Marshall Coll., 1976; BS Labor Rels. and Mgmt., U. Bridgeport, 1978. Dir. ops. Nat. Rec. and Video Studios, NYC, 1978—80; cons., client rep./MTV VCA/Teletronics, NYC, 1979—84, dir. tech. ops., 1980—82, exec. prodr., 1982—85, dir. tech ops. prodr.; artist, art curator Stacey Clarfield Newman Studios, Scarsdale, NY, 1986—. Merchandise dir. Tahari Fashions, NYC, 1985—86; artist mem., jury com. You Gotta Have Art program White Plains Hosp. Ctr., NY, 1990—92; art tchr. collage Scarsdale Adult Edn. Program, 1993—95; artist in residence Scarsdale Elem. Schs., 1995—97; art cons., curator Manhattan Transfer, Inc., NYC, 1997—2000; mem. faculty Young at Art enrichment program, Scarsdale, 2002—; juror Figure and Form Edward Hopper House Mus., NYC, 2004. One-person shows include Quogue Gallery, NY, 1986, Piermont Fine Arts Gallery, NY, 1997-98, 2001, Manhattan Transfer, Inc., 1997, J&W Gallery, New Hope, Pa., 1999, Studio 4 West, 1999, 93 South Gallery, 2000, Adele Greenberg Salon, Cambridge, Mass., 2000, Amb. Galleries, Palm Beach, Fla., 2001, Viridian Gallery, NYC, 2001, 02, 05, Viridian Gallery @ Chelsea, 2002, 04, 05, 08, Walking Man Gallery, Whitefish, Mont., 2008, 09; exhibited in juried group shows: Piermont Fine Art Gallery, 1995, 96, 98, 99, 2000, 01, Anaya Gallery, Scarsdale, 1986, Katonah Gallery, NY, 1986, Gallery at Jamaica, Stratton Mountain, Vt., 1987, CDS Contemporary Art, Albuquerque, 1989, Mari Galleries, Mamaroneck, NY, 1992, Manhattan Transfer, Inc., 1993, 98, 93 South Gallery, Nyack, NY, 1998-99, Bibro Fine Arts Gallery, Chelsea, NY, 1998, Weber Fine Art, Scarsdale, 1998, 2000, J&W Gallery, New Hope, 1998, 99, 2001, 02, Studio 4 West, Hewlett Mus., 2000, Amb. Gallery, Palm Beach, 2000, Viridian Gallery, NYC, 2000-04, Adele Greenberg Salon, 2000, 01, A Pirate Space, Denver, 2001, Contemporary Art Oasis, Denver, 2001, Manhattanville Coll. Gallery, 2002, Nat. Assn. Women Artists, NYC, 2003, Chgo. Fine Arts Bldg. Gallery, 2003, Inklings, Viridian Artists, Chelsea, 2005, 06, News Art, Virdian Artists, 2005, John Jay Coll. Pres.'s Gallery, 2005, Fountain St. Gallery, Cape Girardeau, Mo., 2006, City Lights, Virdian Artists Inc., NYC, 2006, Online Juried Exhibition, 2009, Juried Art Competition, 2009, Viridian Artists Inc., 2007, A Reality, Viridian Artists Inc., NY, 2007, New Art for New Collectors, Viridian Artist, Inc, 2007, Global, Walking Man Gallery, 2008, Walking Man Gallery, 2009, Internet Gallery, 2009; commd. Am. Soc. Plastic and Reconstructive Surgeons, LA Conv. Ctr., 1988, White Plains Hosp. Ctr., 1989, 90, Cystic Fibrosis Found., NYC, 1990, Joan Kroc Found., Calif., 1989-91. 1st v.p., bd. dirs. Internat. Coll. Surgeons Aux., Chgo., 1988—90; mem. Gala com. Juvenile Diabetes Found., 2000; Regional v.p. Am. Cancer Soc., White Plains, 1986—88; bd. dirs. White Plains Hosp. Ctr. Aux.; fund raiser, event planner Holocaust Commn., NYC, 1998; active Scarsdale Tremont Synagogue Gala, 2001, 2002; fund-raiser Alternative Arts and Music Events, Scarsdale Teen Ctr., 2003—; liaison Scarsdale H.S. PTA, Alternative Art and Music Events, Scarsdale Teen Ctr., 2003—05; bd. dirs. com. on spl. edn. Scarsdale Sch. Dist.; fund-raiser Tibet House, NYC, 2008. Recipient Featured Artist Winner, Art Competition, 2009, Online Art Competition prize, 2009; finalist Emerging Artist Competition, 2009. Mem. Internat. Platform Assn., Nat. Mus. Women in Contemporary Arts, Nat. Assn. Women Artists, Inc., Katonah Mus., Nat. Mus. Women in Arts (artist), Nat. Arts Club. Avocations: piano, photography, tennis, kayaking, skiing. Office Phone: 914-725-1174. Personal E-mail: staceyscn21@aol.com.

NEWMAN, STEPHEN ALEXANDER, chemical engineer; b. Auburn, NY, Apr. 12, 1938; s. Solomon and Anna (Reich) N.; m. Mary Ellen Lassow, July 26, 1964; children: Sharon Rose, Lori Suzanne. BSChemE, Rensselaer Poly. Inst., 1960; MSChemE, MIT, 1962; PhD, Rutgers U., 1976. Registered profl. engr., N.J. Rsch. engr. M.W. Kellogg Co., Piscataway, N.J., 1962-67; tech. mgr. Foster Wheeler Energy Corp., Clinton, NJ, 1967—96; prin. engr. Kvaerner Process, Bridgewater, NJ, 1996—99, cons. engr., 1999—, clients have included ABB Lummus Global (Bloomfield, NJ) and Kvaerner Process (Bridgewater, NJ). Organizer, conf./symposium chmn. Nat. Thermodynamics Conf., 1978, World Congress Chem. Engring., Montreal, 1981, CODATA Congress, Jerusalem, 1984; panel NAS, 1980-82; cons. Nat. Bur. Standards, Washington, 1979; chmn. various project coms. U.S. Dept. Energy, 1977-84; spkr. in field. Editor: Thermodynamics of Aqueous Systems with Industrial Applications, 1980, Chemical Engineering Thermodynamics, 1983, Shale Oil Upgrading and Refining, 1983, Acid and Sour Gas Treating Processes, 1985; book and article reviewer Chem. Engring. mag., Gulf Publs., 1980—; contbr. numerous articles to profl. jours. Pres. Mens' Club Temple Israel, Union, N.J., 1980-81. AEC fellow, 1961-62; grantee NSF, 1978, 84. Fellow AIChE (chmn. nat. rsch. com. 1984-85, co-founder Design Inst. Phys. Property Data 1977, vice chmn. 1979-85, award 1989); mem. Am. Petroleum Inst. (chair contractors com. on tech. data 1978-96), Gas Processors Assn. (project monitor 1976-85, tech. com.), Am. Assn. Engring. Socs. Jewish. Home: 941 Douglas Ter Union NJ 07083-6523 Office Phone: 908-688-5167. Personal E-mail: snewman412@yahoo.com.

NEWMAN, STEPHEN MICHAEL, lawyer; b. Buffalo, Jan. 12, 1945; s. Howard A. and Mildred (Ballow) N.; m. Gayle Mallon, May 24, 1969; children: Holly, Deborah. AB, Princeton U., 1966; JD, U. Mich., 1969. Bar: N.Y. 1969, Fla. 1976. Assoc. Hodgson, Russ, Andrews, Woods & Goodyear, Buffalo, 1969-73; ptnr. Hodgson Russ, LLP (formerly Hodgson, Russ, Andrews, Woods & Goodyear), Buffalo, 1973—2004, Nixon Peabody, LLP, Buffalo, 2005—. Lectr. in field. Bd. dirs. Leukemia Soc., United Jewish Fedn. Buffalo Inc., Jewish Ctr. Greater Buffalo Inc., Temple Beth Zion; bd. dirs., chpt. chmn., exec. com. Am. Jewish Com., Buffalo chpt.; bd. advisors Am. Lung Assn., Southeast Fla. chpt. Fellow Am. Coll. Trusts and Estates Coun.; mem. ABA (personal svc. corps. com. tax sect.), N.Y. State Bar Assn. (chair trusts and estates law sect. 2001), Princeton Club of Fla. Office: Nixon Peabody LLP 7121 Fairway Dr Ste 203 Palm Beach Gardens FL 33418 Home Phone: 561-626-4621; Office Phone: 561-691-5424. Business E-Mail: snewman@nixonpeabody.com.

NEWMAN, STEVEN B., hematologist, oncologist; b. Chgo. MD, Tufts U. Sch. of Medicine, Boston, 1977. Cert. Internal Medicine, 1980, Med. Oncology, 1983, Hematology, 1984. Residency in internal medicine U. Chicago Hosp. and Clinics, Chicago, 1977—80; fellowship training in hematology and med. oncology U. Chicago Hosp. and UCLA Med. Ctr., Chicago, 1980—82; faculty mem. UCLA Med. Ctr., 1982—90; staff mem. Northwestern Memorial Hosp., Chicago, 1990—; staff mem. & prof. Robert Lurie Comprehensive Cancer Ctr., Chicago, 1990—; staff mem. Hematology Oncology Assoc. of Ill., 1995—. Fellow: Am. Coll. of Physicians; mem.: Am. Soc. of Hematology, Am. Soc. of Clinical Oncology. Office: Hematology Oncology Assoc 676 N St Clair Ste 2140 Chicago IL 60611 Business E-Mail: steven.newman=@usoncology.com.*

NEWMAN, STEVEN EARL, horticulturist, educator; b. El Paso, Tex., May 29, 1955; s. Clarence Walter and Kay Johnston Newman, Rosemary Johnson Newman (Stepmother); m. Debra Harris Debra Kay Harris; children: Russell Lanier, Thomas Henry. BS, Mont. State U., Bozeman, 1977; MS, U. Nebr. - Lincoln, 1981; PhD, Tex. A&M U., Coll. Sta., 1985. Assoc. prof. dept. nursery & floriculture Miss. State U., Starkville, 1985—94; ext. greenhouse crops specialist & prof. dept. floriculture Colo. State U., Fort Collins, 1994—. Author: (text book) The Commercial Greenhouse, 3E; contbr. scientific papers to numerous profl. jours. Vol. leader Boy Scouts Am., Fort Collins, 2000—. Mem.: Am. Soc. Hort. Sci. (working group chair 1993—2007). Conservative. Roman Catholic. Avocations: fishing, backpacking, gardening. Home: 2312 Hampshire Ct Fort Collins CO 80526 Office: Horticulture & Landscape Architecture Colo State Univ Fort Collins CO 80523-1173 Office Fax: 970-491-7500. Personal E-mail: se.newman@hotmail.com. Business E-Mail: steven.newman@colostate.edu.

NEWMAN, STEVEN L., health care executive; BA, Rutgers U., NJ; MBA, Tulane U., New Orleans; MD, U. Tenn. Intern to resident to fellow Emory U. Sch. Medicine, Atlanta; assoc. prof. pediat. and medicine Wright State U. Sch. Medicine, Dayton, Ohio, 1979—90; dir. gastroenterology and nutrition support Children's Med. Ctr., Dayton, Ohio, 1979—90; sr. v.p., chief med. officer Touro Infirmary, New Orleans, 1990—97; pres., CEO Louisville Healthcare Network Columbia/HCA, 1997—98, pres. Omega Divsn., 1998—99; CEO Audubon Hosp., 1997; v.p. ops. Gulf States Region in Ala., La. and Miss. Tenet Healthcare Corp., 1999—2000, sr. v.p. ops., 2000—03, sr. v.p. Calif. ops., 2003—07, COO. Mem. exec. com. of bd. dirs. Calif. Hosp. Assn. Office: Tenet Healthcare Corp PO Box 809088 Dallas TX 75380-9088 Office Phone: 469-893-2200. Office Fax: 469-893-8600.

NEWMAN, THEODORE ROOSEVELT, JR., Senior Judge, DC Court of Appeals; b. Birmingham, Ala., July 5, 1934; s. Theodore R. and Ruth L. (Oliver) N. AB, Brown U., 1955, LL.D. (hon.), 1980; JD, Harvard U., 1958. Bar: D.C. 1958, Ala. 1959. Atty. civil rights div. Dept. Justice, Washington, 1961-62; practiced law in Washington, 1962-70; assoc. judge D.C. Superior Ct., 1970-76; judge D.C. Ct. Appeals, 1976-91, chief judge, 1976-84, sr. judge, 1991—; bd. dirs. Nat. Center for State Cts., v.p., 1980-81, pres., 1981-82. Visiting lecturer Harvard Law Sch.; adjunct prof. Howard U. Sch. of Law, Georgetown Law Ctr. Trustee Brown U. With USAF, 1958-61. Fellow Am. Bar Found.; mem. Nat. Bar Assn. (past pres. jud. coun., C. Francis Stradford award 1984, William H. Hastie award 1988). E-mail: tnewman@dccappeals.gov.*

NEWMAN, THOMAS, composer; s. Alfred Newman; m. Anne Marie Zirbes; children: Evan, Julia, Jack. Scores include: (films) Grandview, U.S.A., 1984, Reckless, 1984, Revenge of the Nerds, 1984, Girls Just Want to Have Fun, 1985, Desperately Seeking Susan, 1985, The Man with One Red Shoe, 1985, Real Genius, 1985, Gung Ho, 1986, Jumpin' Jack flash, 1986, Quicksilver, 1986, Light of Day, 1987, The Lost Boys, 1987, Less Than Zero, 1987, The Great Outdoors, 1988, The Prince of Pennsylvania, 1988, Cookie, 1989, Men Don't Leave, 1990, Naked Tango, 1990, Welcome Home, Roxy Carmichael, 1990, Career Opportunities, 1991, Deceived, 1991, The Rapture, 1991, Fried Green Tomatoes, 1991, The Linguini Incident, 1992, The Player, 1992, Whispers in the Dark, 1992, Scent of a Woman, 1992, Flesh and Bone, 1993, Josh and S.A.M., 1993, The Favor, 1994, Threesome, 1994, The Shawshank Redemption, 1994 (Acad. award nominee for best original score, 1994), Little Women, 1994 (Acad. award nominee for best original score, 1994), Unstrung Heroes, 1995 (Acad. award nominee for best original score, 1996), How to Make an American Quilt, 1995, Up Close & Personal, 1996, Phenomenon, 1996, American Buffalo, 1996, The People vs. Larry Flynt, 1996, Mad City, 1997, Red Corner, 1997, Oscar and Lucinda, 1997, The Horse Whisperer, 1998, Meet Joe Black 1998, American Beauty, 1999 (Golden Globe award nominee for best original score, 2000, Acad. award nominee for best original score, 2000, Grammy award for best soundtrack album, 2001), The Green Mile, 1999, Erin Brockovich, 2000, My Khmer Heart, 2000, Pay It Forward, 2000, In the Bedroom, 2001, The Execution of Wanda Jean, 2002, The Salton Sea, 2002, Road to Perdition, 2002 (Acad. award nominee for best original score, 2003), White Oleander, 2002, Finding Nemo, 2003 (Acad. award nominee for best original score, 2004), Lemony Snicket's A Series of Unfortunate Events, 2004 (Acad. award nominee for best original score, 2005), Cinderella Man, 2005, La Femme dans la chambre, 2005, Jarhead, 2005, Little Children, 2005, The Good German, 2006 (Acad. award nominee for best original score, 2007), Nothing is Private, 2007, WALL-E, 2008 (Best Instrumental Arrangement, Best Song Written for Motion Picture, Grammy Awards, 2009), Revolutionary Road, 2008; (TV movies) The Seduction of Gina, 1984, Heat Wave, 1991, Those Secrets, 1992, Citizen Cohn, 1992; (TV miniseries) Angels in America, 2003; composed themes for (TV series) Against the Law, 1990, Six Feet Under, 2001 (Emmy award for Outstanding Main Title Theme Music, 2002). Recipient Composer of Yr. award, Hollywood Film Festival, 2004. Office: The Gorfaine Schwartz Agency Inc 4111 W Alameda Ave Ste 509 Burbank CA 91505-4171*

NEWMAN, THOMAS RUBIN, lawyer; b. London, Sept. 7, 1933; BA cum laude, Hofstra U., Hempstead, NY, 1957; LLB, NYU Sch. Law, 1960. Bar: NY 1961, US Dist. Ct. (so. and ea. dists.) NY, US Ct. Appeals (2nd cir.), US Supreme Ct. 1964. Jud. clk. to hon. Charles W. Froessel NY State Ct. Appeals, 1960-62; assoc./ptnr. Sabin, Bermant & Blau (formerly Goldman, Evans & Goldman), 1963—70; founding ptnr. Siff & Newman (formerly Siff, Newman, Rosen & Parker), 1971—87; ptnr. Bower & Gardner, 1971—91; founding mem., pres. Newman & Co., P.C., 1991—99; of counsel Luce, Forward, Hamilton & Scripps LLP, NYC, 1999—2003, Duane Morris LLP, NYC, 2003—. Mem. adv. com. civil practice NY State Office Ct. Adminstrn., 1987—. Author numerous edn1. law handbooks; contbr. articles to profl. jours. Fellow: NY State Bar Assn. (chair com. courts of appellate jurisdiction 1981—85); mem.: ABA, AIDA Reinsurance & Ins. Arbitration Soc., Am. Acad. Appellate Lawyers, Fedn. Ins. & Corp. Counsel, Am. Law Inst. (life), Assn. Bar City of NY (mem. spl. com. on tort litig. 1984—87), Pi Gamma Mu. Office: Duane Morris LLP 1540 Broadway New York NY 10036 Office Phone: 212-692-1028. Office Fax: 212-208-0902. Business E-Mail: TRNewman@duanemorris.com.*

NEWMAN, WILLIAM CLIFFORD, bishop emeritus; b. Balt., Aug. 16, 1928; Attended, St. Mary Sem., Cath. U., Loyola Coll. Ordained priest Archdiocese of Balt., 1954, aux. bishop, 1984—2003, aux. bishop emeritus, 2003—; ordained bishop, 1984. Roman Catholic. Office: Chancery Office 320 Cathedral St Baltimore MD 21201-4421 Address: 6536 Cherry Hill Rd Baldwin MD 21013-9300

NEWMAN, WILLIAM I., geophysicist, astrophysicist, educator; s. Hymie G. and Jessie Newman; m. Deborah A. Juster, Dec. 10, 2006; m. Alice Lynne Sparling (div. June 28, 2006); children: Theodore Ethan, Jennifer Rachel. BSc with first class honors, U. Alta., Edmonton, Can., 1971, MSc, 1972; MS, Cornell U., Ithaca, NY, 1975, PhD, 1979. Mem. Inst. Advanced Study, Princeton, NJ, 1978—80; prof. U. Calif., LA, 1980—. Vis. assoc. prof. Cornell U., 1987—88; Morris Belkin vis. prof. Weizmann Inst., Rehovot, Israel, 2000—01. Named disting. scholar, Los Alamos Nat. Lab., N. Mex., 1990—91; fellow, John Simon Guggenheim Found., 1987-1988. Mem.: Am. Astron. Soc. Divsn. Dynamical Astronomy (chair 2003—04). Office: UCLA Dept Earth & Space Sci 595 C Young Dr E 3806 Geology Bldg Los Angeles CA 90095-1567 Business E-Mail: win@ucla.edu.

NEWMAN, ZELDA KAHAN, linguist; b. NYC, Dec. 9, 1946; d. Julius and Pearl Kahan; m. David Solomon Kahan, Jan. 7, 1973; children: Moshe Shmuel, Yehuda, Yehudit. PhD, U. Mich., 1983. Linguist Hebraic and Judaic studies Lehman Coll., Bronx, NY, 2003—. Contbr. articles to profl. jours. Founder MASLAN, Beer Sheva, Israel, 1990—2003. Mem.: Acad. Theater Awards. Jewish. Avocation: gardening. Home: 600 W 239th St apt 6E Bronx NY 10463 Office: Lehman Coll CUNY 250 Bedford Pk Blvd W Bronx NY 10468 Business E-Mail: zelda.newman@lehman.cuny.edu.

NEWMARK, CRAIG ALEXANDER, Internet company executive; b. Morristown, NJ, Dec. 6, 1952; s. Leon and Joyce Newmark. BS, Case Western Reserve U., 1975, MS in Computer Sci., 1977. Computer programmer IBM, NJ, 1979—93; systems security architect, gen. cons. Charles Schwab, Calif., 1993—95; ind. contractor, software sys. architect Bank of America, Calif., 1995—97, Intel, Calif., 1995—97, Sun Microsystems, Calif., 1995—97; founder, chmn., customer service rep. Craigslist, San Francisco, 1995—. Featured in AP, Wall Street Journal, NY Times, LA Times, USA Today, Business Week, Time Mag., and Esquire Mag. Adv. bd. Climate Theatre, Haight-Ashbury Food Program; supporter of local writers through Grotto Nights. Named #1 Most Efficient US Job Site, Forrester Rsch. Report, Wall St. Jour., 2000, Best Cmty. Website - People's Voice, Webby Awards, 2001, The Elite of the Online Employment Industry, WEDDLE's User's Choice Awards, 2004, 50 online destinations for the quarterlifer, Hatch Mag., 2004, 50 Coolest Websites, Time mag., 2004, Person of the Year, Webby Awards, The Internat. Acad. Digital Arts and Sciences, 2005, Webby Person of Yr., 2005; named one of World's 100 Most Influential People, Time Mag., 2005, 26 Most Fascinating Entrepreneurs, Inc.com, 2005, 50 Most Important People on the Web, PC World, 2007. Fellow: World Tech. Network (World Tech. award-Comm. Tech. 2006). Achievements include millions of people use Craigslist to research subjects such as: jobs, housing, goods & services, events, friendships, and advice; first commercial transmission of a website into space by Deep Space Communications Network, March 11, 2005. Office: Craigslist 1319 9th Ave San Francisco CA 94122-2308 Office Phone: 415-566-6394. Office Fax: 415-504-6394. Business E-Mail: craig@craigslist.org.

NEWMARK, EMANUEL, ophthalmologist; b. Newark, May 25, 1936; s. Charles Meyer and Bella (Yoskowitz) Newmark; m. Tina Steinberg, Aug. 25, 1957; children: Karen Beth, Heidi Ellen, Stuart Jeffrey. BS in Pharmacy, Rutgers U., Newark, 1959; postgrad., U. Amsterdam, The Netherlands, 1960-63, Armed Forces Inst. Pathology, Washington, 1971; MD, Duke U., Durham, NC, 1966; postgrad., Harvard U., Cambridge, Mass., 1967. Diplomate Am. Bd. Ophthalmology. Intern George Washington U. Hosp., Washington, 1966; trainee NIH rsch. U. Fla., Gainesville, 1967—70; resident ophthalmology U. Fla. Hosp., 1967—70; instr. dept. ophthalmology U. Fla., 1970; cons. ophthalmology Gainesville VA Hosp., 1970; clin. instr. ophthalmology U. Tex. Med. Sch., San Antonio, 1971—72; cons. ophthalmology Kerrville VA Hosp., Tex., 1971—72; asst. chief ophthalmology svc. Brooke Army Gen. Hosp., Fort Sam, Tex., 1971—72. Clin. asst. prof. ophthalmology Bexar County Hosp. and Clinics, San Antonio, 1971—72; tchg. faculty Joint Commn. Allied Health Pers. in Ophthalmology, commr., 2004—; sec., treas. Palm Beach Eye Assocs., Atlantis, Fla., 1973—98; pharm. adv. com. Agy. Health Care Adminstrn. Bd. Optometry, 1991—; mem. adv. bd. Fla. east coast chpt. Nat. Sjorgren's Syndrome; chief ophthalmology JFK Med. Ctr., 1984, chmn. CME and edn. com., 2004—; staff ophthalmologist West Palm Beach VA Hosp., 2005—, Regional Eye Inst., 1998—2006. Contbr. chapters to books, articles to profl. jours.; exec. editor Ophthalmic Medical Assisting: An Independent Study Course, 2006. Alumni assoc. Rutgers Coll. Pharmacy, 1990—, chmn. reunion, 1986, 2001, Duke U. Med. Alumni Assn., NC, 1967—; centurian Davison Club-Duke U. Med. Sch., NC, 1982—; campaign chmn., nat. vice chmn. Israel Bonds, Palm Beach County, Fla., 1988—90; participant charitable orgns.; v.p. Palm Beach Liturgical Culture Found., 1994—2000, pres., 2000—01. Decorated Lion of Judea State of Israel; recipient Gates of Jerusalem medal, 1991, Jerusalem medal, 1996, Recognition award, Joint Commn. Allied Health Personnel in Ophthalmology, 2001, 2006, US Army Commendation medal. Fellow: ACS, Am. Acad. Ophthalmology (del. to coun. 1996—2001, allied health edn. com. 1997—2002, editor Refinements 1998—2000, rep. to joint com. allied health pers. in ophthalmology 2004—, Fla. state chmn. ednl. trust, Achievement award 2001, Councillors award 2001, Secretariat award 2005); mem.: AMA, Fla. Soc. Ophthalmology (ethics chmn. 1985—90, pres. 1990—91, James W. Clower Jr. Cmty. Svc. award 1995, Shalar Richardson, MD Svc. to Medicine award 2007), Palm Beach County Ophthal. Soc. (pres. 1984—85, Ophthalmologist of Yr. 2004), Palm Beach County Med. Soc. (chair ethics com. 1997—2000, vice chair ethics com. 2002, bd. dirs. 2003, bd. dirs. mem.-at-large 2003—, coun. on ethical and jud. affairs 2004—, trustee 2005, v.p. svcs. bd. 2008—, Heroes in Medicine award 2009), Fla. Med. Assn. (ho. dels. 1993—95, 2001—06, 2008—), Am. Orgn. for Rehab. Through Tng. Fedn. (nat. exec. com.-campaign cabinet 1987, pres. 1987—90, hon. del. 1993—95, 2001—, Palm Beach Men's Achievement award 1988, Pres. award 1989), Founder's Soc. Duke U. Jewish. Avocation: travel. Home: 180 Palm Cir Atlantis FL 33462-6627 Office: West Palm Beach Vets Med Ctr 7305 Military Trail West Palm Beach FL 33410 Personal E-mail: mannynewmark@msn.com.

NEWMARK, LEONARD DANIEL, linguistics educator; b. Attica, Ind., Apr. 8, 1929; s. Max Jacob and Sophie (Glusker) N.; m. Ruth Broessler, Sept. 16, 1951; children: Katya, Mark. AB, U. Chgo., 1947; MA, Ind. U., 1951, PhD, 1955. Instr. English U. Ill., Urbana, 1951; vis. asst. prof. linguistics U. Mich., Ann Arbor, 1961; assoc. prof. English Ohio State U., 1954-62; assoc. prof. linguistics Ind. U., Bloomington, 1962-63; prof. linguistics U. Calif., San Diego, 1963-91, prof. emeritus, 1992—, chmn. dept., 1963-71, 79-85, head program in Am. lang. and culture, 1979-84, rsch. linguist Ctr. for Rsch. in Lang., 1992—. Author: Linguistic History of English, 1963, Spoken Albanian, 1997, Standard Albanian, 1982, Albanian-English Dictionary, 1998, Albanian Handbook, 1999; founding editor UCSD Emeriti Newsletter: Chronicles, 2001-2004. Mem. Linguistics Soc. Am., Dictionary Soc. N.Am., Phi Beta Kappa. Achievements include invention of memory aid device. Business E-Mail: ldnewmark@ucsd.edu.

NEWMARK, MARILYN, sculptor; b. NYC, July 20, 1928; d. Edward Ellis and Mabel (Davies) Newmark; m. Leonard J. Meiselman, Mar. 15, 1952. Student, Adelphi Coll., 1945—47, Alfred U., NYC, 1949. Sculpture specializing in horses, equestrian figures, dogs, foxes. Exhibited in group shows Derby Mus., Fleischer Mus., Scottsdale, Leigh Yawkey Woodson Art Mus., Wis., Bennington Ctr. for Arts, Vt., NAD, NYC, Nat. Arts Club, NYC, Smithsonian Instn., Washington, Mus. of Horse, Ky., Port of History Mus., Pa., Marietta/Cobb Mus. Art, Wildlife Experience, Denver, Nat. Geog. Soc., Washington, Allegheny Colls. Galleries, Butler Inst. Am. Art; represented in permanent collections Nat. Mus. Racing, Saratoga, NY, Internat. Mus. Horse, Ky. Horse Park, Brookgreen Gardens, S.C.,also pvt. collections. Recipient Anna Hyatt Huntington award, 1970-72, 75, 78, 80-83, 86, 88, 90, 97, 2002, Gold medal, 1973, award Coun. Am. Artists Socs., 1972, 73, 79, 80, Hudson Valley John Newington award, 1973, 77, Gold medal, 1979, Elliot Liskin Meml. award, 1989, 96, Academician NAD Ellin P. Speyer award, 1974, 93, 99, Artist Fund award, 1982, Michael Gressel award, 2006. Fellow Nat. Sculpture Soc. (coun. 1973-75, rec. sec. 1976, 2008, sec. 1977-79, coun. 1981-83, 92-97, 2006-, Bronze medal 1986, Mildred Victor Meml. award 1996, Leonard Meiselman Meml. award 2003), Audubon Artists (Elliott Liskin Meml. award 2000, 02), Am. Artists Profl. League (Gold medal 1974, 77, medal of hon. 1987), Allied Artists Am. (Gold medal 1981, 93, In Memorium award 1994), Pen & Brush Club (Gold medal 1977, Salmagundi Club award 1982, 83, 91, C. Dunwiddie Meml. award 1999, 2004), Draft Horse Classic (Calif.) (Best of Show 2006-07, Best in Metal 2008), Soc. Animal Artists (jury of admissions 1972-75, 90—, bd. dirs. 1991—, v.p. 1998—, Legacy award 2002), Am. Acad. Equine Art (founding mem., dir. sculpture 1980—), Nassau Suffolk Horsemans Assn. (dir. 1968-82), Catherine Lorillard Wolfe Art Club, Smithtown Hunt Club, Meadowbrook Hunt Club,Breckenridge Arts Tex.(Clay Pitzer Mem.award, 2007-08), Red River Art Tex.(IESI award, 2008). Address: 4 Central Dr Glen Head NY 11545 Office Phone: 516-621-5914. Personal E-mail: marilynnewmark@aol.com.

NEWMEYER, FREDERICK JARET, linguist, educator; b. Phila., Jan. 30, 1944; s. Alvin S. and Fritzie B. (Nisenson) N.; m. Carolyn V. Platt, Apr. 28, 1968 (div. 1974); m. Marilyn M. Goebel, Dec. 25, 1993. BA, U. Rochester, 1965, MA, 1967; PhD, U. Ill., 1969. Asst. prof. linguistics U. Wash., Seattle, 1969-75, assoc. prof., 1975-81, prof., 1981—, chair, 1990-2000. Vis. prof. U. London, 1979, Cornell U., 1981, U. Md., 1982, UCLA, 1982-83, La Trobe U., Australia, 1987, adj. prof., U. Brit. Columbia & Simon Fraser U., 2007-. Author: English Aspectual Verbs, 1975, Linguistic Theory in America, 1980, Grammatical Theory, 1983, Politics of Linguistics, 1986, Generative Linguistics, 1995, Language Form and Language Function, 1998, Possible and Probable Languages, 2005; editor: Linguistics: The Cambridge Survey, 1988, Natural Language and Linguistic Theory, 1987-2003; assoc. editor: Language, 1980-85. NEH fellow, 1973-74. Fellow AAAS; mem. Linguistic Soc. Am. (sec.-treas. 1989-94, v.p. 2001, pres. 2002). Office: 1068 Seymour St Vancouver BC V6B 3M6 Canada Home: 428 Beach Crescent # 702 Vancouver BC V6Z 3G1 Canada E-mail: fjn@u.washington.edu.

NEWMEYER, ROBERT J., lawyer; b. Phila., 1958; BA cum laude, Oral Roberts U., 1981; JD, O.W. Coburn Sch. Law, 1986. Bar: Okla. 1986, Calif. 1991; U.S. Dist Ct. (no. dist.) Okla. 1986, U.S. Dist. Ct. (so. dist.) Calif. 1997, U.S. Dist. Ct. Colo., 1998; U.S. Ct. Appeals (8th cir.) 1999, U.S. Ct. Appeals (9th cir.) 1998, U.S. Ct. Appeals (10th cir.) 1998, U.S. Ct. Appeals (7th cir.) 1999, U.S. Ct. Appeals (1st cir.) 1999, U.S. Ct. Appeals (5th cir.) 2000. Police officer Tulsa Police Dept., 1981-83; law clk. Blackstock, Joyce, et al, Tulsa, 1984; research asst. O.W. Coburn Sch. Law, Tulsa, 1984-85; legal intern McCormick, Andrew & Clark, Tulsa, 1985-86; assoc. McCormick Andrew & Clark, Tulsa, 1986-87; law clk. to U.S. Magistrate Judge Jeffrey S. Wolfe U.S. Dist. Ct., Okla., 1987-91, law clk. to chief U.S. Magistrate Judge Roger C. McKee Calif., 1991-97; assoc. Bopp, Coleson & Bostrom, Terre Haute, Ind., 1997—99; sr. law clerk U.S. Dist. Judge Roger T. Benitez, U.S. Dist. Ct. Calif., 2000—. Editor Oral Roberts U. Law Rev., 1986. Lctr. Citizen's Crime Commn., Tulsa, 1982-83. Named Top Atty., San Diego Daily Transcript, 2009. Mem. Calif. Bar Assn., Okla. Bar Assn. Republican. Office: PO Box 800 Jamul CA 91935-0800 Office Phone: 619-446-3589. E-mail: robert_newmeyer@casd.uscourts.gov.

NEWPORT, D. JEFFREY, psychiatrist, researcher; MD, U. SC; MS in Clinical Rsch., Emory U. Resident Emory U. Sch. Medicine, assoc. prof. psychiatry & behavioral sciences, assoc. dir. Emory Women's Mental Health Program. Contbr. chapters to books. Recipient Young Faculty award, Am. Psychiatric Inst. for Rsch. & End., Young Investigator award, Nat. Alliance for Rsch. on Schizophrenia & Depression, Hoechst Marion Roussel award, Am. Soc. Clinical Psychopharmacology, Psychiatry Resident of Yr. award, Pfizer. Fellow: Am. Psychiatric Assn., Am. Coll. Psychiatrists, Soc. Biological Psychiatry. Office: Emory University School of Medicine Emory Clinic Bldg B 1365 Clifton Rd NE Ste 6100 Atlanta GA 30322 Office Phone: 404-778-2524. Office Fax: 404-778-2535. E-mail: wmhp@emory.edu.*

NEWSCHAFFER, CRAIG J., epidemiologist, educator; BA in Pub. Rels., Boston U., 1984, BS in Biology, 1984; SM in Health Policy & Mgmt., Harvard Sch. Pub. Health, 1987; PhD in Chronic Disease Epidemiology, Johns Hopkins U., 1996. Policy analyst Project HOPE Ctr. for Health Affairs, 1987—89, sr. rsch. assoc., 1991—93; rsch. asst. Johns Hopkins Bloomberg Sch. Pub. Health, 1989—93, asst. prof., 1999—2002, dir. Ctr. for Autism & Devel. Disabilities, 2001—06, dir. gen. epidemiology, 2002—06, assoc. prof. dept. epidemiology, 2002—06; asst. prof. cmty. health-epidemiology St. Louis U. Sch. Pub. Health, 1993—96, dir. divsn. epidemiology, 1996, rsch. assoc., 1996—2006, adj. asst. prof. cmty. health-epidemiology, 1996—2006; rsch. assoc. epidemiologist Thomas Jefferson U. Med. Coll., 1996—99, rsch. asst. prof., 1996—99; adj. scholar U. Pa. Med. Ctr., 1997—99; prof. & chmn. dept. epidemiology & biostatistics Drexel U. Sch. Pub. Health, 2006—. Assoc. editor Am. Jour. Epidemiology; editorial bd. mem. Developmental Epidemiology. Mem.: Soc. Gen. Internal Medicine, Gerontological Soc. America, Am. Pub. Health Assn. (epidemiology section coun. mem. 1991—2002, gov. coun. mem. 2002—04), Soc. for Epidemiologic Rsch. Office: Drexel University School of Publich Health 245 N 15th St Mail Stop 660 Philadelphia PA 19102-1192 Office Phone: 215-762-7152. Office Fax: 215-762-4088. E-mail: cnewscha@drexel.edu.*

NEWSOM, GAVIN CHRISTOPHER, Mayor, San Francisco; b. San Francisco, Oct. 10, 1967; s. William and Tessa Newsom; m. Kimberly Guilfoyle Newsom, Dec. 8, 2001 (div. 2006); m. Jennifer Siebel, July 26, 2008. BA in Polit. Sci., Santa Clara U., 1989. Founder PlumpJack Wines Mgmt. Group, San Francisco, 1992—; pres. Pkg. and Traffic Commn., San Francisco, 1996—97; mem. Office of Bd. Suprs., San Francisco, 1996—2004; mayor City of San Francisco, 2004—. Named one of 17 People Who Matter, TIME mag., 2004. Office: City Hall Room 200 1 Dr Carlton B Goodlett Place San Francisco CA 94102 Office Phone: 415-554-6141. Office Fax: 415-554-6160. Business E-Mail: gavin.newsom@sfgov.org.*

NEWSOM, GERALD HIGLEY, astronomy educator; b. Albuquerque, Feb. 11, 1939; s. Carroll Vincent and Frances Jeanne (Higley) N.; m. Ann Catherine Bricker, June 17, 1972; children: Christine Ann, Elizabeth Ann. BA, U. Mich., 1961; MA, Harvard U., 1963, PhD, 1968. Research asst. McMath-Hulbert Obs., Pontiac, Mich., summers 1959, 61; research asst. astronomy dept. U. Mich., Ann Arbor, 1959-61; research asst. Shock Tube Lab. Harvard U., Cambridge, Mass., 1962, 64-68; research asst. dept. physics Imperial Coll., London, 1968-69; asst. prof. astronomy Ohio State U., Columbus, 1969-73, assoc. prof., 1973-82, prof., 1982—2004, acting chmn. dept. astronomy, 1991-93, vice chmn. dept. astronomy, 1993—2004, acting asst. dean, 1985-86; sr. post-doctoral research asst. Physikalisches Institut, Bonn, Fed. Republic of Germany, 1978. Author: Astronomy, 1976, Exploring the Universe, 1979; contbr. articles to profl. jours. Fellow Woodrow Wilson Found., 1961-62, NSF, 1961-63; grantee Noble Found., 1961-64. Mem.: Am. Astron. Soc., Internat. Astron. Union. Home: 46 W Weisheimer Rd Columbus OH 43214-2545 Office: Ohio State U Dept Astronomy 140 W 18th Ave Columbus OH 43210-1173 Home Phone: 614-263-8240. Business E-Mail: gnewsom@astronomy.ohio-state.edu.

NEWSOM, JAMES THOMAS, lawyer; b. Carrollton, Mo., Oct. 6, 1944; s. Thomas Edward and Hazel Love (Mitchell) N.; m. Sherry Elaine Retzloff, Aug. 9, 1986; stepchildren: Benjamin A. Bawden, Holly K. Bawden. AB, U. Mo., 1966, JD, 1968. Bar: Mo. 1968, US Supreme Ct. 1971. Assoc. Shook, Hardy & Bacon, London and Kansas City, Mo., 1972, ptnr., 1976—. Mem. Mo. Law Rev., 1966-68. Lt. comdr. JAGC, USNR, 1968-72. Mem. ABA, Kansas City Met. Bar Assn., U. Mo. Law Sch. Law Soc., U. Mo. Jefferson Club, Order of Coif, Perry (Kans.) Yacht Club, Stone Horse Yacht Club (Harwich Port, Mass.). Avocations: skiing, sailing, auto racing. Office: Shook Hardy & Bacon 2555 Grand Blvd Kansas City MO 64108-2613 Home Phone: 913-381-5605; Office Phone: 816-474-6550. Business E-Mail: jnewsom@shb.com.

NEWSOME, FREDERICK V., medical educator; b. Charleston, W.Va., July 7, 1946; s. Moses and Ruth (Bass) N.; m. Osilo Chindo, Mar. 23, 1974, (dec. Aug. 31, 2008); children: Akasemi, Imhotep, Nubia, Hatshepsut. BA in Chemistry, Harvard U., 1968; MD, W.Va. U., 1972; MSc in Tropical Medicine, London Sch. Hygiene & Tropical Medicine, 1981. Diplomate Am. Bd. Internal Medicine. Instr. in medicine Coll. of Physicians and Surgeons Columbia U., NYC, 1975-78; instr. in medicine Albert Einstein Med. Sch., Bronx, 1979-80; sr. lectr. in medicine U. Jos, Nigeria, 1981-88; clin. prof., head dept. of medicine Coll. of Health Scis. Usmanu Danfodio U., Sokoto, Nigeria, 1988-90; chief ambulatory medicine The Meth. Hosp., Bklyn., 1991-92; assoc. attending physician Harlem Hosp. Ctr.; asst. prof. medicine Columbia U. Coll. Physicians & Surgeons, NYC, 1992—. Author: An African American Philosophy of Medicine, 2005; contbr. articles to profl. jours. Fellow ACP, West African Coll. Physicians, Royal Soc. Tropical Medicine and Hygiene; mem. Nat. Med. Assn., Assn. for Study Afro-Am. Life and History. Office: 15 Prince St New Rochelle NY 10801 Office Phone: 212-939-1411.

NEWSOME, GARY D., hospital operations company executive; BS, Bluefield State Coll., W.Va.; MBA, Butler U., Indpls.; advanced studies, U. Mich. Sch. Bus. Hosp. ops. Humana; divisional v.p. group ops., asst. v.p. group ops., hosp. CEO Health Mgmt. Associates, Inc., 1993—98; v.p. group ops. Cmty. Health Systems, Inc., divsn. pres. hosp. ops.; pres., CEO Health Mgmt. Associates, Inc., 2008—. Bd. dirs. Health Mgmt. Associates, Inc., 2008—. Office: Health Mgmt Associates Inc 5811 Pelican Bay Blvd Ste 500 Naples FL 34108 Office Phone: 239-598-3131.*

NEWSOME, JAMES EUGENE, former mercantile exchange executive; b. 1959; m. Mei Mei Newsome; children: Molly, Riley. BS in Food & Resource Econ., U. Fla., 1982; MS in Animal Sci. & Agrl. Econ., Miss. State U., 1985, PhD in Philosophy, 2001. Exec. v.p. Miss. Cattlemen's Assn. & Beef Coun, 1989—98; commr. Commodity Futures Trading Commn. (CFTC), Washington, 1998—2001, acting chmn., 2001, chmn., 2001—04; pres., CEO NY Merc. Exch., Inc. (NYMEX), NYC, 2004—08. Mem. Pres. Working Group on Fin. Markets, US Corp. Fraud Task Force, Gov's. Task Force on Future Miss. Agrl.; chmn. Miss. Agribus. Coun., pres. Fla. Future Farmers Am., U. Fla. Agrl. Coun., Nat. Futures Assn., Dubai Merc. Exch., bd. dirs. CME Group Inc., 2008-, bd. mgrs. Gavilon Holdings, LLC, 2009- Recipient Disting. Alumnus, U. Fla., Arthur Kaplan award, Futures & Options for Kids; named Person of Yr., Stock Futures & Options; named an Alumni Fellow, Miss. State U. Mem. Assn. Miss. Agrl. Orgns. (pres.).*

NEWSOME, LISA TESTA, anesthesiologist, educator; d. Joseph Salvatore and Jean Marie Testa; m. Albert Ray Newsome; 1 child, Emilie Pierrepont. DMD, U. Pa., Phila., 1987; MD, Vanderbilt, Nashville, 1990. Cert. Examiners NC, 1994. Faculty Wake Forest Anesthesiologist, Winston-Salem, NC, 2001—08; anesthesiologist Somnia, New Rochelle, 2008—. Chair Greensboro Children's Mus., NC, 2008. Business E-Mail: ltn723@triad.rr.com.

NEWSOME, OZZIE, professional sports team executive; b. Muscle Shoals, Ala., Mar. 16, 1956; s. Ethel Newsome and Ozzie Newsome Sr.; m. Gloria Jenkins. BS, U. Ala. Tight end Cleve. Browns, 1978-90, spl. assignment scout, 1991—93, asst. to the head coach, offense, pro pers., 1993, dir. pro pers., 1994—95; v.p. player pers. Balt. Ravens, 1996—99, sr. v.p. football ops., 1999—2002, exec. v.p., gen. mgr., 2002—. Active Big Bros., Athletes in Action; bd. dirs. Police Athletic League. Recipient Byron "Whizzer" White award, 1990; named Offensive Player of Yr., Cleve. Touchdown Club, 1978, 81, 83, 84, 1st Team All-Pro, AP, 1984, NFL Exec. of Yr., 2000; named to Am. Football Conf. Pro-Bowl Team, NFL, 1981, 84, 85, Coll. Football Hall of Fame, 1994, Pro Football Hall of Fame, 1999, Canton Ohio. Mem. Fellowship of Christian Athletes. Office: Balt Ravens Owings Mills Tng Facility 1 Winning Dr Owings Mills MD 21117 Office Phone: 410-701-4000.*

NEWSOME, RANDALL JACKSON, judge; b. Dayton, Ohio, July 13, 1950; s. Harold I. and Sultana S. (Stone) N. BA summa cum laude, Boston U., 1972; JD, U. Cin., 1975. Bar: Ohio 1975, U.S. Dist. Ct. (so. dist.) Ohio 1977, U.S. Ct. Appeals (6th cir.) 1979, U.S. Supreme Ct. 1981. Law clk. to chief judge U.S. Dist. Ct. (so. dist.) Ohio, 1975-77; assoc. Dinsmore & Shohl, Cin., 1978-82; judge U.S. Bankruptcy Ct. (so. dist.) Ohio, 1982-88, U.S. Bankruptcy Ct. (no. dist.) Calif., Oakland, 1988—2004, chief judge, 2004—. Faculty mem. Fed. Jud. Ctr., ALI-ABA, 1987—; mem. Nat. Conf. of Bankruptcy Judges, 1983—, mem. bd. govs., 1987-88, pres., 1998-99; advisor USAID, Kosovo, 2007-08. Contbg. author: Chapter 11 Theory and Practice, 1994—, Collier on Bankruptcy, 1997—. Recipient Disting. Alumus award, U. Cin. Law

Alumni Assn., 2008. Fellow Am. Coll. Bankruptcy; mem. Am. Law Inst., Phi Beta Kappa. Democrat. Office: US Bankruptcy Ct PO Box 2070 Oakland CA 94604-2070 Office Phone: 510-879-3530.

NEWSOME, WILLIAM BRIAN, history professor; s. William Daniel and Ann Newsome; m. Susan Rhea Asbury-Newsome, July 20, 2002; 1 child, Braden Andrew. PhD, U. SC., Columbia, 2002. Asst. prof. history Alfred U., NY, 2003—. Author: (book) French Urban Planning, 1940-1968: The Construction and Deconstruction of an Authoritarian System. Vestry mem. St. Michael's Episcopal Ch., Geneseo, NY, 2006—08. Recipient Excellence Tchg. award, Alfred U., 2006, 2008; Grant, Fulbright Commn., France, 2000—01. Mem.: Western Soc. French History, Soc. French Hist. Studies, NY State Assn. European Historians (v.p. 2008—09), Am. Hist. Assn., Phi Alpha Theta, Phi Kappa Phi. Office: Alfred Univ 1 Saxon Dr Alfred NY 14802

NEWTON, ALEXANDER WORTHY, lawyer; b. Birmingham, Ala., June 19, 1930; s. Jeff H. and Annis Lillian (Kelly) N.; m. Sue Aldridge, Dec. 22, 1952; children: Lamar Aldridge Newton, Kelly McClure Newton Hammond, Jane Worthy Newton, Robins Jeffry Newton. BS, U. Ala., 1952, JD, 1957. Bar: Ala. 1957. Pvt. practice law, Birmingham; assoc. Hare, Wynn & Newell, Birmingham, 1957; ptnr. Hare, Wynn, Newell & Newton, Birmingham, 1961—. Del. U.S. Ct. Appeals (11th cir.) Jud. Conf., 1988, 89, 90, 91; mem. Jefferson County Jud. Nominating Com., 1983-89; mem. Birmingham Airport Authority, 1991-2006; founding dir. First Comm. Bank. Co-author: (with others) Federal Appellate Procedure, 11th Circuit, 1996. Vice chmn. Birmingham Racing Comm., 1984-87; v.p. U. Ala. Law Sch. Found., 1978-79, pres., 1980-82, exec. com., 1987—; mem. Leadership Ala. Class IV; trustee Ala. Trust Fund, 2002; bd. dirs. St. Vincent Hosp. Found.; mem. Jefferson Met. Healthcare Authority, 2005-06. Capt. inf. U.S. Army, 1952-54. Recipient Disting. Alumnus award Farrah Law Soc. U. Ala., 1984, Sam W. Pipes Disting. Alumnus award 1982 Fellow Am. Coll. Trial Lawyers (state chmn. 1983-84, regents' nominatin com. 1984-85), Internat. Soc. Barristers (bd. dirs. 1974-75, sec.-treas. 1976-77, v.p. 1977-78, pres. 1979-80), Internat. Acad. Trial Lawyers (bd. dirs. 1998—); mem. ABA, ATLA, Am. Bar Found., Ala. State Bar (chmn. practices and procedures subsect. 1965, governance com. and pres.'s task force 1984-86, pres.'s com. 1987-88), Birmingham Bar Assn. (exec. com. 1967), Ala. Trial Lawyers Assn. (sec.-treas. 1958-65), Am. Judicature Soc., 11th Cir. Hist. Soc. (trustee 1988-2007), Birmingham Bar Assn. (Lawyer of Yr.), Shoal Creek Club, Birmingham Country Club, Capital City Club (Atlanta), Garden of the Gods Club (Colorado Springs, Colo.), Univ. Club (N.Y.C.), Sigma Chi. Democrat. Presbyterian. Home: 2837 Canoe Brook Ln Birmingham AL 35243-5908 Office: Hare Wynn Newell & Newton 800 Massey Bldg 2025 3d Ave N Birmingham AL 35203-3330 Office Phone: 205-328-5330.

NEWTON, CINDY LYNN, middle school educator, media specialist; b. Frankfort, Ind., Nov. 1, 1954; d. William Max and Barbara Lois Cline; m. Robert Allen Newton, Dec. 28, 1974; children: Amber Lynne Robinson, Amanda Joy Fredericks. BSc, Ind. U., 1994; M in Edn., Ind. Wesleyan U., 1999. Reading Endorsement Ind. U., 1994, Academy of Leadership for Teachers Ind., 1999, cert. media specialist IUPUI, Indpls., Ind., 2009. Elem. tchr. Eastview Elem., Connersville, Ind., 1994—2007; media specialist Connersville Mid. Sch., 2007—. Tech. bldg. go-to Eastview Elem., Connersville, Ind.; armstrong educator Ind. U., 2005—; supervising tchr. Ind. U. East, 1995—; state reading dist. rep. Ind. State Reading Assn., 1998—2006; staff devel. inservice provider Eastview Elem., Connersville, Ind., 1995—. State officer rep. Ind. State Read Assn., 1998—2000; tchr. yr. selection com. Fayette County Schs., Connersville, 2000—07; Sunday sch. tchr. Pk. Pl. Ch. of God, 1981—, dir. 40 Days of Purpose, 2005. Recipient Ind. U. Armstrong Tchr. Educator award, Ind. U., 2005, Citizen's Adv. Achievement award, 3Rivers SWM Dist., 2005, Outstanding Svc. award, Ind. State Reading Assn., 2003, Christel DeHann's Excellence in Edn., Project e, 2000, Outstanding Profl. award, Ind. Wesleyan U., 1999, Tchr. of Yr., Fayette County Sch. Corp., 1998, Three Rivers Solid Waste Mgmt. Environ. Citizen's award; fellow Gifted and Talented Action Rsch. grant, State of Ind., 2000. Master: Connersville Area Reading Coun. (assoc.); mem.: ASCD, Libr. Congress Inst., Internat. Reading Assn. (assoc.), Ind. Computer Educators (assoc.), Ind. State Reading Assn. (assoc.; sec. 2001—02, Outstanding Svc. award 2003), Delta Kappa Gamma. Achievements include development of elementary computer clubs. Office: Connersville Mid Sch 1900 N Grand Ave Connersville IN 47331 Business E-Mail: cnewton@fayette.k12.in.us.

NEWTON, DON ALLEN, economic development consultant; b. Laurel, Miss., Oct. 19, 1934; s. Wilfred L. and Mary (McMullan) N.; m. Coleta Farrell, Oct. 11, 1958; children: Don Jr., Coleta Midge Rast. AA, Meridian CC, Miss., 1954; BA, U. Ala., 1956; postgrad. in Assn. Mgmt., U. NC; postgrad. in Econ. Devel., U. Okla. Asst. mgr. Meridian C. of C., 1956; mgr. Winston County C. of C., Louisville, Miss., 1960—61; asst. dir. Delta Coun. Indsl. and Cmty. Devel. Bd., Stoneville, Miss., 1961—62, dir., 1963—70; exec. v.p. Met. Devel. Bd., Birmingham, Ala., 1970—74; pres. Birmingham Regional C. of C., 1974—99; pub. Birmingham Mag., Birmingham Bus. Mag., 1974—99; pres. Birmingham Area C. of C. Found., Inc., 1988-99, Devel. Assocs. Econ. Devel., 1999. Contbr. articles to profl. jours., newspapers. Former appointee Ala. Export Coun.; bd. dirs. Birmingham Met. Devel. Bd., Ala. Sports Found. Lt. USNR, 1957-60. Named Ala. Mktg. Man of Yr., 1972. Mem.: Sigma Chi. Home: 4156 Glenbrook Dr Birmingham AL 35213 Office: Development Assocs PO Box 530093 Birmingham AL 35253-0093 Home Phone: 205-879-9088.

NEWTON, EDWARD R., obstetrician, educator; Grad., Northwestern U., 1974; MD, Loyola U., 1977. Cert. Ob-Gyn., Maternal-Fetal Medicine, 1984. Intern Chgo. Stritch Sch. Medicine, Loyola U., 1977—78; fellow Tufts U. Sch. Medicine, 1981—83, resident, 1978—81; with dept. ob-gyn. Brody Sch. Medicine, East Carolina U., Greenville, 1998—, prof., chmn. ob-gyn. Office: E Carolina U Brody Sch Medicine Dept Ob-Gyn PCMH Tchg Annex Greenville NC 27834 Office Phone: 252-744-5695. Office Fax: 252-744-2988. E-mail: newtoned@ecu.edu.*

NEWTON, FLOYD CHILDS, III, lawyer; b. Griffin, Ga., Feb. 4, 1955; s. Floyd Childs Jr. and Jean (Hunt) N.; m. Katrina Dalton, Aug. 30, 1986; children: Stephanie, Amanda, Natalie. BA, Princeton U., NJ, 1977; JD, U. Ga., 1980. Bar: Ga. 1980, U.S. Dist. Ct. (no. dist.) Ga. 1980, U.S. Ct. Appeals (11th cir.) 1980. Ptnr. King & Spalding, Atlanta, 1980—. Mem. Nat. Assn. Bond Lawyers (pres. 1998-99). Office: King & Spalding 1180 Peachtree St Atlanta GA 30309 Office Phone: 404-572-4600. Business E-Mail: fnewton@kslaw.com.

NEWTON, FRANCIS CHANDLER, JR., lawyer; b. Boston, Oct. 25, 1925; s. Francis C. and Helen L. (Prentiss) Newton; m. Elizabeth White Newton, June 8, 1950; children: James W., Francis C. III. BA, Amherst Coll., 1949; JD, Boston U., 1952. Bar: Mass. 1952, US Dist. Ct. Mass. 1953, US Ct. Mil. Appeals 1959, US Supreme Ct. 1959, US Ct. Claims 1969, US Ct. Appeals (1st cir.) 1969. Trial counsel Powers & Hall, PC, Boston, 1952—61, ptnr., 1962—66; pvt. practice Boston, 1966—96; judge ODAR SSA, 1996—. Served as col. JAGC, USAR, 1943—82. Mem.: AAJ, ABA, Ancient & Hon. Arty. Co., Mass. Bar Assn., Boston Bar Assn. Home Phone: 978-443-6000; Office Phone: 617-523-4550 ext. 3049. Business E-Mail: francis.c.newton@ssa.gov.

NEWTON, JOHN MILTON, academic administrator, psychologist, educator; b. Schenectady, Feb. 25, 1929; s. Harry Hazleton and Bertha A. (Lehmann) N.; m. Elizabeth Ann Slattery, Sept. 11, 1954; children: Patricia, Peter, Christopher. BS, Union Coll., Schenectady, 1951; MA, Ohio State U., 1952, PhD, 1955. Lic. psychologist, Nebr. Rsch. psychologist Electric Boat divsn. Gen. Dynamics Corp., Groton, Conn., 1957-60; mem. faculty U. Nebr., Omaha, 1960—, prof. psychology, 1966-99, chmn. dept., 1967-74, acting vice chancellor acad. affairs, 1994-95, prof. emeritus, 1999—, dean Coll. Arts and Scis., 1974-94, dean emeritus, 1999—. Cons. in field, 1960-72 Author research papers in field. Served to 1st lt. Med. Service Corps, AUS, 1955-57. Mem. Am. Psychol. Assn., Psychonomic Soc., Midwestern Psychol. Assn. Home: 5611 Jones St Omaha NE 68106-1232 Office: Univ of Nebr-Omaha Dept Psychology Omaha NE 68182-0274 Business E-Mail: jnewton@mail.unomaha.edu.

NEWTON, LISA HAENLEIN, philosopher, educator; b. Orange, NJ, Sept. 17, 1939; d. Wallen Joseph and Carol Bigelow (Cypiot) Haenlein; m. Victor Joseph Newton, June 3, 1972; children: Tracey, Kit, Cynthia Perkins, Daniel Perkins, Laura Perkins. Student, Swarthmore Coll., 1957-59; BS in Philosophy with honors, Columbia U., 1962, PhD, 1967. Asst. prof. philosophy Hofstra U., Hempstead, NY, 1967-69; from asst. prof. to assoc. prof. Fairfield (Conn.) U., 1969—78, prof., 1978—, dir. program applied ethics, 1983—, dir. program environ. studies, 1986—2007; lectr. in medicine Yale U., 1984—. Lectr., cons. in field. Author: Ethics and Sustainability, 2002, Ethics in America, Study Guide, 2d edit., 2003, Ethics in America Source Reader, 2d edit., 2003, Business Ethics and the Natural Environment, 2004, Permission to Steal, 2006; co-author: Watersheds, 1994, 4th edit., 2005, Wake-Up Calls, 2d edit., 2003; co-editor: Taking Sides: Controversial Issues in Business Ethics, 2008; contbr. articles to profl. jours. Mem. exec. bd. Conn. Humanities Coun., 1979—83. Mem.: Internat. Soc. Environ. Ethics (mem. exec. bd.), Assn. Practical Prof. Ethics (exec. bd.), Soc. Bus. Ethics (past pres.), Am. Soc. Bioethics and Humanities, Soc. Ethics Across Curriculum (exec. bd.), Am. Soc. Polit. and Legal Philosophy, Am. Philos. Assn., Am. Soc. Value Inquiry (past pres.), Phi Beta Kappa (local sec.). Home: 1870 Redding Rd Fairfield CT 06824 Office: Fairfield U Program Applied Ethics Fairfield CT 06824 Office Phone: 203-254-4128. Business E-Mail: lhnewton@mail.fairfield.edu.

NEWTON, LLOYD ALFRED, philosopher, educator; b. Midland, Tex., Nov. 1, 1967; m. Lori Ruth Reimer, June 24, 1992; children: Holly Elizabeth, Alexander Nicholas, Mary Margaret. PhD, U. Dallas, Tex., 2003. Assoc. prof. philosophy Benedictine Coll., Atchison, Kans., 2003—. Home: 200 N 2nd Atchison KS 66002 Office: Benedictine Coll 1020 N 2nd Atchison KS 66002

NEWTON, NELL JESSUP, dean, law educator; b. St. Louis, Apr. 30, 1944; d. Robert Edward and Marcella (Boehm) Mier. BA, U. Calif., Berkeley, 1973; JD, U. Calif., Hastings, 1976. Bar: Calif., Washington, U.S. Ct. Appeals (9th crct.), U.S. Supreme Ct. Prof. Cath. U. Sch. Law, 1976-92; prof. Washington Coll. Law Am. U., Washington, 1992—98; dean U. Denver Law Sch., 1998—2000, U. Conn. Sch. Law, Hartford, 2000—06, U. Calif. Hastings Coll. Law, San Francisco, 2006—09; Joseph A. Matson dean U. Notre Dame Law Sch., 2009—. Lectr. Internat. Law Inst., Washington, 1984-89; prof. Pre-Law Summer Inst. for Native Am. Students, U. N.Mex. Law Sch., Albuquerque, 1990, 91, 93; panelist, speaker NEH, 1981; presenter S.W. Intertribal Ct. of Appeals, 1990; panelist Orgn. Am. Historians, 1991; vis. prof. Boston Coll. Law Sch., Hastings Law Sch. Co-author: American Indian Law, 3d edit., 1991; contbr. articles to profl. jours. NEH fellow Harvard Law Sch., 1980. Life fellow Am. Bar Found., Conn. Bar Found.; mem. Soc. of Law Teachers, Law & Soc. Assn., Law Sch. Admissions Coun. Assn., Am. Law Schs. (Native Am. rights sect., mem. exec. com. 1987—, chair 1987-88, oral argument newsletter editor 1987—, mem. women in legal edn. sect. 1987—, chair profl. devel. workshop com. 1992, sec. 1993), Balt.-Washington-Va. Women Law Tchrs. Group (planning com. Symposium on Scholarship I 1985, II 1986), Thurston Soc., Order of Coif. Office: U Notre Dame Law Sch 2100 Eck Hall of Law PO Box 780 Notre Dame IN 46556 Office Phone: 574-631-6789. E-mail: Nell.Newton@nd.edu.*

NEWTON, PAUL GEORGE, musician, retired librarian; b. Syracuse, NY, Dec. 1, 1930; s. Wayland LeRoy and Georgia Crumrine Newton; m. Dahlia Lorraine Brazell, Dec. 24, 1961; children: Jessica Suzanne, Roy Christopher. MusB cum laude, Syracuse U., 1952; MusM, Ind. U., 1954; PhD, U. North Tex., 1968; MLS, U. N.C., 1974. Instr. Augustana Coll., Sioux Falls, SD, 1954—56; prof. Wayland Bapt. Coll., Plainview, Tex., 1956—58, 1960—64; asst. prof. N.W. La. State Coll., Natchitoches, 1958—59, Stephen F. Austin State U., Nacogdoches, Tex., 1964—65, Ark. State U., Jonesboro, 1965—66; orch. dir. Forsyth County Schs., Winston-Salem, NC, 1968—69; music libr. Mars Hill (N.C.) Coll., 1969—83; libr. dir. Martin Meth. Coll., Pulaski, Tenn., 1983—93. Violist Asheville (N.C.) Symphony Orch., 1979—83; archivist Mars Hill Coll., 1979—83. Recipient Merit award, Kennedy-Douglass Mus., Florence, Ala., 1994. Mem.: So. Appalachian Mineral Soc., Am. Musicol. Soc., Ark. Archaeol. Soc. Avocations: travel, art, archaeology, geology, photography. Home: 114 S Sam Davis Ave Pulaski TN 38478 Office: 94 W Ridge Rd Mars Hill NC 28754 E-mail: pgnewton@energize.net.

NEWTON, PAULINE T., humanities educator; d. Geoffrey Paul and Thille Adelaide (Lambert) N. BA, Hollins U., Roanoke, Va., 1996; MA, Am. U., Washington, 1998; PhD, Tulsa U., Okla., 2002. Intern D Mag. Dallas, 1995; tutor Writing Ctr., student asst. coll. rels. Hollins U., Roanoke, 1995—96; tchg. asst. Am. U., 1996—97, asst. word processing and intranet software McCabe Computers and Writing Lab., rsch. asst. English dept., adj. instr., 1997—98; editl. intern Tulsa Studies in Women's Lit. U. Tulsa, 1999—2000, archivist Nimrod Internat. Jour., 1998—2001, grad. asst. computer info. requests Office of Dean of Grad. Sch., 2001—02; lectr. rhetoric Southern Meth. U., Dallas, 2002—, tutor, Writing Ctr., 2007—. Asst. hardware and software computer svcs. Hollins U., Roanoke, 1996; founder, editor U. Tulsa Grad. Rev., 1999—2002; adj. instr. Tulsa C.C., 2000—01; faculty vol. 1st-yr. orientation So. Meth. U., 2003—04; panelist and spkr. in field. Rschr., indexer: Women Coauthors by Holly A. Laird, 2000; author: Around San Antonio, 2001, Transcultural Women of Late-Twentieth-Century US American Literature: First Generation Migrants from Islands and Peninsulas, 2005, numerous poems; contbr. articles and revs. to profl. jours. and mags. Vol. Jubilee Cmty. Ctr., Dallas, 2001, Dallas Scholarship Fund/Tulip Project, 2002—03, chair, 2003—04. Recipient Cornelson-Halsey Leadership award, 1993—94, Hollins Merit award for acads., 1992—96, Jane Cocke Funkhouser award, 1996, Chapman Disting. PhD award, 2000—01, Fulbright-Hays award, 2005, Extra Mile award, SMU, 2008; F. B. Parriott scholar, 1998—2002, John S. Zink fellow, 1999—2002, Sam Taylor fellow, 2003—04. Mem.: Alexander Graham Bell Assn. (publs. and membership asst., coeditor, writer 1996—97, bd. dirs. Tex. chpt. 2003—, chair-elect 2006—08), Omicron Delta Kappa. Avocation: marathons. Office: So Meth Univ PO Box 750435 Dallas TX 75205

NEWTON, RAY C., university official; b. Denver, Colo., Sept. 26, 1935; s. Louis Weiss and Thelma (Sipe) N.; m. Patricia Rae (Boekhaus), Dec. 27, 1956; children: Sheri D., Lynn D., William L. (dec.). Grad., Kans. State U., Ft. Hays, 1957; postgrad., S.D. State U., 1959-61, U. Tex., 1970-72. Tchr., chmn. English dept. LaCrosse (Kans.) High Sch., 1957-59; mem. faculty N.Mex. Highlands U., Las Vegas, 1961-63, instr., asst. dean students, 1963-73, dir. pub. info. and pubs., adminstrv. asst. to pres., 1965-73, asst. prof., then assoc. prof. journalism, 1965-73; mem. faculty No. Ariz. U., Flagstaff, 1973—, prof. journalism, asst. dean creative and communication arts, 1984-87, dean, 1987-88, assoc. to pres., 1988-94. Dir. bilingual mass media program N.Mex. Highlands U., 1972-73; corr. Sta. KGGM-TV, Albuquerque, 1966-71; cons. in field. Author: (with Newsom and Wellert) Media Writing, 1984, (with Vannette and Cervany) Rethinking Global Education, 1993, Building Partnerships with the Forest Service, 1994, Maximizing Benefits Minimizing Tourism Impact, 1996, Regional Planning and Growth Management, 1999, Implementing Verde Valley Open Space Land, 2002, Building Future Leaders, 2003, Monitoring Community Education Needs, 2005, (with C. Penner & J. Penner) Resource Study Guide:My Brother's Voice; editor: Damn The Rejections, 2008, Drawing Straws, 2008; contbr. articles and revs. to profl. jours. and popular mags. Mem. adminstrv. bd. Prescott United Meth. Ch.; mem. exec. council Grand Canyon council Boy Scouts Am.; bd. dirs. Flagstaff Festival of the Arts; ex-officio bd. dirs. Ariz. Alliance for Arts Edn.; bd. dir. Yavapai County Cmty. Found.; bd. dirs. Yavapai Symphony Assn., Yavapai County Edn. Found., 2004—, edn. found., 2004—; pres. Yavapai Coll. Found., 2004-07; past pres. bd. dirs. Diamond Resorts Corp., Sedona, Ariz. Grantee Rotary Found. 1968, Danforth Found., 1969-70; Walter fellow U. Tex., 1971-72; named Journalism Prof. of Yr., Ariz. Newspaper Assn., 1984, Disting. Faculty mem. No. Ariz. U., 1984; recipient Nat. Teaching award Poynter Inst. Media Studies, St. Petersburg, Fla., 1985, Disting. Alumni award Kans. State U., Ft. Hays, 1993. Mem. Assn. Edn. Journalism/Mass Communication, Am. Soc. Journalism Sch. Adminstrs., Am. Soc. Newspaper Editors (mem. minorities edn. com.), Ariz. Press Assn. (mem. bd. dirs., chmn. edn. com.), We. Social Sci. Assn. (v.p. 1979-80, mem. exec. coun., editorial bd.), Am. Assn. Higher Edn., Inter-Am. Press Assn., 1st Amendment Coalition (past bd. dirs.), Soc. Profl. Journalists, Coll. Sports Info. Dirs. Assn., Flagstaff C. of C., Kiwanis, Phi Eta Sigma, Lambda Iota Tau, Phi Delta Kappa (area coord. Ariz., Outstanding Leadership award, 1994), Phi Delta Kappa, Phi Kappa Phi (nat. bd. dirs., Disting. Svc. award 1992), Kappa Tau Alpha. Home: 941 Lupine Ln Prescott AZ 86305-6734

NEWTON, ROGER GERHARD, educator, physicist; b. Landsberg, Germany, Nov. 30, 1924; came to U.S., 1946, naturalized, 1949; s. Arthur and Margaret (Blume) Neuweg; m. Ruth Gordon, June 18, 1953; children: Rachel, Julie, Paul. Student, U. Berlin, Germany; AB summa cum laude, Harvard, 1949, MA, 1950, PhD, 1953. Teaching fellow Harvard, 1951-52; mem. Inst. Advanced Study, Princeton, 1953-55, 79; mem. faculty Ind. U., 1955—, prof. physics, 1960-78, disting. prof. physics, 1978—95, disting. prof. emeritus, 1995—, chmn. dept., 1973-80, chmn. math. physics program, 1965-86, dir. Inst. for Advanced Study, 1982-86. Vis. prof. U. Rome, Italy, 1962-63, U. Montpellier, France, 1971-72 Author: Scattering Theory of Waves and Particles, 1966, 2d edit., 1982, The Complex j-Plane, 1964, Inverse Schrödinger Scattering in Three Dimension, 1989, What Makes Nature Tick?, 1993, The Truth of Sci., 1997, Thinking About Physics, 2000, Quantum Physics, 2002, Galileo's Pendulum, 2004, From Clockwork to Crapshoot, 2007, How Physics Confronts Reality, 2009; assoc. editor: Jour. Math. Physics, 1967—70, 1973—76, 1983—86; editor, 1992—2005; assoc. editor: Am. Jour. Physics, 1986—88, Inverse Problems, 1985—90; internat. adv. panel, 1991—; contbr. articles to profl. jours. Pres. Bloomington Civil Liberties Union, 1968. Served with AUS, 1946-47. Recipient Bowdoin prize Harvard, 1948; Jewett fellow, 1953-55; NSF sr. postdoctoral fellow, 1962-63; C.N.R.S. fellow U. Montpellier, France, 1971-72 Fellow AAAS (coun. 1987-89), Am. Phys. Soc. (chmn. Heinemann prize com. 1991-92); mem. AAUP, NY Acad. Scis., Fedn. Am. Scientists, Phi Beta Kappa (pres. Gamma chpt. 1991-92), Sigma Xi. Personal E-mail: newton@indiana.edu.

NEWTON, TERRY FERNANDO, health facility specialist, writer; b. Miami, Fla., Dec. 10, 1956; s. Julius Lee Newton and Frances Louise Cason; children: Torrence Levine, Patrick Fernando. Student, Fla. Montanari, 1976—78; BATh, 2007; Theology, Prog. Universal Life Ch. Specialist child care Montanari Clin. Sch., Hialeah, Fla., 1976—79; technician mental health Miami Variety Children's Hosp., Coral Gables, Fla., 1979—80; psychiat. nurse technician Cedars of Lebanon Hosp., Miami, Fla., 1980—82; from office asst. dir. of safety to health info. specialist II Jackson Hosp., Miami, 1982—83, health info. specialist II, 1983—. 1st v.p. Lip Tongue & Ear Prodn., Miami, 1999—. Author: A Composition in Verse, 1996, A Cascade of Memories, 1998, America at the Millenium, 2000, Earthbeat, 2002, Theatre of the Mind, 2003, The Dream of Time, 2007. Active media rep. Concern & Committed Bros. Inc., Miami, 2002; bd. dir. BMS Movement, 2001—. Recipient Accomplishment award, Gov. Lawton Chiles, 1997, Renaissance award, Macedonia Ch., 2006, Unsung Hero award, Coconut Grove Negro Women Club, 2006, Coconut Grove Wall Walk of Fame, Land Trust, Inc., 2009; named African Am. Achiever, JM Family Enterprise, Inc., 1998—2003, Cmty. Achiever, Macedonia Ch., 1999; named to Internat. Poetry Hall of Fame, 1997, Miami Dade Office of Mayor, Bd. County Commrs. Mem.: Fla. State Poetry Hosts Coalition (promotor 2003), Concern Bros. Inc. Poetry Club (dir. 2001, Mentor award 1997). Avocations: reading, performing, basketball, birdwatching. Home: 2529 NW 92nd St Miami FL 33147 Home Phone: 786-267-3314; Office Phone: 786-351-5893, 786-683-9144. Personal E-mail: newton.t.f@gmail.com. E-mail: renee@jazzandpoetry.net.

NEWTON, THOMAS, state agency administrator, public health service officer; BA in Environ. Planning and Polit. Sci., U. No. Iowa, Cedar Falls, M in Pub. Policy. Sanitarian Washington County, Iowa, 1996—97; pub. health officer Black Hawk County Health Dept., Iowa, 1997—2000; cmty. health cons. Iowa Dept. Pub. Health, 2000—02, dir. divsn. environ. health, 2002—07, pub. health dir., 2007—. Past pres. Iowa Environ. Health Assn. Named Gov. Golden Dome Leader of Yr., Iowa Dept. Pub. Health, 2004. Mem.: APHA, Iowa Pub. Health Assn., Nat. Environ. Health Assn. Office: Iowa Dept Pub Health Lucas State Office Bldg Des Moines IA 50319-0075 Office Phone: 515-281-7689.*

NEWTON, VIRGINIA, archivist, historian, librarian; d. John Walter and Reba Catherine Newton; m. Alvin Ellis Schmid, 2003. Student, Inst. Tecnológico y de Estudios Superiores de Monterrey, Nuevo Leon, Mex., 1957; AA in Bus. Adminstrn., Stephens Coll., 1958; BA in History, Okla. State U., 1960; M of Librarianship, U. Wash., 1963; cert. in libr. sci., U. Tex., 1968, MA in Latin Am. Studies, History, Archives and Libr. Sci., 1975, PhD in Latin Am. Studies, History, Archives and Libr. Sci., 1983. Libr. Inst. Pub. Affairs U. Tex., Austin, 1963-65, libr. Art Libr., 1965-67;

coord. Sr. Cmty. Svcs. Program Econ. Opportunities Devel. Corp., San Antonio, 1968-69; archivist, spl. collections libr. Trinity U., San Antonio, 1969-73; spl. collections and reference libr. Pan Am. U., Edinburg, Tex., 1974-77; archivist, records analyst Alaska State Archives and Records Svc., 1983-84, dep. state archivist, 1984-87; state archivist Alaska State Archives & Records Mgmt. Svcs., 1988-93; dir. Columbus Meml. Libr. OAS, Washington, 1993—2001. Archives cons. Ford Found. for Brazilian Archivists Assn., 1976, Soc. for Ibero-Latin Thought, 1980, Project for a Notarial Archives Computerized Guide, 1980; chair Alaska State Hist. Records Adv. Bd., 1988-93, coords. steering com., 1991-93; cons. Puerto Rican Hist. Records Adv. Bd., 1997-99. Author: An Archivists' Guide to the Catholic Church in Mexico, 1979. Founder jail libr. Bexar County Jail, San Antonio; hon. dep. sheriff Bexar County, 1972-75; mem. Dem. party; chair Dems. Abroad in Mex., 1979-81; mem. Dems. Abroad Del. The Dem. Nat. Conv., N.Y., 1980; vice- chair Bill Egan Forum Greater Juneau Dem. Precinct, 1986-88 Recipient Commendation award Gov. of Alaska William Sheffield, 1985, Disting. Alumnae award U. Tex. Sch. Libr. and Info. Sci., 1998; Masonic Scholarship for internat. rels. George Washington U., 1960-61; univ. fellow U. Tex.-Austin, 1982-83, post masters fellow U.S. Dept. Edn.-U. Tex., Austin, 1967-68; scholar Orgn. Am. States, 1980, 81, Fulbright-Hays scholar, 1979, 80, scholar Nat. Def. Fgn. Lang.-U. Tex., Austin, 1978-79, scholar Calif. State Libr., 1962-63. Mem. AAUW (bd. dirs. 1983-86, scholar 1983), Nat. Assn. Govt. Archives and Records Adminstrs. (bd. dirs. 1989-93, chair membership com. 1989-93), Alaska Hist. Soc. (bd. treas. 1988-94), Alaska Libr. Assn., Acad. Cert. Archivists (cert. 1989), Rotary, Phi Kappa Phi. Democrat. Avocations: skiing, dance, researching, reading, hiking. Office: 206 Laurel Heights Place San Antonio TX 78212

NEWTON, WILLIAM ALLEN, JR., pediatrician, pathologist; b. Traverse City, Mich., May 19, 1923; s. William Allen and Florence Emma (Brown) N.; m. Helen Patricia Goodrich, Apr. 21, 1945; children: Katherine Germaine, Elizabeth Gale, William Allen, Nancy Anne. BSc cum laude, Alma Coll., Mich., 1943; MD, U. Mich., 1946. Diplomate: Am. Bd. Pathology, Am. Bd. Pediatrics. Intern Wayne County Gen. Hosp., Detroit, 1947; resident in pediatric pathology/oncology/hematology Children's Hosp. Mich., Detroit, 1948-50; resident in pediat. Children's Hosp. Phila., 1950; dir. labs. Children's Hosp. Columbus, Ohio, 1952-88, rsch. pathologist Ohio, 1989—93; mem. faculty Coll. Medicine, Ohio State U., 1952—, prof., 1965—, chief pediatric pathology, 1952-89, chief divsn. pediatric hematology, 1952—82, prof. emeritus, 1989—. Chmn. pathology com. Children's Cancer Study Group, 1965-91; chmn. Pathology Com. Intergroup Rhabdomyosarcoma Study Group; chmn. pathology com. Late Effects Study Group. Contbr. articles to med. jours. Trustee, exec. com. Ohio divsn. Am. Cancer Soc., 1972-86; adv. com. on childhood cancer Am. Cancer Soc.; chmn. exec. com. Consortium for Cancer Control Ohio, 1982-86; sci. adv. com. Armed Forces Inst. Pathology; pres. Cure of Childhood Cancer in China, 2000—. Served to capt. M.C. U.S. Army, 1950-52, brig. gen. Res. ret. Mem. Am. Assn. Cancer Rsch., Ohio State Med. Assn. (com. on cancer), Midwest Soc. Pediatric Research (mem. council 1960-63, pres. 1964-65), Soc. Pediatric Research, Am. Pediatric Soc., Pediatric Pathology Club (pres. 1968-69), Am. Soc. Clin. Oncology, Internat. Soc. Pediatric Oncology, Sigma Xi, Phi Sigma Pi. Republican. Baptist. Home: 2500 Harrison Rd Johnstown OH 43031-9540 Office: PO Box 6957 Columbus OH 43205 Home Phone: 740-927-4647; Office Phone: 614-722-3269. Business E-Mail: wnewton@chi.osu.edu.

NEWTSON, RICHARD L., sociologist, educator; b. Danville, Ill., Apr. 26, 1956; PhD, Iowa State U., Ames, 1994. Lectr. Nat. U. Kyiv Mohyla Acad., Ukraine, 1996—98; prof. Columbus State U., Ga., 1998—. Office: Columbus State Univ 4225 Univ Ave Columbus GA 31907 Office Fax: 706-568-2461. Business E-Mail: newtson_richard@colstate.edu.

NEXSEN, JULIAN JACOBS, lawyer; b. Kingstree, SC, Apr. 14, 1924; s. William Ivey and Barbara (Jacobs) N.; m. Mary Elizabeth McIntosh, Jan. 28, 1948; children: Julian Jacobs Jr. At, The Citadel, Charleston, SC, 1941—43; BS magna cum laude, U. SC, Columbia, 1948, JD magna cum laude, 1950. Bar: S.C. 1950, U.S. Supreme Ct. 1960. Ptnr. firm Nexsen Pruet, LLC, Columbia, SC. Trustee Richland County Pub. Libr., chmn., 1976-77; trustee Providence Hosp., chmn., 1984-86; trustee Providence Found., Providence Ministries, Sisters of Charity of St. Augustine Health Sys.; past bd. dirs. Columbia Music Festival Assn., ARC Richland-Lexington Counties, Ctrl. Carolina Cmty. Found.; mem. U.S.C. Law Sch. partnership bd.; elder Eastminster Presbyn. Ch., trustee Congaree Presbytery, 1967-87, Synod, S.C., 1969-74, mem. Trinity Presbytery Coun. Lt. inf. AUS, 1943-46, ETO, capt., 1950-51, Korea. Decorated Bronze Star with oak leaf cluster; recipient Compleat Lawyer award U. SC Sch. Law, Disting. Pub. Svc. award Order of Coif, 2007. Mem. ABA, SC Bar (treas., bd. govs. 1974-79, House of Dels. 1980-92), Richland County Bar Assn. (pres. 1974-75, Disting. Svc. award 1987), Am. Bar Found., SC Bar Found. (pres. 1971-72), SC Law Inst. (coun., exec. com. 1986—), Am. Law Inst., Am. Coll. Trust and Estate Counsel (regent 1973-82), Am. Judicature Soc., Forest Lake Country Club, Palmetto Club, Kiwanis (bd. dirs. 1972-74, 77-79), Phi Beta Kappa. Home: 2840 Sheffield Rd Columbia SC 29204-2332 Office Phone: 803-771-8900. Business E-Mail: jnexsen@nexsenpruet.com.

NEY, EDWARD N., ambassador, advertising and public relations executive; b. St. Paul, May 26, 1925; s. John Joseph and Marie (Noonan) N.; m. Suzanne Hayes, 1950 (div. 1974); children: Nicholas, Hilary, Michelle; m. Judith I. Lasky, May 24, 1974. BA (Lord Jeffrey Amherst scholar 1942), Amherst Coll., 1947. With Young & Rubicam, Inc., NYC, 1951-86, chmn., pres. CEO, 1970-86; chmn. Paine Webber/Young & Rubicam Ventures, NYC, 1987-89; vice-chmn. Paine Webber, Inc., NYC, 1987-89; amb. to Can., Am. Embassy, Ottawa, Ont., 1989-92; chmn. bd. advisors Burson-Marsteller, NYC, 1992-98; chmn. Marsteller Advt.; chmn. emeritus Young & Rubicam Advt., NYC, 1999—. Mem. Coun. on Fgn. Rels., 1975—; mem. adv. bd. Ctr. for Strategic and Internat. Studies (C.S.I.S.), 1986—; honorary chmn. Advt. Coun.; mem. Advt. Hall of Fame. Life Trustee Amherst Coll., 1979—; Trustee Bush Presidential Libr. Found., James A. Baker III Inst. for Public Policy, Rice U., Museum of TV/Radio (MTR), 1982—. Office: Young Rubicam Advt 285 Madison Ave New York NY 10017-6486 Business E-Mail: ed_ney@yr.com.

NEYLAN, THOMAS COOGAN, psychiatrist; b. Chgo., Ill., Jan. 31, 1957; s. John Francis and Mary Alice Neylan; m. Mary Genevieve De May, Sept. 20, 1986; children: Michael De May, Matthew De May, Kyra De May. MD, Rush U., Chgo., Ill., 1984. Cert. Am. Bd. of Psychiatry and Neurology, 1989. Assoc. prof. psychiatry U. Calif., San Francisco, 2003—; med. dir., PTSD program San Francisco Dept. of VA Med. Ctr. Contbr. scientific papers pub. to profl. jour. Grantee Rsch. Grants, NIH, 1998-present. Achievements include research in Multiple grants from the Nat. Inst. of Health. Office: Univ Calif San Francisco VAMC-116P 4150 Clement St San Francisco CA 94121 E-mail: thomas.neylan@ucsf.edu.*

NE-YO, (SHAFFER C. SMITH), singer; b. Camden, Ark., Oct. 18, 1979; 1 child, Chimere. Singer: (albums) In My Own Words, 2006, Because of You, 2007 (Grammy award, Best Contemporary R&B Album, 2008), Year of the Gentleman, 2008; actor: (films) Save the Last Dance 2, 2006, Stomp the Yard, 2007; singer: (songs) Miss Independent, 2008 (Best Male R&B Vocal Performance, Best R&B Song, Grammy Awards, 2009). Recipient Top New R&B Artist award, Billboard, 2006, Top Hot Male R&B Songs Artist award, 2006, Best New Artist award, Soul Train Music Awards, 2007, Best Male R&B Artist award, BET (Black Entertainment TV) Awards, 2007. Office: c/o Def Jam Recordings 825 8th Ave New York NY 10019

NG, CHAAN S., radiologist, educator; BA, Christ's Coll., Cambridge, Eng., 1979, MA, 1983, MS in Engring., 1993; MBBS with distinction, Royal Free Hosp. Sch. Med., London, 1989. Diplomate in diagnostic radiology Am. Bd. Radiology, 2002. Lectr. cons. U. Cambridge, Addenbrooke Hosp., England, 1998—2001; fellow Chrisrt's Coll., 1999—2001; asst. prof. U. Tex., Md. Anderson Cancer Ctr., Houston, 2001—06, assoc. prof., 2006—. Contbr. articles to profl. jours. Fellow: Royal Coll. Radiologists (Robert & Elma Kemp Harper prize 2002); mem.: RCP, Am. Soc. Clin. Oncology, Am. Roentgen Ray Soc. Office: Md Anderson Cancer Ctr Radiology Unit 368 368 1515 Holcombe Boulevard Houston TX 77030-4009 Office Phone: 713-792-6759. Office Fax: 713-745-1302. Business E-Mail: cng@mdanderson.org.

NG, CHOON HOE, process engineer; b. Kuala Lumpur, Malaysia, Dec. 20, 1975; B in Elec. and Electronic Engring., Robert Gordon U., Eng., 1999; PhD in Elec. Engring., U. Aberdeen, Eng., 2003; MBA in Bus. Adminstrn. with distinction, U. Nottingham, Eng., 2008. Cert. Six Sigma mgr., Six Sigma black belt, project mgmt. Applications and customer devel. engr. Bertda Svcs. Pte Ltd., Singapore, 2003—04; sr. rsch. and devel. engr. Siemens Pte Ltd., Singapore, 2004—06, sys. integration and test lead, 2006—07, process engr., 2007—08; 6 sigma black belt Caterpillar Asia Pte Ltd., 2008—. Spkr. in field. Contbr. articles to profl.jours. Recipient Overseas Rsch. Student award Scheme, Universities UK, 1999—2002, Francis Morrison prize, Robert Gordon U., 1999, Book prize, Tunku Abdul Rahman Coll., 1996—98; Small Grants Fund, U. of Aberdeen, 2003, MTC Found. scholarship, Malaysian Tobacco Co., 1996—98. Mem.: IEEE (licentiate), Project Mgmt. Inst. (licentiate), Instn. Engring. and Tech. (licentiate), Singapore Quality Inst. (licentiate), Bd. Engrs. Malaysia (licentiate). Buddhist. Achievements include breakthroughs in linear and rotary permanent magnet synchronous motor drive research. Office Fax: (65)68808008. Business E-Mail: ng_choon_hoe@cat.com.

NG, DOMINIC, bank executive; b. Hong Kong, Jan. 24, 1959; BBA in Acctg., U. Houston, 1980. CPA Calif., Texas. Dir. Chinese bus. svcs., sr. mgr. Deloitte & Touche, LLP, L.A., Houston, 1980—90; pres., CEO Seyen Investment, Inc., LA, 1990—92, East-West Fed. Bank f.s.b., San Marino, Calif., 1992—. Bd. dirs. Fed. Res. Bank, San Francisco, LA, Mattel Inc. Office: East West Bank 135 N Los Robles Ave 7th Fl Pasadena CA 91101 Office Phone: 626-768-6800. Business E-Mail: carmen.pan@eastwest.com.

NG, KAM WING, mechanical engineer, researcher; s. Wah Ng and Kwon Leung; m. Shirley Yuen, Aug. 18, 1974; children: Melissa Y., Janice Y. BE, Cooper Union, NY, 1973; MME, Rensselaer Poly. Inst., Hartford, Conn., 1975; PhD, U. RI, Kingston, 1988; MBA, Marymount U., Arlington, Va., 2005. Registered profl. engr., Va., 1993. Sr. acoustic engr. Pratt & Whitney Aircraft, East Hartford, Conn., 1973—78; project engr. ITT Grinnell Corp, Providence, 1978—82; mech. engr. Naval Underwater Sys. Ctr., Newport, RI, 1982—92; dep. divsn. dir. Office Naval Rsch., Arlington, Va., 1992—. Mem. cert. bd. Inst. Noise Control Engring., NY, 1980—2002; chmn. sci. planning group in mechanics Office Sec. of Def., Arlington, Va., 2004—06; adj. faculty Cath. U. Am., Washington, 1992—96. Mem. edit. bd.: Jour. Vibration and Control, 1999—2004, Internat. Jour. COMADEM, 1999—; contbr. articles to profl. jours. Sci. fair judge, Va., 1997—2003. Recipient Best Paper award, Soc. Automotive Engring., 2001. Mem.: Soc. Mech. Failure Prevention (dir. rsch. 1998—2002), NATO Rsch. & Tech. (advanced vehicle tech. 2002—07), Am. Soc. Mech. Engr., Phi Beta Delta, Delta Epsilon Sigma, Delta Mu Delta. Achievements include patents in field. Office: Office Naval Rsch 875 North Randolph St Arlington VA 22203 Office Phone: 703-696-0812. Office Fax: 703-696-2556. Business E-Mail: kam.ng1@navy.mil.

NG, KIM (KIMBERLY J. NG), professional sports team executive; b. Wu Peiqin, China, Nov. 17, 1968; m. Tony Markward. BA in Pub. Policy, U. Chgo., 1990. Front office arbitration intern Chgo. White Sox, 1990, spl. projects analyst, 1991, asst. dir., baseball ops., 1991—95; dir. waivers, player records MLB Am. League, 1995—97; v.p., asst. gen. mgr. NY Yankees, 1998—2001; v.p. baseball ops., asst. gen. mgr. LA Dodgers, 2001—, interim dir. player devel., 2004. Named one of 10 to Watch, Baseball America, 2008; named to Young Leaders Forum, Nat. Com. on US-China Rels., 2007—. Office: Los Angeles Dodgers 1000 Elysian Park Ave Los Angeles CA 90012-1199*

NG, LAWRENCE MING-LOY, pediatrician; b. Hong Kong, Mar. 21, 1940; arrived in U.S., 1967, naturalized, 1977; s. John Iu-cheung and Mary Wing (Wong) N.; m. Bella May Ha Kan, June 25, 1971; children: Jennifer Wing-mui, Jessica Wing-yee. MBBS in Medicine, U. Hong Kong, 1965. Diplomate Am. Bd. Pediatrics. House physician Queen Elizabeth Hosp., Hong Kong, 1965-66, med. officer, 1966-67; resident physician Children's Hosp. of Los Angeles, 1967-68, Children's Hosp. Med. Ctr., Oakland, Calif., 1968-70; fellow in pediatric cardiology, 1970-72; now mem. tchg. staff; practice medicine specializing in pediat. and pediatric cardiology, San Leandro, Calif., 1972—, Oakland, Calif., 1982—; mng. ptnr. Pediatric Med. Assocs. of East Bay, 1990—. Chief pediat. Oakland Hosp., 1974-77, Meml. Hosp., San Leandro, 1986-88; chief pediat. Vesper Meml. Hosp., 1977-79, sec. staff, 1984, v.p. staff, 1985; founder Pediatric Assocs. of East Bay, 1990. Active Republican Party. Recipient Small Bus. Leadership award, Oakland Chinatown C. of C., Comty. Svc. award, Ethnic Health Inst., Family Bridges Comty. Svc. award, Spl. Congl. Recognition cert., 2004; Hon. fellow, U. Hong Kong, 2008. Fellow: Am. Acad. Pediatrics; mem.: AMA, Children 1st Med. Group (bd. dirs. 2008—), Chancellor's Assocs. U. Calif. at Berkeley, Children's First Healthcare Network (bd. dirs. 1997—2008, sec. 2006—08), Oakland Chinatown C. of C. (bd. dirs. 1986—91, 1986—91, adv. bd. 1992—, Cmty. Spirit award 2000), Ethnic Health Inst. (bd. dirs. 1998—, Frank Stagger Sr. Cmty. svc. award 2004), Fedn. Chinese Med. Socs. (dir. 1998—2006, sec. 2006—), Chinese-Am. Physicians Soc. (sec. 1980, pres. 1983, exec. dir. 1997—2001, bd. dirs. 2003—, exec. dir. 2008—), Chinese-Am. POlit. Assn. (life), Orgn. Chinese Ams. (chpt. pres. 1984), Smithsonian Assocs., L.A. Pediat. Soc., Alameda County Assn. Primary Care Practitioners (membership chmn. 1993—97, sec.-treas. 1994—97), Am. Heart Assn., Calif. Med. Assn., Family Bridges Inc. (bd. dirs. 2002—, Kenneth Hoh award for cmty. svc. 2004, Outstanding Vol. award 2006, 2009), Hong Kong U. Alumni Assn. (sec. No. Calif. chpt. 1992—96, pres. 1997—2000, chair 2001—), Oakland Asian Cultural Ctr. (dir. 1996—99, treas. 1996—99), Consumer's Union (life), Stanford U. Alumni Assn. (life), Friends of Hong Kong U. (bd. dirs. 2001—, treas. 2003—06, pres. 2007—), U.S. Golf Assn., No. Calif. Golf Assn., San Leandro Golf Club, Commonwealth Club, PGA Tour Ptnrs. Club (life). Republican. Buddhist. Avocations: golf, photography, web design. Office: 345 9th St Ste 204 Oakland CA 94607-4206 also: 101 Callan Ave Ste 401 San Leandro CA 94577-4523 Home Phone: 510-351-4225; Office Phone: 510-357-7077. E-mail: lmn@pedmed.com.

NG, SIAUW-HOI, research scientist; s. Khay Seng Ng and Djoet Joeng Law; m. W.F. Young; 1 child, Felix. BSChemE, Nat. Taiwan U., Taipei, 1964; PhD in Phys. Chemistry, U. NB, Fredericton, Can., 1970. Sci. tchr. PPS-3 (San Shan) HS, Medan, 1960—61; math. tchr. Sutomo HS, Medan, 1961—62; engr. Taiwan Inst. Environment, Taipei, 1964—65; tchg. asst. Nat. Taiwan U., Taipei, 1965—66; rsch. engr. Iron Ore Co. Can., Schefferville, Que., 1970—72, spl. lab. supr. Sept-Iles, Que., 1972—82; rsch. scientist Energy Rsch. Labs., Ottawa, Ont., 1982—94; vis. scholar Syncrude Edmonton Rsch. Ctr., Alta., 1994—95; rsch. scientist Nat. Ctr. for Upgrading Tech., Devon, Alta., 1995—. Mem. PhD adv. bd., dept. chem. engring. U. Western Ont., London, 1990—93; adj. prof. Beijing Inst. Petrochem. Tech., 1997—; PhD rsch. co-supr., dept. chem. engring. China U. of Petroleum, Beijing, 1999—2006, Hanoi U. Tech., Vietnam, 2005—; adj. prof. dept. chem. engring. Ningbo Inst. Tech., Zhejiang U., China, 2006—; mem. editl. bd. Acta Petroki Sinica (Petroleum processing Sect.), Beijing, 2008—. Recipient Merit award, Iron Ore Co. of Can., 1975, 1979, 1980, Energy Rsch. Labs., 1991, Anshan Rsch. Inst. of Thermal Engring., Ministry of Metall. Industry, China, 1994, Nat. Ctr. for Upgrading Tech., 1999, 2002, Energy Tech. and Programs Sector, Natural Resources Can., 2005, Bus. Devel. award, Can. Ctr. Mineral and Energy Tech., 1992, Rsch. Cooperation award, Beijing Inst. Petrochem. Tech., 2005, Leadership award, Fed. Ptnrs. in Tech. Transfer, 2005, Departmental Merit award, Natural Resources Can., 2005, Alumni award of distinction, UNB Associated Alumni, 2007. Mem.: ASTM, Am. Chem. Soc. Achievements include patents for metal trap dispersion technology for fluid catalytic cracking catalysts with extra protection against metals and with prolonged life; development of microactivity (MAT) technology for transfer to Canadian industry; quality improvement of oil-sands-derived heavy gas oils as feeds to fluid catalytic cracking unit; application of process chemistry in support of industrial needs; diversification of the use of oil-sands bitumen for production of petrochemical feedstocks. Avocations: badminton, travel. Office: Nat Ctr for Upgrading Tech 1 Oil Patch Dr Devon AB Canada T9G 1A8 Office Fax: 780-987-5349. Business E-Mail: sng@nrcan.gc.ca.

NG, TSE NGA, research scientist; b. Hong Kong, June 21, 1980; m. Mark Stuart Bailey. BS, Knox Coll., Galesburg, Ill., 2000; PhD, Cornell U., Ithaca, NY, 2006. Rsch. scientist Palo Alto Rsch. Ctr., Calif., 2006—. Personal E-mail: ng_tse_nga@hotmail.com.

NG, YEE SEUNG, physicist; came to U.S., 1970; BS in Engring. Physics, U. Ill., Urbana, 1974; MSEE, Pa. State U., 1977, PhD in Physics, 1980. Rsch. scientist Kodak Rsch. Lab., Rochester, NY, 1980-84, sr. rsch. scientist, 1984-88; rsch. assoc. Kodak Copy Product R&D, Rochester, 1988-97, project chief engr. color demand printing, 1997-99; chief engr. Nexpress Solution, LLC, Rochester, 1999—2003; sr. rsch. assoc. Nexpress Solutions, Rochester, 2003—06; mgr. intellectual property Eastman Kodak Co., Rochester, 2006—. Contbr. articles to profl. jours. Recipient Chester Carlson award Soc. of Imaging Sci. and Tech., 2000. Fellow Soc. Imaging Sci. and Tech., mem. N.Y. Acad. Scis. Achievements include over 90 patents in electrophotographic processes and electronic printing. Office: Eastman Kodak Co 2600 Manitou Rd Rochester NY 14653 E-mail: yeesng@ieee.org.

NGANGA, LYDIAH WANGUI, education educator; arrived in US, 1992; d. Edward Mwangi Kamau and Ziporah Waihiga Mwangi; m. John Nganga Dr. Kambutu, July 13, 1989; children: Evans Kambutu, Timothy Mwangi, Kathleen Njoki. BS in Family and Consumer Sci., U. Wyo., Laramie, 1998, MSc in Family & Consumer Scis., 1998—2000, PhD in Edn., Curriculum & Instrn., 2000—05. Cert. tchr. PTSB Wyo., 2003. Tchr. Mariakani HS, Kenya, 1988—92; faculty residence life Family Housing U. Wyo., 1992—98; asst. prof. elem. & early childhood Casper Ctr. Casper, 2005—; tchr. Natrona County HS, Casper, Wyo., 1999—2005. Bd. mem. Early Learning Ctr., Casper, 2004—; com. mem. Shepherd Social Justice U. Wyo., Laramie, 2005—. Mem.: AERA (corr.), ACEI (corr.), NAEYC (corr.), Golden Key, Phi Upsilon Omcron, Delta Sigma. Home: PO Box 50462 Casper WY 82605 Office: Univ Wyo Casper Ctr PO Box 50462 Casper WY 82605 Office Fax: 307-268-2416. Business E-Mail: lnganga@uwyo.edu.

NGANJE, WILLIAM EVANGE, finance educator; b. Buea Cameroon, Swp, Cameroon, Oct. 13, 1966; s. Simon Elive and Julie Namondo Nganje; m. Annette Enanga Nganje; children: Willann Ikome, Willette Epupa, Elizabeth Enjema, Simon Elive. PhD, U. Ill., Urbana Champaign, 1999. Asst. prof. ND State U., Fargo, 1998—2005, assoc. prof., 2005—06, Ariz. State U., Mesa, Ariz., 2007—. Grantee, USDA, 2006—, ERS, 2007—, Dept. Homeland Security, 2008—. Mem.: Am. Agrl. Economics Assn. (sec., vice chair and chair WERA-72 2005—08). Office: Ariz State Univ 7171 E Sonoran Arroyo Mall Mesa AZ 85212 Office Phone: 480-727-1524. Office Fax: 480-727-1961. Business E-Mail: william.nganje@asu.edu.

NGATA, HALOTI (ETUINI HALOTI NGATA), professional football player; b. Inglewood, Calif., Jan. 21, 1984; m. Christine Adams, 2007. Attended, U. Oreg., Eugene. Nose tackle Balt. Ravens, 2006—. Participant Md. State Police's Ann. Polar Bear Plunge for Spl. Olympics, 2007, 2008, Walk for Juvenile Diabetes, Balt., 2008; host Haloti Ngata Sportsfest for Juvenile Diabetes Found., 2008. Recipient Morris Trophy, PAC 10, 2005; named 1st Team All-Conf., 2005, co-Defensive Player of Yr., PAC-10, 2005, Consensus All-Am., AP, NFL Draft Report, Football Writers Assn. America, Walter Camp Football Found., Sports Illus., ESPN.com, 2005; named to All-Rookie Team, Pro Football Weekly, Profl. Football Writers America, 2006, All-Joe Team, USA Today, 2007; finalist Outland Trophy, 2005, Bronko Nagurski award, 2005. Office: Balt Ravens M&T Bank Stadium 1101 Russell St Baltimore MD 21230*

NGHIEM, PAUL T., dermatologist, educator; AB in Biological Sciences, Harvard U., 1986; MD, Stanford U. Sch. Medicine, 1994, PhD in Cancer Biology, 1994. Assoc. prof. divsn. dermatology U. Wash., assoc. prof. dept. pathology; affiliate investigator clinical rsch. divsn. Fred Hutchinson Cancer Rsch. Ctr. Office: UW Medical Center 815 Mercer St Box 358050 Seattle WA 98195-8050 Office Phone: 206-221-4364. E-mail: pnghiem@u.washington.edu.*

NGUYEN, ANN CAC KHUE, pharmaceutical and medicinal chemist; b. Kieu Moc, Sontay, Vietnam, Nov. 12, 1949; d. Nguyen Van Soan and Luu Thi Hieu. BS, U. Saigon, 1973; MS, San Francisco State U., 1978; PhD, U. Calif., San Francisco, 1983. Tchg. and rsch. asst. U. Calif., San Francisco, 1978-83, postdoctoral fellow, 1983-86, rsch. scientist, 1987—. Contbr. articles to profl. jours. Recipient Nat. Rsch. Svc. award, NIH, 1981-83; Regents fellow U. Calif., San Francisco, 1978-81. Mem.

AAAS, Am. Chem. Soc., N.Y. Acad. Scis., Bay Area Enzyme Mechanism Group, Am. Assn. Pharm. Scientists. Roman Catholic. Home: 1488 Portola Dr San Francisco CA 94127-1409 Office: U Calif PO Box 446 San Francisco CA 94143-0001 Personal E-mail: ann94143@yahoo.com. Business E-Mail: ann.cac.k.nguyen@ucsf.edu.

NGUYEN, BACH-YEN T., medical association administrator; m. Vinh P. Tran. MD, U. Minn., Mpls., 1985. Diplomate Nat. Bd. Med. Examiners, 1986, Am. Bd. Internal Medicine, 1988. Resident internal medicine NY Hos-Cornell Med. Ctr., NYC, 1985—88; infectious diseases med. staff fellow NIH, NIAID, Bethesda, Md., 1988—91; sr. clin. investigator Nat. Cancer Inst., Bethesda, 1991—95; assoc. dir. Merck & Co. Inc., North Wales, Pa., 1995—98, med. dir., 1998—2003, sr. med. dir., 2003—. Office: Merck & Co Inc 351 N Sumneytown Pike North Wales PA 19454-2505 Office Fax: 267-305-6477. Business E-Mail: bachyen_nguyen@merck.com.

NGUYEN, CHARLES CUONG, engineering educator, researcher, dean; b. Danang, Vietnam, Jan. 1, 1956; arrived in U.S., 1978, naturalized, 1978; s. Buoi and Tinh Thi Nguyen; m. Kim-Bang Pham, Aug. 5, 1989; children: Carissa Kim Thuy Duong, Olivia Quynh Duong, Dylan Nhat Khang, Parker Duy Khang. Diploma, Konstanz U., Fed. Rep. Germany, 1978; MS with distinction, George Washington U., 1980, DSc with superiour performance, 1982. Engr. Siemens Corp., Erlangen, Germany, 1977-78; lectr. George Washington U., Washington, 1978-82; asst. prof. engring. Cath. U. Am., Washington, 1982-85, assoc. prof. elec. engring., 1985-92, prof., 1992—, chmn. dept. elec. engring. and computer sci., 1997-2001, dean Sch. Engring., 2001—. Cons. Mitre Corp., Meridian Corp., Jet Propulsion Lab., others; dir. Ctr. Artificial Intelligence and Robotics, 1985—; mem. organizing coms. various robotics confs.; sr. rsch. assoc. NAS, 1990—; program vice chair IEE-Internat. Conf. Robotics 2d Automation, 1997, Internat. Symposium and Robotic Automation, 1997; chmn. organizing com. Robotics Internat., Internat. Symposium Robotics and Mfg. Founding editor, editor-in-chief: Jour. Intelligent Automation and Soft Computing (10th Anniversary award, 2006); editor: (book) Robotics and Manufacturing, Vol. 5, 1994, Intelligent Automation and Soft Computing, Vol. 1, 1994, Intelligent Automation and Soft Computing, Vol. 2, 1994; mem. editl. bd.: Jour. Intelligent and Fuzzy Sys., Engring. Design and Automation, assoc. editor: Computers and Elec. Engring.: An Internat. Jour., 1992—, guest editor: Jour. Robotic Sys., —; contbr. scientific papers to profl. jours. Apptd. by Pres. Bus to bd. dirs. Vietnam Edn. Found., 2004—07. Recipient Leadership award, Internat. Network Engring. Rsch., Excellence in Cmty. Svc. award, Vietnamese Med. Rsch. Found., 2007, Rsch. Initiation award, Engring. Found., 1985, Disting. Alumni Scholar award, George Wash. U., 2002, Lifetime Achievement award, World Automation Congress, 2004, Cmty. Svc. award in Edn., Asia Entertainment Inc., 2004, Lifetime Achievement award, Dist. Columbia Coun. Engring. and Archtl. Socs., 2009; fellow, NASA-Am. Soc. Elec. Engring., 1985, 1986, Goddard Space Flight Ctr., 1994. Mem.: IEEE (sr.; program v.p. Washington chpt.), Soc. Mfg. Engrs. (sr. Robotics Internat.), Internat. Soc. Mini-and Microcomputers, Tau Beta Pi (faculty advisor), Sigma Xi. Roman Catholic. Avocations: guitar, singing, tennis, skiing, ping pong/table tennis. Business E-Mail: nguyen@cua.edu.

NGUYEN, CLIFFORD HAM-THIEM, telecommunications engineer; b. Saigon, Vietnam, Nov. 7, 1962; came to U.S., 1982; s. Nghi Duc Nguyen and Lien Kim Hoang; m. Julie Thach Pham. BSEE, Poly. U., 1988, MSEE, 1989; MA in Stats., Columbia U., 1998. Electronics engr. ARDEC Dept. Def., Dover, NJ, 1989-91; switch engr. Bell Atlantic/NYNEX, NYC, 1991-96, sr. engr., 1996-99, sr. specialist, 1999; ops mgr. Lucent, 1999-2000; mem. tech. staff Bell Labs, NJ, 2000—07; computer scientist RDECOM DOD, 2007—09; portfolio mgr. CECOM LCMC DOD, 2009—. Achievements include research in telecommunications infrastructures; methodologies and tolls for wireline and wireless network planning, design, and deployment decisions; development of network performance analysis on data, voice, optical; planning, designing, engineering telecommunication networks with broad range of technologies and products.

NGUYEN, DAO MINH, thoracic surgeon, director; b. Saigon, Vietnam, Nov. 11, 1961; s. Phu Nguyen and Van Thi Ta; m. Catherinei Thi Nguyen, Aug. 2, 1986; children: Duc Minh, Christopher Minh, Jonathan, Benjamin. Degree in Med., McGill U., Montreal, Que., Canada, 1986. Cert. in gen. surgery McGill U., 1986, diplomate gen. surgery Royal Coll., Am. Bd. Surgeons. Prin. investigator Nat. Cancer Inst., NIH, Bethesda, Md., 1998—2007; dir., thoracic surgery sect. U. Miami, Miller Sch. Medicine, Fla., 2007—. Fellow: ACS; mem.: RCPS. Office: Univ Miami-Jackson Meml PO Box 016960 (R114) Miami FL 33101 Office Fax: 305-547-2185.

NGUYEN, DONG, computer scientist, researcher, software engineer, educator; s. Dao Nguyen and Khau Thi Le; m. Dung Xuan Phi, Dec. 30, 1976; children: Henry Huy, Huy Tuan. BS in Computer Sci. and Engring., Calif. State U., Long Beach, 1985, MS in Computer Sci., 1988; PhD in Computer Engring. and Applied Math., Claremont Grad. U., 2000, exec. MBA, 2002, MS in Math., 1997. Software engr. Info. Internat., Inc., Culver City, Calif., 1984—86; sr. software engr. CAL-COMP, Anaheim, Calif., 1986—90; sr. programmer analyst Sys. Divsn. Ball Aerospace, Huntington Beach, Calif., 1985—87; sr. firmware engr. Micro Tech., Inc., Anaheim, Calif., 1990—92; sr. software engr., sys. engr. Beckman Instruments, Brea, 1990—97; sr. staff engr. B/E Aerospace, Irvine, Calif., 1997—2001; sr. adv. engr., rschr. Kofax Image Products, Irvine, Calif., 2001—03; software engr. mgr. Celerity Group, Inc., Yorba Linda, 2003—. Lectr. Cal State Univ., Longweach, 1998—2000, in field. Prodr.(music concerts): Young Love, 1992—94. Achievements include research in reliability modeling and evaluation in real-time distributed multimedia systems; recovery blocks in real-time distributed systems; failure mode and effect analysis in software reliability; reliability modeling and evaluation in computer networks and distributed systems; development of rasterization algorithm which greatly improved the speed of converting the vector data to raster data in printers/plotters; dynamic camera calibration in real-time without manual operations from users. Personal E-mail: nguyendg@aol.com.

NGUYEN, HIEN TRONG, astrophysicist, researcher; PhD, Princeton U., NJ, 1993. Rsch. scientist JET Propulsion Lab., Calif. Inst. Tech., Pasadena, 1997—. Office: Jet Propulsion Lab 4800 Oak Grove Dr MS169-506 Pasadena CA 91109 Office Fax: 626 296-0844.

NGUYEN, KHANH GIA, medical educator; b. Hanoi, Vietnam, Dec. 17, 1940; arrived in Can., 1972; s. Lien Bich and Lan Chi Nguyen; m. Nga Thi Ho, Dec. 30, 1940; children: Van Thanh Nguyen-Ho, Phong Nguyen-Ho. Cert. of physics, chemistry and biology, Saigon U., 1961, MD, 1969. Diplomate Am. Bd. Pathology, Am. Bd. Pathology in Cytopathology, cert. pathologist Royal Coll. Physicians and Surgeons, Can. Asst. prof. pathology U. Sask., Saskatoon, Canada, 1978—82; pathologist Plains Health Ctr., Regina, Canada, 1978—80; pathologist, head provincial cytology lab. Pasqua Hosp., Regina, Canada, 1980—82; asst. prof. pathology U. Alta., Edmonton, Alberta, Canada, 1982—84, assoc. prof. pathology, 1984—92, prof. lab. medicine and pathology, 1992—2006, prof. emeritus lab. medicine and pathology, 2006—; pathologist U. Alta. Hosp., Edmonton, Alberta, Canada, 1982—2006, pathologist and head of electron microscopy, 1987—2000, pathologist and head of cytology, 1997—2004; pathologist BC Cancer Agy., Vancouver, Canada, 2006—. Cons. pathologist Can. Tumor Reference Ctr., Ottawa, Ontario, Canada, 1982—87. Author: Essentials of Aspiration Biopsy Cytology, 1991, Essentials of Exfoliative Cytology, 1992, Essentials of Cytology: An Atlas, 1993, Critical Issues in Cytopathology, 1996, Essentials of Lung Tumor Cytology, 2007, Essentials of Abdominal Fine-Needle Aspiration Cytology, 2007, Essentials of Head and Neck Cytology, 2009; mem. editl. bd.: Acta Cytologica Jour., 1985—2006, Vietnamese Med. Jour., 2001—06; contbr. articles to profl. jours. Accreditation com. for Can. sch. cytotechnology Can. Med. Assn., Ottawa, Ont., Canada, 1992—2000. Recipient Med. Excellency award, Vietnamese Am. Rsch. Found., Westminster, CA, USA, 2004. Fellow: Internat. Acad. Cytology (assoc.; membership com. 1989—92, editl. com. 1992—95, exam. bd. 1995—2002); mem.: European Acad. Scis., Royal Coll. Physicians and Surgeons of Can., Can. Soc. Cytology (hon.; chmn. 1984—85, sec.-treas. 1985—89), Papanicolaou Soc. Cytopathology (assoc.; member-at-large 1991—99). Achievements include research in cytopathology, pathology, patient care. Personal E-mail: khanhnguyen1730@hotmail.com. Business E-Mail: gknguyen@bccancer.bc.ca.

NGUYEN, LAM HUY, electronics engineer; arrived in US, 1979; s. Quyen Huy Nguyen and Cuc Thi Pham; m. Kim Thu Phan, May 24, 2003; children: Vy Lam, Kim Linh. BSEE, Va. Poly. Inst. and State U., Blacksburg, 1984; MSEE, George Washington U., Washington, 1991; MS in Computer Sci., Johns Hopkins U., Balt., 1994. Design engr. GE, Portsmouth, Va., 1984—85; electronics engr. Harry Diamond Lab., Adelphi, Md., 1985—92; team leader signal processing, microwave br. Army Rsch. Lab., Adelphi, 1992—. Contbr. articles to profl. jours., chapters to books. Recipient R&D Achievement award, US Army, 2006, 2008, Sci. and Engring. Excellence award, Army Rsch. Lab., 2005, 2007, 2008. Mem.: IEEE, Eta Kappa Nu, Phi Kappa Phi, Tau Beta Pi. Achievements include design and development of several versions of ultra-wideband radar; development of algorithms for SAR signal and image processing. Avocations: guitar, photography. Home: 11568 Jamestown Ct Laurel MD 20723 Office: Army Rsch Lab AMSRD-ARL-SE-RU-Microwave Br 2800 Powder Mill Rd Adelphi MD 20783-1197

NGUYEN, LOC H., social services administrator; arrived in US, 1975, naturalized; s. Phuoc H. and Tuyet-Nga T. Nguyen; m. Catherine L. Daly Nguyen; 1 child, Colson T. D. Nguyen. BS, U. Calif., LA, 1992, MPH, 1995, MA in Social Welfare, 1995, DPH, 2002. Program coord. UCLA Ctr. Pub. Health & Disasters, 1997—98, program dir., 1998—99; children's social worker LA County Dept. Children & Family Svcs., Pasadena, 1999—2004, supervising children's social worker, 2004—07, asst. regional adminstr. Covina, 2007—. Vol. Vietnamese refugee camps Cmty. & Family Svcs. Internat., Hong Kong, 1992, Manila, 92; adminstrv. intern & staff asst. US asst. sec. aging US HHS, Washington, 1994; vol. Bosnian refugee camps Suncocret, Stobrec, Croatia, 1995; vol. instr., disaster svcs. Greater LA Chpt. ARC, 1997—2002, chmn. disaster vols., 1998—99. Contbr. articles to profl. jours. County commr. LA County Policy Roundtable Child Care, 2002—05. Fellow Pub. Health Grad. Fellowship, U. Calif., LA Dept. Cmty. Health Scis., 1992—94. Mem.: Delta Omega Nat. Pub. Health. Office: LA County Dept Children & Family Svcs 1373 East Ctr Court Dr Covina CA 91724 Business E-Mail: nguyelc@dcfs.lacounty.gov.

NGUYEN, MADISON, councilwoman; b. Vietnam; BA in History, U. Calif., Santa Cruz; M in Social Sci., U. Chgo. Assoc. ombudsperson County of Santa Clara's Office of Human Rels.; pres. Franklin-McKinley Bd. Edn.; teacher sociology and Vietnamese Am. culture De Anza Cmty. Coll., Evergreen Valley Cmty. Coll.; councilwoman, Dist. 7 San José City Coun., 2005—. Mem. cmty. adv. bd. United Way Silicon Valley; mem. Asian Am. Cmty. Adv. Coun., San Jose State U. Office: San Jose City Coun 200 E Santa Clara St 18th Fl San Jose CA 95113 Office Phone: 408-535-4907. Office Fax: 408-292-6468. Business E-Mail: District7@sanjoseca.gov.*

NGUYEN, MEGAN, pharmacist, educator; d. Trung and En Nguyen; m. Randall Nguyen, May 27, 2000; children: Matthew D.M., Jacob M.Q. BS in Biol. Scis., U. Calif., Irvine, 1995; PharmD, Western U. Health Sci., Pomona, Calif., 2000. Asst. prof. pharmacy practice Western U. Health Sci., 2002—. Cons. pharmacist Cmty. Care Health Ctrs., Huntington Beach, Calif., 2005—08. Vol. Camp Footprints, Huntington Beach, 1997—2007, dir. camper recruitment and treas., 1997—2007. Named Clerkship Preceptor of Yr., Western U. Health Sci., 2007. Office: Western Univ Health Sci 309 E Second St Pomona CA 01854 Business E-Mail: megannguyen@westernu.edu.

NGUYEN, MONIQUE M., optometrist, educator; d. Hop Nguyen and Namkim Le; m. Hung V. Nguyen; children: Kinsey Q., Garran T. OD, Southern. Calif. Coll. Optometry, Fullerton, 2002. Cert. residency in pediatric optometry and vision therapy Southern Calif. Coll. Optometry, 2003. Asst. prof. Southern Calif. Coll. Optometry, Fullerton, 2003—; ind. optometrist A+ Vision Optometry, Ladera Ranch, Calif., 2008—. Fellow: Am. Acad. Optometry; mem.: Orange County Optometric Soc., Calif. Optometric Assn., Coll. Vision Devel., Am. Optometric Assn. Avocations: reading, embroidery. Office: A+ Vision Optometry 777 Corporate Dr Ste 200 Ladera Ranch CA 92694 Office Fax: 949-364-4419.

NGUYEN, QUANG, chemical engineer; BASc, MASc, U. Ottawa, Can., 1977. Pilot plant mgr. Iotech Corp, Ottawa, 1977—81; nuc. tech. supr. ii Ont. Hydro, Tiveron, 1981—85; project engr. Tigney Tech., Edmonton, Alta., 1985—86; rsch. scientist Forintek Can. Corp., Ottawa, 1986—90; sr. rsch. scientist Tembec Inc., Temiscaming, 1990—93; sr. engr. Nat. Renewable Energy Lab., Golden, Colo., 1993—2002; program mgr. Abengoa Bioenergy New Tech., Chesterfield, Mo., 2002—. Mem.: Colo. Engrs. and Land Surveyors, Profl. Engrs. Ont. Achievements include design & construction of pilot an commercial demonstration plants for conversion of cellulosic biomass to ethanol and co-products; patents in field.

NGUYEN, QUE HUONG, physics professor; b. Hanoi, Vietnam, Jan. 26, 1960; d. Thanh Long Nguyen and Minh Nguyet Thi Le; m. Anh Quoc Nguyen, Jan. 6, 1985; children: Nhan Hau Quoc, Nhanvan Quoc. PhD in Physics, CUNY, 2001. Rschr. Hanoi Inst. Physics, Vietnam Acad. Scis. & Techs., 1982—94, Inst. Physics, Moldova Acad. Scis., Kishinev, 1991—92, Physics Dept., City Coll., CUNY, 2001—05; asst. prof. Physics Dept., Marshall U., Huntington, W.Va., 2005—09, assoc. prof., 2009—. Contbr. articles to profl. publs. Mem.: APS. Office: Physics Dept Marshall Univ One John Marshall Dr Huntington WV 25755 Office Fax: 304-696-2494. Business E-Mail: nguyenh@marshall.edu.

NGUYEN, RU, entomologist; b. Nhatrang, Khanh Hoa, Vietnam, Dec. 12, 1944; s. Tam Nguyen and Van Thi Le; m. Kim-Dung Thi Nguyen, Jan. 28, 1981; 1 child, Kim-Anh. BS, Coll. Agr., Saigon, Vietnam, 1966; PhD, U. Fla., 1975. Asst. entomologist U. Fla., Gainesville, 1976—78; rsch. fellow Alexander von Humboldt-Stiftung/U. Bonn, Germany, 1978—79; rsch. entomologist, leader USDA-APHIS-PPQ, Ft. Lauderdale, Fla., 1980—82; rsch. entomologist divsn. plant industry Fla. Dept. Agr., Gainesville, 1982—. Mem. Caribbean fruit fly tech. com. Fla. Dept. Agr., 1983—; mem. citrus leafminer task force U. Fla., Gainesville, 1994—98; mem. nat. genetic resources adv. coun. USDA, Washington, 2000—04. Contbr. articles to profl. jours.; author: (book) Catalog of Aleyrodidae on Citrus and Their Natural Enemies, 1993. Recipient Disting. Svc. to Agr. award, Gamma Sigma Delta Honor Soc. of Agr., 1995, Outstanding Achievement award in developing Fly Free Zone, Fla. Dept. Agr. and Consumer Svcs., 1984. Mem.: Fla. Entomol. Soc. (Team Rsch. award 1997, 2007, Achievement award for rsch. 2002), Internat. Orgn. for Biol. Control, Entomol. Soc. Am. Office: Fla Dept Agr Divsn Plant Industry PO Box 147100 Gainesville FL 32614 Office Phone: 352-372-3505 ext. 430. Personal E-mail: runguyen@aol.com.

NGUYEN, SAN DUY, psychiatrist, educator; b. Langson, Vietnam, Sept. 25, 1932; arrived in Can., 1971, naturalized, 1977; s. Nguyen Duy and Tran Tuyet, Quyen (Trang) San; m. Eddie Jean Ciesielski, Aug. 24, 1971; children: Thuan Le San, Megan Thuloan San, Muriel Mylinh San, Claire Kimlan San, Robin Xuanlan San, Baodan Edward San. MD, U. Saigon, 1960; postgrad, U. Mich., 1970. Intern Cho Ray Hosp., Saigon, 1957—58; resident Univ. Hosp., Ann Arbor, Mich., 1968—70, Lafayette Clinic, Detroit, 1970—71, Clarke Inst. Psychiatry, Toronto, Ont., Canada, 1971—72; chief of psychiatry S. Vietnamese Army, 1964—68; sr. psychiatrist Queen St. Mental Health Ctr., Toronto, 1972—74; unit dir. Homewood San., Guelph, Ont., 1974—80; cons. psychiatrist Guelph Gen. Hosp., Guelph, 1974—80, St. Joseph's Hosp., Guelph; practice medicine specializing in psychiatry Guelph, 1974—80; unit dir. inpatient svc. Royal Ottawa Hosp., Ont., Canada, 1980—84, dir. psychiat. rehab. program, 1985—87; asst. prof. psychiatry U. Ottawa Med. Sch., 1980—85; assoc. prof. psychiatry, 1985—87; bd. dir. Hong Fook Mental Health Svc., Toronto, 1987—; dir. East-West Mental Health Ctr., Toronto, 1987—; chmn., bd. dir. Access Alliance Multicultural Health Ctr., Toronto, 1988—; cons. UN High Commr. for Refugees, 1987—. Author: Etude du Tetanos au Vietnam, 1960, Psycholsomatic Medicine: Theoretical, Clinical, and Transcultural Aspects, 1983, Uprooting, Loss and Adaptation, 1984—87, S.E. Asian Mental Health, 1985, Ten Years Later: Indochinese Communities in Can., 1988, Refugee Resettlement and Well-Being, 1989; co-author: The Psychology and Physiology of Stress, 1969. Served, 1953—68, Army Republic of Vietnam. Mem.: NY Acad. Sci., Internat. Soc. Hypnosis, Am. Soc. Clin. Hypnosis, Am. Psychiat. Assn., Can. Psychiat. Assn., Can. Med. Assn. Buddhist. Office: 2238 Dundas St W Ste 306 Toronto ON Canada M6R 3A9

NGUYEN, THACH NGOC, cardiologist; b. Feb. 2, 1953; s. Sau Ngoc Nguyen and Hanh Hong Tran. Diploma, Hue Med. Sch., 1978. Diplomate Am. Bd. Internal Medicine, Am. Bd. Cardiovasc. Diseases and Interventional Cardiology. Resident internal medicine Bklyn. Hosp., 1982-85, fellow cardiology, 1985-87; clin. asst. prof. medicine Ind. U. Sch. Medicine, 1992—; dir. cardiovascular rsch. St. Mary Med. Ctr., Hobart, Ind., 1997—, dir. cardiology, 2001—, pres. med. staff, 2002—04, 2006—. Editl. cons. Jour. of Interventional Cardiology, 1998, Vietnamese Med. Jour., 2001; sect. editor Mgmt. of Patients, Lesion & Complication; hon. prof. Inst. Geriatric Cardiology, Chinese PLA Ctrl. Hosp., Beijng, 2004—, Chao Yang Red Cross Hosp., 1998—, Beijing Friendship Hosp., Nanjing U. Hosp., 2006, Hanoi Med. Coll., 2007. Editor: Cardiology Today, 1995, Advances and Challenges in Today's Cardiology, 1997, Management of Complex Cardiovascular Problems: The Consultant's Approach, 2002, Spanish edit., 2002, Vietnamese edit., 2002, Practical Handbook of Advanced Interventional Cardiology, 2000;: 3d edit., 2007, Management of Complex Cardiovascular Problems: The Evidence-Based Medicine Approach, 2007, Cardiology of the 21st Century, 2009; co-editor: Jour. Geriatric Cardiology, 2003. Fellow: ACP, Soc. Cardiovasc. Angiography and Intervention; mem.: Am. Coll. Cardiology (internat. com. 2006—09, internat. membership task force 2007, strategic adv. 2009—). Roman Catholic. Address: 200 E 86th Pl Merrillville IN 46410-6258 Home Phone: 219-872-7275; Office Phone: 219-756-1400. E-mail: thachnguyen2000@yahoo.com.

NGUYEN, TIEN MANH, technical executive; b. Saigon, Vietnam, Apr. 5, 1957; came to the U.S., 1975; s. Hung The and Bi Thi (Luu) N.; m. Thu Hang Thi, Dec. 28 1985. BS in Engring., Calif. State U., Fullerton, 1979, MS in Engring., 1980; MSEE, U. Calif., San Diego, 1982; PhD in Elec. Engring., Columbia Pacific U., 1986; MA in Math., Claremont Grad. Sch., 1993, PhD in Engring. Math., 1995; MSEE in Digital Signal Processing, passed comprehensive exam, Calif. State U., Long Beach, 1995. Cert. electro magnetic compatibility engr., mfg. technologist. Tchg. asst. U. Calif., San Diego, 1982-83; chief automated mfg. dept. ITT Ednl. Svcs., West Covina, Calif., 1983-85; tech. staff, NASA rep. to Consultative Com. for Space Data Systems Jet Propulsion Lab., Pasadena, Calif., 1985—96; engring. specialist The Aerospace Corp., El Segundo, Calif., 1996-97, sect. mgr., 1997-2000, assoc. dir., 2000—02, acting dir., 2002—03, prin. tech. staff, 2003—04; engring. fellow, program area chief engr. Raytheon, Space and Airborne Sys., 2005—. Prin. tech. advisor Internat. Consultative Com. for Space Data Systems (CCSDS), Pasadena, 1985-90, 93-96. Editor: Proceedings of Consultative Com. for Space Data Systems, Radio Frequency & Modulation, 1989, 94, VACET Tech. Jour., 1996-97; contbr. 3 chpts. to Wiley Ency. of Elec. and Electronics Engring., 1999-2000; contbr. over 200 articles to profl. jours.; patentee in field. Grad. rep. EECS dept. U. Calif., San Diego, 1982-83; NASA del. to internat. Consultative Com. for Space Data Systems, 1986-96; mem. red team review NASA and govt. projects, 1999—. San Diego fellow, 1980-82, Long Beach Found. scholar Calif. State U.; recipient Bendix Mgmt. Club award, 1987, NASA Hon. award, 1988, 24 NASA Techbrief awards, 1989-96, 2 NASA Hon. awards, 1993, West Bond prize award for best PhD dissertation, 1995, Recognition Honoree, Calif. State U., Cert. Merit, RNC Presdl. Victory Team, 2005, Fullerton, Cert. Spl. Recognition, 2006, 50 Yrs. Commemorative Event, 2007, Cert. Recognition, Calif. State Assembly, 2007, Calif. State Senate, 2007, County of Orange, 2007; Inducted to Eisenhower Commn., 2006. Mem. IEEE (sr., vice chmn. 1987-94, session chmn. internat. symposium on electro magnetic compatibility 1986, internat. conf. on telecomm. 1995, session organizer and chmn., award 1986, 95, student activities chair Orange County Sect., 1996-97, 11 Aerospace Invention Disclosure awards 1998—, 5 Aerospace's Spot awards 1997—, 4 Aerospace Performance awards 1998-04, Asian-Pacific Man of Yr. award 2000, 2 aerospace divsn. team achievement awards 2000—04, session organizer and chmn. Aerospace Conf. 2001, Tech. Program Chmn., award, Yeh. Tech. Conf. 2004), AIAA (sr.), AAAS, Soc. Mfg. Engrs., Am. Math. Soc., Armed Forces Commn. and Electronics Assn., Vietnamese-Am. Sci. and Profl. Engring. Soc. (chmn. bd. dirs. 1995-96, planning chair and tech. program chair conf. 1996, presenter in field, invited presenter math. modeling workshop 1994—, editor VASPES '96 Conf. Proc.), Vietnamese Assn. for Computing, Engring., Tech., and Sci. (gen. co-chmn. Viet-Tech. Internat. Conf. 1996 (editor-in-chief VACETS Tech. Jour. 1996-97, mem. steering com. 1997, elected mem. exec. com. 1997-98), N.Y. Acad. Scis., U.S. Naval Inst., Phi Kappa Phi, Sigma Xi. Republican. Buddhist. Achievements include 10 patents, including technique to resolve phase ambiguity for QPSK systems, carrier synchronization for GMSK and linearization techniques for non-linear power amplifiers; development of new algorithms to design communications systems for space applications; future standards for space data systems. Home: 17501 Edgewood Ln Yorba Linda CA 92886-1951 Office: Raytheon Space and Airborne Sys 2000 E El Segundo Blvd El Segundo CA 90245 Office Phone: 310-607-7603. Personal E-mail: tngyen57@aol.com. Business E-Mail: tien_m_nguyen@raytheon.com.

NGUYEN, TILA (TILA TEQUILA), entertainer, model, singer; b. Singapore, Oct. 24, 1981; Actor: (film) I Now Pronounce You Chuck and Larry, 2007; (TV series) A Shot At Love With Tila Tequila, 2007; contestant: (TV series) Surviving Nugent, 2003, host: Pants-Off Dance-Off, 2006; singer: (albums) Tila Tequila, 2007; co-author (with Sarah Tomlinson): Hooking up with Tila Tequila: A Guide to Love, Fame, Happiness, Success, and Being the Life of the Party, 2008; featured on covers of Stuff, Import Tuner Mag., Maxim and others. Named one of Most Important People on the Web, PC World, 2007. Achievements include being the most popular person on MySpace.

NGUYEN, TRUNG HIEU, internist; b. Bac Lieu, Vietnam, Nov. 12, 1970; s. Quy V. Nguyen and Ha T. Luu; m. Thao L. Dinh, Nov. 1, 1997; children: Matthew T., Gabrielle M. BS in Chemistry, East Carolina U., Greenville, NC, 1996; MD, Brody Sch. Medicine, Greenville, 2007. Scientist GlaxoSmithKline, Research Triagle Pk., 1997—2002, Metrics, Inc., Grenville, NC, 2002—03; physician Kans. U. Med. Ctr., 2007—. Author. Recipient award, Nat. Collegiate Minority Leadership, 1994, 1st. Pl. All Campus Men's Table Tennis, East Carolina U., 1995—96, 2005; named 1st Pl., Pitt CC, 1994. Mem.: Am. Chem. Soc., Am. Med. Student Assn., Internal Medicine Interest Group, Am. Coll. Physicians, ECU Honor Student Orgn., Golden Key Honor Soc. Home: 3316 N Virginia Ave Kansas City MO 64116 Business E-Mail: tnguyen2@kumc.edu.

NGUYEN-DINH, THANH, internist, geriatrician, acupuncturist; b. Saigon, Vietnam; s. Bam and Chanh (Thi Duong) Nguyen-Dinh; m. Kim-Chi Nguyen-Dinh; children: Trung, Kim-Trang, Kim-Trinh, Trong. MD, Free U. Brussels, 1974; Tropical MD, Antwerp Tropical Med. Inst., 1975. Diplomate Am. Bd. Internal Medicine, Am. Bd. Geriat. Medicine, Am. Bd. Forensic Examiners, Am. Bd. Forensic Medicine, Coll. Acupuncture and Neuromuscular Therapy, Am. Assn. Integrative Medicine. Asst. prof. medicine Howard Med. Svc., Washington, 1981—2004; physician dir. St. Elizabeth Unit, D.C. Gen. Hosp., Washington, 1983-94. Co-dir. Howard U. Md. Clinics, D.C. Gen. Hosp., 1990-96. Contbr. articles to profl. jours. Fellow ACP, Am. Assn. Integrative Medicine (diplomate). Avocations: chess, swimming. Office: 6519 Dearborn Dr Falls Church VA 22044-1118 Personal E-mail: drtnd@yahoo.com.

NGUYEN-OGHALAI, TRACY UYENTRANG, medical educator, researcher; d. Thao Nguyen and Yem Thi Cao; m. John Steven Oghalai, Dec. 28, 1996; children: Kevin James Oghalai, Thomas Patrick Oghalai. MD, U. Tenn., Memphis, 1993. Asst. prof. U. Tex. Med. Br., Galveston, 2003—. Recipient Jr. Career Devel. award Geriatric Medicine, Assn. Subspecialty Profs., 2005—; BIRCWH scholar, U. Tex. Med. Br., Ctr. Interdisciplinary Rsch. Women's Health, 2006—. Office: U Tex Med Br 301 Univ Blvd Rte 1165 Galveston TX 77555

NGUYEN-WONG, KHANH-HOA THI, literature and language professor; MA, San Jose State U., 1989. Cert. profl. clear multiple subject tchr. Calif., 1987. Elem. tchr. Oak Grove Sch. Dist., San Jose, 1987—2006; coll. prof. Evergreen Valley Coll., San Jose, 2001—. ESL tchr. East Side Union Sch. Dist., San Jose, 1991—94. Translator: (non-profit refugee ctrs.) Volunteer Work For The Community. Worker homeless, Burlingame, Calif., 1990. Conservative. Buddhist. Avocations: gardening, travel, exercise. Office: Evergreen Valley Coll 3095 Yerba Buena Rd San Jose CA 95135-1598 Business E-Mail: khanh.hoanguyen-wong@evc.edu.

NHO, SHANE JAY, surgeon; b. Chgo., June 30, 1976; s. Jai Jung and Sun Ae Nho. BA, Northwestern U., Evanston, Ill., 2003; MS, Rush U., Chgo., 2003; MD, Rush U., 2003. Lic. orthopedic surgeon NY, 2004. Gen. surgery internship NY Presbyn. Hosp., NYC, 2003—04; orthop. surgery resident Hosp. Spl. Surgery, NYC, 2003—. Contbr. articles to profl. jours. Recipient Hon. Mention in Clin. Rsch. award, Biomedical Rsch. Poster Competition, 2002; nominee Neer award, Am. Shoulder and Elbow Surgeons, 2008; grantee Rsch. grant, Hosp. Spl. Surgery, 2007. Mem.: Am. Medial Assn. (assoc.), NY State Med. Soc. (assoc.), Orthop. Rsch. Soc. (assoc.), Am. Acad. Orthop. Surgeons (assoc.), Alpha Omega Alpha, Sigma Xi (assoc.). Office: Hosp Special Surgery 535 E 70th St New York NY 10021

NI, BUKUO, chemistry professor; s. Faquan Ni and Cainv Zheng; m. Qianying Zhang; 1 child, Wenyan. BS, Zhejiang U., Hangzhou, China, 1999; PhD, Shanghai Inst. Organic Chemistry, Chinese Acad. Sci., 2004. Prof. TAMU-Commerce, Tex., 2009—. Contbr. articles to profl. jours. Achievements include research in Organic Biomolecular Chemistry. Office: TAMU-Commerce Chemistry Dept 2600 S Neal St Commerce TX 75429 Personal E-mail: bukuo.ni@gmail.com. Business E-Mail: bukuo_ni@tamu-commerce.edu.

NI, DAIHENG, engineering educator; PhD, Ga. Inst. Tech., Atlanta, 2004. Asst. prof. U. Mass. Amherst, 2005—. Mem.: TRB Com. Traffic Flow Theory & Characteristics. Office: Univ Mass Amherst 130 Natural Resources Rd Amherst MA 01003 Business E-Mail: ni@ecs.umass.edu.

NI, JESSIE H.-T., research and development company executive, director; d. Yung-Chen Ni and Ing-Ju Ho; m. Cheng-Lung Chang, July 19, 1991; children: Anthony Chang, Casey Chang. PhD, U. Minn., 1995. Rsch. assoc. U. Minn., Minneapolis, 1995—2000; mgr. R&D Sys. Inc., 2000—06, scientist, 2000—06, dir., 2006—. Cons. U. Minn., 2000; dir. Como Student Cmty Coop. Musician: (performance) Minn. Chinese Music Ensemble (Book Award, 1987), translator med. and legal translations. Recipient Brainstorm award, U. Minn., 1999; Cancer Biology tng. grant, Nat. Cancer Inst., 1995—97. Office: R&D Sys Inc 614 McKinley Place NE Minneapolis MN 55413 Office Fax: 612-379-6580. Business E-Mail: jessie.ni@rndsystems.com.

NI, JINLAN, economics professor; married; children: Olivia Guo, Annika Guo. Asst. prof. U. Nebr. at Omaha, 2004—. Recipient Outstanding Grad. Prof., 2009. Office: Univ Nebraska at Omaha 6001 Dodge St Omaha NE 68182 Business E-Mail: jni@mail.unoamaha.edu.

NI, QINGWEN, engineering educator; s. Yongchang Ni and Zhiyian Tang; m. Rena Ren, Apr. 28, 1978; 1 child, Hao. PhD, U. North Tex., Denton, 1991. Postdoc. assoc. Purdue U., West Lafayette, Ind., 1991—93; sr. rsch. scientist South West Rsch. Inst., San Antonio, 1993—2001; assoc. prof. Tex. A&M Internat. U., Laredo, 2001—. With SW Rsch. Inst., San Antonio, 2001—08. Contbr. to publs. Grant, NIH, 2002—05, 2003—07, NSF grant, South Tex. Border Math. and Pre-Engring. Grads., 2003—08, Tex. A&M Internat. U., 2008—. Office: Tex A&M Internat Univ 5201 University Blvd Laredo TX 78045 Business E-Mail: qni@tamiu.edu.

NIBLACK, TRACEY, social studies educator; d. Tom and Katherine Neet; m. Jeff Niblack, June 20, 1998. BS in Edn., U. Mo., Columbia, 1998. Educator Claremore (Okla.) Pub. Schs., 2000—04, Ladue Pub. Schools, St. Louis, 2004—. Class sponsor Claremore HS, 2000—04; club sponsor Ladue Horton Watkins H.S., St. Louis, 2004—; student coun. sponsor Ladue Horton Watkins HS, 2005—06, model UN sponsor, 2006—, religious diversity sponsor, 2007—. Recipient Stuart and Lorton award for Excellence in Tchg. Okla. History, Okla. Hist. Soc., 2003. Office: Ladue Public Schools 1201 S Warson Rd Saint Louis MO 63124 Personal E-mail: tjniblack@yahoo.com.

NIBLOCK, ROBERT A., consumer home products company executive; b. Fla., 1962; m. Melanie Niblock; 2 children. BA in Acctg., U. NC. Acct. Ernst & Young, 1986—93; dir. tax Lowe's Companies Inc., Mooresville, NC, sr. dir. tax Mooreville, NC, v.p., treas., 1997—99, sr. v.p. fin. Mooresville, NC, 1999—2000, sr. v.p., CFO, 2000—01, exec. v.p., CFO, 2001—03, pres., 2003—, CEO, chmn., 2005—. Bd. dirs. Lowe's Companies Inc., 2004—. Office: Lowe's Companies Inc 1000 Lowe's Blvd Mooresville NC 28117*

NICAISE, OLIVIER JEAN-CHARLES, chemistry professor; b. Reims, France, Jan. 24, 1960; s. Hubert and Danielle Nicaise; m. Deborah Jean Lombardi, July 2, 1988; children: Alexandra Marie, Edouard Hubert. PhD, U. Ill., Urbana-Champaign, 1987. Asst. prof. chemistry St. Louis U., 1998—2004, Southern Conn. State U., New Haven, 2004—08; vis. prof. chemistry Trinity Coll., Hartford, Conn., 2008—. Author: (book) Comprehensive Asymmetric Catalysis I-III; contbr. articles to profl. jours. Recipient Excellence Tchg. award, U. Ill., 1988; nominee J. Phillip Smith Outstanding Tchg. award, Southern Conn. State U., 2008. Mem.: Am. Chem. Soc. (chemistry olympiad coord. New Haven sect. 2006—, Travel award 1999, 2001, 2003). Home: 121 Paradise Ave Hamden CT 06514-2011 Office: Trinity Coll Dept Chemistry 300 Summit St Hartford CT 06106-3100 Business E-Mail: olivier.nicaise@trincoll.edu.

NICANDRI, DAVID L., museum director; Grad., SUNY, Plattsburgh; MA in Am. History, U. Idaho, 1972; D (hon.), Gonzaga U., 2001. Curator Wash. State Capitol Mus., 1973—87; dir. Wash. State Hist. Soc. Mus., 1987—. Presenter in field. Author: (books) Olympias Forgotten Pioneers, 1976, Italians in Washington State: Emigration 1853-1924, 1977, Northwest Chiefs: Gustave Sohon's Views of the 1855 Stevens Treaty Councils, 1986; co-author: (book) Washington: Images of a State's Heritage, 1988; exec. editor Columbia: The Mag. of Northwest History; contbr. articles to profl. publs. Mem. Tumwater City Coun., 1978—87. Achievements include research on Lewis & Clark. Office: Wash State Hist Soc Mus 1911 Pacific Ave Tacoma WA 98402 Office Phone: 253-798-5900. Business E-Mail: dnicandri@wshs.wa.gov.

NICANDRI, GREGG THOMAS, orthopedist; b. Rochester, NY, Nov. 28, 1976; s. Stephen Anthony and Patricia Ann Nicandri; m. Katrina Fox, Aug. 6, 2005; 1 child, Lillian Katherine. BA, Pa. State U., Sta. Coll., 1999; MD, Va. Commonwealth U., Richmond, 2003. Contbr. articles to profl. jours. Student dir. Cross Over Free Health Care Clinic, Richmond, 1999—2003. Grantee, AO N.Am., 2006; fellow, Duke U. Sports Medicine, 2008. Mem.: AMA. Achievements include design of reconstructing the medial collateral and posterior cruciate ligaments. Office: Duke Sports Medicine Ctr 317 Finch Yeager Durham NC 27710

NICASTRI, ANN GILBERT, science educator; b. NYC, May 26, 1934; d. Ralph and Ruth Gilbert; m. Anthony D. Nicastri, July 2, 1960; children: RuthAnn, Christina, Catherine, Daniel. BA magna cum laude, Bklyn. Coll., 1954; MA, Columbia U., NYC, 1956. Tchg. asst. Barnard Coll., NYC, 1954—55, Columbia Coll., NYC, 1955; tchr. Midwood HS, Bklyn., 1955—60, tchr. AP biology, rsch., 1986—2004; tchr. Balt. Jr. HS, 1960—61, Balt. Jr. Coll., 1961—62, Julia Richman HS, NYC, 1962—63; adj. faculty fellows program, cons. Bklyn. Coll., 2004—. Sci. judge NYC Sci. and Engring. Fair, 2001—; rsch. coord. student projects Midwood H.S., Bklyn., 2003—04. Recipient ISEF Mentor award, USAF, 2004; fellow, NSF, 1957—58, 1959. Mem.: N.Y. Acad. Sci., Kappa Delta Pi, Phi Beta Kappa. Home: 164 Beach 143rd St Neponsit NY 11694-1105 Personal E-mail: agnicastri@aol.com.

NICASTRO, ANTHONY JOSEPH, academic administrator, educator; s. Anthony Joseph and Elvira Novellino Nicastro. BS in Physics, U. Del., Newark, 1976, BS in Math., 1979, MS in Physics, 1980, PhD in Physics, 1981. Asst. prof. physics Bucknell U., Lewisburg, Pa., 1981—87, assoc. prof. physics, 1987—90, West Chester U. Pa., 1990—2006, chair physics, 2002—, prof., 2006—, asst. dir., Ancient Biomaterials Inst., 2006—. Vis. prof. James Clk. Maxwell Found., 1989. Author: (textbook) Laboratory Astronomy; contbr. scientific papers to profl. jours. Commr. Westtown Twp. Planning Commn., West Chester, 1992—99. Recipient Internat. Course Competition award, Ctr. Theology and Nat. Scis., 2001; grantee, Rsch. Corp., 1984; Local Scis. Initiative grant, Metanexus, 2004—08. Mem.: Am. Phys. Soc., Sigma Xi. Office: West Chester Univ PA Dept Physics 135 Boucher Hall West Chester PA 19383

NICASTRO, CHRIS L., state official, school system administrator; m. Charles Nicastro; 4 children. BA in History, Ind. U., 1973; M in Ednl. Adminstrn., U. Mo., St. Louis, 1982; PhD in Ednl. Adminstrn., St. Louis U., 1991. Social studies tchr. N.W. R-I Sch. Dist., Jefferson County, Mo., 1976, asst. to supt. for personnel; asst. supt. Ritenour Sch. Dist., St. Louis County, Mo., 1984—95, supt., 1995—2002, Hazelwood Sch. Dist., St. Louis County, Mo., 2002—09; commr. edn. Mo. Dept. of Elem and Secondary Edn., 2009—. Mem.: Mo. Assn. Sch. Adminstrs. (MASA) (former pres., Supt. of Yr. 2009). Office: Mo Dept Elem and Secondary Edn 205 Jefferson St PO Box 480 Jefferson City MO 65102 Office Phone: 573-751-4212. Office Fax: 573-751-8613.*

NICCHI, VINCENT, JR., cardiologist; b. Bklyn., Nov. 16, 1955; s. Vincent Sr. and Rosalie (Martino) N.; m. Kathleen Mary Healy, May 26, 1985; children: Kristina Rose, Lisa Marie, Michelle Kathleen, Vincent Michael. BS in Chemistry, Bklyn. Coll., 1977; MD, U. Noreste, Tampico Tamps, Mex., 1981. Diplomate Am. Bd. Internal Medicine, Am. Bd. Cardiovasc. Diseases, Am. Bd. Nuc. Cardiology. Intern Maimonides Med. Ctr., Bklyn., 1982-83, resident, 1983-85; fellow in cardiology Deborah Heart Lung Ctr., Browns Mills, NJ, 1985-87; invasive/interventional cardiologist Ariz. Heart Inst., 1987-96; founder Cardiac Care Consultants, Sun City, Ariz., 1996—; chmn. cardiology sect. Boswell Hosp., Sun City, 2007—, mem. staff. Past chmn. credential com. Del Webb Hosp., Sun City West, Ariz., past mem. med. exec. com. Fellow: Am. Coll. Cardiology; mem.: AMA. Roman Catholic. Office: Cardiac Care Consultants 13634 North 93rd Ave Ste 30 Peoria AZ 85381

NICCOLINI, DIANORA, photographer; b. Florence, Italy, Oct. 3, 1936; arrived in US, 1945, naturalized, 1960; d. George and Elaine (Augsbury) Niccolini. Student, Hunter Coll., 1955—82, Art Students League, 1960, Germain Sch. Photography, 1962; BA magna cum laude, Marymount Manhattan Coll., 1995. Med. photographer Manhattan Eye, Ear and Throat Hosp., 1963—65; organizer med. photography dept. Lenox Hill Hosp., 1965—67, 1st chief med. photographer, 1965—67; organizer, head dept. med. and audio visual edn. St. Clare's Hosp., NYC, 1967—76; mem. Third Eye Gallery, NYC, 1974—76; owner Dianora Niccolini Creations, 1976—. Instr. photography Camera Club NY, 1978—79, Germain Sch. Photography, 1978—79, NY Inst. Photography, 1981—83; instr. comml. photography NY Inst. Tech., 1996—97. One-woman shows include 209 Photo Gallery, Top of the Stairs Gallery, Third Eye Gallery, 1974, 1975, 1977, Photographics Unltd. Gallery, NYC, 1981, W. Broadway Gallery, 1981, Camera Club NY, 1982, Overseas Press Club, NYC, 1983, Impulse Gallery, Provincetown, Mass., 1983, Throckmorton Fine Art Gallery, NYC, 1998, 2001, exhibited in group shows at Photography Over 65, 1978, Jacob Javits Fed. Bldg., 1992, Neikrug Gallery, 1993, Ward-Nasse Gallery, 1996, Internat. Salon, 1996, Curcio-Spector Gallery, 1996, Throckmorton Fine Art, 1997, 2001; pub.: portfolios; author: Women of Vision, 1982, Men in Focus, 1983, Big Fun with Billy, 2001; editor: P. W. P. Times, 1981—82; contbr. photographs to photog. books; Flashcards, Inc., 1988—90; contbg. editor: Functional Photography, 1979—80, NY Photo Dist. News, 1980. Mem.: Profl. Women Photographers (pres. 1980—84), Am. Soc. Picture Profls., Am. Soc. Mag. Photographers, Internat. Ctr. Photography, Biol. Photog. Assn., Women Photographs NY (founder 1974). Home: 356 E 78th St New York NY 10021-2239 Personal E-mail: dianoran@aol.com.

NICE, CARTER, conductor; b. Jacksonville, Fla., Apr. 5, 1940; s. Clarence Carter and Elizabeth Jane (Hintermister) N.; m. Jennifer Charlotte Smith, Apr. 4, 1983; children: Danielle, Christian, Olivia. MusB, Eastman Sch. Music, 1962; MusM, Manhattan Sch. Music, 1964. Asst. condr., concert master New Orleans Philharm., 1967-79; condr., music dir. Sacramento Symphony, 1979-92; music dir., condr. Bear Valley Music Fest., 1985—. Office: 579 Kevington Ct Sacramento CA 95864 Office Phone: 916-973-1138. Personal E-mail: ccniii@aol.com.

NICE, SCOTT DEAN, voice educator; s. Rita A. Zoller; m. Kristen K. Nice, Oct. 24, 1998. BA in Theatre Performance, Western Mich. U., Kalamazoo, 1998; MFA in Acting, Northern Ill. U., DeKalb. Cert. voicework tchr. Catherine Fitzmaurice, 2008. Asst. prof. voice and movement U. Northern Iowa Dept. Theatre, Cedar Falls, 2002—07, UNC, Wilmington Dept. Theatre, NC, 2007—. Resident voice and movement coach Gately, Poole Acting Intensives, DeKalb, Ill., 2002—; owner opporator Studio Nice, Wilmington, 2008—. Choreographer fight (theatrical productions) NYC Actor. Workshop leader Boy Scouts Am., Cedar Falls, Iowa, 2002—07. Office: Univ NC Wilmington 601 S Coll St Wilmington NC 28403-5671 Office Fax: 910-962-2110. Business E-Mail: nices@uncw.edu.

NICELY, OLZA M. (TONY), insurance company executive; b. Va., 1943; BBA, Georgia Coll. Cert. gen. ins. Ins. Inst. Am. Endorsement clk GEICO, 1961—73, asst. v.p., 1973—80; v.p. GEICO Ins. Cos., 1980—85, sr. v.p., 1985—87, exec. v.p., 1987—89, pres., 1989—, CEO, 1991—, chmn. Washington, 1993—. Trustee Geo. Mason Univ. Found. Mem.: Ins. Inst. for Hwy Safety, Property Casualty Insurers Assn. Am. Office: GEICO One Geico Plaza Washington DC 20076-0001*

NICEWARNER, METTA LEE, library director, artist; b. Abilene, Tex., Jan. 17, 1943; d. Ray Escoe and Pauline Oliver Nicewarner; life ptnr. Oscar Pedro La Madrid. BA, Hardin-Simmons U., Abilene, Texas, 1964; MLS, U. Tex., Austin, 1970. Libr. Hardin-Simmons U. Libr., 1966—70; serials cataloger and reference libr. Ariz. State U., Tempe, 1970—75; head, spl. collections and pub. svcs. coord. Tex. Woman's U., Denton, 1984—91; head access svcs. and head interlibr. loan U. Nev., Las Vegas, 1992—96; dir. libr. svcs. Athens Tech. Coll., Ga., 1996—. Libr. cons. Frito-Lay Corp. Tech. Svc. Divsn., Dallas, 1984—85, Cody Libr. Southwestern U., Georgetown, Tex., 1987; adj. faculty on UNLV campus U. Ariz. Grad. Sch. of Libr. and Info. Sci., Las Vegas, Nev., 1994. Contbr. articles to profl. jours. Mem., vol. C. of C. Conv. and Visitor's Bur., Denton, Tex., 1984—88. Named Adm. in the Tex. Navy, Gov. of Tex., 1986. Mem.: ALA, Tech. Coll. Sys. Ga. Libr. Coun. (mem., chair various coms. 1997—2008), N.Ga. Associated Librs. (sec., treas. 1999—2001), Mountain-Plains Libr. Assn. (mem. exec. bd., sec. 1993—97), Assn. Coll. and Rsch. Librs., Libr. Adminstrn. and Mgmt. Assn., Ga. Libr. Assn., Nev. Libr. Assn. (mem. exec. bd., sec. 1996), Mountain-Plains Libr. Assn., Beta Sigma Phi (pres., sec., city coun. rep., city coun. vp 1985—94, Named Woman of Yr. 1987). Democrat. Avocations: designing and making jewellery, reading, gardening. Office: Athens Tech Coll Libr 800 US Hwy 29 N Athens GA 30601 Office Fax: 706-355-5162. Business E-Mail: mnicewarner@athenstech.edu.

NICHOL, GENE RAY, JR., law educator, former academic administrator; b. Dallas, May 11, 1951; s. Gene R. and Dolores (Dumas) N.; m. Janet Castle, Aug. 20, 1973 (div. 1978); m. Glenn George, Nov. 25, 1984. BA in Philosophy, Okla. State U., 1973; JD, U. Texas, 1976. Bar: Alaska 1978. Assoc. Ely, Guess and Rudd, Anchorage, 1976-78; asst. prof. W.Va. U., Morgantown, 1978-80, assoc. prof., 1980-82; prof. law U. Fla., Gainesville, 1983-84; Cutler prof. law, dir. Inst. of Bill of Rights Law Coll. William & Mary, Williamsburg, Va., 1984-88, pres., 2005—07; dean U. Colo. Law Sch., 1988-95; dean, Burton Craige prof. law U. NC Sch. of Law, Chapel Hill, 1999—2005, prof. law, 2008—. Host Culture Wars, KBDI T.V., Denver, 1995-96. Author: (with M. Redish) Federal Courts; columnist: Rocky Mt. News, 1999-2000, Raleigh News and Observer, 2000-04; contbr. articles to profl. jours. Posten research grantee U. W.Va., 1980, 81, 82. Mem. Nat. Lawyers Guild (coms. 1978, vice chair Colo. reapportionment commn.), Am. Law Inst., ACLU (coms. 1978—), Am. Bar Found. Fellows, Order of Coif. Roman Catholic. Avocation: back packing. Office: U NC Sch of Law 5106 Van Hecke-Wettach Hall 100 Ridge Rd Chapel Hill NC 27599 E-mail: gnichol@email.unc.edu.

NICHOL, JOSEPH MCGINTY See MCG

NICHOLAS, CAROLINE JEAN, retired nurse, consultant; b. Lansing, Mich., Feb. 11, 1935; d. Homer Paul and Lucinda Rachel (McDonald) Anderson; m. William C. Nicholas (div.); children: Jan Marie, David Craig, Jill Elizabeth. BSN, Mich. State U., East Lansing, 1956, MA, 1969. RN Mich. Staff nurse MSU, East Lansing, 1956—57; clin. instr. Med. Hosp., 1957—62; nurse, 1962—86; nursing instr. Lansing CC, 1967—79; nurse cons. Mich. Dept. of Pub. Health, 1979—90, ret., 1990. Docent Women's Hist. Soc. and Hall of Fame, Lansing, 1980—; elder, delta Presbyn. Ch. Mem.: Phi Kappa Phi, Sigma Theta Tau, Alpha Omicron Pi. Avocations: travel, reading, sewing, cross stitch. Home: 2734 Trudy Ln Lansing MI 48910-3826

NICHOLAS, FREDERICK M., lawyer; b. NYC, May 30, 1920; s. Benjamin L. and Rose F. (Nechols) Nicholas; m. Eleanore Berman, Sept. 2, 1951 (div. 1963); children: Deborah, Jan, Tony; m. Joan Fields, Jan. 2, 1983. AB, U. So. Calif., 1947; postgrad., U. Chgo., 1949-50; JD, U. So. Calif., 1952. Bar: Calif. 1952, US Dist. Ct. Calif. 1952, US Ct. Appeals (9th cir.) 1952. Assoc. Loeb & Loeb, LA, 1952-56; ptnr. Swerdlow, Glikbarg & Nicholas, Beverly Hills, Calif., 1956-62; pvt. practice Beverly Hills, 1962-80; pres., atty. Hapsmith Co., Beverly Hills, 1980—. Gen. counsel Beverly Hills Realty Bd., 1971—79; founder, pres. Pub. Counsel, LA, 1970—73. Author: Setting Up a Shopping Center, 1960, Commercial Real Property Lease Practice, 1976. Chmn. Mus. Contemporary Art, LA, 1987—93, life trustee, 2002—; chmn. com. Walt Disney Concert Hall, LA, 1987—95; trustee Music Ctr. Los Angeles County, 1987—95, LA Philharm. Assn., 1987—95, Mus. Flying, Santa Monica, Calif., 1991—2002, Frederick R. Weisman Art Found., 2003—, Frederick R. Weisman Philanthropic Found., 2003—, Pitzer Coll., 1992—95, Art Ctr. Coll. Design, 2003—08, life trustee, 2009—; chmn. Calif. Pub. Broadcasting Commn., Sacramento, 1972—78; pres. Maple Ctr., 1977—79; co-developer Ronald Reagan Bldg., Washington, 1998; adminstr. Estate of Sam Francis, 1996—2008, Cedars Sinai Hosp., 2008—. With US Army, 1941—46, capt. US Army, 1946. Recipient Pub. Svc. award, Coro Found., 1988, Medici award, LA C. of C., 1990, Founders award, Pub. Counsel, 1990, Trustees award, Calif. Inst. Arts, 1993, City of Angels award, LA Ctrl. Bus. Assn., Disting. Svc. award, U. So. Calif. Law Sch. Class of 1952, 2002, Parkison Spirit of Urbanism award, U. So. Calif. Archtl. Guild, 2004, Equal Justice Advocacy award, ACLU Found., 2005, Cmty. Svc. award, AIA LA, 2006, Lloyd N. Cutler Lifetime Achievement award, Lawyers Com. Civil Rights Under Law, 2008; named Citizen of the Yr., Beverly Hills Bd. Realtors, 1978, Man of the Yr., Maple Ctr., 1980, Outstanding Founder in Philanthropy, Nat. Philanthropy Day Com., 1990. Mem.: Beverly Hills Bar Assn. (bd. govs. 1970—76, Disting. Svc. award 1974, 1981, Exceptional Svc. award 1986, 2004, Disting. Svc. award 2008, Louis B. Fox Disting. Svc. award 2008), Beverly Hills C. of C. (Man of the Yr. 1983). Home: 1001 Maybrook Dr Beverly Hills CA 90210-2715 Office: Hapsmith Co 3844 Culver Center St Ste B Culver City CA 90232 Business E-Mail: fmnicholas@hapsmithco.com.

NICHOLAS, KERI, real estate agent; b. Atherton, Calif. Residential real estate agent for over 20 years Coldwell Banker, Menlo Park, Calif. Named one of Internat. President's Premier list, Coldwell Banker, the Top 50 Real Estate Agents in the Country, Wall Street Journal. Office: Coldwell Banker 930 Santa Cruz Ave Menlo Park CA 94025 Office Phone: 650-329-6654. Office Fax: 650-329-9450. Business E-Mail: kerinich@aol.com.*

NICHOLAS, LAWRENCE BRUCE, company executive; b. Dallas, Nov. 9, 1945; s. J. W. and Helen Elouise (Whiteacre) N.; m. Virginia Pearl Farmer, Aug. 5, 1967; children: Helen Brooke, John Lawrence, Alexis Bradlee. BBA, So. Meth. U., 1968. Mem. sales staff Nicholas Machinery Co., Dallas, 1963-69; sales mgr. Indsl. and Comml. Rsch. Corp., Dallas, 1969-74; v.p. Precision Concepts Corp., Dallas, 1974-76, gen. mgr., 1976-78, pres. Addison, Tex., 1978-86, INCOR Inc., Addison, 1974-91, dir.; pres. The Octagon Group Corp., 2006—. Pres., dir. Multiple Axis Machine Corp., 1981-96, Investment Svcs. Corp., 1991-93; mem. adv. bd. Consultores Patrimoniales, Mex. City, 1992-2007; pres. Equity Capital Interests, Inc., San Antonio, Tex., 1993—; chmn. bd. dirs. Cross Securities Internat. Corp., San Antonio, 1993-94; pres. Worldwide Exec. Aviation, San Antonio, 1996—; bd. dirs. Sea Hawke Yachte Ltd., Can., 2003-. Served as officer Ordnance Corps, U.S. Army, 1968, N.G., 1968-74. Mem. NRA, Soc. Mfg. Engrs., Nat. Shooting Sports Found., Safari Club Internat., World Affairs Coun. San Antonio, Petroleum Club San Antonio.

NICHOLAS, LYNN B., medical association administrator; b. Tenn. BS in Med. Tech., Tenn. Wesleyan Coll.; M in Mgmt., Cent. Mich. U., 1983. Cert. in healthcare mgmt. Various positions including med. technologist, lab mgr., head lab svcs., sr. v.p. clin./ambulatory svc. Morristown Meml. Hosp., NJ, 1976—95; exec. v.p., COO NJ Hosp. Assn., 1995—2000; pres., CEO La. Hosp. Assn., 2000—04; CEO Am. Diabetes Assn., Alexandria, Va., 2004—06, Mass. Hosp. Assn., 2007—. Former chair La. Health Works Commn. Fellow: Am. Coll. Healthcare Execs. (bd. govs. 2003—06). Office: Mass Hosp Assn 5 New Eng Exec Pk Burlington MA 01803 Office Phone: 703-549-1500, 800-342-2383, 781-262-6000. Office Fax: 703-739-9346.*

NICHOLAS, LYNN HOLMAN, historian, researcher, writer; b. New London, Conn., Nov. 11, 1939; d. William Grizzard Holman and Carol (Ackiss) Wakelin; m. Robert Carter Nicholas III, Dec. 20, 1965; children: William C., R. Carter, Philip H. Student, Radcliffe Coll., 1957-59; diploma, U. Madrid, 1960; BA, Oxford U., Eng., 1964. Mem. adv. panel Presdl. Commn. on Holocaust Assets in the U.S., 1999; mem. US Delegation Holocaust Era Assets Conf. Prague, 2009. Author: The Rape of Europa: The Fate of Europe's Treasures in the Third Reich and the Second World War, 1994 (Nat. Book Critics Circle award 1995), Cruel World: The Children of Europe in the Nazi Web, 2005. Decorated chevalier Légion d'Honneur (France); named Amicus Poloniae, Govt. of Poland, 2003. Personal E-mail: lynnick105@aol.com.

NICHOLAS, NICHOLAS CONSTANTINE, retired military officer; b. Balt., Apr. 20, 1929; s. Constantine and Helene (Kalymnin) Nicholas; m. Sammie Ruth Vick (div.); children: Carolyn H., Lois E. stepchildren: Deborah L., Jana D.; m. Linda Lee Elkins, Sept. 2, 1977. Grad., Balt. City Coll., 1947; BA, U. Md., 1952; MA, U. Okla., 1973; attended, USAF Sch. Aviation Medicine, 1956, USAF Sch. Aerospace Medicine, 1975. Commissioned 2d lt. USAF, Coll. Pk., Md., 1952, group intelligence officer Bryan AFB, Tex., 1952; observor B-36 aircraft Ramey AFB, PR, 1954—56; observor B-36 and B-52 Aircraft; comdr. 4th Physiological Tng. Flight, Carswell AFB, Tex., 1956—63; chief physiological tng. unit Little Rock AFB, Ark., 1963—66; command coord. aerospace physiology Hdqs. Strategic Air Command, Omaha, 1966—70, Pacific Air Force and Comdr. 15th Physiological Training Unit Kadena AFB, 1970—72; chief dept. medicine USAF Sch. of Health Care Scis. Sheppard AFB, 1972—76; chief med. sys. divsn. Office of Sec. of Def., Washington, 1976—78; chief Health Policy and Programs Divsn., 1978—84, Biomed. Sci. Corps.; chmn. Crisis Mgmt. Hdqrs. USAF S.G., 1981—84. Cons. aerospace physiology Surgeons General USAF, Wash., DC, 1977—88, cons. med. edn. and tng., 1977—88; cons. MedTech Comm. Inc., NYC. Author: Use of Modified Partial Pressure Suits to Aleviate Orthostatic Hypotension, 1962; co-author: Human Decompression Tests for B-58 Escape Capsule System, 1964, USAF/USN Physician Assistant Program: Military Medicine, 1977. Pres. Young Dem. Club, Coll. Pk, Md., 1950—52; delegate State Convention Young Dem. Club, Anapolis, Md., 1951, Nat. Convention Young Dem. Club, St. Louis, 1951; mem. Inaugural Gala for Pres. Truman, Wash., DC, 1949. Col. USAF, 1952—84. Decorated Air Force Commendation medal with cluster Air Force, Meritorious Svc. medals with cluster, Air medal, Air Force Outstanding Unit awards with three clusters, Armed Forces Expeditionary medal, Joint Svc. Commendation medal, Legion of Merit, Nat. Defense Svc. medal with cluster, Vietnam Svc. medal with 5 Clusters, Vietnam Gallantry Cross with one Bronze Star, Vietnam Campaign medal with one Silver Star; recipient Men's League award Outstanding Achievement and Svc. to U., U. Md., 1950; nominee One of America's Ten Outstanding Young Men, Fort Worth, Tex., 1963, Little Rock, Ark., 1964. Mem.: Arnold Air Soc., Scabbard and Blade, Aerospace Physiologist Soc., Assn. Mil. Surgeons of US, Mil. Officers Assn. (life), Air Force Assn. (life), Aerospace Medicine Assn. (life), Phi Alpha Theta, Omicron Delta Kappa, Phi Kappa Tau. Episcopalian. Avocations: walking, reading. Home: 8724 Racquet Club Dr Fort Worth TX 76120 Personal E-mail: nicholasn101@charter.net.

NICHOLAS, NICKIE LEE, retired industrial hygienist; b. Lake Charles, La., Jan. 19, 1938; d. Clyde Lee and Jessie Mae (Lyons) Nicholas. BS, U. Houston, 1960, MS, 1966. Tchr. sci. Pasadena (Tex.) Ind. Sch. Dist., 1960-61; chemist FDA, Dallas, 1961-62, VA Hosp., Houston, 1962-66; chief biochemist Baylor U. Coll. Medicine, 1966-68; cheist NASA Johnson Spacecraft Ctr., 1968-73; analytical chemist TVA, Muscle Shoals, Ala., 1973-75; indsl. hygienist, compliance officer OSHA, Dept. Labor, Houston, 1975-79, area dir. Tulsa, 1979-82, mgr. Austin, Tex., 1982-96, ret., 1996. Faculty VA Sch. Med. Tech., Houston, 1963—66. Recipient award for Outstanding Achievement, German Embassy, 1958, Suggestion award, VA, 1968, Group Achievement award, Skylab Med. Team NASA, 1974, Personal Achievement award, Dept. Labor Fed. Women's Program, 1984, Career Achievement award, Federally Employed Women Inc., 1988, Meritorious Performance award, DOL-OSHA, 1990, Asst. Sec.'s Leadership award, 1992, 1996, Disting. Career Svc. award, Dept. Labor, 1991, Sec.'s Exceptional Achievement award, 1991, cert. of Appreciation, OSHA, 1991. Mem.: Fed. Exec. Assn. (pres. 1984—85), Am. Harp Soc., Am. Soc. Safety Engrs., Am. Indsl. Hygiene Assn., Am. Conf. Govtl. Indsl. Hygienists, Am. Assn. Clin. Chemists, Am. Chem. Soc. (dir. analytical group Southeastern Tex. and Brazosport sects. 1971, chmn. elect 1973), Order Eastern Star, Kappa Epsilon. Home: 1603 LCR 706 Kosse TX 76653

NICHOLAS, PETER M., medical products executive; married; 3 children. BS, Duke U.; MS, U. Pa. Former corp. dir. mktg., gen. mgr. med. products divsn. Millipore Corp.; various sales, mktg., and gen. mgmt. positions Eli Lily and Co.; co-chmn. bd. Boston Sci., Natick, Mass., 1979—95, CEO, 1979—99, chmn. bd., 1995—. Chmn. bd. trustees, mem. bd. exec. com. Duke U.; mem. Mass. Bus. Roundtable, Mass. Bus. High Tech. Coun., CEOs for Fundamental Change in Edn., Boys and Girls Club Boston. Named one of World's Richest People, Forbes Mag., 2001—04. Fellow: Nat. Acad. Arts and Scis. (trustee); mem.: Boys and Girls Club, Boston, CEOs Fundamental Change Edn., Mass. Bus. High Tech. Coun., Mass. Bus. Roundtable. Office: Boston Sci 1 Boston Sci Pl Natick MA 01760-1537*

NICHOLAS, RALPH WALLACE, anthropologist, educator; b. Dallas, Nov. 28, 1934; s. Ralph Wendell and Ruth Elizabeth (Oury) N.; m. Marta Ruth Weinstock, June 13, 1963. BA, Wayne U., 1957; MA, U. Chgo., 1958, PhD, 1962. From asst. prof. to prof. Mich. State U., East Lansing, 1964-71; prof. anthropology U. Chgo., 1971—2000, chmn. dept., 1981-82, dep. provost, 1982-87, dean of coll., 1987-92, dir. Ctr. Internat. Studies, 1984-95, William Rainey Harper prof. anthropology and social scis., 1992-2000, William Rainey Harper prof. emeritus, 2000—; pres. Internat. House of Chgo., 1993-2000. Cons. Ford Found., Dhaka, Bangladesh, 1973 Author: (with others) Kinship Bengali Culture, 1977, The Fruits of Worship, 2003, Rites of Spring, 2008; editor: Jour. Asian Studies, 1975-78. Sec. Coun. Am. Overseas Rsch. Ctrs., 2005—; v.p. Am. Inst. Indian Studies, 1974—76, treas., 1993—2001, pres.-elect, 2001—02, pres., 2002—; trustee Bangladesh Found., 1972—2005; dir. Indo-Am. Ctr., Chgo. Ford Found. fgn. area tng. fellow, India, 1960-61; Sch. Oriental and African Studies research fellow, London, 1962-63; sr. Fulbright fellow, West Bengal, India, 1968-69 Fellow AAAS, Am. Anthrop. Assn., Royal Anthrop. Inst. (Eng.); mem. Assn. Asian Studies, India League of Am. Found. (trustee). Office: U Chgo Dept Anthropology 1126 E 59th St Chicago IL 60637-1580 also: Am Inst Indian Studies 1130 E 59th St Chicago IL 60637

NICHOLAS, ROBERT A., lawyer; BA magna cum laude, Amherst Coll., 1976; JD, Columbia U., 1980. Bar: NY 1981, Pa. 1985. Asst. dist. atty. Manhattan Dist. Atty.'s Office, 1980—85; with Reed Smith LLP, 1985—, former head Del. Valley Region litig. group, mng. ptnr. Phila. and Wilmington offices, 2000—07, mem. exec. com., mng. ptnr. NY office, 2007—. Bd. mem. World Affairs Coun. of Phila. Office: Reed Smith LLP 599 Lexington Ave 29th Fl New York NY 10022 Office Fax: 212-521-5450.

NICHOLAS, STEPHEN J., orthopedic surgeon, sports medicine physician; BA in Biology, Harvard U., Cambridge, Mass., 1982; MD, NY Med. Coll., Valhalla, NY, 1986. Dir. Nicholas Inst. Sports Medicine and Athletic Trama, Lenox Hill Hosp., NYC, 2001—; chief, bioskills lab. Lenox Hill Hosp., NYC. With Lenox Hill Hosp.; worked extensively with profl. and collegiate athletes; orthopaedist NY Jets, NY Islanders, Hofstra U., & NJ Galdiators. Mem. NYC Sports Comm.; mem. alumni adv. bd. NY Med. Coll. Mem.: AMA, Am. Orthopaedic Assn., Quigley Orthopedic Soc., Med. Soc. State NY, Am. Orthopedic Soc. for Sports Medicine (mem. publs. com.), Am. Acad. Orthopedic Surgeons. Office: 130 E 77th St New York NY 10075 Office Phone: 212-737-3301.

NICHOLAS, THOMAS ANDREW, artist; b. Middletown, Conn., Sept. 26, 1934; s. Michael and Lena (Sequenzia) N.; m. Gloria R. Spencer, Oct. 11, 1958; 1 child, Thomas Michael. Student of Ernst Lohrmann, 1949-53; scholarship student, Sch. Visual Arts, NYC, 1953-55. Instr. Famous Artists Schs., Inc., Westport, Conn., 1958-60; instr. painting, Rockport, Mass., 1963-66. Commd. by Franklin Mint Gallery Am. Art to produce lithographs of Am. coastline, 1977; one-man shows include Grand Cen. Galleries, NYC, 1962, 64, 66, 68, 70, 78, I.F.A. Galleries, Washington, 1964-92, A. Huney Gallery, San Diego, 1980, 82;, Carolyn Hill Gallery, Soho, NYC, 1988-89, 3 person show, 1992; represented in permanent collections Butler Inst. Am. Art, Youngstown, Ohio, Ga. Mus., Athens, New Britain Art Mus., Conn., U. Utah, Adelphi U., Greenshields Mus., Montreal, Can., Farnsworth Mus., Rockland, Maine, Springfield Art Mus., Mo., Ranger Collection at NAD, Peabody Mus., Salem, Mass., Hispanic Soc. Am., Peter A. Juley and Son Collection, Nat. Mus. Am. Art, 80 images, Smithsonian Inst., Washington, DC. Recipient Key to City, Middlesex County Conn., 1989, Gold medal honor New Eng. Watercolor Soc., Boston, 1985, Acad. Artists Assn., 1985, Emile Lowe award Am. Watercolor Soc. 1961, watercolor prize 1964, Gold medal honor 1969, Clare Stout award 1971, Mary S. Litt award 1972, medal honor for watercolor Knickerbocker Artists 1962, Purchase award watercolor Butler Inst. Am. Art 1962, Henry Ward Ranger Fund purchase watercolor NAD 1962, 71, Obrig prize watercolor 1964, 66, 79, 87, Gold medal honor watercolor Allied Artists Am. 1962, Grumbacher prize 1978, Today Mag. Art medal 1970, 74, Gold medal honor watercolor Am. Artists Profl. League 1964, best landscape award 1974, Gold medal 1978, Edwin S. Webster award honor watercolor Boston Soc. Watercolor 1964, gold medal honor watercolor Hudson Valley Art Assn. 1964, 74, DuMond Meml. award 1971, Isabel Stinschneider Meml. award 1972, Herman Wick Meml. award Salmagundi Club, NYC, 1966, 2d prize 1966, June Justin J. Impasto award 1972, Arthur T. Hill prize 1973, Arthur T. Hill Meml. prize 1975, Louis Z. Seley prize 1978, Gwynne Lennon prize 1979, Gold medal honor oil Rockport Art Assn. 1966, 1969, 1976, 1985, 1996, 1997, 1999, 2002, 03, 04, 07, cash award Wichita Centennial Watercolor 1970, Providence Art Club prize 1972, Gold medal Franklin Mint Competition 1974, Gold medal Honor Acad. Assn. 1976, Grumbacher award watercolor, Acad. Artists Assn., 1990, Grumbacher Gold medal Gouache New Eng. Watercolor Soc., 1992, Gouache Transparent Watercolor, 1995, others; named Knickerbocker Honoree Artist of Yr., 1989; Elizabeth Greenshields grantee, 1961, 62. Mem. NAD (assoc. 1963-70, academician, 1970-, cert. merit watercolor 1992), Am. Watercolor Soc. (ea. v.p. 1994—, Dolphin fellow), Boston Watercolor Soc., Conn. Watercolor Socs., Allied Artists Am., Knickerbocker Artists (dir.'s prize 1971, Gold medal 1989), Boston Guild Artists (Grumbacher Gold medallion award watercolor 1988, No. Shore Arts Assn. award oil 1991), Rockport Art Assn. (George O. Davies Meml. Silver medal 1988, 94, Darrand award oil 1992, Cirino award 1st prize Gouache 1992, Clark Popular award Gouache 1992, Cooley award graphics 1995, Clark Popular award Gouache 1995, Cirino award Gouache 1995, Davis Meml. award watercolor 1996, Mills Meml. award Gouache 1996), Hudson Valley Artists (Gold medal 1974, 85, 94, Huntington Meml. award oil 1995, Bohnert Meml. award oil 1996), Hudson Valley Art Assn. (honoree 2000). Office: Tom Nicholas Gallery 65 Main St Rockport MA 01966-1512 Home Phone: 978-546-2074; Office Phone: 978-546-9647. Personal E-mail: tangallery@aol.com. *I have been fortunate to have been encouraged by my family at an early age and have a number of people to thank for their support, especially my wife. I feel artists must never compromise their ideals and principles, no matter how high their standards. Originality and professional ethics with one's work make goals achieved meaningful. On the one hand, an artist should inwardly feel that there is little he can't accomplish, and yet he must learn to work within his realized limitations.*

NICHOLAS, WILLIAM RICHARD, lawyer; b. Pontiac, Mich., June 19, 1934; s. Reginald and Edna Irene (Bartlett) N.; m. Diana Lee Johnson, Aug. 20, 1960; children: Susan Lee, William Richard Jr. BS in Bus., U. Idaho, 1956; JD, U. Mich., 1962. Bar: 1963. Of counsel Latham & Watkins, Los Angeles, 1962-96. Contbr. numerous articles on taxation. Lt. (j.g.) USN, 1956-59. Mem. Calif. Bar Assn., Los Angeles County Bar Assn., Am. Coll. Tax Counsel. Home: 1808 Old Ranch Rd Los Angeles CA 90049-2207 Office: Latham Watkins 355 S Grand Ave Los Angeles CA 90071-1560 Office Phone: 310-485-1234.

NICHOLAW, CASEY, theater director, choreographer; b. 1962; Performer: (Broadway plays) Crazy for You, 1992, The Best Little Whorehouse Goes Public, 1994, Victor/Victoria, 1995, Steel Pier, 1997, Saturday Night Fever, 1999, Seussical, 2000, Thoroughly Modern Millie, 2002; choreographer (Broadway plays) Spamalot, 2005; dir., choreographer: (Broadway plays) The Drowsy Chaperone, 2006; dir.: To Be or Not to Be, 2008. Mem.: Soc. Stage Directors and Choreographers. Office: c/o David Kalodner William Morris Agy 1325 Ave of the Americas New York NY 10019 Office Phone: 212-903-1148.*

NICHOLL, MATTHEW JAMES, music educator, director; b. Cleve., Feb. 11, 1956; s. Russell J. Nicholl, Joan Severs Nicholl (Stepfather); m. Susan Calhoun, Dec. 29, 1990; children: Leigh Calhoun, John Calhoun. MusB, MusM, U. North Tex., Denton, 1982. Asst. prof., music Western Carolina U., Cullowhee, NC, 1990—96, Berklee Coll. Music, Boston, 1996—2000, assoc. prof., music, 2000—02, chair, contemporary writing and prodn. dept., 2002—. Composer, keyboardist, prodr. (compact disk recording) Windborn, Featuring the Dallas Brass, From Here to There, Matthew Nicholl and Eliot Wadopian, Silent Picture, Nicholl and Farquharson; author: (book) Music Notation, Preparing Scores and Parts.

NICHOLLS, ANTHONY, biophysicist, software company executive; b. Plymouth, England; BS in Physics, Oxford U.; PhD, Inst. for Molecular Biophysics, Fla. State U., 1988. Rschr. Columbia U., NYC, 1989—97; founder, pres. & CEO OpenEye Scientific Software, Santa Fe, 1997—. Achievements include re-writing the electrostatics program DelPhi and writing widely-used graphics software GRASP that displays electric potentials around macromolecules. Office: Openeye Scientific Software 9D Bisbee Ct Santa Fe NM 87508-1338*

NICHOLLS, PETER J., academic administrator; BS in Math., London U., 1967; PhD in Math., Cambridge U., Eng., 1970. Prof. math. scis. No. Ill. U., 1971—91, acting dean Coll. Liberal Arts and Scis., 1988—89, assoc. dean Coll. Liberal Arts and Scis., 1987—88, 1989—91; dean Coll. Arts and Scis. Kans. State U., 1991—2002, prof. math., 1991—2002; provost, acad. v.p. Colo. State U., Ft. Collins, 2002—05; provost, exec. v.p. U. Conn., Storrs, 2005—. Office: Office of the Provost U Conn 352 Mansfield Rd Unit 2086 Storrs Mansfield CT 06269-2086 Office Phone: 860-486-4037.

NICHOLLS, RICHARD AURELIUS, retired obstetrician, gynecologist; b. Norfolk, Va., Aug. 12, 1941; s. Richard Beddoe and Aurelia (Gill) Nicholls; m. Geri Bowden, Feb. 24, 1986. BS in Biology, Stetson U., Deland, Fla., 1963; MD, Med. Coll. Va., 1967. Diplomate Am. Bd. Ob-Gyn. Ret., 1998; intern Charity Hosp. Tulane divsn., New Orleans, 1967—68, resident in ob-gyn., 1968—71; asst. prof. ob-gyn. Tulane Med. Sch., New Orleans, 1973—74, clin. asst. prof., 1974—83; pvt. practice specializing in ob-gyn. Pascagoula, Miss., 1974—89, Ocean Spring, Miss., 1989—98; ret. Mem. staff Singing River Hosp., chmn. surg. and ob-gyn. depts., 1979—80, chmn. ob-gyn. dept., 1984; mem. staff Ocean Springs Hosp., laser com., pharmacy com. and therapeutics com., chmn. ob -gyn. dept., mem. exec. bd., 1990—91, sec., treas. staff, 1991—92, exec. bd., 1991—92, chief staff, 1993—94. Contbr. articles to profl. jours. Bd. dirs. Miss Racing Assn. Maj. US Army, 1971—73. Fellow: ACS, ACOG; mem.: Am. Cancer Soc. (bd. dirs. Jackson County br.), Am. Veneral Disease Soc., Conrald Collins Ob-Gyn Soc., Gulf Coast Ob-Gyn. Soc., New Orleans Ob-Gyn Soc., New Orleans Grad. Me4d. Assembly, So. Med. Soc., AMA, Am. Assn. Gynecol. Laparoscopists, Am. Fertility Soc., Singing River Med. Soc., Miss. State Med. Soc.

NICHOLLS, ROBERT LEE, civil engineer, educator; b. Lincoln, Nebr., June 11, 1929; s. Carrol C. and Claire (McDermet) N.; m. Ruth Ann Allen, Aug. 30, 1958; children: David, Jonathan, Carol. BSCE with high honors, U. Colo., 1951; MSCE, Iowa State U., Ames, 1952, PhD, 1957. Registered profl. engr., Del., Pa., Iowa, Md. Design engr., constrn. supr. U.S. Army Corps Engrs., Japan, Korea, 1953-55; chief materials engr. and hwy. design engr. Gannett & Fleming, Harrisburg, Pa., 1957-59; prof. civil engring. U. Del., Newark, 1959-93. Geotech. engring. and constrn. materials cons. DuPont, Hercules, Thiokol, others; also other engring. cons. Author: Composite Construction Materials, 1976; co-author: Civil Engineering Systems, 1972 (also Polish and Spanish edits.), 2d edit., 2005; author, editor: ASCE Structural Plastics Selection Manual, 1984; also articles; 7 patents in field. Dist. advance chmn. Boy Scouts Am.; vol. cons. concrete products plants Internat. Exec. Svc. Corp., 1993—, cons. airfield and hanger designs, Engring. Ministries

Iternat., 1993—. Fellow ASCE (life; pres. Del. sect. 1974-75, nat. citation for sect. activities 1975), Ops. Rsch. Soc. Am., Internat. Soc. Soil Mechanics, Transp. Rsch. Bd., Am. Concrete Inst. Achievements include design and construction management for mission aviation airstrips and hangars; design and construction management for GPS autopilots for mission aviation unmanned supply drops. Business E-Mail: rnich@udel.edu.

NICHOLLS, TIM S., paper company executive; BBA, Univ. SC, Spartansburg; MBA, Univ. Ga. Fin. mgmt. positions Union Camp Co., 1991—99; various mgmt. positions Internat. Paper, Memphis, 1999—2007, gen. mgr. emerging markets, dir. fin. indsl. packaging, v.p., CFO IP Europe Brussels, pres. Weldwood Canadian pulp & wood bus. Vancouver, v.p. spl. assignment Memphis, sr. v.p., CFO, 2007—. Office: Internat Paper 6400 Poplar Ave Memphis TN 38197

NICHOLS, ALBERT MYRON, retired minister; b. Creston, Iowa, Oct. 17, 1914; s. Albert Maurice and Lou (Myers) N.; m. Phyllis Cochran, June 28, 1939; children: Byron Albert, Phillip Garrett. AB, UCLA, 1936; BS, San Francisco Theol. Sem., 1940; DD, Occidental Coll., 1952. Ordained to ministry United Presbyn. Ch. in U.S.A., 1940. Pastor chs., North Hollywood, Calif., 1940-43; assoc. pastor Pasadena (Calif.) Presbyn. Ch., 1943-57; pastor 1st Presbyn. Ch., Pendleton, Oreg., 1957-82, ret., 1982. Chmn. gen. assembly com. on responsible marriage and parenthood United Presbyn. Ch. in U.S.A., 1959-62, mem. Bd. Christian Edn., 1969-72; mem. 1st coun. Synod of Pacific; moderator Oreg. Synod, 1968, 69; stated clk. Ea. Oreg. Presbytery, 1975-99. Pres. Pasadena Child Guidance Clinic, 1955-57, Glen Eddy Residents Assn., 2004; trustee San Francisco Theol. Sem., 1963-84; life trustee Lewis and Clark Coll., Portland, Oreg.; active Pendleton City Recreation Commn., 1965-2001; founding bd. dirs. Presbyn. Intercommunity Hosp., Whittier, Calif.; mem. State of Oreg. Health Coun., 1985-88, State Trauma Adv. Bd., 1987-91; chmn. City of Pendleton Capital Improvements Commn., 1983-2001. Named 1st Citizen of Pendleton, 1984. Home: 114 Glen Eddy Dr Niskayuna NY 12309 Personal E-mail: nicholsm@gleneddy.com.

NICHOLS, ARGIE NELL, science educator; d. Thurman and Imodel Franklin; m. Bobby Lee Jones, Jan. 8, 2008; children: Traci Davis, Joshua. EdD, U. Ark., Fayetteville, 2006. Assoc. prof. U. Ark., Ft. Smith, 1994—.

NICHOLS, CLYDE RICHARD, minister, consumer products company executive; b. NYC, Apr. 15, 1945; s. William and Novella Nichols; m. Marsha A. Wade, Oct. 11, 1986; children: Forest, Marvin, Anthony, Gerald. BS, Met. State Coll., Denver, 1985; ThD, Berean Bible Coll., Dallas, 1994. Ordained pastor and bishop Fellowship of Deliverance Chs., Inc. Correction officer City and County Denver, 1981-92; sr. pastor, founder Redeeming Love Ch., Denver; sr. dir. M&C Enterprises, Inc., Denver; exec. dir. Josie M. Bedford Found. Dir. membership Greater Metro Denver Ministers Alliance Orgn., Denver, 1997-99. Bd. dirs. Denver Opportunities for Outreach and Reflection 2000—. Recipient award for outstanding cmty. work Cheyenne br. NAACP, Wyo., 1982, award for outstanding cmty. activities 24th Syl Morgan Acad. Arts, Denver, 1992, Juanita Gray award. Avocations: travel, reading, computers. Home and Office: PO Box 31092 Aurora CO 80041-0092 Business E-Mail: mcenterpr31092@aol.com. E-mail: rev98crn@aol.com.

NICHOLS, DANA, literature and language educator; d. Don and Jean Nichols. AA in English and Fgn. Langs., Gainesville State Coll., Ga., 1995; BA in English and Spanish, Mercer U., Macon, Ga., 1997; MA in English, Ga. State U., Atlanta, 1998, PhD in English, 2006. Instrnl. lab asst. Gainesville State Coll., Ga., 1997—2002, asst. prof. English, Spanish, 2002—. Scholar, Phi Theta Kappa, 1995—97. Mem.: Popular Culture Assn. Am., Soc. Study So. Lit. Avocations: travel, horseback riding. Office: Gainesville State Coll PO Box 1358 Gainesville GA 30503 Business E-Mail: dnichols@gsc.edu.

NICHOLS, DENNIS WITT, rector; b. Bedford, Va., Oct. 20, 1955; s. Heenan Witt and Betty C. Nichols; m. Linda Jean Wintersteen, Aug. 8, 1958; children: Ashley Corinne, Ande Catherine. BME magna cum laude, Shenandoah U., Winchester, Va, 1978; MDiv magna cum laude, Gen. Theol. Sem., NYC, 1992. Tchr. Holy Cross Regional Sch., Lynchburg, Va., 1979—85, Bedford County Pub. Schs., Va., 1985—89; pastoral asst. Grace Episcopal Ch., Manhattan, NY, 1990—91; episcopal deacon St. Mark's Episcopal Ch., Queens, NY, 1991—92; organist asst. Gen. Theol. Sem., NYC, 1991—92; organist, choir master St. Marks Episcopal Ch., Queens, 1991—92; rector St. John Wilderness, Gibbsboro, NJ, 1992—95, St. Peter's Episcopal Ch., Clarksboro, NJ, 1995—. Dean Woodbury Episcopal Convocation, Diocese of NJ, NJ, 2001—04; mem. alumni exec. com. Gen. Theol. Sem., 2003—05. Contbr. articles to profl. jours. Del. Oxford Round Table, England, 2007. Scholar, Louise Wilkens Found., 1971—78. Liberal. Episcopalian. Avocations: golf, swimming, chess, travel. Personal E-mail: dn4116@comcast.net. E-mail: stpetes10@verizon.net.

NICHOLS, DONALD ARTHUR, economist, educator; b. Madison, Conn., Dec. 20, 1940; s. Edward Charles and Ruth (Nilson) Nichols; m. Linda Powley, Aug. 19, 1962 (dec. Oct. 1982); children: Charles Spencer, Elizabeth Clarke; m. Barbara Jakubowski Noel, May 22, 1983 (dec. Dec. 26, 2000); m. Jane Bartels, Sept. 26, 2001. BA, Yale U., 1962, MA, 1963, PhD, 1968. Mem. faculty dept. econs. U. Wis., Madison, 1966—2006, prof., 1977—2006, chmn. dept. econs., 1983-86, 88-90, mem. exec. com. faculty senate, 1987-90, chmn., 1989-90, dir. Robert M. LaFollette Sch. Pub. Affairs, 2002—06, Wis. Idea fellow, 2004—06, emeritus prof., 2006—; lectr. Yale U., 1970—71; sr. economist Senate Budget Com., Washington, 1975—76; dep. asst. sec. for econ. policy and rsch. Dept. Labor, Washington, 1977-79; dir. Ctr. for Rsch. on Wis. Economy. Econ. advisor to gov. State of Wis., 1983—86; exec. sec. Gov.'s Coun. Econ. Advisors, 1983—86; mem. Gov.'s Export Strategy Commn., 1994—95, Gov.'s Econ. Growth Coun., 2003—06; mem. acad. adv. coun. Fed. Res. Bank of Chgo., 2004—; bd. dirs. Thompson, Plumb Funds, 1987—, bd. chmn., 2009—; bd. dirs. Sustainable Woods Co-operative, 2001—03; dir. Ctr. for World Affairs and Global Economy, 1995—2000; affiliate Christensen Assocs., Madison, 1999—; cons. in field. Author: (with Clark Reynolds) Principles of Economics, 1970, Dollars and Sense, 1994; contbr. articles to profl. jours. Trustee U. Wis. Bookstore, 1990-95; bd. advisors Am. Players Theatre, Spring Green, Wis., 1993-2001, Taliesin Coun., 2001-04, bd. dirs. Wis. Walnut Coun., 2008- NSF fellow, 1963-66, 70-72; Nat. Commn. Employment Policy rsch. grantee, 1980-82; recipient William H. Kiekhofer Meml. Teaching prize U. Wis., 1973 Mem. Am. Econ. Assn., Royal Econ. Soc.

NICHOLS, EDIE DIANE, real estate broker; b. Grahamstown, Eastern Cape Province, Republic of South Africa, Mar. 28, 1939; arrived in U.S., 1963; d. Cyril Doughtry and Dorothy Ethel (Nottingham) Tyson; m. John F. Nichols, Dec. 16, 1962 (div. Dec. 1978); 1 child, Ian Tyson. Adminstrv. asst. Am. Acad. Medicine, NYC, 1963-64, Jack Lenor Larsen, Inc., NYC, 1964-70; v.p. John Scott Fones, Inc., NYC, 1971-76, Howard J. Rubenstein Assocs. Inc., NYC, 1976-80; dir. comm. Carl Byoir & Assocs., NYC, 1981-83; account supr. Hill and Knowlton, NYC, 1983-85; broker Cross & Brown Co., NYC, 1986-88; v.p. Marc Nichols Assocs., Inc., NYC, 1989-95; mng. ptnr. Nichols Brown Internat., NYC, 1995—2004; real estate broker Citi-Habitats, NYC, 2005—06; v.p. J.C. DeNiro & Assoc., NYC, 2006—. Trustee Ctrl. Pk. Hist. Soc., N.Y.C., 1978-80. Mem. NOW, Internat. Assn. Corp. and Profl. Recruitment, N.Y. Women in Comm. (pub. rels. chair 1980-81, v.p., programs bd. dirs. 1985-87), Fin. Women's Assn. of N.Y. (bd. dirs. 1997-98), City Club of N.Y. (trustee, v.p., fin. and devel. 1987-89). Democrat. Episcopalian. Home: 16 Stuyvesant Oval Apt 10F New York NY 10009 Office: JC DeNiro & Assoc 34 8th Ave New York NY 10014 Office Phone: 212-561-0690, 212-741-3037. E-mail: ednny@aol.com.

NICHOLS, EUGENE DOUGLAS, mathematics professor; b. Rovno, Poland, Feb. 6, 1923; came to U.S., 1946, naturalized, 1951; s. Alex and Anna (Radchuk) Nichiporuk; m. Alice Bissell, Mar. 31, 1951. BS, U. Chgo., 1949, postgrad., 1949-51; MEd, U. Ill., 1953, MA, 1954, PhD, 1956. Instr. math. Roberts Wesleyan Coll., North Chili, N.Y., 1950-51, U. Ill., 1951-56; assoc. prof. math. edn. Fla. State U., 1956-61, prof., head dept., 1961-73; dir. Project for Mathematical Devel. of Children, 1973-77; dir. math program NSF, 1958-61; dir. Math. Inst. Elem. Tchrs., 1961-70; pres. Nichols Schwartz Pub., 1992—; prof. math. edn. Fla. State U., 1974-90. Chmn. U. Ill. Com. on Sch. Math., 1954-55; cons. editor math McGraw-Hill Book Co., 1956 Co-author: Modern Elementary Algebra, 1961, Introduction to Sets, 1962, Arithmetic of Directed Numbers, 1962, Introduction to Equations and Inequalities, 1963, Introduction to Coordinate Geometry, 1963, Introduction to Exponents, 1964, Understanding Arithmetic, 1965, Elementary Mathematics Patterns and Structure, 1966, Algebra, 1966, Modern Geometry, 1968, Modern Trigonometry, 1968, Modern Intermediate Algebra, 1969, Analytic Geometry, 1973, Holt Algebra 1, 1974, 78, 82, 86, 92, Holt Algebra 2, 1974, 78, 82, 86, 92, Holt Geometry, 1974, 78, 82, 86, Holt School Mathematics, 1974, 78, 81, Holt Pre-Algebra Mathematics, 1980, 86, Holt Mathematics, 1981, 85, Elementary School Mathematics and How to Teach It, 1982, Geometry, 1991, Holt Pre-Algebra, 1992, Mathematics Dictionary and Handbook, 1993, 95, 98, 99; author: Pre-Algebra Mathematics, 1970, Introductory Algebra for College Students, 1971, Mathematics for the Elementary School Teacher, 1971, College Mathematics, 1975, College Mathematics for General Education, rev. edit., 1975. Named Fla. State U. Disting. Prof., 1968-69; recipient Disting. Alumni award U. Ill. Coll. Edn., 1970. Mem. Am. Math. Soc., Math. Assn. Am., Sch. Sci. and Math. Assn., Nat. Coun. Tchrs. Math., Coun. Basic Edn., Text and Acad. Authors Assn., Pi Mu Epsilon, Phi Delta Kappa. Home: 3386 W Lakeshore Dr Tallahassee FL 32312-1305 Home Phone: 850-385-9218; Office Phone: 570-253-9362. Personal E-mail: eunichols@aol.com. *Do not look for a career--look for opportunities to do kind things for others. Be honest with yourself and with those around you.*

NICHOLS, FRANK C., dental educator; b. Cherrypoint, NC, Dec. 25, 1951; s. Christine Nichols; m. Nancy Ann Nichols; children: Lynn Michelle, Cynthia Ann. PhD, U. Rochester, NY, 1981. Diplomate in periodontology Am. Bd., 1993. Prof. U. Conn., Farmington, 1985—. Contbr. scientific papers. Recipient Kaiser Permanente tchg. award. Home: 146 Sedgwick Rd West Hartford CT 06107 Office: Univ Conn 263 Farmington Ave Farmington CT 06030 Office Fax: 860-679-2179. Personal E-mail: f.nichols@snet.net. Business E-Mail: nichols@nso.uchc.edu.

NICHOLS, GEORGE LEON, JR., minister; b. Phila., Mar. 7, 1938; s. George Leon Sr. and Elva Grace (Berger) N.; m. K. Diane Hunt, Sept. 21, 1963; children: Katherine J., Stephen J. BS in Bible, Phila. Coll. Bible, 1961; postgrad., Reformed Episcopal Sem., Phila., 1961-63; DD, Fla. Bible Coll, Hollywood, 1976; D of Ministry, Luther Rice Sem., Jacksonville, Fla., 1979; MA, Liberty U., 1988. Ordained to ministry Bapt. Ch., 1961; cert. Christian counselor. Pastor Nicetown Bapt. Ch., Phila., 1961-64, 1st Bapt. Ch., Elmer, N.J., 1964-67; sr. pastor Pennsville Bapt. Ch., Mt. Pleasant, Pa., 1967-87, Faith Bapt. Ch., Wilmington, Del., 1987—. Trustee Phila. Biblical U., Langhorne, Pa., 1987; trustee, Out-Island Ministries, St. Petersburg, Fla., 1975-, pres.; bd. dirs. Mil. Evangelism, Aberdeen, Md. Mem. Am. Assn. Christian Counselors, Bibl. Archeol. Soc., Evang. Theol. Soc. Office: Faith Bapt Ch 4210 Limestone Rd Wilmington DE 19808-2099 Home: 17 Cauline Ct Newark DE 19711 Office Phone: 302-998-4105. Business E-Mail: gnichols@fbcwilmington.com. *To enjoy life we must have a theology that is practical and practiced.*

NICHOLS, GINA LYNN, archivist, writer; d. Mark Charles Kubin and Barbara Josephine (Holtby) Spain; m. Mark James Nichols (div.); 1 child, Hunter Thomas. BA in History, Calif. State U., Northridge, 2002, MA in History, 2006. Archivist USN Seabee Mus., Port Hueneme, Calif., 2004—. Author: The Seabees at Port Hueneme, 2006, The Seabees at Gulfport, 2007. Grantee, U. Corp., Calif. State U., Northridge, 2002; Whitsett scholar, Whitsett Found., 2003. Mem.: Soc. Mil. Historians, Hist. Soc. So. Calif. (Whitsett fellow 2003), Soc. Calif. Archivists (devel. com. 2002—), Soc. Am. Archivists. Office: USN Seabee Mus 99 23rd Ave Port Hueneme Cbc Base CA 93043

NICHOLS, GREGORY DAWSON, playwright, educator; b. Evanston, Ill., Mar. 20, 1967; married. PhD, U. Wash., Seattle, 2004. Playwright (play) Virtual Solitiar (Best Play award, 1998, Best Actor award, 1998). Educator North Seattle CC, 2007—. Recipient Outstanding Instrn. award, Seattle CC Dist., 2008.

NICHOLS, GUY WARREN, retired institute and utilities executive; b. Colchester, Vt., Oct. 27, 1925; s. Guy W. and Gladys (Tomlinson) N.; m. Shirley Hibbard, June 21, 1947; children: Pamela, Gail, Sally. BSCE, U. Vt., 1947; postgrad., Worcester Poly. Inst. Sch. Indsl. Mgmt., 1953-56; MS in Bus. Adminstrn., MIT, 1961. With New. Eng. Electric System, Westborough, Mass., 1947-84, exec. v.p., 1968-70, pres., 1970-84, chief exec. officer, 1972-84, chmn. bd., 1978-84. Bd. dirs. Ameresco Inc. Chmn., trustee Woods Hole Oceanographic Instn., 1985-95. Sloan fellow, MIT, 1961. Fellow Am. Acad. Arts and Scis. Office: 40 Sylvan Rd Ste E-1980 Waltham MA 02451 Personal E-mail: looncall99@comcast.net.

NICHOLS, HARVEY, biology professor; s. Allen and Dorothy Nichols. BA, U. Manchester, 1960; PhD, U. Leicester, Eng., 1964. Biologist Yale U., New Haven, 1963—64; postdoc rsch. scientist U. Wis., Madison, 1964—69; prof. dept. biology U. Colo., Boulder, 1969—. Recipient BFA Excellence Svc. award, U. Colo., 1990, BFA Excellence Tchg. award, 2002—03.

NICHOLS, HENRY LOUIS, retired lawyer; b. Collin County, Tex., Nov. 7, 1916; s. Jesse Cleveland and Leva (Stiff) N.; m. Elaine Guentherman, May 17, 1949; children: David Michael, Martha Marie. LL.B., So. Meth. U., 1940. Bar: Tex. 1939. Asst. city atty., Dallas, 1946-50; pvt. practice, 1951—. Mem. adv. bd. Ctr. for Legal Mcpl. Studies. Served to lt. col. AUS, 1941-46; col. USAR ret. Rsch. fellow Southwestern Legal Found., 1964. Fellow Am. Bar Found.; mem. ABA, Dallas Bar Assn. (pres. 1963), State Bar Tex., Tex. Bar Found. (charter), Park City Club. Home: 3131 Maple Ave Apt 13H Dallas TX 75201-1206 *As a night-school graduate (Law School), I believe the opportunities in America are unlimited for anyone willing to work. Nowhere in the world are such opportunities available. We who live in the U.S.A. are blessed and the most fortunate of all people. We should strive to maintain that which our fathers preserved for us.*

NICHOLS, IRIS JEAN, retired illustrator; b. Yakima, Wash., Aug. 2, 1938; d. Charles Frederick and Velma Irene (Hacker) Beisner; (div. June 1963); children: Reid William, Amy Jo; m. David Gary Nichols, Sept. 21, 1966. BFA in Art, U. Wash., 1978. Freelance illustrator, graphic designer, Seattle, 1966—2004; med. illustrator, head dept. illustration Swedish Hosp. Med. Ctr., Seattle, 1981-86; owner, med. and sci. illustrator Art for Medicine, Seattle, 1986—2003; ret., 2003. Med. illustrator U. Wash., Seattle, 1966-67; part-time med. illustrator, graphic coord. dept. art The Mason Clinic, 1968-78; instr. advanced illustration Cornish Coll. Arts, Seattle, 1988-90; organized, coordinated and gifted the artwork of Prof. Glen E. Alps of U. Wash. after his death in 1996 Illustrator various books including Bryophytes of Pacific Northwest, 1966, Microbiology, 1973, 78, 82, 94, 98, Introduction to Human Physiology, 1980, Understanding Human Anatomy and Physiology, 1983, Human Anatomy, 1984 Regional Anesthesia, 1990, many other med. and sci. books, and children's books on various subjects; exhibited in group shows at Seattle Pacific Sci. Ctr., summer 1979, 82, Am. Coll. Surgeons (1st prize 1974), N.W. Urology Conf. (1st prize 1974, 76, 2d prize 1975); pub. illustrations Constellation Pk. and Marine Res., City Seattle Pk., 1999, Whale Tail Park, Seattle. Pres. ArtsWest (formerly West Seattle Arts Coun.), 1983; chmn. West Seattle (Wash.) H.S. Art Acquisition Com., 2003—. Named to West Seattle H.S. Alumni Hall of Fame, 1986, Matrix Table, 1986-96. Mem. Assn. Med. Illustrators (Murial McLatchie Fine Arts award 1981), Nat. Mus. Women in the Arts (Wash. state com., bd. dirs. 1987-95, pres. 1993-94), Women Painters of Wash. (pres. 1987-89), U. Wash. Alumni Assn., Lambda Rho Art Assn. (pres. alumni assn. 1995-98, treas. 2002-04) Avocations: artwork, printmaking, small books.

NICHOLS, JAMES RICHARD, civil engineer, consultant; b. Amarillo, Tex., June 29, 1923; s. Marvin Curtis and Ethel (Nichols) N.; m. Billie Louise Smith, Dec. 24, 1944; children: Judith Ann, James Richard Jr., John M. BS in Civil Engring., Tex. A&M U., 1949, MS in Civil Engring., 1950; DHum (hon.), Tex. Wesleyan U., 1990. Registered profl. engr., Tex., Okla., N.Mex. Ptnr. Freese & Nichols, Inc., Cons. Engrs., Fort Worth, 1950-76, pres., 1977-88, chmn., 1988—. Former chmn., dir. emeritus Tex. Bd. Profl. Engrs. Former chmn. Ft. Worth Conv. and Visitors Bur., Baylor All Saints Hosp.; bd. dirs. Pub. Comm. Found. North Tex., Tex. A&M Rsch. Found., Tex. Wesleyan U.; co-chmn. Metroplex Mission with Billy Graham. With US Army, 1943—46. Fellow: Am. Cons. Engrs. Coun.; mem.: NSPE, ASCE (hon.), Tex. Water Conservation Assn., Ft. Worth C. of C. (bd. dirs., adv. coun., former chmn.), Rotary, Ft. Worth Club, Exch. Club. Methodist. Office: Freese & Nichols Inc 4055 Internat Plz Ste 200 Fort Worth TX 76109-4895 Home: 1600 Texas St Apt 21602 Fort Worth TX 76102-7512 Office Phone: 817-735-7300. Personal E-mail: jrn@freese.com.

NICHOLS, J(OHN) ALDEN, retired history professor; b. Westerly, RI, Feb. 28, 1919; s. Thomas Pitman and Jennie Althea (Howland) N.; m. Barbara Searles Tuttle, June 8, 1946 (dec. Dec., 1975); children: Catherine Tyler Nichols Thompson, David Alden, Margaret Foster. BA with high honors, high distinction, Wesleyan U., Middletown, Conn., 1941; MA, Columbia U., 1948, PhD, 1951. History instr. Wesleyan U., Middletown, Conn., 1948-50, asst. prof. history, 1959-61, Skidmore Coll., Saratoga Springs, N.Y., 1950-51; fellowship Ford Found., 1951-52; editor Ginn & Co., Boston, 1952-59; assoc. prof. history U. Ill., Champaign-Urbana, 1961-67, prof. history, 1967-89; ret., 1989. Author: (books) Germany After Bismarck, 1958, The Year of the Three Kaisers, 1987; mng. editor Daedalus, 1959-61. Schiff fellow, Columbia U., N.Y.C., 1947, sr. rsch. fellow, Fulbright Program, West Germany, 1963. Mem. AAUP, Am. Hist. Assn., Philosophy Club (U. Ill.). Democrat. Avocations: piano, electronic organ. Home: 505 W Pennsylvania Ave Urbana IL 61801-4922 Home (Summer): 1741 Upper Hollow Rd Dorset VT 05251-9610

NICHOLS, LARRY, medical educator; Assoc. prof. pathology & medicine U. Pitts., 1992—. Office: Univ Pittsburgh Med Ctr 200 Lothrop St Pittsburgh PA 15213

NICHOLS, MARY D., state official, former federal agency administrator; b. Mpls., Apr. 10, 1945; m. John F. Daum; 2 children. BA, Cornell U., 1966; JD, Yale U., 1971. Atty. Ctr. for Law in Pub. Interest, L.A., 1971—74; sec. environ. affairs State of Calif., 1974—78; chief asst. city atty. City of L.A., 1978—79; pvt. cons., 1983—88; sr. staff atty. Nat. Resources Def. Coun., L.A., 1989—93; asst. adminstr. for air & radiation EPA, Washington, 1993—97; sec. resources State of Calif., Sacramento, 1999—2003; prof.-in-residence UCLA. Chair Calif. Air Resources Bd., 1974-78, 1979-1983, 2007-; campaign mgr. TYom Bradlery for Gov. of Calif., 1985-86; bd. commissioners L.A. Dept. Water and Power; instr. U. So. Calif., UCLA; founding trustee Calif. Environ. Trust; bd. dirs. L.A. 2000 Partnership; cons. in field. Office: Calif Air Resources Bd 1001 I St PO Box 2815 Sacramento CA 95812 also: UCLA Box 951476 Los Angeles CA 90095 E-mail: nichols@law.ucla.edu.*

NICHOLS, MICHAEL COOPER, food products executive, lawyer; b. Birmingham, Ala., Feb. 4, 1952; s. F.W. and Jeanette (Cooper) N.; m. Marcia Couch, Sept. 23, 1976; children: Joshua, Jessica, Zachary, Anna. BA with honors, Brown U., 1974; JD, Emory U., 1977. Bar: Ga. 1977, Tex. 1981. Mem. Ga. Ho. of Reps., Atlanta, 1977-81; chief adminstrv. officer Appletree Mktg., Houston, 1988-91; gen. counsel SYSCO Corp., Houston, 1981-88, v.p., 1991—98, v.p., sec., gen. counsel, 1998—, sr. v.p., gen. counsel, corp. sec., 2006—. Pres. Houston Food Bank, Houston, 1990—92; trustee Houston Police Officer Pension Fund; chmn. Houston Civil Svc. Commn.; bd. dirs. Congregation Beth Israel, 1986. Home: 2122 Dunstan Houston TX 77005 Office Phone: 281-584-1471. E-mail: nichols.mike@corp.sysco.com.*

NICHOLS, MIKE, stage and film director; b. Berlin, Nov. 6, 1931; s. Nicholaievitch and Brigitte (Landauer) Peschowsky; m. Patricia Scott, 1957 (div.); m. Margot Callas, 1974 (div.); 1 child; m. Annabel Davis-Goff (div.); 2 children; m. Diane Sawyer, Apr. 29, 1988. Student, U. Chgo., 1950-53; student acting, Lee Strasberg. Ptnr. with Elaine May in comedy act; first appeared at Playwrights Theatre Club, Compass Theatre, Chgo.; NY debut An Evening with Mike Nichols and Elaine May, 1960; acted in A Matter of Position, Phila., 1962; dir.: (plays) Barefoot in the Park, 1963 (Tony award best dir.), The Knack, 1964, Luv, 1964 (Tony award best dir.), The Odd Couple, 1965 (Tony award best dir.), The Apple Tree, 1966, The Little Foxes, 1967, Plaza Suite, 1968 (Tony award best dir.), The Prisoner of 2d Avenue, 1971 (Tony award best dir.), Uncle Vanya (co-adapted), 1973, Streamers, 1976, Comedians, 1976, The Gin Game, 1977, (LA Drama Critics award),

Drink Before Dinner, 1978, Lunch Hour, 1980, Fools, 1981, The Real Thing, 1984 (Tony award 1984,), Hurlyburly, 1984, Social Security, 1984, Elliot Loves, 1990, Death and the Maiden, 1992, The Play What I Wrote, 2003, Whoopi, 2004, Spamalot, 2005 (Outer Critic Cir., outstanding direction of a musical, 2005, Julia Hansen award for excellence in directing, Drama League, 2005, Tony award for best direction of a musical, 2005, Julia Hansen Award excellence in directing, The Drama League, 2005), The Country Girl, 2008; (films) Who's Afraid of Virginia Woolf?, 1966, (Academy award nomination best director 1966), The Graduate, 1967 (Academy award best director 1967), Catch-22, 1970, Carnal Knowledge, 1971, The Day of the Dolphin, 1973, The Fortune, 1975, Heartburn, 1986, Biloxi Blues, 1987, Working Girl, 1988 (Academy award nomination best director 1988), Wolf, 1994; dir., prodr.: Silkwood, 1983 (Academy award nomination best director 1983), Postcards From the Edge, 1990, Regarding Henry, 1991, The Birdcage, 1996, Primary Colors, 1998, What Planet Are You From?, 2000, Closer, 2004, Charlie Wilson's War, 2007; prodr. All the Pretty Horses, 2000; prodr.: (musical) Annie, 1977; dir., exec. prodr. (TV movies) Wit, 2001; (mini-series) Angels in America, 2003 (Emmy award Outstanding Directing for a Miniseries, Movie or Dramatic Special, 2004); performed at NY musical Pres. Johnson's Inaugural Gala, 1965.

NICHOLS, RALPH ARTHUR, retired lawyer; b. Clinton, NY, Jan. 27, 1919; s. Arthur Britcher and Carrie Lena (Pitcher) N.; m. Pamela Crow Bermingham, May 3, 1947 (dec. Feb. 1980); children: Jeremy Nichols Pierce, Ralph A. Jr., Melinda Nichols Mayer; m. Victoria Requa Lalli, Sept. 5, 1981. AB, Hamilton Coll., 1940; LLB, Yale U., 1947. Bar: Conn. 1949, N.Y. 1947, U.S. Dist. Ct. (so. dist.) N.Y. 1949, U.S. Dist. Ct. Conn. 1950, U.S. Supreme Ct. 1959. Assoc. Burke & Burke, NYC, 1947-49, Maguire, Walker & Middleton, Stamford, Conn., 1949-54; assoc., then ptnr. Cummings & Lockwood, Stamford, 1954—2009. Founder, former bd. dirs. Stamford Land Conservation Trust; former bd. dirs. Conservationists Stamford, Inc., Stamford YMCA; former bd. dirs., sec. Stamford Area Commerce and Industry; trustee Stamford YMCA. Lt. USNR, 1942-46, ETO, PTO. Fellow: Am. Coll. Trust and Estate Counsel; mem.: ABA, Yale Club (N.Y.C.), Woodway Country Club (Darien, Conn.), Phi Delta Phi. Republican. Episcopalian. Home: 32 Bank St New Canaan CT 06840-6238 Home Phone: 203-966-6325. E-mail: rnichols@cl-law.com.

NICHOLS, ROBERT HASTINGS, lawyer; b. Mpls., Aug. 22, 1941; s. James Hastings and Judith (Beach) Nichols; m. Jean Christy, Nov. 30, 1968; children: Marc O., Seth J., Ethan D., Rebecca J. AB, Yale U., New Haven, Conn., 1963; JD, U. Chgo., 1967. Bar: Ill. 1967, US Dist. Ct. (no. dist.) Ill. 1967, US Ct. Appeals (7th cir.) 1972, US Dist. Ct. (ea. dist.) Wis. 1975, US Ct. Appeals (8th cir.) 1975, US Ct. Appeals (DC cir.) 1976, US Supreme Ct. 1986; cert. in Pub. Affairs Coro Found., 1964. Ptnr. Cotton, Watt, Jones and King, Chgo., 1967—95; sr. atty. and coord. United Airlines Master Exec. Coun., Air Line Pilots Assn., Internat. AFL-CIO, 1995—. Cons. Govt. of New Zealand, Auckland, 1980; mem. lawyers coord. com. AFL-CIO. Contbr. articles to legal publs. Mem.: Columbia Yacht Club. Democrat. Presbyterian. Home: 1030 E 49th St Chicago IL 60615-1814 Office: 9550 W Higgins Rd Ste 1000 Rosemont IL 60018 Home Phone: 773-373-6151; Office Phone: 847-292-1700. Business E-Mail: nicholsr@alpa.org.

NICHOLS, ROBERT LEIGHTON, civil engineer; b. Amarillo, Tex., June 24, 1926; s. Marvin Curtis and Ethel Nichols; m. Frances Hardison, June 8, 1948; children: Eileen, William C., Michael L. BSCE, Tex. A&M U., Coll. Station, 1947, MSCE, 1948. Grad. asst., instr. Tex. A&M U., 1947-48; assoc. Freese & Nichols (and predecessors), Ft. Worth, 1948-50, ptnr., 1950-77, v.p., 1977-88, pres., 1988-91, vice chmn., 1991-92, pres. emeritus, 1992—. Mem. Bldg. Stds. Commn., 1956—62; pres. Tri-State Water Resource Coalition, 2003—. Chmn. Horn Frog dist. Boy Scouts Am., pres. Longhorn coun., 1990—93, Ozark Trails coun., 1998—99; mem. City Coun., Webb City, Mo., 2004—06. Mem.: NSPE (pres. 1977—78, pres. Ednl. Found.), ASCE, Environ. Task Force Jasper and Newton Counties (pres. 2003—), Tri-state Water Resource Coalition (pres. 2002—), Nat. Inst. Engring. Ethics (pres. 1995—97), Tex. Pub. Works Assn., Tex. Water Utilities Assn., Am. Pub. Works Assn., Water Environ. Assn. Tex. (pres. 1962—63), Water Environ. Fedn., Tex. Water Conservation Assn., Am. Water Works Assn., Tex. Soc. Profl. Engrs. (pres. 1965—66), C. of C. Webb City, Mo. (exec. dir. 1997—2001), Masons, Chi Epsilon, Tau Beta Pi. Methodist. Office Phone: 417-673-7151. Business E-Mail: rln@freese.com.

NICHOLS, RONALD LEE, surgeon, educator; b. Chgo., June 25, 1941; s. Peter Raymond and Jane Eleanor (Johnson) N.; m. Elsa Elaine Johnson, Dec. 4, 1964; children: Kimberly Jane, Matthew Bennett. MD, U. Ill., 1966, MS, 1970. Diplomate Am. Bd. Surgery (assoc. cert. examiner, New Orleans, 1991), Nat. Bd. Med. Examiners. Intern U. Ill. Hosp., Chgo., 1966-67, resident in surgery, 1967-72, instr. surgery, 1970-72, asst. prof. surgery, 1972-74; assoc. prof. surgery U. Health Scis. Chgo. Med. Sch., 1975-77, dir. surg. edn., 1975-77; William Henderson prof. surgery Tulane U. Sch. Medicine, New Orleans, 1977—2002, vice chmn. dept. surgery, 1982-91, staff surgeon, 1977—2002, prof. microbiology, immunology, 1979—, William Henderson prof. surgery emeritus, 2003—; sr. vis. surgeon Med. Ctr. La., New Orleans, 1988—. Cons. surgeon VA Hosp., Alexandria, La., 1978-93, Huey P. Long Hosp., Pineville, La., 1978-2002, Lallie Kemp Charity Hosp., Independence, La., 1977-85, Touro Infirmary, New Orleans, Monmouth Med. Ctr., Long Branch, NJ, 1979-88; sr. vis. surgeon Med. Ctr. La., New Orleans, 1988—; mem. VA Coop. Study Rev. Bd., 1978-81, VA Merit Rev. Bd. in Surgery, 1979-82; sci. program com. 3d Internat. Conf. Nosocomial Infections, Ctr. Disease Control, sci. program and fundraising com. 4th Internat. Conf.; bd. dirs. Nat. Found. Infectious Diseases, 1988-2003, v.p., 1994-97, pres.-elect., 1997-99, pres., 1999-2001, trustee, 2003-2008, bd. dirs., 2008-; hon. fellow faculty Kasr El Aini Cairo U. Sch. Medicine, 1989; adv. com. on infection control Ctrs. for Disease Control, 1991-97; disting. guest, vis. prof. Royal Coll. Surgeons Thailand, 1989, 1992; infectious diseases adv. bd. Roche Labs., 1988-95, Abbott Labs., 1990-92, Kimberly Clark Corp., 1990-99, SmithKline Beecham Labs., 1990-95, Fujisawa Pharm., chmn., 1990-99, Bayer Pharm., 1994-2001, Merck Sharpe Dohme, 1996, Depotech, 1996, Zeneca Pharm., 1997-2000, Rhone-Poulenc Rorer, 1997-99, Wyeth-Ayrest Labs., 1998-2003, Pfizer Pharm., 1999, Searle Pharm., 1999-2001, GlaxoWellcome, 1999, Aventis, 1999-2000, Cubist Pharm., 2000—05, Regent Med., 2003—06, others; study group Prophylaxis Antibiotic Project La. Health Care Rev., Inc., 1995-2000, Nat. Com. Study Blood Borne Disease Transmission make Nat. Policy, Rockefeller Brothers Fund, 2001-03; apptd. by gov. La. commn. HIV and AIDS, 1999-2007; lectr. Royal Coll. Physicians and Surgeons, Can., 1998, Internat. Infectious Disease Soc. Ob-gyn., 1998, 20th NY State Surg. Symposium, 1998, Dept. Surgery, U. Ark., 1998; nat. policy com. study innovative surgery reg. Greenwall Found., 2003—06; lectr. in field. Author: (with Gorbach, Bartlett and Nichols) Manual of Surgical Infection, 1984; author, guest editor: (with Nichols, Hyslop Jr. and Bartlett) Decision Mking in Surgical Sepsis, 1991; guest editor, author: Surgical Sepsis and Beyond, 1993; mem. editl. bd. Current Surgery, 1977-2006, Hosp. Physician, 1980—2006, Infection Control, 1980-86, Guidelines to Antibiotic Therapy, 1976-81, Am. Jour. Infection Control, 1981-99, Internat. Medicine, 1983—, Confronting Infection, 1983-86, Current Concepts in Clin. Surgery, 1984—, Fact Line, 1984-91, Host/Pathogen News, 1984—, Infectious Diseases in Clin. Practice, 1991—2005, surg. sect. editor, 1992-2005, Surg. Infections: Index and Revs., 1991—, So. Med. Jour., 1992-97, ANAEROBE, 1994—, Surg. Infections, 1998—, Clin. Infectious Diseases, 1999—; editl. adv. bd. MD Consult Infectious Diseases, 2002-04; mem. adv. bd. Physician News Network, 1991-95; patentee (with S.G. schoenberger and W.R. Rank) Helical-Tipped Lesion Localization Needle Device; patentee in field. Elected faculty sponsor graduating class Tulane Med. Sch., 1979-80, 83, 85, 87, 88, 91-92; apptd. La. Commn. HIV and AIDS, 1999-2007. Maj. USAR, 1972-75. Recipient House Staff tchg. award U. Ill. Coll. Medicine, 1973, rsch. award bd. trustees U. Health Scis., Chgo. Med. Ctr., 1977, Clin. Prof. of Year U. Health Sci., 1977, Tchg. award Owl Club, 1980-86, 90, Douglas Stubbs Lectr. award Nat. Med. Assn. Surg. Sect., 1987, Prix d'Elegance award Men of Fashion, New Orleans, 1993; named Prof. of Yr. U. Health Sci., Chgo. Med. Sch., 1977, Clin. Prof. of Yr. Tulane U. Sch. Medicine, 1979, Brit. Jour. Surgery Lectr., 1997, 1st Ann. Warren Cole Lectr., 2001; elected to Wall of Fame, Lakeview HS, Chgo., 2006. Fellow Infectious Disease Soc. Am. (mem. FDA subcom. to develop guidelines in surg. prophylaxis 1989-93, co-recipient Joseph Susman Meml. award 1990), Am. Acad. Microbiology, Internat. Soc. Univ. Colon and Rectal Surgeons, ACS (mem. oper. rm. environ. com. 1978-80, vice chair oper. rm. environ. com. 1980-81, chmn. oper. rm. environ. com. 1981-83, sr. mem. oper. rm. environ. com. 1983-87, mem. internat. rels. com. 1987-93, sr. mem. internat. rels. com. 1993-97); mem. AMA, Joint Commn. on Accreditation of Health Care Orgn. (Infection Control adv. group, 1988-98, sci. program com. 3d internat. conf. nosocomial infections CDC/Nat. Found. Infectious Diseases 1990, FDA Subcom. to Develop Guidelines in Surg. Prophylaxis, 1989-93; prophylactic antibiotic study group La. Health Care Rev. Inc. 1996-2000, clin. advisor, mem., 2001-08, AIDS commr. State of La. 1992-94, mem. 1999-2007), 5th Nat. Forum on AIDS (sci. program com.), US Pharmacopeial Convention Inc. (adv. panel surg. drugs and devices 1995-2000, nominating com. The Heinz Awards 1995-96), Assn. Practitioners in Infection Control (physician adv. coun. 1991-98), Internat. Soc. Anaerobic Bacteria, So. Med. Assn. (vice chmn. sect. surgery 1980-81, chmn. 1982-83), Assn. Acad. Surgery, NY Acad. Sci., Warren H. Cole Soc. (pres.-elect 1988, pres. 1989-90), Assn. VA Surgeons, Soc. Surgery Alimentary Tract, Inst. Medicine Chgo., Midwest Surg. Assn., Ctrl. Surg. Assn., Ill. Surg. Soc., European Soc. Surg. Rsch., Collegium Internationale Chirugiae Digestivae, Chgo. Surg. Soc. (hon.), New Orleans Surg. Soc. (bd. dirs. 1983-87), Soc. Univ. Surgeons, Surg. Soc. La., Southeastern Surg. Soc., Phoenix Surg. Soc. (hon.), Hellenic Surg. Soc. (hon.), Ctrl. NY Surg. Soc. (hon.), Tulane Surg. Soc., Alton Ochsner Surg. Soc., Am. Soc. Microbiology, Soc. Internat. de Chirugie, Surg. Infection Soc. (sci. study com. 1982-83, fellowship com. 1985-87, ad hoc sci. liaison com. 1986-89, program com. 1986-87, chmn. ad hoc com. rels. with industry 1990-93, mem. sci. liaison com. 1995-96), Soc. for Intestinal Microbial Ecology and Disease, Soc. Critical Care Medicine, Am. Surg. Assn., Kansas City Surg. Soc., Bay Surg. Soc. (hon.), Cuban Surg. Soc. (hon.), Panhellenic Surg. Soc. (hon.), Tacoma Surg. Club (hon.), Sigma Xi, Alpha Omega Alpha. Episcopalian. Home: 1521 7th St New Orleans LA 70115-3322 Office: 1430 Tulane Ave New Orleans LA 70112-2699 Office Phone: 504-988-5168. Personal E-mail: rlnmd@yahoo.com. Business E-Mail: ronald.nichols@tulane.edu.

NICHOLS, STEVEN PARKS, mechanical engineer, educator, academic administrator, lawyer; b. Cody, Wyo., July 1, 1950; s. Rufus Parks Nichols and Gwen Sena (Frank) Keyes; m. Mary Ruth Barrow, Aug. 5, 1990; 1 child, Nicholas Barrow Nichols. PhD, U. Tex., Austin, 1975, JD, 1983. Assoc. dir. Tex. Space Grant Consortium, Austin, 1989-91, dir. Design Projects Program, 1989—2002; dep. dir. Ctr. for Energy Studies, U. Tex., Austin, 1988-91, dir. of Ctr., 1991-99, acting dir. Ctr. for Electromechanics, 1994-99, assoc. prof. mech. engring., 1996—2000, prof. mech. engring., 2004—, assoc. chair dept. mech. engring., 1999—2002, dir. Ctr. for Energy and Environ. Resources, 1998—, fellow Ctr. for Nano and Molecular Scis., 1998—, dir. Chair of Free Enterprise, 2001—, fellow, 2001—, assoc. v.p. rsch., 2002—06, ASME Internat. vision and strategy task force, 2006—, prof. IC2, 2006—, fellows dir. Advanced Mfg. Ctr. Bd. dirs. Assn. Mfg. Excellence; chmn. Nat. Coun. Space Grant Dirs., NASA, 1989-92; bd. dirs. So. Coalition for Advanced Transp., 1994-99, chair elect 1998-99, chair 1998-00; bd. dirs. Nat. Inst. for Engring. Ethics, 1996-; chmn. mgmt. divsn. ASME Internat., 1999-01, exec. com. engring. and tech. mgmt., 1999-; rsch. integrity officer, 2004-2006. Patentee (with others) pulsed welding techniques, railgun igniter, inert burner, rail thruster, other patents pending. Recipient Olympus Innovation award, 2005. Fellow ASME (Disting. Lectr. award 2004-06, strategic vision com. 2007-), IC2 Inst. (sr.), Ctr. Nano and Biotech.; mem. NSPE, ABA, ASCE (anti-corruption task force 2006-), Am. Soc. Engring. Edn. (Fred Merryfield Design award 2001, Kauffman Outstanding Entrepreneurship award 2007), Nat. Inst. Engring. Ethics (bd. govs. 1987-93, 96-01), NY Acad. Scis. (Tex. gov.'s task force on technology communicalization, 2006—, dir. global idea product program, 2003—). Home: 1400 Lorrain St Austin TX 78703-4023 Office: U Tex Dept Mech Engring Austin TX 78712

NICHOLS, VICKI ANNE, financial consultant, librarian; b. Denver, June 10, 1949; d. Glenn Warner and Loretta Irene (Chalender) Adams; m. Robert H. Nichols, Oct. 28, 1972 (div.); children: Christopher Travis, Lindsay Meredith. BA, Colo. Coll., 1972; postgrad., U. Denver, 1976-77. Treas., controller, dir. Polaris Resources, Inc., Denver, 1972-86; controller InterCap Devel. Corp., 1986-87; treas., controller, dir. Transnat. Cons., Ltd., 1986-91; web coord. Jefferson County Pub. Libr., Colo., 1986—. Dir., owner Nichols Bus. Services. Home: 4305 Brentwood St Wheat Ridge CO 80033-4412 Office: 10200 W 20th Ave Lakewood CO 80215 Business E-Mail: vnichols@jefferson.lib.co.us.

NICHOLS, WILLIAM CURTIS, psychologist, educator, marriage and family therapist, consultant; b. Fayette, Ala., Apr. 16, 1929; s. William Curtis and Eva (Hargett) N.; m. Alice Louise Mancill, May 29, 1954 (dec. 1990); children: Alice Camille, William Mancill, David Paul; m. Mary Anne Pace, Feb. 29, 1992. AB, U. Ala., 1953; EdD, Columbia U., 1960. Diplomate Am. Bd. Profl. Psychology. Asst. prof. sociology U. Ala., Birmingham, 1960-63; postdoctoral fellow Merrill-Palmer Inst., 1963-64, mem. psychotherapy faculty, 1965-69; prof. sociology Samford U., Birmingham, Ala., 1963-65; pvt. practice clin. psychology and marital and family therapy Grosse Pointe, Mich., 1969-73, 76-87; pvt. practice psychology, marital and family therapy Birmingham, Mich., 1976-87; prof. home and family life, dir. marriage and family counseling Fla. State U., 1973-76; exec. dir. Gov.'s Constituency Children, Fla., 1987-89; pvt. practice marital and family therapy S.E. Family Inst., 1989-90; pres. William Nichols Assocs., Organizational Cons., 1990-91; cons., marital and family therapist Atlanta, 1992—97; cons. in field, 1997-98; with The Nichols Group, Inc., 1998. Adj. prof. clin. psychology U. Detroit, 1976-83; adj. prof. family therapy Fla. State U., 1990-91; adj. prof., grad. faculty child and family devel. dept. U. Ga., 1992-05, founder, chair adv. com. Family Therapy Archives, 1993—, The Nichols Group, Inc., 1998-99. Author: Treating People in Families: An Integrative Framework, 1996, Marital Therapy: An Integrative Approach, 1988, Treating Adult Survivors of Childhood Sexual Abuse, 1992, The AAMFT: Fifty Years of Marital and Family Therapy, 1992, Family Therapy Around the World: A Festschrif to Florence Kaslow, 2004; co-author: Systematic Family Therapy, 1986; editor: (with others) Handbook of Family Development and Intervention, 2000; editor The Family Coord., 1970-75, Jour. Marriage and Family Counseling, 1974-76, Contemporary Family Therapy: An Internat. Jour., 1986-2006, Family Therapy News, 1986-91, The Internat. Connection, 1996-99; mem. editl. bd. Internat. Jour. Family Therapy, 1977-85, Jour. Divorce and Remarriage, 1976-83, 85—, Sage Family Studies Abstracts, 1977-99, Family Systems Medicine, 1982-96, Jour. Marital and Family Therapy, 1984—, Jour. Family Psychotherapy, 1990—, Jour. Family Psychology, 1986-90. Mem. mental health and health coms. Detroit Mayor's Commn. on Children and Youth, 1966-69; bd. dir. Family and Children's Svc., Oakland, Mich., 1977-87, chmn., 1984-86, dir. emeritus, 1987—. With C.E., U.S. Army, 1948-49. Recipient Svc. award Ala. Assn. for Mental Health, 1962, Spl. award for Outstanding Contbns. Fla. Assn. Marriage and Family Therapy, 1977, 82, 90; NSF fellow U. Colo., 1963, Disting. Svc. Families award Southeastern Coun. on Family Rels., 1996. Fellow: APA, Am. Assn. Marriage and Family Therapy (dir. 1969—72, founding editor Jour. Marital and Family Therapy 1974—76, chmn. accreditation com. 1976—77, pres.-elect 1979—80, dir. 1979—83, pres. 1981—82, Spl. awards 1976, 1978, Disting. Leadership awards 1982, 1983, Disting. Leadership award 1991, Orgnl. Contbns. award 1992), Am. Psychol. Soc.; mem.: Am. Family Therapy Acad., Internat. Family Therapy Assn. (bd. dirs. 1996—98, editor Internat. Connections 1996—99, pres.-elect 1998—99, pres. 2000—01, pres. elect 2009, pres. 2009—), Ga. Assn. for Marriage and Family Therapy (pres.-elect 1994—95, pres. 1996), Mich. Bd. Marriage Counselors (chmn. 1980—87), Nat. Coun. on Family Rels. (bd. dir., exec. com. 1969—78, pres. 1976—77), Mich. Assn. Marriage Counselors (pres. 1969—71, chmn. profl. liaison com. 1972—73), Mich. Inter-Profl. Assn. on Marriage, Divorce and Family (com. chmn. 1968—71, 1976—86, trustee 1977—80, Orgnl. Contbn. award 1992), Assn. Marital and Family therapy Regulation Bds. (MFT examination adv. bd. 1989—92), Am. Assn. Marriage and Family Therapy Edn. and Rsch. Found. (trustee 1992—94). Home: 755 W Lake Dr Athens GA 30606 Personal E-mail: nicholsw@aol.com.

NICHOLS, WILLIAM FORD, JR., foundation, health science association administrator, educator; b. Palo Alto, Calif., July 4, 1934; s. William Ford and Elizabeth (Woodyatt) N.; m. Rosemary Peterson, 1988; children: Deborah, John, Andrew. AB, Stanford U., 1956, MBA, 1958. CPA, Calif. With Price Waterhouse, San Francisco, 1958-69, Price Waterhouse & Co., Sydney, Australia, 1966; asst. contr. Saga Corp., Menlo Park, Calif., 1969-72, contr., 1972—, asst. treas., 1981-83; assoc. prof. San Jose State U., 1983-88; treas. William and Flora Hewlett Found., Menlo Park, 1985-2000. Trustee Investment Fund for Founds., 1991-2001. Bd. dirs. Lucile Packard Found. for Children's Health, Palo Alto, Calif., 1999—2006; trustee Oreg. Shakespeare Festival Endowment Fund, 2005-, chair 2009-. Mem. AICPA, Calif. Soc. CPA's, Inst. Mgmt. Accts. (nat. v.p. 1974-75, bd. dirs.), Fin. Execs. Inst. (pres. Santa Clara Valley chpt. 1979-80), Palo Alto Club, Alpha Omega Alpha (asst. treas. 1985—). Home: 620 Sand Hill Rd Apt 220-D Palo Alto CA 94304-2098

NICHOLSON, BRUCE J., insurance company executive; BS, St. Olaf Coll., Northfield, Minn., 1968. With Ministers Life Ins. Co., Mpls., 1975-1984, Towers Perrin Co, Mpls., 1984-1990; exec. v.p., CFO Lutheran Brotherhood, Mpls., 1990—97, exec. v.p., COO, 1997—99, pres., COO, 1999—2000, pres., CEO, 2000—02, Thrivent Fin. for Lutherans, Mpls., 2002—05, chmn., pres., CEO, 2005—. Mem. bd. regents St. Olaf Coll.; bd. mem. Luther Sem., Minn. Orchestral Assn., Minn. Bus. Partnership, Fox Cities C. of C. Fellow: Soc. of Actuaries; mem.: Am. Acad. of Actuaries. Office: Thrivent Financial for Lutherans 625 4th Ave S Minneapolis MN 55415*

NICHOLSON, CIE (CYNTHIA NICHOLSON), marketing professional; b. Chgo. BS in Biosci., U. Ill., 1986; MBA in Mktg. and Fin., U. Ind. Kelley Sch. Bus., 1988. Mktg. dir. R.J. Reynolds, 1988—97; dir. innovation, food svc. divsn. PepsiCo, Inc., 1997—99, dir. innovation, 1999—2000, v.p. Mountain Dew divsn., 2000—01, v.p. flavored carbonated beverages, 2001—03, v.p. non-carbonated beverages, 2003—05, sr. v.p., chief mktg. officer, 2005—08; co-founder Pup To Go, LLC, 2008—; prin. strategist GamesThatGive, Inc., 2009—. Recipient Acad. Alumni Fellows award, U. Ind. Kelley Sch. Bus., 2008; named a Woman to Watch, Advt. Age, 2001, Marketer of Yr., Brandweek, 2002; named to The Mktg. 50, Advt. Age, 2003, NYC Acad. Women Leaders, YMCA, 2003. Mem.: Assn. Nat. Advertisers (bd. dirs. 2006—08). Avocation: golf.*

NICHOLSON, COY LEE, language educator, writer; b. Hanford, Calif., Sept. 15, 1936; s. Coy Hargrove and Retha Alice Nicholson. AA, Little Rock Jr. Coll., 1955; BA, Millsaps Coll., Jackson, Miss., 1957; MA, U. Miss., 1959. Cert. in gen. secondary tchg. Calif., 1960. Tchr. Turlock HS, 1959—64; instr. Modesto Jr. Coll., Calif., 1964—96. Author: (book) Common Ground, 2000; author, illustrator: Speakeasy, 2005. Recipient Cert. of Recognition for Achievment in Lit. Arts, Stanislaus County Arts Coun., Calif., 2001; Wallstreet Jour. fellow, Fresno State U., 1961, scholar, Nat. Endowment for the Humanities, 1964, 1978. Avocation: calligraphy. Home: Bethel Retirement Ctr Apt 327 2345 Scenic Dr Modesto CA 95355

NICHOLSON, DOROTHY NELIS, retired pre-school educator; b. Piqua, Ohio, Mar. 26, 1923; d. Frank Allen and Elsie Mamie Nelis; m. Robert Arthur Nicholson, June 17, 1944; children: Paul M., Gary A. BS, Anderson U., Ind., 1946, LittD (hon.), 2006; MS in Edn., Ind. U., Bloomington, 1977. Dir. children's work Nat. Bd. Christian Edn. Ch. of God, Anderson, 1947—48, children's dir. Park Pl., 1948—51; tchr. Park Pl. Nursery Sch., Anderson, 1965—67; dir. Park Pl. Children's Ctr., Anderson, 1967—78; ret., 1978. Curriculum writer, advisor Warner Press, Anderson, 1950—65. Editor: Egermeier's Favorite Bible Stories, 1965; author: Toward Effective Teaching - Young Children, 1970, I Can Choose, 1974, Lord It's Late But I Can't Sleep, 1984, The Cookery Collection, 1989. Bd. dirs. Anderson YWCA, 1984—86; bd. dirs., chair Park Pl. Ch., Anderson, 1984—85. Recipient Lifetime Achievement award, Anderson U., 2001. Mem.: AAUW, Charissa Club (chair, treas. various yrs.). Avocations: travel, needlepoint, exercise. Home: 2727 Crown Pointe Cir Apt 127 Anderson IN 46012

NICHOLSON, GREG POWELL, orthopedist; b. Columbus, Ind., Dec. 22, 1959; m. Margaret Nicholson, May 21, 1988; children: Benjamin, Madeline, Samuel, Isabel. BA with highest distinction in Bio., Ind. Univ., Bloomington, 1982; MD, Ind. Univ. Sch. Med., Indianapolis, 1986. Diplomate Nat. Bd. Med. Examiners. Orthopedist Orthopaedic Specialists Ind., Indianapolis, 1992—95, Orhtopaedics Indianapolis, PC, 1995—2001, Rush Univ. Hosp. Supervisor, resident edn. orthopedic dept. St. Vincent Hosp. for Ind. Univ., 1991—95; physician Ind. Indians AAA Baseball Team, 1992—2001; clin. asst., prof. orthopaedics Ind. Univ.; vice-chmn., dept. orthopaedics St. Vincent Hosp., 1997—2001; prof., dept. orthopaedic surgery Rush Univ. Mem.:

Indpls. Orthopaedic Club, Ind. Orthopaedic Soc., Marion County Med. Soc., AMA, Mid Am. Orthopaedic Assn., Assn. Bone and Joint Surgeons, Am. Shoulder and Elbow Surgeons, Am. Acad. Orthopaedic Surgeons. Office: Midwest Orthopaedics Ste 1063 1725 W Harrison St Chicago IL 60612 Office Phone: 312-432-2332.*

NICHOLSON, HENRY HALE, JR., retired surgeon; b. Statesville, NC, June 22, 1922; s. Henry Hale and Martha Haseltine (Miller) N.; m. Freda Hyams, Sept. 24, 1956; children: Henry Hale III, Thomas Dalton Miller, John Christie, Michael Witherspoon, Freda Amanda, W. Stuart Cooper. BA in Chemistry, Duke U., 1944, MD, 1947; grad., USAF Sch. Aviation Medicine, 1952. Diplomate Am. Bd. Gen. Surgery, Am. Bd. Colon and Rectal Surgery. Rotating intern U. Wis. Gen. Hosp., Madison, 1947-48; resident in gen. surgery Med. Coll. Va., Richmond, 1948-49, Alton Ochsner Hosp. and Clinic, New Orleans, 1949-51, 53-55, inaugeral resident in colon and rectal surgery, 1955-56; resident in gen. surgery Tulane U., La. Charity Hosp., New Orleans, 1949-51, 53-55; pvt. practice gen., colon and rectal surgery, aerospace medicine Charlotte, NC, 1956—2002; sr. surg. staff mem. Carolinas Med. Ctr. and Mercy Hosp., Charlotte; ret., 2002. Sr. surg. staff Presbyn. Hosp., Charlotte, 1956-2002; sr. active teaching staff Carolinas Med. Ctr., 1956-85, cons. staff, 1985—; surg. cons. Surgeon Gen. USAF, 1971-82. Mem. Airport Authority Charlotte/Douglas Internat. Airport, 1992-2009, chmn., 2008-09; mem. Mayor's Com. of 100 to study regional transp. and make appropriate recommendations, 1993-94; sr. examiner FAA, 1952-2007, active pilot; mem. athletic-med. bd. N.C. Shrine Bowl, 1980-2003. With U.S. Army, 1943-46. Maj. flight surgeon USAF, 1951-53, Korea; col. USAFR, 1961-82, NCANG, command air surgeon, 1971-82. Decorated Legion of Merit, Disting. Svc. medal NC; named Flight Surgeon of Yr., USA N.G., 1981, 1st Alternate Flight Surgeon of Yr. award USAF, 1982. Fellow ACS, Am. Soc. Colon and Rectal Surgeons; mem. Mecklenberg County Med. Soc. (pres. 1972), Charlotte Surg. Soc. (pres. 1987), Shriners, Masons (32 degree), Jesters, Alton Ochsner Surg. Soc., Hazel Creek Trout Club, Rotary Internat., Robert Burns Soc., St. Andrews Soc. of Carolina, Air Force Assn., Hound Ears Club (Blowing Rock, N.C.), Charlotte Country Club, Alpha Tau Omega, Phi Chi, Omicron Delta Kappa. Methodist. Avocations: golf, skiing, fly fishing, travel, painting. Home Phone: 704-525-2277.

NICHOLSON, HILTON M., telecommunications industry executive; BSEE, La. Tech U.; MSEE, Clemson U.; MBA, Duke U. V.p., gen. mgr. core switching & routing divsn. Alcatel-Lucent (Lucent Technologies); sr. v.p., product ops. 3com, 2004—06; pres., IP cable bus. unit ADC Telecom. Inc., 2002—04, v.p., pres. network solutions bus. unit, 2006—. Office: ADC Telecommunications Inc 13625 Technology Dr Minneapolis MN 55440 Office Phone: 952-938-8080. Office Fax: 952-917-1717.

NICHOLSON, JACK, actor; b. Neptune, NJ, Apr. 22, 1937; raised by John and Ethel May Nicholson; m. Sandra Knight, June 17, 1962 (div. Aug. 8, 1968); children: Jennifer, Lorraine Broussard. Acting debut: (Hollywood stage prodn.) Tea an Sympathy; actor: (films) Cry-Baby Killer, 1958, Studs Lonigen, 1960, Little Shop of Horrors, 1960, Ensign Pulver, 1964, The Trip, 1967, Easy Rider, 1969 (Acad. award nomination best supporting actor), Five Easy Pieces, 1970, Carnal Knowledge, 1971, A Safe Place, 1971, The Last Detail, 1974 (Cannes Film Festival prize, BAFTA award best actor), Chinatown, 1974 (BAFTA award best actor, Acad. award nomination, NY Film Critics Circle award, Golden Globe award best actor), Tommy, The Passenger, 1975, The Fortune, 1975, One Flew Over the Cuckoo's Nest, 1975 (Golden Globe award best actor, Acad. award for best actor, 1975, NY Film Critics Circle award, BAFTA award best actor), The Missouri Breaks, 1976, The Last Tycoon, 1976, The Shining, 1980, The Postman Always Rings Twice, 1981, Reds, 1981 (BAFTA award best supporting actor, Acad. award nomination best supporting actor), The Border, 1982, Terms of Endearment, 1983 (Acad. award best supporting actor, Golden Globe award best actor), Prizzi's Honor, 1985, Heartburn, 1986, The Witches of Eastwick, 1987, Broadcast News, 1987, Ironweed, 1987 (Acad. award nomination best actor), Batman, 1989, Man Trouble, 1991, A Few Good Men, 1992, Hoffa, 1992, Wolf, 1994, The Crossing Guard, 1995, Mars Attacks!, 1996, The Evening Star, 1996, Blood and Wine, 1996, As Good As It Gets, 1997 (Acad. award best actor, Golden Globe award best actor, SAG award best actor), The Pledge, 2001, About Schmidt, 2002 (Acad. award nomination best actor, Golden Globe award best actor), Anger Management, 2003, Something's Gotta Give, 2003, The Departed, 2006 (MTV Movie award best villain, 2007), The Bucket List, 2007; prodr.: Head, 1968, Ride the Whirlwind, The Shooting; dir.: Drive, He Said, 1971; dir., actor: (films) Goin' South, 1978, The Two Jakes, 1990. Recipient Life Achievement award, Am. Film Inst., 1994, Cecil B. DeMille award, 1999; co-recipient (with Bobby McFerrin) Grammy award for best recording for children, 1987; named to Calif. Hall of Fame, 2008. Office: Bresler Kelly & Assocs 11500 W Olympic Blvd Ste 510 Los Angeles CA 90064-1578*

NICHOLSON, JIM (ROBERT JAMES NICHOLSON), lawyer, former United States Secretary of Veterans Affairs, former ambassador; b. Struble, IA, Feb. 4, 1938; s. Don and Helen Nicholson; m. Suzanne Marie Ferrell; children: Nick, Katie, R.J. BS, US Mil. Acad., West Point, 1961; MA in Pub. Policy, Columbia U., 1969; JD, U. Denver, 1972, LLD (hon.), St. John's U., U. Dallas, Cath. U., Ave Maria U.; PhD in Pub. Svc. (hon.), Regis U., 2001; PhD (hon.), John Cabot U., 2002, Kings Coll. Atty., Denver, 1973-78; founder Nicholson Enterprises, Inc., 1978, Renaissance Homes, Denver, 1987; committeeman from Colo. Rep. Nat. Com., 1986—2000, vice chmn, 1993—97, chmn., 1997—2001; US amb. to The Holy See US Dept. State, Rome, 2001—05; sec. US Dept. Veterans Affairs, Washington, 2005—07; sr. counsel Brownstein Hyatt Farber & Schreck, Washington, 2008—. Chmn. task force presdl. primaries and caucuses Rep. Nat. Com., 1996, chmn. rules com., 1993-97, mem. budget com. Author: (non-fiction) The United States and the Holy See-The Long Road, 2002. Bd. dirs. Daniels Fund, Federated Funds, Horatio Alger Assn. With US Army, 1961—69, with USAR, 1969—91, ret. as col. Decorated Bronze Star, Combat Infantryman's Badge, Meritorious Svc. medal with oak leaf cluster, Vietnamese Cross for Gallantry, 2 Air medals, Horatio Alger award, 2000, Pres. medal, Georgetown U., 2003, Disting. Grad. US Mil. Acad.award, 2005; inducted as a Knight in the Sovereign Mil. Order of Malta, 1999, named a Knight of the Grand Cross of the Order of Pius IX, Pope John Paul II, 2003. Fellow: US C. of C. Office: Brownstein Hyatt Farber Schreck 1350 I St NW Ste 510 Washington DC 20005 Office Phone: 202-296-7353. Business E-Mail: jnicholson@bhfs.com.

NICHOLSON, JOSEPH BRUCE, real estate developer; b. San Jose, Calif., Jan. 21, 1940; s. Wilmot Joseph and Ruth (Russell) N.; m. Susan Knight, Nov. 1963 (div. 1972); children: Kelsey Erin, Craig Wilmot; m. Linda Mirassou, Aug. 1992. BArch, U. Oreg., 1963. Exec. v.p. Nicholson-Brown Inc., Santa Clara, Calif., 1967-80; prin. Nicholson Assocs., Aptos, Calif., 1977—; v.p., gen. mgr. Nicholson-Wilson Co., Santa Clara, 1980-83; prin. The Nicholson Co., Campbell, Calif., 1984—; v.p. Pacific Property Ventures Inc., Campbell, 1988—; pres. Nicholson Constrn. Inc., Campbell, 1989—; v.p. Nicholson Property Mgmt. Inc., Campbell, 1989—; pres. The Nicholson Family Found., 1996—. Bd. dirs. Transmetrics Inc., San Jose, DITZ Bros. Colo. Springs, 2008-. Bd. dirs. Triton Mus., Santa Clara, 1979, Hope Rehab. Svc., San Jose, 1979, United Way Ctrl. Area, San Jose, 1991. Devel. Engring. Rsch. Inst., Carmel, Calif., 1999—, Tannery Art Ctr., Santa Cruz, 2003—; pres. adv. bd. de Saisset Mus., Santa Clara U., 1991; trustee Mus. of Art and History, Santa Cruz, 1993; pres. Cabrillo Festival of Contemporary Music, Santa Cruz, Calif., 2000—. Lt. USN, 1963—67. Mem. Rotary, Commonwealth Club (San Francisco), Tennis Club Rio Del Mar. Republican. Avocations: travel, reading, art, painting, tennis. Home: 218 Shoreview Dr Aptos CA 95003-4621 Business E-Mail: brucenicholson@thenicholsonco.com.

NICHOLSON, KRISTIN E., legislative staff member; b. St. Louis, Mar. 25, 1972; BS, Northwestern U., Evanston, Ill., 1993; JD, U. Colo., Boulder, 1996. Bar: Colo. 1996. Legis. asst. for Rep. Glenn Poshard US House Reps., Washington, 1997, legis. dir., 1997—98, legis. dir. for Rep. David Phelps, 1999—2000, chief of staff for James R. Langevin, 2001—. Jewish. Avocation: languages. Office: Office of Congressman James R Langevin 1030 Longworth House Office Bldg Washington DC 20515 Office Phone: 202-225-2735. Business E-Mail: kristin.nicholson@mail.house.gov.*

NICHOLSON, LARRY T., construction executive; b. 1957; B, Ohio U., 1979. V.p., constrn. Transeastern Properties, Coral Springs, Fla.; v.p. Berman Devel. Corp., 1996; v.p., ops, SE region The Ryland Group, Inc., pres., Orlando divsn., Ryland Homes, 1999—2005, sr. v.p., pres., SE region, Ryland Homes, 2005—07, exec. v.p., COO, 2007—08, pres., COO, 2008—09, pres., CEO, 2009—. Bd. dirs. The Ryland Group Inc., 2009—. Avocation: baseball. Office: The Ryland Group Inc Ste 400 24025 Park Sorrento Calabasas CA 91302 Office Phone: 818-223-7500. Office Fax: 818-223-7667.*

NICHOLSON, LELAND ROSS, retired utilities executive, energy consultant; b. Carrington, ND, Feb. 21, 1924; s. Malcom and Lena May (Kerlin) N.; m. Virginia E. Blair, Mar. 16, 1946; children: Heather Le Nicholson Studebaker, Leland B., Holly Kay. Student, Northwestern U., 1940-41; BSEE, U. N.D., 1949; postgrad. in utility mgmt., U. Minn., 1952. Planning and mktg. engr. Minkota Power Coop., Grand Forks, ND, 1949-54; dir. new bus. Kans. Power & Light Co., Topeka, 1954-64, v.p. mktg., 1964-76, sr. v.p., 1976-80, exec. v.p., 1980-83, also bd. dirs.; pres. Kans. Power & Light Gas Service, Topeka, 1985-88, ret., 1988; pres., chief operating officer The Gas Service Co., Kansas City, Mo., 1983-85. Pres. Indsl. Devel. Corp., Topeka; chmn. Kans. Coun. on Electricity and Environment; exec. com. Kansas City Labor Mgmt. Coun., 1986-89; mem. Mktg. Execs. Conf.; bd. dirs. Gas Service Energy Corp., Kansas City, Merchants Nat. Bank, Topeka. Idea innovator heat pump water heater, photo cell controlled yard light, hydrogen fuel cell, electric grill. Bd. dirs., area relations com. Kansas City Area Econ. Devel. Coun., Mo., 1983-89; bd. dirs. Kansas City Pvt. Industry Coun., 1986-89, Kansas City Downtown Coun.; trustee U. Mo., Kansas City, 1984-91; mktg. chmn. Kansas City Full Employment Council; past chmn., mem. Topeka-Shawnee County Planning Commn.; adult adv. com. Sea Scouts. Master sgt. USMC, 1942-46. Mem. Am. Gas Assn., Midwest Gas Assn. (bd. dirs. 1985-89), Mo. Valley Electric Assn. (chmn. 1979-81), Edison Electric Inst. (mktg. chmn. 1978-80), Assoc. Industries of Mo., Kans. Assn. Commerce and Industry, Greater Kansas City (Mo.) C. of C. (bd. dirs. 1979-82), US Marine Corps League (life), Shawnee Yacht Club (Topeka) (commodore 1972-74), Lake Gaston Assn. (pres. 1993-97), Kansas City Club, Rotary. Republican. Methodist. Avocations: sailing, canoeing, fishing, reading, electronics. Office Phone: 434-689-2066.

NICHOLSON, LESLIE A., federal agency administrator; married; 2 children. Grad., La. State U.; JD, Vanderbilt U. Tchr. advanced comml. real estate seminars Va. Sch. Law; chair litig. dep. law firm; mem. bd. dirs. Am. Coll. Constrn. Lawyers; exec. v.p., gen. counsel local bank; gen. counsel US Gen. Svcs. Adminstrn., 2008—. Mem.: Am. Coll. Real Estate Lawyers. Office: US Gen Svcs Adminstrn 1800 F St NW Rm 4140 Washington DC 20405 Office Phone: 202-501-2200. Office Fax: 202-501-2509. Business E-Mail: leslie.nicholson@gsa.gov.*

NICHOLSON, MARVIN, JR., federal official; b. Ont., Can., 1971; s. John Beatty (Stepfather) and Elizabeth Nicholson. Degree in geography, U. We. Ont., 1993. Former bartender, windsurfing gear shop employee, golf caddie, Mass.; driver, staff mem., personal aide Senator John Kerry, Washington, 2000—04, spl. asst., 2004—07; nat. trip dir. Senator Barack Obama Presdl. Campaign, 2007—08; trip dir. The White House, Washington, 2009—. Democrat. Office: The White House 1600 Pennsylvania Ave NW Washington DC 20500*

NICHOLSON, MYREEN MOORE, artist, researcher; b. Norfolk, Va., June 2, 1940; d. William Chester and Illeen (Fox) Moore; m. Roland Quarles Nicholson Jr., Jan. 9, 1965 (dec. 1986); children: Andrea Joy, Ross (dec. 1965); m. Harold Wellington McKinney II, 1981; 1 child, Cara Isadora. AA, William and Mary Coll., 1960; BA, Old Dominion U., 1962, MA, 1997; MLS, U. N.C., Chapel Hill, 1971; postgrad., The Citadel, 1968-69, Hastie Sch. Art, 1968, Chrysler Mus. Art Sch., 1964, Contemporary Art Ctr., Va., 1972, Old Dominion U., 1997—2000. LCSW Va., 1965, S.C., 1967; cert. tchr. English, art and media Va. English tchr., Chesapeake, Va., 1962-63; dept. head Portsmouth Bus. Coll., Va., 1963-64; tech. writer City Planning/Art Commn., Norfolk, 1964-65; art tchr. Norfolk pub. schs., 1965-67; prof. lit. art Palmer Jr. Coll., Charleston, S.C., 1968; tchr. John's Island, SC, 1968; libr. Charleston Schs., 1968-69; asst. to asst. dir. City Libr. Norfolk, 1970-72; art and audio-visual libr., 1972-75; rsch. libr., 1975-83; libr. dept. fiction, 1983-90; prof. Ctrl. Tex. Coll., 1998—; dir. W. Ghent Arts Alliance, Norfolk, 1978—, Grader SAT's, 2006—. Poet-in-schs., Virginia Beach, Va., 1987. Book reviewer Art Book Revs., Libr. Jour., 1973-76; editor, illustrator Acquisitions Bibliographies, 1970—, (play) Eldorado: The Poes in Norfolk, 1996, West Ghent newsletter, 1995-96; juried exhibits various cities including Grand Hyatt, Mayflower, Washington, by Joan Mondale, Nohra Haime, curator of Freer Gallery, by sr. curator Nat. Mus. Am. Art, curator Phillips Collection, asst. curator, White House and by dir. of Nat. Portrait Gallery; group shows include Contemporary Art Ctr., Va., Va. Beach, 1993, 98, Yorktown Small Works Show, 1996, Tidewater Artists Assn. Portfolio Show, 1996, Suffolk Artists and Writers Invitational Exhibit, 1996, Artists in Virginia, 1996, Peninsula Ann., Juried Art Exhibit, 1996, Hampton Bay Day Juried Art Exhibit, 1996, Trinity Ch. Stations of the Cross, Portsmouth Mus., 1996-97, Hermitage Mus., 1996-2008, Yorktown, Va. On-The-Hill, 1997, 98 (First Place, IPA Printmaking, Washington), Wakefield Art Ctr., 1998, Portlock So No, 2008, Hampton Art League, 2009, Norfolk Internat. Airport, 2002-04, Poet's Domain: Halley's Comet, 2008; contbr. art and poetry to various publs. and anthologies. Mem. Charleston Artists Guild, 1968-70, Virginia Beach Arts Ctr., 1978-98, Suffolk Art League, 1990-2003; bd. dirs. W. Ghent Art/Lit. Festival, 1979; poetry reader Poetry Soc. Va., Va. Ctr. for Creative Arts, Sweetbriar, 1989, Walden Books, 1991, Christopher Newport U., 1994-95, J.M. Prince Books and Coffeehouse, 1995—, Statues St. Mark's Cath. Ch., 1991-92, Statue City of Hampton Va. Devel., 2004-05, Statue of St. Bridget, Oreg., 2005, GaiaFest, 2006-09; graphics of hundreds of celebrities from life; curator Va. Winter Show Life Saving Mus., 1991-92; judge Bornstein art scholarship Chrysler Mus., 1992; mem. staff Mid-Atlantic Antiques Mag., 1993-2008; Nat. Endowment Arts grantwriter, 1975; bd. dirs. Tidewater Literacy Coun., 1971-72, Maine Antiques Digest, 2007; poetry reader GaiaFest, 2006-08. Recipient awards various art and poetry contests; Coll. William and Mary art scholarship, 1958, William & Mary Tricentenial award for Contbns. to the Arts in Va., 1993; recipient Cert. for Vol. Contbns. to Va. by Gov., 1984; named Precinct Capt.-at-Large, 2002-03. Mem. ALA (poster sessions rev. com. 1985-96, pub. relations judge, subcom. com. 1988-90), Pub. Libr. Assn. (com. bylaws and orgns. 1988-90), Va. Libr. Assn. (pub. rels. com. 1984-86, grievance and pay equity com. 1986-88, co-winner Paraprofl. Logo award 1985, chair Pub. Documen ts Forum 1992-93), Southeastern Libr. Assn. (Rothrock award com. 1986-88, com. on coms. 1991-92), Poetry Soc. Va. (v.p. 1986-89, nominating com. 1989-90, editor newsletter 1990-93, dir. publicity 1993-95, 70th Anniversary plaque for Wren Bldg., commn. 75th anniversary poster), Art Librs. Soc. N.Am., Tidewater Artists Alliance (bd. dirs. 1989—, chair grantwriting com. 1990—, pres. 1991-92), Hampton Arts League, Norfolk Hist. Soc., Internat. Platform Assn., Old Dominion U. Alumni Assn. (artistic dir. Silver Reunion), Southeastern Soc. Archtl. Historians, Ikara (pres. 1989—), D'Art Ctr. (bd. dirs. 1991-92), Ex Libris Soc. (charter), Va. Writers Club. Home and Office: Dir Moore Nicholson Arts West Ghent Arts Office 1404 Gates Ave Norfolk VA 23507-1131 Office Phone: 757-282-6982. Personal E-mail: Myreen7@gmail.com.

NICHOLSON, PAMELA M., rental and leasing company executive; b. 1960; BA, U. Mo., 1981. Mgmt. trainee Enterprise Rent-A-Car, St. Louis, 1981—82, asst. br. mgr. to Southern Calif. regional v.p., 1982—94, corp. v.p., 1994—97, gen. mgr. NYC, 1997—99, sr. v.p., N.Am. ops. St. Louis, 1999—2003, exec. v.p., COO, 2003—08, pres., COO, 2008—. Bd. dirs. Energizer Holdings, Inc., 2002—. Former bd. mem. United Way of Bergen County, NJ, INROADS, St. Louis; bd. dirs. Humane Soc., Mo.; com. mem. St. Louis Regional Chamber and Growth Assn.; dir. Enterprise Rent-A-Car Found. Named one of 50 Most Powerful Women in Bus., Fortune mag., 2006, 2007, 2008, 100 Most Powerful Women, Forbes mag., 2008, 2009. Office: Enterprise Rent A Car 600 Corporate Park Dr Saint Louis MO 63105 Office Phone: 314-512-5000.*

NICHOLSON, R. STEPHEN, former cultural organization administrator; b. Radford, Va., Mar. 4, 1926; s. Roy S. and Ethel Dovie (Macy) Nicholson; m. Carol Peterson; 1 child, Suzanne Carpenter. AB, Marion Coll., 1950; MA, Syracuse U., NY, 1956; PhD, Mich. State U., East Lansing, 1971. Pres. Daley Coll., Chgo., 1969-71; prof. Lansing C.C., Lansing, Mich., 1963-66, acad. dean, 1971—76; pres. Clark County C.C. (now So. Nev. C.C.), 1971—76, Mt. Hood C.C., 1976—85; chancellor Oakland C.C., 1985-90; vice chancellor Higher Colls. of Tech., United Arab Emirates, 1990-92; CEO Internat. Christian Leadership, 1992-93, Mercy Corps Internat., 1994—95, chmn. bd. dirs., 1997—2004; corp. bd. dirs. Green Plains Renewable Energy, 2005—. Pres. Creative Futures; bd. dirs. MCI, Green Plains Renewable Energy Corp., 2004—. Sr. fellow for higher edn. M.J. Murdock Trust, 1993—95, 1996—99; chair bd. dir. N.W. Autism Found., 2000—02; bd. dir. Green Plains Reusable Energy, Inc., 2004—. Mem.: Green Plains Renewable Energy (bd. dirs. 2005—08), World Affairs Coun., Am. Acad. Polit. and Social Scis., Am. Sociology Assn., Am. Sch. Adminstrs. Assn., N.W. Assn. Cmty. and Jr. Coll.s (pres. 1976), Am. Assn. Cmty. and Jr. Colls. (pres. Pres.'s Acad. 1982, bd. dirs. 1985—87), Am. Futurist Soc., Japan-Am. Soc., Gresham C. of C. (corp. bd. dir. 1977—79), Rotary Club (pres. 1983, Paul Harris fellow 1986), Phi Delta Kappa. Home and Office: 9685 Irvine Bay Ct Las Vegas NV 89147-8365 Personal E-mail: stephenicholson@cox.net.

NICHOLSON, ROBERT ARTHUR, college president; b. Pepin, Wis., Oct. 13, 1923; s. Arthur W. and Ethel (Weeden) N.; m. Dorothy Nelis, June 17, 1944; children: Paul, Gary. BS, Anderson U., Ind., 1944; MA, NYU, 1946, PhD, 1953. With Anderson U., 1945-90, successively instr., asst. prof., assoc. prof. music, chmn. dept., asst. to dean, 1945-58, dean, 1958-83, v.p., 1964-83, pres., 1983-90, pres. emeritus, 1990—. Author: Handbook to the Hymnal of the Church of God, 1953, So I Said Yes! A Personal Memoir, 2006; editor: Hymnal of the Church of God, 1953, 71. Interim CEO Ch. of God Ministries, Inc., 1998, cons., 1997-99; interim exec. pastor, Park Place Ch. of God, 1995; interim min. of music, 1999-2002; mem. pub. bd. Ch. of God, 1955-80, chmn. commn. higher edn., 1963-70, 83-86, vice chmn., 1970-83, cons., 1990-96; cons. Warner Pacific Coll., Oreg., 1990-98, N.Ind. United Meth. Found., Inc., 1992-95, Anderson Pub. Libr., 1994-95, United Faith Housing Corp., 1994, Hopewell Ctr., 1996, Alexandria Cmty. Ctr., Inc., 1997, Family Network Agy., Inc., 1997-2000, Wilson Boys and Girls Club, 1997, Cmty. Found. Grant County, 1998, United Way Anderson and Madison County, Ind., 1998, 2000, Anderson Area C. of C., 1998, 2001, Christian Ctr., 2001; bd. dirs. Anderson Symphony Orch., 1974-87, 93-94, United Way Madison County, 1985-89, 91-94, Minnetrista Cultural Found., 1988-2002; bd. dirs., v.p. Anderson Internat., 1990-93; bd. dirs. Cmty. Hosp. Madison County, 1986-95, vice chmn., 1988-94, interim pres., CEO, 1991; mem. Madison County Comty. Found., Inc., 1991-2003, pres., 1991-98. Mem. Associated Colls. of Ind., Ind. Colls. and Univs. of Ind. (chmn. 1988-89), Anderson Area C. of C. (bd. dirs. 1985-90, vice chmn. and chmn. elect 1988, chmn. 1989). Home: 2727 Crown Pointe Cir Apt 127 Anderson IN 46012-3265

NICHOLSON, WILL FAUST, JR., bank executive; b. Colorado Springs, Colo., Feb. 8, 1929; s. Will Faust and Gladys Olivia (Burns) N.; m. Shirley Ann Baker, Nov. 26, 1955; children: Ann Louise Nicholson Naughton, Will Faust III. S.B., M.I.T., 1950; MBA, U. Denver, 1956. V.p. Van Schaack & Co., Denver, 1954-66; pntr. N. G. Petry Constrn. Co., Denver, 1966-70; sr. v.p. Colo. Nat. Bankshares, Inc., Denver, 1970-75, pres., 1975-95, chmn. bd., chief exec. officer, 1985-95; chmn. Rocky Mountain Bankcard Sys., Denver, 1995—2001. Bd. dirs. Boys and Girls Clubs of Metro Denver; active Downtown Denver, Inc., Colo. Assn. of Commerce and Industry, chmn. 1990-91, Denver Urban Renewal Authority, 1958-59, Denver Bd. Water Commrs., 1959-65, pres. 1964, 65; Nat. Western Stock Show. With USAF, 1950-53. Mem. Assn. Bank Holding Cos. (bd. dirs. 1979-87, 89-91, exec. com. 1980-85, vice chmn. 1981-82, chmn. 1983-84), US C. of C. (bd. dirs. 1990-2005, chmn. 1999-2000), US Golf Assn. (exec. com. 1974-82, v.p. 1978, 79, pres. 1980, 81), Denver Country Club, Univ. Club Colo., Univ. Club NY, Castle Pines Golf Club, Royal and Ancient Golf Club (St. Andrews, Scotland), Augusta (Ga.) Nat. Golf Club. Republican. Episcopalian. Home: 37 Polo Club Cir Denver CO 80209-3307 Office: Rocky Mountain BankCard Sys Inc PO Box 5168 Denver CO 80217-5168

NICHOLSON, WILLIAM JOSEPH, energy and environmental consultant; b. Tacoma, Aug. 24, 1938; s. Ferris Frank and Athyleen Myrtle (Fesenmaier) Nicholson; m. Carland Elaine Crook, Oct. 10, 1964; children: Courtney, Brian, Kay, Benjamin. SB in ChemE, MIT, Cambridge, Mass., 1960, SM in ChemE Practice, 1961; PhD in ChemE, Cornell U., Ithaca, NY, 1965; MBA, Pacific Luth. U., Tacoma, Wash., 1969. Registered profl. chem. engr., Wash. Sr. devel. engr. Hooker Chem. Co., Tacoma, 1964—69, Battelle N.W., Richland, Wash., 1969—70; planning assoc. Potlatch Corp., San Francisco, 1970—75, mgr. corp. energy svc., 1976—94, dir. corp. energy and environ. svcs.,

1994—2002, ind. energy and environ. cons., 2002—; chair energy coun. Am. Forest and Paper Assn., Washington, 1998—2002. Mem. MIT Ednl. Coun., 1971—; U.S. expert environ. labeling Internat. Stds. Orgn., 1994—2000; adv. bd. Forest Products lab. U. Calif., Richmond, 1992—2003, chmn. adv. bd., 1993—95, 2003, adv. bd. Coll. Natural Resources, 1993—95; adv. com. Fed. Biomass, 2000—05; project peer reviewer USDOE, 2004—06; expert energy mgmt. US Tech. Adv. Group Internat. Stds. Orgn., 2008—. Mem.: AAAS, AIChE (assoc.), Am. Chem. Soc., Commonwealth Club (San Francisco), Sigma Xi. Republican. Avocations: history, genealogy. Home and Office: PO Box 1114 Ross CA 94957-1114 Office Phone: 415-457-2425. Personal E-mail: nicholsonhome@aol.com.

NICHOLSON, WILLIAM NOEL, clinical neuropsychologist; b. Detroit, Dec. 24, 1936; s. James Eardly and Hazel A. (Wagner) N.; m. Nancy Ann Marshall, June 15, 1957; children: Anne Marie, Kristin, Scott. AB, Wittenberg U., 1959; MDiv, Luth. Theol. Sem., Phila., 1962; PhD, Mich. State U., 1972. Diplomate Am. Bd. Forensic Examiners, Am. Bd. Med. Psychotherapists; lic. clin. psychologist, Mich.; ordained to ministry Luth. Ch., 1962; cert. Nat. Register Health Care Providers in Psychology, Assn. of State and Provincial Psychology Bds. Parish pastor Our Saviour Luth. Ch., Saginaw, Mich., 1962-69; intern in psychology Ingham Mental Health Bd., 1971-72; resident in psychology Bay-Arenac Mental Health Bd., 1972-74; dir., psychologist Riverside Ctr., Bay City, Mich., 1974-75; pastor, psychologist Psych Studies and Clergy Consultation of Mich., 1989—2003. Pres. Bay Psychol. Assocs., P.C., Bay City, 1975—2002; cons. Gov.'s Office of Drug Abuse, 1972-74. Author: A Guttman Facet Analysis of Attitude-Behaviors Toward Drug Users by Heroin Addicts and Mental Health Therapists, 1972, An Episcopalian Guide to the Augsburg Confession, 1997; contbr. articles to profl. jours. Mem. APA, Mich. Psychol. Assn. Office: 820 Arlington Ave Ste 2 Petoskey MI 49770 Office Phone: 231-347-4700, 231-347-0117.

NICHOLSON-GUTHRIE, CATHERINE S. See GUTHRIE, CATHERINE

NICHOLS RANDALL, BARBARA LEE, library director, educator; b. Wichita Falls, Tex., Aug. 9, 1951; d. Robert and Margaret Jean Nichols; m. James Edward Randall, Oct. 9, 1976; children: Holly Kim Randall, Gil Adam Randall. BA, SUNY, Brockport, 1973; MLS, U. Albany, NY, 1976. Cert. pub. libr. NY State Edn. Dept., 1976. Tech. specialist, acting asst. editor, Ctrl. Office Libr. Svcs. SUNY, 1976—78, local arrangements co-chair, Librs. Assn., 1998—99; sr. libr., CONSER project rep. NY State Libr., Albany, 1978—85, assoc. libr., collection acquisition and processing, 1985—93, newspaper project dir., 1988—92; spl. coord. faculty grants & rsch. Siena Coll., Latham, NY, 1993—95; automation & catalog specialist, libr. II Washington-Saratoga-Warren-Hamilton-Essex Sch. Libr. Sys., Saratoga Springs, NY, 1995—97; vis. assoc. libr. U. Albany, 1997—99, com. mem., coun. rsch., 1998—99, adj. prof., dept. info. studies, 2003; asst. dir. Guilderland Pub. Libr., NY, 1999—2001, dir., 2001—. Reviewer, nat. leadership grants Inst. Mus. and Libr. Svcs., Washington, 1998—99; steering com. mem. New Yorkers Better Librs. Polit. Action Com., Canton, 2005—. Bd. dirs. mem. Guilderland C. of C., NY, 2007; newsletter editor Internat. Accelerated Missions, Albany, 1994—2000; bldg. com. mem. Our Savior's Luth. Sch., Albany, 2002—08; pres. Korean Am. Families, Albany, 1986—89; sch. bd. mem. Korean Lang. Sch. Greater Albany Area, 1991—96. Mem.: ALA (Chgo.) (fundraising com. mem., ALCTS 1998—99), Dirs. Assn., Upper Hudson Libr. Sys. (chairperson 2005—06), Capital Dist. Libr. Coun., Hudson Mohawk Libr. Assn., NY Libr. Assn. (Albany) (coun. mem. 2000—01, legis. com. mem. 2002—03, 2008—). Lutheran. Avocations: writing, needlecrafts, genealogy. Office: Guilderland Pub Libr 2228 Western Ave Guilderland NY 12084 Home Fax: 518-935-9007. Personal E-mail: bnr51@aol.com. Business E-Mail: randallb@guilpl.org.

NICKEL, ALBERT GEORGE, advertising agency executive; b. Pitts., July 12, 1943; s. Frank George and Dorothy (Wiefling) N.; m. Dana Cooper; children: Mark, Grace, Olivia. AB, Washington and Jefferson Coll., 1965; MBA, Ind. U., 1967. Mktg. rsch. analyst Pfizer, Inc., NYC, 1967, prof. svc. rep., 1967-68, mktg. rsch. mgr., 1968-69, product mgr., 1969-70, USV Internat., Tuckahoe, NY, 1970-71; account supr. Sudler & Hennessey, NYC, 1973-77; sr. v.p. mgmt. group supr. Young and Rubicam, NYC, 1977-79; chmn., pres., COO Dorritie Lyons & Nickel, Inc., NYC; chmn., pres., CEO HMC Group Omnicom, Inc., 1999—2006; chmn., CEO Lyons, Lavey, Nickel, Swift, Inc., 2000—06. Trustee Wilton YMCA, Five Town Found.; bd. dirs. Cancer CARE; bd. dirs., exec. com. Wilton LaCrosse Assn.; trustee Dominican Coll., Healthcare Businesswoman's Assn., Wilton HS Long Range Planning Team, Am. Coun. on Sci. and Health, Cancer Care; co-chmn. TBWA WorldHealth. Capt. USAF, 1969. Recipient Ellis Island medal of honor and honor soc., 2002. Mem. Pharm. Rsch. and Mfrs. Assn. (bd. dirs.), Healthcare Mktg. and Comm. Coun. (bd. dirs.), Vis. Nurses Assn. (sec. found. bd.), Midwest Healthcare Mktg. Assn., Wilton Riding Club (pres.), Shore and Country Club, Silver Spring Country Club. Home: 65 Keelers Ridge Rd Wilton CT 06897-1608 Office Phone: 212-771-3301. Personal E-mail: al_nickel@yahoo.com.

NICKELL, JAKE, internet retail executive, apparel designer; b. Crown Point, Ind., 1980; m. Shondi Nickell, 2004. Attended, Ill. Inst. Art, 1998—2001. Co-founder & pres. SkinnyCorp, Chgo., 2000—. Co-creator (SkinnyCorp websites) Threadless, 2000, Naked & Angry, OMG Clothing, Extra Tasty, Yay Hooray!, 15 Megs of Fame. Named one of 40 Under 40, Crain's Chgo. Bus., 2006. Home: Skinny Corp STE 206 4043 N Ravenswood Ave Chicago IL 60613-2435 Office Phone: 773-878-3557. Office Fax: 888-595-3258. E-mail: info@skinnycorp.com.

NICKELS, GREG, Mayor, Seattle; b. Chgo., Aug. 7, 1955; s. Bob and Kathie Nickels; m. Sharon Nickels; children: Jacob, Carey. Legis. asst. to Council member Norm Rice City of Seattle, 1979—87; mem. King County Coun., 1987—2002; mayor City of Seattle, 2002—. Chair Seattle/King County Bd. Health, 1996—2001; mem. exec. com. & bd. dirs. Dirs. of Sound Transit. Recipient First Ann. Greg Nickels award for Econ. Develop., U. Dist. Bus. Improvement Assn., 2003, First Place City Livability award, US Conf. Mayors, 2005, Charles R. Imbrecht Blue Sky Innovation award, Calstart, 2005, Nat. Conservation Achievement award, Nat. Wildlife Fedn., 2006, Edgar Wayburn award, Nat. Sierra Club award for Environ. Leadership, 2006, Climate Protection award, US EPA, 2006, Global Warming Globie awards, Environ. Def. Fund, 2007, Inaugural Visionary award, Urban League Contractor Develop. & Competitiveness Ctr., 2007, Innovations in Am. Govt. award, Harvard U. John F. Kennedy Sch. Govt., 2007, Ancil Payne Civic Leader of Yr. award, Washington CeaseFire, 2008, Energy Leadership award, Energy Efficiency Forum, 2008, Econ. Develop. Pub. Sector Champion award, EnterpriseSeattle, 2009; named Local Official Yr., Nat. Assn. Home Builders, 2003, Pub. Official of Yr., Nat. Assn. Indsl. and Office Properties, 2005, Low Carbon Leader, Climate Group, 2005; named one of 25 Leaders who are fighting to stave off the planetwide catastrophe: The Pied Piper, Rolling Stone Mag., 2006. Mem.: Am. Soc. Landscape Architects (hon.). Office: Office of the Mayor Seattle City Hall 600 4th Ave 7th Fl Seattle WA 98124 also: City Hall PO Box 94749 Seattle WA 98124-4749 E-mail: gjnickels@seattle.gov.*

NICKELS, RUTH ELIZABETH, band director; b. Warsaw, Ind., Nov. 21, 1955; m. David Brent Nickels, July 7, 2001. MusB in Performance, DePauw U., 1978; MusM in Performance, Ithaca Coll., 1980; cert. in edn., Grace Coll., 1986; post-master credits, Ind. U., 1986. Profl. tchg. lic. music edn. Dir. bands Fairfield Jr.-Sr. H.S., Goshen, Ind., 1986—92; H.S. band dir. Yorktown (Ind.) H.S., 1992—93; dir. bands Orleans (Ind.) Jr.-Sr. H.S., 1993—97, Southwestern Mid., H.S., Hanover, Ind., 1997—. Music judge Ind. State Music Assn., Indpls. Finalist Marching Band Mid-State Champions Class A, 2005, 2007. Mem.: NEA, Ind. State Tchrs. Assn., Ind. Bandmasters Assn., Music Educator's Nat. Conf., Women Band Dirs. Assn., Nat. Band Assn. Avocations: reading, travel, cooking, walking. Home: 3166 S River Bluff Dr Hanover IN 47243 Office: Southwestern Mid and HS 167 S Main Cross St Hanover IN 47243 Personal E-mail: nickelsre@aol.com. Business E-Mail: rnickels@swjcs.k12.in.us.

NICKENS, HARRY CARL, medical association administrator; b. Monterey, Tenn., June 25, 1944; s. Van B. and Martha (Winningham) N.; m. Alicia Beck, Aug. 26, 1967; children: Kimberly, Cassidee, Brad. BS, Tenn. Tech. U., 1966, MS, 1968; EdD, U. Tenn., 1972. Counselor Va. Western C.C., Roanoke, 1972-76, dir. student devel., 1977-78, dean students, 1979-84, exec. dir. community devel. and tng., 1985-89; pres. Coll. Health Scis., Roanoke, 1989—2001; v.p. cmty. rels. and devel. Ephraim McDowell Health, Danville, Ky., 2002—07. Chair Roanoke Valley Chamber's Sch., originator Grad. Ctr.; pres. Ephraim McDowell Health Care Found., 2003-06. Pres. Roanoke Valley Career Edn.; bd. dirs. Va. Cares, Adult Care Ctr., Am. Heart Assn., Va. Amateur Sports, Salvation Army; bd. suprs. Roanoke County; trustee St. Catherine Coll. Mem. Kiwanis (pres. Roanoke chpt. 1990, pres. Danville chpt. 2006). Baptist. Avocation: gardening. Home: 107 Patrick Henry Ct Danville KY 40422 Office: Ephraim McDowell Health 217 South 3rd St Danville KY 40422 Office Phone: 859-239-2632. Business E-Mail: hnickens@emhealth.org.

NICKERSON, GARY LEE, educational consultant; b. Cleve., Nov. 7, 1942; s. Alto Lee and Louisa Evelyn (Watson) Nickerson; m. Barbara Marie Butler, Aug. 17, 1968; 1 child, L'Oreal. BS, Ohio U., Athens, 1966; MA, Atlanta U., 1971. Cert. secondary tchr. Ohio. With Cleve. Pub. Schs., 1966-98; sci. dept. chmn. John F. Kennedy High Sch., Cleve., 1985-98; youth edn. coord. Cleve. Bot. Garden, 1999—2002; sci. mgr. Cleve. Mcpl. Schs., 2002—04; ednl. cons. Ohio Dept. Edn., 2004—. Sci. instr. Std. Oil Elem. Tchg. Retraining Program, 1986, Cleve. Ednl. Found. Elem. Tchg. Retraining Program, 1990—, Baldwin Wallace U. Upward Bound Program, 1992; physics instr. Case Western Res. U., Cleve., 1988, engring. project instr. MEIOP Summer Program, 91; mem. adv. panel Ednl. Devel. Ctr., Inc., Newton, Mass., 1989—98; tchr. trainer Kent State U. Trivet Program, 1991—98; sci. tchr. Gov.'s Inst. Gifted and Talented Cleve. State U., 1992—98. Co-author: curriculum guides. Bd. trustees Earthday Coalition, 2004—, READ, 2006—, Edfocus, 2006—; trustee N.E. Ohio Sci. and Engring. Fair, 2001—04. Recipient cert. of Excellence in Tchg., Rotary, 1990. Mem.: NAACP, Sci. Edn. Coun. Ohio, Nat. Sci. Tchrs. Assn., Cleve. Regional Coun. Sci. Tchrs. (bd. dirs. 1986—87, pres. 2002—06), Metrocabse Assn., Urban League, Kappa Alpha Psi. Democrat. Baptist. Avocations: ice skating, tennis, swimming, singing, weightlifting. Home: 5871 White Pine Dr Cleveland OH 44146-3075

NICKERSON, JERRY EDGAR ALAN, business executive; b. North Sydney, NS, Can., Apr. 28, 1936; s. Jeremiah Beldon and Jean Frances (Innes) N.; m. Jean Frances Ritcey, Sept. 20, 1958; children: Mark Alan, Jerry Ross. B.Commerce, Dalhousie U., 1958. Chmn. bd. H.B. Nickerson & Sons Ltd., North Sydney. Bd. dirs. Gt. West Life & Annuity, Gt. West Life Assurance Co., Great-West Lifeco Inc., London Ins. Group, London Life Ins., Power Fin., Inc., Power Corp. Can., Can. Life Fin. Corp., The Can. Life Assurance Co., Can. Life Capital Corp., The Crown Life Insurance Corp., The Can. Life Insurance Corp., Putnam Investments LLC Mem. Chief Execs. Orgn., Zeta Psi. Office: HB Nickerson & Sons Ltd PO Box 130 North Sydney NS Canada B2A 3M2 Office Phone: 902-794-8008. Personal E-mail: jeanickerson@aol.com.

NICKERSON, JOHN MITCHELL, political science professor; b. Lewiston, Maine, July 1, 1937; s. Elmer Winfield and Marion Gertrude (Howard) N. BA, U. Maine, 1959; MA, Wash. State U., 1966; PhD, U. Idaho, 1971. Commd. 2d lt. US Army, 1959, advanced through grades to capt., resigned, 1967; rsch. assoc. Bur. Pub. Adminstrn. U. Maine, Orono, 1967—68, mem. grad. faculty, 1970—88, asst. prof., assoc. prof. polit. sci. Augusta, 1970—81, prof., 1981—, developer 10 baccalaureate degrees pub. adminstrn.; dir. New Eng. Govtl. Rsch. Inst., Inc., Waterville, Maine, 1971. Lectr. Colby Coll., Waterville, Maine, 1979, Maine State Dedimus Justice; cons. in field. Author: The Control of Civil Disturbances, 1968; Municipal Police in Maine - A Study of Selected Personnel Practices with Emphasis on Recruit Selection and Training, 1969; (with others) A Study of Policy-Making: The Dynamics and Adaptability of the United States Federal System, 1971; editor, author foreward: Is the Municipality Liable for Insufficiently Trained Police? (James P. Murphy), 1968; contbr. articles to profl. jours. Mem. Maine State Police Planning Adv. Group, 1984-87, Maine State Bd. Assessment Rev., 1981-84, Maine Hwy. Safety Com., 1984-87; vice chmn. adv. bd. Salvation Army, Augusta, 1980-85; trustee, treas. Lithgow Library, 1980-85; incorporator Kennebec Valley Med. Ctr., Augusta, 1980-97. Dept. Justice grantee, 1967. Mem. Am. Polit. Sci. Assn., New Eng. Polit. Sci. Assn., Northeastern Polit. Sci. Assn., Acad. Polit. Sci. (life), Am. Acad. Polit. and Social Sci. (life), Am. Soc. for Pub. Adminstrn., ACLU (life), Kennebec Hist. Soc. (life), Kennebec Valley Humane Soc. (life), Maine Civil Liberties Union (life, legis. com.), Pi Sigma Alpha, Pi Alpha Alpha. Home: 190 Capitol St Apt 216 Augusta ME 04330-6237 Office: U Maine at Augusta 46 University Dr Augusta ME 04330 Office Phone: 207-621-3287. Business E-Mail: john.nickerson@maine.edu.

NICKERSON, KENNETH WARWICK, biology professor; b. Attleboro, Mass., Nov. 19, 1942; s. Walter John and Helen Nickerson; m. Ann Weinkauff, July 1, 1972; children: David Warwick, Daniel Patrick. PhD, U. Cin., 1969. Prof., biol. scis. U. Nebr., Lincoln, 1973—. Contbr. articles to profl. jour. Mem.: Am. Acad. Microbiology. Office: Univ Nebr Biol Scis Lincoln NE 68588-0666

NICKITAS, DONNA MARIE, nursing educator, researcher; b. Bklyn., Apr. 28, 1953; d. Jonh L. Costello and Anna Barone; m. Michael N. Nickitas, Oct. 24, 1982; children: Nick M., Catherine Anna, Jon-Philip. AAS Nursing, Kingsborough C.C., Bklyn., NY, 1974; BSN, SUNY, Stonybrook, 1976; MA, NYU, 1980; PhD, Adelphi U., Garden City, NY, 1989. Cert. nursing adminstrn., basic, ANCC, 1982, CNAA, BC, ANCC, 2003. Maj. USAF, Rapid City, SD, 1976—93; grad. splty. coord. Hunter Coll., NYC, 1993—, assoc. prof., 1996—, Grad. Sch., CUNY, 2007—, prof., 2009—; dir. Continuing Edn. Hunter, Belleme Sch. Nursing, 2009—. Cons. NYC Health and Hosp. Corp., 2007—. Author: (book) Quick Reference Guide to Nursing Leadership. Pres. League Women Voters, Greenwich, Conn., 2003—. Fellow, Am. Assn. Colls. Nursing, 2006. Fellow: NY Acad. Medicine; mem.: Sigma Theta Tau. Conservative. Home: 15 Center Rd Old Greenwich CT 06870 Office: Hunter Coll 425 East 25th St New York NY 10010 Office Phone: 212-481-4376. Office Fax: 212-481-4427. Business E-Mail: dnickita@hunter.cuny.edu.

NICKLAUS, JACK WILLIAM, professional golfer, sports apparel executive; b. Columbus, Ohio, Jan. 21, 1940; s. Louis Charles, Jr. and Helen (Schoener) N.; m. Barbara Bash, July 23, 1960; children: Jack William II, Steven Charles, Nancy Jean, Gary Thomas, Michael Scott. Student, Ohio State U., 1957-62, D (hon.) of Athletic Arts, 1972; LLD (hon.), U. St. Andrews, 1984. Chmn., CEO Golden Bear Internat., Inc.; ptnr. Nicklaus Design; owner Nicklaus Golf Equipment Co. Player U.S. Ryder Cup Team, 1969, 71, 73, 75, 77, 81, 83, 87. Author: My 55 Ways to Lower Your Golf Score, 1964, Take a Tip From Me, 1968, The Greatest Game of All, 1969, Jack Nicklaus' Lesson Tee, 1972, Golf My Way, 1974, Jack Nicklaus' Playing Lessons, 1976, On and Off the Fairway, 1978, Play Better Golf, Vols. 1-3, 1980, 81, 83, The Full Swing, 1982, My Most Memorable Shots in the Majors, 1988. Chmn. Ohio divsn. Am. Cancer Soc., 1967; chmn. sports divsn. Nat. Easter Seal Soc., 1967. Recipient Byron Nelson award, 1964, 65, 72, 73, Bob Jones award, 1975, Presdl. Medal of Freedom, The White House, 2005; named PGA Player of Yr., 1967, 72, 73, 75, 76, Dunlop Profl. Athlete of Yr., 1972, Golfer of Yr. Profl. Golfers Assn., 1973, Sportsman of Yr., Sports Illus. mag., 1978, Athlete of the Decade for 1970-79, 1979, Golfer of the '70s, 1979, Golfer of the Century, 1988; named to World Golf Hall of Fame, 1974; named one of Most Influential People in the World of Sports, 2008. Mem. President's Club Ohio State U., Phi Gamma Delta. Achievements include playing on over 105 golf courses on 5 continents, 12 ranked in US Top 100; hosted 185 profl. tournaments 1973—; won 73 ofcl. tournaments; maj. tournaments won include Tournament of Champions, 1963, 64, 71, 73, 77, US Amateur, 1959, 61, US Open, 1962, 67, 72, 80, US Masters, 1963, 65, 66, 72, 75, 86, Brit. Open, 1966, 70, 78, PGA Championship, 1963, 71, 73, 75, 80, Internat. Pro-Amateur, 1973, Tournament Players Championship, 1974, 76, 78, Australian Open, 1964, 68, 71, 75, 76, 78, World Series of Golf, 1962, 63, 67, 70, 76, PGA Seniors Championship, 1991, US Sr. Open, 1991, 93. Office: Golden Bear Golf Inc 11780 US Hwy #1 North Palm Beach FL 33408

NICKLE, DENNIS EDWIN, electronics engineer, consultant, deacon; b. Sioux City, Iowa, Jan. 30, 1936; s. Harold Bateman and Helen Cecilia (Killackey) H. BS in Math., Fla. State U., 1961. Cert. software configuration specialist; ordained deacon Roman Cath. Ch., 1979. Reliability mathematician Pratt & Whitney Aircraft Co., West Palm Beach, Fla., 1961-63; br. supr. Melpar Inc., Falls Church, Va., 1963-66; prin. mem. tech. staff Xerox Data Sys., Rockville, Md., 1966-70; sr. tech. officer WHO, Washington, 1970-76; software tech. mgr. Melpar divsn. E-Sys., Inc., Falls Church, 1976-95; software process improvement mgr. Bell Atlantic, Arlington, Va., 1996-97; sr. software mgr. Litton Denro, Gaithersburg, Md., 1997—2001; cons., 2001—; bd. dirs., treas. BARK Enterprises LLC, 2006—. Lectr. in field; coord. D.C. Software Process Improvement Network, 1995—2001, chair, 1997—2002. Author: Stress in Adolescents, 1986; co-author: Handbook for Handling Non-Productive Stress in Adolescence, Standard for Software Life Cycle Processes, IMPEESA Junior Leader Training Guide, Standard for Software Quality Assurance, 1984-91, Standard for Developing Software Life Cycle Processes, Configuration Management Procedures, Software Quality Assurance Procedures, Software Development Procedures; editor: Mama's Good Italian Cookbook, 2004; contbr. to profl. jours. Chief judge for computers Fairfax County Regional Sci. Fair, 1964-88; scoutmaster, commr. Boy Scouts Am., 1957-92; youth custodian Fairfax County Juvenile Ct., 1973-87; chaplain No. Va. Regional Juvenile Detention Home, 1978-88; moderator Nocturnal Adoration Soc.; parochial St. Michael's Ch., Annandale, Va., 1979-89, Christ the Redeemer, Sterling, Va., 1990-93; mem. Vol. Income Tax Assistance Program, 2004—; counselor Va. Ins. Councellry and Assistance Program, 2004—. With U.S. Army, 1958-60. Recipient Eagle award, Silver award, Silver Beaver award, other awards Boy Scouts Am.; Ad Altare Dei, St. George Emblem, Diocese of Richmond. Mem. Assn. Computing Machinery, Computer Soc., Am. Soc. for Quality Control, CODSIA (chmn. working groups), ORLANDO II (Govt./industry working group), Old Crows Assn., Rolm Mil-Spec Computer Users Group (internat. pres.), San Antonio I (select industry coord. group), Nat. Security Indsl. Assn. (conv. com. 1985-96, software quality assurance subcom., regional membership chmn. 1981-89, nat. exec. vice-chmn. 1989-94, chmn. 1994-96), Am. Security Coun., IEEE (sr., stds. working group in computers 1983—, Outstanding Vol. award 1993, Golden Core 1996), Def. Software Devel. Stds. Adv. Bd. (chmn. 1991-96), Soc. Software Quality, Hewlett-Packard Users Group, Smithsonian Assn., Internat. Platform Assn., NRA (endowment), Nat. Eagle Scout Assn. (life), KC (4 deg.), Alpha Phi Omega (life), Sigma Phi Epsilon. Home: 43245 Preston Ct Ashburn VA 20147-5307 Office Phone: 703-729-2653.

NICKLES, PETER, state attorney general; b. Sept. 26, 1938; BA, Princeton Univ., 1960; EC, Univ. Munich, Univ. Sorbonne; LLB, Harvard Univ., 1963. Bar: Washington, DC 1964. Sr. litig. ptnr. Covington & Burling, Washington; acting atty. gen. DC, 2008, atty. gen., 2008—. Mem. Lawyer's Com. Civil Rights Under Law, Washington, 1964; counsel Jackson St. Task Force and Kent State Task Force, 1968—70; chmn. Neighborhood Local Svc. Program, Washington, 1970—75; adj. prof. Howard Law Sch., Washington, 1980—92. Recipient Pro Bono Svc. award, DC Bar Assn., 1998, Servant of Justice award, Legal Aid Soc., 2003; named one of 75 Best Lawyers in Washington, Washingtonian mag., 2002. Democrat. Office: Office of Atty Gen John A Wilson Bldg Ste 409 1350 Pennsylvania Ave NW Washington DC 20009 Office Phone: 202-724-1305. Business E-Mail: oag@dc.gov.*

NICKLESS, RALPH WALTER, bishop; b. Denver, May 28, 1947; s. Walter and E. Margaret (McGovern) Nickless. BA, St. Thomas, 1969; MA in Pastoral Theology, Pontifical Gregorian U., Rome, 1973, STB, 1972. Ordained priest Archdiocese of Denver, Colo., 1973, vicar gen. Colo.; pastor Our Lady of Fatima Parish, Lakewood, Colo.; bishop Diocese of Sioux City, 2005—; ordained bishop, 2006. Roman Catholic. Office: Diocese of Sioux City 1821 Jackson St PO Box 3379 Sioux City IA 51102-3379 Office Phone: 712-233-7555. Office Fax: 712-233-7557. E-mail: bishopnickless@scdiocese.org.

NICKLIN, EMILY, lawyer; b. Cooperstown, NY, June 24, 1953; d. George Leslie Jr. and Katherine Mildred (Aronson) N.; m. Jay Schleusener, Dec. 28, 1974; children: Max, Lucas, Anna. BA, U. Chgo., 1975, JD, 1977. Bar: Ill. 1977, US Dist. Ct. (no. dist. Ill.) 1979, US Ct. Appeals (7th cir.) 1979. Law clk. to judge US Dist. Ct. (no. dist. Ill.), Chgo., 1977-79; assoc. Kirkland & Ellis, Chgo., 1979-83, ptnr., 1983—, mem. firm mgmt. com., 1995—. Tchr. Ill. Continuing Legal Edn. Bar Prog., Chgo., 1983—; fellow Salzburg Seminar, Austria, 1983; dep. corp. counsel City of Chgo., 1989-91; mem. bd. trustees, U. Chgo., lectr. law, 2001. Named one of Am. Top 50 Women Litigators, Nat. Law. Jour., 2001, 30 Tough Lawyers, Chgo. Mag. Mem. Nat. Inst. Trial Advocacy (tchr., team leader 1982—), Order of Coif, Phi Beta Kappa. Office: Kirkland & Ellis LLP 200 E Randolph Dr Fl 54 Chicago IL 60601-6636 Office Phone: 312-861-2387. Office Fax: 312-861-2200. E-mail: enicklin@kirkland.com.

NICKOLE, LEONIDAS A., performing arts educator, director; s. Anesty Nickole and Olga (Petrakis). BA, MA, Emerson Coll., Boston, LHD (hon.) in Humane Letters; MA, Columbia U., NYC. Dir. Allentown Civic Theatre, Pa., 1952—53; instr. drama Emerson Coll., 1953—60, chmn. dept. theatre edn., 1960—66, prof. dept. theatre arts, 1960—66, 1966—80, chmn. dept. theatre arts, 1960—80, founder musical theatre soc., 1969—2001, dir., 1969—2001, prof., dept. performing arts, 1980—2001, prof. emeritus, dept. performing arts, 2001—. Founder Theatre Co. Saugus, Inc., Saugus, 1969—, dir., 1969—; co-founder BN Prodns. Inc., Mass., 1970—2006; adj. prof. theatre history Boston Conservatory Music, 1980—88; adj. prof. music Northeastern U., Boston, 1967—68. Mem. Saugus Pub. Libr., 2006—; dir. New Wrinkle Theatre, Boston, 1975—80; mem. Saugus Pub. Libr., 1979—99; dir. M.E.G. Found., Saugus, 2007—. Decorated Combat Inf. badge US Army, Two Bronze Stars, DSM USN; recipient award, St. George Greek Orthodox Ch., 1972, Pres. award, Emerson Coll., 1973, Trustees award, 1993, Excellence Tchg. award, Salve Regina Coll., 1991; named one of Hon. Dr. Humane Letters, Emerson Coll., 2001. Fellow: New Eng. Theatre Conf. (pres. 1970—71, Musical Theatre Soc. citation 1970, Coll. Fellows award 1983—); mem.: Theatre Co. Saugus Inc. (life). Home: 123 Forest St Saugus MA 01906 Office: Emerson Coll 120 Boylston St Boston MA 02116 E-mail: leo_nickole@emerson.edu.

NICKON, ALEX, chemist, educator; b. Poland, Oct. 6, 1927; came to U.S., 1955, naturalized, 1961; s. Steve and Maria (Nickon); m. Beulah Monica Godby, Aug. 22, 1950; children— Dale Beverly, Linda Cheryl, Leanne Marie. B.Sc., U. Alta., 1949; MA, Harvard U., 1951, PhD, 1953. Vis. lectr. Bryn Mawr Coll., 1953; postdoctoral fellow Birkbeck Coll., U. London, England, 1953-54, NRC, Ottawa, Canada, 1954-55; NSF sr. fellow; Imperial Coll., London, 1963-64; U. Munich, Germany, 1971-72; mem. faculty Johns Hopkins, 1955—, prof. chemistry, 1964-94, Vernon K. Krieble prof. chemistry, 1975-94, prof. emeritus, 1994—. Vis. assoc. Am. Chem. Soc. on Profl. Tng., 1975-95; mem. medicinal chem. panel NIH, 1966-70; postdoctoral panel NRC, 1968-69. Sr. editor Jour. Organic Chemistry, 1965-71; Am. exec. editor: Tetrahedron Reports, 1978-96. Recipient Md. Chemist award, 1990; Sloan Found. fellow, 1957-61 Fellow N.Y. Acad. Scis.; mem. Am. Chem. Soc. (nat. awards com. 1974-76), Brit. Chem. Soc. Home: 770 Knoll Rd Copper Canyon TX 75077-4802 Personal E-mail: nickontx@yahoo.com.

NICKSON, JULIE L., legislative staff member; B in Psychology, U. Md.; JD, Nova Southeastern U. Shepard Broad Law Ctr., Ft. Lauderdale, Fla. Asst. to the dir. Baptist World Alliance; legal fellow WHO, Switzerland; asst. counsel George Wash. U. Health Plan; sr. legis. asst. Rep. Marcy Kaptur US House of Reps., Washington, legis. dir., adminstrv. asst., Rep. Barbara Lee, 2004—05, chief of staff to Rep. Barbara Lee, 2005—, asst., appropriations com., 2007—. Democrat. Office: 2444 Rayburn House Office Bldg Washington DC 20515 Office Phone: 202-225-2661. Office Fax: 202-225-9817.*

NICKSON, ROBERT FRAZIER, film producer, educator; b. Chgo., Ill., 1942; s. James Joseph and Margaret Hofrichter Nickson. BA, Dartmouth Coll., Hanover, New Hampshire, 1967; MFA, NYU, 1970. Percussionist Holy Modal Rounders, Rounder Records, East Fairfield, Vt., 1971—76; asst. prof. film Hamilton Coll., Clinton, NY, 1978—80, NY U., NYC, 1980—82; asst. prof. art Kirkland Coll., Clinton, NY, 1977—78; assoc. prof. film Newhouse Sch., Syracuse U., NY, 1982—84; prof. film prodn. Grad. Film, NY U., 1984—. Feature film, prodr., financing cons. Orenda Films, NYC, 1986—. Musician: (albums) Have Moicy (Album of the Yr. - Village Voice; Top 20 NYT, 1976); dir.: (plays) The Village (Gurdin Meml. Directing Prize, 1967); prodr.: (films) No Way Home (Deauville Film Festival - Audience Prize, 1996), (line producer) Curtain Call, (co-producer) Auf Wiedersehen Amerika (German Film Awards - Silver Bear, 1995), The Search for One Eye Jimmy, Pen Pals (Best First Film - Tokyo Film Festival, 1991); production controller (films) Jungle Fever, Mo' Better Blues, Do the Right Thing, Streetsmart. Sergeant USAR, 1963—65, South East Asia. Home: Washington Square Vill New York NY 10012 Office: Graduate Film Prog NYU 721 Broadway 10th fl New York NY 10003 Office Fax: 212-995-4063; Home Fax: 212-995-4063. Business E-Mail: orenfilm@tiac.net.

NICOARA, ANDREEA CARINA, mathematics professor; arrived in US, 1991, naturalized, 1996; d. Ioan Lucian Nicoara and Ana Eugenia Bursan. BS in Math. (hon.), Stanford U., Calif., 1997; MA in Math., Princeton U., NJ, 1999, PhD in Math., 2002. Benjamin Peirce asst. prof. math. Harvard U., Cambridge, Mass., 2002—08; asst. prof. U. Pa., 2008—. Contbr. articles to profl. jours. Recipient Boothe prize for Excellence in Writing, Stanford U., 1994, Firestone medal for Excellence in Rsch., 1997, Robert M. Golden medal for Excellence in the Humanities, 1997; Luce fellow, Princeton U., 1997—99, Postdoctoral fellow, NSF, 2003—06. Mem.: Am. Math. Soc. (Waldemar J. Trjitzinsky Meml. Fund award 1996), Kokikai Aikido (instr. 2004, black belt 2004), Phi Beta Kappa. Democrat. Roman Catholic. Avocations: art history, comparative religion, Aikido, fencing, travel.

NICOL, DOMINIK, writer, photographer; b. northern Oltenia, Romania, Sept. 25, 1930; arrived in US, 1969, naturalized, 1976; s. Dumitru and Valentina (Sandulescu) Nicolaescu-Stroe. Diploma in Chemistry and Tech. of Antibiotics, The Tech. Sch., Bucharest, Romania, 1954. Photo-reporter Agerpress, Bucharest, 1950-51; med. photographer Cantacuzino Hosp., Bucharest, 1955-68; ret., 1995. Author, editor: Self Encounter, 1979, Ten Oneiric Sketches, 1980, Rendes-Vous sau Intalnire cu mine insumi, 1987; (play) Vacuum (Colocviu de abis), 1979, Vacuum-Void, 1988, Pe portativul vietii, 1992. Home: 150 Riverside Dr Room 904 Manhattan New York NY 10024

NICOLADIS, MICHAEL F., engineering company executive; b. New Orleans, Aug. 15, 1960; s. Frank and Peggy (Yemelos) N. B in Engring. magna cum laude, Vanderbilt U., 1982; MBA, Duke U., 1984. Assoc. N-Y Assocs., Inc., Metairie, La., 1984-85, v.p., 1985-97, COO, sr. v.p., 1997—. Mem. Holy Trinity Greek Orthodox Cathedral, New Orleans. Fuqua Scholar, Conoco Scholar Duke U. Mem.: ASCE, Martin's Episcopal Sch. (bd. trustee), Am. Pub. Works Assn., Am. Coun. Engring. Cos., Soc. Am. Mil. Engrs., Chi Epsilon, Tau Beta Pi. Avocations: tennis, reading, travel. Office: N-Y Assocs Inc 2750 Lake Villa Dr Metairie LA 70002-6786 Office Phone: 504-885-0500. Business E-Mail: mnicoladis@n-yassociates.com.

NICOLAOU, KYRIACOS COSTA (K. C. NICOLAOU), chemistry professor; b. Karavas, Kyrenia, Cyprus, July 5, 1946; came to U.S., 1972; s. Costa and Helen (Yettimi) N.; m. Georgette Karayianni, July 15, 1973; children; Colette, Alexis, Christopher, Paul. BSc, Bedford Coll., London, 1969; PhD, U. Coll., London, 1972; DSc, U. London, 1994; D (hon.), U. Thessaloniki, 1996, U. Cyprus, 1997, U. Alcala, Madrid, 1998, U. Crete, 1998, Agrl. U. Athens, 2000, U. Patras, Greece, 2002, U. Rome, 2003. Rsch. assoc. Columbia U., NYC, 1972-73, Harvard U., Cambridge, Mass., 1973-76; from asst. prof. to Rhodes-Thompson prof. chemistry U. Pa., Phila., 1976-89; prof. chemistry U. Calif. at San Diego, La Jolla, 1989—; Darlene Shiley prof. chemistry, chmn. dept. The Scripps Rsch. Inst., La Jolla, Calif., 1989—, Aline W. & L.S. Skaggs prof., Skaggs Inst. Chem. Biology, 1996—. Vis. prof. U. Paris, 1986; mem. exec. com. Diann. Cyprus Conf. on Drug Design; mem. med. study sect. D, NIH, 1988-90; mem. internat. adv. bd. Angewandte Chemie, 1994—. Author: (with N. A. Petasis) Selenium in Natural Products Synthesis, 1984, (with E. J. Sorensen) Classics in Total Synthesis, 1996; co-editor: Synthesis, Germany, 1984-90, Chemistry and Biology, 1994; editl. bd. Prostaglandins, Leukotrienes and Medicine, 1978-88, Synthesis, 1990—, Accounts of Chem. Rsch., 1992—, Carbohydrate Letters, 1993—, Chemistry-A European Jour., 1994—, Perspectives in Drug, Discovery and Design, 1994—, Indian Jour. of Chemistry, Sect. B, 1995—; mem. bd. consulting editors Tetrahedron Publs., 1992—; mem. adv. bd. Contemporary Organic Synthesis, 1993—; mem. regional adv. bd. J. C. S. Chem. Comm., 189—, J. C. S. Perkin I, 1991—; contbr. articles to profl. jours.; patentee in field. Decorated Hon. medal Order of the Comdr., Greece, 1998; recipient Japan Soc. for Promotion Sci. award 1987-88, US Sr. Scientist award Alexander von Humboldt Found., 1987-88, Alan R. Day award Phila. Organic Chemists Club, 1993, Pfizer Rsch. award, 1993-94, Paul Janssen prize, 1994, Alexander the Great award Hellenic Cultural Soc. San Diego, 1994, Rhone-Poulenc medal Royal Soc. Chemistry, 1995, Chem. Pioneer Am. Inst. of Chemists, 1996, Inhoffen Medal of Gesellscaft fur Biotechnologische Forschung mbH (GBF) Tech. U. Braunschweig, 1996, Aspirin prize, 1999, Yamada prize, 1999, Max Tischler prize, 2000, Paul Karrer Gold medal, 2000, Schering prize, 2001, Nagoya medal, 2001, Centenary medal Royal Soc. Chemistry, 2001-02, Petrahedron prize, prize Bodossaki Found., 2004, Burkardt-Helferich prize, 2006; fellow A.P. Sloan Found., 1979-83, J. S. Guggenheim Found., 1984; Camille and Henry Dreyfus scholar, 1980-84, Arthur C. Cope scholar, 1987. Fellow NY Acad. Scis., Am. Acad. Arts and Scis., Indian Acad. Scis. (hon.), Chem. Rsch. Soc. India (hon.); mem. Nat. Acad. Scis., Am. Chem. Soc. (Creative Work in Synthetic Organic Chemistry award 1993, William H. Nichols medal 1996, Ernest Guenther award in chemistry of natural products 1996, Linus Pauling award 1996, Esselen award for chemistry in pub. interest 1998, Nobel Laureate Signature award 2003, Auburn G.M. Kosolapoff award 2006), Chem. Soc. London, German Chem. Soc., Japanese Chem. Soc., Acad. Athens (fgn. mem.). Office: Scripps Rsch Inst Dept Chemistry 10550 N Torrey Pines Rd La Jolla CA 92037-1000 also: U Calif San Diego 9500 Gilman Dr La Jolla CA 92093

NICOLAS, KENNETH LEE, import/export company executive; s. Norman L. and Bernice L. (Hameister) N.; m. Anne Vanderwielen, July 5, 1992 (dec.); children: Juliana M., Camille G. BA in Polit. Sci., Calif. State U., Fullerton, 1968; MA in Legis. Affairs/Econs., George Washington U., 1975. Exec. asst. Congressman Richard T. Hanna, Washington, 1970-72; sr. staff assoc. Nat. Assn. Ednl. Broadcasters, Washington, 1972-74; founder, pres. Nicolas Assocs. Internat., Inc., 1972—80; exec. dir. Am. Coll. Nuc. Physicians, Washington, 1974-77; aide to the Pres. White House, Washington, 1977-80; v.p. McSweeney & Co. Consulting, Newport Beach, Calif., 1980-83, L.E. Peterson & Co. Investment Banking, Costa Mesa, Calif., 1983-85; founder, pres. Fin. Strategies Group, Inc., Newport Beach, 1985—; CEO Tradex Internat., Inc., Newport Beach, 1988-94; founder, CEO Trade Access Group, Inc., 1994—. Adj. prof. Orange Coast Coll., Costa Mesa, 1983-97, internat. MBA program U. So. Calif., 1989-90, Thunderbird Sch. Internat. Bus., Orange County, 1990-92, U. Calif., Riverside and Irvine, 1996-98; adj. prof. internat. bus. MBA program Webster U., 1998—. Author: (article series) Business to Business Mag., 1984-87 (Excellence award 1984-87). Bd. dirs., v.p. Leukemia Soc. Am., Orange County, Calif., 1982-88; chmn. Holiday Project, 1992-94; mem. bd. mgrs., chmn. capital devel. com. Orange County YMCA, 2001—, gen. campaign chmn., fedn. chief parent/child program, 2002-; nation chief Orange Blossom Nation, Indian Princess Program; bd. gov. YMCA, 2006-; investment advisor, City of Irvine, Calif., 2006-; democratic party canidate, Orange County, 2007-. With U.S. Army, 1968-70, Vietnam. Recipient Outstanding Svc. award Nat. Holiday Project, 1993, Nat. Svc. Appreciation award Pres. Jimmy Carter, 1980, Excellence award Leukemia Soc. Am., 1988. Mem. Japan Am. Soc. (Orange County chpt. chmn. bd. dirs. 1997-99), Japan Am. Soc. So. Calif. (exec. bd. 1996-98), Surfrider Assn. Democrat. Episcopalian. Avocations: Karate, sailing, travel, chess, swimming.

NICOLÁS, SHERWOOD-DROZ, electrical engineer, researcher, computer engineer, researcher; b. San Juan, Puerto Rico, July 14, 1980; s. Thorne Sherwood and Edna Droz. BS, Worcester Poly. Inst., Worcester, Mass, 2002; MS, 2005. Rschr. Conway Libr., London, 2001, W/S Atkins DK, Copenhagen, 2001, WPI/Raytheon, Worcester, 2003, Cornell U., Ithaca, NY, 2007—. Mem.: Optical Soc. Am., IEEE, Tau Beta Pi, Eta Kappa Nu. Achievements include patents pending for adaptable satellite networking.

NICOLELIS, MIGUEL A. L., neuroscientist, educator; MD, U. Sao Paulo Med. Sch., 1984; PhD, U. Sao Paulo, 1988. Intern U. Sao Paulo, 1983—84, rsch. assoc. dept. pathology, 1985—86, rsch. instr. dept. pathology, 1986—88, asst. prof. dept. pathology, 1988—92; rsch. instr. dept. physiology & biophysics Hahnemann U., 1989—94; asst. prof. dept. neurobiology Duke U. Med. Ctr., 1994—97, assoc. prof. dept. neurobiology, 1998—2001, assoc. prof. biomedical engineering, 1999—2001, assoc. prof. experimental psychology, 1991—2001, prof. nuerobiology biomedical engring & psychological & brain sciences, 2001—, co-dir Ctr. for Neuroengineering, 2001—. Editorial bd. mem. Neuroinformatics, Jour. Neuroscience Methods; editor-in-chief Frontiers in Neuroscience. Mem.: Brazilian Soc. Animal Physiology, Am. Assn. Advance Sci., Internat. Soc. Neuroscience, Soc. Neuroscience. Office: Duke University Medical Center Dept Neurobiology 327 E Bryan Research Bldg Box 3209 Durham NC 27708 Office Phone: 919-684-4580. Office Fax: 919-668-2248. E-mail: nicoleli@neuro.duke.edu.*

NICOLETTI, PAUL LEE, retired veterinarian, educator; b. Goodman, Mo., Oct. 26, 1932; s. Felix and Clarice N.; m. Earlene Blackburn, June 6, 1954; children: Diana, Julie, Nancy. BS in Agr., U. Mo., 1956, DVM, 1956; MS, U. Wis., 1962. Diplomate Am. Coll. Vet. Preventive Medicine. Veterinarian USDA, Mo., Wis., NY, 1956-68, UN FAO, Tehran, Iran, 1968-72, USDA, Jackson, Miss., 1972-75, Gainesville, Fla., 1973-78; prof. vet. medicine U. Fla., Gainesville, 1978—2003, prof. emeritus, 2003—. Recipient awards from Fla. Cattleman's Assn., 1978, Dairy Farmers, Inc., 1978, Borden award, 1979, Gold Star award Fla. Veterinary Medicine Assoc., 1981, 86, U. Austral, Chile, 1981, P.R. Dairy Assn., 1978, faculty alumni award U. Mo., 1987; named Basic Scis. Tchr. of Yr. Nat. Student Am. Vet. Med. Assn., 1994, Alumnus of Yr. award, U. Mo., 2000, U. Fla. Disting. Svc. award, 2003. Mem. Am. Vet. Medicine Assn. (internat. prize 1991), Fla. Vet. Medicine Assn. (pres. 1995-96, veterinarian of yr. 1994, Disting. Svc. award 1999, Lifetime Achievement award 2004), Am. Coll. Vet. Preventive Medicine (pres. 1997-98), Phi Zeta (nat. pres. 1997-99). Home: 2552 SW 14th Dr Gainesville FL 32608-2042 Office: Univ of Fla Coll Vet Medicine PO Box 110880 Gainesville FL 32611-0880 Office Phone: 352-392-2239 ext. 5860. Business E-Mail: nicolettip@vetmed.ufl.edu.

NICOLL, EDWARD J., information technology company executive; b. Aug. 13, 1953; JD, Yale U., 1997. Co-founder, pres. Waterhouse Investor Svcs., Inc. (sold to Toronto-Dominion Bank and became TD Waterhouse), 1979—96; chmn., CEO Datek Online Holdings, Corp., Iselin, NJ, 1999—2002, Instinet, LLC, 2002—07, chmn., 2007—. Trustee New Cmty. Found. Fellow Yale U. Achievements include first to to attend Yale Law without a college degree.

NICOLODI, MARIA, neuropharmacologist, medical researcher; b. Florence, Italy, June 2, 1955; d. Beniamino and Giovanna (Zicari) N. B in Medicine, U. Florence, 1984, PhD, 1992; specialist in neurology, U. Pavia, Italy, 1994. Asst. prof. U. Catania, Italy, 1997-99; fellow U. Florence, 1990-93. Internat. cons. Med. Inst. Treatment of Pain, Santiago, Chile, 1997—; gen. sec. Interuniv. Ctr. Neurochemistry and Clin. Pharmacology of Primary Headaches, Italy; asst. rschr. U. Florence, 1999—; asst. prof. U. Siena, Italy, 2000—; pres. Found. Prevention Primary Pain, 2003—; head physician Ctr. Pain Medicine Villanova Hosp., Florence, 2008. Contbr. over 285 articles to profl. jours.; editor 2 Congress Procs. books; inventor in fields of therapy for chronic headache, primary fibromyalgia and prevention of primary pain in children; patentee in field; referee Jour. Internat. Headache Soc., 1993—, Jour. Am. Assn. Headache, Sci. Cooperator Italian Soc. Study of Headache. Rsch. grantee Glaxo Solvay-Pharma and Florence U., 1994, Nat. Coun. Rsch., Rome, 1995 recipient Internat. Greppi Jr. prize, 1990, Sr. prize, 1995, Migraine Trust prize, 2006. Mem. Internat. Headache Soc., Internat. Club Functional Organic and Non-Organic Nociceptive Diseases (founder, mem. scientific bd. 1991), Found. Prevention and Therapy of Primary Pain and Headache (pres.), World Neurol. Fedn. Avocations: gardening, painting. Office: Via Costa de' Magnoli 28 I-50125 Florence Italy Office Phone: 390552466010, 390552480716. Business E-Mail: info@fondazionesicuterinicolodi.it.

NICOLSON, DAN HENRY, retired plant taxonomist; b. Kansas City, Mo., Sept. 5, 1933; s. John Whitley and LeOna Johanna (Teget) N.; m. Alice Black Crawford, Aug. 22, 1959; children: John Crawford, Sarah Whitley, David Teget. AB, Grinnell Coll., 1955; MBA, Stanford U., 1957; MSc, Cornell U., 1959, PhD, 1964. Asst. curator Smithsonian Instn., Washington, 1964-65, assoc. curator, 1965-74, curator, 1974—2006; ret., 2006. Author: Flora of Dominica, 1991; co-author: An Interpretation Van Rheede's Hortus Malabaricus, 1988, The Forsters and the Botany of the Second Cook Expedition (1772-1775), 2004; co-editor: Flora of the Hassan District, 1976. Mem. Internat. Assn. Plant Taxonomy (v.p. 1987-93, pres. 1993-99, past pres. 1999-2005), Washington Biologists Field Club (treas. 1981-97), Washington Bot. Soc. (pres. 1989-90, treas. 1997-2006). Office: Dept Botany MRC-166 Nat Mus Natural History Smithsonian Instn Washington DC 20013-7012 Office Phone: 202-633-0910. Business E-Mail: nicolson@si.edu.

NICOSIA, MARK, engineering educator; PhD in Mech. Engring., Pa. State U., Univ. Pk., 1997. Assoc. prof. mech. engring. Widener U., Chester, Pa., 2005—. Office: Widener Univ Sch Engring One University Pl Chester PA 19013 Business E-Mail: manicosia@widener.edu.

NICULESCU, PETER S., former mortgage company executive; b. 1959; BA in Economics, Victoria U., Wellington, New Zealand, 1979; Ph.D in Economics, Yale U., 1985. With fixed-income rsch. and portfolio mgmt. Salomon Bros.; with fixed-income rsch. & portfolio mgmt. Sanford C. Bernstein & Co.; joined Goldman Sachs, 1990, mng. dir., co-head fixed-income rsch. and strategy; sr. v.p. portfolio strategy Fannie Mae (Fed. Nat. Mortgage Assn.), Washington, 1999—2002, exec. v.p. capital markets, 2002—08, exec. v.p., chief bus. officer, 2008.

NIDECKER, ANDREAS CORNELIS, radiologist, educator; b. Tiel, The Netherlands, Oct. 1, 1947; s. Hans Jakob and Rosemarie (Huggenberg) Nidecker; children from previous marriage: Florian, Maja, Eva. MD, Med. Sch. U. Basel, Switzerland, 1973. Diplomate Am. Bd. Radiology. Internship Lawrence Gen. Hosp., Toronto, Canada, 1973—74, 1976—79; asst. prof. radiology U. Basel, 1985-99, prof., 1999—; pvt. practice Basel, 1982—. Mem. Arbeitsgruppe Knochentumoren, Deutsches Krebforschungsfentrur; co-owner IMAMED Radiologie Nordwest, Basel. Mem. exec. com., past pres. Internat. Physicians Prevention Nuc. War, 1982—; mem. constl. coun. Basel Canton. Mem.: Swiss Soc. Radiology, Radiol. Soc. N.Am., Internat. Soc. Skeletal Radiology. Avocations: hiking, skiing, travel, music. Office: IMAMED Radiologie Nordwest Untere Rebgasse 18 4058 Basel Switzerland E-mail: anidecker@bluewin.ch, andreas.nidecker@imamed.ch.

NIDZGORSKI, BARBARA HELEN, gifted and talented educator, puppeteer; b. Wilmington, Del., July 15, 1951; d. Joseph Edward and Angela Victoria (Palczewski) N. BFA, U. Del., Newark, 1973; MA, U. Conn., 1980; MFA, Conn. Coll., New London, 1989. Cert. tchr., Conn, art tchr. K-12, Conn. Tchr. grade 4, grade 7/8 algebra Woodland Country Day Sch., Jericho, N.J., 1974-78; tchr. gifted and talented Greenwich (Conn.) Pub. Schs., 1979-80, New London Pub. Schs., 1987-94; tchr. gifted and talented, grades 6-12 Dist. 18 Lyme/Old Lyme, Conn., 1994—2002; tchr. gifted and talented secondary sch. Dist. 4, Deep River, Conn., 2002—. Gen. mgr. nat. puppetry conf. Eugene O'Neill Theatre, Waterford, Conn., 1990—; instr. U. Conn., Storrs, 1982-98. Co-author: (cards for classroom) Mission Possible, 1981-82. Recipient Mark Shedd Excellence award Conn. Consortium for Law and Citizenship in Edn; named to Outstanding Young Women of Am., 1985; named Conn. Tchr.-In-Space, NASA, 1985. Mem. Delta Kappa Gamma (art chair 1991-98, state chair 1994-97), Phi Delta Gamma. Avocations: theater, kayaking, mountain biking, musical instruments, pottery. Home: 41 White Birch Cir Niantic CT 06357-1610 Office: Regional Dist 4 1 Winthrop Rd Deep River CT 06417 Office Phone: 860-526-9546. Personal E-mail: oneillpupconf@aol.com.

NIE, QING, mathematics professor; PhD, Ohio State U., Columbus, 1995. Dickson instr. U. Chgo., 1997—99; asst. to prof. U. Calif., Irvine, 1999—. Office: Univ Calif Dept Math Irvine CA 92697-3875

NIEBRUEGGE, MICHAEL E., lawyer; b. Alton, Ill., Mar. 21, 1952; BA, Harvard U., 1974; JD, Cornell U., 1977. Bar: Ill. 1977, U.S. Dist. Ct. (no. dist.) Ill. 1977, Tex. 1982, U.S. Dist. Ct. (so dist.) Tex. 1988. Lectr. bus. law Northwestern Univ., Chg., Ill., 1979—80; v.p., gen. counsel Gulf Coast Royalty Co., Houston, 1981—82; atty. Mayer, Brown, Rowe & Maw LLP, Chgo., 1977—81, Houston, 1982—84, ptnr., 1984—, ptnr.-in-charge, 1995—. Lectr. Northwestern U., Chgo., 1979-80. Mem. State Bar Tex., Tex. Assn. Bank Counsel. Office: Mayer Brown Rowe & Maw LLP 700 Louisiana St Ste 3400 Houston TX 77002-2798 Office Phone: 713-546-0507. Office Fax: 713-632-1800. Business E-Mail: mniebruegge@mayerbrownrowe.com.

NIEBYL, JENNIFER ROBINSON, obstetrician, gynecologist, educator; BSc, McGill U., Mont., 1963; MD, Yale U., 1967. Diplomate Am. Bd. Ob-Gyn., Am. Bd. Maternal and Fetal Medicine. Intern in Internal Medicine N.Y. Hosp.-Cornell Med. Ctr., 1967-68, resident in ob-gyn., 1968-70, Johns Hopkins Hosp., Balt., 1970-73, fellow in maternal and fetal medicine, 1976-78, mem. staff, 1973—88, U. Iowa Hosps. and Clinics, Iowa City, 1988—; prof., head ob-gyn. dept. U. Iowa Sch. Medicine, Iowa City, 1988—2009, prof. ob-gyn. dept., 2009—. Mem. ACOG, Am. Gynecol. and Obstetrical Soc., Soc. Gynecol. Investigation, Soc. Maternal Fetal Medicine, Inst. Medicine of NAS. Office: U Iowa Hosps & Clinics 200 Hawkins Dr Iowa City IA 52242 Office Phone: 319-356-1976, 319-384-9247.

NIEBYLSKI, DIANNA C., Latin American and comparative literature professor; PhD, Brandeis U., Waltham, Mass., 1988. Asst. prof., Spanish and Humanities Earlham Coll., Ind., 1988—96; vis. prof. Latin Am. lit. U. Chgo., 1998—99; assoc. prof. Latin Am. lit. and social theory U. Ky., 1999—2004; dept. head U. Ill., Chgo., 2004—07, prof. Latin Am. & comp. lit, 2004—. Contbr. scientific papers on gender, humor, globalization and Latin Am. fiction; author: The Poem on The Edge of The Ward, 1991, Humoring Resistance, 1995, Rosarrio Force, 1996. Grant, Social Sci. Found., Nat. Endowment Humanities, 1997—98, Rsch. fellowship, Lilly Corp., 1986, 1988, 1990. Mem.: MLA, IAPL, AILFH, AJHS, ACLA. Office: Univ Ill Chgo S Morgan Chicago IL 60607 Personal E-mail: dcn@uic.edu.

NIED, STACEY JEAN, psychologist; b. Perth Amboy, NJ, May 15, 1966; EdD, Rutgers U., NB, NJ, 2004. Cert. sch. psychologist NJ, 2002. Clinician SERV Ctrs., East Brunswick, NJ, 1993—96; sch. psychologist Cambridge Elem. Sch., Kendall Pk., NJ, 2002—. Cons. Adv. dem. party Move on.org, Princeton, Plainsboro, NJ, 2008. Achievements include research in identity, self studies. Office: Cambridge Elem Sch 35 Cambridge Rd Kendall Park NJ 08824

NIEDERAUER, DUNCAN L., stock exchange executive; b. Sept. 7, 1959; married; 3 children. BA cum laude in Economics, Colgate U., 1981; MBA, Emory U., 1985. Joined Goldman Sachs & Co., 1985, with equities divsn., 1987, ran the Equities E-Commerce effort, global head of portfolio trading, and spent three years in Tokyo in Derivatives and Japanese products, mng. dir., 1997—2000, ptnr., 2000—07, relocated to the headquarters of Spear, Leeds & Kellogg, 2000; co-head equities divsn. execution services franchise The Goldman Sachs Group, Inc., 2005—07; pres., co-COO NYSE Group Inc., NYC, 2007; pres., co-COO, head US cash markets NYSE Euronext, Inc., NYC, 2007, CEO, dir., 2007—. Bd. dirs. EzeCastle Software, 2000—. Bd. trustees Colgate U. Mem.: Omicron Delta Epsilon. Office: NYSE Euronext Inc 11 Wall St New York NY 10005*

NIEDERAUER, GEORGE H., archbishop; b. LA, June 14, 1936; s. George and Elaine N. BA Philosophy, St. John's Seminary, Camarillo, CA, 1959; BA Sacred Theology, Catholic U., Washington, DC, 1962; MA English Lit., Loyola U., LA, 1962; PhD English Lit., USC, 1966. Ordained priest Archdiocese of LA, Calif., 1962; asst. pastor Our Lady of the Assumption Parish, Claremont, Calif., 1962—63; priest in residence Holy Name of Jesus Parish, Los Angeles, 1963—65; instr. English Lit. St. John's Seminary Coll., Camarillo, Calif., 1965—79; instr. of English Lit. Mt. St. Mary's Coll., Los Angeles, 1967—74; English Dept. chmn. St. John's Seminary Coll., Camarillo, 1968—77, spiritual dir., 1972—79; part-time instr. of Spiritual Theology St. John's Seminary Theologate, 1976—79, full-time instr. of Spiritual Theology, 1979—87; part-time instr. of English Lit. St. John's Seminary Coll., 1979—92; rector St. John's Seminary, 1987—92, spiritual dir., 1979—95; co-dir. Cardinal Manning House of Prayer for Priests, Los Angeles, 1992—95; ordained bishop, 1995; bishop Diocese of Salt Lake City, 1995—2005; archbishop Archdiocese of San Francisco, Calif., 2005—. Mem. Nat. Fedn. of Spiritual Dirs., pres., 1975—77; mem. bd. of the Comm. of Priests' Retreat Archdiocese L.A.; mem. select comm. for revision of U.S. Cath. Conf. "Program for Priestly Formation" 3rd edit.; mem. Vatican Visitation Team for Theologates; spkr. World Vision Internat., Fuller Theol. Sem., Calif. Lutheran Coll. Mem.: Camarillo Ministerial Assn., Western Assn. of Spiritual Dirs. (pres. 1973—75), Alpha Sigma Nu (Jesuit Honor Soc. - LMU chpt.). Roman Catholic. Avocations: classical music, stamp collecting/philately, reading, film appreciation. Office: The Roman Catholic Archdiocese of San Francisco One Peter Yorke Way San Francisco CA 94109

NIEDERHOFFER, ROY GARY, hedge fund manager; b. NYC, Mar. 21, 1966; s. Arthur and Elaine (Eisenberg) Niederhoffer. BS in Computational Neurosci., magna cum laude, Harvard U., 1987. Founder Software Innovations Co., NYC, 1980; co-founder Microvations, Inc., NYC, 1982, Niederhoffer Firester, Inc., NYC, 1989—; securities trader, v.p. NCZ Commodities, Inc., NYC, 1987—92; founder, pres. R.G. Niederhoffer Capital Mgmt., Inc., 1993—. Democrat. Jewish. Avocations: classical and jazz music, piano, violin, skiing. Office: RG Niederhoffer Capital Mgmt 1700 Broadway Fl 39 New York NY 10019 Business E-Mail: royn@niederhoffer.com.*

NIEDERHUBER, JOHN EDWARD, federal agency administrator; b. Steubenville, Ohio, June 21, 1938; s. William Henry and Helen (Smittle) Niederhuber; m. Tracey J. Williamson (dec. Dec. 2001); children: Elizabeth Ann, Matthew John. BS, Bethany Coll., W.Va., 1960; MD, Ohio State U. Coll. Medicine, 1964. Diplomate Am. Bd. Surgery. Intern surgery Ohio State U. Hosp., Columbus, 1964-65; vis. fellow divsn. immunology Karolinska Inst., Stockholm, 1970—71; resident surgery U. Mich. Med. Ctr., Ann Arbor, 1971—73, faculty, 1973—87, prof. surgery, prof. microbiolog/immunology, 1980-87, assoc. dean rsch., 1982—85, sr. assoc. dean med. sch., 1983—85, chief divsn. surg. oncology, 1983—86; vis. prof. molecular biology & genetics Johns Hopkins U. Sch. Med., Balt., 1986—87, prof. surgery, oncology, molecular biology & genetics, 1987-91; chief surgery Stanford U. Hosp., Calif., 1991-95; Emile Holman prof. surgery, chair dept. surgery, head sect. surg. scis. Stanford U. Sch. Medicine., 1991-95, prof. microbiology/immunology, 1991-97; asst. dean oncology, dir. Comprehensive Cancer Ctr. U. Wis. Sch. Medicine, Madison, 1997—2002, prof. surgery/oncology, 1997—2005; dep. dir. translational & clin. scis., COO Nat. Cancer. Inst. (NCI), NIH, Bethesda, Md., 2005—06; acting dir. Nat. Cancer Inst., NIH, 2006, dir., 2006—. Cons. Wayne County Gen. Hosp., Mich., 1973—84, Ann Arbor VA Hosp., 1973—87; vis. prof. Howard Hughes Med. Inst., Chevy Chase, Md. Mem. editl. bd. Jour. Immunology, 1981—85, Current Opinion in Oncology, 1989—95, Annals of Surgery, 1991—97, Surg. Oncology, 1991—, Jour. Clin. Oncology, 1993—95, Annals of Surg. Oncology, 1993—, The Oncologist, 1995—, Surgery, 1999—2004; contbr. articles to profl. jours., chapters to books. Mem. awards assembly GM Cancer Rsch. Found., 1988—92, 1998—2003; mem. rsch. adv. com. Burroughs-Wellcome Found., 1999—2006. Capt. US Army, 1965—67. Recipient Disting. Faculty Svc. award, U. Mich., 1978, Alumni Achievement award, Ohio State U. Coll. Medicine, 1989, Disting. Alumni award in medicine, Bethany Coll., 1989, Career Devel. award, USPHS. Fellow: ACS; mem.: Soc. Clin. Surgery, Am. Soc. Clin. Oncology, Am. Assn. Cancer Rsch., Soc. Surg. Oncology (v.p. 1999—2001, pres. 2001—02, 2001—03), Assn. Acad. Surgeons, Soc. Univ. Surgeons, Coller Surg. Soc., Am. Assn. Cancer Insts. (v.p. 1999—2001), Am. Soc. Transplant Surgeons, Am. Assn. Immunologists, Am. Surg. Assn., Transplantation Soc., Inst. Medicine. Avocations: golf, gardening. Office: Nat Cancer Inst NIH 6116 Exec Blvd Rm 3036A Bethesda MD 20892-2590 Business E-Mail: niederhj@mail.nih.gov.*

NIEDERMAN, JAMES CORSON, retired internist, educator; b. Hamilton, Ohio, Nov. 27, 1924; s. Clifford Frederick and Henrietta (Corson) N.; m. Miriam Camp, Dec. 12, 1951; children— Timothy Porter, Derrick Corson, Eliza Orton, Caroline Noble. Student, Kenyon Coll., 1942—45, DSc (hon.), 1981; MD, Johns Hopkins U., 1949. Intern Osler Svc. Johns Hopkins Hosp., Balt., 1949-50; asst. resident in medicine Yale-New Haven Med. Center, 1950-51, assoc. resident, 1953-55; med. ctr. practice specializing in internal medicine, infectious disease and clin. epidemiology New Haven, 1955-97; instr. Yale U., 1955-58, asst. prof., 1958-66, assoc. prof., 1966-76, clin. prof. medicine and epidemiology, 1976-97, emeritus clin. prof. medicine and epidemiology, 1997—, clin. prof. emeritus epidemiology and pub. health, 1998; mem. Nat. Coun. for Johns Hopkins Medicine. Trustee Kenyon Coll., 1974-97, trustee emeritus, 1997—; bd. counselors Smith Coll., 1970-77. Served to 1st lt. M.C. U.S. Army, 1951-53. Fellow Silliman Coll., Yale U. Fellow Am. Coll. Epidemiology; mem. Infectious Diseases Soc. Am., Am. Epidemiol. Soc., Johns Hopkins Med. and Surg. Assn.; mem. The Kenyon Rev. Bd. Trustees, Conn. Soc. Arts and Scis. Clubs: Yale (N.Y.C.); New Haven Lawn. Democrat. Episcopalian. Achievements include research in clin. epidemiology of Epstein Barr virus infections and demonstration of its causal relationship of infectious mononucleosis. Home: 429 Sperry Rd Bethany CT 06524-3544 Home Phone: 203-393-3538. Home Fax: 203-393-1902. E-mail: jcniederman@sbcglobal.net.

NIEDERMAN, MICHAEL STEVEN, physician, educator; b. NYC, Mar. 30, 1953; s. L. Louis and Betty Doris N.; m. Ronna Diane Kay, Aug. 15, 1976; children: Alex, Eric. AB, Boston U., 1974, MD, 1977. Intern Northwestern U. Med. Sch., Chgo., 1977-78, resident, 1978—80; pulmonary medicine fellow Yale U. Sch. Med., New Haven, 1980—83; dir. Med. ICU Winthrop U. Hosp., Mineola, NY, 1983—97, chief pulmonary and critical care medicine, 1997—99, chmn. dept. medicine, 1999—; assoc. prof., then prof. medicine SUNY, Stony Brook, 1990—. Dir. Microbiology Assembly, Am. Thoracic Soc., NYC, 1990—91. Editor: Respiratory Infections (textbook), 1994; editor-in-chief Clin. Pulmonary Medicine, 1994—; mem. editl. bd. Am. Jour. Respiratory and Cridical Care Medicine, 1994—, Chest, 1994—, Critical Care Medicine; contbr. numerous articles to profl. jours. Fellow ACP, Am. Coll. Chest Physicians (credentials com. 1991—), Coll. Critical Care Medicine; mem. Phi Beta Kappa, Alpha Omega Alpha. Avocations: skiing, tennis, golf, jazz music. Office: Winthrop Univ Hosp 222 Station Plz N Ste 509 Mineola NY 11501-3893 Office Phone: 516-663-2381. Business E-Mail: mniederman@winthrop.org.

NIEDERMAYER, SCOTT, professional hockey player; b. Edmonton, Alta., Can., Aug. 31, 1973; m. Lisa Niedermayer; children: Logan John, Jackson Robert, Joshua Leo, Luke Scott. Defenseman NJ Devils, 1991—2005, Anaheim Ducks (formerly Mighty Ducks of Anaheim), 2005—, capt., 2005—07, 2008—. Mem. Team Can., Olympic Games, Nagano, Japan, 1998, Salt Lake City, 2002, Team Can., World Cup of Hockey, 1996, 2004. Recipient James Norris Meml. Trophy, 2004, Mark Messier Leadership Award, 2006, Conn Smythe Trophy, 2007; named to All-Rookie Team, NHL, 1993, Second All-Star Team, 1998, First All-Star Team, 2004, 2006, 2007, NHL All-Star Game, 1998, 2001, 2004, 2007, 2008, 2009. Achievements include being a member of Stanley Cup Champion New Jersey Devils, 1995, 2000, 2003, Anaheim Ducks, 2007; being a member of gold medal winning Canadian Hockey Team, Salt Lake City Olympic games, 2002; being a member of World Cup Champion Team Canada, 2004. Office: c/o Anaheim Ducks 5695 E Katella Ave Anaheim CA 92806*

NIEHAUS, MICHAEL, application developer, consultant; b. Huntingburg, Ind., July 14, 1968; s. Thomas and Janice Niehaus; m. Alayna Kiesel; children: Anya, Grant. BS, Ball State U., Muncie, Ind., 1990. IT cons. Marathon Oil Co., Houston, 1990—2004; sr. software devel. engr. Microsoft, Redmond, Wash., 2004—. Office: Microsoft One Microsoft Way Redmond WA 98052 Business E-Mail: mniehaus@microsoft.com.

NIEHOFF, KARL RICHARD BESUDEN, finance company executive; b. Cin., May 11, 1943; s. Karl George and Jean (Besuden) N.; children: K. Richard B. Jr., Kelly B. BA, U. Cin., 1967. Corp. trust ops. officer 5th-3d Union Trust, Cin., 1968-74; v.p., gen. mgr. Sabina Water Co., Ohio, 1974-76; v.p., sec. Weil, Roth and Irving, Inc., 1974-76; co-mgr., mcpl. fin. dept. Thomson McKinnon Securities, Cin. and NYC, 1976—78; chmn. Cin. Stock Exch., Inc., Cin., 1975, pres., trustee, seat owner, 1976—89; exch. rep., founding mem. Consol. Quote, Consol. Tape Oper. Coms., 1979-90, alt., 1991-92; pres. Fin. Instruments Svcs. Corp., Cin., Chgo., London, 1985-90; sr. v.p. Trading, Trans. and Market Svcs. NASDAQ, Inc., 1990—92; v.p. D.E. Shaw & Co., NYC, 1992-94; pres. D.E. Shaw Securities, LLC, NYC, 1992—94; pres., mng. ptnr. Niehoff and Assocs., NYC, 1994-99; mng. dir., chief of party, developer MDTS OTC Capital Mkt. Devel. Project, Ceto (Subs. Warsaw Stock Exch., Warsaw, 1994—96; advisor Ministry Mass Privatization, Republic of Poland, Warsaw, 1994—96; v.p., dir. Third Market Trading Corp., Chicago, 1994-98; pres., dir. SBX Inc., Cin., Princeton, NJ, 1997-2000; mng. dir. trading and tech. Unified Mgmt. Corp., Indpls., 1999—2000; pres. VSX Techs. Inc., NYC, Indpls., 1999—2000, Mark Securities, Inc., Pelham Manor, NY, 2002—05; pres., CEO Webix, Inc., NYC, 2000—02; chmn. The X-Change Corp., NYC, 2002, pres., 2002; founder, chmn. US OTC Markets, Inc., NYC, 2005—; founder chmn. & CEO Altra Mark Inc., NYC, 2008—; dir., pres., sec., treas. Schuyler Pk. Manor Apts., Pelham Manor, NY, 2000—08; dir. Entrex, Inc., Chgo., 2006—. Witness US House Reps. Consumers Protection and Fin. Com., 1977, other gen. oversight, GAO com. panels and inquiries, 1987—94; panelist to numerous sec. divsn. conf., 1987—2009; v.p. Wit Capital Corp., NYC, 1998—99; pres., COO DSM-Wit, 1998—99; mem. Phila. Stock Exch., 1974—76, Cin. Stock Exch., 1974—89, trustee, 1974—90, chmn. bd. trustees, 1975; developer Nat. Securities Trading Sys., 1976—89; founding mem. dir. Composite Quote Sys., 1977—91, Consolidated Tape Operating Com., 1977—91; mem. trading com. Inter-Market, 1980—90; mem. chief execs. com. Stock Exch., 1988—90; mem. task force com. GLOBEX, 1988—89; founding charter mem. Easdaq, Brussels, 1994—96; vis. lectr. U. Cin. Coll. Bus. Adminstrn., Xavier U. Bus. Adminstrn. Coll., Cin.; long-term planning com. rep. Chgo. Bd. Options Exch., 1987—88; allied mem. NY Stock Exch., 1996—98, mem., 1997; pres. Digital Stock Market, NYC, 1998—99; vis. com. US Info. Agy., NYC, 1992—95; mng. dir. trading and tech. Unified Mgmt. Corp., Inc., Indpls., 1999—2000, NYC, 1999—2000; pres. WEBIX, Inc., 1999—2002; bd. dirs., audit com. Equity Analysts Mutual Funds, LLC, Cin., 2002—05; instl. trading com. Boston Stock Exch., instl. adv. com., 2004. Trustee, sec. Contemporary Arts Ctr., Cin., 1975-83; mem. Young Mens Mercantile Libr. Assn., 1974-90, adv. com., 1974-77; devel. com. Tangeman Gallery of Art, 1981-82; pres., dir. Bermuda High Condominium Assn., Delray Beach, Fla., 1999-06; mem. Boston Securities Traders Assn., 2000-05. Nominee, Great Living Cincinnatian, 2008. Mem.: Securities Traders Assn. NY (chmn. listed trading com. 1993, OTC Bull. Bd. 2002—04, com. chmn. STA trading subcom. 2002—04), India House, Keeneland Assn., Stone House Club, Queen City Mcpl. Bond Club (trustee 1974—80), Cin. Stock and Bond Club (trustee and 1st v.p. 1974—90), NY Athletic Club, NYAC Yacht Club (Pelham Manor), Nat. Arts Club, Phi Alpha Theta.

NIELSEN, ERLAND KOLDING, library director; b. Frederiksberg, Denmark, Jan. 13, 1947; s. Olav and Anna (Kolding) N.; m. Anne Birthe van Holck, 1969 (div. 1981); children: Gudrun, Jens Christian; m. Inger Sørensen, 1982. MA in History, PhD, U. Copenhagen, 1973. Lectr. Royal Sch. Librarianship U. Copenhagen, 1971-80, asst. prof. Inst Contemporary History, 1973-83, head dept. humanities and social scis., 1980-86, head Edn. Research Librarians and Documentalists Royal Sch. Librarianship, 1984-86; dir. gen. Royal Libr., Copenhagen, 1986—. Mem. Nat. Coun. of Librs., 1998—.; mem., chair evaluation coms. for appt. of nat. librarians and libr. dirs. in Scandinavia; mergers with 8 major/minor instns., 1990-2008 including Nat. Libr. Sci. Medicine. Author, editor 13 books in history and library sci.; contbr. articles to profl. jours. Mem. Internat. Fedn. Libr. Assns. and Instns. (sec. standing commn. for nat. librs., 1990-98, chmn. gen. rsch. librs. div., mem. profl. bd. 1991-93), Rsch. Librarian's Council (sec. 1975-79, chmn. 1979-82), Danish Rsch. Libraries Assn. (bd. dirs. 1987—2002, vice chair 1996-98, chair 1998-2002), Danish Libr. Assn. (mem. bd. dirs. 1990—), Adv. Council Rsch. Libraries (bd. dirs. 1987—), Conf. Dirs. Nat. Librarians (vice chair 2004-2008), Nat. Libr. Policy Bd., Conf. European Nat. Librs., Liber (exec. bd. dirs. 1994—, vice-chair 1999—, pres. 2003-2006), Arbeitsgemeinschaft Bibliotheca Baltica (bd. dirs. 1994-98), Arnamagnean Commn., Commn. Literary Sources Danish History (chair 1990—), Electronic Rsch. Libr. Denmark (bd. dirs. 1998—), Nat. Commn. on Export of Cultural Assets (bd. dirs. 1987—, chair 1995—) Danish Memory of the World Com. (chair 1997-). Home: Egholmsvej 1 DK-2830 Virum Denmark Office: Det Kongelige Bibliotek Postboks 2149 DK 1016 Copenhagen Denmark Home Phone: +4545853750; Office Phone: +4533474301. Personal E-mail: ekn@kb.dk.

NIELSEN, FORREST HAROLD, research nutritionist; b. Dancy, Wis., Oct. 26, 1941; s. George Adolph and Sylvia Viola (Blood) N.; m. Emily Joanne Currie, June 13, 1964; children: Forrest Erik, Kistin Emily. BS, U. Wis., 1963, MS, 1966, PhD, 1967. NIH grad. fellow, dept. biochemistry U. Wis., Madison, 1963-67; rsch. chemist, Human Nutrition Rsch. Inst. USDA, Beltsville, Md., 1969-70, rsch. chemist Human Nutrition Rsch. Ctr. Grand Forks, ND, 1970-86, ctr. dir. and rsch. nutritionist, 1986-2001, rsch. nutritionist, 2001—. Adj. prof. dept. biochemistry and molecular biology, U. N.D., Grand Forks, 1971—, speaker in field. Assoc. editor Magnesium and Trace Elements Jour., 1990-93; mem. editl. bd. Jour. Trace Elements in Exptl. Medicine, 1988—2004, Biol. Trace Element Rsch. Jour., 1979—, Jour. Nutrition, 1984-88, Biofactors, 1997—; contbr. articles to profl. jours. Capt. U.S. Army, 1967-69. Recipient Klaus Schwarz Commemorative medal and award Internat. Assn. of Bioinorganic Scientists; named Scientist of Yr. U.S. Dept. Agrl., 1993. Mem. Internat. Soc. Trace Element Rsch. in Humans (gov. bd. 1989—2007, pres. 1992-95), Soc. for Exptl. Biology and Medicine, Am. Soc. Nutrition (fellow), N.D. Acad. Sci. (pres. 1988-89), Internat. Bone and Mineral Soc., Sigma Xi (pres. U. N.D. chpt. 1976-77). Lutheran. Achievements include patent for use of Boron Supplements to Increase in Vivo Production of Hydroxylated Steroids; discovery of the nutritional essentiality of the trace elements boron and nickel. Office: USDA ARS GFHNRC 2420 2 Ave N Stop 9034 Grand Forks ND 58202-9034 Office Phone: 701-795-8455. Business E-Mail: forrest.nielsen@ars.usda.gov.

NIELSEN, GEORGE LEE, architect; b. Ames, Iowa, Dec. 12, 1937; s. Verner Henry and Verba Lucile (Smith) N.; m. Karen Wall, Feb. 28, 1959; children: David Stuart, Kristina, Melissa. B.Arch., Iowa State U., 1961; M.Arch., M.I.T., 1962. Registered arch., Mass., Ohio, N.Y., Ill., Ind., Ky., Miss., Kans., Colo., Mich., Nat. Coun. Archtl. Registration Bds. Designer Perry, Shaw, Hepburn & Dean, Boston, 1961-64, F.A. Stahl & Assos., Cambridge, Mass., 1964-65; project architect Peirce & Pierce, Boston, 1965-70; project mgr. A.M. Kinney Assos., Cin., 1970—, partner, 1978—; sec. A.M. Kinney Assocs., Inc., Ill., 1993—, also dir. Cin.; v.p. A.M. Kinney Inc., Cin., 1992-94, pres., 1994-99, also dir.; sr. prin. A.M. Kinney Inc. Assocs., 1999—. Architect prin. works include Avco Rsch. Lab., Cin. Children's Hosp. Med. Ctr., Square D. Corp., Nalco Chem. Co., Olin Corp., Mead Johnson/Bristol Myers Squib, Cin. Gas and Elec. Co., Novartis Pharm. Corp., Hoechst Celanese, Hoechst Marion Roussel, Martek Bioscis., Witco Corp., Sotheby's, Shell Chem. Co., Bayer Corp., U. Ky. Biomed./Biol. Scis. Rsch. Bldg., U. Ky. Chandler Med. Ctr. Patient Care Facility, Wright Patterson Environ. Hazzards Bldg. and Edwards AFB Sci. Rsch. Bldg. With US Army, 1962—64. Mem.: AIA (design awards 1970—71, 1974, 1978, 1981, 1991, 1994, 1995, 2001, 2002). Episcopalian. Home: 5680 Windridge View Cincinnati OH 45243-2518 Office: A M Kinney Inc 150 E 4th St Fl 6 Cincinnati OH 45202-4131 Home Phone: 513-321-4995; Office Phone: 513-421-2265.

NIELSEN, JAKOB, computer interface engineer; b. Copenhagen, Oct. 5, 1957; arrived in U.S., 1990, naturalized, 2001; s. Gerhard and Helle (Hofner); m. Hannah Kain, Feb. 18, 1984. MS in Computer Sci., Aarhus U., Denmark, 1983; PhD in Computer Sci., T.U. of Denmark, 1988. Rsch. fellow Aarhus U., 1983-84; vis. scientist IBM User Interface Inst., Yorktown Heights, NY, 1985; adj. asst. prof. T.U. Denmark, Lyngby, 1986-90; mem. rsch. staff Bell Comm. Rsch., Morristown, NJ, 1990-94; disting. engr. Sun Microsystems, Mountain View, Calif., 1994-98; principal Nielsen Norman Group, Fremont, Calif., 1998—. Author: Hypertext and Hypermedia, 1990, Usability Engineering, 1993, Multimedia and Hypertext: The Internet and Beyond, 1995, Designing Web Usability: The Practice of Simplicity, 2000, Homepage Usability: 50 Websites Deconstructed, 2001, Prioritizing Web Usability, 2006; editor: Coordinating User Interfaces for Consistency, 1989, Designing User Interfaces for International Use, 1990, Usability Inspection Methods, 1994, International User Interfaces, 1996; mem. editl. bd.: Behavior and Info. Tech., 1989—, Hypermedia Jour., 1989—95, Interacting with Computers, 1989—, Internat. Jour. Human-Computer Interaction, 1989—, Internat. Jour. Man-Machine Studies, 1991—94, ACM Networker, 1997—2000, Personal Technologies, 1997—2004; contbr. articles to profl. jours. Mem.: Assn. for Computing Machinery (papers co-chair internat. conf. 1993, editl. bd. Networker 1997—2000, spl. interest group on computer human interaction). Achievements include holder 79 patents in field; founding of discount usability engineering approach; invention (with R. Molich) of heuristic evaluation method for cost-effective improvement of user interfaces; demonstration (with T.K. Landauer) that user testing and heuristic evaluation both follow same mathematical model; definition of the parallel design method for rapidly exploring user interface alternatives; patents for.

NIELSEN, JENNIFER LEE, molecular ecologist, researcher; b. Balt., Mar. 21, 1946; d. Leo Jay and Mary Marriott (Mules) N.; divorced; children: Nadja Wilson, Allisha Ochs MFA, Ecole des Beaux Arts, Paris, 1968; BS, Evergreen State Coll., 1987; MS, U. Calif., Berkeley, 1990,

PhD, 1994. Artist, Seattle, 1969-78; fish biologist Weyerhaeuser Co., Tacoma, 1978-89; resource cons. Berkeley, 1989-90; rsch. biologist USDA-Forest Svc., Albany, Calif., 1990-99; vis. scientist Stanford U., Pacific Grove, Calif., 1994-99; supr. fisheries Alaska Sci. Ctr., Anchorage, 1999—. Rsch. assoc. Calif. State U. Mosslanding Marie Sta., 1995-99; adj. prof. integrated biology U. Calif., Berkeley, 1998; adj. prof. U. Alaska, Fairbanks, 1999—, U. Alaska Anchorage, 2001-; supervisory rsch. fishery biologist U.S. Geol. Svc., Alaska Sci. Ctr., Anchorage, 1999—. Editor-in-chief: Reviews in Fish Biology and Fisheries, 1999—; editor: Evolution and the Aquatic Ecosystem, 1995, Advisory Editor Environment Biology of Fishes, 1998—; contbr. over 100 articles to profl. jours.; paintings exhibited at Metro. Mus. Modern Art, 1966; represented in numerous pvt. collections, U.S. and Europe. Mem. Am. Fisheries Soc. (pres. chpt. 1993-94, genetics sect. pres. 1999-2001, pres. 2007), Molecular Marine Biology and Biotech. (regional editor 1995), Animal Behaviour Soc. (policy com. 1993-94). Avocations: painting, cooking, gardening, skijoring. Office: USGS Alaska Sci Ctr 4210 University Dr Anchorage AK 99508 Home: 18365 E Twin Hills In Sutton AK 99674 Office Phone: 907-786-7062. Business E-Mail: jlnielson@usgs.gov. E-mail: jennifer_nielsen@usgs.gov.

NIELSEN, KENNETH RAY, academic administrator; b. Oct. 15, 1941; s. Frank and Elinor (Hansen) N.; children: Elizabeth, Mary. BEd, U. Wis., Whitewater, 1965; MS, U. Wis., Stout, 1966; EdD, U. Wyo., 1968. Dir. student activities Cornell U., Ithaca, N.Y., 1968-72; adminstr., prof. Tchr. Tng. Coll., San Juan, P.R., 1974-77; v.p. student affairs Northland Coll., Ashland, Wis., 1972-77; v.p. student life Seattle U., 1977-84; pres. Coll. St. Mary, Omaha, 1984-96, Woodbury U., Burbank, Calif., 1996—. Bd. dirs. Boy Scouts Am., Girl Scouts U.S.A., Nat. Coun. Christians and Jews, Providence Hosp. Found.; chmn. edn. sect. United Way Bd.; mem. Gov.'s Community Svcs. and Continuing Edn. Mem. Am. Coun. Edn., Am. Assn. Higher Edn., Am. Assn. Univ. Adminstrs., Coun. Ind. Colls. Roman Catholic. Avocations: reading, exercise. Office: Woodbury U 7500 N Glenoaks Blvd Burbank CA 91504-1099

NIELSEN, LESLIE, actor; b. Regina, Sask., Can., Feb. 11, 1926; s. Ingvard and Maybelle Nielsen; m. Monica Bayar, 1950 (div. 1955); m. Sandy Ullman, 1958 (div.); children: Thea, Maura; m. Brooks Nielsen, 1981 (div. 1983). Student, Neighborhood Playhouse, NYC. Former announcer, disk jockey, Can. radio; feature films include The Vagabond King, 1956, Forbidden Planet, 1956, Ransom!, 1956, The Opposite Sex, 1956, Hot Summer Night, 1957, Tammy and the Bachelor, 1957, Night Train to Paris, 1964, Harlow, 1965, Dark Intruder, 1965, Beau Geste, 1965, Gunfight in Abilene, 1967, The Reluctant Astronaut, 1967, Rosie, 1967, Counterpoint, 1967, Dayton's Devils, 1969, How to Commit Marriage, 1969, Change of Mind, 1969, The Resurrection of Zachary Wheeler, 1971, The Poseidon Adventure, 1972, Viva, Knievel, 1977, City of Fire, 1979, Airplane!, 1980, Wrong is Right, 1982, Creepshow, 1983, Spaceship, 1983, Soul Man, 1986, The Patriot, 1986, Nuts, 1987, Nightstick, 1987, Home Is Where the Hart Is, 1987, The Naked Gun, 1988, Dangerous Curves, The Repossessed, The Naked Gun 2 1/2: The Smell of Fear, 1991, All I Want for Christmas, 1991, Surf Ninjas, 1993, The Naked Gun 33 1/3: The Final Insult, 1994, Rent-a-Kid, 1995, Dracula: Dead and Loving It, 1995, Spy Hard, 1996; Family Plan, 1997, Mr. Magoo, 1997, Wrongfully Accused, 1998, 2001: A Space Travesty, 1999, Camouflage, 2001, Kevin of the North, 2001, Men with Brooms, 2002, Scary Movie 3, 2003, Scary Movie 4, 2006, Music Within, 2007, Superhero Movie, 2008; TV films include Crime Syndicated, 1952, Man Behind The Badge, 1954, See How They Run, 1964, Shadow Over Elveron, 1968, Hawaii Five-O, 1968, Companions in Nightmare, 1968, Trial Run, 1969, Deadlock, 1969, Night Slaves, 1970, The Aquarians, 1970, Hauser's Memory, 1970, Monty Nash, 1971, They Call It Murder, 1971, Incident in San Francisco, 1972, Snatched, 1973, The Letters, 1973, Can Ellen Be Saved?, 1974, Brinks! The Great Robbery, 1976, Little Mo, 1978, miniseries Back Stairs At the White House, 1979, Institute For Revenge, 1979, Ohms, 1980, The Night The Bridge Fell Down, 1980, Murder Among Friends, 1982, Cave-In, 1983, Blade in Hong Kong, 1985, The Loner, Fatal Confession: A Father Dowling Mystery, Chance of a Lifetime, 1991, Harvey, 1996, Mr. Willowby's Christmas Tree, 1995, Safety Patrol, 1998, Santa Who?, 2000, Noël Noël, 2003; numerous other TV appearances including dramatic series Studio One, Armstrong Circle Theater, Goodyear Playhouse; TV series include The New Breed, 1961, The Bold Ones, 1963-67, Peyton Place, 1965, Bracken's World, 1969-70, Shaping Up, 1984, Police Squad, 1982, The Golden Girls, 1992, (voice) Pumper Pups, 2000, Liography, 2001, Zeroman, 2004; toured country in one man show Darrow, 1979; co-author: The Naked Truth, 1993. With Can. Air Force, WWII. Office: c/o Sandy Bresler Bresler Kelly & Assocs 11500 W Olympic Blvd #352 Los Angeles CA 90064

NIELSEN, MARK FRANCIS, lawyer; b. Racine, Wis., Feb. 16, 1954; s. John Harvey and Kathleen Margaret (Rooney) N.; m. Alice Margrite Shuman, Apr. 28, 1984 (div.). BA, U. Wis., Parkside, 1976; JD, Harvard U., 1979. Bar: Wis. 1979, U.S. Dist. Ct. (ea. and we. dists.) Wis. 1979. Asst. dist. atty. Racine (Wis.) County, 1979-82; assoc. Schwartz Weber & Tofte, Racine, 1982-83; ptnr. Schwartz Tofte & Nielsen, Ltd., Racine, 1989—. Ct. commr. Racine Cir. Ct., 1987—; judge Mcpl. Ct., 2006-. Contbr. articles to profl. jours. Bd. dirs. Racine County Dem. Party, 1979-80, 86-88. Mem. Wis. Bar Assn., Nat. Criminal Def. Lawyers Assn., Assn. Trial Lawyers Am., Wis. Criminal Def. Lawyers Assn. (pres. 1999-2000, dir. Milw. 1986—), NBTA. Unitarian Universalist. Office: Schwartz Tofte & Nielsen Ltd 4d 704 Park Ave Racine WI 53403-1234 Office Phone: 262-637-9655. Office Fax: 262-637-3448. Business E-Mail: mark@stnlaw.com.

NIELSEN, MORTEN ØRREGAARD, economics professor; b. Herning, Denmark, Nov. 14, 1976; arrived in U.S., 2003; s. Jens Ørregaard and Inga Irene Skytte Nielsen. BS in Econs., U. Aarhus, Denmark, 1998, MSc in Econs., 2001, PhD in Econs., 2003; MSc in Econometrics and Math. Econs., London Sch. Econs. and Polit. Sci., 1999. Postdoctoral rsch. fellow Dept. Econ. U. Aarhus, Denmark, 2003—03; asst. prof. economics Dept. Econ. Cornell U., Ithaca, NY, 2003—08; assoc. prof., economics Queen's U., Kingston, Ont., Canada, 2008—, Stephen J.R. Smith faculty fellow, 2008—. Contbr. articles to profl. jours. Mem.: Inst. Math. Stats., Am. Econ. Assn., Econometric Soc. Office: Queen's Univ Economics Dept Dunning Hall 94 University Ave Kingston ON K7L 3N6 Canada

NIELSEN, NANCY H., health organization executive, medical educator; b. Elkins, W.Va., 1942; m. Don Nielsen; 5 children. BA, W.Va. U., 1964; MS in Microbiology, Cath. U., 1967, PhD in Microbiology, 1969; MD, SUNY Medicine and Biomedical Scis., Buffalo, 1976. Past chief med. officer NY State Dept. Health Western Region; former pres. med. staff Buffalo Gen. Hosp.; asst. dean med. edn., clin. prof. medicine U. Buffalo Sch. Medicine and Biomed. Sci., Buffalo; apptd. to serve US Dept. Health and Human Svcs. Adv. Com. on Regulatory Reform, 2002; assoc. med. dir. for quality, interim chief med. officer Independent Health Assn., NY, chief med. officer NY; clin. prof. medicine, sr. assoc. dean med. edn. Sch. Medicine and Biomedical Scis., U. Buffalo. Bd. dir. Med. Liability Mut. Ins. Co., Kaleida Health, Nat. Patient Safety Found.; former trustee SUNY; former mem. Commn. for the Prevention of Youth Violence, Task Force on Quality and Patient Safety. Bd. dirs. Nat. Patient Safety Found. Recipient Samuel P. Capen award, U. Buffalo Alumni Assn., 1996. Fellow: ACP; mem.: AMA (vice spkr. Ho. of Dels. 2000—03, spkr. Ho. of Dels. 2003—07, pres.-elect 2007—08, pres. 2008—, bd. trustee, former mem. Coun. on Sci. Affairs, del. med. sch. sect., liaison to the Coun. on Med. Edn.), Inst. Medicine (Consumer Empowerment Com. of America's Health Information Cmty., Roundtable on Evidence Based Medicine), NY State Soc. Internal Medicine (bd. dir.), Med. Soc. State of NY (spkr. ho. dels. 1995—2000), Erie County Med. Soc. (former pres.). Office: AMA 515 N State St Chicago IL 60610 also: U Buffalo Sch Medicine And Biomedical Scis 40 Biomedical Education Bldg Buffalo NY 14214 Business E-Mail: nielse@buffalo.edu.*

NIELSEN, NIELS CHRISTIAN, JR., retired religious studies educator; b. Long Beach, Calif., June 2, 1921; s. Niels Hansen and Frances (Nofziger) N.; m. Erika Kreuth, May 10, 1958; children: Camilla Regina, Niels Albrecht. BA, George Pepperdine Coll., LA, 1942; BD, Yale U., 1946, PhD, 1951. Ordained to ministry Meth. Ch., 1946. Pastor Woodbury (Conn.) Meth. Ch., 1944-46; instr. religion Yale U., New Haven, 1948-51; faculty Rice U., Houston, 1951—, J. Newton Rayzor prof. religious studies, prof. emeritus, 1991—; Amax presdl. prof. humanities Colo. Sch. Mines, Golden, 1982-83. Author: Philosophy and Religion in Contemporary Japan, 1957, Geistige Landerkunde USA, 1960, A Layman Looks at World Religions, 1962, God in Education, 1966, Solzhenitsyn's Religion, 1975, The Religion of Jimmy Carter, 1977, The Crisis of Human Rights, 1978, Religions of the World, 1982, Revolutions in Eastern Europe: The Religious Roots, 1991, Fundamentalism, Mythos and World Religions, 1993; editor: Religion After Communism in Russia, 1994, God in the Obama Era, 2009: president's religion & ethics from Washington to Barack Obama 2009; contbr. articles to profl. jours. Mem. Am. Acad. Religion, Am. Philos. Soc., Am. Soc. Study Religion (sec. 1977-89), Soc. European Culture, Soc. for Values in Higher Edn. Democrat. Home and Office: 2424 Swift Blvd Houston TX 77030-1806 Office Phone: 713-667-0783. Business E-Mail: niels@rice.edu.

NIELSEN, PAUL DOUGLAS, engineering executive, retired military officer; s. Jack Alton and Shirley Mae (Gillette) N.; m. Dorothy Webb Spragins, May 3, 1975. BS in Physics and Math., USAF Acad., 1972; MS in Applied Sci., U. Calif., Davis, 1973, PhD in Plasma Physics, 1981; MBA, U. N.Mex., 1977; postgrad., Nat. War Coll., 1988-89. Physicist Nat. Security Agency Ft. George G. Meade, Md., 1973—75; space sys. procurement officer nuc. techs. Air Force Weapons Lab., Kirtland AFB, N.Mex., 1975—77; sys. programs mgmt. officer nuc. techs. Air Force Sys. Command, Andrews AFB, Md., 1977—78, aide to comdr., 1977—78; space sys. procurement mgmt. officer Hdqrs. AFSC, Andrews AFB, Md., 1978; mil. rsch. assoc. Dept. Energy Lawrence Livermore Nat. Libr., 1978—81; asst. chief advanced sys., chief Satellite Attitude Control br., Satellite Engring. divsn., sec. Air Force Office Spl. Projects, L.A. Air Force Sta., Calif., 1981—84; sys. program dir. electronics sys. divsn. Command Ctr. Processing and Display Sys. Replacement Program, Hanscom AFB, Mass., 1984—85; sys. program dir. Space Def. Ops Ctr., 1985—87; chief engr. Strat. Sys. Deputate, ESD, Hanscom AFB, Mass., 1987—88; mil. asst., col. Office of Asst. Sec. Def., Washington, 1989-92; comdr. Rome Lab., Griffiss AFB, 1992-95; command dir. Cheyenne Mountain Ops. Ctr., Cheyenne Mountain Air Sta, Colo., 1995—96, chief ops., 1996-97; brig. gen., dir. plans N.Am. Aerospace Def. Command, Peterson AFB, Colo., 1997-99; vice comdr. Aero. Systems Ctr., AFMC, Wright-Patterson AFB, Ohio, 1999-2000; comdr. Air Force Rsch. Lab., Wright-Patterson AFB, 2000—04; CEO, dir. Software Engring Inst. Carnegie Mellon U., Pitts., 2004—. With USAF, 1972, ret. USAF, 2004, 2d lt., 1972, 1st lt., 1974, capt., 1976, major, 1981, lt. col., 1986, col., 1989, brigadier gen., 1997, major gen., 2001. Decorated Def. Superior Svc. medal with oak leaf cluster, Meritorious Svc. medal with two oak leaf clusters, Disting. Svc. medal, Legion of Merit, Def. Meritorious Svc. medal; fellow Hertz Found., Livermore, Calif., 1972-73, 78-81. Fellow AIAA (Hap Arnold award 2002, pres., 2007-08), IEEE; mem. Armed Forces Comm. and Electronics Assn., Air Force Assn. Office: Software Eng Inst Carnegie Mellon Univ 4500 Fifth Ave Pittsburgh PA 15213-3890 Home: 30 Wedgewood Ln Pittsburgh PA 15215-1560 Office Phone: 412-268-7740. Business E-Mail: nielsen@sei.cmu.edu.

NIEMAN, VALERIE GAIL, writer, language educator, journalist; b. Jamestown, NY, July 6, 1955; d. Warner Ernest and Eleanor A. (Aiken); m. Jack Hobbs. Student, Jamestown CC, NY, 1975—76; BS in Journalism, W.Va. U., Morgantown, 1978; MFA in Creative Writing, Queens U., Charlotte, NC. Staff writer W.Va. U News Svc., Morgantown, W.Va., 1978; reporter Dominion Post, Morgantown, 1978, Times West Virginian, Fairmont, W.Va., 1979-92, city editor, 1992-95, exec. editor, 1995-97; asst. city/state editor News & Record, Greensboro, NC, 1997—2004; instr. dept. journalism and mass comm. NC A&T State U., Greensboro, 2000—04, asst. prof. English, journalism, 2004—09, 2009—, assoc. prof., 2009—. Tchr. basic newswriting W.Va. U., Morgantown, 1990, tchr. sci. fiction writing, 1995; lectr., vis. writer tri-state area, 1988-1997; co-founder, co-dir. Kestrel Writers Conf., Fairmont, 1993-97; dir. HBCU Nat. Newspaper conf., 2006, instr. John C. Campbell Folk Sch., Brasstown, NC, 2008-. Author: (novel) Neena Gathering, 1988, Survivors, 2000, (short story collection) Fidelities, 2004, (poetry chpts.) How We Live, 1996, Slipping Out of Old Eve, 1988, (poetry collection) Wake Wake Wake, 2006; founding co-editor: Kestrel lit. jour., Fairmont, 1992-1997, poet facilitator Life Verse, 2009. W.Va. cir. writer W.Va. Humanities Commn., 1994; mem. Leadership Marion, Fairmont, 1995-96. Recipient award in letters Fairmont Arts and Humanities, 1988, 94, Elizabeth Simpson Smith prize, 1998, 2002, Greg Grummer award in poetry George Mason U., 1999, others; fellow in poetry NEA, 1991, fellow in fiction Ky. Found. for Women, 1991, fellow in fiction W.Va. Commn. on Arts, 1992. Mem.: NC Writers Conf., NC Writers Network (instr. 2007—), Am. Sailing Assn., Lake Townsend Yacht Club (chmn Mayor's Cup Regatta 2006, 2009). Democrat. United Ch. Of Christ. Avocations: gardening, hiking, travel, sailing. Office: NC AT&T State U 1601 E Market St Greensboro NC 27411 Business E-Mail: vgnieman@ncat.edu.

NIEMANN, JUDITH A., vocalist, educator; b. Kans. City, Mo., Aug. 13, 1937; d. Jordan E. and Mildred B. Hooton; m. Marvin L. Wenz, Aug. 3, 1957 (div. July 1978); m. Chester S. Niemann, Jr., Mar. 16, 1980; children: Laura, Dan, Scott, Sheryl, Austin, Shaun. MusB, U. Iowa, 1974. Cert. Bds. Edn. Ky, Fla. Music tchr. Jefferson County Bd. Edn., Louisville, 1974—79, St. Lucie County Bd. Edn., Ft. Pierce, Fla., 1979—86, Volusia County Bd. Edn., DeLand, Fla., 1986—89, Ind. River Sch. County, Vero Beach, Fla., 1986—, hon. guest condr., 1985—; choir dir. Meth. Ch., Vero Beach, 1980—82, First United Meth. Ch., DeLand, 1987—2006; voice instr. Daytona State Coll, Fla., 1989—, guest condr., 2007. Mem. Ky. HS Athletic Assn., 1974—79, Fla. Music Edn. Assoc., 1979—89, Music Educators Nat. Conf., 1979—89, Nat. Assn. Tchrs. Singing; co-developer, Internat. Baccalaureate Curriculum Music Volusia County, 1986; dir. Ch. Choirs, DeLand, 2004, DeLand Symphony Chorus, 2006—07. Exhibited in group shows at Louisville Opera, Ky., one-woman shows include Tri-City Symphony, Iowa, U. Iowa, Louisville Youth Orchestra, Dayton Beach Symphony, Fla., Bel Canto Chorus, Daytona, Daytona Beach Coll. Soloist DeLand Benefit Program, Various Chs. Orgn., Iowa, Ky., Fla. Avocations: reading, music, flower arranging, writing. Office: Daytona State Coll 1200 Internat Speedway Blvd Daytona Beach FL 32120 Office Phone: 386-504-4682.

NIEMEIER, CHARLES D., non-profit corporation administrator, accountant; b. 1956; BBA, Baylor U.; JD, Georgetown U. Bar: 1995. Ptnr. Williams & Connolly LLP, Washington, 1988—99; chief acct. enforcement divsn., co-chair fin. fraud task force Securities & Exch. Commn. (SEC), 1999—2002; mem. Pub. Co. Acctg. Oversight Bd. (PCAOB), 2002—, acting chmn., 2003. Office: Pub Co Acctg Oversight Bd (PCAOB) 1666 K St NW Washington DC 20006-2803 Office Phone: 202-207-9100. Office Fax: 202-862-8430.*

NIEMETH, CHARLES FREDERICK, lawyer; b. Lorain, Ohio, Nov. 25, 1939; s. Charles Ambrose and Christine Cameron (Mollison) N.; m. Anne Marie Meckes, Oct. 12, 1968. BA, Harvard U., 1962; JD, U. Mich., 1965. Bar: Calif. 1966, N.Y. 1984. Assoc. O'Melveny & Myers, Los Angeles, 1965-72, ptnr., 1973—2005, Baker & McKenzie, NYC, 2005—. Mem. leadership com. Corp. Fund of Lincoln Ctr. Mem. nat. com. Mich. Law Sch. Fund; trustee Challengers Boys and Girls Club, 1968-83; mem. bus. adv. coun. UCLA, 1979-83; mem. exec. com. Internat. Student Ctr., 1979-83; bd. dirs. Olympic Tower Condominium, 1986-92, N.Y. Philharm.; bd. visitors Mich. Law Sch., mem. Tri-Bar Opinion Com. Mem. Riviera Tennis Club, Regency Club, N.Y. Athletic Club, Field Club (Greenwich, Conn.), Harvard Club (NYC). Democrat. Roman Catholic. Home: 70 Oneida Dr Greenwich CT 06830-7131 Office: Baker & McKenzie 1114 Avenue of the Americas New York NY 10036 Home Phone: 203-622-9312; Office Phone: 212-891-3568. E-mail: charles.f.niemeth@bakernet.com.

NIEMEYER, PAUL VICTOR, federal judge; b. Princeton, NJ, Apr. 5, 1941; s. Gerhart and Lucie (Lenzer) Niemeyer; m. Susan Kinley, Aug. 24, 1963; children: Jonathan K., Peter E., Christopher J. AB, Kenyon Coll., 1962; student, U. Munich, Federal Republic of Germany, 1962—63; JD, U. Notre Dame, 1966. Bar: Md. 1966, US Dist. Ct. Md. 1967, US Ct. Appeals (4th cir.) 1968, US Supreme Ct. 1970, US Dist. Ct. (so. dist.) Tex. 1977, US Ct. Appeals (5th cir.) 1978, US Ct. Appeals (3d cir.) 1980. Assoc. Piper & Marbury, Balt., 1966—74, ptnr., 1974—88; US dist. judge US Dist. Ct. Md., Balt., 1988—90; cir. judge US Ct. Appeals (4th cir.), Balt., 1990—. Lectr. advanced bus. law Johns Hopkins U., Balt., 1971—75; lectr. Md. Jud. Conf., Md. Ct. Clks. Assn.; sr. lecturing fellow in appellate advocacy Duke U. Sch. of Law, 1994—; mem. standing com. on rules of practice and procedure cts. appeals, 1973—88; atty. grievance com.-hearing panel, 1978—81; select com.-profl. conduct, 1983—85; adv. com. on Fed. Rules of Civil Procedure, 1993—2000; chmn., 1996—2000. Author: (book) A Path Remembered, 2006; co-author: Maryland Rules Commentary, 1984, 3d. edit., 2003, Maryland Rules Commentary supplement, 1988; contbr. articles to profl. jours. Recipient Spl. Merit citation, Am. Judicature Soc., 1987. Fellow: Am. Law Inst., Md. Bar Assn. (Disting. Svc. award litigation sect. 1981), Md. Bar Found., Am. Bar Found., Am. Coll. Trial Lawyers; mem.: Lawyers' Round Table, Wednesday Law Club. Republican. Episcopalian. Office: US Cir Ct Md US Courthouse 101 W Lombard St Ste 910 Baltimore MD 21201-2611*

NIEMEYER, SANDRA KAY, retired secondary school educator; b. New Hampton, Iowa, July 25, 1940; d. Wilbert R. and Irene F. (Perske) Remley; m. John Niemeyer, June 3, 1962 (div. Jan. 1981); children: Rebecca Jones, Rachel Herold. BA in English, Wartburg Coll., 1962; MA in English, Iowa State U., 1976; postgrad., U. SC, 1984-87, Southern Univ., 1994. Cert. secondary English educator, SC, Iowa. Tchr. art, speech, French Ocheyedan (Iowa) HS, 1962-63; tchr. basic English Des Moines Area C.C., Ankeny, 1973-76; activities dir. Mitchell Village Care Ctr., Mitchellville, 1981-83; English educator Holly Hill (SC) Roberts High, 1983—2003; freelance writer ACT, 2002—04; ret., 2003. Freelance writer, materials developer, Ankeny, 1975-81; presenter in-strnl. media workshop Santa Clara U. Ext., Mason City, Iowa, 1975; SAT tutor, 1992—; tchg. cons. Stepens Correctional Inst., Columbia, SC, 1986. Vol. Friends of Libr.; tutor Adult Literacy Coun. Fellow Ctr. for Excellence in Writing, Coastal Carolina U., Conway, SC, 1993. Mem. ASCD, Nat. Coun. Tchrs. English, Palmetto State Tchrs. Assn. Lutheran. Avocations: travel, reading, antiques.

NIEMI, ALBERT WILLIAM, JR., economics professor; b. Worcester, Mass., Aug. 30, 1942; s. Albert William and Helen Josephine (Powers) N.; m. Maria de Sano, Feb. 4, 1967; children: Albert III, Edward. AB, Stonehill Coll., 1964; MA, U. Conn., 1965, PhD, 1969. Asst. prof. Terry College of Bus., U. Ga., Athens, 1968-71, assoc. prof., 1971-75, prof., 1975—96, dir. rsch., 1975-96, assoc. dean, 1976-78, chmn. dept. econs., 1981-82, acting dean, 1982-83, dean, 1983—96; dean Coll. Bus. Adminstrn. U. Ala., Birmingham, 1996—97; dean, Tolleson Chair in bus. leadership Edwin L. Cox Sch. Bus., So. Meth. U., 1997—. Author: State and Regional Patterns in American Manufacturing, 1974, Gross State Product and Productivity in the Southeast, 1975, U.S. Economic History, 1975, 80. Mem. exec. com., bd. dirs. World Affairs Coun. of Dallas; mem. internat. adv. coun. Greater Dallas C. of C.; bd. mem. Children's Med. Ctr.; adv. coun. Cath. Found.; pres. coun. Dallas Ctr. for Performing Arts; bd. trustees Stonehill Coll. Mem. Assn. for Univ. Bus. and Econ. Rsch. (sec. 1982-84, pres. 1986), Am. Econ. Assn., Econ. History Assn., So. Econ. Assn., Athens Area C. of C., Beta Gamma Sigma, Phi Kappa Phi, Delta Epsilon Sigma. Office: So Meth U Cox Sch Bus Fincher Bldg, Rm 200 PO Box 750333 Dallas TX 75275 Office Phone: 214-768-3012.

NIEMI, JANICE, retired lawyer, state legislator, judge; b. Flint, Mich., Sept. 18, 1928; d. Richard Jesse and Norma (Bell) Bailey; m. Preston Niemi, Feb. 4, 1953 (div. 1987); children: Ries, Patricia. BA, U. Wash., 1950, LLB, 1967; postgrad., U. Mich., 1950-52; cert., Hague Acad. Internat. Law, The Netherlands, 1954. Bar: Wash. 1968. Assoc. firm Powell, Livengood, Dunlap & Silverdale, Kirkland, Wash., 1968; staff atty. Legal Svc. Ctr., Seattle, 1968-70; judge Seattle Dist. Ct., 1971-72, King County Superior Ct., Seattle, 1973-78; acting gen. counsel, dep. gen. counsel SBA, Washington, 1979-81; mem. Wash. State Ho. of Reps., Olympia, 1983-87, chmn. com. on state govt., 1984; mem. Wash. State Senate, 1987-95; sole practice Seattle, 1981-94; superior ct. judge King County, 1995-2000; chief criminal judge, 1997-2000; ret., 2000; mem. Wash. State Gambling Commn., 2002—08. Mem. White Ho. Fellows Regional Selection Panel, Seattle, 1974—77, chmn., 1976, 77; incorporator Soudn Savs. & Loan, Seattle, 1975. Bd. visitors dept. psychology U. Wash., Seattle, 1983—87, bd. visitors dept. sociology, 1988—98; mem. adv. bd. Tacoma Art Mus., 2008—; mem. Wash. State Gender and Justice Commn., 1987—89; Bd. dirs. Allied Arts, Seattle, 1971—78, Ctr. Contemporary Art, Seattle, 1981—83, Women's Network, Seattle, 1981—84, Pub. Defender Assn., Seattle, 1982—84; Artist's Trust, 2002—05. Named Woman of Yr. in Law, Past Pres.'s Assn., Seattle, 1971, Woman of Yr., Matrix Table, Seattle, 1973, Capitol

Hill Bus. and Profl. Women, 1975. Mem. Wash. State Bar Assn., Wash. Women Lawyers, Am. Arbitration Assn. (panel 2003—). Democrat. Home: PO Box 20516 Seattle WA 98102-1516 Personal E-mail: janicen@aol.com.

NIEMI, RICHARD GENE, political science educator; b. Green Bay, Wis., Jan. 10, 1941; s. Eugene H. and Dorothy M. (Stevens) N.; m. Shirley A. Gill, Aug. 4, 1962; children: Nancy, Patricia, Jennifer, Julie. BA, Lawrence Coll., 1962; PhD, U. Mich., 1967. Asst. prof. polit. sci. U. Rochester, NY, 1967-71, assoc. prof. NY, 1971-75, prof., 1975—99, disting. grad. tchg. prof. NY, 1983-86, chmn. dept. polit. sci. NY, 1979-83, assoc. dean NY, 1986-89, sr. assoc. dean NY, 1989-91, Watson prof. NY, 1999—, now assoc. dept. chair and dir. undergraduate studies NY. Vis. prof. U. Lund, Sweden, 1974, 81, U. Iowa, 1985; vis. rschr. Kobe U., Japan, 1991. Co-author (with M. Kent Jennings): (political science book) The Political Character of Adolescence, 1974; author: Generations and Politics, 1981, How Generations Perceive Each Other, 1974; co-author (with others): Minority Representation and the Quest for Voting Equality, 1992; co-author: (with Jane Junn) (Education Book) Civic Education: What Makes Students Learn, 1998; co-author: (with others) (Political Science Book) Term Limits in the States, 1999; co-editor (with Harold Stanley): (Polit. Sci. Book) Vital Statistics on American Politics, 2003, 9th edit.; co-editor: (with Herbert Weisberg) (Politic. Sci. Book) Controversies in Voting Behavior, 2001; co-editor: (Polit. Sci. Book) Comparing Democracies, 1996, 2d edit, 2002; co-author: Trends in Public Opinion. Grantee, NIMH, 1969—70, Ford Found., 1972—73, NSF, 1974—77, 1980—86, 1994—, Am. Ednl. Rsch. Assn., 1997—98, U.S. Dept. Edn., 1997—99, 2001—02; fellow, Guggenheim Found., 1983—84, Ctr. for Advanced Study in Behavioral Sci., 1989. Fellow Am. Acad. Arts & Scis.; mem. Am. Polit. Sci. Assn., Phi Beta Kappa. Lutheran. Home: 45 Boniface Dr Rochester NY 14620-3333 Office: U Rochester Dept Polit Sci Rochester NY 14627-0146 E-mail: niemi@rochester.edu.

NIEMIEC, DAVID WALLACE, investment company executive; b. Midland, Mich., Dec. 17, 1949; s. George G. and Eleanor (Yack) N.; m. Melanie Taveau Mason, Oct. 4, 1975; children: Elizabeth Street, Margaret Johnson. AB, Harvard U., 1972, MBA, 1974. Assoc. Dillon, Read & Co., Inc., NYC, 1974-78, v.p., 1979-81, sr. v.p., chief adminstrv. officer, 1982-83, mng. dir., chief adminstrv. officer, 1984-97, vice chmn., 1991-97; mng. dir. Saratoga Ptnrs., NYC, 1998—2001, adv., 2001—. Bd. dirs. Emeritus Corp., Seattle, OSI Pharms., Melville, NY; bd. dirs., trustee Templeton Funds, Ft. Lauderdale. Trustee Nightingale-Bamford Sch., N.Y.C., 1993-2004; bd. govs. The Mannes Coll. of Music, N.Y.C., 1996—. Mem. Union Club N.Y.C. Republican. Unitarian Universalist. Office: Saratoga Ptnrs 535 Madison Ave New York NY 10022-4212 Office Phone: 212-906-7044.

NIEMIEC, EDWARD WALTER, retired professional association executive; b. Detroit, Nov. 1, 1936; s. Walter A. and Mary N.; m. Nancy M. Bennett, Aug. 25, 1962; children: Lisa, Julie, Brenda. BS, U. Detroit, 1959, MBA, 1961. With Paine Webber Jackson & Curtis, NYC, 1959-80, exec. v.p., dir. adminstrv. divsn., to 1980; v.p., bd. dirs. Moseley, Hallgarten, Estabrook, Weeden, Inc., 1980-82; also bd. dirs. Moseley, Hallgarten, Estabrook & Weeden Holding Corp.; pres., CEO, dir., mem. exec. com. Securities Settlement Corp. (subs. The Travelers 1982), NYC, 1980-87; pres., dir. Inc. Trading Co. subs. Instinet Corp., 1988-89; COO Instinet Corp. subs. Reuters Holdings Plc., 1988-89; group v.p. AICPA, NYC, 1989—2001. Served with U.S. Army. Roman Catholic.

NIENSTEDT, JOHN CLAYTON, archbishop; b. Detroit, Mar. 18, 1947; s. John and Elizabeth S. (Kennedy) N. BA, Sacred Heart Sem., 1969; BST, Pontifical Gregorian U., 1972; Licentiate in Sacred Theology, Pontifical Inst. of St. Alphonsus, 1977, DST, 1985. Ordained deacon North Am. Coll., Rome, 1972; deacon intern Sacred Heart Parish, Dearborn, Mich., 1973-74, priest, 1974; ordained priest Archdiocese of Detroit, Mich., 1974, vicar gen., 1979—80, aux. bishop, so. region, 1996—2001; assoc. pastor Guardian Angels Ch., Clawson, Mich., 1974-76; sec. to Cardinal John Dearden, 1977-80; prof. moral theol. St. John Provincial Sem., Plymouth, Mich., 1977—78; apptd. minor official of 2nd grade Vatican Secretariate of State, 1980-85; temporary assoc. pastor St. Regis Parish, Birmingham, Mich., 1986; pastor St. Patrick's Parish, Union Lake, Mich., 1986-87; rector Sacred Heart Major Sem., Detroit, 1988—94, asst. prof. moral theol., 1988—2000; pastor Shrine of the Little Flower parish, Royal Oak, Mich., 1994—96; ordained bishop, 1996; bishop Diocese of New Ulm, Minn., 2001—07; coadjutor archbishop Archdiocese of Saint Paul & Mpls., Minn., 2007—08, archbishop, 2008—. Weekend assoc. pastor St. Fabian's Parish, Farmington Hills, Mich., 1977, Our Lady of Sorrow's Parish, Farmington, 1978-80; mem. med. moral com. Mich. Conf. for Cath. Health Facilities, 1977-80; asst. chaplain Baby Jesus Hosp., Rome, Italy 1980-83; chaplain Bros. of Holy Cross assigned to Notre Dame High Sch. for Boys, Rome, 1981-84; instr. religion First Eucharist Program Marymont Internat. Sch., 1980-83; adj. prof. moral theology Orchard Lake Schs., 1986; bd. trustees Madonna Coll., 1989-94, trustee com. acad. affairs, 1989—; mem. Midwest/Western Rector's Conf., 1987—, Wranglers, 1986-90, Archdiocesan Med. Moral Com., 1987; trustee, Cath. Relief Soc., 2005-. Contbr. articles to profl. jours. Apptd. a Chaplain to His Holiness by Pope John Paul II bearing title Monsignor, 1985, a Prelate of Honor by Pope John Paul II, 1990. Mem. Cath. Theol. Soc. Am., Assn. Gov. Bds. of U. and Colls. (workshop theol. sch. trustees, chief execs. Cin. chpt. 1989), Midwest Assn. Theol. Schs. (ann. participation 1988, 89, 90), Assn. Am. Colls. (ann. participation 1990). Roman Catholic. Office: Archdiocese of St Paul & Mpls 226 Summit Ave Saint Paul MN 55102-2197

NIEPORENT, DREW A., restaurant owner; b. NYC, June 4, 1955; m. Ann Nieporent; children: Andrew, Gabrielle. BS in Hotel Mgmt., Cornell U., 1977. Mgmt. Maxwell's Plum, NYC, Tavern On The Green, NYC, Le Périgord, NYC, La Grenouille, NYC, Le Plaza Athénée, NYC; owner Montrachet, NYC, 1985—; co-owner Tribeca Grill, NYC, 1990—; pres., owner Myriad Restaurant Group, NYC, 1993—, Nobu, NYC, Next Door Nobu, NYC, Nobu 57, NYC, Centrico, NYC, Crush Wine and Spirits, NYC, Pulse, NYC, The Coach House, NYC. Guest lectr. Cornell U., NYU, NYC, Syracuse U., New Eng. Culinary Inst., NY Restaurant Assn., New Sch., NYC; dir. American Inst. of Wine and Food. Hon. co-chairperson, master ceremonies Starfish Found., 1995; co-chair Share Our Strength's Taste Nation, NYC, 1997—99; guest honor Tourette Syndrome Assn. Dinner, 1997; culinary chair Momentum Project; hon. chair City Harvest Food Coun.; bd. dirs. Citymeals on Wheels. Recipient Gates Jerusalem medal, Israel Bonds, 1994, Outstanding Svc. award, James Beard Found., 1995, Outstanding Restaurateur award, 2009; named Man of the Yr., Food Beverage Assn., 1993, Humanitarian of the Yr., James Beard Found., 2000, Restaurateur of the Yr., Bon Appetit Mag., 2000. Mem.: Am. Inst. Wine and Food (bd. dirs.). Office: Myriad Restaurant Group 180 Franklin St New York NY 10013 Office Phone: 212-219-9500. Office Fax: 212-219-2380.*

NIESEN, JAMES LOUIS, theater director; b. St. Louis, Feb. 15, 1946; s. James Louis and Emily Elise (Brennecke) N. BFA, Ill. Wesleyan U., 1968; MFA, Ohio U., 1974. Actor Stage South, Columbia, S.C., 1974-75, Long Wharf Theatre, New Haven, 1977-78, Geva Theater, Rochester, N.Y., 1978-79; freelance dir., 1980-83; stage mgr. Roundabout Theater, NYC, 1982-83; artistic dir. Irondale Ensemble Project, NYC, 1983—. Panelist N.Y. Found. on the Arts, N.Y., 1988-89. Author: (book) Game Guide, 1988; contbr. articles to profl. jours.; dir. (play) St. Joan of the Stockyards, 1993, Danton's Death, 1994, You Can't Win, 1994, Andrew Carnegie Presands the Jew of Malta, 1996, The Mother, 1997, Degenerate Art, 1998, The Murals of Rockefeller Center, 2002, The Pope and the Witch, 2000, Brecht on Brecht, 2000, Jungle of Cities, 2001, Peter Pan, 2001, Seuss Centennial Tour, 2004, Outside the Law, 2004, Wasted 2005, 9/11 Voices 2007, Great American Allister Traveling War Medicine 2008, RT Greene 2009. Mem. Actors Equity Assn. Avocations: folk music, country music, tennis. Home: 419 Pacific St Brooklyn NY 11217-2204 Office: Irondale Ensemble Project 85 S Oxford St Brooklyn NY 11217 Office Phone: 718-488-9233. Personal E-mail: jim@irondale.org.

NIETO, ANGELICA BAYLON, principal, educator; b. El Paso, Jan. 17, 1957; d. Roberto Baylon and Teresa Provecio; m. Oscar Rene Nieto, Aug. 7, 1981; children: Cassandra Nieto Licon, Oscar Rene. BE, U. Tex., El Paso, MEd, 1979. Cert. in principalship Tex., 2001. Mentor tchr. spl. edn. programs Ysleta Ind. Sch. Dist., spl. edn. tchr., 1979—93, facilitator spl. edn. programs, 2001—04, coord. spl. edn. programs, 2003—05, prin., 2005—; exec. dir. spl. edn., 2009—; principal, 2005—08. Named Tchr. of Yr., Ysleta Ind. Sch. Dist., 1978, Tech. Prin. of Yr., YISD Instrnl. Tech., 2006—07. Home: 1649 Dick Ritter El Paso TX 79936 Office: Robert F Kennedy Pre-K Acad 9009 Alameda El Paso TX 79907 Office Phone: 915-434-0903. Office Fax: 915-860-7530. Business E-Mail: anieto@yisd.net. E-mail: angelica.nieto@sbcglobal.net.

NIETO, JUAN MANUEL, emergency medicine physician; b. Alpine, Tex., Sept. 24, 1949; s. Edmundo Miguel and Socorro; children: Ana Raquel, Cristina Marie. BS, U. Notre Dame, 1970; MD, U. Colo., 1974. Intern LA County, U. So. Calif. Med. Ctr., 1974-75; physician Cmty. Health Found., LA, 1975-77; physician emergency dept. Physicians Med. Group, Marina Del Ray, Calif., 1977-78; resident in emergency medicine Denver Gen.-St. Anthony Hosp. Sys., 1978-80; mem. staff North Colo. Med. Ctr., Greeley, 1980-83; emergency physician, med. dir. emergency dept. Brackenridge Hosp., Austin, Tex., 1984-85; practice medicine Austin, 1983—. Emergency physician Emergency Physicians Affiliates, 1986-89; assoc. prof. U. Tex. Health Sci. Ctr., San Antonio, 1994—; mem. planning com. Starflight Helicopter Air Transport, 1985; instr. advanced cardiac life support, 1977; bd. dirs. Nat. Chicano Health Orgn., 1971-74; advisor East Los Angeles Hypertension Screening Program, 1978; med. advisor Weld County Ambulance Service, 1980-83; med. dir. Air Life, 1980-83; med. dir. Alamo Heights Emergency Med. Svc., 1988-90, med. dir. AMR Ambulance, 1991-98; amb. Nat. Health Svc. Corps, 2003—. Del. Colo. Med. Soc., 1983. Fellow: Nat. Hispanic Med. Assn., Am. Acad. Emergency Medicine, Am. Coll. Emergency Physicians, NYU Wagner Sch. (leadership fellow 2001); mem.: APHA, Nat. Hispanic Medicine Assn., Soc. Academic Emergency Medicine, Physicians for a Nat. Healthcare Program, Nat. Hispanic Med. Assn., Travis County Med. Soc., Tex. Med. Assn., Nat. Hispanic Med. Assn. (leadership fellow, advisor, board mem. 2001—, mem. adv. bd. 2003—, Leadership award 2006), Amnesty Internat. Office Phone: 210-358-2078. Personal E-mail: jnietomd@sbcglobal.net, juan-nieto@msn.com.

NIETO, LOU, food products executive; b. Tex. BA, U. Chgo., 1977; MBA, Harvard U. Bus. Sch. Adminstrn. Intern Am. Nat. Bank, Chgo.; packaged foods assoc. Quaker Oats Co.; sr. mktg. and strategy assoc. Dean Foods Co., Mission Foods Corp., LA, Kraft Foods, Inc.; pres., CEO Federated Group, Inc.; pres. packaged meats and deli ConAgra Foods, Inc., 2005—06, pres. consumer foods refrigerated bus., 2006—. Bd. dirs. Ryder Sys., Inc. Mem. vis. com. U. Chgo. Recipient Stars award, Hispanic Alliance Career Advancement, 2007. Office: Conagra Foods Inc 215 W Diehl Rd Naperville IL 60563-1278 Office Phone: 630-512-1000.

NIETO HERNÁNDEZ, MARÍA DE LA PURIFICACIÓN, language educator; d. José Nieto Hernández and Catalina Hernández Hernández; m. David Konstan, Aug. 12, 1994. Profl. degree in music, Conservatory of Valladolid, Spain, 1982; BA in Classics, MA in Classics, U. Salamanca, Spain, 1982, PhD in Classics, 1990. Asst. prof. Greek U. Salamanca, 1987—93, assoc. prof. Greek, 1993—94; classics lectr. Brown U., Providence, 1998—2007, sr. classics lectr., 2007—. Dir. grad. study, dept. classics Brown U., 2007—. Contbr. articles to profl. jours. Bd. bd. Fraternity the Love and Peace Christ, Salamanca, 1978—81; founder Fraternity the Most Holy Christ the Redeemer, Salamanca, 1984, sec. of the bd. dirs., 1984—91. Grantee Spl. Rsch. grant, Spanish Ministry Edn. & Sci., 1983—86, Summer Stipend grant, Goethe Inst., 1985. Mem.: Soc. Homeric Studies, Classical Assn. New Eng., Am. Philol Assn., Spanish Soc. Classical Studies (sec. treas. Salamanca sect. 1990—94). Roman Catholic. Avocations: walking, reading, cooking. Office: Brown Univ Box 1856 Providence RI 02912 Business E-Mail: pura_nieto@brown.edu.

NIEUWENDYK, JOE, professional sports team executive, retired professional hockey player; b. Oshawa, Ontario, Can., Sept. 10, 1966; m. Tina Nieuwendyk; children: Kaycee, Tyra, Jackson. Attended, Cornell U., 1984—87. Center Calgary Flames, 1987—95, Dallas Stars, 1995—2002, NJ Devils, 2002—03, Toronto Maple Leafs, 2003—05, Fla. Panthers, 2005—06, spl. cons. to gen. mgr., 2007—08; spl. asst. to gen. mgr. Toronto Maple Leafs, 2008—09; gen. mgr. Dallas Stars, 2009—. Mem. Team Can., Olympic Games, Nagano, Japan, 1998, Salt Lake City, 2002. Recipient Dodge Ram Tough Award, 1988, Calder Meml. Trophy, NHL, 1988, King Clancy Meml. Trophy, 1995, Conn Smythe Trophy, 1999; named Ivy League Rookie of Yr., 1985, NHL Rookie of Yr., Sporting News, 1988; named to East First All-American Team, NCAA, 1986, 1987, First-Team All-Conference Team, ECAC, 1986, 1987, All-Rookie Team, NHL, 1988, NHL All-Star Game, 1988—90, 1004. Achievements include being a member of Stanley Cup Champion Calgary Flames, 1989, Dallas Stars, 1999, New Jersey Devils, 2003; being a member of gold medal Canadian Hockey team, Salt Lake City Olympic Games, 2002. Office: Dallas Stars 2601 Avenue of the Stars Frisco TX 75034*

NIEUWSMA, MILTON JOHN, writer, journalist; b. Sept. 5, 1941; s. John and Jean (Potter); m. Marilee Gordon, Feb. 1, 1964; children: Jonathan, Gregory, Elizabeth. BA, Hope Coll., Holland, Mich., 1963; postgrad., Wayne State U., 1963—65; MA, U. Ill., 1978. Pres. Trans. Am. Syndicate, Inc., Chgo., 1988—97; vis. prof. Rutgers U., New Brunswick, NJ, 1990—95, St. Xavier U., Chgo., 1996—97. Author: Kinderlager, 1998, Surviving Auschwitz, 2005, Second Chance, 2009; writer, co-prodr.: Children of The Shoah, PBS, 2005 (2 Emmy awards, 2006), Defying Hitler, 2006; contbg. editor: Chgo. Tribune, L.A. Times, others. Recipient Hope Coll. Disting. Alumni award, 2009. Home: 2421 Central-Idlewood Beach Holland MI 49424-2277

NIEVAR, ANGELA M., social sciences educator; d. William Haywood and Nadean Jones; m. Billy Wayne Nievar, Dec. 27, 2002; children: Richard William Casady, Margaret Jean Casady, Robert Lee Casady. PhD in Family and Child Ecology, Mich. State U., E. Lansing, 2004. Cert. family life educator Nat. Coun. Family Rels., 2008. Rsch. asst. Mich. State U., 2001—03; asst. prof. U. N.Tex., Denton, 2004—. Mem. Cmty. Workgroup for Devel. Nat. Child Care Accreditation Stds., 1997—98. Contbr. articles to profl. jours. Unit commr. Boy Scouts Am., Denton, 2005—08, cub scout commr. North Tex., 2008—; bd. mem. Family Outreach Am., Denton, 2005—06. Recipient Legislative Advocacy Recognition award, Gov. Michael Leavitt, Utah Assn. Edn. Young Children, and Utah Office Child Care, 1998; grantee Rsch. Grant, Timberlawn Psychiatric Found., 2007—08. Mem.: Soc. Rsch. Human Devel. (conf. registration chair 2005—06), Soc. Rsch. in Child Devel., Tex. Coun. Family Rels. (bd. mem.-at-large 2007—), Nat. Coun. Family Rels., Am. Ednl. Rsch. Assn. (webmaster counseling and human devel. divsn. 2007—). Mem. Lds Ch. Office: Univ N Tex 1155 Union Cir #311335 Denton TX 76203 Office Fax: 940-565-2185. Business E-Mail: angela.nievar@unt.edu.

NIEWIAROSKI, TRUDI OSMERS (GERTRUDE), social studies educator; b. Jersey City, Apr. 30, 1935; d. Albert John and Margaret (Niemeyer) Osmers; m. Donald H. Niewiaroski, June 8, 1957; children: Donald H., Donna, Margaret Anne, Nancy Noel. AB in History and German, Upsala Coll., East Orange, NJ, 1957; MEd, Montgomery County Pub. Schs., Rockville, Md., 1992. Cert. tchr. Md. Tchr. geography Colego Americano, Quito, Ecuador, 1964-66; bd. dirs. Cotopaxi Acad., Quito, 1964-65; tchr. speed reading Escuela Lincoln, Buenos Aires, Argentina, 1966-67; substitute thcr. Montgomery County Pub. Schs., Rockville, 1978-83, tchr. social studies, 1984—. Del. Eisenhower People to People Educators' Del. Vietnam, 1993; pres. Fulbright Meml. Fund Program, 1997; resident tchg. fellow Russia-Ukraine Excellence in Tchg. Program, 1997; resident scholar in Korea The Korea Soc., 1999; Ethiopia site visit Global Poverty Project, 2007. Author curricula; contbr. chpts. to books, articles to profl. jours.; lectr. at workshops. Bd. dirs. Cotopaxi Acad., Quito, 1964-65; pres. Citizens Assn., Potomac, Md., 1977-81; leader Girl Scouts U.S., 1975-76; adv. coun. Milken Found; pres. Fulbright Meml. Fund Program Japan Alumni, 1999-. Recipient Md. Tchr. of Yr. award State of Md. Edn. Dept., 1993, finalist nat. Tchr. of Yr., 1993, Disting. Alumni award Upsala Coll., 1993, Nat. Educator award Milken Found., 1994, Summer Fellowship Korean Studies Program, 1999, Joseph Malone fellowship Sultanate of Oman, 2003, Goethe Inst. fellowship, Germany, 2003; Fulbright fellow, India, 1985, China, 1990, Japan Keizai Koho Ctr. fellow, 1992, Fulbright Meml. Fund Tchr. Program fellow, Japan, 1997, Fulbright fellow, South Africa, 2001, Malone fellow, Oman, 2003, U. Tex. Mideast Inst. fellow, 2005; UMBC-U. Mex. Art and Culture scholar, 1995; mem. Cuba Study Tour, 2004, Dar Al Islam Study Tour, Iran, 2004; fellow U. Pitts. and Freeman Found., China, 2004; Fulbright fellow, China, 2004; Egypt fellow U. Tex. Middle East Inst., 2005. Fellow Korea Soc. (Fellowship to North aand South Korea); mem. AAUW, ASCD, Nat. Coun. Social Studies, Md. Coun. for Social Studies, Asia Soc., Smithsonian Instn., Montgomery County Hist. Soc., Spl. Interest Groups-China, Japan and Korea, Md. Bus. Roundtable for Edn., Nat. Social Studies Suprs. Assn., Kappa Delta Pi. Achievements include first American teacher group to visit North Korea. Avocations: cake and cookie decorating, travel. Office: R Montgomery High Sch Rockville MD 20852 Home Phone: 301-847-7999. Personal E-mail: trudi222@comcast.net. Business E-Mail: trudi_niewiaroski@fc.mcps.k12.md.us.

NIFFENEGGER, AUDREY ANNE, artist, writer; b. South Haven, Mich., June 13, 1963; BFA, Art Inst. Chgo., 1985; MFA, Northwestern U., Evanston, Ill., 1991. Prof. Columbia Coll. Chgo. Ctr. Book & Paper Arts, 1995—. Faculty North Shore Art League, Winnetka, Ill. Author: (novels) The Time Traveler's Wife, 2003 (Publishers Weekly bestseller, NY Times bestseller), (graphic novels) The Three Incestuous Sisters, 2005, The Adventuress, 2006, (short stories) The Night Bookmobile, 2004, Jakob Wywialowski and the Angels, 2004, Prudence: The Cautionary Tale of a Picky Eater, 2006. Office: Columbia Coll Chgo Books & Paper Ctr 1104 S Wabash Rm 200 600 S Mich Ave Chicago IL 60605 Business E-Mail: aniffenegger@popmail.colum.edu.*

NIGAM, HEMANSHU, lawyer, Internet company executive; BA in Polit. Theory, Wesleyan U., Conn., 1987; JD, Boston U. Sch. Law, 1990. Dep. district atty. LA County Dist. Atty. Office, 1990—97; trial atty., criminal divsn. US Dept. Justice, Washington, 1997—2000; v.p., dir. worldwide internet enforcement Motion Picture Assn./Motion Picture Assn. Am., 2000—02; corp. atty., criminal compliance, security & law enforcement affairs, digital integrity group, Microsoft law and corp. affairs Microsoft Corp., Redmond, Wash., 2002—06, dir., consumer security outreach and child safe computing; chief security officer, MySpace.com News Corp., NYC, 2006—. Spkr. in field. Mem.: Washington State Bar Assn., Calif. State Bar Assn. Achievements include being a proven leader in online safety and security; served as a federal prosecutor against Internet child exploitation for the US Department of Justice; an advisor to a Congressional commission on online child safety; an advisor to the White House on cyber stalking. Office: News Corp 1211 Avenue of Americas 8th Fl New York NY 10036

NIGH, JOSEPH AARON, lawyer; B in Psychology, Ohio State U., Columbus, 2001, JD, 2004. Ptnr. Nigh & Zeidan LLC, Columbus, Tyack, Blackmore & Liston Co., LPA, Columbus. Office: Tyack Blackmore and Liston Co LPA 536 S High St Columbus OH 43215 Office Phone: 614-221-1341. Business E-Mail: jnigh@tblattorneys.com.

NIGHTINGALE, BARBRA LYNNE, English language educator, poet; b. Chgo., Aug. 6, 1949; d. Arthur Alfred and Jeri Louise (Smith) Evans; divorced; 1 child, Kimberly Beth. AA, Delgado Jr. Coll., New Orleans, 1974; BS in Health Adminstrn., Fla. Internat. U., 1980; MA in English, Fla. Atlantic U., 1985; EdD in Higher Edn., Fla. Internat. U., 1991. Assoc. prof. English Broward C.C., Pembroke Pines, Fla., 1983—. Advisor south campus Phi Theta Kappa, Pembroke Pines, 1988—; coord. south campus Honors Inst., Pembroke Pines, 1992—. Author: (book of poetry) Lovers Never Die, 1981, Prelude to a Woman, 1986, Lunar Equations, 1993. Recipient Grand prize poetry Nat. Fedn. of State Poetry Socs., 1991. Mem. NEA, Hannah Kahn Poetry Found. (pres. 1994—). Avocations: reading, travel, antique collecting. Home: 2231 N 52nd Ave Hollywood FL 33021-3310 Office: Broward Community Coll 7200 Pines Blvd Pembroke Pines FL 33024-7225

NIGHTINGALE, EDMUND JOSEPH, clinical psychologist, educator, consultant; b. St. Paul, Jan. 10, 1941; s. Edmund Anthony and Lauretta Alexandria (Horejs) N.; m. Marie Arcara, Apr. 9, 1978 (dec. April 1992); 1 child, Edmund Bernard. Student, Nazarath Hall Prep. Sem., 1959—61; AB, St. Paul Sem., 1963; AB magna cum laude, Cath. U. Louvain, Belgium, 1965, MA, 1967, STB cum laude, 1967; postgrad., U. Minn., 1971; MA, Loyola U., Chgo., 1973, PhD of Clin.

Psychology, 1975. Lic. clin. psychologist, Ill., Minn., cert. Nat. Registry Health Svc. Providers in Psychology; diplomate clin. psychology Am. Bd. Profl. Psychology. With Cath. Archdiocese St. Paul and Mpls., 1967—73; intern clin. psychology Michael Reese Hosp. and Med. Ctr., Chgo., 1973—74; with West Side VA Hosp., Chgo., 1974—75; staff psychologist Student Counseling Ctr., Loyola U., Chgo., 1975; staff psychologist, clin. coord. inpatient unit Drug Dependency Treatment Ctr., 1975—80; chief psychology VA Med. Ctr., Danville, Ill., 1980—86, VA Med. Ctr. Mpls., 1986—2006; ret., 2006; cons., 2006—. Mem. pers. bd. Archdiocese St. Paul and Mpls., 1968-70; lectr. psychology, Loyola U., Chgo., 1975; asst. professorial lectr. psychology, St. Paul Xavier Coll., Chgo., 1975-78; adj. asst. prof. psychology in psychology, Abraham Lincoln Sch. Medicine, Med. Ctr. U. Ill., Chgo., 1977-82; adj. prof. psychology Purdue U., 1981-87; asst. prof. psychology Med. Sch., U. Minn., 1987—, clin. assoc. prof. psychology Coll. Liberal Arts, 1986-90; adj. asst. prof., 1990—; clin. asst. prof. U. Ill. Sch. Medicine, Urbana/Champaign, 1982-87; mem. grad. faculty counseling psychology Ind. State U., Terre Haute, 1983-86 Founding editor: Louvain Studies, 1966; editor: VA Dir. Psychology Staffing and Svcs., 1982, 83, 84, 85, 87; ad hoc reviewer, editl. bd. 2008-, Psychol. Svcs., 2006-. Bd. dirs. Inst. Postgrad. Studies, Ill. Psychol. Assn Recipient Exemplary Career award, US Dept. VA, 2006. Fellow APA (clin. psychology, psychotherapy, pub. svc., psychol. hypnosis, fellow Trauma Psychology, sec. treas. pub. svc. 1990-91, coun. reps. 1999-2004, pres. elect pub. svc. 2006, pres. pub. svc. 2007-08, past pres., 2008-09, mem. com. on accreditation, 2006-07, fellowship com. 2008-, Karl F. Heiser Presdl. award for Adv. 2002, divsn. Psychologists Pub. Svc. Disting. Contbns. award 2002); mem. AAAS, Am. Psychol. Soc., Assn. for Advancement Psychology, Ill. Psychol. Assn. (clin. psychology and acad. sects., sec. 1982-83, pres.-elect 1983-84, pres. 1984-85), Am. Group Psychotherapy Assn., Am. Soc. Clin. Hypnosis, Minn. Psychol. Assn. (pub. svc.- pres. 1997-99), Eagle Scout, Assn. VA Chief Psychologists (sec., treas. 1987-90, pres.-elect 1990-91, pres. 1991-92, past pres. 1992-93, Outstanding Leadership award 1992), Minn. Soc. Clin. Hypnosis (bd. dirs. 1999-2001), ULLR Found. (bd. dirs. 2004-, pres. 2006-08), Nat. MS Soc. (bd. trustees, Minn. chpt., 2005-). Home: 28 W Marie Ave West Saint Paul MN 55118 Business E-Mail: night002@umn.edu.

NIGHTINGALE, ELENA OTTOLENGHI, pediatric geneticist, academic administrator, educator; b. Livorno, Italy, Nov. 1, 1932; arrived in U.S., 1939, naturalized; d. Mario Lazzaro and Elisa Vittoria (Levi) Ottolenghi; m. Suart L. Nightingale, July 1, 1965; children: Elizabeth, Marisa. AB summa cum laude, Barnard Coll., 1954; PhD, Rockefeller U., 1961; MD, NYU, 1964. Asst. prof. Cornell U. Med. Coll., NYC, 1965—70, Johns Hopkins U., Balt., 1970—73; fellow in clin. genetics and pediat. Georgetown U. Hosp., Washington, 1973—74; sr. staff officer NAS, Washington, 1975—79, sr. program officer Inst. Medicine, 1979—82, sr. scholar-in-residence, 1982—83; spl. advisor to pres. Carnegie Corp. N.Y., NYC, 1983—94, sr. program officer, 1989—94; scholar-in-residence Inst. of Medicine, NAS, Washington, 1995—. Vis. assoc. prof. Harvard Med. Sch., Boston, 1980—84, vis. lectr., 1984—95; adj. prof. pediat. Georgetown U. Med. Ctr., 1984—, George Washington U. Med. Ctr., 1994—; mem. recombinant DNA adv. com. NIH, Bethesda, Md., 1979—83. Editor: The Breaking of Bodies and Minds: Torture, Psychiatric Abuses and the Health Professions, 1985, Prenatal Screening, Policies and Values: The Example of Neural Tube Defects, 1987, Promoting the Health of Adolescents: New Directions for the 21st Century, 1993, Adolescent Risk and Vulnerability: Concepts and Measurement, 2001; co-author: Before Birth: Prenatal Screening for Genetic Disease, 1990; contbr. numerous sci. articles to profl. publs. Bd. dirs. Amnesty Internat., U.S.A., Washington, 1989—91, Ctr. for Youth Svcs., Washington, 1980—84, Sci. Svc., Inc., Washington, 1985—96. Recipient Walsh McDermott medal, Inst. Medicine, 2006. Fellow: AAAS (chmn. com. on sci. freedom and responsibility 1985—88), N.Y. Acad. Scis.; mem.: Inst. Medicine of NAS (chmn. com. on health and human rights 1987—90), Genetics Soc. Am., Am. Soc. Human Genetics (social issues com. 1982—85), Am. Soc. Microbiology, Sigma Xi, Phi Beta Kappa. Office: NAS 500 5th St NW Washington DC 20001 Business E-Mail: enightin@nas.edu.

NIGHTINGALE, STUART LESTER, public health consultant; b. NYC, Jan. 26, 1938; s. Lester M. Nightingale and Beatrice L. N. Helpern; m. Elena Ottolenghi, July 1, 1965; children: Elizabeth S., Marisa O. BA, Yale U., 1959; MD, NYU, 1964. Diplomate Am. Bd. Internal Medicine. Intern in medicine and surgery Montefiore Hosp. and Med. Ctr., Bronx, 1964—65, resident in internal medicine, fellow in adolescent medicine, 1965—66, resident internal medicine, fellow adolescent medicine, 1967—69, asst. attending physician, 1969—70; resident in anatomical pathology NYU Sch. Medicine, 1966—67; med. dir. drug abuse adminstrn. Dept. Health and Mental Hygiene State of Md., Balt., 1971—72; chief treatment and rehab., office of programs, spl. action office for drug abuse prevention Exec. Office of Pres., Washington, 1972—74, chief office treatment and rehab., spl. action office for drug abuse prevention, 1974—75; dir. divsn. resource devel. Nat. Inst. on Drug Abuse, Rockville, Md., 1974—76; asst. to dir. Bur. Drugs, FDA, Rockville, 1976—79; dep. assoc. commr. for health affairs FDA, Rockville, 1979—82, acting assoc. commr. for health affairs, 1979—82, assoc. commr. for health affairs, 1982—2000; sr. med. adv. to dir. global health affairs Dept. HHS, Washington, 2000—07, chief med. officer Office of the Asst. Sec. for Planning and Evaluation, 2000—03, chief med. officer Office Pub. Health Emergency Preparedness, 2004—07, dep. asst. sec. Office Pub. Health Emergency Preparedness, 2005—07; cons. NIH, HHS, 2007—. Vis. physician Balt. City Hosps., 1970-72; clin. instr. dept. medicine Coll. Medicine SUNY, Bklyn., 1970; asst. physician out-patient dept., instr. dept. medicine Johns Hopkins U. Sch. Medicine, Balt., 1970-72, med. dir. drug abuse ctr., 1970-71, instr. dept. med. care and hosps. Sch. Hygiene and Pub. Health, 1971-74, rsch. program mgr. health svcs. rsch. and devel. ctr., 1970-71; chmn. rsch. involving human subjects com. FDA, 1979-84; liaison mem. Commn. on Fed. Drug Approval Process, U.S. Congress, 1980-81; mem.-at-large U.S. Pharmacopeial Conv., Inc., 1985-95; bd. trustees The Milton Helpern Libr. of Legal Medicine, N.Y.C., 1982-2005; bd. dirs. Nat. Coun. on Patient Info. and Edn., Washington, 1982-2000; mem. forum on drug devel. and regulation Inst. Medicine, NAS, Washington, 1986-2000. Contbg. author Jour. AMA, 1985-99, Am. Family Physician, 1986-99. Capt. M.C., USAR, 1966-72; with USPHS. Recipient Disting. Svc. Spl. Action Office for Drug Abuse Prevention award Exec. Office of Pres., 1975, Pub. Health Superior Svc. award, 1983, Disting. Contbn. award Nat. Coun. Patient Info. and Edn., 1987, Achievement award Am. Assn. Physicians for Human Rights, 1990, Presdl. Meritorious Exec. Rank award, 1990, 2005, Pub. Health Svc. Spl. Recognition award, 1993, Sec.'s Recognition award Dept. HHS, 1999, Surgeon Gen. Exemplary award, 2007. Fellow ACP; mem. AMA, Sr. Execs. Assn., Cosmos Club., Acad. Medicine Wash., FDA Alumni Assn., Med. Adminstrs. Conf. Office: OBA NIH 6705 Rockledge Dr Bethesda MD 20892 Office Phone: 301-496-9838. Business E-Mail: nightins@od.nih.gov.

NIGHTINGALE, WILLIAM JOSLYN, management consultant; b. Mpls., Sept. 16, 1929; s. William Isaac and Gladys (Joslyn) N.; children: Paul, Sara, William Joslyn, Jr., Margaret. BA, Bowdoin Coll., 1951; MBA, Harvard U., 1953. Mktg. mgr. Gen. Mills. Inc., Mpls., 1957-66; sr. assoc. Booz, Allen & Hamilton Inc., NYC, 1966-68; v.p. fin. Hanes Corp., Winston-Salem, NC, 1969; pres. Bali Co. Inc., NYC, 1970—95; founder, pres., chmn., sr. adviser Nightingale & Assocs. LLC, Stamford, Conn., 1975—2000. Bd. dirs. Ring's End Inc. Active numerous charitable orgns.; vestryman St. Luke's Episcopal Ch., 1975-78, sr. warden, 1989-91; mem. Darien Representative Town Meeting, 1971-74. Lt. (j.g.) USNR, 1953-57. Mem. Wee Burn Country Club(Darian Ct), Noroton, Yacht Club(Damery Ct), Harvard Club, NYC. Republican. Home: 195 Rowayton Ave Norwalk CT 06853-1237

NIGHY, BILL FRANCIS, actor; b. Surrey, England, Dec. 12, 1949; life ptnr. Diana Quick; 1 child, Mary. Spokesperson Nat. Soc. for Epilepsy; amb. DebRA, 2006—. Actor: (films) Death Watch, 1979, Eye of the Needle, 1981, Curse of the Pink Panther, 1983, Little Drummer Girl, 1984, The Phantom of the Opera, 1989, Being Human, 1993, True Blue, 1996, Indian Summer (Alive and Kicking), 1996, Fairy Tale: A True Story, 1997, Still Crazy, 1998 (Evening Standard Peter Sellers award, 1998), Guest House Paradiso, 1999, Blow Dry, 2001, The Lawless Heart, 2001 (Best Supporting Actor, LA Critics Cir. award, 2002), Lucky Break, 2001, AKA, 2002, I Capture the Castle, 2003 (Best Supporting Actor, LA Critics Cir. award, 2004), Love Actually, 2003 (Best Supporting Actor, Brit. Acad. Film and TV Arts, LA Critics Cir. award, London Film Critics award, 2004, Best Comdey Performance, Evening Standard Peter Sellers award, 2004), Underworld, 2003, Shaun of the Dead, 2004, Enduring Love, 2004, The Magic Roundabout, 2005, The Hitchhiker's Guide To The Galaxy, 2005, The Constant Gardener, 2005, Underworld: Evolution, 2006, Pirates Of the Caribbean - Dean Man's Chest, 2006, Stormbreaker, 2006, Flushed Away, 2006, Notes on a Scandal, 2006, Disgrace, 2006, Pirates of the Caribbean: At World's End, 2007 (Choice Movie: Villain, Teen Choice Awards, 2007), Valkyrie, 2008, Underworld: Rise of the Lycans, 2009, (voice) G-Force, 2009,: (TV films) Deasey, 1979, Fat, 1979, Little Lord Fauntleroy, 1980, Dreams of Leaving, 1980, Writing On the Wall, 1990, Antonia and Jane, 1991, The Girl In The Café, 2005, Gideon's Daughter, 2006 (Satellite award, 2006, Best Performance by an Actor in a Mini-Series or Motion Picture Made for TV, Golden Globe award, Hollywood Fgn. Press Assn., 2007); (TV series) Agony, 2nd season, 1980, Making News, 1989, The Lost Prince, 2003 (Best Actor, Broadcasting Press Guild award, 2003), The Young Visitors, 2003 (Best Actor in a TV Film, Broadcasting Press Guild award, 2003); (TV miniseries) Reilly - Ace of Spies, 1983, The Last Place on Earth, 1985, The Men's Room, 1991, Eye of the Storm, 1993, God's Messengers, 1994, The Canterbury Tales, 1998, State of Play, 2003 (Best Actor, Brit. Acad. Film and TV Arts, 2004, Best Actor, Broadcasting Press Guild award, 2003), The Canterbury Tales, The Wife Of Bath, 2003, He Knew He Was Right, 2004; (Broadway plays) The Vertical Hour, 2007 (Theatre World award, 2007). Office: c/o Markham and Froggatt Ltd Personal Management 4 Windmill St London W1T 2HZ England*

NIGRO, KENNETH MICHAEL, musician, educator; b. Waterbury, Conn., Nov. 27, 1954; s. Ugo Mario and Antoinette Rose Nigro; m. Karen Lynn Milo, July 17, 1976; 1 child, Kyle Michael. BS in Music Edn., Ctrl. Conn. State U., 1976; MusM in Applied Music, U. Miami, 1980; degree in Adminstrn., Sacred Heart U., 2000. Cert. educator Conn., administrator Conn. Freelance musician, 1979—; lectr. Ctrl. Conn. State U., New Britain, 1982—87; lectr. saxophone, improv and combo, dir. saxophone ensemble U. Conn., Storrs, 1987—2004; tchr. music Wilby HS, Waterbury, Conn., 1997—; woodwind lectr. Naugatuck Valley CC, Waterbury, 2004—. Clinician, performer Yamaha Corp. Am., Indpls., 1998—. Author: The Complete Saxophone; musician: White Nights Jazz Festival, 1995, Fifty-third Presdl. Inaugural, 1997, (albums) New Millenium Jazz Ensemble CD, 1998; composer: (songs) Big Schleps, 2001, 84 Again, 2004, The Complete Saxophone, 2005; contbr. articles to profl. jours. Recipient Saxophone Svc. Performance award, Saxophone Jour., 1977; scholar, U. Miami, 1979—80. Mem.: Nat. Assn. Coll. Wind & Percussion Instrs, Pi Kappa Lambda, Phi Beta Mu. Avocations: bicycling, swimming, running. Personal E-mail: kyamasax@aol.com.

NIGRO, LOUIS J., JR., United States Ambassador to Republic of Chad; PhD in Modern European Hist., Vanderbilt U., Washington. Fulbright-Hays rsch. fellow, Italy; instr. modern European hist. Stanford U., Calif.; officer Calif. Army Nat. Guard; joined Fgn. Svc. US Dept. State, 1980, various positions at US Embassies in the Bahamas, Chad, and Haiti, dep. chief of mission The Holy See, Italy, Guinea, Cuba, various positions with Ops. Ctr., Policy Planning Coun., Office We. European Affairs, and Office Canadian Affairs Washington, US amb. to Chad, 2007—. Prof. internat. rels. US Army War Coll., 2006—07; diplomat in residence U. Houston. Author: The New Diplomacy in Italy: American Propaganda and U.S.-Italian Relations, 1917-1919, 1999. Recipient Superior Honor award, US Dept. State. Office: DOS Amb 2410 Ndjamena Pl Washington DC 20521-2410*

NIGUIDULA, KATHLEEN ANN, musician, educator; b. Upper Darby, Pa., Apr. 5, 1972; d. Faustino Nazario Niguidula and Brenda Marie Maybury; m. Christopher Jordan O'Neill, Aug. 30, 2004; children: Luke O'Neill, Jacquelyn O'Neill. B in Music Edn., Eastman Sch. Music, 1994; MusM in Piano Performance, Boston Conservatory, 1998. Cert. K-12 music tchr. N.Y., Tex., Mass. Music tchr., choir dir. grades 6-8 Aldine Ind. Sch. Dist., Houston, 1994—95; music tchr., choir dir. grades 7-8 Norwood Pub. Schs., Mass., 1998—99; music tchr. K-8 Music On The Move, Chelsea, Mass., 1999—2001; piano tchr. Timeline Music, Wakefield, Mass., 1998—2001; music tchr. Wolf Sch., Providence, 2001—05; piano tchr. Music Sch. R.I. Philharm., Providence, 2001—, registrar, 2005—. Freelance accompanist, Boston, 1996—; choir dir. K-5 after-school programs Wolf Sch., Providence, 2001—; coord. early childhood music Music Sch. R.I. Philharmonic, 2002—04. Music dir., organist Islington Cmty. Ch., Westwood, Mass., 1999—2004. Recipient Excellence in Music award, Sarasota Visual and Performing Arts, 1990, 1st prize Composition, Women's Soc. Sarasota, 1990, 1st prize Music Performance, Shriner's Club, 1990; finalist piano, Florida Concerto Competition, 1989; scholar, Eastman Sch. Music, 1990—94. Mem.: Orff-Schuwerk Assn., Music Educators Nat. Conf., Music Tchrs. Nat. Assn., New Eng. Piano Tchrs. Assn., Chopin Club. Home Phone: 401-359-0545. Personal E-mail: kathleen-o@cox.net.

NIGWEKAR, SAGAR U., dentist, researcher; M, clin. U. Rochester Sch. Medicine & Dentistry, 2006. Rschr. Rochester Gen. Hosp.,U. Rochester Sch. Medicine & Dentistry, 2006—, attending physician, 2006. Primary investigator Rochester Gen. Hosp., 2006—. Recipient award, Rochester Acad. Medicine Primary Care, 2008; grantee Rsch. grant, Nat. Kidney Found. NY; grant, Rochester Health Found., 2008. Achievements include research in natriuretic peptides in acute kidney injury.

NII, SHIRO, director, virologist, educator; b. Naruto, Tokushima, Japan, Jan. 12, 1932; parents Atsushi and Toyo (Toyota) N.; m. Etsuko Tada, Mar. 29, 1960; children: Satoshi, Keiko Maeda, Yoshiko Fujita. MD, Osaka U., 1956, PhD, 1961. Lic. physician. Rsch. assoc. Rsch. Inst. for Microbial Diseases Osaka U., Japan, 1961—66, assoc. prof. Rsch. Inst. for Microbial Diseases, 1966—78; prof. Okayama U. Med. Sch., Japan, 1978—97, dean, 1993—95; prof. emeritus Okayama U., 1997—; prof. Kawasaki Coll. Allied Health Professions, Kurashiki, Japan, 1997—98; pres. Niimi Coll., Japan, 1998—2002; academic adminstr. CAC Rehab. Coll., Hiroshima, 2002—03, dir., 2003—06, dir. emeritus, 2006—. Councilor Okayama U., 1990-92; hon. prof. Jiangxi Med. Coll., China, 1993; guest prof. Dalian Med. Coll., China, 1994; expert adviser Sci. and Tech. Com., 1994; pres. Univ. and Coll. Assn. Okayama Prefecture, 1995, 43d Ann. Meeting of Japanese Virologists, 1995. Co-author: (book) Virology, 1997; editor, co-author: (book) Essentials of Microbiology, 1983, 98; contbr. articles to sci. jours. Mem.: Japanese Assn. Infectious Diseases (auditor 1995—98), Japanese Soc. Virology (hon.). Avocations: reading, baseball, walking. Home: 372-1-206 Hama Okayama 703-8256 Japan E-mail: snii@po12.oninet.ne.jp.

NII, YUKO, artist; b. Tokyo, Toshima-ku, Japan, Oct. 22, 1942; arrived in US, 1963; d. Satoshi and Chieko Nii. BFA, Macalester Coll., St. Paul, Minn., 1965; MFA, Pratt Inst., Bklyn., 1969. Residency Yaddo, Saratoga Springs, NY, 1980, 1982; artist (painter); founder, dir. Williamsburg Art and Hist. Ctr., Bklyn., 1996—. Costume and stage set designer Chiang Ching Dance Company, NYC, 1977—78, Zignal I at La-Mama, 1978—79; contbr. N.Y. Jour., Japan, 1982—83, NY Arts Mag., 2002, 11211 mag., 2004, Friends and Mentors Art Show catalog, 2001. One-woman shows include Elaine Benson Gallery, L.I., 1977, 1986, 1994, Fairleigh Dickenson U., N.J., 1978, Berkshire Mus., Mass., 1979, Monique Knowlton Gallery, N.Y.C., 1979, Vered Internat. Gallery, L.I., 1979, Haber Theodore Gallery, N.Y.C., 1980, Internat. Monetary Fund, Washington, 1980. Recipient Woman of Yr., Office of Bklyn. Borough Pres. Howard Golden, 1998, Office of Gov. of N.Y. State George Pataki, 2001, Office of Bklyn. Borough Pres. Marty Markowitz, 2003, Outstanding Citizen award, N.Y.C. Coun., 2003, Asian Cultural award, Office Bklyn. Borough Pres. Marty Markowitz, 2008; fellow, Pratt Inst., Bklyn., 1966—69; scholar, Macalester Coll., St. Paul, Minn., 1963—65. Home: 385 Clinton Ave Brooklyn NY 11238 Office: Williamsburg Art & Hist Ctr 135 Broadway Brooklyn NY 11211 Home Fax: 718-486-6012. Personal E-mail: wahcenter@earthlink.net.

NIJMAN, JENNIFER T., lawyer; b. Aug. 27, 1962; BA, U. Ill., 1984; JD, U. Chgo., 1987. Bar: Ill. 1987, US Dist. Ct. (no. dist.) Ill. 1987. Ptnr. Nijman Franzetti LLP, Chgo., 2008—; assoc. to ptnr. Winston & Strawn LLP, Chgo., 1994—2007. Bd. dirs. Pub. Interest Law Initiative, Ctr. Conflict Resolution; chair Ill. Legal Needs Study, Ill. Coalition Equal Justice. Contbr. articles to profl. jours. Mem.: ABA (mem. environ. litigation com.), Economic Club Chgo., Ill. State Bar Assn., Chgo. Bar Assn. (pres. 2002—03). Office: Nijman Franzetti LLP 10 S Lasalle St Ste 3600 Chicago IL 60603 Office Phone: 312-251-5590. Office Fax: 312-251-4610. Business E-Mail: jn@nijmanfranzetti.com.

NIKAIDO, HIROSHI, microbiologist; b. Tokyo, Mar. 26, 1932; arrived in U.S., 1962; s. Tatsuya and Ryo Nikaido; m. Kishiko Jokura, Mar. 11, 1963; children: Michio, George. MD, Keio U., Tokyo, 1955, D in Med. Sci., 1961. Assoc. bacteriology Harvard Med. Sch., Boston, 1963-64, asst. prof., 1965-69; assoc. prof. U. Calif., Berkeley, 1969-71, prof., 1971—. Sci. adv. Essential Therapeutics, Mountain View, Calif., 1992—2002. Co-author: Microbial Biotechnology, 1995, 2nd edit., 2007; contbr. articles to profl. jours. Recipient Paul Ehrlich award, Paul Ehrlich Found., 1969, Freedom to Discover Achievement award, Bristol-Myers Squibb, 2004. Fellow: Am. Acad. Microbiology; mem.: Natl. Acad. Sci., Am. Acad. Arts and Scis., Am. Soc. Biochemistry and Molecular Biology, Am. Soc. Microbiology (editor Jour. Bacteriology 1998—2002, Hoechst-Roussel award 1984).

NIKAM, SHIVPRASAD, vascular and endovascular surgeon; b. India; MBBS, B.J. Med. Coll., Pune, India, 1993, MS, 1998; MD, Ednl. Commn. Fgn. Med. Grads., 1999. Diplomate Nat. Bd. Med. Exams. New Delhi, 1998, cert. in gen. surgery Am. Bd. Surgery, 2006, in vascular surgery Am. Bd. Surgery, 2008. Intern Sassoon Gen. Hosps., Pune, Maharashtra, 1993—94, resident surgery, 1995—98, lectr. surgery, 1998—99; clin. observer Meml. Sloan Kettering Cancer Ctr., NYC, 1999; registrar surgery Royal Albert Edward Infirmary, Wigan, England, 2000; resident, surgery Bronx Lebanon Hosp. Ctr., NY, 2001—05, chief resident, 2004—05; fellow, vascular and endovascular surgery Geisinger Med. Ctr., Danville, Pa., 2005—07; vascular and endovascular surgeon Geisinger Wyo. Valley Med. Ctr., Wilkes Barre, Pa., 2007—. Contbr. articles to profl. jours. Recipient Late Minu Mehta Meml. award, 1998, Late Dr. Balawant Narayan Ranade Meml. award, 1998, All India Maratha Samaaj award, 2000. Fellow: ACS, Royal Coll. Surgeons; mem.: Soc. Vascular Surgery. Office: Geisinger Wyoming Valley Medical Ctr 1000 E Mountain Blvd Wilkes Barre PA 18711

NIKIRK, SUSAN SILVA (SUSAN SILVA), minister, writer, dancer, consultant; b. NYC, Mar. 13, 1947; d. Victor and Lina Silva; m. Gerald Eugene Nikirk, Jan. 29, 1988; 1 adopted child, Autumn Victoria Jai Chuan Nikirk. English, City Coll. of N.Y., NYC, 1966; fashion mktg., Fashion Inst. Tech., NYC, 1967; Biblical studies, Heart to Heart Internat., Norwich, Conn., 1993. Rev. Ordination Kingsway Fellowship Internat., Iowa, 1992; championship cert. nat. adjudicator Nat. Dance Coun. Am., 2006, master cert. dance tchr. Nat. Dance Tchrs. Am., 85, Nat. Dance Tchrs. Am., 2006, championship cert. dance tchr. N. Am. Dance Tchrs. Assn., 2006, cert. examiner Arthur Murray Internat., 2007. Profl. dancer Broadway, Off Broadway Theatre & TV, NYC, 1964—72; dir. fashion merchandising sch. Barbizon Sch. of Queens, Rego Pk., Queens, NY, 1973—75; mgmt. cons. RTW Mgmt., NYC, 1975—77; Theatrical Exhbn., Am. Ballroom Dance Champion in US Competitions Fred Astaire, Arthur Murray, Ohio Star Ball, various ind. competitions, 1977—86; profl. ballroom dancer and tchr. Fred Astaire, Arthur Murray, various ind. dance studios, 1977—89; night club act Hamilton & Silva, 1980—85; examiner, coach Arthur Murray Internat., 2007—; profl. ballroom nat. adjudicator Nat. Dance Coun. of Am., Arthur Murray Internat., 2006—; choreographer Ind. Dance Teams, 1977—89, 2006—; author & mktg. cons. Arthur Murray Internat., Coral Gables, Fla., 1985—89; cosmetic cons. Estee Lauder, Inc., Conn., 1989—91; co-founder, ordained min., v.p. bd. dirs. Nikirk Ministries, Colchester, Conn., 1992—; Theatrical, Exhbn., Ballroom coach and choreographer, 2006—. Ordained min., nat. & internat. speaker inter Denom. chs. and confs., USA, Holland, Belgium, Switerland, Germany, Iceland, 1992—; pastor VINE Tng. and Worship Ctr., 1997—2005; dir. founder Watchmen Sch. of Prayer, Colchester, Conn., 1998—. Dancer (discotheque) Beatles Tour, 1965; author: (tchg. video, manual) Arthur Murray Bronze Theatrical Ballroom Syllabus, 1986—88, (tchg. video) Watchmen Sch. of Prayer, 2002; co-host, co-producer (TV series) Voice In New Eng. T.V. Broadcast, 1996—; dance dir. Cinemystic Film; contbr. articles pub. to profl. jour.; choreographer Dance With Me, 2007—. Recipient Profl. Dance Devel. award, Arthur Murray Studios, 1986. Mem.: Arthur Murray Nat. Dance Bd., Nat. Dance Coun. Am., N.Am. Dance Tchrs. Assn., Nat. Dance Tchrs. Assn., Kingsway Fellowship Internat. Messianic Jew. Avocations: gardening, dance. Office: Nikirk Ministries PO Box 211 Colchester CT 06415 Office Phone: 860-537-5881. Business E-Mail: snikirk@nikirkvoice.org.

NIKOLAI, LOREN ALFRED, accounting educator; b. Northfield, Minn., Dec. 14, 1943; s. Roman Peter and Loyola (Gertrude) N.; m. Anita Carol Baker, Jan. 15, 1966; children: Trishia, Jay. BA, St. Cloud State U., 1966, MBA, 1967; PhD, U. Minn., 1973. CPA, Mo. Asst. prof. U. N.C., Chapel Hill, 1973-76; assoc. prof. U. Mo., Columbia, 1976-80, prof., 1980-82, Ernst & Young Disting. prof. Sch. Accountancy, 1982—, dir. masters programs, 2002—08. Author: Financial Accounting: Concepts and Uses, 1988, 3d edit., 1995, Intermediate Accounting, 1980, 11th edit., 2009, Accounting Information for Business Decisions, 2000, updated 2d edit., 2007. Recipient Faculty award of merit Fedn. Schs. of Accountancy, 1989, Disting. Alumni award St. Cloud U., 1990, Coll. of Bus. Faculty Mem. of Yr. award, 1991, Mo. Outstanding Acctg. Educators award, 1993; Kemper fellow U. Mo., 1992, Alumni award MU Faculty, 1996, UM Presdl. awd. for Outstanding Teaching, 1999; Coll. of Bus. Teacher of the Yr., 1999. Mem. AICPA, Am. Acctg. Assn., Mo. Soc. CPAs, Fedn. Schs. of Acctg. (pres. 1994, emeritus prof. 2009). Office: Univ Mo Sch Accountancy 504 Cornell Hall Columbia MO 65211-0001

NIKOLAOU, LAMBIS W., International Olympic Committee board member; b. Nov. 23, 1935; m. Tonia Papapanagiotou; children: Olga, Catherine, Vassilis. BS in Civil Engring., Munich U. Applied Scis.; PhD in Sports Scis. (hon.), Mainz U.; PhD in Humanities (hon.), Phila. U. Civil engr.; pub. works contractor; mem. exec. bd. Internat. Olympic Com., 2001—; mem. Hellenic Olympic Com., Greece, 1985—, pres., 1985—93, 1997—2004. Bd. dirs. various tech. cos.; former vice chmn. bd. dirs. Olmpic Airways; pres. NOC, 1985—93, 1997—; v.p. organizing om. 2004 Olympic Games, Athens, Greece; mem. cultural commn. Internat. Olympic Com., 1988—99, mem. mktg. commn., 1995—, mem. IOC 2000 commn., 1999, mem. culture and Olympic edn. commn., 2000—; mem. exec. bd. European Olympic Coms., 1989—93, 1997—; mem. Bd. of Ephoria of Internat. Olympic Acad., 1989—, v.p., 2001—04; dignitary Ecumenical Patriarchate of Constantinople; officer Order of Honour of Greece. Pres. Depanom, Greece, 1983—89; advisor to Prime Minister Govt. Greece, 1983—89, 1993—96, rep. of Prime Minister to European Union (Commn. for Trans-European Networks). Recipient Coat of Arms, City of Moscow, Key to City, Salt Lake, Beijing, Sophia, Gold Medal to City of Taipei, Pres. Chinese Taipei, Golden Cross of Merit, Athens. Office: Internat Olympic Com Exec Bd Chateau de Vidy 1007 Lausanne Switzerland also: Hellenic Olympic Com D Vikela 52 152 33 Halandri Greece Office Phone: 00 30 210 68 78 881. E-mail: lwnikolaou@ath.forthnet.gr.

NIKOLICH-ZUGICH, JANKO, biomedical scientist, educator; b. Belgrade, Serbia, Serbia-Monteneg (Yugoslavia), Nov. 25, 1960; MD, U. Belgrade, 1984, MS, 1987, PhD, 1993. Cert. gen. practice Yugoslavia, 1985. Rsch. assoc. Scripps Clinic and Rsch. Found., La Jolla, Calif., 1987—90; asst. mem., asst. prof. Meml. Sloan-Kettering Cancer Ctr. and Cornell U. Grad. Sch. Med. Scis., NYC, 1990—96, assoc. mem., assoc. prof., 1996—2000; prof., sr. scientist dept. molecular microbiology & immunology Vaccine & Gene Therapy Inst., Oreg. Primate Rsch. Ctr., Oreg. Health & Sci. U., Portland, 2000—08; prof., head, dept. immunobiology, co-dir., Ariz. Ctr. Aging U. Ariz. Coll. Medicine, Tuscon, 2008—, Elizabeth Bowman prof. med. res., 2008—. Dir. flow cytometry core faculty MSKCC, NYC, 1990—2000. Editor: Intrathymic T-cell Development, 1994; mem. editl. bd.: Cellular Immunology, 1996—, Jour. Immunology, 1996—2002, Jour. Virology, 2007—, Jour. Aging Cell, 2008—, Jour. Gerom Biol. Sci., 2008—; contbr. articles to profl. jours. Recipient Preclincal Prostate Cancer award, Cancer Rsch. Inst., 1999—2002; scholar, PEW Charitable Trust, 1991—95. Mem.: Am. Aging Assn., Am. Assn. Immunologists. Mailing: Univ of Arizona Dept of Immunobiology PO Box 245049 1501 N Campbell Ave Tucson AZ 85724 Office: Univ of Arizona Dept of Immunobiology 1656 E Mabel St Tucson AZ 85724

NIKOLOV, IVAN P., economics professor; b. Berkovitza, Bulgaria, Jan. 8, 1950; s. Peter I. Nikolov and Keranka V. Nikolova; m. Ofelia R Nikolova, Mar. 27, 1983; 1 child, Savina Nikolova. M in Economics, Warsaw Sch. Economics, 1974; PhD, St. Petersburg U. Fin. and Economics, Russia, 1980, Southern Ill. U., Carbondale, 1995. Dir. global edn., prof. Southern Ill. U., 2000—02; exec. dir., ill. internat. hs initiative U. Ill., Champaign, 2002—05; dir. & prof., ctr. int. programs Valdosta State U., Ga., 2005—. Bd. dirs. Internat. Trade Club Chgo., 2002—06; mem. UGS Coun. Internat. Edn., Atlanta, 2005—. Contbr. articles to profl. jours. (Bulgarian Ministry of Edn., 1989). Numerous grants, Nat. Orgns., 1993—2008. Office: Valdosta State Univ 1500 N Patterson St Valdosta GA 31698-0037 Office Fax: 229-245-3849; Home Fax: 229-245-3849. Business E-Mail: inikolov@valdosta.edu.

NIKONOVA, ELENA VLADIMIROVNA, physician, scientist; b. Rostov-on-Don region, Russia; arrived in USA, 1993, naturalized, 2006; m. Sergei Nikonov, 1990; children: Elena, Roman. RN in Family Practice with honors, North Causean R.R. Ministry Sch. Nursing, 1986; MD in Pediat. with honors, Russian State Med. U., 1992. Cert. in Piano Performance Sch. Music, Russia, 1982. Postdoctoral fellow Russian Acad. Med. Scis., Moscow, 1992—95, U. Pa., Phila., 2000—05; staff scientist The Wistar Inst., 2006—. Spkr. in field; workshop participant in field. Contbr. articles to profl. jours. Vol. Ctr. for Sleep, U. Pa., 1998; program performer TCU, Cliburn Piano Inst., Ft. Worth, 2004; fin. donor Ea. Paralyzed VA, Leukemia and Lymphoma Soc., Assn. Mouth and Foot Painting Artists, Del. County Fraternal Police Order, 2001—06; blood donor ARC. Recipient 1st Ann. Biomedical Postdoc Rsch. Symposium Achievement cert., U. Pa., 2002; grantee Young Investigator award, Sleep Medicine Edn. and Rsch. Found., 2002—04; NRSA Postdoctoral fellow, Ctr. for Sleep U. Pa., 2000—03. Mem.: Sleep Rsch. Soc., Mitochondria Rsch. Soc., Am. Acad. Sleep Medicine (Young Investigator award). Russian Orthodox. Avocations: piano, languages, ethnography, classical music, ayurvedic medicine. Office: Wistar Inst Molecular Cellular Oncogenesis Program 3601 Spruce St Rm 303 Philadelphia PA 19104 Office Fax: 215-898-4521.

NIKOPOULOS, BETH, educational association administrator; BA in English, U. Tex., Arlington; MA in Human Services, Nat. U., San Diego. Dir., tutorial services Brookhaven Coll., Dallas, 1998—. Mem.: Assn. Tutoring Profession (pres. 2007—), Coll. Reading Learning Assn., Tex. Tutors' Assn. (former pres.), Nat. Tutoring Assn. (chair, constn. and by-laws 1998—2003). Office: Brookhaven College Bldg S Rm S255 3939 Calley View Ln Farmers Branch Dallas TX 75244-4997 Office Phone: 972-860-4672.

NIKSIC, GWEN M., biology professor; d. Thomas and Kathleen Niksic; m. Lucian Babiarz, Aug. 28, 2006. BS in Animal Sci., U. Ill., Urbana, 1990; MS in Animal Sci., U. Nev., Reno, 1993; postgrad. in Animal Sci., U. NH, Durham, 1996; PhD, U. ND, Grand Forks, 2005—. Tutor hearing impaired program Whitney Young Magnet HS, Chgo., 1985—86; grad. asst. U. Nev., Reno, 1991—93; tchg. and rsch. asst. U. NH, Durham, 1993—96; clk. Melroe, Bismarck, ND, 1997—2001; profl. math. and sci. tutor and lab instr. U. of Mary, Bismarck, 2001—04, asst. prof., 2004—. Recipient Quality Cost/Improvement award, Melroe, 1998. Mem.: Riverside Readers, Sigma Xi. Avocation: reading. Office: U of Mary 7500 University Dr Bismarck ND 58504

NILLES, MATTHEW L., microbiology educator, researcher; b. Fargo, ND, Oct. 29, 1965; s. Carl D. and Diantha R. Nilles; m. Dawnita S. Lepisto, Sept. 13, 1986; 1 child, Alexandra. PhD, Wash. State U., 1995. Postdoctoral rsch. assoc. U. Ky., Lexington, 1995-98; asst. prof. microbiology U. N.D., Grand Forks, 1998—. Contbr. articles to sci. jours., including Microbiology, Jour. Bacteriology, Infection and Immunity. Recipient nat. rsch. svc. award NIH, 1997. Mem. Am. Soc. for Microbiology. Office: U ND 501 N Columbia Rd Grand Forks ND 58203 Personal E-mail: mlnilles@mac.com.

NILOFF, PAUL HYMAN, surgeon, educator; b. Sherbrooke, Quebec, Can., July 1, 1921; arrived in US, 1978; s. Solomon and Mindel Niloff; m. Madelaine Harriet Fromson, Nov. 12, 1952; children: Jonathan, Donna Hirschfeld, Susan Weisz. BA in Biology & Chemistry with honors, Bishop's U., Lennoxville, Quebec, 1940; MD, MCGill U., Montreal, Quebec, CM, 1943, MSc in Exptl. Surgery, 1950, Diploma in Surgery, 1951. Diplomate ACS, 1952, cert. surg. specialist Royal Coll. Surgeons, Can., 1952, Coll. Physicians & Surgeons, Quebec, 1952, diplomate Am. Bd. Surgery, 1952, Am. Bd. Quality Assurance & Utilization Review Physicians, Inc., 1995. Sr. surgeon pvt. practice Sir Mortimer Davis-Jewish Gen. Hosp., Montreal, 1951—78; surgeon-in-chief Reddy Meml. Hosp., Montreal, 1971—76; assoc. prof. surgery MCGill U., 1971—78; pvt. practice Palm Beach Regional, JFK Hosp., Lake Worth, Fla., 1978—2002; physician advisor, surg. svcs. JFK Hosp., Atlantis, 2002—06; assoc. dir. postgrad. surg. edn. Palms West Hosp., Wellington, 2006—08; clin. assoc. prof. NOVA Southeastern U., 2006—08. Pres. Montreal Clin. Soc., 1962. Contbr. articles to profl. jours. Chmn. med. div. Combined Jewish Appeal, Montreal, 1961, Red Feather Campaign, 1962. Capt. Royal Canadian Army Med. Corp., 1942—46, Can. Fellow: ACS, Royal Coll. Surgeons (Can.); mem.: Montreal Clin. Soc. (past pres.), Palm Beach County Med. Soc., Fla. Med. Assn., Am. Hernia Soc. (charter), Canadian Med. Assn., Am. Bd. Surgery. Business E-Mail: pniloff@hotmail.com.

NILSEN, ARTHUR CHRISTIAN, lawyer; b. Rockville Centre, NY, Dec. 30, 1946; s. Arthur and Lillian Alfheld (Christiansen) N.; m. Linda Marie Rom Oleschlager, July 27, 1966 (div. Jan. 1977); children: Christopher James, Karla Lynn; m. Donna Jean Holmes, Apr. 22, 1978; children: Arthur Christian, Arthur Jorgen, Johanna Blanche. BS, Cornell U., 1969; MBA in Fin., JD, Samford U., 1986. Bar: Ala., Ga. Dir. ops. M.D. Anderson Tumor Inst., Houston, 1976-78; dir. exec. svcs./ops. PFM, Inc., St. Louis, 1978-83; atty. Roe & Rowell, Birmingham, Ala., 1983-86; regional ptnr. Hyatt Legal Svcs., Atlanta, 1986-88; atty. Law Offices of Frederick Hanna, Atlanta, 1988-89; mng. atty. Siler & Jonap, Atlanta, 1989-92, Law Offices of Kenneth S. Nugent, P.C., Atlanta, 1995—96, Attys. Kaufman & Assocs., P.A., Atlanta, 2003—06, Dover Law Firm, P.C., Atlanta, 2006—08; supervising atty. Trauner, Cohen & Thomas LLP, 2008—09; mng. ptnr. Jonap & Assocs., Atlanta, 1992-94; mng. ptnr., cons. A.C. Nilsen & Assocs., Atlanta, 1994—; CEO, CFO Thomas W. Malone, P.C., Atlanta, 2001—02; dir. Atlanta Soaerotion Trauner Cohen Thomas LLP, 2008—; mng. dir. Law Firm Travner, Cohent Thomas LLP, 2009—; mng. ptnr. Arthur C. Nilsen & Assocs. P.C., 2009—; mng. attorney, ptnr. TWF Fin. LLC, 2009—. Bd. dirs. Law Offices Richardson, Phoenix, Ariz. Active nat. and local Rep. coms., 1975; mem. Roswell United Meth. Choir, 1978, Bd. Stewards. Mem. ABA, ATLA, Ga. Trial Lawyer's Assn., Masons, Men's Club. Republican. Methodist. Avocations: golf, swimming, fishing, reading, writing. Office: A C Nilsen & Assocs PO Box 243 Roswell GA 30077-0243 Home: 190 Riding Trail Ct Roswell GA 30075-1758 Personal E-mail: art@nilsenlaw.com.

NILSEN, MARTIN JOHN, lawyer; b. NY, Aug. 30, 1949; s. Martin Smith and Eleanor Rita Nilsen; m. Barbara Lillian Primsky, Aug. 5, 1972; children: Dennis Martin, James Patrick, Laura Mary. BA, St. John's U., 1967—71; JD, St. John's U. Sch. Law, 1972—75. Bar: NY 1976, US Supreme Court: 1993. Atty. Lawyers Title Ins. Corp., NYC, 1975—78; coun. The Continental Ins. Cos., New York, NY, 1978—81; assoc. Trubin Sillcocks Edelman & Knapp, New York, NY, 1981—84; coun. LeBoeuf, Lamb, Greene & MacRae, New York, NY, 1984—93; ptnr. Bigham, Englar, Jones & Houston, New York, NY, 1994—95, Wilson, Elser, Moskowitz, Edelman & Dicker, LLP, New York, NY, 1995—99, Edwards & Angell, LLP, New York, NY, 1999—2002; sr. v.p., sec. & gen. coun. Arch Ins. Group, Jersey City, 2002—. Mem. Equestrian Order of the Holy Sepulchre of Jerusalem, Sovereign Mil. Order Malta. Mem.: Assn. of Corp. Coun., ABA. Avocations: music, languages, athletics, horsemanship, travel. Office: Arch Ins Group 300 Plz Three 3rd Fl Jersey City NJ 07311 Office Phone: 201-743-4123. Business E-Mail: mnilsen@archinsurance.com.

NILSEN, MICHELINE CELESTINE, art historian, educator; d. Firmin Joseph Marcel Molle and Marie José Gillard; m. Norman Nilsen, Mar. 29, 1969; children: Svenerik, Saskia Anna Agot. MA, Brown U., Providence, 1975; MLS, Southern Conn. State U., New Haven, 1983; PhD, U. Del., Newark, 2003; BA, U. Pa., Phila., 2005, MLA, 2008. Reference coord. Pratt Inst., Bklyn., 2003—04; asst. prof. art history Ind. U. South Bend, 2004—. Guest curator U. Notre Dame Snite Mus., Ind., 2007—. Author: (book) Railways and the Western European Capitals: Studies of Implantation in London, Paris, Berlin, and Brussels. Recipient Carter Manny award, Graham Found., 2001—02, Robert T. Silver Meml. award, U. Del., 2001; fellow fellowship, Kress Found., 2001—02. Mem.: Soc. Archtl. Historians (Carroll L.V. Meeks fellowship 2000), Coll. Art Assn. (com. mem. 2008—). Office: Ind Univ South Bend-Arts 1700 Mishawaka Ave South Bend IN 46634-7111 Business E-Mail: mnilsen@iusb.edu.

NILSON, GEORGE ALBERT, lawyer; b. NYC, Jan. 15, 1942; s. Howard Seth and Beatrice Ethyl (McCurdy) N.; m. Elizabeth Hughes Logan, July 18, 1942; children: Scott Logan, Douglas George. BA, Yale U., 1963, LLB, 1967, M of Urban Studies, 1967. Bar: Md. 1967, U.S. Dist. Ct. Md., U.S. Ct. Appeals (4th cir.), U.S. Supreme Ct. Assoc. Piper & Marbury, Balt., 1967-73, ptnr., 1982—2006; asst. atty. gen. Md. State Law Dept., Balt., 1973-76, dep. atty. gen., 1976-82; city atty. Legal Dept., Baltimore, Md., 2006—. Chmn. Gen. Assembly Compensation Commn., Annapolis, Md., 1984-93, Commn. to Rev. Md. Elections Laws, Annapolis, 1986-87. Pres. Guilford Assn., Balt., 1990-92. Mem. Rule Day Club, The Wranglers, Sergeants Inn. Democrat. Avocations: fishing, golf. Office: Balt City Dept Law City Hall Ste 101 100 N Holliday St Baltimore MD 21201 Office Phone: 410-396-8393. Business E-Mail: george.nilson@baltimorecity.gov.

NILSSON, EDWARD OLOF, architect; b. Queens, NY, Nov. 10, 1947; s. Gerhard Eugen and Selma Kristina (Landy) N.; m. Frances Britton Stith, Apr. 27, 1974; children: Anders, Peter. BArch, The Cooper Union, 1970; MArch, Harvard U., 1971; MBA, Babson Coll., 1997. Registered architect, Mass., Maine, cert. Conn., NY, RI. Architect The Architects Collaborative, Cambridge, Mass., 1971-77, Anderson Notter Finegold, Inc., Boston, 1977-80; prin. Nilsson Assocs., Marblehead, Mass., 1981-92, Nilsson & Siden Assocs., Inc., Marblehead, 1992—. Author: architect AIA Conf. on Bldg. Redesign and Energy Challenges, 1984; prin. works include Rivervision 2020, Boston, also instnl., comml. and residential projects. Mem. Watertown (Mass.) Planning Bd., 1981-83, Marblehead Planning Bd., 1985-91, 2008-, chmn., 1986-90; mem. Episcopal Times Editl. Bd., Boston, 1986-88, bd. dirs. Gen. Theol. Libr., Boston, 1986-88; bd. trustees Episcopal Div. Sch., Cambridge, 2007-; bd. dirs. Arts Fedn., Inc., 2006-, Historic Salem, Inc., 2007-. Mem. AIA, Boston Soc. Architects, Rotary.

NILSSON, KENT R., federal agency administrator; BS, Lehigh U., Bethlehem, Pa.; MBA, Lehigh U., PhD in Economics and Fin.; JD, Coll. William and Mary, Williamsburg, Va. Bar: DC, NC, Va. Sr. atty. advisor, legal counsel to commr. FCC, dep. chief-policy network svcs. divsn., spl. counsel, dep. chief network tech. divsn., inspector gen., 2006—; chief cost analysis br., acct. and audits divsn. Common Carrier Bur. Office: FCC Rm 2-C762 445 12th St SW Washington DC 20554 Office Phone: 202-418-0476. Office Fax: 202-418-2811. Business E-Mail: Kent.Nilsson@fcc.gov.*

NIMER, STEPHEN DAVID, physician, leukemia researcher; b. Chgo., May 20, 1954; m. Georgia Takigawa, Oct. 18, 1987. BS, MIT, 1975; MD, U. Chgo. Sch. Medicine, 1979. Diplomate Am. Bd. Internal Medicine, Am. Bd. Hematology, Am. Bd. Med. Oncology. Intern, internal medicine UCLA Sch. Medicine, 1979—80, resident, hematologic oncology, 1980—82, fellow, 1983—86, asst. prof. medicine, 1987-92; dir. transplantation biology Jonsson Compr. Cancer Ctr., LA, 1991-92; assoc. mem. Sloan-Kettering Inst., NYC, 1993-99, mem., 1999—; chief hematology svc. Meml. Hosp., NYC, 1993—; head, divsn. hematologic oncology Meml. Sloan-Kettering Cancer Ctr., NYC, 1996—2008, vice chair faculty devel., 2008—; prof. medicine Weill Medical Coll., 2000—; chair Alfred P. Sloan, 2008—. Funded investigator NIH, 1990—. Mem. editl. bd.: Blood, 1997—2002; co-editor: Hematologic Complications of Cancer, 1996; contbr. over 200 sci. articles to profl. jours. Chmn. med. adv. bd. G&P Charitable Found., Gabrielle's Angel Found. for Cancer Rsch., 1998-; bd. dirs. Bone Marrow Found., Aplastic Anemia, Myelodysplastic Syndrome (MDS) Internat. Found., Inc., Myelodysplastic Syndrome (MDS) Found. Recipient Irma T. Hirschl Career Scientist award Cornell U. Med. Sch., 1995. Fellow ACP; mem. Am. Soc. for Clin. Investigation, Am. Soc. for Hematology, Am. Soc. Clin. Oncology, Am. Assn. for Cancer Rsch., Leukemia Soc. Am. (bd. trustees NY chpt. 1998-2004), Aplastic Anemia Found. Am. (bd. med. dirs. 1996—), MDS Found. (med. bd.), Alpha Omega Alpha. Office: Meml Sloan Kettering Cancer Ctr Box 575 1275 York Ave New York NY 10021-6094 Office Phone: 212-639-7871. Business E-Mail: nimers@mskcc.org.

NIMETZ, MATTHEW, lawyer, investment company executive; b. Bklyn, June 17, 1939; s. Joseph L. and Elsie (Botwinik) N.; children: Alexandra Elise, Lloyd. BA, Williams Coll., 1960, LL.D. (hon.), 1979; BA (Rhodes scholar), Balliol Coll., Oxford U., Eng., 1962, MA, 1966; LL.B., Harvard U., 1965. Bar: NY 1966, DC 1968. Law clk. to Justice John M. Harlan, US Supreme Ct., 1965-67; staff asst. to Pres. Johnson, 1967-69; assoc. firm Simpson Thacher & Bartlett, NYC, 1969-74, ptnr., 1974-77; counselor Dept. of State, Washington, 1977-80, acting coord. refugee affairs, 1979-80, under sec. of state for security assistance, sci. and tech., 1980; ptnr. firm Paul, Weiss, Rifkind, Wharton & Garrison, NYC, 1981-2000; mng. dir. Gen. Atlantic LLC, Greenwich, Conn., 2000—. Commr. Port Authority NY and NJ, 1975-77; dir. Weis Markets, Inc., 2007-; mem. NY State Adv. Coun. on State Productivity, 1990-92; presdl. envoy Greece-Macedonian Negotiations, 1994-95, spl. rep. UN Sec. Gen., 1999—. Trustee William Coll., 1981-96; chmn. UN Devel. Corp., 1986-94; bd. dir. Charles H. Revson Found., 1990-98, NY State Nature Conservancy, 1997-2005; chmn. Carnegie Forum in US, Greece and Turkey, 1996-98; chmn. Ctr. for Democracy and Reconciliation in S.E. Europe, 1998—; trustee Ctrl. European U., Budapest, Hungary, 2005—, Levin Inst., 2005—. Mem. Assn. of Bar of City of NY, Coun. on Fgn. Rels. Clubs: Harvard (NYC), Econ. Club NY. Office: Gen Atlantic LLC 3 Pickwick Plz Greenwich CT 06830-5538

NIMKARN, SAROJ, endocrinologist, researcher; MD (hon.), Mahidol U., Bangkok, 1991. Lic. Am. Bd. of Pediats. and Subboard Pediat. Endocrinology. Clin. instr. pediats. dept. pediats. Siriraj Hosp., Mahidol U., Bangkok, 2001—03, asst. prof. pediats. dept. pediats. faculty medicine, 2003—04; asst. prof. pediats. Med. Coll. of Wis., Milw., 2004—05, Mt. Sinai Sch. of Medicine of NYU, NYC, 2005—09, Weill Cornell Med. Coll., 2009—. Recipient Recognition Winning Poster award, Nat. Coop. Growth Study, 1999, Fellowship Rsch. Tng. grant, Lilly Rsch. Labs., Divsn. of Eli Lilly & Co., 1999, Endocrine Soc. Endocrinology award, Endocrine Soc. of Thailand, 2003, Investigator award, 11th Asian Congress of Pediat. and 1st Asian Congress of Pediat. Nursing, 2003, Free Paper award, 44th Siriraj Sci. Ann. Meeting, Faculty of Medicine, Siriraj Hosp., 2004, grant for rsch. devel., Faculty of Medicine, Siriraj Hosp., 2001. Mem.: Pediat. Endocrine Soc. of Thailand, Asia Pacific Pediat. Endocrine Soc., Lawson Wilkins Pediat. Endocrine Soc., Med. Coun. of Thailand, The Endocrine Soc. Office: Well Cornell Med Coll Box 103 525 E 68th St New York NY 10065 Office Phone: 212-746-3462. Business E-Mail: sanrooz@med.cornell.edu.

NIMKIN, BERNARD WILLIAM, retired lawyer; b. NYC, Apr. 15, 1923; s. Myron Benjamin and Anabel (Davidow) N.; m. Jean Horowitz, Feb. 9, 1947; children— David Andrew, Margaret Lee, Katherine. BS cum laude, Harvard U., 1943, LL.B. cum laude, 1949. Bar: N.Y. State bar 1949, U.S. Supreme Ct., 1999. Asso. firm Carter, Ledyard & Milburn, NYC, 1949-58; asso. and partner firm Kaye Scholer, LLP, NYC, 1958-91. Lectr. Practising Law Inst., Banking Law Inst.; Mem. Am. Law Inst.; vis. com. U. Miami Law Sch.; mem. adv. bd. Rev. of Securities Regulation. Contbr. articles to profl. jours. Mem. Conservation Commn., Town of Mamaroneck, N.Y., 1970-74; bd. dirs., sec. United Way of Tri-State, 1985-91. Served to 1st lt. U.S. Army, 1943-46. Mem. ABA (mem. fed. regulation of securities com. 1975—, corp. laws com. 1984-92, legal opinions com. 1989—), N.Y. State Bar Assn. (chmn. sect. banking corp. and bus. law 1979-81, ho. of dels. 1981-84, chmn. corp. law com. 1976-79), Assn. Bar City of N.Y. (chmn. uniform state laws com. 1962-65), Tribar Opinion Com. Democrat. Jewish. Home: 116 E 63rd St New York NY 10065-7325 Office: Kaye Scholer LLP 425 Park Ave New York NY 10022-3506 E-mail: bandjnimkin@earthlink.net.

NIMMANAPALLI, RAMADEVI, veterinarian, educator; d. Sivachandra Reddy Nimmanapalli and Bharathi Yeddula; m. Sreenivasa Reddy Donapaty, Apr. 2, 1994; children: Anjole Donapaty, Pranav Reddy Donapaty. BVSC & AH, Coll. vet. Medicine, Tirupati, India, 1991; MVSc, IVRI, Izatnagar, India, 1994; D. Phil, St. Hilda's Coll., U. oxford, England, 1999. Postdoc. rsch. assoc. Moffitt Cancer Ctr., Tampa, Fla., 2000—05; jr. faculty MD Anderson Cancer ctr., Houston, 2005—06; asst. prof. CVMNAH Tuskegee U., Ala., 2006—. Contbr. scientific papers to profl. jours. Grant, L & L soc., 2001—05, Multiple Myeloma soc., 2004—05. Mem.: Am. Soc. Microbiology, Am. Soc. Hematology, Am. Assn. Cancer Soc. Office: CVMNAH Tuskegee Univ Dept Pathobiology Tuskegee Institute AL 36088 Office Fax: 334-724-4100. Personal E-mail: ramadevi.nimmanapalli@gmail.com.

NIMMER, RAYMOND T., dean, law educator; b. Chgo., May 2, 1944; s. Raymond O. and Helen (Barscz) Nimmer. BA in Math., Valparaiso U., 1966, JD with distinction, 1968. Bar: Ill 1968, Tex. 1984, US Ct. Appeals (5th Cir.) 1984, US Supreme Ct. 1985, US Ct. Appeals (11th Cir.), US Ct. Appeals (Fed. Cir.). Rsch. atty. Am. Bar Found., 1968—75; assoc. dean U. Houston Law Ctr., 1975—85, Leonard H. Childs prof. law, 1979—, acting dean, 1993—95, co-dir. Intellectual Property and Info. Law Program, 1997—, interim dean, 2006—08, dean, 2008—; counsel Sheinfeld, Maley & Kay, Houston, 1985—91, Weil, Gotshal & Manges, Houston, 1992—99; prof. law, co dir. Houston Inst. on Info. & Intellectual Property Law, 1998—. Cons. Law Social Scis. Program NSF, 1979—92; vis. prof. law U. Tex., Austin, 1985, U. Mich. Law Sch., Ann Arbor, 1987, U. Maine Sch. Law, 2001—; cons. US State Dept. Legal Advisors Office, 1990—2001; vis. prof. law Sydney U., Australia, 2003, 08; cons. US Office Tech. Assessment, Washington, 1991—95; chmn. Twenty-Second Century Found., 2004—; chair Annual Computer and Info. Law Inst., 2001—; Fulbright-Fladd disting. chair internat. Commercial law Universidad Catholica Sch. Law, Lisbon, Portugal, 2007—08, disting. chair in residence, 2008—; spkr. in field. Author: Commercial Asset-Based Financing, 1989, The Law of Computer Technology, 2d edit., 1993; co-author: Secured Financing in Personal Property, 1992, Bankruptcy and Creditors Rights, 1992, Modern Licensing Law, 2005-08; bd. editors The Cyberspace Lawyer, 1995-, Computer and Recht Internat., 1999-, Contracts Law Jour., 2008-; mem. bd. advisors Internat Law and Regulation Jour., 1998-; contbr. articles to prof. jours. Recipient 5th Nat. Prize Nathan Burkan Copyright Competition, ASCAP, 1970; Best New Book in Law, Assn. Am. Publishers, 1985; Faculty Svc. Award, U. Houston, 2004 Fellow: Tex. Bar Found., Am. Coll. Comml. Fin. Lawyers; mem.: Computer Law Assn. (bd. dirs. 1994—99), Law and Soc. Assn., Licensing Law Execs. Soc., Am. Law Inst., Am. Intellectual Property Law Assn. Office: Univ Houston Law Ctr 104 BLB 100 Law Ctr Houston TX 77204 Office Phone: 713-743-2100. Office Fax: 713-743-2122. E-mail: lawdean@uh.edu.*

NIMOY, LEONARD, actor, director; b. Boston, Mar. 26, 1931; s. Max and Dora (Spinner) N.; m. Sandi Zober, Feb. 21, 1954 (div.); children: Julie, Adam; m. Susan Bay, 1988. Student (drama scholar), Boston Coll., Pasadena Playhouse, Calif., Jeff Corey, 1960-63; MA, Antioch U., Austin, Tex. Operator drama studio, San Fernando Valley; tchr. Synanon; owner Adajul Music Pub. Co. Actor: (TV appearances) Eleventh Hour, Kraft Theatre, Profiles in Courage, Bonanza, The Twilight Zone, Wagon Train, The Virginian, The Outer Limits, Rawhide, Dr. Kildare, Night Gallery, Columbo, T.J. Hooker, Star Trek: The Next Generation; (TV series) Star Trek, 1966—69, Mission: Impossible, 1969—71, Brave New World, 1998; host (TV series) In Search Of..., 1976—80; actor: (films) Rhubarb, 1951, Queen for a Day, 1951, Kid Monk Baroni, 1952, The Brain Eaters, 1958, The Balcony, 1963, Assault on the Wayne, 1971, Catlow, 1971, Baffled!, 1973, The Alpha Caper, 1973, The Missing Are Deadly, 1975, Invasion of the Body Snatchers, 1978, Seizure: The Story of Kathy Morris, 1979, Star Trek: The Motion Picture, 1979, Star Trek II: The Wrath of Khan, 1982, A Woman Called Golda, 1982, The Sun Also Rises, 1984, Star Trek V: The Final Frontier, 1989, Bonanza: Under Attack, 1995, Carpati: 50 Miles, 50 Years, 1996, Star Trek, 2009, Land of the Lost, 2009; (TV films) Age of Darkness: A Night Gallery Retrospective, 2002; actor, co-prodr. (films) Never Forget, 1991, voice Transformers: The Movie, 1986, The Pagemaster, 1994, A Life Apart: Hasidism in America, 1997, Sinbad: Beyond the Veil of Mists, 2000, Atlantis: The Lost Empire, 2001, dir., actor Star Trek III: The Search for Spock, 1984, dir., co-writer, actor Star Trek IV: The Voyage Home, 1986, exec. prodr., co-writer, actor Star Trek VI: The Undiscovered Country, 1991; dir.: Three Men and a Baby, 1987, The Good Mother, 1988, Body Wars, 1989, Funny About Love, 1990, Holy Matrimony, 1994; (TV series) Deadly Games, 1995; actor: (stage appearances) Dr. Faustus, Stalag 17, Streetcar Named Desire, Cat on a Hot Tin Roof, Deathwatch, Monserrat, Irma La Douce, Visit to a Small Planet, Fiddler on a Roof, The Man in the Glass Booth, 6 Rms Riv Vu, Equus, Love Letters, others; actor, dir., writer (stage appearances) Vincent; composer: (albums) The New World of Leonard Nimoy, other songs; author: (poetry and photography) Will I Think of You, (biography) I Am Not Spock, 1975, We Are All Children, 1977, Come Be With Me, 1979. Mem. ACLU; mem. sch. com. adv. bd. Parents for Peace Western Los Angeles.; del. Dem. Central Com., 1971, 72. Served with AUS, 1954-56. Office: c/o The Gersh Agy Inc 232 N Canon Dr Beverly Hills CA 90210-5302*

NIMS, ARTHUR LEE, III, federal judge; b. Oklahoma City, Jan. 3, 1923; s. Arthur Lee and Edwina (Peckham) N.; m. Nancy Chloe Keyes, July 28, 1950; children: Chloe, Lucy. BA, Williams Coll., 1945; LLB, U. Ga., 1949; LLM in Taxation, NYU, 1954. Bar: Ga. 1949, NJ 1955. Practice law, Macon, Ga., 1949-51; spl. atty. Office Chief Counsel, IRS, NYC and Washington, 1951-55; assoc. McCarter & English, Newark, 1955-61, ptnr., 1961-79; judge US Tax Ct., Washington, 1979-88, chief judge, 1988-92, sr. judge, 1992—. Mem. standing com. Episcopal Diocese of Newark, 1971-75; pres. Colonial Symphony Soc., Madison, NJ, 1975-78. Served to lt. (j.g.) USNR, 1943-46. Recipient Kellogg award Williams Coll., 1990, Career Achievement award The Tax Soc. NYU, 1990. Fellow American Coll. Tax Counsel; mem. ABA (sec. sect. taxation 1977-79), NJ Bar Assn. (chmn. sect. taxation 1969-7l, American Law Inst., J. Edgar Murdock American Inn of Ct. (pres. 1988-92). Office: US Tax Ct 400 2nd St NW Washington DC 20217-0002*

NIMZ, TIMOTHY J., museum director; Dir. Shawnee Town, Kans., 1994—96; former dir., exec. v.p. Nat. Agr. Ctr. and Hall of Fame, Bonner Springs, Kans.; dir. Littleton Hist. Mus., Colo., 2002—. Contbr. articles to profl. jours. Office: Littleton Hist Mus 6028 S Gallup St Littleton CO 80120 Office Phone: 303-795-3950. Office Fax: 303-730-9818. E-mail: mutn@littletongov.org.

NING, CYNTHIA YUMEI, language educator; b. Lahore, Pakistan, Sept. 18, 1952; arrived in US, 1967; d. Chung Fong and Grace Chen Ning; m. Allan Yee (div.); 1 child, Robyn Ning Yee. BA in German, Kalamazoo Coll., Mich., 1973; MA in Chinese, U. Mich., Ann Arbor, 1977, PhD in Chinese, 1986. Instr. Chinese, east Asian langs. U. Hawaii, Honolulu, 1979—83, coord. Ctr. Japanese Studies, 1986—91, assoc. dir. Ctr. Chinese Studies, 1991—, dir. Conficius Inst., 2006—; project adminstr. Nat. Resource Ctr. East Asian Studies, Honolulu, 1983—88; tchr. Chinese Punahou Sch., Honolulu, 1985—86. Host ednl. program Say It In Chinese, Hawaii Pub. TV. Author: Chinese Sentence Book, 1996, Communicating in Chinese, 1993, Exploring in Chinese, 2007. Bd. dirs. US-China People's Friendship Assn., Hawaii, 1995—2000. Recipient award for tchg., U. Hawaii, 1993; grantee, US Dept. Edn., 1987—88, 1989—2002. Mem.: Hawaii Assn. Lang. Tchrs. (pres. 1989—91), Chinese Lang. Tchrs. Assn. (pres. 1998—99, exec. dir. 2000—, 2000—). Avocations: reading, hiking, yoga, films, dance. Home: 1717 Mott-Smith Dr # 3308 Honolulu HI 96822 Office: U Hawaii Ctr Chinese Studies 1890 East-West Rd Honolulu HI 96822 Business E-Mail: cyndy@hawaii.edu.

NING, XUE-HAN (HSUEH-HAN NING), physiologist, researcher; b. Peng-Lai, Shandong, People's Republic of China, Apr. 15, 1936; came to U.S., 1984; s. Yi-Xing and Liu Ning; m. Jian-Xin Fan, May 28, 1967; 1 child, Di Fan. MD, Shanghai 1st Med. Coll., People's Republic of China, 1960; post grad., Chinese Traditional Medicine Coll. for Advanced Study, 1960—61; postgrad. in Physiology, U. Mich., 1984—87. Rsch. fellow, rsch. assoc., leader cardiovasc. rsch. group Shanghai Inst. Physiology, Acad. Sinica, 1973—83, head, assoc. prof. cardiovasc. rsch. unit, 1960—87, prof. and chair hypoxia dept., 1988-90, vice chairperson academic com., 1988-90; NIH internat. rsch. fellow U. Mich., Ann Arbor, 1984-87; prof. and dir. Key Lab of Hypoxia Physiology Academia Sinica, Shanghai, 1989-90. Acting leader, High Altitude Physiology Group, Chinese mountaineering and sci. expdn. team to Mt. Everest, 1975; leader High Altitude Physiology Group, Dept. Metall. Industry of China and Ry. Engring. Corps, 1979; vis. prof. dept. physiology Mich. State U., East Lansing, U. Mich., U. Wash. Med. Sch., 1989-97; affiliate prof., U. Wash., 1997—; rsch. scientist Children's Hosp. and Regional Med. Ctr., Seattle, 1997—. Author: High Altitude Physiology and Medicine, 1981, Reports on Scientific Expedition to Mt. Qomolungma, High Altitude Physiology, 1980, Environment and Ecology of Qinghai-Xizang (Tibet) Plateau, 1982, Self-Health Care at High Altitude, 2006; mem. editl. bd. Chinese Jour. Applied Physiology, 1984-1992, Acta Physiologica, 1988-90, Chinese Jour. Physiology (Taiwan) 2004-; contbr. articles to profl. jours. Recipient Merit award Shanghai Sci. Congress, 1977, All-China Sci. Congress, Beijing, 1978, Super Class award Academia Sinica, Beijing, 1986, 1st Class award Nat. Natural Scis., Beijing, 1987, 2d Class award Acad. Sinica Sci. and Technol. Achievements, Beijing, 1992, # 1 Best Article award Tzu-Chi Med. Jour., Taiwan, 1995. Mem. Am. Physiol. Soc., Am. Heart Assn., Internat. Soc. Heart Rsch., Royal Soc. Medicine, Internat. Soc. for Mountain Medicine. Achievements include first to electrocardiography record at summit of Mt. Everest; research in predictive evaluation of mountaineering performance; characteristics for high altitude adaptation and acclimatization; effect of medicinal herbs on cardiac performance; cardiovascular adaptation and resistance to hypoxia and ischemia; injury threshold of short-cycle-intermittent hypoxia and gene expression in heat; the critical temperature 30 degrees celsius "temperature protectine threshold" for modulating myocardial energy, metabolic pathways, and gene expression to resist ischemia and hypoxia; the 28 degrees celsius "temperature injury threshold" for cardiac contractility in the beating heart in vivo; hypothermic cross adaptation protects heart from subsequent ischema and hypoxia by preserving signaling for mitochondrial biogenesis, activateing stress pathways and inactivating apoptosis to maintain myocardial stability and improve functional recovery during reperfusion and reoxygenation. Home: 7033 43rd Ave NE Seattle WA 98115-6015 Office: Wash Dept Pediats CHRMC 4800 Sand Point Way NE Box G0035 Seattle WA 98105-0371 Business E-Mail: xh@u.washington.edu.

NINIVAGGI, DANIEL A., lawyer, manufacturing executive; b. NYC, June 27, 1964; m. Katie Ninivaggi; children: Caleb, Matthew, Jane, Jack. BA, Columbia U., 1986; MBA, U. Chgo., 1988; JD, Stanford U., 1991. Bar: Ill. 1991, NY 1995, Mich. 2003. Assoc. Skadden, Arps, Slate, Meagher & Flum, Winston & Strawn, LLP, NYC, 1992—98, ptnr., 1998—2003; v.p., sec., gen. counsel Lear Corp., Southfield, Mich., 2003—04, sr. v.p., sec., gen. counsel, 2004—06, exec. v.p., sec., gen. counsel, 2006—07, exec. v.p., chief adminstrv. officer, 2007—09; of counsel Winston & Strawn LLP, Detroit, 2009—. Mailing: Winston & Strawn LLP 200 Park Ave New York NY 10166-4193 Office Phone: 212-294-6787.

NIÑO, DEANNA HOLLYE, lawyer; d. Alfredo and Hollye Niño. BA, U. Vt., 1991; JD, U. Denver, 1995. Atty., pension investigator U.S. Dept. Labor, Boston, 1996—99; atty. Marcia Wagner and Assocs., Boston, 1999—2000, Greenberg Traurig, LLP, NYC, 2000—. Instr. Internat. Found. Employee Benefit Plans, Brookfield, Wis., 2000—; spkr. in field; presenter in field. Contbr. articles to profl. jours. Recipient Good Job award, U.S. Dept. Labor, 1998. Mem.: ABA, N.Y. Bar Assn. Office: Greenberg Traurig LLP Attorneys At Law 200 Park Avenue New York NY 10166 Office Fax: 212-805-9243; Home Fax: 212-805-9243. Business E-Mail: ninod@gtlaw.com.

NINOW, KEVIN J., chemicals executive; With Huntsman Corp., Salt Lake City, 1989—, project engr., process control group leader, mgr. tech., ops. mgr. C4's; plant mgr. C4's; plant mgr. oxides and olefins Huntsman Corp., v.p. internat. mfg., v.p. European Petrochemicals, sr. v.p. European Petrochemicals, 1999—2003, divsn. pres. base chems. and polymers, 2003—. Office: Huntsman Corp 500 Huntsman Way Salt Lake City UT 84108 Office Phone: 801-584-5700.

NIPPERT, CHARLES, engineering educator, department chairman; b. Allentown, Pa., May 10, 1947; s. Charles and Eleanor Nippert; m. Carolyn Cochrane, Nov. 11, 1972; children: Collin, Corinne. BSChemE, Lehigh U., Bethlehem, Pa., 1969, MSChemE, 1972, PhD in Chem. Engring., 1976. Cert. profl. engr., Pa., 1990. Chair, dept. chem. engring. Widener U., Chester, Pa., 2006—. Achievements include development of virtual laboratory for use in education. Office: Widener Univ One University Pl Chester PA 19013-5792 Office Fax: 610-499-4059.

NIRENBERG, DARRYL D., lawyer; b. Middletown, NY, Sept. 23, 1959; s. Alex Jack and Sandra (Levine) Nirenberg. BA cum laude, Colgate U., 1981; JD, George Washington U., 1987. Legis. asst. Senator S.I. Havakawa, Washington, 1981—82; profl. staff Agr. Com. US Senate, 1983—86, assoc. rep. counsel Fgn. Rels. Com., 1987—89, rep. dep. staff dir. Fgn. Rels. Com., 1990—91; chief of staff Senator Jesse Helms, 1991—95; ptnr. pub. policy def. and nat. security practices, hiring ptnr. Patton Boggs LLP. Mem. Moot Ct. Team George Washington U.; vice chmn. NY State Coll. Reps., 1979—80, Fairfax County Young Rep., Va., 1982—83; campaign aide Senator Jacob K. Javits, 1980; counsel Rep. Platform Com., 2000, Presdl. Inauguration Con., 2001. Mem.: Phi Alpha Theta. Jewish. Office: US Senate Com on Fgn Relations 452 Dirksen Bldg Washington DC 20510-0001 also: Patton Boggs LLP 2550 M St Nw Washington DC 20037-1350 Office Phone: 202-457-6022. Office Fax: 202-457-6315. Business E-Mail: dnirenberg@pattonboggs.com.

NIRENBERG, LOUIS, mathematician, educator; b. Hamilton, Ont., Can., Feb. 28, 1925; arrived in U.S., 1945, naturalized, 1954; s. Zuzie and Bina (Katz) Nirenberg; m. Susan Blank, Jan. 25, 1948; children: Marc, Lisa. BSc, McGill U., Montreal, 1945, DSc (hon.), 1986; MS, NYU, 1947, PhD, 1949; DSc (hon.), U. Pisa, Italy, 1990, U. Paris Dauphine, 1990, McMaster U., Can., 2000. Mem. faculty NYU, 1949—, prof. math., 1957—, dir. Courant Inst., 1970—72. Visitor Inst. Advanced Study, 1958; hon. prof. Nannkai U., Zhejiang U. Author rsch. articles. Recipient Crafoord prize, Royal Swedish Acad., 1982, Nat. medal of Sci., 1995; fellow NRC, 1951—52, Sloan Found., 1958—60, Guggenheim Found., 1966—67, 1975—76, Fulbright, 1965. Mem.: NAS, Ukrainian Acad. Sci. (fgn.), Accademia de Scienze e Lettere (fgn.), Istituto Lombardo, Accademia dei Lincei (fgn.), French Acad. Scis. (fgn.), Am. Philos. Soc., Am. Math. Soc. (v.p. 1976—78, M. Bocher prize 1959, L.P. Steele prize 1994), Am. Acad. Arts and Scis., European Acad. Scis. (hon.). Home: 221 W 82nd St New York NY 10024-5406 Office: Courant Inst 251 Mercer St New York NY 10012-1185 Home Phone: 212-724-1069. Business E-Mail: nirenl@cims.nyu.edu.

NIRENBERG, MARSHALL WARREN, biochemist; b. NYC, Apr. 10, 1927; s. Harry Edward and Minerva (Bykowsky) Nirenberg; m. Perola Zaltzman, July 14, 1961. BS in Zoology, U. Fla., 1948, MS, 1952; PhD in Biochemistry, U. Mich., 1957. Postdoctoral fellow Am. Cancer Soc. at NIH, 1957—59; postdoctoral fellow USPHS at NIH, 1959—60; mem. staff NIH, 1960—; rsch. biochemist, chief lab. biochem. genetics Nat. Heart, Lung and Blood Inst., NIH, Bethesda, Md., 1962—. Recipient Molecular Biology award, NAS, 1962, award in biol. scis., Washington Acad. Scis., 1962, medal, HEW, 1964, Modern Medicine award, 1963, Harrison Howe award, Am. Chem. Soc., 1964, Nat. Medal Sci., Pres. Johnson, 1965, Hildebrand award, Am. Chem. Soc., 1966, Research Corp. award, 1966, A.C.P. award, 1967, award merit, Gairdner Found., Can, 1967, Prix Charles Leopold Meyer, French Acad. Scis., 1967, Franklin medal, Franklin Inst., 1968, Albert Lasker Med. Research award, 1968, Priestly award, 1968; co-recipient Louisa Gross Horowitz prize Columbia, 1968, Nobel prize in physiology or medicine, 1968. Fellow: AAAS, NY Acad. Scis.; mem.: NAS, Pontificial Acad. Scis., Leopoldina Deutsche Akademie der Naturforscher, Soc. Devel. Biology, Soc. for Study Devel. and Growth, Washingon Acad. Scis., Harvey Soc. (hon.), Biophys. Soc., Am. Acad. Arts and Scis., Am. Chem. Soc. (Paul Lewis award enzyme chemistry 1964), Am. Soc. Biol. Chemists. Achievements include research in mechanism protein synthesis, genetic code, nucleic acids, regulatory mechanisms in synthesis macromolecules, and neurobiology.*

NIROOMAND, FARHANG, economics professor, researcher; b. Shiraz, Iran, Aug. 20, 1953; s. Nahid and Aziz Niroomand; m. Farnaz Zand. BA, Nat. U. Iran, Tehran, 1974; MA, Mich. State U., East Lansing, 1977, PhD, 1983. Chair, dept. economics & internat. bus. Coll. Bus., U. Southern Miss., Hattiesburg, 1997—99, assoc. dean academic affairs, 1999—2000, dir. grad. programs, 1999—2000, assoc. dean, 2000—07, prof., 2000—07; assoc., ctr. rsch. internat. economics U. Wis., Milwaukee, 2002—; mem. Miss. Dist. Export Coun., Jackson, 2006—. Project dir. US Dept. Edn., 2005—08. Contbr. articles to profl. jour. Bd. mem. Dist. Export Coun., Jackson, Miss., 2006. Recipient Excellence Tchg. award, U. Southern Miss., 1987, 1994, BellSouth Outstanding Faculty award, 1990, Louis K. Brandt Faculty Rsch. award, 1999, Edn. award, Miss. World Trade Ctr., 2008; Title VI-B grant, US Dept. Edn., 2000—03, 2005—08. Fellow: Assn. Global Bus. (jour. editor 2005—07, Best Paper award 2005); mem.: Acad. Internat. Bus., Am. Econ. Soc., Omicron Delta Epsilon (v.p. 2006—07, exec. sec. 2007—, treas. 2007—). Office: Univ Southern Miss 118 College Dr #5072 Hattiesburg MS 39406 Office Fax: 601-266-4920. Personal E-mail: farhang.niroomand@comcast.net. Business E-Mail: farhang.niroomand@usm.edu.

NIRSCHL, ROBERT PHILLIP, orthopedic surgeon; b. South Milwaukee, Wis., Aug. 28, 1933; s. Boyd A. and Helen (Wozny) N.; m. Mary Ann Oleniczak, June 21, 1958; children: Suzanne, Robert C., Julie. Student, Coll. Holy Cross, 1951-53, Marquette U., 1953-54; MD, Med. Coll. Wis./Marquette U., 1958; MS, U. Minn., 1965. Diplomate Am. Bd. Orthop. Surgery. Intern St. Mary's Hosp., Duluth, Minn., 1958-59; resident in orthop. Mayo Clinic, Rochester, Minn., 1959-63; lt. comdr. USN, Washington, 1963-65; pvt. practice Arlington, Va., 1965—. Attending orthop. surgeon Va. Hosp. Ctr., Arlington, dir. Hand Surgery Svc., 1975—85, v.p. med. staff, 1980—83, mem. hosp. med. exec. com., 2006—; chief orthop. surgery No. Va. Cmty. Hosp., 1971—82; founding dir. Nirschl Orthop. Ctr. for Sports Medicine and Joint Reconstrn., 1974—, Nirschl Orthop. Sport Med. Ctr. Orthop. Sports Medicine Fellowship Program Va. Hosp. Ctr., Arlington, 1987—; mem. clin. faculty Georgetown U. Med. Ctr., 1965—; orthop. cons. Pres.'s Coun. Phys. Fitness, Washington, 1981—87; mem. sports sci. com. USTA, NYC, 1987—94; chief orthopedic sports med. cons. Athletic Dept. Marymount U., 2006—; course dir. numerous symposia in field. Author: Arm Care, 1981, rev. edit., 1996, Isoflex Exercise System, 1983; chief med. editor Orthop. Today, 1983-93; mem. editl. bd. The Physician and Sportsmedicine, 1992-2005, The Med. Sentinel, 1996-02, Orthopedics Today, 2003-; creator 10 video programs; contbr. 45 chpts. to books and over 125 articles to profl. publs.; patentee in field. Chmn. Jeffersonian Health Policy Found., Williamsburg, Va., 1994—97; mem. Va. Bd. Medicine, 2000—04; trustee Marymount U., Arlington, 2005—. Grantee Pfizer Inc., 1992-93, Sano Corp, 1993-94, Iomed Corp., 1999-2000, Travanti Pharma Inc, 2008-09. Mem.: AMA, Am. Orthop. Assn., VA Orthop. Soc. (Lifetime Career award 2005), Arlington County Med. Soc. (pres. 1977, chmn. legis. com. 1987—2004, Welburn award 1995), Med. Soc. Va. (chmn. sports medicine com. 1973—84, trustee polit. action com. 1990—2002, legis. com. 1995, liability com. 2005—, trustee polit. action com. 2006—), Va. Orthop. Soc. (pres. 1998—99, career award 2005), Washington Orthop. Soc., Ea. Orthop. Assn., Soc. Tennis Medicine and Sci. (exec. com.), Am. Orthop. Soc. Sports Medicine (ethics com. 1992—97, bd. dels. 2002—), Am. Acad. Orthop. Surgery (health fin. com. 1994—2000, comm. and state soc. coms. bd. of counselors 2000—03, bd. counselors 2000—06), Washington Golf and Country Club. Republican. Roman Catholic. Avocation: fitness activities. Office: Nirschl Orthop Ctr Sports Medicine & Joint Reconstrn 1715 N George Mason Dr Ste 504 Arlington VA 22205-3670 Home Phone: 703-237-8706; Office Phone: 703-525-2200. Personal E-mail: nirschlorthopaedics@comcast.net.

NISE, NORMAN S., engineering educator; m. Ellen L. Becker, June 4, 1961; children: Benjamin E., Alan H., Sharon L. Miller. BSEE, Drexel U., Phila., 1960; MSEE, Lehigh U., Bethlehem, Pa., 1962. Mem. tech. staff Hughes Aircraft Co., Fullerton, Calif., 1961—70, Rockwell Internat., Downey, Calif., 1980—93; prof. emeritus Calif. State Poly. U., Pomona, 1963—. Author: (book) Control Systems Engineering. Mem.: IEEE, ASEE, Eta Kappa Nu, Tau Beta Pi, Tau Epsilon Phi. Office: Calif State Polytechnic Univ 3801 W Temple Ave Pomona CA 91768 Office Fax: 909-869-4687. Business E-Mail: nsnise@csupomona.edu.

NISENHOLTZ, MARTIN ABRAM, telecommunications executive, educator; b. Phila., Apr. 1, 1955; s. Louis William and Rhoda Greta (Koenig) N.; m. Anne Ermine Stockler, July 26, 1987; children: Johanna, Marjorie. BA, U. Pa., 1977, MA, 1979. Research scientist NYU, NYC, 1979-83; mgr. Ogilvy & Mather, NYC, 1983-84, v.p., 1984-89, sr. v.p., 1989-94; dir. content strategy Ameritech Corp., Chgo., 1994-95; pres. N.Y. Times Electronic Media Co., 1995-99; CEO N.Y. Times Digital, 1999—2005; sr. v.p. digital ops. The N.Y. Times Co., 2005—. Mem. ops. Ogilvy & Mather Direct, 1992—94; adj. assoc. prof. NYU, 1983—; bd. dirs. internet advtsg. bur. Ctr. for Comm., 1999; bd. dirs. Yellow Pages Group. Mem. Annenberg Sch. Alumni Bd., 1996—; bd. dirs. N.Y. Leukemia and Lumphoma Soc., 2005—. Recipient Merrill Panott Citizenship award, 1997, Ten award, 2003; grantee Nat. Endowment Arts, 1981. Mem.: Online Pubs. Assn. (founding chmn. 2001—04), Interactive Svcs. Assn. (dir. 1985—94, chmn. 1991, Disting. Svc. award 1994). Office: NY Times Co 620 8th Ave New York NY 10018 Office Phone: 212-556-8879. Business E-Mail: martin@nytimes.com.

NISHAR, DIPCHAND (DEEP NISHAR), Internet company executive; BS with honors, Indian Inst. Tech., Kharagpur; MSEE, U. Ill., Urbana-Champaign; MBA, Harvard Bus. Sch. Various product mgmt., mktg., fin. & engring. positions Cummins Engine Co., Columbus, Ind.;

assoc. Boston Consulting Group; founder Patkai Networks, 2000; founding team mem. Universal Application Network bus. unit Siebel Sys., Inc., Calif.; dir. ads systems automation Google Inc., Mountain View, Calif., 2003—05, dir. wireless products, 2005—07, sr. dir. product mgmt. Asia-Pacific, 2007—08; v.p. product strategy LinkedIn Corp., Mountain View, 2009—. Adv. Airline Intelligence Systems Inc. (AISystems). Recipient Google Founders award. Achievements include patents in field. Office: LinkedIn Corp 2029 Stierlin Ct Palo Alto CA 94303 Office Phone: 650-687-3600. Office Fax: 650-687-0505.*

NISHI, GREGG K., surgeon, educator; BS, U. Calif., Irvine; MD, George Washington U. Sch. Medicine. Intern North Shore U. Hosp., Manhasset, NY; resident Cedars-Sinai Med. Ctr., surgeon Ctr. for Weight Loss, surgeon Surgical Intensive Care Unit & Trauma Surgery Svcs.; asst. clinical prof. surgery UCLA David Geffen Sch. Medicine. Recipient Leo G. Rigler MD award, Cedars-Sinai Med. Ctr., Paul Rubenstein MD Prize for Excellence. Fellow: Am. Coll. Surgeons; mem.: AMA, Soc. Laparoendoscopic Surgeons (Resident Achievement award), Soc. Am. Gastrointestinal Endoscopic Surgeons. Office: 8635 W 3rd St #795-W Los Angeles CA 90048 Office Phone: 310-423-8350. Office Fax: 310-423-4145.*

NISHIHARA, MINORU, surgeon; b. Naha, Okinawa, Japan, July 24, 1962; s. Shigeru and Takako Nishihara; m. Yasuko Ishibashi, July 30, 1967; children: Katsumi, Shiori. MD, Nagasaki U., Japan, 1988, PhD, 1999. Physician Nagasaki U. Sch. Medicine, 1988-93, Nishi-Isahaya Hosp., Nagasaki, 1997-98; chief surgery Nat. Tsushima Hosp., Nagasaki, 1998-99, Heart-Life Hosp., Okinawa, 1999—2003, sub-mgr. surgery, 2003—07, mgr. surgery, 2007—, dir., 2009—. Mem.: Japan Surg. Assn., Japanese Soc. Gastroent. Surgery, Japan Surg. Soc. Achievements include research in parathyroid hormone-related protein; digestive surgery; hepato-biliary-pancreatic surgery. Avocations: kendo player, computers. Office: Heart Life Hosp 208 Iju Nakagusuku-son Nakagami-gun Okinawa 901-2492 Japan Office Phone: 098-895-3255. Office Fax: 098-895-3066. Personal E-mail: minorunish@aol.jp. Business E-Mail: m.nishihara@heartlife.or.jp.

NISHII, LISA, psychology professor; PhD, U. Md., Coll. Pk., 2003. Contbr. articles to academic jours., scientific papers to rsch. publs. (Best Empirical Paper Pub. award, Internat. Assn. Conflict Mgmt., 2004). Mem. Ithaca Asian Am. Assn., NY, 2003—05. Recipient Wallace Reins Best Paper award, Soc. Indsl.-Orgnl. Psychology, 2005, MacIntyre Exemplary Tchg. award, Cornell U., award, SHRM Found., Office Disability Employment Policy, Dept. Labor. Mem.: Internat. Assn. Conflict Mgmt. (com. mem. 1999—2004), Acad. Mgmt. (com. mem. 2004—08), Soc. Indsl. and Orgnl. Psychology (com. mem. 2002—08). Democrat. Avocations: travel, cooking, squash, tennis, swimming. Office: Cornell Univ 363 Ives Hall Ithaca NY 14853

NISHIMURA, JOSEPH YO, retired retail executive, accountant; b. Berkeley, Calif., Nov. 4, 1933; s. Masamoto and Kimiko (Ishihara) N.; m. Joyce Toshiye Mori, Sept. 1, 1956; children: Brenda Joyce, Stephen Lloyd. AB cum laude, Princeton U., 1956; MBA, Stanford U., 1961. CPA, Calif., N.Y.; cert. Employee Benefit Specialist. Audit supr. Touche Ross & Co., San Francisco, 1961-66; contr. Scott Co. of Calif., Oakland, 1966-67, Purity Stores, Inc., Burlingame, Calif., 1967-69; pres. Cubit Sys. Corp., Burlingame, 1969-72; sr. v.p. Golden West Fin. Corp., Oakland, 1972-73; exec. v.p. Victory Mkts., Inc., Norwich, NY, 1973-90; gen. ptnr. Mori Enterprises, 1994—2005. Dir. Carl's Drug Co., Rome, N.Y., 1988-90, mem. site devel. com., Wakefern Food Corp., Edison, N.J., 1996—. V.p., bd. dirs. Chenango Meml. Hosp., Norwich, 1981-87; bd. dirs. United Fund, Norwich, 1984-90, N.Y. State Food Mchts. Assn., 1988-90, Binghamton (N.Y.) Philharmonic, 1988-98, treas., 1990-93; cons. Mori Charitable Unitrust, 2005-. Served to lt. (j.g.) USN, 1956-59; Japan. Mem. AICPA, Calif. Soc. CPAs, Marbella Country Club. Democrat. Presbyterian.

NISHIMURA, PETE HIDEO, oral surgeon; b. Hilo, Hawaii, Aug. 7, 1922; s. Hideichi and Satsuki N.; m. Tomoe Nishimura, June, 1949; children— Dennis Dean, Grant Neil, Dawn Naomi. Student, U. Hawaii, 1940-44; D.D.S., U. Mo., 1947; MSD., Northwestern U., 1949. Practice dentistry specializing in oral surgery, Honolulu, 1952—; pres. Oral Surgery Group, 1978—. Mem. coun. Nat. Bd. Dental Examination; dir. Hawaii Dental Svc., 1962-85, pres., 1970-72, 76-78; pres. State Bd. Dental Examiners, Delta Sigma Delta, Fedn. Dentaire Internat. Served with U.S. Army, 1952-54. Recipient Citation for outstanding pub. svc. toward the devel. of state plan for emergency mgmt. resources, Dir. Emergency Planning, Exec. Office of Pres. of U.S., 1968, Lifetime Achievement award, Hawaii Dental Assn.; named Disting. Alumni, U. Mo. Hawaii, 2004. Fellow Am. Coll. Dentists, Internat. Coll. Dentists; mem. ADA, Hawaii Dental Assn. (past pres., Lifetime Achievement award 2006), Delta Dental Plans Assn. (dir.), Honolulu County Dental Soc., Hawaii Soc. Oral Surgeons, Am. Assn. Oral and Maxillofacial Surgeons, Western Soc. Oral and Maxillofacial Surgeons, Am. Assn. Dental Examiners, Pierre Fauchard Acad. (citation for oustanding contbn. to arts and sci. of dentistry 1987). Democrat. Home: Apt 606 4389 Malia St Honolulu HI 96821 Office: 848 S Beretania St Honolulu HI 96813-2551 Personal E-mail: hilopete@aol.com.

NISHINO, HITOSHI, physics professor; s. Nishino. BSc, U. Tokyo, Hongo, Bunkyo-ku, 1976, MSc, 1978, MSc, 1981. Vis. scientist Internat. Ctr. Theoretical Physics, Trieste, Italy, 1982—84; rsch. assoc. U. Md., College Park, 1984—86, 1990—94, sr. rsch. assoc., 1996—2001; rsch. assoc. Brandeis U., Waltham, Mass., 1986—88, U. NC, Chapel Hill, 1988—90; lectr. Howard U., Washington, 1994—95; jr. faculty mem. Calif. State U., Long Beach, Calif., 2001—. Contbr. scientific papers to profl. jours. Grantee, NSF, 2003—05, 2007—08. Office: CA State Univ 1250 Bellflower Boulevard Long Beach CA 90840 Business E-Mail: hnishino@csulb.edu.

NISHIYAMA, CHIAKI, economist, educator; b. Fukuoka-ken, Japan, Aug. 9, 1924; s. Michiki and Teruko (Tsuji) N.; m. Shigeko Okabe, June 9, 1957; children: Keita, Mikiko. BA in Econs., Rikkyo U., Tokyo, 1950; MA in Polit. Sci., U. Chgo., 1952, PhD in Social Thought, 1960, postgrad. in econs., 1959-60. Instr. U. Chgo., 1955—56, lectr. econs., 1956—57; assoc. prof. Rikkyo U., 1962-64, prof. econs., 1964-90, prof. emeritus, 1990—. Sr. rsch. fellow Hoover Instn., Stanford U., 1977—; prof. econs. Grad. Sch. Internat. Mgmt., U. Japan, 1994-97; lectr. Tng. Inst., Min. Trade and Industry, Japanese Govt., 1964-66, Gakushuin U., 1970-71, Waseda U., 1972-74; exec. dir. Assembly on US-Japan Econ. Policy, 1972-76; prime minister's spl. envoy to White House, 1971, 75; specialist counselor Japan Employers' Assn., 1975-85; fellow Woodrow Wilson Internat. Ctr. for Scholars, 1978-79; del. European Assembly, Strasbourg, France, 1982; world travel for Japanese Min. Fgn. Affairs, Japan External Trade Orgn., 1968-82; lectr. various univs., US and Europe, 1976-94; mem. Am. Citizen to Citizen Econ. and Fin. Mgmt. Del. to USSR, 1991; spl. envoy of Japan to Germany, Czechoslovakia, Hungary, Bulgaria, Ukraine, Russia, 1991. Author numerous books including: Lecture on Modern Economics, 1964, Free Economy, Its Policies and Principles, 1974, The Price for Prosperity, 1974, A Monetary History and Analysis of the Japanese Economy 1968-70, 1974, Reflection on Japanese Economy, 1976, Monetarism, 1976, The Last Chance for Creativity, Liberty and Prosperity, 1981, Human Capitalism, 1982, The Fourth Philosophy, Vol. I, 1982, Vol. II, 1983, No Limits to Growth, 1984, The Essence of Hayek, 1984, The Japanese Economy, 1987, Paradigm Shift, 1987, Japanese Economy and Life Tomorrow, 1988, A New Economics Under a New Paradigm, 1991, The End of Recession, 1994, Depression or New Prosperity, 1998, Market Economy: New Way, 1999, Chicago Boys, 2003, Japan in the New Century and Blackship, 2005, Reason and Its Limits from Asian Paradigm, 2005; editl. bd. Jour. Internat. Money and Fin., 1981—. Hon. fellow Inst. Econ. Affairs, London, 1976—; mem. adv. bd. Econ. Inst. Paris, 1984-86, Carl Menger Inst., Wien, 1984; councilor The Daiwa Securities Welfare Found., 1994—. Recipient Japan Econ. Lit. award Japan Econ. Jour., 1974; Eahart fellow, 1960-61, E.C. Nef fellow, 1958-59; grantee Relm, 1962-64, Ford, 1965-66, Lilly, 1966-67, Bank of Japan, Bankers Assn. Japan, other fin. orgns., 1978-83. Mem. Am. Enterprise Inst. (adj. scholar), Am. Econ. Assn., Econometric Soc., Japan Econs. Assn., Econ. Assn., Statis. Soc., Mont Pelerin Soc. (pres. 1980-82, sr. v.p. 1982-85, hon. v.p. 1986-88), Japan Econ. Rsch. Ctr. (spl. mem. 1964). Episcopalian. Office: Nishiyama-Kenkyushitsu 5-15-18 Kamiuma Setagaya-ku 154-0011 Tokyo Japan Personal E-mail: nichiko@classicmsn.com.

NISKALA, MARKKU, international organization administrator; MPA, Tampere U., 1969. With Finnish Red Cross, 1970—73; various positions including dir. Europe Dept. at Internat. Federation of Red Cross and Red Crescent, 1973—88; sec. gen. Finnish Red Cross, 1988—2003, Internat. Fedn. of Red Cross and Red Crescent, 2003—. Chmn. commn. fin. internat. com. Red Cross, 1992; chmn. red crescent donor forum coord. group Internat. Fedn. Red Cross, 2001—, sec. gen., 2003—; chmn. SCHR, Geneva, 2006. Avocation: languages. Office: Internat Fedn Red Cross and Crescent Soc PO Box 372 CH-1211 Geneva Switzerland Office Phone: 4122 730 4222. Business E-Mail: secretariat@ifrc.org.

NISKANEN, WILLIAM ARTHUR, JR., economist, retired think-tank executive; b. Bend, Oreg., Mar. 13, 1933; s. William Arthur and Nina Elizabeth (McCord) Niskanen; m. Kathyrn Washburn; children: Lia, Pamela, Jaime. BA, Harvard U., 1954; MA, U. Chgo., 1955, PhD, 1962. Staff economist RAND Corp., Santa Monica, Calif., 1957—62; staff dir. US Dept. Def., Washington, 1962—64; divsn. dir. Inst. Def. Analyses, Washington, 1964—70; asst. dir. Office Mgmt. & Budget, Exec. Office of the Pres., Washington, 1970—72; prof. U. Calif., Berkeley, 1972—75; chief economist Ford Motor Co., Dearborn, Mich., 1975—80; prof. UCLA, 1980—81; mem. Coun. Econ. Advisers, Exec. Office of the Pres., Washington, 1981—85; chmn. Cato Inst., Washington, 1985—2008, sr. economist, 2008—. Author: Bureaucracy and Representative Goverment, 1971, Reaganomics, 1988, Policy Analysis and Public Choice, 1998, Going Digital, 1998, Autocratic, Democratic and Optimal Government, 2004, After Enron: Lessons for Public Policy, 2005, Reflection of a Political Economist, 2008; editor: Regulation mag., 1990—96. Founder Nat. Tax Limitation Com. Mem.: Atlantic Econ. Assn. (past pres.), Pub. Choice Soc. (past pres.), Am. Econ. Assn. Republican. Office: Cato Inst 1000 Massachusetts Ave NW Washington DC 20001-5400 Home Phone: 202-546-1097; Office Phone: 202-789-5236. Business E-Mail: wniskan@cato.org.

NISS, BARBARA JOYCE, archivist; b. Malone, NY, Dec. 11, 1958; d. Raymond Paul and Alice Marie St. Mary; m. Michael Allen Niss, July 2, 1983; children: Matthew Raymond, Sarah Rachel. BA, Coll. New Rochelle, NY, 1980; MA, NYU, NYC, 1982. Asst. archivist Archives NY Hosp. Cornell Med. Ctr., NYC, 1982—84; assoc. archivist LaGuardia Archives, NYC, 1984—86; archivist Mt. Sinai Med. Ctr., NYC, 1986—93, 1999—, asst. to libr. dir., 1995—99. Cons. writer Mt. Sinai Alumni, NYC, 1995. Co-author: (non-fiction book) This House of Noble Deeds: The Mount Sinai Hospital (Arline Custer Meml. Award, 2003), Teaching Tomorrow's Medicine Today: The Mount Sinai School of Medicine; contbr. articles to profl. jours. Bd. dirs. Kids SPACE, Rye, NY, 1997—98; bd. mem. Women's Assn. Rye Presbyn. Ch., NY, 2001—06; bd. dirs. Alumnae Assn. Coll. New Rochelle, NY, 1998—2000. Recipient Ursula Laurus, Coll. New Rochelle, 2000, Unsung Hero award, Alumnae Assn. Mt. Sinai Hosp. Sch. Nursing, 2001, award, Mt. Sinai Alumni, 2008. Mem.: Am. Assn. History Medicine, METRO Conservation Preservation Adv. Coun., Archivists Round Table Met. NY (chairperson 1985—86), Mid-Atlantic Regional Archives Conf. (program com. mem. 1988—89), Archivists and Librs. History Health Scis. (steering com. 1992—93), Soc. Am. Archivists. Office: Mt Sinai Med Ctr Box 1102 Levy Libr 1 Gustave Levy Pl New York NY 10029-6574 Office Phone: 212-241-7239. Business E-Mail: barbara.niss@mssm.edu.

NISSEN, CHRISTOPHER KARL, educator; b. Millbrae, Calif., Mar. 29, 1956; m. Margaret Louise Bigley, June 1, 1986 (div. 2002); children: Alexander Bigley, Cameron Forster. PhD, U. Calif., Berkeley, 1987. Assoc. prof. Northern Ill. U., DeKalb, 1988—. Contbr. monographs. Achievements include research in Italian literature. Home: 328 W Roosevelt St Dekalb IL 60115 Office: Northern Ill Univ Dekalb IL 60115-2854 Business E-Mail: cnissen@niu.edu.

NISSEN, STEVEN EVAN, cardiologist, researcher; b. Toledo, Sept. 1, 1948; m. Linda Butler. BS, U. Mich., Ann Arbor; MD, U. Mich. Sch. Medicine, Ann Arbor, 1978. Intern internal medicine Univ. Calif. Davis, Sacramento, resident internal medicine; fellowship in cardiology Chandler Med. Ctr. Univ. Ky., Lexington; cardiologist Cleveland Clinic, 1992—, dir. coronary ICU, 1992—97, sect. head clinical cardiology, 1992—2002, vice chmn. dept. cardiology, 1993—2002, interim chmn., dept. cardiovascular med., 2006, chmn., dept. cardiovascular med., 2006—, dir., Joseph J. Jacobs Ctr. for Thrombosis and Vascular Biology; prof. medicine Cleve. Clinic Lerner Sch. Medicine. Mem. and chmn. CardioRenal adv. panel US FDA; spl. govt. employee US FDA Committees; mem. med. & sci. adv. bd. Forbes Medi-Tech Inc.; vis. prof. at med. colleges and universities internationally and nationally. Contbr. articles to profl. jours., chapters to books; mem. editl. bd. Internat. Jour. Cardiac Imaging, Cardiology Today, Clinical Cardiology; editor: Current Cardiology Reports, 2006—; sr. consulting editor Journal of American College of Cardiology, 2002—. Recipient Award for Outstanding Rsch. in Cardiovascular Rsch., Gill Heart Inst., U. Ky., 2004; named one of The World's Most Influential People, TIME mag., 2007. Mem.: Am. Coll. Cardiology (pres., chmn. bd. trustees 2006—, ednl. products com., info. tech. com.). Achievements include development of intravascular ultrasound imaging; published rsch. on cardiovascular problems caused by Cox-2 inhibitor drugs, such as Vioxx & Celebrex. Avocation: bicycling. Office: Cleveland Clinic Mail Code F 15 9500 Euclid Ave Cleveland OH 44195 Office Phone: 216-445-6852. Business E-Mail: nissens@ccf.org.

NISSEN, VARINA, employment services executive; MBA, Melbourne Bus. Sch., Australia. Dir. corp. svcs. Sydney Airports Corp. Ltd.; CEO Australia, exec. dir. Asia Pacific Burson-Marsteller; mng. dir. Australia and New Zealand Manpower, Inc., 2003—06, sr. v.p. global mktg. and comm., 2006—. Bd. mem. Essendon, Bankstown, Hoxton Pk., Camden Airports, Australia; dir. Com. Econ. Devel., Australia.

NISSENBLATT, MICHAEL JEFFREY, medical oncologist; b. Bronx, NY, June 4, 1948; m. Marlene Nissenblatt; 1 child, Doree; 1 child, Paulina. MD, Columbia P&S, 1973. Diplomate Am. Bd. Internal Medicine. Intern Johns Hopkins, Balt., 1973-74, resident, 1974-75, 75-76, fellow, 1976-78; assoc. dir. med. oncology RW Johnson U. Hosp., New Brunswick, 1996—; staff St. Peter's Med. Ctr., New Brunswick; clin. prof. medicine RW Johnson U. Sch. Medicine, 1996—. Dir. Ctrl. NJ Oncology Ctr., 1981—. Recipient Chamber of Commerce award, 2003, Partners in Caring award, Am. Cancer Soc., 2004. Fellow ACP; mem. AMA, AAAS, Am. Radiol. Soc., Am. Soc. Clin. Oncology, Cancer Chemotherapy Found., Johns Hopkins Med. Surgeons Soc., Maimonides Soc., Middlesex County Med. Soc., N.J. Breast Cancer Coalition, others. Jewish. Avocations: running, astronomy, anthropology, motivational speaking. Office: Ctrl Jersey Oncology Ctr PA 205 Easton Ave New Brunswick NJ 08901-1722 Office Phone: 732-828-9570. Personal E-mail: mjnmotor@aol.com.

NISSENSON, ALLEN RICHARD, physician, educator; b. Chgo., Dec. 10, 1946; s. Harry and Sylvia Lillian (Chapnitsky) N.; m. Charna H. Karp, May 28, 1978; 1 child, Ariel Rose. BS in Medicine, Northwestern U., 1967, MD, 1971. Diplomate Am. Bd. Internal Medicine, bd. cert. internal medicine and nephrology. Intern in medicine Michael Reese Hosp. and Med. Ctr., Chgo., 1971-72, resident in internal medicine, 1972-74; fellowship in nephrology Northwestern U., Chgo., 1974-76; assoc. medicine Northwestern U. Med. Sch., Chgo., 1976-77; asst. prof. medicine UCLA Sch. Medicine, 1977-82, assoc. prof. medicine, 1982-88, prof. medicine, 1988—; dir. dialysis program UCLA Ctr. for the Health Scis., 1977—, med. dir. renal mgmt. strategies, assoc. dean David Geffen Sch. Medicine, 2006—. Adj. attending physician Northwestern Meml. Hosp., Chgo., 1976-77; asst. attending physician UCLA Ctr. for Health Scis., 1977-82, assoc. attending physician, 1988—; attending physician nephrology Wadsworth VA Hosp., 1978—; cons. on peritoneal dialysis Baxter-Travenol Labs., 1981—; mem. nephrology adv. com. Nephrology Nursing Edn. Grant, Calif. State U., 1983-90; vice chmn. Forum of End Stage Renal Disease Networks, 1988-91; mem. sci. adv. bd. Nat. Kidney Found., 1989-91, chmn. coun. on clin. nephrology, dialysis and transplantation, 1989-91; cons. on End Stage Renal Disease reimbursement Rand Corp., 1990—, others. Editor-in-chief Advances in Renal Replacement Therapy, 1993—, Hemodialysis Internat., 2004—, Medscape Nephrology, 2006; mem. editl. bd. Dialysis and Transplantation, 1978—, UCLA Health Insights, 1981-89, Perspectives in Peritoneal Dialysis, 1983—, Internat. Jour. Artificial Organs, 1984—, Seminars in Dialysis, 1987—, Am. Jour. Nephrology, 1989—, Am. Jour. Kidney Diseases, 1989—, Geriat. Nephrology and Urology Jour., 1989—; mem. editl. adv. bd. Contemporary Dialysis, 1983—, Nephrology Practice Today, 1989—, Hematopoietic Therapy Index and Revs., 1993—, Primary Care Reports, 1994—; editl. cons. Am. Jour. Nephrology, 1981-88; contbr. chpts. to books, abstracts and articles to profl. publs. Recipient Nat. Kidney Found. So. Calif. Cmty. Svc. award, 1981, Pres.'s award Nat. Kidney Found., 1998, Lifetime Achievement award in hemodialysis U. Mo., 2007; Robert Wood Johnson policy fellow Office of Sen. Paul Wellstone, 1994-95. Fellow ACP; mem. Am. Soc. for Artifical Internal Organs, Am. Fedn. for Clin. Rsch., Am. Soc. Nephrology, Internat. Soc. Nephrology, Internat. Soc. Artificial Organs, Western Soc. for Clin. Investigation, European Dialysis and Transplant Assn., N.Am. Soc. for Dialysis and Transplantation, Renal Physicians' Assn. (bd. dirs. 1993—, sec. bd. dirs. 1994—, pres. 1999-2001), Calif. Renal Physicians (bd. dirs. 1987—). Office: 601 Hawaii St El Segundo CA 90245 Office Phone: 310-536-2549. E-mail: anissenson@mednet.ucla.edu.

NISSINEN, MIKKO PEKKA, dancer, performing arts company executive, artistic director; arrived in U.S., 1987; Grad., Finnish Nat. Ballet Sch., 1977; postgrad., Leningrad Acad. Ballet Sch., 1979-80. Mem. corps de ballet Finnish Nat. Ballet, Helsinki, 1977-79, soloist, 1980-82; grand sujete Dutch Nat. Ballet, Amsterdam, The Netherlands, 1982-84; soloist Basel (Switzerland) Ballet, 1984-87, San Francisco Ballet, 1987-88, prin. dancer, 1988-96; artistic dir. Marin Ballet, 1996-97, Alberta Ballet, Calgary, Canada, 1998—2002, Boston Ballet, 2001—. Guest artist La Bayadere Nat. Ballet Can., 1989; guest artist Oberlin Dance Collective, 1993; bd. dirs. Le Don Des Etoiles; guest tchr. Royal Acad. Danciang, 1993, Kennedy Ctr. Ednl. Program, 1994, Nat. Ballet Sch., Toronto, 1994; lectr. on dance history and state of dance today Stanford U., Lethbridge U., St. Mary's Coll., Christensen Soc.; artistic com. N.Y. Choreographic Inst.; juror Prix de Lausanne, Benois de la Danse, Helsinki Internat. Ballet Competition, NY Internat. Ballet Competition. Dancer Sleeping Beauty, San Francisco Ballet, Swan Lake, Bizet Pas de Deux, Handel-a Celebration, Haffner Symphony, Variations de Ballet, Rodin, Rodeo, Con Brio, Ballet d'Isoline, Giuliani: Variations on a Theme, Tchaikovsky Pas de Deux, Symphony in C, Theme and Variations, Ballo della Regina, The Nutcracker, Airs de Ballet, Maelstrom, Dark Elegies, Harvest Moon, Napoli, Job, The Wanderer Fantasy, In the middle, somewhat elevated, Calcium Light Night, Le Corsaire Pas de Deux, Dreams of Harmony, Pulcinella, The Dream, Don Quixote, Giselle, A Midsummer Night's Dream, Les Biches, Sleeping Beauty, Pyrrich Dances, Masse, Le Tombeau de Couperin, Symphony in C, The Four Temperaments, The Prodigal Son, Rodin, Pierrot Lunaire, La Fille mal gardée, Swan Lake, Henze, Five Tangos, In and Out, Bits and Pieces, Jeu de Cartes, Gala Des Etoiles, Can. Internat. Ballet Gala, 1989, 1990, 1991, 1992, 1993, 1994, 1995, Reykjavik Arts Festival, 1990, Internat. Ballet Gala, Kuopio, Finland, 1992, Vail, Colo., 1993, Night of Stars Ballet Gala, Helsinki, 1993, choreographer Nutcracker, Marin Ballet, 1996, Alta. Ballet, 2000, Boston Ballet, Nutcracker, 2003—04, Swan Lake, 2004, Raymonda Act III. Recipient 1st prize Nat. Dance Competition, Kuopio, Finland, 1978, Arts and Letters award, Finlandia Found., 2008, Awarded, United Nations Assn., Greater Boston, 2007; fellowship exec. program for non-profit leaders, Stanford Univ. Fellow: Albert Schweitzer Armitage; mem.: Artistic Com. NY Choreographic Inst. (adv. bd. mem.). Office: Boston Ballet 19 Clarendon St Boston MA 02116-6100*

NISTALA, RAVI, nephrologist; s. Gopalakrishna and Vijayalakshmi Nistala; m. Puja Nyayapathi, Dec. 21, 1999; 1 child, Satvika. MBBS, Grant Med. Coll., Mumbai, 1995; MS in Genetics, U. Iowa, 2002. Registered Maharashtra Med. Assn., Mumbai, 1995, diplomate Am. Bd. Internal Medicine, 2008, lic. State Bd. Registration, 2009. Med. officer Oil & Natural Gas Commn., Mumbai, 1995—97; grad. rsch. asst. U. Iowa, 1997—2002, rsch. asst., 2002—03, postdoc. rsch. fellow, 2003—04; resident internal medicine U. Mo.-Columbia, 2005—08, fellow nephrology divsn., 2008—. Vol. Grant Med. Coll., 1990; physician Free Med. Clinic, 2002—03. Mem.: ACP, Nat. Kidney Found., Am. Soc. Nephrology. Achievements include development of genetic manipulation of large p1 phage and bacterial artificial chromosomes to study gene expression, transcription and regulation. Office Phone: 573-882-7992.

NITA, GELU M., physics professor, researcher; s. Ioan and Violeria Nita; m. Daniela Nita; 1 child, Alexandra. PhD, NJ Inst. Tech. and Rutgers, State U. NJ, Newark, 2003. Asst. rsch. prof. NJ Inst. Tech., 2003—. Office: NJ Inst Tech 323 Martin Luther King Blvd Newark NJ 07102-1982 Business E-Mail: gnita@njit.edu.

NITE, SANDRA BONORDEN, mathematics educator; b. Port Lavaca, Tex., Dec. 1, 1954; d. Arthur Henry and Robbie LeNell Bonorden; m. Michael Nite, Dec. 29, 1973; 1 child, Stephanie. BS in Math., Tex. State U., San Marcos, 1975, MS in Math., 1977, MusM in Music Edn., 1997. Cert. Orgn. Am. Kodaly Educators, 1996, secondary math. tchg. Tex. State Bd. Educator, 1979, secondary computer information systems tchg. 1979, secondary biology tchg. 1979, secondary chemistry tchg. 1979, secondary composite sci. tchg. 1979, secondary english lang. Arts tchg. 1999, secondary music tchg. 1999, master math. tchg. 2007. Math. and computer sci. tchr. Sweeny Ind. Sch. Dist., Tex., 1977—83, math. rep., site-based mgmt. com., 1998—2005, math. coord., 1998—2005, math. and sci. tchr., 1996—98; math. instr. Brazosport Coll., Lake Jackson, Tex., 1990—96, adj. math and music instr., 1996—2005; online adj. instr. ITT Tech. Inst., Indpls., 2004—; sr. lectr. Tex. A&M U., Coll. Sta., 2005—, Assoc. dir., ctr. for technology-mediated learning in math., 2008—. Dir. and tchr. Music Forte Studio, Lake Jackson, 1994—98; math. tchg. cons. W.H. Freeman Pub., NYC, 2001—05; math. curriculum contract writer COMAP, Boston, 2001—04; math. contract writer Tex. ESC Region IV, Tex. ESC Region V, Houston, Beaumont, Tex., 2002—05. Cooking and sewing leader 4-H, West Columbia, Tex., 1996—2002; chmn. St. Jude Children's Rsch. Hosp., Memphis, 1990—92; treas. Brazosport Music Tchrs. Assn., Lake Jackson, Tex., 1993—95; co-chrmn., keyboard kapers Brazosport Coll., Lake Jackson, 1994—96; co-chmn., composition festival Brazosport Music Tchrs. Assn., Lake Jackson, Tex., 1995—96; treas. West Columbia Jr. High PTO, West Columbia, Tex., 1995—97, Columbia-Brazoria ISD Bond Promotion Com., West Columbia, Tex., 1998—98, Sweeny H.S. PTO, Sweeny, Tex., 1998—2005; facilities com. mem. Columbia-Brazoria Ind. Sch. Dist., West Columbia, Tex., 1998—2002, suprs. adv. com. mem., 1999—2001, dist. site based mgmt. com. mem., 1999—2001; county fair and youth fair com. Brazoria County Fair Assn., Angleton, Tex., 1998—2002. Recipient Outstanding Svc. award, Tex. A&M U. Dept. Math., 2008; named Outstanding Educator, Tex. A&M U. Coll. Edn. and Human Devel., 2007; nominee Piper Prof., Brazosport Coll., 1995—96; grantee AP Calculus grant, Tex. Edn. Agy., 1999; Computer grant, Brazosport Coll., 1995—96, Ninth Grade Success Initiative grant, Tex. Edn. Agy., 2002—04, Tchr. Quality Algebra II grant, Tex. Higher Edn. Coordinating Bd., 2008—. Mem.: Houston Area Math. Supervisors, Tex. Assn. Supervisors Math., Nat. Coun. Tchrs. Math. Office: Texas A&M Univ TAMU Mail Stop 3368 College Station TX 77843-3368 Office Fax: 979-862-4190. Business E-Mail: snite@math.tamu.edu.

NITECKI, JOSEPH ZBIGNIEW, librarian; b. Dabrowa Górnicza, Poland, Jan. 31, 1922; came to U.S., 1951, naturalized, 1956; s. Henryk W. and Antonina S. N.; m. Sophie V. Zboinski, June 17, 1945; children: Zbigniew H., Danuta A. BA in Philosophy, Wayne State U., 1955; MA, Roosevelt U., 1959; MA in L.S., U. Chgo., 1963. Various profl. and adminstrv. positions in libraries U. Chgo., 1961-63, Chgo. City Coll., 1963-66, U. Wis., Milw., 1967-70, Temple U., Phila., 1970-78; prof., exec. dir. libraries U. Wis., Oshkosh, 1978-80; dir. libraries SUNY, Albany, 1980-88, vis. prof. Sch. Info Sci. and Policy, 1988-90, prof. emeritus, 1990—. Cons. library issues. Author, editor compiler and reviewer in field; ref. and manuscript reader. Served with Polish Armed Forces under Brit. command, 1939-48. Recipient 1st. prize Polish Émigré Poetry Contest, 2001. Mem. ALA, Beta Phi Mu. Home: 430 Coburg Village Way Rexford NY 12148-1461 E-mail: jzniteckisr@aol.com.

NITHYANANDAN, PALLAVI, research scientist; b. Chennai, Tamilnadu, India, Nov. 25, 1978; d. Nithyanandan Rathinam and Jayanthi Nithyanandan; m. Madan Bangalore, Aug. 20, 2004. PhD, U. Md. Balt., 2005. Registered pharmacist Pharmacy Coun. India, 2001. Grad. rsch. asst. U. Md. Balt.; rsch. scientist US Pharmacopeia, Rockville, Md., 2005—. Contbr. articles to scientific jours. Mem.: Am. Assn. Pharm. Scientists, Rho Chi (hon.; inducted mem. 2002). Achievements include research in developed test method for the analysis and prediction of robustness of inhaler devices. Home: 5521 Alderbrook Ct Apt 110 Rockville MD 20851 Office: United States Pharmacopeia 12601 Twinbrook Parkway Rockville MD 20852 Office Fax: 301-816-8518. Personal E-mail: pallavi109@gmail.com. Business E-Mail: pxn@usp.org.

NITIKMAN, FRANKLIN W., lawyer; b. Davenport, Iowa, Oct. 26, 1940; s. David A. and Janette (Gordon) N.; m. Adrienne C. Drell, Nov. 28, 1972. BA, Northwestern U., 1963; LLB, Yale U., 1966. Bar: Ill. 1966, US Dist. Ct. (no. dist.) Ill. 1967, US Tax Ct. 1972, Fla. 1977, DC 1981. Assoc. McDermott, Will & Emery, Chgo., 1966-72, ptnr., 1973—2006, counsel, 2007—. Co-author: Drafting Wills and Trust Agreements, 1990. Bd. dirs. Owen Coon Found., Glenview, Ill., 1985—, Jewish Fedn. Met. Chgo., Jewish United Fund, 1994—2003, Spertus Inst. Jewish Studies, Chgo., 1991—, chmn. bd., 1999—2002. Fellow Am. Coll. Trust and Estate Coun., Am. Bar Found.; mem. Standard Club, Arts Club (Chgo.). Home: 365 Lakeside Pl Highland Park IL 60035-5371 Office: McDermott Will & Emery LLP 227 W Monroe St Ste 4700 Chicago IL 60606-5096 Office Phone: 312-984-7614. Business E-Mail: fnitikman@mwe.com.

NITOWSKY, HAROLD MARTIN, physician, educator; b. Bklyn., Feb. 12, 1925; s. Max and Fannie (Gershowitz) N.; m. Myra Heller, Nov. 28, 1954; children— Fran Ellen, Daniel Howard. AB, N.Y. U., 1944, MD, 1947; MS, U. Colo., 1952. Intern Mt. Sinai Hosp., NYC, 1947-48; resident pediats. U. Colo. Med. Center, 1948-50; USPHS postdoctoral fellow U. Colo., 1950-51; staff Sinai Hosp., Balt., 1953-67, dir. pediat. rsch., 1960-67; faculty Johns Hopkins Sch. Medicine, 1953-67, assoc. prof. ob-gyn., pediats., molecular genetics, 1962-67; prof. pediats. and genetics Albert Einstein Coll. Medicine, 1967—. Cons. Nat. Inst. Child Health and Human Devel., 1966—; Sr. surgeon USPHS, 1951-53 Contbr. articles on nutrition, metabolism, genetics to profl. jours. Mem. Am. Pediat. Soc., Soc. Pediat. Rsch., Am. Soc. Human Genetics. Home: 25 Devonshire Rd New Rochelle NY 10804-3925 Office: 122 Palmer Hill Rd Apt 3334 Stamford CT 06902 Personal E-mail: nidoc@aol.com.

NITTOLY, PAUL GERARD, lawyer; b. Bklyn., July 13, 1948; s. Edward Joseph and Philomena (Lorenzo) Nittoly; m. Maryann Racioppi, May 31, 1970; children: Melissa Beth, Matthew Edward. AB, Rutgers U., 1970; JD, NYLS, 1973. Bar: N.J., U.S. Dist. Ct. NJ 1973, U.S. Supreme Ct. 1979, U.S. Ct. Appeals (3d cir.) 1990, U.S. Dist. Ct. (so. and ea. dist.) NY 1998, cert.: NJ Supreme Ct. (trial atty. civil and criminal law). Asst. prosecutor, sr. trial atty. Essex County Prosecutor's Office, Newark, 1974-79; ptnr. Shanley & Fisher, P.C., Morristown, NJ, 1979-99, Drinker Biddle & Shanley LLP, Florham Park, NJ, 1999—2003, Drinker Biddle & Reath, LLP, Florham Park, 2003—. Moot trial ct. judge Seton Hall Law Sch., Newark, 1982—; lectr. symposium perinatal malpractice ACOG and Rutgers U. Med. Sch., Morristown, NJ, 1984; mem. practitioner's adv. group U.S. Sentencing Commn., 1992—2002. Author: Readings in White Collar Crime, 1991; mem. editl. adv. bd. Corporate Criminal Liability Reporter; contbr. chapters to books. Pres. C. Willard Heckel Am. Inn. of Ct., 1995—97, master; del. adv. Am. Bd. Trial Advs.; pres. Legal Svcs. Found. Essex County, 2007—09; trustee, vol. Lawyers for Justice, 2009—. Capt. US Army, 1972. Named Superlawyers, White Collar Criminal Def., 2005—, Best Lawyers in America, 2008—. Fellow: Am. Coll. Trial Lawyers; mem.: ABA, Assn. Fed. Bar State N.J. (trustee 2000—), Trial Attys. N.J. (pres. 2005—06), Assn. Criminal Def. Attys. N.J., Nat. Assn. Criminal Def. Lawyers, Morris County Bar Assn., Essex County Bar Assn. (pres. 1998—99, Samuel S. Saiber Profl. Achievement award 2005), N.J. Bar Assn., Park Ave. Club (Morristown), Delta Upsilon. Roman Catholic. Home: 275 Meetinghouse Ln Mountainside NJ 07092-1305 Office: Drinker Biddle & Reath LLP 500 Campus Dr Fl 4 Florham Park NJ 07932-1047 Office Phone: 973-549-7180. Business E-Mail: paul.nittoly@dbr.com.

NITZARIM, YOEL DAVID, language educator; b. Chgo., Aug. 29, 1949; s. Maurice and Elaine Pearl Smith; m. Esther Marsha Nitzarim; children: Rachel Sarah, Gavriella Leebah. BA, Northeastern Ill. U., Chgo., 1974, MEd, 1983. Cert. secondary edn. in English Ill. ESL tchr. Kibbutz Newe Eitan Regional H.S., Israel, 1976—77, Kibbutz Maoz Haim Elem. Sch., Israel, 1976—77, Morton Jr. Coll., Cicero, Ill., 1988; ESL tchr. Soviet refugees Truman Coll./ The Jewish Vocat. Svc. Temple Menorah, Chgo., 1989, 1991—92; ESL instr. Rogosin H.S., Migdal Ha'Emeq, Israel, 1978—79, ORT Israel Vocat. H.S., Osefia, Israel, 1978—79; adult English seminar tchr. Cultural Ctr. Kfar Tabor, Israel, 1978—79; prep. seminar course biology Oranim Coll., Tivon, Israel, 1979; Hebrew and Jewish social studies tchr. Jewish Reconstructionist Congregation, Evanston, Ill., 1982—83; Jewish social studies tchr. B'nai Tikvah, Deerfield, Ill., 1982—83; English tchr. Aquinas Cath. H.S., Chgo., 1980—82, St. Benedict H.S., Chgo., 1984—86, Austin Career Edn. Ctr., Chgo., 1989—92; writing tchr. Columbia Coll., Chgo., 1988; asst. prof. English East-West U., Chgo., 1999—2002; instr. English Benedictine U., Lisle, Ill., 2002—03; instr. English composition Coll. Lake County, Grayslake, Ill., 2005—, McHenry County Coll., Crystal Lake, Ill., 2006—08. Author: (essays, poetry, photography, short stories) Affair of the Mind; contbr. articles to profl. jours. Founding mem. Nat. Campaign for Tolerance, a project of the So. Poverty Law Ctr., 2005—; charter mem. US Holocaust Meml. Mus.; founding sponsor Martin Luther King, Jr. Nat. Meml., Washington. Nominee Faculty of Yr. Program award, Coll Lake County Student Govt. Assn., 2008—09. Mem.: Ill. Holocaust Mus. (Skokie) (founding mem.), Assn. for Jewish Theater, English Tchrs. Assn. Israel, Abraham Lincoln Presidential Library Mus. (nat. assoc.), Am. Soc. Yad Vashem, US Holocaust Meml. Mus. Jewish. Avocations: reading, writing, music, travel, skydiving, dogs. Personal E-mail: Ynitzari1@aol.com.

NITZE, WILLIAM ALBERT, government official, lawyer, not-for-profit developer, energy executive; b. NYC, Sept. 27, 1942; s. Paul Henry and Phyllis (Pratt) N.; m. Ann Kendall Richards, June 5, 1971; children: Paul Kendall, Charles Richards. BA, Harvard U., 1964, JD, 1969; BA, Oxford U., 1966. Bar: N.Y. 1970, U.S. Supreme Ct. 1987. Assoc. Sullivan and Cromwell, NYC, 1970-72; v.p. London Arts, Inc., NYC, 1972-73; counsel Mobil South, Inc., NYC, 1974-76; gen. counsel Mobil Oil Japan, Tokyo, 1976-80; asst. gen. counsel exploration and producing divsn. Mobil Oil Corp., NYC, 1980-87; dep asst. sec. for environment, health and natural resources U.S. Dept. State, Washington, 1987-90; pres. Alliance to Save Energy, Washington, 1990-94, Gemstar Group, Washington, 2001—05; asst. adminstr. for internat. activities U.S. EPA, Washington, 1994-2001; chmn. GridPoint, Inc., Washington, 2003—07, Clear Path Technologies, Inc., Corona, Calif., 2007—. Chmn. Oceana Energy Co., Washington, 2006—; mem. adv. com. Sch. Advanced Internat. Studies, Washington, 1982—95, professorial lectr., 1993—94, 2001—; vis. scholar Environ. Law Inst., Washington, 1990. Trustee Aspen Inst., Queenstown, Md., 1988—, Krasnow Inst., Fairfax, Va., 1996—2001, mem. adv. bd., 2004—; bd. dirs. Charles A. Lindbergh Fund, Mpls., 1990—94, Nat. Symphony Orch. Assn., Washington, 1990—2002, Atlantic Coun. US, Washington, 2002—, Galapagos Conservancy, Falls Church, Va., 2001—, vice chmn., 2002—03, chmn., 2003—; bd. dirs. Climate Inst., Washington, 2001—09, vice chmn., 2001—02, chmn., 2002—09, Alliance to Save Energy, 2001—. Mem.: Coun. on Fgn. Rels., Assn. Bar City NY, Knickerbocker Club, Links Club, Cosmos Club, Met. Club. Republican. Episcopalian. Avocations: running, piano, collecting art. Home: 1537 28th St NW Washington DC 20007-3059 Office: Ste 100 1785 Mass Ave NW Washington DC 20036 Office Phone: 202-331-2485. Business E-Mail: wnitze@gridpoint.com.

NIU, FENG, research and development company executive; b. Haixi, Qinghai, China, Aug. 28, 1977; m. Ying Wang. PhD, U. Miami, Fla., 2007. Rsch. asst. U. Miami, 2003—07; R & D engr. Automated Precision Inc., Rockville, Md., 2007—. Vis. scholar Microsoft Rsch. Asia, Beijing, 2002—03. Mem.: IEEE, Soc. Mfg. Engrs. Achievements include research in video-based human activity analysis; patents pending for video segmentation techniques for video summarization.

NIU, GRETA AIYU, language educator; b. Bklyn. d. Gregory Cheng-Chi and Kathleen Chien-Mei Niu; m. Evan Michael Lowenstein, July 21, 2001; 1 child, Lyndon Lowenstein-Niu. BA, Wellesley Coll., Mass., 1991; PhD, Duke U., Durham, NC, 1998. Asst. prof. english SUNY Coll., Brockport, 1999—2004, U. Rochester, NY, 2004—. Bd. mem. Asian, Pacific Islander and Am. History Project Greater Rochester, 2002—; exec. com. mem., asian am. lit. divsn. MLA, NYC, 2004—08; pres. Cir. Asian Am. Lit. Studies, 2008—. DeWitt Wallace-Reader's Digest fellowship, Duke U., 1991—92. Office: Univ Rochester Dept English Rochester NY 14627-0451

NIU, STEVE, director; b. Guyuan, Ningxia, China, Oct. 16, 1962; s. Guoqing Niu and Wanfang Xu; m. Ling Bao, July 18, 1987; children: Jing, Daniel Scott. PhD in Info. Sci., Carleton U., Ottawa, 2001. Database programmer Chan's Food Group, Durham, NC, 1996—97; dir. instml. tech. Shaw U., Raleigh, NC, 2001—. Visitor scientist UN Energy Devel., Salt Lake City, 1994—95; asst. dir. China Partnership Program. Bd. trustee mem. Xian U. Sci. and Tech., Shanxi, China, 2007. Named one of Best Rsch. Scientist, China Coal Indsl. Ministry, 1991. Home: 803 East Oak Dr Durham NC 27705 Office: Shaw Univ 118 East South St Raleigh NC 27601-2341 Office Fax: 919-546-8258; Home Fax: 919-383-4448. Business E-Mail: sniu@shawu.edu.

NIVARTHI, RAJU NAGA, anesthesiology educator; b. Nandyal, India, June 16, 1964; came to U.S., 1993; s. Kameswara Sarma and Suseelamma Nivarthi; m. Aparna Nagaraju Nivarthi; children: Nidhi, Aditya. BSc with Chemistry, Zoology and Botany, Sri Venkateswara U., Tirupati, India, 1984; MSc in Biochemistry, Sri Kirshnadevaraya U., Anantapur, India, 1986; PhD, U. Hyderabad, 1996. Fellow Sch. Life Scis., U. Hyderabad, India, 1987-93; rsch. asst. prof. dept. anesthesiology NYU Med. Ctr., NYC, 1996, scientist, 1996-99, Wyeth-Ayerst Rsch., Pearl River, NY, 1999-2001; sr. scientist, mgr. analytical biochemistry Bristol-Myers Squibb, Syracuse, NY, 2001—05, mgr. immunology and molecular biology, biologics quality control, 2005—08; sr. scientist quality control tech. svc. Genzyme, Framingham, Mass., 2008—. Contbr. articles to profl. jours. Jr. Rsch. fellow Coun. Sci. and Indsl. Rsch., India, 1987, Sr. Rsch. fellow Coun. Sci. and Indsl. Rsch., 1990, Postdoctoral fellow NIH, 1998; recipient cert. of merit Pharmacia & Biotech Prize for Young Scientists, 1997, named 2000 Outstanding Scientist of 20th Century, 1998, Internat. Biographical Ctr. Mem. AAAS, Acad. Med. Cmty., Am. Chem. Soc., Am. Soc. Anesthesiologists, Am. Soc. Biochemistry and Molecular Biology, Internat. Anesthesia Rsch. Soc., Internat. Soc. for Study of Xenobiotics, Nat. Geographic Soc., N.Y. Acad. Scis. Home: 2 Copley Dr Northborough MA 01532-3603 Office: Genzyme 45 New York Ave Framingham MA 01701 Office Phone: 315-432-9612. Personal E-mail: rnivarthi@yahoo.com.

NIVATVONGS, SANTHAT, colorectal surgeon; b. Bangkok, Sept. 28, 1939; arrived in US, 1965; MD, Chulalongkorn Hosp. U., Bangkok, Thailand, 1964. Diplomate Am. Bd. Surgery, Am. Bd. Colon & Rectal Surgey. Intern Wayne County Gen. Hosp., Eloise, Mich., 1965-66; resident Harper Hosp., Detroit, 1966-67, United Hosp., St. Paul, 1967-70; fellow in ColonRectal Surgery U. Minn., Mpls., 1970-71; mem. staff Mayo Clinic, Rochester, Minn.; prof. Surgery Mayo Clinic Coll. Medicine, Rochester. Mem. Am. Col. Surgeons, Am. Soc. Colon Rectal Surgeons, Soc. Am. Gastrointestinal Endoscopic Surgeons, Soc. Surgery of Alimentary Tract. Office: Colon-Rectal Surgery Sec Mayo Clinic Rochester MN 55905-0001

NIVISON, DAVID SHEPHERD, language educator, philosopher; b. Farmingdale, Maine, Jan. 17, 1923; s. William and Ruth (Robinson) N.; m. Cornelia Green, Sept. 11, 1944(dec. June 19, 2008); children: Louise, Helen Thom, David Gregory, James Nicholas. AB summa cum laude, Harvard U., 1946, MA, 1948, PhD, 1953. Instr. Chinese Stanford U., 1948-52, Ford Found. faculty fellow, 1952-53, instr. Chinese and philosophy, 1953-54; Fulbright research scholar Kyoto, Japan, 1954-55; lectr. philosophy Stanford U., 1955-58, asst. prof. Chinese and philosophy, 1958-59, assoc. prof., 1959-66, prof., 1966-88, Walter Y. Evans-Wentz prof. Oriental Philosophies, Religions and Ethics, 1983-88, chmn. dept. philosophy, 1969-72, 75-76, acting chmn. dept. Asian langs., 1985-86, emeritus, 1988—. Author: The Life and Thought of Chang Hsüeh-ch'eng, 1738-1801, 1966, Chinese trans., 2003, 2007; The Ways of Confucianism: Investigations in Chinese Philosophy, 1996, Chinese trans., 2006; co-author: Chinese Lang., Thought and Culture: Nivison and His Critics, 1996, The Riddle of the Bamboo Annals, 2009; editor, co-compiler (with P. J. Ivanhoe): Stanford Chinese Concordance Series, 1979; co-editor (with A. F. Wright): Confucianismi in Action, 1959; co-editor (with Dongfang Shao): Studies on the Modern Text of the Bamboo Annals (in Chinese), 2002; contbr. articles to profl. jours. and encys. Served with AUS, 1943-46. Recipient Prix Stanislas-Julien Inst. de France, 1967; Am. Council Learned Socs. fellow, 1973; John Simon Guggenheim fellow, 1973-74 Mem. Assn. Asian Studies, Am. Philos. Assn. (v.p. Pacific div. 1978-79, pres. 1979-80), Am. Oriental Soc. (Western br. v.p. 1964-65, sec. 1965-70, pres. 1971-72), AAUP (pres. No. Calif. Conf. 1964-66), Internat. Acad. Chinese Culture (Beijing, Peoples Republic of China), Phi Beta Kappa. Home: 1169 Russell Ave Los Altos CA 94024-5066 Business E-Mail: dnivison@stanford.edu.

NIX, BARBARA LOIS, real estate broker; b. Sept. 25, 1929; d. Martin Clayton and Norma (Gunter) Westfield; m. B. H. Nix, July 12, 1968; children: William Martin Dahl, Theresa Irene Dahl stepchildren: Dennis Leon, Denise Lynn. Student, St. Elizabeths Sch. Nursing, Yakima, Wash., 1949-50; AA, Sierra Coll., 1978; student, Calif. State U., Sacramento, 1984. Bookkeeper, office mgr. Lakeport (Calif.) Tire Svc., 1966-69, Dr. K. J. Absher, Grass Valley, Calif., 1972-75; real estate sales and office mgr. Rough and Ready Land Co., Penn Valley, Calif., 1976-77, co-owner, v.p., sec., 1978—, Wildwood West Real Estate, Gateway Real Estate. Co-owner Nix's Antiques, 1996—. Youth and welfare chmn. Yakima Federated Jr. Women's Club, 1957; den mother Cub Scouts, 1959—60; leader Girls Scouts U.S., 1961—62; mem. Sierra, Nev. Meml. Hosp. Found.; adv. bd. dirs., v.p. Roots and Wings Ednl. Found., 1991—95; mem. Nevada County Sch. Dist. Redistricting Bd. Recipient Pres.'s award, Sierra Coll., 1973, others. Mem.: Am. Assn. Univ. Women, Sierra Nev. Meml. Hosp. Aux., Penn Valley (founder, pres. 1978), Lake Wildwood Women's Club, Job's Daus. (life). Republican. Roman Catholic. Home: 19365 Wildflower Dr Penn Valley CA 95946-9735 Office: POBox 191 Penn Valley CA 95946

NIX, J. ELMER, retired orthopedist, surgeon; b. Ellisville, Miss., Oct. 24, 1931; s. Robert Leroy and Gladys Jane (Strahan) Nix; m. Rosemary Jane Cochrane, Nov. 16, 1956; children: Georgia Miller, Susan Hill, James Elmer Jr., Robert L. II. MD, Jefferson Med. Coll., Phila., 1956. Diplomate Am. Bd. Orthop. Surgery, 1965. Intern Hermann Hosp., Houston, 1956—57, resident, 1959—63; orthop. surgeon Am. Acad. Orthop. Surgeons, Chgo., 1965—2007; ret., 2007. Asst. prof. orthop. surgery U. Miss. Sch. Medicine, 1963—. Pres. N.Am. Spine Soc., Chgo., 1986—87; AMA del. Miss. Spine Soc., 1987—99, N.Am. Spine Soc., 1987—99; pres. Clinical Orthop. Soc., 1995—96, Miss. State Med. Soc., Jackson, 1990—91. Capt. USAF, 1957—59. Recipient Clinical Surgery award, Jefferson Med. Coll., 1956, David Selby award, N.Am. Spine Soc., 1997; named Intern of Yr., Hermann Hosp., Houston, 1957, Violet Keller Outstanding Resident, 1963; named one of Am. Top Surgeons, Consumer Rsch. Coun. Am., 2002. Fellow: Am. Bd. Orthop. Surgery, Am. Acad. Orthop. Surgery; mem.: N.Am. Spine Soc. (founder), Walter Scott Club. Republican. Presbyterian. Avocations: golf, reading, poetry, football. Home: 420 St Andrews Dr Jackson MS 39211

NIX, JERRY W., automotive executive; Sr. v.p. fin., CFO Genuine Parts Co., Atlanta, 1979—2000, exec. v.p. fin., CFO, 2000—05, vice-chmn., exec. v.p. fin., CFO, 2005—. Office: Genuine Parts Co 2999 Circle 75 Pkwy SE Atlanta GA 30339-3050

NIX, KELSEY I., lawyer; b. Texarkana, Ark., Jan. 24, 1961; s. Thomas M. and E. E. Nix; m. Claire LaBrunerie Nix, Apr. 28, 1990; children: Sabine A., Simone E., Elodie C., Ines N. BA, Hendrix Coll., Conway, Ark., 1984; BS, Columbia U., NYC, 1984; JD, Duke U., Durham, NC, 1987. Bar: U.S. Dist. Ct. (so. and ea. dist.) N.Y. 1988, U.S. Ct. Appeals (Fed. cir.) 1989, U.S. Ct. Appeals (6th cir.) 2004, U.S. Ct. Appeals (11th cir.) 2006, U.S. Supreme Ct. 1992, N.Y. 1988, U.S. Patent and Trademark Office 1988. Assoc. Fish & Neave, NYC, 1987—96; ptnr. Fish & Neave (now Ropes & Gray), NYC, 1997—2003, Willkie Farr & Gallagher, NYC, 2003—. Lectr. in field. Contbr. articles to profl. jours. Mem.: ABA, Columbia U. Engring. Alumni Assn. (bd. dirs. 2006—, v.p. 2009—), Am. Intellectual Property Law Assn. Avocations: scuba diving, travel, running. Office: Willkie Farr & Gallagher LLP 787 Seventh Ave New York NY 10019

NIX, KEMIE RICHARDS, educational association administrator, editor; b. Atlanta, Dec. 10, 1938; d. James McDowell and Evelyn Knight Richards; m. John Arthur Nix, July 22, 1961; children: Mary Evelyn Nix Hollowell, John Arthur Jr. EdB, Emory U., 1960, EdM, 1970. Tchr. Westminster Schs., Atlanta, 1961—87; founder, dir. Children's Lit. for Children, Atlanta, 1986—2002, Reader-to-Reader, Atlanta, 1986—2002; co-founder, co-dir. Reader-to-Patient, Atlanta, 1990—2000; co-founder Biblioteca Juvenil de Mayaguez; PR, 1991—2001; dir. Reader-to-Reader: Africa, 1990—. Children's book editor Atlanta Jour./Constn., 1976—91, Parents' Choice, 1978—, corr. editor Jour. African Youth and Children's Lit., 1995—. Bd. dirs. US Bd. Books Young People, Wilmington, Del., 1996—98, Children's Lit. Children, Atlanta, 1996—, Mt. Kenya Acad., Nyeri, Kenya, 2002—. Named to Coca-Cola Centennial Olympic Wall, Atlanta, 1996, Kemie Nix Libr. named in her honor,

Primary Sch., Nyeri, 1992, Mt. Kenya Acad., Nyeri, 2001. Mem.: ALA (Newbery com. 1994, Notable Books com. 1998—99, Newbery com. 2002, Caldecott com. 2006), Internat. Reading Assn. Democrat. Presbyterian. Avocations: birdwatching, animals, reading. Home and Office: Reader-to-Reader: Africa 104 Madison Ave Peachtree City GA 30269 Personal E-mail: kemienix@aol.com.

NIX, PATRICIA, artist; d. Nobe Astin Briggs and Lela Mae (Lucas) Rockstrom; m. (dec.); children: Pandora Nix Shaw, William Riley Jr., John Houston. BA, NYU, 1982. One-woman shows include Tower Gallery, Southampton, N.Y., 1978—82, 1985, NYU, 1980, Sutton Gallery, N.Y.C., 1982—83, Baumgartner Gallery, Washington, 1984, S.I. (N.Y.) Mus., 1986, Andre Zarre Gallery, N.Y.C., 1987, S.I. (N.Y.) Mus., 1988, Nerlino Gallery, N.Y.C., 1988, Andre Zarre Gallery, 1991, U. Windsor (Ont., Can.) Mus., Griffin McGear Modern Gallery, N.Y.C., 1989, San Angelo (Tex.) Mus. of Art, 1991, Hurlbutt Gallery, Greenwich, Conn., 1990, Galerie Donguy, Paris, 1994, Dillon Gallery, N.Y.C., 1994—98, numerous group shows including most recently, exhibited in group shows at Merill Chase Galleries, Chgo., 1999, Am. Embassy, Rome, Italy, 1999, Hilligoss Galleries, 2000—03, Tex. Tech. Mus., Lubbock, 2000, Dillin Gallery, NYC, 2006, Ann Norton Mus. Sculptor Garden, West Palm Beach, Fla., 2007; represented in numerous permanent collections, designer sets and costumes (ballets) Petrushka, Pulcinella, Jeu de Cartes, 2002, Totem Altar, Saint Peters Ch., N.Y.C., 2004, Gallerie Mary Claude Goinnard, Paris, France, 2005, Totem Altar, St. John the Devine Cathedral., N.Y.C., 2005, Mary Claude Goinnard, Paris, France, 2005, Hudson Riuer Museum-Travelling to 8 other Museum, 2008. Office Phone: 212-686-3512.

NIXON, AGNES ECKHARDT, television writer, producer; m. Robert Nixon (dec.); 4 children. Student, Sch. Speech, Northwestern U. Writer for radio and TV; freelance writer for: TV programs Hallmark Hall of Fame, Robert Montgomery Presents, Studio One; creator, packager, head writer: daytime TV series All My Children; creator nightime mini-series The Manions of America; creator, packager daytime TV series One Life to Live; creator, packager: daytime TV series Loving; co-creator: daytime TV series As The World Turns; formerly head writer, The Guiding Light, daytime TV series Another World; creator, story cons. The City. Recipient Trustees award Nat. Acad. TV Arts and Sci., 1981, Super Achiever award Jr. Diabetes Found., 1981, Wilmer Eye Inst. award, 1981, Communicator award Am. Women in Radio & TV, 1984, Gold Plate award Am. Acad. Achievement, 1993, Popular Culture Lifetime Achievement award Popular Culture Assn., 1995, Pub. Svc. award Johns Hopkins Hosp., 1995, Humanitarian award Nat. Osteoporosis Found., 1996; inducted into TV Hall of Fame, 1993. Mem. Internat. Radio and TV Soc. Nat. Acad. TV Arts and Scis., Harvard Found. (bd. dirs.), Mus. TV and Radio (bd. dirs.), The Friars Club. Address: All My Children 320 W 66th St New York NY 10023-6304*

NIXON, ARLIE JAMES, gas and oil company executive; b. Ralston, Okla., May 22, 1914; s. James Gordon and Wella May (Platt) N.; m. Wylie Elizabeth Jones, Apr. 21, 1939 (div May 1950); children: Cole Jay, Kathleen (Mrs. S. Brent Joyce); m. Lisa Marie Grant, Dec. 7, 1981 (div. June 1989). BS, Okla. State U., 1935. Airline capt. Trans World Airlines, NYC, 1939-74; pres. Crystal Gas Co., Jennings, Okla., 1960—, Blackburn Gas Co., Jennings, 1964—, Blackberry Oil Co., Jennings, 1969—. Represented U.S. in several ofcl. dels. to internat. aviation tech. meetings, also represented Internat. Fedn. Air Line Pilots Assns. at internat. confs. Lt. (j.g.) USNR, 1935-63. Mem. Internat. Fedn. Air Line Pilots Assn. (regional v.p. 1972), Internat. Platform Assn., Wings Club. Democrat. Office: PO Box 68 Jennings OK 74038-0068 Office Phone: 918-454-2241.

NIXON, BRENDA JOYCE, elementary school educator, small business owner; b. Hazlehurst, Miss., Feb. 6, 1949; d. Archie C. Ashley, Sr. and Joyce B. Ashley; m. W.B. (Benny) Nixon, Jr. (div.); children: Ashley Michelle Nixon Rogers, Christopher Jarrett. BA, William Carey Coll., Hattiesburg, Miss, 1971; post grad., 1987—. CPA; lic. educator Miss. Group leader Ga. Bapt. Children's Home, Palmetto, Ga.; tchr. grade 6 Union Academy, Georgetown, Miss., 1987—95, Windsor Academy, Macon, Ga., 1993—2000, Crystal Springs Mid. Sch., Crystal Springs, Miss., 2000—. Tchr. participant So. Regional Edn. Bd., lead tchr. lang. arts 6th grade; pres. club rep. Avon, 2001—. Vol. fund raiser Bethel Vol. Fire Dept., Hazlehurst, 2004; state level judge Pre Teen Am. Program, 1994—96; music dir. Bethel Bapt. Ch., Hazlehurst, 2000—, mission action dir., 2003—. Named Tchr. of Yr., Macon/Bibb County Fire Dept., 1997—98, Macon Sheriff's Dept., 1998—99, Nat. Honor Roll Outstanding Am. Tchr., 2006. Avocations: reading, painting, music. Office: Crystal Springs Mid Sch 2092 S Pat Harrison Dr Crystal Springs MS 39059-3038 Home: 8157 Hwy 472 Hazlehurst MS 39083 Office Phone: 601-892-2789. Personal E-mail: abcnixon@aol.com.

NIXON, CHARLES WILLIAM, retired acoustician; b. Wellsburg, W.Va., Aug. 15, 1929; s. William E. and Lenora S. (Treiber) Nixon; m. Barbara Irene Hunter, May 19, 1956; children: Timothy C., Tracy Scott. BS, Ohio State U., 1952, MS, 1953, PhD, 1960. Tchr. spl. edn. Ohio and W.Va. Pub. Schs., Wheeling, 1954—56; rsch. audiologist Aeromed Lab., Wright Patterson AFB, Ohio, 1956—67; supervisory rsch. audiologist Armstrong Lab., Wright Patterson AFB, 1967—96, Veridian, Dayton, 1996—2004. Chair W4 Am. Nat. Stds. Inst., NYC, 1968—96; U.S. rep. hearing protection Internat. Stds. Orgn., Geneva, 1968—96; USAF rep. NRC-NAS Hearing Com., Washington, 1976—94; chair robotics panel Joint Dirs. Labs., Washington, 1987—88. Author: reports and book chpts. Cpl. US Army, 1953—55. Recipient Meritorious Svc. medal, U.S. Dept. Def., Dayton, Ohio, 1986, Outstanding Civilian Svc. award, 1996. Fellow: Acoustical Soc. Am.; mem.: Rsch. Soc. Am. Achievements include research in noise exposure, voice communications, hearing protection, sonic boom, active noise reduction, 3-D audio displays, others. Home: 4316 Sillman Pl Dayton OH 45440-1141

NIXON, CYNTHIA, actress; b. NYC, Apr. 9, 1966; d. Walter and Anne Nixon; children: Samantha Mozes, Charles Ezekiel Mozes. BA in English, Barnard Coll., 1988. Founding member The Drama Dept., 1996. Actor: (plays) The Philadelphia Story, 1980 (Theatre World Award, 1981), The Real Thing, 1984, Hurly Burly, 1984, Indiscretions, 1996 (Tony Award nom., 1996, Tony award, best performance by leading actress in a play, 2006), Rabbit Hole, 2006, The Prime of Miss Jean Brodie, 2006; (films) Little Darlings, 1980, Prince of the City, 1981, Tattoo, 1981, I Am the Cheese, 1983, Amadeus, 1984, The Manhattan Project, 1986, O.C. and Stiggs, 1987, Let It Ride, 1989, Through an Open Window, 1992, The Pelican Brief, 1993, Addams Family Values, 1993, Baby's Day Out, 1994, The Cottonwood, 1996, 'M' Word, 1996, Marvin's Room, 1996, Advice From a Caterpillar, 1999, The Out-of-Towners, 1999, Igby Goes Down, 2002, The Paper Mache Chase, 2003, Sex and the City: The Movie, 2008; (TV series) Sex and the City, 1998—2004 (Emmy nom. for Outstanding Supporting Actress in a comedy series, 2002, Emmy award Outstanding Supporting Actress in a Comedy Series, 2004); (TV miniseries) Tanner '88, 1988; (TV films) The Seven Wishes of a Rich Kid, 1979, The Private History of a Campaign That Failed, 1981, Rascals and Robbers: The Secret Adventures of Tom Sawyer and Huck Finn, 1982, My Body, My Child, 1982, Fifth of July, 1982, The Murder of Mary Phagan, 1988, Women & Wallace, 1990, Love She Sought, The, 1990, Face of a Stranger, 1991, Love, Lies and Murder, 1991, Kiss-Kiss, Dahlings!, 1992, Sex and the Matrix, 2000, Papa's Angels, 2000, Stage on Screen: The Women, 2002, Tanner on Tanner, 2004, Warm Springs, 2005. Office: c/o William Morris Agy One William Morris Place Beverly Hills CA 90212

NIXON, DANIEL WALKER, oncologist, researcher; b. Brunswick, Ga., Sept. 8, 1943; s. Marvin Elesberry and Mildred Anita (Whitehead) N.; m. Sandra Gayle Brakefield, July 18, 1970; children: William B., Marvin A. BS, U. Ga., 1965, MD, 1969. Diplomate Am. Bd. Internal Medicine, Am. Bd. Med. Oncology; lic. physician S.C. Asst. prof. Med. Coll. Ga., Augusta, 1973-75; from assoc. prof. to prof. Emory U., Atlanta, 1975-87; assoc. dir. divsn. cancer prevention and control, Nat. Cancer Inst. NIH, Bethesda, Md., 1987-89; v.p., prof. edn. Am. Cancer Soc., Atlanta, 1989-94; Folk prof., assoc. dir. prevention and control Hollings Cancer Ctr., Med. U. S.C., Charleston, 1994—99; pres. Inst. Cancer Prevention, NYC, 1999—2004; rsch. prof. dept. biol. scis. Clemson U., 2008—. Mem. sci. bd. Cancer Treatment Rsch. Found., chmn. bd. sci. counselors, 1999-2008. Author: Cancer Recovery Eating Plan, 1994; editor: Cancer Chemoprevention, 1994; editor-in-chief Preventive Medicine, 1999—2004; contbr. more than 100 articles to med. jours. Capt. USNR. Recipient several found. awards; grantee NIH, 1975—2004. Mem. Army and Navy Club, Fripp Island Golf Club. Achievements include research in cancer prevention and nutrition; chemoprevention and cancer metabolism. Office: Cancer Treatment Ctr America 14200 W Fillmore St Goodyear AZ 85338 Personal E-mail: dnixonun@aol.com.

NIXON, DAVID, dancer; b. Windsor, Ont., Can. Student, The Nat. Ballet Sch. Dancer Nat. Ballet Can., 1978—82, 1st soloist, 1982—84; prin. dancer Deutsche Opera Ballet, Berlin, 1985—90, Komische OperaBallet, Berlin, 1991—93; artistic dir. Ballet met., Columbus, Ohio, 1995—2001, Northern Ballet Theatre, England, 2001—. Various guest appearance including Munich Ballet, 1990-91, Staatsoper, Berlin, 1990, Birmingham Royal Ballet, 1990-93. Dancer Bayerisches Staatsoper Ballet Munich, 1990—91, Alexander Godunov and Stars, 1982, Milw. Ballet, 1984, Sydney Ballet Australia, 1984, World Ballet Festival Tokyo, 1985, 1988, Hamburg Ballet, 1988, 1989, Staatsoper Berlin, 1988—91, Bayerisches Staatsballet, 1988—90, Komische Opera Berlin, 1990—93; prodr.: David Nixon's Dance Theatre, Hebbel Theatre Berlin, 1990, 1991; choreographer Butterfly, 1983, La Follia, 1984, Dangerous Liaisons, 1990, 1996, African Fantasy, 1990, Celebrate Mozart, 1991, Sudden Impulse, 1994, A Summer's Nights Reflections, 1995, Full-Length Nutcracker, 1995, Butterfly, 1996, Beauty and the Beast, 1997, Carmen, 1997, Romeo and Juliet, 1998, Swan Lake, 1998, Dracula, 1999, A Midsummer Nights Dream, 2000—03, A Celebration of Dance with Music by Gershwin, 2001, Wuthering Heights, 2002, Peter Pan, 2004, Undine, 2006, A Sleeping Beauty Tale, 2007, Hamlet, 2008. Recipient Olivier award, 2005, Best Dir. award, 2004, 2006, Patron's award, Critics' Cir. Nat. Dance Awards, 2008. Office: Northern Ballet Theatre West Park Centre Spen Ln Leeds LS16 5BE England

NIXON, DENNIS E., financial company executive; m. Elma (Bavi) H. Nixon; children: Denise, Jonathan, Kristina. BS in Finance, U. Tex., Austin, 1964. Bank examiner Union Nat. Bank, Laredo, Tex., exec. v.p.; pres., CEO Internat. Bancshares Corp., Laredo, Tex., 1975—. Recipient Platinum Corazon award, United Way, Jr. Achievement Bus. Hall of Fame award, Paul Harris Fellow award, Rotary Internat., Eleanor Roosevelt Humanities award, State Israel; named to Tex. Bus. Hall of Fame, 2006. Mem.: US C. of C. (bd. dirs. 2007—). Avocations: fishing, hunting, skiing. Office: Internat Bancshares Corp 1200 San Bernardo Ave Laredo TX 78040-6301

NIXON, EUGENE RAY, chemist, educator; b. Mt. Pleasant, Mich., Apr. 14, 1919; s. William S. and Grace (Brookens) N.; m. Phyllis R. Jones, June 10, 1945; children— Cynthia L., Emily E. Sc.B. summa cum laude, Alma Coll., 1941; PhD, Brown U., 1947. Research chemist Manhattan Project, 1942-46; instr. chemistry Brown U., 1947-49; mem. faculty U. Pa., Phila., 1949-85, prof. chemistry, 1965-85, vice dean grad. sch., 1958-62, acting chmn. dept. chemistry, 1965-66, dir. materials research lab., 1969-72, prof. emeritus, 1985—. Vis. prof. U. London, 1963-64; vis. lectr. Bryn Mawr Coll., 1957-58 Mem. Am. Chem. Soc., Am. Phys. Soc., Soc. Applied Spectroscopy (Jour. award 1965, Spectroscopist of Yr. award Del. Valley sect. 1988), Coblentz Soc. (bd. mgrs.), Sigma Xi. Research, publs. on phys. chemistry, molecular structure and molecular spectroscopy, properties of crystals, intermolecular interactions, laser spectroscopy and laser chemistry. Home: 35 Julio Dr Apt 106 Shrewsbury MA 01545-3049 Home Phone: 508-845-1681.

NIXON, JAY (JEREMIAH NIXON), Governor of Missouri; b. DeSoto, Mo., Feb. 13, 1956; s. Jeremiah and Betty (Lea) Nixon; m. Georganne Nixon; children: Jeremiah, Will. BS in Polit. Sci., U. Mo., 1978, JD, 1981. Ptnr. Nixon, Nixon, Breeze & Roberts, Jefferson County, Mo., 1981—86; mem. Mo. State Senate from Dist. 22, 1986—93; atty. gen. State of Mo., 1993—2009, gov., 2009—. Chmn. select com. ins. reform; creator video internat. devel. and edn. opportunity prog. Recipient Conservation Fedn. Mo award, 1992; named Outstanding Young Missourian, Jaycees, 1994, Outstanding Young Lawyer, Barrister's Mag., 1993. Mem.: Mo. Assn. Trial Attys., Midwest Assn. Attys. Gen., Nat. Assn. Attys. Gen. Democrat. Methodist. Office: Office of Gov Missouri Capitol Bldg Rm 216 Jefferson City MO 65101 Office Fax: 573-751-1588.

NIXON, JUDITH MAY, librarian; b. Gary, Ind., June 14, 1945; d. Louis Robert Sr. and Mable Sophia (Reiner) Vician; m. Cleon Robert Nixon III, Aug. 20, 1967; 1 child, Elizabeth Marie. BS in Edn., Valparaiso U., 1967; MA in LS, U. Iowa, 1974. Tchr. U.S. Peace Corps, Tonga, 1968—69; popular books libr. Lincoln Libr., Springfield, Ill., 1971—73; ref. libr. Cedar Rapids (Iowa) Pub. Libr., 1974—76; ref.coord. U. Wis., Platteville, 1976—82; bus. libr. U. Ariz., Tucson, 1982—84; consumer and family sci. libr. Purdue U., West Lafayette, La., 1984—93, Krannert mgmt. and econs. libr., 1993—2005, humanities, social sci. and edn. head libr., 2005—09, edn. libr., 2009—. Editor: Industry and Company Information, 1991, Organization Charts, 1992, 2d edit., 1996, Hotel and Restaurant Industries, 1993; editor quar. serial Lodging and Restaurant Index, 1985-93. Leader Girl Scouts U.S., Lafayette, 1985—2005. Recipient John H. Moriarty award Purdue U. Librs., 1989. Mem. ALA (chair bus. reference and svcs. sect. 1995-96, GALE Rsch. award for excellence in bus. librarianship 1994). Home: 2375 N 23rd St Lafayette IN 47904-1242 Office: Purdue U Libraries Humanities Social Sci Edn Libr 504 W State St West Lafayette IN 47907-2058 Office Phone: 765-494-2834. Business E-Mail: jnixon@purdue.edu.

NIXON, J.V., cardiologist, educator; children: Sarah, Andrew. MB, ChB; MD, Victoria U. Manchchester, Eng., 1975. Prof. internal medicine, cardiology Va. Commonwealth U., Richmond, 2008—; noninvasive cardiology svcs. Pauley Heart Ctr., VCU Med. Ctr., Richmond, 1987—. Fellow: Am. Coll. Cardiology; mem.: Am. Heart Assn. Office: Pauley Heart Ctr VCU Health System Gateway 2-288 1200 E Marshall St Richmond VA 23298

NIXON, MARNI, singer; b. Altadena, Calif., Feb. 22, 1930; d. Charles and Margaret (Wittke) McEathron; m. Ernest Gold, May 22, 1950 (div. 1969); m. Lajos Frederick Fenster, July 23, 1971 (div. July 1975); m. Albert David Block, Apr. 11, 1983. Student, L.A. City Coll., UCLA, U. So. Calif., Tanglewood, Mass. Dir. vocal faculty Calif. Inst. Arts, Valencia, 1970-72; pvt. tchr., vocal coacn, condr. master classes, 1970—; pvt. voice tchr., coach, condr. master classes, 1970—; head apprentice divsn. Santa Barbara Music Acad. of West, 1980; formerly dir. opera workshop Cornish Inst. Arts, Seattle. Tchr. in field; judge Met. Opera Internat. Am. Music Awards, Nat. Inst. Music Theatre, 1984—87; dialect dir., opera recs. Actor: (musicals) Pasadena (Calif.) Playhouse, 1940—45; (films) Sound of Music, 1964, I Think I Do, 1996; (TV series) Boomerang, 1975; (Broadway plays) My Fair Lady, 1964, 2007, Taking My Turn, 1983, Opal, 1992—94, Cabaret, 1998, Ballymore, 1999, Follies, 2000—01, James Joyce's The Dead, 1999—2001, Nine, 2003, My Fair Lady, 2008; singer (soloist): Roger Wagner chorale, 1947—53; singer: (Operas) New Eng. Opera Co., LA Opera Co., Ford Found. TV Opera, 1948—63, San Francisco Spring Opera, 1966, Seattle Opera, 1971—73, classical recitals and appearances with symphony orchs. throughout U.S., Can., Eng., Israel, Ireland; voice dub: (films) My Fair Lady; The King and I; An Affair to Remember; West Side Story; Disney's Mulan; others; singer: (albums) Columbia, Mus. Heritage Records, Capital, RCA Victor, Ednl. Records, Reference Recs., Varese-Sarabande, Nonesuch; author: I Could Have Sung All Night: My Story, 2006. Recipient 4 Emmy awards for best actress, 2 Action for Childrens TV awards, 1977, Chgo. Film Festival award, 1977, 2 Gold Records for Songs from Mary Poppins and Mulan, VERA award, Voice Found., Phila., 2007; nominee Drama Desk award, 2 Grammy award, NARAS. Mem.: Nat. Assn. Tchrs. Singing (pres. N.Y. chpt. 1994—97, panelist new music). Personal E-mail: singermarnix@aol.com.

NIXON, NICHOLAS, photographer; b. Detroit, 1947; m. Bebe Brown. BA in English, Univ. Mich., 1969; MFA, Univ. N.Mex., 1974. Prof. photography Mass. Coll. Art, 1975—. Photography (books) Photographs From One Year, 1983, Pictures of People, 1988, School, 1998, The Brown Sisters, 2002, Nicholas Nixon Photographs, 2003, Home, 2005, (with Bebe Nixon, David R. Godine) People With AIDS, 1991, (exhibitions) The Brown Sisters, Mus. Modern Art, NYC, Zab Riskie Gallery, NYC, Detroit Art Inst., Victoria and Albert Mus., London, St. Louis Art Mus., San Diego Art Mus., Dallas Art Mus., Chgo. Art Inst., Musee de la ville de Paris, Toledo Art Mus., San Francisco Mus. Modern Art, LA County Mus., Cleve. Art Inst. Recipient Friends of Photog. Peer award, 1988; grantee NEA Fellowship, 1976, 1980, 1987, Guggenheim Fellowship, 1977, 1986. Office: Mass Coll of Art + Design 621 Huntington Ave Boston MA 02115 Office Phone: 617-879-7000. Business E-Mail: nicholas.nixon@massart.edu.

NIXON, RALPH ANGUS, psychiatrist, educator, research neuroscientist; b. Somerville, Mass., Jan. 29, 1947; s. Ralph Angus and Eleanor Nixon; m. Katharine Sangree Faulkner, Aug. 20, 1974; children: Abigail, Rebecca. AB, Brandeis U., 1968; PhD in Cell and Devel. Biology, Harvard U., 1974; MD, U. Vt., 1976. Intern Mass. Gen. Hosp., 1976, Salem Hosp., 1977; resident in psychiatry Mass. Gen. Hosp., 1977-79, McLean Hosp., 1979-80; clin. assoc. in psychiatry Mass. Gen. Hosp., Boston, 1980-97; assoc. in neurosci. Children's Hosp Med. Ctr., Boston, 1982-88; staff physician Rehab. Ctr. for Aged, Boston, 1984-90; asst. prof. psychiatry Harvard Med. Sch., Boston, 1982-86, assoc. prof., 1986-96; assoc. neuropathologist McLean Hosp., Belmont, Mass., 1982-90, assoc. psychiatrist, 1988-93, neuropathologist, 1991; psychiatrist, 1993-97; prof. psychiatry and cell biology NYU Med. Sch., NYC, 1997—, vice chmn. dept. psychiatry, 2001—; dir. rsch. Nathan Kline Inst.-NYU Med. Ctr., Orangeburg, dir. ctr. dementia rsch., 1997—; dir. Silberstein Inst. and Ctr. of Excellence on Brain Aging and Dementia NYU Langone Med. Ctr. Mem. sci. rev. com. Am. Fedn. for Aging Rsch., 1990-92; mem. neurosci., behavior and sociology of aging rev. com., subcom. A, Nat. Inst. on Aging, NIH, 1991-95, chmn., 1994-95; dir. labs. for molecular neurosci. McLean Hosp., 1992; mem. adv. bd. Internat. Congress Alzheimer's Disease, 1993—. Mem. editl. bd. Jour. Neurochemistry, 1986-96, Neurochem. Rsch., 1988—, Harvard Rev. Psychiatry, 1992—, Neurobiology of Aging, 1994—, Alzheimer's Disease Rev., 1997—; contbr. over 200 biol. articles to Sci. Jour. Cell Biology, Jour. Biol. Chem., Annals N.Y. Acad. Sci., Proc. NAS, chpts. to books; Proteases and Protease Inhibitors Banner C Nixon R.A. eds. Annals Acad. Sci. vol. 67, 1992. Hon. bd. dirs. Ch. League for Civic Concerns, Boston, 1987-89. Recipient Merit award NIH, 1990, Leadership and Excellence in Alzheimer Disease award, Nat. Inst. Aging, 1992, Temple Discovery award Alzheimers Assn., 1999, N.Y. State OMH Rsch. award, 1999, Career Leadership award, Nat. Inst. on Aging, 1999, Zenith award, Alzheimer's Assn., 2003; Ethel DuPont Warren fellow, 1979-80, rsch. fellow Med. Found., 1980-82, Alfred P. Sloan Found., 1981-83, Scottish Rite Schizophrenia Rsch. Program, 1983-85. Mem. AAAS, Soc. for Neurosci., Fedn. Am. Scientists, Am. Soc. for Neurochemistry, Internat. Soc. for Neurochemistry, Am. Psychiat. Assn., Am. Soc. for Cell Biology, Am. Assn. for Geriatric Psychiatry, Gerontol. Soc. Am., Am. Assn. Neuropathologists, N.Y. Acad. Sci. Achievements include 5 patents (with others) on diagnosis and treatment of Alzheimer's disease. Office: Nathan Kline Inst NYU Med Ctr 140 Old Orangeburg Rd Orangeburg NY 10962-1157*

NIXON, RONDA LYNN, paralegal; b. Ashland, Ky., Jan. 9, 1971; d. Ronnie Dewey and Sadie Francis Bishop; m. Norman Brian Nixon, May 1, 2004; children: Darren Connors, Shelby Connors, Roni Nixon. AAS in Paralegal Tech., Miller Motte Bus. Coll., Clarksville, Tenn., 1995; BS in Paralegal Studies, Kaplan U., Chgo., 2007. Cert. Paralegal Nat. Assn. of Legal Asst., 2005. Paralegal Pruitt & Thorner, Catlettsburg, Ky., 2003—; legal sec. Robinson & Rice, Ashland, Ky., 2003. Advocate CASA, Ashland, Ky., 2004—06. Mem.: Nat. Assn. of Legal Assistants, Assn. of Trial Lawyers of Am. Home: 102Township Rd 286 Chesapeake OH 45619 Office: Pruitt & Thorner P O Box 352 Catlettsburg KY 41129

NIXON, SCOTT WEST, oceanography science educator; b. Phila., Aug. 24, 1943; s. Robert Scott West and Elizabeth (Wright) West Nixon; m. Pendleton Hall, (div.); children: Carter Hall, Elizabeth Pendleton; m. Virginia Lee. BA, U. Del., 1965; PhD, U. N.C., 1970. Prof. oceanography U. R.I., Kingston, 1970—, dir. sea grant coll. program, 1983-2000. Mem. ocean studies bd. NRC, 1999-2004. Author: (with others) A Coastal Marine Ecosystem, 1978, The New England High Salt Marshes, 1982; co-editor-in-chief Estuaries, 1988—2006; also articles. Recipient Ketchum award Woods Hole Oceanographic Inst., 1992, Achievement award New Eng. Estuarine Rsch. Soc., 2000, Achievement award Nat. Sea Grant Assn., 2001, Lifetime appointment Nat. Assn. of Nat. Academies, 2002; grantee NSF, NOAA, EPA, Office Water Resources Rsch., State of R.I. Mem. Am. Soc. Limnology and Oceanography (governing bd. 1984-87), Estuarine Rsch. Fedn. (Odum award 2003) Office: U RI Bay Campus Dept Of Oceanography Narragansett RI 02882 Office Phone: 401-874-6803. Business E-Mail: swn@gso.uri.edu.

NIYEKAWA, AGNES MITSUE, foreign language professor; b. Tokyo, May 9, 1924; came to U.S., 1949, naturalized; d. Basil Zensaku and Irene (Kano) N.; m. Roy C. Calogeras (div. 1964); children: Erik, Karen. BA in English, Tokyo Women's U., 1945; BA in Sociology, U. Hawaii, 1952; MA in Psychology, Bryn Mawr Coll., 1954; PhD in Psychology, NYU, 1960; postdoc. in Linguistics, Columbia U., MIT, U. Wash., 1963. Rsch. assoc. psychology dept. NYU, 1959-61; asst. prof. ednl. psychology U. Hawaii, Honolulu, 1964-67, from prof. human devel. to chmn. East Asian langs., 1971-81, prof. East Asian langs. and lit., 1973-91, prof. emeritus, 1992—; assoc. prof. ednl. psychology Northeastern U., Boston, 1968-69; from sr. specialist Inst. Advanced Rsch. to assoc. dir. Culture Learning Inst. East West Ctr., Honolulu, 1969-71. Vis. scholar Columbia U., NYC, 1961-63, MIT, Cambridge, 1967-68, Harvard U., Cambridge, 1987, U. Tokyo, 1982, U. Vienna, 1986-87; keynote spkr. Convention of German Speaking Nations' Assn. Japanese Studies, Vienna, 1990. Author: Minimum Essential Politeness, 1992, (with others) Cross-Cultural Learning, 1977, Design for Cross-Cultural Learning, 1987; contbr. numerous articles to profl. jours. USPHS fellow, 1961-63; grantee U.S. Office Edn., 1965-67, Am. Coun. Learned Socs., 1962, 67-68, Fulbright, 1981-82, Social Sci. Rsch. Coun.; recipient Order of the Sacred Treasure (Gold Rays with Rosette), Japanese govt., 1998 Mem. Chamber Music Hawaii (bd. dirs.), Austrian Assn. Hawaii (bd. dirs., Austrian of Yr.). Home: 500 University Ave Apt 2003 Honolulu HI 96826-4941 Personal E-mail: agnesmn@hawaiiantel.net.

NIZIOLEK, ALICE, academic administrator; b. Elmhurst, Ill. BS, Elmhurst Coll., 1999; MA, Concordia U., River Forest, Ill., 2001. Internat. student coord. Elmhurst Coll., 2002—; tchr. German Walther Luth. HS, Melrose Pk., Ill. Chair Study Ill., Chgo., 2008—. Mem.: Alpha Mu Gamma, Phi Kappa Phi, Phi Beta Delta. Avocations: travel, golf, reading. Office: Elmhurst Coll 190 Prospect Ave Elmhurst IL 60126

NJOCK LIBII, JOSUÉ, mechanical engineer, educator; s. Pierre Libii Ndoum and Marthe Ngo Yana Ngo Njock; m. Louise Gezina Magoon, Sept. 22, 1979; children: Kekla Johanna Magoon, Bikobi Njock Libii. PhD, U. Mich., Ann Arbor, 1980. Cert. wind resistance designer, FEMA, 1993, flood protection designer, 1994, earthquake resistant designer, 1995. Asst. prof. Purdue U., Dept. Mech. Engring., Ft. Wayne, Ind., 1984—90, assoc. prof., 1990—. Engring. cons. UN' FAO, Rome, 1983—84. Contbr. articles to profl. jour. Cons. evaluator Higher Learning Commn. North Ctrl. Assn. Coll. and Sch., Chgo., 1993—2008. Decorated Math and Sci. Edn. Outreach US Army. Mem.: Am. Soc. Engring. Edn., Phi Kappa Phi (chpt. pres. 1998—2000). Office: Purdue Univ Ft Wayne 2101 E Coliseum Blvd Fort Wayne IN 46805-1499 Office Fax: 260-481-6880. Business E-Mail: libii@engr.ipfw.edu.

NJOKU, MARY GLORIA, psychology professor, researcher; arrived in US, 1997, naturalized, 2007; d. John Onwuegbuche and Grace Onyewuchi Njoku. BA in Liberal Studies, DePaul U., Chgo., 2001, MA in Psychology, 2005, PhD in Clin. Psychology, 2007. Tchr., asst. dir. Mater Amabilis Nursery/Primary Sch. Isunjaba, Orlu, Imo, 1992—97; family educator Maryville Ctr. Medically Complex Children, Chgo., 1997—2002; direct support profl. Misericordia Heart Mercy, Chgo., 2002—03; grad. asst. DePaul U., 2003—06, adj. faculty, 2005—06, rsch. assoc., psychology instr., 2007—; psychology internship Mercy Health Partners, Toledo, 2006—07. Cons. African Cath. Clergy & Religious Assn., Chgo., 2003—05; regional sec. Daughters Divine Love Congregation, Highwood, Ill., 2005—; communique coord. African Conf. Cath. Clergy & Religious of US, 2006—. Author: (self-help books) My Health Management Manual: A Guide for a Healthy and Happy Life, 2007, I Need Healing: Personality, Anxiety and Mood Disorders, 2003, (book) Education among Nigerian Youths: Can our Educational System be Redeemed?, 2002; contbr. articles to profl. jours. Councillor Daughters Divine Love, Highwood, Ill., 2005; chair orientation com. African Conf. Cath. Clergy & Religious of US, 2007; children & behavioral challenged teenage vol. Orlu, 1992—97; prisoner & mental health challenged vol., 1993—97; com. mem. Ecological-Cmty. Psychology Conf. Planning Com., Chgo., 2002—03; grad. student rep. APA of Grad. Students, DePaul U., DC, 2002—05; diversity & tng. com. mem. DePaul Cmty. Mental Health Ctr., Chgo., 2003—05; organizer chronic illness buddy program Chronic Fatigue Syndrome, Fibromyalgia & Chem. Sensitivity Coalition Chgo., 2005—06; vol. St. Elizabeth Sch., Chgo., 2007; animator DePaul U. Oxford Ho. Initiative, Chgo., 2007; home visitation & pastoral care vol. St. Joseph Cath. Ch. Isunjaba, Orlu, 1992—97; youth spiritual dir. St. Joseph's Ch. Cath. Youth Orgn., Orlu, 1993—97; religious presence activity vol. Cath. Parishes of St. Hyacinth, St. John Vianney & St. James, Archdiocese of Chgo., 1997—2007; pastoral care vol. Highland Pk. Nursing & Rehab., Highwood, 2005—06. Recipient Internat. Travel award, APA, 2006. Mem.: African Conf. Cath. Clergy Religious US, Daughters Divine Love Congregation, Soc. Cmty. Rsch. and Action. Achievements include research in myalgic encephalomyelitis/chronic fatigue syndrome in an African country using recommended methodologies. Avocations: reading, singing, writing. Home: 4117 S Michigan Ave Chicago IL 60653 Office: Center Cmty Rsch 990 W Fullerton Ave Chicago IL 60614 Office Fax: 773-325-4923. Personal E-mail: caelisgloria@aol.com. Business E-Mail: nmgloria@depaul.edu.

NJOKU, SCHOLASTICA IBARI, retired college librarian, writer; d. David Mgbahuruike Njoku and Elizabeth Ekeoma Ukaegbu; divorced; children: Anthony, Emelia, Martina, Iheanyi, Chinedu, Onyekachi. BA cum laude in English, Wiley Coll., 1963; MLS, U. Oreg., 1965, MS in Edn., 1967, PhD in Edn., 1969; diploma in writing for children and teenagers, Inst. Children's Lit., Conn., 1996. Ref. libr. Knapp Libr. Project, Portland, Oreg., 1965—66; asst. edn. libr. Portland State U., 1969—70; assoc. prof. edn. Miss. Valley State Coll., Itta Bena, 1970—72; ref. cons. Oreg. State Libr., Salem, 1974—81, on-line cataloger, 1981—86; ref. libr. Portland C.C., 1986—2003; ret., 2003. Multicultural mentoring com. Portland C.C., 1996—2003, ednl. adv. coun. com., 1999—2003, women history planning com., 1999—2003. Author: The Miracle of A Christmas Doll, 1986, Dog What?, 1989; contbr. poems to poetry anthologies; author (writer, recorder): (CD) Smiling Faces in My Class At School, 2006. Recipient 3d prize Poetry award, Ann. Reader's Digest, United Negro Coll. Fund, 1963. Mem.: ALA, The Willamette Writers, Pacific NW Libr. Assn., Oreg. State Poetry Assn., Am. Assn. Higher Edn., Oreg. Libr. Assn., Delta Sigma Theta (Sisterhood award 2006). Democrat. Roman Catholic. Avocations: gardening, story telling, reading, writing. Home: 307 NE Holland St Portland OR 97211

NJUS, DAVID LARS, biophysicist; b. Honolulu, Oct. 17, 1948; s. Kasper M. and Alice M. Njus; m. Deborah Handrinos, Aug. 18, 1984; 3 children. B.S., MIT, 1970; Ph.D., Harvard U., 1975. Vis. scientist U. Oxford, 1975-78; asst. prof. Wayne State U., Detroit, 1978-82, assoc. prof. biol. scis., 1982-86, prof. biol. scis. 1986—, assoc. dean, 1991-93, 1994-. Contbr. articles to profl. jours. Mem. Founders Soc. Detroit Inst. Arts. Recipient Nat. Research Service award NIH, 1976-78; NSF fellow, 1975; established investigator Am. Heart Assn., 1983-88. Fellow AAAS; mem. Am. Heart Assn., Am. Soc. Biochemistry and Molecular Biology, Biophys. Soc., Nat. Acads. Edn. (fellow life sci. 2004-05). Office: Wayne State U Dept Biol Sci Detroit MI 48202 Business E-Mail: dnjus@wayne.edu.

NKANSAH, FRANKLIN DANIEL, electrical engineer, educator; s. John Benjamin and Rachel Endurance Nkansah; m. Mercy Ekfui Yongkuma, Dec. 27, 1991; children: Claribel, Franklin. PhD, Lehigh U., Pa., 2000. Mem. tech. staff AT&T Bell Labs., Allentown, Pa., 1988—93; wireless device mgr. Motorola Inc, Austin, Tex., 1993—2000; engring. mgr. Advanced Micro Devices, Austin, 2000—06; pres., CEO FDN Enterprises LLC, Buda, Tex., 2002—; prof. elec. engring. Prairie View A&M U., Tex., 2002—. Tech. cons. AWET Group and Holdings, Accra, Ghana, 1999—, overseer strategic directions, 2000—. Contbr. articles to profl. jours. Active Bekom Orphan Ho., Bekom, Cameroon, 2003—07. Mem.: IEEE. Achievements include patents for integrated circuit structure and method therefore; method for forming trench isolation; method of making a semiconductor device using chemicalmechanical polishing having a combination-step process; method of integrated circuit fabrication having planarized dielectrics.

NKOY, FLORY LUMU, medical educator; s. Olenga Nkoy and Zizita Esale; m. Annie Dioko Nkoy, Dec. 18, 1993; children: Joshua A., Jason A. B. U. Kinshasa, Democratic Republic of the Congo, 1984, MD, 1988; MS, MPH, U. Utah, Salt Lake City, 2005. Attending physician gen. medicine Epharza Med. Ctr., Kinshasa, 1989—94; attending physician internal medicine Kimtambo Hosp., Kinshasa, 1989—94; coord. Millcreek Women's Ctr., Salt Lake City, 1996—97; rsch. assoc. Utah Valley Regional Med. Ctr., Provo, Utah, 1997—99; oncology rschr. Intermountain Health Care, Salt Lake City, 2001—06; asst. prof. rsch., rsch. dir. U. Utah, Salt Lake City, 2006—. Cons. Oncodx, Phoenix, 2005. Contbr. articles to profl. jours. Grantee, Deseret Found., Salt Lake City, 2002, 2004; fellow, Intermountain Health Care, 1999—2001. Mem.: Internat. Soc. Quality Life Rsch., Am. Fedn. Med. Rsch., Am. Med. Informatics Assn. Avocations: reading, travel, exercise.

NOBACK, RICHARDSON KILBOURNE, medical educator; b. Richmond, Va., Nov. 7, 1923; s. Gustav Joseph and Hazel (Kilborn) N.; m. Nan Jean Gates, Apr. 5, 1947; children: Carl R., Robert K., Catherine E. MD, Cornell U., 1947; BA, Columbia U., 1993. Diplomate Am. Bd. Internal Medicine. Intern N.Y. Hosp., 1947-48; asst. resident Cornell Med. div. Bellevue Hosp., NYC, 1958-50, chief resident, 1950-52; instr. medicine Cornell U., NYC, 1950-53; asst. prof. medicine SUNY Upstate Med. Ctr., Syracuse, 1955-56; assoc. prof. medicine U. Ky. Med. Ctr., Lexington, 1956-64; exec. dir. Kansas City (Mo.) Gen. Hosp. and Med. Ctr., 1964-69; assoc. dean, prof. medicine U. Mo. Sch. Medicine, Columbia, 1964-69, founding dean Kansas City, 1969-78, prof. medicine, 1969-90, prof. and dean emeritus, 1990—. Cons. U. Tenn., U. Mich., U. Del., Northeastern Ohio Group, U. Mo., Eastern Va. Med. Sch., Tex. Tech. U. Author Realism, Standards, and Performances: Three Essentials in Assessment, Planning, and Action, 2005; contbr. numerous articles to profl. jours. Bd. dirs. Kansas City Gen. Hosp., Truman Med. Ctr., Wayne Miner Health Ctr., Jackson County Med. Soc., The Shepherd's Ctr., Am. Fedn. Aging Rsch., Mo. Gerontol. Inst., The Shepherd's Ctrs. of Am.; dir. Mo. Geriatric Edn. Ctr., 1985-88. With US Army, 1943—46, with USAF, 1953—55. Recipient medal of honor Avila Coll., Kansas City, 1968, merit award Met. Med. Soc., 1991, recognition award Mo. Soc. Internal Medicine, 1993. Mem. AMA, Mo. Med. Assn. (former mem. ho. of dels., v.p. 1992), Am. Geriatric Soc., Alpha Omega Alpha, Phi Kappa Phi. Avocations: photography, writing, travel. Home: 2912 Abercorn Dr Las Vegas NV 89134-7440 Personal E-mail: nanori@embarqmail.com.

NOBE, KEN, chemical engineering professor; b. Berkeley, Calif., Aug. 26, 1925; s. Sidney and Kiyo (Uyeyama) N.; m. Mary Tagami, Aug. 31, 1957; children: Steven Andrew, Keven Gibbs, Brian Kelvin. BS, U. Calif., Berkeley, 1951; PhD, UCLA, 1956. Jr. chem. engr. Air Reduction Co., Murray Hill, NJ, 1951-52; instr. engring. UCLA, 1955—57, asst. prof. chem. engring., 1957-62, assoc. prof., 1962-68, prof., 1968—2004, prof. emeritus, 2004—, chmn. dept. chem., nuclear and thermal engring., 1978-83, founding chmn. chem. engring., 1983-84. Mem. tech. staff Ramo-Wooldridge Corp., El Segundo, Calif., 1958-59 Div. editor: Jour. Electrochem. Soc, 1967-91, Electrochimica Acta, 1977-85 With US Army, 1944—46. Recipient Disting. Tchg. award, UCLA, 1962. Mem. Electrochem. Soc. (Henry B. Linford award 1992), Am. Chem. Soc., Internat. Soc. Electrochemistry, Am. Electroplaters Surfacing Fin. Soc. (Abner Brenner Gold medal 2000), Sigma Xi. Office: UCLA Dept Chemical Engring Los Angeles CA 90095-1592 Business E-Mail: nobe@seas.ucla.edu.

NOBEL, JOEL J., biomedical researcher; b. Phila., Dec. 8, 1934; s. Bernard D. and Golda R. (Nobel) Judovich; m. Bonnie Sue Goldberg, June 19, 1960 (div.); children: Erika, Joshua; m. Loretta Schwartz, Oct. 28, 1979 (div.); 1 child, Adam. AB, Haverford Coll., 1956; MA, U. Pa., 1958; MD, Thomas Jefferson Med. Coll., Phila., 1963. Intern Presbyn. Hosp., Phila., 1963-64; resident in surgery Pa. Hosp., Phila., 1964-65; resident in neurosurgery U. Pa. Hosp., 1965-66; practice medicine specializing in biomed. engring. rsch. and healthcare tech. assessment, hosp. planning and mgmt., Phila., 1968—; dir. research Emergency Care Research Inst., Plymouth Meeting, Pa., 1968-71, dir., pres., 1971—2001; bd. dirs. Consumers Union, 1976—79, 1980—2005, Conflict Interest Com., 2008—; pres. Plymouth Inst., 1979—2002; founder and pres. emeritus ECRI, 2001—; founder, pres. ECRI Bhd, Malaysia, 2001—; CEO The Nobel Group, 2002—, chmn. Arab Health award, 2004—09; mng. dir. IMD, 2006—. Chmn. tech. policy com., exec. bd., chmn. strategiuc planning com. Consumers Union; cons. in field. Publisher Health Devices, 1971-2001, Health Devices Alerts, 1977-2001; contbr. articles to profl. jours. With submarine force USN, 1966—68. Smith, Kline & French fgn. fellow, 1962; grantee HEW, 1968-72; grantee Am. Heart Assn., 1965-66 Mem. AMA, APHA, Assn. Advancement Med. Instrumentation, Critical Care Med. Soc., Pa. Med. Assn., Navy League, US Naval Inst., Brit. Officers Club Phila. Office: ECRI 5200 Butler Pike Plymouth Meeting PA 19462-1298 Home: 361 Righters Mill Rd Gladwyne PA 19035

NOBER, ROGER, rail transportation executive, lawyer; married; 3 children. BA, Haverford Coll., Pa., 1986; JD, Harvard Law Sch., 1989. With Skadden, Arps, Slate, Meagher & Flom, NYC; various positions Com. on Transp. and Infrastructure US House Reps., 1993—97, chief counsel Com. on Transp. and Infrastructure, 1997—2001; counselor to dep. sec. Michael Jackson US Dept. Transp.; chmn. Surface Transp. Bd., 2002—06; ptnr. Steptoe & Johnson, LLP, Washington, 2006; exec. v.p. law, sec. Burlington No. Santa Fe Corp., 2007—. Chmn. Surface Transp. Bd., 2002—06. Republican. Office: Burlington No Santa Fe Corp PO Box 961056 Fort Worth TX 76161-0056 Office Phone: 817-352-1460.*

NOBERT, FRANCES, music educator; b. Winston-Salem, NC, Dec. 12, 1936; d. Henry Carrington and Frances Mozelle (Harrison) Cuningham; m. Jon Marshall Nobert (div. Jan. 1980). BM in Music Edn., Salem Coll., 1959; Fulbright Cert. in Organ, Conservatory of Music, Frankfurt am Main, Germany, 1961; MM in Organ, Syracuse U., 1963; DMA in Choral Music, U. So. Calif., 1980. Organist, choir dir. United Ch., Fayetteville, N.Y., 1961-67; choral, gen. music tchr. Fayetteville Manlius Sch. Dist., 1963-67; vocal music tchr. U.S. Grant HS, Van Nuys, Calif., 1967-80; organist United Ch. Christ Congregational, Claremont, Calif., 1981-83; organist, choir dir. St. Matthias Episc. Ch., Whittier, Calif., 1983-94; organist First United Meth. Ch., Pasadena, Calif., 2000—03, Santa Monica, 2006—07; prof. music, coll. organist Whittier Coll., 1982-98, coord. women's studies, 1995-98, disting. svc. prof. music, 1998—99, prof. emerita, 1999—. Singer L.A. Master Chorale, 1972-86; vis. instr. of key bd. theory, L.A. Valley Coll., Van Nuys, 1980-81, spring 1982; bd. dirs., program chair, sub-dean, dean Pasadena chpt. Am. Guild of Organists, Calif., 1991-95, dean, 1998-99, south coast dist. convenor, 1999-2004, Region IX councillor, 2004—; v.p. Mader Corp., 2005-; resident dir. for Denmark's Internat. Study Program, Whittier Coll., 1994. Faculty Rsch. grantee Whittier Coll., 1984, devel. grantee, 1986, 88, 90, 91, 93. 96, 97, Irvine grantee, 1995. Mem. NOW, Internat. Alliance for Women in Music (treas. 1997-2000, v.p. 2000-03), Am. Guild Organists, Organ Hist. Soc., Rio Hondo Symphony Guild, Whittier Cultural Arts Found., Mader Corp. (v.p. 2005—), Feminist Majority, Pi Kappa Lambda, Mu Phi Epsilon. Episcopalian. Avocations: travel, languages. Personal E-mail: fnobert99organ@aol.com.

NOBIL, JAMES HOWARD, JR., real estate investor, developer, broker, consultant; b. Columbus, Ohio, Mar. 21, 1955; s. James Howard Nobil and Carol Mae (Weisenberger) Greenbaum; m. Elizabeth Ann Corro, Apr. 16, 1983 (div. 1998); children: Jonathan James Michael, Jennifer Carrie Lee. BA in Polit. Sci., Tufts U., Medford, Mass., 1976; postgrad., George Washington U., Washington, DC, 1978—80. Lic. real estate broker Md., Va., D.C., Fla.; sr. cert. leasing specialist ICSC. Account exec. Riviere Securities Corp., Washington, 1977-78; v.p. ops. Fed. Realty Investment Trust, Bethesda, Md., 1978-83; mng. gen. ptnr. NRW Devel. Co., Vienna, Va., 1983-84; v.p. acquisitions Oxford Nat. Properties Corp., Bethesda, 1984-85; 1st v.p. Washington Real Estate Investment Trust, Bethesda, 1985-86; pres. Washington Comml. Properties, Inc., McLean, Va., 1986—, Rent Verification Svcs. (subs. of Washington Comml. Properties, Inc.), McLean, 1986—. Mem. Internat. Coun. Shopping Ctrs., Nat. Assn. Realtors,Greater Washington, DC Comml. Brokers Coun. Avocations: running, boating, skiing, tennis. Office: Washington Comml Properties Inc 6849 Old Dominion Dr 220 Mc Lean VA 22101-3705

NOBLE, ALLEN GEORGE, geography educator; b. Astoria, NY, Jan. 28, 1930; s. Chauncey Helmer and Mary Oliver (Van Allen) N.; m. Jane Sylvia Walter, June 27, 1959; children: Lisa, Matthew, Douglas. BA, Utica Coll., 1951; MA, U. Md., 1953; PhD, U. Ill., 1957. Joined Fgn. Svc., 1957, resigned, 1963; assoc. prof. geography California (Pa.) State Coll., 1963-64; prof. geography and planning U. Akron, Ohio, 1964—99, disting. prof. emeritus Ohio, 2000—. Vis. prof. Laurentian U., U. Tel Aviv, U. Vaasa, Finland. Author: Wood Brick & Stone, 1984, Ethnic Geography of Early Utica, NY: Time, Space and Community, 1999, Traditional Buildings, 2007; co-author: The Old Barn Book, 1995; editor: To Build in a New Land, 1992 (Kniffen prize 1995); co-editor: Barns of the Midwest, 1995, Regional Development and Planning for the 21st Century, 1999, Geography and Planning Research Themes for the New Millenium, 2000, Challenges to Asian Urbanization in the 21st Century, 2003. Fulbright scholar U. Peradeniya, Sri Lanka, 1979. Mem. Am. Geog. Soc., Can. Geog. Assn., Assn. Am. Geographers (Honors award 1989), Ohio Acad. Sci. (pres. 1989-90, Finnish Acad. Sci. and Letters, Centennial Honoree 1991), Pioneer Am. Soc. (exec. dir. 1977-86), Sigma Xi. Office: Dept Geography and Planning U Akron Akron OH 44325-5005 Home Phone: 330-836-9268; Office Phone: 330-972-8038.

NOBLE, ERNEST PASCAL, pharmacologist, biochemist, educator, psychiatrist; b. Baghdad, Iraq, Apr. 2, 1929; came to U.S., 1946; s. Noble Babik and Barkev Grace (Kasparian) Babikian; m. Inga Birgitta Kilstromer, May 19, 1956; children: Lorna, Katharine, Erik BS in Chemistry, U. Calif.-Berkeley, 1951; PhD in Biochemistry, Oreg. State U., 1955; MD, Case Western Res. U., 1962. Diplomate Nat. Bd. Med. Examiners. Sr. instr. biochemistry Western Res. U., Cleve., 1957-62; intern Stanford Med. Ctr., Calif., 1962-63, resident in psychiatry Calif., 1963-66, research assoc., asst. prof. Calif., 1965-69; assoc. prof. psychiatry, psychobiology and pharmacology U. Calif.-Irvine, 1969-71, prof., chief neurochemistry, 1971-76, 79-81; dir. Nat. Inst. Alcohol Abuse and Alcoholism HEW, 1976-78, assoc. adminstr. sci., alcohol, drug abuse and mental health, 1978-79; Pike prof. alcohol studies, dir. Alcohol Research Ctr. UCLA Sch. of Medicine, 1981—. Mem. various med./sci. jour. editorial bds.; contbr. numerous articles to profl. jours., chpts. to books V.p. Nat. Coun. on Alcoholism 1981-84; pres. Internat. Commn. for the Prevention of Alcoholism and Drug Dependency, 1988. Fulbright scholar, 1955-56; Guggenheim fellow, 1974-75; Sr. Fulbright scholar, 1984-85; recipient Career Devel. award NIMH, HEW, 1966-69 Fellow Am. Coll. Neuropsychopharmacology; mem. Internat. Soc. Neurochemistry, Am. Soc. Pharmacology and Exptl. Therapeutics, Research Soc. on Alcoholism. Office: UCLA 760 Westwood Plz Los Angeles CA 90095-8353

NOBLE, HELEN BONNER, artist; b. Northville, Mich., Mar. 27, 1922; d. George Coburn and Helen Josephine (McCambridge) Harper; m. Morton Noble, Jr., June 27, 1943; children: Martha, Kathryn, Elizabeth, John. Student, Wayne State U., Case Western REs. U., 1939-43, Santa Barbar Art Inst. One-woman shows include Gallery 932, Ventura, Calif., 1983, The Oaks Gallery, Ojai, Calif., 1988; group shows include Bradley Galleries, Santa Barbara, Calif., 1978, 79, Meredith Niles Gallery, Santa Barbara, 1980-83, Merida-Rapp Graphics, Louisville, 1986; other exhibits include 3rd Women in Art Exhbn., Springfield, Ill., 1983, 2nd Ann. Nat. Print Exhbn. of Springfield Art Assn., 1982, 24th Ann. Nat. Exhbn. of Prints and Drawings, Oklahoma City, 1982, 40th Ann Nat. Juried Print Exhbn., Clinton, N.J., 1996, others; represented in collections; curated small work exhbn., StoneMetal Press, San Antonio, 2005-06. Office Phone: 805-965-3121.

NOBLE, JOHN W., legislative staff member; Grad., U. Ariz., Tucson; attended, Am. U., Washington, 2000. Staff asst., Rep. Rick Boucher US House of Reps., Washington, 2004—06, press. sec., Rep. Rick Boucher, 2006—08, comm. dir. to Rep. Niki Tsongas, 2008—. Democrat. Office: 1607 Longworth House Office Bldg Washington DC 20515 Office Phone: 202-225-3411. Office Fax: 202-226-0771. Business E-Mail: john.noble@mail.house.gov.*

NOBLE, KENNETH ERIC, lawyer; b. Amboy, Ill., Apr. 24, 1962; BS in Fin., Northen Ill. U., 1984; JD summa cum laude, U. Ill., Champaign, 1990. Cert. mgmt. acct., 1985; bar: Ill. 1991, NY 2002, cert.: Law Soc. Eng. and Wales (solicitor) 2006, Clk. US Supreme Ct. 2002. Assoc. Winston & Strawn, Chgo., 1991—93; equity ptnr. Mayer, Brown, Rowe & Maw LLP, NYC, 1993—2008, Katten Muchin Rosenmon LLP, 2008—. Author: (legal treatise) Lender Liability. Devel. com. Babies Heart Fund, NYC, 2005—07. Mem.: Turnaround Mgmt. Assn., Am.

Bankruptcy Inst. Office: Katten Muchin Rosenman LLP 575 Madison Ave New York NY 10022 Office Phone: 212-940-6419. Business E-Mail: kenneth.noble@kattenlaw.com.

NOBLE, MARY C., state supreme court justice; b. Jackson, Ky., 1949; m. Larry Noble. B., Austin Peay State U., Clarksville, Tenn., 1971, M., 1975; JD, U. Ky. Coll. Law, 1981. Pvt. practice, 1981—91; domestic rels. commr., 1989—91; cir. judge for Fayette County Fayette Cir. Ct., 1991—2006, chief regional cir. judge, 1998—2002; assoc. justice for 5th Supreme Ct. Dist. Supreme Ct. Ky., 2007—; co-founder Ky. Drug Courts, Drug Ct. judge, 1996—2006. Mem.: Nat. Assn. Drug Ct. Professionals (mem. & former pres. congress state drug cts., bd. dirs.). Office: Supreme Court Of Kentucky 300 W Vine St Ste 2201 Lexington KY 40507-1810 Office Phone: 859-246-2220.*

NOBLE, PAMELA LEE, primatologist; b. Honolulu, Aug. 9, 1968; d. Charles Clifford and Patrica Lee (Hammond) Noble; children: Amanda Lee, Griffin Earl. OAS, Pima C.C., 1995; BA in Anthropology and Psychology with honors, U. Ariz., 1999; postgrad., Ga. Inst. Tech., 1999—2000; MBA postgrad, Univ. Phoenix, 2005. Tutor Pima C.C., Tucson, 1993-96; intern, rschr. Jane Goodall Inst., 1996-98, Dian Fossey Gorilla Fund, 1997—; rsch. assoc. TECHLAB, Zoo Atlanta, 1999—2000; sr. rsch. specialist, psychol. Yerkes Primate Center, 2000—03; projects mgr., neurobiology NIMH Intramural Rsch. Programs, 2003—. Guest lectr. grad. level animal behavior U. Ariz., 1997, Monash U. Primate Ctr., Australia, 2008; tax profl. H&R Block, Seasonal. Contbg. author The Scholastic Tradition, 1993, The Jane Goodall Institute World Report, 1997, Ark Animals online mag.; asst. editor ChimpanZoo Newsletter, 1996, 97, asst. editor conf. procs., 1995, 96; contbr. articles to profl. jours. Spkr. Casa Niños Montessori Sch., Tucson, 1996-97. Ariz. State Champion Women's Flying 200 Meter and Women's 500 Meter Track Racing, 1999, Dir.'s award, NIMH, 2007; named 2000 Outstanding Scientists, 2008. Mem. So. Ariz. Mountain Biking Assn., Golden Key Nat. Honor Soc, Am. Soc. Primatologists. Avocations: mountain biking, wine tasting, cooking. Office: NIHAC Bldg 110 Rm 119 16701 Elmer School Rd Poolesville MD 20837 Home: 5522 Upshur Sq Frederick MD 21703 Office Phone: 301-451-2195. Business E-Mail: noblep@mail.nih.gov.

NOBLE, RALPH C., animal scientist, department chairman; s. Willie G. Noble; m. Debra Tazewell; 1 child, Rachel C. BS, Tuskegee U., Ala., 1973, MS, 1975; PhD, U. Ill., Champaign-Urbana, 1981. Cert. artificial insemination technician Ala., forage mgmt. Coop. Ext., Ala., beef quality assurance Coop. Ext., Ala. Instr. Tuskegee U., 1975—77, from asst. to assoc. prof., 1982—2005, acting coord. George Washington Carver agrl. expt. sta., 1985—86, coord. of CSREES animal sci. rsch. program, 1986—97, coord. animal, poultry and vet. scis. program, 2002—05; rsch./tchg. asst. U. Ill., Champaign-Urbana, 1978—81; chmn. dept. animal scis. NC A&T State U., Greensboro, 2005—. Cons. Heifer Internat., Gainsville, Fla., 1990—2005; dir. strategic alliance for the Ala. goat industry Tuskegee U., 2001—05; advisor Ala. Farmers Fedn. Meat Goat and Sheep subcom., Montgomery, 2002—05; bd. dirs. NRCS-AL Grassland Res. com., Auburn, Ala., 2003—05; mem. adv. com. U.S. Poultry & Egg Assn., Atlanta, 2002—03; advisor Nat. Pre-Vet. Medicine Assn., Stillwater, Okla., 2002—04; chair livestock com. Macon County Farmers Orgn., Inc., Tuskegee, 1988—2005; mem. planning com. farmers conf. Tuskegee U. Coop. Ext. Program, 1982—2005; contbg. editor Am. Assn. Animal Sci., Urbana, 1985—86. Vol. eyeglass collection Lions Club, Tuskegee, 1986—90; sec. Sigma Xi, Tuskegee; pres., sec. Gamma Sigma Delta, Tuskegee; mem. Humane Soc. of the Piedmont, Greensboro, 2006—; mem. adv. com. to the bishop ELCA SE Luth. Ch., Atlanta, 1986—88; bd. dirs. St. Luke Luth. Ch., Tuskegee, 1988—98. Recipient Outstanding Faculty Performance award for tchg., Tuskegee U., 1987, 1997, Outstanding Faculty Performance award for svc., 2002, Outstanding Recognition award for tech. assistance to small farmers in the Southea. US, Heifer Project Internat., 2002, Alumni Merit Honor, Tuskegee U. Vet. Alumni Assn., 2005. Mem.: Phi Kappa Phi (licentiate). Office: NC A&T State U Webb Hall Ste 101 1601 E Market St Greensboro NC 27411 Office Fax: 336-334-7288. E-mail: rcnoble@ncat.edu.

NOBLE, RONALD KENNETH, secretary general of Interpol; b. Ft. Dix, NJ, Sept. 24, 1956; s. James L. and Rosemarie Noble. BA cum laude, U. NH, 1979; JD, Stanford U., 1982. Bar: Pa. 1983, NJ, 1983. Sr. law clk. to Hon. A. Leon Higginbotham Jr. US Ct. Appeals (3rd Cir.), Phila., 1982-84; asst. US atty. (ea. dist.) Pa. US Dept. Justice, Phila., 1984-88, spl. counsel & chief of staff criminal divsn. Washington, 1988-89, dep. asst. atty. gen., 1989; asst. prof. law NYU Sch. Law, 1990—92, assoc. prof., 1992—99, prof., 1999—; asst. sec. for enforcement US Dept. Treasury, Washington, 1993-94, under sec. for enforcement, 1994-96; sec. gen INTERPOL (Internat. Criminal Police Orgn.), Lyon, France, 2000—. Pres. Fin. Action Task Force, 1994—; mem. exec. com. INTERPOL (Internat. Criminal Police Orgn.), 1994—; mem. Root-Tilden Scholar Selection Bd., 1990—; chmn. Customs Ops. Adv. Com., 1993—; chmn. Bank Secrecy Act Adv. Com., 1993—. Articles editor Stanford Law Rev., 1981-82. Mem. Am. Law Inst. Office: NYU Sch of Law Vanderbilt Hall 40 Washington Sq S Rm 420 New York NY 10012-1099 also: INTERPOL Gen Secretariat 200 quai Charles de Gaulle 69006 Lyon France

NOBLE, THOMAS FRANCIS, history professor, department chairman; b. Chgo., May 10, 1947; s. Elmer Laverne and Patricia Ruth Noble; m. Linda Lee Jones, Nov. 11, 1967; children: Kirby Anne McClure, Jeremy Andrew. BA, Ohio U., Athens, 1969; MA, Mich. State U., East Lansing, 1971, PhD, 1974. Asst. prof. history Tex. Tech U., Lubbock, 1976—80; prof. history U. Va., Charlottesville, 1980—2000; dir. medieval inst. U. Notre Dame, Ind., 2001—08; prof. and chair Dept. History, Notre Dame, Ind., 2008—. Author: (book) Western Civilization; editor: Soldiers of Christ. Fulbright-Hays, Fulbright Commn., 1972—73, fellow, Nat. Endowment Humanities, 1980, 1993—94, Residential fellowship, Netherlands Inst. Advanced Study, 1999—2000. Fellow: Medieval Acad. Am.; mem.: Inst. Advanced Study, Princeton, Am. Soc. Ch. History, Am. Cath. Hist. Assn. (exec. com. 1988—91), Am. Hist. Assn. Independent. Roman Catholic. Avocations: golf, travel. Home: 50750 Andover Trail Granger IN 46530 Office: Dept History 219 O'Shaugnessy Hall Notre Dame IN 46556 Business E-Mail: tnoble@nd.edu.

NOBLE, WESTON HENRY, music educator; b. Riceville, Iowa, Nov. 30, 1922; s. Merwin Henry and Ruth Lillian (Lappin) N. BA, Luther Coll., 1943; MusM, U. Mich., 1953, postgrad., 1954-57; MusD (hon.), Augustana Coll., Sioux Falls, SD, 1971, St. Olaf Coll., 1996, Westminster Choir Coll., 2005, Carthage Coll., Kenosha, Wis., 2008, Wartburg Coll., Waverly, 2009. Dir. band, choir LuVerne (Iowa) pub. schs., 1946-48; dir. Nordic Choir, Decorah, Iowa, 1948—2005; from instr. to prof. music Luther Coll., Decorah, 1948—; dir. Luther Coll. Concert Band, Decorah, 1948-73. Conducted: 900 music festivals (choirs, bands, orchestras). Recipient Robert McCowen Meml. award Iowa Music Educators Assn., 1968; Presdl. award Ill. Music Edn. Assn., 1992; Citation of Merit award U. Mich. Sch. Music, 1993; named 1 of 10 Outstanding Music Dirs. in U.S., Sch. Musician mag., 1972, 1st Outstanding Music Educator of U.S., Fedn. of High Sch. Assns. 1990, Robert Lawson Show Citation(ACDH), 1999, St. Olaf Medallion award King of Norway, 1998, Medal of Hon., Internat. Band and Orch. Conf.-The Midwest Band and Orch. Clinic, Chgo., 2008, decorated 1948-2005. Fellow Am. Bandmasters Assn., Am. Choral Dirs. Assn. (founding mem.), Coll. Music Soc., Music Educators Nat. Conf, Music Tchrs. Nat. Assn., Iowa Bandmaster Assn.(hon. life mem.) Republican. Lutheran. Avocations: swimming, reading, hiking. Office: Luther Coll Dept Music Decorah IA 52101 Home: 709 Serenity Ct Decorah IA 52101-1564 Business E-Mail: noblewes@luther.edu.

NOBLES, LAURENCE HEWIT, retired geology educator; b. Spokane, Wash., Sept. 28, 1927; s. Harry and Florence (Giffin) N.; m. Barbara Joanne Smith, Aug. 28, 1948; children: Heather C., Laurence F. BS, MS, Calif. Inst. Tech., 1949; PhD, Harvard, 1952. Instr. geology Northwestern U., 1952-55, asst. prof., 1955-61, assoc. prof., 1961-67, prof., 1967-90, prof. emeritus, 1990—, also asst. dean Coll. Arts and Scis., 1966-67, asso. dean, 1968-70; acting dean Northwestern U. (Coll. Arts and Scis.), 1970-72, dean adminstrn., 1972-81, v.p. adminstrn. and fin. planning, 1981-86. Trustee Adler Planetarium, 1980-86, Chgo. Acad. Scis., 1967-87, pres., 1973-78, hon. trustee, 1987—; faculty rep. Big Ten Conf., 1976-81; mem. Port Ludlow Village Coun., 2005—, pres., 2006-07. Mem. Am. Geophys. Union, Geol. Soc. Am. Personal E-mail: lnobles@cablespeed.com.

NOBLES-KNIGHT, DOLORES, pharmacist, educator; PharmD., U. Southern Calif., LA, 1987; MPH, Harvard U., Boston, 2004. Dir., team leader, customer outcomes rsch. Pfizer Inc., NYC, 2001—03, dir., team leader, nat. acct. med. specialists, 2003—05, health policy regional med. specialist, 2005—07; chair, pharmacy practice Chgo. State U. Coll. Pharmacy, 2007—. Mem. Minority Health Coun. Midwest Chpt., AHA, Chgo., 2007. Mem.: APHA, South Suburban Pharmacists Assn. (pres. 2007), ISPOR. Independent. Office: Chgo State Univ Coll Pharmacy 9501 S King Dr Chicago IL 60628-1598 Business E-Mail: dnobles@csu.edu.

NOBOA, ABDIN I., psychologist, educator; arrived in US, 1947; s. Israel and Carmen L. Noboa; m. Migdalia Rivera de Noboa, July 28, 1985; children: Rafael, Maria; m. Patricia L. Hakes; children: Aric, Rene. BA, U. Ill., Urbana, 1969; EdM, Harvard U., Cambridge, 1970; MA, CPhil, U. Calif., Berkeley, 1974, PhD, 1981. Dep. dir. Aspira, Inc. Ill., Chgo., 1970—71; staff psychologist Boston U. Mental Health Ctr., 1971—72; rsch. assoc. Nat. Inst. Edn., Dept. Health, Edn. and Welfare, Washington, 1974—77; dir. rsch. Latino Inst., Reston, Va., 1980—85; dir. rsch., evaluation and planning New Haven Pub. Schs., 1985—87; v.p. rsch. and evaluation Quest Internat., Granville, Ohio, 1987—93; program dir. Ohio Dept. Mental Health, Columbus, 1997—99; rsch. assoc. Cosmos Corp., Bethesda, 2000—01; dir. rsch. and evaluation IQ Solutions, Inc., Rockville, Md., 2002—03; pres. Innovative Consultants Internat., Inc., Washington, 2004—. Mem. Com. Racial and Ethnic Definitions, Washington, 1975; IRB scientific review bd. Danya, Inc., Silver Spring, Md., 2006. Author: (book) Segregation Trends Among Hispanics in the Nation, 1982; editor: Language Policy in the United States, 1982. Rsch. Grant, U. Boricua, 1978, U. Tex., 1980. Independent. Avocations: violin, chess, racquetball. Office: Innovative Consultants Internat 10419 Rodney Rd Silver Spring MD 20903-1133

NOBUHARA, KERILYN, medical educator; Asst. prof. surgery and pediat. U. Calif. San Francisco, 2003—. Office: Univ Calif San Francisco 513 Parnassus HSW 1601 San Francisco CA 94143-0570

NOCE, DAVID D., judge; AB, St. Louis U.; JD, U. Mo., Columbia. Bar: Mo. Law clk. to Hon. H. Kenneth Wangelin US Dist. Ct. (ea. and we. dists.) Mo.; law clk. to Hon. John F. Nangle US Dist. Ct. (ea. dist.) Mo.; asst. US atty. (ea. dist.) Mo US Dept. Justice, St. Louis; magistrate judge US Dist. Ct. (ea. dist.) Mo., St. Louis, 1976—. Adj. prof. law St. Louis U. Sch. Law, Washington U. Sch. Law, St. Louis. Author: Jury Instructions Drafting Workbook West, 1999. Legal Officer, U.S. Army. Mem. ABA, Mo. Bar, Bar Assn. Met. St. Louis, Fed. Magistrate Judges Assn. Office: US Courthouse 17th Flr N 111 S 10th St Saint Louis MO 63102 Office Phone: 314-244-7630.

NOCE, WALTER WILLIAM, JR., hospital administrator; b. Neptune, NJ, Sept. 27, 1945; s. Walter William and Louise Marie (Jenkins) N.; m. Susan Harris, Nov. 6, 2005; children: Krista Suzanne, David Michael. BA, LaSalle Coll., Phila., 1967; M.P.H., UCLA, 1969. Regional coordinator USPHS, Rockville, Md., 1969-71; v.p. Hollywood Presbyn. Hosp., LA, 1971-75; sr. v.p. Hollywood Presbyn. Med. ctr., 1975-77; v.p. adminstrn. Huntington Meml. Hosp, Pasadena, Calif., 1977-83; pres., CEO St. Joseph Hosp., Orange, Calif., 1983-90, Children's Hosp., LA, 1995—2006, vice chmn., 2006—; pres. so. Calif. region St. Joseph Health Sys., 1987-90, exec. v.p., 1990-94. Preceptor UCLA Health Svcs. Mgmt. Program, 1977—; chmn. bd. Health Plan of Am., 1985-91; chmn. Hosp. Coun. So. Calif., 1989. Exec. v.p. Mental Health Assn. in LA County, 1979-82; regional v.p. Calif. Mental Health Assn., 1982-83; vice chmn., bd. trustees Childresn's Hosp. LA, 2006-07. W. Glenn Ebersole finalist Assn. Western Hosp., 1969; recipient USPHS letter commendation, 1971, leadership in health affairs award Healthcare Assn. So. Calif., 1997. Mem. Am. Coll. Hosp. Adminstrs., Am. Hosp. Assn. (ho. of dels. 1994—), Nat. Assn. Children's Hosps. (bd. dirs. 1995—), Calif. Assn. Cath. Hosps. (chmn. 1990-91), Calif. Assn. Hosps. and Health Sys. (chmn. 1992), UCLA Hosp. Adminstrn. Alumni Assn. (pres. 1979-80), Pasadena C. of C. (v.p. 1980-82). Home: 1012 Glen Oaks Blvd Pasadena CA 91105-1108 Office: Childrens Hosp LA 4650 Sunset Blvd Los Angeles CA 90027 Home Phone: 626-796-3809; Office Phone: 323-671-1779. Business E-Mail: wnoce@chla.usc.edu. *Ambition is necessary for success, but success achieved at the expense of others is failure.**

NOCERA, DANIEL G., chemistry professor; BS, Rutgers U., NJ, 1979; PhD, Calif. Inst. Tech., Pasadena, 1984. Asst. prof. Mich. State U., East Lansing, 1984—90, prof., 1990—97; prof. chemistry & Henry Dreyfus prof. energy Mass. Inst. Tech., Cambridge, 1997—. Co-author: Photochemistry and Radiation Chemistry, 1998; editor: Inorganic Chemistry Comm.; chmn. editl. bd.: ChemSusChem; contbr. scientific papers. Recipient Am. Inst. Chemists award, 1979, Prize for Excellence in Undergraduate Tchg., MIT Sch. Sci., 2005, Eni-Italgas prize for energy & the environment, 2005, Inter-Am. Photochemistry award, 2006, Burghausen Chemistry award, 2007, Am. Chem. Soc. award in inorganic chemistry, 2009; named one of The World's Most Influential People, TIME mag., 2009. Mem.: AAAS. Achievements include development of a method of making hydrogen fuel from water. Office: Rm 6-335 Mass Inst Tech 77 Massachusetts Ave Cambridge MA 02139-4307 Office Phone: 617-253-5537. Office Fax: 617-253-7670. Business E-Mail: nocera@mit.edu.*

NOCERA, JOSEPH, columnist; b. Providence, May 6, 1952; married; 3 children. BS in Journalism, Boston U., 1974. Contbg. editor Newsweek; exec. editor New England Monthly, Fortune mag., editorial dir.; editor Wash. Monthly; columnist The Profit Motive column, GQ, Esquire, 1988—90; sr. editor Tex. Monthly mag.; editor-at-large Fortune mag.; columnist Money mag., 1998; fin. columnist The NY Times, 2005—. Anchor PBS Frontline Documentary, Betting on the Market, 1997; master's project adv., grad. sch. journalism Columbia Univ. Contbr. articles to Wall Street Journal, Newsweek, Wash. Monthly; author: Bidness: The Booms and Busts of the Texas Economy, 1986, A Piece of the Action: How the Middle Class Joined the Money Class, 1994 (NY Pub.Libr.Helen Bernstein award for best non-fiction book of yr., 1995), Good Guys and Bad Guys: Behind the Scenes with the Saints and Scoundrels of American Business (and Everything in Between), 2008. Recipient John Hancock award, 1983, 1984, 1991, Gerald Loeb award, 1993, 1996; named one of 100 Business News Luminaries of the Century, The Journalist and Financial Reporting, 2000. Office: The NY Times 620 8th Ave New York NY 10018-1618

NOCHIMSON, DAVID, lawyer; b. Paterson, NJ, June 19, 1943; s. Samuel S. and Mildred (Singer) N.; m. Roberta Maizel, June 5, 1966 (div. 1972); m. Gail Burgess, May 26, 1978. BA, Yale U., 1965; LLB, Columbia U., 1968; LLM, Australian Nat. U., Canberra, 1969. Bar: N.Y. 1970, Calif. 1977. Assoc. Paul, Weiss, Rifkind, Wharton and Garrison, NYC, 1970-72; sr. v.p. Comprop Equities Corp., NYC, 1972-76; assoc. Mitchell, Silberberg and Knupp, LA, 1977-80, ptnr., 1980-83, Ziffren, Brittenham LLP, LA, 1983—. Adv. com. UCLA Entertainment Symposium, 1979-99, co-chmn., 1981-82. Contbr. articles to Encyclopedia of Investments, 1982, profl. jours. Pres. Friends of the L.A. Free Clinic, 1994-96; trustee Santa Monica (Calif.) Mus. of Art, 1995—. Fulbright scholar, Australia, 1968-69. Mem. ABA (forum com. on entertainment and sports industries 1982—, editor The Entertainment and Sports Lawyer 1982-89, chmn. 1989-92), Internat. Bar Assn. (Vice chmn. entertainment com. 1986-90), Am. Bar Found., Beverly Hills Bar Assn. Democrat. Jewish. Avocations: tennis, racquetball, yoga, playing piano, hiking. Office: Ziffren Brittenham LLP 1801 Century Park W Los Angeles CA 90067-6406 Office Phone: 310-552-3388.

NOCHMAN, LOIS WOOD KIVI (MRS. MARVIN NOCHMAN), retired literature educator; b. Detroit, Nov. 5, 1924; d. Peter K. and Annetta Lois (Wood) Kivi; m. Harold I. Pitchford, Sept. 6, 1944 (div. May 1949); children: Jean Wood Pitchford Scott, Joyce Lynn Pitchford Undiano; m. Marvin A. Nochman, Aug. 15, 1953; 1 child, Joseph Asa. AB, U. Mich., 1946, AM, 1949. Tchr. adult edn., Honolulu, 1947, Ypsilanti (Mich.) H.S., 1951—52; spl. instr. English Wayne State U., Detroit, 1953—54; tchr. Highland Park (Mich.) Coll., 1950—51, instr. English, 1954—83; ret., 1983. Mem. exec. bd. Highland Park Fedn. Tchrs., 1963—66, 1973, del. to nat. conv., 64, 1971—74; rep. higher edn. Mich. Fedn. Tchrs. Exec. Com., 1972—76; mem. faculty adv. com. Gov's Commn. Higher Edn., 1973—. Contbr. articles to profl. jours. Tchr. Baha'i Schs., Davison, Mich., 1954—55, 1958—59, 1963—66, Beaulac, Que., Canada, 1960, Greenacre, Maine, 1965; sec. local spiritual assembly Baha'is, Ann Arbor, Mich., 1953, sec. Detroit, 1954, chmn., 1955; mem. nat. com. Baha'is U.S., 1955—58; sec. com. and coun. Baha'i Schs., Davison, Mich., 1956, 1958, 1963—68; Baha'i lectr. subject of local TV show Senior Focus, 1992. Recipient Women's Movement plaque, Women Lawyers Assn. Mich., 1975, Lifetime Achievement award, Mich., 2007. Mem.: MLA, NOW, Nat. Soc. Lit. and Arts, Am. Fedn. Tchrs., Mich. Coll. English Assn., Nat. Coun. Tchrs. English, Women's Equity and Action League (sec. Mich. chpt. 1975—79), Alpha Gamma Delta, Alpha Lambda Delta. Avocation: U.S. Swimming Master Champion.

NOCIONI, ANDRES MARCELO, professional basketball player; b. Santa Fe, Argentina, Nov. 30, 1979; m. Paula Nocioni; 1 child, Laureano. Profl. basketball player Tau Ceramica, Spain, 2003—04; forward Chgo. Bulls, 2004—09, Sacramento Kings, 2009—. Mem. Argentinean Nat. Team, 1999—. Recipient Gold medal, Tournament of the Americas, Neuquen, Argentina, 2001, Gold medal, men's basketball, Athens Olympic Games, Greece, 2004. Office: Sacramento Kings Arco Arena One Sports Pky Sacramento CA 95834*

NODA, NAO-AKI, mechanical engineering educator, researcher; b. Bisai-city, Japan, Dec. 25, 1956; s. Akikatsu and Kayoko (Asai) N.; m. Kaoru Miyoshi Noda, Dec. 23, 1990; children: Kanako, Yoshihisa. B in Engring., Kyushu Inst. Tech., Kitakyushu, Japan, 1979; M in Engring., 1981; PhD in Engring., Kyushu U., Fukuoka, Japan, 1984. Asst. prof. Kyushu Inst. Tech., Kitakyushu, Japan, 1984-87; vis. prof. Lehigh (Pa.) U., 1985-86; assoc. prof. Kyushu Inst. Tech., Kitakyushu, Japan, 1987—2003, prof., 2003—. Vis. lectr. Nishi-Nippon Inst. Tech., Kitakyushu, Japan, 1989-90, Oita (Japan) U., 1990-91, Kyushu Sangyo U., Fukuoka, Japan, 1994-96. Author: Theory of Elasticity Useful for Machine Design; co-author: Safety Engineering, Q&A: Risk based Machine Design; co-editor: Stress Intensity Factors Handbook, vol. 4, Stress Intensity Factors Handbook, vol. 5; contbr. articles to profl. jours. Fellow Japanese Mín. Edn. and Sci., 1985-86; named hon. prof. Shandong (China) U. Tech., 1996, East China Jiaotong U., 2003, Shadong (China) U., 2008; recipient Medal for Outstanding Paper, Japan Soc. Tech. Plasticity, 2008. Mem. Japan Soc. Mech. Engrs., Japan Soc. Material Sci. Achievements include rsch. in stress analysis for notched and stepped bars, cracked bodies, and various shaped inclusions by the application of body-force method coupled with a singular integral equation formulation. Home: 1-2-37 Kawanaka-yutakamachi Shimonoseki 751-0853 Japan Office: Kyushu Inst Tech 1-1 Sensui-cho Tobata Kitakyushu 804-8550 Japan Office Phone: 81938843124. Business E-Mail: noda@mech.kyutech.ac.jp.

NODDINGS, NEL, education educator, writer; b. Irvington, NJ, Jan. 19, 1929; d. Edward A. Rieth and Nellie A. (Connors) Walter; m. James A. Noddings, Aug. 20, 1949; children: Chris, Howard, Laurie, James, Nancy, William, Sharon, Edward, Vicky, Timothy. BA in Math., Montclair State Coll., 1949; MA in Math., Rutgers U., 1964; PhD in Edn., Stanford U., 1973; PhD (hon.), Columbia Coll., SC, 1995; LLD (hon.), Queen's U., Can., 2006; LHD (hon.), Montclair State U., 2006; PhD (hon.), Lewis & Clark Coll., Portland, Oreg., 2007. Cert. tchr. Calif., NJ. Tchr. Woodbury (N.J.) Pub. Schs., 1949-52; tchr. math. dept. Matawan (N.J.) High Sch., 1958-62, chair, asst. prin., 1964-69; curriculum supr. Montgomery Twp. Pub. Schs., Skillman, NJ, 1970-72; dir. precollegiate edn. U. Chgo., 1975-76; asst. prof. Pa. State U., State College, 1973; from asst. prof. to assoc. prof. Stanford (Calif.) U., 1977-86, prof., 1986—, assoc. dean, 1990-92, acting dean, 1992-94, Lee L. Jacks prof. child edn., 1992-98, prof. emeritus, 1998—; prof. philosophy and edn. Columbia U., NYC, 1998—. Bd. dirs. Ctr. for Human Caring Sch. Nursing, Denver, 1986-92; cons. NIE, NSF and various other sch. dists. Author: Caring: A Feminine Approach to Ethics and Moral Education, 1984, Women and Evil, 1989; author: (with W. Paul Shore) Awakening the Inner Eye: Intuition in Education, 1984; author: (with Carol Witherell) Stories Lives Tell, 1991; author: The Challenge to Care in Schools, 1992, Educating for Intelligent Belief or Unbelief, 1993, Philosophy of Education, 1995, Starting at Home: Caring and Social Policy, 2002, Educating Moral People, 2002, Happiness and Education, 2003; editor (with Suzanne Gordon and Patricia Benner): Caregiving, 1996; editor: (with Michael Katz and Kenneth Strike) Justice and Caring, 1999; editor: Educating Citizens for Global Awareness, 2005, Critical Lessons: What Our Schools Should Teach, 2006, When School Reform Goes Wrong, 2007. Mem. disting. women's adv. bd. Coll. St.

Catherine. Recipient Anne Roe award for Contbns. to Profl. Devel. of Women, Harvard Grad. Sch. Edn., 1993, medal for disting. svc. Tchrs. Coll. Columbia, 1994, Willystine Goodsell award, 1997, Laureate chpt. Kappa Delta Pi, Pi Lambda Theta award, 1999, award for disting. leadership in edn. Rutgers U., 2004; Spencer Mentor grantee, Spencer Found., 1995-97. Fellow Philosophy of Edn. Soc. (pres. 1991-92); mem. Am. Ednl. Rsch. Assn. (Div B, 2000, Lifetime achievment award, Inaugural fellow 2009), Am. Philos. Assn., Nat. Acad. Edn. (pres. 2001—), John Dewey Soc. (pres. 1994-96), Phi Beta Kappa (vis. scholar). Avocation: gardening. Home Phone: 732-988-9695; Office Phone: 732-988-9695. Business E-Mail: noddings@stanford.edu.

NODDLE, JEFFREY, retail and food distribution company executive; b. June 1, 1946; BA, U. Iowa, 1969. With Supervalu Inc., Eden Prairie, Minn., 1976—82, v.p. merchandising, 1985—88, sr. v.p. mktg., 1976-92, exec. v.p. mktg., 1992-95, exec. v.p. mktg, pres., COO wholesale food companies, 1995-99, pres., COO, 2000-01, pres., CEO, 2001—04, chmn., CEO, 2004—09, exec. chmn., 2009—. Bd. dirs. General Cable Corp., 1998—2004, Donaldson Co. Inc., 2000—, Supervalu Inc., 2000—, Ameriprise Financial INc., 2005—, Ind. Grocers Alliance Inc., Food Industry Ctr., U. Minn., Acad. Food Mktg., St. Joseph's U., Pa., Donaldson Co. Inc.; chmn. bd. Food Mktg. Inst. Bd. dir. Greater Twin Cities United Way; bd. overseers U. Minn. Carlson Sch. Mgmt.; exec. com. Minn. Bus. Partnership. Office: Supervalu Inc 11840 Valley View Rd Eden Prairie MN 55344-3691*

NODEEN, JANEY PRICE, information technology executive; m. Thomas Nodeen. BS in Info. Sci., Christopher Newport Coll., 1987; grad., Def. Sys. Mgmt. Coll., 1994; grad. advanced mgmt. program, Nat. Def. U., 1995; grad. owner president's program, Harvard Bus. Sch., 2003. Engring. analyst Newport News Shipbldg., Va., 1978-86; mgr. submarine info. resources and computer ops. Dept. of the Navy, Washington, 1986-93, mem. exec. devel. program, 1993-96, sr. staff Navy Acquisition Reform Exec., 1995, dep. program exec. officer Submarines for Acquisition, 1996-97; prin. Burke Consortium, Inc., Springfield, Va., 1997—. Mil. legis. fellow for Congressman Sam Gejdenson, 1994; sr. exec. fellow John F. Kennedy Sch. Govt. Harvard U., class officer, 1994. Office: Burke Consortium Inc Ste 510 5500 Cherokee Ave Alexandria VA 22312

NODLER, CHARLES EDWARD, JR., archivist, history professor; b. Urbana, Ill., Jan. 13, 1949; s. Charles Edward Nodler, Sr. and Beatrice June Nodler. AA, Crowder Coll., 1973; BA in History, Mo. So. State Coll., Joplin, 1975; MA in History, U. Tex., Arlington, 1978; MA in Libr. Sci., U. Mo., Columbia, 1995. Cert. archival Adminstrn. U. Tex., Arlington, 1979, archivist Acad. Cert. Archivists, 2007. Archivist Mo. So. State U., Joplin, 1978—. Project archivist George Washington Carver Nat. Monument, Diamond, Mo., 1981—82; history prof. SW Bapt. U., Kelley U. Coll., Joplin, 1989—90; adj. history prof. Mo. So. State U., Joplin, 2005—06; exec. bd. Gene Taylor Libr. and Mus., Sarcoxie, Mo., 1990—; v.p. George Wash. Carver Birthplace Dist. Assn., Diamond, 1994—; archival cons. Newton County, Mo., Neosho, 2006. Author: Bracing the Cornerpost, 1992, Field of Teams; Baseball in Neosho, 2006; contbr. Committeeman Rep. Party, Neosho, 2002—06; lay leader United Meth. Ch., Neosho, 2000—06. With US Army, 1969—71. Named Outstanding Alumnus, Crowder Coll., 2007; grantee Digitization Grant Riches from the Earth: Geol. and Indsl. History of Jasper County, Libr. Svcs. and Tech. Grant Act, Digital Imaging Grant Program, 2006; Digitization Grant Mining the History SW Mo., Environ. Task Force Jasper and Newton County, 2005—06. Mem.: Pub. History Alliance Mo., Acad. Cert. Archivists, Soc. SW Archivists, Midwest Archives Conf., Soc. Am. Archivists, Newtonia Battlefields Protection Assn. (life), Phi Alpha Theta. Conservative. Methodist. Avocations: collect old sports cards (baseball and football), weight training, running. Home: 1215 Northwest Blvd Neosho MO 64850 Office: Missouri Southern State University 3950 E Newman Rd Joplin MO 64801 Office Fax: 417-625-9734. Business E-Mail: nodler-c@mssu.edu.

NOE, ADRIANNE, museum administrator; PhD in History, U. Del. Assoc. dir. Armed Forces Inst. Pathology; dir. Nat. Mus. Health and Medicine, Washington. Adj. prof. computational biosciences George Mason U., Fairfax County, Va.; v.p. bd. dirs. Nat. Health Sci. Consortium. Fellow, Guggenheim Found.; History fellow, USAF. Mem.: Med. Mus. Assn. (past pres.), Washington Soc. for the History of Medicine (pres.), Acad. Medicine. Office: Nat Mus Health and Medicine Bldg 54 6825 16th St NW Washington DC 20306-6000

NOE, ELNORA (ELLIE), retired chemicals executive; b. Evansville, Ind., Aug. 23, 1928; d. Thomas Noe and Evelyn (West) Dieter. Student, Ind. U.-Purdue U., Indpls. Sec. Pitman Moore Co., Indpls., 1946—60; with Dow Chem. Co., Indpls., 1960-90, pub. rels. asst. then mgr. employee comm., 1970-87, mgr. cmty. rels., 1987-90, DowBrands, Inc., Indpls., 1986-90, vice chmn. Indpls. C. of C. corp. affairs discussion group, 1988—89, chmn., 1989-90; mem. steering com. Learn About Bus. Recipient 2d pl. award as Businesswoman of Yr., Indpls. Bus. and Profl. Women's Assn., 1980, Indpls. Profl. Woman of Yr. award Zonta, Altrusa, Soroptomist & Pilot Svc. Clubs, 1985, DowBrands Great Things Cmty. Svc. award, 1991. Mem. Am. Bus. Women Assn. (Woman of Yr. award 1965, past pres.), Ind. Assn. Bus. Communicators (hon., Communicator of Yr. 1977), Assn. Women in Comm. (Louise Eleanor Kleinhenz award 1984), Zonta (dist. pub. rels. chmn. 1978-80, area dir. 1980-82, pres. Indpls. club 1977-79, bd. dirs. 1993-95, 2000-02, 04-06, v.p. 2006—08, pres., 2008, bd. dir, 2008-), Dow Indpls. Retiree Group (pres. 1995—).

NOE, GUY, retired social services administrator; b. Brussels, Jan. 28, 1934; came to U.S., 1955, naturalized, 1961; s. Marinus Cornelis and Johana Dorothea (Beijne) N.; 1 child, Jeanette Sue. BS, Regional Agrl. Sch., Loiret, France, 1954. Social worker State of Wyo., Casper, 1962-66; dir. Natrona County (Wyo.) Dept. Public Assistance, Casper, 1966-79, Wyo. Div. Mental Health, Cheyenne, 1979-82, asst. adminstr. Divsn. of Youth Svcs., 1992-95; former mgr. Platte County Office Pub. Assistance and Social Svcs., Wheatland, Wyo., dir. low income energy assistance programs, 1994-95. Lectr. in field. V.p. Wyo. chpt. Big Bros., 1976-77; chmn. adv. coun. social svcs. State of Wyo., 1969-79; bd. dirs. Casper United Way, 1970—, Casper Salvation Army, 1970—, Casper chpt. ARC, 1977—; mem. Gov.'s Drug Abuse Adv. Bd., 1992—; pres. State Employees Assn. Named Outstanding Adminstr. State of Wyo., 1976; recipient Youth Svcs. award Wyo. Human Resources Confedn., 1988; named to Wyo. Dept. Family Svcs. Hall of Fame, 2005. Mem. ASPA, Am. Public Welfare Assn. (Wyo. membership chmn.), Wyo. State Employees Assn. (pres. 1996-97), Toastmasters. Democrat. Home: 2731 Deming Blvd Cheyenne WY 82001-5709

NOE, J. MARK, communications educator; m. Sharon N. Noe. PhD, Kans. U., Lawrence, 1985. Assoc. dean Pk. U., Parkville, Mo., 2005—. Contbr. articles to profl. jours. (Outstanding Grad. Faculty award, 2007). Mem.: Coun. Coll. Arts and Scis. Deans. Achievements include founder and developer of the master of arts in communication and leadership. Home: 14070 NW 63rd St Kansas City MO 64152 Office: Pk Univ 8700 River Pk Dr Parkville MO 64152 Business E-Mail: jmark.noe@park.edu.

NOE, JAMES KIRBY, retired computer consultant; b. Denver, June 21, 1951; s. George F. and Fern D. (Wilterdink) N. BSBA in Mgmt. Info., U. No. Colo., 1983. Cert. data processor, systems profl., SAS Base Program. Sys. supr. USN Tactical Support Ctr., Sigonella, Sicily, Italy, 1978-79; tech. mgr. Empire Dispatch of No. Colo., Greeley, 1979-80; cons. Greeley C. of C., 1983; project mgr. software devel. Microhealth Sys. Corp., Denver, 1983-84; database analyst Manville Corp., Littleton, Colo., 1984; leader project devel. Citicorp Diners Club, Englewood, Colo., 1985; cons. Mountain Bell Telephone, Denver, 1985-86; computer programmer Colo. Dept. Revenue, Denver, 1986-87; cons. DST Sys., Inc., Kansas City, Mo., 1987-91, Broadcast Data Sys., Kansas City, Mo., 1991-92, U.S. Sprint, Kansas City, 1992—2001, TEK Sys., Kansas City, 2003—07. Pres. Pine Tree Players, Brunswick, Maine, 1976-77, Sigonella Theatre Co., 1978; bd. dirs. Theatre Assocs. Group, Inc., Denver, 1985-86, v.p., 1987. Petty officer first class, aviation antisubmarine warfare operator USN, 1970—79. Recipient Eagle Scout award Boy Scouts Am., 1964, bronze palm, 1965, 5-Yr. Svc. award Am. Cancer Soc., Brunswick, 1977; named Outstanding Vol. Theatre Assocs. Group, Inc., 1987. Mem. Assn. for Computing Machinery (com. mem. 1984-98, chmn. Denver chpt. 1987), Data Processing Mgmt. Assn. (com. mem. 1984-98), Kansas City Area SAS User Group (com. mem. 1994-, chmn. 2005-07), Internat. Eagle Scout Assoc. Republican. Presbyterian. Avocations: gemology, theater, fishing, reading. Home: 12009 Ash St Apt 27 Overland Park KS 66209 Personal E-mail: jamesknoe@earthlink.net.

NOE, VIRGILIO CARDINAL, cardinal, archbishop; b. Zelata di Bereguardo, Italy, Mar. 30, 1922; D in Church history, Pontifical Gregorian Univ., Rome, 1952. Ordained priest Diocese of Pavia, Italy, 1944; prof. ecclesiastical history Seminaries of Pavia & Tortona; sec. Ctr. for Liturgical Action, Rome, 1964—68; prof. sacred art Pontifical Liturgical Inst. of St. Anselm, Rome, 1964—68; undersecretary Congregation for Divine Worship, 1969—77; Master of Pontifical Ceremonies Rome, 1970; adj. sec. Congregation for Divine Worship & Discipline of the Sacraments, Rome, 1977—82; ordained bishop, 1982; archbishop, sec. Congregation for Divine Worship & Discipline of the Sacraments, Rome, 1982—89; pres. Commn. for Protection of Historical & Artistic Monuments of the Holy See, Rome, 1989—91; elevated to cardinal, 1991; cardinal-deacon S. Giovanni Bosco in via Tuscolana, 1991—2002; pres. Fabric of St. Peter, Rome, 1991—2002, pres. emeritus, 2002—; vicar gen. Vatican City State, Rome, 1991—2002, vicar gen. emeritus, 2002—; archpriest St. Peter Basilica, Rome, 1997—2002, archpriest emeritus, 2002—; cardinal-priest Regina Apostolorum, 2002—. Roman Catholic. Office: Vatican City 00120 Vatican City Italy

NOEL, CAROL ADELE, music educator, opera singer; d. Albert Edgar and Adelaide L. Noel. MusB, Boston Conservation Music, 1962; MusM, Northwestern U., Ill., 1970. Cert. K-12 tchr. Ill., Tex., music and elem. edn., in computer studies program Daley Coll., Chgo., 2008, Daley Coll., Chgo., 2009. Opera singer Lyric Opera Chgo., 1963, State Opera Houses, Rendsburg/Hagen, Germany, 1965—67; soloist Chgo. Wind Ensemble, 1977, Southwest Allied Arts Assn., Chgo., 1982; music tchr. Chgo. Pub. Schs., 1971—. Choir dir. Posen Sch. Choir, Ill., 1982; music dir. Grant Cmty. Acad., Chgo., 1995—98; chorus dir. Thorp Elem. Sch., Chgo., 2005—07; substitute tchr. Office Cath. Schs. Chgo., 2007—, Chgo. Suburban Dists., 2007—. Recipient Alderman Pacini vocal award; grantee Voice Scholarship, Rosary Coll. Mem.: AARP, Chgo. Tchrs. Union, Music Educators Nat. Conf., German Theatre Union, Actors Equity Assn., Am. Guild Musical Artists. Avocations: travel, theater, dance, concerts, museums. Home: 6629 S Whipple St Chicago IL 60629-2915 Personal E-mail: Cancatlady11@aol.com.

NOEL, CRAIG, performing arts company executive, producer; LHD (hon.), U. San Diego. Actor Old Globe Theatre, San Diego, 1937—, dir., 1939—, exec. prodr. Instituted Globe Ednl. Tours, 1974, Old Globe's multicultural theater component Teatro Meta, 1983; established Play Discovery Program, 1974—, Shakespeare Festival, 1949—; founder Calif. Theatre Coun.; former v.p. Calif. Confedn. Arts.; introduced various playwrights, including Beckett and Ionesco, to San Diego at La Jolla Mus. Contemporary Art, then Falstaff Tavern (renamed Cassius Carter Centre Stage, 1969). Dir. more than 200 works; prodr. 290 works; recent prodns. include Morning's at Seven, Shirley Valentine, The Norman Conquests, 1979, Taking Steps, 1984, Intimate Exchanges, 1987, The Night of the Iguana, 1987, The Boiler Room, 1987, The White Rose, 1991, Mr. A's Amazing Maze Plays, 1994. Named Outstanding Citizen, U. Ariz. Alumni Assn., One of 25 Persons Who Shaped City's History, San Diego Union; Recipient Gov.'s award for Arts, San Diego's Living Treasure award, Conservator Am. Arts award, Am. Conservatory Theatre, Headliner award, San Diego Press Club, San Diego Gentlemen of Distinction award, combined tribute, Pub. Arts Adv. Coun. and San Diego County Bd. Suprs., Nat. Medal Arts, 2007; Year proclaimed in his honor, Mayor Maureen O'Connor, San Diego, 1987. Office: Old Globe Theatre PO Box 2171 San Diego CA 92112-2171

NOEL, DON OBERT, JR., retired editor, columnist; b. Elizabeth, NJ, Nov. 27, 1931; s. Don O. and Catherine (Pyle) N.; m. Elizabeth Bradford Foulds, Aug. 29, 1953; 1 child, Emily Rebecca. BA in Am. Studies, Cornell U., 1954. Reporter Hartford (Conn.) Times, 1958-68, asst. mng. editor, 1968-69, editorial page editor, 1969-74, editor in chief, 1974-75; sr. corr. WFSB-TV, host Face the State Post-Newsweek Stas., 1975-84; polit. columnist op-ed page Hartford Courant, 1984-97, ret., 1997. Author: Jamaica memoir, Near a Far Sea, 2006. Bd. sec. Blue Hills Civic Assn., Hartford, 1988-05; bd. dirs. ACLU of Conn., 1998-, chair, 2005-. Served alt. mil. duty Am. Friends Svc. Com., Tokyo, 1954-56. Recipient Sevellon Brown Meml. award New England AP, 1964, Nat. Journalism award AMA, 1972, Nat. Journalism award Am. Soc. Planning Officials, 1972, 74; fellow Alicia Patterson Found., 1966-67; finalist Pulitzer Prize for non-deadline reporting, 1964. Mem. Soc. Of Friends. Avocations: gardening, birdwatching, language study. Home: 141 Ridgefield St Hartford CT 06112-1837 Office Phone: 860-247-2080. Personal E-mail: dononoel@yahoo.com.

NOEL, FRANKLIN LINWOOD, judge; b. NYC, Dec. 7, 1951; s. Charles Alexander and Mayme (Loth) N.; m. Ellen Barbara Perl, Sept. 15, 1979; children: Kate Alexandra, Charles David. BA, SUNY, Binghamton, 1974; JD, Georgetown U., 1977. Bar: D.C. 1977, U. S. Dist. Ct. D.C. 1978, U.S. Ct. Appeals (D.C. cir.) 1978, Pa. 1979, Minn. 1983, U.S. Ct. Appeals (8th cir.) 1983, U.S. Dist. Ct. Minn. 1984. Assoc. Arnold & Porter, Washington, 1977-79; asst. dist. atty. Phila. Dist. Attys. Office, 1979-83; asst. U.S. atty. U.S. Attys. Office, Mpls., 1983-89; U.S. magistrate judge U.S. Dist. Ct., Mpls., 1989—. Legal writing instr. U. Minn., Mpls., 1989-92, adj. prof. Law Sch., 1996—. Mem. League Am. Bicyclists, Phi Beta Kappa. Episcopalian. Avocation: bicycling. Office: US Dist Ct 300 S 4th St Minneapolis MN 55415-1320

NOEL, JAMES ANTHONY, religious studies educator, minister; b. NYC, Jan. 1, 1948; s. James Anthony Noel and Beatrice Lockett; m. Diana Nieves Sanchez; children: Michelle, Kaiya, Daniel, Amada. PhD, Grad. Theol. Union, Berkeley, Calif., 1999. Prof. Am. religion San Francisco Theol. Sem., San Anselmo, 1991—. Paintings, Continuity; contbr. articles to profl. jours. Chmn. Marin City Cmty. Devel. Corp., Calif., 1978—86. Office: San Francisco Theol Sem 105 Seminary Rd San Anselmo CA 94960 Business E-Mail: jnoel@sfts.edu.

NOEL, MARY MARGARET, nutritionist, educator; b. Tacoma, July 13, 1948; d. Webster Young and Mary Leize Barth; m. George W. Noel, June 30, 1973; children: Katherine Mary, Joseph William. BS in Dietetics, Mich. State U., 1969; MPH, U. Mich., 1973; PhD in Family Ecology, Mich. Sate U., 1988. Registered dietitian. Intern in dietetics Barnes Med. Ctr., St. Louis, 1970; nutrition cons. Vis. Nurse Assn., St. Louis, 1970-72; clin. nutritionist U. Mich., Ann Arbor, 1973-76; instr. dietetics Mich. State U., East Lansing, 1975-76; cons. in nutrition East Lansing, 1976-86; exec. dir. Dairy Coun. of Mich., Okemos, 1986-88; asst. prof. dept. family practice, Coll. Human Medicine Mich. State U., East Lansing, 1988-93, assoc. prof., 1993—2000, prof., 2000—, assoc. chair dept., 1997—. Vol. Neighborhood Assn., East Lansing, 1983-97; bd. dirs., treas. Downtown Devel. Authority, East Lansing, 1986-96; vol. East Lansing Pub. Schs., 1982-98. Grantee, NIH, 1997—2001. Mem. Am. Dietetic Assn. (sect. sec. 1970—), Mich. Dietetic Assn. (parliamentarian 1972—, nominating com., Recognized Young Dietitian 1977), Soc. for Tchrs. of Family Medicine, Vis. Nurses of Lansing (vice chair, then chair 1987-91) Office: Mich State U Dept Family Practice Coll Human Medicin B101 Clin Ctr East Lansing MI 48824 Business E-Mail: noel@msu.edu.

NOEL, NANCY W., literature and language professor; b. Buchanan, Va., Dec. 25, 1952; d. Glen Earl Weston and Elizabeth Grace Gruver; m. Peter Jon Vernimb, Nov. 26, 1988. BA in English, Va. Tech, Blacksburg, 1975; MA in English, Va. Commonwealth U., Richmond, 1986. Cert. in post-secondary tchg. Va. Dept. Edn., 1975. English tchr. Hanover County Pub. Schs., Ashland, Va., 1975—82, Henrico County Pub. Schs., Richmond, Va., 1982—91; instr. English Germanna CC, Fredericksburg, Va., 2000—, dept. chair English, 2003—07. Contbr. articles to profl. jours. publs. Therapy dog, disaster, stress relief handler Therapy Dog Internat., Fredericksburg, 1997—2004; Parish com. mem. Fredericksburg United Meth. Ch., Va., 2006—09, ch. coun. mem., 2009—. Recipient Active award, Therapy Dog Internat., 2002—04. Mem.: Two-Yr. Coll. Educators, Nat. Coun. Tchrs. English, Delta Kappa Gamma (chpt. expansion chair 2002—04, gamma alpha chpt., beta eta chpt. pres.), Delta Kappa Gamma Soc. Internat. (alpha tau chpt. pres. 2004—08). Methodist. Avocations: music, theater, reading. Office: Germanna CC 10000 Germanna Point Dr Fredericksburg VA 22408 Business E-Mail: nnoel@germanna.edu.

NOEL, RANDALL DEANE, lawyer; b. Memphis, Oct. 19, 1953; s. D.A. and Patricia G. Noel; m. Lissa Johns, May 28, 1977; children: Lauren Elizabeth, Randall Walker. BBA with honors, U. Miss., 1975, JD, 1978. Bar: Miss. 1978, U.S. Dist. Ct. (no. and so. dists.) Miss. 1978, Tenn. 1979, U.S. Dist. Ct. (we., mid. and ea. dists.) Tenn. 1979, U.S. Ct. Appeals (5th and 6th cirs.) 1984, U.S. Supreme Ct. 1986. Assoc. Armstrong/Allen, PLLC, Memphis, 1978-85, ptnr., 1985—, mgr. litig. practice group, 1990-94; mgmt. com. Armstrong, Allen, Prewitt, Gentry, Johnston & Holmes, Memphis, 1994—97; chief mem. Armstrong/Allen, PLLC, Memphis, 2002—04; ptnr. Butler, Snow, O'Mara, Stevens & Cannada, 2004—, litig. dept. chair, 2007—. Fin. com. Memphis in May Internat. Festival, 1980-81; pres. Carnival Memphis, 1996; bd. dirs. Christ United Meth. Ch., Memphis, 1984-87, 89-91, chmn. bd. trustees, 1995; mem. Leadership Memphis, 1994-95. Fellow Am. Bar Found., Tenn. Bar Found., Memphis Bar Found.; mem. ABA (young lawyers divsn., fellow dir. 1988-90, editor The Affiliate newsletter 1987-88, dir. Affiliate Outreach project 1988—, vice-chmn. Award of Achievement com. 1986, ALI-ABA bd. 1992-97, div. dir. litig. sect., 2002, coun. litig. sect., mem. House of Dels., standing com. fed. judiciary), Am. Counsel Assn. (pres. 1997), Tenn. Bar Assn. (pres. young lawyers divsn. 1990, pres. litig. sect. 1988, bd. govs. 1989—, pres. 1999, Pres.'s Disting. Svc. award 1988-89), So. Conf. Bar Pres. (pres. 2000), Memphis and Shelby Bar Assn. (mem. jud, recommendations, law week nominations and membership coms.), Miss. Bar Assn., Def. Rsch. Inst., Tenn. Def. Lawyers Assn., Am. Judicature Soc. (bd. dirs. 1992-96), Tenn. Legal Cmty. Found. (pres. 1999-2001), Tenn. Supreme Ct. Hist. Soc. (bd. dirs. 2005). Home: 2938 Tishomingo Ln Memphis TN 38111-2627 Office: Butler Snow O'Mara Stevens & Cannada PLLC Ste 500 Crescent Ctr 6075 Poplar Ave Memphis TN 38119 Business E-Mail: randy.noel@butlersnow.com.

NOELL, BEVERLY ANN, music educator; BA in Music Edn., Calif. State U., Fresno, 1989, MA in Music Performance, 1995; EdS in Instrnl. Tech., U. West Ga., Carrollton, 2008. Cert. tchr. Ga. Profl. Stds. Commn. Music tchr. Whitesburg Elem. Sch., Ga., 1998—; flute instr. U. West Ga., Carrollton, 1995—2002. Music program coord. Calif. State U., Fresno, Calif., 1990—95. Mem. Carrollton Youth Orch., Ga., 2005. Recipient Tchr. of Yr., Whitesburg Elem. Sch., 2002, Spirit award, Carroll County Employer Rels. Bd., 2002, Found. Nat. Award for Outstanding Tchg., Mr. Holland's Opus Found., 2006; nominee Outstanding Arts Educator, Woodruff Arts Ctr., 2009. Mem.: Ga. Music Educators Assn., Music Educators Nat. Conf. Office: Whitesburg Elem Sch 868 Main St Whitesburg GA 30185 Business E-Mail: bev.noell@carrollcountyschools.com.

NOESEN, DARLENE DOROTHY, mathematics educator; b. Chgo., July 9, 1947; d. Leonard Michael and Mary Anna Noesen. BA Sociology, Loyola U., 1970; MA Math., Northeastern U., Chgo., 1985. Secondary Tchg.6-12 Ill. State Tchr. Certification Bd., 1985, Elem. Tchg. K-9 Ill. State Tchr. Certification Bd., 1970. Tchr. 1st grade St. Simeon, Bellwood, Ill., 1970—74; tchr. St. Benedict Elem. Sch., Chgo., 1974—87; math. educator St. Benedict H.S., 1987—90; chair math. dept. St. Hilary Sch., Chgo., 1990—98, St. Gregory H.S., Chgo., 1998—. Regional program dir. Sch. Sisters of St. Francis Assoc. Relationship. Dir. nat. office Women-Ch. Convergence, 1995—2001; coord. Chgo. Cath. Women, Chgo., 1982—94; founding mem. Chgo. Women-Ch., 1994—. Master: Nat. Honor Soc. (advisor 1987—). Roman Catholic. Avocations: photography, reading, travel, hiking, bicycling. Home: 2572 W Argyle St Chicago IL 60625-2604

NOFFSINGER, NANCY LEIGH, retired special education educator; b. Princeton, Ky., Oct. 20, 1948; d. Charlie H. and Margaree (Oates) N. BS, Murray State U., Ky., 1980, masters equivalent, 1982, postgrad., 1987. LPN, 1974. Sch. nurse, then spl. edn. tchr. Dawson Springs Bd. Edn., Ky., 1980-83; spl. edn. substitute tchr. various counties, Ky., 1983-85; spl. edn. tchr. Critten County Bd. Edn., Marion, Ky., 1985—98, Christian County Bd. Edn., Hopkinsville, Ky., 1998—2003; ret., 2003; sub. tchr., 2004—09; advertising affilate Singer Edn. Internat. Inc., 2009—. Mem. NEA, ACLU, Ky. Edn. Assn. Ret. (1st dist. pres. 1996-97, human and civil rights state com. 1994—, chair 1997-98), Amnesty Internat., Crittenden County Edn. Assn. (pres. 1992-95, 97-98, chair KePAC legis. chair 1995-97), Christian County Edn. Assn. (bldg.

rep. 1998-2003), Nature Conservancy, World Wildlife Fund, Sierra Club, Nat. Wildlife Fedn. Democrat. Home: 200 N Franklin St Apt 303 Princeton KY 42445-1684 Home Phone: 270-365-6504. Personal E-mail: noffsingern@bellsouth.net.

NOGINA, ELENA Y., mathematics professor, researcher; d. Yuri M. Malinsky and Olga V. Nogina; m. Sergei N. Artemov, Dec. 15, 1984; children: Dmitry Nogin, Aleksey Nogin. M in Math. & Edn., Moscow U., PhD in Math. Vis. prof. U. Montpellier, III, 1992; vis. rschr. U. Amsterdam, 1994; rschr. Acad. Sci., Moscow; prof. Moscow U., CUNY, NYC, 2001—. Math. logic & computability theory dept. chair Moscow U., 1983—97, dir. math. & computer sci. program for liberal arts/linguistics, 1993—97. Contbr. scientific papers. Recipient Svc. in Edn. medal, USSR Parliament, 1987, Sci. Achievements medal, USSR Nat. Exhbn.; Rsch. grant, Internat. Sci. Found., 1993—95, Nat. Grant Program Univs. Russia, 1994—97, Russian Found. Basic Rsch., 1994—97, CCRI, 2004—05, PCS-CUNY, 2005—06. Mem.: NY Acad. Sci., Moscow Matematical Soc., Assn. Symbolic Logic, Am. Math. Soc. Home: 21 S End Ave Penthouse 2V New York NY 10280-1071

NOGUCHI, HIDEO, insurance company executive; b. Kyoto, Jan. 17, 1945; s. Tasao and Ishiko (Tsujii) Noguchi; m. Eleanor Kazuko Horii, May 7, 1970; children: Mark H.Y., Mitchell H.Y. BBA, U. Hawaii, 1969. Buyer RCA Purchasing Co., Tokyo, 1969—73; ins. specialist Continental Ins. Agy., Honolulu, 1973—82; CEO Noguchi & Assocs., Inc., Honolulu, 1983—. Cons. in field. Recipient Nat. New Agt. Leadership award, CNA Corp., 1974, Key Club award, CNA Co., 1975, 1979—81, Nat. New Agt. Leader II, Continental Assurance Co., Can Co., 1975, Aloha Club award, 1983, VIP Club award, Pacific Guardian Life, 1984—86, Persistency Leader of Region award, 1984; named to Coll. Bus. Adminstrn. Alumni Hall of Honor, U. Hawaii, 2004. Mem.: Hawaii Ind. Ins. Agents Assn., Urasenke Hawaii Assn. Profl. Ins. Agents, Rotary (bd. dirs. 1980). Office: 1314 S King St Ste 560 Honolulu HI 96814-1978 Office Phone: 808-596-2700.

NOGUCHI, HIROFUMI, surgeon; b. Fukuyama, Japan, June 23, 1971; s. Yasufumi and Setsuko Noguchi. MD, Okayama U., Japan, 1996, PhD in Medicine and dentistry, 2002. Diplomate Okayama, Japan, 1996. Clin. fellow grad. sch. medicine and dentistry Okayama U., 1996—2002; post doctoral fellow med. sch. Harvard U., Boston, 2002—03; clin. fellow grad. sch. medicine Kyoto U., 2003—05; assoc. dir. Diabetes Rsch. Inst. Kyoto, 2005—06, Diabetes Rsch. Inst. Japan, Toyoake, Japan, 2006—. Vis. assoc. prof. Fujita Health U., Toyoake, Japan, 2006—; asst. prof. Nagoya U., Japan, 2006—; lectr. in field. Grantee, Ministry Edn., Culture, Sports, 2005, Pub. Welfare Trust, 2006, Nagoya U., 2006. Mem.: Japanese Soc. Hepato-Biliary-Pancreatic Surgery (Pres. award 2005, 2006), Japanese Soc. Regenerative Medicine (Excellent Lectr. award 2004), Okayama Med. Soc. (Yuki award 2005), Japan Soc. Promotion of Sci. (2 grants 2005, fellowship 2005—06). Achievements include first to perform islet transplantation from non-heart-beating donor pancreata in Japan; perform successful Islet transplantation from living donor pancreas in worldwide. Office: Baylor Research Institute 3434 Live Oak St Dallas TX 75204 Office Phone: 214-820-9016. Office Fax: 214-820-4952. Business E-Mail: noguchih@med.nagoya-u.ac.jp, hirofumn@baylorhealth.edu.

NOGUERE, SUZANNE, trade association administrator, poet; b. Bklyn., Dec. 1, 1947; d. Eugene R. and Virginia Helene (Braun) N.; m. Henry Grinberg, June 5, 1983. BA in Philosophy magna cum laude with honors, Columbia U., NYC, 1969. Classified ad mgr. Printing News, Melville, NY, 1973—2006, sr. acct. exec., 1999—2006; sr. dir. mem. svcs. Nat. Assn. for Printing Leadership, Paramus, NJ, 2006—07, exec. asst. to CEO and COO, 2008—. Author: (children's books) Little Koala, 1979, Little Raccoon, 1981, (poetry collection) Whirling Round the Sun, 1996; poet (with artist Miriam Adams): (exhibitions) Leaf Lines, 1998, poet (with artist Lesley Nishigawara): (exhibitions) Left Out, 2003; co-author (with James V. Hatch): The Stone House, A Blues Legend, 2000; co-author: (plays) Klub Ka, The Blues Legend, U. Iowa, 2002, La MaMa E.T.C., 2004, U. Md., 2006. Recipient Discovery award The 92nd St. Y Unterberg Poetry Ctr. and The Nation mag., 1996. Mem. Acad. Am. Poets, Poetry Soc. Am. (Gertrude B. Claytor Meml. award 1989), Poets House, Dramatists Guild Am., Authors Guild. Home: 27 W 96th St Apt 12B New York NY 10025-6614 Office: Nat Assn for Printing Leadership 75 W Century Rd Paramus NJ 07652 Office Phone: 800-642-6275 ext. 6304. Personal E-mail: snoguere@napl.org.

NOH, KYOUNG LAE, electronics engineer, researcher; b. Seoul, Republic of Korea, Oct. 5, 1974; s. Seung Hoe Noh and Enha Cho; m. Misun Kim, Dec. 13, 2008. BS in Electronic Comm. Engring., Hanyang U., Seoul, 2000, MS in Electronic Comm. Engring., 2002; PhD, Tex. A&M U., Coll. Sta., 2008. Engr., comm. signal processing lab. Hanyang U., R & D Ctr., SK Telecom, 2002—03; rsch. asst. Tex. A&M U., 2003—08; sr. engr. Samsung Electronics, Seoul, 2008—. Contbr. articles to profl. jours., chapters to books. Achievements include patents for smart antenna, ad-hoc, sensor network; research in wireless communications, sensor networks, cooperative communications. Office: Samsung Electronics Co Ltd Telecom R&D Ctr 416 Maeta-3Dong Seoul 443-370 Republic of Korea Personal E-mail: abigbliss@gmail.com. Business E-Mail: eddie.noh@samsung.com.

NOH, YOO-JEONG, research scientist; b. Busan, Republic Of Korea; PhD in Meteorology, Fla. State U., Tallahassee. Rsch. scientist CIRA Colo. State U., Ft. Collins, 2006—. Mem.: Korean Atmospheric Scientists America, Am. Geoscis. Union, Am. Meteorol. Soc. Achievements include development of snowfall retrieval algorithm using surface microwave satellite observations; satellite detection algorithm of cloud icing conditions; research in aircraft measurements and analyses of mixed-phase clouds regarding icing problems; satellite remote sensing and ground validation of cloud and precipitation. Office: CIRA Colo State Univ 1375 Campus Delivery Fort Collins CO 80523

NOHRNBERG, JAMES CARSON, language educator; b. Berkeley, Calif., Mar. 19, 1941; s. Carson and Geneva Gertrude (Gibbs) N.; m. Stephanie Payson Lamport, June 14, 1964; children: Gabrielle L., Peter Carson L. Student, Kenyon Coll., 1958-60; BA, Harvard Coll., 1962, postgrad., 1965-68; PhD, U. Toronto, 1970. Tchg. fellow dept. English U. Coll., U. Toronto, 1963-64; jr. fellow Soc. of Fellows Harvard U., 1965-68; acting instr. dept. English Yale U., New Haven, 1968-69, lectr., 1969-70, asst. prof., 1970-75, assoc. prof., 1975; prof. English U. Va., Charlottesville, 1975—. Adj. instr. English Harvard U., Cambridge, 1967; Gauss Seminars in Criticism lectr. Princeton U., 1987; lectr. various univs., 1974—. Author: The Analogy of The Faerie Queene, 1976, 80, Like Unto Moses: The Constituting of an Interruption, 1995; mem. editl. bd. Spenser Ency., 1977-90, Spenser Studies, 1977—, Manchester Spenser, 2007—; contbr. articles to profl. jours. and poems to mags.; editor vols. on allegory, Bible, Homer, Dante, Boiardo, Spenser, Raleigh Shakespeare, Milton, Jennyson Thomas Pynchon, Northrop Frye, among others. Recipient Am. Acad. Poets prize Harvard U., 1962; Woodrow Wilson fellow, 1962, jr. fellow Harvard U., 1965-68, Morse fellow Yale U., 1974-75, U. Va. Ctr. for Advanced Studies fellow, 1975-78, Guggenheim fellow, 1981-82, Ind. U. Inst. for Advanced Studies fellow, 1991, U. Va. Sesquicentennial fellow, 2003-2004, Hon. award Renaissance Prose Conf., Purdue U., 2009. Mem.: MLA, Am. Comparative Lit. Assn., Milton Soc., Spenser Soc. (Colin Clont Lifetime Achievement award 2009), Phi Beta Kappa. Presbyterian. Avocations: poetry, collecting books and records. Home: 1874 Wayside Pl Charlottesville VA 22903-1631 Office: U Va Dept English Bryan Hall Charlottesville VA 22903 Office Phone: 434-924-6629. Business E-Mail: jcn@virginia.edu.

NOLAN, CHRISTOPHER ALOYSIUS, III, real estate developer, architect, music promotion; b. Boston, July 17, 1950; s. Christopher Aloysius Nolan Jr. and Gladys Edna Kiely Nolan; m. Deborah Ellen Barham, July 22, 1982 (dec. Feb. 1999). BA, U. Toronto, 1972; MArch, Harvard, 1979; student, Sch. of Museum of Fine Arts, Boston, 1972-75. Registered architect, NY, NJ, Conn. Grad. arch. Russell Architects, Cambridge, 1977—79; arch. Eli Attia and Assocs., NYC, 1979-80, Haines Lundberg Waehler, NYC, 1980-81, Castro-Blanco Piscioneri Feder, NYC, 1981-84; chief arch. Howco Investment Corp., Livingston, NJ, 1984-88; devel. mgr. Hirschfeld Realty, NYC, 1988; mng. dir. Joseph Hilton & Assocs., NYC and Parsippany, NJ, 1988—96; project exec. AJ Contracting Co., Inc., NYC, 1996-2000; dir. devel. LCOR Inc., NYC, 2000—08; cons. Nolan & Assoc., NY, 2009—, Calif. Mem. planning bd. Clermont, NY, 1991-05, town bd., Clermont, NY, 2006-; bd. trustees Madison Sq. Boys and Girls Club, 1993-05, Friends of Clermont State Hist. Site, 2007-; vice chair Columbia County Dem. Com., 2006-07, chair, 2008-; chair Assn. Amis d'Essakane, Mali, 2006-. Mem.: AIA, Harvard Club. Avocations: politics, yoga, music. Office: 123 45th St Newport Beach CA 92663 Office Phone: 518-755-5089. Personal E-mail: chrisanolan3@gmail.com. Business E-Mail: cnolan@theworld.com.

NOLAN, DEANNA NICOLE, professional basketball player; b. Flint, Mich., Aug. 25, 1979; d. Virginia Nolan and Phillip Murphy. Grad. in Child and Family Devel., U. Ga., Athens, 2001. Guard-forward Detroit Shock, 2001—; player (off-season) Zaragoza, Spain, 2003—04, Ramat Hasharon, Israel, 2005—06, Ekater in Burg, Russia, 2007—08. Mem. USA Women's Sr. Nat. Team. Named to All-WNBA Second Team, 2003, Eastern Conf. All-Star Team, WNBA, 2003, 2005—07, All-WNBA First Team, 2005, WNBA All-Defensive Second Team, 2005, WNBA All-Defensive First Team, 2007, WNBA MVP, 2006. Achievements include winning WNBA Championships as a member of the Shock, 2003, 06. Mailing: Detroit Shock Palace Sports & Entertainment 5 Championship Dr Auburn Hills MI 48326 Office Phone: 248-377-0100. Personal E-mail: dnolan14@hotmail.com.

NOLAN, JAMES LAWRY, JR., sociologist; b. LA, Sept. 26, 1962; s. James Lawry and Karen Thorson Nolan; m. Catherine Elizabeth Ballou, June 25, 1988; children: Amy, David, Laura, William. BA, U. Calif., Davis, 1984; MA, U. Va., 1992, PhD, 1995. Lectr. U. Va., Charlottesville, 1995—96; asst. prof. sociology Williams Coll., Williamstown, Mass., 1996—2002, assoc. prof., sociology, 2002—07, prof., sociology, 2007—, chmn. dept. anthropology and sociology, 2002—04, 2009—; vis. Fulbright Sch. Loughborough U, Loughborough, England, 1999—2000; dir Williams-Exeter Programme, Oxford U., 2004—06; tutor for vis. students Exeter Coll., Oxford U., 2004—06; vis. fellow Ctr. for Criminol. Oxford U., 2004—06. Editor: The Am. Culture Wars: Current Contests, Future Prospects, 1996, Drug Courts: In Theory, In Practice, 2002; author: The Therapeutic State: Justifying Gov. at Cent. End, 1998, Reinventing Justice: The Am. Drug Ct. Movement, 2001, Legal Accents, Legal Borrowing: The International Problem - Solving Court Movement, 2009. Fellow, NEH, 1999—2000; Fulbright scholar, Fulbright Found., 1999—2000, Sorokin postdoctoral fellow, 1995—96. Mem.: Am. Sociol. Assoc. Office: Williams College Dept of Anthropology and Sociology 85 Mission Park Dr Williamstown MA 01267 Office Phone: 413-597-2460.

NOLAN, JAMES PAUL, internist, educator, researcher; b. Buffalo, June 21, 1929; s. James Paul and Isabel (Curry) N.; m. Christa Paul, July 23, 1956; children— Lisa, James, Christopher, Thomas. BA, Yale U., 1951, MD cum laude, 1955. Diplomate Am. Bd. Internal Medicine. Instr. in medicine Yale U., New Haven, 1961-63; intern Grace-New Haven Hosp., 1955-56, resident, 1958-60, chief med. resident, 1961-62, asso. physician, 1962-63; asst. prof. medicine SUNY, Buffalo, 1963-67, asso. prof., 1967-69, prof., 1969—, vice-chmn. dept. medicine, 1973-77, acting chmn. dept., 1978-79, chmn. dept., 1979-95, disting. svc. prof., 1996—; chief of medicine Buffalo Gen. Hosp., 1969-80, attending, 1969—; asso. attending Edward J. Meyer Meml. Hosp., Buffalo, 1963-68, attending, 1968-71, cons., 1971—; cons. physician Millard Fillmore Hosp., 1981—, Deaconess Hosp., 1973—. Attending Buffalo VA Hosp., Children's Hosp. Buffalo; cons. Roswell Park Meml. Inst., 1970—; acting dir. dept. medicine Erie County Med. Center, 1978-80, dir. dept., 1980—; trustee Buffalo Gen. Hosp., 1974—; bd. dirs. Kaleid Health, ACP Found. Editl. adv. bd. Jour. Medicine Exptl. and Clin, 1971—; reviewer: Gastroenterology, 1973—; contbr. numerous articles to med. and sci. jours. Served to lt. comdr., M.C. USN, 1956-58. NIH grantee, 1979-86; Hartford Found. grantee, 1981 Mem. ACP (master, chair bd. regents 1994-95), Am. Fedn. Clin. Rsch., AAAS, Am. Gastroent. Assn. (procedures com.), Am. Assn. Study of Liver Disease, Reticuloendothelial Soc., N.Y. Acad. Sci., Am. Clin. and Climatol. Assn., Interurban Club, Ctrl. Soc. Clin. Rsch., Internat. Assn. Study of Liver, Assn. Am. Physicians, Assn. Profs. Medicine (pres. 1993-94), Phi Beta Kappa, Alpha Omega Alpha. Office: 462 Grider St Buffalo NY 14215-3021 Address: 213 Burbank Dr Snyder NY 14226-3938 E-mail: jpnolanmd@yahoo.com.

NOLAN, JAMES W., food products executive; BS, Ithaca Coll., NY. With Procter & Gamble; various positions including chief customer officer PepsiCola N.Am. and sr. v.p. sales and market devel. PepsiCola N.Am. PepsiCo; with PepsiAmericas, 2001—05, exec. v.p. US ops.; exec. v.p., CEO Foodservice Sara Lee Corp., 2005—08, exec. v.p., CEO fresh bakery, 2008—. Office: Sara Lee Corp 3500 Lacey Rd Downers Grove IL 60515 Office Phone: 630-598-6000.

NOLAN, JANIECE SIMMONS, retired health system administrator, consultant; b. Ft. Worth; d. James Coleman and Berenice Johnson Simmons; m. Robert L. Nolan; children: Douglas, Patricia, Nancy, Margaret, Sheffield, Gemini Janiece. BA, U. Tex., 1961, MA, 1963; PhD, Tulane U., 1968; MPH, U. Calif., Berkeley, 1975. Diplomate Am. Coll. Healthcare Execs. Rsch. scientist Tex. Nuc. (Nuc. Chgo.), Austin, 1963-65; head cell biology Gulf South Rsch. Inst., New Orleans, 1968-70; postdoctoral fellow dept. physiology/anatomy U. Calif., Berkeley, 1970-72; rsch. physiologist, acting assoc. chief of staff for rsch. VA Hosp., Martinez, Calif., 1970-75; COO, v.p. adminstrn. John Muir Med. Ctr., Walnut Creek, Calif., 1977-97; pres., CEO John Muir Physician Network, Walnut Creek, 1997—2008; cons., 2008—. Commr. State Commn. Emergency Svcs., Sacramento, 1997—2000; mem. corp. adv. bd. for grad. program in health mgmt. rsch. U. Calif., Berkeley, 2003—08; mem. industry adv. bd. Ctr. Health Mgmt. Rsch., 2004—08, health care cons., 2008—. Capt. USNR, (ret.). Woodrow Wilson fellow, 1960; named Woman of Yr., Women Health Care Execs., San Francisco, 1989, Women's Hall of Fame for leadership, Contra Costa County Commn. for Women, 2008; recipient Navy Commendation medals (3), Humanitarian Svc. medal, Armed Forces Res. medals (2), Disting. Leadership award, Grad. Program Health Mgmt., Alumni Assn., U. Calif., Berkeley, 2009. Mem.: Writers Workshop, Southern Calif. Geneal. Soc., Internat. Soc. Genetic Genealogy, Am. Mil. Surgeons of the U.S., Calif. Geneal. Soc., Naval Res. Assn. (life), U. Sect. Club, U. Calif., Rotary (Paul Harris fellow), Phi Beta Kappa (No. Calif. Assn. bd. dirs. 2005—). Avocations: international travel, genealogy, writing, tap dancing. Office: PO Box 1137 Lafayette CA 94549-1137 Business E-Mail: jn1137@aol.com.

NOLAN, JEANADA H., retired state agency administrator, social worker, educator; b. Fresno, Calif., Aug. 6, 1915; d. John Andrew and Lucille Wallace Hamilton; children: Jay Hamilton, Thomas Joseph. BA, Fresno State Coll., Calif., 1938; MA, Sacramento State Coll., Calif., 1953; PhD, Union Grad. Sch., Cin., 1977. Social worker Fresno County Welfare Dept., Calif., 1935—42; social welfare agt. State Dept. Social Welfare, Sacramento, 1942—45; coord. parent and preschool edn. Sacramento City Unified Sch. Dist., 1951—66, coord. Project Head Start, 1965; chief bur. preschool edn. programs Calif. State Dept. Edn., 1966—72, asst. to assoc. supt. early childhood edn., 1972—74; ret., 1974. Mem. Gov.'s Adv. Commn. Children and Youth, Sacramento, 1959—65; exec. sec. Gov.'s Adv. Com. Child Devel. Programs, 1966—72; parent involvement specialist Nat. Head Start, 1966—69; adv. bd. Parent Participation Preschools Internat., 1966—70; co-chmn., leader child devel. com. Wilson Riles Early Childhood Edn. Program, 1972; vis. lectr. in orgn., mgmt. and adminstrn. preschool and child care programs U. Calif. Ext., 1974—79; prodr. radio series Families are Our Bus., 1954; mem. State Bd. Mgrs. Calif. Congress Parents and Tchr. Contbr. articles to profl. jours. Mem.: Sacramento Soc. Blind (mem. consumer adv. com. 1999—), Sacramento Mental Health Assn. (charter mem.), Calif. Assn. Edn. Young Children, Nat. Assn. Young Children, UN-USA, Ret. Tchrs. Assn., Soroptimist Internat.

NOLAN, JOHN EDWARD, lawyer; b. Mpls., July 11, 1927; s. John E. and Teresa (Franey) Nolan; m. Joan Dobbins, June 3, 1950; children: Carol N. Klatt, John Edward III(dec.), Kelly N. Spencer, Richard Clark, Patricia N. McNeill. BS, U.S. Naval Acad., 1950; JD, Georgetown U., 1955. Bar: DC 1955, US Supreme Ct. 1959, Md. 1961. Law clk. to Justice Clark U.S. Supreme Ct., 1955-56; adminstrv. asst. to Atty. Gen. Robert F. Kennedy, 1963-64; assoc. Steptoe & Johnson, Washington, 1956-62, ptnr., 1962—63, 1965—. Assoc. counsel Cuban families com. Cuban Prisoners Exch., Havana, 1962—63; spl. counsel refugee subcom. Senate Jud. Com., Vietnam, 1967—68; mem. CPR Panel Disting. neutrals, Washington; mediator U.S. Ct. Appeals DC cir.; mem. exec. com. Lawyers Com. Civil Rights Under Law; vis. fellow Wolfson Coll., Cambridge U., England, 1987, 92; bd. dirs. Iomega, Inc., 1993—2008. Trustee Robert F. Kennedy Meml., 1969—; moderator Aspen Inst., 1980—; gen. counsel, bd. dirs. U.S. Naval Acad. Found., 1997—2007; bd. dirs. Fund Dem. Majority. Served from 2d lt. to capt. USMC, 1950—54, Korea. Decorated Silver Star, Bronze Star with combat V, Purple Heart; recipient Disting. Grad. award, US Naval Acad., 2009. Mem.: ABA, Am. Law Inst., DC Bar Assn., U.S. Naval Acad. Alumni Assn. (bd. counsel 1997—2007), Univ. Club (N.Y.C.), Congl. Club, Met. Club (Washington). Democrat. Roman Catholic. Office: 1330 Connecticut Ave NW Washington DC 20036-1704 Office Phone: 202-429-8107. E-mail: jnolan@steptoe.com.

NOLAN, JOHN MICHAEL, lawyer; b. Conway, Ark., June 21, 1948; s. Paul Thomas and Peggy (Hime) N. BA, U. Tex., 1970, JD, 1973; LLM in Taxation, George Washington U., Washington, DC, 1976. Bar: Tex. 1973, DC 1975, US Ct. Mil. Appeals 1973, US Ct. Appeals (DC cir.) 1975, US Tax Ct. 1975, US Supreme Ct. 1975. Chief counsel to chief judge US Ct. Mil. Appeals, Washington, 1976-77; assoc. Winstead, McGuire, Sechrest & Minick PC, Dallas, 1977-81; shareholder Winstead Sechrest & Minick PC, Dallas, 1981—2006, Winstead, Dallas, 2007—. Editor in chief The Advocate, 1973-76. Capt. JAGC, US Army, 1973-76. Named one of Outstanding Young Men in Am. US Jaycees, 1976; Keeton fellow Chancellor Coun.; named among Best Lawyers in Am. Tex. Super Lawyer. Fellow Dallas Bar Found. (life), Tex. Bar Found. (life); mem. ABA (real property, probate and trust sect., real property com., partnerships, joint ventures, and other investment vehicles), Tex. Bar Assn. (real property, probate and trust sect.), DC Bar Assn., Dallas Bar Assn. (real estate group), Tex. Coll. Real Estate Lawyers, Am. Coll. Real Estate Lawyers, Coll. State Bar Tex., Real Estate Coun. (bd. dirs.), Salesmanship Club Dallas, Royal Oaks Country Club. Presbyterian. Home: 6681 Crest Way Ct Dallas TX 75230-2868 Office: Winstead 5400 Renaissance Tower 1201 Elm St Ste 5400 Dallas TX 75270-2199 Office Phone: 214-745-5251. Business E-Mail: jnolan@winstead.com.

NOLAN, JOSEPH THOMAS, journalism educator, communications consultant; b. Waterbury, Conn., Apr. 11, 1920; s. Thomas Francis and Mary Margaret (Gaffney) N.; m. Virginia Theodate Tappin, May 6, 1943; children— Carol Nolan Rigolot, David J., David Nolan AB, Holy Cross Coll., 1942; MA in English Lit., Boston U., 1945; PhD in Econs, NYU, 1973. Washington corr. UPI, 1943-49; writer, copy editor N.Y. Times, NYC, 1949-55; mgr. editorial and press services RCA Corp., NYC, 1955-62; sr. v.p. corporate communications Chase Manhattan Bank, NYC, 1962-74; prof. journalism and pub. affairs U. S.C., Columbia, 1974-76; v.p. pub. affairs Monsanto Co., St. Louis, 1976-85; Gannett vis. prof. communications U. Fla., 1985-86; prof. communications U. North Fla., Jacksonville, 1986-92; adj. prof. bus. and comm. Flagler Coll., St. Augustine, Fla., 1985—95. Contbr. articles to various mags. Fellow Pub. Rels. Soc. Am. Roman Catholic. Home: 30 Park Terrace Dr Saint Augustine FL 32080-5334

NOLAN, LESLIE MARIAN, artist; b. Portland, Mar. 11, 1948; d. John Edward Nolan and Marion May Lindseth; m. K. Steven Halter, May 30, 1979; children: Ryan, Edward, Douglas. BA in French, Portland State U., 1970; MS in spl. studies, George Washington U., DC, 1975; MS in nat. security, Nat. Def. U., DC, 1997. Chief fgn. activities U.S. Info. Agy., Washington, 1979—82, dep. chief physical security, 1982—87, chief overseas support, 1987—93, chief security svc., 1993—96, resource analyst, 1997—99; chief attestation officer of U.S. U.S. Dept. of State, Washington, 1999—2004; artist self-employed, Herndon, Va., 2004—. V.p. programs Fairfax Art League, Va., 2000—04; co-chair hanging Art League, Alexandria, Va., 2005—06. Logo, Fairfax Art League, 2003. Mem.: League of Reston Artists, Potomac Valley Watercolorists, So. Watercolor Soc., League of Women Voters. Avocations: reading, travel, hiking. Home: 11660 Gilman Ln Herndon VA 20170

NOLAN, MARILYN ANN, health facility administrator; b. Brighton, Mass., July 17, 1935; d. Anthony Henry and Anne Claire Nikiel; m. George Francis Nolan; 2 children. BA, Trinity Coll., Washington, 1957; MSS in Social Wk., Boston U., 1959. Diplomate Am. Inst. Hypnotherapy; lic. ind. clin. social worker. Med. social worker Peter Bent Brigham Hosp., Boston, 1959—60; geriatric and psychiat. social worker Modesto State Hosp., Calif., 1960—63; psychiat. social worker, geriatric med. substance abuse therapist, visual impairment svc. coord. VA Med. Ctr., Bedford, Mass., 1966—87, psychiat. social worker, substance abuse therapist, 1989—91, visual impairment svc. team coord. Long

Beach, Calif., 1987—89, St. Petersburg, Fla., 1991—2004; pvt. practice guided imagery, visualization and stress mgmt. Largo, Fla., Wareham, Mass., 2004—. Chmn. disabled people's program Bay Pines VA Med. Ctr., St. Petersburg, 1991—94; field work instr. Boston Coll., 1972—86, Boston U., 1972—86. Recipient Outstanding Contbn. award, Am. Legion, 1990, Tampa Bay Fed. Equal Employment Opportunity, 1993, Blinded Vets. Assn., 2002. Mem.: NASW (bd. cert. diplomate), Nat. Guild Hypnotists (cert.), Acad. Cert. Social Workers. Roman Catholic. Avocations: reading, piano, accordion. Studio: 63 Edgewater Dr Wareham MA 02571 Home Phone: 727-399-0258; Office Phone: 508-291-0507. Personal E-mail: magenol@aol.com.

NOLAN, MIKE, professional football coach; b. Balt., Mar. 7, 1959; s. Dick Nolan; m. Kathy Nolan; children: Michael, Christopher, Laura, Jennifer. Attended, U. Oreg. Asst. coach U. Oreg., 1981—82, Stanford U., 1982—83, Rice U., 1984—85; head coach LSU, 1986; linebackers coach, spl. teams asst. Denver Broncos, 1987—92, defensive coord., 2009—, NY Giants, 1993—96, Wash. Redskins, 1997—99, NY Jets, 2000; wide receivers coach Balt. Ravens, 2001, defensive coord., 2002—04; head coach San Francisco 49ers, 2005—08. Office: Denver Broncos 13655 Broncos Pky Englewood CO 80112*

NOLAN, OWEN, professional hockey player; b. Belfast, Northern Ireland, Feb. 12, 1972; m. Diana Nolan; children: Jordan, Dylan. Right wing Cornwall Royals, 1988—90, Halifax Citadels, 1990—91, Que. Nordiques, 1990—95, Colo. Avalanche, 1995, San Jose Sharks, 1995—2003, Toronto Maple Leafs, 2003—04, Phoenix Coyotes, 2006—07, Calgary Flames, 2007—08, Minn. Wild, 2008—. Mem. Team Can., Olympic Games, Salt Lake City, 2002. Recipient Emms Family Award, Ont. Hockey League (OHL), 1989, Jim Mahon Meml. Trophy, 1990; named to NHL All-Star Game, 1992, 1996, 1997, 2000, 2002. Achievements include being the first overall draft pick in NHL entry draft, 1990; being a member of gold medal Canadian Hockey team, Salt Lake City Olympic Games, 2002. Office: Minn Wild 317 Washington St Saint Paul MN 55102

NOLAN, PETER JOHN, physics professor; b. NYC, Mar. 25, 1934; s. Peter John and Nora (Gleeson) Nolan; m. Barbara Nolan, 2000; children from previous marriage: Thomas, James, John, Kevin. BS in Physics, Manhattan Coll., 1956; cert. in Meteorology, UCLA, 1958; MS in Physics, Adelphi U., 1966, PhD in Physics, 1974. Engr. various corps., NJ, NY, 1956-63; systems analysis engr. on lunar module Gruman Aircraft Engring. Corp., Bethpage, NY, 1963-66; asst. prof. physics SUNY, Farmingdale, 1966-68, assoc. prof. physics, 1968-71, prof. physics, 1971—. Chmn. physics dept. SUNY, Farmingdale, 1970—77. Author: Experiments in Physics, 1982, 2d edit., 1995, Electromagnetic Theory for Electrical Technology Students, 1995, Fundamentals of College Physics, 1993, Italian Version, Fundementi Di Fisica, 1996, (CD Rom) Physics For Students of Science and Engineering. Mem.: Am. Assn. Physics Tchrs. Home: 59 Parnell Dr Smithtown NY 11787-2428 Office: Farmingdale State Coll Dept Physics Farmingdale NY 11735 Office Phone: 631-420-2271. Personal E-mail: pjnolan@optonline.net. Business E-Mail: nolanpj@farmingdale.edu.

NOLAN, RICHARD THOMAS, clergyman, educator; b. Waltham, Mass., May 30, 1937; s. Thomas Michael and Elizabeth Louise (Leishman) N.; m. Robert C. Pingpank, June 4, 2009. BA, Trinity Coll., 1960; Diploma in Theol. Studies, Berkeley Div. Sch., 1960; MDiv. in Theol. Studies, Hartford Sem. Found., 1963; postgrad. in Religious Edn., Union Theol. Sem., 1963; MA in Religion, Yale U., 1967; PhD in Religion, NYU, 1973; postgrad. in Career Assessment, Ctr. Career Devel. and Ministry, 1987; postgrad. in Biomed. Ethics, Harvard U., 1991. Ordained deacon Episcopal Ch., 1963, priest, 1965; cert. in clinical pastoral edn. Conn. Valley Hosp., 1962, in death, dying and bereavement Waterbury Hosp. Health Ctr., Conn., 1977. Instr. Latin and English Watkinson Sch., Conn., 1961-62; instr. math. Choir Sch. of Cathedral of St. John the Divine, NYC, 1962-64; instr. math. and religion, assoc. chaplain Cheshire Acad., Conn., 1965-67; instr. Hartford Sem. Found., Conn., 1967-68, asst. acad. dean, lectr. philosophy and edn., 1968-70; instr. Mattatuck C.C., Waterbury, Conn., 1969-70, asst. prof. philosophy and history, 1970-74, assoc. prof., 1974-78, prof. philosophy and social sci., 1978-92, prof. emeritus, 1992—; vicar St. Paul's Parish, Bantam, Conn., 1974-88, pastor emeritus, 1988—; pres. Litchfield Inst., Conn. and Fla., 1984-96; adj. lectr. in philosophy Palm Beach C. C., Fla., 2000—02. Ethics com. Waterbury Hosp. Health Ctr., 1984—88; vis. and adj. prof. philosophy, theology and religious studies Trinity Coll., Conn., L.I. U., U. Miami, St Joseph Coll., Conn., Pace U., Teikyo Post U., U. Conn., Hartford Grad. Ctr., Ctrl. Conn. State U., 1964—95, Broward C.C., Fla.; lectr. philosophy and theology Barry U., Fla., 1973, 1989—92, 1997—98; adj. assoc. in continuing edn. Berkeley Div. Sch. Yale U., 1987—89; Rabbi Harry Halpern Meml. lectr., Southbury, Conn., 1987; adj. prof. philosophy Fla. Atlantic U., 1998—99; adj. prof. The Union Inst., Fla., 1999; faculty of cons. examiners Charter Oak State Coll., Conn., 1990—93; assoc. for edn. Christ Ch. Cathedral, Hartford, Conn., 1988—94, hon. canon, 1991—; cons. Dept. Def. Activity Non-Traditional Ednl. Support, Ednl. Testing Svc., Princeton, NJ, 1990; vis. scholar Coll. Preachers, Washington Nat. Cathedral, 1994; supply priest Episcopal Diocese of S.E. Fla., 1994—2002; ret. priest-in-residence St. Andrew's Ch., Lake Worth, Fla., 2002—; soc. regents Cathedral Ch. St. John the Divine, 2002—; rsch. fellow med. ethics Yale U., 1978. Author (with H. Titus and M. Smith): Living Issues in Philosophy, 7th edit., 1979, Indonesian edit., 1984, 8th edit., 1986, 9th edit., 1995; author: (with F. Kirkpatrick) Living Issues in Ethics, 1982, 2d edit., 2000, Chinese edit., 1988 (Honored Author for Books Exceeding 100,000 Copies award Wadsworth Pub. Co., 1986); editor, contbr. Diaconate Now, 1968, host Conversations With..., 1987—89; author (with Robert C. Pingpank): Soul Mates: More Than Partners (online), 2004. Notary pub., Fla. Recipient Founder's Day award, NYU, 1973; co-recipient award Exceptional Leadership and Cmty. Svc., ACLU Palm Beach Chpt., 2008. Mem. Am. Acad. Religion, Am. Philos. Assn., Authors Guild, Hemlock Soc. Fla. (adv. bd. 1998-2009), Interfaith Alliance, Integrity, 1635 Soc. Boston Latin Sch. Alumni Assn., Elizabeth S. Taber Soc. Tabor Acad. Alumni Assn., ELMS, Soc. Trinity Coll., Cavalier King Charles Spaniel Club, Yale Legacy Partners, Harwood Soc. Cheshire Acad., Society of The Torch of NYU, Founders Soc. of the Wash. Nat. Cathedral, Lambda Legal, Compass Lake Worth Fla., Compassion & Choices, Phi Delta Kappa. Independent. Episcopalian. Home: 2527 Egret Lake Dr West Palm Beach FL 33413-2161 Personal E-mail: canon@rtnolan.com. *Who am I? By baptism I am a resurrected child of God born to love and be loved; my pilgrimage among others is lived within this baptismal identity, more enduring than any achievement.*

NOLAN, ROBERT B., United States Ambassador to Lesotho; BBA, Villanova U., Phila., 1974; student in bus. adminstrn., George Wash. U., Washington. Joined US Fgn. Svc., 1976; gen. services officer US Dept. State, Conakry, Guinea, 1977—78, adminstrv. officer Antananarivo, Madagascar, 1978—81, Havana, Cuba, 1986—88, Helsinki, 1992—94, dir. office overseas employment, Bur. Human Resources Washington, 1994—96, dir. policy and planning, Office the Under Sec. State for Mgmt., 1996—97, exec. dir., Bur. We. Hemisphere Affairs, 1997—2000, prin. oficer Monterrey, Mexico, 2000—01, dir. office performance evaluation, Bur. Human Resources Washington, 2001—06, dir. office career devel. and assignments, Bur. Human Resources, 2006—07, US amb. to the Kingdom of Lesotho Maseru, 2007—. Recipient Meritorious Honor award, US Dept. State, 1988, Superior Honor award, 1993, 2000, 2004, 2006. Office: DOS Amb 2340 Maseru Pl Washington DC 20521-2340*

NOLAN, STANTON PEELLE, surgeon, educator; b. Washington, May 29, 1933; s. James Parker and Ellen Dubose (Peelle) N.; m. Marion Faro, June 16, 1955; children: Stanton Peelle Jr., Tiphanie Ravenel Clarke. BA, Princeton U., NJ, 1955; MD, U. Va., Charlottesville, 1959, MS, 1962. Diplomate Am. Bd. Surgery, Am. Bd. Thoracic Surgery. Intern U. Va. Med. Ctr., Charlottesville, 1959-60, asst. resident gen. surgery, 1960-61, research fellow surgery, 1961-62, sr. asst. resident gen. surgery, 1962-64, chief resident gen surgery, 1964-65, chief resident thoracic cardiovascular surgery, 1965-66; sr. rsch. assoc. Clinic of Surgery Nat. Heart Inst., NIH, Bethesda, Md., 1966-68; asst. prof. surgery U. Va. Med. Ctr., Charlottesville, 1968-70, assoc. prof. surgery, 1970-74, surgeon in charge div. thoracic cardiovascular surgery, 1970-93, prof. surgery, 1974-81, Claude A. Jessup prof. surgery, 1981-98, clin. prof. surgery, 1998—2004, prof. surgery, 2004—06, med. dir. Thoracic Cardiovascular post-operative unit, 1989-93, prof. emeritus of surgery, 2006—. Established Investigator Am. Heart Assn., 1969-74; mem. surgery A study sect. NIH, Washington, 1972-76, surgery and bioengring. study sect. 1984-87, chmn. 1985-87; cons. thoracic cardiovascular surgery VA Hosp., Salem, Va., 1968-98, Am. Bd. Surgery cons. to qualifying examination com., 1988-91; surg. cons. Bur. Crippled Children, Charlottesville, 1968-93; vis. cons. cardiothoracic surgery Aga Khan U., Karachi, Pakistan, 1995, vis cons. Vol. Health Svcs., Madras, India, 1997, cons. So. Petrochem. Industries Corp. SPIC, Chennai, India 2000; vis. prof. U. Hanover, Germany, 1990; vis. prof. Cardiac Surgerey, U. Wis. 1992; keynote spkr., assoc. surg. physician asst., 2000. Mem. editl. bd. Jour. Surg. Rsch., 1973-79, Annals of Thoracic Surgery, 1979-88; mem. sci. adv. bd. Jour. for Heart Valve Disease, 1993—2006; mem. editl. adv. bd. ECRI Operating Rm. Risk Mgmt., 1992-2006; co-editor: Comprehensive Thoracic Surgery Curriculum, TSDA, 1995; contbr. articles to profl. jours., chpts. to books. Bd. mgrs. Ctrl. Va. Health Network, 2000—05, Westminster Canterbury Blue Ridge, chmn. Residents' Assn., 2004—06, Westminster Canterbury Found. bd., 2007—; bd. dirs. Piedmont Liability Trust, 1989—2005, chmn. claims com., 1989—2006, chmn. bd., 1991—2004. Recipient John Horsley Meml. prize U. Va. Med. Sch., 1962, Merit award Rsch. Forum of Am. Coll. Chest Physicians, 1968, Clyde Watson Disting. Svc. award Pastoral Care and Edn., 2006, Stanton P. Nolan Professorship Thoracic and Cardiovascular Surgery, U. Va. Bd. Visitors, 2006; Rsch. fellow Va. Heart Assn., 1961-62, Am. Cancer Soc., 1963-64; grantee NIH, 1968-84, Am. Heart Assn., 1970-73, Medtronic Corp., 1975-81. Fellow ACS (com. allied health pers. 1996—2004, exec. com. 1997-2000, vice chair), Am. Coll. Cardiology, Am. Surg. Assn.; mem. Am. Assn. Thoracic Surgery, Am. Heart Assn. (coun. on cardiovasc. surgery 1969-99, anesthesiology, radiology and surgery study com. 1991-94), Andrew G. Morrow Soc., Assn. Acad. Surgery, Assn. Advancement of Med. Instrumentation (chair 1998-2000, co-chmn. cardiac valve prostheses stds. com. 1974-2005, mem. internat. stds. strategy com. 1989—2005, bd. dirs. 1990-2000, stds. bd. 1991—2005, edn. com. 1992-93, nominating com. 1996-2000, chair 1998-2000, exec. com. 1996-2000, govt. rels. com. 1996-2000), Internat. Stds. Orgn. (chmn. subcom. on cardiovascular surg. implants 1982-2004), Assn. Clin. Cardiac Surgeons, Halsted Soc. (exec. com. 1985-89), Coord. Com. on Perfusion Affairs (chmn. 1990-2000), Internat. Assn. Cardiac Biol. Implants (sci. com. 1994), Am. Assn. for Vascular Surgery, Muller-Jones Surg. Soc. (pres. 1979), Soc. Internat. de Cirurgie, Soc. Vascular Surgery, Soc. Thoracic Surgeons (ad hoc com. on industry rels. 1992-97, stds. and ethics com. 1993-95, 98-2001, edn. and resources com. 1996-97), Soc. Univ. Surgeons, Southeastern Surg. Congress, So. Surg. Assn. (2d v.p. 1982), Thoracic Surgery Found. Rsch. and Edn. (chair New Century Soc. com. 1997-2000), Va. Surg. Soc. (v.p. 1980-83, pres. 1984), Va. Vascular Soc. (exec. coun. 1985-86), Soc. Critical Care Medicine, Raven Soc., Assn. Am. Med. Colls. (rep. coun. acad. socs. 1992-01), Chevy Chase Club, Alpha Omega Alpha, Omicron Delta Kappa, Commn. on Accreditation Allied Health Education Programs (Award for Exceptional Svc. 2007). Home: #5204 250 Pantops Mountain Rd Charlottesville VA 22911-8702 Office: U Va TCV Surgery PO Box 800679 Charlottesville VA 22908-0679 Business E-Mail: snolan@virginia.edu.

NOLAN, STEPHEN JAMES, United States ambassador to Republic of Botswana; b. Pa. m. Judy Nolan. BS, Villanova U., Pa., 1975; MBA, Am. Grad. Sch. Internat. Mgmt., 1978; grad. sr. seminar, Nat. Fgn. Affairs Training Ctr., Arlington, Va. Joined as fgn. svc. officer US Dept. State, 1976, various assignments Dakar, Berlin, Jerusalem and Washington, supervisory gen. svc. officer Nairobi, Kenya, 1988—91, adminstrv. officer US Embassy Harare, Zimbabwe, 1993—97, counselor adminstrv. affairs Nairobi, 1997—99, consul gen. Cape Town, South Africa, 2000—03, exec. dir., Bur. African Affairs, 2004—08, US amb. to Botswana, 2008—. Recipient Award for Heroism, US Dept. State, Superior Honor award. Office: DOS Amb 2170 Gaborne Pl Washington DC 20521-2170*

NOLAN, STEVE, Mayor, Corona, California; Owner Backwoods BBQ; former chmn. Parks & Recreation Commn.; councilman City of Corona, 2004—08, mayor, 2008—. Rep. Infrastructure & Econ. Devel. Ad Hoc Com., Homeless Shelter Funding Ad Hoc Com. Pres. Corona Youth Sports Found.; dir. Partners for Parks & Recreation Found.; bd. mem. Corona C. of C. Named Citizen of Yr., Corona C. of C., 2003. Mem.: Circle City Rotary. Office: 400 S Vicentia Ave Corona CA 92882 Office Phone: 951-736-2400. E-mail: SNolan@ci.corona.ca.us.*

NOLAN, TED (THEODORE JOHN NOLAN), professional sports team executive, former professional hockey coach; b. Sault Ste. Marie, Ont., Can., Apr. 7, 1958; m. Sandra Nolan; children: Brandon, Jordan. LLD (hon.), Laurentian U., 2002. Left wing Detroit Red Wings, 1981—84, Pitts. Penguins, 1985—86; head coach Sault Ste. Marie Greyhounds, 1988—94; asst. coach Hartford Whalers, 1994-95; head coach Buffalo Sabres, 1995—97; head coach, dir. hockey ops. Moncton Wildcats, 2005—06; head coach NY Islanders, 2006—08; v.p. hockey ops. Rochester Americans, 2009—. Pres., CEO Ted Nolan Found. Recipient Order of Ontario, 1993, National Aboriginal Achievement Award, 1994, Jack Adams Award, NHL, 1997; named Sault Ste. Marie Citizen of Yr., 1990—91. Office: Rochester Americans Blue Cross Arena 1 War Memorial Sq Rochester NY 14614*

NOLAN, THERESA A., retired judge, mediator, arbitrator; b. Washington, Dec. 10, 1930; d. Peter James Sr. and Mary Dorothea (Gerhardt) Hagan; m. Bernard A. Nolan, Jr. (dec.); children: Patrick, Theresa Davis, Mary Ellen Purcell, Joanne Kowalczyk, Frances McKeever, Bernard, Christine, Thomas, Barbara Kristek, William, Kathleen, Joseph; m. Walter G. Planet (dec.). BA, U. Balt., 1973; LLB, U. Balt. Sch. Law, 1975. Bar: Md. 1976. Legal sec. Law & Sinclair, Upper Marlboro, Md., 1961—68, McGrane, Casey, Miller, Lanham, 1968—72; legis. asst. Prince George's County Office Law, Upper Marlboro, 1972—76; ptnr. Sherry, Boyer & Nolan, Bowie, 1977—79; sole practitioner, 1979—80; master domestic rels. causes 7th Jud. Cir. Ct. Md., Upper Marlboro, 1981—85; judge 4th Dist. Ct. Md., 1985—97, civil coordinating judge, 1991—2000; judge 7th Jud. Cir. Ct. Md., 1997—2000; mediator Md. Ct. Sys., 2000—. Instr. paralegal program Prince George's Cmty. Coll., 1980—88, USDA, 1980—88, U. Md. U. Coll., 1985—2000; family law sect. coun. Md. State Bar Assn., 1982—85; mem. Gov.'s Coun. Child Support Enforcement, 1983—86; mem. adv. bd. Dist. Pub. Defender, Upper Marlboro, 1984—; bd. govs. Md. State Bar Assn., 1985—87, 1989—91, local bar liaison, 1986—88; com. on criminal law procedure Md. Jud. Conf., 1987—88, dist. ct. edn. com., 1988—89, exec. com., 1990—91, chair dist. ct. edn. com., 1990—91, faculty, 1990—2000, vice chair, 1991—92, chair, 1992—93, civil law and procedures com., 1992—94, adminstrv. judges com., 1995—96, pub. rels. com., 1996—2000; pres. Prince George's County Women Lawyers Caucus, 1979—80, treas., 1981—82, exec. com., 1989—91; mem. Commn. Future of Md. Cts., 1995—96, chair criminal, juvenile and family matters sub-com. Charter mem. Law Found. Prince George's County; chmn. Prince George's County Cable Television Commn., 1978; mem. sodality Sacred Heart Parish; bd. dir. Prince George's Hosp., Cheverly, Md., 2000—03, Md. Vol. Lawyers Svcs., Inc., 1986—93; adv. bd. Family Crisis Ctr., Prince George's County Hotline and Suicide Prevention Ctr. Recipient Fabulous Forties award, Prince George's Cmty. Coll., 1998, Disting. Svc. award, Prince George's County, 2000, Salute to Women award, Gtr. Bowie C. of C., 2000; named a Woman of History, 1990, Woman of Achievement, Prince George's County, 1994; named one of Md. Top 100 Woment, 1998; named to Women's Hall of Fame, Prince George's County, 1993. Mem.: Am. Judges Assn., Inns of Ct., Md. Cir. Judges Assn., Women's Bar Assn. Md. (pres.-elect 1994—95, treas. 1981—82, bd. dir. 1982—94, nominating com. 1985—87, chmn. elections 1986, exec. com. 1989—90, chmn. awards com. 1989—93, Rita Davidson award 1993), Nat. Assn. Women Judges (sec. 4th dist. 1991—92, treas. 1993—94, pres. 1995—97, chair women in prison com. 2000, women in prison com. 2000—, ret. mem.), Prince George's County Bar Assn. (criminal liaison com. 1978, bd. dir. 1978—90, domestic rels. com. 1980—90, treas. 1981—82, sec. 1982—83, pres.-elect 1983—84, pres. 1984—85, budget com. 1984—86, chair social com. 1985—98, chmn. ABA-MSBA liaison com. 1986, nominating com. 1989—90). Democrat. Roman Catholic. Avocations: dance, golf, theater, book club, travel. Home: 2802 Berth Ter Annapolis MD 21401-7103

NOLAN, WILLIAM C., JR., oil industry executive; b. 1939; BA, Yale U., New Haven, 1961, JD, 1964. Mem. law dept. Murphy Oil Corp., El Dorado, Ark., 1964—69, chmn. bd. dirs., 2002—; founding ptnr. Nolan and Alderson, Attys., El Dorado, 1969—; pres. Noalmark Broadcasting. Office: Murphy Oil Corp PO Box 7000 El Dorado AR 71731-7000 also: Nolan and Alderson Attys 202 W 19th St El Dorado AR 71730

NOLAND, CARRIE JAURÈS, educator; b. NYC, Aug. 18, 1958; d. Aaron and Dorothy Estelle Noland; m. Christopher John Beach, Aug. 29, 1987; children: Julian Michael Beach, Francesca Karin Beach. PhD, Harvard U., Cambridge, Mass., 1990. Asst. prof. Columbia U., NYC, 1990—92; prof. U. Calif., Irvine, 1992—, dir., edn. abroad program Bordeaux, 2006—07. Author: (books) Agency and Embodiment, Poetry at Stake: Lyric Aesthetics and the Challenge of Technology, 1999; co-editor (with Sally Ann Ness): Migrations of Gesture, 2008; co-editor: (with Barret Watlen) Diasporic Avant-Gardes, 2009. Fellow: U. Calif., Irvine, Critical Theory Inst.

NOLAND, KENNETH CLIFTON, artist; b. Asheville, NC, Apr. 10, 1924; s. Harry C. and Bessie (Elkins) N.; m. Cornelia Langer (div.); children: Cady, William L., Lyndon; m. Stephanie Gordon, 1967 (div.); m. Peggy Schiffer; children: Samuel Jesse (div.); m. Paige Rense, 1994. Student, Ozzip Zadkine, Paris, 1948-49; studied, Black Mountain Coll., NC, summers, 1950, 51. Tchr. Inst. Contemporary Arts, 1950-52, Cath. U., 1951-60. One man shows include Galerie Creuze, Paris, 1949, Tibor de Nagy Gallery, N.Y.C., 1957, 58, Jefferson Pl. Gallery, 1958, French & Co., N.Y.C., 1959, Bennington Coll., 1961, Andre Emmerich Gallery, N.Y.C., 15 shows from 1960-83, Andre Emmerich Gallery, Zurich, Switzerland, 1973, 76, 79, 82, David Mirvish Gallery, Toronto, Can., 1965, 67, 74, 76, Jewish Mus., 1965, Salander O'Reilly Galleries, N.Y.C., 1989, Leo Castelli Gallery, N.Y., 1995, Gana Art Gallery, Seoul, 1995-96, also other galleries in Milan, Italy, Paris, Zurich, Dusseldorf, Hamburg and Cologne, Fed. Republic Germany, London, Montreal and Toronto, Can.; retrospective show Guggenheim Mus., N.Y.C., 1977; group shows include Kootz Gallery, N.Y.C., 1954, Norman Mackenzie Art Gallery, Regina, Sask., Can., 1963, Corcoran Gallery, Washington, 1956, 59, 63, 64, 67, 70, 75, Corcoran Gallery Biennial in Italy, 1964, Fogg Art Mus., Cambridge, Mass., 1965, 72, Mus. Modern Art, N.Y.C., 1965, 68, Nat. Gallery, Washington, 1968, U.S. Pavilion Expo 67, Montreal, Art Inst. Chgo., 1962, 70, 72, 76, Balt. Mus., 1957, 70, 77, Jewish Mus., 1963, Tate Gallery, London, 1964, 74, Guggenheim Mus., 1961, 66, 70, 73-74, 76-77, L.A. County Mus., 1964, Inst. Contemporary Art, Boston, 1964, 65, 67, Whitney Mus., N.Y.C., 1961-67, 69-73, 76, Met. Mus. N.Y.C., 1968, 70, Mus. Fine Arts, Boston, 1972, Albright-Knox Gallery, Buffalo, 1978, 80, Ameringer Howard Fine Art, NY, 99; Meredith Long Gall., Houston,Tex., 99; Andre Emmerich, CLosing Exhibition of Gall., NY, 99; CHAC-Mool Gall., CA, 99, Ameringer/Howard Gall., N.Y.C, 1999-2001, Farnsworth Mus. Art, Maine, 2002, Naples (Fla.) Mus., 2002; represented in permanent collections Salander O'Reily Galleries, N.Y.C., Mus. of Fine Arts, Houston, 1994, Ft. Lauderdale, 1994; Arte Metro Roma, Rome Colosseum Ctrl. Subway Mosaic Installed, 1995. Trustee Bennington (Vt.) Coll. Recipient 1st prize Premio Nacional Internat., Inst. Torcuato de Tella, Buenos Aires, 1964, Creative Arts award Brandeis U., 1965, 4th prize Corcoran Biennale, 1967; recipient The N.C. Award/medal of arts, 1995. Office Phone: 207-372-9684. Personal E-mail: kcnbridge@aol.com.

NOLAND, MARIAM CHARL, foundation executive; b. Parkersburg, W.Va., Mar. 29, 1947; d. Lloyd Henry and Ethel May (Beare) Noland; m. James Arthur Kelly, June 13, 1981. BS, Case Western Res. U., 1969; M in Edn., Harvard U., 1975. Asst. dir admissions, fin. aid Baldwin-Wallace Coll., Berea, Ohio, 1969-72; asst. dir. admissions Davidson (N.C.) Coll., 1972-74; case writer Inst. Edn. Mgmt., Cambridge, Mass., 1975; sec., treas., program officer The Cleve. Found., 1975-81; v.p. The St. Paul Found., 1981-85; pres. Community Found. for S.E. Mich., 1985—. Trustee Coun. Mich. Founds., 1988-98, Coun. on Founds., 1994-99, Henry Ford Health System, 1994-2002, 2004— Alma Coll., 1994-2004, John S. and James L. Knight Found., 2002—, Detroit Riverfront Conservancy, 2003—; commr. Detroit 300, 2000-01, trustee Independent Sector, 2008-. Office: Community Found SE Mich 333 W Fort St Ste 2010 Detroit MI 48226-3134 Office Phone: 313-961-6675. Business E-Mail: mnoland@cfsem.org.

NOLAND, MARY RICHERSON, management consultant; b. Lebanon, Ky., Aug. 6, 1925; d. Thomas Wesley and Mary Suda Richerson; m. James Russell Noland, Jr., Dec. 22, 1945; children: James Russell III, Ellen Gay, Mary Elise. Student, U. Louisville, New Haven State U., 1946—47, U. Houston, 1969—70. Exec. dir. vol. svcs. Meml. City

Hosp., Houston, 1971—73; exec. cons. Mgmt. Techs., Inc., Houston, 1975—78, pres. CEO, 1978—98, chmn., 1998—, Personalysis Corp., Houston, 2000—. Editor: Real Estate Focused Newsletter, 1973—75. Organizer, dir. Heart of Houston, 1965—66. Methodist. Avocations: reading, history, politics, music, piano. Home: 13303 Havershire Houston TX 77079 Office: Personalysis Corp 5847 San Felipe 650 Houston TX 77079

NOLAND, THOMAS TURLEY, JR., managed healthcare company executive; b. Norwalk, Conn., July 16, 1953; s. Thomas Turley and Judy (Kwis) N.; m. Vivian Ruth Sawyer, July 17, 1982; children: Andrew Montgomery, Sidney Victoria. Student, Duke U., 1971-73; BA magna cum laude, Yale U., 1975. Staff writer Anniston Star newspaper, Anniston, Ala., 1976-79; spl. correspondent Atlanta Constitution newspaper, Paris, 1979-84; instr. English and journalism Am. Coll. in Paris, 1979-81; inst. English Centre de Perfectionnement Linguistique, Paris, 1981-84, co-dir. Am. dept., 1982-84; mgr. pub. affairs Humana Inc., Louisville, 1984-85, sr. mgr. pub. affairs, 1985-87, dir. communications, 1987-91, v.p. communications, 1991-93; pub. Health Care Industry Group, The Cobb Group, Louisville, 1993-95, Profl. Pub. Course, Stanford U., 1993; pub. Vertical Mkts. Group The Cobb Group, Louisville, 1995-97; v.p. corp. comms. Humana Inc., Louisville, 1997-99, sr. v.p. corp. comms., 1999—. Author: The Permissive Will of God, 1979, The Celestine Travesty, 1996; co-author (play) Columbia Preserved, 1983, (play) The Neglected Few, 2000; editor (book) September 11 2001: Stories from 55 Broad Street, 2002; co-editor Remembering Wendell Cherry, 2003, The Dacian Chronicles, 2006. Chmn. bd. Ky. chpt. Nat. Multiple Sclerosis Soc., Louisville, 1987-88, bd. dirs., 1985-90; bd. dirs. Ky. Shakespeare Festival, 1986-91, U.S.A. Harvest, Louisville, 1989-94; bd. dirs., Filson Club Hist. Soc., Louisville, 1991—, treas., 1994-96. v.p., 1997, pres., 1998-03; bd. dirs., Cabbage Patch Settlement House, Louisville, 1994-97, Ky. Ctr. African-Am. Heritage, 1999-2005, Yale in Ky., 2000-, Ky. Opera, 2002-05; mem. Leadership Louisville Class, 1989-90; vestry Calvary Episc. Ch., 1990-92, jr. warden, 1995, sr. warden, 1996-97, vestry St. Francis in Fields Episc. Ch., 2004-2007; bd. dirs., Louisville Orch., 2006-, chmn. bd., 2008-, Partnership for Creative Economies, 2006-08; bd. dirs., Greater Louisville Fund For Arts, 2006-. Recipient 1st place award feature writing Ala. AP Assn., 1978, Silver Anvil award Pub. Rels. Soc. Am., 1985, 2009. Mem. Health Ins. Assn. Am. (pub. rels. policy com. 1989-93), America's Health Ins. Plans (strategic Commns. com. 1997-2004), Arthur W. Page Soc., Americas Health Insurance Plans(strategic com., 2004-) Republican. Anglican. Avocations: history, travel, French language and literature, running, racquetball. Office: Humana Inc 500 W Main St Louisville KY 40202-4268 Home Phone: 502-895-9635; Office Phone: 502-580-3674. Business E-Mail: tnoland@humana.com.

NOLAN-RIEGLE, MARY CATHERINE, biology professor; b. Ft. Meade, Md., June 8, 1954; BA in Biology, Montclair State U., NJ, 1976; MA in Botany, Rutgers U., New Brunswick, NJ, 1980; PhD in Plant Physiology, Rutgers U., 1983. Adminstrv. dir. Hill Pinckert Archs., 1984—89; chief fin. officer FKS, Inc., Districtly Kids, 1989—92; adj. prof. South Orange County Cmty. Coll., Mission Viejo, Calif., 1991—94; prof. Fullerton Coll., Calif., 1993—. Lead faculty biology Academic Senate Calif. Cmty. Colls., Sacramento, 2003—07, adv. com. numbering project, 2007—, lead faculty biology numbering project. Office: Fullerton Coll 321 E Chapman Ave Fullerton CA 92832 Business E-Mail: mnolanriegle@fullcoll.edu.

NOLASCO, LORI D., literature and language professor; b. Rochester, NY, Feb. 2, 1966; d. Frank J. and Carol A. Dovidio; m. Ramon Antonio Nolasco; children: Naun Antonio, Maher Dabbagh, Lanibel, Dania Dabbagh. BA in English, French, SUNY, Fredonia, 1987; MA in Comparative Lit., Sorbonne Paris IV, 1990; PhD in Comparative Lit., Sorbonne Paris III, 1995. Cert. in tchg. English as fgn. lang. Rutgers U., NJ, 1994, CLEP-Spanish, BA Level Coll. Bds., Princeton, NJ, 2008. Lectr.-multicultural lit. SUNY, Brockport, 2000—, St. John Fisher Coll., Rochester, NY, 2000—; writing ctr. instr. Rochester Inst. Tech., NY, 2006—; grant tutor-English-French-Spanish Monroe CC, Rochester. Translator, interpreter Premier Transl. Svcs., Fairport, NY, 2003—. Vol. Cath. Family Ctr., Rochester, 2007—08, Rochester Womens Network. Mem.: Rochester Internat. Coun., Rochester Poets, Casa Hispana Nazareth Coll. Liberal. Avocations: travel, music, poetry. Home: 66 Robin St Rochester NY 14613 Office: Rochester Inst Tech 1 Lomb Memorial Dr Rochester NY 14623 Personal E-mail: ldnolasco@gmail.com. Business E-Mail: lddelc@rit.edu.

NOLD, CARL RICHARD, museum administrator; b. Mineola, NY, Nov. 26, 1955; s. Carl Frederick and Joan Catherine (Heine) N.; m. Mary Beth Krivoruchka (div.). BA in History magna cum laude, St. John's U., Jamaica, NY, 1977; MA in History Mus. Studies, SUNY, Oneonta, 1982. Pres. Gregory Mus., Hicksville, N.Y., 1977; registrar N.Y. State Hist. Assn., Cooperstown, 1978-80; dir., curator Gadsby's Tavern Mus., Alexandria, Va., 1980-84; dir. State Mus. Pa., Harrisburg, 1984-91; exec. dir. Mackinac State Hist. Parks, Lansing, Mackinac Island, Mich., 1992—2003; pres., CEO Historic New Eng. (Soc. Preservation New England Antiquities), Boston, 2003—. Grant reviewer Inst. Mus. Svcs., Washington, 1982-90, 95—, mus. assessment prog. reviewer, 1985—, panelist, 1992-94; panelist mus. grant program Nat. Endowment for Humanities, 1990-93, panelist challenge grant program, 1997. Co-author: Gadsby's Tavern Mus. Interpretive Master Plan, 1984; contbr. articles to profl. jours. Mem. adv. bd. for Grad. History George Mason U., Fairfax, Va., 1982-84, Ctr. for Great Lakes Culture, Mich. State U., 2000-2002; adv. com. Susquehanna Mus. Art, Harrisburg, 1989-91; bd. dirs. Harrisburg-Hershey-Carlisle Tourism and Visitor Bur., 1987-91, bd. sec., 1990-91; mem. mayor's adv. bd. city of Mackinac Island, 1993-2003; mem. task force Mich. Cultural Tourism, 1998—; mem. Essex Nat. Heritage Commn., 2003-06. Fellow Mass. Hist. Soc.; mem. Assn. of Midwest Mus. (treas. 1998-2000, pres. 2000-2002, Mich. Mus. Assn. (bd. dirs. 1995-98, bd. sec. 1999-2001, Dist. Svc. award, 2002, 06), Am. Assn. Mus. (vis. com. mus. accreditation 1989—, chmn. coun. of regions 2000-01, MAP adv. com. 2002-, bd. dirs. 2003—, chair fin. com. 2005—, bd. vice chmn. 2007-08, bd. chair 2008-), Am. Assn. for State and Local History (elections chmn. 1990, mem. performance measurement program task force 2002-03), Colonial Soc. Mass. (audit com., 2007—), Cooperstown Grad. Assn. (bd. dirs. 1985-87), St. Botolph Club(Boston). Home: 21 Grove St Winchester MA 01890-3837 Office: Hist New Eng 141 Cambridge St Boston MA 02114-2702

NOLEN, ROY LEMUEL, retired lawyer; b. Montgomery, Ala., Nov. 29, 1937; s. Roy Lemuel Jr. and Elizabeth (Larkin) N.; m. Evelyn McNeill Thomas, Aug. 28, 1965; 1 child, Rives Rutledge. BArch, Rice U., 1961; LLB, Harvard U., 1967. Bar: Tex. 1968, U.S. Ct. Appeals (5th cir.) 1969. Law clk. to sr. judge U.S. Ct. Appeals (5th cir.), 1967-68; assoc. Baker Botts LLP, Houston, 1968-75, ptnr., 1976-2000; co-head Corp. Dept., 1985-90; mem. exec. com., 1988-91; adminstrv. ptnr., 1997-2000; ret., 2001. Cmty. rep. instnl. animal care and use com. M.D. Anderson Cancer Ctr., 2001—06. Bd. dirs. Houston Ballet Found., 1980-92, Rice Design Alliance, 1995-96; exec. com. Contemporary Arts Mus., 1990-96, 97-2002; exec. com. Houston Symphony Soc., 1994-99, gen. counsel, 1994-98; trustee Menil Found. (Menil Collection), 1999—, sr. warden Christ Ch. Cathedral, 1991-92, chancellor, 2003-08; chmn. Houston area devel. initiative Episcopal Diocese of Tex., 1997. 1st lt. USMC, 1961-64. Mem.: State Bar Tex., Briar Club, Paul Jones Dancing Club, Allegro, Coronado Club. Episcopalian. Office: Baker Botts LLP One Shell Plz 910 Louisiana St Houston TX 77002-4995 Office Phone: 713-229-1216. Personal E-mail: roynolen@aol.com.

NOLEN, SAMUEL AUGUSTUS, lawyer; b. Circleville, Ohio, Nov. 18, 1954; s. Jake Thomas and Amelia Aerl (Maverick) N.; m. Gail Anne McCurdy, May 17, 1980; children: S. Maverick, Maury McCurdy. Student, U. Regensburg, 1974-75; BA cum laude, Vanderbilt U., 1976; JD, Washington and Lee U., 1979. Bar: Del. 1979, US Dist. Ct. Del. 1980, US Ct. Appeals (3d cir.) 1985, US Supreme Ct. 2004. Law clk. Del. Ct. Chancery, Wilmington, 1979-80; assoc. Richards, Layton & Finger, Wilmington, 1980-86, mem., 1986—. Bd. dirs. Lex Mundi Pro Bono Found., 2006—. Mem. ABA, Internat. Bar Assn. (sect. bus. law), Del. Bar Assn. (sect. corp. law), Coun. Sect. Corp. Law, World Affairs Coun. Wilmington, Inc. (bd. dirs.), Lex Mundi Ltd. (bd. dirs. 2002—, exec. com. 2003—, chair 2007-08, chair emeritus 2008-), Greenville Country Club. Republican. Episcopalian. Office: Richards Layton & Finger 1 Rodney Sq Wilmington DE 19801-3305 Office Phone: 302-651-7752.

NOLEN, WILLIAM GILES, lawyer, accountant; b. Fayetteville, Ark., Aug. 4, 1931; s. William Jefferson and Marie (Giles) N.; m. Carole Turner, Aug. 25, 1957; children: Kathy, Thomas (dec.). BSBA, U. Ark., Fayetteville, 1960; JD, U. Houston, 1980. Bar: Tex. 1980; CPA, Tex. Auditor Arthur Andersen & Co., Houston, 1960-66; sec., treas. Brown & Root (U.K.) Ltd., London, 1966-69; v.p. Highlands Ins. Co., Houston, 1969-73, sr. v.p., 1973-80, dir., 1973-88; v.p. Halliburton Co., Dallas, 1980-82; sr. v.p. Brown & Root, Inc., Houston, 1982-86; exec. v.p. Highlands Ins. Co., Houston, 1986-88; of counsel Whitmore, Sheppard & Pollicoff, Houston, 1988-92, Policoff, Smith & Myres LLP, Houston, 1992-95, Policoff, Smith, Myres & Remels LLP, Houston, 1995-2000, Pollicoff, Smith & Remels, Houston, 2000—02. Maj. USAF, 1951-56. Mem. Am. Assn. Atty. CPAs (past pres., bd. dirs.), Tex. Soc. CPAs (Tex. CPA of Yr. 1961), Mensa. Presbyterian.

NOLEN HOLLAND, NOLA, choreographer; MFA, U. Okla., Norman. Choreographer (over twenty-five dance works) Red and Yellow, Black and White. Mem.: CORPS de Ballet Internat., Inc. (treas. 2008). Office: Slippery Rock Univ Pa Dance Dept 1 Morrow Way Slippery Rock PA 16057-1326 Office Fax: 724-738-4524. Business E-Mail: nola.nolen@sru.edu.

NOLFF, SUSAN D., web site designer, small business owner; b. Highland Park, Mich., Oct. 31, 1963; d. Kenneth A. and Georgia A. Blodick; m. Shawn R. Nolff, Aug. 25, 1984; children: Joshua L., Sheryl L. Slovinski, Daniele J. AAS in Visual Comm., Northwestern Mich. Coll., Traverse City, Mich., 2004; Webmaster Cert. (Level II), Northwestern Mich. Coll., 2005. Registered Gen. Contr., Mich., 1993. Archtl. draftsperson Cmty. Design, Inc., Traverse City, 1988—92; property mgmt./mortgage originator First of Am. Bank, Traverse City, Mich., 1992—95; real estate closer Corp. Title, Traverse City, 1995—97; gen. ptnr./ops. mgr. Countryside Constrn., Grawn, 1995—; paraprofessional-visual imaging tech. dept. Traverse Bay Area Intermediate Sch. Dist., Traverse City, 2003—05; web designer Byte Prodns., LLC, Traverse City, 2005—. Spkr., presenter, mentor Zonta Club, Traverse City, 2006; spreaker, presenter, mentor GirlTech, Traverse City, 2004—05. Recipient Adult Student of Yr. award, Northwestern C.C., 2003, Webmaster Departmental Award, Computer Info. Systems Dept. - Northwestern Mich. Coll., 2005; scholar Women's Coun. Scholarship, Home Builders Assn. Grand Traverse Area - Women's Coun., 2002—04, Edn. Scholarship, Home Builder's Assn. of the Grand Traverse Area, 2003, Home-In-A-Day Scholarship, 2002—04, Honors Scholarship, Northwestern Mich. Coll., 2003. Mem.: Visual Comm. Adv. Bd. (assoc.), Visual Imaging Tech. Adv. Bd. (assoc.), Mensa Soc. - NW Mich. Chpt. (assoc.), Phi Theta Kappa (life). Lutheran.

NOLL, JEANNE C., retired music educator; b. Reading, Pa., Aug. 12, 1935; d. Carl Foreman and Barbara Rebecca (Mengel) Winter; m. Clair W. Noll; children: Eric W., Douglas C. BS Music Edn., Lebanon Valley Coll., Annville, Pa., 1957; music student, West Chester U., Milligan U., Lehigh U., MIT. Cert. tchr. Pa., 1961. Tchr. elem. music North Coventry Elem. Sch., Chester County, Pa., Yokohama Army Sch., Japan, 1957—58; tchr. vocal jr. H.S. Reading Sch. Dist., Pa., 1959—61; organist, choir dir. St. Paul's United Ch. of Christ, Fleetwood, Pa., 1967—2001, organist/choir dir. emerita, 2002—; tchr. vocal music elem., jr. and sr. H.S. Kutztown Area Sch. Dist., Pa., 1981—94, dir. show choir, 1981—94. Accompanist Kutztown Cmty. Choir, 1999—2001, organist, mem., 2001—. Del. 17th congl. dist. Rep. Nat. Conv., NY, 2004, Minn., 2008, del. 6th congl. dist. Phila., 2000; mem. Rep. Com., Fleetwood, 1982—; com. woman Pa. Rep. state com., Harrisburg, 1998—; active Berks Area Muhlenberg Coun. Rep. Women, 1996, 2d v.p., 2006, dir., 2008; vice chair Berk County Rep. Com., 2005—, vice chair, acting chair, 2007—. Mem.: East Penn Valley Kiwanis Club (Dir., Key Club Advisor 1994—, Kiwanian of the Year 2000). Mem. United Ch. Of Christ. Avocations: travel, music, reading, politics.

NOLL, KENNETH EUGENE, air resources engineering educator; b. Brantwood, Wis., Aug. 20, 1936; s. Virgil R. and Pearl (Copland) N; m. Tatiana Gachomnina; children— Michael, Elizabeth. Registered profl. engr., Calif., Tenn., Ill. Sr. air resources engr. State of Calif., 1963-70; prof. air resources U. Tenn., 1970-75; prof. air resources engring. Ill. Inst. Tech., Chgo., 1975-2009, prof., chmn. environ. engring., 1989—97; dir. Regional Air Pollution Tng. Ctr. U.S. EPA. Author: Air Monitoring Survey Design, 1977, Recovery, Recycle and Reuse of Industrial Waste, 1984, Adsorption Technology for Air and Water Pollution Control, 1992, Fundamental Air Pollution Sys., 1999. Chmn. Knox County Air Pollution Control Bd., 1972-75. Served to 1st lt. USAF, 1959-63, Korea. U.S. EPA research fellow, 1968-69. Mem. ASCE, Air Pollution Control Assn. Office: Ill Inst Tech Dept Environ Engring 3201 S State St Dept Environ Chicago IL 60616 Home: 3252 S Canal St Chicago IL 60616-3510

NOLL, MARK A., history professor; BA in English, Wheaton Coll., Ill.; MA, Trinity Evangelical Div. Sch., Ill.; PhD in History of Christianity, Vanderbilt U., Nashville, 1975. Faculty Wheaton Coll., Ill., 1979—, McManis prof. Christian Thought Dept. History, 2006, co-founder and dir. Inst. Study Am. Evangs., 2006; Francis A. McAnaney prof. history U. Notre Dame, 2006—. Vis. lectr. Harvard Div. Sch., Chgo. Div. Sch., Westminster Theol. Sem., Regent Coll., Vancouver, BC. Contbr. articles to religious jours. Recipient Nat. Humanities Medal, NEH, 2006. Fellow: Am. Acad. Arts & Sci. Office: Dept History U Notre Dame 219 OShaughnessy Hall Notre Dame IN 46556 Office Phone: 574-631-7574. E-mail: Mark.Noll.8@nd.edu.

NOLL, RICHARD A., apparel executive; BBA, Pa. State Univ.; MBA with distinction, Carnegie Mellon Univ. CEO U.S. sock bus. Sara Lee Corp., Chgo., 1992—2002, COO bakery group, 2002—03, CEO bakery group, 2003—05, sr. v.p., pres. & COO branded apparel, 2005—06, CEO branded apparel, 2006; CEO Hanesbrands Inc., Winston Salem, NC, 2006—09, chmn., CEO, 2009—. Office: Hanesbrands Inc 1000 E Hanes Mill Rd Winston Salem NC 27105*

NOLL, ROGER GORDON, economist, educator; b. Monterey Park, Calif., Mar. 13, 1940; s. Cecil Ray and Hjordis Alberta (Westover) Noll; m. Robyn Schreiber, Aug. 25, 1962 (dec. Jan. 2000); 1 child, Kimberlee Elizabeth; m. Ann Seminara, Dec. 2, 2001. BS, Calif. Inst. Tech., 1962; AM, Harvard U., 1965, PhD in Econs, 1967. Mem. social sci. faculty Calif. Inst. Tech., 1965-84, prof., 1973-82, inst. prof., 1982-84, chmn. div. humanities and social scis., 1978-82; prof. econs. Stanford U., 1984—2006, Morris M. Doyle centennial prof. of pub. policy, 1990—2002, dir. pub. policy program, 1986—2002, dir. Am. Studies Program, 2001—02, dir. Ctr. for Internat. Devel., 2002—06, prof. emeritus, 2006—; Jean Monnet prof. European U. Inst., 1991; vis. fellow Brookings Instn., 1995-96, non-resident sr. fellow, 1996—2000, vis. scholar, 2003. Sr. staff economist Coun. Econ. Advisors, Washington, 1967—69; sr. fellow Brookings Instn., Washington, 1970—73; mem. tech. adv. bd. Com. Econ. Devel., 1978—82; mem. adv. coun. NSF, 1978—89, NASA, 1978—81, SERI, 1982—90; mem. Pres.'s Commn. Nat. Agenda for Eighties, 1980; chmn. L.A. Sch. Monitoring Com., 1978—79; mem. Commn. Behavioral Social Scis. and Edn. NAS, 1984—90, mem. bd. sci., tech. and econ. policy, 2000—06; mem. energy rsch. adv. bd. Dept. Energy, 1986—89; mem. Sec. Energy Adv. Bd., 1990—94, Calif. Coun. Sci. and Tech., 1995—2000; mem. bd. on sci., tech. and econ. policy NRC, 2001—07. Author: (book) Reforming Regulation, 1971, The Economics and Politics of Deregulation, 1991, The Economics and Politics of the Slowdown in Regulatory Reform, 1999; co-author: Economic Aspects of Television Regulation, 1973, The Political Economy of Deregulation, 1983, The Technology Pork Barrel, 1991; editor: Government and the Sports Business, 1974, Regulatory Policy and the Social Sciences, 1985, Challenges to Research Universities, 1998; co-editor: Constitutional Reform in California, 1995, Sports, Jobs and Taxes, 1997, A Communications Cornucopia, 1998; supervisory editor: Info. Econs. and Policy Jour., 1984—92. Recipient 1st ann. book award, Nat. Assn. Ednl. Broadcasters, 1974; grantee NSF, 1973—82; fellow Guggenheim, 1983—84. Mem.: Am. Econ. Assn. Democrat. Home: 4153 Hubbartt Dr Palo Alto CA 94306-3834 Office: Stanford U Dept Econs Stanford CA 94305 Office Phone: 650-723-2297. Business E-Mail: rnoll@stanford.edu.

NOLL, WALTER, mathematics professor; b. Berlin, Jan. 7, 1925; came to U.S., 1955, naturalized, 1961; s. Franz and Martha N.; m. Helga I. Schönberg, Apr. 1, 1955 (dec. Jan. 1976); children: Virginia, Peter; m. Mary T. Strauss, Jan. 4, 1979 (dec. Nov. 1999); m. Marilyn Smith Marsh, Dec. 30, 2000. Diplom-Ingenieur, Technische U. Berlin, 1951; Lincencié ès Sciences, U. Paris, 1950; PhD, Ind. U., 1954. Sci. asst. Technische U., Berlin, 1951-55; instr. U. So. Calif., 1955-56; assoc. prof. Carnegie-Mellon U., Pitts., 1956-60, prof., 1960—. Vis. prof. Johns Hopkins U., 1962-63, Oxford U. and U. of Pisa, 1984-85; vis. lectr. Soc. for Indsl. and Applied Math., 1969-71 Author: (with C. Truesdell) The Non-Linear Field Theories of Mechanics, 1965, 2d edit. 1992, 3d edit. 2004, (with B.D. Coleman, H. Markovitz) Viscometric Flows of Non-Newtonian Fluids, 1966, The Foundations of Mechanics and Thermodynamics, Selected Papers, 1974, Finite-Dimensional Spaces: Algebra, Geometry, and Analysis, vol. 1, 1987, Five Contributions to Natural Philosophy, 2005. Mem. Soc. for Natural Philosophy (founding, pres. 1973-75), Am. Math. Soc., Math. Assn. Am. Achievements include research in conceptual mathematical foundations of continuum mechanics and thermodynamics. Home: 308 Field Club Ridge Rd Pittsburgh PA 15238-2422 Business E-Mail: wn0g@andrew.cmu.edu.

NOLLER, HARRY FRANCIS, JR., biochemist, educator; b. Oakland, Calif., June 10, 1939; s. Harry Francis and Charlotte Frances (Silva) N.; m. Betty Lucille Parnow, Nov. 25, 1964 (div. 1969); 1 child, Maria Irene; m. Sharon Ann Sussman; 1 child, Eric Francis; stepchildren: Django Sussman, Seb Sussman; m. Laura Lancaster, 2008. AB, U. Calif., Berkeley, 1960; PhD, U. Oreg., 1965. NIH postdoctoral fellow MRC Lab. of Molecular Biology, Cambridge, 1965—66, Inst. Molecular Biology, Univ. Geneva, Switzerland, 1966—68; asst. prof. biology U. Calif., Santa Cruz, 1968-73, assoc. prof., 1973-79, prof. biology, 1979—, Robert Louis Sinsheimer prof. molecular biology, 1987—. Dir. Ctr. Molecular Biology of RNA, 1992-; lectr. in field. Contbr. articles to profl. jours. Recipient Newcomb-Cleve. Prize, 2001, Rosenstiel award in Basic Biomed. Sci., 2002, Judd award, Sloan Kettering, 2003, Massry prize, 2004, Paul Ehrlich and Ludwig Darmstaedter prize, Paul Ehrlich Found., 2007, Gairdner Found. Internat. award, 2007; named Spkr. of Yr., Netherlands Soc. for Biochemistry and Molecular Biology, 2002; Sherman Fairchild Disting. Scholar, Divsn Biology, Calif. Inst. Tech., 1989—90. Fellow Am. Acad. Arts and Scis.; mem. NAS, The RNA Soc. (pres.-elect 1997, pres. 1998, Lifetime Achievement award, 2003), Russian Acad. Scis., Am. Acad. Microbiology, AAAS (Newcomb Cleveland prize, 2002). Office: U Calif Santa Cruz 225 Sinsheimer Laboratories Santa Cruz CA 95064 Office Phone: 831-459-3703. Office Fax: 831-459-3737. Business E-Mail: noller@biology.ucsc.edu.

NOLLES, NIKI, literature and language professor; M, U. Nev., Las Vegas, 1980. Cert. profl. dept. chair Inst. Leadership Tng. and Devel., 1996, in tchg. excellence Outstanding Svc. to Student Tchg. and Learning, 1998. English and lit. faculty Red Rocks CC, Lakewood, Colo., 1990—, accreditation report writer, 2008. Mem.: Phi Kappa Phi. Avocation: travel. Office Phone: 303-914-6377. Business E-Mail: niki.nolles@rrcc.edu.

NOLPH, GEORGIA BOWER, physician; b. Appleton, Minn., Jan. 26, 1938; d. Clarence Walter and Gladys Mae (Hanson) Bower; m. Karl David Nolph, July 26, 1961; children: Erika Lynn, Kristoper Karl. BA, St. Olaf Coll., 1960; MD, Woman's Med. Coll. Pa., 1964. Pvt. practice with G.H. Ferguson MD, Bala-Cynwyd, Pa., 1965-67; civil service Walter Reed Army Med. Ctr., Washington, 1967-69; instr. community health and med. practice U. Mo., Columbia, 1969-70; asst. prof. U. Mo. Med. Sch., Columbia, 1970-77, assoc. prof. family and community medicine, 1977—. Acting med. dir. Family Med. Care Ctr., U. Mo. Hosp. and Clinics, Columbia, 1980—87; med. dir. NBA Lenoir Retirement Cmty., 1987—99, Lenoir bd. dirs., 2000—05, v.p., 2001—03, pres., 2003—05. Assoc. editor. (profl. jour.) Continuing Education for the Family Physician, 1972-73. V.p. Parents for Drug Free Youth, Columbia, Mo., 1985-86, 86-87, pres. 1987-88, 88-89; bd. dir. Columbia Civic Orch. Mem.: Boone County Med. Soc., Mo. State Med. Assn., Am. Bus. Women's Assn. (pres. Boone Belles chpt. 2004—06), Am. Med. Women's Assn. (state dir. 1975—2003, region VII gov. 1996—2003), Boone Belles Social Club (pres. 2006—), Am. Legion Aux. Republican. Methodist. Avocations: music, reading, travel, needlecrafts. Home: 908 Hickory Hill Dr Columbia MO 65203-2320 Office: U Mo Med Sch Dept Family and Cmty Medicine 1 Hospital Dr Columbia MO 65201-5276

NOLTE, NICK, actor; b. Omaha, Feb. 8, 1941; m. Sheila Page, 1966 (div. 1971), m. Sharon Haddad, May 10, 1978 (div. 1983); m. Rebecca Linger, Feb. 19, 1984 (div. 1995); 1 child, Brawley King; 1 child with Clytie Lane Student, Ariz. St. Univ., Eastern Ariz. Coll., Pasadena City Coll., Phoenix City Coll.; studies with, John Paul, Allen Dutton. Actor:

(play) The Last Pad, 1973, (TV movies) Winter Kill, 1974, The California Kid, 1974, Death Sentence, 1974, (TV series) Adams of Eagle Lake, 1975, (TV movies) The Treasure Chest Murder, 1975, The Runaway Barge, 1975, (mini-series) Rich Man, Poor Man, 1976; (films) Return to Macon County, 1975, The Deep, 1977, Who'll Stop the Rain, 1978, North Dallas Forty, 1979, Heart Beat, 1980, Cannery Row, 1982, 48 Hours, 1982, Under Fire, 1983, The Ultimate Solution of Grace Quigley, 1984, Teachers, 1984, Down and Out in Beverly Hills, 1986, Weeds, 1987, Extreme Prejudice, 1987, Farewell to the King, 1988, Three Fugitives, 1988, New York Stories, 1989, Everybody Wins, 1989, Q & A, 1990, Another 48 Hours, 1990, Prince of Tides, 1991, Cape Fear, 1991, Lorenzo's Oil, 1992, The Player, 1992, Blue Chips, 1994, I'll Do Anything, 1994, I Love Trouble, 1994, Jefferson in Paris, 1995, Mulholland Falls, 1996, Mother Night, 1996, Nightwatch, 1997, Afterglow, 1997, U-Turn, 1997, Affliction (also exec. prod), 1998, The Thin Red Line, 1998, The Best of Enemies, 1999, Simpatico, 1999, Breakfast of Champions, 1999, The Golden Bowl, 2000, Trixie, 2000, Investigating Sex (also prod.), 2001, The Good Thief, 2002, Northfork, 2003, The Hulk, 2003, (voice only) Over the Hedge, 2006, Peaceful Warrior, 2006, (voice) The Spiderwick Chronicles, 2008, The Mysteries of Pittsburgh, 2008, Chicago, 2008.

NOLTING, DANIEL LINCOLN, school librarian; b. Waverly, Iowa, Feb. 12, 1963; s. Wendell Leroy and Janice Marie Nolting; children: Wilhelmina Lynn, Josephine Matheson. BFA, U. Northern Iowa, Cedar Falls, 1986; MFA, Pratt Inst., Brooklyn, 1991; MS-LIS, Pratt Inst., NY, 1997. Visual resources cataloger Yale U., New Haven, 1999—2002; head libr. tech. sec. Chatham U., Pittsburgh, 2003. Grantee NEA, Wash., 1993. Mem.: Visual Resources Divsn., Art Lib. Soc. North America (webmaster 2003). Achievements include patents for media control device. Office: Chatham Univ JKM Libr Pittsburgh PA 15232 Business E-Mail: dnolting@chatham.edu.

NOMAKUCHI, TAMOTSU, electronics executive; b. Kagoshima, Japan, Nov. 18, 1940; Postgraduate studies, Kyoto U., 1965; MS, Osaks U., 1975; PhD, Osaku U., 1978. Researcher, Ctrl. Rsach. Lab. Mitsubishi Electric Corp., Japan, 1965—97, dir., info. tech., 1995—97, sr. v.p., v.p., corp. R&D develop. unit, 1997—2001, exec. v.p., v.p. info. tech., 2001—02, pres., CEO, 2002—06, chmn., 2006—. Bd. dir. Mitsubishi Electric Corp., 1995—2005. Mem.: Japan Electronics and Info. Tech. Industries Assn. (vice-chmn. exec. bd., indsl. equipment and social systems), Assn. Radio Industries and Businesses (dir. 2005—), Comm. and Info. Network Assn. Japan (chmn. 2005—). Office: Mitsubishi Electric Corp 2-7-3 Marunouchi Chiyoda-ku Tokyo 100-8310 Japan

NOMURA, JASON T., emergency physician; s. Lloyd T. and Avis F. Nomura. BA, U. Hawaii, Hilo, 1999; MD, John A Burns Sch. Medicine U. Hawaii, Honolulu, 2003. Diplomate Am. Bd. Internal Medicine, 2008. Emergency medicine-internal medicine resident Christiana Care Health Sys., Newark, Del., 2003—08, emergency medicine-internal medicine chief resident, 2007—08, emergency physician, 2008—, internal medicine physician, 2008—, assoc. dir. emergency ultrasound, 2009. Contbr. articles to med. jours. Recipient Paul Shaw Meml. award, Christiana Care Health Sys., 2007, Resident Academic Excellence award, Emergency Medicine Residents Assn., 2008; fellowship, Christiana Care Health Sys., 2009—. Mem.: AMA, ACP, Med. Soc. Del., Soc. Academic Emergency Medicine, Am. Acad. Emergency Medicine, Am. Coll. Emergency Medicine, Am. Inst. Ultrasound in Medicine, Am. MENSA. Office: Christiana Care Health Sys 4755 Ogletown Stanton Rd Newark DE 19718

NONIS, DAVID, professional sports team executive; b. Burnaby, BC, Can., May 25, 1966; m. Susan Nonis; 1 child, Nicholas. BA, U. Maine, 1988, MBA, 1990. Asst. corp. contracts, computer scouting and team svcs. Vancouver Canucks, 1990—94, sr. v.p., dir. hockey ops., 1998—2004, gen. mgr., 2004—08; mgr. hockey ops. NHL, 1994—98; sr. advisor Anaheim Ducks, 2008—. Office: Anaheim Ducks 2695 E Katella Ave Anaheim CA 92806

NONNA, JOHN MICHAEL, lawyer; b. NYC, July 8, 1948; s. Angelo and Josephine (Visconti) N.; m. Jean Wanda (Cleary), June 9, 1973; children: Elizabeth, Caroline, Marianne, Timothy. BA, Princeton U., 1970; JD, NYU, 1975. Bar: NY 1976, US Dist. Ct. (so. dist.) NY, 1978, US Ct. Appeals (2d cir.) 1978, US Ct. Appeals (9th cir.) 1980, US Ct. Appeals (5th cir.) 1997, US Ct. Appeals (7th cir.), US Dist. Ct. Conn. 1988, US Supreme Ct. 1998, US Ct. Appeals (DC cir.) 2007. Law asst. to Hon. D.L. Gabrielli N.Y. Ct. Appeals, Albany, 1975-77; assoc. Reid and Priest, NYC, 1977-84; ptnr. Werner and Kennedy, NYC, 1984-99, LeBoeuf, Lamb, Greene, and MacRae, NYC, 1999—2007, Dewey and LeBeouf, 2008—. Contbr. articles to profl. jours. With Westchester County Bd. Legislators 2008-; dep. mayor, trustee Pleasantville, NY, 1990-95; mayor, 1995-2003; acting justice, 1983-89; fellow, Am. Coll. Trial Lawyers; bd. dirs. Lawyers Com. for Civil Rights Under the Law. With USNR, 1970-75. Mem. U.S. Olympic Team, 1972, 1980; Congr. Medal of Achievement, Paul Harris fellow Rotary Internat. Fellow Am. Bar Found. (life), ABA (torts and ins. practice sect. com. chair 1986-87, 92-93), NY State Bar Assn. (chair comml. and fed. litig. sect. 1998-99, co-editor in chief 2000, NY Ins. Law Practice), Assn. Bar City NY, NY Fencers Club (pres. 1990-93). Avocations: fencing, running, piano. Home Phone: 914-769-8961. Business E-Mail: jnonna@dl.com.

NOONAN, JACQUELINE ANNE, pediatrician, educator; b. Burlington, Vt., Oct. 28, 1928; BA, Albertus Magnus Coll., New Haven, Conn., 1950; MD, U. Vt., Burlington, 1954, DSc (hon.), 1980. Diplomate Am. Bd. Pediatrics, Am. Bd. Pediatric Cardiology. Intern N.C. Meml. Hosp., Chapel Hill, 1954-55; resident in pediatrics Children's Hosp., Cin., 1955-57; rsch. fellow Children's Med. Ctr., Boston, 1957-59; asst. prof. pediatrics State U. Iowa Sch. Medicine, 1959-61; asst. prof. pediatrics cardiology U. Ky. Coll. Medicine, Lexington, 1961-64, assoc. prof., 1964-69, prof., 1969-99, chmn. dept. pediatrics, 1974-92, emeritus prof., 1999—. Mem. embryology and human devel. study sect. NIH, 1973-78; mem. US-USSR Symposium on Congenital Heart Disease, 1975; mem. sub. bd. pediatric cardiology Am. Bd. Pediatrics, 1977-82; examiner, mem. test. com. Nat. Bd. Med. Examiners, 1984-90, exec. com., 1991-95; participant various confs. in field; vis. prof. Vanderbilt U., Nashville, 1987; spkr. in field. Contbr. articles, revs. to med. publs.; mem. editl. bd. Am. Jour. Diseases Children, 1970-80, Am. Jour. Med. Edn., 1975-78, Pediatric Cardiology, 1978-90, Am. Heart Jour., 1994-96, Clin. Pediatrics, 1990-99. Fellow: Royal Coll. Irish Physicians (hon.); mem.: AMA, So. Soc. Pediat. Rsch. (pres. 1972), Soc. Pediat. Rsch., NIH Alumni Assn., Ky. State Med. Assn., Irish-Am. Pediat. Soc. (pres. 1999—2001), Fayette County Pediat. Soc., Am. Pediat. Soc., Assn. Med. Sch. Pediatrics (dept. chmn. exec. com. 1978—81), Am. Coll. Cardiology (gov. Ky. chpt. 1989—92), Am. Acad. Pediatrics (chmn. cardiol. sect. 1972—74). Business E-Mail: jnoonan@uky.edu.

NOONAN, JAMES C., lawyer, mediator, arbitrator; b. Chgo., July 16, 1928; s. T. Clifford and Ethel (Jennett) N.; m. Carol Colbert, Nov. 24, 1954 (div. June 1975); children: James, Christopher, Mary, Anne, Catherine; m. Ardis Niemann, May 24, 1986. AB, U. Notre Dame, 1953, MA in Criminology, 1954; JD, William Mitchell Coll. Law, St. Paul, 1962. Bar: Minn. 1962, U.S. Dist. Ct. Minn. 1963, U.S. Ct. Appeals (8th cir.) 1971, U.S. Supreme Ct. 1969. Probation officer Ramsey County Juvenile Ct., St. Paul, 1954-57; supt. Woodview Detention Home, St. Paul, 1957-63; assoc. Firestone, Fink, Krawetz, Miley, O'Neill, St. Paul, 1963-67; ptnr. Firestone Fink, Krawetz, Miley, Maas and Noonan, St. Paul, 1967-70, Magistad & Noonan, St. Paul, 1971-75; owner James C. Noonan and Assocs., St. Paul, 1975—. Mem. adv. bd. Home of Good Shepherd, St. Paul, 1958-74; mem. citizen adv. bd. Detention and Corrections Authority, St. Paul, 1966-80. Mem. ABA, Minn. State Bar Assn., Ramsey County Bar Assn., St. Paul Amateur Radio Club, Am. Radio Relay League. Roman Catholic. Avocation: amateur radio (w9osn). Home (Winter): 2015 E Edison St Tucson AZ 85719-3801 Home Phone: 651-222-2180, 520-318-6222.

NOONAN, JOHN GERARD, bishop emeritus; b. Limerick, Ireland, Feb. 26, 1951; s. John and Margaret Purcell Noonan. BA, St. John Vianney Coll. Sem., Miami, 1977—79; MDiv, St. Vincent de Paul Regional Sem., Boynton Beach, 1979—83; MEd, Boston Coll., 1993—96. Ordained priest Archdiocese of Miami, 1983; parochial vicar St. Elizabeth of Hungry, Pompano Beach, 1983—89; chaplain Youth Ministry, Broward County, 1985—87; dean of men St. John Vianney Coll. Sem., 1989—93, pres., rector, 1996—; supervising prin. Msgr. Edward Pace High Sch., 1993—94, St. Brendan High Sch., Miami, 1994—96; dir. Priestly Life and Ministry, 2001—; ordained bishop, 2005; aux. bishop Archdiocese of Miami, 2005—. Roman Catholic. Office: Archdiocese of Miami 9401 Biscayne Blvd Miami FL 33138

NOONAN, JOHN T., JR., federal judge, educator; b. Boston, Oct. 24, 1926; s. John T. and Marie (Shea) Noonan; m. Mary Lee Bennett, Dec. 27, 1967; children: John Kenneth, Rebecca Lee, Susanna Bain. BA, Harvard U., 1946, LLB, 1954; student, Cambridge U., 1946—47; MA, Cath. U. Am., 1949, PhD, 1951, LHD, 1980, Holy Cross Coll., 1980, Loyola U., Chgo., 1999; LLD, U. Santa Clara, 1974, U. Notre Dame, 1976, Loyola U. South, 1978, St. Louis U., 1981, Duquesne U., 1995, Valparaiso U., 1996, U. San Diego, 1999, Gonzaga U., 1986, U. San Francisco, 1986. Bar: Mass. 1954, US Supreme Ct. 1971. Mem. spl. staff Nat. Security Council, 1954-55; pvt. practice Herrick & Smith, Boston, 1955-60; prof. law U. Notre Dame, 1961-66, U. Calif., Berkeley, 1967-86, chmn. religious studies, 1970-73, chmn. medieval studies, 1978-79; judge US Ct. Appeals (9th cir.), San Francisco, 1985-96, sr. judge, 1996—. Oliver Wendell Holmes, Jr. lectr. Harvard U. Law Sch., 1972; Pope John XXIII lectr. Cath. U. Law Sch., 1973; Cardinal Bellarmine lectr. St. Louis U. Div. Sch., 1973; Ernest Messenger lectr. Cornell U., 1982; John Dewey Meml. lectr. U. Minn., 1986; Baum lectr. U. Ill., 1988; Strassberger lectr. U. Tex., 1989; chmn. bd. Games Rsch., Inc., 1961—76; overseer Harvard U., 1991—97; Maguire chair in ethics Libr. of Congress, 2002; vis. prof. U. Catania, Sicily, Italy, 2002; vis. Disting. prof. kaw Emory U., 2000; Erasmus lectr. U. Notre Dame, 2003. Author: The Scholastic Analysis of Usury, 1957, Contraception: A History of Its Treatment by the Catholic Theologians and Canonists, 1965, Power to Dissolve, 1972, Persons and Masks of the Law, 1976, The Antelope, 1977, A Private Choice, 1979, Bribes, 1984, The Responsible Judge, 1993, Professional and Personal Responsibilities of the Lawyer, 1997, Canons and Canonists in Context, 1997, The Lustre of Our Country, 1998, Narrowing the Nation's Power, 2002, A Church That Can and Cannot Change, 2005; editor: Natural Law Forum, 1961—70, Am. Jour. Jurisprudence, 1970, The Morality of Abortion, 1970. Chmn. Brookline Redevel. Authority, Mass., 1958—62; cons. Papal Commn. on Family, 1965—66, Ford Found., Indonesian Legal Program, 1968, NIH, 1973, 1974; expert Presdl. Commn. on Population and Am. Future, 1971; pres. Thomas More-Jacques Maritain Inst., 1977—; trustee Population Coun., 1969—76, Phi Kappa Found., 1970—76, U. San Francisco, 1971—75; mem. com. theol. edn. Yale U., 1972—77; cons. U.S. Cath. Conf., 1979—86; sec., treas. Inst. for Rsch. in Medieval Canon Law, 1970—88; trustee Grad. Theol. Union, 1970—73; exec. com. Cath. Commn. Intellectual and Cultural Affairs, 1972—75; bd. dirs. Ctr. for Human Values in the Health Scis., 1969—71, S.W. Intergroup Rels. Coun., 1970—72, Inst. for Study Ethical Issues, 1971—73. Recipient St. Thomas More award, U. San Francisco, 1974, Christian Culture medal, 1975, Laetare medal, U. Notre Dame, 1984, Campion medal, Cath. Book Club, 1987, Alemany medal, Western Dominican Province, 1988; fellow Guggenheim fellow, 1965—66, 1979—80, Ctr. for Advanced Studies in Behavioral Scis. fellow, 1973—74, Wilson Ctr. fellow, 1979—80, Kluge chair in Am. law and govt., Libr. Congress Ctr. for Scholars, 2002. Fellow: Am. Acad. Arts and Scis., Am. Soc. Legal Historians (hon.); mem.: Am. Law Inst., Canon Law Soc. Am. (gov. 1970—72), Am. Soc. Polit. and Legal Philosophy (v.p. 1964), Phi Beta Kappa (senator United chpts. 1970—72, pres. Alpha of Calif. chpt. 1972—73). Office: US Ct Appeals 9th Cir 95 7th St San Francisco CA 94103-1526*

NOONAN, JOSETTE MARIE, music educator; b. Melrose Park, Ill., Mar. 6, 1955; d. Frank Eugene and Barbara Ann Noonan. ADN, Waubonsee Coll., Ill., 1984; MusB, DePaul U., 1990. Registered Profl. Nurse, Ill., 1984; cert. musikgarten educator 1999, dir. music ministries 2005. Music dir. St. Mary's Ch., West Chgo., Ill.; RN surg. resource team Children's Meml. Med. Ctr., Chgo., 1985—90; singer Grant Pk. Symphony Chorus, 1985—90; artist in residence Coll. of DuPage, Glen Ellyn, Ill., 1987—88; asst. dir. Light Opera Works, Evanston, Ill., 1990—91; RN rehab. Oak Pk. Hosp., Ill., 1992—97; soprano soloist and sect. leader First United Meth. Ch. at Chgo. Temple, Chgo., 1993—2004, children's choir dir., 1999—2003; voice tchr. No. Ill. U. Cmty. Sch. of Music, DeKalb, Ill., 1999—2002; music and movement tchr. No. Ill. U. Suzuki Sch., DeKalb, 1999—2002; tchr. voice and strings Countryside Music Sch., Elburn, Ill., 1999—2007; music tchr. Creative Beginning Presch., 2005—07. Violist Celebration String Quartet, Arlington Heights, Ill., 2000—04; dir. Countryside Players, Elburn, Ill., 2002—07, Kindechor and Angeli Musicali Children's Choirs St. Mary's, West Chgo., Ill., 2005—06, St. Mary's Players, 2005—08; choir Kinderchor and Pouth Cancer, 2005—06; founder and adminstr. Patrick Edgar Triplett Meml. Scholarship Program; rehabilitative music specialist Healing Harps, DeKalb, Ill., 2000—03; guest artist German Song Text Workshop, Vienna, 2004, Assisi Music Festival, Italy, 2005—08, Mladi Fest, Medjugorje, Bosnia-Herzegovina, 2005, Accademia Voci d'Estate, Verona, Italy, 2006—08, Art Song Festival, 2006. Composer: (songs) Songs for Children's Worship; arranger (musical) From Mozart to Moulin Rouge; singer: (improvisatory music for dance troupe) The Death of the King, author of poems. Past pres. Ill. Collegiate Music Educators, Mokena, Ill., 2000—01; canvas voters to encourage passage of referendum for schs. Save our Schs., West Chgo., Ill., 1970; fed and clothed homeless people First United Meth. Ch. at Chgo., Chgo., 2000—02; care and concern ministry First United Meth. Ch. at Chgo. Temple, Chgo., 2002—04; mem. Pax Christi, 2005—06, Christian Peacemaker Team, 2005—06, Kairos Retreat Leadership Team, 2006. Recipient Invitation to sing for Martin Katz, DePaul U., 1987, Invited to sing for John Wustman, 1988, Invitation to sing Honors Recitals, 1985—88, Invited to sing and speak at a meml. concert honoring composer, Moses Hogan, Abyssinian Bapt. Ch. NY, 2002, First prize, Italian Cultural Soc. Voice Competition, 1988. Mem.: Nat. Assn. Pastoral Musicians, Nat. Guild Hypnotists (assoc.), Am. Choral Dirs. Assn. (assoc.; treas. local chpt. 1999—2001), Music Educator's Nat. Conf. (assoc.; pres. of ill. collegiate assn. 2000—01), Healing Harps (assoc.). Independent. Achievements include development of music program for autistic children at Northern Illinois University; music and movement program for local preschool; specialist in German Lied interpretation, Gregorian Chant; planned, executed and evaluated a weekend workshop for music education students in the state of Illinois entitled, What I didn't learn in music school. Avocations: backpacking, german language and culture, scuba diving, fiddling, hypnosis, languages. Home: 324 Church St West Chicago IL 60185 Office: St Mary's Church 140 North Oakwood Avenue West Chicago IL 60185 Office Fax: 630-293-2671. E-mail: scotchdiva@aol.com.

NOONAN, PATRICK FRANCIS, conservation executive; b. St. Petersburg, Fla., Dec. 2, 1942; s. Francis Patrick and Henrietta (Donovan) Noonan; m. Nancy Elizabeth Peck, Aug. 15, 1964; children: Karen Elizabeth(dec.), Dawn Wiley. BA, Gettysburg Coll., 1965; M in City and Regional Planning, Catholic U. Am., 1967; MBA, Am. U., 1971. V.p., pres. The Nature Conservancy, 1968—80; founder, dir., chmn. Am. Farmland Trust, 1980—97; founder, chmn., pres. The Conservation Fund, 1985—2003, chmn. emeritus, 2003—. Trustee Nat. Geog. Soc., 1990—; vice chmn. Nat. Geog. Edn. Found., 1995—; trustee Gettysburg Coll., 1978—91, Duke U. Sch. Environment, 1979—, Ind. Sector, 1984—91, Am. Conservation Assn., 1986—, Natural Resources Coun. Am., 1996—2002; dir. Ashland, 1991—2006, Internat. Paper, 1993—2004, Saul Ctrs., 1993—; mem. Pres.' Commn. on Am. Outdoors, 1985—87, Pres.' Commn. on Environ. Quality, 1991—93, Pres.' Commn. on White House Fellows, 2001—08. MacArthur Found. fellow, 1985—90. Home: 3553 Hamlet Pl Chevy Chase MD 20815

NOONAN, PATRICK SUTTON, author management educator; b. Springfield, Ill., July 11, 1955; s. Patrick Arthur and Julia Ann (Sutton) N.; m. M. Jo Howarth, Apr. 27, 1985; children: Paul Howarth, William Prindiville. BS in Engring. Sci., Yale U., 1977, MBA, 1984; MS in Engring. Sci., Harvard U., 1989, PhD in Decision Scis., 1992. Dir. and gen. mgr. East River Consort, Boston, 1977—80; pres. Greenpeace New Eng., Boston, 1980-82; assoc. McKinsey & Co., Inc., NYC, 1984-88; prin. Planning Techs. Group, Inc., Lexington, Mass., 1990—98; assoc. prof. Emory U., 1993—; Fulbright sr. specialist, 2005. Author, Decision and Info. Analysis, 2009; Prodr. record albums, including Laurasia, 1978, Undiscovered Country, 1988, Beat Noir, 1996, Scott's Red Star, 2000; prodr. film Journey to Georges Bank, 1982. Office Phone: 404-727-0549. Business E-Mail: pnoonan@emory.edu.

NOONAN, PEGGY (MARGARET ELLEN NOONAN), columnist, writer; b. Bklyn., Sept. 7, 1950; d. Jim and Mary Jane (Byrne) Noonan; m. Richard Kahn, Nov. 27, 1985 (div. 1990); 1 child, Will. BA in English Lit. & Journalism, Fairleigh Dickinson U., Rutherford, NJ, 1974, PhD (hon.), 1990; D (hon.), St. John Fisher Coll., Adelphi Coll., Miami U., St. Francis Coll. Premium adjuster Aetna Ins. Co., Newark, 1968-70; temp. agy. sec. NYC, 1974; news staffer WEEI Radio (CBS station), Boston, 1974, editl. dir., 1975-77; writer, editor CBS News, NYC, 1977-80, commentary for Walter Cronkite and Dan Rather, 1980-81, full time commentary writer for Dan Rather, 1981-84; White House speech writing tech. for Ronald Reagan, Washington, 1984-86; White House speech writer for George Bush, Washington, 1988-89; now weekly columnist Wall St. Jour. Adj. prof. journalism NYU, 1978—79; bd. trustees Manhattan Inst. Policy Rsch. Author: What I Saw at the Revolution: A Political Life in the Reagan Era, 1990, Life, Liberty and the Pursuit of Happiness, 1994, Simply Speaking: How to Communicate Your Ideas With Style, Substance, and Clarity, 1998, On Speaking Well, 1999, The Case Against Hillary Clinton, When Character Was King: A Story of Ronald Reagan, 2001, A Heart, A Cross And A Flag, 2003, John Paul The Great: Remembering a Spiritual Father, 2005, Patriotic Grace: What It Is and Why We Need It Now, 2008; guest editor Mademoiselle mag.; contbg. editor TIME mag., Good Housekeeping, contbr. (TV series) The West Wing. Named Mother of Yr., Nat. Mother's Day Commn., 1990. Republican. Roman Catholic. Office: Icm Artists 470 Park Ave S New York NY 10016-6819 also: Wall St Jour Editl & Bus Hdqs 200 Liberty St New York NY 10281*

NOONE, ROBERT BARRETT, plastic surgeon; b. Scranton, Pa., Oct. 30, 1939; s. Robert Patrick and Margaret Ann (Barrett) N.; m. Barbara Ellen Atkins, May 29, 1965; children: Robert B. Jr., Megan J., Genevieve C., Rebecca B., Theresa Ann. BS, U. Scranton, 1961; MD, U. Pa., 1965. Diplomate Am. Bd. Surgery, Am. Bd. Plastic Surgery. Rotating intern Hosp. of U. Pa., Phila., 1965-66, resident in surgery, 1966-71, resident in plastic surgery, 1971-73; asst. prof. surgery Sch. Medicine, U. Pa., Phila., 1974-83, clin. assoc. prof. surgery, 1983-89, clin. prof. surgery, 1989—; head sect. on plastic surgery Pa. Hosp., Phila., 1974-80; chief svc. plastic surgery Bryn Mawr (Pa.) Hosp., 1977—2005, chmn. dept. surgery, 1991—2001; chief svc. plastic surgery Lankenau Hosp., Phila., 1980-91; exec. dir. Am. Bd. Plastic Surgery, 1997—. Bd. dirs. Am. Bd. Plastic Surgery, Phila., 1987-94, vice chmn. 1993-94; bd. dirs. Plastic Surgery Ednl. Found., Chgo., 1981-91, pres. 1989-90. Contbr. articles to profl. jours. Bd. dirs., trustee Rosemont Sch. of the Holy Child, Pa., 1983-87, U. Scranton, 1998—2004, vice-chair, 2002-04. Capt. USAF, 1967-69. Recipient Frank J. O'Hara Disting. Alumnus award U. Scranton, 1986, Magee-Woodruff award Bryn Mawr Hosp., 2005. Fellow ACS (bd. govs. 1994-98); mem. AMA (del. plastic surgery 1986-88), Am. Soc. Plastic and Reconstructive Surgery (bd. dirs. 1989-90, 92-95, chmn. bd. trustees 1994-95), Am. Assn. Plastic Surgeons (sec. 1995-98, v.p. 1998-99, pres.-elect 1999-2000, pres. 2000-01, disting. fellow 2006), Northeastern Soc. Plastic Surgeons (pres. 1985-86), Robert H. Ivy Soc. (pres. 1982-83), Merion Cricket Club, Phila. Country Club, Eagles Mere Country Club. Republican. Roman Catholic. Avocations: golf, tennis, photography, swimming, travel, reading. Home: 234 Cheswold Hill Rd Haverford PA 19041-1814 Office: Plastic & Reconstructive Surg Assocs 888 Glenbrook Ave Bryn Mawr PA 19010-2506 Office Phone: 610-527-4833. E-mail: RBNoone@aol.com.

NOONKESTER, JAMES RALPH, retired college president; b. Flatridge, Va., June 10, 1924; s. Reggie L. and Arcie (Parks) N.; m. Naomi Hopkins, June 10, 1947; children: Myron Craig, Lila. BA, U. Richmond, 1944, LLD, 1968; ThM, So. Bapt. Theol. Sem., 1947, PhD, 1949; LHD (hon.), Blue Mountain Coll., 1982; postgrad., Harvard U., 1980. Minister edn. 1st Bapt. Ch., Charlottesville, Va., 1950-52; prof., head div. religion and philosophy William Carey U., Hattiesburg, Miss., 1952-53, acad. dean, 1953-56, pres., 1956-89, pres. emeritus, 1989—. Pres. Miss. Found. Ind. Colls.; mem. Edn. commn. So. Bapt. Conv., chmn., 1983; bd. dirs. Miss. Sch. Bds. Assn. Workers Compensation Trust, 1993-95, chmn., 1994. Chmn. bd. dirs. Am. Cancer Soc., Miss. divsn., 1966; campaign chmn. United Givers Fund, 1975-76, pres. 1976-77; coun. chmn. Boy Scouts Am., dir. Planned Giving Pine Burr area Boy Scouts Am., 1990-93; trustee Hattiesburg Pub. Schs., 1990-95, pres. bd. trustees, 1992-95 Named Outstanding Grad. English U. Richmond, 1944, Hattiesburg's Outstanding Young Man of 1956, Sales and Mktg. Execs. Man of Yr., 1983; recipient Silver Beaver award Boy Scouts Am., 1981, HUB award, 1983 Mem. NEA, Miss. Edn. Assn., Hattiesburg Concert Assn. (bd. dir.), So. Assn. Bapt. Colls. and Schs. (pres.), Miss.

Assn. Colls. (pres.), Hattiesburg C. of C. (pres. 1966), Kiwanis, Phi Beta Kappa, Phi Delta Kappa, Chi Beta Phi, Omicron Delta Kappa. Home: 100 Lesley Ln Hattiesburg MS 39402-2922

NOOR, AHMED KHAIRY, engineering educator, researcher; b. Cairo, Egypt, Aug. 11, 1938; s. Mohamed Sayed and Fatma Mohamed (El-Zeini) N.; m. Zakia Mahmoud Taha, Aug. 18, 1966; 1 child. Mohamed. BS with honors, Cairo (Egypt) U., 1958; M.S., U. Ill., Urbana, 1961, PhD, 1963. Asst. prof. aero. and astronautics Stanford U., 1963-64; sr. lectr. structural mechanics, Cairo (Egypt) U., 1964-67; vis. sr. lectr. structural mechanics U. Baghdad, Iraq, 1967-68; sr. lectr. structural mechanics U. New South Wales, Australia, 1968-71; NRC sen. resident postdoct. res. assoc. NASA Langley Rsch. Center, Hampton, Va., 1971-72; prof. engring. and applied sci. George Washington U., Hampton, Va., 1972-90; Ferman W. Perry prof. aerospace structures and applied mechanics U. Va.; dir. advanced computational tech. ctr. NASA Langley Rsch. Ctr., Hampton, Va., William E. Lobeck prof. acrospace engring., emeritus scholar & dir. Ctr. Advanced Engring. Environments, Old Dominion U., Norflok, Va.; mem. coms. computational mechanics and large space systems Nat. Acad. Engring. Fellow AIAA, ASME, ASCE, Am. Acad. Mechanics, Internat. Assn. for Computational Mechanics (founder mem., pres.), U.S. Assn. for Computational Mechanics, Sigma Xi. Editor-in-chief Jour. Advances in Engineering Software; editor books on structures and solids and computational mechanics; mem. editorial bd. of several tech. jours.; contbr. articles to profl. jours. Home: 31 Towler Dr Hampton VA 23666-2659 Office: Univ Va NASA Langley Rsch Ctr Ms Ctr # 369 Hampton VA 23681-0001 Office Phone: 757-766-5233. Business E-Mail: ankoor@odu.edu.

NOOR, JAWWAD, economics professor; b. Lahore, Pakistan, Sept. 12, 1975; arrived in US, 2000, permanent resident, 2006; s. Noor B. and Talat B.; m. Sabahat Jalil, June 23, 2001. BSc with honors, U. London, 1997; PhD in Econs., U. Rochester, NY, 2005. Prof. econs. Boston U., 2005—. Contbr. articles to profl. jours. Recipient Acad. Achievement award, U. London, 1997, Neu Family award for Teaching Excellence, Boston U., 2008; grantee, Nat. Sci. Found., 2008—; fellow, U. Rochester, 2000—05. Achievements include development of theories of temptation and self-control; theories and experiments on intertemporal choice. Avocations: music, philosophy. Office: Boston Univ 270 Bay State Rd Boston MA 02215

NOOR, RONNY, language educator, writer; MA, Tech. U., Berlin, 1986, Okla. State U., 1989, PhD, 1994. Lectr. Salisbury State U., Md., 1995—96; sr. lectr. U. Tex., Brownsville, 1996—98, asst. prof., 1999—2004, assoc. prof., 2004—. Author: (novel) Snake Dance in Berlin; contbr. essays, short stories, articles to profl. jours. Recipient Exceptional Merit award, U. Tex. Brownville, 2001, 2007, Wall of Tolerance honoree, Nat. Campaign for Tolerance, 2005, Faculty Appreciation award, Student Support Svcs. Program/A Support Program in Reaching Excellence, U. Tex. Brownville, 2005, Student Support Svcs. Program/A Support Program in Reaching Excellence, 2006. Mem.: Nat. Writers Assn., South Ctrl. MLA, Popular Culture Assn. Achievements include research in literature and linguistics. Avocations: piano, tennis. Personal E-mail: noorronny@yahoo.com.

NOORDERGRAAF, ABRAHAM, biophysics educator; b. Utrecht, Netherlands, Aug. 7, 1929; s. Leendert and Johanna (Kool) N.; m. Geertruida Alida Van Nee, Sept. 6, 1956 (div. Jan. 2001); children: Annemiek (Mrs. James A. Young), Gerrit Jan, Jeske Inette, Alexander Abraham. B.Sc., U. Utrecht, 1953, MS, 1955, PhD, 1956; MA (hon.), U. Pa., 1971. Teaching asst. U. Utrecht, 1949-50, asst. dept. physics, 1951-53, research asst. dept. med. physics, 1953-55, research fellow dept. med. physics, 1956-58, sr. research fellow dept. med. physics, 1959-65; tchr. math. and physics Vereniging Nijverheidsonderwijs, Utrecht, 1951; research asst. U. Amsterdam, Netherlands, 1952; vis. fellow dept. therapeutic research U. Pa., Phila., 1957-58; assoc. prof. biomed. engring. Moore Sch. Elec. Engring., U. Pa., 1964-70, acting head electromed. div., 1968-69, prof. biomed. engring., 1970-97, assoc. dir. biomed. engring. tng. program, 1971-76, asso. dir. sch., 1972-74, chmn. grad. group in biomed. electronic engring., 1973-75, chmn. dept. bioengring., 1973-76, chmn. grad. group bioengring., 1975-76, dir. systems and integrative biology tng. program, 1979-84; prof. physiology Sch. Vet. Medicine U. Pa., 1976-97, prof. Dutch culture Sch. Arts and Scis., 1983-97, prof. anesthesia Med. Sch., 1990-97, prof. emeritus, 1997—. Vis. prof. biomed. engring. U. Miami, 1970-79, Erasmus U. Med. Sch., Rotterdam, The Netherlands, 1970-71, Tech. U., Delft, 1970-71, Polish Acad. Scis., Warsaw, 1975; hon. vis. prof. physiology U. Ljubljana, 1994—; mem. cardiovasc. study sect. NIH, 1985-89, temp. mem., 1998—; cons. sci. affairs divsn. NATO, 1973—; participant numerous internat. confs. in field. Author: (with I. Starr) Ballistocardiography in Cardiovascular Research, 1967, Circulatory System Dynamics, 1978; contbg. author: Biological Engineering, 1969; Editor: (with G.N. Jager and N. Westerhof) Circulatory Analog Computers, 1963, (with G.H. Pollack) Ballistocardiography and Cardiac Performance, 1967, (with E. Kresch) The Venous System: Characteristics and Function, 1969, (with J. Baan and J. Raines) Cardiovascular System Dynamics, 1978, (with Reichenbach-Consten) Two Hundred Years of Netherlands-American Interaction; sci. editor Biophysics and Bioengring. Series, 1976-94; contbr. numerous articles to profl. jours.; Referee: Biophys. Jour., 1968—, Physics in Medicine and Biology, 1969—, Bull. Math. Biophysics, 1972-84, Circulation Research, 1973—; Circulation 1995-; mem. editorial adv. bd.: Jour. Biomechanics, 1969-84; assoc. editor: Bull. Math. Biology, 1973-84. V.p. Haverford Friends Sch. PTA, 1968—70. Recipient S. Reid Warren Jr. award U. Pa. Sch. Engring. and Applied Sci., 1986, Christian and Mary Lindback award U. Pa., 1988, Lifetime Achievement award, 2001, Internat. Order of Merit, 2003, Arthur C. Guyton award, 2003. Fellow IEEE (life, mem. adminstrv. com. engring. in medicine and biology group 1967-70, mem. edn. com. group biomed. engring. 1968-70, sec. Phila. chpt. 1974-75, mem. regional coun. profl. group engring. in medicine and biology 1974-77), AAAS, N.Y. Acad. Scis., Explorers Club, Coll. Physicians Phila., Am. Coll. Cardiology, Royal Soc. Medicine London; mem. Nederlandse Natuurkundige Vereniging, Ballistocardiograph Research Soc. U.S.A. (sec.-treas. 1965-67, pres. 1968-70), Biophys. Soc. (charter), European Soc. for Noninvasive Cardiovascular Research (co-founder 1960, sec.-treas. 1960-61, mem. com. on nomenclature 1960-61, officer 1961-62, Herman C. Burger award 1978, Disting. Rsch. Award, 1993), Cardiovascular System Dynamics Soc. (co-founder 1976, pres. 1976-80, hon. life 1986), Franklin Inst., John Morgan Soc., Biomed. Engring. Soc. (founding mem., chmn. membership com. 1978-79, dir. 1972-75), Am. Heart Assn., Instrument Soc. Am. (sr. mem.), Soc. Math. Biology (charter mem.), Am. Physiol. Soc., Microcirculatory Soc., Am. Assn. Med. Systems and Informatics, Pa. Acad. Sci., Sigma Xi, Phi Zeta. Presbyterian. Achievements include discovery (with Maximilian Moser) of impedance-defined flow, generalizing William Harvey's 1628 theory of blood circulation; research in properties of impedance-defined flow, especially with respect to venous return and cardiopulmonary resuscitation. Home: 620 Haydock Ln Haverford PA 19041-1208 Office Phone: 610-649-1242. Business E-Mail: anoor@seas.upenn.edu.

NOOYI, INDRA KRISHNAMURTHY, food products executive; b. Madras, India, Oct. 28, 1955; m. Raj K. Nooyi; children: Preetha, Tara. BS, Madras Christian Coll., India, 1976; MBA, Indian Inst. Mgmt., Calcutta, 1978; MA Pub. & Pvt. Mgmt., Yale U., 1980. Product mgr. Johnson & Johnson, India, Mettur Beardsell, Ltd., India; dir. internat. corp. strategy projects Boston Cons. Group, 1980—86; bus. devel. exec. Motorola, Inc., v.p., dir. corp. strategy and planning, 1986—90; sr. v.p. strategy, planning and strategic mktg. Asea Brown Boveri, 1990—94; sr. v.p. strategic planning PepsiCo, Inc., Purchase, NY, 1994-2000, sr. v.p., CFO, 2000-01, pres., CFO, 2001—06, pres., CEO, 2006—07, chairwoman, pres., CEO, 2007—. Bd. dir. Phoenix Home Life Mut. Ins. Co. Bd. dir. PepsiCo Found.; trustee Convent of Sacred Heart Sch., Greenwich, Conn. Named an Outstanding Am. of Choice, US Dept. State, 2007; named one of 50 Women to Watch, The Wall St. Jour., 2005, 2006, 2008, 100 Most Powerful Women, Forbes Mag., 2005—09, 50 Most Powerful Women in Bus., Fortune mag., 2006, 2007, 2008, The World's Most Influential People, TIME mag., 2007, 50 Who Matter Now, Business 2.0, 2007, America's Best Leaders, US News & World Report, 2008. Fellow: Am. Acad. Arts & Scis. Achievements include being the first woman CEO for PepsiCo, Inc. Avocation: guitar. Office: PepsiCo Inc 700 Anderson Hill Rd Purchase NY 10577-1444*

NOPAR, ALAN S., lawyer; b. Chgo. s. Myron E. and Evelyn M. Nopar; m. Angela P. Yancey, Aug. 26, 2000. BS, U. Ill., 1976; JD, Stanford U., Calif., 1979. Bar: Ariz. 1979, US Dist. Ct. Ariz. 1980, US Ct. Appeals (9th cir.) 1980, US Supreme Ct. 1982, Calif. 1989; CPA, Ill. Assoc. O'Connor, Cavanagh, Anderson, Westover, Killingsworth & Beshears P.A., Phoenix, 1979-85, ptnr., 1985-87; of counsel Tower, Byrne & Beaugureau, Phoenix, 1987-88; ptnr. Minutillo & Gorman, San Jose, Calif., 1989-91, Bosco, Blau, Ward & Nopar, San Jose, 1991-96; exec. v.p., gen. counsel, dir. AmeriNet Fin. Systems, Inc., Ontario, Calif., 1996-97; sole practice law Palo Alto, Calif., 1998-99; ptnr. Bosco, Ward & Nopar, Palo Alto, 2000—04, Bosco & Nopar, Palo Alto, 2004—07, Nopar & Assocs., Palo Alto, 2007—. Mem. Ariz. Rep. Caucus, Phoenix, 1984-88. Mem. AICPA, ABA (bus. law and law practice mgmt. sects., mem. forum com. on franchising), Ariz. Bar Assn. (bus. law sect.), Calif. State Bar Assn. (bus. law sect.). Avocations: golf, skiing, tennis, bicycling. Office: 425 Sherman Ave Ste 100 Palo Alto CA 94306-1849

NORA, AUDREY HART, physician; b. Picayune, Miss., Dec. 5, 1936; d. Allen Joshua and Vera Lee (Ballard) H.; m. James Jackson Nora, Apr. 9, 1966; children: James Jackson Jr., Elizabeth Hart. BS, U. Miss., 1958, MD, 1961; MPH, U. Calif., 1978. Diplomate Am. Bd. Pediat., Am. Bd. Hematology and Oncology. Resident in pediat. U. Wis. Hosp., Madison, 1961-64; fellow in hematology/oncology Baylor U., Tex. Childrens Hosp., Houston, 1964-66, asst. prof. pediat., 1966-70; assoc. clin. prof. pediat. U. Colo. Sch. Medicine, Denver, 1970—; dir. genetics Denver Childrens Hosp., 1970-78; commd. med. officer USPHS, 1978, advanced through grades to asst. surgeon gen., 1983, cons. maternal and child health Denver, 1978-83, asst. surgeon gen. regional health adminstr., 1983-92, dir. maternal & child health bur., health resources and svc. adminstrn., 1992-99. Mem. adv. com. NIH, Bethesda, 1975-77; mem. adv. bd. Metronet Health, Inc., Denver, 1986-92; mem. adv. bd. Colo. Assn. Commerce and Industry, Denver, 1985-92, WIC Adu Bd. USDA, 1989-99; mem. adv. coun. NICHD, 1992-99; bd. mem. RMC for Health Promotion and Edn., pres., 2004-05. Author: (with J.J. Nora) Genetics and Counseling in Cardiovascular Diseases, 1978, (with others) Blakiston's Medical Dictionary, 1980, Birth Defects Encyclopedia, 1990, (with J.J. Nora and K. Berg) Cardiovascular Diseases: Genetics, Epidemiology and Prevention, 1991; contbr. articles to profl. jours. Recipient Virginia Apgar award Nat. Found., 1976. Fellow Am. Acad. Pediat.; mem. Am. Pub. Health Assn. (governing coun. 1990-92, coun. mem. maternal and child health 1990-93), Commd. Officers Assn., Am. Soc. Human Genetics, Teratology Soc., Western Soc. Pediatric Rsch. Presbyterian. Avocations: cooking, hiking, quilting. Office: 1973 S Kenton Ct Aurora CO 80014-4709

NORA, JAMES JACKSON, physician, writer, educator; b. Chgo., June 26, 1928; s. Joseph James and Mae Henrietta (Jackson) N.; m. Barbara June Fluhrer, Sept. 7, 1949 (div. 1963); children: Wendy Alison, Penelope Welbon, Marianne Leslie; m. Audrey Faye Hart, Apr. 9, 1966; children: James Jackson Jr., Elizabeth Hart Nora. AB, Harvard U., 1950; MD, Yale U., 1954; MPH, U. Calif., Berkeley, 1978. Diplomate Am. Bd. Pediat., Am. Bd. Cardiology, Am. Bd. Med. Genetics. Intern Detroit Receiving Hosp., 1954-55; resident in pediat. U. Wis. Hosps., Madison, 1959-61, fellow in cardiology, 1962-64; fellow in genetics McGill U. Children's Hosp., Montreal, Canada, 1964-65; assoc. prof. pediat. Baylor Coll. Medicine, Houston, 1965-71; prof. genetics, preventive medicine and pediat. U. Colo. Med. Sch., Denver, 1971—, prof. emeritus, 1986. Dir. pediatric cardiology and cardiovasc. tng. U. Colo. Sch. Medicine, 1971-78; mem. task force Nat. Heart and Lung Program, Bethesda, Md., 1973; cons. WHO, Geneva, 1983—; mem. U.S.-U.S.S.R. Exch. Program on Heart Disease, Moscow and Leningrad, 1975. Author: The Whole Heart Book, 1980, 2d rev. edit., 1989; author: (with F.C. Fraser) Medical Genetics, 4th Rev. edit., 1994; author: Genetics of Man, 2d rev. edit., 1986, Cardiovascular Diseases: Genetics, Epidemiology and Prevention, 1991, The Upstart Spring, 1989, The Psi Delegation, 1989, The Hemingway Sabbatical, 1996, Songs from a Brazen Bull, 2001, Panacea, 2002, What Every Senior Needs to Know About Health Care, 2004, Half-Open Windows, 2005, Progress Notes, 2005, The 9/11 Dialogues, 2006, Rules of the Game, 2008, Climate, 2008, War Crimes, 2009, By a Truthful Storyteller, 2009. 2nd lt. USAAC, 1945—47. Grantee Nat. Heart, Lung and Blood Inst., Nat. Inst. Child Health and Human Devel., Am. Heart Assn., NIH; recipient Virginia Apgar Meml. award. Fellow: Am. Coll. Med. Genetics, Am. Coll. Cardiology; mem.: Poets and Writers, Acad. Am. Poets, Mystery Writers Am., Authors League Am., Authors Guild. Democrat. Presbyterian. Avocations: writing fiction, poetry.

NORAH, PATRICIA ANN, retired music educator; b. Columbus, Ga., Sept. 1, 1946; d. Tommy T. and Mary Farley Norah; 1 child, Terrence D. Murphy. Student, Spelman Coll., 1964—65, U. Fla., 1972; B Music Edn., Columbus State U., 1971, MEd, 1978. Cert. tchr. Ga. Gen. music tchr. South Columbus Elem. Sch., 1971—78, Matthew Elem. Sch./Ft. Benning Pub. Schs., Columbus, 1986—87; choral dir. Ft. Mid. Sch., Columbus, 1978—84, Baker HS, Columbus, 1987—91, Carver HS, Columbus, 1991—2006; ret., 2006. Vocal coach, Columbus, 1995—; asst. min. music St. Benedict Cath. Ch., Columbus, 1999—; workshop dir. Franchise Ch., Phenix City, Ala., 2004; min. music Spirit Truth Liberty Ministries Internat., 2007—. Performer Columbus Consol. Gov. One Columbus, 2003; active Keep Columbus Beautiful. Recipient Outstanding Ga. Citizen award, Sec. of State Cathy Cox, 2000, Outstanding African-Am. award, Carver HS, Music Tchr. Excellence award, Nat. League Am. Pen Women (Columbus chpt.), 2006; named to Most Outstanding Women Am., 1974. Mem.: NEA, Nat. Music Educators Assn., Ga. Assn. Educators, Ga. Music Educators Assn. (mem.-at-large elem. coun. 1974). Avocations: reading, travel, music. Home: 3633 St Mary's Rd Columbus GA 31906

NORBACK, CRAIG THOMAS, writer; b. Pitts., Nov. 14, 1943; s. Howard George and Maybelle Veronica Montaigne (Cosse) Norback; m. Judith Carol Shaul, Oct. 12, 1976. BS, Washington U., St. Louis, 1967; postgrad., Drew U., 1986—. Author, co-author, compiler, producer over 150 books, including: The Misspeller's Dictionary, 1972, Everything You Can Get from the Government for Free or Almost for Free, 1975, The Dream Machine: The Golden Age of American Automobiles 1946-65, 1976, Great Songs of Madison Avenue, 1976, Great North American Indians, 1977, The Health Care Directory, 1977, The Older American's Handbook, 1977, The Educational Marketplace, 1978, Famous American Admirals, 1978, Newsweek Travel Guide to the U.S., 1978, The Dow Jones-Irwin Guide to Franchising, 1979, The Horseman's Catalog, 1979, The Must Words, 1979, The Practical Inventor's Handbook, 1979, ABC Complete Book of Sports Facts, 1980, ABC Monday Night Football, 1980-81, 1982, The Bible Almanac, 1980, Check Yourself Out, 1980, The Signet Book of World Winners, 1980, The TV Guide Almanac, 1980, The World's Great News Photos (1840-1980), 1980, The Allergy Encyclopedia, 1981, American Expressions, 1981, The Computer Invasion, 1981, The Consumer's Energy Handbook, 1981, 500 Questions New Parents Ask, 1982, Business Week Almanac, 1982, The International Yellow Pages, 1982, The Puzzle King's Bafflers, 1982, The Associated Press Sunday Crossword Puzzle Book, 1983, Chilton's Job Textbook Series: Advertising Management, 1983, Office Management, 1983, It's a Fact, 1983, National Education Association Parent and Child Success Library: Helping Your Child Read, 1983, How Letters Make Words, 1983, How to Prepare Your Child for School, 1983, Learning the Alphabet, 1983, Learning to Add, 1983, The Ultimate Toy Catalog, 1983, U.S. Publicity Directory, various years, Advertising and Promotion Management, 1983, America Wants to Know, 1983, Certified Professional Secretary modules I through VI, 1984, East Coast Publicity Directory, 1984, Human Resources Yearbook, 1987, 88, 89, 90, Princeton Area Job Finder, 1986-87, Career Encyclopedia, 1987, Travel Publicity Directory, 1987, 88, 89, 90, Arthur Young Guide to Venture Capital, 1987, Hazardous Chemicals on File, 1988, Joint Ventures, 1992. Home: 3112 Kaitlyn Ct Princeton Junction NJ 08550-5349

NORBECK, JACK CARL, library exhibitor; b. Greensburg, Pa., Dec. 8, 1940; Cert., Opticians Inst., 1971; Cert. U. Conn., Ratcliffe Hicks Sch. Agr., 1964. Founder, pres. Norbeck Rsch., Coplay, Pa., 1978—. Designer 80 mag. covers. Author: The Encyclopedia of American Steam Traction Engines; contbr. articles to profl. jours.; more than 255 photo exhibits in 42 countries. Recipient 20th Century award, Am. Medal of Honor, 2001, Noble prize, 2001, Internat. Ambs. medal and Gold Record of Achievement, 2001; named Internat. Man of the Yr., 2000—01, Disting. Accomplishment Hall of Fame, Am. Biog. Inst., 2009. Mem.: Internat. Biog. Ctr., YMCA, USA Gymnastics, Am. Legion, Union Hist. Fire Soc., The Authors Guild, Am. Soc. Agrl. Engrs., Hist. Steam Assns. Lutheran. Achievements include design using his photos on 80 magazine covers. Home and Office: Norbeck Research 117 N Ruch St 8 Coplay PA 18037-1712

NORBECK, JANE S., retired nursing educator; b. Redfield, SD, Feb. 20, 1942; d. Sterling M. and Helen L. (Williamson) N.; m. Paul J. Gorman, June 28, 1970. BA in Psychology, U. Minn., 1965, BSN, 1965; MS, U. Calif., San Francisco, 1971, DSN, 1975. Psychiat. nurse Colo. Psychiat. Hosp., Denver, 1965-66, Langley Porter Hosp., San Francisco, 1966-67; pub. health nurse San Francisco Health Dept., 1968-69; prof. U. Calif. Sch. of Nursing, San Francisco, 1975—2003, dean, 1989-99, dept. chair, 1984-89, prof. and dean emeritus, 2003. Chair study sect. Nat. Inst. of Nursing Rsch., 1990-93, mem. editl. bd. Archives of Psychiat. Nursing, 1985-95, Rsch. in Nursing and Health, 1987-2003. Co-editor: Annual Review of Nursing Research, 1996-97; contbr. articles to profl. jours. Mem. ANA, Am. Acad. Nursing, Inst. of Medicine, Sigma Theta Tau.

NORBERG, ARTHUR LAWRENCE, JR., historian, physicist, educator; b. Providence, Apr. 13, 1938; s. Arthur Lawrence Sr. and Margaret Helen (Riley) N.; children: Catherine E. Norberg Morin, Patricia A. Norberg Fetta, Timothy E., Gregory T. BS in Physics, Providence Coll., 1959; MS in Physics, U. Vt., 1962; PhD in History of Sci., U. Wis., 1974. Asst. prof. physics St. Michael's Coll., Winooski, Vt., 1961-63, 64-68; assoc. scientist Westinghouse Electric Co., Pitts., 1963-64; instr. in physics U. Wis., Whitewater, 1968-71; rsch. historian U. Calif., Berkeley, 1973-79; program mgr. NSF, Washington, 1979-81; dir. Charles Babbage Inst. for History of Info. Processing U. Minn., Mpls., 1981—93, 1999—2006, prof. history of sci. and tech., 1995—2005, assoc. prof. computer sci., 1981-95, prof. computer sci., 1995—2005, prof. emeritus, 2005—, consulting historian, 2006—. Del. Am. Coun. Learned Socs., N.Y.C., 1981-87; mem. adv. coun. NASA, Washington, 1988-93; endowed ERA Land Grant chair U. Minn., 1989-93, 99—2006. Editor: Annals of the History of Computing, 1982-93; adv. editor Tech. and Culture, 1985-92, (books) Transforming Computer Technology: Information Processing for the Pentagon, 1996, Computers and Commerce, 2005; contbr. articles to profl. jours Founding pres. City Works-A Tech. Ctr., Mpls., 1987-90; exec. dir. Charles Babbage Found., 1984-94; trustee Charles Babbage Found., 1993-96. Fellow AAAS; mem. History of Sci. Soc. (treas. 1975-80), Brit. Soc. for History of Sci., Soc. for History of Tech., Sigma Xi. E-mail: norberg@cs.umn.edu.

NORBERG, RICHARD EDWIN, physicist, researcher; b. Newark, Dec. 28, 1922; s. Arthur Edwin and Melita (Roefer) N.; m. Patricia Ann Leach, Dec. 27, 1947 (dec. July 1977); children: Karen Elizabeth, Craig Alan, Peter Douglas; m. Jeanne C. O'Brien, Apr. 1, 1978. BA, DePauw U., 1943; MA, U. Ill., 1947, PhD, 1951. Research assoc., control sytems lab. U. Ill., 1951-53, asst. prof., 1953; vis. lectr. physics Washington U., St. Louis, 1954—, mem. faculty, 1955—, prof. physics, 1958—, chmn. dept., 1962-91. Mem. editl. bd. Magnetic Rsch. Rev. Served with USAAF, 1942-46. Co-recipient ISMAR prize, 2004. Fellow Am. Phys. Soc., Internat. Soc. Magnetic Research. Home: 7134 Princeton Ave Saint Louis MO 63130-2308 Office: Washington U Dept Physics PO Box 1105 Saint Louis MO 63188-1105 Business E-Mail: ren@wuphys.wustl.edu.

NORBERG-KING, TERESA JOY, research aquatic biologist; b. Moose Lake, Minn., Feb. 15, 1957; d. William John and Wellma Josephine (Anderson) Norberg; m. Michael B. King, Sept. 29, 1984; children: Nicholas, Alexandra; 1 stepchild, Stephanie. BS in Biology, U. Minn., Duluth, 1980; MS in Zoology and Physiology, U. Wyo., 1987. Clk. stenographer/clk. typist Environ. Rsch. Lab., U.S. EPA, Duluth, 1976-79, biol. lab. aide, 1979-80, biol. lab. technician, 1980-82, biologist, 1982-87, rsch. aquatic biologist, 1987—. Presenter workshops in field; lectr. in field. Contbr. numerous articles/abstracts to profl. jours.; joint editl. bd. Am. Pub. Health Assn., Am. Water Wks. Assn., Water Pollution Control Fedn. Mem. Am. Chem. Soc., Soc. for Environ. Toxicology and Chemistry, Sigma Xi. Office: US EPA Mid Continent Ecology Divsn 6201 Congdon Blvd Duluth MN 55804-2558

NORCEL, JACQUELINE JOYCE CASALE, educational association administrator; b. Nov. 19, 1940; d. Frederick and Josephine Jeanette (Bestafka) Casale; m. Edward John Norcel, Feb. 24, 1962. BS, Fordham

U., 1961; MS, Bklyn. Coll., 1966; 6th yr. cert., So. Conn. State U., 1980; postgrad., Bridgeport U. Elem. tchr. NYC Pub. Schs., 1961-80; prin. Coventry (Conn.) Schs., 1980-84, Trumbull (Conn.) Schs., 1984—2003, Frenchtown Elem. Sch., 2003—. Guest lectr. So. Conn. State U., 1980; cons. Monson (Mass.) Schs., 1984; mem. Conn. State Prin. Acad. Adv. Bd., 1986-88; mem. adj. faculty Sacred Heart U., Fairfield, Conn., 1985—, So. Conn. State U., summer 1991; fed. rels. coord. Nat. Assn. Elem. Sch. Prins., Conn., 1999-2002. Editor: Best of the Decade, 1980; mem. editl. adv. bd. Principal Matters; contbr. articles to profl. jours. Chmn. bldg. com. Trumbull Bd. Edn., 1978-80; chmn. Sch. Benefit Com., Trumbull, 1985-86; catechist Bridgeport Diocese, Roman Cath. Ch., Conn., 1975-85, youth min., 1979-84, coord., evaluator leadership tng. workshops for teens and adults, 1979-84; chairperson dist. wide cultural diversity com., 1990-; mem. St. Stephen's Parish Coun., 1993-97, trustee, 1997—, Eucharist min., 1999—, lector, 1990-; com. mem. New Sch. Bldg. Town of Trumbull, 2001-05. Recipient Town of Trumbull Svc. award, 1982, Nat. Disting. Prin. award, 1988, Joseph Formica Disting. Svc. award EMSPAC, 1994, Named Elem. Sch. of Yr., Conn. Assn. Sch., 2007-08. Mem.: ASCD, Assoc. Tchrs. Math. in Conn., New Eng. Coalition Ednl. Leaders, Ea. Conn. Coun. Internat. Reading Assn., Conn. Assn. Elem. Sch. Prins., Trumbull Adminstrs. Assn. (pres.-elect 1989—91, pres. 1991—93, 2002—), Conn. Assn. Supervision and Curriculum Devel., Nat. Assn. Elem. Sch. Prins. (del. to gen. assemblies 1984—90, zone I dir. 1987—90, del. to gen. assemblies 1999—), Hartford Area Prins. and Suprs. Assn. (local pres. 1981—82), Conn. Assn. Schs. (bd. mem. 2000—05), Adminstrn. and Supervision Assn. (sec. 1980—81, pres. 1981—82, exec bd. 1982—93), Elem. Mid. Sch. Prins. Assn. (pres. 1985—86, state elected rep. 1989—90, fed. rels. coord. 1990—94, dists. 1, 2 and 3 dir. 1995—98, commr. 1997—2000, fed. rels. coord. 1999—2002, Citizen of Yr. award 1991, Pres.'s award 1981—85), N.E. Regional Elem. Prins. Assn. (rep. 1984—86, sec. 1986—87), Delta Kappa Gamma (v.p. 1996—2000), Pi Lambda Theta, Phi Delta Kappa (v.p. rsch. and projects 1993—95, Disting. Fellow award 1992). Home: 5240 Madison Ave Trumbull CT 06611-1016 Office: Frenchtown Elem Sch 30 Frenchtown Rd Trumbull CT 06611 Office Phone: 203-452-4227. Personal E-mail: norcelj98@yahoo.com.

NORCIA, STEPHEN WILLIAM, advertising executive; b. NYC, Jan. 21, 1941; s. William Matthew and Amelia (Marrone) N.; m. Martha Elizabeth Whelan, Apr. 22, 1978; children: Matthew F., Daniel P., Anne E. BA, U. Conn., 1962. Media planner and buyer SSC&B, NYC, 1965-66; account exec. McCann-Erickson Co., Chgo., 1966-68, v.p., dep. mgr. Milw., 1971-72, v.p., mgmt. supr. NYC, 1972-74, sr. v.p., gen. mgr. Atlanta, 1974-78, exec. v.p., gen. mgr. NYC, 1978-81; exec. v.p., mem. exec. policy com., mem. mgmt. com. Lintas, NYC, 1981-94, exec. v.p., 1989-91, world wide client dir., dir. bus. devel., 1991-94, also bd. dirs.; mng. ptnr. Earle Palmer Brown, NYC, 1994-96; dir. global account DDB, NYC, 1996-99, mng. dir., 1998-2000; v.p. bus. devel. Agency-.com, 2000—02; owner cons. co. Norcia Group, 2002—; founder, prin. Topsail Group, 2003. Account exec. Needham, Harper & Steers, Chgo., 1968-70; dir. mktg. product devel. workshop Interpub., N.Y.C., 1970-71; bd. dirs. Communication Counselors Network; adj. prof. Fordham U., Iona Coll. Bd. dirs. U. Ga. Master of Br. Mgmt. Program, 1985, 86, 87, Advt. Edn. Found., 1999-2007; bd. dirs. Spirial Frog, 2006—. 1st lt. U.S. Army, 1962-65. Recipient Robert E. Healy award Interpub. Group Cos., 1975, Effie award Am. Mktg. Assn., 1985, Grand Effie award Am. Mktg. Assn., 1984. Mem. Am. Assn. Advt. Agys., Advt. Club N.Y., Am. Yacht Club, NY Yacht Club, Essex Yacht Club, Old Lyme Country Club. Republican. Roman Catholic. Avocations: tennis, boating, skiing, bicycling. Home: 53 Otter Cove Dr Old Saybrook CT 06475 Office: Topsail Group PO Box 488 Old Saybrook CT 06475 Office Phone: 914-921-3351.

NORCOTT, FLEMMING L., JR., state supreme court justice; b. New Haven, Oct. 11, 1943; BA, Columbia U., 1965, JD, 1968; LLD (hon.), U. New Haven, 1993, Albertus Magnus Coll., 2004. Bar: Conn. 1968. Peace corps vol. U. East Africa, Nairobi, Kenya; legal staff Bedford-Stuyvestant Restoration Corp.; asst. atty. gen. Office Atty. Gen., V.I.; judge Superior Ct., 1979-87, Appellate Ct., 1987-92; assoc. justice Conn. Supreme Ct., Hartford, 1992—. Hearing examiner Conn. Commn. Human Rights and Opportunities; co-founder, exec. dir. Ctr. Advocacy, Rsch. and Planning, Ind., New Haven; lectr. Yale U. Bd. govs. U. New Haven; bd. dirs. Dixwell Community House, Ea. Collegiate Football Officials. Assn., New Haven Football Officials Assn., Long Wharf Theatre; assoc. fellow Calhoun Coll., Yale U.; bd. trustees Yale-New Haven Hosp. Mem. Omega Psi Phi Office: Conn Supreme Ct 231 Capital Ave Hartford CT 06106*

NORD, HENRY J., transportation executive; b. Berlin, May 1, 1917; came to U.S., 1937, naturalized, 1943; s. Walter and Herta (Riess) N.; children: Stephen, Philip. Student, U. Oxford, Eng., 1934, Northwestern U., 1938-40, Ill. Inst. Tech., 1942; JD, De Paul U., 1949. CPA, Ill. Apprentice in export, Hamburg, Germany, 1935- 37; with GATX Corp., Chgo., 1938-85, comptroller, 1961-67, v.p., 1967-71, exec. v.p., 1971-78, sr. v.p., 1978-80, v.p., 1980-82, cons., 1982-84, fin. cons., 1982—, dir., 1964-78. Dir. Planned Lighting, Inc. to 1988. Trustee DePaul U. Served to 1st lt. AUS, 1943—46. Mem. Internat. Law Assn. Clubs: Cliffdwellers (Chgo.). Home: 1000 N Lake Shore Pl Chicago IL 60611-1308 Office: 111 N Wabash Ave Chicago IL 60602-1936

NORD, KEITH DOUGLAS, surgeon, director; MD, Uniformed Svcs. U., Bethesda, Md., 1983. Cert. ABOS, 1992. Lt. col. USAF, March AFB, Calif., 1979—95; pres. & CEO Sports, Orthopedics & Spine, Jackson, Tenn., 1995—; fellowship dir. SOS Ednl. Found., Jackson, 2005—. Instr. Arthroscopy Assn. N.Am., Rosemont, Ill., 2007—. Contbr. articles to profl. jours. Prof. health & human svcs. Lambuth Univ., Tenn., 2007—09. Decorated Meritorious Svc. medal USAF; recipient Pinnacle award, Jackson-Madison County, 2001, 2004, Best Video award, AAOS, 2006, Mayor Jackson, 2007, Disting. Svc. Leadership award, Tenn. Interscholastic Athletic Adminstrs. Assn., 2008; named one of Americas Top Doctors, 2006—08. Mem.: Internat. Soc. Arthroscopy, Knee Surgery & Orthop. Sports Medicine, Arthroscopy Assn. N.Am. (edn. com. mem. 2009—). Lutheran. Achievements include patents for arthrex penetrator & bird beak suture retrievers. Office: Sports Orthop & Spine 569 Skyline Dr Jackson TN 38301

NORD, MYRTLE SELMA, writer, researcher; b. Lane, SD, Mar. 13, 1918; d. Carl Frederick Schaefer and Minna Anna (Meyer) Scandrett; m. Warren E. Nord, Aug. 10, 1938. BA, Fort Lewis Coll., 1972. Sec. Anaconda Mining, Robeau, SD, 1935; waitress Rapid City, SD, 1935-38; office mgr. Farmers Ins. Group, Durango, Colo., 1947-62, ret., 1962. Author: Tell Me a Story, 1956, Inspiring Stories, 1975, Prospectives on Mass Communications, 1982, Main Currents in Communications, 1986, Leadville's Chicken Bill, 1977, The Searcher, 1993-94, Hot Flashes From Writing, 2005, Sestina and Haiku, 2005, The Searcher, 2006, Observations, 2006, To Kill A Bird, 2006, Murder 101, 2006, View Points, 2007, Kip, Boy Pioneer of Am. West, 2007; (plays) Five Under Cover 6, 1983, Celebrations 6, 1986, Virtue of Necessity, 1982, (stage plays) Tomorrow = X2,19, 1968, Sound Another Trumpet, 1976, (serials) Children's Friend, Missing Red Envelope, 1950-51, The Blue Triangle, 1952-53, (musicals) Getting It 2-Gether, 1982, No Patsy Like a Dame, 1985, High Blonde Pressure, 1986, Katie's Capers in the Mining Camp, 1989, (poetry) Hold Dear a Long Time Love, 1998, Story, Out-Guessing Ourselves, 1999 (Palomar Showcase); contbr. articles to popular mags.; chpts. to books. Mem. Nat. League of Am. Pen Women (state pres. 1966-68), Mystery Writers of Am. Avocations: herbs, music, outdoors. Home: Apt 213 11 E Orange Grove Rd Tucson AZ 85704-5555 Personal E-mail: myrtle.nord747@comcast.net.

NORD, NANCY ANN, commissioner; b. Sioux Falls, SD, Sept. 1946; m. James S. Halpern, Mar. 8, 1994. BA, U. Nebr.; JD, George Washington U. Dir. consumer affairs US C. of C., 1972—75; rep. coun. Commerce Com., US Ho. of Reps., 1975—81; gen. counsel White House Coun. on Environ. Quality, 1981—82; exec. dir. Assn. of Corp. Counsel (formerly Am. Corp. Counsel Assn.), 1982—90; atty. FCC, 1991, Jellinek, Schwartz & Connelly, 1991—93; atty. fed. affairs Verner, Liipfert, Bernhard, McPherson and Hand, Washington, 1993—97; dir. fed. govt. rels. Eastman Kodak Co., 1997—2003; commr. US Consumer Products Safety Commn., Bethesda, Md., 2005—, acting chairwoman, 2006—09. Pres. Exec. Women in Govt., 2006. Office: US Consumer Products Safety Commn 4330 E West Highway Bethesda MD 20814 Office Phone: 301-504-7923. Office Fax: 301-504-0124. E-mail: commissionernord@cpsc.gov.*

NORD, WALTER ROBERT, business administration educator, researcher, consultant; b. Mt. Kisco, NY, July 2, 1939; s. Arthur William and Elizabeth (Reimstedt) N.; m. Ann Feagan, June 10, 1967. BA in Econs., Williams Coll., 1961; MS in Organizational Behavior, Cornell U., 1963; PhD in Social Psychology, Washington U., St. Louis, 1967. Asst. prof. organizational psychology Washington U., 1967-70, assoc. prof., 1970-73, prof., 1973-89; prof. mgmt. U. South Fla., 1989—, Disting. Univ. prof., 2001; vis. prof. faculty commerce Northwestern U., 1981, U. B.C. (Can.), Vancouver, 1975-76. Author: (with S. Tucker) Implementing Routine and Radical Innovations, 1987; editor: Concepts and Controversy in Organizational Behavior, 1972, rev. edit, 1976; (with P. Frost and V. Mitchell) Organizational Reality, 1978, rev. edit., 1982, 86, 92; (with H. Meltzer) Making Organizations Humane and Productive, 1982; (with P. Frost and V. Mitchell) Managerial Reality, 1989, HRM Reality, 1992; (with A. Brief) Meanings of Occupational Work, 1990, (with S. Clegg and C. Hardy) Handbook of Organization Studies, 1996 (George Terry Book award 1997), 2d edit., 2006, (with P. Frost and L. Krefting) Managerial and Organization Reality, Stories of Life and Work, 2004, (with S. Clegg, C. Hardy and T. Lawrence) Sage Handbook of Organization Studies, 2006. Fellow APA; mem. Acad. Mgmt. (named Disting. Educator 2002). Home: 6004 Pratt St Tampa FL 33647-1043 Office: U South Fla Sch Bus Tampa FL 33620-5500 Office Phone: 813-974-1787. Business E-Mail: wnord@coba.usf.edu.

NORDBY, EUGENE JORGEN, orthopedic surgeon; b. Abbotsford, Wis., Apr. 30, 1918; s. Herman Preus and Lucille Violet (Korsrud) N.; m. Olive Marie Jensen, June 21, 1941; 1 child, Jon Jorgen BA, Luther Coll., Decorah, Iowa, 1939; MD, U. Wis., 1943. Diplomate Am. Bd. Orthopaedic Surgery. Intern Madison Gen. Hosp., Wis., 1943-44, asst. in orthopedic surgery Wis., 1944-48; practice medicine specializing in orthopedic surgery Madison, Wis., 1948—. Pres. Bone and Joint Surgery Assocs., S.C., 1969—91; chief staff Madison Gen. Hosp., 1957—63; assoc. clin. prof. U. Wis. Med. Sch., 1961—; bd. dirs. Wis. Physicians Svcs., 1958—, chmn. pharmacy dir., 1979—2009, chmn. emeritus, 2009—; bd. dirs. Norweguan Am. Geneal. Ctr., Naeseth Libr.; chmn. Wis. Physicians Svcs., 1979—; dir. Wis. Regional Med. Program, Chgo. Madison and No. R.R.; bd. govs. Wis. Health Care Liability Ins. Plan; chmn. trustees S.M.S. Realty Corp.; mem. bd. attys. Profl. Responsibility of Wis. Supreme Ct., 1992—; bd. dirs. WPS Cmty. Bank, 2008—, chmn. exec. com., 2008—. Mem. editl. bd. Clin. Orthopaedics and Related Research, 1964—, Spine, 1994-2000. Pres. Vesterheim Norwegian Am. Mus., Decorah, Iowa, 1968-97, pres. emeritus, 1997—. Served to capt. M.C., AUS, 1944-46 Decorated Knight 1st class Royal Norwegian Order St. Olav, 1979; named Notable Norwegian Dane County Norwegian-Am. Fest, 1995; recipient Disting. Svc. award Internat. Rotary,1 987, Den Hoyeste Aere award Vesterheim, 1993, Lyman Smith, M.D. and Eugene J. Nordby, M.D. award for minimally invasive spine surgery established N.Am. Spine Soc., 1998, The Nordby Bldg. designated Wis. Phys. Svc. Health Ins. Co., 1998, Internat. Intradiscal Therapy Soc. Lifetime Achievement award, 2006, First World Congress Minimally Invasive Spine Surgery, 2008. Fellow Wisdom Hall of Fame; mem. Am. Acad. Orthop. Surgeons (bd. dirs. 1972-73, 1st chmn. bd. councilors 1972), Clin. Orthop. Soc., Assn. Bone and Joint Surgeons (pres. 1973), Internat. Soc. Study Lumbar Spine, State Med. Soc. Wis. (chmn. 1968-76, treas. 1976-97, Coun. award 1976), Am. Orthop. Assn., N.Am. Spine Soc., Internat. Intradiscal Therapy Soc. (sec. 1987-99, exec. dir. 1996-2006, exec. dir. emeritus 2006—, Eugene J. Nordby Rsch. award established in his honor 1993, Lifetime Achievement award 2006), Wis. Orthop. Soc., Dane County Med. Soc. (pres. 1957), Nat. Exch. Club, Madison Torske Klubben (founder, pres. 1978-98, pres. emeritus 1998—), Norwegian-Am. Orthop. Soc., Am. Acad. Orthop. Surgeons, Am. Orthop. Assn., Norwegian Am. Found., Norwegian-Am. Geneal. Ctr. (bd. mem. 2006-2008), WPS Cmty. Bank Bd. (chmn. exec. com., 2009-), Phi Chi. Lutheran. Home: 7824 Courtyard Dr Madison WI 53719 Office: 304 S Whitney Way Madison WI 53705 Home Phone: 608-831-2356; Office Phone: 608-831-2356. Personal E-mail: ejnor@charter.net. *We must remember no matter how dedicated we are to the accumulation of knowledge, it isn't always what you know that matters but what you can think of in time.*

NORDELL, HANS RODERICK, journalist, retired editor; b. Alexandria, Minn., June 26, 1925; s. Wilbur Eric and Amelia (Jasperson) N.; m. Joan Projansky, Apr. 30, 1955; children: Eric Peter, John Roderick, Elizabeth Sabin. AB magna cum laude, Harvard U., 1948; B Litt, U. Dublin, 1951. Exec. editor World Monitor: The Christian Science Monitor Monthly; with Christian Sci. Monitor, Boston, 1948-93, arts editor, 1968-73, asst. chief editorial writer, 1973-83, home forum editor, 1983-85, feature editor, 1985-87; exec. editor World Monitor: The Christian Science Monitor Monthly, Boston, 1988-93. Bd. dirs. Cmty. Music Ctr., Boston, 1970-94, corp. chair, 1994—; bd. dirs. Young Audiences, 1970-88; mem. Com. for Harvard Theatre Collection, 1977-91; trustee Berklee Coll. Music, 1970-97, trustee emeritus, 1997—. With USMCR, 1943-46. Fellowship Rotary Found., 1950-51. Mem.: Harvard Musical Assn., St. Botolph Club, Phi Beta Kappa. Christian Scientist. Home: 25 Meadow Way Cambridge MA 02138-4635

NORDEN, ERNEST ELWOOD, retired foreign language educator; b. Chgo., July 11, 1938; s. Ernest and Jeleste Katherine (Diggle) N.; m. Janet Louise Burke, June 22, 1963; children: Brent C., Keith R. BS, Purdue U., 1961; MA, U. Oreg., 1963; PhD, U. Calif., Berkeley, 1974. Asst. prof. U. Colo., Boulder, 1969-71, Northeast La. U., Monroe, 1971-72, 73-75; assoc. prof. Baylor U., Waco, Tex., 1975-85, prof., 1985—2006; prof. emeritus, 2006—. Contbr. articles to profl. jours. Vol. Dept. Pub. Health, Waco, 1993-96. Jr. lectr. Fulbright Commn., 1972-73; fellow NEH, 1975, 87, Woodrow Wilson fellowship, 1961. Mem. Am. Assn. Tchrs. Spanish and Portuguese (v.p. Lone Star chpt. 1978-79, pres. 1979-80), Modern Lang. Assn. Am. (bibliographer Spanish sect. 1981-2007, mem. advisory com., 2004-07). Home Phone: 469-467-6938. Personal E-mail: ernest_norden@baylor.edu.

NORDENBERG, MARK ALAN, academic administrator, law educator; b. Duluth, Minn., July 12, 1948; s. John Clemens and Shirley Mae (Tappen) N.; m. Nikki Patricia Pirillo, Dec. 26, 1970; children: Erin, Carl, Michael. BA, Thiel Coll., 1970; JD, U. Wis., 1973. Bar: Wis. 1973, Minn. 1974, U.S. Supreme Ct. 1976, Pa. 1985. Atty. Gray, Plant, Mooty & Anderson, Mpls., 1973—75; prof. law Capital U. Law Ctr., Columbus, Ohio, 1975—77, U. Pitts., 1977—, acting dean Sch. Law, 1985—87, dean Sch. Law, 1987—93, interim sr. vice chancellor & provost, 1993—94, Disting. Svc. prof., 1994—, interim chancellor, 1995—96, chancellor, 1996—. Mem. U.S. Supreme Ct. Adv. Com. on Civil Rules, Washington, 1988-93, Pa. Supreme Ct. Civil Procedure Rules Com., Phila., 1986-92; reporter civil justice adv. group U.S. Dist. Ct., Pitts., 1991-96; bd. dirs. Bank of NY Mellon Corp. Author: Modern Pennsylvania Civil Practice, 1985, 2d edit., 1995. Bd. dirs. Allegheny Conf. on Cmty. Devel., Pitts., Pitts. Coun. on Higher Edn., Pa. Assn. Colls. and Univs., Assn. Am. Univs.; trustee Thiel Coll., Greenville, Pa., 1987—97; bd. dirs. Pitts. Life Scis. Greenhouse, The Tech. Collaborative. Named Vectors Pitts. Person of Yr. in Edn., 1996, Person of Yr., 1997, Pitts. Mag. Person of Yr., 2001, Hon. Consul for Great Britain. Fellow Am. Bar Found.; mem. ABA, Pa. Bar Assn., Allegheny County Bar Assn., Pitts. Athletic Assn., Duquesne Club. Office: U Pitts Cathedral of Learning Pittsburgh PA 15260 Office Phone: 412-624-4200. Business E-Mail: norden@pitt.edu.

NORDGREN, DEBRA, librarian, educator; MSE, U. Wis. Superior; MA, U. Denver. Assoc. prof., libr. sci. U. Wis. Superior, 1989—, libr. dir., 2007—. Mem.: ALA, No. Waters Libr. Svc. Bd., Wis. Libr. Assn. Office: Univ Wis-Superior Belknap & Catlin P O Box 2000 Superior WI 54880 Business E-Mail: dnordgre@uwsuper.edu.

NORDGREN, RONALD PAUL, retired engineering educator, researcher; b. Munising, Mich., Apr. 3, 1936; s. Paul A. and Martha M. N.; m. Joan E. McAfee, Sept 12, 1959; children: Sonia, Paul. BS in Engring., U. Mich., 1957, MS in Engring., 1958; PhD, U. Calif., Berkeley, 1962. Rsch. asst. U. Calif., Berkeley, 1959-62; mathematician Shell Devel. Co., Houston, 1963-68, staff rsch. engr., 1968-74, sr. staff rsch. engr., 1974-80, rsch. assoc., 1980-90; Brown prof. civil and mech. engring. Rice U., Houston, 1989-2000, prof. emeritus, 2001—. U.S. nat. com. on theoretical and applied mechanics NRC, 1984-86, U.S. nat. com. for rock mechanics, 1991-95. Contbr. articles to profl. jours.; assoc. editor Jour. Applied Mechanics, 1972-76, 81-85; patentee in field. Fellow: ASME; mem.: NAE, Sigma Xi. Office: 3989 Pebble Beach Dr Longmont CO 80503-8358 Business E-Mail: nordgren@rice.edu.

NORDHAUS, ROBERT RIGGS, lawyer; b. Albuquerque, Mar. 27, 1937; s. Robert J. and Virginia (Riggs) N.; m. Jean Friedberg, June 27, 1964; children: Ronald E., Hannah E. BA, Stanford U., 1960; LLB, Yale U., 1963. Bar: N.Mex. 1963, D.C. 1981, U.S. Supreme Ct. 1982. Asst. counsel U.S. House Reps., Washington, 1963-74, counsel interstate and fgn. commerce com., 1975-76; asst. adminstr. FEA, Washington, 1977; gen. counsel Fed. Energy Regulatory Commn., Washington, 1977-80; ptnr. Van Ness, Feldman & Curtis, Washington, 1981-93; gen. counsel US Dept. Energy, Washington, 1993-97; ptnr. Van Ness Feldman P.C., Washington, 1997—. Professorial lectr. George Washington Law Sch., Washington, 2001-; bd. mem., PNM Resources, Inc., 2007- 2d. lt. U.S. Army, 1960. Mem. Fed. Energy Bar Assn. (bd. dirs. 1989-92). Office: Van Ness Feldman PC Ste 700 1050 Thomas Jefferson St NW Washington DC 20007-3877 Office Phone: 202-298-1800. E-mail: rrn@vnf.com.

NORDHOFF, HENRY LOUIS (HANK NORDHOFF), biotechnology company executive, investor; b. Feb. 20, 1942; m. Robin Tharp; 4 children. BA in internat. relations and political economy, Johns Hopkins U., 1963; MBA, Columbia U. Sr. positions in Brussels, Seoul, Tokyo and NY Pfizer, Inc., 1970—86; v.p. acquisitions and bus. devel. Sterling Drug Inc. (merged into Kodak); pres., CEO American Biogenetics Sciences, Notre Dame, Ind., TargeTech (merged into Immune Response Corp.), Meriden, Conn., 1992—94; pres. Gen-Probe Inc., San Diego, 1994—2008, CEO, 1994—2009, chmn., 2002—. Bd. dir. MannKind Corp., 2005—. Bd. dirs. Prostate Cancer Found.; chmn. Calif. Healthcare Inst., San Diego Regional Economic Devel. Corp.; advisory bd. mem. Cancer Ctr., Rady Sch. Mgmt., U. Calif. San Diego, Jacob School of Engineering, U. Calif. San Diego; bd. trustees U. San Diego. Officer USN, 1963—67. Avocations: golf, tennis, squash. Office: Gen Probe Inc 10210 Genetic Center Dr San Diego CA 92121*

NORDLAND, GERALD, museum administrator, historian, consultant; b. LA; AB, JD, U. So. Calif. Dean of faculty Chouinard Art Sch., LA, 1960-64; dir. Washington Gallery of Modern Art, 1964-66, San Francisco Mus. Art, 1966-72, Frederick S. Wight Art Galleries, UCLA, 1973-77, Milw. Art Mus., 1977-85; ind. curator, author, editor Chgo., 1985—. Author: Paul Jenkins, 1972, Gaston Lachaise/The Man and His Work, 1974, Richard Diebenkorn, 1987, rev. edit., 2001, Frank Lloyd Wright: In the Realm of Ideas, 1988, Zhou Brothers, 1994, Ynez Johnston, 1996, Lev Syrkin, 1998, Twentieth Century American Drawings, 1998, Jon Schueler: To The North, 2002, In the Spirit of the Times, 2003, Emerson Woelffer: A Solo Flight, 2003, Richard Drebenkorn in New Mexico, 2007, Breaking the Mold, 2007. Gaston Lachaise Found. grantee, 1973-74; John Simon Guggenheim Found. fellow, 1985-86. Home and Office: 645 W Sheridan Rd Chicago IL 60613-3316 Office Phone: 773-348-5133. Personal E-mail: geraldnordland@sbcglobal.net.

NORDLI, DOUGLAS R., neurologist; m. Jo-Anne Tierney. BA, Haverford Coll., Pa.; MD, Columbia U. Coll. Physicians and Surgeons, NYC, 1984. Cert. in pediat. Am. bd. Pediactrics, 1990, in neurology with spl. qualifications in child neurology Am. bd. Neurology Psychiatry, 1990, in neurology with spl. qualifications in clin. neurophysiology Am. bd. Clinical Neurophysiology, 1997. Residency in pediat. Columbia-Presbyn. Med. Ctr., 1986, residency in child neurology, 1988, fellowship in clin. neurophysiology and epilepsy, 1990; asst. prof. child neurology Columbia U., NYC, 1994—99; Lorna S. and James P. Langdon chmn. pediat. epilepsy, dir., attending physician neurology, epilepsy ctr. Children's Meml. Hosp., Chgo., 1999—; assoc. prof. neurology and pediat. Northwestern U. Feinberg Sch. Medicine, Ill.; fellowship program dir. epilepsy Northwestern U. McGaw Med. Ctr., Ill. Asst. bd. examiner Am. Bd. Clin. Neurophysiology; profl. adv. bd. Epilepsy Found., Greater Chgo., Epilepsy Services Northeastern Ill. Editor: Pediatric Neurology; contbr. articles to profl. jours., chapters to books. Mem.: Child Neurology Soc., Am. Epilepsy Soc., Am. Acad. Neurology, Alpha Omega Alpha. Office: Childrens Meml Hosp 2300 Childrens Plz Chicago IL 60614

NORDLIE, ROBERT CONRAD, biochemistry educator; b. Willmar, Minn., June 11, 1930; s. Peder Conrad and Myrtle (Spindler) N.; m. Sally Ann Christianson, Aug. 23, 1959; children: Margaret, Melissa, John. BS St. Cloud State Coll., Minn., 1952; MS, U. N.D., 1957, PhD,

1960. Tchg., rsch. asst. biochemistry U. N.D. Med. Sch., Grand Forks, 1955-60, James J. Hill rsch. prof. biochemistry, 1962-74, Chester Fritz disting. prof. biochemistry, 1974—, Cornatzer prof., chmn. dept. biochemistry and molecular biology, 1983-2000, Chester Fritz disting. emeritus prof., 2000—. Hon. prof. San Marcos U., Lima, Peru, 1981, 82—; emeritus prof., 2000-; NIH fellow Inst. Enzyme Rsch., U. Wis., 1960-61; mem. biochemistry study sect. NIH; merit rev. com. VA, 1994—; cons. enzymology Oak Ridge, 1961—; vis. prof. Tokyo Biomed. Inst., 1984; mem. predoctoral fellowship rev. group Howard Hughes Inst., 1990-93. Mem. editorial bd.: Jour. Biol. Chemistry, Biochimca et Biophysica Acta. Research publs. on enzymology relating to metabolism of various carbohydrates in mammalian livers, regulation blood sugar levels. Served with AUS, 1953-55. Recipient Disting. Alumnus award St. Cloud State U., 1983; recipient Sigma Xi Rsch. award, 1969, Golden Apple award U. N.D., 1968, Edgar Dale award U. N.D., 1983, Burlington No. Faculty Scholar award, 1987, Thomas J. Clifford Faculty Achievement award for excellence in rsch. U. N.D. Found., 1993, Hippocratic Dignity award, 2005. Mem. AAAS, Am. Soc. Biol. Chemistry and Molecular Biology, Am. Chem. Soc., Internat. Union Biochemists, Soc. Exptl. Biology and Medicine, Am. Inst. Nutrition, Sigma Xi, Alpha Omega Alpha. Home: 162 Columbia Ct Grand Forks ND 58203-2947 Office Phone: 701-777-2751. Business E-Mail: rnordlie@medicine.nodak.edu.

NORDLINGER, GERSON, investor; b. Washington, Feb. 2, 1916; s. Gerson and Camille (Bensinger) N. BA, George Washington U., 1935; BCS, Benjamin Franklin U., 1939. Head Navy Dept. Bur. Aeros. Budget, 1946-50; trustee Washington Real Estate Investment Trust, 1961-98; pres. Nordlinger Investment Corp., Washington, 1955—. Chmn. D.C. Arts Commn., 1965-67; v.p. Nat. Symphony Assn., 1953—, Nat. Ballet, 1966-70, Alliance Francaise, 1980—; pres. Prevention of Blindness Soc., 1960-67; treas. Friendship House, 1951-69; vice chmn. D.C. Recreation Bd., 1960-67; trustee Washington Performing Arts Soc., Mt. Vernon Coll., Washington Opera, Cathedral Choral Soc., Phillips Collection; life trustee Nat. Symphony Orch., 1952—; state com. Republican Party, 1952-64. Lt. comdr. Supply Corps, USNR, 1941-46, PTO. Recipient Angel of Arts award, 2001. Mem. D.C. Inst. CPAs, Cosmos Club, Met. Club. Home: 2700 Calvert St NW # 515 Washington DC 20008-2621 also: 3900 Galt Ocean Dr Fort Lauderdale FL 33308-6631 Personal E-mail: gersonn@aol.com.

NORDLINGER, STEPHANIE G., lawyer; b. LA, 1940; BA, UCLA, 1961, MA, 1969, U. Calif., Berkeley, 1962; JD, Loyola U., 1975. Bar: Calif. 1975, U.S. Dist. Ct. (ctrl. dist.) Calif. 1976, U.S. Ct. Appeals (9th cir.) 1976, U.S. Supreme Ct. 1992. Pvt. practice, LA, 1976-77, 89—; dep. pub. defender L.A. County, 1977-79; adj. prof. Calif. State U., Northridge, 1979; pvt. practice Santa Monica, Encino, Calif., 1979-83; assoc. Baltaxe, Rutkin & Levin, Beverly Hills, Calif., 1983-84; pvt. practice Marina del Rey, Calif., 1984-87; exec. dir. Westside Legal Svcs., Santa Monica, 1988. Mem. adv. com. U.S. Ct. Appeals (9th cir.), San Francisco, 1987-90. Cons.: (book) CEB California Civil Writ Practice, 1987. Bd. dirs. ACLU Southern Calif., Beverly Hills-Westwood chpt. pres. ACLU, 1973-74, pres. Westwood Dem. Club, L.A., 1993-95; mem. state ctrl. com. Calif. Dems., 1995-96. Mem. RAND Alumni Assn., L.A. Computer Soc. (pres. 1994, 2000-01, v.p. 2007, dir., editor), L.A. County Bar Assn., Sierra Club. Westwood-Westside Dem. Club (pres. 2005—). Avocations: genealogy, gardening, travel. Office: PO Box 78757 Los Angeles CA 90016-0757 Office Phone: 323-299-3244. Business E-Mail: nordlingeresq@aol.com.

NORDLOH, DAVID JOSEPH, literature and language professor, dean; b. Cin., May 3, 1942; s. Joseph Westerman and Josephine (Fusz) N.; m. Barbara Jane Beddow, June 29, 1968; children: Geoffrey David, Jennifer Ellen Blum. AB in English, Coll. of Holy Cross, 1964; PhD in English, Ind. U., 1969. From asst. prof. to prof. emeritus English Ind. U., Bloomington, 1969—2007, prof. emeritus English, 2007—, assoc. dean faculties, 2003—06. Vis. assoc. prof. U. Va., Charlottesville, 1978; dir. Am. Studies Program, Ind. U., 1987-94. Gen. editor: A Selected Edition of W.D. Howells, 1974-2006; editor: Twayne's United States Author's Series, 1978-90; co-editor: American Literary Scholarship, 1986—; mem. editl. bd. Walter Scott Edition, 1984—; adv. bd. The Writings of James Fenimore Cooper, 1995—. Pres. Bloomington Symphony Orch., 1986-88, 93-94. Fulbright scholar, 1982-83. Mem. Am. Lit. Assn. Home: 1600 Morganton Rd L-3 Pinehurst NC 28374 Personal E-mail: nordloh@indiana.edu.

NORDLUND, DONALD CRAIG, lawyer, electronics executive; b. Chgo., May 23, 1949; s. Donald E. and Jane (Houston) N.; m. Sally Baum, Sept. 7, 1975; children: Courtney Elizabeth, Michael Andrew, Laurie Katherine. AB in Polit. Sci. and Journalism, Stanford U., 1971; JD, Vanderbilt U., 1974. Assoc. Ware & Freidenrich, Palo Alto, Calif., 1974-77; atty. Hewlett-Packard Co., Palo Alto, 1977-87, assoc. gen. counsel, sec., dir., 1987-99; sr. v.p., gen. counsel, sec. Agilent Technologies, Inc., 1999—. Panelist ann. disclosure doc. seminar Practicing Law Inst., 1982—2005, co-chmn., 2002—04; bd. dirs. Addison Ave. Fed. Credit Union, 1985—; sec., dir. Agilent Tech. Found. and various Agilent Tech. subsidiaries, 1999—; mem. corp. law com. ABA, 2005—08. Chmn. bd. dirs. Santa Clara County chpt. Jr. Achievement, 1995-97. Mem.: Assn. Gen. Counsel (pres. 2006—07), Assn. Corp. Counsel (bd. dirs. San Francisco chpt. 1984—2000, pres. 1989—90, nat. bd. dirs. 1995—2001, Founding dir. Bay Area Chapter), Soc. Corp. Sec. and Governance Profl. (pres. San Francisco region 1986—88, bd. dirs. 1987—90, mem. exec. com. 1988—89, chmn. securities law com. 1995—98, nat. chmn. 1999—2000). Avocations: tennis, skiing, sailing, golf. Office: Agilent Technologies Inc 5301 Stevens Creek Blvd Santa Clara CA 95051

NORDLUND, LEIF NIKLAS DENNIS, research scientist; b. Östersund, Jämtland, Sweden, Oct. 26, 1975; s. Claes-Håkan Nordlund and Helen Eriksdotter; m. Lisa Bodil Christina Avestedt, May 11, 2005; children: Ludvig Theo Walter Avestedt Nordlund, Sara Tove Avestedt Nordlund. MS in Engring. Physics, Uppsala U., Sweden, 1998, PhD, 2004, Stockholm U. Postdoc. rschr. Stanford Synchrotron Radiation Lightsource, Menlo Park, Calif., 2005—07, staff scientist, 2008—. Wennergren Postdoc. fellowship, Wennergren Found., 2005—06. Office: SLAC Nat Accelerator Lab 2575 Sand Hill Rd MS69 Menlo Park CA 94025 Office Fax: 1.650.926.4100. Business E-Mail: nordlund@slac.stanford.edu.

NORDMAN, CHRISTER ERIC, chemistry professor; b. Helsinki, Finland, Jan. 23, 1925; came to U.S., 1948, naturalized, 1960; s. Eric Johan and Gertrud (Nordgren) N.; m. Barbara Lorraine Neal, Nov. 28, 1952 (div. 1993); children: Christina, Aleta, Eric, Carl; m. Outi Marttila, Dec. 28, 1994. Dipl. Ing., Finnish Inst. Tech., Helsinki, 1949; PhD, U. Minn., 1953. Research asso. Inst. Cancer Research, Phila., 1953-55; mem. faculty U. Mich., Ann Arbor, 1955—, prof. chemistry, 1964-95; prof. emeritus, 1995—. Mem. U.S. Nat. Com. Crystallography, 1970-72. Served with Finnish Army, 1943-44. NIH spl. fellow, 1971-72; recipient A.L. Patterson award, 1997. Fellow AAAS; mem. Am. Chem. Soc., Am. Phys. Soc., Am. Crystallographic Assn., Finnish Soc. Scis. and Letters. Home: 27 Haverhill Ct Ann Arbor MI 48105-1406 Office: Univ Mich Dept Chemistry Ann Arbor MI 48109 Business E-Mail: cnordman@umich.edu.

NORDSTRAND, NATHALIE ELIZABETH JOHNSON, artist; b. Woburn, Mass., Nov. 6, 1932; d. Edward N. and Ruth Peterson Johnson; m. Robert I. Nordstrand, Jan. 12, 1962. AA, Bradford Jr. Coll., 1952; BA, Columbia U., 1954, Barnard Coll., 1954; studied with with Jay Connaway, Don Stone, Roger Curtis, Paul Strisik. Rsch. assoc. Gerontology Age Ctr. of New Eng., Boston, 1955-64; clk. corp. dir. Johnson Bros. Greenhouses, Inc., Woburn, 1958-84; owner Nordstrand Gallery, Rockport, Mass., 1970-99. Exhibited at Nat. Acad. Galleries, NYC, Springfield Mus. Fine Arts, Hammond Mus., North Salem, NYC, Bhulabha Meml. Inst., Bombay, India, Copley Soc. at Boston Symphony Hall, Hermann Fine Arts Ctr., Marietta, Ohio, Am. C. of C., Hong Kong, 1975-76, Silvermine Guild, Conn., 1976, Wall of Fame, Balt. Watercolor Soc., 1976, Ann. Copley Masters Exhbn. Boston, others; one woman shows include Rockport (Mass.) Art Assn., 1969, Laura Knotts Art Gallery, Bradford Coll., 1982, Reading Pub. Libr. Found., 1997; several invited exhibitions; paintings in Nat. Mus. Am. Art, Smithsonian Inst., 1994, Best of Watercolors, 1995, Best of Oil Painting, 1996, Landscape Inspirations, 1997, Gallery of Marine Art, 1998, St. Botolph Club, Banks Gallery North Conway, 2008. Planning bd. North Suburban Art Festival, 1963—68; chair. planned giving Athena Soc., Barnard Coll., NYC, 2003—04. Recipient Louis E. Seley award, Salma Gundi Art Club, 1974, Excellence in Watercolor award, Rockport Art Assn., 1997, Philip Isenberg Meml. award, Salma Gundi Club, 1997, more than 240 awards in nat. and regional competition, 1960—, Richard Ochs Meml. award, Salmacundi Club, 2008, Joseph C. Santoro Meml. award, Rockport Art Assn., 2008; named Citizen of Yr., Reading chpt. Am. Cancer Soc., 1983. Fellow Am. Artist Profl. League (Gold medal 1971, 75, award 1978-79); mem. Acad. Artists Assn. (Watercolor awards 1973-74, 76-77, New Eng. Heritage award 1993), Copley Soc. Boston (master artist), Hudson Valley, North Shore (bd. dirs. 1964-67, 86-95), Rockport Art Assn. (Lifetime Dedication to Promotion of Art award 1999, Joseph Santoro Meml. award 2005, Robert Dunnelly Meml. award 2007), Affiliated Art Assn. Mass. (v.p. 1980), Reading Art Assn. (charter, program chmn. 1960-86, Pres.'s awards 1973-80), Am. Watercolor Soc. (juror internat. exhbn. 1992), Allied Artists Am. (Watercolor Gold medals 1973-74), New Eng. Watercolor Soc. (2d v.p. 1984-90), Boston Watercolor Soc. (award 1975), Guild Boston Artists (bd. dirs. 1986-99, A. Lassall Ripley award 1993), Reading Assn. Fine and Performing Arts (charter, bd. dirs. 1993), Nat. Mus. Women in Arts (charter mem.), Salmagundi Art Club (40 awards including MacGowin Tuttle Meml. award 1976, 78-79, Elliot Liskin Meml. award 1988, Steven Blackman award 1988, Joseph Hartley award 1989, 2001, 2002, Mortimer Freehof Meml. award 1991, Bruce Crane award 1994, Rita Duis Meml. award 2001, Margery Saroka Meml. award 2003, Thomas Moran award 2004, Ogden Pleissner Meml. award 2006). Methodist. Address: 384 Franklin St Reading MA 01867-1036 Office Phone: 781-944-4252. Personal E-mail: nordstrands@aol.com.

NORDSTROM, BLAKE W., retail executive; b. 1960; With Nordstrom, Inc., Seattle, 1974—, v.p. & gen. mgr. Wash./Alaska region, 1991—95, co-pres. Seattle, 1995—2000, pres., 2000—, bd. dir., 2005—. Office: Nordstrom Inc 1617 Sixth Ave Seattle WA 98101-1742

NORDSTROM, CHERYL K., epidemiologist, researcher; b. Mich., Dec. 1970; d. Charles D. and Beverly A. Nordstrom; m. Randy Semig. BA, U. Mich., Ann Arbor, 1992, MPH, 1995; PhD, U. So. Calif., 2001. Dir. cardiology biostatistics & epidemiology St. John Hosp. & Med. Ctr., Detroit, 2001—03; rsch. assoc. U. Mich., Ann Arbor, 2003—05; asst. prof. Wayne State U., Detroit, 2005—; co-investigator William Beaumont Hosps. Clin. Rsch. Partnership. Co-investigator, methodologist Detroit Med. Ctr., Ctr. for Clin. Rsch., 2005—; evaluation cons. Pasadena Ednl. Found., Pasadena Unified Sch. Dist., Calif., 1998—2000. Contbr. articles to profl. jours. Mem.: Am. Heart Assn., Soc. for Pub. Health Edn., Ctr. for Urban African Amercian Health (assoc.). Office: Wayne State Univ 5557 Cass Ave Rm 318 Detroit MI 48202 Office Fax: 313-577-5777. Business E-Mail: cnordstrom@wayne.edu.

NORDYKE, ELEANOR COLE, demographer, researcher, public health nurse; b. LA, June 15, 1927; d. Ralph G. and Louise Noble (Carter) Cole; m. Robert Allan Nordyke, June 18, 1950 (dec. 1997); children: Mary Ellen Nordyke-Grace, Carolyn Nordyke Cozzette, Thomas J., Susan Nordyke Bell., Gretchen Nordyke Worthington. BS, Stanford U., 1950; P.H.N. accreditation, U. Calif.-Berkeley, 1952; MPH, U. Hawaii, 1969. RN. Pub. health nurse San Francisco Dept. Health, 1950-52; nurse-tchr. Punahou Sch., Honolulu, 1966-67; clinic coordinator East-West Population Inst., East-West Ctr., Honolulu, 1969-75, population rschr., 1975-82, rsch. fellow, 1982-92. Cons. Hawaii Commn. on Population, Honolulu, 1970-83; mem. Hawaii Policy Action Group for Family Planning, Honolulu, 1971-89, chmn., 1976-77; nurse-cons. vol. Straub Clinic and Hosp., 2001—. Author: The Peopling of Hawaii, 1977, 2d rev. edit., 1989, A Profile of Hawaii's Elderly Population, 1984; author: (with Robert Gardner) The Demographic Situation in Hawaii, 1974; author: Pacific Images-Views from Captain Cook's Third Voyage, 1999, 2nd edit., 2008; editor: I'm Third-An American Boy of Depression Years - Memoirs of Robert A. Nordyke, MD, 2003; mem. editl. bd. Hawaiian Jour. History, 1980—; contbr. articles to profl. jours. Bd. dirs. YMCA, Honolulu, 1970-85, YMCA Camp Erdman Br., 1985—, vice-chmn. 1978-79, chmn. YMCA Camp Erdman, 1989-92; bd. dirs. Hawaii Planned Parenthood, 1974-78, Friends of Libr. of Hawaii, 1985-87, 2002-2005; trustee Hawaiian Hist. Soc., 1978-82, Arcadia Retirement Residence, Honolulu, 1978-87; mem. liberal arts coun. Hawaii Pacific U., 1988—. Mem. Population Reference Bur., Hawaii Econ. Assn., Hawaiian Hist. Soc., Friends of East-West Ctr., Friends of Univ. Hawaii Sch. Medicine, Stanford Nurses Alumni Assn., Stanford Alumni Assn. (bd. dirs. Hawaii chpt.), U. Hawaii Sch. Pub. Health Alumni Assn. (life), Gen. Fed. Women's History Club, Adventure Club of Honolulu, Book Reading Clubs, Captain-Cook Soc., Outrigger Canoe Club, Morning Music Club, Caledonian Soc., Phi Beta Kappa. Democrat. Congregationalist. Avocations: music, art, swimming, Hawaiian books, travel. Home: 2013 Kakela Dr Honolulu HI 96822-2158 Office Phone: 808-949-3549.

NORE, NANO ANN, Art History Professor; d. Russell and Lucille Nore; 1 child, Joel Lueders. BFA, Kans. City Art Inst., 1974; MARS, Ctrl. Theol. Sem., Kans. City, 1980; MA, Tex. Woman's U., Denton, 1976, MFA, 1990. K-12 Art Teaching Certification Mo. Dept. of Edn., 1974. Art instr. Kans. City Mo. Sch. Dist., 1974—78, Penn Valley CC, Kans. City, 1975—80; prof. art Pk. U., Parkville, Mo., 1980—83; art history instr. Johnson Co. CC, Overland Pk., Kans., 1986—88; prof. art & art history William Jewell Coll., Liberty, Mo., 1988—. Morocco grant, Fulbright-Hayes, 2008. Mem.: Coll. Art Assn. Democrat. Episcopalian. Office: William Jewell Coll 500 College Hill Liberty MO 64068 Business E-Mail: nanonore@william.jewell.edu.

NORELL, MARK ALLEN, paleontologist, curator; b. St. Paul, July 26, 1957; s. Albert Donald Norell and Helen Louise Soltau; m. Vivian Pan, Nov. 1, 1991; 1 child, Inga Pan. BS, Long Beach State U., 1980; MS, San Diego State U., 1983; PhD, Yale U., 1988. Assoc. curator Am. Mus., NYC, 1989—99, chmn. dept., 1996—99, divsn. chmn., curator, 1999—2005, 2008—. Adj. assoc. prof. dept. biology Yale U., New Haven, 1991-99; adj. prof. Columbia U., 1995—; lectr. in the field. Author: All You Need to Know About Dinosaurs, 1991, Discovering Dinosaurs, 1995, 2d edit., 2000 (recipient Young Readers Book of Yr. award, Scientific American), Searching for Velocirapter, 1996, A Dinosaur and Its Nest, 1999, Unearthing the Dragon, 2005, and several others; contbr. articles to profl. jours. Named Disting. Alumnus, Long Beach State U., 2000, NYC Leader of Yr., NY Times. Fellow: Explorer's Club, Willi Hennig Soc.; mem.: Soc. Vertebrate Paleontology (Romer prize 1987). Achievements include contributing to the investigation of unearthing the remains of a perfectly preserved 130 million-year-old new species of dinosaur in China, which provides a look at how prehistoric creatures slept. Office: Am Museum of Natural History 79th at Central Park W New York NY 10024-5192 Home Phone: 917-710-6399; Office Phone: 212-769-5804. Business E-Mail: norell@amnh.org.

NORELLI, TERIE THOMPSON, state legislator; b. Orange, NJ, July 7, 1952; d. George Russell and Iverna C. (Weber) Thompson; m. Allen M. Norelli, Dec. 31, 1973; children: Gina Marie, Daniel Thompson. BS in Math. summa cum laude, U. NH, 1985. Tchr. math. Winnacunnet High Sch., Hampton, NH, 1985—95; mem. Rockingham, Dist. 16 NH House of Reps., Concord, 1996—, house spkr., 2007—, sci., tech. and energy com., 1996—2003, telecomm. oversight com., 1997—2003; house Dem. leadership NH House Reps., Concord, 1998—2007; asst. Dem. whip NH House of Reps., Concord, 2002—04, asst. Dem. leader, 2005—07, chair clean air subcom., 1998—2003, electric utility restructuring oversight com., 1998—2003, pub. works and hwys. com., 2003—05, rules com., 2003—, chair, 2007—, co-chair reproductive rights caucus, 1996—2005, mem. legis. caucus for children, 1997—2002, mem. fin. com., 2005—06. Participant in devel. series geometry insvc. workshops U. NH, 1986-89. Area team Nat. Abortion Rights Action League of NH, Portsmouth, 1990-94, bd. dirs., Concord, 1996-2000; chair Naral-Prochoice NH Pac, 2001-07; bd. dirs. Sexual Assault Support Svcs., Portsmouth, 1992-96, pres. bd., 1993-95; del. to Joint US-China Conf. on Women's Issues, Beijing, 1995; organizing com. Bringing Back Beijing '95, Statewide Women's Conf., Concord, 1996, Beijing +5 Tri-State Preperation Conf., 1999; adv. bd. Feminist Health Ctr. Ports, Portsmouth, 1996-97; mem. Leadership Seacoast, 1995, bd. dirs. State Legis. Leaders Found., 2007-, chair standing coms. Nat. Coun. State Legis., 2009. Recipient NH Women's Lobby Meritorious Svc. award, 2002, Naral Pro-Choice NH Champion for Choice award, 2003, NASW-NH Legislator of Yr. award, 2004, Friend of Edn. award, 2007, Police Benevolent Assn. Legis. award, 2007, Porchlight award, Sexual Assault Support Svcs, 2007, Pub. Svc. award, Bi-State Primary Care Assn., 2006, Legis. Leadership award, NH Grange, 2008. Mem. Phi Beta Kappa, Phi Kappa Phi, Pi Mu Epsilon. Democrat. Avocations: travel, arts and culture, yoga. Home: 35 Middle Rd Portsmouth NH 03801-4802 Office: State House 107 N Main St Concord NH 03301 Home Phone: 603-436-2108; Office Phone: 603-271-3661. Business E-Mail: terie.norelli@leg.state.nh.us.

NORFLEET, LEONTINE SANDRA, retired biologist; d. James Edward and Dorothy Calloway Norfleet. BS, CUNY, NYC, 1957; MA in Biol. and Physiol. Scis., Hunter Coll., NYC, 1964; MBA in Human Resources Mgmt., Adelphi U., Garden City, NY, 1994. Clin. microbiologist Bklyn. Jewish Hosp., 1957—63; asst. bacteriologist Byrd S. Coler Hosp., Roosevelt Island, NY, 1963—64; med. rschr. LI Jewish Hosp., Ney Hyde Pk., NY, 1964—67; biochemistry assoc. Endo Labs./Dupont-Merck/Bristol Meyers Squibb, Garden City, 1967—2004, quality assurance specialist, scientist, auditor, quality engr. Author: (poem) Speaking for Myself (Editor's Choice award, 2008). Vol. NYC Ballet, 2004—; vol. math tutor, HS Learning Leaders program, NYC, 2007. Mem.: Internat. Soc. Poets, Met. Opera Guild, Am. Ballet Theater Guild, NYC Ballet Guild. Democrat. Roman Catholic. Avocations: exercise, ballet, reading, movies. Home: 111-39 201 St Saint Albans NY 11412

NORGAARD, RICHARD BRUCE, ecological economist, educator, consultant; b. Washington, Aug. 18, 1943; s. John Trout and Marva Dawn (Andersen) N.; m. Marida Jane Fowle, June 19, 1965 (div.); children: Kari Marie, Marc Anders; m. Nancy A. Rader, June 5, 1993; children: Addie Nelle, Mathiesen Rader. BA in Econs., U. Calif., Berkeley, 1965; MS in Agrl. Econs., Oreg. State U., 1967; PhD in Econs., U. Chgo., 1971. Instr. Oreg. Coll. Edn., 1967-68; asst. prof. agrl. and resource econs. U. Calif., Berkeley, 1970-76, assoc. prof., 1976-77, 80-87, assoc. prof. energy and resources, 1987-92, prof. energy and resources, 1992—. Project specialist Ford Found., Brazil, 1978-79; environ. cons. to internat. devel. agencies; sci. com. on problems of the environment U.S. Nat. Rsch. Coun.; founding chmn. bd. Redefining Progress, 1993-97; sci. adv. bd. US EPA, 2000-04; mem. ind. sci. bd. Calif. Bay-Delta Authority, 2007-08, UNEP ind. Panel Sustainable Resource Mgmt., 2009-. Author: Development Betrayed: The End of Progress and a Coevolutionary Revisioning of the Future, 1994; chpt. rev. editor Millenium Ecosys. Assessment, 2004-05; mem. editl. bd. numerous academic jours.; contbr. articles to profl. jours. Active civil rights, environ., and peace orgns. Recipient Kenneth E. Boalding award, Inst. Soc. Ecological Economics, 2006, Faculty Mentoring award, Berkeley Grad. Student Assoc., 2007. Fellow AAAS, mem. Am. Econs. Assn., Internat. Soc. Ecol. Econs. (pres. 1998-2001, past pres. 2002-2003), Fedn. Am. Scientists, Assn. Environ. and Resource Econs., Am. Inst. Biol. Scis. (bd. dirs. 2000-, treas. 2004—). Home: 1198 Keith Ave Berkeley CA 94708-1607 Office: U Calif Energy & Resources Program 310 Barrows Hall Berkeley CA 94720-3050 Business E-Mail: norgaard@berkeley.edu.

NORGLE, CHARLES RONALD, SR., federal judge; BBA, Northwestern U., Evanston, Ill., 1964; JD, John Marshall Law Sch., Chgo., 1969. Asst. state's atty. DuPage County, Ill., 1969-71, dep. pub. defender Ill., 1971-73, assoc. judge Ill., 1973-77, 78-81, cir. judge Ill., 1977-78, 81-84; judge U.S. Dist. Ct. (no. dist.) Ill., Chgo., 1984—2006, Criminal Law Com., Chgo., 2006—. Mem. exec. com. No. Dist. Ill.; mem. 7th Cir. Jud. Coun., 7th Cir. Jud. Conf. planning com., subcom. grant requests Fed. Defender Orgn., Fed. Defender Svcs. Com.; mem. Jud. Conf. Criminal Law Com.; adj. faculty Northwestern U. Sch. Law, John Marshall Law Sch., Chgo.; pres. Atticus Finch Inn Ct. Mem. ABA, Fed. Bar Assn., Fed. Circuit Bar Assn., Ill. Bar Assn., DuPage County (Ill.) Bar Assn., Nat. Attys. Assn., DuPage Assn. Women Attys., Chgo. Legal Club, Northwestern Club. Office: US Dist Ct 219 S Dearborn St Ste 2346 Chicago IL 60604-1802

NORGREN, WILLIAM ANDREW, retired religious denomination administrator; b. Frostburg, Md., May 5, 1927; s. William Andrew and Martha Elizabeth Leona (Richardson) N. BA, Coll. William and Mary, 1948; STB, now STM, Gen. Theol. Sem., NYC, 1953; LittB, Oxford U., Eng., 1959; DD (hon.), Gen. Theol. Sem., NYC, 1984, Berkley Div. Sch., Yale U., New Haven, 1995. Ordained to ministry Episcopal Ch.,

1953. Chaplain Christ Ch. Cathedral, Oxford, 1955-59; exec. dir. Commn. on Faith and Order Nat. Coun. Chs. of Christ in U.S.A., NYC, 1959-71, mem. gen. bd., 1979-95; pastoral asst. Trinity Ch., NYC, 1972-74; assoc. ecumenical officer Episcopal Ch., NYC, 1975-79, ecumenical officer, 1979-94, theol. cons., 1995-2000. Observer 2d Vatican Coun., Roman Cath. Ch., Vatican City, 1963-65; mem. assemblies World Co. Chs., various cities, 1961, 68, 83, 91. Editor: Living Room Dialogues, 1965, Implications of the Gospel, 1988, Toward Full Communion and Concordat of Agreement, 1991; author: Commentary on Called to Common Mission, 1999. Fellow, Gen. Theol. Sem., 1953—55. Democrat. Episcopalian. Avocations: art, music, theater, walking.

NORI, FRANCO MAURO, physicist, researcher; b. Caracas, Venezuela, May 7, 1959; s. Romolo and Maria (Di Natale) N. BS in Physics cum laude, U. Simón Bolívar, Caracas, 1982; MS in Physics, U. Ill., 1983, PhD in Physics, 1987. Conicit fellow U. Ill., Urbana, 1982-84, rsch. asst., 1984-87; postdoctoral rsch. fellow U. Calif., Santa Barbara, 1987-89; asst. prof. U. Mich., Ann Arbor, 1990—96, assoc. prof., 1996—2003, prof., 2004—; lab. head Digital Materials Lab., Inst. Phys. & Chem. Rsch., 2002—08. Lectr. in field. Contbr. articles to profl. jours. Fellow Am. Phys. Soc. (elected fellow), Brit. Inst. Physics, Am. Assn. Advancement Scis.(elected fellow); mem. Am. Assn. of Hispanic Physicists (life). Office: Univ of Mich Dept Physics Ann Arbor MI 48109-1040 also: Digital Materials Lab Advanced Sci Inst 2-1 Hirosawa Wako Shi Saitama 351-0198 Japan

NORIEGA, MELISSA, city councilwoman, educator; b. Phila., 1954; d. Charles and Connie Meisgeier; m. Richard J. Noriega, Feb. 14, 1991; 1 child, Richard J. Jr. 1 stepchild, Alex. BS in Psychology, U. Houston, 1977; MEd, U. Houston Coll. Edn., 1983. Faculty Houston Ind. Sch. Dist., 1981—2005, 2007—, various positions including adminstrv. asst. Title I rsch., mgr. Spl. Projects and Dist. Initiatives, now mgr. Profl. Devel. Svcs.; mem., Dist. 145 Tex. House of Reps., 2005—06; councilwoman-at-large, Position 3 Houston City Coun., 2007—. Mem. exec. com. Parents for Pub. Sch.'s. Active Christ Ch. Cathedral. Recipient Joe E. Moreno Svc. award, Tex. House Reps., 2005, Recognition award, Greater Houston Partnership, 2005, Cmty. Svc. award, Am. Jewish Com., 2006; named Freshman of Yr., Dem. Caucus, 2005. Mem.: East End C. of C. (Svc. award 2005), Eastwood Civic Assn. (past pres.), U. Houston Alumni Assn. (life). Office: City Hall Annex 900 Bagby 1st Fl Houston TX 77002 Office Phone: 832-393-3005. Office Fax: 713-247-2648. Business E-Mail: atlarge3@cityofhouston.net.*

NORIEGA, RICK (RICHARD JOEL NORIEGA), state legislator; b. Jan. 8, 1958; m to Melissa Meisgeier; children: Alexander & Rick Jr. Grad., U. Houston, 1984; MPA, Harvard U. John F. Kennedy Sch. Govt., 1999. Texas State Representative, District 145, 1999-, member, Human Serv & Transportation Committees, 1999-, Corrections, Def Affairs & State-Fed Relations Committees, currently, Texas House Representative.Sr state relations specialist, currently; project manager, Communities in Schools Inc, formerly; teacher, Houston Independent Sch District & Houston Community Col Syst, formerly; joined Houston Industries Inc (now CenterPoint Energy), 1993-, manager economic development, 1998-; director, Catholic Charities, currently. Mem. human svc. & transportation, corrections, def. affairs and state-fed. rels. coms. Tex. House Representatives. Mem. Christ Ch. Cathedral, Houston; Laredo border sector comdr. Operation Jump Start, 2006; incident comdr., Houston's Hurricane Katrina relief efforts George R. Brown Convention Ctr. Named Legislator of Year, Hispanic Journal, 2001; Awards from: Texas Association of Bilingual Educators (TABE), Texas League of United Latin America Citizens (LULAC); selected by the Texas Association of Chicanos in Higher Education (TACHE) and the Hispanic Journal as "2001 Legislator of the Year"; Nat awards included the Legislature Leaders in Education Award from the Nat Col Bd, 2002 and Hispanic Caucus of the America Association for Higher Education (AAHE) for Outstanding Support of Hispanic Issues In Higher Education, 2003; Govt of Mexico, honored with OHTLI Award. Democrat. Mailing: PO Box 230324 Houston TX 77023 Address: 2900 Woodridge Ste 305 Houston TX 77087 Office: Capitol Ext E2 718 Austin TX 78701 Fax: 512-463-5896, 713-649-6454.*

NORIN, LORI ANN, communication educator; b. Long Beach, Calif., Dec. 18, 1956; d. William Henry Clayton and Shirley Anne (Teague) Kelley; m. Kenneth E. Norin, July 25, 1987; 1 child, Alexis Ann. AA, Westark C.C., Ft. Smith, Ark., 1977; BA, Northeastern State U., Tahlequah, Okla., 1979; MA in Comm., Northeastern State U., 1987. Cert. secondary edn. tchr., Okla., Ark. Tchr. journalism Chaffin Jr. H.S., Ft. Smith, 1979-84, Northside H.S., Ft. Smith, 1985-88, Southside H.S., Ft. Smith, 1988-91; instr. journalism Westark C.C., Ft. Smith, 1991—. Cons. various h.s. Ft. Smith, 1985-95; com. chair Mass Media adv. bd., Ft. Smith, 1994-96. Adviser (lit. mag.) A Rainbow Collection (Pacemaker award), 1983; (newspaper) Southworld, 1985 (All Ark. award 1988-91), Lion Pride, Grizzly, Cougar Print; (yearbook) Southerner, 1985 (All Ark. award 1988-91), Numa, Bruin. Yearbook adviser Immaculate Conception Sch., Ft. Smith, 1991-95; Nat. judge sch. pub. Nat. Scholastic Press Assn., 1994—; judge Vet.'s Speech Contest, Ft. Smith, 1994-95. Named Outstanding Adviser Ark. H.S. Press Assn., 1983, 87, Outstanding Young Educators Ft. Smith Jaycees, 1983; Recipient Quality Journalism Instrn. Journalism Edn. Assn., 1996. Mem. Coll. Media Assn., Ark. Coll. Media, Phi Delta Kappa (editor 1996-97). Roman Catholic. Avocation: arts and crafts. Office: Westark C C 5210 Grard Ave Fort Smith AR 72913

NORINS, ARTHUR LEONARD, dermatologist, educator; b. Chgo., Dec. 2, 1928; s. Russell Joseph and Elsie (Lindemann) N.; m. Mona Lisa Wetzer, Sept. 12, 1954; children: Catherine, Nan, Jane, Arthur. BS in Chem. Engring, Northwestern U., 1951, MS in Physiology, 1953, MD, 1955. Diplomate: Am. Bd. Dermatology; subcert. in dermatopathology. Intern U. Mich., Ann Arbor, 1955-56; resident in dermatology Northwestern U., Chgo., 1956-59; asst. prof. Stanford U., 1961-64; prof., chmn. dept. dermatology, prof. pathology Ind. U. Sch. Medicine, Indpls., 1964-93, prof. emeritus, 1993—. Mem. staff Riley Children's Hosp., Univ. Hosp., Wishard Hosp.; cons. VA Hosp. Contbr. articles to profl. jours. Capt. M.C. U.S. Army, 1959-61. Recipient Pres.' award Ind. U., 1979 Fellow ACP; mem. Am. Acad. Dermatology (bd. dirs.), Am. Dermatol. Assn., Soc. Pediatric Dermatology (founder, past pres.), Am. Soc. Dermatopathology, Am. Soc. Photobiology (founder), Soc. Investigative Dermatology, Am. Acad. Dermatology (hon.), 2008 Home: 10100 Torre Ave Apt 211 Cupertino CA 95014-2168 Office: 550 University Blvd Ste 3240 Indianapolis IN 46202-5149

NORKIN, CYNTHIA CLAIR, retired physical therapist; b. Boston, May 6, 1932; d. Miles Nelson and Carolyn (Green) Clair; m. Stanislav A Norkin, Feb. 19, 1955 (dec. 1970); 1 child, Alexandra. BS in Edn., Tufts U., 1954; cert. phys. therapist, Bouve Boston Coll., 1954; MS, Boston U., 1973, EdD, 1984. Instr. Bouve Boston Coll., 1954—55; staff phys. therapist New Eng. Med. Ctr., Boston, 1954—55, Abington (Pa.) Meml. Hosp., 1965—70, Ea. Montgomery Country Vis. Nurse Assn., 1970—72; asst. prof. phys. therapy Sargent Coll./Boston U., 1973—84; assoc. prof. phys. therapy, dir., founder Ohio U. Sch. Phys. Therapy, Athens, 1984—95, ret., 1995. Consult Boston Ctr Independent Living, Cambridge Vis Nurse Asn, Mass Medicaid Cost Effectiveness Project, 1978; secy Health Planning Coun Greater Boston, 1976—78; book, manuscript reviewer F A Davis Co, 1986—; arthritis adv comt Ohio Dept Health. Author (with P Levangie and C Norkin): Joint Structure and Function: A Comprehensive Analysis, 1983, 4th edit., 2005; author: (with D J White) Joint Measurement: A Guide to Goniometry, 1985; author: 4th edit., 2009. Trustee Brimmer and May Sch, 1980. Mem.: APHA, AAAS, Athens County Vis Nurse Asn (secy adv coun 1984—95), Mass Asn Mental health, Mass Physical Therapy Asn (chair quality assurance comt 1980—83), Am Physical Therapy Asn (on site evaluator comn on accreditation 1986—95). Episcopalian.

NORLAND, RICHARD BOYCE, United States Ambassador to Uzbekistan; B, Georgetown U. Sch. Fgn. Svc., 1977; M in Internat. Pub. Policy, Johns Hopkins U. Sch. Advanced Internat. Studies, 1992; M in Nat. Security Strategy, Nat. War Coll., 2002. Joined US Fgn. Svc., 1980; fgn. svc. assignment US Dept. State, Manama, Bahrain, 1981—82, chief US info. office Tromso, 1986—88, polit. officer Moscow, 1988—90, peacekeeping monitor, Conf. on Security and Cooperation Georgia, 1993, peacekeeping monitor Chechnya, 1995, polit. counselor Dublin, 1995—98, sr. Arctic official, 1998—99, polit. officer Mazar-e-Sharif, Afghanistan, 2002—03, dep. chief of mission Riga, Latvia, 2003—05, Kabul, Afghanistan, 2005—07, US amb. to Uzbekistan Tashkent, 2007—; dir. European affairs Nat. Security Coun., Washington, 1999—2001. Office: DOS Amb 7110 Tashkent Pl Washington DC 20521-7110*

NORMAN, ALBERT GEORGE, JR., lawyer; b. Birmingham, Ala., May 29, 1929; s. Albert G. and Ila Mae (Carroll) N.; m. Catherine Marshall DeShazo, Sept. 3, 1955; children: Catherine Marshall, Albert George III. BA, Auburn U., 1953; LLB, Emory U., 1958; MA, U. NC, 1960. Bar: Ga. 1957. Assoc. Moise, Post & Gardner, Atlanta, 1958-60, ptnr., 1960-62, Hansell & Post, Atlanta, 1962-86, Long, Aldridge & Norman, Atlanta, 1986-2000. Dir. Atlanta Gas Light Co., 1976-2000. Served with USAF, 1946-49. Mem. ABA, Ga. Bar Assn., Atlanta Bar Assn., Lawyers Club Atlanta (pres. 1973-74), Am. Law Inst., Am. Judicature Soc. (dir. 1975-78), Old War Horse Lawyers Club, (pres. 1991-92), Cherokee Town and Country Club. Episcopalian. Office: 134 Peachtree St NW Atlanta GA 30303-1802 Personal E-mail: almarnorman@mindspring.com.

NORMAN, BOBBY DON, artist, writer, research scientist; b. Dallas, June 5, 1933; s. Reuben Ray Norman and Bessie Mae Norman-Gregory; m. Mae Pearl Delley (dec. July 8, 2001); 1 child, Parette Michelle. Cert. grad. (hon.), S.W. Sch. Bus. Adminstrn., 1959. Mgr. Mile High Club, Dallas, 1955—57; city distbn. clk. U.S. Post Office, Dallas, 1959—66; office mgr., co-dir. So. Christian Leadership Conf., Dallas, 1969—73; cmty. liaison dir. Planned Parenthood N.E. Tex., Dallas, 1974—76; exec. v.p., gen. mgr. Davis Norman & Zanders, Inc., Dallas, 1977—78; house supr. Fed. Bur. Prisons, Dallas, 1982—83; supr. Halfway House Tex. Dept. Corrections, Dallas, 1983—84; artist, writer, scientist, publ. speaker Dallas, 1955—. Founder, pres. Assn. Advancing Artists and Writers, Inc., Dallas, 1969—76. Author: Artistic Theological Science, 1998, Biblical Geology, 1998, Tectonic Fundamentals of Biblical Geology, 1998, Tectonic Analyses and Notes of Modern Biblical Geology and Earth Science, 1998, Tectonic Verbal Postering and Various Advanced Studies of Earth Science, 1998, Glossary and Cross Reference of Biblical Geology and Tectonics, 1999, Biblical Geology: Events, Writings and Geo-Morality, 2003, Time of Babel: Biblical Geology and Tectonics, 2004; Artistic Theology and Perpendicular Line Compostion, 2005. Commr. Greater Dallas Cmty. Rels. Commn., 1970—72; mem. block partnership com. Greater Dallas Coun. Chs., 1970—71; organizer, tactical negotiator Dallas-Ft. Worth Coalition for the Free Flow of Info., 1970—72. Cpl. USAF, 1951—55, Korea. Recipient Tng. award, So. Christian Leadership Conf., 1969, Svc. award, Greater Dallas Cmty. Rels. Commn., 1972, Art award, Black C. of C., 1973. Baptist. Achievements include research in Biblical geology. Avocations: fishing, art.

NORMAN, CHRISTINA, broadcast executive; b. July 30, 1963; m. Charles Hunt; children: Zoe, Asha. BA in Film Prodn., Boston U., 1985. Freelance prodn. coord MTV Networks, 1986—91, prodn. mgr., 1991—93, supervising prodr., on-air promotions, 1993—94, dir., on-air promotions, 1994—95, v.p., on-air promotions, 1995—97, sr. v.p., on-air promotions, 1997—99, sr. v.p., mktg. & on-air promotion, 1999—2002, pres., 2005—08, VH1, 2004—05, exec. v.p., gen. mgr., 2002—04; CEO Oprah Winfrey Network (OWN), 2009—. Recipient Nat. Pub. Svc. award, Television Acad. Emmy Awards, 2002, Namiq Qasar Vision award, 2003; named one of The 10 Most Powerful Blacks in TV, Ebony mag., 2002, The 100 Most Powerful Women in Hollywood, Hollywood Reporter, 2003, 2006, 2007; named to 40 under 40 list, Crain's NY Bus., 2003.*

NORMAN, DONALD ARTHUR, psychologist, educator; b. NYC, Dec. 25, 1935; s. Noah N. and Miriam F. N.; m. Martha Karpati (dec.); children: Cynthia, Michael; m. Julie Jacobsen; 1 child, Eric. BSEE, MIT, 1957; MSEE, U. Pa., 1959, PhD in Psychology, 1962; degree in psychology (hon.), U. Padua, Italy, 1995; PhD in Indsl. Design (hon.), Tech. U. Delft, The Netherlands, 2006. Lectr. Harvard U., 1962-66; prof. dept. psychology U. Calif.-San Diego, La Jolla, 1966-92, prof. emeritus, 1992—, prof., chair dept. cognitive sci., 1988-92, chair dept. psychology, 1974-78; Apple fellow Apple Computer Inc., Cupertino, Calif., 1993-97, v.p. advanced tech., 1995-97; exec. info. appliances Hewlett Packard, Palo Alto, Calif., 1997-98; co-founder, prin. Nielsen Norman Group, Fremont, Calif., 1998—; pres. learning sys. UNext, 1999—2001; prof. departments elec. engring., computer sci., psychology and cognitive sci. Northwestern U., 2001—; co-dir. Segal Design Inst., 2007—, Kellgy Mc Cornick Program, 2008—; breed prof. Dergn, 2008—; vis. disting. prof. KAIST, Republic of Korea. Cons. to industry on human centered product design. Author: Human Information Processing, 2d edit., 1977, Learning and Memory, 1982, User Centered System Design, 1986, The Psychology of Everyday Things, 1988, The Design of Everyday Things, 1989, 2002, Turn Signals Are the Facial Expressions of Automobiles, 1992, Things That Make Us Smart, 1993, The Invisible Computer, 1998, Emotional Design, 2004, The Design of Future Things, 2007; mem. edtl. bd. Ency. Brit. Recipient Excellence in Rsch. award, U. Calif., 1983, Benjamin Franklin medal in Computer and Cognitive Sci., Franklin Inst., 2006. Fellow: APA, Am. Psychol. Soc. (charter fellow, Franklin V. Taylor award 2005), Assn. Computing Machines (Lifetime Achievement award (Human-Computer Interaction Group)), Cognitive Sci. Soc. (chmn., founding mem.), Human Factors and Ergonomics Soc., Am. Acad. Arts and Scis.; mem.: Sigma Xi. E-mail: norman@nngroup.com.

NORMAN, GREGORY JOHN, professional golfer; b. Mt. Isa, Australia, Feb. 10, 1955; m. Laura Andrassy, July 1, 1981 (div. 2006); children: Morgan-Leigh, Gregory. Profl. golfer, 1976—; chmn., CEO Gt. White Shark Enterprises Inc., Hobe Sound, Fla. Capt. Pres.'s Cup Internat. Team, 2008. Winner Brit. Open Championship, 1986, 93, 20 PGA Tour titles, 68 additional internat. titles; winner Vardon trophy, 1989, 90, 94; recipient Arnold Palmer award for leading money winner, 1995, Byron Nelson trophy for the lowest scoring average, 1995; ranked #1 in World Golf Ranking for 331 Weeks; named PGA Player of Yr., 1995, PGA Tour Player of Yr., 1995; named to World Golf Hall of Fame, 2001. Achievements include being the leading Money Winner PGA Tour 1986, 90. Office Phone: 561-743-8818.

NORMAN, JOHN BARSTOW, JR., graphics designer, educator; b. Paola, Kans., Feb. 5, 1940; s. John B. and Ruby Maxine (Johnson) N.; m. Roberta Jeanne Martin, June 6, 1967; children: John Barstow III, Elizabeth Jeanne. BFA, U. Kans., 1962, MFA, 1966. Designer and illustrator Advt. Design, Kansas City, Mo., 1962-64; asst. instr. U. Kans., Lawrence, 1964-66; art dir. Hallmark Cards, Inc., Kansas City, 1966-69; instr. dept. art U. Denver, 1969-73, asst. prof., 1973-78, assoc. prof., 1978-93, disting. prof., 1980-93, prof. emeritus, 1993—; sr. designer Mo. Coun. Arts & Humanities, 1966-67; cons. designer Rocky Mt. Bank Note Corp., Denver, 1971—. Cons. designer Signage identity System, U. Denver; bd. dirs. comm. U. Denver; tech. cons. Denver Art Mus., 1974—, designed exhbns, 1974-75; adv. cons. Jefferson County (Colo.) Sch. System, 1976—; chmn. Design and Sculpture Exhbn., Colo. Celebration of the Arts, 1975-76. One-man shows include GalleryCortina, Aspen, Colo., 1983; commd. works include Jedda, Saudi Arabia, Synegistics Corp., Denver; represented in permanent collections Pasadena Ctr. for Arts, N.Y. Arts Dirs. Club, Calif. State U./Fiber Collection, Pasadena Ctr. Arts, N.Y. Art Dirs. Club, Midland Art Coun./Fiber Collection, Geologic Soc. Am.; represented in traveling exhbns. L.A. Art Dirs. Show and N.Y. Art Dirs. Show, U.S., Europe, Japan, 1985; featured in Denver Post, 1984, Post Electric City Mag., 1984, Rocky Mt. News, 1984, Douglas County Press, 1984, Mile High Cable Vision, 1985, Sta. KWGN-TV, 1985, Les Krantz's Am. Artists, 1988; illustrated Survey of Leading Contemporaries, 1988, U.S. Surface Design Jour., 1988; co-work represented in film collectin Mus. Modern Art, N.Y.C.; selected fashion show designs displayed Sister City dels., Denver, 1987. Recipient Silver medal award N.Y. Internat. Film and Video Competition, 1976, Design awards Coun. ADvancement and Support Edn., 1969, 71, 73; 76, Honor Mention award L.A. Art Dirs. Club, 1984, Honor Mention award N.Y. ARt Dirs. Club, 1984, Native Am. Wearable Art Competition, 1985, 5th pl. Nat. Wind Sail Am. Banners Competition, Midland, Mich., 1985, also awards for surface designs in Colo. Ctr. for Arts Wearable ARt Competition, 1984-85, Foothills Art Gallery Nat. Wearable Competition, 1984-85, Fashion Group Denver Competition, 1984-85. Mem. Art Dirs. Club Denver (Gold medals 1974-82, Best of Show Gold medal 1983, Honor Mentin award 1984, 3 gold medals 1989), Univ. Dirs. Assn. Home: PO Box 507 Lake George CO 80827-0507 Office Phone: 719-339-1751, 719-216-4990. Personal E-mail: normanranch@earthlink.net.

NORMAN, MARY MARSHALL, academic administrator, alcohol/drug abuse services professional, educator; b. Auburn, NY, Jan. 10, 1937; d. Anthony John and Zita Norman. BS cum laude, LeMoyne Coll., 1958; MA, Marquette U., 1960; EdD, Pa. State U., 1971. Cert. alcoholism counselor. Tchr. St. Cecilia's Elem. Sch., Theinsville, Wis., 1959-60; vocat. counselor Marquette U., Milw., 1959-60; dir. testing and counseling U. Rochester (N.Y.), NY, 1960-62; dir. testing and counseling, dean women, assoc. dean coll. Corning (N.Y.) C.C., Corning (NY) C.C., 1962-68, asst. dean students, dir. student activities, asst. prof. ps University Park, 1962-68; rsch. asst. Ctr. for Study Higher Edn. Pa. State U., University Park, Pa., 1969-71; dean faculty South Campus C.C. Allegheny County, West Mifflin, Pa., 1971-72, campus pres., coll. v.p., 1972-82; pres. Orange County C.C., 1982-86; alcohol counselor Sullivan County Alcohol Drug Abuse Svc., 1985-90; sr. counselor Horton Family Program, 1990-96, ednl. cons., writer, 1996—. Cons. Boricua Coll., N.Y.C., 1976-77; reader NSF, 1977-78; govtl. commn. com. Am. Assn. Cmty. and Jr. Colls., 1976-79, bd. dirs., 1982—; chmn. middle state accreditation teams; chmn. Ernest Boyer, pres. Carnegie Found., 1987, with, com. redefine the Liberal Arts degree, 1982. Contbr. articles to profl. jours. Active Econ. Devel. Seneca County, Seneca County Tourism Bd.; mem. planning bd. Town of Seneca Falls, 2006—; active St. Patrick's Ch.; bd. dirs. Orange County United Way, Orange County Alcoholism and Drug Abuse Coun., 1993—96, Seneca County Hist. Soc., 1997—, Guild and Altar Soc., 1999. Mem. Nat. Women's Hall of Fame. Mem.: Pa. Coun. on Higher Edn., Nat. Am. Coun. on Edn. (Pa. rep. identification women for adminstrn. 1978—82, pres. 1980—96, bd. dirs.), Pitts. Coun. Women Execs. (charter), Pa. Assn. Acad. Deans, Pa. Assn. Two-Yr. Colls., Am. Assn. Women in Cmty. and Jr. Colls. (charter, Woman of the Yr. 1981), Nat. Assn. Women Deans and Counselors, Am. Assn. Higher Edn., Seneca County C. of C. (bd. dirs., mem. tourism com.), Orange County C. of C. (bd. dirs.), Amnesty Internat. (charter mem. women's coun. 2000—), Concerned Citizens for Good Govt. (charter), Kiwanis (bd. dirs. 2002—05, planning bd. Seneca Falls 2006—), Gamma Pi Epsilon. Home: 9 S Park St Seneca Falls NY 13148-1423 Office Phone: 315-568-2392.

NORMAN, RALPH LOUIS, retired physicist, consultant; b. Kingston, Tenn., Mar. 25, 1933; s. Walter Hugh and Helen Irene (Smith) N.; m. Agnes Irene Pickel, Sept. 5, 1964; children: Mark Alan, Max Alvin. BS, U. Tenn., 1959; LL.B., Blackstone Sch. Law, 1967, JD, 1971; certificate, Indsl. Coll. Armed Forces, 1969; MA in Pub. Adminstrn, U. Okla., 1971; D.Sci. (hon.), Apollo Research Inst., 1976. Engr. Chrysler Corp. Missile Div., Huntsville, Ala., 1959-60; physicist Army Rocket & Guided Missile Agy., Redstone Arsenal, Ala., 1960-61; asst. project mgr. Army Missile Command, Redstone Arsenal, 1961-62, project mgr., 1962-89, ret., 1989; cons. to several def. contractors, 1989—; faculty Athens (Ala.) Coll., 1970-71, Calhoun Jr. Coll., Decatur, Ala., 1971-74, 85-90, U. Montevallo, Ala., 1973-74, U. Ala. at Huntsville, 1976-77, Columbia (Mo.) Coll., 1977-79. Cons. firm Bishop and Sexton, 1973—, Athens State Coll., Ala.; reviewer NSF, 1974-76; FAA examiner. Contbr. articles profl. jours. Served with USN, 1951-55. Recipient Dept. Def. commendations, 1961, 65, Dept. Army commendation, 1972 Mem. N.Y. Acad. Scis., Assn. U.S. Army. Home: 102 Nobleton Ln NW Huntsville AL 35806-4014 *I strive to make the knowledge gained through my research benefit all mankind.*

NORMAN, THENA MONTS DURHAM, microbiologist, researcher, health facility administrator; b. Bradenton, Fla., July 10, 1945; d. Turner and Silverrene (Taylor) M.; m. Millard Durham, Aug. 30, 1969 (div. 2001); children: Bryce Vincent-Barnard, Brittanie Yvonne; m. Herman H. Norman, August 6, 2005. BS, Fisk U., 1966; MS, Purdue U., 1968. Rsch. microbiologist Ctrs. for Disease Control, Atlanta, 1968-86, assoc. dir. for programs Nat. Ctr. for Prevention Svcs., 1988-95; program analyst Office Dir. Ctr. for Health Promotion and Edn., 1986-88; dir. exec. secretariat Ctrs. for Dis. Control and Prevention, Atlanta, 1995—2001; dep. dir. for policy Nat. Ctr. for HIV, STD, and TB Prevention for CDC, Atlanta, 2001—05; ret., 2005. Cons. FDA; mem. alumnae adv. com., pres. coun. dept. biol. scis. Purdue U.; bd. dirs. Balm in Gilead, Inc. Contbr. articles to profl. jours. Mem. NAACP, Neighborhood Planning Unit, SCLC/Women Adv. Coun., So. Christian Leadership Council/Women, Atlanta, 2005; bd. dirs. Cmty. Advanced Practices Nurses, Atlanta, 2004. Recipient Sec.'s award for Disting. Svc. Dept. HHS, 2001. Mem. AAAS, Sci. Rsch. Soc., Am. Soc. Microbiologists, CDC Assn. Exec. Women (founder, co-chmn.), Women in Sci. and

Engring., Alumni Adv. Com., Nat. Assn. Broaden and Enchance Images (bd. dirs.). Democrat. Office Phone: 404-753-1322, 678-613-6265. Personal E-mail: thena1@bellsouth.net.

NORMAND, ROBERT, retired lawyer; b. Montreal, Que., Can., Sept. 24, 1936; s. Lucien and Eva (Rochon) N.; m. Madeleine Scott, Sept. 16, 1961; children: Eric, Yves, Genevieve. BA, U. Montreal, 1956; LLL, U. Sherbrooke, Que., 1960; diploma, Inst. d'etudes politiques, Paris, 1962. Bar: Que. 1960. Legal adviser Nat. Assembly, Quebec City, 1962-67, law clk., 1967-71; asst. dep. min. justice Que. Govt., Quebec City, 1970-71, dep. min. justice, 1971-77, dep. min. intergovtl. affairs, 1977-82, dep. min. fin., 1982-87; pres., pub. Le Soleil (Hollinger), Quebec City, 1987-93; v.p. corp. affairs UniMedia Inc., 1993-94, dep. min. internat. affairs, 1994-96; pres., dir. gen. Télé-Québec, 1996-99, ret., 1999. Sec. Study Com. on Expropriation 1965-67; guest prof. legis. law faculty Laval U., Ottawa U., 1971; pres. Que. Police Inst., 1974; chmn. Com. Supervising Olympic Security, 1974-76; chmn. Uniform Law Conf. Can.; dir. Caisse de Dèpot et Placement du Quèbec, 1982-87; v.p. Can. del. Diplomatic Conf. on travel contracts, Brussels, 1970; pres. Can. del. at convs. Internat. Inst. French Lang. law, 1974, 76. V.p. Hosp. du Saint-Sacrement, Quebec City, 1988-94; vice chmn. Inst. Rsch. on Pub. Policy, Montreal, 1988-94; pres. Que. Symphony Orch., Quebec City, 1989-92; consul gen. Sweden, Quebec City, 1989-94; co-pres. United Way Campaign Greater Quebec Region, 1989, hon. chmn. Telethon for Cerebral Palsy, 1990; mem. Citizens Forum, Spicer Commn., 1990-91; chmn. Ec. Nat. de l'Humour, 1997-99. Capt. Can. Army, 1954-60. Named Queen's Counsel, 1971, Comdr., Royal Order of the Polar Star, Sweden, Chevalier de la Legion d'honneur, France; recipient Pub. Adminstrn. award of excellence Nat. Sch. Pub. Adminstrn. Alumni, Quebec City, 1986. Mem. Investment Dealers Assn. Can. (dir. 1989-94), Que. Garrison Club (dir. 1991-96), Profl. Liability Ins. of Que. Bar (dir. 1991-94), Que. Bar (supervisory com. 1988-93), La Commanderie de Bordeaux. Roman Catholic. Avocations: fishing, hunting. Home: 2750 de L'Anse Sainte-Foy PQ Canada G1W 2G5 E-mail: robenorm@videotron.ca.

NORMANDEAU, ANDRE GABRIEL, criminologist, educator; b. Montreal, May 4, 1942; s. Gabriel E. and Laurette D. (Sauve) N.; m. Pierrette La Pointe, Aug. 14, 1965; children: Alain, Louis, Jean. MA in Criminology, U. Pa., Phila., 1965, PhD in Sociology, 1968. Asst. prof. criminology U. Montreal, 1968-71, assoc. prof., 1971-76, prof., 1976—, chmn. dept. criminology, 1970-80, dir. Internat. Ctr. Comparative Criminology, 1983-89, dir. Rsch. Inst. on Police, 1990—. Author: Public Attitudes and Crime, 1970, The Measurement of Crime, 1975, Patterns of Robbery, 1980, Crimes of Violence, 1985, A Vision of the Police, 1990, Crime Prevention, 1993, Justice and Minorities, 1995, Community Policing, 1998, Death Penalty, 2003, Terrorism, 2006, Prisons in Can. and France, 2008. Woodrow Wilson fellow, 1964-68 Mem. Internat. Soc. Criminology, Am. Soc. Criminology, Am. Sociol. Assn., Can. Criminal Justice Assn. Roman Catholic. Avocations: movies, tennis. Home: 3150 Ave Kent Montreal PQ Canada H3S 1N1 Office: Dept Criminology U Montreal Montreal PQ Canada H3C 3J7 Home Phone: 514-345-0038; Office Phone: 514-343-6111 ext 3999. Business E-Mail: andre.normandeau@umontreal.ca. *Happiness is achieved by working for it, not by waiting for it to come to you.*

NORMILE, ROBERT J., lawyer, consumer products company executive; b. July 1959; BA in econ. & philosophy, Fordham U.; JD, NYU. Atty. Latham & Watkins, Sullivan & Cromwell; asst. gen. counsel Mattel Inc., El Segundo, Calif., 1992—94, v.p., asst. gen. counsel, 1994—98, v.p., assoc. gen. counsel, sec., 1998—99, sr. v.p., gen. counsel, sec., 1999—. Office: Mattel Inc 333 Continental Blvd El Segundo CA 90245-5012 Office Phone: 310-252-2000. Office Fax: 310-252-2180.

NORMORE, CALVIN, philosophy professor; BA with honors, McGill U., 1968; MA in Philosophy, U. Toronto, 1969, PhD in Philosophy, 1976. Prof. philosophy UCLA, 1997—2008; Macdonald chair moral philosophy McGill U., Montreal, 2008—. Hon. rsch. prof. U. Queensland, Australia. Fellow: Am. Acad. Arts and Sciences; mem.: Am. Philos. Assn. (past pres. Pacific divsn.). Office: McGill U Dept Philosophy 855 Sherbrooke St W Montreal PQ H3A 2T7 Canada

NORONA, MIKE, automotive parts company executive; married; 2 children. B in Commerce, U. BC. Head fin. Future Shop, Canada; v.p. fin. svcs. Best Buy Co. Inc., pres. fin. svcs., 2007—08; exec. v.p., CFO Advance Auto Parts, Inc., Roanoke, Va., 2008—. Adv. com. mem. MasterCard, First Data; former bd. mem. World Wide Retail Exchange. Mem.: Certified Gen. Accountants of Can. Office: Advance Auto Parts Inc 5008 Airport Rd Roanoke VA 24012*

NORONHA, SILVESTER JOHN, engineer, researcher; married, Nov. 23. PhD, Indian Inst. Sci., Bangalore, 1998. Cert. profl. engr., Va., 2009. Postdoc. rsch. assoc. Oxford U., England, 1999—2001; rsch. assoc., lectr. U. Calif., LA, 2002—07; sr. engr. Areva NP Inc., Lynchburg, Va., 2007—. Mem.: ASME (web master 2008), TMS, MRS. Achievements include research in dynamical basis of repeated yielding phenomena; physical basis of brittle-ductile transition; origin of scatter in fracture toughness measurements. Office: Areva NP Inc 3315 Old Forest Rd Lynchburg VA 24501 Office Fax: 434-382-2343.

NORQUIST, DAVID L., federal agency administrator; b. 1966; BA, MA, U. Mich., Georgetown U. Staff mem. appropriations com. US Ho. of Reps.; dep. under sec. for fin. mgmt., comptr. US Dept. Def., acting prin. under sec., comptr., dep. under sec. for budget and appropriations affairs, comptr.; CFO US Dept. Homeland Security, 2006—. Office: US Dept Homeland Security Seventh and D Streets SW Washington DC 20528 Office Phone: 202-401-4782. Office Fax: 202-772-9646.*

NORQUIST, GROVER GLENN, economist; b. Sharon, Pa., Oct. 19, 1956; s. Warren Elliott and Carol (Lutz) Norquist; m. Samah Alrayyes, Apr. 2, 2005. BA, Harvard U., 1978, MBA, 1981. Exec. dir. Nat. Taxpayers Union, Washington, 1978-79, Coll. Rep. Nat. Com., Washington, 1981-82, Americans for Reagan Agenda, Washington, 1982-83; chief speechwriter U.S. C. of C., Washington, 1983-85; field dir. Citizens for America, Washington, 1985; founder, pres. Americans for Tax Reform, Washington, 1985—. Econ. adv. UNITA, Angola, 1985—88; speech writer presdl. campaigns, 1987, 88; mem. Small Bus. Survival Com., 1994; chmn. emeritus Islamic Free Market Inst. Author: Rock the House, 1995, Leave Us Alone: Getting the Government's Hands Off Our Money, Our Guns, Our Lives, 2008; polit. columnist Am. Spectator mag., 1992—. Named one of The 50 Most Powerful People in DC, GQ mag., 2007, The 25 Most Influential Republicans, Newsmax Mag., 2008. Mem.: NRA (bd. dirs.), Am. Soc. Competitiveness (pres.), Am. Conservative Union (bd. dirs.). Republican. Office: Ams for Tax Reform Ste 200 722 12th St NW Fl 4 Washington DC 20005-3966*

NORRELL, MARY PATRICIA, nursing educator; b. Seymour, Ind., Jan. 03; d. William C. and Mary Elizabeth (Elkins) Ulrey; m. Robert Gerald Norrell, Aug. 17, 1974; children: Shannan, Richard, Trisha. BSN, Ball State U., Muncie, Ind., 1971; MS, Ind. U., Bloomington, 1996. Cert. inpatient obstetrics, TB and CPR instr. Team leader Mt. Sinai Med. Ctr., Miami Beach, Fla., 1971—73; charge nurse Jackson County Schneck Meml. Hosp., Seymour, Ind., 1971, 1973—74; nurse Camp Matoaka, Oakland, Maine, 1973; prof. Ivy Tech. C.C. Ind., Columbus, Ind., 1974—. Item writer Nat. Coun. Licensure Exam. Practical Nurses, 1992; participant Acad. Instrl. Excellence, Ivy Tech. C.C. Ind., 2001-02; practical nursing program chair Ivy Tech. C.C. Ind., 2003-06. Textbook reviewer, cons.: Saunders, 1990—97, textbook reviewer: Prentice-Hall, 2005; textbook reviewer F.A. Davis, 2005—. Bd. dirs. Sr. Ctr., Columbus, Ind., 2005—. Recipient Pres.'s award for instrnl. excellence, 2003. Home: 572 Shawnee Ct Seymour IN 47274-1956 Business E-Mail: mnorrell@ivytech.edu.

NORRID, HENRY GAIL, osteopathic physician and surgeon, researcher, educator, healthcare facility administrator; b. Amarillo, Tex., June 4, 1940; s. Henry Horatio and Johnnie Belle (Combs, Cummins) N.; m. Andreia Maybeth Hudson, Jan. 29, 1966 (dec. 1988); children: Joshua Andrew, Noah Adam; m. Cheryll Diane Payne, Mar. 19, 1989 (div. Aug. 2000); stepchildren: Kim Sheri Payne, Matthew Dominic Payne; m. Carolyn A. Layton, June 8, 2002; stepchildren: Crissey Ann Elizabeth Bruce, David Randall Marshall Bruce. AA, Amarillo Coll., 1963; BA, U. Tex., 1966; MS, W. Tex. State U., 1967; DO, Kirksville Coll., 1973. Diplomate Bd. Osteo. Physicians and Surgeons, Nat. Bd. Examiners Osteo. Physicians and Surgeons; cert. basic sci. tchr. Iowa, Tex., Colo. Intern Interboro Gen. Hosp., Bklyn., 1973-74; attending physician dept. gen. practice Osteo. Hosp. and Clinic N.Y., NYC, 1974-77; gen. practice medicine specializing in osteo. Amarillo, Tex., 1978—; emergency care physician Amarillo Emergency Receiving Ctr. Amarillo Hosp. Dist., 1978-79, Ready Care Emergency Ctr., Arlington and Bedford, Tex., 1990-92, St. Anthony Hosp., Amarillo, 1992; history cons. Tex. Panhandle Heritage Found., 2004—. Emeritus mem. consulting staff physician dept. family practice Northwest Tex. Hosp., Amarillo, 1995; emergency/trauma physician Tex. EM Care, 1995—; mem. mass casualty nat. disaster response team ARC, 1995; contract staff physician Tex. Tech. Univ. Sch. Medicine and Health Scis. Ctr., med. dept. and infirmary Tex. Dept. Corrections, Tex. Dept. Criminal Justice, 1992-94; med. cons. rehab. medicine vocat rehab. divsn. Tex. Rehab. Commn., Plano, 1992-94; cattleman, ranch owner, Van Zandt County, Tex.; lectr. osteo. prins. and practice, The Osteo. Hosp. and Clinic N.Y., 1974-77, mem. credentials com., 1975-76; mem. exec. com. Southwest Osteo. Hosp., Amarillo, 1983-84, chief of staff, 1984-85; sec. dept. family practice Northwest Tex. Hosp., Amarillo, 1981-82, mem. credentials com., 1984-85, joint practice com. dept. family practice, 1986-87; mem. orgnl. com. for devel. of dept. osteo. prins. and practices, chmn. N.Y.C. group N.Y. Coll. Osteo. Med., 1977; mem. founding com. N.Y. Coll. Osteo. Medicine, N.Y. Inst. Tech., Old Westbury L.I., 1976-77; mem. North Tex. Support Group, Dallas; instr. human anatomy and physiology dept. biol. scis. Amarillo Coll., 1998-2001, fall 2003. Contbr. articles to Tex. Jour. Sci., other publs. Scout physician Llano Estecato coun. Boy Scouts Am., Tex., 1978-85; vol. physician Hurricane Katrina, 2005; active Polk St. Meth. Ch., Amarillo. Served to E-4 U.S. Army, 1956-63. Recipient William M. Giltner Meml. Fund award 1972, Humanitarian award Am. Cath. Conf., 1979, Century award Boy Scouts Am., 1982, Pfizer Sr. Med. Student award, 1973; Maxwell D. Warmer Meml. scholar 1973; scholar Kirksville Coll. Osteo. Medicine, 1970; Tex. Legislature scholar, 1969-73; named to Eminent Soc. Border Legionaires, 11th Armored Cavalry Regiment, Germany, 1958. Mem. Am. Coll. Gen. Practitioners, Tex. Osteo. Med. Assn. (life) (pres. dist. I, mem. ho. of dels. 1981-82, 95), Tex. C.C. Tchrs. Assn., SAR, The Sons of Republic of Tex., Am. Osteo. Assn., World Future Soc. (profl.), Gen. Soc. War of 1812, NY Acad. Scis., Ex-Student's Assn. of The U. Tex. (life), 11th Armored Cavalry Regiment Assn., 36th (Tex.) Inf. Divsn. Assn. (life), Baron of the Magna Charta (Somerset chpt. Magna Charta Barrons 1994—), Masons, Am. Legion, Beta Beta Beta, Sigma Sigma Phi (pres. 1972), Alpha Phi Omega, Psi Sigma Alpha, Theta Psi, Theta Psi Clowns (1969-73). Avocations: astronomy, short wave listening, camping, fishing, history.

NORRINGTON, LORRIE M., Internet company executive; b. 1960; BBA, U. Md., 1982; MBA, Harvard U., Cambridge, Mass., 1989. With GE, 1982—2001; pres., CEO GE FANUC Automation; exec. v.p. small bus. and personal fin. Intuit Inc., Mountain View, Calif., 2001—05, mem. Office of CEO, 2003—05; pres., CEO Shopping.com Ltd. eBay Inc., 2005—06, pres. eBay Internat. San Jose, 2006—08, head of marketplace ops., 2008, pres. eBay Marketplaces, 2008—. Mem. adv. bd. Catalyst Group. Named one of 50 Most Powerful Women in Bus., Fortune mag., 2008. Office: eBay Inc 2145 Hamilton Ave San Jose CA 95125*

NORRIS, ALAN EUGENE, federal judge; b. Columbus, Ohio, Aug. 15, 1935; s. J. Russell and Dorothy A. (Shrader) N.; m. Nancy Jean Myers, Apr. 15, 1962 (dec. Jan. 1986); children: Tom Edward Jackson, Tracy Elaine; m. Carol Lynn Spohn, Nov. 10, 1990. BA, Otterbein Coll., 1957, HLD (hon.), 1991; cert., U. Paris, 1956; LLB, NYU, 1960; LLM, U. Va., 1986; HLD (hon.), Capitul U. Law Sch., 2001. Bar: Ohio 1960, US Dist. Ct. (so. dist) Ohio 1962, US Dist. Ct. (no. dist) Ohio 1964. Law clk. to judge Ohio Supreme Ct., Columbus, 1960-61; assoc. Vorys, Sater, Seymour & Pease, Columbus, 1961-62; ptnr. Metz, Bailey, Norris & Spicer, Westerville, Ohio, 1962-80; judge Ohio Ct. Appeals (10th dist.), Columbus, 1981-86, US Ct. Appeals (6th cir.), Columbus, 1986—, sr. judge, 2001—. Contbr. articles to profl. jours. Mem. Ohio Ho. of Reps., Columbus, 1967—80. Named Outstanding Young Man, Westerville Jaycees, 1971; recipient Legislator of Yr. award Ohio Acad. Trial Lawyers, Columbus, 1972. Mem. Ohio Bar Assn., Columbus Bar Assn. Lodges: Masons (master 1966-67). Republican. Methodist. Office: US Ct Appeals 328 US Courthouse 85 Marconi Blvd Columbus OH 43215-2823*

NORRIS, CHARLES HEAD, lawyer, manufacturing executive; b. Boston, Sept. 14, 1940; s. Charles Head and Martha Marie N.; m. Diana D. Strawbridge, July 27, 1974 (div. 1994); children: Margaret Dorrance, Cecilia Walker; m. Ceil T. Walker, Oct. 13, 2001. BA, U. Pa., 1963; JD, 1968; MA, U. Wash., 1965. Mem. Morgan, Lewis & Bockius, Phila., 1968-77; pres., chief exec. Artemis Corp., 1978-79; chmn. bd., chief exec., 1979-91; chmn. exec. com., vice-chmn. bd. Remington Rand Corp., 1979-81; ptnr. Artemis Energy Co., 1980-92; chmn., CEO Norris Investment Co., 1992—. Chmn. Norris Mfg. Co., 1994—, Garret Precision Products, 1996—; chmn., CEO AmTech Engring. Co., 1996—, Triad Tool & Die, 2009-; trustee maj. stockholders' voting trust Campbell Soup Co., 1987-90; bd. dirs. SBSF Funds, Inc., 1988-91, Del. Trust, 1987-91. Mem. Harvard U. Overseas Com. to Visit Libr., 1989—; mem. Pa. Commn. to Crime and Delinquency, 1980-84; mem. Thouron Award Selection Com., 1985-90; mem. Pa. Electoral Coll., 1980; mem. West Pikeland Twp. Suprs., 1969-72; mem. bd. visitors Carnegie Mellon U. Sch. Urban and Pub. Affairs, 1988-90; corp. mem. Belmont Hill Sch., 1990—. Served with USAF, 1960. Mem. ABA, Pa. Bar Assn., Am. Econ. Assn., Phila., Knickerbocker, Vicmead Hunt, Everglades (bd. dirs. 1986-91), Bath and Tennis Club (treas., bd. dirs. 1985-91), Sunningdale Golf Club, The Brookline (Mass.) Country Club, Coral Beach and Tennis Club, Mid Ocean Club, Rolling Rock Club. Office: PO Box 772719 Memphis TN 38177-2719 Address: Clark Tower 5100 Poplar Ave Ste 2700 Memphis TN 38137 Office Phone: 901-322-6049. Business E-Mail: bfoust@norrisinvestmentco.com.

NORRIS, CHUCK (CARLOS RAY), actor; b. Ryan, Okla., Mar. 10, 1940; s. Ray and Wilma Norris; m. Dianne Holochek, Dec., 1958 (div. 1988), children: Mike, Dina, Eric; m. Gena O. Kelly, Nov. 28, 1998; children: Dakota Alan, Danilee; stepchildren: Kelley, Tim. Weekly syndicated columnist World Net Daily, Townhall Human Events. Actor: (films) The Wrecking Crew, 1969, Return of the Dragon, 1972, The Student Teachers, 1973, Slaughter in San Francisco, 1974, Breaker!, Breaker!, 1977, Good Guys Wear Black, 1978, Force of One, 1979, The Octagon, 1980, An Eye for an Eye, 1981, Silent Rage, 1982, Forced Vengeance, 1982, Lone Wolf McQuade, 1983, Missing in Action, 1984, Missing in Action II: The Beginning, 1985, Code of Silence, 1985, Delta Force, 1986, Firewalker, 1986, Hero and the Terror, 1988, Delta Force 2: Operation Stranglehold, 1990, The Hitman, 1991, Hellbound, 1994, Top Dog, 1995, Forrest Warrior, 1996, Bells of Innocence, 2003, Dodgeball: A True Underdog Story, 2004 The Cutter, 2006; actor, co-screenwriter: (films) Invasion, U.S.A., 1985, Braddock: Missing in Action III, 1987; actor, co-exec. prodr. (films) Sidekicks, 1993; actor, exec. prodr. (TV films) Logan's War: Bound by Honor, 1998, The President's Man, 2000, The President's Man: A Line in the Sand, 2001, Walker, Texas Ranger: Trial By Fire, 2005; actor, (TV series) Walker, Texas Ranger, 1993-2001; actor, exec. prodr. (TV series) Walker, Texas Ranger, 1995-2001, Sons of Thunder, 1999; exec. prodr. (films) Birdie and Bogey, 2004; author: The Secret Power Within: Zen Solutions to Real Problems, 1996, Black Belt Patriotism: How to Reawaken America, 2008; co-author: (with Joe Hyams) The Secret of Inner Strength: My Story, 1988, (with Ken Abraham) Against All Odds: My Story, 2004; (novels) (with Ken Abraham & Aaron Norris) The Justice Riders, 2006, Threat to Justice, 2007; host: The Ultimate Stuntman: A Tribute to Dar Robinson. Founder, chmn. United Fighting Arts Fedn.; founder, chmn. Kick Start Found., Houston, 1992; founder, World Combat League, 2005. Profl. world middleweight karate champion, 1968-74; Named Fighter of the Yr., Black Belt mag., 1969, Veteran of the Yr., Am. Veteran awards, 2000 Address: Kick Start Found Ste 203 427 W 20th St Houston TX 77008

NORRIS, DARCY JANELLE, sign language teacher; d. David Harry Norris and Jodene Ann Compton. Assoc. in Arts, Mott C.C., Flint, Michigan, 1991; BS, Ctrl. Mich. U., Mt. Pleasant, Mich., 1994; MS in Higher Edn., Capella U., Minn., 2007. Interpreter deaf Ctrl. Mich. U., 1992—95, faculty, 1996—; interpreter deaf students St. Louis Pub. Sch. Sys., 1992—2000; interpreter Soaring Eagle Casino, Mich., 2000—. Author: Deaf Manual for Hearing People. Tchr sign lang. Sacred Heart Acad., Mt. Pleasant, 2001—. Recipient Gold Pin, Golden Key Nat. Honor Soc., 1994, Svc. awards, Ctrl. Mich. U. Office: Ctrl Mich Univ 2183 Health Professions Building Mount Pleasant MI 48858 Office Phone: 989-774-7294. Personal E-mail: ttymeasl@yahoo.com. Business E-Mail: norri1dj@cmich.edu.

NORRIS, DARELL FOREST, retired insurance company executive; b. Pontiac, Mich., Oct. 19, 1928; s. Forest Ellis and Mabel Marie (Smith) N.; m. Thordis Marie Johansen, Aug. 21, 1955; children: Dara Lee, Jennifer, Lisa, Nancy. BS, U. Kans., 1950. CLU; ChFC. Reporter, mem. sports staff Kansas City (Mo.) Star, 1950-51; pilot TWA, 1955-58; divsn. agy. mgr. Merced (Calif.) region Farmers Group, Inc., 1959-62, sales rep. Colorado Springs (Colo.) region, 1962-64, regional agy. mgr. Aurora, Ill., 1964-66, regional sales mgr. Santa Ana, Calif., 1966-69, mem. mgmt. tng. program staff, dir. agys. LA, 1969—71, regional mgr. Austin, Tex., 1971-73, v.p. sales LA, 1973-76, v.p. field ops. midwestern zone, 1976-79, v.p. field ops. western zone, 1979—. Pres. Farmers New World Mgmt. Co., 1977-81, v.p. staff ops., 1981-85, sr. v.p. life co. ops. and staff support svcs., 1985-90, farmers cons., 1990-93, gen. ins. cons., 1993—, vice chmn., 2. Vice chmn. bd. dirs. Northridge Hosp. Med. Found.; chmn. bd. deacons 1st Bapt. Ch., Granada Hills, Calif., 1977-89, 2003-07; sustaining mem. Rep. Nat. Com. Served with SAC, USAF, 1951-55; capt. Calif. Air N.G., 1958-62. Mem. Am. Soc. CLUs, ChFC, Ins. Edn. Assn. (trustee 1982-84). E-mail: DNorris268@aol.com.

NORRIS, DAVID OTTO, educator; b. Ashtabula, Ohio, Oct. 1, 1939; s. Otto Lee and Thelma Louise (Colledge) N.; m. Kay Linda Wilkinson, July 23, 1966; children: Sara Elizabeth, Linda Kay. BS, Baldwin-Wallace Coll., Berea, Ohio, 1961; PhD, U. Wash., 1966. Asst. prof. biology U. Colo., Boulder, 1966-70, assoc. prof. biology, 1970-76, prof. biology, 1976—; vis. assoc. prof. U. Calif., Berkeley, 1974; vis. prof. Oreg. State U., 1983-84. Author: (with others) Hormones and Reproduction in Fishes, Amphibians, and Reptiles, 1987, Identifying Plant Food Cells in Gastric Contents for Forensic Investigation, 1988, Vertebrate Endocrinology, 4th ed., 2006, Endocrine Disruption: Biological Basics for Health Effects in Wildlife and Humans, 2006; contbr. articles to profl. jours. Grantee NSF, 1968-70, 1976-83, 90-91, 94, 97-99, 2009-, Nat. Inst. Justice, 1984-86, Coun. on Rsch. and Creative Work, 1967, 72, 76, 79, 84, NIH, 1968, 75, 79, 80, 85, 86, US EPA, 2001-08. Mem. Am. Fish Soc., Colo.-Wyo. Acad. Sci., Endocrine Soc., Soc. for Neurosci., Am. Acad. Forensic Sci., Soc. Integrative Comparative Biology, NecroSearch Internat., Sigma Xi. Office: U Colo Dept Integrative Physiology PO Box 354 UCB Boulder CO 80309-0354

NORRIS, DOLORES JUNE, elementary school educator; b. Belmore, NY, Feb. 10, 1938; d. Abe and Doris Cyril (Stahl) Wanser; m. William Dean Norris, June 11, 1960; children: William Dean II, Ronald Wayne, Darla Cyrille. BS in Elem. Edn., So. Nazarene U., 1959; MS in Computer Edn., Nova U., 1988, EdS in Computer Applications, 1990. Cert. elem. edn. and computer sci. tchr., Fla. Tchr. 4th and 5th grades Ruskin (Fla.) Elem. Sch., 1959-61; tchr. 5th grade Emerson Elem. Sch., Kansas City, Kans., 1961-63; tchr. 1st grade Hickman Mills, Mo., 1964-65; tchr. 3d and 4th grades Lake Mary Elem. Sch., Sanford, Fla., 1968-72; tchr. 1st grade St. Charles Cath. Sch., Port Charlotte, Fla., 1976-77; primary tchr. Meadow Park Elem. Sch., Port Charlotte, 1977-89; computer specialist Vineland Elem. Sch., Rotanda West, Fla., 1989-90, Myakka River Elem. Sch., Port Charlotte, 1990—, tech. trainer, 1995—. Reading coun. Charlotte County Schs., Port Charlotte, 1987—, rep., 1989-90, in-svc. com. 1990-93, 98; program planner Meadow Park Elem. Sch., 1988-89; program planner Myakka River Elem. Sch. 1991-93, 2004-05; tech. facilitator Myakka Tiver Elem. Sch., 1999—; instr. in edn. U. Phoenix, 2002—. Mem. Rotary, Punta Gorda, Fla., 1982-86; co-dir. teens Touring Puppet Group, Punta Gorda, 1982-86; puppet co-dir. NOW Teens, Punta Gorda, 1976-80. Mem. Internat. Tech. in Edn., Fla. Assn. Computers in Edn, pres. Southwest Florida Assn. Computers in Edn. Avocations: piano, swimming, travel. Home: 1171 Richter St Port Charlotte FL 33952-2870 Personal E-mail: norrisdj@gmail.com.

NORRIS, GLENN L., lawyer; b. Clarinda, Iowa, Sept. 25, 1946; s. Harold E. and Darlene Louise (Crane) N.; m. Dale Bailey, Jan. 28, 1967 (div. June 1990); m. Tiffinny C. Sparks, Nov. 14, 1998; children: Christopher Steven, Catherine Beth, Glenn Leonard Jr., Janet Darlene. BA, Simpson Coll., 1968; JD with honors, U. Iowa, 1971. Bar: Iowa 1971, So. Dist. Iowa 1971, U.S. Dist. Ct., no. dist., Iowa, 8th circuit,

1972, U.S. Supreme Ct., 1976. Law clerk U.S. Dist. Judge Hanson, Ft. Dodge, Iowa, 1971-73; assoc. Hawkins, Hedberg & Ward, Des Moines, Iowa, 1973-78; ptnr. Hawkins & Norris, P.C., Des Moines, Iowa, 1978—. Editor: Iowa Academy of Trial Lawyers Handbook, 3d edit., 1999. Mem. tech. com. Iowa Supreme Ct. Commn. for Planning for 21st Century, 1996-98, Iowa Supreme Ct. Budget Adv. Com., 1997—; dir. men's chorus Sacred Heart Knights of Columbus. Recipient St. George award for Disting. Svc. to Cath. Scouting, Boy Scouts Am., Eagle Scout. Fellow Iowa Acad. Trial Lawyers; master C. Edwin Moore Am. Inn of Ct. (pres. 1998-2000); mem. Am. Bd. Trial Advs. (cert. civil trial advocate 2000—), Iowa State Bar Assn. (mem. fed. practice com. 1999—), Iowa Assn. Trial Lawyers (bd. govs. 1987-98). Roman Catholic. Home: 6205 Oakwood Hills Dr Johnston IA 50131-1962 Office: Hawkins & Norris PC 2501 Grand Ave Ste C Des Moines IA 50312-5311 E-mail: gnorrislaw@hotmail.com.

NORRIS, JACKIE, federal official, history educator; m. John Norris; children: Hunter, Cole, Sam. BA in Political Sci., SUNY Geneseo, 1992; MA in Political Sci., Iowa State U., 2008. Cert. secondary education teacher certification Iowa State U., 2002. With US Dept. Housing & Urban Devel.; scheduler for v.p. Al Gore The White House, Washington; fin. dir. Tom Vilsack's Campaign for Gov.; polit. dir. Al Gore's Iowa Caucus Campaign, 1999—2000; tchr. Am. govt. and history Ames HS, Johnston HS; sr. advisor, Iowa state dir. Barack Obama Presdl. Campaign, 2007—08; chief of staff to Michelle Obama Obama-Biden Transition Team, 2008—09; chief of staff to First Lady Michelle Obama The White House, Washington, 2009; sr. adviser Corp. for Nat. and Community Service, 2009—. Democrat. Office: Corp National and Community Service 1201 New York Ave NW Washington DC 20525*

NORRIS, JAMES HAROLD, lawyer; b. New Kensington, Pa., Sept. 18, 1953; s. J. Harold and Eleanore Rose (Arch) N.; m. Ann Marie Annase, Nov. 25, 1988; children: Ryan, Scott, Nicholas. BA, Washington Jefferson Coll., 1975; JD, Duquesne U., 1978. Bar: Pa. 1978, U.S. Dist. Ct. (we. dist.) Pa. 1978, U.S. Ct. Appeals (3d cir.) 1994, U.S. Dist. Ct. (no. dist.) W.Va. 1996, U.S. Supreme Ct., 2003. Assoc. Ruffin Hazlett Snyder Brown & Stabile, Pitts., 1979-83; ptnr. Eckert Seamans Cherin & Mellott, Pitts., 1983—; exec. v.p., gen. counsel Academy System; gen. counsel Targe Energy, LLC. Adj. prof. U. Pitts. Sch. Law, 2000—04; chief counsel Allegheny Regional Asset Dist. Bd. dirs. Epilepsy Found. Western Pa., North Hills YMCA, 2002—06. Mem. Allegheny County Bar Assn., Pa. Bar Assn. (chmn. adminstrv. law sect. 1992-94, spl. achievement award 1993). Home: 3475 Palomino Dr Gibsonia PA 15044 Office: Eckert Seamans Cherin & Mellott 600 Grant St Pittsburgh PA 15219-2702 Office Phone: 412-566-6159. Business E-Mail: jnorris@eckertseamans.com.

NORRIS, JOANNE WAREHAM, school counselor; b. Roaring Spring, Pa., Jan. 31, 1953; d. C. Roscoe and Wilma Irene (Allen) Wareham; m. Raymond H. Norris, June 16, 1973; children: Charles (dec.), Joanna. BSEd in Communicative Disorders, West Chester U., Pa., 1981; MEd in Sch. Counseling, U. Del., Newark, 1992. Cert. sch. counselor, Pa., 1992, Md., 1993, trainer Crisis Prevention Inst., 1998; nat. cert. counselor, 1995, nat. cert. sch. counselor Nat. Bd. Cert. Counselors, 1996; lic. profl. counselor, Pa., 2002. Exec. sec. Keystone Auto Club, Phila., 1973-78; office mgr. Holy Family Ch., Newark, Del., 1985-88; staff asst., dean's office U. Del., Newark, 1988-93; child devel. counselor Cecil County Pub. Schs., Elkton, Md., 1993—2002; intervention specialist Lancaster Sch. Dist., Pa., 2002—06; sch. counselor Columbia Boro Sch. Dist., Pa., 2006—. Mem. NEA, Assn. Supervision and Curriculum Devel., Am. Sch. Counselors Assn., Pa. Sch. Counselors Assn., Pa. State Edn. Assn., Columbia Edn. Assn, Kappa Delta Pi (Outstanding Mem. of Yr. U. Del. chpt. 1993). Avocations: travel, computers, desktop publishing. Home: 1121 State Rd Lincoln University PA 19352-1005 Office Phone: 717-684-4010 ext. 302. Business E-Mail: jnorris@columbia.k12.pa.us.

NORRIS, JOHN HART, lawyer, director; b. New Bedford, Mass., Aug. 4, 1942; s. Edwin Arter and Harriet Joan (Winter) Norris; m. Anne Kiley Monaghan, June 10, 1967; children: Kiley Anne, Amy O'Shea. BA, Ind. U., 1964; JD, U. Mich., 1967. Bar: Mich. 1968, U.S. Ct. Mil. Appeals 1969, U.S. Supreme Ct. 1974, U.S. Ct. Claims 1975, U.S. Tax Ct. 1979. From assoc. to ptnr. Monaghan, Campbell, LoPrete, McDonald and Norris, 1970-83; of counsel Dickinson, Wright, Moon, Van Dusen & Freeman, 1983-84, ptnr., 1985—; dep. asst. atty. gen. State of Mich., 1997—. Natural gas law counsel to claims mediator Columbia Gas Transmission Corp.; chpt. 11 bankruptcy procs. Wilmington (Del.) Bankruptcy Ct., 1992—; dep. asst. atty. gen. State of Mich., 1997—; bd. dirs. Prime Securities Corp., Ray M. Whyte Co., Ward-Williston Drilling Co., One Stop Capital Shop. Contbr. articles to profl. jours. Trustee Boys and Girls Clubs Southeastern Mich., 1979—, Mich. Wildlife Habitat Found.; trustee, bd. dirs. African Wildlife Found.; mem. Rep. State Fin. Com.; founder, co-chmn. Rep. Majority Club; trustee Mercy Coll., Detroit, Detroit Hist. Soc., 1984—; trustee, 1st vice chmn. Salk Inst. Fellow: Mich. State Bar Found.; mem.: ABA (litig. and natural resources sects.), Def. Orientation Conf. Assn., Fin. and Estate Planning Coun. Detroit, Am. Arbitration Assn., Detroit Bar Assn. (mem. pub. adv. com.), Oakland County Bar Assn., State Bar Mich. (chmn. environ. law sect. 1982—83, probate and trust law sect., mem. energy conservation task force, mem. oil and gas com.), Mich. Oil and Gas Assn. (mem. legal and legis. com.), Detroit Zool. Soc., Yondotega Club, Bloomfield Hills Country Club, Turtle Lake Club, Prismatic Club, Hundred Club, Thomas M. Cooley Club, Detroit Athletic Econ. Club (Detroit), Blue Key, Phi Delta Phi. Home: 1325 Buckingham Ave Birmingham MI 48009-5881 Office: Dickinson Wright 38525 Woodward Ave Ste 2000 Bloomfield Hills MI 48304-2971 Office Phone: 248-433-7227. Business E-Mail: jnorris@dickinsonwright.com.

NORRIS, LONNIE HAROLD, dean; b. Houston, Nov. 22, 1942; m. Donna M. Farmer, June 18, 1966; children: Marlaina M., Michael A. BA in Chemistry, Fisk U., 1964; DMD, Harvard U., 1976, MPH, 1977. Cert. diplomate Am. Bd. of Oral/Maxillofacial Surgeons. Asst. prof. oral & maxillofacial surgery Tufts U. Sch. Dental Medicine, Boston, 1981-88, assoc. prof., 1988-95, prof., 1995—, interim dean, 1995-96, dean, 1996—. Mem. com. dental accreditation, 1994—2003; chmn. coun. deans Am. Dental Edn. Assn., 2005—06. Named Disting. Practitioner, Nat. Acads. Practice, Dentist of the Yr., New Eng. chpt. Pierre Fauchard Acad. Fellow: Pierre Fauchard Acad., Internat. Coll. Dentists, Am. Bd. Oral/Maxillofacial Surgery, Am. Assn. Oral/Maxillofacial Surgeons, Am. Coll. Dentists, Am. Acad. Dental Sci., Phi Beta Kappa, Omicron Kappa Upsilon. Avocation: travel. Office: Tufts U Sch Dental Medicine 1 Kneeland St Boston MA 02111-1527 Office Phone: 617-636-6636. Business E-Mail: lonnie.norris@tufts.edu.

NORRIS, RICHARD ANTHONY, retired accountant; b. Birmingham, July 6, 1943; s. Albert Edward and Audrey (Rowley) N.; m. Geri M., Jan. 20, 1947; 1 child, Karen Louise. BA, U. Leeds, York, Eng., 1966. Chartered acct., UK, Can. Auditor Price Waterhouse & Co., Bristol, Eng., 1966-70, mgr. Montreal, Que., Can., 1970-78; mgr. corp. acctg., controller Can. Pacific Enterprises, Montreal, Calgary, Alta., Can., 1978-85; v.p. fin. US Ops. Laidlaw Waste Systems Inc., North Richland Hills, Tex., 1986-96; v.p., CFO Nexcycle, Inc., Dallas, 1997-2000; sr. v.p., CFO Casella Waste Systems Inc., Rutland, Vt., 2000—08. Home: 66 Sheffield Ter Marlborough MA 01752-1785

NORRIS, RICHARD PATRICK, museum director, historian, educator; b. Galveston, Tex., May 21, 1944; s. William Gerard and Iris Elsa (Allington) N.; m. Therese Louise Aalid, July 27, 1974; children: William Gerard, John Patrick. BA, Ohio State U., 1966; MA in Polit. Sci., SUNY, Binghamton, 1968; PhD in Am. Studies, U. Minn., 1976. Instr. U. Minn., Mpls., 1970-76; lectr. U. Md., Europe/Asia, 1976-78; dir. Chippewa Valley Mus., Eau Claire, Wis., 1978-80, Kalamazoo Valley Mus., 1985—; curator of history Mus. Sci. & Hist., Fort Worth, 1980-85. Lectr. Tex. Christian U., Fort Worth, Tex., 1981—85; cons. Am. Assn. Mus., Washington, 1979—, NEH, Washington, 1989; adj. prof. We. Mich. U., Kalamazoo, 1986—. Author: History by Design, 1984; book reviewer: Mus. News, History News; contbr. articles to profl. jours. Mem.: Assn. Midwest Mus., Internat. Coun. Mus., Am. Assn. State and Local History, Am. Assn. Mus., Rotary (dir. Kalamazoo club 1991—93, pres. 1999—2000). Office: Kalamazoo Valley Museum PO Box 4070 Kalamazoo MI 49003-4070 Home Phone: 269-345-5295; Office Phone: 269-373-7988. Business E-Mail: rnorris@kvcc.edu.

NORRIS, RUTH ANN FINK, social worker; b. Leavenworth, Kans., Oct. 29, 1955; d. Ival Eugene and Maxine Barbara (Ripper) Scholtz; m. V.W. Rusty Norris, May 21, 1977 (div. 2005); m. Charles Terry Fink, July 11, 2007 BA, Graceland Coll., 1978; MSW, U. Kans., 1988. LCSW. Social worker Okla. Dept. Human Svcs., Miami, 1979-82, Mo. Div. Family Svcs., Kansas City, Mo., 1982-87; clin. social worker Western Mo. Mental Health Ctr., Kansas City, 1988-97; exec. dir., pres. Ctr. for Wholeness Concepts, Independence, Mo., 1992-93; with Norris Counseling Svcs., Independence, 1993—2001; sr. social worker Truman Behavioral Health Network, Kansas City, Mo., 1997—2002; group home dir., numerous divsn. Western Mo. Mental Health Ctr., Kansas City, Mo., 2002—. Named one of Outstanding Young Women Am., 1991. Mem. NASW, Acad. Cert. Social Workers. Avocations: travel, reading. Office: Western Mo Mental Health Ctr Esperanza House 1000 E 24th St Kansas City MO 64108 Home: 10414 E 45th Terr Kansas City MO 64133 Office: Supported Cmty Living Svcs Dept Mental Health 2600 E 12th St Kansas City MO 64127 Personal E-mail: rafmsw2007@yahoo.com. Business E-Mail: ruth.fink@dmh.mo.gov.

NORRIS, SANDRA LOVE, occupational therapy assistant; b. East St. Louis, Ill., Jan. 6, 1956; d. Morrison Love and Sarah (Cameron) Miller; m. Frank Rex Norris, Aug. 15, 1987. AAS, Ill. Ctrl. Coll., 1979. Lic. occupl. therapy asst. Ill. Tchr. asst. Mamie O Stookey Sch., Belleville, Ill., 1980—83; activity therapy asst. Belleville Meml. Hosp., 1983—90, occupl. therapy asst., 1990—95, SSM Good Samaritan Hosp., Mt. Vernon, Ill., 1995—97, Eden Village Therapy Ctr., Glen Carbon, Ill., 1997—2001, Select Therapies, Lebanon Greenville, Highland, Ill., 2002—, So. Ill. Specialized Healthcare Assocs./Anderson Hosp., Maryville, Ill., 2003—06, Staffing Concepts Nat., Inc., Edwardsville, Ill., 2004—. Clin. instr. Eden Village Therapy Ctr., Glen Carbon, 1997—99. Radio reader for blind Radio Info. Svc. Shrine Lady Snows, Belleville, 1984—; vol., Buddy Program Bethany Pl. AIDS Svc. Orgn., Belleville, 1995—96; with Prospect Pk. United Method Ch., heartland Hosp. Clerical Fairview, 2008—, Mind Eye Vs. radio IFO Svc. Avocations: reading, Bingo. Home: 814 N Douglas Ave Belleville IL 62220 Office: Univ Nursing Home 1095 University Dr Edwardsville IL 62025 Office Phone: 618-656-1081.

NORRIS, TIMOTHY JON, lawyer; b. Orlando, Fla., Mar. 30, 1947; s. Robert Elfred and Adeline Ann (Wright) N.; m. Lorena Maria Martinez, Dec. 21, 1985; children: Noele, Kelsey. BA in Philosophy magna cum laude, Athenaeum of Ohio, 1969; JD cum laude, Harvard U., 1975. Bar: Fla. 1975, US Dist. Ct. (so. dist.) Fla. 1976, (mid. dist.) Fla. 1981, US Ct. Appeals (11th cir.) 1981, US Supreme Ct. 1984. Assoc. Thomson, Muraro, Razook & Hart, PA, Miami, Fla., 1975—79, ptnr., 1980—86, 1990—95, Weil, Gotshal & Manges, Miami, Fla., 1986-90, Thomson, Muraro, Razook & Hart, PA, 1995—99; shareholder Buchanan Ingersoll PC, 1999—2003; ptnr. Duane Morris LLP, 2003—. Contbr. articles to law jours. Sgt. U.S. Army, 1969-72, Vietnam. Recipient Best Lawyers in Am., 1991. Mem.: Am. Bankruptcy Inst., Fla. Bar. Office: Duane Morris LLP Ste 3400 200 S Biscayne Blvd Miami FL 33131-2318 Office Phone: 305-960-2241. Office Fax: 305-397-1890. Business E-Mail: tjnorris@duanemorris.com.*

NORRIS, VIRGINIA OAKLEY, secondary school educator; b. LA, Jan. 14, 1928; d. Earl James Taylor Oakley and Florence Marian (Ashley) Guthrie; m. Robert Matheson Norris, Jan. 5, 1952; children: Donald Oakley Norris, James Matheson Norris, Elizabeth Anne-Norris Dodson. AA, UCLA, 1946, BA, 1948. Cert. secondary tchr., Calif. Tchr., art dept. chmn. Anaheim Union H.S., Calif., 1949—51; engring. draftsman Hughes Aircraft, LA, 1951; tchr. Santa Barbara City Schs. and H.S., Santa Barbara, 1963—79; tchr./spinning U. Calif. Santa Barbara Ext., 1973; instr./fiber arts adult edn. Santa Barbara City Coll., 1972—84; demonstrator various schs., mus., chs., confs. and fairs, Calif., 1972—. Workshop for fiberarts groups presenter, Calif., New Zealand, Norfolk Island and Faroe Islands, 1973—. Contbr. articles to profl. jours. Bd. dirs., pres. Arboleda Park Improvement Assn., Santa Barbara, 1960-81; mem. Santa Barbara County Libr. Adv. Com., 1964-72, Goleta Valley Gen. Plan Adv. Com., Santa Barbara, 1973-81. Recipient Best Handspun Wool award Nat. Handcrafted Wool Showcase, 1978. Mem. Wellington Handweavers and Spinners Guild, Santa Barbara Fiber Arts Guild (pres. 1977-79), New Zealand Spinners, Weavers and Woolcraft Soc., Tawa Spinners Guild, UCLA Alumni Assn., U. Calif. Santa Barbara Faculty Women's Club (pres. 1984-86), Chi Omega. Congregationalist. Home: 4424 Nueces Dr Santa Barbara CA 93110-2006

NORSTRAND, IRIS FLETCHER, psychiatrist, neurologist, educator; b. Bklyn., Nov. 21, 1915; d. Matthew Emerson and Violet Marie (Anderson) Fletcher; m. Severin Anton Norstrand, May 20, 1941; children: Virginia Helene Norstrand Villano, Thomas Fletcher, Lucille Joyce. BA, Bklyn. Coll., 1937, MA in Biochemistry, 1965, PhD in Biochemistry, 1972; MD, L.I. Coll. Medicine, 1941. Diplomate Am. Bd. Psychiatry and Neurology, cert. geriat. psychiatry. Intern Montefiore Hosp., Bronx, NY, 1941-42; asst. resident in neurology N.Y. Neurol. Inst.-Columbia-Presbyn. Med. Ctr., NYC, 1944-45; pvt. practice Bklyn., 1947-52; resident in psychiatry Bklyn. VA Med. Ctr., 1952-54, resident in neurology, 1954-55, staff neurologist, 1955-81, asst. chief neurol. svc., 1981-91, staff psychiatrist, 1991-95. Neurol. cons. Indsl. Home for Blind, Bklyn., 1948-51; clin. prof. neurology SUNY Health Sci. Ctr., Bklyn., 1981—; attending neurologist Kings County Hosp., Bklyn., State U. Hosp., Bklyn.; cons. in field. Contbr. articles to profl. jours. Mem. Nat. Rep. Congl. Com., Rep. Senatorial Inner Circle. Recipient Spl. plaque Mil. Order Purple Heart, 1986, Spl. Achievement award PhD Alumni Assn. of CUNY, 1993, Lifetime Achievement award Bklyn. Coll., 1995, others. Fellow Am. Psychiat. Assn., Am. Acad. Neurology, Internat. Soc. Neurochemistry, Am. Assn. U. Profs. Neurology, Am. Med. EEG Soc. (pres. l987-88), Nat. Assn. VA Physicians (pres. l989-91, James O'Connor award l987), N.Y. Acad. Scis., Sigma Xi. Republican. Presbyterian. Avocations: writing, piano, travel, reading. Home: 7624 10th Ave Brooklyn NY 11228-2309

NORTELL, BRUCE, lawyer; b. Nov. 19, 1946; s. Joseph and Dorothy Nortell; children: Adam, Daniel, Anthony. AB, Boston U., 1968; JD, U. Chgo., 1971. Bar: Ill. 1971, U.S. Dist. Ct. (no. dist.) Ill. 1971, U.S. Supreme Ct. 1979. Sole practice, Chgo., 1971—74; asst. dir. legal affairs AMA, Chgo., 1974—81, counsel, sec. jud. coun., 1976—81; dir. tax and fin. planning Loyola U., Chgo., 1981—88, North Ctrl. Coll., Naperville, Ill., 1988—. Contbr. articles to profl. jours.; author two books novels. Mem.: ABA, Chgo. Bar Assn., Ill. Bar Assn. (Lincoln award 1975), Phi Beta Kappa (bd.). Home: 1124 Dickens Ln Naperville IL 60563-4301 Office: 30 N Brainard St Naperville IL 60540-4607 Office Phone: 630-637-5214. Business E-Mail: bnortell@noctrl.edu.

NORTH, CHARLES LAURENCE, poet, educator; b. NYC, June 9, 1941; s. Monroe Daniel and Viola Utstein North; m. Paula De Pillis, June 2, 1963; children: Jill, Michael. BA magna cum laude, Tufts U., 1962; MA with honors, Columbia U., 1964. Poet-in-residence Pace U., NYC, 1982—. Author: (books of poems) Lineups, 1972, Elizabethan and Nova Scotian Music, 1974, Six Buildings, 1977, Leap Year, 1978, The Year of the Olive Oil, 1989, New and Selected Poems, 1999, The Nearness of the Way You Look Tonight, 2001, Cadenza, 2007, Complete Lineups, 2009; (essays) No Other Way, 1998; co-author (with Tony Towle) Gemini, 1981, (with Trevor Winkfield) Tulips, 2004; co-editor: The Green Lake is Awake, 1994, (with J. Schuyler) Broadway, 1979, Broadway 2, 1989. Mem. poetry project St. Mark's Ch. Recipient Poets Found. award Poets Found., NYC, 1972, Fund for Poetry award Fund for Poetry, NYC, 1987, 89, 98, 2005; Creative Writing fellow Nat. Endowment for the Arts, Washington, 1980, 2001; grantee Found. Contemporary Arts, 2008. Mem. PEN, Poetry Soc. Am., Poets House, Phi Beta Kappa. Office: Pace Univ Dept English 1 Pace Plz Dept English New York NY 10038-1598

NORTH, DOUGLASS CECIL, economist, educator; b. Cambridge, Mass., Nov. 5, 1920; s. Henry Emerson and Edith (Saitta) North; m. Elisabeth Willard Case, Sept. 28, 1972; children from previous marriage: Douglass Alan, Christopher, Malcolm Peter. BA, U. Calif., Berkeley, 1942, PhD, 1952; D in Natural Scis. (hon.), U. of Cologne, Federal Republic of Germany, 1988, U. Zurich, Switzerland, 1993, Stockholm Sch. of Econs., Sweden, 1994, Prague Sch. Econs., 1995. Asst. prof. econs. U. Wash., 1950—56, assoc. prof., 1957—60, prof., 1960—83, chmn. dept., 1967—79, prof. emeritus, 1983—; dir. Inst. Econ. Research, 1960—66, Nat. Bur. Econ. Research, 1967—87; Spencer T. Olin prof. in arts and scis. Washington U., St. Louis, 1983—. Pitt prof. Am. history and instns. Cambridge U., 1981—82; fellow Ctr. for Advanced Study on Behavioral Scis., 1987—88; co-founder Internat. Soc. for the New Institutional Econ., 1997. Author: The Economic Growth of the U.S. 1790-1860, 1961, Growth and Welfare in the American Past, 1966; author: (with L. Davis) Institutional Change and American Economic Growth, 1971; author: (with R. Miller) The Economics of Public Issues, 1971, 1974, 1976, 1978, 1980; author: (with R. Thomas) The Rise of the Western World, 1973; author: Structure and Change in Economic History, 1981, Institutions, Institutional Change and Economic Performance, 1990. Recipient Nobel Prize in Econ. Sci., Nobel Found., 1993; grantee, Social Sci. Rsch. Coun., 1962, Rockefeller Found., 1960—63, Ford Found., 1961, 1966, NSF, 1967—73, Bradley Found., 1986—; fellow Guggenheim Found., 1972—73. Fellow: Am. Acad. Arts and Scis.; mem.: Econ. History Assn., The Brit. Acad. (corr.), Am. Econ. Assn. Office: Dept Econ Washington Univ Rm 305 Elliot Hall Box 1208 Saint Louis MO 63130*

NORTH, E(DWARD) LEE, retired writer, former aerospace company professional; b. Englewood, NJ, June 2, 1924; s. Edward Louis North and Genevieve Jean (Smith) North Francais; m. Florence Kirkland Hennen, Aug. 29, 1945; children: Patrick Lee, Diane North Goncalves. BA, Washington and Jefferson Coll., 1946. Sports editor Washington Reporter, Pa., 1947-49; publicity dir. Washington and Jefferson Coll., 1949-51; writer, editor Grumman Aerospace Corp., Bethpage, NY, 1951-78, proposal mgr., 1978-89. Hon. consul Free Polish Govt., London, 1980-95. Author: For This One Hour, 1970, Redcoats, Redskins, and Red-Eyed Monsters: A human-interest history of West Virginia, 1979, Battling the Indians, Panthers, and Nittany Lions, 1991, The Fifty-Five West Virginias, 1998, Mark of the White Wolf, 2000, Snowflakes on the Don, 2002, 2d edit., 2007, Eyes that Haunt, 2005; co-author (with Jane Wyman): Chris, the Rhode Island Wonder Dog, 1993; co-author: (with Arthur Dromerhauser) The History of Bay Shore High School Athletics, 1994. Chmn. Good Govt. Party, Suffolk County, NY, 1956—57; bd. of policy Liberty Lobby, Washington, 1975—2001; chmn. Islip Town (NY) Conservative Party, 1970s; historian Brightwaters Village, 1990—2006. Recipient Gold Cross of Merit Free Poland Govt., 1985. Mem.: The Authors Guild, Football Writers of Am., Am. Edn. Assn. (bd. dirs. 1992—2006), Rep. Nat. Com., Assn. of Pub. Historians of N.Y. State, Phi Kappa Psi. Episcopalian. Avocations: tennis, golf, bridge, Scrabble, study of wolves. Home: 55 Woodland Dr Brightwaters NY 11718 Personal E-mail: north444@aol.com.

NORTH, GARY L., career military officer; B in Polit. Sci., East Carolina U.; MPA, Golden Gate U., 1984, M in Human Resources Mgmt., 1986; M in Nat. Resource Strategy, Nat. Def. U., 1994. Advanced through grades to lt. gen. USAF, 2006; weapons sys. officer 35th tactical fighter squadron Kunsan AB, Republic of Korea, 1978—79; F-4G Wild Weasel elec. warfare officer 561st and 563rd tactical fighter squadrons George AFB, Calif., 1979—80; fighter lead-in training Holloman AFB, N.Mex., 1981—82, Hill AFB, Utah, 1981—82; squadron scheduler, squadron weapons officer19th tactical squadron Shaw AFB, SC, 1982—85, wings weapons officer, 363rd tactical fighter wing SC, 1985—86; F-16 weapons officer, fligt comdr. 526th tactical fighter squadron Ramstein AB, Germany, 1986—87, aide-de-camp, F-16 instr. pilot to Commander-in-Chief of USAF Europe, 1987—89; asst. ops. officer 19th tactical fighter squadron, wing chief standardization and evaluation Shaw AFB, SC, 1990—93, chief wing weapons and safety Operation Desert Storm, comdr. 33rd fighter squadron SC, 1990—93; comdr. 35th ops. group Misawa AB, Japan, 1994—96; comdr. 8th fighter wing Kunsan AB, Republic of Korea, 1999—2000; chief joint requirements divsn., dep. dir. joint matters USAF Hdqs., Washington, 1996—97, dep. dir. politico-military affairs for Asia-Pacific, joint staff, 2002—04; dir. ops. U.S. Pacific command Camp H.M. Smith, Hawaii, 2004—06; comdr. 9th Air Force, U.S. Ctrl. Command Air Forces Shaw AFB, SC, 2006—. Decorated Df. Superior Svc. Medal with two oak leaf clusters, Legion of Merit with oak leaf cluster, Disting. Flying Cross with "V" device and oak leaf cluster, Meritorious Svc. Medal with oak leaf cluster, Air Medal with four oak leaf clusters, Aerial Achievement Medal with wto oak leaf clusters, Air Force Commendation Medal with two oak leaf clusters, Combat Readiness Medal with four oak leaf clusters; recipient Lance P. Sijan USAF Leadership Award, 1993.

NORTH, HELEN FLORENCE, classicist, educator; b. Utica, NY; d. James H. and Catherine (Debbold) N. AB, Cornell U., 1942, MA, 1943, PhD, 1945; LLD (hon.), Rosary Coll., 1982; DLitt (hon.), Trinity Coll.,

Dublin, 1984, Fordham U., 1999; LHD (hon.), La Salle U., 1985, Yale U., 1986. Instr. classical lang. Rosary Coll., River Forest, Ill., 1946-48; faculty Swarthmore Coll., 1948—91, prof. classics, 1961-91, chmn. dept., 1959-91, emerita, 1991—. Centennial prof. classics, 1966-73, 78-91, Kenan prof., 1973-78, sr. rsch. scholar, 2003—. Vis. asst. prof. Cornell U., 1952—; vis. assoc. prof. Barnard Coll., 1954—55; vis. prof. LaSalle Coll., Phila., 1965, Am. Sch. Classical Studies, Athens, 1975, Athens, 87; Blegen disting. vis. rsch. prof. Vassar Coll., 1979. Author: Sophrosyne: Self-Knowledge and Self-Restraint in Greek Literature, 1966, From Myth to Icon: Reflections of Greek Ethical Doctrine in Literature and Art, 1979, (with Mary C. North) The West of Ireland: A Megalithic Primer, 1999, Cork and the Rest of Ireland: A Megalithic Primer II, 2003; translator: John Milton's Second Defense of the English People, 1966; editor: Interpretations of Plato: A Swarthmore Symposium, 1977; co-editor: Of Eloquence, 1970; editor Jour. History of Ideas; mem. editl. bd. Catalogus Translationum et Commentariorum, 1979. Bd. dirs. Am. Coun. Learned Socs., 1977-85; trustee LaSalle U., 1972-2003, chmn. bd. trustees, 1991-93; trustee King's Coll., Am. Acad. in Rome; chmn. com. on Classical Sch. Recipient Harbison prize Danforth Found., 1969, Centennial medal Am. Acad. Rome, 1995; named Distinguished Daughter of Pa., 1989, del. of Am. Philological Assn. to Am. Coun. Learned Socs., 1991-95; grantee Am. Coun. Learned Socs., 1943-45, 73, fellow, 1971-72, 87-88; Mary Isabel Sibley fellow Phi Beta Kappa Found., 1945-46, Ford Fund Advancement Edn. fellow, Fulbright fellow Rome, 1953-54, Guggenheim fellow, 1958-59, 75-76, AAUW, 1963-64; grantee Danforth Found., 1962, Lindbach Found., 1966; Sr. fellow NEH, 1967-68; NEH Coll. Tchrs. fellow, 1983-84; Martin classical lectr. Oberlin Coll., 1972. Mem. Am. Philol. Assn. (dir. 1968—, pres. 1976—, Charles J. Goodwin award 1969, Disting. Svc. medal 1996), Classical Assn. Atlantic States, Catholic Commn. Intellectual and Cultural Affairs (chmn. 1968-69), Am. Acad. Arts and Scis., Am. Philos. Soc., Soc. Religion Higher Edn., Phi Beta Kappa (bd. vis. scholars 1975-76, senate 1991—2003), Phi Kappa Phi. Home: 604 Ogden Ave Swarthmore PA 19081-1131 Personal E-mail: hnorth1@swarthmore.edu.

NORTH, MARJORIE MARY, writer; b. Mt. Clemens, Mich., Oct. 21, 1945; d. Robert Haller and Hilla Beryl (Willard) Wright; m. William B. Hirons; children: Laura, Christina, Angela. Features editor Elizabeth City (N.C.) Daily Advance, 1966-69; news/mng. editor Brandon (Fla.) News, 1977-78; city editor Leesburg (Fla.) Comml., 1978-79; metro editor Sarasota (Fla.) Herald Tribune, 1979-80, Fla. West editor, 1980-85, daily columnist, 1985—2009. Host Weekly Interview Show, SNN-TV, 1997—2005. Author: Sarasota: A City For All Seasons, 1994, (plays) With the Best Intentions, 1994, Back in the Game, 1998. Recipient Layout, Creativity and Overall Publ. awards Fla. Press Assn., numerous comty. awards and citations; winner Fla. shorts competition Fla. Studio Theater New Play Festival, 1994, 98; Paul Harris fellow. Avocations: tennis, entertaining, theater. Office: Sarasota Herald-Tribune PO Box 1719 Sarasota FL 34230-1719 E-mail: mnorth456@gmail.com.

NORTH, OLIVER LAURENCE (OLLIE NORTH), syndicated columnist, retired military officer; b. San Antonio, Oct. 7, 1943; m. Betsy Stuart, Nov. 13, 1968; children: Tait, Dornin, Sarah, Stuart. Student, SUNY, Brockport; BA, US Naval Acad., Annapolis, 1968. Commd. lt. USMC, 1966, advanced through ranks to lt. col., 1983, ret., 1990; dep. dir. polit.-mil. affairs NSC, Washington, 1981—83, counter-terrorism coord., 1983—86; host nat.-syndicated radio program Oliver North Radio Show/Common Sense Radio, 1995—2003; host War Stories with Oliver North, Fox News Channel, 2001—. Founder, hon. chmn. Freedom Alliance, Dulles, Va., 1990—; former co-host Equal Time, MSNBC; regular commentator Hannity & Colmes. Author: Under Fire: An American Story, 1991, War Stories: Operation Iraqi Freedom, 2003, American Heroes: In the Fight Against Radical Islam, 2008; co-author: (with David Roth) One More Mission: Oliver North Returns to Vietnam, 1993, (with Brian Smith) True Freedom: The Liberating Power of Prayer, 2004, (with Sara Horn) A Greater Freedom: Stories of Faith from Operation Iraqi Freedom, 2004, (with Joe Musser) War Stories II: Heroism in the Pacific, 2004, War Stories III: The Heroes Who Defeated Hitler, 2005, Mission Compromised: A Novel, 2002, Jericho Sanction, 2003, The Assassins, 2005. Decorated Silver Star, Bronze Star, Purple Hearts (2). Mem.: NRA (mem. bd. dirs. 1998—). Republican. Office: Freedom Alliance 22570 Markey Ct Ste 240 Dulles VA 20166 Office Phone: 703-444-7940. Office Fax: 703-444-9893.*

NORTH, PETER MACHIN, academic administrator, barrister; b. Nottingham, Eng., Aug. 30, 1936; s. Geoffrey Machin and Freda Brunt (Smith) N.; m. Stephanie Mary Chadwick, Aug. 13, 1960; children: Jane, Nicholas, James. BA, Oxford U., Eng., 1959, BCL, 1960, MA, 1963, DCL, 1976; LLD (hon.), Reading U., Eng., 1992, Nottingham U., 1996, Aberdeen U., 1997, U. New Brunswick, 2002; LHD (hon.), U. Ariz., 2005. Teaching assoc. Northwestern U., Chgo., 1960-61; lectr. U. Wales, Aberystwyth, 1960-63, U. Nottingham, Eng., 1964-65; fellow Keble Coll./Oxford U., 1965-76; law commr. Law Commn., London, 1976-84; prin. Jesus Coll./Oxford U., 1984—2005; vice-chancellor Oxford U., 1993-97; chmn. fin. com. Oxford U. Press, 2005—08. Visitor Ashmolean Mus., 2004—07; mem. Sr. Salaries Rev. Body, 2004—. Author: Occupiers' Liability, 1971, Modern Law of Animals, 1972, Private International Law, 1999, Essays in Private International Law, 1993. Chmn. Rd. Traffic Law Rev., London, 1985-88, Rev. of Parades and Marches in No. Ireland, 1996-97, Independent Com. for Supervision of Stds. of Telephone Info. Svcs., 1999—2006. Lt. English Army, 1954-56. Decorated Knight Bachelor, Comdr. Order Brit. Empire, Queens Counsel. Fellow British Acad.; mem. Inst. Internat. Law, Internat. Acad. Comparative Law. Mem. Ch. Eng. Home and Office: Univ Oxford Jesus Coll Oxford OX1 3DW England E-mail: peter.north@jesus.ox.ac.uk.

NORTH, RICHARD BOYDSTON, neurological surgery educator; b. Summit, NJ, Nov. 28, 1948; s. William Borsum and Geraldine H. (Flitcraft) N.; m. Catherine Basgal Anderson, Nov. 15, 1983; children: Richard B. Jr., Jacqueline R. Student, Harvard U., 1966-68; BA, Johns Hopkins U., 1970, MD, 1973. Diplomate Am. Bd. Neurol. Surgery. Fellow in biomed. engring. Johns Hopkins U., Balt., 1973-78; intern in surgery Duke U. Med. Ctr., Durham, N.C., 1978-79; resident, fellow in neurosurgery Johns Hopkins U., Balt., 1979-83, from instr. to asst. prof. Neurosurgery, 1983-91, assoc. prof. Neurosurgery, 1991-97, prof. neurosurgery, anesthesiology & critical care medicine, 1997—, dir. div. Functional Neurosurgery, co-dir. spine svc., 1991—. Cons. Applied Physics Lab. Johns Hopkins U., Balt., 1974-78. Contbr. articles to profl. jours. Mem. AMA, Assn. for Advancement of Med. Instrumentation (co-chair Implanted Neurosimulator subcom.), Am. Assn. Neurol. Surgeons (past-chmn. sect. on pain), Congress of Neurol. Surgeons, Am. Pain Soc., Internat. Assn. for Study of Pain, Am. Soc. Functional and Stereotactic Neurosurgery, World Soc. Functional and Stereotactic Neurosurgery. Office: Johns Hopkins Hosp Dept Neurosurg Meyer 7-113 600 N Wolfe St Baltimore MD 21287-0005

NORTH, STEVEN EDWARD, lawyer, educator; b. Oct. 16, 1941; s. Irving J. and Barbara (Grubman) N.; m. Sue J. Buznitsky, Dec. 24, 1966; children: Jennifer, Samantha. BA, CCNY, 1963; JD, Bklyn. Law Sch., 1966; LLM, NYU, 1967. Bar: NY 1967, US Dist. Ct. (so. and ea. dists.) NY 1970, US Supreme Ct. 1971. Asst. dist. atty. homicide bur. NY County Dist. Atty. Office, NYC, 1967-71; spl. asst. atty. gen., bur. chief NY State Atty. Gen.'s Office, NYC, 1972-75; pvt. practice NYC, 1975. Mem. adv. com. Ann. Civil Litigation Inst., Practicing Law Inst., 1996; chmn. Assn. Bar Subcom. on Investigation into Imposition of Legis. Limits on Awards for Non-Econ. Damages, 1995; mediator US Dist. Ct. (so. dist.) NY, 1994—, apptd. jud. screening program; mem. adv. coms. solo law practice Practicing Law Inst., 1991, adv. bd. tort litigation, 1989—; vis. faculty Sch. Law, NYU, faculty workshop Cardozo Sch. Law, judge appellate argument, alumni advisor; faculty advisor Trial of Breast Cancer Case, Law Jour. Seminars, 2000, faculty Annual Intensive Trial Program, 1997-; guest lectr. Advanced Medium Malpractice Cases, 2007, Grand Rounds Jacobi Hosp., Bronx, NY, 2001, Mt. Sinai Sch. Medicine, 2006; faculty chmn. Contuining Legal Edn. Programs, commentator, Court TV, Eyewitness News, Talk News TV; lectr. and spkr. in field. Author: Prevention and Detection of Fraud in Industry, 1973, Controlling the Deposition: Winning Your Case Before Trial, 1978, Deposition Strategy, Law and Forms, vol. 1 (Introduction and Law), vol. 5 (Medical Malpractice), vol. 8 (Personal Injury), 1981, (course handbooks) Trial Mechanics, Personal Injury Desbook, 1983, Trial Mechanics and Discovery, 1985, 86, Medical Malpractice Litigation, 1988, Managing the Multi-Million Dollar Case, 1990, Objectifying Brain Damage in Closed Head Injury, 1990, Fundamentals of Medical Malpractice Litigation, 1991, Damage Update, 1992, 93, 94, 95, 96, 97—, Proving & Defending Damages, 1993, Conducting & Defending Depositions, 1993; contbr. chpts. to books; editor: Cancer Litigation Bull., 1994—, Fear of Developing Cancer; contbg. editor: Law and Order mag.; med.-legal editor Perinatology, 1983; coauthor: Medical Malpractice in NY 3rd Edit., 2009, Medical Malpractice Chapter NYS Bar Assoc., 2009; contbr. articles to legal jour., Chapter to Books; commentator Eyewitness News, 1994, Court TV, 1994-98, Talk News TV, 1996. Mem. leadership coun. So. Poverty Law Ctr. Recipient Ten Highest Verdicts award, NY State, Eight Highest Verdicts award, NY Law Jour., 2005, 2008; named NY Times Super Lawyer, 2009; named one of Top 100 Attorneys, NY Times Super Lawyer, 2008, Top NY Lawyers, 2006, NY Super Lawyers, 2008, 2009, Leading Plaintiff Lawyers, 2007, Best Lawyers in NY, 2007. Mem. ATLA, NCCJ (lawyers divsn., ann. dinner com.), NOW (benefits com.), US Holocaust Mus. (charter mem.), Am. Bd. Trial Adv., Soc. Med. Jurisprudence, NY State Bar Assn. (faculty), NY State Trial Lawyers Assn. (bd. dir. 1990—, faculty chmn. Depositions in Action 2000, North's Ninety-Nine Pointers on Advanced Deposition Practices 1999), Lotos Club, Nat. Eagle Scout Assn., State Trial Lawyers Assn. (bd. dir. 1990—, seminar faculty chmn. 1993, faculty decisions program 1991—, Law Day dinner com.), NY County Lawyers Assn. (exec. com. med. malpractice sect., exec. com. gen. tort law sect.), Assn. Bar of City of NY (civil ct. com. 1980-83, legal and continuing edn. com. 1983—, legal referral svc. com., med. malpractice mediator 1994—, chmn. subcom. on imposition of legis. limits to awards for non-econ. damages), Vol. Lawyers for the Arts, Million Dollar Adv. Forum, Vol. Lawyers for the Arts, NY County Supreme Ct. Com. Med. Malpractice Litigation, NY Soc. Anesthesiologist (speaker), NY State Bar Assn. Home: 148 E 74th St New York NY 10021 Office Phone: 212-861-5000. Business E-Mail: north@north.law.com.

NORTH, WILLIAM HAVEN, foreign service officer; b. Summit, NJ, Aug. 17, 1926; s. Eric M. and Gladys (Haven) N.; m. Jeanne Foote, Sept. 2, 1950; children: Jeannette Haven, William Ashby, Charles Eric. BA in History with honors, Wesleyan U., Middletown, Conn., 1949; MA in History, Columbia, 1951. Program officer ICA, Ethiopia, 1953-57; then dep. chief program divsn. ICA (African-European Regional Office), Washington, 1958—61; asst. dir. for program USAID Mission, Nigeria, until 1965; dir. Ctrl. and Western African affairs AID, Washington, 1966-70; mission dir. U.S. AID mission to Ghana, 1970-76; dep. asst. adminstr. Africa Bur. AID, 1976-82, spl. asst. Office of the Adminstr., 1982-83, assoc. asst. adminstr. Ctr. Devel. Info. and Evaluation, 1983-89, ret.; pvt. cons. Internat. Devel. for World Bank, 1989—, UN Devel. Program USAID, 1989—; coord. Evaluation of Global Environ. Facility, 1993, Evaluation Spl. Porgram of Asst. to Africa, 1997-98, Evaluation DAC/OECD Eval. Group, 1998; evaluator UNDP Aid Coordination, 1998—. Evaluator UNDP Global Program for HIV/AIDS, 2000, African Governance Capacity Bldg, UNDP, Danida, Denmark, 2002-03; fellow Ctr. for Internat. Affairs, Harvard U., 1965-66; chmn. experts group on evaluation Devel. Assistance Commn., OECD, 1985-88; vice-chmn. editl. bd. Fgn. Svc. Jour., 1983-86; mem. adv. panel on evaluation Inter-Am. Devel. Bank, 1993-94; prin. evaluator Internat. Fin. Corp.; program dir. U.S. Fgn. Assistance Oral History Program, 1995—; cons. UN Devel. Coop. Policy Branch, 2000-02. Interviewer Iraq, Afghanistan, Sudan for US Inst. Peace and Assn. Diplomatic Studies and Tng., 2005—. Evaluator USAID Program in Iraq, 2003-04. Served with AUS, 1944-46. Recipient Meritorious Svc. award for exemplary achievement in pub. adminstrn., W.A. Jump Honor cert., Superior Honor award for Nigerian Relief Adminstrn., Equal Employment Opportunity award, Disting. Honor award AID, Presdl. Meritorious Svc. medal, Adminstrs. Career Svc. award. Mem. Soc. for Internat. Devel., African Studies Assn., Assn. Diplomatic Studies and Tng., Am. Evaluation Assn., Applachian Mountain Club. Methodist. Home and Office: Internat Development 6748 Brigadoon Dr Bethesda MD 20817-5436 Home Phone: 301-320-4325. E-mail: willnorth@aol.com.

NORTHCUT, TERRY BRUMLEY, social sciences educator; d. Rex and Mary Blythe Brumley; children: Blythe Marie, Samuel Harrison. PhD, Smith Coll., Northampton, Mass., 1991. Lic. Clin. social worker Ill., 1999. Asst. prof. U. Southern. Calif., LA, 1992—96; adj. prof. Smith Coll. Social Work, 1992—2007; dir. doc. program Loyol U. Chgo. SSW, 2003—08. Recipient Faculty Mem. Yr. award, Sch. Social Work, 1998. Mem.: Soc. Social Work Rsch., Ill. Clin. Social Work Soc., CSWE, SEPI, NASW. D-Liberal. Avocations: reading, gardening, cooking, exercise. Office: Loyola Univ Chgo SSW 820 N MI Ave Chicago IL 60611 Business E-Mail: tnorthc@wpo.it.luc.edu.

NORTHCUTT, CLARENCE DEWEY, lawyer; b. Guin, Ala., July 7, 1916; s. Walter G. and Nancy E. (Homer) Northcutt; m. Gwen Barton, Feb. 2, 2009. AB, U. Okla., 1939, LL.B., 1938. Bar: Okla. 1938. Pvt. practice, Ponca City, 1938—. Mem. bd. visitors U. Okla. Served with AUS, 1941-46. Decorated Bronze Star, Air medal with oak leaf cluster, Order St. John of Jerusalem; named Outstanding Citizen of Ponca City, 1982; inducted to Okla. Hall of Fame, 2001. Fellow Am. Coll. Trial Lawyers, Am. Coll. Trust and Estate Attys., Am. Bar Found.; mem. Acad. Univ. Fellows, Internat. Soc. Barristers, Am. Bd. Advocacy, Internat. Acad. Trial Lawyers, Okla. Bar Assn. (pres. 1975, bd. govs.), Ponca City C. of C. (past pres.). Clubs: Mason (32 Degree), Kiwanian. Democrat. Baptist. Office: PO Box 1669 Ponca City OK 74602-1669 Office Phone: 580-762-1655. Business E-Mail: cdnorth@northcuttlawfirm.com.

NORTHCUTT, ELEEN MARIE, secondary school educator; b. Seattle, Aug. 23, 1949; d. Glenn O.N. and Marjorie Eleen (Hays) Riedasch; m. Richard Lee Northcutt, Aug. 12, 1972 (dec. Jan. 1984); children: Brian Lee, Sara Eleen. BA in History, Wash. State U., 1972; MA in Teaching, Whitworth Coll., 1985. Cert. tchr. Wash. Substitute tchr. Spokane (Wash.) Sch. Dist. 81, 1979-84; tchr. talented and gifted in history and English Mead Sch. Dist. 354, Spokane, Wash., 1984—. Chmn. Mead Vocabulary Com., 1989-91, co-adv. Northwood Jr. H.S. Writing Club, Spokane, 1988-90, mem. Secondary Lang. Arts Curriculum, Spokane, 1985-92, edn. svc. dist. 101 mini-grant com., 1986-94, Mead essential learnings com., 1991-92, Mead writing assessment com., 1991—94, mem. exec. com. Learning Across Curriculum, Spokane, 1987-90, co-adv. State History Day Northwood Jr. H.S., 1987-91; presenter Nat. Sci. Conf., 1989, student-tchr. seminar Washington State U., 1991-93; varsity coach girls golf team Mead H.S., 1993—97, Mt. Spokane H.S., 1997—. Mem. Parent Adv. Coun. Woodridge Elem. Sch., Spokane, 1987-88, asst. dir. Wash. Jr. Golf Assn., Spokane, 1988—, v.p. Ascension Luth. Ch. Women, Spokane, 1981-82, asst. supt. Sunday Sch., 1982-84. Mem. Nat. Coun. Tchrs. English, Nat. Coun. Social Studies, Internat. Order Rainbow Girls (adv. bd. pres. 1978-80), Secondary Social Studies Com., Order Ea. Star. Avocations: golf, travel, gardening.

NORTHCUTT, ROBERT F., lawyer; b. Dothan, Ala., Oct. 17, 1951; s. Flowers Glenn and Milbra Brock Northcutt; m. Karen Allen Northcutt, Feb. 23, 1985. BA, Birmingham-So. Coll., Ala., 1974; JD, Cumberland Sch. Law, Birmingham, 1977. Bar: Ala. 1978, US Dist. Ct. (mid. dist.) Ala. 1978, US Dist. Ct. (no. dist.) Ala. 1978, US Dist. Ct. (so. dist.) Ala. 1978, US Ct. Appeals (11th cir.) 1978. Ptnr. Hardwick, Hause, Segrest & Northcutt, Dothan, 1978—87; assoc. gen. counsel West Point Stevens, West Point, Ga., 1987—89; asst. gen. counsel Enstar, Montgomery, Ala., 1989—91; ptnr. Robison & Belser, Montgomery, 1991—2001; shareholder Capell & Howard P.C., Montgomery, 2001—. Dep. atty. gen. State Ala., 1998—2006; gen. counsel Ala. River Reg Solid Waste Authority, Tallassee, Ala., 2002—, Receiver-Ala. Dept. Ins., Montgomery, 2004—; lectr. in field. Named Best Lawyers, America. Mem.: ABA, Def. Rsch. Inst., Am. Inns Ct., Ala. Def. Lawyers Assn., Ala. State Bar, Montgomery County Bar Assn., Rotary (pres. Dothan chpt. 1987, dir. found. Montgomery chpt. 2002—04, dir. Montgomery chpt. 2002—04, Paul Harris fellow), Delta Theta Phi, Sigma Alpha Epsilon (pres.). Home: 3040 Bankhead Ave Montgomery AL 36106 Office: Capell & Howard PC 150 Perry St PO Box 2069 Montgomery AL 36104

NORTHCUTT, WILLIAM MARION, English literature educator; b. Nashville, May 9, 1962; arrived in Germany, 1993; s. James Edward and Lucy Ann (Prater) N.; m. Birgit Kröger, June 27, 1988; children: James Terence, Aura Mae. BA summa cum laude, Tenn. State U., 1989; MA, U. Conn., 1991; postgrad., Miami U., Oxford, Ohio, 1991—. Tchg. asst. English lit. U. Conn., Storrs, 1989-91, Miami U., 1991-93, U. Bayreuth, Germany, 1993—. Socialist. Office: Dyersburg State CC 1510 Lake Rd Dyersburg TN 38024

NORTHEN, CHARLES SWIFT, III, retired bank executive; b. Birmingham, Ala., Jan. 25, 1937; s. Charles Swift and Jennie Hood (Hunt) S.; m. Margaret Carson Robinson, Dec. 27, 1959 (div. 1972); children: Margaret Allen, Charles Swift IV, Bryce Robinson; m. Betty Jean Taylor, Oct. 3, 1981. BA cum laude, Vanderbilt U., 1959, MA, 1961. Chartered fin. analyst. Mem. staff trust dept. Birmingham Trust Nat. Bank, 1960-64; with First Ala. Bank Birmingham, 1964-80, sr. v.p., trust officer, 1975-80, Central Bank of South, Birmingham, 1981-85; exec. v.p. Regions Fin. Corp., 1985—95, corp. investment officer, 1993-95; mng. dir. Sterne, Agee & Leach, Inc., Birmingham, 1995-98, investment cons., 1998—2001; ret. Lectr. So. Trust Sch., Birmingham So. Coll.; pres. First Ala. Investments Inc.; dir. Hubbard Press, Findlay, Ohio. Bd. dirs. United Presbyn. Found., N.Y.C., 1977-86; mem. Birmingham Com. Fgn. Rels., 1970—. Mem. Ala. Security Dealers Assn. (pres.), Ala. Soc. Fin. Analysts (pres.), Inst. Chartered Fin. Analysts, Newcomen Soc., SAR, Kiwanis, Mountain Brook Club, The Club, Soc. Colonial Wars (Ala. gov. 2005-06). Presbyterian. Home: 3024 N Woodridge Rd Birmingham AL 35223-2748

NORTHERN, RICHARD, lawyer; b. Louisville, Dec. 17, 1948; s. James William and Mary Helen (Barry) Northern; m. Mary Lou Grundy, Aug. 28, 1971; children: James Barry, Nancy Hope, Mary Grace. BA in English, U. Louisville, 1970, JD, 1976; MPA, Harvard U., 1977; LHD (hon.), Spalding U., 2006. Bar: Ky. 1976, U.S. Dist. Ct. (we. and ea. dists.) Ky. 1977. Staff writer Courier-Jour., Louisville, 1970-72; dir. planning devel. Jefferson County Govt., Louisville, 1972-76; legis. dir. Office of U.S. Rep. Romano Mazzoli, Washington, 1977-78; spl. asst. U.S. Sec. of Interior, Washington, 1979-80; ptnr., mem. exec. com. Wyatt, Tarrant & Combs, Louisville, 1980—. Bd. dirs. Nugent Sand Co. Chmn. bd. dirs. Cath. Edn. Found., Inc., Louisville, 1998—; chmn. Louisville Devel. Authority, 2005—; chair athletic adv. bd. Spalding U., 2005—; dir. Jewish Hosp. Found., 2006—. White House fellow, 1979, U.S.-Japan Leadership fellow, Japan Soc., Inc., 1988. Democrat. Roman Catholic. Office: Wyatt Tarrant & Combs 2800 Citizens Plz Louisville KY 40202-2898 Office Phone: 502-562-7234. Business E-Mail: rnorthern@wyattfirm.com.

NORTHEY, WILLIAM THOMAS, microbiologist, educator; b. Duluth, Minn., Aug. 10, 1928; s. William Thomas Northey and Mary Ellen Riley; m. Margaret Esparza, July 1, 1972; m. Elizabeth L. Van Laeke, Aug. 12, 1950 (div. June 15, 1970); children: Kathleen, William Northey III, Bruce, Brian, Barry, Brett, Suzanne. BA, U. of Minn., 1950; MA, U. of Kans., 1957, PhD, 1959. Rsch. asst. Abbott Labs., Chgo., 1950—51, Naval Med Rsch. Unit #4, Gt. Lakes, Ill., 1951—55; tchg. and rsch. U. of Kans., Lawrence, Kans., 1955—59; from asst. prof. to prof. emeritus Ariz. State U., Tempe, Ariz., 1959—85, prof. emeritus, 1985—. Cons. Unidynamics Corp., Goodyear, Ariz., 1960—63, AiResearch Corp., Phoenix, 1963—65; pres., dir. Iatric Corp., Tempe, 1960—92. Contbr. articles to profl. jours. Vol. United Fund, Phoenix; grant reviewer Ariz. Heart Assn., Phoenix; bd. dir. Ariz. Br. of Allergy Found. of Ariz., Phoenix. Seaman second USNR, 1946—51. Grantee, NIH, 1960—85, USAF, 1963—68. Fellow: Am. Acad. of Microbiology; mem.: Am. Soc. of Immunology, Am. Soc. of Microbiology (pres. Ariz. chpt. 1963). Achievements include development of scorpion anti-venom; research in aeroallergens in Arizona. Avocations: skiing, swimming, reading. Home: 4818 N 72nd Way Scottsdale AZ 85251-1302 Home Phone: 480-946-9754.

NORTHRIP, ROBERT EARL, lawyer; b. Sleeper, Mo., May 8, 1939; s. Novel and Jessie (Burch) N.; m. Linda Kay Francis, June 15, 1968; children: Robert E. Jr., William F., Darryl F., David F. BA, Southwest Mo. State, 1960; MA, U. N.C., 1965; JD, U. Mo., 1968. Bar: Mo. 1968, U.S. Dist. Ct. (we. dist.) Mo, 1968, U.S. Ct. Appeals (10th cir.) 1976, U.S. Ct. Appeals (8th cir.) 1980, U.S. Ct. Appeals (9th cir.) 1983, U.S. Ct. Appeals (3d cir.) 1987, U.S. Supreme Ct. 1978. Ptnr. Shook, Hardy & Bacon, Kansas City, Mo., 1968—. Active Nelson Art Gallery, Soc. of Fellows, Kans. City, Mo. 1st lt. US Army, 1963-65. Mem. Mo. Bar Assn., Lawyers Assn. Kansas City, Mo. Orgn. Def. Lawyers, Kansas City Met. Bar Assn., U. Mo. Alumni Assn. (past pres. Kansas City chpt.), Nat. Soc. Arts and Letters. Republican. Avocations: baseball, football. Office: Shook Hardy & Bacon 2555 Grand Blvd Kansas City MO 64108-2613 Home: 6439 Wenonga Rd Mission Hills KS 66208 Office Phone: 816-474-6550. Personal E-mail: rnorthrip@gmail.com.

NORTHROP, PEGGY, editor-in-chief; b. 1954; m. Sean Elder; 1 adopted child, Franny. BA in Anthropology, U. Calif., Berkeley, 1980. Reporter, editor San Francisco Examiner Sunday mag.; editor Berkeley

Monthly; with Glamour mag., Vogue Condé Nast Publs.; with Health mag., Real Simple Time Inc.; editor-in-chief Organic Style Rodale Inc., 2002—04; editor-in-chief More mag. Meredith Corp., 2004—07; editor-in-chief Reader's Digest Assn., Inc., 2007—09, global editor-in-chief, 2009—. Contbr. Today Show, CBS Early Show, PBS's To the Contrary, XM radio's MoreTime. Active mem. CARE; mem. adv. bd. Develop - Don't Destroy - Bklyn. Recipient Women Who Get it Right award, Nat. Breast Cancer Coalition, 2006, Nat. Mag. award for Gen. Excellence, Am. Soc. Mag. Editors, 2009; named one of 21 Most Intriguing People, MIN mag., 2003. Mem.: Am. Soc. Mag. Editors (bd. dirs., Ellie award for personal svc.). Office: Readers Digest Assn Inc Hdqs Readers Digest Rd Pleasantville NY 10570 Office Phone: 914-238-1000.*

NORTHRUP, JASON, marriage and family therapist; b. Dallas, Aug. 22, 1980; s. William and Briseida DeLeon Northrup; m. Kirsten Jones, June 5, 2004; 1 child, Madalyn. BS, Abilene Christian U., Tex., 2002, MS in Marriage and Family Therapy, 2004; PhD, Tex. Tech U., Lubbock, 2008. Lic. marriage & family therapist 2009; profl. counselor Tex., 2008. Therapist Employee Assistance Program, Tex. Tech U. Health Scis. Ctr., Lubbock, 2006—08, Chupik Counseling and Consulting, PA, Temple, Tex., 2008—. Aamft supr. candidate, Temple, Tex., 2007—. Small group leader Raintree Christian Ch., Lubbock, 2005—08. Mem.: Am. Assn. Marriage and Family Therapists. Avocations: travel, reading, movies. Office: Chupik Counseling and Consulting PA 3010 Scott Blvd Ste 103 Temple TX 76502 Business E-Mail: jason.northrup@ttu.edu.

NORTHUP, ANNE MEAGHER, commissioner, former United States Representative from Kentucky; b. Louisville, Jan. 22, 1948; d. James L. and Floy Gates (Terstegge) Meagher; m. Robert Wood Northup, Apr. 12, 1969; children: David, Katherine, Joshua, Kevin, Erin, Mark. BA in Econs. and Bus., St. Mary's Coll. Notre Dame, South Bend, Ind., 1970. Mem. Ky. House of Reps., Frankfort, 1987-96, US Congress from 3d Ky. Dist., 1997—2007; commr. US Consumer Product Safety Commn., Bethesda, Md., 2009—. Mem. fin. adv. bd. EPA, 1989-93; mem. home econs. adv. bd. U. Ky. Coll. Agr., 1992— Appeared on Meet the Press, Fox News Sunday, Larry King Live, CNN & Co., Hardball with Chris Matthews. Mem. exec. com. Partnership Ky. Sch. Reform, 1990—; bd. dirs. Greater Louisville Pub. Radio, 1993—, Hospice Louisville, 1994—, Ky. Cancer Consortium, 1992—; mem. cmty. adv. bd. Jr. League Louisville, 1993—; active Holy Spirit Cath. Ch. Named Outstanding Woman of Achievement St. Matthews BPW, 1990; recipient Cath. Schs. Disting. Alumni award, 1991, U. Notre Dame award of the yr. Ky. Alumni Assn., 1991, Clearing the Air award Am. Lung Assn. of Ky., 1991, Svc. Above Self award St. Matthews Rotary Club, 1992, Pub. Svc. award Am. Heart Assn., 1992, Sacred Heart Acad. Alumna award, 1994, Nat. Fedn. of Ind. Bus./Guardian of Small Bus. award, 1996, 97, 98, Legislator of Yr. award Environ. Industry Assn., 1997, Outstanding Freshman Mem. of Congress award Nat. Industries for Blind, 1997, Spirit of Enterprise award U.S. C. of C., 1997, Bulldog award Watchdogs of Treasury, 1998, Jefferson award Citizens for Sound Economy, 1998, Outstanding Support award Am. Printing House for Blind, 1998, Legislator of Yr. award Assn. Equipment Distbrs., 1999, Cmty. Healthcare Champion award Nat. Assn. Cmty. Health Ctrs., Inc., 1999, Spirit of Enterprise award C. of C., 1999, Susan B. Anthony Congl. award, 1999, Pub. Policy Adv. of Yr. award Nat. Assn. Women Bus. Owners, 1999, Honor Roll of Legis. Achievement in Econ. Devel. award So. Econ. Devel. Coun., Inc., 1999, Legislator of Yr. award Nat. Beer Whoesalers Assn., 1999. Mem. Nat. Order Women Legislators, Nat. Conf. State Legislators, Nat. Rep. Legis. Conf., Inst. Rep. Women, So. Legis. Conf. (alternate from Ky. to fiscal affairs and govtl. com.), Nat. Fedn. Ind. Bus. Republican. Roman Catholic. Office: US Consumer Products Safety Commn 4330 East West Highway Bethesda MD 20814*

NORTON, CYNTHIA G., biology professor; b. Kenmore, Ny, Feb. 14, 1958; d. Edward D. and Christine M. Gundaker; m. Jeremy J. Norton, May 21, 1983; children: Jeffrey, Andrew. BA, Smith Coll., Northampton, Mass., 1980; PhD, U. Iowa, Iowa City, 1985. Prof. biology & women's studies Coll. St. Catherine, St. Paul, 1990—. Mem.: Nat. Women's Studies Assn., Soc. Study Evolution, Am. Malacological Soc. Office: Coll St Catherine 2004 Randolph Ave Saint Paul MN 55105 Business E-Mail: cgnorton@stkate.edu.

NORTON, DOUGLAS EVATT, mathematician, educator; b. Danville, Ill., Aug. 2, 1957; s. Luther Hooper and Lucy Evatt N.; m. Kathryn Ann Friggle, Sept. 15, 1979; children: Hannah, Jacob. BS, Wake Forest U., 1979; MA, U. Wis., 1984; PhD, U. Minn., 1989. Asst. prof. math. scis. Villanova (Pa.) U., 1989-96, assoc. prof. math. scis., 1996—, chair dept. math. scis., 2003—. Fulbright lectr., rsch. scholar U. Botswana, 1996-97. Contbr. articles to profl. jours. Co-pres. Haverford H.S. Parent-Tchr. Student Assn., Havertown, Pa., 1999-2000. Rotary fellow 1979-80. Mem. AAAS, AAUP, Am. Math. Soc., Math. Assn. Am., Soc. for Indsl. and Applied Math., Assn. for Women in Math., Nat. Coun. Tchrs. Math., Pa. Acad. Sci., Phi Beta Kappa, Omicron Delta Kappa, Phi Kappa Phi, Sigma Xi. Home: 12 Landaff Rd Havertown PA 19083 Office: Villanova U Dept Math Scis 800 Lancaster Ave Villanova PA 19085 Office Phone: 610-519-4850. Fax: 610-519-6928. E-mail: douglas.norton@villanova.edu.

NORTON, DOUGLAS RAY, former auditor general; b. Portales, N.Mex., Mar. 23, 1933; s. Clayton G. and Lillian W. Norton; m. Wanda Jones, May 23, 1951 (div. July 1979); children: Debbie Norton Goodman, Vicki Norton Hulet, Denise Norton Cummings; m. Robertta J. Andersen, July 31, 1998. BS, U. Ariz., 1963. CPA, Ariz. Staff acct., audit supr. Ernst & Ernst, Tucson, Ariz., 1963-67; ptnr. Baker, Price & Norton, Prescott, Ariz., 1968-75, Lester Witte & Co., Prescott, Ariz., 1975-76; auditor gen. State of Ariz., Phoenix, 1976-99; ret., 1999. Former mem. Profl. Adv. Bd. Sch. Acctg. Ariz. State U., Tempe; former mem. acctg. bd. advisors U. Ariz. Pres. Prescott Bd. Edn., 1976. Served with U.S. Army, 1953-55. Mem. AICPA, Ariz. Soc. CPAs, Nat. Assn. State Auditors, Comptrollers and Treasurers (pres. 1993-94), Nat. State Auditors Assn. (pres. 1982-83), Lions (pres. Prescott chpt. 1973-74). Home: PO Box 3120 Chino Valley AZ 86323-2707

NORTON, DUNBAR SUTTON, economic developer; b. Hoquiam, Wash., Jan. 30, 1926; s. Percy Dunbar and Anna Fedelia (Sutton) N.; m. Kathleen Margaret Mullarky, Dec. 21, 1948 (dec. Apr. 1994); children: Priscilla K., Rebecca C., Jennifer A., Douglas S.; m. Mary Ethel Wolff, May 25, 1996. Student, U. Oreg., 1946—48; diploma, U.S. Army Command & Gen. Staff, 1964. Enlisted U.S. Army, 1944, commd. 2d lt., 1948, advanced through grades to lt. col., ret., 1974; dir. econ. devel. dept. Yuma County C. of C., Ariz., 1974—83; exec. v.p. Lakin Enterprises, Yuma, 1983—87; owner Norton Cons., Yuma, 1987—. Corp. mem. Greater Yuma Econ. Devel. Corp., 1984-96, vice chmn., 1993-95; dir. Lower Colo. River Rsch. Ctr. Ariz. West Coll./No. Ariz. U., 1996-2000 Active Yuma County Indsl. Devel. Authority, 1984-90, 92-2006, pres., 1992-2006; chmn. fundraising com. Yuma Cross Park Coun., 1984-88, sec., 1988-90, v.p., 1990-92, bd. dirs., 1982-96; bd. dirs. Yuma Leadership, 1984-93, Yuma Youth Leadership, 1993-96, Ariz. Partnership Air Transp., 1990-96, v.p., 1993-95; chmn. devel. com. Yuma County Airport Authority, 1985-88, v.p., 1992-2002, pres., 2003-04, chmn. mktg. com., 2004, dir., 2008-09; vice chmn. Yuma Main St. Bd., 1988-90, Yuma County Geog. Info. Sys. Task Force, 1991-95, Yuma Kids Voting, 1990-91; bd. dirs. Yuma County Civic Trusteeship, 1993-95, Ariz. We. Coll. Found. Bd., 2000-02, chmn. scholar awards commn., 2000-02; chmn. The Southwest Inst., 1995-96, What's Best for Our Kids, 1995-96, Yuma Sch. Dist. No. 1 New Elem. Sch. Planning Com., 1996-97, co-chmn. maintain level budget override com., 1999-2001; trustee Yuma County Libr., 1996-02; chmn. Yuma County Complete Count com. U.S. Census, 1990, 95, 2000; com. mem. Yuma County Town Hall, 1999-2005. Decorated Legion of Merit with oak leaf cluster, Bronze Star, Meritorious Svc. and Army Commendation Medal with Oak Leaf Cluster Mem. Ariz. Assn. for Econ. Devel. (bd. dirs. 1975-82, pres. 1982-83, legis. affairs com. 1987-2002, Developer of Yr. 1978, William W. Lampkin award 2001), Yuma Execs. Assn. (sec.-treas., exec. dir. 1987-2009). Republican. Roman Catholic. Avocations: golf, swimming, singing. Home and Office: 12267 E Del Norte Yuma AZ 85367-7356 Home Phone: 928-276-3158. Personal E-mail: yumexec@msn.com.

NORTON, EDWARD, actor; b. Boston, Aug. 18, 1969; s. Edward and Robin Norton. BA in History, Yale U., 1991. Motion picture and stage actor. Actor: (films) Everyone Says I Love You, 1996 (L.A. Film Critics Assn. award, 1996), Primal Fear, 1996 (nominee Best Supporting Actor Oscar, 1996, Chgo. Film Critics Assn. award, 1997, Golden Globe award, 1996, Nat. Bd. Rev. award, 1996), The People vs. Larry Flynt, 1996, Rounders, 1998, American History X, 1998 (nominee Best Actor Oscar, 1999, Chgo. Film Critics Assn. award, 1999, Golden Satellite award, 1999), Fight Club, 1999, The Score, 2001, Death to Smoochy, 2002, Red Dragon, 2002, Frida, 2002, The Italian Job, 2003, Kingdom of Heaven, 2005, Pride and Glory, 2008; actor, co-prodr. 25th Hour, 2002, actor, screenwriter (films) The Incredible Hulk, 2008, dir., prodr. Keeping the Faith, 2000; exec. prodr.: (films) Dirty Work, 2004. Office: c/o Brian Swardstrom Endeavor Talent Agy 9601 Wilshire Blvd Fl 3 Beverly Hills CA 90210

NORTON, EDWARD C., economist, educator; PhD, MIT, Cambridge, 1990. Asst. prof. Harvard Med. Sch., Boston, 1990—93; sr. economist RTI Internat., Research Triangle Park, NC, 1993—96; prof. U. N.C. Chapel Hill, 1996—2008. Recipient Phillip and Ruth Hettleman prize, U. N.C. Chapel Hill, 2003. Mem.: Am. Soc. Health Economists (bd. trustees 2004—08). Office: Univ MI Dept Health Mgmt and Policy Ann Arbor MI 48109

NORTON, ELEANOR HOLMES, Delegate to United States House Representative from District of Columbia, lawyer, educator; b. Washington, June 13, 1937; d. Coleman and Vela (Lynch) Holmes; m. Edward W. Norton (div.); children: Katherine Felicia, John Holmes. BA, Antioch Coll., Ohio, 1960; MA in Am. Studies, Yale U., 1963, LLB, 1964. Bar: Pa. 1965, US Supreme Ct. 1968. Law clk. to Judge A. Leon Higginbotham Fed. Dist. Ct., 1964-65; asst. legal dir. ACLU, 1965-70; exec. asst. to mayor City of NY, 1971-74; chmn. NYC Commn. on Human Rights, 1970-77, EEOC, Washington, 1977-81; sr. fellow Urban Inst., Washington, 1981-82; prof. law Georgetown U., Washington, 1982—; del. (at large) US Congress from DC, 1990—, mem. coms. on govt. reform and transp./infrastructure. Named one of 100 Most Influential Black Americans, Ebony mag., 2006; named to Power 150, Ebony mag. 2008. Democrat. Office: US Ho of Reps 2136 RayburnHo Office Bldg Washington DC 20515-0001 Office Phone: 202-225-8050. Office Fax: 202-225-3002.*

NORTON, ELIZABETH WYCHGEL, retired lawyer; b. Cleve., Mar. 25, 1933; d. James Nicolas and Ruth Elizabeth (Cannell) Wychgel; m. Henry Wacks Norton Jr., July 16, 1954 (div. 1971); children: James, Henry, Peter, Fred; m. James Cory Ferguson, Dec. 14, 1985 (div. Apr. 1988). BA in Math., Wellesley Coll., 1954; JD cum laude, U. Minn., 1974. Bar: Minn. 1974. Summer intern Minn. Atty. Gen.'s Office, St. Paul, 1972; with U.S. Dept. Treasury, St. Paul, 1973; assoc. Gray, Plant, Mooty, Mooty & Bennett, P.A., Mpls., 1974-79, prin., 1980-94, of counsel, 1995-96; ret. Mem. Minn. Lawyers Bd. Profl. Responsibility, 1984-89; mem. U. Minn. Law Sch. Bd. Visitors, 1987-92. Trustee YWCA, Mpls., 1979-84, 89-91, co-chmn. deferred giving com., 1980-81, chmn. by-laws com., bd. dirs., 1976-77, lectr.; treas. Minn. Women's Campaign Fund, 1985; guarantor, 1982-83, budget and fin. com. bd. dirs., 1984-87; trustee Ripley Meml. Found., 1980-84; treas. Jones-Harrison Home, 1967, bd. dirs., 1962-69, 2d v.p., chmn. fin., 1968-69; mem. Sen. David Durenberger's Women's Network, 1983-88. Durant scholar. Fellow Am. Bar Found.; mem. ABA (mediation task force family law sect. 1983-84), Minn. Bar Assn. (human rights com. family law sect., task force uniform marital property act 1984-85), Minn. Bar Found. (dir. 1991-94), Hennepin County Bar Assn. (pres. 1987-88, chmn. task force on pub. edn. 1984, chmn., mem. exec. com. family law sect. 1979-94), Minn. Inst. Legal Edn., Minn. Women's Lawyers (exec. com.), Hemlock Soc. of S.W. Fla. (co-chmn. 1999-2001), U. Minn. Law Sch. Alumni Assn. (dir. 1975-81, exec. com. 1981-83), Wellesley Club (Naples, pres. 2002-04), Phi Beta Kappa. Home: 26 Water Oaks Way Naples FL 34105-7157 Personal E-mail: betsynorton@comcast.net, betsynorton@mac.com.

NORTON, GALE ANN, lawyer, former United States Secretary of the Interior; b. Wichita, Mar. 11, 1954; d. Dale Bentsen and Anna Jacqueline (Lansdowne) N.; m. John Goethe Hughes, Mar. 26, 1990. BA, U. Denver, 1975, JD, 1978. Bar: Colo. 1978, U.S. Supreme Ct. 1981. Jud. clk. Colo. Ct. Appeals, Denver, 1978-79; sr. atty. Mountain States Legal Found., Denver, 1979-83; nat. fellow Hoover Instn. Stanford U., Calif., 1983-84; asst. to dep. sec. USDA, Washington, 1984-85; assoc. solicitor US Dept. Interior, Washington, 1985-87; pvt. practice law Denver, 1987-90; atty. gen. State of Colo., Denver, 1991—99; sr. counsel Brownstein, Hyatt & Farber, P.C., 1999—2000; sec. US Dept. Interior, Washington, 2001—06; gen. counsel Royal Dutch Shell, Colo., 2007—. Lectr. U. Denver Law Sch., 1989; transp. law program dir. U. Denver, 1978-79. Contbr. chpts. to books, articles to profl. jours. Past chair Nat. Assn. Attys. Gen. Environ. Com.; co-chair Nat. Policy Forum Environ. Coun.; candidate for 1996 election to U.S. Senate; chair environ. commn. Rep. Nat. Lawyers Assn. Named Young Career Woman Bus. and Profl. Women, 1981, Young Lawyer of Yr., 1991, Mary Lathrop Trailblazer award Colo. Women's Bar Assn., 1999. Mem. Federalist Soc., Colo. Women's Forum, Order of St. Ives. Republican. Methodist. Avocation: skiing. Mailing: 4582 S Ulster St, #1400 Denver CO 80237

NORTON, JANE ELLEN BERGMAN (JANE BERGMAN), former lieutenant governor; b. Grand Junction, Colo. d. Walter F. and Elinor (Pitman) Bergman; m. Mike Norton; children: Lacee, Tyler. BS in Health Sci., with distinction, Colo. State U., 1976; MS in Mgmt., Regis U. With Med. Group Mgmt. Assn., Englewood, Colo.; mem. Colo. Ho. Reps., 1986—87; regional dir. US Dept. Health and Human Svcs.; exec. dir. Colo. Dept. Pub. Health Environment, 1999—2002; lt. gov. State of Colo., Denver, 2003—07. Chair Colo. Commn. on Indian Affairs; del. Aerospace State Assn., Edn. Commn. of States; co-chair Colo. Space Coalition; Colo. spokesperson Go Red for Women Campaign Am. Heart Assn.; hon. chair Prematurity Campaign Colo. March of Dimes; hon. chair Colo. Freedom Meml. Bd. dirs. Internat. Found. Electronic Systems, Am. Coun. Young Polit. Leaders; nat. bd. adv. Inst. Sci. and Space Studies; adv. bd. women's health U. Colo.; bd. adv. Colo. History Day; co-chair Colo. Health Disparities Commn. Recipient Disting. Veterans Advocate award, United Veterans Com. Colo., Legislator of Yr. award, Persons Living with HIV Action Network of Colo., David M. Clark, S.J. Innovative Leadership award, Regis U., Family Values award, State of Colo., Honor Alumna award, Colo. State U. Coll. Applied Human Sci., US Public Health Svc. award outstanding accomplishment increasing childhood immunization rates, Outstanding Svc. to Seniors award, US Adminstrn. on Aging; named Woman of Distinction, Girls Scouts, 2005, Public Servant of Yr., Rocky Mt. Family Coun. Mem.: Nat. Lt. Governors Assn. (chair-elect 2006), Omicron Kappa Upsilon (hon.). Republican. Avocations: hiking, skiing.

NORTON, JOHN W., JR., chemical engineer, educator; s. John W. and Jill S. Norton; m. Liana C. McDonald, July 17, 1993; children: Gillian, Maris, Benjamin. BCE, U. Cin., 1993, MSE in Environ. Engring., 1995; MSE in Indsl. & Ops. Engring., U. Mich., Ann Arbor, 2004, MS in Geotech. Engring., 2002, PhD in Civil Engring., 2006. N.Am. practice lead, renewable energy MWH Americas, Inc., Chgo., 2007—; instr., chem. engring. U. Mich., Ann Arbor, 2007—. Invited spkr. U. Tokyo, U. Mich., UCLA, Tex. A&M, U. Toledo, Rutgers U., Columbia U., U. Cin., 2001—, UN Inst. Water Forum; closing spkr. Nat. Assn. Clean Water Agys., Cleve., 2007—07; instr., energy sys. Am. Water Works Assn., Denver, guest spkr., San Diego, 2009—; author, lit. rev. Water Environ. Fedn., Alexandria, Va., 2008—, co-author, manual practice 8, 2008—. Contbr. scientific papers. Christ renews parish men's group St. Isaac Jogues, Hinsdale, Ill., 2009. Mem.: Internat. Water Assn. Roman Catholic. Home: 742 Chestnut St Hinsdale IL 60521 Personal E-mail: johnnorton@umich.edu. Business E-Mail: john.w.norton@us.mwhglobal.com.

NORTON, KAREN ANN, accountant; b. Nov. 1, 1950; d. Dale Francis and Ruby Grace (Gehlhar) N. BA, U. Minn., 1972; postgrad., U. Md., 1978; MBA, Calif. State Poly. U., Pomona, 1989. CPA Md. Securities transactions analyst Bur. of Pub. Debt, Washington, 1972-79, internal auditor, 1979-81, IRS, Washington, 1981; sr. acct. World Vision Internat., Monrovia, Calif., 1981-83, acctg. supr., 1983-87; sr. sys. liaison coord. Home Savs. Am. (name changed to Washington Mut.), 1987-97, sys. auditor, 1997-2000, sect. mgr., 2000—02, group mgr., v.p., 2003—04, v.p., 2005—; project mgr. II Indy Mac Bank, 2004—05, v.p., 2005—08; Sr. fin. controls mgr. Kaiser Permanente, 2008—. Author: (poetry) Ode to Joyce, 1985 (Golden Poet award 1985). 2d v.p. chpt. Nat. Treasury Employees Union, Washington, 1978, editor chpt. newsletter; mem. M-2 Prisoners Sponsorship Program, Chino, Calif., 1984-86. Recipient Spl. Achievement award Dept. Treasury, 1976, Superior Performance award Dept. Treasury, 1977-78; Charles and Ellora Alliss scholar, 1968. Mem. Angel Flight, Flying Samaritans, Habitat for Humanity. Avocations: flying, chess, tennis. Office: Kaiser Permanente 393 E Walnut St Pasadena CA 91188 Office Phone: 626-405-3006. Personal E-mail: skypilot@pacbell.net.

NORTON, LARRY, oncologist, researcher; b. Bronx, NY, 1947; MD, Columbia U. Coll. Physicians and Surgeons, 1972. Diplomate Am. Bd. Internal Medicine, Am. Bd. Oncology. Intern Bronx Mcpl. Hosp.-Einstein, NYC, 1972-73, resident, 1973-74; mem. staff Meml. Sloan-Kettering Cancer Ctr., NYC, dep. physician-in-chief breast cancer programs, dir. Specialized Program of Rsch. Excellence in Breast Cancer, med. dir. Evelyn H. Lauder Breast Ctr. and Iris Cantor Diagnostic Ctr., Norna S. Sarofim chair clin. oncology, 1995—. Former chair breast com. Cancer and Leukemia Group B, Nat. Cancer Inst.; mem. cancer clin. investigations review com. NCI, mem., consensus develop. conf. on treatment of early stage breast cancer, 1990, mem, cooperative breast cancer tissue resource registry; prin. investigator Program Project Grant, Nat. Cancer Inst.; Presdl. appointee National Cancer Adv. Bd., NCI, 1998—2004. Contbr. articles to profl. jours.; mem. several editl. bd. Recipient Sci. Achievement Award, Susan G. Komen Found., 1997; co-recipient NYC Award for Advancement of Cancer Medicine, Gilda's Club, 2006. Mem.: Nat. Alliance of Breast Cancer Organs. (pres.), Am. Soc. Clin. Oncology (pres. 2001—02, past found. chair, David A. Karnofsky Meml. award 2004), Alpha Omega Alpha. Achievements include being the co-developer of the Norton-Simon Hypothesis; co-developer of an approach to therapy called dose density. Office: Meml Sloan-Kettering Cancer Ctr 1275 York Ave New York NY 10021-6094 Office Phone: 212-639-5325.*

NORTON, MARGARET SARAH, retired insurance company executive; d. William Leander Norton and Mattie Rice Reed. BA in Speech, Birmingham So. Coll., 1953; postgrad. in speech therapy, Emory U., 1953—54. Registered rep. Nat. Assn. Securities Dealers, 1973. Asst. to dean women Finch Coll., NYC, 1960—64; agent The Equitable Life Assurance Soc. US, Mobile, Ala., 1968—76; asst. dir. Historic Blakeley State Pk., Spanish Ft., Ala., 1978—94; ret., 1994. Pres. Ea. Shore Rep. Women, Fairhope, Ala., 1999—2004; mem. steering com. Baldwin County Rep. Party, Ala., 1999—, mem. exec. com., 1999—, Ala. Rep. Party, 2003—; founding bd. mem. Mobile Ballet; bd. mem. Baldwin County Humane Soc.; v.p, Ea. Shore Rep. Women, Fairhope, 2008—; dir. Dist. 1, Ala. Fedn. Rep. Women; bd. dirs., ho. & hospitality chmn. Mobile Assn. Life Underwriters, 1970—74; bd. dirs., govs. appointee Historic Blakeley Auth., 2003—. Recipient Woman of Yr., Am. Bus. Women's Assn., 1992, resolutions of commendation, Ala. Senate and Ho. of Reps., 2004, day proclaimed in her honor, Gov. Ala. and also Fairhope, Ala., 2004. Mem.: Nat. Assn. Life Underwriters (life), Ea, Shore Federated Women's Club. Republican. Methodist. Avocations: piano, politics, art, public speaking. Home: 402 Fairwood Blvd Fairhope AL 36532 Home Phone: 251-928-1180.

NORTON, MARY BETH, history educator, writer; b. Ann Arbor, Mich., Mar. 25, 1943; d. Clark Frederic and Mary Elizabeth (Lunny) N. BA, U. Mich., 1964; MA, Harvard U., 1965, PhD, 1969; DHL (hon.), Siena Coll., 1983, Marymount Manhattan Coll., 1984, De Pauw U., 1989; DLitt (hon.), Ill. Wesleyan U., 1992. Asst. prof. history U. Conn., Storrs, 1969-71; from asst. prof. to prof. Cornell U., Ithaca, NY, 1971-87, Mary Donlon Alger prof. Am. history, 1987—. Pitt prof. Am. history and instn. U. Cambridge, 2005—06. Author: The British-Americans: The Loyalist Exiles in England, 1774-1789, 1972, Liberty's Daughters: The Revolutionary Experience of American Women, 1750-1800, 1980 (Berkshire prize for Best Book Woman Historian 1980), Founding Mothers and Fathers: Gendered Power and the Forming of American Society, 1996 (finalist Pulitzer prize in history 1997), In the Devil's Snare: The Salem Witchcraft Crisis of 1692, 2002 (Amb. Book award of English-Speaking Union 2003); co-author: A People and A Nation, 1982, 8th rev. edit., 2008; editor: AHA Guide to Hist. Literature, 3d rev. edit., 1995; co-editor: Women of America: A History, 1979, To Toil the Livelong Day: America's Women at Work, 1790-1980, 1987, Major Problems in American Women's History, 1989, 4th rev. edit., 2007; contbr. articles to profl. jours. Trustee Cornell U., 1973-75, 83-88; mem. Nat. Coun. Humanities, Washington, 1979-84. Woodrow Wilson Found. fellow, 1964-65, NEH fellow, 1974-75, Shelby Cullom Davis Ctr. fellow Princeton U., 1977-78, Rockefeller Found. fellow, 1986-87, Soc. for Humanities fellow Cornell U., 1989-90, John Simon Guggenheim Meml. Found. fellow, 1993-94, Starr Found. fellow Lady Margaret Hall, Oxford U., 2000, Mellon postdoctoral fellow Huntington Libr., 2001, LA Times Disting. fellow, 2008-09. Fellow Soc. Am. Hist. (exec. bd. 1974-87, 2003—, v.p. 2007, pres. 2008-09; Allan Nevins prize 1970); mem. Am. Hist. Assn. (v.p. for rsch. 1985-87), Am. Acad. Arts and Sci., Orgn. Am. Hist. (exec. bd. 1983-86), Berkshire Conf. Women Hist. (pres. 1983-85) Democrat. Methodist. Office: Cornell U Dept History 325 Mcgraw Hall Ithaca NY 14853-4601 Business E-Mail: mbn1@cornell.edu.

NORTON, PETER K., retired computer utilities programmer, writer; b. Aberdenne, Wash., Nov. 14, 1943; m. Eileen Harris Norton, 1983 (div. 2000). Programmer, Norton Utilities (sold bus. to Symantec). Co-author (with David Wild): Peter Norton's Computing Fundamentals, 1995; co-author: (with Arthur Griffith) Peter Norton's Complete Guide to Linux, 1999; co-author: (with Scott Clark) Peter Norton's New Inside the PC, 2002, and several others; contbr. articles to profl. jours. Trustee Mus. Modern Art, NYC. Named one of Top 200 Collectors, Artnews Mag., 2004—08. Avocation: Collector of Contemporary Art.

NORTON, STEPHEN ALLEN, earth sciences educator; b. Newton, Mass., May 21, 1940; children: David S., Lisa A., Stephen A. BA, Princeton U., 1962; MA, Harvard U., 1963, PhD, 1967. Prof. emeritus, earth scis. U. Maine, Orono, 1978—, dept. chmn., 1978—82, 1993—99, dean arts and scis., 1984—86. Fellow Geol. Soc. Am.; mem. Am. Soc. Limnology and Oceanography. Office: U Maine Dept Earth Scis Bryand Ctr Orono ME 04469-5790

NORTON, SUSAN E.S., museum director; BA, Coll. William & Mary; MA, George Washington Univ. Mem. editl. staff Nat. Geographic Mag., Washington, 1980—83; grants reviewer, comm. on rsch. & exploration Nat. Geographic Soc., 1983—85; mem. editl. staff, area specialist in archaeology Nat. Geographic Mag., 1985—87; events mgr., pub. affairs specialist Nat. Geographic Soc., 1988—95; dir. Nat. Geographic Soc. Explorers Hall, 1995—; dir. spl. events Nat. Geographic Soc. Adv. Nat. Children's Mus., Washington; developer, exhibition on culture of Mongolia Nat. Mus. Mongolia, Fine Art Mus. Ulaanbaatar, 2004; cons. Suzanne Mubarak Children's Mus., Cairo, 2002; co-developer, exhibition on Sir Edmund Hillary: Everest & Beyond Auckland War Mus., & Nat. Geographic Soc., New Zealand, 2002; cultural fellowship Govt. of Australia, 2001; exhibition developer Tehran Mus. Contemporary Art, Meridian Internat. Ctr., Iran, 2001, City of Petra, Jordan, 1997. Mem.: Am. Assn. Museums, Internat. Women's Media Found., Nat. Press Club. Office: Nat Geographic Soc 1145 17th St NW Washington DC 20036-4688 Office Phone: 202-826-6616. Office Fax: 202-857-5864. Business E-Mail: snorton@ngs.org.

NORTON, TERRY M., veterinarian, director; BS, N.Mex. State U., Las Cruces; DVM, Tufts U. Diplomate Am. Coll. Zoological Medicine, 1992. Small animal medicine and surgery internship, Washington; zoo and wildlife medicine resident U. Fla., Gainesville; dir. vet. svcs. Ga. Sea Turtle Ctr., Jekyll Island; vet. St. Catherines Island Ctr., wildlife vet. Adj. prof. U. Fla., NC State U., U. Ga. Colls. Vet. Medicine; rschr. Ga. Dept. Natural Resources, US Fish and Wildlife Svc. Assoc. editor: Jour. Zoo and Wildlife Medicine; contbr. articles to profl. publs. Office: Ga Sea Turtle Ctr 214 Stable Rd Jekyll Island GA 31527 Office Phone: 912-635-4070. Business E-Mail: tnorton@jekyllisland.com.

NORTON-SMITH, THOMAS MICHAEL, humanities educator; b. Springfield, Ill., Aug. 2, 1954; s. Wilfred and Marilyn R. Smith; m. Linda Lee Norton, Sept. 10, 1983; children: Michael Chandler, Shelley Anne Robinson, Kathryn Greigh. BS in Math., Mo. So. State Coll., Joplin, 1979; MS in Math., Pittsburg State U., KS, 1981; PhD, U. Ill., Urbana-Champaign, 1988. Grad. asst. Pittsburg State U.Dept. Math., 1979—81; instr. Parkland C.C.Dept. Social Scis., Champaign, Ill., 1983—84; instr. dept. philosophy Kent State U. Stark Campus, North Canton, 1985—86, assoc. & asst. prof. philosophy, 1988—; grad. asst. U. Ill.: Dept. Philosophy, 1986—87. Mem. Kent State U. Faculty Senate, Ohio, 2002—04; chair Kent State U. Faculty Senate Exec. Com., 2003—04, Faculty Senate Ethics Com., Kent, 2006—07; sec. Kent State U. Stark Campus Faculty Coun., 1992—95; chair Kent State U.: Dept. Philosophy, 1995—97; treas. Am. Indian Philosophy Assn., 1999—; internat. adv. bd. mem. Can. Jour. Native Studies, 2006—; mem. Am. Philos. Assn. Com. Status Indigenous Philosophers, 2001—04, 2006—, assoc. chair, 2007—08, chair, 2008—; mem. Kent State U. Prof. Standing Com., 1996—2000, 2001—05, chair, 1998—99; mem. Instl. Diversity Scholarship Com., 2002—07. Contbr. articles articles to profl. jours., chapters to books. Mem. Piqua Sept Shawnee Tribe. Recipient Disting. Tchg. award, Kent State U. Stark Campus, 1991, Graduate's Applause, U. Tchg. Coun., 2000; grant, CDC Franklin County Ohio Dept. Edn., 2005, JFS Summit County, Ohio., 2005. Mem.: Am. Philos. Assn., Ohio Philos. Assn., Ctrl. States Philos. Assn., Am. Assn. Philosophy Tchrs., 1999 Am. Indian Philosophy Assn. (treas. 1999—2009), Am. Philos. Assn. Com. Status Indigenous Philosophers (assoc. chair 2007—08, chair 2008—). Independent. Avocation: history. Office: Kent State Univ Stark Campus 6000 Frank Ave NW North Canton OH 44720 Home Phone: 330-499-5185; Office Phone: 330-244-3381. Office Fax: 330-494-6121. Business E-Mail: tnorton@kent.edu.

NORVELL, JOHN EDMONDSON, III, retired neuroscientist, educator; b. Charleston, W.Va., Nov. 18, 1929; s. John Edmondson Jr., and Mathilde (Wood) N.; m. Rosemary Justice, June 2, 1962; children: John Edmondson IV, Scott Justice. BS, U. Charleston, W.Va., 1953; MS, W.Va. U., Morgantown, 1956; PhD, Ohio State U., Columbus, 1966. From asst. to assoc. prof. Med. Coll. Va., Richmond, 1966-76; prof., chmn. Oral Roberts U., Tulsa, 1976-87, prof., 1987-89; prof., chmn. Universidad Central del Caribe, Bayamon, P.R., 1990-91; prof. Oral Roberts U., Tulsa, 1992—98, prof. emeritus, 1998. Lectr. dept. surgery US Naval Hosp., Portsmouth, Va., 1968-1971; invited sci. editor New Eng. Jour. Medicine, 1970; vis. lectr. dept. anatomy U. Va., Hebrew U., Hadassah Med. Sch., Jerusalem, 1974, U. Va., Dept. Anatomy; chmn. Okla. State Anatomical Bd., Tulsa, 1978-89; gov.'s mini-cabinet on health and human resources, Okla., 1980-90; vis. prof. Sch. Medicine U. Nairobi, Kenya, 1982, Sch. Med. Scis., U. Benin, Nigeria, 1989; seminar speaker Zhongshan Med. Coll., Guangzhou, People's Republic of China, 1983; presenter in field. Author: Atlas of Neuroanatomy, 1976, Atlas of Cross Sections of Human Body, 1982; contbr. articles to profl. jours. Mem. Am. Assn. Anatomists, Soc. Neurosci., Transplantation Soc. Sigma Xi. Achievements include research in degeneration and regeneration of the intrinsic nerve fibers of hearts and kidneys after transplantation; aorticorenal ganglion. Home: 7018 E 100th St Tulsa OK 74133-6235 Office: Oral Roberts U Dept Biology 7777 S Lewis Ave Tulsa OK 74171-0003 Personal E-mail: jnorvell9@cox.net.

NORWALK, LESLIE V., federal agency administrator; b. Dayton, Ohio, 1966; B in Economics and Internat. Rels. cum laude, Wellesley Coll.; JD, George Mason U. Atty. Epstein Becker & Green, P.C.; acting dep. adminstr. Ctrs. for Medicare & Medicaid Svcs. (CMS), 2003—04, dep. adminstr., 2004—06, acting adminstr., 2006—. Office: Ctrs Medicare and Medicaid Svcs 200 Independence Ave SW Washington DC 20201

NORWARD, JOSEPHINE NORMA, social work educator, consultant; b. Johannesburg, Jan. 8, 1949; arrived in U.S., 1980; d. Henry and Florence Nxumalo; m. Howard Norward, Sept. 22, 1984 (div. June 1996); children: Nontuthuzelo, Mandisa. Diploma in Social Work, U. Zululand, Empangeni, South Africa, 1972; MSW, U. N.C., Chapel Hill, 1982; PhD, Atlanta U., 1989. Social worker City Coun. Johannesburg, 1972—80; asst. prof. Tampa U., Fla., 1987—89; sch. social worker Hillsborough County Bd. Edn., Tampa, 1989—91; assoc. prof. Kean U., Union, NJ, 1991—. Faculty mentor N.J. Undergrad. Minority Academic Career Program; cons. in field. Contbr. chapters to books. Vol. Edn. Law Ctr., Camden, 2005—. Mem.: Nat. Assn. Sch. Social Workers, Coun. Social Work Edn. Episcopalian. Avocations: travel, yoga, theater, pilates. Office: Kean Univ 1000 Morris Ave Union NJ 07083 E-mail: jnorward@aol.com.

NORWITT, RICHARD ADAM, manufacturing executive; Grad., Georgetown U.; LLB, U. Mich.; MBA, INSEAD, France. Joined Amphenol Corp., 1998, bus. devel. mgr., Asia, 1998, 2000—03, gen. mgr. ea. Asia Elec. tech., 2001—03, dir., interconnect sys. ops., Asia, 2002—03, group gen. mgr., Worldwide RF & Microwave Products Divsn., 2003—06, v.p., 2004—06, sr. v.p., 2006—07, COO, 2007—08, pres., 2007—, CEO, 2009—. Bd. dirs. Amphenol Corp., 2009—. Office: Amphenol Corp 358 Hall Ave Wallingford CT 06492 Office Phone: 203-265-8900. Office Fax: 203-265-8516.*

NORWOOD, BERNARD, economist; b. Boston, Nov. 21, 1922; s. Hyman and Rose (Fink) N.; m. Janet Lippe, June 25, 1943; children: Stephen Harlan, Peter Carlton. BA, Boston U., 1947; MA, Fletcher Sch. Law and Diplomacy, 1948, PhD, 1957. Internat. economist State Dept., 1949-58; joined U.S. Fgn. Svc., 1955; 1st sec. U.S. mission to European Communities, Brussels, Belgium, 1958-62; asst. chief comml. policy and treaties divsn. Dept. State, 1962; chmn. trade staff com. Office Spl. Rep. for Trade Negotiations, Exec. Office Pres., 1963-67; assigned The Nat. War Coll., 1967-68; advisor divsn. internat. fin. bd. govs. Fed. Res. Sys., 1968-75; prin. assoc., sr. cons. Nathan Assocs., Inc., 1975-94. Mem. U.S. del. to negotiations and confs. GATT, Geneva, 1953-67. Served with AUS, 1943-46. Home and Office: 5610 Wisconsin Ave # 21D Chevy Chase MD 20815-4415

NORWOOD, BRANDI AISHA, middle school educator; b. Atlanta, Oct. 17, 1978; d. Sara Clements and David A. Norwood. BS, Tenn. State U., Nashville, 2000; MEd in Ednl. Leadership, Troy State U., Augusta, Ga., 2003; cert. in Ednl. Leadership, U. West Ga., Carrollton, 2004; EdS in Ednl. Leadership, Argosy U., Sarasota, Fla., 2006. 7th grade life sci. tchr. Henderson Mid. Sch., Jackson, Ga., 2001—05; 7th grade life sci. and social sci. tchr. Clements Mid. Sch., Covington, Ga., 2005—. Cheerleading coach Clements Mid. Sch., Covington, 2005—; asst. coach girls basketball Henderson Mid. Sch., Jackson, 2001—05, head coach girls track, 2001—05, cheerleading coach, 2001—05. Mem.: Ga. Assn. Educators (assoc.), Profl. Assn. Ga. Educators (assoc.), Pi Lambda Theta (assoc.). Democrat. Baptist. Avocations: reading, travel. Home: 9129 Carr Cir Covington GA 30014 Personal E-mail: norwoodbrandi@netscape.net.

NORWOOD, DEBORAH ANNE, law librarian; b. Honolulu, Nov. 12, 1950; BA, U. Wash., 1972, M in Law Librarianship, 1979; JD, Willamette U., 1974. Bar: Wash., U.S. Dist. Ct. (we. dist.) 1975, U.S. Ct. Appeals (9th cir.) 1980. Ptnr. Evans and Norwood, Seattle, 1975-79; law libr. U.S. Courts Libr., Seattle, 1980-89; state law libr. Wash. State Law Libr., Olympia, 1989—2002, reporter of decisions, 1994-2001; asst. dir. pub. svcs. Jacob Burns Law Libr. George Washington U., Washington, 2002—. Mem. Freedom to Read Found. Mem. Am. Assn. Law Librs. (chmn. state, ct. and county spl. interest sect. 1995-96, chair legal info. svcs. to pub. spl. interest sect. 2001-02). Office: Jacob Burns Law Libr George Washington U 716-20th St NW Washington DC 20052 Office Phone: 202-994-7338. Business E-Mail: dnorwood@law.gwu.edu.

NORWOOD, JANET LIPPE, economist; b. Newark, Dec. 11, 1923; d. M. Turner and Thelma (Levinson) Lippe; m. Bernard Norwood, June 25, 1943; children: Stephen Harlan, Peter Carlton. BA, Douglass Coll., 1945; MA, 1946; PhD, Fletcher Sch. Law and Diplomacy, 1949; LLD (hon.), Fla. Internat. U., 1979, Carnegie Mellon U., Pitts., 1984, Harvard U., Cambridge, Mass., 1997, Rutgers U., 2003; D, State US. Instr. Wellesley Coll., 1948-49; economist William L. Clayton Ctr., Tufts U., 1953-58; with Bur. Labor Stats., U.S. Dept. Labor, Washington, 1963-91; dep. commr., then acting commr. Bur. Labor Stats. Dept. Labor, Washington, 1975-79, commr. labor stats., 1979-92; sr. fellow The Urban Inst., Washington, 1992-99; counselor, sr. fellow N.Y. Conf. Bd., 2001—09. Dir. Nat. Opinion Rsch. Ctr., chair adv. coun. unemployment compensation, 1993—96; pres. COSSA, 2001—02; mem. bd. sci. counselors Nat. Ctr. Health Stats., 1975—77; chair panel on offshoring Nat. Acad. Pub. Adminstrn., 2005—07. Author: Organizing to Count: Change in the Federal Statistical System, 1995; contbr. scientific papers in field. Recipient Disting. Achievement award, Dept. Labor, 1972, Spl. Commendation award, 1977, Philip Arnow award, 1979, Elmer Staats award, 1982, Pub. Svc. award, 1984, Presdl. Disting. Exec. Rank, 1988, Elizabeth Scott award, Com. Pres.'s Statis. Assns., 2002; named Hall Disting. Alumni, Rutgers U., 1987. Fellow: AAAS, Nat. Assn. Bus. Economists, Royal Statis. Soc., Am. Statis. Assn. (pres. 1989, Founder's award 1997); mem.: Nat. Inst. Statis. Sci. (bd. trustees 1991—2000), Nat. Acad. Sci. (assoc.), Nat. Acad. Pub. Adminstrn., Internat. Assn. Ofcls. Stats., Internat. Statis. Inst., Douglass Coll. Soc. Disting. Achievement, Cosmos Club (pres. 1995—96). Home: 5610 Wisconsin Ave Ph 21-d Chevy Chase MD 20815-4444 Home Phone: 301-951-8581. Personal E-mail: janetnor@aol.com.

NOSBUSCH, KEITH D., multi-industry high-technology company executive; BS in Elec. and Computer Engring., U. Wis., Milw., 1974, MBA, 1976. Joined Allen-Bradley (subs. Rockwell Internat.), Milw., 1974; mktg. devel. specialist, indsl. control div. Rockwell Automation, 1978, sr. market planner, corp. planning, 1980, mgr. bus. planning, motion ctrl. div., 1982, devel. engring. mgr., motion ctrl. div., 1983, dir. prod. planning and devel., motion ctrl. div., 1985, v.p., presence sensing, automation group, 1988, v.p. control logix, automation group, 1994, pres. Automation Control Sys., 1998—2004, pres., CEO, 2004—, chmn., 2005—. Bd. dirs. Manitowoc Co., 2003—, Met. Milw. Assn. of Commerce. Advisory coun. U. Wis., Milw. Sch. Bus.; bd. trustees Boys & Girls Club of Milw. Mem.: Nat. Elec. Mfrs. Assn. (bd. govs.), Mfrs.' Alliance (bd. trustees). Office: Rockwell Automation 1201 2d St Milwaukee WI 53204

NOSÉ, YUKIHIKO, surgeon, educator; b. Iwamisawa, Hokkaido, Japan, May 7, 1932; came to U.S., 1962; s. Minoru and Haru (Murakami) N.; m. Bonnie Jean MacDonald, Mar. 15, 1965 (div. 1987); children: Kimi Wilhelmina, Ken Willem, Kevin Scott; m. Ako Funakoshi, May 5, 1990. MD, U. Hokkaido, Sapporo, Japan, 1957, PhD, 1962. Surgeon in charge sect. artificial organs U. Hokkaido Sch. Medicine, 1961-62; rsch. assoc. Maimonides Hosp., Bklyn., 1962-64; postgrad. fellow dept. artificial organs Cleve. Clinic Found., 1964-66; mem. staff dept. artificial organs Cleve. Clinic, 1966—89, chmn. dept. artificial organs, 1970—90, chmn. emeritus, 1990—; prof. surgery Baylor Coll. Medicine, Houston, 1991—. V.p. Internat. Ctr. Artificial Organs and Transplantation, Cleve., 1979—; cons., mem. surgery and bioengring. study sect. NIH, 1981-87; assoc. dean Asian region Internat. Faculty Artificial Organs, 1992—; prof. Bologna (Italy) U. Sch. Medicine, 1994—. Author: Manual on Artificial Organs: Volume I-The Artificial Kidney, 1969, Volume II-The Oxygenator, 1973, Cardiac Engineering, 1970, Die Kunstliche Niere, 1974, Plasmapheresis, Historical Perspective, Therapeutic Applications and New Frontiers (with Kambic), 1983, Future Perspective for the Development of Artificial Organs (with Kolff), 1988; contbr. to numerous profl. publs. Fellow Am. Inst. Med. and Biol. Engring., N.Y. Acad. Sci.; mem. AMA, AAAS, Internat. Soc. Artificial Organs (trustee, past pres.), Am. Soc. Artificial Internal Organs (past pres., trustee), World Apheresis Assn. (congress pres. 1994), Am. Soc. Testing Materials (chair subcom. on cardiovascular prosthesis in med. and surg. materials and devices, Moses award 1979), Am. Heart Assn., Am. Soc. Apheresis, Am. Soc. Artificial Internal Organs (pres. 1992, congress pres. 1994), Am. Soc. Biomaterials, Assn. Advancement Med. Instrumentation. Achievements include development of various types of artificial organs including cardiac prosthesis, artificial kidney, hepatic assist, respiratory assist, plasmapheresis, biomaterials. Home: 1111 Hermann Dr Houston TX 77004-7142 Office: Baylor Coll Medicine One Baylor Plaza Dept Surgery Houston TX 77030 Office Phone: 713-798-4434. Business E-Mail: ynose@bcm.tmc.edu.

NOSKI, CHARLES H., former telecommunications executive; b. Aug. 1952; Degree, Calif. State U., Northridge, 1973, degree, 1995. Corp. v.p., controller Hughes Elec. Corp., 1990—92, senior v.p., CFO, 1992—99, vice chmn., 1996—97; with Haskins & Sells (now Deloitte & Touche), 1973-83, ptnr., 1983-90; pres., COO At&T Corp., NYC, 1997—99, sr. exec. v.p., CFO, 1999—2002; vice chmn. bd. dirs. AT&T Corp, 2002; corp. v.p., CFO Northrop Grumman Corp., 2003—05. Past mem. standing adv. group Pub. Co. Accounting Oversight Bd.; past mem. Fin. Accounting Standards Adv. Coun.; bd. dirs. Northrop Grumman Corp., 2002—05, Microsoft Corp., 2003—, Air Products and Chemicals Inc., 2000—04, 2005—, Morgan Stanley, 2005—, Automatic Data Processing Inc., 2008—; sr. advisor Blackstone Group, 2003. Bd. dir. Performing Arts Ctr. of LA County. Mem.: Fin. Execs. Internat., Am. Inst. CPAs.

NOSKO, MICHAEL GERRIK, neurosurgeon, educator; b. Montreal, Feb. 24, 1957; came to U.S., 1991; s. Joseph John and June Elizabeth (Salter) N.; m. Deborah Anne Branciere, May 23, 1981; children: Douglas Joseph, Denise Elizabeth, Keith Michael. BS, McMaster U., 1978; MD, U. Toronto, 1982; PhD, U. Alberta, 1986. Intern U. Toronto Gen. Hosp., Ont., Canada, 1982—83; resident U. Alberta Hosps., Edmonton, Canada, 1986—91; assoc. prof. neurosurgery Robert Wood Johnson Med. Sch., New Brunswick, NJ, 1991—, chief, neurosurgery divsn., 1991—. Cons. and presenter in field. Contbr. articles to profl. jours., chpts. to books. Rsch. fellow Alberta Heritage Found., 1983-86; Chancellor' scholar McMaster U., 1975, Univ. scholar, 1976, Edwin Marwin Dalley Meml. scholar, 1977; recipient Acad. award Am. Acad. Neurol. Surgery, 1986. Fellow Am. Coll. Surgeons (Resident Rsch. award 1986), Royal Coll. Surgeons Can., Acad. Medicine N.J.; mem. AMA, Am. Assn. Neurol. Surgeons, Can. Neurosurg. Soc., N.J. Neurosurg. Soc., N.Y. Acad. Scis., Middlesex County Med. Soc., Soc. Critical Care Medicine, Congress Neurol. Surgeons, Alpha Omega Alpha. Anglican. Avocations: instructing/flying aircraft and helicopters, fishing. Office: Divsn Neurosurgery 125 Paterson St Ste 2100 New Brunswick NJ 08901-1962 Office Phone: 732-235-7756. Business E-Mail: nosko@umdnj.edu.

NOSONOVSKY, MICHAEL, research scientist; s. Iosif and Galina Nosonovsky; m. Nadya Nosonovsky, Aug. 3, 1998; children: Mark Mordecai, Ariel. PhD, Northeastern U., Boston, 2001. Vis. scholar Ohio State U., Columbus, 2002—05; NRC postdoc. fellow Nat. Inst. Stads. and Tech., Gaithersburg, Md., 2005—07; rsch. scientist Stevens Inst. Tech., Hoboken, NJ, 2007—. Contbr. articles to profl. publs. Mem.: ASME (Burt L. Newkirk award 2008, Best Reviewer 2006). Home: 120-23 84th Ave Kew Gardens NY 11415 Office: Stevens Inst Tech Castle Pt on Hudson Hoboken NJ 07030 Office Fax: 201-216-8315. Business E-Mail: michael.nosonovsky@stevens.edu.

NOSSEIR, NAGY SABET, engineering educator; b. Cairo, Mar. 28, 1948; s. Sabet Nosseir and Florance Gobran; m. Halla Hashim, Dec. 31, 1991; children: Lara, Rami. PhD, U. Southern Calif., LA, 1979. Rsch. assoc. U. Toronto, Ont., Canada, 1973—75, U. Southern Calif., 1975—79; prof. San Diego State U., 2000—. Cons. Gen. Dynamics Co., San Diego, 1983—90. Contbr. articles to profl. jours. Grant, Office Naval Rsch., 1984—88, Grad. Rsch. and Tng. award, NASA, 1988—90. Fellow: AIAA. Office: San Diego State Univ College Engring San Diego CA 92182-0001 Business E-Mail: nosseir@mail.sdsu.edu.

NOTARIANNI, PHILIP FRANK, historian, program coordinator; b. Salt Lake City, July 24, 1948; s. Filippo and Carmela (Angotti) N.; m. Maria Teresa Maletta, Apr. 9, 1983. BS in History, U. Utah, 1970, MA in History, 1972, U. Minn., 1976, PhD, 1980. Teaching asst. U. Utah, Salt Lake City, 1972-73; archivist U. Minn., Mpls., 1973-76; history cons. Utah State Hist. Soc., Salt Lake City, 1976-77, preservation historian, 1977-83, coord. mus. svcs., 1983-90, coord. pub. programs, acting assoc. dir., dir., 2003—. Assoc. prof. U. Utah; mem. temp. faculty cultural anthropology U. Calabria, Italy. Author: ...The Tintic Minig District, 1982, (with others) The Avenues of Salt Lake City, 1980 (Merit award 1981); editor: Carbon County..., 1981; contbr. articles to profl. jours. Mem. Italian-Am. Civic League, Salt Lake City, 1990—. Unico/Rockefeller Found. grantee, 1973-76, Fulbright Rsch. grantee Italy, 1987-88; recipient Merit award Utah Heritage Found., 1981, Utah Endowment for the Humanities, 1986. Mem. Am.-Italian Hist. Assn. (com. 1990—), Utah State Hist. Soc., Utah Mus. Assn. (pres., bd. dirs. 1983-87). Roman Catholic. Avocations: photography, jogging, travel. Office: Utah State Hist Soc 300 S Rio Grande St Salt Lake City UT 84101-1106 Office Phone: 801-533-3515. Office Fax: 801-533-3567. Business E-Mail: pnotarianni@utah.gov.

NOTARO, GERALD ANTHONY, university librarian; b. Buffalo, June 25, 1950; s. Sebastian Frank and Rosalie Patricia Notaro. BA, Canisius Coll., Buffalo, 1972; MLS, SUNY, Buffalo, 1976. Cert. sch. libr. media specialist NY, 1975, pub. libr. NY, 1976. Head to instrnl. media Franklin Coll., Ind., 1981—85; libr. U. South Fla., St. Petersburg, 1985—. Contbr. various media reviews. Founder and sec. Kenwood Neighborhood Assn., St. Petersburg, Fla., 1985—88; rev. com. mem. Charter Rev. Com., City St. Petersburg, St. Petersburg, Fla., 2001—02; founder and chair FLA LBGT Libr. Services Support Group, Orlando, Fla., 2003—; bd. mem. Pinellas County ACLU, St. Petersburg, Fla., 1986—2000; bd. mem. and sec. St. Pete Pride, St. Petersburg, Fla., 2003—06. Recipient Professorial Excellence Program award, U. South Fla., 1997. Mem.: Fla. Libr. Assn. (two sect. chairs 1986—, founder, media svcs. librs. 1986—2003, chair, media svcs. librs 1986—2003). Democrat. Unitarian Universalist. Office: Univ South Florida 140 7th Ave S Saint Petersburg FL 33701 Office Fax: 727-873-4127; Home Fax: 727-873-4127. Business E-Mail: notaro@mail.usf.edu. E-mail: notaro@stpt.usf.edu.

NOTESTINE, GREG, dentist; BS, Wright State U.; DDS, Ohio State U. Gen. practice resident Miami Valley Hosp., Dayton, Ohio; pvt. practice gen. and cosmetic dentistry Beavercreek, Ohio. Mem.: ADA, Am. Acad. Cosmetic Dentistry, Dayton Dental Soc., Ohio Dental Assn., Wright State U. Alumni Assn. Office: 2149D N Fairfield Rd Beavercreek OH 45431 Office Phone: 937-431-9916. E-mail: drgreg@gregnotestine.com.

NOTH, CHRIS, actor; b. Madison, Wis., Nov. 13, 1954; 1 child, Orion Christopher. Grad., Yale Sch. Drama. Co-owner The Cutting Room, NYC, 1999—. Actor: (films) Smithereens, 1982, Waitress!, 1982, Off Beat, 1986, Baby Boom, 1987, Jakarta, 1988, Naked in New York, 1993, Burnzy's Last Call, 1995, The Deli, 1997, Cold Around the Heart, 1997, The Broken Giant, 1998, The Confession, 1999, Getting to Know You, 1999, A Texas Funeral, 1999, Pigeonholed, 1999, The Acting Class, 2000, Cast Away, 2000, Double Whammy, 2001, The Glass House, 2001, Searching for Paradise, 2002, Mr. 3000, 2004, Tooth Fairy, 2004, The Perfect Man, 2005, Sex and the City: The Movie, 2008, My One and Only, 2009; (TV films) Killer in the Mirror, 1986, Apology, 1986, At Mother's Request, 1987, In the Shadows, Someone's Watching, 1993, Where Are My Children, 1994, Nothing Lasts Forever, 1995, Abducted: A Father's Love, 1996, Born Free: A New Adventure, 1996, Rough Riders, 1997, Medusa's Child, 1997, Julius Caesar, 2002, This Is Your Country, 2003; actor, writer (TV films) Exiled, 1998, actor, prodr. The Judge, 2001, actor, exec. prodr. Bad Apple, 2004; actor: (TV series) Hill Street Blues, 1986, Law & Order, 1990—95, Sex and the City, 1998—2004, Law & Order: Criminal Intent, 2005—07; (TV miniseries) I'll Take Manhattan, 1987; (Broadway plays) The Best Man, What Didn't Happen; (plays) American Buffalo. Office: The Cutting Room 19 W 24th St New York NY 10010 also: c/o United Talent Agy 9560 Wilshire Blvd Ste 500 Beverly Hills CA 90212-2401*

NOTHAFT, FRANK EMILE, economist; b. Jersey City, Apr. 10, 1956; s. Frank Emil and Rita Johanna (Laer) N.; m. Lisa Beth Greenfield, June 13, 1981; children: Frank Austin, Daniel Blake, John Paul. BA, N.Y.U., 1976; MA, Columbia U., 1977, MPhil, 1979, PhD, 1986. Economist Bd. Govs. Fed. Reserve System, Washington, 1983-86; sr. economist Freddie Mac, McLean, Va., 1986-88, dep. chief economist, 1988-90, dir., office of chief economist, 1990—2001, chief economist, 2001—, v.p., 2004—. Contbr. articles to profl. jours. Sec., bd. dirs. Falls Church Housing Corp., Va., 1988-91. Sloan Found. grantee, 1982; Columbia U. fellow, 1976-79; recipient Founders' Day award, N.Y.U., 1976. Mem. Am. Real Estate Urban Econs. Assn. (bd. dirs. 1990-92, 2002-04, v.p. 2006-08, pres. 2008—09), Fin. Mgmt. Assn. (bd. dirs. 2006-08), Am. Real Estate Soc. Office: Freddie Mac 8200 Jones Branch Dr Mail Stop 484 Mc Lean VA 22102-3110

NOTHOM, THEODORE JOHN, professor; s. Paul Nothom and Angeline Van Der Plaat; m. Susan Kowitz, Nov. 30, 1968; children: Jennifer R. Vocale, Joshua R. BA, St. Cloud State U., St. Cloud, Minn., 1976; MA, New Mex State U., Las Cruces, 1986. Instr. El Paso CC, Tex., 1986—93; asst. prof. New Mex State U. Dona Ana, Las Cruces, 1994—. Office: New Mexico State Univ Dona Ana 3400 S Espina St Las Cruces NM 88003

NOTHOMB, CHARLES FERDINAND, Belgian government official, minister; b. May 3, 1936; married; 3 children. LLD, U. Louvain, 1957, B Econ. Scis., 1958. Counselor Dept. Social and Econ. Affairs UN, NYC, 1961—62; dep. rsch. Ctr. de Recherches Sociologiques U. Louvain, 1962—65; charge of mission Office Min. of French Culture, 1965—68; mem. Ho. of Reps., Dist. Arlon-Marche-Bastogne, 1968—99, European Coun. and Parliamentary Assembly, Western European Union, 1968—73; nat. leader Social Christian Party, 1972—79; chmn. Ho. of Reps.; mem. European Parliament; min. of fgn. affairs, 1980—81; vice-prime min., min. interior and pub. svc. Belgium, 1981—86; spkr. Fed. Ho. of Reps., 1988—95; mem. Belgian Senate, 1995—99; v.p. Internat. European Movement, 2000—07; chmn. Medea Inst. for Euro Arab Cooperation. Mem.: Assn. European Prospective (chmn.). Office: rue du Paradis 1 - 6720 Habay-la-Neuve Belgium Office Phone: 00 32 63 42 23 20. Personal E-mail: cfn@hotmail.com. E-mail: cfn@nothomb.org.

NOTKIN, LEONARD SHELDON, architect; b. NYC, Apr. 1, 1931; s. Murry and Evelyn (Mofshatz) N.; m. Ann Mathilda Stefanko, Nov. 24, 1956; children: Jennifer, Mead. BArch, U. Pa., 1954. Registered architect, N.Y., Mass., Ohio, Pa., Nat. Coun. Archtl. Registration Bds. Architect, Percival Goodman (Architect), NYC, 1956-58; Architect Bloch and Hesse (Architects), NYC, 1958-59, Resnick and Green (Architects), NYC, 1959-60; architect, prin., v.p. The Architects Collaborative, Inc., Cambridge, Mass., 1960-95; chief design critic Boston Archtl. Center, 1964-69; mem. Lexington (Mass.) Design Adv. Com., 1970-73, chmn., 1972; profl. studio critic Harvard Grad. Sch. Design, 1974-76; pres. Boston Design Assocs., Inc., Waltham, Mass., 1995—. Major recent works include Intermediate Sch. 137, Bronx, N.Y., 1976, Visual Arts Instructional Facility SUNY, Purchase, 1976, Lahey Clinic Med. Ctr., Burlington, Mass., 1976—, W. Penn Hosp., Pitts., 1977, St. Francis/St. George Hosp., Cin., 1978, Blue Cross/Blue Shield of Conn. Hdqrs., North Haven, Temple U. Hosp., Phila., composite hosp. Loring AFB, Limestone, Maine, Med. Facilities, Fort Drum, N.Y., Health Care Internat. Ltd., Glasgow, Scotland, Intensive Care Hosp. and Hotel, U. Ky. Cancer Rsch. Ctr., Children's Hosp. Med. Ctr. Rsch. Lab., Cin., new main entrance, lobby and admissions facilities Hosp. of U. Pa., Phila., Childrens Hosp., Kuwait, 1996, Health Facilities, Algiers, Algeria, 1996, Nigeria, 2003, Office Building/Auburn, Mass., Greenfield Comty. Coll., Mass. Served with U.S. Army, 1954-56. Recipient Design award for IBM Hdqrs., Gaithersburg, Md. Progressive Architecture mag., 1964; 1st pl. award for Worcester (Mass.) Community Center AIA, 1966; Design award for Worcester Found. Exptl. Biology bldg. Mass. chpt. AIA, 1968; Design award NIH Rsch. Lab., Bethesda, Md. GSA, 1972; Best Bldg. of Yr. award for Norwalk HS Assn. for Better Cmty. Design, Conn., 1972; Honor award Conn. Soc. Architects AIA, 1974. Mem. AIA, Mass. State Assn. Architects, Boston Soc. Architects (dir. 1976-79, spl. design citation 1993). Office: Boston Design Assocs Inc 393 Totten Pond Rd Waltham MA 02451-2003 Office Phone: 781-259-9190. Personal E-mail: leonardnotkin@comcast.net.

NOTO, JOHN, engineering executive; b. NYC, Mar. 25, 1967; s. Anthony and Dorothy Noto. BS in Physics and Astronomy, U. Rochester, NY, 1989; MS in Physics, Tufts U., Medford, Mass., 1991; PhD, Boston U., 1997. Dir. engring. Sci. Solutions, Chelmsford, Mass., 1995—2000, pres., 2000—. Grad. student rsch. fellow Air Force Geophysics Lab., Bedford, Mass., 1990; vis. scientist Arecibo Obs., PR, 1995—. Recipient Photonics Cir. Excellence award, Laurin Pub., 2001. Mem.: SPIE, Smaller Bus. Assn. (New England), Am. Geophys. Union. Office: Sci Solutions Inc 55 Middlesex St North Chelmsford MA 01863

NOTO, LUCIO A., investment company executive, retired oil industry executive; b. Apr. 24, 1939; m. Gwendolyn Louise Noto. BS in Physics, U. Notre Dame, 1959; MBA, Cornell U.; Woodrow Wilson Fellowship, U. Notre Dame; Bache Fellowship, Cornell U. With Mobil Corp., 1962—2002; pres. Mobil Saudi Arabia, 1981—85, chmn., 1985—86; v.p. planning & economics Mobil Oil Corp., 1986—88; CFO Mobil Corp., 1989—93, pres., COO, 1993—94, chmn., CEO, 1994—99; vice chmn. Exxon Mobil Corp., 1999—2001; mng. ptnr. Midstream Partners LLC, 2001—. Bd. dirs. Mobil Oil Corp., 1986—88, Mobil Corp., 1988—99, ExxonMobil Oil Corp., 1999—2001, IBM Corp., 1995—, Stem Cell Innovations Inc., 2001—, Penske Automotive Group, Inc., 2001—, Shinsei Bank, 2005—, Philip Morris Internat., Inc., 2008—, UAG Inc., Comml. Internat. Bank Egypt. Dir. Am. Petroleum Inst. Pub. Policy Com., The Bus. Coun., The Coun. on Fgn. Rels. and Bus. Roundtable. Named Petroleum Exec. of the Yr., 20th Oil & Money Conf., 1999.*

NOTOPOULOS, ALEXANDER ANASTASIOS, JR., lawyer; b. Altoona, Pa., Jan. 29, 1953; s. Alexander Anastasios Sr. and Christine (Economou) N.; m. Alexis J. Anderson, Aug. 4, 1984. BA summa cum laude, Amherst Coll., 1974; JD magna cum laude, Harvard U., 1977. Bar: Mass. 1978. Law clk. to judge U.S. Ct. Appeals (3d cir.), Phila., 1977-78; assoc. Sullivan & Worcester, Boston, 1978-85, ptnr., 1985—. Mem., bd. dir. Newton Presbyn. Ch. Nursery Sch., 1992—94. Recipient Mass. Super Lawyer, Boston Magazine, 2004—08, Best Lawyers in Am., 2007. Mem.: ABA, Am. Coll. Investment Counsel, coun. Harvard Law Sch. Assn. 1987-1991., Comml. Fin. Svcs. & Fed. Regulation Securities Com. Bus. Law Sect. Aba., Uniform Comml. Code, Boston Bar Assn. Home: 96 Shornecliffe Rd Newton MA 02458-2421 Office: Sullivan & Worcester LLP One Post Office Sq Boston MA 02109 Office Fax: 617-338-2880. Business E-Mail: anotopoulos@sandw.com.

NOTTAGE, LYNN, playwright; b. Bklyn., 1964; BA, Brown. U., Providence, 1986; MFA, Yale Sch. Drama, New Haven, 1989. Vis. lectr. playwriting Yale Sch. Drama. Author: (plays) A Walk Through Time, A Stone's Throw, Fabulation (Obie award for playwriting, Village Voice mag., 2005), Intimate Apparel (NY Drama Critics' Cir. award for best play, 2004), Las Meninas, Mud, River, Stone, Por' Knockers, Crumbs from the Table of Joy (NAACP Theatre award for performance), Poof! (Heideman award), Ruined (Pulitzer prize for drama, 2009, NY Drama Critics' Cir. award for Best Play, 2009, Drama Desk award for Best Play, 2009, Obie award for best new Am. play, Village Voice, 2009); plays produced regionally by The Acting Co., Actors Theatre Louisville, Alliance Theatre Co, Capital Repertory Theatre, Crossroads Theatre, Freedom Repertory Theatre, Playwrights Horizons, San Jose Repertory Theatre, Second Stage Theatre, Steppenwolf Theatre Co., Studio Arena Theatre, Vineyard Theatre, Yale Repertory Theatre, Playwrights Horizons, Off Broadway, others. Mem. adv. bd. NY Found. Arts. Recipient Steingberg New Play award, Am. Theatre Critics', 2004, PEN/Laura Pels award for drama, 2004, John Gassner award for best playwright, 2004, August Wilson playwriting award, Nat. Black Theatre Festival, 2005; grantee NEA/Theater Comm. Group; fellow NY Found. Arts, 1994, 2000, John Simon Guggenheim Meml. Found., 2005, John D. & Catherine T. MacArthur Found., 2007, Lucille Lortel Found., 2007. Mem.: New Dramatists. Mailing: c/o Gersh Agency Peter Hagan/Frank Wuliger 41 Madison Ave 33rd Fl New York NY 10010 Office Phone: 212-634-8115.*

NOTTENBURG, RICHARD N., former communications executive; b. 1954; BSEE, Polytechnic Inst. NY; MSEE, Colo. State U.; PhD elec. engring., Ecole Polytechnique Federale de Lausanne, Switzerland. Mem. tech. staff Bell Laboratories, 1984—90, disting. mem. tech. staff, interim dept. head, 1990—91; assoc. prof. elec. engring. U. So. Calif., 1991—98; co-founder, pres., CEO Multilink Tech. Corp., 1995—2003; v.p., gen. mgr. Vitesse Semiconductor Corp., 2003—04; strategic adv. Motorola, Inc., Schaumburg, Ill., 2004, sr. v.p., chief strategy officer, 2004—05, exec. v.p., chief strategy officer, 2005—07, exec. v.p., chief strategy officer, chief tech. officer, 2007—08; pres., CEO Sonus Networks Inc., Westford, Mass., 2008—. Contbr. articles to profl. jours. Achievements include patents in field. Office: Sonus Networks Inc 7 Technology Park Dr Westford MA 01886*

NOTTER, ROBERT H., biomedical researcher, educator; s. Dr. Harley A. and Margaret T. Notter; m. Barbara B. Notter; m. Mary Francis Dolsky Notter (dec.); children: Becket A., Tracy M., Kelley C., Sarah A., Emily Blake. BS, Stanford U., 1964, MS, 1965; PhD, U. Wash., 1969; MD, U. Rochester, 1980. Prof. pediat., environ. medicine and chem. engring. U. Rochester, NY, 1989—2001, prof. pediat. and environ. medicine, 2001—. Dir., biomedical engring. program U. Rochester, 1984—95; dir. neonatology rsch. U. Rochester, 1989—2000; dir. NIH Spl. Ctr. Rsch. in Lung Biology and Disease in Infants and Children, U. Rochester, 1989—97. Author: Lung Surfactants: Basic Science and Clinical Applications, 2000; editor: Lung Surfactant Replacement Therapy, 1989, Lung Injury: Mechanisms, Pathophysiology and Therapy, 2005; contbr. over 250 articles and abstracts to profl. jours. Recipient Rsch. Career Devel. award, NIH, 1981, Health Leadership award, March of Dimes, 2005; grantee multiple grants, NIH, 1975—. Mem.: Soc. for Pediatric Rsch. Achievements include research and development of surfactant-based therapies for lung disease and injury. Office: U Rochester Sch of Med 601 Elmwood Ave Rochester NY 14642

NOTTERMAN, DANIEL A., pediatrician, educator; BA, Cornell U., 1973; MA in Philosophy, Tufts U., 1977; MD, NYU, 1978. Diplomate Am. Bd. Pediatrics. Intern, resident NYU Med. Ctr., NYC, 1978—81, chief resident in pediat., 1981—82; rsch. fellow clin. pharmacology Cornell Med. Ctr., NYC, 1983—84; dir. divsn. pediatric critical care medicine N.Y. Hosp. Cornell Med. Ctr., NYC, 1985—97; postdoc. rschr., prof. Princeton U., NJ, 1992—2001, prof., dept. molecular biology, 2007—, chair, com. health professions, 2007—; chair, dept. pediats. Robert Wood Johnson Med. Sch., 2001—07, chief pediat. svc., 2001—07. Home: 7 Symmes Ct Cranbury NJ 08512 Office: Princeton Univ 229 Lewis Thomas Princeton NJ 08544 Office Phone: 609-258-7185. Business E-Mail: dan1@princeton.edu.

NOTTI, DONNA BETTS, special education educator; b. Manassas, Va., Sept. 4, 1968; d. William Jackson and Christine Joan (Fant) B.; m. David L. Notti, Oct. 14, 1995. BS in Spl. Edn., Old Dominion U., Norfolk, Va., 1990. Tchr., counselor Southeastern Cooperative Ednl. Programs, Norfolk, Va., 1991—2004; vol. tutor Tonelson Teaching and Learning Ctr., Norfolk, Va., 1989; secondary spl. edn. tchr. Chesapeake City Schs., Va., 2004—. Chair child study com. Oscar Smith HS, Chesapeake, Va., 2006—07, chair spl. edn. dept., 2007—. Mem. Coun. for Exceptional Children (v.p. 1989-90), Coun. for Children With Behavior Disorders, Coun. for Exceptional Children-Mental Retardation, Am. Re-ED Assn., Va. State Reading Assn., Chesapeake Reading Coun. Lutheran. Office: 1994 Tiger Dr Chesapeake VA 23320 Personal E-mail: dbnotti@yahoo.com.

NOTTINGHAM, EDWARD WILLIS, JR., former federal judge; b. Denver, Jan. 9, 1948; s. Edward Willis and Willie Newton (Gullett) N.; m. Cheryl Ann Card, June 6, 1970 (div. Feb. 1981); children: Amelia Charlene, Edward Willis III; m. Janis Ellen Chapman, Aug. 18, 1984 (div. Dec. 1998); 1 child, Spencer Chapman. AB, Cornell U., 1969; JD, U. Colo., 1972. Bar: Colo. 1972, U.S. Dist. Ct. Colo. 1972, U.S. Ct. Appeals (10th cir.) 1973. Law clk. to presiding judge US Dist. Ct. Colo., Denver, 1972-73; assoc. Sherman & Howard, Denver, 1973-76, 78-80, ptnr., 1980-87, Beckner & Nottingham, Grand Junction, Colo., 1987-89; asst. US atty. (dist. Colo.) US Dept. Justice, Denver, 1976-78; judge US Dist. Ct. Colo., Denver, 1989—2008, chief judge, 2007—08. Mem. Jud. Conf. of the U.S. Com. on Automation and Tech., 1994-2000, chmn., 1997-2000. Bd. dirs. Beaver Creek Met. Dist., Avon, Colo., 1980-88, Justice Info. Ctr., Denver, 1985-87, 21st Jud. Dist. Victim Compensation Fund, Grand Junction, Colo., 1987-89. Mem. ABA, Colo. Bar Assn. (chmn. criminal law sect. 1983-85, chmn. ethics com. 1988-89), Order of Coif, Denver Athletic Club, Delta Sigma Rho, Tau Kappa Alpha. Episcopalian.

NOTTINGHAM, JAMES M., surgeon, educator; m. Deborah Nottingham, June 14, 1998; 1 child, Sidney William. MD, Med. Coll. Va., Richmond, 1987. Diplomate Am. Bd. Surgery, 2006. Prof. surgery U. SC, Columbia, 1998—. Fellow: ACS. Office: Univ Specialty Clinics Surgery 2 Richland Medical Pk Ste 402 Columbia SC 29203 Business E-Mail: james.nottingham@uscmed.sc.edu.

NOTTINGHAM, WILLIAM JESSE, retired religious organization administrator, minister; b. Sharon, Pa., Nov. 22, 1927; s. Jess William and Alice May (Green) Nottingham; m. Patricia Clutts, Feb. 1, 1949; children: Theodore Jess, Deborah Joan Selke, Nancy Alice, Gregory Philip. BA, Bethany Coll., W.Va., 1949, DD (hon.), 1987, BD, Union Theol. Sem., NYC, 1953; PhD, Columbia U., 1962; DD (hon.), Christian Theol. Sem., Indpls., 1984. Ordained to ministry Christian Ch. (Disciples of Christ), 1945, ministerial standing United Ch. of Christ. Machinist apprentice Westinghouse, 1943—45; pastor Ch. of Christ, Canoe Camp and Covington, Pa., 1949-50; field worker Ch. of the Master, NYC, 1950-53; assoc. min. Nat. City Christian Ch., Washington, 1954-58; fraternal worker Coun. on Christian Unity, France, 1958-65; with CIMADE and Centre de Glay; with youth dept. World Coun. of Chs., Geneva, 1965-68; exec. sec. for Latin Am. and Caribbean Christian Ch. (Disciples of Christ) and United Ch. Christ, Indpls., 1968-76; exec. sec. East Asia and Pacific Divsn. Overseas Ministries, Christian Ch. (Disciples of Christ), 1976-83; pres., exec. sec. Europe Divsn. Overseas Ministries Christian Ch. (Disciples of Christ), Indpls., 1984-94, pres. emeritus, 2004; ret., 1994; affiliate prof. mission Christian Theol. Sem., 1995—2005. Author: Christian Faith and Secular Action: An Introduction to the Life and Thought of Jacques Maritain, 1968, The Practice and Preaching of Liberation, 1986, The Social Ethics of Martin Bucer 1491-1551, 1962; translator: God's Underground, 1970, Prayer at the Heart of Life, 1975, Materialist Approaches to the Bible, 1985, Madeleine Barot, 1991; contbr. articles to theol. jours. Mem. Ind. Faith and Labor Network, Com. To Free Lori Berenson, Eagle Scout, 1946. Chaplain USNR, 1954—65. Recipient Disting. Alumnus award, Union Theol. Sem., 1999, Martin Luther King, Jr. Drum Major for Justice award, 2003; Fulbright scholar, Strasbourg, France, 1953—54. Mem.: Assn. Am. Indian Affair, Disciples Justice Action Network, United Christian Missionary Soc., Assn. Disciples for Theol. Discussion, Indpls. Peace and Justice Ctr., Sierra Club, Kappa Alpha. Democrat. E-mail: nottingham50@q.com.

NOTTIS, KATHARYN E.K., educational psychologist, researcher; b. Fountain Hill, Pa., Mar. 23, 1951; d. Robert Lewis and Lorelei Zimmerman Ketter; m. Gary Neil Nottis, Aug. 6, 1995; children: Colleen Ebehi Ross, Timothy Earl Ross, David Evan Ross. BSED, Buffalo State Coll., NY, 1973; MSED, 1976; PhD, State U. NY at Buffalo, 1996. Katharyn E. Ross NY, 1976. Tchr. Cantalician Ctr. for Learning, Buffalo, 1973—75, 1980—83, Assn. for Retarded Children, Buffalo, 1975—80, Bornhava, Buffalo, 1983—88; edn. specialist nat. Ctr. for Earthquake Engring. Rsch., Buffalo, 1988—95; asst. prof. Bucknell U., Lewisburg, Pa., 1995—2002, assoc. prof., 2002—. Common learning coord. Bucknell U., Lewisburg, Pa., 2005—07. Bd. mem. CMSU Devel. Supports and Services Adv. Bd., Danville, Pa., 2005—08. Recipient Lindback award for Disting. Tchg., Bucknell U., 2004; grantee Collaborative Rsch. with Prince, Vigeant, Miller, NSF, 2007—. Mem.: Nat. Assn. Geoscience Tchrs., Northeastern Ednl. Rsch. Assn. (bd. mem. 2005—), Kappa Delta Pi, Delta Kappa Gamma Internat., Sigma Chpt. Achievements include research in inquiry-based activities to repair persistent student misconceptions of critical engineering concepts. Avocations: birdwatching, hiking, reading. Office: Bucknell Univ 463 Olin Science Bldg Lewisburg PA 17837

NOTTURNO, MARK AMADEUS, philosopher; PhD, Columbia U., NYC, 1982. Prof. Soros Founds., Vienna, 1994—99; fellow Interactivity Found., Parkersburg, W.Va., 2002—. Author: (book) Science and The Open Society, Objectivity, Rationality, and the Third Realm; editor: Knowledge and the Body-Mind Problem, Knowledge and the Mind-Body Problem, The Myth of the Framework, Perspectives on Psychologism. Home: 71 Randolph Pl NW Washington DC 20001 Office: Interactivity Found Parkersburg WV 26101 Personal E-mail: manotturno@comcast.net.

NOTZ, JOHN KRANZ, JR., arbitrator, mediator, retired lawyer; b. Chgo., Jan. 5, 1932; s. John Kranz and Elinor (Trostel) N.; m. Janis Wellin, Apr. 23, 1966; children: Jane Elinor Notz, John Wellin Notz. BA, Williams Coll., Williamstown, Mass., 1953; JD, Northwestern U., Chgo., 1956. Bar: Ill. 1956, Fla. 1957, Wis. 1989, U.S. Supreme Ct. 1960. Assoc. 1st Nat. Bank Chgo., 1954, 1956; from assoc. to ptnr. Gardner, Carton & Douglas, Chgo., 1960-95, of counsel, 1990-95; ret., 1996. Arbitrator, mediator Am. Arbitration Assn., Chgo. Internat. Dispute Resolution Assn., FINRA Inc., Nat. Futures Assn. Contbr. articles to profl. jours. Mem. Sec. of State Corp. Acts Adv. Com., 1982-95, chmn., 1987-89; pres. Chgo. Lit. Club, 1996-97; mem. Ill. Inst. Continuing Legal Edn., 1980-91, chmn., 1990-91; former pres. Black Point Historic Preserve, Inc.; trustee Graceland Cemetery; former treas. Soc. Archl. Historians; bd. dirs. Libr. Am. Landscape History, Geneva Lake Conservancy. 1st lt. USAF, 1957-60. Recipient Svc. award Northwestern U., 1978 Fellow Am. Bar Found. (life), Ill. Bar Found. (life), Chgo. Bar Found. (life); mem. Am. Law Inst., Ill. State Bar Assn., Chgo. Bar Assn., Wis. State Bar, Lawyers Club City Chgo., Racquet Club Chgo., Lake Geneva (Wis.) Country Club, Tower Club (Chgo.), Literary Club (Chgo.), Caxton Club (Chgo.), Cliff Dwellers (Chgo.), The Antiquarian Soc., Asian Arts Coun., Art Inst. Chgo., Anthropology Alliance, The Field Mus.(Chgo.). Office: 191 N Wacker Dr 3700 Chicago IL 60606-1698

NOUJAIM, FARES DOURID, investment company executive; b. Kuwait, 1964; arrived in US, 1972; married; 3 children. BS in Quantitative Economics, Pace U., NYC. Analyst Goldman Sachs & Co., 1985—87; fin. mgmt. positions through vice chmn. & global head of capital markets group The Bear Stearns Companies Inc., 1987—2008; pres. Middle East & No. Africa Merrill Lynch & Co. Inc., NYC, 2008—09; vice chmn. corp. & investment banking Bank of America Corp., 2009—. Office: Bank of America Corp 100 N Tryon St Charlotte NC 28255*

NOURYEH, CHRISTOPHER, humanities educator; BA in Humanities, Damascus U., Syria, 1965; MA in English Lit., CUNY, 1968, PhD in Comparative Lit., 1975. Instr. Columbia U., NYC, 1967-69; from instr. to asst. prof. York and Medgar Evers Colls. CUNY, 1972-76; asst.

prof. writing and lit. Touro Coll., NYC, 1980-86, 91-92, mem. faculty senate and curriculum com., 1983-86, dir. advisement and retention, 1986-91; asst. prof. humanties Canton Coll. Tech. SUNY, 1992—. Adj. asst. prof. CUNY, summers 1980-83; adj. prof. Iona Coll., Yonkers, N.Y., 1977-92; book reviewer Ararat, World Lit. Today, 1980—; attendee numerous confs., 1974-87, reviewer, Manuscripts. Author: Translation and Critical Study of Ten Pre-Islamic Odes: Traces in the Sand, 1993; translator: (Arabic poetry) Contemporary Writings from the Middle East, 1979, The Literature of Modern Arabia: An Anthology, 1988. Recipient scholarship CUNY, 1966-68, fellow, 1971-73; fellow Internat. House, 1968-70, Damascus U., 1961-65. Mem. MLA, Medieval Club N.Y., Alumni Assn. CUNY (past bd. dirs.). Home: 85 Judson St Canton NY 13617-1147

NOVA, CRAIG, writer; b. Los Angeles, July 5, 1945; s. Karl and Elizabeth (Sinclair) N.; m. Christina Barnes, July 2, 1977; children: Abigail, Tate. BA, U. Calif.-Berkeley, 1967; M.F.A., Columbia U., 1969. Disting. prof. humanities U. N.C., Greensboro, 2005—. Author: Turkey Hash, 1972, The Geek, 1975, Incandescence, 1978, The Good Son, 1982, The Congressman's Daughter, 1986, Tornado Alley, 1989, Trombone, 1992, The Book of Dreams, 1994, The Universal Door, 1997, Brook Trout and the Writing life, 1999, Wetware, 2001, Cruisers, 2004. Recipient Harper-Saxton prize Harper and Row, Pubs., 1972; recipient award in lit. Am. Acad. and Inst. Arts and Letters; Guggenheim Found. fellow, 1977; fellow Nat. Endowment for Arts, 1973, Nat. Endowment for Arts, 1975, Creative Artists Pub. Service, 1976; NEA fellow, 1985; story included in Best Am. Short Stories, 1987. Office Phone: 919-732-1857. E-mail: nova@sover.net.

NOVACEK, JAY MCKINLEY, retired professional football player; b. Martin, SD, Oct. 24, 1962; BS in Indsl. Edn., U. Wyoming, 1986. With St. Louis Cardinals, 1985-87, Phoenix Cardinals (formerly St. Louis Cardinals), 1988-89; tight end Dallas Cowboys, 1990—96; ret., 1997; owner Jay Novacek's Upper 84 Ranch, Brady, Nebr., 1997—. Named NFL All-Pro, 1990—92, 1993—95; named to NFL Pro Bowl, 1991—95, U. Wis. Hall of Fame, 1993, Coll. Football Hall of Fame, 2008. Achievements include being a member of the Dallas Cowboys Super Bowl XXVII, 1993, XXVIII, 1994, XXX, 1996 winning teams. Office: Jay Novacek's Upper 84 Ranch 12475 S Brady Mrefield Rd Brady NE 69123-2925 Office Phone: 308-584-3759.

NOVACK, ALVIN JOHN, physician; b. Red Lodge, Mont., Mar. 11, 1925; s. John and Anna Geraldine (Maddio) N.; m. Betty P. Novack, Jan. 10, 1952; children— Vance, Deborah, Michelle, Mitchel, Craig, Brad, Mary Ellen, Garth. MD, U. Wash., 1952. Intern Harper Hosp., Detroit, 1952, resident in surgery, 1953; resident in otolaryngology Johns Hopkins U., 1954-57; resident in surgery Columbia-Presbyn. Med. Center, NYC, 1957-60, fellow head and neck surgery, 1957-60; dir. head and neck surgery Swedish Hosp., Seattle, 1960-91; dir. otolaryngology Children's Orthopedic Hosp., Seattle, 1965-78; ret., 1991. Contbr. articles to med. jours. Served to lt. AUS, 1940-43. Nat. Cancer Inst. fellow, 1957-60 Fellow A.C.S.; mem. AMA, Am. Acad. Otolaryngology and Head and Neck Surgery, Soc. Head and Neck Surgeons, North Pacific Surg. Assn., Pacific Coast Surg. Assn., Seattle Surg. Soc.

NOVACK, KENNETH JOSEPH, lawyer; b. Boston, Aug. 25, 1941; s. Hyman and Dorothy Ruth N.; m. Marianne Margaret Lefebvre; children: Laura Ann, Sara Elizabeth, Emily Kate, Jeffrey Nicholas. BA (Rufus Choate scholar), Dartmouth Coll., 1963; LL.B., Harvard U., 1966. Bar: Mass. 1966, D.C. 1972. With Mintz, Levin, Cohn, Ferris, Glovsky and Popeo, P.C., Boston, 1996—98, 2004—, named ptnr., 1970, mem. exec. com., 1972—98, mng. ptnr Boston, 1972—78, pres., CEO, 1991-94, sr. counsel, 2004—; vice chmn. AOL Inc. (AOL and Time Warner merge, 2001), 1998—2001, Time Warner Inc. (formerly AOL Time Warner), 2001—04. Bd. dirs. Time Warner Inc., 2001—, Paratek Pharms., 2002—. Vice chmn. Mus. Sci., Boston, Combined Jewish Philanthropies, Tufts-New England Med. Ctr., trustee emeritus; trustee Novack Family Found., Appleton Ptnrs., Inc., BBN Technologies, Inc., Energizing, Inc., Leerink Swan, Co., Premalies, Inc. Mem. ABA, Internat. Bar Assn., Boston Bar Assn. (co-chmn. securities law com. 1970-85), D.C. Bar Assn., Am. Law Inst. Clubs: St. Botolph, Harvard of Boston, Algonquin Club. Office: Mintz Levin Cohn Ferris Glovsky and Popeo PC 1 Financial Ctr Fl 42 Boston MA 02111

NOVAK, ALFREDO ERNEST, bishop emeritus; b. Dwight, Nebr., June 2, 1930; Ordained priest Congregation of the Most Holy Redeemer, 1956; ordained bishop, 1979; aux. bishop Archdiocese of São Paulo, Brazil, 1979—89; bishop Diocese of Paranagua, Brazil, 1989—2006, bishop emeritus, 2006—. Roman Catholic. Office: Diocese of Paranagua CP 531 Rua Conselheiro Sinimbu 498 83203-050 Paranagua Brazil

NOVAK, BARBARA, art history educator; b. NYC; d. Joseph and Sadie (Kaufman) N.; m. Brian O'Doherty, July 5, 1960. BA, Barnard Coll., 1951; MA, Radcliffe Coll., 1953, PhD, 1957; PhD (hon.), Columbia U., 2007. TV instr. Mus. Fine Arts, Boston, 1957-58; mem. faculty Barnard Coll., Columbia U., NYC, 1958-98, prof. art history, 1970—, Helen G. Altschul prof., 1984-98, prof. emeritus, 1998—. Vis. Mellon prof. U. Pitts., 1971; mem. adv. coun. Archives of Am. Art, NAD Author: American Painting of the 19th Century, 1969, 3d edit., 2007, Nature and Culture, 1980, 3d edit., 2007, Voyages of the Self, 2007, The Thyssen-Bornemisza Collection 19th Century American Painting, 1986, Alice's Neck, 1987, The Margaret-Ghost, 2003, (novels) The Ape and the Whale, 1995, (play) The Ape and the Whale: Darwin and Melville in Their Own Words, 1987 (performed at Symphony Space 1987), Dreams and Shadows: Thomas H. Hotchkiss in 19th Century Italy, 1993; co-editor: Next to Nature, 1980; mem. editl. bd. Am. Art Jour. Commr. Nat. Portrait Gallery. Recipient disting. tchg. award, Coll. Art Assn., 1997, Lawrence Fleishman award for outstanding scholarship, Archives Am. Art, 1999, medal of distinction, Barnard Coll., 2002; Fulbright fellow, Belgium, 1953—54, Guggenheim fellow, 1974, Nat. Book Critics nominee, 1980, L.A. Times Book Award nominee, 1980, Am. Book Award paperback nominee, 1981. Fellow Soc. Am. Historians, Phila. Atheneum; mem. Soc. Am. Historians, Am. Antiquarian Soc., Coll. Art Assn. (dir. 1974-77, Disting. Tchg. of Art History award 1997), PEN. Achievements include honored with Barbara Novak professorship in art history at Barnard Coll. and Columbia U., 2004; Barbara Novak Acquisition Fund at Nat. Portrait Gallery.

NOVAK, B.J. MANALY (BENJAMIN JOSEPH NOVAK), actor, television producer, scriptwriter; b. Newton, Mass., July 31, 1979; s. William Novak. Degree in Eng. and Spanish Lit., Harvard U., Cambridge, Mass. Writer (TV series) Raising Dad, 2001, writer, producer, actor The Office, 2005— (Writers Guild of Am. award, 2007, Outstanding Performance by an Ensemble in a Comedy Series, SAG, 2008); actor: (films) Unaccompanied Minors, 2006, Reign Over Me, 2007, Knocked Up, 2007, Inglourious Basterds, 2009. Office: NBC Network 30 Rockefeller Plz New York NY 10112

NOVAK, CAMILLE, small business owner, consultant; d. Edward Sherrill Arnold, Sr. and Nila Ruth (Grow) Arnold; m. Robert Novak, Nov. 1, 1975. AA, St. Louis C.C., St. Louis, Mo., 1996; BA in Media Comm., Webster U., St. Louis, Mo., 1998, BA in History, 1998, MA in Media Comm., 2000. Paralegal Cert.: Nat. Acad. of Paralegals 1991; Leadership Devel. Cert. Phi Theta Kappa Internat. Honor Soc., 2001. Exec. adminstrn. Christian Appalachian Project, Lancaster, Ky., 1974—77, St. William's Cath. Ch., Lancaster, 1974—77; comm. adminstr. First Bapt. Ch. of St. John, St. Louis, 1978—82; writer: features, film/theatre rev., oped, edn. The Montage Newspaper, 1993—98; adminstrn. mgmt. Lyss Fine Arts, 1993—2003; adminstr. social and behavioral scis.,history and govt. tutor program St. Louis CC, 1996—2000; intern Ky. filmmakers collection U. of Ky. Spl. Collections and Archives, Lexington, 1998—98; adminstrn. St. Louis ARC, 1999—2004, bus. mgr., 2005—07; adminstrv. support Meramec Global Studies Program St. Louis CC Dist., 2000—01; instr. St. Louis CC Dist., 2000—02; bus. mgr. Tower Hills Claims Mgmt. Inc., St. Louis, 2004—05; office adminstr. Stites and Harbison PLLC, 2007—. Owner Novak Enterprises, St. Louis, 1982—. Actor: (A World of Their Own), (The Big Brass Ring), (King of the Hill), (Soul of the Game); prodr.: (graphic design) The New Millennium (The Eichling Yearbook Internat. Award, 2000); dir.(editor, cinemtographer): (film) The Star-True life acctg. about an Appalachian African Am. youth with cognitive & phys. disabilities who taught the true meaning of life to a class of misfits (Mind over TV Best of Camille show 1997, Meramec Classic Film Festival, 1997, various U.S. film and video festivals, 1997); author: (journalistic writing) Body of Work (Internat. Bus. Communicators Assn. Award, 1996, The Press Club of Met. St. Louis Milton Ferman Meml. Award, 1997), (novels) The Stewart Chronicles, The Star, Lights, Camera, Propaganda Starring American Film as Propaganda Tool: 1938-1945; prodr.(animator): (animated film emphasizing global unity) Scarlet Ribbons (Presented at Meramec Classic Film Festival and Mind Over TV Best of Camille show, 1997), (editor) (documentary) Psalm 23-an alternative reading of 20th Century hist. as filtered through post- modern media. Founder/prodr./dir./steering com. Meramec Classic Film Festival, St. Louis, 1999—2000; founder/prodr./dir. Dollars for Scholars Scholarship programming, St. Louis, 1997—2002, Petey K. Bear Says Reading is FUN! state-wide literacy project, St. Louis, 1998—99. Recipient Most Disting. Chpt. Advisor, Mo. Phi Theta Kappa, 2002, Mo. State All-Academic First Team, Mo. CC Assn., 1997, US Achievement Acad. All-American Scholar, 1997, Meramec Honors Program Honors Grad. (and Scholarship Recipient), 1993-2000; Graduate in 1996, 1997, Commencement Spkr., SLCC-Meramec Coll., 1996, Horizon Award for Advisors, Mo. Phi Theta Kappa, 2002, Paralegal Student of Mo., Nat. Acad. of Paralegal Studies, 1992, Nat. Acad. for Paralegal Studies Scholarly Distinction of Merit, NAPS, 1992, West Ednl. Pub. Paralegal Student Award, West Ednl. Pub. Co., 1992, Nat. Deans List, 1996, 1997, 1998, 1999, 2000, Campus Deans List, SLCC and Webster U., 1993-2000, Phi Theta Kappa Internat. Paragon Award for New Advisors Nominee, Phi Theta Kappa Internat., 2002, Honors Program Instr. Recognition Award, Forest Pk. CC Honors Program, 2002, Rotary Internat. Amb. of Goodwill Alt., Rotary Internat. of Mo., 1997, Phi Theta Kappa Internat. Disting. Regional Officer Award, 1999, Phi Theta Kappa Internat. Disting. Chpt. Pres. Award, 1997; named All-USA Today Academic Team Scholar Campus Representative, St. Louis CC, 1997; nominee Presidents Merit Award for Excellence in Academics, SLCC-Meramec Campus Pres., 1996; scholar Guistwhite Scholar, Phi Theta Kappa Internat., 1997, Hites Scholar, St. Louis CC, 1997, Am. Bus. Women's Assn. Scholar, ABA, 1996, St. Louis Journalism Found. Scholar, 1996-1997-1998-only 3 time awardee, Phi Theta Kappa Transfer Scholar, Webster U., 1996-1998, A. E. Hotchner Scholar, Scholarship Found. of St. Louis, 1996—2002, Alpha Kappa Alpha, 1997. Master: The Spirit of St. Louis Alumni Assn. (life; assn. advisor 2002—03); mem.: Nat. Assn. Profl. and Exec. Women (Woman of Excellence award 2008), Assn. Legal Adminstrs. (nat. & Ky. chpt. 2008—), Soc. HR Mgmt. (nat. & Ky. chpt. 2008—), Phi Theta Kappa (life; chpt. & regional pres. 1996—99, chpt. advisor 2000—02, Mo. Region Disting. Chpt. & Regional Pres., Advisor 1996—99, Internat. Disting. Regional Officer Award (99) & Internat. Disting. Chpt. Pres. Award (97) 1999, 1997 respectively). Home: 628 Mannington Pl Lexington KY 40503 Office Phone: 859-226-2318. Business E-Mail: cnovak@stites.com.

NOVAK, DAVID, theology studies educator, rabbi; b. Chgo., Aug. 19, 1941; s. Syd and Sylvia (Wien) N.; m. Melva Ziman, July 3, 1963; children: Marianne, Jacob George. AB in Classics and Ancient History, U. Chgo., 1961; M in Hebrew Lit., Jewish Theol. Sem. Am., 1964; PhD, Georgetown U., 1971. Ordained rabbi, 1966. Rabbi Shaare Tikvah Congregation, 1966—69; dir. Jewish chaplaincy St. Elizabeths Hosp., 1966—69; rabbi Emanuel Synagogue, Oklahoma City, 1968—72, Beth Tfiloh Congregation, Balt., 1972—77, Congregation Beth El, Norfolk, Va., 1977—81, Congregation Darchay Noam, Far Rockaway, NY, 1981—89; Edgar M. Bronfman prof. modern Judaic studies U. Va., Charlottesville, 1989—97; J. Richard and Dorothy Shiff chair of Jewish studies U. Toronto, 1997—. Lectr. philosophy Oklahoma City U., 1969-72, New Sch. for Social Rsch., 1982-84; lectr. Jewish studies Balt. Hebrew Coll., 1972-77; adj. asst. prof. philosophy Old Dominion U., 1977-81; vis. assoc. prof. Talmud Jewish Theol. Sem. Am., 1986-88; adj. assoc. prof. Baruch Coll., CUNY, 1984-88, adj. prof., 1989; founder, v.p., coord. panel Halakhic Inquiry Union Traditional Judaism/Inst. Traditional Judaism; disting. vis. prof. religion and corp. ethics Drew U., 1995; Yarnton/Lancaster lectr. Oxford U., 1996; Charles E. Test, MD Disting. vis. scholar Princeton U., 2004, vis. prof. religion, 2006. Contbg. editor First Things. Sec.-treas. Inst. on Religion and Pub. Life. Essay winner Hyman G. Enelow prize Jewish Theol. Sem. Am., 1975; recipient Rabbi Jacob B. Augus award Jewish Theol. Sem. Am., 1984, Best Book Constructive Religious Thought award Am. Acad. of Religion, 2000; Woodrow Wilson Internat. Ctr. for Scholars fellow, 1992-93. Fellow Acad. for Jewish Philosophy, Am. Acad. for Jewish Rsch.; mem. Am. Theol. Soc., Assn. for Jewish Studies, Am. Acad. Religion, Assisted Human Reprodn, Canada Dean Tikvah Fund Summer Seminar Princeton U. Office: Univ Coll 15 King's College Cir Toronto ON Canada M5S 3H7

NOVAK, DAVID C., restaurant company executive; b. 1952; m. Wendy Novak. BA, U. Mo., 1974. Sr. v.p., mktg. Pizza Hut, 1986—90; exec. v.p., mktg. and nat. sales Pepsi-Cola Co., 1990—92, COO, N. Am., 1992—94; pres., CEO N. Am. Kentucky Fried Chicken, 1994—97; group pres., CEO, Pizza Hut, KFC Tricon Global Restaurants, Inc. (now Yum! Brands Inc.), Louisville, 1996—97; vice-chmn. Yum! Brands Inc., Louisville, 1996—97, pres., 1997—, CEO, 2000—, chmn., 2001—. Bd. dirs. Yum Brands, Inc., 1997—, J.P. Morgan Chase & Co., 2001—. Co-author (with John Boswell): The Education of an Accidental CEO: Lessons Learned from the Trailer Park to the Corner Office, 2007. Office: Yum Brands Inc 1441 Gardiner Ln Louisville KY 40213-1914*

NOVAK, GILES ANTHONY, astrophysicist; b. Kans. City, Oct. 12, 1959; s. Henry Julius and Constance Anne (Troop) N.; m. Barbara Elizabeth Glaessner, Apr. 7, 1990; children: Lillian Glaessner, Rosa Glaessner. BS in Physics, MIT, 1981; PhD, U. Chgo., 1988. Postdoctoral rsch. assoc. dept. physics and astronomy U. Mass., Amherst, 1988-91; instr. dept. physics Princeton (N.J.) U., 1991-93; asst. prof. dept. physics and astronomy Northwestern U., Evanston, Ill., 1993—99, assoc. prof., 1999—2008, prof., 2008—. Harper fellow U. Chgo., 1986; recipient Career award NSF, 1997. Mem. Am. Astron. Soc. Office: Northwestern U Dept Physics and Astronomy 2145 Sheridan Rd Evanston IL 60208-0834 Office Phone: 847-491-8645.

NOVAK, GORDON S., JR., computer scientist, educator; b. Colo., 1947; m. Susan Raye Strawn, May 7, 1977; children: Genevieve, Courtney. BSEE, U. Tex., 1969, MA in Computer Sci., 1971, PhD in Computer Sci., 1976. Mgr. sys. programming Tracor Inc., Austin, Tex., 1966-76; instr. U. Tex., Austin, 1976-77, asst. prof., 1978-81, 83-84, assoc. prof., 1984-98; prof., 1998—; dir. Artificial Intelligence Lab. U. Tex., Austin, 1984-99; computer sci. SRI Internat., Menlo Park, Calif., 1977-78. Vis. asst. prof. Stanford (Calif.) U., 1981-83. Contbr. articles to profl. jours. Office: U Tex Dept Computer Sci Austin TX 78712

NOVAK, GREGORY, marketing professional; b. Johnstown, Pa., Oct. 19, 1949; s. Eugene F. and Joan (Tross) N.; m. Naomi Sosia Wall; children: Rebecca, Jeffrey, Jacqueline. BA, U. Vt., 1971. Project dir. Dun & Bradstreet, NYC, 1973-74; sr. analyst Colgate Palmolive, NYC, 1974-76; mgr. brand rsch. R.J. Reynolds, Winston-Salem, NC, 1976-77, mgr. group new brand rsch., 1977-80, dir. new bus., 1980-81, dir. group mktg., 1981-84; nat. dir. mktg. Deloitte Haskins & Sells, NYC, 1984-90; pres. Novak Mktg. Inc., 1990—. Office: Novak Mktg Inc 29 Brandon Dr Mount Kisco NY 10549-3720 Business E-Mail: greg@novakmarketing.com.

NOVAK, JAMES EDMUND, nephrologist; s. James Ballaz and Beverly Joan Novak; m. Jessica Eve Shill. MD, U. Mich., Ann Arbor, MI, PhD, 2002. Bd. cert. in nephrology Am. Bd. Internal Medicine, 2007, cert. in internal medicine Am. Bd. Internal Medicine, 2005, med. license State of Mich., 2008, State of NC, 2006. Sr. staff nephrologist Henry Ford Health Sys., Detroit, 2008—, dir., nephrology med. student curriculum, 2008—. Recipient Individual Nat. Rsch. Svc. award, Nat. Institutes Mental Health, 1999; Med. Scientist Tng. Program fellowship, U. Mich., NIH, 1994—2002, Pharmacological Scientist Tng. Program fellowship, U. Mich., 1997—98. Mem.: Am. Soc. Nephrology, Alpha Omega Alpha.

NOVAK, JASON, music educator; s. James Novak and Sandra Corbett. MusB, Wright State U., Dayton, Ohio, 1999. Asst. dir. of bands London City Schs., Ohio, 2000—02; dir. of bands Brookville Local Schs., Ohio, 2002—. Mem.: Ohio Edn. Assn., Music Educators Nat. Conf., Ohio Music Edn. Assn. (pres. elect). R-Consevative. Lutheran. Avocations: hiking, travel. Home: 4894 Fishburg Rd Dayton OH 45424-5305 Office Fax: 937-833-6302. Personal E-mail: jasnovak9@aol.com. E-mail: bvjrjnovak@mdeca.org.

NOVAK, JASON P., secondary school educator; b. Joliet, Ill., Oct. 12, 1971; s. Gerald and Susan Novak. BA, Ea. Ill. U., Charleston, 1998. Tchr., coach Unity H.S., Tolono, Ill., 1998, Knox Jr. H.S., The Woodlands, Tex., 1998—2001, The Woodlands H.S. McCullough Campus, 2001—01, St. Pius X H.S., Houston, 2002—. With USAF, 1989—93. Decorated Air Force Commendation award USAF, Liberation Kuwait medal, SW Asia Svc. with three Bronze Stars, Nat. Def. Svc. medal, Air Force Good Conduct medal, Air Force Longevity medal. Mem.: Oxford Round Table, Nat. Cath. Ednl. Assn., Am. Inst. Archaeology, Nat. Coun. Social Studies. Achievements include small arms expert. Office: St Pius X High School 811 West Donovan St Houston TX 77091 E-mail: novakj@stpiusx.org.

NOVAK, JOHN G., construction executive; Ind. residential contractor; pres. Novak Constrn. Co., Chgo., 1980—, CEO. Achievements include leading Novak Construction Company when it was named one of the 50 fastest growing companies in the Chicago area by Crain's Chicago Business, 2007. Office: Novak Constrn Co 3423 N Drake Ave Chicago IL 60618 Office Phone: 773-278-1100. Office Fax: 773-278-1119.

NOVAK, JOYCE KEEN, artist, secondary school educator; d. Clifford Patrick and Mildred Ella Keen; m. Jack Janis, Dec. 15, 1950 (div. July 16, 1954); m. William John Moore, Oct. 28, 1955 (div. Feb. 26, 1965); children: Robert John, William Keen, Marilyn Joyce, James Clifford; m. Robert Novak, May 7, 1966; stepchildren: Susan Grace, Nina Louise. BS of Bus. Edn., U. Mich., 1954, MS of Bus. Edn., 1950. Tchr. Southfield HS, Highland Pk., Mich., 1954—56, Wayne Meml. HS, 1955—57, Dist. 214 HS, Wheeling, Ill., 1963—66; profl. fine artist Arlington Heights, Ill., 1966—89, Palatine, Ill., 1989—95, Nokomis, Fla., 1995—. Pres. Contemporary Art Ctr., Arlington Heights, Ill., 1984—86; adv. bd. Space 900, Chgo., 1992—95. 40 solo exhbns. Pres. N.W. Suburban Panhellenic Assn., Chgo.; sister city emissary Village Arlington Heights, Zoazhuang, China, 1989. Recipient numerous nat., regional and local art awards. Mem.: Nat. League Am. Pen Women Inc., Fla. Artists Group (v.p. 2003—05, pres. 2005—07), Women's Contemporary Artists (life). Presbyterian. Avocations: swimming, tai chi, bridge. Home: 1066 Truman St Nokomis FL 34275 Personal E-mail: jnart@comcast.net.

NOVAK, LESLIE HOWARD, lawyer; b. Chgo., May 10, 1944; s. Sidney and Sadie (Jensky) N.; m. Nancy Ruth Sherman, July 2, 1967; children: Heidi Ellen, Shani Beth. BS in Bus. with high distinction, U. Minn., 1966, JD cum laude, 1969. Bar: Minn. 1970, U.S. Dist. Ct. Minn. 1970, U.S. Ct. Appeals (8th cir.) 1974, U.S. Supreme Ct. 1995. Assoc. Robins, Kaplan, Miller & Ciresi, Mpls., 1969-77, ptnr., 1977-92, Mackall, Crounse & Moore, PLC., Mpls., 1992—, mng. ptnr., 1997-99. Bd. dirs. Am. Israel C. of C. and Industry of Minn., Mpls., 1981—, founding pres., 1981-91; founding sec., founding bd. dir. Assn. N.Am.-Israel Chambers Commerce, Inc., 1993—; bd. dirs. United Jewish Fund and Coun., St. Paul, 1986-2007; founding dir. Illusion Theater and Sch.; past bd. dirs., past pres. Jewish Family Svc. St. Paul; past bd. dirs. Mt. Zion Temple. Named Leading Am. Atty., Am.'s Registry Outstanding Profls. Mem. Oakridge Country Club, Gopher Golf Boosters Club, Phi Delta Phi, Beta Gamma Sigma. Avocations: biking, golf, tennis, skiing. Office: Mackall Crounse & Moore PLC 1400 AT&T Tower 901 Marquette Ave Minneapolis MN 55402-2859 Home Phone: 952-471-7575; Office Phone: 612-305-1460. Business E-Mail: lhn@mcmlaw.com.

NOVAK, MARK, lawyer; b. Buffalo, Jan. 28, 1952; s. Eugene Francis and Joan (Tross) N.; m. Charlene Mary Ingoglia, Sept. 2, 1972; children: Jason Charles, Jennifer Rose. BA, U. Rochester, 1974; JD, Loyola U., Chgo., 1977. Bar: Ill. 1977, U.S. Dist. Ct. (no. dist.) Ill. 1977, U.S. Ct. Appeals (7th cir.) 1978. Assoc. Anesi, Ozmon & Lewin, Ltd., Chgo., 1977—83; ptnr. Anesi, Ozmon, Rodin, Novak & Kohen, Ltd., Chgo., 1983—, pres., 2006—; bd. chmn. Novak Family Found., 2007—. Fundraiser Christmas is for Kids Charity, Chgo., 1992—. Mem. ATLA (product liability sect. 1985—), ABA, Ill. Trial Lawyers Assn., Trial Lawyers for Pub. Justice, Chgo. Bar Assn. (jud. evaluation com. 1995—). Home: 1212 N Lake Shore Dr Chicago IL 60610-2371 Office: Anesi Ozmon Rodin Novak & Kohen Ltd 161 N Clark St Fl 21 Chicago IL 60601-3206 Office Phone: 312-372-3822.

NOVAK, MAXIMILLIAN ERWIN, retired English literature professor; b. NYC, Mar. 26, 1930; s. George and Elsie (Loewy) Novak; m. Estelle Gershgoren, Aug. 21, 1966; children: Ralph, Daniel, Rachel. PhD, UCLA, 1958; D.Phil., St. John's Coll., Oxford U., Eng., 1961. Asst. prof. English, U. Mich., Ann Arbor, 1958-62; prof. English UCLA, 1962—2001, Clark Library prof., 1973-74, 2003—04, disting. prof. emeritus, 2001—. Author: Economics and the Fiction of Daniel Defoe, 1962, Defoe and the Nature of Man, 1963, Congreve, 1971, The Wild Man Within, 1972, English Literature in the Age of Disguise, 1977, Realism, Myth and History in the Fiction of Daniel Defoe, 1983, Eighteenth-Century English Literature, 1983, Passionate Encounters, 2000, Daniel Defoe Master of Fictions, 2001, Enchanted Ground, 2004, Approaches to Robinson Crusoe, 2005; editor: Augustan Reprint Society Dryden: Works, vol. 10, 1970, vol. 13, 1984, Southerne Oroonoko, 1976, Stoke Newington Daniel Defoe, 1999—, Age of Projects, 2008. Fulbright fellow, 1955—57, Guggenheim fellow, 1965—66, 1985—86, Am. Philos. Soc. fellow, 1979, NEH fellow, 1980—81, Beinecke Libr. fellow, 1991, Pres.' fellow, U. Calif., 1991—, Huntington Libr. fellow, 1991. Mem.: MLA, Western Soc. Eighteenth Century Studies, Johnson Soc. So. Calif., Am. Soc. 18th Century Studies. Democrat. Jewish. Home: 451 S El Camino Dr Beverly Hills CA 90212-4221 Office Phone: 310-825-4173. E-mail: novak@humnet.ucla.edu.

NOVAK, MICHAEL (JOHN), religion educator, author, editor; b. Johnstown, Pa., Sept. 9, 1933; s. Michael John and Irene (Sakmar) N.; m. Karen Ruth Laub-Novak, June 29, 1963; children: Richard, Tanya, Jana. AB summa cum laude, Stonehill Coll., North Easton, Mass., 1956; BT cum laude, Gregorian U., Rome, 1958; MA, Harvard U., 1966; LLD, Keuka Coll., NY, 1970, Stonehill Coll., Mass., 1977, Thomas More Coll., 1992; LHD, Davis and Elkins Coll., W.Va., 1971, LeMoyne Coll., NY, 1976, Sacred Heart U., 1977, Muhlenberg Coll., 1979, D'Youville Coll., 1981, Boston U., 1981, New Eng. Coll., 1983, Rivier Coll., 1984, Marquette U., 1987; D en Ciencias Sociales, U. Francisco Marroquin, Guatemala, 1993, Jacksonville U., 1994; HHD, Saint Xavier U., 1995. Tchg. fellow Harvard U., 1961-63; asst. prof. Stanford U., 1965-68; assoc. prof. philosophy and religious studies SUNY, Old Westbury, 1968-71; assoc. dir. humanities Rockefeller Found., NYC, 1973-75; provost Disciplines Coll., SUNY, Old Westbury, 1969-71; vis. prof. Jan. session Carleton Coll., Northfield, Minn., 1970, Immaculate Heart Coll., Hollywood, Calif., 1971, U. Calif., Santa Barbara, 1972, Riverside, 1975; Ledden-Watson disting. prof. religion Syracuse U., 1977-79; journalist nat. elections Newsday, 1972; writer in residence The Washington Star, 1976, syndicated columnist, 1976-80, 84-89; columnist Forbes Mag., 1989—94; resident scholar Am. Enterprise Int., Washington, 1978—83; George Frederick Jewett chair pub. policy and religion Am. Enterprise Inst., Washington, 1983—, dir. social and polit. studies, 1987—; chmn. working seminar on family and Am. welfare policy Ind., 1986; faculty U. Notre Dame, Ind., 1986-87, vis. W. Harold and Martha Welch Prof. Am. Studies Ind., 1987, 88. Judge Nat. Book awards, 1971, DuPont Broadcast Journalism awards, 1971-80; speechwriter nat. polit. campaigns, 1970, 72; mem. Bd. Internat. Broadcasting, 1983—; mem. Presdl. Task Force Project Econ. Justice, 1985-87, Council Scholars Library of Congress, 1986—; mem. monitoring panel UNESCO, 1984; vice chmn. Lay Commn. Cath. Social Teaching and U.S. Economy, 1984-86; U.S. Ambassador to Experts Meeting on Human Contacts of the Conf. On Security and Cooperation in Europe, Bern, Switzerland, 1986; U.S. rep. to human rights commn. UN, 1981-83; hon. prof. U. Cuyo, Argentina, 1992. Author: (novel) The Tiber was Silver, 1961, A New Generation, 1964, The Experience of Marriage, 1964, The Open Church, 1964, Belief and Unbelief, 1965, 3d edit., 1994, A Time to Build, 1967, A Theology for Radical Politics, 1969, American Philosophy and the Future, 1968, Story in Politics, 1970, (with Brown and Herschel) Vietnam: Crisis of Conscience, 1967, Naked I Leave, 1970; Politics: Realism & Imagination, 1971, Ascent of the Mountain, Flight of the Dove, 1971, A Book of Elements, 1972, All the Catholic People, 1971, The Experience of Nothingness, 1970, The Rise of the Unmeltable Ethnics, 1972, Choosing Our King, 1974, The Joy of Sports, 1976, The Guns of Lattimer, 1978, The American Vision, 1978, Rethinking Human Rights I and II, 1981, 82, The Spirit of Democratic Capitalism, 1982, Confession of a Catholic, 1983, Moral Clarity in the Nuclear Age, 1983, Freedom with Justice, 1984, Human Rights and the New Realism, 1986, Will It Liberate? Questions About Liberation Theology, 1986, Character and Crime, 1986, The New Consensus on Family and Welfare, 1987, Taking Glasnost Seriously: Toward an Open Soviet Union, 1988, Free Persons and the Common Good, 1989, This Hemisphere of Liberty, 1990, The Spirit of Democratic Capitalism, 1991 (Anthony Fisher award 1992), Choosing Presidents, 1992, The Catholic Ethic and the Spirit of Capitalism, 1993, Awakening from Nihilism, 1995, Joy of Sports, rev. 1995; Belief and Unbelief, rev., 1995; Business as a Calling, 1996, The Fire of Invention, 1997, with daughter Jana Novak, Tell Me Why: A Father Answers His Daughter's Questions About God, 1998, On Cultivating Liberty, 1999, To Empower People, anniv. ed, 1995, A Free Society Reader, 2000, Three in One, 2001 (essays on Dem. Capitalism 1976-2000), On Two Wings, 2002; numerous other articles and books transl. into all maj. langs.; assoc. editor Commonweal mag., 1966-69; contbg. editor Christian Century, 1967-80, Christianity and Crisis, 1968-76, Jour. Ecumenical Studies, 1966-77, This World, 1982-89, First Things, 1990; religion editor Nat. Rev., 1979-86; founder, pub. Crisis, 1982-1996, editor-in-chief, 1993-95. Decorated K.M.G., Soverign Mil. Order of Malta, 1987, Order of the Byzantine Cross Republic of Slovakia, 1996; Kent fellow, 1961-65; fellow Hastings Inst., 1970-76; named Most Influential Prof. Sr. Class Stanford U., 1967, 68; Man of Yr. Johnstown, Pa., 1978; recipient Faith and Freedom award Religious Heritage Am., 1978, HIAS Liberty award, 1981, Friend of Freedom award, 1981; Newman Alumni award CCNY, 1984; George Washington Honor medal, 1984; award of Excellence, Religion in Media, 8th annual Angel Awards, 1985, Ellis Island Honor medal, 1986, Anthony Fisher award, 1992, Wilhelm Weber Prize, 1993, Templeton prize for progress in religion, 1994, Internat. prize Inst. World Capitalism, 1994, Award for the Arts City of Bratislava, 1998, Gold Medal Slovak Acad. Scis., 2000, Masaryk award Czech Republic, 2000, IDI Award for Econs., Fondazione Istituto Dirigenti, Rome, 2000, Cezanne medal City of Aix-en-Provence, 1998, Boyer award Am. Enterprise Inst., 1999, Internat. Prize for Cath. Culture, Italy, 1999, Gold medal Pa. Soc., 2001, Milan R. Stefanik award Slovak-Am. Cultural Ctr., 2002, Maritain medal for Scholarly Excellence, Am. Maritain Assn., 2002; diploma as vis. prof. U. Francisco Marroquin, 1985; named acad. corr. mem. from U.S., Argentina Nat. Acad. Scis., Morals & Politics, 1985, others. Mem. Soc. Religion in Higher Edn. (ctrl. com. 1970-73), Am. Acad. Religion (prog. dir. 1968-72), Coun. Fgn. Rels., Cath. Theol. Soc., Soc. Christian Ethics, Inst. Religion and Democracy (dir. 1981—), Nat. Ctr. Urban and Ethnic Affairs (dir. 1982-86). Office: Am Enterprise Inst 1150 17th St NW Washington DC 20036-4603 E-mail: mnovak@aei.org. *Many persons have found a certain emptiness at the heart of human life — an experience of nothingness. Hidden in it, implicit in it, are prior commitments to honesty, courage, freedom, community. To increase the frequency of such acts in our lives is to grow, and to feel them diminish is to wither.*

NOVAK, MICHAEL, physician, otologist; BS, Ohio State U., Columbus, 1971; MD, Baylor Coll. Medicine, Houston, 1974. Cert. ACGME Am. Bd. Otolaryn. Head and Neck Surgery, 1979. Attending otologist Carle Clinic Assn., Urbana, Ill., 1981—; asst. clin. prof. surgery U. Ill. Coll. Medicine, Urbana, 1981—. Med. dir. Carle Expanding Children's Hearing Opportunities Program, Urbana, 1987—. Contbr. chapters to books. Bd. mem. Alexander Graham Bell Assn. Deaf and Hard of Heariing, Washington, 2003—08. Maj. USAF, 1979—81, Biloxi, Miss. Fellow: Am. Acad. Otolaryngology, Head and Neck Surgery. Achievements include development of adult cochlear implant program, 1984; co-investigator multiple FDA clinical trials. Office: Carle Clinic Assn 602 W University Ave NCE 4 Urbana IL 61801 Business E-Mail: michael.novak@carle.com.

NOVAK, RANDI RUTH, systems engineer, computer scientist; b. Chgo., July 10, 1954; d. Bernard Richard and Shirley Ann (Fiedorczyk) Novak; children: Rona Rachel Reich, Bonnie Shaina Reich. BS in Math., U. Calif., Santa Cruz, 1976, BA in Econs. with honors, 1976; postgrad., U. Rochester, 1976-78. Rsch. asst. U. Calif., Santa Cruz, 1974-76; Russian translator U. Chgo., 1977—78; intern economist Congl. Budget Office, Washington, 1977; engr. Lockheed MSC, Sunnyvale, Calif., 1978-82; software engr. contractor Silicon Valley Systems, Belmont, Calif., 1982, 83-84, Data Encore (subs. of Verbatim), Sunnyvale, 1982-83; systems programmer CompuPro/Viasyn Corp., Hayward, Calif., 1984-87; mem. tech. staff Network Equipment Techs., Redwood City, Calif., 1987-89; v.p. engring., founder Segue Setups, Burlingame, Calif., 1989-92, ptnr., 1992—; sr. tech. staff NEC Am., San Jose, Calif., 1992—94; sr. systems engr. Hitachi Computer Products, Santa Clara, Calif., 1994-96; prin. engr. Rapid-City Comms./Bay Networks/Nortel Networks, Santa Clara, Calif., 1996—2002, Trapeze Networks, Pleasanton, Calif., 2002—04; prin. engr. tech. staff Foundry Networks, San Jose, 2004—. Fellow Dept. Treasury, 1974-76, NSF, 1977-78, U. Rochester, Rush Rhees fellow. Mem. IEEE Computer Soc., Am. Math. Assn., Computer Profls. for Social Responsibility, Soc. for Computing and Info. Processing, Internat. Platform Assn., Calif. Scholarship Fedn. (life). Avocations: piano, oboe, music, photography, mathematics. Home: 4166 School St Pleasanton CA 94566-6218 Office Phone: 408-207-1528. Personal E-mail: rrnovak@comcast.net.

NOVAK, RAYMOND FRANCIS, environmental services administrator, pharmacology educator; s. Joseph Raymond and Margaret A. (Cerutti) N.; m. Frances C. Holy, Apr. 12, 1969; children: Jennifer, Jessica, Janelle, Joanna. BS in Chemistry, U. Mo., St. Louis, 1968; PhD in Phys. Chemistry, Case Western Res. U., 1973. Assoc. in pharmacology Northwestern U. Med. Sch., Chgo., 1976-77, asst. prof. pharmacology, 1977-81, assoc. prof., 1981-86, prof., 1986-88; prof. pediat., pharmacology Wayne State U. Sch. Medicine, Children's Hosp. Mich., Detroit, 1988—; dir. Inst. Environ. Health Scis. Wayne State U., Detroit, 1988—2008, dir. EHS Ctr. in Molecular and Cellular Toxicology with Human Application, 1994—2008, dir. interdisciplinary grad. program in Molecular and Cellular Toxicology, 1994—2008; ad hoc bd. mem. sci. counselors Nat. Toxicology Program, NIH Nat. Inst. Environ. Sci., 2008—. Mem. toxicology study sect. NIH, Bethesda, Md., 1984-88, mem. and chair numerous grant review com.; adj. sci. Inhalation Toxicology Rsch. Inst., Lovelace Biomed. and Environ. Rsch. Inst., 1991-98; program leader Epidemiology and Environ. Carcinogenesis, Karmanos Cancer Inst. and Comprehensive Cancer Ctr., 1996-98. Assoc. editor Toxicol. Applied Pharmacology, 1992-96, Toxicol. Scis., 2004—09; editor Drug Metabolism and Disposition, 1994-2000; mem. editorial bd. Jour. Toxicology and Environ. Health, 19 87-92, In Vivo, 1986—, Toxic Substances Jour., 1993-98; mem. bd. pub. trustees Am. Soc. Pharmacology and Experimental Therapeutics, 1994-2000; publr. over 140 sci. manuscripts, review articles and book chpt. in profl. jour. and books. Co. comdr., field grade officer (Major) USAR, 1968—99. Recipient Disting. Alumni award U. Mo., St. Louis, 1988; grantee Nat. Inst. Environ. Health Sci., 1979—2009, Gen. Medicine sect. NIH, 1979-82, 89-94. Mem. Am. Soc. for Biochem. and Molecular Biology, Soc. Toxicology (councilor 1996-98, chmn. cont. edn. com. 1995-96), Am. Assn. for Cancer Rsch., Am. Soc. for Pharmacology and Exptl. Therapeutics (bd. publ. trustees 1994-99), Am. Soc. Hematology, Internat. Soc. for Study Xenobiotics. Achievements include patents in field. Office: Children's Hosp Mich Dept Pediat Divsn Clin Pharmacology & Toxicology Rm 3N47 3901 Beanbian St Detroit MI 48201-2119 Office Phone: 313-745-5767. Business E-Mail: R.Novak@wayne.edu.

NOVAK, ROBERT LOUIS, civil engineer, pavement management consultant; b. Chgo., Feb. 29, 1928; s. Louis and Frances (Kucera) N.; m. Virginia Staas, Jan. 22, 1955 (div. 1962); children: Susan Grace, Nina Louise; m. Joyce Eloise Keen, May 7, 1966; stepchildren: Robert John Moore, William Keen Moore, Marilyn Joyce Moore, James Clifford Moore. BCE, Ga. Inst. Tech., 1948. With Am. Bridge Co., 1948-49; soils engr. Soil Testing Svc., Chgo., 1952-54; chief materials engr. Skidmore Owings and Merrill USAF Acad., Colorado Springs, 1954, dir. field invest; asst. dir. engring. O'Hare field constrn. Naess & Murphy, Chgo., 1958-60; pres. Novak, Dempsey & Assocs., Palatine, Ill., 1960-85; ptnr. Infrastructure Mgmt. Svcs., Arlington Heights, Ill., 1985-89, cons., 1989—. Contbr. articles to profl. jours. With U.S. Army, 1950-52. Mem. ASTM, Am. Pub. Works Assn. (life; Meritorious Svc. award 1990), Transp. Rsch. Bd. Achievements include a pioneer in field of pavement mgmt. and development of one of the first pavement management computer software programs. Home: 1066 Truman St Nokomis FL 34275-4401

NOVAK, RYNELL STIFF, retired academic administrator; b. Collin County, Tex., May 24, 1929; d. Roy Odus and Wilma (Vermillion) Stiff; m. Joseph Robert Novak, May 11, 1954; children: Robert David, Daniel Allan, Timothy Criswell, Rebekah Novak Proctor, Elisabeth Novak Richards. BA, U. North Tex., Denton, 1949, cert. in libr. studies, 1965, MA, 1973, PhD, 1975, postdoctoral studies, 1975—78, Tex. A&M U., College Station, 1987; MRE, S.W. Bapt. Theol. Sem., 1953. cert. profl. in human resources. Tchr. Plainview (Tex.) Ind. Sch. Dist., 1949-50; draftsman Convair, Ft. Worth, 1951-52; rsch. assoc. U. North Tex., Denton, 1974-79; text editor Home Mission Bd. So. Bapt. Conv., Atlanta, 1979-83; staff assoc. Tex. A&M U. System, College Station, 1984—94. Instr. in speech Blinn Coll., Brenham, Tex., 1988-95. Author: The Novak Connection, 1983. Dist. officer Tex. PTA, 1966—71; v.p. Tex. Bapt. Student Union, 1948—49; mem., dir. Missions Coun. Bapt. Ch.; mem. exec. bd. Bapt. Gen. Conv. Tex., 1974—79. Mem.: Vermillion Family Reunion (officer, spkr.), Altoga Cemetery Assn. (pres.), Stephen Williams Chpt. US Dau. 1812 (pres.), Stiff Chapel Cemetery Assn. (pres.), Hist. Park Found. of Denton County (pres.), Denton County Hist. Commn. (vice chmn. 2009—), Descs. of Washington's Army at Valley Forge (Tex. brigade comdr. 1991—95, comdr.-in-chief 2004—06), Tex. Brigade, Mensa, United Daus. of the Confederacy, Tex. Soc. DAR (regent La Villita chpt. 1990—92, 1994—95, regent Benjamin Lyon chpt. 2000—01, state chmn. 2006—09), Nat. Soc. US Daus. 1812 (nat. treas. 2003—09), Tex. Soc. US Daus. 1812 (hon. state pres.). Avocations: genealogy, photography, travel. Home: 2500 Hinkle Dr 27 Denton TX 76201 Personal E-mail: rsnovak@juno.com.

NOVAK, TERRY LEE, dean, educator; b. Chamberlain, SD, Sept. 1, 1940; s. Warren F. and Elaine M. N.; m. Barbara Hosea, Aug. 29, 1981; 1 child, David. B.Sc., S.D. State U., 1962; postgrad. (Rotary fellow), U. Paris, 1962-63; M.P.A., Colo. U., 1965, PhD, 1970. Asst. city mgr. City of Anchorage, 1966-68; city mgr. City of Hopkins, Minn., 1968-74, City of Columbia, Mo., 1974-78, City of Spokane, Wash., 1978-91; v.p. bus. and fin. Ea. Wash. U., Cheney, 1991—94, prof. public adminstrn., 1992—, dir. grad. program pub. adminstrn., 1994-95; dir. Spokane Joint Ctr. for Higher Edn., 1995-98; bus. mgr. Riverpoint campus Wash. State U., 1998-99; prof pub. adminstrn. Eastern Wash. U., 1999—. Asst. adj. prof. U. Mo., Columbia, 1975, 77; adj. instr. Gonzaga U., Spokane, 1986-88; mem. nat. adv. coun. on environ. policy and tech. EPA. Author: Special Assessment Financing in American Cities, 1970; contbr. articles to profl. jours. Mem. ASPA, Internat. City Mgrs. Assn. (Acad. Profl. Devel.). Episcopalian. Office: 668 N Riverpoint Blvd Spokane WA 99202-1677 E-mail: tnovak@terrynovak.net.

NOVALES, RONALD RICHARDS, zoologist, educator; b. San Francisco, Apr. 24, 1928; s. William Henry and Dorothy (Richards) N.; m. Barbara Jean Martin, Dec. 19, 1953; children: Nancy Ann, Mary Elizabeth. BA, U. Calif., Berkeley, 1950, MA, 1953, PhD, 1958; postgrad., UCLA, 1951-52. Asst. prof. biol. scis. Northwestern U., Evanston, Ill., 1958-64, assoc. prof., 1964-70, prof., 1970-80, prof. neurobiology and physiology, 1981-93, prof. biology 6 yr. med. program, emeritus prof. neurobiology and physiology, 1993—. Cons. A.J. Nystrom Co., 1969 Mem. editorial bd.: The American Zoologist, 1969-73; Contbr.: articles to profl. jours. Ency. Brit. Book of Year. Served with U.S. Army, 1953-55. NSF research grantee, 1959-73, 75-78 Fellow AAAS. Unitarian Universalist. Home: 2008 Mcdaniel Ave Evanston IL 60201-2125 Home Phone: 847-491-9819. *Remember not to "die on the barbed wire" of all the conflicting demands of your work. It is possible for you to cut through the individual strands and to make a successful rush for the enemy's trench.*

NOVASCONE, TODD, legislative staff member; s. Jack and Marilyn Novascone; m. Sarah Novascone. BA in Acctg., Baylor U., Waco, Tex., 2004. Various sales positions Am. Bldg. Supply, 1995—2005; mem. Dist. 99 Kans. House of Reps., 2000—05; chief of staff to congressman Jerry Moran US House of Reps., Washington, 2005—. Republican. Mailing: US House Reps 2202 Rayburn House Office Bldg Washington DC 20515 Office Phone: 202-225-2715. Office Fax: 202-225-5124. Business E-Mail: todd.novascone@mail.house.gov.*

NOVELLO, ANTONIA COELLO, pediatric nephrologist, former state health commissioner, former United States Surgeon General; b. Fajardo, PR, Aug. 23, 1944; d. Antonio and Ana D. (Flores) Coello; m. Joseph R. Novello, May 30, 1970. BS, U. P.R., Rio Piedras, 1965; MD, U. P.R., San Juan, 1970; MPH, Johns Hopkins Sch. Hygiene, 1982; DrPh, Johns Hopkins U., 2000; DSc (hon.), Med. Coll. Ohio, 1990, U. Ctrl. Caribe, Cayey, PR, 1990, Lehigh U., 1992, Hood Coll., 1992, U. Notre Dame, Ind., 1991, N.Y. Med. Coll., 1992, U. Mass., 1992, Fla. Internat. U., 1992, Cath. U., 1993, Washington Coll., 1993, St. Mary's Coll., 1993, Ea. Va. Med. Sch., 1993; Ctrl. Conn. State U., 1993, Georgetown U., 1993, U. Mich., 1994, Mt. Sinai Sch. Medicine, 1995; LHD (hon.), Alvernia Coll., 1996; HHD (hon.), Kings Coll., 1996; D in Health Sci. (hon.), Ponce Sch. of Medicine, 1996; D in Law (hon.), Gannon U., 1997; LHD (hon.), Loyola U., 1997; DSc (hon.), U. North Tex., Ft. Worth, 2002, Howard U., 2003, NYU, 2003, Pace U., 2003, Coll. New Rochelle, NY, 2003, Chatham Coll., Pitts., 2005; LHD (hon.), Coll. St. Rose, NY, 2004, Setton Hall U., 2006, Nova Southeastern U., 2007. Diplomate Am. Bd. Pediatrics. Intern in pediatrics U. Mich. Med. Ctr., Ann Arbor, 1970-71, resident in pediatrics, 1971-73, pediatric nephrology fellow, 1973-74, Georgetown U. Hosp., Washington, 1974-75; project officer Nat. Inst. Arthritis, Metabolism and Digestive Diseases NIH, Bethesda, Md., 1978-79, staff physician, 1979-80; exec. sec. gen. medicine B study sect., div. of rsch. grants NIH, Bethesda, 1981-86; dep. dir. Nat. Inst. Child Health & Human Devel., NIH, Bethesda, 1986-90; surgeon gen. US Dept. Health & Human Services, Washington, 1990-93; spl. rep. for health and nutrition UNICEF, NYC, 1993—96; vis. prof. health policy and mgmt. Johns Hopkins U. Sch. of Hygiene and Pub. Health, 1996—99; commr. of health State of NY, 1999—2007; v.p. Women and Children's Health and Policy Affairs, Fla. Children's Hosp., 2008—; exec. Disney Children's Hosp., Orlando, Fla., 2009—. Clin. prof. pediatrics Georgetown U. Hosp., Washington, 1986, 89, Uniformed Svcs. U. of Health Scis., 1989; adj. prof. pediatrics and communicable diseases U. Mich. Med. Sch., 1993; adj. prof. internat. health Sch. Hygiene and Pub. Health, Johns Hopkins U., Balt.; prof. dept. health policy mgmt. and behavior SUNY, 1999—; clin. prof. pediats. U. Rochester, N.Y., 1999—; mem. Georgetown Med. Ctr. Interdepartmental Rsch. Group; legis. fellow U.S. Senate Com. on Labor and Human Resources, Washington, 1982-83; mem. Com. on Rsch. in Pediatric Nephrology, Washington; participant grants assoc. program seminars Nat. Inst. Arthritis, Diabetes and Digestive and Kidney Diseases, NIH, Bethesda, 1980-81; pediatric cons. Adolescent Medicine Svc., Psychiat. Inst., Washington, 1979-83; nephrology cons. Met. Washington Renal Dialysis Ctr. affiliate Georgetown U. Hosp., Washington, 1975-78; phys. diagnosis class instr. U. Mich. Med. Ctr., Ann Arbor, 1973-74; chair Sec.'s Work Group on Pediatric HIV Infection and Diseases, DHHS, 1988; cons. WHO, Geneva, 1989; mem. Johns Hopkins Soc. Scholars, 1991. Contbr. numerous articles to profl. jours. and chpts. to books in field; mem. editorial bd. Internat. Jour Artificial Organs, Jour. Mexican Nephrology. Served in USPHS, 1978-99. Recipient Intern of Yr. award U. Mich. Dept. Pediatrics, 1971, Woman of Yr. award Disting. Grads. Pub. Sch. Systems, San Juan, 1980, PHS Commendation medal HHS, 1983, PHS Citation award HHS, 1984, Cert. of Recognition, Divsn. Rsch. Grants, NIH, 1985, PHS Outstanding medal HHS, 1988, PHS Unit Commendation, 1988, PHS Surgeon Gen.'s Exemplary Svc. medal, 1989, PHS Outstanding Unit citation, 1989, DHHS Asst. Sec. for Health Cert. of Commendation, 1989, Surgeon Gen. Medallion award, 1990, Alumni award U. Mich. Med. Ctr., 1991, Elizabeth Blackwell award, 1991, Woodrow Wilson award for disting. govt. svc., 1991, Congl. Hispanic Caucus medal, 1991, Order of Mil. Med. Merit, 1992, Washington Times Freedom award, 1992, Charles C. Shepard Sci. award, 1992, Golden Plate award, 1992, Elizabeth Ann Seton award, 1992, Ellis Island Congl. Medal of Honor, 1993, Legion of Merit medal, 1993, Athena award Alumnae Coun., 1993, Nat. Citation award Mortar Bd., 1993, Disting. Pub. Svc. award, 1993, Healthy Am. Fitness Leaders award, 1994, Pub. Leadership Edn. Network Mentor award, 1994, Disting. Svc. award Nat. Coun. Cath. Women, 1995, James E. Van Zandt Citizenship award, 1995, Ronald McDonald Children's Charities Excellence award, 1995, Hispanic Heritage Leadership award, 1998, Disting. Alumnus award Am. Assn. of State Colls. and Univs., 1997, Humanitarian award Am. Cancer Soc., 2001, James Smithson Bicentenial medal Smithsonian Inst., 2002; named Health Leader of Yr., COA, 1992; inductee Nat. Women's Hall of Fame, 1994, Internat. Pediatric Hall of Fame Miami Children's Hosp., 1996, Am. Med. Women Assn. Hall of Fame, 2002. Fellow Am. Acad. Pediatrics (Excellence Pub. Svc. award 1993); mem. AMA (Nathan Davis award 1993, Meritorious Svc. award 1993, Luther L. Terry award, 2000), Inst. Medicine Nat. Acad. Scis., Internat. Soc. Nephrology, Am. Soc. Nephrology, Latin Am. Soc. Nephrology, Soc. for Pediatric Rsch., Am. Pediatric Soc., Assn. Mil. Surgeons U.S., Am. Soc. Pediatric Nephrology, Pan Am. Med. and Dental Soc. (pres.-elect, sec. 1984), D.C. Med. Soc. (assoc.), Johns Hopkins U. Soc. Scholars, Alpha Omega

Alpha. Achievements include being the first woman and first Hispanic to serve as surgeon general. Avocation: collecting antique furniture. Office Phone: 407-303-1976, 407-489-6835. Business E-Mail: antonia.novello.md@flhosp.org.

NOVEY, DONALD W., physician, health facility administrator; b. Chgo., Feb. 4, 1951; s. Theodore B. and Elaine (Lewitz) N.; m. Judy Novey, July 28, 1990; 1 child, Miguel. BA in Psychology with honors, Ind. U., 1973; MD, U. Ill., 1977. Diplomate Am. Bd. Family Practice. Resident in family practice So. Ill. U., Meml. Hosp., Carbondale, 1977-78; staff physician Murphysboro (Ill.) Health Ctr., 1979; assoc. prof. medicine Dr. William M. Scholl Coll. Podiatric Medicine, Chgo., 1979-87; pres. Med. Media Syss., Chgo., 1984—; instr. medicine Northwestern U. Med. Sch., Chgo., 1989-91; asst. med. dir. AMA, Chgo., 1989-91; resident in family practice U. Ill., Ravenswood Hosp. Med. Ctr., 1991-93; mem. full-time attending faculty family practice residency program Luth. Gen. Hosp., Park Ridge, Ill., 1993—; dir. Ctr. for Complementary Medicine, Advocate Med. Group, Park Ridge, Ill., 1998—. Presenter in field. Prodr. videotapes; author Clinician's Complete Reference to Complementary and Alternative Medicine. Recipient 1st prize Health Edn. Media Assn., 1985, Silver cert. John Muir Med. Film Festival, 1986, 90, Bronze award Brit. Med. Assn., 1986, Norman W. Shapiro Meml. award Am. Podiatric Med. Assn., 1987, 3rd prize Health Scis. Comm. Assn., 1987, Gold award Worldfest-Charleston Internat. Film and Video Festival, 1994, Silver award, 1995, Golden Eagle award CINE, 1995, Gold award Worldfest-Houston Internat. Film and Video Festival, 1995, 2 Gold awards Brit. Med. Assn. Med. Film Festival, 1996, Med. Edn. award, 1996. Mem. Am. Acad. Family Physicians, Ill. Acad. Family Physicians, Internat. TV Assn. (Recognition award 1985, Silver medal 1989), Phi Beta Kappa. Office: Ctr for Complementary Medicine 1775 Ballard Rd Park Ridge IL 60068 Office Phone: 847-318-2860.*

NOVICH, BRUCE ERIC, chemicals executive; b. Phila., Mar. 15, 1957; s. Samuel David and Vivian Rose Novich; m. Susan S. Novich, Sept. 5, 1982; children: Scott, Spencer, Corey. BA, Colgate U., 1979; BSChemE, MIT, 1980, MS in Geology, 1982, MSCE, 1982, ScD in Materials Processing, 1984. V.p. R & D and engring. Ceramics Process System, Milford, Mass., 1984-95; global bus. dir. electronics-zebralink PPG Industries, Pitts., 1995-2000; global bus. dir. Fujifilm Electronic Materials, 2000—04, Fuji Film Electronic Materials, Inc., Kingstown, RI, 2004—; sr. v.p. Fujifilm Corp., 2007—. Contbr. articles to profl. jours. Recipient 2 R & D 100 awards. Achievements include 25 patents in ceramics, composites and electronic packaging. Office: Fuji Film Electronic Materials Inc 80 Circuit Dr N North Kingstown RI 02852 Home Phone: 401-996-2333. Business E-Mail: bruce_novich@fujifilm-ffem.com.

NOVICH, NEIL S., metals distribution company executive; BA in Physics summa cum laude, Harvard U., 1974; MS in Nuclear Engring., MIT, 1979, MS in Mgmt., 1981. Former dir. Bain & Co.; COO Ryerson Inc., Chgo., 1994—99, chmn., pres., CEO, 1999—. Dir. W.W. Grainger, Inc. Trustee Field Mus. Natural History, Children's Home & Aid Soc. Ill.; mem. vis. com. Divsn. Phys. Scis., U. Chgo. Nat. Sci. Found. scholar, Ford scholar. Mem. Phi Beta Kappa. Office: Ryerson Inc 2621 W 15th Pl Chicago IL 60608

NOVICK, BARBARA, investment adviser; b. Glen Cove, NY, Sept. 5, 1960; d. Howard and Libbijane (Rolnick) G.; m. Barry Roy Novick, Dec. 26, 1981; 1 child, Abigail. BA cum laude, Cornell U., 1981. Analyst Morgan Stanley, NYC, 1982-85; v.p. First Boston, NYC, 1985-88; ptnr. Blackstone Fin. Mgmt., NYC, 1988—94; founding ptnr. BlackRock, Inc., NYC, 1994—, vice chmn., 2006—, sr. advisor, 2008—. Sec. Blackstone Target Term Trust, N.Y.C., 1988—. Avocations: skiing, biking, swimming, reading. Office: BlackRock Inc 40 E 52nd St New York NY 10022*

NOVICK, JULIUS LERNER, theater critic, educator; b. NYC, Jan. 31, 1939; s. Solomon Joseph and Ethel (Lerner) N.; m. Phyllis Belle Spaeth, May 27, 1983; 1 child, Ilana BA, Harvard U., 1960; D.F.A., Yale U., 1966. Theatre critic WNDT-TV, Channel 13, NYC, 1968-70; asst. prof. English NYU, NYC, 1969-72; assoc. prof. lit. SUNY-Purchase, 1972-80, prof., 1980—2001, prof. emeritus, 2002—; theatre critic The Village Voice, NYC, 1958-89, The N.Y. Observer, NYC, 1987-91, Newsday, NYC, 1992-94, Kempner Disting. prof., 1997-99. Vis. lectr, drama div. Juilliard Sch., N.Y.C., 1968-71; dramaturg The Acting Co., N.Y.C., 1971-73; vis. critic Dartmouth Summer Repertory Co., Hanover, N.H., 1976, 79, 80, 82, 83, 84; master critic Nat. Critics Inst., Waterford, Conn., 1971— Author: Beyond Broadway, The Quest for Permanent Theatre, 1968, Beyond the Golden Door, Jewish Am. Drama and Jewish Am. Experience, 2008 Fulbright scholar, 1960-61; Woodrow Wilson fellow, 1961-62; Guggenheim fellow, 1977; recipient George Jean Nathan award for dramatic criticism, 1981-82 Mem.: Am. Theatre and Drama Soc., Assn. for Theatre in Higher Edn., Assn. for Jewish Studies, Am. Theatre Critics Assn., Am. Soc. for Theatre Rsch. Jewish. E-mail: Jluddite@aol.com.

NOVICK, NELSON LEE, dermatologist, internist, consultant, cosmetic dermasurgeon, writer; b. Bklyn., June 27, 1949; s. Benjamin and Vivian (Meltzer) N.; m. Meryl Sohnis, June 20, 1971; children: Yonatan, Yoel, Ariel, Daniel, Avraham, Shmuel, Yehudah. BA in Biology magna cum laude, Bklyn. Coll., 1971; MD, Mt. Sinai Sch. Medicine, 1975. Diplomate Am. Bd. Internal Medicine, Am. Bd. Dermatology, Am. Bd. Med. Examiners. Resident internal medicine Mt. Sinai Med. Ctr., NYC, 1975—78, postgrad. preceptee, 1980—83, outpatient dept. clinic chief, dermatology svc., 1983—2003, attending, 2004—; resident Skin and Cancer Unit NYU Med. Ctr., NYC, 1978—80; clin. prof. Mt. Sinai Sch. Medicine, NYC, 2004—. Cons. Westwood-Squibb Skin Care Info. Ctr., Vaseline Intensive Care Rsch., Bausch & Lomb, Schering-Plough, Sandoz Internat., Procter & Gamble, Lever-2000, Novartis, Bradley Pharms., Merz Pharms., Inst. for Med. Info., Collagenesis Corp., PediFix, Biocell Tech. Network, others; skin health and beauty expert, Runner's World Mag., 2000-02; expert cons. Dermatology, Guidelines Expert, Nitron Advisors Healthcare Circle of Experts, 2003-, various med. websites; mem. MSSM spkrs. bureau, 2003-. Author: Saving Face, Skin Care for Teens, Super Skin, Baby Skin, You Can Do Something About Your Allergies, You Can Look Younger at Any Age, Diseases of the Mucus Membranes, (novel) In the Path of the Wolf, (audiotape series) Keeping That Baby Skin Look, Healthier and Younger-Looking Skin, Lunchtime Beauty Fixes for a Prettier Face, Breathing Easier, Fido, Food and Fumes; co-author: The External Ear; reviewer Annals Internal Medicine, Jour. Am. Acad. Dermatology, Jour. Dermatol. Surgery, Internat. Jour. Dermatology; editl. advisor Exec. Health's Good Health Report, Snyder Comm., Your Baby Wallboard Program; former med. editor Current Podiatric Medicine, Jour. Am. Analgesia Soc., Consumer Rsch. Coun. America's Guide to America's Top Physicians, 2003, Consumer Research Council of America's Guide to America's Top Dermatologists, 2007-08; contbr. articles to profl. jours. Regent's Coll. scholar, 1971, Max and Leah Strauss Fund scholar, 1971, Grand St. Found. scholar, 1971; recipient Dept. Dermatology award for contbg. to edn. of residents, 2000-01, Dept. Dermatology award for exceptional svc. in patient care, 2001-02; Dept. Dermatology award for two decades of outstanding svc., 2003, Dermatology award for Excellence, 2006-07. Fellow ACP (direct election), Am. Acad. Dermatology (Leadership Cir. 2006-08), Am. Soc. Dermatol. Surgery, Am. Acad. Cosmetic Surgery, Skin Cancer Found. (hon.); mem. AMA, AAAS, Soc. Investigative Dermatology, Skin Phototrauma Found., Internat. Soc. for Androgenic Disorders, Skin Cancer Found. (charter), N.Y. Acad. Scis., N.Y. County Med. Soc., Am. Soc. Dermatologic Surgery, Am. Analgesia Soc. (past bd. dirs.), Am. Soc. Cosmetic Dermatology & Aesthetic Surgery (charter), Nature Conservancy, Audubon Soc., Nat. Geog. Found., N.Y. Zool. Soc., Am. Mus. Natural History, Smithsonian Instn., Nat. Wildlife Fedn., The Wilderness Soc., Author's Guild, Author's League Am., Phi Beta Kappa. Jewish. Office: 328 E 75th St New York NY 10021-3317 also: CosMediSpa 49 Hahayil St Raanana 077-2100818 Israel Office Phone: 212-772-9300. Personal E-mail: nnovickmd@aol.com. E-mail: CosMediSpa@gmail.com. *The true measure of a person's success in life is not how much he accomplished, but how much of his God-given potential he has used.*

NOVICK, PETER J., cell biologist, educator; PhD, U. Calif., Berkeley, 1981. Prof. cell biology Yale U., New Haven. Contbr. articles to profl. jours. Fellow: Am. Acad. Arts & Scis. Office: Dept Cell Biology Yale U Sch Medicine 333 Cedar St PO Box 208002 New Haven CT 06520-8002 E-mail: Peter.Novick@yale.edu.

NOVICK, RICHARD PAUL, research scientist, public health institute administrator; b. NYC, Aug. 10, 1932; s. Samuel and Mollie (Foster) N.; m. Barbara Zabin, June 1, 1958; children— Lynn Judith, Dorothy Ruth BA magna cum laude, Yale U., 1954; MD with honors in Microbiol., NYU, 1959. Intern dept. medicine Yale U., New Haven, 1959—60; postdoctoral fellow Nat. Inst. Med. Rsch., London, 1961—62; asst. resident dept. medicine Vanderbilt U. Hosp., Nashville, 1962—63; special postdoctoral fellow Rockefeller U., NYC, 1963-65; assoc. Pub. Health Rsch. Inst. of City of NY, 1965-69, assoc. mem., 1969-75, mem., chmn. dept. plasmid biology, 1975-81, dir., 1981—91; prof. depts. microbiol. and medicine NYU Sch. Medicine, 1993—. Adj. prof. dept. microbiol. Sch. Medicine, NYU, 1966—1993; mem. recombinant DNA adv. com. NIH, Bethesda, Md., 1979-82; head sci. adv. com., applied genetics div. Pub. Health Rsch. Inst., 1983 Editor-in-chief Plasmid Jour., 1977; adv. editor Internat. Rev. Cytology, 1979; editl. cons. biol. abstracts, 1984; Contbr. articles to profl. jours. Bd. dirs. Alliance for Prudent Use of Antibiotics, Boston, 1982, sci. adv. bd.; Com. for Responsible Genetics, Boston, 1983; mem. adv. com. on microbiol. and virology Am. Cancer Soc., NYC, 1983 Named 1st ann. W.A. Altemeier lectr. Surg. Infections Soc., Boston, 1982, Selman A. Waksman hon. lectr. Rutgers U., 1983 Mem. Am. Soc. Microbiol., Am. Genetics Soc., Harvey Soc., Phi Beta Kappa, Alpha Omega Alpha, NAS. Avocations: woodworking, skiing, culinary mycology. Home: 10 W 86th St New York NY 10024-3606 Office: Skirball Inst of Biomolecular Medicine 2nd floor Labs 1 and 2 540 First Ave New York NY 10016

NOVICK, ROBERT T., lawyer; b. Oct. 6, 1958; BA, Bucknell Univ., 1980; JD cum laude, Am. Univ., 1983. Bar: DC 1984, US Ct. Internat. Trade. Assoc. Steptoe & Johnson LLP, Washington, 1983—90, ptnr., 1991—97; counselor Office of U.S. Trade Rep., Washington, 1997—99, gen. counsel, 1999—2001; ptnr., chmn. Trade dept. Wilmer Cutler Pickering Hale & Dorr, Washington, 2001—. Commr. Adv. Commn. on Electronic Commerce, U.S. Congress. Editor (exec.): Am. Univ. Law Rev. Office: Wilmer Cutler Pickering Hale & Dorr 1875 Pennsylvania Ave NW Washington DC 20006 Office Phone: 202-663-6140. Office Fax: 202-663-6363. Business E-Mail: robert.novick@wilmerhale.com.

NOVIELLO, DONALD, science educator; s. Peggy Grace Noviello; m. Paulette Louise Gerardi; children: Cristopher Andrew, Vincent Michael. Degree, Pa. Coll. Tech., Williamsport, 1991; BA, Bucknell U., Lewisburg, Pa., 1992, MEd, 1995. Assoc. Pa. Coll. Tech., 1988—90, tutor, 1989—, faculty, 1995—. Employee steering com. Williamsport Area Sch. Dist., 1995—97. Chairperson Mayor's Adv. Coun., Williamsport, 2008—. Recipient Cert. Recognition, Pa. Coll. Tech., 1989, 1st Paper award, Phi Alpha Theta, 1995. Mem.: Internat. Honor Soc. History, Kappa Delta Pi. Avocations: golf, tennis, skiing, fishing. Office: Pa Coll Tech One College Ave Williamsport PA 17701 Business E-Mail: dnoviell@pct.edu.

NOVIKOV, SERGEI PETROVICH, mathematician; b. Gorky, Russia, Mar. 20, 1938; s. Peter Sergeevitch and Ludmila Vsevolodovna (Keldysh) N.; m. Eleonora Vikentievna Tsoi, Oct. 2, 1962; children: Irina, Maria, Peter. B.Math., Moscow State U., 1960; PhD in math., Steklov Math. Inst., Moscow, 1964; PhD (hon.), U. Athens, 1988, U. Tel Aviv, 2000. Jr. rschr. Steklov Math. Inst., Moscow, 1963—65, sr. rschr., 1965—75; chmn. math. dept. Landau Inst. Theoretical Physics, Moscow, 1971—93, prin. rschr., 1993—. Chmn. dept. geometry and topology Steklov Math. Ins., 1983—, Moscow State U., 1983—; vis. prof. U. Md., Coll. Pk., 1992-96, disting. univ. prof., 1997-. Contbr. articles to profl. jours. Recipient Moscow Math. Soc. Young Mathematicians prize, 1964, Lenin Prize, 1967, Fields medal Internat. Math. Union, 1970, Lobachevskii Internat. Prize, Acad. of Sci. of the USSR, 1981, Wolf prize in math. Wolf Found., Israel, 2005. Mem. Moscow Math. Soc. (pres. 1985-96), Internat. Assn. of Math. Physicists (v.p. 1986-90), London Math. Soc. (hon. mem.), Serbian Acad. of Sci. and Art (hon. mem.), Acad. of Sci of the USSR (corresponding mem. 1966-81, full mem. 1981—), elected foreign mem. of the Academia de Lincei, Italy, 1991, mem. Academia Europea, 1992, foreign mem. of the NAS, 1994, mem of the Pontifical Acad. of Sci. (Vatican), 1996. Office: Landau Inst Kosygin St 2 Moscow Russia also: Dept of Math Math Bldg U of Maryland College Park MD 20742-4015

NOVIKOVA, TATYANA, music educator; b. Gomel, Belarus, Nov. 13, 1951; arrived in U.S., 1992; d. Sergei Saveliy Novikov and Julia Alexander Novikova; m. Yevgeniy Sagalchik, Apr. 26, 1977; 1 child, Marsha. BA, Gomel State Coll., Belarus, 1972; MusM, Belarus State Conservatory, Minsk, 1979. Instr. Gomel Music Sch., Belarus, 1974—76, Minsk Pub. Sch., 1976—92, Minsk State Coll., 1977—92, Stamford Project Music, Stamford, 1993—94, Ctrl. Music Sch., Stamford, 1994—2002; tchr. Ridgefield Acad., Conn., 1997—99, Greenwich Cath. Sch., Conn., 1999—. Mem.: Nat. Assn. Music Edn., Conn. State Music Tchrs. Assn., Schubert Club. Mailing: Apt 10 41 Rock Spring Rd Stamford CT 06906-1936

NOVITCH, MARK, physician, retired pharmaceutical executive; b. New London, Conn., Apr. 23, 1932; s. Charles Weinger and Mary (Margolick) N.; m. Katherine Louise Henderson, Oct. 9, 1971; 1 dau., Julia Drummond. AB, Yale U., 1954; MD, N.Y. Med. Coll., 1958. Intern, asst. resident in medicine Boston City Hosp., 1958-60; rsch. fellow Harvard Med. Sch., 1960-62, asst. in medicine, 1962-64, instr. medicine, 1964-67; mem. med. staff Peter Bent Brigham Hosp., Boston, 1962-67; asst. physician Univ. Health Svcs., Harvard U., 1961-67; asst. to dep. asst. sec. for health and sci. affairs HEW, Washington, 1967-71; dep. assoc. commr. for med. affairs FDA, Washington, 1971-78, assoc. commr. for health affairs, 1978-81; dep. commr. food and drugs HHS, 1981-85; corp. v.p. The Upjohn Co., Kalamazoo, 1985-86, sr. v.p. sci. adminstrn., 1986-88, exec. v.p., 1989-90, vice-chmn. bd. dirs., 1991-93; prof. health scis. George Washington U., Washington, 1994-97. Adj. prof. George Washington U., 1997—2001; chmn. bd. dirs. Food and Drug Law Inst., 2001—02; pres. U.S. Pharmacopeial Conv. Inc., 1990—95, trustee, 1990—2000. USPHS fellow, 1960-62; Brookings Instn. fed. exec. fellow, 1970-71 Mem. Mass. Med. Soc. Home: 3558 Albemarle St NW Washington DC 20008-4214

NOVITZ, CHARLES RICHARD, broadcast executive, reporter; b. Chgo., Oct. 25, 1934; m. Eve Krzyzanowski, Feb. 11, 1988; 1 child, Alexandra Maris. BS in Journalism, U. Ill., Champaign-Urbana, 1956; MS, Columbia U., 1960; MPA, NYU, 1971. Reporter, writer, editor City News Bur., Chgo., 1956-57, UPI, Chgo., 1957-59; editor, writer, field producer NBC News, NYC and Chgo., 1959-60; with ABC News, 1960-79; mgr. ABC News (TV network syndication), 1973-79; mng. dir. Ind. TV News Assn., NYC, 1979-81; producer, exec. NBC News, NYC, 1982-85, 87; assoc. Rowan & Blewitt, Inc./Exec. TV Workshop, NYC, 1985-95; pres. NovaNews Comm. Cons., NYC, 1994—. On-air talent Money Call News, 1988; freelance TV producer, cable and pub. TV series, 1985—; adj. instr. LIU, 1967-69, NYU, 1969-70; asst. adj. prof. Lehman Coll., 1970-71; adj. prof., producer interactive televised course CUNY, 1972-75 Mem. Silurians, Broadcast Pioneers, Radio TV News Dirs. Assn., Alumni Assn. Columbia Grad. Sch. Journalism (pres. 1979), Deadline Club N.Y.C. (pres. 1969), Deadline Club Found. (pres. 1999—), Soc. Profl. Journalists-Sigma Delta Chi (pres. 1981-82). Office: 160 West End Ave Apt 29D New York NY 10023-5616 also: 392 Moonstone Beach Rd Wakefield RI 02879-5102 Home Phone: 212-787-6908; Office Phone: 212-787-6908. Personal E-mail: evevideo@earthlink.net.

NOVOGRATZ, MICHAEL E., hedge fund manager; b. Nov. 26, 1964; m. Dora Caceres; 4 children. BA, Princeton U., NJ. Various positions Goldman Sachs, including head fixed income, currencies & commodities risk Asia, 1992—99, ptnr. NYC, 1998—2002, pres. L.Am.; pres., prin., head global funds Fortress Investment Group LLC, 2002—, bd. dirs., 2006—. Bd. dirs. Sch. for Strings, Acumen Fund; chmn. bd. dirs. Beat the Streets Wrestling Inc.; bd. trustees NYU Med. Ctr. Helicopter pilot US Army, NJ Nat. Guard. Named to 'The World's Billionaires' list, Forbes mag. Office: Fortress Investment Group LLC 1345 Ave Americas New York NY 10105 Office Phone: 212-798-6100.*

NOVOGROD, NANCY GERSTEIN, editor; b. NYC, Jan. 30, 1949; d. Max and Hilda (Kirschbaum) Gerstein; m. John Campner Novogrod, Nov. 7, 1976; children: James Campner, Caroline Anne. AB, Mt. Holyoke Coll., 1971. Sec. fiction dept. The New Yorker, NYC, 1971-73, reader, 1973-76; asst. editor Clarkson Potter/Pubs., NYC, 1977-78, assoc. editor, 1978-80, editor, 1980-83, sr. editor, 1984-86, exec. editor, 1987; sr. editor HG (House & Garden mag.), NYC, 1987-88, editor-in-chief, 1988-93, Travel + Leisure, NYC, 1993—; editl. dir. Am. Express Pub., NYC, 2000—. Bd. dirs. Am. Soc. Mag. Editors, 2000—07. Bd. dirs. NY Bot. Garden, 1991—2008; exec. com., bd. dirs. Mount Holyoke Coll., 1992—97; adv. bd. Breast Cancer Rsch. Found., 1993—2009; co-chair, bd. dirs. NY Ctr. Children, NYC, 2003. Office: Travel + Leisure 1120 Avenue of the Americas New York NY 10036-6700 Personal E-mail: nancy.g.novogrod@aexp.com.

NOVOGRODER, MICHAEL, pediatric endocrinologist; b. NYC, Dec. 22, 1943; MD, SUNY Health Sci. Ctr., Coll. Medicine, Syracuse, 1969. Cert. in pediat. 1974, in pediatric endocrinology 1980. Internship in pediat. Bronx Mcpl. Hosp. Ctr., NY, 1969—70, residency in pediat., 1970—72, residency in pediatric endocrinology, 1972—73; fellowship NY Presbyn. Hosp. Weill Cornell Med. Ctr., NYC, 1975—76; staff physician Columbia Presbyn. Med. Ctr., NYC; clin. prof. pediat. Morgan Stanley Children's Hosp. NY Presbyn. Babies & Children's Hosp., NYC; endocrinologist Met. Pediat. Group, Teaneck, NJ. Contbr. articles to profl. jours. Fellow: Am. Acad. Pediat., Endocrine Soc., Lawson Wilkins Pediatric Endocrine Soc. Office: Met Pediat Group 704 Palisade Ave Teaneck NJ 07666 Office Phone: 201-836-4301. Office Fax: 201-836-5110.

NOVOTNY, DAVID JOSEPH, lawyer; b. Melrose Park, Ill., Oct. 3, 1953; s. Joseph F. and Dorothy E. (Erickson) N.; m. Gladys Ruth Korynecky, May 1, 1982. BSc, DePaul U., 1975, JD, 1978. Bar: Ill. 1978, U.S. Dist. Ct. (no. dist.) Ill. 1978, U.S. Ct. Appeals (7th cir.) 1985, U.S. Dist. Ct. (no. dist.), Ind. 1995, U.S. Dist. Ct. (cen. dist.) Ill. 1999. Law clk. to justice Ill. Appellate Ct., Chgo., 1978-80; assoc. Rooks, Pitts & Poust, Chgo., 1980-83, Peterson, Ross, Schloerb & Seidel (now Peterson & Ross), Chgo., 1983-88, ptnr., 1988—. Arbitrator Am. Arbitration Assn., 1987—, Cir. Ct. Cook County Ct.-Annexed Arbitration, 1990—. Exec. editor DePaul Law Rev., 1978. Mem. ABA, Ill. State Bar Assn., 7th Cir. Bar Assn., Soc. Trial Lawyers, Asia-Pacific Lawyers Assn., Lawyer-Pilots Bar Assn., Legal Club Chgo., Def. Rsch. Inst. Office: Peterson Ross 200 E Randolph St Ste 7200 Chicago IL 60601-7719

NOVOTNY, DONALD WAYNE, electrical engineer, educator; b. Chgo., Dec. 15, 1934; s. Adolph and Margaret Novotny; m. Louise J. Eenigenburg, June 26, 1954; children: Donna Jo Kopp, Cynthia Mason. BEE, Ill. Inst. Tech., 1956, MS, 1957; PhD, U. Wis., 1961. Registered profl. engr., Wis. Instr. Ill. Inst. Tech., 1957-58; mem. faculty U. Wis., Madison, 1958—, prof. elec. engring., 1969-96, Grainger prof. power electronics, 1990—96, prof. emeritus, 1996—, chmn. dept. elec. and computer engring., 1976-80. Vis. prof. Mont. State U., 1966, Eindhoven (The Netherlands) Tech. U., 1974, Tech. U. Louvain, Belgium, 1986; Fulbright lectr. Tech. U. Ghent, Belgium, 1981; diw. Wis. Elec. Machines and Power Electronics Consortium, 1981—96; assoc. dir. Univ.-Industry Rsch. Program, 1982—93; chmn. elec. engring. program Nat. Technol. U., 1989—2003; cons. to industry. Author: Introductory Electromechanics, 1965, Vector Control and Dynamics of AC Drives, 1996; assoc. editor: Electric Machines and Power Systems, 1976—99; contbr. scientific papers to profl. jours. Recipient Outstanding Paper award, Engring. Inst. Can., 1966, Outstanding Achievement award, IEEE-IAS, 1998; named Disting. Lectr., 1995; grantee, numerous industries and govt. agys.; fellow, GE, 1956, Ford Found., 1960. Fellow: IEEE (prize paper award 1983, 1984, 1986, 1987, 1990, 1991, 1993, 1994, 3d Millennium medal 2000, Nikola Tesla award 2009); mem.: Am. Soc. Engring. Edn., Rotary, Sigma Xi, Eta Kappa Nu, Tau Beta Pi. Congregationalist. Home: 1421 E Skyline Dr Madison WI 53705-1132 Office: U Wis Dept Elec and Computer Engring 1415 Engineering Dr Madison WI 53706-1607 Office Phone: 608-262-6926. Business E-Mail: novotny@engr.wisc.edu.

NOVOTNY, F. DOUGLAS, lawyer; b. Mineola, NY, Mar. 10, 1952; s. Frank Joseph and Eleanor Evans (Rose) N.; m. Norma R. Federici, Sept. 7, 1991; children: Nicholas, Christina, Alexander. BA cum laude, SUNY, Albany, 1974; postgrad., NYU, Hofstra U., Hempstead, NY, C.W. Post U.; JD cum laude, Albany Law Sch., 1979. Bar: NY 1980, US Dist. Ct. (no. dist.) NY 1980. Confidential law asst. Appellate Divsn. 3d Dept., Albany, 1979-80; ptnr. DeGraff, Foy, Conway, Holt-Harris & Mealey, Albany, 1980-91; pvt. practice Saratoga, NY, 1991-93; mng. atty. Law Offices of F. Douglas Novotny, 1993—, Am. Internat. Group, Inc.,

1993—2006; ptnr. Wilson, Elser, Moskowitz, Edelman & Dicker, 2006—. Mem. Albany County Arbitration Panel, 1984—. Editor Albany Law Rev., 1978-79; contbr. articles to profl. jours. Mem. ATLA, Justinian Soc., Assn. Trial Lawyers Am., Capital Dist. Trial Lawyers Assn. Presbyterian. Home: 27 Mallard Lndg S Waterford NY 12188-1037 Office: 677 Broadway Albany NY 12207 Office Phone: 518-449-8893. Business E-Mail: douglas.novotny@wilsonelser.com.

NOVOTNY, ROGER, state banking agency administrator; s. A. M. and Ida Novotny; m. Nila DeWald; 2 children. Dir. motor fuel tax divsn. SD Dept. Revenue, 1972—76, dir. sales tax divsn., 1976—93, dir. bus. tax divsn., 1993—95; govt. rels. mgr. Aman Collection Svc., Aberdeen, SD, 1995, v.p. contract collections, 1998—2001, sr. v.p., COO; dir. divsn. banking SD Dept. Revenue & Regulation, 2004—. Office: SD Divsn Banking 217 1/2 W Missouri Ave Pierre SD 57501 Office Phone: 605-773-3421. Office Fax: 605-773-5367. E-mail: roger.novotny@state.sd.us.*

NOVOTNY, THOMAS EDWARD, healthcare educator, consultant; b. Omaha, May 3, 1947; s. Anton Joseph and Anne Prazan Novotny; m. Andrea Borges Sereno, July 9, 2004. BS, U. Nebr., Lincoln, 1969; MD, U. Nebr. Med. Ctr., Omaha, 1973; MPH, Johns Hopkins Bloomberg Sch. Pub. Health, Balt., 1991. Diplomate Calif., 1974. Adm. US Pub. Health Svc., Washington, 1979—2002; family physician Nat. Health Svc. Corps, Guerneville, Calif., 1979—84; med. epidemiologist Ctr. Disease Control Prevention, Atlanta, 1984—91; asst. dean, pub. health practice U. Calif., Berkeley, Calif., 1992—97, prof., epidemiology and biostatistics San Francisco, 2002—08; cdc liaison World Bank, Washington, 1997—99, cons., 2002—; dep. asst. sec. internat. refugee health US HHS, Washington, 1999—2002. Author: (book) Global Health Diplomacy; contbr. articles to med. & sci. jours. Decorated Surgeon Gens. Exemplary Svc. medal US Pub. Health Svc. Fellow: Am. Coll. Preventive Medicine. Liberal. Avocations: saxophone, sailing, kayaking, scuba diving, travel. Office: San Diego State Univ Hardy Tower 119 5500 Campanile Dr San Diego CA 92182-4162 Office Fax: 619-594-6112. Business E-Mail: tnovotny@mail.sdsu.edu.

NOVOTOROV, ANDREW, educator; b. Nizhniy Novgorod, Russian Fedn., Mar. 18, 1960; married. Doctoral, Iowa State U., Ames, 2001. Asst. prof. Dickinson State U., ND, 2003—06, Ft. Hays State U., Kans., 2006—. Adj. faculty William Penn U., West Des Moines, Iowa, 2001—03. Home: 106W 38th St Hays KS 67601 Office: Fort Hays State Univ 509 S Campus Dr Hays KS 67601 Business E-Mail: avnovotorov@fhsu.edu.

NOWACKI, JAMES NELSON, lawyer; b. Columbus, Ohio, Sept. 12, 1947; s. Louis James and Betty Jane (Nelson) N.; m. Catherine Ann Holden, Aug. 1, 1970; children: Carrie, Anastasia, Emma. AB, Princeton U., 1969; JD, Yale U., 1973. Bar: Ill. 1973, N.Y. 1982, U.S. dist. Ct. (no. dist.) Ill. 1973, U.S. Ct. Appeals (7th cir.) 1978, U.S. Ct. Appeals (6th cir.) 1987, U.S. Supreme Ct. 1992. Assoc. Isham, Lincoln & Beale, Chgo., 1976-79; ptnr. Kirkland & Ellis, Chgo., 1980—. Mem. Winnetka Sch. Bd. Dist. 36, Ill. 1983-91, bd. pres., 1989-91; mem. New Trier Sch. Bd., 1997-99, pres., 1997-98. Harlan Fiske Stone prize Yale U., 1972. Mem. ABA (forum com. on constrn. industry, litigation sect.), Skokie Country Club. Home: 708 Prospect Ave Winnetka IL 60093-2320 Office: James Nelson Nowacki Kirkland & Ellis LLP 300 N Lasalle St Chicago IL 60654 Office Phone: 312-861-2174. Business E-Mail: jnowacki@kirkland.com.

NOWAK, JERRY (GERALD C. NOWAK), music educator, Musician Writer Conductor; b. Detroit, Mich., Apr. 16, 1936; s. John and Lucille Nowak; m. Judith C. Christian, Sept. 30, 1937; children: Amy Elizabeth DeGrgorio, Christopher Gerald. BS in Music Edn., Coll. of N.J., 1954—58, MA, 1968. Music tchr. Hunterdon Ctrl. Regional H.S., Flemington, NJ, 1958—69; prof. emeritus Bucks County C.C., Newtown, Pa., 1969—2005. Co-author: Conducting Music, Not the Musicians, 2002, The Art of Expressive Playing, 2004, musician (founding mem.) Phila. Saxophone Quartet, N.J Saxophone Quartet; musician: (composer, arranger) more than 1000 pub. compositions and arrangements for instrumental and vocal ensembles; condr.: rec. sessions in N.Y.C., Phila., Washington and London. Pres. Raritan Twp. Athletic Assn., Flemington, NJ, 1980—82. Mem.: ASCAP. Home: 42 Madison Ave Flemington NJ 08822 Office Phone: 908-782-5128. Personal E-mail: jerrynowak@comcast.net.

NOWAK, JERZY, educational association administrator, horticulture professor, director; m. Jocelyne Couture-Nowak (dec.); children: Francine Dulong, Sylvie Couture-Nowak. MSc in Plant Biochemistry, Agrl.-Tech. U., Olsztyn, Poland, 1968, PhD in Plant Physiology & Biochemistry, 1973, Dr. Habil in Biochemistry, 1980. Jr. rsch. asst. Inst. Potato Rsch., Gdansk, Poland, 1968—69, rsch. asst., 1971—73; postdoctoral fellow molecular biology Max-Planck Soc., Goettingen, Germany, 1974—75; postdoctoral fellow enzyme tech. Alex v. Humboldt Found., Braunschweig, Germany, 1977—78; adj. prof. Agrl.-Tech. U., Olsztyn, Poland, 1980; Alex v. Humboldt rsch. fellow GBF, Braunschweig, Germany, 1980—83; vis. sr. lectr. U. Lagos, Nigeria, 1980—82; vis. rsch. sci. U. Alberta, Edmonton, Alta., Canada, 1983—84; assoc. prof. Nova Scotia Agrl. Coll., Truro, NS, Canada, 1984—88, prof. plant sci., 1988—2000, dept. head plant sci., 1997—2000; hon. rsch. fellow Biology Dept. Dalhousie U., Halifax, NS, Canada, 1985—91, adj. prof., 1991—2001; prof. horticulture Va. Tech. U., Blacksburg, 2000—, dept. head horticulture, Coll. Agrl. and Life Scis., 2000—08, founding dir. Ctr. for Peace Studies and Violence Prevention, 2008—; founder Inst. Sustainable and Renewable Resources, Danville, Va., 2001—05, co-dir., 2003—05; interim dir. rsch., tech. devel. and transfer Inst. Advanced Learning and Rsch., Danville, Va., 2005. Contbr. articles to profl. jours. Office: Va Tech U 301 Saunders Hall Blacksburg VA 24061 Office Phone: 540-231-9836. E-mail: jenowak@vt.edu.

NOWAK, JOHN E., law educator; b. Chgo., Jan. 2, 1947; s. George Edward and Evelyn (Bucci) N.; m. Judith Johnson, June 1, 1968; children: John Edwin, Jeffrey Edward. AB, Marquette U., 1968; JD, U. Ill., 1971. Law clk. Supreme Ct. of Ill., Chgo., 1971-72; asst. prof. U. Ill., Urbana, 1972-75, assoc. prof., 1975-87, law prof., 1978—2008, grad. coll. faculty, 1982—2008, Baum prof. Law, 1993—2008. Prof. constl. law Loyola U., Chgo., 2008—, simon chair constl. law, 2008—; chmn. Constl. Law Sch. Sect.; faculty rep. Big Ten Intercollegiate Conf., 1981—91; vis. prof. law U. Mich., Ann Arbor, 1985; Lee disting. vis. prof. Coll. William and Mary, 1993; Williams vis. prof. law U. Richmond, 2003. Co-author: Treatise on Constitutional Law 4th edit., 2008, supplement, 2009; editor: Story's Commentaries on the Constitution, 1987, Constitutional Law, 8th edit. 2009, Principles of Constitutional Law, 2004, 3d edit., 2007. Scholar-in-Residence, U. of Ariz., Tucson, 1985, 87. Mem. Assn. of Am. Law Schs. (chmn. constl. law sect., accreditation com.), Nat. Collegiate Athletic Assn. (mem. infractions com. 1987-91), Am. Law Inst., Am. Bar Assn., Ill. Bar Assn., Order of the Coif (Triennial Book award com.). Roman Catholic. Home: 1701 Mayfair Rd Champaign IL 61821-5522

NOWAK (JAROSZ), LINDA THERESE, special education educator, consultant; b. Buffalo, Nov. 25, 1954; d. Joseph John Sr. and Theresa E. Jarosz; m. Raymond John Nowak, Sr., June 18, 1982; 1 child, Raymond John Jr. BS in Edn., Buffalo State Coll., 1988, MEd, 1994, Niagara U., NYC, 1998. Cert. sch. dist. adminstr. N.Y., sch. adminstrn. and supervision N.Y., spl. edn. tchr. N.Y., elem. edn. tchr. N.Y. Spl. edn. cons. tchr. West St. Elem. Sch. Niagara Wheatfield Cen. Sch. Dist., Sanborn, NY, 1989—, prin. summer sch., 1999—2000, head tchr. summer sch., 2001—04. Adj. prof. edn. Niagara U., 2004—08. Fundraiser, supporter United Spinal Assn., Milford, NH, 2003—05; vol. Am. Cancer Soc., Amherst, NY, 2001—03; bd. dirs., mem. devel. com. Niagara Frontier Ctr. for Ind. Living, Niagara Falls, 2002—05., Orleans/Niagara Tchr. Ctr. grantee, 2002—04. Mem.: ASCD (assoc.), Am. Fedn. Tchrs., NY State United Tchrs., Coun. for Exceptional Children, Delta Kappa Gamma (assoc.). Democrat. Roman Catholic. Avocation: collecting antiques. Home: 5761 Dunnigan Rd Lockport NY 14094 Office: West St Elem Sch 5700 West St Sanborn NY 14132 Personal E-mail: ltnowak82@verizon.net. Business E-Mail: lnowak@nwcsd.org.

NOWAK, PATRICIA CARI, lawyer; b. Chgo., May 29, 1956; d. Joseph A. and Elaine R. Cari; m. Robert W. Nowak, Aug. 9, 1985. BSN, Loyola U., Chgo., 1978, JD, 1986; MSN, Boston Coll., Chestnut Hill, Mass., 1980; postgrad., U. Notre Dame, South Bend, Ind., 1983—84. Bar: Ill. 1986, U.S. Dist. Ct. (no. dist.) Ill. 1986. Staff nurse Rush Presbyn. St. Lukes Med. Ctr., Chgo., 1978—79; nursing instr. Christ Hosp., Oaklawn, Ill., 1980—81; nurse mgr., clin. supr. Loyola U. Med. Ctr., Maywood, Ill., 1981—83; assoc. Rooks Pitts Chgo., 1986—92, ptnr., 1993—2003, Dykema, Chgo., 2003—. Lector, eucharistic minister St. Paul of Cross Ch., Park Ridge, Ill., 2002—; v.p. Apostolate Women, 2008—. Mem.: ABA, ARDC (com. mem. 2008—), Chgo. Bar Assn. (chair investigations jud. evaluation com. 2002), Ill. Bar Assn. Democrat. Roman Catholic. Avocations: skiing, sailing, hiking. Home: 1210 Beau Dr Park Ridge IL 60068 Office: Dykema 10 S Wacker Dr Ste 2300 Chicago IL 60606 Office Phone: 312-627-2141, 312-876-1155. Business E-Mail: pnowak@dykema.com.

NOWAK-FABRYKOWSKI, KRYSTYNA TERESA, early childhood education educator; m. Jacek Wiktor Fabrykowski; children: Marta Chrisitna, Olga Victoria. PhD, U. Warsaw, Poland, 1996; MEd, U. Lodz, Poland. Asst. prof. Mt. Union Coll., Alliance, Ohio, 1998—2002, John Carroll U., Univ. Heights, Ohio, 2002—07; assoc. prof. early childhood edn. Coastal Carolina U. Spadoni Coll. Edn.Conway, SC, 2007—. Mem.: Am. Ednl. Rsch. Assn. Office: Ctrl Mich Univ Dept Tchr Edn & Profl Devel Mount Pleasant MI 48859 Office Fax: 989-774-3152. Business E-Mail: nowaklk@cmich.edu.

NOWAKOWSKI, MICHAEL, Councilman; m. Delia Nowakowski; children: Victor, Michael Ray, Irene, Carlos Raul, Raymond Casmir. BA in Religious Studies, Ariz. State U. Gen. mgr. non-profit radio station; former asst. dir. Cath. Diocese Phoenix Office of Youth and Young Adult Ministry; councilman, Dist. 7 Phoenix City Coun. Chmn. Census Com.; mem. Downtown & Aviation, Housing & Neighborhoods Coms. Founding mem. Mayor's Anti-Graffiti Task Force; mem. City of Phoenix Census, 2000, Police Chief Adv. Bd.; co-chmn. City of Phoenix Hist. Bond Com., 2006; chmn. Santa Rosa Neighborhood Coun.; supt. adv. bd. Phoenix Union High Sch. Office: 200 W Washington St 11th Fl Phoenix AZ 85003 Office Phone: 602-262-7492. Office Fax: 602-534-4816. Business E-Mail: council.district.7@phoenix.gov.*

NOWAKOWSKI, RICHARD STANLEY, medical educator, director; b. Milw., Oct. 21, 1950; s. Charles Edward and Felice Rose Nowakowski; m. Nancy Lynn Hayes, Aug. 18, 1971; 1 child, Alexandra Catherine. BA, U. Wis., Madison, 1971; PhD, Harvard U., Cambridge, Mass., 1976. Grad. student Harvard U.; rsch. asst. Wis. Regional Primate Rsch. Ctr., Madison, 1969—71; postdoc. fellow Duke U., Durham, NC, 1976—79; wissenschaftlicher asst. Max Planck Inst. Biophysical Chemistry, Goettingen, Germany, 1979—81; asst. prof. Med. Ctr., U. Miss., Jackson, 1981—85; assoc. mem. Keck Ctr. Collaborative Neurosci., Rutgers U., Piscataway, 2005—; prof. U. Medicine and Dentistry NJ, Robert Wood Johnson Med. Sch., Piscataway, 1985—, dir., postdoc. career devel. program, 2007—. Mem. Nat. Postdoctoral Assn., Washington, 2009—. Mem.: IBANGS, Nat. Postdoc. Assn., Complex Trait Consortium, Soc. Neurosci. Office: Univ Medicine and Dentistry NJ Robert Wood Johnson Med Sch 675 Hoes Ln Piscataway NJ 08854 Business E-Mail: rsn@umdnj.edu.

NOWE, RONALD JOHN, state legislator, small business owner; b. Gloucester, Mass., Feb. 7, 1946; children: Ronald Jr., Miguel. Student, Hesser Coll., 1976. Owner, mgr. Now Ins. Agy., Epping, N.H., agy. mgr.; propr., mgr. Kamper Kampania Kampground, 3d Street Grocery; mgr., propr. Oak Grove Golfing; mem. N.H. Ho. of Reps. Mem., chmn. wildlife and marine resources com., com. whip, legis. adminstrn. chmn., chmn. sheriff com., mem. long range planning com. Mem. Pub. Water Access Adv. Bd.; vice chair Epping Planning Bd. Mem. DAV (jr. vice. comdr. 1983-94), VFW, Am. Legion, Masons. Republican. Home: PO Box 327 Epping NH 03042 Office: Legis Office Bldg Rm 308 Concord NH 03301

NOWEIR, MADBULI HAMED, chemical engineer, educator; b. Menuf, Menufia, Egypt, Dec. 4, 1934; s. Hamed Ali and Nageya Ahmad (Abdel-Fattah) Noweir; m. Safaa Abdel-Hameed Sharouda, Mar. 31, 1960; children: Hanan, Ashraf, Ahmad. BSChemE, U. Alexandria, Egypt, 1955, MSc in Hygiene, 1959; DSc in Indsl. Hygiene, U. Pitts., 1964; postgrad., U. Cin., 1967-69. Factory insp., Cairo, 1955-57; instr. U. Alexandria, 1957-64, from asst. to assoc. prof. Inst. Pub. Health, 1964-74, prof. indsl. hygiene and safety, 1974-89, founder, dir. NIOSH-HIPH Rsch. Ctr., 1979-89; prof. Coll. Engring. King Abdul Aziz U., Jeddah, Saudi Arabia, 1989—. Cons. WHO, 1970—, temp. advisor, 1973—; Egyptian rep. numerous confs. and meetings; mem. permanent com. and internat. conf. Occ.H., 1970—, WHO Occupl. Health Experts Panel, Geneva, Alexandria, 1971—, Permanent Coun. Environment, Egypt, 1983—. Author: 2 books; contbr. articles to profl. jours. Founder, chmn. Islam Cultural and Sci. Soc., Alexandria, 1982—89. Recipient cup of Achievement, NIOSH, 1974, Kuwait Sci. Achievement award, Kuwait Found. Advancement Sci., 1983; grantee, NIOSH, EPA, AID, 1969—89, others. Mem.: Syndicate Engrs. Egypt, Am. Conf. Govt. Indsl. Hygienists, Am. Indsl. Hygiene Assn. (Yant Meml. award 1979). Muslim. Avocations: reading, music, travel, gymnastics. Home: 1 Maksoud Pasha St Somouha Alexandria Egypt Office Phone: 0966-2-6952252. Personal E-mail: madbuli@yahoo.com.

NOWEL, ANDREW F., academic administrator; s. Bernard and Marjorie Nowel; m. Melissa Hand Nowel, Oct. 4, 1997. MS in Economics, NC State U., Raleigh, 1986; BS in Bus., U. NC, Wilmington, 1984. Sr. academic advisor, coord. curriculum Coll. Mgmt., NC State U., 1992—.

NOWELL, LINDA GAIL, not-for-profit executive; b. Ft. Worth, Apr. 24, 1949; d. Jesse Wayne and Bennie Dale (Flint) Stallings. BA in English, U. North Tex., 1970. Cert. secondary edn. tchr. Tex. Tchr. pub. sch., 1970—77; ind. sales rep. Jostens Printing & Pub. Div., Owatona, Minn., 1980—84; v.p. Nowell Equipment Co., Cranfils Gap, Tex., 1984—89; edn. coord. Tex. Farm Bur., Waco, Tex., 1987—90; account exec. MAC Printing, Las Vegas, Nev., 1991—94; mgr. frontier health outreach program Nev. Rural Health Ctrs., Inc., 1994—97; state coord. Nev. 5-A-Day Coalition, 1995—96; exec. dir. No To Abuse, Pahrump, Nev., 1999—2005; v.p. cmty. devel. United Way So. Nev., Las Vegas, 2005—07; coord., programs & svc. Nat. MS Soc., 2009—. Active Landmark Edn., Inc. Mem.: NAFE. Home Phone: 702-880-9696. Personal E-mail: graymare@cox.net.

NOWELL, PETER CAREY, pathologist, educator; b. Phila., Feb. 8, 1928; s. Foster and Margaret (Matlack) Nowell; m. Helen Worst, Sept. 9, 1950; children: Sharon, Timothy, Karen, Kristin, Michael. BA, Wesleyan U., Middletown, Conn., 1948; MD, U. Pa., 1952. Intern Phila. Gen. Hosp., 1952—53; resident pathology Presbyn. Hosp., Phila., 1953—54; med. tchg., rsch. specializing in cancer Phila., 1956—; from instr. to prof. pathology Sch. Medicine U. Pa., 1956—, chmn. dept. pathology, 1967—73, dir., Cancer Ctr., 1973—75. Lt. M.C. USNR, 1954—56. Recipient Rsch. Career award, USPHS, 1964—67, Parke-Davis award, 1965, Lindback Disting. Tchg. award, 1967, Passano award, 1984, Rous-Whipple award, Am. Assn. Pathology, 1986, de Villers award, Leukemia Soc. Am., 1987, Mott prize, GM Cancer Rsch. Found., 1989, 3M award, FASEB, 1993, Lasker-DeBakey Clin. Med. Rsch. award, Lasker Found., 1998. Mem.: Am. Acad. Arts & Sciences. Home: 345 Mount Alverno Rd Media PA 19063-5313 Office: U Pa Sch Medicine Dept Pathology & Lab Medicine Philadelphia PA 19104-6082 Office Phone: 215-898-8066. Business E-Mail: nowell@mail.med.upenn.edu.

NOWICK, ARTHUR STANLEY, metallurgy and materials science educator; b. NYC, Aug. 29, 1923; s. Hyman and Clara (Sperling) N.; m. Joan Franzblau, Oct. 30, 1949; children: Jonathan, Steven, Alan, James. AB, Bklyn. Coll., 1943; A.M., Columbia U., 1948, PhD, 1950. Physicist NACA, Cleve., 1944-46; instr. U. Chgo., 1949-51; asst. prof., then assoc. prof. metallurgy Yale U., 1951-57; mgr. metallurgy research IBM Corp Research Center, Yorktown Heights, NY, 1957-66; prof. metallurgy Columbia U., 1966-90, Henry Marion Howe prof. metallurgy and materials sci., 1990-95, prof. emeritus, 1996—. Adj. prof. chem. engring. and materials sci. dept. U. Calif., Irvine, 2001; Frank Golick lectr. U. Mo., 1970; vis. prof. Technion, Haifa, Israel, 1973; co-chmn. Internat. Conf. Internal Friction, 1961, 69; cons. in field. Author: Crystal Properties Via Group Theory, 1995; co-author: Anelastic Relaxation in Crystalline Solids, 1972; co-editor: Diffusion in Solids, 1975, Diffusion in Crystalline Solids, 1984; contbr. articles to profl. jours. Named David Turnbull lecturer Materials Rsch. Soc., 1994; gold medalist Internat. Conf. Internal Friction, 1989. Fellow AIME, Am. Phys. Soc.; mem. Materials Rsch. Soc. (Turnbull lectr. 1994), Sigma Xi (pres. Kappa chpt. 1983-85). Home: 24 Hillsdale Dr Newport Beach CA 92660-4234 Office: U Calif Irvine 916 Engineering Tower Irvine CA 92697-2575 Business E-Mail: anowick@uci.edu.

NOWICKI, KENNETH ROBERT, physics professor; b. Detroit, Dec. 17, 1963; s. Robert Anthony and Rita Mae Nowicki; m. Melinda Kaye Patterson, Aug. 9, 1986; children: Krystin Michelle, Kayla Danielle, Kensley Brielle. MS, U. Miss., Oxford, 1999. Sci. instr. & coach Pontotoc HS, Pontotoc, Miss., 1987—99; physics instr. Itawamba CC, Fulton, 1999—. Chmn. deacons West Heights Bapt. Ch., Pontotoc, 2007—08. Named Coach of Yr., MHSAA, 1998—99, Meritorous Tchr. of Yr., Phi Delta Kappa & ICC, 1997, 2003. Home: PO Box 493 Pontotoc MS 38863 Office: Itawamba CC 602 West Hill St Fulton MS 38843 Business E-Mail: krnowicki@iccms.edu.

NOWICKI, STACY A., library director; b. Ill. m. Anders J Dahlberg, Oct. 13, 2002. BA, Oberlin Coll., Ohio, 1995; MusM, Northwestern U., Evanston, Ill., 1997; MA in Libr. and Info. Sci., Dominican U., River Forest, Ill., 1997; PhD, Nova Southeastern U., Fort Lauderdale, Fla., 2002. Dir. instrnl. tech. Calumet Coll. St. Joseph, Whiting, Ind., 1997—2000; libr. dir. Kalamazoo Coll., 2006—. Chair Mich. Libr. Assn. Info. Literacy Roundtable, Lansing, 2006—07. Office: Kalamazoo Coll 1200 Academy St Kalamazoo MI 49006

NOWIK, JOHN DAVID, musician, educator; b. Allentown, Pa., Aug. 26, 1960; s. Stanley John and Helen Mary Nowik; m. Martha Elizabeth Huddleston, Jan. 9, 1982; children: Elizabeth J., Anna M., Krystyna H., Sofia M., Katerina T., Lucia F., Johanna C., Alexander S., Monica R., Clare Magdalena. MusB, Westminster Choir Coll., 1982; MusM, Emory U., 1996. Organist, choir dir. St. Joseph the Worker Ch., Fallsington, Pa., 1980—83; instr., organist St. Joseph's Prep. Sem., Princeton, NJ, 1981—85; cathedral organist, dir. music Cathedral St. Francis of Assisi, Metuchen, NJ, 1983—2001; univ. organist Seton Hall U., South Orange, NJ, 1996—; dir. music, organist Immaculate Conception Sem., South Orange, NJ, 1996—. Dir. concerts, arts Cathedral Concert Series, Metuchen, NJ, 1984—2001; assoc. condr. Brunswick Symphony Orch., New Brunswick, NJ, 1985—2001. Editor (contributor) hymnal. Recipient Excellence in Achievement award, Middlesex County Cultural and Heritage Commn., 1993; scholar, Emory U., 1995—96. Mem.: Conf. Roman Cath. Cathedral Musicians, Am. Guild Organists (dean 1993—95). Roman Catholic. Avocations: composing, music, bicycling, stamp collecting/philately. Office: Seton Hall U 400 South Orange Ave South Orange NJ 07079

NOWITZKI, DIRK WERNER, professional basketball player; b. Würzburg, West Germany, June 19, 1978; s. Joerg and Helen Nowitzki. Forward Dallas Mavericks, 1998—. Served in German Army, 1997—98. Named NBA MVP, 2007; named to All-NBA Second Team, 2002, 2003, 2008, All-NBA First Team, 2005—07, 2009, Western Conf. All-Star Team, NBA, 2002—09. Achievements include winning All-Star 3-point Contest, 2006. Avocations: reading, saxophone. Mailing: Dallas Mavericks 2500 Victory Ave Dallas TX 75219*

NOWLAND, JAMES FERRELL, lawyer; b. Talladega, Ala., Dec. 7, 1942; s. James Franklin and Wilma Delene (Dean) N.; m. Faye Roberts, Aug. 28, 1964; children: Angela Roschelle, James Ferrell II. BS, Jacksonville State U., Ala., 1967; BS in Med. Technology, U. Ark., 1972; grad., U. Ark. Med. Ctr., 1974; JD, Oglethorpe U., 1983. Bar: Ga. 1984, U.S. Dist. Ct. (no. dist.) Ga. 1984, U.S. Ct. Appeals (11th cir.) 1984, U.S. Supreme Ct. 1988. Chemist U.S. Army C.E., Marietta, Ga., 1972-97; pvt. practice Cobb County, Ga., 1984—. Capt. USAF, 1967-72. Mem. ABA, Ga. Bar Assn., Cobb County Bar Assn. Home: 50 Mt Calvary Rd Marietta GA 30064-1918 Office: PO Box 1847 Marietta GA 30061-1847 Office Phone: 770-425-0601. Personal E-mail: jim1nowland@msn.com.

NOYES, RICHARD HALL, bookseller; b. Evanston, Ill., Feb. 12, 1930; s. George Frederick and Dorothy (Hall) N.; m. Judith Claire Mitchell, Oct. 10, 1953; children— Catherine, Stephanie, Matthew. BA, Wesleyan U., Middletown, Conn., 1952. Tng. program, elementary-high sch. salesman Rand McNally & Co., Colo., Utah, Idaho, Wyo., 1955-59; founder, owner, mgr. The Chinook Bookshop, Colorado Springs, Colo., 1959—. Contbr. to A Manual on Bookselling, 1974, The Business of Book Publishing, 1984; contbr. articles to newspapers and trade jours.

Co-chmn. Colo. Media Coalition, 1974—; bd. dirs. Colorado Springs Fine Arts Ctr., 1977-81, Citizens Goals for Colorado Springs, 1976-88; trustee Fountain Valley Sch., 1979-81; vice chmn. Colorado Springs Charter Rev. Commn., 1991-92; mem. adv. com. U. Colo., Colorado Springs, 1997—, Downtown Partnership, 1998—. Served with AUS, 1952-54. Recipient Intellectual Freedom award Mountain Plains Librs. Assn., 1977, Disting. Svc. award U. Colo., 1980, Recognition award Pikes Peak Arts Coun., 1989, Charles S. Haslam award, 1990), Entrepreneur of Yr. award U. Colo., 1992, Gordon Saull award for outstanding bookseller Mountains and Plains Booksellers Assn., 1996. Mem. Am. Booksellers Assn. (pres., dir.) Home: 1601 Constellation Dr Colorado Springs CO 80906-1609

NOYES, ROBERT EDWIN, publisher, writer; b. NYC, June 22, 1925; s. Clarence A. and Edith (LaDomus) N.; m. Janet Brown, Mar. 24, 1952 (div. June 1963); children— Keith, Steven, Mark, Geoffrey; m. Mariel Jones, July 24, 1964; children— Rebecca, Robert. BSChemE, Northwestern U., 1945. Chem. engr. Am. Cyanamid Co., Pearl River, NY, 1947; sales exec. Titanium Pigment Corp., NYC, 1948-55; market research mgr. U.S. Indsl. Chem. Co., NYC, 1956-58; sales mgr. atomic energy Curtiss Wright Export, NYC, 1958-60; founder, pres., chmn. bd. Noyes Data Corp., Westwood, NJ, 1960-99; pub. Noyes Press, Noyes Publs., Westwood, 1961-99, Noyes Strategic Pubs., Saddle River, NJ, 1999—2008. Served to lt. (j.g.) USNR, 1945-47. Mem.: AIAA, Am. Inst. Chem. Engrs., Am. Chem. Soc., N.Y. Yacht Club. Episcopalian. Home: 224 W Saddle River Rd Saddle River NJ 07458-2620 Home Phone: 201-327-9489.

NOYMER, ANDREW, medical educator, researcher; AB, U. Harvard, Cambridge, Mass., 1995; MSc, London Sch. Hygiene & Tropical Medicine, 1996; PhD, U. Calif., Berkeley, 2006. Asst. prof. U. Calif., Irvine, 2006—; rsch. scientist IIASA, Laxenburg, Austria, 2006—. Contbr. articles to profl. jours. Office: Univ Calif 3151 Social Sci Plz Irvine CA 92697-5100

NOZIK, ARTHUR JACK, research physical chemist; b. Springfield, Mass., Jan. 10, 1936; s. Morris and Lillian (Golden) N.; m. Rhoda Ann Fisher, Sept. 6, 1958; children: Eva Sue, Jane Marla. B Chem. Engring., Cornell U., 1959; MS, Yale U., 1962, PhD in Phys. Chemistry, 1967. Rsch. engr. McDonnell-Douglas Aircraft Co., Santa Monica, Calif., 1958-60; staff engr. Am. Cyanamid Co., Stamford, Conn., 1961-64, staff scientist, 1967-74; group leader Allied-Signal Corp., Morristown, NJ, 1974-78; sr. scientist Nat. Renewable Energy Lab. (formerly Solar Energy Rsch. Inst.), Golden, Colo., 1978—80, br. chief, 1980—85, sr. rsch. fellow, 1985—. Lectr. in field; mem. sci. rev. coms. US Dept. Energy and NSF; disting. lectr. Dept. Energy and Am. Western Univs., Salt Lake City, 1990; prof. adjoint chemistry, U. Colo., Boulder, 1998-. Co-author: Surface Electron Transfer Processes 1994; editor: Photoeffects at Semiconductor-Electrolyte Interfaces, 1981; sr. editor: Jour. Phys. Chemistry, 1993-2005; co-editor: Nanostructured and Photoelectrochemical Systems for Solar Photon Conversion, 2008; mem. editorial bd. Jour. Solar Energy Materials, 1982—, Energy and Environment Science, 2007-; contbr. articles to profl. jours., sci. papers, book chapters; patentee in field. Recipient Outstanding Achievement award Solar Energy Rsch. Inst., 1984, H.M. Hubbard award, 1991, MRI Hubbard award, 1992, Dir.'s award, Nat. Renewable Energy Lab., 1993, Van Morris award Midwest Rsch. Inst., 1985, MRI Chmn.'s award, 2007, Eni award, 2008, Sci. Tech. award, Intergovtl. Renewable Energy Orgn., 2009. Fellow: AAAS, Am. Phys. Soc.; mem: Am. Chem. Soc., Electrochemical Soc. (chmn. energy tech. group 1984-85, Rsch. award, 2002), Materials Rsch. Soc., Sigma Xi. Avocations: hiking, skiing, biking. Office: Nat Renewable Energy Lab 1617 Cole Blvd Golden CO 80401 Office Fax: 303-384-6655.

NRIAGU, JEROME OKON, environmental geochemist; b. Ora-eri Town, Anambra, Nigeria, Oct. 24, 1942; arrived in U.S., 1993; s. Martin and Helena (Anaekwe) N.; children: Chinedu Delbert, Uzoma Vivian, Osita Jide. BSc with honors, U. Ibadan, Nigeria, 1965, DSc, 1992; MS, U. Wis., 1967; PhD, U. Toronto, Ont., 1970. Rsch. scientist Environment Can., Burlington, Ont., 1970-93; prof. environ. chem. sch. of pub. health U. Mich., Ann Arbor, 1993—; dir. environ. health scis. program, 1996-99; rsch. prof. Ctr. for Human Growth and Devel., U. Mich., 1997—. Adj. prof. U. Waterloo, Ont., 1985—96; vis. scientist NOAA, Ann Arbor, 1992; bd. dirs. Ecology Ctr. Mich., Alliance to End Childhood Lead Poisoning, Washington, 1998—. Author: Lead and Lead Poisoning in Antiquity, 1983; editor: (book series) Advances in Environmental Science and Technology, 1982—, Trace Metals in the Environment, 1996—, 29 books on various environ. topics, 1979—, Sci. of the Total Environment, 1983—; mem. editl. bds.: 9 jours.; contbr. articles to profl. jours. Recipient Rigler medal, Can. Soc. Limnologists, 1988; Fulbright sr. fellow, 2002. Fellow: Royal Soc. Can. (Romanowski medal 1999); mem.: AAAS, Am. Pub. Health Assn. Roman Catholic. Avocations: photography, reading (African authors), travel. Office: Univ Michigan Environ/Indsl Health 109 Observatory St Ann Arbor MI 48109-2029

NSIAH, CHRISTIAN, economics professor, consultant; s. Alexander Yaw and Vida Gifty Nsiah. PhD in Economics, Mid. Tenn. State U., Murfreesboro, 2005. Asst. prof. Black Hills State U., Spearfish, SD, 2005—; coord. economics/fin. program Coll. Bus. and Tech., Black Hills State U., Spearfish, SD, 2008. Nat. adv. bd. mem. Economics Praxis Exam, Ednl. Testing Services, Princeton, Nebr., 2008; vis. prof. Mont. Dakota Utilities Co., Fargo, ND, 2007. Contbr. articles to numerous profl.jours. Mem.: Am. Econs. Assn., Acad. Econs. and Fin. Office: Black Hills State Univ 1200 Univ Str Unit 9064 Spearfish SD 57799-9064 Business E-Mail: christiannsiah@bhsu.edu.

NSOULI, TALAL MOUNIR, physician, allergist, immunologist; b. Mexico City, Feb. 21, 1952; s. Mounir Saleh and Suad (Murebey) Nsouli; m. Susan Lynn Dandy, Sept. 19, 1982; children: Mounir, Suad, Ameed, Samir. Brevet diploma, Lycee Francais, Brussels, 1968; BS, Lycee Francais, 1973; MD, U. Brussels, 1981; MD in Allergy and Immunology, Georgetown U., 1986. Research fellow Georgetown Sch. Medicine, Washington, 1983—; clin. fellow Georgetown U. Hosp., Washington, 1983-85, attending physician, 1985—, clin. assoc. prof., 1986—, prof. Pediat. Allergy, 2000—; med. dir. Watergate Asthma and Allergy Ctr., Washington, 1985—. Rschr. ICISI Georgetown U. Hosp., 1984—; pvt. allergist to Pres. Bill Clinton, 1992—2001; dist. clin. scientist Internat. Ctr. Interdisciplinary Studies of Immunology, Washington, 1986—. Editl. bd.: Annals of Allergy, Asthma and Immunology; contbr. articles to profl. jour. Active mem. Am. Med. Polit. Action, Washington, 1983—. Fellow: Am. Coll. Allergy, Asthma and Immunology (chmn. Wash. chpt. asthma screening program); mem.: AAAS, AMA (Physician award 1986), Med. Soc. D.C. (bd. communicable diseases 1986—), N.Y. Acad. Sci., Am. Thoracic Soc., Am. Acad. Allergists, Cosmos Club. Avocations: Karate, automobile safety engring. Home: 8924 Holly Leaf Ln Bethesda MD 20817-2653 Office: Watergate Asthma & Allergy 2600 Virginia Ave NW Washington DC 20037-1905

NTAIMO, LEWIS, engineering educator, researcher; b. Kitwe, Zambia, May 21, 1973; s. Laso and Alice Bwalya Ntaimo; m. Chloe Agnes Balfour; children: Joseph Mulenga, Claire Mumba, Ceanah Bwalya. PhD in Systems and Indsl. Engring., U. Ariz., Tucson, 2004. Rsch. asst. dept. mining and geol. engring. U. Ariz., Tucson, 1999—2000, rsch. asst. dept. sys. and indsl. engring., 2001—04; asst. prof. dept. indsl. and sys. engring. Tex. A&M U., College Station, 2004—. Grantee, NSF, 2005—. Mem.: Inst. Indsl. Engrs. (assoc.; faculty advisor student chpt. 2005—06). Office: Tex A&M U 3131 Tamu College Station TX 77843 Office Fax: 979-847-9005. Business E-Mail: ntaimo@tamu.edu.

NTZIACHRISTOS, VASILIS, radiology, bioengineering educator; Diploma in Elec. Engring., Aristotle U., 1993; postgrad., U. Copenhagen Med. Sch., 1994—95; MS in Bioengring., U. Pa., 1998, PhD in Bioengring., 2000. Asst. prof. Harvard U. Med. Sch.; head lab. for biooptics and molecular imaging Mass. Gen. Hosp. Editor (assoc.): IEEE Transactions on Med. Imaging, 2005—. Recipient Solomon R. Pollack award, U. Penn., 2002; named one of Top 100 Innovators, MIT Tech. Review, 2004; Damon Runyon Cancer Rsch. Found. fellowship, 2001. Mem.: Optical Soc. Am. (chair biomed. optical imagineg group 2004—, chair biomed. topical mtgs. 2006—). Office: Harvard Med Mass Gen Hosp Rm 5406 Radiology 149 13th St Charlestown MA 02129 Business E-Mail: vasilis@helix.mgh.harvard.edu.

NUAIMI, MARK N., Mayor, Fontana, California; m. Susanne Nuaimi; children: Jessica, Marcus, Davis. BS in Elec. Engring., Calif. State Poly. U., Pomona; MA in Bus. Adminstrn., U. LaVerne. Chmn. Fontana Industrial Devel. Authority; current asst. mgr. City of Colton, Calif.; chmn. City of Fontana Area Coun., 1998—; mayor City of Fontana, Calif., 2002—. Rep. I-10 Corridor Com., Fontana Unified Sch. Dist. Sub-Com., Route 30 Corridor Com., City of Fontana Annexation and Pub. Rels., City of Fontana Recreation, City of Fontana C. of C., San Bernardino Associated Govt., Southern Calif. Assn. Govts. Mem.: Fontana Boys & Girls Club (pres. 1995—97, treas. 1997—99). Avocation: youth sports coach. Office: City Hall 8353 Sierra Ave Fontana CA 92335 Office Phone: 909-350-7600. Business E-Mail: mnuaimi@fontana.org.*

NUCCIARONE, A. PATRICK, lawyer; b. Denville, NJ, Aug. 29, 1947; s. H. Joseph and Alice Marie (McGuirk) N. BA, U. So. Calif., 1969; JD, George Washington U., 1973. Bar: N.J. 1973, N.Y. 1981, Vt. 1984, U.S. Dist. Ct. N.J. 1973, U.S. Dist. Ct. (no. dist.) Ohio 1986, U.S. Ct. Appeals (3d cir.) 1976, U.S. Supreme Ct. 1995. Com. staff asst. U.S. House of Reps., Washington, 1971-72; staff asst. Exec. Office of Pres. of U.S., Washington, 1972-73; asst. U.S. Atty. Office of U.S. Atty., Newark, 1974-83, chief environ. sect., 1978-83; spl. asst. Atty. Gen. Office of Atty. Gen., Montpelier, Vt., 1984; ptnr. Hannoch Weisman, Roseland, NJ, 1984-91, Dechert, Price & Rhoads, Princeton, NJ, 1991-95; fed. monitor U.S. Dist. Ct., NY, 2001—. Co-chmn. N.J. Hazardous Task Force, Trenton, 1978-83; supr. Rutgers U. Environ. Law Clinic, Newark, 1978-83; mem. Environ. Expn. Adv. Bd., Trenton, 1985-90; chmn. ann. seminar on impacts of environ. law bus. trans. Practicing Law Inst., 1986-92, mem. adv. com. on environ. law, 1986—; mem. faculty NYU Summer Inst. on Environ. Law, 1991-94. Contbr. articles to profl. jours. Recipient Outstanding Service award U.S. Dept. Justice, Washington, 1980, Spl. Achievement awards U.S. Dept. Justice, 1978, 79, Presdl. Citation for Excellent Performance Exec. Office of Pres., Washington, 1973. Mem. ABA (vice chmn. sect. on natural resources, energy and environ. law 1987-93), N.J. State Bar Assn. (bd. dirs. environ. law sect. 1985-89). Office: 1540 Hwy 138 Ste 107 Wall NJ 07719-3766 Office Phone: 732-280-4800.

NUCHI, LIOR O., lawyer; b. Tiberius, Israel, Aug. 8, 1960; BA, Columbia Univ., 1982; JD, NYU, 1987. Bar: Calif. Sr. bus. ptnr. Bingham McCutchen, East Palo Alto, Calif.; ptnr., chmn. Cross-Border Transactions group & Israel practice Pillsbury Winthrop Shaw Pittman, Palo Alto, Calif., 2004—. Mem.: Nat. Assn. of Corp. Directors, Silicon Ventures, Calif.-Israel C. of C. Office: Pillsbury Winthrop Shaw Pittman 2475 Hanover St Palo Alto CA 94304-1114 Office Phone: 650-233-4803. Office Fax: 650-233-4545. Business E-Mail: lior.nuchi@pillsburylaw.com.

NUCHTERN, JED G., surgeon, educator; b. NYC, Mar. 3, 1956; m. Sharon E. Plon. AB, Princeton U., NJ, 1979; MD, Harvard Med. Sch., Boston, 1985. Diplomate Am. Bd. Surgery, 1993. Prof. dept. surgery Baylor Coll. Medicine, Houston, 1995—.

NUCKOLLS, JOHN HOPKINS, physicist, researcher; b. Chgo., Nov. 17, 1930; s. Asa Hopkins and Helen (Gates) N.; m. Ruth Munsterman, Apr. 21, 1952 (div. 1983); children: Helen Marie, Robert David; m. Amelia Aphrodite Liaskas, July 29, 1983. BS, Wheaton Coll., 1953; MA, Columbia U., 1955; DSc (hon.), Fla. Inst. Tech., 1977. Physicist U. Calif., Lawrence Livermore Nat. Lab., 1955—2007, assoc. leader thermonuclear design divsn., 1965-80, assoc. leader laser fusion program, 1975-83, divsn. leader, 1980-83, assoc. dir. physics, 1983-88, dir., 1988-94, assoc. dir. at large, 1994-97, dir. emeritus, 1997—, Lawrence Livermore Nat. Security, 2007—. Mem. emeritus U.S. Strategic Command Strategic adv. group; tech. adv. bd. Network Physics, Inc.; cons. def. sci. bd. Dept. Def., Intellectual Ventures; mem. adv. coms. to dir. CIA, 1989-99. Recipient E.O. Lawrence award Pres. and AEC, 1969, Fusion Leadership award, 1983, Edward Teller medal Am. Nuc. Soc., 1991, Resolution of Appreciation, U. Calif. Regents, 1994, Sec. of Def. Outstanding Pub. Svc. medal, 1996, Disting. Assoc. award U.S. Dept. Energy, 1996, Career Achievement award Fusion Power Assocs., 1996, Spl. award, 2008. Fellow: AAAS, Am. Phys. Soc. (J.C. Maxwell prize 1981); mem.: NAE. Office: Lawrence Livermore Nat Lab PO Box 808 Livermore CA 94551-0808

NUCKOLS, FRANK JOSEPH, psychiatrist; b. Akron, Ohio, Apr. 7, 1926; s. William Alexander, Jr. and Jean (Harrison) Nuckols; m. Jane Fleetwood McIntosh, June 16, 1948; children: Claud Alexander, John Andrew. BA, U. Louisville, Ky., 1946; MD, U. Ala., Birmingham, 1951. Diplomate Am. Bd. Psychiatry and Neurology, 1959, cert. med. profl. Nat. Assn. Disability Examiners, 2005. Intern Holy Name Jesus Hosp., Gadsden, Ala., 1951; ward physician Ala. State Hosp., Tuscaloosa, 1951-52; resident U. Louisville, USPHS Hosp., Lexington, Ky., 1953-56; mem. faculty dept. psychiatry U. Ala. Med. Ctr., Birmingham, 1958-68, dir. tng. psychiat. residents, 1964-68, head div. community psychiatry, 1964-68, head continuing psychiat. edn. for physicians, 1964-68; chief psychiat. staff in-patient svc. U. Hosp., Birmingham, 1966-68; dir. tng. Hill Crest Hosp., Birmingham, 1975-79; pvt. practice Birmingham, 1968-93; cons. Ala. Div. Disability Determinations, Birmingham, 1993—. Staff Med. Ctr. East Hosp., Birmingham, Bapt. Med. Ctr. Montclair, Birmingham; cons. staff St. Vincent's Hosp., Birmingham, Lloyd Noland Hosp., Birmingham, South Highland Hosp., Birmingham; vis. faculty, mem. interuniv. forum cmty. psychiatry Harvard U., Boston, 1963—66; vis. faculty Baylor U. Med. Sch., Houston, 1967—71. Sr. surgeon USPHS, 1956—. Ensign USNR, 1943—45. Fellow: So. Psychiat. Assn., Am. Psychiat. Assn. (life; disting.); mem.: Nat. Assn. Disability Examiners (cert. med. prof. 2005, State Ala. Med. Cons. of Yr. 2005, Commr.'s citation 2005), Mental Health Assn. State Ala. (chmn. profl. adv. com. 1961), Jefferson County Med. Soc., Jefferson County Mental Health Assn. (v.p. 1960), So. Med. Assn., Med. Assn. Ala., Tau Kappa Epsilon, Phi Beta Pi. Home and Office: 300 Royal Towers Dr Apt 720 Vestavia AL 35209

NUECHTERLEIN, KEITH H., psychology professor; b. Akron, Ohio, Sept. 23, 1948; s. Harold F. and Frieda D. L. Nuechterlein; m. Nancy Alexander Nuechterlein, Apr. 27, 1981. BA, U. Minn., 1970, PhD, 1978. Cert. psychologist Bd. of Psychology, Calif., 1980. Asst. prof. dept. psychiatry UCLA, 1978—85, assoc. prof. dept. psychiatry and psychology, 1985—89, prof., 1989—. Dir. UCLA Aftercare Rsch. Program, 1980—; co-chair MATRICS Neurocognition Com., LA, 2002—06; dir. UCLA Ctr. for Neurocognition and Emotion in Schizophrenia, 2003—. Contbr. articles to profl. jours. Recipient Joseph Zubin Meml. Fund award, N.Y. State Psychiat. Inst., 1995, Disting. Sci. Achievement in Psychology, Calif. Psychol. Assn., 1997; grantee Devel. Processes in Schizophrenic Disorders, NIMH, 1983—, Transmission of Vulnerability Factors in Schizophrenia, 1994—, Ctr. Neurocognition and Emotion in Schizophrenia, 2003—. Fellow: Am. Psychopathological Assn., Am. Psychol. Soc.; mem.: AAAS, APA, Soc. for Psychophysiological Rsch., Soc. for Rsch. in Psychopathology (pres. 2006—07). Achievements include research in MATRICS Consensus Cognitive Battery for Clinical Trials in Schizophrenia; development of Degraded-Stimulus Continuous Performance Test; 3-7 Continuous Performance Test; research in Cognitive Domains in Schizophrenia; Attentional Deficits in Schizophrenia. Office: UCLA Dept Psychiatry 300 UCLA Medical Plz Rm 2240 Los Angeles CA 90095-6968 Office Fax: 310-206-3651. Business E-Mail: keithn@ucla.edu.

NUERNBERG, WILLIAM RICHARD, lawyer; b. Pitts., July 7, 1946; s. William W. and Frances (Hubler) N. BA cum laude, Denison U., 1968; JD cum laude, U. Mich., 1971. Bar: Pa. 1971, U.S. Dist.Ct. (we. dist.) Pa. 1971, Fla. 1995. Mem. Eckert Seamans Cherin & Mellott LLC, 1981-98; ptnr. Duane Morris LLP, Miami, 1999—. Bd. govs. Big Bros. Big Sisters Greater Miami. Pitt fellow U. Pitts. Sch. Bus., 1987-88. Mem. ABA, Pa. Bar Assn., Fla. Bar Assn., Miami City Club. Office: Duane Morris LLP 200 S Biscayne Blvd Ste 3400 Miami FL 33131-2318

NUESSE, CELESTINE JOSEPH, retired university official; b. Sevastopol, Wis., Nov. 25, 1913; s. George and Salome Helen (Martens) N.; m. Margaret O'Donoghue, 1969. B.E., Central State Tchrs. Coll., Stevens Point, Wis., 1934; MA, Northwestern U., 1937; PhD, Cath. U. Am., 1944, LHD (hon.), 1982; LLD (hon.), Merrimack Coll., 1960. Tchr. social studies Pub. High Sch., Antigo, Wis., 1934-40; instr. sociology Coll. St. Catherine, St. Paul, 1943, Marquette U., Milw., 1943-45; instr. Cath. U. Am., Washington, 1945-48, asst. prof., 1948-52, assoc. prof., 1952-64, prof., 1964-81, prof. emeritus, 1981—, dean Sch. Social Sci., 1952-61, exec. v.p., 1967-81, provost, 1968—78, provost emeritus, 1981—. Spl. rep. in Germany, Nat. Cath. Welfare Conf., 1950-51; mem. U.S. Nat. Commn. for UNESCO, 1950-56, 63-69, exec. com., 1954-56; mem. gov. bd. UNESCO Youth Inst., Munich, Germany, 1955-59; mem. U.S. Bd. Fgn. Scholarships, 1954-58, chmn., 1956-58; mem. D.C. Commr.'s Coun. on Human Relations, 1958-64, D.C. Commn. on Postsecondary Edn., 1975-80 Author: The Social Thought of American Catholics, 1634-1829, 1945, The Catholic University of America: A Centennial History, 1990; co-author, co-editor: The Sociology of the Parish, 1951; staff editor New Cath. Ency., 1963-66, chmn. editl. bd. supplements, 1973-79; contbr. articles to profl. jours. Mem. Am. Cath. Hist. Assn., Am. Cath. Sociol. Soc. (pres. 1954), Am. Sociol. Assn., Cath. Assn. Internat. Peace (pres. 1954-56), Cath. Commn. Intellectual and Cultural Affairs, Inst. Internat. Sociologie, Internat. Conf. on Sociology of Religion (past v.p.), Nat. Cath. Ednl. Assn., Cath. Interracial Council Washington (pres. 1962-66), Cosmos Club (Washington), KC, Phi Beta Kappa (hon.), Alpha Kappa Delta, Pi Gamma Mu, Sigma Tau Delta, Phi Sigma Epsilon. Home: 9101 River Crescent Dr Annapolis MD 21401 Home Phone: 410-224-0773.

NUFFER, MONIKA, pharmacist, educator; d. Paul W. and Dagmar Majer; m. Wes A. Nuffer; 1 child, Tyler A. PharmD, U. Colo., Denver, 2003. Clin. pharmacist Kaiser, Aurora, 1999—; pharmacy resident VA, Albuquerque, 2003—04; instr. and coord., exptl. edn. U. Colo., 2007—. Office: Univ Colo Denver SOP 12700 E 19th Ave Aurora CO 80045 Office Fax: 303-724-3732.

NUGENT, ALAN F., software company executive; With Hewlett-Packard Co.; v.p., software develop., chief tech. officer Xerox Corp.; sr. v.p., chief tech. officer, chief info. officer American Re-Insurance Co.; consulting chief technologist, chief software architect BellSouth Corp.; exec. v.p., chief tech. officer, chief info. officer Vectant, Inc.; sr. v.p., chief tech. officer Novell, Inc.; with CA, Inc., Islandia, NY, 2005—, sr. v.p., gen. mgr., enterprise systems, Unicenter bus. unit, 2005—06, exec. v.p., chief tech. officer, 2006—. Office: CA Inc One CA Plaza Islandia NY 11749

NUGENT, GEORGE ROBERT, neurosurgeon; b. Yonkers, NY, Feb. 6, 1921; s. George Fitzsimmons and Alberta Belle (Wolven) N.; m. Virginia Ellen Hayes, July 3, 1947; children: Dana A., Robert W., Leslie Ellen, Barnes L., Courtney A. BA, Kenyon Coll., 1950; MD, U. Cinn., 1953. Diplomate Am. Bd. Neurol. Surgery. Resident Duke U. Med. Ctr., Durham, 1958, instr. of neurosurgery, 1957-58; asst. dir. Divsn. Neurosurgery U. Cinn. Coll. Medicine, 1958-61; asst. prof. neurosurgery to prof. neurosurgery W. Va. U. Med. Ctr., Morgantown, 1961—, chmn. dept. neurosurgery, 1970-85, prof. neurosurgery, 1985—. Cons. VA Hosp., Clarksburg, W.Va., 1961-93, Pa. Trauma Found., Pittsburgh, 1991-92; participant seminars in field; guest prof. various univs. Exhibitor various sci. exhibits, 1973-79; contbr. articles to profl. jours. and publs. Team physician W. Va. U. Mountaineers, Morgantown, 1966—. Lt. (j.g.) U.S. Maritime Svc., 1943-45. Fellow Am. Bd. Neurol. Surgery; mem. Am. Assn. Neurol. Surgeons, Congress Neurol. Surgeons, So. Neurosurg. Soc. (v.p. 1970-96), Soc. Neurol. Surgeons. Democrat. Avocations: tennis, woodworking, travel, cooking, reading. Office: Robert Byrd Health Scis Ctr Morgantown WV 26506 Office Phone: 304-293-5041. Fax: 304-292-4944.

NUGENT, HELEN JEAN MCCLELLAND, history professor; b. Indpls., Oct. 14, 1934; d. John Isaac and Ruth Augusta (Mather) McClelland; m. Paul Thomas Nugent, Aug. 19, 1935; children: Paula Jean Nugent Barickman, Thomas J. Nugent II, Ruth E. B. Nugent Simard. BA, Franklin Coll., 1956; MA, U. Ill., 1965, Ind. U., 1971; PhD, Mich. State U., 1983. Lifetime cert. in secondary edn., Ind. Tchr. grades 9-12 Union City HS, Ind., 1956—57, Seven Mile HS, Ohio, 1957—58; tchr. history St. Rose Acad., Vincennes, Ind., 1962—64; instr. history Margaret Hall Sch., Versailes, Ky., 1964—66; lectr. history Ind.U./Purdue U., Columbus, 1976—82; vis. lectr. Ind. U./Purdue U., Columbus, 2001; dir. Can. studies Franklin Coll., Ind., 1984—95, chair dept. history, 1996—99, prof. emerita history, dir. emerita Can. studies, 1999—. Contbr. numerous articles, papers to profl. jours., chpts. to books. Mem. Franklin Coll. Alumni Coun., 2002—05; judge consistory ct. Anglican Cath. Ch., 2006—09. Recipient Alumni award Franklin Coll., 1997. Mem. Mid West Assn. Can. Studies (v.p. 1990-92, exec.

coun. 1992-94), Assn. Can. Studies U.S. (exec. bd. 1993-97), Ind. Hist. Soc., Assn. Can. Studies, Phi Alpha Theta, Theta Alpha Phi, Delta Kappa Gamma, Phi Kappa Phi. Anglican Catholic.

NUGENT, NELLE, theater, film and television producer; b. Jersey City, May 24, 1939; d. John Patrick and Evelyn Adelaide (Stern) N.; m. Donald G. Baker, June 6, 1960 (div. 1962); m. Benjamin Janney, June 22, 1969 (div. Apr., 1980); m. Jolyon Fox Stern, Apr. 7, 1982; 1 child, Alexandra Fox Stern. BS, Skidmore Coll., 1960, DHL (hon.), 1981. Chmn. bd. McCann & Nugent, Prodns. Inc., NYC, 1976-86; pres. Foxboro Prodns., Inc., NYC, 1985-94; pres., CEO Foxboro Entertainment, 1990-94; pres. The Foxboro Co., Inc.; co-prin. Golden Fox Films, Inc. Adj. faculty NYU, NYC, 2003—. Stage mgr. various off-Broadway shows, 1960-64; stage mgr. Broadways plays Any Wednesday, 1963-64, Dylan, 1964, Ben Franklin in Paris, 1964-65; v.p., prodn. supr. Theatre Now, 1966-69; prodn. supr., then gen. mgr., 1969-76, assoc. mng. dir. Nederlander Corp., operating theaters and producing plays in, NYC and on tour, 1970-76; co-founder McCam & Nugent Prodns., Inc., 1976; prodr.: Dracula, 1977 (Tony award), The Gin Game (Tony nomination), The Elephant Man, 1978 (Tony award, Drama Critics award), Morning's at Seven, 1980 (Tony award), Home, 1980 (Tony nomination), Otherwise Engaged, Amadeus, 1981 (Tony award); also produced: Rose and Piaf, 1980, Otherwise Engaged, The Life and Adventures of Nicholas Nickleby, 1981 (Tony award, Drama Critics award), The Dresser (Tony award nominee), 1981, Mass Appeal, 1981; The Lady & The Clarinet, 1982; The Glass Menagerie (revival), 1983; Painting Churches (Obie award), 1983; Total Abandon, 1983; All's Well That End's Well, 1983 (Tony nomination); Pilobolus Dance Company, 1983; Pacific Overtures (revival), 1984; Much Ado about Nothing/Cyrano de Bergerac (repertory) (Tony award nominees), 1984; Leader of the Pack (Tony award nominee), 1985, The Life and Adventures of Nicholas Nickleby (revival) (Tony award nominee), 1986; prodr.: TV spls.: Morning's At Seven, Piaf; Pilobolus; prodr. A Fighting Choice, 1986-88, A Conspiracy of Love, 1987, The Final Verdict, 1990 (Cable Ace award nominee Best Picture); exec. prodr. (TV pilot) Morning Maggie, 1987, Dick Clark Prodns., 1988-90, (feature films) Student Body, 1993, Getting In, 1994, Jane Doe, 1996; (TV films) In the Presence of Mine Enemies, 1995-96 (Houston Festival Silver Star award), A Town Has Turned to Dust, 1997 (World Festival Silver medal 1998), After the Storm (Best Feature Film NY Internat. Independent Film & Video Festival, 2000), Angelciti Festival (Best Feature 2001), Houston Worldfest (Platinum award, Best Film Made for TV 2001), (Broadway prodn.) The Smell of the Kill, 2002, Sly Fox, 2004, A Mother, A Daughter and a Gun, 2005, And Then There Were None, London, West End, 2005, American Buffalo, 2008, Masterharord and the Boys Feature failure, 2009, Little House on the Prairie Musical, Nat. Tour, 2009. Mem.: Acad. TV Arts and Scis., Prodrs. Guild Am. East (exec. bd., co-founder), League Am. Theaters and Producers. Avocations: sailing, gardening, opera. Office: 234 W 44th St Ste 1005 New York NY 10036

NUGENT, PAULINE, ancient language educator; PhD, U. Tex., Austin, 1992. First grade tchr. Primary Schs., San Antonio, 1958—64; tchr. Incarnate Word HS, San Antonio, 1975. French prof. Incarnate Word Coll., Dunmore, Ireland, 1975—79; prof. classics Mo. State U., Springfield, 1992—. Recipient Gov. award, State Gov. Mo., 1997. Mem.: North Am. Patristic Soc., Am. Assn. Tchrs. French, Classical Assn. Mid., West & South, Am. Philol Assn., Phi Kappa Phi. Home: 1931 S Virginia Ave Springfield MO 65807 Office: Mo State Univ 901 S Nat Ave Springfield MO 65897 Office Fax: 417-836-7626. Business E-Mail: paulinenugent@missouristate.edu.

NUGENT, RACHEL A., economist; b. Topeka, Sept. 27, 1957; d. Walter Terry and Katherine Cleary Nugent; m. Brian N. Baird; children: Walter Franklin Baird, William Washington Baird. PhD, George Wash. U., 1994. Assoc. prof. Pacific Luth. U., Tacoma, 1991—97; sr. devel. economist UN FAO, Rome, 1997—2001; program dir. US NIH, Bethesda, Md., 2001—04; economist Ctr. Global Devel., Washington. Office: Ctr Global Devel 1800 Mass Ave NW Washington DC 20036 Business E-Mail: rnugent@cgdev.org.

NUGENT, S. GEORGIA, academic administrator; m. Thomas J Scherer. B cum laude, Princeton U., 1973; PhD in classics, Cornell U. Instr. Swarthmore Coll.; assoc. prof. Brown U., 1985; asst. prof. Princeton U., 1979, dean, Harold McGraw Jr. Ctr. for tchg. and learning, asst. to pres., 1992—95, assoc. provost, 1995; pres. Kenyon Coll., 2003—. Author books. Recipient Wriston award for excellence in tchg. Office: Office of Pres Ransom Hall Kenyon Coll Gambier OH 43022 Office Phone: 740-427-5111. Office Fax: 740-427-2335. Business E-Mail: nugent@kenyon.edu.*

NUGENT, TED (THEODORE ANTHONY NUGENT), musician, radio personality; b. Detroit, Dec. 13, 1948; s. Warren Henry and Marion (Johnson) Nugent; m. Sandra Janowski, Jan. 30, 1971 (div. Dec. 31, 1979); children: Sasha Emma, Theodore Tobias, Starr; m. Shemane Deziel, Jan. 21, 1989; 1 child, Rocco. Student, Oakland Community Coll., Detroit. Guitarist Amboy Dukes, 1967—75, Damn Yankees, 1989—96; solo artist, 1975—; Mich. County Sheriff dep., 1978—; host, Ted Nugent Morning Show WWBR, Detroit. Pres. Ted Nugent United Sportsmen of Am. Guitarist: (albums with Amboy Dukes) Ted Nugent and the Amboy Dukes, 1968, Migration, 1969, Journey to the Center of the Mind, 1969, Marriage on the Rocks, 1970, Call of the Wild, 1973, Survival of the Fiittest, 1974, Tooth, Fang, and Claw, 1974, Dr. Slingshot, 1975; (solo albums) Ted Nugent, 1975, Free for All, 1976, Cat Scratch Fever, 1977, Double Live Gonzo, 1977, Weekend Warriors, 1978, State of Shock, 1979, Scream Dream, 1980, Great Gonzos/The Best of Ted Nugent, 1981, Intensities in Ten Cities, 1981, Nugent, 1982, Penetrator, 1984, Little Miss Dangerous, 1986, The Ultimate Collection, 1987, If You Can't Lick 'Em...Lick 'Em, 1988, Call of the Wild, 1991, Out of Control, 1993, Spirit of the Wild, 1995, Motor City Madness, 1996, Live at Hammersmith '79, 1997, Super Hits, 1998, Over the Top, 1998, On the Edge, 1998, Loaded for Bear: The Best of Ted Nugent, 1999, Noble Savage, 2001, Full Blontal Nugity, 2001, Take No Prisoners, 2002, The Ultimate Ted Nugent, 2002, Take Two, 2002, Craveman, 2002, The Ultimate Ted Nugent, 2002, Hunt Music, 2003, Love Grenade, 2007, Sweden Rocks, 2008; (with Damn Yankees) Damn Yankees, 1990, Don't Tread, 1992; author: Blood Trails: The Truth about Bowhunting, 1991, God, Guns and Rock 'n' Roll, 2000, Blood Trails II: The Truth about Bowhunting, 2004, Ted, White & Blue: The Nugent Manifesto, 2008; co-author: (with Shemane Nugent) Kill It and Grill It: A Guide to Preparing and Cooking Wild Game and Fish, 2002; appeared in: (TV reality series) Surviving Nugent, 2003-04, SuperGroup, 2006; editor, publisher Ted Nugent Adventure Outdoors Mag.; creator, prodr. Ted Nugent Spirit of the Wild, PBS; contbr. articles to profl. jours. Sheriff dep. Mich. County, 1978—; founder Ted Nugent Kamp for Kids; appointee Mich. State Parks Found.; bd. dirs. Lyme Alliance. Recipient Nat. Arbor Day Conservation Award, 1999, ATV Image Award, 2004; named Man of Yr., Mich. Recreation and Parks Assn., Mich. Conservationist of Yr., 1999; named to The Native Am. Strongheart Soc. Mem.: ASCAP, Safari Club Internat., Native Am. Strongheart Soc., Quality Deer Mgmt. Assn. of Mich. (dir.), Ducks Unlimited (life sponsor), Mich. Bowhunters (life), Nat. Trappers Assn. (life), Nat. Rifle Assn. (life; bd. dirs. 1995—). Office: Nugent USA 4008 W Michigan Ave Jackson MI 49202*

NUGENT, WALTER TERRY KING, historian; b. Watertown, NY, Jan. 11, 1935; s. Clarence A. and Florence (King) Nugent; m. Suellen Hoy, 1986; children from previous marriage: Katherine, Rachel, David, Douglas, Terry, Mary. AB, St. Benedict's Coll., 1954, DLitt, 1968; MA, Georgetown U., 1956; PhD, U. Chgo., 1961. Instr. history Washburn U., 1957—58; asst. prof. Kans. State U., 1961—63, Ind. U., Bloomington, 1963—64, assoc. prof., 1964—68, prof., 1968—84, assoc. dean Coll. Arts and Scis., 1967—71, dir. overseas study, 1967—76, chmn. history dept., 1974—77; Andrew V. Tackes prof. history U. Notre Dame, 1984—2000, Andrew V. Tackes prof. emeritus, 2000—. Paley lectr., Fulbright vis. prof. Hebrew U., Jerusalem, 1978—79; summer seminar dir. NEH, 1979, 84, 86; vis. prof. U. Hamburg, U. Warsaw, 1982; Mary Ball Washington Fulbright prof. U. Coll., Dublin, 1991—92. Author: (book) The Tolerant Populists, 1963, Creative History, 1967, The Money Question During Reconstruction, 1967, Money and American Society 1865-1880, 1968, Modern America, 1973, From Centennial to World War: American Society 1876-1917, 1977, Structures of American Social History, 1981, Crossings: The Great Transactlantic Migrations 1870-1914, 1992; author: (with Martin Ridge) The American West: The Reader, 1999, Into the West: The Story of Its People, 1999 (Caughey award, 2000); author: Making Our Way: A Family History, 2003, Habits of Empire: A History of American Expansion, 2008. Bd. dirs. U.S.-Israel Ednl. Found., 1985—89. Recipient medal of Merit, Warsaw U., 1992; Newberry Libr. fellow, 1962, Guggenheim fellow, 1964—65, Huntington Libr. fellow, 1979, 1985, Beinecke fellow, Yale U., 1990. Mem.: Soc. Historians the Gilded Age and Progressive Era (pres. 2000—02), Soc. Am. Historians, Western Hist. Assn. (pres. 2005—06, hon. life mem.). Democrat. E-mail: wnugent@nd.edu.

NUGENT, WILLIAM C., cardiothoracic surgeon; b. Oct. 17, 1949; BS, Franklin & Marshall Coll., Lancaster, Pa., 1971; MD in Medicine, cum laude, Albany Med. Sch., NY, 1975. Diplomate Am. Bd. Thoracic Surgery, Am. Bd. Surgery, lic. NH. Intern internal medicine Boston U., 1975—76; resident gen. surgery Beth Israel Hosp., Boston, 1976—79, chief resident gen. surgery, 1979—80, emergency unit staff surgeon, 1980—81; surgical rsch. fellow cardiothoracic surgery Mass. Gen. Hosp., Boston, 1980—81; resident thoracic surgery U. Mich., Ann Arbor, 1981—83; chief cardiothoracic surgery Dartmouth-Hitchcock Med. Ctr., Lebanon, NH, 1983—. Surg. rsch. cons. AVCO Med. Rsch. Lab., Everett, Mass., 1980—81; staff surgeon Mary Hitchcock Meml. Hosp., Hanover, NH, 1983—; cons. VA Hosp., White River, Vt., 1983—; asst. prof. surgery Dartmouth Med. Sch., Hanover, NH, 1983—92, assoc. prof. surgery, 1992—98, prof. surgery, 1998—, prof. cmty. family medicine, 2001—; assoc., Ctr. Evaluative Clin. Sci. Dartmouth-Hitchcock Med. Ctr., 1994—; clinical oncology affiliate, Norris Cotton Cancer Ctr. Dartmouth Hitchcock Med. Ctr., 2004—. Contbr. articles to profl. jours. Recipient Daggett Trust prize for Profl. Conduct, 1975, Frederick D. McAndless prize for Psychiatry, 1975, Chmn. award, Dartmouth Hitchcock Med. Ctr., 1997; Sheridan-Alley Scholar, Thoracic Surgery Found. Rsch. Edn., 1998. Mem.: Soc. Thoracic Surgeons, Gen. Thoracic Surg. Club, Cardiothoracic Surgery Network, Am. Assn. Thoracic Surgery, Alpha Omega Alpha. Avocations: fly fishing, flying, computers. Office: Dartmouth-Hitchcock Med Ctr Dept Cardiothoracic Surgery One Medical Ctr Dr Lebanon NH 03756 Office Phone: 603-650-8572. Office Fax: 603-650-6346. Business E-Mail: william.c.nugent@hitchcock.org.

NUGTEREN, CORNELIUS, air force officer; b. Colton, SD, Feb. 7, 1928; s. Adrian Joe and Marie Johanna N.; m. Liane Albrecht, Sept. 22, 1956; children: Cecile, Aneli. BA, Central Coll., Pella, Iowa, 1951. Commd. 2d lt. USAF, 1953, advanced through grades to maj. gen., 1980; advisor Vietnam Air Force, 1970-71; served in Germany, 1971-77; vice comdr. (Air Logistics Center), Utah, 1977-79; comdr. (Aerospace Rescue and Recovery Service), Scott AFB, Ill., 1979-81; chief (Joint U.S. Mil. Aid Group), Greece, 1981-82; comdr. Air Logistics Ctr., Robins AFB, Ga, 1983-88; ret.; cons. for def. industries Warner Robins, Ga., 1988-94; v.p. Chem. Tech. Internat., Warner Robins, Mercer U. Engring. Rsch. Ctr., Warner Robins, 1996—. Decorated D.S.M., Legion of Merit, Bronze Star, Superior Service medal; recipient USAF EEO award, 1979; named to Ga. Aviation Hall of Fame, 2004. Mem. Air Force Assn., Order Daedalians, Internat. Order Hansen, Order of the Sword. Office: 114 Holly Dr Warner Robins GA 31088-6615 Office Phone: 478-953-6810. Personal E-mail: gennewt@aol.com. *Service to one's country is not just a job...it's a calling. Integrity to and within the institution to which you belong is an absolute necessity. Loyalty to peers and subordinates is equally important as loyalty to your superiors. Attitude toward life, humankind and profession is key determinant to success. Goals should be set high enough so as to be unattainable. Standard of conduct must always include duty, honor, country.*

NUJOMA, SAM DANIEL, President of Namibia; b. Etunda Village, Ongandjera, Namibia, May 12, 1929; s. Daniel Uutoni and Helvi Mpingana (Kondombolo) N.; m. Kovambo Theopoldine Katjimune, May 6, 1956; 4 children. LLD (hon.), Ahmadu Bello U., Zaria, Nigeria, 1982, U. Lincoln, 1990; D of Tech. (hon.), Fed. U. Tech., Minna, Nigeria, 1992; EdD (hon.), U. Namibia, 1993; LLD, Roma U., Maseru, Lesotho, 1993; LLD (hon.), Ohio Ctrl. State U., 1993, State U. N.J., 1997; JD (hon.), Rutgers U., 1997; D (hon.), Acad. Coun. Russian Econ. Acad., 1998, People's Friendship U., Russia, 1998; D of Pub. Svc. (hon.), La Roche Coll., 1999; LLD (hon.), U. Zimbabwe, 1999. Elected leader Ovamboland People's Orgn., 1959; pres. South West Africa People's Orgn. of Namibia (SWAPO), Windhoek, 1960—; pres. of Namibia, Windhoek, 1990—; re-elected, 1994, 1999; comdr.-in-chief of def. force Indep. Rep. of Namibia, 1990—2005; founding pres., founding father Republic Nambia, 2005—. Founding chancellor U. Namibia, 1993. Recipient Lenin Peace prize, 1973, Frederic Joliot Curie gold medal for svc. rendered to struggle for freedom, 1980, Medaglia Pontificia, 1980, 91, Cert. of Honour U. Ibadan, Nigeria, 1986, Ho Chi Minh award World Peace Coun., 1986, Masters Degree Order of Brasilia Fed. Dist. Govt. Brasilia, 1987, Grant Master Order Merit Grant Cruz, Order of Brazil, 1988, Namibia Freedom award, Calif. State U., 1988, Indira Gandhi Peace prize for Disarmament and Develop., 1990, Ordre du Merite Congo, 1991, Jose Marti, Cuba, 1991, Chief of Golden Heart, Kenya, 1992, Order of Nat. Flag First Class, DPRK, 1992, Grand Master Order of Welwitschia, Namibia, 1995, Order of Liberty Highest Cross, Portugal, 1995, Africa prize for leadership, N.Y., 1995, Order of Good Hope Gold, S. Africa, 1996, Global Marketplace award, 1999, Order of Friendship award, Vietnam, 2002; named citizen of Silvester, mayor, Calif., 1965, hon. citizen of Atlanta, San Fransisco, Chgo., N.Y.C., East Palo Alto, 1988; decorated Grand Cordon, Tunisia, 1994. Avocations: reading, swimming, fishing, gardening. Office: Sam Nujoma Found Robert Mugabe Ave Windoek 13220 Namibia Business E-Mail: jnauto@iway.na.

NULAND, ANTHONY C. J., lawyer; b. NYC, 1943; AB cum laude, Princeton U., 1965; JD, NYU, 1968. Bar: N.Y. 1969, D.C. 1977, Ga. 1978. Asst. dir. divsn. market regulation SEC, 1975-76, assoc. dir. divsn. market regulation, 1976-77; now ptnr. Seward & Kissel, NYC, 1977—. Office: Seward & Kissel 1200 G St NW Ste 350 Washington DC 20005-3881 Office Phone: 202-737-8833.

NULAND, SHERWIN, surgeon, writer; b. NYC, Dec. 8, 1930; s. Meyer and Violet (Lutsky) N.; m. Sarah Peterson, May 29, 1977; children: Victoria Jane, Andrew Meyer, William Peterson, Amelia Rose. BA, NYU, 1951; MD, Yale U., 1955. Surgeon Yale-New Haven Hosp. (Conn.), 1962—92; clin. prof. surgery Yale Sch. Medicine, New Haven, 1962—; rsch. affiliate history sci. and medicine program Yale U. Author: The Origins of Anesthesia, 1983, Doctors: The Biography of Medicine, 1988, Medicine: The Art of Healing, 1991, How We Die: Reflections on Life's Final Chapter, 1994 (Nat. Book award for non-fiction, 1994, Pulitzer prize finalist, 1995), The Wisdom of the Body: How We Live, 1997, The Mysteries Within: A Surgeon Reflects on Medical Myths, 2000, Leonardo da Vinci, 2000, Lost in America, 2003, The Doctors' Plague, 2003, Maimonides, 2005, The Art of Aging, 2007, The Uncertain Art: Thoughts on a Life in Medicine, 2008; contbg. editor The New Republic, mem. editl. bd. Perspectives in Biology and Medicine. V.p. Conn. Hospice, New Haven, 1978-80; bd. dirs. Hastings Ctr. Hastings Ctr. fellow. Fellow AAAS, ACS; mem. New Eng. Surg. Soc., Assocs. of Yale Med. Sch. Libr. (chmn. 1982-94), Yale-China Assn. (chmn. med. 1988-93), History of Medicine and Allied Scis. (chmn. bd. jour. 1979-2002). Democrat. Jewish. Avocation: tennis. Home: 29 Old Hartford Tpke Hamden CT 06517-3523 Office: PO Box 6356 Hamden CT 06517-0356 Office Phone: 203-776-5635. Personal E-mail: snuland@comcast.net.

NULAND, VICTORIA J., former United States permanent representative to NATO; b. Conn., 1961; d. Sherwin B. Nuland; m. Robert Kagan; children: Elena, David. BA, Brown U., 1983. With Am. Embassy US Dept. State, Moscow, 1991—93, chief of staff to dep. sec., 1993—96, dep. dir. for former Soviet Union affairs, 1997—99, US dep. permanent rep. to NATO Brussels, 2000—03, US permanent rep. to NATO, 2005—08; prin. dep. nat. security adv. to v.p. The White House, Washington, 2003—05. State Dept Fellow Coun. Fgn. Rels., 1996—97, "Next Generation" fellow, 1999—2000. Recipient Disting. Civilian Svc. medal, US Dept. Def.

NULL, WILLIAM SETH, lawyer; b. NYC, Apr. 15, 1954; s. Douglas P. Null and Barbara M. (Black) Schacker; m. Lauren E. Thaler, May 10, 1981; children: Danielle, Evan. BA, Hampshire Coll., 1977; JD, Yeshiva U., 1980. Bar: N.Y. 1981, U.S. Dist. Ct. (ea. and so. dists.) N.Y. 1981, U.S. Supreme Ct. 1987. With Null & Null, P.C., Garden City, N.Y., 1980-83, Kraver & Martin, NYC, 1983-85, Cuddy & Feder LLP, White Plains, NY, 1985—, mng. ptnr., 1999—. Dir. The Housing Partnership, Elmsford, NY, 1995—2001, White Plains Bridge of Friendship Found., 1994—; dir. Westchester chpt. Juvenile Diabetes Rsch. Found. Internat., 1998—, pres., 2004—06; dir. Gilda's Club Westchester, 2001—, The Briarcliff Manor Edn. Found., 2001—03, White Plains Hosp. Ctr., 2002—. Office: Cuddy & Feder LLP 445 Hamilton Ave 14th Fl White Plains NY 10601 Office Phone: 914-761-1300. Business E-Mail: wnull@cuddyfeder.com.

NULTON, WILLIAM CLEMENTS, retired lawyer; b. Pittsburg, Kans., Feb. 22, 1931; s. Perley Edgar and Mary Celia (Anderson) N.; m. Vicki Smith, Aug. 20, 1956; children: Carnie, Erica. BA, Kans. U., 1953, LLB with honors, 1958; postgrad., NYU, 1953-54. Bar: Kans. 1958, Mo. 1959. Sr. atty. Great Lakes Pipe Line Co., Kansas City, Mo., 1958-66, asst. sec., 1961-66; assoc. Blackwell, Sanders, Matheny, Weary & Lombardi, Kansas City, 1966-68, ptnr., 1968-81; assoc. Shughart Thomson & Kilroy, Kansas City, 1981-83, ptnr., 1983-94. Contbr. articles to profl. jours. Bd. dirs. Corinth Hills Home Assn., Shawnee Mission, 1974-76, Faith Friends, 1999-2004, Front Porch Alliance, 1999—2006, Ivanhoe Neighborhood Coun., 2003—, Kansas City Civil Rights Consortium, 1993-2005, Marillac Acad., 1994-99; pres. Beta Theta Pi Kansas City Alumni Assn., 1977 (Man of Yr. award 2002); mem., elder Village United Presbyn. Ch., Prairie Village, Kans., 1976—, trustee, 1992-94, endowment bd., 1997-2001; bd. dirs. Prairie Village Mcpl. Found., 1987—, v.p., 2000-05, pres., 2005-2007; Kans. adv. com. U.S. Civil Rights Commn., 1994-2006, acting chmn., 1998; Shawnee Mission Unified Bd. Edn., 1969-73, v.p., 1973; pres. Corinth Elem. Bd. Edn., Johnson County, Kans., 1969; chmn. Full Employment Task Group on Employment Disabled, Kansas City, 1987. Summerfield scholar, Kans. U., 1949—53, Root-Tilden scholar, NYU, 1953—54. Mem. ABA (mgmt. chmn. labor and employment law sect., com. on arbitration and collective bargaining 1989-92), Am. Acad. Hosp. Attys. (co-chmn. task group on bylaws for small rural hosps. 1992-93), Mo. Bar Assn. (chmn. labor law com. 1982), Nat. Health Lawyers Assn. (co-chmn. task group on alternative dispute resolution in health care field 1990-91), Phi Beta Kappa, Order of Coif. Republican. Home: 7908 El Monte St Shawnee Mission KS 66208-5047

NUMMINEN, TEPPO, professional hockey player; b. July 3, 1968; Defenseman Phoenix Coyotes (formerly Winnipeg Jets), 1998—2003, Dallas Stars, 2003—05, Buffalo Sabres, 2005—. Player NHL All-Star Game, 1999—2001. Achievements include being a member of silver medal winning Finnish Hockey Team, Torino Olympics, Italy, 2006. Office: Buffalo Sabres HSBC Arena One Seymour H Knox III Plaza Buffalo NY 14203-3096*

NUMOTO, TAKESHI, computer software company executive; LLB, U. Tokyo; MBA, Stanford U., Calif. Pub. servant Ministry Internat. Trade and Industry, Japan; joined Microsoft Corp., Redmond, Wash., 1997, bus. devel. mgr. Windows NT program mgmt. team, bus. devel. mgr. Microsoft bus. divsn., corp. v.p. Office product mgmt. group, 2009—. Office: Microsoft Corp One Microsoft Way Redmond WA 98052-6399*

NUMRICH, RICHARD, economics professor; b. Pasaic, Nj, Apr. 30, 1957; m. Sharon Numrich. PhD, SUNY Albany, NY, 1986. Prof. economics CSN, Las Vegas, Nev., 1995—2008. Office: Coll Southern Nevada 6375 W Charleston Blvd Las Vegas NV 89146 Personal E-mail: numrich@cox.net. E-mail: rich.numrich@csn.edu.

NUNAMAKER, SUSAN SUN, mathematics professor; d. Chin-tse and Jean Hwei-Lan Sun; m. Michael Edward Nunamaker; 1 child, Marina. BS in Math., U. Ill., Urbana-Champaign, 1982, BS in Civil Engring., 1982, MS in Applied Math., 1984. Rsch. asst. Ill. State Water Survey, 1979—81; tchg. and rsch. asst. U. Ill., 1982—86; math. prof. DeVry U., Addison, Ill., 1997—2006; math instr. Triton Coll., River Grove, Ill., 1997, Waubonsee CC, Sugar Grove, Ill., 2005—, Coll. DuPage, Glen Ellyn, Ill., 2006—; owner Sunflower Bear R & D, Urbana-Champaign, 1993—96, cons., 2006—. Computing analyst Minnow Bear Computers, Urbana-Champaign, 1984—93; engring. technician US Corps Engring. Rsch. Lab, Urbana-Champaign, 1979—80; instr. Waubimsee C.C., Sugar Grove, Ill., 2006—. Recipient Book award, Harvard U., 1976,

Lazarus Human Rels. award, Am. Jewish Cmty., 1977; Engring. scholarships, U. Ill., 1977, Math scholarships, 1978. Mem.: Ill. Math. Assn. CC, Math. Assn. Am., Am. Math. Soc. (assoc.). Home: 5 South 370 Vest Naperville IL 60563 Office: Coll DuPage 425 Fawell Blvd Glen Ellyn IL 60137 also: Waubonsee CC Route 47 at Waubonsee Dr Sugar Grove IL 60554 Personal E-mail: susan@nunamaker.com. Business E-Mail: nunama@cdnet.cod.edu.

NUNES, ANTHONY S., language educator; b. Taunton, Mass., Jan. 7, 1950; s. Alice A. Nunes; m. Maria A. Dinis, June 6, 1970; children: Jonathan Anthony, Jennifer E. Howard, Joshua E. MA, Brown U., Providence, 1983; MEd, Boston Coll., Chestnut Hill, Mass., 1992—95. Dean students Coyle and Cassidy HS, Taunton, 1990—95, tchr. Portuguese and Spanish, 2002—, tchr. and dept. chairperson, 2002—; prin. Bishop Connolly HS, Taunton, 1995—2002; vis. lectr. Portuguese Bridgewater State Coll., Mass., 2004—. Translator RENEW Internat., Newark, 2004—. Translator: (hist. and religious) Our Lady of Sorrows. V.p. scholarship com. Portuguese Am. Scholarship Found., Fall River, Mass., 1996—2006; v.p. Fundacao Faialense, Inc., East Providence, 2002—. Recipient Portuguese Heritage award, Mass. Mem.: Nat. Cath. Edn. Assn., Am. Assn. Tchrs. Spanish and Portuguese. Avocation: travel. Office: Coyle and Cassidy HS 2 Hamilton St Taunton MA 02780 Business E-Mail: asnunes@coylecassidy.com.

NUNES, DEVIN, United States Representative from California; b. Tulare, Calif., Oct. 1, 1973; m. Elizabeth Tamariz. BS in Agrl. Bus., Calif. Poly. State U., 1995, MS in Agrl., 1996. Cert. Calif. Agr. Leadership Fellowship Prog., 2000. Farmer, mgr. Nunes Dairy, 1998—2000; Calif. state dir. USDA, 2001; mem. US Congress from 21st Calif. dist., 2002—, mem. ways and means com., former asst. majority whip. Mem. Western Caucus, Rep. Main Street Partnership, Prescription Drug Action Team, Portuguese Caucus, Ho. Impact Aid Coalition, Congl. Youth Civic Caucus, Congl. Working Grp. Combat Govt. Waste, Congl. Wine Caucus, Congl. Mining Caucus, Congl. Farmer Cooperative Caucus, Congl. Caucus to Fight/Control Methamphetamine, Congl. Caucus Am. Issues; mem., former co-chair Congl. Hispanic Caucus; chair Dairy Caucus. Mem. bd. trustees Coll. Sequoias, 1996—2002. Republican. Roman Catholic. Office: US Ho Reps 1013 Longworth Ho Office Bldg Washington DC 20515-0521*

NUNEZ, OSCAR, actor; b. Cuba, Nov. 18, 1958; m. Carla Nunez. Attended, F.I.T., Parsons Sch. Design, NYC; grad., Magna Inst. Dental Tech. Cert. Dental Tech. Former mem. Shock of the Funny Comedy Troupe, Groundlings Sunday Co. Actor: (films) The Italian Job, 2003, When Do We Eat?, 2005, The Chipotle Diamonds, 2005, Glory Road, 2006, Reno 911!: Miami, 2007, The Proposal, 2009; (TV series) Resurrection Blvd., 24, Arrested Development, The Steve Harvey Show, That's Life, Ally McBeal, Curb Your Enthusiasm, 2000, The Bad Girl's Guide, 2003, Reno 911!, 2004—06, The Office, 2006— (Outstanding Performance by an Ensemble in a Comedy Series, SAG, 2007, 2008); actor, exec. prodr. (TV series) Halfway Home, 2007—. Office: OmniPop Talent Group Ste 201 4605 Lankershim Blvd Toluca Lake CA 91602*

NUNEZ-LAWTON, MIGUEL G., financial analyst; b. Havana, Cuba, Feb. 8, 1949; came to U.S., 1964; s. Miguel Nunez-Cancio and Silvia Lawton-Alfonso. BSBA, Georgetown U., 1971, postgrad. in Econs., 1973. Asst. treas. Deltec Securities Corp., NYC, 1971; debt specialist internat. econs. dept. World Bank, Washington, 1973-95; internat. cons. Miami, Fla., 1996—; World Bank del. Paris Club Debt Renegotiation for Senegal, 1982. UN Conf. in Trade and Devel. cons. Nat. Bank Angola, Luanda, 2000, Geneva; chief tech. adviser UN Conf. Trade and Devel. Bur. Treasury, Manila, 1989—90. Bd. dirs., treas. Friends of Art Mus. of the Americas, OAS, Washington, 1988-90; bd. dirs. Friends of Peru, 1991-1996, Amigos of the Cuban Heritage Collection, Richter Library, U. Miami, 2003—; panel mem. The Lawrenceville Sch., 1992; mem. Presdl. Inaugural Com., Washington, 1997. Roman Catholic. Avocations: art collecting, genealogy. Home: 8860 SW 123rd Ct Apt K106 Miami FL 33186-4152 Office Phone: 305-606-0983. Personal E-mail: mnlawton@hotmail.com.

NUNEZ-PORTUONDO, RICARDO, investment company executive; b. NYC, June 9, 1933; s. Emilio and Maria (Garcia) N-P.; m. Dolores Maldonado, Sept. 7, 1963; children— Ricardo Jose, Emilio Manuel, Eduardo Javier. LL.D., U. Havana, Cuba; postdoctoral in law, U. Fla., 1975. Bar: Cuba, Fla. Editor Latin Am. div. USIA, Miami, Fla., 1961-71, editor Washington, 1961-71; nat. dir. Cuban Refugee Program, Washington, 1975-77; pres. Cultural Pub., Inc., Miami, 1994—, Central Investment Trust, Coral Gables, Fla., 1977—; chmn. bd. Interstate Bank of Commerce, Miami, 1986-88; v.p. Century 21, Coral Gables, 1989—; adv. Miami-Dade County Commr. Jimmy L Morales, 1996—; litigation cons. Cohen & Kandell, P.A. Attorneys at Law, 1998—. Author: A Critique on the Linowitz Report, 1975, Cuba: La Otra Imagen, 1994, Un Procer Cubano, 1994, Cuban Refugee Program, The Early Years, 1995. Dir. Nat. Hispanic Scholarship Fund, San Francisco, 1978—; dir. COSSMHO, Washington, 1980—; trustee emeritus Fla. Internat. U., 1984—; pres. Mercy Hosp. Found., Miami, 1985—; bd. dirs. ARC, Greater Miami. Recipient numerous awards for civic contbns. including day named in honor Ricardo Nunez Day, Miami, 1975. Mem. Cuban Lawyers Assn., Cuban Acad. History, Metro. Club, Lyford Cay Club, Ocean Reef Club, Key Biscayne Yacht Club, Big Five Club, 200 Club. Republican. Roman Catholic. Office: PO Box 141720 Coral Gables FL 33114-1720

NUNIS, DOYCE BLACKMAN, JR., historian, educator; b. Cedartown, Ga., May 30, 1924; s. Doyce Blackman and Winnie Ethel (Morris) N. BA, UCLA, 1947; MS, U. So. Calif., 1950, M.Ed., 1952, PhD, 1958. Lectr. U. So. Calif., 1951—56; instr. El Camino Coll., 1956—59; asst. prof. edn. and history UCLA, 1959—65; assoc. prof. history U. So. Calif., 1965—68, prof., 1968—89, disting. prof. emeritus, 1989—; asst. rsch. historian UCLA, 1959—63; assoc. U. Calif., 1963—65, lectr., 1960—61, asst. prof. edn. and history, 1961—64, assoc. prof., 1964—65. Author: Andrew Sublette, Rocky Mountain Prince, 1960, Josiah Belden, 1841 California Overland Pioneer, 1962, The Golden Frontier: The Recollections of Herman Francis Rinehart, 1851-69, 1962, The California Diary of Faxon Dean Atherton, 1836-39, 1964, Letters of a Young Miner, 1964, The Journal of James H. Bull, 1965, The Trials of Isaac Graham, 1967, The Medical Journey of Pierre Garnier in California, 1851, 1967, Past is Prologue, 1968, Hudson's Bay Company's First Fur Brigade to the Sacramento Valley, 1968, Sketches of a Journey on Two Oceans by H.J.A. Alric, 1850-1867, 1971, San Francisco 1856 Vigilance Committee: Three Views, 1971, The Drawings of Ignatio Tirsh, Los Angeles and Its Environs in the 20th Century, A Bibliography, 1973, A History of American Political Thought, 2 vols, 1975, The Mexican War in Baja California, 1977, Henry Hoyt's A Frontier Doctor, 1979, Los Angeles from the Days of the Old Pueblo, 1981, The 1769 Transit of Venus, 1982, The Missionary Letters of Jacob Baegert, 1982, Men, Medicine and Water, 1982, Southern California Historical Anthology, 1984, George Coe's Frontier Fighter, 1984, Life of Tom Horn, 1987, A Guide to the History of California, 1989, Great Doctors of Medicine, 1990, The Bidwell-Bartleson Party, 1991, The Life of Tom Horn Revisited, 1992, Southern California's Spanish Heritage, 1992, Southern California Local History, A Gathering of W.W. Robinson's Writings, 1993, From Mexican Days to the Gold Rush, 1993, Tales of Mexican California, 1994, Women in the Life of Southern California, 1996, Hispanic California Revisited, 1996, The Presidio of San Francisco under Spain and Mexico, 1775-1848, 1996, Mission San Fernando, Rey de España: A Bicentennial Tribute, 1997, A Parochial and Institutional History of the Diocese of Oakland, 1999, The Founding Documents of Los Angeles: A Bilingual Edition, 2005, Journal of a Hide and Tallow Sea Captain's Wife, 2005; editor So. Calif. Quar., 1962-2004; contbr. articles to profl. jours. Trustee Mission Santa Barbara Archives-Libr., 1970-2007, pres., 1972-2007, life hon. trustee, 2007—. Decorated Benemereti, Papal medal, 1984; recipient Distinction award Calif. Com. for Promotion of History, 1985, Merit award Calif. Conf. Hist. Socs., 1986, Franciscan Hist. award, 1990, Disting. Emeritus award U. So. Calif., 1993, Knight Comdr. of St. Gregory, 1993, Order of Isabel the Cath. (Spanish Govt.), 1995, Oscar Lewis award Book Club of Calif., 1996, Benefactor award Franciscans, Province of St. Barbara 1999, Svc. award, 2007, Norman Neuenburg award Calif. Mission Studies Assn., 2005; Henry E. Huntington Libr. grantee-in-aid, 1960, Am. Philos. Soc. grantee, 1969; Guggenheim fellow, 1963-64. Fellow Calif. Hist. Soc. (trustee 1987-93, v.p. 1989-93, Henry R. Wagner award 1988), Hist. Soc. So. Calif.; mem. Am. Antiquarian Soc., Am. Hist. Assn., Orgn. Am. Historians, We. Hist. Assn., Zamorano Club, L.A. Corral Westerners, Phi Alpha Theta, Pi Sigma Alpha, Phi Kappa Phi.

NUNLEY, RYAN M., orthopaedic surgeon; BA in Economics, Vanderbilt U., Nashville, 1998; MD, U. NC, Chapel Hill, 2002. Lab asst. Vanderbilt U., 1996—98, Duke U. Med. Ctr., Durham, 1997; musculoskeletal course instr. Washington U. Sch. Medicine, St. Louis, 2004—, asst. prof., 2008—. Mem.: Mid-America Orthop. Assn., Am. Orthop. Assn., Am. Assn. Orthop. Surgeons. Office: Washington Univ Sch Medicine 660 S Euclid Campus Box 8233 Saint Louis MO 63110

NUNN, CHARLES BURGESS, retired religious organization administrator; b. Richmond, Va., May 1, 1931; s. Charles Burgess Sr. and Virginia Atkinson (Goode) N.; m. Helen Agnes Parker, Sept. 1, 1957; children: Patsy Virginia, Catherine Louise, Stephen Charles, Stewart Gavin. BA in Econs., Randolph Macon Coll., 1953; BD, Southwestern Bapt. Theol. Sem., 1959, MDiv, 1969; DMin, Pitts. Theol. Sem., 1979. Ordained to Gospel ministry, 1954. Pastor Warwick Rd. Bapt. Chapel, Richmond, Va., 1952-53, Garrett's Bluff Bapt. Ch., Arthur City, Tex., 1954-56, Plymouth Haven Bapt. Ch., Alexandria, Va., 1959-68, First Bapt. Ch., Bluefield, W.Va., 1968-77; exec. dir. missions Richmond (Va.) Bapt. Assn., 1977-97; adminstr., treas. So. Bapt. Conf./Assoc. Dirs. Missions, 1997—2003, ret., 2003. Trustee Bluefield (Va.) Coll., 1972-82, U. Richmond, Va., 1989-93; first v.p. Va. Bapt. Gen. Bd., Richmond, 1974-75; dir. Home Mission Bd., So. Bapt. Conv., Atlanta, 1976-84. Author: (children's book) Following Jesus, 1968. Commr. Bluefield (W.Va.) Urban Renewal Authority, 1971-74; chmn. Bluefield (W.Va.) Beautification Commn., 1972-73; pres. North Chamberlayne Civic Assn., Richmond, 1989-91. Recipient Disting. Svc. award City of Bluefield, 1970, Disting. Alumnus award Alumni Soc. Randolph Macon, Ashland, Va., 1992, Vol. Missions award Richmond Regional Devel. Coun. of the Fgn. Mission Bd., So. Bapt. Conv., 1995. Mem. Richmond Rotary Club (bd. dirs. 1990-92), Sandston Rotary Club, Pawleys Island Rotary Club, Omicron Delta Kappa. Avocations: travel, fishing, photography, baseball. Personal E-mail: cbnunnjr@aol.com.

NUNN, DONALD RAY, plastic surgeon; b. Mt. Airy, NC, Sept. 22, 1953; BS in Biochemistry/Nutrition, Va. Poly. Inst. and State U., Blacksburg; DDS, Med. Coll. Va./Va. Commonwealth U., Richmond, 1979, MD, 1992. Cert. Am. Bd. Oral/Maxillofacial Surgery, 1985, Am. Bd. Otolaryngology, 1998, Am. Bd. Plastic Surgery, 2001. Resident maxillofacial plastic surgery U. NC, Chapel Hill, 1979—82; intern surgery Med. Coll. Va. Hosps., Richmond, 1992—93; resident otolaryngology Ea. Va. Med. Sch., Norfolk, 1993—97; resident plastic surgery UCLA, 1997—99; fellow Manhattan Eye, Ear and Throat Hosp., NYC, 1999—2000; active staff mem. plastic surgery Northside Hosp., Atlanta, 2001. Featured: magazines Atlanta Style & Design, Jezebel. Mem.: Am. Assn. Oral and Maxillofacial Surgeons, Am. Soc. Aesthetic Plastic Surgery, Am. Soc. Plastic Surgeons. Office: 5673 Peachtree Dunwoody Rd NE Ste 870 Atlanta GA 30342 Office Phone: 404-255-2975. Office Fax: 404-255-2276. E-mail: donaldrnunn@aol.com.

NUNN, GRADY HARRISON, retired political science professor; b. Arlington, Tex., Apr. 12, 1918; s. William Roy and Floy Brooke (Dugan) N.; m. Ann Torrey Welsh, June 15, 1951 (dec. 1980); 1 child, Therese von Hohoff.; m. Virginia Cotton Chivington, Dec. 18, 1982 (dec. 2009). BA, U. Okla., 1939, MA, 1941; PhD (Penfield fellow), N.Y.U., 1961. Instr. N.Y.U., 1946-49; from instr. to asso. prof. U. Ala., Tuscaloosa, 1949-65, prof., chmn. dept. polit. sci. Birmingham, 1969-83, prof. emeritus, 1983—; vis. asst. prof. Ind. U., 1960-61; asst. prof., asso. prof. U. Pitts. at Ahmadu Bello U., Nigeria, 1964-68; assoc. prof. U. Pitts., 1968, Auburn U., 1968-69. Bd. dirs. Unitarian Universalist Service Com., 1978-84, v.p., 1981-82 Assoc. editor: Background on World Politics, 1957-62; Contbr. to: Readings in Government in American Society, 1949, Federalism in the Commonwealth, 1963, The Politics and Administration of Nigerian Government, 1965; editorial bd.: Jour. of Politics, 1971-74. Mem. Birmingham Regional Planning Commn., 1995-2000. Capt. F.A., AUS, 1942-46. Ford Found. Fgn. Area fellow, 1956-57 Mem. Am. Polit. Sci. Assn., So. Polit. Sci. Assn. (exec. council 1974-77), Royal African Soc., AAUP (pres. Ala. conf.), Phi Beta Kappa, Pi Sigma Alpha, Phi Eta Sigma, Alpha Tau Omega, Omicron Delta Kappa. Unitarian Universalist. Home: 5723 Belmont Place Birmingham AL 35210 Personal E-mail: ghnunn@aol.com.

NUNN, MARTHA ELIZABETH, dental educator, director; b. Memphis, Aug. 7, 1954; d. Marvin Nathan and Nancy Partlow Nunn; m. James Neighbors Johnson; children: James Christopher Johnson, Mary Catherine Johnson. BS in Chemistry, U. Tenn., Knoxville, 1976, MS in Stats., 1991; DDS, U. Tenn., Memphis, 1981; PhD in Biostats., U. Wash., Seattle, 1997. Asst. prof. Baylor Coll. Dentistry, Dallas, 1997—2000; assoc. prof. Boston U., 2000—. Dir., biometry core NE Ctr. Rsch. Evaluate and Eliminate Dental Disparities, Boston, 2001—. Recipient Arthur H. Wuehrmann prize, Am. Acad. Oral and Maxillofacial Radiology, 2001; Biometry Core grant, NIH NIDCR, 2001—08, Rsch. grant, 2004—06, 2005—07. Mem.: Am. Dental Edn. Assn., Internat. Biometric Soc., Am. Statis. Assn., Am. Acad. Periodontology (Clin. Rsch. award 1997), Internat. Assn. Dental Rsch. (sec. & treas. salivary rsch. group 2006—08). Independent. Office: Boston Univ 715 Albany 560 Boston MA 02118 Business E-Mail: nunn@bu.edu.

NUNN, PATARICA DIAN, poet; b. Arkadelphia, Ark., Aug. 10, 1951; m. Freddie Lee Nunn, Mar. 16, 1979; children: Katarica Lakisha, Roshonda Lanae, Ophelia Lorraine, Opal Laverne. Student, Ouachita Bapt. U., 1971—72. Dir. assistance operator Southwestern Bell Tel. Co., Hot Springs, Ark., 1978—2003; ret., 2003. Songwriter My Moment of Miles, Time, 1998, Mellow Drifting, 2002, Sassy Sassy Lady, 2003; author: (poetry) Sacred Memories, 1996, A True Mother's Love, 1997, A True Father's Love, 1998, Out in Left Field, 1998, A Breathe of Fresh Air, 2002. Bd. dirs., mem. adv. com. Nat. Libr. Poetry. Named to Internat. Poetry Hall of Fame, 1997, Internat. Hall of Fames's Mus. Mem.: Poetry Guild, Nat. Author's Registry. Democrat. Home: PO Box 191608 Little Rock AR 72219-1608

NUNN, SAM (SAMUEL AUGUSTUS NUNN JR.), think-tank executive, former United States Senator from Georgia, lawyer; b. Perry, Ga., Sept. 8, 1938; s. Samuel Augustus and Elizabeth (Cannon) N.; m. Colleen O'Brien, Sept. 25, 1965; children: Michelle, Brian. Student, Ga. Inst. Tech., 1956-59; AB, LL.B., Emory U., 1962. Bar: Ga. 1962. Legal counsel armed services com. US Ho. Reps., 1963; mem. firm Nunn, Geiger & Rampey, Perry, Ga., 1964-73; mem. Ga. Ho. Reps., 1968-72; US Senator from Ga., 1972-96; chmn. US Senate Armed Services Com., 1987—95; ptnr. King & Spalding LLP, Atlanta, 1997—2003; Disting. prof. Ga. Inst. Tech. Sam Nunn Sch. Internat. Affairs, Atlanta, 1997—; co-chmn., CEO Nuc. Threat Initiative, Washington, 2003—; chmn. bd. trustees Ctr. Strategic & Internat. Studies, Washington. Mem. Senate Select Com. on Secret Mil. Assistance to Iran and the Nicaraguan Opposition, 1987; bd. dirs. Texaco, 1997-2001, ChevronTexaco Corp., 2001-05, Chevron Corp., 2005-, The Coca-Cola Co., 1997-, Gen. Electric Co., 1997-, Dell Inc. (formerly Dell Computer Corp.), 1999-Served in USCG, 1959—68. Democrat. Methodist. Office: Nuc Threat Initiative 1747 Pennsylvania Ave NW Ste 700 Washington DC 20006*

NUNNALLY, ALLEN C., lawyer; BA, Amherst Coll., 1999; JD, Boston U., 2002. Bar: Mass. 2003, D.C. 2005, U.S. Dist. Ct. Mass. 2003, US Ct. Appeals Federal Cir. 2008. Mng. editor Boston U. Jour. Sci. and Tech. Law, 2001—02; litigation assoc. Wilmer Cutler Pickering Hale and Dorr LLP, Boston, 2002—. Contbr. chapters to books, articles to profl. jours. Vol. tchr. discovering justice Citizen Schs. Mock Trial Legal Apprenticeship Program, 2002—; bd. trustees Cmty. Charter Sch. Cambridge, 2007—; regional legal coord. Mass. Obama Am., 2008; vol. legal counsel Kerry-Edwards Campaign Dem. Nat. Com., 2004; bd. dirs. Friends of the Children, Boston, 2006—, treas., 2007—. Edward F. Hennessey scholar, Boston U. Sch. Law, 2002. Mem.: ABA, Mass. Bar Assn., Boston Bar Assn. Avocations: politics, reading, personal fitness, Boston sports enthusiast. Office: Wilmer Cutler Pickering Hale and Dorr 60 State St Boston MA 02109

NUNNALLY, CHARLES LYNN, biology and agriculture professor; b. Jacksonville, Tex., June 30, 1954; s. Macion Diehl Nunnally and Virdie Mae Douglas; m. Rita Kay Yarbrough, June 22, 1984. AA, Tyler Jr. Coll., Tex., 1974; BS, Sam Houston State U., Huntsville,Tex., 1976; MA, 1978; Degree Ministerial Course Study, Perkins Sch. Theology, Dallas, 2007. Lic. local pastors United Methodist Ch., 1990. Instr. agr. Wharton County Jr. Coll., Tex., 1978—84, dir. hutchins rsch. farm, 1983—84; demonstration aide Tex. Agr. Ext. Svc., Coll. Sta., Tex., 1983; instr. horticulture Trinity Valley CC, Athens, Tex., 1984—98, prof. biology & agr., 1998—; pastor Adams Chapel, Bethel United Methodist Chs., Rusk, Tex., 1990—. Adv. bd. Resource Conservation Devel., Tex., 1982—84. Den leader Cub Scouts, Jacksonville, 1995—99. Recipient Bronze Cross award, Son of Confederate Veterans, Tex. Div., 2007, Silver Cross award, Confederate Veterans, Tex. Div., 2008. Mem.: Tex. Jr. Coll. Agr. Assn, Tex. CC. Tchrs. Assn. Methodist. Avocations: antique farm equipment, music, gardening, history. Home: 1141 County Rd 3110 Jacksonville TX 75766 Office: Trinity Valley CC PO Box 2530 Palestine TX 75802 Office Phone: 903-729-0256 238. Office Fax: 903-729-2325. Business E-Mail: Cnunnally@tcc.edu.

NUNNALLY, WAVERLY EARL, religious studies educator, writer; b. Richmond, Va., Dec. 7, 1955; s. Waverly Earl Nunnally Sr. and Bertha Mae Nunnally; m. Lacey Ann Curtis, Aug. 26, 1978; children: Jacob Israel, Abbey Rene Hibbert. BA, Miss. Coll., Clinton, 1978; MA, Jerusalem U. Coll., Israel, 1983, Ref. Theol. Sem., Jackson, 1986; MPhil, Hebrew Union Coll., Cin., Ohio., 1991, PhD, 1992. Prof. early judaism & christian origins Ctrl. Bible Coll., Springfield, Mo., 1992—2002, Evangel U., Springfield, 2002—. Translator: (book) The Book of Acts; contbr. articles to profl. jours. Mem.: Soc. Bibl. Lit., Grad. Sch. Alumni Assn. (pres. 2000—03). Office: Evangel Univ 1111 N Glenstone Springfield MO 65802 Office Fax: 417-865-9599. Business E-Mail: nunnallyw@evangel.edu.

NUNNERY, PAMELA L., literature and language educator; d. Darrell D. and Wilmeth K. Edwards; m. Dale E. Nunnery, June 2, 1979; children: Laura N., Benjamin D. MA, U. Mo., Columbia, 1980; BSE, SE Mo. State U., Cape Girardeau, 1977. English tchr. Caruthersville HS, Mo., 1977—78; tchg. asst. U. Mo., Columbia, 1978—80; english coord. Three Rivers CC, Poplar Bluff, Mo., 2005—. Mentor Claudia Found., Poplar Bluff, Mo., 1998—2008; scholarship chmn. Chpt. KB PEO, Poplar Bluff, Mo., 2006—08; mem. First Bapt. Ch., Poplar Bluff, Mo., 1982—2008. Recipient Govs. award, Coordinating Bd. Higher Edn., 2002, Tchr. of Yr., NISOD, 2007. Mem.: Mo. CC Assn. Republican. Baptist. Office: Three Rivers CC 2080 Three Rivers Blvd Poplar Bluff MO 63901 E-mail: pnunn@trcc.edu.

NUOVO, BETTY A., state legislator, lawyer; b. Englewood, NJ, Dec. 10, 1931; m. Victor L. Nuovo, 1953; 2 children. BS in Edn., Bucknell U., Lewisburg, Pa., 1953. Tchr., 1953—57; pvt. practice atty. Middleury, Vt., 1974—; mem. Dist. Addison-1 Vt. House of Reps., 1981—90, 1996—. Jud. com. Vt. House of Reps., 1981-88, chmn. 1985-88, chmn. jud. rules com. 1985-86, adminstrv. rules com. 1985-88, vice-chmn. 1987-88, ways and means com. 1989-90, Middlebury natural resources and energy com., 1996-2000, jud. com., 2001-02, agr. com., 2003-04, ways and means com., 2005-06, ranking mem. natural resources and energy com., 2007—. Chair Vt. State Dem. Platform Com., Middlebury Charter Comn., Vt., Addison County Dem. Com.; mem. Addison County Regional Planning Commn., 1975-1978, bd. dirs., exec. bd., 1976-1978; bd. selectmen Middlebury, 1995-1998; bd. dirs. Vt. YMCA; mem. Middlebury LWV. Democrat. Congregationalist. Mailing: PO Box 1113 Middlebury VT 05753-0347 Office: State House 115 State St Montpelier VT 05633 also: 20 South Pleasant St Middlebury VT 05753 Home Phone: 802-388-2024; Office Phone: 802-828-2231. Business E-Mail: bnuovo@leg.state.vt.us.*

NURENBERG, DAVID, retired oil company executive; b. NYC, Mar. 25, 1939; s. Abraham S. and Katherine G. N.; m. Brenda G. Schwait, Sept. 1963; children— Jill Suzanne, Brian Michael. BS in Marine Engring, U.S. Mcht. Marine Acad., 1960; MS in Indsl. Mgmt, Columbia U., 1963, PhD in Mgmt. Sci, 1965. With Exxon Corp., 1963-67; employee relations mgr. Esso Pappas, Athens, Greece, 1968-72; labor relations and compensation mgr. Esso Europe, London, 1972-77; corp. sec. Esso Eastern Inc., Houston, 1977-82; mgr. exec. compensation Exxon Corp., NYC, 1982-90, mgr. compensation and exec. programs Irving, Tex., 1990-98; ret. Past mem. conf. exec. compensation Conf. Bd., past chmn.; adj. prof. Union Inst. Past mem. exec. edn. adv. bd. Wharton Sch., U. Pa.; past mem. adv. bd. Ctr. for Effective Orgns., U. So. Calif. Mem. Am. Compensation Assn. (bd. dirs., chmn., exec. comp. coun., bd. steering com.), Am. Contract Bridge League (silver life master).

NURICK, CARL J., author, consultant, poet; b. Harrisburg, Pa., Mar. 29, 1934; s. Gilbert and Sylvia Nurick; m. Elizabeth Parker Nurick; children: Kim, Scott, Todd, Craig. BA, Pa. State U., 1955; postgrad., Mich. State U., Columbia U. Area v.p. AT&T, Phila., 1982—86; internat. v.p. Internat. Alliance, 1987—93; exec. v.p. Transnet, Huntington Valley, Pa., 1993; v.p. OutSource Internat., 1995—96; pres. and COO Vircom, West Chester, Pa., 1996—97; freelance author Nokomis, Fla., 1998—; cons. world religions and military. Mem. MBA adv. bd. Pa. State U. and Bloomsburg U., 1974—86; mktg. adv. bd. Drexel U., Phila., 1974—78. Author: The Truth About Islam, 2003, Living To Die, 2003, The World According to Green Street Boy, 2006, poetry. Bd. dirs. Suburban Gen. Hosp., Norristown, Pa., 1979—80. Surface warfare officer USN, 1955—70. Mem.: Fairview Lake Assn., U.S. Naval Inst., Inlets Assn., US Navy League. Avocations: reading, fitness, boating, music.

NURKO, SAMUEL, gastroenterologist, researcher; b. Mexico city, Dec. 31, 1956; s. Abraham and Bertha Nurko; m. Rebeca Rosengaus, Dec. 13, 1980; children: Ariela, Uri, Yael. MD, U. Nat. Autonoma Mex., 1981; MPH, Harvard Sch. Pub. Health, Boston, 2000. Cert. in pediat. Am. Bd. Pediat., 1987, in pediat. gastroenterology 1990. Intern, pediat. Boston City Hosp., 1981—82, jr. resident, pediat., 1982—83, chief resident, pediat., 1984—85; sr. resident, pediat. Mass. Gen. Hosp., 1983—84; chief gastroenterology Hosp. Infantil de Mex., 1988—93; fellow, padiatric gastroenterology Children's Hosp., Boston, 1985—88, dir. ctr. motility and functional gastrointestinal disorders, 1993—; assoc. prof. pediat. Harvard Med. Sch., Boston, 2005—. Contbr. 120 peer reviewed publs. and chpt. Rsch. grantee, NIH, founds., industry, 1988—. Mem.: Am. Motility Soc., N.Am. Soc. for Pediatric Gestroenterology, Hepatology and Nutrition (chmn. internat. com. 2001—03). Office: Children's Hosp Boston 300 Longwood Ave Boston MA 02115 Office Phone: 617-355-6055.

NURMIKKO, ARTO VEIKKO, engineering educator; b. Finland; BSEE, MSEE, PhD, Univ. Calif., Berkeley. Engring. faculty Brown Univ., Providence, 1975—, L. Herbert Ballou Univ. prof. engring., physics, 1994—, dir., Ctr. Adv. Advanced Materials Rsch., 1989—2001. Author: more than 300 scientific jour. articles. Grantee Guggenheim Fellowship. Fellow: IEEE, Optical Soc. Am., Am. Phys. Soc., Am. Acad. Arts & Scis.; mem.: AAAS, Phi Beta Kappa. Office: Dept Physics Divsn Engring Brown Univ Providence RI 02912 Office Phone: 401-863-2869. Business E-Mail: Arto_Nurmikko@brown.edu.

NURNBERG, CHARLES GORDON, publishing executive; b. Newark, Nov. 16, 1947; s. Max and Eleanor (Gordon) Nurnberg; m. Barbara Ann Goldstein, Dec. 20, 1970; children: Jeremy, Peter, David. BA, Syracuse U., 1969. Proofreader Frederick Fell Pub., Inc., NYC, 1969, editor, 1970-72, sales, 1972-74, sales mgr., 1974-75, v.p. sales, 1975-77, exec. v.p., 1977-78, pub., 1978; pub. paperbacks Sterling Pub. Co., Inc., NYC, 1978-80, v.p., dir. mktg., 1980-82, sr. v.p., 1982-89, exec. v.p., 1990—2003, pres., 2003—08, CEO, 2003—08, pub., 2003—08; pres. & pub. Imagine Pub. Inc., 2008—. Com. mem. Book Industry Study Grp., 1992—95. Mem.: Assn. Am. Pubs. (mktg. com. 1970—73, chmn. pubs. forum com. 1973—79), Marlboro Soccer Assn. (bd. dirs., coach 1974). Avocations: writing, travel, exercise. Personal E-mail: charlesnurnberg@hotmail.com. Business E-Mail: cnurnberg@imaginebks.com.

NURSE, SIR PAUL M., academic administrator; m. Anne Nurse; children: Sarah, Emily. BSc, U. Birmingham, 1970; PhD, East Anglia, 1973. Dir. rsch. Imperial Cancer Rsch. Fund, 1993—96, dir. gen., 1996—2002; chief exec. Cancer Rsch. U.K., London, 2002—03; pres. Rockefeller U., NYC, 2003—, pres. lab. yeast genetics and cell biology, 2003—, prof., dept. molecular, cellular and develop. biology, 2003—. Chair microbiology U. Oxford, 1988—93. Recipient Internat. award, Gairdner Found., 1992, Royal medal, Royal Soc., 1995, H. P. Heineken prize for biochemistry and biophysics, Royal Netherlands Acad. Arts & Scis., 1996, Dr. Josef Steiner prize, Cancer Found., Bern, Switzerland, 1996, Alfred P. Sloan Jr. prize, GM Cancer Rsch. Found., 1997, Albert Lasker award for Basic Med. Rsch., Lasker Found., 1998, Berkan Judd award, 1998, Nobel Prize in Physiology or Medicine, Nobel Found., 2001; named one of 25 Leaders Reshaping NY, Crain's NY mag., 2008. Fellow: Am. Acad. Arts & Scis., Royal Soc. (Copley medal 2005); mem.: NAS (foreign assoc.). Avocations: hiking, flying. Office: Rockefeller U 1230 York Ave New York NY 10021-6399 Business E-Mail: nurse@rockefeller.edu.*

NUSBACHER, GLORIA WEINBERG, lawyer; b. NYC, July 22, 1951; d. Murray and Doris Weinberg; m. Burton Nusbacher, Aug. 4, 1974; 1 child, Shoshana. BA magna cum laude, Barnard Coll., 1972; JD with hons., Columbia U., 1975. Bar: N.Y. 1976. Assoc. Hughes Hubbard & Reed LLP, NYC, 1975-83, counsel, 1983-91, 2008—, ptnr., 1991—2008. Lectr. in field. Mem. Columbia Law Rev.; contbr. articles to profl. jours. Troop leader, leader trainer Girl Scouts USA, 1991-97. Fellow Am. Coll. Employee Benefits Counsel; mem. ABA (employee benefits and exec. compensation com. 1987—, fed. regulation securities com., subcom. employee benefits, exec. compensation and sect. 16, 1983—, task force Sect. 16, 1991-97, vice-chair com. employee benefits and exec. compensation 2001-03, chair subcom. fed. and state securities laws of com. employee benefits and exec. compensation 1994-2001, 03-, mem. task force exec. compensation 1992-94). Office: Hughes Hubbard & Reed LLP 1 Battery Park Plz New York NY 10004-1482 Office Phone: 212-837-6719. Business E-Mail: nusbache@hugheshubbard.com.

NUSS, DANIEL WEHRMANN, surgeon, educator; b. New Orleans, Nov. 21, 1955; s. Warren Philip and Celina (Seghers) N.; m. Wilma Rowley, June 23, 1978; 1 child, Olivia Emily. BS, La. State U., 1977, MD, 1981. Diplomate Am. Bd. Otolaryngology; lic. physician La., Pa. Resident in gen. surgery Charity Hosp. of La., New Orleans, 1981-83; resident in surg. oncology of head and neck M.D. Anderson Hosp. and Tumor Inst., U. Tex. Med. Ctr., Houston, 1984; resident in otolaryngology-head and neck surgery La. State U. Med. Ctr., New Orleans, 1984-87; clin. fellow in surgery of cranial base dept. otolaryngology Ctr. for Cranial Base Surgery, U. Pitts. Sch. Medicine, 1989-90, rsch. fellow in surgery of cranial base dept. otolaryngology, 1990-91; instr. otolaryngology-head and neck surgery La. State U. Med. Ctr., 1987, asst. prof. otolaryngology-head and neck surgery, 1988-89, 91-92, asst. prof. neurosurgery, 1991-92, assoc. prof. otolaryngology-head and neck surgery/neurosurg., 1992-96, dir. residency program dept. otolaryngol.-head & neck surg., 1993—, chmn. dept. otolaryngology-head & neck surgery, 1996—, prof. dept. neurosurgery/otolaryngology-head and neck surg., 1996—. Reviewer manuscripts Head and Neck Jour., 1990—, Skull Base Surgery Jour., 1992—; corr. editor, reviewer manuscripts skull base surgery sect. Otolaryngology-Head and Neck Surgery Jour., 1994—; contbr. articles to profl. jours. Named one of Top Drs. in New Orleans, New Orleans Mag., 1995; recipient Upjohn award for excellence in medicine, 1982; Blanco-Loustalot Meml. scholar, 1979-81. Fellow ACS, Am. Acad. Otolaryngology-Head and Neck Surgery (Cert. of Honor 1995); mem. AMA, N.Am. Skull Base Soc., Soc. Head and Neck Surgeons, So. Med. Assn., Soc. Univ. Otolaryngologists, Assn. Acad. Depts. of Otolaryngology-Head and Neck Surgery, La. Acad. Otolaryngology-Head and Neck Surgery (elected mem.-at-large), La. State Med. Soc., Greater New Orleans Soc. for Otolaryngology-Head and Neck Surgery (treas. 1992-94, v.p. 1994-96, pres.-elect 1995-96, pres. 1996-98), Orleans Parish Med. Soc. Office: La State U Med Ctr 2020 Gravier St Dept New Orleans LA 70112-2272

NUSS, LAWTON R., state supreme court justice; b. Salina, Kans., Dec. 30, 1952; m. Barbara Nuss; 5 children. BA in English and History, U. Kans., 1975, JD, 1982. Atty. Clark Mize & Linville, 1982—2002; special prosecutor City of Salina, 1994—96; justice Kans. Supreme Ct., Topeka, 2002—. Former mediator U.S. Dist. Ct., Kans. Combat engring. officer USMC. Mem.: Kans. Assn. Def. Counsel (pres.), Kans. Bar Assn. (chmn. bd. editors jour.). Office: Kans Jud Ctr 301 SW 10th Topeka KS 66612-1507*

NUSS, ROGER CHARLES, otolaryngologist, director; b. Abington, Pa., July 31, 1962; m. Kim Wilson; children: Charles Wilson, Julia Elizabeth, Emily Alyson, Sarah Ruth. BS, Swarthmore Coll., Pa., 1984; MD, Harvard Med. Sch., Boston, 1988. Diplomate Am. Bd. Otolaryngology, 1994. Resident dept. otolaryngology Harvard, 1989—93; fellow pediat. otolaryngology Children's Hosp. Boston, 1993—94, asst. otolaryngology, 1996—, dir. pediat. voice clinic, 1997—; asst. otolaryngology Mass. Eye & Ear Infirmary, Boston, 1994—96. Contbr. scientific papers to numerous profl. jours. V.p. Wayland Swim & Tennis Club, Mass., 2009—; marathon runner Boston Marathon. Fellow: ACS, Am. Academy Otolaryngology (head & neck surgery 1994); mem.: Am. Soc. Pediat. Otolaryngology. Avocations: swimming, running. Office: Children's Hosp Boston 300 Longwood Ave Boston MA 02115 Office Phone: 617-355-5116.

NUSSBAUM, BENNETT L., food products executive; BS in Econs., U. Pa. Wharton Sch. Bus., Phila., 1969; MBA, Columbia U., 1971. Exec. PepsiCola Internat.; sr. v.p., CFO Kinko's Inc., Ventura, Calif.; exec. v.p., CFO Burger King Corp., 2001—03; sr. v.p., CFO Winn-Dixie Stores, Inc., 2003—. Office: Winn Dixie Stores Inc 5050 Edgewood Ct Jacksonville FL 32254 Office Phone: 904-370-6655. Business E-Mail: bennettnussbaum@winn-dixie.com.

NUSSBAUM, CHARLES OLIVER, philosopher, educator; b. NYC, July 25, 1946; s. Nathan and Sara Gisela Nussbaum; m. Sherry Renee Smith; 1 child, Brittany Renee. PhD, Emory U., Atlanta, 1988. Vis. asst. prof. philosophy Northern Mich. U., Marquette, 1990—91; assoc. prof. philosophy U. Tex., Arlington, Tex., 1991—. Mem.: Am. Soc. Aesthetics, Am. Philos. Assn. Office: Univ Tex Arlington Dept Philosophy & Humanities Arlington TX 76019 Office Phone: 817-272-3217. Office Fax: 817-272-5807. Business E-Mail: nussbaum@uta.edu.

NUSSBAUM, MICHAEL SCOT, physician, medical educator; b. Cleve., Nov. 4, 1956; s. Fritz S. and Elaine (Sukenik) N.; m. Sue Ellen Weinstein, Aug. 6, 1983; children: Jaclyn, Rachel. BA, Northwestern U., 1977; MD, U. Pa., 1981. Intern dept. surgery U. Cin., 1981-82, resident dept. surgery, 1982-86, chief resident dept. surgery, 1985-86; dir. surg. edn. Jewish Hosp., Cin., 1986-90; asst. prof. surgery U. Cin., 1986-96, assoc. prof. surgery, 1996—, asst. prof. molecular and cellular physiology, 1991—, prof. surgery, 2006—; attending physician dept. parenteral and enteral nutrition U. Cin. Hosp., 1989—, dir. surg. endoscopy and laparoscopy, 1993—2000, chief sect. gen. surgery, 1999—2003, chief of staff, 2000—08, vice chmn. clin. affairs, 2003—08, asst. dean for hosp. affairs, 2003—06, interm chair dept. surgery, 2006—07; prof. U. Fla. Coll. Med. Jacksonville Dept. Surgery, 2008—, chair, 2008—. Med. records com. Jewish Hosp. Cin., 1986-88, med. incident rev. com., 1986-92, intensive care com., 1986-2000, CPR com., 1986-92, course dir. ACLS, 1987-92, chmn. nutrition support com., 1988-2000; chmn. adverse drug reaction com. U. Cin. Hosp., 1988-92, edn. coordinating com., 1990-93, oper. rm. adv. com. 1992-2000, patient care rev. com., 1992-2000, chmn. pharmacy and therapeutics com., 1992-2000, med. co-dir. collaborative care unit, 1993—, clin., tech. and support design team, 1994—, others; ACLS subcom. Am. Heart Assn.-Southwestern Ohio Chpt., 1988-95, affiliate faculty ACLS, 1988-95; assoc. examiner The Am. Bd. Surgery, 1990, 94, 96; trauma adv. com. Ohio Emergency Med. Svcs. Bd., 1993-2000; intern chair dept. surgery, U. Cin., 2006-. Editor-in-chief: The Mont Reid Handbook, The University of Cincinnati Surgical Manual, 1987; editl. bd. mem. Current Summaries in the Jour. Parenteral and Enteral Nutrition, 1991-97; contbr. chpts. to books and articles to profl. jours. Bd. mem. Yavneh Day Sch., Cin., 1992-95. Fellow ACS (com. on trauma, instr. advanced trauma life support 1987—, Ohio chpt. chmn. resident essay contest 1994—, sec. Ohio chpt. 1997-2000, chair local arrangements 1996 annual meeting); mem. Am. Soc. for Parenteral and Enteral Nutrition (liaison com. 1993-95), Am. Trauma Soc., Assn. for Acad. Surgery (com. on edn. 1989-91, nominating com. 1992, com. on issues 1992-94, councilor 1994-96), Assn. for Surg. Edn., Ctrl. Surg. Assn. (sec. 2006-2009, pres. elec. 2009-), Cin. Acad. Medicine, Cin. Surg. Soc. (treas. 1990-92), Collegium Interatn. Chirurgia Digestivae, Mont Reid Surg. Soc. U. Cin., Ohio Soc. for Parenteral and Enteral Nutrition (dir.-at-large 1990, pres.-elect 1991, pres. 1991-92), Ohio State Med. Assn., Pancreas Club, Inc., Soc. Am. Gastrointestinal Endoscopic Surgeons (resident edn. com. 1998-2006, rsch. com. 1998-2005, 2001-2006, membership com. 2001--), Am. Bd. Surgery, 2000-2006, Soc. Critical Care Medicine, Soc. for Parenteral Alimentation, Soc. for Surgery of the Alimentary Tract, Surg. Infection Soc., Soc. Univ. Surgeons (com. on surg. edn. 1998-2002, chair 1999-2002), Am. Surg. Assn., Halsted Soc., Alpha Omega Alpha. Office: Univ FL Jacksonville Coll Medicine Dept Surgery 653 W 8th St 3rd Fl Faculty Clinic Jacksonville FL 32209 Office Phone: 904-244-5502. Business E-Mail: michael.nussbaun@jax.ufl.edu.

NUSSBAUM, MICHEL ERNEST, physician; b. LA, Nov. 7, 1947; s. Schymen and Jeannette Eleanor (Pequignot) N.; m. Joyce Wendy Laudon, Nov. 1, 1981; children: Eleanor, Anna. BA, Cornell U., 1969; MD, Free U. Brussels, 1977. Intern internal medicine NY Hosp. Queens, Flushing, 1977-78, resident, 1978-80, fellow gastroenterology, 1980-82, attending physician, 1982—; physician pvt. practice, Flushing, NY, 1982—; attending physician Flushing Hosp. Med. Ctr., 1987—; clin. instr. medicine Weill Med. Coll. Cornell U., NYC, 1994-98, clin. asst. prof. medicine, 1998—, clin. assoc. prof. medicine, 2009—; med. dir. Franklin Ctr. for Nursing and Rehab., Flushing, 1995-99. Dir. endoscopy NY Hosp. Queens, 1990—, asst. dir. gastroenterology, 1998-2004, assoc. dir. gastroenterology, 2004—, pres. med. staff soc., 1992-96, chmn. med. bd., 1997-2003, trustee, 1998-2003 Fellow: ACP, Am. Gastroent. Assn., Am. Coll. Gastroenterology. Office: 142-43 Booth Memorial Ave Flushing NY 11355-5343 Office Phone: 718-886-1919.

NUSSBAUM, PAUL STOWELL, retired urologist; b. St. Louis, Mo., Sept. 25, 1930; s. Paul Beckman and Claire Stevenson Nussbaum; m. Joyce Lee Linebarger, May 27, 1955; children: Paul Stevenson, John Michael, David Matthew, Barbara Lee. Academic diploma, Castle Heights Mil. Acad., Lebanon, Tenn., 1948; AB in Biol. Scis., S.E. Mo. State Coll., Cape Girardeau, 1952; MD, U. Tenn. Coll. Medicine, Memphis, 1955. Cert. Am. Bd. Urology. Chief urology U.S. Army Hosp., Ft. Leonard Wood, Mo., 1961—64; pvt. practice urology Cape Girardeau, Mo., 1965—67; program dir. urology Scott White Meml. Hosp., Temple, Tex., 1967—77; pvt. practice urology Santa Fe, 1977—87; ret. Cons. urology U.S. Vets. Adminstrn., Marion, Ill., 1965—69, Temple, Tex., 1969—77. Author: (med. jour.) Surgery, Gynecology and Obstretics. Maj. US Army, 1957—64. Fellow: ACS; mem.: Am. Urol. Assn. (sr.), Masonic, Scottish Rite, Order of Ea. Star (Santa Fe #19, Past Patron). Republican. Methodist. Avocations: flying, hunting, fishing, sailing, golf. Home: 102 Pinehurst Meadowlakes TX 78654-6416

NUSSBAUM, SAMUEL R., healthcare insurance company executive, medical educator; MD, Mt. Sinai Sch. Medicine. Prof. Harvard Med. Sch.; sr. v.p. health care delivery Blue Cross Blue Shield Mass.; pres., CEO Physician Partners of New Eng.; CEO health plan, pres. med. grp. BJC Health Sys., 1996—2000, exec. v.p. med. affairs and sys. integration, 1996—2000; exec. v.p., chief med. officer WellPoint, Inc., Indpls., 2001—. Chmn. Nat. Com. Quality Health Care; chair Chief Med. Officer Leadership Coun. Am.'s Health Ins. Plan, bd. mem.; chmn. health care data and quality subcommittee Ind. Commn. on Excellence in Health Care; prof. clin. medicine Washington U. Sch. Medicine; adj. prof. Washington U. Olin Sch. Bus. Recipient Physician Exec. Award of Excellence, Am. Coll. Physician Execs. and Modern Physician mag., 2004. Mem.: Disease Mgmt. Assn. Am. Office: WellPoint Inc 120 Monument Cir Indianapolis IN 46204*

NUSSENZWEIG, MICHEL CLAUDIO, immunologist, educator; BA, NYU; PhD, Rockefeller Univ., NYC; MD, NYU Med. Sch. Faculty Rockefeller Univ., 1990—, Sherman Fairchild prof. immunology, and head, immunology sect., 2001—; also investigator Howard Hughes Med. Inst., 1990—. Recipient Solomon A. Berson award for basic sci., Huang Found. Meritorious Career award, Am. Assn. Immunologists. Fellow: Am. Acad. Arts & Scis. Office: Rockefeller Univ 1230 York Ave New York NY 10021 Office Phone: 212-327-8000. Business E-Mail: nussen@rockefeller.edu.

NUSSLE, JIM (JAMES ALLEN NUSSLE), former United States Representative from Iowa; b. Des Moines, June 27, 1960; s. Mark S. and Loma Kay (Fisher) Nussle, Mark S. and Lorna Kay (Fisher) Nussle; m. Leslie J. Harbison, Aug. 23, 1986 (div. July 2, 1996); children: Sarah, Mark; m. Karen Chiccehitto, 2001. BA, Luther Coll., Decorah, Iowa, 1983; JD, Drake U., Des Moines, 1985. Bar: Iowa 1985. Pvt. practice law, Manchester, Iowa, 1986; state atty. Del. County, Manchester, 1986-90; mem. US Congress from 2nd Iowa dist., Washington, 1991—2002, mem. house ways & means com., chmn. budget com., 2001—07; mem. US Congress from 1st Iowa dist., Washington, 2003—07; dir. Office Mgmt. & Budget Exec. Office of the Pres., Washington, 2007—09; spl. adviser Growth Energy, 2009—. Adv. Rudolph Guiliani Presdl. Exploratory Com., NYC, 2007; bd. dirs. Growth Energy, 2009—. Recipient Taxpayer's Friend Award, Nat Taxpayers Union, Superheros Award, Citizens Against Govt. Waste, Golden Plow Award, Am. Farm Bur. Mem.: Del. Farm Bur. Republican. Lutheran. Avocation: guitar. Office: Growth Energy 1900 K St NW Ste 100 Washington DC 20006 Office Phone: 202-496-7306. Office Fax: 202-496-7066.*

NÜSSLEIN-VOLHARD, CHRISTIANE, medical researcher; b. Magdeburg, Germany, Oct. 20, 1942; d. Rolf Volhard and Brigitte (Haas) Volhard. Diploma in Biochemistry, U. Tübingen, 1968, PhD, 1973; ScD (hon.), Yale U., Oxford Univ., 2005. Rsch. assoc. lab. of Dr. Schaller Max-Planck Inst. for Devel. Biology, Tübingen, 1972-74; postdoctoral fellow lab. of Dr. W. Gehring, Biozentrum, Basel, Switzerland, 1975-76; postdoctoral fellow lab of Dr. K. Sander U. Freiburg, 1977; head rsch. group European Molecular Biology Lab., Heidelberg, 1978-80; rsch. group leader Friedrich-Miescher Lab. Max-Planck-Gesellschaft, Tübingen, 1981-85; sci. mem. Max-Planck Assn., dir. Max-Planck Inst. for Devel. Biology, Tübingen, 1985-90, dir. genetics dept., 1990—. Hon. prof. U. Tübingen. Author: Von Genen und Embryonen, 2004, Das Werden des Lebens, 2004, Coming to life, 2006; contbr. numerous articles to profl. jours. Recipient Albert Lasker award for Basic Med. Rsch., Lasker Found., 1991, Louisa Gross Horowitz prize Columbia U., 1992, Forderpreis award Deutschen Forschungsgemeinschaft, 1986, Franz Vogt prize U. Giessen, 1986, Carus medal German Acad. Leopoldine, 1989, Schering prize, Berlin, 1993, Rosenstiel medal Brandeis U., Nobel prize in physiology or medicine, 1995, L'oréal-UNESCO Tribute award (for UNESCO's 60th anniversary), 2006. Mem. European Molecular Biology Orgn., Berlin Brandenburgische Acad., Am. Philosophical Soc. Achievements include rsch. in using embryos, created a series of genetic screens that led to the identification of most of the genes responsible for the organism's body segment development, establishing that genes encode signaling molecules that tell cells where they are in the organism's overall structure and what their function is to be. Office: Max-Planck-Institut fur Entwicklungsbiologie Abt III Genetik Spemannstr 35 72076 Tübingen Germany*

NUTAN, MOHAMMAD TAWHIDUL HAQUE, pharmacy educator, researcher; s. Enamul and Fatema Haque; m. Manna Salowa, 2000; 1 child, Mohammad Muhitul Haque (Arnob). B of Pharmacy, U. Dhaka, Bangladesh, 1994, PharmM, 1997; PhD, Tex. Tech U. Health Scis. Ctr., Amarillo, 2004. Cert. FPGE Nat. Assn. of Bds. of Pharmacy, 2004. Lectr. dept. pharmacy U. Asia Pacific, Dhaka, Bangladesh, 1997; lectr. pharmacy discipline Khulna U., Bangladesh, 1997—2000; tchr, rsch. asst. sch. pharmacy Tex. Tech U. Health Scis. Ctr., Amarillo, 2000—04; grad. pharmacy intern Walgreen Co., Miami, Fla., 2004—06; asst. prof. Tex. A&M U. Health Scis. Ctr., Irma Lerma Rangel Coll. Pharmacy, Kingsville, Tex., 2006—. Chair, pharms. faculty search com. Tex. A&M U. Health Scis. Ctr. Coll. Pharmacy, Kingsville, 2006—, mem., acad. credentialing com., 2006—, mem., curriculum affair com., 2006—, advisor PharmD students, 2006—. Contbr. articles to scientific jours. Named Tchr. Of Year, Tex. A&M Coll. Pharmacy, 2007—08. Mem.: Am. Assn. Coll. Pharmacy, Am. Assn. Pharm. Scientists, Bangladesh Pharm. Soc., Pharmacy Grad. Assn. Bangladesh, Sigma Xi. Achievements include research in developed a controlled release multi-particulate formulation coated with starch acetate; developed a limonene-based coenzyme Q-10 self-nanoemulsified dosage form; developed an enteric dual-controlled gastrointestinal therapeutic system of salmon calcitonin; developed a cellulose acetate butyrate dispersion for controlled release coating; discovery of isolated a new alkaloid, Bismurrayafoline E, from plant source. Avocations: astronomy, geography, reading, travel, movies. Office: Texas A&M Coll Pharmacy 1010 West Ave B MSC 131 Kingsville TX 78363

NUTI, WILLIAM R., computer services company executive; married; 1 child. BS in Fin. and Economics, Long Island U., 1986. Various sales positions to sr. sales staff mem. IBM, 1982—88; sales mgr. Network Equipment Technologies, 1988—90, Netrix Corp., 1990—92; with Cisco Systems, 1992—2002, v.p. then pres. Greater Asia Pacific region, sr. v.p., pres. Europe, Middle East and Africa ops. London, 1999—2001, sr. v.p. worldwide service provider bus. and US theatre ops., 2001—02; pres., COO Symbol Tech., Holtsville, NY, 2002—03, pres., CEO, 2003—05; pres. & CEO NCR Corp., Dayton, Ohio, 2005—07, chmn., pres., CEO, 2007—. Bd. dir. Opus 360, 1999—, Sprint Nextel Corp., 2008—. Bd. dir. Fair Media Council; trustee Long Island U. Office: NCR Corp 1700 S Patterson Blvd Dayton OH 45479

NUTT, HOUSTON DALE, JR., college football coach; b. Little Rock, Ark., Oct. 14, 1957; s. Houston Dale and Emogene Nutt; m. Diana Nutt; children: Houston, Hailey, Hanna, Haven. BA in Phys. Edn., Okla. State U., Stillwater, 1981. Grad. asst. Okla. State U. Cowboys, 1981—83, receivers coach, 1984—89, offensive coord., 1989—90; asst. coach U. Ark. Razorbacks, 1983—84, wide receivers coach, 1990—93, head coach, 1998—2007, Murray St. U. Racers, 1993—96, Boise State U. Broncos, 1996—98, U. Miss. Rebels, 2008—. Office: U Miss PO Box 1848 University MS 38677*

NUTTALL, RICHARD NORRIS, management consultant, physician; b. Hamilton, Ont., Can., Feb. 7, 1940; s. James William and Margaret Gay (Walsh) N.; m. Ethel Jane Pickering, July 9, 1977; children: Andrew Richard, John Patrick. BSA, U. Toronto, 1961; MPA, Harvard U., 1964; MB, BS, U. London, 1974; MPH, James Cook U., 2003; MSc, U. Western Ont., 2005. Cert. mgmt. cons. Zone dir. Health and Welfare Can., Prince Rupert, B.C., 1977-79, regional dir. Edmonton, Alta., 1980-82; pres. Rutland Consulting Group, Ltd., Vancouver, B.C., Canada, 1982-87, Richmond Assocs. Internat., Vancouver, 1988-90; med. health officer Govt. N.W. Ters., Yellowknife, B.C., Canada, 1990-93, Regina (Can.) Health Dist., 1993-97; pres. Anjohn Med. Svcs., Inc., Victoria, Canada, 1997—. Staff physician Royal Jubilee Hosp. Fellow Am. Coll. Preventive Medicine, Am. Coll. Healthcare Execs., Can. Coll. Health Svc. Execs., Coll. Family Physicians Can. Office: 1186 Eaglenest Pl Victoria BC V8Y 3C7 Canada Office Phone: 250-598-5158. Business E-Mail: rnuttall@shaw.ca.

NUTTER, JAMES RANDALL, management educator; b. Stephenville, Tex., Nov. 11, 1945; s. Coleman Evan and Mary Frances (Jay) N.; m. Marilyn Grace Marotta, Aug. 23, 1969; children: Heather Elizabeth, Susan Mary, Katherine Grace. BS, No. Ill. U., DeKalb, 1968, MEd, 1969; DSc, Nova U., Davie, Fla., 1991; DBA, Nova S.E. U., Davie, 1995. Cert. master fin. profl. Tchr. social studies Hinsdale (Ill.) South H.S., 1968-69, Govt. U.S. V.I., St. Thomas, 1969-71; dir. employee rels. Shuron divsn. Textron Corp., Rochester, N.Y., 1971-73; dir. corp. tng. Sybron Corp., Rochester, 1973-75; dir. human resources Red Wing Co., Fredonia, N.Y., 1975-82; assoc. prof., dept. chair Liberty U., Lynchburg, Va., 1982-92; prof., chair bus. dept., dir. grad. bus. studies Geneva Coll., Beaver Falls, Pa., 1992—. Pres. Nutter/Forbus Group, Inc., Lynchburg, 1982-92; bd. dirs. Lynchburg Preheater Inc.; commr. Assn. Collegiate Bus. Schs. and Programs, 1998—; mem. acad. adv. coun. Pacific Inst. for Bus. Mgmt.; vis. prof. Peoples Republic of China Fgn. Experts Bur., 1999-, N.W. Nazarene U. MBA Mex. and Korea Program, vis. prof. bus. Southeast U. Nanjing, China, 2008-. Nat. examiner Malcomb Baldrige Nat. Quality Program, quality sys. & accreditation cons. Fellow Am. Acad. Fin. Mgmt.; mem. Am. Mgmt. Assn., Soc. Strategic Mgmt., Acad. Mgmt., Soc. Human Resource Mgmt. (faculty advisor 1972—), Christian Bus. Faculty Assn., Assn. Collegiate Bus. Schs. and Programs (nat. chair 2002-03, bd. dirs. 2002-, Malcolm Baldrige Nat. Quality Award examiner, 2008). Republican. Avocations: fishing, travel, reading. Home: 437 Woodward Ridge Dr Mount Holly NC 28120 Office Phone: 724-847-6615. Business E-Mail: jrn@geneva.edu.

NUTTER, MICHAEL ANTHONY, Mayor, Philadelphia, former councilman; b. Phila., June 29, 1957; m. Lisa Nutter, 1991; children: Olivia, Christian. BS, Wharton Sch. Bus., U. Pa., 1979. Investment mgr. Pryorm Counts & Co., Inc.; campaign mgr. Rendell for Gov. Campaign; city councilman Dist. 4 City of Phila., 1992—2006, mayor, 2008—. Chmn. Comms. and Econ. Devel. Com., Pa. Convention Ctr. Authority, 2003-07; vice chmn. Lic. and Inspections and Appropriations Coms.; mem. Pub. Property Com., Pub. Works Com., Transp. and Pub. Utilities Com., Pub. Safety, Ethics and Whole Com. Leader Dem. 52nd Ward. Named to Power 150, Ebony mag., 2008. Democrat. Office: City Hall Rm 215 Philadelphia PA 19107

NUTTER, SUSAN K., librarian, academic administrator; b. Boston, Aug. 9, 1944; m. Joe Hewitt, 1982; stepchildren: Kirsten Elizabeth Hewitt(dec.), Stephen A. Hewitt. BS, Colby Coll., Waterville, Maine, 1966; MLIS, Simmons Coll., Boston, 1968. Libr. intern to libr. Project INTREX MIT, 1966—73, assoc. head engring. libraries, assoc. dir. libraries collection mgmt. and technol. services, 1980—87; Coun. on Libr. Resources Academic Libr. Mgmt. Intern U. NC, Chapel Hill, 1979—80; dir. libraries NC State U., Raleigh, 1987—, vice provost, 1995—. Mem. steering com. NC Libraries for Virtual Edn. (NC LIVE); mem. exec. com., governing bd. Triangle Rsch. Libraries Network. Recipient Alumni Achievement Award, Simmons Coll., 1995, Hugh C. Atkinson Meml. Medal, Assn. College & Rsch. Libraries, 1999; named Libr. of Yr., Libr. Jour., 2005. Mem.: Assn. Rsch. Libraries (pres. 1993). Office: DH Hill Libr NC State U Campus Box 7111 Raleigh NC 27695-7111 Office Phone: 919-515-7188. Office Fax: 919-515-3628. Business E-Mail: susan_nutter@ncsu.edu.

NUTTER, ZOE DELL LANTIS, retired public relations executive; b. Yamhill, Oreg., June 14, 1915; d. Arthur Lee Lantis and Olive Adelaide (Reed) Lantis-Hilton; m. Richard S. West, Apr. 30, 1941 (div. Nov. 1964); m. Ervin John Nutter, Dec. 30, 1965. Assoc. in Bus., Santa Ana Jr. Coll., 1944. Cert. spl. emergency secondary tchr., Calif.; FAA cert. lic. commercial, instrument, single/multi engine land airplanes pilot. Promoter World's Fair & Comml. Airlines Golden Gate Internat. Expn., San Francisco, 1937-39; pirate theme girl, official hostess Treasure Island's World Fair, San Francisco, 1939-40; prin. dancer San Francisco Ballet, 1937-41; artist, 1941-45; program dir. Glenn County H.S., Willows, Calif., 1952-58; pub. rels. Monarch Piper Aviation Co., Monterey, Calif., 1963-65; pilot, pub. rels. Elano Corp., Xenia, Ohio, 1968-85. Bd. dirs. Nat. Aviation Hall of Fame, Dayton, Ohio, pres., chmn., 1989-92, bd. trustees, 1976—, chmn. bd. nominations, 1992—; bd. trustees Ford's Theatre, Washington, Treasure Island Mus., San Francisco; charter mem. Friends of First Ladies, Smithsonian, Washington, 1990-93. Assoc. editor KYH mag. of Shikar Safari Internat., 1985-87; contbg. columnist Scripps Howard San Francisco News, 1938. Bd. dirs. Cin. May Festival, 1976-80, San Francisco Aero. Soc., 1997-; cen. com. Glenn County Rep. Party, Willows, 1960-64; state cen. com. Rep. Party, 1962-64; adv. bd. Women's Air & Space Mus., Dayton, 1987-94. Warrant officer, Civil Air Patrol, 1967-69. Recipient Civic Contbn. Honor award Big Brothers/Big Sisters, 1991, John Collier Nat. award Camp Fire Girls & Boys, 1988, Tambourine award Salvation Army, 1982, State of Ohio Gov.'s award for Volunteerism, 1992, Spirit of Innovation award Wright State U., 2001, Amb. award Wright Bros. Heritage Benefit, 2001, East Ann. Zoe Dell Nutter Dayton Air Show award, 2003, In grateful appreciation of contbn. 1909 Wright Flyer Monument award Inventing Flight (orgn. charted by Congress), 2003, Deeds-Kettering award Outstanding Contbn., Engrs. CLub Dayton, 2004; named Most Photographed Girl in World, News Burs. & Clipping Svcs., 1938-39. Mem., founder Dancers Over 40, NYC; Fellow Pres.'s Club U. Ky., Ohio State U., Wright State U.; mem. 99's Internat. Women Pilots Orgn. (life, hospitality chmn. 1968), San Francisco Aeronaut. Soc. (bd. dirs. 1997—), Monterey Bay Chapter 99's (mem. chmn. 1964-65), Walnut Grove Country Club, Rotary (Paul Harris fellow 1987), Shikar Safari Internat. (host com. 1976), Country Club of the North. Achievements include established ann. Zoe Dell Nutter Dayton Air Show award, 2003. Avocations: aviation, flying, horseback riding, hunting, shooting, fashion. Home: 986 Trebein Rd Xenia OH 45385-9534

NUTTING, PAUL JOHN, city manager; b. Oswego, NY, July 6, 1952; s. Robert Truman and Joan Violet (Joyce) N. BA, SUNY Oswego, 1974; MPA, SUNY Albany, 1977. Adminstrv. asst. City of League City, Tex., 1978—79, acting city adminstr., 1979—80, 1981, asst. city adminstr., 1980—81, exec. asst. to mayor, 1981—82, city adminstr., 1982—95; city mgr. City of Springfield, Tenn., 1995—. Bd. dir. Tenn. Energy Acquisition Corp., 1996-2004, Five Rivers Resource Conservation and Devel. Coun.; mem. exec. bd. Nashville Area Met. Planning Orgn., 2003-05, alt. bd. mem., 2005-; alt. bd. mem. Regional Transp. Authority, 2003-; bd. dirs. Tenn. Mcpl. League, 2005-07. Bd. dir. League City Family Welfare Coun., 1978-89; chmn. United Way, Robertson County, 2003; mem. exec. bd. Mainland Communities United Way, Texas City, Tex., 1991-94; adv. dir. League City Mchts. and Bus. Assn., 1989-95, North Galveston County C. of C., Dickinson, Tex., 1989-95. Mem. Internat. City and County Mgmt. Assn., Tenn. City Mgmt. Assn., Texas City Mgmt. Assn., Am. Soc. for Pub. Adminstrn. (pres. Houston area chpt. 1991-93, dir. 1990-91, 93-95), Robertson County C. of C., Springfield Rotary Club (pres. 2006-07), League City Rotary Club (pres. 1985-86, 93-94), Rotary. Roman Catholic. Avocations: golf, history. Home: 333 Walnut St Springfield TN 37172-2125 Office: City Of Springfield PO Box 788 Springfield TN 37172-0788 Office Phone: 615-382-2200.

NUTZELL, NATALIE, financial analyst; b. Memphis, Sept. 1, 1981; d. Michael G. and Amy McNatt Nutzell. Degree, U. Tenn., Martin, 2000, Degree, 2002. Admin. asst. Internat. Paper, Memphis, 1999—2002; legal asst. Glassman, Edwards, Wade Wyatt, P.C., 2002—05; compliance analyst 21st Century Holding Co., Ft. Lauderdale, Fla., 2007—. Participant Walk Furthe Animals, Ft. Lauderdale, 2009. Mem.: FAIA, Nat. Campaign Tolerance (founder 2004—), Zeta Tau Alpha. Avocations: horseback riding, dog breeding.

NUTZLE, FUTZIE (BRUCE JOHN KLEINSMITH), artist, writer, animator; b. Lakewood, Ohio, Feb. 21, 1942; s. Adrian Ralph and Naomi Irene Kleinsmith; children: Adrian David, Ariel Justine and Tess Alexandra (twins); m. Halina Pochron Kleinsmith. Author: Modern Loafer, Thames and Hudson, 1981, (authobiography) Futzie Nutzle, 1983, Earthquake, 1989, Run the World: 50 Cents Chronicle Books, 1991; illustrator: The Armies Encamped Beyond Unfinished Avenues (Morton Marcus), 1977, Box of Nothing, 1982, The Duke of Chemical Birds (Howard McCord), 1989, Book of Solutions, 1990, Fact and Friction, 1990, Managing for the 90s, 1992, Soundbites for Success, 1994; feature cartoonist Rolling Stone, N.Y.C., 1975-80, The Japan Times, Tokyo and L.A., 1986-98, The Prague Post, Czechoslovakia, 1991-92; contbr. exhbns. include Inaugural, 1966, Cupola, 1967, Rolling Renaissance, San Francisco, 1968, 100 Acres, O.K. Harris 1971, N.Y.C., San Francisco Mus. Art, 1972, Indpls. and Cin. Mus. Art, 1975, Leica, L.A., 1978, Santa Barbara Mus. Annex, Calif., 1978, Swope, Santa Monica, West Beach Cafe, Venice, Calif., 1985, Les Oranges, Santa Monica, Correspondence Sch., NY Correspondence Sch., 1968-75, 1st Ann. Art-A-Thon, N.Y.C., 1985, Am. Epiphany with Phillip Hefferton, 1986, Polit. Cartoon Show, Braunstein, San Francisco, Komsomolskaya Pravda, 1988, retrospective Eloise Packard Smith, 1990, exemplary contemporary, Cowell, U. Calif. Santa Cruz, 1991, Silicon Graphics Inc., Computer Graphics for NAB, Las Vegas, 1993, Prague Eco-Fair, 1991; represented in pvt. and pub. collections Mus. Modern Art, N.Y.C., San Francisco Mus. Modern Art, Oakland Mus., San Francisco Mus. Cartoon Art, Whitney Mus. Am. Art, N.Y.C., Aromas (Calif.) Libr., San Juan Bautista Libr., contbr. The Redwood Coast Review, (bugle) Art Secundas Artists Periodical Scottsdale, Ariz., Santa Cruz Weekly Newspaper Letters, Weekly Mgs, rep. Winfield Gallery Address: Fools Gold 34A Polk St PO Box 1083 San Juan Bautista CA 95045 Office Phone: 831-623-9275. Personal E-mail: fnutzle@aol.com.

NUWAL, TARA C., economics professor; b. Banera, Rajasthan, India, Sept. 4, 1945; s. Banshilal and Mohan Nuwal; m. Rajan Nuwal, Mar. 7, 1977; children: Tushar, Tapas. MA in Economics, U. Jodhpur, India, 1968, PhD, 1974. Prof. LNM Coll. Bus. Mgmt., Muzaffarpur, Bihar, India, 1975—98, contr., exam., 1994—98; lectr. U. Houston, 2003—. Contbr. articles. V.p. MMNA South West Chpt., Houston, 2009. Home: 17111 Carshalton Ct Houston TX 77084 Office: Coll Bus Univ Houston 320 N Main St Ste 462 Houston TX 77002 Personal E-mail: nuwaltc@yahoo.com. Business E-Mail: nuwalt@uhd.edu.

NUWER, HENRY JOSEPH (HANK NUWER), journalist, educator; b. Buffalo, Aug. 19, 1946; s. Henry Robert and Teresa (Lysiak) N.; m. Alice May (Cerniglia), Dec. 28, 1968 (div. Mar. 1980); 1 child, Henry Christian; m. Jenine (Howard), Apr. 9, 1982 (div. 2004); 1 child, Adam.; m. Lizabeth Klein, Aug. 9, 2005 (div. 2009). BS in English, State U. Coll. NY, Buffalo, 1968, DHL, 2006; MA in English, Highlands U., Las Vegas, 1971; PhD Equivalency, Ball State U., Muncie, Ind., 1988. H.S. tchr., NY, 1968—69, N.Mex., 1970—71; freelance author, journalist, 1969—; asst. prof. Clemson U., SC, 1982—83; assoc. prof. Ball State U., Muncie, Ind., 1985—89; sr. editor Rodale Press, Emmaus, Pa., 1990—91; editor in chief Arts Ind. Mag., Indpls., 1993—95; assoc. prof. journalism U. Richmond, Va., 1995—97. Expert lectr. Hazing, 1990—; hazing cons. NBC Movie-of-the-Week, Moment of Truth: Broken Pledges, Indpls., 1994, U.S. Dept. Edn., 2002—; adj. prof. journalism Ind. U. Sch. Journalism, Indpls., 1995-2008; Anderson U., 1998-2002; asst. prof. journalism, Franklin (Ind.) Coll., 2002—; nat. advisor NCAA study and survey on hazing in coll. athletic groups Alfred U., 1999, adv. bd. security on campus, 2006, bd. dirs. HazingPrevention website, 2007. Author: Steroids, 1990; Broken Pledges: The Deadly Rite of Hazing, 1990; How to Write Like an Expert, 1995; The Legend of Jesse Owens, 1998; Wrongs of Passage, 1999, rev. edit., 2002; High School Hazing, 2000, To the Young Writer, 2002, The Hazing Reader, 2003, At the Crest, 2004; The Freelance Writer's Desktop Companion, 2008, One Long Wild Conversation, 2009; mem. editl. staff Reporter Dispatch, 1969-70, Chic Mag., 1976-77; contbr. articles to profl. jour. Grantee: Nat. Endowment for the Arts, 1976; Idaho Humanities Coun., 1985; Gannett Found., 1988; named New Mag. Adviser of Yr., Coll. Media Advisers, 1988; Disting. Alumnus, Buffalo State Coll., 1999, Faculty Scholar of Yr. Franklin Coll. Mem.: SAR, Investigative Reporters and Editors, Soc. Profl. Journalists (3d pl. Best Bus. Article Ind. competition 2002), Sons of Am. Legion, Sigma Tau Rho, Alpha Lambda Delta, Phi Kappa Phi. Democrat. Roman Catholic. Office: Franklin Coll Journalism Dept 101Branigin Blvd Franklin IN 46131-2598 Business E-Mail: hnuwer@hanknuwer.com.

NUYAN, SEYHAN, control engineer; b. Adana, Turkey, Apr. 25, 1948; s. Edip and Iclal Nuyan; m. Debra Diane Black, Feb. 8, 1980. BS, Mid. East Tech. U., 1972; MS, U. S.C., 1974, PhD, 1978. Grad. rsch. asst. U. S.C., Columbia, 1972—77, instr., 1977—78; sr. control design engr. Sentrol Sys. Ltd., Toronto, Ont., Canada, 1979—83, mgr. application design, 1983—91; mgr. paper applications Valmet Automation Ltd., 1991—94, dir. paper expertise ctr., 1994—97, dir., N.Am. ctr. of excellence Richmond Hill, Ont., 1997—2000; dir. product tech. Metso Automation Ltd., Richmond Hill, 2000—02; bus. mgr. Metso Automation Oy., Helsinki, Finland, 2002—05, dir. paper process Norcross, Ga., 2006—08; dir. Paper Applications, 2008—. Mgmt. team mem. Metso Automation, Richmond Hill, Ontario, Canada, 1994—2002; rsch. & devel. bd. mem. Metso Automation Oy., Helsinki, Finland, 1994—2002. Actor: Theatre Ensemble of Turkish Culture and Folklore Soc. Can.; president (cultural, art, history, etc.) Turkish Culture and Folklore Soc. Can., (cultural & community representation) Federation of Can. Turkish Assn.; contbr. articles to profl. jours. Pres. Fedn. of Can. Turkish Assn., Toronto, Ontario, Canada, 2000—03. Recipient Medal of Honor, Knight, First Class, Order of the Lion of Finland; grantee Fullbright, US Dept. of State, 1972-1978; J.F. Kennedy scholar, Mid. East Tech. U., 1970-1972, Ctrl. Treaty Orgn.-Mid. East Tech. U. scholar, 1969-1970. Mem.: IEEE, Tech. Assn. Pulp & Paper Industry, Pulp & Paper Tech. Assn. Can., Knight Order Lion Finland, Turkish Culture and Folklore Soc. Can., Sigma Xi (life). Achievements include patents for Method and apparatus for controlling spectral reflectance of a material; Multivariable control loop assessment; invention of Spectral color control by spectral responses; first to commercialization of cross directional optimization of paper and plastics; development of Many online control and measurement applications for paper production; research in New control and measurement techniques for on-line industrial applications; first to Application of self-tuning regulators to paper industry; development of Expert systems for troubleshooting cross-machine directional problems. Avocations: theater (on- and off-stage), classical music, history, travel, swimming. Address: 10960 Abbotts Station Dr Duluth GA 30097 Office: Metso Automation USA Inc 2900 Courtyards Dr Norcross GA 30071 Home Phone: 678-575-0448; Office Phone: 770-263-2078. Business E-Mail: seyhan.nuyan@metso.com.

NUZZO, ANTHONY GERALD, bank executive; b. New Haven, Aug. 9, 1951; s. Michael Anthony and Theresa Mary (Aitro) N.; m. Julie Nuzzo, Mar. 22, 1975; children: Beth, Michael, Cortney. BA, Boston Coll., 1973; MBA, Columbia U., 1975. CLU, cert. in long-term care. Brand asst. Procter & Gamble, Cin., 1975-76, sales rep., 1976, asst. brand mgr., 1976-77; asst. product dir. Johnson & Johnson, New Brunswick, NJ, 1977-78, spl. project dir., 1978-79, product dir. Milltown, NJ, 1979-82, group product dir., 1982-84; v.p. Am. Express Travel Related Svcs., NYC, 1984-87; v.p., exec. com. Am. Express Can., Inc., Markham, Ont., 1987-88; v.p. internat. mktg. Am. Express, NY, 1988; v.p. Chem. Bank, NYC, 1988-90, sr. v.p., 1990-91; pres., CEO Chem. Bank Del., Wilmington, 1991-92; pres., founder Advanced Mktg. Assocs., Inc., East Brunswick, NJ, 1992-93; pres., CEO Fidelity Trust Co., Salt Lake City, 1993-98, chmn., 1998-99; pres., CEO Fidelity TempWorks/TempSource, Boston, 1998-99; chmn., pres., CEO @Bank, Framingham, Mass., 1999-2000; pres., CEO Engage, Andover, Mass., 2000—01; pres., CEO, founder The Nuzzo Group, Inc., Wellesley, Mass., 2001—05; fin. adviser The Commonwealth Fin. Group, Newton, Mass., 2002—05; sr. v.p. Citizens Bank, Norwood, Mass., 2005—06, TD Banknorth, Burlington, Mass., 2007—. Mem. Visa Mktg. Advisors, 1989—92, 1993—98. Editor: Physiology, 1984. Dir., co-chair, co-founder Citizens Against UnSafe Environments, East Brunswick, 1981-93; bd. dirs. Utah Bd. Fin. Instns., 1995-98. Named to PS&D Merchandising Hall of Fame Procter & Gamble, Cin., 1977, named Scholar of the Coll., Boston Coll., 1973; recipient Bus. Sch. Svc. award Columbia U., 1975, Excellence award Package Designer Coun., NYC, 1980, Clio Creative Excellence award Clio Adv. Body, NYC, 1981, Effie award, NYC, 1989. Mem. Boston Coll. Alumni Assn., Columbia Bus. Sch. Alumni Assn. (dir. NY club 1975), Utah Bankers Assn. (bd. dirs. 1996-98), Utah Assn. Fin. Svcs. (bd. dirs. 1993-98, treas. 1995-96). Avocations: golf, skiing, reading. E-mail: agnuzzo@aol.com.

NUZZO, JENNIFFER BRONWYN, epidemiologist; d. Penelope Nuzzo. MS, Harvard Sch. Pub. Health, Boston, 2001; Attending, Johns Hopkins Sch. Pub. Health, Balt., 2005. Pub. health epidemiologist NYC Dept. Environ. Protection, NYC, 2002—03; cons. DAI, Inc.-USAID, Bethesda, Md., 2007; assoc. Ctr. Biosecurity, Balt., 2003—. Project adv. coun. mem. Am. Water Works Assn. Rsch. Found., Denver, 2006—07; assoc. editor Biosecurity Bioterrorism, Balt., 2003—; coun. mem. US EPA Nat. Drinking Water Adv. Coun., Washington, 2006—. Founding mem. Mcpl. Environ. Com., Northvale, NJ, 1993—95. Pub. Health Trainee fellowship, Harvard Sch. Pub. Health, 2000—01, Charlotte Silverman Epidemiology fellowship, Johns Hopkins Sch. Pub. Health, 2007. Office: Ctr Biosecurity 621 E Pratt St Ste 210 Baltimore MD 21202 Office Phone: 443-578-3304.

NWABUZOR, AUGUSTINE M., global strategy educator, consultant; b. Issele-Mkpitime, Delta, Nigeria, Aug. 17, 1943; m. Bridget Enwelim Aninyei Nwabuzor, Sept. 29, 1968; children: Eunice, Claire, Augustine, Benedict, Henry, Charles. BS summa cum laude, NYU, NYC, 1966; MBA with distinction, Harvard U., Cambridge, 1968, DBA, 1974. Divisional mgr. UAC Nigeria, Lagos, 1971—74; gen. mgr. Bendel Steel Structures, Warri, Nigeria, 1974—79; dep. gen. mgr. Fed-Govt. Nigeria, Ajaokuta Steel Co., 1986—95; chair. dept. bus admin. Enugu State U., Nigeria, 1996—97; prof. Lahore U. Mgmt. Sci., Pakistan, 1997—99, Jackson State U., Miss., 1998—, Fla. A & M U., Tallahassee, 1999—. Contbr. articles to numerous profl. jours.; author: (books) Business-Govt Relations, 1989, Administrative Theory and Practice, 1994. Grand knight KC, Tallahassee, 2005. Mem.: Acad. Internat. Bus. Independent. Roman Catholic. Avocations: soccer, cricket. Home: 2529 Lemon Ln Tallahassee FL 32308 Office: Sch Bus and Ind FAMU 1 SBI Plz Tallahassee FL 32307 Office Phone: 850-412-7735. Personal E-mail: nwabuzor@embarqmail.com.

NWACHUKU, LEVI AKALAZU, social sciences and behavioral studies educator; b. Okpala, Nigeria, Aug. 23, 1940; came to U.S., 1963; s. Moses Akalazu and Evangeline (Enwere-Uzo) N.; m. Ugochi Justina Nwachuku, Dec. 19, 1981; children: Uchenna, Nneka, Chimereze, Chinomso, Enyinna. BA, Lincoln U., Pa., 1967; MA, Howard U., 1969; PhD, Mich. State U., 1973. V.p. acad. Shorter Coll., Little Rock, 1977; assoc. prof. U. Mich., Flint, 1977-81, dir. Black studies, 1973-81; reader history U. Maiduguri, Nigeria, 1981-88; coord. African Am. studies Lincoln U., 1989-94, chair dept. history, 1993—2002, chair dept. history, polit. sci., 2003—, dean faculty social scis., 1994-97. Co-author: Exploring the African-American Experience, 1995, Troubled Journey: Nigeria Since the Civil War, 2004; editor: Lincoln Jour. Social and Polit. Thought, 2001—, Lincoln U. Press, 2007-; lead editor: Exploring the African American Experience, 2006. Recipient Christian R. and Mary F. Lindback Tchg. award, 2005; named Outstanding Male Faculty Mem., NAACP, 1995, Prof. of Yr., Lincoln U., 2004. Mem. Phi Alpha Theta, Alpha Phi Alpha. Home: PO Box 153 Lincoln University PA 19352-0153 Office: Lincoln U Lincoln University PA 19352 Office Phone: 484-365-8126.

NWAGBARAOCHA, JOEL ONUKWUGHA, academic administrator, educator; b. Victoria, Cameroons, Nov. 21, 1942; came to U.S., 1964; naturalized, 1974; s. John O. and Christiana (Ihejeihu) N.; m. Patsy Coleman, Aug. 27, 1977; children: Jason, Jonathan, John, Eric. BS in Math., Norfolk State U., 1969, cert. in physics, 1969; EdM, Harvard

U., 1970, EdD (Univ. fellow), 1972. Tchr. math. and physics Emmanuel Coll., Owerri, Nigeria, 1960-64; asst. dir. Manpower Rsch. Inst./Norfolk (Va.) State Coll., 1969-70; rsch. assoc. Harvard U. Grad. Sch. Edn., 1969-72; assoc. dir. co-op acad. planning program Inst. for Svcs. to Edn., Washington, 1972-74, dir. instnl. planning and mgmt. program, 1974-76, dir. divsn. acad. planning and faculty devel., 1976-78; assoc. prof. edn., v.p. planning and ops. analysis Morgan State U., Balt., 1978-87; v.p. acad. affairs Voorhees Coll., Denmark, S.C., 1987-80; pres. Barber-Scotia Coll., Concord, N.C., 1990-94; prof. edn., bus. adminstrn. Strayer U., Washington, 1994—, dir. grad. studies, 2000—02, dean grad. sch., 2005—07, interim pres., 2006—07, provost, chief academic officer, 2007—. Dean Tacoma Park Campus, Strayer Coll., Washington; interim pres., Strayer U., 2006-; cons. in higher edn. planning and evaluation system devel., 1972—. Co-author: Operational Manual for ollege Planning Development, 1977, Planning Management and Evaluation System, 1979; mem. editl. bd. Spartan Echo, 1967-69; contbr. articles to profl. jours. Mem. AAAS, Am. Coun. on Edn., Nat. Coun. on Social Studies, Am. Assn. for Higher Edn., Am. Humanist Assn., Soc. for Coll. and Univ. Planning, Am. Assn. Univ. Adminstrs., Am. Mgmt. Assn., Higher Edn. Group of Washington, Smithsonian Nat. Assoc., Alpha Kappa Mu, Phi Beta Sigma, Beta Kappa Chi, Phi Delta Kappa. Home: 10928 Battersea Ln Columbia MD 21044-2701 Office: Strayer Univ Washington DC Campus 1133 15th St NW Washington DC 20005-2601 Business E-Mail: jon@strayer.edu.

NWALA, KINGSLEY, economics professor; s. Chief Innocent and Celine Nwala; m. Eunice Ike; children: Prince, Monique, Reginald, Precious. PhD, Howard U., Washington, 1995. Prof. economics Elizabeth City State U., NC, 1997—. Contbr. articles to profl. jours. Avocations: swimming, soccer, tennis. Office: Elizabeth City State Univ 1704 Weeksville Rd Elizabeth City NC 27909 Personal E-mail: nwala@cox.net. Business E-Mail: knnwala@mail.ecsu.edu.

NWANEGBO, EDWARD, epidemiologist, researcher; s. Edward A. and Juliana A. Nwanegbo; m. Annasstasia Nwanegbo; children: Edward E., Francis C. MD, U. Nigeria, Enugu, 1995; MPH, U. Pitts., 2008. Diplomate Nigeria Med. and Dental Coun., 1996, ECFMG, 2003, lic. Iowa Bd. Medicine, 2008; cert. diploma Katz Grad. Sch. Bus. Studies, 2007. Med. officer Umuaka Cmty. Hosp., Orlu Nigeria, 1997—99; rsch. physician Med. Rsch. Coun., Banjul, Gambia, 1999—2001; rsch. assoc. U. Pitts., 2001—08; res. physician SLMEF, U. Iowa, Sioux City. Reviewer (book) Micro-competition with Foreign DNA and Origin of Chronic Diseases; contbr. chapters to books, articles to numerous sci. jours. Vol. Pitts. AIDS Task Force, 2001—03. Recipient Merit award, 1997, Pitts. Innovator award, 2006. Mem.: AMA, Am. Soc. Gene Therapy. Achievements include patents pending for new treatment for epidemic keratoconjuctivitis; discovery of SARS vaccine; design of use of flow cytometry for adenoviral neutralization studies; application of MALDI-TOFF mass spectrometry in adenoviral serotypes screening. Office: SLMEF Univ Iowa 2501 Pierce St Sioux City IA 51104

NWANERI, SAM O., science educator; s. Humphrey S. and Evelyn O. Nwaneri; married; 1 child, Uchenna Sam. BA in Math., Harding U., Searcy, 1989; M in Urban & Regional Planning, Ala. A & M U., Normal, Huntsville, 2003; PhD, Ala. A & M U., Huntsville, 2008. Product devel. mgr. Network Internat. Inc, Little Rock, 1996—2001; GIS lab. mgr. Ala. A & M U., 2001—03; asst. prof. Acorn State U., Miss., 2008—. Project coord. Trinity Group-Planners & Engrs., Huntsville, Ala., 2003—08. Referee Nat. Assn. Soccer Ofcl., Chgo., 1989—2009. Recipient Ark. Traveler award, Office Gov. Ark. Sec. State, 2007; named Hon. Citizen of Ark., Bd. Dirs. City Little Rock, 2007. Mem.: Huntsville Land Trust. Home: 4059 Braeswood Dr Apt 9 Huntsville AL 35802 Business E-Mail: integer7@netzero.net.

NWOMEH, BENEDICT C., pediatric surgeon; b. Ozara, Enugu State, Nigeria, Mar. 3, 1965; arrived in US, 1994; s. Peter and Margaret Nwomeh; m. Henrietta A. Osodi, Dec. 6, 1999; children: Chiedozie, Chukwuemeka, Chioma. MB, U. Lagos, Nigeria, 1981, MD, 1986. Intern Med. Coll. Va. Commonwealth U., 1994—95, jr. resident, 1995—96, rsch. fellow, 1996—98, sr. resident, 1998—2000, chief resident, 2000—01; asst. prof. surgery Ohio State U., Columbus, 2003—; attending pediat. surgeon Columbus Children's Hosp., Ohio, 2003—. Dir. surg. edn. Columbus Children's Hosp., 2004—, surg. dir. Ctr. for Pediat. and Adolescent Inflammatory Bowel Disease, 2005—. Editor: Paediatric Trauma Care in Africa: A Practical Guide, 2006; contbr. articles to profl. jours. Bd. mem. First Love Inc., Columbus, 2005—. Recipient Residents Rsch. prize, Va. Soc. Plastic Surgery, 1997, David Hume Rsch. award, Humera Surg. Soc., Med. Coll. Va., 1999, Outstanding Surgeon award, Children's Hosp. Pitts. Critical Care Staff, 2003, Gold Found. Little Apple Tchg. award, U. Pitts. Sch. Medicine, Class 2004, 2004, Ohio Health Policy Rsch. award, Health Policy Inst. Ohio, 2006; named Young Investigator of Yr., Wound Healing Soc., 1997—98. Fellow: ACS, Royal Coll. Surgeons Eng., Royal Coll. Physicians and Surgeons Glasgow, Am. Acad. Pediat., Assn. for Surg. Edn., Royal Coll. Surgeons Edinburgh, West African Coll. Surgeons, Soc. Black Academic Surgeons (mem. publs. com. 2006); mem.: Ctrl. Ohio Pediat. Soc., Internat. Pediat. Endosurgery Group, Brit. Med. Assn., Assn. Pediat. Surgeons Nigeria. Achievements include described the dynamics of the matrix metalloproteinases MMP-1 and MMP-8 in acute open human dermal wounds; research in Contrast extravasation predicts the need for operative intervention in children with blunt splenic trauma; racial and socioeconomic disparity in perforated appendicitis among children; discovery of MMP-8 is the predominant collagenase in healing wounds and nonhealing ulcers. Office: Nationwide Childrens Hospital 700 Childrens Drive ED379 Columbus OH 43205

NYBERG, DONALD ARVID, oil industry executive; b. Ridgewood, NJ, Aug. 23, 1951; s. Arvid H. and Rita T. (Tenwick) N.; m. Susan Radis, Feb. 16, 1985; children: Matthew D., Ryan T. BA, St. Lawrence U., 1973; MBA, Harvard U., 1975. Mgr. marine ops. Standard Oil, LA, 1982-83, mgr. ops. planning Cleve., 1984-85, dir. strategic studies, 1986; divsn. mgr. Brit. Petroleum, Ltd., London, 1987-88; v.p., gen. mgr. U.S. gas bus. BP Exploration, Houston, 1989, v.p., gen. mgr. tech., 1990, v.p. comml., 1991-94; pres., CEO BP Pipelines, Anchorage, 1991-94; pres. Marya Resources, Houston, 1994—; v.p. MAPCO, Tulsa, 1996; pres. Tesoro Marine Svcs., Houston, 1996—2003; CEO, bd. dirs. McDonough Marine, 2004—07; CEO Champion Elevators, 2005—07, bd. dirs., 2004—07; prof. mgmt., program dir. San Jacinto Coll., 2008—. Bd. dirs., exec. com. Boys and Girls Country Houston, Asst. League Houston. Mem. Forest Club, Bentwater Country Club. Avocations: running, weightlifting, reading. Office Phone: 713-553-1880. Personal E-mail: don.nyberg@yahoo.com.

NYBERG, KAREN L., astronaut; b. Parkers Prairie, Minn., Oct. 7, 1969; d. Kenneth and Phyllis Nyberg. BS in Mech. Engring. (summa cum laude), U. ND, 1994; MS in Mech. Engring., U. Tex., Austin, 1996, PhD in Mech. Engring., 1998. Co-op working in a variety of areas Johnson Space Ctr., 1991—95; environ. control sys. engr. Crew and Thermal Sys. Divsn., 1998—2000; mission specialist NASA, 2000—. Technical duties, crew support astronaut (Expedition 6 crew), astronaut office station ops. br. NASA, 2002, duties with space shuttle and exploration branches; mission specialist STS-124 Mission (Discovery), mission to Internat. Space Station to launch components to complete Japanese Kibo Lab., 2008. Recipient U. ND Sch. Engring. & Mines Meritorious Svc. award, 1991—92, D.J. Robinson award for Academic Achievement, 1992, Space Act award, 1993, NASA Tech Briefs award, 1993, NASA Johnson Space Ctr. Patent Application award, 1993, Joyce Medalen Soc. Women Engrs. award, 1993—94, NASA Johnson Space Ctr. Cooperative Edn. Spl. Achievement award, 1994, U. ND Young Alumni Achievement award, 2004. Achievements include patents for Robot Friendly Probe and Socket Assembly, 1991; being the 50th woman to fly in space (STS-124 Mission aboard the Discovery, 2008). Avocations: art, running, volleyball, sewing, backpacking, piano. Office: Astronauts Office/CB NASA Lyndon B Johnson Space Ctr 2101 NASA Pkwy Houston TX 77058

NYBERG, STANLEY ERIC, research scientist; b. Boston, Jan. 30, 1948; s. Leroy Milton and Anna Maria (Olson) N. PhD, SUNY, Stony Brook, 1975; MBA, Yale U., 1984. Postdoctoral fellow U. Calif., Berkeley, 1975-76; asst. prof. North Park Coll., Chgo., 1976-79, Barnard Coll., Columbia U., NYC, 1979-82; sys. mgmt. Interactive Data Corp., Lexington, Mass., 1984-88, Dept. of Revenue, Commonwealth of Mass., Boston, 1988-2000; with Dept. of Environ. Protection, Commonwealth of Mass., 2000—01; registrar vital records and stats. Commonwealth of Mass., 2001—. Co-author: Human Memory: An Introduction to Research and Theory, 1982. Bd. dir. Childrens Home Cromwell, Conn., 1988-94, Decade Fund, Yale U. Sch. Mgmt., 1984-1985; ch. coun. Luth. Ch. of Redeemer, Woburn, Mass., 1991-1997, West Roxbury Rugby Football Club, 1984-1987; v.p., sec. L Street Running Club, South Boston, 1987—; mem. divsn. ecumenism New Eng. Synod, Evang. Luth. Ch. in Am., 1997—2002; bd. dir. Scandinavian Charitable Soc. Greater Boston, 2000—, v.p. 2002-2004, pres., 2004-06. Fellow Assn. Psychol. Sci.; mem. APA, Soc. Applied Rsch. in Memory and Cognition, Ea. Psychol. Assn., Midwestern Psychol. Assn. Personal E-mail: snyberg@aol.com.

NYBORG, VANESSA MARIE, psychologist, researcher, educator; b. San Francisco, Mar. 1, 1972; d. Milton and Beatrice Nyborg. BA, UCLA, 1995; PhD, Duke U., 2001. Postdoctoral rsch. fellow Brown Med. Sch., Providence, 2001—03; rschr. Ctr. for Sch. Based Youth Devel., U. Calif., Santa Barbara, 2003, asst. rschr., adj. prof. Gevirtz Sch. Edn., 2003—. Grantee, NIH, 2003—. Mem.: APA, Psi Chi. Office: U Calif Gevirtz Grad Sch Edn Santa Barbara CA 93106 Business E-Mail: vnyborg@education.ucsb.edu.

NYBORG, WESLEY LEMARS, physics professor; b. Ruthven, Iowa, May 15, 1917; s. Isaac and Leva (Larson) N.; m. Beth Woolsey, Sept. 8, 1945; 1 dau., Elsa Beth. BA, Luther Coll., 1941; MS, Pa. State U., 1944, PhD, 1947. Asst. prof. physics Pa. State U., University Park, 1948-50; asst. prof. Brown U., Providence, 1950-54, asso. prof., 1954-60; prof. U. Vt., Burlington, 1960-86, acting chmn. physics dept., 1978-79, prof. emeritus, 1986—. Vis. scientist Oxford (Eng.) U., 1960-61, Univ. Coll., Cardiff, Wales, 1969, U. of Rochester, 1987; Exec. council Am. Inst. Ultrasound in Medicine, 1972-74, 76-78, chmn. bioeffects com., 1976-78; adv. bd. Bur. Radiol. Health, 1972-75; cons. FDA, 1976—; chmn. sci. com. 66 Nat. Council Radiation Protection and Measurements, 1980—; mem. working group on biol. effects ultrasound, WHO, 1982, 85, 88; mem. study sect. diagnostic radiology NIH, 1982-85; adv. mem. Rochester Ctr. for Biomed. Ultrasound, 1986; Lauriston S. Taylor lectr. Nat. Coun. Radiation Protection and Measurements, Bethesda, Md., 2001. Author: Intermediate Biophysical Mechanics, 1975; co-editor: Biological Effects of Ultrasound, 1985, (with J. Wu) Emerging Therapeutic Ultrasound, 2006; mem. editl. bd.: Ultrasound in Medicine and Biology, Jour. Ultrasound in Medicine; co-editor Proc. Symposium on Safety and Standardization in Med. Ultrasound, 2d World Fedn. Ultrasound in Medicine and Biology, 1989; contbr. to profl. jours. Recipient Presdl. recognition award Am. Inst. Ultrasound in Medicine, 1977, Univ. scholar award in phys. scis. U. Vt., 1984, Disting. Svc. award Luther Coll., 1996, Vt. Acad. Sci. and Engring., 1997, Lauriston S. Taylor Lectr. award 2001, P.P. Lele award, 5th Internat. Symposium, 2005; USPHS fellow MIT, 1956-57; research grantee NIH, 1955—. Fellow AAAS, Acoustical Soc. Am. (exec. coun. 1965-68, Silver medal 1990), Am. Inst. Ultrasound in Medicine (Joseph H. Holmes award 1985, W.J. Fry Lecture award 1990), Ultrasonic Soc. India (hon.); mem. Nat. Acad. Engrs., Am. Phys. Soc., Biophys. Soc., Am. Assn. Physics Tchrs., Sigma Xi, Sigma Pi Sigma. Home: 2 Stirling Pl Burlington VT 05408-2634 Business E-Mail: wesley.nyborg@uvm.edu.

NYCE, JOHN DANIEL, lawyer; b. York, Pa., Sept. 7, 1947; s. Harry Lincoln and Dorothy (Wagner) Nyce; m. Deborah Dvorak; children: Joshua David, Laura Kimberly. BA, SUNY, Buffalo, 1970; JD, U. Miami, 1973. Bar: Fla. 1973, U.S. District Ct. (so. dist.) Fla. 1973, U.S. Dist. Ct. (middle dist.), Fla. 1973, U.S. Ct. Appeals (5th and 11th cirs.) 1986, U.S. Supreme Ct. 1984. Assoc. Ralph P. Douglas, Pompano Beach, Fla., 1974, Coleman, Leonard & Morrison, Ft. Lauderdale, Fla., 1975-78; sole practice Ft. Lauderdale, 1979—. Adj. prof. bus. law, inernat. bus. law Lynn U., Boca Raton, Fla., 2001—. Author: Proof of God's Existence in the Seven C's and Christian Handbook of Lists, 2003, ApoloVangelism, 2006. Mem. Social Register Ft. Lauderdale; mem. Broward County Right to Life, Operation Rescue, South Fla., Beach Street Aid to the Homeless of Ft. Lauderdale, Legis. Adv. Coun. on Adoptions, Am. Assn. Adoption Attys., Nat. Right to Life Com., Inc.; founder Broward County Christian Lawyers Assn., past pres., bd. dirs.; founder Am. Assn. Adoption Attys., past pres., bd. dirs.; mem. Christian Legal Soc.; mem. exec. com. Broward County Rep. Party; Broward Citizens bd. U. Miami; mem. Conservative Caucus of Broward County; bd. dirs. Shepherd Care Ministries, Inc.; co-founder Christian Adoption Svcs. of Shepherd Care Ministries, Inc.; cert. trainer Evangelism Explosion III Internat., Inc.; legal counsel and evangelism trainer Coral Ridge Presbytn. Ch., Christ the Rock Cmty. Ch., First Bapt. Ch., West Hollywood, Fla., Calvary Chapel of Ft. Lauderdale Ch., New Covenant Presbyn. Ch.; bd. dirs. Alliance for Responsible Growth, Inc. Mem.: Am. Assn. Adoption Attys., Nat. Acad. Elder Law Attys., Attys. Title Ins. Fund, NRA, Am. Numismatic Assn., U. Miami Alumni Assn., SUNY Buffalo Alumni Assn., S.D. Rifle and Hunting Assn., Holiday Park Tennis Ctr., U.S. Tennis Assn., U. Miami Hurricane Club, Sports Fitness Clin., Palm Aire Golf and Country Club. Republican. Presbyterian. Office: PO Box 11071 Fort Lauderdale FL 33339-1071 Office Phone: 954-567-3305. E-mail: miamijd73@gmail.com.

NYDEGGER, RICK D., lawyer; b. Salt Lake City, Apr. 24, 1949; s. A. Don and Jean Virginia (Hansen) N.; m. Denise Winegar, Oct. 22, 1970; children: Dan L., Chad E., Kurt D., Brittney Smith, Trent R. BSEE cum laude, Brigham Young U., Provo, Utah, 1974, JD cum laude, 1977. Bar: Utah 1977, US Dist Ct. (ctrl. dist.) Utah 1977, US Patent Office 1977, US Ct. Appeals (5th and 10th cirs.) 1980, US Supreme Ct. 1990, US Ct. Appeals (fed. cir.) 1994. Assoc. Fox, Edwards, & Gardiner, 1977-81, shareholder, dir., 1981-84; founding shareholder, dir., officer Workman, Nydegger, Salt Lake City, 1984—. Adj. prof. S.J. Quinney Coll. Law, U. Utah, 1988-99, J. Reuben Clark Law Sch., Brigham Young U., 1998-2002. Contbr. articles to profl. jours.; author: US and internat. intellectual property profl. programs. Eagle scout, Boy Scouts Am., 1953; chair lawyers centennial com., Utah State Centennial Commn., 1996-97; pres. Nat. Inventors Hall of Fame, 2000-05; bd. dirs. NIHF Found., 1998-2006, pres.; trustee Am. Intellectual Property Law Edn. Found., 2001-03; chair patent pub. adv. com. US Patent & Trademark Office, 2003-06. Named Hon. Alumnus of Yr., U. Utah S.J. Quinney Coll. Law, 2004, Alumnus of Yr., Brigham Young U. J. Rueben Clark Law Sch., 2005; named one of Best Lawyers in America, 1990—; named to Chambers USA Band I Ranking, 2008—. Fellow Am. Intellectual Property Law Assn. (founding mem., chmn. electronic computer law com. 1990-93, bd. dirs. 1993-96, editl. bd. quar. jour., vice-chmn. ad hoc com. PCT practice, 1994-98, chmn. nominations com. 2005, chmn. mid-winter Inst. 2000 planning com., 2d v.p. 2000-01, 1st v.p. 2001-02, pres-elect 2002-03, pres. 2003-04); mem. ABA, Utah State Bar (chmn. patent, trademark, copyright sect. 1985-87), Fed. Cir. Bar Assn., US Supreme Ct. Hist. Soc. (bd. dirs. 1993-94, trustee 2005-), Nat. Coun. Intellectual Property Law Assn. (chmn. 2000-01), Order of Coif (hon. J. Rueben Clark Law Sch. Chpt.), Eta Kappa Nu. Avocations: fishing, tennis, reading. Office: Workman Nydegger 60 E South Temple Ste 1000 Salt Lake City UT 84111-1011 Home Phone: 801-756-4751; Office Phone: 801-533-9800. Business E-Mail: rnydegger@wnlaw.com.

NYDEN, TAMMY MARIE, philosopher, educator; b. Waukegan, Ill., May 3, 1971; d. Raymond Charles and Mary Beatrice Nyden; m. James Andrew Bullock; children: Cole Xavier Bullock, Jonah Garrison Bullock. BA in Philosophy, U. Nev., Las Vegas, 1993; MA in philosophy, Baylor U., Waco, Tex., 1994; PhD in Philosophy, Claremont Grad. U., Calif., 2003. Asst. prof. philosophy Grinnell Coll., Iowa, 2005—. Sec. - treas. Iowa Philos. Soc., 2005—. Mem. ethics com. Mayflower, Grinnell, Iowa, 2008—08. Rsch. grant, Am. Philosophical Soc. Franklin. Fellow: Kristeller-Popkin, Am. Coun. Learned Socs., Netherland-America Found.; mem.: North Am. Spinoza Soc., Am. Philos. Assn. Democrat. Office: Grinnell Coll Philosophy Dept Grinnell IA 50112 Business E-Mail: nydenbul@grinnell.edu.

NYE, BERNARD CARL, educational administrator; b. Newark, Ohio, Nov. 25, 1927; s. Bernard Harry and Eralie Juanita (Hupp) N.; m. Nancy Ann Otterman, June 10, 1950; children: Vicki, Linda, Patricia, Terri, Steven, Melanie, Michael, Brian, James. BSc, Ohio State U., 1950, PhD, 1967; MSc, Bowling Green State U., Ohio, 1955. Cert. Completion Instr. Seminar, Frontline Leadership, Essentials of Mgmt. Course, Mgmt. Principals Am. Mgmt. Assn. Salesman (part-time) McDonnell's Shoe Store, 1942-62, co-mgr., 1950-52; mktg. and distributive edn. coord. Napoleon HS, Ohio, 1952-54, Newark HS, Ohio, 1954-62; asst. vocat. dir., mktg. and distributive edn. svcs. Vocat. div. State Dept. Edn., Ohio, 1962-83; dean bus. pub. svcs. div. Columbus State CC, 1984-85, bus. and industry rep., 1985-89; OTTO rep. Cen. Ohio Tech. Coll., Newark, 1990-91, continuing edn. coord., 1991-95, asst. dean continuing edn., 1995—98; ret., 1998. Adj. bus. dept. instr. Ctrl. Ohio Tech. Coll., 1986-, Columbus State CC, 1978-83; selected as first adj. instr. Ctrl. Ohio Tech. Coll., 2006; taught summer courses at U. Mass, U. South Fla., U. NC, Chapel Hill, U. SC, U. Wash., Marshall U., W.Va., Mankato State Coll., Minn. Author Product Planning; co-author Management Development, 1966; contbr. articles to profl. jours. Chair Job Svcs. Employer Com., Newark, 1991-93; mem. Licking County Econ. Devel. Adv. Com., 1991-94; bd. dirs. Licking/Knox Counties Goodwill Industries, 1992-2000, pres., 1998-2000, emeritus trustee; bd. dirs. Licking County Big Bros./Big Sisters, 1993-95; bd. dirs. Friends of Citizens With Disabilities, 1998-2000, pres. 1998-2000; bd. dir. SCORE, 1990-98, chair 1996-98; sponsored children (with wife) in the US who were from Africa, Brazil, China, Egypt, France, Hungary, India, Indonesia, Korea, Malaysia, East and West Pakistan, Phillipines, Portugal, and Spain. Recipient Disting. Alumni Svc. award Ohio State U., 1970, Nat. Distributive Mktg. Edn. Profl. Devel. award, 1980; recipient of plaque, Newark, Ohio DECA Chpt. which was named Bernard C. Nye Chpt. May 23, 1985, Tchr. Extraordinaire plaque, Newark HS Class of 1957, Outstanding Svc. award, DECA, Cert. Achievement, SCORE, Licking County Chpt., Cert. Induction, DECA Hall of Fame, Achievement for Outstanding Accomplishment in the fields of Archeology and Budgetectomy, Appreciation from US Postal Svc. Guest Spkr. Newark, Ohio, Lion's Club, Entitled to membership in Nat. Assn. Distributive Edn. Tchrs., Acknowledgement from Ron Willingham for completing profl. skills workshop, Cert. Appreciation, Am. Legion Dept. Ohio Svc. Nation USA, Appreciation award, Ohio Bur. Employment Svcs., Cert. Recognition of Yrs. Dedicated Svc., Newark Campus Ohio State U., Ctrl. Ohio Tech. Coll., Columbus State Coll., Cert. Recognition, Help Hospitalized Vets., 2005, A Donor of Yr., Help Hospitalized Vets., 2006, 2007, Patriot of Yr. award, Help Hospitalized Vets., 2007, Mus. Founding Mem. Cert. Appreciation, Nat. Law Enforcement Officers Meml. Fund., 2006, Cert. Appreciation, Food for the Poor, VFW, 2006, Am. Legion. Dept. Ohio, 2006. Mem. Ohio Vocational Assn. (life), Coshocton C. of C., Knox C. of C., Masons (The Grand Lodge of Free and Accepted Masons of Ohio Fifty Year award). Methodist. Avocations: fishing, boating, gardening. Home Phone: 740-763-2756.

NYE, DAN, former internet company executive; BA in Polit. Sci., Hamilton Coll., 1988; MBA, Harvard Bus. Sch., 1994. Mem. brand mgmt. Procter & Gamble, 1988—92; various positions including, v.p., gen. mgr. internat. divsn., dir. mktg. for small bus. products and svcs., v.p., gen. mgr., small bus. divsn. Intuit, Inc., 1995—2001; exec. v.p., gen. mgr., investment mgmt. Advent Software, 2002—07; CEO LinkedIn Corp., Mountain View, Calif., 2007—09. Bd. mem. Constant Contact, 2009—. Office: Constant Contact 1601 Trapelo Rd Ste 329 Waltham MA 02451

NYE, DOROTHY MAE, freelance journalist, educator; d. Robert Nathan and Marinda Josephine Nye; m. Joseph Arlo Westby, Nov. 20, 1955 (div.); children: Timothy Scott Westby, Pamela Kay Westby, Lisa Maureen Westby Peltier, Thomas Oscar Westby, Theodore Edward Westby, Erik Charles Westby. BA, U. Denver, 1999—2001, Combined Licensure & Master's Program, 2002—03. Administrator's Credential Nat. Assn. Edn. of Young Children (NAEYC) & Red Cross, 1993, Montessori Certification Nat. Ctr. for Montessori Edn., 1992. Asst. to v.p. of sales Morton Buildings, Morton, Ill., 1971—83; assoc. dir. of admissions Parks Coll., Denver, 1984—86; dir. of admissions Denver Tech. Coll., 1986—90; primary tchr. Montessori Inst., Houston, 1991—93; sales team mgr. Time Warner, Denver, 1993—96; counselor Open Door, Valley City, ND, 1996—99; communicatons specialist Theodore Roosevelt Medora Found., Medora, ND, 1999—2000; ednl. specialist for elderly Life Care of Am., Aurora, Colo., 2001—04; h.s. english tchr. Life Skills Charter Sch. of Colo. Springs, 2004—. Coord. for internat. program U. of ND & Mexican Universities, Valley City, ND, 1997—99. Com. monitor Majority Caucus Colo. Ho. of Representatives, Denver, 1993—95. Mem.: Pi Lambda Phi, Sigma Tau Delta. Business E-Mail: dorothy.nye@lifeskillscenters.com. E-mail: grand_ma10@msn.com.

NYE, ERIC W., English language and literature educator; b. Omaha, July 31, 1952; s. William Frank and Mary Roberta (Lueder) N.; m. Carol Denison Frost, Dec. 21, 1980; children: Charles William, Ellen Mary. BA, St. Olaf Coll., 1974; MA, U. Chgo., 1976, PhD, 1983; postgrad., Queens' Coll., Cambridge, England, 1979-82. Tutor in coll. writing com.

U. Chgo., 1976-79, tchg. intern, 1978; tutor Am. lit. Cambridge (Eng.) U., 1979-82; asst. prof. English and religious studies U. Wyo., Laramie, 1983-89, assoc. prof., 1989—, dir. English honors program, 1985—89, 1992—93, 2002—04, 2008—. Pres., bd. dirs. Plainview Tel. Co., Nebr., Nyecom Telesvcs., Inc.; hon. vis. fellow U. Edinburgh (Scotland) Inst. for Advanced Studies in the Humanities, 1987; guest lectr. NEH summer Inst., Laramie, Wyo., 1985, Carlyle Soc. of Edinburgh, 1987, Wordsworth summer Conf., Grasmere, Eng., 1988, cons. NEH. Contbr. articles and reviews to profl. jours. Elected mem. Wyo. Coun. for Humanities, 1992—96, mem. exec. com., 1993—94; mem. adv. bd. Wyo. Ctr. for the Book, 1995—, chair, 2006—08; mem. Peripatetics, 1989—, The Grolier Club, 2007—; leader Boy Scouts Am., 1999—2005. Nat. Merit scholar St. Olaf Coll., 1970-74; Amb. fellow Rotary Found., 1979-80; grantee Am. Coun. Learned Socs., 1988; recipient Disting. Alumnus award Lincoln (Nebr.) East H.S., 1986, Slater Tchg. award 2000, Extraordinary Merit Tchg. award 2006, Extraordinary Merit Adv. award 1999. Mem.: MLA (del. assembly 1991—93), Guild Book Workers, Bibliog. Soc. London (hon. treas. for N.Am. 2002—), Soc. History of Authorship, Reading, and Pub., Am. Acad. Bookbinding, Assn. Literary Scholars and Critics (life), Gen. Soc. Mayflower Descendents, Royal Oak Found., Charles Lamb Soc., Coleridge Soc. (life), Friends of Dove Cottage (life), Jane Austen Soc. N.Am. (life; judge essay contest 2007—), Carlyle Soc. (life), Wyo. State Hist. Soc. (life), Tennyson Soc. (life), Friends of Cambridge U. Libr. (life), The Victorian Inst., Penn Club (London), Am. Friends Cambridge U., Am. Trust for the Brit. Libr., Queens' Coll. Club (Cambridge), The Grolier Club, Phi Beta Kappa (rep. Triennial Coun. 1988, pres., v.p., sec. Wyo. chpt. 1988—, rep. Triennial Coun. 1994, 2000, 2003, 2006, 2009, Dedicated Svc. award 1997). Home: 1495 Apache Dr Laramie WY 82072-6966 Office: U Wyo Dept English 3353 1000 E U Ave Laramie WY 82071 Office Phone: 307-766-6452. Business E-Mail: nye@uwyo.edu.

NYE, GLENN CARLYLE, III, United States Representative from Virginia; b. Phila., Sept. 9, 1974; B, Georgetown U. Sch. Fgn. Svc., Washington. Asst. to the US dir. European Bank Reconstrn. and Devel.; fgn. svc. officer US Embassy, Macedonia and Kosovo, fgn. svc. officer, Afghan Constl. Convention Kabul, Afghanistan, fgn. svc. officer Singapore; mgr., West Bank and Gaza US Agy. Internat. Devel. (USAID); ops. dir. Transitional Nat. Assembly Election, Iraq; mem. US Congress from 2nd Va. Dist., 2009—. Lectr. in field. Recipient Superior Honor award, US State Dept., 2001. Democrat. Presbyterian. Office: US Congress 116 Cannon House Office Bldg Washington DC 20515-4602 also: Dist Office 4772 Euclid Rd Ste E Virginia Beach VA 23462 Office Phone: 202-225-4215, 757-497-6859. Office Fax: 202-225-4218, 757-497-5474.*

NYE, JOHN VINCENT CANIZARES, economics professor; s. Walter S and Pacita C Nye; m. Lirong Huang; children: Michael Walter, Andrew James. BS in Physics, Calif. Inst. Tech., Pasadena, 1981; MA, Northwestern U., Evanston, Ill., PhD in Economics, 1985. Prof. economics Wash. U., St. Louis, 1985—2008, George Mason U., Fairfax, Va., 2007—; frederic bastiat prof. polit. economy Mercatus Ctr., Arlington, Va., 2007—. Author: (book) War, Wine, and Taxes; editor: Frontiers of the New Institutional Economics. Nat. fellowship, Hoover Instn., Stanford U., 1996—97. Mem.: Internat. Soc. New Instl. Economics, Econ. History Assn. Office: George Mason Univ 4400 University Dr Fairfax VA 22030

NYE, JOSEPH SAMUEL, JR., political science professor; b. South Orange, NJ, Jan. 19, 1937; s. Joseph S. and Else (Ashwell) N.; m. Molly Harding, June 10, 1961; children: John Bundy, Joseph Benjamin, Daniel Tupper AB in Pub. Affairs, Princeton U., 1958; BA in Philosophy, Politics and Econs., Oxford U., Eng., 1960; PhD in Polit. Sci., Harvard U., 1964. Prof. govt. Harvard U., Cambridge, Mass., 1964—95, dean, John F. Kennedy Sch. Govt., 1995—2004, univ. disting. svc. prof., 2004—, Sultan of Oman prof. internat. rels., 2005—; dep. undersec. state, security assistance, sci. & tech. US Dept. State, Washington, 1977-79, cons., 1979; asst. sec. def., internat. security affairs US Dept. Def., Washington, 1994—95. Cons. US Dept. Energy, Washington, 1979; US rep. UN Adv. Bd. on Disarmament; chmn. Nat. Intelligence Coun., 1993-94; vis. prof. Balliol Coll., Oxford, Eng., 2005. Author: Pan Africanism and East African Integration, 1965, Peace in Paris: Integration and Conflict in Regional Organization, 1971 (with Robert O. Keohane) Power and Interdependence: World Politics in Transition, 1977, The Making of America's Soviet Policy, 1984, (with Graham Allison and Albert Carnesale) Hawks, Doves and Owls: An Agenda for Avoiding Nuclear War, 1985, Nuclear Ethics, 1986, Bound to Lead: The Changing Nature of American Power, 1990, (with Kurt Biedenkopf and Motoo Shiina) Global Competition After the Cold War: A Reassessment of Trilateralism, 1991, Understanding International Conflicts: An Introduction to Theory and History, 1993, The Paradox of American Power: Why the World's Only Only Superpower Can't Go It Alone, 2002, (with Yukio Satoh and Paul Wikinson) Addressing the New International Terrorism: Prevention, Intervention, and Multilateral Cooperation, 2003, Soft Power: The Means to Success in World Politics, 2004, The Power Game: A Washington Novel, 2004, The Powers to Lead, 2008; co-editor: Canada and the United States: Transnational and Transgovernmental Relations, 1974, Energy and Security, 1980, Global Dilemmas, 1985, Seeking Stability in Space: Anti-Satellite Weapons and the Evolving Space Regime, 1987, On The Defensive? The Future of SDI, 1988, Fateful Visions: avoiding Nuclear Catastrophe, 1988, democracy.com?: Governance in a Networked World, 1999, Governance in a Globalizing World, 2000, For the People: Can We Fix Public Service, 2003; contbr. book chapters, articles to profl. jours., newspaper op-eds. Recipient: US Dept. State Disting. Honor award, 1979, Intelligence Cmty. Disting. Svc. medal, 1994, Dept. Def. Disting. Svc. medal with Oak Leaf Cluster, 1995, Charles E. Merriam award Am. Polit. Sci. Assn., 2003, Woodrow Wilson award Princeton U., 2004; Rhodes scholar Oxford U., 1958-60; fellow, Woodrow Wilson Internat. Ctr., Smithsonian Inst., 1993, hon. fellow, Exeter Coll, Oxford, 1996; Montague Burton Professorship, U. Edinburgh, 1990. Fellow Am. Acad. Arts and Scis., Aspen Inst. Humanistic Study (sr. fellow, 1983-93); mem. AAAS (mem. com. on sci., arms control, and nat. security, 1984-90), Am. Coun. on Germany (bd. dirs., 1985-93), Atlantic Inst. Internat. Affairs, (bd. govs., 1974-77), Internat. Inst. Strategic Studies (coun. mem.), Coun. Fgn. Rels. (bd. dirs.), Trilateral Commn., Am. Acad. Diplomacy. Office: Harvard Univ John F Kennedy Sch Govt 79 JFK St Mailbox 124 Cambridge MA 02138 E-mail: joseph_nye@harvard.edu.*

NYE, LINDA PURCELL, secondary school educator; d. George T and Sara Jane Purcell; m. Stephen Christopher Nye, Aug. 5, 2001; children: Levi, Clifton. MusB in Edn., U. of Puget Sound, Tacoma, Wash., 1975; MEd in Counseling, U. of Puget Sound, 1986; Cert. of Vocal Mastery, Austro-Am. Inst. of Edn., Vienna, Austria, 1972—73. Choir/dramateacher White River Sch. Dist., Buckley, Wash.; choir/drama tchr. Clover Pk. Sch. Dist., Lakewood, Wash., 1986—96; choir/drama/English tchr. Evergreen Sch. Dist., Vancouver, Wash., 1996—2009, Redmond Sch. Dist., Oreg.; high sch. choir dir.; musical theatre dir. Dir.: Best in the Northwest Festival (Best Dir., 1992); (plays) Grease (Outstanding Theatre Prodn. in Pierce County, 1989); choreographer (plays) He's Risen! (Best Artistic Design, 1993). V.p. Adelphian Concert Choir, pres., 1974—75; treas. Puyallup Bus. and Profl. Women, Puyallup, Wash., 1977—78. Recipient Inspirational award, Adelphian Concert Choir/ U. of Puget Sound, 1974; named Outstanding Woman in Pierce County, Bus. and Profl. Women, 1979; scholar Four Yr. Vocal scholar, U. of Puget Sound Sch. of Music, 1971—75. Fellow: NEA (assoc.); mem.: Am. Choral Dirs. Assn. (organizing chmn. women's hon. choir N.W. divsn. 1988), EEA, Wash. Edn. Assn., Music Educator's Nat. Conf. (assoc.; dist. pres. 1979—83, v.p. 1979—83, organizing chmn. all-N.W. choir), Mortar Bd. (life), Sigma Alpha Iota Alumnae Assn. (assoc.; pres. 1974—84, v.p. 1974—84, treas. 1974—84, Ruby Sword of Honor/ Nu Province Leadership Award 1976). Liberal. Avocations: travel, singing. Personal E-mail: lnye525@bendbroadband.com.

NYE, MARGARET BIEN, middle school educator; b. Tali, Yunnan, China, Sept. 18, 1945; came to U.S., 1950; d. George Sung-Nien and Jane Feng-Chen (Ng) Bien; m. Rodman Fuller Nye, Mar. 3, 1974. AB, San Diego State U., 1969. Cert. elem. tchr., Calif. Tchr. LaJolla Elem. Sch., San Diego, 1969-71, McCabe Union Sch., El Centro, Calif., 1971-73, Taipei (Taiwan) Am. Sch., 1974-76, Hamlin Sch. for Girls, San Francisco, 1979-85, Horace Mann Middle Sch., San Francisco, 1985—96, 1997—2002, Beijing Internat. Sch., Beijing, 1996—97; pres. Presidio Mid. Sch., San Francisco, 2002—. Participant Project 2061, San Francisco, 1989-94. Recipient Star Tchr. award, 1990, Mentor Tchr. award, 1988-94. Mem. ASCD, NSTA, Nat. Coun. Tchrs. Math., Calif. Math. Coun., San Francisco Math. Tchrs. Assn. (v.p. 1989-91), Assn. Chinese Tchrs., United Educators San Francisco, Peer Assistance and Rev. (mem. panel 2001-04, math/sci. collaborative, 2000-04, Met Life fellow, 2004-05). Office: 450 30th Ave San Francisco CA 94121 Business E-Mail: nyem@sfusd.edu.

NYE, TRACY D., psychologist; b. Mountain View, Calif., July 3, 1980; d. Daniel A and Diana L Nye. Cert. sch. psychology specialist Western Ill. U., Macomb, 2005; sch. psychologist Oreg., 2008. Sch. psychologist Forest Grove Sch. Dist., Oreg., 2007—, Sherwood Sch. Dist., Oreg., 2005—07. Mem. Oreg. Sch. Psychologist Assn., Portland, Oreg., 2005—08. Mem. New Thought Ministries Oreg., Beaverton, 2007—08. Mem.: Oregon Sch. Psychologist assn. Democrat. Avocation: travel. Office: Forest Grove Sch Dist 1255 Pacific Ave Forest Grove OR 97116 Personal E-mail: tracynye98@yahoo.com. Business E-Mail: tnye@fgsd.k12.or.us.

NYE, W. MARCUS W., lawyer; b. NYC, Aug. 3, 1945; s. W.R. and Nora (McLaren) N.; m. Eva Johnson BA, Harvard U., 1967; JD, U. Idaho, 1974. Bar: Idaho 1974, U.S. Dist. Ct. Idaho 1974, U.S. Ct. Appeals (9th cir.) 1980; lic. pilot. Ptnr. Racine, Olson, Nye, Budge & Bailey, Pocatello, Idaho, 1974—. Vis. prof. law U. Idaho, Moscow, 1984; pres. Idaho State U. Found., 2001-03, U. Idaho Coll. Law Found. Commr., Idaho State Centennial Found., 1985-90. Recipient Alumni Svc. award U. Idaho, 1988, Bartz award Idaho State U, 2004; named Dist. Lawyer of Yr., Idaho State Bar, 2005. Fellow ABA (bd. govs. 1997-2000), Am. Bar Found. (stat. chmn. 1992-95); mem. Am. Bd. Trial Advs. (nat. bd. dirs.), Am. Coll. Trial Lawyers, Idaho State Bar Assn. (pres. 1987-88), Idaho Def. Counsel Assn. (pres. 1982), 6th Dist. Bar Assn. (pres. 1982). Avocation: travel. Home: 173 S 15th Ave Pocatello ID 83201-4056 Office: Racine Olson Nye Budge & Bailey PO Box 1391 Pocatello ID 83204-1391 Office Phone: 208-232-6101. Business E-Mail: nye@racinelaw.net.

NYENHUIS, JACOB EUGENE, academic administrator; b. Mille Lacs County, Minn., Mar. 25, 1935; s. Egbert Peter and Rosa (Walburg) N.; m. Leona Mae Van Duyn, June 6, 1956; children: Karen J. Louwsma, Kathy J. Kurtze, Lorna J. Cook, Sarah Van Duyn N. AB in Greek, Calvin Coll., 1956; AM in Classics, Stanford U., 1961, PhD in Classics, 1963; LittD (hon.), Hope Coll., 2001. Asst. in classical langs. Calvin Coll., Grand Rapids, Mich., 1957-59; acting instr. Stanford (Calif.) U., 1962; from asst. prof. to prof. Wayne State U., Detroit, 1962-75, dir. honors program, 1964-75, chmn. Greek and Latin dept., 1965-75; prof. classics, dean for humanities Hope Coll., Holland, Mich., 1975-78, dean for arts and humanities, 1978-84, provost, 1984—2001, prof. and provost emeritus, 2001—; sr. rsch. fellow A.C. Van Raalte Inst., 2001—02, dir., 2002—. Cons. Mich. Dept. Edn., Lansing, 1971-72, Gustavus Adolphus Coll., St. Peter, Minn., 1974, Northwestern Coll., Orange City, Iowa, 1983, Whitworth Coll., Spokane, Wash., 1987, The Daedalus Project, 1988, Albion Coll., 2002-03, Kalamazoo Coll., 2003—04; reviewer NEH, Washington, 1986-87, panelist, 1991; reviewer Lilly Endowment, Indpls., 1987-89, U.S. Dept. Edn., 1993, Mich. Humanities Coun., 1999-2001, 2006; vis. assoc. prof. U. Calif., Santa Barbara, 1967-68, Ohio State U., Columbus, 1972; vis. rsch. prof. Am. Sch. Classical Studies, Athens, Greece, 1973-74, mng. com.; vis. scholar Green Coll. Oxford U., 1989; mem. editl. adv. bd. Christianity and The Arts, 1998-2001, chmn., 1999-2001. Co-author: Latin Via Ovid, 1977, rev. edit., 1982, A Dream Fulfilled: The Van Raalte Sculpture in Centennial Park, 1997; editor: Petronius: Cena Trimalchionis, 1970, Plautus: Amphitruo, 1970, A Goodly Heritage: Essays in Honor of the Reverend Dr. Elton J. Bruins at Eighty, 2007; co-editor: Dutch-American Arts and Letters in Historical Perspective, 2008; author: Centennial History of 14th Street Christian Reformed Church, Holland, Michigan, 2002, Myth and the Creative Process: Michael Ayrton and the Myth of Daedalus, the Maze Maker, 2003; contbr. articles to profl. jours. Elder Christian Ref. Ch., Palo Alto, Calif., 1960—62, elder, clk. Grosse Pointe, Mich., 1964—67, Holland, Mich., 1976—85, v.p., 1988—91, exec. com., 1994—95; trustee Calvin Theol. Sem., 2001—07, mem. exec. com., 2002—07, v.p., 2003—07; chmn. human rels. coun. Open Housing Com., Grosse Pointe, 1971—73. Mem. Am. Philol. Assn., Danforth Assocs. (chmn. regional com. 1975-77), Mich. Classical Conf. (1st v.p. 1965-66, pres. 1966-67), Mich. Coun. Humanities (bd. dirs., 1976-84, 88-92, 96-99, chmn. 1980-82, Disting. Svc. award 1984), Nat. Fedn. State Humanities Couns. (bd. dirs. 1979-84, pres. 1981-83), Gt. Lakes Colls. Assn. (bd. dirs. 1991-93), Coun. on Undergrad. Rsch. (councilor-at-large 1993-99), Green Coll. Soc., Mortar Board, Phi Beta Kappa, Eta Sigma Phi. Democrat. Avocations: photography, carpentry. Office: Hope Coll Van Raalte Inst PO Box 9000 Holland MI 49422-9000 Office Phone: 616-395-7171. Business E-Mail: nyenhuis@hope.edu.

NYERGES, ALEXANDER LEE, museum director; b. Rochester, NY, Feb. 27, 1957; s. Sandor Elek and Lena (Angeline) N.; m. Kathryn Gray; 1 child, Robert Angeline. BA, George Washington U., 1979, MA, 1981. Intern The Octagon, Washington, 1976-79; archeol. asst. Smithsonian Instn., Washington, 1977; curatorial intern Nat. Mus. Am. History, 1978-79; adminstrv. asst. George Washington U., Washington, 1979-81; exec. dir. DeLand Mus. Art, Fla., 1981-85, Miss. Mus. Art, Jackson, 1985-92; dir. Dayton Art Inst., 1992—2006, Va. Mus. Fine Arts, Richmond, 2006—. Mem. grants panel Nat. Endowment for the Arts, 1988—; field surveyor Inst. Mus. Svcs., Washington, 1985-88, nat. review panel, 1990-92; treas., bd. dirs. Volusia County Arts Coun., Daytona Beach, Fla., 1983-85. Author: Selections from the Permanent Collection, 1999, In Praise of Nature: Ansel Adams and Photographers of the American West, The Harold W Shaw Collection: Pre Columbian Treasures, 2003, Edward Weston: A Photographer's Love of Life, 2004; contbr. articles to profl. jours. Bd. dirs. West Volusia Hist. Soc., 1984-85; pres. Miss. Inst. Arts and Letters, 1987-88; trustee Cultural Arts Ctr., DeLand, 1984-85, Miami Valley Cultural Alliance, 1993-95, Intermus. Conservation Lab., 1993-99, Montgomery County Arts and Culture Dist., 1994-2001; trustee, chmn. Dayton-Montgomery County Conv. and Visitors Bur.; bd. trustees Assn. Art Mus. Dirs., 2007—. U.S. Dept. Edn. scholar, 1973. Mem. DeLand Area C. of C. (bd. dirs., tourist adv. com. 1984-85), Assn. Art Mus. Dirs., Am. Assn. Mus. (S.E. regional rep. to non-print media com. 1983-85, nat. legis. com. 1986-93), Miss. Mus. Assn., Southeastern Mus. Conf. (bd. dirs. 1991-92), Fla. Mus. Assn., Fla. Art Mus. Dirs. Assn., Cultural Roundtable (pres. 1993-95), Ohio Mus. Assn. (trustee 1993-98), Phi Beta Kappa. Avocations: photography, music, writing, sports, scuba diving. Office: Virginia Mus Fine Arts 200 N Blvd Richmond VA 23220 Office Phone: 804-340-1504. E-mail: anyerges@aol.com.

NYGAARD, RICHARD LOWELL, federal judge; b. Thief River Falls, MN, 1940; BS cum laude, U. So. Calif., 1969; JD, U. Mich., 1971. Mem. Orton, Nygaard & Dunlevy, 1972—80; judge Ct. Common Pleas, 6th Dist. Pa., Erie, 1981—88, US Ct. Appeals (3d cir.), Erie, Pa., 1988—2005, sr. judge, 2005—; sr. lecturer Penn State Univ., 1999—2003. Councilman Erie County, Pa., 1977—81. With USNR, 1958—64. Mem.: ABA, Erie County Bar Assn., Pa. Bar Assn. Office: James A Byrne Courthouse 601 Market St Rm 2100 Philadelphia PA 19106 also: 17 S Park Row Ste B-230 Erie PA 16501-1164*

NYGREN, MALCOLM ERNEST, minister; b. Portsmouth, Ohio, Sept. 12, 1925; s. Gustav Henning and Alma Marie (Viberg) N.; m. Betty Sue Perry, May 14, 1950 (dec. Oct. 1996); children: Melinda (Mrs. Robert Pierce), Nancy; m. Mimi Cozad, Oct. 12, 1999. AB, Hanover Coll., Ind., 1949; BD, McCormick Theol. Sem., Chgo., 1952; STD, San Francisco Theol. Sem., 1980. Ordained to ministry Presbyn. Ch. (USA), 1952. Sr. pastor 1st Presbyn. Ch., Champaign, Ill., 1952-90; ret., 1990. Author: Lord of the Four Seasons, 1986; author: (book)Shades Of Life, 2007, syndicated columnist Champaign News Gazette, others; contbr. religious and humorous articles to periodicals. Bd. dirs. Kemmerer Village, Assumption, Ill., 1976-82; pres., fellow Charles W. Christie Found., Champaign, 1975-86; mem. instl. rev. bd. U. Ill., Urbana-Champaign, 1991-97. With inf. U.S. Army, 1943-46, ETO. Mem. Rotary. Office Phone: 217-356-8124. Personal E-mail: malnygren@gmail.com. *We are all citizens of two worlds-and the world we can't see is more significant than the one we do.*

NYGREN, WILLIAM C., investment company executive; BS in acctg., Univ. Minn., 1980; MS in fin., Univ. Wis., Madison, 1981. Cert. CFA. Fin. analyst Northwestern Mutual Life. Ins. Co., 1981—83; investment analyst Harris Associates L.P., Chgo., 1983—90, dir. rsch., 1990—98, ptnr., portfolio mgr. Oakmark Select Fund, 1996—, portfolio mgr. Oakmark Fund, 2000—, portfolio mgr. Oakmark Global Select Fund, 2006—. Named Domestic Stockpicker of the Yr., Morningstar, 2001. Office: Harris Associates LP Ste 500 2 N LaSalle St Chicago IL 60602 Office Phone: 312-621-0600.

NYHAN, WILLIAM LEO, pediatrician, educator; b. Boston, Mar. 13, 1926; s. W. Leo and Mary N.; m. Christine Murphy, Nov. 20, 1948; children: Christopher, Abigail. Student, Harvard U., 1943-45; MD, Columbia U., 1949; MS, U. Ill., 1956, PhD, 1958; doctorate (hon.), Tokushima U., Japan, 1981. Intern Yale U.-Grace-New Haven Hosp., 1949-50, resident, 1950-51, 53-55; asst. prof. pediatrics Johns Hopkins U., 1958-61, assoc. prof., 1961-63; prof. pediatrics, biochemistry U. Miami, 1963-69, chmn. dept. pediatrics, 1963-69; prof. U. Calif., San Diego, 1969—, chmn. dept. pediatrics, 1969-86. Mem. FDA adv. com. on Teratogenic Effects of Certain Drugs, 1964-70; mem. pediatric panel AMA Council on Drugs, 1964-70; mem. Nat. Adv. Child Health and Human Devel. Council, 1967-71; mem. research adv. com. Calif. Dept. Mental Hygiene, 1969-72; mem. med. and sci. adv. com. Leukemia Soc. Am., Inc., 1968-72; mem. basic adv. com. Nat. Found. March of Dimes, 1973-81; mem. Basil O'Connor Starter grants com., 1973-93; mem. clin. cancer program project rev. com. Nat. Cancer Inst., 1977-81; vis. prof. extraordinario U. del Salvador (Argentina), 1982. Author (with E. Edelson): The Heredity Factor, Genes, Chromosomes and You, 1976; author: Genetic & Malformation Syndromes in Clinical Medicine, 1976, Abnormalities in Amino Acid Metabolism in Clinical Medicine, 1984, Diagnostic Recognition of Genetic Diseases, 1987; author: (with P. Ozand) Atlas of Metabolic Diseases, 1998; author: (with B. Barshop and P. Ozand) 2d edit., 2005; author: (with G. Hoffmann, J. Zschocke, S.G. Kahler and E. Mayatepek) Inherited Metabolic Diseases, 2001; editor: Amino Acid Metabolism and Genetic Variation, 1967, Heritable Disorders of Amino Acid Metabolism, 1974; mem. editl. bd.: Jour. Pediat., 1964—78, Western Jour. Medicine, 1974—86, King Faisal Hosp. Med. Jour., 1981—85, Annals of Saudi Medicine, 1985—87, mem. editl. com.: Ann. Rev. Nutrition, 1982—86, mem. editl. staff: Med. and Pediat. Oncology, 1975—83. Served with U.S. Navy, 1944-46; U.S. Army, 1951-53. Nat. Found. Infantile Paralysis fellow, 1955-58; recipient Commemorative medallion Columbia U. Coll. Physicians and Surgeons, 1967, Guthrie award Am. Assn. Mental Retardation, 1998, Pool of Bethesda award Bethesda Luth. Homes and Svcs., 1999. Fellow: Inst. Medicine of Nat. Acad. Scis., Am. Acad. Pediat. (Borden award 1980, Lifetime Achievement award 1999, Leonard Tow Humanism Medicine award Arnold P. Gold Found. 2008); mem.: AAAS, Biochem. Soc., Am. Coll. Med. Genetics, Am. Assn. Clin. Chemists, Am. Soc. Human Genetics (dir. 1978—81), Am. Soc. Clin. Investigation, Soc. Exptl. Biology and Medicine, Am. Inst. Biol. Scis., South African Human Genetics (hon.), Nat. Acad. Scis. Inst. Medicine (hon.), Inst. Investigaciones Citologicas (Spain) (corr.), Soc. Francaise de Pediatrie (corr.), Am. Pediatric Soc., Western Soc. Pediatric Rsch. (pres. 1976—77), Am. Soc. Pharmacology and Exptl. Therapeutics, Am. Assn. Cancer Rsch., Soc. Pediatric Rsch. (pres. 1970—71), Am. Chem. Soc., Am. Fedn. Clin. Rsch., Alpha Omega Alpha, Sigma Xi. Office: U Calif San Diego Dept Pediatrics # 0830 9500 Gilman Dr La Jolla CA 92093-0830 Office Phone: 619-543-5237. Business E-Mail: wnyhan@ucsd.edu.

NYIKOS, STACY ANN, publishing executive; d. Michael J. and Martha Nyikos; m. Rainer Kohrs, Dec. 1, 1994; children: Alysia Bella Kohrs, Sophia Johanna Kohrs. BA, U. Notre Dame, 1990; MA, Christian Albrecht U., Germany, 1994; PhD, U. Va., 2000. Gen. mgr. Stonehorse Pub., Tulsa, Okla., 2004—07; stats. lab coord. U. Okla., Tulsa, 2004—06. Author: (children's lit.) Squirt, 2005, Shelby, 2006, Dizzy, 2007, Dragon Wishes, 2008. Organizer Okla. involvement Screentime Awareness, Internat. TV Turnoff Week. Recipient Moms Choice award, 2007; named winner, Ariz. Author's Literacy Contest, 2006; finalist Foreword Bk. of Yr. award, 2006; grantee, Fulbright Com., 1998—99; Dissertation Improvement grantee, NSF, 1999—2001, President's fellow, U. Va., 1995—98, Dumas Malone Traveling fellow, 1998—99. Liberal. Roman Catholic. Avocations: running, travel. Office: Stonehorse Pub LLC Ste D1 Rm 296 6528 E 101st St Tulsa OK 74133 Office Fax: 888-867-1927. Business E-Mail: snyikos@stonehorsepublishing.com.

NYIRI, JOSEPH ANTON, sculptor, art educator; b. Racine, Wis., May 24, 1937; s. Joseph Anton Nyiri and Dorothy Marion (Larson) Zinki; m. Laura Lee Primeau, Aug. 29, 1959 (dec. Mar. 1982); children: Krista, Nicole, Page; m. Melissa Trent, July 28, 1985. BA, U. Wis., 1959, MS,

1961. Tchr. art Madison Sch. Dist., Wis., 1959-62; art cons. San Diego Unified Schs., 1962-65, dist. resource tchr., 1965-73, regional tchr. occupational art, 1973-76, mentor tchr., 1985-95; sculptor San Diego, 1962—; fine arts cons., 1966—; head dept. art edn. Serra H.S., San Diego, 1976—; tchr. art Zool. Soc. San Diego, 1991—. Fine art restorer, 1963—; lectr. art and art edn., 1964—; pvt. art tchr. San Diego City Zoo, 1965—; instr. art U. Calif., San Diego, 1967—80, San Diego State U. Ext., 1969—; cons. gifted and talented edn. program San Diego City Schs., 1995—; cons. gifted programs Escondido, Calif. and Poway, Calif. Schs., 1995—, Boston Schs., 1996—98, Romona, Calif. Pub. Schs., 1996—. Exhibitions include sculptures in numerous one-man, two-person, juried and invitational shows, 1960—, U. Mex., Baja, Calif., 1983; reviewer: Calif. Art Rev., 1989. Active Art Guild San Diego Mus. Art; bd. dir. San Diego Art Inst. Sgt. Wis. N.G., 1955—61. Recipient Creativity award, Pacific Inst., 1969; named Secondary Tchr. of the Yr., San Diego City Schs., 1982; named an 3 Tchrs. of Yr., San Diego County, 1983; named one of Outstanding Art Tchrs. in US, RISD, 1984; named to Horlick HS Grads of Distinction, Racine. Mem.: Allied Craftsmen San Diego, Arts/Worth: Nat. Coun. Art (charter), Zool. Soc. San Diego, Internat. Platform Assn. Democrat. Avocations: running, hiking, travel, reading, poetry. Office: Zool Soc San Diego Edn Dept PO Box 551 San Diego CA 92112-0551 Office Phone: 619-295-3049. Personal E-mail: mnyiri@cox.net. Business E-Mail: mnyiri@sandiegozoo.org. *Personal philosophy: Love others, exercise everyday, be creative, live life and enjoy, be able to receive pleasure and give pleasure and live life as if you are going to die tomorrow.*

NYIRJESY, ISTVAN, retired obstetrician, gynecologist; b. Budapest, Hungary, Nov. 14, 1929; came to U.S., 1954, naturalized, 1960; s. Sandor D. and Margit (Bertalan) N.; m. Michelle Shoepp, June 16, 1956; children: Francis, Paul, Christine. MD, Catholic U. Louvain, Belgium, 1955. Diplomate: Am. Bd. Ob-Gyn. Intern Cath. U. Louvain and Little Co. Mary Hosp., Evergeen Park, Ill., 1954-55; resident in gynecology obstetrics, 1960-63; chief obstetrical research Nat. Naval Med. Center, Bethesda, Md., 1966-68; ret., 1968; practice medicine specializing in Ob-Gyn Bethesda, 1968—2008; tchr. Georgetown Med. Sch. Clin. prof. Ob-Gyn Georgetown U., 1968—; cons. NIH, 1974—, FDA, 1977-88. Lit. editor Breast Disease: contbr. articles to med. jours.; author: Prevention and Detection of Gynecologic and Breast Cancer, 1994. Pres., Internat. Found. for Gynecol. Cancer Detection and Prevention, 1993—. Officer M.C. USN, 1956-68; advanced through grades to comdr. Recipient Sword of Hope pin Am. Cancer Soc., 1973, Vicennial medal Georgetown U., 1988. Fellow ACOG (Host award 1964), Hungarian Gynecologic Soc. (hon.), Internat. Coll. Surgeons; mem. Montgomery County (Md.) Med. Soc. (chmn. profl. edn. com. 1971-72), Am. Soc. of Breast Disease (past pres.), Assn. Profs. Ob-Gyn., Am. Soc. Reproductive Medicine, Washington Gynecol. Soc. (v.p. 1993-94, 1st v.p. 1994-95, pres. 1996-97).

NYKANEN, DAVID GORDON, pediatrician, cardiologist, consultant; b. Toronto, Ont., Can., Mar. 20, 1962; s. Paul Allan Nykanen and Elizabeth Anne Fulton; m. Lori Michelle Grigg; children: Colin, Lauren, Stephanie. MD, U. Calgary, Alta., Can., 1986. Asst. prof. U. Toronto, 1993—2000; active staff Hosp. for Sick Children, Toronto, 1993—2000, program dir. - cardiology, 1994—2000; dir. cardiac catherization and interventions Miami (Fla.) Children's Hosp., 2001—. Cons. Bayliss Med. Co., Mississauga, Ont., 1998—, WL Gore Med., Flagstaff, Ariz., 2000—; presenter in field. Contbr. chapters to books, articles to profl. jours. Fellow: Soc. Cardiac Angiography and Interventions, Royal Coll. Physicians and Surgeons Can.; mem.: Can. Pediat. Cardiology Assn., Can. Cardiovasc. Soc. Office: Congenital Heart Inst 50 W Sturtevant St Orlando FL 32806 Office Phone: 407-649-6907. Business E-Mail: david.nykanen@orlandohealth.com.

NYLANDER, JANE LOUISE, museum director, educator, writer; b. Cleve., Jan. 27, 1938; d. James Merritt and Jeannette Cayford; m. Daniel Harris Giffen, 1963 (div. 1970); children: Sarah Louise, Thomas Harris; m. Richard Conrad Nylander, 1972: 1 child, Timothy Frost. AB, Brown U., Providence, RI, 1959; MA, U. Del., Newark, 1961; postgrad., Attingham Summer Sch., Eng., 1970; DFA (hon.), New Eng. Coll., Henniker, NH, 1994. Curator Hist. Soc. York County, Pa., 1961-62, N.H. Hist. Soc., Concord, 1962-69; instr. New Eng. Coll., Henniker, NH, 1964-65, Monadnock C.C., Peterborough, NH, 1966-69; curator of textiles and ceramics Old Sturbridge Village, Mass., 1969-85; adj. assoc. prof. Boston U., 1978-85; sr. curator Old Sturbridge Village, 1985-86; dir. Strawbery Banke Mus., Portsmouth, NH, 1986-92, Soc. for Preservation of New Eng. Antiquities, Boston, 1992-93, pres., 1993—2002, pres. emerita, 2002—. Adj. prof. art history and Am. studies Boston U., 1993—96; mem. adv. bd. Concord (Mass.) Mus., 1986—94, Wentworth-Coolidge Commn., 1991—96, mem. adv. com., 1996—2004; mem. adv. bd. John Nicholas Brown Ctr. for Am. Studies, Providence, 1995—2003; mem. adv. bd. dept. Am. decorative arts Mus. Fine Arts, Boston, 1971—99, Art of the Ams., 1999—2000; mem. adv. com. Lakes Region Conservation Trust, 2002—04, Charles S. Parsons Fund, 2004—06; advisor house com. Moffatt Ladd House, 1973—; mem. nat. coun. Strawbery Banke Mus., 2004—, mem. steering com. Ctr. for Study of Cmty., 2004—05; cons. in field. Author: Fabrics for Historic Buildings, 4th edit., 1990, Our Own Snug Fireside: Images of the New England Home 1760-1860, 1993, paperback edit., 1994, Windows on the Past, 2000, The Art of Family, 2002; author: (with Richard C. Nylander) Fabrics and Wallpaper for Historic Buildings, 2005; mem. editl. bd.: Hist. N.H., 1993—, The Dublin Seminar, 1984—; contbr. numerous articles to profl. jours. Trustee Worcester (Mass.) Hist. Mus., 1978—84, Hist. Deerfield (Mass.) Inc., 1981—94, 2003—, chair strategic planning com., 2003—, hon. trustee, 1994—2003, Hist. Mass., Inc., 1991—93, Decorative Arts Trust, 1991—, Portsmouth Athenaeum, 1988—90, Japan Soc. N.H., 1988—92, Fort Ticonderoga, 2000—02, Coun. Colonial Soc. Mass., 1993—96; mem. adv. bd. New Eng. Heritage Ctr., 1993—2002; active State Ho. Adv. Com., Boston, 1984—85, Gov.'s Coun. for Wentworth Coolidge Mansion, Concord, 1964—66; mem. Com. for Preservation of N.H. State Flags, 1989—92; mem. H.F. duPont award com. Winterthur Mus., 1993—, mem. Mt. Vernon adv. com. for 1999, 1996—99; designator The Henderson Found., 1992—2004. Recipient Charles F. Montgomery prize, Decorative Arts Soc., 1985, Disting. Sophomore Book prize, Boston U., 1993, (with Richard C. Nylander) The Anne and Roger Webb award, Historic Mass., Inc., 1996, John F. Ayer award, The Bay State League, 2002, Boston History award, Bostonian Soc., 2003, award for outstanding contbn. to decorative arts, Iris Found., 2005, Lifetime Achievement award (with Richard C. Nylander), Victorian Soc. Am., 2005, Roll of Honor, Nat. Soc. Colonial Dames of Am., N.H., 2006, Pres.'s award, Old Sturbridge Vill., 2009. Mem.: NH Hist. Soc. (interpretation com. 2003—05, exbns. and pubs. com. 2005—, trustee 2007—, exhbns. & publs. com. chair 2007—), Costume Soc. Am. (bd. dirs. 1977—83), New Eng. Hist. Geneal. Soc., NH Humanities Coun., Soc. Preservation of NH Forests, Soc. Winterthur Fellows, Mass. Hist. Soc., Portsmouth Athenaeum, Royal Oak Assn., Nat. Trust for Hist. Preservation, Am. Assn. for State and Local History (Cert. of Commendation 2001, 2008), Am. Antiquarian Soc. (elected 1984), N.H. Preservation Alliance, Friends of Hist. Deerfield, Nat. Soc. Colonial Dames in NH (bd. dirs. 1967—73, program chair 2002—, Roll of Honor 2006), Am. Inst. Architects (hon.; hon. elected mem. NH chpt. 2007, hon. elected mem., nat. 2009), Colonial Soc. Mass., Lakes Region Conservation Trust (Advisor 2002—04), Castle Preservation Soc. (vice chair 2004—07, bd. dirs. 2004—08), Friends of the Moffatt Ladd House, Brown Club NH (trustee 1988—93). Episcopalian. Home: 17 Franklin St Portsmouth NH 03801-4501

NYMADAWA, PAGBAJABYN, physician, public health administrator; b. Barunburen, Selenghe, Mongolia, Jan. 11, 1947; s. Makhbolyn Pagbajab and Serenengyin Chimid; m. Tumur-ochiryn Oyunbat; children: Naranbaatar, Naranbat, Naranbold. Dr., Med. U., Ulaanbaatar, Mongolia, 1971; MD, Humboldt U., Berlin, 1977; DSc, Acad. Med. Scis., Moscow, 1989; MD (hon.), Rangsit U., Thailand, 1994. Lectr., chair physiology Med. U., 1971-74; postgrad. fellow Inst. Applied Virology, Berlin, 1974-77; head dept. virology Nat. Inst. Hyg. Epid. Microbiology, Ulaanbaatar, 1978-85; WHO fellow Med. Rsch. Inst., Eng., 1980; dep. dir. rsch. and devel. Nat. Inst. Hyg. Epid. Microbiology, Ulaanbaatar, 1985-87; dep. min. Ministry of Health, Ulaanbaatar, 1987-90; min. health Govt. of Mongolia, Ulaanbaatar, 1990—96, 2000—04; social policy advisor Pres. of Mongolia, 1998—2000; M.P. Mongolia. V.p. 43d World Health Assembly, Geneva, 1990; pres. 44th World Health Assembly, Geneva, 1991; chmn. Subassembly Med. Scis., Mongolian Acad. Sci., 1997—. Author 20 books. Recipient medal for 70th and 80th Jubilee of People's Revolution in Mongolia, Pres. of Mongolia, 1991, Order of the Polar Star, 1996. Mem. WHO (mem. exec. bd. 1992-95), Acad. Scis. Mongolia, Mongolian Med. Scis. (mem. editorial bd. jour. 1987-90, editor-in-chief 1990-2000), N.Y. Acad. Scis. Home: Central Post PO Box 596 Ulaanbaatar 13 Mongolia Office: Mongolian Acad Scis PO Box 596 Central Post Ulaanbaatar 13 Mongolia Home Phone: 976-11-345599; Office Phone: 976-11-450267. Personal E-mail: nymadawa@gmail.com.

NYOCHEMBENG, LEOPOLD M., plant pathologist, educator; m. Evelyn B. Nkea; children: Sherrel E., Vanessa N., Mikayla A, Leanna F. BS in Agrl. Engring. Works, U. Dschang, Cameroon, 1988; MS, Ala. A & M U., Normal, 1994, PhD, 2001. Recipient Thomas Jefferson award, USAID, 1993—94; Organic Rsch. grant, EPA, 2007—, USDA, 2007—, Ala. Agrl. Land Grant Alliance, 2008—. Mem.: Internat. Soc. Plant Pathology, ASA-CSSA-SSSA, Am. Phytopathological Soc. Achievements include research in differential expression of peroxidase in roots of cocoyam inoculated with pythium myriotylum. Office: Alabama A & M Univ 4900 Meridian St Normal AL 35762 Office Fax: 256-372-4208. Personal E-mail: leopold_fiona@hotmail.com, lnyochem@gmail.com.

NYOKKA, SUZETTE, artist, natural health educator; b. Meadowbrook, Pa., June 10, 1961; d. Barbara Louise and adopted d. Walter H. Schmitz, Thomas Ziemba; children: Gaelen Ishi Nyokka Morrell, Emily Luna Rose Nyokka Morrell. BA, Calif. Inst. Integral Studies, 2001. Advanced Massage Therapies, Natural Health Educator Inst. of Ednl. Therapy, Heartwood Inst., 1988, cert. in Jin Shin Jyutsu 2005. Founder Heartwood Garden, Garberville, Calif., 1984—89; creator/artist Island Mt. Basketry, Garberville, 1986—; massage therapist/ educator Advanced Massage Therapies, Woodside, Menlo Park, Calif., 1989—2005, massage therapist/educator Garberville/Novato, 2005—; ednl. activist So. Humboldt Cmty. Sch. Dist., Garberville, 1984—; dir. Skyfish Sch. Permaculture Program, Garberville, 1997—2005; artistic dir. Teen's Radio, Redway, Calif., 2005—; instr. permacuture design, adj. advisor Skyfish Sch., Briceland, 1997—. Prodr.: (storytelling festivals) Live Performances; co-creator (cd) All Spirits Sing (Best Native Am. Rec., 1998). Co-coord. Arts and Ecology Ctr., Garberville, Calif., 2005—; developmennt coord. KMUD Teen's Cmty. Radio, Garberville, Calif., 2004—05; vp So. Humboldt Youth and Cmty. Ctr., Garberville, Calif.; pres. Trees Found., Garberville, Calif., 1996—98; participant in a cross cultural sharing Nat. Storytelling Assn., San Francisco, 2002, China, 2002. Grant, Music For Little People Found., 2002, Humboldt Area Found., 2004, Calif. Inst. of Integral Studies, 2000. Mem.: So. Humboldt Cmty. Parks and Garden Club (life). Democrat-Npl. Avocations: reading, photography, language, film, travel. Home: 352 Meadowview Rd Garberville CA 95542 Personal E-mail: suzette@asis.com.

NYQUIST, CORINNE ELAINE, librarian; b. Minnesota Falls, Minn., Nov. 1, 1935; d. Clair Francis and Ebba Ingeborg Johnson; m. Thomas Eugene Nyquist, Dec. 22, 1956; children: Jonathan Eugene, Lynn Marie. BA (cum laude), Macalester Coll., 1956; MALS, U. Minn., 1971; PhD (hon.), U. Albany, 2004. Asst. librarian U. Minn., Mpls., 1959-60, Evanston (Ill.) Pub. Library, 1962-64, Skokie (Ill.) Pub. Library, 1965-66; asst. librarian, research asst. Rhodes U., Grahamstown, Republic of South Africa, 1967; asst. librarian to librarian SUNY, New Paltz, 1968—, ombudsman, 1983-85. Co-project dir. human rights documentation project Ford Found., 1986-88; cons. N.Y. State Edn. Dept., Albany, 1980-82; chmn. internat. librs. com. SUNY, 1984-86. Contbr. articles to profl. jours. Chmn. Town Dem. Com., New Paltz, 1984-86, 2007—; adv. com. on awards SUNY, 1989-94. Recipient Chancellor's award, 1986; grantee SUNY Rsch. Found., 1975, 84-86, Ford Found., 1986. Mem. ALA (chmn. human rights task force 1989-91, exec. internat. rels. task force 1987-92, interlibr. loan code revision com. 2006—08, codes, guidelines and tech. stds. com. 2007—), African Studies Assn., NY African Studies Assn. (co-editor newsletter 1974-99, v.p. 1991-92, pres. 1992-93), Ulster County Librs. Assn. (exec. com. 1984-94), Sojourner Truth Inst. (bd. dirs. 1997-2001), SUNY Librs. Assn., Beta Phi Mu, NY African Studies Assn.(dir. secretariat, 2008-) Avocations: reading, hiking, cross country skiing, travel. Office: SUNY Sojourner Truth Libr New Paltz NY 12561-2493 Home: 140 Huguenot St New Paltz NY 12561-1018 Office Phone: 845-257-3681. E-mail: nyquistc@newpaltz.edu.

NYROP, DONALD WILLIAM, air transportation executive; b. Elgin, Nebr., Apr. 1, 1912; s. William A. and Nellie (Wylie) N.; m. Grace Cary, Apr. 19, 1941; children: Nancy, William, Karen, Kathryn. AB, Doane Coll., 1934; JD, George Washington U., 1939. Bar: D.C. 1938. Atty. Gen. Counsel's Office, CAA, Washington, 1939-41; exec. officer to chmn. CAB, 1942, chmn., 1952; rep. U.S. airlines; mem. ofcl. U.S. delegations Internat. Civil Aviation Orgn. Assemblies, 1946, 47; dep. adminstr. for ops. CAA, 1948-50, adminstr., 1950-51; chmn. CAB, 1951-52; pres. Northwest Airlines, Inc., 1954-78. Served with Air Transport Command USAAF, 1942-46. Decorated Legion of Merit. Mem.: Mpls. Club. Home: 4505 Golf Ter Minneapolis MN 55424-1510

NYSETH, ELIZABETH ANN, retired secondary school educator; b. St. Paul, Nov. 4, 1948; d. Herbert John and Dagna Mabel (Eimon) Borgert; m. Gary Lynn Nyseth, Dec. 7, 1988; children: Robert, Catherine, Mark; stepchildren: Jeff, Amy, Pete, Christopher. BS in Home Econs. Edn., U. Wis.-Stout, Menomonie, 1970, MS in Clothing, Textiles and Related Art, 1984. Cert. home econs. tchr., Wis. Tchr. Chippewa Falls (Wis.) Schs., 1970—, student tchr. supr. with U. Wis.-Stout, 1973—, curriculum asst. for family/consumer edn., bus. and mktg., 1990—2004, ret., 2004; owner Lamb's Creek Sewing Co., 2006—. Advisor Future Homemakers of Am., 1972—; mem. curriculum devel. pilot project Wis. Dept. Pub. Instrn., Madison, 1983-91, workshop facilitator, 1985-91; curriculum cons., 1989-91; adj. instr. U. Wis., Stout, 2004-05. Contbg. mem.: Wis. Mid. Sch. Curriculum Guide for Family and Consumer Edn., 1983—91; author: Sewing Tech., 2001. Recipient Cert. of Appreciation Wis. Dept. Pub. Instrn., 1991, U. Wis.-Stout, 1992, 93. Mem.: ASCD, Chippewa Falls Fedn. Tchrs. (v.p. 1993—, bldg. steward), Wis. Family and Consumer Edn. (State award for Dedicated Svc. 2004), N.W. Wis.Edn. Assn. Lutheran. Avocations: sewing, crafts, boating, fishing. Home: 1255 Jeffery Blvd Cumberland WI 54829 Personal E-mail: boatnsew@centurytel.net.

NYTES, JACKIE (M. JACQUELINE NYTES), councilwoman; m. Michael O'Brien; 1 child, Patrick. BA in Polit. Sci., U. Wis., Madison, M in Libr. Sci. Pub. libr., Ill., Wis., Carmel Clay Pub. Libr., Indpls.; assoc. dir., CFO Indpls.-Marion County Pub. Libr.; councillor, dist. 9 Indpls.-Marion County City-County Coun. Adj. prof. Ind. U.-Purdue U. Indpls.; former pres. Ind. Econ. Devel. Coun. Host family, fgn. exch. program Homestay Internat.; mem. adv. com. State Ind. Pub. Employees Retirement Fund 1977; candidate, Marion County auditor Dem. Party, 2002; former bd. mem. St. Richards Sch., Mid-North Ch. Coun.; chair French market St. Joan of Arc Ch.; exec. dir. Mapleton-Fall Creek Devel. Corp., former bd. mem., Mapleton-Fall Creek Neighborhood Assn., Horizon's Urban Summer Enrichment Program, Ind. Repertory Theater; bd. mem. The Internat. Ctr., Indpls. Symphony Orch. Recipient Citizen of Yr. award, Ind. Libr. Assn., 2005, Frank and Judy O'Bannon Equality award, Stonewall Democrats, 2005, Chris Gonzales award, ACLU, 2006, Lambda Legal Leadership award, 2006. Democrat. Office: 3444 Washington Blvd Indianapolis IN 46205-3717 also: Indpls Marion County City County Coun 241 City County Bldg 200 E Washington St Indianapolis IN 46204 Office Phone: 317-370-6184, 317-327-4242. Business E-Mail: jnytes@indygov.org.*

NZEH, OKOROAFOR OGBAJIE, director; m. Fidelia Nkeiruka Nzeh. BS, Ala. A&M, Ga., 1980; MS, Huntsville, 1983; MBA, 1987; PhD, Clark Atlanta U., 1994. Pres. African Christian Fellowship Chpt., Augusta, Ga.; Dir. accreditation self study Paine Coll., 1998—2008, chair divsn. bus. adminstrn., 1997—. Home: 779 Locks Way Ct Augusta GA 30907 Office: Paine Coll 1235 15th St Augusta GA 30901

O, KENNETH KYONGYOP, engineering educator; s. Sang-Chol and Yong-Ae O; m. Hyun-Joo Nam, Dec. 28, 1991; children: Stephen Tae-Jin, Daniel Tae-Su, Andrew Tae-Yoon. BS, MS, MIT, 1984, PhD, 1989. Sr. process engr. Analog Devices Inc, Wilmington, Mass., 1989—94; prof. U. Fla., Gainesville, Fla., 1994—, Rsch. Found. Prof., 2004—06. Chief tech. officer Global Communication Device, North Andover, Mass., 2002—03. Recipient Faculty Partnership award, IBM, 1995, 1997, 2000, Copper Design Challenge award, Semiconductor Rsch. Corp., 1999, Career Devel. award, NSF, 1996, Copper Design Challenge award, Semiconductor Rsch. Corp., 1999; Materials Processing Ctr. fellow, MIT, 1985. Mem.: IEEE, Sigma Xi. Achievements include development of RF silicon bipolar process technology; first to show CMOS technology can be used to produce RF integrated circuits for WLAN applications which are competitive to those fabricated using the SiGe technology; development of Aaproaches to improve on-chip inductors and varactors in silicon integrated circuits; first to show on-chip antennas can be used for communication within and between IC's; development of Schottky diodes with cut-off frequency greater than 1 THz in CMOS technology; research in 200-GHz CMOS oscillator. It holds the highest operating frequency silicon based circuits. Office: U Florida Dept ECE 539 New Engineering Building Gainesville FL 32611 Office Fax: 352-392-8381. Business E-Mail: kko@tec.ufl.edu.

OAKES, DAVID, statistician; b. Stockport, England, May 8, 1947; came to U.S., 1983; s. Norman Edward and Kathleen O.; m. Peggy Foster, Apr. 23, 1977; 1 child, William Foster. MA, U. Cambridge, 1972; PhD, London U., 1972. Asst. prof. Harvard U., Cambridge, Mass., 1977; sr. lectr. London Sch. Hygiene & Tropical Medicine, 1977-83; from assoc. prof. to prof. statistics & biostatistics U. Rochester, N.Y., 1983—. Chair dept. statistics U. Rochester, 1989-95, chair dept. biostatistics, 1995-2002. Co-author: Analysis of Survival Data, 1984; contbr. articles to profl. jours. Fellow Am. Statis. Assn., Internat. Statis. Inst., Inst. Math. Stats. Office: U Rochester Dept Biostatistics 601 Elmwood Ave Rochester NY 14642-0001

OAKES, ELLEN RUTH, psychotherapist, health facility administrator; b. Bartlesville, Okla., Aug. 19, 1919; d. John Isaac and Eva Ruth (Engle) Harboldt; m. Paul Otis Oakes Sr., June 12, 1937 (div. April 1974); children: Paul Otis Jr., Deborah Ellen, Nancy Elaine Masters; m. Siegmar Johann Knopp, Nov. 24, 1975 (div. Feb. 1998). BA in Sociology, Psychology summa cum laude, Oklahoma City U., 1961; MS in Clin. Psychology, U. Okla., 1963, PhD, 1967. Lic. clin. psychologist, Okla. Chief psychometrist Okla. U. Guidance Ctr., Norman, 1962; psychology trainee VA Hosp., Oklahoma City, 1962-64, Cerebral Palsy Ctr., Norman, Okla., 1964-65; psychology intern Guidance Service, Norman, 1965-66, staff psychologist, 1966-67; asst. prof. psychology Okla. U. Med. Sch., Oklahoma City, 1967-70; supr. psychology interns Okla. Univ. Health Scis. Ctr., 1967-80; founder, dir. Timberridge Inst., Oklahoma City, 1970-90, pres., 1980-90; pvt. practice clin. psychologist Oklahoma City, 1970-92. Instr. Okla. U. extension course, Tinker AFB, Oklahoma City, 1963, U. Okla., 1965-66; discussion leader Inst. for Tchrs. of Disadvantaged Child Oklahoma City Sch. System, 1966; leader group therapy sessions Asbury Meth. and Westminster Presbyn. Chs., Oklahoma City, 1966; mem. psychology team confs. for hearing disorders, Okla. U. Med. Sch., 1967-70; cons. Oklahoma City Pub. Schs., 1970-72; cons., group leader halfway house, 1972; mem. Okla. State Bd. Examiners Psychologist, 1974, 75; lectr. chs., PTAs, hosps.; reviewer Am. Psychol. Assn. Civilian Health and Med. Program of the Uniformed Svcs., 1978-89. Workshop conductor on Shame & Sexuality, Zurick Jungian Inst. winter seminar, 1992; attended Européen Congrés de Gestalt Thérapie in Paris, 1992; contbr. articles to profl. jours. Speaker Okla. County Mental Health Assn. Annual Worry Clinic, St. Luke's Ch., Oklahoma City, 1968-92, psychology dept. Sorosis Club, St. Luke's Ch.; charter mem. English spkg. Christian Congregation mission outreach Pauluskirche, Bochum, Germany, 1993-97, exec. coun., 1996-97. Mem. APA (peer rev. project with CHAMPUS, 1978-89), Okla. Psychol. Assn. (life, pres. 1975-76, named Pioneer Psychologist of Okla. by exec. com. 1998). Avocations: art, travel, poetry, photography, walking.

OAKES, JAMES, history professor; b. NYC, Dec. 19, 1953; s. Frank and Joan Oakes; m. Deborah Bohr, June 10, 1980; 1 child, Daniel Augustin. PhD, Berkeley, Calif., 1981. Asst. prof. Purdue U., W. Lafayette, Ind., 1981—82, Princeton U., NJ, 1982—86; prof. Northwestern U., Evanston, Ill., 1986—98; disting. prof. CUNY Grad. Ctr., NYC, 1998—. Author: (history) Slavery and Freedom: An Interpretation of the Old South, The Ruling Race: A History of American Slaveholders. Recipient Lincon prize, Civil War Inst. Gettysburg Coll., 2008; fellow, Inst. Advanced Study in Behavioral Scis., 1990; fellowship, NEH, 1982. Office: CUNY Grad Ctr 365 Fifth Ave New York NY 10016

OAKES, LESTER CORNELIUS, retired electrical engineer, consultant; b. Knoxville, Oct. 11, 1923; s. Charles Vaughn and Maude Cornelia (Harrison) O.; m. Kathleen Clark, Dec. 27, 1947; children: Michael, Richard, Cynthia, Melissa. BS in E.E., U. Tenn., 1949, MS, 1962. Registered profl. engr., Tenn. Engr. Fairchild Engring. and Aircraft, Oak

Ridge, 1949-51; engr. I&C div. Oak Ridge Nat. Lab., 1951-68, dep. head I&C div., 1968—, asst. dir. I&C div., 1971-90; cons. Oak Ridge Nat. Lab., electric Power Rsch. Inst., Nuclear Regulatory Commn., 1990—. Contbr. articles to profl. jours.; patentee in field. Served with USAF, 1943-46. Martin Marietta Corp. fellow. Fellow IEEE Presbyterian. Home: 710 Pleasant Hill Rd Maryville TN 37803-7337 Personal E-mail: lesoakes@earthlink.net.

OAKES, PAMELA R., retired elementary school educator; d. Frederick O. and Virginia Hoover Abrams; m. F. Michael Oakes, Oct. 4, 1958; children: Michael, Lisa Poole, Gigi Kershner, Gina Korsi. AA, Jefferson C.C., Louisville, 1971; BS in Edn., U. Louisville, 1979, postgrad., 1979—80, U. St. Thomas, Houston, 1992—94. Cert. ESL and gifted and talented tchr. Tchr. spl. edn. Jefferson County Sch. Dist., Louisville, 1979—80; tchr. 5th/6th grade St. Thomas Acad., West Hartford, Conn., 1980—82; tchr. 5th grade Our Lady of Victory, Victoria, Tex., 1982—84, St. Gregory the Great, San Antonio, 1984—85; tchr. 2d grade Houston Ind. Sch. Dist., 1985—89; tchr. 5th grade Cypress-Fairbanks Ind. Sch. Dist., Houston, 1989—2005, ret., 2005. Demonstration tchr. Houston Ind. Sch. Dist., 1988; coord. spelling bee Matzke Elem. Sch., 1995—2005. Mem.: Tex. Edn. Assn., Ky. Cols., Kappa Delta Pi. Roman Catholic. Avocations: sewing, interior decorating. Office: Cypress-Fairbanks ISD Matzke Elem 13102 Jones Rd Houston TX 77070 Home: 3106 Arroyo Pass San Antonio TX 78259-3402

OAKES, ROBERT JAMES, physics and astronomy professor; b. Mpls., Jan. 21, 1936; s. Sherman E. and Josephine J. (Olson) O.; children: Cindy L., Lisa A. BS, U. Minn., 1957, MS, 1959, PhD, 1962. NSF fellow Stanford U., 1962-64; asst. prof. physics, 1964-68; assoc. prof. physics Northwestern U., 1968-70, prof. physics, 1970-76, prof. physics and astronomy, 1976—. Vis. staff mem. Los Alamos Sci. Lab., 1971-92; vis. scientist, user Fermi Nat. Accelerator Lab., 1975-2006, CERN, 1966-67; mem. Inst. for Advanced Study, Princeton, 1967-68; vis. scientist DESY, 1971-72; faculty assoc. Argonne Nab. Lab., 1982—2002; U.S. scientist NSF-Yugoslav joint program, 1982-92; panelist Nat. Rsch. Coun., 1990-98. A.P. Sloan fellow 1965-68; Air Force Office Sci. Rsch. grantee, 1969-71, NSF grantee 1971-87, Dept. Energy grantee, 1987—; named Fulbright-Hays Disting. prof. U. Sarajevo, Yugoslavia, 1979-80; recipient Natural Sci. prize China, 1993. Fellow Am. Phys. Soc., AAAS; mem. N.Y. Acad. Sci., Ill. Acad. Sci., Sigma Xi, Tau Beta Pi. Office: Northwestern U Dept Physics 2145 Sheridan Rd Evanston IL 60208-0834

OAKES, TERRY LOUIS, resident real estate broker; b. Denver, June 12, 1953; s. Robert Walter and Stella Marie (Ray) O.; m. Cynthia Alison Bailey, Jan. 10, 1981; children: Madeleine Bailey, Robert Alan. BBA, So. Meth. U., 1975. Dept. mgr. Woolf Bros., Dallas, 1975-76; buyer I.K.O. Dry Goods, Denver, 1976-79, gen. sales mgr., 1979-81, exec. v.p., mdse. mgr., 1981-86; nat. sales mgr. Fresh Squeeze div. Bayly Corp., Denver, 1986-88; owner, pres. Bolderdash, Denver, 1988—2008; broker residential real estate Fuller Sotheby's Internat. Realty, 2008—. Tchr., mem. adv. bd. fashion mdse. divsn. Colo. Inst. Art., Denver, 1991-98. Bd. dirs. Cherry Creek North Bus. Improvement Dist., 1996-2008; v.p. Sunwood, Vail, Colo. Mem. Vail Racquet Club (bd. dirs.). Democrat. Presbyterian. Home: 5390 S Geneva St Englewood CO 80111-6205 Office: Fuller Sotheby's Internat Realty 3033E 1st Ave #500 Denver CO 80206 Office Phone: 303-809-9259. Personal E-mail: toakes@fullerproperties.com.

OAKLANDER, ANNE LOUISE, medical educator; MD, Albert Einstein Coll. Medicine, Bronx, NY, PhD, 1987. Diplomate Nat. Bd. Med. Examiners, 1988, Am. Bd. Psychiatry and Neurology, 1990. Assoc. prof. Harvard Med. Sch., Boston, 2006—. Grantee Beeson Physician Faculty Scholar award, Am. Fedn. Aging Rsch., 1999—2004. Office: Mass Gen Hosp 275 Charles St Warren 310 Boston MA 02114

OAKLEY, ANDREW ARTHUR, journalist, educator; b. Chgo., Oct. 22, 1958; s. Arthur George and Dolores Margarite (Hernandez) O.; m. Suzanna Pinter, Sept. 7, 1985; children: Glen Matthias, Ryan Arthur. BS in Journalism, Northwestern U., 1980, MS, 1981. Reporter Woodstock Daily Sentinel, Ill., 1980-81; police reporter Herald-Palladium, St. Joseph, Mich., 1981-82; city hall reporter Daily Herald, Arlington Heights, Ill., 1982-84; instr. journalism Oakton CC, Des Plaines, Ill., 1984-85; features editor North Shore Mag., Winnetka, Ill., 1985-86; news editor City and State, Chgo., 1986-93; journalism editor P.O. Publ. Co., Port Murray, NJ, 1993-2000; newsletter editor All Aboard for Hackettstown, NJ, 1996-98. Lectr. Northwestern U., Evanston, Ill., 1990-96; columnist Daily Herald, Arlington Heights, Ill., 1995-96; copy editor Full Time Dads Mag., Clifton, NJ, 1997-2000; corr. Daily Herald, Arlington Heights, 1995-2009; English tchr. North Warren Regional HS, Blairstown, NJ, 2009-. Author: Eighty-Eight, 1988, Issues Confronting City and State Governments, 1992, Beginning Journalism Packet, 1994; cons. editor P.O. Pub. Co., Skokie, Ill., 1988-92. Lifetime mem. N Club, 1980—; commr. Skokie Human Rels. Commn., 1987-94; advisor Mcpl. Alliance Lit. Club, 1997-98; U.S. Soccer Fedn. coach, referee, 1999—; edn. chmn. Charleston (Ill.) Alliance Ch., 2000-04; v.p. Blairstown Little League, 2005-07. Mem. MLA, NJ Edn. Assn., Nat. Coun. Tchrs. English, Medill Alumni Assn., Wilderness Soc., North Warren United Soccer Club, Appalachian Mountain Club, Nature Conservancy, Population-Environ. Balance, Paulinskill Valley Trail Com. E-mail: nwarrenunited@aol.com.

OAKLEY, CAROLYN LE, state legislator, city manager, director; b. Portland, Oreg., June 28, 1942; d. George Thomas and Ruth Alveta Victoria (Engberg) Penketh; children: Christine, Michelle. BS in Edn., Oreg. State U., 1965. Educator Linn County (Oreg.) Schs., 1965-76; owner Linn County Tractor, 1965-90; mem. Oreg. Legis. Assembly, Salem, 1989—, asst. majority leader, 1993—, majority whip, 1994; apptd. regional dir. region 10 Dept. Health and Human Svcs., Seattle, 2002—. Mem. exec. bd. Oreg. Retail Coun., 1987-90. Chmn. Linn County Rep. Ctrl. Com., 1982-84; chmn. bd. dirs. North Albany Svc. Dist., 1988-90; chair Salvation Army, Linn and Benton Counties, 1987—; vice chmn. bd. trustees Linn-Benton C.C. Found., 1987—; pres. Women for Agr., Linn and Benton Counties, 1984-86; mem. STRIDE Leadership Round Table, 1991—; state chair Am. Legis. Exch. Coun., 1991-96; nat. bd. dirs., 199-99, exec. com., 1995, 1st vice chair, 1998; mem. Edn. Commn. of the States, 1991—, com. policies and priorities, 1993—, steering com., 1998—, exec. com., 1998; mem. Leadership Coun. on Higher Edn., 1995—; mem. nat. policy bd. Danforth Found., 1995—; state dir., Women in Govt., 1996—; state dir., Nat. Order Women Legislators, 1993—; hon. mem. Linn-Benton Compact Bd., 1993—; active Linn County Criminal Justice Coun., 1994—; vol. Good Samaritan Hosp. Found., State Land Trust for Affordable Housing, Majestic Theater; bd. trustees Good Samaritan Found., 2006—; pres. Benton County Rep. Women, 2000-02. Named Woman of Yr. Albany chpt. Beta Sigma Phi, 1970. Mem. Nat Conf. State Legislators (chmn. edn. com. 1992—), Albany C. of C. (bd. dirs. 1986-93, 96—), Linn County Rep. Women (legis. chmn. 1982-91, pres. 2006—), Greater Corvallis Rotary Club (bd. dirs., 2004-), Delta Kappa Gamma Soc. Internat. Republican. Avocations: gardening, camping, volunteering. Home: 3197 NW Crest Loop Albany OR 97321-9627 Office Phone: 541-928-7745. Personal E-mail: cloakley@juno.com.

OAKLEY, DEBORAH JANE, educator; b. Jan. 31, 1937; d. George F. and Kathryn (Willson) Hacker; m. Bruce Oakley, June 16, 1958; children: Ingrid Andrea, Brian Benjamin. BA, Swarthmore Coll., 1958; MA, Brown U., 1960; MPH, U. Mich., 1969, PhD, 1977. Dir. teenage and adult programs YWCA, Providence, 1959-63; editl. asst. Stockholm U., 1963-64; rsch. investigator, lectr. dept. population planning U. Mich., 1971-77, asst. prof. cmty. health programs Ann Arbor, 1977-79, asst. prof. nursing rsch., 1979-81, assoc. prof., 1981-89, prof., 1989—2002, interim dir. Ctr. Nursing Rsch., 1988-90, acting dir. Ctr. Nursing Rsch., 1998, prof. emeritus, 2002—, interim dir. Health Asian Ams. program, 2005. Vis. prof. Beijing Med. U., 1996-2002; prin. investigator NIH, CDC and pvt. found. funded rsch. grants and contracts on family planning, women's health and health care in China, nat. adv. com. nursing rsch., 1993-97; adv. workshop on Nat. Survey on Family Growth, 1994-97; co-chair Mich. Initiative for Women's Health, 1993-95. Author: (with Leslie Corsa) Population Planning, 1979; contbr. articles to profl. jours. Bd. dirs. Planned Parenthood Fedn. Am., 1975-80. Recipient Margaret Sanger award Washtenaw County Planned Parenthood, 1975, Outstanding Young Woman of Ann Arbor award Jaycees, 1970, Dist. Faculty award Mich. Assn. Gov. Bds., 1992, Blue Cross Blue Shield Found. of Mich. award for Excellence in Health Policy, 1996. Mem. APHA (chmn. population sect. coun.), Internat. Union Sci. Study Population, Midwest Nursing Rsch. Soc., Population Assn. Am., Delta Omega, Sigma Theta Tau (hon.). Democrat. Home: 5200 S Lake Dr Chelsea MI 48118-9481 Office: U Mich Sch Nursing Ann Arbor MI 48109-5482 E-mail: doakley@umich.edu.

OAKLEY, FRANCIS CHRISTOPHER, historian, educator; b. Liverpool, Eng., Oct. 6, 1931; arrived in U.S., 1957, naturalized, 1968; s. Joseph Vincent and Siobean (NiCurean) O.; m. Claire-Ann Lamenzo, Aug. 9, 1958; children: Deirdre, Christopher, Timothy, Brian. BA, Corpus Christi Coll., Oxford U., 1953, MA, 1957; postgrad., Pontifical Inst. Medieval Studies, Toronto, 1953—55; MA, Yale U., 1958, PhD, 1960; LLD, Amherst Coll., 1986, Wesleyan U., 1989, U. Notre Dame, 2006; LHD, Northwestern U., 1990, North Adams State Coll., 1993, Bowdoin Coll., 1993; LittD, Williams Coll., 1994. Mem. faculty Yale U., 1959-61, Williams Coll., Williamstown, Mass., 1961—2002, prof. history, 1970—2002, dean faculty, 1977-84, Edward Dorr Griffin prof. history of ideas, 1984—85, pres., 1985-94, pres. emeritus, 1994—, Edward Dorr Griffin prof. history of ideas, 1994—2002, prof. emeritus, 2002—; interim pres. Am. Coun. Learned Socs., 2002—03, pres. emeritus, 2003—; hon. fellow Corpus Christi Coll., Oxford U., 1991—; sr. fellow Oakley Ctr. Humanities, Williams Coll., 2002—. Vis. lectr. Bennington (Vt.) Coll., 1967; Sir Isaiah Berlin vis. prof. Oxford U., 1999-2000; Merle Curti lectr. U. Wis., Madison, 2001; Étienne Gilson lectr. Pontifical Inst. Medieval Studies, Toronto, 2002; mem. Inst. Advanced Study Princeton, 1981-82; fellow Nat. Humanities Ctr., 1991; guest scholar Woodrow Wilson Internat. Ctr. for Scholars, 1994; chair bd. dirs. Am. Coun. Learned Socs., 1993-97; trustee Sterling and Francine Clark Art Inst., 1985—, pres. bd. trustees, 1998-2005; trustee MassMoCA Found., 1995-2004, Willamstown Art Conservation Ctr., 1995-98, Williamstown Theatre Festival, 1985-93; trustee Nat. Humanities Ctr., 1996-02, 2003-07, chmn. bd. trustees, 2004-07, Lake Forest Coll., 1997-2001; trustee Inst. Advanced Cath. Studies, 1998-2005, vice chair, 2002-05; mem. MassMoCA Cultural Devel. Commn., 1988-2007; mem. adv. coun. Ctr. for Study of Religion, Princeton U., 1999—. Author: The Political Thought of Pierre d'Ailly: The Voluntarist Tradition, 1964, Kingship and the Gods: The Western Apostasy, 1968, Council over Pope?, Towards a Provisional Ecclesiology, 1969, Medieval Experience: Foundations of Western Cultural Singularity, 1974, rev. England edit., The Crucial Centuries, 1979, Spanish edit., 1980, 95, Medieval Acad. edit., 1988, 93, The Western Church in the Later Middle Ages, 1979, rev. edit., 1985, 88, 91, Natural Law, Conciliarism and Consent in the Late Middle Ages, 1984, Omnipotence, Covenant and Order: An Excursion in the History of Ideas, 1984, Community of Learning: The American College and the Liberal Arts Tradition, 1992, Scholarship and Teaching: A Matter of Mutual Support, 1996, Politics and Eternity: Studies in the History of Medieval and Early Modern Political Thoughts, 1999, The Leadership Challenges of a College Presidency, 2002, The Conciliarist Tradition, 2003, 2nd edit., 2007 (Roland H. Bainton History prize, 2004); Paperback Editor: Natural Law, laws of Nature and Natural Rights, 2005, Kingship: The Politics of Enchantment, 2006; editor: (with Daniel O'Connor) Creation: The Impact of an Idea, 1969, (with Bruce Russett) Governance, Accountability and the Future of the Catholic Church, 2003; contbr. articles to profl. jours. Lt. Brit. Army, 1955-57. Goldsmith's Co. London fellow, 1953-55, Social Sci. Rsch. Coun. fellow, 1963, Am. Coun. Learned Socs. fellow, 1965, 69-70, Weil Inst. fellow, 1965, Folger Shakespeare Libr. fellow, 1974, NEH fellow, 1976, 81-82, Mellon emeritus rsch. fellow, 2005, Academic fellow, Carnegie Corp. NY, 2003-05; recipient Wilbur Lucius Cross medal Yale Grad. Sch., 1997. Fellow Medieval Acad. Am. (pres. fellows 1999-2002), Am. Acad. Arts and Scis.; mem. Am. Hist. Assn., Am. Cath. Hist. Assn., Am. Ch. History Soc., New Eng. Medieval Conf. (pres. 1983-84), The Century Assn., Am. Cusanus Soc. (adv. bd. 1997—). Democrat. Roman Catholic. Office: Williams Coll Oakley Ctr Humanities & Soc Sci Williamstown MA 01267 Office Phone: 413-597-2149. Business E-Mail: foakley@williams.edu.

OAKS, SUNNY, child and family advocate, consultant, author, lyricist; b. Cardston, Alta., Can., Aug. 21, 1944; d. Willard Glen Hansen and Priscilla Pearl Hansen-Wallace; m. Guy Eugene Williams (dec.); children: Shelley, Jason; m. Michael Oaks, Jan. 28, 1984; children: Brian, Anna, Bethany, Christen. Grad high sch., Moses Lake, Wash. Bus. leader Shaklee Wholesale Distbn., 1972—92; founder, dir. Adults Supporting Kids, Wenatchee, Wash., 1995—96, CARE for Kids, 1997—99; founder, CEO, dir. trainer. grant writer HOME Connection, 1998—99; pvt. practice East Wenatchee, 1999—2008. Mem. adv. bd. Home Connection, Care for Kids, Adults Supporting Kids. Author: Secrets, 1992; singer, composer: albums Sunny's Song, 1987. Recipient High Volume award, Shaklee; grantee, Cmty. Found., 1997, Cmty. Network, 1997—98, Target Stores, 1997—98, Washington Assn. Prevention of Child Abuse and Neglect, 1998, Alcoa, 2000. Mem.: Shaklee Pres.' Club (Altus award). Avocations: writing, music, sewing, swimming. E-mail: healthyhorizons@verizon.net.

OATES, JAMES CALDWELL, rheumatologist, physician, research scientist; b. Nashville, Jan. 5, 1964; s. John Alexander III and Meredith (Stringfield) O; m. Jennifer Goodwin; children: Evan Edward, Aubrey Elizabeth. BS in Chemistry, Bates Coll., 1986; MD, Johns Hopkins U., 1991. Intern Duke U. Med. Ctr., Durham, N.C., 1991-92, resident, 1992-94, fellow in rheumatology, 1994-96, Med. U. S.C., Charleston, 1996-97, asst. prof. medicine, 1997—2000, assoc. prof. medicine, 2000—, assoc. dir., Clin. Translational Rsch. Ctr., 2007—; chief rheumatology Ralph H. Johnson VA Med. Ctr., 2007—. Mem. Am. Coll. Rheumatology, Am. Fedn. Med. Rsch., Southern Soc. Clin. Rsch., Nitric Oxide Soc., Soc. Free Radical Biology and Medicine. Office: Med U SC MSC 637 Charleston SC 29425-6370

OATES, JANE, federal agency administrator; b. Pa., 1953; BA in Edn., Boston Coll., 1975; MEd in Reading, Arcadia U., Phila., 1983. Pub. sch. tchr., Boston, Phila.; field rschr. Ctr. Rsch. in Human Devel. and Edn. Temple U., Phila.; sr. policy advisor to Mass. Senator Edward Kennedy US Senate Com. Health, Edn., Labor, & Pensions Com., 1997; sr. advisor to Gov. Jon Corzine State of NJ, 2006; exec. dir. NJ Commn. Higher Edn., 2006; asst. sec. Employment & Tng. Adminstrn. (ETA) US Dept. Labor, Washington, 2009—. Mem. NJ State Employment and Tng. Commn., NJ State Commn. on Adult Literacy and Edn., NJ High School Redesign Task Force, Pub. Sector Work Group; chair NJ State Educators Health Benefits Commn., Gov.'s Schs. Bd. Overseers. Office: Employment and Tng Adminstrn US Dept Labor Frances Perkins Bldg 200 Constitution Ave NW Washington DC 20210*

OATES, JOHN ALEXANDER, III, medical educator; b. Fayetteville, NC, Apr. 23, 1932; s. John Alexander and Isabelle (Crowder) O.; m. Meredith Stringfield, June 12, 1956; children: David Alexander, Christine Larkin, James Caldwell. BS magna cum laude, Wake Forest Coll., 1953; MD, Bowman Gray Sch. Medicine, 1956. Intern, asst. resident medicine N.Y. Hosp.-Cornell U. Med. Center, NYC, 1956-58, 61-62; from clin. assoc. to sr. investigator Nat. Heart Inst., 1958-63; faculty Vanderbilt U. Sch. Medicine, Nashville, 1963—, prof. medicine and pharmacology, 1969—, Werthan prof. investigative medicine, 1974-84, chmn. dept. medicine, 1983-97, Thomas F. Frist Sr. prof. medicine, 1984—. Drug rsch. bd. Nat. Acad. Scis.-NRC, 1967-71; chmn. pharmacology and toxicology tng. com. Nat. Inst. Gen. Med. Scis., 1969-70; adv. coun. Nat. Heart, Lung and Blood Inst., 1985-89. Master ACP; fellow Am. Acad. Arts and Scis., Am. Assn. Advancement Sci.; mem. Am. Fedn. Clin. Rsch. (pres. 1970-71), Am. Soc. Clin. Investigation (v.p. 1976-77), Assn. Am. Physicians (pres. 1981-82), Am. Soc. Pharmacology and Exptl. Therapeutics (chmn. exec. com. divsn. clin. pharmacology 1967-69), Inst. of Medicine. Achievements include co-discovery of antihypertensive effect of methyldopa, elucidation of a number of interactions between drugs in humans; research in biochemistry and pathophysiology of eicosanoids. Home: 2032 Sunset Hills Terr Nashville TN 37215 Office: Vanderbilt Med Ctr 536 RRB Nashville TN 37232-6602 Home Phone: 615-665-1976; Office Phone: 615-343-4845. Business E-Mail: john.oates@vanderbilt.edu.

OATES, JOYCE CAROL, writer, educator; b. Lockport, NY, June 16, 1938; d. Frederic James and Caroline (Bush) Oates; m. Raymond Joseph Smith, Jan. 23, 1961 (dec. Feb. 18, 2008). BA, Syracuse U., NY, 1960; MA, U. Wis., Madison, 1961. Instr. English U. Detroit, 1961-65, asst. prof., 1965-67; prof. English U. Windsor, Ont., Canada, 1967-87; writer-in-residence Princeton U., NJ, 1978-81, prof., 1987—2008, Roger S. Berlind '52 prof. humanities/prof. creative writing, 2008—. Author: (novels) With Shuddering Fall, 1964, A Garden of Earthly Delights, 1967 (M.L. Rosenthal award, Nat. Inst. Arts & Letters, 1968), Expensive People, 1968, Them, 1969 (Nat. Book award, 1970), Wonderland, 1971, Do with Me What You Will, 1973, The Assassins: A Book of Hours, 1975, Childwold, 1976, Son of the Morning, 1978, Cybele, 1979, Unholy Loves, 1979, Bellefleur, 1980, Angel of Light, 1981, A Bloodsmoor Romance, 1982, Mysteries of Winterthurn, 1984, Solstice, 1985, Marya: A Life, 1986, You Must Remember This, 1987, American Appetites, 1989, Because It Is Bitter, and Because It Is My Heart, 1990, Foxfire: Confessions of a Girl Gang, 1993, What I Lived For, 1994, Zombie, 1995 (Bram Stoker award, 1996, Fisk Fiction prize, Boston Book Review, 1996), We Were the Mulvaneys, 1996, Man Crazy, 1997, My Heart Laid Bare, 1998, Broke Heart Blues, 1999, Blonde, 2000, Middle Age: A Romance, 2001, I'll Take You There, 2002, The Tattooed Girl, 2003, The Falls, 2004 (Prix Femina Etranger, France, 2005), Missing Mom, 2005, Black Girl / White Girl, 2006, The Gravedigger's Daughter, 2007, My Sister, My Love, 2008, (under pseudonym Rosamond Smith) Lives of the Twins, 1987, Soul/Mate, 1989, Nemesis, 1990, Snake Eyes, 1992, You Can't Catch Me, 1995, Double Delight, 1997, Starr Bright Will Be With you Soon, 1999, The Barrens, 2001, (under pseudonym Lauren Kelly) Take Me, Take Me With You, 2003, The Stolen Heart, 2005, Blood Mask, 2006, (novellas) The Triumph of the Spider Monkey, 1976, I Lock My Door Upon Myself, 1990, The Rise of Life on Earth, 1991, Black Water, 1992, First Love: A Gothic Tale, 1996, Beasts, 2002, Rape: A Love Story, 2003, The Corn Maiden: A Love Story, 2005, (short story collections) By the North Gate, 1963, Upon the Sweeping Flood And Other Stories, 1966, The Wheel of Love And Other Stories, 1970, Marriages and Infidelities, 1972, The Goddess and Other Women, 1974, The Poisoned Kiss And Other Stories from the Portuguese, 1975, The Seduction & Other Stories, 1975, Crossing the Border: Fifteen Tales, 1976, Night-Side, 1977, All the Good People I've Left Behind, 1979, A Sentimental Education: Stories, 1980, Last Days: Stories, 1984, Wild Saturday, 1984, Raven's Wing: Stories, 1986, The Assignation: Stories, 1989, Oates In Exile, 1990, Heat And Other Stories, 1991, Where Is Here?, 1992, Where Are You Going, Where Have You Been?: Selected Early Stories, 1993, Haunted: Tales of the Grotesque, 1994, Demon and Other Tales, 1996, Will You Always Love Me? And Other Stories, 1996, The Collector of Hearts: New Tales of the Grotesque, 1998, Faithless: Tales of Transgression, 2001, I Am No One You Know: Stories, 2004, The Female of the Species: Tales of Mystery and Suspense, 2006, High Lonesome: New & Selected Stories, 2006, The Museum of Dr. Moses: Tales of Mystery and Suspense, 2007, Wild Nights!, 2008, (young adult fiction) Big Mouth & Ugly Girl, 2002, Small Avalanches and Other Stories, 2003, Freaky Green Eyes, 2003, Sexy, 2005, After the Wreck, I Picked Myself Up, Spread My Wings, and Flew Away, 2006, (children's fiction) Come Meet Muffin!, 1998, Where Is Little Reynard?, 2003, (poetry) Women In Love and Other Poems, 1968, Anonymous Sins & Other Poems, 1969, Love and Its Derangements, 1970, Angel Fire, 1973, The Fabulous Beasts, 1975, Women Whose Lives Are Food, Men Whose Lives Are Money, 1978, Invisible Woman: New and Selected Poems, 1982, The Time Traveler, 1989, Tenderness, 1996, (plays) Miracle Play, 1974, Three Plays, 1980, In Darkest America, 1991, I Stand Before You Naked, 1991, Twelve Plays, 1991, The Perfectionist and Other Plays, 1996, New Plays, 1998, Dr. Magic: Six One Act Plays, 2004; contbr. numerous essays, short stories and works of criticism to various pubs. Recipient O. Henry award, 1967, 1973, Heidemann award, 1990, Rea award for Short Story, 1990, PEN/Malamud award for Excellence in Art of Short Story, 1996, Chgo. Tribune Lit. prize, 2006; named Humanist of Yr., Am. Humanist Assn., 2007; grantee NEA, 1966, 1968. Office: c/o John Hawkins Agy 71 W 23rd St Ste 1600 New York NY 10010-4102 also: Princeton U Lewis Ctr Arts 185 Nassau St Princeton NJ 08544-0001 Office Phone: 609-258-4705. Business E-Mail: jcsmith@princeton.edu.*

OATES, STEPHEN BAERY, retired historian; b. Pampa, Tex., Jan. 5, 1936; s. Steve Theodore and Florence (Baer) O.; divorced; children: Gregory Allen, Stephanie. BA magna cum laude, U. Tex., 1958, MA, 1960, PhD, 1968; Litt.D. (hon.), Lincoln Coll., 1981. Prof. history U. Mass., Amherst, 1971—98, Paul Murray Kendall prof. biography, 1980—98, adj. prof. English, 1981—98, ret. prof. emeritus. Author: Confederate Cavalry West of the River, 1961, Rip Ford's Texas, 1963, Republic of Texas, 1968, Visions of Glory, 1970, To Purge This Land With Blood: A Biography of John Brown, 1970, Portrait of America, 2 vols., 1973, rev. edits., 2007, The Fires of Jubilee: Nat Turner's Fierce Rebellion, 1975, With Malice Toward None: The Life of Abraham

Lincoln (Christopher award for outstanding lit., Barondess/Lincoln award N.Y. Civil War Round Table 1977), Our Fiery Trial: Abraham Lincoln, John Brown, and the Civil War Era, 1979, Let the Trumpet Sound: The Life of Martin Luther King, Jr., 1982 (Christopher award, Robert F. Kennedy Meml. Book award), Abraham Lincoln, The Man Behind the Myths, 1984, Biography as High Adventure: Life Writers Speak on Their Art, 1986, William Faulkner: The Man and the Artist, 1987, A Woman of Valor: Clara Barton and the Civil War, 1994, The Approaching Fury: Voices of the Storm, 1820-1861, 1997, The Whirlwind of War: Voices of the Storm, 1861-1865, 1998; contbr. articles and essays to periodicals; lectr. Presdl. Writers award, 1985; Master Tchr. award U. Hartford, 1985; Silver Medal award Case Council for Advance and Support of Edn., Prof. of Yr., 1986, 87, Kidger award New Eng. History Tchrs. Assn., Nevins-Freeman award Chgo. Civil War Round Table, 1993, Lifetime Achievement award, Lincoln Group NY, 2009; Guggenheim fellow, 1972; sr. summer fellow NEH, 1978. Fellow Tex. State Hist. Assn.; mem. Tex. Inst. Letters, Soc. Am. Historians, Am. Antiquarian Soc., Phi Beta Kappa. Office: U Mass Dept History Amherst MA 01003

OATES, WILLIAM ARMSTRONG, JR., investment company executive; b. Pitts., July 27, 1942; s. Wiliiam Armstrong and Margaret (Nichols) O.; m. Elizabeth Dick Macy, Sept. 7, 1968; children: Elizabeth N., Katherine M., Emily E.A. BA, Colby Coll., 1965; MBA, Harvard U., 1972. Asst. treas. Morgan Guaranty Trust, NYC, 1966—2004; pres. N.E. Investors Growth Fund, Boston, 1980—; ptnr. N.E. Investment Mgmt. Inc., Boston, 1984—. Dir. Horn Corp., Ayer, Mass., Furman Lumber Co., Boston, Clifford Inc., Bethel, Vt. Pres. bd. trustees Groton (Mass.) Sch., 1979; trustee, treas. Roxbury Latin Sch., West Roxbury, Mass., 2005; trustee Colby Coll., Waterville, Maine, 2005. 2d lt. Army N.G., 1966-70. Mem.: Country Club, Somerset Club, Harvard Club. Republican. Episcopalian. Home: 201 Village Ave Dedham MA 02026-4230 Office: NE Investment Mgmt Inc 150 Federal St Ste 1000 Boston MA 02110-1745

O'BAIRE-KARK, MARIKA, nurse, educator, writer; b. Manila, Oct. 3, 1947; d. Gerald John and Giovanna (BelForti) Barry; m. Pieter Kark, Oct. 3, 2004; children from previous marriage: Matthew Plocharczyk, Alexei Plocharczyk, Rita Higgins, D. Patrick Higgins. Student, U. Conn., 1964—65; diploma, Ellis Hosp. Sch. Nursing, 1977; BSN, Russell Sage Coll., 1980, postgrad., 1983, postgrad., 1994; grad. ontological design, Logonet Inc. ODC-J, 1993; postgrad. humanities, Calif. State U., Dominguez Hills, 1995; postgrad., U. Dundee, 2000; postgrad. in Writing, Stanford U., 2006—; MSc in Health Sci., Disaster and Emergency Mgmt. with summa cum laude, 2007. RN NY, Calif., in med. surgery, OMSRN, 2007; lic. avatar master/wizard Star's Edge Internat. Tchr. English Lang. Inst., Taipei, Taiwan, 1971—73; team leader, staff nurse acute psychiatry Samaritan Hosp., Troy, NY, 1978—80; staff nurse pediat. ICU Albany Med. Ctr., NY, 1980—84, 1997—; rsch. nurse Commn. on Quality Care for Mentally Disabled, Albany, 1984; staff nurse Columbia-Greene Med. Ctr., Catskill, NY, 1984—89; night charge nurse Conifer Park, Scotia, NY, 1991—92; nursing educator St. Clare's Hosp., Schenectady, NY, 1992—96; adj clin. educator Albany Med. Ctr. So. Vt. Coll., Bennington, 1997—2001; nurse, specialized surg. pre-ICU Stanford U. Hosp., 2005—07. On-call nurse Cmty. Hospice Saratoga, NY, 1998—2004; founder Future Design: Create What You Prefer, Avatar Tech. and Skills, 1999—, Favorite Nurses, Colonie, NY, 2002—. Author: (novels) Dragon, 2002, Future Joyous, 2002, (short stories) About Love, (screenplays) Syin; contbr. articles to Echo Mag. Past vol. curriculum designer gifted and talented programs; firefighter Cazenovia, NY. Mem.: Ontological Design Cmty., Upstate Ind. Filmakers/Screenwriters, Childreach Plan Internat., Toastmasters Internat. Office Phone: 650-380-1597. Personal E-mail: mobaire@yahoo.com.

OBAMA, BARACK HUSSEIN, JR., 44th President of the United States; b. Honolulu, Aug. 4, 1961; s. Barack Obama Sr. and Shirley Ann (Dunham); m. Michelle Robinson, Oct. 18, 1992; children: Malia Ann, Natasha. Attended, Occidental Coll., 1979—81; BA in Polit. Sci., Columbia U., 1983; JD magna cum laude, Harvard U., 1991; LLD (hon.), Knox Coll., 2005, Northwestern U., 2005, U. Mass., 2006, Xavier U., 2006, So. New Hampshire U, 2007, Harvard U., 2007, Wesleyan U., 2008, U. Notre Dame, 2009. Editor-in-chief Harvard Law Review; writer, fin. analyst Bus. Internat. Corp., 1984—85; dir. Developing Communities Project, 1985—88; exec. dir. PROJECT VOTE!, Ill., 1992; assoc. Davis, Miner, Barnhill & Galland, P.C., 1993—96, of counsel, 1996—2004; mem. Ill. State Senate from Dist. 13, Springfield, 1997—2005, mem. judiciary & local govt. com., chmn., pub. health & human services com.; US Senator from Ill., 2005—08; mem. US Senate Environment & Pub. Work. Com., Fgn. Rels. Com., Veterans Affairs Com., 2005—08; pres. US, 2009—. Sr. lecturer U. Chgo. Law Sch., 1993—2004; keynote speaker Dem. Nat. Convention, Boston, 2004; Dem. presdl. nominee US, 2008. Author: Dreams From My Father: A Story of Race and Inheritance, 1995 (Publishers Weekly bestseller, Grammy award for Best Spoken Word or Non-Musical Album, Recording Acad., 2006), Audacity of Hope: Thoughts on Reclaiming the American Dream, 2006 (Best Literary Work in Nonfiction, NAACP Image awards, 2007, Grammy award for Best Spoken Word Album, Recording Acad., 2008, Publishers Weekly bestseller), Change We Can Believe In: Barack Obama's Plan to Renew America's Promise, 2008. Bd. dirs. Chgo. Lawyers Com. for Civil Rights Under the Law and Pub. Allies, Joyce Found., 1994—, Woods Fund Chgo., Ctr. for Neighborhood Tech., Chgo. Annenberg Challenge, Lugenia Burns Hope Ctr.; chmn. Chgo. Lawyers Com. for Civil Rights Under the Law. Recipient 40 Under 40 award, Crains Chgo. Bus., 1993, Monarch award for Outstanding Public Service, 1994, "Legal Eagle" award for Litigation, IVI-IPO, 1995, Freshman Legis. award, Ind. Voters of IL Ind. Precinct Organizations, 1997, Outstanding Legis. award, Campaign for Better Health Care-IL Primary Health Care Assn., 1998, Legis. award, Associated Firefighters of IL, 2004, Chmn.'s award, NAACP, 2005, Harvard Law Sch. Assn. award, 2005, Howard Blake Walker award, Christopher House, 2005, Lifetime Achievement award, Detroit, Mich. chapter NAACP, 2005, Congl. Leadership award, Nat. Urban League, 2006; named The Most Fascinating Person of 2008, Barbara Walters, Person of the Yr., TIME mag., 2008; named one of The World's Most Influential People, 2005—09, The Most Influential Black Americans, Ebony mag., 2006, The 50 Most Powerful People in DC, GQ mag., 2007, The Global Elite, Newsweek mag., 2008, The Top 25 Market Movers, US News & World Report, 2009; named to Power 150, Ebony mag., 2008. Mem.: vis. com., Irving B. Harris Grad. Sch. Pub. Policy Studies, U. Chgo., IL Bar Assn., Cook County Bar Assn. Democrat. Ch. Christ. Achievements include becoming the first African-American to be elected President of the United States, Nov. 4, 2008. Office: The White House 1600 Pennsylvania Ave NW Washington DC 20500*

OBAMA, MICHELLE LAVAUGHN ROBINSON, First Lady of the United States, former hospital administrator; b. Chgo., Jan. 17, 1964; d. Fraser and Marian Robinson; m. Barack Hussein Obama, Jr., Oct. 18, 1992; children: Malia Ann, Natasha. BA cum laude, Princeton U., 1985; JD, Harvard U., 1988. Assoc. mktg. and intellectual property Sidley and Austin LLP, Chgo., 1988—91; asst. to mayor, asst. commr. planning and devel. City of Chgo., 1991—93; founding exec. dir. Pub. Allies - Chgo., 1993—96; assoc. dean students, dir. cmty. svc. U. Chgo., 1997—2005; exec. dir. cmty. and external affairs U. Chgo. Med. Ctr., 2002—05, v.p. cmty. and external affairs, mgr. bus. diversity program, 2005—08; First Lady of the U.S., 2009—. Bd. dirs. TreeHouse Foods, Inc., 2005—07, Chgo. Coun. on Global Affairs. Former bd. mem. Commn. on Chgo. Landmarks; bd. mem. Otho S.A. Sprague Meml. Inst., Facing History and Ourselves, Muntu Dance Co. Named a Woman to Watch, Crain's Chgo. Bus., 2008; named one of The World's 25 Most Inspiring Women, Essence mag., 2006, The World's Most Influential People, TIME mag., 2009, 100 Most Powerful Women, Forbes mag., 2009. Mem.: Alpha Kappa Alpha (hon.). Democrat. Protestant. Office: The White House 1600 Pennsylvania Ave NW Washington DC 20500*

OBAMOGIE, MERCY A., physician; b. Lagos, Nigeria, Jan. 18, 1954; d. Godwin I and Janet E. (Amiolemen) O.; m. Abiodun O. Odunmbaku, June 20, 1980 (div. 1995); children: Abisola, Adenike, Abiodun. BS, Columbia U., 1980; MD, U. Medicine and Dentistry N.J., Piscataway, 1984; MPH, Johns Hopkins U., 1987; MBA, U. Calif., Irvine, 2000; JD, Thomas Cooley Law Sch., Lansing, MI, 2006. Diplomate Am. Bd. Family Practice, Nat. Bd. Med. Examiners. Intern in internal medicine Muhlenberg Hosp., Plainfield, NJ, 1984-85; resident in gen. preventive medicine Johns Hopkins U., Balt., 1985-86; resident in family practice Georgetown U./Providence Hosp., Washington, 1986-89; pvt. practice Washington, Greenbelt, Md., 1989—; med. dir. Doctors Slim and Fitness Ctr., Greenbelt, 1996-98. Med. adv. bd. Metra Health Ins. Co., 1992-94; utilization com. Aetna Ins. Co., 1993-95, credentialing com., 1996; med. adv. com. United HealthCare, 1997; mem. planning com. Providence Hosp., Washington, 1996-98; with Prince George's Hosp. Ctr., Cheverly, Md., Howard U. Hosp., Washington, Doctors Cmty. Hosp., Lanham, Md., Providence Hosp., Washington; pres., med. dir. Mercy Med. Ctr., Benin City, Nigeria, 1996—; pres., CEO ASAKI Corp., Greenbelt, Md., 2000—. Contbr. articles to profl. jours. Office: 7323 Hanover Pkwy Ste A Greenbelt MD 20770-3617 Home: 6600 Manton Way Lanham MD 20706 Office Phone: 301-345-5900. Business E-Mail: obamogim@cooley.edu.

OBED, LEONORA RITA VILLEGAS, writer, educator; b. Manila, Philippines, May 22, 1971; arrived in US, 1973; d. Reynaldo Nera and Josefina Kalaw (Villegas) Obed. BA in English Lit. and Philosophy, St. Joseph's U., 1993; MA in English Lit., U. Toronto, 1994; postgrad. cert. in 18th Century Lit. with honors, Coll. of NJ, Trenton, 1993; postgrad. in English Lit., U. Edinburgh. Cert. Ind. Study in 18th Century Lit. Trenton State Coll., Ewing, 1993; NJ Agrl. Experiment Sta., Office Continuing Profl. Edn., 2008, voice curriculum level I Trenton Cmty. Music Sch. Tchr. seminar M courses U. Toronto, Canada, 1994—95; pvt. tutor, 1996; tchr., Religious Edn. (Grade 7-8) Our Lady Good Counsel Ch., lector, 2005—; election ofcl. NJ Bd. Elections, Trenton, clk.; asst. editor Newsletter Thornton Wilder Soc.; mentor Native Am. Children Futers for Children. Spkr., presenter in field; reader various radio broadcasts, 2006, Lib. for Blind and Handicapped, 2006. Author: (short stories) The Apprehension of Magic Realism: The Short Story in the Philippines, U. Iowa, 1996, The Invention of Candles, 2001, I Won't Send Roses, 2001, (plays) Epitome, 2003, Supporter: The Robert Burns Birth Place Museum, Scotland; contbr. scientific papers, articles to profl. jours.; performer: (pub. reading) Werewolf of West Trenton, 2007; exhbn. and auction, Flemington Rocks, 2006, art exhbn., 2007, doll exhbn., Internat. and Collectors' Dolls and Toys: Enchantment for Overscheduled, Ewing Libr., NJ, 2007, one-woman shows include Poets and Play Wrights for Pen-Persons, 2009, Ctr. Pennington NJ, 2009. Vol. Jane Ausen Soc. North Am. Ann. Gen. Meeting, Phila., 2009; religious edn. tchr. Our Lady Good Counsel Ch., Trenton, NJ, 2007—; vol., donor Blue Mountain Festival Music, Trinity Cathedral, Trenton, NJ, 2009; supporter Ujmid Women's Ctr., Ewing, NJ. Creative Writing fellowship, Vt. Studio Ctr., 2008. Mem.: Stuttering Found., Nat. Trust Scotland, Edinburgh, Lakota Wolf Reserve, Columbia, NJ, Wolf Pk., Battlefield Grounds, IN, Wolf Hollow, Ipswich, MA, Culloden Battlefield Meml. Project, Scotland, Martin Luther King Meml., Wash., DC (charter and founding mem.), Nat. Women's Mus. (charter and founding mem.), Wolf Hollow, Ipswich, Oxford Soc., NYC, St. Joseph's U. Reunion Com., U. Toronto Alumni, NYC, Friends of Ewing Libr., Steinway Soc. Greater Princeton, Jane Austen Soc. N.Am., Princeton, NYC, Phila., Gerard Manley Hopkins Soc., Monasterevan, Ireland, Yeats Soc., Sligo, Ireland, Waterford Crystal Soc., Modern Lang. Assn., Greater Princeton Steinway Soc., Jane Austin Soc. Easton Pa., Hopkins Soc., Yeats Soc., NYC, Oscar Wilde Soc., Lee Middleton Doll Collector's Club. Achievements include articles, novels, plays. Avocations: piano, dance, stamp collecting/philately, horseback riding, wine tasting. Home and Office: 10 Michelle Ct Trenton NJ 08628-2924 Office: Coll NJ PO Box 7718 Trenton NJ 08628-0718 also: C/O Dr Lincoln Konkle Coll NJ PO Box 7718 Trenton NJ 08628-0718 Home Phone: 609-771-0158; Office Phone: 609-213-4434, 609-558-0771. Personal E-mail: leonora.obed@hotmail.com.

OBENAUF, STEVEN D., microbiologist, educator; s. Henry C. and Beryl Obenauf; m. Gail Pucci, May 13, 1978; children: Lauren, Adam S. PhD, U. Miami Coll. Medicine, Fla., 1982. Registered microbiologist Am. Soc. Microbiology, 1989. Asst. prof. dept. microbiology health scis. divsn. Nova Southeastern U., North Miami Beach, 1987—93; assoc. prof. dept. biol. scis. Broward Coll., Davie, Fla., 1993—, faculty senate pres., 1997—99, gen. edn. task force chair, 2003—, assoc. academic dean dept. biol. scis., 2008—. Sec. Fla. Br., Am. Soc. Microbiology, 1985—95. Pres. Laurel Woods Homeowners Assn., Sautee, Ga., 2006—. Recipient Golden Apple award, Southeastern Coll. Osteo. Medicine, 1991—96; named Prof. of Yr., Broward Coll. Ctrl. Campus, 1996—2001, Endowed Tchg. Chair of Yr., Broward Coll. Found., 1997—2004. Mem.: Nat. Assn. Biology Tchrs. Office: Broward Coll 3501 SW Davie Rd Davie FL 33331 Business E-Mail: sobenauf@broward.edu.

OBENG, KOFI, science educator; s. Kwaku Anane Simpeh and Amma Boaduah; m. Eunice Annette Jones; 1 child, Efua Boaduah. BSc, U. Sci. and Tech., Kumasi, Ghana, 1973; MUP, McGill U., Montreal, Can., 1977; MA, U. Pa., Phila., 1979, PhD, 1981. Asst. prof. NC A&T State U., Greensboro, 1982—86, assoc. prof., 1986—92, prof., 1992—. Advisory county transp. issues Cmty. Transp. Adv. Bd., Greensboro, 2008. Mem.: Am. Econ. Assn., Am. Soc. Transp. and Logistics, Transp. Rsch. Forum. Democrat. Episcopalian. Avocations: travel, fishing. Home: 2100 Needleleaf Ln Greensboro NC 27411 Office: NC A&T State Univ 1601 E Market St Greensboro NC 27411 Office Fax: 336-334-7093. Business E-Mail: obengk@ncat.edu.

OBER, DORIS ANN, writer, editor, consultant; b. NY, Nov. 21, 1944; d. Emil Howard and Betty Novick Ober; m. Richard Kirschman, Sept. 13, 2001. Student, Tex. Western Coll., El Paso, Tex., 1962, Syracuse Univ., Syracuse, NY, 1963—64. Acct. exec. D.L. Blair Corp., NYC, 1960—62; promotion, mkgt. asst. mgr. Arlans Dept. Stores, NYC, 1968—69; ptnr., bus. mgr. One Age Graphics, Tucson, 1970—77; publ. rels. dir. Oakland Ballet, Oakland, Calif., 1977—79; self-employed San Fransicso/Dogtown, 1980—. Cons. in field. Ind. editor The World Rushed In: California Gold Rush Experience, 1981, And the Band Played On: Politics, People and the Aids Epidemic, 1987, The Bug in the Martini Olive, 1991, Simple is Powerful: Anecdotes for a Complex World, 1992, Conduct Unbecoming: The Homosexual Subculture in the U.S. Military, 1993, The Seven States of California, 1995, Tales of Two Cities, A Persian Memoir, 1996, I Love A Cop: What Police Families Need to Know, 1997, 45 Effective Ways for Hiring Smart: How to Predict Winners and Losers in the Incredibly Expensive People Reading Game, 1998, Games Companies Play, 2000, Secrets of Six-Figure Women, 2002, Stagecoach, 2002, I Love a Firefighter: What the Family Needs to Know, 2004, Overcoming Underearning, 2006, The Earthquake and Firestorms of 1906, 2005, Walter Stegner and the American West, 2008, Remember Who You Are, 2008, We Never Lost Hope, 2008; collaborator: American Daughter Gone to War: On the Front Lines with an Army Nurse in Vietnam, 1992, Covarrubias, 1994, Thousands of Words You Already Know in Spanish, 1995, Finding Hope When a Child Dies, 1999, Make a Name for Yourself: The Eight Steps to Becoming an Unforgettable Brand in Your Business, 2000, Ordinary People Doing the Exraordinary: The Story of Ed and Joyce Koupal and the Initiative Process, 2002, TransFats: The Hidden Killer in Our Food, 2004; mng. editor West Marin Review, 2008—09. E-mail: ober@marincounty.net.

OBER, RICHARD FRANCIS, JR., lawyer, director, banker; b. Balt., Dec. 12, 1943; s. Richard Francis and Caroline Fisher Ober; m. Carol Laycock Munger, Aug. 25, 1973; children: Julia Keyser Allen, Margaret Delancey. AB cum laude, Princeton U., 1965; LLB, Yale U., 1968. Bar: Md. 1968, Pa. 1970, N.J. 1977. Law clk. to chief judge Md. Ct. Appeals, Annapolis, 1968; assoc. Ballard, Spahr, Andrews & Ingersoll, Phila., 1969-75; gen. counsel Summit Bancorp, Princeton, NJ, 1975—2001; v.p., gen. counsel, sec. TerraCycle, Inc, Trenton, NJ, 2004—08. Sec. Summit Bancorp, Princeton, 1978-2001, sr. v.p., 1982-88, exec. v.p., 1988-2001; bd. dirs. sec. Summit Credit Life Ins. Co., Summit Credit Corp.; sec. Summit Bank, Summit Leasing Co., Summit Venture Capital, Inc. Fire commr. South Brunswick Fire Dist. 3, NJ, 1981-85; Republican county committeeman, 1975-04; v.p. Republican Assn. Princeton, 1995-96; trustee Princeton Day Sch., 1986-92, treas., 1988-92, vice-chmn., 1990-92; trustee Yale Law Sch. Assn. N.J.; first vice-chmn., dir N.J. Spl. Olympics; co-facilitator Trinity Jobseekers, 2005—; ombudsman NJ Com. Employer Support Guard and Res., 2005-. Mem. ABA, Bank Corp. Counsel Com. (chmn. 1979-80), NJ Bar Assn. (gen. coun. 1982-85, 93-94, exec. com. banking law sect. 1979-94, sec. sect. 1980-81, vice-chmn. 1981-82, chmn. 1984-85, exec. com. pro bono com. 1982-85, vice-chmn. 1984-85), NJ Corp. Counsel Assn. (exec. com. 1980-91, 2d v.p. 1982-85, pres. 1985-86, chmn. banking and fin. instns. com. 1984-85), Am. Bankers Assn. (exec. com. bank counsel unit 1990-95, vice-chmn. 1993-94, chmn. 1994-95), NJ Bankers Assn. (chmn. bank lawyers coun. 1993-94, chmn. legal and tax com. 1994-95), NJ Bus. and Industry Assn. (legis. affairs com.), Pa. Bankers Assn. (legal affairs com.), Assn. Corp. Counsel (contbr. articles to profl. jours.), Princeton Bar Assn., Fin. Svcs. Roundtable, Lawyers Coun., Bedens Brook Club (Princeton). Episcopalian.

OBER, RUSSELL JOHN, JR., lawyer; b. Pitts., June 26, 1948; s. Russell J. and Marion C. (Hampson) O.; children: Lauren Elizabeth, Russell John III; m. Sandi J. Antill. BA, U. Pitts., 1970, JD, 1973. Bar: Pa. 1973, U.S. Dist. Ct. (we. dist.) Pa. 1973, (ea. dist.) Pa. 2007, (ea. dist.) Wis. 1997, (dist.) DC 2006, U.S. Tax Ct. 1982, U.S. Ct. Appeals (4th cir.) 1976, U.S. Ct. Appeals (3d cir.) 1979, U.S. Ct. Appeals (D.C. cir.) 1985, U.S. Ct. Appeals (2d cir.), 1990, U.S. Ct. Appeals (7th cir.) 1993, U.S. Ct. Appeals (6th cir.) 2000, U.S. Supreme Ct. 1976. Asst. dist. atty. Allegheny County, Pitts., 1973-75; ptnr. Wallace Chapas & Ober, Pitts., 1975-80, Rose, Schmidt, Hasley & DiSalle, Pitts., 1980-92, Meyer, Unkovic & Scott, Pitts., 1992—. Bd. dirs. Parent and Child Guidance Ctr., Pitts., 1983-90, treas., 1985-86, pres., 1986-88; bd. mgmt. South Hills Area YMCA, 1989-91; mem. Mt. Lebanon Traffic Commn., 1976-81; bd. dirs. Whale's Tale Youth Family Counseling Ctr., 1990-95. Mem. ABA (discovery com. litigation sect. 1982-88, ho. of dels. young lawyers div. 1982-83), Pa. Bar Assn. (ho. of dels. 1983-2004), Allegheny County Bar Assn. (chmn. young lawyers sect. 1983, bd. govs. 1984, fin. com. 1984-88, mem. coun. civil litigation sect. 1991-93, judiciary com. 2004—), Nat. Bd. Trial Advocacy (diplomate), Acad. Lawyers Allegheny County (fellow 1983—, bd. govs. 1988-90) U. Pitts. Law Alumni Assn. (bd. govs. 1984-89, v.p. 1985-87, pres. 1987-88), Rivers Club Office: Meyer Unkovic & Scott 1300 Oliver Bldg Pittsburgh PA 15222 Office Phone: 412-456-2806. Business E-Mail: rjo@muslaw.com.

OBER, STUART ALAN, investment advisor, writer; b. NYC, Oct. 2, 1946; s. Paul and Gertrude E. (Stollerman) Ober; m. Allison Craig; children: Erik Kenneth, Alexander Gabriel. BA, Wesleyan U., Middletown, Conn., 1968; postgrad., U. Sorbonne, Paris, 1972, CUNY, 1976—77. Accredited investment fiduciary analyst, cert. fraud examiner. Specialist tax investment Fidelity Mutual Life, NYC, 1972—73; sr. assoc. mktg. ENI Corp., 1973; with mktg. and analysis J.F. Crowley and Co., Inc., 1974; co-mgr. Tax Investment Dept. Moseley, Hallgarten & Estabrook, NYC, 1974; co-dir. mktg. NFC Petroleum, NYC, 1975; specialist tax investment Loeb, Rhoades & Co., NYC, 1976—77; divisional dir. Dept. Tax Investment Josephthal & Co., Inc., NYC, 1977—78; founder, mgr. Dept. Tax Investment Bruns, Nordeman, Rea & Co., NYC, 1978—79; pvt. practice cons. NYC, 1979—81; founder, pres. Securities Investigations, Inc., Woodstock, NY, 1981—. Arbitrator Nat. Futures Assn., 2003—, Am. Arbitration Assn.; chmn. NASD, NYSE; cons. in field; expert witness in field; lectr. in field. Author: Everybody's Guide to Tax Shelters; editor-in-chief: Ober Income Letter, 1983-88; pub.: Tax Shelter Blue Book, 1983—. Bd. dirs., v.p. Woodstock Playhouse Assn., 1985-87; trustee Maverick Concerts, 1986—; chmn. Woodstock Arts and Cultural Com., 1988. Mem.: Inst. Cert. Fin. Planners (fin. products stds. bd. 1986—90, treas. 1988—90). Office: PO Box 888 Woodstock NY 12498-0888 Home Fax: 845-679-2301.

OBERBILLIG, MOLLY CASTLEMAN, utilities executive; b. Gibraltar, Feb. 11, 1934; arrived in U.S., 1935; d. William Ferguson and Mary Castleman (Davis) Cavenaugh; m. Gary Joel Oberbillig, Nov. 8, 1961; children: Andrew Ferguson, Julie Anne. Student, Reed Coll., Portland, Oreg., 1951—53, Antioch Coll., Yellow Springs, Ohio, 1953—54, U. Wash., Seattle, 1954—55, San Jose State Coll., 1963—64. Conservation mgr. Mason County Pub. Utility Dist., 1975—90. Contbr. articles to profl. jours. Founding sponsor Martin Luther King Jr. Nat. meml., Wash., DC, 2005—; founding trustee Anne Williston Scholarship, Seattle, 1988—2007; sec. Mason Coun. Fire Dist., Lilliwaup, Wash., 1979—81; mem. leadership coun. So. Poverty Law Ctr., 1992—; founder and chmn. Youth Diversity Award Thurston Coun. Cultural Diversity and Human Rights, 1995—; sustainer Rural Advancement Fund Internat., 1995—; charter mem. Nat. Women's History Mus., 2003—; mem. Nordiska Folkdance Exhibition Team, 1953—61; founding mem. Prog. Patriots Club; vice chmn. Dem. Ctrl. Com., Shelton, Wash., 1991—92. Mem.: Thurston Diversity Coun., Thurston Coun. Cultural Diversity and Human Rights. Avocations: gardening, ethical investing, sustainability environmental concerns. Home: 1907 Parkwood Dr SE Olympia WA 98501

OBERDORSTER, GUNTER, toxicologist, educator; b. Cologne, Germany, Feb. 27, 1939; came to U.S., 1979; s. Ewald and Liesel (Selbach) O.; m. Ingeborg Gerda Karden, Mar. 22, 1968; children: Jan. Eva, Uta. DVM, U. Giessen, 1964, PhD (DVM), 1966. Diplomate in pharmacology and toxicology. Scientist Pharm Industry, Cologne, Fed. Republic Germany, 1965-67; asst. prof. U. Cologne, 1968-71; mem. sci. staff Fraunhofer Inst., Grafschaft, Fed. Republic Germany, 1971-79; assoc. prof. toxicology U. Rochester, N.Y., 1979-89, prof. N.Y., 1989—, head divsn. respiratory biology and toxicology N.Y. Mem. contact group heavy metals European Commn., Brussels, 1977-79; cons. WHO, Geneva, 1983—, sci. adv. bd. EPA, Washington, 1984—, UNEP, Geneva, 1985, N.Y. State Health Dept., 1987. Mem. editl. bd. Jour. Aerosols in Medicine, Inhalation Toxicology; contbr. articles to profl. jours. Recipient John von Fraunhofer prize, 1982; grantee EPA-Dept. Energy, 1979-81, NIH, 1982—. Mem. Am. Thoracic Soc., Soc. Toxicology (Career Achievement award inhalation splty. sect. 1996), Am. Conf. Govtl. and Indsl. Hygienists, Internat. Soc. Aerosols in Medicine. Avocations: literature, skiing, rowing. Office: U Rochester Dept Environ Medicine 575 Elmwood Ave Rochester NY 14620-2945

OBERFIELD, SHARON ELEFANT, pediatric endocrinologist; b. NYC, Aug. 14, 1950; d. Nicholas and Anna (Weiss) Elefant; m. Richard A. Oberfield; 2 children. AB in Biology, Cornell U., 1970, MD, 1974. Diplomate in pediat. and pediatric endocrinology Am. Bd. Pediat. Intern in pediat. The NY Hosp., 1974-75, resident in pediat., 1975-76, fellow in pediatric endocrinology, 1976-79, asst. attending pediatrician, 1979-84; asst. attending pediatrician endocrinology Meml. Sloan Kettering Cancer Ctr., NYC, 1986—2001. Provisional pediatrician to outpatient dept. NY Hosp., 1976-79; assoc. attending pediatrician St. Luke's-Roosevelt Hosp. Ctr., NYC, 1984-91, Presbyn. Hosp., NYC, 1991, Tisch Hosp., Bellevue Hosp., NYC, 1992—; attending pediatrician Children's Hosp. of NY-Presbyn. Hosp., 1998—; asst. attending pediatrician Meml. Sloan Kettering Cancer Ctr., 1979-84; asst. prof. pediat. Cornell U. Med. Coll., NYC, 1979-84, Columbia U. Coll. Physicians & Surgeons, NYC, 1984-91, assoc. prof. clin. pediat., 1991, prof., 1998—, dir. pediat. endocrinology, 2004—. Grantee NIH, 1978-84, 2005-, Hoffman-LaRoche, 1985-89, Eli Lilly, 1986-92. Children's Brain Tumor Found., 1995-98; recipient Mitchell Spivak Meml. prize in pediatrics, 1974. Mem. Am. Med. Women's Assn. (citation 1974), NY Acad. Scis., NY Pediatric Soc., Soc. Pediatric Rsch., Endocrine Soc., Lawson Wilkins Soc., Pediatric Endocrinology, Alpha Omega Alpha. Office: Divsn Pediat Endocrinology Columbia Univ 630 W 168th St PH-5E-522 New York NY 10032 Office Phone: 212-305-6559. Business E-Mail: seo8@columbia.edu.

OBERG, LYLE, physician, academic administrator; b. Forestburg, Alberta, Can. m. Evelyn Oberg; children: Jillian, Scott. Pre-med studies, Red Deer Coll.; MD, U. Alberta, Can. Physician Gen. Practice, Alberta; elected to legis. assembly Alberta Parliament, Edmonton, 1993—, appointed minister of learning, 1999—2004, appointed minister infrastructure and transp., 2005—06, minister fin., 2006—. Chmn. standing policy com. on health restructuring Alberta Legis. Assembly, Edmonton, Canada, 1995—97, minister of family and social svcs., 1997—99; Alberta rep. Ministerial Coun. on Social Policy Renewal; mem. treasury bd, and standing com. on learning and employment Alberta Legislative Assembly, 1999—. Avocations: golf, hunting, sailing. Office: 408 Legislative BGldg 10800 97th Ave Edmonton AB T5K 2B6 Canada Office Phone: 780-427-8809.

OBERHAUS, GEOFFREY LUTHER, lawyer; b. Bowling Green, Ohio, Dec. 15, 1969; s. Luther and Cindy Oberhaus. BChemE, U. Detroit, 1992; JD, Rutgers U., 1998. Bar: Ohio 1998. Environ. engr. Occidental Chem. Corp., Burlington, NJ, 1992—98; ptnr. Dinsmore & Shohl LLP, Cin., 1998—. Named one of Ohio's Rising Stars, Super Lawyers, 2006. Mem.: Ohio State Bar Assn., Cin. Intellectual Property Law Assn., Cin. Bar Assn., ABA, Am. Intellectual Property Owners Assn., Am. Intellectual Property Lawyers Assn. Office: Dinsmore & Shohl LLP 255 East 5th St Cincinnati OH 45202 Office Fax: 513-977-8141. Business E-Mail: geof.oberhaus@dinslaw.com.

OBERHAUSER, ANDRES F., medical educator, researcher; b. Santiago, Chile, Nov. 11, 1961; life ptnr. Marcela Videla. PhD, U. Chile, Santiago, 1988. Asst. prof. Mayo Clinic, Rochester, Minn., 1997—2002; assoc. prof. U. Tex. Med. Br., Galveston. Grantee, NIH, 2006. Mem.: Biophys. Soc. Achievements include research in single molecule force spectroscopy. Home and Office: Univ Tex Med Br 301 University Blvd Galveston TX 77555 Business E-Mail: afoberha@utmb.edu.

OBERHELMAN, DOUGLAS RAY, tractor company executive; b. 1953; BA, Millikin U. With Caterpillar Inc., Peoria, Ill., 1975—, mng. dir., Shin Caterpillar Mitsubishi Tokyo, 1991—94, v.p., CFO Peoria, Ill., 1995—98, v.p., dir. engine products divsn., 1998—2001, group pres., 2001—. Bd. dirs. Nat. Assn. Manufacturers, Ameren Corp., 2003—, Caterpillar Inc., 2003—, Eli Lilly & Co., 2008—. Trustee, past chmn. Millikin Univ.; bd. dir. Ill. chpt., Nature Conservancy, Forest Park Found., Cordell Hull Inst. Office: Caterpillar Inc 100 NE Adams St Peoria IL 61629-0002*

OBERHELMAN, HARLEY DEAN, retired educator; b. Clay Center, Kans., June 30, 1928; s. Gideon Alfred and Anna (Vittetoe) O.; m. Hope Constance Nansen, Sept. 9, 1954; children: Richard Alfred, David Dean. BS, U. Kans., 1950, MA, 1952, PhD, 1958. Instr. in Spanish Lawrence (Kans.) Pub. Schs., 1950-55, dir. fgn. langs., 1956-58; instr. U. Kans., Lawrence, 1955-56; mem. faculty Tex. Tech. U., Lubbock, 1958—, prof., 1963—, chmn. dept. classical and Romance langs., 1963-70, chmn. Latin Am. area studies, 1969-76, Paul Whitfield Horn prof. romance langs., 1992—2005, ret., 2005. Fulbright lectr. English as fgn. lang. Nat. U. Tucuman, Argentina, 1961; lectr. in Argentina for NDEA, 1962, 63, 64; leader Rotary Internat. Study Team, Chile, 1970, Finland, 1973 Author: (with Agnes M. Brady) Espanol Moderno, I and II, 1964, 65, Ernesto Sabato, 1970, The Presence of Faulkner in the Writings of Garcia Marquez, 1980, Gabriel Garcia Marquez: A Study of the Short Fiction, 1991; assoc. editor Hispania, 1953-65. Tex. Research grantee in Uruguay, 1962; Tex. Research grantee Colombia, 1977, 87; Fulbright travel grantee to Colombia, 1988, 91. Mem. Am. Assn. Tchrs. Spanish and Portuguese, SW Coun. Latin Am. Studies, Assn. Colombianists, Sigma Delta Pi Hispanic Honor Soc. (Don Quijote Honor award 2008). Home: 6215 Louisville Dr Lubbock TX 79413-5428

OBERHELMAN, HARRY ALVIN, JR., surgeon, educator; b. Chgo., Nov. 15, 1923; s. Harry Alvin and Beatrice (Babel) O.; m. Betty Jane Porter, June 12, 1946; children: Harry Alvin III, James I., Robert P., Thomas L., Nancy L. Student, Yale U., 1942-43; BS, U. Chgo., 1946, MD, 1947. Diplomate: Am. Bd. Surgery. Intern U. Chgo. Clinics, 1947—48, resident surgery, 1948—51, 1952—57; asst. prof., assoc. prof. surgery U. Chgo. Sch. Medicine, 1957—60; mem. faculty Stanford Sch. Medicine, Calif., 1960—, prof. surgery, 1964—95, emeritus prof. surgery, 1995—; med. dir. Stanford Internat. Med. Svc., 2006—. Mem. div. licensing Calif. Bd. Med. Quality Assurance, 1970-82 Author papers in field. Served with USAF, 1951-53. Mem. AMA, Calif. Med. Assn., Soc. Univ. Surgeons, Am., Western, Pacific Coast surg. assns., Soc. Alimentary Tract, Halsted Soc., Fedn. State Med. Bds. U.S. (bd. dirs. 1979-82) Home: 668 Cabrillo St Stanford CA 94305-8404 Office Phone: 650-736-7964. Personal E-mail: hoberhelman@hotmail.com.

OBERHOLTZER, J. CARL, pathologist, researcher; MD, Jefferson Med. Coll.; PhD in Biochemistry, U. Pa. Assoc. dir. training, Office of Ctrs., Training, and Resources NIH, Bethesda, Md., 2006—08, chief Lab. of Pathology, Ctr. Cancer Rsch., Nat. Cancer Inst., 2008—. Office: Nat Cancer Ctr Bldg 10, Rm 2N208 10 Center Dr Bethesda MD 20892 Office Phone: 301-594-1884. Office Fax: 301-402-0043. E-mail: oberholtzerc@mail.nih.gov.*

OBERHOLTZER, LYDIA S., economist, consultant; 1 child, Daniel. MS in Land Resources, U. Wis., Madison, 1996. Rschr., program mgr. Wallace Ctr. Winrock, Rosslyn, Va., 1997—2004; rschr. US Dept. Agr., Economic Rsch. Svc., Pa. State U., Washington, 2004—. Cons., Takoma Park, Md., 2004—. Office: US Dept Agr Economic Rsch Svc PA State Univ 1800 M St NW Washington DC 20036 Personal E-mail: lydia.oberholtzer@gmail.com.

OBERING, TREY (HENRY A. OBERING II), federal agency administrator, career military officer; BS cum laude, U. Notre Dame, 1973; disting. grad., Squadron Officer Sch., Maxwell Air Force Base, 1977; MS in astronautical engring., Stanford U., 1980; grad., Defense Systems Mgmt. Coll., 1984; disting. grad., Air Command and Staff Coll., 1988, Indsl. Coll. of Armed Forces, 1993. Advanced through the ranks to lt. gen. USAF, 2004; student, undergraduate pilot training Craig Air Force Base, Ala., 1973—75; student pilot, F-4E Replacement Training Unit MacDill Air Force Base, Fla., 1975—76; operational F-4E pilot, chief aircraft maintenance unit, base exec. officer Moody Air Force Base, Ga., 1976—79; design mgr., space shuttle ground support; chief, space shuttle vehicle integration Vandenberg Air Force Base, Calif., 1980—82; engr., NASA Orbiter Project Kennedy Space Ctr., Fla., 1982—84; space shuttle project engr.; dir. shuttle engring. Western Space and Missile Ctr., Vandenberg Air Force Base, 1984—87; chief, spl. projects inspections Norton Air Force Base, Calif., 1988—90; program element monitor, Air Force Medium Space Launch Vehicles Program; dep. chief, Space Systems Div. Office of Sec. of Air Force for Acquisition, Washington, 1990—91; exec. officer to asst. sec. Office of Sec. of Air Force for Acquisition, the Pentagon, 1991—92; mission area dir., information dominance Office of Sec. of Air Force for Acquisition, 1999—2001; dep. dir., Acquisition and Tech. Group Defense Mapping Agency, Washington, 1993—96; prog. dir., spl. projects, Electronic Systems Ctr., Air Force Materiel Command Hanscom Air Force Base, Mass., 1993—96, dir., Expeditionary Forces Experiment System Program Office, 1997—99; dep., Force Structure Integration and Deployment; prog. dir., Battle Mgmt. Command and Control Missile Defense Agency, Washington, 2001—03; dir. Joint Nat. Integration Ctr., 2003—04, Missile Defense Agency, 2004—. Top Gun, Air-to-Air F-4E Replacement Training Unit. 2nd. lt. USAF, 1973, 1st lt., 1975, captain, 1977, major, 1986, lt. col., 1989, col., 1994, brigadier gen., 2000, major gen., 2004. Decorated Defense Superior Service Medal, Def. Disting. Svc. medal, Legion of Merit with oak leaf cluster, Meritorious Service Medal with three oak leaf clusters, Air Force Commendation Medal, Air Force Achievement Medal. Mailing: Military Defense Agency 7100 Defense Pentagon Washington DC 20301-7100*

OBERLANDER, MICHAEL I., lawyer, consumer products company executive; AB, U. Chgo.; JD, Vanderbilt U. Bar: Mo. 1993, Ill. 1994. Atty. Bryan Cave LLP, 1993—2000; v.p., gen. counsel Brown Shoe Co., Inc., St. Louis, 2000—01, 2001—06, sr. v.p., gen. counsel, corp. sec., 2006—. Office: Brown Shoe Co, Inc 8300 Maryland Ave Saint Louis MO 63105 Office Phone: 314-854-4119. E-mail: moberlander@brownshoe.com.

OBERLY, KATHRYN ANNE, judge; b. Chgo., May 22, 1950; d. James Richard and Lucille Mary (Kraus) Oberly; 1 child, Michael W. Goelzer; m. Haynes B. Johnson, June 29, 2002. Student, Vassar Coll., 1967—69; BA, U. Wis., 1971, JD, 1973. Bar: Wis. 1973, D.C. 1981, N.Y. 1995. Law clk. U.S. Ct. Appeals, Omaha, 1973-74; trial atty. U.S. Dept. Justice, Washington, 1974-77, spl. asst., 1977-81, spl. litig. counsel, 1981-82, asst. to Solicitor Gen., 1982-86; ptnr. Mayer, Brown & Platt, Washington, 1986-91; assoc. gen. counsel Ernst & Young LLP, Washington, 1991-94, vice-chair, gen. counsel NYC, 1994—2009; assoc. judge DC Ct. Appeals, Washington, 2009—. Bd. dirs. Appleseed Found., 2003—04. Named one of 50 Most Influential Women Lawyers in Am., Nat. Law Jour., 1998; recipient Aiming High award, Legal Momentum, 2007. Mem. ABA, Am. Law Inst. (coun. mem.), Am. Acad. Appellate Lawyers, Wis. Bar Assn., D.C. Bar Assn., NY Bar Assn. Democrat. Office: DC Ct APpeals 430 E St NW Washington DC 20001 Office Phone: 202-879-2791. Business E-Mail: koberly@dcappeals.gov.*

OBERMAN, MICHAEL STEWART, lawyer; b. Bklyn., May 21, 1947; s. Hyman Martin and Gertrude O.; m. Sharon Land, Oct. 8, 1975; 1 child, Abigail Land. AB, Columbia U., 1969; JD, Harvard U., 1972. Bar: N.Y. 1973, U.S. Dist. Ct. (so. and ea. dists.) N.Y. 1973, U.S. Ct. Appeals (2d cir.) 1973, U.S. Supreme Ct. 1976, Calif. 1981, U.S. Dist. Ct. (no. dist.) Calif. 1981, U.S. Ct. Appeals (9th cir.) 1981, U.S. Dist. Ct. (so. and cen. dists.) Calif. 1982, U.S. Ct. Appeals (5th cir.) 1989, D.C. 1992, U.S. Ct. Appeals (7th cir.) 1993. Law clk. to Hon. Milton Pollack, U.S. Dist. Ct. (so. dist.) N.Y., 1972-73; assoc. Kramer Levin Naftalis & Frankel LLP, NYC, 1973-79, ptnr., 1980—. Contbr. articles to profl. jours Recipient Nathan Burkan prize ASCAP, 1973. Mem. N.Y. State Bar Assn. (mem. ho. of dels. 1989-91, exec. com. comml. and fed. litigation sect.). Office: Kramer Levin Naftalis & Frankel LLP 1177 Avenue of the Americas New York NY 10036-1003 Office Phone: 212-715-9294. Business E-Mail: moberman@kramerlevin.com.

OBERMANN, RICHARD MICHAEL, governmental technology and policy analyst; b. May 21, 1949; s. Baird J. and Phyllis L. (Weber) Obermann; m. Grace Karaffa; children: Pearl Louise, John Baird. BS of Engring. in Aerospace and Mech. Scis. cum laude, Princeton U., 1971, PhD in Engring., Aerospace and Mech. Scis., 1977; MS of Engring. in Astronautics and Aeros., Stanford U., 1972; postgrad., Va. Poly. Inst. and State U., Am. U., Harvard U., 1993. With MITRE Corp., McLean, Va., 1977-88, engr. transp. systems analysis, transp. energy analysis, telecommunications, project leader, mem. tech. staff in communications and system design; sr. staff officer aeros. and space engring. bd. NRC, Washington, 1988-90, study dir. and analyst technol. and policy issues; mem. profl. staff for space subcom. US Ho. of Reps. Com. on Sci., Space and Tech., Washington, 1990-95; minority staff dir., space and aeronautics subcom. US Ho. of Reps. Com. on Sci., Washington, 1995—2007; staff dir. space and aeronautics subcom. US Ho. of Reps. Com. on Sci. and Tech., Washington, 2007—. Lectr. in field; presenter in field. Contbr. articles to profl. jours.; reviewer for jours.:. Fellow AIAA (internat. activities com., pub. policy com.), Brit. Interplanetary Soc., Am. Astronaut. Soc. (bd. dirs., exec. com., internat. policy com.); mem. IEEE, AAAS, NY Acad. Sci., Asia Soc., Nat. Space Club, Pacific Telecomms. Coun., Women in Aerospace (bd. dirs.), Internat. Acad. Astronautics, World Affairs Coun. Avocations: languages, sports, trumpet.

OBERMAYER, HERMAN JOSEPH, newspaper publisher; b. Phila., Sept. 19, 1924; s. Leon J. and Julia (Sinsheimer) O.; m. Betty Nan Levy, June 28, 1955; children: Helen O. Levy-Myers, Veronica O. Atnipp, Adele O. Malpass, Elizabeth O. Weintraub. Student, U. Geneva, Switzerland, 1946; AB cum laude, Dartmouth Coll., Hanover, NH, 1948. Reporter L.I. Daily Press, Jamaica, NY, 1950-53; classified advt. mgr. New Orleans Item, 1953-55; asst. to pub. Standard-Times, New Bedford, Mass., 1955-57; editor, pub. Long Branch Daily Record, NJ, 1957-71, No. Va. Sun, Arlington, 1963-89; adj. prof. journalism U. Md., 1989-93; vis. lectr. U. West Indies, Jamaica, 1994-95; publ. com. Commentary Mag., 1989—2006. Pulitzer Prize juror, 1983, 84; lectr. publs. mgmt. Hungary, Poland, Lithuania, Latvia, Estonia, Ukraine, Moldova, Slovenia, Macedonia, Russia, Croatia, Serbia, 1990-2002, Internat. Ctr. Journalists, 1992-2002. Author: Jews in the News, 2001, Soldiering for Freedom: A GI's Account of World War II, 2005, Rehnqvist: A Personal Portrait of the Distinguished Chief Justice of the US, 2009; contbr. articles to popular mags., local newspapers. Bd. dirs. Monmouth Med. Ctr., 1958-71; exec. coun. Monmouth Boy Scouts Am., 1958-71, exec. com. Nat. Capital coun., 1971-79, v.p., 1974-77; mem. Va. Legis. Alcohol Beverage Control Study Commn., 1972-74, Arlington Arts Ctr., 2008-; trustee Arlington (Va.) Bicentennial Commn., Am. Jewish Com. Cmty. Svc. award, 1986, nat. bd. govs., 1989-96, nat. coun., 1996—; trustee Jewish Inst. for Nat. Security Affairs, 1996—. With AUS, 1943-46, ETO. Rhineland Campaign Star; Recipient Silver Beaver award Boy Scouts Am., 1977, Knight Internat. Press fellow, 1994-95. Mem. Am. Soc. Newspaper Editors, So. Newspaper Pubs. Assn. (dir. 1981-84), Mont. Pelerin Soc., Nat. Press Club (Washington), Cosmos Club (Washington), Washington Golf and Country Club (Arlington, Va.), Dartmouth Club (NYC), Sigma Chi. Jewish. Rotarian.

OBERN, VIVIAN MARIE HAPEMAN, volunteer; b. Park Ridge, Ill., May 26, 1921; d. Vaughn Webber and Beatrice Beckwith Hapeman; m. Earl George Obern, Dec. 4, 1942; children: George Vaughn, Dale Marie, Reade Webber. BA, Principia Coll., Elsah, Ill., 1942. Vol. SBCRATAC, 1967—2009; exec. sec. Santa Barbara County Trails Coun., 1966—2007; co-chmn. Am. Revolutionary Bicentennial Com., 1974—77; chair Bicentennial Re-enactment Santa Barbara County, 1974—78; chmn. County Christopher Columbus Quincentennial, 1992; pres. Santa Barbara Trust for Hist. Preservation, 1989—91; leader Girl Scouts Am., 1960—66; mem. Calif. Recreational Trails Com., Sacramento, 1971—76; vol. Hope House, 1969—2009; mem. adv. com. to suprs. Santa Barbara County Riding and Hiking Trails, Calif., 1967—; mem. Santa Barbara Courthouse Docents Coun., 1974—2006. Recipient Hon. Life Svc. award, PTA, 1968, 1976, Disting. Alumna award, Principia Coll., 1996, Lifetime Achievement award, Calif. Recreational Trails, 1997, Environ. award, Santa Barbara County Trails Coun., 1997, Pearl Chase Hist. Preservation award, Santa Barbara Trust for Hist. Preservation, 1998, Wildlife Sanctuary award, 2002, Obern Bikeway/Trail named in her honor, 2004, Environ. Studies Cmty. Svc. award, U. Calif., Santa Barbara, 2006; named Woman of Yr., Santa Barbara Advt. Club, 1989, George and Vie Obern Preservation Stewardship award in her honor, Santa Barbara Trust for Historic Preservation, 2006. Mem.: Daus. of Union Vets. (pres. Daughters of Union Vet. Santa Barbara 1992—93, pres. dept. Calif., Nev. 1993—95). Christian Scientist. Avocations: equestrian activities, baking, horseback riding, travel. Home: 4140 Marina Dr Santa Barbara CA 93110 E-mail: viegeoobern2@cox.net.

OBERNAUER, MARNE, securities company executive; b. Pitts., Mar. 6, 1919; s. Arthur H. and Anna (Somerman) O.; m. Joan Strassburger, Aug. 1, 1941; children: Marne Jr., Wendy Damon. Grad., Cornell U., 1941. Vice chmn. Beverage Distbrs. Corp. and BDH Inc., Aurora, Colo.; pres. Doric Securities Co. Bus. cons., pvt. investor. Pres., bd. dirs. The Obernauer Found., Inc. Served to lt. USNR, 1942-45. Mem. Concordia Club (Pitts.), Century Country Club (Purchase, N.Y.), Banyan Golf Club (Palm Beach, Fla.). Home: 2 North Breakers Row Palm Beach FL 33480 Office: 60 E 42d St Ste 1912 New York NY 10165 Fax: 561-659-2132.

OBERNDORF, MEYERA E., Former Mayor, Virginia Beach, Virginia; m. Roger L. Oberndorf; children: Marcie, Heide. BS in Elem. Edn., Old Dominion U., 1964, LLD (hon.), 1999. Broadcaster Sta. WNIS, Norfolk, Va.; chair Pub. Libr. bd., Va.; mem. city coun. City of Virginia Beach, Va., 1976—88, vice-mayor Va., 1986—88, mayor Va., 1988—2008. Mem. exec. bd. Tidewater coun. Boys Scouts Am.; bd. dirs. Va.Beach Pub. Libr., 1966-76, chmn. bd., 1967-76; past pres. Va. Muncipal League; bd. dir. Hampton Roads Partnership; Econ. Develop. Alliance; adv. com. Va. Inst. of Gov. Recipient Women's Achievement award, Zonta Club of Hampton Roads, 2002; named Outstanding Woman of Va., Am. Legion Aux., Newsmaker of the Yr., Va. Press Women, 1997; named one of 25 Most Dynamic Mayors in the US, Newsweek. Mem. AAUW, U.S. Conf. Mayors (trustee), Va. Mcpl. League (exec. bd.), Nat. League Cities (vice-chmn., mem. adv. bd., past chair Energy, Environ., and Natural Resources Steering Com.), Princess Anne Women's Club; chair Standing Com. on Internat. Affairs. Jewish.*

O'BERRY, PHILLIP AARON, retired veterinarian; b. Tampa, Fla., Feb. 1, 1933; s. Luther Lee and Marjorie Mae (Mahlum) O'B.; m. Terri Martin, July 31, 1960; children: Kelly, Eric, Holly, Danny, Andy, Toby. BS in Agr., U. Fla., Gainsville, 1955; DVM, Auburn U., Ala., 1960; PhD, Iowa State U., Ames, 1967. With Agrl. Rsch. Svc. USDA, 1956—2003, asst. to dir. vet. scis. rsch. div. Beltsville, Md., 1967-72; asst. dir. Nat. Animal Disease Ctr., Ames, Iowa, 1972-73, dir., 1973-88, tech. transfer coord., 1988—2003; prin. scientist Office Agr. Biotech., USDA, 1988-90; ret., 2003. Adj. prof. Coll. Vet. Medicine, Iowa State U., 1973—; expert panel livestock infertility FAO; sci. adv. com. Pan Am. Zoonosis Ctr., Buenos Aires; mem. Fed. Coun. Sci. and Tech.; com. animal health, world food and nutrition study NRC; cons. Govt. of Italy, Govt. of Mex., USDA, Govt. of Egypt; nat needs grad. fellowship rev. panel USDA, 1989-91, cons. agr. biotech. rsch. adv. com.; sci. adv. bd. Biotech. R&D Corp., 1992-2001, sci. review bd. Am. Jour. Vet. Rsch., 1990-92; mem. USDA Patent Review Com., 1988-2003. Author 27 rsch. publs.; mem. editl. adv. bd. Food Safety mag. Recipient Cert. Merit, Agrl. Rsch. Svc., 1972, 84, 2005, Alumni Merit award Iowa State Club Chgo., 1982, Cert. Appreciation, 1988, Tech. Transfer award 1989, 2004, USDA, Disting. Alumnus award Auburn U., 1991; named Hon. Diplomate Am. Coll. Vet. Microbiologists, 1995, Ames Citizen the Yr., 2000, Iowa Gov.'s Vol. award, 2001, Philanthropy award, 2006. Mem. APHA, AVMA, AAAS, Nat. Assn. Fed. Vets., Iowa Vet. Med. Assn., NY Acad. Scis., Conf. Rsch. Workers Animal Diseases, Am. Soc. Microbiology, Am. Assn. Lab. Animal Sci., US Animal Health Assn., Am. Assn. Bovine Practitioners, Livestock Cons. Inst., Sigma Xi, Phi Zeta, Phi Kappa Phi, Gamma Sigma Delta (Alumni award Merit 1976), Alpha Zeta, Spades, Blue Key. Democrat. Home: 1612 Woodhaven Cir Ames IA 50010-4170 Personal E-mail: terrioberry@mchsi.com.

OBERST, CONOR MULLEN, singer, musician; b. Omaha, Feb. 15, 1980; s. Matthew and Nancy Oberst. Band mem. Commander Venus, 1994—97; drummer Park Ave., 1996—98; lead singer Bright Eyes, 1997—; singer & guitarist Desaparecidos, 2000—; founding mem. Saddle Creek Records, Omaha, Team Love Records, NYC, 2003—. Singer: (albums) (with Bright Eyes) Letting Off the Happiness, 1998, Fevers and Mirrors, 2000, Lifted, or The Story is in the Soil, Keep Your Ear to the Ground, 2002, Digital Ash in a Digital Urn, 2005, I'm Wide Awake, It's Morning, 2005, Cassadaga, 2007, Motion Sickness, 2007, (with Desaparecidos) Read Music/Speak Spanish, 2002, (with Conor Oberst and Mystic Valley Band) Conor Oberst, 2008. Office: c/o Chloe Walsh or Jill Strominger Press Here Publicity 138 W 25th St 7th Fl New York NY 10001 also: c/o Team Love 151 1st Ave #115 New York NY 10003 Office Phone: 212-246-2640. E-mail: info@saddlecreek.com, info@pressherepublicity.com.

OBERSTAR, JAMES LOUIS, United States Representative from Minnesota; b. Chisholm, Minn., Sept. 10, 1934; s. Louis and Mary (Grillo) O.; m. Jo Garlick, Oct. 12, 1963 (dec. July 1991); children: Thomas Edward, Katherine Noelle, Anne-Therese, Monica Rose; m. Jean Kurth, Nov. 1993; stepchildren: Corinne Quinlan Kurth, Charles Burke Kurth, Jr. BA summa cum laude, St. Thomas Coll., 1956; postgrad. in French, Laval U., Que., Can.; MS in Govt. (scholar), Coll. Europe, Bruges, Belgium, 1957; postgrad. in govt, Georgetown U. Adminstrv. asst. to Rep. John A. Blatnik US Congress, 1963-74; adminstr. US House Pub. Works Com., 1971-74; mem. US Congress from 8th Minn. Dist., 1975—; ranking minority mem. US House Transp.& Infrastructure Com, 2005—07; chmn. US House Transp.& Infrastructure Com., 2007—. Trustee Kennedy Ctr., 1995—; bd. mem. Mineta I.I.STPS Inst., 1995—. Mem.: Am. Polit. Sci. Assn. Dfl. Roman Catholic. Office: US Congress 2365 Rayburn House Office Bldg Washington DC 20515-2308 also: 231 Federal Bldg Duluth MN 55802*

OBERSTE, STEVE, microbiologist; b. Nebr., 1957; married. PhD, U. Fla., Gainesville, 1988. Rsch. microbiologist CDC, Atlanta, 1996—2006, chief picornavirus lab., 2007—.

OBERT, JEANNE L., alcohol/drug abuse services professional, director; d. W. L. Piguet and Mary Jane Lemere Piguet. MA in Marriage, Family and Child Therapy, Azusa Pacific, Calif., 1981; MS in Mgmt., Lesley Coll., Cambridge, Mass., 1995. Cert. LMFT Calif., 1984, supervisor Am. Assoc. Marriage & Family Therapy, 1992. Co-founder Matrix Inst. Addictions, LA, 1994—, exec. dir., 1999—. Cons. Substance Abuse & Mental Health Svcs. Adminstrn., Rockville, Md., 1990—. Contbr. articles to profl. jours. Active Human Interaction Rsch. Inst., Encino, Calif., 2006; sci. adv. bd. mem. Phoenix House, NYC, 2007. Mem.: Am. Assn. Marriage & Family Therapists. Office: Matrix Inst Addictions 1849 Sawtelle Blvd 100 Los Angeles CA 90025 Office Fax: 310-207-4404. Business E-Mail: jlobert@matrixinstitute.org.

OBERT, PAUL RICHARD, lawyer, manufacturing executive; b. Pitts. s. Edgar F. and Elizabeth T. Obert. BS, Georgetown U., 1950; JD, U. Pitts., 1953. Bar: Pa. 1954, D.C. 1956, Ohio 1972, Ill. 1974, U.S. Supreme Ct. 1970. Sole practice, Pitts., 1954-60; asst. counsel H.K. Porter Co., Inc., Pitts., 1960—62, sec., gen. counsel, 1962-71, Addressograph-Multigraph Corp., Cleve., 1972-74; v.p. law Marshall Field & Co., Chgo., 1974-82, sec., 1976-82; v.p., gen. counsel, sec. CF Industries, Inc., Long Grove, Ill., 1982—, also officer, dir. various subs. Served to lt. col. USAF. Mem. ABA (corp. gen. counsel com.), Pa. Bar Assn., Allegheny County Bar Assn., Ill. Bar Assn., Chgo. Bar Assn., Am. Soc. Corp. Secs., Am. Retail Fedn. (bd. dirs. 1977-80), Georgetown U. Alumni Assn. (bd. govs.), Pitts. Athletic Assn., Univ. Club (Chgo.), Delta Theta Phi. Office: CF Industries Inc 1 Salem Lake Dr Long Grove IL 60047-8401

OBERTON, WILLARD D., industrial supply company executive; Grad., St. Cloud Tech. Coll. V.p., COO Fastenal Co., Winona, Minn., 1997—2002, bd. dir., 1999—, exec. v.p., COO, 2000—01, pres., COO, 2001—02, pres., CEO, 2002—. Bd. dir. Wincraft Inc., Donaldson Co. Inc. Trustee Coll. St. Benedict. Office: Fastenal Co 2001 Theurer Blvd Winona MN 55987

OBEY, DAVID ROSS, United States Representative from Wisconsin; b. Okmulgee, Okla., Oct. 3, 1938; s. Orville John and Mary Jane (Chellis) Obey; m. Joan Therese Lepinski, June 9, 1962; children: Craig David, Douglas David. BS in Polit. Sci., U. Wis., Madison, 1960; MA in Soviet Politics, U. Wis., 1962. Mem. Wis. State Gen. Assembly, 1963-69, asst. minority leader, 1967-69; mem. US Congress from 7th Wis. Dist., 1969—; ranking mem. US House Appropriations Com., 1995—2007, chmn., 1994—95, 2007—. Mem. adminstrv. com. Wis. Dem. Com., 1960-62 Author: Raising Hell for Justice: The Washington Battles of a Heartland Progressive, 2007. Named Edn. Legislator of Yr., Rural div. NEA, 1968; recipient Legis. Leadership award Eagelton Inst. Politics, 1964, Award of Merit Nat. Coun. Sr. Citizens, 1976, Citation for Legis. Statesmanship Coun. Exceptional Children, 1976. Democrat. Office: US Congress 2314 Rayburn House Office Bldg Washington DC 20515-4907 also: District Office First Star Plaza 401 5th Street, Suite 406 Wausau WI 54403 Office Phone: 202-225-3365.*

OBIELODAN, JAMES BOLANLE, management information systems educator; s. Micah and Serah Obielodan; m. Doni Roseline Ifiabor; children: Olufunmilola Aimalohi, Olufemi Emmanuel. BTh, Igbaja Theol. Sem., Kwara State, Nigeria, 1977; BA in Speech Communication, Wheaton Coll., Ill., 1983; MA in Telecom., Wheaton Coll. and Grad. Sch., 1984; MA, Mich. State U., East Lansing, 1986, PhD in Ednl. Sys. Devel., 1996, MBA, 2000. Asst. prof. MIS Sch. Bus., Ky. State U., Frankfort, 2001—08, interim chair, 2005—08. Mgr., faculty facility for creative computing Computer Lab, Mich. State U., 1993—2001. Contbr. conf. paper. Sunday adult sch. tchr. Assemblies God, Frankfort, 2005—08. Recipient Faculty Appreciation award. Mem.: Assn. Info. Tech. Profls. Office: Kentucky State Univ 400 East Main St Frankfort KY 40601 Business E-Mail: james.obielodan@kysu.edu.

OBIOZOR, GEORGE ACHULIKE, former ambassador; b. Nigeria, Aug. 15, 1942; married. BA in Polit. Sci. and Hist., U. Puget Sound, Tacoma, Wash.; M in Internat. Affairs, Columbia U., NYC, 1971, M of Philos. in Internat. Affairs, 1974, PhD in Internat. Affairs, 1976. Lectr. Pratt Inst., NYC, 1971—75; asst. prof. polit. sci. CUNY Medgar Evers Coll., 1975—79; Ralph Bunche Rsch. Fellow in UN CUNY Grad. Ctr., 1977—78; spl. asst. Office of Polit. Adv. to Pres., Nigeria, 1980—83; sr. rsch. fellow Nigerian Inst. Internat. Affairs, Lagos, Nigeria, 1984—87; spl. adv. to Min. of Fgn. Affairs Nigeria, 1988—89; spl. asst. to pres. of Nigeria on internat. affairs, 1990; dir. gen. Nigerian Inst. Internat. Affairs, 1991—99; Nigerian amb. to Israel and high commr. to Cyprus, 1999—2003; Nigerian amb. to US Washington, 2004—07. Chmn. Commonwealth Tech. Meeting, Abuja, 1996; vis. prof. internat. affairs African Inst., Russian Acad. Sci., Moscow, 1998. Author and editor of numerous profl. books. Recipient Ugwumba 1 of Orlu, 1991; grantee Albert Schweitzer fellowship, 1969—71, Alice Stetten fellowship, Columbia U. Sch. Internat. Affairs, 1969—71.

OBIOZOR, WILLIAMS EMEKA, special education educator; b. Nsukka, Enugu, Nigeria, May 19, 1966; s. Raymond Offorkansi and Martha Abiose Obiozor; m. Obiageli Mary Onwudiegwu; 1 child, Kenechi Raymond. EdD, Wilmington U., Delaware, 2004. Cert. leadership & innovation edn. Wilmington U., Del., 2007. Spl. edn. tchr. Md. Pub. Schs., Balt., 2002—07; asst. prof. Bloomsburg U., Pa., 2007—, asst. dir. Frederick Douglass Inst. Academic Excellence, 2008—; vis. prof. Penn State U., Hazelton, Pa., 2008—. Author: (novels) White For Black (Excellence award, 2008), Waves Of Passion: Celebrating African Romance & Fantasies. Coord. Dorchester Cmty. Reading Program, Cambridge, Md., 2003—07; project vol. NE Alliance Homelessness, Bloomsburg Town-Pa., 2007; organizing coord. Black History Month & Africana Rsch. Forum, Bloomsburg, 2007; adviser Heavenson Internat. Bus. Sch., Banjul, Kmc Area, 1997—2000. Recipient award, Senate Md., City Balt. & Md. Ho. Representatives, 2003, Ednl. Leader & Mentor award, Congl. Youth Leadership Coun., Washington, 2006, Legacy Black Achievements award, Bloomsburg U. Africana Forum, 2007. Mem.: Nat. Educators Assn., Igbo Studies Assn., Nat. Coun. Black Studies, Coun. Exceptional Children, Phi Lambda Theta. Office: Bloomsburg Univ 400 East 2nd St Bloomsburg PA 17815 Office Fax: 570-389-3980. Personal E-mail: emekkah@yahoo.com. Business E-Mail: wobiozor@bloomu.edu.

O'BLACK, SEAN, legislative staff member; Online comm. specialist, legis. correspondent, Senator Joe Lieberman US Senate, Washington, 2004, comm. asst., Senator Christopher Dodd, 2004—06; press sec., Rep. Adam Schiff US House of Reps., Washington, 2006—08, comm. dir. to Rep. Adam Schiff, 2008—. Democrat. Office: 2447 Rayburn House Office Bldg Washington DC 20515 Office Phone: 202-225-4176. Office Fax: 202-225-5828.*

OBLER, GERI, small business owner, artist, educator; b. NY, May 1, 1942; m. Arnold Obler, June 30, 1963; children: Nancy, Gary. BFA, Pratt Inst., 1963; MA, Hunter Coll., 1966; EdD, T.C. Columbia U., 1974. Tchr. art John Bowne H.S., Flushing, NY, 1963—74; prin., owner Geri Obler Fine Arts, NYC, 1985—. Assoc. website Sotheby's Auction Ho., NYC, 2000—03. Author: (catalogue introduction) Mel Ramos: His Graphic Work, 2002; exhibitions include Geri Obler Fine Arts. Mem.: Nat. Assn. Women Artists. Home: 26 Brokaw Ln Great Neck NY 11023 Office: Geri Obler Fine Arts 153 E 57th St New York NY 10022 Office Phone: 917-913-4244. Personal E-mail: oblerart@aol.com.

OBLINGER, DIANA G., educational association administrator; BS, MS, Iowa State U., PhD in Plant Breeding and Cytogenetics. Faculty mem. Mich. State U.; faculty mem., academic adminstr. U. Mo.-Columbia; with IMB; exec. dir. higher edn. Microsoft; v.p. info. resources, chief info. officer U. NC Sys.; cons., sr. fellow Ctr. for Applied Rsch. EDUCAUSE, 2000—02, v.p., 2004—07, dir. Learning Initiative, pres., 2008—. Adj. prof. adult and CC edn. NC State U.; bd. mem. Directorate of Edn. and Human Resources, NSF, Nat. Academies Forum on Info. Tech. and Rsch. Univs., U. Tex. TeleCampus; chair Nat. Vis. Com., Nat. Sci. Digital Libr. Project, NSF; bd. dirs. ACT, Inc., Iowa City, 2007—. Co-editor: The Learning Revolution: The Challenge of Information Technology in the Academy, 1997, The Future Compatible Campus: Planning, Designing, and Implementing Information Technology in the Academy, 1998, Renewing Administration: Peparing Colleges and Universities for the 21st Century, 1999, E is for Everything, 2000; co-author (with Anne-Lee Verville): What Business Wants from Higher Education, 1998; contbr. articles to profl. jours. Recipient Disting. Svc. Award, Nat. Univ. Telecommunications Network (NUTN), 2006. Mem.: Sigma Xi, Phi Kappa Phi, Phi Beta Kappa. Office: EDUCAUSE 1150 18th St, NW, Ste 1010 Washington DC 20036 Office Phone: 919-306-4191. E-mail: doblinger@educause.edu.

OBLINGER, JAMES L., former academic administrator; b. Ashland, Ohio, Nov. 3, 1945; s. Richard Bruce and Pauline (Frary) Oblinger; m. Diana G. Oblinger; 4 children. BA in Bacteriology, DePauw U., Greencastle, Ind., 1967; MS in Food Tech., Iowa State U., 1970, PhD in Food Tech., 1972. Asst. prof. to prof. food sci. and human nutrition U. Fla., Gainesville, 1972-84; assoc. dean, dir. resident instrn. Coll. Agr. U. Mo., Columbia, 1984-86; assoc. dean, dir. acad. affairs Coll. Agr. and Life Sci. NC State U., Raleigh, 1986—97, dean, exec. dir. for agrl. programs, 1997—2003, provost, exec. vice chancellor for acad. affairs, 2003—04, chancellor, 2005—09. Contbr. articles to profl. jours., chpts. to books. Recipient Award of Merit, Inst. of Food and Agrl. Scis., 1981, William V. Cruess Nat. Award, 1983, Disting. Educator Award, Nat. Assn. Colls. and Tchrs. of Agriculture, 1994, Iowa State Disting. Alumni Achievement award, 2006. Mem. Inst. Food Technologists (Wm. V. Cruess Nat. Award Excellence 1983), Coun. for Agrl. Sci. and Tech. (pres. 1990-91), Am. Assn. Higher Edn., Sigma Xi, Phi Kappa Phi, Gamma Sigma Delta, Phi Tau Sigma, Phi Epsilon Phi, Phi Beta Kappa. Episcopalian. Office Phone: 919-515-2191. Business E-Mail: james_oblinger@ncsu.edu.

O'BLOCK, ROBERT, association, publishing executive; BS in Sociology, Pitts. State U., Kans., 1972, MS in Sociology, 1973, EdS, 2001; PhD, Kans. State U., 1976; MA in Psychology, Newport U., 1998, PsyD in Psychology, 2000; MDiv, Trinity Coll., 2001, DMin, 2003; STD (hon.), St. Elins Sch. Orthodox Theology, 2003. Ordained deacon So. Episcopal Ch., 1999; ordained priest So. Episcopal Ch., 2002. Patrolman Frontenac (Kans.) Police Dept., 1971-73; probation officer Crawford County Juvenile Ct., 1973-74; supr. Children's Ct. Ctr., 1974; adminstrv. asst. to dean student affairs/cmty. svc. Labette Cmty. Jr. Coll., 1976; dir. night sch. Marymount Coll., 1976; asst. prof. dept. adminstrv. justice Wichita State U., 1977-79; assoc. prof. dept. criminal justice/polit. sci. Appalachian State U., Boone, NC, 1979-89; prof. and chair dept. adminstrn. justice Coll. Ozarks, Point Lookout, Mo., 1989—93; exec. dir. Am. Coll. Forensic Examiners, Springfield, Mo., 1994—. Founder Am. Bd. Forensic Medicine, Am. Bd. Forensic Examiners, Am. Bd. Forensic Psychol.; lectr., cons. in field. Author: Criminal Justice Research Sources, 1983, 4th edit., 1992, (with others) Security and Crime Prevention, 2d edit., 1990, The 7 Steps to the Cure of Souls, 2005; founder, pub. The Forensic Examiner, Annals of the Am. Psychotherapy Assn., contbr. articles to profl. jours., holder 25 U.S. fed. trademarks. Adv. bd. Larnard State Hosp. Named Knight Chevalier, Sovereign Military Order of Temple of Jerusalem, 2001; grantee, Gov.'s Commn. on Criminal Adminstrn., 1976—77. Mem.: Am. Assn. Integrative Medicine (co-founder, CEO), Am. Coll. Forensic Examiners (founder), Am. Psychotherapy Assn. (founder, chmn., CEO). Office: 2750 E Sunshine St Springfield MO 65804-2047 Home: 3686 E Kingswood Dr Springfield MO 65809-4635 Home Phone: 417-848-8119; Office Phone: 417-881-3818. Personal E-mail: rloblock@aol.com.

O'BLOCK, ROBERT PAUL, management consultant; b. Pitts., Mar. 9, 1943; s. Paul Joseph and Mary Elizabeth (Galicic) O'B.; m. Megan Marie. BSME, Purdue U., 1965; MBA, Harvard U., 1967. Rsch. and tchg. fellow in fin., econs. and urban mgmt. Harvard U., 1967-70; assoc. in real estate mgmt. and fin. McKinsey & Co., Inc., Boston, 1969-78; gen. and mng. ptnr. Freeport Ctr., Clearfield, Utah, 1971—; prin. McKinsey & Co., Inc., Boston, 1979-84, dir., 1984-98, McKinsey Adv. Coun., Boston, 1998—. Vis. lectr. urban econs. Yale Law Sch., Princeton U.; cons. Mass., N.J. housing fin. agys., Rockefeller Assn., HUD, 1968-76; chmn. mgmt. com. Snowbird Lodge (Utah), 1974-86. Contbr. articles to profl. jours. Mem. nat. adv. bd. Snowbird Arts Inst., 1977-83; mem. budget com. N.Y. Pub. Libr., 1977-79; mem. adv. bd. Internat. Tennis Hall of Fame, 1986-89, bd. dirs., 1989-95; mem. bd. overseers Boston Symphony Orch., 1988-2000, vice-chmn. bd. overseers, 1992-95, chmn., 1995-2000, trustee, 2000—, vice chmn. bd. trustees, 2002—; trustee U.S. Ski Ednl. Found., 1989-2001, Park Sch., 1997—2003; bd. dirs. Bankrate, Inc. Mem. Devon Yacht Club, Maidstone Club, Nat. Golf Links Am., The Country Club (Brookline), Univ. Club Boston. Office: 60 Cramond Rd Chestnut Hill MA 02467-2803

OBLOY, LEONARD GERARD, priest; b. Cleve., Sept. 1, 1951; s. Henry Joseph and Ruth Elsie (Walter) Obloy. AB, Borromeo Coll. of Ohio, 1973; MDiv, St. Mary's Sem., 1977; SSL, Pontifical Bibl. Inst., Rome, 1983, postgrad., 1984. Ordained priest Roman Cath. Ch., 1977. Assoc. pastor St. Helen Parish, Newbury, Ohio, 1977-80, St. Rose of Lima Parish, Cleve., 1984-88; vice-rector Mt. St. Mary's Sem., Emmitsburg, Md., 1988-97, asst. prof. sacred scripture and computer sci., 1988-99, dir. aux. svcs., 1997-99; assoc. pastor St. Francis of Assisi Parish, Gates Mills, Ohio, 1999—2002; pastor St. William Parish, Euclid, Ohio, 2002—. Adj. prof. St. Mary's Sem., Cleve., 1984—88, Cleve., 1999—; dean grad. divsn. Cath. Distance U., Hamilton, Va., 1995—2003, dean emeritus, 2003—; guest lectr. Our Lady of Holy Cross Coll., New Orleans, 1998—2003; lectr. in field. Author, narrator pub. TV series And God Said, Witness; author various pamphlets, audio casettes for Cath. Distance U. Mem.: IEEE Computer Soc., Vatican Radio, Sacred Congregation for Doctrine of Faith, Nat. Cath. Edn. Assn., Corp. for Pub. Broadcasting, Cath. Bibl. Fedn., NY Acad. Scis., Assn. Computing Machinery, GTO Assn. Am. Avocations: computers, audio engineering, audio recording, auto dragracing. Office: St William Parish 367 E 260th St Euclid OH 44132 Office Phone: 216-731-1515. Personal E-mail: lgobloy@aol.com. Business E-Mail: info@saintwilliameuclid.org.

OBNINSKY, VICTOR PETER, lawyer; b. San Rafael, Calif., Oct. 12, 1944; s. Peter Victor and Anne Bartholdi (Donston) Obninsky; BA, Columbia U., NYC, 1966; JD, U. Calif., Hastings, 1969. Bar: Calif. 1970. Sole practice, Novato, Calif., 1970-2001, Tiburon, Calif., 2001—02, Sonoma, Calif., 2003—. Arbitrator Marin County Superior Ct., San Rafael, 1979—; superior ct. judge pro tem, 1979—; lectr. real estate and partnership law; facilitator Sonoma County Superior Ct., 2008-. Author: The Russians in Early California, 1966. Bd. dir. Calif. Young Reps., 1968-69, Richardson Bay San. Dist., 1974-75, Marin County Legal Aid Soc., 1976-78, vol., 2003-; baseball coach Little League, Babe Ruth League, 1970-84; mem. nat. panel consumer arbitrators Better Bus. Bur., 1974-88; leader Boy Scouts Am., 1970-84; permanent sec. Phillips Acad. Class of 1962, 1987—; mem. Phillips Acad. Alumni Coun., 1991-95; bd. cmty. advisors Buck Ctr. Rsch. on Aging, 1990-2001. Recipient Diploma of Honor, City Mus. Obninsk, Russia, 2004. Mem.: BBB, ABA, State Bar Calif., Marin County Bar Assn. (bd. dirs. 1985—91, treas. 1987—88, pres.-elect 1989, pres. 1990), Sonoma Bar Assn., Global Alliance Internat. Advancement (hon.), Russian Nobility Assn. Am., Inc., Phi Gamma Delta, Phi Delta Phi. Republican. Russian Orthodox. Avocations: travel, reading, politics. Home and Office: 21453 Shainsky Sonoma CA 95476-8412 Office Phone: 707-935-7422. Personal E-mail: vpobninsky@comcast.net. *An all-out intellectual attempt to understand baseball thoroughly may give sufficient insight to understand oneself; the so-called "designated hitter" rule should be abolished immediately.*

OBOGEANU, MADALINA MARIA, reporter; arrived in U.S., 1997; d. Vasile and Calina Obogeanu. BA in polit. sci, German studies (spl. hons.), Hunter Coll., NYC, 2004. Analyst UNICEF, UN, NYC, 2000; rsch. asst. Dept. Econ. Affairs, UN, NYC, 2001; asst. prodr. Clear Channel, NYC, 2003; rsch. analyst Hunter Coll., NYC, 2004; reporter Instl. Investor, NYC, 2004—. Mem.: German Academic Exch. Svc. (Scholarship 2002), The Acad. Polit. Sci. Avocations: tennis, skiing, reading. Office: Instl Investor Inc 225 Park Ave S New York NY 10003

OBOLENSKY, IVAN, investment banker, foundation administrator, writer; b. London, May 15, 1925; s. Serge and Alice (Astor) O. Bouverie (parents Am. citizens); m. Claire McGinnis, 1949 (div. 1956); children: Marina Ava, Ivan Serge, David; m. Mary Elizabeth Morris, 1959; 1 child, Serge. AB, Yale U., New Haven, Conn., 1947. Pres. Hotel Investments, Inc., NYC, 1950-58; dir. Silver Bear Inc., Atla., 1947—69; v.p., treas. Serge Obolensky Assocs., 1952-75; pres. Ivan Obolensky Inc. and Astor Books, Ivan Obolensky Inc., pubs., 1956-65; ptnr. A.T. Brod & Co., investment bankers, 1960—65, Dominick & Dominick Inc., investment bankers, 1965-70, Middendorf Colgate, investment bankers, 1970-73; v.p. C.B. Richard, Ellis/Moseley Hallgarten, investment bankers, 1974-81, Sterling Grace & Co., investment bankers, NYC, 1982-87; sr. v.p. Jesup, Josephthal & Co., investment bankers, NYC, 1987-90; principal Astor Capital Mgmt. Assocs. LLC, 1980—; v.p. Capital Mgmt. Assocs., NYC, 1990—, Shields & Co., NYC, 1990—. Bd. dirs. Gold Canyon Resources, 1996—, HiEnergy Technologies, 2005-06, Uranian Energy Corp., 2007-; cons. and lectr. in field. Author: Rogues' March, 1956; contbr. to Nihon Keizai Shimbun, Tokyo, on precious metals, 1985—, program com. NY Soc. of Security Analysts for pub., aerospace, metals and mining, nuc. power, oil and gas; contbr. articles to profl. publs. Bd. dirs. Police Athletic League, NYC, 1975-85, exec. com., 1980-85, 96—, U.S.O., 1987—2004, Audubon Canyon Ranch, Calif., 1989—, Tolstoy Found., 1994-2000, Soldiers', Sailors', Marines', Coast Guard' and Airmen's Club, 1976—, pres., 1987-2000, chmn., ceo, 2000—, Russian Nobility Assn. in Am., 1990—, treas., 1991—, v.p., 1995—, Musicians Emergency Fund, 1985-93, pres.1987-92, Children's Blood Found., NY Hosp., 1952—, pres., 1981-95, pres. emeritus, 1995—; pres., dir. Josephine Lawrence Hopkins Found., 1971-; pres. Whitemarsh Found., 1980-, Masonic Toys for Tots Found., 2003-; bd. dirs. Masonic Brotherhood Found., 1996—. Lt. (j.g.) USNR, 1943-45, ret., 1980. Published works by James Agee: A Death in the Family and Tad Mosel: All the Way Home, which received Pulitzer prizes, 2 Caldecott awards. Mem. Am. Legion, Mil. Order Loyal Legion US (sr. vice-comdr. 1955, comdr. 1967-70), St. Elmo Soc., Met. Mus. Art (life), Knickerbocker Club, NY Yacht Club, New Eng. Soc. NY, St. George's Soc. NY, The Navy League, The Naval Inst., The Naval Order, Army and Navy Club, The Pilgrims, Order of Lafayette, Explorer's Club: Masons (Holland #8 master 1981, dist. dep. grand master 1st Manhattan 1983-84, grand ledge NY, grand treas. 1994-96), DeMolay (hon. mem.), Masonic Brotherhood Found. (chmn. fin. oversight com. 1999-, chmn. com. endowments, 2004-), Grand Lodge State of NY. Office: Shields & Co 140 Broadway New York NY 10005-1101 Office Phone: 212-320-3000. Personal E-mail: iobolensky@aol.com. Business E-Mail: ivan.obolensky@shieldsandco.com.

OBOT, ISIDORE SILAS, public health scholar; s. Silas and Jane Obot; m. Theresa Isidore Adadiaha, Dec. 1, 1984; children: Ifiok Isidore, Aniekan Isidore, Ubong Isidore, Tete Isidore. BA, Loyola Coll., Balt., 1976, MA, 1978; PhD, Howard U., Washington, 1982; MPH, Harvard U., 1984. From lectr. to sr. lectr. psychology U. Jos, Nigeria, 1985—2001; rsch. fellow Johns Hopkins U. Sch. Pub. Health, Balt.,

1998—2000; scientist substance abuse WHO, Geneva, 2002—06; prof. sch. pub. health and policy Morgan State U., Balt., 2006—, chmn. dept. behavioral health scis., 2006—. Bd. dirs. Centre for Rsch. and Info. on Substance Abuse, Jos, 1990—2002. Editor: African Jour. Drug and Alcohol Studies. Rsch. and Writing grant, John D. and Catherine T. McArthur Found., 2000—01. Mem.: Internat. Soc. Addiction Jour. Editors (bd. dirs. 2004—), Kettil Bruun Soc. for Alcohol Rsch. (steering com. 2003—), Coll. on Problems of Drug Dependence, Beta Kappa Chi, Psi Chi. Roman Catholic. Avocations: travel, reading, music, walking. Office Fax: 443-885-8309. Personal E-mail: obotis@gmail.com.

O'BOYLE, CHRISTINA, science educator; b. Cleve. d. Tom and Elaine O'Boyle. MS in Geology, Kent State U., Ohio. Assoc. geologist Tetra Tech., Pasadena, Calif., 2004; assoc. prof. geology LA City Coll., 2004—. Mem.: Geol. Soc. America. Avocations: travel, literature. Office: LA City Coll 855 N Vermont Los Angeles CA 90029

O'BOYLE, MICHAEL WILLIAM, psychology educator; b. Chgo., Mar. 29, 1952; s. Eugene James and Mildred Mable (Swanson) O'B. BS in Psychology, Loyola U. Chgo., 1975; MA in Psychology, U. Nevada, Las Vegas, 1977; PhD in Psychology, U. So. Calif., 1982. Asst. prof. psychology Iowa State U., Ames, 1982-89, assoc. prof. psychology, 1989-98, prof. psychology, 1999—. Ad hoc reviewer Am. Jour. Psychology, Brain and Cognition, Brain and Lang., Devl. Neuropsychol., Jour. Internat. Neuropsychol. Soc., Laterality., Econ. and Social Rsch. Coun. Gt. Britain, James S. McDonnell Found., Nat. Sci. Found.; participant in inaugaral James S. McDonnell Found. Summer Inst. in Cognitive Neurosci., Harvard U., Cambridge, Mass., 1988; vis. scholar U. Melbourne, Parkville, Victoria, Australia, 1991-92. Contbr. over 35 articles to profl. jours. including Jour. Psycholinguistic Rsch., Neuropsychologia, Behavioral and Neural Biology, Brain and Cognition, Brain and Lang., Cortex, others; presentations to sci. confs. and meetings; guest editor: spl. issue Devel. Neuropsychology: Intelligence, Learning Disability and Related Brain Characteristics. Recipient Outstanding Educator award Torch chpt. Mortar Board, Iowa State U., 1989; grantee Sigma Xi, 1982, Midwest Transp. Ctr., 1991-92, 94-95, Ricoh Corp., 1989-90, 91-92, 92-93, 93-94, 94-95, 95-96. 96-97. Mem. Internat. Neuropsychol. Soc., Iowa Acad. Sci. (sect. chair psychology 1989-90. 93-94), Midwestern Psychol. Assn., Psychonomic Soc. Democrat. Achievements include contributions to the understanding of the specialized functions of the left and right cerebral hemispheres and how they serve as neurological basis for individual differences in higher-order thinking processes, particularly as they relate to handedness, sex and intellectual giftedness; study of neurologically damaged patients and the study of how their impairments reveal fundamental principles about how perception, memory and language are subserved by, and organized in the human brain. Office: Iowa State U Psychology Dept Ames IA 50011-0001

OBRAMS, GUNTA IRIS, clinical research administrator; b. Düsseldorf, Germany, Sept. 2, 1953; came to U.S., 1961; d. Robert and Olga (Baltins) O.; m. Malcolm DeWitt Patterson, Dec. 22, 1975; 1 child, Andrew McDougal Patterson. BS in Biology cum laude, Rensselaer Poly. Inst., 1977; MD, Union U., Albany, NY, 1977; MPH, Johns Hopkins U., 1982, PhD, 1988. Resident in obstetrics and gynecology Ea. Va. Grad. Sch. Medicine, Norfolk, 1977-78; community physician Southampton Meml. Hosp., Franklin, Va., 1978-81; resident in gen. preventive medicine sch. hygiene and pub. health Johns Hopkins U., Balt., 1981-84, project dir., 1983-85, med. dir., 1985-86; med. officer divsn. cancer etiology Nat. Cancer Inst., Bethesda, Md., 1986-89, dep. chief, 1989-90, chief, 1990-96, dir. extramural epidemiology & genetics program, 1996-2001; mgmt. US Coast Guard Health Svcs., 2001—05; med. officer divsn. clin. resources NIH, Bethesda, 2005—. Editor: (with M. Potter): The Epidemiology and Biology of Multiple Myeloma, 1991; contbr. articles to profl. jours. With USPHS, 1987—. Recipient Nat. Cancer Inst. Nat. Rsch. Svc. award, 1981, Rsch. Career award Nat. Inst. Occupational Safety & Health; scholar Am. Med. Women's Assn., 1977. Mem. Phi Beta Kappa, Delta Omega, Alpha Omega Alpha. Office: DCRR NCRR NIH 6701 Democracy Blvd MSC-4874 Bethesda MD 20892 Office Phone: 301-435-0768. Personal E-mail: go4wellness@comcast.net.

O'BRIAN, JONATHAN D., recreation director, story educator, language educator, educator; b. Jamestown, NY, Feb. 16, 1968; s. John Daniel O'Brian and Margaret Ann Martin. AA, Jamestown C.C., 1985; B in History, SUNY at Fredonia, 1987; cert., Sorbonne U., 1988; M in History, SUNY at Buffalo, 1991. Instr., asst. prof. Jamestown C.C., Jamestown, NY, 1992—. Dir. camp Jamestown YMCA, 1987—. Trustee Fenton History Ctr., Jamestown, 1999—; bd. dirs. Scandinavian Studies Program, Jamestown. Named Outstanding Young Men Am., 1987, Jr. Citizen of Yr., Optimist Club, 1979. Mem.: Orgn. Am. Historians, Fenton Hist. Soc. (bd. dirs.), Phi Theta Kappa (co-advisor 2000—). Democrat. Roman Catholic. Avocations: travel, writing, water-skiing, camping. Office: YMCA Camp Onyahsa 101 E Fourth St Jamestown NY 14701

O'BRIEN, ADRIENNE GRATIA, communications educator; b. NYC, Nov. 19, 1935; d. John Robert and Regina C. (Murphy) O'B.; m. David G. Salten, Dec. 21, 1987 (dec. Oct. 2006). AB, Hunter Coll., NYC; MA, MA, Villanova U., Pa.; PhD, Syracuse U. Faculty Cabrini Coll., Radnor, Pa., 1962-68, dir. R & D, 1971-72; prof., chair MA program NY Inst. Tech., Old Westbury, 1974-78, dean Sch. Media and Arts, 1979-91, prof. comm. arts, 1992—. Pres. AID Assocs., NYC, 1972-74, Creative Cons., Port Washington, NY, 1992—; reviewer Nat. Coun. Humanities, Washington, 1981; pres. Women in Instrnl. Tech., Washington, 1981. Editor: Computer Based Training Today, 1987; prodr., dir. (video) Then and Now, 1995 (Communicator award, 1996), Legacy of Mother Ursula, 1996 (Communicator award, 1997), Maritime Mus. of L.I., founder, exec. prodr. L.I. News tonight, 1984; reviewer: Jour. Staff Devel., 1990. Mem. project steering com. Where Are the Women?, 2002; bd. dirs. Girl Scouts of Nassau County, 2002—. Recipient Instrnl. Nat. Leadership award, Assn. Ednl. Comm. and Tech., Washington, 1989, Comm. award, Maritime Mus. L.I., 2001, L.I. Top 50 Women award, L.I. Bus. News, 2002, 2009, Lifetime Achievement award, Pub. Rels. Profls. L.I., 2005, Cmty. Svc. award, Patron of the Arts, NY, 2005, Women on the Job Achievement in Edn. award, 2005, Adult Recognition award for cmty. svc., Girl Scouts Nassau County, 2007, Juliet Law Disting. award, 2008; named one of 90 Women for 90 Yrs., Girl Scouts of Nassau County, 2001. Mem.: Women on the Job (v.p. 1995—2004), Alpha Epsilon Rho (hon.). Avocation: videography. Office: NY Inst Tech Old Westbury NY 11568

O'BRIEN, ANDREA MAXWORTHY, education teacher; b. Racine, Wis., Oct. 14, 1952; d. Vernon Edward and Irma Elida Giese; m. Kevin Robert O'Brien; 1 child, Sean Michael. BA, U. Wis.-Parkside, Racine, 1974; MS, U. Wis.-Madison, 1983, PhD, 1990. Assoc. prof. curriculum & instrn. U. Wis.-Whitewater, 1988—. Contbr. articles to profl. jours. Recipient Audrey Z. McClellan Endowed Tchr. Distinction, Coll. Edn., 2008—09. Office: Univ Wis-Whitewater 800 W Main St Madison WI 53704

O'BRIEN, BARBARA, Lieutenant Governor of Colorado; b. Apr. 18, 1950; m. Rick O'Brien; children: Jared, Connor. BA, U. Calif., LA, 1972; PhD, Columbia U., NYC, 1981. Project asst. Inst. for Urban and Minority Edn., Columbia U., 1977—79; head speechwriter, dep. dir. Policy Office of Gov., Gov. Richard Lamm, 1983—85; dir., Campus Affairs U. Colo. Denver, 1985—88; exec. dir. Inst. Internat. Bus., Colo. U. Denver, 1988—90; pres. Colo. Children's Campaign, 1990—; lt. gov. State of Colo., 2007—. Mem. Mayor's Leadership Team on Early Edn., Governor's Commn. on Children and Families, Nat. Kids County Steering Com., Tony Grampsas Youth Services Fund; founder, co-chair Kids Caucus. Democrat. Office: Lieutenant Governor 130 State Capital Denver CO 80203 Office Phone: 303-866-2087. Office Fax: 303-866-5469. Business E-Mail: Ltgovernor.obrien@state.co.us.

O'BRIEN, BONNIE JEANNE, counseling administrator; b. Winsted, Conn., Oct. 10, 1970; d. Charles Joseph and Jeannette Grace O'Brien. BA in Psychology, Ctrl. Conn. State U., 1993, MSc, 2000; postgrad., Sacred Heart U., 2004—05. Cert. elem. edn. tchr. 1997. Child devel. counselor Kaburne Sch., New Marlborough, Mass., 1990—92; pre-sch. tchr. Kindercare, Conn., 1992—95; tchr. Lake Tahoe (Calif) Elem., 1996—97; learning specialist Ctrl. Conn. State U., New Britain, Conn., 1997—2000; sch. counselor intern Avon (Conn.) Pub. Schs., 1996—2000; sch. counselor Woodbury (Conn.) Mid. Sch., 2000—. Cheerleading & field hockey coach Woodbury Mid. Sch., 2000—. Mem.: Am. Sch. Counselor Assn., Conn. Counseling Assn., Conn. Sch. Counselor Assn. (Sch. Counselor award 2004), Phi Delta Kappa (bd. mem.). Avocations: travel, kayaking, cooking. Office: Woodbury Mid Sch 67 Washington Ave Woodbury CT 06798

O'BRIEN, CHRISTOPHER BLACKBURN, gastroenterologist, director; b. Va., Apr. 25, 1954; s. Gérard Joseph and Mildred O'Brien; m. Michele Porcaro, May 1990. BS, U. Fla., 1976; MD, Johns Hopkins, Balt., 1980. Lic. Fla., 1983, diplomate Am. Bd. Internal Medicine, 1984, in transplant hepatology 2009, cert. in hepatology U. Miami, 1984, in internal medicine 1981, resident 1983, diplomate Am. Bd. Gastroenterology, 1985, cert. in gastroenterology U. Pa., 1986, in clin. nutrition U. Pa., 1986. Rsch. assoc., gastroenterology U. Pa., Phila., 1986—87, asst. prof., medicine, 1987—97; clin. transplant hepatologist Hosp. U. Pa., 1987—90, clin. dir., liver ctr., 1990—97, acting chief, gastrointestinal sect., 1992—92, dir., clin. activities, gastrointestinal sect., 1992—94, med. dir., liver transplantation, 1994—95; UNOS dir., liver transplant Children's Hosp. Phila., 1988—90; dir., hepatitis lab., gastroenterology divsn. U. Pa. Med. Ctr., Phila., 1994—97; prof., clin. medicine U. Miami, Fla., 1997, assoc. prof., clin. medicine, 1998—2005, chief, clin. hepatology, 2006—, co-dir., hepatitis lab. Author: Primary Sclerosing Cholangitis with Multiple Myeloma, Baseline Characteristics and HBV DNA Levels at Week 24 Predict the Outcomes of Two Years Treatment with Telbivudine. Gastroenterology, Dynamic Evolution of Lab Approaches to Liver Disease.; contbr. articles to profl. jours. Co-dir., med. Hep-C Alert, Miami, 2002—; mem. Am. Liver Found., Phila., 1990—97. Recipient award, America's Top Physician's, 2004—06, Fla. Super Drs., 2008—; named Rschr. of Yr., Del. Valley Chpt. Am. Liver Found., 1992, Best Doctors, Phila. Mag., 2004; fellowship, Am. Coll. Gastroenterology, 2009. Mem.: RCP (Ireland) (fellowship 2009). Office: Univ Miami 1500 NW 12th Ave Miami FL 33136

O'BRIEN, CLARE, lawyer; b. Ireland, 1961; children: Una, Lucy. BA summa cum laude, Trinity Coll., 1982. Bar: Ireland, NY 1986, U.S. Dist. Ct. NY (so. dist.) 1987. Atty. Eugene F. Collins & Son, Brady & Tarpey, 1987—88, Shearman & Sterling LLP, NYC, 1988—95, mem., mergers & acquisitions group, 1989—, ptnr., 1995—. Bd. dirs. Am. Assn. Internat. Commn. Jurists. Named Dealmaker of Yr., Am. Lawyer mag., 2006. Office: Shearman & Sterling LLP 599 Lexington Ave New York NY 10022-6069 Office Phone: 212-848-8966. Office Fax: 212-848-7179. E-mail: cobrien@shearman.com.

O'BRIEN, CONAN, talk show host, writer, performer; b. Brookline, Mass., Apr. 18, 1963; m. Liza Powel, Jan. 2002; children: Neve, Beckett. BA Am. Hist., Lit., Harvard U., 1985. Staff mem. The Harvard Lampoon, 1981-85 (pres. 1983, 84); head Conaco. Stage appearances with: The Groundlings (LA) 1985-87; writer, performer The Happy Happy Good Show (LA, Chgo.) 1988; writer (TV series) Not Necessarily the News (HBO) 1985-87, Saturday Night Live, 1988-91 (NBC, Emmy Outstanding Writing in Comedy series 1989), Lookwell (NBC) 1991; writer, prodr. The Simpsons (Fox) 1991-93, The Wilton North Report (syndicated) 1987; writer, prodr., host Late Night with Conan O'Brien (NBC) 1993-2009 (Best Writing in Comedy/Variety Show Writer's Guild award 1997, TV award Writers Guild Am. 2000, 2002, 2003, 2005, 2006, Primetime Emmy for Outstanding Writing for a Variety, Music or Comedy Prog., Acad. TV Arts and Scis., 2007); host Tonight Show with Conan O'Brien, 2009-; host (TV Specials) Emmy Awards 2002; film appearances include Tomorrow Night, 1998, Barenaked in America, 1999, Vanilla Sky, 2001, Bewitched, 2005, The Great Buck Howard, 2008; TV appearances include (voice) The Simpsons, 1994, The Single Guy, 1996, Arli$$, 1996, (voice) Dr. Katz, Professional Therapist, 1997, Veronica's Closet, 1998, Spin City, 1998, LateLine, 1999, Space Ghost Coast to Coast, 1999, (voice) Futurama, 1999, Tomorrow Night, 1998, (voice) Robot Chicken, 2005. Named one of 25 Most Intriguing People, People Mag., 50 Funniest People Alive, Entertainment Weekly. Office: NBC Universal Tonight Show 100 Universal City Plz Universal City CA 91608

O'BRIEN, DANIEL J., lawyer; b. Los Alamos, N.Mex., Nov. 18, 1951; BS, U. N.Mex., 1975, MBA, 1980, JD, 1983. Bar: N.Mex. 1983, Tex. 1993, U.S. Dist. Ct. N.Mex. 1984, U.S. Ct. Appeals (10th cir.) 1987. Ptnr. O'Brien & Ulibarri, P.C., Albuquerque, shareholder. Mem.: ABA, Albuquerque Bar Assn., N.Mex. Trial Lawyers Assn., N.Mex. Def. Lawyers Assn. (pres. 1999—2000), State Bar N.Mex. (bd. commrs. 1994—2000, v.p. 2002, pres. 2004). Office: O'Brien & Ulibarri PC 6000 Indian Sch NE Ste 200 Albuquerque NM 87110 Office Phone: 505-883-8181. Office Fax: 505-883-3232. Business E-Mail: dobrien@obrienlawoffice.com.

O'BRIEN, DANNY, legislative staff member; With Office of Pub. Liason The White House, Washington; Nev. state dir. Al Gore presdl. campaign, 2000; chief of staff Senator Robert Torricelli, Washington, 2001—02, Senator Joe Biden, Washington, 2003—08, Senator Robert Menendez, Washington, 2008—. Office: Office of Senator Robert Menendez Senate Hart Office Bldg Washington DC 20510-3006 Office Phone: 202-224-4744. E-mail: danny_obrien@menendez.senate.gov.*

O'BRIEN, DAVID MICHAEL, law educator; b. Rock Springs, Wyo., Aug. 30, 1951; s. Ralph Rockwell and Lucile O'Brien; m. Claudine M. Mendelovitz, Dec. 17, 1982; children: Benjamin, Sara, Talia. BA, U. Calif., Santa Barbara, 1973, MA, 1974, PhD, 1977. Fulbright lectr. Oxford (Eng.) U., 1987-88; lectr. U. Calif., Santa Barbara, 1976-77; asst. prof. U. Puget Sound, Tacoma, Wash., 1977-79; Spicer prof. U. Va., Charlottesville, 1979—. Fulbright rschr., Tokyo, Kyoto, Japan, 1993-94, Fulbright chair, Bologna, Italy, 1999; jud. fellow U.S. Supreme Ct., Washington, 1982-83; Fulbriht lectr., Oxford U., England, 1987-1988; vis. postdoctoral fellow Russell Sage Found., NYC, 1981-82; lectr. USIA, Burma, Japan, France, 1994-95. Author: Supreme Court Watch, 1991—, Constitutional Law and Politics, 2 vols., 6th edit., 2005, Storm Center: The Supreme Court in American Politics, 7th edit., 2005, To Dream of Dreams: Constitutional Politics in Postwar Japan, 1996, To Dream of Dreams: Religious Freedom in Postwar Japan, 1996, Animal Sacrifice & Religious Freedom, 2004; editor: Views from the Bench, 1985, Judges on Judging, 1997, Government by the People, 22nd edit., 2005. Rappatour, jud. selection 20th Century Fund Task Force, N.Y., 1986-87. Tom C. Clark Jud. Fellow, Jud. Fellows Commn., Washington, 1983. Mem. ABA (Silver Gavel award 1987), Am. Judicature Soc., Am. Polit. Sci. Assn., Supreme Ct. Hist. Soc. (editl. bd. 1982—), Internat. Polit. Sci. Assn. Democrat. Avocations: painting, travel. Home: 916 Tilman Rd Charlottesville VA 22901-6338 Office: U Va 232 Cabell Hall Charlottesville VA 22901 Office Phone: 434-994-3358.

O'BRIEN, DENIS P., utilities executive; m. Carolyn O'Brien; 3 children. B in Indsl. Engring., Rutgers U., NJ; M in Bus., Drexel U., Phila. V.p. ops. Exelon Corp., sr. v.p., pres. PECO Energy, exec. v.p., pres. & CEO PECO, 2007—. Bd. mem. Energy Assn. Pa., Am. Gas Assn., Pa. Bus. Roundtable, Pa. Economy League, Greater Phila. C. of C., Select Greater Phila., Franklin Inst., WHYY, Inc., Greater Phila. YMCA; bd. trustees Drexel U. Office: PECO Energy 2301 Market St PO Box 8699 Philadelphia PA 19101 Office Phone: 800-494-4000.*

O'BRIEN, DENISE DIANE, medical/surgical nurse, perianesthesia nurse; b. Caro, Mich., Mar. 2, 1953; d. James Howard and Donna June (McLane) Chapin; m. Michael K. O'Brien, Aug. 25, 1973; children: Matthew, Bridget. BSN, U. Mich., 1975; MSN clin. nurse specialist, Adult Health, Madonna U., 2003. Cert. post anesthesia nurse; cert. ambulatory perianesthesia nurse, clincial nurse specialist cert. adult health. Gen. surgery staff nurse U. Mich. Hosps., Ann Arbor, 1975-77, clin. nurse in post anesthesia care unit, 1977-90, ednl. nurse coord., 1991—2003, clin. nurse specialist perianesthesia care areas, 2003. Editor Jour. Post Anesthesia Nursing, 1988-93; interim editor Jour. Perianesthesia Nursing, 1999-2000. Fellow, Am. Acad. Nursing, 2004. Mem. Am. Soc. Perianesthesia Nurses (exec. com. 1988-90, pres. 1994-95). Business E-Mail: dedeo@umich.edu.

O'BRIEN, DENNIS M., state legislator; b. 1952; m. Bernadette Benson; children: Dennis Jr., Brendan, Joseph. BS in Labor Rels., La Salle U., Phila., 1982. Mem. Dist. 169 Pa. House of Reps., Harrisburg, 1977—80, 1983—, spkr. of the House, 2007—08. Republican. Office: 312 Main Capitol Bldg PO Box 202169 Harrisburg PA 17120-2169 also: Dist Office 9811 Academy Rd Lower Level Philadelphia PA 19144-1715 Office Phone: 717-787-5689, 215-632-5150. Office Fax: 717-787-1339, 215-281-2094.

O'BRIEN, EDWARD IGNATIUS, corporate financial executive, director, investor, lawyer; b. NYC, Sept. 15, 1928; s. Edward I. and Marguerite (Malone) O'B.; m. Margaret M. Feeney, June 29, 1957; children: Edward Ignatius III, Margaret Mary, Thomas Gerard, John Joseph. AB, Fordham U., 1950; LLB, St. John's U., 1954; grad., Advanced Mgmt. Program, Cornell U., 1965. Bar: N.Y. 1954. With firm Hale, Kay & Brennan, NYC, 1954-55; with Bache & Co., Inc., NYC, 1955-74, gen. counsel, 1960, gen. ptnr., 1964, sec., 1968, v.p., 1965-68, sr. v.p., mem. exec. com., 1969, exec. v.p., 1969, chmn. exec. com., 1971-74; pres. Securities Industry Assn., 1974-93; retired, 1993. Bd. dirs. 8 corps.; lectr. Am. Law Inst., Practising Law Inst., Am. Mgmt. Assn.; exch. ofcl. Am. Stock Exch., 1972; mem. adv. bd., mem. exec. com. Securities Regulation Inst., U. Calif., 1975—. Mem. Cardinal's com. Laity Cath. Archdiocese N.Y., mem. Cardinal's com. for edn.; chmn. Fordham U. Coun., 1971-73; bd. dirs. 3 non-profit orgns.; chmn. corp. devel. com. Fordham U.; trustee, chmn. bd. trustees Fordham Prep. Sch., 1975-77, Capt. USAR. Mem. NY State Bar Assn,. Am. Arbitration Assn., Am. Soc. Internat. Law, Guild Cath. Lawyers, Securites Industry Assn. (chmn. publicly owned firms com. 1972), Nat. Assn. Securities Dealers (dist. com. 1973-74), Shenorock Shore Club (Rye, NY), Town Club (Scarsdale, NY). Home and Office: 12 Woods Ln Scarsdale NY 10583-6408

O'BRIEN, EDWARD JOHN, musician, vocalist; b. Oxford, England, Apr. 15, 1968; Student in Econs., Manchester U., Eng. Barman; photographer's asst.; guitarist, vocalist Radiohead, 1992—. Musician (and vocalist): (albums) Pablo Honey, 1993, The Bends, 1995, OK Computer, 1997 (Grammy award for Best Alternative Music Performance, 1997), Kid A, 2000 (Grammy award for Best Alternative Music Performance, 2000), Amnesiac, 2001, I Might Be Wrong: Live Recordings, 2001, Hail to the Thief, 2003, In Rainbows, 2007 (Grammy award for Best Alternative Music Album, 2009). Office: Capital Records 1750 North Vine St 10th Fl Hollywood CA 90028*

O'BRIEN, EDWIN FREDERICK, archbishop; b. Bronx, NY, Apr. 8, 1939; s. Edwin Frederick and Mary Winifred O'Brien. BA, St. Joseph's Sem., Yonkers, NY, 1961, MDiv, 1964, MA, 1965; STD, Angelicum Univ., Rome, 1976. Ordained priest Archdiocese of NY, 1965, vice chancellor, 1976—81, dir. comm., 1981—83, sec. Cardinals Terence Cooke, John O'Connor, 1983—85, aux. bishop, 1996—97; parish priest, chaplain US Mil. Acad., West Point, NY, 1965—70; commd. 2d lt. US Army, 1970, advanced through grades to capt., 1973; chaplain 82nd Airborne Divsn., Ft. Bragg, NC, 1970—71, 173rd Airborne Brigade, 1st Cavalry Brigade, Vietnam, 1971—72; post chaplain Ft. Gordon, Ga., 1972—73; assoc. pastor St. Patrick's Cathedral, NYC, 1976—81; rector St. Joseph's Sem., Dunwoodie, NY, 1985—89, 1994—97, Pontifical North America Coll., Rome, 1990—94; ordained bishop, 1996; coadjutor archbishop Ordinariate of USA Military, Washington, 1997, archbishop, 1997—2007, Archdiocese of Balt., Md., 2007—. Bd. dirs. Nat. Conf. Cath. Bishops, Basilica Nat. Shrine Immaculate Conception; Trustee St. Joseph's Sem., Pontifical Coll. Josephinum; chmn. bd, trustees Pontifical North American Coll. Mem.: Fellowship Cath. Scholars. Roman Catholic. Office: Archdiocese of Balt 320 Cathedral St Baltimore MD 21201

O'BRIEN, ELMER JOHN, librarian, educator; b. Kemmerer, Wyo., Apr. 8, 1932; s. Ernest and Emily Catherine (Reinhart) O'B.; m. Betty Alice Peterson, July 2, 1966. AB, Birmingham So. Coll., 1954; Th.M., Iliff Sch. Theology, 1957; MA, U. Denver, 1961. Ordained to ministry Methodist Ch., 1957; pastor Meth. Ch., Pagosa Springs, Colo., 1957—60; circulation-reference librarian Boston U. Sch. Theology, 1961—65; asst. librarian Garrett-Evang. Theol. Sem., Evanston, Ill., 1965—69; librarian, prof. United Theol. Sem., Dayton, Ohio, 1969—96, prof. emeritus, 1996—; abstractor Am. Bibliog. Center, 1969—73; dir. Ctr. for Evang. United Brethren Heritage, 1979—96; acting libr. Iliff Sch. Theology, 2000—01. Chmn. div. exec. com. Dayton-Miami Valley Libr. Consortium, 1983-84; rsch. assoc. Am. Antiquarian Soc., 1990. Author: Bibliography of Festschriften in Religion Published Since 1960, 1972, Religion Index Two: Festschriften, 1960-69; contbg. author: Communication and Change in American Religious History, 1993, Essays in Celebration of the First Fifty Years, 1996; pub. Meth. Revs. Index, 1818-1985, 1989-91; contbr. articles to profl. jours. Recipient theol. and scholarship award Assn. Theol. Schs. in U.S. and Can., 1990-91; Libr. Staff Devel. grant Assn. Theol. Schs. in U.S. and Can.,

1976-77, Rsch. grant United Meth. Ch. Bd. Higher Edn. and Ministry, 1984-85 Mem. ALA, Acad. Libr. Assn. Ohio, Am. Theol. Libr. Assn. (head bur. personnel and placement 1969-73, dir. 1973-76, v.p. 1977-78, pres. 1978-79), Am. Antiquarian Soc. (rsch. assoc. 1990), Delta Sigma Phi, Omicron Delta Kappa, Eta Sigma Phi, Kappa Phi Kappa. Clubs: Torch Internat. (v.p. Dayton club 1981-82, pres. 1982-83). Home: 4840 Thunderbird Dr Apt 281 Boulder CO 80303-3829 Personal E-mail: ejobr@aol.com.

O'BRIEN, EVA FROMM, lawyer; b. Herne, Germany, May 6, 1956; came to U.S., 1959; d. Georg and Eva (Aust) F.; m. John J. O'Brien, Feb. 12, 2000. BS in Chem. Engring., Syracuse U., 1978; JD, U. Houston, 1985. Bar: Tex. 1985, U.S. Dist. Ct. (so. dist.) Tex. 1987, U.S. Ct. Appeals (5th cir.) 1997. Engr. Chrysler Corp., Deer Park, Mich., 1978-79; process engr. Mobay Chem. Co., Baytown, Tex., 1980, ETI Engrs. Inc., Houston, 1981-82; engr. Petromas Inc., Houston, 1982-83; sr. chem. engr. NUS Corp., Houston, 1983-84; briefing clk., assoc. Hill Parker Franklin Cardwell & Jones, Houston, 1985-86; assoc. Fulbright & Jaworski LLP, Houston, 1986-93, ptnr., 1994—, and head, environ. law dept. Author, editor: Texas Environmental Law Handbook, 1989, 5th edit., 2000, (book chpt.) Environmental Aspects of Real Estate Transactions, 2d edit., 1999. Mem. ABA (co-chair real estate and probate sect., underground storage tank and RCRA com. 1994-95), Houston Bar Assn. (co-chair legal line com. 1988-90; sec. environ. law sect. 1991, vice-chair 1992, chair 1993). Office: Fulbright & Jaworski LLP 1301 McKinney St Ste 5100 Houston TX 77010-3031 Office Phone: 713-651-5151. Office Fax: 713-651-5246. Business E-Mail: eobrien@fulbright.com.

O'BRIEN, GEORGE DENNIS, retired academic administrator; b. Chgo., Feb. 21, 1931; s. George Francis and Helen (Fehlandt) O'B.; m. Judith Alyce Johnson, June 21, 1958; children: Elizabeth Belle, Juliana Helen, Victoria Alyce. AB in English, Yale, 1952; PhD in Philosophy, U. Chgo., 1961. Tchr. humanities, Carnegie rsch. fellow U. Chgo., 1956-57; from instr. to asst. prof., asst. dean Princeton (N.J.) U., 1958-65; on leave in Athens, Greece, 1963-64; spl. honors seminars LaSalle Coll., spring 1963, fall 1964, spring 1965; assoc. prof. philosophy Middlebury (Vt.) Coll., 1965-71, prof., 1971-76, dean of men, 1965-67, dean of coll., 1967-74, dean faculty, 1975-76; pres. Bucknell U., 1976-84, U. Rochester, NY, 1984-94; ret., 1994. Author: Hegel on Reason in History, 1975, God and the New Haven Railway, 1986, What to Expect from College, 1991, All the Essential Half-Truths About Higher Education, 1997, The Idea of a Catholic University, 2002, Finding The Voice Of The Church 2007; contbr. articles to profl. jours. Trustee LaSalle Coll., Phila., 1965—2009; bd. dirs. Union Theol. Sem., 1985-90, Rsch. Librs. Group, 1994-96; chair Commonweal Found., 2002—. Fellow Am. Coun. Learned Socs., London, 1971-72; Nat. Phi Beta Kappa scholar, 1996-97. Mem. Am. Philos. Assn., Phi Beta Kappa. Home: 153 Wildflower Ln Middlebury VT 05753-9172 Office Phone: 802-388-1376. Business E-Mail: gdob@middlebury.edu.

O'BRIEN, GERALD JAMES, utilities executive; b. St. Paul, May 1, 1923; s. Dewey Joseph and Henrietta Elizabeth O'B.; m. Patricia Margaret McCorison, Feb. 23, 1946; children: Kathleen, Thomas, John, Andrew. Student, St. Thomas Coll., 1940-41, 45-46; B.C.S., Drake U., 1948. Staff acct. Haskins & Sells, Mpls., 1948-50; with Donovan Cos., Inc., St. Paul, 1950-81, sec., asst. treas., 1977-81; utility rate cons., 1981-84. Dir. Alumbaugh Coal Co., Donovan Constrn. Co., So. Tier Gas Corp., Gas Distbrs. Info. Service. Served with U.S. Army, 1942-45. Decorated Purple Heart. Address: 11111 River Hills Dr Apt 234 Burnsville MN 55337

O'BRIEN, GRACE WILHELMINA EHLIG, retired educational administrator, genealogical consultant, psychologist, writer; b. Los Angeles, Aug. 27, 1922; d. Max Carl and Janette (Rentchler) Ehlig; AA, Pasadena City Coll., 1942; BA, UCLA, 1944, postgrad., 1944-46; postgrad. Riverside City Coll., 1946; postgrad. Calif. State U., LA, 1954-66, 68-78, MA in Guidance, 1964; m. Louis J. O'Brien, Nov. 8, 1947; children: Carol Jean, Lawrence John, Perry Lewis. Tchr., Perris Union HS, Calif., 1945-46; tchr., counselor, psychometrist, psychologist LA City Schs., 1946-66, cons. counselor, sch. psychologist Elem. Secondary Edn. Act, Edn. and Guidance program, 1966-68; head counselor, asst. prin. Garden Gate Opportunity Sch., 1968-73; vice prin. Markham Jr. HS, 1973, Belvedere Jr. HS, 1974; asst. prin. Garfield HS, 1974-75, Mt. Vernon Jr. HS, 1975-76, Gage Jr. HS, 1976-77; prin. Garden Gate HS, 1977-80, Johnson HS, 1980-84; LDS libr. and tchr, 1984-05; geneal. cons., 1984-. Den mother chmn. Cub Scouts, 1964-66. Recipient Spl. Svc. award Boy Scouts, 1964. Mem. DAR (regent, Dist. X Dir., treas.), Daus. of Am. Colonists (bd. dirs. 1994—), Calif. Tchrs. Assn., UCLA Alumni Assn., Associated Adminstrn. LA, Calif. Assn. Sch. Adminstrs., Phi Delta Kappa, Pi Lambda Theta, Chi Delta Phi. Presbyterian (supt. Sunday sch. 1953-54). Home: 3880 Shadow Grove Rd Pasadena CA 91107-2240 Personal E-mail: ljobrien@earthlink.net.

O'BRIEN, GREGORY MICHAEL ST. LAWRENCE, academic administrator; b. NYC, Oct. 7, 1944; s. Henry Joseph and Mary Agnes (McGoldrick) O'B.; m. Mary K. McLaughlin, Dec. 28, 1968; children: Jennifer Jane, Meredith Kathleen. BA with honors, Lehigh U., 1966; MA, Boston U., 1968, PhD, 1969. Assoc. in psychology Lab. Community Psychology, Harvard Med. Sch., Boston; dir. Human Svcs. Design Lab., Sch. Applied Social Scis., Case Western Res. U., Cleve., 1970-74; dean, prof. Sch. Social Welfare, U. Wis., Milw., 1974-78; provost, prof. psychology U. Mich.-Flint, 1978-80; prof. social work and psychology, v.p. acad. affairs U. South Fla., Tampa, 1980-83, provost, 1983-87, prof. mgmt., 1986-87; chancellor U. New Orleans, 1987—2003; interim supr. New Orleans Paris Schs., 1999; pres. Argosy U. Sys., 2004—07, pres. emeritus, 2008—. Bd. dirs. WLAE-TV (PBS), Bank One New Orleans Region, Entergy New Orleans, Nat. Coalition for Advanced Mfg., Nat. Assn. State Univs. and Land-Grant Colls. Contbr. chpts. to books, articles to profl. jours. State of La. Econ. Devel. Coun., 1997—; vice chmn. State of La. Film and Video Commn., 1993-94, mem., 1993-2003; chmn. Metro. Coun. Govts. MetroVision, 1992-1994; adv. mem. Bus. Coun. New Orleans and the River Region; bd. dirs. The Chamber/New Orleans and the River Region, 1988-2003; mem. Kellogg Commn. on Future of Land Grant Colls. and State Univs., 1996-1998. NIMH fellow, 1968-69 Fellow Am. Coll. Mental Health Adminstrs. (founding fellow, pres. 1984-86); mem. NCAA (chair pres. commn. 1992-93), Nat. Assn. Social Workers, Nat. Conf. Social Welfare, Soc. Gen. Systems Research, Am. Psychol. Assn., Am. Public Health Assn., Metrovision Partnership Found. (1992-93), Council Social Work Edn, (presdl. task force on structure of assn.), Indsl. Relations Research Assn. Roman Catholic. Office: 900 Gulf Shore Dr # 1022 Destin FL 32541 Home: 900 Gulf Shore Dr Unit 1022 Destin FL 32541-3208

O'BRIEN, J. WILLARD, lawyer, educator; b. NYC, Oct. 19, 1930; s. J. Willard and Anna C. (Carroll) O.'B.; m. Peggy J. O'Brien. BS, Fordham U., 1952, JD, 1957. Bar: N.Y. 1957. Assoc. Cahill, Gordon, Reindel & Ohl, NYC, 1957-62; asst. prof. law Syracuse U. Coll. Law, 1962-65; prof. law Villanova (Pa.) U. Sch. Law, 1965-98, dean, 1972-83, dir. Connelly Inst. Law and Morality, 1983-95, dean and prof. of law emeritus, 1998—. Mem. Pa. Fed. Jud. Nominating Commn., 1977-80, vice chmn., 1978-80; mem. Pa. Law and Justice Inst., 1972-73, chmn. exec. com., 1973-75, pres., 1975-77 Editor-in-chief Fordham Law Rev, 1956-57. Bd. dirs. Nat. Inst. on Holocaust, 1984-85; bd. dirs. Phila. Coordinating Council on the Holocaust, 1983—2003. Served with USAF, 1952-54; Served with N.Y. Air N.G., 1954-58. Mem.: ABA, Pa. Bar Assn. Roman Catholic.

O'BRIEN, JACK GEORGE, artistic director; b. Saginaw, Mich., June 18, 1939; s. J. George and Evelyn (MacArthur Martens) O'B. AB, U. Mich., 1961, MA, 1962. Asst. dir. APA Repertory Theatre, NYC, 1963-67, asso. dir., 1967-69; worked with San Diego Nat. Shakespeare Festival, 1969-82, A.C.T., 1970-80, Loretto Hilton, 1975, Ahmanson, Los Angeles, 1978-80, San Francisco Opera, Houston Grand Opera, Washington Opera Soc.; artistic dir. N.Y.C. Opera, 1982, Old Globe Theatre, San Diego, 1981—. Dir.: (Broadway plays) Cock-A-Doodle Dandy, 1969, The Time of Your Life, 1975, Porgy and Bess, 1976, 1983, The Most Happy Fella, 1979, Two Shakespearean Actors, 1992, Damn Yankees, 1994—95, Getting Away With Murder, 1996, The Little Foxes, 1997, More to Love, 1998, The Full Monty, 2000—02 (Tony nom. best dir. of a musical, 2001), Imaginary Friends, 2003, Hairspray, 2002 (Tony award best dir. of a musical, 2003), Henry IV, 2003—04 (Tony award best dir. of a play, 2004), The Coast of Utopia, 2006 (Outer Critics Cir. award outstanding dir. of a musical, 2007, Tony award best dir. of a play, 2007, Drama Desk award outstanding dir. of a play, 2007); art. dir. (Broadway plays) Into the Woods, 1987—89, Rumors, 1988—90, The Piano Lesson, 1990—91, Two Trains Running, 1992, Redwood Curtain, 1993, Play On!, 1997, Oldest Living Confederate Widow Tells All, 2003. Mem. Actors' Equity, Am. Soc. Composers and Performers, Soc. Stage Dirs. and Choreographers, Dirs. Guild Am. Office: Old Globe Theatre PO Box 122171 San Diego CA 92112-2171

O'BRIEN, JAMES EDWARD, surgeon; b. Hartford, Conn., June 15, 1963; s. James Edward and Joan O'Brien; m. Lina Maheswata Pattanayak, Jan. 10, 1998; children: Lauren Maya, Connor Rajan, Christine Mira. BS, Rensselaer Polytechnic Inst., Troy, NY, 1985; MD, U. Conn., Farmington, 1989. Resident Thomas Jefferson U. Hosp., 1989—99, Children's Hosp. Phila., 1999—2001; pediatric cardiothoracic surgeon Children's Mercy Hosp., Kans. City, Mo., 2001—. Contbr. articles to profl. jours. Fellow: ACS; mem.: AMA, So. Thoracic Surg. Assn., Am. Heart Assn., Soc. Thoracic Surgeons. Avocations: swimming, golf, travel. Office: Children's Mercy Hosp 2401 Gillham Rd Kansas City MO 64108 Office Fax: 816-802-1245. Business E-Mail: jobrien@cmh.edu.

O'BRIEN, JAMES J., manufacturing executive; b. Circleville, Ohio; Degree in Acctg., Fin., Ohio State U., MBA. Exec. asst. to chmn. Ashland Inc., 1992—94; v.p., gen. mgr. branded mktg. Ashland Petroleum Co., 1994; v.p. Ashland Inc.; pres. Valvoline, 1995—2001; with Ashland Inc., 1976—, sr. v.p., 1997, group oper. officer, pres., COO, 2002, chmn., CEO, 2002—. Bd. dir. Humana Inc., 2006—. Nat. bd. dirs. Big Bros. Big Sisters Am.; adv. bd. sch. bus. Ohio State U.; chmn. bd. trustees Midway Coll. Ky. Mem.: Am. Chemistry Coun., Assn. Governing Bds. Univ. Colls. Office: 50 E River Ctr Blvd Covington KY 41012-0391

O'BRIEN, JAMES JEROME, construction management consultant; b. Phila., Oct. 20, 1929; s. Sylvester Jerome and Emma Belle Filer (Fulforth) O'B.; m. Carmen Hiester, June 10, 1952 (div. Aug. 1, 1984); children: Jessica, Michael, David; m. Rita F. Gibson, Nov. 1, 1984 BCE, Cornell U., 1952; postgrad., U. Houston, 1957-58. Registered profl. engr., NY, NJ, Pa., Ga. Project engr. Rohm & Haas, Phila. and Tex., 1955-59, RCA Corp., Moorestown, NJ, 1959-62; cons. Mauchly Assocs., Fort Washington, Pa., 1962-65; founding ptnr., exec. v.p. Meridian Engring. Co., Phila., 1965-68; pres. MDC Systems, Cherry Hill, 1968-72; ptnr. James J. O'Brien P.E., Cherry Hill, 1972-77; pres. O'Brien-Kreitzberg & Assocs., NYC, Pennsauken, San Francisco, 1977-80, chief exec. officer, 1980-89, chmn. bd. dirs., 1989-93, vice chmn., 1993—2002; cons. in field, 2002; prin. James J. O'Brien P.E., 2003—. Author: CPM in Construction Management-Scheduling by the Critical Path Method, 1965; co-author: CPM in Construction Management-Project Management with CPM, 7th edit., 2009, Management Information Systems-Concepts, Techniques and Applications, 1970, Management with Computers, 1972, Construction Inspection Handbook, 1974, 4th edit., 1997, Value Analysis in Design and Construction, 1976, Construction Delay-Risks, Rsponsibilities and Litigation, 1976, Preconstruction Estimating: Budget to Bid, 1994, Construction Documentation, 3d edit., 1995; co-author: Construction Management: A Professional Approach, 1974; editor: Recollections (L.D. Miles), 1987; author, editor: Scheduling Handbook, 1969, Contractor's Management Handbook, 1971, 2d edit., 1990, Standard Handbook of Heavy Construction, 3d edit., 1996, Construction Change Orders, 1998; contbr. articles to profl. jours. Lt. USN, 1952—55. Recipient Profl. Mgr. award, N.Y. Chpt. Soc. Advancement Mgmt., 1969. Fellow: ASCE (v.p. 1985, pres. South Jersey br. 1985, pres. NJ sect. 1987—89, com. on quality in civil engring. profession 1990—97, Constrn. Mgmt. award 1976, Disting. Engr. South Jersey br. 1986), Cornell Soc. Engrs. (dean's adv. com. sch. civil and environ. engring. 1986—87), Const. Mgmt. Assn. Am. (bd. dirs. 1990—92, Fellow award 1993, Constrn. Mgr. of Yr. award NY-NJ chpt. 1994, Ch. Time Mgt. Com 2008), Project Mgmt. Inst. (sec. 1971, v.p. 1972, pres. 1973, chmn. bd. 1974—75, project mgmt. profl. 1984, v.p. edn. 2002—08, editor Time Mgmt. chpt. PMBOK 3d edit. 2004, charter mem. Coll. Scheduling, award for contbn. to project mgmt. 1983, Fellow award 1989, Coll. Scheduling 1st Jim O'Brien Achievement in Life award 2005); mem.: Regional Alliance Small Contractors (bd. dirs. 1989—95), Port Authority NY and NJ, Miles Value Found. (bd. dirs. 1987—90, trustee 1990—99, bd. dirs. 1999), Soc. Am. Value Engrs. (v.p. NE region 1986—87, cert. value specialist, Fallon Value-in-Life award 1993, fellow 2005), Chi Epsilon, Tau Beta Pi. Home and Office: 2 Linden Ave Riverton NJ 08077-1124 Office Phone: 856-786-8287. Personal E-mail: jimobriendd527@aol.com.

O'BRIEN, JAMES PHILLIP, lawyer; b. Monmouth, Ill., Jan. 6, 1949; s. John Matthew and Roberta Helen (Cavanaugh) O'B.; m. Laurene Reason, Aug. 30, 1969 (div. 1980); m. Lynn Florsheim, Sept. 5, 1987 (dec. May 2005). BA, Western Ill. U., 1971; JD, U. Ill., 1974. Bar: Ill. 1974. Asst. atty. gen. State Ill., Springfield, 1974-75; jud. clerk Ill. Appellate Ct., Springfield, 1975-76; assoc. Graham & Graham, Springfield, 1976-81; corp. counsel Am. Hosp. Assn., Chgo., 1981-84; ptnr., chmn. health care dept. Katten, Muchin Rosenman, Chgo., 1984—. Task force med. malpractice reform legislation Am. Hosp. Assn., 1983-84, tax adv. com., 1987-91, tax reporting and compliance com., 1990-91; spkr. in field. Contbr. numerous articles to profl. jours. Recipient cert. recognition Ill. Dept. Children and Family Svcs., 1981; Edward Arthur Mellinger Found. scholar, Western Ill. U. 1971. Mem.: Am. Arbitration Assn. (Task Force Health Care Dispute Resolution 1982—84), Am. Health Lawyers Assn. Office: Katten Muchin Rosenman 525 W Monroe St Ste 1900 Chicago IL 60661-3693 Home Phone: 312-943-9460; Office Phone: 312-902-5630. Business E-Mail: phillip.obrien@kattenlaw.com.

O'BRIEN, JANE MARGARET, academic administrator; b. Washington, Nov. 17, 1953; d. Thomas and Edith (Pedersen) O'B; m. James A. Grube, June 28, 1975; children: William Howard Grube-O'Brien, Harold Thomas Grube O'Brien. BS in Biochemistry, Vassar Coll., 1975; PhD in Chemistry, U. Del., 1981. Rsch. asst. U. Vt., Burlington, 1978-79; asst. prof. chemistry Middlebury (Vt.) Coll., 1980-88, assoc. provost, 1988-89, assoc. prof. chemistry, 1988-91, dean of faculty, 1989-91; pres. Hollins Coll., Roanoke, Va., 1991—96, St. Mary's Coll., Md., 1996—. Ednl. chmn. biology task force New Eng. Consortium Undergraduate Sci., 1988-91; project mgr. H. Hughes Med. Inst. Instl. Awards, 1988-91; mem. steering com. Sloan New Liberal Arts Initiative, 1988-91; bd. dir. Norfolk Southern Corp., So. Md. Navy Alliance, Nat. Outdoor Leadership Sch.; mem. NCAA Div. III Pres. Council. Implementation com. Vermont EPSCoR, 1989-91; bd. dirs. Coun. Ind. Colls. in Va., 1991-96, Va. Found. for Ind. Colls., 1991-96; ednl. adv. com. Rainforest All, 1991—; bd. dir. Md. Citizens for the Arts Found., Univ. Mobility. Grad. fellow U. Del., 1975-76, Kellogg fellow W.K. Kellogg Found., 1989-92, Internat. fellow Assoc. Am. Colls., 1990-91, Regional fellow finalist White House Fellowship, 1991; Eisenhower Fellow, 1999. Mem.: Phi Beta Kappa, Sigma Xi. Office: St Mary's College Office of the President 18952 E Fisher Rd Saint Marys City MD 20686-3001

O'BRIEN, JIM, professional basketball coach; b. Phila., Feb. 11, 1952; m. Sharon O'Brien; children: Jack, Shannon, Caitlyn. B in Mgmt. & Mktg., St. Joseph's U., 1974; MBA, U. Md., 1981. Asst. coach Wheeling Jesuit Coll., 1974—75, Pembroke State Coll., 1975—76, U. Md., 1976—77, St. Joseph's U., 1977—78, U. Oreg., 1978—82, NY Knicks, 1987—88, U. Ky., 1994—97; head coach Wheeling Jesuit Coll., 1982—87, U. Dayton, 1989—94; interim head coach Boston Celtics, 2001, head coach, 2001—04, Phila. 76ers, 2004—05, Ind. Pacers, 2007—. Recipient Markward award, 1970; named to St. Joseph's U. Hall of Fame, 1988, Big Five Hall of Fame, 1989. Office: Ind Pacers 125 S Pennsylvania St Indianapolis IN 46204*

O'BRIEN, JOHN FEIGHAN, investment banker; b. Cleve., Aug. 8, 1936; s. Francis John and Ann (Feighan) O'B.; m. Regina Quaid Harahan, June 27, 1959 (div. 1976); children: Regina, Victoria, Julie, John Jr.; m. Marilyn E. Schreiner, 1977. BS, Georgetown U., 1958. Salesman Appliance Mart, Cleve., 1958-59, ptnr., 1960-66; investment broker McDonald & Co. Investments, Cleve., 1966-71, ptnr., 1971-83, exec. v.p., 1983-88, mng. dir., 1988-91, sr. mng. dir., 1993—2007; investment assoc. UBS, 2007—. Bd. dirs. Hitchcock House, Cleve., 1978-89, Recovery Resources; chmn. Alcoholism Svcs. of Cleve., 1989-92, Alcohol and Drug-Addiction Svcs. Bd. of Cuyahoga County, 1992-98; trustee St. Edward H.S., Lakewood, Ohio, Alumnus of Yr., 1997, chmn. capital campaign, 1993-95; grand jury foreman Cuyahoga County, 2000. Named Good Fellow of Yr., Irish Good Fellows Club Cleve., 1996, Benefactor of Yr., St. Edward HS, 2003. Mem. Leadership Cleve., Greater Cleve. Growth Assn., Georgetown U. Alumni Assn. (alumni bd. senator, John Carroll award 1999), Cleve. Yacht Club, Lago Mar Club, Stella Maris (bd. mem., 2007-). Home (Winter): 1800 S Ocean Dr Fort Lauderdale FL 33316-3704 Office: UB5 Investments 18500 Lake Rd Ste 300 Rocky River OH 44116-1744 Personal E-mail: jfeighanob@aol.com.

O'BRIEN, JOHN WILFRID, economist, educator, retired university president; b. Toronto, Ont., Can., Aug. 4, 1931; s. Wilfred Edmond and Audrey (Swain) O'B.; m. Joyce Helen Bennett, Aug. 4, 1956; children: Margaret Anne, Catherine Audrey. BA, McGill U., 1953, MA, 1955, PhD, 1962, LLD, 1976; postgrad., Inst. Polit. Studies, Paris, 1954; DCL, Bishop's U., 1976; LLD, Concordia U., 2004. Lectr. econs. Sir George Williams U., Montreal, 1954-57, asst. prof., 1957-61, assoc. prof., 1961-63, asst. dean U., 1961-63, dean arts, 1963-68, vice-prin. acad., 1968-69, prof., 1965-96, prin., vice chancellor, pres., 1969-74; rector, vice chancellor, pres. Concordia U., Montreal, 1974-84, rector emeritus, 1984—. Provincial ednl. TV com. Dept. Edn. Que., 1962-66, dep. chmn., 1965-66, mem. tchr. tng. planning com., 1964-66; mem. Gauthier Ad Hoc Com., Univ. Operating Budgets, 1965-68, Council Univs., 1969-76; pres. Conf. Rectors and Prins. Que. Univs., 1974-77; mem. council Assn. Commonwealth Univs., 1975-78; bd. dirs. Assn. Univs. and Colls., Can., 1977-79; mem. Conseil Consultatif sur l'Immigration, Que. Gov., 1977-79, Corp. Higher Edn. Forum, 1983-84; bd. govs. Montreal YMCA, 1969-89, Vanier Coll., 1975-79, Fraser-Hickson Inst., 1975-00, pres. 1989-92, Que. div. Can. Mental Health Assn., 1977-79, Montreal World Film Festival, 1985-2004; sec., treas., Cinematheque Can., 1988-96, bd. dirs.; sec., treas. World Film Fest. Found., 1989-96; exec. mem. Alliance Que., 1989-96, chmn., 1990-96, bd. dirs.; hon. mem. Corp. Higher Edn. Forum, 1984-00; hon. v.p. Que. Provincial council Boy Scouts Can., 1974-90; hon. councillor Montreal Mus. Fine Arts, 1969-2003. Author: Canadian Money and Banking, 1964, (with G. Lermer) 2d edit., 1969.

O'BRIEN, JOHN WILLIAM, JR., management consultant; b. Bronx, NY, Jan. 1, 1937; BS, MIT, 1958; MS, UCLA, 1964. Sr. assoc. Planning Rsch. Corp., LA, 1962—67; dir. fin. systems group Synergetic Scis., Inc., Tarzana, Calif., 1967—70; dir. analytical svcs. divsn. James H. Oliphant & Co., LA, 1970—72; chmn. bd., CEO, pres. Wilshire Assocs. (formerly O'Brien Assocs. Inc.), Santa Monica, Calif., 1972—75; v.p. A.G. Becker Inc., 1975—81; chmn., CEO Leland O'Brien Rubinstein Assocs., 1981—97; mng. dir. Credit Suisse Asset Mgmt., NYC, 1997—2000; adj. prof. fin. U. Calif. Berkeley Haas Sch. Bus., 2000—. Recipient Graham and Dodd award Fin. Analysts Fedn., 1970, Matthew McArthur award Investment Mgmt. Consultants Assn., 2004; named Businessman of Yr. Fortune Mag., 1987. Mem.: Delta Upsilon. Home: 119 Jasmine Creek Dr Corona Del Mar CA 92625-1418 Office Phone: 510-643-1396. Personal E-mail: obrien@jwobrien.com. Business E-Mail: obrien@haas.berkeley.edu.

O'BRIEN, KENNETH PAUL, historian, educator; b. NYC, Oct. 26, 1943; s. Patrick Cornelius and Dorothy May O'Brien; m. Diane Barbara Stiso, Sept. 10, 1966; 1 child, Meghan Kathleen Doherty. PhD, Northwestern U., Evanston, Ill., 1970. Assoc. prof. history SUNY Coll., 1985—, dir., coll. honors program, 2001—. Contbr. chapters to books. Recipient SUNY Chancellor's award, SUNY, 1981, 2006, Edward Winslow award, NY State Historian's Office, 1994. Mem.: SUNY Faculty Senate (senator 2003—, pres. 2000—02). Avocations: golf, basketball, movies. Home: 17 Carolin Dr Brockport NY 14420 Office: SUNY Coll Brockport Honors 219 Holmes Hall Brockport NY 14420 Business E-Mail: kobrien@brockport.edu.

O'BRIEN, KEVIN D., medical educator; BS summa cum laude, U. Idaho, 1980; MD honors, U. Wash., 1984. Diplomate Am. Bd. Internal Medicine, Cardiovascular Diseases Am. Bd. Internal Medicine. Intern, resident U. Wash., Seattle, 1984—87, chief med. resident, 1987—88, prof., medicine, 2008—; atteding physician U. Wash. Med. Ctr., Seattle, 1988—. Med. student rsch. fellow Fred Hutchinson Cancer rsch. Ctr., Seattle, 1981. Contbr. articles to profl. jours. Recipient Sheard-Sanford award, Am. Soc. Clin. Pathologists, 1983. Fellow: Am. Heart Assn.; mem.: Western Soc. Clin. Investigation (pres. 2007—, councilor 2003—06, Outstanding Investigator award 2003), Am. Fedn. Med.

Rsch. (pres. 2001—02, found. pres. 2002—03). Office: Univ Wash Med Ctr Campus Box 356422 1959 NE Pacific St Seattle WA 98195-6422 Office Phone: 206-685-3930. Business E-Mail: cardiac@u.washington.edu.

O'BRIEN, KEVIN JAMES, museum director; b. St. Cloud, Minn., 1954; m. Grace Benedict. BFA, U. Notre Dame, 1977; MFA, Tulane U., 1979. Dir. Community Ctr. for Arts, Michigan City, Ind., 1981-85, So. Ohio Mus. and Cultural Ctr., Ohio Arts Coun., 1985-88, Pensacola (Fla.) Mus. Art/Fla. Arts Coun., 1988-91, Everhart Mus., Scranton, Pa., 1991, Pa. Coun. Arts, 1994; exec. dir. Key West Art & Hist. Soc., 1995—2000, Tippecanoe County Hist. Assn., Lafayette, Ky. Mus. Art and Craft, Louisville, 2006—. Office: Ky Mus Art and Craft 715 W Main St Louisville KY 40202 Office Phone: 502-589-0155 ext. 201. Business E-Mail: kevinobrien@kentuckyarts.org.

O'BRIEN, LAWRENCE FRANCIS, III, (LARRY O'BRIEN), lobbyist, lawyer; b. Springfield, Mass., Dec. 31, 1945; s. Lawrence Francis and Elva (Brassard) O'Brien; m. Helen Marie Powell; children: Lawrence L., Peter F. BA, Harvard U., 1967; JD, Columbia U., 1972. Bar: NY 1973, DC 1979. Assoc. atty. Breed, Abbott & Morgan, NYC, 1972-77; dep. tax. asst., sec. treas. US Treas. Dept., Washington, 1977-79; ptnr. Breed, Abbott & Morgan, Washington, 1979-83, Dewey, Ballantine, Bushby, Palmer & Wood, Washington, 1983-93, O'Brien Calio, Washington, 1993—2001, OB-C Group LLC, Washington, 2001—. Served to 1st lt. US Army, 1968-70. Democrat. Roman Catholic. Office: OB-C Group LLC 1350 I St NW Washington DC 20005*

O'BRIEN, MARK STEPHEN, pediatric neurosurgeon; b. West New York, NJ, Jan. 2, 1933; s. Mark Peter and Hannah (Dempsey) O'B.; m. Mary Morris Johnson, June 3, 1961 (div.); children: David, Derek, Marcia; m. Karen-Marie Sampson, June 1, 1984; children: Blythe, Blake, Lauren-Blair, Connor. AB cum laude, Seton Hall U., 1955; MD, St. Louis U., 1959. Diplomate Am. Bd. Neurol. Surgery, Am. Bd. Pediat. Neurol. Surgery. Intern St. John's Hosp., St. Louis, 1959-60, resident in surgery, 1960; resident in neurology Charity Hosp., New Orleans, 1962-63; resident in neurosurgery St. Vincent's Hosp., NYC, 1963-64, resident in surgery, 1965; sr. resident, chief resident Cin. Children's Hosp., U. Cin., 1965-68, research fellow in neurosurgery, 1966-67, 67-68; NIH spl. fellow in neuroradiology Albert Einstein Coll. Medicine, NYC, 1968-69; mem. faculty dept. surgery Emory U. Sch. Medicine, Atlanta, 1969—2003, prof. surgery, assoc. prof. pediatrics, 1979—2003; chief neurosurgery Henrietta Egleston Hosp. for Children, Atlanta, 1971—2003; prof. neurosurgery U. Ark. for Med. Scis., Little Rock, 2005—. Trustee Elaine Clark Center for Exceptional Children; mem. med. adv. bd. Nat. Found., March of Dimes; trustee Henrietta Egleston Hosp. for Children; mem. profl. adv. panel Spina Bifida Assn. Am. Editorial bd. Pediatric Neurosurgery; contbr. chpts. to books, articles to med. jours. Served with USNR, 1960-62. Mem. Am. Assn. Neurol. Surgeons, Soc. Neurol. Surgeons, Congress Neurol. Surgeons, Internat. Soc. Pediatric Neurosurgery, Greater Atlanta Pediatric Soc., Med. Soc. Atlanta, AMA, ACS, Ga. Neurosurg. Soc., Am. Acad. Pediatrics, Am. Soc. Pediatric Neurosurgery, Pediatric Oncology Group, Am. Bd. Pediatric Neurol. Surgery (sec.), Acad. Pediatric Neurosurgeons. Home: 5720 Hawthorne Rd Little Rock AR 72207 Office: Ark Childrens Hosp 800 Marshall St Slot 838 Little Rock AR 72202 Office Phone: 501-364-1448. Personal E-mail: mobrien33@aol.com. Business E-Mail: obrienmark@uams.edu.

O'BRIEN, MARY DEVON, communications executive, consultant; b. Buenos Aires, Feb. 13, 1944; came to U.S., 1949, naturalized, 1962; d. George Earle and Margaret Frances (Richards) Owen; m. Gordon Covert O'Brien, Feb. 16, 1962 (div. Aug. 1982); children: Christopher Covert, Devon Elizabeth; m. Christopher Gerard Smith, May 28, 1983 BA, Rutgers U., 1975, MBA, 1976. Project mgmt. cert., 1989. Contr. manpower Def. Comm. divsn. ITT, Nutley, NJ, 1977-80, adminstr. program, 1977-78, mgr. cost, schedule control, 1978-79, voice processing project, 1979-80; mgr. project Avionics divsn. ITT, Nutley, 1980-81, sr. mgr. projects, 1981-93, cons. strategic planning, 1983-95; pres. Anamex, Inc., 1995—. Bd. trustees South Mountain Counseling Ctr., 1987-98, chmn. bd. trustees, 1994—; bd. dir. N.J. Eye Inst.; session leader Internet Conf., Florence, Italy, 1992; session moderator, panel mem. MES Conf., Cairo, Egypt, 1993, spkr., session leader Vancouver, 1994, keynote spkr. New Zealand, 1995; lectr. in field Author: Pace: System Manual, 1979, Voices, 1982; contbr. articles to profl. jours. and Maplewood Community calendar. Chmn. Citizens Budget Adv. Com., Maplewood, N.J., 1984-87, chmn. recreation, libr., pub. svcs., 1982-83, 94-96, chmn. pub. safety, emergency svcs., 1983-84, chmn. schs. and edn., 1984-85, chmn. gen. gov. and fin., 1998-2000; first v.p. Maplewood Civic Assn., 1987-89, pres., 1989-91, 2000—, sec. 1993-94, bd. dirs., officer, 1984—; chmn. Maple Leaf Svc. award Com., 1987-89, 94—, Community Svc. Coun. of Oranges and Maplewood Homelessness, Affordable Housing, Shelter Com., 1988—; chmn. speaker's bur. United Way, 1989-93; bd. trustees United Way Essex and West Hudson Cmty. Svc. Coun., 1988—; v.p. mktg. United Way Community Svc. Coun. of Oranges and Maplewood, 1990-93, v.p. 1994; mem. Maplewood Zoning Bd. of Adjustment, 1983-95; officer, mem. exec. bd. N.J. Project Mgmt. Inst., 1985—, pres., 1987-88, 95-2000, v.p. adminstrn., 1994-95; bd. dirs. Performance Mgmt. Assn.; chmn. Charter Com.; chmn. Internat. Project Mgmt. Inst. Jour. and Membership survey, 1986-87, mktg. com., 1986-89, long range planning and steering com., 1987—; bd. dir., vice chmn. Coun. Chpt. Pres. Interaction Com., 1986-90, chmn., 1991—, pres. Internat. Project Mgmt. Inst., 1991, chmn., 1992, v.p. Region II, 1989-90; adv. bd. Project Mgmt. Jour., 1987-90, N.J. PMI Ednl., 1987—; liaison officer, PMI internat. liaison to Australian Inst. of Project Mgmt. and Western Australia Project Mgmt. Assn.; apptd. fellow Leadership N.J., 1993—, Internat. Project Mgmt. Inst. and Performance Mgmt. Assocs.; mem. MCA/N.J. Blood Bank Drive; chmn. Maplewood Community Calendar, 1990-98; trustee community svc. coun. and edn. program United Way Essex and West Hudson, 1988—, also, chmn. leadership div., chmn. speakers bur., 1991— and mem. communications com.; mem. bd. dirs. Governing Inst. N.J.; chmn. Maplewood Rep. County Com., 1996—; chair, sec. Essex County Rep. County Com. Recipient Spl. commendation for Cmty. Svc. Twp. Maplewood, 1987; First Place award Anti-Shoplifting Program for Distributive Edn. Club Am., 1981, N.J. Fedn. of Women's Clubs, 1981, 82, Retail Mchts. Assn., 1981, 82; Commendation and Merit awards Air Force Inst. Tech., 1981; Pres.'s Safety award ITT, 1983; State award 1st Pl. N.J. Fedn. of Women's Clubs Garden Show, 1982; Cert. Spl. Merit award N.J. Fedn. of Women's Clubs, 1982, Disting. Contbn. award United Way, 1990, Pursuit of Exellence Cost Savs. Achievement award ITT Avionics, 1990, Maple Leaf award outstanding cmty. svc., 1992, Phoebe and Benjamin Shackelford award United Way, 1992, U.S. Ho. Reps. citation, 1992, N.H. Gen. Assembly Senate resolution Cmty. Leadership and Svc., 1992, resolution of Appreciation Township of Maplewood, Maplewood C. of C. Disting. Svc. award, 2005; N.J. Leadership fellow, 1993, awarded fellow of Internat. Project Mgmt. Inst., 1995. Mem. NAFE, Internat. Platform Speakers Assn., Grand Jury Assn., Telecomms. Group and Aerospace Industries Assn., Women's Career Network Assn., Nat. Security Indsl. Assn., Assn. for Info. and Image Mgmt., Internat. Project Mgmt. Inst. (liaison officer pres. 1991—, Outstanding Svc. and Contbrn. award 1986-87, Outstanding Pres. award 1988, Meritorious Svc. Recognition award 1989-1990), Performance Mgmt. Assn, Indsl. Rels. Rsch. Assn., ITT Mgmt. Assn., Rutgers Grad. Sch. Bus. Mgmt. Alumni Assn., Maplewood LWV (chair women and family issues com., voter registration bd. dir.), Maplewood Women's Evening Membership Div. (pres. 1980-82), Lions (Maplewood dir. 1992-95, program chmn. 1991-92, treas. 1994-95, N.J. dist. 16E zone gov., chmn. 1992-93, 95-96, cabinet sec. internat. dist., region chmn. 1993-94, 96-98, trustee Eye Bank N.J., internat. dist. 16-E cabinet sec. 1994-95, dist. 16-E chmn. peace poster contest 1995-99, pres. Newark 1995-97, sec. 1997—, N.J. State chmn. youth outreach and quest 1995-98, internat. dist. 16-E gov., 1999—, dist. MD16 treas., 1999—, youth oppportunities chmn. N.J dist. MD-16, coun. chmn. 2003-2004, state advisor 2004-, trustee Eye Bank of Delaware Valley, sec.-treas. 2003-05, 3d vice chmn. 2005-). Home: 594 Valley St Maplewood NJ 07040-2616 Office: 21 Madison Plz Ste 152 Madison NJ 07940-2354

O'BRIEN, MARY ELLEN CHRISTINA, artist, educator; b. Caribou, Maine, Nov. 15, 1928; d. Richard Stephen and Caroline Elizabeth (McGuire) Sullivan; m. John Michael O'Brien, May 15, 1965; children: Maureen-Caroline, Kathleen. Cert. in arts, Cambridge Sch. of Design; student, Crafts Students League, 1958, Paul Puzinas Art Studio, 1959, Penland Sch. of Crafts, 1994. Freelance designer MIT and Harvard U., Cambridge, Mass., 1954-55; arts and crafts dir. Cambridge coun. Girl Scouts U.S., 1955, Spl. Svcs., U.S. Army, Ft. Devens, Mass., 1956-57, Ft. Totten, N.Y., 1957-61, Europe, 1961-64; art tchr. Red Feather Agys., Boston, 1955-56; freelance comml. artist Jordon March, Boston, 1955-56; art tchr. Most Holy Redeemer Sch., Tampa, Fla., 1971-78, Acad. of Holy Names, Tampa, 1986-94; art specialist City of Tampa, 1979-81. Pvt. tchr., 1981-86; creative art dir. polit. campaign Dem. Party, Tampa. 1970's. Cover design artist The Patron Sts., 1959; one-woman shows include Methodist Adminstrn. Bldg., Realistic Artist Gallery, Fed. Bank Bldg.; exhibitions include Busch-Reisinger Mus., Cambridge, Mass., 1955, Portland Art Mus., Maine, Art League LI Gallery Puzinas Studio, Gt. Neck, NY, Living Design Studio, Manchester, NH, NY Pub. Libr. Sys. Bayside Br., LI, The Studio Gallery, LI, NY, First Presbyn. Ch. Temple Terrace, Stewart Art Show, Gasparilla Outdoor Art Show, Lowry Park Outdoor Art Show, Vets. Adminstrn. Hosp., Fla., St. Joseph's Art Gallery, Fla., 1978, Rental Gallery of Tampa Bay Art Ctr., Fla., 1973, Mus. of Art., Fla., Performing Art Ctr., Fla., Fla. Craftsmen Gallery, St. Petersburg, Kotler Art Gallery, Tampa, Fla., 2008, and numerous others; jurined internat. shows include Ratner Mus., Bethesda, Md., Sandy Springs Mus., Md., Kohler Gallery, Tampa, Fla., 2008, Carollwood Cultural Ctr. Gallery, 2008-08, Eustis Mus., Fla., 2008, Lacy Gallery, Tampa, 2008, Deltona art Ctr., Fla., 2008, Brandon Art Ctr., Fla., 2007-08. Albequerque Balloon Mus., 2008-09. Mem. delegation to Japan to observe art in schs. People to People Delegation, 1995; docent Mus. Art, 1974-85, 94—; vol. Performing Arts Ctr. Mem. Nat. League Am. Pen Women (pres. 1984-85, chair nat. art competition), Sick Painters, Alpha Delta Kappa. Roman Catholic. Avocations: sewing, reading. Home: 10801 N Edison Ave Tampa FL 33612-6501 Personal E-mail: artlover621@verizon.com.

O'BRIEN, MICHAEL J., lawyer, advertising executive; Ptnr. O'Sullivan LLP, Goodwin Procter LLC, 2002—03; sr. v.p., gen. counsel, sec. Omnicom Group Inc., NYC, 2003—. Office: Omnicom Group Inc 437 Madison Ave New York NY 10022 Office Phone: 212-415-3640. Fax: 212-415-3530.

O'BRIEN, MORGAN EDWARD, communications executive, lawyer; b. Washington, Dec. 14, 1944; AB Classical with honors, Georgetown U., 1966; JD, Northwestern U., 1969. Bar: Ill. 1969, Washington 1971. Lawyer Mobile Svcs. divsn. Common Carrier Bur. FCC, Washington, 1970-72; asst. bur. chief Spectrum Mgmt. Pvt. Radio Bur. FCC, Washington, 1976-87; co-founder, chmn. bd. Nextel Comm., Inc., Reston, Va., 1987-96, vice chmn., 1996—2005; co-founder, chmn. Cyren Call Comms., McLean, Va., 2006—. Ptnr. Jones, Day, Reavis & Pogue, Washington, 1986-90; pvt. practice, Washington, 1979-90.

O'BRIEN, NANCY PATRICIA, librarian, educator; b. Galesburg, Ill., Mar. 17, 1955; d. Leo Frederick O'Brien and Yvonne Blanche (Uhlmann) O'Brien Tabb; 1 child, Nicole Pamela. AB in English, U. Ill., 1976, MS in LS, 1977. Vis. instr. U. Ill., Urbana, 1977-78, asst. prof. libr. adminstrn., 1978-84, assoc. prof., 1984-91, prof., 1991—, serials bibliographer, 1977-78, social sci. bibliographer collection devel. div., 1979-81, project dir. Title II-C grant, 1987-88, acting libr. and info. sci. libr., 1989-90, head Edn. and Social Sci. Libr., 1994—, coord. social scis. divsn., 1996—2003, edn. subject specialist, 1981—. Discussion leader Ill. White House Conf. on Libr. and Info. svcs., 1990; mem. nat. adv. bd. Office Ednl. Rsch. and Improvement, US Dept. Edn., 1989-91; grant proposal reviewer NEH, 1991; mem. adv. bd. Ctr. for Children's Books, 1992-97; cons. Ark. Coll., 1989; chmn. rev. team Instrnl. Materials Ctr., U. Wis., Madison, 1989; chair exec. com. Nat. Edn. Network Nat. Libr. Edn. US Dept. Edn., 1998—2002; mem. ERIC Steering Com., Inst. Edn. Sci., US Dept. Edn., 2007- presenter in field. Author: Test Construction: A Bibliography of Resources, 1988, (with Emily Fabiano) Core List of Books and Journals in Education, 1991; Education: A Guide to Reference and Information Sources, 2d edit., 2000, (with Paul Fehrmann) Directory of Test Collections in Academic, Professional, and Research Libraries, 2001, (with John Collins III) Greenwood Dictionary of Edn., 2003; (with Kate Corby) Education in Resources in College Libraries, 2006, (with Jeannie Kamerman and Sharon K. Naylor) Education in Guide to Refernce, 2008; co-editor Media/Microforms column Serials Rev., 1979-82; mem. editl. bd. Bull. Bibliography, 1982-90; asst. editor Libr. Hi Tech., 1983-85; editor EBSS Newsletter, 1990-91; contbr. articles to profl. jours., chpts. to books. Mem. ALA (Whitney-Carnegie grantee 1990-91), Am. Ednl. Rsch. Assn. (mem. spl. interest group libr. resources and info. tech.), Assn. Coll. and Rsch. Librs. (mem. access policy guidelines task force 1990-95, vice chmn., chmn.-elect edn. and behavioral scis. sect. 1993-94, chmn. 1994-95, mem. acad. status com. 1996-2000, Disting. Edn. and Behavioral Scis. Libr. award 1997, mem. new pubs. adv. bd. 2004-07, chair disting. edn. and behavioral sci. libr. award com., 2004-07), Libr. Adminstrn. and Mgmt. Assn. (mem. edn. and tng. com. pub. rels. sect. 1990-95), Resources and Tech. Svcs. Divsn.(mem. micropub. com. 1982-85, chmn. 1983-85, cons. 1985-87). Office: U Ill Edn & Social Sci Libr 100 Main Libr 1408 W Gregory Dr Urbana IL 61801-3607 Office Phone: 217-333-2408. Business E-Mail: npobrien@illinois.edu.

O'BRIEN, PATRICK D., telecommunications industry executive; BSEE, Iowa State U.; MBA, U. St. Thomas. Worked in network planning capacity Contel Tel. (now Verizon); product mgr., DSX products unit ADC Telecom. Inc., 1993—2002, held several positions in the product mgmt. area, including v.p., gen. mgr., copper & fiber connectivity products, pres., copper & fiber connectivity bus. unit, 2002—04, pres., regional dir., Americas region, pres., global connectivity solutions bus. unit, 2004—. Bd.dirs., chmn.(compensation com.) Krone Comm. Ltd., 2007—; mng. dir. ADC GMbH, Germany, 2007—; mng dir. (EMEA) ADC Telecomm. Inc., 2007—. Office: ADC Telecommunications Inc 13625 Technology Dr Minneapolis MN 55440 Office Phone: 952-938-8080. Office Fax: 952-917-1717.*

O'BRIEN, PATRICK T., lawyer; b. NYC, Nov. 14, 1942; BS, Wheeling Coll., 1964; MA in Criminal Justice, John Jay Coll., 1976; JD cum laude, Univ. Miami, 1990. Bar: Fla. 1990, US Ct. Internat. Trade 1996. Spl. agent US Customs Svc.; now shareholder, tech., media, telecom. Greenberg Traurig LLP, Ft. Lauderdale, Fla. Mem.: ABA (Fla. regional subcom. on white collar crime), Fla. Bar Assn., Assn. Cert. Anti-Money Laundering Specialists, Interactive Gaming Counsel. Office: Greenberg Traurig LLP Ste 2000 401 E Las Olas Blvd Fort Lauderdale FL 33301-2296 Office Phone: 954-768-8221. Office Fax: 954-765-1477. Business E-Mail: obrienp@gtlaw.com.

O'BRIEN, RAYMOND FRANCIS, transportation executive; b. Atchison, Kans., May 31, 1922; s. James C. and Anna M. (Wagner) O'B.; m. Mary Ann Baugher, Sept. 3, 1947; children: James B., William T., Kathleen A., Christopher R. BS in Bus. Adminstrn., U. Mo., 1948; grad., Advanced Mgmt. Program, Harvard, 1966. Accountant-auditor Peat, Marwick, Mitchell & Co., Kansas City, Mo., 1948-52; contr., treas. Riss & Co., Kansas City, Mo., 1952-58; regional contr. Consol. Freightways Corp. of Del., Indpls., also, Akron, Ohio, 1958-61; contr. Consol. Freightways, Inc., San Francisco, 1961—, v.p., treas., 1962-63, bd. dirs., 1966, v.p. fin., 1967-69, exec. v.p., 1969-75, pres., 1975—, chief exec. officer, 1977-88, 90-91, chmn., 1988—; now chmn. emeritus Conway Transportation. Pres. CF Motor Freight subs. Consol. Freightways, Inc., 1973; dir. Transam. Corp., Watkins-Johnson, Inc.; past chmn. Western-Hwy. Inst., Champion Road Machinery, Ltd. Former mem. bus. adv. bd. Northwestern U., U. Calif., Berkeley, Menlo Country Club; bd. dirs., regent, former chmn. bd. trustees St. Mary's Coll.; bd. dirs., regent Charles Armstrong Sch., 1991—; mem. Pres.'s Adv. Herbert Hoover Boys and Girls Club; dir. Boy Scouts Am. Bay Area Coun. Served to 1st lt. USAAF, 1942-45. Recipient Disting. Svc. Citation Automotive Hall Fame, 1991; named Outstanding Chief Exec. five times Financial World Mag.

O'BRIEN, RAYMOND VINCENT, JR., banker; b. Bronx, NY, Sept. 23, 1927; s. Raymond Vincent and Blanche (Harper) O'B.; m. Theresa Sweeney, Mar. 29, 1952 (dec. June 1981); children: Susan, Raymond, Christopher, Sean, Carol, Nancy Meisenzahl; m. Ellen Boyle, July 24, 1982. BA, Fordham U., 1951, JD, 1958; postgrad., Harvard U. Advanced Mgmt. Program, 1969. With Chase Manhattan Bank, N.A., NYC, 1953-74; chief exec. officer, chmn. bd. Emigrant Savs. Bank, NYC, 1978—93, pres., 1974-77. Trustee Fordham U., 1979-92; chmn. bd. trustees Regis H.S., 1988-92; past chmn. Cmty. Bankers Assn., N.Y., Nat. Assn. Cmty. Bankers. Served with AUS, 1946-47, 51-53. Mem. Guild Cath. Lawyers, Navesink Country Club (Middletown, N.J.), Plantation Country Club (Ponte Vedra, Fla.), K.M., Friendly Sons St. Patrick. Republican. Roman Catholic. Home: 102 Lands End Ponte Vedra Beach FL 32082-3906

O'BRIEN, RICHARD L(EE), physician, educator, academic administrator; b. Shenandoah, Iowa, Aug. 30, 1934; s. Thomas Lee O'B. and Grace Ellen (Sims) Parish; m. Joan Frances Gurney, June 29, 1957; children: Sheila Marie, Kathleen Therese, Michael James, Patrick Kevin. MS in Physiology, Creighton U., 1958, MD, 1960. Diplomate Nat. Bd. Med. Examiners. Intern and resident Columbia med. divsn. Bellevue Hosp., NYC, 1960-62; postdoctoral fellow in biochemistry Inst. for Enzyme Rsch., U. Wis., 1962-64; asst. prof. to prof. pathology Sch. Medicine, U. So. Calif., LA, 1966-82, dep. dir. Cancer Ctr., 1975-80, dir. rsch. and edn. Cancer Ctr., 1980-81, dir. Cancer Ctr., 1981-82; dean Sch. Medicine Creighton U., Omaha, 1982-92, acting v.p. health scis., 1984-85, v.p. health scis., 1985-99, prof. health policy and ethics, Univ. prof., 2002—, dir. office of interprofl. edn., 2002—05. Vis. prof. molecular biology U. Geneva, 1973-74; mem. cancer control rsch. grants rev. com. NIH, Nat. Cancer Inst.; mem. Cancer Ctr. Support grant rev. com. Nat. Cancer Inst., 1984-88, chmn. 1987-88; co-chmn. United Way/CHAD Pacesetter campaign, 1988, 94; bd. dirs. Health Future Found., 2003—; cons. in field. Contbr. articles to profl. jours.; editor various profl. jours. Bd. dirs. Opera Omaha, 1994-2001, 04—, pres., 1998-2000, Opera Omaha Found., 2000—06, chmn., 2004—06; co-chair, Building Bright Futures Adolescent Behavioral Health Task Force, 2007-, NE Medical Assn. Health Care Reform Task Force, 2007-. Capt. US Army, 1964-66. Recipient Disting. Svc. award Met. Omaha Med. Soc., 1987, Silver Rose Opera Omaha, 2000; Spl. fellow Nat. Cancer Inst., 1967-69; named Citizen of Yr. Combined Health Agys. Drive-Health, 1986. Mem. ACP, Am. Assn. Pathologists, Am. Assn. Cancer Rsch., Am. Assn. Cancer Edn., AAAS, Am. Assn. Cancer Insts. (dir. 1982-83), Assn. Am. Med. Colls. (chmn. MCAT evaluation panel 1987-88, liaison com. on med. edn., 1988-93, co-chmn, 1989-93, adv. panel Strategic Planning Health Care Reform 1992-96), Assn. Acad. Health Ctrs. (long-range planning com. 1986, 2000, nominating com. 1987, 96, Task Force Health Care Delivery 1992, mem. task force on leadership and instl. values 1993-99, bd. dirs. 1998-99), Am. Cancer Soc. (adv. com. Inst. Rsch. Grants 1977-80, Outstanding Leadership award 1981, dir. Calif. divsn. 1980-82, dir. Nebr. divsn. 1992-96), Am. Hosp. Assn. (com. on med. edn. 1986-89), Alpha Omega Alpha. Home: 9927 Essex Dr Omaha NE 68114-3873 Office: Creighton Univ California At 24th Omaha NE 68178-0001 Home Phone: 402-392-0331; Office Phone: 402-280-2017. Business E-Mail: rlo@creighton.edu.

O'BRIEN, RICHARD T., mining executive; BA in Economics, U. Chgo., 1976; JD, Lewis and Clark Coll., Northwestern Sch. Law, 1985. Joined PacificCorp, 1983; CFO, sr. v.p. PacifiCorp, Portland, Oreg., 1995—98, CFO, exec. v.p., 1998; v.p. Mirant (formerly S. Energy, Inc.), 2000—01, pres., Mirant Capital Mgmt., 2000—01; sr. v.p., CFO AGL Resources, 2001, exec. v.p., CFO Atlanta, 2001—05; sr. v.p., CFO Newmont Mining Co., Denver, 2005—06, exec. v.p., CFO, 2006—07, pres., CEO, 2007—. Office: Newmont Mining 1700 Lincoln St Denver CO 80203

O'BRIEN, ROBERT BROWNELL, JR., banker, consultant, yacht broker, opera company executive, museum director; b. NYC, Sept. 6, 1934; s. Robert Brownell and Eloise (Boles) O'B.; m. Sarah Lager, Nov. 28, 1958; children: Robert Brownell III, William Stuart, Jennifer. BA, Lehigh U., 1957; postgrad., NYU, Am. Inst. Banking. Asst. treas., credit officer, br. locations officer Bankers Trust Co., NYC, 1957-63; v.p., dir. bus. devel. George A. Murray Co., gen. contractors, NYC, 1964; also v.p. Bowery Savs. Bank, 1964-69; dir., chief exec. officer Fed. Savs. & Loan Ins. Corp., Washington, 1969-71; chmn. exec. com. Fed. Home Loan Bank Bd., 1969-71; v.p. Bowery Savs. Bank, NYC, 1972; exec. v.p. First Fed. Savs. & Loan Assn., NYC, 1973-75; chmn., chief exec. officer Carteret Savs. Bank, Morristown, 1975-91, also bd. dirs.; mng. dir. Printon Kane Group Inc., Short Hills, NJ, 1991-94; dir., former chief exec. officer Govs. Bank Corp., West Palm Beach, 1992-94; pres., CEO Hubert Johnson Inc., 1998—. Bd. dirs. Fed. Home Loan Bank N.Y., Govs. Bank Corp., Ocean Med. Ctr. Found., Ocean County Atty. Ethics Com.; vice chmn. 1st Mortgage Capital Corp., Vero Beach, Fla.; chmn. Neighborhood Housing Svcs. Am., 1972-91; vice chmn., bd dirs. U.S. League Savs. Instns., Washington, O'Brien Yacht Sales. Contbr. articles to trade mags. Trustee Trinity Pawling Sch., Palm Beach County Housing Partnership, Lehigh U., Ocean Med. Found., Tuckerton Seaport; devel. cons. Ocean County Coll., Toms River, N.J.; chmn. Housing Opportunities Found.; trustee, pres. Toms River Seaport Soc., N.J. Mus. Boating; trustee, pres., past chmn. Cmty. Found. of N.J., 1987—; trustee, pres. Bay Head Hist. Soc.; vice chmn., bd. dirs. Dalt Found.; chmn. adv. bd. Palm Beach Maritime Mus., Peanut Island, Fla.; active Nat. Commn. on Neighborhoods, The Kemp Commn.; past chmn., exec. dir. N.J. State Opera. Mem. Nat. Coun. Savs. Instns. (past chmn.), Essex County Savs. and Loan League (past chmn.), NJ Savs. League (past chmn.), NJ Hist. Soc. (past chmn.), Greater Newark C. of C. (bd. dirs.), NJ C. of C. (bd. dirs.), Union League Club, Delray Beach Yacht Club (past commodore), NY Yacht Club, Morris County Golf Club, Somerset Hills Golf Club, Palm Beach Yacht Club, Bay Head Yacht Club (past commodore), Bay Head Fire Co. #1. Republican. Episcopalian. Home: 500 Club Dr Bay Head NJ 08742-5016 Office Phone: 732-295-2072. Personal E-mail: bob@woodenboatsnj.com.

O'BRIEN, ROBERT CHARLES, lawyer; s. Robert Charles and Judith Lorie O'Brien; m. Louisa Maria Thuynsma, May 9, 1988; children: Margaret Elizabeth, Robert Christopher, Lauren Marie. BA, UCLA, 1988; JD, U. Calif., Berkeley, 1991. Bar: Calif. 1991. Legal officer UN Compensation Commn., Geneva, Vaud, 1996—98; ptnr. O'Brien Abeles LLP, LA, 1999—2006; US alt. rep. to UN Gen. Assembly US Dept. State, NYC, 2005—06; ptnr. Arent Fox LLP, LA, 2006—. Co-chmn. Lawyers Bush Cheney, Calif., 2004; co-chair US Dept. State Pub. Pvt. Ptnr. Justice Reform, Afghanistan, 2007—; mem. nat. steering com. Lawyers for Mitt Romney, Boston, 2007—08, US Cultural Adv. Com., 2008—. Maj. US Army, 1992—2005. Mem.: State Bar Calif. (exec. com., internat. law sect. 1999—2002), J. Reuben Clark Law Soc. (chmn. LA chpt. 2003—05). Mem. Lds Ch. Office: Arent Fox LLP 555 W 5th St 48th Floor Los Angeles CA 90013-1065 Office Phone: 213-629-7400. Office Fax: 213-629-7401. E-mail: obrien.robert@arentfox.com.

O'BRIEN, ROBERT JOHN, JR., public relations executive, former government official, air force officer; b. Wheeling, W. Va., Apr. 16, 1935; s. Robert John and Martha Virginia (Hunter) O'B.; m. Margaret Eugenia Schultz BS in Journalism, Northwestern U., Evanston, Ill., 1957; MA in Journalism, U. Wis., Madison, 1970; grad., Indsl. Coll. Armed Forces, 1977. Comnd. officer U.S. Air Force, 1957, advanced through grades to col.; dir. pub. affairs N. Am. Air Def. Command, Colorado Springs, Colo., 1977-80, Air Force Systems Command, Camp Springs, Md., 1980-82; dir. def. info. Office Sec. Def., Washington, 1982-83, dep. asst. sec. def., 1983-86; dir. pub. rels., Washington McDonnell Douglas Corp., Arlington, Va., 1986-97; v.p. pub. rels. The Boeing Co., Arlington, Va., 1997-99. Decorated D.S.M., Legion of Merit, Bronze Star, Air medal, Honor medal (Republic Vietnam) Mem. Air Force Assn., Pub. Rels. Soc. Am., Aviation/Space Writers Assn., U.S. Space Found., Ret. Officers Assn., Williamsburg Nat. Golf Club. Republican. Methodist. Avocations: golf, stamp collecting/philately, model railroading.

OBRIEN, SCOTT, entrepreneur; b. Buffalo, Jan. 20, 1963; s. James M. and Bonnie L. OBrien; m. Kristen N. Nolle; children: Brandon William, Kaetlin Gail, Kerick Scott James. Fl. covering OBrien Fl. Covering, East Aurora, NY, 1980—2000; sales and mktg. Healthy Coffee Today, Holland, NY, 2006—. Home and Office: Yes Marketing 9343 Warner Gulf Rd Holland NY 14080 Office Fax: 509-357-9979. Business E-Mail: askscottobrien@gmail.com.

O'BRIEN, SOLEDAD, news anchor; b. St. James, NY, Sept. 19, 1966; m. Brad Raymond; children: Sofia, Cecilia, Charlie, Jackson. Degree in English and Am. Lit., Harvard U.; hon. degree, Siena Coll., Mercy Coll. Prodr. Second Opinion, reporter Health Week in Review Sta. KISS-FM, Boston; assoc. prodr., newswriter Sta. WBZ-TV, Boston; prodr. NBC News, 1991—93; co-host The Know Zone Discovery Channel; chief East Bay bur. Sta. KRON-TV, San Francisco, reporter, 1993—96; co-host The Site, Nightly News, Weekend Today MSNBC, 1996—99; anchor, Weekend Today NBC, 1999—2003; co-anchor, American Morning CNN, 2003—07; anchor, spl. corr. CNN: Spl. Investigations Unit. Bd. dirs. Harlem Sch. the Arts. Recipient Emmy award as a co-host on Discovery Channel's The Know Zone, Women of Power award, Nat. Urban League, 2006, Mickey Leland Humanitarian award, Nat. Assn. Minorities in Cable, 2006, President's award, NAACP Image Awards, 2007, Clara Barton Humanitarian award, Am. Red Cross, Mass. Bay, 2007, Gracie Allen award, Found. Am. Women in Radio and TV, 2007, Soledad O'Brien Freedom's Voice award, Cmty. Voices at the Morehouse Sch. Medicine, 2007; named one of 50 Most Beautiful People, People Mag., 2001, People en Español, 2004, Crain's Bus. Reports', Essence Mag. & Black Enterprise, "40 under 40", Top 100 Irish Americans (several times), Irish Am. Mag. Mem.: Nat. Assn. Hispanic Journalists, Nat. Assn. Black Journalists. Office: CNN One CNN Ctr Atlanta GA 30348

O'BRIEN, TERRENCE LEO, federal judge; b. Lincoln, Nebr., Aug. 8, 1943; s. Leo James and Luella Mildred (Benting) O'B.; m. Dorothy Marguerite Driskill, Mar. 30, 1966; children: Sean Brendan, Heather Kathleen. BS in Acctg., U. Wyo., 1965, JD with honors, 1972. Bar: Wyo. 1972. Staff atty. Land and Natural Resources-US Dept. Justice, Washington, 1972-74, Omohundro & O'Brien, Buffalo, Wyo., 1974—80; judge 6th Jud. Dist. Wyo., Gillette, 1980—2000; pres. Visionary Communications Inc, 2000—01; private practice Wyo., 2001—02; judge US Ct. Appeals (10th cir.), 2002—. Justice of Peace Johnson County, Buffalo, 1975-80. Mem. Wyo. Community Coll. Commn., 1978-80. Capt. US Army, 1966-69. Mem.: Rotary. Republican. Office: US Courthouse 2120 Capitol Ave Rm 2141 Cheyenne WY 82001 Office Phone: 307-443-2400.*

O'BRIEN, TERRENCE P., ophthalmologist, educator; b. Mar. 3, 1959; BS summa cum laude, U. Mich., 1981, MD, 1985. Diplomate Nat. Bd. Med. Examiners, Am. Bd. Ophathology. Intern dept. medicine and surgery William Beaumont Hosp., Royal Oak, Mich., 1985—86; resident The Wilmer Eye Inst., Johns Hopkins Hosp., Balt., 1986—89; fellow Cullen Eye Inst., Baylor Coll. Medicine, Houston, 1989—90; asst. chief svc. The Wilmer Eye Inst., Johns Hopkins Hosp., Balt., 1990—91, dir. Ocular Microbiology Lab., 1991—, dir. refractive eye surgery, 1996—, asst. prof. ophthalmology, 1991—98, assoc. prof. ophthalmology, 1998—. Presenter in field. Mem. editl. bd.: Taking Care, 1995—, Ocular Surgery News, 1996—, Eye World, 1996—, Clin. Signs in Ophthalmology, 1997, Ocular Infection and Hygiene, 1997—, Vision & Aging, 2001—, Refractive Surgery Quarterly, 2001—, Cataract and Refractive Surgery Today, 2001—, cons.: Rev. Ophthalmology, 1996, ad hoc reviewer: Am. Jour. Ophthalmology, Archives Ophthalmology, Cornea, Current Eye Rsch., Investigative Ophthalmology and Visual Sci., Jour. Infectious Diseases, Jour. Catarat and Refractive Surgery, Jour. Refractive Surgery, Ophthalmology, Retina, Rev. Ophthalmology, Revs. Infectious Disease; contbr. articles to profl. jours. James B. Angell scholar. Fellow: Am. Acad. Ophthalmology (mem. in tng. 1986—90, program chair refractice surgery interest group 2002—03, subspecialty day com. mem. 2002—, bd. dirs. refractive surgery interest group 1998—); mem.: Wilmer Residents' Assn., Md. Soc. Eye Physicians and Surgeons, Balt. City Med. Soc. (trustee 1993), Rsch. to Prevent Blindness, Am. Soc. Cataract and Refractive Surgeons, Assn. Univ. Profs. in Ophthalmology (assoc.), Contact Lens Assn. Ophthalmologists (faculty 1988, 1995), Ocular Microbiology and Immunology Group (bd. dirs. 1997—), Assn. for Rsch. in Vision and Ophthalmology, Internat. Soc. Ocular Pharmaceutics (bd. dirs. 1994—), Internat. Conf. Ocular Infections (exec. bd./program com. 1992—), Sigma Xi, Alpha Omega Alpha, Phi Beta Kappa. Office: Wilmer Eye Inst at Green Spring Station Ste 305 10753 Falls Rd Lutherville MD 21093

O'BRIEN, THOMAS FRANCIS, microbiologist, director; s. Francis Noonan and Mary Gertrude O'Brien; m. Ruth Reardon, Aug. 23, 1958; children: Neal Francis, Luke Gavin, Conan Christopher, Kate Bartlett, Jane O'Brien Garvey, Justin Powers. AB, Coll. Holy Cros, Worcester, Mass., 1950; MD, Harvard Med. Sch., Boston, 1954. Diplomate Am Bd. Internal Medicine, 1961. Dir. divsn. infectious diseases Peter Bent Brigham Hosp., Boston, 1962—75; med. dir. microbiology lab. Brigham and Women's Hosp., Boston, 1975—, co-dir. WHO Collaborating Ctr. Surveillance Antimicrobial Resistance, 1985—. Capt. USAR, 1957—59, Brooke Army Med. Ctr., San Antonio. Mem.: Alliance Prudent Use Antibiotics (v.p. 1986). Achievements include co-development and global deployment of WHONET software. Office: Microbiology Brigham and Women's Hosp 75 Francis St Boston MA 02115

O'BRIEN, THOMAS GEORGE, III, lawyer; b. NYC, Aug. 26, 1942; s. Thomas George Jr. and Margaret Patricia (Arctander) O'B.; m. Alison Marie Rich, Aug. 26, 1967; children: Christian Arctander, Kylin Stafford. AB magna cum laude, U. Notre Dame, 1964; LLB, Yale U., 1967; MA in Theology summa cum laude, St. Vincent de Paul Regional Sem., 2003. Bar: N.Y. 1967, Fla. 1988. Assoc. Carter, Ledyard & Milburn, NYC, 1971-78; assoc. gen. counsel Frank B. Hall & Co. Inc., Briarcliff Manor, NY, 1978-79, v.p., sec., gen. counsel, 1979-86; exec. v.p., sec., gen. counsel CenTrust Savs. Bank, Miami, 1986-87; of counsel Steel Hector & Davis, Miami, 1987-88, ptnr. West Palm Beach, Fla., 1988—2001. Author: Florida Law of Corporations and Business Organizations, 1990, 92-98. Trustee Bus. Vols. for Arts, Miami, 1986—88, Fla. Repertory Theatre, West Palm Beach, 1989—91, chmn., 1990—91; vestry mem. Episcopal Ch., Bethesda-by-the-Sea, 1991—94, sr. warden Bethesda-by-the-Sea, 1992—94; bd. dirs. Palm Beach Fellowship Christians and Jews, 1993—97, sec., 1996—97; chmn. Diocesan Sch. Christian Studies Bd., 2003—; lay dep. Episcopal Ch. Gen. Conv., 2004—, mem. program, budget and fin. com., 2005—; mem. exec. bd. Episcopal Diocese of S.E. Fla., 2001—04, sec., 2006—08; bd. dirs. Bus. Devel. Bd. Palm Beach County, 1991—98, sec., 1992—93, chmn., 1993—94; bd. dirs. Directions 21st Century, 1995—98, chmn., 1996—98; bd. dirs. Toward a More Perfect Union, 2000—09, sec., 2000—01, 2005—06, chair, 2003—05. Mem.: ABA (com. on legal opinions 1992—2001, negotiated acquisitions com. 1998—2001), Am. Soc. Corp. Secs. (sec. N.Y. regional group 1984—86), Fla. Bar Assn. (chmn. com. on opinion stds. 1988—95, mem. corps./securities law com. 1988—2002, vice-chmn. 1989—90, exec. coun. bus. law sect. 1989—93, chmn. 1990—91), PGA Nat. Club. Home: 272 Eagleton Estates Blvd Palm Beach Gardens FL 33418-8423 Personal E-mail: tgobrien@comcast.net.

O'BRIEN, THOMAS M., travel company executive; BS in econ. cum laude, Wharton Sch. Univ. Pa., 1988. Sr. mgr. Arthur Andersen LLP, 1988—96; v.p. Reit Mgmt., 1996—2006; treas., CFO Hospitality Properties Trust, 1996—2002, exec. v.p., 2002—03; pres. RMR Advisors Inc., 2003—07; pres., CEO RMR Funds, 2003—07; sr. v.p. Reit Mgmt. & Rsch. LLC, 2006—; mng. dir. TravelCenters of America LLC, Westlake, Ohio, 2006—, pres., CEO, 2007—. Bd. dir. VirnetX, 2007—. Office: Travel Centers of America Ste 200 24601 Center Ridge Rd Westlake OH 44145-5639*

O'BRIEN, THOMAS PETER, lawyer, former prosecutor; Grad., US Naval Acad., 1981; JD, U. San Diego, 1993. Clk. LA County Dist. Atty.'s Office, prosecutor hardcore gang divsn.; chief criminal divsn., asst. US atty. (ctrl. dist.) Calif. US Dept. Justice, 2000—07, US atty. (ctrl. dist.) Calif., 2007—09; ptnr. Paul, Hastings, Janofsky & Walker LLP, L.A., Calif., 2009—. Radar intercept officer USN. Recipient Atty Gen.'s Award for Exceptional Svc., US Dept. Justice, 2007. Republican. Office: Paul Hastings Janofsky & Walker LLP 515 S Flower St 25th Fl Los Angeles CA 90071 Office Phone: 213-683-6000. Office Fax: 213-627-0705.*

O'BRIEN, TIMOTHY ANDREW, journalist, writer, lawyer, educator; b. NYC, July 11, 1943; s. Timothy Andrew and Hildegarde J. (Schenkel) O'B.; m. Maria de Guadalupe Margarita Moreno, Jan. 15, 1971; children: Theresa Marie, Tim A. BA in Comm., Mich. State U., 1967; MA in Polit. Sci., U. Md., 1972; postgrad., Tulane U., 1974-75; JD, Loyola U., New Orleans, 1976. Bar: La. 1976, D.C. 1977, U.S. Supreme Ct 1981. News writer, reporter, anchor WKBD-TV, Detroit, 1968-69, WTOP-TV, Washington, 1969-72, WDSU-TV, New Orleans, 1972-74, WVUE-TV, New Orleans, 1974-77; law corr. ABC News, 1977-99; corr. Cable News Network (CNN), 2001—. Leo Goodwin Prof. Law Southeastern U., 1997; disting. prof. law Hofstra U., Sch. Law, 2000, St. Thomas Sch. Law, Miami, 2001, Nova U., 2002; disting. vis. prof. law, Nova Southeastern U., 1999, 2001, Loyola Sch. of Law, 2003. Contbr. articles to profl. jours. Bd. govs. Woodward Acad., College Park, Ga.; bd. visitors Loyola U. Sch. Law., 1997—. Recipient AP award for outstanding reporting of extraordinary event, 1976, New Orleans Press Club award for non-spot news reporting, 1976, Emmy award for documentary on D.C., 1969, ABA awards of merit, 1979 (2), 80, 85, Gavel award for documentary, 1980, Nat. award for human rights reporting Women in Comm., 1981, Disting. Alumnus award Mich. State U., 1996. Mem. Am. Law Inst., Radio-TV Corrs. Assn. Washington, Am. Judicature Soc. (bd. dirs. 1991-97). Home Phone: 301-942-1036.

O'BRIEN, TIMOTHY JAMES, lawyer; b. Detroit, Nov. 4, 1945; m. Hyon Baek, Jan. 31, 1970; children: Jean, Jane. AB, Yale U., 1967; JD, Harvard U., 1976. Bar: N.Y. 1977, Hong Kong, 1999. Assoc. Cleary, Gottlieb, Steen & Hamilton, NYC, 1976-80; ptnr. Coudert Bros., NYC and Hong Kong, 1980—2005, mng. ptnr. Hong Kong office, 2002—05; sr. fgn. legal counsel Shin & Kim, Seoul, 2005—06; sr. counsel Kim & Chang, Seoul, Republic of Korea, 2006—. Lectr. US law, Korean Judicial Rsch. and Tng. Inst., 2005-06; dir. MetLife Korea, Ltd. Co-author: Corporate Governance in Korea at the Millennium, 2002; mem.: Harvard Law Rev., 1975—76; contbr. articles to profl. jours. Assoc. dir., vol. Peace Corps, Republic of Korea, 1967-73. Mem. ABA (vice-chmn. Aisia Pacific com. internat. section., co-chmn. conf. on Korea-U.S. trade and investment 1990-92), Assn. of Bar City of N.Y. (internat. law com., Asian affairs com. 1989-94), Korea Soc. (N.Y., sec., bd. dir. 1996-99). Office: Kim & Chang Seyang Bldg 223 Naeja-dong Jongno-gu Seoul Republic of Korea Home Phone: 82-2-796-7479.

O'BRIEN, WALTER JOHN, retired artist management executive, writer; b. Elizabeth, NJ, Dec. 25, 1951; s. Walter Francis and Marie Carmella (Valvano) O'B.; m. Andrea Lapides, Sept. 15, 1973 (div. Apr. 1975). Dir. album promotions JEM Div. Passport Records, South Plainfield, NJ, 1973-75, ATV/Pye Records, NYC, 1975-77; label mgr. Passport Records, South Plainfield, 1977-78; dir. artist devel. Genesis Hit and Run Music Mgmt., NYC, 1978-80; gen. mgr. Hannibal Records, NYC, 1981; founder, label mgr. Relativity/Combat Records div. Important Records, Jamaica, 1981-84; founder, pres. Concrete Mgmt. Inc., NYC, 1984—; co-founder, pres., v.p. Concrete Mktg. Inc., 1987—90; pres. Piranha Bros. Prodns. Inc., NYC, 1990-95. Telecomm. trainer IMC Computer Network, NYC, 1984-86; adv. bd. dirs. dept. music bus. NYU, 1985-90, lectr., 1985—2003, SUCO, Oneonta, NY, 1987—2003; NARAS/Grammy award rock adv. com. mem., 1992-94. Columnist: Music & Sound Output mag, 1980-83, Keyboards, Computers, Software mag., 1985-87; freelance writer, photographer Courier News, Gannett Inc., 2005-07, staff writer, reporter 2007-. Recipient Excellence in Math. award Math. Assn. Am., Princeton, N.J., 1969. Avocations: computers, amateur radio, shortwave. Office: Courier News 92 E Main St Somerville NJ 08876 Office Phone: 908-243-6613. Personal E-mail: walterobrien@me.com. Business E-Mail: wobrien@gannett.com.

O'BROCHTA, DAVID A., molecular biologist, researcher; b. Apr. 26, 1955; BS in Biology, U. Kans., 1977; PhD in Devel. & Cell Biology, U. Calif., Irvine, 1984. Fellow in molecular genetics & plant biology U. Calif., San Diego, 1985; fellow in insect molecular genetics USDA, Gainesvile, Fla., 1987; asst. prof. Ctr for Agricultural Biotechnology U. Md. Biotechnology Ctr., 1989, assoc. prof. Ctr for Agricultural Biotechnology, 1995, prof. Ctr. for Biosystems Rsch., 2004—. Editorial bd. Molecular Insect Biology, 1995—. Office: University of Maryland Biotechnology Institute 5115 Plant Sciences Bldg College Park MD 20742-4450 Office Phone: 301-405-7680. Office Fax: 301-314-9075.*

O'BRYAN, MARGARET SUNDBERG, music educator; b. Potsdam, NY, Dec. 18, 1957; d. Randell Llewellyn and Marion Hamlin Sundberg; m. Thomas Henry O'Bryan, Aug. 25, 1984. MusB, Crane Sch. of Music, Potsdam, 1980, MusM, 1986. Cert. tchr. music K-12 NY. Tchr. vocal music Somersworth City Schs., Somersworth, NH, 1980—81, Central Square Ctrl. Sch., NY, 1983—84, Harpursville Ctrl. Sch., NY, 1984—2001, St. Regis Falls Ctrl. Sch., NY, 2001—. Dist. rep. Broome County Music Educators Assn., Harpursville, 1986—2001, county music festival chair; Chenango County vocal adjudicator Assn. Chenango Area Music Tchrs., Harpursville, 1988—2000, county music festival chair; mem. policy bd. St. Regis Falls Ctrl. Sch. Mem. St. Regis Falls Sports Boosters, PTO, St. Regis Falls, 2002—05, Olympic Chorus, Lake Placid, NY, 1980; mem. adv. bd. No. Gateway, 2006—; founder, instr. Harpursville Juggling Club, 1998—2001, St. Regis Falls Juggling Club, 2002—. Regents scholar, NY State, 1976—80. Mem.: Inst. Learning Centered Edn., Franklin County Music Educators Assn. (chair vocal music festival 2006—), NY State United Tchrs., St. Regis Falls United Tchrs. (co-organizer benefit auction 2004), NY State Sch. Music Assn., Music Educators Nat. Conf., Internat. Jugglers Assn. Mem. Lds Ch. Avocations: juggling, genealogy, landscape photography, travel. Home: PO Box 109 Port Kent Rd Nicholville NY 12965 Office: St Regis Falls Ctrl Sch 92 N Main St Saint Regis Falls NY 12980 Business E-Mail: mobryan@mail.fehb.org.

O'BRYANT, DANIEL R., consumer products company executive; BS in Mgmt. Sci., Calif. State Polytechnic U., Pomona, Calif.; MBA, U. So. Calif. Fin. mgmt. positions Baker Hughes; dir. cap. planning Avery Dennison, Pasadena, Calif., 1990—91, dir. fin. spl. tape div. Belgium, 1991—92, group fin. dir. Netherlands, 1992—94, v.p. fin. European ops., 1994—95, v.p. ops. planning Pasadena, Calif., 1995—96, v.p. ops. audit, 1996—97, v.p. gen. mgr. Fasson Roll div. Painesville, Ohio, 1997—2001, sr. v.p. fin., CFO, 2001—05, exec. v.p. fin., CFO, 2005—. Office: Avery Dennison Corp Ctr 150 North Orange Grove Blvd Pasadena CA 91103-3596

O'BRYON, JAMES FREDRICK, defense consultant; b. Schenectady, NY, Oct. 1, 1941; s. Frederick Stanley and Elizabeth Mary O'B.; m. Margaret Adina Bell, Oct 23, 1965; children: Daniel, Douglas, Cris, Kera. BS in Math., King's Coll., Briarcliff, NY, 1964; MSA in Ops. Rsch., George Washington U., 1973; SM in Elec. Engring., MIT, 1975. Mathematician Ballistics Rsch. Lab. Aberdeen Proving Ground, Md., 1966-74, asst. to dir. Ballistics Rsch. Lab., 1975-76, ops. rsch. analyst smart munitions group Ballistics Rsch. Lab., 1976-79, chmn. red-on-blue working group Joint Tech. Coord. Group, 1979-85, chief combat survivability and tech. U.S. Army Materiel Systems Analysis Activity, 1985-86; asst. dep. undersec. def. Office Sec. Def., Washington, 1986-88, dir. live-fire testing, 1988-95, dep. dir. operational test and evaluation, 1995—2001; chmn. O'Bryon Group, 2001—. Dir. Live Fire Test Program, Washington, 1986-2001; mem. Conventional Sys. Com., Washington, 1987—; panel mem. NAS, 2000-05, chmn. com. 2005—07; newscaster, radio personality WRBS-FM, Balt., 1965-80; chmn. Mobius Bus. Solutions, 2002-04, Cons. Svc. Engring. Co., 2002-; cons. Inst. Def. Analysis, 2005-, ORSA Corp., 2005-, Scitech Corp., 2006-, Space Micro Corp., 2007-, SRA Corp, 2003 Musician (albums) Until Then, 1968, Portrait of a Man, 1972, My Favorite Song, 1977, Celebration of Praise, 1982; author: I Fail to Miss Your Point, 2007, Red-on-Blue Weapons, Effects, 1983, Lessons Learned From Live Fire Testing, 2006, I Fail to Miss Your Point, 2007; co-author: Non-traditional War & Peace: Twenty-First Century Challenges and Solutions, 2009; contbr. articles to profl. jours. Active edn. coun. MIT, Cambridge, 1980—; chmn. Sch. Ministries, Inc., 2008-; mem. adv. bd. N.Y. Theol. Sem. With U.S. Army, 1964-66. Named Outstanding Young Man in Am., Jaycees, 1970, Disting. Lectr., Def. Aquisition U., 1988; fellow Ctr. Advanced Engring. Study MIT. Mem. AIAA, NAS/NRC (com. mem., chmn.), Nat. Def. Indsl. Assn. (chmn. Test and Evaluation divsn., 1993-, Arthur Stein award, 2002, Walter Hollis award, 2007, NDIA Gold medal 1997), Internat. Test and Evaluation Assn., Am. Inst. Aeronautics & Astronautics, Internat. Bible Soc. Found. (bd. mem. 2000-09). Home: 1608 S Tollgate Rd Bel Air MD 21015-5825 Office Phone: 443-528-2711. Business E-Mail: jamesobryon@obryongroup.com.

OBSITNIK, VINCENT, United States Ambassador to Slovakia; b. Moravany, Slovakia, 1938; married; 4 children. Grad. with honors, US Naval Acad., Annapolis, Md., 1959; MBA in Fin., Am. U., Washington; attended, IBM Advanced Mgmt. Sch., Sands Point, LI, IBM Advanced Mgmt. Sch., La Hulpe, Belgium; attended Unisys exec. program, U. Pa. Wharton Sch., Phila. Various position in mktg., sales, mfg., engring. and program mgmt. IBM Corp.; mgmt. positions in mfg. IBM World Trade Corp.; v.p., internat. Litton Corp.; pres. systems devel. divsn. Unisys Corp.; founder, pres. Internat. Investments Inc. Apptd. mem. US Commn. for the Preservation of America's Heritage Abroad, 2001—06; apptd. mem., US presdl. del. Austrian State Treaty Anniversary, 2005, Commemoration of the 65th Anniversary of the Tragedy in Babyn Yar, Ukraine, 2006. Officer USN, 1959—64. Avocations: running, tennis, squash. Office: DOS Amb 5840 Bratislava Pl Washington DC 20521-5840

OBYDOL-ALEXANDRE, KAREEN, literature and language professor; d. Simon Rodolphe Obydol and Ursule Jeanne Alexandre-Nairay. MA, Sorbonne Nouvelle, Paris, 1992. French tchr., advisor Newark Acad., Livngston, NJ, 1997—. Recipient Tech. Award, Newark Acad., 2004. Mem.: AATF. Office: Montclair State Univ 1 Normal Ave Montclair NJ 07042 Home Fax: 973-992-8962. Business E-Mail: obydolk@mail.montclair.edu.

O'BYRNE, MICHAEL, retired management consultant; b. Butte, Mont., Dec. 26, 1938; s. Michael E. and Margaret F. (Turner) O'B.; m. Penny L. Graham, Nov. 14, 1964; children: Jennifer L. McLellan, Gregory M. O'Byrne, Andrew G. O'Byrne. BSME, U. Wash., 1961. Cert. engr., Wash. V.p. PACCAR, Inc., Bellevue, Wash., 1969-84; pres. Mobi-Dock, Inc., Mercer Island, Wash., 1985-86; ptnr. The Catalyst Group, Mercer Island, 1986-89; pres. Raima Corp., Bellevue, 1988-89, Pacific North Equiptment Co., Kent, Wash., 1990-95; cons. Master Performance, Inc., Bellevue, 1995-2000, Vehicle Monitor Corp., Redmond, Va., 1996—2004; ret. Council mem. Hunts Point, Wash., 1980-97; mem. bd. dirs. Mcpl. League of King County, Seattle, 1994-95; dist. chmn. Boy Scouts Am., Seattle, 1994-98; pres. USO Puget Sound Area, 1997-2004. Lt. comdr. USN, 1961-69. Mem. Soc. Automotive Engrs., Assoc. Equipment Distributors (chpt. pres. 1994-95), Rotary Internat., Seattle Yacht Club. Republican. Avocations: sailing, skiing, fishing. E-mail: michael.obyrne@comcast.net.

O'CARROLL, PATRICK P., JR., federal agency administrator; BS, Mount Saint Mary's Coll., Emmitsburg, Md.; M in Forensic Scis., George Washington U. With US Secret Svc.; asst. inspector gen. for investigations US Social Security Adminstrn., Washington, asst. inspector gen. for external affairs, inspector gen., 2004—. Chair investigation com. Pres.'s Coun. on Integrity and Efficiency. Mem.: Assn. Govt. Accountants, Internat. Assn. Chiefs of Police. Office: US Social Security Adminstrn Office of Inspector Gen PO Box17768 Baltimore MD 21235*

OCASIO, BILLY, state official, former alderman; b. Humboldt Park, Ill., Apr. 26, 1961; s. Antonio and Gladys Ocasio; m. Veronica Ocasio; children: Ismael, Gabriel, Antonio. Attended, U. Ill., Urbana-Champaign; BA, Northeastern U., 1993. Edn. counselor Aspira, Inc., Ill.; exec. dir. Ctr. Cmty. and Leadership Devel.; rehab. dir. Latin United Cmty. Housing Assn.; pres. Colectiva Latina; alderman, 26th ward Chgo. City Coun., 1992—2009; adv. to Gov. Pat Quinn State of Ill., Chgo., 2009—. Chmn. human rels. com. Chgo. City Coun. Organizer, host Roberto Clemente HS Youth Summit, 1983; mem. Puerto Ricans Organized for Chgo., 1989; bd. dirs. Aspira, Inc.; v.p. bd. dirs. Bickerdike Redevel. Corp. Democrat. Office: Office of the Governor James R Thompson Ctr 100 W Randolph 16-100 Chicago IL 60601 Office Phone: 312-814-2121.*

OCCHIATO, MICHAEL ANTHONY, municipal official; b. Pueblo, Colo. s. Joseph Michael and Joan Occhiato; m. Peggy Ann Stefonowicz, June 27, 1964 (div. Sept. 1983); children: Michael, James, Jennifer. BBA, U. Denver, 1961; MBA, U. Colo., 1984; postgrad., U. So. Colo. Grad. Real Estate Inst., 1996, cert. residential specialist 2000. Sales mgr. Tivoli Brewing co., Denver, 1965-67, acting brewmaster, prodn. control mgr., 1967-68, plant mgr., 1968-69; adminstrv. mgr. King Resources Co., Denver, 1969-70; ops. mgr. Canners Inc., Pepsi-Cola Bottling Co., Pueblo, 1970-76; pres. Pepsi-Cola Bottling Co., Pueblo, 1978-82; gen. mgr. Pepsi-Cola Bottling Group div. PepsiCo., Pueblo, 1982, area v.p., 1982-83; ind. cons. Pueblo, 1983—; with Die Mktg. Devel. Lambs Info. Sys., 1983—85; broker assoc. Sound Venture Realty, Pueblo, 1996-98, Jones Healy Better Homes & Gardens, 1998—; with Coldwell Banker Partners, 2006—; pres. council Bergamo, Italy, 2007. V.p. Colo. Soft Drink Assn., 1978, pres., 1979; regional dir. Pepsi Cola Mgmt. Inst. divsn. Pepsi Co., 1979-82; pres. Ethnic Foods Internat. dba Taco Rancho, Pueblo, Exodus 20, 1996—; chmn. Weifang (China) Sister City Del., 1991—; bd. dirs. Pueblo Diversified Industries, Pueblo Crime Stoppers, Pueblo Regional Bldg; rancher, 1976—; land devel. real estate broker assoc., 1996—. Mem. Pueblo City Coun., 1978—93, 2001—, pres., 1986—87, 1991, 1992, 2003, 2006, 2007; mem. Pueblo Bd. Health, 1978—80, Pueblo Regional Planning Commn., 1980—81, Pueblo Action Inc., 1978—80, Pueblo Planning and Zoning Commn., 1985; chmn. Pueblo Area Coun. Govts., 1980—82, 1984—85; mem. Pueblo Econ. Devel. Corp., 1983—91; chmn. fundraising Pueblo chpt. Am. Heart Assn., 1983—; active Earth Wise Pueblo, 1991; pres. Pueblo City Coun., 2002; active Pueblo Regional Bldg. Bd., 2003—; rep. in signing Sister City Agreement with Bergamo, Italy City of Pueblo, 2004; pres. Pueblo City Coun., 2006—; bd. dirs. Pueblo Urban Renewal Authority, 1993—, Pueblo Crime Stoppers, 2001—, El Pueblo Boys Ranch; v.p. Colo. Soft Drink Assn., 1979—80, pres., 1980—81; del. 1st World Conf. Local Elected Ofcls. to 1st UN Internat. Coun. for Local Environ. Initiative. Lt. USN, 1961—65. Named Italian Citizen of Yr., Pueblo, Colo., 2008. Mem. So. Colo. Emergency Med. Technicians Assn. (pres. 1975), Am. Saler Assn., Am. Quarter Horse Assn., Colo. Cattle Assn., Pueblo C. of C., Rotary, Pi Kappa Alpha (v.p. 1960). Home and Office: 11 Harrogate Ter Pueblo CO 81001-1723

OCH, DANIEL S., hedge fund manager; b. Jan. 27, 1961; m. Jane Och. BS in Fin., U. Pa. Wharton Sch., 1982. With Goldman, Sachs & Co., NYC, 1982—94, mem. risk arbitrage group, 1982, head proprietary trading group, co-head US equities trading; founder, CEO, exec. mng. dir., chmn. bd. dirs. Och-Ziff Capital Mgmt. Group, 1994—, also chief investment officer; officer, dir. Och-Ziff Mgmt. Europe Ltd., Och-Ziff Capital Mgmt. Hong Kong Ltd., Och-Ziff Japan Ltd., Och-Ziff India Pvt. Ltd. Trustee NY Presbyn. Med. Ctr.; bd. dirs. UJA Fedn. NY Wall St. divsn., Am. Jewish Com. (AJC), Birthright Israel Found., Robin Hood Found., Say Yes to Edn., Inc. Office: Och-Ziff Capital Mgmt Group 9 W 57th St, 39th Fl New York NY 10019 Office Phone: 212-790-0000.*

OCHMANEK, DAVID ALAN, defense analyst; b. Oak Park, Ill., Apr. 10, 1951; s. Edwin Joseph and Phyllis Jean (Straass) O.; m. Barbara Jane Larson, June 16, 1973; children: James Edwin, Anne Skaaden. BS in Internat. Affairs, Polit. Sci., USAF Acad., 1973; MPA in Pub. Affairs and Internat. Rels., Princeton U., 1980. Fgn. svc. officer U.S. Dept. State, 1980-85; profl. staff The Rand Corp., 1985-93, 95—; dep. asst. sec. of def. for strategy Washington, 1993-95; sr. def. analyst The RAND Corp., Washington, 1995—. Author: Military Operations Against Terrorist Groups Abroad, 2003, NATO's Future: Implications for U.S. Military Capabilities and Force Posture, 2000; co-author: (with Edward L. Warner III) Next Moves: An Arms Control Agenda for the 1990's, 1989, (with Christopher Bowie et al) The New Calculus, 1993, (with Zalmay Khalilzad) Strategic Appraisal, 1997, (with Edward Harshberger el at) To Find and Not to Yield, 1998, (with Anthony Lake) The Real and the Ideal, 2001, (with Andrew R. Hoehn) A New Divsn. Labor: Meeting America's Security Challenges Beyond Iraq, 2007, (with Lowell Schwartz) The Challenge of Nuclear Armed Regional Adversaries, 2008; contbr. articles to profl. jours., chpts. to books. Capt. USAF, 1973-78. Lutheran. Office: The RAND Corp 1200 S Hayes St Arlington VA 22202-5050 Home Phone: 202-543-5896; Office Phone: 703-413-1100.

OCHOA, ARMANDO XAVIER, bishop; b. Oxnard, Calif., Apr. 9, 1943; Attended, Ventura Coll., Calif., St. John's Coll., Camarillo, Calif. Ordained priest Archdiocese of LA, 1970, aux. bishop, vicar gen., 1987-96; ordained bishop, 1986; bishop Diocese of El Paso, Tex., 1996—. Roman Catholic.

OCHOA, ARTHUR J., lawyer, hospital administrator; b. LA, Calif., Sept. 16, 1968; s. Arthur P. and Josephine E. Ochoa; m. Daniele J. Worth, Jan. 25, 1998; children: Madeleine Worth, Eloise Worth. BA, U. of So. California, 1986—90; JD, Yale Law Sch., 1992—95. Bar: State of Calif. 1995. Policy coord. Youth Svc. Am., Washington, 1990—92; assoc. O'Melveny & Myers LLP, LA, Calif., 1995—98; atty. Irell & Manella LLP, Century City, 1998—2001; dir. planned giving Cedars-Sinai Med. Ctr., LA, 2001—04, sr. v.p. cmty. rels. and devel., 2004—. Mem. and sec., bd. of directors Youth Svc. Am., Washington, 1997—98; adj. faculty mem., mba program U. of Judiasm, LA, 2001—03; adv. bd. mem. Neopets Found., Glendale, 2001—06. Chmn. tax exempt orgn. com. LA County Bar Assn., 2004; mem., bd. of trustees Mexican Am. Bar Found., LA, 2002—. Mem.: Ctr. Early Edn., West Hollywood (bd. trustees 2008—), Nat. Eagle Scout Assn., Jonathan Club (L.A.), Yale Club N.Y.C., Phi Beta Kappa. Office: Cedars-Sinai Med Ctr 8700 Beverly Blvd Ste 2416 Los Angeles CA 90048 E-mail: ochoaa@cshs.org.

OCHOA, LORENA, professional golfer; b. Guadalajara, Mex., Nov. 15, 1981; d. Javier and Marcela Ochoa. Student, U. Ariz. Profl. golfer LPGA Tour, 2003—. Five-time U.S. 8-12 Jr. World Championship winner; NCAA Player of Yr., 2001; NCAA Freshman of Yr., 01; finished second NCAA Championships, 2001; finished first place Futures Tour money list, 2002. Founder The Lorena Ochoa Found., Mexico, 2004—. Recipient Nat. Sports award, Mex., 2001, Nancy Lopez award for Outstanding Amateur Accomplishments, 2002, Louise Suggs Rolex Rookie of Yr. award, LPGA, 2003, Rolex Player of Yr. award, 2006, Player of Yr. award, 2007, ESPY award, Best Female Internat. Athlete, ESPN, 2008, Mickey Wright award, Golf Digest, 2008; named Female Player of Yr., Golf Writers Assn. of America, 2006, Female Athlete of Yr., AP, 2006, 2007; named one of 100 Most Influential People in the World, TIME mag., 2008, 100 Most Powerful Celebrities, Forbes.com, 2008. Achievements include winner LPGA Tour events including Franklin Am. Mortgage Championship, 2004, Wachovia LPGA Classic, 2004, Wegmans LPGA, 2005, 07; LPGA Takefuji Classic, 2006, Sybase Classic, 2006, 07, Wendy's Championship for Children, 2006, Corona Morelia Championship, 2006, Samsung World Championship, 2006, 07, Tournament of Champions, 2006; Safeway Internat., 2007, Women's British Open, 2007, Can. Women's Open, 2007, Safeway Classic, 2007, ADT Championship, 2007, Kraft Nabisco Championship, 2008. Avocations: triathalons, marathons, mountain climbing, tennis, basketball, accordion. Office: c/o LPGA 100 International Golf Dr Daytona Beach FL 32124-1092*

OCHOA, RUBEN, artist; b. Oceanside, Calif., 1974; Student, Parsons Sch. Design, NYC, 1996; BA, Otis Coll. Art and Design, LA, 1997; MFA, U. Calif., Irvine, 2003. One-man shows include Vox Alta Projects, San Diego, 2004, Lizabeth Oliveria Gallery, LA, 2006, LAXART, 2006, Hallwalls Contemporary Art Ctr., Buffalo, NY, 2007, Susanne Vielmetter LA Projects, 2007, Susanne Vielmetter Berlin Projects, 2008, exhibited in group shows at Better Look Twice, Pasadena City Coll. Art Gallery, 2002, Calif. Biennial, Orange County Mus. Art, 2004, 25 Bold Moves, Campari Emerging Artists Exhbn., LA, 2006, The Newstand Project, 2006, Phantom Sightings, LA County Mus. Art, 2008, Whitney Biennial, Whitney Mus. Am. Art, NYC, 2008. Recipient Institutional Rsch. award, U. Calif., 2002; Durfee Found. grant, 2004, Visual Arts grant, Creative Capital Found., 2005, Emerging Artist fellowship, Calif. Cmty. Found., 2004, Media Arts fellowship, Rockefeller Found., 2006, Guggenheim fellowship, 2008. Office: c/o Susanne Vielmetter LA Projects 5795 W Washington Blvd Culver City CA 90232

OCHOA-BRILLEMBOURG, HILDA MARGARITA, investment banker; b. July 8, 1944; BS in Econs., U. Catolica Andres Bello, Caracas, Venezuela; MPA, Harvard U.; postgrad. in fin., Harvard Bus. Sch. Chief investment officer, pension investment div. World Bank, 1976—87; mng. dir. Emerging Markets Investment Corp.; founder, pres., CEO Strategic Investment Group, 1987—. Bd. dirs. Harvard Mgmt. Co., Gen. Mills, Inc., McGraw-Hill Inc.; treas. C.A. Luz Electrica de Venezuela, Caracas, 1967—71; lectr. U. Catolica Andres Bello, 1970; ind. cons. in econs. and fin. Published articles in Fin. Analyst Jour. and Pensions & Investments. Bd. dirs. Washington Nat. Opera; chmn. bd. dirs. Youth Orch. of the Americas; vice chair, Group of 50 Carnegie Endowment for Internat. Peace; mem. adv. com. Rockefeller Ctr. for Latin Am. Studies; bd. dirs. Fulbright Found., Atlantic Coun. US. Fulbright-Hays fellow. Office: 1001 19th St N 16th Fl Arlington VA 22209-1722 Office Phone: 703-243-4433.

OCHOCINCO, CHAD (CHAD JAVON JOHNSON), professional football player; b. Miami, Fla., Jan. 9, 1978; Student, Langston U., Okla., 1996; grad. in Phys. Ed., Oreg. State U., 2000. Wide receiver Cin. Bengals, 2001—. Named 1st Team All-Pro, NFL, 2005—06; named to Am. Football Conf. Pro Bowl Team, 2003—07, All-AFC Team, Pro Football Weekly, 2004. Achievements include leading the AFC in receiving yards, 2003, 2004, 2005; leading the NFL in receiving yards, 2006. Office: Cin Bengals 1 Paul Brown Stadium Dr Cincinnati OH 45202*

OCHS, CAROL REBECCA, theologian, writer, theology studies educator, philosopher; b. NYC, May 7, 1939; d. Herman and Clara Florence (Michaels) Blumenthal; m. Michael Ochs, Sept. 27, 1959; children: Elisabeth Amy, Miriam Adina. BA, CUNY, 1960, MA, 1964; PhD, Brandeis U., 1968. Philosophy lectr. CUNY, 1964-65; from asst. prof. to prof. philosophy Simmons Coll., Boston, 1967-92, prof. emerita, 1992—. Adj. faculty Grad. Sch. Union Inst., Cin., 1992—97, Hebrew Union Coll.-Jewish Inst. Religion, NYC, 1994—97, dir. grad. studies, vis. prof. philosophy, 1997—2001, dir. grad. studies, adj. prof. Jewish Religious Thought, 2001—; cons. Inst. for Svc. to Higher Edn., Chestnut Hill, Mass., 1972, St. Mary's Coll., South Bend, Ind., 1980; scholar-in-residence Hollins Coll., Roanoke, Va., 1987, numerous temples and synagogues; mem. selection com. Kent Postdoctoral Fellowships Bunting Inst., Radcliffe Coll.; lectr. in field. Author: Behind the Sex of God: Toward a New Consciousness Transcending Matriarchy and Patriarchy, 1977, Women and Spirituality, 1983, 2d edit., 1997, An Ascent to Joy: Transforming Deadness of Spirit, 1989, The Noah Paradox: Time as Burden, Time as Blessing, 1991, Song of the Self: Biblical Spirituality and Human Holiness, 1994, Jewish Spiritual Guidance, 1997, Our Lives as Torah: Finding God in Our Own Stories, 2001, Reaching Godward: Voices from Jewish Spiritual Guidance, 2004; contbr. articles to profl. jours. Mem. Jewish-Cath. Dialogue, Boston, 1989-93; mem. Cath.-Jewish com. Archdiocese of Boston, 1989-93. Fellow NEH, 1976, 88, Nat. Humanities Inst., U. Chgo., 1978-79, Danforth Found., 1981-86, Coolidge Rsch., Colloquium, 1985, Resource Theologian, 1995-99. Fellow Soc. for Values in Higher Edn. (bd. dirs. 1982-88, chair ctrl. com. 1985-87, 2003—, v.p. 2004-), Assn. for Religion and Intellectual Life (mem. editl. bd. 1986—1992). Office: Hebrew Union Coll 1 W 4th St New York NY 10012 Office Phone: 212-824-2267. Personal E-mail: cochs@earthlink.net.

OCHS, MICHAEL, editor, librarian, music educator; b. Cologne, Germany, Feb. 1, 1937; came to U.S., 1939, naturalized, 1945; s. Isaac Julius and Claire (Baum) O.; m. Carol Rebecca Blumenthal, Sept. 27, 1959; children— Elisabeth Amy, Miriam Adina BA, CCNY, 1958; MS, Columbia U., 1963; A.M., NYU, 1964; D.A., Simmons Coll., 1975. Cataloguer CCNY, 1963-65, lectr. in music, 1964; music libr. Brandeis U., Waltham, Mass., 1965-68, creative arts libr., 1968-74; asst. prof. libr. sci. Simmons Coll., Boston, 1974-78; libr. Eda Kuhn Loeb Music Libr., Harvard U., Cambridge, Mass., 1978-88, Richard F. French libr., 1988-92; lectr. music Harvard U., Cambridge, Mass., 1978-81, sr. lectr. music, 1981-92, also libr. cons., 1977-78; music editor W. W. Norton and Co., NYC, 1992-2001; pres. Ochs Editl., 2001—. Libr. cons. Biblioteca Berenson, Florence, Italy, 1983, Columbia U., 1987; project dir. U.S. Répertoire International des Sources Musicales Manuscript Inventory Ctr. at Harvard U., NEH, Cambridge, Mass., 1985-88. Editor Notes, Jour. Music Libr. Assn., 1987-92, Music Librarianship in America, 1991; contbr. articles to profl. jours., 1976—. Mem. Am. Musicol. Soc. (bd. dirs. 2000-02), Internat. Assn. Music Librs. (pres. rsch. librs. br. 1987-90), Music Libr. Assn. (bd. dirs. 1976-78, pres. 1993-95). Office Phone: 212-987-1089. Personal E-mail: mochsed@gmail.net.

OCHS, PETER WARREN, religion educator; b. Boston, Jan. 26, 1950; s. Sidney and Ruth (Adelman) O.; m. Vanessa Lynn Yablin, June 16, 1974; children: Juliana, Elizabeth. BA summa cum laude, Yale U., 1971, PhD, 1979; MA, Jewish Theol. Sem., 1974. Dir. Jewish Theol. Sem. Pre-High Sch., NYC, 1972-74; counselor to Jewish students Colgate U., Hamilton, N.Y., 1979-86, asst. prof. religion, 1979-86; advisor Colgate-Hamilton Jewish Community, Hamilton, N.Y., 1979—; Wallerstein vis. assoc. prof. Jewish studies Drew U., Madison, N.J., 1988-90, Wallerstein assoc. prof. Jewish studies, 1990—. Fulbright sr. lectr. in philosopy The Hebrew U. of Jerusalem, 1988; lectr. in field. Author: Knowledge Under the Mast, 1970, Talk of the Sea—Oral Navigational Lore on Puluwat, 1971, Learning Sea Lore on Puluwat Atoll, 1975, (with others) Understanding the Rabbinic Mind: Essays on the Hermeneutic of Max Kadushin, 1990; mem. editorial bd. Cross Currents—Religion and Intellectual Life; contbr. articles to profl. jours. Mem. Labor Zionist Alliance, Israel, 1981—, Nitivot Shalom, Jerusalem, 1981—, edn. com. Sch. Bd. of Hebrew Acad. Morris County (chairperson). NEH grantee, 1971, 73, 74, Smithsonian Instn. fellow, 1969, Kent fellow, 1974, Yale U. fellow, 1977, Colgate U. rsch. grantee, 1980, 81, 82. Mem. Soc. for Values in Higher Edn., Am. Acad. Religion, Am. Philos. Assn., Charles S. Peirce Soc., Assocs. for Religion in Intellectual Life, Assn. for Advancement of Am. Philosophy, Acad. for Jewish Philosophy, B'nai Brith. Office: Drew U Dept Religion Madison NJ 07940

OCHS, SIDNEY, neurophysiology researcher, educator; b. Fall River, Mass., June 30, 1924; s. Nathan and Rose (Kniaz) O.; m. Bess Ratner; children: Rachel F., Raymond S. Susan B. PhD in Physiology, U. Chgo., 1952. Rsch. assoc. Ill. Neuropsychiat. Inst., Chgo., 1952-54; rsch. fellow Calif. Inst. Tech., Pasadena, 1954-56; asst. prof. dept. physiology U. Tex. Med. Br., Galveston, 1956-58; assoc. prof. dept. physiology Ind. U., Indpls., 1958-61, prof., 1961-94, prof. emeritus, 1994—. Author: Elements of Neurophysiology, 1965, Axoplasmic Transport and Its Relation to Other Nerve Functions, 1982, A History of Nerve Functions: From Animal Spirits to Molecular Mechanisms, 2004; founding editor, editor-in-chief: Devel. Neurobiology (formerly Jour. Neurobiology), 1969-76, assoc. editor, 1977-86. With US Army, 1943—45. Mem. Internat. Brain Rsch. Orgn., Internat. Soc. Neurochemistry, Internat. Soc. Hist. Neurosciences, Am. Physiol. Soc., Soc. Neurosci., Am. Soc. Neurochemistry, Peripheral Nerve Soc., Hist. Sci. Soc. Democrat. Jewish. Avocations: amateur radio, history. Office: Ind U Med Ctr Dept Cellular & Integ Physiology 635 Barnhill Dr Indianapolis IN 46202-5126 Office Phone: 317-274-7940. Business E-Mail: sochs@iupui.edu.

OCHS, WALTER J., civil engineer, consultant; b. Springfield, Minn., May 20, 1934; s. Walter Minrod and Cleo (Schultz) O.; m. Connie Mae Strate, Sept. 15, 1956; children: Julie, Brian. BS in Agrl. Engring., South Dakota State U., 1957. Registered profl. civil engr., Mich. Engr. in training USDA, Soil Conservation Svc., Watertown, S.D., 1957-58, project engr. Britton, S.D., 1958-61, area engr. Sioux Falls, S.D., 1961-63, asst. state conservation engr. East Lansing, Mich., 1963-66, state conservation engr., 1966-69, asst. state conservationist Saint Paul, Minn., 1969-71, nat. drainage engr. Washington, 1971-86; drainage adviser World Bank, Washington, 1986-96; internat. ind. water mgmt. cons., 1996—98; co-owner Water Mgmt. Engrs., LLC, 1998—. Bd. dirs. Internat. Inst. for Land Reclamation and Improvement Postgrad Land Drainage Course, The Netherlands, 1990-98; particpated in project work over 30 countries; mem. Internat. Commn. Irrigation and Drainage. Contbr. to profl. jours. Named Fed. Engr. of Yr., NSPE, 1982; recipient Outstanding Alumnus award S.D. State U., 1977, Outstanding Contbn. award Corrugated Plastic Tubing Assn., 1981, Svc. to the Profession award U.S. Com. on Irrigation and Drainage, 2004; named to Internat. Drainage Hall of Fame, 1996. Fellow: Am. Soc. Agrl. Engrs.; mem.: ASCE (chmn. drainage com. 1975—76, Royce J. Tipton award 2001). Office: 6731 Fern Ln Annandale VA 22003-1903 E-mail: wochs@hotmail.com.

OCHSENDORF, JOHN, structural engineer, educator; BSc in Structural Engring., Cornell U., 1986; MSc in Civil Engring., Princeton U., 1998; PhD, Cambridge U., 2002. Rsch. asst. Structural Engring. Lab. Cornell U., 1993—96, tchg. asst. Sch. Civil and Environ. Engring., 1995—96; tchg. asst. Dept. Civil Engring. Princeton U., 1996—98; structural engr. Guy Nordenson and Assocs., NYC, 1997—98; undergrad. supr. Dept. Engring. U. Cambridge, England, 1998—2002, vis. lectr. Dept. Architecture, 1999—2000; asst. prof. bldg. tech. MIT, Cambridge, 2002, now assoc. prof. Named MacArthur Fellow, The John D. and Catherine T. MacArthur Found., 2008; fellow NSF; Fulbright Scholar. Office: MIT Dept Architecture 77 Massachusetts Ave Cambridge MA 02139-4307 Office Phone: 617-253-4087. E-mail: jao@mit.edu.

OCHSNER, JOHN LOCKWOOD, thoracic-cardiovascular surgeon; b. Madison, Wis., Feb. 10, 1927; s. Edward William Alton and Isabel (Lockwood) O.; m. Mary Lou Hannon, Mar. 20, 1954; children: John L., Joby Hannon, Katherine Lockwood, Frank Hannon. MD, Tulane U., 1952; hon. diploma (hon.), U. Delgado, San Salvador, El Salvador, 1999. Diplomate Am. Bd. Thoracic Surgery (chmn. 1993-95), Am. Bd. Surgery, Am. Bd. Vascular Surgery. Intern Univ. Mich. Hosp., Ann Arbor, 1952-53, resident, 1953-54, Baylor U. Affilliated Hosp., Houston, 1956-58, 1958-59; chief surg. resident Tex. Children's Hosp., 1959-60; instr. Baylor U., Houston, 1960-61; mem. staff Ochsner Clinic, New Orleans, 1961—, chmn. dept. surgery, 1966-87, chmn. emeritus dept surgery, 1987—; clin. asst. prof. Tulane U., New Orleans, 1961-65, clin. assoc. prof., 1965-70, clin. prof. surgery, 1970—. Vis. prof. to more then 40 univs. and colls. Author: (with others) Coronary Artery Surgery, 1978. Pres. Tennis Patrons Assn. New Orleans, 1972; image amb. City of New Orleans, 1982; bd. dirs. Internat. Trade Mart, New Orleans, 1983. Capt. USAF, 1954-56. Recipient award, Life Mag., 1961, Golden Plate Acad. Achievement award, 1962, award of distinction, Am. Heart Assn. La., 1976, Svc. award, Cystic Fibrosis Rsch. Found., 1977—78, medal of honor, Ecuador, 1981, Crystal Achievement award, Child's Wish of Greater New Orleans, 1987, Young Leadership Coun. award, 1987, medal of honor, Czechoslovakian Surg. Soc., 1996, Honor of Achievement, Am. Heart Assn., 1997, Internat. Recognition award, Denton A. Cooley Cardiovasc. Surg. Soc., 1998, Outstanding Alumnus award, Tulane Sch. Medicine, 1998, Spirit of Love award, Ronald McDonald House Charities, 1999, DeBakey award, DeBakey Internat.

Surg. Soc., 2000, Outstanding Physician award, Orleans Parish Med. Soc., 2002, Weiss Brotherhood award, New Orleans chpt. Nat. Conf. for Cmty. and Justice, 2002, Outstanding Person award, Family Svc. Greater New Orleans, 2004, DeBakey medal, Covenant Heart Inst., 2007, Order of the Plimsoll Mark, World Trade Ctr.; named Rex, King of Carnival, Mardi Gras, New Orleans, 1990, Grand Marshall, Oktoberfest, 1990, 1992. Mem. Am. Assn. Thoracic Surgery (sec. 1979-83, pres. 1992-93), New Orleans Surg. Soc. (pres. 1977-78), So. Surg. Assn. (pres. 1991), So. Assn. for Vascular Surgery (pres. 1983), Boston Club, La. Club, New Orleans Country Club, City Club, Alpha Omega Alpha. Republican. Office: Ochsner Clinic Found 1514 Jefferson Hwy BH 231 New Orleans LA 70121-2483 Home: 170 Walnut St 9-H New Orleans LA 70118

OCHSNER, OTHON HENRY, II, importer, restaurant critic; b. Chgo., May 19, 1934; s. Othon Henry and Louise Catherine (Schlichenmaier) Ochsner. Legal staff Walgreen Co., Chgo., 1961-65; sales mgr. Porsche Car Imports, Senpeir Tire Divsn., Northbrook, Ill., 1966-67; nat. sales mgr. Pirelli Tire Corp., NYC, 1968-73; pres., CEO Ochsner Internat., Chgo., 1974—; mng. dir. Oberhallu Warehousing, Lake Buff, Ill. Bd.dirs., pres. Swiss-U.S.A. Racing Team, Chgo., 1976—. Author: Ochsner Pocket Guide to the Finest Restaurants and Hotels in the World, 12th edit.; author Ochsner Restaurant Newsletters, 1986—, Ochsner Restaurant Guide on Web, 2000- Pres., exec. dir. Louise Catherine Schlichenmaier and Othon Henry Ochsner I Charitable Family Found., 2000—; founder Ochsner Art, Automobile, and Bicycle Mus., Lake Buff. With U.S. Army, 1957-59. Mem. The Am. Inst. Wine and Food, Am.-Swiss C. of C., Swiss-Am. Hist. Soc., Swiss Gourmet Soc. (pres. U.S. chpt.), Swiss Travel Club, Swiss Club Chgo., The Bagatelle Club, Conf. de la Chaine des Rotisseurs, Ordre des Canariers. Baptist. Avocation: visiting and reviewing world class French and Swiss restaurants worldwide. Home: 701 Bluff Rd Lake Bluff IL 60044-2116 Office: Oberhallu Warehousing 86 Albrect Dr Lake Bluff IL 60044 Home Phone: 847-295-2027; Office Phone: 847-465-8200.

OCKERMAN, HERBERT W., agricultural and international studies educator; b. Chaplin, Ky., Jan. 16, 1932; m. Frances Ockerman (dec.). BS with Distinction, U. Ky., 1954, MS, 1958; PhD, N.C. State U., 1962; PhD (hon.), Wyzial U., Poland, 2004; PhD in Humanities (hon.), Cavite U., Philippines, 2008; postgrad., Air U., 1964-70, Ohio State U., 1974, postgrad., 1983, postgrad., 1987, postgrad., 2001, postgrad., 2003—. Asst. prof. Ohio State U., Columbus, 1961-66, assoc. prof., 1966-71, prof., 1971—. Former mem. Inst. Nutrition and Food Tech.; judge regional and state h.s. sci. fairs, 1965—, Ham Contest, Ky. State Fair, Sausage and Ham Contest, Ohio Meat Processing Groups, 1965; cons. Am. Meat Inst., 1977-88, USDA, 1977-2003, CRC Press., Inc., 1988—; bd. examiners U. Calcutta, 1987-88; examiner U. Mysore, India, 1990-97, U. We. Sydney, Australia, 2005, U. Newcastle, Australia, 2005-07; expert witness, various firms, 1992—, UN expert 95; expert cons. com. FAO/WHO, 2003-; hon. mem. vet., med. faculty Assiut U., Egypt; adv. bd. Bull. Vet. Inst. Poland, 2004—; chmn. sci. bd. Egyptian Jour. Meat Sci. and Tech.; presenter, cons. in field. Chmn. sci. bd.: Egyptian Jour. Molecular Sci. and Tech., 2002; contbr. more than 223 articles to profl. jours., more than 128 chpts. to books. Comdr. pilot USAF, 1955-58. Fisher Packing scholar; named Highest Individual in Beef Grading, Kansas City Meat Judging Contest, 1952, Hall of Disting. Alumni, U. Ky., 1995; recipient Am. Soc. Animal Sci. Meat Rsch. award Lilly Rsch. Labs., 1987, Appreciation cert. Ohio Assn. Meat Processors, 1987-2009, Profl. Devel. award Cahill Faculty, commendation Ohio Ho. of Reps., Merit Svc. badge Polish Govt., plaque Argentina Nat. Meat Bd., Animal Sci. award Roussel UCALF, France, U. Assiuit, Egypt, Silver Platter award Nat. Meat Bd., Sec. Agr., Livestock and Fishery, Argentina, Svc. award Coun. Grad. Students, Pomerance Tchg. award, Outstanding Alumni award U. Ky., Outstanding Ednl. Achievements award Argentine Soc. Agr., Coop. award Vet. Faculty. U. Cordoba, Svc. award Panoma Legis. Br., Brazil; Vet. Faculty award U. Cordoba, Spain, 1982, 94, award Nat. Chung-Hsing U., 1982, 95, You Are The Best award INTA Sci., 1997, award Vet. Mus. Ciechanowcu, Poland, Internat. award Assn. Nat. Tech. en Alimentos de Mexico, Can. Indst. Food Sci. and Tech., 1998, Appreciation plaque Republic of Argentina, 1999, Candle Stick of Knowledge award Ludhiana U., Punjab, India, 1999, Internat. award Am. Meat Sci. Assn., 1999, 2000, Appreciation plaque Am. Coll. Commerce, Taiwan, 1999, plaque Selcuk U., Turkey, 1999, Folklore and Cultural memento Sudanese Socs., Sudan U., 1999, Homage and Acknowledgment award Argentine Sec. Agr., 2000, Internat. award Am. Most. Sci. Assn., 2000, Most Honored Guest award Weifang, China, 2001, World History award Jhadong U., China, 2001, plaque Congress of Ham, Cordoba, Spain, 2001, Michal Oczapowski award Polish Acad. Sci., 2002, Sausage Maker award Poland, 2001, Great Educator award China, 2001, Silver Medallion award INTA Argentina, 2001, Pub. award Taiwan, 2002, Animal Sci. plaque, China, 2002, Food award China, 2002, Publ. award Dayeh U., Taiwan, 2003, Coop. award Cath. U., Argentina, 2004, Lifetime Achievement award PAU India, 2005, Sci. award Argentina Nat. Acad., 2006, The World is your Classroom award DaYeh U., 2006, Lifetime Achivement Alumni award Ag & HES Alumni Assn., North Ctrl. Reagan, U. Ky., Ednl. (Producing Good Students) Tree award Da Yea U., Taiwan, 2007, Porcelain award, 2007, Embroidered Plaque for Presenting 7 Presentations Agrl. Conf. Changsha, China, 2007, Chinese Yoke for Caring Students, 2007, numerous others; co-recipient 2 plaques Al Falat HS, India, 2006; plaque Tangai U., Taiwan; plaque for 36,000 books Da Yeh U., Yunnan U., China, Symobolism award U. Turkey, Predsl. plaque Chkurova, Da Yeh U. Mem. NAS, NCR, ASTM, Am. Meat Sci. Assn., Am. Soc. Animal Sci. (Rsch. award 1987), Reciprocal Meat Conf., European Meeting of Meat Rsch. Workers, Polish Vet. Soc. (hon.), Inst. Food Technologists (nat. and OVS chpts.), Inst. Food Tech. (Internat. award 1998, 2000), Can. Meat Sci. Assn., Internat. Congress Meat Sci. and Tech., Rsch. in Basic Sci., Nat. Acad. Agronomy and Vet. Medicine Argentina(corr. academic), Phi Beta Delta (treas. 1987, pres. 1991, Internat. scholar award 1991, Internat. Faculty award 1991, Presdl. medallion award), Gamma Sigma Delta (Rsch. award 1977, Internat. award of merit 1988), Sigma Xi (outstanding advisor in coll. award 1995), Phi Beta Kappa (Outstanding Tchg. award 1997, Extension Diversity award 1997, Pomerene Tchg. Enhancement award 1997, Outstanding Internat. Faculty award 1997), Internat. Gamma Sigma Delta (Disting. Achievement Nat. award 1998), Phi Kappa Phi, CAVITE U., U. Philippines (life 2008, Appreciation Cert., 2007, Plaque of Recognition, 2007). Achievements include american coordinator for memorandum of understanding between OSU and Assiut University Egypt, 2007; dedication of Ockerman-Hansan Hall CIVIT University, Philippines. Only the 2nd international university building dedicated to an OSU professor, 2007; outstanding volunteer recognition from the United Nations and the International Voluntary Organizations, 2007. Office: Ohio State U Meat Lab Animal Sci 2029 Fyffe Rd Columbus OH 43210-1007 Office Phone: 614-292-4317. Business E-Mail: ockerman.2@osu.edu.

OCKEY, RONALD J., lawyer; b. Green River, Wyo., June 12, 1934; s. Theron G. and Ruby O. (Sackett) O.; m. Arline M. Hawkins, Nov. 27, 1957; children: Carolyn S. Ockey Baggett, Deborah K. Ockey Christiansen, David, Kathleen M. Ockey Hellewell, Valerie Ockey Sachs, Robert. BA, U. Utah, Salt Lake City, 1959, postgrad., 1959-60; JD with honors, George Wash. U., Washington, DC, 1966. Bar: Colo. 1967, Utah 1968, US Dist. Ct. Colo. 1967, US Dist. Ct. Utah 1968, US Ct. Appeals (10th cir.) 1969, US Ct. Claims 1987. Missionary to France for Mormon Ch., 1954-57; law clk. to judge U.S. Dist. Ct. Colo., 1966-67; assoc. ptnr., shareholder, v.p., treas., dir. Jones, Waldo, Holbrook & McDonough, Salt Lake City, 1967-91; mem. Utah Ho. of Reps., 1988-90, Utah State Senate, 1991-94; of counsel Mackey Price & Williams, Salt Lake City, 1995-98; asst. atty. gen. Utah, 1998—. Trustee SmartUtah, Inc., 1995-2002; trustee Utah Tech. Fin. Corp., 1995-98; lectr. in securities, pub. fin. and bankruptcy law. Mem. editl. bd. Utah Bar Jour., 1973-75; mem. staff and bd. editors George Washington Law Rev., 1964-66; contbr. articles to profl. jours. State govtl. affairs chair Utah Jaycees, 1969; del. state Rep. Convs., 1972-74, 76-78, 80-82, 84-86, 94-96, del. Salt Lake County Rep. Conv., 1978-80, 88-92; sec. Wright for Gov. campaign, 1980; legis. dist. chmn. Utah Rep. Party, 1983-87; trustee Food for Poland, 1981-85, pres., trustee Unity to Assist Humanity Alliance, 1992-95; bd. dirs. Utah Opera Co., 1991-94; trustee Utah Info. Tech. Assn., 1991-2000. Lt. US Army, 1960-66, to capt. JAG, USAR, 1966-81. Mem. ABA, Utah State Bar Assn. (various coms.), Nat. Assn. Bond Lawyers (chmn. con. on state legislation 1982-85), George Washington U. Law Alumni Assn. (bd. dirs. 1981-85), Order of Coif, Phi Delta Phi. Home Phone: 801-278-3809; Office Phone: 801-366-0359. Business E-Mail: rockey@utah.gov.

O'CLAIR, KATHERINE CLEMENS, library and information scientist; m. Tim O'Clair, 2005. BS in Environ. Sci., Nazareth Coll., 2001; MS in Libr. and Info. Sci., Fla. State U., 2004. Intern Fletcher Libr. Ariz. State U., asst. libr., sci. reference libr. Life Sciences, Noble Sci. and Engring. Libr., 2005—. Named one of the Movers & Shakers, Libr. Jour., 2007. Mem.: Ariz. Libr. Assn. (co-chair Coll. and Univ. Divsn.), Spl. Libraries Assn. (New Mem. of Yr. 2005). Office: Univ Libraries Ariz State Univ PO Box 871006 Tempe AZ 85287 Office Phone: 480-965-5964. E-mail: katherine.oclair@asu.edu.

O'CONNELL, BRIAN, community organizer, educator, writer; b. Worcester, Mass., Jan. 23, 1930; s. Thomas J. and Mary (Carroll) O'C.; m. Ann C. Brown, July 11, 1953; children: Todd, Tracey, Matthew. BA, Tufts Coll., Medford, Mass., 1953; postgrad., Maxwell Sch. Citizenship and Pub. Adminstrn., 1953-54; also numerous hon. degrees. Field rep. Am. Heart Assn., Pa., 1954-56, Md. exec. dir., 1956—61, Calif. exec. dir., 1961—66; exec. dir. Nat. Assn. Mental Health, 1966-78, dir. emeritus, 1978—; pres. Nat. Council on Philanthropy, 1978-80; exec. dir. Coalition of Nat. Vol. Orgns., 1978-80; pres. Ind. Sector, 1980-95, founding pres., pres. emeritus, 1995—; prof. pub. svc. Tufts U., Medford, Mass., 1995—2006. Mem. U.S. Pres.'s Com. Employment of Handicapped, 1966-68; chmn. Liaison Group Mental Health, 1969-72. Author: Effective Leadership in Voluntary Organizations, 1976, Finding Values That Work: The Search for Fulfillment, 1977, America's Voluntary Spirit, A Book of Readings, 1983, The Board Members Book, 1985, Philanthropy in Action, 1987, Our Organization, 1987, Volunteers in Action, 1989, People Power: Service Advocacy, Empowerment, 1994, Board Overboard, 1995, Powered By Coalition: The Story of Independent Sector, 1997, Voices from the Heart: In Celebration of America's Volunteers, 1999, Civil Society: The Underpinnings of American Democracy, 1999, Fifty Years in Public Causes: Stories From a Road Les Traveled, 2005. Mem. Alumni Coun. Tufts U., 1970-80, trustee, 1988-2000, trustee emeritus, 2000—, chmn. pres. search com., 1992; trustee Points of Light Found., 1989-95; bd. dirs. Hogg Found., 1990-95; chmn. organizing com., 1st chmn. Civicus: World Alliance for Citizen Participation, 1992-96; bd. dirs. E.M. Kauffman Found., 1994—2003, BridgeSpan Group, 1999—, Cape Cod Found., 2003—. Recipient outstanding agy. prof. award United Way Am., 1979, Lincoln Filene Citizenship award, 1985, John W. Gardner Leadership award, 1994, Gold Key award Am. Soc. Assn. Execs., 1994, Chmns. award, NSFRE, 1994, The Tiffany award, 1998. Fellow Am. Pub. Health Assn., Nat. Acad. Pub. Adminstrn. (trustee 1993-2000), Nat. Com. Patients' Rights (chmn. 1975-77). Home: 50 Chase St Chatham MA 02633-2404

O'CONNELL, CARMELA DIGRISTINA, appraisal executive, consultant; b. Johnstown, Pa., Nov. 8, 1925; d. Salvatore and Josephine (Riggio) Digristina; m. Maurice F. O'Connell, Sept. 21, 1974 (dec. Feb. 1984); children: Geraldine, John, Bernard. Diploma, Eastern Secretarial Sch., NYC, Sch. Interior Design. From typist to sec.-treas. Philip P. Masterson Co., NYC, 1942-72; exec. v.p., bd. dirs. Masterson & O'Connell Inc., NYC, 1972-80, cons., 1981—; founder, pres. N.Y. Appraisal Corp., NYC, 1971-80; co-founder, pres. Park Ave. Appraisal, NYC, 1981—. Mem. N.Y. Rep. Com., 1974—, Met. Opera Guild, N.Y.C., 1986; chmn. Ch. of Our Saviour, N.Y.C., 1986; mem. Ladies of Charity, Cath. Charities Archdiocese of N.Y., 1990; bd. dirs. 80 Park Avenue Condominiums, 1997—. Recipient Amita award for Bus. Woman of Yr., 1977, Lena Madesin Phillips award N.Y. League/Fortune 500 Bus. and Profl. Women, 1989. Mem. Nat. Fedn. Bus. and Profl. Women's Clubs Inc. (2d v.p. 1964, 1st v.p. 1966). Roman Catholic. Home: 2421 Old Collier Rd Land O Lakes FL 34639 Office Phone: 813-948-8941.

O'CONNELL, DANIEL CRAIG, retired psychologist, educator; b. Sand Springs, Okla., May 20, 1928; s. John Albert and Letitia Rutherford (McGinnis) O'C. BA, St. Louis U., 1951, Ph.L., 1952, MA, 1953, S.T.L., 1960; PhD, U. Ill., 1963. Joined Soc. of Jesus, 1945; asst. prof. psychology St. Louis U., 1964-66, asso. prof., 1966-72, prof., 1972-80, trustee, 1973-78, pres., 1974-78; prof. psychology Loyola U., Chgo., 1980-89, Georgetown U., Washington, 1990-98, emeritus, 1998—, chmn., 1991-96. Vis. prof. U. Melbourne, Australia, 1972, U. Kans., 1978-79, Georgetown U., 1986, Loyola U., Chgo., 1998-2003; Humboldt fellow Psychol. Inst. Free U. Berlin, 1968; sr. Fulbright lectr. Kassel U., W. Ger., 1979-80. Author: Critical Essays on Language Use and Psychology, 1988, Communicating with One Another, 2008; contbr. articles to profl. jours. Recipient Nancy McNeir Ring award for outstanding teaching St. Louis U., 1969; NSF fellow, 1961, 63, 65, 68; Humboldt Found. grantee, 1973; Humboldt fellow Tech. U. of Berlin, 1987. Fellow: APA, Mo. Psychol. Assn.; mem.: AAAS, AAUP, Mo. Acad. Sci., N.Y. Acad. Sci., Psychonomic Soc., Eastern Psychol. Assn., Southwestern Psychol. Assn., Midwestern Psychol. Assn., Soc. Scientific Study of Religion, Psychologists Interested in Religious Issues, Phi Beta Kappa. Home and Office: 4517 W Pine Blvd Saint Louis MO 63108-2109 Home Phone: 314-758-7179; Office Phone: 314-758-7143. Business E-Mail: doconnell@jesuits-mis.org. *Were it over, it would have been more than my expected share already. The challenge of learning to serve others has moved it along at a quick pace, and I am grateful that I have always received more than I've been able to give in return—from the Lord and from many good people.*

O'CONNELL, DANIEL FRANCIS, lawyer; b. Orange, NJ, May 5, 1943; BS with honors, Villanova U., 1965; JD, Rutgers U., 1968. Bar: NJ 1968, NY 1980, US Supreme Ct. 1980. Ptnr. Lanigan & O'Connell PC, Basking Ridge, NJ, 1969—85; ptnr. mng. ptnr. Shanley & Fisher PC, Morristown, NJ, 1985—99; ptnr., bus. fin. dept., ptnr.-in-charge Drinker Biddle & Reath LLP, Florham Pk., NJ, 1999—2009, mng. ptnr., mem. mgmt. com., 1999—2009. Dist. VII ethics com. Supreme Ct. NJ, 1978-83, sec., 1980-83; chmn. NJ Commn. Legal and Ethical Problems in the Delivery of Health Care, 1986-90. Mem. ABA (labor and employment law sect., antitrust law sect., health law sect. 1977—), NJ State Bar Assn. (labor law sect., health and hosp. law sect.), Somerset County Bar Assn. (exec. com. 1977-81, pres. 1979), Am. Health Lawyers Assn., Am. Hosp. Assn. Office: Drinker Biddle & Reath LLP 500 Campus Dr Florham Park NJ 07932-1047 Office Phone: 973-549-7160. Office Fax: 973-360-0771. Business E-Mail: daniel.oconnell@dbr.com.

O'CONNELL, DANIEL JAMES, lawyer; b. Evergreen Park, Ill., Aug. 14, 1954; s. Edmund J. and Kathryn J. (Hanna) O'C.; m. Nancy L. Eichler, March 21, 1992; children: Kelly Jacklyn, Kirby Kathryn. BS, Millikin U., 1976; JD, IIT, 1980; postgrad., DePaul U., 1981, U. Mich., 1997—2001; MPH, U. Ill., 2005, postgrad., 2006—. Bar: Ill. 1980, US Dist. Ct. (no. dist.) Ill. 1980, US Dist. Ct. (ctrl. dist.) Ill. 2000, US Dist. Ct. Ariz. 1989. Ins. regulatory counsel Kemper Group, Long Grove, Ill., 1980-81, environ. claims counsel, 1981-82; sr. home office claim counsel Zurich Ins. Cos., Schaumburg, Ill., 1982-83; assoc. Clausen, Miller, Gorman et al, Chgo., 1983-86; ptnr. environ. toxic tort litigation O'Connell & Moroney, P.C., Chgo., 1986-90; ptnr. toxic tort litigation Burditt, Bowles & Radzius, Chgo., 1990-91; ptnr. Daniel J. O'Connell & Assocs., P.C., Elgin, Ill., 1991—2002, O'Connell & O'Sullivan, P.C., Elgin, 2002—03, Daniel J. O'Connell & Assocs., P.C., Elgin, 2003—05, O'Connell, Tivin, Miller & Burns, LLC, 2006—. James S. Kemper Found. scholar, 1972—76. Mem.: ABA, APHA, AAAS, Soc. Risk Analysis, British Occupl. Hygiene Soc., Ill. Bar Assn., Kane County Bar Assn., Def. Rsch. Inst., NY Acad. Scis. Home: 177 Macintosh Ct Glen Ellyn IL 60137-6478 Office Phone: 847-741-4603. E-mail: doconn3@uic.edu.

O'CONNELL, DAVID M., academic administrator, priest; b. Phila., Apr. 21, 1955; BPh magna cum laude, Niagara U., 1978; ThM, Mary Immaculate Seminary, 1981, DivM, 1983; PhD in Canon Law, Cath. U., 1987; Licentiate in Canon Law, Cath. U. Am., 1990; PhD (hon.), Franciscan U. Steubenville, St. Thomas Aquinas Coll., St. Charles Sem., St. John's U. Ordained Cath. priest 1982. Religion tchr., dir. student activities Archbishop Wood H.S. for Boys, Warminster, Pa.; registrar, asst. acad. dean, asst. prof. philosophy, homiletics and canon law Mary Immaculate Seminary, Northampton, Pa., 1987—90; prof. theology St. John's U., Jamaica, NY, 1990—98, acad. dean, dean faculty Coll. Liberal Arts and Scis., 1991—98, assoc. v.p., 1996—98; interim acad. v.p. Niagara U., 1994—95; pres. Cath. U. Am., Washington, 1998—, John Joseph Keane U. prof., 2006—. Canonical cons. and ecclesiastical judge on the tribunals Diocese of Harrisburg, Pa., Diocese of Birmingham, Ala., Diocese of Scranton, Pa.; co-host, commentator during papal visit to U.S. CBS-TV, 1995; trustee Consortium Univs. Washington Met. Area; cons. Vatican Congregation for Cath. Edn., 2005—. Contbr. articles to profl. jours. Trustee Cath. U. Am., St. John's U., Archbishop John Carroll H.S., Washington, Basilica of the Nat. Shrine of the Immaculate Conception; active Greater Washington Bd. Trade; mem. adv. bd. U. St.Thomas, St. Paul. Recipient President's medal, St. John's U., St. Elizabeth Ann Seton award, Nat. Cath. Ednl. Assn., 2006. Mem.: Assn. Cath. Colls. and Univs., Ea. Regional Canon Lawyers Assn., Canon Law Soc. Am. Office: Office Pres Cath Univ Am Nugent Hall 620 Michigan Ave NE Washington DC 20064 Office Phone: 202-319-5100. E-mail: cua-president@cua.edu.*

O'CONNELL, DAWN C. MYERS, legislative staff member; Legis. counsel for Rep. John Spratt, US House of Reps., Washington, 2000—04, legis. dir., 2004—07, chief of staff, 2007—. Office: Office of Congressman John Spratt 1401 Longworth House Office Bldg Washington DC 20515 Office Phone: 202-225-5501. Office Fax: 202-225-0464. E-mail: dawn.oconnell@mail.house.gov.*

O'CONNELL, EDMOND J., chemist, educator, chemist, consultant; b. Providence, Apr. 26, 1939; s. Edmond J. and Katherine G. O'Connell; m. Genevieve S. O'Connell, July 24, 1965; children: Shannon, Edmond, Daniel, Sean, Kevin, Timothy. BS, Providence Coll., 1960; PhD, Yale U., 1964. Sr. rsch. chemist E.I. DuPont Co., Wilmington, Del., 1964—67; chemistry prof. Fairfield (Conn.) U., 1967—, Yale U., New Haven, 1974—. Cons. in field. Contbr. articles to profl. jours. Grantee, Am. Chem. Soc., 1968, Rsch. Corp., 1972, NSF. Mem.: Sigma Xi. Roman Catholic. Avocation: marathon running. Home: 161 Harbor St Branford CT 06405 Office: Chemistry Dept Fairfield Univ Fairfield CT 06430

O'CONNELL, EDWARD JAMES, JR., psychologist, educator, systems administrator, consultant; b. Sterling, Ill., Aug. 15, 1932; s. Edward James and Elizabeth E. (Clapham) O.; m. Pamelia Canon Floyd, Aug. 21, 1959; children— Edward James III, John Matthew BS in Psychology, Ill. Inst. Tech., 1958; MA in Psychology, Northwestern U., 1961, PhD in Psychology, 1962. NSF postdoctoral fellow Carnegie Inst. Tech., Pitts., 1962-63, asst. prof. psychology, 1963-65; psychology faculty Syracuse (N.Y.) U., NY, 1965-93, prof., 1975-93, prof. emeritus, 1993—. Cons. Rand Corp., Santa Monica, Calif., 1962-64, Abt Assocs., Boston, 1970-73, Marcy Psychiat. Hosp., N.Y., 1979-82 Served to cpl. U.S. Army, 1952-54 NSF predoctoral fellow, 1959-62: NSF postdoctoral fellow, 1962-63; Northwestern U. predoctoral fellow, 1958-59 Mem. Sigma Xi. Democrat. Avocations: billiards, computer programming. Address: PO Box 570 Cashiers NC 28717-0570 Office Phone: 828-743-3257. Personal E-mail: ejoconn@dnet.net.

O'CONNELL, HUGH MELLEN, JR., retired architect; b. Oak Park, Ill., Nov. 29, 1929; s. Hugh M. and Helen Mae (Evans) O'C.; m. Frances Ann Small, Apr. 13, 1957; children: Patricia Lynn, Susan Marie, Jeanette Maureen. Student mech. engring., Purdue U., 1948-50; BS in Archtl. Engring, U. Ill., 1953. Registered architect, Ariz., Calif., La., Nev., Nat. Council Archtl. Registration Bds. Designer John Mackel; structural engr. Los Angeles, 1955-57; architect Harnish & Morgan & Causey, Ontario, Calif., 1957-63; pvt. practice Ventura, Calif., 1963—69; architect Andrews/O'Connell, Ventura, 1970-78; dir. engring. div. Naval Constrn. Bn. Center, Port Hueneme, Calif., 1978-91, supervisory architect, 1991-93; ret., 1993. Mem. tech. adv. com. Ventura Coll., 1965-78; sec. Oxnard Citizens' Adv. Com., 1969-79, v.p., 1970-72, pres., 1972—; chmn. Oxnard Beautification Com., 1969, 74, Oxnard Cmty. Block Grant adv. com., 1975-76; mem. Oxnard Planning Commn., 1976-86, vice chmn., 1978-79, chmn., 1980-81. Mem. Oxnard Art-in-Pub. Places Commn., 1988-93, 2003—. Served with AUS, 1953-55. Mem. AIA (emeritus, pres. Ventura chpt. 1973), Am. Concrete Inst., Soc. Am. Registered Architects (Design award 1968, dir. 1970), Am. Legion, Soc. for Preservation and Encouragement of Barbershop Quartet Singing in Am. (chpt. pres. 1979, chpt. sec. 1980-83), Acad. Model Aeros. (#9190 1948—), Channel Islands Condors Club (treas. 1986-99), Sports Flyers Assn., Alpha Rho Chi (Anthemios chpt.). Presbyterian (elder 1963, deacon 1967). Lodges: Kiwanis (pres. 1969, div. sec. 1974-75), Elks. Home and Office: 520 Ivywood Dr Oxnard CA 93030-3527 Personal E-mail: hughoarch@msn.com.

O'CONNELL, JACK T., state official, school system administrator; b. Glen Cove, NY, Oct. 8, 1951; m. Doree O'Connell; 1 child, Jennifer Lynn. BA in History, Calif. State U., Fullerton; cert. secondary tchr.,

Calif. State U., Long Beach, 1975. Tchr. various high schs.; mem. Calif. State Assembly, 1982—94, Calif. State Senate, 1994—2002; state supt. pub. instrn. State of Calif., 2002—. Mem. Santa Barbara County Sch. Bd. Democrat. Office: Calif Dept Edn Ste 5602 1430 N St Sacramento CA 95814 Office Phone: 916-319-0800.*

O'CONNELL, JEANNE, financial planner, insurance broker; b. Stoneham, Mass., Dec. 9, 1951; d. Kenneth Edward and Frances Evelyn (Matulewicz) O'C.; 1 child, Ryan Sulloway. Student, U. Oreg., 1971-72; BFA cum laude, U. Mass.-Amherst, 1974, U. Calif.-Sacramento, summer 1973; postgrad., Northeastern U., 1975; MBA, Suffolk U., 1984. CPCU, CLU; chartered fin. cons.; assoc. in underwriting; enrolled agt. designation. Ins. clk. S.B. Swaim & Co., Boston, 1969-72, Hollis Perrin & Co., Boston, 1972; underwriting asst. Pub. Svc. Mut. Ins. Co., Newton, Mass., 1974-77; personal lines analyst Comml. Union Ins. Co., Boston, 1977-80, sr. personal lines analyst, 1980-83, tech. specialist, 1983-88; pvt. practice fin. cons., brokerage Boston, 1988—. Instr. ins. and fin. planning Ins. Libr. Boston, 1988—2003; speaker in field; ind. tax preparer; pub. arbitrator FIMRA; founder, dir. Red Dragon Arts Coop., Boston, 1983, Ebay Store-Reddragonarts, 2005-; potter, artist Radcliffe Pottery Studio, Boston, 1980-85. Mem. exec. student adv. bd. Suffolk U., 1982—83, student liaison mem. between Exec. MBA Program and regular MBA Program and dean's adv. bd., coord. Exec. MBA Program Policy Seminar Weekend, 1983; v.p., trustee Friends Waltham Pub. Libr., 1998, 1999, asst. treas., 2000, 2000—. Fellow Nat. Tax Practice Inst.; mem. Nat. Soc. Enrolled Agts., Nat. Soc. Accts., Nat. Assn. Tax Preparers, Waltham Garden Club (photographer 1997-2004), Garden Club Fedn. Mass. (photographer 2007-), Delta Mu Delta. Avocations: reading books on tape, photography, rubber stamps, gardening. Studio: 229 School St Waltham MA 02451-4546 Office Phone: 781-891-1721. Personal E-mail: reddragonarts@yahoo.com.

O'CONNELL, JEFFREY, law educator; b. Worcester, Mass., Sept. 28, 1928; s. Thomas Joseph and Mary (Carroll) O'C.; m. Virginia Kearns, Nov. 26, 1960 (dec. 1994); children: Mara, Devin. Grad. cum laude, Phillips Exeter Acad., 1947; AB cum laude, Dartmouth Coll., 1951; JD, Harvard U., 1954. Bar: Mass. 1954, Conn. 1954, Va. 1983, hon. admittance to Ark. and Minn. bar. Instr. speech Tufts U., 1953-54; assoc. Sherburne, Powers & Needham, 1954-57, Hale & Dorr, Boston, 1958-59; asst. prof., then assoc. prof. law U. Iowa Coll. Law, 1959-62; assoc. dir. automobile claims study Harvard Law Sch., 1963-64; assoc. prof. law U. Ill. Coll. Law., 1964-65, prof., 1965-79; prof. law U. Va. Law Sch., 1980-83, John Allan Love prof., 1983-90, Samuel H. McCoy II prof., 1990—, Class of 1948 rsch. prof., 1994-97. Summer vis. prof. Northwestern U., 1963, U. Mich., 1966, 75, So. Meth. U., 1972, U. Tex., 1977, U. Wash., 1979; John Marshall Harlan vis. prof. N.Y. Law Sch., 1991; vis. fellow Centre for Socio-Legal Studies, Wolfson Coll., Oxford (Eng.) U., 1973, 79; Thomas Jefferson vis. fellow Downing Coll. Cambridge U., Eng., 1989; mem. U. Va. Ctr. for Advanced Study, 1980-83. Author: (with R.E. Keeton) Basic Protection for the Traffic Victim, 1965, After Cars Crash: The Need for Legal and Insurance Reform, 1967, (with Arthur Myers) Safety Last: An Indictment of the Auto Industry, 1966, (with R.E. Keeton, John McCord) Crisis in Car Insurance, 1968, (with Wallace Wilson) Car Insurance and Consumer Desires, 1969, The Injury Industry, 1971, (with Rita James Simon) Payment for Pain and Suffering, 1972, Ending Insult to Injury: No-Fault Insurance for Products and Services, 1975, (with Roger Henderson) Tort Law, No-Fault and Beyond, 1975, The Lawsuit Lottery: Only the Lawyers Win, 1979, (with C. Brian Kelly) The Blame Game: Injuries, Insurance and Injustice, 1986, (with Lester Brickman and Michael Horowitz) Rethinking Contingency Fees: A Proposal to Align the Contingency Fee System with its Policy Roots and Ethical Mandates, 1994, (with Peter Bell) Accidental Justice: The Dilemmas of Tort Law, 1997, (with Thomas E. O'Connell) Friendships Accross Ages: Johnson and Moswell, Holmes and Laski, 2007,(with Christopher J. Robinette) A Reipe Belanced Tort Reform,2008 Mem. Nat. Hwy. Safety Adv. Com., 1967-70; edn1. adv. bd. John Simon Guggenheim Found., 1973-87; bd. dirs. Consumers Union, 1970-76; mem. com. on competitive safeguards and med. aspects of sports NCAA, 1985-87. Served as 1st lt. USAF, 1954-57. Recipient Robert B. McKay award for ins. scholarship Tort and Ins. Practice sect. ABA, 1992; Guggenheim fellow, 1972-73, 79-80. Mem. ABA, Va. Bar Assn., Casque and Gauntlet, Farmington Country Club, Phi Beta Kappa, Psi Upsilon. Democrat. Roman Catholic. Home: 505 Oak Cir Charlottesville VA 22901-3220 Office: U Va Sch Law 580 Massie Rd Charlottesville VA 22903-1738 Home Phone: 434-979-8330; Office Phone: 434-924-7809. Business E-Mail: jo@virginia.edu.

O'CONNELL, JOHN BERNARD, JR., medical educator, department chairman; b. Chgo., July 27, 1949; s. John B. O'Connell; m. Mary Owens, Jan. 12, 1980; children: Jessica, Moira, Claire, Sheila, John. BS, U. Ill., Chgo., 1971; MD magna cum laude, Loyola U., Maywood, Ill., 1974. Diplomate Nat. Bd. Med. Examiners, Am. Bd. Internal Medicine, Am. Bd. Cardiovascular Disease. Intern Loyola U. Med. Ctr., Maywood, 1975-76, resident in internal medicine, 1976-78, chief resident in internal medicine, 1977-78, fellow in cardiology, 1978-80, staff physician emergency dept., 1979-81, attending cardiologist, 1980-86, med. dir. Cardiac Transplantation Program, 1984-86; clin. instr. in medicine Loyola U., Stritch Sch. Medicine, Maywood, 1977-80, asst. prof. medicine, 1980-85, assoc. prof. medicine, 1985-86; asst. chief med. svc. Hines VA Hosp., Maywood, 1981-83; attending cardiologist LDS Hosp., Salt Lake City, 1986-91, U. Utah Med. Ctr., Salt Lake City, 1986-91; assoc. prof. medicine Sch. Medicine, U. Utah, Salt Lake City, 1986-91, prof., 1991; attending physician Univ. Hosp., U. Miss. Med. Ctr., Jackson, 1991—97; prof. medicine U. Miss. Med. Sch., Jackson, 1991—97, chmn. dept. medicine, 1991—97; prof., chair dept. internal medicine Wayne State U., Detroit, 1997—2005; prof. cardiology Feinberg Sch. Medicine, Northwestern U., Chgo., 2005—; assoc. dir., dir. network devel. Bluhm Cardiovasc. Inst., Northwestern Meml. Hosp., Chgo., dir. Ctr. Heart Failure, 2005—. Cons. Salt Lake VA Med. Ctr., Salt Lake City, 1988-91, Primary Children's Med. Ctr., Salt Lake City, 1988-91; med. dir., chmn. exec. com. UTAH Cardiac Transplant Program, Salt Lake City, 1986-91; chmn. adv. bd. Exptl. Organ Transplantation Procedures, apptd. by Gov. of Ill., 1985-86; mem. working group on myocarditis Nat. Heart, Lung and Blood Inst., 1985; com. mem. Internat. Symposium Inflammatory Heart Disease, Snowmass, Colo., July, 1988; mem. sci. coun. Internat. Soc. and Fedn. Cardiology, 1990—; mem. spl. study sect. NIH, 1990; mem. sci. bd. Internat. Congress of Cardiology on Cardiovascular Pharmacotherapy and Cardiomyopathies, Greece, 1990; mem. adv. com. Miss. Health Scis. Info. Network, 1992-94; med. dir. Miss. Organ Procurement Agy., 1992-93; mem. sci. com. Internat. Workshop on the Cardiomyopathies, LaCoruna, Spain, 1993. Co-editor (monographs): Myocarditis: Precursor of Cardiomyopathy, 1983, Drug Therapy of Dilated Cardiomyopahty and Myocarditis, 1988, Intrathoracic Transplantation 2000, 1993; mem. editorial bd. Jour. Heart and Lung Transplantation, 1986—, Internat. Jour. Cardiology, 1992—, Transplantation, 1993—; manuscript cons. numerous publs.; contbr. articles to profl. jours. Recipient Norris L. Brookens Outstanding Resident award Ill. Soc. Internal Medicine, 1978, Robert Kark, M.D. Rsch. award Chgo. Soc. Internal Medicine, 1981, Outstanding Young Citizen award Chgo. Jr. Assocs. Commerce and Industry, 1985, Shinshu U. medal Matsumoto City, Nagano, Japan, 1992; grantee Earl M. Bane Charitable Trust, 1979-83, Fraternal Order Eagles, 1983-86, BRSG, 1983-84, NHLBI, 1986-91, Deseret Found., 1987-91, Bristol Myers Squibb, 1988-91, Burroughs Wellcome, 1992—, Otsuka Pharm., 1993—, Smith Kline Beecham Pharm., 1993—. Fellow ACP, Am. Coll. Chest Physicians, Am. Coll. Cardiology (cardiac transplantation com. 1991—, conf. steering com. 1991-92), Am. Coll. Angiology; mem. AMA, AAAS, Assn. of Profs. of Medicine (bd. dirs. 1997—, treas. 1998-2001, pres.-elect 2001-02, pres. 2002-03), Am. Soc. Transplant Physicians (mem. tng. and manpower com. 1990—, mem. pub. policy com. 1993—, numerous others), N.Y. Acad. Scis., Internat. Soc. Heart and Lung Transplant (mem. sci. program com. 1987, 89, 90, councilor 1989-91, pres.-elect 1991-92, pres. 1993-94, past pres. 1993-94, others), Transplantation Soc., Assn. Profs. Medicine, Rsch., Miss. (bd. dirs.), Jackson Acad. Medicine, So. Soc. Clin. Investigation, Am. Fedn. Clin. Rsch. (sen. midwest sect. 1983-86), So. Soc. Clin. Rsch., Ctrl. Soc. Clin. Rsch., Miss. State Med. Assn., Ctrl. Med. Soc., Am. Heart Assn. (bd. dirs. West Cook County 1982-86, v.p. 1985-86, chmn. 1990-92, numerous others), United Network for Organ Sharing (mem. coalition on organ doning 1991-92, mem. thoracic com. 1992—, mem. sci. adv. com. 1993—), Alpha Omega Alpha. Office: Northwestern U Med Sch Galter 10-240 201 E Huron St Chicago IL 60611 Office Phone: 313-745-8244, 312-695-1105. Office Fax: 312-695-1434. Business E-Mail: joconnel@med.wayne.edu. E-mail: joconnell@northwestern.edu.

O'CONNELL, KEVIN, lawyer; s. Michael Frederick and Kathryn Agnes (Kelley) O'Connell; m. Mary Adams, July 14, 1990; children: Tiffany W., Elizabeth H., Dana A., Lisel E. AB, Harvard, 1955, JD, 1960. Bar: Calif. 1961. Assoc. firm O'Melveny & Myers, LA, 1960-63; asst. U.S. atty. criminal div. Ctrl. Dist. Calif., LA, 1963-65; staff counsel Gov. Calif. Commn. to Investigate Watts Riot, LA, 1965-66; ptnr. Tuttle & Taylor, LA, 1966-70, Coleman & O'Connell, LA, 1971-75; pvt. practice law LA, 1975-78; of counsel firm Simon & Sheridan, LA, 1978-89; ptnr. Manatt, Phelps & Phillips, LA, 1989—. Adj. prof. law U. So. Calif. Law Sch., 2002—. Bd. editors Harvard Law Rev., 1958—60. Bd. dirs. Calif. Supreme Ct. Hist. Soc.; mem. Los Angeles County Dem. Ctrl. Com., Calif., 1973—74. Lt. USMCR, 1955—57. Recipient Best Lawyers in Am. Mem.: Pacific Coun. on Internat. Policy, Am. Law Inst. Avocations: hiking, reading. Home: 426 N Mccadden Pl Los Angeles CA 90004-1026 Office: Manatt Phelps & Phillips Trident Ctr E Tower 11355 W Olympic Blvd Los Angeles CA 90064-1614 Home Phone: 323-935-2116; Office Phone: 310-312-4222. Business E-Mail: koconnell@manatt.com.

O'CONNELL, MARY-KATHLEEN, lawyer; BA cum laude, Yale U., 1977; JD, NYU, 1981. Bar: Mass. 1981. With Goodwin Procter LLP, Boston, 1981—, ptnr., chair, trusts & estate planning practice, mem., investment com. Staff NYU Law Rev. Mem.: ABA, Estate Planning Coun., Women's Bar Assn., Mass Bar Assn., Boston Bar Assn. Office: Goodwin Procter LLP Exchange Pl 53 State St Boston MA 02109 Office Phone: 617-570-1391. Office Fax: 617-523-1231. Business E-Mail: moconnell@goodwinprocter.com.

O'CONNELL, MAURICE DANIEL, lawyer; b. Ticonderoga, NY, Nov. 9, 1929; s. Maurice Daniel and Leila (Geraghty) O'C.; m. Joan MacLure Landers, Aug. 2, 1952; children: Mark M., David L., Ann M., Leila K., Ellen A. Grad., Phillips Exeter Acad., 1946; AB, Williams Coll., 1950; LLB, Cornell U., 1956. Bar: Ohio 1956. Since practiced in, Toledo; assoc. Williams, Eversman & Black, 1956-60; ptnr. Robison, Curphey & O'Connell, 1961-95, of counsel, 1996—; spl. hearing officer in conscientious objector cases U.S. Dept. Justice, 1966-68. Mem. complaint rev. bd. Bd. Commrs. on Grievance and Discipline of Supreme Ct. Ohio, 1987. Mem. Ottawa Hills Bd. Edn., 1963-66, pres., 1967-69; former trustee Toledo Soc. for Handicapped; past trustee Woodlawn Cemetery; past trustee Toledo Hearing and Speech Center, Easter Seal Soc.; mem. alumni council Phillips Exeter Acad. Served to 1st lt. USMCR, 1950-53. Life fellow Ohio State Bar Found.; mem. NW Ohio Alumni Assn. of Williams Coll. (past pres.), Ohio Bar Assn., Toledo Bar Assn. (chmn. grievance com. 1971-74), Kappa Alpha, Phi Delta Phi. Clubs: Toledo. Home: 3922 W Bancroft St Toledo OH 43606-2533 Office: 9th Flr Four SeaGate Toledo OH 43604

O'CONNELL, PATRICIA ELLEN, musician, educator; b. Endicott, NY, Jan. 12, 1955; d. Harold Seymour Arnold and Sylvia Patricia Russell; m. William Harry O'Connell, July 1, 2006; children: Jennifer Lynn Kotski, William Hancock Ellis, Matthew Charles Ellis. Regents diploma, Owego Free Acad., NY, 1973; MusB, Crane Sch. Music, Potsdam, NY, 1977; MusM, Ithaca Coll. Sch. Music, 1983. Cert. music edn. K - 12 N.Y. State. Band dir. LaFargeville (N.Y.) Cen. Sch., 1977—78, Newark Valley (N.Y.) Mid. Sch., 1978—90, Vestal (N.Y.) Jr. H.S., 1990—92; band and chorus dir. Vestal Sr. H.S., Vestal, 1992—97, band dir., 1997—; dir. Vestal Marching Band, 1992—2002, co-dir., 2004—; pit orch. condr. Damn Yankees, Carousel Vestal HS. French horn performer Binghamton (N.Y.) Philharm. Orch., 1978—; prin. horn Tri Cities Opera Orch., Binghamton, 1978—, Jubilee Arts Concerts; French horn performer Glimmerglass Opera Orch., Cooperstown, NY, 1979—, Fair Winds Woodwind Quintet, 2004—, Brass Menagerie Brass Quintet, 2005—; guest condr. Band Festival, Sullivan County, Pa., 1990, 98; founder So. Tier Comty. Band Workshops; former condr. The Kirby Band; chmn. HS band Broome County Music Educators, 2003, 07. Contbr. sch. band and orch. mag. Warden St. Paul's Episcopal Ch., Owego, 2004—06; bd. dirs. Spectrum Drum and Bugle Corps, Corning, NY, 1994—98, Owego, NY. Recipient Solo Performer award, Binghamton Cmty. Orch., 1995, Midi Sta. grant, Vestal Schools Found., 1996. Mem.: N.Y. State Sch. Music Assn., Am. Fedn. Musicians (orch. rep. 1998—2008), N.Y. State Band Dirs, Assn., Music Educators Nat. Conf. Episcopalian. Avocations: ferrets, needlework, yardwork, walking. Home: 132 Southside Dr Owego NY 13827 Office: Vestal H S 205 Woodlawn Dr Vestal NY 13850 Personal E-mail: peoconnell@stny.rr.com.

O'CONNELL, PATRICK, chef; Attended, Catholic U. Am. Proprietor, co-owner, chef Inn at Little Washington, Wash., Va., 1978. Author: (cookbooks) The Inn at Little Washington: A Consuming Passion, 1996, Patrick O'Connell's Refined American Cuisine: The Inn at Little Washington, 2004. Recipient 2008 Am.'s Top Restaurants award for Inn at Little Washington, Zagat Survey, 2007, Mondavi award for Culinary Excellence, Robert Mondavi; named Best Chef: Mid-Atlantic, James Beard Found., 1993, Outstanding Chef in Am., 2001. Mem.: North Atlantic Relais Gourmand (pres., internat. bd. dirs.). Office: Inn at Little Washington Middle and Main St Washington VA 22747 Office Phone: 540-675-3800. Office Fax: 540-675-3100.

O'CONNELL, RALPH ANTHONY, dean, psychiatrist, educator; b. NYC, Jan. 26, 1938; s. Ralph E. and Agnes H. (O'Connell) O'C.; m. Jane Burke, June 15, 1963; children: Ralph E. III, Ellen C., John B. AB cum laude, Coll. of Holy Cross, Worcester, Mass., 1959; MD, Cornell U., 1963. Diplomate Am. Bd. Psychiatry and Neurology. Intern St. Vincent's Hosp. and Med. Ctr. N.Y., NYC, 1963-64, resident, 1964, 67-69, rsch. psychiatrist, 1969-71, chief inpatient dept. psychiatry, 1971-76, clin. dir. and vice chmn. psychiatry, 1974-95; prof. psychiatry N.Y. Med. Coll., Valhalla, 1984—, dean and provost, 1996—. Editor-in-chief Comprehensive Psychiatry, 1983-96. Served to capt. U.S. Army, 1965-66. Fellow Am. Psychiat. Assn., N.Y. Acad. Medicine (trustee 1989—). Clubs: Univ. (N.Y.C.). Roman Catholic. Office: NY Med Coll Valhalla NY 10595 Office Phone: 914-594-4900.

O'CONNELL, RICHARD (JAMES), English literature educator, poet; b. NYC, Oct. 25, 1928; s. Richard James and Mary Ellen (Fallon) O'C.; BS, Temple U., 1956; MA, Johns Hopkins, 1957. Instr. English Temple U., Phila., 1957-61, asst. prof., 1961-69, assoc. prof., 1969-86, sr. assoc. prof., 1986-93, assoc. prof. emeritus, 1993; guest lectr. poetry dept. writing seminars Johns Hopkins U., 1961-74; participant Poetry in Schs. Program, Pa. Coun. Arts, 1971-73; Fulbright lectr. Am. lit. U. Brazil, Rio de Janeiro, 1960, U. Navarre, Pamplona, Spain, 1962-63. Served with USN, 1948-52. Recipient prize Contemporary Poetry Press, 1972. Mem. PEN, MLA, Assocs. Writing Programs, Walt Whitman Poetry Ctr. (dir. 1975-84), Lit. Fellowship Phila. Author: From an Interior Silence, 1961, Cries of Flesh and Stone, 1962, New Poems and Translations, 1963, Brazilian Happenings, 1966, Terrane, 1967, Thirty Epigrams, 1971, Irish Monastic Poems (transl.), 1975, The Word in Time (selected transl. of Antonio Machado), 1975, Sappho (selected transl.), 1975, Lorca (selected transl.), 1976, Middle English Poems (transl.), 1976, More Irish Poems (transl.), 1976, Epigrams from Martial (transl.), 1976, One Hundred Epigrams from the Greek Anthology (trans.), 1977, Hudson's Fourth Voyage, 1978, The Epigrams of Luxorius (transl.), 1984, Temple Poems, 1985, Hanging Tough, 1986, Battle Poems, 1987, Selected Epigrams, 1990, Lives of The Poets, 1990, New Epigrams From Martial (transl.), 1991, The Caliban Poems, 1992, RetroWorlds, 1993 (transl.) Simulations, 1993, Voyages, 1995, The Bright Tower, 1997, American Obits, 2001, Fractals, 2002, Dawn Crossing, 2003, Waiting for the Terrorists, 2006; editor: Apollo's Day, 17th Century Songs, 1969, Atlantis Edits., 1962—, Poetry Newsletter, 1971-86. Home: 1147 Hillsboro Mile Apt 510 Hillsboro Beach FL 33062-1720 Personal E-mail: rocon100@comcast.net.

O'CONNELL, RICHARD JOHN, geophysicist, educator; b. Helena, Mont., Aug. 27, 1941; BS in Physics, Calif. Inst. Tech., 1963, MS in Geology, 1966, PhD in Geophysics, 1969. Rsch. fellow in geophysics Calif. Inst. Tech., 1969-70; rsch. geophysicist Inst. of Geophysics and Planetary Physics UCLA, 1970-71; asst. prof. dept. geol. scis. Harvard U., 1971-74, assoc. prof., 1974-77, prof. geophysics, 1977—, mem. Ctr. for Earth and Planetary Physics, 1971—86, dir. Ctr. for Earth and Planetary Physics, 1983-86. Cons. Rockwell Internat., 1984-87, AMOCO Tulane Rsch. Ctr., 1984—; vis. staff mem. Los Alamos Nat. Lab., 1980—. Contbr. numerous articles to profl. jours. Fellow Am. Geophys. Union (Inge Lehmann Medal, 2000), AAAS, Am. Acad. Arts & Scis.; mem. Geological Soc. Am. (Arthur L. Day Medal, 2001), Royal Astron. Soc., Sigma Xi. Office: Dept Earth & Planetary Sci Harvard U 20 Oxford St Cambridge MA 02138-2902 Business E-Mail: oconnell@geophysics.harvard.edu.

O'CONNELL, ROBERT FRANCIS, physics professor; b. Athlone, Ireland, Apr. 22, 1933; came to U.S., 1958; s. William and Catherine (O'Reilly) O'C.; m. Josephine Molly Buckley, Aug. 3, 1963; children: Adrienne Molly, Fiona Catherine, Eimear Kathleen. BSc, Nat. U. Ireland, Galway, 1953, DSc, 1975; PhD, U. Notre Dame, 1962. Telecommunications engr. Dept. Posts and Telegraphs, Dublin, Ireland, 1954-58; scholar Inst. Advanced Studies, Dublin, 1962-63; systems analyst IBM, Dublin, 1963-64; sr. rsch. assoc. Inst. Space Studies, NYC, 1966-68; asst. prof. physics La. State U., Baton Rouge, 1964-66, assoc. prof., 1966-69, prof., 1969-86, Boyd prof., 1986—. Editor for theoretical physics Hadronic Jour.; former bd. mem. Phys. Rev. A; contbr. articles to profl. jours. Named Disting. Rsch. Master, La. State U., 1975; NAS-NRC fellow, 1966-68, Sci. Rsch. Coun. (Eng.) sr. vis. fellow, 1976. Fellow Am. Phys. Soc.; mem. Am. Astron. Soc., Internat. Astronomy Union, Internat. Soc. Gen. Relativity and Gravitation. Republican. Roman Catholic. Avocation: tennis. Home: 522 Bancroft Way Baton Rouge LA 70808-4807 Office: La State Univ Dept Physics And Astronomy Baton Rouge LA 70803-0001

O'CONNELL, SHARON KAY, media specialist; d. Gilford Erskin and Mildred Elinor Alexander; m. James J. O'Connell, Aug. 10, 1984; children: James Alexander, Daniel Joseph. BA, U. Wyo., Laramie, 1968; MA, U. Northern Colo., Greeley, 1975; MLS, Syracuse U., NY, 1992. School Media Specialist NY, 1995. Libr. media specialist Skaneateles Ctrl. Sch., NY, 1985—. Proj. mgr. Paper Crane Project. Recipient Antje Lemtke Book award, Syracuse U., 1992, Nat. Info. Infrastructure Hon. Mention award, 1995. Office: Skaneateles Middle Sch 35 East St Skaneateles NY 13152 Business E-Mail: soconnel@skanschools.org.

O'CONNELL, TAAFFE CANNON, actress, publishing executive; b. Providence; d. Joseph Ceril and Edith Ethelyn (Dent) O'C. BA, MFA, U. Miss., University. Regional supr. Gloria Marshall Figure Salons, SC; v.p., co-founder Doc Sox Inc., Pacific Palisades, Calif., 1988-90; pres., founder Canoco Pub., LA, 1991—, 1-800-266-DYNE, LA, 1992-93. Founder Rising Star Distbn., Yes I Can Actor's Workshops, 2001—, Get Inside the Agent's Head Seminars, 2003, Actors Acing Hollywood Seminars, 2006; exec. prodr. Beanie/Twigg 1999—, Canoco Prodn. Appeared in films, including Men Without Dates, Dangerous, Hot Chili, Cheech & Chong Nice Dreams, Rocky II, Galaxy of Terror, New Years Evil, Rich Man Poor Man Book I, Caged Fury; TV appearances include Malubu Branch, General Hospital, Dangerous Women, Dallas, Knight and Daye, The New Gidget, Knight Rider, Three's Company, Dr. Joyce Brothers Show, Blansky's Beauties, Peter Lupus Show, Fix-It City, Happy Days, Laverne & Shirley, Wonder Woman, The Incredible Hulk; theater appearances include Too True to be Good, Damn Yankees, Anastasia, Star Spangled Girl, The Beaux Stratagem, The Canterbury Tales; founder, pub. The Caster, 1991, Power Agent, 1993; Jan. founder Rising Star Distbn. and Canoco Prodns., 1999—, Get Inside the Agents' Head Seminars, Yes I Can Actors Workshops, Actors Acing Hollywood Seminars, 2005—; exec prodr.: Beanie & Twigg, Paranormal Private Eyes, Inside the Industry, 2000, Hollywood DVD, Actors Acting Hollywood DVD Series, 2009. Mem. Screen Actors' Guild, Am. Fedn. TV Radio Artists, Actor's Equity, Actor's Forum (bd. dirs. 1985-94). Avocations: singing, spinning, sailing, travel. Office: Canoco Pub 11611 Chenault St Ste 118 Los Angeles CA 90049-4574 Office Phone: 310-471-2287. Personal E-mail: industryedge@adelphia.net.

O'CONNELL, WILLIAM EDWARD, JR., retired finance educator; b. NYC, Sept. 16, 1937; s. William Edward and Helen Margaret (Brazel) O'Connell; m. Janet Elinor Shields, Aug. 15, 1965; children: William Edward III, Cathleen Anne. AB, Manhattan Coll., Riverdale, NY, 1959; MBA, Columbia U., NYC, 1961; DBA with honors, Ind. U., Bloomington, 1967; JD, Coll. William and Mary, Williamsburg, Va., 1974. Fin. analyst Pfizer, Inc., NYC, 1962-64; asst. prof. U. Conn., Storrs, 1967-69; Morris prof. banking U. Va., Charlottesville, 1988; Chessie prof. bus. Coll. William and Mary, Williamsburg, Va., 1969—2005. Mem. faculty Va. Bankers Sch., Charlottesville, 1975—99, Stonier Grad Sch. Banking, Newark, 1977—91, Bank Adminstrn. Inst., Madison, Wis., 1978—97; bd. dirs. C. & F Fin. Corp., Citizens & Farmers Bank. Author: Asset & Liability Management, 1979, Advanced Financial

Planning, 1984, Financial Planning for Credit Unions, 1989, Strategic Financial Managment for Commercial Banks, 1993. Mem.: Fin. Mgmt. Assn., Am. Fin. Assn., Fords Colony Country Club, Omicron Delta Epsilon, Beta Gamma Sigma. Roman Catholic. Home: 102 Overlook Dr Williamsburg VA 23185-4434 Office: Coll William & Mary Mason Sch Business PO Box 8795 Williamsburg VA 23187-8795 Home Phone: 757-229-1587; Office Phone: 757-221-2950. Business E-Mail: william.oconnell@mason.wm.edu.

O'CONNELL, WILLIAM RAYMOND, JR., educational consultant, retired academic administrator; b. Richmond, Va., Jan. 4, 1933; s. William Raymond and Mary Helen (Wenenger) O'C.; m. Peggy Annette Tucker, June 29, 1957; 1 child, William Raymond III. B of Music Edn., Richmond Profl. Inst., 1955; MA, Columbia U., 1962, EdD, 1969; HLD (hon.), New Eng. Coll., 1995. Asst. to provost Richmond Profl. Inst., Va., 1955-57, dean of men, 1957-59, dean of students, dean of men, 1959-61; asst. to provost, dir. student info. ctr. Tchrs. Coll. Columbia U., NYC, 1962-65, rsch. asst. inst. of higher edn. Tchrs. Coll., 1965-66; rsch. assoc. So. Regional Edn. Bd., Atlanta, 1966-69, dir. spl. programs, 1969-73, project dir., undergrad. edn. reform, 1973-79; dir. curriculum and faculty devel. Assn. Am. Colls., Washington, 1979-80, v.p. for programs, 1980-82, v.p., 1982-85; pres. New Eng. Coll., Henniker, NH, 1985-95, pres. emeritus, 1995—; vis. sr. fellow Assn. Am. Colls. and Univs., 1995—97; dir. health edn. and leadership program Nat. Assn. Student Pers. Adminstrs., 1996—2002, 2003—05. Cons. Coun. for Advancement Small Colls., 1975; adv. com. project on instnl. renewal through improvement of tchg. Soc. for Values in Higher Edn., 1975-78; evaluator NH Postsecondary Edn. Commn., 1987-95, vice chmn., 1990-92, chmn., 1992-94; evaluator Nat. Ctr. for Rsch. to Improve Postsecondary Tchg. and Learning, 1987-90, New Eng. Assn. Schs. and Colls., 1988, 91; higher edn. rev. panel awards for pioneering achievements in higher edn. Charles A. Dana Found., 1988, 89. Author, editor: articles to profl. publs. Pres. Richmond Cmty. Amb. Project, 1958-60, bd. dirs., 1960-61; bd. dirs. Alumni Assn. Acad. divsn. Va. Commonwealth U., 1970-73; chmn. fundraising com. Atlanta Boys Choir, Inc., 1976-77, trustee 1978-79; trustee Atlanta Coun. for Internat. Visitors, 1973-76, 78-79; pres. UN Assn., Atlanta, 1976-77; steering com. Nat. Coun. chpt., divsn. pres. UN Assn. US, 1977-79, nat. coun., 1980-90; steering com. Leadership Concord, 1992-95, chmn., 1994-95. Named Cmty. Amb. to Sweden Cmty. Amb. Project of the Experiment in Internat. Living, 1956. Fellow Royal Soc. of the Arts UK (life); mem. NH Coun. on World Affairs (bd. dirs. 1993-95), Williamsburg AIDS Network (bd. dirs., 2006-08), Greater Concord C. of C. (bd. dirs. 1989-93), Coordinating Coun. for Internat. Univs. (bd. dirs. 2001-06), Va. Commonwealth U. Alumni Assn. (bd. dirs. 2006-09), Phi Delta Kappa. Methodist. Avocations: antiques, travel. E-mail: wroconn@cox.net.

O'CONNOR, ANAHAD S., journalist; b. NYC, May 23, 1982; B, Yale U., 2003. Intern NY Times, 1999, CAP Advisors, St. Vincent's Hosp., Dublin; staff reporter Yale Daily News; health & fitness columnist NY Times, 2003—. Author: Never Shower in a Thunderstorm: Surprising Facts and Misleading Myths About Our Health and the World We Live In, 2007. Office: NY Times Science & Health Desk 620 8th Ave New York NY 10018-1618 Office Phone: 212-556-7141. Office Fax: 212-556-7306.

O'CONNOR, BRIAN D.A., music educator, French horn musician; b. Albuquerque, Dec. 6, 1951; s. Joseph Fredrick and Mary Adger (King) O'Connor; m. Coral Lynn Johnson, Sept. 21, 1972 (dec. July 1993); 1 child, Sean Adger. Student, New Eng. Conservatory of Music, Boston, 1970—72; BFA, Calif. Inst. of the Arts, Valencia, 1973. Recording musician French horn L.A. Recording Orch., 1974—; prof. horn UCLA, 1998—. Horn clinician Calif State Music Edn., LA, 2001—; French horn performer Pacific Serenades, LA, 2000—, UCLA Faculty Chamber Group, Westwood, 2001—. Musician (horn, soloist): (more than 1,900 films, including) Flicka, The Notebook, The Rock, Crimson Tide, Contact, Backdraft, Star Trek-First Contact, others, (films) Cinderella Man, (TV series) Star Trek, others, The Pacifier, Star Trek: Enterprise. Mem.: Recording Musicians Assn. of L.A. (pres. 1999—2005). Avocations: soccer, running, flying, bicycling. Office: 20335 Ventura Blvd Ste 400 Woodland Hills CA 91364 Personal E-mail: horn51@aol.com.

O'CONNOR, BRIDGET, investment company technology officer; b. 1964; A, Middlesex County Coll., NJ. With AT&T Bell Labs, 1985—91, Lehman Bros., 1991, chief info. officer, head global bus., 2002—. Contbr. articles to profl. jours. Named one of The 100 Most Influential Women in NYC Bus., Crain's NY Bus., 2007. Mem.: YWCA NYC Acad. Women Leaders. Mailing: Lehman Bros Holdings Inc 745 7th Ave New York NY 10019 Office Phone: 212-526-7000. Office Fax: 212-526-8766.

O'CONNOR, CHARLES EDWARD, JR., state government official, lawyer; b. Phila., Feb. 21, 1960; s. Charles Edward O'Connor, Ruth Pauline Cardamone-O'Connor; m. Lori Marie Ruszkiewicz; 1 child, Charles Henry. BA, LaSalle Coll., Phila., 1982; JD, Widener U., Wilmington, Delaware, 1988. Election clk. County Commrs. Office, Phila., 1978—81; parcel post machine clk. U.S. Postal Svc., Phila., 1982—83, letter carrier Abington, Pa., 1983—85; bail interview supr. Common Pleas Ct. Phila., 1985—89; law clk. to Hon. John T.J Kelly Jr. Superior Ct. Pa., Phila., 1989—92, chief law clk. to Hon. John T.J Kelly Jr., 1992—97, dep. prothonotary for ea. dist. Pa., 1997—2005; exec. dir. 2001 Legis. Reapportionment Commn., Harrisburg, Pa., 2001—02. Mem. 2d Dist. Police Adv. Coun., Phila., 1998—2004, 24th Dist. Police Adv. Coun., 1989—92; counsel Summerdale Boys Club, Phila., 1993—97. Co-author: (book) Practical Tips for Navigating Appellate Courts, 2006. Mem. 53d Ward Rep. Exec. Com., Phila., 1978—82, 25th Ward Rep. Exec. Com., Philadelphia, 1988—89; pres. Friends of Summerdale Civic Assn., Phila., 1999—2004. Mem.: Nat. Assn. Appellate Ct. Cks., Brehon Law Soc., Order Sons of Italy in Am., Grand Army of The Republic Mus., Custodes Pacis Lodge, Ancient Order of Hiberians (First Degree 2000). Roman Catholic. Avocation: Pennsylvania History, Neighborhood Clean-up/Graffiti Removal, Old Car Repair and Restoration, Urban Affairs. Office: Superior Ct Pa 530 Walnut St Ste 315 Philadelphia PA 19106 Home: 3628 E Thompson St Philadelphia PA 19134-5512 Office Phone: 215-560-5795, 215-560-5801. Business E-Mail: charlie.o'connor@pacourts.us.

O'CONNOR, CHRISTOPHER JOHN, information technology manager, consultant; b. Stoughton, Mass., Jan. 29, 1967; s. James Edward and Sally Anne O'Connor; m. Martha Treichel O'Connor, Apr. 6, 2002; children: Brigid Grace, Brendan Padraig. BS, US Mil. Acad., West Point, NY, 1989. Sr. analyst Teledyne Brown Engring., Arlington, Va., 1999—2000; sr. cons. BearingPoint/KPMG Consulting, Alexandria, Va., 2000—04; program mgr. Kepler Rsch., Inc, Arlington, 2004—09; founder/pres. Change 1 Person, Alexandria, 2006—; founder, COO Nat. Continuity Inst., 2007—; assoc. Booz Allen Hamilton McLean, 2009—. Maj. US Army, 1989—99. Decorated Bronze Star medal US Army; recipient Meritorious Svc. medal, 1999. Mem.: Project Mgmt. Inst. (life cert. project mgmt. profl.), Six Sigma Black Belt. Republican. Roman Catholic. Avocations: soccer, hockey, running. Home: 8612 Pilgrim Ct Alexandria VA 22308 Office: 13200 Woodland Park Rd Herndon VA 20171 Office Phone: 703-984-1055 ext 90102. Personal E-mail: chrisoconnor@change1person.org. Business E-Mail: oconnor_christopher@bah.com.

O'CONNOR, CHRISTOPHER M., cardiologist; b. Dec. 8, 1957; MD, U. Md., 1983. Cert. Internal Medicine, 1988, Cardiovasc. Disease, 1989. Resident in internal medicine/cardiology Duke U. Med. Ctr., Durham, NC, 1983—86, 1986—87, 1988—89, exec. dir. cardiology, dir. Heart Ctr. Office: Duke Sch Medicine 129 Davison Bldg DUMC 3356 Durham NC 27710 Office Phone: 919-681-5816, 919-681-3447. Office Fax: 919-681-7755.*

O'CONNOR, DORIS JULIA, not-for-profit fundraiser, consultant; b. Apr. 30, 1930; 1 child: Kim C. BA cum laude in Econs., U. Houston, 1975. Adminstrv. asst. Shell Cos. Found. Inc., NYC, 1966-71, asst. sec. Houston, 1971-73, sec., 1973-76, sr. v.p., dir., mem. exec. com., 1976-93; prin. Doris O'Connor & Co., 1993—. Corp. assoc. United Way of Am., Washington, 1976-93; corp. advisor Bus. Com. of Arts, N.Y.C., 1976-91, del., 1982-87; dir. Ind. Sector, Washington, 1981-89, vice chmn., 1983-87; mem. contbns. coun. Conf. Bd., N.Y.C., 1976-93; advisor Coun. of Better Bus. Burs., Washington, 1975-94, vice chmn., 1983-87; commr. adv. commn. on work-based learning, Dept. Labor, 1991-93; mem. Houston/Harris County Arts Task Force, 1991-93, Houston Ind. Sch. Dist. Task Force, 1991-93; trustee Houston Grand Opera, 1993-99, Houston Symphony Soc., 1993-99, Soc. Performing Arts, 1993-99, Cultural Arts Coun., 1993-96, Greater Houston Coalition Edn. Excellence, 1993-96; mem. adv. bd. Houston Zool. Soc., 1993-99; mem. Mus. Fine Arts, Houston. Mem. Houston Com. Fgn. Rels., Houston World Affairs Coun., Houston Philos. Soc., Plaza Club (bd. givs. 1987-89), Omicron Delta Epsilon. Office Phone: 713-522-3278.

O'CONNOR, EDWARD GEARING, lawyer; b. Pitts., May 5, 1940; s. Timothy R. and Irene B. (Gearing) O'C.; m. Janet M. Showalter, June 17, 1972; children: Mark G., Susan M. BA, Duquesne U., 1962, JD, 1965. Bar: Pa. 1965, US Dist. Ct. (we. dist.) Pa. 1965, US Ct. Appeals (3d cir.) 1968, US Supreme Ct. 1976. Assoc. Eckert, Seamans, Cherin & Mellott, Pitts., 1965-72, ptnr., 1973-99, sr. counsel, 2000—. Mem. adv. com. on appellate ct. rules Supreme Ct. Pa., 1986—92, mem. procedure rules com., 1998—2004; bd. dirs., mem. audit com., compliance com. Federated Investors, Inc. Editor Duquesne U. Law Rev., 1964-65. Chmn. Hampton Twp. Planning Commn., Pa., 1986—87; mem. Hampton Twp. Zoning Hearing Bd., 1997—; bd. dirs. Duquesne U., 1995—2007. Recipient Disting. Alumni award Duquesne U. Law Rev., 1985, Disting. Law Alumni award Duquesne U. Sch. Law, 1991, Disting. Svc. award Hampton Twp., 1991, McAnurlty Svc. award Duquesne U., 1992; named Century Club Disting. Alumni, Duquesne U., 1985. Fellow: Pa. Bar Found., Am. Bar Found.; mem.: St. Thomas More Soc. Allegheny County, Ally City Bar Found. (chair fellows com. 2000—01), Acad. Trial Lawyers Allegheny County (bd. govs. 1986—89, 1998—), Pa. Bar Assn. (ho. of dels. 1985—90), Pitts. Athletic Assn., Duquesne U. Alumni Assn. (pres. 1980—82, 1988—90, bd. govs. 1982—90, bd. dirs. 1988—89), Duquesne Club. Republican. Roman Catholic. Home: 4288 Green Glade Ct Allison Park PA 15101-1202 Office: Eckert Seamans Cherin & Mellott 600 Grant St Ste 44th Pittsburgh PA 15219-2702 Office Phone: 412-566-6053. Business E-Mail: eoconnor@eckertseamans.com.

O'CONNOR, EDWARD JOSEPH, neurologist; b. LA, Jan. 12, 1944; s. Edward Joseph and Claire Smith O'Connor; m. Laura Davidson Folks, Mar. 6, 1982; children: Charles, Kevin, Andrew. BS, U. Notre Dame, Ind., 1966; MD, UCLA, 1970. Diplomate Am. Bd. Neurology and Psychiatry, Am. Bd. Electrodiagnostic Medicine. Intern U. Calif. Affiliate Hosps., 1970—71; resident internal medicine Wadsworth VA Hosp., LA, 1971—72; resident neurology U. N.Mex., 1974—76; chief resident UCLA, 1976—77; registrar Inst. Neurology, London, 1977—78; chief section neurology White Meml. Hosp., LA, 1979—86; owner Nerol. Assocs. West LA, Santa Monica, Calif., 1986—. Assoc. prof. neurology USC & UCLA. Bd. dirs. UCLA Rugby. Recipient UCLA Rugby Hall of Fame, 2008; named to Santa Monica Rugby Club Hall of Fame, 2009. Fellow: Am. Acad. Neurology. Democrat. Roman Catholic. Office: Neurol Assocs West LA 2811 Wilshire Blvd # 790 Santa Monica CA 90403

O'CONNOR, EDWARD VINCENT, JR., lawyer; b. Yokosuka, Japan, Nov. 9, 1952; s. Edward Vincent and Margaret (Robertson) O'C.; m. Kathy J. Hunt, May 23, 1992. BA, Duke U., 1975; JD, N.Y. Law Sch., 1981. Bar: Va. 1982, D.C. 1983. Assoc. Lewis, Kinsey, Dack & Good, Washington, 1982-87; ptnr. Lewis, Dack, Paradiso & Good, Washington, 1988-89, Lewis, Dack, Paradiso, O'Connor & Good, Washington, 1989-94, The Lewis Law Firm, 1994, Byrd, Mische, Bevis, Bowen, Joseph & O'Connor, Fairfax, Va., 1995—2003; pvt. practice Fairfax, 2003—. Arbitrator DC Superior Ct.; neutral case evaluator and conciliator Fairfax County Cir. Ct.; lectr. in field. Bd. dirs., treas. Potomac Legal Aid Soc., 2001—. Named One of Best 50 Divorce Lawyers Washingtonian mag., 1995, 2000, Va. Super Lawyer, 2007-09. Mem. Va. State Bar (spl. com. on access to legal svcs. 1994-04, 5th dist. discipline com. 2001-03, sec., 2003-04, vice chair, 2004-06, bar coun. 2005—), DC Bar, Fairfax County Bar Assn. (vice chair family law sect. 1995-96, continuing edn. com. 1988-95, chair 1995, pub. svc. com. 1995, chair 1996-98, cir. ct. com. 1994-96, 99-01, jud. selection com., pro bono com., James Keith award for pub. svc. 1999), Legal Svcs. No. Va. (bd. dirs., chmn. pro bono com., sec.-treas. 1998-02, pres. 2002-03, treas. 2003-06, pro bono award for outstanding svc. 1997), Potomac Legal Aid Soc. (treas. 2003—). Home Phone: 703-437-4414; Office Phone: 571-432-0555. Personal E-mail: eddie52911@hotmail.com. Business E-Mail: evojr@cox.net.

O'CONNOR, FRANCIS X., financial executive; b. Bklyn., May 7, 1929; s. Richard B. and Mary (McCafferty) O'C.; m. Leona A. Windorf, June 30, 1951; children: Francis X., Edward K., Brendan T., Richard B. III, A. Bruce, Marianne, Margaret, Leona. BS, St. Peter's Coll., 1951. CPA, N.Y., N.J. Audit mgr. Coopers & Lybrand, NYC, 1951-65; controller Ward Foods, Inc., NYC, 1965-66, v.p. fin., CFO, 1966-72, also bd. dirs., 1968-73; v.p. fin., CFO UMC Industries, Inc., NYC, 1973-76; v.p. fin. and corp. devel., CFO SKF Industries, Inc., King of Prussia, Pa., 1976-87; v.p. corp. fin. Moore & Schley Securities Corp., Morristown, NJ, 1987-89; mng. dir. Sterling Manhattan Corp. Investment Bankers, NYC, 1989-93. Adv. bd. Boyden Cons. Corp. Mem. AICPA, AIM, N.Y. State Soc. CPAs. Fin. Excs. Inst., Nat. Conf. on Power Transmission (trustee), Machinery and Allied Products Inst. Fin. Coun., St. Peter's Coll. Alumni Assn. (trustee, past pres. Monmouth chpt.), Navy League U.S., Spring Lake Golf Club, (past pres., trustee), Seaview Country Club (N.J.), Green Gables Croquet Club (past pres.), Legacy Golf Club (Ft. Pierce, Fla.), Yacht and Country Club (Stuart, Fla.). Home: 2355 NE Ocean Blvd Stuart FL 34996-2945 Office: 16 St Clair Ave Spring Lake NJ 07762

O'CONNOR, GAIL, legislative staff member; Dep. press sec., Senator Dianne Feinstein US Senate, Washington, 2006—08; press sec., Rep. Nydia Velazquez US House of Reps., 2008—, press sec., small bus. com., 2008. Democrat. Office: 2466 Rayburn House Office Bldg Washington DC 20515 Office Phone: 202-225-2361. Office Fax: 202-225-0327. Business E-Mail: gail.oconnor@mail.house.gov.*

O'CONNOR, GORDON JAMES, Canadian government official; b. Toronto, Ont., Can., May 18, 1939; married; 2 children. BS in Math. and Physics, Concordia U.; BA in Philosophy, York U. Mem. House Commons, Canada, 2004—; min. nat. def. Govt. of Canada, Ottawa, 2006—07, min. nat. revenue, 2007—. Served over 30 years as military officer Canadian Army, 2nd lt. to Brigadier Gen. Armour Br. Office: Parliament Hill House of Commons 157 East Block Ottawa ON K1A 0A6 Canada also: District Office 101-240 Michael Cowpland Dr Kanata ON K2M 1P6 Canada Office Phone: 613 992 1119, 613 592 3469. Office Fax: 613 992 1043, 613 592 4756. E-mail: oconng@parl.gc.ca, mp@gordonoconnor.ca.

O'CONNOR, JAMES E., waste management executive; b. May 14, 1949; m. Cathy O'Connor; children: Kerry O'Connor Stiles, James, Kevin. BS, DePaul Univ., 1972. Staff acct. Waste Mgmt., Oakbrook, Ill., 1972-78, with, 1982-87, v.p. southeastern region, 1987-91, sr. v.p. N.Am., 1991-92, area pres., 1992-98; CEO Republic Svcs., Inc., Ft. Lauderdale, Fla., 1998—2003, chmn., CEO, 2003—. Bd. dirs. Broward Workshop, Children's Cardiac Found.; mem. bd. advisors Broward Econ. Devel. Coun., Broward County Make-A-Wish Found.; trustee Fla. Tax Watch, Mus. Art, St. Thomas Aquinas H.S. Found. Recipient Tree of Life award Jewish Nat. Fund, 1995. Office: Republic Svcs Inc 110 SE 6th St 28th Fl Fort Lauderdale FL 33301

O'CONNOR, JAMES JOHN, retired utility company executive; b. Chgo., Mar. 15, 1937; s. Fred James and Helen Elizabeth O'Connor; m. Ellen Louise Lawlor, Nov. 24, 1960; children: Fred, John (dec.), James, Helen Elizabeth. BS, Holy Cross Coll., 1958; MBA, Harvard U., 1960; JD, Georgetown U., 1963. Bar: Ill. 1963. With Commonwealth Edison Co., Chgo., 1963-98, asst. to chmn. exec. com., 1964-65, comml. mgr., 1966, asst. v.p., 1967-70, v.p., 1970-73, exec. v.p., 1973-77, pres., 1977-87, chmn., 1980-98, CEO, also bd. dirs., 1998; chmn., CEO Unicom Corp., Chgo., 1994-98, ret., 1998. Bd. dirs. Corning, Inc., United Air Lines, Smurfit-Stone Container Corp., Armstrong World Industries. Bd. dirs. Lyric Opera, Joffrey Ballet, Helen Brach Found.; bd. dirs., trustee Mus. Sci. and Industry, Chgo. Symphony; past chmn. Met. Savs. Bond Campaign; trustee Northwestern U.; bd. dirs., past chmn. Chgo. Urban League, Chicagoland C. of C.; past chmn. bd. trustees Field Mus. Natural History; life trustee Adler Planetarium, Mus. Sci. and Industry; mem. exec. bd. Chgo. Area coun. Boy Scouts Am.; chmn. Big Shoulders Fund; exec. v.p. The Hundred Club Cook County; dir., past pres. Cath. Charities; past chmn., hon. dir. Am. Cancer Soc., Chgo. Conv. and Tourism Bur. With USAF, 1960-63.

O'CONNOR, JOHN JOSEPH, information technology manager; b. Smyrna, Tenn., June 1, 1959; s. John O'Connor and Dolores Jane (Bell) Brem; m. Lea Ann Bradford, Sept. 6, 1986; 1 child, Colleen Michelle. BS, Tex. A&M U., 1981. Cert. marine engr. 3rd asst. engr. Marine Engrs. Beneficial Assn., Houston, 1981-84; asst. engr. Biehl Ship Mgmt., Houston, 1984; balance technician Hickham Industries, Inc., LaPorte, Tex., 1984-86, prodn. scheduler/Sulzer, 1986-87, project engr./Sulzer, 1987-88, engring. mgr./Sulzer, 1988-89, ops. mgr./Sulzer Huntington Beach, Calif., 1989-93, sr. engr., corp. mergers and acquisitions La Porte, Tex., 1993-94; tech. and field svc. mgr. Sulzer Turbosys. Internat., Houston, 1994-98; engring. projects mgr. Hickham Industries, Inc., LaPorte, Tex., 1998—. Guest speaker Tex. A&M U., Galveston, Tex., College Station, Tex., 1981-89, U. Houston, 1986-89; moderator Power Machinery and Compressor Conf., Houston, 1989. Prin. engr. inventions in field (Achievement awards 1989); author: Steam Turbine Overhaul and Repair Specifications, 1994. Bd. dirs. Cedar Lawn Assn., pres., 1998-2001; bd. dirs. East End Presch., pres., 1998-99; bd. dirs. (pres.) Galveston Alliance of Island Neighborhoods, 1998-2003; adv. bd. Galveston Hist. Found., 1999. Recipient Outstanding Records in Engring., Gulf Oil Corp., Galveston, 1981. Mem. ASME (guest speaker convs.), Pacific Energy Assn. (guest speaker convs. 1990-92), Assn. of Former Students/Tex. A&M. Avocations: hiking, camping, travel, automotive restoration, litigation. Business E-Mail: john.oconnor@sulzerhickham.com.

O'CONNOR, JOHN JOSEPH, JR., academic administrator; b. Augusta, Maine, Sept. 5, 1954; s. John Joseph and Elizabeth (Devine) O'Connor; m. Michelle K. Sonn, Nov. 15, 1980; 1 child, Carolyn Elizabeth. BA, U. Notre Dame, 1976; MS in Pub. Adminstrn., NYU, 1987. Press sec., spl. asst. to majority whip US House Reps., Washington, 1976—81; assoc. v.p. for external affairs NYU, NYC, 1981—87, exec. asst. to the pres., 1987—91, v.p. univ. rels., 1988—95; pres. Ballintober Group, 1995—96; acting vice chancellor, sec. SUNY Sys., Albany, 1996—97, vice chancellor, sec., 1997—, pres. Rsch. Found. of the State Univ., 2000—, officer-in-charge, 2008—. Bd. dirs. Greenwich Village Alliance, NYC, King Juan Carlos I of Spain Found., Am. Ditchley Found.; dir. Wall St. Jour. Found., Washington, 1988—91; chairperson Washington Square Coalition, NYC, 1989. Contbr. articles to profl. jours. Justice of the peace State of Maine, Augusta, 1972—86; dir. NYU-NY Police Dept. Watch Team, NYC, 1991; chmn. bd. trustees Saint Mary's Coll., Notre Dame, Ind. Recipient Edn. award, Am. Legion, Augusta, 1972. Fellow: British Royal Soc. for the Arts, Manufactures and Commerce; mem.: Coun. for Advancement and Support of Edn., Greenwich Village C. of C., NYU Alumni Assn. Roman Catholic. Office: SUNY Officer-In-Charge State University Plaza Albany NY 12246 Office Phone: 518-443-5355.*

O'CONNOR, JOHN MORRIS, III, retired humanities educator; b. Evanston, Ill., Sept. 21, 1937; s. John Morris and Clare Evelyn (Merrick) O'Connor; m. Mary Bittner, Dec. 30, 1960 (div.); 1 child, Emily; m. Miranda E. P. Ind, Aug. 14, 1971 (div.); 1 child, Amanda; m. Beate A. Schiwek, July 3, 2006. Student, Georgetown U., 1955—56; BA, Cornell U., 1959; MA, Harvard U., 1962, PhD, 1965. Instr. Vassar Coll., 1964-66, asst. prof. philosophy, 1966-68; asst. prof. Case Western Res. U., Cleve., 1968-70, assoc. prof., 1970-77; exec. sec. Am. Philos. Assn. U. Del., Newark, 1977-84, assoc. prof., 1977-83; asst. dir. programs Nat. Humanities Ctr., Research Triangle Park, NC, 1983-87; dean Sch. Humanities William Paterson Univ., Wayne, NJ, 1987—91, dean Sch. Humanities, Mgmt. and Social Scis., 1991-92, coord. spl. projects Office of Provost, 1992-93, prof. philosophy, 1992-2001; ret., 2001. Editor (with others): Introductory Philosophy, 1967, Modern Materialism, 1969, Moral Problems in Medicine, 1976; contbr. articles to profl. jours. Woodrow Wilson Nat. fellow, 1959—60. Home: 523 Guilford Ave Chambersburg PA 17201

O'CONNOR, KAREN, political science professor, researcher, writer; b. Buffalo, Feb. 15, 1952; d. Robert J. and Norma (Wilton) O'Connor; m. Allen McDonogh, June 7, 1974 (div. 1986); 1 child, Meghan; m. Richard Cupitt, July 31, 1992. BA, SUNY, Buffalo, 1973, JD, 1977, PhD, 1979. Bar: Ga. 1978. Instr. polit. sci. Emory U., Atlanta, 1977—78, asst. prof., 1978—83, assoc. prof., 1983—88, prof., 1988—95, Am. U., Washington, 1995—2006, Jonathan N. Halfat disting. prof., 2006—. Editor Women & Politics, 1999—2004; mem. editl. bd. Law & Policy,

1982—2005, Jour. of Politics, 1984—87, Am. Politics Quar., 1987—90; founder and dir. Women & Politics Inst., 1999, emeritus founder and dir., 2009. Author: Women's Organization's Use of the Courts, 1980; author: (with N.E. McGlen) Women's Rights, 1983; editor: Women and Congress, 2002; co-author (with McGlen): Women, Politics and American Society, 2004; co-author: (with L. Sabato) American Government, 10th edit., 2009; co-editor (with S. Brewer and M. Fisher): Gendering Politics, 2005; mem. editl. bd. Women, Politics & Public Policy; contbr. articles to profl. jours. Mem.: Nat. Capitol Area Polit. Sci. Assn. (pres. 2001—02), So. Polit. Sci. Assn. (pres. 2000—01), Women and Politics (pres. organized sect. 2006—07), Am. Polit. Sci. Assn. (exec. coun. 1985—87), Cosmos Club. Home: 4383 Westover Pl NW Washington DC 20016-5555 Office: Dept of Govt American Univ 4400 Massachusetts Ave NW Washington DC 20016 Office Phone: 202-885-6237. Business E-Mail: oconn@american.edu.

O'CONNOR, KARL WILLIAM (GOODYEAR JOHNSON), retired lawyer; b. Washington, Aug. 1, 1931; s. Hector and Lucile (Johnson) O'C.; m. Sylvia Gasbarri, Mar. 23, 1951 (dec.); m. Judith Ann Byers, July 22, 1972 (div. 1983); m. Eleanor Celler, Aug. 3, 1984 (div. 1986); m. Alma Hepner, Jan. 1, 1987 (div. 1996); children: Blair, Frances, Brian, Brendan; m. Allie O'Connor, Jul. 15, 2000. BA, U. Va., 1952, JD, 1958. Bar: Va. 1958, D.C. 1959, Am. Samoa 1976, Calif. 1977, Oreg. 1993. Law clk. U.S. Dist. Ct. Va., Abingdon, 1958-59; practice law Washington, 1959-61; trial atty. U.S. Dept. Justice, Washington, 1961-65; dep. dir. Men's Job Corps OEO, Washington, 1965-67; mem. civil rights div. Dept. of Justice, chief criminal sect., prin. dep. asst. atty. gen., 1967-75, spl. counsel for intelligence coordination, 1975; v.p., counsel Assn. of Motion Picture and Television Producers, Hollywood, Calif., 1975-76; assoc. justice Am. Samoa, 1976; chief justice, 1977-78; sr. trial atty. GSA Task Force, Dept. Justice, 1978-81; insp. gen. CSA, 1981-82; spl. counsel Merit Systems Protection Bd., Washington, 1983-86; U.S. atty. for Guam and the No. Marianas, 1986-89; pvt. practice Medford, Oreg., 1989—; Am. counsel O'Reilly Vernier Ltd., Hong Kong, 1992-93; ptnr. O'Connor & Vernier, Medford, Oreg., 1993-94; emeritus, 1994. Served with USMC, 1952-55. Mem. Oreg. Bar Assn., D.C. Bar Assn., Va. Bar Assn., Calif. Bar Assn., Am. Samoa Bar Assn., Soc. Colonial Wars, Phi Alpha Delta, Sigma Nu. Home: Box 126 6743 Griffin Ln Jacksonville OR 97530

O'CONNOR, KATHLEEN MARY, lawyer; b. Camden, Jan. 14, 1949; d. John A. and Marie V. (Flynn) O'C. BA, U. Fla., 1971, JD, 1981. Bar: Fla. 1981, US Ct. Appeals (11th cir.) 1982, US Supreme Ct. 1987. Atty. Walton, Lantaff, Schroeder & Carson, Miami, Fla., 1981-84, Thornton, Davis & Murray PA, Miami, 1984-98, Thornton, Davis & Fein, P.A., Miami, 2002—07; pvt. practice, 2007—. Exec. editor U. Fla. Law Rev., 1981; contbr. articles to profl. jours. Legal advocate Miami Project to Cure Paralysis, 1992-97. Mem. ABA, Dade County Bar Assn. (chmn. appellate cts. com. 2004—05), Def. Rsch. Inst., Fla. Def. Lawyers Assn., Fla. Assn. for Women Lawyers (bd. dirs. Miami-Dade County chpt. 2002—), Fla. Bar (mem. appellate rules com. 2002—08, cert. 1995—), 3rd Dist. Ct. Appeal Hist. Soc. (charter pres. 2008-09, bd. mem. 2008-). Home: 7445 SW 147 St Palmetto Bay FL 33158 Office Phone: 305-278-9596. Personal E-mail: kmomiami@bellsouth.net.

O'CONNOR, KEVIN, computer programming executive; BSEE with honors, U. Mich. Co-founder ICC Software Co., Atlanta, 1983—91; chief tech. officer, v.p. rsch. DCA, Atlanta, 1992—95; funded and built ISS Group, Atlanta, 1995, chmn. bd. dirs., 1995—; co-founder, chief exec. officer Internet Advt. Network, 1995—; co-founder, pres., chief exec. officer DoubleClick, NY, 1996—. Office: DoubleClick 111 Eighth Ave 10th Fl New York NY 10011 Office Phone: 212-683-0001, 212-271-2542. Office Fax: 212-287-1203.

O'CONNOR, KEVIN, professional sports team executive; b. Bronx, NY; m. Linda O'Connor; children: Katie, Adam, Lindsay, Brian(dec.). Grad. in econs. and bus., Belmont Abbey Coll., NC, 1969. Asst. coach Va. Poly. Inst. and State U., 1972—74, Va. Mil. Inst., 1974—76, U. Colo., 1976—79, UCLA, 1979—84; scout LA Clippers, Portland Trail Blazers, NJ Nets, 1990—94, Utah Jazz, 1994—97, v.p. basketball ops., 1999—2002, sr. v.p. basketball ops., 2002—07, exec. v.p. basketball ops., gen. mgr., 2007—; dir. player pers. Phila. 76ers, 1997—99. Mem. Men's Sr. Nat. Team Com. USA Basketball. Served in US Army, 1969—71. Office: Utah Jazz 301 W South Temple Salt Lake City UT 84101*

O'CONNOR, KEVIN JAMES, lawyer, former federal agency administrator; b. Hartford, Conn., May 3, 1967; s. Dennis Edmund and Mary Theresa (Leahy) O'Connor. BA with honors, U. Notre Dame, 1989; JD with high honors, U. Conn., 1992. Conn. 1992, NY 1993, US Dist. Ct. Conn. (so. and ea. dists.) NY 1994, US Ct. Appeals (2d cir.) 1994. Law clk. to Hon. William H. Timbers US Ct. Appeals (2nd Cir.), NYC, 1992-93; litigation assoc. Cahill, Gordon & Reindel LLP, NYC, 1993-95; staff atty., sr. counsel Divsn. Enforcement SEC, Washington, 1995-97; ptnr. Day Berry & Howard LLP, Hartford, 1999—2002; corp. counsel Town of West Hartford, 1999—2001; US atty. Dist. Conn. US Dept. Justice, Hartford, 2002—08, assoc. dep. atty. gen. Washington, 2007, chief of staff to atty. gen., 2007, assoc. atty. gen., 2008—09; ptnr. Bracewell & Giuliani LLP, Hartford, Conn., 2009—. Adj. prof. George Washington U. Law Sch., Washington, 1996-97, U. Conn. Law Sch., 1998—; chair, US Dept. Justice Intellectual Property Task Force, 2007-08; trustee, Fed, Bar Coun., 2008- Bd. mem., adv. U. Notre Dame Monogram Club, 2001—; corporator Hartford Hospital, 2001—08, St. Francis Hosp., 2008—. Recipient Impact Award, Conn. Law Tribune, 2002, Disting. Grad. award, U. Conn. Sch. Law, 2008, Edmund J. Randolph award, US Dept. Justice, 2009; named The Irish Person of the Yr., Ctrl. Conn. Celtic Cultural Com., 2004. Republican. Roman Catholic. Office: Bracewell & Giuliani LLP 225 Asylum St Ste 2600 Hartford CT 06103 Office Phone: 860-256-8602. Office Fax: 860-256-8610. E-mail: kevin.oconnor@bgllp.com.*

O'CONNOR, KEVIN THOMAS, religious organization administrator; b. Dubuque, Iowa, Oct. 9, 1950; s. Francis John and Marion Helen (Rhomberg) O'C.; m. Abbie J. O'Connor, July 17, 1993; 1 child, Sean Francis. BS, Regis Coll., Denver, 1973. Spl. agt. Northwestern Mut. Life, Denver, 1973-78; account exec. Blue Cross/Blue Shield of Colo., Denver, 1978-82; pres., owner O'Connor Ins. Cons., Denver, 1982-92; dir. devel. Archdiocese of Denver, 1992-95, mgr. Cath. appeal, 1995-96; dir. devel. Archdiocese of L.A., 1996—2006; exec. dir. devel. Archdiocese of Washington, 2006—. Chmn. Regis Coll. Telefund, Denver, 1987-88, 90-91; treas., 1st vice chmn. Serra Trust Fund for Vocations, 1988-93, chmn., 1993-96; mem. fin. coun. St. James Parish, 1988-95, chmn. autumn bazaar, 1985, 87, mem. choir, 1993-95; sec. Mother Teresa Com., 1989; mem. choir St. Bede The Venerable, La Canada, Calif., 2001-06. Recipient Share Serra Comm. award Serra Internat., 1989, Spl. Project award Dist. 6, 1986, 88, Spl. Recognition award, 1989, Outstanding Serran award, 1995, Jan Berbers award, 1996, Alumni Svc. award Regis Coll., 1990, Disting. Alumnus award Wahlert H.S., 1994. Mem. Serra Internat. (trustee 1997-2003, sec. bd. 1998-2001, chmn. internat. vocation com. 2000-01, v.p. 2001-03, co-founder Pueblo chpt., 1992, Colo. Springs chpt., 1995, Greeley chpt., 1996, pres. Denver chpt., 1991-92, dist. 6 gov., 1995-96). Roman Catholic. Avocations: golf, tennis, mountain climbing, handball, running. Home: 406 Calloway Ct Silver Spring MD 20905 Office: Archdiocese 5001 Eastern Ave Hyattsville MD 20782-3447 Home Phone: 301-421-1172; Office Phone: 301-853-4574. Personal E-mail: oconnorak@verizon.net. Business E-Mail: koconnor@adw.org.

O'CONNOR, MARILYN JANE, paralegal; b. Reno, Sept. 17, 1947; d. William James and Elizabeth Lillian (Gordon) Weiss; m. Dennis Lindley O'Connor, May 18, 1969 (div. Jan. 20, 1984); children: John Kelly, Stephanie Lynne. Cert.: U. Nev., Reno (in paralegal studies) 2003. Complex litigation specialist, 1980—2006; document rev., content acquisition specialist Ajilon Legal, assoc., 2006—08, Fullerton Design Co., 2009—. Mem. Nat. Women's History Mus. Achievements include precedent-setting court challenge that secured right of non-attorneys to use state-funded law libraries. Personal E-mail: marilynoconnor2005@sbcglobal.net.

O'CONNOR, MAUREEN, state supreme court justice; b. Washington, Aug. 7, 1951; d. Patrick and Mary E. O'Connor; children: Alex, Ed. BA, Seton Hill Coll., 1973; postgrad., SUNY, 1975-76; JD, Cleve. State U., 1980. Pvt. practice, 1981-85; magistrate Summit County Probate Ct., 1985-93; judge Summit County Ct. of Common Pleas, 1993-95; prosecuting atty. Summit County, 1995-99; lt. gov., dir. Dept. Pub. Safety State of Ohio, 1999—2003; justice Ohio Supreme Ct., Ohio, 2003—. Dir. Summit County Child Support Enforcement Agy.; former chair Ohio Security Task Force, Building Security Review Com.; spkr. in field. Parishioner St. Vincent's Ch.; vol. Comty. Drug Bd., Am. Cancer Soc., bd. dirs.; bd. dirs. Victim Assistance, St. Edward Home, Fairlawn, Furnace St. Mission. Recipient MADD Law Enforcement award, 1997, Cleve. State Disting. Alumnae award for Civic Achievement, 1997. Mem. MADD, Nat. Dist. Attys. Assn., Nat. Child Support Enforcement Assn., Nat. Coll. Dist. Attys. Assn., Ohio Prosecuting Attys. Assn. (exec. com.), Ohio Family Support Assn., Atty. Gen.'s Prosecutor Liaison Com., Summit County Police Chiefs Assn., Summit Forum, Summit County Child Mortality. Republican. Office: Ohio Supreme Ct 65 S Front St Columbus OH 43215*

O'CONNOR, MICHAEL E., lawyer; b. Syracuse, NY, Sept. 15, 1948; s. Leo T. and Geraldine (Hager) O'Connor; m. Margaret A. Soplop, June 3, 1972. AA, Auburn CC, NY, 1968; BA, SUNY, Buffalo, 1970; JD, Syracuse U., 1974. Bar: N.Y. 1975, U.S. Supreme Ct. 1983. Assoc. Coulter, Fraser, Bolton, Bird & Ventre, Syracuse, 1975-80, ptnr., 1981-90, Hancock & Estabrook, 1990-94, DeLaney & O'Connor LLP, 1994—. Pres. Onondaga Title Assn., 1979, Ctrl. N.Y. Estate Planning Coun., 1981; adj. prof. law Syracuse U. Law Sch.; pres. Most Holy Rosary Home Sch. Assn., 1985—86, Aurora CNY Inc., 1988—90, 2007—08. Bd. dirs. Syracuse Symphony Orch.; chmn. bd. CNY Cmty. Found.; pres. Citizens Found., Inc., 1983—85. Fellow: Am. Coll. Trust and Estate Counsel (state chair 1997—2002); mem.: ABA, Onondaga County Bar Assn. (chmn. estate and surrogates ct. com. 1981—87, bd. dirs. 1984—86), N.Y. State Bar Assn. (ho. of dels. 1982—85, chair elder law sect. 1999—2000, chair trusts and estates sect. 2005), Century Club of Syracuse, Lions (pres. 1984—85). Republican. Roman Catholic. Home: 154 Robineau Rd Syracuse NY 13207-1644 Office: DeLaney & O'Connor LLP One Lincoln Ctr Syracuse NY 13202 Office Phone: 315-476-8450. Business E-Mail: oconnor@delaneyoconnor.com.

O'CONNOR, OTIS LESLIE, retired lawyer, director; b. Charleston, W.Va., July 6, 1935; s. Robert Emmett and Julia Elizabeth (Aultz) O'C.; m. Elizabeth Frances Morris, Aug. 7, 1965; children: Otis Leslie, James M. AB, Princeton U., 1957; JD, Harvard U., 1963; MBA, W.Va. Coll. Grad. Studies, 1979; MA, Trinity Theol. Sem., 2003. Bar: W.Va. 1963, U.S. Dist. (so. dist.) W.Va. 1963. Assoc. Steptoe & Johnson, Charleston, 1963-69, ptnr., 1969—2008. Pres. Daymark, Inc., 1981—82. With USN, 1957—60, served to comdr. JAGC USNR, 1960—81. Mem. ABA, W.Va. Bar Assn., Kanawha County Bar Assn., Res. Officers Assn., Rotary Internat. Club (Charleston). Presbyterian. Home: 890 Chester Rd Charleston WV 25302-2817 Home Phone: 304-342-6248.

O'CONNOR, PATRICK J., alderman; b. June 21, 1954; BA, Loyola U., Chgo.; JD, Loyola U. Sch. Law, Chgo., 1979. Atty., Chgo.; alderman, 40th ward Chgo. City Coun., 1983—; Dem. committeeman 40th Ward, Chgo., 1984—. Chmn. edn. com. Chgo. City Coun. Panelist, Raising Healthy Children and Families The White House, 2002; mem., chmn. Hawthorne Scholastic Acad. Sch. Coun., 1989—91. Mem.: Nat. League Cities Coun. on Youth, Edn. and Families (chmn. 2002). Democrat. Office: 5850 N Lincoln Ave Chicago IL 60659-4694 also: City Hall 121 N La Salle St Rm 305 Chicago IL 60602 Office Phone: 773-769-1140, 312-744-6858. Office Fax: 773-769-3804. Business E-Mail: ward40@cityofchicago.org.*

O'CONNOR, PAUL DANIEL, lawyer; b. Paterson, NJ, Nov. 24, 1936; s. Paul Daniel and Anne Marie Christopher O'C.; children: Steven Paul, Sheryl Lynn, Laura Ann. BS in Engring, U.S. Naval Acad., 1959; LLB, U. Va., 1965. Bar: N.Y. 1965, Calif. 1995. Assoc. firm Winthrop, Stimson, Putnam & Roberts, NYC, 1965-72, partner, 1972-80; sr. v.p., gen. counsel Singer Co., Stamford, Conn., 1980-86; CEO Citation Builders, 1986—95; trustee Valley Trusts, Oakland, Calif., 1986—; gen. coun. Berg Holdings, Sausalito, Calif., 2007. 1st lt. USAF, 1959-62. Mem.: Assn. Bar City NY, Bar Assn. San Francisco. Home Phone: 415-516-3693; Office Phone: 510-874-4300.

O'CONNOR, R. D., retired healthcare executive; BS in Psychology and Sociology, U. So. Miss., 1960, MS Adminstrv. Pers., 1961, PhD Mgmt. and Orgnl. Comm., 1983. Asst. dean student affairs Holmes Jr. Coll., Goodman, Miss., 1961-64, Dept. Edn., Jackson, Miss., 1964-65; asst. adminstr. Hinds Gen. Hosp., Jackson, Miss., 1965-68; adminstr. Rankin Gen. Hosp., Brandon, Miss., 1968-76; v.p. Human Resources/ Mktg. Delta Mgmt. Systems, Metairie, La., 1976-79; asst. to pres. Bapt. Med. Ctr., Jacksonville, Fla., 1979-82; pres. RiverGroup Riverside Hosp., Rivercorp Inc., Riverside Found., Jacksonville, Fla., 1982-87; owner O'Connor & Assocs., Jacksonville, Fla., 1987-91; pres. Fla. 1st: Managed Health Care, Winter Haven, Orlando & Tampa, Fla., 1991-94; dir. orgn. devel. Mid Florida Med. Svcs. Inc., Winter Haven, Fla., 1994-97. Instr. U. So. Miss., Hattiesburg, Ms.; tchr., lectr. various univs., C.C.s, military acads.; grad. faculty coord. Webster U.; online instr. for univs. Contbr. articles to profl. jours. and books. Commr. Cleary Heights Sewer Dist., 1978-79; pres'. selective task force Induction Procedures, 1969; chmn. personnel com. San Jose Baptist Ch., 1981-86, strategic planning com., 1986-87; gov's. com. Statewide Planning Vocat. Rehab., 1968; bd. dirs. Rankin County C. of C., 1970-73, exec. com., chmn. health affairs com., 1970-72, chmn. highway com. 1970-74, fin. com. 1971-73), Family Blood Assurance Program, 1972-77, v.p. 1977, Vol. Action Coun., 1973-76, United Givers Fund, 1973-76. With Army Security Agy., Air Nat. Guard, Med. Svc. Corps., ret. Fellow Am. Coll. Healthcare Execs. (life); mem. Fla. Hosp. Assn. (com. chmn. 1984), Greater Jacksonville Area Hosp. Coun. (chmn. 1985), Jackson-Vicksburg Hosp. Coun. (chmn. 1974), Nat. Assn. Mental Health (bd. dirs. 1973-74), Miss. Assn. Mental Health (pres. 1972-74), Miss. Hosp. Assn. (bd. dirs.1973-76, exec. devel. com. 1972-75, mgmt. engring. adminstrv. bd. 1973, fin. com. 1972-74, chmn. nominating com. 1971, coord. divsn. profl. practice 1970). Office Phone: 904-268-4560.

O'CONNOR, RALPH STURGES, investment company executive; b. Pasadena, Calif., Aug. 27, 1926; s. Thomas Ireland and Edith Masury (Sturges) O'Connor; m. Alice Maconda Brown, Apr. 28, 1950; children: George Rufus, Thomas Ireland III, Nancy Isabel, John Herman. BA, Johns Hopkins U., Balt., 1951; postgrad., Harvard U., Cambridge, Mass., 1967. With Highland Resources, Inc., Houston, 1951-87, exec. v.p., 1961-64, pres., 1964-87; pres., CEO Ralph S. O'Connor and Assocs., Houston, 1987—. Chmn. bd. dirs. Amaud's Restaurant, New Orleans. Pres. Marian and Speros Martel Found., Houston, 1983—2003; trustee emeritus Rice U., Johns Hopkins U., Oldfields Sch., Glencoe, Md. With USAAF, 1943—46. Mem.: NAS, Presdl. Counselors, Houston Landmen's Assn. (past pres.), All Am. Wildcatters, Am. Assn. Petroleum Landmen, Johns Hopkins Instns., Players Club, River Oaks Country Club, Bayou Club. Home: 5627 Indian Cir Houston TX 77056-1006 Office: Ralph S O'Connor & Assocs 10000 Memorial Dr Ste 510 Houston TX 77024-3422 Office Phone: 713-682-3441.

O'CONNOR, REED CHARLES, federal judge; b. Houston, 1965; BS, U. Houston, 1986; JD, South Tex. Coll. Law, 1989. Bar: Tex. 1990. Assoc. Vinson & Elkins, LLP, 1989—94; asst. dist. atty. Tarrant County Dist. Atty.'s Office, 1994—98; asst. US atty. (no. dist.) Tex. US Dept. Justice, 1998—2007; mem. US Senate Com. on Judiciary, 2003—07; judge US Dist. Ct. (no dist.) Tex., 2007—. Mem.: South Tex. Law Review. Office: US Dist Ct 1100 Commerce St Dallas TX 75242

O'CONNOR, ROD, chemist, consultant, inventor; b. Cape Girardeau, Mo., July 4, 1934; s. Jay H. and Flora (Winters) O'C.; m. Shirley Ann Sander, Aug. 7, 1955; children: Mark Alan (dec.), Kara Ann, Shanna Suzanne, Timothy Patrick. BS, S.E. Mo. State Coll., 1955; PhD, U. Calif., Berkeley, 1958. Asst. prof. chemistry U. Omaha, 1958-60, Mont. State Coll., 1960-63; assoc. prof. chemistry Mont. State U., Bozeman, 1963-66; assoc. prof., coordinator gen. chemistry Kent (Ohio) State U., 1966-67; prof., dir. 1st year chemistry U. Ariz., Tucson, 1968-72; staff assoc. Adv. Council on Coll. Chemistry Stanford (Calif.) U., 1967-68; vis. prof. Wash. State U., Pullman, 1972-73; prof. chemistry Tex. A&M, College Station, 1973-86; pres. Texas ROMEC Inc., College Station, 1983-98; prof. environ. studies Baylor U., Waco, Tex., 1996-99. Cons. insect venoms Hollister-Stier Labs., Spokane, Wash., 1963-67; lab. separates editor W.H. Freeman Co., 1968-78; ednl. cons. TUCARA-4 Media Resources, Inc., 1971-74; mem. Coll. Chemistry Cons. Service; vis. scientist, tour lectr. Am. Chem. Soc., 1970-86. Author: (with T. Moeller) Ions in Aqueous Systems, 1972, Fundamentals of Chemistry, 1981, (with C. Mickey and A. Hassell) Solving Problems in Chemistry, 1981, (with L. Peck and K. Irgolic) Fundamentals of Chemistry in The Laboratory, 1981, (with T.E. Taylor and P. Glenn) Toward Success in College, 1981, (with A. Hassell and C. Mickey) Advanced Problems in Applied Chemistry, 2000; films Laboratory Safety, 1971; Contbr. articles to profl. jours.; patentee in field Recipient nat. teaching award Mfg. Chemists Assn., 1978; 4 regional teaching awards. Fellow AAAS, Am. Inst. Chemists, Sigma Xi; mem. Internat. Soc. Toxinology, Am. Chem. Soc. Office: Chem Consulting Svcs 1300 Angelina Cir College Station TX 77840-4855 Office Phone: 979-693-5804. E-mail: docroc34@hotmail.com.

O'CONNOR, RORY, pharmaceutical company executive, medical director; b. Liverpool, United Kingdom, July 21, 1955; m. Catherine Doyle, Aug. 12, 1995; children: Mairead, Ruairi, Ciara, Niamh. MB ChB, U. Liverpool, Faculty Medicine, 1973—78. Mfpm Faculty Pharm. Medicine, Royal Coll. Physicians, UK, 1996. Med. dir. Pfizer Ctrl. Rsch., Sandwich, England, 1994—96; v.p. med. affairs Pfizer Pharms. Group, NYC, 1996—. Office: Pfizer Inc 235 E 42nd St New York NY 10520 E-mail: oconnor1@pfizer.com.

O'CONNOR, SANDRA DAY, retired United States supreme court justice; b. El Paso, Tex., Mar. 26, 1930; d. Harry A. and Ada Mae (Wilkey) Day; m. John Jay O'Connor, III, 1952; children: Scott, Brian, Jay. BA with great distinction, Stanford U., 1950, LLB, 1952. Bar: Calif., Ariz. Dep. county atty., San Mateo, Calif., 1952—53; civilian atty. Q.M. Market Ctr., Frankfurt am Main, Germany, 1954—57; pvt. law practice Maryvale, 1958—60; asst. atty. gen. State of Ariz., 1965—69; mem. Ariz. State Senate, 1969—75, majority leader, 1972—75, chmn. com. on state, county and mcpl. affairs, 1972—73; judge Maricopa County Superior Ct., Phoenix, 1975—79, Ariz. Ct. Appeals, 1979—81; assoc. justice US Supreme Ct., Washington, 1981—2006; chancellor Coll. William & Mary, Williamsburg, Va., 2005—; vis. judge US Ct. Appeals (2nd circuit), NYC, 2006—. Mem. Maricopa County Bd. Adjustments and Appeals, 1963—64, Ariz. Criminal Code Commn., 1974—76, Nat. Defense Advisory Com. on Women in Svcs., 1974—76; chmn. vis. bd. Maricopa County Juvenile Detention Home, 1963—64; chmn. Ariz. Supreme Ct. Com. to Reorganize Lower Cts., 1974—75, Maricopa County Superior Ct. Judges Tng. and Edn. Com., 1977—79; vice chmn. Ariz. Select Law Enforcement Review Commn., 1979—80; served on Legislative Coun., Probate Code Commn., Ariz. Advisory Coun. on Intergovernmental Rels.; mem. Iraq Study Group, 2006. Mem. bd. editors: Stanford (Calif.) U. Law Review; co-author (with H. Alan Day): (memoir) Lazy B: Growing Up on a Cattle Ranch in the American Southwest, 2002; author (with Dan Andreasen, illustrator): (children's books) Chico: A True Story from the Childhood of the First Woman Supreme Court Justice, 2005; developer (video game) Our Courts, 2008. Trustee Rockefeller Found.; mem. adv. bd. Smithsonian Nat. Mus. Natural History, 2006—; mem., selection com. Okla. City Nat. Meml. and Mus., 2005—; co-chair nat. adv. coun. Campaign for Civic Mission of Schs., 2005—; mem. Cathedral Chpt. Wash. Nat. Cathedral, 1991—99. Recipient Annual award, NCCJ, 1975, Disting. Achievement award, Ariz. State U., 1980, Gimble Nat. award, Gimble Phila. awards Com., 1982, Elizabeth Blackwell award, Hobart & William Smith Coll., 1985, Award of Merit, Stanford Law Sch., 1990, OH State Law award, OH State U., 1992, Fordham-Stein Ethics prize, Fordham U., 1992, Sara Lee Frontrunner award, 1997, ABA medal, 1997, Thomas Jefferson award of Law, U. Va., 1987, AAUW Achievement award, 1988, William Green award for Profl. Excellence, U. Richmond, 1990, Presdl. Medal of Freedom, The White House, 2009; named Woman of Yr., Phoenix Advt. Club, 1972, National Women's Hall of Fame, 1995; named one of The Most Powerful Women, Forbes mag., 2005. Fellow: American Acad. Arts & Sciences; mem.: Anglo-American Exchange, Ariz. State Personnel Commn., Stanford Ctr. Ethics (adv. bd. 2005—), American Soc. Internat. Law (adv. com. 2001—), Ariz. Women Lawyer's Assn., Nat. Assn. Women Judges, Advisory Com. for Judiciary Leadership Development Coun. (hon.), Ariz. Judges' Assn., Calif. Bar Assn., Maricopa County Bar Assn. (chmn. Lawyer Referral Svc. 1960—62), Ariz. Bar Assn. (former mem. Com. Legal Aid, former mem. Com. Public Relations, former mem. Com. Lower Ct. Reorganization, former mem. Com. Continuing Legal Edn.), ABA (exec. bd. Ctrl. European and Eurasian Law Initiative 1990—, exec. com. Mus.

Law 2000—, adv. commn. Standing Com. on Law Library of Congress 2002—, mem. Commn. on Civic Edn. and Seperation of Powers 2005—). Office: Coll of William & Mary PO Box 8795 Williamsburg VA 23187-8795*

O'CONNOR, SEAN M., diversified financial services company executive; CEO Standard New York Securities, 1994—2002; exec. dir. Standard Bank London Ltd., 1999—2002; CEO Internat. Assets Holding Corp., 2002—. Bd. dir. Internat. Assets Holding Corp., 2002—. Office: Internat Assets Holding Corp Ste 2060 200 E Ctrl Pkwy Altamonte Springs FL 32701*

O'CONNOR, SHERYL BRODERICK, retired literature and language educator; b. Macon, Ga., Apr. 14, 1943; d. Charles Robert and Gloria Broderick; children: Kimberly O'Connor Biss, Broderick Jeffrey. BA, Mt. Holyoke Coll., South Hadley, Mass., 1965; MA in Tchg. English, Smith Coll., Northampton, Mass., 1965. Cert. tchr. English Mass., tchr. secondary English N.J. Tchr. Sweeney Meml., Chicopee, Mass., 1966—69; tchr., jr. sch. chair MacDuffie Sch., Springfield, Mass., 1969—72; instr. critical reading Camden County Coll., Blackwood, NJ, 1987—90; tchr. East Camden Mid. Sch., Camden, NJ, 1984—2009. Mem. curriculum adv. com. Camden Bd. Edn., 1996; mem., v.p. Bd. Edn., Medford, NJ, 1979—89. Contbr. poetry to mags. Fellow: Rotary Found. of Rotary Internat.; mem.: Camden Edn. Assn. (rep. 2000—), Mensa, Cherry Hill Rotary (pres. 2000—01). Republican. Anglican. Home: 2 Andover Ct Southampton NJ 08088

O'CONNOR, STANLEY JAMES, Asian studies educator; b. Des Moines, July 1, 1926; s. Stanley James and Marion (Stout) O'C.; m. Janet Raleigh, Sept. 4, 1952; children: Stanley James, Janet, Cynthia. BA, Cornell U., 1951, PhD, 1964; MA, U. Va., 1954. Sr. analyst U.S. Govt., Washington, 1952-60; fgn. area tng. fellow Cornell U., 1961-63, prof., 1964—, chmn. dept. Asian studies, 1966-69, chmn. dept. art history, 1970-76, dir. S.E. Asia program, 1979-84. Cons. Ford Found.; adv. bd. Andrew D. White Mus., Ithaca, 1969-73, Herbert F. Johnson Mus., 1974-76. Author: Hindu Gods of Peninsular Siam, 1972, (with T. Harrisson) Excavation of the Prehistoric Iron Industry in West Borneo, 1969, Gold and Megalithic Activity in Prehistoric and Recent West Borneo, 1970; guest editor Asian Art and Culture, 1995; mem. editl. bd. Indonesia, Studies on Southeast Asia, 1985-2008. Bd. dirs. Historic Ithaca, 1981-82, Am. Com. for South Asian Art, 1982-85, 89-92; mem. adv. bd. Asia Soc. Gallery, 1989-93, Wells Coll. Book ARts Ctr., 1999—. With AUS, 1946-47. JDR 3d Found. fellow, 1966; NEH sr. fellow, 1973-74; vis. fellow Inst. for Southeast Asian Studies, Singapore, 1973-74 Fellow Explorers Club; mem. Assn. Asian Studies (S.E. Asia coun. 1978-81), Royal Asiatic Soc. (Malaysian br.), Siam Soc. Home: 617 Highland Rd Ithaca NY 14850-1411 Business E-Mail: sj02@cornell.edu.

O'CONNOR, THOMAS C., energy executive; b. 1955; m. Diane O'Connor; 3 children. BS cum laude in Biology, U. Mass., Lowell, 1977, MS in Environ. Studies, 1980. Dir. mktg. svcs., dir. bus. devel. Tex. Ea. Transmission Corp.; pres. PanEnergy Devel. Co.; supr. environ. compliance to mgr. environ. compliance to mgr. market devel. Algonquin Gas Transmission Duke Energy Corp., Charlotte, NC, 1987—89, sr. v.p. mktg. and capacity mgmt., v.p. mktg., v.p. east coast mktg. NE pipeline group, 1994—2002, pres., CEO Duke Energy Gas Transmission's US ops., 2002—05, group v.p. corp. strategy, 2005—06, group exec., COO US Franchised Electric and Gas, group exec., pres. comml. business, 2006—07; chmn., pres., CEO DCP Midstream, LLC, Denver, 2007—. Mem. sci. devel. bd. U. Mass Lowell Coll. Arts & Scis. Office: DCP Midstream LLC 370 17th St Ste 2500 Denver CO 80202

O'CONNOR, TOM, corporate executive, management consultant; b. Boston, June 11, 1942; s. Thomas Henry and Blanche (Cosgrove) O'C.; m. Mary Alice Kelly; 1 child, Michael Kelly O'Connor. BA in econs., U. Mass., 1971; postgrad., U. Wis., Milw., 1971-73, U. Del., 1978, Am. U., 1980. Economist Interstate Commerce Commn., Washington, 1973-74; mgr. planning U.S. Railway Assn., Washington, 1974-75; cons. transp. R.L. Banks & Assocs., Washington, 1975-77; asst. dir. Conrail, Phila., 1977-79; asst. v.p. econs. Assn. Am. R.R.'s, Washington, 1979-82; v.p. DNS Assocs., Inc., Washington, Lexington (Mass.), 1982-88; v.p., ptnr. Snavely, King, Majoros, O'Connor & Lee, Inc., Washington, 1988—. Chmn. surface freight transport regulation com. Transp. Rsch. Bd., 1994—. Pres. Green Briar Civic Assn., Fairfax, Va., 1985, Greenbriar Dem. Club, Fairfax, 1984-89, Greenbriar Community Ctr., Fairfax, 1984; v.p. Greenbriar West PTA, Fairfax, 1986-88. Sgt. U.S. Army, 1963-66. Mem. Am. Econ. Assn., Am. Statis. Assn., Coun. Logistics Mgmt., Transp. Rsch. Forum (pres. Washington chpt. 1987-89), Nat. Def. Assn. (bd. dirs. 1991-94), Air Force Assn., Phi Beta Kappa, Phi Kappa Phi. Democrat. Roman Catholic. Avocations: camping, reading, counseling. Home: 13222 Point Pleasant Dr Fairfax VA 22033-3515 Office: Snavely King Majoros O'Connor & Lee Inc 1111 14th St Ste 300 Washington DC 20005-4050 Office Phone: 202-371-9149. Fax: 202-842-4966. Personal E-mail: skmoltom1@aol.com. Business E-Mail: toconnor@snavely-king.com.

O'CONNOR, WILLIAM MICHAEL, search company executive; b. Chgo., Sept. 28, 1947; s. Maurice Francis and Margaret (Brand) O'C.; m. Karen Jean Gipson, Jan. 30, 1972; children: Sean, Mary, William, David. BA in History, Loyola U., Chgo., 1970. Interviewer Ill. State Employment Svc., Chgo., 1970-73; ins. agt. Equitable Life Assurance Soc., Chgo., 1973-76; recruiting officer U.S. Army, Chgo., 1977-78; profl. employment rep. GTE Network Systems, Northlake, Ill., 1978-81; employment mgr. Molex, Inc., Lisle, Ill., 1981-85, Rand McNally & Co., Skokie, Ill., 1986; v.p. Richards Cons., Ltd., Chgo., 1987-88; v.p., ptnr. Chestnut Hill Ptnrs., Deerfield, Ill., 1988-95; v.p. Kennedy & Co., Chgo., 1995-2001; pres. Edgewood Internat., Woodridge, Ill., 2001—. Mem. Art Inst. Chgo., Smithsonian Inst., Field Mus. Natural History, Rep. Nat. Com., 1984—. Lt. col. USAR, 1971-99. Decorated Chevalier, Sovereign Mil. Order of Temple of Jerusalem, 1998—. Mem. Res. Officers Assn., U.S. Armor Assn. (Order of St. George), Mil. Police Assn., 337th Cavalry Regiment (Order of the Spur), Bus. Mobilized for Loyola U. Roman Catholic. Home: 3018 Edgewood Pky Woodridge IL 60517 Office: Edgewood Internat 3018 Edgewood Pkwy Woodridge IL 60517 Office Phone: 630-985-6067. E-mail: wocatedgewood@aol.com.

OCVIRK, OTTO GEORGE, artist; b. Detroit, Nov. 13, 1922; s. Joseph and Louise (Ekle) O.; m. Betty Josephine Lebie, June 11, 1949; children: Robert Joseph, Thomas Frederick, Carol Louise. B.F.A., State U. Iowa, 1949, M.F.A., 1950. Advt. artist apprentice Bass-Luckoff Advt. Agy., Detroit, 1941; engring. draftsman Curtiss-Wright Aircraft Corp., Buffalo, 1942; faculty Bowling Green (Ohio) State U., 1950—, assoc. prof., 1960-65, prof. art, 1965-85, prof. emeritus, 1985—. Exhibited in group shows at, Denver Mus. Art, 1949, 50, 53, Detroit Inst. Art, 71948, 49, 50, 53, 56, Dayton (Ohio) Art Inst., 1950, 51, 56, Ohio State U., 1953, Walker Art Center, Mpls., 1948, 49, Library of Congress, Washington, 1949, Bklyn. Mus., 1949, Joslyn Mus., Omaha, 1949, Colorado Springs Fine Arts Center, 1949; represented in permanent collections, Detroit Inst. Arts, Dayton Art Inst., Friends of Am. Art, Grand Rapids, Mich., State U. Iowa, Iowa City, Bowling Green State U.; (Recipient 24 nat., regional juried art exhbn. awards 1947-57, others.); Author: (with R. Stinson, P. Wigg, R. Bone and David Cayton) Art Fundamentals— Theory and Practice, 1960-97, 7th edit., 1994, 8th edit., 1997, 9th edit., 2001, 10th edit., 2005. Scoutmaster Toledo Area council Boy Scouts Am., 1960-63, asst. scoutmaster, 1963-74, dist. commr., 1978-80. Served with AUS, 1943-46. Recipient Silver Beaver award Boy Scouts Am., 1976, Magnifico award Medici Circle, Bowling Green State U., 1987. Mem. Delta Phi Delta (hon.) Methodist. Home and Office: 231 Haskins Rd Bowling Green OH 43402-2206 Home Phone: 419-352-6749. *"Freedom for expression" keys creative thought into a productive whole.*

O'DAY, PAUL THOMAS, trade association executive; b. May 2, 1935; s. James Thomas and Jeannette Irene (Deschenes) O'D.; m. Nancy Frances Eitler, June 16, 1962; children: Kathleen, Maureen, Michael, Ellen. BA, Am. Internat. Coll., Springfield, Mass., 1958; JD, Georgetown U., 1963; MPA, Am. U., 1967; D of Pub. Adminstrn. honoris causa, Am. Internat. Coll., 1997. Bar: D.C. 1964, Va. 2005, U.S. Supreme Ct. 1974. Patent examiner US Patent Office, Washington, 1959-62; exec. sec. panel high-speed ground transp., auto. air poll. Dept. Commerce, Washington, 1965-66, staff asst. to sec., 1967-69, exec. asst. to sec., 1969-71, dep. dir. bur. domestic commerce, 1972-74; dep. dir. Nat. Bus. Coun. for Consumer Affairs, Washington, 1971-72; cons. to Gen. Counsel GE, Fairfield, Conn., 1974-75; asst. trade rep. Exec. Office of the Pres., Washington, 1975-77; dep. asst. sec. US Dept. Commerce, Washington, 1978-84; pres. Am. Fiber Mfrs. Assn., Washington, 1984—. Chmn. Fiber Econs. Bur., 1984—; pres. Eisenhower World Affairs Inst., 1993-99, exec. com., 2000-06. Corporator Am. Internat. Coll., 1974—; mem. governing coun. Shakespeare Theater Guild, 1989-2001. Recipient Constl. Law award Georgetown U. Law Ctr., 1962; Alumni award Am. Internat. Coll., 1970; Pres.'s Meritorious Exec. award., 1984; Nat. Inst. Pub. Affairs fellow Princeton U., 1964 Mem.: AAAS, Am. Constitution Soc., Nat. Assn. Mfrs. (bd. dirs. 2006—), Am. Chem. Soc., Jussi Bjorling Soc. USA (charter), O'Dea Clan Assn. (Corofin, Ireland), Cosmos Club. Home: 8261 Private Ln Annandale VA 22003-4471 Office: Am Fiber Mfrs Assn 1530 Wilson Blvd Ste 690 Arlington VA 22209 Home Phone: 703-425-7727.

ODDEN, ALLAN ROBERT, education educator; b. Duluth, Minn., Sept. 16, 1943; s. Robert Norman and Mabel Eleanor (Bjornnes) Odden; m. Eleanor Ann Rubottom, May 28, 1966; children: Sarina, Robert. BS, Brown U., 1965; MDiv, Union Theol. Sem., 1969; MA, Columbia U., 1971, PhD, 1975. Tchr. N.Y.C. Pub. Schs., 1967-72; rsch. assoc. Teachers' Coll. Columbia U., NYC, 1972-75; dir. policy Edn. Commn. of the States, Denver, 1975-84; prof. U. So. Calif., LA, 1984-93, U. Wis., Madison, 1993—; co-dir. Strategic Mgmt. Human Capital, 2008—. Rsch. dir. Sch. Fin. Commns., Conn., 1974—75, SD, 1975—76, Mo., 1975—76, Mo., 1993, Mo., 94, NY, 1978—81, NJ, 1991—92, Ark., 2003, Ark., 2005—06, Wyo., 2005, Wyo., 05, Wyo., 06, Wash., 2005—06, Wis., 2005—07; co-dir. Consortium Policy Rsch. Edn., Strategic Mgmt. Human Capital Pub. Edn., 2008—; cons. Nat. Govs. Assn., Nat. Conf. State Legislatures, US Sec. Edn., US Senate, US Dept. Edn., many state legislatures and govs.; mem. task force sch. fin. equity adequacy and productivity NRC, 1996—99; ct. master Superior Ct. NJ in Abbott V. Burke Sch. Fin. Case, 1997—98. Author: (book) Education Leadership for America's Schools, 1995; co-author: (books) Financing Schools for High Performance, 1998, Paying Teachers for What They Know and Do, 1997, 2d edit., 2002, School Finance: A Policy Perspective, 1992, 4th edit., 2007, Reallocating Resources: How to Boost Student Achievement Without Spending More, 2001, How to Create World Class Teacher Compensation, 2007, Doubling Student Performance and Finding the Resources to Do It, 2009, Ten Strategies for Doubling Student Performance, 2009; editor: Education Policy Implementation, 1991, Rethinking School Finance, 1992, School-Based Financing, 1999; contbr. articles to profl. jours., chapters to books. Mem. L.A. Chamber Edn. and Human Resources Commn., 1986, Gov.'s Sch. Fin. Commn., Calif., 1987, Calif. Assessment Policy Com., Gov.'s Edn. Task Force, Wis., 1996, Carnegie Corp. Task Force Edn. in the Early Yrs., 1994—96; mem. nat. rsch. coun. com. sch. fin. equity, adequcy and productivity, 1996—99; mem. Gov.'s Blue Ribbon Commn. State and Local Partnerships 21st Century, Wis., 2000. Grantee, Dept. Edn., Carnegie Corp., Spencer Found., Ford Found., Atlantic Philanthropic Svcs., Mellon Found., Carnegie Corp., Pew Charitable Trusts, Rockefeller Found., Joyce Found., Bill & Melinda Gates Found. Mem.: Politics Edn. Assn., Am. Ednl. Fin. Assn. (pres. 1979—80), Am. Ednl. Rsch. Assn. Avocations: Lionel training collecting, youth soccer, baseball coach. Office: U Wis Sch Edn Wis Ctr Edn Rsch 1025 W Johnson St # 653E Madison WI 53706-1706 Home: 360 W Washington Ave Unit 1002 Madison WI 53703-2766 Home Phone: 608-233-8720. Business E-Mail: arodden@wisc.edu.

ODDI, MARIE CAPORALE, educational administrator; b. New Haven, July 27, 1927; d. Michael and Rose (Monaco) Caporale; BA cum laude, Brown U., 1949; MS, So. Conn. State U., 1968, postgrad., 1974—; m. Frank Oddi, Apr. 2, 1951; children— Laura, Frank, Elissa. Service rep. So. New Eng. Tel. Co., New Haven, 1949-54; tchr. Hamden Pub. Schs., Conn., 1964-73, prin., 1973-87; prin. Beecher Rd. Sch., Woodbridge, Conn. 1987—92; consortium mem. Charles Kettering Found. and Nat. Assn. Elem. Sch. Prins.; grant reader NEH; curriculum adv. and developer; charter adv. bd. mem. Conn. Prin. Acad., co-chair mentor program, mentor prin. Fellow Inst. for Devel. of Ednl. Activities (Acad. of Fellows Disting. Educator award); mem. Elem. and Middle Sch. Prins. Assn. of Conn. (recipient Joseph J. Formica Disting. Service award 1980, Pres.'s award 1978, 79, 81, 82, 84), Nat. Assn. Elem. Sch. Prins., Assn. Hamden Public Sch. Adminstrs., Adminstrn. and Supervision Assn. of So. Conn. State U., LWV Phi Delta Kappa (pres. So. Conn. State Coll. chpt. 1981-82), Delta Kappa Gamma. Author: (with Gilbert Rebhun) Looking in on an Open Space Classroom; contbr. articles in field to profl. jours.; editor Elem. and Middle Sch. Prins. Assn. of Conn. News Forum, 1978-82. Home: 26 Parmalee Dr Hamden CT 06514-2008

ODDIS, JOSEPH ANTHONY, health associations executive; b. Greensburg, Pa., Nov. 5, 1928; s. Giacinto and Felicetta (D'Amico) O.; m. Jeanne Trevena, July 10, 1954; children: Joseph Michael, Marie Theresa/ BS, Duquesne U., 1950; DSc (hon.), Mass. Coll. Pharmacy, 1975, Phila. Coll. Pharmacy and Sci., 1975, Albany Coll. Pharmacy, Union U., 1976, Duquesne U., 1989, Mercer U., 1995; LHD (hon.), L.I. U., 1991. Staff pharmacist Mercy Hosp., Pitts., 1950-51, asst. chief pharmacist, 1953-54; chief pharmacist Western Pa. Hosp., Pitts., 1954-56; staff rep. hosp. pharmacy Am. Hosp. Assn., Chgo., 1956-60; dir. div. hosp. pharmacy Am. Pharm., Washington, 1960-62; exec. v.p. Am. Soc. Health-System Pharmacists, Washington, 1960-98. Pres. Am. Soc. Hosp. Pharmacists Research and Edn. Found., 1986-98. Active Boy Scouts Am., Camp Fire Girls; Sec. Am. Soc. Health-System Pharmacists Research and Edn. Found., 1970-86. Served with AUS, 1951-53. Recipient 1st cert. Honor award Duquesne U. Sch. Pharmacy, 1969, named Outstanding Alumnus, 1978; recipient Harvey A.K. Whitney award Am. Soc. Hosp. Pharmacists, 1970, Julius Sturmer Meml. Lecture award Rho Chi soc, Phila., 1971, Howard C. Newton Lecture award 1977, Samuel Melendy Lecture award, 1978, Hugo H. Schaefer award, 1983, Reed and Alice Henninger Lecture award, 1984, Donald E. Francke medal, 1986, Remington medal award, 1990. Fellow AAAS; mem. Am. Pharm. Assn., Am. Soc. Hosp. Pharmacists, Am. Inst. History Pharmacy, Internat. Pharm. Fedn. (pres. hosp. pharmacy sect. 1977-81, v.p. 1984-86, pres. 1986-90), Drug Info. Assn., Am. Soc. Assn. Execs., Can. Soc. Hosp. Pharmacists (hon.), Soc. Hosp. Pharmacists Australia (hon.), Pharm. Soc. Gt. Britain (hon.), Pharm. Soc. Nigeria (hon.), Nat. Coun. Patient Info. and Edn. (sec. 1982-85), Israel Pharm. Soc. (hon.), Rho Chi, Kappa Psi (hon.), Duquesne U. Century Club (charter). Home: 6509 Rockhurst Rd Bethesda MD 20817-1661 Office: Am Soc Health-System Pharmacists 7272 Wisconsin Ave Bethesda MD 20814-4836 Personal E-mail: jao@ashp.org.

ODDO, JAMES S., city councilman, lawyer; b. NYC; BA, Fordham Univ., 1988; JD, NY Law Sch., 1991. Bar: NY 1991. Chief of staff to NY City Councilman John Fusco, 1992—94; counsel to NY City Coun. Minority Leader Thomas V. Ognibene, 1995—98; city councilman Dist. 50 NY City Coun., 1999—. Minority Leader NY City Coun., 2002—. Mem.: ABA, NY Bar Assn., NJ Bar Assn., Richmond County Bar Assn. Republican. Mailing: 94 Lincoln Ave Staten Island NY 10306 Office Phone: 718-980-1017, 212-788-7159. Office Fax: 718-980-1051. Business E-Mail: oddo@council.nyc.ny.us.*

ODDONE, PIERMARIA JORGE, physicist; b. Arequipa, Peru, Mar. 26, 1944; came to US, 1961; s. Pietro Giovanni and Maria Vittoria (Jona) O.; m. Barbara S. Oddone, Aug. 27, 1965; children: Gian Michele, Alessandra. BS in Physics, MIT, 1965; PhD in Physics, Princeton U., 1970. Postdoctoral fellow Calif. Tech. Inst., Pasadena, 1970-72, Lawrence Berkeley Nat. Lab., Calif., 1972-76, staff scientist Calif., 1976-78, sr. staff scientist Calif., 1978-87, dir. physics div. Calif., 1987-91, lab. dep. dir. Calif., 1990—2005; dir. Fermi Nat. Accelerator Lab., Batavia, Ill., 2005—. Head initial positron electron project Accelerator Stanford Linear Accelerator Ctr., 1976—82, leader, sci. coord. Time Project Chamber collaboration, 1984—87. Recipient Panofsky award, Am. Phys. Soc., 2005. Fellow Am. Phys. Soc., Am. Acad. Arts & Scis. Achievements include research in in high energy physics; development of Time Projection Chamber and Asymmetric B-Factory (a particle collider). Office: Fermilab PO Box 500 Batavia IL 60510-0500 Office Phone: 630-840-3211. Business E-Mail: pjoddone@fnal.gov.

ODDSSON, DAVID, former Prime Minister of Iceland, bank executive; b. Reykjavik, Iceland, Jan. 17, 1948; s. Oddur Olafsson and Ingibjörg Kristin (Ludviksdottir) O.; m. Astridur Thorarensen, 1970. Grad., Reykjavik Sec. Grammar Sch., 1970; grad. lawyer, U. Iceland, 1976. Chief clk. Reykjavik Theatre, 1970-72; parliamentary reporter Morgunbladid newspaper, 1973-74; with Almenna Bokafelagid Pubs., 1975-76; office mgr. Reykjavik Health Ins. Fund, 1976-78, mng. dir., 1978-82; mayor City of Reykjavik, 1982-91; elected vice-chmn. Independence Party, 1989, elected chmn., 1991; M.P. Althing, 1991; prime min. Govt. of Iceland, Reykjavik, 1991—2004, min. fgn. affairs & external trade, 2004—05, min. statistical bureau, 2004—05; gov. and chmn. govs. Ctrl. Bank of Iceland, 2005—. Prodr. numerous radio programs Iceland State Broadcasting Svc., 1968-75; bd. dirs. Almenna Bokafelagid Pubs. Author: Sjalfstaedisstefnan (The Independence Movement), 1981, (plays) (with T. Eldjarn and H. Gunnlaugsson) Eg Vil Audga Mitt Land (For My Country's Benefit), 1974, (with H. Gunnlaugsson) Islendingaspjoll (Icelandic Confabulations), 1975, (TV dramas) Robert Eliasson Kemur Heim fra Utlondum (Robert Eliasson Returns from Abroad), 1977, Kusk a Hvitflibbanum (Stains on the White Collar), 1981, author two best-selling collections of short stories; translator: Eistland-Smathjod undir Oki Erlends Valds (Estonia, a Small Nation under the Yoke of a Foreign Power, by Anders Küng), 1973, A Couple of Days Without Gudny, 1997, Stolen from the Author of the Alphabet, 2002. Bd. dirs. Independence Party Youth Fedn., 1973-75, Vardberg (Assn. for Western Cooperation), 1973-77, Reykjavik Mcpl. Youth Summer Sch., 1974-82; mem. Reykjavik City Coun., from 1974, mem. exec. com., from 1980, chmn., from 1982, mem. supervisory com., 1978-80; mem. negotiating com. State Social Security Inst., others, 1976-81; mem. exec. com. Independence Party, 1979—; mem. Reykjavik Traffic Com., 1974-78, Reykjavik Mcpl. Bd. Edn., 1974-82; bd. dirs. Kjarvalsstadir Art Mus., Reykjavik, 1974-82, vice-chmn., 1974-78; mem. Reykjavik Youth Coun., 1974-82, chmn., 1974-78; mem. Reykjavik Bd. Freshwater Fisheries & Pisciculture, 1974-82, vice chmn., 1974-78; chmn. exec. com. Reykjavik Arts Festival, 1976-78; mem. negotiating com. for merger of Landsvirkjun (Nat. Power Co.) and Laxarvirkjun Power Co., 1980-81; mem. bldg. com. Reykjavik Mcpl. Theatre, 1975-79, 82-91, vice chmn., 1975-79, chmn., 1982-91; chmn. bd. dirs. Shop and Office Workers' Pension Fund, 1982-91; mem. editorial com. History of Reykjavik, 1981-91, chmn., 1982-91. Recipient Golden Plate award, Acad. Achievement, 2004. Office: Ministry Fgn Affairs Rauoararstigur 25 150 Reykjavik Iceland also: Central Bank Iceland Kalkofnsvegi 1 150 Reykjavik Iceland Office Phone: 354 569 9600. Business E-Mail: sedlabanki@sedlabanki.is. E-mail: postur@for.stjr.is.

O'DEA, J. DAVID, psychologist, educator; b. Ellsworth, Kans., Feb. 17, 1924; m. Teresa Eleanor Cordova. BS in Psychology, Emporia State U., 1948, MS in Psychology, 1949; PhD in Psychology, Oreg. State U., 1952. Lic. psychologist Fla. Assoc. prof. Fla. State U., Tallahassee, 1953—56; sr. staff assoc. IBM, Dunedin, Fla., 1956—82. Cons. psychologist, Dunedin, 1982—92; vis. prof. Notre Dame U., South Bend, Ind., 1953, U. Va., Charlottesville, 1956, Oreg. State U., Corvallis, 1964, U. Miami, 1969—70; chmn. bd. Caladesi Nat. Bank, Dunedin, 1967—72, Clearwater (Fla.) Oaks Bank, Clearwater, 1973—82. Contbr., author: book Counseling Selected Readings, 1962; contbr. articles to profl. jours. and mags. Mem. adv. counsel for pres. Berea (Ky.) Coll.; mem. Eagle Scout; bd. dirs. Dunedin Pub. Libr., 1991—; bd. dirs. past mem. Dunedin Coun. Orgns.; bd. dirs. Mease Hosp., Dunedin. With USN, 1942—45, WWII. Named Ky. col., Hon. Order of Ky. Cols., 1982; named to Sr. Citizen Hall of Fame, Dunedin, Fla., 2006. Mem.: VFW, APA (life; Fla. state pres. 1969—70), Ye Mystic Krewe of Neptune (charter mem. Tampa Bay, dir. 1979—), KC (4th degree, Family of Month 1980), Elks (life). Roman Catholic. Avocations: travel, reading, civil volunteering, genealogy. Home: 509 Baywood Dr S Dunedin FL 34698 Home Phone: 727-733-7535.

O'DEA, PATRICK J., food products executive; m. Holly O'Dea; 4 children. BS in bus. administration, U. Albany. With Procter & Gamble, 1984—95; v.p., gen. mgr. specialty cheese divsn. Stella Foods, 1995—97; CEO, pres. Mother's Specialty Foods Corp., 1997; CEO Archway, Mother's Cookies and Mother's Cake and Cookie Co., 1997—2001; CEO, pres. Peet's Coffee & Tea Inc., 2002—, dir., 2002—. Mem.: Nat. Coffee Assn. (bd. trustees), Calif. C. of C. (bd. trustees). Avocation: triathlon. Office: Peet's Coffee & Tea 1400 Park Ave Emeryville CA 94608*

O'DEA, THOMAS JOSEPH, clinical engineer, medical physicist; b. NYC, July 7, 1938; s. Patrick Jostph O'Dea and Beatrice Gaffney; m. Kathryn Jean O'Dea, July 11, 1970; children: Christine, Patrick. BA, Cath. U. Am., 1961; MA, SUNY, Buffalo, 1967; PhD, U. Minn., 2001. Registered profl. engr., Minn., cert. in clin. engring., Internat. Cert. Commn. Physics tchr. Christian Bros., NYC, 1961—67; dir. med. physics Evanston (Ill.) Hosp., 1968—77; dir. engring. U. Minn. Hosp.,

Mpls., 1977—97; prin. Tom O'Dea Health Care Engring., St. Paul, 1997—. Ptnr. Hemoxy LLC, Mpls., 1998—; adj. prof. med. physics and elec. engring. U. Minn., 2007; cons. in field. Contbr. articles to profl. jours. Mem. Telecomm. and Tech. Com., Shoreview, Minn., 2000—. Recipient Best Mgmt. article, Biomed. Inst. and Tech., 1997, Best Rsch. Article award, 2001; grantee, NSF, 1967, NIH, 1968. Mem.: Assn. Advanced Med. Physics, Assn. Advanced Med. Inst. (various offices), Am. Coll. Clin. Engring (chmn. advocacy 1984—, award 2002). Roman Catholic. Achievements include patents for device for measuring O2 diffusion from red blood cells; non invasive measurement gastric lumen and non invasive mucus expulsion from lungs; an improved HFCC device for cyotic febrosis & a device for measuring gastric lumen. Avocation: swimming. Home and Office: 925 Arbogast St Shoreview MN 55126 Office Phone: 651-283-8542. Personal E-mail: tomkayjodea@comcast.net.

ODEEN, PHILIP A., communications executive; b. SD, 1935; BA in Govt., U. SD, 1957; MA in Polit. Sci., U. Wis., 1959. V.p. Wilson Sporting Goods Co., 1973—78; with Coopers & Lybrand, 1978—92; pres., CEO BDM Internat., Inc., 1992—97; exec. v.p., gen. mgr. TRW Systems & Info. Tech., 1997—99; exec. v.p. Wash. ops. TRW, Inc., 1998—2000, chmn., 2002; acting CEO, chmn. Reynolds & Reynolds Co., 2004—05, non-exec. chmn., 2005—06; CEO QinetiQ N. Am., 2005—06; chmn. Avaya, Inc., 2006—07; non-exec. chmn. Convergys Corp., Cin., 2007—. Bd. dirs. Convergys Corp., 2000—, Avaya, Inc., 2002—, Northrop Grumman Corp., 2003—. Office: Convergys Corp PO Box 1638 201 E Fourth St Cincinnati OH 45201

O'DELL, CONNIE VINCENT, special education educator; b. Talladega, Ala., Oct. 15, 1951; d. Ernest Wesley and Mildred Malone Vincent; m. Ronnie Michael O'Dell, May 19, 1973; children: Lorrie Storm, Ashley Michelle. BS, U. Ala., 1973; MA, U. Ala., Tuscaloosa, 1979. Cert. tchr. State of Ala., State of Ga. Spl. edn. tchr. Childersburg (Ala.) H.S., 1974, Eden Sch., Pell City, Ala., 1974—77; learning disabilities tchr. Ashville (Ala.) HS, 1977—2001; tchr. Oak Mountain Youth Svcs., Pelham, 2001—02; spl. edn. tchr. Temple (Ga.) HS, 2002—. Sponsor, advisor Ashville H.S. Jr. Beta Club, 1996—98; cheerleader coach Ashville H.S., 1984—91. Organist Blue Eye Bapt. Ch., Lincoln, 2001—05, ch. clk., sec., 2002—05; bd. dirs. Blue Eye Cemetery Bd., Lincoln, Ala., 2002—05. Mem.: NEA, Ga. Assn. of Educators, St. Clair County Edn. Assn. (pres., v.p., sec. 1981—84), Ala. Edn. Assn. Baptist. Avocations: reading, piano, travel. Home: 1605 Blue Eye Springs Rd Lincoln AL 35096 Office: Temple H S 589 Sage St Temple GA 30179 E-mail: connie.odell@carrollcountyschools.com.

O'DELL, DOUGLAS V., JR., federal agency administrator, retired military officer; b. 1948; m. Judith O'Dell; 5 children. BA in History and Latin Am. Studies, Rutgers U., NJ, 1971; grad., NATO Def. Coll. Sr. Res. Officers Course, Rome, US Army War Coll.; grad. Sr. Res. Component Officers Course, Carlisle; grad. Sr. Exec. Course, Harvard U.; grad., Capstone. Enlisted USMC, 1968, advanced through grades to maj. gen., 2004; rifle platoon comdr. 1st Battalion, 7th Marines; platoon comdr., co. exec. officer, hdqs. comdt. 3rd Battalion, 5th Marines; served with 4th Svc. Battalion, USMCR, Freemansburg, Pa., 1974—75; co. exec. officer, weapons co. comdr., fire support coord., battalion ops. officer 2nd Battalion, 25th Marines, 1975—85; ops. officer 1st Battalion, 23rd Marines, 1985, 1/23 to commdg. officer, 1987; served with Detachment 2, Hdqs., 4th Marine Divsn.; G-3 plans 2nd Marine Expeditionary Brigade, Camp Lejeune, 1989, 1993—98; served with II MEF staff, Operation Desert Storm, 1990—91; exec. officer to commdg. officer 25th Marines, Worcester, Mass., 1992—93; dep. chief staff Marine Forces Res., 1998—2001; asst. divsn. comdr. 4th Marine Divsn., New Orleans, 1999—2001; comdr. 4th Marine Expeditionary Brigade (Anti-Terrorism), Camp Lejeune, NC, 2001—04, 4th Marine Divsn./ Joint Task Force Katrina/Rita, New Orleans, 2004—07; ret., 2007; coord. Recovery & Rebuilding in the Gulf Coast Region US Dept. Homeland Security, New Orleans, 2008—. Regional v.p. AIM Investments, 1988—93, ptnr., 1993—2001. Achievements include a 28-year career in business with investment management positions in the private sector as well as USMC duty; as commanding general in New Orleans when Hurrican Katrina hit in 2005, he employed 2,700 marines and sailors and assisted in rescuing and evacuting civilians and restoring basic functions to the city. Office: Coord Gulf Coast Rebuilding US Dept Homeland Security Washington DC 20528*

ODELL, HERBERT, lawyer; b. Phila., Oct. 20, 1937; s. Samuel and Selma (Kramer) O.; m. Valerie Odell; children: Wesley, Jonathan, James, Sarah, Samuel. BS in Econs., U. Pa., 1959; JD magna cum laude, U. Miami, 1962; LLM, Harvard U., 1963. Bar: Fla. 1963, Pa. 1968, D.C. 2002. Trial atty. tax div. U.S. Dept. Justice, Washington, 1963-65; assoc. Walton, Lantaff, Schroeder, Carson & Wahl, Miami, Fla., 1965-67; from assoc. to ptnr. Morgan, Lewis & Bockius, Phila., 1967-89; ptnr. Zapruder & Odell, Phila., 1989-98, Odell & Ptnrs., Phila., 1998-99, Miller & Chevalier, Chartered, Phila., 2000—06, Chamberlain, Hrdlicka, White, Williams & Martin, 2007—. Adj. prof. U. Miami, Villanova U.; lectr. various tax insts. Contbr. articles to profl. jours. Ford fellow, 1962-63. Mem.: ABA, D.C. Bar Assn., Phila. Bar Assn., Pa. Bar Assn., Fla. Bar Assn., Harvard Club, Beta Alpha Psi, Omicron Delta Kappa, Phi Kappa Phi. Avocations: sailing, running, tennis, scuba diving, fishing. Office: Chamberlain Hrdlicka et al Ste 570 300 Conshohocken State Rd West Conshohocken PA 19428 Home Phone: 610-827-0967; Office Phone: 610-772-2310. Business E-Mail: hodell@chamberlainlaw.com.

ODELL, JOHN STEPHEN, political scientist; b. San Antonio, Aug. 25, 1945; s. Earl T. Odell and Jeraldine Busby; m. Margaret Gonder, Jan. 16, 1971. BA, U. Tex., 1967; MA, U. Wis., 1968, PhD, 1976. Lectr. Southwest Tex. State U., 1968—69; asst. prof. dept. govt. Harvard U., Cambridge, Mass., 1976-82; assoc. prof. Sch. Internat. Rels. U. So. Calif., LA, 1982-90, dir. Ctr. for Internat. Studies, 1989-92, prof. Sch. Internat. Rels., 1990—; dir. L.Am. policy devel. Office of U.S. Trade Rep., Exec. Office of Pres., Washington, 1984-85. Vis. fellow Inst. for Internat. Econs., Washington, 1985-87, Rsch. Inst., Ministry Internat. Trade and Industry, Tokyo, 1989; cons. Inst. Tch. Autonoma Mex., Mexico City, 1991; cons. World Bank, Asia Found., U.S. Dept. State. Author: U.S. International Monetary Policy, 1982; author: (co-author) Anti-Protection: Changing Forces in U.S. Trade Policies, 1987; co-editor: International Trade Policies: Gains From Exchange Between Economics and Political Science, 1990; author: Negotiating the World Economy, 2000; editor: Internat. Orgn., 1992—96, Negotiating Trade, 2006. 1st lt. U.S. Army, 1969-71, Vietnam. Rsch. grantee Carnegie Endowment for Internat. Peace, 1975, Ford Found., 1979-82, 89-90; Fellow Coun. on Fgn. Rels., 1984-85, Social Sci. Rsch. Coun., 1987-89, Stanford U., 1994-95. Mem. Am. Polit. Sci. Assn., Coun. on Fgn. Affairs, Pacific Coun. on Internat. Policy, Internat. Studies Assn. Office: U So Calif Sch Internat Rels Los Angeles CA 90089-0043 Office Phone: 213-740-4298. Fax: (213) 742-0281. E-mail: odell@usc.edu.

ODELL, PATRICK LOWRY, retired mathematics professor; b. Watonga, Okla., Nov. 29, 1930; s. Max Vernon and Pamela (Massey) Odell; m. Norma Lou Maddox, Aug. 16, 1958 (dec. May 1980); children: James M., David L., Michael R.L., Julie K., Patricia L., Deborah L.; m. Dovalee Dorsett, Aug. 3, 1985. BS, U. Tex., 1952; postgrad., UCLA, 1953-54; MS, Okla. State U., 1958, PhD, 1962. Mathematician White Sands (N.Mex.) Proving Grounds, 1952-53, Kaman Nuclear, Albuquerque, 1958-59, U.S. Naval Nuclear Ordnance Evaluation Unit, 1959-62, Ling-Temco Vought Aeros., 1962; asst. prof. math. U. Tex., Austin, 1962-66; prof., chmn. dept. math. Tex. Technol. U., Lubbock, 1966-71, coordinator insts., dir. rsch., Coll. Arts and Sci., 1971-72; prof math. scis. and environ. scis. U. Tex., Dallas, 1972-88, prof. emeritus, 1988—; prof. emeritus math. sci. Baylor U., Waco, Tex., 1988—2001; exec. dean grad. studies and rsch. U. Tex., Dallas, 1972-75. Assoc. dir. Tex. Ctr. for Rsch., Austin, 1964—66; rsch. scientist Def. Rsch. Lab., 1963—65; cons. math. statistician, 1962—. Capt. USAF, 1953—57. Fellow: Am. Statis. Assn., Tex. Acad. Sci. (Disting. Tex. Scientist award 1994). Home: 1117 Deer Run Rd Valley Mills TX 76689 Personal E-mail: pat_odell@baylor.edu.

ODELL, STANLEY JACK, retired philosopher professor; b. Lawrence, Va., Apr. 22, 1933; m. Barbara Reed Bradford, Dec. 12, 1991; children: Lynn A., Erin A. Bradley. PhD, U. Ill., Champagne-Urbana, 1966. Emeritus prof. U. Md., Coll. Pk., Md., 1966—2008. Author: (book) The Philosophy of Language, Consequentialist Ethics, Bertrand Russell, Schopenhauer, G. E. Moore. Fellow, NSF, 1965. Home: 19385 Cypress Ridge Ter Leesburg VA 20176-5168 Office: Univ Md College Park MD 20742-3105 Business E-Mail: sjodell@umd.edu.com.

ODEN, DEREK, history professor; b. Kirksville, Mo., Aug. 11, 1972; s. Robert Malcolm and Sue Ellen Oden; m. Jennifer Oden, June 5, 1999; children: Luke, Caleb. BA, Wartburg Coll., Waverly, Iowa, 1995; MA, U. Nebr., Omaha, 2000; PhD, Iowa State U., Ames, 2006. Lectr. Iowa State U., 2004; site supr. Living History Farms, Urbandale, Iowa, 2005—07; instr. William Penn U., Urbandale, 2005—07; asst. history prof. Del Mar Coll., Corpus Christi, Tex., 2007—, 2007—. Contbr. articles to numerous profl. jours. Recipient Rsch. Excellence award, Iowa State U., 2006, Everett E. Edwards award, Agrl. History Soc., 2005, Pres. Excellence award, William Penn U., 2006; named History Grad. Student of Yr., U. Nebr., 2000, Phi Alpha Theta Grad. Rsch. Paper of Yr., Iowa State U., 2001. Office: Del Mar Coll 101 Baldwin Blvd Corpus Christi TX 78404 Business E-Mail: doden@delmar.edu.

ODEN, GLORIA, language educator, poet; b. Yonkers, NY, Oct. 30, 1923; d. Redmond Stanley and Ethel (Kincaid) Oden. BA in History, Howard U., 1944, JD, 1948. Faculty New Sch. for Social Rsch., NYC, 1966; vis. lectr. dept. English SUNY, Stony Brook, 1969-70; asst. prof. English U. Md., Balt., 1971—75, assoc. prof., 1975—83, prof., 1983—96. Sr. editor IEEE proc. and tech. mags., 1966—67; supr. math./sci. books Appleton-Century-Crofts, 1967—68; project dir. lang. arts books Hold, Rinehart and Winston, 1968—72, sr. editor coll. dept., 1968—71; editor Am. Inst. Physics/Am. Jour. Physics, 1961—66; lectr. in field; condr. numerous poetry readings; juror fiction panel Mass. Cultural Coun., 1994; juror poetry panel N.J. State Coun., 1993, 94; numerous others; cons. Reel Deal Prodns. Co., NEH, 1984, 87. Author: (poems) Resurrections, 1978, The Tie that Binds, 1980, Appearances, 2003; contbr. poetry to mags., newspapers, audio, anthologies, articles to profl. jours. Recipient Disting. Black Women's award, Towson U., 1984; NEH Summer grantee, 1974, Breadloaf Writers scholar, 1960, Creative Writing fellow, John Hay Whitney Found., 1955—56, Yaddo fellow, 1956. Mem.: PEN Am. Ctr., Poetry Soc. Am. (bd. govs. 1981—82, v.p. 1983—84). Home: 707 Maiden Choice Ln Apt 8119 Catonsville MD 21228-4185

ODEN, GREG, professional basketball player; b. Buffalo, Jan. 22, 1988; s. Greg Oden, Sr. and Zoe Oden. Student in Bus. Adminstrn., Ohio State U., Columbus, 2006—07. Draft pick Portland Trail Blazers, Oreg., 2007. Mem. USA Basketball Men's Sr. Nat. Team, 2007—. Recipient Arthur L. Trester Mental Attitude award, Ind. Boy's Basketball Class 4A, 2005—06, Morgan Wootten award (McDonald's All-Am. Player of Yr.), 2006; named USA Today Player of Yr., 2005, 2006, Parade Mag. Player of Yr., 2005, 2006, Gatorade Ind. and Nat. Player of Yr., 2005, 2006, Gatorade Nat. HS Male Athlete of Yr., 2006, Player of Yr., Nat. HS Coaches Assn., 2006, Ind. Mr. Basketball, Indpls. Star, 2006, Atlanta Tipoff Club 2006 Naismith Prep Player of Yr.; named a McDonald's All-Am., 2006. Achievements include being the number one pick in the 2007 NBA Draft. Office: Portland Trail Blazers Rose Quarter One Center Ct Portland OR 97227*

ODEN, JEAN P(HIFER), special education educator; b. Chgo., May 2, 1936; d. Dillard James and Lena (Conner) Phifer; m. James Edward Oden, Apr. 26, 1959; 1 child, Eric James. BE, Chgo. Tchrs. Coll., 1958; MEd in Learning Disabilities, Chgo. State U., 1973; postgrad., Nat. Coll. Edn., Evanston, Ill., 1986—, cert. advance studies, 1987; EdD, Nat.-Louis U., 1995. Tchr. elem. schs. Chgo., 1958-73, tchr. learning disabilities elem. schs., 1973-81, cons. spl. edn., ind. edn. program facilitator, 1981; learning disability specialist Phillips HS, Chgo., 1982—87, Englewood HS, Chgo., 1987—94, Harold Washington Elem. Sch., Chgo., 1994-98. Mem. Ill. Guidelines for Learning Disabilities Devel. Com., Springfield, Ill., 1981-82, Com. to Devel. State Test for Learning Disabilities Tchrs., Springfield, 1986—; speaker Who's Who Congress, Cambridge, Eng., 1992; mem. del. to Vietnam, 1993, China, 1994, Oxford U., 1997, South Africa, 2001; mem. African Affairs Adv. Coun. to Chgo. Human Rels. Commn., 1999-, People to People Internat. Worldwide Conf., 2002—; chair edn. com. Chgo. Southside NAACP, 2000, sec. 2003. Sec. Nat. Urban League NYC conf., 1980-2005, Chgo. Southside br., 2003—; mem. Congl. Victory Fund, Chgo., 1985, SCLC Met. Chgo., 1979-81, Mayoral Summit Parent-Community Coun. on Ednl. Reform, 1987—, Chgo. Mayor's Edn. Summit on Sch. Reform, 1988; charter mem. Rep. Presdl. Adv. Task Force, 1989, Rep. Inner Circle, 1991, Ctr. for Study of the Presidency, 1998; mem. Coalition Black Trade Unionists, 1991—, cons. pool Nat. Juvenile Justice Resource Ctr., 1991—, NAACP; state chair African Am. Econ. Devel. Task Force, Ill. Legis. Black Caucus, 1992—; bd. dirs., African Scientific Rsch. Mus. Inst., 2003. US Dept. Edn. grantee, 1986; recipient Citizenship award Chgo. mayor, 1984, Cert. merit NAACP South Side Br., 1978; named state advisor US Congl. Adv. Bd., 1985; speaker edn. seminar 19th Congress on Arts and Communicatiion, Cambridge, Eng. Mem. ASCD, LWV, NAACP (chair edn. com. 2000, sec. Chgo. Southside br., 2003), Minority Mainstream, United Neighborhoods Intertwined for Total Equality (founder, exec. dir., rschr.), Assn. for Citizens with Learning Disabilities, Coun. for Exceptional Children (liaison to state bd. Ill. Divsn. for Citizens with Learning Disabilities 1980), Spl. Edn. Tchrs. Assn. (1st pres., founder), Black Parents United for Edn. and Related Svcs. (founder), Kappa Delta Pi, Lehigh (Fla.) Country Club, Thousand Trails Club (Ottawa, Ill.). Mem. Carter C.M.E. Ch. Avocations: hiking, racketball, travel, camping. Office Phone: 773-821-6122. Office Fax: 773 821-4456. *Personal philosophy: Those of us in society who are fortunate to reach levels of influence should share skills and talents with the less fortunate. A society which maintain masses of people in an undeveloped state is doomed to class conflict and cultural extinction. Those who don't study history are bound to repeat it.*

ODEN, JOHN TINSLEY, engineering educator, mathematician, consultant; b. Alexandria, La., Dec. 25, 1936; s. John James and Sara Elizabeth (Lyles) O.; m. Barbara Clare Smith, Mar. 19, 1965; children: John Walker, Elizabeth Lee. BS, La. State U., 1959; MS, Okla. State U., 1960, PhD, 1962; DSc (hon.), Tech. U. Lisbon, Portugal, 1986; Doctorate (hon.), Polytechnique de Mons, Belgium, 2000, Tech. U. Krakow, Poland, 2001, Ecole Normale Superior Cachan, 2006. Registered profl. engr., Tex., La. Teaching asst. La. State U., Baton Rouge, 1959; asst. prof. Okla. State U., Stillwater, 1961-63; sr. structures engr. Gen. Dynamics, Fort Worth, 1963-64; prof., head dept. engring. mechanics U. Ala., Huntsville, 1964-73; prof. U. Tex., Austin, 1973—, Carol and Henry Groppe prof. engring., Ernest and Virginia Cockrell chair in engring. Austin, 1987-93, Cockrell Family Regents chair engring., 1993—. Prof. Coope U. Fed., Brazil, 1974; dir. Inst. Computational Engring and Sci., 2003, assoc. v.p. for rsch., 2003—; mem. Sci. Rsch. Coun. vis. scholar Brunel U., Eng., 1981; com. on computational mechanics NRC; chmn. U.S. Nat. Com. on Theoretical and Applied Mechanics, 1992-94; founder, CEO computational Mechanics Co., Inc., 1982-96; Peter O'Donnell Jr. chair in computer sys., 2003. Author, editor 45 books; editor Jour. Computer Methods in Applied Mechanics and Engring., 1980—; contbr. over 500 articles to profl. jours. Decorated Chevalier Ordre des Palms Academique (France); recipient rsch. award Southeastern Conf. on Theoretical and Applied Mechanics, 1978, Lohmann medal Okla. State U., 1991, Hocott Rsch. award, 1992, Computational Mechanics Medal Japan Soc. Mech. Engrs., 1993, Presdl. Citation, U. Tex. Austin, 2004 Fellow ASCE (life; Outstanding Svc. award 1968, Walter Huber rsch. award 1973, Theodore von Karman medal 1992, Joe J. King Prof. Engring. award 1994), ASME (hon. mem., Worcester Reed Warner medal 1990, Timoshenko medal 1996), NAE, Soc. Engring. Sci. (pres. 1978, Eringen medal 1991), Am. Acad. Mechanics (pres. 1990-94, Disting. Svc. medal 1995), Internat. Assn. Computational Mechanics (pres. 1990-94, Congress-Gauss-Newton medal 1994), Am. Acad. Arts and Sciences; mem. Soc. Indsl. and Applied Math., U.S. Assn. Computational Mechanics (pres. 1990-92, John Von Neumann medal 1993), Soc. Natural Philosophy, Nat. Acad. Engring. Mex., Nat. Acad. Engring. Brazil, World Innovation Found. (hon. 2004), Polish Assn. Computational Mechanics (Zienkiewicz medal, 2007). Office: Univ Tex Austin ICES Campus Code CO200 Austin TX 78712 Home: 7403 W Rim Dr Austin TX 78731-2044

ODEN, ROBERT A., JR., academic administrator; m. Teresa Oden; children: Robert, Katherine. BA in History and Lit., Harvard Coll.; MA in Religious Studies/Oriental Langs., Cambridge U.; MA in Theology, Harvard Divinity, 1972; PhD in Near Eastern Langs. and Lit., Harvard U., 1975; MA (hon.), Dartmouth Coll., 1987. Faculty Dartmouth Coll., 1975—89, prof., 1985—89, chair dept. of religion, 1983—89; dir., founder Dartmouth's Humanities Inst.; headmaster Hotchkiss Sch., Lakeville, Conn., 1989—95; pres. Kenyon Coll., Gambier, Ohio, 1995—2002, Carleton Coll., Northfield, Minn., 2002—. Chmn. com. on orgn. and policy Dartmouth Coll., com. on admissions and fin. aid; lectr. in field. Author: The Bible Without Theology, 1987. Mem.: Conn. Assn. Ind. Schs. (bd. dirs.). Avocations: fishing, running, religious studies, archaeology. Office: Carleton Coll 1 North College St Northfield MN 55057 Office Phone: 507-646-4305. E-mail: president@acs.carleton.edu.*

ODEN, WILLIAM BRYANT, bishop, educator; b. McAllen, Tex., Aug. 3, 1935; s. Charles Alva and Evea (Bryant) O.; m. Marilyn Brown, July 12, 1957; children: Danna Lee Oden Bowen, William Dirk, Valerie Lyn, Charles Bryant. BA, Okla. State U., 1958; MDiv, Harvard U., 1961, postgrad., 1964; ThD, Boston U., 1964; DD (hon.), Oklahoma City U., 1980; LHD (hon.), Centenary Coll., 1990. Ordained to ministry Meth. Ch., 1961. Pastor Aldersgate United Meth. Ch., Oklahoma City, 1963-69, St. Stephen's United Meth. Ch., Norman, Okla., 1969-76, Crown Heights United Meth. Ch., Oklahoma City, 1976-83; prof. Phillips Grad. Sem., Enid, 1976-88; pastor 1st United Meth. Ch., Enid, 1983-88; bishop United Meth. Ch., La., 1988-96, Dallas area, 1996—2004, Ecumenical del. to Lambeth Conf., 1998. Pres., United Meth. Coun. Bishops, 2000-01; pres. SCJ Coll. of Bishops, 1989-90; del. Gen. Conf., 1976, 80, 84, 88; chmn. Okla. Del. to Gen. and Jurisdictional Confs., 1984, 88; Jackson lectr. Perkins Sch. Theology, So. Meth. U., 1975, Wilson lectr. SCJ Bishop's Week, 1989; co-chair World Meth.-Anglican Dialogue, 1991-95; bd. dirs. Wesley Works Project; pres. Gen. Bd. Higher Edn. & Ministry, 1996-01; pres. comm., United Meth. Comm., 2000-04; Ecumenical officer, head communion, 2004-. Author: Oklahoma Methodism in the Twentieth Century, 1968, Liturgy as Life Journey, 1976, Wordeed: Evangelism in Biblical and Wesleyan Perspective, 1978; contbr.: Send Me: The Iteneracy in Crisis, 1991, Vision and Supervision, 2003. Trustee Oklahoma City U., 1980-88, Southwestern U., Winfield, Kans., 1983-88, Centenary Coll., 1988-96, Dillard U., 1988-96, So. Meth. U., 1996—2004. Recipient Outstanding Alumni award, Harvard Divinity Sch., 2005; named to U. Hall of Fame, Okla. State, 2003; Charles E. Merrill fellow, Harvard U., 2003. Mem. Am. Acad. Homiletics. Methodist. Avocations: writing, reading biographies, mountain climbing, backpacking. Home: PO BOX 866188 Plano TX 75086-6188 Personal E-mail: wbo8@earthlink.net.

ODENIGBO, INNOCENT CHUKWUNWIKE, linguist, writer, consultant; b. Nri, Anambra State, Nigeria, Sept. 28, 1941; arrived in U.S., 1998; s. Lazarus Okonkwo and Rosaline Ama Odenigbo; m. Monica Chinwe Akpu, Oct. 6, 1996; m. Felicia Umekwulu Egesi, Sept. 26, 1967 (div. Sept. 16, 1996); children: Uchenna Zephyrina, Ifeanyi Innocent, Chukwuemeka John-Mary, Uzoamaka Assumpta. BA in Languages, U. Grenoble, 1971; postgrad., U. Besancon, 1974—75, U. Aston, Birmingham, Eng., 1981—82, CIRNEA, Paris, 1990—94; PhD in Languages, Am. West U., 2002; MBA, Dowling Coll., 2002. Lang. prof. Inst. Mgmt. and Tech., Enugu, Nigeria, 1971—73; rsch. officer Nigerian Nat. Supply Co., London, 1973—78; sr. news presenter Nigerian TV Authority, Enugu, Nigeria, 1979—81; chief editor, anchorman Anambra Broadcasting Svc., Awka, Nigeria, 1983—98; pres. IMC Info. Svcs., Newark, 2003—. Cons. IMC Info. Services, Newark, 2003—. Author: (poetry) Thank God for America, (autobiography) A Human Comedy; prodr.: (TV Documentaries) Les Halles de Paris, 1990, Le Louvre du Pouvoir, 1992, L'enfant qui Prolonge La Vie, 1994. Patron French Lang. Students Assn. Nnamdi Azikiwe U., Awka, Nigeria. Recipient Best Broadcaster award, Nigeria Union Journalists, 1984. Mem.: Nigerian Inst. Mgmt., Nigerian Inst. Pub. Rels., Soc. Nigerian Broadcasters, Inst. Linguists London, Soc. Profl. Journalists, Internat. Soc. Poets (Disting. Mem. 2000, 2001). Personal E-mail: odenigbo@inosaint.com.

ODENWELLER, ROBERT PAUL, philatelist, trade association administrator, retired pilot; b. Sept. 19, 1938; s. Charles Joseph and Robina Katharine (Watson) O.; m. Jane Blackistone Rawlings, June 24, 1965; 1 stepchild, Joy McCorriston; 1 child, Liesl Hasbrouck. BS, US Air Force Acad., 1960. Commd. USAF, 1956, advanced through grades to capt., 1963, resigned, 1956-66. Mem. Collectors Club Inc., NYC, 1964—, gov. 1969—, program chmn., 1970-80, 2004-, mem. editl. bd., 1975-2004, editor 2005-, sec. 1979-82, v.p. 1983-86, pres. 1987-90, trustee, 1992-98, Honorary mem., 2007; trustee, vice chmn. then chmn. expert com. Philatelic Found., NYC, 1970—. Author: The FIP Guide to Exhibiting and Judging Traditional and Postal History Exhibits, 1993; author, editor: Philatelic Vocabulary in Five Languages, 1978 (Vermeil medal 1979); editor: Opinions VI, 1992 (Gold medal), The Stamps and Postal History of Nineteenth Century Samoa, 2004 (Gold medal, Nat. Grand award, Internat. Gold medal, 2005, Spl. prize, 2005, Best in Show, 2005), The Collectors Club Philatelist, 2005- (3 Gold medals, Vermeil medal 2006, Diane Boehret award Am. Philatelic Congress, 2006); contbr. articles to profl. jours. Recipient Grand Prix d'Honneur, Zeapex Orgn., 1980; selected to sign Roll of Disting. Philatelists, Brit. Philatelic Fedn., 1991, US Philatelist Classics Soc., 2009, mem. bd. election, Alfred Lichtenstein Meml. award Collectors Club, NY, 1993, TWA Flight Ops. Meritorious Achievement award 1995, award of Excellence, 1995, 2000. Fellow Royal Philatelic Soc. London (hon., spl. rep. for US 2003—, conduct com. 2004—, Crawford medal, 2005), Royal Philatelic Soc. N.Z. (elected hon. life fellow, 2008, Collins award 2005); mem. Fedn. Internat. de Philatelie (pres. commn. traditional philately 1978-96; Grand Prix d'Honneur 1980, Svc. medal 1996, Rsch. medal 2006), Am. Philatelic Soc. (bd. dirs. 1981-84, 89-90, 2007- named Champion of Champions 1973, Luff award 1996, chmn. 2003-07), Assn. Internat. Des Experts Philateliques (expert 1980-, bd. dirs. 1987-), Fedn. New Zealand Philatelic Socs., Grand Prix Club Internat. (sec., treas. 1980-89, bd. dirs. 1989-92, 94-00, v.p. 1994-96, pres. 1996-2000), Soc. Australasian Specialists (pres. 1969-72), US Chess Fedn., European Acad. Philately (elected hon. mem., 2008), Smithsonian Instn. Coun. Philatelists; mem. Brit. Philatelic Fedn., RDP Trust (bd. of election, 2006-). Republican. Episcopalian. Avocations: stamp collecting/philately, photography, languages, chess, bridge. Home: Chalon Round Top Rd Bernardsville NJ 07924 Office: Collector's Club Inc 22 E 35th St New York NY 10016-3806 Office Phone: 908-766-5460. Business E-Mail: ccpeditor@yahoo.com.

ODERMATT, DIANA B., development consultant; b. Hollywood, Calif., Nov. 25, 1938; d. Harold and Mary H. (Wilson) Birtwistle; m. Robert Allen Odermatt, June 9, 1960; children: Kristin Odermatt Lee, Kyle David Odermatt. BA, Mills Coll., 1960. Assoc. dir. admissions Mills Coll., Oakland, Calif., 1978-82, dean admissions and fin. aid, 1982-85; dir. devel. Head-Royce Sch., Oakland, 1985-91; major gift officer univ. rels. U. Calif., Berkeley, 1992-95, cons. Coll. Environ. Design, 1995-96; dir. devel. Bentley Sch., Oakland, 1996-99. Tchr., trainer Coun. for the Advancement and Support of Edn., Washington, 1980-93; bd. mem. European Coun. Ind. Schs., Washington, 1982-85; cons. The Coll. Bd., N.Y.C., 1985-92. Contbr. articles to profl. jours. Home: 39 Drury Ln Berkeley CA 94705-1615 E-mail: dbomatt@aol.com.

ODERMATT, ROBERT ALLEN, architect; b. Oakland, Calif., Jan. 3, 1938; s. Clifford Allen and Margaret Louise (Budge) O.; m. Diana Birtwistle, June 9, 1960; children: Kristin Ann, Kyle David. BArch, U. Calif., Berkeley, 1960. Registered architect, Calif., Oreg., Nev., Colo., Hawaii; cert. Nat. Coun. Archtl. Registration Bds. Draftsman Anderson Simonds Dusel Campini, Oakland, 1960-61; architect James R. Lucas, Orinda, Calif., 1961-62, ROMA Architects, San Francisco, 1962-76, architect, pres., 1976-84; prin. ROMA Design Group, San Francisco, 1962-92; pres. The Odermatt Group, Berkeley, Calif., 1992—. Prin. spkr. Internat. Conf. on Rebuilding Cities, Pitts., 1988; mem. U.S. Design in Am. Program, Sofia, Bulgaria, Armenian Disaster Assn. Team, 1989, NA Collateral Internship Mgmt. Com.; prin. State of Calif. Bay Arera Facilities Plan, 1992, Greece Resort Privatization Program, 1993. Prin. designer U.S. Embassy, Bahrain, Grand Canyon Nat. Park, 1977, Yosemite Nat. Park, 1987; prin. planner hotel complex Westin Hotel, Vail, Colo., 1982, Kaanapali Resort, 1987, Las Montanas Resort, San Diego; master plan U. Calif., Berkeley, 1988, Kohanaiki and Mauna Lani resorts, 1989, Calif. State Strategic Real Estate Plan, 1992, Greek Resort/Marina Privatization Program, 1993, Tektronix Strategic Plan, 1994, United Labs, Manila Master Plan, 1995, State of Calif. Real Estate Orgn. Plan, 1996, Ford Island Pearl Harbor Master Plan, 1996, Pearl Harbor Visitor Ctr. Plan, 1997, Albiano Resort Study, 1998; master plans include Trefethen Vineyards, Bell Garden, Napa Valley Expo. Bd. dirs. Nat. Archtl. Accrediting Bd., 2003—, pres., 2005; mem. Koa Ridge Urban Design Plan, Santa Monica LRT Urban Design Plan, Santa Cruz Downtown Assessment, Eisenhower E. Plan, Alexandria, Va., Upper Potomac W. Plan, Alexandria, King St. Revitalization Study, Alexandria, 2004, Oakland Mayor's Com. on High Density Housing, 1982, Oakland Gen. Plan Congress, 1994; mem. waterfront plan adv. com. City of Oakland, 1996, Westpark Town Ctr., 2003, Koa Ridge Cmty., Oahu, Hawaii, King St. Retail Plan, Alexandria; mem. adv. com. Queen Emma Founds. Lands of Waikiki Plan, 2004—05; mem. adv. com. land use, circulation plan City of Santa Monica, 2007—08. Recipient Leslie M. Boney Spirit of Fellowship award. Fellow AIA (dir. East Bay chpt. 1969-71, pres. 1980-81, dir. Calif. coun. 1979-81, Disting. Svc. award Calif. chpt., 1991, nat. dir. 1983-86, nat. v.p. 1986-87, chair AIA internat. steering com. 1993-94, graphic stds. adv. com. 1991-92, U. Calif. archtl. review commn. 1992-96, exec. com. Coll. Fellows 1996-98, vice chancellor Coll. Fellows 1999, chancellor 2000, East Bay medal 1997, Edward C. Kemper medal for outstanding svc. 2004), Am. Archtl. Found. (regent, bd. dirs.), Nat. Archt. Accreditation Bd. (pres.). E-mail: raomatt@aol.com.

ODERWALD, SUSAN, professional society administrator; BS in Internat. Rels. and Russian Studies, Wheaton Coll.; MBA, Loyola Coll. Exec. dir. Soc. Music Librs., Nat. Assn. of Remodeling Industry, US Agrl. Export Devel. Coun.; dir. internat. trade Am. Forest & Paper Assn., Washington; v.p., co-founder Kimball Assocs., McLean, Va.; dep. exec. dir. Soc. Plastic Engrs., Brookfield, Conn., 2001—04, exec. dir., 2004—. Office: Soc Plastic Engrs 14 Fairfield Dr PO Box 403 Brookfield CT 06804-0403 Office Phone: 203-740-5471. Office Fax: 203-775-8490. E-mail: seoderwald@4spe.org.

O'DESKY, ILYSE HOPE, psychologist, educator; b. Newark, Oct. 27, 1964; d. Sheldon O'Desky and Leona Brenner; m. Leonard Brian Garber, June 28, 1992. D in Clin. Psychology, Yeshiva U., Bronx, NY, 1992. Asst. prof. Kean U., Union, NJ, 2001—; pediatric neuropsychologist Neuropsychological Testing Ctr., Springfield, 2003—; chief psychology SCMC, 2006—. Med. staff St. Barnabas Med. Ctr., Livingston, NJ, 1997—. Invited spkr. Nat. NLD Orgn., San Francisco, 2006. Grantee, Kean U., 2001—02, 2005—06, 2007—. Mem.: APA, NJ Psychol. Assn. (sec. to academic and sci. affairs com. 2003—06, Rschr. of Yr. award 2003), NJ Neuropsychological Soc. (exec. bd. 2002—04); Nat. Acad. Neuropsychology. Achievements include patents for the board games, Line by Line and Boxed In; research in the overdiagnosis of attention deficit/hyperactivity disorder; the misdiagnosis of attention deficit/hyperactivity disorder and NLD. Office: 26 Linden Avenue Springfield NJ 07081

ODGERS, RICHARD WILLIAM, lawyer; b. Detroit, Dec. 31, 1936; s. Richard Stanley and Elsie Maude (Trevarthen) O.; m. Gail C. Bassett, Aug. 29, 1959; children: Thomas R., Andrew B. AB, U. Mich., 1959, JD, 1961. Bar: Calif. 1962. Assoc. Pillsbury, Madison & Sutro, San Francisco, 1961—69, ptnr., 1969—87, 1998—2000; exec. v.p., gen. counsel Pacific Telesis Group, 1987-98; ptnr. Pillsbury Winthrop Shaw Pittman, San Francisco, 2001—. Mem. Calif. Task Force Lawyer Support for Legal Svcs. Dir. Legal Cmty. Against Violence; dir., sec. Van Loben Sels/RembeRock Charitable Found.; bd. dirs. Immigrant Legal Resource Ctr., Fed. Dist. Ct. Hist. Soc.; mem. Calif. Legal Svcs. Trust Fund Commn. With USNR. Fellow Am. Bar Found., Am. Judicature Soc., Am. Coll. Trial Lawyers; mem. ABA, Am. Law Inst., Bar Assn. San Francisco (past dir., co-chair task force charitable giving). Office: Pillsbury Winthrop Shaw Pittman 50 Fremont St San Francisco CA 94105 Office Phone: 415-983-1202. Office Fax: 415-983-1200. Business E-Mail: richard.odgers@pillsburylaw.com.

ODHIAMBO, DAVID NANDI, literature and language educator; b. Nairobi, Kenya, June 24, 1965; s. Barack Wellington and Florence Engasia Odhiambo; m. Seonagh Maria Copperthorne, Aug. 15, 1999. BA, McGill U., Montreal, 1987; MFA, U. Mass., Amherst, 2004. Prof. Cumberland County Coll., Vineland, NJ, 2006. Author: (novel) Kipligat's Chance, The Reverend's Apprentice.

ODIERNO, RAYMOND T., career military officer; b. Rockaway, NJ, 1954; s. Raymond J. and Helen Odierno; m. Linda Odierno; children: Anthony, Kathrin, Michael. BS, U.S. Mil. Acad., West Point, NY, 1976; MS in Nuc. Effects Engring., N.C. State U.; MA in Nat. Security and Strategy, U.S. Naval War Coll. Commd. lt. US Army, advanced through grades to gen., 2008, nuc. rsch. officer, chief acquisition support divsn. Def. Nuc. Agy., 1986—87, various positions, commdr. 2d bat., 1992—94, commdr. artillery divsn. Ft. Hood, Tex., 1995—97, dir. requirements & force mgmt. Office Dep. Chief Staff Ops. & Plans Washington, commdg. gen., 4th Infantry Divsn. (Mechanized) Ft. Hood, Tex., 2002—04, commdg. gen. III Corps. & Ft. Hood, 2006—08; asst. to the Chmn. of the Joint Chiefs of Staff US Dept. Def., Washington, 2004—06; comdr. Multi-Nat. Corps-Operation Iraqi Freedom, Baghdad, Iraq, 2006—08, Multi-Nat. Force-Iraq, Baghdad, 2008—. Decorated Army Disting. Svc. medal, Def. Superior Svc. medal, Legion of Merit with 5 oak leaf clusters, Meritorious Svc. medal with 3 oak leaf clusters, Def. Meritorious Svc. medal. Office: Multi-Nat-Forces-Iraq 7115 S Boundary Blvd MacDill AFB Tampa FL 33621*

ODISHOO, SARAH A., literature and language professor, writer, poet; b. Chgo., July 12, 1939; d. Saul Eshoo and Nanajan Odishoo; divorced; children: Elizabeth, Leslie. BA in English Lit., Ill. Wesleyan U., 1961; MA in Poetry and English Lit., N.E. Ill. U., 1980. Instr. English composition No. Ill. U., 1982—85; prof. English, world lit., mythology and writing Columbia Coll., Chgo., 1985—, prof. lit., 1992—. Co-dir. freshman writing program, dir. profl. writing program and seminars Columbia Coll., 1985-89, pres. faculty orgn., 1990-92, dir. myth. workshops, 1998, guest poet/collaborator CD/sound collaboration, dept. sound, 1999, liaison to bd. trustees, CCFO rep., 1999-2000; faculty adv. coun. Ill. Bd. Higher Edn., 1985-89; coord. PEN Midwest Reading Series, 1988-89; archeol. dig for study of mythology of early Jewish and Christian nomadic cultures, Nitzana, 1992; artist in-residence Nitzana (Israel) Ednl. Project, dept. history Ben Gurion U. Negev, 1993, U. Wyo., 1999, Byrdcliffe Colony, Woodstock (NY) Guild, 2000; lectr. River Oaks Art Coun., Oak Pk., Ill., 2000, Chgo. Cultural Ctr., 2003; guest tchr. Hyde Sch., Bath, Maine, 2003; Mythic Path Instr., Hyde Sch., Bath, Maine, 2003. Contbr. articles to profl. jours. Office: Columbia Coll Chgo 600 S Michigan Ave Chicago IL 60605 Office Phone: 312-344-8124. Business E-Mail: sodishoo@colum.edu.

ODLAND, STEVE, consumer products company executive; BBA, U. Notre Dame, Ind., 1980; M in Mgmt., Northwestern U., 1981. Various positions Quaker Oats Co.; sr. v.p., gen. mgr. snacks divsn. Sara Lee, 1996—98, pres. bakery foodservice. divsn., 1997—98; pres., CEO Tops Markets, Inc., 1998—2000; COO Ahold USA, Inc., 2000—01; chmn., pres., CEO AutoZone Inc., Memphis, 2001—05; chmn., CEO Office Depot, Inc., Delray Beach, Fla., 2005—. Chmn. corp. governance task force Bus. Roundtable, 2004; bd. dirs. Gen. Mills, Inc. Named Top New CEO, Bloomberg Markets Mag., 2002. Office: Office Depot Inc 6600 N Military Trl Boca Raton FL 33496-2434

ODLE, ROBERT CHARLES, JR., lawyer; b. Port Huron, Mich., Feb. 15, 1944; s. Robert Charles and Elizabeth Dagmar (Lassen) O.; m. Lydia Ann Karpinol, Aug. 2, 1969. BA, Wayne State U., Detroit, 1966; JD, Detroit Coll. Law, 1969, LLD (hon.), 1992. Staff asst. to pres. of US, 1969-71; dir. adminstrn. Com. Re-election of President, 1971-73; dep. asst. sec. HUD, 1973-76; Washington corp. affairs rep. Internat. Paper Co., 1976-81; asst. sect. Dept. Energy, 1981-85; ptnr. Weil, Gotshal & Manges, 1985—. Mem. Mich. Bar Assn., DC Bar Assn., Delta Theta Phi. Clubs: University (Washington). Republican. Roman Catholic. Home: 476 S Union St Alexandria VA 22314-3826 Office: Weil Gotshal & Manges LLP Ste 900 1300 Eye St NW Washington DC 20005 Office Phone: 202-682-7180.

O'DOHERTY, BRIAN, writer; b. Ballaghadereen, Ireland; came to U.S., 1957; m. Barbara Novak, 1960. MB BCh, Univ. Coll. Dublin, Nat. U. Ireland, 1952, DPH with honors, 1955; MS in Hygiene, Harvard U., 1958. TV host Invitation to Art, Mus. Fine Arts, Boston, 1958-61; art critic N.Y. Times, 1961-64; host Dialogue, WNBC, 1961-64; vis. prof. Berkeley U., 1967; dir. visual arts Nat. Endowment for Arts, 1969-76, dir. media arts, 1976-94; dir. Millennium Projects, 1994-96. Art and architecture critic Today Program, 1971-77; adj. prof. Barnard Coll., 1969-96; editor-in-chief Art in Am., 1971-74; Univ. prof. fine arts and media L.I. U., 1997—2007. Author: (art book) Object and Idea: A New York Art Journal, 1961-67, 1967; editor: (museum study) Museums in Crisis, 1972, (art books) American Masters, The Voice and the Myth, 1973, 2d edit., 1995, Inside the White Cube, 1986, revised edit., 1999, Studio and Cube, 2007, (novels) The Strange Case of Mile P., 1992 (Saggitarius award, 1993), The Deposition of Father McGreevy, 1999 (Booker prize short list, 2000); dir.: (films) Hopper's Silence, 1981; contbr. articles to profl. jours. Recipient Mpls. Citizens award, 1961, Eire Soc. Gold medal for contbns. to culture, 1963, Grand Prix Montreal Internat. Festival of Arts Film award, 1982, Emmy nominations; Smith-Mundt fellow. Fellow Royal Coll. Physicians Ireland (hon.); mem. Am. Irish Hist. Soc. (bd. dirs.), Whitney Mus. Am. Art (bd. dirs. 1996-2000), Coll. Art Assn. (life; Mather award 1964). Office: 15 W 67th St New York NY 10023-6226

ODOM, FLOYD CLARK, surgeon; b. Cisco, Tex., 1946; MD, U. Tex., San Antonio, 1972. Diplomate Am. Bd. Colon & Rectal Surgery, Am. Bd. Surgery. Intern Bexar County Hosp., San Antonio, 1972-73, resident in gen. surgery, 1973-77; fellow in colon & rectal surgery Baylor Med. Ctr., Dallas, 1977-78; colorectal surgeon Presbyn. Hosp., Dallas, 1997—. Fellow ACS, Am. Soc. Colon and Rectal Surgeons. Office: 8220 Walnut Hill Ln Dallas TX 75231-4406 Home Phone: 214-360-0364; Office Phone: 214-739-5758.

ODOM, G. DAVID (DAVE ODOM), retired men's college basketball coach; b. Oct. 9, 1942; m. Lynn A. Odom; children: Lane, Ryan. BA, Guilford Coll., 1965; MEd, East Carolina U., 1969. Asst. coach Goldsboro HS, 1965—67, head coach, 1967—69, Durham HS, 1969—76; asst. coach Wake Forest U. Demon Deacons, 1976—79, head coach, 1979—82, 1989—2001; asst. coach U. Va. Cavaliers, 1982—89; head coach U. SC Gamecocks, 2001—08; ret. Asst. coach USA Basketball Jr. World Championship Team, 1999; bd. dirs. Nat. Assn. Basketball Coaches. Vol. coach US svc. men and women basketball tournament Operation Hardwood, Kuwait, 2005. Recipient Lifetime Alumni Contbr. award, U. SC, 2007, Lifetime Achievement award, SC State Hall of Fame, 2008; named Coach of Yr., Atlantic Coast Conf., 1991, 1994, 1995, Dist. Coach of Yr., 1991, 1993, 1994, Nat. Coach of Yr., 1995, Coach of Yr., Southeastern Conf., 2004; named to Hall of Fame, Guilford Coll. Athletic, 1998. Achievements include led the Wake Forest University men's basketball team to the National Invitation Title in 2000 and the University of South Carolina men's basketball team in 2005 and 2006; holds a 392-260 head coaching record.

ODOM, LAMAR JOSEPH, professional basketball player; b. Jamaica, NY, Nov. 6, 1979; Student, UNLV; grad., U. Rhode Island, 2001. Player LA Clippers, 1999—2003, Miami Heat, 2003—04, LA Lakers, 2004—. Mem. US Olympics Basketball Team, Athens, Greece, 2004. Named to All-Rookie First Team, 2000. Achievements include member of NBA Championship winning Los Angeles Lakers, 2009. Office: c/o LA Lakers 555 N Nash St El Segundo CA 90245*

ODOM, MARJORIE MILDRED MORGAN, retired librarian; b. Lavernia, Tex., July 22, 1924; d. Andrew Jackson and Estella Fledia (Phillips) Morgan; m. Steven Odom, Jr. (dec.). Cert. in cosmetology, C.J. Walker Beauty Coll., 1943; BA in Libr. Sci., Our Lady of Lake U., San Antonio, 1964, MA in Edn., 1979. Ordained deacon Bapt. Ch., 1985. Mgr. Mme. C.J. Walker Beauty Salon, San Antonio, 1944—52; propr. Ross Hotel Beauty Salon, San Antonio, 1952—63; asst. supr. children's dept. San Antonio Pub. Libr., 1964—65; secondary sch. libr. San Antonio Ind. Sch. Dist., 1965—90; ret., 1990. Past sponsor Libr. Reading Club, San Antonio; past mem. Tex. Senator's adv. coun. on legis. affairs; del. Bexar County Presdl. Senatorial Dist. Conv., 1984, 1988; mem. Dist. 19 Tex. Dem. conv., Ft. Worth, 1990; del. Dem. State Conv., El Paso, 2002; elected Dem. Precinct chair, 2002—08; del. Tex. State Dem. Convention, 2004; chmn. evangelism com. Corinth Bapt. Ch., San Antonio, 1983—86, mem. evangelism and witnessing team, 1984—, Sunday sch. tchr., 1983—2008; trainer Evangelism Explosion, 1987—2008. Recipient outstanding award analysis and design, Kappa Pi Sigma, 1978, appreciation plaque, PTA, 1981, cert., Internat. Ctr. Learning, 1982—83, Nat. Sunday Sch. and Bapt. Temperance Union Congress, 1967—70. Mem.: NEA (life), Delcrest Area Neighborhood Assn. (com. chmn. yard of month com. 2007), San Antonio Area Ret. Tchrs. Assn. (telephone com. 2003—, scholarship com. 2004—05). Democrat. Home: PO Box 8374 San Antonio TX 78208-0374

O'DONNELL, AMY L., legislative staff member; Grad., Pa. State U., 2002; JD, Temple U. Sch. Law, Phila., 2005. Legis. asst., Rep. Albert Wynn US House of Reps., Washington, 2007, legis. asst., Rep. John B. Larson, 2007, tax counsel, Rep. John B. Larson, 2007—08, chief of staff to Rep. John B. Larson, 2008—. Democrat. Office: 106 Cannon House Office Bldg Washington DC 20515 Office Phone: 202-225-2265. Office Fax: 202-225-1031.*

O'DONNELL, BERNARD JOSEPH, JR., lawyer; s. Bernard Joseph and Afkam O'Donnell. BA in English, Mary Washington Coll., Fredericksburg, Va., 1993; MA in English, Loyola U. Chgo., 1996; JD summa cum laude, Fla. State U., 2000. Bar: Fla. 2000, US Dist. Ct. (mid. dist.) Fla. 2003, US Ct. Appeals (9th cir.) 2006. Adj. prof. English Palm Beach Atlantic Coll., West Palm Beach, Fla., 1997—98, Fla. State U., Tallahassee, 1998—2000, U. Fla., Gainesville, 2000—03; pvt. practice law Gainesville, 2000—03; assoc. Henderson, Franklin, P.A., Ft. Myers, Fla., 2003—06; sr. assoc. Newmeyer & Dillion, LLP, Newport Beach, Calif., 2006—; v.p. legal svcs. Innodata Isogen, Hackensack, NJ, 2006—07; spl. aide to gov. Charlie Crist Tallahassee, 2007—. Pro-bono atty. Guardian Ad Litem, Ctrl. Fla., 2001—03; vis. prof. English U. Fla., 2006; presenter in field. Author: Fun and Games, 1995; contbr. articles to profl. jours. Bd. dirs. S.W. Fla. Symphony, 2003—06, Hospitality Beverage Inst., Tallahassee, 2007—, Shelter, Tallahassee, 2007—. Recipient Excellence in Tchr. award, U. Fla., 2002, Excellence in Tchg. award, U. Fla. Anderson Scholars, 2002, 2003; Lester Crow scholar in edn., 1993, Dean's scholar in law, 1998, Katzentine-Simon scholar in law, 1999, Grinter fellow in English, 2000—03. Mem.: ABA, MLA, Fla. Def. Lawyers Assn., Fla. Bar Assn., Order of the Coif. Roman Catholic. Avocations: reading, basketball, guitar. Office: 703 N Main St Ste A Gainesville FL 32601 Home: 1114 SW 7th Ave #8 Gainesville FL 32601 Personal E-mail: bodlaw1@yahoo.com.

O'DONNELL, BRENNAN PATRICK, academic administrator, literature and language professor; b. Wilkes-Barre, Pa., Feb. 23, 1958; s. Charles Edward and Mary Patricia (Brennan) O'D.; m. Angela Gina Alaimo, May 30, 1981; children: Charles Brennan, Patrick Aloysius, William Michael. BA in English, Pa. State U., 1981; MA, U. NC, 1983, PhD in English and Am. Lit. and Lang., 1987. Tchg. asst. Dept. English U. NC, Chapel Hill, 1983-86; asst. prof. English Loyola Coll. of Md., Balt., 1987-93, assoc. prof. English, 1994, dir. honors program, 1999—2004; dean Fordham Coll. at Rose Hill, 2004—09; pres. Manhattan College, 2009—. Bd. dirs. Collegium, Fairfield, Conn. Author: Numerous Verse: A Guide to the Stanzas and Metrical Structures of Wordsworth's Poetry, 1989, The Passion of Meter: A Study of Wordsworth's Metrical Art, 1995; contbr. articles to profl. jours. Sec. parish coun. St. Francis of Assisi Roman Cath. Ch., Balt., 1997—, baseball coach, 1996—. Pogue fellow U. NC, 1981-82, 82-83, Grad. Sch. Dissertation fellow U. NC, 1987. Mem. MLA, Nat. Seminar on Jesuit Higher Edn., N.Am. Soc. for Study of Romanticism, Phi Beta Kappa. Avocations: classical guitar, coaching baseball. Office: Manhattan Coll Office of Pres Bronx NY 10471 Office Fax: 718-817-4700, 718-817-4720. E-mail: brodonnell@fordham.edu.*

O'DONNELL, CHRIS, actor; b. Winnetka, Ill., June 26, 1970; m. Caroline Fentress, Apr. 19, 1997; children Lilly Ann, Christopher Jr., Charles, Finley BA in Mktg., Boston Coll., 1995. Actor: (films) Men Don't Leave, 1990, Fried Green Tomatoes, 1991, Scent of a Woman, 1992 (Golden Globe award nomination best supporting actor 1992), School Ties, 1992, The Three Musketeers, 1993, Blue Sky, 1994, Circle of Friends, 1995, Mad Love, 1995, Batman Forever, 1995, In Love and War, 1996, The Chamber, 1996, Batman & Robin, 1997, Cookie's Fortune, 1999, Vertical Limit, 2000, 29 Palms, 2002, Kinsey, 2004, The Sisters, 2005, Kit Kittredge: An American Girl, 2008, Max Payne, 2008; actor, prodr. (films) The Bachelor, 1999; actor: (TV films) The Amazing Westermans, 2004; actor:(TV appearances) The Practice, 2003, Two and a Half Men, 2004, Head Cases, 2005, Grey's Anatomy, 2005; prodr. (TV films) The Triangle, 2001, Miracle on the 17th Green, 1999

O'DONNELL, CHRISTINE T., political commentator, marketing consultant; b. Phila., Aug. 27, 1969; Degree in English and Comm., Fairleigh Dickinson U., Madison, NJ, 1991. Mktg. cons. Rep. Nat. Com., Washington, 1994; with Intercollegiate Studies Inst., Del., 2003. Regular appearances on Fox News Channel, CNN, C-SPAN, FNC's O'Reilly Factor, Hannity & Colmes, MSNBC's Hardball with Chris Matthews, Entertainment Tonight, ABC's Politically Incorrect with Bill Maher, others. Past bd. dirs. Birthright of Del. Recipient Abraham

Lincoln Grad. Fellowship, Claremont Inst., Calif., 2002. Mem.: Del. Press Assn. Republican. Office: 459 StoneBridge Blvd New Castle DE 19720 Office Phone: 302-299-8066.*

O'DONNELL, COLIN I., statistician, researcher; b. Springfield, Mass., Sept. 4, 1956; s. Charles P. and Coline W. O'Donnell; m. Casey M. Dills; children: Brandon Odell Dills, Oisín Richard. Attending in Biostatistics, U. Colo. Denver, 2009. Cert. in collaborative instl. training initiative Fred Hutchinson Cancer Rsch. Ctr., U Maimi, 2008, HIPAA Research U. of Colo. Health Sciences Ctr., 2008. Math. instr. Met. State Coll. Denver, 2002—05; statistician Dept. Urologic Oncolgy, Aurora, Colo., 2002—; computer programmer to database mgr. Nat. Lung Screening Trial, Aurora, 2003—; statis. analyst Power and Sample Size Methods Mammography Trials, Aurora, 2006—; biostatistician Etiology Rheumatiod Arthritis, Aurora, 2008—; study coord. Proportion Women High Lifetime Risk Breast Cancer, Aurora, 2008—. Statis. cons. Global Edn. Group, Littleton, Colo., 2009. Recipient COMAP Hon. Mention award, NSA, 1996, Marvin Porter award, Dept. Preventative Medicine and Biometrics, 2007, Maurice Davies award, 2008. Office: Univ Colo Denver Rm W3125 13001 E 17th Pl Mail Stop C245 Aurora CO 80045 Business E-Mail: colin.odonnell@ucdenver.edu.

O'DONNELL, DANIEL E., lawyer, information technology executive; b. Newark, 1948; m. Linda O'Donnell. Grad., Coll. Holy Cross, Worcester, Mass., 1969; JD, Coll. William & Mary, Williamsburg, Va., 1974. V.p., asst. gen. counsel and corp. sec. IBM Corp., Armonk, NY. Office: IBM Corp 1 New Orchard Rd Armonk NY 10504 Office Phone: 914-499-7050. Business E-Mail: odonnell@us.ibm.com.*

O'DONNELL, EDWARD FRANCIS, JR., lawyer; b. Waterbury, Conn., May 13, 1950; s. Edward Francis and Dorothy Patricia (Breheny) O'D.; m. Jayne Ann DeSantis, Dec. 29, 1972; children: Ryan Anderson, Brooke Stires. BA, St. Anselm Coll., Manchester, NH, 1972; JD, U. Conn., 1977. Bar: S.C. 1978, Conn. 1977, U.S. Dist. Ct. S.C. 1978, U.S. Dist. Ct. Conn. 1980, U.S. Ct. Appeals (1st and 2d cirs.) 1980. Assoc. Ogeltree, Deakins, Nash, Smoak & Stewart, Greenville, S.C., 1977-79; ptnr. Siegel, O'Connor, Zangari, O'Donnell & Beck, P.C., Hartford, Conn., 1979—. Contbr. articles to profl. jours. Mem. ABA, Conn. Bar Assn., S.C. Bar Assn., Hartford Bar Assn., Hartford Club, Phi Alpha Theta. Roman Catholic. Office: Siegel O'Connor O'Donnell & Beck PC 150 Trumbull St Fl 5 Hartford CT 06103-2400 Office Phone: 860-727-8900. Business E-Mail: eodonnell@siegeloconnor.com.

O'DONNELL, F. SCOTT, former state agency administrator; b. Brownsville, Pa., Sept. 20, 1940; s. Francis Horner and Rebecca (Warren) O'D.; m. Ann Bukmir, Dec. 30, 1976. BA, Grove City Coll., Pa., 1962; postgraduate student, U. Wis. Grad. Sch. Banking, 1970, Internat. Sch. Banking, U. Colo., 1972. Nat. bank examiner Comptr. Currency, Cleve., 1965—71; sr. v.p. First Nat. Bank, Steubenville, Ohio, 1971—75; supt. banks State of Ohio, Columbus, 1975-77; exec. v.p. Heritage Bancorp, Steubenville, 1977-80; from v.p. to exec. v.p. Soc. Corp., Cleve., 1980-95; dep. tax commr. State of Ohio, Columbus, 1996-99; supt. fin. instns. divsn. Ohio Dept. Commerce, 1999—2006. Mem. state banking bd. Div. of Banks, Columbus, 1979-85, govt. affairs com. Ohio Bankers Assn., 1982-84. Served with USCG, 1963-69. Mem. Columbus Athletic Club, Pitts. Univ. Club, Belmont Hills Country Club, Lakewood Country Club. Avocations: travel, politics, antiques.

O'DONNELL, JAMES FRANCIS, retired health scientist administrator; b. Cleve., July 22, 1928; s. John Michael and Mary Louise (Hayes) O'D.; m. Winifred Locke, Sept. 10, 1955; children— Anne Catherine, Patrick John, Mary Elizabeth BS in Biology, St. Louis U., 1949; PhD in Biochemistry, U. Chgo., 1957. Asst., then. assoc. prof. biol. chemistry and exptl. medicine Coll. Medicine, U. Cin., 1957—68; grants assoc., divsn. rsch. grants NIH, Bethesda, Md., 1968—69; program dir. population and reprodn. grants br. Ctr. for Population Research, Nat. Inst. Child Health and Human Devel., NIH, 1969—71; asst. dir. divsn. rsch. resources NIH, Bethesda, 1971—76, dep. dir. divsn. rsch. resources, 1976—90, acting dir. divsn. rsch. resources, 1981—82, dir. Office of Extramural Programs, Office of the Dir., 1990-99; ret., 1999. Sci. cons. Commonwealth Health Rsch. Bd., Richmond, Va., 1999—. Served with U.S. Army, 1950-52 Home: 11601 Bunnell Ct S Rockville MD 20854-3603 Home Phone: 301-299-9378. Personal E-mail: jfwlodonnell@erols.com.

O'DONNELL, JAMES JOSEPH, insurance company executive, economics professor; b. Boston, Nov. 12, 1951; s. James Joseph and Regina Doris O'Donnell; m. Carol Ann O'Donnell, Aug. 18, 1984; children: Rebecca Ann Iantuonno, Elizabeth Ann Stewart. BA, Olivet Coll., Miss., 1973; LLB, La Salle U., Chgo., 1976; PhD, MBA, Calif. Coast U., Santa Ana, 1983. Cert. casualty claims law assoc. Am. Ednl. Inst., 1993, fraud claims law assoc. 1995, property claims law assoc. 1996, sr. claims law assoc. 1997, worker compensation claims law assoc. 1997. V.p. claims Peninsula Ins. Cos., Salisbury, Md., 1992—; adj. prof. economics & risk mgmt. Salisbury U., 2000—. Musician (master, dir.): Lifeteen Choir (Vol. of Yr. Diocese Wilmington, 2008). Exec. dir. Parish Pastoral Coun., Dover, Del., 1997—2003; bd. mem. Holy Cross Elem. Sch., Dover, 1998—2002, St. Thomas Moore Cath. HS, Magnolia, Del., 2000—02. Mem.: KC, Assn. Am. Trial Lawyers. Home: 223 Fairway Cir E Smyrna DE 19977 Office: Peninsula Ins Co 112-120 E Market St Salisbury MD 21803 Business E-Mail: jodonnell@peninsulainsurance.com.

O'DONNELL, JAMES V., apparel executive; Mgmt. positions The Gap Inc., 1980—87, exec. v.p., bd. dir., 1987—92, COO, 1989—92; CEO Computer Aided Systems Inc., 1992—97; project cons. C. Everett Koop Found., 1997—2000; dir. merchant banking Colmen Capital Adv. Inc., 1997—2002; pres., COO Lyte Inc., 1999—2000; COO Am. Eagle Outfitters, Warrendale, Pa., 2000—03, bd. dir., 2000—, co-CEO, 2002—03, CEO, 2003—08, pres., CEO, 2008—. Mem. adv. bd. Coll. Commerce & Fin. Villanova Univ. Office: American Eagle Outfitters 150 Thorn Hill Dr Warrendale PA 15086

O'DONNELL, JOHN SETEL, energy executive; 3 children. BS in Computer Sci., Yale U., 1976. With Princeton U. Plasma Physics Lab.; co-founder, v.p. engring. Multiflow Computer, 1984—90; co-founder, chief tech. officer Equator Techs., 1996—2005; v.p. tech. and bus. devel. Pixelworks, 2005—06; pres. Tsugino, 2006; exec. v.p. Ausra, Inc., 2006—. Achievements include development of the world's first VLIW computers; Field of Mirrors, a solar thermal plant that can provide large amounts of electricity at low cost without emitting gases attributed to global warming. Avocations: bicycling, flying. Office: Ausra Inc 2585 E Bayshore Rd Palo Alto CA 94303 Office Phone: 650-424-9300. Office Fax: 650-494-3893.

O'DONNELL, KATHLEEN C., artist; b. Clifton, NJ, Nov. 15, 1919; d. George Francis and Alvina Rose (Munzell) Denzel; m. John Joseph O'Donnell, Feb. 17, 1942; children: John Joseph, Sharon Rose. BA cum laude, Montclair State U., NJ, 1983. Designer Denzell Mfg. Co., Passaic, NJ, 1937—38, clk., 1939—41; sec. Marschalk Ins., Clifton, NJ, 1941—42; clk. The Fair, Passaic, 1968—69; designer Arise Ministry, Lakewood, NJ, 1983—91; assoc. NJ Bell, Clifton & Totowa, 1969—85. Represented in numerous pvt. collections, group and one-woman shows. Mem.: Roxbury Assn. Art, Clifton Assn. Artists, Bell Atlantic Pioneers. Roman Catholic.

O'DONNELL, KATHLEEN MARIE, lawyer; b. Methuen, Mass., Dec. 16, 1955; d. John Joseph and Helen Miriam (McCormack) O'D. BA magna cum laude, Wheaton Coll., Norton, Mass., 1977; JD cum laude, Suffolk U., 1980. Bar: Mass. 1981, U.S. Dist. Ct. Mass. 1982, U.S. Ct. Appeals (1st cir.) 1982. Instr. Suffolk U., Boston, 1980-82; assoc. Law Office Albert J. Marcotte, Lowell, Mass., 1982—. Bd. dirs. Greater Lowell Pastoral Gounseling Ctr., 1987—, Greater Lowell Rape Crisis Ctr., Sohier Park Com., York, Maine, 1989—, co-chair, 1991—; bd. govs. Mass. Acad. Trial Attys. Mem. ATLA, ABA, Mass. Bar Assn. (v.p. 2001, treas. 2002, pres.-elect 2003, pres. 2004), Mass. Acad. Trial Attys.(treas. 1995, pres. 1996), Greater Lowell Bar Assn. (treas. 1987, sec. 1988, v.p. 1989, pres. 1990), Am. Bd. Trial Advocates, Phi Delta Phi. Democrat. Roman Catholic. Office: Law Office Albert Marcotte 45 Merrimack St Lowell MA 01852-1729 Home Phone: 978-458-2724; Office Phone: 978-458-1229. E-mail: mlfko@aol.com.

O'DONNELL, KEVIN, retired metal products executive; b. Cleve., June 9, 1925; s. Charles Richard and Ella (Kilbane) O'Donnell; m. Ellen Blydenburgh, Aug. 16, 1965; children: Kevin, Susan, Michael, John, Maura, Neil, Megan, Hugh. AB, Kenyon Coll., Gambier, Ohio, 1947, PhD (hon.) in Law, 1980; MBA, Harvard U., 1947; PhD in Econs. (hon.), Pusan Nat. U., Korea, 1970; PhD in Humanities (hon.), Ohio Wesleyan U., 1972. Gen. sales mgr. Steel Improvement & Forge Co., Cleve., 1947-60; mgmt. cons. Booz, Allen and Hamilton, Cleve., 1960-62; gen. mgr., dir. Atlas Alloys-Rio Algom Corp., Cleve., 1963-66; dir. Peace Corps, Seoul, Republic of Korea, 1966-70, dir. adminstrn. and fin., then acting dep. dir., 1970-71; assoc. dir. internat. ops. ACTION, 1971-72; exec. v.p. SIFCO Industries, Inc., Cleve., 1972-75, pres., chief oper. officer, 1976-83, pres., chief exec. officer, 1983-89, chief exec. officer, 1989-90, chmn., exec. comm., 1990-94; ret., 1994. Bd. dirs. Ctrl. Pk. Media Corp., NYC, Doyle Pacific Industries, Ltd., Hong Kong; adv. dir. Capital Strategies, Inc., Cleve. Mem. Washington Inst. Fgn. Affairs, Cleve. Com. Fgn. Rels., chmn., 1979—82, CCWA, 1982—89; pres. Guest House Inc., 1990—92; trustee Alcohol Svcs., Cleve., 1993—, Cleve. Coun. World Affairs, Nat. Peace Corps. Assn. Decorated Order Civil Merit Republic of Korea; recipient Disting. Internationalist award, Cleve. Coun. World Affairs, 2007. Mem.: Harvard Bus. Sch. Alumni Assn. (dir. Boston 1991—94), Army-Navy Club (Washington), Westwood Country Club, Union Club, 50 Club, First Friday Club, Harvard Bus. Sch. Club Cleve., Knights of Malta (master knight). Republican. Roman Catholic. Avocations: golf, reading. Office Phone: 216-226-3505. Personal E-mail: kevodoncle@aol.com.

O'DONNELL, LAURENCE GERARD, retired managing editor; b. Bklyn., June 30, 1935; s. Thomas Edward and Dorothy (Clark) O'D.; m. Joan M. Coniglio, Jan. 9, 1960; children: Christopher, Carolyn, Jeffrey, Anthony. AB, Holy Cross Coll., Worcester, Mass., 1957. Reporter Wall Street Jour., NYC, 1958-66, chief Detroit Bur., 1966-74, asst. mng. editor, 1974-77, mng. editor, 1977-83; assoc. editor Dow Jones & Co., Inc., NYC, 1983-90, cons., 1991-99. Pres. Dow Jones Newspaper Fund, 1988-93, bd. dirs.; vis. lectr. Queens Coll./CUNY, 1992-99. Trustee Holy Cross Coll., 1982-90, adv. bd. 2006-; journalism adv. bd. Queens Coll./CUNY, 1989-2003; juror Pulitzer Prize, 1982, 83; bd. dirs. Interam. Press Assn., 1986-2001. Mem. Am. Soc. Newspaper Editors. Mem. Natl. adv. com., Robert Wood Johnson Found., 2002-. Office: Dow Jones Newspaper Fund PO Box 300 Princeton NJ 08543-0300

O'DONNELL, LAWRENCE, III, waste management executive; BS in Archtl. Engring., U. Tex., 1980; JD cum laude, U. Houston, 1983. Bar: Tex. 1983. Assoc. Wood, Campbell, Moody & Gibbs, Houston, 1983-84; ptnr. Campbell & Riggs, Houston, 1984-91; dep. gen. counsel Baker Hughes Inc., Houston, 1991-94, corp. sec., 1991-96, v.p., gen. counsel, 1995-2000, Baker Hughes Oilfield Ops., Houston, 1993-95; sr. v.p., gen. counsel, sec. Waste Mgmt., Inc., Houston, 2000—01, exec. v.p., gen. counsel, corp. sec., 2001, exec. v.p. western ops., 2001—03, exec. v.p. ops. support, chief adminstrv. officer, 2003—04, pres., COO, 2004—. Bd. dirs., mem. exec. com. Spring Br. Edn. Found.; bd. dirs. Am. Arbitration Assn., U. Tex. Med. Br.; mem. energy planning coun. State of Tex., 2004. Trustee Houston Police Activities League; mem. adv. bd. Brookwood. Mem.: ASCE, ABA, Houston Bar Assn., Tex. State Bar, Order of Barons, Phi Delta Phi. Avocations: golf, sailing, skiing. Office: Waste Mgmt Inc 1001 Fannin St Ste 4000 Houston TX 77002-6711

O'DONNELL, MARK PATRICK, writer, drama educator; b. Cleve., July 19, 1954; s. Hubert John and Frances (Novak) O'D. BA magna cum laude, Harvard U., 1976. Faculty dept. drama NYU, NYC, 1984—; faculty New Sch., NYC, 1984—, Yale U., 1998—2003. Author: Elementary Education, 1985, Vertigo Park, 1992, Getting Over Homer, 1996, (plays) Fables for Friends, 1980, That's It, Folks!, 1983, The Nice and the Nasty, 1986, Strangers on Earth, 1988, Vertigo Park, 1990, Scapin, 1996, Let Nothing You Dismay, 1998, (Broadway plays) Hairspray, 2002 (Tony award for Best Book of a Musical, 2003, Drama Desk award for Outstanding Book of a Musical, 2003, Laurence Olivier Best New Musical award for London prodn., 2008), Cry-Baby, 2008; contbg. editor Esquire mag., 1977-78, Spy mag., 1987—, Seven Days mag., 1988-90. Cons. Nat. Gay Task Force, Washington, 1987. Recipient Le Comte Du Nuoy prize, 1980; Guggenheim fellow, 1986. Mem. Dramatists Guild, Writers Guild Am. Home and Office: 202 Riverside Dr Apt 8E New York NY 10025-7280

O'DONNELL, MATTHEW, electrical engineering, computer science educator, dean; b. Bronxville, NY, Dec. 18, 1950; s. Hubert Bernard and Loretto Anne (Schmidt) O'D.; m. Catharine Gleason, Jan. 3, 1976; children: Brendan Gleason, Sean Gleason. BS in Physics with honors, U. Notre Dame, 1972, PhD in Solid State Physics, 1976. Grad. rsch. and teaching fellow in physics U. Notre Dame, Ind., 1972-76; postdoctoral fellow in physics Washington U., St. Louis, 1976-78, sr. rsch. assoc. in physics, rsch. instr. medicine, 1978-80; physicist Rsch. and Devel. Ctr., GE Co., Schenectady, N.Y., 1980-90; prof. elec. engring. and computer sci. U. Mich., Ann Arbor, 1990—2006, Levin prof. engring., 1998—2006, chair bio. engring. dept., 1999—2006; dean sch. engring., computer sci. U. Wash., Seattle, 2006—. Rsch. fellow elec. engring. Yale U., New Haven, Conn., 1984-85; presenter in field, profl. cons. Gen Electric, 1990-2000, Endosonics 1993-2003, Acuson/Siemens 1995-2002, Microsound Sys. 1995-1997, Q-Dot, 1995-2000, Pangea Med., 1998-1999, Focus Surgery, 1998-2002, Tetrad, 1999-, Pixel Velocity, 2001-, Vascular Imaging, 2003-, Sonetics, 2003-. Editorial bd.: Ultrasonic Imaging; contbr. articles to Phys. Rev. Letters, Solid State Communications, Jour. Acoustical Soc. Am., Ultrasound in Medicine, Am. Jour. Physiology, Circulation Rsch., Jour. Applied Physics, Am. Jour. Cardiology, Ultrasonic Imaging, others. Recipient Whitney award for Internal Rsch., Gen. Electric, 1990—91, EECS Tchg. award, Univ. Mich., 1995. Fellow IEEE; mem. Am. Phys. Soc., Sigma Xi, Am. Inst. Med. Bio. Engring. Achievements include 40 patents including Collimation of Ultrasonic Linear Array Transducer, Method for Imaging Blood Flow Using Multiple-Echo, Phase-Contrast NMR, Method and Apparatus for Fully Digital Beam Formation in a Phased Array Ultrasonic. Office: UW Coll Engring Loew Hall Box 352180 Seattle WA 98195-2180

O'DONNELL, MICHAEL W., energy company executive; BS in Econ., Temple U. With Columbia Sys., 1971—, v.p. fin. svcs. Svc. Corp., 1983, sr. v.p. distbn. companies, asst. CFO Columbus, Ohio, 1987—93; sr. v.p., CFO Columbia Energy Corp., Reston, Va., 1993—2000; exec. v.p., CFO NiSource Inc., Merrillville, Ind., 2000—08, exec. v.p., 2008—. Office: NiSource Inc 801 E 86th St Merrillville IN 46410

O'DONNELL, MICKIE LOUISE, religious educator; b. Jamestown, NY, Jan. 30, 1950; d. Robert Hunt and Charlotte Anne (Newberg) O'Donnell; children: Rachel, Sarah, Joel, Joshua. BA, U. Aberdeen, 1982, MA, 1984; MRE, Trinity Divinity Sch., 1991, postgrad. Dir. christian edn. The Village Ch., Northbrook, Ill., 1985-95; dir. children's ministries Christ's Ch. of Oakbrook, Ill., 1995—99; exec. dir. Children's Ministries of Am. Adj. prof. Trinity U., 1999-2001, Deerfield, Ill., 1986-1999; dir. radio program Unshackled, Chgo., 1995—2008; cons. David C. Cook Publ., Colo. Springs, Colo., 1986—, At Large, 1986—; spkr. in field; mins. Spiritual Formation Westminster Presbyterian Ch.; pres. Lord and King Assn., 2001-. Author: Children of War, 1994; Co-Author: Workshop Wondors, 2005; contbr. articles to profl. jours. Bd. dirs. Girl Scouts, Northbrook, 1988-90, Northbrook Citizens for Drug and Alcohol Awareness, Northbrook, 1988-93. Mem. ASCD, AFTRA Presbyterian. Avocations: reading, music, movies, spectator sports, theater. Home: 2050 W Ill Ave Aurora IL 60506

O'DONNELL, NORAH, news correspondent; b. Washington, Jan. 23, 1974; m. Geoff Tracy, June 2001; children: Grace, Henry, Riley Norah. BA in Philosophy, Georgetown U., MA in Internat. Affairs. Staff writer covering Congress Roll Call newspaper; contbr., news analyst MSNBC, 1997—99, chief Washington corr., 2005—, anchor MSNBC Live; corr. NBC News, 1999—, White House corr., 2003—05, contbg. corr. 'Today'. Contbr. numerous broadcasts NBC Nightly News, The Today Show, Dateline NBC; regular sub. host Hardball with Chris Matthews, The Chris Matthews Show, The Situation with Tucker Carlson; co-host NYC St. Patrick's Day Parade, WNBC, 2007—. Recipient Sigma Delta Chi award for Breaking News Coverage, Soc. Profl. Journalists, 2001; named one of Top 100 Irish Americans, Irish Am. Mag., 2000, Washington's 100 Most Powerful Women, Washingtonian Mag. Office: NBC News 30 Rockefeller Plaza New York NY 10112*

O'DONNELL, PATRICIA EILEEN, art educator; b. July 14, 1952; MFA, U. Mass., 1986. Asst. prof. So. Conn. State U., New Haven, 1986-87, U. Maine, Farmington, 1987-93, assoc. prof., 1993—, chair dept. humanities, 1994—. Contbr. stories to New Yorker, 1984, Prairie Schooner, 2000. Address: PO Box 438 Wilton ME 04294-0438 Office Phone: 207-778-7419.

O'DONNELL, PATRICK EMMETT, lawyer; b. NYC, Mar. 17, 1937; s. Emmett and Lorraine Antoinette (Muller) O'D.; m. Janet Eve Mottershead, Sept. 21, 1968; children: Patrick Justin, Hollace Tobin, Darcy Tanner. Student, Georgetown U., 1955-58; LLB, Am. Univ., 1962. Bar: D.C. 1962. Asst. corp. counsel City of Washington, 1962-69; spl. asst. to the pres. The White House, Washington, 1971-76; legal counsel to chmn. FCC, Washington, 1969-71; Washington counsel Gen. Electric Co., Washington, 1976-78, J.C. Penney Co., Inc., Washington, 1978-80; regional polit. dir. Howard Baker for Pres., Washington, 1980; asst. dir. legis. affairs Ronald Reagan for Pres., Washington, 1980-81; ptnr. O'Connor & Hannan, Washington, 1981—2001; ptnr., legislative, govtl. affairs Venable LLP, Washington, 2001—07. Vice chmn. fin. George Bush Com., Washington, 1988; economic affairs counsel Rep. Nat. Com., Washington, 1976-80; bd. dirs. Radio Marti (Presdl. Commn.), Washington, 1981-84. Mem. USO (bd. dirs. 1978-91). Republican. Roman Catholic. Office: Squire Sanders & Dempsey LLP 1201 Pennsylvania Ave NW Ste 500 Washington DC 20004 Office Phone: 202-344-4702, 202-626-6249. Office Fax: 202-344-8300. Personal E-mail: podonnell@ssd.com. Business E-Mail: peodonnell@venable.com.

O'DONNELL, PETER, JR., foundation administrator; m. Edith O'Donnell. LHD (hon.), So. Meth. U., 2008. Co-founder, pres. O'Donnell Found., Dallas, 1956—; former dir. Dallas Biomedical Corp., Interfirst Bank, Stadium Associates; dir., exec. com. Univ. Med. Ctr., Inc. Recipient Disting. Svc. award, U. Tex. Austin Alumni Assn., 2003. Fellow: Am. Acad. Arts and Sciences; mem.: Acad. Medicine, Sci. and Engring. of Tex. (founding mem.), Nat. Acad. Medicine (Pres.'s cir.). Office: O'Donnell Found Ste 1660 100 Crescent Ct Dallas TX 75201

O'DONNELL, ROSIE, television personality, actress, comedienne; b. Commack, NY, Mar. 21, 1962; m. Kelli Carpenter, Feb. 26, 2004; children: Parker Jaren, Chelsea Belle, Blake Christopher, Vivienne Rose. Student, Dickinson Coll., Boston U. Host The Rosie O'Donnell Show, 1995—2002; editor Rosie mag., 2000—02; co-host The View, 2006—07; host Rosie Radio, 2009—. Actress (films) A League of Their Own, 1992, Sleepless in Seattle, 1993 (American Comedy award nomination for best supporting female in a motion picture, 1994), Another Stakeout, 1993 (American Comedy award nomination for best actress in a motion picture, 1994), Car 54, Where Are You?, 1994, I'll Do Anything, 1994, The Flintstones, 1994, Exit to Eden, 1994, Now and Then, 1995, Beautiful Girls, 1996, Harriet the Spy, 1996, A Very Brady Sequel, 1996, Wide Awake, 1996, Get Bruce, 1999, Jackie's Back, 1999, Tarzan (voice only), 1999, Flintstones in Viva Rock Vegas, 2000, (TV films) The Twilight of the Golds, 1997, (TV series) Gimme A Break, 1986—87, Stand By Your Man, 1992, Women Aloud, 1992, (Broadway plays) Grease, 1994, Seussical the Musical, 2001, Fiddler on the Roof, 2005, host, comedienne (TV series) Stand-up Spotlight, VH-1, 1993 (American Comedy award nomination for best female performer in a TV special, 1994, Cable ACE award nomination for best entertainment host, 1994), actress, exec. prodr. (TV films) Riding the Bus with My Sister, 2005; exec. prodr.: (TV films) Kids are Punny, 1998; (films) Mina & the Family Treasure, 2004; (Broadway plays) Taboo, 2003—04; TV appearances include Ally McBeal, 1999, Third Watch, 2000, The Practice, 2000, Will & Grace, 2002, Judging Amy, 2003, Queer as Folk, 2005, Nip Tuck, 2006—07; author: Find Me, 2002, Celebrity Detox: (the fame game), 2007. Recipient Daytime Emmy awards for The Rosie O'Donnell Show, 1997—2001; named one of The World's Most Influential People, TIME mag., 2007.

O'DONNELL, TERRENCE, lawyer, multi-industry company executive; b. NYC, Mar. 3, 1944; s. Emmett and Lorraine (Muller) O'Donnell; m. Margaret Lynne Kidder; children: Stephanie T., Erin K., Victoria L. BS, USAF Acad., Colo., 1966; JD, Georgetown Law Sch., 1971. Bar: DC 1971, US Ct. Appeals (DC cir.) 1978, US Ct. Appeals (4th cir.) 1987, US Dist. Ct. Md. 1986, US Ct. Mil. Appeals 1990, US Ct. Fed. Claims, US Supreme Ct., others. Commd. 2d lt. USAF, 1966, advanced through grades to capt., various positions Washington and Republic of Vietnam, 1966-72, resigned, 1972; dep. spl. asst. to Pres. The White House,

Washington, 1972—74, spl. asst. to Pres., 1974—77, appointments sec., 1974-77; assoc. Williams & Connolly LLP, Washington, 1977-82, ptnr., 1982-89, 1992—; gen. counsel US Dept. Def., Washington, 1989-92; exec. v.p., gen. counsel Textron Inc., 2000—. Presdl. appointee to bd. visitors US Air Force Acad., Colorado Springs, 1982-87, chmn., 1985-86; US corr. and rep. UN Prog. to Prevent Crime, Washington and NYC, 1977-81; bd. dirs. IGI Inc., ePlus, Inc. Trustee Gerald R. Ford Found., Grand Rapids, Mich., 1987—; mem. Adminstrv. Conf. US, 1991-92; mem. adv. com. US Ct. Fed. Claims; mem. code com. US Ct. Mil. Appeals for the Armed Forces, 1993-95; bd. dirs. Falcon Found., 1988—. Decorated Bronze star; recipient Disting. Pub. Svc. medal US Dept. Def., 1992, Atty. Gen.'s Disting. Svc. award US Dept. Justice, 1992. Mem. ABA, DC Bar Assn., Bar of US Supreme Ct., and others. Office: Textron Inc 40 Westminster St Providence RI 02903 Office Phone: 202-434-5678. Personal E-mail: todonnell@wc.com. Business E-Mail: todonnell@textron.com.*

O'DONNELL, TERRENCE, state supreme court justice; b. Cleve., Feb. 11, 1946; m. Mary Beth O'Donnell; children: Terrence, Michael, Colleen, Nora. BA in Polit. Sci., Kent State U., Ohio, 1968; JD, Cleve. State U., 1971. Bar: Ohio 1971. Instr. speech and debate Cuyahoga Cmty. Coll., 1968—70; instr. grades 7 & 8 St. Brendan Sch., North Olmstead, 1970; law clerk to Judge Justice J.J.P. Corrigan Supreme Ct. Ohio, 1971—72; law clerk to Judge John M. Manos and Judge V. Corrigan 8th Dist. Ct. Appeals, 1972—74; dir. program paralegal edn. David M. Myers Coll., 1974—76; atty. Marshman, Snyder & Corrigan, 1976—80; judge Cuyahoga County Ct. Common Pleas, 1980—95, 8th Dist. Ct. Appeals, 1995—2003; justice Ohio Supreme Ct., 2003—. Vis. judge counties throughout Ohio, 2003—; chmn. Ohio Legal Rights Svc. Commn.; instr. CPA bus. law rev. Cleve. State U.; instr. several continuing legal edn. programs; mem. Ohio Supreme Ct. Commn. on Professionalism. Past pres. Legal Eagles; former mem. bd. trustees Magnificat HS, Rocky River, past pres. Father's Club; exec. dir. emeritus St. Patrick's Day Parade, Cleve.; coach Little League Baseball, Rocky River; instr. pub. sch. religion program St. Bernadette Ch., Westlake; mem. St. Bernadette Parish, Westlake, Ohio; mem. bd. dirs. Our Lady Wayside. Mem.: Ohio Supreme Ct., Ohio State Bar Assn. (mem. pub. understanding law sect.), Cleve. Bar Assn. (chmn. law related edn. com., Pres.'s award 1989—99), Cath. Lawyer's Guild Cleve. (officer). Office: Ohio Supreme Ct 65 S Front St Columbus OH 43215-3431*

O'DONNELL, THOMAS LAWRENCE PATRICK, lawyer; b. Taunton, Mass., Aug. 12, 1926; s. Patrick Francis and Ellen Balfe (Brady) O'D.; m. Carol Hodgdon, Feb. 16, 1952; children: Ellen, Thomas, Janet Gael, Christopher Hodgdon AB magna cum laude, Harvard U., 1947, LL.B., 1949. Bar: Mass. 1950. Assoc. Ropes & Gray, Boston, 1949-52, 54-61, ptnr., 1962-97, chmn., 1984-90, of counsel, 1998—. Dir. Rath & Strong, Inc., 1985-96. Trustee, Trustees of Reservations, 1970—, chmn. bd., 1975-76, life trustee, 2007; bd. dirs. Mass. Land Conservation Trust, 1975-2002, chmn. bd., 1986-2002; bd. dirs. Mass. Taxpayers Found., 1972—, chmn. bd., 1977-79, 93-95, mem. exec. com., 1976—; bd. dirs. Boston Mcpl. Rsch. Bur., 1965—, chmn. bd., 1967-72; mem. pub. pension task force Mass. Bus. Roundtable, 1983-86; bd. dirs., sec. Jobs for Mass., Inc., 1981-83; moderator Town of Hingham, 1967—; del. Rep. Nat. Conv., 1972, all Rep. State convs., 1960-94; overseer Harvard U., 1986-92; bd. dirs. United Way Mass. Bay, 1987—, mem. exec. com. 1993—, chmn. bd. 1997-2000. Lt. USNR, 1944-45, 52-54. Recipient Cushing award Labor Guild of Archdiocese Boston, 1973, Humanitarian award The Nat. Conf. Greater Boston, 1997, The Harvard medal, 1997; mem. Knights of Malta, 1983— Fellow Am. Bar Found.; mem. ABA, Mass. Bar Assn., Boston Bar Assn., Indsl. Rels. Rsch. Assn. (pres. Boston chpt. 1980), Harvard Alumni Assn. (bd. dirs. 1978-81, 1st marshal class of 1947), Harvard Club Boston (bd. govs. 1985-91), Union of Boston Club, Hingham Yacht Club, Comml. Club. Roman Catholic. Home: 7 South Ln Hingham MA 02043-2446 Office: Ropes & Gray LLP 1 International Pl Boston MA 02110-2624 Office Phone: 617-951-7455. Business E-Mail: todonnell@ropesgray.com.

O'DONNELL, TOM, legislative staff member; b. Apr. 5, 1964; Degree, Syracuse U., NY, 1983; BA in Polit. Sci., SUNY, Plattsburgh, 1986. Cert. non-resident seminar program Naval War Coll., Newport, RI, 1995. Mil. legis. asst. for Rep. Patricia Schroede US House of Reps., Washington, 1987—89, mil. legis. asst. for Rep. Lane Evans, 1989—93, legis. dir., 1993—2002, chief of staff for Rep. Rush Holt, 2007—08, chief of staff for Rep. Phil Hare, 2008—; profl. staff mem. US House Vets. Affairs Com.; v.p. congl. affairs Continental Consulting Group, 2002—07. Roman Catholic. Office: Office of Congressman Phil Hare 428 Cannon House Office Bldg Washington DC 20515-1317 Office Phone: 202-225-5905. Business E-Mail: tom.odonnell@mail.house.gov.*

O'DONNELL, WILLIAM DAVID, retired construction firm executive; b. Brockton, Mass., Aug. 21, 1926; s. John Frank and Agnes Teresa (Flanagan) O'D.; m. Dixie Lou Anderson, Jan. 31, 1951; children—Craig Patrick, Ginger Lynn BS, U. N.Mex., 1953. Registered profl. engr., Ill., 1958. Engr. State of Ill., 1953-59; with Gregory-Anderson Co., Rockford, Ill., 1959—, gen. mgr., 1960-61, sec., 1961-81, pres., 1981-94; ret. Bd. dirs. Growth Enterprise, Davis Meml. Park, BankOne, Rockford. Dir. St. Anthony Med. Ctr., Youth Svcs. Network, Cath. Conf. of Ill.; bd. dirs. Rockford YMCA, pres., 1984. Served with USN, 1943-47 Recipient Friend of the Boy award Optimist Club, 1966, Excalibur award for cmty. svc. Rockford Register Star, 1971; named Titan of Yr., Boylan H.S., 1974, Papal Knight Order of St. Gregory the Great; fellow Wisdom Hall of Fame. Fellow: NSPE, ASCE, Soc. Am. Mil. Engrs.; mem.: VFW (life), No. Ill. Bldg. Contractors, Amateur Trapshooting Assn., World Future Soc., Aircraft Owners & Pilots Assn., Balloon Fedn. Am., Am. Polar Soc., Nat. Sporting Clays Assn., Old Antarctic Explorers Assn., Forest Hills Country (Rockford), Metropolitan Club (Chgo.); Adventurers (Chgo.), Adventurers Club, Metropolitan Club, Forest Hills Country Club, Rotary (Service Above Self award 1972; v.p. Rockford chpt. 1983, pres. 1984), Rotary (v.p. Rockford chpt. 1983, pres. 1984, Svc. Above Self award 1972), Am. Legion (life), Tau Beta Pi, Chi Epsilon, Sigma Tau. Home: 2004 Bradley Rd Rockford IL 61107-1258 Office: PO Box 900 Rockford IL 61105-0900 Personal E-mail: wdodonnell@sbcglobal.net.

O'DONNELL, WILLIAM JAMES, engineering executive; b. Pitts., June 19, 1935; s. William James and Elizabeth (Rau) O'D.; m. Joanne Mary Kusen, Jan. 31, 1959; children: Suzanne, Janice, William, Thomas, Kerry, Amy. BSME, Carnegie Inst. Tech., 1957; MSME, U. Pitts., 1959, PhD, 1962. Jr. engr. Westinghouse Research Lab., 1957-58, asso. engr., 1958; with Westinghouse Bettis Atomic Power Lab., West Mifflin, Pa., 1961-70, adv. engr., 1966-70; pres., chmn. bd. O'Donnell & Assos., Inc., Pitts., 1970—. Contbr. numerous articles on engring. and mechanics to profl. jours.; holder patents on processes and devices. Served with C.E. AUS, 1963-64. Recipient Machinery's Achievement award as outstanding mech. designer, 1957, Pi Tau Sigma Gold medal for achievements in engring., 1967, Pressure Vessel and Piping award ASME, 1994, Disting. Alumni award U. Pitts. Sch. Mech. Engring., 1996, Disting. Achievement award, Carnegie Mellon U., 2004. Fellow ASME (nat. award for outstanding contbn. to engring. profession 1973, internat. award for best publ. in pressure vessels and piping 1988, Engr. of Yr. award 1988, Pressure Vessel and Piping medal 1994); mem. NSPE, AAAS, ASTM, Soc. Exptl. Mechanics, Am. Nuclear Soc., Am. Soc. Metals Internat., The Minerals, Metals and Materials Soc., Sigma Xi. Home: 121 Sunrise Ln Venetia PA 15367 Office: O'Donnell Consulting Engrs 2940 S Park Rd Pittsburgh PA 15102 Office Phone: 412-835-5007. Business E-Mail: wjo@odonnellconsulting.com.

O'DONOVAN, CORMAC A., neurologist, educator; 2 children. BS, U. Coll. Galway, Ireland, 1982, MD, 1985. Assoc. prof. neurology Wake Forest U. Sch. Medicine, Winston-Salem, NC, 1995—. Med. dir., dir. eeg and evoked potential labs., assoc. prof. internal medicine-cardiology Wake Forest U. Sch. Medicine. Fellow: Am. Clin. Neurophysiology; mem.: AMA, Am. Acad. Sleep Medicine, Irish Neurol. Assn., So. Epilepsy and Ctrl. EEG Soc., Am. EEG Soc., Am. Epilepsy Soc., Am. Acad. Neurology. Office: Wake Forest Univ Sch of Medicine Medical Center Blvd Winston Salem NC 27157 Business E-Mail: odonovan@wfubmc.edu.

O'DOWD, DONALD DAVY, retired university president; b. Manchester, NH, Jan. 23, 1927; s. Hugh Davy and Laura (Morin) O'D.; m. Janet Louise Fithian, Aug. 23, 1953; children: Daniel D., Diane K., James E., John M. BA summa cum laude, Dartmouth Coll., 1951; postgrad. (Fulbright fellow), U. Edinburgh, Scotland, 1951-52; MA, Harvard U., 1955, PhD, 1957. Instr., asst. prof. psychology, dean freshmen Wesleyan U., Middletown, Conn., 1955-60; assoc. prof., prof. of psychology, dean Univ. Oakland Univ., Rochester, Mich., 1960-65, provost, 1965-70; pres. Oakland U., Rochester, Mich., 1970-80; exec. vice chancellor SUNY, Albany, 1980-84; pres. U. of Alaska Statewide System, 1984-90. Carnegie Corp. fellow, 1965—66. Mem. APA, AAAS, Phi Beta Kappa, Sigma Xi. Home and Office: 801 A Senda Verde Santa Barbara CA 93105

O'DRISCOLL, MARGARET MILLAR (PEGGY O'DRISCOLL), real estate broker; b. Hollywood, Calif., Aug. 2, 1925; d. Russell Hartney and Marion Scott (Macarthur) Millar; m. William Harrington Walker, Jan. 10, 1949 (dec. Dec. 22, 1968); children: William Russell Walker, Elizabeth Howland, Hiram Scott Walker; m. James O'Driscoll, Oct. 17, 1970. Student UCLA, 1942-44. Lic. ins. solicitor, real estate broker, Calif. Salesman, Carol Smart Real Estate, Del Mar, Calif., 1966-68, Bernard & Assocs., Solana Beach, Calif., 1968-70; owner Town and Country Real Estate, Rancho Santa Fe, Calif., 1970—; pres. Peggy O'Driscoll Enterprises, Inc. Mem. publicity com. Rancho Santa Fe Republican Women, 1950-58; mem. San Dieguito Citizens Planning Group, 1977-78; mem. vestry St. Peter's Episcopal Ch., Del Mar, 1976-78; bd. dirs. Rancho Santa Fe Cmty. Svcs. Dist., 1982-85, chmn., 1985, mem., 1986—. Mem. San Dieguito Bd Realtors (v.p. 1980-82, pres. 1983-84), Calif. Assn. Realtors (hon. life mem., bd. dirs. 1981-86, ins. trustee 1982-86, regional v.p. dist. 29 1986), Rancho Santa Fe Cmty. Ctr., Rancho Santa Fe Hist. Soc. (bd. dirs. 1985-86), San Diego County Coun. Real Estate Bds., Rancho Santa Fe Club, The Country Friends, The Gold Diggers (San Diego, Gifts of Loving Donors), Garden Club (publicity chmn. 1965-74), Rancho Santa Fe Women's Golf Club (founding mem.). Home: PO Box 457 Rancho Santa Fe CA 92067-0457 Home Phone: 858-756-1528; Office Phone: 858-756-1422.

O'DRISCOLL, SEAMAS STIOFAN, literature and language professor; BA, Stanford U., Calif., 1988; PhD, Harvard U., Cambridge, Mass., 2005. Asst. prof. Northwestern U., Evanston, Ill., 2005—.

ODUBER, NELSON ORLANDO, Prime Minister of Aruba; b. Aruba, Feb. 7, 1947; s. Urbano and Carmen Oduber; m. Glenda Croes, 1974; children: Glenson, Danguillaume, Nelson Jr. BA in Pub. Adminstrn., U. Tilburg, The Netherlands, 1970, MA in Constl. Sci., 1972. Mem. People's Electoral Movement, 1975—, M.P., leader, 1986—; commr. Exec. Coun. Aruba, 1975-85; mem. Island Coun., 1979-85; prime min. Aruba, 1989—94, 2001—. Named Man of Yr., Diario newspaper, 1980, Revista Amistad mag., 1980, Orden Francisco de Miranda Primera Clase, Orden del Liberador Promera Clase. Office: Office of Prime Min Oranjestad Aruba

ODUJEBE, OLADAPO A., toxicologist, educator, emergency physician; s. Henry A. and Owodoye I. Odujebe; m. Olubukola B. Dada, Sept. 27, 2006; children: Oluwamayowa A., Baby Girl. BS, Rutgers U. & UMDNJ SHRP, Newark, NJ, 1997; MD, NJ. Med. Sch., Newark, 2002. Cert. residency emergency medicine Albert Einstein Med. Ctr., 2006. Fellow med. toxicology NY U., 2006—08; asst. prof. and med. toxicologist Emory U., Atlanta, 2008, 2008—. Mem.: AMA, Am. Acad. Clin. Toxicologists, Soc. Acad. Emergency Medicine, Am. Coll. Emergency Physicians. Office: Emory Univ Hosp 49 Jesse Hill Jr Dr SE #316 Atlanta GA 30303

ODUM, JEFFERY NEAL, mechanical engineer; b. Bristol, Tenn., Sept. 11, 1956; s. Herschel S. and Minnie Lee (Carrier) O.; m. Stacy Elaine Ferrell, mar. 18, 1989; 1 child, Charles Wesley Ferrell. BSME, Tenn. Technol. U., 1978; MS in Engring., U. Tenn., 1983. Sr. project engr. TVA, Knoxville, 1978-81; sr. constrn. engr. Stone & Webster Engring. Corp., Boston, 1981-84; div. engr. E.I. DuPont de Nemours & Co., Aiken, S.C., 1984-89; engring. mgr. Flour Daniel, Greenville, S.C., 1989-92; mgr. of projects, Pharmaceutical Bus. Group CRS Sirrine Engrs., Inc., Raleigh, N.C., 1992-93; sr. project mgr. Gilbane Bldg. Co., Raleigh, 1993-95; dir. engring. Gilbane Process Group, Vacaville, Calif., 1995-98; biopharm. office leader Clark, Richardson and Biskup, Cons. Engrs., Cary, NC, 1998—2005; prin. NC Biosource, 2005—; dir. validation acad. NC Cmty. Coll. Sys. Author: Sterile Product Facility Design and Project Management, 1996, 2d edit., 2004, Large Scale Biomanufacturing, 2004, Advances in Large Scale Biomanufacturing-Capital Projects, 2004, 07, Advanced Technologies For Biopharmaceutical Processing, 2005; contbr. articles to profl. jours Vol. Spl. Olympics, Habitat for Humanity; mem. bd. govs. U. Tenn., 2002—06. Recipient DuPont Engring. Achievement award 1986, 88, 89, Nat. Svc. Alumni award Univ. Tenn. Mem. Parenteral Drug Assn., Internat. Soc. Pharm. Engrs. (bd. dirs., pres. Carolina chpt. 1996-97, chair N.Am. Chpt. Coun. 1998, chair publs. com. 2000-01, chair chpt. excellence 2000-01, chair tng. 2002, Svc. award 1999, 2001, 2003, 2005, chmn. N. Am. edn. com. 2004, Richard Purdy Outstanding Achievement award 2002, edn advisor N.Am.), ISPE Tng. Faculty (N.Am. edn. advisor 2006—), U. Tenn. Nat. Alumni Assn. (pres. Augusta chpt. 1987-89, bd. govs.), Order Engr., Kappa Sigma Republican. Presbyterian. Avocations: sports, biking, cooking, writing, skiing. Office: NCBiosource 1213 Enoerbury Dr Raleigh NC 27614 Office Phone: 919-341-3565. E-mail: jodum@ncbiosource.com.

ODUM, MARVIN E., oil industry executive; b. 1958; married; 3 children. BS in Mech. Engring., U. Tex., 1982; MBA, U. Houston. Engr. Shell Oil Co., 1982, gas and power dir. for Americas London, 2001; v.p. bus. devel. & tech. Shell Exploration & Prodn., Houston, exec. v.p. Americas, 2005—; pres. Shell Oil Co., 2008—; CEO InterGen, 2003—05; bd. dirs. upstream Americas unit Royal Dutch Shell, 2009—. Adv. bd. mem. U. Tex. Coll. Engring.; bd. dirs. Am. Petroleum Inst., chmn. upstream com.; mem. deans coun. Harvard U. JFK Sch. Govt. Bd. dirs. Palmer Drug Abuse Prog.; bd. visitors Univ. Cancer Foundation, M.D. Anderson Cancer Center. Office: Shell Oil Co 910 Louisiana St Houston TX 77210 Office Phone: 713-241-6161. Office Fax: 713-241-4044.*

ODYA, GREGORY MATTHEW, musician, educator; b. Bloomington, Ind., Apr. 22, 1980; s. Charles Ervin and Martha Fortenberry Odya; m. Erin Catherine Stapleton, June 23, 2001. Degree in instrumental music edn., Ind. U., 2004. Lic. tchr. Ind. Weekend coord., program asst. Christole, Inc., Bloomington, Ind., 2000—02; asst. program coord. Edgewood H.S. Marching Band, Ellettsville, Ind., 2000—03; instr. Bloomington H.S. North Marching Band, 2002; instrumental music arranger, instr. and performer Edgewood H.S. Show Choirs, 2002—04; assoc. instr. The PA Inst., MSD Lawrence Twp., Indpls., 2004; assoc. dir. of bands Decatur Ctrl. H.S. MSD Decatur Twp., Indpls., 2004—. Adjudicator Edgewood H.S. Contest of Champions, 2004. Music performer St. John the Apostle Cath. Ch., Bloomington, 2003—04. Mem.: Ind. State Tchrs. Assn., Music Educators Nat. Conf., Phi Lambda Theta, Golden Key, Nat. Soc. Collegiate Scholars. Avocations: running, swimming, music composition, music performance. Personal E-mail: gmodya@gmail.com.

ODZA, RANDALL M., lawyer; b. Schnectady, May 6, 1942; s. Mitchell and Grace (Mannes) O.; m. Rita Ginness, June 19, 1966; children: Kenneth, Keith. BS in Indsl. and Labor Rels., Cornell U., 1964, LLB, 1967. Bar: N.Y. 1967, U.S. Ct. Appeals (2d cir.) 1970, U.S. Dist. Ct. (so. and ea. dists.) N.Y. 1969, U.S. Dist. Ct. (we. dist.) N.Y. 1970. Assoc. Proskauer, Rose, Goetz & Mandelsohn, NYC, 1967-69, Jaeckle, Fleischmann & Mugel, Buffalo, 1969-72, ptnr., 1972—. Sec. bd. trustees Buffalo Philharm. Orch. Soc.; past trustee, legal counsel, treas. Temple Beth Am. Recipient Western NY Retail Mchts. Assn., 1980. Fellow Coll. Labor and Employment Lawyers; mem. ABA, Labor and Employment Relations Assn. Western NY, Erie County Bar Assn., NY State Bar Assn. Office: Jaeckle Fleischmann & Mugel 12 Fountain Plz Rm 700 Buffalo NY 14202-2292 Home Phone: 716-636-8893; Office Phone: 716-843-3877. Business E-Mail: rodza@jaeckle.com.

ODZE, ROBERT D., pathologist; s. Walter Karl Odze and Helen Natasha Menkes. BSc, McGill U., Montreal, 1980, MDCM, 1984. Cert. anatomic pathology. Staff pathologist Mount Sinai Hosp., Toronto, Canada; instr. pathology U. Toronto Med. Sch., Canada, 1991—93; cons. GI pathology New Eng. Deaconess Med. Ctr., Boston, 1994—99, Beth Israel Deaconess Med. Ctr., Boston, 1996—99; dir. GI pathology svc. Brigham and Women's Hosp., Boston, 1997—; assoc. prof. pathology Harvard Med. Sch., Boston, 1999—; cons. pathologist Dana Farber Cancer Inst., Boston, 2004—. Author, editor: Surgical Pathology GI Tract, Liver, Bilary Tract and Pancreas, 2003, assoc. editor: Am. Jour. Gastroenterology, 2003—, mem. editl. bd.: Human Pathology, 2001—, Gastrointestinal Endoscopy, 2001. Recipient MRC award, McGill U. Dept. Sci., 1980, CIBA prize for anatomy, McGill U. Med. Sch., 1981, MRC award, 1981, Joseph Morley Drake prize for pathology, 1982, Outstanding Surgery Student award, ACP and McGill U. Med. Sch., 1983, Pathology Finlayson Rsch. award, McGill U., 1988; grantee, Am. Coll. Gastroenterology, 1994—95, 1998—99, Stanley Robbins Rsch. Award, 1996—97; Univ. scholar, McGill U. Dept. Sci., 1981, Faculty scholar, McGill U. Med. Sch., 1982. Mem.: Arthur Purdy Stout Soc. Surg. Pathologists, U.S. and Can. Acad. Pathology Gastrointestinal Pathology Soc., U.S. and Can. Acad. Pathology, Am. Gastroenterol. Assn., Am. Coll. Gastroenterology, Crohn's Colitis Found. Am. Home: 1175 Chestnut St Unit 3 Newton MA 02464 Office: Brigham & Womens Hosp 75 Francis St Boston MA 02115

OECHLER, HENRY JOHN, JR., lawyer; b. Charlotte, NC, Apr. 9, 1946; s. Henry J. and Convere Jones (McAden) O. AB, Princeton U., 1968; JD, Duke U., 1971. Bar: N.Y. 1972, U.S. Ct. Appeals (2d cir.) 1974, U.S. Ct. Appeals (D.C. cir.) 1975, U.S. Ct. Appeals (8th cir.) 1986, U.S. Ct. Appeals (9th cir.) 1995. Assoc. Chadbourne & Parke, NYC, 1971-80, ptnr., 1980—2006, of counsel, 2006—. Avocation: studying airline schedules. Office: Chadbourne & Parke 30 Rockefeller Plz Fl 31 New York NY 10112-0129

OEHLER, JUDITH JANE MOODY, retired counselor; b. Farner, Tenn., Mar. 5, 1942; d. William Henry and Peggy (Lindsey) Moody; m. Carl Bailey Oehler, June 1, 1963; children: David W., Paul E. BS in Elem. Edn., U. Tex., 1964; MEd, Tex. Christian U., 1976. Lic. profl. counselor, Nat. Bd. Cert. counselor. Elem. tchr. Arlington (Tex.) Ind. Sch. Dist., 1965-78, elem. counselor, 1979—96, ret., 1996. Mem. Arlington Women's Club. Fellow AACD; mem. Nat. Soc. DAR (regent 2000-02), Tex. Assn. Counseling and Devel., North Ctrl. Tex. Assn. Counseling and Devel. (sec. 1995-96, Caring award 1995), Tex. State Tchrs. Assn. (life mem.), Arlington Assn. Tex. Profl. Educators (sec. 1994—95), Retired Sch. Employees Arlimgton, Aux. Tex. Soc. Profl. Engrs. (pres. Mid-Cities chpt. 1992-94, state sec. 1993-94, v.p. Region V 1994-95, state pres. 1997-98), Encore Club (1st v.p. 2004-05), Arlington Woman's Club (sec. travel dept., antique dept. chmn. 2003-05, club photographer 2005-07, 1st v.p. 2007-2008), Nat. Soc. US Daus 1812, United Daughter of The Confrederacy, Daus. Am. Colonists (sec. 2007-08), Nat. Soc. Tex. Colonial Dames XVII Century (sec. 2007-08), Nat. Huguenot Soc., Nat. Soc. Magna Charta Dames, Nat. Soc. Dames of Court of Honor, Ill. State Soc., Arlington Women Rotary, Phi Delta Kappa. Methodist. Avocations: travel, reading, swimming, gardening, walking. Home: 2408 Westwood Dr Arlington TX 76012-2905

OEHLER, MICHAEL GLENN, humanities educator, social sciences educator, researcher, administrator; b. Reno, Nev., Aug. 1957; s. Charles Frederick and Beverly May Oehler; m. Annámaria Szigeti, July 1999; children: András Michael, Anna Krisztina, Kai Erik, Rachel Anna, Matean (Tay) Adam. BA, Whitworth Coll., Spokane, Wash., 1979; MA in Tchg., Sch. for Internat. Tng., Brattleboro, Vt., 1988; D in Ministry (conflict mgmt.) with high distinction, Trinity Theol. Seminary (in conj. with U. Liverpool, Liverpool, Eng.), Newburgh, Ind., 2003. Cert. in tchg. fgn. lang. Ednl. Solutions, Inc., NYC, 1985, in children and their books Oxford U. and Fla. State U., joint program, Oxford, Eng., 1991, Summer Inst. English and Applied Linguistics, Cambridge U. Rsch. Ctr., English and Applied Linguistics, Cambridge, Eng., 1991, founds. in intercultural tng. Internat. Soc. Intercultural Edn., Tng. and Rsch., Wash. DC, 1992, in tng. design for internat. and multicultural programs Summer Inst. Intercultural Comm., Portland, 1992, postgrad. cert. in pragmatics and cross-cultural comm. Australian Nat. Ctr. English Lang. Tchg. and Rsch., 1993; anti-terrorism officer cert., assessing terrorism-related risk cert., attack at Jedawal: critical lessons for AT professionals cert., and maritime security awareness cert. S2 Safety and Intelligence Inst., Clearwater, Fla., 2006, Live Response Psychological Impact of Terrorism cert. Saint Petersburg Coll. Nat. Terrorism Preparedness Inst., Fla., 2006, bomb threat mgmt. cert. S2 Safety and Intelligence Inst., Clearwater, Fla., 2007, identification of Iraqi chem-bio munitions cert. S2 Safety and Intelligence Inst., Clearwater, Fla., 2008, cert. in conflict analysis US Inst. Peace, DC, 2008. Remedial instr. Marist Brothers Internat. Sch., Kobe, Japan, 1979—80, ESL dept. coord. and head tchr., 1980—82; lectr. Tokai Women's Coll. and Jr. Coll., Kagamigahara,

Japan, 1983—89; tchr. trainee Harvard U., Cambridge, Mass., 1988, instr., 1994; vis. lectr., vis. asst. prof., vis. assoc. prof., vis. prof. Aichi Prefectural U., Nagoya, Japan, 1989—2005; adj. grad., undergrad. lectr. Nagoya Nat. U., 1989—2005; assoc. prof. Meikai U., Urayasu, Japan, 2005—; v.p. global ops. Nihon Homeland Security K.K., Tokyo, 2008—. Profl. academic presentations and consultations in field; intercultural del., Russia and Lithuania People to People Amb. Programs, Spokane, Wash., 1993; doctoral rsch. Oxford Ctr. Mission Studies, Oxford, England, 1995—97. Contbr. papers to academic jours. Organizer and distributor Disaster Relief Program, Kobe, Japan, 1995; mem. Tokyo Union Ch., 2005—. Mem.: Omicron Psi (Gold mem.). Protestant. Avocations: travel, reading, sports, history. Business E-Mail: oehler@meikai.ac.jp, moehler@nihon-homelandsecurity.com.

OEHLER, RICHARD WILLIAM, lawyer; b. NYC, Nov. 24, 1950; s. John Montgomery and Florence Mae (Jahn) O.; m. Linda Tyson. BA, Dartmouth Coll., 1972; JD, Harvard U., 1976. Bar: Calif. 1976, Wash. 1987, D.C. 1988, U.S. Dist. Ct. (no. dist.) Calif. 1976, U.S. Dist. Ct. Wash. 1987, U.S. Claims Ct. 1979, U.S. Ct. Appeals (fed. cir.) 1982. Assoc. Pillsbury, Madison & Sutro, San Francisco, 1976-78; trial atty. U.S. Dept. Justice, Washington, 1978-87; of counsel Perkins Coie, Seattle, 1987-90, ptnr., 1990—. Mem. ABA, Nat. Contract Mgmt. Assn. (Spl. Achievement award 1990-92), Wash. State Bar Assn. Office: Perkins Coie 1201 3rd Ave Fl 40 Seattle WA 98101-3029 Office Phone: 206-359-8419. Business E-Mail: roehler@perkinscoie.com.

OEHLERT, WILLIAM HERBERT, JR., cardiologist, administrator, educator; b. Murphysboro, Ill., Sept. 11, 1942; s. William Herbert Sr. and Geneva Mae (Roberts) O.; m. L. Keith Brown, Mar. 14, 1976; children: Emily Jane, Amanda Elizabeth. BA, So. Ill. U., 1967; MD, Washington U., St. Louis, 1967; M in Med. Mgmt., Tulane U., 1998. Diplomate Nat. Bd. Med. Examiners, Am. Bd. Internal Medicine, Am. Bd. Cardiovascular Disease, North Am. Soc. Pacing and Electrophysiology, Am. Coll. Physician Execs. Med. intern Union Meml. Hosp., Balt., 1967-68, resident, 1968-69, U. Iowa, Iowa City, 1969-70, cardiology fellow, 1970-72; asst. prof. medicine, dir. coronary care units U. Okla. Health Sci. Ctr., Oklahoma City, 1972-74, asst. clin. prof. medicine, 1974-82, assoc. clin. prof. medicine, 1982-88, clin. prof. medicine, 1988—; chmn. dept. cardiology Bapt. Med. Ctr., 1992-95; pvt. practice Oklahoma City, 1974—. Med. dir. cardiovasc. svcs. Integris Bapt. Med. Ctr., 1993-98; pres. Cardiovasc. Clinic, Oklahoma City, 1987-91, chmn. exec. com., 1987-91; med. dir. Cardiovasc. Imaging Svcs. Corp., Oklahoma City, 1987-92; v.p. Plaza Med. Group, 1992-93; CEO W.H. Oehlert, MD, P.C., 1993—; prin. clin. coord Okla. Found. Med. Quality, 1998-2002, med. clin. coord., 2002-06. Author: Arrhythmias, 1973, Cardiovascular Drugs, 1976; contbr. articles to profl. jours. Fellow ACP, Am. Heart Assn. (nat. program com. 1979-82, pres. Okla. affiliate 1985-86, bd. dirs. 1974-88, ACLS nat. affiliate faculty 1987-90, bd. dirs. Oklahoma City 1999-2005), Am. Coll. Cardiology; mem. AMA (del. 2007—), ACP-Am. Soc. Internal Medicine, Nat. Assn. Residents and Interns, Am. Coll. Physician Execs. (cert.), Am. Diabetes Assn. (western coun. 2000-03, ea. coun. 2000-01), Okla. State Med. Assn. (pres., 2007—08, trustee 2001—, chmn. Physicians Campaign for Healthier Okla., 2003-04, chmn. CME accreditation rev. com. 2003—04, chmn. CME planning com. 2004-07), Okla. City Clin. Soc., Okla. Cardiac Soc. (pres. 1978-79), Osler Soc., Soc. Nuc. Medicine, Okla. Found. for Med. Quality (bd. dirs. 1995-98), Okla. County Med. Soc. (chmn. quality of care com. 1990-91, pres. 2006), Wilderness Med. Soc., Stewart Wolf Soc., Sportman's Club (bd. dirs. 2003-09), Okla. Blood Inst. (bd. dirs. 2007-), Phi Eta Sigma, Phi Kappa Phi. Home: 3017 Rock Ridge Pl Oklahoma City OK 73120-5713 Office Phone: 405-751-5224. Personal E-mail: woehlert@cox.net.

OEHME, REINHARD, physicist, researcher; b. Wiesbaden, Germany, Jan. 26, 1928; arrived in U.S., 1954, permanent resident, 1956; s. Reinhold and Katharina (Kraus) Oehme; m. Mafalda Pisani, Nov. 5, 1952. Diplom Physiker, U. Frankfurt am Main, Germany, 1948; doctoral student of Werner Heisenberg, Max Planck Inst. Physik and U. Goettingen, 1949—51; Dr. rer. nat., U. Goettingen, Germany, 1951. Asst. Max Planck Inst. Physics, Goettingen, 1949—54; research asso. Fermi Inst. Nuclear Studies, U. Chgo., 1954-56; mem. faculty dept. physics and Fermi Inst., 1958—, prof. physics, 1960—; mem. Inst. Advanced Studies, Princeton, 1956-58. Vis. prof. Inst. de Física Teórica, São Paulo, Brazil, 1952-53, U. Md., 1957, U. Vienna, Austria, 1961, Imperial Coll., London, Eng., 1963-64, U. Karlsruhe, Fed. Republic Germany, 1974, 75, 77, U. Tokyo, 1976, 88; vis. scientist Internat. Centre Theoretical Physics, Miramare-Trieste, Italy, Brookhaven Nat. Lab., Lawrence Radiation Lab., U. Calif., Berkeley, CERN, Geneva, Switzerland, Max Planck Inst., Munich, Fed. Republic Germany, Rsch. Inst. for Fundamental Physics, Kyoto (Japan) U. Author articles in field, chpts. in books. Guggenheim fellow, 1963-64; recipient Humboldt award, 1974, Japan Soc. for Promotion of Sci. Fellowship awards, 1976, 88. Fellow: Am. Phys. Soc. Achievements include discovery of chargeconjugation non-invariance; the fundumental importance of CP-transformations; formulation and proof of Edge of the Wedge theorem, and of hadronic dispersion relations and sum rules; reduction of quantum field theories using renormalization group methods, supersymmetric theories as particular solutions; superconvergence relations for propagators and their implications for the confinement of gluons and quarks. Office: U Chgo Enrico Fermi Inst 5640 S Ellis Ave Chicago IL 60637-1433 Office Phone: 773-702-7299. Business E-Mail: oehme@theory.uchicago.edu.

OEHME, WOLFGANG WALTER, landscape architect; b. Chemnitz, Germany, May 18, 1930; came to the U.S., 1957; s. Walter Gustav and Elisabeth Elsa (Neumann) O.; 1 child, Roland. Degree in horticulture, Bitterfeld Trade Sch., 1950; degree in landscape architecture, U. Berlin, 1954. Exch. student Waterer & Sons Nurseries, Bagshot, United Kingdom, 1954-56; landscape architect Baltimore County Planning, Towson, Md., 1958-65, The Rouse Co., Columbia, Md., 1965-66; asst. prof. U. Pa., Phila., 1962-64, U. Ga., Athens, 1965; pvt. practice Balt., 1965-74; CEO Oehme, Van Sweden and Assocs., Inc., Washington, 1974—. Co-author: Bold Romantic Gardens, 1990, Gardening with Water, 1995, Process Architecture, 1996, Gardening with Nature, 1997. Recipient Spl. Resolution for Disting. and dedicated vol. svc. Baltimore County Coun., 2003; named to Hall of Fame, Towson Devel. Corp., 1995; named Man of Yr., German Soc. Md., 1996. Fellow Am. Soc. Landscape Architects; mem. Perennial Plant Assn. (Disting. Svc. 1988), Garden Writers Assn. (Quill and Trowel award 1991). Mass. Hort. Soc. (George Robert White medal of honor 2002). Home: 511A W Joppa Rd Baltimore MD 21204-3819 Office: 800 G St SE Washington DC 20003-2816 Office Phone: 202-546-7575. Business E-Mail: oehme@ovsla.com.

OEI, LOK S., digital communications systems and DSP engineer, researcher; BSEE, U. Mich., 1973, MA in Math., 1973; DSc, Washington U., 1977. Mem. tech. staff Mitre Corp., McLean, Va., 1977—81; staff engr. Hughes Aircraft Co., Fullerton, Calif., 1981—86; prin. sys. engr. Lockheed Martin, Sunnyvale, Calif., 1986—94; sr. prin. engr. Boeing/Raytheon/Hughes Electronics Sys., El Segundo, Calif., 1994—2006. Mem.: IEEE, AIAA, Sigma Xi, Phi Kappa Phi, Eta Kappa Nu, Tau Beta Pi. Home: PO Box 1186 Mountain View CA 94042 Office: PO Box70191 Sunnyvale CA 94087 Personal E-mail: lsoei@ieee.org.

OELBERG, DAVID GEORGE, neonatologist educator, researcher; b. Waukon, Iowa, May 26, 1952; s. George Robert and Elizabeth Abigail (Kepler) O.; m. Debra Penuel, Aug. 4, 1979; children: Anna Elizabeth, Benjamin George. BS with highest honors, Coll. William and Mary, 1974; MD, U. Md., 1978. Diplomate in pediat. and in neonatal-perinatal medicine Am. Bd. Pediat. Intern U. Tex. Med. Br., Galveston, 1978-79, resident, 1979-81, house pediat. staff, 1978-81; postdoctoral fellow in neonatal medicine U. Tex. Med. Sch., Houston, 1981-84, asst. prof. dept. pediat., 1984-90, assoc. prof., 1990-93; assoc. prof. pediat., head perinatal rsch. Ctr. Pediat. Rsch. Ea. Va. Med. Sch., 1993-2001, prof., interim chmn. dept. pediat. Ctr. Pediat. Rsch., 2001—, dir. divsn. neonatal-perinatal medicine. Mem. hosp. staff Hermann Hosp., Houston, 1983-93; physician Crippled Children's Svcs. Program, Houston, 1985-93; mem. hosp. staff Lyndon B. Johnson County Hosp., 1990-93; vis. prof. Wyeth-Ayerst Labs., 1992; med. dir. Office Rsch., Children's Hosp. of King's Daus., 1993—, v.p. for acad. devel., 2001—; med. dirs. Office of Rsch., Sentara-Norfolk Gen. Hosp., 1993—, pres. med. staff. Mem. editl. adv. bd. jour. Neonatal Intensive Care; contbr. articles to profl. jours.; ad hoc reviewer profl. jours.; patentee in field. Physician cons. Parents of Victims of Sudden Infant Death Syndrome, Houston, 1984; chmn. Instl. Animal Care and Use Com. Recipient award in analytical chemistry Am. Chem. Soc., 1974, NIH Clin. Investigator award NHLBI, 1989-94; rsch. grantee Am. Lung Assn., 1989-90, NIH, 1989-94. Fellow Am. Acad. Pediat. NY Acad. Scis.; mem. AMA, NAS, Soc. Exptl. Biology and Medicine, So. Soc. Pediatric Rsch. (councilor, pres., sec.-treas.), Soc. Pediatric Rsch. Achievements include development of a method for optical measurement of bilirubin in tissue and ion channel proteins in pulmonary surfactant. Home: 1624 W Little Neck Rd Virginia Beach VA 23452-4720 Office: Ea Va Med Sch Ctr Pediatric Rsch 855 W Brambleton Ave Norfolk VA 23510-1005 Office Phone: 757-668-7456. Business E-Mail: doelberg@chkd.org.

OELBERG, ROBERT NATHAN, landscape architect; b. Washington, May 7, 1956; s. George Robert and Elizabeth Abigail (Kepler) Oelberg; m. Katherine Jane Shoffner, Nov. 9, 2002; stepchildren: Forrest Dungan, Katelyn Dungan. BA in Art magna cum laude, Maharishi Internat. U., Fairfield, Iowa, 1981; M.Landscape Arch., U. Va., Charlottesville, 1985. Registered landscape architect NC. Landscape architect, sr. project mgr. Land Design Inc., Alexandria, Va., 1985-93; owner Robert N. Oelberg ASLA PA, Boone, NC, 1994—97, 1999—2005, 2008—; dir. HMR Land Planning and Landscape Arch., Boone, 1997-99, v.p. planning Ginn NC region, 2005—08. Chmn. Boone Country Dancers; bd. dir. Wilkes Vocational Svcs. With USMC, 1974—76. DuPont fellow, 1984. Mem.: Am. Soc. Landscape Architects. Democrat. Episcopalian. Office: 782 Little Laurel Rd Ext Boone NC 28607 Home: 782 Little Laurel Rd Ext Boone NC 28607-8915 Home Phone: 828-264-4297; Office Phone: 823-264-4149. Business E-Mail: bob@oelbergla.com.

OELLERICH, MICHAEL, clinical chemistry professor, chemical pathologist; b. Heidelberg, Germany, July 15, 1944; s. Friedrich W. and Roswitha (Kamner) O.; m. Pushpa Singh, Mar. 12, 1976; children: Mark Oellerich, Thomas, Diana. MD, U. Heidelberg, 1970; Habilitation, Med. U. Hannover, 1978; DHC, Bulgarian Nat. Acad. Medicine, Sofia, 1998. Cert. FFPath RCPI, FRCPath. Intern U. Heidelberg, 1971—72; resident in internal medicine U. Düsseldorf, Germany, 1973—75; resident Inst. for Clin. Chemistry, Med. U. Hannover, Germany, 1972—73, 1975—79, head physician, 1979—82, dep. chmn., 1982—91; prof. clin. chemistry U. Hannover/Göttingen, Germany, 1982—; dir. dept. clin. chemistry, ctrl. lab. Ctr. Internal Medicine U. Göttingen, 1991—, dean faculty medicine, 1996—98, vice dean faculty medicine, 1998—99; dep. chief exec. for rsch. and tchg. Georg-August U., Göttingen, 1999—2004. Mem. DFG Commn. for Clin. Toxicol. Analysis, 1984-89; mem. coun. faculty medicine, U. Göttingen, 1993—, habilitation com., 1993-98; chmn. 4th Internat. Congress of Therapeutic Drug Monitoring and Clin. Toxicology, Vienna, 1995; steering com. Eurolife, 1999—; Path Ctr. vis. lectr. Western Austria, 2004; lectr. in field. Mem. editl. bd. Jour. Clin. Chemistry and Clin. Biochemistry, 1985—88, Therapeutic Drug Monitoring, 1987—2002; editor: Therapeutic Drug Monitoring, 2003—; assoc. editor Clin. Biochemistry, 1996—2007, Clin. Chemistry, 2007—; contbr. 350 articles to profl. jours., chapters to books. Recipient Ludolf-Krehl prize, S.W. German Soc. for Internal Medicine, 1971, Traveling Lectureship award, Can. Soc. Clin. Chemists, 2002, Prof. Landbeck award, 2004. Fellow: Royal Coll. Pathology, Royal Coll. Physicians Ireland (hon.); mem.: German United Assn. Clin. Chemistry and Lab. Medicine (pres. 2003—05), World Assn. Soc. Pathology and Lab. Medicine (sec.-treas. 2005—07, pres. 2009—), Bulgarian Nat. Acad. Medicine, Internat. Assn. Therapeutic Drug Monitoring and Clin. Toxicology (pres.-elect 1995—97, pres. 1997—99, award for exceptional contbns. 1999, C.E. Pippenger award 2001), Am. Assn. for Clin. Chemistry, German Soc. for Clin. Chemistry (bd. dirs. 1984—86), German Assn. Lab. Medicine (pres.-elect 1999—2000, pres. 2001—02). Lutheran. Achievements include invention of hypoglycemic hydrazonopropionic acid and of the MEGX liver function test. Office: Georg-August Univ Dept Clin Chemistry Robert-Koch-Str 40 D-37075 Göttingen Germany Office Phone: 49-551-398561. Business E-Mail: michael.oellerich@med.uni-goettingen.de. E-mail: moeller@med.uni-goettingen.de.

OEMKE, MARK PAUL, biology professor, researcher; s. Harold Edward and Virginia Louise Oemke; m. Amy Lynn Peterson, Apr. 20, 1995; children: Virginia Louise, Rebecca, Arthur Challenger, Holly Elizabeth. PhD in Natural Sci., Mich. State U., East Lansing, 1983. Aquatic biologist State Mich., Dept. Environ. Quality, Lansing, 1988—2001; prof. biology Alma Coll., Mich., 2001—. Contbr. articles to profl. jours. Mem.: Sigma Xi. Office: Alma Coll 614 W Superior St Alma MI 48801 Office Fax: 989-463-7076. Business E-Mail: oemke@alma.edu.

OERTEL, GOETZ KUNO HEINRICH, physicist, professional society administrator; b. Stuhm, Germany, Aug. 24, 1934; arrived in US, 1957; s. Egon F.K. and Margarete W. (Wittek) O.; m. Brigitte Beckmann, June 17, 1960; children: Ines M.H. Oertel Downing, Carsten K.R. Abitur, Robert Mayer, Heilbronn, Fed. Republic Germany, 1953; vordiplom, U. Kiel, Fed. Republic Germany, 1956; PhD, U. Md., College Park, 1963. Aerospace engr. Langley Ctr. NASA, Hampton, Va., 1963-68, chief solar physics Washington, 1968-75, policy analyst for sci. advisor to Pres. and Office Mgmt. and Budget, 1974-75; head astronomy divsn. NSF, Washington, 1975; dir. def. and civilian nuc. waste programs US Dept. Energy, Washington, 1975-83; acting mgr. sav. river ops. office Aiken, SC, 1983-84; dep. mgr. ops. office Albuquerque, 1984-85; dep. asst. sec. of energy for EH, Washington, 1985-86; pres., CEO Assn. Univs. for Rsch. in Astronomy, Inc., Washington, 1986-99, pres. emeritus; also bd. dirs. Assn. Univs. for Rsch. in Astronomy, Inc. (AURA, Inc.), Washington, disting. advisor, 2000—. Cons. Los Alamos Lab., N.Mex., 1987-92, Westinghouse Electric, 1988-99, Lampadia Found., Fundacion Andes of Santiago de Chile, Vitae Found. Sao Paulo, Brazil; bd. dirs. Inst. for Sci. and Soc., Ellensburg, Wash., IUE Corp.; mem. bd. internat. sci. orgns. NAS, 2001-06; bd. mem. Sch. of Computational Sci., George Mason U., 1995-2007, chair, 2002-03, bd. mem. Coll. Sci., 2006-07; mem. US Com. for CODATA, 1993-03, chmn. 1997-2000; US nat. del. CODATA ICSU, 1999-2001; mem. peer rev. com. ASME, 1996-2000; cons. conicyt, Govt. of Chile, 2000-04, VITAE Found., Brazil, 2001-04, Fundacion Andes, Chile, 2000-03; chmn., bd. dirs. Ctr. of Excellence for Hazardous Materials Mgmt., Carlsbad, N.Mex., 2003-04; lifetime nat. assoc. Nat. Acads. Washington, 2003—; trustee FLF Trust, 2006—. Contbr. articles to profl. jours. Recipient ASME Dixy Lee Ray prize, 2005; Fulbright grantee, 1957; Exceptional Svc. medal NASA, 1973, Bronze medal Dept. Energy, 1983, Silver medal, 1985, Disting. Svcs. award NSF, 1999; asteroid named in his honor, Internat. Astronomical Union, 2006. Fellow AAAS; mem. Am. Phys. Soc., Am. Astron. Soc., Internat. Astron. Union (named minor planet Goetzoertel in honor), NY Acad. Scis., Philos. Soc. Washington, Internat. U. Exch., Inc. (bd. dirs.), Cosmos Club (admissions com. 2004-07, awards com. 2007—, chair 2008-), Sigma Xi. Lutheran. Achievements include patents in field. Avocations: exercise, chess, computing, genealogy. Address: 8833 Watts Mine Terr Potomac MD 20854-5439 Office Phone: 301-365-1061. Business E-Mail: goetz@oertel.org.

OERTEL, MICHAEL, researcher, medical educator; b. Berlin, May 6, 1971; arrived in U.S., 2001; s. Dieter and Heiderose Oertel. Diploma in Biology, U. Leipzig, 1995, PhD, 2000. Postdoctoral fellow Inst. Clin. Immunology U. Leipzig, Germany, 2000—01; rsch. assoc. Albert Einstein Coll. Medicine Yeshiva U., Bronx, NY, 2001—03, instr. medicine Marion Bessin Liver Rsch. Ctr., 2004—. Contbr. articles to profl. jours. Mem.: German Assn. for the Study of the Liver, Am. Assn. for Study of Liver Diseases, German Transplantation Soc. Avocations: reading, music, chess, horseback riding, travel. Office: Albert Einstein Coll Medicine Yeshiva U Marion Bessin Liver Rsch Ctr 1300 Morris Park Ave Ullm 605 Bronx NY 10461 Office Phone: 718-430-3310. Business E-Mail: moertel@aecom.yu.edu.

OERTEL, YOLANDA CASTILLO, pathologist, educator; b. Lima, Peru, Dec. 14, 1938; came to U.S., 1966; d. Leonardo A. and Dalila (Ramirez) C.; m. James E. Oertel, Sept. 24, 1969. MD, Cayetano Heredia, Lima, 1964; Dr. honoris causa, U. Peruana Cayetano Heredia, 1999. Diplomate Am. Bd. Pathology (mem. test com. for cytopathology 1988-94). Internat. postdoctoral fellowship NIH, Bethesda, Md., 1966-68; asst. prof. pathology Sch. Medicine George Washington U., Washington, 1975-78, assoc. prof., 1978-84, prof., 1984-98, prof. emerita, 1998—. Adj. prof. pathology and lab. medicine MCP Hahnemann U. Sch. Medicine; cons. Registry Cytology Armed Forces Inst. Pathology, Washington, 1981—. Author: Fine Needle Aspiration of the Breast, 1987; contbr. chpts. to books, articles to profl. jours. Decorated comendador de la Orden Cayetano Heredia, 1999; recipient Francisco A. Camino prize Peruvian Med. Assn., 1965, cert. Meritorious Svc. Armed Forces Inst. Pathology, 1974; named Disting. Alumna Cayetano Heredia Med. Sch., 1989. Mem. Assn. Mil. Surgeons (hon.), Colombian Soc. Pathology (hon.), Argentinian Soc. Pathology (hon.), Peruvian Soc. Pathologists (hon.), Argentinian Soc. Cytopathology, (hon.), Am. Soc. Cytopathology, Internat. Acad. Pathology, Soc. Latinoamericana Patologia, Am. Soc. Clin. Pathologists (coun. on cytopathology 1982-88), Coll. Am. Pathologists, Arthur Purdy Stout Soc. Surg. Pathologists, Am. Thyroid Assn., L.Am. Thyroid Soc. Avocations: reading, opera. Office: Washington Hosp Ctr Pathology Dept Washington Cancer Inst 110 Irving St NW Washington DC 20010-2975 Home Phone: 703-836-0639; Office Phone: 202-877-2740. Office Fax: 202-877-0197. Business E-Mail: Yolanda.C.Oertel@medstar.net.

OERTER, CYNTHIA LYNN, medical technologist; b. Waupaca, Wis., Mar. 8, 1948; d. Lavern Charles and Geraldine Mae (Huffcutt) Trinrud; m. Gregory Van Oerter, June 8, 1968; children: Nathan, Justin. BS, U. Wis., Oshkosh, 1971; MS, Cardinal Stritch Coll., 1993. Cert. Am. Soc. Clin. Pathologists. Med. technologist Mercy Med. Ctr., Oshkosh, Wis., 1970-76, Iola (Wis.) Hosp., 1978-86, wellness cons., 1985-86, Riverside Med. Ctr., Waupaca, Wis., 1986—95, med. technologist, hematology supr., insvc. coord., 1987-95; pres. Pro Health Consul, Inc., Waupaca, Wis., 1994—; bus. ptnr., adminstr. Garden Park House, 1994—2000, owner, adminstr., 2000—; owner Back Door Bakery, 2003—, Secret Garden Cafe, 2003—. Tchr. Fox Valley Coll., Appleton, Wis., 1986, 87; organizer Overeaters Anonymous, Iola, 1985-89; owner Green Fountain Inn, 1995—; com. mem. Cmty Clinic, 2008- Mem. parent's com. gifted and talented Waupaca Sch. Sys., 1984, charter mem. edn. employment coun., 1989-92, mem. adv. com. guidance program K-12, 1992; vol. Nat. Wellness Inst., 1986-97, Am. Lung Assn., 1986-87; tchr. smokeless program Am. Inst. Preventative Medicine, 1988-93; com. mem. Main St. Design, 1999-01. Mem. NAFE, Nat. Platform Assn., Am. Sch. Health Assn. (com. mem.), Waupaca C. of C. (tourism com. 2002—, Athena award 2003), Rotary (sec. 1996-98, bd. dirs. 1995-04, 2006—, pres. 2000-01). Republican. Lutheran. Avocations: gardening, gourmet cooking, sailing, Bible study.

OESTERLE, ERIC ADAM, lawyer; b. Lafayette, Ind., Dec. 2, 1948; s. Eric Clark and Germaine Dora (Seelye) Oesterle; m. Carolyn Anne Scherer, Sept. 16, 1973; children: Adam Clark, Allison Margaret. BS, U. Mich., 1970, JD, 1973. Bar: Ill. 1973, US Dist. Ct. (no. dist.) Ill. 1973, US Ct. Appeals (7th cir.) 1987, US Supreme Ct. 1986. Assoc. Sonnenschein, Carlin, Nath & Rosenthal, Chgo., 1973—80; ptnr. Sonnenschein Nath & Rosenthal, Chgo., 1980—2007, Miller Shakman & Beem, LLP, Chgo., 2007—. Major gifts com. U. Mich. Law Sch., 2002—. Fellow: Am. Bar Found.; mem.: ABA, Chgo. Bar Assn. Home: 645 Lake Rd Glen Ellyn IL 60137-4249 Office: Miller Shakman and Beem LLP 180 N La Salle, Ste 3600 Chicago IL 60614 Business E-Mail: eoesterle@millershakman.com.

OESTERLE, STEPHEN N., medical products executive, cardiologist, educator; b. LaGrande, Oreg., Mar. 3, 1951; BA summa cum laude, Harvard Univ., 1973; MD, Yale Univ., 1977. Intern & resident Mass. Gen. Hosp., 1977—80; fellowship in cardiology Stanford Univ., 1981—83; cardiologist Good Samaritan Hosp., LA, 1986—91; cardiologist, med. educator Georgetown Univ., 1991—92; assoc. prof. med. & dir. cardiac catheterization & coronary intervention labs Stanford Univ. Med. Ctr., 1992—98; assoc. prof. med. Harvard Med. Sch., 1998—2002; dir. invasive cardiology svc. Mass. Gen. Hosp., 1998—2002; sr. v.p. medicine & tech. Medtronic Inc., Mpls., 2002—. Office: Medtronic Inc 710 Medtronic Pkwy Minneapolis MN 55432-5604

OESTERLIN, LOVYE GWENDOLYN, retired chemist, educator, retired educational consultant; b. Cheraw, SC, Aug. 26, 1932; d. John Eliot Davis and Lucile Monica (Davis) McIver; m. Rudolf Oesterlin, Dec. 29, 1956; children: Monika Oesterlin Wiltshire, Barbara Oesterlin Heath, Michael, Margrete Oesterlin Jean-Louis. BS, Bennett Coll., Greensboro, NC, 1953; MS, N.Mex. Highlands U., Las Vegas, 1966. Chem. technician Sloan-Kettering Inst., NYC, 1953; rsch. chemist sanitary engring. U. Calif., Berkeley, 1955—59; phys. sci. tchr. Hamilton Jr. H.S., Oakland, Calif., 1960—63; tchr. chemistry Columbia H.S., East Greenbush, NY, 1967—93, SUNY, Albany, 1988—93, ret., 1993; field supr. of student tchrs. Cabrini Coll., Radner, Pa., 1994—2001. Cons. State Edn. Dept., N.Y. State, Albany, NY, 1973—93. Recipient Belle Tobias award, Bennett Coll., 1949; grantee, NSF, 1960, 1962, 1981; Fulbright grant, State Dept., Washington, 1953. Mem.: NSTA (evaluator), Am. Chem. Soc., East Greenbush Tchrs. Assn., State Tchrs. Assn. N.Y. State (Sci. Fair dir.), Nat. Assn. Biology Tchrs. (dir.), Sci. Tchrs. Assn. N.Y. (rep. to bd. regents, Svc. award), The Links, Inc. (Svc. award), Delta Sigma Theta. Democrat. United Methodist. Avocations: reading, piano, quilting, travel, opera. Home Fax: 610-469-1047. E-mail: loveBBS@aol.com.

OESTREICH, CHARLES HENRY, retired university president; b. Columbus, Ohio, June 8, 1932; s. Henry F. and Martha (Schwartz) O.; m. Rhoda J. Haseley, Aug. 26, 1957; children: Martha, Mary, David. BS, Capital U., 1954; MS, Ohio U., 1956, PhD, 1961; LLD, Capital U., 1986. Instr. chemistry Va. Mil. Inst., 1956-57, Capital U., Columbus, 1960-62, asst. prof., 1962-64, assoc. prof., 1965-69; acad. dean Tex. Luth. U., Seguin, 1969-76, interim pres., 1976-77, pres., 1977-94, pres. emeritus Seguin, 1995—. Postdoctoral rsch. fellow Vanderbilt U., 1965-66 Bd. dirs., past pres. Mid-Tex. Symphony; bd. dirs. St. Luke's Health Ministries, Eden Home, Inc. Mem. Rotary (past pres. Seguin). Home and Office: 2269 S Abbey Loop New Braunfels TX 78130-8965 E-mail: charleso@satx.rr.com.

OESTREICH, DEAN, manufacturing executive; BS in Agronomy, U. Minn., 1974. Corn breeder Pioneer Hi-Bred Internat., Inc., 1974—80, various positions in information mgmt. for rsch., N.Am. sls. and supply mgmt., 1980—90, dir. worldwide parent seed, 1990—93, supply mgmt. dir., 1993—99, v.p. & dir. for Africa, Middle Ea., Asia and Pacific ops., 1999—2001, v.p. & dir. supply mgmt., 2001—02, v.p. & bus. dir. N. Am. ops., 2002—04, pres., 2004—07, chmn., 2007—, v.p., gen. mgr. DuPont. Dir. Chinese Cultural Ctr. of Am.; mem. Iowa Bus. Council; mem. exec. com. Biosciences Alliance of Iowa; trustee Civic Ctr. of Greater Des Moines. Mem.: Am. Seed Trade Assn. (dir.-at-large). Office: Pioneer Hi-Bred Internat Inc PO Box 1000 Johnston IA 50131-0184*

OETTGEN, HERBERT FRIEDRICH, physician; b. Cologne, Germany, Nov. 22, 1923; came to U.S., 1958; s. Peter and Minna (Kaul) O.; m. Trudi Hesberg, Feb. 16, 1957; children: Hans Christoph, Joerg Peter, Anne Barbara. MD, U. Cologne, 1951. Diplomate Bd. Internal Medicine, Fed. Republic of Germany. Resident in pathology City Hosp., Cologne, 1952-54, resident in medicine, 1955-58; fellow Meml. Sloan-Kettering Cancer Ctr., NYC, 1958-62, assoc. to assoc. mem., 1963-69, mem., 1972—, attending physician, 1971—; prof. medicine Cornell U. Med. Coll., NYC, 1972—. Assoc. dir. Cancer Rsch. Inst., N.Y.C., 1985—. Author over 350 publs. in hematology, cancer rsch., immunology and clin. oncology. Recipient award for cancer rsch. Wilhelm Warner Found., Hamburg, Fed. Republic Germany, 1970, Lisec-Artz award Friedrich Wilhelm U., Bonn, Fed. Republic of Germany, 1982. Presbyterian. Avocations: violin, woodworking. Home: 48 Overlook Dr New Canaan CT 06840-6825 Office: Meml Sloan-Kettering Cancer Ctr 1275 York Ave New York NY 10021-6094 Home Phone: 203-966-5709; Office Phone: 212-639-7505. Business E-Mail: oettgenh@mskcc.org, hoettgen@licr.org.

OETTGEN, J. PETER, cardiologist, researcher; came to U.S., 1963; s. Herbert F. and Gertrud Oettgen; m. Susan Elizabeth Purdy; children: C. Phillip, Thomas. MD, U. Conn., Farmington, 1987. Diplomate in cardiology Am. Bd. Medicine, 2003. Dir., preventive cardiology Beth Israel Deaconess Med. Ctr., Boston, 1997—2008, assoc. chief, molecular and vascular medicine, 2008—. Dir. Cardiovascular Health and Lipid Ctr., Beth Israel Hosp., Boston. Sarnoff fellow Sarnoff Found. for Cardiovascular Rsch., 1985-86. Fellow Am. Coll. Cardiology. Office: Beth Israel Deaconess Med Ctr 330 Brookline Ave RN-270D Boston MA 02115 Business E-Mail: joettgen@bidmc.harvard.edu.

OETTINGER, ANTHONY GERVIN, mathematician, educator; b. Nuremberg, Germany, Mar. 29, 1929; came to U.S., 1941, naturalized, 1947; s. Albert and Marguerite (Bing) O.; m. Marilyn Tanner, June 20, 1954; children: Douglas, Marjorie. AB, Harvard U., 1951, PhD, 1954; Henry fellow, U. Cambridge, Eng., 1951-52; Litt.D. (hon.), U. Pitts., 1984. Mem. faculty Harvard, 1955—, asso. prof. applied math., 1960-63, prof. linguistics, 1963-75, Gordon McKay prof. applied math., 1963—2007, chmn. program on info. resources policy, 1972—, mem. faculty of govt., 1973—2004, prof. info. resources policy, 1975—2007, rsch. prof., 2007—. Mem. command control comm. and intelligence bd. Dept. Navy, 1978-83; mem. sci. adv. group Def. Comm. Agy., 1979-90; chmn. bd. visitors Nat. Def. Intelligence Coll., 1986—; chmn., dir. Nat. Intelligence Sci. Adv. Bd., 1994—; cons. Arthur D. Little, Inc., 1956-80, Office Sci. and Tech., Exec. Office of Pres., 1960-73, Bellcomm, Inc., 1963-68, Sys. Devel. Corp., 1965-68, Nat. Security Coun., Exec. Office of Pres., 1975-81, Pres.'s Fgn. Intelligence Adv. Bd., 1981-90; chmn. Computer Sci. and Engring. Bd., Nat. Acad. Scis., 1968-73; mem. Mass. Cmty. Antenna TV Commn., 1972-79, chmn., 1975-79; mem. rsch. adv. bd. Com. for Econ. Devel., 1975-79; trustee Babbage Inst., 1991—; panel mem. Naval Studies Bd. NAS/NRC, 1993-95; mem. banking and fin. team Pres.' Commn. on Critical Infrastructure Protection, 1998; mem. Def. Sci. Bd., 2003—. Author: A Study for the Design of an Automatic Dictionary, 1954, Automatic Language Translation: Lexical and Technical Aspects, 1960, Run Computer Run: The Mythology of Educational Innovation, 1969, High and Low Politics: Information Resources for the 80s, 1977, Behind the Telephone Debates, 1988, Mastering the Changing Information World, 1993; editor: Proc. of a Symposium on Digital Computers and Their Applications, 1962; contbr. chpts. to The Information Resources Policy Handbook: Research for the Information Age, 1999. Fellow Am. Acad. Arts and Scis., AAAS, IEEE, Assn. Computing Machinery (mem. coun. 1961-68, chmn. com. U.S. Govt. Rels. 1964-66, editor computational linguistics sect. Commn. 1964-66, pres. 1966-68); mem. Soc. Indsl. and Applied Math. (mem. coun. 1963-67), Coun. on Fgn. Rels., Phi Beta Kappa, Sigma Xi. Clubs: Cosmos (Washington); Harvard (N.Y.C.). Home: 65 Elizabeth Rd Belmont MA 02478-3819 Office: Harvard U Maxwell Dworkin 125 33 Oxford St Cambridge MA 02138-2901 Office Phone: 617-495-4114. Business E-Mail: anthony@seas.harvard.edu.

O'FALLON, ANDREW STEVEN, software engineer, educator; b. Pullman, Wash., May 20, 1979; s. James V. and Elaine O'Fallon. MS in Computer Sci., Wash. State U., Pullman, 2004. Instr. software engring. Wash. State U., 2004—. Contractor Digilent Inc., Pullman, 2007—. Contbr. several conf. to profl. publs. Recipient Outstanding Tchg. Asst. in Computer Sci. award, Coll. Engring. and Architecture, Wash. State U., 2003, Outstanding Tchg. Computer Sci. award, 2006. Mem.: Sch. Elec. Engring. & Computer Sci. (excellent com. tchr.), Golden Key Nat. Honor Soc., Tau Bita Pi. Office: Washington State Univ EECS PO Box 642752 Pullman WA 99164-2752 Office Fax: 509-335-3818. Business E-Mail: aofallon@eecs.wsu.edu.

O'FARRELL, MARK THEODORE, religious organization administrator; b. Milw., Apr. 13, 1948; s. Theodore Wolfred and Ernestine (Shelhammer) O.; m. Phillis Gilley, Sept. 18, 1948; children: Gwen, Kevin. BA, Columbia Bible Coll., 1970; DD, Toccan Falls Coll., 1996. Asst. pastor 1st Alliance Ch., Macon, Ga., 1970-71, sr. pastor Port Charlotte, Fla., 1981-86, Belle Glade (Fla.) Alliance Ch., 1971-81; asst. to dist. supt., ext. dir. Southeastern Dist. of Christian and Missionary Alliance, Orlando, Fla., 1986-93, dist. supt., 1993—2005; pres. Trinity Coll. Fla., New Port Richey, 2005—. Recipient Spiritual Aims award Kiwanis, Antioch award Ch. Planting Nat. Office: Trinity Coll Fla 2430 Welbilt Blvd New Port Richey FL 34655 Office Phone: 727-376-6911.

O'FARRILL, ARTURO, composer; b. Havana, Cuba, Oct. 28, 1921; s. Arturo O'Farrill Alvarez and Teresa (Theye) Ajuria; m. Alison Deane; children: Zachary, Adam. Grad. high sch., Gainesville, Ga.; trained, Manhattan Sch. Music, Bklyn. Coll. Conservatory, Queens Coll. Aaron Copland Sch. Music. Pianist Carla Bley Big Band, 1979—83; composer, arranger Benny Goodman Orch., 1948-49, Stan Kenton Orch., Dizzy Gillespie Orch., Count Basie Orch., Machito Orch., others; dir. Chico O'Farrill's Afro-Cuban Jazz Orch., NYC, 1995; founder, dir. Afro Latin Jazz Orch., NYC, 2002—, Afro Latin Jazz Alliance, 2007—. Alan and Wendy Pesky artist in residence Lafayette Coll.; vis. artist Haystack Mountain Sch. Crafts, 2007; asst. prof. jazz U. Mass., Amherst, 2007—08; dir. Purchase Latin Jazz Orch. SUNY Purchase, 2008—. Numerous compositions for jazz ensembles, classical orchs., and chamber groups; alubms include Blood Lines, 1999, A Night in Tunisia, 2000, Cumana, 2004, Live in Brooklyn, 2005, Song for Chico, 2008 (Grammy award for Best Latin Jazz Album, 2009), In These Shoes, 2008. Recipient Outstanding Achievement award, Latin Jazz USA, 2003, Disting. Alumnus medal, Bklyn. Coll. Mem. ASCAP. Office: Afro Latin Jazz Alliance 364 14th St Brooklyn NY 11215-5010 also: SUNY Purchase Conservatory of Music 735 Anderson Hill Rd Purchase NY 10577*

OFFENBERGER, ALLAN ANTHONY, retired electrical engineering educator; b. Wadena, Sask., Can., Aug. 11, 1938; s. Ivy Viola (Hagglund) O. (dec.); m. Margaret Elizabeth Patterson, Apr. 12, 1963; children: Brian, Gary. BS, U. B.C., 1962, MS, 1963; PhD, MIT, 1968. Asst. prof. U. Alta., Edmonton, Canada, 1968—70, assoc. prof., 1970—75, prof., 1975—95, prof. emeritus, 1996—. Vis. prof. UK Atomic Energy Agy., Abingdon, Oxon, 1975-76, U. Oxford, UK, 1992, U. Osaka, Japan, 2000; project dir. Laser Fusion Project, Edmonton, 1984-91; mem. strategic adv. com. Nat. Fusion Program, Atomic Energy Can. Ltd., Chalk River, Ont., 1987-96; Cons. Lawrence Livermore Nat. Lab., Calif., 1996-2007; served on several execs. bds., sci. adv. and rsch. grant committees; hosted internat. scholars; invited lectr., cons. in field. Mem. editorial bd. Laser and Particle Beams, 1987-2004; contbr. over 150 sci. articles on lasers and plasma physics Killam Rsch. fellow Can. Coun., 1980-82. SERC rsch. fellow, Eng., 1992. Mem. Can. Assn. Physicists (exec. officer, v.p. elect 1987-88, pres. 1989-90), Am. Phys. Soc., Sigma Xi. Achievements include establishing a major center for high power laser research and development (particularly krypton fluoride lasers) for fusion energy and other applications. Home: 412 Lessard Dr Edmonton AB Canada T6M 1A7 Office: U Alta Dept Elec Computer Engring Edmonton AB Canada T6G 2V4 Office Phone: 780-492-3939. Business E-Mail: aao@ece.ualberta.ca.

OFFEREINS, DIANE M., finance company executive; BBA, Loyola Univ., New Orleans. Positions through v.p., dir. application devel. Southeast Bank, Miami, Fla.; v.p. retail delivery systems Bank of Am., San Francisco; sr. exec. v.p. MBNA Am.; exec. v.p., CIO Discover Fin. Services, Riverwoods, Ill., 1999—2005, exec. v.p., chief adminstrv. & tech. officer, 2005—. Bd. mem. Loretto Hosp. Found. Named one of Top 20 Nonbank Women in Fin., US Banker, 2008. Office: Discover Fin Services 2500 Lake Cook Rd Riverwoods IL 60015*

OFFIELD, MARTIN F., biology professor; b. Ft. Worth, Tex., Dec. 14, 1965; s. Claud F. and Betty J. Offield; m. Donna L. Hart, Apr. 25, 1992. BS, Liberty U., Lynchburg, Va., 1988; PhD, Vanderbilt U., Nashville, 1996. Rsch. scientist U. Va., Charlottesville, 1996—2002; assoc. prof. Liberty U., 2002—. Contbr. articles to profl. jours. including Trends in Genetics. Mem.: Soc. Devel. Biology. Achievements include research in mouse and frog genetics. Office: Liberty Univ 1971 University Blvd Lynchburg VA 24502 Office Fax: 434-582-2488.

OFFIT, MORRIS WOLF, investment company executive; b. Balt., Jan. 22, 1937; s. Michael and Rhea (Wolf) O.; m. Nancy Silverman, Nov. 26, 1959; children: Ned S., Daniel W. BA in History, Johns Hopkins U., 1957, LHD (hon.), 1996; MBA in Fin., U. Pa., 1959. V.p. investment dept. Mercantile Safe Deposit and Trust, Balt., 1960—68; gen. ptnr. Salomon Bros. Inc., NYC, 1968-80; pres. Julius Baer Securities, NYC, 1980-82; now CEO Offit Hall Capital Mgmt. LLC, 2002—; CEO Offit Assoc. Inc., NYC, 1983—2001. Trustee, former chmn. bd. trustees Johns Hopkins U.; chmn. adv. coun. Nitze Sch. Advanced Internat. Studies; trustee Jewish Mus., former chmn.; trustee Jewish Theol. Sem., Thirteen-WNET, United Jewish Appeal Fedn. N.Y., Am. Jewish Com. Mem. Coun. on Fgn. Rels. Office: Offit Hall Capital Mgmt LLC 65 E 55th St New York NY 10022

OFFIT, PAUL ALLAN, pediatrician; b. Balt., 1951; BS in Psychology, Tufts U., 1973; MD, U. Md. Sch. Medicine, 1977. Cert. Pediat. Resident, pediat. Children's Hosp., Pitts., 1977—80, chief, divsn. infectious diseases Phila., 1982—, dir., Vaccine Edn. Ctr.; prof. pediat. U. Pa. Sch. Medicine, Maurice R. Hilleman Prof. Vaccinology. Mem. adv. com. on immunization practices Ctr. for Disease Control. Contbr. several articles to profl. jours.; co-author: Breaking the Antibiotic Habit: A Parent's Guide to Coughs, Colds, Ear Infections, and Sore Throats, 1999, Vaccines: What Every Parent Should Know, 1999, Vaccine Handbook: A Practical Guide for Clinicians, 2003, Vaccines: What You Should Know, 3rd edit., 2003; author: Cutter Incident: How America's First Polio Vaccine Led to Today's Growing Vaccine Crisis, 2005, Vaccinated: One Man's Quest to Defeat the World's Deadliest Diseases, 2007, Autism's False Prophets: Bad Science, Risky Medicine, and the Search for a Cure, 2008. Recipient J. Edmund Bradley prize for Excellence in Pediat., U. Md. Med. Sch., Young Investigator award in Vaccine Develop., Infectious Diseases Soc. Am., Rsch. Career Develop. award, NIH. Achievements include being co-inventor of a rotavirus vaccine, RotaTeq. Office: Divsn Infectious Diseases Abramson Rsch Bldg Rm 1202D 34th St and Civic Center Blvd Philadelphia PA 19104 Office Phone: 215-590-2020. Office Fax: 215-590-2025. Business E-Mail: offit@email.chop.edu.*

OFFIT, SIDNEY, writer, educator; b. Balt., Oct. 13, 1928; s. Barney and Lillian (Cohen) O.; m. Avodah Crindell Komito, Aug. 8, 1952; children: Kenneth, Michael Robert. BA, Johns Hopkins U., Balt., 1950; DHL (hon.), LI U., 1999. Editorial staff Mercury Publs., NYC, 1952-53, Macfadden Publs., NYC, 1953-54; contbg. editor Baseball mag., Washington, 1955-58; faculty NYU, 1964—2003; assoc. editor Intellectual Digest, 1970-72, sr. editor, 1972-74; adj. prof. creative writing NYU, 1977—2003. Lectr. creative writing New Sch. U., 1965—; curator George Polk Awards for Journalism, 1977—; commentator Channel 5 TV, NYC, 1975-85, Channel 11 TV, 1992. Author: He Had it Made, 1959, The Other Side of the Street, 1962, Soupbone, 1963, Topsy Turvey, 1965, The Adventure of Homer Fink, 1966, The Boy Who Made a Million, 1968; short stories Not All the Girls Have Million Dollar Smiles, 1971; Only a Girl Like You, 1972, What Kind of Guy Do You Think I Am?, 1977, Memoir of the Bookie's Son, 1995, Friends, Writers and Other Countrymen, 2008; book editor: Politics Today, 1978-80. Selection com. Dist. Sch. Bd., NYC, 1968; exec. bd. Lexington Democratic Club, 1957-60, NY Dem. County Com., 1966-; chmn. 19th Precinct Cmty. Coun. NYC, 1964-80. Recipient Disting. Alumni award Valley Forge Mil. Acad., 1961, Otty Cmty. Svc. award, 1975, Tchg. Excellence award NYU, 1981, commendation for achievment as teacher, scholar, communicator NY State Legislature, 1983, proclamation for contbns. to city, NYC Coun., 1983, Police Athletic League citation for svc. to children of NYC, 1991, 96, 2002, 04, Honors Convocation award Marymount Manhattan Coll., 1994, Detlev W. Bronk award Johns Hopkins Alumni Assn., 1994, Disting. Univ. Tchg. award New Sch. U., 2000, Poets and Writers award Writers for Writers, 2005 Mem. Tudor and Stuart Club, Authors Guild Found. (pres. 1993—), Authors Guild (coun. 1970-77, 79—, v.p. 1993-95), Authors League (nat. coun. 1976-), Authors League Fund (v.p. 1998—, acting pres. 2004-05), Am. Ctr. PEN (exec. com. 1969, 2003—, v.p. 1970-74, internat. del. 1971-72, 74), Club Century Assn.(NYC), Coffee House Club (NYC). Home: 23 E 69th St New York NY 10021-4919 *I have been guided by a strong devotion to my family and friends and moderate ambition. In both these priorities I have been influenced by my parents. With my writing I have tried to fulfill my own needs, and for the most I have been satisfied by the reception. I do not aspire to fame or great fortune, and this leaves me free to enjoy the sharing of experiences with my friends and family. I consider myself a lucky man and this keeps me grateful to whatever forces there are that contrive man's fortune.*

OFFNER, ERIC DELMONTE, lawyer; b. Vienna, June 23, 1928; came to U.S., 1941, naturalized, 1949; s. Sigmund J. and Kathe (Delmonte) O.; m. Julie Cousins, 1955 (dec. 1959); m. Barbara Ann Shotton, July 2, 1961; 1 son, Gary Douglas; m. Carol Sue Marcus, Jan. 12, 1980 (dec. 1983) BBA, CCNY, 1949; JD in Internat. Affairs, Cornell U., 1952. Bar: NY 1952. Assoc. Langner, Parry, Card & Langner, NYC, 1952-57; ptnr. Haseltine, Lake, Waters & Offner, NYC, 1957-77; sr. ptnr. Offner & Kuhn, 1978-83; pvt. practice NYC, 1965—. Instr. George Washington U. Law Sch., Cornell U. Law Sch.; spl. prof. law Hofstra Law Sch., 1974-92; jazz disc jockey ProgressiveRadioNetwork.org.; jazz record prodr. Author: International Trademark Protection, 1964, Japanese edit., 1977, International Trademark Service, Vols. I-III 1970, Vol. IV, 1972, Vol. V., 1973, Vol. VI, 1976, Vol. VII, 1981, Vols. I-VII, 2d edit., 1981, Legal Training Course on Trademarks, 1982; editor in chief: Cornell Law Forum, 1950-51; mem. editorial bd.: Trademark Reporter, 1961-64, 69-72; book reviewer Jour. Humanism and Ethical Religion; contbr. articles to profl. jours.; prodr. jazz concerts N.Y.C., 1996—, jazz video and jazz CDs. V.p. Riverdale Mental Health Clinic, N.Y.C., 1966-67; pres. Riverdale Mental Health Assn., 1967-69, pres. Ethical Culture Soc., Riverdale-Yonkers, 1964-67, pres. Ethical Cultural Retirement Ctr., 1975-94; trustee Am. Ethical Union, 1967-73, Internat. Alliance of Holistic Lawyers; bd. dirs. Fit Kids; pres. The Sidney Bechet Soc., Ltd., 1997—. Mem. N.Y. Patent Law Assn. (assoc. editor Bull. 1961-66, gov. 1973-76), ABA, City N.Y. Bar Assn. (sec. 1962-64), U.S. Trademark Assn., World Peace Through Law (charter), Trademark Soc. Washington (charter), Inst. Trade Mark Agts. (London), Sidney Bechet Soc. Ltd. (pres. 1997—), Australian Patent Inst., Internat. Assn. Protection Indsl. Property, Nat. Coun. Patent Law Assn., Internat. Patent, Trademark Assn., Phi Alpha Delta. Home: 20 Joy Dr New Hyde Park NY 11040-1109 Office Phone: 516-627-6334. Personal E-mail: eoffner@optonline.net. *Do unto others so as to elicit the best in them and thereby the best in yourself.*

OFLAZOGLU, EZOGELIN, oncologist, science administrator; PhD, SUNY, Buffalo, Roswell Pk. Cancer Inst., 2002. Grad. rsch. assoc. Roswell Pk. Cancer Inst., 1997—2002; postdoc. scientist Immunex, Amgen, Seattle, 2002—04; scientist Seattle Genetics, Inc., Bothell, Wash., 2004—06, sr. scientist, 2006—08, program mgr., 2008—. Adj. prof. Seattle U., 2007. Mem.: Drug Info. Assn., Am. Assn. Immunologist, Am. Assn. Cancer Rsch. Achievements include research in cancer, autoimmune and inflammatory disease; patents for methods of treating neoplastic, autoimmune and inflammatory diseases. Office: Seattle Genetics Inc 21823 30th Dr SE Bothell WA 98021 Business E-Mail: eoflazoglu@seagen.com.

OFNER, WILLIAM BERNARD, investor, speechwriter; b. LA, Aug. 24, 1929; s. Harry D. and Gertrude (Skoss) Ofner; m. Florence Ila Maxwell, Apr. 13, 1953 (div. 1956). AA, LA City Coll., 1949; BA, Calif. State U., LA, 1953; JD, Loyola U., LA, 1965; postgrad., Sorbonne, 1951, U. So. Calif., 1966, Glendale CC, 1986-92; cert. de Langue Francaise, 1987. Bar: Calif. 1966, U.S. Dist. Ct. Calif. 1966, U.S. Supreme Ct. 1972. Assoc. Thomas Moore and Assoc., LA, 1967-69; pvt. practice LA, 1969-70, 74—; assoc. Peter Lam, LA, 1981-94, mng. atty., 1993—99. Assoc. C. M. Coronel, 1986—87, Jack D. Janofsky, 1987—89, Mario P. Gonzalez, 1990—92, Genaro Legorreta, Jr., 1997—98; lectr. Van Norman U., 1975; property mgr., 1982—2004; investor, 1984—; speechwriter, 2008—. Electronics instr. USNR, 1949—54. Mem.: LA Fitness Athletic Club, Inst. Gen. Semantics, Toastmasters. Democrat. Avocations: photography, linguistics, tutoring, painting, walking. Office: 2935 E Chino Ave Ste E-5 Chino Hills CA 91709 Home Phone: 909-590-4484.

OFTE, DONALD, retired nuclear energy industry executive; b. NYC, Aug. 23, 1929; s. Sverre and Ingeborg Ofte; m. Margaret Mae McHenney, July 23, 1955; children: Marc Christian, Nancy Carolyn Appleby, Kirk Donald Jr. BA in Chemistry, Dana Coll., 1952; postgrad. study metall. engring., Ohio State U., 1958-60. Jr. chemist Inst. Atomic Rsch., Ames, Iowa, 1952-53; sr. rsch. chemist Monsanto Rsch. Corp., Miamisburg, Ohio, 1958-66; ops. engr. AEC, Miamisburg, 1966-69, br. chief, div. dir. ops. office Albuquerque, 1969-73, mgr. Pinellas area office Largo, Fla., 1973-79; mgr. Rocky Flats area office Dept. Energy, Golden, Colo., 1979-82, asst. mgr. devel. and prodn. Albuquerque, 1982-83, dep. mgr. ops. office, 1983-84; prin. dep. asst. sec. Dept. Energy Defense Programs, Washington, 1984-87; mgr. ops. office Dept. Energy, Idaho Falls, Idaho, 1987-89; mgmt. cons. Idaho Falls, 1990—92; v.p. govt. ops. United Engrs. & Constructors (Raytheon Engrs. & Constrn.), Denver, 1992-93; v.p. Adv. Scis., Inc., Albuquerque, 1993-94; pres. FERMCO (also known as Fluor Daniel, Fernald), Cin., 1994-96; chmn., bd. mgrs. Washington Group BWXT Oper. Svcs., LLC, 2004—05; ret. V.p. Fluor-Daniel, Inc., 1994—96; affiliate prof. Idaho State U., 1990—92; cons. in field. Author: (with others) Plutonium 1960, 1965, Physicochemical Methods in Metals Research; contbr. articles to profl. jours. on metallurgy and ceramics. Campaign chmn. United Way Pinellas, St. Petersburg, Fla., 1978; vice chmn. Denver Fed. Exec. Bd., 1981; bd. dirs. Bonneville County United Way, Idaho Rsch. Found.; mem. adv. bd. Teton Peaks Council Boy Scouts of Am., 1987-92, Eastern Idaho Tech. Coll.; chmn. Excellence in Edn. Fund Com., 1990-92; vice chmn., bd. dirs. Rio Grande Ch. ARC, Albuquerque, 1982-84; trustee, bd. dirs. Nat. Atomic Mus., 1999—2003. Served to lt. (j.g.) USN, 1953-57. Recipient citation AEC for Apollo 12 SNAP 27 Radioisotope Generator, 1969, High Quality Performance award AEC, 1968, Group Achievement award NASA, 1972; Meritorious Svc. award Dept. Energy, 1985, Disting. Career Svc. award, 1989. Mem. Am. Chem. Soc. (emeritus), Am. Nuclear Soc., Am. Soc. Metals, Nat. Contract Mgmt. Assn., Am. Soc. Pub. Adminstrs., Suncoast Archeol. Soc., Idaho

Falls C. of C. (bd. dirs., cmty. svc. award 1990), Rotary Internat. (Paul Harris fellow). Avocations: reading, bridge, gardening, golf. Home: 1129 Salamanca St NW Albuquerque NM 87107-5643 Personal E-mail: dofte@aol.com.

OGAN, RUSSELL GRIFFITH, real estate broker; b. Reading, Pa., Nov. 20, 1923; s. Russell John and Edna Gwendlyn (Griffith) O.; m. Gloria Mae Withers, Oct. 30, 1943; children: Susan Ann (Mrs. Greg Gunn), Russell Lee. Student, Wyomissing Polytech. Inst., 1942, Air Command Staff Coll., 1948; grad., Nat. War Coll., 1963. Enlisted as pvt. U.S. Army, 1942; advanced through grades to brig. gen. USAF, 1970; fighter squadron comdr. Dover AFB, Del., 1951; dir. combat operations (11th Air Div.), Ladd AFB, Alaska, 1951-53; dir. (Combat Operations Center), Hamilton AFB, Calif., 1953-56; with (Hdqrs. Air Def. Command), Ent AFB, Colo., 1956-60; dir. (Aerospace Def. Systems Office, Air Force Ballistic Missile Div.), 1960-62; from dep. dir. plans to comdr. Sector Operation Ctr. NATO, Germany, 1963-66; dep. dir. personnel data and records (USAF Mil. Personnel Center), Randolph AFB, Tex., 1966-68; comdr. 71st Missile Warning Wing, then vice comdr. (14th Aerospace Force), Ent AFB, Colo., 1968-71; dep. dir. personnel programs Hdqrs. USAF, Washington, 1971-72; dir. Prisoner of War and Missing in Action Affairs, Office Sec. Def., Washington, 1972-74; former pres. Vacation Interval Mktg.; real estate broker Fishermen's Village, Punta Gorda, Fla. Decorated D.S.M., Legion of Merit with bronze oak leaf cluster, Air medal with 1 silver and 1 bronze oak leaf cluster. Mem. Daedalians, T.R.O.A., Kingsway Country Club. Flew 62 missions as fighter pilot over France and Germany, 1944-45. Home (Winter): 12413 SW Kingsway Cir Lake Suzy FL 34269 Personal E-mail: ogan43@aol.com.

O'GARA, PATRICK THOMAS, internist, cardiovascular physician; b. Chgo., Apr. 17, 1952; s. Thomas E. and Eileen L. (Lamb) O.; m. Laura A. Daniel, Oct. 10, 1981, children: Brian, Grady, Katherine. BA, Yale U., 1974; MD, Northwestern U., 1978. Diplomate Am. Bd. Internal Medicine, Am. Bd. Cardiovascular Medicine. Intern in med. Mass. Gen. Hosp., Boston, 1978—79, resident in internal med., 1979—81, fellow in cardiology, 1981-83, chief resident internal medicine, 1984; rsch. fellow Nat. Heart Lung and Blood Inst./NIH, 1985-86; assoc. prof. medicine Harvard Med. Sch., Boston; dir. clinical cardiology Brigham & Womens Hosp., Boston, vice-chmn. clinical affairs dept. medicine. Co-editor Cardiology in Review; mem. editl. bd. Chest. Fellow: AHA (mem. sci. advance com.), Am. Coll. Cardiology (bd. trustees). Office: Brigham & Womens Hosp Cardiovasc Divsn 75 Francis St Boston MA 02115 Office Phone: 857-307-1990. Office Fax: 857-307-1955. Business E-Mail: pogara@partners.org.

OGARD, KAREN, investment advisor, financial planner; b. Duluth, Minn., Sept. 17, 1957; d. Norris and Sofia Ogard. BSBA, U. N.D., 1979. CFP. Joined A.G. Edwards and Sons, Cheyenne, Wyo., 1983, sr. v.p. investments, CFP Englewood, Colo. Bd. dirs. Credit Union, Cheyenne, Wyo., 1981-83; tchr. adult edn. cmty. colls., 1983-85; lectr., spkr. in field. Contbr. Rsch. Cancer Found., Safe House, and others, 1979—; youth group leader Good Shepherd Ch., Englewood, 1994-95; bd. dirs., fund raiser Kenyan Children's Found., Denver, 1998—. Named one of The Top 100 Women Fin. Advisors, Barron's, 2008. Mem. Internat. Bd. CFPs, Zonta Club, Milestone Club. Avocations: water-skiing, boating, theater, travel. Office: Ag Edwards 1200 17th St Ste 2500 Denver CO 80202-5837

O'GARDEN, IRENE, writer, actress; b. Mpls., Dec. 23, 1951; d. Donald Edward and Betty O'Brien; m. John Leonard Pielmeier, Oct. 9, 1982. BA in Theatre and English, U. Minn., 1974; grad. student, State Coll. Pa., 1996. Actress Guthrie Theatre, Mpls., 1975—76; freelance actress NYC, 1976—80. Bd. dirs. Philipstown Performing Arts, Garrison, NY, Periwinkle Theatre Youth; sec. Philipstown Performing Arts; founder, host Art Garden Seasonal Peforming Literary Mag., 1987—; creator various writing workshops, Giving Voice Monologue Writing Workshop. Author (illustrator): Fat Girl: One Woman's Way Out, 1993; author: Maybe My Baby, 1995, The Scrubbly Bubbly Carwash, 2003 (Best Book award, 2004, Alice Curtis Desmond Children's Lit. award, 2009), (plays) Women On Fire, 2003—04 (nominee Lucille Lortel award, 2004), Little Heart, 2006; performer (poetry): Nuyorican Poets Cafe, Bowery Poetry Club, Hudson Valley Poet's Festival; contbr. poetry to jours.; performer: (films) The Capture of the Green River Killer (Lifetime Movie Network). Grantee, Poets and Writers, N.Y., 1984, 1985, 1997, 2003, 2005; Berilla Kerr Playwrighting fellow, Millay Colony Arts, 2004, New Harmony Play Project fellow, 2005. Mem.: Philipstown Depot Theatre (bd. mem.), Periwinkle Theatre Youth (bd. mem.), Soc. of Scribes, The Authors Guild, The Dramatists Guild, Actors Equity Assn. Avocations: calligraphy, bookbinding, gardening.

OGATA, KATSUHIKO, engineering educator; b. Tokyo, Jan. 6, 1925; came to U.S., 1952; s. Fukuhei and Teruko (Yasaki) O.; m. Asako Nakamura, Sept. 6, 1961; 1 son, Takahiko. BS, U. Tokyo, 1947; MS, U. Ill., 1953; PhD, U. Calif., Berkeley, 1956. Research asst. Sci. Research Inst., Tokyo, 1948-51; fuel engr. Nippon Steel Tube Co., Tokyo, 1951-52; mem. faculty U. Minn., 1956—, prof. mech. engring., 1961—; prof. elec. engring. Yokohama Nat. U., 1960-61, 64-65, 68-69. Author: State Space Analysis of Control Systems, 1967, Modern Control Engineering, 1970, 2009, Dynamic Programming, 1973, Ingenieria de Control Moderna, 1974, 1998, Metody Przestrzeni Stanow w Teorii Sterowania, 1974, System Dynamics, 1978, 2003, Engenharia de Controle Moderno, 1982, 2003, Teknik Kontrol Automatik, 1985, Discrete-Time Control Systems, 1986, 1995, Gendai Seigyo Riron, 1986, Dinamica de Sistemas, 1987, Solving Control Engineering Problems with MATLAB, 1994, Gendai Seigyo Kogaku, 1994, Designing Linear Control Systems with MATLAB, 1994, Kejuruteraan Kawalan Moden, 1996, Sistemas de Control en Tiempo Discreto, 1996, Projeto de Sistemas Lineares de Controle com MATLAB, 1996, Solucao de Problemas de Engenharia de Controle com MATLAB, 1997, MATLAB for Control Engineers, 2007. Recipient Outstanding Adv. award Inst. of Tech., U. Minn., 1981, John R. Ragazzini Edn. award Am. Automatic Control Coun., 1999. Fellow ASME; mem. Sigma Xi, Pi Tau Sigma. Personal E-mail: kogata02@comcast.net.

OGATA, SHIJURO, retired central banker; b. Tokyo, Nov. 16, 1927; s. Taketora and Koto (Hara) O.; m. Sadako Nakamura, Jan. 21, 1961; children: Atshushi, Akiko. BA, U. Tokyo, 1950; MA, Fletcher Sch. of Law/Diplomacy, 1955. Joined Bank of Japan, 1950, asst. rep. in London, 1962—64, rep. in New York, 1975—78, adv. to Gov., 1978—79, dir. Fgn. Dept., 1979—81, exec. dir., 1981—84, dep. gov. internat. rels. Tokyo, 1984-86; dep. gov. Japan Devel. Bank, Tokyo, 1986-91; dir. Barclays PLC & Barclays Bank PLC, London, 1991-95, Fuji Xerox, 1991—2001; advisor in Japan Swire Group, London, 1991-98, Yamaichi Securities, 1991—97; co-chmn. Study Grp. on UN Financing, 1992—93; chmn. Barclays Trust & Banking Co. (Japan) Ltd., 1993-97; dir. Horiba, Kyoto, 1995—2006; mem. internat. coun. JPMorganChase, NYC, 2001—02; auditor Fuji Xerox, 2001—02. Advisor Imperial Hotel, Tokyo, 1991-2001. Contbr. numerous articles to profl. jours. Recipient Japan Soc. award, 1992. Mem. Group of Thirty. Avocations: reading, writing. Home: 3-29-18 Denenchofu Tokyo 145-0071 Japan

OGAWA, AYAKO, language educator, writer; b. Saihaku-cho, Tottori Prefacture, Japan, Feb. 20, 1938; arrived in US, 1990; d. Haruzo and Yaeko Endo; m. Tadaaki Ogawa, Nov. 6, 1961; 1 child, Yuki. EdD, U. Cin., 1998. Dir. Xavier U., Cin., 1992—97, instr. Japanese program, 1992—97; dir. Japanese lang. program Raymond Walters Coll, U. Cin., 2007—, asst. prof. Japanese lang. program, 2007—. Author: (novels) Across the Milky Way, (travel) See You at the Opposite Ends of the Globe, (essay book) Still Waters Run Deep I, Still Waters Run Deep II, Suddenly like a flame; contbr. scientific papers. Recipient Pres. award, World Coun. Curriculum Instrn., 1998. Mem.: Japan Internat. Edn. Soc. Avocations: travel, writing.

OGDEN, C(HESTER) ROBERT, insurance company executive; b. Clarksburg, W.Va., Aug. 11, 1923; s. Daniel Miller and Mary Elizabeth (Maphis) O.; m. Margaret Ellen Martin; children: David M., Robert J., Douglas H. SB, Harvard U., 1946; vet.'s cert., Harvard Bus. Sch., 1947; JD, Yale U., 1950. Bar: N.Y, 1952, Wash., 1957. Assoc. Chadbourne & Park, NYC, 1950-53, Hawkins, Delafield & Wood, NYC, 1953-57, Preston, Thorgrimson & Horowitz, Seattle, 1957-58; v.p. R.J. Martin & Co./R.J. Martin Mortgage Co., Spokane, Wash., 1958-84; pres. R.J. Martin Mortgage Co., Spokane, 1984—; exec. v.p. Great N.W. Life Ins. Co., Spokane, 1963, pres., 1964; pres., gen. counsel North Coast Life Ins. Co., Spokane, 1965—2007, chmn. bd., 2007—. Mem. Nat. Adv. Coun. US Regional Med. Programs, US Dept. HEW, 1973-74, Spokane City County Historic Landmarks Commn., 1988-96, chmn., 1991-96; bd. dirs. Wash. Trust for Historic Preservation, 1989-95; pres. Spokane Cmty. Found., 1981-83, Spokane Rotary, 1978, Spokane Symphony, 1983-85, mem., 1958-; bd. mem. 1978-85, Wash. Alaska Regional Med. Program, 1966-74, chmn. 1969-73; pres. bd. St. George's Sch., Spokane, 1972-76; sec. Wash. State Republician Ctrl. Commn., 1973-75. 1st lt. USAAC, 1943-45, ETO. Mem. ABA, Wash. State Bar Assn., Spokane Club. Republican. Episcopalian. Home: 216 W Sumner Ave Spokane WA 99204-3651 Office: North Coast Life Ins Co 1116 W Riverside Ave Spokane WA 99201-1198 Office Phone: 509-838-4235.

OGDEN, DANIEL MILLER, JR., public official, educator; b. Clarksburg, W.Va., Apr. 28, 1922; s. Daniel Miller and Mary (Maphis) O.; m. Valeria Juan Munson, Dec. 28, 1946; children: Janeth Lee Martin, Patricia Jo Hunter, Daniel Munson. BA in Polit. Sci., Wash. State U., 1944; MA, U. Chgo., 1947, PhD, 1949. From instr. to assoc. prof. Wash. State U., Pullman, 1949-61; staff asst. resources program U.S. Dept. Interior, 1961-64; asst. dir. U.S. Bur. Outdoor Recreation, 1964-67; dir. budget U.S. Dept. Interior, Washington, 1967-68; dean Coll. Humanities and Social Scis. Colo. State U., Ft. Collins, 1968-76; disting. vis. prof. Lewis and Clark Coll. and Portland (Oreg.) State U., 1977-78; dir. Office of Power Mktg. Coordination U.S. Dept. Energy, 1978-84; mgr. Pub. Power Coun., Portland, Oreg., 1984-88, ret., 1988. Mem. profl. staff com. interstate and fgn. commerce U.S. Senate, 1956-57; spll. asst. to chmn. Dem. Nat. Com., 1960-61; lectr. Mgmt. Devel. Ctrs., U.S. Office Pers. Mgmt., 1966-2004. Co-author: Electing the President, rev. edit., 1968, American National Government, 7th edit., 1970, American State and Local Government, 5th edit., 1972, Washington Politics, 1960, How National Policy is Made, 7th edit., 2009. Committeeman Wash. Dem. Ctrl. Com., 1952-56; chmn. Whitman County Dem. Ctrl. Com., 1958-60; chmn. 49th Legis. Dist. Dem. Com., 1990-94; chmn. Clark County Dem. Ctrl. com., 1994-98, 1999-2000, vice chair, 1998-99. With inf. U.S. Army, 1943-46. Mem. Phi Beta Kappa, Phi Kappa Phi, Pi Sigma Alpha, Sigma Delta Chi. Mem. Unitarian Ch. Home: 2916 NE 88th Ct Vancouver WA 98662-6836 Office Phone: 360-254-8886.

OGDEN, DAVID WILLIAM, federal agency administrator; b. Washington, Nov. 12, 1953; s. Horace Greeley and Elaine Celia (Condrell) O.; children: Jonathan Smith, Elaine Smith. BA summa cum laude, U. Pa., 1976; JD magna cum laude, Harvard U., 1981. Bar: D.C. 1983, Va. 1986, U.S. Dist. Ct. D.C. 1984, U.S. Dist. Ct. (ea. dist.) Va. 1988, U.S. Ct. Appeals (D.C. cir.) 1984, U.S. Ct. Appeals (4th cir.) 1986, U.S. Ct. Appeals (1st cir.) 1989, U.S. Ct. Appeals (10th cir.) 1991, U.S. Supreme Ct. 1987, U.S. Ct. Appeals (5th and 9th cirs.) 2000. Law clk. to Hon. Abraham D. Sofaer US Dist. Ct. (so. dist.) N.Y., NYC, 1981-82; law clk. to Assoc. Justice Harry A. Blackmun US Supreme Ct., Washington, 1982-83; assoc. atty. Ennis, Friedman, Bersoff & Ewing, Washington, 1983-85; ptnr. Ennis, Friedman & Bersoff, Washington, 1986-88, Jenner & Block, Washington, 1988-94; legal counsel, dep. gen. counsel US Dept. Def., Washington, 1994-95; assoc. dep. atty. gen. US Dept. Justice, Washington, 1995-97, counselor to the atty. gen., 1997-98, chief of staff to atty. gen., 1998-99, acting asst. atty. gen. for civil divsn., 1999-2000, asst. atty. gen. for civil divsn., 2000-2001, dep. atty. gen., 2009—; ptnr., co-chair, govt. & regulatory litigation practice group Wilmer Hale (formerly Wilmer Cutler Pickering Hale and Dorr LLP), Washington, 2001—09. Adj. prof. law Georgetown U. Law Ctr., 1992-95. Author: (with Jerald A. Jacobs) Legal Risk Management for Associations, 1995. Recipient Disting. Pub. Svc. medal US Dept. Def., 1995, Atty. Gen.'s medallion, US Dept Justice, 1999, Edmund J. Randolph award in Recognition of Outstanding Svc. US Dept. Justice, 2001, The Nat. Law Jour. Pro Bono award, 2006; named of the Top Washington Lawyers Washington Bus. Jour., 2006; named a Washington DC Super Lawyer, 2007 Mem. ABA, Am. Bar Found., D.C. Bar Assn., Phi Beta Kappa. Democrat. Office: US Dept Justice 950 Pennsylvania Ave NW Rm 4111 Washington DC 20530 Office Phone: 202-514-2101.

OGDEN, JOHN CLIFTON, III, environmental scientist, director; b. Nashville, Tenn., Nov. 18, 1938; s. John Clifton Ogden, Jr. and Mary Ruth McKay; m. Maryanne Biggar, Sept. 12, 1975; m. Mary Ann Hollingsworth (div.); children: Laura Ann, Nicholas Alan. BA, George Peabody Coll., Nashville, 1961. Rsch. biologist Nat. Pk. Svc., Homestead, Fla., 1965—74, chair ecology working team, Man & the Biosphere Everglades team, 1993—94, coord. Fish & Wildlife Svc. wood stork recovery group, 1988—90, sr. rsch. scientist, 1988—95; mem. Fish & Wildlife Svc. crocodile recovery team Nat. Audubon Soc., Tavernier, Fla., 1974—78, sr. rsch. biologist, 1974—88, pres., Colonial Waterbird Soc., 1976—79, co-dir. Calif. condor recovery program Ventura, 1980—85, mem. Fish & Wildlife Svc. condor recovery team, 1980—88, dir. ornithol. rsch. unit Tavernier, Fla., 1986—88; adj. prof. U. Miami, Rosensteil Sch. Marine & Atmospheric Sci., 1996—2001; lead environ. scientist South Fla. Water Mgmt. Dist., West Palm Beach, 1995—2003; co-chair sci. coordination team South Fla. Ecosystem Restoration Task Force, West Palm Beach, 2003—04; chief environ. scientist South Fla. Water Mgmt. Dist., West Palm Beach, 2003—. Co-editor: (Everglades sci. rev.) Everglades. The Ecosystem and its Restoration, 1994; author: (two book chapts.) Monitoring Systems: Interdisciplinary Approaches, 2003; author: (lead coord.) 13 papers in Wetlands Jour., 2005; author: (and co-editor) (conf. proceedings) Wading Birds, National Aubudon Society Report 7, 1972; author: (and sr. editor) Transactions North American Osprey Conference, 1978; author: (and co-author) White Stork. Status and Conservation, 1980. Mem. Fla. Ornithol. Soc., 1986—88. Recipient Ann. Conservationist of Yr., Everglades Coalition, 1994, Disting. Svc. award, Colonial Waterbird Soc., 1996, Palladium medal, Am. Assn. Civil Engrs. & Nat. Audubon Soc., 1999, Charles Brookfield award for Exceptional Contbn. to South Fla. Conservation, Tropical Audubon Soc., 2004; fellow, Fla. State U., 1962—64, Am. Ornithologists Union, 1992. Mem.: Waterbird Soc. (life; pres. 1976—79). Democrat. Avocations: canoeing, hiking, birdwatching, collecting Florida landscape art, collecting orchids & palms. Home: 17390 Avocado Dr Homestead FL 33030 Office: S Florida Water Mgmt Dist 3301 Gun Club Rd West Palm Beach FL 33406 Personal E-mail: palmlodge@aol.com. Business E-Mail: jogden@sfwmd.gov.

OGDEN, MAUREEN BLACK, state legislator; b. Vancouver, BC, Nov. 1, 1928; came to U.S., 1930; d. William Moore and Margaret Hunter (Leitch) Black; m. Robert Moore Ogden, June 23, 1956; children: Thomas, Henry, Peter. BA, Smith Coll., 1950; MA, Columbia U., 1963; M in City and Regional Planning, Rutgers U., 1977. Researcher, staff asst. Ford Found., NYC, 1951-56; staff assoc. Fgn. Policy Assn., NYC, 1956-58; mem. Millburn (N.J.) Twp. Com., 1976-81; mayor Twp. of Millburn, N.J., 1979-81; mem. N.J. Gen. Assembly, Trenton, 1982-96. Chmn. Assembly Environment Com., N.J. Gen. Assembly; chmn. Energy and Pub. Utilities Com., Coun. State Govts., 1991-92; mem. adv. bd. Sch. Policy and Planning, Rutgers Univ., New Brunswick, N.J., 1992-96, vice chair Nat. Affairs and Legis. Com. Energy Sources. Author: Natural Resources Inventory, Township of Millburn, 1974. Bd. govs. N.J. Hist. Soc., Newark, 1992-2000; trustee NJ chpt. The Nature Conservancy, 1994-99; hon. trustee Paper Mill Playhouse, Millburn, 1990—; former trustee St. Barnabas Med. Ctr., Livingston, NJ; former pres. NJ Drug Abuse Adv. Coun.; chair Gov.'s Coun. on NJ Outdoors, 1996-99; mem. Palisades Interstate Park Commn., 1996-99; chair Garden State Preservation Trust, 1999—; co-chair policy com. NJ Conservation Found., 2000-, trustee, 2006-; mem. steering com. Highlands Coalition of NJ-NY-Conn. Recipient citation Nat. Assn. State Outdoors Recreation Liaison Officers, 1987, cert. appreciation John F. Kennedy Ctr. for the Performing Arts, The Alliance for Art Edn., 1987, disting. svc. award Art Educators N.J., 1987, ann. environ. quality award EPA Region II, 1988, citation Humane Soc. U.S., 1989, award N.J. Hist. Sites Coun., 1989, N.J. Sch. Conservation, 1990, pres.'s award The Nature Conservancy, 1995, pub. policy award Nat. Trust for Hist. Preservation, 1995. Mem.: Garden Club Am. (vice chair, energy sources, nat. affairs and legislation com. 2005—). Republican. Episcopalian. Home: 59 Lakeview Ave Short Hills NJ 07078-2240 Personal E-mail: mrogden@worldnet.att.net.

OGDEN, VALERIA MUNSON, management consultant, state representative; b. Okanogan, Wash., Feb. 9, 1924; d. Ivan Bodwell and Pearle (Wilson) Munson; m. Daniel Miller Ogden Jr., Dec. 28, 1946; children: Janeth Lee Ogden Martin, Patricia Jo Ogden Hunter, Daniel Munson Ogden. BA magna cum laude, Wash. State U., 1946. Exec. dir. Potomac Coun. Camp Fire, Washington, 1964-68, Ft. Collins (Colo.) United Way, 1969-73, Designing Tomorrow Today, Ft. Collins, 1973-74, Poudre Valley Community Edn. Assn., Ft. Collins, 1977-78; pres. Valeria M. Ogden, Inc., Kensington, Md., 1978-81; nat. field cons. Camp Fire, Inc., Kansas City, Mo., 1980-81; exec. dir. Nat. Capital Area YWCA, Washington, 1981-84, Clark County YWCA, Vancouver, Wash., 1985-89; pvt. practice mgmt. cons. Vancouver, 1989—; mem. Wash. Ho. of Reps., 1990—2002, spkr. pro tempore, 1999—2002. Mem. adj. faculty pub. adminstrn. program Lewis and Clark Coll., Portland (Oreg.) State U., 1979-94; mem. Pvt. Industry Coun., Vancouver, 1986-95; mem. regional Svcs. Network Bd. Mental Health, 1993-03. Author: Camp Fire Membership, 1980. Mem. Wash. State Coun. Vol. Action, Olympia, 1986—90; county vice-chair Larimer County Dems., Ft. Collins, 1974—75; spkr. pro tem Wash. Ho. of Reps., 1999—2002; rep. Gov. Chris Gregoire S.W. Wash., 2005; mem. precinct com. Clark County Dems., Vancouver, 1986—88; treas. Mortar Bd. Nat. Found., Vancouver, 1987—96; bd. dirs. Clark County Coun. for Homeless, Vancouver, 1989—2004, chmn., 1994; bd. dirs. Wash. Wild Life and Recreation Coalition, 1995—2002, Human Svcs. Coun., 1996—2002, Wash. State Hist. Soc., 1996—2006, State Legis. Leaders Found., 2001—02, Columbia Springs Environ. Edn. Ctr. Found., 2003—06, Clark County Skill Ctr. Found., 2003—06; emeritus mem.; bd. dirs. S.W. Wash. Child Care Consortium, 2003—; chair arts and tourism com. Nat. Conf. State Legis., 1996—97; chair Affordable Cmty. Environments, 1998—2009, Wash. State Interagy. Com. for Outdoor Recreation, 2003—09, Wash. State Historic Preservation Fund, 2003—06, S.W. Wash. Ctr. for the Arts, 2003; pres. Nat. Order of Women Legislators, 1999—2001; mem. exec. com. Nat. Conf. State Legis., 2000—02; mem. adv. bd. Wash. State U., Vancouver, 2002—. Named Citizen of Yr. Ft. Collins Bd. of Realtors, 1975, State Legislator of Yr., Wash. State Labor Coun., 2000, Citizen of Yr., Vancouver, Wash., 2002, First Citizen, Clark County, 2006; recipient Gulick award Camp Fire Inc., 1956, Alumna Achievement award Wash. State U. Alumni Assn., 1988; named YWCA Woman of Achievement, 1991, 100 Most Powerful Women, Clark County, 2007, Caring Heart award, 2009. Mem. AAUW, Internat. Assn. Vol. Adminstrs. (pres. Boulder 1989-90), Nat. Assn. YWCA Exec. Dirs. (nat. bd. nominating com. 1988-90), Sci. and Soc. Assn. (bd. dirs. 1993-97), Women in Action, Philanthropic and Ednl. Orgn., Soroptimists, Phi Beta Kappa. Democrat. Avocations: hiking, travel. Home: 2916 NE 88th Ct Vancouver WA 98662-6836 Office Phone: 360-254-8886. Personal E-mail: repval@comcast.net.

OGG, WILSON REID, lawyer, retired judge, poet, curator, publishing executive; b. Alhambra, Calif., Feb. 26, 1928; s. James Brooks and Mary (Wilson) Ogg. Student, Pasadena Jr. Coll., 1946; AB, U. Calif., Berkeley, 1949; JD, U. Calif., 1952; Cultural D in Philosophy of Law, World U. Roundtable, 1983. Bar: Calif. 1955. Assoc. trust dept. Wells Fargo Bank, San Francisco, 1954-55; pvt. practice Berkeley, 1955—. Instr. Taegu English Lang. Inst., 1954, 25th Sta. Hosp., Taegu, Republic of Korea, 1954; rsch. atty., legal editor dept. of continuing edn. bar U. Calif., 1958—63; curator-in-residence, Pinebrook, 1964—; adminstv. law judge, 1974—93; real estate broker, cons., 1974—; trustee World U., 1976—80; dir. admissions internat. Soc. Phil. Enquiry, 1981—84; dep. dir. gen. Internat. Biog. Ctr., England, 1986—; dep. gov. Am. Biog. Inst. Rsch. Assn., 1986—; owner Pinebrook Press, Berkeley, Calif., 1988—; sci. faculty Cambridge U., 2000—. Author: The Enfolding Universe, 1995, Constitutional Law. Constitutional Crisis Facing American Democracy, 2005, Collective Essays of Wilson Ogg, 2005, numerous poems; contbr. articles to profl. jours. With AUS, 1952—54. Recipient Internat. Peace prize, Auth. of United Cultural Conv., U.S., 2002, Auth. of United Culture Conv., U.S., 2005, 50 Yr. Commemorative medal, Albert Schweitzer Assn., 2003, World medal Freedom, 2006; named to Internat. Poetry Hall of Fame, Nat. Libr. Poetry, 1997. Mem.: ACLU, ASCAP, ABA, VFW, AAAS, London Diplomatic Acad., Inst. Noetic Scis., Intertel, Calif. Soc. Psychical Study (pres., chmn. bd. 1963—65), Am. Arbitration Assn. (nat. panel arbitrators), San Francisco Bar Assn., State Bar Calif., Internat. Soc. Individual Liberty, Internat. Platform Assn., Faculty Club of the U. Calif. at Berkeley (emeritus), Men's Inner Cir. Achievement, Amnesty Internat., Marines Meml. Club, Elks, Shriners, Masons, Am. Legion. Unitarian Universalist. Home and Office: 1663 Britannia Ave Henderson NV 89014-3423 Home Fax: 510-540-6052. Business E-Mail: wilsonogg@cal.berkeley.edu.

OGGEL, YNÉS M., language educator, director; d. Gaudencio and América Cardoso; m. James D. Cardoso, July 1996; children: Kristopher Mark Byam, Hayley, Christian. PhD, Mich. State U., Lansing, 1986. Assoc. prof. Buena Vista U., Storm Lake, Iowa, 1993—96; prof. Briar Cliff U., Sioux City, Iowa, chair spanish, 2007—. Chair bd. dirs. Mercy

Med. Ctr., Sioux City. Translator: (book) The Royal Roman Road. Mem. United Way, Sioux City, 1996—99, Art Ctr., Sioux City, 1998—2002, Sioux City Symphony Orch., 1998—2002, Boys and Girls Home, Sioux City, 1998—2002, Crittenton Ctr., Sioux Ctiy, 2001—03, Mercy Med. Ctr., Sioux City, 2000—08, pres., 2006—08. Nominee Best Hispanic Educator, State Mich. Bd. Edn., 1992. Mem.: MLA, ACTFL. Office: Briar Cliff Univ 3303 Rebecca Sioux City IA 51104 Business E-Mail: ynes.oggel@briarcliff.edu.

OGGINS, ROBIN S., history professor; b. Paris, Oct. 30, 1931; s. Isaiah and Nerma Berman Oggins; m. Virginia Darrow, Mar. 17, 1956; children: Jean, Cy, Katherine Ertle. BA, MA, U. Chgo., PhD, 1967. Instr. Harpur Coll., 1962—67; asst. prof. SUNY, Binghamton, 1967—74, assoc. prof., 1974—2004; assoc. prof. emeritus Binghamton U., 2004—. Author: (non-fiction books) Castles and Fortresses, Cathedrals, The Kings and Their Hawks: Falconry in Medieval England. Mem. Vestal Libr. Bd. Trustees, NY, 1979—. Fellow: Royal Historical Soc. Home and Office: 412 Pierce Hill Rd Vestal NY 13850 Business E-Mail: roggins@binghamton.edu.

OGILBY, BARRY RAY, lawyer; b. Dixon, Ky., Jan. 19, 1947; s. Jesse Bryan and Ann (Sutton) O; m. Carolyn Cowser, May 30, 1969 (div. 1973); m. Charlene Marie Coehlo, July 2, 1983(div. 2008); children: Kevin Glenn, Brandon Jesse. BS in Geology, U. Ky., 1969; JD, U. Memphis, 1972. Bar: Tenn. 1972, Tex. 1972, Ky. 1973, Calif. 1985, U.S. Dist. Ct. (cen. and no. dists.) Calif. 1987, U.S. Ct. Appeals (9th cir.) 1989; cert. mediator. Litigation atty. Exxon U.S.A., Houston, 1972-74, mktg. atty. Memphis, 1975-76, labor, environ. atty. LA, 1976-78, refinery atty. Benicia, Calif., 1978-81; asst. gen. counsel Exxon Pipeline Co., Houston, 1981-84; assoc. div. atty. Exxon Co. USA, Thousand Oaks, Calif., 1985-86; pvt. practice Calabasas, Calif., 1986—91; gen. counsel Marine Spill Response Corp., 1991-94; of counsel Bingham McCutchen LLP, Walnut Creek, Calif., 1995—; ptnr. Cooper, White & Cooper, LP, Walnut Creek, 2004—. Adj. prof. environ. law La Verne Coll., 1989-90; lectr. Am. Labor Inst.-ABA legal Edn. Seminar, San Francisco, 1980, 82, 2002-03. Contbr. articles to profl. jours. Mem. ABA (nat. resources law com., marine resources com. 1998—). Office: Cooper White & Cooper Ste 450 1333 N California Blvd Walnut Creek CA 94596 Office Phone: 925-935-0700. Business E-Mail: bogilby@cwclaw.com.

OGILVIE, KELVIN KENNETH, academic administrator, chemist, educator; m. Emma Roleen; children: Kristine, Kevin. BS with honors, Acadia U., 1964, DSc (hon.), 1983; PhD, Northwestern U., 1968; DSc (hon.), U. N.B., Can., 1991, McGill U., 1998. Assoc. prof. U. Man., Winnipeg, 1968-74; prof. chemistry McGill U., Montreal, 1974-88, Can. Pacific prof. biotech., 1984-87; bd. dirs. Sci. Adv. Bd., Biologicals, Toronto, Ont., 1979-84; dir. Office of Biotech. McGill U., 1984-87; prof. chemistry Acadia U., Wolfville, N.S., 1987—2008, v.p. acad. affairs, 1987—93, pres., vice-chancellor, 1993—2003. Invited lectr. on biotech. Tianjin, People's Republic of China, 1985; Snider lectr. U. Toronto, 1991; Gwen Leslie Meml. lectr., 1991; Centennial Mossman lectr. McGill U., 1998; mem. Nat. Adv. Bd. Sci. and Tech., 1994-95; chair selection com. Indsl. Postgrad. Scholarship program NSERCC, 1994; mem. Coun. N.S. Univ. Pres. 1993-2003; mem. Coun. of Applied Sci. and Tech. for N.S., 1988-93; mem. Nat. Biotech. Adv. Com., 1988-99; mem. Fisher Biotech. Adv. Ctr., Can., 1989-92; mem. sci. adv. bd. Allelix Biopharms., 1991-93; chair adv. bd. NRC Inst. for Marine Bioscis., 1990-93, 2007—; mem. steering com. on biotech. labor Can., 1990-92; mem. Atlantic regional com. Prime Min.'s Awards for Tchg. Excellence in Sci., Tech. and Math., 1993-2004; chair regional planning forum for a pharm. industry, Atlantic, Can., 1993; mem. Atomic Energy Control Bd., Can., 1997-99; chair sci. adv. bd. Quanta Nova Can., 1998-2001; mem. Can. Electronic Bus. Roundtable, 1999-2002, Can. Global Bus. Dialogue on Electronic Commerce, 1999, Coun. of Ministers Com. on Online Learning, 2000-01; mem. IBM Global Edn. Policy Coun., 2000-03, The Can. e-Bus. Initiative, 2002-04; chair Premier's Coun. on Innovation, N.S., 2003-06, AIMS Sr. fellow on Postsecondary Edn., 2004—; chair adv. bd. Atlantic Innovation Fund, 2009—; bd. dirs. Genome Can., 2005—; mem. Independent Panel of Experts Review Fed. Labr., Canada, 2007-08, mem. adv. bd. Terragon Environ. Techs. Inc., 2007-. Mem. editl. bd. Nucleosides and Nucleotides, 1981-92; contbr. over 150 articles to profl. jours.; holder 14 patents. Decorated Knight of Malta, 1985, Order of Can., 1991; recipient Commemorative medal for 125th Anniversary of Confedn. Can., 1992, Buck-Whitney medal, 1983, Manning Prin. award, 1992, Queen Elizabeth Golden Jubilee medal, 2002; named Hon. Col. 14th Air Maintenance Squadron, RCAF, 1995-2000; named to McLean's Honor Roll of Canadians Who Made a Difference, 1988, NS Discovery Ctr. Sci. and Tech. Hall of Fame, 2002; E.W.R. Steacie Meml. fellow, 1982-84. Fellow Chem. Inst. Can.; mem. Am. Chem. Soc., Assn. Univs. and Colls. Can. (standing com. on rsch. 1993-2000), Atlantic Univ. Athletic Assn. (pres. 1995-97). Achievements include inventing of BIOLF-62 (ganciclovir), antiviral drug used worldwide; developer general synthesis of RNA; developer original 'gene machine'; developer complete chemical synthesis of large RNA molecules; developer Acadia Advantage Program. Home: PO Box 307 Canning NS Canada B0P 1H0 Office: K2O Consulting PO Box 307 Canning NS Canada B0P 1HO E-mail: kelvin.ogilvie@acadiau.ca.

OGILVIE, LLOYD JOHN, clergyman; b. Kenosha, Wis., Sept. 2, 1930; s. Vard Spencer and Katherine (Jacobson) O.; m. Mary Jane Jenkins, Mar. 25, 1951 (dec. Apr. 2003), Doris Kaiser (Somner), Apr. 19, 2005. BA, Lake Forest Coll., 1952, DD, 1997; MA, Garrett Theol. Sem., 1957; postgrad., New Coll., U. Edinburgh, Scotland, 1955-56; LHD, U. Redlands, 1974, Seattle Pacific U., 1995; DD, Whitworth Coll., 1973, Westmount Coll., 1997, Lehigh U., 1999, Azusa Pacific Coll., 2001, U. Edinburgh, 2003, Carthage Coll., 2004; LLD, Ea. U., 1988, George Fox U., 1997, Pepperdine U., 1998, Belhaven Coll., 2001; HHD, Moravian Coll., 1975, Dickinson Coll., 1998; DST, Roberts Wesleyan Coll., 2000; DD, Asbury Coll., 2008; LittD, Kings Coll., 2008. Ordained to ministry Presbyn. Ch., 1956; student pastor Gurnee, Ill., 1952-56; first pastor Winnetka (Ill.) Presbyn. Ch., 1956-62; pastor 1st, Presbyn. Ch., Bethlehem, Pa., 1962-72, 1st Presbyn. Ch., Hollywood, Calif., 1972—95. Preacher Chgo. Sunday Evening Club, 1963—1989; radio and TV personality weekly syndicated TV & Radio program Let God Love You. Chaplain US Senate, 1995-2003, ret. 2003. Author: A Life Full of Surprises, 1969, Let God Love You, 1974, If I Should Wake Before I Die, 1973, Lord of the Ups and Downs, 1974, You've Got Charisma, 1975, Cup of Wonder, 1976, Life Without Limits, 1976, Drumbeat of Love, 1977, When God First Thought of You, 1978, The Autobiography of God, 1979, The Bush Is Still Burning, 1980, The Radiance of the Inner Splendor, 1980, Congratulations, God Believes in You, 1981, Life as it Was Meant to Be, 1981, The Beauty of Love, The Beauty of Friendship, 1981, The Beauty of Caring, The Beauty of Sharing, 1981, God's Best for My Life, 1981, God's Will in Your Life, 1982, Ask Him Anything, 1982, Commentary on Book of Acts, 1983, Praying with Power, 1983, Falling into Greatness, 1983, Freedom in the Spirit, 1984, Making Stress Work For You, 1984, The Lord of the Impossible, 1984, Why Not Accept Christ's Healing and Wholeness, 1984, If God Cares, Why Do I Still Have Problems?, 1985, Understanding the Hard Sayings of Jesus, 1986, 12 Steps to Living Without Fear, 1987, A Future and a Hope, 1988, Enjoying God, 1990, Silent Strength, 1990, The Lord of the Loose Ends, 1991, Conversation with God, 1992, The Greatest Counselor in the World, 1994, Perfect Peace, 1997, Quiet Moments with God, 1998, The Red Ember In the White Ash, 2006, The Essence of His Presence, 2007, god's: Best For Your Life, 2008; gen. editor: Communicator's Commentary Series of the Bible, 32 vol., 1982, 1978-1995; host: (TV and radio program) Let God Love You. Pres. Leadership Unlimited Fuller Theol. Sem., Lloyd John Ogilvie Inst. of Preaching. Recipient Disting. Svc. Citation, Lake Forest Coll., Silver Angel award, Gold Medallion Book award, 1985, Angel award, Religion in Media, 1986—, William Booth award, Salvation Army, 1992; named Preacher of Yr., Religion in Media, 1982; named one of 12 Most Effective Preachers in the English-Speaking World, Baylor U. Office: 10112 Empyrean Way Los Angeles CA 90067 Office Phone: 310-203-3085. Business E-Mail: logilvie@sbcglobal.net.

OGILVIE, RICHARD IAN, clinical pharmacologist; b. Sudbury, Ont., Can., Oct. 9, 1936; s. Patrick Ian and Gena Hilda (Olson) O.; m. Ernestine Tahedl, Oct. 9, 1965; children— Degen Elisabeth, Lars Ian. MD, U. Toronto, 1960. Intern Toronto (Ont.) Gen. Hosp., 1960-61; resident Montreal Gen. and Univ. Alta. hosps., 1962-66; fellow in clin. pharmacology McGill U., Montreal, 1966-68, asst. prof. medicine, pharmacology and therapeutics, 1968-73, assoc. prof., 1973-78, prof., 1978-83, chmn. dept. pharmacology and therapeutics, 1978-83. Prof. emeritus, U. Toronto, 2002-, clin. pharmacologist Montreal Gen. Hosp., 1968-83, dir. div. clin. pharmacology, 1976-83; prof. medicine and pharmacology U. Toronto, 1983—2002; dir. div. cardiology Toronto Western Hosp., 1983-88, div. clin. pharmacology, 1983-91; mem. pharm. grants com. Med. Research Coun. Can., 1977-82, chmn. 1980-82; mem. med. adv. com. Que. Heart Found., 1976-82, chmn. 1977-81. Editor Hypertension Canada, 1989-2008. Bd. dirs. PMAC Health Care Found., 1986-92; hon. sec.-treas. Banting Research Found., 1984-87, chmn. grant rev. com., 1985-86 Decorated knight comdr. Sovereign Mil. Order St. John of Jerusalem, Knights of Malta, 1987, nat. chmn., recipient prize in med. ethics, 1988-98, sci. advisor to the prior, 1987—, Knight Grand Cross, 1990; jury mem. Can. Prix Galien, 1994-99; grantee Can. Kidney Found., J.C. Edwards Found., Med. Rsch. Coun., Que. Heart Found., Can. Found. Advancement Therapeutics, Conseil de la recherche en sante du Que. Fellow ACP, Royal Coll. Physicians of Can.; mem. Can. Soc. Clin. Investigation (coun. 1977-80), Can. Hypertension Soc. (bd. dirs. 1979-81, 89-94, 96—, v.p. 1991-92, pres. 1992-93, Disting. Svc. award, 2002), Can. Found. Advancement Clin. Pharmacology (dir. 1978-86), Canadian Soc. for Clin. Pharmacology (pres. 1979-82, Sr. Investigator award 1993), Internat. Union Pharmacology (coun. mem. clin. pharmacology sect. 1981-84, chmn. 1984-87), Pharm. Soc. Can., Can. Cardiovascular Soc., Am. Soc. Pharmacology and Exptl. Therapeutics, Am. Soc. Clin. Pharm., Toronto Hypertension Soc. (pres. 1988-98). Home: 79 Collard Dr King City ON Canada L7B 1E4 Office: Toronto Western Hosp 399 Bathurst St Toronto ON Canada M5T 2S8 Office Phone: 416-603-5176.

OGILVIE, T(HOMAS) FRANCIS, marine engineering educator; b. Atlantic City, Sept. 26, 1929; s. Thomas Fleisher and Frances Augusta (Wilson) O.; m. Joan Husselton, Sept. 11, 1950; children: Nancy Louise, Mary Beth, Kenneth Stuart. BA in Physics, Cornell U., 1950; M.Sc. in Aero. Engring., U. Md., 1957; PhD in Engring. Sci., U. Calif., Berkeley, 1960; D in Naval Arch./Marine Engring. (hon.), Nat. Tech. U. Athens, 1996. Physicist, David Taylor Model Basin, Dept. Navy, Bethesda, Md., 1951-62, 64-67; liaison scientist Office of Naval Research, London, 1962-63; asso. prof. naval architecture and marine engring. U. Mich., Ann Arbor, 1967-70, prof. fluid mechanics, 1970-81, chmn. dept. naval architecture and marine engring., 1973-81; prof. ocean engring. MIT, Cambridge, 1982-96, prof. emeritus, 1996—, head dept., 1982-94, young investigator ocean engring. endowed lectureships, 1994—. Vis. prof. naval architecture Osaka (Japan) U., 1976; vis. prof. math. U. Manchester, Eng., 1976; founding mem. Ariz. Sr. Acad., Tucson, 1997. Contbr. articles to profl. jours. Recipient Meritorious Pub. Svc. award U.S. Dept. of Transp., 1982. Fellow Soc. of Naval Architects and Marine Engrs. (coun. 1977-82, exec. com. 1978-80, 83-84, William H. Webb medal 1989); mem. Sigma Xi, Phi Beta Kappa. Home: 7559 S Eliot Ln Tucson AZ 85747-9627

OGINTZ, EILEEN, travel writer; m. Andy Ogintz; children: Matt, Reggie, Melanie. Masters in Journalism, U. Mo. Reporter, nat. corr., feature writer Chgo. Tribune, 1978—92; newspaper reporter Anniston Star, Record, Hackensack, NJ, Des Moines Register, Chicago Tribune; column writer, family travel expert Taking the Kids (Taking the Kids.com), 1992—. Has taught journalism at Northwestern U., NYU, Colo. Coll. and Quinnipiac U.; spkr., cons. in field. Quoted in USA Today, Wall Street Journal, New York Times, and parenting and women magazines on travel., guest appearences 48 Hours, The Today Show, Good Morning America, Oprah and other local radio and TV news programs.; author: Are We There Yet?, 1996, A Kid's Guide to New York City, 2004, A Kid's Guide to Cruising Alaska, 2004. Recipient Parents' Choice for Taking the Kids series, Southam award for Taking the Kids on a Sailing Adventure and Taking the Kids to a Quirky Caribbean Resort, 2006. Office: Taking the Kids 478 post Road East #566 Westport CT 06880 Office Phone: 203-227-9180. Office Fax: 203-227-9185. Business E-Mail: eileen@takingthekids.com.*

OGIRRI, ESTHER O., Academic Librarian; d. Beatrice Iyevbele; children: Osi O., Aghie I., Pete O. BA, MA, W.Va. U., Morgantown, 1989; MLIS, U. SC, Columbia, 1994. Cert. tchr. NC Bd. Edn., 1990. Reference svc. libr. Wake Tech CC, Raleigh, NC, 2001—03, interim libr. dir., 2003—04; libr. Northern Wake Campus, Wake Tech CC, Raleigh, 2007—. Tchr. Charlotte Mecklenburg Sch., NC, 1990—92; head, acquisitions dept. Johnson C. Smith U., Charlotte, 1994—98; reference libr. Ctrl. Piedmont CC, Charlotte, 1998—2000, adj. instr., 1999—2000; with Conducted Several Rsch. Presentation, North Carolina CC. Won Internet Infrastructure grant, Libr. Svc. Tech. Act. Grant, 2003—04. Home: PO Box 542 Garner NC 27529 Office: Wake Tech CC 6600 Louisburg Rd Raleigh NC 27616-6328 Personal E-mail: estherogirri@att.net. Business E-Mail: eoogirri@waketech.edu.

OGLE, JAMES DAVID, lawyer; b. Kirksville, Mo., Mar. 23, 1968; s. John Charles and Elizabeth Ann Ogle; m. Laura Kerr Ogle, Aug. 14, 1993; children: Taylor, Jackson. BSc Okla. State U., Stillwater; JD, Okla. City U., Okla. Bar: Okla. 1997, US Dist. Ct. (no., ea., and we. dists.) 1997, US Ct. Appeals (10th cir.) 1998, US Supreme Ct. 2004. Various sales, mktg. positions G.D. Searle, Skokie, Ill., 1990—93, Carter Healthcare, Okla. City, 1993—95; atty. Martin Law Office, 1995—2003, Ogle & Welch, P.C., 2003—. Spkr. in field. Mem., assoc. Okla. City Art Mus., Okla., 1997—2002; trustee Okla. County Law Libr. Named one of Top Okla. Lawyers, 2006, 2007. Mem.: Okla. County Bar Assn. (pres.), Okla. Criminal Def. Assn., Nat. Assn. Criminal Def. Lawyers (life). Office: 100 Park Ave Ste 500 Oklahoma City OK 73102 Office Phone: 405-605-6644. Office Fax: 405-605-6633. Business E-Mail: david@oglelaw.net.

OGLE, ORRETT E., oral surgeon; s. O. Ogle; m. J. Ogle; children: Kerry, Cherise. DDS, Columbia U., NYC, 0974. Diplomate Am. Bd. Oral and Maxillofacial Surgery, 1983. Staff maxillofacial surgeon Mama Yemo Hosp. and Nat. U. Zaire, Kinshasa, 1977—79; chief, oral and maxillofacial surgery Woodhull Hosp., Bklyn., 1982—; attending oral and maxillofacial surgeon Harlem Hosp., Columbia U., NYC, 1985—94; chief: oral and maxillofacial surgery Lincoln Hosp., NY Med. Coll., Bronx. Author: (text book) Atlas Minor Of Oral Surgery. Organizer People People Ethiopia, NYC, 2001—02; med. vol. and organizer med. assistance fgn. trips ENAHPA, Detroit, 2002—. Mem.: Am. Assn. Oral And Maxillofacial Surgeons. Democrat-Npl. Avocations: travel, reading. Office: Woodhull Med And Mental Health Ctr 760 Broadway Brooklyn NY 11206 Office Fax: 718-630-3244; Home Fax: 516-483-1373. Personal E-mail: oeogle@aol.com. Business E-Mail: orrett.ogle@woodhullhc.nychhc.org.

OGLE, SARAH JEAN, retired educational consultant, educator; d. Henry Albert and Myra Jane Smith; m. Melvin David Ogle, May 27, 1972; children: Melvin Keith, Lynnette J. Ogle Davidson. BA, Belmont U., 1967; M in Edn. Adminstrn., U. Tex., Arlington, Tex., 2000; student, Baylor U., Tex. Wesleyan U. Cert. tchr. Tex., 1992, tchr. ESL Tex., 1995, mid-mgmt. adminstr. Tex., 1999. Adminstrv. asst. Weldon Aston & Co. CPA, Ft. Worth, 1973—90; tchr. South Hills Elem. Sch., Ft. Worth, 1990—97; instrl. specialist Briscoe Elem. Sch., Ft. Worth, 1997—98; asst. prin. Greenbriar Elem., Ft. Worth, 1998—2001; prin. Souder Elem. Sch., Everman, Tex., 2001—04; asst. prin. Hubbard Heights Elem. Sch., Ft. Worth, 2004—06, Luella Merrett Elem., 2006—08. Exchange tchr. Japan Sister Cities Ft. Worth. Past pres. Adolescent Pregnancy Prevention, Ft. Worth, 1988—89; mem. Broadway Baptist Ch., Stephen Minister Leader; tchr. U. Bapt. Ch. Named Tchr. of Week, Dillards, Outstanding Tchr., South Hills. Mem.: PTA (life), Delta Kappa Gamma. Home: 5504 Winifred Dr Fort Worth TX 76133 Home Phone: 817-292-4810. Personal E-mail: ogle5504@swbell.net.

OGLESBY, CHARLES R., automotive executive; BBA in Mktg., U. Ga. COO First Am. Automotive, Inc., San Francisco; pres., North Point Automotive Group. Asbury Automotive Group., Inc., Little Rock, 2002—06, pres., Nalley Automotive Group. Atlanta, 2004—06, sr. v.p., COO NYC, 2006—07, pres., CEO, 2007—. Bd. dirs. Asbury Automotive Group., Inc., 2006—. Office: Asbury Automotive Group Inc 622 Third Ave 37th Fl New York NY 10017 Office Phone: 212-885-2500.

OGLESBY, ELAINE SUE, elementary school educator; b. Rensselaer, Ind., Dec. 11, 1958; d. Richard E. and Lois I. Oglesby. BS in Natural Resources and Environ. Sci., Purdue U., 1981; MEd, Ind. U., 1988, MLS, 2005. Tchr. Indpls. Pub. Schs., 1986—2004, digital coach, 2004—. Recipient Shining Star, Indpls. Pub. Schs., 1993—94, Spirit of Harshman, Harshman Mid. Sch., 1998, Tchr. of the Yr. award, 2003, Top Ten Tchr. award, Indpls. Pub. Schs., 2003; grantee, Eli Lily Found., 1993. Mem.: Ind. Mid. Level Educators (assoc.), Nat. Mid. Sch. Assn. (assoc.), Ind. Libr. Fedn. (assoc.), Assn. Curriculum and Devel. (assoc.).

OGLETREE, CHARLES J., JR., law educator; b. Calif., Dec. 31, 1952; m. Pamela Barnes, 1975; children: Charles III, Rashida. BA in Polit. Sci., Stanford U., 1974, MA in Polit. Sci., 1975; JD, Harvard U., 1978; LLD (hon.), NC Ctrl. U., New Eng. Sch. Law, Tougaloo Coll., Amherst Coll., 2002, U. Miami Sch. Law, 2003, Wilberforce U., 2003. Bar: DC 1979, US Supreme Ct. 1983. Staff atty. DC Pub. Defender Svc., tng. dir., 1982—83, trial chief, 1983—84, dep. dir., 1984—85; joined Jessamy, Fort & Ogletree, 1985; of counsel Jordan, Keys & Jessamy, Washington; lectr. law Harvard Law Sch., Cambridge, Mass., 1984, vis. prof. law from practice, 1985—89, Edward R. Johnston Lectr. Law, 1989, asst. prof. law, 1989—93, dir. Criminal Justice Inst., 1990, prof. law., 1993—, faculty dir. clin. progs., 1996, Jesse Climenko Prof. Law, 1998—, assoc. dean clin. progs., 2002—03, vice dean clin. programs, 2003, dir. Charles Hamilton Houston Inst. Race and Justice, 2004—. Adj. prof. Am. U., Washington, 1983—85; moderator various nationally televised forums; guest commentator various nat. and local TV and radio progs. Co-author: Beyond the Rodney King Story: An Investigation of Police Conduct in Minority Communities, 1995; author: All Deliberate Speed: Reflections on the First Half-Century of Brown v. Board of Education, 2004; co-editor: Brown at 50: The Unfinished Legacy, 2004; contbr. articles to profl. jours., chapters to books. Chmn. bd. trustees U. DC; chmn. bd. dirs. B.E.L.L. Found.; mem. bd. trustees Stanford U., chmn. Stanford Fund. Recipient Charles Hamilton Houston Medallion of Merit, Washington Bar Assn., 2001, Equal Justice award, Nat. Bar Assn., 2002, Tribune Soc. Justice award, Courts of NY State, 2003, Universal Humanitarian award, NAACP, 2003; named one of 100 Most Influential Lawyers in Am., Nat. Law Jour., 2000, 50 Most Influential Minority Lawyers in America, 2008, 100 Most Influential Blacks in Am., Black Enterprise mag., 2003, Savoy mag., 2003; named to Power 150, Ebony mag., 2007, 2008. Office: Harvard Law Sch 1563 Massachusetts Ave Cambridge MA 02138 Office Phone: 617-495-5097. Office Fax: 617-496-3936. E-mail: ogletree@law.harvard.edu.*

OGLETREE, GLENDA L., education educator; b. Birmingham, Ala., Feb. 16, 1954; children: Alison L. Brady, Derek N. PhD in Elem. Edn., U. Ala., Tuscaloosa, 2007. Tchr. Jefferson County Bd. Edn., Birmingham, 1987—90, Shelby County Bd. Edn., Alabaster, Ala., 1990—2006, Calhoun County Bd. Edn., Anniston, Ala.; asst. prof. Armstrong Atlantic State U., Savannah, Ga., 2008—. Recipient Honor Societies, KDP, Pinnacle, Golden Key, 2003-2006. Mem.: NSTA, Kappa Delta Pi (Ga.) (sponser 2003). Home Phone: 205-835-0385; Office Phone: 912-344-2602.

OGLETREE, THOMAS WARREN, retired religious studies educator; b. Arab, Ala., June 17, 1933; s. John Warren and Carrie Elizabeth (Brown) Ogletree; m. Mary-Lynn Rimbey Ogletree; children: Thomas Rimbey, Kathryn Rimbey; m. Marilyn Brittain Rice (div. 1971); children: David Franklin, Julia Brittain, Lauren Bernick. BD, Garrett Theological Sem., Evanston, Ill., 1959; PhD, Vanderbilt U., Nashville, Tenn., 1963; postdoc. degree, Free U., West Berlin, Germany, 1969, Sorbonne U., Paris, 1974, Cambridge U., Eng., 1987; BA, Birmingham Southern Coll., Ala., 1955, DD (hon.), 1991; MA (hon.), Yale U., New Haven, 1990; LLD (hon.), Livingston Coll., 1995. Asst. prof., philosophy & religion Birmingham Southern Coll., 1963—65; asst. to assoc. prof. theology Chgo. Theological Sem., 1965—70; assoc. to prof. theological ethics Div. Sch., Vanderbilt U., 1970—81; dean, prof., theological ethics Theological Sch., Drew U., Madison, 1981—90, Yale U., Div. Sch., 1990—96, prof., ethics and religious studies, 1996—2008. Editor soundings Interdisciplinary Jour., Nashville, 1975—80; founding editor Annual Soc. Christian Ethics, 1981; assoc. editor Jours. Religious Ethics, 1980—90, trustee, 1990—, chair trustee, 2008—. Co-author (with Herbert Aptheker and Shepherd Bliss): (book) From Hope to Liberation: Towards a New Marxist-Christian Dialogue; co-editor (with George Lucas Jr.): Lifeboat Ethics: The Moral Dilemmas of World Hunger; contbr. articles to profl. jours. Leader Civil Rights Movement, Nashville, 1961—62; faculty, cons. Operation Breadbasket Leadership Jesse Jackson, Chgo., 1966—68; ordained min. United Meth. Ch.; founding pastor Vestavia Hills United Meth. Ch., Birmingham, 1952—62. Mem.: Soc. Values Higher Edn. (bd. dir. exe. com. 1978—84, chairperson ctrl. com. program and planning 1978—82), Soc. Christian Ethics (pres. 1983—84, v.p. 1982—83, exe. com. bd. dir. 1982—84, pubs. com., chairperson 1980—81), Clare Hall Cambridge U. (life). Democrat. Avocations: running, soccer, baseball, racquetball. Home: 78 Nut Plains Rd W Guilford CT 06437

OGLIARUSO, MICHAEL ANTHONY, retired chemist, educator, actor; b. Bklyn., Aug. 10, 1938; s. Andrea and Anna (Bianco) O.; m. Basila Gallo, Apr. 2, 1961; 1 child, Michael Dana. BS, Poly. Inst. Bklyn., 1960, PhD, 1965. Postdoctoral rsch. assoc. UCLA, 1965-67; asst. prof. chemistry Va. Poly. Inst. and State U., Blacksburg, 1967-72, assoc. prof., 1972-78, prof., 1978-95, assoc. dean Coll. Arts and Scis., 1984-95; ret. Coll. Arts and Scis.; profl. actor. Contbr. articles to profl. jours. Served with C.E. U.S. Army, 1960-61. Mem. Am. Chem. Soc., Va. Acad. Sci., Sigma Xi, Phi Lambda Upsilon. *I have been fortunate to be associated with the most personally rewarding profession available today, the professional education of young men and women. This career is best suited to persons who wish to remain young in spirit, since regardless of your age you are always surrounded with students who are between 18 and 22 years old. This is the best way I know to remain spiritually young.*

OGNIBENE, ANDRE JOHN, internist, educator, retired military officer; b. NYC, Nov. 18, 1931; s. Morris S. and Josephine C. (Macaluso) O.; m. Margaret A. Haug, Apr. 21, 1957; children: Judy, Andrea, Adrienne, Marc, Eric. BA cum laude, Columbia U., 1952; MD, NYU, 1956. Diplomate Am. Bd. Internal Medicine, Am. Bd. Geriatrics, Am. Bd. Med. Mgmt. Intern in medicine Bellevue Hosp., NYC, 1956-57, resident in medicine, 1957-59; commd. capt. US Army M.C., 1957, advanced through grades to brig. gen., 1978; resident in medicine Manhattan VA Hosp., NYC and chief resident in medicine, 1959-60; chief med. service US Army Hosp., Nurnburg, Germany, 1961-62, chief dept. medicine, 1962-64; fellow in cardiology Walter Reed Gen. Hosp., Washington, 1964-65, asst. in cardiology, 1965-66, asst. chief dept. medicine, 1969-72; chief dept. medicine, chief profl. services US Army Hosp., Ft. Meade, Md., 1966-68; cons. in medicine Hdqrs. US Army, Vietnam, 1969; asst. chief dept. medicine Walter Reed Army Med. Ctr., 1970-72; from chief dept. medicine to dir. med. edn. Brooke Army Med. Ctr., Ft. Sam Houston, Tex., 1972-78, dir. med. edn., 1976-78, dep. comdr. and chief profl. services, 1976-78, comdr., commanding gen., 1978-81; hosp. dir. San Antonio State Chest Hosp., 1981-85; program dir. internal medicine Canton, Ohio, 1985-95; prof. medicine NE Ohio U., Rootstown, 1985-98, prof. emeritus, 1998—, chmn. dept. medicine, 1989-98, assoc. dean for med. edn., 1989—98; med. dir. Mercy Med. Ctr., 1995—98; v.p., treas. Majomed Corp., San Antonio, 1999—2008. Instr. medicine NYU, 1960; assoc. clin. prof. Georgetown U., 1970-72; clin. prof. U. Tex. Health Sci. Ctr., San Antonio, 1973-85, mem. postgrad. adv. com., 1977-78; mem. Instl. Rev. Bd., 1981-85; pres. Bexar Met. unit Am. Cancer Soc., 1984; dir. Eisenhower Nat. Bank; bd. dirs. Cancer Therapy and Rsch. Ctr.; chmn. South Tex. Epilepsy Found., 1985. Contbr. articles to med. publs. and chpts. to books; editor, prin. author Internal Medicine in Vietnam, Vol. II, 1982; editor-in-chief: Internal Medicine in Vietnam, vol. I, 1977. Trustee Regina Health Ctr., 1992-97; mem. med. adv. bd. Access Health Inc., 1998-2000. Decorated DSM, Legion of Merit; named among Am. Top Physicians, Consumer Rsch. Coun., 2003-05. Master ACP (laureate, master tchr.); fellow Am. Coll. Physician Execs. (cert.), Am. Coll. Angiology; mem. NY Acad. Scis., Am. Fedn. Clin. Rsch., Bexar County Med. Soc., Stark County Med. Soc., Assn. Profs. Medicine, Tex. Med. Found., Alpha Omega Alpha. Home and Office: 27671 Ramblewood St San Antonio TX 78261-2013 Personal E-mail: aognibene@satx.rr.com. *Compassion must remain the universal prescription in medical practice. Technology can provide no solutions in the absence of humanity.*

OGNIBENE, FREDERICK PETER, internist; b. Jamestown, NY, Aug. 30, 1953; s. Vincent Larry and Alma Linda (Martinelli) O. BA, U. Rochester, 1975; MD, Cornell U., 1979. Diplomate Am. Bd. Internal Medicine, Am. Bd. Internal Medicine-Critical Care. From intern to resident N.Y. Hosp./Cornell Med. Ctr., 1979-82; from med. to sr. staff fellow Critical Care Medicine Dept. NIH, Bethesda, Md., 1982-87, sr. investigator, 1987—, fellowship dir., 1998—2003. Assoc. clin. prof. George Washington U., Washington, 1996—; adj. assoc. prof. U. Md., 2000—; dir. clin. rsch. tng. program NIH, 2000—, dir. office clin. rsch. tng. and med. edn., 2003—, dep. dir. ednl. affairs and strategic partnerships Clin. Ctr., 2009-. Manuscript reviewer; contbr. articles to profl. jours., chpts. to books. Mem. bd. dirs. Washington Project Arts, 2007-; bd. dirs. Cultural Devel. Corp. D.C., 2003—06, Curator's Cir. Hirshhorn Mus. and Sculpture Garden, 2004-. Capt. USPHS, 1985-2007. Fellow ACP, Am. Coll. Critical Care Medicine (chair credentials com. 1992-94, bd. regents 1994-2000); mem. Cornell U. Med. Coll. Alumni Assn. (bd. dirs.), Am. Fedn. Clin. Rschs. (nat. coun. 1987-95, sec.-treas. ea. sect. 1987-91, chair-elect 1991-92, chair 1992-93), Am. Fedn. Clin. Rsch. Found. (trustee), Soc. Critical Care Medicine (co-chair symposium 1998, governing coun. 2000-04, sec. 2004-05, pres. 2007), Alpha Omega Alpha. Democrat. Roman Catholic. Avocations: travel, studying Italian language, collecting contemporary American art. Home: 1661 Crescent Pl NW Apt 308 Washington DC 20009 Office: NIH Rm BIL 403 9000 Rockville Pike Bldg 10 Bethesda MD 20892 Office Phone: 301-496-9425, 301-402-0563. Business E-Mail: fognibene@cc.nih.gov.

OGORA, JANE, university librarian; d. James Herbert and Zipporah Arisa Achola; m. Evans Ogora; children: Masongo, Kwamboka. BA in English, U. Eastern Africa, Eldoret, Kenya, 1991; MLS, State U. NJ, Rutgers, 2000. Libr. trainee NY Pub. Libr., 1999; reference libr. St. Peter's Coll., Jersey City, 1999—2005; evening-weekend reference libr. Fairleigh Dickinson U., Teaneck, NJ, 2002—05; access svc. libr. Wash. Adventist U., Takoma Pk., 2005—. Mem.: ALA, Md. Libr. Assn. Adventist. Office: Columbia Union Coll 7600 Flower Ave Takoma Park MD 20912 Business E-Mail: janogora@cuc.edu.

OGRA, PEARAY L., pediatrician, educator; b. Srinagar, Kashmir, India, Mar. 19, 1937; came to U.S., 1961, naturalized, 1969; s. Govinda Kaul and Gunvati (Daftari) O.; children: Sanjay, Monica. MB, Christian Med. Coll., Ludhiana, India, 1961. Intern Binghamton (N.Y.) Gen. Hosp., 1962-63; resident U. Chgo., 1963-64, N.Y. U.-Bellevue Med Center, 1964-66, fellow in infectious diseases, 1966-68; asst. prof. pediatrics SUNY, Buffalo, 1968-71, assoc. prof. pediatrics and microbiology, 1972-74, prof., 1974-91; John Sealy disting. chair, prof. U. Tex. Med. Br., Galveston, 1991-2000, chmn. dept. pediatrics, 1991-99; prof. pediatrics Children's Hosp., Buffalo, 2000—. Dir. divsn. virology Children's Hosp. Buffalo, 1969-81, chief dept. infectious diseases, 1970-91; dir. Clin. Labs. Children's Hosp., 1985-90; mem. study sect. NIH, 1979-85, maternal child health com., 1987-91; mem., chmn. bd. Internat. Pediat. Rsch. Found., Inc., 1984-89; mem. com. on vaccines for 21st century Inst. of Medicine NAS, 1997-2000, com. in infant formula, 2002; adv. bd. Internat. Vaccine Inst., Seoul, Rep. Korea, 2003—, Merck scholar-in-residence, 2006—; chmn. external rev. group Program on Mucosal Vaccines, European Commn., 2005—. Recipient E. Mead Johnson award for Pediatric Research Am. Acad. Pediatrics, 1978; Kalhana award Kashmir Sci. Culture and Soc., 1984; Stockton Kimball award SUNY, 1985; Buswell fellow, 1968-71. Fellow Royal Soc. Medicine, Assn. Am. Physicians, Am. Acad. Pediatrics, Am. Acad. Microbiology; mem. Am. Soc. Clin. Investigation, Soc. Pediatric Rsch., Infectious Disease Soc. Am., Soc. Exptl. Biology and Medicine, Am. Assn. Immunologists, Am. Soc. Microbiology, AAAS, Am. Fedn. Clin. Rsch., Am. Soc. Virology, Pediatric Infectious Disease Soc. (chmn. com. internatl health 2006—). Home: 163 Troy Del Way Williamsville NY 14221-4505 Office Phone: 716-878-7407. Business E-Mail: pogra@upa.chob.edu. E-mail: plogra@buffalo.edu.

O'GRADY, BARBARA VINSON, retired community health nurse, administrator; b. Alhambra, Calif., July 6, 1928; d. Weston Wright and Merdith Alyda (Noble) Vinson; m. Joseph Putnam O'Grady, Oct. 24, 1952; children: Joseph Jr., Jeffrey, Kent, Kimberly, Kathryn; m. John Mark Prebish, June 28, 1997. BS, UCLA, 1951; MS, U. Minn., 1972. Staff public health nurse San Diego Co. Health Dept., 1952; staff nurse U. Minn. Hosp., 1954-56; staff public health nurse Family Nursing Svc., St. Paul, 1972; asst. prof. Gustavus Adolphus Coll., St. Peter, Minn., 1972-77; dir. Ramsey County Public Health Nursing Svc., St. Paul, 1977-88; health staff Senator Dave Durenberger, Mpls., 1988; cons. pvt. practice, Waterville, Minn., 1989-97, ret., 1998. Mem. bd. govs. U. Minn. Hosp. and Clinic, Mpls., 1983-91, chair, 1985-87; clin. faculty Sch. Pub. Health, 1984-88. Author: (with others) Computer Applications in Medical Care, 1982, Nursing and Computers, 1989, NCNIP: Models for the Future of Nursing, 1989, Procs. of Impact of DRG's on Nursing Conf., 1988; mem. editl. bd. Jour. Cmty. Health Nursing, 1984-94. Mem. Mpls. Charter Commn., 1967-72; co-chair Minn. GOP Issues Devel., 1968, Minn. GOP Constn. Com., 1966-70; chair Dick Erdall Campaign Com., 1965-71; bd. dirs. Presbyn. Homes of Minn., St. Paul, 1982-88; bd. dirs. Living at Home/Block Nurse Program, 1986-98, chair external rels. com., 1988-98; sec. Women's Environ. Watch, Santa Ynez Valley, Calif., 2001-; adminstrv. asst. to coord., Valley Mentoring Program, 2003-. Recipient Outstanding Contbn. Midwest Alliance in Nursing, 1984, Outstanding Achievement award Bd, of Ramsey County Commrs., 1987; Annie Yates scholar L.A. County General Hosp. Alumni Assn., 1948; Living At Home grantee The Commonwealth Fund, 1986. Fellow Am. Acad. of Nursing; mem. ANA, APHA, Nat. League for Nursing, Minn. Public Health Assn., Sigma Theta Tau. Republican. Presbyterian. Avocations: swimming, reading, travel. Home: PO Box 624 Santa Ynez CA 93460-0624 Personal E-mail: barbandjohn624@gmail.com.

O'GRADY, DENNIS JOSEPH, lawyer; b. Hoboken, NJ, Nov. 16, 1943; s. Joseph A. and Eileen O'Grady; m. Mary Anne Amoruso, Sept. 9, 1966 (div. Apr. 1984); 1 child, Kara Anne. AB, Seton Hall Coll., 1965; MA, U. So. Calif., 1969; JD, Rutgers U., 1973. Bar: N.J. 1973, U.S. Ct. Appeals (3d cir.) 1975, U.S. Dist. Ct. N.J., U.S. Supreme Ct. 2000. Ptnr. Riker, Danzig, Scherer, Hyland & Perretti, NYC, 1974—, Trenton and Morristown, NJ, 1974—. Adj. asst. prof. of bus. law St. Peter's Coll., Jersey City, 1973—; adj. prof. law Rutgers U. Law Sch., 1997—. Recipient First Tier, Chambers Leading Lawyers NJ, 2006—; named to, Best Lawyers in Am., 2003—. Fellow: Am. Coll. Bankruptcy Lawyers; mem.: ABA (bus./bankruptcy sect.), NJ Turnaround Assn. (bd. dirs.), Am. Bd. Cert. (faculty subcom.), Am. Bankruptcy Inst. (health care subcom., bd. profl. cert.), Fed. Bar Assn., N.J. State Bar Assn. (debtor/creditor sect.). Democrat. Roman Catholic. Office: Riker Danzig Scherer Hyland & Perretti 1 Speedwell Ave Morristown NJ 07960-6823 Office Phone: 973-538-0800. Business E-Mail: dogrady@riker.com.

O'GRADY, JOHN JOSEPH, III, lawyer; b. NYC, Mar. 21, 1933; s. John Joseph and Terese (O'Rourke) O'G.; m. Mary E. McHugh, June 28, 1958; children: Glennon, Ellen, Carol, Paul. AB, Holy Cross Coll., 1954; JD, Harvard U., 1957. Bar: N.Y. 1958. Assoc. Cadwalader, Wickersham & Taft, NYC, 1958-66, ptnr., 1966-96, counsel, 1997—. Office: Cadwalader Wickersham & Taft One World Fin Ctr New York NY 10281 Office Phone: 212-504-6000.

O'GRADY, LIAM, federal judge; b. Newark, 1950; BA, Franklin & Marshall Coll., 1973; JD, George Mason U., 1977. Pvt. practice, Va., 1979—82; asst. commonwealth's atty. Commonwealth of Va., 1982—86; asst. US atty. (ea. dist.) Va. US Dept. Justice, 1986—92; ptnr. Finnegan, Henderson, Farabow, Garrett, & Dunner, LLP, 1992—2003; magistrate judge US Dist. Ct. (ea. dist.) Va., Alexandria, 2003—07, judge, 2007—. Office: Albert V Bryan US Courthouse 401 Courthouse Sq Alexandria VA 22314 Office Phone: 703-299-2121.

O'GRADY, RICHARD T., science administrator; Grad. in Zoology, McGill U., Montreal; PhD, U. BC, Vancouver, 1987. Postdoctoral fellow Smithsonian Instn. Nat. Mus. Natural History; pub. BioScience; exec. dir. Am. Inst. Biol. Scis., Washington, 1997—. Office: Am Inst Biol Scis 1444 I St NW Ste 200 Washington DC 20005 Office Phone: 202-628-1500 ext. 258. Office Fax: 202-628-1509. E-mail: rogrady@aibs.org.

OGSBURY, JAMES STANLEY, III, neurosurgeon, educator; s. James Stanley and Lucile (Becker) Ogsbury; m. Kathleen McBride Ogsbury. BS, Denison U., 1965; MD, Cornell U. Med. Coll., 1969. Diplomate Am. Bd. Neurosurgery. Intern, resident N.Y. Hosp., NYC, 1969—71; resident U. Colo. Health Sci. Ctr., Denver, 1973—77, clin. asst. prof. neurosurgery, 1977—; clin. neurosurgeon Luth. Med. Ctr., Wheat Ridge, Colo., 1977—, St. Anthony's Hosp., Denver, 1977—. Med. dir. Colo. Low Back Colaborative, 2009—. Maj. USAF, 1971—73. Mem.: Colo. Neurosurg. Soc. Avocations: skiing, bicycling. Office: Rocky Mountain Neurosurgical Consultants LLC 2460 W 26th Ave Bldg C Ste 220-C Denver CO 80211 Office Phone: 303-431-6678. Business E-Mail: rmns@guest.net.

OGUCHI, TAKASHI, geoscientist, educator; b. Matsumoto, Japan, Mar. 13, 1963; s. Kimpei and Taeko Oguchi; m. Chiaki T. Oguchi, Mar. 14, 1993; children: Kei, Risa. BA, U. Tokyo, 1985, MSc, 1987, DSc, 1996. Asst. prof. U. Tokyo, 1991—98, assoc. prof., 1998—2009, prof., 2009—. Adj. grad. faculty mem., dept. earth sci. U. Memphis, 2007—. Editor in chief: Geomorphology, 2003—, mem. editl. bd.: Catena, 1997—, Geomorphology, 1999—2002, Geographical Research, 2004—, Geography Compass, 2006—, Open Geology Jour., 2007—. Mem. steering com. IGU Commn. on Land Degradation, 2004—, Trans Asiatic Geog. Info. Sci. Soc., 2006—; v.p. IAG Working Group on Human Impact on the Landscape, 2006—. Recipient Comland award, IGU, 2008; named Excellent Young Geographer award, Assn. Japanese Geographers, 1995. Achievements include GIS applications in geomorphology. Office: CSIS Univ Tokyo 5-1-5 Kashiwanoha Kashiwa 277-8568 Japan Business E-Mail: oguchi@csis.u-tokyo.ac.jp.

OGUNLADE, ABIMBOLA ADEGOKE, systems engineer; b. Ado-Ekiti, Ekiti State, Nigeria, Apr. 23, 1979; s. Adekunle Babatunde and Ibiyinka Ogunlade. B in Electronics, Elec. Engring. with honors, U. Ado-Ekiti, Nigeria, 2002; M in Engring. Mgmt. and Devel., North West U., South Africa, 2008. MCSE Microsoft, 2003, cert. LPIC 1 Linux Profl. Inst., 2004, adminstr. Citrix, 2005, Solaris 9 Sun Microsyst., 2005, IBM, 2005, sys. expert. xSeries Linux IBM, 2005. Instrumentation, control sys. trainee Sasol-Chevron Escravos Gas-to-Liquids Project, Sasolburg, Free State, South Africa; indsl. trainee Nigerian Nat. Petroleum Corp., Products and Pipeline Mktg. Co. Ltd., Ore Depot, Ondo State, Nigeria, 2000—01; sys. engr. Roe Nigeria Ltd., Victoria Island, Lagos State, Nigeria, 2004—05; enterprise systems engr. Dimension Data, Victoria Island, 2005—06. With Nat. Youth Svc. Corps., 2003—04. Mem.: Internat. Coun. Sys. Engring., Project Mgmt. Inst., Inst. Engring. and Tech. Anglican. Achievements include design of Schmitt Triggered Light Operated Switch for automatic control of street lighting systems; research in comparative cost-benefit analysis of renewable energy resources for rural community development in Nigeria; implementation of Integrated Systems Engineering Learning System at North West University, South Africa. Avocations: travel, music, reading, computers. Home: Flat H4 Kollege Pk Harry Smith St PO Box 264 Free State Sasolburg 1947 South Africa Office: Chevron Nigeria Ltd EGTL 2 Chevron Dr Lagos State Lekki Peninsula 00234 Nigeria Personal E-mail: bimbo_ogun@yahoo.com.

OGURCAK, JANICE L., museum director, educator; b. Hershey, Pa., Jan. 4, 1956; d. Christian S. and Lillian K. Seaman; m. Richard S. Ogurcak, Aug. 27, 1977; children: Christiann Ogurcak Bodwell, Jesse. BJ, Pa. State U., 1977. News reporter Sun-Gazette, Williamsport, Pa., 1977—91, lifestyle editor, 1991—2005; mus. dir. Peter J. McGovern Little League Mus., Williamsport, Pa., 2005—. Coll. newspaper advisor Lycourier of Lycoming Coll., Williamsport, Pa., 2000—; adj. coll. instr. Lycoming Coll., Williamsport, Pa., 2002—. V.p. Am. Bus. Women's Assn., Williamsport, Pa. Recipient Story of the Yr. award, Am. Cancer Soc., Pa., 1992; named Woman of the Yr., Am. Bus. Women's Assn., 1991. Mem.: Am. Assn. for State and Local History, Internat. Assn. of Sports Museums and Halls of Fame, Internat. Sports Heritage Assn., Small Museums Assn., Pa. Fedn. of Museums and Hist. Orgns., Am. Assn. of Museums. Office: Peter J McGovern Little League Mus PO Box 3485 525 Rte 15 Hwy South Williamsport PA 17701

OH, ALLEN JAMES, lawyer; b. Warren, Mich., Feb. 5, 1973; s. Kong Ping and Soo Khuan Oh; m. Tiffany Ann Millay, June 16, 2001; children: Madison Rose Kathleen, Mikyla Renee. BS in Elec. Engring., U. Mich., 1993; JD, U. Pa., 1996. Bar: Minn. 1996, Mich. 1998, U.S. Patent and Trademark Office 1998. Assoc. Merchant & Gould PC, Mpls., 1996—98, Rader, Fishman & Grauer PLLC, Bloomfield Hills, Mich., 1998—99, Schwegman, Lundberg, Woessner & Kluth, P.A., Mpls., 1999—2001, Shumaker Sieffert, Woodbury, Minn., 2001—02; patent atty. Allen J. Oh Law Office, Maple Grove, Minn., 2002—03, 2007—, Moore & Hansen, PLLP, Mpls., 2003—07. Bd. dirs. EECS Alumni Soc. U. Mich., Ann Arbor, Mich.; presenter in field. Mem.: IEEE (sr.), Minn. State Bar Assn. (mem. assembly 2005—), Tau Beta Pi, Eta Kappa Nu (v.p. 1992—93). Libertarian. Episcopalian. Office: Law Office 7200 Forestview Ln Ste U204 Maple Grove MN 55369 Business E-Mail: allen@ajoiplaw.com.

OH, CHANG, chemical engineer, consultant; b. Seoul, Kyeong-Ki, Republic Of Korea, Apr. 28, 1946; m. Theresa Oh, Mar. 26, 1976; children: Paul J., John E. MS, U. Fla., Gainesville, 1979; PhD, Wash. State U., Pullman, 1985. R & D engr. Korea Inst. Sci. & Tech., Seoul, 1974—77; process engr. Ethyl Corp., Baton Rouge, 1979—82; consulting engr. Idaho Nat. Lab., Idaho Falls, 1985—. Recipient Best Paper award, Am. Nuc. Soc., 2008. Fellow: ASME. Independent. Office: Idaho Nat Lab 2525 N Fremont Ave Idaho Falls ID 83415 Office Fax: 208-526-0528. Business E-Mail: chang.oh@inl.gov.

OH, CHANG KOOK, civil engineer, researcher; b. Seoul, Republic Of Korea, July 8, 1973; s. Tae June Oh and Soon Ock Hong; m. Hee Jo Bang, Mar. 24, 2007. BS with honors, Seoul Nat. U., 1998, MCE, 2000; PhD in Civil Engring., Calif. Inst. Tech., Pasadena, 2007. Rsch. asst. Seoul Nat. U., 1998—2000, Calif. Inst. Tech., 2002—07; asst. structural engr. Hyundai Engring. & Constrn. Co. Ltd., Seoul, 2000—01; rschr. Korea Earthquake Engring. Rsch. Ctr., Seoul, 2001—02; postdoc. scholar Carnegie Mellon U., Pitts., 2007—. Contbr. chapters to books & articles to profl. jours. Choir mem. Somang Presbyn. Ch., Seoul, 1997—2002. With Ministry Nat. Def. ROK Army, 1994—95, Seoul. Recipient Charles D. Babcock award, Calif. Inst. Tech., 2004; Harold Hellwig fellowship, 2002—07. Mem.: ASCE, Korean Soc. Civil Engrs., Earthquake Engring. Soc. Korea, Earthquake Engring. Rsch. Inst. Avocations: racquetball, swimming, travel. Office: Carnegie Mellon Univ 119 Porter Hall Pittsburgh PA 15213 E-mail: ockoogi@gmail.com.

OH, HONG KEUN, medical educator, physician; b. Suncheon, Korea (South), June 4, 1950; s. Gil Yeon Oh and Deuk Up Huh; m. Soon Hwa Choi, Sept. 19, 1980; children: Dong Hoon, Yoon Ju. MB, Kyung Hee U., Seoul, Republic of Korea, 1975; M in Medicine, Kyung Hee U., 1978, PhD, 1984; Naturopathic Dr., Can. Coll. Naturopathic Medicine, Toronto, Can., 1991; M in Healing Ministry, United Theol. U., Seoul, 1999. Cert. Dr. Ministry of Health and Welfare, 1975, Naturopathic Dr. Assn. Naturopathic Medicine, 1991. Prof. Sch. of Medicine, U. Toronto, 1986—88; mem. Physician and Surgeon of Ont., 1986—88; pres. Korea Soc. Comprehensive and Alternative Medicine, Seoul, 1997—; dean, prof. Jeonju U., Republic of Korea, 2005—. Pres. Korea Aromatherapy Assn., Seoul, Cheonra Buk Do, 1997—, Korea Soc. Stress Sci., Seoul, 1999—2001; chmn. World Orgn. Aromatherapy, Tokyo, 2002—04; pres. Dr. Oh's Neuropsychiatric Hosp., Seoul, 1997—2000. Author: (medical textbook) Dr. Oh's Naturopathic Medicine, (health book) Handbook of aromatherapy, (book) Dr. Oh's Aromatherapy textbook; contbr. scientific papers. Dir. Korean Mental Health Ctr., Toronto, 1986—89. Maj. 57 Mil. Army Hosp., 1980—83, Eujungbu, Korea. Presbyterian. Achievements include patents for effective composition of essential oils. Avocations: travel, bicycling, swimming, skiing, hiking. Office: Jeonju U 1200 Hyoja Dong Wansan Gu Chonra Buk Do Jeonju 560-757 Republic of Korea Office Fax: 82 63 220 2054.

OH, JAE KUEN, cardiologist, consultant, medical educator, director; b. Taejon, Korea (South), May 17, 1952; m. Terry Oh; 1 child, Phillip S. Maj. in BioChemistry, U. Pa., Phila., 1971—75; MD, Pa. State U., Hershey, 1975—79; Residency, Mayo Grad. Sch. Medicine, Rochester, Minn., 1979—82; Fellowship, Mayo Grad. Sch. of Medicine, Rochester, Minn., 1982—85. Board Certified Internal Medicine Splty. Bd., 1982, Cardiovasc. Splty. Bd., 1985, The Nat. Bd. Echocardiography, 2000; Nat. Bd. Exam, 1981. Residency Mayo Clinic, Rochester, Minn., 1979—82, fellowship, 1982—85, cons., 1985—. Cons. Mayo Clinic, Rochester, Minn., 1988—, prof. medicine, 1998—, dir. echo core lab, 1999—, co-director echocardiography lab., 2003—. Author: (book) The Echo Manual. Grantee NIH U01, NIH, 2002. Fellow: Am. Coll. Cardiology, Am. Heart Assn. (grant 2001, 2003); mem.: Am. Soc. Echocardiography. Avocations: golf, travel, movies, writing. Office: Mayo Clinic 200 First St SW Rochester MN 05905

OH, JOHN KIE-CHIANG, political science professor, academic administrator; b. Seoul, Nov. 1, 1930; came to U.S., 1954, naturalized, 1971; s. Sung-Jun and Duk-Cho (Kim) O.; m. Bonnie Cho, Sept. 5, 1959; children: Jane J., Marie J., James J. BS, Marquette U., 1957; postgrad., Columbia U., 1957-58; PhD, Georgetown U., 1962. Asst. prof. St. Thomas Coll., St. Paul, 1962-66; assoc. prof. polit. sci. Marquette U., Milw., 1967-71, prof., chmn., 1971-77, dean grad. sch., 1977-85; acad. v.p. Cath. U. Am., Washington, 1985-89, Banigan scholar, prof. dept. politics, 1990-2001, prof. emeritus, 2001—. Adviser Republic of Korea Embassy, 2001—03; nat. chmn. Asian Sect. Fulbright Hays Program. Author: Korea: Democracy on Trial, 1968, (with Peter Cheng et al) Emerging Roles of Asian Nations in the 1980's, 1979, Democratization and Economic Development in Korea, 1990, Korean Politics: The Quest for Democratization and Economic Development, 1999, Thai transl., 2004, The Korean Embassy in America, 2003; contbr. articles to profl. jours. Chmn. scholarship com. World Affairs Coun., 1976-78; mem. Wis. Gov.'s Commn. for UN, Madison, 1971-74; chmn. Korean Studies com., Assn. Asian Studies, 1975-76. Grantee Hill Found., 1963, Relm Found., 1968, Social Sci. Rsch Coun., 1973, Am. Coun. Learned Socs., 1973. Mem. Am. Polit. Sci. Assn., Assn. Asian Studies, Internat. Polit. Sci. Assn., Midwest Conf. Asian Affairs (pres. 1970-71), Assn. Cath. Colls. and Univs. (bd. dirs. 1983-87), Indian Spring Country Club (bd. govs. 2000). Roman Catholic. Home: 807 Davis St 1506 Evanston IL 60201 Personal E-mail: jnboh@aol.com.

OH, JUNG EUN JEN, transportation executive, researcher; b. Seoul, Republic of Korea, Aug. 18, 1977; d. Chi Hang Oh and Hea Jung Choi. BS in Civil Engring., Seoul Nat. U., 2000, MS in Civil Engring., 2002; MS in Economics, Purdue U., West Lafayette, Ind., 2007, PhD in Civil Engring., 2008. Grad. rsch. asst. Seoul Nat. U., 2000—02; jr. rschr. Korea Transport Inst., Goyang, Gyeonggi, Republic of Korea, 2002—04; rschr., tchg. asst. Purdue U., 2004—08; transport specialist World Bank, Washington, 2008—. Exec. leader Internat. Rd. Fedn., 2008. Contbr. scientific papers. Recipient Eldon J. Yoder Meml. award, Purdue U., 2007. Mem.: Transp. Rsch. Bd. Achievements include research in evaluation of transportation systems and their impact on economic, social development. Office: World Bank 1818 H St NW Washington DC 20433 Personal E-mail: jenishere77@gmail.com.

OH, JUNG HUN, computer engineer; b. Jeonnam, Korea (South), Dec. 25, 1971; s. Seung Ok Oh and Dong Jin Choi; m. Young Bun Kim, Dec. 1, 1972; 1 child, Yu Na. BS, Soongsil U., Seoul, 1995, MS, 1997; PhD in Computer Sci. & Engring., U. Tex., Arlington, 2008. Sys. engr. Jinro Industries, Seoul, Republic of Korea, 1997—98; sr. software engr. Willtech, Seoul, 1997—2002, Sk C&C, Seoul, Republic of Korea, 2002—03; rsch. scholar U. Tex., Arlington, 2004—08; postdoc. rsch. assoc., dept. radiation oncology Washington U., St. Louis, 2009—. Software engring. tng. Satyam, Hyderabad, India, 2003; product edn. Willtech, Seoul, Korea (South), 1998—2002. Contbr. articles to profl. jours. Fellow Hermann fellow, U. Tex. at Arlington, 2003; scholar Grad. Study Abroad scholar, Korea Sci. and Engring. Found., 2003. Mem.: IEEE, Internat. Assn. Engring. Democrat-Npl. Christian. Avocations: travel, golf, basketball. Home: 4907 W Pine Blvd 107 Saint Louis MO 63108 Personal E-mail: ojh1225@gmail.com.

OH, KYUNG SUK (DAN OH), electrical engineer; b. Pusan, Republic Of Korea, June 24, 1965; s. Bong Do Oh and KumBok Lee; m. Myung Sook Jun, July 26, 1992; children: Christopher, Terry. PhD in Elec. Engring., U. Ill., Urbana-Champaign, 1995. Devel. engr. III AMP Inc., Harrisburg, Pa., 1995—96; mem. tech. staff Synopsis, Inc., Mountain View, Calif., 1996—2000; sr. engring. mgr. Rambus Inc., Los Altos, 2000—. Contract cons. Cadence Inc., Chemsford, Mass., 1994. Contbr. articles to more than 40 profl. jours. Recipient Bronze Tablet award, U. Ill., 1991. Mem.: IEEE. Achievements include patents in field; patents pending in field. Home: 10219 Palo Vista Rd Cupertino CA 95014 Office: Rambus Inc 4440 El Camino Real Los Altos CA 94022 Office Fax: 650-947-5001. Personal E-mail: ksoh@yahoo.com. Business E-Mail: doh@rambus.com.

OH, MARK EDWARD, minister; s. Kap Soo and Boonhak Oh; m. Rosemary McGuire, Aug. 20, 1965; children: Christopher Douglas, Jonathan David. BA, Keimyung U., 1958; MA, San Francisco Theol. Sem., 1963; MRE, New Orleans Bapt. Theol. Sem., 1964; MDiv, We. Sem. Portland, 1968; PhD, Calif. Grad. Sch. Theology, 1971; D of Ministry, Fuller Theol. Sem., 1988. Ordination Crescent-Bay Bapt. Assn., CA, 1968. Pastor Internat. Bible Ch., LA, 1972—. Pres. Christ Bible Coll., LA, 2001—. Mem.: Am. Assn. Christian Counselors (charter).

OH, MYOUNGHO, computer scientist, educator; b. Pusan, South Korea, Dec. 11, 1960; s. Suntae Oh and Bokcheol Baek; m. Kyungyoon Shim, Aug. 27, 1989; children: Hyunju, Hyunwoo. BS, Korea Mil. Acad., Seoul, 1984; MS, Oreg. State U., Corvallis, 1988; PhD, KAIST, Daejon, 1996. Chmn. dept. computer sci Korea Mil. Acad., 2000—04, assoc. prof. computer sci., 2000—06, prof. info. sci., 2006—, head prof. info. sci., 2009—. Asst. mgr. acad. bd. Korea Mil. Acad., Seoul, 1990—91, asst. dir. computer ctr., 1997—98, dir. ednl. development, 2005—06; vis. scholar dept. sys. sci. Washington U., St. Louis, 1999—2000; rsch. bd. advisors Am. Biog. Inst., 2005—; planning mgr. Hwarangdae Rsch. Inst., 2006—08; bd. advisors Def. Agy. Tech. and Quality, 2006—07, Republic of Korea Army Hdqs., Office Analysis & Evaluation, 2007—09. Author: (books) Differential Equation, 1991, Improvement of Computer Efficiency, 2002, Introduction to Computer Science, 2003, Computer Network, 2003, C Language, 2003, Practical Use of Computers, 2004, Computer Science, 2005, Introduction to Information Science & Technology, 2008, NCW & Unmanned Combat Systems, 2008, Military Information Network, 2009; contbr. articles to profl. jours. Col. South Korea Mil. Decorated True Soldier of Yr. Korean Army; recipient Award of Excellence, 2007—08, Ministry of Nat. Def., 2005, Honor Prize, Prime Min. of Korea, 1984, Edn. award, Korea Mil. Acad., 2001, Best Achievement Prof. award, 2002, 2003, 2006. Mem.: Korea Info. Soc., Korea Inst. of Mil. Sci. and Tech., Korea Math. Soc. Buddhism. Avocations: running, swimming. Office: Korea Mil Acad Dept Electronics & Info Sci Gongneung-dong Nowon-gu Seoul 139-799 Republic of Korea Business E-Mail: mhoh@kma.ac.kr.

OH, SANDRA, actress; b. Nepean, Ont., Can., July 20, 1971; m. Alexander Payne, Jan. 1, 2003 (div. Dec. 21, 2006). Actor: (films) Double Happiness, 1994, Bean, 1997, The Princess Diaries, 2001, Big Fat Liar, 2002, Full Frontal, 2002, Long Life, Happiness & Prosperity, 2002, Rick, 2003, Under the Tuscan Sun, 2003, Break a Leg, 2003, Wilby Wonderful, 2004, Sideways, 2004 (Screen Actors Guild Award, outstanding performance by cast in motion picture, 2005), 8 Minutes to Love, 2004, Hard Candy, 2005, Break a Leg, 2005, Cake, 2005, 3 Needles, 2005, Sorry, Haters, 2005, The Night Listener, 2006, For Your Consideration, 2006, Falling, 2007, Blindness, 2008; (TV series) Arli$$, 1996—2002 (CableACE Award, 1997), Grey's Anatomy, 2005— (Best Performance by an Actress in a Supporting Role in a Series, Mini-Series or Motion Picture Made for TV, Hollywood Fgn. Press Assn. (Golden Globe), 2006, Outstanding Performance by a Female Actor in a Drama Series, Screen Actors Guild award, 2006, Outstanding Performance by an Ensemble in a Drama Series, SAG, 2007); (TV miniseries) Further Tales of the City, 2001.

OH, SANGYOON, assistant professor; b. Seoul, Republic of Korea, July 7, 1971; s. Choonjae Oh and Sunmin Park. BS in Engring., Sungkyunkwan U., Seoul, Republic of Korea, 1994; MS, Syracuse U., NY, 1999; PhD, Ind. U., Bloomington, 2006. Project engr. Hansol Paper Co., Seoul, Republic of Korea, 1995—96; rsch. asst. NE Parallel Archs. Ctr. Syracuse U., 1999—2000; rsch. asst. computational sci. and info. tech. Fla. State U., Tallahassee, 2000—01; rsch. asst. cmty. grids lab. Ind. U., Bloomington, 2001—06; rsch. scientist SK Telecom, Seoul, Republic of Korea, 2006—07; asst. prof. computer engring. Ajou U. Contbr. articles to profl. jours. V.p. young adult group Korean United Meth. Ch., Bloomington, 2003—04, youth min., 2005—06. Pvt., 1991, Republic of Korea Mil. Grad. Rsch. scholar, Syracuse U., 1999—2000, Fla. State U., 2000—01, Ind. U., 2001—06. Mem.: IEEE. Achievements include design of handheld flexible representation architecture for web service on mobile devices; development of handheld message service for light weight messaging on mobile devices; tango interactive collaboration system; research in collaboration framework for universal accessibility. Avocations: golf, tennis, history. Office: Ajou Univ Sans Woncheon-dong Yeongtong-gu Suwon 443-749 Republic of Korea Home Phone: 82-31-219-2633. Business E-Mail: syoh@ajou.ac.kr.

OH, SEACHEON, chemical engineer, educator; b. Seoul, Republic of Korea, Mar. 6, 1965; s. Sanghwan Oh and Gumsun Lee; m. Sunmi Lee, Feb. 14, 1993; 1 child, Minseok. BS in Chem. Engring., Hanyang U., Seoul, Republic of Korea, 1987, MS in Chem. Engring., 1989, PhD in Chem. Engring., 1997. Rschr. Hanil Synthetic Fiber Co., Ltd., Masan, Republic of Korea, 1994—98; project manage Hyundai Engring. Co., Ltd., Seoul, 1998—99; sr. rschr. rsch. inst. indsl. sci. Hanyang U., Seoul, 1999; asst. prof. Cheonan Nat. Tech. Coll., Republic of Korea, 2000—04; assoc. prof. Kongju Nat. U., Cheonan, 2005—. Mem. rsch. com. Korea Energy Mgmt. Corp., Yongin, Republic of Korea, 2005—; mem. estimation com. new environ. tech. Korea Inst. Environ. Sci. and Tech., Seoul, 2004—; mem. estimation com. Korea Inst. Indsl. Tech., Seoul, 2004—. Contbr. articles to profl. jours. Mem. com. Local Agenda 21 Cheonan, 2001—02. Mem.: Korean Soc. Waste Mgmt., Korean Soc. Environ. Engrs., Korean Soc. Indsl. and Engring. Chemistry, Korean Inst. Chem. Engrs. (mem. com. energy and environ. sect. 2004—05), Korean Fedn. Environ. Movement. Achievements include patents for pyrolysis method of plastic wastes using tubular reactor; pyrolysis reactor of plastic wastes. Home: 101-704 Keyryong 1078 Dujeong-dong Cheonan 330-210 Republic of Korea Office: Kongju National Univ Dept Environ Engring 275 Budae-dong Cheonan 330-717 Republic of Korea Office Fax: 82-41-552-0380. Personal E-mail: oh1965@hanmail.net. Business E-Mail: ohsec@kongju.ac.kr.

OH, SOOJIN SUSAN, elementary school educator; b. Seoul, July 7, 1980; d. Hyun Kyung and Eunsim Oh. BA summa cum laude, U. Pa., Phila., 2003, MS in Edn., 2004; doctoral candidate in Edn., Harvard Grad. Sch. Edn., Cambridge, Mass., 2007—. Cert. tchr. elem. edn. Pa. Info. tech. asst. mgr. Coll. Ho. Computing, U. Pa., Phila., 1999—2003; acad. and career advisor U. Pa., Phila., 2000—03; product mgmt. intern Chubb Group of Ins. Cos., Washington, 2001; pub. svc. intern Korean Am. Coalition, Washington, 2001; tchg. asst. Wharton Sch., U. Pa., Phila., 2002—03; strategic mktg. intern Toyota Motor Corp., Torrance, Calif., 2002; rsch. analyst U. Pa. Grad. Sch. Edn., Phila., 2004; head tchr. grade 1 Abington Friends Sch., Jenkintown, Pa., 2004—; ednl. cons. Laurus Enterprise, Seoul, 2005. Mem. math curriculum planning and devel. com. Abington Friends Sch., Jenkintown, Pa., 2004—, mem. acad. planning com., 2004—, internat. intern liaison; ethnographer Hist. Soc. Pa., Phila., 2004; transl., interpreter interviews, press confs., articles; fellow Klingenstein Summer Inst., Columbia U., 2006; presenter in field. Editor rev. bd.: Urban Edn. Jour.; editl. bd. Dear Theopilus Newsletter; contbr. articles to profl. jours. Local area coord. Habitat for Humanity, Reseda, Calif., 1995—99; liaison Tree People, Beverly Hills, 1995—99; chpt. mem. UNICEF, Phila., 2003—; curriculum developer Quo Vadis West Philly Edn. Outreach Program, Phila., 2004—; vol. nursery, maternity, oncology, pediat., newborn ICU Valley Presbyn. Hosp., Van Nuys, Calif., 1993—99; liaison Salvation Army, Canoga Park, Calif., 1995—99; pub. svc. intern Korean Am. Coaltion, Washington, 2001—; women's ministry, small group ministry leader Emmanuel Ch. in Phila., 1999—; pianist, ministry dir., youth group pres. Calvary Presbyn. Ch., Granada Hills, Calif., 1992—99. Recipient Korean Am. Student Leader of the Yr. award, Korean Heritage Found., Nat. Leadership and Svc. award, USAA Ednl. Found., 1997, Nat. Math. award, U.S. Acade. Achievement, 1997, Nat. Prudential Leadership award, Prudential Fin., 1998, Leadership award, Korean Sr. Citizens Mut. Club, 2001; grantee, Samuel S. Fels Fund, 2004, U. Pa. Grad. Sch. of Edn., 2004; fellow, Columbia U. Tchrs. Coll., 2000, Roothbert Fund, 2007; scholar, Boston U., 1999, UCLA Chancellor, 1999, UCLA Alumni Assn., 1999, U. Calif. Berkeley Regents, 1999, Korean Am. Scholarship Found., 2000, 2001, 2002, 2003, 2004, Korea Times, 2000, 2002, Central Daily News, 2001, Ca. Golden State; All Am. scholarship, USAA Ednl. Found., 1996, Toyota Cmty. scholarship, Toyota Motor U.S.A., 1999—2003, Tylenol Cmty. scholarship, Johnson & Johnson, 1999, Nat. AP scholar, Edn. Testing Svcs., 1999, Penn Alumni scholarship, U. Pa., 1999—2003, Nat. Merit Commended scholar, Edn. Testing Svcs., 1999, Korean Ambassadorial scholarship, Embassy of Republic of Korea, 2003, Scott Kyungmo Kim Scholarship, 2004. Mem.: North Am. Reggio Emilia Alliance (assoc.), Nat. Assn. for Edn. of Young Children (assoc.), Key Club Internat. (life; pres., v.p., dist. rep. 1995—99, Kiwanis Internat. Cmty. Leadership award 1999, Disting. Leader of the Yr. award 1995), Kiwanis (pres. local chpt. Key Club 1995—99), Pi Gamma Mu (life), Ephebian Honor Soc. (life), Golden Key Internat. Honor Soc. (life; pres. 2002—03), Psi Chi (life; pres., v.p., fin. dir. 2000—03). Achievements include research in educational policy, research and practice across K-12 schools and higher education institutions in China; key factors that facilitate effortless recall, accuracy and memory retention for simple multiplication; historical, cultural, and sociopolitical forces that have shaped the West Philadelphia neighborhood; featured in various newspapers such as: LA Times, Korea Times, Dong-A Daily News, Central Daily News. Avocations: photography, travel, interior design, literature, classical concerts. Office: Abington Friends Sch 575 Washington Ln Jenkintown PA 19046

OH, SOON YOUNG, researcher; s. Do Kwang Oh and Joo Young Lee; m. Mi Hyeon Kim; 1 child, Hee Wan. PhD, U. Calif., LA, 2008. Grad. student rschr. U. Calif., 2003—. Office: Univ Calif 4732 Boelter Hall Los Angeles CA 90034

OH, TAI KEUN, business educator, consultant; arrived in US, 1958, naturalized, 1969; m. Gretchen Brenneke Oh, Dec. 26, 1964; children: Erica, Elizabeth, Emily. BA, Seijo U., 1957; MA, Northern Ill. U., 1961; MLS, U. Wis., 1965, PhD, 1970. Asst. prof. mgmt. Roosevelt U., Chgo., 1969—73; assoc. prof. Calif. State U., Fullerton, 1973—76, prof. mgmt., 1976—2001, prof. mgmt. emeritus, 2001—; vis. prof. U. Hawaii, 1983—84, U. Nuertingen, Germany, 1996—97, 1999; advisor Pacific Asian Mgmt. Inst., U. Hawaii; internat. referee Asia-Pacific Jour. Mgmt., 1990—; cons. Calty Design Rsch. Inc.; subs. Toyota Motor Corp.; guest lectr. Chiba U. Commerce, Japan; cons., spkr. in field. Editl. bd. Acad. Mgmt. Rev., 1978—81, contbg. author Ency. Profl. Mgmt., 1978, Handbook of Management, 1985; contbr. articles to profl. jours. Recipient award, Calif. State U., 1987; named Outstanding Prof., Bus. Adminstrn. & Economics, Calif. State U., 1976, 1978; grantee, NSF, 1968—69. Mem.: Acad. Mgmt. Achievements include helped over 100 organizations solve complex human resource and management problems over the course of his career. Home: 2044 E Eucalyptus Ln Brea CA 92821-5911 E-mail: toh@fullerton.edu.

OH, WILLIAM, physician; b. The Philippines, May 22, 1931; came to U.S., 1958, naturalized, 1970; s. Bun Kun and Chay Suat (Lim) Oh; m. Mary Oh, June 4, 1960; children: Kenneth Albert, Kerstin Amy. MD, U. Santo Tomas, Phillipines, 1958; MA (hon.), Brown U., 1974; DSc (hon.), R.I. Coll., 1985. Diplomate Am. Bd. Pediatrics, Am. Bd. Neonatal Perinatal Medicine. Intern Deaconess Hosp., Milw., 1958-59; resident in pediatrics Michael Reese Hosp., Chgo., 1959-63; fellow in neonatology Kavolinska Inst., Stockholm, 1963-65; dir. neonatology Michael Reese Hosp., Chgo., 1965-69; dir. neonatology, assoc. prof. pediatrics UCLA, 1969-73, prof., 1973-74; prof. pediatrics and obstetrics Brown U., Providence, 1974-88, Sylvia Kay Hassenfeld prof. pediatrics, chmn. dept., 1989—2003; pediatrician-in-chief Women and Infants Hosp. of R.I., Providence, 1974—89, R.I. Hosp.; prof., chmn. dept. pediatrics Brown U., 1989—2003; prof. pediat. Women and Infants' Hosp., Brown U., 2003—. Mem. NIH study sect. on human embryology and devel., chmn., 1985-93; mem. pediatric test com. Bd. Med. Exam., 1985-89; mem. sub-bd. of neonatal-perinatal medicine Am. Bd. Pediatrics, 1982-88; chair com. on Fetus and Newborn, Am. Acad. Pediatrics; mem. Nat. Adv. Coun. for Child Health, 1995-99. Author book in field; contbr. chpts. to books, numerous articles to profl. jours.; editor profl. jour. Adv. com. Nat. Found. of March of Dimes. NIH grantee. Mem. Am. Pediatric Soc., Am. Acad. Pediatrics (fetus and newborn com. 1986-90), Soc. Pediatric Research, Perinatal Research Soc. (pres. 1981), Am. Inst. Nutrition, Fedn. Am. Socs. Exptl. Biology. Roman Catholic. Home: 24 Robbins Dr Barrington RI 02806-2612 Office: Dudley Providence RI 02905-4923 Office Phone: 401-274-1100. Business E-Mail: woh@wihri.org.

OH, WILLIAM KYU, oncologist; b. Inchon, Korea (South), Aug. 14, 1965; s. Daniel K and Esther A Oh; m. Easter Chiu, Oct. 18, 1997; children: Christopher J, Andrew M. BS, Yale U., 1983—87; MD, NY U., 1988—92. Diplomate Internal Medicine and Medical Oncology Am. Bd. of Internal Medicine, 1997, lic. Medical Doctor Mass., 1992. Intern Brigham and Women's Hosp., Boston, 1992—93, resident, 1993—95, assoc. physician; fellow Harvard Med. Sch., Boston, 1992—97, instr. medicine, 1997—2000, asst. prof. medicine, 2000—07, assoc. prof. medicine, 2007—; fellow Dana-Farber Cancer Inst., Boston, 1995—98, clin. dir., Lank Ctr. Oncology, 2002—09. Mem.: Cancer and Leukemia Group B, Am. Soc. Clin. Oncology (mem., cancer edn. com. 2004—). Office: Dana-Farber Cancer Inst Mailstop D1230 44 Binney St Boston MA 02215 also: Mount Sinai Sch Medicine One Gustave L Levy Pl Box 1079 New York NY 10029 Business E-Mail: william.oh@mssm.edu.*

O'HAGAN, JAMES JOSEPH, lawyer; b. Chgo., Dec. 29, 1936; s. Francis James and Florence Agnes (Dowgialo) O'H.; m. Suzanne Elizabeth Wiegand, June 28, 1958; children: Timothy, Karen, Peggy, Kevin. B in Commerce, De Paul U., 1958, JD, 1962. Sr. ptnr. O'Hagan Spencer, Chgo., 2006—. Mem. Cook County Pres.'s Com. on the Cts. for the 21st Century, chmn. suburban subcom., 1998—2000; lawyer Chgo. Claim Mgrs. Assn., 1992—2006; chmn. USLaw Network, Inc., 2001—03, mem. exec. com., 2001—06; founding mem. Profl. Lines Atty. Network. Mem. ABA, Ill. Bar Assn. Chgo. Bar Assn., Am. Bd. Trial Advocates, Internat. Assn. Def. Coun., Def. Rsch. Inst., Profl. Liability Underwriters Soc. Avocations: golf, physical conditioning, painting, reading. Office: O'Hagan Spencer 1 East Wacker Dr Ste 3400 Chicago IL 60601 Home Phone: 847-292-1266; Office Phone: 312-422-6121. Business E-Mail: johagan@ohaganspencer.com.

O'HAIR, SEAN, professional golfer; b. Lubbock, Tex., July 11, 1982; s. Marc and Brenda O'Hair; m. Jackie Lucas, 2002; children: Molly, Luke. Profl. golfer, 1999—. Writer (blog) pgatour.com, 2008. Achievements include winning PGA Tour events: John Deere Classic, 2005, PODS Championship, 2008, Quail Hollow Championship, 2009. Office: PGA Tour 100 PGA Tour Blvd Ponte Vedra FL 32082*

O'HALLORAN, PATRICK, psychologist; b. Elizabeth, NJ, May 29, 1972; s. Peter and Barbara O'Halloran. BA, Moravian Coll., Bethlehem, Pa., 1994; MA, Seton Hall U., South Orange, NJ, 1995, MA, 2006, EdD, 2008. Cert. edn. specialist Seton Hall U., 1999, ednl. adminstrv. NJ., 2008. Sch. psychologist Long Hill Twp., Millington, NJ, 1999—2001, Watchung Hills Regional HS, Warren Township, NJ, 2001—08. Mem.: NASP. Office: Watchung Hills Regional High Sch 108 Stirling Rd Warren NJ 07059 Business E-Mail: pohalloran@whrhs.org.

O'HALLORAN, THOMAS ALPHONSUS, JR., retired physicist, researcher; b. Bklyn., Apr. 13, 1931; s. Thomas Alphonsus Sr. and Nora (Sheehan) O'H.; m. Barbara Joyce Hug, June 9, 1954; children: Theresa Joyce, Maureen Ann, Kevin Thomas, Patrick Joseph. Student, San Jose State U., 1948-50; BS in Physics & Math., Oreg. State U., 1953, MS in Physics, 1954; PhD, U. Calif., Berkeley, 1963. Rsch. asst. Lawrence Berkeley Lab., U. Calif., 1963-64; rsch. fellow Harvard U., Cambridge, Mass., 1964-66; asst. prof. physics U. Ill., Urbana, 1966-68, assoc. prof., 1968-70, prof., 1970-93, prof. emeritus, 1993—; vis. scholar U. Utah, Salt Lake City, 1990-93, rsch. prof. physics, 1993-97; ret., 1997. Vis. scientist Lawrence Berkeley Lab., U. Calif., 1979-80. Contbr. numerous articles on elem. particle physics to profl. jours. Lt. USNR, 1954-58. Guggenheim fellow, 1979-80. Fellow Am. Phys. Soc. Home: 4614 Ledgemont Dr Holladay UT 84124-4735 Personal E-mail: tomohal@comcast.net.

OHAMA, GARY LOUIS, dental ceramist; b. Abington, Pa., Dec. 9, 1948; s. Benjamin Saburo and Kuniko Hirokawa Ohama; m. Susanne Louise Clinton; stepchildren: Philip, Holly, Hana; 1 child from previous marriage, Jennifer Suzanne. BS, Pa. State U., 1971. Owner, ceramist Ohama Dental Studio, Inc., Abington, 1973—91; finisher Nakashima Woodworkers, New Hope, Pa., 2000—02; dental ceramist Ft. Washington (Pa.) Dental Lab., 2002—. Cons., lectr. on dental ceramics N.Y. Dental Lab. Congress, Dentsply Internat., Ney Co., Sterngold, Colo., others. Aikido instr. Served with USAR, 1971—77. Recipient Outstanding Alumni award, Pa. State U., 1982, Eagle Scout award. Lutheran. Achievements include development of internal translucency and effects of refractive index in dental ceramics; of special oil, and oil/polyurethane wood finishing processes; research in breath dynamics and biomechanical movements and body functions; effects of breathing and spinal cord alignment on bio-mechanical performance. Avocation: Aikido instructor. Home: 402 Fretz Rd Perkasie PA 18944 Home Phone: 215-249-1614; Office Phone: 215-628-4944. Personal E-mail: gary.ohama@gmail.com.

OHANIAN, BERNARD JAY, writer, editor; b. Tokyo, Apr. 22, 1956; came to U.S., 1956; s. Abraham Sam and Bernadine Jeanette (Preis) O.; m. Catharine Greta Vollmer, July 2, 1983 (div. 1990); m. Kathleen Karen Kelly, Aug. 14, 1994; children: Rafael Kelly, Sofia Kelly. Student, U. Degli Studi, Pisa, Italy, 1977-78; BA, U. Calif., Berkeley, 1980. Editor Newsfront Internat., Oakland, Calif., 1978-81; editor-in-chief Mediafile, San Francisco, 1981-83; corr. RKO Radio, Rome, 1983-84; English lang. editor Inter Press Svc., Rome, 1983-84; sr. editor Rip N Read News Svc., San Francisco, 1984-85, Mother Jones mag., San Francisco, 1985-88; sr. editor, features MacWeek mag., San Francisco, 1988-89; editl. dir. RX Media Publs., Sausalito, Calif., 1989-90; mem. editl. staff Nat. Geographic mag., Washington, 1992-95, editl. dir. internat. edits. to assoc. editor, 1995—2006; v.p. content integration AARP Publications. Freelance editl. cons., 1990—; vis. faculty mem. Sch. of Journalism U. Calif., Berkeley, 1990. Author (books) Baseball in America, 1991, A Day in the Life of Italy, 1990; editor (books) The Power to Heal, 1990, A Day in the Life of Ireland, 1991; caption writer (book) In Pursuit of Ideas, 1992; editorial cons., caption writer: The Face of Mercy, 1993. Bd. dirs. Media Alliance, San Francisco, 1986-93, pres., 1988-92. Recipient Best Feature Article award Western Publs. Assn., 1990. Mem. Am. Soc. Mag. Editors, U. Calif. Berkeley Alumni Assn. (life). Avocations: travel, basketball, photography, current affairs, opera. Office: AARP Publications 601 E St NW Washington DC 20049 Personal E-mail: bernardohanian@aol.com.

OHANIAN, MIHRAN JACOB, nuclear engineer, educator, dean, researcher; b. Istanbul, Turkey, Aug. 7, 1933; came to U.S., 1956, naturalized, 1967; s. Mark and Mary Catherine (Sayabalian) O.; m. Sandra Jean Blair, Apr. 22, 1962; children: Heather Jean Allen, Holly Lynn Welty. BSE.E. with high honors, Robert Coll. Engring. Sch., Istanbul, 1956; M.E.E., Rensselaer Poly. Inst., 1960, PhD in Nuclear Engring. and Sci., 1963. Lectr. nuclear engring. Rensselaer Poly. Inst., 1963, instr., 1958-62; asst. prof. nuclear engring. U. Fla., Gainesville, 1964-67, assoc. prof., 1967-70, prof., 1970-2001, prof. emeritus, 2001—, chmn. dept., 1969-79, assoc. dir. Engring. and Indsl. Expt. Sta., 1977-99, assoc. dean for rsch., 1979-90, assoc. dean for adminstrn. and planning, 1990-91, assoc. dean for rsch. and adminstrn., 1991-98, interim v.p. rsch., dean of grad. sch., 1998-99, pres. Rsch. Found., 1998-99, interim dean Coll. of Engr., assoc. v.p. Engring. and Indsl. Experiment Station, 1999-2001; sabbatical leave Inst. Energy Analysis, Oak Ridge, 1976-77, on assignment, 1977-78. Cons. Fla. Power Corp., Batelle Meml. Inst., Fla. Nuc. Assocs., Oak Ridge Nat. Lab., Inst. Energy Analysis, Argonne Nat. Lab., Savannah River Lab., U. Va., Tex. Higher Edn. Bd., NSF; U. Fla. rep. U.S. Nuc. Energy Inst., 1972-2001, mem. adv. coun., 1972-80; U. Fla. rep. to Oak Ridge Assoc. Univs., 1972-76; mem. engring. accreditation commn. Accreditation Bd. Engring. and Tech., 1984-88; mem. rev. com. reactor analysis and safety divsn. Argonne Nat. Lab, 1982-88, chmn. 1986-87, mem. rev. com. reactor engring. divsn., 1992-2001; mem. adv. com. Consol. Fuel Reprocessing Program Oak Ridge Nat. Lab., 1982-88; mem. com. on univ. rsch. reactors Energy Engring. Bd., NRC, 1986-88; mem. U.S. Dept. Energy's Adv. Com. on Nuc. Facility Safety (ACNFS), 1988-90; bd. dirs., chmn. Fla. Inst. Phosphate Rsch., 1990-2001. Contbr. articles to profl. jours. Trustee Fla. Defenders of the Environment, 1969-71, treas., 1969-70, mem., 1969—80. Recipient valor medal Am. Legion, 1966, Disting. Faculty award Fla. Blue Key, 1984; Alumnus fellow Rensselaer Poly. Inst., 1994. Fellow AAAS, Am. Nuclear Soc. (v.p., pres.-elect 1989-90, pres. 1990-91, bd. dirs. 1974-77, 84-93, vice chmn., chmn. edn. divsn. 1975-76, exec. com. nuc. fuel cycle divsn. 1978-81, mem. profl. devel. and accreditation com., chmn. tech. program internat. conf. Washington, 1980, mem. nominating com., 1980-81, 87-88, chmn., 1991-92, exec. com., 1986-92, honors and awards com. 1997—, chmn. 2004—07, Exceptional Svc. award 1980, adv. editor Nuclear Sci. and Engring. Jour. 1989— hon. chmn. ann. conf. 1997, hon. chmn. 10th Internat. Conf. on Robotics, 2004), Engr. Coun. Profl. Devel. (dir. 1976-78), Am. Assn. Engring. Soc. (awards com. 1985-86, bd. dir. 1990-91, exec. com. 1990-95, sec.-treas., 1992, chair-elect 1993, chair 1994, chair nominating com. 1995, chair awards com. 1996), Am. Soc. Engring. Edn. (adv. com. Ford Found. Resident Fellow Program 1971-79, sec.-treas. nuc. engring. divsn. 1981-82, vice chmn. 1982-83, chmn. 1983-84, projects bd. 1981-87, chmn. awards com. 1985-87); mem. Nat. Audubon Soc. (pres. 1965-66), Ret. Faculty U. Fla. Inc. (pres. 2004—05), Rotary (Paul Harris fellow), Sigma Xi, Tau Beta Pi (eminent engr.), Alpha Nu Sigma (pres. 1981-83), Eta Kappa Nu, Phi Kappa Phi, Epsilon Lambda Chi. Presbyterian. Home: 6095 Twin Lakes Rd Keystone Heights FL 32656-9728 Business E-Mail: johanian@ufl.edu.

OHANJANIAN, RUZANNA, clinical psychologist; d. Vladimir and Nina Ohanjanian; 1 child, Irene Gyulnazarian. BA in Linguistics & Lit. with honors, Leninakan Ednl. Inst., 1977; MA in Psychology, Yerevan P. State U., 1981; PhD, Moscow Acad. Scis., 1985; postdoctoral, U. San Francisco Med. Ctr., 1996. Cert. trauma specialist, Traumatic Incident Reduction Calif., 1991, lic. clin. psychologist Bd. Psychology, Calif., 1999. Clin. psychologist Dept. Pub. Health, San Francisco, 1998—2002, Family Svcs., Palo Alto, Calif., 1998—2002, Multilingual Psychology Cons., Mountain View, Calif., 1996—98, UCSF Med. Ctr., Mt. Zion Hosp., San Francisco. Nat. disaster team mem. Min. Health, Armenia, 1989—91; assoc. prof. Yerevan State U., Armenia, 1990—92, vis. prof., 1992; presenter State of World Forum, San Francisco, 1997; crisis mgmt. team mem. Family Enterprise Internat. Behavioral Health, 1999—. Contbr. over 30 publs. and presentations in field. Chmn. Irene Gyulnazarian Ednl. Fund for Armenia, Los Gatos, Calif., 2003—. Recipient Appreciation award, FEI Behavioral Health, 2000, Alaska Airlines, 2000, Make a Difference award, Total Employee Assistance and Mgmt. Inc., 2002, Employee Assistance Program Appreciation award, Pacific Care Behavioral Health; named Hon. Dr., Yerevay State U., 2005. Mem.: APA, Armenian Profl. Soc. Avocations: painting, piano. Office: Ohanjanian Ruzanna POBox 320652 Los Gatos CA 95032 Personal E-mail: irachka2@hotmail.com.

O'HANLON, CAROL ANN, minister; b. Jacksonville, Fla. d. Oscar Lee Miller and Elsie (Beecher) Simpson; m. Arthur Francis, July 16, 1963; 1 child, Arthur Patrick. BA, Montreat, 1956; M of Religious Edn., Union Sem., 1959, MDiv, 1963; MS in Counseling, L.I. U., 1977, Profl. Diploma, 1980. Ordained to ministry United Meth. Ch., 1965; cert. Christian edn. min., expert in traumatic stress; nat. cert. counselor; cert. hypnotherapist; registered behavioral therapist. Asst. pastor, minister edn. Kings Hwy. United Meth. Ch., Bklyn., 1961-63; asst. pastor Bellmore (L.I.) United Meth. Ch., 1964-66; assoc. pastor Farmingdale (L.I.) United Meth. Ch., 1966-80; assoc. pastor, coord. food pantry Babylon (N.Y.) United Meth. Ch., 1980-95; pastor United Meth. Ch., Bellmore, NY, 1995—98; interim pastor Bridgehampton United Ch., 1999; counselor Mental Health Faculty Mercy Haven Inc., 2000—08. Coord. children's work United Meth. Ch., L.I., 1966-78, chmn. dist. edn., 1978-85, 87-91, dist. dir. Sch. Faith and Life, 1980-92, coord. adult ministries, 1983-85, founder dist. edn. com, 1979-93, dist. bd. ministry, 1990-95, dist. nominating com., 1983-91, dist. coun. on ministries, 1966-93. Author: The Knockout Punch - Facets and Ways of Coping with a Sudden Death, 1999. Mem.: Am. Acad. ExpertsTraumatic Stress, Am. Assn. Profl. Hypnotherapists, N.Y. Mental Health Counselors Assn., Suffolk Coalition. Home: 275 N Grand St Cobleskill NY 12043

OHANYAN, ANNA, political science professor; d. Suren and Susanna Ohanyan; m. Aram Adourian, Aug. 23, 2003; children: Isabelle Ani Adourian, Elise Mariam Adourian. MS in Conflict Resolution, Nova Southeastern U., Ft. Lauderdale, Fla., 1998; MA in polit. sci., Syracuse U., NY, 1999, PhD, 2004. Rsch. fellow Harvard U., Kennedy Sch. Govt., Cambridge, Mass., 2002—04; asst. prof. Polit. Sci. Dept. Stonehill Coll., Easton, Mass., 2004—; vis. asst. prof. Simmons Coll., Boston, 2004—05; resident scholar Woodrow Wilson Internat. Ctr. Scholars, Washington, 2007. Cons. Acad. Ednl. Devel., Washington, 1998—2001, UN Found., 1999, Md. U., 2000, Carter Ctr., Atlanta, 2001. Contbr. articles to profl. jours. Internat. educator Eurasia Internat. U., Yerevan, Armenia, 1998—2008; faculty fellow Martin Inst. Law and Soc., Easton, Mass., 2008. Grantee Rsch. Grant, Eurasia Found., 2006—07, Stonehill Coll., 2006, Woodrow Wilson Internat. Ctr. Scholars, 2007. Mem.: Arm. Internat. Women's Assn., Internat. Studies Assn. Office: Stonehill Coll 325 Washington St North Easton MA 02357 Business E-Mail: aohanyan@stonehill.edu.

O'HARA, JOHN PAUL, III, orthopedic surgeon; b. Detroit, June 10, 1946; m. Randy Baird, Mar. 11, 1987; children: Riley Anne, Nolan Baird, Evan John. BA, U. Mich., Ann Arbor, 1968, MD, 1972. Resident U. Va. Med. Ctr., Charlottesville, 1973-77; fellow Nuffield Orthopaedic Ctr., Oxford, Eng., 1977; practice medicine specializing in orthopaedic surgery Southfield, 1978—; staff Providence Hosp., Southfield, Mich., 1978—, pres. elect med. staff, 1990, pres. med. staff, 1991; sect. chief orthopedics; pres. Porretta Orthopedic Ctr., 1996—, med. dir., 2001—; pres. Providence Med. Group, 2005—07. Pres. Providence Hosp. Med. Staff Research Found., 1984-85, bd. dirs., 1982—85; bd. dirs. Mich. Master Health Plan, Southfield, 1982. Contbr. articles to profl. jours. Pres. Birmingham (Mich.) Little League Baseball. Recipient Disting. Alumni award Brother Rice High Sch., 1986. Fellow Am. Acad. Orthopaedic Surgery, Mid Am. Orthopaedic Soc.; mem. Detroit Orthopaedic Soc., Mich. Orthopaedic Soc., Detroit Acad. Orthopaedic Surgeons (past pres.), Oakland Hills Country Club (Birmingham, Mich.), Beverly Hills (Mich.) Club. Avocations: earthwatch vol., travel, sports. Home: 627 Waddington St Bloomfield Hills MI 48301-2346 Office Phone: 248-349-7015.

O'HARA, KELLI, singer, actress; b. Tulsa, Apr. 16, 1976; m. Greg Naughton, July 28, 2007. MusB in Vocal Performance/Opera, Okla. City U. Performer: (Broadway plays) Jekyll & Hyde, 2000—01, Follies, 2001, Sweet Smell of Success, 2002, Dracula, the Musical, 2004, The Light in the Piazza, 2005, The Pajama Game, 2006, South Pacific, 2008 (Outstanding Musical Revival, Drama Desk Awards, 2008), (plays) My Life with Albertine, 2003, The Light in the Piazza, 2004, Sunday in the Park with George, 2007, My Fair Lady; actor: (films) The Dying Gaul, 2005, The Key to Reserva, 2007; singer: (albums) Wonder in the World, 2008. Mem.: Gamma Phi Beta. Office: care Randi Goldstein The Gersh Agy 41 Madison Ave 33rd Fl New York NY 10010 also: care Erica Tuchman Onentertainment 12 W 57th St PH New York NY 10019

O'HARA, MICHAEL M., theater educator; b. Princeton, NY, Oct. 10, 1959; s. Francis James and Patricia Ann (Smith) O'H.; m. Karen Marie Marks, Sept. 27, 1987 (div. June 1990); m. Mary Ellen Durant, Dec. 30, 1992. BA in English, Fordham U., 1982; MA in Theatre History, Critisim, U. Md., 1990, postgrad., 1990—. Tchr. English, Latin, drama The Canterbury Sch., Ft. Myers, Fla., 1985-86; tchr. English, drama West Nottingham Acad., Colora, Md., 1986-87; asst. box office mgr. U. Md. Dept. Theatre, College Park, 1990; critic, instr. Nat. Critic's Inst., Ithica, N.Y., 1991-93; edit. asst. theatre survey U. Md. Dept. Theatre, 1991-93, grad. teaching asst., 1988—. Adminstrv. asst. to chair U. Md., 1992—; guest lectr., coord. workshop, treas., grad. student assn., 1989. Contbr. articles to profl. jours. Fellow Nat. Critic's Inst., 1990. Mem. Omicron Delta Kappa, Pi Kappa Delta. Office: U Md Dept Theatre Tawes Fine Arts Rm 0202 College Park MD 20742-0001

O'HARA, PATRICIA ANNE, law educator, former dean; BA summa cum laude, Santa Clara U., 1971; JD summa cum laude, Notre Dame, 1974. Bar: Calif. 1974. Assoc. Brobeck, Phleger & Harrison, 1974—79, 1980—81; assoc. prof. law Notre Dame Law Sch., 1981, prof., 1990—, v.p. student affairs, 1990—99, Joseph A. Matson dean, law educator, 1999—2009. Chair nominating com. Am. Assn. Law Schools, 2005—06, chair, sect. law sch. deans, 2007. Contbr. chapters to books, articles to law jours. Mem.: Law Sch. Admissions Coun. (bd. trustees). Office: U Notre Dame 203 Law Sch PO Box 780 Notre Dame IN 46556-0780 Office Phone: 574-631-6789. Office Fax: 574-631-8400. E-mail: Patricia.A.O'Hara.3@nd.edu.*

O'HARA, PATRICIA BERNADETTE, chemistry professor; d. John Lawrence and Ruth Janet O'Hara; m. Richard Alan Blatchly, Sept. 27, 1980; children: Sarah Blatchly, Rebecca Blatchly. PhD, Columbia U., NY, 1981. Prof. chemistry Amherst Coll., Mass., 1983—, advisor dean faculty, 2008—. Adv. bd. Amherst Regional Mid. Sch., 2008—; edn. dir. Wesley United Meth. Ch., Hadley, Mass.; mem. Ctr. Civic Engagement Amherst Coll., 2008—. Mem.: Women Sci., Biophysical Soc., Am. Chem. Soc., Phi Beta Kappa. Liberal. Methodist. Achievements include research in macromolecular systems. Avocations: singing, running. Office: Amherst Coll Merrill Sci Ctr Amherst MA 01002 Office Fax: 413-542-2732. Business E-Mail: pbohara@amherst.edu.

O'HARA, SABINE U., academic administrator, dean, economist, educator; b. Ludwigsburg, W. Germany, Oct. 29, 1955; d. Wolfgang E. and Margarete Maier; m. Philip O'Hara, Mar. 17, 1983; children: Daniel, David, Dennis. Doctorate, U. Gottingen, Germany, 1984. Dir. pub. policy N.Y. State Coun. Chs., Albany, 1990—93; asst. prof. econs. Rensselaer Poly. Inst., Troy, NY, 1994—99, dir. grad. studies in econs., 1996—99; provost and prof. econs. Green Mountain Coll., Poultney, Vt., 1999—2002; v.p. acad. affairs and dean Concordia Coll., Moorhead, Minn., 2002—04; pres. Roanoke Coll., Salem, Va., 2004—06; exec. dir. Coun. Internat. Exchange of Scholars (Fulbright), 2006—; v.p. Internat. Inst. Edn. Lectr. in field. Author: (books) Economic Theory for Environmentalists, 1996; contbr. articles to profl. jours. Steering com. Downtown Revitalization Initiative, Poultney, 2001—02; bd. dirs. Girls Inc. of Greater Capital Dist., Albany, 1998—2000, Employee Ownership Project, Albany, 1997—2000; vice chair Schenectady Econ. Devel. Initiative, NY, 1994—97. Recipient Outstanding Paper award for excellence, Internat. Jour. Social Econs., 1996, 2000, Outstanding Svc. award, N.Y. State Coun. Chs., 1997; grantee Rsch. grantee, Froehlich Found., Sloan Found.;, Hewlett Found. Mem.: Am. Econ. Assn., Internat. Assn. Feminist Econs., Assn. Social Econs., Internat. Soc. Ecol. Econs. Home: 5036 Nebraska Ave Nw Washington DC 20008-2937 Business E-Mail: ohara@roanoke.edu.

O'HARA, SARA MARIE, radiologist; d. John Francis and Claire Annastasia O'Hara; m. Jeffrey Brian Betts, Sept. 6, 1997; children: Sailor Delaney Betts, Sanibel Star Betts. BS in Chemistry and Physics, Georgetown U., Washington, 1984, MD, 1988. Diplomate Am. Bd. Radiology, 1993, CAQ pediat. radiology Am. Bd. Radiology, cert. spl. competance in nuc. medicine Am. Bd. Radiology. Intern Riverside Meth. Hosp., Columbus, 1989; resident Georgetown U. Med. Sch., 1990; resident in diagnostic radiology U. Cin. Med. Ctr., 1990—93; fellow in pediatric radiology Cin. Children's Hosp., 1993—94; tng. in nuc. medicine DC Children's Hosp.; head pediatric nuc. medicine Duke U. Med. Ctr.; chief ultrasound divsn. Cin. Children's Hosp., 2000—. Recipient Outstanding Contribution to Dept. Morale, Cin. Children's Hosp., 2003—04, Radiology Editor's Recognition award, 2004. Mem.: Soc. Uroradiology, Soc. Nuc. Medicine, Radiol. Soc. North America, Soc. Pediatric Radiology, Soc. Radiologists in Ultrasound, Ohio Med. Soc., NC Med. Soc., Assn. U. Radiologists, Am. Roentgen Ray Soc., Am. Coll. Radiology, Am. Inst. Ultrasound in Medicine, Alpha Omega Alpha. Avocation: travel. Office: Cincinnati Childrens Hosp Radiology 3333 Burnet Ave MLC 5031 Cincinnati OH 45229 Business E-Mail: sara.ohara@cchmc.org.*

O'HARE, DENIS, actor; b. Kansas City, Mo., Jan. 17, 1962; BA, Northwestern U. Actor: (Broadway plays) Racing Demon, 1995, Cabaret, 1998, Major Barbara, 2001, Take Me Out, 2003 (Drama Desk award outstanding featured actor in a play, 2003, Tony award best featured actor in a play, 2003, Clarence Derwent award, 2003, Outer Critics Circle award, OBIE award, Village Voice, Lucille Lortel award), Assassins, 2004, Sweet Charity, 2005 (Drama Desk award outstanding featured actor in a musical, 2005), Inherit the Wind, 2007; (films) St. Patrick's Day, 1997, River Red, 1998, Sweet and Lowdown, 1999, The Anniversary Party, 2001, 21 Grams, 2003, Garden State, 2004, Heights, 2004, Derailed, 2005, Stephanie Daley, 2006, Half Nelson, 2006, The Babysitters, 2007, Michael Clayton, 2007, The Proposal, 2009; (TV films) St. Maybe, 1998, Hamlet, 2000, Angel, 2005, Once Upon a Mattress, 2000; (TV series) The Young Indiana Jones Chronicles, 1993, Law & Order: Special Victims Unit, 2000, 100 Centre Street, 2001, Law & Order, 1993, 1996, 1997, 2003, Justice, 2006.*

O'HARE, JAMES RAYMOND, energy executive; b. Evergreen Park, Ill., July 20, 1938; s. Raymond Clarence and Helen (Nickel) O'H.; m. Nan Jane Raleigh, Sept. 18, 1965; children: Joan, Daniel, Colleen, Patrick. BS, Marquette U., 1960; MBA, U. Calif. at Los Angeles, 1961. C.P.A., Ind., Ill., Ky., Calif., Tex. Mgr. Peat, Marwick, Mitchell & Co., Chgo., 1961-68, South Bend, Ind., 1968-69; controller Essex Internat., Inc., Fort Wayne, Ind., 1969-76, Am. Air Filter Co., Inc., Louisville, 1976-80; fin. v.p. and treas. Petrolane Inc., Long Beach, Calif., 1980-85; treas. Tex. Eastern Corp., Houston, 1985-87, v.p., treas., 1987-88; sr. v.p. fin. and adminstrn. Tex. Ea. Gas Transmission Co., Houston, 1988—89; v.p., CFO Enclean Inc., Houston, 1991—93; fin. cons., 1993—97; v.p., CFO Ascendant Healthcare Group, Inc., Houston, 1997, John March Ptnrs., Inc., Houston, 1998—2004, Sensor Microsystems, Inc., San Antonio, 2004; gen. ptnr. Connemara Ventures, LLC, The Woodlands, 2004. Controller Afras USA, Inc., 2005. Served with USNR, 1962-68. Mem. Evans Scholars, Fin. Execs. Inst., The Woodlands Country Club, Beta Gamma Sigma. Personal E-mail: johare@swbell.net.

O'HARE, JOSEPH ALOYSIUS, priest, editor-in-chief, former academic administrator; b. NYC, Feb. 12, 1931; s. Joseph Aloysius and Marie Angela (Enright) O'H. AB, Berchmans Coll, Cebu City, Philippines, 1954, MA, 1955; STL, Woodstock Coll., Md., 1962; PhD, Fordham U., 1968; DHL (hon.), Fairfield U., 1980, Rockhurst Coll., Kansas City, Mo., 1984, Ateneo de Manila U., 1990, CUNY, 1991, Coll. of St. Rose, Albany, NY, 1995, St. Francis Coll., Bklyn., 1996, St. Peter's Coll., 1997, Albertus Magnus Coll., 2004; DLitt (hon.), Coll. New Rochelle, 1984; D.D. (hon.), Muhlenberg Coll., 1998; DLitt (hon.), Fordham U., 2003. Joined S.J., 1948, ordained priest Roman Cath. Ch., 1961. Instr. Ateneo de Manila U., 1955-58, prof. philosophy, 1968-72; assoc. editor Am. Mag., NYC, 1972-75, 2003—, editor-in-chief, 1975-84; pres. Fordham U., Bronx, NY, 1984—2003, Regis HS, NYC, 2004—05. Author weekly column Of Many Things (Best Original Column award Cath. Press Assn. 1976, 78, 81, 84) Office Phone: 212-581-4640. Business E-Mail: johare@fordham.edu.

OHASHI, YOJI, air transportation executive; b. Jan. 21, 1940; BA in Law, Keio U., 1964. Joined All Nippon Airways Co., 1964, dir., engring., maintenance, 1992—93, sr. dir., gen. mgr., 1995—97, mng. dir., 1997—99, sr. exec. v.p., sales, mktg., 1999—2001, pres., CEO, bd. dirs., 2001—05, chmn., bd. dir., 2005—. Office: All Nippon Airways Ltd 5-2 Higashi-Shinbashi 1 chome Minato-ku Tokyo 105-7133 Japan

O'HAYNES, DELILAH FERNE, literature and language professor; BS, East Tenn. State U., Johnson City, 1977; MS, Radford U., Va., 1983; EdD, U. Tenn., Knoxville, 1992. Instr., english East Tenn. State U., 1986—92; prof., english Concord U., Athens, W.Va., 1992—. Pres. & owner Walk Free Press, Athens, 2005—. Author: (book of poetry and photography) The Character of Mountains, (book of non-fiction) Walk Free From Fear of Cancer, (novels) (appalachian humor) Home Town Folks, (book of poetry therapy) Rise, Woman. Rise; editor: (anthology) Appalachia's Last Stand; prodr.: (cd teachings) teaching companion to Rise, Woman. Rise.; author: (book of non-fiction) Messiah Manifest. Resource mem. Holston Conf. Native Am. Ministry Team, Knoxville, 1992—; speaker's bur. Concord U., 2000—, founder, sexual assault response team, 2000—; sec. WindHorse Healing Arts Ctr., Bluefield, 2004—07; invited mem. Stop Abusive Family Environments, Kimball, 2009—. Fellowship, Radford U., 1982—83. Mem.: Appalachian Ctr. Poets & Writers, Appalachian Authors Guild (workshop leader 2009—), W.Va. Writers, Appalachian Writers Assn. (scholarship chair, fiction judge 2000—), Inkslingers Writers Group. Christian Ch. Avocations: gardening, hiking, reading. Office: Concord Univ Vermillion St PO Box 1000 Athens WV 24712 Office Phone: 304-384-5261. Business E-Mail: dohaynes@concord.edu.

OHAYON, MAURICE M., research center administrator, psychiatrist; b. Casablanca, Morocco, June 22, 1948; arrived in Can., 1990; MD, U. Aix Marseille II, France, 1979, Cert. d'Etudes Spéciales Psychiatry, 1980, D in Computer Scis., 1992; PhD in Human Biology, U. Calude Bernard, Lyon, France, 1997. Resident in psychiatry and neurology C.H.U. Marseille, 1975-77; hosp. psychiatrist France, 1980-90; sci. dir. Rsch. Ctr. Fernand Seguin, Montreal, Que., Can., 1990-92; dir. rsch. ctr. Inst. Philippe Pinel, Montreal, 1992—; rsch. coord. U. Montreal, 1992-96; pres. Ctr. Evaluation and Statistics, Montreal, 1998—; project dir. Ctr. for Human Sleep Rsch. Stanford (Calif.) U. Med. Ctr. Assoc. prof. U. Que. Trois-Rivières, 1993—; sci. conseiller Ctr. Hos. Vinatier, France, 1994—; vis. clin. scientist St. Mary's Hosp., London, 1995—; cons. prof. psychiatry Stanford U., 1995—; adj. prof. psychiatry NYU, 1998—. Author: Intelligence Artificielle et Psychiatrie, 1989, Apprentissage, Adaptation et Réadaptation: Etat de la Recherche, 1995; Dis-moi comment tu dors, 1997. Mem. APHA, Can. Psychol. Assn., N.Y. Acad. Scis. Office: Ctr Rsch Philippe Pinel 10905 Henri Bourassa E Montreal PQ Canada H1C 1H1

OHAYON, MAURICE MOYSES, medical educator, director; MD, DSc in Math & Computer Scis., PhD in Biology. Cert. in psychiatry France, 1981. Prof. Stanford U., Palo Alto, Calif., 2008—; dir. Stanford Sleep Epidemiology, 2008—. Contbr. scientific papers. Office: Stanford Sleep Epidemiology Rsch Ctr 3430 W Bayshore Palo Alto CA 94303 Business E-Mail: mrcohayon@stanford.edu.

O'HEARN, ROBERT RAYMOND, stage designer; b. Elkhart, Ind., July 19, 1921; s. Robert Raymond, Sr. and Ella May (Stoldt) O'H. BA, Ind. U., 1939-43; student, Art Students League, 1943-45. Designer Brattle Theatre, Cambridge, Mass., 1948-52; prof. stage design, chmn. design dept. Sch. Music Ind. U., 1989—. Instr. Studio and Forum Scenic Design, 1968-88. Stage designer: Broadway shows The Relapse, 1950,

Loves Labor's Lost, 1953, Othello, Festival, 1955, The Apple Cart, Child of Fortune, 1956; asst. designer: Broadway shows Kismet, 1953, Pajama Game, 1955, My Fair Lady, 1956, West Side Story, 1958; designer: for film A Clerical Error, 1955; designer prodns. Central City Opera House, 1959-63, Opera Soc. Washington, 1958-61, L'Elisir D'Amore at Met. Opera House, 1960, Die Meistersinger, 1962, Aida, 1963; stage designer: As You Like It, Stratford, Conn., 1961, Troilus and Cressida, Stratford, 1961, Kiss Me Kate, Los Angles Civic Light Opera, 1964, N.Y.C. Center, 1965, Samson and Delila, Met. Opera, 1964, La Sylphide, Am. Ballet Theatre, 1964, Italian Symphony, 1971, Adam Cochrane, Broadway, 1964, Pique Dame, Met. Opera, 1965, La Ventana, 1966, Die Frau Ohne Schatten, 1966, Porgy and Bess, Vienna Volksoper, 1965, Bregenzer Festspiele, 1971, Otello, Boston Opera, also Hamburg State Opera, 1967, Hansel and Gretel, Met. Opera, 1967, Nutcracker Ballet, San Francisco Ballet, 1967, L.A. Ballet, 1979, La Traviata, Santa Fe Opera, 1968, Rosalinda, L.A. Civic Light Opera, 1968, Der Rosenkavalier, Met. Opera, 1969, Tallis Fantasia, N.Y.C. Ballet, 1969, Boris Godunov (unproduced), Met. Opera, 1970, Parsifal, Met. Opera, 1970, Porgy and Bess, Bregenz Festspiel, Austria, 1971, Falstaff, Marriage of Figaro, Gianni Schicci, Central City Opera House, 1972, Barber of Seville, 1973, The Enchanted, Kennedy Center, 1973, The Mind with the Dirty Man, Los Angeles, 1973, Midsummer Night's Dream, Central City Opera, 1974, Coppelia, Ballet West, 1974, Carmen, Strasbourg, 1974, The Pearl Fishers, Miami Opera, 1974, N.Y.C. Opera, 1980, Don Pasquale, Miami Opera, 1976, Scipio Africanus, Central City Opera, 1975, Swan Lake, Strasbourg, 1975, Marriage of Figaro, Met. Opera, 1975, Die Meistersinger, Karlsruhe, Germany, 1975, Girl of the Golden West, Houston Opera, 1976, N.Y.C. Opera, 1977, Vienna Staatsoper, 1976, Boris Godunov, Strasbourg, 1976, Der Rosenkavelier, Karlsruhe, 1976, Don Quixote, Ballet West, 1977, Die Meistersinger, Chgo. Lyric Opera, 1977, Adriana Lecouvreur, Miami Opera, 1978, La Boheme, 1978, Coppelia, Pacific N.W. Dance, Seattle, 1978, Andrea Chenier, N.Y.C. Opera, 1978, Der Rosenkavelier, Can. Opera Co., Toronto, 1978, Taming of the Shrew, Pa. State U., 1980, Die Fledermaus, Miami Opera, 1980, Tosca, Miami Opera, 1981, West Side Story, Bregenz Festspiel, Austria, 1981, Mich. Opera Theatre, 1985; Pique Dame, San Francisco Opera, 1982, La Traviata, Miami Opera, 1982, Of Mice and Men, Miami Opera, 1982, Carousel, Annie Get Your Gun, Miami Opera, 1984, Lucia di Lammermoor, 1984, L'Italiana in Algeri, 1985, Porgy and Bess, Met. Opera, 1985, West Side Story, Mich. Opera Theatre, 1985, Aida, Don Giovanni, Opera Colo., 1986, My Fair Lady, Mich. Opera Theatre, 1986, Samson and Delilah, Manon Lescaut Opera Colo., 1987, Annie Get Your Gun, Paper Mill Playhouse, 1987, Peter Grimes, Ind. U., 1987, Madama Butterfly, N.J. State Opera, 1990. Mem. vis. com. Costume Inst., Met. Museum. Recipient Robert L. B. Tobin award for lifetime achievement in theatrical design, 2005. Mem. United Scenic Artists. Home: 2604 E 2nd St Bloomington IN 47401-5351

O'HERN, JANE SUSAN, psychologist, educator; b. Winthrop, Mass., Mar. 21, 1933; d. Joseph Francis and Mona (Garvey) O'H. BS, Boston U., 1954, EdD, 1962; MA, Mich. State U., 1956. Instr. Mercyhurst Coll., 1954-55, Hofstra Coll., 1956-57, State Coll., Salem and Boston, 1957-60; asst. prof. Boston U., 1962-67, assoc. prof., 1967-75, prof. edn. and psychiat. (psychology), 1975-95, prof. emeritus, 1995—, chmn. dept. counseling psychology, 1972-75, 88-89, dir. mental health edn. program, 1975-81, dir. internat. edn., 1978-81, asst. v.p. internat. edn., 1981; prof. emeritus mental health and behavioral medicine program Boston U. Sch. Medicine, 2001—. Pres. ASSIST Internat., Inc., 1989—98; adv. bd, Internat. Study Cons., 1994—98; founder BettyBoston LLC, 2002—. Contbr. articles to profl. jours. Trustee Boston Ctr. Modern Psychoanalytic Studies, 1980-92. Recipient grants U.S. Office Edn., NIMH, Dept. of Def. Mem. Assn. Counselor Edn. and Suprs., Am. Counseling Assn., North Atlantic Assn. Counselor Edn. and Supervision (past pres.), Mass. Psychol. Assn., Am. Psychol. Assn., Mortar Bd., Pi Lamda Theta, Sigma Kappa, Phi Delta Kappa, Phi Beta Delta. Home: 111 Perkins St Apt 287 Boston MA 02130-4324 Office Phone: 617-414-2325. Personal E-mail: assistint@aol.com. Business E-Mail: johern@bu.edu.

OHGA, NORIO, retired electronics executive; b. Numazu, Shizuoka, Japan, Jan. 29, 1930; s. Shoichi Ohga and Toshi Mizuno; m. Midori Matsubara, 1957. Grad., Tokyo Nat. U. Fine Arts and Music, 1953, Kunst U., Berlin, 1957; Dr hc music (hon.), Rochester U., 1996, McGill U., 1999. Cons., advisor Tokyo Tsushin Kogyo (later Sony Corp.), 1953-59; gen. mgr. tape recorder divsn., product planning divsn., indsl. design divsn. Sony Corp., Tokyo, 1959; originally trained as an opera singer; bd. dirs. Sony Corp., Tokyo, 1964-72, mng. dirs., 1972-74, sr. mng. dir., 1974-76, dep. pres., 1976-82, pres., chief oper. officer, 1982-89, pres. and CEO, 1989-95, chmn. and CEO, 1995-99, chmn., rep. dir., 1999-2000, chmn. bd., 2000—03, hon. chmn., 2003—; CEO Nobuyuki Idei. Sr. mng. dir. CBS/Sony Group, Inc., 1968-70, pres., 1970-80, chmn., 1980-91; chmn. Sony Corp. Am., 1988-98; vice chmn. Keidanren, 1998. Decorated Cmdr. Cross First Class of the Order of Merit of the Rep. of Austria, 1987, Medal of Honor with Blue Ribbon by J.M. the Emperor of Japan, 1988, Comdr.'s Cross Order of Merit of Germany, 1994, Officier de l'Ordre Nat. de la Legion d'Honneur France, 1996, Grande Ufficiale dell'Ordine Al Merito della Repubblica Italiana award Pres. Italian Republic, 1998, Grand Decoration of Honour in Silver with Star of the Rep. of Austria, 1999, Order of Panglima Jasa Negara of Malaysia, 1999, Knight Comdr.'s Cross (Badge and Star, FRG, 2001, First Class Order of the Sacred Treasure of Japan, 2001. Mem. Japan Fedn. Econ. Orgn. (vice-chmn. 1998), Tokyo C. of C. and Industry (vice chmn.). Avocations: yachting, flying. Office: Sony Corp 6-7-35 Kitashinagawa 6-chome Shinagawa-ku Tokyo 141 Japan also: Sony Corp Am 550 Madison Ave New York NY 10022-3211

OHL, JOAN ESCHENBACH, federal agency administrator; b. Harrisburg, Pa. m. Ronald E. Ohl. Grad., U. Del., 1967; EdM, SUNY, Buffalo, 1969; post grad., Pa. State U. Dir. women's housing Colo. Coll., Colo. Springs, 1969; positions at U. Ark., Pa. State U.; asst. to v.p. Fairleigh Dickinson U., Rutherford, NJ, 1975—82; v.p. Independent Coll. Fund of NJ; cons. to C.E. "Jim" Compton of FIVE-J Energy Inc. & Grafton Coal Co., 1984—93; sec. Dept. Health and Human Resources, W.Va., 1997—2001; commr. Adminstrn. Children, Youth and Families Adminstrn. Children and Families, HHS, Washington, 2002—. Bd. mem. W.Va. Health Care Cost Rev. Authority, 1993—97. Recipient Disting. West Virginian award, 2000, Joan E. Ohl Rural Health Leadership award, W.Va. Rural Health Assn., 2000, Leadership award, Multi-CAP, Inc., 2000, Bateman award, W.Va. Hosp. Assn., 2000, Leadership award, W.Va. Pub. Health Assn., 2000, James Hansen Humanitarian award, U. Buffalo, 2004. Office: HHS Adminstrn Children, Youth and Families 1250 Maryland Ave SW Suite Washington DC 20424*

OHLAND, MATTHEW WILLIAM, engineering educator, consultant; s. Theodor Charles and Nancy Ann Ohland; m. Emily Mara Herrington, Aug. 19, 1989; children: Charlotte Elise, Carson Herrington, Charlotte Elise, Carson Herrington, Anders William. BA in Religion, Swarthmore Coll., Pa., 1989, BS in Engring., 1989; MS in Mech. Engring., Rensselaer Poly. Inst., Troy, NY, 1992, MS in Materials Engring., 1992; PhD in Civil Engring., U. Fla., Gainesville, 1996. Assoc. prof. Purdue U. Engring. Edn., West Lafayette, Ind., 2006—. Mem.: Tau Beta Pi (pres. 2002—06). Office: Purdue Univ Engring Edn 701 W Stadium Ave West Lafayette IN 47907

OH-LEE, JUSTIN DOHOON, psychology professor; b. Seoul, Republic of Korea, May 23, 1963; arrived in US, 1979; s. Myung Suck and Bong Sun Oh; m. Connie Chong Lee, Mar. 31, 1996; 1 child, Grace Nara. Degree in chemistry with distinction, Colo. Coll., 1986; PhD in Psychology, UCLA, 1995. Postdoctoral fellow Nat. Inst. Neurol. Disorders and Stroke, NIH, Bethesda, Md., 1995—99, rsch. fellow clin. pharmacology, 1999—2001; faculty psychiatry and psychology Found. for Advanced Edn. in the Scis., NIH, Bethesda, 1999—2001; assoc. prof. psychology Ctrl. Mich. U., Mount Pleasant, 2001—. Spl. vol., cons. Nat. Inst. Neurol. Disorders and Stroke, NIH, Bethesda, Md., 2001—03. Contbr. chapters to books, articles to profl. jours. Faculty advisor Adventist Students for Christ, Mount Pleasant, 2003—05; sci. advisor Parkinson's Support Group, Mount Pleasant, 2002—05. Recipient Outstanding Rsch. award, Assn. Korean Neuroscientist Assn., Grad. Divsn. award, UCLA, Grad. Divsn. Travel Grant Rsch. award, 1990—91, Pres. AA Fellowship award, 1993, Coll. Letters and Sci. Grad. Student award, 1993, Disting. Svc. award, NINDS ACUC, NIH, 1999, Spl. Act/Svc. award, U.S. Dept. Health and HUman Svcs., 2000, Rsch. Professorship award, Ctrl. Mich. U., 2003; named Hon. Recognition for Outstanding Rsch., Nat. Inst. Neurol. Disorders and Stroke; grantee, NIH, 2001, 2005, Pres. Rsch. Investment Fund grantee, Ctrl. Mich. U., 2002; fellow, Nat. Parkinson Found. Ctr. Excellence, 2003; Rsch. Enhancement Award grantee, NIH, NINDS, Summer Faculty scholar, CHSBS, Ctrl. Mich. U., 2003. Mem.: APA, NIH, Asian and Pacific Islanders Am. Orgn., Soc. for Neuroscience, Am. Psychol. Soc. (faculty advisor Student Caucus, Ctrl. Mich. U. 2002—05). Home: 1412 Abbey Ln Mount Pleasant MI 48858 Office: Central Michigan Univ Psychology 1280 E Campus Dr HP 2181 Mount Pleasant MI 48859 Office Fax: 989-774-2553; Home Fax: 989-774-2253. Business E-Mail: oh1jd@cmich.edu.

OHLEMEYER, WILLIAM S., lawyer; b. St. Louis, 1959; BS in Bus. Adminstrn., U. Mo., 1981; JD cum laude, U. Mo.-Columbia Sch. Law, 1984. Bar: US Ct. Appeals 8th Cir., US Dist. Ct. We. Dist. Mo. Law clk. to chief judge US Dist. Ct. (we. dist.) Mo.; products liability divsn. lawyer Shook, Hardy, & Bacon LLP, Kans. City, Mo., 1986, ptnr., 1991, pro bono com., hiring com., exec. com., 1998; from atty. to v.p., assoc. gen. counsel Altria Group, Inc., NYC, 1999—2008; ptnr. Boies, Schiller & Flexner LLP, NYC, 2008—. Named one of Nation's Top 10 Trial Lawyers, Nat. Law Jour., 1998. Mem.: Order of Coif. Office: Boies, Schiller & Flexner LLP 575 Lexington Ave 7th Fl New York NY 10022 Office Phone: 212-446-2300. Office Fax: 212-446-2350.

OHLSON, DOUGLAS DEAN, artist, educator; b. Cherokee, Iowa, Nov. 18, 1936; s. Lloyd E. and Effie O. (Johnson) O. BA, U. Minn., 1961. Prof. art Hunter Coll., NYC, 1964—2001; ret., 2001. One man shows include Fischbach Gallery, N.Y.C., 1964, 66-70, 72, Susan Caldwell Gallery, N.Y.C., 1974, 76, 77, 79, 81, 82, 83, Portland (Oreg.) Ctr. for Visual Arts, 1977, Ruth Siegel Gallery, N.Y.C., 1985, 87, Andre Zarre Gallery, N.Y.C., 1985, 90, 92, 93, 95, 2000, 04, 09, Gallery 99, Nina Freudenheim Gallery, Buffalo, 1986, Jaffe Gallery, Miami, 1989, Elaine Baker Gallery, Boca Raton, 1986, 2003, Doug Ohlson 20 Years of Painting: 1982-2002, Lorel Tracy Galy Red Bank, NJ, 2006, Elaine Baker Galy, Boca Raton, 2007; group shows include Mus. Modern Art, N.Y.C., 1968, Tate Gallery, London, 1969, Whitney Mus., N.Y.C., 1969, 71, Corcoran Gallery, Washington, 1972, 73, UCLA, 1975, Born in Iowa: The Homecoming, 1986-87, Hunter Coll./Times Sq. Gallery, N.Y.C.; invitational Am. Acad. Arts and Letters, 1992, 94, 97, 2002; represented in permanent collections Met. Mus. Art, N.Y.C., Nat. Gallery Art, Washington, Am. Fedn. Art, Mus. Modern Art, Frankfurt, Fed. Republic Germany, Lowe Art Mus., Miami, Fla., Karl Ernst Osthaus Mus., Hagen, Germany, Mus. Contemporary Art, Helsinki, Mpls. Inst. Art, Dallas Mus., Bklyn. Mus., Whitney Mus., N.Y.C., Harvard Art Mus., Cambridge, Mass. Served with USMC, 1955-58. Guggenheim fellow, 1968; Creative Artists Public Service grantee, 1974; Nat. Endowment for Arts grantee, 1976 Home: 35 Bond St New York NY 10012-2426

OHM, HERBERT WILLIS, agronomy educator, agriculturist; b. Albert Lea, Minn., Jan. 28, 1945; s. Wilhelm Carl and Lena Ann (Finkbeiner) O.; m. Judy Ann Chrisinger, Aug. 8, 1964; children: Cari Lynn, David William. BS in Agrl. Edn., U. Minn., St. Paul, 1967; MS in Plant Breeding, N.D. State U., 1969; PhD in Plant Genetics and Breeding, Purdue U., 1972. Cert. agronomist. Asst. prof. Purdue U., West Lafayette, Ind., 1972-77, assoc. prof. agronomy, 1977-83, prof., 1983—2004, disting. prof., 2004—. Team leader Interdisciplinary Wheat and Oat Genetics and Breeding Program, West Lafayette, 1980—, Interdisciplinary Purdue/AID Devel. Program, Burkina Faso, West Africa, 1983-85; mgr. hard red winter wheat rsch. Pioneer Hi-Bred Internat., Inc., Hutchinson, Kans., 1980. Contbr. book chpts. Recipient Soils and Crops Merit award Ind. Crop Improvement Assn., 1988, Merit award Orgn. of African Unity, 1989, Meritorious Svc. award Sci., Tech. and Rsch. Commn., 1989, Agronomic Achievement award American Soc. of Agronomy, 1994, Sch. of Agr. Team award, 2000, Distinction cert. Purdue Agr. Alumni Assn., 2005. Fellow: AAAS, Crop Sci. Soc. Am. (chmn. divsn. 1991), Am. Soc. Agronomy; mem.: Am. Registry Cert. Profls. in Agrl. Crops and Soils (cert.), Coun. Agrl. Sci. and Tech., Nat. Oat Improvement Coun. (chmn.), Am. Oat Workers Conf. (chmn.). Avocations: woodworking, music. Office: Purdue U Dept Agronomy Lilly Hall Life Scis West Lafayette IN 47907-1150 Office Phone: 765-494-8072. Business E-Mail: hohm@purdue.edu.

OHM, SEONG K., consumer products company executive; b. South Korea; m. Michael Ohm; children: Jessica, Nicholas. BS in Neurosci., U. Rochester, NY, MBA in Fin. and Mktg. Mktg. consumer divsn General Electric Co.; dir. product mgmt. and sales ops. AT&T Inc.; dir. sales ops. Agere Systems; v.p., divisional mdse. mgr. electronics and tech. products Sam's Club/Wal-Mart Stores, Inc., 2003—05, sr. v.p., gen. mdse. mgr., 2005—. Office: Wal Mart Stores Inc Hdqs 702 SW 8th St Bentonville AR 72716 Office Phone: 479-273-4000. Office Fax: 479-277-1830.

OHMAN, E. MAGNUS, cardiologist, educator; s. Karl-Erik Ohman and Maj-Britt Borjeson; m. Elspeth O'Reilly-Hyland, June 12, 1987; children: Edward, Elsa-Maria, Henry. MB, BCh, MD, Royal Coll. of Surgeons in Ireland, Dublin, 1981. Resident gen. internal med. St. Laurence's Hosp., St. Vincent's Hosp., Dublin, 1981—84; rsch. fellow in cardiology St. Laurence's Hosp., Dublin, 1984—87; fellow in cardiology Duke U. Med. Ctr., Durham, NC, 1987—91, asst. prof. medicine, 1991—96, assoc. prof. medicine, 1996—2001; prof. medicine U. NC, Chapel Hill, NC, 2001—05, Duke U. Med. Ctr., Durham, NC, 2005—. Dir. Heart Ctr. U. of N.C., Chapel Hill, 2001—05. Contbr. articles to profl. jours.; editor (assoc.): Am. Heart Jour. Recipient Edith Walsh award, Brit. Med. Assn., 1985. Fellow: Am. Coll. Cardiology, European Soc. Cardiology, Royal Coll. Physicians of Ireland, Soc. of Cardiac Angiography and Intervention; mem.: Am. Coll. Chest Physicians (chmn. Peer Rev. Com.), AMA (chmn. Acute Cardiac Care Com.). Achievements include patents for Methods patent for assessing reperfusion in heart attacks. Office: Duke Univ Med Ctr DUMC 3126 Erwin Rd Durham NC 27710 Office Phone: 919-681-2069. Office Fax: 919-681-0811.

OHNAMI, MASATERU, mechanical engineering educator; b. Kyoto, Apr. 6, 1931; s. Eijiro and Hisae Ohnami; m. Hiroko Ohnami, Oct. 10, 1959; 1 child, Masahiro. B in Engring., Ritsumeikan U., Kyoto, Japan, 1954; D in Engring., Kyoto U., 1960; D in Internat. Rels. (hon.), Am. U., Washington, 1995; LLD (hon.), U. BC, Can., 1997; DSc (hon.), Macquarie U., Australia, 1999. Asst. prof. Kyoto U., 1955-61; assoc. prof. Ritsumeikan U., Kyoto, 1961-67, prof., 1967—2000, dean acad. affairs, 1978-80, dean faculty sci. and engring., 1988-90, pres., 1991-98, emeritus prof., 1999—, emeritus exec.; prof., pres. Kyoto Tachibana U., 2000—04, emeritus prof., 2004—. Vis. rsch. prof. Columbia Univ, NYC, 1963—64; mng. dir. Japan Assn. Pvt. Colls. and Univs., Tokyo, 1991—99; v.p. Japan U. Accreditation Assn., Tokyo, 1997—2001, pres., 2001—03; mem. sci. coun. Ministry Edn., Tokyo, 1984—86, 1988—91, regular mem. Coun. Colls. and Univs., 1995—97; regular mem. Univ Formation Coun., 1993—2002; mem. steering com. Ctr. Entrance Exam (DNC), 1996—2001; hon. consul Republic Philippines, Kyoto, 1997—2003. Author: (book) Plasticity and High Temperature Strength of Materials, 1988, Fracture and Society, 1992. Mem.: INQAAHE, Sci. Coun. Japan (material research liaison com. 1988—94), Japanese Soc. Strength and Fracture Materials (hon.; bd. dir. 1984—99), Soc. Materials Sci. Japan (hon.; bd. dir. 1971—74, 1981—84, 1985—88, Prize 1971). Avocations: painting, reading. Home: 8-10 Hyugacho Osaka Takatsuki 569-0024 Japan

OHNO, APOLO ANTON, Olympic athlete; b. Seattle, May 22, 1982; Mem. US Elite Short Track Speedskating Team. Performer: Dancing with the Stars, 2007 (Named Champion, 2007). Recipient US Champion, 1999, 2001, 2002, 1500 meter Gold medal, 2002 Olympic Games, 1000 meter Silver medal, 1000 meter Bronze Medal, 2006 Winter Olympic Games, Men's Short Track Relay Bronze Medal, Gold Medal 500 meter Speed Skating, 2006 Winter Olympics; named US Champion, 1997, World Jr. Short Track Champion, 1999, World Cup Overall Champion, 2001, 500 meter champion, 2001, 1000 meter champion, 2001, 1500 meter champion, 2001; named to Asian-Am. Hall of Fame, 2007. Achievements include was a national champion and record holder in indoor inline skating, earned a state championship as a swimmer in the breaststroke. Avocations: music, badminton, basketball, break dancing. Address: US Speedskating PO Box 18370 Kearns UT 84118-0370

O'HOP, SUZANNE ELIZABETH, educator; b. San Antonio, Apr. 24, 1967; d. Paul A. Sr. and Florentine A. O'H. BA in English cum laude, Dickinson Coll., 1989; MA in English Lit., Millersville U., 1993; PhD in English Lit., U. R.I., 1997. Tchr. English Dover (Pa.) Area H.S., 1989-90, Mechanicsburg (Pa.) Area H.S., 1990-92, Snowflake (Ariz.) H.S., 1994-98; prof. English Northland Pioneer Coll., Snowflake, 1998—. Dept. chair Northland Pioneer Coll., 1998—. Contbr. articles to profl. jours.; chpt. to book. NEH grant, 1996. Mem. MLA, Sigma Tau Delta. Roman Catholic. Avocations: hiking, fishing, writing, physical fitness. Office: Northland Pioneer Coll PO Box 610 Holbrook AZ 86025-0610 Personal E-mail: wfseo@northand.cc.az.us. Business E-Mail: sohop@npc.edu.

OHRENSTEIN, ROMAN ABRAHAM, economist, educator, rabbi; b. Slomniki, Poland, June 12, 1920; arrived in U.S., 1951, naturalized, 1957; s. Joseph Barukh and Gena (Fiefkopf) O.; m. Ruth Silberstein, Aug. 30, 1953; children: Gena Ann, Ilana Rose. MA in Econs., U. Munich, 1948, PhD in Econs. cum laude, 1949, postgrad. in medicine, 1949—51; MHL, Jewish Theol. Sem. Am., 1955; postgrad., Columbia U., 1963—64. Ordained rabbi, 1955. Rabbi, Auburn, NY, 1955—57, Pittsfield, Mass., 1957—60, Atlanta, 1960—62, NYC, 1962—66; prof. econs. Nassau Coll., SUNY, Garden City, 1964-99, chmn. econs. dept., 1976-78, 82-84, prof. emeritus, 1999—, campus chaplain, 1970—; chaplain Nassau County Civic Preparedness, NY, 1965—; mem. Coll. Coun. Am. Coll. Jerusalem, 1967-73, prof. econs., 1968-73. Vis. prof. U. Newcastle, Australia, 1985, vis. rsch. prof., 1989; past chaplain Kiwanis, Police Dept. Cayuga County, NY, 1955-57, Mt. Sinai Hosp., NYC, 1963-64; mem. Coun. of Orgns., U.S.A., 1978-85; mem. spl. com. on Jewish law Rabbinical Assembly, 1971; condr. seminars U. Queensland, Sydney U., Nat. U., Australia, 1989, Sorbonne, Paris, 1990; lectr., guest spkr. Jewish civic and profl. orgns. Author: (series) Economic Thought in Talmudic Literature, 1968, 70, 83, 86, 87, 89, 91-93, 96, 2003, 07 (citation Am. Biog. Inst. 1985), Inventories During Business Fluctuations, 1973, Inventory Control as an Economic Shock Absorber, 1975, Economic Analysis in Talmudic Literature, 1992, ed edit., rev. and enlarged, 2003, rev. 3rd edit., 2009; contbr. chpt. to anthology: Ancient and Medieval Economic Ideas, 1998; mem. editl. adv. bd. Internat. Rev. Econs. and Ethics; columnist Algemeiner Jour., NYC; contbr. articles to profl. jours on Talmudic Economics. Mem. nat. exec. comm. Am. Profs. for Peace in the Mid. East, 1971-73; mem. adv. bd. Am. Acad. Alliance for Israel, 1995—. Recipient 1st Faculty Disting. Achievement award Nassau Coll., SUNY, 1992, 95, Citation of Excellence, Anbar Electronic Intelligence, Eng., 1996, Poineering Rsch. in Talmudic Economics, 1968; SUNY fellow, 1968, 70, Merit Cert., Am. Jour. Economics and Sociology, 2007. Mem.: Rabbinical Assembly NY Bd. Rabbis, Am. Econ. Assn., History of Econs. Soc., Assn. Social Econs., Learned Soc., NY Acad. Scis., Internat. Soc. for Intercommunication New Ideas, Literati Club (Eng.). Home: 28-74 208th St Bayside NY 11360-2421 Personal E-mail: ohrenste@aol.com. *I kept my faith in God coupled with loyalty to tradition, sharpened my mind while maintaining discipline of the heart; tenacity in the face of adversity, turning stumbling blocks into stepping stones while never losing sight of life's supreme purpose: to leave the world a little better than I found it.*

OHRING, GEORGE, meteorologist; b. NYC, June 20, 1931; s. Aron and Anna (Wasserman) O.; m. Jean Ohring, Dec. 19, 1953; children: Marshall, Peter, Richard. BS, CCNY, 1952; MS, NYU, NYC, 1954, PhD, 1957. Asst. meterologist NYU, NYC, 1953-57; atmospheric physicist Air Force Cambridge Rsch. Lab., Bedford, Mass., 1957-60; mgr. meteorology lab. GCA Corp., Bedford, 1960-71; assoc. prof. Tel Aviv (Israel) U., 1971-83; chief land scis. br. NOAA, Washington, 1983-84, chief satellite rsch. lab., 1984-96, chief climate rsch. and applications divsn., 1996—2000, cons., 2001—. Chmn. Commn. A. of Com. on Space Rsch., Paris, 1986-92. Author: Weather on the Planets, 1966; contbr. articles to profl. jours. Grantee U.S. Army, NOAA, U.S.-Israel Bi-Nat. Sci. Found., Israel Acad. Scis., 1970's. Fellow AAAS, Internat. Assn. Meteorology and Atmospheric Physics (exec. com. 1988-96), Am. Meteorology Soc., Am Geophys. Union. Home: 6100 Wpd College Park MD 20740 Office: NOAA Nat Environ Satellite Data & Info Svc Washington DC 20233-0001

OHRN, NILS YNGVE, chemistry and physics educator; b. Avesta, Sweden, June 11, 1934; came to U.S., 1966; s. Nils E. and Gerda M. (Akerlund) O.; m. Ann M.M. Thorsell, Aug. 24, 1957; children: Elisabeth, Maria. MS, Uppsala U., 1958, PhD, 1963, F.D., 1966. Research assoc. Uppsala (Sweden) U., 1963-66; assoc. prof. U. Fla., Gainesville, 1966-70, prof. chemistry and physics, 1971—, assoc. dir.

Quantum Theory Project, 1976-77, dir. Quantum Theory Project, 1983-98, chmn. dept. chemistry, 1977-83. Editor: Internat. Jour. Quantum Chemistry, 1970—. Fulbright grantee Com. for Internat. Exchange of Scholars, Washington, 1961-63; recipient Bicentennial Gold medal King of Sweden, 1980; Fla. Acad. Scis. medal, 1984; named Tchr./Scholar of Yr., U. Fla., 2003-04. Fellow Am. Phys. Soc., Chaire Francqui Interuniversitaires Belgium; mem. Am. Chem. Soc. (Fla. award 1997), Royal Acad. Scis. Uppsala Sweden (fgn.), Finnish Acad. Scis. (fgn.), Royal Danish Acad. Scis. (fgn.), Sigma Xi, Phi Beta Kappa. Home: 1823 NW 11th Rd Gainesville FL 32605-5323 Office: U Fla Quantum Theory Project 2301 NPB Bldg # 92 Gainesville FL 32611-8435 Business E-Mail: ohrn@qtp.ufl.edu.

OHRT, COLIN, pharmacologist, department chairman; s. Bonnie and Delwin Ohrt; m. Suwan Ohrt. MD, Wash. U., St. Louis, 1987. Cert. Tex. State Bd. Med. Examiners, 1989, diplomate Am. Bd. Internal Medicine, 2000, Am. Bd. Clin. Pharmacology, 2003. Chief, dept. clin. pharmacology & transnat. medicine Walter Reed Army Inst. Rsch., Exptl. Therapeutics Divsn., Silver Spring, Md., 1991—. Office: Walter Reed Army Inst Rsch 501 Robert Grant Ave Silver Spring MD 20910 Office Fax: 301-319-9449.

OHSFELDT, ROBERT L., health economist, educator; b. Houston, July 30, 1956; s. Ronald A. and Mildred A.O.; m. Peggy J. Moon, May 18, 1985; children: Erika K., Michael E, Britta A. BS, U. Houston, 1977, PhD, 1983. Rsch. assoc. Southwest Ctr. for Urban Rsch., Houston, 1979-81; asst. prof. Ball State U., Muncie, Ind., 1982-86; rsch. economist Am. Med. Assn., Chgo., 1983-84; asst. prof. Ariz. State U., Tempe, 1986-89; assoc. prof./prof. Sch. of Pub. Health U. Ala., Birmingham, 1989—98, scientist Injury Control Rsch. Ctr., 1989—98, scholar Lister Hill Ctr. Health Policy, 1990—98; health econs. rsch. scientist Eli Lilly and Co., Indpls., 1998—2001; prof. Coll. Pub. Health, U. Iowa, Iowa City, 2001—05, Tex. A and M Health Sci. Ctr., College Station, 2005—. Vis. asst. prof. La. Tech. U., Ruston, 1981-82; mem. rev. com. grant proposals NIH, Dept. Vet. Affairs, Agy. Health Care Policy and Rsch.; jour. reviewer Am. Econ. Rev., Rev. Econs. and Statistics, Jour. Health Econs., JAMA, So. Econ. Jour., among others. Author numerous chpts. for books; co-author: The Business of Health, 2007; co-editor: Socioeconomic Characteristics of Medical Practice, 1984; mem. editl. bd. Jour. Managed Care Pharmacy, 2005-,contbr. articles to profl. jours. Named Robert Wood Johnson Found. Faculty Fellow in Health Care Fin., Johns Hopkins U., Balt., 1987-88. Mem. Internat. Health Econ. Assn., Internat. Soc. Pharmacoeconomics and Outcomes Rsch., Acad. Managed Care Pharmacy.

OHST, WENDY JOAN, government agency administrator, educator; b. Muskegon, Mich., Feb. 20, 1949; d. Edward John Barron, Jr. and Mable Barron; m. Terrence Duane Ohst, Oct. 21, 1972; children: Heather Lynn Reyes, Holly Ann Garratt. AA, Muskegon CC, Mich., 1969; BS, Calif. Coast U., 1994; BBA, Baker Coll., 1998; MPA, Grand Valley State U., 2001. Contract asst. Teledyne Continental Motors, Muskegon, 1968; bookkeeper, teller FMB Lumberman's Bank, Muskegon, 1969—72; adminstrv. svcs. supr. Muskegon (Mich.) County Dept. of Employment & Tng., 1972—94, dep. dir., 1994—. Adj. prof. Baker Coll., Muskegon, Mich., 2002—; cons., presenter in field. Pres. local chpt. Nat. Fedn. of Bus. & Profl. Woman, Muskegon, 1990—91; campaign coord. United Way, 1990—2001; bd. dir. Muskegon (Mich.) Schs. Health & Human Svcs. Adv. Bd., 2002—03, Baker Corp. Svcs. Adv. Bd., 1999—. Mem.: Muskegon (Mich.) C.of C., Mich. Works Assn., Nat. Assn. Workforce Devel. Profls., Pi Alpha Alpha, Phi Kappa Phi, Delta Mu Delta. Lutheran. Avocations: travel, reading. Office: Department of Employment & Training 1611 Oak Avenue Muskegon MI 49442 Business E-Mail: ohst@co.muskegon.mi.us.

OHTANI, HIROKO, automotive professional; PhD in Chemistry, U. Calif., Berkeley, 1988. Sr. tech. specialist Ford Motor Co., Dearborn, Mich., 1995. Office: Materials and Nanotechnology Dept 2101 Village Rd Dearborn MI 48121 Office Phone: 313-594-1728. Office Fax: 313-323-1129. Business E-Mail: hohtani@ford.com.

O'HURLEY, JOHN, actor; b. Kittery, Maine, Oct. 9, 1954; m. Eva LaRue Callahan, 1992 (div. 1994); m. Lisa Mesloh, Aug. 14, 2004; 1 child, William Dylan. BA, Providence Coll., 1976, DFA, 2006. Co-owner J. Peterman Co., bd. dirs.; principal ptnr. Heritage Capitol Advisors, Atlanta, Round One Investments, Los Angeles. Actor: (TV series) The Edge of Night, 1983—84, Loving, 1984—86, All My Children, 1988, The Young & the Restless, 1989—91, Santa Barbara, 1990—91, Scorch, 1992, General Hospital, 1992, Valley of the Dolls, 1994, A Whole New Ballgame, 1995, Seinfeld, 1995—98, Lost on Earth, 1997, Over the Top, 1997, Cursed, 2000—01, The Mullets, 2003—04; (TV films) Something is Out There, 1988, Billy the Kid, 1989, White Hot: The Mysterious Murder of Thelma Todd, 1991, Seduction: 3 Tales from the "Inner Sanctum", 1992, My Son is Innocent, 1996, The Secret, 1997, Murder Live!, 1997, Blood on Her Hands, 1998, Tempting Fate, 1998, Life of the Party: The Pamela Harriman Story, 1998, Wild Grizzly, 1999, Three Secrets, 1999; (films) Night Eyes II, 1992, Mirror Images, 1992, The Power Within, 1995, Love Stinks, 1999, Slammed, 2001, Firetrap, 2001, Race to Space, 2001, Teddy Bears' Picnic, 2002, Buying the Cow, 2002, Knuckle Sandwich, 2004; voice actor: (TV series) Mickey Mouse Works, 1999—2000; Buzz Lightyear of Star Command, 2000; House of Mouse, 2001—02; Duck Dodgers, 2003—; Father of the Pride, 2004; (films) Tarzan & Jane, 2002; host: (TV series) Extraordinary World of Animals, 1999; Get Golf with the PGA Tour!, 2000; To Tell the Truth, 2000—01; NBC National Dog Show, 2001—; Family Feud, 2006—; contestant Dancing with the Stars, 2005; composer: (albums) Peace of Our Minds, 2005; author: It's Okay To Miss the Bed On The First Jump, 2006 (NY Times Bestseller), Before Your Dog Can Eat Your Homework, First You Have To Do It, 2007. Named one of sexiest men alive, People mag., 2005. Avocations: golf, tennis, carpentry, interior design, wine collection. Office: 11611 San Vicente Blvd #104 Los Angeles CA 90049

OINAS, VALDAR, aerospace scientist; b. Tartu, Estonia, Feb. 12, 1942; s. Felix Johannes and Lisbet Oinas. PhD, Caltech., Pasadena, Calif., 1972. Asst. prof. U. Nebr., Lincoln, 1972—74; prof. Queensborough Comm. Coll., Bayside, NY, 1974—98; rsch. scientist Goddard Inst. Space Studies, NYC, 1978—. Contbr. articles to profl. jours. Office: Goddard Inst Space Studies 2880 Broadway New York NY 10025 Office Fax: 212-678-5552. Business E-Mail: voinas@giss.nasa.gov.

OIWA, HIROSHI, surgeon; b. Saijo, Ehime, Japan, Aug. 26, 1958; s. Oiwa Yoichi and Oiwa Haruko; m. Fumiko Tanino, 1988; 1 child, Nao Oiwa. MD, Okayama U., Japan, 1984. Cert. Japanese Bd. Surgery, 1988, Japanese Bd. Thoracic Surgery, 1991, Japanese Bd. Cardiovasc. Surgery, 2004. Resident Okayama U. Hosp., Japan, 1984—88, Tokyo U. Hosp., 1988—92, staff, 1992—98, Kanagawa Children's Med. Ctr., Yokohama, Japan, 1998—99, Okayama U. Hosp., 2003—05; asst. prof. Kyorin U., Tokyo, 1999—2003, Teikyo U., Tokyo, 2005—07; chief medicine Tokiwadai Surg. Hosp., Tokyo, 2007—; staff Kitagawa Hosp., Okayama, 2008—; dir. of establishment Shin-Kurashiki Peach Clinic, 2008—. Achievements include invention of systematic traction techniques for pediatric minimally invasive cardiac surgery. Office: Shin-Kurasiki Peach Clinic 1513 Tamashimayashima Kureshiki 713-8113 Japan Office Fax: +81-864-427-0054. Personal E-mail: hiroshioiwa@hotmail.com.

OJAKLI, ZIAD S., lobbyist, automotive executive; b. Brooklyn, NY, June 28, 1967; BA in American Govt., Georgetown U., 1989; MA in American Govt., Johns Hopkins U. Legis. asst. to Senator Dan Coats US Senate, Washington, 1988—94, policy dir. & chief of staff to Senator Paul Coverdell, 1998—2000; chief of staff to Rep. Mark Souder US Congress, Washington, 1995—98; Senate liason Bush-Cheney Transition Team, Washington, 2000; dep. asst. to the Pres. for legis. affairs The White House, Washington, 2001—02, prin. dep. asst. to Pres. for legis. affairs, 2002—03; group v.p. govt. & cmty. rels. Ford Motor Co., Dearborn, Mich., 2004—. Bd. mem. Alliance of Automobile Manufacturers, Arab-Am. Mus. Adv. Bd., Arab-Am. Ctr. for Econ. & Social Services, Fabretto Children's Found., Henry Ford Learning Inst., NAM; del. World Econ. Forum's Young Global Leaders; bd. mem. Mich. Manufacturers Assn., Washington Ctr. for Internships. Republican. Office: Ford Motor Co 1 American Rd Dearborn MI 48126*

OJALVO, MORRIS, civil engineer, educator; b. NYC, Mar. 4, 1924; s. Nissim and (Fanny) O.; m. Anita Bedein, Dec. 26, 1948; children: Lynne, Joseph, Howard, Isobel. B.C.E., Rensselear Poly. Inst., Troy, NY, 1944, M.C.E., 1952; PhD, Lehigh U., Bethlehem, Pa., 1960; JD, Ohio State U., Columbus, 1978. Bar: Ohio 1979. Draftsman Am. Bridge Co., Elmira, N.Y., 1946-47; tutor civil engring. CCNY, 1947-49; instr. Rensselear Poly. Inst., 1949-51; asst. prof. Princeton U., 1951-58; research instr. Lehigh U., 1958-60; mem. faculty Ohio State U., 1960—, prof. civil engring., 1964-82, prof. emeritus, 1982—; vis. prof. U. Tex.-Austin, 1982-83. Author: Thin-Walled Bars With Open Profiles, 1990; contbr. papers in field; patentee warp restraining device. With USN, 1943—46. Mem.: ASCE, Structural Stability Rsch. Coun. Home and Office: 1024 Fairway Ln Estes Park CO 80517-7156 Office Phone: 970-577-0237. E-mail: morris_ojalvo@yahoo.com.

OJEDA, ANA MARIA, therapist, clinical caseworker; b. Miami, Feb. 1, 1980; d. Juan Bruno and Daisy Irene Ojeda. BSc in Psychology and Elem. Edn., U. Miami, Coral Gables, Fla., 2002, MSc in Mental Health Counseling, 2004; MA in Clin. Psychology, Regent U., 2006. Milieu therapist Miami Children's Hosp., 2001—03; therapist Psychsolutions, Miami, 2002; psychotherapist Miami Children's Hosp., 2003—04; residential counselor The Pines Residential Treatment Ctr., Portsmouth, Va., 2004—05, therapist/clin. caseworker, 2005—06. Assoc. tchr. U. Miami, Hialeati, 2002, rsch. asst., Coral Gables, 03. Recipient academic merit, U. Miami, 2004, certificate of appreciation, Miami Children's Hosp., 2003; named to Provost's Honor Roll, U. Miami, 2001—02, Dean's List, 2001—02; nominee Excellence award, Miami Children's Hosp., 2003. Mem.: APA, Pi Lambda Theta. Republican. Catholic. Avocations: travel, bicycling, running, reading. Office: The Pines Residential Treatment Ctr 825 Crawford Pkwy Portsmouth VA 23704 Home: 2820 ALHAMBRA CIR Coral Gables FL 33134-6254 Personal E-mail: anamojeda@aol.com.

OJEDA, JOSEPH A., psychotherapist; b. NYC, Mar. 25, 1950; s. Benigno Ojeda and Maria Luisa Ayala; children: Kenneth, Lorraine. D of Naturopathy, Westbrook U., Weirton, W.Va., 2004; PhD in Hypnotherapy, LaSalle U., Mandeville, La., 2002; DD, U. of Universal Life, Modesto, Calif., 1975; M in Holistic Healing, Westbrook U., 1996. Diplomate Am. Coll. Forensic Examiners, 1997, Am. Psychotherapy Assn., 1998, bd. cert. Am. Acad. of Experts in Traumatic Stress. Psychotherapist/clergy Counseling Ch. of the Universal Living God, Jamaica, NY, 1972—97; psychotherapist Holistic Healing, Hypnotherapy & Psychotherapy Family, Middletown, 1998—. Marriage officiant Counseling Ch. of the Universal Living God, 1976—, pastoral counseling, 1976—; free counseling walk-in clinic, Counseling Ch. of the Universal Living God, 1972—97. Author: (book) Re-education & Reprogramming with Hypnotherapy..., 2001, Integration of Behavioral & Relaxation Approaches..., 2002, Application of Self-Hypnosis Reprogramming Procedure..., 2002, Secrets of Clairvoyance, Explanation & Instructions, 2007. Recipient award for poem Mysterious Woman, Nat. Libr. of Poetry, 1997, Medal of Merit for cmty. involvement, Pres. Ronald Reagan, 1986, award letter for emergency control ctr. assistance, Commr. Joseph V. Terrenzio, Dept. of Hosp. Bur., 1970. Fellow: Am. Acad. of Experts in Traumatic Stresss. Home and Office: 27 Sproat Street Middletown NY 10940 Personal E-mail: hypnotex@juno.com.

OJEDA EISELEY, JAIME DE, former Spanish ambassador, educator; b. Aug. 5, 1933; BL maxima cum laude in Law, U. Madrid, Spain, 1957; grad., Internat. Acad. of The Hague, The Netherlands; student, Naval War Coll. and Sr. Ctr. for Nat. Def. Studies, Madrid, Spain. Prof. polit. law Complutense U. Madrid, Spain, 1958; joined diplomatic svcs., 1958; served Embassy of Spain, Washington, 1962—69; min. counselor Peking, China, 1973—76; consul-gen. of Spain Hong Kong and Macao, 1976-79; fellow Ctr. Internat. Rels., Harvard U., Cambridge, Mass., 1979-80; dep. permanent rep. NATO, 1982-83, permanent rep., 1983-90; amb. to U.S.A., Spanish Embassy, Washington, 1990-97; pres. high level coun. fgn. affairs Min. F.A. Madrid, 1997. Vis. scholar Johns Hopkins U., Washington, 1997; amb.-in-residence Shenandoah U., Winchester, Va., 1997—; disting. adj. fellow CSIS, Washington, 1997. Translator: Alice in Wonderland and Through the Looking Glass, by Lewis Carroll, 1971—74, Spain and America: The Past and Future, 1994, El 98 en el Congreso y en la Prensa de los Estados Unidos, 1999. Lt. Reserve Marine Corps. Spanish Navy, 1957. Decorated Great Cross Mil. Merit, Great Cross of Civil Merit, Order of Charles III. Home: PO Box 57 3770 Leeds Manor Rd Markham VA 22643-1817

OJO-AMAIZE, EMMANUEL ADE, immunologist; s. Frederick Ojo and Grace Bare; m. Meley TesfaMichael, Dec. 18, 1981; 1 child, Taamrat Ohihon Amaize. PhD, U. Uppsala, Sweden, 1978. Cert. in microbiology Uppsala U. BioMedicum, 1979. Rsch. technician Meloy Labs., Springfield, Va., 1972—74; dir. immunology Splty. Labs. Inc., Santa Monica, Calif., 1991—98; rsch. assoc. City Hope Med. Ctr., Duarte, Calif., 1974—76; lectr. U. Ife, Health Scis., Ile, Oyo, Nigeria, 1978—80; rockefeller postdoc. fellow Uppsala U. Biomedical Ctr., Sweden, 1980—81; world health orgn. fellow NY U. Med. Ctr., 1981—83; postdoc. scientist U. Md. Animal Scis., Coll. Pk., Md., 1984—86; sr. nat. Insts. health nih fellow UCLA Sch. Medicine, 1986—87; dir. immunology ICN Pharms., Costa Mesa, Calif., 1987—89; rsch. asst. prof. USC Sch. Medicine, LA, 1989—91. Founder Immune Modulation, Inc.,Paraquest, Bloomington, Calif., 1998—, pres., 1998—, ceo, 1998—. Contbr. articles to profl.jours. (NIH Fellowship, 1986). Grant, Calif. State AIDS Task Force, 1987. Mem.: Scandinavian Soc. Immunology, AAAS. Independent. Achievements include patents for the discovery of a new drug for anti-cancer, anti-viral, anti-inflammatory and anti-parasitic indications. Avocations: travel, tennis, reading, dance. Office: Immune Modulation Inc-Paraquest Inc PO Box 998 Bloomington CA 92316-0998 Office Fax: 909-823-3963. Business E-Mail: ojoamaize@aol.com.

OJOGHO, OKECHUKWU N., surgeon, educator; m. Tammie A. Ojogho; children: Brittani, Brandon, Bailee. BSc in Microbiology, Immunology, San Diego State U., 1982; MD, U. Calif. San Francisco, 1986; MS in Med. Mgmt., Marshall Sch. Bus., U. Southern Calif., LA, 2007. Dir., adult and pediatric kidney, pancreas transplantation Loma Linda U. Sch. Medicine, Calif., 1996—2005, assoc. prof. surgery, 2004—07, prof. surgery, 2007—. Dir. and surgeon-in-chief Transplantation Inst., Loma Linda U. Med. Ctr., Calif., 2005—08. Mem., bd. dirs. Faculty Physicians & Surgeons, Loma Linda, 2005—08, Southern Calif. Renal Disease Coun., LA, 2007—09; vice chair bd. dirs. OneLegacy Organ Procurement Orgn., LA, 2008—09; mem., unos minority affairs com. United Network Organ Sharing, 2006—08; mem., kidney, pancreas adv. bd. Am. Soc. Transplantation, 2007—09. Recipient, Phi Kappa Phi Nat. Honor Soc., 1981, Naurice M. Nesset Rsch. Forum, 1993, Centennial Vanguard award, Loma Linda U., 2006. Fellow: ACS; mem.: Healthcare Fin. Mgmt. Assn., Am. Coll. Physician Executives, Am. Soc. Transplant Surgeons. Avocations: soccer, golf, travel, bicycling. Office: Loma Linda Univ Med Ctr 11234 Anderson St Rm 1405 Loma Linda CA 92354 Office Fax: 909-558-0110. Business E-Mail: oojogho@llu.edu.

OJWANG, J.G.O., research scientist; s. John W. Onango and Martha Atieno; m. Madona Ojwang; 1 child, Richard. BSc., Jomo Kenyatta U., Kenya, 1998; MSc in Physics and Astronomy, Groningen State U., Netherlands, 2004; degree, Eindhoven U., Netherlands, 2009—. Guest rschr. Caltech, Pasadena, Calif., 2006—; postdoc fellow Carnegie Geophys. Lab., Washington, 2009—; vis. scientist Eindhoven U., 2009—. Physics examiner Kenya Nat. Exams. Coun., Nairobi, Kenya, 1999—2002. Recipient Best Lecture award, 2007; fellowship, NUFFIC, Netherlands, 2002—04. Mem.: European Phys. Soc., Am. Phys. soc. Achievements include research in hydrogen storage solutions elucidation of the role of alanes in mass transport of aluminum atoms during the thermal decomposition of sodium alanate.

OK, EFE A., economics professor; b. Ankara, Turkey, Jan. 12, 1969; s. Gurkan Hasan Ok and Birol Turker; m. Berna Falay, Aug. 10, 2007. PhD, Cornell U., Ithaca, NY, 1995. Prof. economics NYU, 1995—. Author: (profl. book) Probability with Economic Applications, Mathematical Methods for Economics, Real Analysis with Economic Applications; contbr. articles to profl. jour. Grantee Rsch. grant, NSF, 1995—2008. Mem.: Jour. Econ. Theory.

OKABE, KATSUMI, retired special education educator; b. Osaka, Japan, Dec. 14, 1937; s. Kumataro and Sumiko Okabe; m. Toshiko Nishimori Okabe, Sept. 7, 1974; children: Katsushi, Katsuro. BE, Ehime U., Matsuyama, 1964; MA, Wayne State U., 1975, PhD, 1977. Cert. tchg. Ehime Prefectural Bd. Edn. Elem. sch. tchr. Mcpl. Bd. Edn., Matsuyama, 1964—68; chief speech, lang. pathologist Prefectural Bd. Edn., Matsuyama, 1969—71, Chikamori Hosp., Kochi, Japan, 1980—82; faculty U. Tsukuba, 1982—97, prof., 1997—2001, Seirei Christopher U., Hamamatsu, Japan, 2001—02; ret., 2002. Dir. Japanese Assn. Psychology Human Svcs., Yachiyo-shi, Japan, 2003—05. Author: Educational Rehabilitation and Nursing for Aphasics, 1997, Educational Rehabilitation and Nursing for Aphasics in Japan, 2005, Creating Family Harmony Through Tanka-- An Appeal for Educational Reform in the 21st Century, 2007. Host Chikamori Hosp., Kochi City, 1981. Grantee, Ehime Prefectural Bd. Edn., 1968; Grad. Profl. scholarships, Wayne State U., 1974—77. Mem.: Japan Soc. Study Edn., Japaneses Assn. Spl. Edn., Japanese Assn. Comm. Disorders. Achievements include coordinating the agreement for academic exchange and cooperation between the University of Southern Indiana and the University of Tsukuba in Japan. Avocation: bicycling. Home: 3-25-46 Inodai Toride shi 302-0015 Japan Home Phone: 81-297-73-0181. Personal E-mail: k_m_okabe@ybb.ne.jp.

OKADA, ELLIE, business educator; b. Kobe, Hyogo, Japan, Mar. 25, 1958; d. Suteo and Yoko Okada. AB in Commerce, Kwansei Gakuin U., 1984; MBA, Kobe U., 1986, DBA, 1999. Assoc. prof. Yokohama Nat. U., Kanagawa, Japan, 1990—2003, prof. Internat. Grad. Sch. Social Scis., 2003—. Vis. scholar Ctr. Japanese Economy and Bus., Columbia U. Bus. Sch., NYC, 1993, 2008—09; dir. Ted Impact, Tokyo, 2007—08; rsch. assoc. Program US Japan Rels. Weatherhead Ctr. Internat. Affairs, Harvard U., 2009—. Mem. steering com.: jour. Knowledge Forum. Com. mem. sect. intellectual properties policy Coun. Econ. and Indsl. Policy, Japanese Govt., Tokyo, 2002—06, com. mem. sect. growth policy, 2004—06; expert com. Coun. Sci. and Tech. Policy, Japanese Govt., Tokyo, 2007—08. Recipient Meritorious Svc. award, Japan Patent Office, 2005. Fellow: Knowledge Mgmt. Soc. Japan (rsch. prize 2005), Intellectual Property Assn. Japan; mem.: Rsch. Consortium Intellectual Asset Mgmt. (Paris club 2006—). Roman Catholic. Achievements include first to subleader of formulating Disclosure Guideline of Intellectual Properties; patent in field. Avocation: music. Office: Yokohama Nat U 79-4 Tokiwadai Hodogaya-ku Yokohama Kanagawa 240-8501 Japan

OKADA, RONALD SHIG, lawyer; b. Cleve., June 11, 1960; s. Shig and Mary Mariko (Machida) O.; m. Ann (Haugan) Aug. 18, 1984; children: Lauren Mariko, David Ryon, Julia Elise. BA, Carleton Coll., 1982; JD, U. Mich., 1985. Bar: Ohio 1985, U.S. Dist. Ct. (no. dist.) Ohio 1985, U.S. Ct. Appeals (6th cir.) 1988, (11th cir.), 1998, U.S. Supreme Ct., 1999. Assoc. Baker & Hostetler LLP, Cleve., 1985-92, ptnr., litigation dept., 1993—, mem. policy com., 2002—07. Mem. ABA, Ohio Bar Assn., Cleve. Bar Assn., Carleton Coll. Alumni Club (no. Ohio). Office: Baker & Hostetler LLP 3200 National City Ctr Cleveland OH 44114-3485 Home Phone: 440-572-6514; Office Phone: 216-861-7645. Office Fax: 216-696-0740. Business E-Mail: rokada@bakerlaw.com.

OKAFOR, EMEKA (CHUKWUEMEKA NOUBUISI OKAFOR), professional basketball player; b. Houston, Tex., Sept. 28, 1982; BA in Fin., U. Conn., Storrs, 2004. Ctr. Charlotte Bobcats, 2004—09, New Orleans Hornets, 2009—. Mem. US Olympics Basketball Team, Athens, Greece, 2004. Named First Team Academic All-American, 2003—04, Most Outstanding Player, NCAA Final Four, 2004, Co-Nat. Player of Yr., NABC, 2004, First Team All-American, AP, 2004, Big East Player of Yr., 2004, Defensive Player of Yr., 2004, Rookie of Yr., NBA, 2005, First Team All-Rookie, 2005. Achievements include member of NCAA men's basketball national championship winning University of Connecticut Huskies, 2004. Office: New Orleans Hornets 1250 Poydras St Fl 19 New Orleans LA 70113*

OKAFOR, MARTIN OKECHUKWU, physics professor, educational consultant; arrived in US, 1981, naturalized; m. Nwakego N. Okafor, July 19, 1986; 1 child, Uzoma O. MS in Physics, Ga. Inst. Tech., Atlanta, 1983. Asst. prof. physics Dekalb Coll., Decatur, Ga., 1983—2002, Ga. Perimeter Coll., Clarkston, 1983—2002, chair math & sci. dept., 1993—2007, chair sci. dept., 1997—99, distance edn. fellow, 2001—, assoc. prof. physics, 2002—. Chair academic adv. com. physics & astronomy U. Sys. Ga., Atlanta, 1999—2000, faculty assoc. academic affairs, 2000—01; chief exec. officer, prin. cons. Lifelong Literacy Concepts, Stone Mountain, Ga., 2007—. Nat. pres. Mbieri Nwaotuoke USA, Stone Mountain, 2000—; gen. sec. Nigerians In Diaspora Orgn.,

Washington, 2000—03; ranking trustee All Nigerian Am. Congress, Washington, 2005—. Grantee K-12 Sci. Safety Grant, GA Dept. Edn. Math Sci. Partnership, 2005—06, Phys. Sci. Course Mid. Sch. Sci. Tchrs., GA Dept. Edn., 2006—07. Mem.: Ga. Acad. Sci., Am. Assn. Physics Tchrs., South East Sect. Am. Phys. Soc. (life), Sigma Pi Sigma (life). Democrat. Episcopalian. Office: Ga Perimeter Coll 555 N Indian Creek Clarkston GA 30021 Business E-Mail: mokafor@gpc.edu.

OKAMOTO, YOSHI, science educator; b. Osaka, Japan, May 10, 1926; s. Jen Okamoto; m. Michiko Tsuchiya, Aug. 10, 1960; 1 child, Ken. PhD, Purdue U., Lafayett, Ind., 1958. Prof. Polytecnhic Inst. NYU, NYC, 1960—. Dir.: (chem. devel.) Preparetion Novel Polymer Materials; contbr. scientific papers. Home: 3 Horizon Rd Fort Lee NJ 07024 Office: 6 Metrotech Ctr 1 Brooklyn NY 11201 Office Fax: 718-260-3508. Business E-Mail: yokamoto@poly.edu.

O'KANE, BARBARA LYNN, research psychologist; b. Jersey City, Sept. 7, 1950; d. Herbert and Pearl Clair Sandick; m. David Dean O'Kane, June 25, 1988; 1 child, Nathan Sean. BS, Suffolk U., 1976; PhD, Brandeis U., 1982. Rsch. psychologist U.S. Army Natick R&D Ctr., Natick, Mass., 1979-85; R&D insp. U.S. Army Material Command, Alexandria, Va., 1985-89; engring. rsch. psychologist U.S. Army Night Vision and Electronic Sensors Directorate, Ft. Belvoir, Va., 1985—. Author: (chpt.) Vision Models for Target Detection and Recognition, 1995, Childrens Science Book Seeing Heart; contbr. articles to profl. jours. Avocations: music, public speaking, creation science, skiing. Home: 6117 Burnett St Alexandria VA 22310-2662 Office: US Army Night Vision Lab Burbeck Rd Fort Belvoir VA 22060 Business E-Mail: okane@nvl.army.mil.

OKARMA, JEROME D., lawyer, manufacturing executive; b. 1952; m. Pam Okarma; 2 children. BA in History, Western Ill. U., 1974; JD, Northwestern U., 1977. Bar: Ill. 1977, Wis. 1989. Atty. Inland Steel Co., 1977—82; asst. sec., sr. atty. Borg-Warner Corp., 1982—89; asst. gen. counsel Johnson Controls, Inc., Milw., 1990—2000, dep. gen. counsel, 2000—04, v.p., 2003—, gen. counsel, sec., 2004—. Bd. mem. United Way Leadership Team, Legal Divsn. Recipient Disting. Alumni award, We. Ill. U., 2004. Office: Johnson Controls Inc 5757 N Green Bay Ave Milwaukee WI 53209 Office Phone: 414-524-1200. E-mail: jerome.d.okarma@jci.com.*

OKARMA, THOMAS BERNARD, biotechnology company executive; b. 1946; AB, Dartmouth Coll., 1968; MD, Stanford U., 1972, PhD in Pharmacology, 1974; exec. MBA, Stanford Grad. Sch. Bus., 1997. Asst. prof., dept. medicine Stanford U. Sch. Medicine, 1980—85; scientific founder Applied Immune Sciences, Inc., 1985; v.p. R&D to, chmn., CEO, bd. dir. Applied Immune Sciences, Inc.(acquired by Rhone-Poulene Rorer in 1995); sr. v.p. Rhone-Poulene Rorer, 1995—96; with Geron Corp., Menlo Park, Calif., 1997—, v.p., cell therapies, 1997—98, v.p. R&D, 1998—99, pres., CEO, 1999—, pres., oncology drug develop, 2008—. Bd. dirs. Geron Corp., Menlo Park, Calif., 1999—, Geron Bio-Med Ltd., TA Therapeutics, Ltd., BIO (Biotechnology Industry Orgn.); spkr. in field. Contbr. several articles to profl. jours. Chmn., bd. overseers Dartmouth Med. Sch., 2000—07. Achievements include patents in field. Avocations: scuba diving, water and snow skiing, fishing, anything outdoors. Office: Geron Corp 230 Constitution Dr Menlo Park CA 94025 Office Phone: 650-473-7700. Office Fax: 650-473-7750. E-mail: info@geron.com.*

OKAZAKI, MASAHARU, chemist; s. Kikuji and Hama Okazaki; m. Hideyo Satoh, Mar. 26, 1977; children: Yohsuke, Hiroko. Grad., Osaka U., Japan, 1971, PhD, 1981. Postdoctoral rschr. U. BC, Vancouver, Canada, 1981—83; asst. prof. Ehime U., Matsuyama, Japan, 1984—87; assoc. prof. Inst. Molecular Sci., Okazaki, Aichi, Japan, 1989—91; sr. rschr. Nat. Inst. Advanced Indsl. Sci. and Tech., Chubu Br., Nagoya, Aichi, Japan, 1987—. Scholar, Yukawa Found., 1976. Achievements include invention of product yield detected ESR (spectroscopy) and fluid dynamics in the nanospace of mesoporous silica. Home: 5-3-66 Takakuradai Kasugai Aichi 487-0017 Japan Office: Nat Inst Advanced Indsl Sci and Tech 2266-98 Shimoshidami Moriyama-ku Nagoya Aichi 463-8560 Japan Office Fax: 81-52-736-7066. Business E-Mail: masa-okazaki@aist.go.jp.

OKAZAWA, HIROMI, school librarian; b. Kawanishi, Hyogo, Japan, May 16, 1980; d. Shinji and Sachiko Okazawa; m. Richard Tseng. MA in Asian Studies, U. Ill., Champaign, 2006; MLIS, U. Ill., 2008. Libr. asst. U. Libr., Champaign, 2006—. Author: (novel) Comic stories from old Japan. Home: 2515 B Leeper Dr Champaign IL 61822

O'KEEFE, FRANCIS RONALD, lawyer; b. Oct. 7, 1950; AB, Georgetown U., 1972; JD, Cleve.-Marshall Coll., 1977. Bar: Ohio 1977, U.S. Dist. Ct. (no. dist.) Ohio 1978, U.S. Supreme Ct. 2002. Pvt. practice, 1977—86; sec. and gen. counsel Broadview Fin. Corp., 1986—89; ptnr. Hahn, Loeser & Parks LLP, 1989—. Recipient Sindell Tort Competition prize, Cleve.-Marshall Law Sch., 1977, Most Useful to Practicing Attys. Law Rev. Article award, 1977; named Ohio Super Lawyer, Cin. mag., 2004, 2005; named to Best Lawyers in Am. in corp. law, 2001—. Mem.: ABA, Soc. Corp. Governance Profls., Met. Cleve. Bar Assn., Ohio State Bar Assn. Office: Hahn Loeser & Parks LLP 200 Public Sq Ste 2800 Cleveland OH 44114-2301 Office Phone: 216-274-2396. E-mail: frokeefe@hahnlaw.com.

O'KEEFE, GARY RAYMOND, actor; b. Riverside, Calif., Oct. 3, 1940; s. Harold Clarence and Geraldine Amelia (Richardson) O'K.; m. Annette Barbara Dimeo, June 2, 1967. Grad. high sch., Santa Monica, Calif. Actor, LA, 1969—. Appeared in over 200 movies, TV shows and on stage. Chmn. Gower Gulch Neighbor Assn., Hollywood, Calif., 1978-79. Sgt. U.S. Army, 1960-66, Europe, Korea, Vietnam. Decorated Purple Heart with oak leaf cluster, Combat Infantryman's Badge. Mem. SAG, AFTRA, VFW (life), 28th Inf. Assn. Democrat. Avocation: ironman triathlons (finished 5 times). E-mail: rayclb@sbcglobal.net.

O'KEEFE, JAMES WILLIAM, JR., investment manager and banker; b. Troy, NY, Oct. 23, 1948; s. James William and Antoinnette (Shannon) O'K.; m. Ann Palmer Ghiglione, June 4, 1977; 1 child, Courtney Anne. BA, Georgetown U., 1970; MBA, Harvard U., 1972. Mng. dir. Morgan Stanley & Co. Inc., NYC, 1972-87, Kidder, Peabody & Co. Inc., NYC, 1987-92; CEO Aetna Realty Investors, Inc., 1993—96; CEO, Allegis Realty Investors, Hartford, Conn., 1996—99; mng. dir., head of global real estate UBS Global Asset Mgmt., 1999—. Pres., mem. Nat. Coun. Real Estate Investment Fiducaries, 2009. Mem. Urban Land Inst., Nat. Assn. Real Estate Investment Trusts, NY Athletic Club, Fishers Island Club, Knickerbocker Club. Avocation: golf.

O'KEEFE, JOHN DAVID, brokerage house executive; b. NYC, Nov. 16, 1941; s. Timothy J. and Agnes V. (Timlin) O.; m. Stefanie Carreau Keegan, Jan. 28, 1978; children: Douglas G., Hillary C., John M., Meredith B. BBA, Iona Coll., 1963; MBA, L.I. U., 1968. Analyst L.I. Lighting Co., Mineola, NY, 1965-69, Pershing and Co., NYC, 1969-72; mng. dir. Kidder, Peabody and Co., Inc., NYC, 1972-89; v.p. Smith Barney, NYC, 1989—. Bd. dirs. Heisman Found. Sgt. USMC, 1963-65. Mem.: Marine Corps. League, Union Club NYC, Downtown Athletic Club (gov. 1986, chmn. Heisman Trophy com. 1987—88, gov. 1988). Republican. Home: 31 Linden Tree Rd Wilton CT 06897-1613 Office: Smith Barney 200 Nyala Farms Rd Westport CT 06880-6267 Office Phone: 203-221-6082. Business E-Mail: john.d.okeefe@smithbarney.com.

O'KEEFE, KATHLEEN MARY, state official; b. Butte, Mont., Mar. 25, 1933; d. Hugh I. and Kathleen Mary (Harris) O'Keefe; m. Nick M. Baker, Sept. 18, 1954 (div. 1970); children: Patrick, Susan, Michael, Cynthia, Hugh, Mardeen. BA in Comm., St. Mary Coll., Xavier, Kans., 1954. Profl. singer, mem. Kathie Baker Quartet, 1962-72; rsch. cons. Wash. Ho. of Reps., Olympia, 1972-73; info. officer Wash. Employment Security Commn., Seattle, 1973-81, dir.pub. affairs, 1981-90, video dir., 1990-95, ret., 1995. Freelance writer, composer, producer, 1973—. Author: Job Finding In the Nineties, The Third Alternative, handbook on TV prodn., (children: So You Want to be President, 1995; composer numerous songs, also writer, dir., prodr. numerous spots. Founder, pres. bd. Eden, Inc., visual and performing arts, 1975—; pub. rels. chmn. Nat. Women's Dem. Conv., Seattle, 1979, Wash. Dem. Women, 1976-85; bd. dirs., composer, prodr., dir. N.Y. Film Festival, 1979; Dem. candidate Wash. State Senate, 1968. Recipient Silver medal Seattle Creative Awards Show for composing, directing and producing Rent A Kid, TV Pub. Svc. spot, 1979. Mem. Wash. Press Women. Roman Catholic. Home: 1325 138th St SE Mill Creek WA 98012-5505 Office Phone: 425-337-0356. E-mail: kathie@nwrain.com.

O'KEEFE, LINDA LEE, physical education educator; b. Mojave, Calif., Apr. 28, 1947; d. Edward and Betty June O'Keefe. BS in Phys. Edn., U. Dayton, Ohio, 1971, MS in Phys. Edn., 1976. Tchr. Bellehaven Elem. Sch., Dayton, 1971—72, Meadowdale HS, Dayton, 1972—78; prof. Sinclair CC, Dayton, 1979—, coach, 1979—2003. Spkr., event organizer Am. Cancer Soc., Dayton, 2000—. Recipient Excellence in Tchg. award, Nat. Inst. Staff Devel., 2003, Faculty Excellence and Innovation award, Southwestern Ohio Coun. Higher Edn., 2003; named Coach of Yr., Sinclair CC, 1979—2003; named one of Ohio's Top Educators, Ohio Mag., 2003; named to Hall of Fame, Dayton Tennis Commn., 1987, Nat. Jr. Coll. Athletic Assn., 1996. Mem.: AAHPERD, Am. Assn. Health Educators, Ohio Assn. Health, Phys. Edn., Recreation and Dance. Avocations: reading, bicycling, tennis, hiking, gardening. Home: 1100 Stanwick Beavercreek OH 45430 Office: Sinclair CC 444 W 3d St Dayton OH 45430 Office Phone: 937-512-2287. Fax: 937-512-3056. Business E-Mail: linda.okeefe@sinclair.edu.

O'KEEFE, MICHAEL DANIEL, lawyer; b. St. Louis, Jan. 3, 1938; s. Daniel Michael and Hanoria (Moriarty) O'K.; m. Bonnie Bowdern, July 11, 1964; children: Collen Coyne, Daniel Michael. AB, LLB, St. Louis U., 1961; postgrad., George Washington U., 1963. Bar: Mo. 1961, U.S. Ct. Appeals (8th cir.) 1961, U.S. Dist. Ct. (ea. dist.) Mo. 1961, Ill. 1975, U.S. Dist. Ct. (so. dist.) Ill. 1975, U.S. Ct. Appeals (5th and 7th cirs.) 1983, (10th cir.) 1995. Asst. cir. atty., St. Louis, 1961—62, 1964—65; pvt. practice, 1964-67; ptnr. Lucas, Murphy & O'Keefe, St. Louis, 1967-74, Thompson & Mitchell, St. Louis, 1974-96, Thompson Coburn, St. Louis, 1996—. Adj. prof. trial practice Sch. of Law, St. Louis U., 1992—. Editor: American Maritime Cases, 1985—. Trustee St. Louis U. Capt. USAF, 1962-64. Fellow Am. Coll. Trial Lawyers; mem. Internat. Assn. Def. Counsel, Fedn. Ins. and Corp. Counsel, Maritime Law Assn., Nat. Assn. Railroad Trial Counsel, Am. Law Inst. Democrat. Roman Catholic. Avocations: reading, tennis, fencing, archaeology, microbiology. Home: 372 Walton Row Saint Louis MO 63108-1909 Office: Thompson Coburn One US Bank Plz Saint Louis MO 63101-1643 Office Phone: 314-552-6092. Business E-Mail: mokeefe@thompsoncoburn.com.

O'KEEFE, PATRICK WILLIAM, research scientist; BS, U. Coll., Dublin; MS, Cornell U., Ithaca, NY, 1967; PhD, Oreg. State U., Corvallis, 1971. Rsch. scientist Battelle Pacific NW Labs., Richland, Wash., 1971—73; food scientist ITT Continental Baking, Rye, NY, 1973—74; rsch. fellow Harvard U., Cambridge, Mass., 1974—78; rsch. scientist Wadsworth Ctr., NY State Dept. Health, Albany, 1979—; assoc. prof. Sch. Pub. Health, SUNY, Albany, 2000—. Grantee, NIEHS Basic Superfund Rsch. Program, 1992—95, 1995—2000. Mem.: Soc. Environ. Toxicology and Chemistry, Am. Chem. Soc. Achievements include research in the environmental chemistry and analysis of pharmaceuticals, personal care products, dioxins and related compounds. Office: NY State Dept Health PO Box 509 Empire State Plz Albany NY 12201

O'KEEFE, SEAN CHARLES, manufacturing executive, former academic administrator; b. Monterey, Calif., Jan. 27, 1956; s. Patrick Gordon and Patricia Carlin O'Keefe; m. Laura Jean McCarthy, Oct. 7, 1978; children: Lindsey, Jonathan, Kevin. BA, Loyola U., New Orleans, 1977; MPA, Syracuse U., 1978. Budget analyst US Dept. Def., Washington, comtr., CFO, 1989—92, sec. of Navy, 1992—93; profl. staff US Senate Appropriations Com., Washington; staff dir. US Def. Appropriations Subcommittee, Washington; asst. to sr. v.p. for rsch., dean grad. sch. Pa. State U., prof., bus. adminstrn. University Park; Louis A. Bantle Prof., business and govt. policy Maxwell Sch. Citizenship and Pub. Affairs, Syracuse U., 1996, endowed chair, 1996; dir., Nat. Security Studies Partnership, Syracuse U. and John Hopkins U., 1996; dep. dir. Office of Mgmt. & Budget, Washington, 2000—01; adminstr. NASA, Washington, 2001—05; chancellor La. State U. and A&M Coll., Baton Rouge, 2005—08; v.p. Washington ops. GE Aviation, Washington, 2008—. Bd. dirs. E. I. du Pont de Nemours & Co., 2005-, Battele Meml. Inst., Sensis Corp.; vis. scholar Wolfson Coll. U. Cambridge. Co-author: The Defense Industry in Post Cold War Era: Corporate Strategies and Public Policy Perspectives, 1998; contbr. articles to profl. jours.; chpts. to books. Staff rep. platform com. Rep. Nat. Com., New Orleans, 1988, advisor, Washington, 1994-97, mem. bd. adv. Naval Postgraduate Sch. Recipient Disting. Pub. Svc. award, 1993, Navigator award, Potomac Inst. for Policy Studies, 2005; named Honorary Engr., Engrs. Coun., 2005; named one of Top 100 Irish Americans, Irish Am. Mag., 2003—04, the Stars of the South, 2006; named to, La. Polit. Hall of Fame, 2007. Fellow Nat. Acad. Pub. Adminstrn., Internat. Acad. Astronautics; mem. Ft. Ticonderoga Assn., Cavalry Club. Republican. Roman Catholic. Avocations: golf, fishing. Office: GE Aviation 1601 N Kent St # 1013 Arlington VA 22209 Office Phone: 703-351-5890.*

O'KEEFE, TAMRA LYNN, psychologist, school system administrator, director; b. Elkhart, Ind., Sept. 26, 1965; d. Leland Ray and Joan Marie Trapp; m. David Gerard O'Keefe, June 2, 1990; 1 child, Rachel Jack. BA in Spanish, Fine-Arts, Ind. U., Bloomington, 1987; MS in Sch. Psychology, Memphis State U., 1994; post masters, U. Whitewater, Wis., 1996. Cert. sch. psychologist Wis., NC, 2001. Sch. psychologist Charlotte Mecklenburg Schs., NC, 2001—02, Union Cmty. Schs., Monroe, NC, 2002—05, Kohler Pub. Schs., Wis., spl. edn. coord., 2005—, dir. spl. edn., 2008—. Choir mem. Bethany Luth. Ch., Kohler, 2008—. Mem.: Kappa Delta Pi. Independent. Avocations: swimming, gardening, reading, art, crafts. Home: 512 E Riverside Dr Kohler WI 53044 Office: Kohler Pub Schs 333 Upper Rd Kohler WI 53044 Business E-Mail: o'keefet@kohler.k12.wi.us.

O'KEEFE, THOMAS MICHAEL, academic administrator; b. St. Cloud, Minn., Mar. 25, 1940; s. Thomas William and Genevieve B. (McCormick) O'K.; m. Kathleen Marie Gnifkowski, Aug. 20, 1966; children: Steven Michael, Ann Catherine. Student, Marquette U., 1961-65, BS, 1965; MS in Nuclear Physics, U. Pitts., 1968; DHL, Hamline U., 1989. Dir. edn. planning HEW, Washington, 1969-70, dep. asst. sec., 1977-80; v.p. Carnegie Found. for Advancement of Teaching, Washington, 1980-83; pres. Consortium for Advancement Pvt. Higher Edn., Washington, 1983-89; exec. v.p. McKnight Found., Mpls., 1989-99; commr. Dept. Human Svcs., State Minn., St. Paul, 1999—2002; pres. Mpls. Coll. Art and Design, 2002—09. Dir. Washington internships in edn. George Washington U., 1970-73; dir. policy analysis and evaluation U. Ill., Chgo., 1973-74, assoc. v.p. acad. affairs, 1974-77; head U.S. del. to Orgn. Econ. Coop. and Devel., 1979, 80; mem. Carnegie Forum on Edn. and the Economy, 1985-88; mem. N.J. Commn. on Ind. Higher Edn., 1986-88; mem. task force on ind. higher edn. Edn. Commn. States, 1987-89; co-chair Edn. Program, The Aspen Inst., 1987—. Contbr. articles to profl. jours.; contbg. editor: Change mag., 1985—2001; bd. dirs.: Editl. Project in Edn., 1984—93. Bd. dirs. The Edn. Resources Inst., Boston, 1987-94, Minn. Coun. on Founds., 1994-99, Minn. Pub. Radio, 1999—, Alliance Excellent Edn., 2004-; trustee Buena Vista Coll., Storm Lake, Iowa, 1984-90; mem. Coun. on Fgn. Rels., 1995-99; bd. regents U. Minn., 1996-02. Democrat. Office: Mpls Coll Art and Design 2501 Stevens Ave S Minneapolis MN 55404

OKEKE, CHRISTIAN NWACHUKWU, law educator; b. Obinofia, Enugu, Nigeria, June 8, 1941; s. Stephen Agueze and Sussana Nwaduvu Okeke; m. Justina Nwanagu Okeke. LLM Summa Cum Laude, Kiev State U., Ukraine, 1969; PhD, Free U., Holland, 1973. Lic. Nigerian Coun. Legal Edn. Sr. Lectr. U. Nigeria, Enugu, Nigeria, 1974—85; pioneer dean emeritus Nnamdi Azikiwe U., Awka, Nigeria, 1985—91; dep. vice chancellor, dean of law emeritus Enugu State U. of Sci. Tech., Enugu, Nigeria, 1991—95; fellow MaxPlanck Inst., Heidelberg, Germany, 1994—95; law prof. Golden Gate U., San Francisco, 1996—. Ptr. ILegbune, Okeke & Co., Enugu, Nigeria, 1980—94; cons. African Network for Prevention of Child Abuse and Neglect, Enugu, 1974—; trustee mem. Internat. First Aid Soc., Enugu, 1974—. Author: Expansion of New Subjects of International Law, 1973, Controversial Subject of Contemporary International Law, 1974, Theory & Practice of International Law in Nigeria, 1986. Exec. dir. Internat. First Aid Soc., Inc., Antioch, Calif., 1994—. Rsch. fellowship, Hague Acad. of Internat. Law, 1970, fellowship, Cambridge U., England, 1971. Mem.: Nigerian Bar Assn., Nigerian Soc. of Internat. Law. Home: 4320 Mink Ct Antioch CA 94531 Office: Golden Gate U Sch of Law 536 Mission St San Francisco CA 94105 Office Phone: 415-442-6695. Office Fax: 415-442-6756. E-mail: cokeke@ggu.edu.

OKEKE, CONSTANCE O., ophthalmologist, educator; 2 children. MD, Yale Sch. Medicine, New Haven, Conn., 2000; MSCE, U. Pa., Phila., 2008. Cert. in ophthalmology residency Johns Hopkins Wilmer Eye Inst., Md., 2004. Ophthalmologist Va. Eye Consultants. Office: Va Eye Consultants 241 Corp Blvd Norfolk VA 23502 Office Phone: 757-622-2200. Business E-Mail: cokeke@vec2020.com.

O'KELLEY, WILLIAM CLARK, federal judge; b. Atlanta, Jan. 2, 1930; s. Ezra Clark and Theo (Johnson) O'K.; m. Ernestine Allen, Mar. 28, 1953; children: Virginia Leigh O'Kelley Wood, William Clark Jr. AB, Emory U., 1951, LLB, 1953. Bar: Ga. 1952. Pvt. practice, Atlanta, 1957-59; asst. U.S. atty. No. Dist. Ga., 1959-61; partner O'Kelley, Hopkins & Van Gerpen, Atlanta, 1961-70; U.S. dist. judge No. Dist. Ga., Atlanta, 1970—, chief judge, 1988-94. Mem. com. on adminstrn. of criminal law Jud. Conf. U.S., 1979-82, exec. com., 1983-84, subcom. on jury trials in complex criminal cases, 1981-82, dist. judge rep. 11th cir., 1981-84, mem. adv. com. of fed. rules of criminal procedure, 1984-87; bd. dirs. Fed. Jud. Ctr., 1987-91, adv. com. history program, 1989-91, com. on orientation of newly appointed dist. judges, 1985-88; mem. Com. Jud. Resources, 1989-94; mem. Jud. Coun. 11th Cir., 1990-96, exec. com., 1990-96; mem. Fgn. Intelligence Surveillance Ct., 1980-87; mem. Alien Terrorist Removal Ct., 1996—; corp. sec., dir. Gwinnett Bank & Trust Co., Norcross, Ga., 1967-70. Mem. exec. com., gen. counsel Ga. Republican Com., 1968-70; mem. fin. com. Northwest Ga. Girl Scout Coun., 1958-70; trustee Emory U., 1991-97, mem. fin. com., 1994-2007; mem. Emeritus Adv. Com. to pres. and chmn. bd., 2008-. Served as 1st lt. USAF, 1953-57; capt. USAFR. Mem. Fed. Bar Assn., Ga. State Bar, Atlanta Bar Assn., Dist. Judges Assn. 5th Cir. (sec.-treas. 1976-77, v.p. 1977-78, pres. 1978-80), Lawyers Club Atlanta, Kiwanis (past pres.), Atlanta Athletic Club, Sigma Chi (named Significant Sig 1983), Phi Delta Phi, Omicron Delta Kappa. Baptist. Home: 550 Ridgecrest Dr Norcross GA 30071-2158 Office: US Dist Ct 1942 US Courthouse 75 Spring St SW Atlanta GA 30303-3309 Office Phone: 404-215-1530.

O'KELLY, CRYSTAL KATHLEEN, secondary school educator, television producer; b. Pomona, Calif., Dec. 10, 1957; d. Guy Lewis and Doris Lowell (Schmidt) O. BS in Comm., Calif. Poly. U., 1984. Cert. tchr. Calif. Trainer, server CNC Orgn., Rancho Cucamonga, Calif., 1977-84; cons. Grubb & Ellis, Ontario, Calif., 1985; salesperson Nordstrom, Montclair, Calif., 1986; sr. analyst Gen. Dynamics, Pomona, 1986-90; asst. dir. Crystal Cathedral, Garden Grove, Calif., 1996; prodr., on-air talent Claremont (Calif.) Pub. Access TV, 1991—; substitute tchr. Claremont Unified Sch. Dist., 1993—2005; English tchr. H.S. Porrona Unified Sch. Dist., 2005—. Staff writer Poly Post, Pomona, 1981-82; chmn. bd., 1995-97, bd. mem. Claremont Pub. Access TV, 1994—; summer sch. tchr., Webb Pvt. Sch., 2000-05. Ind. prodr., dir., host, writer, editor, TV show People to Know, a show dedicated to excellence in TV and the arts, 1994—; creator, producer Miss O'Kelly's Story Time, 1999. Vol., co-host fundraiser Claremont Pub. Access TV, 1991—, Sta. CPAT and The Prodrs. Club, Claremont, 1991-93; various other cmty. and mun. projects. Recipient Calif. State scholar, 1976, Basic Edn. Opportunity grantee, 1978. Mem. Toastmasters (v.p. 1997, pres. 1999—), Toastmasters Club 12, Pomona Valley Art Assn., Claremont Tennis Club. Protestant. Avocations: painting, dance, acting, art collecting, photgraphy. Office: People to Know PO Box 992 Claremont CA 91711-0992

OKEN, EMILY, physician, educator; AB, Princeton U., NJ, 1991; MD, Harvard Med. Sch., Boston, 1996; MPH, Harvard Sch. Pub. Health, 2003. Registered physician Mass., 1996, diplomate Am. Bd. Pediat., 2000, Am. Bd. Internal Medicine, 2000. Clin. fellow Mass. Gen. Hosp., Boston, 1996—2000; fellow Harvard Med. Sch., 2001—03, instr., 2003—06, asst. prof., 2007—. Office: Harvard Med Sch 133 Brookline Ave 6th Fl Boston MA 02215 Business E-Mail: emily_oken@harvardpilgrim.org.

OKERLUND, ARLENE NAYLOR, academic administrator, writer; b. Emmitsburg, Md., Oct. 13, 1938; d. George Wilbur and Ruth Opal (Sensenbaugh) Naylor; m. Michael Dennis Okerlund, June 6, 1959 (div. Apr. 1983); 1 dau., Linda Susan. BA, U. Md., 1960; PhD, U. Calif.-San Diego, 1969. Instr. sci. Mercy Hosp. Nursing Sch., Balt., 1959-63; prof. English San Jose (Calif.) State U., 1969—2005, dean humanities and arts, 1980-86, acad. v.p., 1986-93. Cons. Ednl. Testing Svc., Berkeley,

Calif., 1976—80. Author: Elizabeth Wydeville: The Slandered Queen, 2005, Elizabeth Of York, 2009; editor San Jose Studies, 1975—80; contbr. articles on the humanities to profl. jours. Bd. dirs. World Forum Silicon Valley, Peninsula Banjo Band. Grantee NEH, 1979; grantee San Jose State U., 1971-72. Mem.: MLA (del. to assembly, west coast rep. 1976—77), Am. Beethoven Soc. (v.p. bd. dirs. 1983—2006), Calif. Coun. Fine Arts Deans (pres. 1984—86), Internat. Coun. Fine Arts Deans, Philol. Assn. Pacific Coast (sec.-treas. 1975—78). Democrat. Office: San Jose State U Dept English Washington Sq San Jose CA 95192-0090 Office Phone: 408-924-4425. Business E-Mail: okerlund@email.sjsu.edu.

OKERSON, ANN SHUMELDA LILLIAN, librarian; d. Jacob and Alexandra Tereshtshenko Shumelda. MLS, U. Calif. Libr. Simon Fraser U., Vancouver, B.C., Canada, 1970—85; dir. libr. svcs. Jerry Alper Inc., Eastchester, N.Y., 1985-90; sr. program officer Assn. of Rsch. Libraries., Washington, 1990-95; assoc. univ. libr., collection develop and mgmt. Yale U., New Haven, 1995—, assoc. univ. libr., collections and technical services, 1999—, assoc. univ. libr., collections and internat. programs, 2003—. Adj. faculty mem., grad. sch. info. U. Mich., 1995; private investigator, project coord. Liblicense, 1997—; worked over the years on numerous projects, adv. boards, and speaking engagements. Author (synopsia chpt.) Andrew W. Mellon study University Libraries and Scholarly Communications, 1992; creator, pub., Directory of Electronic Journals, Newsletters and Academic Discussions Lists, 1991-95; co-editor (with James O'Donnell) Scholarly Journals at the Crossroads: a Subversive Proposal for Electronic Journal Publishing, 1995; co-owner, co-moderator, NewJour, 1993-; Editor numerous books; contbr. articles to profl. publs. Named Alumni of Yr., Mt. View Acad., 1995, Serials Libr. Yr., ALA, 1993; recipient Best Article in the area of serials, acquisitions, and/or collections award, ALA, 1988, 93, Libr. Info. Tech. Assn.(LITA)/High Tech award, 1999; numerous grants. Avocations: chocolate, travel, reading. Office: Yale U Libr PO Box 208240 New Haven CT 06520-8240 Office Phone: 203-432-1764. Business E-Mail: ann.okerson@yale.edu.

OKIISHI, THEODORE HISAO, mechanical engineering educator; b. Honolulu, Jan. 15, 1939; s. Clifford Muneo and Dorothy Asako (Tokushima) O.; m. Rae Wiemers, May 28, 1963; children: Christopher Gene, John Clifford, Mark William, Kenneth Edward. Student, U. Hawaii, 1956-57; BS, Iowa State U., 1960, MS, 1963, PhD, 1965. Registered profl. engr., Iowa, Ohio. Asst. prof. to prof., assoc. dean coll. engring. Iowa State U., Ames, 1967—2007, interim v.p., rsch. and econ. devel., 2008—09. Cons. on fluid dynamics Contbr. articles to profl. jours. Served to capt. C.E., U.S. Army, 1965-67 Decorated Joint Services Commendation award; named Outstanding Prof., Iowa State U. student sect. ASME, 1983, Mech. Engring. Dept. Prof. of Yr., Iowa State U., 1977, 86, 90; recipient award for research NASA, 1975; Ralph R. Teetor award Soc. Automotive Engrs., 1976, Engring. Coll. Superior Teaching award Iowa State U., 1987, Cardinal Key Iowa State U., 1991. Fellow ASME (Melville medal 1989, 98, dedicated svc. award, 2001, R. Tom Sawyer award, 2008); mem. AIAA, Sigma Xi. Republican. Mem. Ch. of Jesus Christ of Latter-day Saints. Club: Osborn Research Home: 2940 Monroe Dr Ames IA 50010-4362 Office: Iowa State U 2610 Beardshear Hall Ames IA 50011-0001 Office Phone: 515-232-0997. Business E-Mail: tedo@iastate.edu.

OKINAGA, LAWRENCE SHOJI, lawyer; m. Carolyn Hisako Uesugi, Nov. 26, 1966; children: Carrie, Caryn, Laurie. BA, U. Hawaii, 1963; JD, Georgetown U., 1972. Bar: Hawaii 1972, U.S. Dist. Ct. Hawaii 1972, U.S. Ct. Appeals (9th cir.) 1976. Adminstrv. asst. to Congressman Spark Matsunaga, Honolulu, 1964, 65-69; law clk. to chief judge U.S. Dist. Ct. Hawaii, Honolulu, 1972-73; assoc. Carlsmith Ball, Honolulu, 1973-76, ptnr., 1976—. Mem. Gov.'s Citizens Adv. Com. Coastal Zone Mgmt., 1974—79; sec. Hawaii Bicentennial Corp., 1975—77, vice chmn., 1983—85, chmn., 1985—87; mem. Jud. Selection Commn., State of Hawaii, 1979—87, vice chmn., 1986; mem. consumer adv. coun. Fed. Res. Bd., 1984—86; chmn. Jud. Conduct Commn., State of Hawaii, 1991—94; apptd. mem. Fed. Savs. and Loan Adv. Coun., Washington, 1988—89; mem. nat. adv. coun. U.S. SBA, 1994—2000; mem. adv. coun. Fed. Res. Bank, San Francisco, 1995—2002. Pres., bd. dirs. Moiliili Cmty. Ctr., Honolulu, 1965—68, 1973—86, trustee, 1993—; bd. dirs. Pub. Sch. Hawaii Found., 2004—; chmn. Carole Kai Charities Inc., 2001—; mem., bd. dirs. Japan America Soc. Hawaii, 2004—; chmn. Hawaii Fed. Jud. Selection Commn., 2009—; bd. visitors Georgetown U. Law Ctr., 1993—; trustee Kuakini Med. Ctr., 1984—88, 1989—96. Capt. USAFR, 1964—72, capt. USAFR, 1974—76. Mem.: ABA (ho. of dels. 1991—94, mem. standing com. jud. selection tenure and compensation 1993—96, mem. standing com. jud. independence 1999—2002), Am. Judicature Soc. (bd. dirs. 1986, treas. 1995—97, pres. 1997—99), Hawaii Bar Assn. (sec., bd. dirs. 1981), Georgetown U. Law Alumni Assn. (bd. dirs. 1986—91), Omicron Delta Kappa. Office: Carlsmith Ball PO Box 656 Honolulu HI 96809-0656 E-mail: lso@carlsmith.com.

OKITA, GEORGE TORAO, retired pharmacologist; b. Seattle, Jan. 18, 1922; s. Kazuo and Fusao (Muguruma) O.; m. Fujiko Shimizu, Nov. 29, 1958; children: Ronald Hajime, Sharon Mariko, Glenn Torao. Student, U. Cin., 1943-44; BA, Ohio State U., 1948; PhD, U. Chgo., 1951. Rsch. asst., rsch. assoc., instr., then asst. prof. U. Chgo., 1949-63; assoc. prof. Northwestern U. Med. Sch., 1963-66, prof. pharmacology, 1966—90, acting chmn. pharmacology, 1968—70, 1976—77; prof. emeritus molecular pharmacology and biol. chemistry, 1990—. Contbr. articles to profl. jours.; Asst. editor: Jour. Pharmacology and Exptl. Therapeutics, 1965-68. Served with AUS, 1944-46. NIH Postdoctoral fellow, 1952 Mem. AAAS, AAUP, Am. Soc. Pharmacology and Exptl. Therapeutics, Internat. Soc. Biochem. Pharmacology, Am. Heart Assn., Cardiac Muscle Soc., Sigma Xi. Achievements include research in med. field. Home: 95-1058 Kihene St Mililani HI 96789 Personal E-mail: gtoki@aol.com.

OKOAMPA-AHOOFE, KWAME, language educator, historian; arrived in US, 1985; s. Kwame and Adwoa Aninwaa Okoampa-Ahoofe; m. Dolly D. Mensah, June 24, 2004; children: Abena Aninwaa, Kwame III, Yaw Sintim. BA with honors, CCNY, 1990; MA, Temple U., Phila., 1993, PhD, 1998. Instr. English Tech. Career Inst., NYC, 1991—93; instr. history Ind. State U., Terre Haute, 1994—95; asst. prof. English SUNY-Nassau CC, Garden City, 1997—2007, assoc. prof., 2007—. Curator-at-large Okyeman Archives, Kibi, Ghana, 2006—. Author: Atumpan, 2004, The New Scapegoats, 2005, Dr. J.B. Danquah, 2005, Nananom, 2005; reporter, book critic/editor: NY Amsterdam News, 1987—2002, asst. editor, spl. corr./columnist: African Profiles Internat., 1991—95, dep. editor: Terra Haute Vanguard, 1994—95, columnist: NY Beacon, 2003—05, Harlem Times, 2003—04, Accra Mail, 2005—07; contbr. articles to profl. jous. Mem. Okyeman Coun., Ghana, 2006—. Recipient John J. Reyne Artistic Achievement award for English poetry, CCNY, 1988, Best Essay award, Nassau Rev., Nassau C.C., SUNY, 1999; Ford Found. undergrad. fellow, City Coll. CUNY, 1987—90. Mem.: MLA, Nat. Coun. Tchrs. English. Independent. Presbyterian. Avocations: journalism, debating political and social issues. Office: Nassau CC SUNY One Education Dr Garden City NY 11530 Home: 4 Fordham Hill Oval Apt 1C Bronx NY 10468-4717 Office Phone: 516-572-8121.

OKOGBAA, GEOFFREY OBITOR, engineering educator; s. Frederick Owhondaa and Janet Mbara Okogbaa; m. Elizabeth Yakubu; children: Janet Nendaa Precious, Timothy Federick, Jennifer Hechi-Taye, Jeffrey Ndago-Kehinde. BS in Indsl. & Sys. Engring., Ohio State U., Columbus, 1977, MS, 1979; PhD in Mech. & Indsl. Engring., U. Cin., 1984. Asst. prof. indsl. engring. U. Cin., 1984—89; prof. indsl. engring. U. South Fla., Tampa, 1990—. CEO Nitron Global Svcs. Corp., Tampa, 2008—. Contbr. articles to profl. jours. Recipient Best Paper award, RAMS, 2006; grant, NSF, US Dept. Edn. Fellow: Inst. Indsl. Engrs. (dir., QCRE divsn. 1990—91, Excellence Award 1991); mem.: SME, ASQ, Reliabiablity and Maintainability Symposium (bd. dirs. mem.). Office: Univ South Fla 4202 E Fowler Ave ENB 118 Tampa FL 33620-5350 Office Fax: 813-974-5953; Home Fax: 813-977-0056. Personal E-mail: okogbaa@aol.com. Business E-Mail: okogbaa@eng.usf.edu.

OKON, TOMASZ R., palliative medicine physician, educator; b. Olsztyn, Poland, Aug. 25, 1963; s. Tadeusz Jerzy and Stanislawa Okon; m. Jennifer Bible, Aug. 8, 1997; 1 child, Nicholas Tadeusz. MD, Med. Coll. Ohio, Toledo, 1997. Instr. U. Va., Charlottesville, 2000—02; clin. asst. prof. U. Wis., Madison, 2002—; palliative medicine fellowship dir. Marshfield Clinic, Wis., 2002—. Assoc. med. dir., palliative care unit St. Joseph's Hosp., Marshfield, 2002—. Donor Little Sisters of Poor, Va., 2000—07. Mem.: Alpha Omega Alpha, Am. Acad. Hospice and Palliative Medicine. Office: Marshfield Clinic 1000 N Oak Marshfield WI 54449 Business E-Mail: okon.tomasz@marshfieldclinic.org.

OKONEDO, SOPHIE, actress; b. London, Jan. 1, 1969; 1 child, Aoife. Grad., Cambridge U. Actor: (films) Young Soul Rebels, 1991, Go Now, 1995, Ace Ventura: When Nature Calls, 1995, The Jackel, 1997, This Year's Love, 1999, Mad Cows, 1999, Peaches, 2000, Once Seen, 2001, Dirty Pretty Things, 2002, Cross My Heart, 2003, Hotel Rwanda, 2004 (Oscar Nominee for Best Performance by an Actress in a Supporting Role, 2005, Nominee Image award for Outstanding Supporting Actress in a Motion Picture, 2005), Aeon Flux, 2005, Stormbreaker, 2006, Scenes of a Sexual Nature, 2006, Martian Child, 2007, The Secret Life of Bees, 2008; (TV films) Age of Treason, 1993, Deep Secrets, 1996, Never Never, 2000, Sweet Revenge, 2001, Dead Casual, 2002, The Inspector Lynley Mysteries: In the Presence of the Enemy, 2003, Alibi, 2003, Whose Baby?, 2004, Born with two Mothers, 2005, Tsunami: The Aftermath, 2006 (Actress in a TV movie, miniseries or dramatic special, NAACP Image Awards, 2007); (TV miniseries) Doctor Who: Scream of the Shalka, 2003; (TV series) Staying Alive, 1996, The Governor, 1996, In Defiance, 2000, Clocking Off, 2000, Jackanory Junior, 2007, (video) Flashing Flames, 2006. Office: c/o Markham and Froggatt Ltd 4 Windmill St London W1T 2HZ England

O'KONSKI, MARJORIE KATHERINE, music educator; d. Robert Thomas and Katherine Josephine Kilbride; m. James Edward O'Konski, July 15, 1972; children: Mary Elizabeth, Katherine Helena, Robert Michael, Brian James, Richard Joseph. MusB in Piano Performance, U. Mo., Kansas City, 1968; MusM in Piano Performance, U. Mich., Ann Arbor, 1970; MusM in Edn. and Music Therapy, U. Kans., Lawrence, 1996. Tchg. asst. U. Mich., Ann Arbor, 1968—70; instr. piano Wash. State U., Pullman, 1970—71, Southwestern Coll., Winfield, Kans., 1971—72, O'Konski Piano Studio, Bradenton, Fla., 1973—79, Olathe, Kans., 1979—89, Lawrence, 1990—97; music therapist Wichita Falls State Hosp., Tex., 1996—97; instr. piano O'Konski Piano Studio, Topeka, 1997—2003; dir. music therapy clin. tng. and activities Midwest Health Svcs., 1997—2003; music therapist O'Konski Music Therapy Contract Svcs., 2002—03; dir. music therapy program Wartburg Coll., Waverly, Iowa. Advisor music therapy majors Wartburg Coll. Music Therapy Program, Waverly, Iowa, 2003—; mem. Wartburg Coll. Human and Animal Rsch. Com., 2004—06, Wartburg Coll. Faculty Interest Group, 2006—, Wartburg Coll. Instrnl. Resources Com., 2006—; advisor Southwestern Coll. Female Athletes, Winfield, Kans., 1971—72; coord. quality assurance Lexington Pk. Nursing and Post-Acute Care Facility, Topeka, 2001—03; mem. practice analysis com. Certification Bd. Music Therapists, Kansas City, Mo., 2003—03; advisor Wartburg Coll. Cath. Knights, 2003—, Wartburg Music Therapy Student Assn., 2003—; adj. faculty Washburn U., Tokepa, 1998—2003; presenter, spkr. in field. Performer: (soloist) Kansas City Philharmonic, Bach Concerto for Four Harpsichords, (piano accompanist) Washburn U. Faculty Recital, Saxophone, Graduate Recital, Saxophone, Washburn U. Student Recital, voice, Washburn U. Studio Recital, Violin, Violin Music for Memorial Service, Washburn University Faculty Recital, Voice, Senior Recital, Violincello, Senior Recital, Trumpet, Senior Recital, Percussion, Auditions for Washburn Univ.Honors Recital, (soloist) Kansas City Youth Symphony, Symphonic Variations, C. Frank, (piano accompanist) Honors Recital, Washburn University, Studio Recital, Trumpet, Student Recital, Washburn University, Washburn University Senior Recital, Voice, Washburn University Faculty Recital, Voice, Senior Recital, Violincello, Student Recital, Washburn University, Regional Voice Competition, NATS, Washburn University Joint Faculty Recital, Opera Selections, (soloist) Concerto in A Minor, R. Schumann, (piano accompanist) Studio Recital, Violin, Washburn University Student Recital, Opera Selections, Topeka Opera Society (KS), Masterclass, Violincello, Student Recital, Washburn University, Senior Recital, Viola, Wartburg College Faculty Recital, Voice, Benefit Concert, Violincello, (piano soloist) Fundraiser (Dinner), Wartburg Symphony, (piano accompanist) Wartburg College Scholarship Auditions, (soloist) Southwestern Coll. Orch., Concerto in A Major, W. A. Mozart, (piano accompanist) Wartburg College Senior Recital, Bassoon, Wartburg College Junior Recital, Voice, Student Recitals, Wartburg College, Voice Audition, Wartburg Faculty Position, (symphony pianist) Topeka Symphony Orchestra Concerts, Wartburg Community Symphony Concerts; piano adjudicator (performance evaluation) Student Day Auditions, FSMTA (Florida), Student Day Auditions, KMTA (Kansas); performer: (piano) Chorale Fantasy, L. van Beethoven, (piano soloist) Salon Music at Lexington Park, (piano accompanist) University of Kansas Faculty Recital, Trombone, Violin Studio Recital (KS), University of Kansas Senior Recital, Student Compositions. Mem. Lawrence Civic Choir, Kans., 1991—94; sec., mem. Wartburg Cmty. Symphony, Waverly, 2003—06. Recipient Activity Dir. Yr., Kans. Health Care Assn., 1999, Aging Rsch. Devel. Support award, Wartburg Coll., 2005; grantee, Midwest Health Svcs., Kans., 2000, 2002, Wartburg Coll., 2005; fellow, Robert F. Unkefer Acad. Neurologic Music Therapy, Colo. State U., 2005. Mem.: AAUW (assoc.), AAUP (assoc.), Topeka Activity Dirs. Assn. (sec. 1999—2000, pres. 2000—01, sec., treas. 2001—03), Am. Music Therapy Assn. (assoc.; mem. rep. midwestern region 2003—06), Pi Kappa Lambda, Mu Phi Epsilon (life; pres., Alpha Kappa chpt. 1966—68, Outstanding Sr. 1968). Conservative. Roman Catholic. Achievements include development of comprehensive music therapy program for long-term care, Midwest Health Services (Kansas); six-month national roster music therapy internship program at Midwest Health Services (KS); Tone Bar Chimes Performing Ensemble For Long-Term Care Residents; Performances Within Facility, Local Community, And Adjoining Communities; Uniform Concert Attire; Compact Discs And Videos Produced; intergenerational performing ensemble; choreography, singing, playing instrument, spoken dialogue included; costumes, set designs, original scripts; music arranged by Marjorie O'Konski. Avocations: reading, travel, hiking, cryptography, solving sudoku puzzles. Home: 1209 Charlene Street Waverly IA 50677-9631 Office: Wartburg College 100 Wartburg Boulevard Waverly IA 50677-0903 Office Fax: 319-352-8501. E-mail: marj.okonski@wartburg.edu.

OKORN, NCHOR BICHENE, political science professor; b. Bendeghe Ekim, Etung, Nigeria, Apr. 4, 1956; s. Nta Bichene Okorn Tanya and Late Lily Adek Ndifon; m. Anthonia Nchor Obiem; children: Bichene Nchor, Ejenenorb Nchor, Niyenodo Nchor, Ekebnta Nchor, Ogar Nchor. BBA, MA, MBA, Ctrl. State U.; PhD in Polit. Sci., Atlanta U., 1989. Asst. prof. polit. sci. Selma U., Ala., 1983—84; prof. polit. sci. Dillard U., New Orleans, 1990—. Founder & CEO African World Network Orgn. Inc., New Orleans, 1993—. Supervising bd. policy making Bendeghe Ekim, Cmty. Babk, Nigeria, 1995—2005. Named one of America's Best Tchrs., Nat. Am. Tchrs. Assn., 2000, 2005. Mem.: Nat. Assn. Black Polit. Scientisrs. Home: 4115 Piedmont Dr New Orleans LA 70122 Office: Dillard Univ 2601 Gentilly Blvd New Orleans LA 70122 Office Fax: 504-816-4701; Home Fax: 504-945-7331. Personal E-mail: tanya56565@aol.com. Business E-Mail: nokorn@dillard.edu.

OKOSHI-MUKAI, SUMIYE, artist; b. Seattle; One-woman shows include Gallery Internat., N.Y.C., 1970, Miami Mus. Modern Art, 1972, Galerie Saison, Tokyo, 1982, St. Peter's Ch., Living Room Gallery, N.Y.C., 1987, Viridian Gallery, 1987, 1992, 1996, 1999, Port Washington (N.Y.) Pub. Libr., 1985, NAS, Washington, 1991—92, exhibited in group shows at Bergen Mus. Art and Scis., 1983, Am. Acad. Arts and Scis., 1984, Port Washington Pub. Libr., 1985, Hudson River Mus., 1985, Sao Paulo and N.Y. Culture Exch., 1988, Hyundai Gallery, Pusan, Korea, 1988, Gary Snyder Fine Art, N.Y.C., 2002, Represented in permanent collections The Mitsui & Co., N.Y., Hotel Nikko, Atlanta, Bank of Nagoya, N.Y., Palace Hotel, Guam Island, Port Washington Pub. Libr., Lowe Gallery-U. Miami, Miami Mus. Modern Art, Nat. Women's Edn. Ctr., Saitama-ken, Japan, NAS, Hammond Mus., North Salem, N.Y., The Jane Voorhees Zimmerli Art Mus., N.J., Asian Traditions Modern Expressions; included in Collage-Techniques, 1994. Mem. Nat. Women Artists Assn. (Belle Cramer award Zluta and Joseph Fund award, Ralph Mayer Meml. award, Doris Kreindler Meml. award 2002), Nat. Mus. Women in the Arts (charter mem. 1994).

OKOSI, NSIKAK PAULINUS, physics professor; b. Etinan, Akwa Ibom State, Nigeria, Dec. 1, 1970; s. Paulinus Udo and Sarah Paulinus Okosi; children: NsongUrua Princess NsikakOkosi, Mfoniso Stacia-Danielle NsikakOkosi. BSc in Physics, U. Calabar, Nigeria, 1992; MSc in Radiation Biophysics, Ahmadu Bello U., Zaria, Nigeria, 1998. Adj. faculty, dept. physics Ahmadu Bello U., Zaria, Kaduna State, Nigeria, 1994—96; reseach asst. Strahlenzentrum, Justus Liebig U., Giessen, Germany, 1996—98; tchg. asst. Kans. state U., Manhattan, 1998—2000; tchr. Ygnacio Valley HS, Concord, Calif., 2002—06; radiology specialist US Army, Fort Sam Houston, Tex., 2006—07; adjuct prof. Diablo Valley Coll., Pleasant Hill, Calif., 2007—. Contbr. scientific papers. Presiding officer Nigerian Nat. Youth Svc. Corpers Forum, Akwa Ibom State lineage, Kaduna State Chapter, 1991—92, Nat. Assn. Physics Students, Calabar, Cross River State, Nigeria, 1991—92. With Army, 2005—06, Fort Sam Houston. Fellowship, DAAD. Home: 148 Viking Way Pittsburg CA 94565 Office: Diablo Valley Coll Sci Engring Div 321 Golf Club Rd Pleasant Hill CA 94523 Personal E-mail: npokosi@yahoo.com. Business E-Mail: nokosi@dvc.edu.

OKOUNKOV, ANDREI, mathematics professor; b. Moscow, 1969; 2 children. BA in Math., PhD in Math., Moscow State U. Rsch. fellow, Dobrushin Math. Lab. Inst. for Problems of Info. Transmission, Russian Acad. Sciences; instructor U. Chgo.; asst. prof. U. Calif., Berkeley; prof., math. dept. representation theory Princeton U., 2002—. Mem. Inst. for Advanced Study, Math. Sciences Rsch. Inst., Berkeley. Recipient Sloan Research Fellowship, 2000, Fields medal, Internat. Math. Union, 2006. Office: Princeton U Dept Math 701 Fine Hall Washington Rd Princeton NJ 08544-1000 Office Phone: 609-258-5186. Office Fax: 609-258-1367. E-mail: okounkov@Princeton.edu.

OKOYE-JOHNSON, OGO, education educator; d. Michael and Paulina Okoye; children: Paulina Johnson, Chinyelu Johnson, Chinonso Johnson, Chike Johnson. BA in Edn. & English with honors, U. Nigeria, 1985; MEd in Ednl. Adminstrn., U. Lagos, Nigeria, 1988; PhD in Urban Svcs., Old Dominion U., Notfolk, 1999. Cert. adminstrn. and English prof. Calif., 2006. Asst. prin. LA Unified Sch. Dist., 2005—; asst. prof. Calif. State U., Northridge, 2006—. Multicultural edn. spkr., 2008—. Author: (story book) Oma The Faithful Daughter. Mem. Sound Body, Sound Mind, LA, 2008. Grant, Coll. Sci. and Behavioral Sci., Calif. State U., 2007—08. Master: Sr. High Asst. Prins. Orgn. (pres. 2008—). Conservative. Christian. Avocations: travel, reading.

OKPODU, CAMELLIA MOSES, biology professor, researcher; children: Samelia, Elizabeth, Koren. PhD, NC State U., Raleigh, 1994. Endowed chair Elizabeth City State U., NC, 2000—02; chair biology Norfolk State U., Va., 2001—08. Youth coach Norfolk Soccer League, Va., 2005—07. Fellow, Am. Coun. Edn., 2007. Mem.: AAUW. Achievements include invention of microgravity plant module for NASA Glenn. Avocations: reading, soccer, travel, baking. Office: Norfolk State Univ 700 Park Ave Norfolk VA 23504

OKRENT, DAVID, engineering educator; b. Passaic, NJ, Apr. 19, 1922; s. Abram and Gussie (Pearlman) O.; m. Rita Gilda Holtzman, Feb. 1, 1948 (dec. June 2005); children: Neil, Nina, Jocelyne. ME, Stevens Inst. Tech., 1943; MA, Harvard, 1948, PhD in Physics, 1951. Mech. engr. NACA, Cleve., 1943-46; sr. physicist Argonne (Ill.) Nat. Lab., 1951-71; regents lectr. UCLA, 1968, prof. engring., 1971-91, prof. emeritus, rsch. prof., 1991—. Vis. prof. U. Wash., Seattle, 1963, U. Ariz., Tucson, 1970-71; Isaac Taylor chair Technion, 1977-78 Author: Fast Reactor Cross Sections, 1960, Computing Methods in Reactor Physics, 1968, Reactivity Coefficients in Large Fast Power Reactors, 1970, Nuclear Reactor Safety, 1981; contbr. articles to profl. jours. Mem. adv. com. on reactor safeguards AEC, 1963-87, also chmn., 1966; sci. sec. to sec. gen. of Geneva Conf., 1958; mem. U.S. del. to all Geneva Atoms for Peace Confs. Guggenheim fellow, 1961-62, 77-78; recipient Disting. Appointment award Argonne Univs. Assn., 1970, Disting. Service award U.S. Nuclear Regulatory Commn., 1985. Fellow Soc. for Risk Analysis, Am. Phys. Soc., Am. Nuclear Soc. (Tommy Thompson award 1980, Glenn Seaborg medal 1987, George C. Lawrence Pioneering award 2007), Nat. Acad. Engring. Home: 439 Veteran Ave Los Angeles CA 90024-1956 Business E-Mail: okrent@ucla.edu.

OKTAY, MAJA HRZENJAK, medical educator; b. Zagreb, Croatia, May 20, 1965; arrived in US, 1992; d. Vjekoslav and Terezija Hrženjak; m. Kutluk Han Oktay, Aug. 5, 1995; children: Isabelle, Kenan, Lara. MD, U. Zagreb, 1989; MSc, U. Natural Scis., Zagreb, 1992; PhD, U.

Zagreb and U. Tex., San Antonio, 1995. Bd. cert. anatomical pathology, bd. cert. cytopathology. Intern U. Hosp. Petrova, Zagreb, 1989—90; postdoctoral fellow Meml. Sloan-Kettering Cancer Ctr., NYC, 1996—97, clin. scholar biomed. rsch. training, 1997—98; anatomical pathology resident Yale New Haven Hosp., 1998—2001; cytopathology fellow Montefiore Med. Ctr., Bronx, NY, 2001—02; asst. prof. Albert Einstein Coll. Medicine, Montefiore Med. Ctr., Bronx, 2002—. Contbr. chapters to books, articles to profl. jours. Recipient Outstanding Achievement in Autopsy Pathology award, Dr. Halina Goldstein Fund, 1999; Charles A. Dana fellow, Sloan-Kettering, NY, 1997—98, Clin. scholar, Biomed. Rsch. fellow, grantee, Nat. Cancer Inst., 1997—98. Mem.: US and Can. Acad. Pathology, Coll. Am. Pathologists. Avocations: swimming, jogging, tennis, skiing. Home: 152 Florence Ave Rye NY 10580 Office: Montefiore Headache Center 1575 Blondell Ave Ste 225 Bronx NY 10461-2662

OKTEM, OZGUR, medical doctor, researcher; b. Kars, Turkey, Aug. 1, 1971; s. Lutfi and Fatma Oktem. MD, Erciyes U. Sch. of Medicine, Turkey, 1996. Cert. obstetrics and gynecology Marmara U. Hosp., 2001. Residency obstetrics and gynecology Marmara U. Hosp., Istanbul, Turkey, 1997—2001; rsch. fellow in reproductive medicine Ctr. For Reproductive Medicine and Infertility, Weill Med. Coll. of Cornell U., New York, NY. Dir., chief attending clinician of obgyn Pendik Sifa Hosp., Istanbul, Turkey, 2001—03. Mem.: Postdoctoral Assn. NY, Nat. Geographic Soc., NY Acad. Sci., Soc. Gynecologic Investigations, Am. Soc. Reproductive Medicine (Best Rsch. Study award 2005). Achievements include research in three dimention follicle culture, xenografting human ovary, ovarian transplantation. Avocations: guitar, astronomy. Office Fax: 212-746-8848. Personal E-mail: ozo2001@med.cornell.edu.

OKUHARA, TETSU, artist, photographer; b. LA, Mar. 3, 1940; Student, U. Chgo., 1958-61, The Cooper Union, 1970-71. Lectr., workshop leader Otis Coll., L.A., Hartwick Coll., Oneonta, N.Y., NYU, Rutgers U., New Brunswick, N.J., Sch. Visual Arts, N.Y.C., New Sch., N.Y.C., Wesleyan U., Middletown, Conn, Cornish Inst., Seattle. Exhibited in one person and group shows at L.A. County Mus., 2002, Small Works, NYU, 1999, Fotomassan, Goteborg, Sweden, Chgo. Cultural Ctr., 1997, Gotland Konst Mus., Sweden, 1995, San Francisco Camera Work, 1994, Art Inst. Boston, 1994, Artist Space, N.Y.C., 1992, Chgo. Art Inst., 1991-92, Art in General, N.Y.C., 1990, Cleve. Mus. Art, 1978, San Francisco Mus. Modern Art, 1979, 2003, Tokyo Met. Mus. Photography, 2005, numerous others; represented in permanent collections Mus. Modern Art, N.Y.C., Met. Mus. Art, N.Y.C., Hasselad Collection, Goteborg, Sweden, Tokyo Met. Mus. Photography, Art Inst., Chgo., San Francisco Mus. Modern Art, L.A. County Mus., numerous others. Grantee Creative Artist Pub. Svc., 1973-74, 75-76, N.Y. Found. for the Arts, 1988-89, Nat. Endowment for the Arts, 1988-89, La Napoule Found./Nat. Endowment for the Arts, France, 1989, Intercambio, San Juan, P.R., 1991, James P. Phelan Art Award, San Francisco, 1993-94; Guggenheim fellow, 1975-76, N.Y. Found. for Arts fellow, 2000. Home: 202 E 42nd St New York NY 10017-5808 Office Phone: 212-986-0356. Personal E-mail: tetsuokuhara@yahoo.com.

OKULEWICZ, STEVEN CHARLES, geologist, educator; b. SI, NY, June 25, 1952; s. Sybil Okulewicz. AS, Coll. SI, 1972; BS, Bklyn. Coll., 1975, MA, 1979. Cert. Am. Inst. Profl. Geologists, 1994, profl. geologist Pa., 1995. Phys. sci. technician Dept. Treasury Bur. Mint US Assay Office, NYC, 1980—82; asst. prof., geology Fairleigh Dickinson U., Madison, NJ, 1982—85; instr., geology Hunter Coll., NYC, 1984—89; curatorial asst., dept. mineral scis. Am. Mus. Natural History, NYC, 1985—87; sr. geologist Halliburton NUS, Edison, NJ, 1989—93; adj. lectr., geology Coll. SI, 1991—; sr. geologist instr. Tetra Tech. NUS, Edison, 1993—2005; adj. instr., geology Kingsborough CC, Bklyn., 2006—07; assoc. geologist Weston Solutions, Edison, 2006—; adj. prof., geology Hofstra U., Hempstead, 2009—. Contbr. numerous sci. papers to profl. jours., chapters to books. Founder and past pres. SI Geol. Soc., 1972—75. Named to Alumni Hall of Fame, Coll. SI, 1994. Mem.: Geol. Soc. America, Soc. Am. Magicians. Home: 63 Raymond Ave Staten Island NY 10314 Office: Coll SI 2800 Victory Blvd Staten Island NY 10314 Personal E-mail: geologyprof@aol.com.

OKUN, DEANNA TANNER, federal official; b. Jeffrey City, Wyo., Feb. 8, 1963; m. Bernard Robert Okun; children: Rachel, Kelsi. BA in Polit. Sci., Utah State U., 1985; JD, Duke U. Sch. Law, NC, 1990. Intern Nat. Assn. Realtors, Washington, 1985; rsch. assoc. Competitive Enterprise Inst., Washington, 1985—87; summer assoc. Miller & Chevalier PC, Washington, 1988, Hogan & Hartson LLP, Washington, 1989, Gibson Dunn & Crutcher, L.A, 1989; assoc., mem. Internat. Trade Group Hogan & Hartson LLP, Washington, 1990—93; counsel for internat. affairs to Senator Frank Murkowski, US Senate, 1993—2000; commr. US Internat. Trade Comm., 1999—, vice chmn., 2000—02, 2004—06, chmn, 2002—04. Mem. Chi Omega Alumni Assn., 1985—, Duke U. Alumni Assn., 2000—, Utah State Alumni Assn., 2001—, Wash. Internat. Trade Assn., 2000—, Trade Policy Forum, 1995, The Assn. of Women in Internat. Trade, 2000—. Recipient Alumnus of Yr., Utah State U., 2000. Mem.: Fed. Cir. Bar Assn., DC Internat. Trade Bar Assn., DC Bar Assn., Chesterbrook Swim & Tennis Club, New Dominion's Women's Club. Republican. Office: US Internat Trade Commission 500 E Street SW Washington DC 20436

OKUN, HERBERT STUART, diplomat, educator; b. NYC, Nov. 27, 1930; s. Irving and Ida Muriel (Levine) O.; m. Lorraine Joan Price, Dec. 5, 1954 (div. 1985); children: Jennifer, Elizabeth, Alexandra; m. Enid Curtis Bok, Dec. 27, 1990. AB with great distinction, Stanford U., 1951; postgrad., Syracuse U., 1951—52, Princeton U., 1952; Hochschule fuer Politische Wissenschaft, Munich, 1956—57; MPA, Harvard U., 1959; M Naval Warfare, Naval War Coll., 1969. Mem. US Fgn. Svc., 1955—91, Munich vice consul, 1955—57; with Bur. Intelligence and Rsch., Dept. State Office Soviet Union Affairs, Washington, 1959-61, alt. dir., 1971-73; 2d sec. Am. Embassy, Moscow, 1961-63; consul, prin. officer Am. Consulate, Belo Horizonte, Brazil, 1964-65; 1st sec., prin. officer Am. Embassy, Brasilia, Brazil, 1965-66, counsellor embassy, prin. officer, 1967-68; assigned to Naval War Coll., 1968-69; spl. asst. to sec. of state Dept. State, Washington, 1969-71, dep. chmn. U.S. Del., U.S.-USSR Talks on Prevention Incidents at Sea, 1971-72; polit. advisor and spl. asst. for internat. affairs to comdr.-in-chief NATO So. Command, Naples, Italy, 1973-74; min.-counsellor, dep. chief mission Am. Embassy, Lisbon, Portugal, 1975-78; dep. chmn. U.S. del. Strategic Arms Limitation Talks with Soviet Union, Geneva, 1978-79; vice chmn. U.S. del. to trilateral U.S.-U.K.-USSR Talks on comprehensive test ban treaty, Geneva, 1979-80; amb. to German Dem. Rep. Berlin, 1980—83; amb.-in-residence Aspen Inst., Washington, 1983-85; amb., dep. permanent rep. of U.S. to the UN NYC, 1985-89. Rep. of US to Gen. Assembly UN, to UN Security Coun., 1985-89, to Com. on Peaceful Uses of Outer Space, 1986-87, to Disarmament Commn. UN, 1985-89, to Commn. Human Rights, 1985-89, to com. on program and coordination of Econ. and Social Coun., 1987, 89; amb. in residence Carnegie Corp. NY, 1989-90; US mem. UN Sec. Gen's. Expert Group on Enhancing UN Structure for Drug Abuse Control, 1990, UN Internat. Narcotics Control Bd., Vienna, Austria, 1992-2002, v.p. 1997; founding exec. dir. Fin. Svcs. Vol. Corps, NYC, 1990-97; vis. lectr. Yale Law Sch., New Haven, 1991-2002; professorial lectr. in internat. rels., internat. law and instns. Johns Hopkins. U. Sch. Advanced Internat. Studies, Washington, 2002—09; spl. adviser, dep. personal envoy of the sec. gen. UN, Former Yugoslavia and Nagorno-Karabakh, 1991-92; spl. adv., dep. co-chmn. Internat. Conf. on former Yugoslavia, 1992-93; UN mediator Dispute between Greece and Former Yugoslav Republic of Macedonia, 1993-97; adv. bd. Minority Rights Group USA; spl. advisor Carnegie Commn. on Preventing Deadly Conflict. Commr. U.S.-Poland Action Commn; mem. Internat. Coun., Found. Inter-Ethnic Rels., The Hague, Netherlands, 1995—, mem. Adv. Com., Human Rights Watch, N.Y., 1995—; mem. group internat. advisors Internat. Com. Red Cross, Geneva, 1996-2000; bd. overseers Curtis Inst. Music, Phila.; adv. bd. internat. security studies Yale U., New Haven; mem. adv. bd. Portuguese-Am. Leadership Coun.; bd. dirs. Internat. Ctr. N.Y., 2004-. Served with AUS, 1952-54. Recipient Meritorious Honor award Dept. of State, 1972, Superior Honor award Dept. of State, 1980, Presdl. Meritorious Svc. award, 1983. Mem. Am. Fgn. Policy (nat. com.), Am. Acad. Diplomacy, Lawyers Alliance World Security (nat. bd. dirs.), Washington Inst. Fgn. Affairs, Phi Beta Kappa. Home: 970 Park Ave 6-N New York NY 10028-0324 Home Phone: 212-472-4240.

OKUN, NEIL JEFFREY, vitreoretinal surgeon; b. St. Louis, Nov. 21, 1957; s. Edward and Barbara J. (Braham) O.; m. Joan A. Sosnoff, May 19, 1984; children: David E., Sarah E. AB, Dartmouth Coll., 1980; MD, Washington U., 1984. Diplomate Am. Bd. Ophthalmology. Intern internal medicine Jewish Hosp. at Washington U., St. Louis, 1984-85; resident ophthalmology Washington U. Med. Ctr., St. Louis, 1985-88; fellow vitreoretinal Retina Cons., Ltd., Washington U., St. Louis, 1988-89; vitreoretinal surgeon Fla. Retina Inst., Jacksonville, Fla., 1990-91, Retina Assocs. Ctrl. Fla., Orlando, 1991—2004, Ctrl. Fla. Retina, Orlando, 2004—08, Eye Specialists Mid-Fla., Winter Haven, Fla., 2008—. Instr. dept. ophthalmology Washington U. Sch. Medicine, St. Louis, 1988-89; clin. asst. prof. dept. ophthalmology U. South Fla., Tampa, 1992—; chmn. dept. ophthalmology Fla. Hosp. Orlando, 1996-97 Recipient Upjohn Achievement award for endocrinology and metabolism Washington U. Sch. Medicine, St. Louis, 1984. Fellow ACS, Am. Acad. Ophthalmology; mem. AMA (Physicians's Recognition award for continuing med. edn. 1992—), Am. Soc. Retina Specialists, Assn. for Rsch. in Vision and Ophthalmology, Fla. Med. Assn., Fla. Soc. Ophthalmology, Ctrl. Fla. Soc. Ophthalmology, Polk County Med. Soc., Vitreous Soc., Paul Cibis Club. Avocations: music, art. Office: Eye Specialists Mid-Fla 407 Ave K SE Winter Haven FL 33880 Office Phone: 863-294-3504.

OKUR, MEHMET, professional basketball player; b. Yalova, Turkey, May 26, 1979; s. Abdullah and Nimet Okur; m. Yeliz Caliska, 2004. Profl. basketball player Turkish League Oyak Renault, Turkey, 1997—98, Turkish League Tofas Bursa, Turkey, 1998—2000, Turkish League Efes Pilsen, Turkey, 2000—02; draft pick NBA Detroit Pistons, 2001, ctr./power forward, 2002—04, NBA Utah Jazz, 2004—. Named to Western Conf. All-Star Team, NBA, 2007. Achievements include member of Turkish National Cup winning Tofas Bursa, 1999; member of NBA Finals Championship winning Detroit Pistons, 2004. Mailing: Utah Jazz 301 W South Temple Salt Lake City UT 84101*

OKURA-MARSZYCKI, MINDY EMI, editor; b. Honolulu, July 15, 1976; d. Gary and Gail Okura; m. Brian Marszycki, Mar. 27, 2004. BA in English and Psychology, Boston Coll., Chestnut Hill, Mass., 1998; MS in Pub., NYU, NYC, 2003; MA in English, St. John's U., Queens, NY, 2008. Web content editor/mktg. assoc. PhysicianEd, Boston, 1998—2001; lit. agt. asst. Liza Dawson & Assocs., NYC, 2002; editl. asst. Columbia U. Press, NYC, 2002, Taylor and Francis, NYC, 2002; book editor Other Press, NYC, 2003—07, Springer Sci. & Bus. Media, NYC, 2007—. Grad. Student Dean's fellow, NYU, 2001. Mem.: Young to Pub. Group, NYU Pub. Alumni Steering Com., Sigma Tau Delta. Office: Springer Sci & Bus Media 233 Spring St 7th Fl New York NY 10013 Business E-Mail: mindy.okura-marszycki@springer.com.

OLADUNNI, OLUTAYO O., consultant; b. Lagos, Nigeria, Apr. 20, 1977; BS, Richmond Coll., London, 1998; MS, U. Okla., Norman, 2002, PhD, 2006. Rsch. assoc. Purdue U., W Lafayette, Ind., 2007; cons. Accenture, Chgo., 2007—. Grad. asst. U. Okla., 2005—06; adj. faculty Sch. Ind. Engr. U. Okla., 2006. Recipient Outstanding Tchg. Asst., Sch. Indsl. Engring., U. Okla., 2005, Best Paper award, Internat. Conf. Computer, 2006. Mem.: INNS, ASEE, NSBE. Personal E-mail: dr_o_olad@hotmail.com.

OLAFSON, FREDERICK ARLAN, philosophy educator; b. Winnipeg, Man., Can., Sept. 1, 1924; s. Kristinn K. and Fredericka (Björnson) O.; m. Allie Lewis, June 20, 1952 (dec.); children— Peter Niel, Christopher Arlan, Thomas Andrew. AB, Harvard U., 1947, MA, 1948, PhD, 1951. Instr. philosophy and gen. edn. Harvard U., 1952-54; asst. prof. philosophy, then assoc. prof. Vassar Coll., 1954-60; assoc. prof. Johns Hopkins U., 1960-64; prof. edn. and philosophy Harvard Grad. Sch. Edn., 1964-71; prof. philosophy U. Calif., San Diego, 1971-91, chmn. dept., 1973-76, assoc. dean grad. studies and research, 1980-85. Author: Principles and Persons, 1967, Ethics and Twentieth Century Thought, 1973, The Dialectic of Action, 1979, Heidegger and the Philosophy of the Mind, 1987, What Is A Human Being?, 1995, Heidegger and the Ground of Ethics, 1998, Naturalism and the Human Condition, 2001. Served to lt. (j.g.) USNR, 1943-46. Mem. Nat. Acad. Edn. Home: 6081 Avenida Chamnez La Jolla CA 92037-7404 Business E-Mail: folafson@ucsd.edu.

OLAFSSON, OLAF, communications executive; b. Reykjavik, Iceland, 1962; Grad. in Physics, Brandeis U. With Sony Corp., 1985—97, founder, pres., CEO Sony Interactive Entertainment, Inc., 1991; bd. dirs. Advanta Corp., 1997, pres., 1998; vice chmn. Time Warner Digital Media Time Warner Inc., exec. v.p. NYC. Author: Absolution, 1994, The Journey Home, 2000, Walking Into the Night, 2003. Office: Time Warner Inc 1 Time Warner Ctr New York NY 10019-8016*

OLAGUNJU, AMOS OMOTAYO, computer science educator, consultant, computer science educator, consultant; b. Igosun, Kwara, Nigeria, Nov. 27, 1954; came to U.S., 1980; s. Solomon Atoyebi and Ruth Ebun (Adegoke) O.; m. Janet; 1 child, Amanda. EdD, U. N.C., Greensboro, 1987; PhD, Kensington U., 1990; cert. in cryptography and info. systems, MIT, 1996, cert. in design and analysis experiments, 1999, cert. in digital comm. networks, 1999, cert. in bioinformatic principles, 2001. Cert. bioinformatic prins. MIT, 2001. Dir. mgmt. info. sys. Barber-Scotia Coll., Concord, NC, 1981-82; lectr. NC A&T State U., Greensboro, NC, 1982-87, asst. prof., 1987-90; mem. tech. staff Bell Comm. Rsch., Piscataway, NJ, 1986-90; vis. prof. Mich. State U., East Lansing, Mich., 1990-91; coord. acad. computing, assoc. prof. Del. State U., 1991-92, prof., chair dept. math. and computer sci., 1992—2001; collegiate prof. UMUC-Asia, 2001—02; prof. computer networking and applications St. Cloud State U., Minn., 2002—; dean grad. studies, chief rsch. officer Winston Salem State U., NC, 2006—07; interim dean undergrad studies St. Cloud State U., Minn., 2008—. Cons. NSF, Washington, 1991-93, Edn. Testing Agy., Princeton, NJ, 1995—. Author: Lecture Notes Series in Language C, Systems Programming, Database Systems, Theoretical Aspects of Computing, File Structures, Introduction to Computer Science and Scientific and Engineering Applications of Fortran, 1991-96; mem. editl. bd. Sci. World Jour., 2003—; contbr. articles to Software Metrics, Automatic Indexing, Perfect Hashing, Number Theory, Efficient Statis. Algorithms, Del. State News. Pres. Ahmadu Bello Assn. Computer Univ. Students, Zaria, Nigeria, 1976, Orgn. United Africans, Concord, NC, 1982. Recipient Queen's Grad. award Queen's U., Kingston, Ont., 1979; Navy-Am. Soc. for Engring. Edn. fellow, 1997, sr. fellow 1998, 2000. Mem. Internat. Assn. Sci. Tech. Devel. (reviewer 2001—), Assn. for Modelling and Simulation in Enterprises (program chair 1989-90, editor), Assn. for Computing Machinery (reviewer), NC Acad. Sci. (program chair 1991—, mem. editl. bd. 1999—), NY Acad. Sci. Achievements include invention of the Bell Communication research software report, analysis measurement system and generic administrative quantitative decision support system. Home: 1617 Highland Trail Saint Cloud MN 56301 Home Phone: 320-240-9061. Personal E-mail: blessamos@yahoo.com.

OLAH, GEORGE ANDREW, chemist, educator; b. Budapest, Hungary, May 22, 1927; arrived in U.S., 1964, naturalized, 1970; s. Julius and Magda (Krasznai) Olah; m. Judith Agnes Lengyel, July 9, 1949; children: George John, Ronald Peter. PhD, Tech. U. Budapest, 1949, D (hon.), 1989; DSc (hon.), U. Durham, 1988, U. Munich, 1990, U. Crete, Greece, 1994, U. Szeged, Hungary, 1995, U. Veszprem, 1995, Case Western Res. U., Cleve., 1995, U. So. Calif., 1995, U. Montpellier, 1996, SUNY, 1998, U. Pecs, Hungary, 2001, U. Debrecen, 2003; DSc, U. We. Hungary, 2007, Ohio State U., 2009. Mem. faculty Tech. U. Budapest, 1949—54; assoc. dir. Ctrl. Chem. Rsch. Inst., Hungarian Acad. Scis., 1954—56; rsch. scientist Dow Chem. Can. Ltd., 1957—64, Dow Chem. Co., Framingham, Mass., 1964—65; prof. chemistry Case Western Res. U., Cleve., 1965—69, C.F. Mabery prof. rsch., 1969—77; Donald P. and Katherine B. Loker disting. prof. chemistry, dir. Hydrocarbon Rsch. Inst., U. So. Calif., LA, 1977—, dist. prof. engring., 2008—. Vis. prof. chemistry Ohio State U., 1963, U. Heidelberg, Germany, U. Colo., 1969, Swiss Fed. Inst. Tech., 1972, U. Munich, 1973, U. London, 1973—79, Louis Pasteur U., Strasbourg, France, 1974, U. Paris, 1981; hon. vis. lectr. U. London, 1981—95; cons. to industry. Author: Friedel-Crafts Reactions, Vols. I-IV, 1963—64; author: (with P. Schleyer) Carbonium Ions, Vols. I-V, 1969—76; author: Friedel-Crafts Chemistry, 1973, Carbocations and Electrophilic Reactions, 1973, Halonium Ions, 1975; author: (with Goeppertm Prakash and J. Sommer) Superacids, 1984; author: (with G. Prarash, R.E. Williams, L.D. Field and K. Wade) Hypercarbon Chemistry, 1987; author: (with R. Malthotra and S.C. Narang) Nitration, 1989; author: Cage Hydrocarbons, 1990; author: (with Wade and Williams) Electron Deficient Boron and Carbon Clusters, 1991; author: (with Chambers and Prakash) Synthetic Fluorine Chemistry, 1992; author: (with Molnar) Hydrocarbon Chemistry, 1995; author: (with Laali, Wang, Prakash) Onium Ions, 1998; author: A Life of Magic Chemistry, 2001; author: (with Prarash) Across Conventional Lines, 2003; author: (with Goeppert and Prakash) Beyond Oil and Gas: The Methanol Economy, 2006; author: (with Klumpp) Superelectrophiles and Their Chemistry, 2008; author: (with Prarash, Molnar and Sommer) Superacid Chemistry, 2009; contbr. chapters to books, articles to profl. jours. Recipient Alexander von Humboldt Sr. US Scientist award, 1979, Calif. Scientist of Yr. award, 1989, Pioneer of Chemistry award, Am. Inst. Chemists, 1993, Mendeleev medal, Russian Acad. Scis., 1992, Nobel prize in Chemistry, 1994, Kapitsa medal, Russian Acad. Natural Scis., 1995, Order of the Hungarian Corvin-Chain, 2001, Albert Einstein medal, Russian Acad. Natural Scis., 2002, Bolyai prize, Hungarian Acad. Sci., 2002, Order of Merit with Cross of Star, Republic of Hungary, 2006, Hon. Citizen Budapest, Budapest; Guggenheim fellow, 1972, 1988. Fellow: AAAS, Chem. Inst. Can., Brit. Chem. Soc. (hon.; hon./centenary lectr. 1978, Centenary lectr. 1978); mem.: NAS, NAE, Indian Nat. Acad. Sci. (fgn.), Can. Royal Soc., Royal Soc. Sci. Arts Barcelona, Royal Acad. Sci. and Arts, Am. Acad. Arts and Sci., Chem. Soc. Japan (hon.), Italy Chem. Soc. (hon.), Royal Chem. Soc. (hon.), Hungarian Acad. Sci. (hon.), German Chem. Soc. (hon.), Am. Philos. Soc., Am. Chem. Soc. (award petroleum chemistry 1964, Leo Hendrik Baekeland award N.J. sect. 1966, Morley medal Cleve. sect. 1970, award Synthetic Organic Chemistry 1979, Roger Adams award in organic chemistry 1989, Arthur C. Cope award 2001, Priestley medal 2005), European Acad. Arts, Sci. and Humanities, Royal Soc. London (fgn. mem.), Italian Nat. Acad. Sci. Lincei, Grand Cordon of the Order of the Rising Sun (Japan). Achievements include numerous publications and patents in field. Office: U So Calif Loker Hydrocarbon Rsch Inst Los Angeles CA 90007 Office Phone: 213-740-5976. Business E-Mail: olah@usc.edu. *America still is offering a new home and nearly unlimited possibilities to the newcomer who is willing to work hard for it. It is also where the "main action" in science and technology remains.*

OLAMA, MOHAMMED, research scientist; s. Mohsen Mustafa Olama and Naemeh Hasouneh; m. Suzan Saleh, Dec. 23, 2005; 1 child, Omar. B, U. Jordan, Amman, 1998, M with honors, 2001; PhD, U. Tenn., Knoxville, 2007. Elec. engr. Nat. Electric Power Co., Amman, 1999—2001; rsch. asst. U. Tenn., Knoxville, 2003—07; rsch. assoc. Oak Ridge Nat. Lab., Tenn., 2007—. Contbr. articles to profl. sci. jours. (Scholarly Activities Rsch. Incentive award, 2006, Best paper award, 2008). Recipient Overall 4.0 GPA award, Applied Sci. Dept., U. Ark., Little Rock, 2003, Elec. and Computer Engring. Dept., U. Tenn., 2007, Significant Event award, 2007. Mem.: IEEE, Inst. Math. Stats., Phi Kappa Phi (Knoxville). Achievements include development of new time-varying channel models for mobile wireless networks. Avocations: swimming, soccer, reading, travel, stamp collecting/philately. Office: Oak Ridge Nat Lab 1 Bethel Valley Rd Oak Ridge TN 37831 Office Fax: 865-576-0003. Personal E-mail: aulama2000@yahoo.com. Business E-Mail: olamahussemm@ornl.gov.

OLATUNJI, THABITI SHAWKI (REVEREND THABITI), executive director, motivational speaker, advisor, educator; s. Marquette Alexander Williams Jr. and Virginia Mae Chavis; 1 child, Tabatha Josephine. Student in Bus. Adminstrn., U. Iowa, Iowa City, 1982—85; student in Physics, Maharishi Internat. U., Fairfield, Iowa, 1981—82; student in Electronics Engring., Camden County Coll., Blackwood, NJ, 1980—81; DD (hon.), U. Magi, Golden, Colo., 1992, D (hon.) in Metasymbology, 1995. Ordained min. Order of Magi, 1992. Owner, founder The Supreme Oracle, Superior, 1992—; pres., founder U. of Magi, Golden, 1995—; owner, v.p. LoveTheName.com, Superior, Colo., 2005—; owner, exec. dir. ThePower.org, Superior, 2005—; radio sta. owner, CEO ThePower.com, 2009—. Founder Divine Sci. The Supreme Oracle, 1990; prodr. radio show host Empowerment Hour, Denver, 2003—, Empowerment Hour, alltalkradio.net, 2008—. Author: The Card Basics Manual, 1993, The Scripture of 52 Cards presents The Salvation of the World, 1994, Grand Solar Spreads, 1995, Planetary Interpretations, 1995, All About You, 2000, Empowerment Column, Colo. Daily, Boulder, 2003. Math tchr. Colo. State HS, 2006; chief min. all possibilities r&d World Congress Assn., Fairfield, Iowa, 1981—. E-4 USN, 1976—80. Named Grand Master, Order of Magi, 1992. Mem.: Internat. Forum on New Scis., Global Sci. Congress, Capitols for Age Enlightenment. Achievements include invention of the World's 1st

Personal Time-Map. Avocations: meditation, yoga, fasting. Home and Office: The Supreme Oracle PO Box 772 Superior CO 80027 Business E-Mail: 2Victory@ThePower.org, ceo@thepower.com.

OLBERMANN, KEITH THEODORE, news analyst, sportscaster; b. NYC, Jan. 27, 1959; BS in Comm. Arts, Cornell U., NYU, 1979. Sports reporter UPI Radio, NYC, 1979-80, RKO Radio, NYC, 1980-82, WNEW-AM, NYC, 1980-83; nat. sports reporter, anchor CNN, NYC, 1981-84, WCVB-TV, Boston, 1984; weeknight sports anchor, reporter KTLA-TV, LA, 1985-88; sports commentator KNX-AM, LA, 1996-91; sports anchor, host The Keith Olbermann Show KCBS-TV, LA, 1988-91; weekend co-host ESPN Sports Radio, 1992-93; co-anchor, co-host SportsCenter, ESPN, Bristol, Conn., 1992-97; co-anchor SportsNight, ESPN2, 1993-94; anchor, exec. prodr. Fox Sports Net, 1998—2001; columnist Salon.com, 2002—03; host Countdown with Keith Olbermann, MSNBC, 2003—; co-host ESPN Radio, 2005—07; co-host Football Night in America, NBC Sports, 2007—. Author: The Worst Person in the World: And 119 More Strong Contenders, 2006, Truth and Consequences: Special Comments on the Bush Administration's War on American Values, 2007; co-author (with Dan Patrick): The Big Show: Inside ESPN's Sport Center, 1997. Recipient Cable Ace award for Best Sportscaster, Nat. Acad. Cable Programming, 1995, Edward R. Murrow award, 2002, Golden Mike award for Best Sportscaster (11); named Best Sportscaster, Calif. Radio & TV News Assn., Sportscaster of Yr., Calif. AP, 1985, 1987, 1989. Office: MSNBC Cable LLC 30 Rockefeller Plz Fl 38 New York NY 10112-3899*

OLBERT, STANISLAW, physicist; b. Lwow, Poland, May 9, 1923; m. Norma Louise DeVivo, 1954; children: Elizabeth, Thomas. Student, U. Munich, 1946-49; PhD, MIT, 1953. Rsch. scientist divsn. sponsored rsch. MIT, Cambridge, Mass., 1953-57, from asst. prof. to prof. emeritus, 1957-88, prof. emeritus, 1988—, cons. ctr. ednl. computing initiatives, 1999—2003. Vis. prof. U. Rome, 1986, 87, U. Florence, 1986, 87, Inst. Cosmic Studies, Warsaw, Poland, 1991. Co-author: Introduction to the Physics of Space, 1970; contbr. articles to profl. jours. Office: MIT Ctr Space Rsch 77 Massachusetts Ave Cambridge MA 02139 Personal E-mail: stanolbert@comcast.net.

OLBRANTZ, JOHN PAUL, museum director, art historian; b. Tacoma, June 19, 1950; s. Walter John and Theresa Christine (Hill) Olbrantz; m. Pamela Ann Southas Olbrantz, Apr. 12, 1980; children: Aaron Michael, Sarah Jessica. BA, Western Wash. U., 1972; attended, U. Calif., Santa Barbara, 1973—74; MA, U. Wash., 1976. Cert. in arts adminstrn. & mgmt. U. Calif., Berkeley, 1984. Dirs. Bellevue Art Mus., Wash., 1976—85, San Jose Mus. Art, Calif., 1985—87; dep. dir. Whatcom Mus. History & Art, Bellingham, Wash., 1987—98; Maribeth Collins dir. Hallie Ford Mus. Art, Willamette U., Salem, Wash., 1997—98; lectr. in field. Exhibitions include Eye for Eye: Egyptian Art and Inscriptions, 1978, 5,000 Years of Faces, 1982, Dale Chihuly: A Decade of Glass, 1984, Two Centuries of Afro-American Art, 1989, Robert Colescott: A Retrospective, 1987, A Different War: Vietnam in Art, 1989, Clearly Art: Pilchuck's Glass Legacy, 1992, Jacob Lawrence: American Printmaker, 2000, In the Fullness of Time: Masterpieces of Egyptian Art from American Collections, 2002; contbr. articles to profl. publs. J. Paul Getty Trust scholar, 1984. Mem.: We. Mus. Assn., Am. Assn. Mus. (v.p. 1990—94), Archaeol. Inst. America (v.p. 1978—79, pres. 1979—80). Independent. Office: Hallie Ford Mus Art Willamette Univ 900 State St Salem OR 97301

OLCER, NURI YELMAN, engineering researcher, educator; b. Gaziantep, Turkey, July 22, 1932; arrived in U.S., 1958; s. Samet and Besire Olcer. MS, Tech. U. Istanbul, 1956; PhD, Northwestern U., 1964. Rsch. engr. Ordnance Engring. Assocs., Chgo., 1960—66; assoc. prof. Ill. Inst. Tech., Chgo., 1966—69; mgr. engring. mechanics OEA, Inc., Des Plaines, Ill., 1970—84, v.p. engring. mechanics, 1984—97; cons., 1998—. Resident rsch. fellow Argonne Nat. Lab., Ill., 1962—64. Author: Recoilless Rifle Weapon Systems, 1976; contbr. articles to profl. jours., Fulbright Scholar, 1958—59, Walter P. Murphy Rsch. fellow, Northwestern U. Tech. Inst., 1960—62. Mem.: AIAA, ASME (Calvin Rice Meml. scholar 1959), Soc. Engring. Sci., Am. Soc. Engring. Edn., Can. Math. Soc., N.Y. Acad. Scis., Soc. Nat. Philosophy, Math. Assn. Am., Am. Math. Soc., Am. Acad. Mech., Sigma Xi, Pi Tau Sigma. Avocations: rare book collecting, stamp collecting/philately, hiking, travel. Home: 9756 East Maplewood Cir Englewood CO 80111 Office Phone: 303-773-3659.

OLCESE, JAMES MICHAEL, neuroscientist, educator; b. Panama City, Fla., Apr. 17, 1953; Arrived in Germany, 1988; s. Charles Patrick and Marta (Windisch) O.; m. Ursula Walach, Dec. 21, 1984; children: Erik Maximilian, Phillip Alexander. BS, Emory U., 1974; PhD in Physiology, Marquette U., 1979. Vis. asst. prof. Marquette U., Milw., 1979-80; asst. prof. Rhodes Coll., Memphis, 1980-87, assoc. prof., 1987-88; vis. scientist U. Copenhagen, Denmark, 1988-89; Alexander von Humboldt fellow U. Hamburg, Germany, 1989-90, group leader, 1990—2003; assoc. prof. Fla. State U., 2003—. Vis. scientist U. Mainz, Germany, 1983-85. Mem. editl. bd.: Jour. Pineal Rsch., 1993-2000, Jour. Endocrinology, 2000-06; contbr. chpts. to books and articles to profl. jours. Recipient Rsch. grants NIH, 1986-88, Bundesministerium Forschung/Tech., Germany, 1992-98, Deutsche Forschlungsgemeinschaft, Germany, 1993-2001. Mem.: European Pineal and Biol. Rythms Soc., European Pineal Soc. (sec.-treas. 1990—96). Avocations: music, sailing, camping, tennis. Office: Florida State Univ College of Medicine 3300 MSR MC4300 1115 W Call St Tallahassee FL 32306 Office Fax: 850-644-5781. Business E-Mail: james.olcese@med.fsu.edu.

OLCOTT, JOHN WHITING, air transportation executive; b. Orange, NJ, Oct. 20, 1936; s. Egbert Whiting and Marion Richmond (Braillard) Olcott; m. Hope Bennett Phillips, May 14, 1966 (div. Feb. 1987); children: David Whiting, Bradley Philips, Carter Howell; m. Isobel Waxman Ritter, Nov. 25, 1989. BS in Aero. Engring., Princeton U., 1960, MS in Aero. Engring., 1964; MBA in Gen. Mgmt., Rutgers U., 1970. Cert. Internat. Std. Bus. Aircraft Ops. Auditor Accreditation 2003, 2005. V.p. Linden Flight Svc., NJ, 1960-66; flight rsch. specialist Princeton U., NJ, 1966-68; v.p. corp. devel., sr. cons. Aero. Rsch. Assocs. Princeton, Inc., 1968-74; v.p., group pub., editorial dir. McGraw-Hill Aviation Week Group, Rye Brook, NY, 1973-92; pres. Nat. Bus. Aviation Assn., Inc., 1992—2003, Gen. Aero Co., Inc., 2003—. Rsch. engring. and devel. adv. com. FAA, 1990—2003; mem. bd. govs. Flight Safety Found., 1992—2000; bd. dirs. aerospace tech. adv. com. NASA, 1998—2003, mem. small aircraft transp. sys. coun., 2002—06; co-chair safer skies program FAA, 1999—2003; chmn. Be a Pilot, 2003—05; bd. dirs. Nat. Coalition Aviation Mobility, 2004—06; chmn. bus. aviation adv. bd. Airbus, 2005—; auditor Internat. Std. Bus. Aircraft Ops., 2003—. Chmn. panel gen. aviation and commuter tech. NASA, Washington, 1974—86; chmn. panel gen. aviation safety FAA, Washington, 1983—88; crew chief, mem. New Vernon Vol. First Aid Squad, NJ, 1974—92; bd. dirs. Aviation Rsch. and Edn. Found., Washington, 1988—92; mem. bd. visitors Aircraft Owner and Pilots Assn. Air Safety Found., Frederick, Md., 1988—93; mem. New Vernon Bd. Adjustment, 2003—; mem. integrated devel. team Joint Program and Devel. Office; mem. airports and integrated product team Agile ATC Sys., 2005—; trustee Embry-Riddle Aero. U., Daytona Beach, Fla., 1988—93, 1995—97. Recipient Meritorious Svc. award, Flight Safety Found., 1983, 2003, Dir.'s award, FAA Ctrl. Region, 1984, Am. Spirit award, Nat. Bus. Aviation Assn., 2003, Commendation cert., FAA, 1984, Gill Robb Wilson award, Embry-Riddle Aero. U., 1986, Journalism award, Helicopter Assn. Internat., 1990, William F. Shea award for Disting. Contbn. to Aviation, 2004, Turning Goals into Reality award, NASA, 2005, Langley Rsch. Ctr. Team award, 2005, Elder Statesman award, Nat. Aeronautics Assn., 2006; named to NJ Aviation Hall of Fame, 2001. Mem.: Nat. Air Transp. Assn., Aircraft Owners and Pilots Assn., Soc. Exptl. Test Pilots, Nat. Bus. Aviation Assn., NJ Aviation Assn. (pres. 2005—06). Republican. Presbyterian. Office: Gen Aero Co Hangar One 1 Airport Rd Morristown NJ 07960 Office Phone: 973-734-9994. Business E-Mail: jack@generalaerocompany.com.

OLD, LLOYD JOHN, cancer biologist; b. San Francisco, Sept. 23, 1933; s. John H. and Edna A. (Marks) Old. BA, U. Calif., Berkeley, 1955; MD, U. Calif., San Francisco, 1958; MD (hon.), Karolinska Inst., Stockholm, 1994, U. Lausanne, Switzerland, 1995, Univ. Coll. London, 1997. Rsch. fellow Sloan-Kettering Inst. Cancer Rsch., NYC, 1958—59, rsch. assoc., 1959—60, assoc., 1960—64, assoc. mem., 1964—67, mem., 1967—, acting assoc. dir. research planning, 1972, v.p., assoc. dir., 1973—76, v.p., assoc. dir. sci. devel., 1976—83; rsch. assoc. biology Cornell U. Grad. Sch. Med. Scis., NYC, 1960—62, asst. prof. biology, 1962—66, assoc. prof. biology, 1966—69, prof. biology, 1969—81, prof. immunology, 1981—; assoc. dir. rsch. Meml. Sloan-Kettering Cancer Ctr./Meml. Hosp., NYC, 1973—83, William E. Snee Chair cancer immunology, 1983—. Sci. dir. Ludwig Inst. Cancer Rsch., 1971—86, chmn. sci. com., 1988—2006, bd. dirs., 1989—, dir. NY unit, 1990, CEO, 1995—2004, dir. Cancer Vaccine Collaborative, 2001—, chmn. bd. dirs., 2006—; lectr. Harvey Soc., 1972, G.H.A. Clowes Meml., 1980; assoc. med. dir. NY Cancer Rsch. Inst. Inc., 1970; med. dir. Cancer Rsch. Inst., Inc., 1971—74, dir. sci. adv. coun., 1974—; vis. prof. clin. investigation GM Cancer Rsch. Found., Dana-Farber Cancer Inst.; vis. prof. pathology Harvard U., 1986; fgn. adj. prof. med. faculty Karolinska Inst., 1994—. Adv. editor: Jour. Exptl. Medicine, 1971—76, 1990—95, Progress in Surface and Membrane Sci., 1972—74, assoc. editor: Virology, 1972—74, mem. editl. adv. bd.: Cancer Rsch., 1967—70, Cancer, 1968—71, Recent Results in Cancer Rsch., 1972, mem. editl. bd.: Immunobiology, 1987—. Mem. med. & sci. adv. bd., trustee Leukemia Soc. America Inc., 1970—73; mem. sci. adv. bd. Jane Coffin Childs Meml. Fund Med. Rsch., 1970—75; mem. rsch. coun. Pub. Health Rsch. Inst. NYC, 1977—80, bd. dirs., 1979—89, vice chmn. exec. com., 1984—89; adv. bd. biology divsn. NY Hall of Sci. Recipient Roche award, 1957, Alfred P. Sloan award for cancer rsch., 1962, Lucy Wortham James award, James Ewing Soc., 1970, Louis Gross award, 1972, Founders Tumor Immunology award, Cancer Rsch. Inst., 1975, Rabbi Shai Shacknai Meml. award, 1976, Rsch. Recognition award, Noble Found., 1978, Robert Roesler de Villiers award, 1981, NY Acad. Medicine medal, 1985, Robert Koch prize, 1990, Pres.'s medal, Johns Hopkins U., 2004, Dean's award, Stanford U. Sch. Med., 2004, Charles Rodolphe Brupbacher Cancer Rsch. award, Switzerland, 2007. Mem.: AAAS, NAS, Acad. Cancer Immunology (presdl. mem. 1998—), Inst. Medicine, Am. Assn. Immunologists, Am. Assn. Cancer Rsch. (bd. dirs. 1980—83), Am. Acad. Arts & Scis., NY Acad. Scis., Harvey Soc., Alpha Omega Alpha, Sigma Xi, Phi Beta Kappa. Office: Cancer Rsch Inst Nat Hdqs One Exchange Plaza 55 Broadway Ste 1802 New York NY 10006*

OLDAKER, GUY BROOKLYN, III, lawyer; b. Washington, June 18, 1950; s. Guy B. and Elisabeth H. Oldaker; m. Cynthia L. Keiser, Aug. 3, 1980; children: Guy B. IV, Mary Elisabeth. BA in Chemistry, U. Va., 1972; PhD in Chemistry, Va. Polytech. Inst. & State U., 1978; JD, W.Va. U., 1995. Bar: N.C. 1996, U.S. Dist. Ct. (mid. dist.) N.C. 1996. Tchr. Albemarle H.S., Charlottesville, Va., 1972—75; instr. Va. Polytech. Inst. and State U., Blacksburg, Va., 1977—78; sr. project mgr. Entropy Environmentalists, Inc., Raleigh, NC, 1978—85; sr. staff R&D chemist R.J. Reynolds Tobacco Co., Winston-Salem, 1985—92, cons., 1992—95; exec. dir. Ctr. for Indoor Air Rsch., Winston-Salem, NC, 1987—88; assoc. Gordon & Nesbit, PLLC, 1996—97; pvt. practice Winston-Salem, 1997—2009; with Parrish & Smith, LLC, 2009—. Asst. coach cross country and track Albemarle H.S., Charlottesville, Va., 1972—75; sci. illustrator pvt. practice, Blacksburg, 1978; environ. cons., Morgantown, NC, 1993—95; vocalist Piedmont Opera, Winston-Salem, 2001—; expert witness. Contbr. articles to profl. jours. Pres. Winston-Salem Youth Symphony, 1997—99. Mem.: Forsyth County Criminal Def. Trial Lawyers Assn. (v.p. 2005), N.C. Acad. Trial Lawyers, Winston-Salem Symphony Chorale, Alpha Chi Sigma. Republican. Episcopalian. Achievements include patents for device for sampling indoor air. Avocations: reading, music, calligraphy, pen and ink drawing. Office: Ste 109 250 Executive Park Blvd Winston Salem NC 27103 Home Phone: 336-945-9681; Office Phone: 336-725-2346. Personal E-mail: oldakerlaw@triad.rr.com. Business E-Mail: goldaker@psrlaw.com.

OLDANI, LOUIS JOSEPH, literature educator; b. St. Louis, Mar. 1, 1933; s. Louis Vincent and Angela Josephine (Ponciroli) O. AB, St. Louis U., 1957, MA, 1962; PhD, U. Pa., 1972. Clergyman, Soc. of Jesus, 1951—; ordained priest, 1964. Instr. Rockhurst U., Kansas City, Mo., 1971-73, asst. prof., 1973-77, assoc. prof., 1977-85, prof., 1985—. Chmn. Rockhurst Libr. Bd., 1973-80, 93-95; mem. Rockhurst Rank and Tenure com., Kansas City, 1979-84, 87-91; pres. Rockhurst Faculty Demos, Kansas City, 1989-91, 93-95. Editor: (books) Introduction to Jesuit Theater, 1983, Jesuit Theater Englished, 1989; contbr. articles to profl. publs. Rsch. grantee Lilly Found., 1975,77, sabbatical grantee Rockhurst Coll., 1986-87, 96-97; Mellon Sr. fellow U. Kans., Lawrence, 1979; recipient Disting. Tchg. award Alpha Sigma Nu, 1995. Mem. MLA, Am. Lit. Sect. MLA, AAUP (pres. Rockhurst chpt. 1993-95), Nat. Coun. Tchrs. of English, Theodore Dreiser Soc. Democrat. Roman Catholic. Avocations: writing, travel, walking, cinema. Office: Rockhurst U 1100 Rockhurst Rd Kansas City MO 64110-2561 Office Phone: 816-501-4033. Business E-Mail: louis.oldani@rockhurst.edu.

OLDEN, KEVIN WILLIAM, medical researcher; b. NYC, Aug. 18, 1948; s. William and Josephine Olden; m. Sylvia Suikam Hom, Apr. 23, 1983; 1 child, Kimberly Jane. AB, NYU, 1971; MD, SUNY Downstate Med. Sch., 1976. Diplomate Am. Bd. of Internal Medicine with subspecialties in gastroenterology and addiction medicine, Am. Bd. of Psychiatry and Neurology. Intern categorical medicine UCLA-San Fernando Valley Med. Program, Sepulveda, Calif., 1976—77, resident internal medicine, 1977—79; resident psychiatry Mass. Gen. Hosp., Boston, 1979—81; postdoctoral fellow substance abuse and gastroenterology DVA Med. Ctr., Palo Alto, Calif., 1981—83; dir. alcohol rehab. unit Calif. Pacific Med. Ctr., San Francisco, 1983—86; asst. prof. medicine and psychiatry U. Calif., Davis, 1986—91, assoc. prof. medicine and psychiatry San Francisco, 1991—98, Mayo Med. Sch., Scottsdale, Ariz., 1998—2005; Levy prof. medicine, chair divsn. gastroenterology U. Ark., Little Rock, 2006—. Cons. Rome Internat. Working Teams on Functional GI Disorders, Rome, 1994—; fellow gastroenterology DVA Med. Ctr., Martinez, Calif., 1988—89; assoc. prof. medicine and psychiatry U. South Ala. Sch. Medicine, Mobile, 2005—06. Editor: (book) Handbook of the Functional Gastrointestinal Disorders, Chronic Abdominal Pain: A Comprehensive Approach; guest editor (med. jour.) Psychiat. Annals, Seminars in Gastroenterology, Jour. Psychosomatic Rsch., editl. bd. Am. Jour. Drug and Alcohol Abuse, Medicine and Psychiatry, Am. Jour. Gastroenterology. Med. advisor Internat. Found. for Functional Gastrointestinal Disorders, Milw., 1997—2003, Cyclic Vomiting Assn., Scottsdale, Ariz., 1998—2003; med. cons. Med. Bd. of Calif., San Francisco, 1986—98; med. advisor Physician Diversion Program State of Calif., 1986—97. Capt. USNR, 1978—2003. Recipient Harvard Macy scholar in Med. Edn., Harvard Med. Sch., 2000, Clin. Scholar award, Am. Coll. of Gastroenterology, 1999, Outstanding Physician Educator (Rsch.), Mayo Clinic Scottsdale, 2000, Outstanding Physician and Educator, St. Mary's Med. Ctr., 1992—93, Clinician Engaged in Edn., Mayo Clinic Scottsdale, 1999—2000. Fellow: Acad. of Psychosomatic Medicine, ACP, Am. Coll. of Gastroenterology, Am. Psychiat. Assn.; mem.: Calif. Soc. Addiction Medicine (pres. 1990—92), Calif. Med. Assn. (chair chem. dependency 1986—98), Am. Gastroent. Assn. (pres. functional brain-gut rsch. group 2001—03). Avocations: fishing, scuba diving. Office: Univ Ark Sch Medicine Mail Slot 567 4301 W Markham Little Rock AR 72205-7199 Office Phone: 501-686-5175. Office Fax: 501-686-6248. Business E-Mail: kwolden@uams.edu.

OLDENBURG, CLAES THURE, artist; b. Stockholm, Jan. 28, 1929; s. Gosta and Sigrid (Lindforss) O.; m. Patricia Joan Muschinski, Apr. 13, 1960 (div. Apr. 1970); m. Coosje van Bruggen, July 22, 1977. BA, Yale, 1951; student, Art Inst., Chgo., 1952—54, US Citizen, 1953; degree (hon.), Oberlin Coll., 1970, Art Inst. Chgo., 1979, Bard Coll., 1995, Royal Coll. Art, London, 1996; degree with Coosje van Bruggen (hon.), Calif. Coll. Arts and Crafts, 1996, U. Teesside, Middlesbrough, England, 1999, Nova Scotia Coll. Art and Design, 2005, Coll. Creative Studies, Detroit, 2005. One-man shows include Judson Gallery, NYC, 1959, Reuben Gallery, 1960, Green Gallery, 1962, Sidney Janis Gallery, 1964—70, Galerie Ileana Sonnabend, Paris, 1964, Robert Fraser Gallery, London, 1966, Moderna Museet, Stockholm, 1966, 1977, Mus. Contemporary Art, Chgo., 1966, 1977, Irving Blum Gallery, L.A., 1968, Mus. Modern Art, NYC, 1969, Stedelijk Mus., Amsterdam, 1970, 1977, Tate Gallery, London, 1970, Pasadena Art Mus., 1971, Nelson-Atkins Mus., Kansas City, Mo., 1972, Art Inst. Chgo., 1973, Leo Castelli Gallery, NYC, 1974, 1976, Margo Leavin Gallery, LA, 1975, 1976, 1978, 1988, 1989, Walker Art Ctr., Mpls., 1975, 1992, Art Gallery Ont., Toronto, 1976, Ctr. Georges Pompidou, Paris, 1977, Rijksmus. Kröller-Muller Otterlo, 1979, Mus. Ludwig, Cologne, 1979, Wave Hill, Bronx, N.Y., 1984, Solomon R. Guggenheim Mus., NYC, 1986, 1995, Mus. Haus Esters Krefeld, Germany, 1987, Kunstmus., Basel, 1992, exhibited in group shows at Pace Gallery, 1992, 1994, Nat. Gallery Art, Washington, 1995, Mus. Contemporary Art, LA, 1995, one-man shows include Kunst und Ausstellungshalle der Bundersrepublik Deutschland, Bonn, 1996, exhibited in group shows at Hayward Gallery, London, 1996, Whitney Mus. Am. Art, NYC, 2002, two person show with Coosje van Bruggen, No. Ctr. Contemporary Art, Sunderland, 1988, Leeds City Art Gallery, 1988, Palais des Beaux-Arts, Brussels, 1988, IVAM Ctr. Julio González, Valencia, 1988, Galleria Christian Stein, Milan, 1990, Guggenheim Mus. SoHo, NYC, 1993, Leo Castelli Gallery, 1980, 1986, 1990, Pace Gallery, 1994, Mus. Correr, Venice, 1999, Mus. Serralves, Porto, Portugal, 2001, Met. Mus. Art, NYC, 2002, Paula Cooper Gallery, 2004, two person show with Coosje van Bruggen, Frederick Meijer Gardens and Scupture Park, Grand Rapids, Mich., 2002, Whitney Mus. Am. Art, 2002, Chinati Found., Marfa, Tex., 2003, Paula Cooper Gallery, NYC, 2004, PaceWildenstein, 2005, Konrad Fischer Galerie, Düsseldorf, 2005, Castello di Rivoli Mus. Contemporary Art, Rivoli-Turin, 2006, Fundació Joan Miró, Barcelona, 2007, Waddington Gallery, London, 2007, exhibited in group shows at Martha Jackson Gallery, NYC, 1960, 1961, Dallas Mus. Contemporary Art, 1962, Sidney Janis Gallery, NYC, 1962, 1964, Inst. Contemporary Arts, Lndon, 1963, Art Inst. Chgo., 1962—63, Mus. Modern Art, NYC, 1963, 1988, 1990, 1991, Washington Gallery Modern Art, 1963, Am. Pavilion, Venice, Biennale, 1964, 1968, Moderna Museet, Stockholm, 1964, Whitney Mus. Am. Art, NYC, 1964, 1965, 1968, 1970, 1974, 1981, 1984, 1999, 2002, Solomon R. Guggenheim Mus., 1965, Inst. Contemporary Art, Boston, 1966, Mus. Fridericianum, Kassel, 1968, 1972, 1977, 1982, Richard Feigen Gallery, Chgo., 1968, 1969, Met. Mus. Art, 1969, Minami Gallery, Tokyo, 1975, Mus. Contemporary Art, Chgo., 1980, Art Gallery NSW, Sydney, 1985, Mus. Ludwig Cologne, 1986, U. Art Mus., UC Berkeley, 1987, Westfälisches Landesmus. für Kunst und Kulturegeschichte, Münster, 1987, 1997, Musée nationale d'arte moderne, Ctr. Georges Pompidou, Paris, 1989, La Grande Halle-La Villette, 1989, Royal Acad. Arts, London, 1991, Mus. Contemporary Arts, LA, 1992, exhibited in group shows, Venice Biennale, 1997, Mus. Nat. Modern Art, Ctr. Georges Pompidou, 1989, La Grande Halle-La Villette, Paris, 1989, exhibited in group shows, Royal Acad. Arts, London, 1991, Mus. Contemporary Art, L.A., 1992, exhibited in group shows, Guggenheim Mus., NYC, 1993, Nat. Gallery, London, 2000, Represented in permanent collections Solomon R. Guggenheim Mus., NYC, Mus. Modern Art, Albright-Knox Art Gallery, Buffalo, Ctr. Georges Pompidou, Stedelijk Mus., Tate Gallery, Mus. Ludwig, Moderna Museet, Rose Art Mus. Brandeis U., Waltham, Mass., Oberlin Coll., Nat. Gallery Art, Canberra, Art Gallery Ont., Art Inst. Chgo., Hirshorn Gallery and Sculpture Garden, Whitney Mus. Am. Art, Mus. Contemporary Art, LA, numerous permanent collections, exhibitions include numerous sculptures with Coosje van Bruggen Rijksmus. Kröller-Muller, Otterlo, The Netherlands, 1979, exhibitions include public exhibitions and sculptures with Coosje van Bruggen Nollen Plz. Civic Ctr., Greater Des Moines, Iowa, 1984, Vitra Internat. AG, Weil am Rhein, 1988, Mpls. Sculpture Garden, Walker Art Ctr., Mpls., 1990, Parc de la Villette, Paris, 1993, Ctrl. Gardens, Middlesbrough, Eng., 1994, Nelson-Atkins Mus. Art, Kansas City, Mo., 1996, Tokyo Internat. Exhbn. Ctr., 1996, Guggenheim Found., 2000, Piazzale Cadorna, Milan, 2000, Eindhoven, The Netherlands, 2001, Neumarkt Galerie, Cologne, Germany, 2001; author: Store Days, 1967, Notes in Hand, 1971, Raw Notes, 1973, Multiples in Retrospect, 1991; co-author (with Coosje van Bruggen): Claes Oldenburg: Sketches and Blottings Toward the European Desk Top, 1990, Large-Scale Projects, 1994, Claes Oldenburg Coosje van Bruggen, 1999, Down Liquidambar Lane: Sculpture in the Park, 2001, Images à la Carte, 2004, Sculpture by the Way, 2006; co-author: (with Coosje van Bruggen and Frank O. Gehry) Il Corso del Coltello, 1985; numerous mus. collections. Recipient Sculpture award, Brandeis U., 1971, Skowhegan Sculpture medal, 1972, award, Art Inst. Chgo., 1976, medal, AIA, 1977, Wilhelm-Lehmbruck prize, Germany, 1981, Wolf prize in arts (sculpture), Wolf Found., Israel, 1989, Creative Arts award, Brandeis U., Jack I. and Lillian Poses medal, 1993, Coosje Van Bruggen: Lifetime Achievement award, Internat. Sculpture Ctr., 1994, award, Rolf Schock Found., Stockholm, 1995, Nathaniel S. Saltonstall award, ICA, Boston, 1996, Nat. Medal Arts, Wash., 2000; co-recipient Distinction in Sculpture, Sculpture Ctr., 1994, Ptnr. Edn. award, Solomon R. Guggenheim Mus., 2002, Medal award, Sch. Mus. Fine Arts, Boston, 2004. Mem.: Am. Acad. Arts and Scis., Am. Acad. Inst. Arts & Letters.

OLDENBURG, RICHARD ERIK, auction company executive; b. Stockholm, Sept. 21, 1933; came to U.S., 1936, naturalized, 1959; s. Gösta and Sigrid Elisabeth (Lindforss) O.; m. Harriet Lisa Turnure, Dec. 17, 1960 (dec. Apr. 1998); m. Mary Ellen Meehan, June 11, 2003. AB, Harvard U., 1954. Mgr. design dept. Doubleday & Co., Inc., NYC,

1958-61; mng. editor trade div. Macmillan Co., Inc., NYC, 1961-69; dir. publs. Mus. Modern Art, NYC, 1969-72, dir., 1972-94, dir. emeritus, hon. trustee, 1995—; chmn. Sotheby's North and South America, NYC, 1995-2000, hon. chmn., 2000—06, cons., 2006—. Served with AUS, 1956-58. Home: 447 E 57th St New York NY 10022-3064

OLDER, JAY JUSTIN, ophthalmic plastic surgeon; b. Jersey City, Feb. 7, 1940; m. Lois Rosner; children: Benjamin, Jessica. AB, Rutgers U., 1961; MD, Stanford U., 1966. Diplomate Am. Bd. Ophthalmology. Intern, resident in internal medicine Cornell U./Bellevue Hosp. Ctr., NYC, 1968; resident in ophthalmology Stanford (Calif.) U., 1973; fellow in ophthalmic plastic and reconstructive surgery Stanford U., San Francisco, 1974; pvt. practice Tampa, Fla., 1974—. Clin. prof. ophthalmology U. South Fla. Coll. Medicine, Tampa, 1975—, dir. oculoplastic svc., 1974—99. Author: Eyelid Tumors: Clinical Diagnosis and Surgical Treatment, 1987, 2d edit., 2003. Fellow Am. Acad. Ophthalmology (Sr. Honor award 1995), Am. Soc. Ophthalmic Plastic and Reconstructive Surgery (pres. 1987, sec. 1983-84), ACS; mem. Phi Beta Kappa (v.p. Greater Tampa Bay Assn. 1995-96). Office: Older & Slonim Eyelid Inst 4444 E Fletcher Ave Ste D Tampa FL 33613-4937

OLDERMAN, GERALD, retired medical device company executive; b. NYC, July 16, 1933; s. Cass and Hilda (Klein) O.; m. Myrna Ruth Schwartz, Aug. 3, 1958; children: Sharon, Neil, Lisa. BS in Chemistry, Rensselaer Poly Inst., Troy, NY, 1958; MS Phys. Chemistry, Seton Hall U., South Orange, NJ, 1971, PhD, 1972. Rsch. chemist Nat. Cash Register, Dayton, Ohio, 1958-61; tech. mgmt. positions Johnson & Johnson, New Brunswick, NJ, 1961-75, dir. R & D, bd. dirs. surg. products hosp. divsn., 1972-75, v.p. R & D, Surgikos divsn., 1975-78; v.p. R & D, bd. dirs. Am. Convertors divsn. Am. Hosp. Supply corp., Evanston, Ill., 1978-85; v.p. internat. R & D Pharmaseal divsn. Baxter Healthcare Corp., Valencia, Calif., 1985-91; v.p. R & D, bd. dirs. cardiopulmonary divsn. C.R. Bard, 1991-96; cons. R.F. Caffrey & Assoc., Inc., Brownsville, Vt., 1996—; exec. v.p. R&D tech. and commercialization, bd. dirs. Quick-Med Techs., Inc., Wilmington, Del., 1998—. With USMC, 1954-56. Recipient Robert Wood Johnson medal, Johnson & Johnson, 1969. Fellow Am. Inst. Chemists; mem. Assn. Advancement Med. Instrumentation, INDA, Assn. Nonwovens Industry (bd. dirs., corp. rep. 1986, 87), Nat. Fire Protection Assn. (industry rep.), Am. Soc. Artificial Internat. Organs. Home: 17 Pickman Dr Bedford MA 01730-1009 Office: RF Caffrey & Assoc Inc PO Box 319 Brownsville VT 05037-0319 also: Quick Med Techs Inc 401 NE 25th Terr Boca Raton FL 33431 Office Phone: 781-271-9893, 888-835-2211 ext. 102. Personal E-mail: jolderman@aol.com. Business E-Mail: jolderman@quickmedtech.com.

OLDERSHAW, LOUIS FREDERICK, retired lawyer; b. New Britain, Conn., Aug. 30, 1917; s. Louis A. and Annie Louise (Bold) O.; m. Virginia Wakelin, Nov. 30, 1940; children: Peter W., Robert L., David L. AB, Dartmouth Coll., 1939; LLB, Yale U., 1942. Bar: Mass. 1946, Fed. 1947. Mem. legal staff Army Ordnance Dist., Springfield, Mass., 1942-43; with firm Lyon, Green, Whitmore, Doran & Brooks, Holyoke, Mass., 1947-49; ptnr. firm Davenport, Millane & Oldershaw, Holyoke, 1949-64; treas. Nat. Blank Book Co., Inc., Holyoke, 1964-65, pres., 1965-78, chmn. bd., 1978-83; group v.p., dir. Dennison Mfg. Co., Framingham, Mass., 1967-82; counsel Bulkley, Richardson & Gelinas, Springfield, Mass., 1983—2003; ret., 2003. Mem. editl. bd.: Yale Law Jour, 1941-42. Trustee Mt. Holyoke Coll., 1966-76, Greater Holyoke YMCA; bd. dirs. emeritus Holyoke C.C. Found., Sta. WGBY-TV. Lt. USNR, 1943-47. Mem.: Abenakee Club, Orchards Golf Club, Rotary, Colony Club. Republican. Mem. United Congl. Ch. Home: 30 Bayon Dr South Hadley MA 01075 Office: Baybank Tower 1500 Main St Ste 2700 Springfield MA 01115-0001 Personal E-mail: louolder@aol.com.

OLDFIELD, EDWARD HUDSON, neurosurgeon, researcher; b. Mount Sterling, Ky., Nov. 22, 1947; s. Ellis Hudson Oldfield and Amanda Caroline Miller; m. Susan Shawler Wachs Oldfield, June 8, 1974; 1 child, Caroline Talbott. BA in Physics, U. Ky., 1969, MD, 1973. Diplomate Am. Bd. Neurol. Surgery. Pvt. practice, Lexington, Ky., 1980—81; senior staff fellow NIH, Bethesda, Md., 1981—83, dep. chief clin. neurosurgery, 1983—84, chief neurosurgery, 1984—2007; Crutchfield prof. neurosurgery, internal medicine prof. U. Va., 2007—, med. dir. neuro endocrine program. Med. dir. VHL disease Family Alliance, 1993—; adv. bd. brain cancer McDonnell Found., 1997—2004. Mem. editl. bd. Jour. Neurosurgery, 1994—2002, assoc. editor (jour. Neurosurgery), 2009—. Recipient The Grass Award, Soc. Neurol. Surg., 1995, Farber Award, Am. Assn. Neurol. Surg., 1999, Cushing medal, Am. Assn. Neurol. Surgeons, 2009. Mem.: Soc. Neurological Surgery (pres. 2008—09). Achievements include patents in field of convective-enhanced drug distribution to the Central Nervous System; advances in the understanding and treatment of brain tumors, pituitary tumors, syringomyelia, spinal arteriovenous malformations, and drug delivery to the brain and spinal cord. Home: PO Box 309 Philomont VA 20131 Office: Univ Virginia Dept Neurosurgery PB 800212 Charlottesville VA 22908 Home Phone: 540-338-3607.

OLDFIELD, JAMES EDMUND, retired nutrition educator; b. Victoria, BC, Can., Aug. 30, 1921; came to U.S., 1949; s. Henry Clarence and Doris O. Oldfield; m. Mildred E. Atkinson, Sept. 4, 1942; children: Nancy E. Oldfield McLaren, Kathleen E. Oldfield Sansone, David J., Jane E. Oldfield, Richard A. BSA, U. B.C., 1941, MSA, 1949; PhD, Oreg. State U., 1951. Faculty Oreg. State U., Corvallis, 1951-90, head dept. animal sci., 1967-83, dir. Nutrition Rsch. Inst., 1986-90; ret., 1990. Mem. nat. tech. adv. com. on water supply U.S. Dept. Interior, Washington, 1967-68; bd. dirs. Coun. for Agrl. Sci. and Tech., Ames, Iowa, 1978-84; mem. nutrition study sect. NIH, Bethesda, Md., 1975-80, 85-87; cons. Selenium Tellurium Devel. Assn., Grimbergen, Belgium, 1990-2002. Editor: Selenium in Biomedicine, 1967, Sulphur in Nutrition, 1970, Selenium in Biology and Medicine, 1987; author: Selenium in Nutrition, 1971, Selenium World Atlas, 1999. Served to maj. Can. Army, 1942-46, ETO. Decorated Mil. Cross Can.; Fulbright Rsch. scholar U.S. Dept. State, 1974, Massey U., New Zealand; recipient Klaus Schwarz medal Internat. Assn. Bioinorganic Scientists, 1998. Fellow Am. Soc. Animal Sci. (pres. 1966-67, Morrison award 1972), Am. Inst. Nutrition; mem. Am. Chem. Soc., Am. Registry Profl. Animal Scientists (pres. 1990, editor: Profl. Animal Scientist 1993-96), Fedn. Am. Socs. Exptl. Biol., Pacific Fisheries Technologists (pres. 1966), Kiwanis (pres. 1964, lt. gov. 1986). Republican. Episcopalian. Office: Oreg State Univ Dept Animal Sci Corvallis OR 97331 Home: 4766 SW Birdsong Dr Corvallis OR 97333 Office Phone: 541-737-1894. Office Fax: 541-737-4174. Business E-Mail: james.e.oldfield@oregonstate.edu.

OLDHAM, CHERYL A., federal agency administrator; BA, Tex. Christian U.; JD, St. Mary's U. Dir. Office of White House Liaison, Washington; exec. dir. Sec. Edn.'s Commn. on Future of Higher Edn. US Dept. Edn., Washington, 2003, chief of staff to under sec. edn., acting asst. sec. Office of Postsecondary Edn., 2008—. Office: US Dept Edn Sec's Commn on Future of Edn 400 Maryland Avenue, SW, Rm 7E317 Washington DC 20202-0160 Office Phone: 202-205-8741. E-mail: Cheryl.Oldham@ed.gov.*

OLDHAM, DARIUS DUDLEY, lawyer; b. Beaumont, Tex., July 6, 1941; s. Darius Saran and Mary Francis (Carraway) O.; m. Judy J. White, Jan. 23, 1965; children: Steven, Michael BA, U. Tex., Austin, 1964; JD, U. Tex., 1966. Bar: Tex. 1966, U.S. Dist. Ct. (so., no., ea. and we. dists.) Tex. 1966, U.S. Supreme Ct. 1974, U.S. Ct. Appeals (3rd, 5th and 11th cirs.) 1968; cert. arbitrator and mediator. Assoc. Fulbright & Jaworski, Houston, 1966—74, ptnr., 1974—2006, of counsel/ret. ptnr., 2007—, mem. policy com., 1980—97, 2001—04, mem. exec. com., 1997—2000, mem. litigation mgmt. com., 1998—2004, chair, 2001—02. Mem. faculty grad. litigation program U. Houston; adv. com. Nat. Ctr. State Cts.; mem. chancellors coun. exec. com. U. Tex.; lectr. in field. Former mem. bd. editors Aviation Litigation Reporter, Personal Injury Def. Reporter, Internat. Ins. Law Rev.; contbr. articles to profl. jours. Adv. coun. Nat. Jud. Coll., Inst. Molecular Medicine, U. Tex. Health Sci. Ctr.; former mem. Liberal Arts Adv. Coun., U. Tex.; past bd. dirs. FDCC Found., Houston Pops Orch. Fellow Am. Coll. Trial Lawyers (chair complex litigation and jud. com.), Tex. Bar Found. (life), Am. Bar Found. (life), Houston Bar Found. (life), Am. Bd. Trial Advs. (pres. Houston chpt. 1999); mem. ABA (mem. ho. of dels. 1996-98, chair tort and ins. practice sect. 1994-95, mem. coun. tort and ins. practice sect. 1988-98, presdl. emissary 1993-95, chmn. Standing Com. on Independence of the Judiciary 2001-04, chmn. Select Commn. on Jud. Campaign Fin. 2000-01, standing com. fed. jud. improvements, chmn. John Marshall award selection com. 2004-05), U. Tex. Law Sch. Alumni Assn. Exec. Com., 2003—, Tex. Bar Assn. (chmn. liaison fed. jud. com. 1989-90, pattern jury charges Vol. IV com. 1988-92), Tex. Young Lawyers Assn. (bd. dirs., chmn.), Fed. Def. and Corp. Counsel (pres. 1989-90, chmn. bd. 1990-91, exec. com. 1988-91), Tex. Assn. Def. Counsel, Maritime Law Assn. U.S., Am. Counsel Assn. (bd. dirs. 1982-83, 89-94), Def. Rsch. Inst. (chmn. aerospace com. 1984-87, Presdl. Achievement award 1987, bd. dirs. 1989-92, exec. com. 1991-92), Lawyers for Civil Justice (bd. dirs. 1988-98, chmn. 1998, exec. com. 1990-98, pres. 1997), Nat. Ctr. for State Cts. Lawyers Commn., U. Tex. Health Sci. Ctr. (adv. coun. mem., Inst. Molecular Medicine), River Oaks Country Club, Houston Ctr. Club, Sigma Chi (Significant Sig), Phi Delta Phi. Office: Fulbright & Jaworski 1301 Mckinney St 51st Fl Houston TX 77010-3031 Home Phone: 713-465-5804; Office Phone: 713-651-5397. Personal E-mail: doldham@fulbright.com.

OLDHAM, DEWEY LINDON (SPOONER OLDHAM), musician, songwriter; b. Ala., June 14, 1943; Played at FAME Studios, Muscle Shoals Sound Studios; co-founder Muscle Shoals Rhythm Section; formed songwriting partnership with Dan Penn Chips Moman's Am. Studios, Memphis, 1967. Musician (keyboardist): (songs) When a Man Loves a Woman, Mustang Sally, You Better Move On, I Never Loved a Man (The Way I Love You); songwriter: Do Right Woman, Cry Like a Baby, A Woman Left Lonely, many others. Named to Rock & Roll Hall of Fame, 2009. Home: 21 Pine Cir Rogersville AL 35652 E-mail: booking@spooneroldham.com.*

OLDHAM, JOHN MICHAEL, physician, psychiatrist, educator; b. Muskogee, Okla., Sept. 6, 1940; s. Henry Newland and Alice Gray (Ewton) O.; m. Karen Joan Pacella, Apr. 24, 1971; children: Madeleine Marie, Michael Clark. BS in Engring., Duke U., 1962; MS in Neuroendocrinology, Baylor U., 1966, MD, 1967. Licensed physician NY, NJ, SC, Tex.; diplomate in psychiat. and forensic psychiatry Am. Bd. Psychiatry and Neurology; cert. Am. Psychoanalytic Assn. Intern pediatrics St. Luke's Hosp., NYC, 1967-68; resident psychiat. Columbia U. Dept. Psychiat., N.Y.S. Psychiatric Inst., NYC, 1968-70; chief resident in psychiatry Columbia U., NY State Psychiat. Inst., 1970-71; grad. Columbia Psychoanalytic Ctr., NYC, 1977; dir. psychiatric emergency svcs. Roosevelt Hosp., NYC, 1973-74, dir. residency tng. dept. psychiat., 1974-77; dir. short term diagnostic and treatment unit NY Hosp. Westchester Divsn., White Plains, NY, 1977-80, dir. divsn. acute treatment svcs., 1980-84; deputy dir. NY State Psychiatric Inst., NYC, 1984-89, acting dir., 1989-90, dir., 1990—2002; assoc. chmn. dept. psychiatry Columbia U. Coll. Physicians & Surgeons, NYC, 1986-96, vice chmn., 1996-2000, acting chmn., 2000—02; chief med. officer NY State Office Mental Health, Albany, 1989—2002; prof. psychiatry Med. U. SC, 2002—07, chmn. dept. psychiatry and behavioral sci., 2002—07, exec. dir. Inst. Psychiatry, 2002—07; sr. v.p., chief of staff The Menninger Clinic, 2007—; prof., exec. vice chmn. clin. affairs and devel., Menninger Dept. of Psychiatry and Behavioral Scis. Baylor Coll., 2007. From instr. clin. psychiatry to prof. clin. psychiatry Columbia U. Coll. P&S, 1974-96, 1988-96, Elizabeth K. Dollard profl clin. psychiatry medicine and law, 1996-2002; asst. prof. psychiatry Cornell U. Med. Coll., NYC, 1977-83, assoc. prof. clin. psychiatry, 1983-84; attending staff dept. psychiatry Roosevelt Hosp., NYC, 1973-77; assoc. attending in psychiatry, NY Hosp., 1977-84, Presbyn Hosp., NYC, 1984-88, attending in psychiatry, 1988-2002; tng. and supervising psychoanalyst Columbia Psychoanalytic Ctr., NYC, 1983-2002; coord. med. student edn., dept. psychiatry Cornell U. Med. Coll., Westchester Divsn., White Plains, NY, 1977-84; coord. clin. clerkships in psychiatry Roosevelt Hosp., Columbia U. Coll. P&S, NYC, 1974-77; spl. adv. bd. Freedom From Fear, Inc.; examiner Am. Bd. Psychiatry and Neurology; chmn. acute divsn. rsch. group, Westchester Divsn., NY Hosp., 1981-84, co-project dir. borderline rsch. group, 1982-84, co-prin. investigator familial transmission DSM III personality disorders, 1982-84; prin. investigator personality disorders in bulimia, NYS. Psychiat. Inst., 1985-90, structured DSM III assessment psychoanalytic patients, Columbia Psychoanalytic Ctr., 1986-91; co-prin. investigator validity DSM III R personality disorders, NY State Psychiat. Inst., 1987-94; co-investigator NIMH, 1996-2002; Hall-Mercer vis. scholar, dept. psychiatry, U. Pa., 2004; Judge Bernard Thompson Meml. Lectr., dept. psychiatry, North Shore U. Hosp., 2004; Albert M. Biele MD vis. prof. in psychiatry, Jefferson Med. Coll., 2005; Wolfe-Adler Lectr., SHeppard Pratt Health Sys., 2006; Ferald R. Klerman MD Meml. Lectr., Payne Whitney Clinic, NYC, 2007. Author: (with L.B. Morris) The Personality Self-Portrait, 1990; editor Jour. Psychia. Practice; editor bd. Jour. Personality Disorders; dep. editor Am. Psychiat. Pub., Inc.; reviewer Arch Gen. Psychiatry, Am. Jour. Psychiatry, Psychiat. Svcs.; contbr. numerous articles to profl. jours.; presentations in field. Major USAF, 1971—73. Recipient John J. Weber prize Excellence in Psychoanalytic Rsch. Columbia Psychoanalytic Ctr., 1990, Dorothea Dix Award Mental Illness Found., 1996, Spl. Comm.'s award NY State Office Mental Health, 1997, Spl. Presdl. commendation Am. Psychiat. Assn., 1999, 2005, Payne Whitney Clin. award for Extraordinary Pub. Svc., 2002; Spl. Citation conferred by Governor George E. Pataki, State of NY, 2002; Paul Hoch award for Disting. Leadership, NY State Office Mental Health, 2002. Fellow Am. Coll. Psychiatrists (Bowis award 2007), Am. Psychiat. Assn. (pres. NY County dist. br., 1989-90, com. rsch. psychiat. treatment 1987-93, coun. rsch., steering com. practice guidelines, chmn. sci. program com. 1992-95, chmn. com. quality indicators 1999-2003, chmn. coun. quality care 2003—06), Am. Psychopath. Assn., NY Acad. Medicine; mem. AMA, Am. Psychoanalytic Assn. (cert.), Assn. Psychoanalytic Medicine (pres. 1989-91), Internat. Psychoanalytical Assn., NY Acad. Sci., Assn. Rsch. Personality Disorders (bd. dirs.), Internat. Soc. for Study of Personality Disorders (pres. 2000—03), SC Psychiat. Assn. (pres. 2006-07), Houston Psychiatric Soc. Office: Menninger Clinic PO Box 809045 Houston TX 77280-9045 Office Phone: 713-275-5016. Office Fax: 713-275-5117. Business E-Mail: joldham@menninger.edu.

OLDHAM, MAXINE JERNIGAN, real estate broker; b. Whittier, Calif., Oct. 13, 1923; d. John K. and Lela Hessie (Mears) Jernigan; m. Laurance Montgomery Oldham, Oct. 28, 1941; 1 child, John Laurence. AA, San Diego City Coll., 1973; student Western State U. Law, San Diego, 1976-77, LaSalle U., 1977-78; grad. Realtors Inst., Sacramento, 1978. Mgr. Edin Harig Realty, LaMesa, Calif., 1966-70; tchr. Bd. Edn., San Diego, 1959-66; mgr. Julia Cave Real Estate, San Diego, 1970-73; salesman Computer Realty, San Diego, 1973-74; owner Shelter Island Realty, San Diego, 1974—. Author: Jernigan History, 1982, Mears Geneology, 1985, Fustons of Colonial America, 1988, Sissoms. Mem. Civil Svc. Commn., San Diego, 1957-58. Recipient Outstanding Speaker award Dale Carnegie. Mem. Nat. Assn. Realtors, Calif. Assn. Realtors, San Diego Bd. Realtors, San Diego Apt. Assn., Internationale des Professions Immobilieres (internat. platform speaker), DAR (vice regent Linares chpt.), Colonial Dames 17th Century, Internat. Fedn. Univ. Women. Republican. Roman Catholic. Avocations: music, theater, painting, genealogy, continuing edn. Home: 3348 Lowell St San Diego CA 92106-1713 E-mail: lilyham@coxs.com.

OLDHAM, SEAN MICHAEL, medical educator, consultant; s. Michael and Linda Oldham; m. Suzanne Marie Graham, Aug. 5, 1995; children: Francesca, Califia, Kamala, Keana. PhD, U. NC, Chapel Hill, 1997. Prof. Burnham Inst. Med. Rsch., La Jolla, Calif., 2002—. Rsch. grant, NIH, Rsch. fellowship, AHA, CIRM. Mem.: Genetics Soc. America. Achievements include patents pending for methods to block insulin resistance diseases; methods to prevent stem cell aging. Avocations: skiing, travel, scuba diving. Office: Burnham Inst Med Rsch 10901 N Torrey Pines Rd La Jolla CA 92037 Business E-Mail: soldham@burnham.org.

OLDHAM, SPOONER See **OLDHAM, DEWEY**

OLDHAM, TERRY L., museum director; b. Kansas City, Kans. BS in Aerospace Engring., U. Kans., MA in Art Mus. Edn. with honors; MBA, U. Hawaii. Interim asst. dir. Spencer Mus., Lawrence, Kans.; dir., curator edn. Mus. Art, Tallahassee; dir. Albrecht-Kemper Mus. Art, 1999—. Command pilot USAF, Vietnam, Desert Storm. Decorated Aerial Achievement medal, Bronze Star, Disting. Flying Cross. Office: Albrecht-Kemper Mus Art 2818 Frederick Ave Saint Joseph MO 64506 Office Phone: 816-233-7003. Office Fax: 816-233-3713.

OLDHAM, TODD, fashion designer; b. Corpus Christi, Tex., Oct. 22, 1961; s. Jack and Linda Oldham. Founder Times 7, Dallas; founder, designer Todd Oldham, NYC, 1989; design dir. Escada, Munich, 1994; dorm room furniture designer Target Corp., 2001—03; furniture designer La-Z-Boy Inc., 2002—. Host, dir. Todd Time MTV House of Style, 1993-96; host Top Design, Bravo TV, 2007-;guest Tracy Takes On with Tracy Ullman, 1994, The Nanny, 1996, Roseanne, 1996; designer spl. collection for Batman Forever, 1995, MTV's Choose or Lose bus, 1996, GM Bravada to raise money for cancer rsch., 1997; music video co-dir. (with Hype Williams) Maxi Priest's That Kind of Girl, 1996; music video dir. Us3's Come on Everybody, 1997. Active Design Industries Found. for AIDS, People for the Ethical Treatment of Animals, POWARS, Pet Pals. Recipient Rising Star award Internat. Apparel Mart, Dallas, 1991, Fashion Execellence award Internat. Apparel Mart, Dallas, 1993; named Designer of Yr. Calif. Fashion Industry Friends of AIDS Project, 1996. Mem. Coun. Fashion Designers Am. (Perry Ellis award for new fashion talent 1991). Office: Todd Oldham Store NY 120 Wooster St Frnt 3 New York NY 10012-5200*

OLDING, MICHAEL, plastic and reconstructive surgeon; b. Celina, Ohio, July 4, 1950; s. Paul Robert and Virginia Lee (Hierholzer) O. BS, U. Dayton, 1972; MD, U. Ky., 1980. Diplomate Am. Bd. Plastic Surgery. Intern N.Y. Hosp./Cornell Med. Ctr., NYC, 1980-81, resident in surgery, 1981-82, McGill U., Montreal, Canada, 1982-83, fellow, plastic and reconstructive surgery, 1983-85; assoc. prof. surgery divsn. plastic/reconstructive surgery George Washington U., Washington, 1985—; chief divsn. plastic and reconstructive surgery, dir. Cosmetic Surgery & Laser Ctr., George Washington Univ. Med. Faculty Assoc., Washington. Staff privileges George Washington U. Med. Ctr., Sibley Hosp., Children's Hosp., Washington; served on numerous FDA adv. panels; lectr. in field; presenter King Fisal Hosp., Riyadh, Royal Coll. Surgeons Traveling Fellowship and Plastic Surgery Rsch. Coun., London. Author: Clinicians Pocket reference, 1986; contbr. articles to profl. jours. Annals of Plastic Surgery, Plastic Reconstructive Surgery; featured on Discovery Channel, interviewed by CBS, ABC, FOX, WUSA, Washington Post, Washington Times, NY Times Style mag., Boston Globe; quoted in online articles at ABCnews.com, Forbes.com, CNN.com and participated in an online forum with Washingtonpost.com Bd. dirs. D.C. Ballet Co., 1995—. Named a Top Doc, Washingtonian mag., 1989-, Washington Consumers' Checkbook. Fellow ACS; mem. Northeastern Soc. Plastic Surgery (bd. dirs.), Nat. Capitol Soc. Plastic Surgeons, McGill Plastic Surgery Soc. (bd. dirs.), Am. Soc. Plastic Surgeons, Am. Soc. Aesthetic Plastic Surgeons. Office: George Washington Univ Hosp 2150 Pennsylvania Ave NW Washington DC 20037-3201 Office Phone: 202-741-3241. Office Fax: 202-741-3183.

OLDMAN, GARY, actor; b. London, Mar. 21, 1958; m. Lesley Manville, 1987 (div. 1990); 1 child, Alfie; m. Uma Thurman, Oct. 1, 1990 (div. Apr. 30, 1992); m. Donya Fiorentino, Feb. 16, 1997 (div. Apr. 13, 2001); children: Gulliver Flynn, Charlie John; m. Alexandra Edenborough, 2008. BA, Rose Buford Coll. Speech and Drama, 1979. Actor:(theatre) Massacre at Paris, 1980, Chinchilla, 1980, Desperado Corner, 1980, A Waste of Time, 1980, Summit Conference, 1982, Rat in the Skull, 1984, The Pope's Wedding, 1984 (Drama Mag. Best Actor award 1985, Fringe Best Newcomer award 1985-86), The War Plays, 1985, The Desert Air, 1985, Women Beware Women, 1986, Real Dreams, 1986, Serious Money, 1987; (TV movies) Meantime, 1984, Honest, Decent and True, 1985, Fallen Angels: Dead End for Delia, 1993 (Cable Ace award, Actor in a Dramatic Series), The Firm, 1988, Heading Home, 1991, Jesus, 1999; (TV miniseries) Who Was Lee Harvey Oswald, 1992; (films) Remembrance, 1982, Sid and Nancy, 1986, Prick Up Your Ears, 1987 (Brit. Acad. Film and TV Arts nomination 1988), Track 29, 1988, We Think the World of You, 1988, Criminal Law, 1988, Paris by Night, 1989, Chattahoochee, 1989, Henry & June, 1990, State of Grace, 1990, Rosencrantz and Guildenstern Are Dead, 1990, JFK, 1991, Bram Stoker's Dracula, 1992, True Romance, 1993, Romeo is Bleeding, 1993, The Professional, 1994, Immortal Beloved, 1994, Murder in the First, 1995, The Scarlet Letter, 1995, Basquiat, 1996, The Fifth Element, 1997, Air Force One, 1997, Lost in Space, 1998, Quest for Camelot (aka Magic Sword), 1998, Nobody's Baby, 2001, Hannibal, 2001, Interstate 60, 2002, The Hire: Beat the Devil, 2002, Sin, 2003, Harry Potter and the Prisoner of Azkaban, 2004, Who's Kyle, 2004, Batman Begins, 2005, Harry Potter and the Goblet of Fire, 2005, The Dark Knight, 2008; actor, exec. prodr.: The Contender, 2000; dir., writer, prodr.: Nil By Mouth, 1998 Recipient Outstanding Brit. Film award Brit. Acad., Best Screenplay award Brit. Acad., Dirs. prize Edinburgh Festival Channel Four, Best Dir. prize Cannes Film Festival, Best Actor and Best Newcomer, Brit. Ind. Film Awards Best Actors. Office: c/o Douglas J Urbanski Douglas Mgmt Inc 9713 Little Santa Monica Blvd Beverly Hills CA 90210

OLDS, GLENN RICHARD, medical educator, department chairman; b. Grand Island, Nebr., June 10, 1950; s. Glenn Alvero and Eva Belle Olds; m. Jackie Elaine Lach; children: Glenn Richard Jr., John Michael, Trevor Nathanel. BA, Willamette U., Salem, Oregon, 1972; MD, Case Western Res. U., Cleve., 1976. Diplomate Am. Bd. Internal medicine, 1979, infectious diseases Am. Bd. Internal medicine, 1982. Internal medicine resident Mass. Gen. Hosp., Boston, 1976—78; chief med. resident U. Hosp., Cleve., 1980—81; geog. medicine & infectious disease fellow U. Hosp. & Case Western Res. U., Cleve., 1978—80, asst. prof. medicine, 1981—84; asst., assoc. prof. medicine, founding dir. internat. health inst. Brown U., Providence, 1984—92; prof. & chair dept. medicine Metrohealth Campus Case Western Res. U., Cleve., 1992—2000, Med. Coll. Wis., Milw., 2000—. Chmn., working com. WHO, Geneva, 1992—95, mem., 2001—; mem., schistosomiasis vaccine devel. program adv. com. Egyptian Ministry of Health, Cairo, 1997—2002; mem., internal medicine ACP, Phila., 2002—; bd. trustees & chair Schistosomiasis Control Initiative-Gates Found., London, 2001—. Quality, fin. & exec. com. AIDS Resourse Ctr. Wis., Milw., 2005—. Recipient Mastership, ACP, 2009. Office: Med Coll Wisconsin 9200 W Wisconsin Ave Milwaukee WI 53226

OLDS, JACQUELINE, psychiatrist, educator; b. Springfield, Mass., Jan. 4, 1947; d. James and Marianne (Ejier) O.; m. Richard Stanton Schwartz, Aug. 26, 1978; children: Nathaniel Leland, Sarah Elizabeth. BA, Radcliffe Coll., 1967; MD, Tufts U., 1971. Diplomate Am. Bd. Psychiatry and Neurology. Resident in adult psychiatry Mass. Mental Health Ctr., Boston, 1974; resident in child psychiatry McLean Hosp., Belmont, Mass., 1976, assoc. attending child psychiatrist, 1979—; psychiatrist-in-charge inpatient unit McLean Hall-Mercer Children's Ctr., Belmont, 1976-79; assoc. child psychiatry Beth Israel Hosp., Boston, 1979—; cons. in child psychiatry Mass. Gen. Hosp., Boston, 1994—. Instr. psychiatry Harvard U. Med. Sch, Boston, 1976-86; asst. prof. clin. psychiatry, 1986-2000, assoc. clin. prof. psychiatry, 2000—; bd. dirs. Guidance Ctr., Inc. Author: Overcoming Loneliness in Every Day Life, 1996, Marriage in Motion, 2000, The Lonely American: Drifting Apart in the Twenty-first Century, 2009, editor Clin. Challenges column in Harvard Rev. of Psychiatry; contbr. articles to profl. jours.; author (translator into Spanish): Matrimonio in Moviemento. Recipient Mentoring award Mass. Gen. Hosp. Dept. Child Psychiatry, 1998. Disting. fellow, Am. Psychiat. Assn.; mem. Mass. Psychiat. Soc. (ethics com. 1988-93, mem. pub. affairs com. 1992—), Am. Acad. Child Psychiatry, Am. Psychoanalytic Assn., New England Coun. Child and Adolescent Psychiatry (bd. dirs.). Democrat. Avocations: piano, writing, cooking, watercolors. Office Phone: 617-547-5920. Business E-Mail: jolds@partners.org.

OLDS, JOHN THEODORE, banker; b. NYC, Dec. 24, 1943; s. Richard J. and Barbara (Moses) O.; m. Candace Rose; children: Richard W., Samantha. Grad., Hill Sch., 1961; BA, U. Pa., 1965. Mng. dir. J.P. Morgan & Co., NYC, 1972-97; vice chmn., CEO Devel. Bank Singapore, 1988—2001, advisor to chmn., 2001; sr. advisor Newbridge Capital LLC, San Francisco, 2004—. Bd. dirs. RiskMetrics Group, San Francisco. Bd. dirs. Singapore Millennium Found., Asia Soc. No. Calif.; trustee Singapore Civil Svc. Coll., Calif. Hist. Soc.; bd. dirs. Internat. Monetary Conf. Mem. Bedford Golf and Tennis Club, Mid-Ocean Club, Knickerbocker Club. Episcopalian. Office: Newbridge Capital LLC Ste 3300 LLC345 California St San Francisco CA 94104

OLEARCHYK, ANDREW, cardiothoracic surgeon, educator; b. Peremyshl, Ukraine, Dec. 3, 1935; s. Symon and Anna (Kravéts) O.; m. Renata M. (Sharan), June 26, 1971; children: Christina N., Roman A., and Adrian S. Grad., Med. Acad., Warsaw, Poland, 1961, U. Pa., Phila., 1970. Diplomate Am. Bd. Surgery, Am. Bd. Thoracic Surgery. Chief divsn. anesthesiology, asst. dept. surgery Provincial Hosp., Kielce, Poland, 1963-66; resident in gen. surgery Geisinger Med. Ctr., Danville, Pa., 1968-73; resident in thoracic, cardiac and vascular surgery Allegheny Gen. Hosp., Pitts., 1980-82; pvt. practice medicine splty. in cardiac, thoracic and vascular surgery Phila. and Camden, NJ, 1982—. Author: A Surgeon's Universe, 2003, 2d edit., 2006; contbr. articles to profl. jours. Achievements include description of mimicking of the subclavian steal syndrome (2004); application of the ultrasonic Doppler flow detector to localize an intramyocardial coronary artery to perform coronary artery bypass surgery on a beating heart in the presence of neoplastic pericarditis aiming to preserve cellular immunity (2003); recognition of a triad of the severe atherosclerosis of the aortic valve, a low incidence of coronary artery disease and rheumatic fever in patients with a congenital bicuspid aortic valve (2002); modification of a vertical reduction aortoplasty by a distal external synthetic grafting for surgical treatment of aneurysms of the ascending aorta (2002); treatment of a bullous emphysema of the lung by a conservative resection of bullae and a local application of a biological glue (2001); noted association between congenital diaphramatic defect with peritoneopericardial communication and congenital bicuspid aortic valve (2000); applied a staged treatment of the left subclavian steal syndrome and coronary artery disease by the left carotid-subclavian and coronary artery bypasses (1999); establishing that in patients with coronary artery disease, the causes of congestive heart failure in those with a mild to moderate reduction of the left ventricular ejection fraction were hypertension, myocardial infarction or ishemic insufficiency of the mitral valve, and in those with severe reduction of the left ventricular ejection fraction were left ventricular dysfunction alone, or in combination with ischemic mitral regurgitation (1999); repair of a pseudoaneurysm of the ascending aorta on a beating heart (1997); ligation of bilateral coronary-pulmonary artery fistulas on a beating heart (1996); internal repair of the coronary sinus (Valsalva) aneurysm (1996); grafting of the internal thoracic to coronary arteries without touching the atherosclerotic ascending aorta, on cardiopulmonary bypass with a beating, warm and vented heart and bradycardia induced by beta-blockers (1994); design of Olearchyk R Triple Ringed Cannula Spring Clip to secure vein grafts over blunted cannulas in coronary artery bypass surgery (1989); combined right femoral and iliac retroperitoneal surgical approach to remove retained intraaortic balloon device (1989); technique a side graft during replacement of the ascending aorta in proximal aortic dissection (1989); intro. of endarterectomy and external prosthetic grafting of ascending and transverse aorta under hypothermic circulatory arrest (1987); first to combine insertion of the inferior vena cava filter with a protected iliofemoral venous thrombectomy (Olearchyk's operation, 1986); pioneering promotion of grafting of diffusely diseased coronary arteries with the internal thoracic artery (1980-82) and of the left anterior descending coronary artery sys. during resection of cardiac aneurysms (1979-80); used an inflated Foley balloon catheter to control hemorrhage from cardiac wounds and to infuse fluids through it to replace blood loss before and during suture repair (1978); description of a combined treatment of advanced gastric carcinoma by resection and chemotherapy (1975); recognized that alcoholism and smoking were common habits of patients with stomach cancer (1975); demonstration of safety of simultaneous use of fluothane and curare as gen. anesthesia (1966); description of combined treatment of advanced testicular seminoma with chemotherapy, resection and radiotherapy (1961). Personal E-mail: asolearchyk@yahoo.com.

O'LEARY, DANIEL E., museum program director; m. Hilary Bassett. MBA in mktg and mgmt., U. Mich.; PhD in art hist., Princeton U. Exec. dir. Artrain, Ann Arbor, Mich.; asst. dir. Minn. Inst. Arts, 1988—93; dir. Portland Mus. Art, Maine, 1993—2008, dir. Winslow Homer Studio project Maine, 2008—. Office: Portland Mus Art Seven Congress Sq Portland ME 04101 Office Phone: 207-756-1102. Office Fax: 207-773-7324. E-mail: doleary@portlandmuseum.org.

O'LEARY, DENNIS SOPHIAN, accrediting body executive; b. Kansas City, Mo., Jan. 28, 1938; s. Theodore Morgan and Emily (Sophian) O'L.; m. Margaret Rose Wiedman, Mar. 29, 1980; children: Margaret Rose, Theodore Morgan. BA, Harvard U., 1960; MD, Cornell U., 1964. Diplomate Am. Bd. Internal Medicine, Am. Bd. Hematology. Intern U. Minn. Hosp., Mpls., 1964-65, resident, 1965-66, Strong Meml. Hosp., Rochester, NY, 1966—67, chief resident and hematology fellow, 1967—68; asst. prof. medicine and pathology George Washington U. Med. Ctr., Washington, 1971-73, assoc. prof., 1973-80, prof. medicine, 1980-86, assoc. dean grad. med. edn., 1973-77, dean clin. affairs, 1977-86; pres. Joint Commn., Oakbrook Terrace, Ill., 1986—2007, pres. emeritus, 2008—. Med. dir. George Washington U. Hosp., 1974-85, v.p. Univ. Health Plan, 1977-85; pres. D.C. Med. Soc., 1983. Chmn. editl. bd. Med. Staff News, 1985-86; contbr. articles to profl. jours. Founding mem. Nat. Capital Area Health Care Coalition, Washington, 1982; trustee James S. Brady Found., Washington, 1982-87; bd. dirs. Nat. Quality Forum, 2001-07, bd. dirs. Nat. Patient Safety Found., 2006-, Nat. Adv. Coun. Agy. for Healthcare Rsch. and Quality, 2002-04., bd. dirs. inst. healthcare Improvement, 2008-, Defense Health Bd., 2008-, Maj. U.S. Army, 1968-71. Recipient Community Service award D.C. Med. Soc., 1981, Key to the City, Mayor of Kansas City, Mo., 1982. Master ACP; fellow Am. Coll. Physician Execs.; mem. AMA (Resolution commendation 1981, Disting. Svc. award 2005), Am. Hosp. Assn. (del. 1984-86, Resolution commendation 1981). Avocation: tennis. Home: 5624 Buena Vista Fairway KS 66205

O'LEARY, HAZEL ROLLINS, academic administrator, former United States Secretary of Energy, lawyer; b. Newport News, Va., May 17, 1937; d. Russell E. and Hazel (Palleman) Reid; m. John F. O'Leary, Apr. 23, 1980 (dec. Dec. 19, 1987); 1 child, Carl G. Rollins. BA, Fisk U., Nashville, 1959; JD, Rutgers U., Newark, 1966. Bar: NJ 1967, DC 1985; cert. fin. planner. V.p., gen. counsel O'Leary & Associates, Inc., Washington, 1981-89, pres. Chevy Chase, Md., 1997—; exec. v.p. corp. affairs No. States Power Co., Mpls., 1989-93; adminstr., dep. adminstr. econ. regulatory commn. US Dept. Energy, Washington, 1977—81, sec., 1993-97; COO Blaylock & Partners LLP, NYC, 1997—2002; pres. Fisk U., 2004—. Trustee AES Copr., ICF Kaiser, Inc. Trustee Morehouse Coll., Africare, Ctr. Democracy, Keystone Ctr. Mem. Phi Beta Kappa. Office: Fisk U 1000 17th Ave N Nashville TN 37208-3051 Office Phone: 615-329-8555.

O'LEARY, JOSEPH P., energy executive; b. Chgo., 1954; BBA in Acctg., U. Notre Dame, Ind., 1976. V.p. tower leasing 360 Degree Comm., 1998—99; v.p. fin. United Stationers Corp., 1999—2001; sr. v.p., CFO Integrys Energy Group, Inc., 2001—, sr. v.p., CFO Wis. Pub. Svc. (subs.), 2001—; sr. v.p., CFO, bd. dirs. Peoples Gas Light & Coke Co., Peoples Energy Corp., North Shore Gas Co., 2007—. Mem.: Am. Inst. CPA's, Inst. Mgmt. Accountants, Fin. Execs. Internat. Office: Integrys Energy Group Inc 130 E Randolph Dr Chicago IL 60601 Business E-Mail: jpo'leary@integrysgroup.com.*

O'LEARY, MARY ELIZABETH, retired nursing educator, college dean; b. Holyoke, Mass., Apr. 10, 1932; Diploma, Providence Hosp. Sch. Nursing, 1952; BS in Nursing, Boston Coll., 1954, MS in Nursing, 1958; JD, Western New England Coll., 1966; EdD, U. Mass., 1979. Assoc. degree nursing program, Springfield Tech. CC. Head, practical nursing program Holyoke Pub. Sch. System; dir. edn. Providence Hosp. Sch. Nursing; instr. Boston Coll. Sch. Nursing; clin. instr. med.-surg. nursing Holyoke Hosp. Sch. Nursing; educator Bur. Vocat. Edn., Mass.; staff nurse oper. rm. Mt. Sinai Hosp., NYC, Holyoke (Mass.) Hosp., Providence Hosp., Holyoke; med.-surg. staff nurse St. Elizabeth's Hosp, Brighton, Mass.; med. staff nurse Boston City Hosp.; chairperson Div. Nursing Springfield Tech. CC, Mass., 1969-80, dean Health/Human Svcs. Div. sch., 1980—97, dean emeritus, 1997—; writer, adminstr. practical nursing program City of Holyoke. Rep. Nat. Voc. Edn. Conf., Ohio. 1965, Iowa 1967, Health Issues Adv. Panel Commn. Med. Mal-Practice, 1971; lectr. in field. Author: (with others) Textbook of Practical Nursing, 1974; contbr. articles to profl. jours. Holyoke Health Planning Com., 1960-70, Holyoke Dept. Health Edn. Com. 1964-68, bd. dirs. Holyoke Mcpl. Home Hosp., 1971-72. Grantee Springfield Tech. C.C. and Coll. Our Lady of Elms, 1989-93, Springfield Tech. C.C.-DNS (LSI)-OTA, 1994-95. Mem. Med. Malpractice Tribunal (sec. 1977), Am. Assn. Law and Medicine, Nat. Assn. Higher Edn. Adminstrs., Sigma Theta Tau. Achievements include research in ultrasound, massage therapy. Home: 159 Homestead Ave Holyoke MA 01040-1033

O'LEARY, PATRICK J., manufacturing executive; BS in Acctg. and Law, U. Southampton, England. From acct. to ptnr. Boston (Mass.) Office Deloitte & Touche, 1978—88, ptnr. Boston (Mass.) Office, 1988—94; CFO, dir. Carlisle Plastics, Inc., 1994—96; v.p. fin., treasurer, CFO SPX Corp., Charlotte, NC, 1996—2004, exec. v.p., CFO, 2004—. Bd. dir. Pulte Homes Inc. Office: SPX 13515 Ballantyne Corporate Pl Charlotte NC 28277

O'LEARY, PAUL GERARD, retired insurance company executive; b. Boston, June 22, 1935; s. Gerard Paul and Marie Agnes (Hennessey) O'Leary; m. Elizabeth Jane Pollins, Oct. 14, 1961; children: Paul Hennessey, William Gerard, Mary Elizabeth Conroy, James Daniel. AB cum laude, Harvard U., 1956; MBA, U. Pa., 1958. Alumni dir. Wharton Grad. Sch., U. Pa., Phila., 1958-60; asst. to pres. Colonial Trust Co., NYC, 1960; asst. sec. Empire Trust Co., NYC, 1960-65; sr. investment analyst Blyth & Co., Inc., NYC, 1965-70; v.p. William D. Witter, Inc., NYC, 1970-76, also bd. dirs.; investment sr. v.p. Prudential Ins. Co. Am., Newark, 1977—2002. Instr fin Univ Pa, 1957—60. V.p. Prudential Found., Newark, 1986—96. 1st lt. artillery US Army Nat. Guard, 1953—60. Mem.: Ireland House NYU, NY Hist. Soc., Boston Latin Sch. Alumni Assn., NY Property Ins. Underwriting Assn. (mem. investment com. 1994—2002), Ins. Inst. Hwy. Safety (mem. investment com. 1983—2002), Assn. Ins. and Fin. Analysts (pres. 1973—74), Am. Nuc. Insurers (chmn. investment com. West Hartford, Conn. 1989—96), Inst. Chartered Fin. Analysts, Am. Irish Hist. Soc. (NYC), Hobbyists Unltd. (Ridgewood, NJ), Harvard Club (NYC), Upper Ridgewood Tennis Club, Harvard Club (NJ) (pres. 1983—84). Roman Catholic. Avocations: tennis, philately, cartography, history. Home: 719 Belmont Rd Ridgewood NJ 07450-1300 Personal E-mail: ploleary@yahoo.com.

O'LEARY, PRENTICE LEE, retired lawyer; b. LA, May 6, 1942; BA, UCLA, 1965, JD, 1968. Bar: Calif. 1969. Of counsel Sheppard, Mullin, Richter & Hampton, LA, 1974—2005; ret., 2005. Bd. dirs. Legal Aid Found. LA, 1987—93, Legal Aid Found. L.A., 2000—06. Mem. ABA (bus. bankruptcy com.), State Bar Calif., Los Angles County Bar Assn. (chmn. bankruptcy com., chmn. comml. law and bankrupt sect. 1985-86), Am. Coll. Bankruptcy Profls., Order of Coif. Office: Sheppard Mullin Richter & Hampton 333 S Hope St Fl 48 Los Angeles CA 90071-1406 Home Phone: 310-458-1357; Office Phone: 213-359-9094. E-mail: prenticeo@gmail.com.

O'LEARY, ROBERT WILLIAM, design educator, lighting designer; MFA in Scene Design, Va. Commonwealth U., Richmond, 2004. Head scenic and lighting design Fla. Sch. Arts, Palatka, 2004—. Mem.: Southeastern Theatre Conf. Office: Fla Sch Arts 5001 Saint Johns Ave Palatka FL 32177 Business E-Mail: robertoleary@sjrcc.edu.

O'LEARY, THOMAS MICHAEL, lawyer; b. NYC, Aug. 16, 1948; s. James and Julia Ann (Connolly) O'L.; m. Luise Ann Williams, Jan. 13, 1978; 1 child, Richard Meridith. BA, CUNY, 1974; JD, Seattle U., 1977. Bar: Wash. 1977, U.S. Ct. Mil. Appeals 1978, U.S. Ct. Appeals (9th cir.), U.S. Supreme Ct. 1983. Dep. pros. atty. Pierce County, Tacoma, 1978; commd. 1st lt. U.S. Army, 1978, advanced through grades to capt., 1978; chief trial counsel Office of Staff Judge Adv., Ft. Polk, La., 1978-79, trial def. counsel, trial def. svc., 1979-81; chief legal advisor Office Insp. Gen., Heidelberg, Fed. Republic of Germany, 1981-82; sr. def. counsel Trial Def. Svc., Giessen, Fed. Republic of Germany, 1982-84; asst. chief adminstrv. law U.S. Army Armor Ctr., Ft. Knox, Ky., 1984-85, chief adminstrv. law, 1985, chief legal asst., 1985-86; ret. U.S. Army, 1996; sr. trial atty. Immigration and naturalization Svc., Phoenix, 1987; sector counsel, spl. asst. U.S. atty., U.S. Border Patrol, Tucson, 1987-90; enforcement counsel U.S. Immigration and Naturalization Svc., Tucson, 1990-95, asst. dist. counsel Phoenix litigation, 1995-97. Apptd. U.S. Immigration Judge, U.S. Immigration Ct., Imperial, Calif., 1997-2000, apptd. sr. U.S. Immigration Judge, Tucson, 2000—; adj. prof. Embry-Riddle Aero. U., Tucson, 2002- Decorated Purple Heart, Cross of Gallantry (Vietnam). Mem. Judge Advs Assn., Wash. State Bar Assn., Order Ky. Cols. (commd. col. 1985). Home: 9080 E 25th St Tucson AZ 85710-8675 Office: US Immigration Ct 160 N Stone Ave Rm 300 Tucson AZ 85701 Office Phone: 520-670-5212. Business E-Mail: thomas.o'leary@usdoj.gov.

OLEJNICZAK, BERNARD CHARLES, education educator; b. Green Bay, Wis., Aug. 23, 1930; s. Bernard Clement and Helen Josephine (LeClair) Olejniczak; m. Mary Jean Barrett-Terry, Oct. 13, 1956 (div. Dec. 1979); children: Ann Marie, Mary Rose, Patrick James, Thomas Bernard; m. Margaret Jean Olson, Sept. 19, 1980. BA in Philosophy, St. Norbert Coll., 1953; MA in Counseling, U. Wis., 1966. Tchr. in Latin, French and journalism Pulaski H.S., Wis., 1957—71; adminstr. Pulaski Elem. Schs., 1971—92; ednl. cons., 1993—96; tech. lectr. U. Wis., Oshkosh, 1996—2007. Chmn. curriculum U. Wis. Learning in Retirement, 1997, 2004—, Winnebago Co. Literacy Control Bd., 2005—09. Editor (newsletter): Polish Heritage, 1993—2006, Wisconsin Counselor, 1995—2005. Pres. Village Bd., Pulaski, 1965—70; v.p. Bd. Edn., Pulaski, 1992—96; sec. Pulaski C. of C., 1958—64; pres. Brown County Libr. Bd., Green Bay, Wis., 1985—96, Nicolet Fed. Libr., Green Bay, Wis., 1987—92. Recipient Profl. Writing award, Wis. Counselors Assn., 1999; named Trustee of Yr., Wis. Libr. Assn., 1997. Mem.: Lions Club (newsletter editor, sec. 1993—2004), Phi Delta Kappa. Democrat. Roman Catholic. Avocations: reading, computers. Home: 1625 Graber St Oshkosh WI 54901 Business E-Mail: olejnicz@uwosh.edu.

OLEKSY, JOZEF, former Prime Minister of Poland; b. Nowy Sacz, Poland, June 22, 1946; married; 2 children. B, Warsaw Sch. Econs., 1969, PhD in Econs., 1977. Sci. worker Warsaw Sch. Econs., 1969—78; min., mem. Coun. Mins., Warsaw, 1989; dep. to Sejm, 1989—2005; prim. min. Govt. of Poland, 1995—97; chmn. Social-Democratic Party, Warsaw, 1996—97, 2004—05; minister Internal. Affairs, 2004. Spkr. Parliament, 1993-95, 2004-05; chmn. European Commmn. of the Sejm; vice prime minister, 2004; min. of domestic affairs, 2004. Contbr. articles to profl. jours. Avocations: walking, history, futurology, global challenges. Office: ul Rozbrat 44 A 00-419 Warsaw Poland

OLENCHAK, FRANK RICHARD, retired music educator, musician; b. Scranton, Pa., Aug. 5, 1928; s. Francis Richard and Helen Anita Olenchak; m. Patricia Maye Ingram, June 15, 1949; children: Francis Richard III, Rebecca Lynn, Jeffrey Stuart. MusB, James Madison U., 1950; MEd, Pa. State U., 1957; CASE, postgrad., Johns Hopkins U., 1965; PhD in Music: Music Edn., U. Mich., 1977. Cert. music tchr. Md., Va. Supr. of music, band dir. Galax Pub. Schs., Va., 1950—54; dir. h.s. band Harford County Schs., Bel Air, Md., 1954—58, Balt. City Schs., 1958—61; tchr. elem. instrumental music Balt. County Schs., Towson, Md., 1961—66; emeritus prof. edn. and profl. devel. We. Mich. U., Kalamazoo, 1966—84; adj. coord. student tchg. Ea. Mich. U., Ypsilanti, 1984—85; dir., CEO Music on the Move of Mich., Ann Arbor, 1985—87; chair dept. of music Allen U., Columbia, SC, 1989—2005, ret., 2005; CEO, record prodr. Myrtle Records, Columbia, 1997—. Postdoctoral rschr. Columbia U., 1981; vis. scholar U. Mich., Ann Arbor, 1981—82. Author: Exploratory Music, (periodical) The Instructor, 1968; editor: (newsletter) Michigan Association of Teacher Educators, (books) SchoolMATES, 3 vols., 1981, 1982, The Instructor, 1968. Choir dir. Trinity Luth. Ch., Columbia, 1999—2002; dir. of music 3d Luth. Ch., Balt., 1960—62. Recipient doctoral tchg. fellowship, U. of Mich., 1969—70, acad. scholarship, Shenandoah Conservatory of Music, 1947. Mem.: Am. Fedn. Musicians, Assn. Tchr. Educators (pres., comms. chair 1978—83, Meritorious Svc. award 1980), Phi Delta Kappa (pres. 1978—87, 1991—94, Disting. Svc. Key 1985). Achievements include creating NUMCOMPO, a system for teaching musical notation to children with no prior knowledge of music. Avocations: sports, bridge, checkers, record collecting, travel. Personal E-mail: myrtrec@hotmail.com.

OLENDER, JACK HARVEY, lawyer; b. McKeesport, Pa., Sept. 8, 1935; m. Lovell Olender. BA summa cum laude, U. Pitts., 1957, JD, 1960; LLM, George Washington U., 1961. Bar: DC 1961, US Supreme Ct. 1965, Md. 1966, Pa. 1985; diplomate Am. Bd. Trial Advocates. Pvt. practice, Washington, 1961-79; prin. Jack H. Olender & Assocs., P.C., Washington, 1979—. Contbr. articles to profl. jours. Active World Peace through Law, Washington; with Nat. Capital Area Boys Scout America. Named to Hall of Fame Nat. Assn. Black Women Attys., 1987, DC Hall of Fame, 2000, Washington Bar Assn. Hall of Fame, 2000, Nat. Bar. Assn. Hall of Fame, 2005, Attys. of Yr., Boy Scout, 2009; recipient Presdl. award Nat. Bar Assn., 1996, 2000, 02, 04, Advocate for Justice award Nat. Bar Assn., 2000, Internat. B'nai B'rith Pursuit of Justice award, 2001, named one of 30 Best Lawyers in Washington, Washingtonian survey mag., 2005, Champion Justice award Trial Lawyers Assn., DC, 2004, Charles Hamilton Houston medallian award Washington Bar Assn., 2005, 90 Greatest Washington Lawyers, Legal Times Atty., 2009,Attys. of Yr. Good Scout award Boy Scouts America Nat. Capital Area Divsn., 2009. Fellow Am. Coll. Trial Lawyers, Internat. Acad. Trial Lawyers and Inner Cir. Advs.; mem. Trial Lawyers Assn. Met. Washington (pres. 1969-1970); Am. Coll. Legal Medicine; ATLA, Nat. Bar Assn. (adv. for justice 2000), Am. Bd. Profl. Liability Attys. (sec. 1989—), Trial Lawyers Pub. Justice (bd. dirs.), Internat. Assn. Jewish

Lawyers and Jurists (bd. dirs.), Bar Assn. DC (pres. 1999-2000). Office: Jack H Olender & Assocs PC 888 17th St NW Fl 4 Washington DC 20006-3939 Office Phone: 202-879-7777. Business E-Mail: jhop.c@olender.com.

OLENDORF, WILLIAM CARR, JR., small business owner; b. Albany, NY, Oct. 3, 1945; s. William Carr Sr. and Mary Zilpha (Gillies) O.; m. Barbara Kay Cowan, Aug. 14, 1966; children: Mark, Julie, Jennifer. Student, Columbia Coll., 1964—65, So. Ill. U., 1965—66. Prodn. asst. Sta. WTTW-TV, Chgo., 1962-64; radio announcer Sta. WERX, Wyoming, Mich., 1967-68; sales rep. Sta. WCFL, Chgo., 1968-70, Sta. WJJD-AM & FM, Chgo., 1970-72; v.p. Promotion Network, Chgo., 1972-74; account exec. AVCO-TV, Chgo., 1974-76, Peters, Griffin & Woodward, Chgo., 1976-82, Petry TV, Chgo., 1982-83; owner, pres. Point South KOA Resort, Yemassee, S.C., 1983—. Commr. Point South Pub. Svc. Dist., 1987-88, Lowcountry & Resort Island Tourism Commn., 1994—; mem. tourism tax adv. bd. Jasper County, S.C., 1985—; chmn. Jasper County Hist. Preservation Commn., S.C., 1994-99; trustee S.C. Battleground Preservation Trust, Inc., 1994-98, 2003-2004; mem. Low Country Revolutionary War Trail Commn. Recipient SC Honor award for Historic Preservation, Palmetto Trust for Historic Preservation, SC Dept. Archives and History, 1997, SC Amb. for Econ. Devel. award, 2007. Mem. Nat. Campground Owners Assn. (campground nat. adv. bd. 1989-93, Take Pride in Am. award 1992), Kampground Owners Assn. (S.C. regiona pres. 1994-97, Award of Merit 1990), S.C. Campground Assn. (pres. 1987-88), Point South Mchts. Assn. (pres. 1990—), Jasper County Hist. Soc., Jasper County C. of C. (bd. dirs. 2001-2003), Beaufort Yacht and Sailing Club. Republican. Episcopalian. Avocations: amateur radio operator, sailing. Home and Office: 14 Campground Rd Yemassee SC 29945-1760

OLES, DOUGLAS STUART, lawyer; b. Seattle, Nov. 10, 1954; s. Stuart G. and Ilse (Hanewald) O.; m. Alida Ou Li, Sept. 27, 1998. AB in History with honors and distinction, Stanford U., 1976; JD with honors, U. Wash., 1979. Bar: Wash. 1979, U.S. Dist. Ct. (we. dist.) Wash. 1979, U.S. Dist. Ct.(w.d.wa). Law clk. to Hon. Barbar Rothstein, Seattle, 1979-81; assoc. Oles, Morrison, Rinker, Stanislaw & Ashbaugh, Seattle, 1981-87; ptnr. Oles, Morrison, Rinker & Baker LLP, Seattle, 1988—. Exec. editor U. Wash. Law Rev., 1978-79; chief editor: The Constrn. Lawyer, ABA, 1997-2000. Mem. Diocese Olympia Council, Western Wash., 1985-89, canon com. chair, 1983- Fellow Am. Bar Found., Am. Coll. Constrn. Lawyers; mem. ABA (constrn. forum chair internat. constrn. divsn. 1993-97, nat. chair 2005-06), Internat. Bar Assn., Wash. State Bar Assn., Seattle-King County Bar Assn., Am. Arbitration Assn. (panel arbitrators), Rainier Club (pres. 2007—), Phi Beta Kappa, JAMS(panel neutral) Episcopalian. Avocations: classical archaeology, German language. Personal E-mail: oles@oles.com.

OLES, STUART GREGORY, lawyer; b. Seattle, Dec. 15, 1924; s. Floyd and Helen Louise (La Violette) O.; m. Ilse Hanewald, Feb. 12, 1954; children: Douglas, Karl, Stephen. BS magna cum laude, U. Wash., 1947, JD, 1948. Bar: Wash., 1949, US Supreme Ct. 1960. Dep. pros. atty. King County, Wash., 1949, chief civil dept., 1949—50; gen. practice law Seattle, 1950—95; sr. ptnr. firm Oles, Morrison & Rinker and predecessor, 1955—90, of counsel, 1991—95. Author: A View From the Rock, 1994, On Behalf of My Clients--A Lawyer's Life, 1998. Chmn. Seattle Cmty. Concert Assn., 1955; pres. Friends Seattle Pub. Libr., 1956; mem. Wash. pub. Disclosure Commn., 1973-75; trustee Ch. Divinity Sch. of Pacific, Berkeley, Calif., 1974-75; mem. bd. curators Wash. State Hist. Soc., 1983; former mem. Seattle Symphony Bd.; pres. King County Ct. House Rep. Club, 1950, U. Wash. Young Rep. Club, 1947; Wash. conv. floor leader Taft, 1952, Goldwater, 1964; Wash. chmn. Citizens for Goldwater, 1964; chmn. King County Rep. convs., 1966, 68, 76, 84, 88, 90, 92, 96, Wash. State Rep. Conv., 1980. Served with USMCR, 1943-45. Mem. ABA (past regional vice-chmn. pub. contract law sect.), Wash. Bar Assn., Order of Coif, Am. Legion, Am. Highland Cattle Assn. (v.p. and dir.), Phi Beta Kappa, Phi Alpha Delta. Home: 22715 SE 43rd Ct Issaquah WA 98029-5200 also: Cape St Mary Rnch Lopez Island WA 98261 also: RR 2 Pahoa HI 96778-9802

OLESEN, ROBERT LIND OLE, electrical engineer; s. Henning Lind and Birte Olesen; m. Janet Marie Reilly, Nov. 5, 1994; children: Peter Abner, Hannah Marie. BSEE, U. Mass., Amherst, Mass., 1980; MSEE, Poly. U., Bklyn., 1988; MBA with honors, Hofstra U., Hempstead, NY, 2006. Lic. ham radio operator FCC, 2003. Engr. Charles Stark Draper Lab., Boston, 1980—82, TRW Corp., San Jose, Calif., 1982—84; project engr. Eaton AIL Corp., Commack, NY, 1984—88; prin. engr. Mission Scis., Commack, NY, 1988—90, APS Corp., Commack, NY, 1990—91; staff scientist Target Sys. Tech. Corp., Stony Brook, NY, 1991—99; sr. mgr. InterDigital Comm. Corp., King of Prussia, Pa., 1999—. Adj. prof. Suffolk C.C., Selden, NY, 1995—96. Contbr. articles to profl. jours. Recipient CTO Patent award, InterDigital Comm. Corp., 2005. Mem.: IEEE, Am. Soc. Engring. Mgmt., Internat. Soc. Photographers (award 2006). Achievements include patents for wireless communications support for development of training programs. Avocations: photography, sailing, web site development. Home: 3 Country Club Dr Huntington NY 11743 Office: InterDigital Communications Corporation 2 Huntington Quadrangle Melville NY 11747 Personal E-mail: rolesen@mac.com.

OLESHKO, VLADIMIR P., physical chemist, nanoscience researcher; s. Pavel F. and Olesja I. Oleshko; m. Irina N. Zezjulina, Dec. 16, 1978; children: Alexei V., Marina V. BS, Moscow State U., 1974, MS with honors, 1976, PhD, 1982. Invited scientist-rsch. asst. U. Antwerp, Belgium, 1993—99; postdoc. rsch. assoc. Ariz. State U., Tempe, 1999—2000; sr. scientist Polaroid, Waltham, Mass., 2000—01; sr. rsch. scientist U. Va., Charlottesville, 2002—06; engr. Intel, Phoenix, 2006—08; sr. analytical chemist Sion Power, Tucson, 2008—; adj. rsch. prof., dept. materials sci. & engring. U. Ariz., Tucson. Contbr. articles to profl. jours., chapters to books. Recipient Traveling Poster Exhibit award, Microscopy Soc. America, 2003, 2nd Pl. award, Internat. Metallographic Soc., 2005, Tech. Support awards, Intel, 2006—07; Rsch. fellowship, Belgian Prime Min., 1995—96, Union Carbide, Dow Chem., 1999—2000, Rsch. grant, Russian Found. Basic Rsch., 1995—96, Divsn. Materials Sci. & Engring., Office Sci., US Dept. Energy, 2002—06. Mem.: Materials Rsch. Soc., Belgian Soc. Microscopy, European Microanalysis Soc., Soc. Imaging Sci. and Tech., Microscopy Soc. America. Achievements include invention of technique for detection of color coupler microdispersion drop shapes and sizes in photographic materials; patents pending for integrated method to analyze crystal deposit; research in situ real-time environmental TEM of gas phase Ziegler-Natta catalytic polymerization of propylene; electronic, dielectric and optical properties of individual composite tabular AgX emulsion microcrystals using cryo-EELS and LMTO-ASA techniques; physical properties of metastable and equilibrium precipitates using valence electron energy-loss spectroscopy and energy-filtering TEM; size confinement effects on electronic and optical properties of silver halide nanocrystals as probed by cryo-EFTEM and EELS; non-aggregated Pd nanoparticles deposited onto catalytic supports; aperiodic core structures of Pd and Pt giant clusters chemically stabilized with diphenyl phosphide ligands; metal particle growth during glucose hydrogenation over Ru/SiO_2 evaluated by X-ray absorption spectroscopy and electron microscopy. Office: Sion Power 2900 E Elvira Rd Tucson AZ 85756-7129 Home Phone: 480-299-1730; Office Phone: 520-799-7518. Office Fax: 520-799-7501. Personal E-mail: vladimiroleshko@yahoo.com. Business E-Mail: voleshko@sionpower.com.

OLESKO, KATHRYN MARY, historian; AB, MA, PhD, Cornell U., Ithaca, NY. Faculty mem. Clarkson U., Potsdam, NY, 1980—81, Georgetown U., Washington, 1981—; vis. faculty mem. Cornell U., Ithaca, NY, 1983, Princeton U., NJ, 1988. Dir., program sci., tech. & internat. affairs Georgetown U., Washington, 1993—97, co-dir., Ctr. Environment, 1996—97, dir., MA in German and European studies program, 2004—06, dir., program sci., tech., & internat. affairs, 2006—07. Contbr. articles to profl. jours. Founding mem. Children Kibera, Washington, 2007. Recipient Constantine E. McGuire Outstanding Svc. award, Edmund A. Walsh Sch. Fgn. Svc., Georgetown U., 1997, Vicennial medal, Georgetown U., 2001; grantee, 1984, 1986, 1988, 1990—2000; fellow, Nat. Endowment Humanities, 1984—85, 1991—93, NSF, 1984—85, 1987, 1991—92; Vis. scholar, Max-Planck-Inst. Wissenschaftsgeschichte, 1998, 2008. Fellow: AAAS; mem.: Brit. Soc. History Sci., Am. Hist. Assn., Soc. History Tech., History Sci. Soc. Office: Georgetown Univ Dept History Washington DC 20057-1035 Business E-Mail: oleskok@georgetown.edu.

OLEY, JODI DYAN, lawyer; d. Lori E. Britton; m. James David Oley, Sept. 18, 2004. BA in Internat. Politics, Pa. State U., State College, 2001; JD, Dickinson Sch. Law, Carlisle, Pa., 2004. Bar: Pa. 2004, US Dist. Ct. (ea. dist.) Pa. 2004, US Dist. (mid. dist.) Pa. 2004, NJ 2005, US Dist. Ct. NJ 2005, US Supreme Ct. 2007. Assoc. Daller Greenberg & Dietrich, LLC, Conshohocken, Pa., 2004—06, Eckert Seamans Cherin & Mellot, LLC, Phila., 2006—. Mem.: Def. Rsch. Inst., Am. Bar Assn., Phila. Bar Assn., Pa. Bar Assn. Office: Eckert Seamans Cherin & Mellot LLC Two Liberty Pl 50 South 16th St Philadelphia PA 19102 Office Fax: 215-851-8383. Personal E-mail: joley@eckertseamans.com.

OLGIN, GREGORY B., pharmacy technician, educator; s. Rose M. Malloy. BA in Biology, U. Toledo, Ohio, 2004. Lifeguard Lorain County Family YMCA, Ohio, 1990—2003; adj. faculty Lorain County CC, Elyria, Ohio, 2004—; pharmacy technician Rite Aid Ohio, Sheffield Lake, 2005—. Instr. ARC, Elyria, 1982—; scout leader Heart Ohio Coun. BSA, Sheffield Lake, 1988—, scoutreach commr., 1998—2008; mem. Sheffield Lake Civic Coun., 2004—. Named Man of Yr., Sheffield Lake Civic Coun., 2007. Mem.: United Food and Comml. Workers. Avocations: swimming, camping, hiking, reading. Office Fax: 440-949-6368.

OLIAN, JOANNE CONSTANCE, curator, art historian; b. NYC; d. Richard Edward and Dorothy (Singer) Wahrman; m. Howard Olian; children: Jane Wendy, Patricia Ann; m. Gerald Weintraub; 1 child, Amy Rose Olian Weintraub. Student, Syracuse U.; BA, Hofstra U., 1969; MA, NYU Inst. Fine Arts, 1972. Grad. internship Met. Mus., NYC, 1973; asst. curator Mus. City of N.Y., 1974, curator costume collection, 1975—91; cons. curator Costume Collection, 1992—95, curator emeritus, 1995—. Lectr. Parsons Sch. Design; vis. lectr. Musée des Arts Decoratifs, Paris, summers, 1983—85; co-curator Art and Fashion Nassau County Mus. Art, 2006, assoc. trustee, 2007—; curator Rare Bird of Fashion, Nassau County Mus. Art, 2008. Author: The House of Worth: The Gilded Age, 1860-1918, 1982; editor: Authentic French Fashions of the Twenties, 1990, Everyday Fashions of the Forties, 1992, Children's Fashions from Mode Illustrée 1860-1914, 1994, Wedding Fashions, 1862-1912, 1994, Everyday Fashions, 1909-1920, 1995, La Mode Illustrée, 1997, Victorian and Edwardian Fashions, 1998, 80 Godey's Full-Color Fashions Plates, 1838-1880, 1998, Full-Color Victorian Fashion, 1870-1893, 1999, Everyday Fashions of the Sixties, 1999, Parisian Fashions of the Teens, 2002, Everyday Fashions of the Fifties, 2002, Children's Fashions, 1900-1950, 2003; contbr. articles to profl. jours., chpts. to books Assoc. trustee Nassau County Mus. Art, 2007—; mem. Landmarks Commn. Village of Sands Pt., NY, 1990—2002. Mem. Internat. Coun. Mus. (costume com.), Costume Soc. Am. (dir. 1976-79, 83-86), Fashion Group (bd. dirs. 1985-86), Centre Internat. d'Etude des Textiles Anciens, Cosmopolitan Club N.Y.C Home and Office: 2 Shepherds Ln Sands Point NY 11050 Personal E-mail: joanneolian1@aol.com.

OLIAN, JUDY D., dean, management educator; b. Australia; BS in Psychology, Hebrew U., 1974; MS in Indsl. Rels., U. Wis., 1977, PhD in Indsl. Rels., 1980. Lectr. to full prof. mgmt. and orgn. Robert H. Smith Sch. Bus., U. Md., 1979—2000, sr. assoc. dean, 1999—2000; fellow Am. Coun. Edn. Fellow to pres. U. Md., 1990—91, special asst. to pres., 1991—92, founder, dir. IBM-TQ Project, 1991—92; dean, prof. mgmt. Smeal Coll. Bus., Pa. State U., 2000—; dean UCLA Anderson Sch. Mgmt., 2006—. Exec. com. Personnel and Human Resources divsn. Acad. Mgmt., 1984—87, 1991—94; exec. com. bd. dirs. Assn. to Advance Collegiate Sch. Bus., 2000—01. Author: (syndicated weekly column) About Business; past mem. editl. bd.: Jour. Quality and Mgmt., Acad. Mgmt. Review. Bd. dirs. The Second Mile, Penn State Found. Recipient award for curriculum innovation, Md. Assn. for Higher Edn., 1996. Office: Office of Dean UCLA School Mgmt F 407 Box 951481 Los Angeles CA 90095 Office Phone: 310-825-7982. E-mail: judy.olian@anderson.ucla.edu.*

OLIAN, ROBERT MARTIN, lawyer; b. Cleve., June 14, 1953; s. Robert Meade and Doris Isa (Hessing) Olian; m. Terri Ellen Ruther, Aug. 10, 1980; children: Andrew Zachary, Alix Michelle, Joshua Brett. AB, Harvard U., 1973, JD, 1977, M in Pub. Policy, 1977. Bar: Ill. 1977, U.S. Dist. Ct. (no. dist.) Ill., U.S. Ct. Appeals (7th cir.) 1983, U.S. Dist. Ct. (no. dist. trial bar) Ill. 1992, U.S. Dist. Ct. (we. dist.) Mich. 1994, U.S. Dist. Ct. (cen. dist.) Ill. 2004. Assoc. Sidley & Austin, Chgo., 1977-84; ptnr. Sidley Austin LLP, Chgo., 1985—. Editor: (book) Illinois Environmental Law Handbook, 1988, 1997. Panel atty. Chgo. Vol. Legal Svcs., 1983—; bd. dirs. Friends IDF, 2003—07; trustee North Shore Congregation Israel, 1990—, sec., 1995—96, v.p., 1996—2003, first v.p., 2004—05, pres., 2005—09; mem. regional strategic/mktg. com. Alexian Bros. Ill., Inc., Elk Grove, 1985—88; mem. dean's alumni leadership coun. Harvard Kennedy Sch., 2003—. Mem.: ABA, Chgo. Bar Assn., Harvard Club (Chgo.), Std. Club. Jewish. Home: 85 Oakmont Rd Highland Park IL 60035-4111 Office: Sidley Austin LLP One S Dearborn # 2800 Chicago IL 60603-2302 Home Phone: 847-432-5662; Office Phone: 312-853-7208. Business E-Mail: rolian@sidley.com.

OLICK, PHILIP STEWART, lawyer; b. NYC, Oct. 2, 1936; s. Jack and Anita (Babsky) O.; m. Alice D. Chait, Mar. 25, 1961; children: Jonathan A., Jeffrey K., Diana M. BA, Columbia U., 1957; LLB, NYU, 1960. Bar: N.Y. 1961, Mo. 1966. Ptnr. Benjamin, Galton, Robbins & Flato, NYC, 1961-65; gen. counsel, v.p., sec. Nat. Bellas Hess, Inc., Kansas City, Mo., 1965-69, dir., 1970-76; ptnr. Burke & Burke, NYC, 1970-73, Townley & Updike, 1973-89, Moses & Singer, 1989—. Bd. arbitrators N.Y. Stock Exch. Bd. dirs. Univ. Glee Club NYC, pres. 2005-07; bd. dirs. Young Peoples Chorus NYC. With AUS, 1960-61. Mem. Assn. of Bar of City of N.Y., Univ. Club (N.Y.C.), Columbia Club. Home: 860 5th Ave 19J New York NY 10065-5856 also: 4 Rosebud Ln East Quogue NY 11942-3627 Office: The Chrysler Bldg 405 Lexington Ave New York NY 10174-1299 Office Phone: 212-554-7891. E-mail: polick@mosessinger.com.

OLIKER, DAVID WILLIAM, healthcare management administrator; b. Elkins, W.Va., Mar. 29, 1948; married; 3 children. BA in Sociology and Anthropology, East Carolina U., 1970; MA in Social Anthropology, Am. U., 1973; Cert. in Healthcare Adminstrn., George Washington U., 1977. Health svcs. specialist United Mine Workers Am. Health and Retirement Funds, 1976-78; health planner Health Sys. Agy. Western Md., Cumberland, 1978-79; ops. mgr. Md.-Individual Practice Assn., Inc., Rockville, 1979-81; project dir. N.Y. Health Maintenance Plan, Inc., NYC, 1981-82; pres., CEO MVP Health Plan, Schenectady, NY, 1982—, Preferred Care (merger with MVP Health Plan), Rochester, NY, 2005—. Mem. bd. dir. Schenectady 2000, Albany Colonie Regional C. of C., Twin Rivers Boy Scout Coun. Mem. APHA, Am. Assn. Health Plans, N.Y. State HMO Conf. (bd. dirs.), Nat. Managed Care Inc. (chmn.). Office: MVP Health Plan PO Box 2207 Schenectady NY 12301-2207 also: Preferred Care 259 Monroe Ave Rochester NY 14607*

OLIKER, VLADIMIR, mathematician, educator; b. Ulianovsk, Russia, Oct. 7, 1945; came to U.S. 1975, naturalized 1980; s. Yosef and Sonia (Bakelman) Oliker; m. Elena Matis, Mar. 20, 1969; children: Olga, Aviva, Yosef Matis. MS, Leningrad U., Russia, 1967; PhD, Leningrad U., 1971. Sr. researcher Hydrometeorological Inst., Leningrad, Russia, 1970-72; group leader Dept. Transportation, 1972-74; vis. prof. Temple U., Phila., 1975-77; assoc. prof. to prof. U. Iowa, Iowa City, 1977-80, 80-84; prof. math. Emory U., Atlanta, 1984—. Vis. mem. Math Scis. Research Inst., Berkeley, Calif., 1983; vis. prof. U. Florence, Italy, 1983, Technische U., Berlin, 1982, U. Heidelberg, Fed. Republic Germany, 1981 Contbr. articles to profl. jours. Jewish. Home: 1565 Adelia Pl NE Atlanta GA 30329-3805 Office: Emory U Dept Math And Computer Sci Atlanta GA 30322-0001 Business E-Mail: oliker@mathcs.emory.edu.

OLIMPIO, SUZANNE M., psychologist; b. Kearny, NJ, May 10, 1963; d. John and Arlene Onnembo; m. Edward Olimpio; children: Alyssa, Alexander. BA, Villanova U., Pa.; MA in Counseling, Rider Coll.; diploma in Sch. Psychology, Jersey City U., NJ; cert. in Supr., Seton Hall U. Psychologist Monteville (N.J.) Bd. Edn., 1992—95; dir. Spl. Edn. Boonton (N.J.) Bd. Edn., 1995—97; psychologist Mi Arlington (N.J.) Bd. Edn., 2001—. Coach Girls Travel Soccer, Montville, 2004—. Mem.: N.J. Sch. Psychology Assn., Nat. Assn. Sch. Psychologists, Morris County (N.J.) Psychol. Assn. (v.p. 1992—95), Valhalla Civic Assn. (v.p. 2003—05, bd. dirs. 2001—03). Home: 5 Patrick Ct Boonton NJ 07005-9051

OLIN, MARILYN, secondary school educator; b. Rochester, NY; BA in English, Nazareth Coll. Rochester, 1965; MS in English Edn., SUNY, Brockport, 1971. Nat. bd. cert. tchr. 1999. Tchr. Rochester Diocese Cath. Schs., 1965—68, Rochester Pub. Schs., 1968—71, Duval County (Fla.) Pub. Schs., 1972—, Paxon Sch. for Advanced Studies, Jacksonville, Fla., 1996—. Mem.: Nat. Forensic League, Nat. Bd. for Profl. Tchg. Stds. Office: Paxon Sch for Advanced Studies 3239 Norman E Thagard Blvd Jacksonville FL 32254 Office Phone: 904-693-7583 ext 161.

OLIN, WILLIAM HAROLD, orthodontist, educator; b. Menominee, Mich., Mar. 7, 1924; s. Harold H. and Lillian (Hallgren) Olin; m. Bertha Spitters, May 6, 1950; children: William Harold, Paul Scott, Jon Edward. DDS, Marquette U., 1947; MS, U. Iowa, 1948. Asst. prof. orthodontics Univ. Hosps., U. Iowa, Iowa City, 1948, assoc. prof., 1963-70, prof., 1970-93, prof. emeritus, 1995—. Chmn. bd. dirs. Hills Bank. Author: (book) Cleft Lip and Palate Rehabilitation, 1960; contbr. articles to profl. jours. Fund raiser, participant Ops. Smile. Served to capt. US Army, 1952—54. Mem.: Am. Cancer Soc. (peer reviewed com. mem. 2004, dist. Iowa alumni 2009), Hope Lodge (adv. bd. mem. 2004, cancer bd. 2009), Boy Scout Coun., Am. Acad. Sports Dentistry (bd. dirs., sec./treas. 1989—95), Am. Cleft Palate Assn. (pres. 1970), Iowa Orthodontic Soc. (pres. 1959), Midwest Orthodontic Soc. (pres. 1968—69), Angle Orthodontic Soc. Midwest (pres. 1982), Univ. Athletic Club (bd. dirs.), Rotary (pres. Iowa City). Republican. Methodist. Avocations: collecting political memorabilia, music box collecting, sports, travel, politics, coin collecting/numismatics. Home: 426 Mahaska Dr Iowa City IA 52246-1610 Personal E-mail: w.olin@mchsi.com.

OLINGER, CHAUNCEY GREENE, JR., investment company executive, editorial consultant; b. Long Beach, Calif., Jan. 16, 1933; s. Chauncey Greene and Cora Blount (Urquhart) O.; m. Carla R. Dragan, May 30, 1981. BA in Philosophy with honors, U. Va., Charlottesville, 1955; MA, Columbia U., NY, 1971. Cert. fin. planner Cert. Fin. Planning Bd. Standards. Coadjutant in philosophy Rutgers U., New Brunswick, NJ, 1968—72; rep. NY World Federalists, USA, NYC, 1970; dir. subcom. U.S. sec. of state adv. com. Dept. of State, Washington, 1972; editl. cons. Columbia U., NYC, 1973—82; editor, pres. Met. Rsch. Co., NYC, 1982—91; investment exec. First Albany, NYC, 1991—92, Janney Montgomery Scott LLC, NYC, 1992—2009. Sec. univ. seminar Columbia U., NYC, 1968—72, mem. increase corp. philanthrophic giving com., 1980—83, founder, co-chmn. u. seminar, 1998—2004, chmn. u. seminar, 2005—. Editor: World Enough, (Margaret Mead and Ken Heyman), 1975, A Celebration of Thanksgiving For the Life of I. I. Rabi, 1991, Columbia and the City: The University's Commitment to New York City, 1993, Courtney C. Brown: In Memory, 1995; author: New York City: An Economic Resource Profile, 1989, The I.I. Rabi Memorial Room, 1996; contbr. articles to profl. pubs. Pres. Fellowship of Young Churchmen, Episcopal Diocese of So. Va., 1950-52; trustee Cathedral Ch. St. John the Divine, 1988; nat. chmn. Coalition to Stop SST Environmental Damage, NY, 1975-78; NGO rep. Friends of Earth at UN, 1977-1986; pub. mem. human rights in rsch. com. NY Hosp.-Cornell Med. Ctr., 1975-80; pres. grad. faculty alumni Columbia U., NY, 1977-81, pres. student coun.Columbia U., NY 1963-64; bd. dirs. Bar Harbor (Maine) Festival, 1969-74, Bloomingdale House of Music, NYC, 1976-81. Lt. (j.g.) USN, 1955—58. Recipient Conspicuous Alumni Svc. medal Columbia U., 1980, Svc., Loyalty and Dedication award Grad. Faculty Alumni of Columbia U., 1988. Mem. Am. Philos. Assn., Nat. Inst. Social Scis. (dir. 1988-92, 2005—, pres. 2006-), Fin. Planning Assn., Pilgrims of the US, Am. Soc. Most Venerable Order of Hosp. of St. John of Jerusalem, St. Andrew's Soc. of the State of NY (sec. 1991-95), St. George's Soc. NY, Century Assn., Emeritus Profs. in Columbia (assoc.), The Ch. Club of NY (v.p. 1985-86, 88-89, 96-97, pres. 1997-2000, trustee 1983-89, 93-2000, 2001-04), Laymen's Club of the Cathedral of St. John the Divine (pres. 1988, gov. 1982-2006, 1st v.p. 2004—06), Ft. Ticonderoga Assn., Ctr. UN Reform Edn. (bd. dirs.). Episcopalian. Avocations: reading, writing, walking, theater, ballet, sculpture.

OLINS, ROBERT ABBOT, communications research executive; b. Cambridge, Mass., Sept. 25, 1942; s. Harry and Janice Olins; m. Irma Westrich, June 16, 1967; 1 son, Matthew Abbot. Student, Hobart Coll., 1961-62, San Francisco Art Inst., 1962; BA, U. Mass., 1967; postgrad., U. Tampa, 1968; MA, U. Mo., 1969, PhD, 1972. With Marsteller, 1972,

N.W. Ayer, 1972, Post, Keys & Gardner, Chgo., 1973, Young & Rubicam, Chgo., 1973-76, mng. dir. comm. rsch. divsn., 1976-77; pres., CEO, subs. Comm. Rsch. Inc., Chgo., 1978—, owner, chmn., 1979—. Pres., CEO Insights, Chgo., 1976—; assoc. prof. Howard Univ., 2004— Contbr. articles to profl. jours. Recipient Chgo./4 award for creative excellence, 1974; winner Chgo. Mackinac race, 1981; Am. Assn. Advt. Agys. grantee, 1968-71 Mem.: Mid North Assn. (bd. dirs., chmn. planning), Am. Mktg. Assn., Chgo. Yacht Club, Lake Mich. Yachting Assn., U.S. Sailing Club, Skyline Club. Avocations: skiing, sailing, power boating.

OLIPHANT, CHARLES ROMIG, retired physician; b. Waukegan, Ill., Sept. 10, 1917; s. Charles L. and Mary (Goss) R.; m. Claire E. Canavan, Nov. 7, 1942; children: James R., Cathy Rose, Mary G., William D. Student, St. Louis U., 1936-40, MD, 1943; postgrad., Naval Med. Sch., 1946. Intern Nat. Naval Med. Ctr., Bethesda, Md., 1943; pvt. practice medicine and surgery San Diego, 1947-99; ret., 1999. Bd. dirs. Midway Med. Enterprises; former chief staff Balboa Hosp., Doctors Hosp., Cabrillo Med. Ctr.; chief staff emeritus Sharp Cabrillo Hosp.; mem. staff Mercy Hosp., Children's Hosp., Paradise Valley Hosp., Sharp Meml. Hosp.; sec. Sharp Sr. Health Care, S.D., 1985-98; mem. exec. bd., program chmn. San Diego Power Squadron, 1985-93, 95; charter mem. Am. Bd. Family Practice. Served with M.C., USN, 1943-47. Recipient Golden Staff award Sharp Cabrillo Hosp. Med. Staff, 1990; inducted Wisdom Hall of Fame (Medicine), 2003. Fellow Am. Geriatric Soc. (emeritus), Am. Acad. Family Practice, Am. Assn. Abdominal Surgeons; mem. AMA, Calif. Med. Assn., Am. Acad. Family Physicians (past pres. San Diego chpt., del. Calif. chpt.), San Diego Med. Soc., Pub. Health League, Navy League, San Diego Power Squadron (past comdr.), SAR, San Diego Yacht Club, Douglas County Scottish Soc. Home: Riverview Terr Unit # 109 1971 W Harvard Ave Roseburg OR 97470-2746

OLITSKY, SCOTT ERIC, ophthalmologist; b. Bellefonte, Pa., Aug. 27, 1963; s. Allan and Gwen Olitsky; m. Andrea Rosenfeld, May 28, 1988. AB Summa Cum Laude, Bowdoin Coll., Brunswick, Maine, 1984; MD, Jefferson Med. Coll., Phila., Pa., 1988. Cert. Am. Bd. of Ophthalmology, 1993. Chief of ophthalmology Children's Hosp. of Buffalo, Buffalo, 1998—2002; assoc. prof. SUNY, Buffalo, 1998—2002; chief ophthalmology Children's Mercy Hosp. and Clinics, Kansas City, Mo., 2002—05; assoc. prof. U. Mo.-Kans. City, Kans. City, Mo., 2002—; clin. assoc. prof. U. Kans., Kans. City, Kans., 2002—. Residency program directory of ophthalmology SUNY, Buffalo, 1997—2002. Editor: (textbook) Harley's Pediatric Ophthalmology; author: Nelson's Textbook of Pediatrics; editor: Ophthalmology Clinics of North America; author: Secrets of Ophthalmology, Yearbook of Ophthalmology. Bd. mem. Children's Ctr. for the Visually Impaired, Kans. City, Mo., 2003—05, Kadimah Sch. of Buffalo, 1999—2002, Western NY Ctr. for the visually impaired, Buffalo, 1996—2002; chmn. Am. Assn. of Pediatric Ophthalmology and Strabismus, 2003—05. Mem.: Am. Assn. of Pediatric Ophthalmology and Strabismus (assoc.), Am. Acad. of Ophthalmology (assoc.). Achievements include design of Olitsky Calibrated Needle Holder. Office: Children's Mercy Hosp 2410 Gillham Rd Kansas City MO 66224 Office Fax: 816-855-1793.

OLIVE, DAVID L., endocrinologist, educator; b. Washington, Feb. 25, 1954; s. Jerrald L. and Leah R. (Solomon) O.; m. Sherry Ann Alexander, Jan. 9, 1974 (div. Jan. 1979); m. Katherine Mary Otto, Sept. 27, 1981; children: Zachary, Matthew, Alexander. BS, MIT, 1975; MD, Baylor Coll. Medicine, 1979; MS (hon.), Yale U., 1997. Diplomate Am. Bd. Ob-Gyn. spl. competence gynecology-reproductive endocrinology; cert. Accreditation Coun. for Gynecologic Endoscopy-Advanced Operative Laparoscopy and Advaned Operative Hysteroscopy. Resident in ob-gyn. Northwestern U., Chgo., 1979-83; fellow in reproductive endocrinology and infertility Duke U., Durham, N.C., 1983-85; assoc. dept. ob-gyn. divsn. repro. endocrinology/infertility Duke U. Med. Sch., Durham, 1983-84, asst. prof. dept. ob-gyn., 1985-86; asst. prof., dir. divsn. repro. endocrinology dept. ob-gyn. U. Ark. for Med. Scis., Little Rock, 1985-86, residency dir. dept. ob-gyn., 1985-86; from asst. prof. to assoc. prof. dept. ob-gyn. U. Tex. Health Sci. Ctr., San Antonio, 1987-92, residency dir. dept. ob-gyn., 1990-92; assoc. prof., chief div. repro. endocrinology dept. ob-gyn. Yale U. Sch. Medicine, New Haven, 1992-96, fellowship dir. divsn. repro. endocrinology, 1992—, prof., chief divsn. repro. endocrinology dept. ob-gyn., 1996—. Cons. Cape Fear Valley Hosp., Fayetteville, N.C., 1983-85, Cabarrus County Hosp., Concord, N.C., 1983-85; attending staff Duke U. Med. Ctr., Durham, 1983-85, U. Hosp., Little Rock, 1985-86, Humana Women's Hosp., San Antonio, 1987-92, Yale-New Haven Hosp., 1992—, Hosp. of St. Raphael, New Haven, 1992—; consulting staff Bapt. Med. Ctr., Little Rock, 1986; courtesy staff Middlesex Hosp., Middletown, Conn., 1994—, Meriden-Wallingford Hosp., Meriden, Conn., 1995—; rschr. MIT Network News Study Group, 1973; presenter in field. Contbg. writer: Pulse, 1978; editor Code Blue sect. Resident Staff and Physician, 1980-81; founding editl. bd. mem. Jour. of Soc. for Gynecologic Investigation, 1994; inaugural editl. bd. mem. Jour. of Gynecologic Treatment, 1994; author, editor: (CD-ROM) Cryomyolysis, 1996; mem. editl. bd. Jour. Am. Assn. of Gynecologic Laparoscopists, 1996—, Jour. Soc. for Laparoscopic Surgeons, 1997—; ad hoc reviewer: Acad. Medicine, Am. Jour. Ob-Gyn., Internat. Jour. Gynecology and Obstets., Gynecol. Endocrinology, others; contbr. articles to profl. jours., chpts. to books. Mosby scholar Baylor Coll. Medicine, 1979; James Kennedy fellow Am. Assn. Obstetricians and Gynecologists Found., 1982-83, Serono Symposia In-Tng. award Pacific Coast Fertility Soc., 1995; recipient numerous rsch. grants. Mem. AMA (adv. com. on undergrad. med. edn. student rep. 1978-79, sec. resident physicians' sect. 1980-81, vice-chairperson resident physicians' sect. 1981, chairperson-elect resident physicians' sect. 1982, chairperson resident physicians' sect. 1982-83, mem. adv. panel Women in Medicine Project 1984-89), ACOG (mem. subcom. on reproductive endocrinology), Am. Soc. for Reproductive Medicine (practice com. 1996—, CME com. 1996—, 1st pl. award for reproductive immunology spl. interest group prize paper 1995, 1st pl. award for video competition 1995, Prize paper of reproductive immunology spl. interest group 1996), Am. Assn. Gynecologic Laparoscopists (bd. trustees 1996-98, mem. tech. bull. com. 1996—, chmn. classification com. 1996—, 1st pl. postgrad. prize paper 1995, 2d pl. postgrad. prize paper 1995), Soc. Reproductive Endocrinologists, Soc. for Gynecologic Investigation, Soc. Reproductive Surgeons, Soc. Laparoendocscopi Surgery, Def. Women's Health Rsch. Panel (reproductive health mem. study sect.). Democrat. Jewish. Avocations: bicycling, running, coaching. Office: Wisc Fertility Inst 3146 Deming Way Middleton WI 53562

OLIVE, DAVID MICHAEL, journalist, editor; b. Toronto, Ont., Can., Nov. 9, 1957; s. Harold Leslie and Alison Linton (Black) O.; m. Margaret Anne O'Reilly, Feb. 13, 1982 (div. June 1992). B of Applied Arts in Journalism, Ryerson Polytech. U., 1979. Copy editor Toronto Life Mag., 1979-81; assoc. editor Can. Bus. Mag., Toronto, 1981-84; sr. writer Report on Bus. Mag., Toronto, 1984-87, Toronto Life Mag., 1988-90; editorial writer The Globe and Mail, Toronto, 1990-91, current affairs columnist, 1991-92, bus. ethics columnist, 1996-98; editor Report on Bus. Mag., 1991-97, sr. writer, 1997-98, Fin. Post, 1998, Nat. Post, Toronto, 1998—2001; bus. columnist Toronto Star, 2001—. Dir. Can. Ctr. for Ethics and Corp. Policy, 1988-91, Jessie's Ctr. for Teenagers, 1994—; pres. Jessie's Ctr. Non-Profit Homes Corp., 1994—; pres. Nat. Mag. Awards Found., 1988-90. Author: Just Rewards: The Case for Ethical Reform in Business, 1987, White Knights and Poison Pills: A Cynic's Dictionary of Business Jargon, 1990, Political Babble: The 1,000 Dumbest Things Ever Said by Politicians, 1992, Gender Babble: The Dumbest Things Men Ever Said About Women, 1993, Canadian Political Babble: A Cynic's Dictionary of Political Jargon, 1993, More Political Babble: The Dumbest Things Ever Said by Politicians, 1996, Canada Inside Out: How We See Ourselves, How Others See Us, 1996, No Guts, No Glory: How Canada's Greatest CEOs Built Their Empires, 2000, A Devil's Dictionary of Business Jargon, 2001, The Quotable Tycoon: A Treasury of Business Quotations, 2002, An American Story, The Speaches of Barack Obana. Recipient Silver, Nat. Mag. awards, 1987, Gold, 1988, hon. mention, 1983, 1985, 1987, 1989, 1996, Nat. Bus. Book awards, 2001, Nat. Nerwspaper awards, 2005. Mem. Can. Soc. Mag. Editors, Ethics Practitioners Assn. Can.

OLIVEIRA, KATRINA R.K., educator; d. Frank Oliveira and Maryann Nakoa, Jacob Barros (Stepfather). PhD, U. Hawaii, Manoa, Honolulu, 2006. Instr. Hawaiian U. Hawaii, 2001—09, asst. prof. Hawaiian, 2004—, dir., 2007—. Contbr. chapters to books. Pres. Hale Kuai, Honolulu, 2000—04, sec., 2000—04, co-dir., 2000—04. Recipient Laeoo award, Native Hawaiian Edn. Assn., 2007; Pacific fellowship, AAUW, 1998—99. Mem.: Hawaii Lang. Tchrs. Assn. (treas. 2008—09), Am. Ednl. Rsch. Assn., Ka Pa Hula o Kauanoe o Waahila, Anuenue Canoe Club, Bishop Mus. (assoc.).

OLIVER, ANDREA LAKAYE, history professor; b. Buffalo, July 6, 1972; d. Andre Ricardo and Margaret Louise Howard; m. Eddie John Oliver, Sept. 21, 2002; 1 child, Julia Jeanelle. BS in Polit. Comm., Fla. State U., Tallahassee, 1993, MS in Social Sci. Edn., 1995, ABD in Am. History, 2008. Cert. in social studies Fla. Dept. Edn., 1995. Sec., edn. commr. Doug Jamerson Fla. Dept. Edn., Tallahassee, 1994—95; tchr., advanced Am. history Swift Creek Mid. Sch., Tallahassee, 1995—98, tchr., 2002—03, dir., alternative edn., 2002—03; site mgr., about face Paxen Group, Tallahassee, 1998—2000; asst. prof., history North Fla. CC, Madison, 2003—06, Tallahassee CC, 2006—. Contbr. articles. Mem. Tallahassee Film Festival, 2007—08. Recipient Fla. Commendation medal, 1999; named Minority Educator of Yr., Leon County Schs., 1997. Mem.: Sigma Gamma Rho Sorority Inc. Avocations: exercise, swimming, cooking, travel. Home: 2350 Phillips Rd 7108 Tallahassee FL 32308 Office: Tallahassee CC 444 Appleyard Dr Tallahassee FL 32304 Business E-Mail: olivera@tcc.fl.edu.

OLIVER, CARL RUSSELL, science educator; b. Ft. Lewis, Wash., Feb. 23, 1941; s. Ralph L. and Dorothy F. Oliver; m. Dianne Maree Larson, Apr. 24, 1965; 1 child, Carol Anne. MBA, Calif. Luth. U., Thousand Oaks, 1989; BA in Psychology, Stanford U., 1962; MA in Orgn. Devel., Fielding Grad. U., Santa Barbara, Calif., PhD in Human and Orgn. Devel., 2004. Spl. agt. Air Force Office Spl. Investigations, Washington, 1962—68, dir. contact mgmt., 1971—85; asst. prof. Stanford U., Stanford, Calif., 1968—71; corp. ethics process adminstr. Northrop Grumman Corp., Century, Calif., 1985—2006; lectr. Loyola Marymount U., LA, 2008—; adj. faculty U. Redlands, 2008—. Editl. bd. mem. Forensic Sci. Digest, Washington, 1978—79; dir. Consortium Advanced Tech. Edn., Newbury Pk., Calif., 1987—89; judge Bus. Ethics Fortnight Intercollegiate Competition, LA, 2000—. Author: (book) Plane Talk, Panama's Canal; contbr. articles to profl. jours. With Tournament Roses Parade, Pasadena, Calif., 1995—99; operator Ventura County Emergency Radio Svc., Thousand Oaks, Calif., 1995—99. Lt. col. US Air Force, 1962—85, Washington, DC. Mem.: APA, Assn. Psychol. Sci. Home: PO Box 4888 Thousand Oaks CA 91359-1888 Office: 1 Loyola Marymount Univ Dr Los Angeles CA 90045

OLIVER, DALE HUGH, lawyer; b. Lansing, Mich., June 26, 1947; s. Alvin Earl and Jean Elizabeth (Stanton) Oliver; m. Sarah Elyse Sanders, Mar. 18, 2001; children: Nathan Corey, John Franklin. BA, Mich. State U., 1969; JD cum laude, Harvard U., 1972. Bar: DC 1973, Calif. 1991, US Dist. Ct. (DC dist.) 1973, US Ct. Appeals (DC cir.) 1976, US Supreme Ct. 1980, US Ct. Appeals (fed. cir.) 1983, US Ct. Claims 1983. Assoc., ptnr. Jones, Day, Reavis & Pogue, Washington, 1975—79; ptnr. Crowell & Moring, Washington, 1979—84, Gibson, Dunn & Crutcher, Washington, 1984—87, Jones, Day, Reavis & Pogue, Washington, 1987—92, Quinn Emanuel Urquhart & Oliver, LA, 1992—. Editor: (jour.) Pub. Contracts Law, 1980—86; contbr. articles to profl. jours. Spl. counsel 1980 Presdl. Inaugural Com., Washington, 1980; bd. dirs. LA coun. Boy Scouts Am., 1991—; bd. dirs. Armory Ctr. for Arts, 2006—. Capt. USAF, 1973—75. Mem.: ABA (mem. pub. contract sect. 1979—), Pasadena Arts and Cultural Commn. (commr. 2006—, com. chmn. 2008—), Nat. Security Indsl. Assn., Nat. Contract Mgmt. Assn., Harvard Law Sch. Assn., Mich. State U. Alumni Club of Washington (pres., dir. 1984—88). Office: Quinn Emanuel Urquhart & Oliver & Hedges 865 S Figueroa St 10 Fl Los Angeles CA 90017-2543 Office Phone: 213-443-3154. E-mail: daleoliver@quinnemanuel.com.

OLIVER, DOMINICK MICHAEL, business educator; b. Niagara Falls, NY, Apr. 12, 1962; s. Dominick Jr. and Priscilla (Prenatt) O.; m. Vicki Anne Sellig, May 18, 1991. AAS, Niagara County C.C., Sanborn, NY, 1982; BS in Bus., Niagara U., NYC, 1984, MS in Edn., 1986. Lic. tchr. bus. and distributive edn., N.Y.; bus. sch. lic. bus., mgmt., acctg., gen. academics, N.Y. Temporary instr. Niagara County C.C., Sanborn, 1986-87; tchr. on spl. assignment LaSalle Sr. H.S., Niagara Falls, NY, 1986-87; instr. St. Joseph Parochial Elem. Sch., Niagara Falls, 1987-88; instr., acad. dean Kelley Bus. Inst., Niagara Falls, 1988-91; instr. Cheryl Fell's Sch. Bus., Niagara Falls, 1991-92; instr., advisor Bryant and Stratton Bus. Inst., Buffalo, 1992—99, sr. mentor, portfolio textbook curriculum com., 1996—99; sr. instr., math coordinator The Huntington Learning Ctr., 1999—2000; adj. instr. comp. sci. SUNY Buffalo, 2000—, Niagara County Cmty. Coll., 2001—; asst. prof. office mgmt. and admin. Erie Cmty. Coll., 2002—; with adult cmty. edn. program Kenmore-Town Tonawanda Sch. Dist., 2005—. Bus. mgr. Dove Artworks, Buffalo, 1996—; instr. Adopt-A-H.S., Seneca Vocat. H.S., Kensington H.S., Lafayette H.S., Riverside H.S., Buffalo, 1996-1999; evaluator Empire State Coll., 2003—. Life mem. Buffalo and Erie County Naval and Servicemen's Park, Buffalo, 1991—. Republican. Roman Catholic. Avocations: baseball, football, hockey, political history of US, reading. Home: 119 Wendover Ave Buffalo NY 14223-2731

OLIVER, DONNA H., academic administrator, former secondary school educator; AB, Elon Coll., 1972; MEd, U. NC, Greensboro, 1978; MS, NC Agrl. and Tech. State U., 1987; PhD, U. NC, 1995. Tchr. biology Hugh M. Cummings High Sch., Burlington, NC; v.p. academic affairs Bennett Coll., Greensboro, NC, 1989—. Named Nat. Tchr. Yr., 1987. Office: Bennett College 900 E Washington St Greensboro NC 27401

OLIVER, EDWARD CARL, state legislator, insurance company executive, small business owner; b. St. Paul, May 31, 1930; s. Charles Edmund and Esther Marie (Bjugstad) O.; m. Charlotte Severson, Sept. 15, 1956; children: Charles E., Andrew T., Peter A. BA, U. Minn., 1955. Sales rep. Armstrong Cork Co., NYC, 1955; registered rep. Piper, Jaffray & Hopwood, Mpls., 1958; mgr. Mut. Funds Inc., subs. Dayton's, Mpls., 1964, NWNL Mgmt. Corp. subs. Northwestern Nat. Life Ins. Co., Mpls., 1968-72, v.p., 1972-81, pres., dir., 1981-90; mem. Minn. State Senate, 1992—2003, asst. minority leader, 1998—2003; owner Oliver Fin., 2003—. Arbitrator/mediator, FINRA Dispute Resolution, 1988—; bd. dir. 1st Minn. Bank, N.A. Mem. Gt. Lakes Commn., 1993—; bd. dirs., vice chmn. Minn. State Arts Bd., 2003—. Mem. Internat. Assn. Fin. Planners (past pres. Twin City chpt., nat. governing com.), Psi Upsilon, Mpls. Athletic Club. Home: 20230 Cottagewood Rd Excelsior MN 55331-9300 Office: 464 2d St Ste 203 Excelsior MN 55331 Office Phone: 952-380-0107. E-mail: oliverfinancial@earthlink.net.

OLIVER, GEORGE CHARLES, medical educator, cardiologist; b. Gainesville, Fla., Sept. 30, 1931; s. George Charles and Louise Vivian (Jackson) O.; m. Joan Miles, Aug. 31, 1958 (div.); 1 child, Paul Erskine; m. Maralyn La Verdiere, Sept. 29, 1979. AB, Harvard U., 1953, MD, 1957. Diplomate Am. Bd. Internal Medicine, Am. Bd. Cardiovascular Disease. Intern and resident Stanford Med. Ctr., Palo Alto, Calif., 1957-60, Evelyn Neizer fellow in cardiology, 1960-61; USPHS rsch. fellow Guys Hosp., London, 1963-65; fellow in cardiology Washington U. Med. Sch., St. Louis, 1965-66, instr. medicine, 1966-67, asst. prof. medicine, 1967-70, assoc. prof. medicine, 1970-75, prof. medicine, 1975-81, clin. prof. medicine, 1981—2003, prof. emeritus clin. medicine, 2003—. Chief of cardiology Jewish Hosp., St. Louis, 1971-81, Faith Hosp., St. Louis, 1981-90; sr. cardiologist St. Charles (Mo.) Clinic, 1981-99; cardiologist County Cardiology Inc., 199-. Contbr. articles to profl. jours.; editor: Practical Revs. in Cardiology. Mem. US, USSR Working Group on Sudden Cardiac Death, Policy Bd. for Clin. Trials of Thrombolytic Agents NHLBI, 1973; pres. St. Louis Heart Assn., 1978-80. Capt. USAF, 1961-63. Grantee NHLBI. Fellow Am. Coll. Cardiology (gov. Mo. chpt. 1977-80). Avocations: tennis, chess. Office: County Cardiology Inc 10004 Kennerly Rd Ste 247 Saint Louis MO 63128 Home Phone: 314-432-7645. Personal E-mail: charles_oliver@prodigy.net.

OLIVER, GEORGIANNA WHITE, technology consulting company executive; b. Tulsa, Okla., Sept. 14, 1966; m. Jack Oliver; 1 adopted child, Teddy. BS in Polit. Sci., Okla. State U. Legis. asst. US House Ways and Means Com., 1991; with The Nat. Affordable Housing Mgmt. Assn.; v.p. for real estate mgmt. firm; founder, CEO Evergreen Solutions, Washington, DC, 2000—. Gov. Okla. Intercollegiate Legislature; congl. aide Congressman Bill K. Brewster. Mem.: Vistage. Democrat. Methodist. Office: 1325 E 15th St Ste 205 Tulsa OK 74120 Office Phone: 918-585-8886. Office Fax: 918-585-8889. Personal E-mail: gwoliver2008@gmail.com. Business E-Mail: info@oliverforuscongress.com.

OLIVER, HARRY MAYNARD, JR., retired brokerage house executive; b. Kansas City, Mo., Jan. 21, 1921; s. Harry Maynard and Marie (Curtin) O. BA, Williams Coll., 1943. Pres. M.A. Gesner & Co., Marsh & McLennan Co., Chgo., 1947-88. Chmn. Chgo. Commn. for Sr. Citizens, 1960-69; mem. Chgo. Bd. Edn., 1966-69; pres. Vol. Agys. Chgo., 1956-86; mem. vis. com. Sch. Edn. and div. of social scis., U. Chgo.; pres., bd. dirs. Benton House Settlement, 1953-58; bd. dirs. Adult Edn. Council Greater Chgo., Nat. Fedn. Settlements and Community Centers, 1961-67; trustee Old Peoples Home Chgo., Pub. Sch. Tchrs. Pension and Retirement Fund Chgo., 1966-69, George M. Pullman Ednl. Found., Field Mus. Natural History, 1971-75. Served to lt. (j.g.) USNR, World War II. Mem. Chgo. Club, Racquet Club, Commonwealth Club, Onwentsia Club (Lake Forest, Ill.), Chi Psi. Home: 1948 N Lincoln Ave Chicago IL 60614-5476 also: PO Box 1319 Big Pine Key FL 33043 also: New Richmond PO Box 100 Fennville MI 49408-0100

OLIVER, JACK ERTLE, geophysicist, educator; b. Massillon, Ohio, Sept. 26, 1923; s. Chester L. and Marie (Ertle) O.; m. Gertrude van der Hoeven, Apr. 16, 1964; children: Cornelia Oliver, Amy Oliver. AB, Columbia U., 1947, MA, 1950, PhD, 1953; DSci (hon.), Hamilton Coll., 1988. Rsch. asst., then rsch. assoc. Columbia, 1947-55, mem. faculty, 1955-73, prof. geology, 1961-71, chmn. dept., 1969-71, adj. prof., 1971-73; Irving Porter Church prof. engring. dept. geol. scis. Cornell U., 1971-93, prof. emeritus, 1993—, chmn. dept., 1971-81; chmn. exec. com. COCORP. Terrestrial physicist USAF Cambridge (Mass.) Rsch. Labs., 1951; dir. Inst. for Study of the Continents, 1981-88; cons. AEC, 1969-72, ACDA, 1962-74, USAF Tech. Applications Ctr., 1959-65; mem. Polar Rsch. Com., 1959-71, also nat. commn. uppermantle program, 1963-71; mem. panel solid earth problems NAS, 1962; mem. adv. com. U.S. Coast and Geodetic Survey, 1962-66, on seismology, 1960-72, chmn., 1966-70; mem. Geophysics Rsch. Bd., 1969-70; U.S. coord. 2d U.S.-Japan Earthquake Prediction Conf., Palisades, 1966; earth sci. panel NSF, 1962-65; mem. USAF Sci. Adv. Bd., 1960-63, 64-69; mem. geophysics adv. panel Office Sci. Rsch., USAF, 1961-74, chmn., 1966-68; U.S. del. Test Ban Conf., Geneva, Switzerland, 1958-59; intergovtl. meeting seismology and earthquake engring., mem. exec. com. IASPEI, 1968-71; mem. governing com. Internat. Seismol. Summary Commn., 1963-67, 75-76; mem. exec. com. UNESCO, Paris, France, 1964, U.S.-Japan Earthquake Prediction Conf., Tokyo, 1964; mem. UNESCO Joint Com. on Seismology and Earthquake Engring., 1965-71; chmn. exec. com. Office Earth Scis., NRC, 1976-79, Internat. Seismol. Centre, 1976-78; mem. U.S. Geodynamics Com., 1979-87, chmn., 1984-87; mem. Geol. Scis. Bd., Assembly of Math. and Phys. Scis., NRC, 1981-84; Cabot Disting. vis. scholar U. Houston, 1985-86; commn. on phys. scis., math. and resources NRC, 1987-90, commn. on geoscis., environ. and resources, 1990—. Served with USNR, 1943-46. Recipient Hedberg award Inst. for Study of Earth and Man, So. Meth. U., 1990. Fellow Am. Geophys. Union (pres. seismology sect. 1964-68, Walter H. Bucher medal 1981), Geol. Soc. Am. (coun. 1970-73, v.p. 1986, pres. 1987, Woollard medal 1990, Penrose medal 1998), Geol. Soc. London (hon.); mem. AAAS (chmn. geol. geog. sect. 1993), NAS, Seismol. Soc. Am. (pres. 1964-65, bd. dirs. 1961-70, 72-76, Eighth medal 1984), Soc. Exploration Geophysicists (Virgil Kauffman Gold medal 1983), European Union Geoscis. (hon. fgn. fellow), Sigma Xi. Home: 340 Savage Farm Dr Ithaca NY 14850 Home Phone: 607-257-7554; Office Phone: 607-255-2377. Business E-Mail: oliver@geology.cornell.edu.

OLIVER, JAMIE, chef, television personality; b. Essex, England, May 1, 1975; s. Trevor and Sally Oliver; m. Juliette Norton; children: Poppy Honey, Daisy Boo, Petal Blosssom Rainbow. Grad., Westminster Catering Coll., London. Head pastry chef Neal Street Restaurant, London, 1991—97; chef River Cafe, London, 1997—99; consulting chef Monte's, London, 2000; founder, owner Fifteen Restaurant, London, 2002—. Former columnist GQ mag.; former feature writer The Times Mag., London; designer cookware & tableware line Royal Worcester. Host, chef (TV series) The Naked Chef, 1999-2001 (BAFTA award 2001), Jamie's Kitchen, 2002-04, Oliver's Twist, 2004-, Jamie's School Dinners, 2006- (Best Factual Series award, Outstanding Presenter award, BAFTA 2006), Jamie at Home, 2008-; author (cookbooks) The Naked Chef, 1999, The Return of The Naked Chef, 2000, Happy Days with The Naked Chef, 2001, Jamie's Kitchen, 2003, Jamie's Dinners, 2004, Jamie's Italy, 2005. Founder Fifteen Found., 2002. Decorated MBE;

recipient GQ Best Chef award, 2000, Tatler Best Restaurant award (for Fifteen Restaurant), 2003, Excellence award, Tio Pepe Carlton London Restaurant Awards, 2003, Time Out special award for outstanding achievement, 2003, Glenfiddich Food and Drink award, 2003; named GQ Man of the Yr., 2000. Office: Fifteen Restaurant & Fifteen Found Westland Place London N1 7LP England also: c/o Penguin Publicity 80 Strand WC2R 0RL London England*

OLIVER, JERRY ALTON, former police chief; 5 children. BS in Criminal Justice, Ariz. State U., MS in Pub. Adminstrn., 1988; postgrad., Police Exec. Rsch. Forum, Washington. From patrolman to supr. Phoenix Police Dept., from supr. to asst. chief of police, 1971-90; dir. drug policy Memphis Mayors Office; chief of police Pasadena (Calif.) Police Dept., 1991—94, Richmond (Va.) Police Dept., 1995—2002, Detroit, Mich., 2002—03; spl. policy advisor Ariz. Atty. Gen., 2004—05; dep. dir. Ariz. Dept. Admin., 2005—06; dir. Ariz. Dept. Liquor Lics. & Control. Founder Spl. Friends Project, Richmond, 1988—. Inductee Ariz. State U. Coll. Pub. Programs Hall of Fame, 1989; recipient Phoenix chpt. Image award NAACP, 1990, People of Yr. award Law Enforcement News, 1999, Richmonder of Yr. award Richmond Style Mag., 1999, U.S. Atty. Gen.'s award for outstanding contbns. to cmty. partnership for pub. safety, 2000, othrs. Home Phone: 480-840-1313; Office Phone: 602-542-1932. E-mail: jaoxfive@hotmail.com.

OLIVER, KENTON L., library director; BA in Am. Hist., Washburn U., Topeka; MLS, Emporia State U., Kans. Dir. branch svcs. Johnson County Libr., Overland Park, Kans.; libr. dir. Olathe Pub. Libr., Kans.; head pub. svcs. Daniel Boone Regional Libr., Columbia, Mo.; exec. dir. Stark County Dist. Libr., Canton, Ohio, 2001—. Elected bd. mem. Freedom to Read Found. Mem.: ALA (exec. bd.), Pub. Libr. Assn. (intellectual freedom com., nominating com., membership com., Libr. Video award jury, Gordon M. Conable award jury), Mo. Libr. Assn. (past. pres.), Am. Libr. Assn. (budget analysis & review com., com. on orgn., chair resolutions com.), Kans. Libr. Assn. (past pres.). Office: Stark County Dist Libr 715 Market Ave N Canton OH 44702*

OLIVER, KERRYN HINRICHS, music and religious studies educator; b. Webster City, Iowa, Dec. 1, 1954; d. Lowell K and Kathryn Rosa Hinrichs; m. Michael L. Oliver, Dec. 16, 1978; children: Erin Michelle Bandow, Mark Michael. AA, Ellsworth Coll., Iowa Falls, 1985; MusB, U. Northern Iowa, Cedar Falls, 1997. Lic. pastor NE Assn. UCC/Iowa, 2005, NW Assn. UCC/Iowa, 2005; cert. Level I in Kodaly Drake U., Iowa, 2003. Pvt. piano/vocal tchr., Alden, Iowa, 1980—; music dir. Immanuel Meml. United Ch. of Christ, Alden, Iowa, 1985—2006, christian educator/assoc. pastor, 2005—; vocal music tchr. Alden Elem., Alden, 1999—, Iowa Falls-Alden Schs., Iowa, 1999—; adj. vocal instr. Ellsworth Coll., Iowa Falls, 2003—05; christian educator/pastor Jewell United Ch. of Christ, 2005—; ctr. dist. chair Iowa Choral Dir. Assn., 2006—, rep. bd. dir., 2006—. Workshop leader/cons. Nebr. Conf. United Ch. of Christ, Lincoln, 2003—05, Iowa Conf. United Ch. of Christ, Des Moines, 2005—; ptnr. in edn. United Ch. of Christ, Cleve. and Des Moines, 1997—. Contbr. article/workshop. Vol. music tchr. Alden Cmty. Presch., Iowa, 2001. Mem.: Iowa State Edn. Assn., NEA, Iowa Choral Dirs. Assn., Am. Choral Dirs. Assn., Alden Edn. Assn. (membership chair 2003—04), Phi Theta Kappa, Pi Kappa Lambda Music, Kappa Delta Pi Edn., Golden Key, Omicron Delta Kappa, Sigma Alpha Iota. United Church Of Christ. Avocations: reading, perennial gardens, backyard bird watching/feeding, travel. Home: P O Box 63 712 Hardin St Alden IA 50006-0063 Personal E-mail: olivers@iowatelecom.net.

OLIVER, KIMBERLY, primary school educator; b. Wilmington, Del. BA in English Arts, Hampton U.; MEd in elem. edn., Wilmington Coll. Cert. Nat. Bd. Profl. Teaching Standards, 2004. Kindergarten teacher Broad Acres Elem., Silver Spring, Md., 2000—. Recipient Greenblatt Excellence Teaching award, Greenblatt Edn. Fund, award for tchg. excellence, Concerned Black Men Nat. caucus, 2006; named Md. Tchr. of Yr., 2006, Nat. Tchr. of the Yr., Coun. Chief State Sch. Officers, 2006.

OLIVER, LEANN MICHELLE, government official; d. George L. and Laura Maxine (Jennings) O. BS, Willamette U., 1977; MPA, SUNY, Albany, 1980; cert., Nat. Comml. Lending Sch. of Am. Bankers Assn., Norman, Okla., 1982. Mgmt. trainee U.S. GAO, Albany, 1979-80; presdl. mgmt. intern U.S. SBA, Washington, 1980-83, fin. analyst, policy program devel., 1983-89, acting dir. Office Rural Affairs Econ. Devel., 1995, dir. divsn. Program Devel., 1995-2000, dep. assoc. adminstr. fin. assistance, 2000—05; dep. dir. program devel. Office Econ. Devel., 1989-92; dep. dir. Office Rural Affairs Econ. Devel., 1992-94; acting dir. One Stop Office, Capital Shop Project, 1994; acting dep., assoc. dep. adminstr. Entrepreneurial Devel., 2006; dep. adminstr., coop. programs USDA Rural Devel., 2006—. Bd. dirs. Lafayette Fed. Credit Union, Washington, 1986-2007, treas., 1997-2000, asst. treas., 2000-04, treas., 2004-07. Roman Catholic. Office: USDA Rural Development 1400 Independence Ave SW Mail Stop 3250 Rm 4016 Washington DC 20250 Office Phone: 202-720-7558. Personal E-mail: lmoliver@verizon.net. Business E-Mail: leann.oliver@wdc.usda.gov.

OLIVER, LOUISE V., United States Ambassador to UNESCO; m. Daniel Oliver; 5 children. BA with distinction, Smith Coll. Apptd. commr. Nat. Commn. on Children, 1989; pres. Oliver Mgmt. Consultants; permanent US rep. to UNESCO US Dept. State, Paris, 2004—09. Chmn. Philanthropy Roundtable, Washington, Intercollegiate Studies Inst.; co-founder New Atlantic Initiative; bd. dirs. Independent Women's Forum. Mem.: Phi Beta Kappa. Office: 2 Avenue Gabriel 75382 Cedex 08 Paris France Office Phone: 2023301022. E-mail: parisunesco@state.gov.

OLIVER, MARINA GOODFIELD, University Librarian; d. Silvana Del Piero; m. Roy Michael Oliver, Jan. 2, 1983; 1 child, Michelle Goodfield. MLS, U. North Tex., Denton; MS in Geosci., Tex. Tech. U., Lubbock. GIS, map libr. Tex. Tech. U. Librs., 1999—2001, head, acquisitions, 2003—06, librs. promotion & tenure com. chair, 2005—07, head, electronic resources & assessment, 2006—, TTU librs. copyright specialist, 2006—, pres.'s strategic planning coun. mem., 2008—. Advisor Lubbock Christian U. Libr., 2006—07; faculty senator Tex. Tech. Faculty Senate, Lubbock, 2007—; SFX, metalib conf. program chair Ex Libris Users N.Am., 2007. Contbr. articles to profl. jours. ER&L conf. program planning com. Electronic Resources and Librs., 2007—09; mentor Tex. Tech. MentorTech, 2007—08. Mem.: Gt. Western Libr. Alliance. Office: Tex Tech Univ Librs 18th & Boston Ave Lubbock TX 79409-0002

OLIVER, MARY, poet; b. Maple Heights, Ohio, Sept. 10, 1935; d. Edward William and Helen Mary (Vlasak) O. Student, Ohio State U., 1955—56, Vassar Coll., 1956—57. Chmn. writing dept. Fine Arts Work Ctr., Provincetown, Mass., 1972-73, mem. writing com., 1984; Banister poet-in-residence Sweet Briar Coll., 1991-95. William Blackburn vis. prof. creative writing Duke U., 1995; Catharine Osgood Foster prof. Bennington Coll., 1996-2001. Author: No Voyage and Other Poems, 1963, enlarged edit., 1965, The River Styx, Ohio, 1972, The Night Traveler, 1978, Twelve Moons, 1979, American Primitive, 1983, Dream Work, 1986, House of Light, 1990, New and Selected Poems, 1992, Vol. 2, 2005, A Poetry Handbook, 1994, White Pine, 1994, Blue Pastures, 1995, West Wind, 1997, Rules for the Dance, 1998, Winter Hours, 1999, The Leaf and the Cloud, 2000, What Do We Know, 2002, Owls and Other Fantasies, 2003, Why I Wake Early, 2004, Long Life, 2004, Blue Iris, 2004, New and Selected Poems, Vol. 2, 2005, Thirst, 2006, Our World, 2007, Red Bird, 2008, the Truro Bear and Other Adventures, 2008, Evidence, 2009; contbr. to Yale U. Rev., Kenyon Rev., Poetry, Atlantic, Harvard mag., others. Recipient Shelley Meml. award, 1970, Alice Fay di Castagnola award, 1973, Cleve. Arts prize for lits., 1979, Achievement award Am. Acad. and Inst. Arts and Letters, 1983, Pulitzer prize for poetry, 1984, Christopher award, 1991, L.L. Winship award, 1991, Nat. Book award, 1992, Lannan award, 1998; Nat. Endowment fellow, 1972-73; Guggenheim fellow, 1980-81. Mem. PEN. Home: PO Box 619 Provincetown MA 02657-0619

OLIVER, NURIA MARIA, computer science researcher; b. Alicante, Spain; BS, Tech. U. Madrid, 1992, MS, 1994; PhD in Media Arts & Scis., MIT, 2000. Rsch. asst. engr. Siemens F&E, 1992—93; software engr. Telefonica R&D, Spain, 1994—95; rsch. asst. Media Lab, MIT, 1995—2000; rschr. adaptive systems & interaction group Microsoft Rsch., 2000—. Named one of 40 Most Promising Young Spanish Persons, El Pais, 1999, Top 100 Young Innovators, MIT Tech. Review, 2004; fellow, La Caixa Found., 1995; Motorola fellow, 1997. Mem.: ACM, IEEE. Avocations: ballet, dance, yoga, swimming, art.

OLIVER, PATRICIA, lawyer; b. Erie, Pa. m. Jim Oliver; 3 children. BA magna cum laude in Polit. sci., Allegheny Collge; JD, Case Western Reserve U. Sch. Law, Cleve. Atty. Squire, Sanders & Dempsey, Cleve.; gen. counsel BB&T Corp, Winston-Salem, NC, 2004—. Founder Women in Family Bus. Seminar Series, Cleve. Pres. Children's Aid Soc. Recipient Rainmaker (community svc.), No. Ohio Live Magazine, 2003, Profl. Woman of Excellence, Cleve. YMCA. Office: BB&T Corp 200 W 2nd St Winston Salem NC 27101

OLIVER, ROBERT BRUCE, retired investment company executive; b. Brockton, Mass., Aug. 1, 1931; s. Stanley Thomas and Helen (Sabine) O.; m. Sylvia E. Bell, Feb. 17, 1954; children: Susan Pamela, Robert Bruce. AB, Harvard U., 1953; postgrad., Bus. Sch., 1971, Boston U. Law Sch., 1955-57; MA, Mich. State U., 1958. Ret. chmn., pres., chief exec. officer John Hancock Income Securities Trust, Boston, 1989. Ret. chmn., pres. chief exec. officer John Hancock Investors Trust, John Hancock Bond Trust, John Hancock Growth Trust, John Hancock Tax Exempt Cash Mgmt. Trust, John Hancock Govt. Securities Trust, John Hancock Tax Exempt Income Trust, John Hancock Cash Mgmt. Trust, John Hancock Spl. Equities Trust, John Hancock Global Trust, John Hancock World Trust, John Hancock High Income Trust, John Hancock Tax Exempt Series Trust; chmn., dir. John Hancock Distbrs.; vice chmn., chief exec. officer John Hancock Advisers, Inc.; chmn., mng. dir. John Hancock Advisers Internat. Ltd. 1st lt. USMCR, 1953-55. Mem. Marine Corps League, Haile Plantation Country Club. Home: 9271 SW 29th Ave Gainesville FL 32608 Personal E-mail: rboliver72@aol.com.

OLIVER, TERRY JAMES, retired electronics engineer, communications engineer; b. Greensboro, NC, Sept. 5, 1949; s. William Alfred and Elizabeth Ellen (Baker) O.; m. Janice Marie Jones, Mar. 16, 1974 (div. May 1989); 1 child, Shonn Aaron; m. Janice Marie Meris, Nov. 25, 1990; children Jennifer G. Meris, Kelly Cervero. MS, St. John's U., 1981; PhD, Pacific Western U., 1985; AA, Thomas A. Edison State Coll., 1986, AS, 1987; BS, USNY, Albany, 1988, USNY, 2006. Cert. tchr., N.C., sr. electronics technician, sr. biomed. electronics technician, video photographer, open water diver; lic. tchr. NC Dept. Pub. Instrn. Pub. edn. officer Civil Affairs and Signal Corps USAR, Greensboro, NC, 1975—79; comms.-electronic technician U.S. Army, 1968-75; sound systems engr. Soundak Engineered Systems, Greensboro, 1975-76; electronics tchr. Guilford County Sch. System, Greensboro, 1976-79; commn. electronics engr. U.S. Army, Washington, 1979-86; dir., prof. photoelectronics Randolph C.C., Asheboro, NC, 1986—99; prof. electronics, computers and telecomms. ECPI Coll. Tech., Greensboro, NC, 1999—2004; ret., 2004. Faculty rep. N.C. Assn. Educators, Guilford County, N.C., 1976-79; cons. Guilford Tech. CC New Industry Tng., Greensboro, 1988-90. Mem. Guilford County PACE, 1977-79; party nominee N.C. Ho. of Reps., 1992, N.C. State Senate, 1996; candidate Guilford County Bd. Edn., 1993, N.C. State Senate, 1994; appt. ad large mem. Guilford County Bd. Environ. Quality, 1999-2004. With USAR, 1975-79. Mem. Nat. Soc. Profl. Engrs., Internat. Soc. for Optical Engrs., Soc. Am. Mil. Engrs., Photo Mktg. Assn. Democrat. Moravian. Avocations: scuba diving, tennis, bicycling, walking. Home: 7310 Shellford St Greensboro NC 27406-9165 Personal E-mail: t_oliver5@bellsouth.net.

OLIVER, THORNAL GOODLOE, retired health care executive; b. Memphis, Aug. 26, 1934; s. John Oliver and Evelyn Doris (Goodloe) Mitchell; m. Pauline Reid, Oct. 1, 1959. B.S., Tenn. State U., Nashville, 1956; M.H.A., Washington U., St. Louis, 1973. Cert. nursing home adminstr., Mo. Asst. dir., King Meml. Hosp., Kansas City, Mo., 1973-75; evening mgr. Truman Med. Ctr., Kansas City, Mo., 1975-77; asst. adminstr. Mid-Am. Radiation Ctr. U. Kans. Coll. Health Sci., Kansas City, Kans., 1977-81; dir. CHS, Inc., Leawood, Kans., 1981-82; adminstr. Poplar Bluff Hosp., Mo., 1982-83; adminstr. The Benjamin F. Lee Health Ctr., Wilberforce, Ohio, 1983-86; asst. clin. prof. Dept. Community Medicine, Wright State U., Dayton, 1986-89; asst. patent adminstr. Munson Army Hosp., Ft. Leavenworth, Kans., 1987-2004, ret., 2004; cons. Urban Health Assocs., Nashville, 1986-87, others. Contbr. articles to profl. jours. Served with U.S. Army, 1957-59, USAR, 1959-63. Fellow Am. Coll. Hosp. Adminstrs.; mem. Am. Hosp. Assn., Nat. Assn. Health Services Execs., Am. Med. Record Assn., Mo. League of Nursing Home Adminstrs. Home: 10641 N Grand Ave Kansas City MO 64155-1655

OLIVER, WILLIAM, councilman; Councillor, dist. 10 Indpls.-Marion County City-County Coun., 2004—, minority whip. Democrat. Office: 4712 E 34th St Indianapolis IN 46218 also: Indpls Marion County City County Coun 241 City County Bldg 200 E Washington St Indianapolis IN 46204 Office Phone: 317-546-7467, 317-327-4242. Business E-Mail: woliver@indygov.org.*

OLIVER, WILLIAM DONALD, orthodontist; b. Montreal, Ont., Can., Dec. 14, 1946; s. Austen William and Margaret Kay (Donald) O. BS in Physics, Mt. Allison U., 1964; DDS, McGill U., 1968; MSD in Orthodontics, U. Pa., 1970. Pres. Orthodontic Enterprises Internat., Geneva, 1973—78; orthodontist Barrington, RI, 1979—94; pvt. practice Everett, Wash., 1993—. Instr. Frankfurt Carolinium, 1972-74; witness Senate Armed Svcs. Com., 1975. Inventor Piezo Electric Bone Healing; contbr. articles to profl. jours. Mem. Olympic Ski Team, Squaw Valley, 1960. Served with USAF, 1970-73. Recipient Carter Meml. award, 1964, M.T. Dohan prize, 1966. Mem. ADA, Can. Assn. Orthodontists, Am. Assn. Orthodontists, European Orthodontic Soc., Can. Dental Assn., Fedn. Internat. d'Automobile, Wash. State Soc. Orthodontists, Royal Ocean Racing Club. Republican. Office: 10812 19th Ave SE Everett WA 98208-5153 Office Phone: 425-338-5414. Business E-Mail: braces@seanet.com.

OLIVER, WILLIAM JOHN, pediatrician, educator; b. Blackshear, Ga., Mar. 30, 1925; s. John Wesley and Katherine (Schalwig) O.; m. Marguerite Bertoni, May 28, 1949; children: Ralph Scott, Catherine, Susan. Student, Ga. Southwestern Coll., 1942-43, Mercer U., 1943-44; MD cum laude, U. Mich., 1948. Diplomate Am. Bd. Pediatrics (examiner), Subsplty. Bd. Pediatric Nephrology. Intern, resident U. Mich. Med. Center, 1948-53, dir. pediatric labs., 1959-67; pvt. practice medicine specializing in pediatrics Ann Arbor, Mich., 1953—; instr. dept. pediatrics U. Mich., 1953-56, asst. prof., 1956-61, assoc. prof., 1961-65, prof., 1965, chmn. dept. pediatrics, 1967-79; chief pediatric service Wayne County Hosp., 1958-61. Co-chmn. task force on recent advances of coordinating com. on continuing edn. and recertification Am. Bd. Pediats. and Am. Acad. Pediats., 1977-80; mem. task force for pediatric rev. edn. program, 1980-88; mem. com. program for renewal certification in pediat. Am. Bd. Pediat., 1989-91, mem. exam writing com. for cert. pediatric nephrology, 1989-93, PRCP pilot test com., 1993-96; mem. rev. and question writing com. for Pediat. in Rev. Am. Acad. Pediat., 1991-97; cons. U. Riyadh, Saudi Arabia, 1980, Rsch. Rev. Com. on Pediat., 1989; ednl. cons. dept. pediat. Stanford U. Hosps., 1991-98; mem. self-assessment program for Pediat. in Rev., 1990-98; investigator adaptation primitive So. Ams. Indians, 1976—, African Pygmies, 1987—, worldwide primitive socs., 1997. Author: Primitive Peoples Without Salt, 1998, Amerindian Children: Mortality Study--Human Behavior and Evolution Society, 2005, child abuse study, 2006; mem. editl. bd. IRCS Jour. Med. Sci., 1975-90. Pres. Mich. Kidney Disease Found., 1969, Washtenaw County br. Mich. Childrens Aid Soc., 1964; trustee Ann Arbor Hands-On Mus., 1983-88; pres. bd. trustees Perry Nursery Sch., Ann Arbor, 1989-90. With USNR, 1950-52. Fellow Am. Acad. Pediatrics (chmn. com. med. edn. 1974-80, chmn. coun. on pediatric edn. 1975-80, chmn. task force oversight of pediatric rev. and edn. program 1984-88, Clifford G. Grulee award 1979); mem. Soc. Pediatric Rsch., Midwest Soc. Pediatric Rsch. (pres. 1968), Am. Soc. Nephrology, Assn. Med. Sch. Pediatric Dept. Chairmen (mem. coun. 1977-79), Soc. for Exptl. Biology and Medicine, Am. Pediatric Soc., Alpha Omega Alpha, Gamma Sigma Epsilon. Home: 2892 Bay Ridge Dr Ann Arbor MI 48103-1704 Home Phone: 734-761-5169. Personal E-mail: wjoandmbo@aol.com.

OLIVERA, BALDOMERO M., biology professor; BS summa cum laude, Univ. Philippines, 1960; PhD, Calif. Inst. Tech., 1966; postdoctoral study, Stanford Univ., 1966—68. Rsch. assoc. prof. biochemistry Univ. Philippines Coll. Medicine; vis. rsch. prof. Univ. Kans.; assoc. prof. Univ. Utah, 1970—73, prof., 1973—92, disting. prof. biology, 1992—. Fellow: Am. Acad. Arts & Scis. Office: Molecular Biology Program EIHG 533 Rm 1400 15 N 2030 E Salt Lake City UT 84112-5330 Office Phone: 801-581-5207. Business E-Mail: olivera@biology.utah.edu.

OLIVERI, EUGENE ALFRED, gastroenterologist; b. NYC, Apr. 30, 1937; children: Gregory, Lisa, Michelle. Student, Bklyn. Coll., 1954-56, 58-60; DO summa cum laude, Kansas City Coll., 1964; LHD, U. Health Scis., 2000; MSc, Trinity So. U., 2003; D of Osteopathic Edn., U. New Eng., Biddeford, Maine, 2007. Diplomate Am. Bd. Internal Medicine, Am. Bd. Gastroenterology. Intern Detroit Osteo. Hosp., 1964-65; resident in internal medicine Botsford/Ziegler Hosps., 1965-67; fellowship in gastroenterology VA Hosp., East Orange, NJ, 1967-68; asst. dean Coll. Osteo. Medicine Mich. State U. Prof. dept. internal medicine sect. of gastroenterology Botsford Gen. Hosp., assoc. program dir. gastroenterology residency emeritus; mem., courtesy staff emeritus dept. of internal medicine Huron Valley Hosp. Trustee Pikeville (Ky.) Coll., 1998—2004, U. New Eng., Biddeford, Maine, 2001—. With US Army, 1956—58. Recipient Highest Acad. Achievement award Mead-Johnson, 1964, Outstanding Alumni Achievement award U. for Health Scis., Coll. Osteo. Medicine, 1991, Dr. J.O. Watson Disting. Lecr. Ohio Osteo. Assn., 1991, Walter Patenge medal for humanitarian svc. MSU, 1999, Galusha Meml. lectr., 1999, FSMB A.T. Still Meml. Lecture award, ADA, 2009, Phillips medal Pub Svc., Ohio U., 2002; named Physician of Yr. Mich. chpt. Ileitis and Colitis Found., 1985, Botsford Profl. Staff, 1994. Fellow Am. Coll. Osteo. Internists (pres. 1982-83, Disting. Svc. award 1982, Disting. Lectr. award 1983); fellow Am. Coll. Internists (master); mem. Am. Osteo. Assn. (pres. 1999-2000, trustee mem. bd., Disting. Svc. certificat 2005), Mich. Assn. Osteo. Physician and Surgeons (pres. 1991-92), Oakland County Osteo. Assn., Am. Coll. Gastroenterology, Am. Soc. Gastrointestinal Endoscopy, Am. Soc. Addiction Medicine, Am. Osteo. Found. (bd. dirs., past pres. bd. dirs., com. on awards), Mich. Osteo. Coll. Found. (chair, trustee, bd. dirs.), Crohn's and Colitis Found. Am. (Physician of Yr. 1991), Psi Sigma Alpha, Sigma Sigma Phi. Avocations: cooking, health policy. Home: 844 Old Milford Farms Milford MI 48381-3363 Personal E-mail: docoli@aol.com.

OLIVERI, MICHAEL STEVEN, art educator; s. Frank Thomas and Suzanne Oliveri; m. Laura Hoffman, Mar. 5, 2000; 1 child, Bianca Isabella. MFA, UCLA, 1995. Vis. artist prof. Fla. State U., Tallahassee, 1999—2001; assoc. prof. U. Ga., Athens, 2001—. Photography, micrographs, Innerspace, installation, Ultraviolet Aquiescence and Deep Space Drip Culture, Fast Food Hydrocarbons and Waves in Outerspace, El Pollo Doh Loco. Bd. mem. Artpapers, Atlanta, Ga., 2005. Achievements include patents pending for cigarette butt recepticle. Office: Univ GA Athens GA 30602 Personal E-mail: moliveri101@gmail.com.

OLIVERI, PAUL FRANCIS, lawyer; b. Far Rockaway, NY, Feb. 27, 1954; s. Alphonse J. and Rita (Gregorace) O.; m. Debra Lynn Malkin, Aug. 7, 1977; children: Jason, Evan, Rebecca. BA, NYU, 1976; JD, St. John's U., Queens, NY, 1978. Bar: N.Y. 1979, U.S. Dist. Ct. (ea. and so. dists.) N.Y. 1980. Assoc. Fuchsberg & Fuchsberg, NYC, 1979-83; ptnr. Oliveri & Schwartz, NYC, 1983—. Mem. N.Y. State Bar Assn., Am. Trial Lawyers Assn., N.Y. State Trial Lawyers Assn. (dir. emeritus). Avocations: music, coin collecting/numismatics. Office: Oliveri & Schwartz 1825 Pk Ave 9th Fl New York NY 10035-1914 Office Phone: 212-608-7080. E-mail: poliveri@oliveriandschwartz.com.

OLIVERIO, PIERLUIGI, councilman; Degree, San José State U. With semiconductor and software industry; councilman, Dist. 6 San José City Coun., 2007—. Mgr. Libr. Measure E Campaign. Involved with Willow Glen Neighborhood Assn., Next Door Solutions Battered Women's Shelter, San Jose Anti-Litter Program, San Jose Downtown Assn., Joint Venture Silicon Valley Coun. on Tax & Fiscal Policy, Neighborhood Tree Planting. Office: San Jose City Coun 200 E Santa Clara St San Jose CA 95113-1905 Office Phone: 408-535-4906. Office Fax: 408-292-6465. Business E-Mail: Pierluigi.Oliverio@sanjoseca.gov.*

OLIVERIO, PONZIO, protective services official, educator; b. San Diego, Calif., June 14, 1958; s. Ponzio and Harriet Jean Oliverio; m. Amy Amber Edsall, Nov. 19, 1983; children: Giulia Marie, Giana. BA in Humanities, Thomas Edison Coll., Trenton, NJ, 1992; JD, U. San Diego Sch. Law, 1996. Bar: Calif. 1997; cert. in hostage negotiations FBI, 2004. Dep. sheriff San Diego County Sheriff, 1985—; prof. Nat. U., San Diego, 1999—; adj. faculty San Diego Regional Police Acad., 2000—; prof. U. Phoenix, San Diego, 2003—, faculty advisor; guest lectr., criminal procedure U. San Diego Sch. Law; instr. USN, Master-at-Arms Sch., San Diego. Uniform com. mem. San Diego Sheriff, 1993—95, process improvement team mem., 2003—, tng. officer, sheriff recruiting team, recruiting com., profl. standards com. Columnist The Silver Star Holding Court, San Diego County Herald Cuff Links; co-author: (training manual) Crime-Free Mobile Housing Man., (anthology publ. in True Blue) Jimmy, 2004. Moot ct. judge U. San Diego Sch. Law, 2002—04; com. mem. State Bar Domestic Violence Com., Santa Ana, Calif.; facilitator Domestic Violence Restraining Order Clinic, San Diego, 1995—96. Recipient Letter of Appreciation, Calif. Dept. Corrections, 2000, Chula Vista, Calif. Police Dept., 2000, U.S. Border Patrol, 2001, Award of Exemplary Performance, San Diego Sheriff, 2000, Medal of Valor, 2001, Cert. Recognition, Calif. State Assembly, 2003, Calif. State Senate, 2004, Cert. Spl. Recognition, US Congress, 2004. Mem.: Dep. Sheriff's Assn. San Diego (bd. dirs., v.p., chmn. polit. action com., chmn. legal def. com.), Statewide Calif. Coalition for Battered Women (assoc.), Dep. Sheriff's Assn. (assoc.), Fraternal Order of Police (assoc.). Conservative. Avocations: hunting, fishing. Home: 2208 Boulders Ct Alpine CA 91901 Personal E-mail: ponzio2@cox.net.

OLIVER LEAHY TINEN KAEHLER, JEANNETTE See LEAHY, JEANNETTE

OLIVEROS, PAULINE, composer, performer; b. Houston, May 30, 1932; Studies with, Erickson and Nee; D of Mus. Arts (hon.), U. Md., Balt., 1986. Mem. San Francisco Tape Music Ctr., Mills Coll., 1961-67; Darius Milhaud prof. Mills Coll., 1996. Dir. Tape Music Ctr., Mills Coll., 1966; prof. music. U. Calif. at San Diego; dir. Ctr. for Music Experiment, U. San Diego, 1967-81; founder The Oliveros Found., Inc., 1985—; co-founder Good Sound Found. Author: Software for People: Collected Writings 1963-80, The Roots of the Moment: Collected Writings, 1997; composer: I of IV, Sonic Meditations, El Relicario de los Animales, Tashi Gomang, The Well, Gathering Together, The Wheel of Time, Tara's Room, The Roots of the Moment; founder Deep Listening Crone Music; commd. by Meet the Composer For the Susan Marshall Dance Co. Contenders. Artistic dir. Deep Listening, 1985—. Recipient Beethoven prize City of Bonn, 1977, Letter of Distinction Am. Music Ctr., 1990, Bessie award, 1991, award Found. for Contemporary Performance, 1994; Guggenheim fellow, 1972-73, N.Y. Found. For the Arts fellow, 1989. *I kept doing what I wanted to do until I was paid for it.*

OLIVER-WARREN, MARY ELIZABETH, retired library science educator, library and information scientist; b. Hamlet, NC, Feb. 23, 1924; d. Washington and Carolyn Belle (Middlebrooks) Terry; m. David Oliver, 1947 (div. 1971); children: Donald D., Carolyn L.; m. Arthur Warren, Sept. 14, 1990 (dec. Feb. 1995). BS, Bluefield State U., 1948; MS, South Conn. State U., 1958; student, U. Conn., 1977. Cert. tchr., adminstr. and supr., Conn.; cert. pub. sch. substitute tchr., K-12, NJ. Media specialist Hartford Pub. Schs., Conn., 1952—86; with So. Conn. State U., New Haven, 1972—, asst. prof. Sch. Libr. Sci. and Instructional Tech., 1987—95, ret., 1995; substitute tchr. K-12 Windsor, Conn., 1999—2004, Grady County Pub. Schs., Cairo, Ga., 2004—. Mem. dept. curriculum com. So. Conn. State U., 1987-95, adj. prof., 1995—; cert. substitute tchr. Somerset County Pub. Schs., 1997—; cert. substitute tchr. Windsor, Conn. Sch. Sys., 1999-. Author: My Golden Moments, 1988, The Elementary School Media Center, 1990, Text Book Elementary School Media Center, 1991, I Must Fight Alone, 1991, (textbook) I Must Fight Alone, 1994. Mem. ALA, Conn. Ednl. Media Assn., Black Librs. Network NJ Inc., Assn. Ret. Tchrs. Conn., Black and Hispanic Consortium, So. Conn. State U. Women's Assn., Cicuso Club (v.p.), Friends Club (v.p.), Delta Kappa Gamma, Alpha Kappa Alpha. Avocations: reading, music, piano, walking. Home: 3633 Howard Dr Apt 133 College Park GA 30337

OLIVIER, LEON J., utilities executive; m. Bernadette Olivier. MBA, Northeastern Univ.; D in pub. svc. (hon.), Bridgewater State Coll. Mgmt. positions through v.p. nuclear Boston Edison; sr. v.p., chief nuclear officer Northeast Nuclear Energy Co., 1998—2001; sr. v.p. Entergy Nuclear Northeast, 2001; pres., COO Conn. Light & Power Co., 2001—05; pres. transmission group Northeast Utilities Sys., Hartford, Conn., 2005, exec. v.p. ops., 2005—08, exec. v.p., COO, 2008—. CEO Conn. Light & Power Co., Pub. Svc. Co. NH, We. Mass. Elec. Co., Yankee Gas Services Co. Bd. mem. Lawrence & Meml. Hosp., New London, Ea. Conn. C. of C., Spl. Olympics Conn., World Affairs Council Conn. Mailing: Northeast Utilities Sys PO Box 270 Hartford CT 06141-0270

OLIVIER, LEONARD JAMES, bishop emeritus; b. Lake Charles, La., Oct. 12, 1923; Attended, St. Mary's Sem., Techny, Ill. Ordained priest Soc. of Divine Word, 1951; asst. dean Divine Word Missionary, dean of seminarians, rector; sec. studies US Divine Word seminaries, 1974—82; rector religious cmty. Divine Word Sem., Epworth, Iowa, 1974—82; pastor St. Anthony's Parish, Lafayette, La.; vicar for black Catholics Diocese of Lafayette, vicar, 1986—88; ordained bishop, 1988; aux. bishop Archdiocese of Washington, 1988—2004, aux. bishop emeritus, 2004—. Mem.: KC, Knight of St. John, Knight of St. Peter Claver. Roman Catholic.

OLIVO, FRANK J., alderman; m. Karen Olivo; children: Frank Jr., Dana, Anthony. Alderman, 13th ward Chgo. City Coun. Founder 13th Ward Graffiti Removal Program, Chgo., Southwest Real Estate Anti-Solicitation Program, Chgo. Active St. Mary Star of the Sea Parish, Chgo. Office: 6500 S Pulaski Rd Chicago IL 60629-5136 also: City Hall 121 N La Salle St Rm 209 Office 17 Chicago IL 60602 Office Phone: 773-581-8000, 312-744-3076. Business E-Mail: folivo@cityofchicago.org.*

OLIVO, KAREN, actress; b. Bronx, NY, Aug. 7, 1976; d. Rick Olivo and Penny Brown; m. Matt Caplan. Attended, U. Cin. Coll. Conservatory Music. Actor: (Broadway plays) Rent, 1996—2008, Brooklyn, 2004—05, In the Heights, 2008 (Drama Desk award, Outstanding Ensemble Performance, 2007), West Side Story, 2009— (Tony award, Best Featured Actress in a Musical, 2009); (TV series) All My Children, 2005, Law & Order, 2005, Conviction, 2006, Law & Order: Special Victims Unit, 2007; (films) Adrift in Manhattan, 2007, The New Twenty, 2009. Office: c/o West Side Story The Palace Theatre 1564 Broadway Btwn 46th & 47th St New York NY 10036

OLKINETZKY, SAM, artist, educator, retired museum director; b. NYC, Nov. 22, 1919; s. Isidor and Jennie Olkinetzky; m. Sammie Lee Sturdevant, Dec. 20, 1959; children: Jov Shan, Tova Shana. BA, Bklyn. Coll., 1942; postgrad., Inst. Fine Arts, N.Y. U., 1946-47. Asst. prof. art and humanities Okla. A&M U., Stillwater, 1947-57; vis. asst. prof. art U. Okla., Norman, 1957-58; assoc. prof. art Mus. of Art, 1959—; dir. Mus. Art U. Okla., Norman, 1959-83. Vis. prof. art and humanities U. Ark., Fayetteville, 1962—63, Fayetteville, 1967—68, Langston U., Okla., 1969—70; art cons. Kerr-McGee Industries, Inc.; advisor State of Okla. Visual Arts; mem. State Art Collection Com., Norman Arts and Humanities Coun. One-man shows include Arts Pl. II, Okla. Art Ctr., Firehouse Art Ctr., Norman, 1989, exhibitions include Mus. Non-Objective Art, NYC, Mus. Modern Art, 50-Yr. Retrospective Exhbn., 1942—92, Norick Art Ctr., Oklahoma City, 1992, Represented in permanent collections Mus. Art U. Okla., Philbrook Art Mus., Tulsa, Oklahoma City Mus. Art. With USAAF, 1942—45. Recipient Gov.'s Art award, 1981, St. Gaudens medal, Alexander medal, NYC. Mem.: Art Mus. Assn., Am. Assn. Mus., Mountain-Plains Mus. Assn., Internat. Coun. Mus., Okla. Mus. Assn. (pres. 1978—79).

OLLEY, ROBERT EDWARD, economist, educator; b. Vendun, Que., Can., Apr. 16, 1933; s. Edwin Henry and Elizabeth (Reed) O.; m. Shirley Ann Dahl, Jan. 19, 1957; children— Elizabeth Anne, George Steven, Susan Catherine, Maureen Carolyn BA, Carleton U., Can., 1960; MA, Queen's U., Can., 1961, PhD in Econs., 1969. Vis. asst. prof. Queen's U., Kingston, Canada, 1967-68; asst. prof. econs. U. Sask., Saskatoon, Canada, 1963-67, 68-69, assoc. prof., 1969-71, 73-75, prof., 1975-93, prof. emeritus, 1993—; pres. Gen. Econs Ltd., 1993—. Dir. rsch. Royal Commn. on Consumer Problems and Inflation, 1967-68; econ. advisor Bell Can., Montreal, Que., 1971-73, 78-79, Can. Telecom. Carriers Assn., 1978-85, Sask. Power Corp., 1980-83; econ. advisor AT&T, 1980-90, Waste Mgmt., Inc., 1990-92, SaskTel, 1989-93; chmn. adv. com. on consumer stds. Stds. Coun. Can., 1992-93; Can. rep. to ISO/COPOLCO, Geneva, 1992-93. Author, editor: Consumer Product Testing, 1979; Consumer Product Testing II, 1981; Consumer Credit in Canada, 1966; Economics of the Public Firm: Regulation, Rates, Costs, Productivity Analysis, 1983, Total Factor Productivity of Canadian Telecommunications, 1984; Consumer Reps. Conf. Procs., 1st-4th, 1982-91. Bd. dirs. Can. Found. for Econ. Edn., 1974-82, Can. Gen. Stds. Bd., 1977-81; v.p. Niagara-on-the-Lake Hosp. Found., 2000-03, bd. dirs., 1998-. Recipient Silver Jubilee medal Her Majesty The Queen, 1977, Can.'s Jean P. Carriere Exptl. Contbr. Vol. Standardization award, 1995. Mem. Royal Econ. History Soc., Royal Econs. Assn., Econ. History Assn., Am. Econ. Assn., Can. Econ. Assn., Consumers Assn. Can. (v.p. 1967-75, chmn. 1975-77), Can. Stds. Assn. (dir., exec. com. 1971-93, vice chmn. 1985-87, chmn. 1987-89, Award of Merit 1995), Consumer's Assn. Found. Can. (v.p. 1989-95), Can. Comm. Rsch. Ctr. (dir. 1992-97), Internat. Telecom. Soc. (bd. dirs. 1986-2004), Shaw Guild, Niagara Hist. Soc. (bd. dirs. 1997-99), Niagara-on-the-Lake Golf Club (bd. dirs. 2001-05, v.p. 2002-05) Home and Office: PO Box 1040 374 Queen St Niagara-on-the-Lake ON Canada L0S 1J0 Office Phone: 905-468-0530. Personal E-mail: olley@niagara.com.

OLLILA, JORMA JAAKKO, telecommunications industry executive; b. Seinäjoki, Finland, Aug. 15, 1950; m. Liisa Annikki Metsola; children: Jaakko, Anna, Matti. MSc in Polit. Sci., U. Helsinki, 1976; MSc in Econs., London Sch. Econs., 1978; MSc in Engring., Helsinki U. Tech., 1981; PhD (hon.), U. Helsinki, 1995; DSC (hon.), Helsinki U. Tech., 1998. Account mgr. Citibank N.A., London, 1978-80; acct. officer Citibank Oy, 1980—82, mem. bd. mgmt., 1983—85; v.p. internat. ops. Nokia Corp., 1985—86, mem. group exec. bd., 1986—, sr. v.p. fin., 1986—89, dep. mem. bd. dirs., 1989-90, pres., Nokia Mobile Phones Salo, Finland, 1990-92, pres., CEO Finland, 1992-99, chmn. group exec. bd., 1992—2006, also bd. dir., 1995—, chmn. bd. dirs., CEO, 1999—2006, chmn., 2006—. Royal Dutch Shell, 2006—; v.p. EU Reflection Group, 2007—. Bd. dirs. Ford Motor Co., 2000-08, ICL plc, 1992-2000; mem. MTV Oy, chmn. bd., 1993-97, European Roundtable of Industrialists, 1997—, internat. bd. United World Colls., 1995—, UN Information and Comm. Technology Task Force, GBDe Business Steering Com., 1999-, and others; mem. supr. bd. Tietotehdas Oy, 1992-95, Pohjola Ins. Co. Ltd., 1992-97, NKF Holding N.V., 1992-99, Oy Rastor Ab, 1992-93, Sampo Ins. Co. Ltd., 1993-2000, Pension-Varma Mutual Ins. Co., 1993-98, Merita Bank Ltd.(former Union Bank of Finland, Ltd.), 1994-2000; chmn. bd. dir. and supervisory bd., Finnish Business and Policy Forum EVA, 2004-, Rsch. Inst. Finnish Economy ETLA, 2004-; vice-chmn. bd. dirs. UPM-Kymmene Corp., 2008, Otava Books and Mags. Group Ltd., 1996-; non-exec. chmn. Shell, 2006 Mem. Planning Bd. for Def. Econ., 1992-96, Ministry of Trade and Industry, Tech. Delegation, 1992-95, Sci. and Tech. Policy Coun. Finland, 1993-2002, Dean's coun. John F. Kennedy Sch. Govt. Harvard U., 1995-; mem. supr. bd. Found. Pediat. Rsch., 1993-98, Savonlinna Opera Festival Promotional Assn. Ch. Del., 1993-2002, chmn., 1996-, Assn. Finnish Cultural Found., exec. bd., 1993-; bd. dir. and exec. com. Confederation of Finnish Industry and Employers (TT), 1992-2002, dep. chmn. bd. 1995-2002, WWF Finland, 1995-97; mem. coun. State Tech. Rsch. Ctr., 1992-93, Ctr. for Finnish Bus. and Policy Studies EVA, 1993-2001; bd. dir. Econ. Information Bur., 1993-97; vice-chmn. bd. Internat. C.of C.(Finnish Sect.), 1993-97; chmn. supr. bd. Finnish Fgn. Trade Assn., 1993-98; mem. coun. supervisors, Rsch. Inst. of Finnish Economy ETLA, 1993-2000; vice-chmn. adv. com. 1993-95, Helsinki U. Technology, chmn. 1996-; coun. mem. Helsinki Sch. Econ. and Bus. Adminstrn., 1993-98; mem. exec. bd.Assn. for the Finnish Cultural Found., 1993-99; mem. del., Finnish-Swedish C.of C., 1993-; overseas adv. trustee, Am.-Scandinavian Found., 1994-; mem. Competitiveness Adv. Group, European Commn., 1995-96; mem. internat. bd., United World Coll. 1995-. Order of White Star, Estonia, 1995, Commdr. of Order of Orange-Nassau, 1995, Order of Merit of the Hungarian Republic, Officer's Cross, 1996, Commdr., knight 1st Class of Order of the White Rose of Finland, 1996, Decorated Commdr.'s Cross of the Order of Merit, Fed. Republic of Germany, 1997, Poland, 1999, named Hon. Citizen, Beijing, 2002. Mem. IEEE (hon.), Confedn. Finnish Industries and Employers (mem. bd. dirs. exec. com. 1992-, dep. chmn. 1995-2002), Finnish-Swedish C. of C., Assn. Finnish Cultural Found, State Tech. Rsch. Ctr., Econ. Info. Bur., Ctr. for Finnish Bus. and Policy Studies EVA, Sci. and Tech. Policy Coun., Min. Trade and Industry (tech. del.), Savonlinna Opera Festival Promotional Assn., Am.-Scand Found. (overseas adv. trustee), Nat. Union Finnish Students (chmn. 1973-74), Planning Bd. Def. Econ., State Tech. Rsch. Ctr., Finnish Fgn. Trade Assn. (chmn. supr. bd. 1993-98), Internat. C. of C. (vice-chmn. bd. Finnish sect. 1993-97), others; fellow (hon.) London Sch. of Econs. and Polit. Sci. Avocations: languages, tennis. Office: Nokia Oyi Keilalahdentie 2-4 PO Box 226 FIN-00045 Helsinki Finland also: Nokia Corp care of Carola Kiikka-Miettunen Keilalahdentie 4 02150 Espoo Finland

OLLINGTON, DAVID MCKENNA, performing arts educator; b. Chapel Hill, Nc, May 28, 1961; s. Marc Hilton Ollington and Becky Boling; life ptnr. Cim Roesener. MFA, Tex. Christian U., Fort Worth, 1989; BA, Kans. State U., Manhattan, 1983. Prin. dancer Starlight Theatre, Kans. City, Mo., 1986—96; choreographer Lyric Opera Kans. City, 1992—93, Seattle Children's Theatre, Wash., 2005—05, Coterie Theatre, Kansas City, 2008—; founder/co. mem. Aha! Dance Theatre, Kansas City, 1994—98; artist in residence Shawnee Mission East H.S., Kans., 1997—2000; theatre and dance columnist eKC Mag., Kansas City, 2001—; assoc. prof. Kans. State U., Manhattan, 2001—; actor,dir-.,choreographer Gt. Plains Theatre, Abilene, Kans., 2001—08; columnist EKC Mag., Kansas City, 2001—; core faculty Mo. Fine Arts Acad., Springfield, 2006—. Grant cons. Salina Arts Commn., Kans., 2008—08. Choreographer (theatre) Urinetown (Commendation from the Kennedy Ctr. Am. Coll. Theatre Festival, 2006), Pippin (Commendation from the Kennedy Ctr. Am. Coll. Theatre Festival, 2005); author: (arts writing) eKC Magazine (KC Press Club, Best Entertainment Writing, 2003); choreographer (theatre) The Full Monty (Nomination, Ostrander award, 2006). Treasure,pres. elect MidAmerica Dance Network, Mo., 1990—93; advisor 940 Dance Co., Lawrence, Kans., 2007—08. Mem.: Fathers Sons and Bros. (life). Office: Kans State Univ 129 Nichols Hall CSTD KSU Manhattan KS 66506 Personal E-mail: ollington@aol.com. E-mail: dollingt@ksu.edu.

OLMOS, EDWARD JAMES, actor; b. LA, Feb. 24, 1947; m. Kaija Keel, Dec. 29, 1972 (div. 1992); children: Mico, Bodie; m. Lorraine Bracco, Jan. 28, 1994 (div. Mar. 4, 2002). AA in Sociology, East Los Angeles City Coll.; postgrad., Calif. State U., LA; degree (hon.), U. Colo., Whittier Coll., Calif. State U., Fresno, Occidental Coll., Film Inst., Hollywood, Calif. Exec. dir. Lives in Hazard Ednl. Project, nat. gang prevention program. Performed in exptl. theater, L.A.; actor (play) Zoot Suit (Tony nominee, Los Angeles Drama Critics Circle award, Theatre World award), Broadway and Los Angeles, 1978-80; actor, producer film The Ballad of Gregorio Cortez, 1982, Triumph of the Spirit, 1989; actor, co-producer film Stand and Deliver, 1988 (nominee best actor Acad. Awards 1988); actor films Wolfen, 1981, Zoot Suit, 1981, Blade Runner, 1982, (also assoc. prodr., composer, music adapter) The Ballad of Gregorio Cortez, 1983, Saving Grace, 1986 (also prodr.) Stand and Deliver, 1988, Triumph of the Spirit, 1989, Talent for the Game, 1991, (also dir., prodr.) American Me, 1992, A Million to Juan, 1994, My Family, 1995, Caught, 1996, Selena, 1997, Death in Granada, 1997, The Wonderful Ice Cream Suit, 1998, The Wall, 1998, Gossip, 1999, (voice) The Road to El Dorado, 2000, Gossip, 2000, Jack and Marilyn, 2002, (voice) Beverly Hills Chihuahua, 2008; (TV series) Miami Vice, 1984-89 (Emmy award for best supporting actor in drama series 1985, Golden Globe award 1986); Battlestar Galactica, 2004- (Actor in a television series, drama, ALMA Awards, 2008); (TV miniseries) The Fortunate Pilgrim, 1988, Menendez: A Killing in Beverly Hills, 1994, The Burning Season, 1995 (Golden Globe award for Best Supporting Actor in a TV Movie, Miniseries or Series 1994), Mirage, 1995, Slave of Dreams, 1995, Roosters, 1995, American Family, 2002, Battlestar Galactica, 2003, The Batman, 2004; (TV movies) The Princess and the Barrio Boy, 2000, The Judge, 2001, In the Time of the Butterflies, 2001; star ABC miniseries Dead Man's Walk (prequel to Lonesome Dove), 1996; co-star TV movie 12 Angry Men, 1997; prodr., dir. (TV documentary) Lives in Hazard, 1994, The Limbic Region, 1995. U.S. goodwill amb. UNICEF; nat. spokesman for voter registration, Juvenile Diabetes Found., AIDS Awareness Found.; bd. dirs. Heal L.A., Recruiting New Tchrs., 20th Century Fund, UCLA Sch. Film and Theater, Miami Children's Hosp., L.A. Children's Hosp., Nat. Coun. on Adoption, Children's Action Netowrk, Hollywood Supports, Nat. Hispanic U., Plaza del Raza, Whittier Coll.; spkr. at numerous chs., charities and juvenile instns. throughout U.S. Address: Olmos Productions 18034 Ventura Blvd Ste 288 Encino CA 91316-3516 Office: AA Creative Artists Agency 830 Wilshire Blvd Beverly Hills CA 90210

OLMSTEAD, CECIL JAY, lawyer; b. Jacksonville, Fla., Oct. 15, 1920; s. Cecil Jay Sr. and Bessie (Irby) O.; m. Frances Hughes (dec. 2006); children: Cecil Jay III, Frank Hughes, Jane Olmstead Murphy, Amy Olmstead Vanecek. BA, U. Ga., 1950, LLB, 1951; Sterling Grad. fellow, Yale Law Sch., 1951-52; LLD (hon.), U. Hull, Eng., 1978. Bar: Ga. 1950, U.S. Supreme Ct 1964, D.C. 1978. Asst. to legal adviser Dept. State, counsel Mut. Security Agy., counsel Hoover Commn. on Orgn. Exec. Br. of Govt., 1952-55; dir. Middle East Inst., Wash., DC, 1972—78, Inter-Am. Law Inst., 1958—61; prof. N.Y. U. Sch. Law, 1953-61; adj. prof. law Inter-Am. Law Inst., 1961-69; atty. Texaco, Inc., NYC, 1961-62, asst. to chmn. bd., 1962-70, v.p., asst. to chmn. bd., 1970, v.p., asst. to pres., 1970-71, v.p., asst. to chief exec. officer, 1971-73, exec. dept., v.p., 1973-80; bd. dir. Arahan, 1978—79; mem. firm Steptoe & Johnson, Washington, 1980—. Vis. prof. Columbia U. Sch. Law, 1959; Wang Disting. vis. prof. St. Johns U., 1987-90; mem. adv. panel on internat. law to sec. state; adv. com. law of sea State Dept.; also adv. com. transnat. enterprise; U.S. del. UN Com. on Law of Sea, 1972-73; U.S. del. UN Conf. on Law of Sea, 1974-76; Eisenhower lectr. Nat. War Coll., 1973; mem. U.S. del. UN Conf. on Code of Conduct for Transnat. Corps., ann. 1984-90; mem. World Bank's panel of conciliators of the Internat. Ctr. for Settlement of Investment Disputes, 1988-95; vis. fellow All Souls Coll., Oxford U., 1988; vis. scholar Yale Law Sch., 1990-91. Co-Author with Robert McKay: Freedom to Travel (1968), numerous law review articles. With USAF, 1943-46, 8th and 20th Air Forces. ETO, PTO. Recipient Gold medal City of Brussels (Belgium, 1973, Gold medal City of Paris (France), 1984; named Commdr. Brit. Empire (hon.), 1990. Mem. Internat. Law Assn. (pres. and chmn. Am. br. 1966-73, vice chmn. exec. coun. internat. hdqtrs. London, 1975-86, chmn. exec. coun. 1986-88, 1st Disting. Svc. award,Am. Br. 2004), Am. Law Inst. (assoc. reporter Restatement of the Fgn. Rels. Law of US, 1st edit. 1964, advisor 3d edit.), Coun. on Fgn. Rels., Washington Inst. Fgn. Affairs, Nat. Fgn. Trade Coun. (dir. 2004), Am. Coun. on Germany (hon. dir.), Coun. on Ocean Law (dir.), Nickerbocker Club NYC, Yale Club, Fairfield County Hunt Club (Westport), Cosmos Club (Washington), Order of Coif, Phi Beta Kappa. Home: 4 Sprucewood Ln Westport CT 06880-4021 Office: 1330 Connecticut Ave NW Washington DC 20036-1704 Office Phone: 202-429-6483.

OLMSTEAD, LUCINDA SUE, English professor; b. Gloversville, NY, July 1, 1941; d. Albert Pellegrino and Lois Beverly Harding; m. Robert Lloyd Olmstead, Dec. 23, 1964; children: Kimberly Joy Woloszyn, Kelly Olmstead Masline. BA, Barrington Coll., RI, 1963; MA, SUNY, Albany, NY, 1990. Cert. tchr. N.Y. State Tchr. Certification Assn., 1990. Instr. English Gloversville (N.Y.) Sch. Dist., 1963—64, Johnstown (N.Y.) Sch. Dist., 1967—68; instr. English and history Liverpool (N.Y.) Sch. Dist., 1964—66; substitute tchr. Capital Region Schs., NY, 1968—90; prof. English Bryant & Stratton Coll., Albany, NY, 2001—. Chmn. English dept. Bryant & Stratton Coll., 2001—, advisor Drama Club, 2001—. Author: (children book) But not on my Ice Cream Please, 2008. Mem.: Nat. Coun. Tchrs. English (life). Avocations: singing, music, acting, writing. Home: 233 Shaker Park Dr Loudonville NY 12211 Office: Bryant & Stratton College 1259 Central Avenue Albany NY 12205 Personal E-mail: lusings@nycap.rr.com. Business E-Mail: lsolmstead@bryantstratton.edu.

OLMSTEAD, WILLIAM EDWARD, mathematics professor; b. San Antonio, June 2, 1936; s. William Harold and Gwendolyn (Littlefield) Olmstead; m. Adele Cross, Aug. 14, 1957 (div. 1967); children: William Harold, Randell Edward. BS, Rice U., 1959; MS, Northwestern U., 1962, PhD, 1963. Mem. rsch. staff S.W. Rsch. Inst., San Antonio, 1959—60; Sloan Found. postdoctoral fellow Johns Hopkins, 1963—64; prof. applied math. Northwestern U., Evanston, Ill., 1964—, chmn. dept. engring. scis. and applied math., 1991—93. Vis. mem. Courant Inst. Math. Scis. NYU, 1967—68; faculty visitor U. Coll. London, 1973, Calif. Inst. Tech., 1987, 90; editor Options Prof. Newsletter, Spear Capital Mgmt., 2003—07. Contbr. articles to profl. jours. Recipient Award for Tchg. Excellence, Northwestern Alumni Assn., 1993; named Technol. Inst. Tchr. of Yr., 1980, Charles Deering McCormick prof., 1994—97. Mem.: Am. Contract Bridge League (silver life master), Soc. Indsl. and Applied Math. (editl. bd. jour. 1998—), Am. Phys. Soc., Am. Math. Soc., Am. Acad. Mechanics, Soc. Engring. Sci. (bd. dirs.

1998—2000), John Evans Club, Sigma Tau, Tau Beta Pi, Sigma Xi. Episcopalian. Home: 153 E Laurel Ave #203 Lake Forest IL 60045 Office: Northwestern U Dept Engring Scis And Applie Evanston IL 60208-0001

OLMSTED, JENNIFER, interior design consultant; BS, East Tenn. State U., Johnson City, 1998, grad. cert. Bus. Adminstrn., 1999; cert. med. transcription, Edn. Direct, Scranton, Pa., 2003. Grad. asst. East Tenn. State U., 1998; agy. mgr. Farmer's Ins., Patrick Becker Agy., Boulder, Colo., 2000; med. records mgr. Boulder Internal Medicine, 2000—01; med. transcriptionist Boulder Orthopedics, LLC, 2001—03, Healthcare Employee Services, LLC, Carlsbad, Calif., 2004—05, Lab. Corp. America, San Diego, 2005—06; bus. owner Idle Hando, San Maros, Calif., 2004—. Scholarship, Southern Adventist U., 1994—95, East Tenn. State U., 1995—99. Mem.: Am. Soc. Interior Designers, Phi Theta Kappa, Eta Sigma Gamma, Gamma Beta Phi, Phi Kappa Phi, Alpha Xi Delta.

OLMSTED, JERAULD LOCKWOOD, telephone company executive; b. Des Moines, Aug. 26, 1938; s. George Hamden and Virginia (Camp) O.; m. Mary Karen Autenrieth, June 20, 1962 (div. Dec. 1986); children: Scott H., Victoria L., Jerauld; m. Gisele A. Child, June 17, 1988. BS, Iowa State U., 1961; MBA, George Washington U., 1979; Cert. mgmt. accountant. Vice-pres. First Nat. Bank of Washington, 1969; v.p., dir. Intermediate Credit Corp., 1969-73, Internat. Gen. Industries, Inc., 1974-79, pres., dir., 1980-82, IB Credit Corp., 1982-85, N.Am. Communications, Inc., Bethesda, Md., 1985—. Sr. v.p., dir. Internat. Bank, 1978-85. Bd. govs. Iowa State U. Found., 1980—; chmn. corporate adv. bd. div. arts and humanities U. Md., 1982—86; sec.-treas. George Olmsted Found., 1970—85. Served with US Army, 1961-63. Decorated Knight of Malta, Order of St. John Mem. Fin. Execs. Inst., Mensa, Soc. Cincinnati, Met. Club, Georgetown Club, Bethesda Country Club, Beta Alpha Psi., Beta Gamma Sigma. Republican. Episcopalian. Home and Office: 7735 Arrowood Ct Bethesda MD 20817-2821 Office Phone: 301-365-7225.

OLMSTED, THOMAS JAMES, bishop; b. Oketo, Kans., Jan. 21, 1947; BS in Philosophy, St. Thomas Sem. Coll., 1969; MA in Theology, 1977, PhD in Canon Law, 1979. Ordained priest Diocese of Lincoln, Nebr., 1973; assoc. pastor Cathedral of Risen Christ, Lincoln, Nebr., 1973—76; asst. Secretariat of State of Holy See Pontifical N.Am. Coll., Rome, 1979—88; pastor St. Vincent de Paul Parish, Seward, Nebr., 1989—93; dean personal formation Pontifical Coll. Josephinum, Columbus, Ohio, 1993—97, rector, 1997—99; ordained bishop, 1999; coadjutor bishop Diocese of Wichita, Kans., 1999—2001, bishop, 2001—03, Diocese of Phoenix, 2003—; apostolic adminstr. Diocese of Gallup, N.Mex., 2008—09. Com. mem. US Conf. Cath. Bishops, 1999—; mem. adminstrv. com. US Bishops, mem. com. consecrated life; bd.dir. Cath. Legal Immigration Network. Roman Catholic. Office: Diocese of Phoenix 400 East Monroe St Phoenix AZ 85004-2336*

OLNESS, KAREN NORMA, medical educator; b. Rushford, Minn., Aug. 28, 1936; d. Norman Theodore and Karen Agnes (Gunderson) O.; m. Hakon Daniel Torjesen, 1962. BA, U. Minn., 1958, BS, MD, 1961. Diplomate Am. Bd. Pediat., Am. Bd. Med. Hypnosis, Develop. & Behavioral Pediatrics. Intern Harbor Gen. Hosp., Torrance, Calif.; resident Nat. Children's Hosp. Med. Ctr., Washington; asst. prof. George Washington U., Washington, 1970-74; assoc. prof. U. Minn., Mpls., 1974-87; prof. pediat., family medicine and internat. health Case Western Res. U., Cleve., 1987—. Named Outstanding Woman Physician, Minn. Assn. Women Physicians, 1987; recipient Christopherson award Am. Acad. Pediat., 1998, Aldrich award, Am. Acad. Pediat., 1999, Ann. award Soc. Devel. and Behavioral Pediat., 2003, Outstanding Alumni award U. Minn., 2007, Hon. Doc. award, Khon Kaen U., 2007, Tow Humanism award, 2008; named to Cleve. Med. Hall of Fame, 2000. Fellow: Soc. Clin. and Exptl. Hypnosis (pres. 1991—93), Am. Soc. Clin. Hypnosis (pres. 1984—86), Am. Acad. Pediat. (chair internat. health sect. 2001), Am. Acad. Family Physicians; mem.: Internat. Hypnosis Soc. (pres. 2003—06), Northwestern Pediat. Soc. (pres. 1977), Soc. Devel. and Behavioral Pediat. Office: Case Western Res U 11100 Euclid Ave Cleveland OH 44106-6038 Office Phone: 216-368-4368. Business E-Mail: karen.olness@case.edu.

OLNEY, GISELE CELESTE, engineering educator, consultant; b. Omaha, Nebr., Dec. 12, 1955; d. Eugene Lee Olney and Dorothy Beatrice Harbour; m. Richard John Buhman, Aug. 22, 1979 (dec. July 9, 2005); children: Anna Louise Buhman, Katharine Rose Lynn Buhman, Zachary John Henry Buhman. MS, U. Nebr., Omaha, 2002. Cert. in lean enterprise, Dept. Commerce, NIST, 2000, U. Nebr., 2001; in enterprise resource planning Wright, 1996, trainer MEPU, 2002, growth coach Eureka Ranch, 2008. Engring. mgr. Lozier Corp., Omaha, 1989—91, prodn. inventory control mgr., 1992—98, project mgr., 1994—98; pres. Value Links, Yutan, Nebr., 1998—2008, CEO, 1998—2008; cons. U. Nebr., 1998—, adj. prof., 2003—. Bd. mem. Signs and Shapes, Omaha, 2000—04. Com. chair Rotary Club Omaha, 2003—08; mem. Fine Arts Booster, Yutan, 1997—2008. Mem.: TWHBEA (bd. mem. 2006—08), North Hills Hunt (hon.; huntman 1980—86, Recognition 1984). Avocations: horseback riding, hunting, bicycling, skiing, hiking. Home: 1451 County Rd 4 Yutan NE 68073 Office: Univ Nebr Omaha 6001 Dodge St Omaha NE 68182 Office Fax: 402-554-6260. Business E-Mail: golney@unomaha.edu.

OLNEY, JOHN WILLIAM, psychiatry professor; b. Marathon, Iowa, Oct. 23, 1931; married, 1957; 3 children. BA, U. Iowa, 1957, MD, 1963. Diplomate Am. Bd. Psychiatry, Am. Bd. Neurology. Intern Kaiser Permanente Found., San Francisco, 1963-64; resident, 1964-68; from instr. to assoc. prof. psychiatry Washington U., St. Louis, 1968-77, prof. psychiatry and neuropathology Sch. Medicine, 1977—. NIMH biol. sci. trainee Washington U., 1966-68; asst. psychiatrist Barnes Hosp., 1968—; cons. psychiatrist Malcolm Bliss Mental Health Ctr., 1968—; elected to Inst. Medicine/NAS, 1996. Recipient Wakeman award Rsch. Neurosci., 1992; co-recipient Charles A. Dana award for Pioneering Achievements in Health, 1994. Mem. APA, Am. Assn Neuropathology, Soc. Neurosci. Assn. Rsch. Nervous & Mental Disorders, Psychiatric Rsch. Soc. Achievements include research in role of excitatory neurotoxins in disorders of the nervous system. Office: Washington U Dept Psychiatry Sch Med Saint Louis MO 63110

OLNEY, ROBERT CALDWELL, pediatrician, researcher; s. John Mclean and Pauline Harcourt Olney; m. Carolyn Sue Puckett, Mar. 22, 1997. MD, U. Calif. San Diego Sch. Medicine, La Jolla, 1988. Diplomate Am. Bd. Pediat., 1992, in pediat. endocrinology 1995. Pediat. intern and resident Stanford U. Med. Ctr., Calif., 1988—91, pediat. endocrinology fellow, 1991—94, rsch. fellow, 1994—95; physician, rschr. Nemours Children's Clinic, Jacksonville, Fla., 1995—, dir. pediat. endocrinology tng. program, 2005—. Contbr. articles to profl. jour. Grant, NIH, 1999—2004. Fellow: Am. Acad. Pediat.; mem.: Lawson Wilkins Pediat. Endocrine Soc. Office: Nemours Children's Clinic 807 Children's Way Jacksonville FL 32207

OLOFSON, TOM WILLIAM, technology company executive; b. Oak Park, Ill., Oct. 10, 1941; s. Ragnar V. and Ingrid E. Olofson; m. Jeanne Hamilton, Aug. 20, 1960; children: Christopher, Scott. Various mgmt. positions Bell Telephone Co. of Pa., Pitts., 1963-67; sales mgr. Xerox Corp., Detroit, 1967-68, nat. account mgr. Rochester, NY, 1968, mgr. govt. planning, 1969, mgr. Kansas City (Mo.) br., 1969-74; corp. v.p. health products group Marion Labs., Inc., Kansas City, 1974-78, sr. v.p., mem. Office Pres., 1978-80; exec. v.p., dir. Electronic Realty Assocs., Inc., 1980-83; chmn. bd., CEO Emblem Graphic Sys., Inc., 1983-88, EPIQ Sys., Inc., 1988—. Dir. DemoGraFX, Elinco Internat., Access Industries, Inc., Saztec Internat., Capital Ptnrs. Bd. visitors U. Pitts., Joseph M. Katz Grad. Sch. Bus.; past trustee Barstow Sch.; past chmn. bd. trustees Village United Presbyn. Ch.; chmn. Tom. W. and Jeanne H. Olofson Found., 2001-. Mem. Carlton Club (Chgo.), Kansas City Club, Omicron Delta Kappa, Sigma Chi. Republican. Presbyterian. Office: EPIQ Sys Inc 501 Kansas Ave Kansas City KS 66105-1309

OLOFSSON, JOHN ARNDT, engineering educator; b. NYC, Aug. 9, 1946; s. John Arndt and Gerd Olofsson; life ptnr. Diane Marie Erickson; children: Jennifer Rebecca Powers, Kaarin Alissa Milne. PhD in Civil Engring., U. Maine, Orono, 1977. Prof. U. Alaska Anchorage, 1990—2008. Home: 4315 Elkhorn Dr Eagle River AK 99577 Office: Univ Alaska Anchorage 3211 Providence Dr Anchorage AK 99508 Personal E-mail: john.a.olofsson@gmail.com. Business E-Mail: afjao@uaa.alaska.edu.

OLONI, ANTHONY OLUSHEGUN, medical association administrator, director; s. James Bolaji and Deborah Funmi Oloni. MBBS, U. Ilorin, Nigeria, 1987; grad. cert. in Pub. Health Informatics, U. Ill., 2006, MPH in Informatics, 2004. Med. intern Mil. Hosp., Yaba, Lagos, Nigeria, 1988—89; med. rsch. assoc. Coll. of Medicine, U. Lagos, 1989—90; med. dir. Mc'Lonie Indsl. Clin., Lagos, 1990—92; pub. health cons. Phila. Dept. Pub. Health, 1994—99; pres., CEO, med. dir. Pub. Health Informatics Cons., Atlanta, 2000—; med. dir. Preventive Medicine Assoc., Atlanta, 2000—03. Directorship Nat. Black Leadership Initiative on Cancer, Phila., 1997—99; chaiman Metro-Atlanta Coalition for Cancer Awareness, Atlanta, 2001—02; dir., health adminstr. Project Flow, Mayors Office Cmty. Svcs.; chief health coord. Your Health. Recipient Ujama award for Cmty. Economics. Mem.: Am. Med. Informatics Assn. (assoc.). Achievements include design of patient electronic health record sys. Home: 1862 Hickory Creek Ct Acworth GA 30102 Office: Public Health Informatics Cons PO Box 2822 Acworth GA 30102 Home Fax: 678-355-0462. Business E-Mail: anthony.oloni.md@phicon.org.

OLOPADE, OLUFUNMILAYO FALUSI (FUNMI OLOPADE), geneticist, educator, oncologist, hematologist; b. Nigeria, Apr. 29, 1957; m. Christopher Sola Olopade; 3 children. MD with distinction, U. Ibadan, Nigeria, 1980. Diplomate Am. Bd. Internal Medicine, Am. Bd. Med. Oncology, Am. Bd. Hematology; lic. MD Ill., Ind. Med. officer Nigerian Navy Hosp.; intern in medicine, surgery, pediatrics, ob-gyn. Univ. Coll. Hosp., Ibadan, 1980—81; intern in internal medicine Cook County Hosp., Chgo., 1983—84, resident in internal medicine, 1984—86, chief resident in medicine, 1986; clin. instr. U. Ill. Abraham Lincoln Sch. Medicine, Chgo., 1986—87; postdoctoral fellow jt. sect. hematology/oncology U. Chgo., 1987—91, asst. prof. hematology/oncology, Pritzker Sch. Medicine, 1991—2002, mem. Cancer Rsch. Ctr., 1991—, mem. Cancer Biology com., 1994—, mem. Genetics com., 1996—, assoc. prof. medicine, prof. medicine and human genetics Ill., 2002—, dir. Ctr. for Clinical Cancer Genetics, Cancer Risk Clinic Ill., 1992—, dir. Hematology/Oncology Fellowship Program Ill., 1998—. Attending physician Cook County Hosp., Chgo., 1987; mem. steering com., cooperative family registry for breast cancer studies, Nat. Cancer Inst., also mem. adv. com. Cancer Genetics Network and bd. scientific counselors; mem. adv. bd. Cancerandcareers.org; lectr. in field. Ad hoc reviewer Jour. AMA, Genes, Chromosomes and Cancer, Genomics, Human Molecular Genetics, Cancer Rsch., Blood, Molecular Carcinogenesis, Jour. Clin. Oncology, New Eng. Jour. Medicine; contbr. articles to profl. jours.; contbr. to book chpts. and abstracts on topics including genetics of cancer. Mem. med. adv. bd. Young Survival Coalition. Recipient Sir Samuel Manuwa Gold medal for Excellence in Clin. Sciences, 1980, Scholar award, James S. McDonnell Found., 1992, Doris Duke Disting. Clin. Scientist award, 2000, Phenomenal Women award, 2003, People Are Today's Heroes (PATH), Gov. Rod R. Blagojevich, presented by First Lady Patti Blagojevich, State Ill., 2005, Heroes In Healthcare award, Access Cmty. Network, 2005; named a Top Doctor, Chicago Mag., 1997; named an Outstanding Woman of Achievement, YWCA Metropolitan Chgo., 2008; fellow John D. and Catherine T. MacArthur Found., 2005; Ellen Ruth Lebow Fellowship, Assn. for Brain Tumor Rsch., 1990. Mem. AAAS, Inst. Medicine, Am. Assn. Cancer Rsch. (membership credentialing com. 1994-95, program com. carcinogenesis subcom. 1993; Minorities in Cancer Rsch. Jane Cooke Wright lectureship, 2006), Am. Soc. Clin. Oncology (mem. program com. subcom. tumor biology and genetics 1997, Young Investigator award, 1991), Am. Assn. Preventive Oncology, Women in Cancer Rsch., Am. Soc. Hematology, Am. Coll. Physicians, Am. Soc. Breast Disease, Am. Soc. Hematology, Assn. Am. Professors, Nigerian Med. Assn., Am. Cancer Soc. (adv. com. cancer control investigations, epidemiology, diagnosis, therapy 1994-97). Office: U Chgo Med Ctr 5841 S Maryland Ave # MC2115 Chicago IL 60637-1463 Office Phone: 773-702-1632, 773-702-6149. Office Fax: 773-702-0963. Business E-Mail: folopade@medicine.bsd.uchicago.edu.*

O'LOUGHLIN, JOHN KIRBY, retired insurance executive; b. Bklyn., Mar. 31, 1929; s. John Francis and Anne (Kirby) O'L.; m. Janet R. Tag, July 5, 1952; children: Robert K., Steven M., Patricia A., John A. BA in Econs., St. Lawrence U., Canton, NY, 1951. State agt. Royal Globe Ins. Group, 1953-58; with Allstate Ins. Co., 1958—, mktg. v.p., group v.p., then exec. v.p., 1972—; pres. Allstate Life Ins. Co., 1977—; chmn. bd. Allstate Ins. Co. and Life Co. Can., 1976—, sr. exec. v.p., chief planning officer, 1980-90; ret. Bd. dirs. all cos. in Allstate Ins. Group and Allstate Enterprises, Inc.; former pres. Allstate Enterprises, Inc.; pres., CEO Royal Link Ventures, Ltd., Pinehurst, N.C. Trustee St. Lawrence U.; bd. trustees, pres. U.S. Marine Corps U. Found., Inc.; bd. dirs. Marine Corps Assn., Am. Ireland Fund, USMC Scholarship Found. Inc., Coun. on Ind. Colls.; past chmn. No. Suburban Chgo. United Way; elder 1st United Presbyn. Ch. Capt. USMCR, 1951-53. Mem. Sales and Mktg. Execs. Internat. (bd. dirs., past chmn., pres.), Whispering Woods Golf Club, Pinehurst Country Club, Lahinch Club, Country Club of N.C., Army-Navy Club, Washington. Office: Royal Links Ventures Ltd PO Box 3579 Pinehurst NC 28374-3579

O'LOUGHLIN, KATHLEEN T., dental association administrator; BA in Biology, cum laude, Boston U., 1973; DMD summa cum laude, Tufts U. Sch. Dental Medicine, Medford, Mass., 1981; MA in Health Care Mgmt., Harvard Sch. Pub. Health, Boston, 1998. Tchg. cert. Suffolk U., Boston. Pvt. practice gen. dentistry, Medford, 1981—2001; pres., CEO Dental Svcs. Mass. Inc./Delta Dental Mass., 2002—07; chief dental officer, v.p. quality & care mgmt. United Healthcare, Columbia, Md.; exec. dir., COO ADA, 2009—. Asst. clin. prof. Tufts U. Sch. Dental Medicine, 1996—, bd. trustees, 2006—; clin. instr. Boston U. Goldman Sch. Grad. Dentistry; bd. dirs. Children's Dental Health Project, Washington, Oral Health America; past pres. Oral Health Found. Mass. Mem.: ADA, Tufts U. Sch. Dental Medicine Alumni Assn., East Middlesex Dist. Dental Soc., Pierre Fouchard Acad., Mass. Dental Soc., Am. Assn. Women Dentists, Internat. Coll. Dentists, Am. Coll. Dentists, Omicron Kappa Upsilon. Office: ADA 211 E Chgo Ave Chicago IL 60611 Office Phone: 312-440-2500.

O'LOUGHLIN, KATIE EILEEN BRIDGET, poet; m. Scott Koblish, July 26, 2003; 1 child, Violet Ophelia Koblish-O'Loughlin. AA in Theater and Early Childhood Edn., Palomar Coll., San Marcos, Calif., 1984; BS in Computer and Info. Sci., Coleman Coll., La Mesa, Calif., 1986. Poetic License Poetry Slam Inc., 2001. Ind. creator, prodr., host 6 Women Revealed and 6 Men Revealed, Hollywood, Calif., 1999—2000. Poet in the schs. mid. sch. and HS, East Los Angeles, Calif., 2001—. Author: (book of poetry) I Can't Pull it Together Enough to Look Like My Poster; author: (performer) (spoken word poetry slam performance) Unknown Man with Soft, Soft skin (1st Pl. (tie) BBC Radio Scotland Internat. Poetry Slam, Edinburgh/Glasgow, Scotland, 2002), They Always Said You're Gonna be Like Your Momma When You Grow Up (3rd Pl. Bristol Poetry Festival 2002 Internat. Poetry Slam in Bristol, Eng., 2002), Skinny be Damned, Concave Bellies Don't Bear Babies, Compassion, Being Tempted to Fall from Grace (3rd Pl. Bristol Internat. Poetry 2000 Slam, 2000), They Always Said You're Gonna be Like Your Momma, Snow Globe, Compassion (2nd Pl. Urban Grind San Diego Poetry Slam, 2003), Snow Globe, They Always Said Your Gonna be Like Your Momma, Being Tempted to Fall from Grace (1st Pl. Orange County Big Damn Poetry Slam, 2003), Compassion, Exact Shade, Skinny be Damned, Concave Bellies Don't Bear Babies (1st Pl. Long Beach Big Damn Poetry Slam, 2002), Being Tempted to Fall From Grace, Exact Shade, Skinny be Damned, Concave Bellies Don't Bear Babies (1st Pl. Urban Grind San Diego Poetry Slam, 2002), Exact Shade, Compassion, Being Tempted to Fall from Grace (2nd Pl. Los Feliz Pig Slam, 2002), Being Tempted to Fall from Grace, Compassion, Exact Shade (1st Pl. Long Beach Big Damn Poetry Slam, 2001); author: (book of poetry) For My Sisters; author: (performer) (spoken word poetry slam performance) Skinny be Damned, Concave Bellies Don't Bear Babies, Compassion, Being Tempted to Fall From Grace (2nd Pl. Urban Grind San Diego Poetry Slam, 2001), (spoken word poetry performance) A Woman Revealed (Acceptance into the LA Women's Theatre Festival 2001, 2001). Performer for benefit show Sojourner Ho. for Abused Women and Children, LA, Calif., 2001. Mem.: Poetry Slam Inc. Avocations: travel, scuba diving. Personal E-mail: writeonmomma@yahoo.com.

O'LOUGHLIN, SANDRA S., lawyer; b. Buffalo, Jan. 15, 1942; BA summa cum laude, Rosary Hill Coll., 1973; JD cum laude, U. Buffalo, 1978. Bar: N.Y. 1979. Atty. Hiscock & Barclay, LLP, Buffalo, 1978-79, ptnr., 1990—. Chmn. character and fitness com. appellate divsn. 4th dept. 8th jud. dist. N.Y. Supreme Ct., 1986—2006; adj. prof. SUNY Law Sch., Buffalo; mem. numerous publs., 2002—08. Note editor Buffalo Law Rev., 1977-78. Mem. Erie County Legis. Task Force Mental Health, 1979-81; mem. adv. bd. Congregation of Sisters of St. Joseph, 1987—. Mem. ABA (bus. law com.), Nat. Assn. Bond Lawyers, N.Y. State Bar Assn. (ethics com. 1984-94, 2000-03, vice chmn. 1987-92, unauthorized practice of law com. 1998-2002, mem. com. on securities regulation 1999—, com. standards atty. conduct 2004—), Erie County Bar Assn. (ethics com. 1984-87, chmn. 1987-89, corp. law com. 1984-, grievance com. 1993—). Office: Hiscock & Barclay LLP 1100 M&T Ctr 3 Fountain Plaza Buffalo NY 14203-1414 Business E-Mail: soloughlin@hiscockbarclay.com.

O'LOUGHLIN-BROOKS, JENNIFER L., psychology professor; married; children: Jon, Trenton. BA in Psychology and Speech/Comm., Tex. Christian U., 1991; MS in Exptl. Psychology, Emporia State U., 1994. Assoc. prof. Collin County CC, Tex., 1995—2002, prof. psychology Tex., 2002—. Assoc. editor: Jour. Psychol. Inquiry. Recipient US Prof. of Yr. award, Carnegie Found. for Advancement of Tchg. and Coun. for Advancement and Support of Edn., 2006. Mem.: Tex. Jr. Coll. Tchr.'s Assn., Southwestern Tchrs. of Psychology Assn., Southwestern Psychol. Assn., APA, Psi Beta. Office: Collin County CC 4800 Preston Park Blvd Plano TX 75093 E-mail: jbrooks@ccccd.edu.

OLSCHKI, ALESSANDRO, book publishing executive; b. Florence, Italy, Feb. 12, 1925; s. Aldo Manuzio and Rita (Roster) Olschki; m. Gigliola Serroni, Mar. 26, 1949 (dec. 1985); children: Daniele, Costanza; m. Lydia Boretti, Nov. 20, 1985. Student, Coll. Alla Querce, Florence. Asst. head Leo S. Olschki Publs., Florence, Italy, 1945—63, head, 1963—. Author: Underwater Spearfishing, 1962, 2d. edit., 1965, Visto Si Stampi, 1995, Centotredici Anni, 1999, Marcella, 2002, Scritti subacquei, 2005. Recipient Italian Underwater Spearfishing Champion, 1956, World Champion Underwater Spearfishing, 1957, 1960. Mem.: Underwater Tech. and Sci. Rsch. Group (pres. 1966—), Acad. Underwater Scis., Hist. Diving Soc. (hon.). Home: Via di S Piero in Palco 3 50126 Florence Italy Office: Casa Editrice Leo S Olschki, Viuzzo del Pozzetto no 8 50126 Florence Italy Home Phone: +39-0556530683; Office Phone: +39-0556530684. Business E-Mail: alessandro@olschki.it.

OLSCHWANG, ALAN PAUL, lawyer, crossword and variety puzzle author; b. Chgo., Jan. 30, 1942; s. Morton James and Ida (Ginsberg) O.; m. Barbara Claire Miller, Aug. 22, 1965; children: Elliot, Deborah, Jeffrey. BS, U. Ill., Champaign Urbana, 1963, JD, 1966. Bar: Ill. 1966, NY 1984, Calif. 1992. Law clk. Ill. Supreme Ct., Bloomington, 1966-67; assoc. Sidley & Austin and predecessor firm, Chgo., 1967-73; with Montgomery Ward & Co. Inc., Chgo., 1973-81, assoc. gen. counsel, asst. sec., 1979-81; ptnr. Seki, Jarvis & Lynch, Chgo., 1981-84, dir., mem. exec. com.; dir., exec. v.p., gen. counsel Mitsubishi Electric & Electronics USA, Inc. and predecessors, NYC, 1983-91, Cypress, Calif., 1991—, sr. legal advisor, 2009—. Mem. ABA, Am. Corp. Counsel Assn., Calif. Bar Assn., Ill. Bar Assn., Chgo. Bar Assn., NY State Bar Assn., Am. Arbitration Assn. (panel arbitrators). Office: Mitsubishi Elec & Electronics USA Inc PO Box 6007 5665 Plaza Dr Cypress CA 90630-0007 Business E-Mail: alan.olschwang@meus.mea.com.

OLSEN, ALFRED JON, lawyer; b. Phoenix, Oct. 5, 1940; s. William Hans and Vera (Bearden) O.; m. Susan K. Smith, Apr. 15, 1979. BA in History, U. Ariz., 1962; MS in Acctg., Ariz. State U., 1964; JD, Northwestern U., 1966. Bar: Ariz. 1966, Ill. 1966, U.S. Tax Ct. 1970, U.S. Supreme Ct. 1970; C.P.A., Ariz., Ill. cert. tax specialist. Acct. Arthur Young & Co., C.P.A.s, Chgo., 1966-68; dir. firm Ehmann, Olsen & Lane (P.C.), Phoenix, 1969-76; dir. Streich, Lang, Weeks & Cardon (P.C.), Phoenix, 1977-78; mgr. Olsen-Smith, Ltd., Phoenix, 1978—. Chmn. tax adv. commn. Bd. Legal Specialization, 1990-92. Bd. editors: Jour. Agrl. Law and Taxation, 1978-82, Practical Real Estate Lawyer, 1983-95. Mem. Phoenix adv. bd. Salvation Army., 1973-81. Fellow: Am. Coll. Tax Counsel, Am. Coll. Trust and Estate Counsel (state chair 2002—03, regent 2005—); mem.: ABA (chmn. com. on agr., sect. taxation 1976—78, chmn. CLE com. sect. taxation 1982—84), AICPA, Internat. Acad. Estate and Trust Law (exec. coun. 1994—99), Nat. Cattlemen's Assn. (tax com. 1979—88), Am. Law Inst. (life; chmn. tax planning for agr. 1971—82), Ctrl. Ariz. Estate Planning Coun. (pres. 1972—73), State Bar Ariz., Ariz. Soc. CPAs, Phi Beta Kappa, Phi Kappa Phi, Beta Gamma Sigma, Sigma Nu Internat. (pres. 1986—88). Office: 3300 Virginia Fin Pla 301 E Virginia Ave Phoenix AZ 85004-1218 Office Phone: 602-254-1040.

OLSEN, ASHLEY FULLER, actress, apparel designer; b. Sherman Oaks, Calif., June 13, 1986; d. David and Jarnette Olsen, Mackenzie Olsen (Stepmother). Student, NYU, 2004—. Co-founder, prin. Dualstar Entertaiment, Calif., 1993—; co-editor-in-chief Mary-Kate and Ashley Mag. Co-design cons. (with sister Mary-Kate) The Row, Elizabeth and James, 2007—. Actor: (films) To Grandmother's House We Go, 1992, Double, Double, Toil and Trouble, 1993, The Little Rascals, 1994, How the West Was Fun, 1994, It Takes Two, 1995 (Kid's Choice award for Favorite Movie Actress, 1996), The Challenge, 2003, Charlie's Angels: Full Throttle, 2003; (TV films) Billboard Dad, 1998; (TV series) Full House, 1987—95, Two of a Kind, 1998 (Kid's Choice award for Favorite TV Actress, 1999); actor, prodr.: So Little Time, 2001; Mary-Kate and Ashley in Action!, 2001; actor, prodr., prodr.: (films) Switching Goals, 1999; actor, prodr. Passport to Paris, 1999; Our Lips are Sealed, 2000; Winning London, 2001; Holiday in the Sun, 2001; Getting There, 2002; When In Rome, 2002; New York Minute, 2004; (video series) The Adventures of Mary-Kate and Ashley; You're Invited to Mary-Kate and Ashleys; prodr.: (TV series) Tough Cookie, 2002, Fashion Forward: Spring 2001, 2001; co-author (with Mary-Kate Olsen): Influence, 2008. Recipient Franchise Performers award, DVD Exclusive Awards, 2003, Star on Walk of Fame, 2004; named one of The 100 Most Powerful Women in Hollywood, Hollywood Reporter, 2003. Office: c/o Dualstar Entertainment Group 1801 Century Park East Los Angeles CA 90067

OLSEN, BARBARA A., literature and language professor, classicist, educator; BA, Cornell U., Ithaca, NY, 1990; PhD, Duke U., Durham, NC, 2004. Vanderpool fellow Am. Sch. Classical Studies, Athens, Greece, 1996—97; asst. prof. classics Vassar Coll., Poughkeepsie, NY, 2002—; vis. asst. prof. classics Bard Coll., Annandale-on-Hudson, NY. D-Liberal. Office: Vassar Coll 124 Raymond Ave Box 504 Poughkeepsie NY 12604

OLSEN, DAVID TENG, performing arts educator; b. Seattle, Wash., Mar. 26, 1977; s. Gary David Olsen and Shu Hua Teng; m. Kassie Asmann. BFA, U. Wash., Seattle, 1999; MA, U. Wis.-Madison, 2005, MFA, 2006. Vis. asst. prof. Wellesley Coll., Mass., 2006—. Co-founder Siamesebirds.com, Seattle, 2000—. Exhibitions include Big Dirty. Home: 6 Norfolk Terrace #1 Wellesley MA 02482

OLSEN, DENNIS E., veterinarian, director; b. Lovell, Wyo., Apr. 1, 1957; m. DeAnn Shaw, May 18, 1979; children: Timothy M., Ryan Spencer, Chad Douglas, Sandra Kay Westover, Ronald Shaw. BS, Weber State Coll., Ogden, Utah, 1982, Wash. State U., Pullman, 1985; MS, Colo. State U., Ft. Collins, 1995; DVM, Oreg. State U., Corvallis, 1986. Diplomate Am. Coll. Vet. Surgeons, Md., 1996. Instr. surgery U. Ga., Athens, 1995—96, Va. Tech., Blacksburg, 1996—97; asst. prof. surgery Kans. State U., Manhattan, 1997—2002; program dir. Coll. Southern Nev., Las Vegas, 2002—. Small animal surg. specialist Small Animal Surg. Splty. and Consulting, Las Vegas, 2002—. Contbr. chapters to books, articles to numerous jours. Staff counselor Sky High Hope Camp, Ft. Collins, 1993—94; master Boy Scouts America, Manhattan, Kans., 2000—02, merit badge counselor Henderson, Nev., 2002—08; animal adv. com., chair Clark County, Las Vegas, 2004—06. Recipient Carl J. Norden Disting. Tchr. award, Phizer, Inc. Animal Health, 1999, NISOD Excellence Tchg. award, Coll. Southern Nev., 2006; Pet Trust Faculty fellowship, Kans. State U., 2002. Mem.: Am. Coll. Vet. Surgeons (resident credentialing com. chair 2002—03). Avocations: archery, fishing, camping, reading. Office: Coll Southern Nev 6375 W Charleston Blvd Las Vegas NV 89146-1164 Business E-Mail: dennis.olsen@csn.edu.

OLSEN, EDGAR OLIVER, economics professor; b. New Orleans, La., Mar. 13, 1942; s. Edgar Oliver and Georgie Walker (Thompson) Olsen; m. Barbara Elliott Beasley, June 4, 1966; children: Robert Buckner, Melanie Guerry. BA, Tulane U., 1963; PhD, Rice U., 1968. Postdoctoral fellow Ind. U.-Bloomington, 1967—68; from asst. prof. to assoc. prof. U. Va., Charlottesville, 1970—83, prof., 1983—, chmn. dept. econs., 1993—96. Vis. assoc. prof. econs. U. Wis., Madison, 1975—76, vis. prof., 1982—84; economist Rand Corp., Santa Monica, Calif., 1968—70; vis. scholar HUD, Washington, 1978—79, cons., 1973—2003; bd. editors Am. Econ. Rev., Princeton, NJ, 1985—91; cons. GAO, Washington, 1999—2001; v.p. So. Econ. Assn., 2003—05; bd. dirs. Am. Real Estate and Urban Economics Assn., 1998—2000, 2005—07. Contbr. articles to profl. publs. Congl. Testimony, 2001, 2003, 2006, 2008. Recipient Cert. Spl. Achievement, HUD, 1979; NIH fellow, 1983. Mem.: Am. Real Estate and Urban Econ. Assn., Am. Econ. Assn., Assn. Pub. Policy Analysis and Mgmt., So. Econ. Assn. Home: 1606 Jamestown Dr Charlottesville VA 22901 Office: Univ Va Dept Economics PO Box 400182 Charlottesville VA 22904-4182 Office Phone: 434-924-3443. Business E-Mail: eoo@virginia.edu.

OLSEN, EDWARD JOHN, geologist, educator, curator; b. Chgo., Nov. 23, 1927; s. Edward John and Elizabeth (Bornemann) O.; children—Andrea, Ericka. AB, U. Chgo., 1951, MS, 1955, PhD, 1959. Geologist Geol. Survey Can., 1953, U.S. Geol. Survey, 1954—, Canadian Johns-Manville Co., Ltd., 1956, 57, 59; asst. prof. Case Inst. Tech., also Western Res. U., 1959-60; curator mineralogy Field Mus. Natural History, 1960-91, chmn. dept. geology, 1974-78; research assoc. prof. dept. geophys. scis. U. Chgo., 1977—. Adj. prof. U. Ill., Chgo. Circle, 1970-91. Assoc. editor Geochim. et Cosmochim. Acta., 1985-91. Fellow Mineral. Soc. Am.; mem. Mineral. Assn. Can., Geochem. Soc., Meteoritical Soc. Achievements include spl. research stability relations of minerals in earth's mantle and meteorites. Home: 437 Wild Indigo Ln Madison WI 53717-2148 Office: U Chgo Dept Geophys Sci Chicago IL 60637

OLSEN, GLEN A., church musician, educator; b. Orange, NJ, Jan. 7, 1965; s. Peter Albert and Joan C Olsen; m. Amy Hastings, Aug. 6, 1988; children: Kristen A, Timothy C, Melissa C. BA, Wheaton Coll., 1983—87; MusM, Rutgers U., 1987—89; LittD, Drew U., 1998—2001, MA, 2006. Organist/choir dir. Heritage Bapt. Ch., West Orange, NJ, 1981—83; youth and music dir. North Fork Bapt. Ch., Mattituck, NY, 1983; organist Wheaton Christian Ref. Ch., Ill., 1985—87; min. of music and worship Montvale Evang. Free Ch., NJ, 1987—88; min. of music Lafayette Federated Ch., NJ, 1988—93; min. of music and worship Calvary Evang. Free Ch., Trumbull, Conn., 1993—95; dir. of choral activities Hawthorne Christian Acad., NJ, 1995—2005; dir. of music and organist United Meth. Ch., Madison, NJ, 1995—2005; adj. asst. prof. Drew U., Madison, NJ, 2001—; dir. music Calvary Bapt. Ch., Manhattan, NY, 2005—07. Vol. Calvary Evang. Free Ch., Essex Fells, NJ, 1980. Recipient Outstanding Young Men of Am., 1989; Bard Thompson scholarship, Drew U., 2003—. Mem.: Fellowship of Christian Art Music Composers, Forum on Music and Christian Scholarship, Am. Guild of Organists, Am. Choral Directors Assn. Evangelical Free Church. Avocations: travel, architecture. Personal E-mail: olsenglen@aol.com.

OLSEN, HANS PETER, lawyer; b. Detroit, May 21, 1940; s. Hans Peter and Paula M. (Olsen) O.; m. Elizabeth Ann Gayton, Sept. 14, 1968; children: Hans Peter, Heidi Susanne, Stephanie Elizabeth BA, Mich. State U., 1961; JD, Georgetown U., 1965; LLM, NYU, 1966. Bar: Mich. 1967, Pa. 1969, R.I. 1974. Law clk. Monaghan, McCrone, Campbell & Crawmer, Detroit, 1964, U.S. Ct. of Claims, Fed. Appellate Ct., Washington, 1966—68; assoc. Pepper, Hamilton & Scheetz, Phila., 1968—72; ptnr. Hinckley, Allen, & Snyder, Providence, 1974—2008; prin. Sansiveri, Kimball & McNamee, LLP, 2009—. Adv. planning com. U. R.I. Fed. Taxation Inst.; continuing legal edn. adv. bd., tax symposium adv. bd. Bryant Coll.; mem. Gov.'s State Task Force, R.I. Pub. Expenditure Coun.; cons. Bur. Nat. Affairs; liaison Bar Assn. and North Atlantic region IRS; tax adminstrs. adv. com. R.I.; lectr. tax insts. and other profl. groups N.Y., L.A., Phila., Boston, R.I.; advisor R.I. Econ. Policy com. Contbr. articles to profl. jours. Fellow Am. Bar Found.; mem. ABA (sect. taxation, exempt orgns. com., subcom. healthcare, corp.-shareholders rels. com., partnerships com.), R.I. Bar Assn. (sect. taxation, sec.-treas. 1977-80, liaison with CPAs, specialization com., mem. various coms.), Providence C. of C., R.I. C. of C. (chmn. com. on bus. taxes and public spending, mem., past chmn. legis. action council), Mich. State Bar, Pa. State Bar, RI Bar Assn. Home: 274 Olney St Providence RI 02906-2305 Office: 55 Dorrance St Providence RI 02903-2220 Office Phone: 401-752-0545. Personal E-mail: hpeterolsen@cox.net. Business E-Mail: holsen@sansiveri.com.

OLSEN, HAROLD FREMONT, lawyer; b. Davenport, Wash., Oct. 17, 1920; s. Oscar E. and Dorothy (Sprowls) O.; m. Jeanne L. Rounds, Aug. 30, 1942; children: Eric O., Ronald R., Margaret Ruth. BA, Wash. State U., 1942; LLB, Harvard U., 1948. Bar: Wash. 1948, U.S. Ct. Claims 1970, U.S. Supreme Ct. 1982; CPA, Wash. Instr. Oxford Bus. Sch., Cambridge, Mass., 1946-47; examiner Wash. State Dept. Pub. Utilities, 1948; with firm Perkins Coie (and predecessors), Seattle, 1949—, ptnr., 1954-88, of counsel, 1989—. Trustee Exec. Svcs. Corp. Wash., 1990-96. Bd. dirs. Northwest Hosp. Found., Northwest Hosp., 1980-90; trustee Wash. State U. Found., chmn. 1986-88; mem. adv. coun. Wash. State U. Sch. Bus. and Econs., 1978-90; trustee, mem. exec. com., pres. Mus. of Flight, 1991-92, chmn., 1993; trustee Horizon House, 1994-97. Maj. USAAF, 1942-45, NATOUSA, Mid. East, ETO. Decorated Silver Star. Mem. ABA, Wash. Bar Assn., Seattle Bar Assn., Aircraft Industry Assn. (chmn. legal com. 1957), Phi Beta Kappa, Phi Kappa Phi, Tau Kappa Epsilon, Rainier Club, Queenstown (New Zealand) Golf Club, Seattle Golf Club (pres. 1986-87), Sr. N.W. Golf Assn. Congregationalist. Office: 1201 3rd Ave Ste 4500 Seattle WA 98101-3029 Home: 900 University St Apt 501 Seattle WA 98101 Personal E-mail: h7olsen@comcast.net. Business E-Mail: holsen@perkinscoie.com.

OLSEN, INGER ANNA, retired psychologist; b. Copper Mountain, BC, Can., Dec. 25, 1926; BS, Wash. State U., 1954, MS, 1956, PhD, 1962. Psychiat. nurse Provincial Mental Health Svcs. B.C., 1947-51, psychologist, 1956-58, Vancouver (B.C.) City Met. Health Svcs., 1958-60; psychologist Student Counseling Ctr., Wash. State U., Pullman, 1960—62; sr. psychologist Met. Health Svcs., Vancouver, 1962-66; instr. psychology Langara Coll., Vancouver, B.C., 1966—87; ret., 1987. Contbr. articles to profl. jours. Docent Vancouver Aquarium Assn.; bd. dirs. Second Mile Soc., 1975—89. Mem. APA, Gerontol. Soc. Am., Can. Assn. Gerontology, Phi Beta Kappa, Sigma Xi, Alpha Kappa Delta. Home: 1255 Bidwell St Apt 1910 Vancouver BC Canada V6G 2K8

OLSEN, JØRN, epidemiology educator, researcher; b. Odense, Denmark, May 20, 1946; s. Svend Aage and Irma (Lund) O.; m. Ulla Sig; children: Janne, Uffe, Ole. MD, U. Aarhus, Denmark, 1979, PhD, 1982. Prof. epidemiology U. Aarhus, 1984—; head Danish Epidemiology Scis. Ctr., Aarhus, 1994—2006; chmn. Dept. Epidemiology Sch. Pub. Health U. Calif., LA, 2006—. Mem. med. research council, Denmark, 1985, comac-Epid European Union, Belgium, 1986—, working party WHO/European Union, Belgium, 1988—, HRP/WHO, Geneva, 1990-2001; mem. sci. coun. IARC, Lyon, 1998—; chmn. Nat. Inst. Pub. Health; cons. Nat. Bd. Health, Denmark; mem. Com. for Sci. Rsch., Greenland Editor Scand Social Medicine, 1984-96; author books and numerous articles. Mem. IEA. Office: UCLA Pub Hlth Epid BOX 951772 71 264 CHS Los Angeles CA 90095-1772 Home: 1300 Midvale Ave #402 Los Angeles CA 90024 Office Fax: 310-206-6039. Personal E-mail: jo@soci.au.dk. Business E-Mail: jo@ucla.edu.

OLSEN, KATHIE LYNN, science foundation director; b. Portland, Oreg., Aug. 3, 1952; d. Roland Berg and Gladys Elizabeth (Eldreth) O. BS, Chatham Coll., 1974; PhD, U. Calif., Irvine, 1979. Postdoct. fellow Harvard Med. Sch., Boston, 1979-80; rsch. scientist Long Island Rsch. Inst., Stony Brook, N.Y., 1980-83; rsch. asst. prof. SUNY, Stony Brook, 1982-85, asst. prof., 1985-89; assoc. program dir. NSF, Washington, 1984-86, program dir., 1988, leader neurosci., 1991; legis. fellow Brookings Instn., Washington, 1996—97; chief scientist NASA, 1999—2002; acting assoc. adminstr. Enterprise in Biological and Physical Research, 2000—02; assoc. director, tech. Off. Science & Tech. Policy, Washington, 2002—05; dep. dir. NSF, Washington, 2005—. Adj. assoc. prof. George Washington U., Washington, 1989—; cons. editor Hormones and Behavior, 1988—. Contbr. articles to profl. jours, chapters to books. Recipient Dir. Superior Accomplishmentaward, NSF, Barry M. Goldwater Educator award, Am. Inst. of Aeronautics & Astronautics -Nat. Capital Section, Outstanding Leadership medal, NASA, Internat. Behavioral Neuroscience Soc. award, Soc. for Behavioral Endocrinology award, Barnard medal of Distinction. Mem. Soc. Neurosci., Endocrine Soc., Women in Neurosci., Sod. Study of Reproduction, Internat. Acad. Sex Rsch. Office: NSF 4201 Wilson Blvd Arlington VA 22230

OLSEN, KENNETH HAROLD, geophysicist, astrophysicist, historian; b. Ogden, Utah, Feb. 20, 1930; s. Harold Reuben and Rose (Hill) O.; m. Barbara Ann Parson, June 15, 1955; children: Susan L., Steven K., Christopher P., Richard S. BS, Idaho State Coll., 1952; MS, Calif. Inst. Tech., 1954, PhD, 1957. Grad. rsch. asst. Calif. Inst. Tech., Mt. Wilson and Palomar Obs., Pasadena, 1952-57; staff mem., group leader Los Alamos (N.Mex.) Nat. Lab., 1957-89, lab. assoc., 1989-95; geophys. cons. Lynnwood, Wash., 1989—. Vis. rsch. fellow Applied Seismol. Group, Swedish Nat. Def. Inst., Stockholm, Sweden, 1983; sr. vis. scientist fellow Norwegian Seismic Array, Oslo, Norway, 1983; vis. scholar Geophysics Program, U. Wash., Seattle, 1989-91. Author, editor: Continental Rifts: Evolution, Structure, Tectonics, 1995; contbr. articles to profl. jours. Mem. Am. Geophys. Union, Geol. Soc. Am., Seismol. Soc. Am., Am. Astron. Soc., Royal Astron. Soc. Home: 1029 187th Pl SW Lynnwood WA 98036-4986 Personal E-mail: barbolsen@verizon.net.

OLSEN, M. KENT, lawyer, educator; b. Denver, Mar. 10, 1948; s. Marvin and F. Winona (Wilker) O.; m. Shauna L. Casement; children: Kristofor Anders, Alexander Lee, Nikolaus Alrik, Amanda Elizabeth Hill. BS, Colo. State U., 1970; JD, U. Denver, 1975. Bar: Colo. 1975, U.S. Dist. Ct. Colo. 1982, U.S. Tax Ct. Law clk. Denver Probate Ct., 1973-75; assoc. ptnr. Johnson & McLachlan, Lamar, Colo., 1975-80; assoc. Buchanan, Thomas and Johnson, Lakewood, Colo., 1981-82, William E. Myrick, P.C., Denver, 1982-83; referee Denver Probate Ct., Denver, 1983-89; ptnr. Haines & Olsen, P.C., Denver, 1989-95; pvt. practice Denver, 1995—2001; ptnr. Olsen & Traeger, LLP, 2001—. Adv. bd. Denver Career Coll., 1993—2004, Elder Law Inst., 1994—. Active Gov.'s Commn. on Life and the Law, Denver, 1991-2000; bd. dirs. Adult Care Mgmt., Inc., Denver, 1985-95, Colo. Guardianship Alliance, Denver, 1990-91, Arc of Denver, Inc., 1990—, pres., 1995-97, 2004-06; bd. dirs. Arc of Colo., 2004-, Colo. Fund for People with Disabilities, 1994—, pres., 1994-2000. Recipient Outstanding Vol. Svc. award Adult Care Mgmt., 1990, Outstanding Svc. award The Arc of Denver, 1991, Vol. Svc. award Colo. Gerontol. Soc., 1997, Pres.'s award Arc of Denver, 1998, 2002; named one of Colo. Super Lawyers, Law and Politics, 2006-. Mem. ABA, Colo. Bar Assn. (past chair probate sect.), First Jud. Dist. Bar Assn., Nat. Acad. Elder Law Attys., Colo. Assn. Homes and Svcs. to the Aging, Denver Bar Assn., Denver Estate Planning Coun., Denver C. of C. Avocations: running, skiing, racquetball, art, hiking. Home: 3030 S Roslyn St Denver CO 80231-4153 Office: 650 S Cherry St Ste 850 Denver CO 80246-1805 Home Phone: 303-306-6185; Office Phone: 303-329-4670. Business E-Mail: mkolsen@olsentraeger.com.

OLSEN, MARTIN E., obstetrician, educator; b. Morgantown, W.Va., 1959; m. Natalie Ann Maschmann, June 25, 1985; 1 child, Karen Rebeca. BS, Muskingum Coll., New Concord, 1981; MD, Med. Coll. Ohio, Toledo, 1981. Diplomate Am. Bd. Ob-Gyn. Resident in family practice Akron (Ohio) Gen. Med. Ctr., 1985-88; resident in ob-gyn. U. Tenn., Chattanooga, 1989-91; mem. faculty E. Tenn. State U., Johnson City, 1992—, chmn. dept. ob-byn., 1999—2009; dir. residency program Johnson City Med. Ctr., 1994—. Contbr. articles to profl. jours. Office: PO Box 70569 Johnson City TN 37614-1707 Office Phone: 423-439-8097. Business E-Mail: olsen@etsu.edu.

OLSEN, MARY-KATE, actress, apparel designer; b. Sherman Oaks, Calif., June 13, 1986; d. David and Jarnette Olsen, Mackenzie Olsen (Stepmother). Student, NYU, 2004—05. Co-founder, prin. Dualstar Entertainment, LA, 1993—; co-editor-in-chief Mary-Kate and Ashley Mag. Co-design cons. (with sister Ashley) The Row, Elizabeth and James, 2007—. Actor: (films) To Grandmother's House We Go, 1992, Double, Double, Toil and Trouble, 1993, The Little Rascals, 1994, How the West Was Fun, 1994, It Takes Two, 1995 (Kid's Choice award for Favorite Movie Actress, 1996), The Challenge, 2003, Charlie's Angels: Full Throttle, 2003, The Wackness, 2008; (TV films) Billboard Dad, 1998; (TV series) Full House, 1987—95, Two of a Kind, 1998 (Kids' Choice award for Favorite TV Actress, 1999), Weeds, 2007; actor, prodr.: (films) Switching Goals, 1999; Passport to Paris, 1999; Our Lips are Sealed, 2000; Winning London, 2001; Holiday in the Sun, 2001; Getting There, 2002; When In Rome, 2002; New York Minute, 2004; (TV series) So Little Time, 2001; Mary-Kate and Ashley in Action!, 2001; (video series) The Adventures of Mary-Kate and Ashley; You're Invited to Mary-Kate and Ashley's; prodr.: (TV series) Tough Cookie, 2002, Fashion Forward: Spring 2001, 2001; co-author (with Ashley Olson): Influence, 2008. Recipient Franchise Performers award, DVD Exclusive Awards, 2003, Star on Walk of Fame, 2004; named one of 100 Most Powerful Women in Hollywood, Hollywood (Calif.) Reporter, 2003. Office: Dualstar Entertainment Group 1801 Century Park East Los Angeles CA 90007

OLSEN, R. NILLS, law educator, former dean; BA, U. Wis., 1969; JD, Columbia U. Sch. Law, 1974. Law clerk to Chief Justice Thomas E. Fairchild Seventh Cir. U.S. Ct. Appeals, Chgo.; law lectr. and clin. fellow U. Chgo. Sch. Law; assoc. prof. to prof. law U. Buffalo Law Sch., SUNY, 1978—, vice dean, 1994—98, dean, 1998—2007, dir. clin. edn. Mem. Lewiston-Porter sch. bd.; bd. dirs. N.Y. State Environmental Activists, Youngstown Free Libr., Great Lakes United. Office: Univ Buffalo Law Sch SUNY 413 O'Brian Hall, N Campus Buffalo NY 14260-1100 Office Phone: 716-645-3193. Business E-Mail: nolsen@buffalo.edu.*

OLSEN, REX NORMAN, trade association executive; b. Hazeltown, Idaho, Apr. 9, 1925; s. Adolph Lars and Pearl (Robbins) O. B.J., BA in English, U. Mo., 1950. Editor Clissold Pub. Co., Chgo., 1950-54; copy editor Am. Peoples Ency., Chgo., 1955; asst. editor Am. Hosp. Assn., Chgo., 1956-59, mng. editor, 1959-64, dir. jours. div., 1964-69, dir. publs. bur., 1969-75, exec. editor, asso. pub., 1975-79; v.p., treas. Am. Hosp. Pub., Inc., 1980-85; pres. Words Ltd., 1985—. Dir. publs. ETNA Comms., Chgo., 1997—. Served with USNR, 1943-46. Mem. Soc. Nat. Assn. Pubs. (sec. 1975-76, 2d v.p. 1976-77, 1st v.p. 1977-78, pres. 1978-79), Chgo. Bus. Publs. Assn. (dir. 1974-78, 4th v.p. 1978-79), Sigma Delta Chi. Home and Office: 5510 N Sheridan Rd Unit 12-A Chicago IL 60640-1630 Personal E-mail: rexorudy@aol.com.

OLSEN, RICHARD GALEN, biomedical engineer, consultant; b. Colorado Springs, Colo., Aug. 10, 1945; s. Floyd Edwin and Ruth Elizabeth (Robinson) O.; m. Karen Fidler Brubaker, June 17, 1973 (dec.); children: Kathryn Elizabeth, Nickolas Robert. BSEE, U. Mo., Rolla, 1968; MS, U. Utah, 1970, PhD, 1975. Registered profl. engr., Fla. Engr. Bendix Corp., Kansas City, Mo., 1968-69; elec. engr. Naval Aerospace Med. Rsch. Lab., Pensacola, Fla., 1975-79, chief engring. systems divsn., 1979-82, head bioengring. divsn., 1982-94; head bioengring. dept. Naval Health Rsch. Ctr. Detachment, Brooks AFB, Tex., 1994-2000; cons. in bioelectromagnetics Pensacola, 2001—. Tech. cons. Naval Sea Sys. Command, Arlington, Va., 1989—91, Naval Surface Warfare Ctr., Dahlgren, Va., 1989—95, Armstrong Lab. USAF, 1991—99, Naval Command, Control and Ocean Surveillance Command, San Diego, 1996—97, Selicor, Inc., 2001—. Contbr. articles to profl. jours. and books. With U.S. Army, 1970-72. Recipient Fred A. Hitchcock award Aerospace Physiologist Aerospace Med. Assn., 1987, Award for Excellence in Tech. Transfer, Fed. Lab. Consortium, 2004; named Engr. of the Yr., N.W. Fla. Engrs. Coun., 1991. Mem. IEEE (sr., chmn. Pensacola sect. 1982-83, SCC-28 and SCC-34 coms. 1982-2000, cert. of appreciation 1983), Bioelectromagnetics Soc. (charter, editl. bd. 1990-96), Sigma Xi, Eta Kappa Nu, Tau Beta Pi, Phi Kappa Phi. Achievements include conducting the first shipboard measurements of specific absorption rate (SAR) and of electromagnetic pulse (EMP) induced body current; patents in RF medical device to treat vascular insufficiency, elastic wire conductor, RF coil for hypothermia resuscitation, RF dosimetry system, personal microwave and RF detector, and RF warming of submerged extremities. Office: Selicor Inc 420 Towne Park Trl Austin TX 78751-4727 Personal E-mail: olsen116@bellsouth.net. *Live an ordinary life except in attainment.*

OLSEN, RICHARD JAMES, artist, educator; b. Milw., Nov. 15, 1935; s. Edward Marinus and Ann Frances (Keymar) Olsen; m. Nina Marsh Civilette-Olsen, July 25, 1969; children: Dayna Kim, Dawn Beth(dec.), Josh Keymar. BS, U. Wis., 1958, MFA in Painting and Printmaking, 1966. Tchg. asst. U. Wis., 1965-66; art tchr. grade 8 Winnequah Grade Sch., Monona, Wis., 1966-67; instr. printmaking Oper. Area Arts, Green

Bay, Wis., 1967-69; from instr. painting and drawing to prof. emeritus U. Ga., Athens, 1969—2000, Gen. Sandy Beaver tchg. prof., 1998—2000, emeritus prof., 2001—; represented by Berman Gallery, Atlanta, 1986-97, Novus Inc., Atlanta, 1990—, Maurine Littleton Gallery, Washington, 1990, Miriam Perlman Gallery, Chgo., 1991, EDL & Assocs., Atlanta, 1994, Elements of Art, Columbus, Ohio, 1995, Ellen Wallace-Paushter, Art Cons., Chgo., 1999, Mercury Art Works, Athens, Ga., 2001—. Wrestling coach Monona Grove (Wis.) H.S., 1966-67; panelist Steinham Arts Festival St. Lawrence U., N.Y., 1987, Crossroads in Cultural Studies, Tampere, Finland, 1996; head praparator Reflexes and Reflections Russell Rotunda Capitol Hill, Washington, 1983, Lincoln Ctr., N.Y.C., 1984. One-man shows include Claywork Gallery, Atlanta, 1986, H. Smith Gallery U. SC, Spartanburg, 1991, Nat. Vietnam Vets. Art Mus., Chgo., 1999, Mercury Art Works, Athens, Ga., 2003, 2008, Floataway Complex, Atlanta, 2005, Augusta State U., Ga., 2007, numerous group shows including most recently, exhibited in group shows at Peace Mus., Chgo., 2002, Aurora (Ill.) Hist. Ctr., 2003, U. N.Mex., 2004, Children of War, Nat. Vietnam Vets. Art Mus., 2005, Wis. Vets. Mus., Madison, 2006, Athens Acad., Ga., 2007, Represented in permanent collections Nat. Vietnam Vets. Art Mus., Chgo., Nat. Mus. Fine Art, Hanoi, Vietnam., Ga. World Congress Ctr., Atlanta, U. Ga. Complex Carbohydrate Rsch. Ctr., Bank South Ga., Tifton, Ga., Western Carolina U., Cullowhee, NC, Chastain Bldg., Athens, Ga, Chastain Ins. Agy. Collection; featured (in over 150 mags.). With U.S. Army, 1959-63, Vietnam. Decorated Purple heart, 1963; Visual Arts fellow So. Arts Fdn./NEA, 1988; Sr. Faculty grantee U. Ga. Rsch. Found., Inc., 1991-93, 96-98, Individual Artist grantee Ga. Coun. Arts, 1993-94; recipient Purchase award 8th Annual Maine/Maritime Internat. Flatworks Exhibn., 1990, Merit award Three Works 29th Juried Exbhn., Lyndon House Arts Center, Athens, Ga., 2004. Mem. VFW, Mil. Order of the Purple Heart (comdr. 1999-2000), Vietnam Helicopter Pilots Assn. Home: 165 Springdale St Athens GA 30605-1237 Personal E-mail: richard.j.olsen@att.net.

OLSEN, STEVEN LLOYD, museum administrator, educator; b. Salt Lake City, Sept. 25, 1950; s. Lloyd V. and Mary (Jensen) O.; m. Kathi L. Brening, Apr. 6, 1979; children: Michael, Daniel, Emily, Sarah, Chelsea. BS summa cum laude, Brigham Young U., 1975; AM, U. Chgo., 1978, PhD, 1985. Sr. instr. Stanley H. Kaplan Ednl. Ctr., Salt Lake City, 1979—92; sr. researcher LDS Ch. Hist. Dept., Salt Lake City, 1979-82; supr. of rsch. Mus. Ch. History & Art, Salt Lake City, 1982-86, mgr. collections and rsch., 1986-89, mgr. ops., 1989—2003; adj. prof. dept. anthropology Brigham Young U., Salt Lake City, 1990—2004; assoc. mng. dir. family and ch. history dept. Ch. Jesus Christ of LDS, Salt Lake City, 2003—. Mem. spkrs. bur. Utah Endowment for Humanities, Salt Lake City, 1990; co-chair Gov.'s Initiative on Museums, 1991—92; mem. Gov.'s Task Force on History and Heritage, 1992—93; mem. adv. bd. Utah State Office Mus. Svcs., 1993—2000, Charles Redd Ctr. for Western Studies, Brigham Young U., 1997—2003; bd. mem. Utah Humanities Coun., 2007—. Contbr. articles to profl. jours. Bd. dirs. Salt Lake City Bd. of Edn., 1989. NSF fellow, 1976-79. Mem.: Am. Soc. Ch. History (coun. mem. 2008—), Nat. Alliance State Museums Associations (mem. steering com. 1998—2003), Western Museums Assn. (first v.p. 1994—96, pres. 1996—98, Directors Chair award 2007), Utah Museums Assn. (v.p. 1988—90, pres. 1990—92). Mem. Lds Ch. Avocations: reading, bicycling, photograhy. Office: Mus of Ch History & Art 45 N West Temple Salt Lake City UT 84150-3810 Office Phone: 801-240-4648. Office Fax: 801-240-5342. Business E-Mail: olsensl@ldschurch.org.

OLSEN-ESTIE, JEANNE LINDELL, golf course owner; b. Everett, Wash., July 17, 1946; d. Carmen David Lindell and Violet Louise (Harrison) Johnson; m. Wayne William Olsen, Dec. 22, 1984 (dec. Apr. 1993); children: Kenda, Justin; m. John Gary Estie, Nov. 5, 1994. Grad., Lee Sch. Cosmetology, 1966, Everett Beauty Sch., 1968, Everett Plz. Sch. Cosmotology, 1987. With Marysville Police Dept., Wash., 1967—72, Durham Transp., 1979—87; owner, mgr. Olsen's Riverside Golf Course and Olsen's Golf Equipment, 1979—. Author of poems. Active Maryfest, Marysville, 1976-78; bd. dirs. Snohomish County Camp Fire Boys and Girls. Recipient Editors Choice award for outstanding achievement in poetry, 1999. Mem. Nat. Granite Ware Collectors, Everett Antique Club, Hummel Club Collectors,Everett Elks (officer lodge #479, Exalted Ruler of Yr. 2004). Achievements include pubished in third book of poetry; second woman Exalted Ruler of Elks Lodge #479 since 1899; Perfect Attendance Award, Elks Lodge, 2004. Avocations: golf, collecting and restoring antiques, singing. Home and Office: PO Box 5609 Everett WA 98206-5609

OLSHAKER, MARK BRUCE, scriptwriter, filmmaker; b. Washington, Feb. 28, 1951; s. Bennett and Thelma A. (Abramson) O.; m. Carolyn M. Clemente, Aug. 28, 1977. BA, George Washington U., Washington, 1972. Spl. correspondent St. Louis Post Dispatch, Washington Bur., 1974-75; writer, author, film maker Washington Area, 1972—. V.p. Unicorn Projects, Inc., Washington, 1983—, Mindhunters, Inc. Vienna, Va., 1995—; bd. dirs. Shakespeare Guild, Washington. Author: (novels) Einstein's Brain, 1981, Unnatural Causes, 1986, Blood Race, 1989, The Edge, 1994, Mindhunters: Broken Wings, 1999; (anthology) Unusual Suspects, 1996; (non-fiction) The Instant Image, 1978; co-author (with John Douglas), Mindhunter, 1995 (Anthony award nomination, Brit. Gold Dagger nomination, Edgar nomination, Mystery Writers of Am.), Unabomber: On the Trail of America's Most-Wanted Serial Killer, 1996, Journey into Darkness, 1997, Obsession, 1998, The Anatomy of Motive, 1999, The Cases That Haunt Us, 2000; (with C.J. Peters) Virus Hunter, 1997; contbr. (textbook) Forensic Emergency Medicine; (screen writing) Stormchasers, 1995, (CINE Golden Eagle), The Edge, 1996 (TV Writing and Prodn.) We All Came to America, 1974, A Moment in Time, 1975, Patent Pending, 1975 (silver medal Inst. Film & TV Festival N.Y.), Lewis Mumford: Toward Human Architecture, 1979, Castle, 1983 (Am. Film Festival Red Ribbon), Cathedral, 1985 (Am. Film Festival Blue Ribbon, Cine Golden Eagle) Pyramid, 1988 (CINE Golden Eagle, Nat. Ednl. Film and Video Festival Gold Apple), What's Killing the Children?, 1990, Discovering Hamlet, 1990 (Am. Film Festival Red Ribbon, Bronze medal Inst. Film & TV Festival N.Y.), Mind of a Serial Killer, 1992 (Emmy nomination news and documentary 1993), Roman City, 1994 (Emmy award), Bridge, 1998, Mill Times, 2001, Bioterror: Dealing with a New Reality, 2001, Avoiding Armageddon, 2003, Flashpoints USA: God and Country, 2004; contbr. articles to newspapers, mags., wrote exhibition films for Nat. Park Svc., and Nat. Bicentennial Grand Parade, 1976. Media advisor, NEH, Corp. Pub. Broadcasting, Washington, 1984, 89, 91, 98, DC Comm. Arts and Humanities; hearing com. DC Ct. of Appeal Bd. on Profl. Responsibility, 1988-91; judge Helen Hays Theater Awards, 2007-. Mem. Am. Coll. Forensic Examiners, Writers Guild of Am. East, The Authors Guild, The Cosmos Club, Cosmos Club Found. (chmn.), English-Speaking Union. Office: PO Box 1957 Vienna VA 22183-1957

OLSHAN, JUDD DAVID, human ecologist; s. Marc Allen and Toni Peckham Olshan; m. Hannah Joy Spencer, Sept. 14, 2002. BA in Human Ecology, Coll. of the Atlantic, Bar Harbor, Maine, 1992; MA in Resource Mgmt., Ctrl. Wash. U., 1997; BA in History, SUNY Cortland, 2005. Lic. real estate salesperson Mass., 2001. Tour leader Trek Am., Gardena, Calif., 1994—2000; tchr. Nature's Classroom, Charlton, Mass., 1993—2004; program dir. Regional Environ. Coun., Worcester, Mass., 2000—02; program mgr. Cornell Coop. Ext., Ithaca, NY, 2002—03. Ranger Greater Worcester Land Trust, Worcester, Mass., 2001—02; chair Youth Environ. Svc. Corps Adv. Bd., Worcester, Mass., 2001—02. Contbr. articles to encys. Mem., vol. Greater Worcester Land Trust, 2001—06, Lime Hollow Nature Ctr., Cortland, NY, 2002—06. Recipient Alumni Acheivment awards, SUNY Cortland Alumni Assn., 2004—05, All Coll. Writing award, 2005, Summer Grad. fellow; fellow Univ. fellow, Syracuse U., 2005—; scholar Adult Learner scholar, SUNY Cortland, 2004. Mem.: Am. Hist. Assn. (assoc.), Golden Key Honor Soc., Alpha Sigma Lambda, Tau Sigma, Phi Alpha Phi, Phi Kappa Phi. Democrat. Avocation: back country canoeing. E-mail: jolshan@syr.edu.

OLSHEVSKY, GEORGE, editor; b. Karlsruhe, Germany, June 12, 1946; arrived in U.S., 1947; s. George Eugene and Catherine Sergeyevna Olshevsky; m. Andrea Marie Matyas, Aug. 25, 1982. BSc, MIT, Cambridge, Mass., 1967; MSc, U. Toronto, Ontario, Can., 1970. Computer programmer U. Toronto Computer Ctr., Canada, 1967—77; freelance writer, publisher Official Marvel Comics Index, Toronto, San Diego, Calif., 1976—84; freelance writer The Official Index to Marvel Comics, NYC, 1984—88, Dino Frontline Mag., Tokyo, 1992—96, Dino Press Mag., Tokyo, 2000—02; indexer self employed, 1989—. Author: (book) Mesozoic Meanderings #3, 2000; co-author (cons. with Howard Zimmerman): (children's book) Dinosaurs! The Biggest, Baddest, Strangest, Fastest, 2000; author: Encyclopedia of Dinosaurs, 2001; co-author (cons.): (childrens books series) Discovering Dinosaurs, 2002; contbr. articles to books and mags. on dinosaurs. Office: Publs Requiring Rsch PO Box 161015 San Diego CA 92176-1015 Personal E-mail: dinogeorge@aol.com.

OLSON, ALLISON W., social studies educator; b. Provo, Utah, Mar. 4, 1965; d. Donald Jex and Kelly (Duke) Woolley; m. Steven W. Olson, Dec. 15, 1986; children: Christopher, Cameron, Rylee, Paige. BS Elem. Edn. and Spl. Edn., Brigham Young U., Provo, 1988; postgrad., U. Phoenix. Cert. Social Studies Endorsement Colo. Dept. Edn., type D endorsement administr., prin. lic. Resource specialist Highlands Elem. Sch. Salt Lake City Sch. Dist., 1988—89; resource specialist, tchr. 4th grade Bancroft Elem. Sch. LaMesa/Spring Valley Sch. Dist., San Diego, 1991—94; tchr. 5th grade Stafford Elem. Sch. Stafford County Schs., Va., 2000—03; tchr. 6th grade Heritage Elem. Sch. Douglas County Sch. Dist., Highlands Ranch, Colo., 2003—04; tchr. 8th grade AP Social Studies Liberty Mid. Sch. Cherry Creek Sch. Dist., Aurora, Colo., 2004—. Pvt. tutor, Salt Lake City, 1989—90; tutor Sylvan Learning Ctr., Spring Valley, Calif., 1994—96; mem. Excellence in Equity com. Liberty Mid. Sch., Aurora, 2005—06, coord. Social Studies Dept., 2005—06. Mem.: ASCD, Nat. Coun. Social Studies. Republican. Mem. Lds Ch. Avocations: boating, gardening, volleyball, basketball. Office: Liberty Mid Sch 2500 Dry Creek Rd Aurora CO 80016

OLSON, BARBARA FORD, physician; b. Iowa City, June 15, 1935; d. Leonard A. and Anne (Swanson) Ford; m. Robert Eric Olson, 1959 (div. 1973); children: Katherine Gee, Eric Ford, Julie Marie. BA, Gustavus Adolphus Coll., 1956; MD, U. Minn., 1960. Diplomate Am. Bd. Family Medicine, Am. Bd. Geriat. Medicine, added qualification geriat. medicine. Intern St. Paul-Ramsy Med. Ctr., 1960-61; resident in anesthesiology U. Hosp. Cleve., 1961-62, U. Minn. Hosp., Mpls., 1962-63; pvt. practice anesthesiology St. Johns Hosp. and Devine Redeemer Hosp., St. Paul, 1963-67, Mercy Hosp., Coon Rapids, Minn., 1967-74; staff physician Oak Terrace Nursing Home, Minnetonka, Minn., 1974-88; staff physician, med. dir. geriatric evaluation clinic VA Med. Ctr., St. Cloud, Minn., 1988—. Pres. Alpha Epsilon Iota Med. Found., Mpls., 1980—86, bd.dirs., 1980—86, 2003—. Mem. Minn. Med. Assn., Minn. Women Physicians (pres. 1981-82, bd. dirs. 2003—). Office: VA Med Ctr 4801 8th St N Saint Cloud MN 56303-2015 Home: P O Box 27187 Minneapolis MN 55427 Business E-Mail: Barbara.Olson@va.gov.

OLSON, BETTYE JOHNSON, artist, retired educator; b. Mpls., Jan. 16, 1923; d. Emil Antonious and Irene Irina (Wandtke) J.; m. Howard Einar Olson, July 16, 1949; children: Martha, Jeffrey, Barbara, Virginia. BS in Art Edn., U. Minn., 1945, MEd in Art Edn., 1949; student, U. N.Mex., Summer Sch., Taos, 1947, Cranbrook Summer Art, Mich., 1948. Tchr. art grades 3-12 Summit Sch. for Girls, St. Paul, 1945-47; instr. art U. Minn., Mpls., 1947-49; instr. painting and design Concordia U., St. Paul, 1975-78, 83-84; instr. painting summer sch. Augsburg Coll., Mpls., 1983—89, instr. painting prints, 1988—89; lectr. art Augsburg Coll. of 3rd Age, Mpls., 1984—2009, dir., 1992—98; ret.; instr. painting Elder Learning Inst. U. Minn., 2000—04. Mem. staff Walker Art Ctr., summer 1947; instr. Grunewald Guild, Wash., summer 1990; lectr. women in liturgical arts Luther Northwestern Sem., 1985, lectr. theology and the arts, 1987, 89; lectr. art and lit. series AAUW, 1986-89, 2005-06; artist-in-residence Holden Village Luth. Retreat Ctr., Chelan, Wash., summers 1967-68, 70-71, 74, 78-79, 86-90, 94-96; curriculum bd. Elder Learning Inst., U. Minn., 2000-04. 55 one-woman shows include Unitarian Ch. Gallery, Mpls., 1958, 1990, Met. Med. Ctr., Mpls., 1974, Concordia U., St. Paul, 1975, St. Olaf Coll., Northfield, Minn., 1977, West Lake Gallery, 1964, 67, 71, 75, 78, 82, Inver Hills Coll., Inver Grove Heights, Minn., 1978-, House of Hope Ch., St. Paul, 1978, 1998, Plymouth Congl. Ch., Mpls., 1978-97, Jerome Gallery, Aspen, Colo., 1978, Osborn Gallery, St. Paul, 1979, Augsburg Coll., 1979, 96, Luther Coll., Decorah, Iowa, 1980, Wilson Libr., U. Minn., 1981, St. Paul Campus Gallery, U. Minn., 1981, Am. Swedish Inst., 1978, 1982, Smaland Mus., Vaxjo, Sweden, 1982, Luth. Brotherhood Co., 1983, Phipps Gallery, Hudson, Wis., 1985, Luther Sem., St. Paul, 1998, Berge Gallery, Stillwater, Minn., 1995, 2001, Johnson Heritage Gallery, Grand Marias, Minn., 2002, Undercroft Gallery St. Matthews Ch., 2005, St. Catherines U., 2006; retrospective 60 yrs. participant juried exhbns., including Walker Art Biennial, 1947, Mpls. Art Inst., 1947, St. Paul Gallery, 1961 (Merit award), Sky Gallery, 1975, Minn. Arts Assn., 1975 (Merit award 1975, 76), 76, Minn. Mus. Art, 1976, Watercolor U.S.A., Springfield, Mo., 1977, Minn. State Fair, 1947, 64, 66-68, 74-79, 90, 93 (Merit award 1976, 3rd prize 1977, 93), Lakewood Coll., White Bear Lake, Minn., 1974-79, 81 (Grand prize 1977, Purchase prize 1977), Butler Inst. Am. Art, Youngstown, Ohio, 1977, Women Art Registry Minn. Invited Exhbn Group, 1977, Calif. Women's Conf., Pasadena, Calif., 1978, AAUW, Boston U., 1981; exhibited in group shows at Friends of Art Inst., 1979, West Lake Gallery, 1964-83, Kuopio Art Mus., Finland, 1982, St. Paul Co., 1983, Augsburg Coll., 1988, 89, Minn. Mus. Art, 1988, Modena Italy, 1989, Nash Gallery, U. Minn., 1994, Hill Mansion-History Soc., 1995, 96, 8 Womens Sosin and Sosin gallery, Mpls., 2002, Stillwater Print Show, 2002, Best of Show St. Matthew Comm, 2004-; represented in permanent collections: 3M Co., Minn. History Soc., Minn. Mus. Am. Art, St. Paul, Weisman Mus., Employers Ins. Co. of Wausau, Concordia U., No. States Power Co., Cray Rsch., Pillsbury World Headquaters, Luther Coll., Kuopio Art Mus. Finland, Am. Swedish Inst., Smaland Mus. Sweden, Augsburg Coll., Luther Sem., St. Paul Private, and many others., St. Catherine Coll. Women's Collection. Mem. bd. congl. life Evang. Luth. Ch. Am., St. Paul, 1989-91; coop. mem. West Lake Gallery, Mpls., 1964-84; mem. Mpls. Art Inst., 1945—, Minn. Mus. Am. Art, Walker Art Ctr.; juror, Minn. State Fair, 2001. Mentor protogee program tchg. scholar Met. Arts Coun. to Woman's Art Registry Minn., St. Paul, 1990-94; grantee liberal arts programs Minn. Humanities Commn., Augsburg Coll Third Age, Mpls., 1995-96, 97-98, Elmer Anderson Found., 2006. Mem. AAUW (bd. dir. 1992-94), Woman's Art Registry Minn. (bd. dir. 1992-95). Avocations: attending concerts, theater, skiing, hiking, reading. Home: 1721 Fulham St Apt H Saint Paul MN 55113-5251

OLSON, BYRON LOUIS, biochemist, educator; s. Louis Nels and Mary Virginia Olson; m. Patricia Ann Thomas, June 28, 1969; children: Ann Marie, Michael David. BS, U. of Akron, 1964; PhD, Case Western Res. U., Cleve., 1970. Asst. prof. of preventive dentistry and biochemistry Ind. U. Schools of Dentistry and Medicine, Indpls., 1972—79, assoc. prof. of preventive and cmty. dentistry and biochemistry and molecular biology, 1979—92, prof. of oral biology, biochemistry and molecular biology, 1992—2009. Pres. faculty coun. Ind. U. Sch. Dentistry, 2000—01; chair faculty coun. campus planning com. Ind. U.-Purdue U., Indpls., 1997—99. Contbr. articles to profl. jours. Mem. and bd. chair Ind. Fedn. of Communities for Drug-Free Youth, Inc., Zionsville, 1991—95. 1st lt. US Army, 1964—66. Recipient Tchg. Excellence awards, Ind. U. Sch. of Dentistry, 1997—99; grantee numerous grants. Mem.: Am. Assn. for Dental Rsch. (assoc.; pres. Ind. sect. 1991—92), Internat. Assn. for Dental Rsch. (assoc.), Royal Soc. of Chemistry (assoc.), Am. Dental Edn. Assn. (assoc.; chair biochemistry and nutrition sect. 1992—93, chair, oral biology sect. 1997—99), Am. Chem. Soc. (assoc.; chair, Ind. sect. 1996), Omicron Kappa Upsilon (hon.; chpt. pres. 1998). Roman Catholic. Avocations: swimming, travel, reading, music, fishing. Home: 16 Lake Front Dr Akron OH 44314 Personal E-mail: byrols@att.net. Business E-Mail: bolson@iupui.edu.

OLSON, CHARLES ERIC, economist; b. Wausau, Wis., June 2, 1942; s. Roland Anthony and Lois (Erickson) O.; m. Pamela Ann Templin, July 1, 1967 (div. Oct. 1973); children: Sonja Anne, Erika Christine; m. Carole Emily Collesian, Dec. 1, 1973 (div. Oct. 1990); children: Cora Elizabeth, Sarah Emily; m. Jeanne Esther Katz, Apr. 14, 1991. Student, U. Wis., Marathon County, 1960-62; BBA with honors, U. Wis., Madison, 1964, MS, 1966—67; PhD, U. Wis., 1968. Instr. U. Wis., Madison, 1966-68; asst. prof. U. Md., College Park, 1968-71, assoc. prof. bus., 1971-76; sr. economist H. Zinder & Assocs., Washington, 1976-77, v.p., 1977-79, sr. v.p., 1979—80, pres., 1986-2000, Olson & Co., Inc., 1980-86; Tyser tchg. fellow R.H. Smith Sch. Bus. U. Md., College Park, 2000—07, prof. practice, 2008—. Cons. Devel. Adv. Service, atty. gens. N.C., Minn., Ky., Mass., Va. U.S. Postal Rate Commn., Dept. Def., numerous electric and gas utlities in U.S. and Can. Testified numerous pub. utility rate cases, before Senate Subcom. on Inter-govtl. Relations; mem. advisory com. research and devel. and energy conservation Fed. Power Commn., 1973-74, vice chmn. rate design task force, 1976—. Author: Cost Considerations for Efficient Electricity Supply, 1970; contbr. chpts. to books, articles to profl. jours. Mem. Prince Georges County (Md.) Citizens Airpark Advisory Com., 1970-71. Grantee Inst. Pub. Utilities, 1967-68; U. Md. 1970, 76. Mem. Transp. and Pub. Utilities Group. Home: 10822 Alloway Dr Rockville MD 20854-1503 Office: RH Smith Sch Bus Univ Md College Park MD 20742 Business E-Mail: colson@rhsmith.umd.edu.

OLSON, CHERYL KAY, public health consultant, educator; b. Mpls., Jan. 29, 1960; d. Harley and Renae Olson; m. Lawrence Alan Kutner, Oct. 30, 1988; 1 child, Michael S. Kutner. BA, U. Minn., Mpls., 1981, MPH, 1986; ScD, Harvard Sch. of Pub. Health, Boston, 1995. Cert. in pharmaceutical medicine European Ctr. of Pharm. Medicine, 2001. Co-founder Health Comm. Consultants, Inc., Belmont, Mass., 1985—; co-dir. Harvard Med. Sch. Ctr. Mental Health and Media, Waltham, 2001—; instr. pub. health dept. of psychiatry Mass. Gen. Hosp. Harvard Med. Sch., Boston, 2000—; strategic comm. cons. F. Hoffmann-La Roche Ltd., Basel, Switzerland; prof. Harvard Med. Sch.; co-dir Harvard Med. Sch. Ctr. for Mental Health and Media. Young scholar Johann Jacobs Found., Zurich, Switzerland, 1992, liaison young scholar program, 93; columnist Parents Mag., NYC, 1993—98; evaluation cons. Calif. Dept. Health, Berkeley, 1996—99; vis. prof. pediatric neuropsychiatry U. Medicine and Pharmacy, Timisoara, Romania, 1997—97; vis. scholar Elliot-Pearson Dept. Child Devel. Tufts U., Medford, Mass., 2004—; cons. in field. Co-author: Real-World Fitness, 1999; co-author: (with Lawrence Kutner) Grand Theft Childhood: The Surprising Truth About Violent Video Games and What Parents Can Do, 2008; editor: Proactive Parenting: Guiding Your Child from Two to Six, 2003, If You Decide to Quit Smoking., 2004; contbr. articles to profl. jours. Recipient 2 CINE Golden Eagle awards; grantee prin. investigator, Office of Justice Programs U.S. Dept. of Justice, 2003—. Office: HMS Ctr Mental Health Media Mass Gen Hosp Wang 812 Parkman St Boston MA 02114 E-mail: colson@hms.harvard.edu.

OLSON, DALE C., public relations executive; b. Fargo, ND, Feb. 20, 1934; s. Arthur Edwin and Edith (Weight) Olson Neubauer. Sr. v.p., prin., pres. motion picture divsn. Rogers and Cowan, Inc., Beverly Hills, Calif., 1967-85; prin. Dale C. Olson & Assocs., Beverly Hills, 1985—; mktg. dir. Hollywood History Mus., 2003. Cons. Filmex, L.A., 1972-83; U.S. del. Manila Film Festival, 1982-83. Editor L.A. edit. Theatre ann. Best Plays, 1963-67, 2007; prodr. Rollesgesby. V.p. Diamond Cir. City of Hope, Duarte, Calif., 1980-83; mem. adv. bd. Calif. Mus. Sci. and Industry, L.A., 1975-81; mem. bd. govs. Film Industry Workshops, Inc., 1965-80; pres. Hollywood Press Club, 1963-66; assoc. Los Angeles County Art Mus., 1981-83; bd. trustees Hollywood Arts Coun.; chair 1999 jury USA Film Festival, Dallas; cons. L.A. 2000. Recipient Golden Key, Pub. Rels. News, 1982, Les Mason and pub. svc. awards Publicists Guild, Golden Satellite award for lifetime achievement Internat. Press Acad., 1999, Prism award for pub. svc. Entertainment Industries Coun., 2000, Named in his honor, Dale Olson Lobby, Actors' Fund L.A. Office, 2005. Mem. NATAS, Acad. Motion Picture Arts and Scis. (chmn. pub. rels. coordinating com. 1982—), Actors Fund Am. (chmn. Western coun. 1991, trustee 1992, exec. com. 1998), Hollywood Arts Coun. (bd. dirs.), Pres.'s Club, Thalians. Lutheran. Office Phone: 323-876-9331. Personal E-mail: dolson2000@earthlink.net.

OLSON, DAVID JOHN, political science professor; b. Brantford, ND, May 18, 1941; s. Lloyd and Alice Ingrid (Black) O.; m. Sandra Jean Crabb, June 11, 1966; 1 dau., Maia Kari. BA, Concordia Coll., Moorhead, Minn., 1963; Rockefeller fellow fellow, Union Theol. Sem, NYC, 1963-64; MA (Brooklings Instn. predoctoral rsch. fellow 1968-69), U. Wis., Madison, 1966, PhD (univ. fellow 1967), 1971. Cmty. planner Madison Redvel. Authority, 1965-66; lectr. U. Wis., 1966-67; from lectr. to asso. prof. polit. sci. Ind. U., Bloomington, 1969-76; prof. polit. sci. U. Wash., Seattle, 1976—2005, chmn. dept., 1983-88, Harry Bridges endowed chairlabor studies, 1992-94; bd. dirs. Harry Bridges Inst.; Disting. lectr. in labor studies San Francisco State U., 1994; dir. Ctr. Labor Studies U. Wash., Seattle, 1992-94, prof. emeritus polit. sci., 2005—. Vis. prof. U. Bergen, 1987, Harvard U., 1988-89, U. Hawaii, 1989, U. Calif., Berkeley, 1996, U. Wales, 2006. Co-author: Governing the United States, 1978, Commission Politics, 1977, To Keep the Republic, 1975, Black Politics, 1971; co-editor: Theft of the City, 1974. Recipient Disting. Tchg. award, Ind. U., 1973, Alumni Achievement award, Concordia Coll., 1998, S. Sterling Munro Disting. Tchg. award,

2005, Disting. Tchg. award, U. Wash., 2005, knight, Harold V of Norway, 2006, Outstanding Civic Educator award, Wash. State Senate, 2007; named faculty fellow, Ind. U., 1973. Mem. Am. Polit. Sci. Assn., Western Polit. Sci. Assn. (v.p. 1984, pres. 1985), Midwest Polit. Sci. Assn., So. Polit. Sci. Assn. Democrat. Lutheran. Home: 6512 E Green Lake Way N Seattle WA 98103-5418 Office: U Wash Dept Polit Sci Seattle WA 98195-0001 Office Phone: 206-543-7948. Business E-Mail: davidols@u.washington.edu.

OLSON, DAVID LOUIS, management educator, researcher; b. Sioux Falls, SD, Oct. 4, 1944; s. Ervin Wilfred and Lillian Helen Marjory (Severtson) O.; m. Meri Silver Olson, June 5, 1965; children: David Lewis, Daria Silver, Debra Susan, Daniel Dean. BS in Math., S.D. Sch. Mines & Tech., Rapid City, 1966; MBA, Kearney State U., Nebr., 1978; PhD in Bus. Adminstrn., U. Nebr., 1981. Indsl. engr. U.S. Steel Corp., Gary, Ind., 1966-67; officer U.S. Army Corps Engrs., Germany and Vietnam, 1967-70; engr. Mo. Valley Constrn., Grand Island, Nebr., 1970-79; instr. U. Nebr., Lincoln, 1979-81, prof., 2001—, Tex. A&M U., College Sta., 1981—2001. Presenter in field. Author: Decision Aids for Selection Problems, 1996, Introduction to Information Systems Project Management, 2001, Managerial Issues of Enterprise Resource Planning Systems, 2004; co-author: (with D. Wu) Enterprise Risk Management. Singapore: World Scientific, 2008, New Frontiers in Risk Management. Heidelberg, 2008, (with D. Delen) Advanced Data Mining Techniques. Heidelberg, 2008, and many others.; contbr. over 100 articles to profl. jours. Lt. col. USAR, 1967. Richard D. Irwin Dissertation fellow Irwin Pub., 1980. Fellow Decision Scis. Inst. (v.p. 1989-91, 94-96, 2003-2005, coord. PhD curricular affairs 1996, nat. program chair 1997); mem. Inst. for Ops. Rsch. and the Mgmt. Scis., Soc. for Multiple Criteria Decision Making. Avocation: history. Office: Univ of Nebraska Dept of Mgmt 256 CBA UNL 68588-0491 Lincoln NE 68588

OLSON, DEANNA, school librarian; married. BA, Bemidji State U., Minn., 1987. Receiving specialist Carleton Coll. Bookstore, Northfield, Minn., 1988—97, cataloging specialist, 1997—99; sci. libr. assoc. St. Olaf Coll., Northfield, 1999—. Office: Saint Olaf Coll 1520 St Olaf Ave Northfield MN 55057 Business E-Mail: olsondd@stolaf.edu.

OLSON, DEANNA HELEN, ecologist, researcher; b. Ann Arbor, Mich., Feb. 10, 1958; d. Deane Everett and Jo (Eva Jane) Olson; m. Michael King McDowell, Sept. 4, 1982; children: Shannon Amanda Olson McDowell, Matthew Thomas Olson McDowell. PhD, Oreg. State U., Corvallis, 1988. Rsch. fisheries biologist US Forest Svc., Corvallis, 1990—94, rsch. ecologist, 1994—. Instr. Oreg. State U., 1989—90, courtesy & adj. faculty, 1990—; assoc. editor Northwestern Naturalist: Soc. Northwestern Vertebrate Biology, Corvallis, 1993—2000, SSAR Herpetological Rev., Corvallis, 1996—; instr. Linfield Coll., McMinnville, Oreg., 1989—89. Editor: (book) Amphibians of the Pacific Northwest, Sampling Amphibians in Lentic Habitats. Vol. Salmonwatch, Corvallis, 1994—; artist Wildcat Pk., Corvallis, 2008. Recipient Cert Appreciation, US Forest Svc., 1993—2008; nominee Chief's award, 2005, Chief's Honor award, 2008; Riparian Buffer Study Rsch. grant, US Forest Svc. and Bur. Land Mgmt., 1995—. Mem.: Soc. Northwestern Vertebrate Biology (assoc. editor 1993—2000, pres. 2003—05), Declining Amphibian Populations Task Force (regional co-chair 1991—2005), Ptnrs. Amphibian and Reptile Conservation (regional co-chair 1999—2009, nominee Nat. Co-chair 2009), Soc. Study Amphibians and Reptiles (assoc. editor 1996—). Achievements include design of headwater forests of linkage area; development of conservation assessments for northwestern amphibian species; assisted in development of new partners in amphibian and reptile conservation working group. Office: Pacific NW Rsch Sta USFS 3200 SW Jefferson Way Corvallis OR 97331

OLSON, DONALD RICHARD, mechanical engineering educator; b. Sargent, Nebr., Dec. 26, 1917; s. Harry T. and Gyneth E. (Wittemyer) O.; m. Nancy Walker Benton, June 17, 1944; children: Walter H., Sally, Timothy W. BS, Oreg. State U., 1942; M.Engring., Yale U., 1944, D.Engring., 1951. Profl. engr., Conn. Asst. prof., asso. prof. mech. engring. Yale U., New Haven, 1951-62; prof. mech. engring. Pa. State U., University Park, 1962-83, prof. emeritus, 1983—; head underwater power plants Applied Research Lab., 1962-72, head dept. mech. engring., 1972-83; mem. engring. accreditation commn., 1979-82. Contbr. tech. papers in field to publs. Mem. ASME, Soc. Automotive Engrs. (dir. 1968-71), Sigma Xi. Home: 1930 Cliffside Dr State College PA 16801 E-mail: dro@psu.edu.

OLSON, ERIC THOR, career military officer; b. Tacoma, 1952; married; 2 children. Grad., USN Acad., 1973; MA in Nat. Security Affairs, Naval Postgraduate Sch. Advanced through grades to adm. USN, 2007, asst. dep. chief naval ops. (plans, policy & ops.), comdr. Naval Spl. Warfare Command San Diego, dir. strategy & policy divsn., N51, Office Chief Naval Ops.; dep. comdr. US Spl. Ops. Command (USSOCOM), MacDill AFB, Fla., 2003—07, comdr., 2007—. Decorated Disting. Svc. medal, Silver Star, Bronze Star with V device. Achievements include participating in Operation Restore Hope in Mogadishu, Somalis where he led a recue team to the crash site of two downed Black Hawk helicopters. Office: US Spl Ops Command 7701 Tampa Point Blvd MacDill AFB Tampa FL 33621*

OLSON, GARY ANDREW, academic administrator, English language professor; b. Waterbury, Conn., Dec. 12, 1954; s. Joseph David and Charlotte (Anderson) O.; m. Marlyne Salisbury, June 3, 1978 (div. June 1993); m. Lynn Worsham June 19, 2004. BA, Kings Coll., 1976; MA, U. Conn., 1978; PhD, Indiana U. of Pa., 1980. Instr. U. Ala., Tuscaloosa, 1980-82; asst. prof. U. NC, Wilmington, 1982-85, U. South Fla., Tampa, 1985-87, assoc. prof., 1987-92, prof. English, 1992—, coord. grad. program in rhetoric and composition, 1995—2002, interim dir. Univ. Pubs. Coun., 1995—98, chief academic officer St. Petersburg, 2002—04; dean Coll. Arts & Scis. Ill. State U., Normal, 2004—09; provost, v.p. academic affairs Idaho State U., 2009—. Mem. exec. com. Conf. on Coll. Composition and Comm., 1992-; monthly columnist Chronicle Higher Edn., 2006-. Editor Writing Centers: Theory and Administration, 1984, Journal Advanced Composition, 1985-95, Philosophy, Rhetoric, Literary Criticism: (Inter)Views, 1994, Composition Theory for the Postmodern Classroom, 1994, Women Writing Culture, 1995, Landmark Essays on Advanced Composition, 1996, Publishing in Rhetoric and Composition, 1997; co-editor: The Process Reader, 1985, Advanced Placement English, 1989, The Gender Reader, 1990, (Inter-)Views: Cross Disciplinary Perspectives on Literacy, 1991, Composition Theory for the Postmodern Classroom, 1994; co-author: Style and Readability in Technical Writing. Founding pres. Southeastern Writing Ctr. Assn., 1981-83. Recipient Award for Outstanding Contbn. to English Tchrs. of N.C., 1983, Internat. award for disting. retiring editor Coun. Editors Learned Jours., 1993. Mem. MLA, Nat. Coun. Tchrs. English, Conf. on Coll. Composition and Comm., Assn. Tchrs. of Advanced Composition, Rhetoric Soc. Am. (bd. dirs. 1990-94), South Atlantic MLA. Democrat. Avocations: short wave radio, chess, flute playing, jazz and classical music. Office: Idaho State U Office of Provost 921 S 8th Ave Administrn Bldg 10 Ste 264 Pocatello ID 83209-8063 Home: 1898 Arlington Dr Pocatello ID 83204 Office Phone: 208-282-2171. Office Fax: 208-282-4487. Business E-Mail: golson@isu.edu.

OLSON, GREGORY BRUCE, materials science and engineering educator, academic director; b. Bklyn., Apr. 10, 1947; s. Oscar Gustav Fritz and Elizabeth Rose (Dorner) Olson; m. Jane Ellen Black, May 10, 1980; 1 child, Elise Marie. BS, MS in Materials Sci. and Engring., MIT, 1970, ScD in Materials Sci. and Engring., 1974. Rsch. assoc. dept. materials sci. and engring. MIT, Cambridge, 1974-79, prin. rsch. assoc., 1979-85, sr. rsch. assoc., 1985-88; prof. materials sci. and engring. Northwestern U., Evanston, Ill., 1988—, Wilson-Cook prof. engring. design, 1999—. Cons. Army Materials Tech. Lab., Watertown, Mass., 1975-88, Lawrence Livermore (Calif.) Nat. Lab., 1983-89; Jacob Kurtz Exchange Scientist Technion-Israel Inst. Tech., 1979; SERC vis. prof. U. Cambridge, 1992; assoc. chmn. dept. materials sci. and engring. Northwestern U., 1992-98, dir. materials tech. lab.-steel rsch.group, 1985—; founding mem. Questek Innovations LLC, 1997—. Editor: Innovative UHS Steel Technology, 1990, Martensite, 1992; contbr. numerous papers and articles to jours., encys., and symposia; inventor hydrogen-res. UHS steels, stainless bearing steel, ultrahard carburizing steels. Fellow AMAX Found., 1972-74; named N.Mex. Disting. lectr. in Materials, 1983; recipient Creativity Extension award NSF, 1983-85; Wallenberg grantee Jacob Wallenberg Found., Sweden, 1993; recipient Tech. Recognition award NASA, 1994, Tech. of Yr. award Industry Week mag. 1998, Pollution Prevention Project of Yr. award, Strategic Environ. R & D Program, 2003, Innovation of Yr. award Sun-Times Chgo., 2003. Fellow ASM (chmn. phase transformation com. 1987-90, Boston chpt. Saveur Meml. lectr. 1986, Phila. chpt. 1998, Alpha Sigma Mu lectr. 1996), TMS-AIME (student affairs com., M.R. Tenebaum award 1993); mem. AAAS, Materials Rsch. Soc., Internat. Soc. Martensitic Transformation, Assn. Univ. Related Rsch. Parks (Tech. Transfer award 1998). Lutheran. Avocations: sports cars, jazz, trumpet. Office: Northwestern U Dept Materials Sci and Engring 2220 Campus Dr Evanston IL 60208-3108

OLSON, JACK CONRAD, JR., geriatrician; b. Muskegon, Mich., 1955; BS in Chemistry, Mich. State U., 1977, BA in English, 1977; MD, U. Mich., 1984. Bd. cert. internal medicine, bd. cert. geriatric medicine. Intern U. Wis. Hosps. and Clinics, Madison, 1984—85, resident internal medicine, 1985—87, fellow geriatrics, 1987—89; assoc. med. dir. Mendota Mental Health, U. Wis., 1989—92; dir. Windermere Sr. Health Ctr., U. Chgo., 1992—99; asst. clin. prof., fellowship dir. Rush U. Med. Ctr., Chgo., 1999—. Office: 1725 W Harrison St Ste 955 Chicago IL 60612 Office Phone: 312-942-7030. Business E-Mail: jolson@rush.edu.

OLSON, JAMES RICHARD, retired transportation executive; b. Alexandria, Minn., Mar. 11, 1941; s. Orie D. and Theresa Marie (Erickson) O.; m. Ronna Lee, Feb. 1, 1969 (dec.); 1 child, Trevor James. BS, N.D. State U., 1963; LLD, U. Minn., 1966; MBA, Harvard U., 1968. Asst. to v.p. finance Cargill Inc., Mpls., 1968-69; with Graco Inc., Mpls., 1969-75, v.p. finance, 1972-75; exec. v.p. finance Ponderosa System, Inc., Dayton, Ohio, 1975-77; v.p. planning Pillsbury Co., Mpls., 1977-79, v.p. restaurant group, 1979-80; group v.p.-restaurants The Carlson Cos., Inc., Mpls., 1981-83; exec. v.p., chief fin. and adminstrv. officer Schneider Nat., Inc., 1983-87, pres. van group, 1987-92, pres. transp. sector, 1992-98. Bd. dirs., chair compensation com. Meritex Enterprises, Inc. Mem. Harvard Bus. Sch. Club Minn. (past pres.) Lutheran. Home: 1103 Winslow House 100 2d St SE Minneapolis MN 55414-2157 Office Phone: 612-617-8869. Personal E-mail: jrolson1111@gmail.com.

OLSON, JOHN RICHARD, power industry electrician; b. St. Paul, Sept. 6, 1956; s. Arthur Norman and Viola Ann Olson; m. Diane Evelyn Steen-Hinderlie, July 21, 1989; stepchildren: Peder Donald Hinderlie, Erik Steen Hinderlie. Degree in electrical, Dunwoody Indsl. Inst., Mpls., 1977. Properties mgr. First Lutheran Ch., St. Louis Pk., 1984—86; journeyman, wireman, occasional job steward, foreman Internat. Brotherhood Electrical Workers, Mpls., 1977—. Editor Viking Age Club Newsletters, 2001—07. Coach Baseball Assn., St. Louis Pk., 1992—98; pres. Sons Norway Lodges Joint Com., Twin Cities, 2000—02; treas. Sons Norway Lodges Joint Com., 2002—; pres. Syttende Mai Lodge, 2000—02, St. Louis Pk. Historical Soc., 2002—. Named to Coaches Hall of Fame, Baseball Assn., 1998. Mem.: Trinity Congregation (coord. Thrivent Fin. grants 2005—), Chgo. Northwestern Hist. Soc., Nat. Railroad Passenger Assn., Nat. Model Railrd. Assn., Soo Line Historical Soc. Dfl. Lutheran. Avocations: model building, photography, bowling. Home: 2829 Yosemite Ave S Minneapolis MN 55416

OLSON, KEITH WALDEMAR, historian, educator; b. Poughkeepsie, NY, Aug. 4, 1931; s. Ernest Waldemar and Elin Ingeborg (Rehnstrom) O.; m. Marilyn Joyce Wittschen, Sept. 10, 1955; children: Paula, Judy. BA, SUNY, Albany, 1957, MA, 1959; PhD, U. Wis., 1964; PhD (hon.), U. Tampere, Finland, 2000. Mem. history faculty Syracuse U., NY, 1963-66; mem. history faculty U. Md., College Park, 1966—2008, prof. emeritus history. Fulbright prof. U. Tampere, 1986-87, 2004, U. Oulu, Finland, 1993, U. Jyväskylä, Finland, 1994. Author: The G.I. Bill, the Veterans and the Colleges, 1974; Biography of a Progressive: Franklin K. Lane, 1979, Watergate: The Presidential Scandal That Shook America, 2003. Pres. Am. Scandinavian Found., Washington, 1977-79. Served with U.S. Army, 1952-54. U.S. Office Edn. grantee, 1965-66; U. Md. grantee, 1971, 76, 78. Mem. Am. Hist. Assn., Orgn. Am. Historians, Wis. Hist. Soc., Swedish Am. Hist. Soc., Finnish Hist. Soc. (hon.), Soc. Historians of Am. Fgn. Rels., Cen. Study of Presidency, Am. Scandinavian Assn. (pres. 1998-99). Unitarian Universalist. Home Phone: 802-985-0710; Office Phone: 301-405-4286. Business E-Mail: kwolson@umd.edu.

OLSON, LEROY CALVIN, retired educational administration educator; b. Kane, Pa., Mar. 7, 1926; s. Vernon Reinhold and Gertrude Viola Olson; m. Miriam Marie Vogler, June 19, 1954; children— David Lee, Thomas Edward, Steven Andrew. BS, Clarion State Coll., 1949; M.Ed., Pa. State Coll., 1950; Ed.D., Pa. State U., 1962; postgrad., U. Del., Newark, 1964-65. Tchr.-counselor Boiling Springs H.S., Pa., 1950-52, Gordon Jr. H.S., Coatesville, Pa., 1952-54; guidance dir. Ctrl. Dauphin Sch. Dist., Harrisburg, Pa., 1954-57; coordinator pupil personnel services, asst. supt. for instrn. and personnel, acting supt. Alfred I. duPont Sch. Dist., Wilmington, Del., 1957-65; prof. ednl. adminstrn. Temple U., Phila., 1965-92, prof. emeritus, 1992—. Cons. to schs. bds. and dists., also Nat., Wis., Pa. sch. bds. assns. Contbr. articles to profl. jours. Trustee Luth. Ch., 1963-66, chmn. bd., 1976-78, chmn. various coms., discussion groups. Served with USNR, 1944-46, PTO. Recipient Disting. Alumni award, Clarion State Coll., 1972. Mem. Am. Personnel and Guidance Assn., AAUP, Am. Assn. Sch. Personnel Adminstrs., Assn. Supervision and Curriculum Devel., Council Profs. Instrn. Supervision, Nat. Staff Devel. Council, Am. Legion, Phi Delta Kappa, Phi Kappa Phi. Republican. Home: 211 Azalea Lane West Grove PA 19390 *God's gift of life is a marvelous thing. My attempt to make the best use of that gift is to try to live an integrated and balanced life. This means that active attention must be paid to the physical, social, spiritual, psychological, mental, and recreational aspects as well as to the work or career dimension. It also means we must share that gift through loving and caring about others.*

OLSON, LINDA ANN SALMONSON, minister; b. Charleston, Ill., Apr. 12, 1951; d. Kenneth Emmett and Helen Startzum Salmonson; m. Sheldon Ellis Olson, Sept. 18, 1971; children: Jeffery Ellis, Steven Eric, Ingrid Ann Olson Douglas, Karin Melinda. BSN, Oreg. Health Scis. U., 1973; MDiv, Pacific Luth. Theol. Sem., Berkeley, Calif., 1997. RN Calif., cert. diplomate, Am. Bd. Quality Assurance and Utilization Rev.; ordained Evang. Luth. Ch. in Am., 1997. Intensive care charge nurse St. Vincent Hosp. and Med. Ctr., Portland, Oreg., 1973—75; med. rev. specialist Multnomah Found. Med. Care, Portland, 1975—77; rehab. specialist Internat. Rehab. Assocs., Portland, 1979—81; nursing cons. SAIF Corp., Eugene, Oreg., 1981; med. rev. analyst Blue Cross/Blue Shield of Oreg., Portland, 1981—83; quality assurance mgr. Good Samaritan Hosp. and Med. Ctr., Portland, 1983—84; unit mgr., dist. mgr., nat. product dir. Intracorp, Wayne, Pa., 1984—91; dir. quality svcs. Golden State Rehab. Hosp., San Ramon, Calif., 1991—93; parish pastor Our Savior's Luth. Ch., Ferndale, Calif., 1997—2002; hospice chaplain VITAS Healthcare Corp. of Calif., San Diego, 2002—07, Tri-City Hospice, Vista, Calif., 2007—. Spkr. in field healthcare, ins., hospice. Contbr. articles to profl. jours. Bd. dirs. Luth. Home for Aging of Humboldt County, Fortuna, Calif., 1998—2002, Newburg Retirement Ctr., Fortuna, 1998—2002, Mt. View Village, Fortuna, 1998—2002; mem. Chaplaincy Svcs. Bd. of John Muir Hosp. and Med. Ctr., Walnut Creek, Calif., 1993—97; chair social concerns com. Resurrection Luth. Ch., Dublin, Calif., 1992—94; pres. bd. dirs. Thirvent Fin. Lutherans, No. San Diego County chpt., 2005—. Recipient 2d pl. nat. photography contest, Luth. Brotherhood, 1986, 1st pl. photography contest, Cat Fanciers Assn., Bend, Oreg., 1991; scholar, Luth. Brotherhood, 1993—97, Aid Assn. for Luths., 1993—97. Republican. Avocations: photography, gardening, poetry. Office: Tri-City Hospice 2095 W Vista Way Ste 217 Vista CA 92083 Personal E-mail: prlinda@cox.net.

OLSON, LUTE (ROBERT LUTHER OLSON), retired men's college basketball coach; b. Mayville, ND, Sept. 22, 1934; s. Albert E. and Alinda E. (Halvorson) O.; m. Roberta R. Russell, Nov. 27, 1953 (dec. 2001); children: Vicki, Jody, Gregory, Christi, Steven m. Christine Jack Toretti, 2003 (div., 2008) BA, Augsburg Coll., Mpls., 1956; MA, Chapman Coll., Orange, Calif., 1964. Cert. counselor. Head basketball coach Mahonomen HS, Minn., 1956-57, Two Harbors HS, Minn., 1957-61; dean of boys Baseline Jr. HS, Boulder, Colo., 1961-62; head basketball coach Loara HS, Anaheim, Calif., 1962-64, Marine HS, Huntington Beach, Calif., 1964-69, Long Beach City Coll., Calif., 1969-73, Long Beach State U., 1973-74, U. Iowa, Iowa City, 1974-83, U. Ariz. Wildcats, 1983—2008, head coach NCAA Men's Basketball Tournament champions, 1997; ret., 2008. Author: Passing Game Offense, 1980, Multiple Zone Attack, 1981, Pressure Defense, 1981, Match-up Zone, 1983. Crusade chmn. Am. Cancer Soc., Iowa, 1982. Named Coach of Yr. Orange League, 1964, Sunset League, 1968, Yr. Met. Conf. Calif., 1970-71, PCAA, 1974, Big Ten Conf., 1979, 80, PAC-10 Conf., 1986, 87, 89, 93, 94, 98, 2003; inducted to Naismith Meml. Basketball Hall of Fame, 2002. Mem. Nat. Assn. Basketball Coaches (Coach of Yr. 1980) Lutheran.

OLSON, MARIAN KATHERINE, management consultant; b. Tulsa, Okla., Oct. 15, 1933; d. Sherwood Joseph and Katherine M. (Miller) Lahman; m. Ronald Keith Olson, Oct. 27, 1956 (dec. May 1991). BA in Polit. Sci., U. Colo., 1954, MA in Elem. Edn., 1962; EdD in Ednl. Adminstrn., U. Tulsa, 1969. Tchr. pub. schs., Wyo., Colo., Mont., 1956-67; tchg. fellow, adj. instr. edn. U. Tulsa, 1968-69; asst. prof. edn. Eastern Mont. State Coll., 1970; program assoc. rsch. adminstrn. Mont. State U., 1970-75; on leave with Energy Policy Office of White House then with Fed. Energy Adminstrn., 1973-74; with Dept. Energy and predecessor, 1975—, program analyst, 1975-79, chief planning and environ. compliance br., 1979-83; regional dir. Region VIII Fed. Emergency Mgmt. Agy., 1987-93; exec. dir. Search and Rescue Dogs of the U.S., 1993—. Pres. Marian Olson Assocs., Bannack Pub. Co Contbr. articles in field. Bd. dirs. Disaster Preparedness and Emergency Response Assn. Internat.; incorporator Jeffco Citizens League. Grantee Okla. Consortium Higher Edn., 1969, NIMH, 1974. Mem. Internat. Assn. Emergency Mgrs., Am. Soc. for Info. Sci., Am. Assn. Budget and Program Analysis, Assn. of Contingency Planners, Nat. Inst. Urban Search and Rescue (bd. dirs.), Nat. Assn. for Search and Rescue, Colo. Search and Rescue, Search and Rescue Dogs of U.S., Colo. Emergency Mgmt. Assn., Front Range Rescue Dogs, Kappa Delta Pi, Phi Alpha Theta, Kappa Alpha Theta. Republican. Home: 203 Iowa Dr Golden CO 80403-1337 Office: Marian Olson Assocs 203 Iowa Dr Ste B Golden CO 80403-1337 Personal E-mail: mlolson@ix.netcom.com.

OLSON, MARK WALTER, former non-profit corporation administrator; b. Fergus Falls, Minn., Mar. 17, 1943; s. Walter Roland and Agnes Marie (Peterson) Olson; m. Renee Irene Korda, July 5, 1980; children: Benjamin, Stephanie. BA in Econs., St. Olaf Coll., Northfield, Minn., 1965. Joined First Bank Sys., St. Paul, 1966, named officer, 1969; legis. asst. banking issues Congressman Bill Frenzel, Washington, 1971—72, dir. Minn. dist. office, 1974—76; with Andrews Allen Co., St. Paul, 1972—74; pres., CEO Security State Bank, Fergus Falls, Minn., 1976—88; ptnr. Ernst & Young LLP (formerly Arthur Young & Co.), 1988—99, nat. dir. regulatory consulting practice; staff dir. Securities Subcommittee US Senate Banking Housing & Urban Affairs Com., 2000—01; mem. bd. govs. Fed. Res. Sys., 2001—06, adminstrv. gov., 2002—06; chmn. Pub. Co. Acctg. Oversight Bd. (PCAOB), 2006—09. Bd. dirs. Pioneer Home, Fergus Falls, 1977—86, Lake Region Hosp., Fergus Falls, 1978—88, Fergus Falls Area YMCA, 1977—83. Named a Disting. Alumni, St. Olaf Coll., 2003. Mem.: Am. Bankers Assn. (chmn. govt. rels. coun., bd. dirs. 1982—84, pres. 1986—87), C. of C. (bd. dirs. 1980—84). Lutheran.*

OLSON, MAXINE LOUISE, artist, lecturer; b. Kingsburg, Calif., June 29, 1931; d. Alfred and Lena A. Marshall; divorced; children: Todd Olson, Terry Olson. BA summa cum laude, Calif. State U., Fresno, 1973, MA with distinction, 1975. Asst. prof. U. Ga., Athens, 1986—89; lectr. Coll. of Sequoias, Visalia, Calif., 1973-96. Lectr. Fresno City Coll., 1990, Calif. State U., Fresno, intermitently 1973-96; tchr. Inst. Allende, San Miguel de Allende, Mex., 1973, U. Ga., Cortona, Italy, 1987, 93, UCLA Arts Rsch. Program, Corcoran State Prison, 1996; 6th Annual MicroPubl. Graphics, San Francisco, 1998, The World's Women On-Line United Nations Conf., Beijing, China, 1995. Exhibitions include Oakland Mus., Palazzo Casali, Venice, Italy, Forum Gallery, NYC, Soho 20, The World's Women on-line/UN 4th World Conf. on Women, Beijing, William Sawyer Gallery, Palm Springs Mus., Calif., Silicon Gallery, Pa., Calif. Dept. Fish and Game, Fresno, 2001, The Great 8 - Patterson Bldg., 2004, Fresno.ca, Chait Galleries, Iowa City, Iowa, 2005, Fresno Art Mus. Exhibition- Fast in Translation, 2006, Peninsula Mus. Art, Belmont, Calif., 2007, Spectrum Gallery, 2008; contbr.: Women Artists of American West (Susan Ressler); mural, Kingsburg, Calif.; designer book cover The Portuguese Californian Immigrants in Agriculture (Alvin Graves); exhibitions include San Francisco Mus. Modern Art, Artist's Gallery, 2001, The Great 8, Patterson Bldg., Fresno, Calif., 2004, UMAR, Azores Islands "Yr. of Women", 2008, U. Calif. Can. exhibition U. Calgary, Can., 2008, exhibitions include portuguese artist Boston Pub. Libr., Mass., 2009, exhibitions include Internat. Mus. Women, San Francisco, 2009, Centralism, Gallery 25, Fresno, Calif.,

2009, numerous exhbn., 2006—08. Recipient Harold J. Cleve. Meml. award, 20th Nat. jury Show, Chautauqua, NY, 1977, Juror's award, Ann. Riverside Art Mus., Calif., 1977, Gold award Art of Calif. Mag., 1992, IDN Design award, 1997-98. Mem. Coll. Art Assn., Rotary Club Mural Centennial Design (Kingsburg), Internat. Mus. Women (San Francisco), Coll. Art Assoc., Kingsburg Rotary Club Centennial Mural Design, Friends Libr. Mural Design, Phi Kappa Phi. Roman Catholic. Avocations: painting, drawing, digital art. Home: 1555 Lincoln St Kingsburg CA 93631-1804 Home Phone: 559-897-4586. Personal E-mail: maxineolson@sbcglobal.net.

OLSON, MAYNARD V., science educator, researcher; Grad., Calif. Inst. Tech.; PhD in Chemistry, Stanford U. Faculty mem. Dartmouth Coll., Washington U., St. Louis; prof. genetics and medicine U. Washington, Seattle, 1992—, adj. prof. computer science and engring. Chmn., Genome Rsch. review com. NIH Genome Rsch. Inst. Recipient Genetics Soc. Am. medal, 1992, Gairdner Found. Internat. award, 2002. Mem.: NAS. Office: U Washington 225 Fluke Hall Genome Ctr Box 352145 Seattle WA 98195 Office Phone: 206-685-7346, 206-685-7336. Office Fax: 206-685-7344. Business E-Mail: mvo@u.washington.edu.*

OLSON, NORMAN FREDRICK, not-for-profit developer, retired food science educator; b. Edmund, Wis., Feb. 8, 1931; s. Irving M. and Elva B. (Rhinerson) O.; m. Darlene Mary Thorson, Dec. 28, 1957; children: Kristin A., Eric R. BS, U. Wis., 1953, MS, 1957, PhD, 1959. Asst. prof. U. Wis.-Madison, 1959-63, assoc. prof., 1963-69, prof., 1969-93, dir. Walter V. Price Cheese Research Inst., 1976-93; dir. Ctr. Dairy Research, 1986-93; disting. prof. U. Wis.-Madison, 1993-97, prof. emeritus, 1997—; dir. outreach Shama, Inc., 2007—. Cons. to cheese industry, 1997—. Author: Semi-soft Cheeses; inventor enzyme microencapsulation; sr. editor Jour. Dairy Sci., 1996-2000. Lt. U.S. Army, 1953-55. Recipient Laureate award Nat. Cheese Inst., 1998, Disting. Svc. award Coll. Agrl. Life. Sci., U. Wis., 2002; named Highly Cited Rschr. ISI, 2002. Fellow Inst. Food Technologists (Macy award 1986), Am. Dairy Sci. Assn. (v.p. 1984-85, pres. 1985-86, Pfizer award 1971, Dairy Rsch. Inc. award 1978, Borden Found. award 1988, Hon. award 1997); mem. Inst. Food Technologists. Democrat. Lutheran. Avocation: cross country skiing. Home: 114 Green Lake Pass Madison WI 53705-4755 Office: U Wis Dept Food Sci Babcock Hall Madison WI 53706 Business E-Mail: nfolson@wisc.edu.

OLSON, PAMELA FAITH, lawyer, former federal agency administrator; b. Fargo, ND, July 6, 1954; d. Norman Clifford and Inga (Larson) O.; m. Grant Douglas Aldonas, Apr. 12, 1980; children: Nicole Helen, Kirsten Inga, Noah Grant. BA magna cum laude, U. Minn., 1976, JD, 1980, MBA, 1984. Bar: DC 1981. Instr. U. Minn., Coll. Bus. Adminstrn., Mpls., 1979; atty., Office of Chief Counsel, IRS US Dept. Treasury, Washington, 1981—86; assoc. Skadden, Arps, Slate, Meagher & Flom, LLP, Washington, 1986-90, ptnr., 1990—2001, 2004—; dep. asst. sec. for tax policy US Dept. Treasury, Washington, 2001—02, asst. sec. for tax policy, 2002—04. Bd. dirs. Tax Analysts, 2005-, So. Fed. Tax Inst., 2005-; mem. advisory bd. NYU Inst. on Fed. Taxation Fellow Am. Bar Found., Regent Am. Coll. Tax Counsel; mem. ABA (coun. dir. sect. on taxation 1993-95, vice chair sect. taxation 1995-98, chair-elect sect. on taxation 1999-00, chair sect. on taxation 2000-01, bd. dirs. retirement funds 2004-), Equipment Leasing Assn., DC Bar Assn. (chmn. legis. and regulations com.), U. Minn. Law Sch. Alumi Assn. (bd. dirs. 1992-97), Phi Beta Kappa. Avocations: children, volunteering, cooking, softball, skiing. Office: Skadden Arps Slate Meagher & Flom LLP 1440 New York Ave NW Ste 600 Washington DC 20005-6000 Business E-Mail: pamela.olson@skadden.com.

OLSON, PATRICIA HAGEY, retired elementary school educator; b. South Bend, Ind., Mar. 16, 1926; d. George Lee and Catherine Blakeman Hagey; m. Robert Anderson Olson; children: Cathy Lee, Keith Alan. BS, Purdue U., West Lafayette, Ind., 1947; MA, Loyola U., Chgo., 1955; MEd, U. Ariz., Tucson, 1972, PhD, 1975. Substitute tchr. Chgo. Bd. Edn., 1949—55; tchr. 6th grade Deerfield Pub. Schs., Ill., 1955—59, Palatine Pub. Schs., Ill., 1959—63, tchr. audio lingual spanish grade 3-8; tchr. Spanish Lake Geneva HS, Wis., 1963—66; tchr. 3d grade LA Pub. Schs., 1968—71; tchr. 6th grade Tucson Pub. Schs., 1972—75; instr., edn. dept. U. Ariz., 1975; ret. Home: 324 Linden Apt 105 Wilmette IL 60091 Home Phone: 847-256-8451. Personal E-mail: pjho@mac.com.

OLSON, PAULA SUE, director, educational consultant; b. Sabetha, Kans., July 30, 1950; d. Raymond Eugene and Ivena Orene Legler; m. Carl Arthur Olson, Oct. 3, 1986; 1 child, Matthew Wesley Smith. BS in Edn., Troy State U., Ala., 1975; MS in Edn., U. Ariz., 1985, EdS in Adminstrn., 1983. ESL tchr., Republic of Korea, 1975—76; tchr. freshman English, Cochise Coll., 1976—77; classroom tchr. Sierra Vista Pub. Schs., Ariz., 1977—85, Sunnyside Schs., 1985—89; program facilitator Esperanza Elem. Sch., Tucson, 1989—93; Title I dir. fed. funds for at-risk students Sunnyside Sch. Dist., Tucson, 1993—94; elem. sch. prin. Craycroft Elem. Sch., Tucson, 1994—96; lang. arts and reading instr. Apollo and Challenger Mid. Schs., Tucson, 1996—2003; program facilitator Challenger Mid. Sch., Tucson, 2003—07; ednl. cons., 2007—. Tchr. cons. Nat. Geographic. Author: (interactive textbook) Arizona!. Named Outstanding Ariz. Law-Related Educator of Yr., 1993, Mid. Sch. Educator of Yr., 1994. Mem.: Pi Lambda Theta. Personal E-mail: psolson@dakotacom.net. Business E-Mail: paulao@susd12.org.

OLSON, PETE, United States Representative from Texas, former congressional aide; b. Ft. Lewis, Wash., Dec. 9, 1962; m. Nancy Olson; children: Kate, Grant. BA in Computer Sci., Rice U., 1985; JD, U. Tex. Austin, 1988. Naval liason officer US Senate, 1995—98, staff mem. to Senator Phil Gramm, 1998—2002, chief of staff to Senator John Cornyn, 2002—07; mem. US Congress from 22nd Tex. Dist., 2009—. Officer USAR, naval aviator USN. Decorated Joint Chiefs of Staff Badge, Southwest Asia Svc. medal, Armed Forces Expeditionary medal, Navy & Marine Corps Achievement medal, Joint Svc. Achievement medal, Joint Svc. Commendation medal. Mem.: Tex. Lyceum (dir.), Chancellor's Coun. and Littlefield Soc., Tex. State Soc., R Assn., Rice U., NRA. Republican. Office: US Congress 514 Cannon House Office Bldg Washington DC 20515-4322 also: Dist Office 1650 Hwy 6 Ste 150 Sugar Land TX 77477 Office Phone: 202-225-5951, 281-240-3700. Office Fax: 202-225-5241, 281-240-2959.*

OLSON, PETER W., former publishing executive; b. Chgo., May 1, 1950; m. Candice Carpenter, Sept. 8, 2001. AB in History, magna cum laude, Harvard Coll., 1972; JD cum laude, Harvard Law Sch.; MBA, Harvard Bus. Sch. Assoc. Baker & Botts LLP, Wash., DC, 1976—77, Hamada & Matsumoto, Tokyo, 1977—79; officer, internat. group Dresdner Bank, Frankfurt, 1979—81, deputy mgr., corp. bus. dept. Tokyo, 1981—84, mgr., credit dept., 1984—87; v.p. planning dept., treasury div. Frankfurt, Germany, 1987—88; mgr. Bertelsmann AG, 1988, sr. v.p., Doubleday Book and Music Clubs Garden City, NY, 1989—90, pres., Bertelsmann, Inc., 1990—92, exec. v.p., CFO, Bantam Doubleday Dell Pub. Group, 1992—94, exec. v.p., chief admin. officer, Bantam Doubleday Dell Pub. Group, 1992—94, chmn, CEO Bertelsmann book group N. Am., 1994—98, mem. exec. bd., Bertelsmann Book AG, 1994—98, chmn., CEO, Random House Inc. NYC, 1998—2008, exec. bd. mem., trade book pub. worldwide, 2001—08. Exec. com. The Quills. Mem.: Phi Beta Kappa.

OLSON, RICHARD DAVID, psychology professor; b. Reading, Pa., Oct. 10, 1944; s. Milton Stuart and Sarah Ellen (Moyer) O.; m. M. Gayle Augustine, Aug. 26, 1967. BA, U. Redlands, 1966; MS, St. Louis U., 1968, PhD, 1970. Lic. psychologist, La. Asst. prof. psychology U. New Orleans, 1970-74, assoc. prof., chmn. dept. psychology, 1974-79, prof., chmn. dept., 1979-81, assoc. dean Grad. Sch., 1981-82, dean, 1982-88, vice chancellor, 1984-88, rsch. prof., 1988—2000, prof. emeritus, 2000—; chmn. dept. psychology, 1995—2000. Cons. psychologist, New Orleans, 1973—2002; pres. Statis. Cons. of New Orleans, 1977-82 Editor: Learning in the Classroom, 1971, The Comma After Love, The Selected Poems of Raeburn Miller, 1994, The Collected Poems of Raeburn Miller, 1997; contbr. articles to profl. jours. Grantee HEW, 1976-81 Fellow APA, Am. Psychol. Soc.; mem. Soc. for Neuroscis., Am. Statis. Assn. Home: 40 Infinity Dr Poplarville MS 39470 Office: U New Orleans Dept Psychology Lake Front New Orleans LA 70148 Office Phone: 601-795-4838. Business E-Mail: richardolson@hughes.net.

OLSON, RICHARD GUSTAVE, United States Ambassador to the United Arab Emirates; b. Orange, NJ, Nov. 3, 1959; s. Richard Gustave and Barbara Jean (Hawkins) O. AB in Law and Society, History, Brown U., Providence, 1981. Mgmt. trainee European Am. Bank, NYC, 1982; vice consul Am. Consulate Gen., Ciudad Juarez, Mexico, 1983—84; polit. officer Am. Embassy, Uganda, 1985—86; ops. officer US Dept. State, Washington, 1987; NATO desk officer Fgn. Svc., US Dept. State, 1988, Arabic tng. officer, 1988—90; polit. mil. officer Am. Embassy, Riyadh, Saudi Arabia, 1990—92, polit. econ. chief Addis Ababa, Ethiopia, 1992—94; dep. dir. State Dept. Ops. Ctr., Washington, 1994—96; polit. officer Israel Desk, State Dept., Washington, 1996—97, dep. dir., 1997—98; spl. asst. to amb. Am. Embassy, Addis Ababa, 1999—2001, US consul gen. Dubai, United Arab Emirates, 2001—03; dep. chief US mission NATO, 2006—08; US amb. to the United Arab Emirates US Dept. State, Abu Dhabi, 2008—. Recipient Exceptional Civilian Svc. award, Sec. Def., Superior Honor award, US Dept. State. Mem. Am. Fgn. Svc. Assn. Avocations: bicycling, sailing, travel. Office: DOS Amb 6010 Abu Dhabi Pl Washington DC 20521-6010*

OLSON, ROBERT EDWARD, coal mining executive; b. Phila., Aug. 5, 1927; s. Oscar E. and Marie B. (Kilgallon) O.; m. Jean Emilie Wadsworth, Dec. 31, 1955 (dec. Aug. 1997); children: Grace Olson, Nancy Olson Ashcraft, Karen Olson Culbertson. Student, U. Richmond, 1945, Duke U., 1945-46, U. Pa., 1946; BS in Mining Engring., Pa. State U., 1952. Registered profl. engr., Pa., W.Va. Indsl. engr. Island Creek Coal Co., Holden, W.Va., 1952-55; dir., treas., sr. assoc. Coal Standards, Inc., mgmt. cons., Charleston, W.Va., 1955-61; v.p. adminstrn. Rochester & Pitts. Coal Co., Indiana, Pa., 1961-81; pres., COO Valley Camp Coal Co., Oil City, Pa., 1981-86, vice chmn., dir., mem. exec. com., 1986-88, ret., 1988. Past pres., chmn., dir Kanawha and Hocking Coal & Coke Co., Kelley's Creek and Northwestern R.R. Co., Valley Camp Coal Sales Co.; pres., chief exec. officer Gt. Lakes Coal & Dock Co.; chmn., dir. Donaldson Mine Co., Elm Grove Coal Co., Shrewsbury Coal Co., Helen Mining Co., Valley Camp of Utah Inc.; chmn., CEO Pa. and W.Va. Supply Co. Bd. dirs. United Way of Venango County, 1983-88; pres. bd. trustees Venango County Cmty. Area Found., 1988-94, former dir.; mem. Ind. County C. of C., 1973-81, pres., 1976-77; mem. vestry Christ Episc. Ch., Oil City, 1989-92, 98; charter mem. Haverford (Pa.) State Hosp. Task Force, 1999-2002; mem. Haverford Twp. Environ. Adv. Com., 2002-05. With USN, 1945-47. Mem. Ind. Rotary (club pres. 1979-80), Merion Cricket Club, Theta Delta Chi, Sigma Phi Sigma.

OLSON, ROBERT EUGENE, physician, biochemist, educator; b. Minn., Jan. 23, 1919; s. Ralph William and Minnie (Holtin) O.; m. Catherine Silvoso, Oct. 21, 1944; children: Barbara Lynn, Robert E., Mark Alan, Mary Ellen, Carol Louise. AB, Gustavus Adolphus Coll., 1938; PhD, St. Louis U., 1944; MD, Harvard, 1951; MD (hon.), Chiang Mai U., Thailand, 1983. Diplomate: Nat. Bd. Med. Examiners, Am. Bd. Nutrition (pres. 1962-63). Postgrad. research asst. biochemistry St. Louis U. Sch. Medicine, 1938-43, asst. biochemistry, 1943-44, Alice A. Doisy prof. biochemistry, chmn. dept. biochemistry, 1965-82, asso. prof. medicine, 1966-72, prof. medicine, 1972-82; vis. prof. (sabbatical) dept. biochemistry U. Freiburg, Breisgau, West Germany, 1970-71; also Hoffman-La Roche Co., Basel, Switzerland, 1970-71; instr. biochemistry and nutrition Harvard Sch. Pub. Health, 1946-47; research fellow Nutrition Found., 1947-49, Am. Heart Assn., 1949-51, established investigator, 1951-52; house officer Peter Bent Brigham Hosp., Boston, 1951-52; prof., head dept. biochemistry and nutrition Grad. Sch. Pub. Health U. Pitts.; lectr. medicine Sch. Medicine, 1952-65; mem. panel malnutrition Japan-U.S. Med. Scis. Program, 1965-69; dir. Nutrition Clinic, Falk Clinic, 1953-65; mem. sr. staff Presbyn. Hosp., dir. metabolic unit, 1960-65; mem. staff St. Louis U. Hosp., 1965-81; prof. biochemistry, prof. medicine, assoc. dean acad. affairs U. Pitts. Sch. Medicine, 1982-84; prof. medicine, prof. pharm. scis. SUNY-Stony Brook, 1984-90, prof. emeritus, 1990—; prof. pediatrics U. South Fla., Tampa, 1994—. Cons. Mercy Hosp., U. Pitts. Med. Center; assoc. in medicine St. Margaret's Meml. Hosp., Pitts., dir. metabolic unit, 1954-60; cons. divsn. rsch. grants USPHS, 1954-69, 72-76; dir. Anemia and Malnutrition Center, Chiang Mai, Thailand, 1967-77; vis. scholar dept. biochemistry Oxford (Eng.) U., 1961-62; vis. prof. dept. biochemistry U. Freiburg, West Germany, 1970-71; food and nutrition bd. NRC, 1977-83; adv. council Nat. Inst. Arthritis, Diabetes, Digestive and Kidney Diseases, 1981-85; William A. Noyes lectr. U. Ill., Urbana, 1980. Author: Perspectives in Biological Chemistry, 1970, Methods in Medical Research, 1970, Protein-Calorie Malnutrition, 1975, Balanced Nutrition, 1989; assoc. editor Nutrition Revs., 1954-56, editor, 1978-88; assoc. editor Am. Jour. Medicine, 1956-65, Circulation Rsch., 1956-76, Am. Heart Jour., 1958-65, Am. Jour. Clin. Nutrition, 1960-66, Methods in Med. Rsch., 1963-70, Biochem. Medicine, 1967-90, Molecular and Cellular Cardiology, 1967-78, Ann. Rev. Nutrition, 1979-84, editor, 1984-94; co-editor: Vitamins and Hormones, 1975-81; author 236 original sci. papers in peer-reviewed jours.; contbr. 114 chpts. in books and major reviews to profl. jours. Bd. dirs. Nat. Nutrition Consortium, 1977-81, Am. Council on Sci. and Health, 1984-91. Lt. (j.g.) USNR, 1944-46. Recipient Fulbright award, 1961-62, Guggenheim Found. award, 1961-62, 70-71, McCollum award, 1965, Joseph Goldberger award, 1974; named Atwater Meml. lectr., 1978; Geiger Meml. lectr., 1979, William A. Noyes lectr. U. Ill., 1980, H. Brooks James lectr. N.C. State U., 1981, Virginia Beal lectr. U. Mass., 1990. Fellow ACP, Internat. Acad. Cardiovasc. Scis., Am. Pub. Health Assn. (chmn. food and nutrition sect. 1960-61), Am. Inst. Nutrition (pres. 1981-82, Conrad Elvehjem award 1998), Assn. Am. Physicians; mem. AAAS (sec. med. scis. N. sect. 1965-67), Am. Assn. Cancer Research, Am. Heart Assn., AMA (mem. council food and nutrition 1959-67, vice chmn. 1962-67), Royal Soc. Health (London), N.Y. Acad. Scis., Am. Fedn. Clin. Research, Am. Soc. Clin. Investigation, Boyleston Med. Soc., Am. Chem. Soc. (pres. biochemistry group Pitts. sect. 1960-61), Am. Soc. Biol. Chemists, Soc. Exptl. Biology and Medicine, Am. Soc. Clin. Nutrition (pres. 1961-62, McCollum award 1965, Herman award 2002), Assn. Med. Sch. Depts. Biochemistry (pres. 1979-80), Pa., St. Louis, Allegheny County med. socs., Am. Soc. Study Liver Diseases, Phi Beta Kappa, Sigma Xi, Phi Lambda Upsilon, Alpha Omega Alpha, Alpha Sigma Nu. Clubs: Cosmos (Washington), Countryside Country Club (Clearwater, Fla.). Home: 2673 Camille Dr Palm Harbor FL 34684-2217 Office: U South Fla Dept Pediatrics 17 Davis Blvd Ste 200 Tampa FL 33606-3438 Office Phone: 813-259-8700. Personal E-mail: roberteolsonr@cs.com. Business E-Mail: rolson@hsc.usf.edu.

OLSON, ROBERT HOWARD, lawyer; b. July 6, 1944; s. Robert Howard and Jacquiline (Wells) O.; m. Diane Carol Thorsen, Aug. 13, 1966; children: Jeffrey, Christopher. BA in Govt. summa cum laude, Ind. U., 1966; JD cum laude, Harvard U., 1969. Bar: Ohio 1969, Fla. 1980, Ariz. 1985, Calif. 2001, U.S. Supreme Ct. 1973. Assoc. Squire, Sanders & Dempsey, L.L.P., Cleve., 1969, 70-71, 76-81, ptnr., 1981—, Phoenix, 1985—2002, Squire, Sanders & Dempsey, San Francisco, 2002—; sr. law clk. U.S. Dist. Ct., No. Dist., Ind., 1969-70; chief civil rights divsn. Ohio Atty. Gen.'s Office, Columbus, 1971-73, chief consumer protection, 1973-75, chief counsel, 1975, 1st asst. (chief of staff), 1975-76. Instr. Ohio State U. Law Sch., Columbus, 1974; bd. dirs. Orpheum Theater Found., 1989—2002, sec., 1989—90, pres., 1990—97, exec. com., 1997—99, The Ariz. Ctr. for Law in the Pub. Interest, 1989—2001, treas., 1992—93, 1997—2001, v.p., 1993—94; mem. Ariz. Ctr. for Disability Law, 1994—96, treas., 1994—95; mem. Valley Leadership Class XIV; rsch. com. Ariz. Town Hall, 1998—2002; co-chair Calif. Pub. Fin. Conf., 2006; co-chair, hon. prof. Hosp. Fin. Conf., 2007. Contbr. articles to profl. jours. Bd. dirs. 1st Unitarian Ch. Phoenix, 1987-89, 98-2001, v.p., 1987-89, 2000-2001, pres. 1998-99, Mt. Diablo Unitarian Ch., 2009-, 1st Unitarian Ch. Found., 1987-93, pres., 1990-93; bd. dirs. Mt. Diablo Unitarian Universalist Ch., 2009-; exec. com. San Francisco (Calif.) Heartwalk, Am. Heart Assn., 2005. Named Arts Advocate of Yr. Bus. Vols. Arts/Phoenix, 1997, Super Lawyer, 2008, 09. Mem. Ariz. State Bar Assn., Calif. Bar Assn. Phi Beta Kappa. Office: Squire Sanders & Dempsey LLP One Maritime Plaza Suite 300 San Francisco CA 94111-3492 Office Phone: 415-393-9819.

OLSON, ROBERT WILLIAM, writer, retired counselor; b. Chgo., Feb. 5, 1930; s. Milton Olaf Olson and Leonore Stillman; m. Seiko Itoyama, Jan. 16, 1955. BA, George Williams Coll., 1952; MA, U. Chgo., 1959; 7th yr. cert. counselor-cons., Oreg. State U., 1967. Tchr. 6th grade Matteson Elem. Sch., Ill., 1956—59; cons., sch. counselor elem. schs., jr. and sr. h.s., various cities Ill., Wash., 1959—91; instr. counseling U. Wash., Seattle, 1979—81; family counselor Seattle, 1980—91. Behavioral rschr., U. Wash., 1979-81. Author: Memories with a Christmas Attitude, 1994, Rich Memories with a Christmas Spirit, 2005; editor FOKUS Newsletter, 1998—; contbr. numerous articles to profl. counseling jours. Vol. Love and Forgiveness Seminar, Monroe Penitentiary, 1996—; pres. King County Guidance Assn., Wash., 1978—79; bd. mem. Children Around the World Resource Ctr. With US Army, 1952—56, Korea and Japan. Mem. NEA (life), Wash. Edn. Assn., Internat. Assn. Near-Death Studies, King County Jail (vol. 1998-), Eastside Writers Assn. (hospitality chmn. 1999—), Northwest Christian Writers Assn. Avocations: ceramics, storytelling, swimming. Home and Office: 252 168th Ave SE Bellevue WA 98008 Office Phone: 425-747-3879. Personal E-mail: membob@comcast.net.

OLSON, RONALD LEROY, lawyer; b. Carroll, Iowa, July 9, 1941; s. Clyde L. and Delpha C. (Boyens) Olson; m. Jane Tenhulzen, June 21, 1964; children: Kristin, Steven, Amy. BS, Drake U., 1963; JD, U. Mich., 1966; Diploma Law, Oxford U., Eng., 1967. Bar: Wis. 1966, Calif. 1969, US Dist. Ct. (cen. dist.), Calif. 1969, US Dist. Ct. (so. dist.),Calif. 1973, US Ct. Appeals (9th cir.) 1974, US Ct. Appeals (10th cir.) 1980, US Ct. Appeals (5th cir.) 1982, US Supreme Ct. 1976, US Dist. Ct., Alaska 1983. Atty. civil rights divsn. US Dept. Justice, 1967; law clk. to chief judge David L. Bazelon US Ct. Appeals (DC cir.), Washington, 1967—68; ptnr. Munger, Tolles & Olson LLP, Los Angeles, Calif., 1968—; lawyer del. Ann. 9th Cir. Conf., 1984—89; lectr. in field; mem. editorial bd. Alternatives, 1983—. Mem. bd. dirs. The Wash. Post Co., 2003—. Contbr. articles legal jour. Recipient Burton scholar, U. Mich.; named one of 100 Most Influential Lawyers, Nat. Law Jour., 2006; fellow Am. Coll Trial Lawyers. Fellow: Am. Bar Found., Ford Found. Oxford U.; mem.: 9th Cir. Jud. Conf. (exec. com. 1984—89), Chancery, LA County Barristers (pres. 1976), Assn. Bus. Trial Lawyers (mem. adv. com. trial ct. improvement fund for Calif. jud. coun. 1988—), State Bar Calif. (bd. dir. 1985, v.p. 1986—87), LA County Bar Assn., Am. Arbitration Assn. (bd. dir. 1983, comml. panel 1983), LA Bar Found. (bd. dir. 1977), Am. Judicature Soc., Human Rights (editorial bd., publ. sect. ind. rights and responsibilities 1986—), Soviet Exchange Program (litig. sect. com. 1983—), ABA (litig. sect. council 1976, chmn. sp. com. on dispute resolution 1976—86, chmn. litig. section 1981—82, chmn. standing com. on fed. judiciary 1991—92), Skid Row Housing Trust of LA (mem. 1986—), U. Mich. Law Sch. (com. visitors 1986—), Salzburg Seminar (bd. dir.), Legal Aid Found. LA (bd. dir. 1975—86, pres. 1984—85), Claremont U. Ctr. and Grad. Sch. (chmn. bd. fellows 1984—94), Sequoia Nat. Pk. Natural History Assn., Drake U. (trustee 1977), Alternatives (mem. editorial bd. 1983—88), LA Arts Festival (sec. 1985), Lawyers Alliance for Nuclear Arms Control (adv. com. Los Angeles and Orange Counties chpt.), Frat. of Friends of Music Ctr. (bd. dir., pres. 1978), Omicron Delta Kappa, Phi Eta Sigma, Beta Gamma Sigma. Democrat. Episcopalian. Office: Munger Tolles & Olson LLP 355 S Grand Ave Fl 35 Los Angeles CA 90071-1560 E-mail: Ron.Olson@mto.com.

OLSON, ROY ARTHUR, retired government official; b. Dec. 8, 1938; s. Elof Herman and Beatrice Lorraine (Dolezal) O.; m. Elisabeth Rigge Behrens, June 24, 1967; children: Heather Elisabeth, Peter Roy. BS, Northwestern U., 1960. Writer, editor Chgo. Am., 1956-68; pres. Roy Olson Pub. Rels. Co., Oak Park, Ill., 1968-70; asst. regional adminstr. SBA, Chgo., 1970-95; Chgo. spokesman Ill. Dept. Transp., 1995—2003. Bd. dirs. Am. Food Industries, Chgo., Covenant Village Retirement Ctr., Northbrook, Ill., Brandel Care Ctr., Northbrook. Author: From Bistros to Bible Study, 2006. Chmn. Northbrook Covenant Ch., 1980-81, 97-2000. Mem. Soc. Profl. Journalists, Art Inst. Chgo., City Club (media com.), Execs. Club, Chgo. Press Club, Chgo. Headline Club (past dir. 1964-66), Northwestern Club. Home: 2015 Prairie St Glenview IL 60025-2824 E-mail: olsons2015@yahoo.com.

OLSON, RUE EILEEN, retired librarian; b. Chgo., Nov. 1, 1928; d. Paul H. and Martha M. (Fick) Meyers; m. Richard L. Olson, July 18, 1964; children: Catherine, Karen. Student, Herzl Coll., 1946-48, Northwestern U., 1948-50, Ill. State U., 1960-64, Middle Mgmt. Inst. Spl. Librs. Assn., 1985-87. Acct. Ill. Farm Supply Co., Chgo., 1948-59; asst. libr. Ill. Agrl. Assn., Bloomington, 1960-66, libr., 1966-86, dir. libr. svcs., 1986-96, ret., 1996. Bd. dirs. Corn Belt Libr. Sys., 1989-94, sec., 1991-94; mem. area com. Nat. Libr. Week, 1971, area steering com., 1972; mem. steering com. Illinet/OCLC, 1985-87; mem. adv. coun. of librs. Grad. Sch. Libr. Sci. U., Ill., 1976-79; mem. Ill. State Libr. Adv. Com. for Interlibr. Cooperation, 1979-80; del. Ill. White Ho. Conf. on Libr. and Info. Svcs., 1978; coord. Vita Income Tax Assistance, Bloomington, Ill., 1986-89, 95-99, preparer, 1978—2002; sec. Hawthorn Village Homeowner's Assn., 1995-2002, v.p., 2002—04; congl. sec. Good Shepherd Luth. Ch., 1999-2001, newsletter editor, 1994-96. Mem.

Am., Ill., McLean County (pres. 1970-71), Libr. Assns., Spl. Libs. Assn. (pres. Ill. chpt. 1977-78, first to be named Disting. Mem. food, agr. and nutrition divsn. 1989), Ill. OCLC Users Group (treas. 1988-90, bd. dirs. 1991-92), Internat. Assn. Agrl. Librs. and Documentalists, Am. Soc. Info. Sci., Am. Mgmt. Assn., USIN, Mended Hearts, Inc. (sec. Ill. chpt. 250, 1994-95, v.p. 1995-96, pres. 1996-98), Zonta (pres. 1987-89), Bloomington Club, Am. Heart Assn. (McLean County divsn., midwest affiliate, sec. 1998-2000). Home: 8 Aspen Ct Bloomington IL 61704-2781

OLSON, SCOTT M., civil engineer, educator; PhD, U. Ill., Urbana-Champaign. Profl. engring. lic., Mo., 2005. Geotech. engr. URS Corp., St. Louis, 1995—2004; civil engring. asst. prof. U. Ill., 2004—. Office: Univ Ill 205 N Mathews Ave Urbana IL 61801

OLSON, STANLEY WILLIAM, physician, educator, dean; b. Chgo., Feb. 10, 1914; s. David William and Agnes (Nelson) O.; m. Lorraine Caroline Lofdahl, June 26, 1936; children: Patricia Ann, Richard David, Robert Dean. BS, Wheaton Coll., 1934, LLD (hon.), 1956; MD, U. Ill., 1938; MS in Medicine (fellow), U. Minn., 1943; ScD, U. Akron, 1979, N.E Ohio U., 1985, Morehouse Sch. Medicine. Diplomate: Am. Bd. Internal Medicine. Intern Cook County Hosp., Chgo., 1938-40; asst. dir. Mayo Found., from 1947; cons. medicine Mayo Clinic, 1947—; instr. medicine grad. sch. U. Minn., 1947-50; dean and prof. coll. medicine, med. dir. Rsch. and Ednl. Hosp. U. Ill., 1950-53; dean and prof. Coll. Medicine Baylor U., Tex. Med. Ctr., Houston, 1953-66; prof. medicine Vanderbilt U.; clin. prof. medicine Meharry Med. Coll., 1966-68; dir. Tenn. Mid-South Regional Med. Program, 1967-68; dir. Div. Regional Med. Programs Svc. USPHS, 1968-70; pres. S.W. Found. for Rsch. and Edn., San Antonio, 1970-73; provost Coll. Medicine N.E. Ohio U., 1973-79, cons. med. edn. Morehouse Coll. Medicine, 1980-81; dean Morehouse Sch. Medicine, Atlanta, 1985-87. Past chmn. med. bd., chief staff Ben Taub Hosp., Jefferson Davis Hosp., Houston; nat. adv. council for health research facilities NIH, 1963-68; rev. panel constrn. med. schs. USPHS, 1964-65; spl. cons. div. Regional Med. Programs NIH, 1966-68; med. cons. bd. trustees. SUNY, 1949; cons. to Hoover Commn., 1954; mem. bd. trustees. Wheaton Coll., Ill., 1953-68. Contbr. articles to profl. jours. Capt., M.C. AUS, 1943-46. Mem. AMA, Houston Philos. Soc. (pres. 1962-63), Tex. Philos. Soc., Assn. Am. Med. Colls., Alumni Assn. Mayo Found., Sigma Xi, Alpha Kappa Kappa, Alpha Omega Alpha. Baptist. Home: 6401 Newburg Rd Apt 128 Rockford IL 61108-4322

OLSON, STEPHEN M(ICHAEL), lawyer; b. Jamestown, NY, May 4, 1948; s. Charles R. and Marilyn (Dietzel) O.; m. Linda C. Hanson, Aug. 24, 1968; children: Kevin, Darren. AB cum laude, Princeton U., 1970; JD, U. Chgo., 1973. Bar: Pa. 1973, U.S. Dist. Ct. (we. dist.) Pa. 1973, U.S. Ct. Appeals (3d cir.) 1975, U.S. Ct. Appeals (1st and D.C. cirs.) 1986, U.S. Ct. Appeals (7th cir. and 8th cir. 1988), U.S. Supreme Ct. 1986. Assoc. Kirkpatrick & Lockhart Preston Gates Ellis LLC, Pitts., 1973-81, ptnr., 1981—. Mem.: Princeton Alumni Assn. West Pa., Duquesne Club. Avocations: photography, bicycling. Office: K & L Gates LLP Henry W Oliver Bldg 535 Smithfield St Pittsburgh PA 15222-2312 Office Phone: 412-355-6496. Business E-Mail: stephen.olson@klgates.com.

OLSON, STEVEN ARTHUR, orthopaedic surgeon; b. St. Louis, Feb. 10, 1960; MD, U. Mo., 1986. Cert. in orthopaedic surgery. Intern U. Mo. Hosps., Columbia, 1986-87, resident in orthopaedics, 1987-91; fellow in orthopaedics and trauma U. Calif.-Davis, Sacramento, 1991-92; fellow in pelvic trauma Good Samaritan Hosp., LA, 1993; assoc. prof. U. Calif.-Davis, 1993—. Mem. Am. Acad. Orthopaedic Surgery, Calif. Orthopaedic Assn. Office: U Calif-Davis Med Ctr Dept Orthopaedics 2230 Stockton Blvd Dept Sacramento CA 95817-1419

OLSON, STEVEN THOMAS, medical researcher; b. Oak Park, Ill., Aug. 14, 1948; s. Harry Olson and Joan McCord; life ptnr. Peter Gregory Wolfgang Gettins. PhD, U. Mich., Ann Arbor, 1979. Staff investigator Henry Ford Hosp., Detroit, 1979—93; prof. U. Ill., Chicago, 1994—. Grant, NIH, 1986—2008. Office: Univ Il Chgo Rm 530C 801 S Paulina St Chicago IL 60612 Office Fax: 312-413-1604. Business E-Mail: stolson@uic.edu.

OLSON, THEODORE BEVRY (TED OLSON), lawyer, former federal agency administrator; b. Chgo., Sept. 11, 1940; s. Lester W. & Yvonne Bevry Olson; 2 children; m. Lady Booth, Oct. 21, 2006. BA cum laude, U. Pacific, 1962; LL.B., U. Calif.-Berkeley, 1965. Bar: Calif. 1965, DC 1982. Assoc. Gibson, Dunn & Crutcher LLP, Los Angeles, 1965—71, ptnr., 1972—81, 1984—2001, 2004—, co-chair, appellate & constitutional law practice group, 2004—; asst. atty. gen. US Dept. Justice, Washington, 1981—84, solicitor gen., 2001—04. Panelist Gen. Counsel Leadership Series, 2007; vis. scholar Nat. Constn. Ctr. and U. Pa. Sch. Law, 2007. Mem. Calif. Law Review, 1964-1965, Calif. Commn. on Uniform State Laws, 1972-74, Privacy and Civil Liberties Oversight Bd, 2005-07; del. Republican Nat. Conv., 1976, 80; co-chair Knight Commn., 2008-; mem. bd. trustee Ronald Reagan Presdl. Found. Recipient Edmund J. Randolph award, US Dept. Justice, 1984, 2004, Disting. Pub. Svc. medal, US Dept. Def., 2004; named one of 100 Most Influential Lawyers in America, Nat. Law Jour., 2006. Fellow Am. Acad. Appellate Lawyers, Am. Coll. Trial Lawyers; mem. ABA, Order of the Coif. Republican. Office: Gibson Dunn & Crutcher LLP 1050 Connecticut Ave NW Washington DC 20036 Personal E-mail: tolson@gibsondunn.com.

OLSON, WALTER JUSTUS, JR., management consultant; b. Paterson, NJ, July 27, 1941; s. Walter Justus and Viola Patricia (Trautvetter) O. BS, BA, Brown U., 1964; MBA, Columbia U., 1967. CPA Va. Design engr. Rockwell Internat., Inc., Downey, Calif., 1964-65; mgmt. officer CIA, Washington, 1969-73; sr. cons. Booz, Allen and Hamilton, Inc., Washington, 1973-78; corp. planning coordinator Washington Gas Light Co., Washington, 1978-82; prin. Walter J. Olson & Assoc., McLean, Va., 1982-83; dep. asst. sec. for export adminstrn. U.S. Dept. Commerce, Washington, 1983-86; prin. Walter J. Olson & Assoc., Washington, 1986—; sr. rsch. analyst U.S. House Select Com. Technology Transfer to PRC, Washington, 1998-99. Vice-chmn. fin. com. Fairfax County Reps., Va., 1982-83. Served to 1st lt. USAF, 1967—69. Mem. AICPA, Greater Wash. Soc. CPAs, Strategic Leadership Forum (pres. Washington chpt. 1990-91). Republican. Episcopalian. Home: 7348 Dartford Dr Mc Lean VA 22102-7348 Office: 370 Maple Ave West Ste 4 Vienna VA 22180-5615 Office Phone: 703-356-6919. Personal E-mail: walterolson@mindspring.com.

OLSON, WILLIAM CHARLES, psychology professor; b. Rock Hill, SC, Dec. 16, 1967; s. John B. and Sally S. Olson; m. Vickie Morats Olson; 1 child, Adara Leena. MS, Winthrop U., Rock Hill, 2005. Cert. A+ COMPTIA, 1997. Part time instr. Rowan Cabarrus C.C., Kannapolis, NC, 2006—07; instr. Ctrl. Piedmont C.C., Charlotte, 2007—. Elder Rock Hill Bible Fellowship Ch., 2009—. Christian Ch. Avocations: singing, reading, birdwatching. Office: Ctrl Piedmont CC 3210 CPCC Harris Campus Dr Charlotte NC 28208

OLSON-HELLERUD, LINDA KATHRYN, elementary school educator; b. Wisconsin Rapids, Wis., Aug. 26, 1947; d. Samuel Ellsworth and Lillian (Dvorak) Olson; m. H. A. Hellerud, 1979; 1 child, Sarah Kathryn Hellerud. BS, U. Wis., Stevens Point, 1969, tchg. cert., 1970, MST, 1972; MS, U. Wis., Whitewater, 1975; EdS, U. Wis., Stout, 1978. Cert. reading specialist, technology tng., reading Resdissance Learning. Clk. U. Counseling Ctr. U. Wis., Stevens Point, 1965—69; elem. sch. tchr. Wisconsin Rapids, 1970—76; sch. counselor, 1976—79; dist. dir. elem. guidance, 1979—82; tchr. elem. and reading, 1982—; model reading tchr. Renaissance Learning. Instr. Summer Remedial Reading Program; cons. in field. Advocate Literacy Mentoring Program; active St. Luke's Luth Ch. Mem.: NEA, Ctrl. Wis. Reading Assn., Internat. Reading Assn., Wood County Lit. Coun. (cons.), Wis. Reading Assn. Avocations: literacy activities and research, piano, aerobics, Spanish. Home: 120 11th St N Wisconsin Rapids WI 54494-5371 Office: Howe Elem Sch Wisconsin Rapids WI 54494

OLSSEN, JENNIFER LEIGH, elementary school educator; b. Owensboro, Ky., Apr. 6, 1978; d. Jerry Ray and Mary Alicia Wells; m. Scott Patrick Olssen, Oct. 8, 2005. BS, Ky. Wesleyan Coll., Owensboro, 1998—2001; MS, Ind. Wesleyan U., Marian, 2005—06. Cert. elem. edn. tchr. Ky., 2006. Tchr. Owensboro 5-6 Ctr., 2001—06; math intervention tchr. Sutton Elem. Sch., Owensboro, 2006—; 3rd grade tchr. Sutton Elementary Sch., Owensboro, 2008—. Mem.: NEA, Nat. Coun. Tchrs. Math. D-Conservative. Roman Cath. Avocations: travel, reading. Office: Sutton Elem Sch 2060 Lewis Ln Owensboro KY 42301 Personal E-mail: jolssen@roadrunna.com. Business E-Mail: jennifer.olssen@owensboro.kyschools.us.

OLSSON, CARL ALFRED, urologist, department chairman; b. Boston, Nov. 29, 1938; s. Charles Rudolph and Ruth Marion (Bostrom) O.; m. Mary DeVore, Nov. 4, 1962; children: Ingrid, Leif Eric. Grad., Bowdoin Coll., 1959; MD, Boston U., 1963. Diplomate Am. Bd. Urology (trustee 1988-94, pres. 1993-94). Asst. prof. urology Boston U. Sch. Medicine, 1971-72, assoc. prof., 1972-74, prof., chmn. dept., 1974-80; dir. urology dept. Boston City Hosp., 1974-77; chief urology dept. Boston VA Med. Ctr., 1971—75; urologist-in-chief Univ. Hosp., Boston, 1971-80; John K. Lattimer prof., chmn. dept. urology Coll. Phys. and Surgs., Columbia U., NYC, 1980—2005, chmn. emeritus, 2005—. Dir. Squier Urol. Clinic, urology service Presbyn. Hosp., 1980-2005, chief med. officer, 2008-, integrated med. profls, 2008-, NYC; lectr. surgery Tufts U. Sch. Medicine. Boston Interhosp. Organ Bank, 1976-79; mem. working cadre Nat. Prostate Cancer Project, Nat. Cancer Inst., 1979-84; mem. adv. coun. Nat. Inst. Diabetes, Digestive Disease and Kidney; mem. integration panel for prostate cancer rsch. Dept. of Def., 1998-2002, chmn., 2000-01. Editl. bd. Jour. Prostate, World Jour. Urology, Jour. Urodynamics and Neurourology, Jour. Urology; asst. editor Jour. Urology, 1978-2004; contbr. chpts. to books, articles to med. jours. Recipient Disting. Alumnus award Boston U., 1985, Boston U. Alumni award, 2007. Fellow ACS; mem. Am. Urol. Assn. (hon., coord. continuing med. edn. New Eng. sect. 1977-80, del. rsch. com., bd. dirs. 2001-06, exec. com. 2002-06, sec. 2000-06, found. operating bd. 2005-06, Gold Cystoscope award 1979, Grayson-Carroll award 1971, 73, Hugh Hampton Young award 2001), Boston Surg. Soc. (exec. com. 1976-80), Am. Assn. Clin. Urologists, Am. Surg. Assn., Am. Assn. Genitourinary Surgeons (pres. 2007), Clin. Soc. Genitourinary Surgeons (pres. 2009-), Transplantation Soc., Soc. Urologic Oncology (pres. 1993), Soc. Pelvic Surgeons, Soc. Univ. Urologists (pres. 1990), N.Y. Sect. Am. Urol. Assn. (pres. 2002), AMA, Assn. Acad. Surgery, Am. Soc. Artificial Internal Organs, Am. Soc. Transplant Surgeons, Assn. Med. Colls., Can. Urol. Assn., Societe Internationale d'Urologie, Internat. Urodynamics Soc., Mass. Med. Soc., Soc. Govt. Urologists, Australasian Urol. Soc. (hon.), SE. Sect., AUA (hon.), SC. Sect. A (hon.), New Eng. Handicapped Sportsmen's Assn. (exec. com. 1977-81), U.S. Yacht Racing Union, Yacht Racing Union L.I. Sound, N.Y. Yacht Club, Cottage Park Yacht Club, Larchmont Yacht Club, Storm Trysail Club, Alpha Omega Alpha, Am. Found. Urol. Diseases (bd. dirs. 2002-05, exec. coun. 2002-05), NY Acad. Scis. (Valentine award medal 2006). Episcopalian. Office: Columbia-Presbyn Hosp Irving Pavilion 161 Ft Washington Av New York NY 10032-3702 Office Phone: 516-394-9610. Office Fax: 516-869-3015. E-mail: colsson@impplc.com.

OLSSON, CURT GUNNAR, banker; b. Mjallby, Sweden, Aug. 20, 1927; s. N.E. and Anna (Nilsson) O.; m. Asta Engblom, 1954; two daughters. BS in Econs., Stockholm Sch. Econs., 1950, D in Econ. honoris causa, 1992. Mng. dir. Skandinaviska Enskilda Banken, Stockholm, 1972-76, mng. dir., chief exec. officer, head office, 1976-82, first dep. chmn. bd., group dir., 1982-84, chmn. bd., 1984-96. Consul gen. h.c. for Finland, 1989—99. Knight of Order of Vasa, 1976; King Carl XVI Gustaf's Gold medal 1982; comdr. Royal Norwegian Order of Merit, 1985; comdr. 1st class, Order Lion of Finland, 1987. Mem.: Royal Swedish Acad. Engring. Sci. Office: Styrmansgatan 52 5 tr S 114 60 Stockholm Sweden

OLSTAD, ROGER GALE, science educator; b. Mpls., Jan. 16, 1934; s. Arnold William and Myra (Stroschein) O.; m. Constance Elizabeth Jackson, Aug. 20, 1955; children: Karen Louise, Kenneth Bradley. BS, U. Minn., 1955, MA, 1959, PhD, 1963. Instr. U. Minn., Mpls., 1956-63; asst. prof. U. Ill., Urbana, 1963-64; mem. faculty U. Wash., Seattle, 1964—, asso. prof. sci. edn., 1967-71, prof., 1971-95, asso. dean grad. studies Coll. Edn., 1971-85; prof. emeritus, 1995—. Bd. trustees Shoreline C.C., 2006—, chair, 2009—. Chair environ. quality commn. City of Lake Forest Park, Wash., 1997-2000, city coun., 2000-2007, mayor pro tempore, 2006-2007. Fellow AAAS; mem. NSTA (bd. dirs.) Wash. Sci. Tchrs. Assn. (pres. 1973-74), Nat. Assn. Rsch. Sci. Teaching (pres. 1977-78, bd. dirs.), N.W. Sci. Assn. (chmn. 1966-68), Assn. Edn. Tchrs. in Sci. (regional pres. 1966-68, pres. 1991-92), Nat. Assn. Biology Tchrs., Biol. Scis. Curriculum Study (chmn., bd. dirs. 1989-94), U. Wash. Faculty Club, Phi Delta Kappa. Home: 20143 53rd Ave NE Seattle WA 98155-1801 Office: U Wash Coll Edn Seattle WA 98195-0001 Personal E-mail: rolstad@earthlink.net. Business E-Mail: rolstad@u.washington.edu.

OLSTEIN, ROBERT A., investment company executive; BA in math & statistics, Mich. State Univ.; MBA in acctg., Eli Broad Coll. Bus. Mich. State Univ., 1966. CPA. Acct. Arthur Andersen; co-founder Quality of Earnings Report svc., 1971; fin. mgmt. positions through sr. v.p. & sr. portfolio mgr. Smith Barney, 1981—95; founder, chmn., chief investment officer Olstein Capital Mgmt. L.P., Purchase, NY, 1995—; portfolio mgr. Olstein Fin. Alert Fund, 1995—. Frequent commentator on CNBC, Bloomberg News, Fox News Channel, PBS. Recipient Graham & Dodd Scroll award. Fellow: Fin. Analysts Fedn.; mem.: NY Soc. Securities Analysts (sr.). Office: Olstein Capital Mgmt LP Ste 102 4 Manhattanville Rd Purchase NY 10577

OLSTER, STACEY MICHELE, literature and language professor; b. NYC, Aug. 8, 1953; d. Abraham Jacob Olster and Adeline Esther Meister. PhD, U. Mich., Ann Arbor, 1981. Prof., English Stony Brook U., NY, 2002—. Recipient Pres. award, SUNY (Stony Brook), 1986—87, Chancellor's award, SUNY Office Chancellor, 1987—88, fellowship, Fulbright, 1989—90;, Eli Lilly Found., 1986—87. Office: Dept English Stony Brook Univ Stony Brook NY 11794-5350 Business E-Mail: stacey.olster@stonybrook.edu.

OLSZEWSKI, CHRIS MICHAEL, science educator, director; b. Great Falls, Mont., Oct. 15, 1973; s. Albert and Dolores Olszewski; m. Holly Storrusten, July 17, 1998; 1 child, Hannah. BS in Gen. sci., U. Gt. Falls, 1996; MEd, Our Lady of the Lake U., 2002. Cert. tchr. Mont. Mid. sch. sci. tchr. SW Enrichment Ctr., San Antonio, 1997—2002; secondary sci. tchr. Cut Bank (Mont.) Mid./High Sch., 2002—03; dir. Golden Triangle Curriculum Coop., Shelby, Mont., 2003—. Home: 421 Riverview Dr E Great Falls MT 59404-1553

OLSZEWSKI, JANET, state agency administrator, public health service officer; B sociology, Boston Univ.; MSW, Univ. Mich., 1975. With Mich. Office Svc. to the Aging, 1977—85; mgmt. positions Mich. Dept. Public Health, 1985—91, acting dir. divsn. svc. for crippled children, 1991—92, dir. managed care quality assessment divsn., 1992—97, dir. Medicaid quality improvement & customer svc., 1998—2000; v.p. govt. programs & regulation M-CARE, Univ. Mich., 2000—03; dir. Mich. Dept. Cmty. Health, Lansing, 2003—. Office: Dept Cmty Health 7th Fl Capitol View Bldg 201 Townsend St Lansing MI 48913*

OLTARSH, KENNETH S., lawyer; b. NYC, May 21, 1924; s. Abraham L. and Annabelle W. Oltarsh; m. Naomi D. Oltarsh, Aug. 19, 1955; children: Valerie Oltarsh-McCarthy, Frederic D. BA, Ohio State U., Columbus, 1946; JD, Harvard U., Cambridge, Mass., 1949. Bar: NY 1949, US Ct. Appeals (2d cir.), NY 1956. Atty. Leve Hecht Hadfield & McAlpin, NYC, 1950—52, US Atomic Energy Commn., NYC, 1952—54; ptnr. Duncombe, Oltarsh & Schott, NYC, 1955—62, Solinger & Gordon, NYC, 1962—82, Hall Dickler, LLP, NYC, 1982—2003; of counsel Siller Wilk LLP, NYC, 2003—. Dir. 55 E 66th St. Tenants Corp., NYC, 1981—94, 69th Tenants Corp., NYC, 2001—06; trustee Coldbrook South Unit Owners Trust, Lenox, Mass., 1995—98. Air force cadet USAF, 1943, Maine. Mem.: ABA, Assn. Bar NY, Phi Beta Kappa. Avocation: tennis. Office: Siller Wilk LLP 675 Third Ave New York NY 10017 Office Phone: 212-981-2332. Business E-Mail: koltarsh@sillerwilk.com.

OLTON, PATRICIA MCKINLEY, media specialist; b. Warner Robins, Ga., May 16, 1962; d. James Edward and Mary Joyce McKinley; m. Mark Perry Olton, June 23, 1990; children: Mary Scout, Ann Perri. BA, Mercer U., Macon, Ga., 1983. Cert. educator Ga. Profl. Stds. Commn., 1983. Tchr. Warner Robins HS, 1983—85, Appling Mid. Sch., Macon, 1986—90, E.T. Booth, Woodstock, Ga., 1990—96, Woodstock Mid. Sch., 1996—2005, media specialist, 2005—08, Woodstock HS, 2008—. Named Tchr. of Yr., Woodstock Mid. Sch., 2007. Independent. Roman Catholic. Avocations: reading, travel. Office: Woodstock HS 2010 Towne Lake Hills S Dr Woodstock GA 30189 Business E-Mail: pati.olton@cherokee.k12.ga.us.

OLUFOWOTE, JAMES, communications educator; b. Ibadan, Nigeria; PhD, Purdue U., West Lafayette, Ind., 2005. Asst. prof. Boston Coll., Chestnut Hill, Mass., 2005—. Mem.: Nat. Comm. Assn., Internat. Comm. Assn. Office: Boston Coll Campanella 547 140 Commonwealth Ave Chestnut Hill MA 02467 Business E-Mail: olufowot@bc.edu.

OLUWOLE, OLUWAYEMISI OLUWI, chemical engineer, researcher; s. Moses and Oladoyin Oluwole. BS in Chem. Engring. summa cum laude, Mich. State U., East Lansing, 2001; PhD in Chem. Engring., MIT, Cambridge, 2006. Sr. chem. engr. Aerodyne Rsch., Inc., Billerica, Mass., 2006—. Prodn. process engr. Solutia, Inc., Trenton, Mich., 1998—2000; undergrad. rsch. Nat. Superconducting Cyclotron Lab., East Lansing, 1999—2000; undergrad. rsch. team leader Mich. State U., 2001; doctoral rsch. MIT, 2002—06, grad. tchg. asst., 2002—04, academic tutor, 2005. Contbr. articles to profl. jours. Youth band dir. vineyard Christian Fellowship, Cambridge, Mass., 2004; music dir., youth mentor, spl. programs coord. Redeemed Christian Ch., 2005—07. Recipient Recognition award, Sandia Nat. Labs., 2005. Mem.: AIChE, Nat. Def. Indsl. Assn., Combustion Inst., Am. Chem. Soc., Golden Key, Tau Beta Pi Engring. Honor Soc., Sigma Xi Sci. Rsch. Soc. Achievements include innovative scientific research, discoveries and journal publications on portal-based knowledge environment for collaborative science; research in obtaining accurate solutions using reduced chemical kinetic models: a new model reduction method for models rigorously validated over ranges; an error-controlled adaptive chemistry method for reacting flow simulations; understanding and reducing complex physicochemical model systems; rigorous valid ranges for optimally-reduced kinetic models; rigorous error control in reacting flow simulations using reduced chemistry models; collaborative informatics infrastructure for multi-scale science; new approaches for collaborative sharing of chemical model data and analysis tools; development of RIOT web service and information technologies to enable mechanism reduction for HCCI simulations. Avocations: languages, music, sports, literature. Office: Aerodyne Rsch Inc 45 Manning Rd Billerica MA 01821-3976 Personal E-mail: oluwoleo@gmail.com. Business E-Mail: oluwoleo@aerodyne.com.

OLUYITAN, EMMANUEL FUNSO, communications educator; b. Efon-Alaye, Nigeria, July 25, 1940; BA cum laude in Polit. Sci., Bowie State U., Md., 1972; MPA in Policy Analysis and Journalism, Ind. U., 1975, EdD in Instructional Tech., 1980. News reporter Nigerian Nat. Press, Lagos, 1964-65; music libr., news translator, news reporter Nigerian Broadcasting Corp., 1965-69; pub. info. coord. Aerospace Rsch. Ctr., Sch. Pub./Environ. Affairs, Ind. U., Bloomington, 1973-75; victim assistance officer Indpls. Police Dept., 1975-76; prin. lectr. Nigerian TV Authority, Lagos, 1978-81; assoc. prof. dept. edn. Ahmadu Bello U., Zaria, Nigeria, 1981-88, asst. dean postgrad. studies, 1985-88, head instructional tech. divsn., 1983-88; program officer Nat. Assn. for Equal Opportunity in Higher Edn., Washington, 1988-93; dir. Office of Pub. Rels. and Pubs. Lincoln University, Pa., 1993-96; dir. integrated info. tech. Bennett Coll., Greensboro, N.C., 1996-97; prof. comm. Wilberforce U., Ohio, 1997—2006. Staff writer Office of Pub. Info., Bowie State U., 1973; vice chmn. bd. Adventures in Health, Edn. and Agrl. Devel., Inc., Rockville, Md., 1993—; bd. dirs. Anthony J. Cebrun Journalism Ctr., Nashville; CEO, ASE African Ctr., Dayton, Ohio. Author: Africa Yesterday & Today; photographer, fgn. news editor: Ebony Tree, 1970-72; editor: African Insight, 1973, Nigeria Audio-Visual Newsletter, 1982-86, Nigeria Audio-Visual Jour., 1982-86, Global Vision, 1988-93, Update, 1988-93; assoc. editor: Black Excellence, 1988-93; editor-in-chief: Weekly Calendar, 1993-96, LU Newsletter, 1993-96, The Lincoln Lion, 1993-96, The Lincoln-Jour., 1993-96; contbr. articles to profl. jours., newspapers; contbr. photographs to books, jours.; prodr. numerous ednl. materials (videos, slides, pictures). Recipient Dir. Gen.'s Commendation, Nigerian TV Authority, 1987, Fed. Govt. of Nigeria's Postgrad. award, 1977-80, Award of Accomplishment and Worthiness, Indpls. Police Dept., 1976, Contr.'s Citation, Nigerian Broadcasting Corp., 1967. Mem. Assn. of Nigerians Against Corruption (founder), Nigerian Assn. for Ednl. Media and Tech., Internat. Assn. Black Profls. in Internat. Affairs, Assn. of Ednl. Comm.

and Tech., Oxford Rotary Club (v.p. 1995-96). Avocations: tennis, ping-pong, photography, travel. Office: ASE African Ctr 4550-A Salem Ave Trotwood OH 45416 Personal E-mail: iyabοase@aol.com.

ÖLVECZKY, PETER CSABA, science educator; b. Budapest, Hungary, Apr. 10, 1945; s. Miklós and Cecilia Ölveczky; m. Elisabeth Lien, Mar. 29, 1972. DSc, U. Bergen, Norway, 2000. Assoc. prof. U. Oslo, 2001—; vis. scholar U. Ill., Urbana-Champaign, 2008—.

OLVER, JOHN WALTER, United States Representative from Massachusetts; b. Honesdale, Pa., Sept. 3, 1936; s. Helen Fulleborn Olver; m. Rose Alice Richardson, Sept. 12, 1959; 1 child, Martha. BS, Rensselaer Poly. Inst., 1955; MS, Tufts U., 1956; PhD, MIT, 1961. Asst. prof. chemistry U. Mass., Amherst, 1962-67; mem. Mass. Ho. of Reps., Boston, 1969-72, Mass. Senate, 1973-91, U.S. Congress from 1st Mass. dist., 1991—, mem. com. on appropriations, mem. subcoms. on transp. and mil. constrn., mil. appropriations, asst. whip, 1991—. Contbr. articles to profl. jours. Democrat. Avocations: hiking, gardening, tennis. Office: US House Reps 1111 Longworth House Office Bldg Washington DC 20515-2101 Office Phone: 202-225-5335. Office Fax: 202-226-1224.*

OLYPHANT, TIMOTHY, actor; b. Honolulu, Hawaii, May 20, 1968; m. Alexis Knief; 3 children. Student, U. So. Calif. Actor: (films) The First Wives Club, 1996, A Life Less Ordinary, 1997, Scream 2, 1997, Nineteen Ninety-Nine, 1998, Go, 1999, No Vacancy, 1999, Advice From a Caterpillar, 1999, The Broken Hearts Club: A Romantic Comedy, 2000, Gone in Sixty Seconds, 2000, Auggie Rose, 2000, Head Over Heels, 2001, Doppelganger, 2001, The Safety of Objects, 2001, Rock Star, 2001, Coastlines, 2002, Dreamcatcher, 2003, A Man Apart, 2003, The Girl Next Door, 2004, Catch and Release, 2006, Live Free or Die Hard, 2007, Bill, 2007, Hitman, 2007, Stop-Loss, 2008; (TV films) Ellen Foster, 1997, When Trumpets Fade, 1998, Shadow Realm, 2002; (TV series) Deadwood, 2004—06, (TV appearances) Mr. & Mrs. Smith, 1996, High Incident, 1997, Sex in the City, 1998, Night Visions, 2002, My Name Is Earl, 2006, Sammantha Who?, 2008.

O'MALLEY, ANN S., research scientist; Cert. in medicine NY, 1991, in public health Md., 1993, in preventive medicine 1995. Sr. health rschr. Ctr. Studying Health Sys. Change, Washington, 2005—. Asst. prof. Georgetown U. Med. Ctr., Washington, 1996—2004. Contbr. articles to profl. jour. Office: Ctr Studying Health Sys Change 600 Maryland Ave SW Washington DC 20024

O'MALLEY, BERT WILLIAM, cell biologist, educator, physician; b. Pitts., Dec. 19, 1936; s. Bert Alloysius O'M.; m. Sally Ann Johnson; children: Sally Ann, Bert A., Rebecca, Erin K. BS, U. Pitts., 1959, MD summa cum laude, 1963; DSc (hon.), N.Y. Med. Coll., 1979, Nat. U. Ireland, 1985; MD (hon.), Karolinska Inst., Stockholm, 1984. Intern, resident Duke U., Durham, N.C., 1963-65; clin. assoc. Nat. Cancer Inst., NIH, Bethesda, Md., 1965-67, head molecular biology sect., endocrine br., 1967-69; Lucius Birch prof., dir. Reproductive Biology Ctr. Vanderbilt U. Sch. Medicine, Nashville, 1969-73; Tom Thompson prof., chmn. dept. cell biology Baylor Coll. Medicine, Houston, 1973—, Disting. Svc. prof., 1985, dir. Baylor Ctr. for Reproductive Biology, 1973—. Mem. endocrine study sect., NIH, 1970-73, chmn., 1973-74; chmn. CETUS-UCLA Symposium on Gene Expression, 1982; con., mem. coun. rsch. and clin. investigation awards Am. Cancer Soc., 1985-87. Author: (with A.R. Means) Receptors for Reproductive Hormones, 1973, (with L. Birnbaumer) Hormone Action, vols. I and II, 1977, vol. III, 1978, (with A.M. Gotto) The Role of Receptors in Biology and Medicine, 1986; co-author: Methods in Enzymology: Hormone Action: Calmodulin and Calcium-Binding Proteins, 1983, Mechanism of Steriod Hormone Regulation of Gene Transcription, 1994; editor: Gene Regulation: UCLA Symposium on Molecular Cellular Biology, 1982; contbg. author to over 400 publs. Lt. comdr. USPHS, 1965-69. Recipient Ernst Oppenheimer award Am. Endocrine Soc., 1975, Gregory Pincus medal, 1975, Lila Gruber Cancer award, 1977, Disting. Achievement in Modern Medicine award, 1978, Borden award Assn. Am. Med. Colls., 1978, Dickson prize for Basic Med. Rsch., 1979, Philip S. Hench award U. Pitts., 1981, Axel Munthe Reproductive Biology award, Capri, Italy, 1982, Bicentennial Medallion of Distincton U. Pitts., 1987, Carl G.Hartman award, 2007, 2007 Nat. Medal Sci. Mem. AAAS, NAS, Inst. Med. NAS, Am. Soc. Biol. Chemists, Am. Acad. Arts and Scis., Endocrine Soc. (pres. 1985, Fred Conrad Koch medal 1988), Am. Soc. Clin. Investigation, Am. Inst. Chemists, Fedn. Clin. Rsch., Harvey Soc., Alpha Epsilon Delta, Phi Beta Kappa, Alpha Omega Alpha. Democrat. Roman Catholic. Office: Baylor Coll Medicine Interdepartmental Program in Cell & Molecular Biology One Baylor Pla Houston TX 77030 Office Phone: 713-798-6205. Office Fax: 713-798-5599. Business E-Mail: berto@bcm.edu.

O'MALLEY, CARLON MARTIN, judge; b. Phila., Sept. 7, 1929; s. Carlon Martin and Lucy (Bol) O'M.; m. Mary Catherine Lyons, Aug. 17, 1957; children: Carlon Martin III, Kathleen B. O'Malley Aikman, Harry Tighe, John Todd, Cara M. O'Malley Colombo. BA, Pa. State U., 1951; LLB, Temple U., 1954. Bar: Pa. 1955, Fla. 1973, U.S. Supreme Ct. 1973. Practiced law, 1957-61; asst. U.S. atty. for Middle Dist. Pa., Dept. Justice, 1961-69, U.S. atty., 1979-82; ptnr. O'Malley & Teets, 1970-72, O'Malley, Jordan & Mullaney (and predecessor firms), 1976-79; pvt. practice Pa. and Fla., 1972-79, 82-87; judge Ct. Common Pleas of Lackawanna County (45th Judicial Dist.), 1987-97, sr. judge, 1998—. Dir. pub. safety City of Scranton, 1983-86; lectr. Lackawanna Coll., 1982-86. Editorial bd.: Temple Law Rev, 1952-53. Pres. Lackawanna County (Pa.) unit Am. Cancer Soc., 1966-67; bd. dirs. Pa. Cancer Soc., 1967-68, Lackawanna county chpt. ARC, 1967-69; mem. solicitation team, govtl. divsn. Lackawanna United Fund, 1963-68; chmn. profl. divsn. Greater Scranton (Pa.) YMCA Membership Drives; trustee Everhart Mus., Scranton, 1987—. Pilot USAF, 1955-57, Pa. N.G., 1957-59. Mem. Am. Judges Assn., Nat. Assn. Former U.S. Attys., Pa. Bar Assn., Lackawanna County Bar Assn. (bd. dirs., fin. sec.), Fla. Bar Assn., Country Club of Scranton, Elks (pres. Pa. chpt. 1978-79, judiciary com. 1985-89, justice Grand Forum 1991, 1995-97, chief justice 1992-93, nat. pres. 1997-98), K.C., Phi Kappa (pres.), Delta Theta Phi (pres.). Democrat. Office: Judges Chambers Lackawanna County Courthouse Scranton PA 18503 Office Phone: 570-963-6882.

O'MALLEY, JOHN DANIEL, lawyer, educator, banker; b. Chgo., Dec. 18, 1926; s. William D. and Paula A. (Skaugh) O'M.; m. Caroline Tyler Taylor, July 12, 1958; children: John Daniel, Taylor John. Grad., St. Thomas Mil. Acad., 1945; BS, Loyola U., Chgo., 1950, MA, 1952, JD, 1953; grad., U.S. Army Intelligence Sch., 1962, Command & Gen. Staff Coll., 1965. Bar: Ill. 1953, Mich. 1954, U.S. Supreme Ct. 1962. Asst. prof. law Loyola U., 1953-59, asso. prof., 1959-65; formerly spl. counsel and bond claims mgr. Fed. Ins. Co.; prof. law Loyola U. Grad. Sch. Bus., 1965—, chmn. dept. law, 1968-86. Trust officer, v.p. First Nat. Bank Highland Park (Ill.), Marina City Bank, Chgo., Hyde Park Bank & Trust Co., 1970-75; exec. v.p. Harris Bank Winnetka, Ill., 1975-95. Author: Subrogation Against Banks on Forged Checks, 1967, Common Check Frauds and the Uniform Commercial Code, 1969; Contbr. articles to profl. jours. and law revs. Served to maj. AUS, 1945-47, 61-62. Decorated Knight Grand Cross Papal Order of Holy Sepulchre, Knight Comdr. with star Constantinian Order of St. George (Italy), Knight of Malta. Mem. ABA, Chgo., Ill., Mich. bar assns., Chgo. Crime Commn., French Nat. Hon. Soc., Am., Chgo. bus. law assns., Mil. Govt. Assn., Order of St. Maurice and St. Lazarus (Italy, officer). Home: 1630 Sheridan Rd 6-L Wilmette IL 60091-1830 Office: Loyola Univ 516 1E Pearson St Chicago IL 60611-2147

O'MALLEY, JOHN PATRICK, dean; b. Hoosick Falls, NY, Nov. 27, 1928; s. Thomas Joseph and Mary Alice (Mulvihill) O.'M.; m. Margaret Parlin, June 24, 1989. BA, Villanova U., 1950; MA, PhD, Cath. U., 1969. Tchr. Archbishop Carroll High Sch., Washington, 1954-68, prin., 1987-89; asst. prof. Cath. U., Washington, 1968-69, Merrimack Coll., North Andover, Mass., 1969-74, dean humanities, 1976-78; chair edn. dept. Emmanuel Coll., Boston, 1974-76; dean coll. arts and scis. Villanova (Pa.) U., 1978-84; provost St. Thomas U., Miami, Fla., 1985-86; assoc. prof. Widener U., Chester, Pa., 1990-99, ret., 1999; lectr. Taconic Learning Ctr., 2000—. Editor: Non-Fiction, Books I and II, 1968. Home: PO Box 586 Norfolk CT 06058-0586 Home (Summer): 4207 Burt Lake Burt Lake MI 49717 Home Phone: 231-548-2375. Personal E-mail: jmlly@comcast.net.

O'MALLEY, KEVIN FRANCIS, lawyer, educator, writer; b. St. Louis, May 12, 1947; s. Peter Francis and Dorothy Margaret (Cradick) O'M.; m. Dena Hengen, Apr.2, 1971; children: Kevin Brendan, Ryan Michael. AB, St. Louis U., 1970, JD, 1973. Bar: Mo. 1973, U.S. Ct. Appeals D.C. 1974, U.S. Ct. Appeals (8th cir.) 1979, Ill. 1993. Trial lawyer U.S. Dept. Justice, Washington, 1973-74, Los Angeles, 1974-77, Phoenix, 1977-78, asst. U.S. atty. St. Louis, 1978-83. Adj. prof. law St. Louis U., 1979—85; lectr. Ctrl. and Ea. European Law Initiative, Russian Fedn., 1996, Poland, 99. Author: (with Devitt, Blackmar, O'Malley) Federal Jury Practice and Instruction, 1990, 92, (with O'Malley, Grenig & Lee), 1999-2001, 08, 09, handbook: Criminal Composition federal Jesus Practier & Anstructions; contbr. articles to law books and jours. Cmty. amb. Expt. in Internat. Living, Prague, Czechoslovakia, 1968; bd. dirs. St. Louis-Galway (Ireland) Sister Cities. Capt. U.S. Army, 1973. Recipient Atty. Gen.'s Disting. Svc. award, US Dept. Justice, 1977, John J. Dwyer Meml. Scholarship award, 1967—70; named one of Best Lawyers in Am., 2005—. Fellow Am. Coll. Trial Lawyers; mem. ABA (chmn. govt. litigation counsel com. 1982-86, chmn. jud. com. 1986-87, chmn. com. on ind. and small firms, chmn. trial practice com. 1991-94, health care litigation 1994-98, mem. task force on fed. practice 2005-06), Am. Law Inst., Met. Bar Assn. St. Louis (chmn. criminal law sect.), Nat. Inst. Trial Advocacy, Mo. Athletic Club. Roman Catholic. Office: Greensfelder Hemker & Gale PC 10 S Broadway Ste 2000 Saint Louis MO 63102-1747 Office Phone: 314-345-4753.

O'MALLEY, MARTIN JOSEPH, Governor of Maryland, former mayor, lawyer; b. Washington, Jan. 18, 1963; m. Catherine (Katie) Curran, 1990; children: Grace, Tara, William, Jack. BA, Cath. U., 1985; JD, U. Md. Sch. Law, Balt., 1988; D (hon.), Strayer U. Legis. fellow, state field dir. Staff of US Senator Barbara Mikulski, 1987—88; asst. state's atty. City of Balt., 1988-90, mem. city coun., 1991—99, mayor, 1999—2007; gov. State of Md., Annapolis, 2007—. Co-chmn. task force on fed.-local law enforcement US Conf. Mayors. Former state coord. Senator Bob Kerrey Dem. Primary. chmn. Com. Taxation and Fin., chmn. Legis. Investment. Recipient Svc. to Humanity award Md. Jaycees, 1994, Legis. Achievement Award, Balt. Bd. Realtors. Mem.: Md. Bar Assn., Friendly Sons St. Patricks. Democrat. Roman Catholic. Office: Office of Gov 101 State Cir Annapolis MD 21401-1925

O'MALLEY, SEAN PATRICK CARDINAL, cardinal, archbishop; b. Lakewood, Ohio, June 29, 1944; s. Theodore and Mary Louise O'Malley. Attended, St. Fidelis Sem., Herman, Pa., Capuchin Coll., Washington; MA in Religious Edn., Catholic U., PhD in Spanish & Portuguese, 1978. Ordained priest Roman Cath. Ch., 1970, Order of Friars Minor Capuchin, 1970; prof. Catholic U., Washington, 1969—73; exec. dir., Centro Catolico Hispano Archdiocese of Washington, 1973—78, episcopal vicar of priests serving Portuguese, Haitian & Hispanic communities, 1978-84; ordained bishop, 1984; coadjutor bishop Diocese of St. Thomas, VI, 1984—85, bishop VI, 1985—92, Diocese of Fall River, Mass., 1992—2002, Diocese of Palm Beach, Fla., 2002—03; archbishop Archdiocese of Boston, 2003—; elevated to cardinal by Pope Benedict XVI, 2006; cardinal-priest S. Maria della Vittoria, 2006—. Mem.: US Catholic Conf. of Catholic Bishops (chmn., Com. on Consecrated Life). Roman Catholic. Office: Archdiocese Of Boston 66 Brooks Dr Braintree MA 02184-3839

O'MALLEY, SUSAN, former professional sports team executive; d. Peter and Jan O'Malley. BS in Bus. and Fin., Mt. St. Mary's Coll., 1983; law degree, Georgetown U., 2007. With Earl Palmer Brown Advt., 1983—86; dir. advt. Washington Bullets, 1986—87, dir. mktg., 1987—88, exec. v.p., 1988—91, pres., 1991—96, Washington Wizards, 1996—2007, Washington Sports and Entertainment, 1991—2007. Recipient Americanism award, Alexandria-Olympic Boys and Girls Club, 1997, Adj. Prof. of Yr. award, Georgetown U., 2002. Achievements include becoming first female president of an NBA franchise. Avocations: tennis, travel.

O'MALLEY, THOMAS ANTHONY, gastroenterologist, internist; b. St. Helens, Lancashire, Eng., Jan. 21, 1932; s. Michael and Margaret (Melia) O'M.; m. Margaret Mary O'Kane, Apr. 7, 1958 (dec. Apr. 1985); m. Marianne Rapier, Jan. 23, 1988; children: Anne, Patricia, Katherine, Jane, Margaret. MBChB, U. Liverpool, Eng., 1956; Lic. Medicine, U. State N.Y., 1964. Diplomate Am. Bd. Internal Medicine, State Bd. Med. Examiners Fla. House physician Royal Infirmary, Liverpool, 1956-57; house surgeon Royal Liverpool Children's Hosp., 1957; resident in medicine C.S. Wilson Meml. Hosp., Johnson City, NY, 1957-58; fellow internal medicine Lahey Clinic, Boston, 1958-59; USPHS trainee in gastroenterology U. Rochester (N.Y.), Strong Meml. Hosp., 1959-60; chief resident medicine/Segal Watson fellow gastroenterology Genesee Hosp., Rochester, 1960-61; gastroenterologist Cancer Clinic, Regina, Sask., Canada, 1963; asst. dir. med. edn. Genesee Hosp., U. Rochester, 1964—66; pvt. practice Rochester, NY, 1967—72; clin. asst. prof. medicine U. Rochester, 1967—72; clin. assoc. prof. medicine U. South Fla., Tampa, 1972—. Chief medicine Sarasota (Fla.) Meml. Hosp., 1973, Doctors Hosp., Sarasota, 1985. With RAF, 1961-62. Recipient Physician of Yr. award Doctors Hosp. Sarasota, 1985; listed among Best Dr.'s of Am., 1998. Fellow: ACP, Am. Coll. Gastroenterology; mem.: Cavalieri del Vini Nobili (amb. 1989—, pres. 1997—), Chevalier du Tastevin (comdr. 1985—, officieur comdr. 2001—). Office: O'Malley & Hall MD PA 2650 Bahia Vista St Sarasota FL 34239-2635 Office Phone: 941-366-8960. Personal E-mail: t.omalley10@comcast.net.

OMAN, DOUG, healthcare educator; s. Joseph Wallace and Mary Jane Oman. BA in Math., U. Calif., Berkeley, 1982, PhD in Biostatistics, 1998. Adj. prof. U. Calif., Sch. Pub. Health, 2003—. Contbr. scientific papers to profl. jours. Achievements include research in shared & distinctive effects from passage meditation, a method compatible with all major faiths, based on texts from scriptures or exalted spiritual models; health effects of psychosocial & spiritual factors. Home: PO Box 108 Tomales CA 94971-0108

OMAN, HENRY, retired electrical engineer, engineering executive; b. Portland, Oreg., Aug. 29, 1918; s. Paul L. and Mary (Levonen) O.; m. Winifred Eleanor Potter, June 17, 1944 (dec. Nov. 1950); m. Earlene Mary Boot, Sept. 11, 1954; children: Mary Janet, Eleanor Eva, Eric Paul. BSEE, Oreg. State U., 1940, MSEE, 1951. Registered profl. engr., Wash. Application engr. Allis Chalmers Mfg. Co., Milw., 1940—48; rsch. engr. Boeing Co., Seattle, 1948—63, engring. mgr., 1963—91; ret., 1991. Author: Energy Systems Engineering Handbook, 1986; co-author: Electric Bicycles, a Guide to design and Use, 2005; contbr. numerous articles to profl. jours. Mem. team that restarted amateur radio communication to the outside world from the People's Republic of China, 1981. Recipient prize paper award Am. Inst. Elec. Engrs., 1964. Fellow IEEE (founder power electronics sys. confs., 1970—, v.p. Aerospace and Electronics Sys. Soc. 1984-88, Harry Mimno award 1989, Third Millenium medal 2000, editor-in-chief Aerospace and Electronic Sys. mag. 1995-99/rated in top two by Inst. for Sci. Info.), AIAA (assoc. fellow); mem. AAAS (bd. dir. Pacific divsn.). Republican. Methodist. Achievements include development of concepts for solar power satellite which generates power in geo-synchronous orbit 24 hours per day and beams it to the Earth surface with a microwave beam; research in simple battery-powered electric bicycles for low-cost, pollution-free transportation in developing nations. Home and Office: 19221 Normandy Park Dr SW Seattle WA 98166-4129 Home Phone: 206-878-4458; Office Phone: 206-878-4458. Personal E-mail: h.oman@ieee.org.

OMAN, MARK C., bank executive; b. Cedar Falls, Iowa; B, U. No. Iowa. CPA. With Delooitte, Haskins & Sells, Des Moines, Norwest Corp., 1979; CEO Wells Fargo Home Mortgage, Inc., 1989—97, chmn., 1997—; exec. v.p. mortgage svcs. Norwest, 1997—98; group exec. v.p. home and consumer fin. Wells Fargo & Co., 2002—. Office: Wells Fargo & Co 420 Montgomery St San Francisco CA 94163*

OMAN, RICHARD HEER, retired lawyer; b. Columbus, Ohio, Jan. 4, 1926; s. B. R. Oman and Marguerite H. (Oman) Andrews; m. Jane Ellen Wert, Oct. 5, 1963; children: Sarah M., David W. BA, Ohio State U., 1948, JD, 1951; D in Cmty. Leadership (hon.), Franklin U., 2005. Bar: Ohio 1951. Atty. Ohio Nat. Bank, Columbus, 1951-55; ptnr. Isaac, Postlewaite, O'Brien & Oman, Columbus, 1955-71; dir. Columbus Found., 1955-77, counsel, 1955—2005; ptnr. Porter, Wright, Morris and Arthur (and predecessor firm), Columbus, 1972-89; of counsel Vorys, Sater, Seymour and Pease, Columbus, 1990, ptnr., 1991-96, of counsel, 1997—2004, ret., 2005. Mem. Columbus Airport Commn., 1960-64; trustee Reinberger Found., Cleve., 1980—, Columbus Acad., 1981-87, Grant Hosp., 1978-86, Harding Hosp., 1978-86; sr. warden Trinity Episc. Ch., 1985-88; counsel Columbus Jewish Found., 1985-2005, Wexner Ctr. Found., 1990-2005, Found. Cath. Diocese, Columbus, 2000-2005. Fellow Ohio State Bar Found.; mem. ABA, Am. Coll. Trust and Estate Counsel, Ohio State Bar Assn. (past mem. bd. govs. probate and trust law sect.), Columbus Bar Assn., Columbus Club, Rocky Fork Hunt and Country Club, Nantucket (Mass.) Yacht Club, Kit Kat Club. Republican. Episcopalian. Office: Vorys Sater Seymour & Pease LLP PO Box 1008 52 E Gay St Columbus OH 43215-3161 Home Phone: 614-755-4843; Office Phone: 614-464-6453. Fax: 614-714-4731. Business E-Mail: rhoman@vssp.com.

OMAN, TERINA LOUISE, nursing educator; MSN, SUNY, Binghamton, 1991. Cert. nurse practitioner, W.Va. U., Morgantown, 1999. Nurse educator W.Va. U. Hosps., 1991—95, nursing faculty, 1995—2001; nursing prof. Bloomsburg U., Pa., 2001—06. Office: Bloomsburg Univ 200 E 2nd St Bloomsburg PA 17815 Office Fax: 570-389-3417. Business E-Mail: toman@bloomu.edu.

OMAR, SALEM, physician, gastroenterologist, researcher; b. Kuala Lumpur, Wilayah Persekutuan, Malaysia, Nov. 17, 1968; s. Omar Joni and Salina Abdullah; m. Joanna Abdul Karim, Mar. 22, 1997; 1 child, Edina Salem. MB, BChir with distinction in Pharmacology, U. Malaya, 1993, M in Internal Medicine, 1999. Fellow endoscopic ultrasound Dept. Interdisciplinary Endoscopy U. Hosp. Hamburg-Eppendorf, Germany, 2002—06; lectr. U. Malaya, Kuala Lumpur, 1999—2007, assoc. prof., 2008—. Contbr. articles to profl. jours. Mem.: Parenteral and Enteral Nutrition Soc. Malaysia (asst. sec. 2000—02), Malaysian Soc. Gastroenterology and Hepatology (life). Home: 18 Jalan P8B/2 Presint 8 62250 Putrajaya Malaysia Office Fax: 603-79604190. Personal E-mail: salemomar@yahoo.com.

O'MARA, JOHN ALOYSIUS, bishop emeritus; b. Buffalo, Nov. 17, 1924; arrived in Can., 1940; s. John Aloysius and Anna Theresa (Schenck) O'Mara. Student, St. Augustine's Sem., Toronto, Ont., Can., 1944-51; JCL, St. Thomas U., Rome, 1953. Ordained priest Archdiocese of Toronto, Ont., 1951, mem. chancery Canada, 1953-69; pres., rector St. Augustine's Sem., Toronto, 1969-75; pastor St. Lawrence Parish, Scarboro, Ont., Canada, 1975-76; ordained bishop, 1976; bishop Diocese of Thunder Bay, Ont., 1976-94, Diocese of St. Catharines, Ont., 1994—2001, bishop emeritus, 2001—. Pres. Ont. Conf. Cath. Bishops, 1986—92. Mem. Ont. Hosp. Svcs. Commn., 1964—69; bd. dirs. Ont. Hosp. Assn., 1961—65. Named Hon. Prelate of Papal Household with title Monsignor, 1954; Hon. fellow, U. St. Michael's Coll., Toronto, 1997. Mem.: Cath. Health Assn. Ont. (bd. dirs. 1982—86, 1988—92, 1996), Cath. Ch. Ext. Soc. (bd. dirs. 1992—96). Roman Catholic. Home: Holy Rosary Rectory 21 Queen St S Thorold ON Canada L2V 3M7 Home Phone: 905-227-0912. E-mail: holyrosary@cogeco.her.

O'MARA, THOMAS PATRICK, manufacturing executive; b. St. Catharine's, Ont., Can., Jan. 17, 1937; s. Joseph Thomas and Rosanna Patricia (Riordan) O'M.; m. Nancy Irene Rosevear, Aug. 10, 1968; children: Patricia Catharine, Tracy Irene, Sara Megan. BS, Allegheny Coll., 1958; MS, Carnegie Inst. Tech., 1960. Mktg. analyst U.S. Steel Corp., Pitts., 1960-65; dir. info. systems AMPCO Pitts. (formerly Screw & Bolt Corp.), Pitts., 1965-68; v.p., gen. mgr. Toy div. Samsonite Corp., Denver, 1968-73; regional mgr. Mountain Zone, Hertz Corp., Denver, 1973-75; asst. to chmn. Allen Group, Melville, NY, 1975-76; group exec. v.p. fin. and adminstrn. Bell & Howell Co., Chgo., 1976-77, corp. controller, 1977-78, corp. v.p., 1978-85, pres. visual communications, 1978-85; pres., chief operating officer, dir. Bridge Product Inc., Northbrook, Ill., 1985-87; chmn., chief exec. officer Micro Metl Corp., Indpls., 1987-91; chmn. Omara Ptnrs., 1992—; CEO Engineered Materials Corp., 2002—. Bd. dirs. Loyola U. Press; chmn. Plastics Group, ABC Windows. Mem. Lake Forest H.S. Bd., 1989-96, pres. 1993-96. With USAR, 1961-66. Mem. Econs. Club Chgo., Newcomen Soc. U.S., Sigma Alpha Epsilon, Knollwood Club. Home: 1350 Inverleith Rd Lake Forest IL 60045-1540 Office Phone: 847-302-2328. Business E-Mail: tomara@omarapartners.com.

OMARI, BASSAM O., cardiothoracic surgeon; s. Omar and Munawwar Omari; m. Rana Azhari, Sept. 30, 2004. MD, Am. U. Beirut, 1984. Cert. Am. Bd. Thoracic Surgery, 1996, Am. Bd. Surgery, 1992. Chief divsn. cardiothoracic surgery Harbor-UCLA Med. Ctr., Torrance, Calif., 1994—. Contbr. scientific papers to profl. jours. Fellow: ACS; mem.: Western Thoracic Surg. Assn., Soc. Thoracic Surgery. Office: Harbor-UCLA Med Ctr 1000 W Carson St Torrance CA 90509 Office Fax: 310-320-2129. E-mail: bomari@ucla.edu.

OMATSU, GLENN, Asian American studies professor; b. Cleve., 1947; Grad., East Los Angeles Coll., U. Calif., Santa Cruz. Assoc. editor Amerasia Jour., 1985—2002; editor CrossCurrents, 1985—2002; prof. Asian Am. studies UCLA, Calif. State U., Northridge, Pasadena City Coll. Co-editor: Asian Americans: The Movement and the Moment, 2001. Mem. New Otani Workers Support Com., Koreatown Restaurant Workers Support Com. Recipient Cmty. Svc. award, Japanese Am. Hist. Soc. of So. Calif., Cmty. Activism award, Korean Immigrant Workers Advocates of L.A. Office: CSUN EOP 18111 Nordhoff St Northridge CA 91330-8366 Business E-Mail: glenn.omatsu@csun.edu.

O'MEALEY, JIMMY DEE, finance educator; b. Kaw City, Okla., Apr. 18, 1949; s. Harold Raymond and Beatrice Irene O'Mealey; m. Shelly Elizabeth Mann, Apr. 13, 1985; children: Melissa Farrall, Gary Burton. MBA, Okla. State U., Tulsa, 2000. Exec. dir. Green Country Mktg. Assn., Tulsa, 1982—2000; chmn. Mktg. Resources Inc., Muskogee, Okla., 2000—05; asst. prof. Tulsa CC, 2005—. 1st lt. USAF, 1971—75, Barksdale AFB, La. Office: Tulsa CC 7505 W 41st St Tulsa OK 74107 Office Fax: 918-595-8198.

O'MEARA, ONORATO TIMOTHY, academic administrator, mathematician; b. Cape Town, Republic of South Africa, Jan. 29, 1928; arrived in U.S., 1957; s. Daniel and Fiorina (Allorto) O'M.; m. Jean T. Fadden, Sept. 12, 1953; children: Maria, Timothy, Jean, Kathleen, Eileen. B.Sc., U. Cape Town, 1947, M.Sc., 1948; PhD, Princeton U., 1953; LLD (hon.), U. Notre Dame, 1987. Asst. lectr. U. Natal, Republic South Africa, 1949; lectr. U. Otago, New Zealand, 1954-56; mem. Inst. for Advanced Study, Princeton, NJ, 1957-58, 62; asst. prof. Princeton U., 1958-62; prof. math. U. Notre Dame, Ind., 1962-76, chmn. dept., 1965-66, 68-72, Kenna prof. math., 1976-98, provost, 1978-96, provost emeritus, 1996—, Kenna prof. emeritus, 1998—. Vis. prof. Calif. Inst. Tech., 1968; Gauss prof. Göttingen Acad. Sci., 1978; mem. adv. panel math. scis. NSF, 1974-77, cons., 1960—. Author: Introduction to Quadratic Forms, 1963, 71, 73, 2000, Lectures on Linear Groups, 1974, 2d edit., 1977, 3d edit., 1988, Russian translation, 1976, Symplectic Groups, 1978, 82, Russian translation, 1979, The Classical Groups and K-Theory (with A.J. Hahn), 1989; contbr. articles on arithmetic theory of quadratic forms and isomorphism theory of linear groups to Am. and European profl. jours. Mem. Cath. Commn. Intellectual and Cultural Affairs, 1962—, Commn. on Cath. Scholarship, 1997-99; life trustee U. of Notre Dame, 1996—. Recipient Marianist award U. Dayton, 1988; Alfred P. Sloan fellow, 1960-63. Mem. Am. Math. Soc., Am. Acad. Arts and Sci., Collegium (bd. dirs. 1992-96). Roman Catholic. Home: 1227 E Irvington Ave South Bend IN 46614-1417 Office: U Notre Dame Office of Provost Emeritus 255B Hurley Hall Notre Dame IN 46556 Personal E-mail: omeara1227@sbcglobal.net.

O'MEARA, PATRICK O., political science professor; b. Cape Town, South Africa, Jan. 7, 1938; came to U.S., 1964. s. Daniel and Fiorina (Allorto) O'M. BA, U. Capetown, 1960; MA, Ind. U., 1966, PhD, 1970; D (hon.), Nat. Inst. Devel. Adminstrn., Bangkok, 2005. Dep. dir. African studies program, asst. prof. polit. sci. Ind. U., Bloomington, 1970-72, dir. African studies program, 1972—, assoc. prof. polit. sci. and pub. and environ. affairs, 1972-81, prof. polit. sci. and pub. and environ. affairs, 1981—, dean office of internat. programs, 1993—97, v.p. internat. affair, 2007—. Mem. Ind. Gov.'s Asia Delegation, 2005; cons. in field. Author: Rhodesia: Racial Conflict or Coexistence?, 1975; editor (with Gwendolen M. Carter): Southern Africa in Crisis, 1977; editor: African Independence: The First Twenty-Five Years, 1985, Southern Africa: The Continuing Crisis, 1979, International Politics in Southern Africa, 1982; editor: (with Phyllis M. Martin) Africa, 1977, 3d edit., 1995; editor: (with C.R. Halisi and Brian Winchester) Revolutions of the Late Twentieth Century, 1991; editor: (with Howard D. Mehlinger and Matthew Krain) Globalization and the Challenges of a New Century, 2000; editor: (with Howard D. Mehlinger and Roxanna Ma Newman) Changing Perspectives on International Education, 2001; contbr. articles to profl. jours., chapters to books. Decorated Cross of St. George (Catalonia, Spain); recipient John D. Ryan award Ind. U., 1993, Thomas Hart Benton medallion Ind. U., 1994, Medal of Warsaw U., 2001, Amicus Poloniae, Embassy of Poland, 2003, Founders award Soc. Coll. and Univ. Planning, 2005, Gold Cross of Merit, Republic of Hungary, 2007. Mem. African Studies Assn., Pi Alpha Alpha. Roman Catholic. Office: Ind U Bryan Hall 205 Bloomington IN 47405 Office Phone: 812-855-5021. Business E-Mail: omeara@indiana.edu.

O'MEARA, THOMAS FRANKLIN, priest, educator; b. Des Moines, May 15, 1935; s. Joseph Matthew and Frances Claire (Rock) O'M. MA, Aquinas Inst, Dubuque, Iowa, 1963; PhD, U. Munich, Germany, 1967. Ordained priest Roman Cath. Ch., 1962. Assoc. prof. Aquinas Inst. of Theology, Dubuque, Iowa, 1967-79; prof. U. Notre Dame, South Bend, Ind., 1981-84, William K. Warren prof. of theology, 1985—. Author 14 books, including: Romantic Idealism and Roman Catholicism, 1983, Theology of Ministry, 1985, revised edit., 1999, Church and Culture, 1991, Thomas Aquinas: Theologian, 1997, Erich Przywara, S.J., His Theology and His World, 2002, A Theologian's Journey, 2002, God in the World: Karl Rahnen's Theology. Mem. Catholic Theol. Soc. Am. (pres. 1980). Roman Catholic. Office: St Thomas Aquinas Priory 7200 Division St River Forest IL 60305 Office Phone: 708-771-9341. Personal E-mail: tomeara@nd.edu.

O'MEARA, VICKI A., lawyer; b. Mpls., May 13, 1957; d. James Michael and Joan Kathleen (Shepers) O'M.; children: Joseph O'Meara Masterman, Nicolas James Reisinger O'Meara. BA in Polit. Sci. cum laude, Cornell U., 1979; JD, Northwestern U., Chgo., 1982; MA in Environment & Natural Resource, George Washington U., Washington, 1987. Bar: Minn. 1982, D.C. 1983, Ill. 1989. Asst. to Army gen. counsel U.S. Army-Pentagon, Washington, 1982-86; spl. asst. to White House Counsel The White House Fellows Program, Washington, 1986-87; dep. exec. sec., domestic policy counsel, cabinent affairs The White House, Washington, 1987; dep. gen. counsel litigation and regional ops. U.S. EPA, Washington, 1987; ptnr. Jones, Day, Reavis & Pogue, Chgo., 1988-92, 93—; asst. atty. gen. U.S. Dept. Justice, 1992; exec. vice-pres., chief corp. ops., gen. counsel Ryder Systems Inc., Miami, Fla., 1997, pres. US Supply Chain Sol.; exec. v.p., chief legal & compliance officer Pitney Bowes Inc., Stamford, Conn., 2008—. Faculty mem. Army Logistics Management Inst., Ft. Lee, Va., 1982—86; guest lctr. Nat. ALI ABA progs., 1984—97; adj. prof. Union Inst., Cin., 1994—95. Author rev. Nat. Wetlands Newsletter, 1990; contbr. articles to profl. jours. Bd. dirs. Northwestern U. Alumni Assn., Chgo., 1988-90, Laidla Inc., 2003-04, Health Management Assn.; dir. Defenders of Property Rights, Zoological Soc. S.Fla.; mem. com. Chgo. Coun. Fgn. Rels, Cornell Pres. Coun. Women, Fla. Coun. Econ. Edn. Mem. Chgo. Econ. Club Chgo. (com. fgn. affairs). Office: Pitney Bowes inc 1 Elmcroft Rd Stamford CT 06926-0700

O'MEILIA, DAVID E., prosecutor, lawyer; b. July 1951; Grad. Okla. State U.; grad. in Law, Tulsa Coll. Atty. Tulsa County Dist. Atty.'s Office, 1980—84; asst. US atty. US Atty.'s Office, Tulsa, Okla., 1986—96; atty. Nichols, Wolfe, Stamper, Nally, Fallis & Robertson, 1996—99; ptnr. Lyons, Clark, Danielson & O'Meilia, Tulsa, Okla., 1999—2001; US atty. (no. dist.) Okla. US Dept. Justice, 2001—. Office: US Attys Office 110 W 7th St Ste 300 Tulsa OK 74119*

OMEL, JUNE M., elementary school educator; b. Spring Grove, Minn., June 4, 1945; d. Ernest W. Jameson and Norma L. Wiste; m. Alexander A. Omel, July 13, 1968 (dec.); children: Andrei A., Peter E. BA, Luther Coll., Decorah, Iowa, 1967; postgrad., South Conn. State U., New Haven, 1968—95, Ctrl. Wash. U., Ellensburg, 1968—95, Eastern Wash. U., Cheney, 1968—95, Antioch U., Seattle, 1968—95, Fresno U., Calif., 1968—95, Portland State U., Oreg., 1968—95. Tchr. 2d grade Turkey Hill Sch., Orange, Conn., 1967—69; tchr. 4th grade Kiona-Benton Elem. Sch., Benton City, Wash., 1979—81, tchr. 2d grade, 1981—91, tchr. 3d grade, 1991—2008. Chmn. Young Aus. Com., Benton City; mem. Safe and Civil Schs. Com., Benton City. Contbr. articles to newspapers. Mem. Yale-New Haven (Conn.) Chorale, 1968, Redeemer Oratorio Choir, New Haven, 1968, Chancel Choir, Richland, Wash., 1996—2000. Mem.: ASCD, NEA, Wash. Tchrs. Assn. Republican. Avocations: music, art, writing, reading, gardening. Office: Kiona-Benton Elem Sch 1107 Grace Ave Benton City WA 99320 Home Phone: 509-375-1255; Office Phone: 509-588-3217.

OMENN, GILBERT STANLEY, academic administrator, internist, scientist; b. Chester, Pa., Aug. 30, 1941; s. Leonard and Leah (Miller) O.; m. Martha Darling; children: Rachel Andrea, Jason Montgomery, David Matthew. AB, Princeton U., 1961; MD, Harvard U., 1965; PhD in Genetics, U. Wash., 1972. Lic. Mass., Washington, Bd. Internal Medicine Part 1(1970), Part 2, (1972), Specialty Bd. Med. Genetics-Clin. Genetics, 1982. Intern Mass. Gen. Hosp., Boston, 1965-66; tchg. fellow in medicine Harvard U., 1966-67; rsch. assoc., Nat. Inst. Arthritis and Metabol Diseases NIH, Bethesda, Md., 1967-69; fellow, divsn. med. genetics U. Wash., 1969-71, asst. prof. medicine Seattle, 1971—74, assoc. prof. medicine, 1974—79, dir., Robert Wood Johnson Clin. Scholars Program, 1975—77, investigator Howard Hughes Med. Inst., 1976-77, prof. medicine, 1979-97, prof. environ. health, 1981—, chmn. dept. environ. health, 1981-83; dean U. Wash. Sch. Pub. Health and Cmty. Medicine, 1982-97, dean emeritus, 1997—; CEO health sys. U. Mich. Health Sys., Ann Arbor, 1997—2002; exec. v.p. med. affairs U. Mich., 1997—2002, prof. internal medicine, human genetics and pub. health, 1997—, dir. ctr. biomedical proteomics, 2002—, dir. ctr. computational medicine and biology, 2005—. Bd. dirs. CNA Armune BioSci., US Civilian A D Fedn. Ctr Pub. Intregrity, Population Svcs. Internat. Salzburg Global Seminar, civilian res. dev. fdn. Ctr. Pub. Integrity; sci. adv. bd. 3M, Motorola, Divergence, Compendix Bioscis., Pac N.W. Nat. Lab.; attending staff, U. Hosp., Harborview Med. Ctr., VA Hosp, Providence Hosp., cons. staff, Children's Hosp. and Med. Ctr., Seattle, 1971-97, attending staff, U. Mich. Health Sys., 1997-; White House fellow/spl. asst. to chmn. AEC, 1973-74; asst. dir., 1977-78, assoc. dir., for Human Resources and Social and Economic Svcs, Office Sci. and Tech. Policy, The White House, 1977-80; assoc. dir. human resources Office Mgmt. and Budget, 1980-81; vis. sr. fellow Woodrow Wilson Sch. Pub. and Internat. Affairs, Princeton U., 1981; sci. and pub. policy fellow Brookings Instn., Washington, 1981-82; joint mem. Fed Hutchinson Cancer Rsch. Ctr., Seattle, 1983-; cons. govt. agys., Lifetime Cable Network; mem. Nat. Commn. on the Environment, Rene Dubos Ctr. for Human Environments, AFL-CIO Workplace Health Fund., Electric Power Rsch. Inst., Carnegie Commn. Task Force on Sci. and Tech. in Jud. and Regulatory Decision Making, adv. com. to dir., Ctrs. Disease Control, 1992-95, adv. com. Critical Technologies Inst., RAND; mem. Pres.'s Coun., U. Calif., 1992-97; chair, Pres. Congrl. Commn. on Risk Assessment and Risk Mgmt., 1994-97; mem. Nat. Enterprise for the Environment. Co-author: Clearing the Air, Reforming the Clean Air Act, 1981. Editor: (with others) Genetics, Environment and Behavior: Implications for Educational Policy, 1972; Genetic Control of Environmental Pollutants, 1984; Genetic Variability in Responses to Chemical Exposure, 1984, Environmental Biotechnology: Reducing Risks from Environmental Chemicals through Biotechnology, 1988, Biotechnology in Biodegradation, 1990, Biotechnology and Human Genetic Predisposition to Disease, 1990, Annual Review of Public Health, 1991-97, Clinics in Geriatric Medicine, 1992, Oxford Textbook of Public Health, 1997; editor: Exploring the Human Plasma Proteome, 2006; mem. bd. Jour. Proteome Research, Proteomics; contbr. articles on cancer prevention including proteomics for cancer biomarkers, human biochem. genetics, prenatal diagnosis of inherited disorders, susceptibility to environ. agts., clin. medicine and health policy to profl. publs. Mem. Pres. Coun. on Spinal Cord Injury; mem. Nat. Cancer Adv. Bd., Nat. Heart, Lung and Blood Adv. Coun., Wash. State Gov.'s Commn. on Social and Health Svcs., Ctr. for Excellence in Govt.; chmn. awards panel Gen. Motors Cancer Rsch. Found., 1985-86; chmn. bd. Environ. Studies and Toxicology, Nat. Rsch. Coun., 1988-91; mem. Bd. Health Promotion and Disease Prevention, Inst. Medicine; mem. adv. com. Woodrow Wilson Sch., Princeton U., 1978-84; mem., Report Review Com., NAS, 2001-; chair & mem., various com. of Nat. Rsch. Coun. and Inst. Medicine, NAS; trustee Pacific Sci. Ctr., Fred Hutchinson Cancer Rsch. Ctr., Seattle Symphony Orch., Seattle Youth Symphony Orch., Seattle Chamber Music Festival, Santa Fe Chamber Music Festival, Univ. Mus. Soc., Ann Arbor, United Way Washtenaw County, Mich.; chmn. rules com. Dem. Conv., King County, Wash., 1972. Served with USPHS, 1967-69. U.S. Pub. Health Svc. Spl. Fellow, 1969-71, Nat. Genetics Found. Fellow, 1971-72, White House fellow, 1973-74; recipient Research Career Devel. award USPHS, 1972-76. Fellow ACP, AAAS (pres.-elect, pres., chmn. bd. dirs. 2004-07), Hastings Ctr. Inst. Soc., Ethics and Life Sciences, Collegium Ramazzini; mem. Nat. Acad. Social Ins., Western Assn. Physicians, Inst. Medicine of NAS (medal 2008), White House Fellows Assn. (John W. Gardner Legacy of Leadership award 2004), Am. Soc. Human Genetics, Am. Med. Informatics Assn., Assn. Am. Physicians, Am. Acad. Arts and Scis., Am. Assn. for Advancement of Humanities, Am. Occupational Medicine Assn., Phi Beta Kappa, Sigma XiAlpha Omega Alpha. Jewish. Home: 3340 E Dobson Ann Arbor MI 48105-2583 Office: Univ Mich Med Sch 2017 F Palmer Commons 100 Washtenaw Ave Ann Arbor MI 48109-2218 Office Phone: 734-763-7583. Business E-Mail: gomenn@umich.edu.

OMER, GEORGE ELBERT, JR., retired orthopaedic surgeon, educator; b. Kansas City, Kans., Dec. 23, 1922; s. George Elbert and Edith May (Hines) O.; m. Wendie Vilven, Nov. 6, 1949; children: George Eric, Michael Lee. BA, Ft. Hays Kans. State U., 1944; MD, Kans. U., 1950; MSc in Orthopaedic Surgery, Baylor U., Waco, Tex., 1955. Diplomate Am. Bd. Orthopaedic Surgery, 1959, (bd. dirs. 1983-92, pres. 1987-88), re-cert. orthopaedics and hand surgery, 1983, cert. surgery of the hand, 1989. 2nd lt. US Army, 1945, advanced through grades to col., 1967, ret., 1970; rotating intern Bethany Hosp., Kansas City, 1950-51; resident in orthopaedic surgery Brooke Army Hosp., San Antonio, 1952-55, William Beaumont Army Hosp., El Paso, Tex., 1955-56; chief surgery Irwin Army Hosp., Ft. Riley, Kans., 1957-59; cons. in orthopaedic surgery 8th Army, chief orthop. surgery 121st Evacuation Hosp. Republic of Korea, 1959-60; asst. chief orthopaedic surgery, chief hand surgeon Fitzsimons Army Med. Center, Denver, 1960-63; dir. orthopaedic residency tng. Armed Forces Inst. Pathology at Walter Reed Army Med. Ctr., Washington, 1963-65; chief orthopaedic surgery and chief Army Hand Surg. Center, Brooke Army Med. Center, 1965-70; cons. in orthopaedic and hand surgery Surgeon Gen. Army, 1967-70; prof. orthopaedics, surgery, and anatomy, chmn. dept. orthopaedic surgery, chief div. hand surgery U. N.Mex., 1970-90, med. dir. phys. therapy, 1972-90, acting asst. dean grad. edn. Sch. Medicine, 1980-81. Mem. active staff U. N.Mex. Hosp., Albuquerque, 1970—2005, chief of med. staff, 1984-86; cons. staff other Albuquerque hosps.; cons. orthopedic surgery USPHS, 1966-85, US Army, 1970-92, USAF, 1970-78, VA, 1970-2000; cons. Carrie Tingley Hosp. for Crippled Children, 1970-99, interim med. dir., 1970-72, 86-87, mem. bd. advisor 1972-76, chair, 1994-96. Mem. bd. editors Clin. Orthopaedics, 1973-90, Jour. AMA, 1973-74, Jour. Hand Surgery, 1976-81; trustee Jour. Bone and Joint Surgery, 1993-99, sec., 1993-96, chmn., 1997-99; contbr. more than 300 articles to profl. jours., numerous chpts. to books. Decorated Legion of Merit, Army Commendation medal with oak leaf cluster; recipient Alumni Achievement award Ft. Hays State U., 1973, Recognition plaque Am. Soc. Surgery Hand, 1989, Recognition plaque N.Mex. Orthopaedic Assn., 1991, Recognition award for hand surgery Am. Osteo. Acad. Orthopaedics, 1982, Pioneer award Internat. Socs. for Surgery Hand, 1995, Rodey award U. N.Mex. Alumni Assn., 1997, Cornerstone award U. N.Mex. Health Scis. Ctr., 1997; recognized with Endowed Professorship U. N.Mex. Sch. Medicine, 1995; recognized with named Annual Orthop. Seminar and Alumni Day Brooke Army Med. Ctr., 1999. Fellow ACS, Am. Orthopaedic Assn. (pres. 1988-89, exec. dir. 1989-93), Am. Acad. Orthopaedic Surgeons, Assn. Orthopaedic Chmn., N.Mex. Orthopaedic Assn. (pres. 1979-81, 1999-2000), La. Orthopaedic Assn. (hon.), Korean Orthopaedic Assn. (hon.), Peru Orthopaedic Soc. (hon.), Caribbean Hand Soc., Am. Soc. Surgery Hand (pres. 1978-79), Am. Assn. Surgery of Trauma, Assn. Bone and Joint Surgeons, Assn. Mil. Surgeons US, Riordan Hand Soc. (pres. 1967-68), Sunderland Soc. (pres. 1981-83), Soc. Mil. Orthopaedic Surgeons, Brazilian Hand Soc. (hon.), S.Am. Hand Soc. (hon.), Groupe D'Etude de la Main, Brit. Hand Soc. (hon.), Venezuela Hand Soc. (hon.), South African Hand Soc. (hon.), Western Orthopaedic Assn. (pres. 1981-82), AAAS, Russell A. Hibbs Soc. (pres. 1977-78), 38th Parallel Med. Soc. (Korea) (sec. 1959-60); mem. AMA, Phi Kappa Phi, Phi Sigma, Alpha Omega Alpha, Phi Beta Pi. Achievements include pioneer work in hand surgery. Home: 316 Big Horn Ridge Rd NE Sandia Heights Albuquerque NM 87122 Personal E-mail: geoomer@juno.com.

OMER, SELMA, biochemist, educator; b. New Castle Upon Tyne, Eng., Aug. 25, 1978; d. Mohamed Ibrahim Omer and Zeinab Mahmoud; m. John Wallace Showalter, Aug. 12, 2007. BS in Biochemistry, Reading U., Eng., 1999, PhD in Molecular Endocrinology, 2002. Postdoc. rschr. Oxford U., England, 2003—06; med. edn. fellow U. Calif. San Francisco, 2006—08, basic sci. edn. coord., 2009—. Office: Univ Calif San Francisco 50 Beale St San Francisco CA 94105 Office Fax: 415-597-8299. Business E-Mail: omers@globalhealth.ucsf.edu.

OMERY, ANNA, nursing administrator; D in Nursing Sci., Boston U., 1982. Cert. ANCC, 2008. Contbr. articles to profl. jours. (Excellence & Achievement award, 2003). Symptom Mgmt. fellow, U. Calif., San Francisco, 2003. Mem.: Sigma Theta Tau, Am. Orgn. Nurse Execs. (Rsch. Seed grant 2007). Office: Kaiser Permanente 393 E Walnut St Pasadena CA 93065 Business E-Mail: anna.k.omery@kp.org.

OMHOLT, BRUCE DONALD, product designer, mechanical engineer, consultant; b. Salem, Oreg., Mar. 27, 1943; s. Donald Carl and Violet Mae (Buck) Omholt; m. Mavis Aronow, Aug. 18, 1963 (div. July 1972); children: Madison, Natalie; m. Darla Kay Faber, Oct. 27, 1972; 1 child, Cassidy. BSME, Heald Coll. Engring., San Francisco, 1964. Real estate salesman R. Lea Ward and Assocs., San Francisco, 1962—64; sales engr. Repco Engring., Montebello, Calif., 1964; various mfg., engring. and mgmt. positions Ford Motor Co., Rawsonville, Saline, Owosso, Ypsilanti, Mich., 1964—75; chief engr. E.F. Hauserman Co., Cleve., 1975—77; dir. design and engring. Am. Seating Co., Grand Rapids, Mich., 1977—80; pres. Trinity Engring., Grand Rapids, 1980—81, Rohnert Park, Calif., 1981—. Cons. in mfg., carrier rack apparatus, motorcycle improvements. Achievements include patents for a vertical mitre machine; a merchandise display unit; underwater breathing apparatus.

OMI, PHILIP NORI, retired forestry professor; BA, U. Calif., Berkeley, 1969, MS, 1973, PhD, 1977. Prof. Colo. State U., Fort Collins, 1986—2003, prof. emeritus, 2004—. Asst. prof. Colo. State U., 1977—80, assoc. prof., 1980—86, acting dir., ctr. applied studies Am. ethnicity, 1992—93, interim assoc. provost, 1992—93, dir., western forest fire rsch. ctr., 1992—2006, asst. v.p. acad. affairs; guest instr. Humboldt State U., Arcata, Calif., 2006—; cons. Omi Assocs., Sebastopol, Calif., 2000—; vis. prof. wildland fire mgmt. U. Wash., Seattle; sr. academic specialist Wash. Inst., 2009. Contbr. scientific papers to profl. jours. Grantee, Nat. Sci. Found., 1981; fellow, NATO, 1984—86; grant, Joint Fire Sci. Program, 1998—2008. Mem.: Soc. Am. Foresters. Achievements include research in forest fire science & service to wildland fire managers. Office: Omi Associates PO Box 854 Sebastopol CA 95473 Business E-Mail: philip.omi@colostate.edu.

OMIDI, C. JULIAN, plastic surgeon; b. July 25, 1968; MD, 1996. Cert. in dermatology 2000, in dermatol. surgery 2000, diplomate Am. Bd. Dermatology. Chief resident St. Louis Sch. Medicine; private practice Calif. Lectr. in field. Contbr. articles in profl. jours.; featured on Dr. 90210. Fellow: Am. Acad. Dermatology; mem.: Am. Acad. Cosmetic Surgery, Am. Soc. Dermatol. Surgery. Office Phone: 661-949-6000.

OMIDI, MICHAEL M., plastic surgeon; b. July 19, 1970; MD with distinction in rsch. (magna cum laude), 1997. Diplomate Am. Bd. Surgery, 2004. Tng. in general surgery, plastic & reconstructive surgery, burn surgeon, breast cancer surgeon, facial aesthetic surgery, pediatric/craniofacial reconstructive surgery; resident and fellowship tng. Northwestern U. Meml. Hosp. and Med. Ctr., U. Ill., Chgo. Med. Ctr., Cook County Hosp. Trauma Ctr. and Burn Ctr., U. Miami Med. Ctr. and Miami Children's Hosp. (pediatric plastic surgery and craniofacial surgery); chief staff, dir. surgery Pacific Surgical and Laser Inst., Beverly Hills, Calif. Lectr. and rschr. in field; instructor, lectr. Internat. Acad. for Laser Medicine & Surgery, Ann. Internat. Laser Conf., Florence, Italy; instr. surgery Northwestern U. Meml. Hosp. and Med. Ctr. Contbr. articles to profl. jours.; featured on Dr. 90210, featured in People Mag. and Starr TV. Vol. mem. Interplast Assn. Mem.: Am. Soc. Maxillofacial Surgeons. Avocations: travel, skiing, painting. Home: 9001 Wilshire Blvd Ste 106 Beverly Hills CA 90211-1839 Office Phone: 866-423-2889.*

OMIDYAR, PIERRE M., Internet company executive; b. Paris, June 21, 1967; arrived in U.S., 1973; m. Pam Kerr; 3 children. BS in Computer Sci., Tufts U., 1988. With developer rels. Gen. Magic, Inc.; software developer Claris (subsidiary of Apple Computer), 1988—91; co-founder Ink Devel. Corp., 1991; founder, chmn. eBay, Inc., 1995—. Trustee Tufts U., mem. adminstrn. and finance com., mem., com. on trusteeship.; trustee Santa Fe Inst. Co-founder, chair bd. dirs. Omidyar Found., 1998—; co-founder, CEO Omidyar Network; bd. dir. Meetup-.com. Recipient Light on the Hill award (with Pam Omidyar), Tufts U.; named one of World's Richest People, Forbes, 1999—2007, 50 Most Generous Philanthropists, Fortune Mag., 2005, Forbes Richest Americans, 2006. Office: eBay Inc 2125 Hamilton Ave San Jose CA 95125-5905

OMINSKY, HARRIS, lawyer; b. Phila., Sept. 14, 1932; s. Joseph and Lillian (Herman) O.; m. Rosalyn Rita Rutenberg; children— Michelle, David. BS in Econs., U. Pa., 1953, LLB cum laude, 1956. Bar: Pa. 1956. Ptnr. Ominsky & Ominsky, Phila., 1958-64; ptnr. Blank, Rome, Comisky & McCauley, Phila., 1964—2003, Blank Rome LLP, 1964—2003; co-chmn. real estate dept. Blank, Rome, Comisky & McCauley, Phila., 1988-93. Lectr. Law Sch., Temple U., Phila., 1969-71, lectr. Real Estate Inst., 1996—. Author: Real Estate Practice: New Perspectives, 1996, Real Estate Practice: Breaking New Ground, 2001, If I'm Still Around, I Can't Be Dead, 2002, Real Estate Lore, 2006; contbr. columns to newspapers and mags.; contbr. numerous articles to profl. jours. Pres. bd. Phila. Singing City Choir, 1984-88; chmn. zoning com. Merion Civic Assn., Pa., 1984-91. Fellow Am. Bar Found.; mem. ABA (Harrison Tweed Spl. Merit award 1988), Pa. Bar Assn. (ho. of dels. 1984—2004), Pa. Bar Inst. (bd. dirs. 1981—, exec. com. 1986-93, v.p. 1988-89, pres. 1989-90, lectr., planner 1969—), Phila. Bar Assn. (chmn. real estate taxes subcom. 1984-85, real property sect. 1991-92, Leon J. Obermayer Edn. award 1989, Good Deed award real property sect. 1999), Am. Coll. Real Estate Lawyers (bd. govs. 1993-95), Order of Coif. Home: 526 Baird Rd Merion Station PA 19066-1302 Office: Blank Rome LLP One Logan Sq Philadelphia PA 19103-6998 Home Phone: 610-664-8063; Office Phone: 215-569-5668. Business E-Mail: ominsky@blankrome.com.

OMOHUNDRO, WILLIAM ADDISON, research marketing executive; b. Richmond, Va. s. Floyd Alvin and Mary Elizabeth (Gilliam) O.; m. Delight V. Dixon; children: William A., Jeffrey F., Robert L. BA, U. Va.; M Indsl. Engring., Ga. Tech. U.; MS, Columbia U. Mgr. new product devel. Gen. Electric, Bridgeport, Conn., mgr. new product engring.; mgr. product strategy Sperry Rand, Bridgeport, Conn.; dir. mktg. research Carrier Corp., Syracuse, NY, 1979—. Bd. dirs. Megafax, Inc., Syracuse. Patentee home hair dryer, negative ion generator, others. Pres. Stony Point Assn., Westport, Conn., 1978. Mem.: Am. Mktg. Assn. Republican. Home: 2211 Fleet Landing Blvd Miami FL 33233 Business E-Mail: waoresearch@aol.com.

OMOLE, DUNCAN WAMBOGO, information scientist, corporate communications specialist; b. Nairobi, Kenya, Mar. 18, 1973; arrived in U.S., 2003; s. Henry Omole Omero and Rosemary Akello Omole; m. Edwina Adhiambo Wambogo, Apr. 3, 1999; children: Kimberly Nyagaya, Davin Wambogo. BEd in Arts with 1st class honors, Kenyatta U., Nairobi, 1997. Info. officer Inst. French Rsch. in Africa, Nairobi, 1999—2000; project mgr. African Coun. Comm. Edn., Nairobi, 2000—01; cons. UN High Commn. for Refugees, Nairobi, 2002; info. analyst World Bank Group, Washington, 2003—. Recipient Spot award, World Bank, 2003, 2004, Recognition Cert., 2005; Ibiscus fellow, Fgn. Ministry Govt. of France, Paris, 1999. Mem.: Am. Soc. Info. Sci. and Tech. (program. chmn. 2004—05, chmn. internat. paper contest 2005—, chair internat. info. issues 2006—). Avocations: Scrabble, badminton. Office: World Bank Group 1818 H St NW Washington DC 20433

O'MORCHOE, CHARLES CHRISTOPHER CREAGH, anatomist, surgeon, educator; b. Quetta, India, May 7, 1931; came to U.S., 1968; s. Nial Francis C. and Jessie Elizabeth (Joly) O'M.; m. Patricia Jean Richardson, Sept. 15, 1955; children: Charles Eric Creagh, David James Creagh. BA, Trinity Coll., Dublin U., Ireland, 1953, MB, BCh, BAO, 1955, MA, 1959, MD, 1961, PhD, 1969, DSc, 1981. Resident Halifax Gen. Hosp., England, 1955-57; lectr. in anatomy Sch. Medicine Trinity Coll., Dublin (Ireland) U., 1957-61, 63-65, lectr. in physiology, 1966-67, assoc. prof. in physiology, 1967-68; instr. in anatomy Harvard Med. Sch., Boston, 1962-63; vis. prof. physiology U. Md. Sch. Medicine, Balt., 1961-62, assoc. prof. anatomy, 1968-71, prof. anatomy, 1971-74; chmn. anatomy bd. State of Md., 1971-73; prof., chmn. dept. anatomy Stritch Sch. Medicine Loyola U., Maywood, Ill., 1974-84; dean Coll. Medicine, U. Ill., Urbana-Champaign, 1984-98, prof. anat. scis. and surgery, 1984-98, emeritus dean and prof., 1998—. WHO cons., vis. prof. physiology Jaipur, India, 1967, S.M.S. Med. Coll., U. Rajasthan, vis. prof. anatomy, 1971; vis. scholar, dept. medicine divsn. oncology U. Wash. Sch. Medicine, 2003-06, affiliate prof., 2007-. Assoc. editor: Anatomical Record, 1978-98, Am. Jour. Anatomy, 1987-91, Lymphology, 2004—; contbr. articles to profl. jours. Elected fellow Trinity Coll., Dublin U., 1966; named faculty mem. of yr. Loyola U., Chgo., 1982. Mem. N.Am. Soc. Lymphology (v.p. 1982-84, pres. 1984-86, sec. 1993-98, Cecil K. Drinker award 1992), Am. Assn. Anatomy Chairmen (emeritus), Am. Assn. Anatomists (dir. placement svc. 1981-91), Internat. Soc. Lymphology (exec. com. 1987-97, pres. 1993-95, Presdl. award 2001), Alpha Omega Alpha. Mem. Church of Ireland. Home: 5645 NE Lincoln Rd East Poulsbo WA 98370-7756 Office: U Ill Coll Medicine 190 Med Sci Bldg 506 S Mathews Ave Urbana IL 61801-3618 Business E-Mail: cccom@uiuc.edu.

OMOTOSO, EDWARD, diplomat, author, journalist; 3 children. LLB with honors, London Sch. Econs. and Polit. Sci., U. London, 1966; MS, Columbia U., NYC, 1967; postgrad., Kennedy Sch. Govt. Exec. Edn., Harvard U., Cambridge, Mass., 2004. Exec. sec., conf. establishing internat. fund agrl. devel. UN, Rome, 1974—77, sec. world food coun., 1975—80, resident coord., resident rep. Maseru, Lesotho, 1998—2001; head, external rels. Orgn. Petroleum Exporting Countries, Vienna, 1980—85; dir. divsn. external rels. UN Devel. Program, NYC, 1992—98, sr. spl. advisor, 2003—. Pub., editor-in-chief: quar. mag. Esa-Oke Today; author: A Life Around the World: Surprise International Career Leads to Global Odyssey, 2008. Mem.: Assn. Former Internat. Civil Servants (pres. 2008—). Home: 214-46 Whitehall Ter Queens Village NY 11427 Office: UN Devel Program United Nations Plz New York NY 10017 Personal E-mail: edomotoso@post.harvard.edu. Business E-Mail: omotoso@un.org. E-mail: edomotoso@gmail.com.

OMRAN, ELSAYED M., language educator, consultant; b. Port-said, Egypt; BA, Ain-shams U., Cairo, 1968; MA, U. Newcastle, England, 1974; PhD, Georgetown U., 1983. Prof. Villanova U., Pa., 1983—2008. Author: (books) Documentation of Arabic Grammar: Problems and Reform Efforts. Office: Villanova Univ 800 Lancaster Ave Villanova PA 19085 Office Fax: 610-649-5613. Personal E-mail: sayedomraneg@yahoo.com.

OMTVEDT, CRAIG P., consumer products executive; m. Jane Omtvedt. Degree, U. Minn. Dir. of audit Fortune Brands, Inc., Lincolnshire, Ill., 1989-92, dep. contr., 1992-97, v.p., chief acctg. officer, 1997-99, sr. v.p., CFO Deerfield, Ill., 1999—. Bd. dir. Gen. Cable. Mem. Fin. Exec. Inst., Inst. of Mgmt. Accts., Tax Exec. Inst. Office: Fortune Brands Inc 520 Lake Cook Rd Deerfield IL 60015

OMTVEDT, IRVIN THOMAS, academic administrator, educator; b. Rice Lake, Wis., June 12, 1935; s. Thomas and Irene M. (Nelson) O.; m. Wanda Ruth Rank, Aug. 15, 1959; children: Mark, Penny. BS in Agr., U. Wis., Madison, 1957; MS in Animal Science, Okla. State U., Stillwater, 1959, PhD in Genetics and Animal Breeding, 1961. Fieldman livestock program, Meat and Animal Science Dept. U. Wis., 1956-57; grad. rsch. asst., Animal Science Dept. Okla. State U., 1958-61; extension livestock specialist U. Minn., 1962-64; assoc. prof. animal science Okla. State U., 1964-70, prof. animal science, 1970-73; asst. dean agr., assoc. dir. Ala. Agrl. Experiment Sta. Auburn U., 1973-75; grad. faculty fellow U. Nebr., Lincoln, 1975—2000, prof. animal science, 1975-2000, head animal science dept., 1975-82, dean agrl. rsch., dir. Nebr. Agrl. Experiment Sta., 1982-88, interim vice chancellor for agr. and natural resources, 1987-88, vice chancellor Inst. Agr. and Natural Resources, 1988-2000, v.p. agr. and natural resources, 1992-2000, interim sr. vice chancellor for acad. affairs, 1996-97, vice chancellor for extended edn., 1997-99; prof. emeritus animal sci., 2000—. Commr. Nebr. Rural Devel. Commn., 2000—03; sec. Agr. Builders of Nebr., 2000—; mem. task force NASULGC Food & Soc. Project, 2000—05; bd. dirs. UNL Emeriti Assn., 2001—07, Nebr. Cmty. Found., 2003—05; mem. Agriculture Builders Nebr. Inc., 1982—. Author: 1 textbook; contbr. numerous articles to profl. jours. Bd. dirs. St. Mark's United Meth. Ch. Found., 1989-95, 2006—, Staff Parish Com., 2000-05, adminstrv. bd., 2000-05; bd. dirs. Nebr. Human Resources Found., 1990-91, ADEC Distance Ed Consortium, 1989-95. Recipient Appreciation award, Nebr. SPF, 1981, Booster award, Nebr. Pork Producers, 1983, Agrl. Achievement award, Ak-Sar-Ben, 1989, ADEC Leadership award, 1995, NE Rural Radio Assn. Svc. to Agr. award, 1999, Pound-Howard Disting. Career award, U. Nebr., Lincoln, 2000, NE Agribus. Club Svc. to Agr. award, 2001, NE Farm Bur. Silver Eagle award, 2001, NE Hall Agr. Achievement honoree, 1997; named to NE Hall Agr. Achievement, 1982. Fellow AAAS, Am. Soc. Animal Sci. (editl. bd. Jour. Animal Sci. 1970-73, intersociety coun. rep. 1984-86, mem. bd. dirs. 1980-86, sec.-treas. 1980-83, pres. 1984-85); mem. Nat. Assn. State Univ. and Land Grant Colls. (bd. dirs. bd. on agr. 1992-97), Am. Registry of Profl. Animal Scientists (gov. bd. 1985-88, pres. 1986-87), Coun. for Agrl. Sci. and Tech. (bd. dirs. 1986-89, chair nat. concerns com. 1986-89), Kiwanis (bd. dirs. Lincoln-Capital-City, 1980-83, 2002-06, pres. 1981-82, 2004-05, lt. gov., 2006-07, dist. edn. com. chair, 2007-, dist. found. star, Hixon fellow 2006), Kiwanis Internat. Found. (life) Innocents Soc. U. Nebr.-Lincoln (hon.), Lincoln Agribusiness Club, Lincoln Friendship Home (bd. dirs., 2008-) Sigma Xi, Alpha Zeta, Gamma Sigma Delta (Merit award 1993), Phi Beta Delta. Avocations: travel, gardening. Office Phone: 402-472-0272, 402-472-0272. E-mail: iomtvedt1@unl.edu.

OMURA, GEORGE ADOLF, medical oncologist; b. NYC, Apr. 30, 1938; s. Bunji K. and Martha (Pilger) O.; m. Emily Fowler, Dec. 27, 1962; children: June Ellen, Susan, Ann, George Fowler. BA magna cum laude, Columbia U., 1958; MD, Cornell U., 1962. Intern Bellevue Hosp., NYC, resident, 1965-67; fellow Meml. Sloan Kettering Cancer Ctr., NYC, 1967-70; asst. prof. medicine U. Ala., Birmingham, 1970-73, assoc. prof. medicine, 1973-78, prof. medicine, 1978-95, prof. emeritus, medicine, 1995—, prof. ob-gyn., 1991-95; v.p. clin. devel. BioCryst Pharms., Inc., Birmingham, 1995-99, med. dir., 1996-99; prof. emeritus, ob-gyn U. Ala., Birmingham, 1996—. Cons. Nat. Cancer Inst., 1975-97; chmn. Southeastern Cancer Study Group, 1983-87; cons. to FDA, 1994-95; cons. to pharm. industry, 2000—; prin. investigator cancer and leukemia Group B for Ala., 1986-95. Contbr. articles to profl. jours. Served with USNR, 1963-65. Am. Cancer Soc. jr. faculty clin. fellow, 1971-74. Fellow: ACP; mem.: Am. Assn. Cancer Rsch., Am. Soc. Hematology, Am. Soc. Clin. Oncology, Gynecol. Oncology Group (co-prin. investigator Ala. 1988—2003, bd. dirs. 2003—07), Soc. Gynecologic Oncologists (hon.), Alpha Omega Alpha, Phi Beta Kappa. Home and Office: 3621 Crestside Rd Birmingham AL 35223-1514

OMURA, SATOSHI, research scientist, administrator; b. Nirasaki, Yamanashi, Japan, July 10, 1935; s. Yoshio and Fumiko Omura; m. Fumiko Akiyama, 1962; 1 child, Ikuyo. BS, Yamanashi U., Kofu, 1958; MS, Sci. U. Tokyo, 1963; PhD, U. Tokyo, 1968, Sci. U. Tokyo, 1970; PhD (hon.), Lajos Kossuth U., Debrecen, Hungry, 1991, Wesleyan U., U.S.A., 1994. Rsch. assoc. Yamanashi U., 1963-65; rschr. The Kitasato Inst., Tokyo, 1965-71; assoc. prof. Kitasato U., Tokyo, 1968-75, prof., 1975—84, dir., 1985—; prof The Kitasato Inst., Tokyo, 1984—, exec. v.p., 1984-90, pres., 1990—; prof. Grad. Sch. of Infection Control Sciences, 2002—. Author, editor: Macrolide Antibiotics - Chemistry, Biology and Practice, 1984, The Search for Bioactive Compounds from Microorganisms, 1992, 20 others; patentee in field. Recipient Hoechst-Roussel award Am. Soc. for Microbiology, 1985, Pharm. Soc. Japan award, 1986, Uehara prize Uehara Meml. Found., 1986, Japan Acad. prize Japan Acad., 1990, Purple Ribbon medal Japanese Govt., 1992, Fujihara Found. Sci. award, Naranishi Prize 2000, award Chemistry and Natural Sci., Am. Chem. Soc., 2005. Mem. Deutsche Acad. Naturforscher Leopoldina, Am. Acad. Microbiology; Fgn. Mem. Académie des sciences, France Avocations: golf, skiing, collecting paintings and poetry. Home: 3-12 Okamoto 3-chome Setagaya Tokyo 157 Japan Office: The Kitasato Inst 9-1 Shirokane 5-chome Minatoku Tokyo 108 Japan Office Phone: 813-5791-6101. Office Fax: 813-444-8360. E-mail: omura-s@kitasato.or.jp.

OMURA, YOSHIAKI, medical educator; b. Tomari, Toyama-ken, Japan, Mar. 28, 1934; arrived in U.S., 1959, naturalized, 1979; s. Tsunejiro and Minako (Uozu) Omura; m. Rose Ninon Alexander, Sept. 8, 1962 (separated 1983); children: Alexander Kenji, Vivienne Midori, Richard Itsuma. A degree, Nihon U., 1952—54; BSc in Applied Physics, Waseda U., 1957; MD, Yokohama City U., 1958; postgrad. exptl. physics, Columbia U., 1960—63; ScD (Med.), Coll. Physicians and Surgeons, Columbia U., 1965. Diplomate Internat. Coll. Acupuncture and Electro-Therapeutics, Am. Acad. Pain Mgmt., Am. Bd. Forensic Medicine, Am. Acad. Experts in Traumatic Stress. Rotating intern Tokyo U. Hosp., 1958, Norwalk (Conn.) Hosp., 1959; rsch. fellow cardiovasc. surgery Columbia U., NYC, 1960; resident physician in surgery Francis Delafield Hosp., Cancer Inst., Columbia U., 1961—65; asst. prof. pharmacology and instr. surgery N.Y. Med. Coll., 1966—72; vis. prof. (summers) U. Paris, 1973—77; Maitre de recherche, Disting. Fgn. Scientist program of INSERM Govt. of France, 1977. Rsch. cons. orthop. surgery Columbia U., 1965—66; part-time emergency rm. physician Englewood Hosp., 1965—66; rsch. cons. pharmacology dept. NY Downstate Med. Ctr., SUNY, 1966; co-founder, cons. Lincoln Hosp. Acupuncture Drug Detoxification Program, 1974—75; chmn. Columbia U. Affiliation and Cmty. Medicine com., Cmty. Bd. Francis Delafield Hosp., 1974—75; vis. rsch. prof. dept. elec. engring. Manhattan Coll., 1960—99; chmn. Sci. Divsn. Children's Art & Sci. Workshops, NYC, 1971—92; dir. med. rsch. Heart Disease Rsch. Found., Bklyn., 1972—; adj. prof. dept. pharmacology Chgo. Med. Sch., 1982—93; vis. prof. physiology Sch. Med. Showa U., Tokyo, 1988—96; adj. prof. preventive medicine NY Med. Coll., 1997—; vis. prof. Inst. Anesthesiology and Reanimation U. Padua, Italy, 1999; prof. dept. non-orthodox medicine Ukrainian Nat. Med. U., Kiev, 1993—; attending physician dept. neurosci. LI Coll. Hosp., 1980—88; cons. NY Pain Ctr., 1988—92, NIH Rsch. Grant Evaluation, 1994—96; v.p. Internat. Kirlian Rsch. Assn., 1981—94; mem. NY State Bd. Medicine, 1984—94; mem. alumni coun. Coll. Phys. and Surg. Columbia U., 1986—; vice chair Am. Bd. Forensic Medicine, 2002—07. Author: 7 books; mem. editl. bd. Alternative Medicine, 1985—93, Scandinavian Jour. Acupuncture and Electrotherapy, 1987—, Functional Neurology, 1988—2002; founder, editor-in-chief: Acupuncture & Electro-Therapeutics Rsch. Internat. Jour., 1974—; editl. cons. Jour. Electrocardiology, 1980—86, Am. Jour. Traditional Chinese Medicine, 2006—; contbr. chapters to books, over 220 articles to profl. jours. Recipient Acupuncture Scientist of Yr. award, Internat. Congress of Chinese Medicine, 1989, World 1st Qi Gong Scientist of Yr. award, Internat. Congress of Chinese Medicine & Qi Gong, 1990; grantee, Am. Cancer Soc. Inst., 1961—63, John Polacek Found., 1966—72, NIH, 1967—72, Heart Disease Rsch. Found., 1972—; fellow, Columbia U., 1960. Fellow: Internat. Coll. Angiology, NY Cardiol. Soc., Am. Coll. Angiology, Am. Assn. Integrative Medicine (diplomate) (life; vice chair 2002—07), Am. Coll. Forensic Examiners (life; vice chair sect. forensic medicine 2002—07), Royal Soc. Medicine (life), Internat. Coll. Acupuncture and Electro-Therapeutics (pres. 1980—), Am. Coll. Acupunture (life); mem.: NY Japanese Med. Soc. (pres. 1963—73), Am. Soc. Artificial Internal Organs, Japan Bi-Digital O-Ring Test Med. Soc. (pres. 1990—), Japan Bi-Digital O-Ring Test Assn. (pres. 1986—), NY Acad. Sci., Internat. Assn. for Study of Pain (founding mem. 1975—). Achievements include 7 US and 7 Japanese patents in medical field; originator of Bi-Digital O-Ring test. Home and Office: 800 Riverside Dr Ste 8I New York NY 10032-7400 Office Phone: 212-781-6262. Business E-Mail: icaet@yahoo.com.

ONCHOKE, KEFA K., science educator; s. Johnson Onchoke Karimu and Yunuke Kerubo nee Mogaka. BS, U. Nairobi, Kenya, 1989; MS, Hampton U., Va., 2000; PhD, Ohio State U., Columbus, 2006. Adj. instr. Columbus State CC, Ohio, 2000, Stephen F. Austin State U., Nacogdoches, Tex., 2006—. Ch. mem., Tex. Grantee award, Minority Intro. Rsch. Tng. NIH. Mem.: Am. Chem. Soc. Achievements include research in interphasing experiment and theory. Office: Stephen F Austin State Univ PO Box 13006 SFA Station Nacogdoches TX 75965-3006

ONDERDONK, ANDREW BRUCE, microbiologist; b. Hatford, Conn., July 5, 1947; s. Arthur Bruce and Jacqueline Onderdonk; m. Juliet Ann Wherry, June 2, 1969; children: Mark Andrew, Sara Beghane, Abby Hillman. PhD, U. Mo., 1973. Med. dir. clin. microbiology Brigham and Women's Hosp., Boston, 1990; prof. of pathology Harvard Med. Sch., 1990—. Sch. com. Westwood Pub. Schs., Westwood, Mass., 1994—2000; water commr. Dedham Westwood Water, Dedham, Mass., 1989—93; trustee MacMurray Coll., Jacksonville, Ill., 2001. Recipient Alumni of Yr., MacMurray Coll., 2000; Infectious Diseases fellow, USPHS, 1975—75. Office: Brigham and Women's Hosp 75 Francis St Boston MA 02115 Personal E-mail: aonderdonk@partners.org.

ONDREJCAK, SALLY SUZANNE, psychotherapist; b. Pitts., Oct. 5, 1947; d. William Thomas and June Klose Barnes; m. Michael John Fachetti, Nov. 25, 1986; children: Jillian Leigh Kerr, William Paul. BA, Penn State U., U. Pk., Pa., 1969, MA, MEd, 1971; MS in Profl. Psychology, Edinboro U., Pa., 1993. Spl. edn. resource cons. Coburn Sch. Dist., Pa., 1970—71; asst. prof. psychology Juniata Coll., Huntingdon, Pa., 1973—82; chairwoman marriage and family studies Mercyhurst Coll., Erie, Pa., 1982—; sch. psychologist Edinboro, 1990—95; staff psychologist Dr. Theresa Upton Erie, 1990; therapist Psychol. Svcs., Edinboro, 1993—. Bd. dirs. Licensure Infant Care, Huntingdon, 1971—76; mem.youth ministries Ch. Nazarene, Edinboro, 1990—; internat. adoption cons. Bethany Svcs., Pitts., 2005—; domestic and wildlife rehab. Multiple, Huntingdon, Pa., 1980—, Edinboro, Pa.; mem. aspberger's adv. com. Mercyhurst Coll., Erie, 2008—. Mem.: Youth Ministry and Performing Arts Worship Team (dir.,activity leader 1997—99). Avocation: writing. Office: Mercyhurst Coll 509 E38th St Johnstown PA 15906 Business E-Mail: sondrejcak@mercyhurst.edu.

ONDROVIC, LEO E., medical researcher, educator; s. John Stephen and Clara Anna Ondrovic. PhD, U. South Fla., Tampa, 2001. Biomed. engring. technician James Haley Vets. Hosp., Tampa, 1984—90; engr. U. South Fla., 1990—95, lab. dir., dept. surgery LVAD project, 1990—95, assoc. rschr., dept. surgery, 1995—, lab. dir., dept. surgery, 1995—; asst. prof., physics and biology St. Leo U., Fla., 2005—, pre-med. undergrad. advisor, 2007—. Contbr. scientific papers (Charles S. Neer award, 2001). Recipient Bausch and Laumb Sci. award, Tampa Cath. HS, 1976; nominee Congertional USAF Acad., US Congressman Sam Gibbons, 1976. Mem.: AAAS, Internat. Union Pure and Applied Chemistry, Am. Chem. Soc. Democrat. Roman Catholic. Achievements include research in magnetically activated left ventricular assist device. Avocations: motorcycling, backpacking, kayaking. Office: Saint Leo Univ Math and Sci PO Box 6665 Saint Leo FL 33574-6665 Business E-Mail: leo.ondrovic@saintleo.edu.

O'NEAL, CYNTHIA ANN, lawyer; b. Smithfield, NC, Apr. 24, 1974; d. Jasper and Azzie O'Neal. BA, Duke U., Durham, NC, 1992; JD, Duke U. Law Sch., Durham, NC, 1999. Law clk. NC Supreme Ct., Raleigh, 1999—2000; assoc. Smith Helms Mulliss & Moore, LLP, Raleigh, 2000—02, Taylor Penry Rash & Riemann, PLLC, Raleigh, 2003—07; ptnr., gen. counsel GCS Constrn. Co., Durham, 2007. Author: (book rev.) Fidelity & Surety Law Committee Newsletter. Vol. Habitat for Humanity, Raleigh, 2005—06, Wake County Bar Assn. Lunch with Lawyer Prog., Raleigh, 2005—06, Duke Connect, Durham, 2006—; legal dir. PLM Families Together, Inc., Raleigh, 2006—07. Recipient Leadership award, Triangle Bus. Jour., 2006. Mem.: ABA, NC Assn. Women Attys., Bus. and Profl. Women (chair NC dist. 2006—, Young Careerist award 2006), Associated Gen. Contractors America, United Books Minority Contractors NC, Triangle Comml. Real Estate Women, Nat. Assn. Women in Constrn. (corr. sec. 2006—, Pres. award 2005—06), NC Bar Assn. (lawyers in schools com. 2005—). Achievements include First African-American woman elected to the council of the North Carolina Bar Association construction section. Office: PO Box 457 Zebulon NC 27597 Office Fax: 919-682-0257, 919-269-2997. Personal E-mail: cynoneal@yahoo.com. Business E-Mail: gcs_nc@yahoo.com, coneal@concallaw.com.

O'NEAL, HANK, entertainment producer, small business owner; b. Kilgore, Tex., June 5, 1940; s. Harold Lee and Sarah (Christian) O'N.; m. Shelley M. Shier, May 14, 1985. BA, Syracuse U., 1962. With CIA, Washington and NYC, 1963-76; exec. v.p. Hammond Music Enterprises, NYC, 1980-83; pres., owner Chiaroscuro Records Co./Downtown Sound recording studio, NYC, 1970-80, 85—; exec. v.p. HOSS, Inc., NYC, 1983—, Broadway Bound, Inc., 1998—; v.p. Festival Network, Inc., NYC, 2007—. Instr., dept. head New Sch. for Social Rsch., N.Y.C., 1970-92; bd. dirs. The Jazz Found. Am., N.Y.C., The Jazz Gallery, N.Y.C.; chair bd. govs. Jazz and Contemporary Music, New Sch. U.; pres. SOS Prodns., Wilkes Barre, Pa., 1987—. Author: Eddie Condon

Scrapbook of Jazz, 1973, A Vision Shared, 1976, Berenice Abbott-American Photographer, 1982, Djuna Barnes 1978-81, 1990, Charlie Parker/The Funky Blues Date, 1995; author/photographer: The Floating Jazz Festival, 1985, The Ghosts of Harlem, 1997, Hank O'Neal, 2000, Gay Day, 2006; photographer: (books) Allegra Kent's Water Beauty Book, 1976, All the King's Men, 1990; prodr., cover photographer/designer numerous record albums, 1967—. Capt. U.S. Army, 1963-67. Recipient various awards and prizes for books. Mem. Phi Gamma Delta. Home: Glenside PO Box 101 Thornhurst PA 18424-0101 Office: Chiaroscuro Records 830 Broadway New York NY 10003-4827 Home Phone: 212-598-4325; Office Phone: 212-674-0265. Personal E-mail: chiarohank@aol.com.

O'NEAL, JERMAINE, professional basketball player; b. Columbia, SC, Oct. 13, 1978; s. Angela Ocean. Forward, center Portland Trail Blazers, 1996—2000, Ind. Pacers, 2000—08, Toronto Raptors, 2008—09, Miami Heat, 2009—. Owner Bogota Entertainment, Atlanta. Active Boys & Girls Club. Named NBA's Most Improved Player, 2001—02; named to All-NBA 2nd Team, 2003—04, Ea. Conf. All-Star Team, NBA, 2002—07. Achievements include being the youngest person to play in an NBA game, 1996. Avocations: bowling, billiards, video games. Office: Miami Heat Am Airlines Arena 601 Biscayne Blvd Miami FL 33132*

O'NEAL, KATHLEEN LEN, communications executive, writer, management speaker, financial consultant; b. Ft. Riley, Kans., May 24, 1953; d. Leonard Arthur and Mary (Modlin) O'Neal. BS with honors, U. Mo., 1975; MBA, Calif. Coast U., Santa Ana, 1991. Cert. secondary teacher. Tchr. math. Killian Sr. H.S., Miami, Fla., 1975-78; mfg. supr. Western Electric Co., Lee's Summit, Mo., 1978-79, prodn. control supr., 1979-81; dept. mgr. Lee Wards Co., Independence, Mo., 1981-83; materials mgmt. specialist Northrup-Wilcox Electric, Kansas City, Mo., 1983-84; bus. resource planning mgr. AT&T, Lee's Summit, 1984-85, product mgr. Berkeley Heights, N.J., 1985-87, fin. mgr. Bedminster, N.J., 1987-89, info. sys. devel. mgr. Piscataway, N.J., 1989-90, sr. fin. mgr. Jacksonville, Fla., 1990-91, asst. treas., 1992-95, sr. procurement mgr., 1995-96, procurement system design dist. mgr., 1997-98, payroll dist. mgr., 1998—2001; pres. Kathy O'Neal Speaks, Inc, 2001—; bd. mem., CFO and treas. Genesis Orlando Inc., 2003—05; treas. Parson Pub. Inc., 2004—05; CFO Avancen, LLC, 2005—, Ecofill Sys., 2008—, Avancen MOD Corp., 2008—. Faculty advisor to chair dept. digital game design and devel. bachelor's degree program Internat. Acad. Design and Tech., 2005—06. Recipient Spec Recognition Award, United Way, 1980. Mem.: NOW. Avocations: reading, antique button collecting. Business E-Mail: kathy@mycfoforsuccess.com.

O'NEAL, LYMAN HENRY, biology educator; b. Princeton, Ind., Jan. 18, 1942; s. Henry and Eleanor Anne (Reibold) O'N.; m. Cynthia Sue Woods, June 13, 1964; children: Michael Lyman, Cheri Sue. BA, Oakland City U., 1963; MS, U. Minn., 1970, PhD, 1973. Secondary sch. tchr. Francisco HS, Ind., 1963-66; prof. biology Oakland City U., 1973-89, Edison State Coll., Punta Gorda, Fla., 1989—. Rsch. asst. U. Minn., St. Paul, 1967-73; adj. prof. Henderson CC, Ky. 1982, Fla. So. Coll., Port Charlotte, 1989, Fla. Gulf Coast U., 1998—; bd. dirs. Ecol. Consortium Mid Am. Hancock Biol. Sta. Murray State U., 1982-89; mem. validation study panel Ind. State Dept. Edn., 1986; mem. Mote Marine Lab. Charlotte Harbor Adv. Coun., 1994—; mem. curriculum task force Fla. Gulf Coast U., 1994—. Contbr. articles to profl. jours. Mem. cmty. adv. bd. Fawcett Meml. Hosp. Mem. Am. Inst. Biol. Sci., Fla. Acad. Scis., Nat. Sci. Tchrs. Assn., Nat. Assn. Biology Tchrs. Avocations: bass guitar, painting, multimedia, cartooning. Home: 23 Amazon Dr Punta Gorda FL 33983-5208 Office: Edison State Coll 26300 Airport Rd Punta Gorda FL 33950 Office Phone: 941-637-5614. Business E-Mail: loneal@edison.edu.

O'NEAL, MICHAEL RALPH, state legislator; b. Kansas City, Mo., Jan. 16, 1951; s. Ralph and Margaret; m. Cindy O'Neal; children: Haley, Austin. BA in English, U. Kans., 1973, JD, 1976. Bar: Kans. 1976, US Dist. Ct. Kans. 1976, US Ct. Appeals (10th cir.) 1979. Intern Legis. Counsel State of Kans., Topeka, 1975-76; assoc. Hodge, Reynolds, Smith, Peirce & Forker, Hutchinson, Kans., 1976—79; ptnr. Reynolds, Peirce, Forker, Suter, O'Neal & Myers, Hutchinson, Kans., 1979—88; adminstrv. ptnr. Gilliland & Hayes, P.A., 1988—; mem. Dist. 104 Kans. House of Reps., Kans., 1985—, minority whip Kans., 1991-92, majority whip Kans., 1995-96, spkr. of the house Kans. Instr. Hutchinson CC, 1977-88; com. mem., chmn. jud. com. Kans. Ho. Reps., 1997—, fiscal oversight com., 1997-2001, tax, commerce, transp. and jud. budget com., 2003-06, vice-chmn. house select com. sch. fin., 2005-06, vice-chmn. house rules com., 2005-, vice chmn. house edn. budget sub-com., 2007-; vice-chmn. Kans. Jud. Performance Commn., 2006-. Vice chmn. Rep. Ctrl. Com., Reno County, Kans., 1982-86; bd. dirs. Reno County Mental Health Assn., Hutchinson, 1984-89, YMCA, 1984-86, Crime Stoppers (ex-officio), Hutchinson; chmn. adv. bd. dirs. Wesley Towers Retirement Cmty., 1984-96; mem. Kans. Travel and Tourism Commn., 1990-94; bd. govs. U. Kans. Law Sch., 1991-94; mem. Kans. Sentencing Commn., 1997-2000, Tax Transp. Jud. Budget subcom., 2003-06. Recipient Leadership award Kans. C. of C. and Industry, 1985; named one of Outstanding Young Men Am., 1986. Mem. ABA, Nat. Conf. State Legislatures (criminal justice com.), Kans. Assn. Def. Counsel, Def. Rsch. Inst., Kans. Bar Assn. (prospective legis. com., Outstanding Svc. award), Hutchinson C. of C. (ex-officio bd. dirs., Leadership award 1984), Am. Coun. Young Polit. Leaders (del. Atlantic conf. biennial assembly), Kans. Jud. Coun., Commn. Uniform State Laws. Republican. Protestant. Avocations: basketball, tennis, golf. Office: Gilliland & Hayes PA 2d Flr Box 2977 20 W 2nd Ave Hutchinson KS 67504-2977 also: 300 SW 10th St Rm 390-W Topeka KS 66612 Office Phone: 620-662-0537, 620-663-9181, 785-296-2302, 620-662-0537. Office Fax: 620-669-9426. Business E-Mail: moneal@gh-hutch.com, mike.oneal@house.ks.gov.

O'NEAL, RODNEY, automotive company executive; b. Dayton, OH, Aug. 27, 1953; s. James H. and Ida B. O'Neal; m. Pamela Estell O'Neal, Aug. 20, 1983; children: Heather Marie, Damien Cain. B Indsl. Adminstrn., GM Inst., 1976; MBA (Sloan fellow), Stanford U., 1991. Various engring. and mfg. pos. GM Inland Divsn., Dayton, Portugal, and Can., 1976—91; dir. indsl. engring. Chevrolet-Pontiac-GM of Can. Group, 1991—92; dir. mfg. GM Automotive Components Group Worldwide, Troy, Mich., 1992—94; gen. dir. warehousing and distbn. GM Svc. Parts Ops., 1994—97; v.p. GM, 1997—98; pres. Delphi Interior Systems, Troy, Mich., 1998—2000, exec. v.p. Safety, Thermal and Elec. Arch. sector, 2000—03; pres. dynamics, propulsion and thermal Delphi Corp., Troy, Mich., 2003—05, pres., COO, 2005—06, pres., CEO, 2007—. Bd. dir. Goodyear Tire & Rubber Co., 2004—, Delphi Corp., 2005—, Sprint Nextel Corp., 2007—; mem. Exec. Leadership Coun. Adv. bd. Focus: HOPE. Recipient Lifetime Achievement in Industry award, Nat. Soc. Black Engineers, 2002. Office: World Hdqrs Delphi Corp 5725 Delphi Dr Troy MI 48098-2815

O'NEAL, RONDALD ANSON, finance educator; s. Sidney James O'Neal; m. Gwenelle Marine Styles, Apr. 29, 1981; children: Eavvon Styles, Taila Jenelle, Rondald Anson O'Neal, Jr., Marc Damon, Philip Amiri. BS, CUNY, Bronx, 1978; MBA, Rutgers U., Camden, NJ, 1992; DBA ABD attending, U. Phoenix, 2003—. Cert. in supervision asbestos abatement projects Ga. Inst. Tech., 1991, in cmty. & econ. devel. Harvard U. John F. Kennedy Sch. Govt., 1996. Exec. dir. City Demonstration Agy., Mt. Vernon, NY, 1972—76; regional tech. rep Union Carbide Corp, Moorestown, NJ, 1981—92; pres. Camden CC, Blackwood, NJ, 1994—95, assoc. prof., 1994—. CEO Grace Cmty. Devel. Corp, Mt. Vernon, 1976—78. Contbr. articles to profl. jours. Vice chair Zoning Bd. Appeals, Camden, NJ, 1982—83, Empowerment Zone Commn., Camden, 1995—96; chmn. Nat. Model Cities Directors' Assn., NY, 1974—75. Recipient Lindback Minority Faculty award, Lindback Found., 1996. Mem.: Nat. Black MBA Assn. Avocations: travel, opera, bicycling, photography. Home: 131 Waverly Ave Mount Laurel NJ 08054 Office: Camden CC PO Box 200 College Dr Blackwood NJ 08012 Office Fax: 856-374-5011. Business E-Mail: roneal@camdencc.edu.

O'NEAL, SHAQUILLE RASHAUN, professional basketball player; b. Newark, Mar. 6, 1972; s. Philip A. Harrison and Lucille O'Neal; m. Shaunie Nelson, Dec. 26, 2002 (separated 2007); children: Shareef Rashaun, Amira Sanaa, Shaquir Rashuan, Me'arah Sanaa. BS, La. State U., Baton Rouge, 2000; MBA, U. Phoenix, 2005; student in broadcasting, Sportscaster U. at Syracuse U. S.I. Newhouse Sch. Pub. Comm., NY, 2009. Ctr. Orlando Magic, Fla., 1992—96, LA Lakers, 1996—2004, Miami Heat, Fla., 2004—08, Phoenix Suns, 2008—09, Cleve. Cavaliers, 2009—. Mem. US men's basketball team World Championships, Toronto, Canada, 1994, Olympic Games, Atlanta, 1996; owner, clothing line and record label TWIsM. Actor: (films) Blue Chips, 1994, Kazaam, 1996, Steel, 1997, The Wash, 2001, After the Sunset, 2004, The Year of the Yao, 2004, Scary Movie 4, 2006; performer: (albums) Shaq Diesel, 1993, Shaq Fu: Da Return, 1994, You Can't Stop the Reign, 1995, The Best of Shaquille O'Neal, 1996, Shaquille O'Neal Presents his Superfriends, Vol. 1, 2002. Res. officer Miami Beach Police Dept., Fla.; vol. Tempe Police Dept., Ariz.; res. dep. officer Bedford County Sheriff's Dept., Va., 2004—07; spl. dep., col. Maricopa County Sheriff's Dept., Ariz., 2006—08. Recipient Gold medal, men's basketball, World Championships, 1994, Atlanta Olympic Games, 1996; named 1st Team All-Am., Sporting News, 1991, 1992, NBA Rookie of Yr., 1993, NBA All-Star Game MVP, 2000, 2004, NBA All-Star Game co-MVP, 2009, NBA MVP, 2000, NBA Finals MVP, 2001, 2002; named one of 50 Greatest Players in NBA History, 1996, The Most Influential People in the World of Sports, Bus. Week, 2007, 100 Most Powerful Celebrities, Forbes.com, 2008; named to Eastern Conf. All-Star Team, NBA, 1993—96, 2005—07, Western Conf. All-Star Team, 1997, 1998, 2000—04, 2009, All-NBA 2nd Team, 1995, 1999, All-NBA 1st Team, 1998, 2000—06, NJ Hall of Fame, 2008. Achievements include being first overall pick in the NBA Draft, 1992; member of NBA Championship winning: Los Angeles Lakers, 2000-2002; Miami Heat, 2006; leading the NBA in: field goals, 1994, 1995, 1999-2001; field goal attempts, 1995; field goal percentage, 1994, 1998-2002, 2004-06; free throw attempts, 1995, 1999-2002, 2004; points, 1995, 1999, 2000; points per game, 1995, 2000. Office: Cleve Cavaliers One Center Ct Cleveland OH 44115*

O'NEAL, SUSAN, library director; b. ALexandria, Va., 1947; d. Albert Jackson and Alice O'Neal; 1 child, Terrence J. Crocker. BA, U. NC, Greensboro, 1969; MSLS, U. NC, Chapel Hill, 1971. Head, acquisitions dept Pub. Libr. Charlotte & Mecklenburg Cty, NC, 1973—78; dir. Lee Meml. Libr., Allendale, NJ, 1981—84; dir., info. ctr. Nat. Assn. Purchasing Mgmt., Oradell, NJ, 1984—87; mgr., info. ctr. Catalyst, NYC, 1987; dir. Franklin Lakes Pub. Libr., NJ, 1987—2000, Middletown Twp. Pub. Libr., NJ, 2000—. Mem.: ALA, NJ Libr. Assn. (exec. bd.). Office: Middletown Twp Pub Library 55 New Monmouth Rd Middletown NJ 07748 Office Fax: 732-671-5839. Business E-Mail: soneal@mtpl.org.

O'NEAL, TATUM, actress; b. LA, Nov. 5, 1963; d. Ryan O'Neal and Joanna Cook Moore; m. John McEnroe, Aug. 1, 1986 (div. 1994); children: Kevin, Sean, Emily. Actress (films) Paper Moon, 1973 (Acad. award for Best Supporting Actress, Golden Globe award for New Star of Yr.-Actress), The Bad News Bears, 1976, Nickelodeon, 1976, International Velvet, 1978, Circle of Two, 1980, Little Darlings, 1980, Prisoners, 1981, Certain Fury, 1985, Little Noises, 1992, Basquiat, 1996, The Scoundrel's Wife, 2002, The Technical Writer, 2003, My Brother, 2006, Saving Grace, 2006, (TV films) 15 and Getting Straight, 1989, Fab Five: The Texas Cheerleader Scandal, 2008, Woman on the Run: The Lawrencia Bambenek Story, 1993, (TV miniseries) Wicked Wicked Games, 2006, TV appearances include Shelley Duvall's Faerie Tale Theatre, 1984, Sex and the City, 2003, 8 Simple Rules...for Dating My Teenage Daughter, 2004, Law and Order: Criminal Intent, 2004, Rescue Me, 2006, (appearance as celebrity contestant) Dancing with the Stars, 2006; author (autobiography): A Paper Life: My Story, 2004. Office: c/o Untitled Entertainment 1801 Century Park E Ste 700 Los Angeles CA 90067*

O'NEAL-SERALATHAN, CRESCENTIA, advocate; d. Andrew and Mary Patricia O'Neal; m. Muthiah Seralathan, Aug. 18, 1984; children: Ashanthi Meena Seralathan, Chithra Andasi Seralathan. JD, CWRU, Cleve., 1983. Sr. rschr. Roosevelt Ctr. Am. Policy Studies, Ill. Sch. Reform Project, Chgo., 1984; allocations mgr. United Way of Buffalo and Erie County, 1985—86; we. regional dir. N.Y. Civil Liberties Union, Buffalo, 1986—90; owner, fundraising and program devel. cons. Meendasi, Potomac, Md., 1990—. Planning com. UN 1985 Internat. Youth Yr., Washington, 1981—85; mem. task force women's issues NY State Assembly, Albany, 1986—91; adv. bd. Erie County Task Force on Women, Buffalo, 1986—91, Erie County Task Force on Homeless, Buffalo, 1987—91, NY State Divsn. Human Rights, Buffalo, 1987—90; founder, chmn. We. NY Coalition Against the Death Penalty, Buffalo, 1989—91; del. UN Internat. Conf. on Population and Devel., Cairo, 1994; planning com. UN 4th Internat. Conf. on Women, NYC, 1994—95; del. UN 4th Internat. Conf. On Women, Beijing, China, 1995; fed. grant reviewer LCG, Washington, 2002—; e-commerce exec. Distinctly Yours, Potomac, Md., 2005—, My Kidz Got Syle. Bd. dirs. Ams. for Dem. Action, 1996—97, Nat. Student Christian Leadership Consultation, Atlanta, 1981—85. Recipient Vol. Clearinghouse Vol. Activist award, Govt. of D.C., 1983, Congl. Cert. of Appreciation, U.S. Congress, Ho. Spkr. Thomas P. O'Neal, 1981, Cmty. Leader award, SCLC, 1989; L.B.J. Internship fellow, Congressman Walter E. Fauntroy, 1980. Mem.: UN Assn. (bd. dirs., resource and devel. com. chair 1994—2001). Avocations: jazz, reading, politics, movies, travel. Business E-Mail: crescentia@mykidzgotstyle.com.

ONEGA, ESTHER E., librarian; d. Ronald J. and Mary M. Onega; m. Mitchell G. Farish, May 14, 2005. BA, Va. Tech, Blacksburg, 1982; MLS, U. Md., Coll. Pk., 1989. Legis. libr. Md. Gen. Assembly, Annapolis, 1990—91; law libr. US Dept. Justice, Washington, 1991—95, Fed. Res. Bd., Washington, 1995—97; libr. Sch. of Continuing & Profl. Studies U. Va., Charlottesville, 1997—2005, libr. instrn. and outreach in humanities & social scis., 2005—07, on-site google project mgr., 2007—. Mem.: ALA. Office: Univ Va Alderman Libr Charlottesville VA 22903 Business E-Mail: eeb4n@virginia.edu.

O'NEIL, HAROLD FRANCIS, psychologist, educator; b. Columbia, SC, Jan. 26, 1943; s. Harold Francis Sr. and Margaret Mary O'Neil; m. Eva L. Baker, Sept. 15, 1984; children: Tristan, Christopher. PhD, Fla. State U., 1969; MS, Hollins Coll., 1970. Asst., assoc. prof. U. Tex., Austin, 1971-75; program mgr. Def. Advanced Rsch. Projects Agy., Arlington, Va., 1975-78; from team chief to dir. tng. rsch. lab. sr. exec. svc. Army Rsch. Inst., Alexandria, Va., 1978—85; prof. U. So. Calif., LA, 1985—. Cons. Army Rsch., 1985—, Inst. Def. Analyses, Alexandria, 1985—, Amry Sci. Bd., Washington, 1994—2001, Def. Sci. Bd. Task Force on Tng., Washington, 1999—2002. Editor: (book) Academic Press Education and Technology Series, 1977—92; editl. adviser Lawrence Erlbaum Assocs., Inc., Pubs., 1992—; contbr. chapters to books, articles to profl. jours.; founding editor Japanese Jour. Edn. Fellow: APA, Am. Psychol. Soc. Achievements include research in role of cognition and affect in computer-based instruction, role of motivation in testing, cross-cultural rsch. in Japan on the role of test anxiety and performance; Taiwan and Korea on the role of self-regulation anc achievement, games for tng; development of measures for metacognition, effort, and anxiety. Office: Univ So Calif 600 Wph University Park Los Angeles CA 90089-0001 Business E-Mail: honeil@usc.edu.

O'NEIL, JOHN JOSEPH, lawyer; b. Detroit, July 20, 1943; s. John J. and Dora J. (Collins) O'N.; children: Meghan, Kathryn. BA, Trinity Coll., 1965; LLB, U. Va., 1968. Bar: N.Y. 1969, U.S. Ct. Appeals (2d cir.) 1969, Fla. 1979, D.C. 1982. Assoc. Jackson & Nash, NYC, 1968-71, Paul, Weiss, Rifkind, Wharton & Garrison, NYC, 1971-77, ptnr., 1977—. Fellow Am. Coll. Trusts and Estates Counsel; mem. ABA (com. on spl. problems of aged), N.Y. State Bar Assn. (com. on taxation, trusts and estates sect.), Assn. Bar City N.Y. (com. on trusts and estates), Pi Gamma Mu. Office: Paul Weiss Rifkind Wharton & Garrison Ste 3221 1285 Avenue Of The Americas Fl 21 New York NY 10019-6064 Fax: 212-373-3379. E-mail: joneil@paulweiss.com.

O'NEIL, JOSEPH, pediatrician; b. South Haven, Mich., Sept. 24, 1956; s. Maryhelen O'Neil Cooler; m. Carolyn York, June 13, 1992. Degree in Medicine, Ind. U. Sch. Medicine, Indpls., 1989, MPH, 2006. Diplomate in neurodevel. pediat. Am. Bd. Pediat., 2005. Neurodevel. pediatician Riley Hosp. Children, Indpls., 2002—. Contbr. articles to profl. jour. Fellow: Am. Acad. Pediat. (injury chair 2003—). Office: Riley Hosp Children 702 Barnhill Dr Indianapolis IN 46202

O'NEIL, KATHERINE HUFF, lawyer; B, Stanford U., Calif.; JD, Lewis & Clark Law Sch., Portland, Oreg. Bar: Oreg. 1977. Ptnr. Graff & O'Neil, Portland. Mem. panels US Arbitration & Mediation Svc., Nat. Assn. Securities Dealers, Oreg. Appellate Settlement Conf., Multnomah County Cir. Ct. Arbitration Panel; past pres. Oreg. Law Found.; past. pres. Profl. Liability Fund; founding pres. Oreg. Women Lawyers; Oreg. chair of lawyers reps. Ninth Cir. Jud. Conf.; mem. gender bias task force Fed. Dist. Ct. Oreg.; mem. State-Fed. Jud. Coun. Recipient Award of Merit, Oreg. State Bar, Lifetime Svc. Award, US Dist. Ct. Hist. Soc., 2005, Disting. Alumni Award, Lewis & Clark Law Sch., 2005, Women of Achievement Award, Oreg. Commn. Women, Justice Betty Roberts Award, Oreg. Women Lawyers. Mem.: ABA (bd. govs. 13th dist. 2007—, mem. standing com. on gavel awards, mem. Latin Am. law initiative coun. adv. com., mem. bar svcs. com., mem. commn. on women in profession, Oreg. state del. to house dels., chair house dels. tech. com.). Office: Graff & O'Neil 2121 SW Broadway Portland OR 97201 Office Phone: 503-222-4545.

O'NEIL, MICHAEL C., lawyer; b. Pitts., Nov. 21, 1961; BA with high honors, Bklyn. Coll., 1986; JD with honors, DePaul Univ., 1989. Bar: Ill. 1989. Ptnr., chmn. Privacy Litigation practice group DLA Piper Rudnick Gray Cary, Chgo. Editor (articles & notes): DePaul Law Rev., 1988—89. Office: DLA Piper Rudnick Gray Cary Suite 1900 203 N LaSalle St Chicago IL 60601-1293 Office Phone: 312-368-4098. Office Fax: 312-236-7516. Business E-Mail: michael.oneil@dlapiper.com.

O'NEIL, MICHAEL JOSEPH, opinion survey executive, marketing research consultant; b. Springfield, Mass., June 22, 1951; s. James Francis and Mary Helen (Apolis) O'N.; children: Heather Rose, Sean Michael, Ryan Joseph, Matthew James. BA, Brown U., 1974, MA, 1975; PhD, Northwestern U., 1977. Faculty Northwestern U., 1976-77, U. Ill., Chgo., 1977, U. Mich., Ann Arbor, Mich., 1977-79, fellow Survey Rsch. Ctr., Inst. Social Rsch., 1977-79; dir. Pub. Opinion Rsch. Ctr. Ariz. State U., Tempe, Ariz., 1979-81; pres. O'Neil Assoc., Tempe, Ariz., 1981—; ptnr. Social Venture Ptnrs., 2003—06. Reviewer grant proposals NSF, Washington, 1977—; mem. mktg. com. Phoenix Art Mus., 1992-96; bd. dir. Phoenix Children's Hosp. Found., vice-chmn., 1999-2002. Manuscript reviewer Social Problems, 1977—, Pub. Opinion Quar., 1977—, Urban Affairs Quar., 1977—, Jour. Ofcl. Statistics, 1990—, Sociological Methods and Rsch., 1993; contbr. articles to profl. jours. Chmn. Tempe Union HS Dist. Bus. Edn. adv. com., 1986-88; mem. mktg. com. Mesa Assn. Retarded Citizens, 1985-87; bd. dirs. East Valley Camelback Hosp., Mesa, 1985-90, v.p., 1988-90; bd. dirs. Valley Leadership, Ariz., 1997-99; active Acad./Ariz. Town Halls, Maricopa County Citizens' Jud. Adv. Coun.; v.p. Ariz. Coalition for Tomorrow, 1998-99, pres., 1999-2001, 06—; mem. Phoenix Pride Commn., 1991-94. Mem. Am. Mktg. Assn., Am. Assn. Pub. Opinion Rsch., Alumni Assn. Brown U. (nat. bd. dirs. 1985-90, Ariz. pres. 1984-2005), Phoenix City Club (bd. dirs. 1987-93, pres. 1990-91), East Valley Partnership (mem. bd. dirs. 1993—), Phi Beta Kappa. Independent. Avocation: tennis. Office: O'Neil Assocs 412 E Southern Ave Tempe AZ 85282-5212 Personal E-mail: mike.oneil@alumni.brown.edu. Business E-Mail: oneil@oneilresearch.com.

O'NEIL, MICHELLE MAY, lawyer; b. Ft. Worth, Tex., June 27, 1968; d. Charles Richard and Sandra May; m. O'Neil John L., July 2, 2006. BBA, Baylor U., 1989, JD, 1991. Bar: Tex. 1992, U.S. Supreme Ct. 1999, cert.: Tex. (bd. cert. family law) 1997. Pvt. practice, Belton, Tex., 1992—97; assoc. Erwin A, Cain, P.C., Dallas, 1997-98, McCurley, Kinser, McCurley Nelson Orsinger, LLP, Dallas, 1998—2000, Downs Stanford PC, Dallas, 2000—02, McCurley, Kinser, McCurley, Nelson Orsinger LLP, Dallas, 2002—03, The May Firm, 2003—09, O'Neil Anderson, 2009—. Mem. Tex. Bar Assn., Dallas Bar Assn. (dir. family law sect. 2003-05), Tex. Acad. Family Law Specialists, Annette Stewart Inns Ct. Office: 5420 LBJ Freenay Ste 500 Dallas TX 75240 Office Phone: 972-852-8000. Business E-Mail: michelle@oneilanderson.com.

O'NEIL, ROBERT MARCHANT, law educator; b. Boston, Oct. 16, 1934; s. Walter George and Isabel Sophia (Marchant) O'N.; m. Karen Elizabeth Elson, June 18, 1967; children— Elizabeth, Peter, David, Benjamin AB, Harvard U., 1956, AM, 1957, LLB, 1961; LLD, Beloit Coll., 1985, Ind. U., 1987. Bar: Mass. 1962. Law clk. to Justice William J. Brennan Jr. U.S. Supreme Ct., 1962-63; acting assoc. prof. law U. Calif.-Berkeley, 1963-66, prof., 1966-67, 69-72; exec. asst. to pres., prof. law SUNY-Buffalo, 1967-69; provost, prof. law U. Cin., 1972-73, exec. v.p., prof. law, 1973-75; v.p., prof. law Ind. U., Bloomington, 1975-80; pres. U. Wis. System, 1980-85; prof. law U. Wis.-Madison, 1980-85, U. Va., Charlottesville, 1985—2007, pres., 1985-90, dir. Thomas Jefferson Ctr. for Protection of Free Expression; gen. counsel AAUP, 1970-72, 91-92. Author: Civil Liberties: Case Studies and the

Law, 1965, Free Speech: Responsible Communication Under Law, 2d edit., 1972, The Price of Dependency: Civil Liberties in the Welfare State, 1970, No Heroes, No Villians, 1972, The Courts, Government and Higher Education, 1972, Discriminating Against Discrimination, 1976, Handbook of the Law of Public Employment, 1978, 2d rev. edit., 1993, Classrooms in the Crossfire, 1981, Free Speech in the College Community, 1997, The First Amendment and Civil Liability, 2001, Academic Freedom in the Wired Wotld, 2008; co-author: A Guide to Debate, 1964, The Judiciary and Vietnam, 1972, Civil Liberties Today, 1974. Trustee Tchrs. Ins. and Annuity Assn.; bd. dirs. Commonwealth Fund, Nat. Coalition Against Censorship, Am. Law Inst. Home: 1839 Westview Rd Charlottesville VA 22903-1632 Office: Thomas Jefferson Ctr Protection Free Expression 400 Peter Jefferson Pl Charlottesville VA 22911-8691 Office Phone: 434-295-4784. Business E-Mail: rmo@virginia.edu.

O'NEIL, THOMAS FRANCIS, III, lawyer; b. Fairfield, Conn., Apr. 8, 1957; s. Thomas F. Jr. and Carmen A. (Therrien) O'N.; m. Nancy D., Aug. 14, 1982; children: Caley Elizabeth, P. McGee. AB magna cum laude, Dartmouth Coll., 1975-79; JD, Georgetown U., 1979-82. Bar: Md. 1982, Washington, NY, U.S. Dist. Ct. Md. 1983, U.S. Ct. Appeals (4th cir.) 1983, D.C. 1992, NY. Legis. asst. Congressman Stewart B. McKinney, Washington, 1980-82; law clk. Hon. Alexander Harvey II U.S. Dist. Ct. Md.; assoc. Venable, Baetjer & Howard, Balt., 1984-86; asst. U.S. atty. U.S. Dept. Justice, Balt., 1986-89; assoc. Hogan & Hartson, Balt., 1990-91, ptnr., 1992-95; chief litig. counsel MCI Comms. Corp., Washington, 1995-98; sr. v.p., chief legal counsel MCI, 1999—2001; sr. v.p., gen. counsel MCI Group, 2001—02; sr. ptnr. Piper Rudnick LLP, 2002—04; joint global leader legis. and regulatory group, chmn. govt. affairs practice group, co-chmn. govt. controversies practice group DLA Piper, Washington, 2005—08; sr. v.p., gen. counsel, sec. WellCare Health Plans, Inc., Tampa, Fla., 2008—09, vice chmn., 2009—. Bd. regents mem. Georgetown Univ., 2005—; mem., bd. visitors Georgetown Univ. Law Ctr., 1999—; mem. adv. bd. Georgetown Corp. Counsel Inst.; bd. govs. Fed. Bar Assn., Balt., 1992; ex officio trustee Walters Art Mus., 1995—96, trustee, 1997—2002; mem. adv. bd. Marbury Inst., 2000—02; pres. bd. trustees The Contemporary Mus., Balt., 2005. Contbr. articles to profl. jours. Recipient Chief Postal Insps. Spl. award U.S. Postal Svc., Washington, 1988, Letter of Commendation award Bur. of Investigation, Washington, 1989, Spl. Achievement award U.S. Dept. Justice, 1989. Mem. Internat. Bar Assn., Serjeants Inn Law Club. Republican. Roman Catholic. Office: DLA Piper 1200 19th St NW Washington DC 20036-2412 Business E-Mail: thomas.oneil@dlapiper.com.*

O'NEIL, WAYNE, linguist, educator; b. Kenosha, Wis., Dec. 22, 1931; s. L.J. and Kathryn (Obermeyer) O'N.; married; children: Scott Leslie, Patrick Sean, Elizabeth Erla. AB, U. Wis., 1955, AM, 1956, PhD, 1960; AM (hon.), Harvard U., 1965. Asst. prof. linguistics and lit. U. Oreg., 1961-65; prof. linguistics and edn. Harvard U., 1965-68, lectr. edn., 1968-72, vis. prof. edn., 1978-86; prof. linguistics MIT, 1968—, chmn. lit. faculty, 1969-75, chmn. linguistics program, 1986-97, head dept. linguistics and philosophy, 1989-97. Lectr. human devel. Wheelock Coll., Boston, 1991—; lectr. Beijing Normal U., 1980, Beijing and Shanghai Fgn. Lang. Insts., 1981; lectr. linguistics Shandong (China) U., 1982-83, prof., 1984—; prof. Summer Inst. on Lang. Change, NEH, 1978; vis. prof. Tsuda Coll., Tokyo, 1983, Kanda U. Internat. Studies, Makuhari, Japan, 1997, Am. Indian Lang. Devel. Inst., 2000-2004, Kanazawa Inst. of Tech., Japan, 2001-2007, Navajo Lang. Acad., 2007-; co-dir. MIT-Japan Sci. and Tech. mind articulation project, 1996-2002. Author: (in Chinese) English Transformational Grammar, 1981, Linguistics and Applied Linguistics, 1983, (with S.J. Keyser) Rule Generalization and Optionality in Language Change, 1985, (with S. Flynn) Linguistic Theory in Second Language Acquisition, 1988, (with S. Flynn and G. Martohardjono) The Generative Study of Second Language Acquisition, 1998, (with A. Marantz and Y. Miyashita) Image, Language, Brain, 2000, (with M. Honda) Understanding First and Second Language Acquisition, 2004, (with M. Honda) Thinking Linguistically, 2007, (with M. Honda) Developing Materials and Activities Language Teaching, 2008; mem. editl. group Radical Tchr., 1975—. Mem. steering com. Resist, 1967—, Peoples Coalition for Peace and Justice, 1970-72; co-founder, mem. Linguistics for Nicaragua, 1985—. With U.S. Army, 1952-54. Fulbright fellow in Iceland, 1961; Am. Council Learned Socs. study fellow M.I.T., 1964-65; George Watson fellow U. Queensland, Brisbane, Australia, 1998. Mem. AAAS, Linguistic Soc. Am., Nat. Coun. Tchrs. English, Am. Assn. Applied Linguistics, Assembly for the Tchg. English Grammar. Achievements include development of materials and a theory of second language acquisition and activities in support of native language revitalization. Office: MIT Dept Linguistics and Philosophy Cambridge MA 02139-4307 Business E-Mail: waoneil@mit.edu.

O'NEIL, WILLIAM FRANCIS, academic administrator; b. Worcester, Mass., Mar. 26, 1936; s. John J. and Mary A. (Trahant) O'N.; m. Mary Elizabeth Dillon, Aug. 22, 1959; children: Kathleen, Mary Elizabeth. BS, Boston U., 1960; MEd, Worcester State Coll., 1963; diploma, U. Conn., 1970; EdD, Wayne State U., 1972; PhD in Pub. Edn. (hon.), Bridgewater State Coll., 2002; BFA (hon.), Montserrat Coll. Art, 1994. Tchr. Worcester Pub. Schs., 1960—68, cmty. sch. dir., 1968—73; assoc. prof., dir. community edn. devel. ctr. Worcester State Coll., 1973-75, dir. community svc., 1975—77, dean grad. and continuing edn., 1977—83, exec. v.p., 1983—85, Mass. Coll. Art, Boston, 1985—86, acting pres., 1986—87, pres., 1987—96; exec. officer Mass. State Coll. Coun. Pres., 1996—2002. Contbr. articles to profl. jours. Former mem. Worcester Dem. City Com., Ward I Dem. Com., 1980-2005; pres., trustee Worcester Pub. Libr., 1977-82; mem. Mass. Bd. Libr. Commrs., 1984-89; bd. dirs. Worcester State Coll. Found., 2001—, Worcester Pub. Libr. Found., 2003—. Recipient Outstanding Alumni award field of edn. Worcester State Coll., 1996, citation Mass. Ho. of Reps., 1977, key City of Worcester, 1982; Mott fellow Charles Stewart Mott Found., 1971; Godine Cmty. Svc. medal, Mass. Coll. Art, 2002. Mem. Mass. Pub. Colls. and Univs. Pres. and Chancellors Assn. (chair 1991-92), Assn. Ind. Colls. Art and Design (bd. dirs. 1988-96), Mass. Cmty. Edn. Assn. (life; bd. dirs. 1972-77), Mass. State Colls. Pres. Assn. (chair 1992-93), Profl. Arts Consortium (v.p. Boston 1986-96, pres. 1993-94). Roman Catholic. Home: 47 Harvest Cir Holden MA 01520-3401

O'NEILL, ALBERT CLARENCE, JR., lawyer; b. Gainesville, Fla., Nov. 25, 1939; s. Albert Clarence and Sue Virginia (Henry) O'N.; m. Vanda Marie Nigels, Apr. 26, 1969; 1 child, Heather Marie. BA with high honors, U. Fla., 1962; LL.B. magna cum laude, Harvard U., 1965. Bar: Fla. 1965. Law clk. to judge U.S. Dist. Ct. (mid. dist.) Fla., Jacksonville, 1965-66; assoc. Fowler, White, Collins, Gillen, Humkey & Trenam, Tampa, Fla., 1966-69; ptnr. Trenam, Simmons, Kemker, Scharf & Barkin, Tampa, 1970-77; mem. firm Trenam, Kemker, Scharf, Barkin, Frye, O'Neill & Mullis (P.A.), Tampa, 1977—, also bd. dirs. Vis. lectr. law Stetson Law Sch., 1970-73; mem. adv. coun. IRS, 2001-03. Exec. editor Harvard Law Rev., 1964-65; contbr. articles to profl. jours. Bd. dirs. Fla. Gulf Coast Symphony, Inc., 1975-86, U. Fla. Found., Inc., 1976-84, 97-2001, 03-, Fla. Orch., 1988-2005, Gator Boosters, Inc., 2002—. Mem. ABA (chmn. tax sect. 1992-93), Am. Law Inst., Am. Coll. Tax Counsel, Fla. Bar (chmn. tax sect. 1975-76), Am. Bar Retirement Assn. (pres. 2000-01, bd. dirs. 1995-04), Phi Beta Kappa. Office: Trenam Kemker Scharf Barkin Frye O'Neill & Mullis 101 E Kennedy Blvd Ste 2700 Tampa FL 33602-5150 Office Phone: 813-227-7437. Business E-Mail: aconeill@trenam.com.

O'NEILL, ARTHUR JOSEPH, bishop emeritus; b. East Dubuque, Ill., Dec. 14, 1917; Student, Loras Coll., Dubuque, Iowa, St. Mary's Sem., Balt. Ordained priest Diocese of Rockford, Ill., 1943; ordained bishop, 1968; bishop Diocese of Rockford, Ill., 1968—94, bishop emeritus, 1994—. Roman Catholic. Office: Diocesan Chancery 1245 N Court St Rockford IL 61103-6201

O'NEILL, BEVERLY LEWIS, former mayor, college president; b. Long Beach, Calif., Sept. 8, 1930; d. Clarence John and Flossie Rachel (Nicholson) Lewis; m. William F. O'Neill, Dec. 21, 1952 AA, Long Beach City Coll., 1950; BA, Calif. State U., Long Beach, 1952, MA, 1956; EdD, U. So. Calif., 1977. Elem. tchr. Long Beach Unified Sch. Dist., 1952-57; instr., counsellor Compton (Calif.) Coll., 1957-60; curriculum supr. Little Lake Sch. Dist., Santa Fe Springs, Calif., 1960-62; women's advisor, campus dean Long Beach City Coll., 1962-71, dir. Continuing Edn. Ctr. for Women, 1969-75, dean student affairs, 1971-77, v.p. student svcs., 1977-88, supt.-pres., 1988—93, exec. dir. LBCC Found.; mayor City of Long Beach, Calif., 1994—2006. Mem. New Commn. Skills Am. Workforce; bd. dirs. Internat. City Bank, 2007-. Advisor Jr. League, Long Beach, 1976—, Nat. Coun. on Alcoholism, Long Beach, 1979—; bd. dirs. NCCJ, Long Beach, 1976—; Meml. Hosp. Found., Long Beach, 1984-92, Met. YMCA, Long Beach, 1986-92, United Way, Long Beach, 1986-92. Named Woman of Yr., Long Beach Human Rels. Commn., 1976, to Hall of Fame, Long Beach City Coll., 1977, Disting. Alumni of Yr., Calif. State U., Long Beach, 1985, Long Beach Woman of Yr. Rick Rackers, 1987, Assistance League Aux., 1987, Woman of Yr., Calif. Legislature 54th Dist., 1995; recipient Hannah Solomon award Nat. Coun. Jewish Women, 1984, Outstanding Colleague award Long Beach City Coll., 1985, NCCJ Humanitarian award, 1991, Woman of Excellence award YWCA, 1990, Community Svc. award Community Svcs. Devel. Corp., 1991, Citizen of Yr. award Exch. Club, 1992, Pacific Regional CEO award Assn. Community Coll. Trustees, 1992, EDDY award, 1999, Long Beach Excellence in Leadership, 1999. Mem. Assn. Calif. Community Coll. Adminstrs. (pres. 1988-90, Harry Buttimer award 1991), Calif. Community Colls. Chief Exec. Officers Assn., Rotary, Soroptomists (Women Helping Women award 1981, Hall of Fame award 1984), U.S. Conf. Mayors (trustee, 2001-, pres. 2005-06), League Calif. Cities (pres. 2002-). Democrat.

O'NEILL, BRIAN DENNIS, lawyer; b. Phila., Feb. 21, 1946; s. Harry William and Margaret Elizabeth (Miller) O'N.; m. Bonnie Anne Ryan, Aug. 17, 1968; children: Aimee Kathleen Fulchino, Catherine Margaret O'Sullivan. BA, Fla. State U., 1968, JD, 1971. Bar: Fla. 1971, D.C. 1975, U.S. Ct. Appeals (D.C. cir.) 1978, U.S. Ct. Appeals (5th, 10th and 11th cirs.) 1981, U.S. Ct. Appeals (10th cir.) 1985, U.S. Supreme Ct. 2003. Trial atty. Fed. Power Commn., Washington, 1972-75; assoc. Farmer, Shibley, McGuinn & Flood, Washington, 1975-80; ptnr. LeBoeuf, Lamb, Greene & MacRae LLP, 1980—2007, mng. ptnr. DC office, 1998—2003, chmn. energy/utilities dept., co-chmn. Natural Gas Practice Group; of coun. Dewey & LeBoeuf, 2007. Lectr. in field. Editorial bd. Energy Law Jour., Washington, 1983-84; contbr. articles to profl. jours. Bd. dirs. Immaculata Coll., Rockville, Md., 1989-91; bd. trustees Acad. of Holy Cross, Kensington, Md., 1994-2005, chmn. 2001-02; bd. visitors Fla. State U. Coll. of Law, 1994-; 2d lt. USAF, 1971-72. Mem.: ABA (chmn. coun., pub. utilities, comm. and transp. law sect.), Energy Bar Assn. (chmn. coms. 1983—84), Fla. Bar, Congl. Country Club (Bethesda, Md. bd. govs. 2002—08), Phi Alpha Delta. Democrat. Roman Catholic. Office: Dewey & Le Boeuf LLP 1101 New York Ave NW Washington DC 20005-4213 Home Phone: 301-365-3554; Office Phone: 202-986-8012. Office Fax: 202-986-8102. Business E-Mail: boneill@dl.com.

O'NEILL, BRIAN J., councilman; b. Phila., Dec. 23, 1949; m. Joy Moran; children: Tarrah, Megan, Beth. BS, St. Joseph's U., Phila., 1971; JD, Widener U., Chester, Pa., 1975. Juvenile probation officer; law clk. Ct. of Common Pleas, Pa.; spl. counsel Fox, Rothschild, O'Brien & Frankel; councilman, dist. 10 Phila. City Coun., 1979—, minority leader. Chmn. tech. and info. services com. Phila. City Coun. Bd. dirs. Temple U., Franklin Inst., Shalom, Inc., Opera Co. Phila.; bd. dirs., mem. exec. com. Phila. Airport Adv. Com., Phila. Convention and Visitors Bur.; bd. chmn. Pub. Tech. Inst., Washington; chmn. Northeast Airport Adv. Coun. Recipient Appreciation award Walton Pk. Civic Assn., Emerald Edn. Com., Liberty Bell Youth Orgn., Svc. award Mcpl. War Vets., Comcast Cablevision Phila. Mem. St. Joseph's U. Law Alumni, Nat. League Cities (past pres., mem. exec. com.; Appreciation award), Pa. League Cities and Municipalities (past pres., mem. exec. com.). Republican. Office: Phila City Coun City Hall Rm 562 Philadelphia PA 19107-3290 Office Fax: 215-686-1939. Business E-Mail: brian.O'neill@phila.gov.*

O'NEILL, CHARLES K., lawyer; b. Mineola, NY, June 12, 1947; BA, U. Pa., 1969; JD, Fordham U., 1972. Bar: NY 1973, US Dist. Ct. (So. Dist.) NY 1974, US Dist. Ct. (Ea. Dist.) NY 1974, US Ct. Appeals (2nd Cir.) 1977, US Supreme Ct. 1979, US Ct. Appeals (DC Cir.) 1979, US Ct. Appeals (9th Cir.) 1980. Ptnr. Chadbourne & Parke LLP, NYC, mng. ptnr., mgmt. com., 1998—. Dir. Chadbourne & Parke Found. Lectr. in field; mem. editl. bd.: Fordham Law Rev. Bd. dirs. CAMBA Legal Svcs., NYC; trustee NY Meth. Hosp., NYC. Mem.: Assn. Bar City NY, Fed. Bar Coun., NY State Bar Assn., ABA. Office: Chadbourne & Parke LLP 30 Rockefeller Plz Fl 31 New York NY 10112-0129 Office Phone: 212-408-5365. Office Fax: 212-541-5369. Business E-Mail: co'neill@chadbourne.com.

O'NEILL, CHARLES KELLY, marketing professional, retired advertising executive; b. Springfield, Mo., Apr. 2, 1933; s. Charles Chester and Frances (Kelly) O'N.; m. Kyoko Hirano, June 2, 1981. B.J., U. Mo., 1955. With Galvin-Farris-Alvine, Kansas City, Mo., 1957-58, copy chief, 1958; with Potts-Woodbury, Inc., Kansas City, 1958-61, chief time buyer, 1960-61; with Gardner Advt. Co., St. Louis, 1962-88, assoc. media dir., 1964-65, media dir., 1965-69, v.p., 1966-76, corp. media dir., dir. co., 1969-88, sr. v.p., 1976-78, pres., 1978-88; gen. mgr. Advanswers div., 1971-72; pres. Advanswers Media/Programming, Inc., 1973-78, chmn., 1978-88; v.p. Wells, Rich, Greene, NYC, 1974-88, exec. v.p., 1979-88, dir., 1978-88; vice chmn. WRG-USA, 1981-88; chmn. O'Neill Mktg., Honolulu, 1988—; exec. v.p. Kyoko O'Neill, Inc., 1993—; dir. Colony Surf Ltd., Honolulu, 1990-94, chmn., bd. dirs., 1994. Bd. dirs. Waialae Iki Ridge Cmty. Assn., Honolulu, 1991—, 1st v.p., 1993-94. Lt. (j.g.) USN, 1955-57. Mem. St. Louis Advt. Club (gov. 1981-83), Outrigger Canoe Club (Honolulu), N.Y. Athletic Club, St. Louis Club, St. Louis Racquet Club, The Bridge (Navy League of the U.S.-Honolulu), Labrador Retriever Club of Hawaii, Sigma Chi, Alpha Delta Sigma. Episcopalian. Home: 1594 Hoaaina St Honolulu HI 96821-1345

O'NEILL, HARRIET, state supreme court justice; b. Apr. 20, 1957; m. Kerry Cammack; children: Carolina, Hailey. BA, Converse Coll., 1978; studied, U. Coll., Oxford, England; JD, U. S.C., 1982; PhD (hon.), Converse Coll., 2001. Practice law, Houston; atty. Porter & Clements, Morris & Campbell; pvt. practice, 1982-92; judge 152d Dist. Ct., Houston, 1992—95; justice 14th Ct. Appeals, Houston, 1995—98, Tex. Supreme Ct., Austin, 1998—. Lectr. continuing edn. courses; adv. bd. CLE Inst., 1996; panelist Tex. Ctr. Advanced Jud. Studies., Austin, 1993. Contbr. articles to profl. publs. Mem. U. S.C. academic honors soc.; founder Jud. Outreach for Literacy Training. Named Appellate Justice of Yr., Tex. Assn. of Civil Trial & Appellate Specialists, 2002, 2006. Mem.: Harris County Bar Assn., ABA. Republican. Office: Supreme Ct Texas PO Box 12248 Austin TX 78711-2248*

O'NEILL, HARRY WILLIAM, retired research market and opinion company executive; b. Atlantic City, Jan. 30, 1929; s. Harry William and Marian Elizabeth (Kuhl) O'N.; m. Carmel Gullo, Sept. 21, 1952; children: Sharon Ruth, Randal Bruce. BA, Colgate U., 1950; MS, Pa. State U., 1951. Lic. practicing psychologist, N.J. Research analyst Prudential Ins. Co., Newark, 1957-62; with Opinion Research Corp., Princeton, NJ, 1962-87, sr. v.p., 1970-73, exec. v.p., 1973-80, pres., 1980-85, vice chmn., 1985-87, NOP World, Princeton, NJ, 1988—2005. Mem. co-adj. faculty Rutgers U., 1959-64; vis. lectr. Woodrow Wilson Sch., Princeton U., 1980-82; mem. part-time faculty Rutgers U., 1999—2005. Editor Marketing Research: A Magazine of Management & Applications, 1988-93. Pres. Nat. Coun. Pub. Polls, 1984-94, trustee, 1994—; bd. dirs. Roper Ctr. for Pub. Opinion Rsch., 1984—, chmn., 1994—2004; bd. dirs. Coun. Am. Survey Rsch. Orgns., 1981-83, chmn., 1982-83; vice chmn. Rsch. Industry Coalition, 1993-94, chmn., 1994-95; bd. dirs. Market Rsch. Inst. Internat., 1999—2005; mem. Highland Park (N.J.) Human Rights Commn., 1973-77; bd. dirs. Del-Raritan Lung Assn., 1974-88, v.p., 1977-82, chmn., 1982-84; fin. chmn. Highland Park Rep. Orgn., 1977-89. With USAF, 1951-54. Recipient Maroon citation, Colgate U., 1975, induction into Market Rsch. Coun. Hall of Fame, 1997, Lifetime Achievement award, Coun. Am. Survey Rsch. Orgns., 2001. Mem. Am. Psychol. Assn., Ea. Psychol. Assn., Am. Assn. Pub. Opinion Rsch. (Exceptionally Disting. Achievement 2007, Outstanding Achievement award NY chpt. 1997, Exceptionally Disting. Nat. Achievement award, 2007), Assn. Consumer Rsch., Am. Mktg. Assn., Market Rsch. Coun., Highland Park Rep. Club, Masons, Elks. Presbyterian. Personal E-mail: honeill536@aol.com.

O'NEILL, HEATHER MUNRO, economics professor; b. Phila., Dec. 7, 1954; m. Michael Andrew O'Neill; children: Ian A., Ross M., Bryn A., Lisle E. BA in Economics, U. Vt., Burlington, 1976, BS in Math., 1976; PhD, Georgetown U., Washington, 1986. Prof. economics Ursinus Coll., Collegeville, Pa., 1986—. Recipient Lindback Outstanding Tchg. award. Mem.: Pa. Economics Assn. (bd. mem. 2005—08), Am. Economics Assn. Home: 616 Penllyn Pike Lower Gwynedd PA 19002 Office: Ursinus Coll Dept Economics Main St Collegeville PA 19426 Business E-Mail: honeill@ursinus.edu.

ONEILL, JOHN ROBERT, library director; b. Jamestown, ND, Jan. 25, 1947; s. Robert John and Irene Mae (Lavoy) O'Neill; m. Alicia Kay Unwin. Degree in English Lit., Eastern Wash. U., Cheney, 1970. Cert. in tchg. Wash., 1970. Pvt. practice, Wash., 1974—83, Ariz., 1974—83; libr. dir. City of Cottonwood, Ariz., 1983—. Mem. Cottonwood Bookmarks, 1983—. With USAR, 1972—74, Germany. Mem.: ALA. Libertarian. Avocations: running, reading, baseball. Home: 405 Main St Clarkdale AZ 86324 Office: Cottonwood Pub Libr 100 S 6th St Cottonwood AZ 86326-4238 Office Fax: 928-634-0253. Business E-Mail: joneill@ci.cottonwood.az.us.

O'NEILL, JOSEPH, writer; b. Cork, Ireland, Feb. 23, 1964; m. Sally Singer; 3 children. Grad., Girton Coll., Cambridge, Eng. Former barrister, England and Wales; practiced bus. law The Temple, London. Author: (novels) This Is the Life, 1991, The Breezes, 1996, Netherland, 2008 (named one of NY Times 10 Best Books of 2008, PEN/Faulkner award for Fiction, 2009), (non-fiction) Blood-Dark Track: A Family History, 2001 (NY Times Notable Book, 2002, Economist mag. Book of Yr., Irish Times Book of Yr.), (short fiction anthologized in) Phoenix Irish Short Stories, 1999, Dislocation: Stories from a New Ireland, 2003, Faber Book of Best New Irish Short Stories, 2007; regular contbr. The Atlantic mag. Mailing: c/o Pantheon Books Random House Inc 1745 Broadway New York NY 10019*

O'NEILL, JUNE ELLENOFF, economist; b. NYC, June 14, 1934; d. Louis and Matilda (Liebstein) Ellenoff; m. Sam Cohn, 1955 (div. 1961); 1 child, Peter; m. David Michael O'Neill, Dec. 24, 1964; 1 child, Amy. BA, Sarah Lawrence Coll., Bronxville, NY, 1955; PhD, Columbia U., 1970. Econs. instr. Temple U., Phila., 1965-68; rsch. assoc. Brookings Instn., Washington, 1968-71; sr. economist Pres.'s Coun. Econ. Advisors, Washington, 1971-76; chief human resources budget Congl. Budget Office, Washington, 1976-79; sr. rsch. assoc. The Urban Inst., Washington, 1979-86; dir. Office Policy and Rsch. U.S. Commn. Civil Rights, Washington, 1986-87; prof. econs. and fin., dir. Ctr. for Study Bus. and Govt. Baruch Coll., CUNY, 1987—; Morton Wollman Prof. Econs. Zicklin Sch. Bus. Baruch Coll., 1999—; dir. Congl. Budget Office U.S. Congress, Washington, 1995-99. Adj. scholar Am. Enterprise Inst., 1994-95, 99—; mem. Nat. Adv. Com., The Poverty Inst., U. Wis., 1988-95; chair bd. sci. counselors Nat. Ctr. for Health Stats., 2003—; mem. Nat. Bur. Econ. Rsch., 2004—. Contbr. articles to profl. jours. Mem. Am. Econs. Assn. (v.p. 1998-99), Nat. Acad. Social Ins. Republican. Jewish. Home: 420 Riverside Dr New York NY 10025-7773 Office: CUNY Baruch Coll Ctr Study of Bus and Govt 17 Lexington Ave New York NY 10010-5518 Home Phone: 212-662-1784; Office Phone: 646-312-3540. E-mail: june_oneill@baruch.cuny.edu.

O'NEILL, JUNE F., political organization administrator, county official; m. Ronald O'Neill; 1 child, Victoria Hayes. Attended, Crane Sch. of Music, SUNY, Potsdam. Dem. chair St. Lawrence County, NY, 1978—83, 2001—; North country regional rep. Office of Gov. Mario Cuomo, 1983, dir. Office of Rural Affairs; clk. bd., county auditor, county budget officer, election commr., head social welfare examiner, county adminstr. St. Lawrence County Govt.; dir. training and intergovernmental rels. NY State Office of State Comptroller; regional coord. Spitzer/Paterson Gubernatorial Campaign, NY, 2006; asst. treas. NY State Dem. Com., 2005, chairwoman, 2007—. Mem.: Dem. Rural Conf. Democrat. Office: NY State Dem Com 461 Park Ave S New York NY 10016 Office Phone: 212-725-8825. Office Fax: 212-725-8867.*

O'NEILL, KATHERINE TEMPLETON, journalist, former nursing educator, museum administrator; b. Moline, Ill., Jan. 13, 1949; d. Morris John and Patricia (Collins) Templeton; 1 child by previous marriage, Carolyn Patricia Coquillette; m. William James O'Neill Jr., July 18, 1987; stepchildren: Alec, Sara, Jessie, Laura. BSN, U. Mich., 1971; postgrad., St. Clare's Hall, Oxford, Eng., 1971-72; MSN, Boston U., 1974. RN Ohio, Mass. Instr. Mass. Gen. Hosp., Boston, 1974-76; assoc. prof. Ursuline Coll., Cleve., 1976-81; dir. devel. and pub. rels. Ohio Coll. Podiatric Medicine, Cleve., 1985-87; dir. Chisholm Halle Costume Wing We. Res. Hist. Soc., Cleve., 1988-90; fashion editor Chagrin Valley Times, 1989-2000. Vice-chair bd. dirs., hon. trustee Healthspace Cleve., 1983-2000, Cleve. Music Sch. Settlement, 1983-97. Bd. dirs. Hathaway Brown Sch., 2006—, pres. alumnae bd. dirs., 1984—86; bd. dirs. Cleve. Ballet, 1987—95, Cleve. Inst. Music, 1994—2008, Cleve.

Scholarship Programs, 1995—2003, Mus. Arts Assn. The Cleve. Orch., 1995—; mem. adv. bd. Francis Paine Bolton Sch. Nursing and Mandel Sch. Applied Social Scis., Case Western Res. U., Cleve., 1990—2006, GAMUT, Cleve. State U., 1992—93; bd. dirs. Dress for Success, Cleve., 1998—2000, Cleve. Publs. Yearbook, 1993—95, Vis. Nurse Assn. Healthcare Partners of Ohio, 1995—, Cleve. Cmty. Bldg. Initiative, 2001—04; founding trustee, vice chair Generation Found., Cleve., 1998—; mem. disbursements com. WMJ and Dorothy K. O'Neill Found., 1993—; trustee Cuyanhoga C.C. Found., 2001—; bd. dirs. Cleve. Inst. Art, 2002—08, Gt. Lakes Sci. Ctr., 1999—2009, Ursuline Coll., 1996—, La Confrerie des Chavaliers du Tastevin, 2003, Cleve. State U. Found., 2007—. Avocations: singing, gourmet cooking, orchidology. Office: Clanco Mgmt Pepper Pike OH 44124 Office Fax: 440-893-0325.

O'NEILL, KEVIN, men's college basketball coach; b. Jan. 24, 1957; m. Chelsea Hoffman; 1 child. BA in Edn., McGill U., 1979; EdM, Marycrest Coll., 1983. Head basketball coach Ctrl. HS, Hammond, NY, 1980, North County CC Saints, Saranac, NY, 1980—82, Marycrest Coll. Eagles, Davenport, Iowa, 1982; asst. coach U. Del. Fightin' Blue Hens, 1983—85, U. Tulsa Golden Hurricane, Okla., 1985, U. Ariz. Wildcats, 1986—89, 2007—08; head basketball coach Marquette U. Golden Eagles, 1989—94, U. Tenn. Volunteers, 1994—97, Northwestern U. Wildcats, Ill., 1997—2000; asst. coach NY Knicks, 2000—01, Detroit Pistons, 2001—03; head coach Toronto Raptors, 2003—04; asst. coach Ind. Pacers, 2004—06; asst. coach, spl. asst. to the gen. mgr. Memphis Grizzlies, 2008—09; head basketball coach U. So. Calif. Trojans, 2009—. Office: Univ So Calif Galen Ctr 3400 S Figueroa St Los Angeles CA 90089-2360*

O'NEILL, MARY JANE, not-for-profit administrator, consultant; b. Detroit, Feb. 24, 1923; d. Frank Roger and Kathryn (Rice) Kilcoyne; m. Michael James O'Neill, May 31, 1948; children: Michael, Maureen, Kevin, John(dec.), Kathryn. PhB summa cum laude, U. Detroit, 1944; postgrad., U. Wis., Madison, 1949—50. Editor East Side Shopper, Detroit, 1939—45; club editor Detroit Free Press, 1945—48; reporter UP, Milw. and Madison, 1949; dir. pub. rels. Fairfax-Falls Church Cmty. Chest, Va., 1955—60; copy editor Falls Church Sun-Echo, 1958—60; freelance writer Washington, 1960—63; assoc. editor Med. World News, Washington, 1963—66; dir. publ. rels. Westchester Lighthouse N.Y. Assn. for Blind, 1967—71; dir. pub. edn. The Lighthouse, NYC, 1971—73, dir. pub. rels., 1973—80; exec. dir., CEO Eye-Bank for Sight Restoration, Inc., 1980—2000; ret., 2000. Mem. N.Y. State Transplant Coun., 1991—2002; mem. instl. rsch. rev. bd. Manhattan Eye, Ear and Throat Hosp., 1981—2008; Lenox Hill Hosp., 2008—09; bd. dirs. N.Y. Organ Donor Network, 1997—2003, Pro Mujer, 1997—2003, mem. adv. coun., 2004—. Named to Top 100 Irish Ams., Irish Am. Mag., 1999. Mem.: Pan Am. Eye Bank Assn. (bd. dir.), Women Execs. in Pub. Rels. (dir. 1982—88, pres. 1986—87, found. bd. dir. 2002—08, treas. 2004—08), Eye Bank Assn. Am. (lay adv. bd. 1981—83, dir. 1983—86, pres. N.E. Region 1993—96, exec. com. 1994—96, EBAA Heise award 1997), Women in Comm. (pres. NY chpt. 1980—81), Cosmopolitan Club. E-mail: maryjaneoneill@aol.com.

O'NEILL, MAURA LOUISE, legislative staff member, environmentalist; b. Saratoga, Calif., Sept. 6, 1956; d. Robert John O'Neill and Sunie Cabanne (Birdsall) Creegan; m. Vaho Rebassoo, Nov. 29, 1980; children: Finn, Liisa-Devlin. Student, UCLA, 1973-75; BA magna cum laude, U. Washington, 1977, PhD candidate, 2007; MBA, U. Calif., Berkeley, 2004, Columbia U., NYC, 2004; postgrad., NATO Advanced Study Inst. Legis. intern to Assemblyman Tom Bane, 1974; rsch. asst. King County Pros. Atty.'s Office, 1975-76, Office of Environ. Mediation, 1976-77; environ. analyst Seattle City Light, 1977-78; asst. dir. Consumer Action Now, 1977-80; asst. dir program devel. NYC Mayor's Energy Office, 1980-82; pres., energy and environ. cons. O'Neill & Co., Inc., Seattle, 1982—95; pres., CEO ConneXt, 1995—97; chmn., CEO ImproveMyBusiness.com, 1999—2001; founding CEO Explore Life, 2003—04; chmn. Fourteen40, 2005—08; chief of staff to Senator Maria Cantwell US Senate, Washington, 2008—. Lectr. U. Calif. Haas Sch. Bus., Berkeley, 2005—, Columbia U. Sch. Bus., 2006—, London Sch. Bus. Chair City of Seattle Pub. Safety Civil Svc. Commn., 1987-91; endorsement chair Washington State Women's Polit. Caucus, 1991, chair, 1992-93; treas. Washington Environ. Found.; chair strategic planning com. ARC King County, Seattle, 1995—, mem. bd. dirs. 1994—; pres. Wash. State Dem. Leadership Coun., 1995, v.p., 1994; mem. bd. dirs. Greater Seattle C. of C., 1995, Am. Rovers, 1994—. Named Bus. Person of Yr. Seattle C. of C., 1989 Mem.: Seattle Rotary # 4 (chair environ. com., Environ. Excellence award 1992). Office: 511 SDOB Washington DC 20510-0514 Office Phone: 202-224-3441. Business E-Mail: maura_oneill@cantwell.senate.gov.*

O'NEILL, MEGAN O., biology professor; d. Thomas P. O'Neill; 1 child, Kaitlyn Renee Baur-O'Neill. MSc, Calif. Poly. State U, San Luis Obispo, 2002. Lectr. Calif. Poly. State U., 1999—; instr. Cuesta CC, San Luis Obispo, 1999—.

O'NEILL, MICHAEL JAMES, editor, author; b. Detroit, Nov. 19, 1922; s. Michael J. and Ellen Mary (Dacey) O'Neill; m. Mary Jane Kilcoyne, May 31, 1948; children: Michael, Maureen, Kevin, Kathryn. BA, U. Detroit, 1946, LHD (hon.), 1977; postgrad., Fordham U., 1946—47. Writer Standard News Assn., NYC, 1946—47; with UPI, 1947—56; Washington corr. N.Y. Daily News, 1956—66, asst. mng. editor, 1966—68, mng. editor, 1968—74, v.p., 1971—79, exec. editor, 1974—75, editor, 1975—82, exec. v.p., 1979—82, dir. Freelance writer; lectr., 1983—. Author (with L. Tanzer): The Kennedy Circle, 1961; author: (with K.M. Cahill) Preventive Diplomacy, 1996; author: China Today, 1976, Terrorist Spectaculars: Should TV Coverage Be Curbed, 1986, The Roar of the Crowd, How TV and People Power are Changing the World, 1993. Mem. Nat. Adv. Coun. Health Professions Edn., 1967—71; chmn. Fund of City of N.Y., 2003—06. With US Army, 1943—45, ETO. Decorated Bronze Star; recipient Nat. Affairs Reporting award, Nat. Headliner's, 1956. Mem.: Coun. Fgn. Rels., Am. Soc. Newspaper Editors (pres. 1981—82), Overseas Writers (pres. 1965), Century Club (N.Y.C. chpt.). Address: 23 Cayuga Rd Scarsdale NY 10583-6941

O'NEILL, MICHAEL JAMES, retired special education educator; s. Jean Marie O'Neill; life ptnr. Frank Joseph Correia. BS, Edinboro State Coll., Pa., 1968; MS, San Francisco State U., 1971. Cert. learning specialist Chancellors Office Calif. CC, 1991. Tchr. San Francisco Unified Sch. Dist., 1969—79, program specialist, 1979—85, program adminstr., 1985—90; prof. learning specialist Coll. Desert, Palm Desert, Calif., 1990—2008, coord. disabled students programs & svc. dept., prof., 1997—2008. Recipient WHO award, Calif. CC Assn., 1995, Outstanding Faculty award, Alumni Assn. Coll. Desert, 2003, Faculty Mem. of Yr., Faculty Senate Coll. Desert, 2008. Mem.: NEA. Avocations: travel, yoga. Home: 1455 Twin Palms Dr Palm Springs CA 92264 Business E-Mail: moneill@collegeofthedesert.edu.

O'NEILL, MICHELLE, federal agency administrator; m. Marshall Mills; 1 child. BA, Sweet Briar Coll., 1985; MA, LBJ Sch. Pub. Affairs, 1987. With Office of Antidumping and Countervailing Duty Investigations, 1987—90; mem. internat. econ. policy team White House Office of Policy Develop., 1991—91; exec. asst. to dep. under sec. for internat. trade US Dept. Commerce, Washington, 1992—95; dep. asst. sec. for info. tech. industries Internat. Trade Adminstrn., Washington, 2000—04; chief of staff to under sec. for internat. trade US Dept. Commerce, 1998—2000, dep. under sec. for tech., 2004—05, dep. under sec. for internat. trade, 2005—; legis. fellow House Ways and Means Trade Sub-com., Washington, 1995; comml. attache US Mission to Orgn. for Econ. Cooperation and Develop. (OECD), Paris, 1995—98. Recipient William A. Jump award, 2001, Silver medal, Dept. Commerce, 2001, 2004, Bronze medal, 2003. Office: US Dept Commerce 1401 Constitution Ave, NW Washington DC 20230 Office Phone: 202-482-3917.

O'NEILL, MOLLY ANN, federal agency administrator; d. Vincent and Pam O'Neill. BS in Biology, Va. Tech. Environ. biologist; environ. cons. to exec. mgmt. of state environ. depts.; with Environ. Coun. of the States, 2002—06, state dir. Nat. Environ. Info. Exchange; chief info. officer, asst. adminstr. for environ. info. EPA, 2007—. Named Civilian IT Exec. of Yr., Govt. Computer News, 2007. Office: USEPA Ariel Rios Bldg AR 1200 Pennsylvania Ave NW Washington DC 20004*

O'NEILL, PATRICIA TYDINGS, performing arts educator, language educator; b. Prince Frederick, Md., Dec. 16, 1953; d. James Martin and Mary Evelyn O'Neill, Edward Joseph Pineault (Stepfather); children: Lauren Ann Veneziani, Scott Martin Veneziani. M in English, Pa. State U., State College, 1976; M in Edn., Shenandoah U., Winchester, Va., 2004. Cert. Nat. Bd. Profl. Tchg. Stds., 2005. Theatre/English tchr. No. H.S., Owings, Md., 1976—. Theatre dir. No. High. Dir. Parks and Recreation Summer Theatre for Children, Owings, 1999—2005. Recipient Tchr. of Yr., No. H.S., 1996, Shakespeare Tchr. of Yr., English Speaking Union Wash. DC Area Br., 2004, Outstanding Sch. in Theatre, Md. HS Theatre Assn., 1996, 2000, 2006; named Outstanding Theatre Educator, 2007. Mem.: NEA/CEA (assoc.), Delta Kappa Gamma (life). Avocations: travel, directing plays. Office: Northern HS 2950 Chaneyville Rd Owings MD 20736 Office Fax: 410-257-1530.

O'NEILL, PAUL ANDREW, sportscaster, retired professional baseball player; b. Columbus, Ohio, Feb. 25, 1963; BS, Otterbein Coll. Outfielder Cin. Reds, 1985-92, NY Yankees, 1993—2001; ret., 2001; analyst, NY Yankees broadcasts YES Network, NYC, 2002—. Named to Nat. League All-Star Team, Maj. League Baseball, 1991, Am. League All-Star Team, 1994—98. Achievements include member of the World Series Championship winning Cincinnati Reds, 1990, New York Yankees, 1996, 1998-2000; leading the American League in: batting average, 1994. Office: YES Network LLC The Chrysler Bldg 405 Lexington Ave 36th Fl New York NY 10174-3699*

O'NEILL, PAUL HENRY, former United States Secretary of the Treasury; b. St. Louis, Dec. 4, 1935; s. John Paul and Gaynald Elsie (Irvin) O'N.; m. Nancy Jo Wolfe, Sept. 4, 1955; children: Patricia, Margaret, Julie, Paul Henry. BA, Fresno State Coll., 1960; Haynes Found. fellow, Claremont Grad. Sch., 1960-61; postgrad., George Washington U., 1962-65; MPA, Ind. U., 1966; DSc (hon.), Clarkson U., 1993, Georgetown U., 2005; D Pub. Svc. (hon.), Edinboro U., 1997, California U. Pa., 1998; D Bus. Leadership (hon.), Duquesne U., 1999; LHD (hon.), Calif. State U., 1999; D Pub. Svc. (hon.), U. Pitts., 2003; D Pub. Policy (hon.), Carnegie-Mellon U., 2003; PhD in Pub. Policy (hon.), Pardee RAND, 2004. Site engr. Morrison-Knudsen, Inc., Anchorage, 1955-57; systems analyst VA, Washington, 1961-66; budget examiner Bur. of Budget, Washington, 1967-69; chief human resources program divsn. Office Mgmt. & Budget, Exec. Office of the Pres., Washington, 1969-70, asst. dir., 1971-72, assoc. dir., 1973-74, dep. dir., 1974-77; v.p. Internat. Paper Co., NYC, 1977-81, sr. v.p., 1981-85, pres., dir., 1985-87; CEO Alcoa Inc., Pitts., 1987-99, chmn., 1987-2000; founding co-chair Pittsburgh Regional Healthcare Initiative, 1997—2005; sec. US Dept. Treasury, Washington, 2001—02; sr. advisor The Blackstone Group, L.P., NYC, 2003—. Chmn. Pres.'s Edn. Policy Adv. Com., 1989—92; bd. dirs. Eastman Kodak, 2003—06, Ctr. for Global Devel., 2004—, Celanese Corp., 2004—, Nalco Co., Qcept, TRW Automotive Holdings, RAND, 2003—, mem. bd. of health, 2003—, bd. adv., 2003—, former chmn.; sr. advisor Blackstone Group, 2003—; mem. nat. bd. visitors Calif. State U., Fresno; mem. Nat. Quality Forum, 2003—. Trustee Coun. for Excellence in Govt., 2003—; bd. visitors Heinz Sch., 2004—; active Riverlife Task Force, Pitts., 2003—; bd. dirs. Gerald R. Ford Found., 1981—, chmn. fin. com. Recipient Nat. Inst. Pub. Affairs Career Edn. award, 1965, William A. Jump Meritorious award, 1971, Health Quality award, Nat. Com. Quality Assurance, 2003; Fellow Nat. Inst. Pub. Affairs, 1966. Fellow Nat. Acad. Pub. Adminstrn.; mem. Am. Acad. Arts and Sci., Nat. Acad. Social Ins. (founding mem., hon. advisor), Peterson Inst. (bd. dirs. 2003—). Republican. Methodist. Office: Ste 100 One North Shore Ctr Pittsburgh PA 15212 Home Phone: 412-683-6867; Office Phone: 412-553-1238. Personal E-mail: jceledoniapa@aol.com.

O'NEILL, PHILIP DANIEL, JR., lawyer, arbitrator, educator; b. Boston, Sept. 19, 1951; s. Philip Daniel Sr. and Alice Maureen (Driscoll) O'N.; m. Lisa G. Arrowood, June 25, 1983; children: Alexander Edwin, Sean Matthew, Madeleine Clarice. BA, Hamilton Coll., 1973; JD cum laude, Boston Coll., 1977. Bar: Mass. 1977, N.Y. 1985, R.I. 1988. Assoc. Hale and Dorr, Boston, 1977—83, ptnr., 1983—87, Edwards Angell Palmer & Dodge LLP, Boston, 1987—. Cons. Arms Control and Disarmament Agy. U.S. Dept. Def., 1983—84; adj. rsch. fellow John F. Kennedy Sch. Govt., Ctr. for Sci. and Internat. Affairs Harvard U., Cambridge, Mass., 1983—86; adj. prof. law Boston U., 1992, 2001—, Boston Coll., 1988—, Fletcher Sch. Law and Diplomacy, 2007; Nomura lectr. Harvard U. Law Sch., Cambridge, 2005; panelist in internat. and domestic legal programs; lectr. in field; arbitrator in field. Contbr. articles to profl. jours., chapters to books. Fellow Chartered Inst. Arbitrators (Eng.), Am. Bar Found., Coll. Comml. Arbitrators & Truman Project; mem. ABA (vice-chmn. nat. security and arms control com. 2002-05), Internat. Law Assn. (chmn. Am. br. arbitration com. 1985-89, rep. internat. arbitration com. 1989—), Boston Bar Assn. (chmn. internat. law sect. 1994-96, past chmn. internat. litig. and arbitration com.), Am. Soc. Internat. Law, Nat. Security Network, Truman Project (sr. fellow). Home: 11 Blackburnian Rd Lincoln MA 01773-4317 Office: Edwards Angell Palmer & Dodge LLP 111 Huntington Ave Boston MA 02199-7613

O'NEILL, ROBERT E., prosecutor; Grad., Fordham U.; JD, NY Law Sch. Prosecutor US Dist. Ct. (so. dist.) NY; joined US Dept. Justice, Tampa, 1993, chief criminal divsn. (mid. dist.) Fla., 2002—, interim US atty. (mid. dist.) Fla., 2007—08. Co-owner Four Green Fields. Independent. Office: US Attys Office 400 N Tampa St, Ste 3200 Tampa FL 33602 Office Phone: 813-247-6000. Office Fax: 813-247-6246.

O'NEILL, SALLIE BOYD, educational consultant, sculptor, small business owner; b. Ft. Lauderdale, Fla., Feb. 17, 1926; s. Howard Prindle and Sarah Frances (Clark) Boyd; m. Roger H. Noden O'Neill, July 8, 1945; children: Stephanie Ann Ballard, Ross Hopkins Noden; m. Russell R. O'Neill, Jun 30, 1967. AA, Stephens Coll., 1945. Course coord. UCLA Ext., 1960—72, specialist continuing edn. dept. human devel., acad. appointment, 1972—83; pres. Learning Adventures Inc., 1985—86; v.p., CFO Learning Network Inc., 1985—86, ednl. cons., 1986—, sculptor, 1987—. Bd. dirs. Valley Inst. Visual Art, Sherman Oaks, Calif., Everywoman's Village, Sherman Oaks, Calif., 1988—98, v.p., 1993—95; bd. dirs. Valley Inst. Visual Art, Sherman Oaks, 2004—07. Mem.: Women in Bus. (founding mem., v.p., bd. dirs. 1976—77, 1986—87), Calif. Art Club (sculpting patron), UCLA Women's Faculty Club. Democrat. Home: 15430 Longbow Dr Sherman Oaks CA 91403-4910 Business E-Mail: sallie_oneill@hotmail.com.

O'NEILL, TERRY ANNE, feminist organization executive, lawyer; 1 child. JD, Tulane U., New Orleans, 1980. Law clk. US Ct. Appeals, Chicago; atty. New Orleans; tchr. law U. Calif. Davis; prof. law Tulane U., 1989—2001; chief of staff for Duchy Trachtenberg Montgomery County Coun., Md. Mem.: Nat. Coun. Women's Orgns. (exec. dir., co-chair domestic priorities task force), NOW (membership v.p. 2001—05, pres. 2009—, pres. La. chpt., pres. New Orleans chpt., mem. nat. bd., mem. nat. racial diversity com.). Office: NOW 1100 H St NW 3rd Fl Washington DC 20005*

O'NEILL, WILLIAM LAWRENCE, retired history professor; b. Big Rapids, Mich., Apr. 18, 1935; s. John Patrick and Helen Elizabeth (Marsh) O'N.; m. Elizabeth Carol Knollmueller, Aug. 20, 1960; children: Cassandra Leigh, Catherine Lorraine. AB, U. Mich., 1957; MA, U. Calif., Berkeley, 1958, PhD, 1963. Asst. prof. history U. Colo., 1964—66; asst. prof. U. Wis., 1966—69, assoc. prof., 1969—71; prof. Rutgers U., New Brunswick, NJ, 1971—2006; ret., 2006. Vis. asst. prof. U. Pitts., 1963-64; vis. asso. prof. U. Pa., 1969-70 Author: Divorce in the Progressive Era, 1967, Everyone Was Brave: The Rise and Fall of Feminism in America, 1969, rev. and repub. as: Feminism in America: A History, 1989, Coming Apart: An Informal History of America in the 1960's, 1971, 2005, The Last Romantic: A Life of Max Eastman, 1978, 2d edit., 1991, A Better World: The Great Schism: Stalinism and the American Intellectuals, 1982, repub. as: A Better World: Stalinism and the American Intellectuals, 1989, American High: The Years of Confidence, 1945-60, 1986, A Democracy at War: America's Fight at Home and Abroad in World War II, 1993, A Bubble in Time: America During The Interwar Years, 1989-2001, 2009. Nat. Endowment Humanities fellow, 1979-80 Mem.: Hist. Soc. Office: Rutgers U Dept History New Brunswick NJ 08903 Personal E-mail: wlohp@aol.com.

O'NEILL, WILLIAM M. (BILL O'NEILL), former appellate judge; m. Shaylah O'Neill (dec.); 4 children. BJ, Ohio U., 1969; JD, Cleve. State U. John Marshall Sch. Law. Reporter Sandusky Register, Sta. WLW-T Channel 4; comm. dir. Ohio Civil Svc. Employees Assn.; asst. dir. Comm. Workers America AFL-CIO; asst. atty. gen. State of Ohio; RN, pediat. emergency dept. Hillcrest Hosp.; appellate judge 11th Dist. Ct. of Appeals, Ohio, 1997—2007. Candidate Ohio Supreme Ct., 2004, 06. 2nd lt. US Army, Vietnam, lt. col. US Army Nat. Guard, ret., 2001. Decorated Bronze Star, Army Commendation Medal, Humanitarian Svc.award. Democrat. Mailing: PO Box 601 Chagrin Falls OH 44022

O'NEILL, WILLIAM PATRICK, lawyer; b. Joplin, Mo., Sept. 14, 1951; s. Fred Charles and Dorothy Isabel (Snyder) O'N.; m. Mary Louise Richardson, June 17, 1989. BA, U. Kans., 1973; JD, U. Mich., 1976. Bar: Ill. 1976, U.S. Dist. Ct. (no. dist.) Ill. 1976, U.S. Dist. Ct. D.C. 1982. Assoc. Kirkland & Ellis, Chgo., 1976-81, Sidley & Austin, Chgo., 1982-85, Skadden, Arps, Slate, Meagher & Flom, NYC, 1986-87, Crowell & Moring, Washington, 1987-88, ptnr., 1988—2000, Latham & Watkins, 2001—. Gen. counsel Ill. Common Cause, Chgo., 1979-81. Editor, author: (with others) Successfully Acquiring A U.S. Business, 1990; editorial chmn. Antitrust Law Jour., 1984-89. Mem. University Club of Chgo. Office: Latham & Watkins 555 11th St NW Washington DC 20004-2595 Business E-Mail: williamoneill@lw.com.

O'NEILL, WILLIAM WALTER, dean, cardiologist, educator; b. Nov. 24, 1951; BS, U. Mich., 1972; MD, Wayne State U., 1977. Diplomate Am. Bd. Internal Medicine, Am. Bd. Cardiology. Intern internal medicine U. Wis., Madison, 1977—78; resident internal medicine Wayne State U., Detroit, 1978—80; fellow U. Mich., Ann Arbor, 1980-82, instr. internal medicine, 1982-83, asst. prof., 1983-86, assoc. prof., 1986-87; dir. cardiac catheterization lab. U. Mich. Hosp., Ann Arbor, 1984-87; dir. divsn. cardiovascular disease William Beaumont Hosp., Royal Oak, Troy, Mich., 1987—2006, corp. chief cardiology, 2002—06, vice chair Dept. Internal Medicine for Rsch., 2003; co-dir. Beaumont Heart Ctr., 1999—2006; prof. medicine, exec. dean clin. affairs Miller Sch. Medicine, U. Miami, 2006—. Attending cardiologist VA Hosp., Ann Arbor, 1982-90; chmn. govt. rels. subcom. Nat. Cardiovasc. Network; rsch. peer rev. com. Am. Heart Assn. Mich., 1988-89; chmn. publs. com. Mansfield Scientific Balloon Valvuloplasty Registry; bd. govs. William Beaumont Hosp. Rsch. Inst.; presenter in field. Author: Myocardial Revascularization by Coronary Angioplasty or Bypass Surgery During MI in Acute Myocardial Infarction: New Approaches to Evaluation and Therapy, 1986, (chpt.) Acute Coronary Intervention, 1987, Current Perspective in Coronary Care, 1987, Interventional Cardiovascular Medicine, 1994, Acute Coronary Care, 2d edit., 1995; co-author: (chpts.) Cardiovascular Review, 6th edit., 1985, 8th edit., 1987, Tissue Plasminogen Activator in Thrombolytic Therapy, 1987, Techniques and Applications in Interventional Cardiology, 1991, Atherectomy, 1992, Emergency Medicine: A Comprehensive Study Guide, 3d edit., 1992, Adjunctive Therapy for Acute Myocardial Infarction, 1992, Manual of Interventional CArdiology, 1992, Cura Intensiva Cardiologica, Primary Coronary Angioplasty in Acute Myocardial Infarction; author, co-author: (chpt.) Interventional Cardiovascular Medicine, 1994; editl. cons. Jour. Intervention Cardiology; mem. editl. bd. Catheterization Cardiovasc. Diagnosis; contbr. over 400 articles to profl. publs. Grantee Smith/Kline Beecham, 1989-90, 90—, Advanced Cardiovasc. Sys., Inc., 1988-90, 90—, Midwest Heart Rsch. Found., Abbott Labs., 1990—, Duke U., 1990—, William Beaumont Hosp. Rsch. Inst., 1990—. Fellow Am. Coll. Cardiology (chpt. sec.-treas. 1993-94, reimbursement com.), Am. Coll. Chest Physicians, Coun. Clin. Cardiology; mem. AMA, ACP, Internat. Andreas Gruentzig Soc. Office: U Miami / Divsn Cardiology RMSB 1122A 1600 NW 10th Ave Miami FL 33136 Office Phone: 305-243-9483. E-mail: woneill@med.miami.edu.

O'NEIL MUNDINGER, MARY, nursing educator; MA, Columbia U., 1974, DrPH, 1981. Dean Columbia U. Sch. Nursing, 1986—, prof. health policy. Bd. mem. Cell Therapeutics Inc., 1997—, UnitedHealth Group, 1997—, Gentiva, 2002—, Welch Allyn Inc, 2002—. Mem.: NY Acad. of Medicine, Inst. of Medicine, Am. Acad. Nursing. Office: 617 W 168 St Rm 129 New York NY 10032 Office Phone: 212-305-3582. Office Fax: 212-305-1116. E-mail: mm44@columbia.edu.*

ONEK, JOSEPH NATHAN, lawyer; b. NYC, Jan. 9, 1942; s. Jacob J. and Doris (Aaronson) O.; m. Margot Debrah Piore, June 29, 1963; children: David, Matthew. A.B. magna cum laude, Harvard Coll., 1962; M.A., London Sch. Econs., 1964; LL.B. magna cum laude, Yale Law Sch., 1967. Bar: DC 1968. Law clk. to chief judge David L. Bazelon, US

Ct. Appeals (DC cir.), 1967-68; law clk. Justice William J. Brennan, US Supreme Ct., 1968-69; staff Senate Adminstrv. Practice and Procedure Subcom., Senate Labor and Pub. Welfare Commn., 1969-71; dir., atty. Ctr. for Law and Social Policy, 1971-76; adj. prof. U. Md. Law Sch., Health Care Law, 1976-77; dir. health policy analysis Carter-Mondale Transition Planning Group, 1976-77; assoc. dir. for health and human resources Domestic Policy Staff, White House, 1977-79; dep. counsel to Pres., White House, 1979-81; ptnr. Onek, Klein & Farr, Washington, 1981-91; ptnr. Crowell & Moring, 1991—; presdl. appointee to DC Jud. Nominating Com., 1994—; prin. dep. assoc. atty. gen. US Dept. Justice, 1997-99; sr. coord. Rule of Law US Dept. State, 1999—. Marshall scholar, 1962. Mem. ABA, Phi Beta Kappa. Home: 3723 Ingomar St NW Washington DC 20015-1819

ONES, DENIZ S., psychologist, educator; b. Istanbul, Turkey, Aug. 12, 1965; d. Somer and Ulker (Saime) Ones; m. Ates Haner, July 5, 1993; 1 child, Daria M. Haner. BA, Augustana Coll., 1988; PhD, U. Iowa, 1993. Asst. prof. U. Houston, 1993—96; Hellervik Prof. indsl. psychology U. Minn., Mpls., 1996—; founder Thetametrics LLP, Maple Grove, Minn., 2004—. Author: Handbook of Industrial, Work and Organizational Psychology. Recipient Cattell Award for Outstanding Early Career Contbns., Soc. of Multivariate Exptl. Psychology, 2003, Ernest J. McCormick Award for Disting. Early Career Contbns., Soc. for Indsl. and Orgnl. Psychology, 1998; Fellow of Divsn. 14 (Indsl. and Orgnl. Psychology), APA, 1999, Fellow of Divsn. 5 (Measurement, Stats., and Evaluation), 1998. Achievements include research in meta-analyses of integrity tests, managerial selection, police selection, employment testing. Office: Thetametrics LLP 6427 Ranchview Ln N Maple Grove MN 55311 E-mail: ones@thetametrics.com.

ONESTI, SILVIO JOSEPH, psychiatrist; b. San Francisco, Jan. 3, 1926; s. Silvio Joseph and Johanna (Kristoffy) Onesti; m. Jean Thomas, May 12, 1956; children: Sally Joanna, Stephen Thomas. BS, Stanford U., 1947; MD, McGill U., 1951. Diplomate Am. Bd. Psychiatry and Neurology. Instr. pediatrics Yale Med. Sch., New Haven, 1956-58; career tchr. psychiatry NIMH, Harvard Med. Sch., Beth Israel Hosp., Boston, 1963-65; head child psychiatry unit Beth Israel Hosp., Boston, 1965-73; dir. child and adolescent psychiatry McLean Hosp., Belmont, Mass., 1973-91, dir. Hall-Mercer Ctr. for children and adolescents, 1973-91; dir. child and adolescent psychiat. tng., 1973-92; dir. clin. svcs. McLean Hosp., Belmont, 1981-83; asst. prof. psychiatry Harvard Med. Sch., Boston, 1969—. Contbr. articles to profl. jours. With USN, 1944—46. Fellow: Am. Coll. Psychiatrists, Am. Acad. Child and Adolescent Psychiatry, Am. Psychiat. Assn.; mem.: Mass. Med. Soc., Boston Psychoanalytic Soc. and Inst. (faculty 1971—81), Group Advancement Psychiatry (bd. dirs. 1987—89, fellow 1959—61), Alpha Omega Alpha. Home: 4 Gray Gdns W Cambridge MA 02138-2312 Office: McLean Hosp 115 Mill St Belmont MA 02478-1048 Home Phone: 617-354-3704; Office Phone: 617-855-2801.

ONG, BRUCE NELSON, communication skills consultant; b. Elkhart, Ind., Oct. 31, 1950; s. Richard and Mary Alice (Glace) O.; m. Joanne Marie Bruschi, Aug. 11, 1979; 1 child, Christopher. BA, Wabash Coll., 1973, Oxford U., Eng., 1975, MA, 1980; PhD, U. Va., 1985. Assoc. prof. politics Coll. New Rochelle, N.Y., 1980—, chair divsn. social scis. N.Y., 1992—. Comm. specialist Booz, Allen & Hamilton, N.Y.C., 1986-91, Profl. Devel. Internat., New Rochelle, 1992—. Mem. Nat. Assn. Scholars (nat. sec. 1989—, bd. dirs. 1989—), Am. Polit. Sci. Assn., Intercollegiate Studies Inst. (faculty assoc.). Office: Profl Devel Internat 157 Liberty Ave New Rochelle NY 10805-2303 Personal E-mail: nelson.ong@verizon.net.

ONG, HAN CHUAN, biology professor; b. Georgetown, Penang, Malaysia, Apr. 29, 1977; s. Shin Tiad Ong and Sew Bee Loi; m. Laura Elizabeth Ong, Sept. 28, 2002; 1 child, Noah Ting-Wei. BA, Wabash Coll., Crawfordsville, Ind., 2000; PhD, Ind. U., Bloomington, 2006. Postdoc. rschr. U. Wash., Seattle, 2006—07; asst. prof. biology Lyon Coll., Batesville, Ark., 2007—09. Contbr. articles to profl. jours. publs. Advisor Zeta Beta Tau frat., Batesville, 2007—09; asst. coach Kiwanis Youth Football League, Batesville, Ark., 2007—09; singer Bloomington Chamber Singers, Ind., 2004—06, Batesville Choral Soc., Ark., 2007—09; educator Northctrl. Ark. HS Sci. Tchrs., Batesville, 2008—09. Genome Tng. grant, NIH, 2006—07, Rsch. Infrastructure grant, NASA Space Grant Consortium, 2008—09. Mem.: Soc. Molecular Biology & Evolution. Achievements include discovery of long-term survival of pseudogenes in mitochondrial genoms.

ONG, JOHN DOYLE, former ambassador, retired manufacturing executive; b. Uhrichsville, Ohio, Sept. 29, 1933; s. Louis Brosee and Mary Ellen (Liggett) O.; m. Mary Lee Schupp, July 20, 1957; children: John Francis Harlan, Richard Penn Blackburn, Mary Katherine Caine. BA, MA, Ohio State U., 1954; LLB, Harvard, 1957; LHD, Kent State U., 1982; HHD (hon.), Ohio State U., 1996; LHD (hon.), U. Akron, 1996; D in pub. svc. (hon.), SD State U., 2002. Bar: Ohio 1958. Asst. counsel B.F. Goodrich Co., Akron, 1961-66, group v.p., 1972-73, exec. v.p., 1973-74, vice chmn., 1974-75, pres., dir., 1975-77, pres., COO, 1978-79, chmn. bd., pres., CEO, 1979-84, chmn. bd., CEO, 1984-96, chmn. bd., 1996-97, chmn. emeritus, 1997—; US amb. to Norway Oslo, 2002—05. Chmn. Bus. Roundtable, Washington, 1992—94; mem. Ohio Bus. Roundtable, Columbus, Ohio, 1994—97. V.p. exploring Great Trail coun. Boy Scouts Am., 1974-77; bd. dirs. Nat. Alliance of Bus., 1981-94, chmn., 1984-86, 91; trustee Mus. Arts Assn., Cleve., 1975-, chmn., 1995-2002; Bexley Hall Sem., 1974-81, Case Western Res. U., 1980-92, Ft. Ligonier Assn., 1997-, Kenyon Coll., 1983-85, Hudson Libr. and Hist. Soc., Ohio, trustee, 1967-80, pres., 1971-72, Western Res. Acad., Hudson, 1975-95, pres. bd. trustees, 1977-95; nat. trustee Nat. Symphony Orch., 1975-83, John S. and James L. Knight Found., 1995-2002; mem. bus. adv. com. Transp. Ctr. Northwestern U., 1975-78, Carnegie-Mellon U. Grad. Sch. Indsl. Adminstrn., 1978-83; life trustee U. Chgo., 1991—; chmn. Ohio Bus. Roundtable, 1994-97; trustee Ohio Hist. Soc., 1998-2002; dir. New Amn. Schs., 1991, chmn., 1998-2002. Mem. RTI Internat. (sr. vis. policy fellow, 2006-), Ohio Bar Assn. (bd. govs. corp. counsel sect. 1962-74, chmn. 1970), Rubber Mfrs. Assn. (bd. dirs. 1974-84), Chem. Mfrs. Assn. (bd. dirs. 1988-91, 94-97), Conf. Bd., Coun. Ret. Chief Execs., Coun. Am. Ambs., Bohemian Club, Chagrin Valley Hunt Club, Portage Country Club, Rowfant Club, Union Club, Links, Union League, Ottawa Shooting Club, Met. Club, Rolling Rock Club, Castalia Trout Club, Phi Beta Kappa, Phi Alpha Theta. Episcopalian. Office Phone: 330-665-3830.

ONGKINGCO, FLORENCE KAGAHASTIAN, health facility educator; b. Laguna, The Philippines, July 29, 1945; d. Leopoldo Kagahastian and Cresenciana Quesada; m. Prospero Ongkingeo, July 10, 1976; 1 child Michelle Ann. Diploma in nursing with honors, Philippine Gen. Hosp. Sch. Nursing, 1966; BSN, U. Philippines, 1967; MA in Nursing, NYU, 1975; cert. in computer programming, Queens Computer Coll., 1986. RN, N.Y.; cert. profl. in healthcare quality. Supr., clin. instr. Operations Brotherhood, Vientiane, Laos; team leader NYU Med. Ctr., NYC; coord. nursing care Luth. Med. Ctr.; clin. instr. Queens Hosp. Ctr., Jamaica, N.Y.; dir. staff devel. St. John's Queen's Hosp., Elmhurst, N.Y.; dir. quality assurance and staff devel. Westchester Sq. Med. Ctr., Bronx, N.Y.; dir. nursing edn., staff devel. Booth Meml. Med. Ctr., Flushing, NY; dir. Edn. Cabrini Ctr. for Nursing and Rehab., NYC; nurse educator Stern Family Ctr. for Extended Care and Rehab., Manhasset, NY. Mgmt. devel., workshop leader nursing process and nursing standards; amb. to Nursing Spectrum; presenter in field. Producer, dir. slide-tape program, video program in field. Mem. Ednl. Assn. Hartford Inst. for Geriatric Nursing, Internat. Honor Soc. of Nursing, Sigma Theta Tau.

ONISHI, ANNA TOKIKO, marketing professional; b. Richland, Wash., July 28, 1975; d. Yasuo and Esther Anna Onishi. BA, Smith Coll., 1997. CFA. Sr. rsch. assoc. Fidelity Investments, Merrimack, NH, 1997—2000; sr. analyst Digitas, Boston, 2000—04; exec. dir. rsch. and mktg. strategy Legal Sea Foods, 2004—06; v.p., dir. strategic analysis Muller Advertising, 2006—09; mgr. Web Analytics Liberty Mutual, 2009—. Mem. at large N.H. bd. dirs. Girls Inc., Nashua, 1999—2000; asst. fund agt. class of 1997 Smith Coll. Alumnae, Northampton, Mass., 1999—2002, spl. gifts chair class of 1997, 2002—; bd. mem. Boston Smith Coll. Club, 2009—. Mem.: Assn. Investment Mgmt. and Rsch. Avocations: crew, running, sailing, skiing, volunteering. Office: Liberty Mutual Group personal Maarkets 175 Berkeley St 02H Boston MA 02116

ONISHI, DEIDRE, theater educator, director; d. Raymond John and Doloros Ann (Bowman) Lammers; children: Kosuke Jacob, Genji Thomas, Kengo McKinley. BA in Asian Studies, Carleton Coll., Northfield, Minn., 1979; MA in Theatre and Drama, U. Hawaii-Manoa, Oahu, 1981; MPhill in Theatre and Film, Columbia U., NYC, 1987; PhD in Theatre and Drama, U. Wis.-Madison, 2007. Asst. prof., head drama program Ching I Coll., Taichung, Taiwan, 1981—83; adj. instr. Doshisha Tanki U., Tanabe, Kyoto-fu, Japan, 1987—88, Shukugawa Coll., Kobe, Japan, 1987—88; instr. writing program and ESL program Elmira Coll., NY, 1999—2001, head ESL program, 2001—02, adj. instr. theatre and drama, 2004—05; vis. tchg. fellow dept. theatre and dance Colby Coll., Waterville, Maine, 2005—06; vis. instr. dept. humanities U. Minn., Morris, 2007—08. Dir. theatre maj. Czech Internat. Music Camp Youth, Horni Jeleni, 2001—; musical theatre dir. Blue Lake Fine Arts Camp, Twin Lake, Mich., 2008—. Dir.: (noho theatre group) Naucht und Traume; actor: (performance) Rokumeikan, Susigigawa; composer: (performance) The Soul Shall Dance. Brander Mathews fellowship, Columbia U., 1984—85. Mem.: Internat. Assn. Theater Children and Young People, Am. Soc. Theatre Rsch. Home: 316 Fall Creek Dr Ithaca NY 14850 Business E-Mail: daonishi@wisc.edu.

ONISHI, LISA, chemical engineer, researcher; b. Richland, Wash., Aug. 14, 1978; d. Yasuo and Esther Onishi. BS in Chem. Engring., U. Wash., Seattle, 2000; attending, U. Calif. Berkeley, 2009. Principle engr. UTC Fuel Cells, South Windsor, Conn., 2000—03. Contbr. articles to profl. jours. Com. mem. United Way UTC Fuel Cells, 2001—02. Recipient award, Golden Key Internat. Honor Soc., Most Popular Poster Presentation award, Gorden Rsch. Conf., 2002, Outstanding Performance award, UTC Fuel Cells, 2002, Achievement award, 2003. Mem.: AIChE, Soc. of Women engrs., Am. Chem. Soc., Electrochem. Soc. Achievements include resolving a 104 year old thermodynamic paradox called Schroeder's Paradox. Office: Univ California Berkeley 301B Gilman Hall Berkeley CA 94720 Mailing: PO Box 4337 Berkeley CA 94704

ONISKO, BRUCE CHARLES, mass spectroscopist; b. Erie, Pa., June 24, 1951; s. Anthony Andrew and Dorothy (Merschrod) O. BS in Chemistry, Case Western Res. U., 1973; PhD in Biochemistry, U. Wis., 1978. NRC postdoctoral fellow Ames Research Ctr., Mountain View, Calif., 1979-81; prin. rsch. chemist Zeneca, Inc., Richmond, Calif., 1981—. Contbr. articles to profl. jours.; patentee in field. Mem. Am. Chem. Soc., Am. Soc. Mass Spectrometry, Bay Area Mass Spectrometry. Avocations: bicycling, swimming, baritone. Home: 330 Berkeley Park Blvd Kensington CA 94707-1239 Office: Zeneca Inc 1200 S 47th St Richmond CA 94804-4610

ONLEY, SISTER FRANCESCA, academic administrator; Prin. Nazareth Acad. H.S.; asst. to pres. Holy Family U., Phila., 1980—81, pres., 1981—. Chair Internat. Assn. of U. Pres., UN Commn. on Disarmament Edn., Conflict Resolution and Peace. Office: Holy Family U Office of Pres 9801 Frankford Ave Philadelphia PA 19114 Office Phone: 215-637-7700 3220. E-mail: fonley@holyfamily.edu.

ONN, AMIR, medical educator, researcher; b. Rehovot, Israel, Nov. 19, 1959; arrived in U.S., 2000; s. Itzhak and Nitza Onn; m. Elizabeth E. Half, July 18, 1989; children: Lior, Dana, Alon, Yuval. BA, Hebrew U., Jersalem, MD, 1990. Intern Tel-Aviv Med. Ctr., Tel Aviv Sch. Medicine, resident internal medicine, fellow pulmonary medicine; postdoctoral fellow U. Tex. MD Anderson Cancer Ctr., Houston, fellow interventional pulmonary oncology; asst. prof. medicine and cancer biology U. Tex. M.D. Anderson Cancer Ctr., Houston, 2000—. Recipient Physician Scientist award, U. Tex. MD Anderson Cancer Ctr., 2004—. Home: 4926 N Braeswood Blvd Houston TX 77096-2708 Office Fax: 713-794-4922; Home Fax: 713-729-8700. Business E-Mail: amironn@mdanderson.org.

ONNE, MADELEINE, performing company executive, dancer; b. Stockholm, Sept. 9, 1960; married; 2 children. Mem. co. Royal Swedish Ballet, 1978—81, dance soloist, 1981, prin. dancer, 1984—2002, artistic dir., 2002—08; appointed Royal Ct. dancer Sweden, 1996; founder, dir. Stockholm 59 Degrees North, 1996—2002; artistic dir. Hong Kong Ballet, 2009—. Recipient Litteris et Artibus Royal medal, The Royal Palace, Stockholm, 1999, Gold medal of honor, Royal Swedish Opera House, 2009. Office: Hong Kong Ballet G/F 60 Blue Pool Rd Happy Valley Hong Kong Office Phone: 852-2723 1640. Business E-Mail: madeleine_onne@hkballet.com.*

ONO, SANTA JEREMY, immunologist, educator, administrator; b. Vancouver, BC, Can., Nov. 23, 1962; came to U.S., 1964; s. Takashi Ono and Sachiko Morita; m. Gwendolyn H. Yip, Aug. 12, 1989; 1 child, Juliana Miwa Yip-Ono. BA in Biology, U. Chgo., 1984; PhD in Exptl. Medicine, McGill U., 1990. Rsch. assoc. Harvard U., Cambridge, Mass., 1990-92, assoc. prof., 1996—; asst. prof. Johns Hopkins U., Balt., 1992-96; dir. immunity, inflammation and transplantation Schepens Eye Rsch. Inst., Boston, 1998—; immunologist Brigham and Women's Hosp., Boston, 1999—; Cumberlege prof. biomed. sci., head dept. immunology Univ. Coll., U. London, Inst. Ophthalmology, 2001—. Sci. advisor Santen Pharm. Corp., Nara, Japan, 1999—; vis. prof. Japan Soc. for Promotion of Sci., Kyoto, 1997; panel mem. Arthritis Found., Cellular Immunology Study Sect., 1998-00. Assoc. editor Jour. Immunology, Bethesda, Md., 1999—; editor Jour. Leukocyte Biology, 2000—; mem. editl. bd. Jour. Allergy and Clin. Immunology, 2001—; contbr. articles to profl. jours. Recipient Pharmacia Internat. award in allergy rsch. Pharmacia Rsch. Found., 1998, Career Devel. award Am. Diabetes Assn., 1993-95, Helen Hay Whitney award Whitney Found., 1989-92, Investigator award Nat. Arthritis Found., 1993, Roche award in rsch. Roche Pharms., 1988; inductee life mem. Collegium Internationale Allergologicum, 2000. Home: 7 Blueberry Ln Sharon MA 02067-1004 Office: Harvard Med Sch SERI 20 Staniford St Boston MA 02114-2508 Fax: (617) 912-0127. E-mail: sjono@vision.eri.harvard.edu.

ONO, YOKO, conceptual artist, singer, recording artist; b. Tokyo, Feb. 18, 1933; U.S. citizen; m. Toshi Ichiyanagi, 1956 (div. 1962); m. Tony Cox, Nov. 28, 1962 (annulled March 1, 1963), remarried, June 6, 1963 (div. Feb. 2, 1969) children: Kyoko Chan; m. John Ono Lennon, Mar. 20, 1969 (dec. Dec. 8, 1980); 1 child, Sean Taro, 1 stepchild, Julian; m. Sam Havadtoy, 1981,(separated 2002) Student, Peers' Sch., Gakushuin U., Tokyo, Sarah Lawrence Coll., Harvard U.; PhD (hon.), Art Inst. Of Chicago, 1997, Liverpool U., 2001, Bard College, 2002. One-woman shows include Alchemical Wedding, Albert Hall, London, 1967, Evening with Yoko Ono, Birmingham, 1968, Event, U. Wales, 1969, Everson Mus., Syracuse, N.Y., 1971, Yoko Ono: Objects, Films, Whitney Museum of Amer. Art, 1989, Yoko Ono: A Piece of Sky, Galleria Stefania Miscetti, Rome, 1993, Endangered Species, Wacoal Art Center/Spiral Garden, Tokyo, 1993, Yoko Ono and Fluxus, Royal Festival Hall, South Bank Centre, London, 1997, Have You Seen The Horizon Lately?, Museum Of Modern Art, Oxford, 1997, Open Window, Umm El-Fahem, Israel, 2000, YES Yoko Ono, Japan Society, 2001, My Mommy Was Beautiful, Shoshana Wayne Gallery, Santa Monica, 2002, Yoko Ono Women's Room, Musée d'Art moderne de la Ville de Paris, 2003, Yoko Ono: Odyssey of a Cockroach, Inst. Contemporary Arts, London, 2004, Imagine Peace, 2007, Yoko Ono, Gemalde/Paintings, 2008, Kunsthalle Bremen, 2007; group shows include Fluxshoe, Sch. Art, Falmouth, Cornwall, Eng., 1972, Liverpool Biennial Contemporary Art, 2004, Techniques of the Visible, Shanghai 5 Biennial, 2004, Do You Believe in Reality? Taipei Biennial, 2004, At the Mercy of Others: The Politics of Care, Whitney Mus. Am. Art, 2005, Experiencing Duration, Biennale de Lyon, 2005, Looking at Words, Andrea Rosen Gallery, NY, 2005, To the Human Furture, Flight from the Dark Side, Art Tower, Mito ATM, Mito, The Expanded Eye, Kunsthaus, Zurich, 2006; (albums with John Ono Lennon) Two Virgins, 1968, Life With Lions, 1969, Wedding Album, 1970, Live Peace in Toronto (1969), 1970, Some Time in New York City, 1972, Double Fantasy, 1980 (Grammy award Album of Yr., 1982), Milk and Honey, 1984); (solo albums) Yoko Ono Plastic Ono Band, 1970, Fly, 1971, Approximately Infinite Universe, 1973, Feeling the Space, 1973, Welcome: The Many Sides Of Yoko Ono, 1973, Season of Glass, 1981, It's Alright (I See Rainbows), 1982, Every Man Has A Woman, 1984, Starpeace, 1985, Walking On Thin Ice, 1992, Rising, 1995, New York Rock, 1995, Rising Mixes, 1996, Blueprint For A Sunrise, 2001, Yes, I'm a Witch, 2007, Open Your Box, 2007; co-prodr. Gimme Some Truth - The Making Of John Lennon's Imagine Album, 2001 (Grammy award best long form music video, 2001); exec. prodr. Come Together: A Night for John Lennon's Words & Music, 2001; composer numerous songs including Don't Worry Kyoko, Mummy's Only Looking for her Hand in the Snow, Walking on Thin Ice (Grammy award nomination Best Female Rock Performance on Single 1981), Don't Be Sad; author: Grapefruit, 1964, A Hole to See the Sky Through, 1971, Just Me! (Tada No Atashi), 1986, Sometime In New York City, 1995, Acorns, 1996,; author 6 film scripts, Tokyo, 1964, 13 film scores, London, 1967, John & Yoko Calendar, 1970; appeared in (documentaries) Let it Be, 1970, Imagine: John Lennon, 1988, The Rolling Stones Rock and Roll Circus, 1996 Recipient Helen Caldicott leadership award, 1987, Skowhegan award, 2002, Lifespire award, 2002, MOCA award, 2003, Artist award for Disting. Body of Work, Coll. Art Assn., 2008. Office: c/o John Hendricks 488 Greenwich St New York NY 10013-1313*

ONOCHIE, FLORENCE N., accountant; b. Lagos, Nigeria, Apr. 27, 1961; arrived in U.S., 1987; d. Francis Wilcock E. and Mary Nwamaka E. Okolo; m. Henry Chuks Onochie; children: Chuks, Chizo, Kosi, Ndo's, Kenn. Degree in Fin., U. Tech. Enugu, Nigeria, 1985; BS in Acctg., U. Indpls., 1991. Reconciler Peoples Bank and Trust Co., Indpls., 1988—92; field examiner Ind. State Bd. Accounts, Indpls., 1992—94; acct., pres. HCO, Inc., Indpls., 1992—2001; auditor RGIS, Indpls., 1993—94; reconciler Bank One, Indpls., 1994; acct., pres. FNO, Inc., Indpls., 2001—. Mem. Inst. Bus. Fin. and Estate Planning. Former v.p. Rotary Club Nigeria; bd. mem. Profl. Womens Adv. Bd., Indpls., 2000. Named Woman of Yr., 2000, 2004. Mem.: NAFE, Greater Indpls. C. of C., Ind. Assn. Black Accts., Nat. Assn. Black Accts. (v.p. 2005—), Ind. Soc. Pub. Accts., Nat. Assn. Pub. Accts. Home: 8836 Worthington Cir Indianapolis IN 46278 Office: FNO Profl Svcs Inc Ste 130 3921 N Meridian St Indianapolis IN 46278 Office Phone: 317-872-3437.

ONOFRE-MADRID, MARIA DE LOS SANTOS, language educator; d. Jose Isabel and Rosa Elia Onofre; m. Arturo Madrid, July 28, 1990; 1 child, Eliamaria Madrid-Onofre. BA, Angelo State U., San Angelo, Tex., 1976; MA, U. Tex., Arlington, 1978; ABD, U. Tex., Austin, 1984. Grad. tchg. asst. U. Tex., Arlington, 1976—78; instr. Spanish Angelo State U., 1978—80, asst. instr. Spanish, 1984—, U. Tex., 1980—84. Coord. Mex. exch. program Internat. Studies, San Angelo, 2001—; faculty advisor Ctr. Academic Excellence, San Angelo, 2005—. Contbr. articles to profl. jours. Vol. Rape Crisis Svcs., San Angelo, 1988—91, Teencapp, San Angelo, 1989—91; vol., presented program Spanish media Child Assault Prevention Project, San Angelo, 1989—91; lit. tutor Adult Lit. Coun., San Angelo, 1989—91; cmty. vol. Jefferson Award Com., 1990; mentor San Angelo ISD Mentor Program, 1993—96; parent vol., jr. troop 245 adult sponsor El Camino Girl Scouts, San Angelo, 1997—2003; vol. Ct. Apptd. Spl. Adv., San Angelo, 2003—05; lector, mem. St. Mary's Cath. Ch., San Angelo, 1973—; min. word and eucharistic min. Cath. Newman Ctr., Angelo State U., 1984—; bd. mem. Concho Educators Fed. Credit Union, San Angelo, 1991—2000; dir. San Angelo Schs. Found., San Angelo, 1994—98; freshman mentor Angelo State Univ.'s Retention and Mgmt. Sys., San Angelo, 1994—95; mem., coord., pres. Bowie Elem. Sch. PTA, San Angelo, 1998—2004. Recipient Twenty-Five Yr. Svc. award, Angelo State U., 2007. Mem.: Tex. Assn. Chicanos Higher Edn., Tex. Assn. Coll. and U. Lang. Supervisors, Rotary Internat. (mem., Profl. Women Group Study Exch. 1988), Kappa Delta Pi (San Angelo), Alpha Chi, Alpha Mu Gamma, Sigma Delta Pi (faculty sponsor 1997—).

ONOKPISE, OGHENEKOME UKRAKPO, agronomist, educator, forester, geneticist; b. Lagos, Nigeria, May 10, 1951; came to U.S., 1981; s. Jerome Esagwu and Margaret E. (Agbanobi) O.; m. Lucy Omotaka Edemo, Jan. 31, 1977; children: Oghenemaro, Omurhu, Oghogho, Onoriode. BS, U. Ife, Ile-Ife, Nigeria, 1974; MS, U. Guelph, Ont., Can., 1980; PhD, Iowa State U., 1984. Tutor Sch. Agrl., Yandev, Nigeria, 1974—75; rsch. officer Rubber Rsch. Inst. Nigeria, Benin City, 1975—81; rsch. asst. Iowa State U., Ames, 1981—85; rschr. Ohio State U., Wooster, 1985—86; asst. prof. Fla. A&M U., Tallahassee, 1986—91, assoc. prof., 1991—94, prof., 1994—. Mem. Germplasm Collection Team Internat. Rubber R&D Bd. London, Eng. in Brazil, 1981; team leader Cocoyam Breeding Team USAID, Cameroon, Republic of West Africa, 1988-90, coord. weed control project, Ghana, 1996—; sabbatical leave Inst. Forest Genetics and Tree Breeding U. Gottingen, Germany, 2002; faculty exch. program U. Nat. Resources and Applied Life Scis., Vienna, 2007; faculty exchange visitor U. Boku, Vienna. Author: Growing Up: Tony Joins the System, 2004; contbr. articles to Commonwealth Forestry Rev. Jour., Annals Applied Biology, Plant Breeding,

Acta Agronomca, Seed Sci. and Tech., African Jour. Genetics, Am. Jour. Enology and Viticulture, Indian Jour. Plant Breeding and Genetics, Silvae Genetica, Agronomie, Jour. Plantation Crops, African Tech. Forum, Women in Natural Resources Jour., Natural Resources, Salem Press, Restoration Ecology, Internat. Jour. Tropical Agr., Econ. Botany, West African Jour. Applied Ecology, 2006; Jour. Environ. Monitoring Restoration, 2007; Am.-Eurasian Jour. Agrl. Environ. Sci., 2007; Fla. Entomologist, 2007; African Jour. Biotech., 2008. Editor Pack 104 Club Scouts Newsletter, Boy Scouts Am., Tallahassee, 1986-88; mem. Parish Coun. St. Louis Parish, Tallahassee, 1987-88; tutor Bapt. H.S., Buea, Cameroon, 1988-89; mem. choir St. Louis Cath. Ch., 1991—. Recipient Sci. Paper award Assn. Rsch. Dirs., Washington, 1987, Stephen Spurr award Fla. Divsn. Soc. Am. Foresters, 2008; named Best Agrl. Instr., Agrl. Sci. Club FAMU Students, Tallahassee, 1988, 93; grantee USAID-FAMU, Cameroon, 1988-90, NASA-Fla. A&M U., 1988-91, Internat. Paper Co., 1994, USAID-Fla. A&M U.-U. Fla., Ghana, 1996-98, USDA-Fgn. Agrl. Svcs.-Fla. A&M U., Ghana, 1998—, USDA-Rsch. and Sci. Exch. Divsn.-Fla. A&M U., Ghana, 1999—; German Acad. Faculty Exch. fellow, 2002. Fellow Indian Soc. Genetics and Plant Breeding; mem. Am. Soc. Agronomy, Commonwealth Forestry Assn., Soc. of Am. Foresters (campus faculty rep., diversity com.). Achievements include development of concepts of moving forest for the tropical rain forest; growth of carrots in hydroponic system within growth chambers, inbreeding depression in polyploids with emphasis on forages; biological control of invasive species using native species, Gonts in silvopastoral systems. Home: 2810 Kennesaw Pl Tallahassee FL 32303-1202 Office: Fla A&M U Martin Luther King Blvd Tallahassee FL 32307 Office Phone: 850-561-2217. E-mail: o.onokpise@worldnet.att.net, oghenekome.onokpise@famu.edu.

ONORATO, NICHOLAS LOUIS, retired program director, economist; b. South Barre, Mass., Feb. 24, 1925; s. Charles and Amalia (Tartaglia) O.; m. Elizabeth Louise Settergren, July 19, 1947; children: Gary, Deborah, Nicholas, Jeffrey, Glenn, Charles (dec.), Lisa. Assoc., Becker Jr. Coll., Worcester, Mass., 1949; BS in Pub. Rels., Boston U., Mass., 1951; MA in Econs, Clark U., Worcester, Mass., 1952, PhD, 1959. Mem. faculty Becker Jr. Coll., Worcester, Mass., 1952-54; prof. econs. Worcester Poly. Inst., 1955-68, chmn. dept. econs., govt., bus., 1968-74, dir. Sch. Indsl. Mgmt., 1972-99; prof. emeritus Worcester (Mass.) Poly Inst., 1994. Vis. prof. Clark U., Worcester, 1964-66; fin. cons. Coz Chem. Co., Northbridge, Mass., 1959-95. Contbr. to newspapers and mags. Trustee Bay State Savs. Bank, Worcester. Served with USNR, 1943-46. Mem. Torch Club (pres. Worcester 1967, 87, 95). Home: 39 Knollwood Dr Shrewsbury MA 01545-3329

ONSTOTT, TULLIS, microgeologist, geology professor; b. Carlsbad, N.Mex, Jan. 12, 1955; BS in Geophysics, Calif. Inst. Tech., 1976; MA, PhD in Geology, Princeton U., 1980. Rsch. asst. U.S.G.S. Flagstaff, Ariz., 1974—76; post-doctoral fellow Princeton U., 1980—83; rsch., study Physics Dept., U. of Toronto, 1980—82; rsch. assoc. Princeton U., 1983—85, asst. prof., 1985—91, assoc. prof., 1991—2001, prof., 2001—. Mem. multiple NASA workshops on Mars drilling/sampling. Recipient Presdl. Young Investigator award, Nat. Sci. Found., 1985—89, Jubilee Medal, Geological Soc. South Africa, 1988, Award for Meritorious Accomplishments in Subsurface Microbiology, US Dept. Energy, 1996, Award for Meritorious Achievements, 1998, Appreciation award for Rsch. Excellence, 2002; named one of The World's Most Influential People, TIME mag., 2007. Office: Princeton U Dept Geoscis B79 Guyot Hall Princeton NJ 08544 Office Phone: 609-258-7678. E-mail: tullis@princeton.edu.

ONTON, ANN LOUISE REUTHER, chemist; b. Bridgeport, Conn., Sept. 29, 1943; m. Aare Onton, 1965; children: Alan David, Daryl John, Julie Ann. BS in Chemistry, Purdue U., 1965. Lab. chemist Great Lakes Chem. Corp., 1965-67; rsch. asst. Geigy Chem. Corp., 1967-70; abstractor Chem. Abstracts Svc., 1970-72; rschr. Cancer Prevention II Study, 1980-90; chemist Prototek Enzyme Sys. Products, 1992-93; rsch. assoc. Applied Biotech Concepts, Inc., 1995-98, Genaissance Pharms., 1999-2000; mgr. rsch. devel. and prodn. AllExcel, Inc., 2000—03; lab. asst. U. San Diego, 2003—05; lab. mgr. TheraCour Pharma, Inc., 2005—06; sr. scientist NanoViricides Inc., 2006—. NIH grantee, 1996, 97. Mem. NAFE, AAUW, Am. Chem. Soc., Assn. for Women in Sci. Achievements include co-inventor on patent pending for solubilization and targeted delivery of therapeutic drugs with amphiphilic polymers; first to isolate, sequence and clone A Nidulans ahr asparaginase gene; development of novel materials and methods for improved electrophoresis and DNA sequencing technologies; development of methodologies for purification and testing of enzymes, U.S.A. Nat. and world medalist in Masters and Senior Olympic Swimming. Office Phone: 203-937-6137. Business E-Mail: annonton@snet.net.

ONU, CHUKUEMEKA N., chemistry professor, researcher; b. Ozuzu, Nigeria, May 18, 1952; arrived in US, 1975; s. William Ihemenachi and Evelyn Nwurasi Onu; m. Eunice Njoku Onu, May 3, 1997; children: Adamma Kara, Amara Urbam. BS in Chemistry, Ala. A&M U., Normal, 1979, MS in Molecular Biology, 1981; D in Chemistry Edn., U. Mass., Amherst, 1988. Chemistry lectr. II U. Ibadan Coll. Edn., Port Harcourt, Nigeria, 1991—97, chemistry lectr. I, 1997—2000, sr. lectr. chemistry, 2000—; chemistry prof. Holyoke Cmty. Coll., Mass., 2005—. Vis. assoc. prof. dept. civil and environ. engring. U. Mass., Amherst, 2002—03. Recipient Outstanding Tchrs. award, U. Ibadan, Rivers State Coll. Edn., 1999; named Outstanding Upward Bound Tchr., 1988. Mem.: Am. Ednl. Rsch. Assn., Mass. Tchrs. Assn., Chem. Soc. Nigeria (regional sec. 2000—01), Am. Chem. Soc. Avocations: bicycling, swimming, lawn tennis, soccer. Home: 253 Amherst Rd Apt 5A Sunderland MA 01375 Office: Holyoke Cmty Coll 303 Homestead Ave Holyoke MA 01040 Business E-Mail: conu@hcc.mass.edu.

ONUKWULI, FRANCIS OSITA, computer scientist, secondary school educator, mathematician; b. Warri, Nigeria, Aug. 5, 1955; arrived in U.S., 1977; s. Chief Mathias Nwafor and Mercy (Okonkwo) O.; m. Sandra Anthonia Mgbemena, Oct. 12, 1986; children: Francis Osita, Victor Chinedu, Anthony Tochukwu, Precious Chinenye. BS in Math. and Physics, Philander Smith Coll., Little Rock, 1981; MS in Computer Sci., Atlanta U., 1983; EdD in Ednl. Leadership Secondary and Higher Edn., Clark Atlanta U., 1990. Billing and credit supr. Standard Bank Nigeria Ltd., Benin, 1975-77; tutor, counselor Philander Smith Coll., 1978-81; math. rsch. asst. Atlanta U., 1982-83; instr. computer sci. Spelman Coll., Atlanta, 1983-86; asst. prof. computer sci., mgr. computer and info. sci. lab. Morris Brown Coll., Atlanta, 1986-96, assoc. prof, chmn. computer sci. dept., 1991-92; gifted math. tchr. Lovejoy (Ga.) H.S., 1998—. Cons. PBT Engring. Co., Atlanta, 1985-86; judge Ga. Sci. Fair, 1989, 90, 93, 94, 95, 99, 2001. Co-author: Computer Applications for the Twenty-First Century; author microcomputer materials for calculus students. Recipient Tchr. of the Yr. award, Parent-Tchr.-Student Assn., 2005—06; named Man of Yr., Atlanta Met. Coll., 2002, Prof. of Yr., 2002, Coca Cola Tchr. of Yr., 2004—05, Tchr. of Yr., Lovejoy H.S., 2004—05, STAR Tchr. of Yr., Lovejoy HS, 2008, Clayton County Pub. Schs., 2009. Mem. NSF (co-chair proposal review panelist 1989-90), Math. Assn. Am., Assn. Computing Machinery, Am. Math. Soc., Internat. Devel. Edn. Coun. (sec. 1987), Igbo Union (pres. Atlanta chpt. 1986-91), Umuoji Improvement Union (nat. v.p. U.S. and Can. 2000—04, pres. Atlanta chpt. 2001-07), Anambra State Assn. (nat. edn. com. chmn.), Knights of Columbus (adv. Jonesboro coun. 2005-08), Idemili United Atlanta Inc.(pres. 2008-), Notre Dame Old Boys Assn.(sec., 2006-), Idemili United Atlanta(pres., 2008-) Democrat. Roman Catholic. Home: 7544 Sedona Dr Jonesboro GA 30236-2740 Office: Lovejoy HS 1587 McDonough Rd Lovejoy GA 30250 Home Phone: 678-230-8864; Office Phone: 770-473-2920. Personal E-mail: Dronukwuli@aol.com. E-mail: fonukwuli@clayton.k12.ga.us.

ONUNKWO, EMMANUEL NWAFOR, retired economics professor; b. Ogbunike, Anambra, Nigeria, July 21, 1933; came to U.S., 1966; s. Justin Binyelum and Susannah (Anoma) O.; m. Hazel Herbalene Johnson, June 7, 1969. BA in Econs., U. Durham, Eng., 1960; M Pub. and Internat. Affairs, U. Pitts., 1968; MA in Econs., Georgetown U., 1970, PhD in Econs., 1973. Sr. asst. sec. Ministry of Econ. Planning, Enugu, Nigeria, 1971-73, prin. asst. sec., 1973-74, chief planning officer, 1974, acting asst. contr. of planning, 1974-75; asst. prof. econ. Ft. Valley State Univ., Ga., 1975-78; asst. prof. econs. S.C. State U., Orangeburg, SC, 1978-82, assoc. prof. econs., 1982—87, prof. econs., 1987—2003, dept. chmn., 1988—92. Mem. Nigerian delegation World Bank, 1971; dir. Ctr. for Econ. Edn., 1986-88, S.C. State Coun. on Econ. Edn., DEEP adv. com., 1988-90. Mem. Nat. Econ. Assn., Ea. Econ. Assn., Nigerian Econ. Soc. Anglican/Methodist. Avocations: photography, reading, music. Personal E-mail: eno1427@aol.com.

ONWUDIWE, EBERE, humanities educator, writer; arrived in USA, 1979; s. Onwudiwe Simon and Nwangbede Magdalene Achigaonye; children: Chinwe, MbaMemme Ohiaeri, Obiawo. BA, U. Sci. and Tech., Okla., 1980; MA in Internat. Rels., Fla. State U., Tallahassee, 1981, MS in Econs., 1983, PhD in Polit. Sci., 1986. Sr. fellow program on ethnic & fed. studies U. Ibadan, Nigeria, 2002—; prof. behavioral scis. Ctrl. State U., Wilberforce, Ohio, 1986—; columnist Newswatch Mag., Lagos, Nigeria. Cons. in field. Editor: (jour.) International Journal of African Studies, 1994—, (books) Nigerian Federalism in Crises, Nigeria's Struggle for Democracy and Good Governance, The Management of the National Question in Nigeria, Afro-optimism, 2003; contbr. articles to profl. jours. V.p. Nigerian Scholars for Dialogue, Buffalo. Recipient Officer of Order of Mono, Govt. of Rep. of Togo, 2002. Avocations: tennis, soccer, travel, swimming, movies. Office: Ctrl State Univ 1400 Brush Row Rd Wilberforce OH 45384 Home Fax: 937-376-6257. Personal E-mail: eonwudiwe@csu.ces.edu. Business E-Mail: eondwudiwe@centralstate.edu.

ONYEJI, BENSON CHINEDU, political science professor; s. Philip Nwokejezi and Bernice Onyejindu Onyeji; m. Violet Anikpe Oyathelemi (dec.); children: Adaku Bernice, Chinedu Umunna, Nkechi Ijeoma, Nnenna Kate. PhD, U. Denver, Colo., 1990. Asst. prof. Bates Coll., Lewiston, Maine, 1990—91; assoc. prof. polit. sci. Manchester Coll., Ind., 1991—. Contbr. articles to profl. publs. Mem.: Internat. Studies Assn. (life). Avocations: travel, swimming, running, soccer. Home: 10301 Bitterroot Ct Fort Wayne IN 46804 Office: Manchester Coll 604 E Coll Ave North Manchester IN 46962 Office Fax: 260-982-5043; Home Fax: 260-982-5043. Business E-Mail: bconyeji@manchester.edu.

ONYIDO, JOHN CHIKE, lawyer; b. Ihiala, Anambra State, Nigeria, Feb. 14, 1969; s. John Paul and Clara Chibuogu Onyido; m. Bertha Fountain-Onyido. LLB, U. Benin, Nigeria, 1989; BL, U. Lagos, Nigeria, 1990, MA in Internat. Law and Diplomacy, 1998, LLM, 1994, Cardozo Sch. Law, 2009. Bar: Nigerian Supreme Ct. 1990, N.Y. 2005, So. and Ea. Dist., NY, US Supreme Ct.; cert. notary pub. Nassau County, 2005. Assoc. ptnr. Allan * Ogunkeye, 1992—99; sr. assoc. counsel The Law Union, 1999—2001, head Dept. Intellectual Property Law and Litig., 1999—2001; ptnr. R.U. Metu and Assocs., 2001—05, Jones, Lewis & Simpson Ptnrs., 2001—07, Cravath, Swaine & Moore LLP, 2007—. Contbr. articles to profl. jours. Named Resource Person on Fgn. Investment and Nigerian Intellectual Property Laws, South Africa, 2000. Mem.: ABA, Nigerian Bar Assn., Internat. Bar Assn., Am. Soc. Internat. Law, N.Y. County Lawyers Assn., N.Y. State Bar Assn. Business E-Mail: johnonyido@optonline.net.

OOGURI, HIROSI, physics professor; DSc, U. Tokyo. Prof. physics U. Calif., Berkeley, 1994—2000; Fred Kavli prof. theoretical physics Calif. Inst. Tech., Pasadena, 2000—. Prin. investigator Inst. Physics and Math. Universe, U. Tokyo, Kashiwa, Chiba, 2007—. Recipient Leonard Eisenbud Math. and Physics prize, Am. Math. Soc., 2008, Rsch. award, Alexander von Humboldt Found., Germany, 2008. Mem.: Am. Phys. Soc., Am. Math. Soc.

OOMMEN, THOMAS, research scientist; s. C G. Oommen and V T. Annamma; m. Selin Philip Oommen, June 10, 2004; children: Hannah Leanne, Serah Ann. BE, M S Ramaiah Inst. Tech., Bangalore, 1999; MS, U. Alaska, Fairbanks, 2007; PhD, Tufts U., Medford, 2009. Project engr. Bharat Susamachar Samiti, Dehradun, Uttarkhand, India, 1999—2003, dir. infrastructure devel., 2004—05; project mgr. Shelter for Life, Kabul, Afghanistan, 2004—05; tech. cons. Shelter Life, 2004—05; grad. rsch. asst. Alaska Fairbanks, 2005—06, Tufts U., Medford, Mass., 2007—. Contbr. articles to profl. jours. (Outstanding Student Paper award, 2005). Youth coord. Indian Pentecostal Assembly Boston, Waltham, Mass., 2008. Recipient prize, NE Geotechnical Grad. Rsch. Symposium, 2007, award, Assn. Environ. & Engring. Geologists, 2008. Mem.: ASCE, Internat. Marine Minerals Soc., Am. Soc. Agrl. & Biol. Engrs., Assn. Environ. & Engring. Geologist, IEEE Geoscience & Remote Sensing Soc., Seismol. Soc. Am., Am. Geophys. Union, Sigma Xi Sci. Rsch. Soc. Avocations: swimming, travel. Office: Tufts Univ 200 College Ave Medford MA 02155 Office Phone: 617-924-2976. Business E-Mail: thomas.oommen@tufts.edu.

OORT, ABRAHAM HANS, meteorologist, researcher, educator; b. Leiden, The Netherlands, Sept. 2, 1934; came to U.S., 1961; s. Jan Hendrik and Johanna Maria (Graadt Van Roggen) O.; m. Bineke Pel, May 20, 1961; children: Pieter Jan, Michiel, Sonya. MS, MIT, 1963; PhD in Meteorology, U. Utrecht, The Netherlands, 1964. Rsch. meteorologist Koninklyk Nederlands Meteorologisch Instituut, De Bilt, Netherlands, 1964-66, Geophys. Fluid Dynamics Lab/NOAA, Washington, 1966-68, Princeton, NJ, 1968-77, sr. rsch. meteorologist, 1977-96, ret., 1996. Prof. dept. geol. and geophys. scis. Princeton U., 1971-96; Shiatsu tchr. Kushi Inst. for Macrobiotic Studies, Becket, Mass., 1999--. Author: Physics of Climate, 1992; contbr. monographs in field. 2nd lt. Netherlands Air Force, 1959-61. NATO sci. fellow MIT, Cambridge, 1961-63; 10th Victor P. Starr Meml. lectr. MIT, 1988; recipient Gold medal U.S. Dept. Commerce, Washington, 1979. Fellow N.Y. Acad. Scis., Am. Meteorol. Soc. (Jule G. Charney award 1993), Royal Meteorol. Soc.; mem. Am. Geophys. Union. Democrat. Avocations: sculpture, shiatsu, meditation.

OOSTERHUIS, PAUL WILLIAM, lawyer; b. Webster, Iowa, Nov. 5, 1946; m. Bronson Clayton, Jan. 21, 1978; children: Elizabeth, Christopher. BA magna cum laude, Brown U., 1969; JD cum laude, Harvard U., 1973. Bar: D.C. 1973, U.S. Tax Ct. 1989. Legislation staff atty. joint com. on tax. U.S. Congress, Washington, 1973-76, legislation counsel, 1977—78; assoc. Hogan & Hartson, Washington, 1979-80, ptnr., 1981-88; ptnr., internat. and corp. tax law Skaddon, Arps, Slate, Meagher & Flom, LLP, Washington, 1988—. Adj. prof. lae Georgetown U. Law Ctr., 1977—83. Contbr. articles to profl. publs.; author and co-author (books and articles). Office: Skadden Arps Slate Meagher & Flom LLP 1440 New York Ave NW Ste 600 Washington DC 20005 Office Phone: 202-371-7130. Office Fax: 202-661-8232. Business E-Mail: poosterh@skadden.com.

OOT, MICHAEL P., lawyer; b. Denver, Oct. 12, 1949; s. Lawrence J. Oot; m. Ann Oot; 5 children. BA, Alfred U., NY, 1972; JD, We. New Eng. Sch. Law, 1976. Atty. Oot and Associates, FKA Oot and Fallon, 1976—95, Oot and Stratton, 1995—. Mem. Stockbridge Valley Ctrl. Sch. Dist. Bd. Edn., 2001—02, pres., 2002—07; committeman Madison County NY Dem. Party; dir., v.p. Stockbridge Valley Edn. Found., Inc. Mem.: Onondaga County Bar Assn., NY Bar Assn., Injured Workers Bar Assn., Ctrl. NY Workers Compensation Bar Assn., Am. Assn. Justice. Democrat. Presbyterian. Office: Oot & Stratton 4983 Brittonfield Pwy East Syracuse NY 13057 Office Phone: 315-449-4306. Office Fax: 315-449-4358.

OPAITS, DMITRY FLORIEVICH, research scientist; b. Chernovsty, Ukraine, Nov. 1, 1983; s. Flory Alexandrovich and Paraskeva Dmitrievna Opaits. BS (hon.), Moscow Inst. Physics and Tech., Russia, 2004; MA, Princeton U., NJ, 2008. Rsch. asst. Princeton U., 2005—. Mem.: AIAA. Achievements include research in dielectric barrier discharge plasma actuators for flow control. Office: Princeton Univ Olden St Princeton NJ 08540 Business E-Mail: dopaits@princeton.edu.

OPALA, MARIAN PETER, state supreme court justice; b. Lódz, Poland, Jan. 20, 1921; JD, Oklahoma City U., 1953, BSB in Econs., 1957, LLD (hon.), 1981; LLM, NYU, 1968; HHD, Okla. Christian U. Sci. & Arts, 1981. Bar: Okla. 1953, US Supreme Ct. 1970. Asst. county atty., Oklahoma County, 1953—56; practiced law Oklahoma City, 1956—60, 1965—67; referee Okla. Supreme Ct., Oklahoma City, 1960—65; prof. law Oklahoma City U. Sch. Law, 1965—69; asst. to presiding justice Supreme Ct. Okla., 1967—68; administrv. dir. Cts. Okla., 1968—77; presiding judge Okla. State Indsl. Ct., 1977—78; judge Workers Compensation Ct., 1978; justice Okla. Supreme Ct., 1978—, chief justice, 1991—92. Adj. prof. law Okla. City U., 1962—, U. Okla. Coll. Law, 1969—; prof. law U. Tulsa Law Sch., 1982—; mem. permanent faculty Am. Acad. Jud. Edn., 1970—; mem. NYU Inst. Jud. Adminstrn.; mem. faculty Nat. Jud. Coll., U. Nev., 1975—; chmn. Nat. Conf. State Ct. Adminstrs., 1976-77; mem. Nat. Conf. Commrs. Uniform State Laws, 1982—. Co-author: Oklahoma Court Rules for Perfecting a Civil Appeal, 1969 Mem. Adminstrn. Conf. US, 1993-95. Recipient Herbert Harley award, Am. Judicature Soc., 1977, Disting. Alumni award, Oklahoma City U., 1979, Americanism medal, Nat. Soc. DAR, 1984, ABA/Am. Law Inst. Harrison Tweed Spl. Merit award, 1987, Humanitarian award, NCCJ, 1991, Jour. Record award, 1995, Constn. award, Rogers State U., 1996, Jud. Excellence award, Okla. Bar Assn., 1997, Leo H. Whinery Disting. Svc. award, 1999, Lifetime Achievement award, Oklahoma City Univ. Sch. Law, 2000, First Amendment award, FOI Okla., Inc., 2002; inductee Okla. Hall of Fame, 2000. Mem. ABA (edn. com. appellate judges conf. 1984-93), Okla. Bar Assn. (Earl Sneed Continuing Legal Edn. award 1988, Jud. Excellence award 1997), Okla. County Bar Assn., Am. Soc. Legal History, Oklahoma City Title Lawyers Assn., Am. Judicature Soc. (bd. dirs. 1988-92), Am. Law Inst. (elected), Order of Coif, Phi Delta Phi (Oklahoma City Alumni award). Office: Okla Supreme Ct State Capitol Rm 238 Oklahoma City OK 73105 Office Phone: 405-521-3839.*

OPAR, MICHAEL E., engineering educator, department chairman; b. Elmhurst, Ill., July 8, 1964; m. Veronica Opar. BSIE, Purdue U., West Lafayette, Ind., 1987; MSIE, Bradley U., Peoria, Ill., 1991; PhD, U. Iowa, Iowa City, 2000. Prof., chair St. Ambrose U., Davenport, Iowa, 1993—. Office: Saint Ambrose Univ 518 W Locust St Davenport IA 52803

OPARIL, SUZANNE, cardiologist, educator, researcher; b. Elmira, NY, Apr. 10, 1941; d. Stanley and Anna (Penkova) Oparil. AB, Cornell U., 1961; MD, Columbia U., 1965. Diplomate Am. Bd. Internal Medicine. Intern in medicine Presbyn. Hosp., NYC, 1965—66; sr. asst. resident in medicine Mass. Gen. Hosp., Boston, 1967—68, clin. and rsch. fellow in medicine, cardiac unit, 1968—71; asst. prof. medicine Med. Sch., U. Chgo., 1971—75, assoc. prof., 1975—77; assoc. prof. dept. medicine U. Ala., Birmingham, 1977—81, asst. prof. physiology and biophysics, 1980—81, assoc. prof., 1981—, prof. medicine, 1981—, dir. vascular biology and hypertension program, 1985—, prof. med. physiology and biophysics, 1993—. Mem. vis. faculty Nat. High Blood Pressure Edn. Program, 1974—, Joint Nat. Com. on Detection, Evaluation and Treatment High Blood Pressure, 1991; mem. bd. sci. advisors Sterling Drug, Inc., 1988—91; lectr. in field; Selkurt lectr. Ind. U. Sch. Medicine, 1994; hon. prof. Peking Union Med. Coll., 1994; Louis Gross-Harold Segall lectr. Jewish Gen. Hosp., Montreal, Que., 1995; Joy Goodwin Disting. lectr. Auburn U., 1996; A Ross McIntyre award U. Nebr., 1996. Author books on hypertension; editor: Am. Jour. Med. Scis., 1984—94; assoc. editor: Hpertension, 1979—83, mem. editl. bd.:, 1984—, assoc. editor: Am. Jour. Physiology-Renal, 1989—91, mem. editl. bd.: Jour. Hypertension, 1989—98; contbr. over 450 articles to profl. jours., chapters to books. Recipient Young Investigator award, Internat. Soc. Hypertension, 1979, ann. award, Med. Coll. Pa., 1984; fellow, Am. Coll. Cardiology, 1992. Fellow: Am. Coll. Cardiology; mem.: AAAS, Am. Fedn. for Clin. Rsch. (midwest councillor 1974—75, nat. councillor 1975—78, sec.-treas. 1978—80, pres. 1981—82), Assn. Am. Physicians, So. Soc. for Clin. Investigation (Founder's award 1995), Soc. Exptl. Biology and Medicine (councillor 1993—), Am. Soc. for Clin. Investigation (sec.-treas. 1983—86), Am. Physiol. Soc. (clin. physiology advd. com. 1992—, Carl Ludwig disting. lectr. 2002), Am. Heart Assn. (coun. for high blood pressure rsch. 1973—, coun. on basic scis. 1978—, mem.-at-large, exec. com. 1979—81, chmn. Louis B. Katz Prize com. 1984—86, exec. com. 1985—90, vice chmn. 1986, v.p. Ala. affiliate 1986—87, pres.-elect Ala. affiliate 1987—88, pres. Ala. affiliate 1988—89, chmn. 1988—90, chmn. budget com. 1990—91, mem.-at-large bd. dirs. 1992, Lewis K. Dahl Meml. lectr. 1993, pres.-elect Ala. affiliate 1993—94, nat. pres.-elect 1993—94, nat. pres. 1994—, Arthur C. Corcoran Meml. lectr. 1998, Irving Page-Alva Bradley Lifetime Achievement award 2002), Assn. for Women in Sci., Am. Soc. Hypertension (sci. program com. 1990—92, pub. policy com. 1990—), Inter-Am. Soc. Hypertension, Endocrine Soc., Inst. Medicine of NAS (corr. com. on human rights 1992, chmn. com. adviser Dept. Def. 1993 Breast Cancer Rsch. Program), Phi Kappa Phi, Alpha Omega Alpha (mem. nat. bd. dirs., dir.-at-large 1991, treas. 1993), Sigma Xi, Phi Beta Kappa. Avocations: horseback riding, tennis, hiking, travel. Office: U Ala 703 S 19th St ZRB 1034 Birmingham AL 35294-0007 E-mail: soparil@uab.edu.

OPAT, MATTHEW JOHN, lawyer; b. Riceville, Iowa, Nov. 5, 1952; s. Wesley John and Dolores Genevieve (Ludwig) O.; m. Therese Ann Dusheck, Aug. 13, 1977; children: Michael, Kristin, Steven. BA in

History, U. Iowa, 1974; JD, Hamline U., 1977. Bar: Iowa 1977, Minn. 1977. Prin. Opat Law Office, Chatfield, Minn., 1977—. Atty. Fillmore County, 1997-2003. Mem. Fillmore County Bar Assn. (pres. 1984-85), Minn. State Bar Assn. (bd. dirs. 1985-87), Tenth Dist. Bar Assn. (chmn. ethics com. 1989-96, pres. 2001-2002, 2004-2005) Office: 22 2nd St SE PO Box 455 Chatfield MN 55923-1203 Office Phone: 507-867-4080.

OPDENBOSCH, PATRICK, mechanical engineer, researcher; s. Guy and Gysele Opdenbosch; married. BS in Mech. Engring., Ga. Inst. Tech., Atlanta, 2002, MS in Mech. Engring., 2005, PhD in Mech. Engring., 2007. Rsch. asst. Ga. Inst. Tech., 2002—07, robotics tchr. asst., 2006—07; rsch. engr. HUSCO Internat., Waukesha, Wis., 2005—06, Caterpillar Inc., Peoria, Ill., 2008—. Contbr. scientific papers to profl. jours. (Fluid Power Motion Control Ctr. Rsch. award, 2004), articles. Mem.: ASME, IEEE. Achievements include development of auto-calibration learning algorithm; research in auto-calibration & learning control for electro-hydraulic valves. Home: 2401 W Alta Rd 2603 Peoria IL 61615 Personal E-mail: patrick.opdenbosch@gatech.edu.

OPDYCKE, LEONARD EMERSON, retired literature and language educator, publishing executive, writer; b. Boston, May 22, 1929; s. Leonard and Frances (Prescott) O.; m. Susan Wolcott, 1951 (div.); children: Susan, Deborah, Margot; m. Jeanne Bernhard, 1963 (div.); children: Sarah, Frances; m. Sandra S. Auchincloss, 1976. BA, Harvard U., 1951; MA, U. Rochester, 1965. Tchr. Southfield Sch., Shreveport, La., 1952-53, Dedham (Mass.) Country Day, Harley Sch., Rochester, NY, 1956-64; dir. Poughkeepsie (NY) Day Sch., 1965-72; chair English dept. Rhinebeck (NY) HS, 1973—76; adj. prof. Marist Coll., Poughkeepsie, 1976—84. Co-chair citizen's adv. com. Poughkeepsie Sch. Dist., 1994—2002. Author: French Aeroplanes before the Great War, 1999; editor, pub. WWI Aero, 1961-2007, Skyways, 1987-2007. Bd. dirs. Cmty. Family Devel. Day Care Ctr., 1984—, Hudson River Housing, 2003—05. Mem. Phi Beta Kappa. Avocations: aviation history, linguistics, education. Home and Office: 15 Crescent Rd Poughkeepsie NY 12601-4405 Home Phone: 845-473-3679.

OPEL, PAMELA LYNN, elementary school educator; d. Richard Gene and Virginia Beaty Opel; 1 child, Thomas Wendolin. BA, U. So. Miss., Hattiesburg, 1977, MEd, 1997. Cert. Nat. Bd. Profl. Tchg. Stds. Educator Biloxi Pub. Sch., Miss., 1986—87, Vernon Parish Sch., Ft. Polk, La., 1987—90; tech. editor XMCO, Sterling Heights, Mich., 1991—94; educator Gulfport Sch. Dist., Miss., 1994—2007, specialist, 2007—. Substitute tchr. Northside Ind. Sch. Dist., San Antonio, 1994—95; adj. faculty U. So. Miss., Long Beach, 1997—2004, chair 504 com., 2005—06; assessor Nat. Bd. Profl. Tchg. Stds., San Antonio, 2004, San Antonio, 05, Mobile, Ala., 2004—; editor, manuscript evaluator Corwin Press, 2006. Grantee, Miss. Dept. Edn., 2003. Mem.: Miss. Profl. Educators Assn., Assn. Edn. Therapists, Phi Kappa Phi, Pi Lamba Theta, Phi Delta Kappa. Avocations: reading, sketching, travel, spelunking. Office: Gulfport Sch Dist 37 Pass Rd Gulfport MS 39507 Office Phone: 228-865-4619. Business E-Mail: popel@gulfportk12.ms.us, pam.opel@gulfportschools.org.

OPEL, WILLIAM, medical research administrator; BA, Pepperdine U., Malibu, Calif., 1968; MBA, U. So. Calif., LA, 1993; PhD, Claremont Grad. U., Calif., 1998. Staff Pasadena Found. Med. Rsch., Calif., 1961-63, rsch. assoc., 1964-70, asst. to dir., 1970-72, adminstr., 1972-76, exec. dir., 1976-82; acting exec. dir. Huntington Med. Rsch. Inst., Pasadena, 1978-82, exec. dir., 1982—. Lectr. tech. mgmt. Pepperdine U.; adj. prof. tech. mgmt. Claremont Grad. U.; bd. dirs. Pasadena Biosci. Collaborative. Pres. Pasadena City Coll. Found. Mem.: Phi Kappa Phi, Beta Gamma Sigma. Achievements include launch of one of the country's first clinical magnetic resonance programs, which has won great acclaim in imaging applications development and in clinical spectroscopy, as well as in training of radiologists and other clinicians. Office: Huntington Med Rsch Insts 734 Fairmount Ave Pasadena CA 91105-3104*

OPENSHAW, LINDA LEEK, social worker; b. Provo, Utah, Oct. 30, 1948; d. Kenneth Frank and Della Mae (Williams) Leek; BA in English, U. Utah, 1971, MSW, 1974, DSW, 1981; m. David Byron Openshaw, July 10, 1975; children: Amy Elizabeth, Alison Rebecca, Lauren Jane, Patrick David, Lindsay Marrie. Tchr. English, Strategakis Sch., Athens, Greece, 1972; psychiat. social worker Stanislaus Mental Health, Brief Treatment Program, Modesto, Calif., 1974-76; instr. Chapman Coll., Merced, Calif., 1975; psychiat. social worker Weber Mental Health, Intake Team, Ogden, Utah, 1976-77; women's group coordinator YWCA, Ogden, 1976-77; juvenile ct. alcohol sch. instr., Salt Lake City, 1978-80; sch. social worker East HS, Salt Lake Sch. Dist., Salt Lake City, 1977-80, Highland HS, 1983—; contract clinician Latter-Day Saints Social Svcs., Salt Lake City, 1984-85; trainer for tchrs. Salt Lake Sch. Dist., 1979-80, Utah Divsn. Alcohol and Drugs, 1982-84, social worker, Mesquite Independent Sch. Dist. Sch., 1994-2001, assoc. prof. social work, NSW program dir., Tex. Adminstrn. U. Commerce. Author. Social Work in School Principals & Practice, 2008. Del., Utah Dem. Conv., 1974. Lic. clin. and cert. social worker, Utah. Mem. Utah Coun. Sch. Social Workers (pres. 1979-80), Nat. Assn. Social Workers (cert., chmn. chpt. nominating com. 1982-83, com. inquiry 1984-87), Phi Kappa Phi, Alumni Bd. U. Utah Sch. Social Work (sec. 1983). Democrat. Mem. Ch. of Jesus Christ of Latter-day Saints. Home: 2601 Harborview Blvd Rowlett TX 75088-1861

OPFER, GEORGE JOSEPH, federal agency administrator; b. NYC, May 12, 1947; m. Elizabeth Opfer; 3 children. BS in Mgmt., St. John's U., 1969. With US Secret Svc., US Dept. Treasury, Washington, 1969—94, spl. agt., asst. dir. Office of Investigations; inspector gen. Fed. Emergency Mgmt. Agy. (FEMA), Washington, 1994—2002; dep. insp. gen. US Dept. Labor, 2002—05; inspector gen. US Dept. Veterans Affairs, Washington, 2005—. Recipient Presdl. Rank of Meritorious Exec. award Sr. Exec. Svc., 1992. Office: US Dept Veterans Affairs 810 Vermont Ave NW Rm 1114 Washington DC 20420*

OPITZ, JOHN MARIUS, clinical geneticist, pediatrician; b. Hamburg, Germany, Aug. 15, 1935; came to the U.S., 1950, naturalized, 1957; s. Friedrich and Erica Maria (Quadt) O.; m. Susan O. Lewin; children: Lea, Teresa, John, Chrisanthi, Felix(dec.), Emma; Marian C. Ohden. BA, State U. Iowa, 1956, MD, 1959; DSc (hon.), Mont. State U., 1983, Ohio State U., 2007; MD (hon.), U. Kiel, Germany, 1986, U. Bologna, Italy, 1999, U. Copenhagen. Diplomate Am. Bd. Pediat., Am. Bd. Med. Genetics. Intern State U. Iowa Hosp., 1959-60, resident in pediat., 1960-61; resident, chief resident in pediat. U. Wis. Hosp., Madison, 1961-62; fellow in pediat. and med. genetics U. Wis., 1962-64, asst. prof. med. genetics and pediat., 1964-69, assoc. prof., 1969-72, prof., 1972-79; founder dir. Wis. Clin. Genetics Ctr., 1974-79; clin. prof. med. genetics and pediat. U. Wash., Seattle, 1979—; prof. pediat., human genetics, pathology and ob-gyn. U Utah, SLC, 1997—. Adj. prof. medicine, biology, history and philosophy, vet. rsch. and vet. sci. Mont. State U., Bozeman, 1979-94, McKay lectr., 1992, univ. prof. med. humanities, 1994—; adj. prof. pediat., med. genetics U. Wis., Madison, 1979—, Class of 1947 Disting. prof., 1992; coord. Shodair Mont. Regional Genetic Svcs. Program, Helena, 1979-82; chmn. dept. med. genetics Shodair Children's Hosp., Helena, 1983-94; dir. Found. Devel. and Med. Genetics, Toledo, Ohio, 1994-96; pres. Heritage Genetics P.C., Helena, 1996; Farber lectr. Soc. Pediat. Pathology, 1987; Joseph Garfunkel lectr. So. Ill. U., Springfield, 1987, McKay lectr. Mont. State U., 1992; Warren Wheeler vis. prof. Columbus (Ohio) Children's Hosp., 1987, 2001; Bea Fowlow lectr. in med. genetics U. Calgary, 1996; 1st vis. prof. Hanseatic U. Found. of Lübeck, 1996; Lew Barness lectr. U. South Fla., 2001; Enid Gilbert Barness lectr. U. Wis., 2001; vis. prof. U. Cattolica del Sacro Cuore, Rome, 2001-02. Editor, author 14 books; founder, editor in chief Am. Jour. Med. Genetics, 1977-2000, emeritus assoc. editor; mng. editor European Jour. Pediat., 1977-85; contbr. numerous articles on clin. genetics. Chair Mont. Com. for Humanities, 1991. Recipient Pool of Bethesda award for excellence in mental retardation rsch. Bethesda Luth. Home, 1988, Med. Alumni citation U. Wis., 1989, Disting. Alumni award, U. Iowa, 2009 Col. Harlan Sanders Lifetime Achievement award for work in field of genetic scis. March of Dimes, Purkinje medal Czech Soc. Medicine, Mendel medal Czech Soc. Med. Genetics, 1996, Internat. prize Phoenix-Anni Verdi for Genetic Rsch., 1996. Fellow AAAS, Am. Coll. Med. Genetics (founder); mem. German Acad. Scis. (Leopoldina), Brazilian Acad. Sci., Am. Soc. Human Genetics, Am. Pediat. Soc., Soc. Pediat. Rsch., Am. Bd. Med. Genetics, Am. Inst. Biol. Scis., Am. Soc. Zoologists, Teratology Soc., Genetic Soc. Am., European Soc. Human Genetics, Soc. Study Social Biology, Am. Acad. Pediat., German Soc. Pediat. (hon.), Western Soc. Pediat. Rsch. (emeritus), Italian Soc. Med. Genetics (hon.), Israel Soc. Med. Genetics (hon.), Russian Soc. Med. Genetics (Hon.), So. Africa Soc. Med. Genetics (hon.), Japanese Soc. Human Genetics (hon.), Sigma Xi, German Soc. Human Genetics(honor medal), Soc. Pediat. Pathol-.(hon.) Democrat. Roman Catholic. Achievements include First Evangeline Heaton lectr. in human genetics, U. Colo. Med. Ctr. Home: 2930 E Craig Dr Salt Lake City UT 84109-3636 Office: U Utah Sch Medicine 50 N Mario Capecchi Dr Salt Lake City UT 84132 E-mail: john.opitz@hsc.utah.edu.

OPPEDAHL, JOHN FREDERICK, newspaper publisher, executive; b. Duluth, Minn., Nov. 9, 1944; s. Walter H. and Lucille (Hole) Oppedahl; m. Alison Owen, 1975 (div. 1983); m. Gillian Coyro, Feb. 14, 1987 (div. 2002); 1 child, Max. BA, U. Calif., Berkeley, 1967; MS, Columbia U., 1968. Reporter San Francisco Examiner, 1967; reporter, asst. city editor Detroit Free Press, 1968-75, city editor, 1975-80, exec. city editor, 1981, exec. news editor, 1981-82, asst. mng. editor, 1983; nat. and fgn. editor Dallas Times Herald, 1983-85, asst. mng. editor, 1985-87; mng. editor/news L.A. Herald Examiner, 1987-89; mng. editor Ariz. Republic, Phoenix, 1989-93; exec. editor Phoenix Newspapers, Inc., 1993-95; pub., CEO The Republic, 1996—2000; chmn., pub., CEO San Francisco Chronicle, 2000—03. Chmn. bd. The Daily Californian. Mem.: Am. Soc. Newspaper Editors. Personal E-mail: joppedahl@yahoo.com.

OPPEDAHL, PHILLIP EDWARD, computer company executive; b. Renwick, Iowa, Sept. 17, 1935; s. Edward and Isadore Hannah (Gangstead) O.; m. Sharon Elaine Ree, Aug. 3, 1957 (dec. Aug. 1989), m. Karen Suzanne Ungar, July, 4, 2004; children: Gary Lynn, Tamra Sue, Sue Ann, Lisa Kay. BS in Naval Sci., Navy Postgrad. Sch., 1963, MS in Nuclear Physics, 1971; MS in Sys. Mgmt., U. S.C., 1978. Commd. ensign U.S. Navy, 1956, advanced through grades to capt., 1977; with Airborne Early Warning Squadron, 1957-59, Anti-Submarine Squadron, 1959-65; asst. navigator USS Coral Sea, 1965-67; basic jet flight instr., 1967-69; test group dir. Def. Nuclear Agy., 1972-74; weapons officer USS Oriskany, 1974-76; program mgt. for armament Naval Air Sys. Command, Washington, 1977-79; test dir. Def. Nuclear Agy., Kirtland AFB, N.Mex., 1979-82, dep. comdr., 1982-83; pres., CEO Am. Systems, Albuquerque, 1983—. Bd. dirs. BASIS Internat., 1991— Author: Energy Loss of High Energy Electrons in Beryllium, 1971, Understanding Contractor Motivation and Incentive Contracts. Decorated Def. Superior Svc. medal; recipient Alumni Disting. Svc. award Waldorf Coll., 2006. Mem. Naval Inst., Aircraft Owners and Pilots Assn., Assn. Naval Aviation, Navy League, Exptl. Aircraft Assn. Lutheran.

OPPENHEIM, ALAN VICTOR, electrical engineering educator; b. NYC, Nov. 11, 1937; s. Sydney and Dorothy (Arenz) Oppenheim; m. Phyllis Arnold, June 20, 1964; children: Justine Ruth, Jason Philip. SB, SM, MIT, 1961, ScD, 1964; D (hon.), Tel Aviv U., 1995. Asst. prof. dept. elec. engring. MIT, 1964-69, assoc. prof. dept. elec. engring. and computer scis., 1969-76, prof., 1976-90, Disting. prof. elec. engring., 1990-96, Ford prof. engring., 1996—, MacVicar faculty fellow, 1997—2007; staff scientist Lincoln Lab., 1967-69, assoc. head data systems divsn., 1978-80. Cons. Lincoln Lab., Atlantic Aerospace Inc., Sanders Assocs., Inc. Co-author: Digital Signal Processing, 1975, Signals and Systems, 1983, 2d edit. 1997, 3rd edit. 2009, Discrete-Time Signal Processing, 1989, others; editor: Applications of Digital Signal Processing, 1978, (with others) Advanced Topics in Signal Processing, 1988; contbr. articles to profl. jours. Guggenheim fellow, 1972-73 Fellow IEEE (Edn. medal 1988, Jack S. Kilby Signal Processing Medal 2007); mem. NAE, Sigma Xi, Eta Kappa Nu, Tau Beta Pi.

OPPENHEIM, CHARLES B., lawyer; b. NYC, Oct. 18, 1962; s. Barry J. and Jean Elizabeth (Reeve) O.; m. Lydia Vitlacil, July 25, 1992; children: Calvin, Dean. BA, Cornell U., 1984; JD, Fordham U., 1988. Bar: Calif. 1988. Assoc. Skadden Arps et al., San Francisco, 1988-90, McDermott & Trayner, Pasadena, Calif., 1991-93, Weissburg and Aronson, LA, 1993-95; ptnr. Weissburg & Aronson, LA, 1996, Foley, Lardner, Weissburg & Aronson, LA, 1996, Foley & Lardner LLP, LA, 1996—2009, Hooper, Lundy & Bookman, LA, 2009—. Co-editor: Health Care Law Sourcebook, 1995-2000; contbr. articles to profl. jours. Bd. trustees The Accelerated Sch., LA, 2000—. Recipient Nat. Philanthropy Day medallion, L.A., 2001. Mem. Am. Health Lawyers Assn., Calif. Soc. Healthcare Attys., LA County Bar Assn. (treas. health law section). Office: Hooper Lundy & Bookman Inc 1875 Century Pk E Ste 1600 Los Angeles CA 90067 Office Phone: 310-551-8110. Business E-Mail: coppenheim@health-law.com.

OPPENHEIM, IRWIN, chemical physicist, educator; b. Boston, June 30, 1929; s. James L. and Rose (Rosenberg) O.; m. Bernice Buresh, May 18, 1974; 1 child, Joshua Buresh. AB summa cum laude, Harvard U., 1949; postgrad., Calif. Inst. Tech., 1949-51; PhD, Yale, 1956. Physicist Nat. Bur. Standards, Washington, 1953-60; chief theoretical physics Gen. Dynamics/Convair, San Diego, 1960-61; assoc. prof. chemistry MIT, Cambridge, 1961-65, prof., 1965—. Lectr. physics U. Md., 1953-60; vis. assoc. prof. physics U. Leiden, 1955-56, Lorentz prof., 1983; vis. prof. Weizmann Inst. Sci., 1958-59, U. Calif., San Diego, 1966-67; Van der Waals prof. U. Amsterdam, 1966-67. Author: (with J.G. Kirkwood) Chemical Thermodynamics, 1961; editor: Phys. Rev. E, 1992-2001. Recipient Hildebrand award, 1998. Fellow Am. Phys. Soc., Am. Acad. Arts and Scis., Washington Acad. Sci.; mem. Phi Beta Kappa, Sigma Xi. Achievements include research in quantum statis. mechanics, statis. mechanics of transport processes, thermodynamics. Home: 140 Upland Rd Cambridge MA 02140-3623 Office: MIT 77 Massachusetts Ave #6-223 Cambridge MA 02139-4307 Office Phone: 617-253-1478. Business E-Mail: irwin@mit.edu.

OPPENHEIM, JOOST J., allergist, immunologist, researcher; b. Venlo, The Netherlands, Aug. 11, 1934; MD, Columbia U., 1960. Diplomate Am. Bd. Allergy & Immunology. Intern King County Hosp., Seattle, 1960-61; resident U. Wash. Hosp., Seattle, 1961-62; fellow in immunology U. Birmingham, England, 1965-66; sr. investigator Lab. Biochemistry Nat. Inst. Dental Rsch., NIH, 1966, chief Cellular Immunology Sect., 1970—83; chief Lab. Molecular Immunoregulation Ctr. Cancer Rsch., Nat. Cancer Inst., NIH, Frederick, Md., 1983, also head Cellular Immunology Group, dep. chief Cancer and Inflammation Program. Mem. Am. Acad. Immunology, Assn. Am. Physicians, Am. Soc. Clin. Investigation, Rsch. Soc. Office: Ctr Cancer Rsch Lab Molecular Immunology PO Box B Bldg 560 Rm 21-89A Frederick MD 21702-1201 Office Phone: 301-846-1551. Office Fax: 301-846-7042. E-mail: oppenhei@ncifcrf.gov.*

OPPENHEIM, MARTHA KUNKEL, pianist, educator; b. Port Arthur, Tex., June 25, 1935; d. Samuel Adam and Grace (Moncure) Kunkel; m. Russell Edward Oppenheim, June 18, 1960; children: Lauren Susan, Kristin Lee Oppenheim Mortenson. MusB with honors, U. Tex., 1957, MusM, 1959; diploma in piano, Juilliard Sch. Music, 1960; student, Am. Conservatory, Fontainebleau, France, 1956, student, 1958. Soloist Amarillo (Tex.) Symphony, Austin (Tex.) Symphony, U. Tex. Orch., San Antonio Symphony, Dallas Symphony, Heilbronner Kammer Orch., Heilbron, Germany. Solo and chamber music recitals in Tex., N.Y., France; mem. Halcyon Trio, 1974—77; tchg. asst. U. Tex., 1957—59, 1968—69; pvt. piano tchr., San Antonio, 1962—; pianist in duo with cellist Dan Zollars, 1991—. Recipient 1st place award, Internat. Piano Rec. Festival, Nat. Guild Piano Tchrs., 1956, 1956, Tuesday Mus. Club Young Artist Competition, 1956, 1st place award Young Artist Competition, Amarillo Symphony, 1959, 1st place award G.B. Dealey competition, Dallas Symphony and Dallas Morning News, 1959; scholar, U. Tex., Juilliard Sch. Music. Mem.: San Antonio Music Tchrs. Assn., Tex. Music Tchrs. Assn., Music Tchrs. Nat. Assn., Tuesday Musical Club (San Antonio, bd. dirs.), Pi Kappa Lambda, Sigma Alpha Iota. Presbyterian. Home and Office: 9118 E Valley View Ln San Antonio TX 78217-5160 E-mail: moppenheim@satx.rr.com.

OPPENHEIM, ROBERT, beauty industry executive; b. NYC, May 21, 1925; s. Hyman and Hannah (Lieberman) O.; m. Ruth Wigler, Feb. 7, 1954; children: Nancy Ellen, David Paul, Howard P. BS cum laude, Syracuse U., 1950. Product sales specialist McKesson & Robbins, Yonkers, NY, 1950-55; asst. sales mgr. Clairol, Inc., NYC, 1955-60, pres. Salon div., 1976-83, chmn. Profl. Products div., 1983-87; dir. mktg. Haircolor div. Revlon, Inc., NYC, 1960-68, dir. mktg. and sales Salon div., 1968-70; exec. v.p. Milton R. Barrie Co., Inc., 1970-71; pres. Oppenheim Communications, NYC, 1987—2001; marketing cons. Procter & Gamble, 1989—2001. Pub. Beauty Salon Newsletter, NYC, 1971—83, Salon Update, 1988—95, The Oppenheim Letter, 1988—95; mgmt. cons., 1988—; contbg. commentator Beauty Store Bus., 1998—2004, cons., 1988—2001; contbg. commentator Profl. Beauty Mfr., 1998—99; bd. dirs. Cosmetology Advancement Found., 1995—98, Internat. Haircolor Exch., 1995—96. Author: 101 Salon Promotions, 1999. With AUS, 1942-44, ETO. Decorated Purple Heart; recipient Spirit of Life award City of Hope, 1989, Showman Wall of Fame award Internat. Beauty Show, 1994; inducted into Nat. Cosmetology Assn. Hall of Fame, 1994, Barber & Beauty Supply Inst. Hall of Leaders, 1998. Mem. Nat. Beauty and Barber Mfrs. Assn. (pres. 1984-85), Am. Beauty Assn. (pres. 1985-86), Masons. Address: 1755 York Ave # 22C New York NY 10128-6871 Personal E-mail: robertoppenheim@gmail.com.

OPPENHEIM, TOM, performing company executive; b. NYC, 1960; s. Ellen Adler and Dave Oppenheim; 1 child, Sofia. Pres., artistic dir. Stella Adler Studio of Acting, NYC, 1998—. Actor: (films) Wolf, 1994, Dodgeball, 1995, Going Nomad, 1998, Virgin, 2003. Office: Stella Adler Studio of Acting 3rd Fl 31 W 27th St New York NY 10001 E-mail: info@stellaadler.com.

OPPENHEIM, WILLIAM L., pediatric orthopedist; b. Bangor, Maine, Jan. 4, 1945; BS in Chemistry, U. Md., Coll. Park, 1966; MD magna cum laude, Georgetown U., Washington, DC, 1970. Cert. Am. Bd. Orthop., 1980. Intern in surgery San Francisco Gen. Hosp.; resident in orthop. surgery U. Wash., Seattle; fellow Nuffield Orthop. Ctr., Oxford, England, 1977; fellow in pediatric orthopedics LA Orthop. Hosp., 1979; dir. UCLA/Orthopaedic Hosp. Ctr. Cerebral Palsy; Margaret Jones Kanaar chair, cerebral palsy UCLA Sch. Medicine, prof., chief pediatric orthopedics; cons. LA Shriner's Hosp. Mem. bd. dirs. Temple Beth Shir Shalom, Santa Monica, LA Soc. for Prevention of Cruelty to Animals, 1990—2000. Recipient White Swan award, Abilities First/Jones Kennar Found., 2000; named to America's Best Doctors, 1999, 2004. Fellow: Am. Orthop. Foot and Ankle Soc., Am. Acad. Cerebral Palsy and Devel. Medicine (mem. bd. dirs., sec., webmaster), Am. Acad. Orthop. Surgery, Am. Acad. Pediat. (mem. bd. dirs.), Pediatric Orthop. Soc. North America; mem.: Am. Orthop. Assn., State Orthop. Soc., State Med. Soc., AMA, Western Orthop. Assn. LA Chpt. (pres.). Office: Luskins Children's Clinic La Orthop Hosp 1530 Arizona St Santa Monica CA 90404 Office Phone: 310-206-6345, 310-395-4814. Office Fax: 310-206-0063, 310-395-4943. Business E-Mail: woppenhe@ucla.edu.

OPPENHEIMER, DAVID GRAY, botanist, educator; s. Glen E. and Betty A. Oppenheimer; m. Paris Hannah Grey. BS, U. Minn., Twin Cities, 1982, PhD, 1987. Assoc. prof. biol. sciences U. Ala., Tuscaloosa, 1994—2003; assoc. prof. botany U. Fla., Gainesville, 2003—. Mem.: Japanese Soc. Plant Physiologists, Soc. for Devel. Biology, Genetics Soc. Am., Am. Soc. Plant Biologists, Am. Soc. for Cell Biology. Office: Univ Fla 1376 Mowry Rd Gainesville FL 32610

OPPENHEIMER, DEANNA WATSON, bank executive; b. 1958; m. John Oppenheimer; 2 children. Degree cum laude in Polit. Sci. & Urban Affairs, U. Puget Sound, 1980. Mktg. and govt. rels. officer Washington Mutual Inc., Seattle, 1985—89, mgr. corp. relations divsn., 1989—93, exec. v.p., 1993—95, exec. v.p., consumer banking and corp. rels., 1995—2000, pres., banking and fin. svcs. group, 2000—03, overseer, corp. R&D & corp. rels., 1999—2005, pres., consumer group, 2003—05; COO, UK retail banking Barclays PLC, London, 2005—06, CEO, UK retail banking, 2006—. Bd. dir. Catellus Devel. Corp., U. Puget Sound. Pres. Seattle Children's Theatre Bd.; bd. dir. Corp. Coun. Arts, Greater Seattle YMCA. Recipient Double Halo award, Seattle Advt. Fedn.; named Person of Yr., Media Inc.; named one of 25 Women to Watch, US Banker, 2006, 25 Most Powerful Women in Banking, 2007, 2008. Mem.: Mktg. Comm. Execs. Internat. (pres.). Office: Barclays PLC 1 Churchill Place London E14 5HP England*

OPPENHEIMER, FRANZ MARTIN, lawyer; b. Mainz, Germany, Sept. 7, 1919; s. Arnold and Johanna (Mayer) O.; m. Margaret Spencer Foote, June 17, 1944; children: Martin Foote, Roxana Foote, Edward Arnold. BS, U. Chgo., 1942; student, U. Grenoble, France, 1938-39; LL.B. cum laude (note editor Law Jour. 1945), Yale U., 1945. Bar: N.Y. 1946, D.C. 1955. Rsch. asst. com. human devel. U. Chgo., 1942-43; law clk. to Judge Swan, U.S. Circuit Ct. of Appeals, NY, 1945-46; assoc. atty. Chadbourne, Wallace, Parke & Whiteside, NYC, 1946-47; atty. IBRD, Washington, 1947-57; individual practice law, 1958-59; ptnr. firm

Leva, Hawes, Symington, Martin & Oppenheimer, 1959-83, Fort & Schlefer, Washington, 1984-94; pvt. practice Washington, 1995—2001; sr. of counsel Swidler Berlin Shereff Friedman (formerly Swidler & Berlin), Washington, 1996—2001; individual consulting and law practice, 2001—. Contbr. articles to profl. and other jours, chpts. to books. Founding mem. Company of Christian Jews. Decorated officer's cross Order of Merit (Fed. Republic Germany), chevalier Nat. Order of Merit (France). Mem. ABA, Am. Soc. Internat. Law (hon. v.p., treas. 1964-76), Coun. Fgn. Rels., Yale Club, Century Assn. (N.Y.), City Tavern, Met. Club (Washington). Anglican. Home: 3248 O St NW Washington DC 20007-2847 Personal E-mail: franzmfmo@aol.com.

OPPENHEIMER, JOHN JACOB, allergist, immunologist; b. Boston, June 22, 1960; BA, Lafayette Coll.; MD, Temple U., 1986. Diplomate Am. Bd. Allergy and Immunology, Am. Bd. Internal Medicine. Intern Robert Wood Johnson U. Hosp., New Brunswick, N.J., 1986-87, resident in internal medicine, 1987-89; fellow in allergy and immunology Nat. Jewish Ctr., Denver, 1989-91, staff, 1991-92; mem. staff Morristown (N.J.) Meml. Hosp., 1992—; pvt. practice, 1992-98. Asst. dir. U. Medicine and Dentistry N.J.-N.J. Med. Sch. Bd. dirs. clin. rsch. Pulmonary and Allergy Assn. Mem. Pulmonary and Allergy Assn. (dir. clin. rsch.). Home: 12 N Ridge Rd Denville NJ 07834-9629 Office: 1 Springfield Ave Summit NJ 07901 Office Phone: 973-267-9393. E-mail: nallopp@pol.net.

OPPENHEIMER, MAX, JR., foreign language educator, consultant; b. NYC, July 27, 1917; s. Max and Louise (Pourfuerst) O.; m. Christine Backus, Oct. 14, 1942; children: Edmund Max, Carolyn Christine Oppenheimer. Bachelier ès Lettres, U. Paris, 1935; BA cum laude, NYU, 1941; MA, UCLA, 1942; PhD, U. So. Calif., 1947. Instr. fgn. langs. San Diego State Coll., 1947-49; asst. prof. Romance langs. Washington U., St. Louis, 1949-51; assoc. prof. modern langs. Fla. State U., Tallahassee, 1958-61; prof., chmn. dept. Russian U. Iowa, Iowa City, 1961-67; prof. SUNY, Fredonia, 1967-76, prof. emeritus, 1976—, chmn. dept. fgn. langs., 1967-74; prof. English Yunnan Normal U., Kunming, Peoples Republic of China, 1985-86. Intelligence officer CIA, 1956—58. Translator: Collective Interaction Processes in Polymer, 1961; author: Outline of Russian Grammar, 1962; translator: Theory of Molecular Excitons (Davydov), 1962, Theory of Ship Waves and Wave Resistance (Kostyukov), 1968, The Fake Astrologer (Calderón de la Barca), 1976, 94, The Lady Simpleton (Lope de Vega), 1976, Don Juan (Tirso de Molina), 1976, Swim First and Last, 1981, An Innocent Yank at Home Abroad, 2000, Is That What It Means?, 2004, Is That What It Means? II, 2007, Is That What It Means? III, 2009, Cultivating Gratitude and Playing Your Cards as They are Dealt, 2009; contbr. articles to scholarly and profl. jours. Active YMCA, 1936—. Served to lt. col. M.I., AUS, 1942-46, 51-56, lt. col. Res. ret. Decorated Bronze Star; Fla. State U. grantee, 1961, Office Naval Rsch. grantee, 1965, SUNY grantee, 1973, french Jubilee Liberty medal. Mem.: MLA, Am. Soc. Geolinguistics (pres. 1975—76), Nat. Order Battlefield Commns., Dobro Slovo, Am. Mensa Ltd., Mil. Officers Assn. Am., Am. Soc. Dowsers, Elks, Phi Beta Kappa, Alpha Mu Gamma, Pi Delta Phi (nat. pres. 1946—51), Sigma Delta Pi. Avocation: swimming. Home: 10963 W Coggins Dr Sun City AZ 85351-3346 Home Phone: 623-876-0861. Personal E-mail: maxojr@azquik.com. *When you speak, always say what you think, not what you think you should say for the sake of expediency. Steadfastly, stubbornly, cling to your ideals, principles and beliefs, but be flexible enough to change whenever changing them reflects wisdom, not weakness or compromise. Avoid ego trips or being awed by your own alleged accomplishments.*

OPPENHEIMER, MICHAEL, physicist; b. Bklyn., Feb. 28, 1946; s. Harry and Shirley Oppenheimer; m. Leonie Haimson, Dec. 31, 1986; children: Chloe, Nathaniel. S.B., MIT, 1966; PhD, U. Chgo., 1970. Research fellow Harvard Coll., 1971-73; lectr. astronomy Harvard U., 1973-81; physicist Harvard-Smithsonian Center for Astrophysics, Harvard U., 1973-81, Environ. Def., NYC, 1981—2001, chief scientist, 1996-2001; Albert G. Milbank prof. geoscis. and internat. affairs Princeton U., 2002—, dir. program on sci. tech. and environ. Mem. panels on atmospheric effects of aviation NAS, 1995—99, climate variability and change, 2005—06, alleviate liquid transportation fuels, 2007—08; lead author 3rd and 4th assessments Intergovernmental Panel on Climate Change. Author: Dead Heat: The Race Against the Greenhouse Effect, 1990; contbr. articles to profl. jours. Fellow, Union Carbide, 1969—70, A.F. Morrison, 1979, Guggenheim, 1978—79; vis. scholar, Russell Sage Found., 2005—06. Mem.: AAAS, Internat. Glaciological Soc., Am. Meteorol. Soc., Am. Geophys. Union, Am. Phys. Soc. Office: Princeton U Robertson Hall 448 Princeton NJ 08544 Business E-Mail: omichael@princeton.edu.

OPPENHEIMER, PAUL, literature educator, poet; b. NYC, May 1, 1939; s. Fred R. Oppenheimer and Gertrude Samuels; m. Assia Nakova; children: Julie Sarah, Ben. BA, Princeton U., 1961; MA, Columbia U., 1963, PhD, 1970. Lectr. Hunter Coll. CUNY, NYC, 1964-67, lectr., poet-in-residence City Coll., 1967-70, from asst. prof. to assoc. prof. City Coll., 1970-84, prof. City Coll., 1984—; prof. comparative lit. The Grad. Ctr./CUNY, 2001—. Exch. prof., dir. CUNY student exch. program Sorbonne nouvelle, Paris, 1984-85; exch. prof. U. North London, Eng., 1989-90, Univ. Coll. London German Dept., 1993, 95, 97, 99; Fulbright prof. U. Osnabrück, Germany, 1993-94. Author: Before a Battle and Other Poems, 1967, Beyond the Furies, 1985, The Birth of the Modern Mind: Self, Consciousness, and the Invention of the Sonnet, 1989, Evil and the Demonic: A New Theory of Monstrous Behavior, 1996, An Intelligent Person's Guide to Modern Guilt, 1997, Rubens: A Portrait, 1999, 2002, Blood Memoir, or the First Three Days of Creation, 1999, Infinite Desire: A Guide to Modern Guilt, 2000, The Flame Charts, new poems, 2002; translator: Till Eulenspiegel: His Adventures, 1972, 4th edit., 2001. Woodrow Wilson fellow, 1961-62, Alfred Hodder fellow, 1969-70, Fulbright sr. fellow, Germany, 1993-94; recipient Eisner Scholars award Rifkind Ctr. for the Humanities, 1998. Mem. Dante Soc. Am. Home: 50 W 67th St New York NY 10023-6227 Office: CCNY Dept English and Comparative Lit NAC 138 St and Convent Ave New York NY 10031 Also: The Graduate Ctr CUNY Dept Comparative Lit 365 Fifth Ave New York NY 10016 Office Phone: 212-650-6322. Personal E-mail: pauloppenheimer@hotmail.com.

OPPENHEIMER, PETER, computer company executive; BA with honors, Calif. Polytechnic U.; MBA with honors, U. Santa Clara. Former mgr. info. tech. cons. practice Coopers and Lybrand; former CFO automatic data processing Apple Computer Inc., controller Americas, 1996—97, v.p. worldwide sales controller to corp. controller, 1997—2004; sr. v.p. fin., CFO Apple Inc. (formerly Apple Computer Inc.), 2004—. Office: Apple Inc 1 Infinite Loop Cupertino CA 95014 Office Phone: 408-996-1010.*

OPPENHEIMER, RANDY (MARK RANDALL OPPENHEIMER), lawyer; b. Balt., 1952; AB summa cum laude, Harvard U., 1974; JD, U. Chgo., 1977. Bar: Calif. 1977. Ptnr., co-chair Entertainment, Sports, and Media practice O'Melveny & Myers LLP, LA. Mem.: ABA. Office: O'Melveny & Myers LLP 1999 Ave of Stars, 7th Fl Los Angeles CA 90067-6035 Office Phone: 310-246-6722. Office Fax: 310-246-6779. E-mail: roppenheimer@omm.com.

OPPERMAN, DWIGHT DARWIN, retired publishing company executive; b. Perry, Iowa, June 26, 1923; s. John H. and Zoa L. (Opperman); m. Jeanice Wifvat, Apr. 22, 1942 (dec. 1993); children: Vance K., Fane W. JD, Drake U., 1951, LLD (hon.), 1998, Hamline U. Bar: (Iowa 1951, U.S. Supreme Ct. 1976, U.S Ct. Internat. Trade, 1988.). Editor, asst. editorial counsel West Pub. Co., St. Paul, 1951-64, mgr. reporters and digest depts., 1964-65, v.p., 1965-68, pres., 1968-93, CEO, 1978-96, chmn., 1993-96; chmn. emeritus West Group, Eagan, 1996—; chmn. Key Investment, Mpls.; owner Phoenix New Millennium, 2007—. Dir. Inst. Judicial Adminstrn. Dir. Inst. Jud. Adminstrn., Minn. D.A.R.E. Inc., Brennan Ctr. for Justice; trustee NYU Law Sch.; dir. Nat. Legal Ctr. for Pub. Interest, Nat. Ctr. for State Cts., Supreme Ct. Hist. Soc.; bd. govs. Drake U., Des Moines, founder, Opperman Lecture in Constl. Law. With US Army, WWII. Recipient Toni House award, Conf. of Pub. Info. Officers, 1st George Wickersham Founder's award, Friends of Law Libr. of Congress, 1993, Lifetime Achievement award, Minn. State Bar Assn., 1997, Outstanding Alumni award, Drake U. Law Sch.; named one of 400 Richest Ams., Forbes mag., 2002, 2004, 2006. Fellow: Am. Bar Found.; mem.: ABA, Nat. Ctr. for State Cts. (bd. dirs. 1999—2003, mem. Warren E. Burger Soc., Disting. Svc. award 2004), Am. Law Inst., Am. Judicature Soc. (past bd. mem., past mem. exec. com., Herbert Harley award 1984, Justice award 1992), Fed. Bar Assn., Mpls. Club, Minn. Club, Drake U. Nat. Alumni Assn. (disting. svc. award 1974, Centennial award 1981, Outstanding Alumni award 1988). Achievements include having Drake University's Opperman Hall and law library named in his honor, 1984; having an award named in his honor by the American Judicature Society. Office: Key Investment 601 2nd Ave S Minneapolis MN 55402-4317 Office Phone: 612-333-6700.

OPPERMAN, ROSANNA RESENDEZ, vice principal; b. LA, Apr. 06; d. Victor Thomas and Dolores Resendez Mendez; m. Daniel Charles Opperman, Aug. 3, 1974; children: Joshua Mendez, Timothy Mendez, Laura Mendez. BA in Exptl. Psychology, U. Calif., Santa Barbara, Calif., 1976; degree in Multiple Subject Tchg., Azusa Pacific Coll., 1979; MA in Ednl. Leadership, Calif. State U., Sacramento, 2005. Admin. Svcs. Credential Calif. State U., Sacramento, 2003. From instr. to coord. ABE Program Fremont Sch. for Adults, Sacramento, 1989—2002, coord. ESL Program, 2002—04, Wasc accreditation co-chair, 2002—03; from coord. to vice prin. Winterstein & Bella Vista Adult Ctrs., Sacramento, 2004—; chair Wasc, 2000; vice prin. to dist. migrant coord. Alisal Union Sch. Dist. Awards chmn. no. sect. Calif. Coun. Adult Edn., Sacramento, 1997—99, pres. no. sect., 1999—2000, v.p. no. sect., 1999—2000. Cmty. adv. co-chair Fremont Sch. for Adults, Sacramento, 1999—2000; caravans dir. Nazarene Ch., Sacramento, 1988—94. Recipient Outstanding Leadership award, Calif. Coun. Adult Edn., 1997—2001, Excellence in Tchg. award, 1998. Mem.: Adult Basic Educators (assoc.), Calif. Assn. Tchrs. English to Spkrs. Other Langs. (assoc.). Home: 1431 Via Marettimo Monterey CA 93940 Office Phone: 831-796-3910 3680. Personal E-mail: rosanna.opperman@alisal.org.

OPPERWALL, STEPHEN GABRIEL, lawyer; s. Raymond and Helen Bertha Opperwall; m. Kathleen O'Neill, Oct. 27, 1990; children: Christopher Stephen, Scott O'Neill. BA, Calvin Coll., 1975; JD, U. Santa Clara, 1981. Bar: Calif. 1981, U.S. Dist. Ct. (no., ea., ctrl. and so. dists.) Calif. 1981, U.S. Tax Ct. 1994, U.S. Ct. Appeals (9th cir.) 1984; cert. in creditor's rights, Am. Bd. Cert. Tchg. asst. U. Santa Clara (Calif.) Sch. Law, 1979; judge's law clk. U.S. Ct. Appeals, 9th Cir., San Francisco, 1980; assoc. Pitto & Ubhaus, San Jose, Calif., 1980-82, Germino, Layne & Brodie, Palo Alto, Calif., 1982-87, Tarkington, O'Connor & O'Neill, San Jose, 1988-90, Smith & Smith, San Jose, 1990-92; pvt. practice Law Offices of Stephen G. Opperwall, Pleasanton, Calif., 1992—. Judge pro tem Santa Clara County Cts., 1986—, Alameda County (Calif.) Cts., 1992-. Editor Santa Clara Law Review, 1980. Mem. bd. dirs. Fremont Symphony, 1994; meme. adv. bd. Fremont Bank, Calif., 1996. Mem. Coml. Law League Am., Pleasanton C. of C., Am. Bankruptcy Inst. Avocations: golf, tennis, computers, gardening, music. Office: 4900 Hopyard Rd Ste 100 Pleasanton CA 94588-3149 Office Phone: 925-417-0300. Office Fax: 925-417-0301. E-mail: lawofcsgo@aol.com.

OPPMANN, ANDREW JAMES, newspaper editor; b. Hopkinsville, Ky., Apr. 3, 1963; s. Patrick George Oppmann and Elizabeth Anne (Freeman) Peace; m. Emily Elise Wey, Oct. 8, 1988; children: Emily Katherine, Sarah Elizabeth. BA in Journalism, U. Ky., 1985. Staff writer The Orange County Register, Santa Ana, Calif., 1985-86; copy editor, staff writer Lexington (Ky.) Herald-Leader, 1986-87, bur. chief, asst. metro editor, 1988-91; urban affairs writer The Knoxville (Tenn.) News-Sentinel, 1987-88; asst. city editor The Houston Post, 1991-92, dep. met. editor, 1992, asst. to mng. editor, 1992, met. editor, 1992-94; Ky. editor The Cin. (Ohio) Enquirer, 1994-97; supervising editor The Ky. Enquirer, Ft. Mitchell, 1994-97; mng. editor Montgomery (Ala.) Advertiser, 1998-2001; exec. editor The Post-Crescent, Appleton, Wis., 2001—. Bd. vis. U. Ky. Sch. Journalism, 1994-97. Fellow U. Ky., 1984; recipient Gannett Newsroom Supr. Recognition award, 1995, 2000. Mem. U. Ky. Journalism Alumni Assn. (v.p. 1997-2000, pres. 2001-03), Soc. Profl. Journalists (bd. dirs. Queen City chpt. 1995-97), Ala. AP Mng. Editors (bd. dirs. 1998—), U. Ky. Nat. Alumni Assn. (bd. dirs. 1998-2001). Office: The Post-Crescent PO Box 59 Appleton WI 54912 E-mail: oppedit@aol.com.

OPRE, THOMAS EDWARD, retired editor, film company executive; b. Evansville, Ind., Nov. 6, 1943; s. William Jennings and Ruth (Strouss) O.; children: Thomas Andrew, William Hartley. AB in Journalism, Ind. U., 1965. Writer sports and outdoors Decatur (Ill.) Herald and Rev., 1965-66; outdoor editor Detroit Free Press, 1966—91; field editor Midwest div. Field and Stream mag., 1971-81; editorial dir. Gt. Lakes Sportsman mag., 1972-75; editor-at-large and sports vehicles editor Outdoor Life mag., 1981-93; pres. Tom Opre Prodns., 1967—2004. Pres. TOP Safaris, Inc., 1986—2004. Author numerous articles in outdoor and travel fields. Recipient James Henshall award Am. Fish Tackle Mfrs. Assn., 1969, Teddy award Internat. Outdoor Travel Film Festival, 1973, Environ. award EPA, 1977, Nat. Writer's award Safari Club Internat., 1977, Deep Woods Writing award OWAA, 1977, Conservation Service award Ducks Unltd., 1977; World Wildlife Found. award, 1981; named to Internat. Fishing Hall of Fame, 1968, Conservation Communicator of Yr., 1985. Mem. Outdoor Writers Assn. Am. (past dir., pres., v.p., chmn. bd.), Assn. Gt. Lakes Outdoor Writers (past dir., chmn. bd., pres., v.p.), Mich. Outdoor Writers Assn. (v.p., pres., chmn. bd. dirs.), Alpha Tau Omega. Home and Office: 255 Powers Cv NE Marietta GA 30067-1503 Personal E-mail: topsafaris@aol.com.

OPRI, DEBRA ANN, lawyer; b. Paterson, NJ, June 10, 1960; BFA, NYU, 1982; JD, Whittier Coll., 1987. Bar: Calif. 1989, NJ 1991, DC 1991. Founder, ptnr. Opri & Assoc., Beverly Hills, Calif., 1989—. Legal/polit. analyst and commentator 97.1 FM Talk, LA, Fox News, Inside Edition; columnist The Opri Opinion, www.debraopri.com. Author: Video Rentals and the First Sale Doctrine: The Deficiency of Proposed Legislation, 1986. Mem.: ATLA, Calif. Trial Lawyers Assn., LA Trial Lawyers Assn. Office: Opri & Associates 8383 Wilshire Blvd Ste 830 Beverly Hills CA 90211 Office Phone: 213-658-6774. Office Fax: 213-658-5160.

OPRSAL, NANCY UPSHAW, retired elementary school educator; b. Dallas, Tex., July 10, 1931; d. Banks and Catherine Richards (Butler) Upshaw; m. George Oprsal, Apr. 23, 1957 (dec.); 1 child, Paul Oprsal (dec.). BS in elem. edn., No. Tex. State U., 1952; MA in edn., George Peabody Coll. for Teachers, 1953. Pre-sch. music tchr. Greenhill Sch., Dallas, 1948—53; tchr. Denver Pub. Schools, 1953—55; music tchr. Ft. Worth Pub. Schools, Tex., 1955—57; tchr. Dallas Ind. Sch. Dist., 1957—60, Del Paso Heights Sch. Dist., Sacramento, 1960—62, San Juan Sch. Dist., Sacramento, 1966—96; ret. Guest tchr. San Juan Sch. Dist., Sacramento, 1996—. Server Loaves and Fishes; mem. Green Sanctuary and Social Responsibility Coms.; ch. sch. tchr. Unitarian Univeralist Soc. of Sacramento, 1960—; receptionist and docent Effie Yeaw Nature Ctr., Carmichael, Calif., 1980—; sec. Carmichael Garden Club, 1962—66; coord. Family Promise Interfaith Hospitality Network, 2004—. Democrat. Unitarian Universalist. Avocations: gardening, hiking. Personal E-mail: noprsal@aol.com.

OQILOV, OQIL GHAYBULLOYEVICH, Prime Minister of Tajikistan; b. 1944; Prime min. Tajikistan, 1999—; mem. People's Dem. Party, Tajikistan; min. constrn. Tajikistan Govt. Office: Secretariate of the Prime Minister pr Rudaki 80 734023 Dushanbe Tajikistan Office Phone: 372 21 18 71. Office Fax: 372 21 51 10.

O'QUINN, JOHN M., lawyer; b. 1941; BS, U. Houston, 1965, JD magna cum laude, 1967. Bar: Tex. 1967, US Supreme Ct. 1972, US Ct. Appeals (5th cir.) 1984, US Dist. Ct. (so. and ea. dists. Tex.) 1986. Founding ptnr. O'Quinn, Kerensky, McAninch & Laminack, Houston, 1981—. Mem. adv. com. Tex. State Supreme Ct., 1984-94; trustee U. Houston Law Found., 1985—; adj prof. law, U. Houston, So. Tex. Coll. Law, Tex. So. Coll. Law. Regent U. Houston, 1993-99. Named one of Top 10 Trial Lawyers in Am., Nat. Law Jour., 1993, 2004, 100 Most Influential Lawyers in US, 1994, 100 Legal Legends of Tex., Tex. Lawyer, 5 Best Tex. Trial Lawyers of the Century, Houston Chronicle. Am. Trial Lawyers Assn., Tex. Trial Lawyers Assn. (dir.), Houston Trial Lawyers Assn. (dir.), Houston Bar Assn., State Bar Tex., U. Houston Law Alumni Assn. (pres. 1978). Office: O'Quinn Law Firm 2300 Lyric Ctr Bldg 440 Louisiana St Houston TX 77002-1639 Office Phone: 713-223-1000. Office Fax: 713-222-6903.

O'QUINN, JOSIE LU, nursing educator; BSN, Tex. Christian U., 1960; MS in Nursing, U. Tex., 1976, PhD, 1989. Nurse cons. Bd. Nurse Examiners, 1977-87; assoc. prof. Sch. Nursing U. Tex., Arlington, 1988—2004, dir. BSN progrm, 1996—2000, assoc. dean, 2000—04; ret., 2004. Adj. assoc. prof. U. Tex., Arlington, 2004—09; cons., presenter in field. Contbr. articles to profl. jours. Mem. Tarrant County Clin. Coordinator Coun., 1988-2000, chair, 1989-92, 97—2000; Sch. Nursing rep. United Way, 1989; active adminstrv. bd. Trinity United Meth. Ch., Arlington, 1993-95, mem. mental health task force, 1992, 93, greeter/usher, 1992—00, mem. mental health bd., 1994; mem. nursing rsch. com. Parkland Meml. Hosp., 1989-96; bd. dirs. Arlington adv. com. Tarrant County chpt. ARC, 1989-95, mem. health svcs. of Tarrant County chpt., 1988-95, sec., 1992; team capt. heart walk Am. Heart Assn., 1991; elected mem. Leadership Arlington, 1992-93, chair Parks and Recreation com.; pres. Sunday sch. class First United Meth. Ch., 1989-90, greeter, 1988, 89, 90, 91, mem. adult-family coun., 1990, 91, chair parish nurse ministry panel, 1991-92; bd. dirs. ARC, 1989-95, sec., 1992-93, mem. exec. com., 1992-95; bd. dirs. Cancer Survivors Day Am. Cancer Assn., 1994, 95, Arlington Hist. Soc., 1999—. Recipient Svc. award ARC, 1994, Faculty Recognition award, 1993, U. Tex.-Arlington Recognition award, 1994; named one of Great 100 Nurses, 1996, named to Acad. Disting. Tchrs., U. Tex.-Arlington, 2003, named Ft. Worth Bus. Press Health Care Hero, 2004; grantee Jr. League of Arlington, 1991. Mem. ANA, Nat. League Nurses, Tex. Nurses Assn. (mem. govt. affairs com. 1990-91, chair dist. 3 bylaws com. 1991-92, mem. membership com. 1990, elected mem. nominating com. 1992-93, elected del. 1993, 2001, elected chair nominating com. 1993-94), Tex. League Nurses (mem. membership com. 1989-90), So. Nursing Rsch. Soc., Alumni Assn. Sch. of Nursing, Phi Kappa Phi, Sigma Theta Tau (elected mem. nominating com. 1993-94), UTA Retives Club Avocations: self-development, aerobics, gardening, bowling, golf. Home: 1003 W Lovers Ln Arlington TX 76013-3945 Office Phone: 817-272-2776.

ORAM, FERN AMY, content director; b. Phila., May 19, 1965; d. Linda Shirley and Stuart Jerome Oram; m. David Adam Riegelhaupt, Oct. 5, 2002. Listings editor TVSM, Horsham, Pa., 1986—87, listings mgr., 1987—97, listings dir., 1997—99; prodn. mgr. Peterson's, Lawrenceville, Pa., 1999—2003, editl. dir., 2003—08. Mem.: So. Poverty Law Ctr., Eta Theta Chpt. of Kappa Delta at Villanova U. (chair 2004—08, chpt. adv. bd.), Phila. Suburban West Alumna Assn. of Kappa Delta (pres. 1997—2004), Kappa Delta. Office: Petersons 2000 Lenox Dr Lawrenceville NJ 08648 Home: 707 Manton St Philadelphia PA 19147-5117 Personal E-mail: thinkspink@verizon.net. Business E-Mail: fern.oram@petersons.com.

ORAN, ELAINE SURICK, physicist; b. Rome, Ga., Apr. 16, 1946; d. Herman E. and Bessye R. (Kolker) Surick; m. Daniel Hirsh Oran, Feb. 1, 1969. AB in Physics and Chemistry, Bryn Mawr Coll., 1966; MPh in Physics, Yale U., 1968, PhD in Solid State Physics and Statistical Mechanics, 1972; Doctorate (hon.), Ecole Ctrl. Lyon, France, 2006. Rsch. physicist Naval Rsch. Lab., Washington, 1972-76, supervisory rsch. physicist, 1976-88, sr. scientist reactive flow physics, 1988—. Head Ctr. for Reactive Flow and Dynamical Systems, 1985-87; mem. adv. bd. NSF; cons. to U.S. govt., agys., NATO.; mem. Aero. Adv. Coun. NASA, 1995-97; adj. prof. dept. aerospace engrng. U. Mich., 2005—. Author: Numerical Simulation of Reactive Flow, 1987, 2d edit., 2001, Numerical Approaches to Combustion Modeling, 1991; assoc. editor Jour. Computational Physics, 1992-2002; mem. editl. bd. Prog. Ener. Comb. Sci., 1990-2005; mng. editor Shock Waves, 1998-2002; editor-in-chief AIAA Jour., 2003-; contbr. numerous articles to profl. jours., chpts. to books. Recipient Arthur S. Flemming award, 1979, Women in Sci. and Engring. award, 1988, Oppenheim prize, 1999, Zeldovich Gold medal, 2000; named hon. prof., U. Wales, 2001—05; named to Hall of Fame, Women in Tech. Internat., 2002; grantee, USN, NASA, USAF, Def. Advanced Rsch. Projects Agy. Fellow AIAA (publs. com. 1986-2002, v.p. publs. 1993-97, Dryden Disting. lectr. 2002, editor-in-chief AIAA Jour.), Am. Phys. Soc. (exec. com. fluid dynamics divsn. 1986, 96, exec. com. computational physics 1989-97, chair 1991-92); mem. NAE, Am. Geophys. Union, Combustion Inst. (bd. dirs. 1990-2002), Inst. Dynamics of Energetic Sys. (bd. dirs. 1989—, pres.), Soc. Indsl. and Applied Math., Soc. Women Engrs.(Achievement award 2006), Sigma Xi. Office: Naval Rsch Lab Code 6404 6004 Washington DC 20375 Office Phone: 202-767-2960. Business E-Mail: oran@lcp.nrl.navy.mil.

ORANSKY, IVAN, writer, editor; b. Nyack, NY, Aug. 20, 1972; s. Stanley Howard and Lesley Marsha Oransky. BA, Harvard U., 1994; MD, NYU, 1998. Editor-in-chief Praxis Post, NYC, 2000—02; web editl. dir. The Scientist, Phila., 2002—04, dep. editor, 2004—08; mng. editor Online, Sci, Am., 2008—09; exec. editor Reuters Health, 2009—. Adj. asst. prof. journalism NYU, NYC, 2002—, clin. asst. prof. medicine, 2005—; adj. asst. prof. journalism CUNY, 2007—. Author: Insider's Guide to Medical Schools, 1999, Appleton & Lange's Review of Psychiatry, 6th edit., 2001, 9th edit., 2007, Common Symptom Answer Guide, 2005; contbr. The Lancet. Mem.: Online News Assn., Assn. for Health Care Journalists (bd. dirs. 2002—), Nat. Assn. Sci. Writers. Personal E-mail: ivan-oransky@erols.com. Business E-Mail: ivan.oransky@thomsonreuters.com.

ORATZ, RUTH, physician; d. Murray and Rosalyn Oratz; m. Hank B. Ridless, Nov. 1, 1993. AB in History and Philosophy of Sci., Harvard U., 1977; MD, Albert Einstein Coll. Medicine, 1982. Diplomate in internal medicine and med. oncology Am. Bd. Internal Medicine. Assoc. prof. clin. medicine NYU Sch. Medicine, NYC, 1997—. Mem. adv. bd. breastcancer.org, cancerandcareers, sharsheret. Named Physician of Yr., Cancer Care, 2005. Fellow: ACP; mem.: Am. Assn. for Cancer Rsch., Am. Soc. Clin. Oncologists. Office: Womens Oncology and Wellness Practice Ste 202 345 E 37th St New York NY 10016 Office Phone: 212-400-4904. E-mail: contact@thewomenspractice.org.

ORAVEC, JO ANN ROSE, computing and public policy educator; b. Chgo., Apr. 18, 1954; d. Joseph John and Marion Lena (Koneman) O. MS, U. Wis., 1982, MA, 1984, MBA, 1986, PhD, 1992. Lectr. computer sci. and mgmt. U. Wis., Madison, 1984—94; asst. prof. Baruch Coll., Sch. Pub. Affairs, NYC, 1994—. Author: Interactions in Science and Society, 1991, Virtual Individuals, Virtual Groups, 1996; editor spl. issue Jour. Sys. and Software, 1992. First chair Privacy Coun. of the State of Wis., Madison, 1994-95. Grantee ICEC fellow, Carnegie Mellon, 1986. Mem. Computer Profls. for Social Responsibility (spkr.). Avocation: multimedia development and internet research. Office: Univ of Wisconsin- Whitewater 800 W Main Whitewater WI 53190 Home: PO Box 481 Whitewater WI 53190 Business E-Mail: oravecj@uww.edu.

ORBACH, RAYMOND LEE, physicist, researcher, former federal agency administrator; b. L.A., July 12, 1934; s. Morris Albert and Mary Ruth (Miller) O.; m. Eva Hannah Spiegler, Aug. 26, 1956; children: David Miller, Deborah Hedwig, Thomas Randolph. BS, Calif. Inst. Tech., Pasadena, 1956; PhD, U. Calif., Berkeley, 1960; PhD in Policy Analysis (hon.), The Rand Grad. Sch., Santa Monica, Calif., 2002; PhD in Engring. (hon.), Colo. Sch. Mines, Goldon, 2005. NSF postdoctoral fellow Oxford U., 1960-61; asst. prof. applied physics Harvard U., 1961-63; prof. physics UCLA, 1963-92, asst. vice chancellor acad. change and curriculum devel., 1970-72, chmn. acad. senate L.A. divsn., 1976-77, provost Coll. Letters and Sci., 1982-92; chancellor U. Calif., Riverside, 1992—2002, chancellor emeritus, Disting. prof. physics emeritus, 2002—; dir. Office Sci. US Dept. Energy, Washington, 2002—09, under sec. for sci., 2006—09. Mem. physics adv. panel NSF, 1970-73; mem. vis. com. Brookhaven Nat. Lab., 1970-74; mem. materials rsch. lab. adv. panel NSF, 1974-77; mem. Nat. Commn. on Rsch., 1978-80; chmn. 16th Internat. Conf. on Low Temperature Physics, 1981; Joliot Curie prof. Ecole Superieure de la Physique et Chimie Industrielle de la Ville de Paris, 1982, chmn. Gordon Rsch. Conf. on Fractals, 1986; Lorentz prof. U. Leiden, Netherlands, 1987; Raymond and Beverly Sackler lectr. Tel Aviv U., 1989; faculty rsch. lectr. UCLA, 1990; Andrew Lawson lectr. U. Calif., Riverside, 1992; mem. external rev. com. Nat. High Magnetic Fields Lab., 1994-01. Author: (with A.A. Manenkov) SpinLattice Relaxation in Ionic Solids, 1966; divsn. assoc. editor Phys. Rev. Letters, 1980-83, Jour. Low Temperature Physics, 1980-90, Phys. Rev., 1983-87; contbr. articles to profl. jours. Recipient Whitney M. Young Humanitarian award Urban League of Riverside and San Bernardino, 1998, El Sol Azteca award La Prensa Hispana, 2000, Disting. Alumni award Calif. Inst. Tech., 2005; Alfred P. Sloan Found. fellow, 1963-67; NSF sr. postdoctoral fellow Imperial Coll., 1967-68; Guggenheim fellow Tel Aviv U., 1973-74. Fellow AAAS (chairperson steering group physics sect.), Am. Phys. Soc. (chmn. nominations com. 1981-82, counselor-at-large 1987-91, chmn. divsn. condensed matter 1990-91); mem. NSF (mem. rsch. adv. com. divsn. materials 1992-93), Phys. Soc. (London), Univ. Rsch. Assn. (chair coun. pres. 1993), Sigma Xi, Phi Beta Kappa, Tau Beta Pi. Personal E-mail: rorbach@earthlink.net.*

ORBEN, JACK RICHARD, investment company executive, director; b. Bklyn., June 16, 1938; s. Stanley Souza and Helena Emily (Hall) O.; m. Patricia Wells, Dec. 17, 1960; children: Stacey Souza, Stephanie Anne, Bradford Richard. AA, Valley Forge, Pa., 1956; BA, Tufts U., Medford, Mass., 1960. Sales mgr. nat. accts. NY Tel. Co., 1960—66; founder, exec. v.p. Facts, Inc., 1966—69; chmn., CEO Fiduciary Alliance, Inc., NYC, 1970—; chmn. Oaktree Asset Mgmt., LLC, NYC, 2004—05. Chmn., CEO, pres. Fiduciary Counsel, Inc., 1979-04; chmn. White Plains Charter Revision Commn.; fin. com. City of White Plains; past pres. White Plains Child Day Care Assn., Thomas Slater Ctr.; past chmn., bd. dirs. YMCA Ctrl. and No. Westchester Sec., treas., bd. dirs., Indsl. Devel. Agy. Town of Riverhead, NY. With USNG, 1960-66. Mem. Am. Inst. Econ. Rsch., Fgn. Policy Rsch. Inst., Econ. Club. NY, The Pilgrims, Larchmont Yacht Club, NY Yacht Club, Union League Club, Windemere Island Club, Univ. Club, Down Town Assn., North Fork Country Club. Home: 61 Harbor Rd Riverhead NY 11901 Office Phone: 631-722-5649. Personal E-mail: jrorben@aol.com.

ORBEN, ROBERT, scriptwriter, writer; b. NYC, Mar. 4, 1927; s. Walter August and Marie O.; m. Jean Louise Connelly, July 25, 1945. Humor and speech writer for entertainment personalities, bus. execs., politicians, 1946—; writer Jack Paar Show, NYC, 1962-63, Red Skelton Hour, Hollywood, Calif., 1964-70; editor Orben's Current Comedy, Wilmington, Del., 1971-89; cons. to Vice Pres. Gerald R. Ford, Washington, 1974; speechwriter Pres. Gerald R. Ford, Washington, 1974-75; spl. asst. to pres., dir. White House speechwriting dept., Washington, 1976-77; speaker on uses of humor in communication, 1977—. Author: 2500 Jokes to Start 'Em Laughing, 1979, 2100 Laughs for All Occasions, 1983, 2400 Jokes to Brighten Your Speeches, 1984, 2000 Sure-Fire Jokes for Speakers, 1986, Speechwriter's Handbook of Humor, 2007, others. Recipient World Humor award Workshop Libr. on World Humor, 1992, Humor award Gliner Humor Ctr., U. Md., 2005; Literary fellow Acad. Magical Arts, 1996. Mem. Writers Guild Am. Clubs: Nat. Press (Washington). Unitarian Universalist. Avocations: travel, theater. Home: 3709 S George Mason Dr Apt 205E Falls Church VA 22041-3700 *I have spent most of my lifetime creating laughter and consider it a lifetime well spent. Laughter is one of the glories of the human experience. It warms, amuses, instructs, and opens emotional doors. For me, laughter has been a living and a loving as well.*

ORBISON, JAMES ARCHER, JR., cardiologist, surgeon; b. Dryden, Mich., Aug. 22, 1914; s. James Archer Sr. and Florence (Thomas) Orbison; m. Pil-Sook Lee Orbison, Nov. 7, 1988; m. Helen Alice Bentley (dec.); children: Carole Ann Seeley, James Archer Obison III. Student, U. Denver, 1933—34; BA, U. Mich., 1937, MD, 1940. Diplomate Am. Bd. Internal Medicine, Am. Bd. Cardiovascular Disease, lic. physician Hawaii, Mich. Intern Harper Hosp., 1940—41; commd. 2d lt. US Army, 1941, advanced through grades to col., 1968; resident in internal medicine Oliver Gen. Hosp., Augusta, Ga., 1947—49; asst. prof. clinical medicine Med. Coll. Ga., Augusta, 1949—50; fellow in cardiovascular disease Walter Reed Gen. Hosp., Washington, 1951—52; asst. clin. prof. medicine U. Colo. Sch. Medicine, Denver, 1960—64; cons. tchg. internal medicine Queen's Med. Ctr., Honolulu, 1964—67, attending staff, 1970—88; assoc. clin. prof. medicine U. Hawaii Sch. Medicine, 1967—; assoc. clin. prof. John Burns Sch. Medicine, Honolulu, 1967—88. Presenter in field. Contbr. articles to profl. jours. Decorated Commendation medal US Army, Legion of Merit, Am. Def. medal; recipient Cardiology Laureate award, Hawaii Heart Assn., 1988; grantee, US Army R & D Command, 1959. Fellow: Am. Coll. Cardiology (program com. annual meeting 1962, Hawaii gov. 1971—74); mem.: ACP (life; program com. Colo. regional meeting 1960—64, program com. annual meeting 1963, program com. Hawaii regional meeting 1964), Hawaii Med. Soc. (med. edn. com. 1971—, chronic illness com. 1972—), Assn. for Hosp. Med. Edn., Am. Soc. Clinical Pharmacology and Therapeutics, Am. Fedn. Clin. Rsch. (sr.), Honolulu County Med. Soc. (postgrad. com. 1970—), Hawaii Heart Assn. (bd. dirs. 1964—, 2d v.p. 1972—73, exec. com. 1972—, pres.-elect 1973—). Republican. Presbyterian. Avocations: fishing, tennis, golf, photography, football. Home: 1994 San Antonio Ave Berkeley CA 94707-1620

ORCE, KENNETH W., lawyer; b. Yonkers, NY, Apr. 3, 1943; s. Edmund John and Helen (Mulcahy) Orce; m. Helene Mary Sparti, Aug. 20, 1966; children: Kenneth W., Kimberley J., Brian C. BS with honors, Manhattan Coll., 1965; LLB cum laude, Harvard U., 1968. Bar: NY 1969. Assoc. Cahill Gordon & Reindel LLP, NYC, 1968—76, ptnr., 1976—91, mem. exec. com., 1991—. Editor: Harvard Law Rev., 1966—68. Mem.: Down Town Assn., Hudson Nat. Golf Club, Met. Opera Club. Office: Cahill Gordon & Reindel LLP 80 Pine St New York NY 10005-1702 Office Phone: 212-701-3215. Office Fax: 212-378-2324. Business E-Mail: korce@cahill.com.

ORCHARD, ROBERT JOHN, theater producer, educator; b. Maplewood, NJ, Dec. 3, 1946; s. Robert Orchard and Beatrice (Gould) Todd; m. Pamela Marcy Pritchard, Sept. 6, 1969; children: Christopher, Katherine. Student, The Lawrence Acad., 1965; BA, Middlebury Coll., 1969; MFA, Yale U., 1972. Gen. mgr. Peterborough (N.H.) Players, 1967-70; asst. mng. dir. Yale Repertory Theatre, 1971-72, artistic admistr., 1972-73; instr. Yale Sch. Drama, 1972-73; mng. dir. Yale Repertory Theatre and Sch. Drama, 1973-79, Am. Repertory Theatre, Cambridge, Mass., 1979—2002, exec. dir., 2002—. Assoc. prof., co-chmn. theatre adminstrn. tng. program Yale Sch. Drama, 1975-79; mng. dir. Loeb Drama Ctr., Harvard U., 1979-2000, dir., 2000—, mng. dir. Inst. for Advanced Theatre Tng., 1979-2002, exec. dir., 2002—; orgn. ptnr. Inst. Arts and Civic Dialogue at Harvard U. Former mem. bd. dirs. Theatre Comms. Group; pres. bd. Mass. Cultural Edn. Collaborative, Am. Arts Alliance, Peterborough Players, Cambridge Multi-Cultural Arts Ctrs.; former exec. com. League of Residents Theatres; chmn. NEA, Profl. Theatre Cos., Opera/Mus. Theatre Panels. Office: Am Repertory Theatre 64 Brattle St Cambridge MA 02138-3443

ORCUTT, BEN AVIS, retired social work educator; b. Falco, Ala., Oct. 17, 1914; d. Benjamin A. and Emily Olive Adams; m. Harry P. Orcutt, 1946 (dec.). AB, U. Ala., 1936; MA, Tulane U., 1939, MSW, 1942; DSW, Columbia U., 1962. Social worker ARC, Lagarde Gen. Hosp., New Orleans; social worker, acting field dir. Fort Benning (Ga.) Regional Hosp., 1942-46; chief social work svc. VA Regional Office, Phoenix, 1946—51; chief social work svc. unit outpatient office VA, Birmingham, Ala., 1954-57, 58; rsch. asst. Rsch. Ctr. Sch. Social Work, Columbia U., NYC, 1960-62, field advisor social work, 1962, assoc. prof. social work, 1965-76, La. State U., Baton Rouge, 1962-65; prof. social work, dir. doctoral program U. Ala., University, 1976-84; ret. Rsch. cons. Tavistock Centre, London, 1972; cons. sch. social work U. Houston, 1990, Troy State System, 1992. Author: Science and Inquiry in Social Work Practice, 1990, (with Harry P. Orcutt) America's Riding Horses, 1958, (with Elizabeth R. Prichard, Jean Collard, Austin H. Kutscher, Irene Seeland, Nathan Lefkowitz) Social Work with the Dying Patient and the Family, 1977, (with others) Social Work and Thanatology, 1980; editor: Poverty and Social Casework Services, 1974; mem. editl. bd. Jour. Social Work, 1982-84; contbr. articles to profl. books and jours. Mem. alumni bd. Sch. Social Work Columbia U., 1985—88, 1991—94. Recipient Centennial award for edn. Columbia U. Sch. Social Work, 1998; named to Ala. Social Work Hall of Fame, 1999; NIMH fellow, 1957-60; Ben Avis Adams Orcutt doctoral scholar in social work named in her honor, U. Ala. Mem. Group for Advancement Doctoral Edn. (steering com., editor newsletter 1980-83). Episcopalian. Office: PO Box 870314 Tuscaloosa AL 35487-0314 Home: 1199 Valley View Dr Andalusia AL 36424

ORD, KEITH J., finance educator; b. Grimsby, Eng., Nov. 28, 1942; s. Kenneth and Edith Ord; m. Janice Derr, May 24, 1980; children: Jane Foor, Lawrence. PhD, London Sch. Economics, London, 1966. Prof. Pa. State U., State Coll., 1980—99, Georgetown U., Washington, 1999—. Recipient Hon. Geographer award, Am. Assn. Geographers, 2004. Fellow: Internat. Inst. Forecasters, Royal Statis. Soc., Am. Statis. Assn. Avocation: running. Home: 7838 Oracle Pl Potomac MD 20854 Office: Georgetown Univ 37th and O St NW Washington DC 20057 Personal E-mail: keith.ord@comcast.net. Business E-Mail: ordk@msb.edu.

ORDAL, CASPAR REUBEN, retired executive; b. Martell, Wis., May 5, 1922; s. Zakarias John and Sina Carlovna (Wulfsberg) O.; m. Ann Elizabeth Brady, June 7, 1947; Christopher Rolf, Peter Stuart. BS, Harvard Coll., 1946; M.P.A., Harvard U., 1947. Supr. central indsl. relations staff Ford Motor Co., Dearborn, Mich., 1947-53; dir. orgn. planning and mgmt. devel. Colgate-Palmolive Co., NYC, 1953-65; v.p., gen. mgr. New Holland div. Sperry Rand Corp., (Pa.), 1965-76; corp. v.p. personnel Norton Simon Inc., NYC, 1976-78; sr. v.p. adminstrn. Max Factor & Co., Hollywood, Calif., 1978-85. Served to 1st lt. USAAF, 1943-46. Mem. Personnel Round Table (chmn. 1983-84), Am. Mgmt. Assn. (adv. coun. 1977-82), Lancaster (Pa.) Country Club, Phi Beta Kappa. Lutheran.

ORDEMANN, WILLIAM, energy executive; BSChemE, Va. Tech. U., Blacksburg. V.p. Shell Midstream Enterprises, 1997—98, Tejas Natural Gas Liquids, LLC, 1998—99, Enterprise GP Holdings LP, 1999—2001, sr. v.p., 2001—07, exec. v.p., COO, 2007—; sr. v.p. Tex. Ea. Products Pipeline Company, LLC, 2005. Office: Enterprise GP Holdings LP 1100 Louisiana St Houston TX 77002 Office Phone: 713-381-6500.*

ORDIN, ANDREA SHERIDAN, lawyer; m. Robert Ordin; 1 child, M. Victoria; stepchildren: Allison, Richard. AB, UCLA, 1962, LLB, 1965. Bar: Calif. 1966. Dep. atty. gen. Calif., 1965-72; So. Calif. legal counsel Fair Employment Practices Commn., 1972-73; asst. dist. atty. L.A. County, 1975-77; U.S. atty. Central Dist. Calif. LA, 1977-81; adj. prof. UCLA Law Sch., 1982; chief asst. atty. gen. Calif. LA, 1983-90; sr. counsel Morgan, Lewis & Bockius, LA, 1993—. Mem. L.A. County Bar Assn. (past pres., past exec. dir.). Office: Morgan Lewis & Bockius 300 S Grand Ave Ste 2200 Los Angeles CA 90071-3109 Office Phone: 213-612-1090. Business E-Mail: aordin@morganlewis.com.

ORDOG, TAMAS, research scientist, educator; b. Nagykanizsa, Hungary, Feb. 8, 1964; arrived in US, 1992, permanent resident, 1996; s. Ferenc Ordog and Julianna Domjan; m. Katalin Malek; 1 child, Norbert. MD, U. Pecs, Hungary, 1988. Rsch. fellow neurophysiology rsch. group Hungarian Acad. Scis., Pecs, 1989—92; rsch. fellow U. Tex.-Houston Health Sci. Ctr., 1992—95, sr. rsch. fellow, 1995—97; rsch. asst. prof. U. Nev. Reno Sch. Medicine, 1997—2003, asst. prof., 2003—06; sr. assoc. cons., assoc. prof. Mayo Clinic, Rochester, Minn., 2006—. Contbr. articles to profl. jours. Recipient Young Investigator award, Am. Motility Soc., 2000, 2002, Alvarez award, Internat. Electrogastrography Soc., 2005, Masters award for basic or clin. rsch. digestive scis., 2008, PriCara Eisai; grantee, Am. Motility Soc. and Janssen Pharmaceutica, 2002—03, NIH, 2002—; scholar, Republic of Hungary, 1984—88; Rsch. fellow, Hungarian Acad. Scis., 1989—91. Mem.: AAAS, Soc. for Neuroscience, Internat. Electrogastrography Soc. (treas.), Am. Neurogastroenterology and Motility Soc., Am. Gastroenterol. Assn., The Endocrine Soc. Achievements include research in gastrointestinal cell biology; Diabetic gastroenteropathy; neuroendocrine regulation of reproduction. Office: Mayo Clinic Guggenheim 10 200 1st St SW Rochester MN 55905 Business E-Mail: ordog.tamas@mayo.edu.

ORDON, ANDREW PAUL (DREW ORDON), plastic surgeon; b. Chgo., Dec. 9, 1950; s. V. Anthony and Jay Mary (Lacka) O.; m. Robyn Lee, July 20, 1985; children: Matthew, Shannon. BS with honors in Biol. Scis., U. Calif., Irvine, 1972; MD with honors, U. So. Calif. Medicine, 1979. Diplomate Am. Bd. Plastic Surgery, Am. Bd. Otolaryngology, Head and Neck Surgery, Am. Bd. Cosmetic Surgery, Am. Bd. Med. Examiners. Gen. surgery resident U. So. Calif., LA, 1979-80; otolaryngology, head and neck surgery, facial surgery resident Loma Linda-White Meml., LA, 1980-82, otolaryngology, head and neck surgery, facial surgery chief resident, 1982-83; plastic surgery resident Lenox Hill Hosp., NYC, 1983-84, plastic surgery chief resident, 1984-85; asst. prof. head and neck N.Y. Med. Coll., 1987-90; asst. clin. prof. plastic surgery U. Conn. Sch. Medicine, Farmington, 1990—, UCLA Sch. Medicine, 2004—, Darthmouth Med. Coll., 1999—2004. Fellow aesthetic surgery Beverly Hills Med. Ctr., 1983; chief plastic surgery Med. Arts Ctr. Hosp., N.Y.C., 1985-90; attending surgeon Lenox Hill Hosp., N.Y.C., 1987, N.Y. Eye and Ear Infirmary, N.Y.C., 1987, Beth Israel North Med. Ctr., N.Y.C., 1987. Author: Revealing the New You, A Guide to Plastic Surgery, 1994, Everything You Wanted to Know About Plastic Surgery, 1988, Otoplasty in Facial Aesthetic Plastic Surgery; guest appearances on 20/20, 48 Hours, CNN, Sally Jesse Raphael, Phil Donahue, Leeza, Maury Povitch, Entertainment Tonight, Inside Hollywood, NBC News, ABC News, British Broadcasting Corp., USA Today, Allure, Glamour, Mademoiselle, On-line surgery.com. Grantee NSF, 1972. Fellow ACS, Internat. Coll. Surgeons, Am. Acad. Facial Plastic and Reconstructive Surgery, Liposuction Soc. Am., mem. Am. Soc. Plastic/Reconstructive Surgeons, Am. Soc. Plastic Surgeons, Am. Soc. Aesthetic Plastic Surgery, Internat. Soc. Aesthetic Plastic Surgery, Phi Beta Kappa (calif. Chpt.) Republican. Episcopalian. Avocations: tennis, golf, skiing, boating, travel. Office: 465 N Roxbury Dr #1001 Beverly Hills CA 90210 Office Phone: 310-248-6250. Office Fax: 310-248-6258.

ORDONEZ, MAGGLIO JOSE, professional baseball player; b. Caracas, Venezuela, Jan. 28, 1974; m. Dagly Ordonez; children: Magglio Jr., Maggliana, Sophia. Outfielder Chgo. White Sox, 1997—2004, Detroit Tigers, 2005—. Mem. Venezuelan nat. team World Baseball Classic, 2006, 09. Recipient Silver Slugger award, 2000, 2002, 2007; named MVP, Venezuelan Winter League, 1996, Tiger of Yr., 2007, Am. League Batting Champion, 2007; named to Winter League All-Star Team, Baseball Am., 1997, Am. League All-Star Team, 1999—2001, 2003, 2006—07. Achievements include becoming the second Venezuelan-born player ever to hit 1,000 RBI's, 2008. Mailing: c/o Detroit Tigers Comerica Pk 2100 Woodward Ave Detroit MI 48201*

ORDORICA, STEVEN ANTHONY, obstetrician, gynecologist, educator; b. NYC, Jan. 4, 1957; s. Vincent and Rose (Goiricelaya) O. BA magna cum laude, NYU, 1979; MD, Stony Brook U., 1983. Diplomate Am. Coll. Obstetrics and Gynecology, speciality cert. maternal-fetal medicine; lic. Nat. Bd. Med. Examiners. Resident obstetrics and gynecology NYU-Bellevue Hosp. Ctr., 1983-87, fellow maternal-fetal medicine, 1987-89, instr. obstetrics-gynecology, 1989-91; clin. instr. obstetrics-gynecology NYU, 1986-89, asst. prof. ob/gyn., 1989—2001, clin. assoc. prof. ob/gyn., 2001—; dir. perinatal clinics and prenatal diagnostic unit Gouverneur Hosp., NYC, 1989-94. Perinatal cons. Bellevue Hosp. Ctr., N.Y.C., 1989—; faculty mem. perinatal div. NYU Med. Ctr., 1989—; presenter in field. Contbr. articles to Surgery, Am. Jour. Obstetrics and Gynecology, Am. Jour. Perinatal, Surgery, Obstetrics and Gynecology, Jour. Reproductive Medicine, Acta Geneticae Medicae et Gemellologiae, Jour. Rheumatology. Recipient Founder's Day award, NYU, Wash. Sq. Alumni award; named NYU scholar. Mem. Am. Coll. Obstetrics and Gynecology, Soc. Perinatal Obstetricians, N.Y. Acad. Scis., N.Y. State Perinatal Soc., AMA, Phi Beta Kappa, Beta Lambda Sigma. Achievements include research in investigating aspects of maternal-fetal physiology. Office: NYU Med Ctr 530 1st Ave Ste 10Q New York NY 10016-6402

ORDWAY, ELLEN, biologist, educator, entomologist, researcher; b. NYC, Nov. 8, 1927; d. Samuel Hanson and Anna (Wheatland) Ordway. BA, Wheaton Coll., Mass., 1950; MS, Cornell U., 1955; PhD, U. Kans., 1965. Field asst. N.Y. Zool. Soc., NYC, 1950-52; rsch. asst. Am. Mus. Natural History, NYC, 1955-57; tchg. asst. U. Kans., Lawrence, 1957-61, rsch. asst., 1959-65; asst. prof. U. Minn., Morris, 1965-70, assoc. prof. biology, 1970-85, prof., 1986-97, prof. emeritus, 1997—2005, acad. advisor, 1997—. Cooperator, cons. USDA Bee Rsch. Lab., Tucson, 1971, Tucson, 83. Contbr. articles to profl. jours. Lectr. Morris area svc. clubs, 1972—2004; mgr. preserves Nature Conservancy, Mpls., 1975—; bd. dirs. county chpt. ARC, 1998—2003; vol. Stevens County Hist. Mus., 2005—; bd. dirs. U. Minn. Morris Retirees Assn., 1997—2003, sec., treas., 1998—2003. Mem.: AAAS, Ecol. Soc. Am., Internat. Bee Rsch. Assn., Kans. Entomol. Soc., Sigma Xi. Episcopalian. Avocations: travel, photography. Office: U Minn Div Sci And Math Morris MN 56267

ORDWAY, ERIC, lawyer; b. NYC, Dec. 9, 1949; BA, Princeton Univ., 1971; JD cum laude, Brooklyn Law Sch., 1986. Bar: NY 1987, US Ct. (So. Dist.) NY. Ptnr. Weil Gotshal & Magnes LLP, NYC. Contbr. articles to law jours. Mem.: ABA (chmn. trial practice com. 1987—91). Office: Weil Gotshal & Manges LLP 767 Fifth Ave New York NY 10153 Office Phone: 212-310-8609. Business E-Mail: eric.ordway@weil.com.

ORDWAY, FREDERICK IRA, III, science educator, consultant, researcher, writer; b. NYC, Apr. 4, 1927; s. Frederick Ira and Frances Antoinette (Wright) O.; m. Maria Victoria Arenas, Apr. 13, 1950; children: Frederick Ira IV, Albert James, Aliette Marisol. SB, Harvard U., Cambridge, Mass., 1949; postgrad., U. Alger, 1950, U. Paris, France, 1950-51, 53-54, U. Barcelona, Spain, 1953, U. Innsbruck, Austria, 1954,

Air U., 1952-63, Alexander Hamilton Bus. Inst., 1952-58, Indsl. Coll. Armed Forces, 1953-63; DSc (hon.), U. Ala., 1992. Various geol., engring. positions Mene Grande Oil Co., San Tome, Venezuela, 1949-50, Orinoco Mining Co., Cerro Bolivar, Venezuela, 1950, Reaction Motors, Inc., Lake Denmark, NJ, 1951-53; with guided missiles divsn. Republic Aviation Corp., 1954-55; pres. Gen. Astronautics Rsch. Corp., Huntsville, Ala., 1955-59, 65-66; v.p. Nat. R & D Corp., Atlanta, 1957-59; asst. to dir. Saturn Systems Office, Army Ballistic Missile Agy., Huntsville, 1959-60; chief space info. systems br. George C. Marshall Space Flight Ctr. NASA, 1960-64; prof. sci. and tech. applications Sch. Grad. Studies and Rsch., U. Ala. Rsch. Inst., 1967-73; cons. Sci. and Tech. Policy Office, NSF, 1974-75; cons. ops. analysis divsn. Gen. Rsch. Corp., 1974-75; asst. to adminstr. ERDA, 1975-77, Dept. Energy, 1977-94, policy/internat. affairs dir. spl. projects office, cons., 1994—; also participant internat. energy devel. program Office of Asst. Sec. Internat. Affairs, Dept. Energy, 1978-79. Cons. to industry, Ency. Britannica, Am. Coll. Dictionary of English Lang., M.G.M. film 2001: A Space Odyssey, 1965-66, Paramount Picture Corp., The Adventurers, 1968-69; internat. lectr. space flight and energy programs. Author: (with C.C. Adams) Space Flight, 1958, (with Ronald C. Wakeford) International Missile and Spacecraft Guide, 1960, Annotated Bibliography of Space Science and Technology, 1962, (with J.P. Gardner, M.R. Sharpe, Jr.) Basic Astronautics: An Introduction to Space Science, Engineering and Medicine, 1962, (with Adams, Wernher von Braun) Careers in Astronautics and Rocketry, 1962, (with Gardner, Sharpe, R.C. Wakeford) Applied Astronautics: An Introduction to Space Flight, 1963, (with Wakeford) Conquering the Sun's Empire, 1963, Life in Other Solar Systems, 1965, (with Roger A. MacGowan) Intelligence in the Universe, 1966, (with W. von Braun) History of Rocketry and Space Travel, 1966, 1969, 1975, L'Histoire Mondiale de l'Astronautique, 1968, 70, (with W. von Braun) Rockets' Red Glare, 1976, (with C.C. Adams, M.R. Sharpe) Dividends from Space, 1972, Pictorial Guide to Planet Earth, 1975, (with W. von Braun) New Worlds, 1979, (with M.R. Sharpe) The Rocket Team, 1979, 2d edit., 2003, 3rd edit. 2007, (with F.C. Durant and R.C. Seamans) Between Sputnik and the Shuttle, 1981, (with E.M. Emme) Science Fiction and Space Futures, 1982, (with von Braun, Dave Dooling) Space Travel: A History, 1985, (with Ernst Stuhlinger) Wernher von Braun: Aufbrach in den Weltraum, 1992, Wernher von Braun: Crusader for Space (2 vols.), 1994, rev. 1996, single vol. edit., 1996, (with Randy Liebermann) Blueprint for Space, 1992, Visions of Spaceflight, 2001; editor: Advances in Space Science and Technology, vols. I-XII, 2 supplements, 1959-72, (with R.M.L. Baker, N.W. Makemson) Introduction to Astrodynamics, 1960, (with others) From Peenemünde to Outer Space, 1962, Astronautical Engineering and Science, 1963; mem. editl. bd.: IX Internat. Astronautical Congress procs., 2 vols, 1959, Xth Congress procs., 2 vols, 1960; guest editor: Acta Astronautica, 1985, 94, History of Rocketry and Astronautics, Vol. IX, 1989, Digital book Mars: Target for Tomorrow Microsoft Network & Internet, 1996; Co-developer of biographical film He Conquered Space, 1996, History of Astronautics Video, 1996, inter-active CD Rom, 1997, rev., 2001, interactive CD ROM and video versions) Mars: Past, Present, Future, 1998; contbr. articles to profl. jours., chpts. to books; organizer Blueprint for Space exhbn., 1991-95, US Space and Rocket Ctr., IBM Gallery of Sci. and Art, NASA Vis. Ctr., Houston, Spaceport USA, Cape Canaveral, Fla., Nat. Air and Space Mus., Washington, Va. Air and Space Ctr., Hampton exhibit Shaping The Vision exhibit Art Inst. Chgo., 2001, Bruce Mus. Art and Scis., Greenwich, Conn., 2001, Mus. Flight, Seattle, 2002, others. Served with USNR, 1945. Co-recipient diplôme d'honneur French Commn. d'Histoire, Arts et Letters, Paris, 1969, citation Arthur C. Clarke Found., 2005; commended for contbns. to US Space and Rocket Ctr., Ala. Space Sci. Exhibit, US Space Walk of Fame Found. Fellow: AAAS, AIAA (assoc.; history com. 1975—, internat. activities com. 1980—89, sel. com. hons. and awards 1996—, 2003 Centennial of Flight Ctr. 1998, Hermann Oberth award 1977, K.E. Tsiolkowski award 1988), Brit. Interplanetary Soc. (guest editor 1992—96); mem.: US Space and Rocket Ctr. (Saturn V rocket restoration com., mus. com., sci. adv. coun., co-chmn. explorer 50th anniversery celebration 2008, Legacy award 2008), Acta Astronautica (guest editor 1994, 1997), Eurasian Acad. Scis., Nat. Space Soc. (bd. dirs. 1986—95, publs. com. 1987—88, nominating com. 1990—92, awards com. 1992—, bd. govs. 1997—, Ctr. for Lunar Rsch. com. 1998—), Am. Astron. Soc. (Emme award 1994, Nat. Space Club award 1997), Internat. Acad. Astronautics (history of astronautics com. 1983—, space activities and soc. com. 1986—, peer rev. com. 1995—, Luigi Napolitano Lit. award 1992), Arthur C. Clarke Found. (bd. dirs. 2000—, commendation 2005), Washington Golf and Country Club, Harvard Club NY, Cosmos Club (bd. mgmt. 1986—91, v.p. 1988—90, award 2001). Achievements include donation of spaceflight, lunar & planetary astronomy & rocketry collection to the Centre Library & Archives of the US Space & Rocket Centre in Huntsville; Alabama consisting of more than 180 lots transferred from 1978 to the present; energy research & development collection & some spaceflight material to the M. Louis Salmon Library of the University of Alabama in Huntsville; space fiction collection to the Harvard College Library, Cambridge, Massachusetts & family material to the Dyer Library & Saco Museum, Saco, Maine. Home and Office: 2401 N Taylor St Arlington VA 22207-4021 also: 3423 Lookout Dr SE Huntsville AL 35801 Personal E-mail: ordmars@aol.com.

ORDWAY, JOHN DANTON, retired pension fund administrator, lawyer, accountant; b. Mpls., Mar. 19, 1928; s. John Dunreath Ordway and Inez Adelaide (Stahl) Larson; m. Mary E. Bateman, June 16, 1951 (div. 1978); 1 child, David; m. Patricia A. Nagle, Dec. 27, 1996. BBA, Am. U., 1963, JD, 1965. CPA Minn.; bar: US Dist. Ct. DC 1966. Dir. ins. Nat. Automobile Dealers Assn., Washington, 1957—69; v.p. Edward H. Friend and Co., Washington, 1969—74; exec. v.p., CEO pension bd. United Ch. of Christ, NYC, 1974—96; ret., 1996. Mem. Planning Bd., Stamford, Conn., 1982—86. With US Army, 1946—47. Mem.: AICPA, Black Hall Club (Old Lyme, Conn.), Quail Run Golf Club (Naples, Fla.), Westwood Country Club (Vienna, Va.), Kena Temple. Republican. Mem. United Ch. Of Christ. Home: 7565 Citrus Hill Ln Naples FL 34109 Personal E-mail: uccpb@yahoo.com.

ORDWAY, MARK FRANKLIN, cinematographer; s. Harold Keith and Phoebe Katherine Ordway; m. Michele Marion, Mar. 17, 1990. MS, Ariz. State U., Phoenix, 2003. Tech. photographer Ford Motor Co., Dearborn, Mich., 1987—89, Exponent, Inc., Phoenix, 1989—. Editor (cinematographer): (documentary film) August in April, Pioneer Award Ceremonies Ariz. State U. West, Phoenix, 2004—08. Photographic equipment repair technician USAF, 1983—87, Vandenberg AFB, Calif.

O'REAR, CLARENCE MICHAEL, engineering company executive; b. Chattanooga, Dec. 16, 1940; s. Harry Crawford and Hazel Mae O'Rear; m. Gloria Dianne Pendergrass; children: Clarence Michael Jr., Sharon Leigh Farist. BS, U. Memphis, 1973; MS, U. Memphia, 1975; PhD, Ga. State U., Atlanta, 1995. Cert. professional engr., Ga., 1990. Program chair State Tech. Inst., Memphis, 1969—79; assoc. dept. mgr. Sharp Electronics Mfg. Co., Memphis, 1979—84; dept. mgr. ctv engring. Sanyo Mfg. Co., Forrest City, Alaska, 1984—86; lead instr. engring. tech. Chattahoochee Tech. Coll., Austell, Ga., 1986—. Pvt. practice, Jasper, Ga., 1990. V.p. and bd. mem. Ga. Biomedical Instrumentation Soc., Atlanta, 1990. Spc US Army, 1959—62, Germany. Decorated Commendation medal Ga. N.G. Home: 575 Phila Dr Jasper GA 30143 Office: Chattahoochee Tech Coll 1578 Veterans Meml Hwy Austell GA 30168 Office Fax: 770-732-5904. Business E-Mail: morear@chattcollege.com.

O'REGAN, RUTH, oncologist, educator; b. Dublin; MD, U. Coll., Dublin. Resident & fellow Mater Hosp., Dublin; fellow Northwestern U.; asst. prof. Northwestern U. Hosp.; assoc. prof. hemtology & oncology Emory U.; dir. translational breast cancer rsch. program Winship Cancer Inst. Recipient Compassionate Care award, Women's Bd. Northwestern Hosp., NSABP Young Clinical Investigator award, 2001. Mem.: Am. Soc. Clinical Oncology (breast cancer scientific com.). Office: 1365 Clifton Rd Bldg C Atlanta GA 30322 also: Emory University School of Medicine Department of Biomedical Engineering 101 Woodruff Cir Ste 2007B Atlanta GA 30322*

O'REGGIO, TREVOR EVAN, history professor; s. Ethlyn Wilson; m. Anna Maria Simpson, June 23, 1985; children: Jonathan Carlyle, Elena Maria, Rachel Renee. PhD, U. Chgo., 1997; DMin, Gordon-Conwell, Boston, 2006. Assoc. prof. history Andrews U., Berrien Springs, Mich.; 1998—2008. Capt. US ARMY, 1996—98, Fort Jackson. Mem.: Soc. Bibl. Lit. Avocations: swimming, reading, cycling, soccer. Office: Andrews Univ US 31 Berrien Springs MI 49104 Business E-Mail: toreggio@andrews.edu.

O'REILLY, BILL (WILLIAM O'REILLY JR.), commentator, writer; b. NYC, Sept. 10, 1949; s. William J. and Angela Winifred (Drake) O'Reilly; m. Maureen McPhilmy; children: Madeline, Spencer. BA in Hist., Marist Coll., Poughkeepsie, NY, 1971; MA in Broadcast Journalism, Boston U., 1976; MA in Pub. Policy, Harvard U., 1996. HS tchr., Miami, Fla.; reporter WNEP-TV, Scranton, Pa., WFAA-TV, Dallas, KMGH-TV, Denver, WFSB-TV, Hartford, WCBS-TV, NYC, 1980; fgn. correspondent CBS News; anchor CBS, Boston, ABC, Boston, KATU-TV, Portland; correspondent World News Tonight, ABC, 1986—88; sr. correspondent Inside Edition, 1988, anchor, 1989—95; host, exec. prodr. The O'Reilly Factor, FOX News Channel, 1996—; host Radio Factor, 2002—. Author: Those Who Trespass: A Novel of Television and Murder, 1998, The O'Reilly Factor: The Good, the Bad and the Completely Ridiculous in American Life, 2000, The No Spin Zone: Confrontations with the Powerful and Famous in America, 2001, Who's Looking Out for You?, 2003, The O'Reilly Factor for Kids: A Survival Guide for America's Families, 2004, Culture Warrior, 2006, Bold Fresh Piece of Humanity: A Memoir, 2008 (Publishers Weekly bestseller); co-author (with Charles Flowers): Kids Are Americans Too, 2007. Recipient Disting. Alumni award, Boston U., 2001. Office: FOX News Channel 1211 Avenue of the Americas New York NY 10036*

O'REILLY, DAVID J., oil industry executive; b. Dublin, Jan. 1947; BS ChemE, University Coll., Dublin, 1968, D (hon.) of Sci., 2002. Process engineer Chevron Corp., 1968—71, process engineer, operating assist., 1971—75, adviser, foreign operations, 1976—78, planning mgr., chemical div., 1979, mgr. agricultural chem., 1980—82, mgr. Salt Lake Refinery, 1983—85; mgr. manufacturing Chevron Chemical Co., 1985; gen. mgr. El Segundo Refinery, 1986—88; sr. v.p. Chevron Chemical Corp., 1989—90; v.p. Chevron Corp., 1991—94; pres. Chevron Products Co., San Francisco, 1994—98; dir., vice-chmn. Chevron Corp., San Francisco, 1998—2000, chmn. bd. dirs., CEO, 2000—01; CEO, chmn. ChevronTexaco Corp. (now Chevron Corp.), San Francisco, 2001—. Bd. govs. San Francisco Symphony, Bay Area Coun. Mem.: Am. Soc. Corp. Execs., Bus. Coun., Nat. Petroleum Coun., Am. Petroleum Inst. (treas., bd. dirs.). Office: Chevron Corp 6001 Bollinger Canyon Rd San Ramon CA 94583-2324*

O'REILLY, GERARD P., engineering company executive; s. Vincent and Della O'Reilly; m. Marianne O'Reilly, 1970; children: Peter, Stephen, Kathryn Harmon. BS, Manhattan Coll., NY, 1969; Eng.Sc.D, Columbia U., NY, 1975. Disting. mem. tech. staff Bell Labs. Rsch., Murray Hill, NJ, 2007—08, LGS - Bell Labs. Innovations, Florham Pk., 2008—. Tech. mgr. & dist. mgr. Bell Labs. & AT&T Labs, Holmdel, 1977—98; mem. tech. staff Bell Labs. Applied Rsch., 2000—07. Recipient Doctoral Support award, Bell Labs., 1974—75, Best Paper award, Design Reliable Comm. Conf., 2005. Roman Catholic. Avocation: golf. Office: LGS - Bell Labs Innovations 15 Vreeland Ave Florham Park NJ 07932 Business E-Mail: goreilly@lgsinnovations.com.

O'REILLY, HEATHER ANN, Olympic athlete; b. East Brunswick, NJ, Jan. 2, 1985; Student, U.N.C. Mem. U.S. Women's Nat. Soccer Team, 2002—, U.S. Women's Olympic Soccer Team, Athens, 2004, Beijing, 2008. Named National High School Player of the Yr., 2002; named to NCAA All-Tournament Team, 2003. Achievements include being a member of NCAA Champion University of North Carolina Tar Heels Women's Soccer Team, 2003; being a member of gold medal US Women's Soccer Team, Athens Olympic Games, 2004. Office: c/o US Soccer Federation 1801 S Prairie Ave Chicago IL 60616

O'REILLY, JAMES THOMAS, lawyer, educator, writer; b. NYC, Nov. 15, 1947; s. Matthew Richard and Regina (Casey) O'R.; children: Jean, Ann. BA cum laude, Boston Coll., 1969; JD, U. Va., 1974. Bar: Va. 1974, Ohio 1974, U.S. Supreme Ct. 1979, U.S. Ct. Appeals (6th cir.) 1980. Atty. Procter & Gamble Co., Cin., 1974-76, counsel, 1976-79, sr. counsel for food, drug and product safety, 1979-85, corp. counsel, 1985-93, assoc. gen. counsel, 1993-98; adj. prof. in adminstrv. law U. Cin., 1980-97, vis. prof. law, 1998—. Cons. Adminstrv. Conf. U.S., 1981-82, 89-90, Congl. Office of Compliance, 1995-96; arbitrator State Employee Rels. Bd.; mem. Ohio Bishops Adv. Coun., Mayor's Infrastructure Commn., Cin. Environ. Adv. Coun.; Vice Mayor, City Wyoming, Ohio. Author: Federal Information Disclosure, 1977, Food and Drug Administration Regulatory Manual, 1979, Unions' Rights to Company Information, 1980, Federal Regulation of the Chemical Industry, 1980, Administrative Rulemaking, 1983, Ohio Public Employee Collective Bargaining, 1984, Protecting Workplace Secrets, 1985, Emergency Response to Chemical Accidents, 1986, Product Defects and Hazards, 1987, Protecting Trade Secrets Under SARA, 1988, Toxic Torts Strategy Deskbook, 1989, Complying With Canada's New Labeling Law, 1989, Solid Waste Management, 1991, Ohio Products Liability Handbook, 1991, Toxic Torts Guide, 1991, ABA Product Liability Resource Manual, 1993, RCRA and Superfund Practice Guide, 1993, Clean Air Permits Manual, 1994, United States Environmental Liabilities, 1994, Elder Safety, 1995, Environmental and Workplace Safety for University and Hospital Managers, 1996, Indoor Environmental Health, 1997, Product Warnings, Defects & Hazards, 1999, Accident Prevention Manual, 2000, Food Crisis Management Manual, 2002, Police Racial Profiling, 2002, Homeland Security Deskbook, 2004, Ohio Tort Reform, 2005, Ohio Personal Injury Practice, 2006, Gangs and Law Enforcement, 2007, Brownreds Cleanup, 2008, Consumer Product Safety, 2008, Punishing Corporate Crime, 2009; mem. editl. bd. Food and Drug Cosmetic Law Jour.; contbr. articles to profl. jours. Trustee Regional Coun. of Govts.; mem. Hamilton County Dem. Ctrl. Com. With US Army, 1970—72. Mem. ABA (chmn. AD law sect.), FBA, Food and Drug Law Inst. (chair program com.), Leadership Cin. Democrat. Roman Catholic. Office: 24 Jewett Dr Cincinnati OH 45215-2648 Office Phone: 513-556-0062. Personal E-mail: joreilly@fuse.net. Business E-Mail: james.oreilly@uc.edu.

O'REILLY, MARY, environmental scientist, educator; b. NYC, Aug. 3, 1948; d. Luke Edward and Regina (Mahoney) O'Reilly; m. Jonathan Haney; children: Robert Brophy, Sara Brophy, Lena Reid. Student, Fordham U., 1966—68; BS, U. Mich., 1970, MS, 1972, PhD, 1979. Rsch. asst. prof. Health Sci. Ctr., Syracuse, NY, 1979-84; environ. toxicologist Syracuse Rsch. Corp., 1984-86; pres. ARLS Cons., Inc., Syracuse, 1993—; sr. indsl. hygienist N.Y. State Dept. Labor, Syracuse, 1987—2000; environ. specialist N.Y. State Dept. Transp., Binghamton, 2000—. Adj. asst. prof. SUNY Sch. Pub. Health, Albany, 1990—; dir. Am. Bd. Indsl. Hygiene, Lansing, Mich., 1995—2001; adj. prof. chemistry LeMoyne Coll., 2000; mem. Z10 com. Am. Nat. Stds. Inst., 2001—05; mem. adv. bd. N.Y. State Inst. Health and Environment, 2001—; bd. dirs. Am. Conf. Govt. Indsl. Hygienists, 2006—09; mem. NY State Occupl. Health Clinics Oversight Commn., 2009—. Author: An Ergonomics Guide to VDTs, 1994; author: (with others) Occupational Ergonomics, 1996; co-author: ILO's Encyclopedia of Occupational Health and Safety, 1998, Implications of Hormesis for Industrial Hygienists, 2003, Health Risk Assessment at Brownfield Redevelopment Sites, 2003, Groundwater Effects from Highway Tire Shreds, 2004, An Ergonomics Guide to Computer Workstations, 2007, Canasawacta Creek Watershed Initiative, 2007, Phytoremediation of TCE, 2009, others; contbr. articles to profl. jours. Mem. Syracuse Peace Coun. Mem.: N.Y. State Assn. Transp. Engrs., Human Factors and Ergonomics Soc., Am. Assn. Govtl. Indsl. Hygienists, Am. Indsl. Hygiene Assn. Avocations: Karate, fly fishing, irish harp. Home: 7705 Farley Ln Manlius NY 13104-9571 Home Phone: 315-682-3064; Office Phone: 607-721-8138. Business E-Mail: moreilly@dot.state.ny.us, moreilly@albany.edu.

O'REILLY, MICHAEL, insurance company executive; BS, NYU; MBA, Pace U. Securities analyst investment dept. The Chubb Corp., 1969, chief investment officer, 1986, interim CFO, 2002—03, vice chmn., 2002—, CFO, 2003—. Served in US Army, 1966—67, capt. USAR, 1968—71. Office: The Chubb Corp 15 Mountain View Rd Warren NJ 07059 Office Phone: 908-903-3764. Office Fax: 908-903-2027. E-mail: moreilly@chubb.com.

O'REILLY, RICHARD JOHN, pediatrician; b. Bklyn., Apr. 29, 1943; s. John Russell and Margaret (Cronin) O'R.; m. E. Jean Capitano, Nov. 1984; children from previous marriage: John, Steven. BS, Coll. Holy Cross, 1964; MD, U. Rochester, 1968. Diplomate Am. Bd. Pediat. Intern U. Minn. Hosp., Mpls., 1968-69; resident in pediatrics Children's Hosp. Med. Ctr. and Beth Israel Hosp., Boston, 1971-72; with dept. pediatrics Meml. Sloan Kettering Cancer Ctr., NYC, 1973—; attending pediatrician, chmn. dept. pediatrics Meml. Hosp., NYC, 1986—; mem. dept. immunology Sloan-Kettering Inst. Cancer Research; prof. pediatrics Cornell U. Med. Coll., 1980, Lila Acheson Wallace prof. pediatric research, 1980, Claire L. Tow, chair in pediat. oncology rsch., 2004; chief marrow transplantation svc. Meml. Sloan-Kettering Cancer Ctr., 1981—. Pres. Damon Runyon-Walter Winchell Cancer Fund, 1991-96. Editor-in-chief BBMT, 1995-2001; assoc. editor Cancer Rsch., Clin. Cancer Rsch., 1994-2002. Served with USPHS, 1969-71. Recipient Louise and Allston Boyer-Young Investigator award for clin. rsch., 1980, Boarhaave medal Leiden U., Pediat. Oncology award ASCO, Lifetime Achievement award ASEMT. Mem. AAAS, Am. Pediatric Soc., Am. Assn. Immunologists, Am. Acad. Pediat., Am. Assn. Pathologists, Soc. Pediatric Rsch., NY Transplantation Soc., NY Acad. Scis., Am. Assn. Clin. Radiology, Am. Soc. Hematology, Am. Soc. Blood and Marrow Transplantation (sec. 1993-95, v.p.-elect 1999, pres. 2001). Democrat. Roman Catholic. Achievements include first successful application of marrow transplantation from unrelated donors and from genetically mismatched donors, 1973. Office: Meml Sloan-Kettering Cancer Ctr 1275 York Ave New York NY 10021-6094

O'REILLY, TERENCE JOHN, lawyer; b. Farnborough, Eng., Apr. 12, 1945; came to U.S., 1960, naturalized, 1965; s. Arthur Francis and Doris Eileen (Burden) O'R.; m. Katharine Van Dyke Wallace, Sept. 26, 1970, Andrea Pierceall, 05 21, 2007; children: Tobin Cooper, Matthew Wallace. BA, Loyola U., 1966; JD, U. Calif., Berkeley, 1969. Bar: Calif. 1970. Assoc. Voegelin, Barton, LA, 1969-70, Walkup, Downing & Sterns, San Francisco, 1970-75; mem. Walkup, Shelby, Bastian, Melodia, Kelly & O'Reilly, San Francisco, 1975-87; prin. O'Reilly & Colliss, San Mateo, Calif., 1987—. Lectr. Kennedy Law Sch., Moraga, Calif., 1975-76, Inner Cir. of Advocates, 1998—; bd. govs. Consumer Attys. of Calif., 1995-2009, bd. govs., diplomate Am. Bd. Profl. Liability Lawyers, 1989—; pres. Western Trial Lawyers, 2008-09. V.p. No. Calif. Rugby Football, San Francisco, 1975-80, bd. dirs., 1975—; trustee U.S. Rugby Football Found., 1987—; trustee The Philip Brooks Sch., 1986-89, Coun. of Bancroft Libr., U. Calif.; bd. dirs. San Francisco Traditional Jazz Found., 2002— Mem. Boalt Hall Alumni (bd. dirs. 1982-85), Assn. San Mateo Trial Lawyers (dir. 1992—, pres. 2003), Bohemian Club, Pacific Union Club. Roman Catholic. Office: 1900 O'Farrell St Ste 360 San Mateo CA 94403 Business E-Mail: toreilly@oreillylaw.com.

O'REILLY, TIM, computer book publishing company executive, open sourcer advocate; b. Cork, Ireland, 1954; BA in Classics (cum laude, Harvard Coll., 1975. Founder, pres. O'Reilly & Associates (now called O'Reilly Media, Inc.), Sebastopol, Calif., 1978—. Former bd. dir. Macromedia; bd. dir. CollabNet; spkr. in field. Co-author UNIX Text Processing (with Dale Dougherty and Howard Sams), 1987, (with Grace Todino) Managing UUCP and USENET, (with Valerie Quercia) The X Window System Users' Guide, (with Adrian Nye) The X Toolkit Intrinsics Programming Manual, (with Jerry Peek and Mike Loukides) UNIX Power Tools, (with Troy Mott) Windows 98 in a Nutshell; editor, (with O'Reilly & Associates) major contbr. in the development of many of other titles, including UNIX in a Nutshell, Programming Perl, Sendmail, Essential System Administration, and The Cathedral and the Bazaar; O'Reilly Media Inc. published The Whole Internet User's Guide & Catalog (First popular book about the internet, selected by NY Pub. Libr. as one of the most signicant books of the 20th Century), 1992; introduced Safari Books Online (first web-native svc. for online book content), 2000; writer (web blog) radar.oreilly.com Recipient Industry Achievement award for advocacy on behalf of the open source community, InfoWorld, 1998; named one of 50 Who Matter Now, CNNMoney.com Bus. 2.0, 2006, 2007, 50 Most Important People on the Web, PC World, 2007. Mem.: Electronic Frontier Found. (bd. trustee), Internet Soc. (bd. trustee). Achievements include O'Reilly's Global Network Navigator site (GNN, sold to American Online in 1995) was the first web portal and the first true commerical site on the World Wide Web in 1993. Office: O Reilly Media Inc 1005 Gravenstein Hwy N Sebastopol CA 95472-2811 Office Phone: 707-827-7000. Office Fax: 707-829-0104.

OREN, GLENN M., healthcare educator, consultant; s. Oren and Lund; married; children: Natasha, Joshua, Jacob. PhD, Iowa State U., Ames, 1994. Prof. Mercy Coll. Health Scis., Des Moines, 2004—08. Home: 1598 Kiwi Ave Boone IA 50036 Office: Mercy Coll of Health Scis 928 6th Ave Des Moines IA 50309 Business E-Mail: goren@mercydesmoines.org.

OREN, IDO, political science professor; b. Tel Aviv, Oct. 25, 1958; s. Pinhas and Miriam Oren; m. Jodi Barkin, Aug. 6, 1985; children: Avigail S., Maya, Eytan Z. PhD, U. Chgo., 1992. Asst. prof. polit. sci. U. Fla., Gainesville, 1999—2004, assoc. prof. polit. sci., 2004—. MacArthur Found. fellowship, Social Sci. Rsch. Coun., 1995—97, grant, US Dept. State, 2008. Jewish. Avocations: travel, jazz. Office: Univ Fla Polit Sci Box 117325 Gainesville FL 32611-7325 Office Fax: 352-392-8127. Business E-Mail: oren@ufl.edu.

ORENDER, DONNA, sports association executive; m. M.G. Orender; children: Jacob, Zachary stepchildren: Morgan, Colleen. Grad., Queens Coll., NY, 1978; postgraduate student in Social Work, Adelphi U. Player (Women's Profl. Basketball League) NY Stars, 1978—79, NJ Gems, 1979—80, Chgo. Hustle, 1980—81; with ABC Sports, SportsChannel; owner Primo Donna Prodns.; with NBA Entertainment, PGA Tour, 1988—2001, sr. v.p. strategic devel., 2001—05; pres. WNBA, NYC, 2005—. Prodr.: Insided the PGA Tour. Bd. mem. Beth El - The Beaches Synagogue, Monique Burr Found. for Children, Inc., Jacksonville Film & TV Adv. Coun., Maccabi USA/Sports for Israel. Named one of The Most Influential People in the World of Sports, Bus. Week, 2007. Mem.: Women's Basketball Coaches Assn. (bd. dirs.). Office: WNBA Olympic Tower 645 Fifth Ave New York NY 10022 Office Phone: 212-688-9622, 212-750-9622. E-mail: dorender@wnba.com.*

ORENGO-NANIA, SILVIA, ophthalmologist; b. Detroit, June 24, 1961; d. Antonio and Christina Orengo; m. Jay Nania, Aug. 8, 1992; children: Christina Nania, Jason Nania, Julia Nania. Med. degree, Baylor Coll. of Medicine, Houston, 1983. Exec. eye care line Michael E. DeBakey Vets. Affair Med. Ctr., Houston, 1998—2006; prof. Baylor Coll. of Medicine, Houston, 2006—. Achievements include research in Central Corneal Thickness and Intraocular Pressure. Office: Cullen Eye Inst 6565 Fannin NC205 Houston TX 77030

ORENSTEIN, FRAN M., small business owner, writer, editor; b. Bklyn., Oct. 31, 1939; s. Nathan Gitterman and Gertrude Celia Chall-Gitterman; m. Walter Orenstein, Dec. 21, 1958 (div. Jan. 1977); children: James, Susannah, Peter. BA, Bklyn. Coll., 1960; MEd, Coll. NJ, 1976; EdD, Nova Southeastern U., Ft. Lauderdale, Fla., 1993. Lic. tchr. NY, NJ, guidance NJ, Calif., cert. pub. mgr. NJ. Tchr. Pub. Sch. 256-NYC Bd. Edn., Bklyn., 1960—63, Hilltop Acad., Morganville, NJ, 1973—74; editor, writer Univ. Comms., Rahway, NJ, 1975—79; tchr., content specialist East Windsor Regional Schs., NJ, 1979—80; sr. rehab. counselor NJ Divsn. Vocat. Rehab., Trenton, 1980—88; disability officer Americorps NJ Dept. Edn., Trenton, 1998—2002; program devel. specialist NJ Dept. Cmty. Affairs, Trenton, 1988—98, 2002—; author, poet, editor, founder Sunwriter LLC; dir, Edtl. Svc. Triad Publishing Group. Presenter local, nat., and internat. confs. on gender equity in schs., violence prevention in schs., sexual harassment in schs and the workplace, and; cons., presenter Ednl. Visions Group, East Windsor, NJ, 1990—98. Author, editor: Bus. World for Women / Men mag., 1975—78 (Navy citation, 1977), SACC Talk, 1991—92; author: (books) The Ghost Under Third Base, 2007, The Book of Mysteries: Wizard of Balalac, 2008, Fat Girls From Outerspace, 2008, Five, Six, Pick-Up Sticks, 2008, Destiny in From The Shadows, 2008, The Goblin Murder Mystery, 2008, (poetry) 5 Poems in Essential Verse, a Love and Romance Poetry Anthology. Founding bd. dirs. Ctrl. NJ Breast Cancer Coalition, 2000—02, Am. Cancer Soc. Chpt. N.J. Breast Cancer Coalition, Manalapan, 1973—77, Am. Cancer Soc. Chpt. NJ Breast Cancer Coalition, Freehold, 2000—; bd. dirs., newsletter editor Women's Agenda/NJ Law, 1993—96; vol. bd. dirs. Susan B. Komen Race for the Cure, Princeton, NJ, 1995—99. Mem.: AAUW (1st Pl. in Short Story Category, 2nd Pl. in Poetry Catagory, Writer's Contest, Fla. 2008, honorable mention poetry 2009), Am. Assn. U. Women, Soc. Children's Book Writers and Illustrators, Am. Mensa (Ariz. proctor coord., S.C., Ga., Tampa, Sorasota Fla. proctor), Phi Delta Kappa, Kappa Delta Pi. Avocations: reading, gardening, writing, poetry. Personal E-mail: franoren2@yahoo.com.

ORENTLICHER, JOHN, video research educator, artist; b. Roanoke, Va., June 7, 1943; s. Herman and Jeanette (Levin) O. BA, Goddard Coll., 1968; MFA, Sch. Art Inst. Chgo., 1970. Asst. prof. Ea. Mich. U., Ypsilanti, 1970-76; assoc. prof. Syracuse U., NY, 1976—, chmn. exptl. studios, 1978-81, chmn., prof. art media studies Coll. of Visual and Performing Arts, 1981-85, 87-89, chair dept. transmedia, 2004—08. U.S. curator, 1st Internat. Video Festival Invitational, 1986, 2nd Internat. Video Festival, Mus. de Arte Medellin, Colombia, 1988; Fulbright Hays sr. lectr., Santiago Club, Colombia, 1985, 93; exec. producer WHAT-TV, Syracuse, 1983; video artist. Vol. Peace Corps, Aisen Province, Chile, 1964-66; curator 2d bi-ann. Internat. Video Festival, Medellin, Colombia, Athens Internat. Film and Video Festival-Ann. Kingdom, 2007, Internat. Black Film & Video Festival, 2008, Video Distribution-V-Tape, Toronto, Ont. Exhibitions include Recontre's Paris/Berlin, 2006—07, Athens Internat. Film Video Festival, 2007, exhibitions include travelling Black Maria Internat. Finha & Video Festival, Jersey City, NJ, 2008—09. N.Y. State Coun. grantee, 1984, grantee Rockefeller Found., Nat. Endowment Arts; recipient ACE award. Avocation: music. Home: 6074 Sewickley Dr Jamesville NY 13078-9464 Office: Syracuse U Dept Transmedia 102 Sheffer Bldg Syracuse NY 13244 Office Phone: 315-443-1033. E-mail: jorentli@syr.edu.

ORESKES, IRWIN, biochemistry educator; b. Chgo., June 30, 1926; s. Herman and Clara (Rubenstein) O.; m. Susan E. Nagin, June 18, 1949; children: Michael, Daniel, Naomi, Rebecca. BS in Chemistry, CCNY, 1949; MA in Phys. Chemistry, Bklyn. Coll., 1956; PhD in Biochemistry, CUNY, 1969. Cert. clin. lab. dir. NYC, NY State. Chemist Tech. Tape Co., Bronx, NY, 1949; technician NYU Sch. Medicine, 1950-51; phys. chemist Kingsbrook Jewish Med. Ctr., 1951-56; rsch. fellow Poly. Inst., NY, 1957-58; rsch. assoc. Mt. Sinai Hosp., NYC, 1959-68, dir. arthritis lab., 1961-90; rsch. asst. prof. Mt. Sinai Sch. Medicine, NYC, 1969-74, rsch. assoc. prof., 1974-91; assoc. prof. Hunter Coll. Sch. Health Scis., CUNY, 1969—74, prof., 1974—2002, prof. emeritus, 2002—, dean, 1977-80; mem. doctoral faculty in biochemistry Grad. Ctr., CUNY, 1970—2002, emeritus, 2002—. Vis. prof. Johns Hopkins U. Sch. Health Svcs., 1976-77; cons. to diagnostic reagent and instrument mfrs., 1953-; mem. Internat. Sci. Coun., Albert Einstein Rsch. Inst., Buenos Aires, 1969-79; mem. bd. examiners for clin. labs. NYC Dept. Health, 1973-75; sr. cons. Biotech. Rev. Assocs., 1983-92. Co-editor: Rheumatology for the Health Care Professional, 1991; contbr. numerous articles to profl. jours. Served with U.S. Army, 1944-46. Nat. Inst. Arthritis and Metabolic Diseases grantee, 1961-69; Arthritis Found. grantee, 1961-65, 69, 72; Lupus Found. grantee, 1975-76; CUNY Found. grantee, 1982-83. Mem. Am. Chem. Soc., Am. Coll. Rheumatology, AAAS, NY Acad. Scis., Am. Assn. Immunologists, Am. Assn. Clin. Chemistry, Harvey Soc., Nat. Acad. Clin. Biochemistry, Acad. Clin. Lab. Physicians and Scientists, Clin. Immunology Soc., Sigma Xi, Phi Lambda Upsilon. Home: 670 West End Ave New York NY 10025-7313 Office: Hunter Coll Sch Health Sci 425 E 25th St New York NY 10010-2547 Office Phone: 212-481-5115. *I have always tried to live and work by the idea that strength is not harshness, caring is not sentimentality, and honesty is not vulnerability.*

ORESKES, MICHAEL H., editor, journalist; b. May 1954; m. Geraldine Baum; 2 children. BA, CUNY. Reporter edn., police and labor NY Daily News, 1975, City Hall bur. chief; metro reporter NY Times, 1981, bur. chief Albany, NY, Congl. corr., nat. polit. reporter Washington, 1987—91, city editor, 1991, bur. chief Washington, 1997—2001, asst. mng. editor, dir. electronic news, 2001—04, dep. mng. editor, 2004—05; exec. editor Internat. Herald Tribune NY Times Co., Paris, 2005—08; mng. editor US News AP, 2008—. Co-author (with Eric Lane): The Genius of America: How the Constitution Saved our Country and Why it Can Again, 2007. Office: AP 450 W 33rd St New York NY 10001 Office Phone: 212-621-1500.

ORESKES, NAOMI, science historian; b. NYC, Nov. 25, 1958; d. Irwin Oreskes and Susan Eileen Nagin Oreskes; m. Kenneth Belitz, Sept. 28, 1986; children: Hannah Oreskes Belitz, Clara Oreskes Belitz. BSc with honors, Imperial Coll., London, 1981; PhD, Stanford U., 1990. Geologist We. Mining Corp., Adelaide, Australia, 1981—84; rsch. and tng. asst. Stanford U., Calif., 1984—89; vis. asst. prof. Dartmouth Coll., Hanover, NH, 1990—91, asst. prof., 1991—96; assoc. prof. Gallatin Sch. NYU, 1996—98, U. Calif., San Diego, 1998—2005, prof., 2005—, provost, sixth coll., 2008—. Consulting geologist Western Mining Corp., 1984-90; consulting historian Am. Inst. Physics, N.Y.C., 1990-96. Author: The Rejection of Continental Drift, 1999, Theory and Method in American Earth Science, 1999; editor: Plate Tectonics: An Insider's History of the Modern Theory of the Earth, 2001; contbr. articles to profl. jours. Recipient Lindgren prize Soc. Econ. Geologists, 1993, Young Investigator award NSF, 1994-99, George Sarton Lectr. award AAAS, 2004; fellow NEH, 1993. Mem. Geol. Soc. Am., History Sci. Soc., History Earth Scis. Soc. (pres.). Jewish. Office: Univ Calif San Diego Sixth Coll 9500 Gilman Dr La Jolla CA 92093-0054 Office Phone: 858-822-5951. Business E-Mail: noreskes@ucsd.edu.

ORFALEA, PAUL JAMES, investment company executive, former printing company executive; b. L.A., Nov. 28, 1947; s. Al and Virginia Orfalea; m. Natalie Orfalea; children: Mason, Keenan. BS in Fin., U. So. Calif., 1971; LLD (hon.), Babson Coll., Mass., 2004; Ph.D (hon.), Lebanese Am. U., 2006, Cal Poly U., 2007. Founder, CEO, chmn. Kinko's, Santa Barbara, Calif., 1970—2000, chmn. emeritus, 2000—04; co-founder West Coast Asset Mgmt., Ventura, Calif., 2000—. Cofounder The Orfalea Foundations, Santa Barbara, Calif., 2000—; lectr. Univ. So. Calif., Univ. Calif., Davis, Santa Barbara; adv. bd. Stone Canyon Venture Ptnrs. LP; bd. dirs. Espresso Royale, DataProse. Co-author (with Ann Marsh): Copy This: Lessons from a Hyperactive Dyslexic Who Turned a Bright Idea into One of America's Best Companies, 2005; co-author: (with Lance Helfert, Atticus Lowe, & Dean Zatkowsky) The Entrepreneurial Investor: The Art, Science and Business of Value Investing, 2007. Bd. trustee Univ. Calif. Santa Barbara Found. Recipient Entrepreneur of Yr. award, Univ. So. Calif. Marshall Sch. Bus., 1998, Philanthropist of Yr., 2000, Conrad Hilton Entrepreneur award, 2001, Friend of Calif. Cmty. Colleges, 2003, R.O.S.E. award, Univ. So. Calif., 2003, Hello Friend award, Ennis William Cosby Found., 2003, Lifetime Achievement award, Santa Barbara News Press, 2005, Beta Gamma Sigma Medallion for Entrepreneurship, Sally award, Salvation Army, Ellis Island Medal of Honor; named Lifetime Philanthropist of Yr., Assn. Funding Professionals, 2005; named to CEO Hall of Fame. Office: The Orfalea Foundations 1283 Coast Village Cir Santa Barbara CA 93108 also: West Coast Asset Mgmt Ste 1000 1205 Coast Village Rd Santa Barbara CA 93108-2718 Office Phone: 805-653-5333. Office Fax: 805-648-6466.

ORFIELD, ANTONIA MARIE, optometrist, researcher; d. Alfred Anthony and Eva Swenson Stoll; m. Gary Allan Orfield, May 24, 1963 (div. 2005); children: Amy Elizabeth, Sonia Marie, Rosanna Antonia. BA in History, Smith Coll., 1963; MAT in History/Social Studies, U. Chgo., 1966; BS in Visual Sci., Ill. Coll. Optometry, 1987, OD, 1989. Lic. Mass. Bd. Optometry. Optometrist Michael Reese HMO, Chgo., 1989—91, Eye Exam 2000, Chgo., 1989—91; behavioral optometrist Harvard U. Health, Cambridge, Mass., 1991—. Asst. prof. New Eng. Coll. Optometry, Boston, 1991—2000, dir., chief investigator, clin. preceptor Mather Sch. Vision and Learning Rsch./Svc. Clinic, 1993—99; pvt. practice behavioral optometrist, Cambridge, 1996—; spkr. in field. Author: Eyes for Learning: Preventing and Curing Vision Related Learning Problems, 2007; contbr. articles to profl. jours. Parent rep. Kenwood Acad. Sch. Coun., Chgo., 1989—91. Grantee, State Street Bank, N.E. Congress Optometry, Mass. Soc. Optometrists, Am. Found. Vision Awareness, Friends of the Sensorily Deprived. Fellow: Coll. Optometrists in Vision Devel., Am. Acad. Optometry; mem.: Neurooptometric Rehab. Assn. (charter), Internat. Coll. Applied Kinesiology. Democrat. Achievements include research in children in poverty have a great number of vision problems that interefere with learning; near point glasses can raise test scores; tracking problems are correlated with reading failures; vision therapy is correlated with improvement in grades. Avocations: study of homeopathic medicine, sports vision training, study of educational kinesiology, study of nutrition and vision, swimming. Office: Harvard Univ Health Svc 75 Mt Auburn St Cambridge MA 02138 also: Ste 205 678 Massachussetts Ave Cambridge MA 02139 also: 312 Maryland Ave NE Washington DC 20002-5712 Personal E-mail: antoniaorfield@yahoo.com.

ORFIELD, ROBERT ALLEN, special education director; b. Elizabethton, Tenn., May 28, 1958; s. Hubert Allen Orfield and Peggie Jean West; m. Vicki Lynn Gardner, Aug. 20, 1982; children: Marcus Allen, Megan Lynn. Degree in early childhood edn., East Tenn. State U., Johnson City, 1981, BS, 1984; MS in Mid. Grades Edn., West Ga. U., Carrollton, 1994, degree in Ednl. Leadership, 2001; EdS, Lincoln Meml. U., Harrogate, Tenn., 2006. Lic. administr. Ga. Profl. Standards Commn., 2006, cert. in tchg. gifted Ga. Profl. Standards Commn., 2001. Pulmonary lab technician Vets. Hosp., Johnson City, 1981—84; tchr. Neva Elem. Sch., Mountain City, Tenn., 1984—87, Calhoun Mid. Sch., Ga., 1987—2002, asst. prin., 2002—06; prin. calhoun mid. sch. Calhoun City Schs., 2006—09; special edn. dir. Calhour City Schs., 2009—. Tchr. gov.'s math. sci. initiative North Ga. RESA, Rome, 2001—02; coord. sci. fair Calhoun Mid. Sch., 1994—2000, chmn. sci. dept., 1994—2000, coord. math league, 1987—94. Youth leader Whitfield Bapt. Ch., Dalton, Ga., 1996—98. Second class petty officer USN, 1976—81. Decorated Unit commendation USN, Expeditionary medal, Sea Svc. Deployment ribbon; named Teacher of Year, Calhoun Mid. Sch., 1996. Mem.: Kwanis (assoc.). Republican. Baptist. Avocations: fishing, sports. Home: 123 Holcomb Rd NW Adairsville GA 30103 Office: Calhoun Mid Sch 380 Barrett Rd Calhoun GA 30701 Office Phone: 706-629-3340, 706-602-6609. Office Fax: 706-629-0236, 706-629-3235; Home Fax: 706-629-0236. Business E-Mail: orfieldr@calhounschools.org.

ORFORD, ROBERT RAYMOND, physician, consultant; b. Winnipeg, Manitoba, Can., Apr. 18, 1948; came to U.S., 1988; s. Robert Raymond and Sarah Gloria L. (Gullden) O.; m. Dale Laura Stuart, June 2, 1972; children: Carolyn Tiffany, Andrew Craig, Loren Brent. BS, McGill U., 1969, MD, 1971; MS, U. Minn., 1975; MPH, U. Wash., 1976. Assoc. prof. cmty. medicine U. Alberta, Edmonton, Can., 1978-88; dir. med. svcs. Govt. of Alberta, Edmonton, Can., 1979-81, exec. dir. occupational health svcs., 1981-85, deputy min. cmty. occupational health, 1985-88; med. dir. employee health U. Alberta Hosp., Edmonton, Can., 1988; sr. assoc. cons. Mayo Clinic, Rochester, Minn., 1988-91, cons. preventive medicine, 1991-96, Scottsdale, Ariz., 1996—. Asst. prof. Mayo Med. Sch., Rochester, 1988—; mem. Alberta Energy Resource Conservation Bd., 1988-89; chmn. divsn. preventive and occupl. medicine, dir. exec. health program, Mayo Clinic, Scottsdale, 1999-2007, cons. exec. health program, 2008—. Contbr. articles to profl. jours. Mem. Olmsted County Environ. Commn., Rochester, 1991-96, chair, 1994. Govt. of Can. Nat. Health fellow, 1975-76. Fellow Royal Coll. Physicians and Surgeons Can., Am. Coll. Occupational and Environ. Medicine (pres. 2008-09), Am. Coll. Preventive Medicine, Aerospace Med. Assn.; mem. Internat. Commn. Occupational Health Medicine (nat. sec. 2001—), Ariz. Med. Assn., Am. Med. Assn. Presbyterian. Avocations: languages, fitness, travel. Home: 15516 E Acacia Way Fountain Hills AZ 85268-3158 Office: Mayo Clinic Scottsdale Divsn Preventive Medicine 13400 E Shea Blvd Scottsdale AZ 85259-5499 Office Phone: 480-301-7379. Office Fax: 480-301-7569. Business E-Mail: rorford@mayo.edu.

ORGAN, RITA C., museum administrator, consultant; b. Omaha, Aug. 7, 1965; d. Claude Harold and Elizabeth Lucille Organ. BFA, Calif. Coll. Arts & Crafts, 1987; attended, Ind. U., 1987—90. Curator African-Am. materials Children's Mus., Indpls., 1990—96; dir. exhibits & collections CHW Mus. African-Am. History, Detroit, 1996—2000, Nat. Underground Railroad Freedom Ctr., Cin., 2000—04; exec. dir. Ind. Mus. African-Am. History, Indpls., 2004—06. Bd. pres. Assn. African-Am. Mus., Detroit, 1999—2002; bd. mem. Assn. Study of African Am. Life and History, Washington, 2000—02; mem., mus. cons. adv. bd. The Freedom Ctr., Cin., 2005—. Author: (preface) Black History Resource Guide, 1998. Mem.: Nat. Coun. Negro Women, Assn. Midwest Mus., Assn. African Am. Mus. Avocations: hiking, bicycling, cooking.

ORGILL, MARYKAY, chemistry professor; BS, Brigham Young U., Provo, UT; MS, Purdue U., West Lafayette, Ind., 1999, PhD, 2003. Asst. prof., sci. edn. and biochemistry U. Mo. Columbia, 2003—04; asst. prof., chemistry U. Nev., Las Vegas, 2004—. Recipient Disting. Tchr. award, UNLV Coll. Scis., 2008, Faculty Excellence award, Consol. Students U. Nev., 2008. Mem.: Nat. Assn. Rsch. Sci. Tchg., Am. Chem. Soc. (divsn. chem. edn. program com. 2007—). Office: Univ Nev Las Vegas 4505 S Maryland Pky MS 4003 Las Vegas NV 89154 Office Fax: 702-895-4270. Business E-Mail: marykay.orgill@unlv.edu.

ORIANI, RICHARD ANTHONY, metallurgical engineer, educator; b. El Salvador, July 19, 1920; arrived in U.S., 1929, naturalized, 1943; s. Americo and Berta (Siguenza) Oriani; m. Constance Amelia Gordon, June 26, 1949; children: Margaret, Steven, Julia, Amelia. B in Chem. Engring, CCNY, 1943; MS, Stevens Inst. Tech., 1946; MA, Princeton U., 1948, PhD, 1949. Lab. asst. CCNY, 1943; chemist Bakelite Corp., Bloomfield, NJ, 1943-46; instr. physics Miss Fine's Finishing Sch., Princeton, NJ, 1946-47; rsch. assoc. GE Rsch. Lab., Schenectady, 1949-59; asst. dir. U.S. Steel Corp. Rsch. Lab., Monroeville, Pa., 1959-80; prof. U. Minn., Mpls., 1980-89, dir. Corrosion Rsch. Ctr., 1980-87, prof. emeritus, dir. emeritus, 1989—. Cons. in field. Contbr. articles to profl. jours., chapters to books. Founder, mem. Foxwood Civic Assn., Monroeville, 1959—80; founder, v.p. Monroeville Pub. Libr., 1960—80. Recipient Alexander von Humboldt Sr. Scientist award, 1984, W. R. Whitney award, 1987. Fellow: Electrochemical Soc., Nat. Assn. Corrosion Engrs., N.Y. Acad. Scis., Am. Inst. Chemists, Am. Soc. Metals; mem.: AAAS, Am. Inst. Metall. Engrs., Am. Phys. Soc. Republican. Home: 7250 Lewis Ridge Pky # 305 Edina MN 55439 Office: U Minn 112 Amundson Hall 221 Church St SE Minneapolis MN 55455-0113 Office Phone: 612-625-5862. E-mail: orian001@umn.edu.

ORIGITANO, THOMAS CHARLES, neurological surgeon; BS in Chemistry and Biology, MacMurray Coll., 1976; PhD, Loyola U., Chgo., 1981; MD, Loyola-Stritch U., Maywood, Ill., 1984. Diplomate Am. Bd. Neurol. Surgery, 1995. Intern gen. surgery Loyola U. Med. Ctr., Maywood, 1984—85, resident neurol. surgery, 1985—90, asst. prof., 1990—96, assoc. prof., 1996—98, prof., 1998—, chmn. neurol. surgery med. ctr., 1998—. Home and Office: Loyola Univ Med Ctr 2160 South First Ave Maywood IL 60153

ORIKRI, TIMOTHY UFUOMAEFE, landscape artist; b. Delta State, Nigeria, Nov. 9, 1965; BFA, Delta State U., 1991. Free lance artist Orikridesigns Studio, Detroit, 2001—. Achievements include design of multiple works of art exhibitions. Home: 17603 Cherry Lawn St Detroit MI 48221 Personal E-mail: tim@timothyorikri.com.

ORINGER, KENNETH M., chef, restaurant owner; b. Paramus, NJ, Aug. 8, 1965; Degree in Hotel and Restaurant Mgmt., Bryant Coll.; grad., Culinary Inst. Am. Cook River Cafe, NYC; pastry chef Al Forno, Providence; sous chef Le Marquis de Lafayette, Boston; owner, chef Terra Trattoria, Greenwich, Conn.; chef de cuisine Silks, San Francisco, 1992; chef, ptnr. Tosca, Hingham, Mass.; exec. chef, owner Clio, Boston, 1997—, Uni Sashimi Bar, Boston, Toro, Boston, 2005—, La Verdad, Boston, 2007—, KO Prime, Boston, 2007—. Named Best New Chef, San Francisco Chronicle, Rising Star Chef, Restaurant Hospitality, Best Chef in Boston, Boston Mag., 2000, Best Chef in N.E., James Beard Found., 2001. Office: Restaurant Clio 370 Commonwealth Ave Boston MA 02215

ORKAND, DONALD SAUL, management consultant; b. NYC, Mar. 2, 1936; s. Harold and Sylvia (Wagner) O.; children: Dara Sue, Katarina Day; m. Kim Lim Sang, July 22, 2001; 1 child, Aaron J. BS summa cum laude, NYU, 1956, MBA, 1957, PhD, 1963. Statistician Western Electric Co., NYC, 1956-58; group v.p. Ops. Rsch., Inc., Silver Spring, Md., 1960-69; pres. Ops. Rsch. Industries, Ltd., Ottawa, Ont., Canada, 1968-69; CEO Orkand Corp., Tysons Corner, Va., 1970—2004; ptnr. DC Ventures and Assocs. LLC, Mc Lean, Va., 2004—. Bd. dirs. U. Md. Found., Inc., College Park, 1993-2002. Bd. vis. Univ. Coll., 2002—; trustee Suburban Hosp., 1994-2000. 1st lt. Ordnance Corps, USAR, 1958-60. Mem. Am. Econs. Assn., Am. Statis. Assn. Republican. Jewish. Avocations: reading, theater, travel, exercise. Office: Dc Ventures Associates PO Box 10625 Mc Lean VA 22102-8625

ORKIN, JENNA, writer; b. NYC; d. Harvey Orkin; 1 child, One. BA, Hunter Coll., NYC; JD, NY Law Sch., NY; BA/MA, Oxford U., England. Interviewer Exploring Post One, New York, NY, 1984—86; educator Juilliard, New York, NY, 1978—83; press chairperson 911 Environ. Action, NYC, 2002—04; founder World Trade Ctr. Environ. Orgn., 2002—. Moderator 1st Peak Oil Conf., NYC, 2005. Author: (poem) Dubya's Lament (Best of 2005).

ORKIN, LOUIS RICHARD, physician, educator; b. NYC, Dec. 23, 1915; s. Samuel David and Rebecca (Rish) O.; m. Florence Fine, Mar. 5, 1938; 1 dau., Rita. BA, U. Wis., 1937; MD, NYU, 1941; AAS in Marine Tech., Kingsborough Coll., 1992. Intern Bellevue Hosp., NYC, 1942, resident anesthesiology, 1946-48; practice medicine specializing in anesthesiology Bronx, NY, 1946—48; dir. anesthesiology Backus Hosp., Norwich, Conn., 1948-50; asst. prof. anesthesiology NYU Coll. Medicine, 1950-55; prof., chmn. dept. anesthesiology Albert Einstein Coll. Medicine, 1955-82, Disting. univ. prof., 1982-86, dist. univ. prof. emeritus, 1986—. Vis. prof. depts. bioengring., anesthesiology U. Calif., San Diego, 1971; Cons. VA, USPHS, USN; mem. com. anesthesiology Nat. Acad. Scis., 1964-69; mem. com. anesthetic drugs FDA, Dept. Health, Edn. and Welfare, 1970— Author: Patient in Shock, 1965, Physiology of Obstetrical Anesthesia, 1969; Contbr. articles to profl. jours. V.p. and trustee Wood Library Mus. Served to capt. M.C. AUS, 1942-45. Decorated Bronze Star; honoree Albert Einstein Coll. Medicine, 2005. Fellow Am. Coll. Chest Physicians, NY Acad. Sci., NY Acad. Medicine, Am. Coll. Anesthesiology (past chmn. bd. govs.); mem. NY State Soc. Anesthesiologists (past pres.; Disting. Svc. award 2000). Home: 11 Stuyvesant Oval Apt 11F New York NY 10009-2001 Office Phone: 212-473-0023. Personal E-mail: Louis_Orkin@hotmail.com.

ORLANDO, LORI ANN, medical researcher, educator, physician; d. Geraldine Sainthill and Roy Charles Orlando; m. Bradley F. Mann, May 19, 1995. BS, U. N.C., 1990—2001; MD, Tulane Med. Ctr., 1998; M in health sci., Duke U. Med. Sch., 2004. Diplomate Am. Bd. Internal Medicine. Resident in internal medicine Tulane Med. Ctr., New Orleans, 1998—2001, chief resident in internal medicine, 2001—02; internal medicine fellow Duke U. Med. Ctr., Durham, NC, 2002—04, assoc. in medicine, 2004—06, asst. prof. in medicine, 2006—; rsch. assoc. Durham VA Med. Ctr., NC, 2002—. Contbr. articles to profl. jours. Recipient Rsch. internship, Harvard U., Brigham and Women's Hosp., Dept. of Pathology, 1987, Med. Student Achievement award, Endocrine Soc., 1998, Owl Club award for Outstanding Med. Resident, 2000, 2001, Outstanding Trainee award, so. sect. Am. Fedn. Med. Rsch., 2002, Milton W. Hamuisky award outstanding jr. faculty presentation, 2005, Best Sci. Abstract award, 2005. Mem.: Soc. of Gen. Internal Medicine (assoc.; chair planning com.). Achievements include research in describing chronic kidney disease and evaluating interface between generalist and specialist care.

ORLANSKI, ISIDORO, meteorologist, researcher; b. Buenos Aires, June 6, 1939; s. Samuel and Sara Orlanski; m. Beatriz Gojchgilerint; children: Diego Javier, Guillermo, Elisa Rosana Orlanski Ours. Licensure in Physics, U. Buenos Aires, 1964; PhD, MIT, Cambridge, 1967. Instr. Faculty Scis., U. Buenos Aires, 1963—65; rsch. asst. MIT, Cambridge, 1965—67; rsch. meteorologist GFDL, NOAA, Washington, 1967—68, GFDLl, NOAA, Princeton, NJ, 1968—84, dept. dir., 1980—83, meterologist, 1984—2007; sr. rschr. Princeton U., 2007—. Sesame stering com. mem. NOAA, Washington, 1978—85; chmn., mesoscale working group, IAMAP Internat. Union Geodesy and Geophysics, 1978—85; editl. adv. bd. atmospheric sci. libr. series. D.Reidel Pub. Co., Dordrecht, Netherlands, 1981; mem. internat. com. dynamic meterology Internat. Assn. Meteorology and Atmospheric Physics, 1983—84; funder dir. Ctr. Atmospheric and Oceanic Rsch., Buenos Aires, 1987—89. Mem., US nat. com. Internat. Assn. Meteorology and Atmospheric Physics, Washington, 1986—88; cons. UN Devel. Program, Buenos Aires, Buenos Aires, 1987—88. Recipient Carl-Gustaf Rossby award, 1968, NOAA Outstanding Sci. Paper award, 1977, NOAA Administartor award, 1985. Fellow: Am. Meteorol. Soc. Jewish. Achievements include research in advances in the dynamics of the atmosphere and Oceans. Office: Princeton University Forrestal Campus Rte 1 Princeton NJ 08540 Business E-Mail: orlanski@princeton.edu. E-mail: isidoro.orlanski@noaa.gov.

ORLEBEKE, WILLIAM RONALD, retired lawyer, writer; b. El Paso, Tex., Jan. 5, 1934; s. William Ronald and Frances Claire (Cook) O.; children: Michelle, Julene, David; m. Susan K. Nash, 2000. BA, Willamette U., Salem, Oreg., 1956, JD, 1966; MA, U. Kans., Lawrence, 1957. Bar: Calif. 1966, US Dist. Ct. (no. dist.) Calif. 1967, US Ct. Appeals (9th cir.) 1967, US Ct. Appeals (7th cir.) 1989, US Dist. Ct. (no. dist.) Ill. 1989, US Dist. Ct. (cen. dist.) Calif. 1989. Mem. staff Travelers Ins. Co., Sacramento, 1957-61; br. claim mgr. NY Life Ins. Co., 1961-62; branch claim mgr. Transamerica Ins. Co., San Francisco, 1962-63; spl. investigator Oregon State Police, 1963—65; assoc. Eliassen & Postel, San Francisco, 1966-69; ptnr. Coll, Levy & Orlebeke, Concord, Calif., 1969-77, Orlebeke & Hutchings, Concord, Calif., 1977-89; prin. Law Offices W. Ronald Orlebeke, 1989-98; hearing officer Contra Costa County, Calif., 1981-98; arbitrator Contra Costa County Superior Ct., 1977-98, US Dist. Ct. No. Calif., 1978-98, Mt. Diablo Mcpl. Ct., 1987-89; ret., 1998. Judge pro tem Mt. Diablo Mcpl. Ct., 1973-75; criminology prof. Pioneer-Pacific Coll., 2002-03; instr. Am. history & modern European history Salem Ctr., 2009-. Author: Orlebeke Family in Europe and America, 1570-1990, 1988, Don't Tell Me I Can't, 2003, (novels) Code Jeremiah, 2004, Lightning, 2004. Alumni bd. dir. Willamette U., 1978-81, trustee, 1980-81 scholar chmn. Concord Elks, 1977-79; del. Joint US/China Internat. Trade Law Conf., Beijing, 1987. With USMCR, 1952-59. Sr. scholar Willamette U., 1955-56; Woodrow Wilson fellow Kans. U., 1956-57, US Bur. Nat. Affairs fellow, 1966, others. Mem. SAR, Sons of Confederate Vets. (Merit award 1989), Sons of Union Vets. Civil War, First Marine Divsn. Assn., Order Ea. Star (worthy patron 1980), Masons (sec. Capitol Masonic Ctr., 2001-04, corp. sec. Oreg. Masonic Low Twelve Club, Inc 2005-07, spl. trustee Oreg. chpt. 2006-07), Elks, Rotary (charter pres. Clayton Valley/Concord Sunrise club 1987-88, chmn. dist. 5160 Calif. membership devel. 1989-90, dist. gov. liaison dist. 5160 1990-92, dist. Rotarian of Yr. 1989-90, Paul Harris fellow 1988, 1992 dist. conf. chmn. benefactor 1990, Merit award 1990), Shriners (v.p. Salem Shrine Club 2004-07, pres. 2008—). Republican.

ORLIN, KAREN J., lawyer; b. Washington, Apr. 2, 1948; d. Hyman and Lenore O.; 1 child. AB Summa Cum Laude, in math., U. Pa., 1969; JD, Harvard U., 1972. Bar: N.Y. 1973, U.S. Dist. Ct. (so. and ea. dists.) N.Y. 1973, U.S. Ct. Appeals (2d cir.) 1973, Fla. 1982. Assoc. Kronish, Lieb, Weiner & Hellman LLP, NYC, 1972-81; sr. assoc. Valdes-Fauli, Bischoff, Kriss and Mandler, Miami, 1981-82, ptnr., 1982-83; sr. assoc. Ruden, Barnett, McClosky, Smith, Schuster & Russell, P.A., Ft. Lauderdale, Fla., 1983-85, Shea & Gould, NYC and Miami, Fla., 1985-87; of counsel Thomson, Muraro, Razook and Hart P.A., Miami, Fla., 1987—88; sr. v.p.-assoc. counsel, asst. sec. Am. Savs. of Fla., F.S.B., Miami, 1988—95; ptnr. Berman, Rennert Vogel & Mandler Pa., Miami, 1995—97; mem. Zack Kosnitzky, Miami, 1997—99; of counsel Akerman Senterfitt & Eidson Pa., Miami, 1999—2002; counsel Stearns Weaver Miller Weissler Alhadeff & Sitterson Pa., Miami, 2002—03; sr. atty. Rutherford Mulhall Pa., Boca Raton, Fla., 2004—05; ptnr. Wasserstrom Weinreb & Wealcatch Pl., Hollywood, Fla., 2005—06; pvt. practice & expert witness corp. gov., 2006—; v.p. & gen. legal counsel Pacific Nat. Bank, Miami, Fla., 2007; ptnr. Rothstein Rosenfeldt Adler Pa., Ft. Lauderdale, Fla., 2007—08. Instr. bus. law South Fla. U. Contbr. articles to profl. jours. Mem. Fla. Bar (corps. and securities com. 1999—, chair 2004-06, vice chair, 2001-04), Fla. Bar Com. with CPAs & PIC Pa. (vice chair 2007-08), Fla. Bar Profls., Am. Mensa Ltd., Phi Beta Kappa, ABA (bus. law sect.), NY City Bar Assn., Rotary Club, Downtown Miami Chpt., Cosal Gables C. of C., U. Pa. Dade Alumni Club (sec., 1991-93, pres., 1993-95) Office: PO Box 430620 Miami FL 33243-0620 Office Phone: 305-794-6387. Office Fax: 305-668-7072. Personal E-mail: kjorlin@bellsouth.net, korlin@anstalaw.com.

ORLOV, ALEXEI G., economics professor, researcher; PhD, U. Va., Charlottesville. Assoc. prof. Radford U., Va., 2006—. Office: Radford Univ Dept Economics Radford VA 24142 Business E-Mail: aorlov@radford.edu.

ORLOW, SETH J., dermatologist; b. Bklyn., Dec. 23, 1958; AB magna cum laude, Harvard Coll., 1979; MD, PhD Molecular Pharmacology, Albert Einstein Coll. Medicine, 1986. Diplomate Nat. Bd. Dermatology, Nat. Bd. Med. Examiners. Intern in pediat. Mt. Sinai Med. Ctr., NYC, 1986-87; resident in dermatology Yale-New Haven Hosp., New Haven, 1987-89, fellow in dermatology, 1989-90; asst. prof. dermatology and cell biology NYU Sch. of Medicine, NYC, 1990-94, assoc. prof. dermatology and cell biology, 1994—2000; Weinberg prof. pediat. dermatology, prof. cell biology and pediat. NYU Sch. Medicine, NYC, 2000—, vice chair for rsch. dermatology, 2004—07. Dir. pediat. dermatology, Tisch Hosp., NYC, 1990-2007, chmn. dept. dermatology, 2006—; dir. pediat. dermatology Bellevue Hosp., NYC, 1990—, Lenox Hill Hosp., NYC, 1994—. Editorial bd. Archives of Dermatology, Boston, 1995—, Pigment Cell Rsch., 1995—; ad hoc jour. reviewer numerous publs. Rsch. grantee William T. Morris Found., 1990-92, Evans Found., 1991-92, NIH, 1993-94, 94-98, 94-97; recipient Irma T. Hirschl Career Scientist award, 1995-2000, others. Fellow Am. Acad. Dermatology, Am. Acad. Pediat.; mem. Soc. Investigative Dermatology (bd. dirs. 1988-90), Soc. Pediatric Dermatology, Pan Am. Soc. Pigment Cell Rsch., Assn. for Rsch. in Vision and Ophthalmology, Dermatol. Soc. Greater NY, others. Office: NYU Med Ctr SKI 7 Ste 7R 530 First Ave New York NY 10016 Office Phone: 212-263-5889.

ORLOWSKI, JAMES PHILLIP, pediatrician; b. Washington, Oct. 14, 1947; s. Stanley and Letha Everett Orlowski; m. Linda Dale Donaldson, June 14, 1969; 1 child, James Anders Christensen. MD, Case Western Res. U., 1974. Dir. pediat. ICU Cleve. Clinic Found., Cleve., 1978—93, U. Cmty. Hosp., Tampa, Fla., 1993—. Clin. assoc. prof. pediat., ethics, and critical care U. of South Fla., Tampa, 1994—. Editor: (book) Ethics in Critical Care Medicine. Mem.: Am. Acad. of Pediat., Am. Coll. of Chest Physicians, Am. Coll. of Critical Care Medicine. Office: U Cmty Hosp 3100 E Fletcher Ave Tampa FL 33613 Personal E-mail: jameso@mail.uch.org.

ORM, SALLY S., music educator, piano vocal coach; d. Harvey Jacob and Lucille Mae Seyler; children: Andrea Summer Orm-Gilbert, Jonathan D. Gilbert, Jennifer E. Seager. Student, Eastman Sch. Music. With FBI, Washington, 1970—75; owner Orm Music Studios, 1976—, All Things Music, LLC. Founder keyboard donations Orm Music Studios, Neenah, Wis., 2001—. Treas. Regional Domestic Abuse, Oshkosh, Wis., 1984—86, pres., 1986—88; treas. Audubon Soc., Appleton, 1985—86; Gold award coord. Fox Valley Area Girl Scouts, Appleton, Wis., 1995—99. Recipient Mem. of Yr. award, Fox Valley Keyboard Tchrs., 2001; named Mem. of the Yr. award, Fox Valley Area Girl Scouts, 1999. Mem.: Fin. Foxes (sec. 2008—), Wis. Music Tchrs. Assn. (found. chair 2006—), Music Tchrs. Nat. Assn., Fox Valley Keyboard Tchrs. (v.p., program dir. 1999—2003, Mem. of the Yr. award 2002), World Piano Pedagogy Conf., Keyboard Music Educators Assn. (adjudicator keyboard competition 2002—). Presbyterian. Avocations: gardening, travel. Office: Orm Music Studios 749 S Commercial St Neenah WI 54956 Business E-Mail: sormusic@aol.com.

ORMAN, LEONARD ARNOLD, lawyer; b. Balt., June 15, 1930; s. Samuel and Bertie (Adler) O.; m. Barbara Gold, June 9, 1978; children: Richard Harold, Robert Barton. AB summa cum laude, U. Md., 1952, JD, 1955. Bar: Md. 1955, U.S. Ct. Appeals (4th cir.) 1956, U.S. Dist. Ct. Md. 1955, Ct. Appeals Md. 1955, U.S. Supreme Ct. 1977, U.S. Ct. Claims 1990, D.C. Ct. Appeals 1987. Law clk. Hon. Frederick W. Brune, Chief Judge Md. Ct. of Appeals, 1955-56; mem. dept. legis. reference Md. Legislature, 1957-58; mem. Gov.'s Commn. to Revise Criminal Code, 1958-59; pvt. practice law Balt., 1956—. Lectr. in trial tactics. Mem. editl. bd. Md. Law Rev., 1953-55; contbr. articles to profl. jours. Pres. Young Dems. 2d Dist., Balt., 1960-63. With AUS, 1948-49; lt. col. USAF Res. ret. Rosco Pound Inst. fellow, trustee. Mem. Nat. Bd. Trial Advocacy (cert. civil trial adv.), Am. Bd. Trial Advs., Md. State Bar Assn., Balt. City Bar Assn., Nat. Coll. Trial Advocacy (trustee), AAJ (nat. committeeman 1976-80, bd. govs. 1985—2006, exec. com. 1988-90, chmn. orgn. rev. com., home office and budget com., orgn. and home office com., election com., key man com., past steering com., past publ. com., past ednl. adv. group 1989-90, chmn. Stalwarts Hall of Fame com., past vice-chair ABA-ATLA liaison com., M Club, co-chair conv. site planning com., co-chair polit. insight com., long-range planning com., auth-hwy. adv. com., toy safety conf., med. malpractice adv. com., product liability adv. com., co-chair home office capital improvements adv. com., co-chmn. conv. planning com. Washington, Wiedmann/Wysocki award 1989-90, 1996, 2002), Acad. Trial Adv., Trial Lawyers for Pub. Justice, Md. Trial Lawyers Assn. (bd. govs., pres. 1984-85, Lifetime Achievement award 2002), Order of Coif, Masons, Simon E. Sobeloff Soc. Home: 2 Celadon Rd Owings Mills MD 21117-3010 Office: 26 South St Baltimore MD 21202-3215 Office Phone: 410-962-0400. Business E-Mail: lorman@triallaw.com.

ORMAN, SUZE (SUSAN LYNNE ORMAN), news correspondent, writer; b. Chgo., June 5, 1951; d. Morry and Ann Orman; life ptnr. Kathy Travis. BA in Social Work, Ill. U., 1976, LHD (hon.), 2009. Cert. fin. planner. Account exec. Merrill Lynch, 1980—83; v.p. investments Prudential Bache Securities, 1983—87; dir. Suze Orman Fin. Group, 1987—97. Former fin. contbr. NBC News' Today; host QVC Fin. Freedom hour. Contbr. to Self mag.; author: (PBS spl.) The Road to Wealth; co-prodr.: (PBS spl.) The Road to Wealth; host (PBS spl.) The Road to Wealth; author: (PBS spl.) The Courage to Be Rich; co-prodr.: (PBS spl.) The Courage to Be Rich; host (PBS spl.) The Courage to Be Rich; author: (PBS spl.) The 9 Steps to Financial Freedom; co-prodr.: (PBS spl.) The 9 Steps to Financial Freedom; host (PBS spl.) The 9 Steps to Financial Freedom; contbg. editor: O: The Oprah Mag.; host (nat. syndicated radio talk show) The Suze Orman Show; author: The 9 Steps to Financial Freedom: Practical & Spiritual Steps so You Can Stop Worrying, 1997 (NY Times bestsellers), The Courage to Be Rich: Creating a Life of Material and Spiritual Abundance, 1999 (NY Times bestsellers, Motivational book award Books for a Better Life, 1999), The Road to Wealth: Suze Orman's Complete Guide to Your Money, 2001 (NY Times bestsellers), The Laws of Money, the Lessons of Life: Keep What You Have and Create What You Deserve, 2003, The Money Book for the Young, Fabulous & Broke, 2005 (Publishers Weekly Bestseller), Women and Money: Owning the Power to Control Your Destiny, 2007, Suze Orman's 2009 Action Plan, 2008 (Publishers Weekly bestseller); co-author (with Linda Mead): You've Earned It, Don't Lose It: Mistakes You Can't Afford to Make When You Retire, 1995. Named Top 30 Power Brokers Who Most Influenced Mutual Fund Industry and Affected Money, Smart Money mag., 1999, Outstanding Svc. Show Host for Suze Orman: For the Young, Fabulous & Broke, Nat. Acad. TV Arts and Sciences, Daytime Emmy award, 2006; named one of The World's Most Influential People, TIME mag., 2008, 2009; named to 100th issue as those "who have revolutionized the way Am. thinks about money", Worth mag., 2001. Democrat. Office: CNBC 2200 Fletcher Ave Ste 5 Fort Lee NJ 07024 Mailing: c/o Amanda Urban ICM 40 W 57th St New York NY 10019 Office Phone: 201-585-2183.*

ORME, ANTONY RONALD, geography educator; b. Weston-Super-Mare, Somerset, Eng., May 28, 1936; came to U.S., 1968; s. Ronald Albert and Anne (Parry) O.; m. Amalie Jo Brown, Nov. 18, 1984; children: Mark Antony, Kevin Ronald, Devon Anne. BA with 1st class honors, U. Birmingham, 1957, PhD, 1961. Lectr. Univ. Coll., Dublin, Ireland, 1960-68; mem. faculty UCLA, 1968—, prof. geography, 1973—, dean social scis., 1977-83. Cons. in field. Editor-in-chief Phys. Geography. Recipient Award of Merit Am. Inst. Planners, 1975, Outstanding Svc. award USAF, 1977-80, Founders' medal Brit. Soc. for Geomorphology Mem. Geol. Soc. Am., Assn. Am. Geographers (Disting. Career award), Assn. Geography Tchrs. Ireland (pres. 1964-68), Inst. Brit. Geographers, Internat. Geog. Union. Home: 5128 Del Moreno Dr Woodland Hills CA 91364-2426 Office: UCLA Dept Geography Los Angeles CA 90095-1524 Business E-Mail: orme@geog.ucla.edu.

ORMES, JONATHAN FAIRFIELD, astrophysicist, researcher, educator; b. Colorado Springs, Colo., July 18, 1939; s. Robert Manly and Suzanne (Viertel) O.; m. Karen Lee Minnick, Dec. 26, 1960 (div.); 1 child, Laurie Kylee; m. Janet Carolyn Dahl, Sept. 12, 1964; children: Marina, Nicholas. BS, Stanford U., 1961; PhD, U. Minn., 1967. NRC assoc. Goddard Space Flight Ctr., NASA, Greenbelt, Md., 1967-69, astrophysicist, 1969, head cosmic radiations br., 1981-82, head nuclear astrophysics br., 1983-87, assoc. chief lab. for high energy astrophysics, 1987-90, chief lab. for high energy astrophysics, 1990-2000, project sci. for gamma ray astronomy obs., 1998—2004, dir. space scis., 2000—04; rsch. prof. U. Denver, 2004—; dir. Denver Rsch. Inst., 2005—09. Acting head high energy astrophysics NASA hdqrs., Washington, 1982-83, mem. high energy astrophysics mgmt. ops. working group, 1975-83, cosmic ray program working group, 1984-91; com. on space and solar physics, com. on cosmic ray physics Nat. Acad. Sci., Washington, 1991-94; adj. prof. U. Md. Balt., 2000-, U. Utah, 2001—. Editor: Essays in Space Science, 1987; assoc. editor astrophysics Phys. Rev. Letters, 1991-93; contbr. Astrophysics Jour., Phys. Rev. Letters, Astronomy and Astrophysics. Trustee Paint Br. Unitarian Universalist Ch., Adelphi, Md., 1987-88, chair bd. trustees, 1989, numerous positions, 1972—. Recipient Meritorious Exec. Award (presdl. rank), 2001. Fellow: Am. Phys. Soc. (various divsn. offices); mem.: Am. Geophys. Union, Am. Astron. Soc. (sec.-treas. High Energy Astrophysics divsn. 1985—87), Internat. Astron. Union. Achievements include discovery of unusual isotopic abundance of Ne in galactic cosmic rays; research on composition and energy spectra of cosmic rays, antiprotons and gamma rays from the Milky Way galaxy. Office: U Denver Dept Physics & Astronomy Denver CO 80208-0001 Office Phone: 303-871-3552. Business E-Mail: jonathan.ormes@du.edu.

ORMOND, JULIA, actress; b. Surrey, Eng., Jan. 4, 1965; m. Rory Edwards, Apr. 1989 (div. 1994); m. Jon Rubin, 1999 (separated, 2007); 1 child, Sophie Grad., Webber Douglas Acad. Drama Art, 1988; attended, West Surrey Coll. Art and Design. Founder prodn. co. Indican. Actress: (films) The Baby of Macon, 1992, Legends of the Fall, 1994, Nostradamus, 1994, Captives, 1994, First Knight, 1995, Sabrina, 1995, Smilla's Sense of Snow, 1997, Sibirsky Tsiryulnik, 1998, The Prime Gig, 2000, Resistance, 2003, Inland Empire, 2006, The Way, 2006, I Know Who Killed Me, 2007, Kit Kittredge: An American Girl, 2008, The Curious Case of Benjamin Button, 2008; (TV movies) Young Catherine, 1991, Stalin, 1992, (voice only) Animal Farm, 1999, Varian's War, 2001, Iron Jawed Angels, 2004; (TV mini-series) Traffik, 1990, Beach Girls, 2005; (TV appearances) Ruth Rendall Mysteries, 1990; stage appearances include Faith, Hope and Charity, 1989 (London Critics best newcomer award); prodr.: Calling the Ghosts, 1996. Recipient Female Star of Tomorrow award Sho West Awards, 1995. Office: Endeavor Talent Agy 9601 Wilshire Blvd 10th Fl Beverly Hills CA 90210*

ORMOND, PAUL A., healthcare company executive; b. Aurora, Ill. B in economics with honors, Stanford U., 1971, MBA, 1973. Mem. corp. staff, positions with glass container divsn. Owens-Ill., Inc., 1973-77, nat. mktg. mgr. soft drinks, glass container divsn., 1977-78; mgr. Atlanta sales dist., glass container divsn. Owens-Ill. Inc., 1978-80, asst. gen. mgr. Gerresheimer Glas (internat. affiliate Owens-Ill. Inc.) Germany, 1980-82, v.p. glass container group, 1982-84, v.p. packaging ops., dir. market strategy and devel., 1984-91, corp. v.p., 1986-91; pres., CEO Health Care and Retirement Corp. (HCR) (subs. Owens-Ill. Inc.), Toledo, 1986-91; chmn., pres., CEO Health Care and Retirement Corp. (HCR) (now ind. co.), Toledo, 1991—98; pres., CEO HCR Manor Care Inc., Toledo, 1998—99, Manor Care, Inc., Toledo, 1999—2001, chmn., pres., CEO, 2001—. Office: Manor Care 333 N Summit St Toledo OH 43604-2617*

ORMSBY, ERIC LINN, writer, educator; b. Atlanta, Oct. 16, 1941; s. Robert and Virginia (Haire) O.; m. Dorothy Louise Hoffmann, July 22, 1967; children: Daniel Paul, Charles Martin. BA summa cum laude, U. Pa., 1971; MA, Princeton U., 1973, PhD, 1981; MLS, Rutgers U., 1978. Near East bibliographer libr. Princeton (NJ) U., 1975-77, Near East curator libr., 1977-83; libr. dir. Cath. U. Am., Washington, 1983-86, McGill U., Montreal, Canada, 1986-96, assoc. prof. Inst. Islamic Studies, 1986-96, prof., 1996—2005; prof., chief libr. Inst. Ismaili Studies, London, 2005—. Cons. NYU, 1981-82; mem. libr. com. Mid. East Inst., Washington, 1985-87, Al Akhawayn U., Morocco, 1994-95, Saudi Arabian Monetary Agy., Riyadh, 1995-96; chmn. continuing edn. com. Washington Consortium, 1983-86; mem. bd. Ctr. Rsch. Librs., 1989-95. Author: Theodicy in Islamic Thought, 1984 (Choice Mag. award 1984), Bavarian Shrine and Other Poems, 1990 (QSPELL award for poetry 1991), (poems) Coastlines, 1992, (with others) Handlist of Arabic Manuscripts, 1986, For a Modest God: New and Selected Poems, 1997, (poems) Araby, 2001, (poems) Daybreak at the Straits, 2004, Time's Covenant: Selected Poems, 2007, (essays) Facsimiles of Time, 2001, Ghazali: The Revival of Islam, 2008; editor: Moses Maimonides and His Time, 1989; contbr. articles and book revs. to profl. jours., poetry and essays to various mags., including New Republic, New Yorker, Grand St., Shenandoah, The New Criterion, The NY Times Book Review, The Yale Rev., The Times Lit. Supplement, So. Rev. and Chelsea; weekly columnist N.Y. Sun, 2004—. Instr. Princeton Adult Sch., 1978-80. DAAD fellow German Acad. Exch., 1973-74; recipient Ingram Merrill award, 1993. Fellow Templeton-Cambridge, 2006; Mem. Mid. East Librs. Assn. (v.p. 1981-82, pres. 1982-83), Societe des Amis de Jean de la Fontaine, Can. Assn. Rsch. Librs. (v.p. 1988-89), Can. Libr. Assn., Assn. pour l'Avancement des Scis. et des Techniques de la Documentation, Conseil des recteurs et des principaux des univs. du Québec, Sous-Comité des Bibliotheques (pres. 1989-91). Roman Catholic. Address: 22 Belsize Park Gardens Flat 2 London NW3 4LH England Office: Libr Inst Ismaili Studies 42-44 Grosvenor Gardens London SW1W 0EB England Office Phone: 44 207 881 6045. E-mail: eric.ormsby@btinternet.com.

ORNATO, JOSEPH P., emergency physician, educator; MD, Boston U. Cert. Internal Medicine, 1974, Cardiovascular Disease, 1977, Emergency Medicine, 1997. Resident in internal medicine Mt. Sinai Hosp., NYC; fellow in cardiology Cornell U.; prof. and chair emergency medicine Va. Commonwealth U., Richmond; med. dir. Richmond Ambulance Authority. Mem.: Inst. Medicine. Office: Va Commonwealth U Med Ctr Dept Emergency Medicine 1200 Marshall Ave Richmond VA 23223 E-mail: jornato@mcvh-vcu.edu.*

ORNELLAS, LORRAINE B. (LORI ORNELLAS), small business owner; b. Honokaa, Hawaii, Apr. 19; d. Joseph R. and Maria (Sampaia) Bugado; m. Herbert P. Ornellas, July 1, 1928; children: Kenneth Herbert, Brenda Jane. AS in Business, U. Hawaii, Hilo, 1976, AA, 1996, BA in Counseling Psychology, 1997, BA in Speech Comm., 1997, AS in Adminstrn. Justice, 2000, BA in Elem. Edn., 2002. Cert. agent Vitousek Real Estate Sch., 1986. Owner 50th St. Bar, Hilo, Hawaii, 1956-83; real estate sales rep. Hicks Homes, Hilo, 1972-73; owner, mgr. Gift-Wrap Hawaii, Hilo, 1982—96, Martins & Martins Realty, 1983—87; realty assoc. Big Island Land Co., Ltd., Hilo, 1987—88; agt. Alakai Realty, 1988—; profl. tutor elem. math and reading, 2003—. Vol. Frank Fasi for Mayor Campaign, Honolulu, 1977, Dante Carpenter for Mayor Campaign, Hilo, 1985. Mem. Am. Bus. Women's Assn., Hawaii Bus. Women's Network, Hawaii Island Bd. Realtors, Hawaii Island Portuguese C. of C., Hawaii Island C. of C. Clubs: Hilo Women's. Democrat. Roman Catholic. Avocations: reading, photography, coin collecting/numismatics, cooking, ballroom dancing, dance. Office: Alakai Realty 688 Kinole St Hilo HI 96720 Home Phone: 808-959-7295.

ORNELLAS, MAILE LOUISE, filmmaker, educator; b. Stockton, Calif., Nov. 18, 1948; d. Henry Alexander and Janet Evelyn Ornellas; 1 child, Maia An. BA in Psychology, U. Calif., Berkeley, 1971, MJ in Journalism, 1977; MA in Psychology, San Jose State U., Calif., 1972. Freelance reporter A Closer Look, KQED, San Francisco, 1977—77; prodr. pub. affairs KPIX TV, San Francisco, 1978; prof. film/TV dept. Solano CC, Fairfield, Calif., 1979—; documentary prodr./reporter -capital news bur. PBS, Sacramento, 1979—79; prodr., audio visual cons. Burdick Group, San Francisco, 1980—83; lectr. Am. cultures ethnic studies U. Calif., Berkeley, 1995; fulbright scholar/lectr. Am. studies coll. fogn. langs. Hue U., Hue City, Vietnam, 2007—. Co-dir., writer, editor: (documentary film) Like Any Child, Only More So, 1977 (Student Acad. award for documentary, selected for permanent collection Libr. of Congress, LA Regional Emmy nominee); dir., writer, editor (public affairs program) All Together Now, 1978 (San Francisco Regional Emmy nominee). Judge Am. Film Festival, Student Acad. Awards, Mill Valley Film Festival; VN culture camp panelist, steering com. Bay Area Families Children From Vietnam; pres. bd. dirs. G.R.O.U.P., Berkeley, 1973—76. Fulbright scholar, Ctr. Internat. Exch. of Scholars/J. William Fulbright Scholarship Bd., 2007. Mem.: Solano Coll. Calif. Tchrs. Assn (life; pres. 1988—89, W.H.O. award 1989). Avocations: travel, dance, cross country skiing. Office: Solano CC 4000 Suisun City Fairfield CA 94585 Business E-Mail: maile.ornellas@solano.edu.

ORNISH, DEAN, medical association administrator and educator; MD, Baylor Coll. Medicine. Resident in internal medicine Mass. Gen. Hosp., Boston, 1981-84; clin. fellow in medicine Harvard Med. Sch., 1981-84; clin. prof. medicine U. Calif., San Francisco, 1984—; founder, pres. Preventive Medicine Rsch. Inst., Sausalito, Calif., 1984—; also bd. dirs. Physician cons. to Pres. Bill Clinton, U.S. Congress, others; U.S. bd. dirs. UN High Commn. on Refugees. Author: 5 books including Dr. Dean Ornish's Program for Reversing Heart Disease, 1990, Eat More, Weigh Less, 1993, Love & Survival: The Scientific Basis for the Healing Power of Intimacy, 1998; contbr. numerous articles to profl. jours. Bd. dirs. Quincy Jones Listen Up Found. Recipient Outstanding Young Alumnus award U. Tex., 1994, U.S. Army Surgeon Gen. medal, Beckmann medal German Soc. Prevention and Rehab. Cardiovascular Diseases, 1996. Mem. Calif. Acad. Medicine. Office: Preventive Med Rsch Inst 900 Bridgeway Sausalito CA 94965-2100 Office Phone: 415-332-2525. Fax: 415-332-5730. Business E-Mail: info@pmri.org.

ORNSTEIN, DAVID, urologist; b. Stanford, Calif., Feb. 4, 1966; m. Tracy Taylor Ornstein, June 3, 2003; 1 child, Harrison. MD, Wash. U., St. Louis. Diplomate Am. Bd. Urology, 2002. Med. dir. Vanguard Urologic Rsch. Found., Houston, Tex., 2008—. Recipient Young Investigator award, Soc. Urologic Oncology, 2007, Physician in Excellence, Orange County Med. Assn., 2008; named one of Best Drs. in Am., 2006—08. Office: Vanguard Urologic Inst 6400 Fanin St Ste 2300 Houston TX 77030 Office Fax: 713-366-7993. Business E-Mail: david.ornstein@vanguardurology.com.

ORNSTEIN, NORMAN JAY, political scientist, columnist; b. Grand Rapids, Minn., Oct. 14, 1948; s. Joseph and Dorothy (Latz) O.; m. Judith Linda Harris, May 29, 1977; children: Matthew, Daniel BA, U. Minn., 1967; MA, U. Mich., 1968, PhD, 1972; LLD (hon.), U. Minn., 2007. Asst. prof. Johns Hopkins U., Bologna, Italy, 1971-72; prof. Cath. U. Am., Washington, 1972-84; staff mem., staff dir. Senate Com. on Com. Sys., Washington, 1976-77; fellow Ctr. for Advanced Study in Behavioral Scis., Palo Alto, Calif., 1979-80; resident scholar Am. Enterprise Inst., Washington, 1980—; columnist, bd. contbrs. USA Today, Washington, 1996—2005; columnist Roll Call, 1993—; sr. counselor Continuity Govt. Commn., 2002—; co-dir. Times Mirror-Gallup Study: The People, the Press and Politics, 1987-90, Times Mirror Ctr. for People and Press (now Pew Rsch. Ctr.), 1991—, Renewing Congress Project, Washington, 1992—, AEI-Brookings Election Reform Project, 2005—. Polit. editor Lawmakers program Sta. WETA-TV, Washington, 1980-84; cons. CBS News Election Unit, N.Y.C., 1982—; commentator, cons. MacNeil/Lehrer News Hour, Washington and N.Y.C., 1983—; moderator Calif. Congl. Report, Sta. KCET-TV, L.A., 1983. Author: Interest Groups Lobbying and Policy, 1978: (with others) The New Congress, 1981, Debt and Taxes, 1994, The Permanent Campaign and Its Future, 2000, The Broken Branch: How Congress Failing America, 2006; writer, editor, co-host: (TV series) Congress: We the People, 1984 (cert. of merit 1985). Fortieth Anniversary Fulbright Disting. fellow, 1986-87. Fellow. Am. Acad. Arts & Sci. Mem. Coun. on Fgn. Rels., Am. Polit. Sci. Assn. (coun. 1984-86, Congl. fellow 1969-70, Goodnow award, 2006), Nat. Commn. Pub. Svc. (bd. dirs., Volcker commn. 1987-90), Pub. Broadcasting Svc., Phi Beta Kappa (vis. scholar 1986-87). Jewish. Office: American Enterprise Institute 1150 17th St NW Washington DC 20036-4603 Office Phone: 202-862-5893. Business E-Mail: nornstein@aei.org.*

ORO, FELISA PANAL, education supervisor; b. Maasin, The Philippines, Apr. 23, 1918; d. Alberto L. and Restituta Saludo P.; m. Braulio Kangleon (dec.). BEd, ETC elem. tchr. cert., Cebu Normal Sch., 1940; BSSE in secondary ed., U. Visayas, Cebu City, The Philippines, 1949; MA, U. Visayas, 1985, LLB magna cum laude, 1960. Emergency tchr., 1938-39; critic tchr., 1941; supr. instrn. elem. and high sch., 1949-51; supr. instrn. coll., 1960; supr. interns, 1965-72, 96—; dean coll. commerce, 1972-76; v.p. adminstrn. U. Visayas, 1994-96, adminstrv. officer Grad. Sch., 1996-98, acad. cons., 1998—. Home: Bacayo Guadalupe M Veloso St Cebu City 6000 Philippines

ORONA, JOSEPH RYAN, information technology executive; b. Albuquerque, N.Mex., Aug. 10, 1967; s. Jose Ramon Jorge Orona and Maria Melinda Sanchez. BS in Aero. Studies, Embry-Riddle Aero. U., 1989. Pres. Retis Techs., Inc., Albuquerque, 1993—. Presdl. scholar, U. N.Mex, 1985. Mem.: Aircraft Owners and Pilots Assn. (life). Independent. Roman Catholic. Achievements include design of Scientific collaborative networks and data visualization. Avocations: flight, global travel, mountain biking, wine making, photography. Office: Retis Techs Inc PO Box 40305 Albuquerque NM 87196 Office Fax: 505-247-2473.

O'RORKE, JAMES FRANCIS, JR., lawyer; b. NYC, Dec. 4, 1936; s. James Francis and Helen (Weber) O'R.; m. Carla Phelps, Aug. 6, 1964. AB, Princeton U., 1958; JD, Yale U., 1961. Bar: N.Y. 1962. Assoc. Davies, Hardy & Schenck, 1962-69; ptnr. Davies, Hardy, Ives & Lawther, 1969-72, Skadden, Arps, Slate, Meagher & Flom, NYC, 1972—2006, of counsel, 2007—. Dir. Clinipad Corp.; mem. adv. bd. Chgo. Title Ins. Co. N.Y. Trustee Mus. Am. Indian-Heye Found., 1977-80; dir. James Lenox House Assn., Inc., 1998-02, dir. Keen Theatre Co. Inc., 2001-. Mem. ABA, N.Y. State Bar Assn., Assn. Bar City N.Y., Am. Coll. Real Estate Lawyers, Princeton Club N.Y.C. Office: Skadden Arps Slate Meagher & Flom 4 Times Sq Fl 24 New York NY 10036-6595 Address: C/O Skadden Arps 4 Times Sq Rm 44200 New York NY 10036-6522 Home Phone: 212-262-0362; Office Phone: 212-735-2620. Business E-Mail: jororke@skadden.com.

O'ROURKE, JAMES LOUIS, lawyer; b. Bridgeport, Conn., July 5, 1958; s. James G. and Margaret Elizabeth (Fesco) O'Rourke; m. Margaret C. DiCicco, Sept. 18, 1994. BS, U. Bridgeport, 1984, JD, 1987. Bar: Conn. 1988, U.S. Dist. Ct. Conn. 1989, Mashantucket Pequot Tribal Bar 1995, U.S. Supreme Ct. 1998. Pvt. practice, Stratford, Conn., 1987—. With USN, 1976—79. Mem.: ATLA, ABA, Greater Bridgeport Bar Assn., Conn. Bar Assn., Conn. Trial Lawyers Assn. Roman Catholic. Avocations: boating, gardening, fishing, bicycling, swimming. Office: The Barnum Profl Bldg 1825 Barnum Ave Ste 201 Stratford CT 06614-5333 Home Phone: 203-925-9118; Office Phone: 203-381-9800. Personal E-mail: js.orourke@snet.net.

O'ROURKE, MAUREEN A., dean, law educator; BS summa cum laude, Marist Coll.; JD, Yale Law Sch. With IBM, 1985—93; assoc. prof. Boston U. Sch. Law, 1993—98, prof., 1998—, assoc. dean adminstrn., 2001—03, assoc. dean academic affairs, 2003—04, interim dean, 2004—06, dean, 2006—. Vis. prof. U. Victoria Law Sch., British Columbia, British Virgin Islands, 1999, Columbia U. Sch. Law, 1999, La Trobe U., Australia, 2002. Co-author: Copyright in a Global Economy; contbr. articles to law jours. Recipient Metcalf Award, 2002. Mem.: Marist Coll. Pre-Law Adv. Bd., Inst. for Study of Info. Techn. and Soc., Am. Law Inst., Alpha Chi. Mailing: Boston U Sch Law 765 Commenwealth Ave Boston MA 02215 Office Phone: 617-353-3123. Office Fax: 617-353-3077. Business E-Mail: morourke@bu.edu. E-mail: lawdean@bu.edu.

O'ROURKE, P.J. (PATRICK JAKE O'ROURKE), writer, political satirist, journalist; b. Toledo, Ohio, Nov. 14, 1947; s. Clifford Bronson and Delphine (Loy) O'Rourke; m. Amy Lumet, 1990 (div. 1993); m. Tina O'Rourke, 1995; 3 children. BA, Miami U., Oxford, Ohio, 1969; MA in English, Johns Hopkins U., Balt., 1970. Writer, mng. editor Nat. Lampoon mag., 1973—81; freelance writer, 1981—; writer, then fgn. affairs desk chief Rolling Stone mag., 1981—2001; H. L. Mencken rsch. fellow Cato Inst., Washington. Regular commentator Real Time with Bill Maher; regular corr. Atlantic Monthly, Am. Spectator, The Weekly Standard; frequent panelist Wait Wait... Don't Tell Me!, NPR. Author: Ferrari Refutes the Decline of The West, 1979, Modern Manners, 1983, The Bachelor Home Companion, 1986, Republican Party Reptile, 1987, Holidays in Hell, 1989, Parliament of Whores, 1991 (#1 NY Times bestseller), Give War a Chance, 1992 (#1 NY Times bestseller), All the Trouble in the World, 1994, Age and Guile: Beat Youth, Innocence, and a Bad Haircut, 1995, The American Spectator's Enemies List, 1996, Eat the Rich, 1999, The CEO of the Sofa, 2001, Peace Kills: America's Fun New Imperialism, 2004, On the Wealth of Nations: Books That Changed the World, 2007; co-author: (with Doug Kenney) National Lampoon's 1964 High School Yearbook Parody, 1974, (with John Hughes) National Lampoon's Sunday Newspaper Parody, 1978. Office: Cato Inst 1000 Massachusetts Ave NW Washington DC 20001*

O'ROURKE, ROBERT A., cardiologist, educator; b. San Francisco, Calif., June 12, 1936; m. Suzann Reiter, June 8, 1963; children: Michael, Kevin, Sean, Kathleen, Ryan. Student, Santa Clara U., 1954-55; BS, Creighton U., 1957, MD, 1961. Diplomate Am. Bd. Internal Medicine, 1968, Am. Bd. Cardiology, 1969. Straight med. internship Georgetown U. Hosp., Washington, 1961-62, jr. asst. resident internal medicine, 1962-63, sr. asst. resident internal medicine, 1963-64, med. houseofficer internal medicine, 1961-65, fellow cardiology dept., 1964-65; fellow U. Calif Cardiovasc. Rsch. Inst., Washington, 1965-66; staff cardiologist Madagan Army Hosp., Washington, 1966-68; instr. in medicine cardiology Georgetown U. Hosp., Washington, 1968-69; asst. prof. medicine cardiology coll. medicine U. Ariz., Tucson, 1969-70; asst. prof. medicine cardiology, dir. clin. cardiology section, dir. heart station U. Calif., San Diego, 1970-73, assoc. prof. medicine cardiology, dir. clin. cardiology section, dir. coronary care unit, assoc. dir. myocardial infarction rsch. unit, 1973-76; acting chief medicine Audie L. Murphy Vets. Adminstrn. Hosp., 1977-78; Charles Conrad Brown disting. prof. cardiovasc. disease, dir. cardiovasc. divsn. U. Tex. Health Sci. Ctr., San Antonio, 1976—. Cons. in field for various hosps.; vis. professorships to various med. ctrs./univs. Mem. editl. bd.: Jour. Am. Coll. Cardiology, 1983-87, Am. Jour. Cardiology, 1976-81, 83—, Am. Heart Jour., 1980—, Clin. Cardiology, 1985—, Jour. Intensive Care Medicine, 1985—, Internat. Jour. Cardiology, 1981—, Annals of Internal Medicine, 1979-82, Med. Month, 1983—, Weekly Update: Cardiology, 1978-80, Cardiovasc. Medicine, 1976-80, Cardiologic Consultation, 1980—, Cardiovasc. Drugs and Therapy, 1989-90, Coronary Artery Disease, 1990—, Cardiology, 1990—, Jour. Heart Valve Disease, 1992, Current Problems in Cardiology, 1975—, assoc. editor, 1980-83, editor-in-chief, 1984—, Circulation, 1977-80, 81-83, 83-86, 86—, consulting editor, 1993, Yr. Book Cardiology, 1986-92, assoc. editor, 1986-92; assoc. editor: Jour. Applied Cardiology, 1985-90, Am. Jour. Cardiovasc. Pathology, 1985—. Recipient Sinsheimer award for Cardiovasc. Rsch., 1969-70; grantee from various sponsors. Fellow Am. Coll. Physicians, Am. Coll. Cardiology; mem. Am. Soc. Clin. Investigation, Am. Fedn. Clin. Rsch., Am. Heart Assn., Am. Physiological Soc., Assn. Army Cardiologists, Southern Soc. Clin. Rsch., Am. Soc. Echocardiography, Assn. U. Cardiologists, Alpha Omega Alpha, others. Office: The Univ Tex Health Sci Ctr VAH Rm C644 7703 Floyd Curl Drive San Antonio TX 78229-3900 Office Phone: 210-617-5100. Office Fax: 210-567-4687.

O'ROURKE, SHEILA GAIL, anthropologist; b. Sacramento, June 28, 1950; d. Nell Kathleen O'Rourke and Jock Jocoy; children: Boris Temujin Jocoy, Dard Magnus Rossell. BA, MFA, U. Calif., San Diego, 1996; PhD, U. Calif., Irvine, 2006. Lectr. anthropology U. Calif., 2006—. Artist (experimental video) Hayat/Hayalet, She Left When Ezanay Shut Down, Sonance Six, (costume design) A Stranger in the House (Best Costume Design, 1994). Recipient Third Coll. award, U. Calif., San Diego, 1990, Delta Tau Delta award, Chapman U., 2005; Regents Fellowship, U. Calif., 1993, 1994, 1996, 1998. Mem.: Am. Ethnol. Soc., Soc. Cultural Anthropology, Mid. East Studies Assn., Am. Anthrop. Assn., Phi Beta Kappa. Business E-Mail: sorourke@uci.edu.

O'ROURKE, THOMAS DENIS, civil engineer, educator; b. Pitts., July 31, 1948; s. Lawrence Robert and Adele Mildred (Moloski) O'R.; m. Patricia Ann Lane, Aug. 12, 1978; 1 child, Adele Christina. BSCE, Cornell U., Ithaca, NY, 1970; MSCE, U. Ill., Urbana, 1973, PhD, 1975. Geotech. engr. Dames & Moore, NYC, 1970; rsch. asst. U. Ill., Urbana, 1970-75, asst. prof., 1975-78, Cornell U., Ithaca, NY, 1978-80, assoc. prof., 1981-87, prof., 1987-98, Thomas R. Briggs prof. engring., 1999—. With Nat. Acad. Engring., 1993. Recipient Trevithick prize, Brit. Instn. Civil Engrs., 2002, Outstanding Paper award, Japan Gas Assn., 2003, Engr. Dist. Svc. award, U. Ill., 2005; named Rankine Lectr., Brit. Geotech. Assn., 2008. Fellow: AAAS; mem.: ASTM (C.A. Hogentogler award 1976), ASME, NAE, ASCE (pres. Ithaca sect. 1981—82, chair exec. com. tech. coun. lifeline earthquake engr. 1998—99, Collingwood prize 1983, Huber prize 1988, C. Martin Duke award 1995, Stephen D. Bechtel pipeline engring. award 1997, Ralph B. Peck award 2005), U.S. Com. on Tunnelling Tech. (chmn. 1987—88), Internat. Soc. Rock Mechanics, Internat. Soc. Engring. Geology, Earthquake Engring. Rsch. Inst. (bd. dirs. 1998—2000, v.p. 2000, pres. 2003—04, Outstanding Paper award 1996). Home: 10 Twin Glens Rd Ithaca NY 14850-1041 Office: Cornell U Sch Civil Environ Engring 273 Hollister Hall Ithaca NY 14853-3501 Office Phone: 607-255-6470. Business E-Mail: tdo1@cornell.edu.

O'ROURKE, WILLIAM ANDREW, literature and language professor, writer; b. Chgo., Dec. 4, 1945; s. William Andrew and Elizabeth (Kompare) O'R.; m. Marion Teresa Ghilarducci, July 9, 1986; 1 child, Joseph Ghilarducci. BA, U. Mo. at Kansas City, 1968; M.F.A., Columbia U., 1970. Instr. journalism Kean Coll., Union, NJ, 1973; asst. prof. English Rutgers U., 1975-78, Mount Holyoke Coll., 1978-81, U. Notre Dame, Ind., 1981-87, assoc. prof. Ind., 1987-94, prof. Ind., 1994—. Writer-in-residence Thurber House, Columbus, Ohio, fall 1984 Author: The Harrisburg 7 and the New Catholic Left, 1972, The Meekness of Isaac, 1974, Idle Hands, 1981, Criminal Tendencies, 1987, Signs of the Literary Times: Essays, Reviews, Profiles 1970-92, 1993, Notts, 1996,Campaign America '96: The View From the Couch, 1997, Campaign America 2000: The View From the Couch, 2001, On Having a Heart Attack: A Medical Memoir, 2006; editor: On the Job, 1977, Notre Dame Review: The First Ten Years, 2009. Fine Arts Work Ctr. fellow, Provincetown, Mass., 1970-72; recipient Creative Artists Pub. Svc. award N.Y. State Coun. on Arts, 1975; Nat. Endowment for Arts creative writing fellow, 1981-82, 90-91. Mem. Authors Guild, PEN Am. Ctr., Nat. Book Critics Cir. Office: U Notre Dame Dept English 356 O'Shag Notre Dame IN 46556 Office Phone: 574-631-7377.

O'ROURKE-KAPLAN, MARIAN, dean; b. Walla Walla, Wash., Jan. 3, 1951; d. William Robert O'Rourke Jr. and Bernice Alice O'Rourke; m. Robert Kaplan, Oct. 19, 1991; children: Allison Kaplan, Craig Kaplan. BFA in Fashion Design, Stephens Coll., Columbia, MO, 1971; MBA, Nat. U., San Diego, 1978. Designer Jennifer Dallas, 1971—72, Jerrell, Dallas, 1972—73; instr. Bauder Fashion Coll., Arlington, Tex., 1973—77; ops. mgr. Jay Jacks Internat., Dallas, 1978—82; designer-operation mgr. Lynn French Inc., Dallas, 1982—90; design-owner MOR Originals, Dallas, 1989—91; lectr. U. North Tex., Denton, Tex., 1992—93, asst. prof., 1993—98, chair divsn. design, 1998—2002, assoc. prof., 1998—2008, assoc. dean academic and sudent affairs, 2006—. Designer (suit constructed of zippers) Zippety Yea!, (wool suit) Timely & Tailored (Hon. Mention Ready to Wear -Houston MFA, 1999), (mohair jacket) Fraying at the Edges (Most Successful Design Threads Mag., 2000), (denim dress with handknit accents) Knit Witty (Finalist in Threads mag. Challenge, 2002), (silk day dress) She Earned Her Stripes (FInalist in Thread Mag. challenge, 2004), (conceptual fashion design) 15 Yds. of Muslin and the Path to Sanity (2nd Pl. in 3-D design D.E.N.E exhbn., 2006), (silk evening gown) Moroccan Dream (Audience Choice Award Threads Mag. Challenge, 2008). Mem.: Assn. Sewing and Design Profl. (regional dir. 2007—08), Internat. Textile and Apparel Assn. Avocations: travel, movies, reading. Office: Univ of North Tex 1155 Union Cir #305100 Denton TX 76203-5107 Business E-Mail: orourke@unt.edu.

OROZCO, JORGE, rehabilitation hospital administrator; Physical therapist Rancho Los Amigos Nat. Rehab. Ctr., Downey, Calif., 1989, chief of rehab. therapy, 2001, COO, 2005, interim CEO, 2007, CEO, 2008—. Adj. instr. Clinical Physical Therapy USC, mem. bd. councilors, divsn. biokinesiology and physical therapy, 2002—. Recipient Diversity award, American Physical Therapy Assn., 2003. Office: Rancho Los Amigos 7601 E Imperial Hwy Downey CA 90242*

OROZCO, MARC PETER, secondary school educator; b. Lynwood, Calif., Jan. 16, 1948; s. Marc Saldivar and Corinne Francis Orozco; m. Sylvia Castillo. BA, San Jose State U., Calif., 1976; MA, Calif. Luth. U., Thousand Oaks, 1999. Cert. in tchg. credential San Jose State U., 1975. Tchr. Fillmore Unified Sch. Dist., Calif., 1982—. Therapist intern Coalition End Family Violence, Oxnard, Calif., 2000—05. Bd. mem. City of Fillmore Pks. and Recreation Commn., 1994—98, Palmer Drug Abuse Program, Ventura, Calif., 1990—94, Santa Clara Valley Neighborhood Learning, Santa Paula, Calif., 2005—08. Home: 257 Del Valle Dr Fillmore CA 93015 Office: Fillmore Unified Sch Dist 532 North A St Fillmore CA 93015 Personal E-mail: porozco@dslextreme.com. Business E-Mail: porozco@fillmore.k12.ca.us.

ORPETT, MITCHELL A., lawyer; BA, U. Ill., 1974; cert., Exeter Coll., Oxford, Eng., 1974; MA, U. Ill., 1975, JD, 1978. Dir. Tribler Orpett & Meyer, Chgo. Author numerous law articles. Mem.: ABA (mem.-at-large bd. govs. for tort trial and ins. practice sect. 2008—, mem. audit com. 2008—, house dels. 2005—, Spirit of Racial Justice Award 2002, Andrew C. Hecker Meml. Award 2004, TIPS Staff Counsel Com.'s First Excellence Award), Decalogue Soc. Lawyers (bd. mgrs., exec. officer 1979—88, pres. 1987—88, Intra-Soc. Award of Merit 1983), AIDA Reinsurance and Ins. Arbitration Soc., Ill. State Bar Assn. (chair task force on alternative billing and litig. costs), Ill. Assn. Def. Trial Counsel, Internat. Bar Assn., Fedn. Def. and Corp. Counsel. Office: Tribler Orpett & Meyer 225 W Washington St Ste 1300 Chicago IL 60606 Office Phone: 312-201-6413. E-mail: maorpett@tribler.com.

ORPHAN, VICTORIA JEANNE, science educator; b. La Jolla, Calif., Mar. 10, 1972; d. John Orphan Victor and Threse Orphan Jeanne. PhD, U. Calif. Santa Barbara, 2001. NRC postdoc. fellow NASA Ames Rsch. Ctr., Moffett Field, Calif., 2002—04; asst. prof. Caltech, Pasadena, Calif., 2004—. Recipient Moore Young Investigator award, Gordon and

Betty Moore Found., 2005—. Achievements include patents for process for separating microorganisms. Office: Calif Inst Tech Mail Code 100-23 Pasadena CA 91125 Office Fax: 626-683-0621. Business E-Mail: vorphan@gps.caltech.edu.

ORPHANIDES, NORA CHARLOTTE, ballet educator; b. NYC, June 4, 1951; d. M.T. and Mary Elsie (Tilly) Feffer; m. James Mark Orphanides, July 1, 1972; children: Mark, Elaine Orphanides Mastrosimone, Jennine. BA, CUNY, 1973; student, Joffrey Ballet Sch., NYC, 1970-75; postgrad., Princeton Ballet Sch., 1976-86. Cert. speech and hearing handicapped tchr. With membership dept. M.M.A., NYC, 1987—2002; mem. faculty Princeton (N.J.) Ballet Sch., 1983—, trustee emeritus, 1992—. Master tchr. ballroom dance. Mem. cast Princeton Ballet ann. Nutcracker, 1985-90, now Am. Repertory Ballet Co., 1993—; appeared in Romeo & Juliet, 1995-96, 2000. Fundraising gala chmn. Princeton Ballet, 1985, 86, 91-92, chmn. spl. events, 1987—, trustee, 1986—, chmn. Nutcracker benefit, 1990—, Dracula benefit, 1991, honoree, 1999; dept. chmn. June Fete to benefit Princeton Hosp., 1988, 90-92, 96, 2000, trustee, 1995-99; vol. Nat. Hdqrs. Recording for the Blind, 1991-93; dinner chmn. Nassau Ch. Music Festival, 1992, Handel Festival, Nassau Ch., 1993, Princeton Chamber Symphony, 1993; hon. chmn. Princeton Ballet Gala, 1993, Art First to benefit U. Med. Ctr., 2006; chmn. Christmas Boutique, Princeton Med. Ctr., 1993; trustee, Princeton Med. Ctr. Aux. Bd., 1992-2002, trustee 1995—, pres., 1997-99, past pres., 2000-2002; found. bd. dirs. U. Med. Ctr. Princeton, 2004—; choreographer Stuart Country Day Sch., Princeton, 1996-99, 2001; chmn. benefit dinner Eden Inst., 2000; sponsor, co-chair Am. Ballet Theatre Spring Gala, NYC, 2007. Named honoree Princeton Ballet, 1999, recipient Edward R. and Irene D. Farley Cmty. Stewardship award Eden Inst. Found., 2003. Democrat. Avocations: piano, skiing, tennis. Office: 301 N Harrison St Princeton NJ 08540-3512

ORR, AMY J., sociologist, educator; d. Jody Ann Klute; m. A. Erik Svec, July 5, 1996; 1 child, Hunter Phoenix. BS with highest distinction, Nebr. Wesleyan U., Lincoln, 1993; MA, U. Notre Dame, 1996, PhD, 2000. Vis. asst. prof. sociology U. Notre Dame, Notre Dame, Ind., 2000—01; asst. prof. sociology Linfield Coll., McMinnville, Oreg., 2001—. Bd. mem. Multicultural Adoption Adv. Program, Inc., McMinnville, Oreg., 2003—05. Contbr. articles to profl. jours. and encys., chapters to books. Founding mem. Nat. Campaign for Tolerance (So. Poverty Law Ctr.), Montgomery, Ala., 2001—03; friend of the Ctr. So. Poverty Law Ctr., Montgomery, Ala., 2003—; mem. bd. trustees Pi Gamma Mu, Kans., 2008—; mem. Coun. Undergrad. Rsch., Washington. Recipient Samuel Graf Faculty Achievement award, 2006; grantee, Carnegie Scholarship of Tchg. Program and the Kaneb Ctr. for Tchg. and Learning, 2000, Nat. Coun. Teachers English, 2001. Mem.: AAUW, NAACP, ACLU, Pacific Sociol. Assn. (mem. program com. 2003—05, mem. membership com. 2005—), Am. Sociol. Assn. (soe nominations com. 1996—97), Nat. Women's History Mus. (charter). Achievements include research on the effects of wealth (net worth) race marital status and gender on academic achievement. Business E-Mail: aorr@linfield.edu.

ORR, ANDREW S., landscape artist; b. Albuquerque, N.Mex., June 17, 1969; s. Harold R and Merle Y. Orr; life ptnr. William L. Ringer. BA, Okla. Christian U., 1991. Paintings, Woodstock Hollyhocks. Mem.: So. Vt. Arts Ctr., Am. Artists Profl. League, Oil Painters Am. (assoc. Barbara Carter Fine Gilded Frames award 2008), Salmagundi Club (NY) (Arthur T. Hill award 2008). Democrat. Home: 202 Bentley Ave Poultney VT 05764 Personal E-mail: artsteph1@aol.com.

ORR, BOBBY (ROBERT GORDON ORR), retired professional hockey player, sports agent; b. Parry Sound, Ont., Can., Mar. 20, 1948; m. Peggy Orr; children: Darren, Brent. Defenseman Boston Bruins, 1966—76, Chgo. Blackhawks, 1976—77, 1978, asst. coach, 1976—77; cons. Hartford Whalers, NHL; spokesman Nabisco Brands, Inc., NYC, Bay Banks, Inc., Boston; asst. to the pres. Pandick New Eng.; host Hockey Legends CBC; agent ORR Hockey Group, 2002—. Recipient Calder Meml. Trophy, 1967, James Norris Meml. Trophy, 1968—75, Art Ross Trophy, 1970, 1975, Hart Meml. Trophy, 1970—72, Conn Smythe Trophy, 1970, 1972, Loy Marsh Trophy, 1970, Lester B. Pearson Award, 1975, Lester Patrick Trophy, 1979; named Male Athlete of Yr., Can. CP Poll, 1970, Athlete of Yr., Sport Mag., Sports Illustrated, MVP, Canada Cup, 1976, Officer of Order of Can., 1979; named to World Sports Hall of Fame, 2008. Achievements include being a member of Stanely Cup Champion Boston Bruins, 1970, 1972; being inducted into the Hockey Hall of Fame, 1979; having his number, 4, retired by Boston Bruins, 1979. Office: ORR Hockey Group PO Box 290836 Charlestown MA 02129 Office Phone: 617-886-0404. Office Fax: 617-886-5040.

ORR, DOMINIC P., information technology company executive; b. 1951; m. Teresa Orr (div. 1999); children: Alvin, Adria. BS in Physics, CUNY; MS, Calif. Inst. Tech., PhD in Neurobiology. With HP; v.p. product mgmt. Bay Networks (formerly Synoptics), 1994—96; pres., CEO Alteon Web Sys., 1996—2000; pres. Nortel Networks, Intelligent Internet Web Systems, 2000—01, cons., 2001—02; chmn. Aruba Networks, Sunnyvale, Calif., 2002—06, pres., CEO, 2006—. Bd. dirs. Aruba Networks, 2002—. Mem. sciences bd. visitors UCLA. Office: Aruba Networks 1322 Crossman Ave Sunnyvale CA 94089

ORR, ETHAN, non-profit organization executive; b. 1974; BA in Hist., U. Ariz., BA in Polit. Sci., MPA. Empowerment Zone adminstr. Office of Econ. Devel., Tucson; coun. aid City of Tucson City Coun.; exec. dir. Linkages Inc. Adj. faculty Polit. Sci. dept., U. Ariz., Bus. dept., Pima Cmty. Coll.; faculty mentor Flinn Found. of Ariz. Mem. Faith Christian Ch. Make A Difference Day projects; mem Ariz. Joint Legis. Com. on Homelessness; mem. Fred G. Acosta Cmty. Rels. Coun. Named one of 40 Under 40, Tucson Bus. Edge, 2006. Mem.: Southern Ariz. Job Developers Assn. (co-chair). Office: Linkages Inc Goodwill Bldg Ste 201 1920 E Silverlake Rd Tucson AZ 85710 Office Phone: 520-571-8600.

ORR, KENNETH BRADLEY, academic administrator; b. Charlotte, NC, Mar. 15, 1933; s. Frank Wylie and Kate Harriett O.; m. Ruth Douglas Currie; children: Kevin, Jeffrey, Jonathan. BA, Duke U., 1954; MDiv, Union Theol. Sem., 1960, ThM, 1961; PhD, U. Mich., 1978; LittD, Carroll Coll., 1990; DD, Presbyn. Coll., 1997. Ordained to ministry, Presbyn. Ch., 1961. Minister West End Presbyn. Ch., Roanoke, Va., 1961-64; asst. to pres. Union Theol. Sem., Richmond, Va., 1964-68, v.p., 1968-74; pres. Presbyn. Sch. Christian Edn., Richmond, 1974-79, Presbyn. Coll., Clinton, S.C., 1979-97, pres. emeritus, 1997—; sr. v.p. John McRae & Assocs., Atlanta, 1997—. Past mem. coun. presidents Nat. Assn. Intercollegiate Athletics, Kansas City, Mo., chmn. S. Atlantic Conf., 1989—91; mem. nat. adv. com. on instnl. quality and integrity U.S. Dept. Edn., 1995—2001. Contbr. to religious and ednl. publs. Mem. Assn. Presbyn. Colls. and Univs. (pres. 1994, exec. com.), Coun. Ind. Colls. (bd. dirs. 1993-96), Laurens County C. of C. (past pres.), Kiwanis. Democrat. Avocations: reading, travel, classical music.

ORR, MARCIA, primary school educator, consultant, director; b. Anamosa, Iowa, Mar. 2, 1949; d. Harold Edward Eiben and Clara Elizabeth (Hubbard) E.; m. Robert J. Orr, Sept. 6, 1969; 1 child, Jennifer. Student, U. Iowa, 1977; BS, St. Xavier U., Chgo., 1981; MEd in Early Childhood Leadership, Nat. Louis U., 1996. Bookkeeper Monticello State Bank, 1967-69; exec. sec. Davenport Bank and Trust, 1969-73; asst. educator Elisabeth Ludeman Devel. Ctr., Park Forest, Ill., 1979; tchr. Flossmoor Hills (Ill.) Elem. Sch., 1980-1984; exec. dir. Co-Care, Inc., Park Forest, 1984-89; child devel. rschr., Flossmoor, Ill., 1989—; tchr. Nazarene Nursery Sch. and Kindergarten, Chicago Heights, Ill., 1991; child care ctr. cons. Matteson Sch. Dist. 162, Park Forest, 1991—, adv. mem. project early start, 1991—, home-sch. coord., 1992—; founder, pres., exec. dir. Before and After Sch. Enrichment, Park Forest, 1991—. Grant writer Matteson Sch. Dist. 162 and Before and After Sch. Enrichment, Inc., founder, pres., exec. dir. Child Care Enrichment Ctr. and pre-sch.; officer Boleo Childcare Ctr., Iowa City, 1975-77; mentor to dirs. child care programs early childhood edn. dept. Nat.-Louis U., Ill, 1994—; co-founder Reaching New Horizons, Inc., 1996—; mem. oversight and coord. com. Ill. State Bd. Edn. Early Learning Coun., 2007-, adv. mem. evaluation Com. Early Childhood Programe, State Ill. Contbr. articles pub. to profl. jour. Tchr. religion Infant Jesus of Prague Ch., Flossmoor, Ill., 1982—; mem. Flossmoor PTO, 1987-89; music chmn. Dist. 161 PTO, 1980-90; exec. dir. Before and After Sch. Enrichment, Inc.; parent resource coord. Matteson Sch. Dist. 162. McCormick fellow, 1995—; recipient Golden Achievement award Nat. Sch. Pub. Rels. Assn., 2001; named Best Practices and Best Programs, Louis U., Evanston, Ill., 2001. Mem. NAFE, Nat. Assn. for Edn. Young Children (validator), Women Employed Orgn., Internat. Platform Assn., Parent Inst., South Suburban Small Bus. Assn. (charter). Democrat. Roman Catholic. Avocations: piano, classical music, travel. Home: 9411 Fox Run Ct Frankfort IL 60423-1380 Office: Before and After Sch Enrichment 210 Illinois St Park Forest IL 60466-1100 Office Phone: 708-606-5426. Business E-Mail: base@base-inc.net.

ORR, ROBERT DAVID, clinical ethicist, educator, physician; b. Mooers, NY, Mar. 16, 1941; s. Willard Joseph and Nina Elizabeth (Bell) O.; m. Joyce Lorraine Wirick, June 9, 1962; children: Shirley Ann, Ronald Lee, Robin Lisabeth. BS cum laude, Houghton Coll., 1962; MD, Chirurgee Magistrum, McGill U., Montreal, Que., Can., 1966. Diplomate Am. Bd. Family Practice. Intern U.S. Naval Hosp., Bethesda, Md., 1966-67, resident Jacksonville, Fla., 1967-69, med. officer Roosevelt Roads, P.R., 1969-71; pvt. practice Brattleboro, Vt., 1971-89; fellow clin. ethics U. Chgo., 1989-90; prof. Loma Linda U., Calif., 1990—. Clin. co-dir. Ctr. for Christian Bioethics, Loma Linda, 1991—; chair adv. bd. Ctr. Bioethics and Human Dignity, Bannockburn, Ill., 1994—; prof. U. Vt., 2000-, Grad. Coll., Union U., Schenectady, NY, 2005-. Co-author: Life and Death Decisions, 1990, The Changing Face of Health Care, 1998, Medical Ethics: A Primer for Students, 2001, Aging, Death of the Quest for Immortality, 2004, Basic Questions on Healthcare, 2004; author: Medical Ethics of the Faith Factor, 2009; contbr. numerous articles to profl. jours., chapters to books. Pres. Brattleboro Area Hospice, 1981-84; mem., elder Cmty. Luth. Ch., Burlington, Vt. Lt. comdr. USN, 1966-71. Named Vt. Family Dr. of Yr., Vt. State Med. Soc., 1989. Mem. AMA (Isaac Hayes and Sun Bell award, 1999), Christian Med. and Dental Soc. (mem. ethics commn., chmn. ethics commn. 1991-94), Calif. Med. Assn. (mem. com. on bioethics), Soc. for Bioethics Cons. (bd. dirs. 1996—). Avocations: skiing, reading, racquetball.

ORR, SAN WATTERSON, JR., lawyer; b. Madison, Wis., Sept. 22, 1941; s. San Watterson and Eleanor Augusta (Schalk) Orr; m. Joanne Marie Ruby, June 26, 1965; children: San Watterson III, Nancy Chapman. BBA, U. Wis., 1963, JD, 1966. CPA Wis.; bar: Wis. 1966. Bd. dirs. Yawkey Lumber Co., Wausau, Wis., 1971—, pres., 2008, Forewood, Inc., Wausau, 1979—, also bd. dirs.; dir. Marshall & Ilsley Bank, Wausau, 1988—2008, Marshall & Ilsley Corp., 1994—; chmn. bd. dirs. Wausau Paper Corp., 1997—. Editor: U. Wis. Law Rev., 1962—63. Bd. dirs. Aytchmonde Woodson Found., Inc., Wausau, 1966—2006, Leigh Yawkey Woodson Art Mus., Inc., Wausau, 1981—; pres. Woodson YMCA Found., Wausau, 2002, Nancy Woodson Spire Found., Inc., 2000, Aspirus Health Found., Inc., Wausau, 1998—; chmn. U. Wis. Found., Madison, 2003—05, chmn. emeritus; bd. dirs. Wis. Taxpayers Alliance, Madison, 1983—2006, Wis. Mfrs. and Commerce, 2001—04, Woodson YMCA Found., Wausau, 1979—, Nancy Woodson Spire Found., Inc., 1980—, Aspirus Health Found., Inc., Wausau, 1981—, U. Wis. Found., Madison, 1991—, Wis. Policy Rsch. Inst., Milw., 1995—2006; bd. regents U. Wis. Sys., Madison, 1993—2000, pres., 1998—2000; bd. dirs. Lynde and Harry Bradley Found., 2006—. Mem.: Am. Law Inst., Wis. Bar Assn., Ocean Club Fla., Country Club Fla., Minocqua Country Club. Office: Yawkey Lumber Co 500 3rd St Ste 602 Wausau WI 54403-4857

ORR, TERRENCE S., dancer, ballet master, artistic director; b. Berkeley, Calif., Mar. 12, 1943; m. Cynthia Gregory (div.); m. Marianna Tcherkassky. Student, San Francisco Ballet Sch. With San Francisco Ballet, 1959-65; with Am. Ballet Theatre, NYC, 1965-97, soloist, 1967-72, rehearsal asst., 1970-73, prin. dancer, 1972-78, assoc. ballet master, 1973-78, ballet master, 1978-97; artistic dir. Pitts. Ballet Theatre, 1997—. Prodr. Royal Winnipeg Ballet, Nat. Ballet of Mexico, Teatro alla Scala in Millan, Nat. Ballet de Nancy in France, Teatro Colon in Buenos Aires, Pitts. Ballet Theatre, Boston Ballet, Ballet West, Dance Theatre of Harlem, N.Y.C. Ballet, Cleve./San Jose Ballet, San Francisco Ballet, Ballet Ariz., Sadler's Wells Royal Ballet, Paris Opera Ballet, Australian Ballet. Dancer (ballets) The Nutcracker, San Francisco Ballet, Fantasma, Divertissement d'Auber, Jeu des Cartes, Con Amore, Billy the Kid, Am. Ballet Theatre, Coppelia, La Fille Mal Gardee, Petrouchka, The River, Rodeo, Don Quixote, At Midnight, Dark Elegies, Fancy Free, Graduation Ball, Harbinger, Variations for Four, Pulcinella Variations, Brahms Quintet, Schubertiade, Mendelssohn Symphony, Polyandrion, Giselle, Swan Lake, La Sylphide, Gartenfest, Ontogeny; prodr., dir. Gala Performance, 1984; prodr.: La Sylphide, Rodeo; performer: Fancy Free; prodr.: Graduation Ball, Etudes, Billy the Kid, Fall River Legend, Giselle, Coppelia, Don Quixote, Swan Lake. Office: Pitts Ballet Theatre 2900 Liberty Ave Pittsburgh PA 15201-1511

ORR, TRACY CLIFFORD, anatomy, physiology professor; b. Champaign, Ill., Aug. 27, 1950; s. Clifford Eugene and Joyce Ruth Orr; children: Regan Sue, Jamie Marie, Tracy Ryan, Kimberly Payge, Brittany Nicole, Tristan Colby. BS in Biology, Ill. State U., Normal, 1972; MS in Biol. Scis., Southern Ill. U., Carbondale, 1975. Microbiologist Ctrl. Soya, Gibson City, Ill., 1975—83; aerospace physiologist, various bases USAF, 1983—91; project mgr. biologist U.S. Army Corps Engrs., Galveston, Tex., 1991—2003; asst. prof., anatomy, physiology Coll. Mainland, Tex. City, 2003—. Vol. Animal Alliance Galveston County, Tex. City, 2003—09; vol. coord. Tex. Gen. Land Office, 2007—09. Capt. USAFR, 1983—91, Various AF Bases. Decorated Meritorious Svc., Outstanding Unit award US Air Force; recipient Yearly Commendation awards, US Army Corps Engrs., 1991—2003; named one of Outstanding Instr. of Yr., Coll. Mainland, 2008. Home: PO Box 1144 Texas City TX 77592 Office: Coll Mainland 1200 Amburn Rd Texas City TX 77591 Home Phone: 409-457-5745; Office Phone: 409-938-1211 575. Office Fax: 409-935-1046; Home Fax: 409-935-1046. Business E-Mail: torr@com.edu.

ORR, ZELLIE, entrepreneur, educator, writer, researcher; b. Holly Ridge, Miss., May 12, 1951; d. Leonard and Lucille Rainey; m. Foster G. Orr Jr., Feb. 28, 1976 (div. July 14, 1998); children: Kai A., Nia Haley. Student, L.A. City Coll., 1970—71, U. Calif., Northridge, 1971—73; cert., Airline Schs. Pacific, 1974, CMLS Inst., 1979; MA in Human Letters, U. Metaphysics, 1983. Cert. real estate salesperson, Ga., 1979, pub. notary, Ga, 1985. Personal lines underwriter Kemper Ins. Co., LA, 1976—78, Comml. Union Ins. Co., Atlanta, 1980—82, Moore Group ins. Co., Atlanta, 1982—85; lic. real estate agent Wofford Realty, Riverdale, Ga., 1979—81; owner Traffic Jam Lounge and Restaurant, Sunflower, 1986—89; documentation specialist Windsor Group, Atlanta, 1989—2001, mem. billing and collection mgmt. sys., 1991; pres., founder Comm. Unltd., Austell, Ga., 1995—. Mem. rsch. bd. advisors Am. Biog. Inst., Raleigh, NC, 1992—93. Co-author: Treasured Poems of America, 1989 (Editor's Choice award, 1989), The Best Poems & Poets of the 20th Century, 2000 (Editor's Choice award, 2000), Theatre of The Mind, 2003; author: numerous poems; contbr. to numerous TV shows. Co-organizer Sunflower County Civil Rights and Cmty. Reunion, Indianola, 1999; founder Charles E. Scattergood Meml. Found., Marietta, Ga., 2000; mem. So. Poverty Law Ctr., Habitat for Humanity, Feed the Children. Recipient Cert. Appreciation, Superior Ct., Calif., 1976, Cert. Recognition, CME Ch., Indianola, 1999, Disting. Svc. award, Nat. Mus. of Tuskegee Airmen, 2004, Disting. Svc. and Dedication award, Alva N. Temple chpt. Tuskegee Airmen Inc., 2005, Presdl. award, Tuskegee Airmen, Inc., 2006, Pioneers of Indianola Sch. Desegregation Cert. of Recognition, Martin Luther King Jr. Steering Com., 2007; named 1967 Pioneer of Sch. Desegregation, Mayor of Indianola, Miss., 2007. Mem.: NAACP, NAFE, Am. Metaphys. Drs. Assn., Nat. Trust Hist. Preservation, Nat. Mus. Women in Arts, Internat. Soc. Poets, Nat. Black MBA Assn. Avocations: stamp collecting/philately, reading, coin collecting/numismatics, antiques, chess. Home: 3285 Doyle Ln Marietta GA 30060 Office: HIP Ware Inc PO Box 4372 Alpharetta GA 30023 Personal E-mail: orrs@artsonwheels.com. E-mail: orrz@bellsouth.net.

ORRAJ, CRAIG ALLEN, lawyer; BS magna cum laude in Justice Studies, Ariz. State U., Tempe, 1985; JD, U. Ariz., Tucson, 1988. Bar: N.Mex., Tex. Ptnr. Acosta & Assocs., Albuquerque; mng. ptnr. Law Offices of Craig A. Orraj, Albuquerque; staff counsel Farmers Ins. Exch. & Affiliates. Mem.: ABA (bd. govs. 12th dist. 2008—, vice chair staff counsel com. Tort Trial and Ins. Practice sect., former cabinet mem. Young Lawyers Divsn.), N.Mex State Bar (commr. 2002—, pres.-elect 2006—08, pres. 2008). Office: Ste 525 500 Marquette Ave NW Albuquerque NM 87102-5301 Office Phone: 505-242-8654, 505-246-2924. E-mail: craig.orraj@farmersinsurance.com.

ORRINGER, JEFFREY S., dermatologist, educator; b. Balt., Dec. 7, 1967; s. Mark B. and Susan M. Orringer; m. Kelly A. Orringer, May 1, 1994; children: Matthew J., Kate A. BA with honors, Brown U., 1990; MD, Harvard Med. Sch., 1994. Diplomate Am. Bd. Dermatology. Resident U. Mich., Ann Arbor, 1994—2000, fellowship in Mohs surgery and cosmetic dermatology, 2000—02, assoc. prof. dept. dermatology, 2002—; dir. Cosmetic Dermatology and Laser Ctr., Ann Arbor, 2002—. Contbr. articles to profl. jours. Patient-Directed Investigation grantee, Dermatology Found., 2001—02, Clin. Career Devel. grantee, 2002—05. Fellow: Am. Acad. Dermatology, Am. Soc. Dermatologic Surgery, Am. Coll. Mohs Micrographic Surgery and Cutaneous Oncology, Am. Soc. Laser Medicine and Surgery; mem.: Assn. Acad. Dermatologic Surgeons. Achievements include research in laser therapy and cosmetic dermatology. Office: U Mich Dept Dermatology 1500 E Medical Center Dr Ann Arbor MI 48109

ORRINGER, NELSON ROBERT, Spanish and comparative literature educator; b. Pitts., Nov. 9, 1940; s. Harry Baer and Alta Ruth (Moses) O.; m. Stephanie Ruth Limberg, June 12, 1965; children: Elise, David, Neal. AB, Dartmouth Coll., 1962; MA, Brown U., 1965, PhD, 1969. Lectr. in Spanish Williams Coll., Williamstown, Mass., 1968-70, asst. prof. Spanish, 1970-74; assoc. prof. Spanish U. Conn., Storrs, 1974-80, prof. Spanish and Comparative Lit., 1981—2003, prof. emeritus, 2003—, chair program of comparative lit., 1991—96, chair Spanish PhD program, 1994—2003. Author: Ortega and His German Sources, 1979, New German Sources of Ortega's Philosophy, 1984, Unamuno and Liberal Protestants, 1985, Angel Ganivet (1865-1898), 1998, Hermann Cohen (1842-1918), 2000; co-author: Spanish Philosophical Legacy of the Twentieth Century, 2009; co-editor: Xavier Zubiri Rev., 2000-02; translator: Xavier Zubiri, Dynamic Structure of Reality, 2003; mem. editl. bd. Letras Peninsulares, East Lansing, Mich., 1988, La. Confs. on Hispanic Langs. and Lits. Selected Procs., Tulane U., New Orleans, 1987, 93; editor in Spanish, translator in English of Miguel de Unamuno, Treatise on Love of God, 2007; guest editor Bulletin of Spanish Studies, Glasgow, Scotland, 2002. Postdoctoral rsch. grantee Fulbright, 1981, 89; named Disting. Vis. Alumni Scholar, Brown U., 1981. Mem. AAUP, Sem. on History of Spanish Philosophy, Spanish Soc. Phenomenology, Twentieth-Century Spanish Soc., Internat. Assn. of Hispanists (organizing com. 1982-83), Soc. of Sci. and Lit. Avocations: swimming, travel, study of history of medicine and medical anthropology. Home: 42 Ellise Rd Storrs Mansfield CT 06268-1424 Office: U Conn Dept Modern and Classical Langs PO Box U-1057 Storrs Mansfield CT 06269-1057 Personal E-mail: nelson_orringer@yahoo.com.

ORRIS-MODUGNO, MICHELE MARIE, public relations, marketing and advertising consultant; b. Norwalk, Conn., Feb. 23, 1958; d. Stephen Joseph and Arcenia (Rodriguez) O. Student, U. N.Mex., Albuquerque, 1976-78; BA with honors, U. Bridgeport, Conn., 1980, postgrad., 1981-83. Tchr. Norwalk Pub. Schs., 1981-83; head tchr. presch. Norwalk YMCA, 1983-84; exec. dir. Norwalk Seaport Assn., 1984-86; cons., 1986-87, Barnum Festival, Bridgeport, Conn., 1987-88, P.T. Barnum Found., Bridgeport, 1987; mgr. communications Human Resources Inc., Stamford, Conn., 1987; owner, mgr. Michele Orris, Norwalk, Conn., 1988—. Dir. pub. rels. YWCA of Stamford (Conn.), 1989-90; pres. Fairfield Woods Mid. Sch. PTSA, 2009-. Past sec., pres. Marvin Beach Assn., East Norwalk; asst. dir. pub. rels. Conn. Women's Celebration, 1986; chmn. subcom. auditorium com. New City Hall, Norwalk; active numerous other civic orgns.; bd. dirs. Southwestern Conn. coun. Girl Scouts U.S., 1987-88, Cmtys. In Schs. of Norwalk, Inc., 2000-01; gdn. dirs. Levitt Pavilion Performing Arts, Westport, Conn., 1991-93; mgr. Orch. New Eng., 1993-95; mem. Unquowa Parents Assn., 2000-05; pres. Unquowa Parents' Assn., 2002-04; youth ministry leader St. Pius X Parish, 2006- Recipient award City of Norwalk, 1987. Mem. Greens Farms Acad. Alumni Assn. (pres., class sec.), Phi Sigma Iota (life). Democrat. Roman Catholic. Avocations: reading, tennis, bicycling, golf, art museums. Home and Office: 455 Primrose Ln Fairfield CT 06825-2343 Home Phone: 203-259-8232; Office Phone: 203-259-8232. Business E-Mail: entmom@optonline.net.

ORRO, MARGARITA B., language educator; d. José M. and Norma A. Orro. PhD, CUNY, 1993. Assoc. prof. Miami Dade Coll., Fla., 1989—. Office: Miami Dade Coll 11380 NW 27th Ave Miami FL 33167 Business E-Mail: morro1@mdc.edu.

ORSI, ROBERT, religious studies educator; PhD, Yale U., 1983. Prof. Fordham U., 1981—88; prof. religious studies Ind. U., 1988—2001; Charles Warren prof. history of religion in America Harvard Divinity Sch. and Harvard U., 2001—07; prof. religion Northwestern U., 2007—, Grace Craddock Nagle chair Cath. studies, 2007—. Author: The Madonna of 115th Street: Faith and Community in Italian Harlem, 1880-1950, 1985 (John Gilmary Shea prize, Am. Cath. Hist. Assn., Jesuit Nat. Book award), Thank You, Saint Jude: Women's Devotion to the Patron Saint of Hopeless Causes, 1996 (Merle Curti award in Am. Social History, Orgn. Am. Historians), Between Heaven and Earth: The Religious Worlds People Make and the Scholars Who Study Them, 2004 (Am. Acad. Religion award for Excellence in the Study of Religion); editor: Gods of the City: Religion and the American Urban Landscape, 1999. Fellow Guggenheim Found., 2000, NEH, Fulbright Found. Fellow: Am. Acad. Arts and Sciences; mem.: Am. Acad. Religion (v.p. 2000—01, pres. elect 2001—02, pres. 2002—03). Office: Northwestern U Dept Religion Crowe Hall 1860 Campus Dr 4-139 Evanston IL 60208-2164 Office Phone: 847-467-5157. E-mail: r-orsi@northwestern.edu.

ORSILLO, JAMES EDWARD, computer engineer, information technology executive; b. Elmira, NY, Oct. 30, 1939; s. Giacomo and Irene (Heppy) O.; 1 child, June Lynne. BEE, RCA Insts., 1962; BS in Elec. Engring. and Math., Ind. Inst. Tech., 1964; MS, Rensselear Poly., 1968; BS in Nuclear Engring., Capital Radio Electronic Inst., 1974. Communications engr. Bell Telephone Labs., Holmdel, N.J., 1962-63; video engr. Westinghouse, Elmira, N.Y., 1965-66; computer engr. GE, Pittsfield, Mass., 1966-67; systems specialist Control Data Corp., Mpls., 1968-70; software specialist Computer Sci. Corp., Morristown, N.Y., 1970-72; prin. cons. Computer Cons. Assocs., Elmira, 1972-78; CEO ORTHSTAR, Inc., Elmira, 1974—; acquired Hughes Tng., Inc. Rail Simulation Bus., 1996—. Owner, pres. Shadowstand Properties, Inc. (FKA O-K Properties), Elmira, 1984—, Thundering Hooves Stables, Elmira, 1985—. Author: Mindstorm, 2004. Mem. IEEE, Am. Nuclear Soc., Soc. Indsl. and Applied Math., Am. Helicopter Soc., Army Aviation Assn. Am., Internat. Flying Engrs., USAF Assn., U.S. Naval League, U.S. Polo Assn. Republican. Achievements include invention of Integrated Data Acquisition System (IDAS), of Thread Algebra used in simulation development, of Extended Sentient Non-linear Ensemble (ESNE). Office: ORTHSTAR Inc Airport Corp Park PO Box 459 Big Flats NY 14814-0459 Home Phone: 607-562-8737; Office Phone: 607-562-2100. Business E-Mail: orsillo@orthstar.com.

ORSINI, JAMES A., veterinarian, educator, author, surgeon, editor; s. Salvatore A. Orsini; m. Antoinette B. Orsini, Dec. 26, 1970; 1 child, Colin B. DVM, Cornell U., Ithaca, NY, 1977. Diplomate Am. Coll. Vet. Surgeons, 1986. Assoc. prof. surgery U. Pa., Phila., 1992—, dir., Laminitis Inst. Pa. Vet., 2007—. Author (editor): (book) Equine Emergencies: Treatment and Procedures. Pres. United Way Southen Chester County, Kennett Sq, Pa., 1999—2001. Recipient Disting. Svc. award, PVMA, 2008. Office: Univ Pa 382 W Street Rd Kennett Square PA 19348-1692

ORSON, BARBARA TUSCHNER, actress; b. NYC, May 19, 1929; d. Jonah Tuschner and Rebecca Traceman; m. Jay M. Orson, June 24, 1956; children: Beth-Diane, Theodore. Student, Dramatic Workshop, NYC, 1948-50. Leading soubrette Am. Savoyards, NYC, 1950-51, 53-55; actress Trinity Repertory, Providence, 1964—2002. Founding mem. Trinity Sq. Repertory Co., Providence, 1964—2001. Actress Edinburgh Festival, Scotland, 1968, Am. Repertory Theatre, Cambridge, Mass., 1981-85, Williamstown (Mass.) Theatre, 1985-89, Dallas Theatre Ctr., 1985, Yale Repertory Co., New Haven, Conn., 1991; appeared in: (films) Mission Hill, Code of Ethics, My One and Only, Swimming Upstream, Mr. North, Strangers in Transit (TV) Theatre in America, Feasting with Panthers, Life Among the Lowly, House of Mirth, Camera Three, RI Demon Murder, Miller's Court, Conflict of Interest (Am. premiere) The Suicide, 1980, (world premiere) Grown Ups, 1981, God's Heart, 1995; founding mem., appeared in over 100 prodns. Trinity Sq. Repertory Co., Providence, 1964—; (radio) House of Mirth, Masterpiece Radio Theatre with Jane Alexander; guest artist (Lady Macbeth), Brown U. Recipient Adrian Hall award, Trinity Repertory Co., RI, 2002. Mem. Am. Fedn. Radio and TV Artists, Screen Actors Guild, Actor's Equity Assn., Trinity Rep. Co. (founder). Home: 281 Hillside Ave Pawtucket RI 02860-6119

ORSZAG, PETER RICHARD, federal official, economist; b. Boston, Dec. 16, 1968; s. Steven Alan and Reba (Karp) O.; children: Leila Madeleine, Joshua Nathaniel AB summa cum laude, Princeton U., 1991; MS, London Sch. Econs., 1992, PhD, 1997. Econ. adv. Ministry of Fin., Moscow, 1992-93; staff economist Coun. Econ. Advisers, Exec. Office of the Pres., Washington, 1993-94, sr. economist, 1995-96, sr. adv., 1996; prof. rsch. staff London Sch. Economics, 1994-95; sr. econ. adv. Nat. Econ. Coun., 1997, spl. asst. to Pres for econ. policy, 1998; pres. Sebago Assocs., 1998—2007; dir. Congressional Budget Office (CBO), Washington, 2007—08, Office Mgmt. & Budget (OMB), Exec. Office of the Pres., Washington, 2009—. Lectr. in econs. U. Calif., Berkeley, 1999—2000; rsch. assoc. Ctr. Retirement Rsch., Boston Coll., 2000—07. Marshall scholar, 1991-92. Mem. Inst. Medicine, Nat. Acad. Social Ins., Phi Beta Kappa. Office: Office Management & Budget Eisenhower Executive Office Bldg 1650 Pennsylvania Ave NW Rm 252 Washington DC 20503 Business E-Mail: peter.orszag@cbo.gov.

ORSZAG, STEVEN ALAN, applied mathematician, educator; b. NYC, Feb. 27, 1943; s. Joseph and Rose (Siegel) O.; m. Reba Karp, June 21, 1964; children: J. Michael, Peter Richard, Jonathan Marc. BS, M.I.T., 1962; postgrad. (Henry fellow), St. John's Coll., Cambridge U., Eng., 1962-63; PhD, Princeton U., 1966. Mem. Inst. Advanced Study, Princeton, NJ, 1966—67; prof. applied math. MIT, 1967—84; prof. applied and computational math. Princeton U., 1984—98, dir., 1990—92, Hamrick prof. engring., 1989—98; Smith prof. math. Yale U., New Haven, 1998—, chmn. applied math., 1999—2003. Founder Flow, CHI, Ibrix, Inc., Vectek, Inc.; cons. in field. Author: Studies in Applied Mathematics, 1976, Numerical Analysis of Spectral Methods, 1977, Advanced Mathematical Methods for Scientists and Engineers, 1978; contbr. numerous rsch. publs. in field. A.P. Sloan Found. fellow, 1970-74, Guggenheim fellow, 1989-90. Fellow Am. Inst. Physics (Otto Laporte award 1991), AIAA (Fluid and Plasmadynamics award, 1986), Soc. Indsl. and Applied Math., Soc. Engring. Sci. (G.I. Taylor medal, 1995). Business E-Mail: orszag@math.yale.edu.

ORT, SHANNON, lawyer; b. Appleton, Wis. BA in Criminal Justice/Legal Studies, magna cum laude, Hamline U., 1998; JD magna cum laude, William Mitchell Coll. Law, 2001. Bar: Minn. 2001, Wis. 2002. Assoc. Steffens & Rasmussen; assoc. atty. litig. dept. Rider Bennett, LLP, Mpls.; founder, ptnr. Terzich & Ort, LLP, Mpls., 2007—. Named a Rising Star, Minn. Super Lawyers mag., 2006—09. Mem.: Hennepin County Bar Assn., Minn. State Bar Assn. Office: Terzich and Ort LLP Ste # 5 8525 Edinbrook Crossing Minneapolis MN 55443 Office Phone: 763-391-7412. Business E-Mail: sort@tolawoffice.com.

ORTALDO, JOHN R., immunologist, researcher; b. West Chester, Pa., Apr. 22, 1945; BS, St. Francis Coll., Loretto, Pa., 1967; MS in microbiology, Villanova U., 1969; PhD in microbiology/immunology, George Washington U., 1979. Mil. svc. in immunohematology Walter Reed Army Inst., 1969—71; microbiologist Dept. Agriculture, Dover, Del.; rsch. biologist Cellular and Tumor Immunology Sect., Lab. Cell Biology Nat. Cancer Inst., NIH, 1971, post-doctoral training Lab. Immunodiagnosis, named sr. investigator Lab Immunodiagnosis, 1980, head Natural Immunity Sect., Biol. Therapeutics Br. Frederick, chief Lab. Exptl. Immunology, 1985, acting head Leukocyte Cell Biology Sect. Mem.: Soc. Natural Immunology, Soc. Biol. Therapy, Reticuloendothelial Soc., Am. Assn. Immunology, Am. Assn. Cancer Rsch. Office: Lab Exptl Immunology Nat Cancer Inst at Frederick PO Box B Bldg 560 Rm 31-93 Frederick MD 21702-1201 Office Phone: 301-846-1323. Office Fax: 301-846-1673. E-mail: ortaldo@ncifcrf.gov.*

ORTEGA, KENNY, television director, choreographer; b. Palo Alto, Calif., Apr. 18, 1950; Dir.: (films) Newsies, 1992, Hocus Pocus, 1993; (TV films) High School Musical, 2006 (Outstanding Directorial Achievement in Children's Programs, Dir. Guild Am., 2007), The Cheetah Girls 2, 2006, High School Musical 2, 2007 (Am. Music award for Favorite Soundtrack, 2007); (TV series) Fame LA, 1997, Chicago Hope, 1998—99, Ally McBeal, 2001, Gilmore Girls, 2002—06; choreographer (films) Xanadu, 1980, One From the Heart, 1982, St. Elmo's Fire, 1985, Pretty in Pink, 1986, Ferris Bueller's Day Off, 1986, Dirty Dancing, 1987, Salsa, 1988, Shag, 1989, To Wong Foo Thanks for Everything, Julie Newmar, 1995, (TV films) The Way She Moves, 2001; supervising choreographer, artistic dir. co-prodr. Salt Lake Winter Olympic Games 2002 Opening Ceremony (Emmy award outstanding dir. for a variety, music or comedy spl., Emmy award outstanding choreography), dir., exec. prodr., choreographer (films) High School Musical 3: Senior Year, 2008. Recipient Golden Eagle award lifetime achievement, Nosotros. Office: c/o Andy Patman Paradigm LA 360 N Crescent Dr N Bldg Beverly Hills CA 90210

ORTEGO, GILDA BAEZA, library director, educator; b. El Paso, Tex., Mar. 29, 1952; d. Efren and Bertha (Singh) Baeza; m. Felipe de Ortego y Gasca, Dec. 21, 1986. BA, Tex. Woman's U., 1974, PhD, 2001; MLS, U. Tex., 1976, postgrad., 1990-93; cert:, Hispanic Leadership Inst., 1988. Stack maintenance supr. El Paso Libr. U. Tex., 1974-75; pub. svcs. libr. El Paso Community Coll., 1976-77; ethnic studies libr. U. N.Mex., Albuquerque, 1977-81; br. head El Paso Pub. Libr., 1981-82; dep. head Mex.-Am. Svcs., El Paso Pub. Libr., 1982-84; libr. Mex.-Am. Studies U. Tex. Libr., Austin, 1984—86; libr. Phoenix Pub. Libr., 1987-89; assoc. libr., west campus Ariz. State U., Phoenix, 1989-90; Proyecto Leer libr. Tex. Woman's U., Denton, 1991-92; dean divsn. learning resources Sul Ross State U., Alpine, Tex., 1992—99; dir. univ. libr., Tex. A&M U., Kingsville, 1999—. Speaker and cons. in field. Founding editor jour. La Lista, 1983-84; founding indexer Chicano Periodical Index, 1981-86; reviewer jour. Voices of Youth Advocates, 1988-90; contbr. poetry and articles to books and jours. Recipient Silver award, Nat. Commn. Library and Info. Sci., 1996. Mem. ALA (com. on standing of women in profession, com. on profl. edn.), MLA, Assn. for Libr. and Info. Sci. Edn., Tex. Libr. Assn., Ariz. State Libr. Assn. (pres. svcs. Spanish speaking Roundtable 1988-90), Reforma (pres. El Paso chpt. 1983, pres. Ariz. chpt. 1989-90, nat. v.p. 1993-94, natpres. 1994-95), Unltd. Potential, Inc. (treas. 1988-89), Hispanic Leadership Inst. Alumni Assn. Home: PO Box 5148 Silver City NM 88062-5148

ORTENBERG, TOM, film company executive; m. Edie Ortenberg; children: Jason, Andrew. Grad., Pa. State U., 1982. With Columbia Pictures, 1985, Hemdale Film Corp., pres. distbn. and mktg.; founder LA office Lionsgate Entertainment, Santa Monica, 1996, pres. theatrical films, The Weinstein Co., LA, 2009—. Trustee Brit. Acad. Film and TV Arts, East Coast; mem. bd. dirs., treas. Film Ind. Mem. bd. dirs. Hope For Heroes. Recipient Leadership award, Hollywood Film Festival; named #2 in Indy Power Issue, The Hollywood Reporter. Mem.: Acad. Motion Pictures Arts and Scis. Office: The Weistein Co 345 Hudson St 13th Fl New York NY 10014*

ORTENZIO, ROBERT A., health and medical products executive; V.p. Rehab Hosp. Svcs. Corp.; sr. v.p. Continetal Med. Systems, Inc., Mechanicsburg, Pa., 1986—88, COO, 1988—95, pres., 1995—96; exec. v.p., dir. Horizon/CMS Healthcare Corp.; co-founder, pres., COO Select Medical, Mechanicsburg, Pa., 1997—2001, pres., 2001—04, CEO, 2001—. Bd. dir. US Oncology, Inc. Office: Select Medical 4716 Old Gettysburg Rd Mechanicsburg PA 17055 Office Phone: 717-972-1100.*

ORTENZIO, ROCCO ANTHONY, health products executive; b. Steelton, Pa., Nov. 28, 1932; s. Rocco and Minnie Ortenzio; m. Nancy Miller, Jan. 29, 1955; children: John, Robert, Martin. BS, West Chester U., 1955; postgrad., U. Pa., 1955—56. Pvt. practice phys. therapy, Harrisburg, Pa., 1957—69; founder, pres., CEO Rehab. Corp., Harrisburg, 1969—77, Pa. Health Corp., Mechanicsburg, Pa., 1977—79, Rehab. Hosp. Svc. Corp., Mechanicsburg, 1979—85; co-founder, chmn, CEO Continental Med. Sys., Inc. (merged with Horizon Healthcare Corp.), Mechanicsburg, 1986—95, Select Medical, Mechanicsburg, Pa., 1997—2001, exec. chmn., 2001—. Bd. dirs. Continental Med. Sys., Inc., PNC, N.A., AMSCO Internat., Quorum Health Group, Inc. Mem.: World Pres. Orgn. Republican. Roman Catholic. Office: Select Material 4716 Old Gettysburg Rd Mechanicsburg PA 17055 Office Phone: 717-972-1100.*

ORTH, DAVID NELSON, endocrinologist, educator, sculptor, potter; b. East Orange, NJ, Mar. 5, 1933; s. John Joseph and Marjorie Adelaide (Wauters) O.; m. Linda Diana D'Errico, June 9, 1979; children by previous marriage: John Randall (dec.), Jennifer Stewart, Julie Thomas. ScB in Chemistry, Brown U., 1954; MD, Vanderbilt U., 1962. Intern, Osler med. service Johns Hopkins Hosp., Balt., 1962-63, fellow in medicine, 1962-65; asst. resident John Hopkins Hosp., Balt., 1963-65; mem. faculty dept. medicine Vanderbilt U. Sch. Medicine, Nashville, 1965—, prof., 1975-98, prof. emeritus, 1998—, joint dir. endocrinology div. dept. medicine, 1968-81, dir. cancer research and treatment ctr., 1972-77, dir. div. endocrinology, 1984-96; sculptor and potter, 1998—. Scholar-in-residence Rockefeller Found. Bellagio Study and Conf. Ctr., Italy, 1989; vis. scientist Vollum Inst. for Advanced Biomed. Rsch., Oreg. Health Scis. U., Portland, 1993-94. Contbr. numerous articles in field of endocrinology to med. jours. Served with U.S. Navy, 1954-57. John and Mary R. Markle scholar, 1968-73; Howard Hughes Med. Inst. investigator, 1969-75 Mem. AAUP, AAAS, ACP, Assn. Am. Physicians, Am. Soc. Clin. Investigation, Endocrine Soc. (sec.-treas. 1989-94, pres. 1997-98), N.Y. Acad. Scis., Am. Fedn. Clin. Rsch., So. Soc. Clin. Investigation. Personal E-mail: orth@comcast.net.

ORTH, SUSAN LYNN, judge; b. Evansville, Ind., Nov. 15, 1958; d. Orville William and A. Margaret Orth; m. Terrance D. Becker; 1 child, Brandy L. Orth Becker. BSc, Ind. State U., Terre Haute, 1981; MSc, U. Louisville, Ky., 1982; JD, Salman P. Chase Coll. Law, Ky., 1985. Cert.: (mediator advanced family and civil tng.). Chief dep. prosecutor Floyd County Prosecutor's Office, New Albany, Ind., 1987—2002; sr. prosecutor So. Dist. Ind., 2002—04; judge Floyd County Superior Ct., New Albany, 2004—. Instr. Nat. Dist. Attys. Assn., Columbia, SC, 1998—2002; mem. faculty Ind. Prosecuting Attys. Coun., Indpls., 1998—2002, Ind. Jud. Ctr., Indpls., 2005—; mem. state bd. law examiners com. on character and fitness, local com. on race and gender fairness Ind. Supreme Ct. Atty. New Albany City Coun., 1992—95; mem. judiciary and media com. Ind. Supreme Ct., 2004—; vol. Success by Six Metro United Way, New Albany, 2006; mem. bd. So. Christian Leadership Conf., 1998—, Metro United Way, 2004—; mem. Leadership So. Ind. Class of 2006. Recipient Drum Major award, So. Christian Leadership Conf., 1999; named Citizen of Yr., New Albany Mayor's Office, 2002. Mem.: Sherman Minton Inns of Ct. (pres. exec. bd. 2006—07), Am. Justice Inst. (mem. exec. bd. 2004—), Bus. and Profl. Women. Office: Floyd Superior Ct Room 200 City/G Bldg New Albany IN 47150

ORTHNER, DENNIS K., social sciences educator, consultant; b. Fresno, Calif., Feb. 7, 1945; s. Gordon and Brunhilde Orthner; m. Barbara Fields, July 12, 1968; children: Jason, Melissa, Kristen Maness. PhD, Fla. State U., Tallahassee, 1974. Prof. social sci. Tallahassee CC, 1968—74; asst. to assoc. prof. U. NC, Greensboro, 1974—82; dir. human services rsch. ctr. SRA Corp., Washington, 1982—83; prof. child and family devel. U. Ga., Athens, 1983—88; prof. social work and pub. policy U. NC, Chapel Hill, NC, 1988—. Sr. ptnr. Orthner and Associates, Raleigh, NC, 1983—. Author: (book) Intimate Relationships: An Introduction to Marriage and the Family, (monograph) Pastoral Counseling: Caring and Care-giving Among United Methodist Clergy; contbr. chapters to books. Congl. testimony on mil. families US Senate and Ho. Armed Svcs. Coms., Washington, 1982—2005; congl. testimony U.S. Senate Caucus on the Family, Washington, 1985—87; cons. and rschr. Ministry Labor and Social Affairs, Israel, 1999—2007; spl. asst to the sec. NC HHS, Raleigh, 1994; dir. Citizen-Soldier Support Program; elder and treas. Raleigh Vineyard Christian Fellowship, 1994—2005. Fellow, Nat. Coun. on Family Relations, 2000. Master: Family Coun. NC (pres. 1992—94); mem.: Nat. Mil. Family Assn. (adv. bd. mem. 1986—94), Nat. Coun. on Family Rels. (life; chair, theory constrn. and rsch. methodology workshop 1989—90, chair, family policy sect. 1999—2001). Achievements include research in Career Start, a school and career engagement strategy for lifting children from poverty; organizational learning and client, staff and agency impacts; development of Life Skills for Healthy Marriage, a family readiness program; design of program for Air Force family support centers. Avocations: hiking, photography. Office: Univ NC Chapel Hill Sch Social Work and Public Policy Chapel Hill NC 27599-3550 Office Fax: 919-962-1486. E-mail: orthner@email.unc.edu.

ORTIZ, ALEXIS, physical therapist, educator; b. San Juan, Nov. 10, 1975; s. Luis Ortiz and Gloria Rodriguez; m. Heidi Liam Venegas, July 12, 1998; children: Alex, Joseph. BS in Physical Therapy, U. Puerto Rico, San Juan, 2000; MS in Physical Therapy, Tex. Woman's U., Houston, 2003; PhD in Physical Therapy, Tex. Woman's U., 2006. Lic. physical therapy Tex. Bd. Phys. Therapy Examiners, 2000, cert. strength and conditioning specialist Nat. Strenth and Conditioning Assn., 2002, lic. physical therapist Puerto Rico Bd. Phys. Therapy, 2006, cert. sports clin. specialist Am. Bd. Phys. Therapy Specialists, 2007. Asst. prof. med. scis. U. PR, 2006—, phys. therapist, athletic dept. Recipient Young Investigator award, National Strength and Conditioning Assn., 2007. Office: Univ PR Physical Therapy Program PO Box 365067 San Juan PR 00936 Office Fax: 787-765-2165. Business E-Mail: alexisortiz@cprs.rcm.upr.edu.

ORTIZ, ANGEL VICENTE, church administrator; b. LA, Nov. 9, 1956; s. Benjamin and Petra (Santiago) O.; m. Michele Annette Gaunt, May 5, 1979; children: Angela Nicole, Michael David. BS in Bibl. Studies, Ft. Wayne (Ind.) Bible Coll., 1982. Ordained to ministry Christian and Missionary Alliance, 1987. Pastor, ch. planter Christian and Missionary Alliance, Chula Vista, Calif., 1983-90, supt. Spanish western dist. Escondido, Calif., 1991-96, also nat. conf. spkr., evangelist; asst. to the pres. for program devel. Nyack (N.Y.) Coll., 1996-97, v.p. student devel., dean students, 1997—2002; sr. pastor First Ch. Christian and Missionary Alliance, NYC, 2002—. Republican. Mem. Christian And Missionary Alliance Ch. Avocations: camping, woodworking, refinishing, travel, teaching. Office Phone: 212-604-0300. Business E-Mail: angelortiz@firstchurchnyc.org.

ORTIZ, CHRISTINE, engineering educator; married. BS in Materials Sci. and Engring., Rensselaer Poly. Inst., Netherlands, 1992; MS in Materials Sci. and Engring., Cornell U., Ithaca, 1994, PhD in Materials Sci. and Engring., 1997. Post-doc. rsch. assoc. U. Groningen, Netherlands; asst. prof., materials sci. and engring. MIT, Cambridge, Mass., 1999—2004, assoc. prof., materials sci. and engring., 2004—, faculty dir., 2007—. Contbr. articles to numerous profl. jours. (Cover of Issue). Mem. MIT Diversity Initiative Com., Cambridge, Mass., 2007—08. Recipient Hadassah Appreciation Medal, Hebrew U., 2008, PECASE Award, NSF, 2002, Award, MIT, 2001, CAREER Award, NSF, 2000; named Dow Disting. Lectr., U. Calif., Santa Barbara, 2007; Fellowship, NSSEFF, 2008, Lady Davis Fellowship, Hebrew U. Jerusalem, 2008. Mem.: Am. Chem. Soc. Office: Mass Inst Tech 77 Massachusetts Ave Rm 13-4022 Cambridge MA 02139 Office Fax: 617-258-6936. Business E-Mail: cortiz@mit.edu.

ORTIZ, DAVID (DAVID AMERICO ORTIZ ARIAS), professional baseball player; b. Santo Domingo, Dominican Republic, Nov. 18, 1975; naturalized, US, 2008; s. Americo Ortiz and Angela Rosa Arias; m. Tiffany Brick; children: Jessica, Alexandra, D'Angelo. Designated hitter Minn. Twins, 1997—2002, Boston Red Sox, 2003—. Mem. Dominican Republic nat. team World Baseball Classic, 2006, 09. Co-author (with Tony Massaroti): Big Papi: The Story of How My Baseball Dreams Came True, 2007; guest appearance: (TV series) Judging Amy, 2005. Recipient Edgar Martinez award, 2003—07, Silver Slugger award, 2004—07, Hank Aaron award, 2005; named Am. League Championship Series MVP, 2004; named to Am. League All-Star Team, 2004—08. Achievements include being a member of the World Series Champion Boston Red Sox, 2004 and 2007; being the first player in Red Sox franchise history to hit 40 or more home runs in three consecutive seasons (2004-2006); setting a new Red Sox single-season home run record with 54 in 2006. Office: Boston Red Sox 4 Yawkey Way Boston MA 02215-3496*

ORTIZ, GEORGE, artist; b. 1927; Exhibitions include The State Hermitage Mus., St. Petersburg, 1993, The State Pushkin Mus. Fine Arts, 1993, Royal Acad. Arts, 1994, Altes Mus., 1996. Named one of Top 200 Collectors, ART News Mag., 2004—08. Avocation: collecting art. Mailing: Chougny Fontaine CH 1253 Vandoeuvres Switzerland E-mail: george@ortiz.ch.

ORTIZ, GERARDO, physicist, researcher; b. Buenos Aires, Nov. 28, 1960; s. Gonzalo O. and Adelaida Elena Perez; m. Sandra Mariel Alicino, Feb. 27, 1987; Federico Ezequiel, Nicole Chloe, Matthias Alexander. M in Physics, Inst. Balseiro, Bariloche, Argentina, 1986; PhD in Theoret. Physics, Swiss Fed. Inst. Tech., Lausanne, Switzerland, 1992. Asst. doctorant Swiss Fed. Inst. Tech., Lausanne, Switzerland, 1988-92; postdoct. rsch. asst. U. Ill., Urbana, 1992-96; John Robert Oppenheimer fellow Los Alamos (N. Mex.) Nat. Lab. Adj. prof. U. Ill., Urbana-Champaign; prof. physics Ind. U., Bloomington. Fellow Swiss Nat. Found., 1988-92. Fellow Inst. Physics; mem. Am. Phys. Soc. Avocation: soccer. Office: Ind Univ Dept Physics 727 E Third St Bloomington IN 47405-7105 Business E-Mail: ortizg@indiana.edu.

ORTIZ, JOSEPH M., literature and language professor, writer; BA in English, Yale U., 1995, BA in Math., 1995; PhD in English Lit., Princeton U., 2003. Asst. prof. SUNY, Brockport, 2005—. Postdoc. fellowship, Cornell U. Soc. Humanities, 2004—05. Home: 10 Atkinson St Rochester NY 14608 Office: State Univ NY 350 New Campus Dr Brockport NY 14420 Business E-Mail: jmortiz@brockport.edu.

ORTIZ, MANUEL, lobbyist; b. San Juan; BA, JD, U. Kans., Lawrence. Transactional atty. Verner Liipfert Bernhard McPherson & Hand, Greenberg Traurig LLP; lobbyist Quinn Gillespie & Assocs., Washington, 2003—. Polit. commentator MSNBC, Telemundo, Univision. Nat. fin. vice chmn., co-chair Hispanic steering com. Senator John Kerry's Presdl. Campaign, 2004. Democrat. Office: Quinn Gillespie & Assocs 1133 Connecticut Ave NW 5th Fl Washington DC 20036 Office Phone: 202-457-1110. Office Fax: 202-457-1130.*

ORTIZ, MICHAEL, engineering educator; BS in Civil Engring., Univ. Madrid, 1977; MS, Univ. Calif., Berkeley, 1978, PhD, 1981. Rsch. asst. Univ. Calif., Berkeley, 1979—82; postdoctoral fellow Ministry of Public Works Rsch. and Experimentation Ctr., Madrid, 1982—83; rsch. sci. Dept. Coasts and Harbors, Ministry of Public Works, Madrid, 1983—84; asst. prof. engring Brown Univ., Providence, 1984—87, assoc. prof., 1987—90, prof., 1990—95; prof., aeronautics Calif. Inst. Tech., 1995—2004, Dotty and Dick Hayman prof. aeronautics, mech. engring., 2004—. Recipient Humboldt Rsch. award for Senior US Scientists, 2002; Fulbright Scholarship, 1977—78. Fellow: Internat. Assn. Computational Mechanics (Awards for Rsch. 2002), US Assn. Computational Mechanics, Am. Acad. Arts & Sciences; mem.: Am. Soc. Mech.Engrs., Am. Acad. Mechanics. Office: 115 Firestone MC 105-50 Calif Inst Tech Pasadena CA 91125 Office Phone: 626-395-4530. Business E-Mail: ortiz@aero.caltech.edu.

ORTIZ, ORLANDO, radiologist, department chairman; s. Ana Delia Ortiz; m. Cecilia Sacoto, Oct. 20, 1990; children: Alexander Orlando, Maria Esperanza, Raquel Esmeralda, Esteban Antonio. BA, Columbia Coll., NY, 1981; MD, Harvard Med. Sch., Boston, 1985; MBA, W.Va. U., Morgantown, 1997. Diplomate Am. Bd. Radiology, 1990, cert. in neuroradiology Am. Bd. of Radiology, 1996. Dir. diagnostic and interventional neuroradiology, dept. radiology W.Va. U. Med. Ctr., Morgantown, 1992—97; vice chmn. bus. affairs, dept. radiology U. Md. Med. Ctr., Baltimore, 1999—2000; chmn., dept. radiology Winthrop U. Hosp., Mineola, NY, 2000—, fundraising, 2000—. Editor: (comprehensive multi-media text) Vertebroplasty-CD. Patron Garden City Turkey Trot, Garden City, NY, 2008, Hispanic Counseling Ctr., Hempstead, NY, 2005—09, Circulo de la Hispanidad, Long Beach, NY, 2005—09, LI Fight Charity, Old Bethpage, NY, 2005—08. Recipient Tchr. of Yr., Winthrop-U. Hosp. Dept. Radiology, 1999, Cmty. Svc. award, Hempstead Coalition Cmty. Well Being, 2000, Circulo de la Hispanidad, NY, 2006, Latino Alumni Assn. Columbia U. Heritage award, 2006; named Humanitarian of Yr., Hispanic Counseling Ctr., LI, 2004; named one of Am. Best Doctors, 2001—02, 2005—08. Fellow: Am. Coll. Radiology; mem.: NY State Radiol. Soc. (councilor 2002—04), Am. Soc. Spine Radiology (pres. 2002—03), Am. Soc. Neuroradiology (tech. exhibits com. mem. 2007—09). Roman Catholic. Office: Winthrop Univ Hosp 259 First St Mineola NY 11501

ORTIZ, PABLO, composer; b. Buenos Aires; Grad., Cath. U. Argentina; Masters in music composition, PhD in music composition, Columbia U. Co-dir Electronic Music Studio, prof. composition U. Pitts., 1990—94; prof. music U. Calif. Davis, 1994—. Composer: numerous instrumental and vocal works, (plays) Dance of Death, 1983, El Campo, 1984, El sol naciente, 1984, (films) Gracias por el fuego, 1984, My Sin Was To Love You, 1988, (Operas) Parodia, 1997, Una voz en el viento, 1998. Recipient ASCAP award, 1994, Acad. award, AAAL, 2008; fellow Wellesley Composers Conf., 1986, Guggenheim Found., 1993; Charles Ives fellow, AAAL, 1996. Office: UC Davis Dept Music 1 Shields Ave Davis CA 95616 Office Phone: 530-752-7509. E-mail: pvortiz@ucdavis.edu.

ORTIZ, PATRICK T., lawyer; b. 1950; BA, Coll. Santa Fe; JD, Georgetown U. Bar: N.Mex. 1976. Dep. gen. counsel ins. dept. N.Mex. State Corp. Commn., gen. counsel; asst. atty. gen. energy and utilities sect. Atty. Gen.'s Office, N.Mex.; staff counsel N.Mex. Public Svc. Commn., chief commn. counsel, commr.; atty. Mountain States Telephone & Telegraph Co.; chief counsel US West Comm.; sr. v.p., gen. counsel, sec. PNM Resources, Albuquerque, 1991—. Bd. dirs. N.Mex. Bar Bus. Law Sect.; corp. exec. bd. Gen. Counsel Roundtable. Bd. trustees PNM Found.; pro bono counsel Challenge N.Mex.; bd. dirs. Archdiocese Santa Fe Catholic Found., Nat. Hispanic Cultural Ctr. Found.; mem. bd. visitors Coll. Santa Fe. Named one of Most Influential Hispanics, Hispanic Bus. Mag., Corp. Elite, 2007. Mem.: Chief Legal Officers Assn. (mem. exec. com.), Am. Law Inst., N.Mex Hispanic Bar Assn., Oliver Seth Am. Inn of Ct. (master of bench), Edison Elec. Inst. (mem. legal com.), Am. Gas Assn. (mem. legal com.). Office: PNM Resources Inc Alvarado Sq MS2822 Albuquerque NM 87158-0001

ORTIZ, SOLOMON PORFIRIO, SR., United States Representative from Texas; b. Robstown, Tex., June 3, 1937; children: Yvette, Solomon P. Cert., Inst. Applied Sci., Chgo., 1962; student, Del Mar Coll., Corpus Christi, Tex., 1965—67, Nat. Sheriff's Tng. Inst., LA, 1977. Constable Neuces County, Tex., 1965—68, commr. Tex., 1969-76, sheriff Tex., 1977—83; mem. US Congress from 27th Tex. dist., 1983—, mem. resources com., mem. armed svcs. com., ranking minority mem. readiness subcommittee, dean Congl. Hispanic Caucus. Served in 61st Mil. Police Co. US Army, 1960—62. Named Man of Yr., Internat. Order Foresters, 1981, one of Hispanic Bus. 100 Most Influential Hispanics in US, Hispanic Bus. Mag., 1999. Mem. Nat. Dep. Sheriff's Assn., Sheriff's Assn. Tex., ARC, United Way, Impact Aid Coalition; hon. mem. Corpus Christi Rotary Club. Democrat. Office: US House Reps 2470 Rayburn House Office Bldg Washington DC 20515-4327 Office Phone: 202-225-7742.*

ORTIZ APONTE, SALLY, retired literature and language professor; BA in Edn., U. PR, Rio Piedras, 1954, MA in Hispanic Studies and Humanities cum laude, 1966; PhD in Spanish Philology cum laude, U. Complutense, Madrid, 1974; diploma in Writing for Children and Teenagers, 2008. English tchr. Ctrl. HS, San Juan, 1957—62; tchr. Spanish lang. and lit. U. PR, Rio Piedras, 1963—92, honor program prof., 1993—94. Book evaluator U. PR Press, 1975; mem. adv. bd. PR Coun. Higher Edn., 1979—80, mem. adv. bd. in gen. studies, 1984—90; rep. before U. PR, Inst. Puerto Rican Lit., Pres. U. PR, 1982—89; mem. lit. panel Ateneo de PR, 1976, Pen Club, 1991, Spanish Dept., 1992; evaluator Arecibo Regional Coll. Dir. on Spanish prof. evaluations; U. PR Spanish dept. rep. PR Coun. Higher Edn., Mid. States Assn. and Ana G. Mendez Found., 1980; chair for spl. emphasis subcom. faculty assessment Mid. States Assn., 1982—85; children's lit. and lang. arts del. to China Citizen Amb. Program, 1994. Author: Las Mujeres de Clarin, 1971—73, La Esoteria en la Narrativa Hispanoamericana, 1977; contbr. articles to profl. jours. Named Woman of Yr. in Edn., C. of C., PR, 1980; honor scholar and univ. ring, Hispanoam. Coll. Juan Roncalli, Madrid, 1974. Mem.: MLA, Internat. Reading Assn., PR Acad. Arts and Scis. (bd. dirs. rep. before U. PR, Inst. Puerto Rican lit. 1989—91), Nat. Geog. Soc. Mailing: PO Box 135453 Clermont FL 34713 Home: 505 Ella Mae Dr Davenport FL 33897-4411

ORTIZ-TAYLOR, SHEILA, retired English language educator; b. LA, Sept. 25, 1939; d. John Santray and Juanita Loretta (Shrode) T.; m. John Leonard Clendenning, Aug. 27, 1958 (div. 1971); m. Joy Lynn Lewis, Mar. 16, 1991; children: Andrea, Laura, Jessica, Will, Lynn. BA, Calif. State U., Northridge, 1963; MA, UCLA, 1964, PhD, 1973. Lectr. Calif. State U., Northridge, 1964-70; prof. emerita English Fla. State U., Tallahassee, 2006—. Author: (novels) Faultline, 1982, Spring Forward/Fall Back, 1985, Southbound, 1990, Coachella, 1998, Outrageous, 2006, Assisted living, 2007, (book of poetry) Slow Dancing at Miss Polly's, 1989 (memoir) Imaginary Parents, 1996. Recipient Fulbright fellowship Fulbright Assn., 1991; fellowship Nat. Endowment for the Arts, 2008. Democrat. Personal E-mail: sortiztaylor@fsu.edu.

ORTIZ-WALTERS, ROWENA, management educator; d. Ortiz and Rivera; m. Carl Allan Walters, May 14, 1999; children: Ethan Andrew Walters, Noah Daniel Walters. BS Chemistry, U. Conn., 1996; MBA, U. New Haven, 1999; PhD Mgmt., U. Conn., 2005. Chemist Uniroyal Chem. Corp., Middlebury, Conn., 1996—99; instr. bus. mgmt. U. Conn., Storrs, 2000—; asst. prof. entrepreneurship Quinnipiac U., 2004—. Asst. dir. Wolff Family Program in Entrepreneurship, Storrs, 2000—; pres. Mgmt. Doctoral Student Assn., 2001—02; advisor Quinnipiac U. Entrepreneurial Success team; presenter in field. Contbr. articles to profl. jours. Recipient 40 Under 40 award, Bus. Times, 2006; named Best Teaching Asst. of Yr., U. Conn., 2002, Best Student Tchr. of Yr., 2003; grantee, Quinnipiac U., 2005. Mem.: Mgmt. Doctoral Student Assn., Ea. Acad. Mgmt., Acad. Mgmt. Assn. (chair mentoring com., Best Symposium award 2004). Avocations: hiking, snowshoeing, reading, travel.

ORTLUND, ANNE (ELIZABETH ANNE ORTLUND), writer, musician; b. Wichita, Kans., Dec. 3, 1923; d. Joseph Burton and Mary Elizabeth (Weible) Sweet; m. Raymond Carl Ortlund, Apr. 27, 1946; children: Sherrill Anne, Margot Jeanne, Raymond Carl, Nels Robert. Student, Am. U., 1941—43; AA, Am. Guild Organists, 1944; MusB, U. Redlands, Calif., 1945. Organist Old-Fashioned Revival Hour and Joyful Sound, Radio World-Wide, 1960—75; spkr. Orgn. Renewal Ministries, Newport Beach, Calif., 1980—; composer hymns, anthems NYC, 1963—77. Composer: Macedonia, 1966, 250 hymns; author: Up with Worship, 1975, Disciplines of the Beautiful Woman, 1977, The Gentle Ways of the Beautiful Woman, 1998, How Great Our Joy, 2001, Up With Worship, rev. and updated, 2001, A Fresh Start for Your Friendships, 2001; author: (with Raymond Carl Ortlund) The Best Half of Life, 1976, Discipling One Another, 1979, Children Are Wet Cement, 1981 (Christie award Christian Booksellers Assn., 1982), Joanna: A Story of Renewal, 1982, Building a Great Marriage, 1984; author: (with Raymond C. Ortlund) Staying Power, 1986, Disciplines of the Heart, 1987, Renewal, 1989, Confident in Christ, Disciplines of the Home, 1990, Fix Your Eyes on Jesus, 1991, My Sacrifice His Fire, 1993, In His Presence, 1995, Lord, Make My Life a Miracle, rev. and updated, 2002. Recipient SESAC award, Gospel Musicians, 1978, award, Commd. Conservative Congl. Christian Conf., 2008; named Profl. Woman of Yr., Pasadena Bus. and Profl. Women, 1975. Home: 601 Lido Park Dr Apt 6E Newport Beach CA 92663-4403 Office: Renewal Ministries 151 Kalmus Dr Ste E160 Costa Mesa CA 92626-8828 Office Phone: 714-668-0818. E-mail: anne@ortlund.org.

ORTMAN, GEORGE EARL, artist; b. Oakland, Calif., Oct. 17, 1926; s. William Thomas and Anna Katherine (Noll) O.; m. Conni Whidden, Aug. 5, 1960 (dec.); 1 stepson, Roger Graham Whidden. Student, Calif. Coll. Arts and Crafts, 1947-49, Atelier Stanley William Hayter, 1949, Acad. Andre L'Hote, Paris, 1949-50, Hans Hoffman Sch. Art, 1949-50. Co-founder Tempo Playhouse, NYC, 1954; Instr. painting and drawing NYU, 1962-65; co-chmn. fine arts Sch. Visual Arts NYC, 1963-65; artist-in-residence Princeton U., 1966-69, Honolulu Acad. Art, 1969; head painting dept. Cranbrook Acad. Art, Bloomfield Hills, Mich., 1970-92. One-man exhbns. include Tanager Gallery, 1954, Wittenborn Gallery, 1955, Stable Gallery, 1957, 60, Howard Wise Gallery, 1962, 63, 64, 66, 69, Gimpel-Weitzenhoffer Gallery, 1972 (all N.Y.C.), Swetzoff Gallery, Boston, 1961-62, Fairleigh Dickinson U., 1962, Mirvish Gallery, Toronto, Can., 1964, Walker Art Center, Mpls., 1965, Milw. Art Center, 1966, Dallas Mus. Art, 1966, Portland Mus. Art, 1966, Akron Inst. Art, 1966, U. Chgo., 1967, Princeton U. Art Mus., 1967, Honolulu Acad. Art, 1969, Reed Coll., 1970, Cranbrook Acad. Art, 1970, 92, Indpls. Mus. Art, 1971, J.L. Hudson Gallery, Detroit, 1971, Gimpel-Weitzenhoffer, N.Y.C., 1972, 73, Gertrude Kasle Gallery, Detroit, 1976, Lee Hoffman Gallery, Detroit, 1977, Flint (Mich.) Mus. Art, 1977; other one-man exhbns. include Cranbrook Mus. Art, 1982; exhibited numerous group shows including Whitney Mus. Am. Art Annual, 1962, 63, 64, 65, 67, 73, Carnegie Internat., Pitts., 1964, 67, 70, Jewish Mus., N.Y.C., 1964, Corcoran Mus., Washington, 1964, Mitchell Algus Gallery, N.Y.C., 2002, 07, others; represented permanent collections, Walker Art Center, Mpls., Mus. Modern Art, Whitney Mus. Am. Art, (both N.Y.C.), Guggenheim Mus., N.Y.C., Albright-Knox Mus., Buffalo, NYU, Christian Theol. Sem., Indpls., Indpls. Mus. Art, Cleve. Mus. Art, Mus. Am. Art, Washington, Honolulu Acad. Art, Newark Mus. Art, Container Corp. Am., Chgo. Ind. U. Music Bldg., Wausau (Wis.) Hosp. Center, Unitarian Ch., Princeton, Mfr. Hanover Trust Bldg., Albert Kahn & Assos., Detroit, Renaissance Center, Detroit, Mich. State Univ. Performing Arts Ctr., East Lansing, Detroit Inst. Arts. Guggenheim fellow, 1965-66; Ford Found. grantee, 1966, Lee Krasner Found. grantee; One of five Am. artists selected for 1965 Japanese Bi-ann.; Sculpture grant Adolph Gottlieb Found.; recipient Gov. NJ's Purchase award 2d ann. exhbn. art, 1967, Krasner Found. award, 2003, Lifetime Achievement award; Best of Show Religion in Art Exhbn., Birmingham, Ala., 1966. Mem. Nat. Acad. of Design. Office Phone: 212-794-6551.

ORTNER, BONNIE, media specialist, librarian; b. Havre, Mont., Aug. 31, 1967; d. George and Linda Ortner; children: Shayna, Hiram Williams. EdM, U. Mont., Missoula. Cert. in spl. edn. endorsement Mont., in libr., K-12 endorsement Mont. 7th and 8th grade English tchr. Ft. Benton Pub. Schs., Mont., 2000—01, Huntley Project Schs., Worden, Mont., 2001—04, libr. media specialist, 2004—. V.p. Mont. Forensics Educators Assn., Mont., 2008—. Named Coach of Yr., Mont. Forensics Educators Assn., 2002.

ORTNER, CHARLES B., lawyer; b. Bklyn., Apr. 19, 1945; AB, Washington U., 1967; JD, Bklyn. Law Sch., 1971. Bar: NY 1972. Aide to mayor, NYC, 1970-71; legal asst. to US Atty. US Attys. Office (so. dist.), NY, 1971-72; ptnr. Paul, Hastings, Janofsky & Walker, NYC, Proskauer Rose LLP, NYC. Mem. panel arbitrators Am. Arbitration Assn. Mem. bd. editors: The Computer Lawyer, 1989-92, Entertainment Law and Finance, 1988-92. Named one of 100 Power Lawyers, Hollywood Reporter, 2007; named to Best Lawyers in America, 2005—08, NY Super Lawyers, 2006, 2007. Fellow Am. Bar Found.; mem. ABA (co-advisor to Nat. Conf. Commrs. on Uniform State Laws 1992, mem. coun. sect. sci. and tech. 1987, 1991-92, chmn. computer law divsn. 1988-92, chmn. contracting for computers com. 1981-89), N.Y. State Bar Assn. (chmn. trade secret com. intellectual property law sect. 1991-92, mem. action unit # 2 on reform of state legislature 1974-79), Assn. Bar City N.Y. (chmn. subcom. on pub. law 1975, mem. spl. com. computers and law 1980-83). Office: Proskauer Rose LLP 1585 Broadway New York NY 10036-8299

ORTNER, DONALD J., biological anthropologist, educator; b. Stoneham, Mass., Aug. 23, 1938; s. A. W. and Marie B. (Schweizer) Ortner; m. Joyce E. Walker, Sept. 4, 1960; children: Donald J. Jr., Allison A. May, Karen L. BA, Columbia Union Coll., 1960; MA, Syracuse U., 1967; PhD, U. Kans., 1970; DSc (hon.), U. Bradford, England, 1995. Asst. curator Smithsonian Instn., Washington, 1969-71, assoc. curator, 1971-76, curator, 1976—, chmn. anthropology, 1988-92; acting dir. Nat. Mus. Natural History, Washington, 1994-96. Vis. prof. U. Bradford, 1988—; pres. Paleopathology Assn., 1999—2001. Author: Identification of Pathological Conditions in Human Skeletal Remains, 1981, 2d edit., 2003; editor: How Humans Adapt, 1983; co-editor: Human Paleopathology, 1991; co-author: The Early Bronze Age I Tombs and Burials of Bab Edh-Dhra, Jordan, 2008; mem. editl. bd. Jour. Paleopathology, 1988—, Internat. Jour. Osteoarch, 1990—. Mem.: Paleopathology Assn., Internat. Skeletal Soc., Am. Assn. Phys. Anthropology (mem. exec. com. 1987—90). Office: Smithsonian Inst Nat Mus Natural History 10th & Constitution Ave NW Washington DC 20560-0112 Office Phone: 202-633-1979. Personal E-mail: ortnerdj@verizon.net. Business E-Mail: ortner@si.edu.

ORTNER, EVERETT HOWARD, magazine editor, writer; b. Lowell, Mass., Aug. 25, 1919; s. Herman and Anne (Ehrenhaus) O.; m. Evelyn Frances Gelbman, Jan. 1, 1953. BA, U. Ark., 1939. Editor Popular Publs., NYC, 1946-52; assoc. editor Popular Sci., NYC, 1953-56, copy chief, 1956-70, group editor, 1970-76, mng. editor, 1976-80, editor, 1980-85. Pres. Brownstone Revival Coalition N.Y., 1968-76, chmn., 1986-2002, chmn. emeritus, 2002; founder, pres. Back to the City, Inc., N.Y.C., 1974-83, chmn. bd., 1983—; v.p. L.I. Hist. Soc., Bklyn., 1979-83; chmn. bd Preservation Vols. Inc., 2000—. Lt. U.S. Army, 1942-46, ETO. Recipient Cinderella award Bklyn. Union Gas Co., 1978, Honor citation Borough Pres. Bklyn., 1983, Disting. Citizen award City Louisville, 1979, Quality of Life award Kings County Hosp. Ctr., Bklyn., 1976, Spirit of Life award N.Y. Congl. Home, 1994, Excellence in Hist. Preservation award Preservation League NY State, 2002, Grassroots Preservation award Hist. Dists. Coun., 2002, Lifetime Achievement award Victorian Soc. in Am., 2005, Disting. Alumni award U. Ark., 2006, Lucy G. Moses Preservation award N.Y. Landmarks Conservancy, 2006. Mem. Overseas Press Club, Montauk Club, Ft. Hamilton Officers Club. Home: 272 Berkeley Pl Brooklyn NY 11217-3904

ORTOLANO, RALPH J., engineering consultant; b. Phila., Apr. 12, 1931; BS in Marine Engring., U.S. Mcht. Marine Acad., 1954; MBA, Santa Clara U., 1969. Registered profl. engr., Calif. Engring. watch officer USN, 1954-56; sr. design engr. marine divsn. Westinghouse, Lester, Pa., 1956-64, Sunnyvale, Calif., 1964-69; mgr. project engring. corp. cost recovery dept. Litton Ship Systems, Inc., LA, 1969-72; consulting engr., scientist So. Calif. Edison Co., Rosemead, Calif., 1972-92, chief cons., 1993—. Formed Turbine RESCUE, 1984; cons. more than 100 power cos., numerous others, U.S. and abroad; presenter seminars in the field. Contbr. more than 100 articles to profl. jours.; holder 22 U.S. patents in field. Recipient William R. Gould award SCE, 1992, Meritorious Alumni Svc. award USMMAAA, 1989, Outstanding Profl. Achievement award USMMAAA, 1994; named to USMMA Athletic Hall of Fame, 1990; USMMA rifle range named Ortolano Rifle and Pistol Range in honor of being selected to 1952 and 1953 All-Am. Rifle Teams, and 1952-54 All-Am. Pistol Teams, 1999. Fellow ASME (life, past dir. ASME-SCAC power chpt., past chmn. steam turbine com., past chmn. power divsn., mem. exec. com., co-chmn. steam turbine course 1984-99, George Westinghouse Gold medal 1991, past chmn. EEI steam turbine crack prevention task force). E-mail: turbinerescue@hotmail.com.

ORTON, GEORGE FREDERICK, aerospace engineer; b. Flushing, NY, Aug. 8, 1941; s. Harry and Evelyn (Brostrom) O.; m. Susan K., Dec. 21, 1962; children: Karen, Kevin, Kristen. BS in Aero. Engring., U. Md., 1964; MS in Engring. Mechanics, St. Louis U., 1971. Engr. propulsion McDonnell Douglas Co. (now The Boeing Co.), St. Louis, 1964-73, sr. engr. propulsion, 1973-77, unit chief propulsion, 1977-81, sect. chief propulsion, 1981-86, br. chief nat. aerospace plane, 1986-90, staff dir. nat. aerospace plane, 1990-92, dir. space programs, 1992-93, program mgr. Hypersonics Ctr. Excellence, 1993—, mem. air force sci. adv. bd., 2000—02. Mem. adv. bd. Ga. Inst. Tech., 1998—; guest lectr. USAF Acad., 2000—. Contbr. articles to profl. jours. Advisor Explorer Post 9005, St. Louis, 1980-87; sci. advisor University City (Mo.) Schs. Recipient Silver award, Boeing, 2004, world speed record for X-43A; named to Acad. Disting. Alumni, U. Md., 2003. Fellow AIAA (assoc., mem. liquid propulsion tech. com. 1980-84, 91-96, mem. hypersonics program com. 1994—, Best Paper award 1986), St. Louis Head Injury Assn. Methodist. Achievements include patent for propellant acquisition device for zero-g engine starts, patent for propellant resupply system, NASA technology cash award for work on shuttle auxiliary propulsion. Office: The Boeing Co PO Box 516 Mailcode S 2454055 Saint Louis MO 63166-0516 E-mail: george.f.orton@boeing.com.

ORTON, KYLE, professional football player; b. Altoona, Iowa, Nov. 14, 1982; s. Byron. BA in History, Purdue U., 2005. Quarterback Chgo. Bears, 2005—09, Denver Broncos, 2009—. Recipient Big Ten Offensive Player Yr, Sporting News, 2004. Office: Denver Broncos 13655 Broncos Pky Englewood CO 80112 Office Fax: 847-295-6600.*

ORUC, YAVUZ A., engineering educator, researcher; b. Amasya, Turkey, Apr. 21, 1953; s. Tomris and Ismail Oruc. PhD, Syracuse U., NY, 1983. Asst. prof. Rensselaer Poly. Inst., Troy, NY, 1983—87; prof. rschr. U. Md., College Park, 1988—; vis. prof. Bilkent U., Ankara, Turkey, 1996—97. Program dir. NSF, Arlington, Va., 2000—02; advisor to pres. Sci. and Technol. Rsch. Coun. of Turkey, Ankara, Turkey. Contbr. scientific papers to profl. jours. Achievements include invention and implementation of codemill programming language and technology; invented a method to perform algebraic operations on a permutation network. Business E-Mail: yavuz@eng.umd.edu.

ORULLIAN, B. LARAE, retired bank executive; b. Salt Lake City, May 15, 1933; d. Alma and Bessie (Bacon) O. Cert., Am. Inst. Banking, 1961, 63, 67; grad. Nat. Mortgage Sch., Ohio State U., 1969-71; DHL (hon.), Whittier Coll., Calif., 2004. With Tracy Collins Trust Co., Salt Lake City, 1951-54, Union Nat. Bank, Denver, 1954-57; exec. sec. Guaranty Bank, Denver, 1957-64, asst. cashier, 1964-67, asst. v.p., 1967-70, v.p., 1970-75, exec. v.p., 1975-77, also bd. dirs.; chair, CEO, pres. The Women's Bank N.A., Denver, 1977-97, Colo. Bus. Bankshares, Inc., 1980-97; pres. Guaranty Corp., Denver, 1998—2007, vice chair; ret. Pres., bd. dirs. Lange Golf Co.; chmn. bd. dirs. Frontier Airlines; bd. dirs. KBDI Channel 12TV; trustee Delta Dental Colo., 2005—, Women's Found. Colo.; vice-chair Fronteer Holdings Inc. Treas. Girl Scouts U.S., 1981-87, 1st nat. v.p., chair exec. com., 1987-90, nat. pres., 1990-96; 1st vice chair world bd. World Assn. Girl Guides Girl Scouts, London. Recipient Woman Who Made a Difference award Internat. Women's Forum, 1994, Ultimate Woman of Colo. award, 2005, Women Enterprise award U. Denver, 2005; named to Colo. Women Hall of Fame, 1988; named Colo. Entrepreneur of Yr., Inc. Mag. and Arthur Young and Co., 1989, Woman of Yr., YWCA, 1989, Citizen of Yr., EMC Lions Club, 1995, laureate Colo. Bus. Hall of Fame, 1999. Mem. Bus. and Profl. Women Colo. (3d Century award 1977, Unique Woman of Colo. 2005, Colo. Woman of Enterprise 2005), Internat. Women's Forum, Com. of 200. Independent. Mem. Lds Ch. Home: 6650 W 10th Pl Lakewood CO 80214

ORWIG, MATTHEW DANE, lawyer, former prosecutor; b. Ardmore, Okla., Jan. 2, 1959; s. Richard R. and Mary E. (Pyle) O.; m. Melissa L. Vaughan, July 11, 1981; children: Joshua Matthew, Rachel Elizabeth, Jacob Andrew. BS, Tex. Tech. U., 1981, JD, 1984. Bar: Tex. 1985, US Dist. Ct. (no. dist.) Tex. 1985, US Ct. Appeals (5th cir.) 1985. Legal intern for no. dist. Tex. US Dept. Justice, Dallas, 1983; briefing atty. for judge US Dist. Ct., Lubbock, Tex., 1984-86; ptnr. Jones, Flygare, Galey, Moody and Brown, Lubbock, Tex., 1986-89; asst. US atty. (ea. dist.) Tex. US Dept. Justice, Dallas, 1989—2001, US atty., 2001—07; mng. ptnr., nat. chair govt. litig. & investigations group Sonnenschein Nath & Rosenthal LLP, Dallas, 2007—. Adj. prof. So. Meth. U. Law Sch, 1990—, Tex. Wesleyan U. Sch. Law, 1990—; legal advisor Exec. Office of U.S. Atty., Office of Legal Counsel, 1997—. Mem. ABA, State Bar Tex., Lubbock County Bar Assn., Lubbock County Young Lawyers Assn. (bd. dirs. 1987-89), Tex. Trial Lawyers Assn. Methodist. Office: Sonnenschein Nath & Rosenthal LLP 1717 Main St 34th Fl Dallas TX 75201 Office Phone: 214-259-0990. Business E-Mail: morwig@sonnenschein.com.

ORWOLL, CHRISTOPHER D., museum administrator, military officer; BS, US Navel Acad.; MA in Strategic Studies, Air War Coll.; MS in Engring. Mgmt., Cornell U. Divsn. officer, tactical sys. officer USS Ohio, 1988—91; navel sci. instr. Navel Reserve Officers Training Corps Unit, Cornell U., 1991—93; ops. officer USS Tucson, 1994—97; spl. projects officer, staff comdr. US Navel Forces, Europe, London, 1997—2000; exec. officer USS Dolphin, 2000—02; commdg. officer Navel Reserve Officer Training Coprs, U. Kansas, 2003—06; pres., CEO Kans. Cosmosphere and Space Ctr., Hutchinson, Kans., 2007—. Office: Kans Cosmosphere and Space Ctr 1100 N Plum Hutchinson KS 67501 Office Phone: 620-662-2305. E-mail: chriso@cosmo.org.

ORWOLL, GREGG S.K., lawyer; b. Austin, Minn., Mar. 23, 1926; s. Gilbert M. and Kleonora (Kleven) O.; m. Laverne M. Flentie, Sept. 15, 1951; children: Kimball G., Kent A., Vikki A., Tristen A., Erik G. BS, Northwestern U., Evanston, Ill., 1950; JD, U. Minn., Mpls., 1953. Bar: Minn. 1953, US Supreme Ct. 1973. Assoc. Dorsey & Whitney, Mpls., 1953-59, ptnr., 1959-60; assoc. counsel Mayo Clinic, Rochester, Minn., 1960-63, gen. counsel, 1963-87, sr. legal counsel, 1987-91, sr. counsel, 1991-92. Gen. counsel, dir. Rochester Airport Co., 1962-84, v.p., 1981-84; gen. counsel Mayo Med. Svcs., Ltd., 1972-90; bd. dirs., sec. and gen. counsel Mayo Found. for Med. Edn. and Rsch., 1984-90; gen. counsel Mid-Am. Orthop. Assn., 1983-2009, Minn. Orthop. Soc., 1985-95; counsel Norwegian Am. Orthopaedic Soc., 1999—, Intl. Soc. of Amyloidosis 2002—; asst. sec./sec. Mayo Found., Rochester, 1972-91; sec. Mayo Emeritus Staff, 1998-99, vice chair, 1999-2000, chair, 2000-2001; bd. dirs. Charter House, 1986-90; dir., officer Travelure Motel Corp., 1968-86; dir., v.p. Echo Too Ent., Inc.; dir., v.p. Oberhamer Inc., 1989-99; bd. dirs. Am. Decal and Mfg. Co., 1989-93, sec., 1992-93; adj. prof. William Mitchell Coll. Law, 1978-84. Contbr. articles to profl. jours., chpts. to books; mem. editl. bd. Minn. Law Rev., 1952-53, HealthSpan, 1984-93 Trustee Minn. Coun. on Founds., 1977-82, Mayo Found., 1982-86; trustee William Mitchell Coll. Law, 1982-88, 89-98, mem. exec. com. 1990-98; bd. visitors U. Minn. Law Sch., 1974-76, 85-91; mem. U. Minn. Regent Candidate Adv. Coun., 1988-99, Minn. State Compensation Coun., 1991-97. With USAF, 1944-45. Recipient Outstanding Svc. medal, US Govt., 1991. Mem. ABA, AMA (affiliate), Am. Corp. Counsel Assn., Minn. Soc. Hosp. Attys. (bd. dirs. 1981-86), Minn. State Bar Assn. (chmn. legal/med. com. 1977-81), Olmsted County Bar Assn. (v.p., pres. 1977-79), Rochester C. of C., U. Minn. Law Alumni Assn. (bd. dirs. 1973-76, 85-91), Rochester U. Club (pres. 1977), The Doctors Mayo Soc., Mid Am. Orthop. Assn. (hon.), Mayo Alumni Assn. (hon.), Phi Delta Phi, Phi Delta Theta. Republican. Home: 2233 5th Ave NE Rochester MN 55906-4017 Office: Mayo Clinic 200 1st St SW Rochester MN 55905-0002 Home Phone: 507-282-4880; Office Phone: 507-284-2691.

ORY, MARCIA GAIL, social science researcher; b. Dallas, Feb. 8, 1950; d. Marvin Gilbert and Esther (Levine) O.; m. Raymond James Carroll, Aug. 13, 1972. BA magna cum laude, U. Tex., 1971; MA, Ind. U., 1972; PhD, Purdue U., 1976; MPH, Johns Hopkins U., 1981. Rsch. asst. prof. U. N.C., Chapel Hill, 1976-77, from adj. asst. prof. to assoc. prof. sch. pub. health, 1978-88; rsch. fellow U. Minn., Mpls., 1977-78; asst. prof. Sch. Pub. Health U. Ala., Birmingham, 1978-80; program dir. biosocial aging and health Nat. Inst. on Aging, Bethesda, Md., 1981-86, chief social sci. rsch. on aging, 1987—2001; prof. Sch. Rural Pub. Health Tex A&M U. Sys., College Station, 2001—, regent prof., 2007—. Dir. RWJF Nat. Program Office on Increasing Phys. Activity in the 50 Plus, 2001—, Program on Health Promotion and Aging. Contbr. articles, editor vols. to profl. jours. Mem. several nat. task forces on aging and health issues; leadership coun., Healthy Aging Rsch. Collaborative, Health Found. South Fla.; bd. dirs. Ctr. for Health Improvement. Recipient Dept. HHS award, 1984, 1985, 1988, Dir.'s award, NIH, 1995, Merit award, 1999, 2001, Dir's Lifetime Achievement award, 2000, Polisher award, Gerontol. Soc. Am., 2001, Excellence in Program Innovation award, Archstone Found., 2005, Excellence in Rsch. award, Sch. Rural Pub. Health, 2005—06, Disting. Mentor award, Gerontological Soc. Am., 2007, Betty J. Cleckley Excellence in Minority Health and Ageing Hon. Mention award, 2007, Highest Cited Paper; named Disting. Alumna, Purdue U.; named one of 5 Industry Innovators in Active Aging, Internat. Coun. on Active Aging, 2003; named to McKnights Long Term Care News 100, 1997; fellow, Inst. for Advanced Study, LATrobe U.,vMelbourne, Australia, 2004. Fellow: Soc. Behavioral Medicine (program chmn. pub. health track 1988—89, program com. 1991—92, program chair lifespan/devel. track 2001—02), Acad. for Behavioral Medicine Rsch., Gerontol. Soc. Am.; mem.: APHA (program chmn. 1986, gov. coun. 1986—88, chmn.-elect 1989—91, chmn. 1992—93, leadership group 1996—, chair older women's interest group), Am. Acad. Health Behavior, Am. Sociol. Assn. (regional reporter 1984—94, program com. 1986, nominations com. 1987, councilor-at-large 1992—93), Delta Omega, Omicron Nu, Phi Kappa Phi. Avocations: walking, birding, travel. Office: Sch Rural Pub Health 1266 TAMU College Station TX 77843-1266 Office Phone: 979-458-1373.

ORY, STEVEN JAY, physician, educator; b. Houston, Aug. 4, 1950; s. Edwin Marvin and Norma Gertrude O.; m. Kathleen Higgins, Jan. 10, 1981; children: Eleanor Claire, Edward Michael. BA, Washington and Lee U., 1972; MD, Baylor Coll., 1976. Diplomate Am. Bd. Obstetrics and Gynecology, subsplty. cert. in Reproductive Endocrinolgy and Infertility. Asst. prof. Duke U., Durham, NC, 1981-82, Northwestern U., Chgo., 1982-85; assoc. prof., cons. Mayo Clinic, Rochester, Minn., 1985-95, chmn. sect. reproductive endocrinology and infertility, 1985-95; pvt. practice reproductive endocrinology and infertility; mem. ob-gyn. staff Internat. U., Margate, Fla., 1995—; prof. ob-gyn. Fla. Internat. U., Miami, 2008—; vol. assoc. prof. obstets. and gyn. U. Miami, Fla., 1999—. Assoc. dir. Am. Soc. Reproductive Medicine, Birmingham, Ala., 1986-87; bd. trustees Northwest Med. Ctr., Margate, Fla., 2003—, chair 2009. Asst. editor: Fertility and Sterility, 1988-96, assoc. editor, 2009-; contbr. articles to profl. jours. Mem.: Ft. Lauderdale Ob-Gyn. Soc. (pres. 1998—2000), Soc. Reproductive Endocrinologists (sec.-treas., pres. 2001—02), Am. Soc. Reproductive Medicine (chmn. practice com. 1998—2000, bd. dirs. 1999—2002, v.p. 2004—05, pres.-elect 2005—06, pres. 2006—07, past pres. 2008—09), Soc. for Humanism in Medicine (bd. dirs. 1999—2002, v.p. 2004—05, pres.-elect 2005—06, pres. 2006—07). Office Phone: 954-247-6200.

OSAKWE, CHRISTOPHER, lawyer, educator; b. Lagos, Nigeria, May 8, 1942; arrived in U.S., 1970, naturalized, 1979; s. Simon and Hannah (Morgan) Osakwe; m. Maria Elena Amador, Aug. 19, 1982; 1 child, Rebecca E. LLB, Moscow State U., Lomonosov, 1967; PhD, Moscow State U., 1970; JSD, U. Ill., 1974. Bar: Moscow 1967, Kazakhstan 1997. Prof. sch. law Tulane U., New Orleans, 1972-81, 86-88; Eason-Weinmann prof. comparative law, dir. Tulane U., Eason-Weinmann Ctr. Comparative Law, New Orleans, 1981-86; ptnr. Riddle and Brown, New Orleans, 1989—. Vis. prof. U. Pa., 1978, U. Mich., 1981, Washington and Lee U., 1986, Lomonosov Moscow State U., 1999—2008; vis. fellow St. Anthony's Coll. Oxford (Eng.) U., 1980, vis. fellow Christ Ch. Coll., 1988—89; cons. U.S. Dept. Commerce, 1980—85. Author: The Participation of the Soviet Union in Universal International Organizations, 1972, The Foundations of Soviet Law, 1981, Joint Ventures with the Soviet Union: Law and Practice, 1990, Soviet Business Law, 2 vols., 1991, The Russian Civil Code Annotated: Translation and Commentary, 2000, Comparative Law in Diagrams: General and Special Parts, 2000, 2d edit., 2002, Comparative Law: Diagrammatic Commentary, 2008, Russian Civil Code: Text and Analysis, 2008; author: (with others) Comparative Legal Traditions in a Nutshell, 1982, Comparative Legal Traditions - Text, Materials and Cases, 1985, 2d edit., 1994; editor: Am. Jour. Comparative Law, 1978—86, Jour. Fgn. Legis. and Comparative Law, 2006—; mem. editl. bd.: Am. Jour. Legal Edn., 1983—85. Carnegie fellow, Hague Acad. Internat. Law, 1969, Russian Rsch. fellow, Harvard U., 1972, USSR Sr. Rsch. Exch. fellow, 1982, Rsch. fellow, Kennan Inst. Advanced Russian Studies, 1988. Mem.: ABA, Soc. de Legis. Comparée, Supreme Ct. Hist. Soc., Am. Soc. Internat. Law, Am. Law Inst., Order of Coif. Republican. Roman Catholic. Home: 339 Audubon Blvd New Orleans LA 70125-4124 Office: 201 S Charles Ave Ste 3100 New Orleans LA 70170 Office Phone: 504-861-1272. Personal E-mail: osakwec@aol.com.

OSAROGIAGBON, RAY UYIOSA, oncologist, educator; b. Benin, Edo, Nigeria, May 11, 1967; s. Gabriel Ehigiamusoe and Christiana Edoghaye Osarogiagbon; m. Hilda Eteh Lori-Skinn, Dec. 27, 1994; children: Taylor Ophelia, Iyare Louis, Ifueko Nadine, Osagie Miles. MBBS, U. Ibadan, Nigeria, 1988. Diplomate in internal medicine Am. Bd. Internal Medicine, 1995, in hematology and med. oncology 1999. Chief in-medicine Amarillo VA Med. Ctr., Tex., 2002—05; asst. prof. U. Tenn., 2005—, dir., multidiscplinary thoracic oncology programm and adult sickle cell disease program, Cancer Inst., 2006—, hematology-med. oncology fellowship program dir., 2008—. Contbr. scientific papers to med. jours. Mem. bd. dirs. Germantown Arts Alliance, Tenn., 2008, Tenn. Shakespeare Co., Memphis, 2008. Recipient Cert. of Commendation, Nat. Youth Svc. Corps. Nigeria, 1990, Louis Evans Bruce award, Tex. Tech. U., 2004, Memphis Mag. Best Dr. award, 2008; named Outstanding Resident of Yr., Tex. Tech. U. Health Scis. Ctr., 1995. Mem.: Alpha Omega Alpha Honor Med. Soc. Anglican. Avocations: literature, art, music. Office: Univ Tenn Cancer Inst 1331 Union Ave Memphis TN 38104 Office Fax: 901-722-0542. Business E-Mail: rosarogi@utmem.edu.

OSBALDESTON, GORDON FRANCIS, finance educator, retired federal agency administrator; b. Hamilton, Ont., Can., Apr. 29, 1930; s. John Edward and Margaret (Hanley) O.; m. Geraldine Keller, Oct. 3, 1953; children: Stephen, David, Robert, Catherine B.Commerce, U. Toronto, Ont., Can., 1952; MBA, U. Western Ont., London, 1953, LL.D., 1984, York U., Toronto, 1984, Dalhousie U., Halifax, NS, 1985, Carleton U., Ottawa, Ont., Can., 1987. Fgn. service officer Dept. Trade and Commerce, Ottawa, 1953-54, vice consul, asst. trade commr. Sao Paula, Brazil, 1954-57, Chgo., 1957-60, consul, trade commr. Los Angeles, 1960-64, asst. dir., personnel trade commr. service Ottawa, 1964-66, asst. dir. ops. trade commr. service, 1966-67, exec. dir. trade commr. service, 1967-68; asst. dep. minister Dept. Consumer and Corp. Affairs, Ottawa, 1968-70, dep. minister, 1972-73; dep. sec. Treasury Bd. Secretariat, Ottawa, 1970-72, sec., 1973-76; dep. minister Dept. Industry, Trade and Commerce, Ottawa, 1976-78; sec. Ministry of State for Econ. Devel., Ottawa, 1978-82; undersec. of state Dept. External Affairs, Ottawa, 1982; clk. privy council, sec. to cabinet Privy Council Office, Ottawa, 1982-86; mem. Queen's Privy Coun. for Can., 1986; prof. emeritus Western Bus. Sch. U. Western Ont., 1986—. Mem. Robarts Rsch. Coun., 2004. Author: Keeping Deputy Ministers Accountable, 1989, Organizing to Govern, 1990. Decorated officer Order of Can., companion, 1997; recipient Outstanding Achievment award Can. Govt., 1981, Vanier medal Inst. Pub. Adminstrn., 1990. Mem. London Hunt and Country Club, Psi Upsilon Roman Catholic. Avocations: stamp collecting/philately, golf. Home: 1353 Corley Dr N London ON Canada N6G 4L4 Personal E-mail: gordon5304@aol.com.

OSBERG, GREGORY JOHN, mobile video company executive, former publishing executive; b. Jamestown, NY, June 12, 1957; s. John Raymond and Nancy (Jones) Osberg; m. Linda Burton, Aug. 22, 1981; children: Eric Burton, Alexander Gregory. BS in Mktg., Colo. State U., 1979. Regional mgr. Chilton Pub., Radnor, Pa., 1979-81; account mgr. US News & World Report, NYC, 1981-84, v.p. advt. sales, 1985-90; account mgr. Fortune, NYC, 1984-85; assoc. advt. dir. Newsweek, 1990—94, v.p., assoc. pub., 1994—97; pres. sales and mktg. CNET, Inc., 1997—99; pres. BrassRing, Inc., 1999—2000; exec. v.p. Newsweek, 2000—07, worldwide pub., 2000—07, pres., COO, 2007—08; CEO Buzzwire, Inc., Denver, 2008—. Chmn. Careers in Comm., Pitts., 1980—81; bd. dirs. Internat Advt. Bur. Mem. global leadership coun. Colo. State U. Coll. Bus. Mem.: Mag. Publishers America, Advt. Club NY, Bedens Brook Club. Avocations: golf, tennis, squash, jogging, skiing. Office: Buzzwire Inc 1123 Auraria Pkwy Denver CO 80204*

OSBEY, BRENDA MARIE, literature and language professor; d. Lawrence C. Osbey and Lois Emelda Hamilton; life ptnr. James B. Borders IV. MA, U. Ky., Lexington, 1980; LittD (hon.), Dickinson Coll., Carlisle, Pa. Author: (book) All Saints: New and Selected Poems. Recipient Loring-Williams prize, Acad. Am. Poets, 1980, ICA Internat. Comm. Agy. Rsch. award, Dillard U., 1980, Poetry award, Associated Writers & Writing Programs, 1984, Am. Book award, Columbus Found., 1998, Poet Laureate, State La., 2005—07, award, La. Writers Found., 2006, La. Bd. Regents, 2008—, Atlas award, 2008; Bernadine Scherman fellowship, MacDowell Colony, 1984, Bunting fellowship, Bunting Inst. Radcliffe Coll., Harvard U., 1985—86, Writing fellowship, Ky. Found. Women, 1986—87, Millay Colony Arts, 1987, Va. Ctr. Creative Arts, 1987, Fine Arts Work Ctr. Provincetown, 1987—88, Creative Writing fellowship, Nat. Endowment Arts, 1990, La. Divsn. Arts, 1994, Maxi grant, New Orleans Jazz & Heritage Found., 1993, fellowship, Camargo Found., 2004, Manship Summer fellowship, La. State U., 2008. Mem.: Am. Acad. Poets.

OSBORN, DONALD ROBERT, lawyer; b. NYC, Oct. 9, 1929; s. Robert W. and Ruth C. (Compton) Osborn; m. Marcia Lontz, June 4, 1955 (div.); children: David, Judith, Robert; m. Marie A. Johnson, Sept. 11, 1986. BA, Cornell U., 1951; LLB, Columbia U., 1957. Bar: NY 1957, US Tax Ct. 1958, US Ct. Claims 1961, US Ct. Appeals (2d cir.) 1974, US Ct. Appeals (8th cir.) 1974, US Dist. Ct. (so. and ea. dists.) NY 1975, US Supreme Ct. 1975. Assoc. Sullivan & Cromwell LLP, NYC, 1957—64, ptnr., 1964—96, sr. counsel, 1997—. Mem. coun. White Burkett Miller Ctr. Pub. Affairs, 1976—82; bd. dirs., pres. Stevens Kingsley Found., 1967—2005; sec., treas. Dunlevy Milbank Found., 1974—2009; bd. dirs. Spanel Found., 1978—88; trustee Hamilton Coll., 1978—88, Mus. Broadcasting, 1975—80; trustee, treas. Kirkland Coll., 1969—78. With USN, 1951—54. Mem.: ABA, NY State Bar Assn., Assn. Bar City of NY, Am. Bar Found., India House, Regency Whist Club, Country Club of the Rockies. Presbyterian. Home: 1049 Park Ave New York NY 10028-1061 Office: Sullivan & Cromwell LLP 125 Broad St Fl 32 New York NY 10004-2498 Office Phone: 212-558-3724. Personal E-mail: dromao@aol.com.

OSBORN, HOWARD A., retired mathematics professor; s. Harry Willman and Florence Dickson Osborn; m. Jean E. Henderson, Mar. 24, 1951; children: Mark, Stephen, Adrienne, Emily. PhD, Stanford U., Palo Alto, Calif., 1955. Instr. U. Calif., Berkeley, 1954—56; prof. dept. math. U. Ill., Urbana, 1956—93. Cons. Rand Corp., Santa Monica, Calif., 1956—63. Contbr. scientific papers to numerous profl. jours. Musician Champaign-Urbana Symphony, 1960—2007. Mem.: Am. Math. Soc. Liberal. Achievements include research in differential geometry. Avocation: violin. Office: Univ Ill Dept Math 273 Altgeld Hall MC 382 Urbana IL 61801

OSBORN, JOHN EDWARD, lawyer, pharmaceutical industry executive, government official; b. Davenport, Iowa, Sept. 4, 1957; s. Edward Richard and Patricia Anne (O'Donovan) O.; m. Deborah Lynn Powell, Aug. 11, 1984; children: Delaney Powell, Keeley Rush. Student, Coll. William and Mary, 1975—76; BA, U. Iowa, 1979; JD, U. Va., 1983; MIPP, Johns Hopkins U., 1992; postgrad., Princeton U., 1997—99. Bar: Mass. 1985, U.S. Supreme Ct. 2001. Staff US Rep. Jim Leach, 1978, Congl. Budget Office, 1979—80, US Senator John Heinz, 1981; law clk. to Hon. Albert V. Bryan US Ct. Appeals (4th cir.), Alexandria, Va., 1983-84; assoc. McDermott, Will & Emery, Chgo., Washington, 1981, Sidley & Austin, Chgo., 1982, Hale and Dorr, Boston, Washington, 1983—88, Dechert Price & Rhoads, Phila., 1988-89; spl. asst. to legal adviser US Dept. State, Washington, 1989-92; sr. counsel DuPont Merck Pharm. Co., Wilmington, Del., 1992-94, assoc. gen. counsel, 1994-96, v.p., assoc. gen. counsel, asst. sec., 1996—97; v.p. legal affairs Cephalon, Inc., Frazer and West Chester, Pa., 1997—98, sr. v.p., 1998—2005, gen. counsel, 1998—2008, sec., 1998—2008, exec. v.p., 2006—08; advisor McKinsey & Co., NY, 2007—08. Mem. Northern Ireland Adv. Group, US Dept. State, Washington, 2005—08, US Adv. Commn. Pub. Diplomacy, Washington, 2008—; vis. scholar East European studies Woodrow Wilson Internat. Ctr. for Scholars, Washington, 1991; vis. lectr. Ross Sch. Bus. U. Mich., 1997—; vis. lectr. U. Pa. Law Sch., 2004—07; vis. fellow politics, rsch. collaborator Princeton U., 2002—08; vis. rsch. fellow Ctr. Socio Legal Studies U. Oxford, 2008—; sr. mem. Wadham Coll., Oxford. Contbr. articles to numerous profl. jours. and newspapers; articles editor Va. Jour. Internat. Law, 1982—83. Trustee Siasconset Beach Preservation Fund, 2004—, Tower Hill Sch., Wilmington, Del., 1997—2009, Del. Art Mus., 1999—2006; bd. govs. East-West Ctr., Honolulu, 2004—07; del. Rep. Nat. Conv., San Diego, 1996; rsch. aide, speechwriter George Bush for Pres. Com., 1980, 1988. Recipient Lawdragon 500 Leading Lawyers in Am., 2007; Eisenhower fellow, Ireland and No. Ireland, 1998, Alumni fellow, U. Iowa Coll. Liberal Arts and Sci., 2008. Fellow Am. Law Inst.; mem. Am. Bar Found., Atlantic Coun. US, Brookings Coun., Coun. Fgn. Rels., Oxford and Cambridge Club, Princeton Club NY, Congl. Country Club, Cosmos Club, Met. Club Washington, Sankaty Head Golf and Beach Club, Siasconset Casino Assn., Bidermann Golf Club, Vicmead Hunt Club, Raven Soc., Mortar Bd., Phi Beta Kappa, Phi Delta Phi, Omicron Delta Kappa, Omicron Delta Epsilon. Republican. Roman Catholic. Avocations: golf, tennis, skiing.

OSBORN, JOHN ROBERT, retired engineering educator; b. Kansas City, Mo., Aug. 11, 1924; married, 1945; 3 children. BS, Purdue U., 1950, MS, 1953, PhD in Mech. Engring., 1957. Jr. engr. Thiokol Chem. Corp., 1950-51; asst. Purdue U., West Lafayette, Ind., 1951-57, from asst. prof. to assoc. prof. mechanical engring., 1957-61, prof., 1961-70, 71-79, prof. aero. astronautical engring., 1980—89, prof. emeritus aero. astronautical engring., 1989—2006; br. chief Ballistics Rsch. Lab. Aberdeen Proving Ground, 1970-71. Mem.: AIAA (assoc. fellow, Wyld Propulsion award 1995), Soc. Automotive Engrs. Achievements include research in combustion instability in rockets; high frequency response instrumentation; combustion in solid rockets and interior ballistics. Home: 40 Stayman Ct Lafayette IN 47905-4446 E-mail: josborn@purdue.edu.

OSBORN, JOHN SIMCOE, JR., lawyer; b. Louisville, Jan. 14, 1926; s. John S. and Ruby (Pinnell) O.; m. Mary Jo Fishback, Sept. 6, 1947; children— Robert, John, Donna LLB, U. Louisville, 1949. Bar: Ky. 1949, U.S. Dist. Ut. (ea. and we. dists.) Ky. 1952. Exec. v.p., gen. counsel Louisville Title Ins. Co., 1954-72; ptnr. Tarrant Combs & Bullitt (name changed to Wyatt Tarrant & Combs 1980), Louisville, 1972—. Chmn. bd. Beargrass Corp. Capt. JAGC, U.S. Army, 1952-54. Fellow Am. Bar Found.; mem. Ky. Bar Assn., Louisville Bar Assn., ABA, Am. Land Title Assn., Am. Coll. Real Estate Lawyers, Rotary. Democrat. Lutheran. Office: Wyatt Tarrant & Combs 2800 Citizens Plz Louisville KY 40202 Office Phone: 502-562-7584, 502-589-5235. Business E-Mail: josborn@wyattfirm.com.

OSBORN, JUNE ELAINE, pediatrician, microbiologist, educator, foundation administrator; b. Endicott, NY, May 28, 1937; d. Leslie A. and Dora W. (Wright) Osborn; children: Philip I. Levy, Ellen D. Levy, Laura A. Jana. BA, Oberlin Coll., Ohio, 1957; MD, Western Res. U., 1961; DSc (hon.), U. Med. Dental Sch. N.J., 1990, Emory U., 1993, Oberlin Coll., 1993, Rutgers U., 1994, Case Western Res. U., 1997, SUNY, Stony Brook, 1999, U. Wis., 2004; DMS (hon.), Yale U., 1992; LHD (hon.), Med. Coll. Pa., 1994. Intern, resident in pediatrics Harvard U. Hosp., 1961—64; fellow Johns Hopkins, 1964—65, U. Pitts., 1965—66; prof. med. microbiology and pediat. U. Wis. Med. Sch., Madison, Wis., 1966—84, prof. pediat. and microbiology, 1974—84, assoc. dean Grad. Sch., 1975—84; dean Sch. Pub. Health U. Mich. Sch. Pub. Health, 1984—93; prof. epidemiology, pediat. and communicable diseases U. Mich. Sch. Pub. Health and Med. Sch., 1984—96, prof. emeritus, 2008—. Pres. Josiah Macy, Jr. Found., 1997—2007; pres. emeritus; mem. rev. panel viral vaccine efficacy FDA, 1973—79, mem. vaccines and related biol. products adv. com., 1981—85; mem. exptl. virology study sect. Divsn. Rsch. Grants, NIH, 1975—79; mem. med. affairs com. Yale U. Coun., 1981—86; chmn. life scis. associateships rev. panel NRC, 1981—84; mem. U.S. Army Med. R&D Adv. Com., 1983—85; chmn. working group on AIDS and the Nation's Blood Supply NHLBI, 1984—89; chmn. WHO Planning Group on AIDS and the Internat. Blood Supply, 1985—86. Contbr. articles to profl. jours.; mem. editl. bd.: Jour. AMA, 2002—. Active task force in AIDS, Inst. of Medicine, 1986; adv. com. Robert Wood Johnson Found. AIDS Health Svcs. Program, 1986—91; nat. adv. com. on health of pub. program Pew and Rockefeller Founds.; active Global Commn. on AIDS, WHO, 1988—92; chmn. Nat. Commn. on AIDS, 1989—93; trustee Kaiser Found., 1990—98, Case Western Reserve U., Cleve., 1993—97; nat. vaccine adv. com. HHS, 1995—98; adv. coun. Nat. Inst. on Drug Abuse, 1995—98; internat adv. bd. Nat. Acads., 2002—05; bd. dirs. Legal Action Ctr., 1994—2001, Ctr. for Health Care Strategies, 1998—2003, The Mind Inst., 2003—05, US Pharmacopeia Bd., 2005—. Recipient NIH Pub. Svc. award, 2000, Scientific Freedom and Responsibility award, AAAS, 1994, Lifetime Achievement award; grantee NIH, 1969, 1972, 1974—75, Nat. Multiple Sclerosis Soc., 1971, Nat. Med. fellowship, 2008. Fellow: Infectious Diseases Soc. Am., Am. Acad. Microbiology, Am. Acad. Arts and Scis., Am. Acad. Pediat.; mem.: Inst. Medicine (health promotion and disease prevention bd. 1987—90, coun. mem. 1995—2000), Soc. Pediat. Rsch., Am. Assn. Immunologists. Personal E-mail: jeosborn@aol.com.

OSBORN, KENNETH LOUIS, financial executive; b. Belleville, Ill., Jan. 9, 1946; s. William Arthur and Louise Mary (Brueggemann) Osborn; m. Roberta Marie Vodicka, Oct. 23, 1971; 1 child, David Anthony. BBA, U. N. Mex., 1968. Auditor Ernst & Ernst, Albuquerque, 1968; budget mgr. Rockwell Internat., Chgo, 1970—74; mgr. internat. acctg. Allied Van Lines, 1974—76; fin. mgr. Sealy, Inc., 1976—79; sr. fin. analyst Newark Electronics, 1979—80, internat. dir. credit, 1980—82; bus. mgr. Prime Computer, Ill., 1982—90; acctg. mgr. and CFO Flexonics, Inc., 1990—96; contr. and CFO Jackson Industries, Ill., 1996—. Fin. cons. Am. European Express. Rep. Nat. Com.; presdl. task force. With US Army, 1968—70. Decorated Air medal. Mem.: Inst. Mgmt. Accts., Soc. Am. Baseball Rsch., Mensa Soc.

OSBORN, LA DONNA CAROL, clergywoman; b. Portland, Oreg., Mar. 13, 1947; d. T.L. and Daisy (Washburn) O.; m. Cory A. Nickerson, Dec. 11, 1981; children: Tommy O'Dell, LaVona Thomas, Daneesa O'Dell, Donald O'Dell. Student, Assemblies of God Coll., 1963; BA, Okla. City U., 1994; DD, Bethel Coll., 1995; Doctor of Humane Letters (hon.), Wesley Synod, 1998; MA, Oral Roberts U., 2000; D in Ministry, Am. Christian Coll. and Sem., 2001; DD, Zoe Univ., 2001. Fgn. mission corr., purchaser, personnel agt. Osborn Found., Tulsa, 1969-75, exec. asst., 1975-76, internat. gen. mgr., 1976-81, internat. editor-in-chief, 1981-86, corp. pres., 1986-93; assoc. pastor Internat. Gospel Ctr., Tulsa, 1986-89, sr. pastor, 1989-94, sr. pastor, overseer, 1994-97; founder, presiding bishop Internat. Gospel Fellowship, Tulsa, Okla., 1997—; v.p., CEO OSBORN Ministries, 1998—2009, pres., 2009—; founder, pres. Women Internat. Network, 2003—. Internat. minister, religious tchr., and motivational spkr. Nigeria, Kenya, Uganda, Colombia, Papua New Guinea, France, Russia, Belarus, Kazakhstan, Kyrgyzstan, Ukraine, Russia, Sweden, Eng., Brazil, Holland, Can., India, Zambia, Ecuador, China, Brazil, Mizoram, Guatemala, Mexico, Canada, Myanmar, Indonesia, Angola, Congo, US; internat. spiritual advisor Christian Women's Fellowship Internat. Nigeria; founder Believers' Network Internat. Author: Jesus & Women, 2000, God's Big Picture, 2001, Cross-Cultural Communication in a Multicultural Church, 2002, New Miracle Life Now, 2004, Peace is a Lifestyle, 2005; author: (and editor) Bible tng. courses. Independent. Home: 3111 E 89th St Tulsa OK 74137-3362 Home Phone: 918-299-8045; Office Phone: 918-743-6231. Personal E-mail: drladonna@osborn.org.

OSBORN, LUCY MORIN, pediatrician, educator; b. Kansas City, Mo., 1946; MD, Northwestern U., Evanston, Ill., 1972. Cert. in pediat. Am. Bd. Med. Specialties, in pub. health & gen. preventive medicine Am. Bd. Med. Specialties, 1984. Intern in pediat. U. Wash., Seattle, 1972—73, resident, 1973—74; resident in preventative medicine U. Utah, Salt Lake City, 1974—75, fellow, 1978—80; pediatrician U. Utah Med. Ctr.; prof. pediat. U. Utah Health and Sci. Ctr. Mem.: Am. Acad. Pediat.

OSBORN, MALCOLM EVERETT, lawyer; b. Bangor, Maine, Apr. 29, 1928; s. Lester Everett and Helen (Clark) O.; m. Claire Anne Franks, Aug. 30, 1953; children: Beverly, Lester, Malcolm, Ernest. BA, U. Maine, 1952; postgrad., Harvard U., 1952-54; JD, Boston U., 1956, LLM, 1961. Bar: Maine 1956, Mass. 1956, U.S. Dist. Ct. Mass. 1961, U.S. Tax Ct. 1961, U.S. Claims Ct. 1961, N.C. 1965, U.S. Supreme Ct. 1979, U.S. Ct. Appeals (4th cir.) 1980, Va. 1991. Tax counsel State Mut. Life Assurance Co., Worcester, Mass., 1956-64; v.p., gen. tax counsel Integon Corp. and other group cos., Winston-Salem, NC, 1964-81; ptnr. House, Blanco & Osborn, P.A., Winston-Salem, NC, 1981-88; v.p., gen. counsel, dir. Settlers Life Ins. Co., Bristol, Va., 1984-89; prin. Malcolm E. Osborn, P.A., Winston-Salem, 1988—. Lectr. The Booke Seminars, Life Ins. Co., 1985-87; adj. prof. Wake Forest U. Sch. Law, Winston-Salem, N.C., 1974-82; disting. guest lectr. Ga. State U., 1965; guest lectr. NYU Ann. Inst. Fed. Taxation, 1966, 68, 75, 80; gen. counsel Blue Ridge Mutual Assn., Inc., Galax, Va., 1989—; adj. instr. bus. law Forsyth Tech. C.C., Winston-Salem, N.C., 2004—. Com. editor The Tax Lawyer, ABA, 1974-76; author numerous articles in field. Trustee N.C. Coun. Econ. Edn., 1968-76; bd. dirs. Christian Fellowship Home, 1972-80; co-founder Bereaved Parents Group Winston-Salem, 1978—. Mem. ABA (chmn. com. ins. cos. of taxation sect. 1980-82, chmn. subcom. on continuing legal edn. and publs. 1982-88), Am. Bus. Law Assn. (mem. com. fed. taxation 1968—, chmn. 1972-75), Assn. Life Ins. Counsel (com. on co. tax, tax sect. 1965—), N.C. Bar Assn. (com. taxation 1973—), Fed. Bar Assn. (taxation com. 1973—), Maine State Bar Assn., Va. State Bar Assn., Internat. Bar Assn. (com. on taxes of bus. law sect. 1973—), AAUP, Southeastern Acad. Legal Studies in Bus., Masons (Lincoln, Maine). Office: PO Box 5192 Winston Salem NC 27113-5192 Home Phone: 336-765-5749; Office Phone: 336-659-0613.

OSBORN, MARVIN GRIFFING, JR., educational consultant; b. Baton Rouge, Sept. 7, 1922; s. Marvin Griffing and Mamie (Hester) Osborn; m. Sarah Fleming Osborn, Aug. 3, 1945; children: Jane Fleming, Charles Porter. BA, La. State U., 1942, MA, 1946; LLD, St. Xavier U., 1971; DHum, Phillips U., 1977. Pub. relations counsel La. State U., 1945-47, acting dir. bur. pub. service, 1947; assoc. prof., chmn. dept. journalism and dir. pub. relations Howard Coll. (now Frank Samford U.), 1947-49; dir. pub. relations, lectr. journalism Miss. State Coll. (now Miss. State U.), 1949-53; dir. information Washington U., 1953-58, pub. relations adviser, 1955-58, dir. Devel. Funds, 1958-61; cons. coll. and univ. adminstrn., 1961—, Drake U., Phillips U., Duke U., Tex. Christian U., others, Christian Ch. Found., Nat. Meth. Found. Christian Higher Edn., Lexington Theol. Sem., Memphis Theol. Sem., Nat. Benevolent Assn. Christian Ch., Sisters of Loretto; interim pres. St. Xavier Coll. (now St. Xavier U.), 1968—69; pres. Marvin Osborn, Inc., 1979—94. Mem. planning com. Conf. Advancement Understanding and Support Higher Edn., White Sulphur Springs, W.Va., 1958. Mem., co-chair Cypress Village Devel. Coun., Jacksonville, 1992—98; chair first trustee ballot com. Cypress Village Residents Coun., 2005; mem. Fiers-Brown Soc. Christian Ch. Found., 1991; mem. nat. fundraising com. Disciples World, 2002—04; mem. exec. com. program and arrangements com. Gen. Assembly Christian Ch., 1977, 1987—89; trustee National City Christian Ch. Corp., 1981—85; bd. dirs., mem. exec. com., sec. divsn. higher edn. Christian Ch., 1973—77; mem. panel study fin. procedures Disciples of Christ, 1987—89; bd. dirs. St. Louis Heart Assn., 1969—75, Fla. Christian Ctr., 1986—88. Capt. US Army, 1942—45, ETO. Recipient Harry T. Ice Disting. Svc. award for Excellence in Philanthropy, Christian Ch. Found., 1991. Mem.: Soc. Profl. Journalists, Nat. Benevolent Assn. (amb. 1992—98), Am. Coll. Pub. Rels. Assn. (v.p. dists. 1951—52, v.p. membership 1952—53, sec.-treas. 1953—55, pres. 1959—60), Sigma Chi, Omicron Delta Kappa. Home: 13655 Myrica Ct Jacksonville FL 32224-6626

OSBORN, MARY JANE MERTEN, biochemist, educator; b. Colorado Springs, Colo., Sept. 24, 1927; d. Arthur John and Vivien Naomi (Morgan) Merten; m. Ralph Kenneth Osborn, Oct. 26, 1950. BA, U. Calif., Berkeley, 1948; PhD, U. Wash., 1958. Postdoctoral fellow, dept. microbiology NYU Sch. Medicine, NYC, 1959-61, instr., 1961-62, asst. prof., 1962-63; asst. prof. dept. molecular biology Albert Einstein Coll. Medicine, Bronx, NY, 1963-66, assoc. prof., 1966-68; prof. dept. microbiology U. Conn. Health Ctr., Farmington, 1968—, dept. head, 1980—2002, prof. dept. molecular, microbial and structural biology, 2003—. Mem. bd. sci. counselors Nat. Heart, Lung and Blood Inst., 1975-79; mem. Nat. Sci. Bd., 1980-86; adv. coun. Nat. Inst. Gen. Med. Sci., 1983-86, divsn. rsch. grants NIH, 1989-94, chair, 1992-94; trustee Biosci. Info. Systems, 1986-91, chair, 1990-91; mem. German Am. Acad. Coun., 1994-97; mem. space scis. bd. NRC, 1994-2000, chair com. space biology and medicine, 1994-2000; cochair com. on indications for waterborne pathogens, 2002-03. Assoc. editor Jour. Biol. Chemistry, 1978-80; contbr. articles in field of biochemistry and molecular biology to profl. jours. Mem. rsch. com. Am. Heart Assn., 1972-77, chair, 1976-77. NIH fellow, 1959-61; NIH grantee, 1962-95; NSF grantee, 1965-68; Am. Heart Assn. grantee, 1968-71 Fellow Am. Acad. Arts and Scis. (coun. 1988-91), NAS (coun. 1990-93, com. sci. engring. and pub. policy 1993-96); mem. Am. Acad. Microbiology (bd. govs. 1994-2000), Am. Fedn. Soc. Exptl. Biology (pres. 1982-83), Am. Soc. Biol. Chemists (pres. 1981-82), Am. Soc. Microbiology. Democrat. Office: U Conn Health Ctr Dept Molec Micro and Struct Biology MC3205 Farmington CT 06030-0001 Office Phone: 860-679-4206.

OSBORN, SHANE, state treasurer; b. SD, 1974; m. Teri Osborn, 2003; 2 children. BS in Math. & Statistics, Univ. Nebr., 1996. State treas. State of Nebr., 2007—. Pilot, World Watchers Fleet Air Reconnaissance Squadron One USN, 1996—2005, Iraq, Iran, Afghanistan, S. Am., Asian Pacific. Decorated Disting. Flying Cross for heroism and extraordinary achievement in flight. Mem.: CAP. Office: State Treasurer Rm 2005 State Capitol Bldg PO Box 94788 Lincoln NE 68509-4788 Office Phone: 402-471-2455. Office Fax: 402-471-4390. Business E-Mail: info@treasurer.org.*

OSBORN, WILLIAM A., investment company executive; b. Culver, Ind., Oct. 14, 1947; married; 2 children. BA, Northwestern U., 1969, MBA, 1973. Joined No. Trust Corp., 1970, sr. exec. v.p., commercial banking Chgo., pres., COO, 1993—95, chmn., pres., CEO, 1995—2007, chmn., 2008—. Bd. dirs. No. Trust Corp., 1994—, Nicor, Inc., 1999—2006, Caterpillar Inc., 2000—, The Tribune Co., 2001—; Class A dir. Fed. Reserve Bank Chgo. Bd. trustees Mus. Sci. and Industry, Chgo., Northwestern U., Chgo.; bd. dirs. Chgo. Symphony Orch., Northwestern Meml. HealthCare, Chgo. Urban League, Chgo. Horticultural Society, Lyric Opera Chgo., United Way Metropolitan Chgo.; bd. mgrs. YMCA Metropolitan Chgo.; advisory bd. J.L. Kellogg Grad. Sch. Mgmt., Northwestern. Mem.: Commercial Club of Chgo. (chmn., vice chmn. civic com.), Chgo. United (bd. dirs.), Chgo. Coun. Foreign Relations (bd. dirs.), Financial Services Roundtable, Chgo. Club, Executives' Club (bd. dirs.), Economic Club (bd. dirs.). Office: No Trust Co 50 S Lasalle St Chicago IL 60675-0001

OSBORNE, BURL, retired publishing executive; b. Jenkins, Ky., June 25, 1937; s. Oliver and Juanita (Smallwood) Osborne; m. Betty S. Wilder, Feb. 14, 1974; 1 child, Burl Jonathan. Student, U. Ky.; BA in Journalism, Marshall U., Huntington, W.Va., 1960; MBA, LI Univ. Sch. Bus., 1984; grad. advanced mgmt. prog., Harvard Bus. Sch. Reporter Ashland Daily Ind., Ky., 1957-58; reporter, editor Sta. WHTN-TV, Huntington, W.Va., 1958-60; corr. AP, Bluefield, W.Va., 1960-62, statehouse corr. Charleston, W.Va., 1963-64, corr. Spokane, Wash., 1964-67, news editor Denver, 1967-70, chief Ky. bur., 1970-72, chief Ohio bur., 1972-74, asst. chief Washington bur., 1974-76, mng. editor world hdqs. NYC, 1977-80; exec. editor Dallas Morning News, 1980-83, v.p., 1981, sr. v.p., editor, 1983-84, pres., editor, 1985-90, pub., editor, 1991—2001, pub. emeritus, 2001—07; ind. dir. Freedom Comm. Inc., 2004—, interim CEO, 2009—. Bd. dirs. Belo Corp., 1987—2002, pres. publ. divsn., 1995—2002; bd. dirs. AP, 1993—2007, chmn., 2002—07; bd. dirs. SW Transplant Alliance, 2001—07, chmn., 2007; bd. dirs. JC Penney Co., 2003—, GateHouse Media Inc., 2006—; journalism adv. com. Knight Found., 2001—07. Bd. dirs. Pulitzer Prize Com., 1986—95, co-chmn. bd. dir., 1994—95; bd. dirs. Recommended Reading, Inc., Nat. Kidney Found. Recipient Disting. Alumnus award, Marshall U., 1997, Freedoms Found. Next Millinium award, 1999; named Newspaper Exec. of Yr., Nat. Press Found., 1992; named to Ky. Journalism Hall of Fame, 1994. Mem.: Newspaper Assn. America (bd. dirs. 1996—2004), World Assn. Newspapers (mem. exec. com. 1998—2001, bd. dirs.), So. Newspaper Pub. Assn. (bd. dirs. 1995—2003, pres. 2000—01), Tex. Daily Newspaper Assn. (bd. dirs. 1982—92, pres. 1993), Am. Press Inst. (chmn. 1988—93), Am. Soc. Newspaper Editors (bd. dirs. 1982—91, pres. 1990—91), Orgn. Profl. Journalists. Office: Freedom Comm 17666 Fitch Irvine CA 92614 Personal E-mail: burlosborne@gmail.com.*

OSBORNE, C. KENT, oncologist, educator; AB, U. Mo.; MD, U. Mo. Med. Sch. Cert. Nat. Bds. Parts 1, 2 & 3, diplomate Am. Bd. Internal Medicine, 1975, medical oncology Am. Bd. Internal Medicine, 1977. Intern & resident Johns Hopkins Hosp.; dir. Baylor Coll. Medicine Breast Ctr., Baylor Cancer Ctr.; prof. medicine & cellular & structural biology Baylor Coll. Medicine. Recipient Breull Meml. award, Cleveland Clinic, 1992, Belsky Meml. award, NYU, 1994, Scientific Distinction award, Susan G. Komen Breast Cancer Assn., 1994. Fellow: Nat. Cancer Inst.; mem.: Am. Soc. Clinical Oncology, Am. Assn. Cancer Rsch., Assn. Am. Physicians, Endocrine Soc., Alpha Omega Alpha, Phi Beta Kappa. Office: Lester & Sue Smith Breast Center One Baylor Plaza BCM-600 Houston TX 77030 Office Phone: 713-798-1641. Office Fax: 713-798-1642. E-mail: kosborne@breastcenter.tmc.edu.*

OSBORNE, CHARLES KENT, oncologist, researcher; b. St. Louis, Mar. 8, 1946; married. MD, U. Mo., Columbia, 1972. Diplomate Am. Bd. Internal Medicine, 1975. Dir., Lester and Sue Smith Breast Ctr. Baylor Coll. Medicine, Houston, 1999—, dir., Dan L. Duncan Cancer Ctr., 2005—. Mem.: Am. Soc. Breast Diseases, Am. Assn. Physicians, Am. Soc. Clin. Oncology, Am. Assn. Cancer Rsch. Office: Baylor Coll Medicine One Baylor Plz BCM 600 Houston TX 77030

OSBORNE, DANNY, psychologist, researcher; b. Roseville, Calif., Aug. 3, 1981; s. Denver and Becky Osborne; m. Sheryl Metheney, May 25, 2008. BA, Calif. State U., Bakersfield, 2003, MA, 2005, U. Calif., LA, 2006, PhD student, 2005—. Rsch. fellow U. Calif., 2005—. Rsch. Mentorship fellowship, U. Calif., 2008—. Office: Univ Calif LA 1285 Franz Hall 502 Portola Plz Los Angeles CA 90095 Business E-Mail: dannyosborne@ucla.edu.

OSBORNE, EDWARD C., history professor; s. Irving and Vera Osborne; m. Dorothy Throo, June 1, 1968; children: Lisa Ann Guzman, Amy Renee. MEd, U. Miami, Coral Gables, Fla., 1970; EdS in Asian History, Fla. Atlantic U., Boca Raton, 1975, MA in Diplomatic History, 1996. Chief master sgt. USAFR, Homestead Air Reserve Base, 1980—2002; dept. head social studies Western HS, Fort Lauderdale, Fla., 1998—2001; adj. prof. history Broward Coll., South Campus, Pembroke Pines, Fla., 2005—. Mem.: Soc. Historians Am. Fgn. Rels., Jour. Hist. Soc.

OSBORNE, GLENNA JEAN, health facility administrator; b. East Rainelle, W.Va., Jan. 5, 1945; d. B.J. and Jean Ann (Haranac) Osborne; m. Thomas Joseph Ferrante Jr., June 11, 1966 (div. Nov. 1987); 1 child, Thomas Joseph Osborne; m. Brian Mark Popp, Aug. 13, 1988 (div. Oct. 1999). BA cum laude, U. Tampa, 1966; MA, Fairleigh Dickinson U., 1982; cert., Kean Coll., 1983. Cert. English, speech, dramatic arts tchr., prin./supr.; cert. nursing child assessment feeding scale and nursing child assessment tchg. scale, DENVER II cert., HOME cert. Tchr. Raritan H.S., Hazlet, N.J., 1966, Keyport (N.J.) Pub. Schs., 1968-86, coord. elem. reading and lang. arts, 1980-84, supr. curriculum and instrn., 1984-86; prin. Weston Sch., Manville, N.J., 1986-88, The Bartle Sch., Highland Park, N.J., 1988-91, Orange Ave. Sch., Cranford, N.J., 1991-92; dir. The Open Door Youth Shelter, Binghamton, N.Y., 1992-94; child protective investigator supr. Dept. Health and Rehab. Svcs., Orlando, Fla., 1994-95; program supr. Children's Home Soc., Sanford, Fla., 1995; clin. supr. Healthy Families-Orange, Orlando, Fla., 1995-98; dir. program ops. Children's Home Soc., Tavares, Fla., 1998—2004; adminstr. Lifestream Acad., Fla., 2004—. Regional trainer Individualized Lang. Arts, Weehawken, N.J., 1976-86; cons. McDougal/Littel Pubs., Evanston, Ill., 1982-83; chair adv. bd. women's residential program Ctr. for Drug Free Living, Orlando, 1996. Contbr. chpt.: A Resource Guide of Differentiated Learning Experiences for Gifted Elementary Students, 1981. V.p. Sch. Readiness Coalition for Lake County, 1999; mem. adv. coun. Lake Cmty. Action Agy., Head Start, 1999; bd. dir. Mt. Dora Cmty. Trust, 2002—04, Leadership Lake County, 2004; hon. chairperson, bus. adv. coun., bd. dir., sec. Ctrl. Healthy Start Coalition, 1999—2004; bus. adv. coun. Nat. Rep. Congl. Com., 2005; Sunday sch. tchr. Reformed Ch., Keyport, 1975—80, supt. Sunday sch., 1982—84. Mem.: Elks, Order Ea. Star, Mt. Dora Kiwanis (bd. dirs. 2000, pres. 2002—03, 2002—03, internat. Hixson fellow 2003, Divsn. 9 Lt. Gov.'s award outstanding svc. to club and cmty. 2003), Phi Delta Kappa. Republican. Methodist. Avocation: writing. Office: Lifestream Academy PO Box 491000 Leesburg FL 34749-1000

OSBORNE, JAMES ALFRED, religious organization administrator; b. Toledo, July 3, 1927; s. Alfred James and Gladys Irene (Gaugh) O.; m. Ruth Glenrose Campbell, Nov. 26, 1945; 1 child, Constance Jean (Mrs. Donald William Canning). Grad., Salvation Army Coll., 1947; student, U. Chattanooga, 1954-55; D of Pub. Svc. (hon.), Gordon Coll., 1991. Corps officer Salvation Army, Magness, Nashville, 1947, Southside, Memphis, 1948, Owensboro, Ky., 1949-54, comdg. officer Chattanooga, 1954-61, city comdr. Miami, Fla., 1961-65, divisional sec. Ky.-Tenn. Div., 1965-68, gen. sec. N.C. and S.C. Div., 1968-70, pub. rels. sec. 15 so. states, D.C. and Mex., 1970-71, divisional comdr. Md. and No. W.Va. Div., 1971-73, divisional comdr. Nat. Capital and Virginias Div. Washington, 1973-78, divisional comdr. Fla. Div., 1978-80, chief sec. Western Ter., 1980-84, nat. chief sec. Verona, NJ, 1984-86, territorial comdr. so. states Atlanta, 1986-89; nat. comdr., Republic of Marshall Islands, Guam, P.R., Virgin Islands Salvation Army USA, 1989-93. Chmn. Salvation Army Nat. Planning and Devel. Commn., 1974-76, 84-86; exec. bd. Vision Interfaith Satellite Network, Nat. Assn. Evangelicals, Christian Children's Fund Inc.; chmn. bd. Christian Mgmt. Assn., 1993-94; exec. com. religious alliance Against Pornography; rep. Salvation Army to numerous orgns. Bd. dirs. Nat. Law Ctr. for Children and Families; sec. Tenn. Conf. on Social Welfare, 1959, v.p., 1960; pres. Fla. Conf. on Social Welfare, 1965; pres. Ky. Welfare Assn., 1970. Mem. Chattanooga Pastors Assn. (pres. 1958), Va. and W. Va. Welfare Confs., Rotary. Personal E-mail: jim@jaruosborne.com.

OSBORNE, JOHN EDWARD, retired finance educator; b. Wheeling, W.Va., May 31, 1941; s. John Griswold Osborne and Ann Louise Laupp; m. Susan Darlene Niehaus, Sept. 15, 1981; children: John Mark, Benjamin William, Matthew Laupp, Kaitlin Luise; m. Gretchen Elsbeth Webb, Aug. 25, 1962 (div. Feb. 20, 1979). BA, Bethany U., W.Va., 1963; MS, MIT, Cambridge, 1965; degree in Stanford Exec. Program, Stanford U., Palo Alto, Calif., 1990. Fin. analyst Std. Oil Calif., San Francisco, 1965—69; dir. sys. Irving Lundborg & Co., San Francisco, 1969—70; mktg. mgr. IBM, San Francisco, 1970—80; v.p. sales & mktg. Elect Air Tool Inc., Palo Alto, 1980—81; area sales dir. Apple Computer, Menlo Pk., Calif., 1981—85, dir. field ops. Cupertino, Calif., 1986—88, dir. fin., 1988—90, CFO, enterprise sys. divsn., 1991—94, sr. dir. sales & mktg., 1994—97; exec. search cons. Devine & Virnig, Sunnyvale, Calif., 1998—2004; v.p. Essential Solutions Inc., San Jose, Calif., 2004—07; prof. economics Bethany Coll. Recipient Golden Cir. award, IBM, 1972, Golden Apple award, Apple Computer, 1982—85; named Editor Sloan Mgmt. Rev., MIT, 1963—65, Dir. of Yr., Apple Computer, 1984—85. Mem.: Symposiarchs.

OSBORNE, JOHN WALTER, historian, educator, author; b. Bklyn., Aug. 19, 1927; s. Douglas Walter and Gertrude Ann (Purcell) O.; m. Frances Patricia Hannon, Aug. 2, 1958; 1 son, David. BA, Rutgers U., 1957, MA (Louis Bevier fellow), 1959, PhD, 1961. Asst. prof. history Kean Coll. of N.J., 1961-63, N.J. Inst. Tech., 1963-64; asst. prof. Rutgers U., New Brunswick, NJ, 1964-66, assoc. prof., 1966-69, prof., 1969-93, prof. emeritus, 1993—. Author: William Cobbett-His Thought and His Times, 1966, The Silent Revolution: The Industrial Revolution in England as a Source of Cultural Change, 1970, John Cartwright, 1972; co-author: Cobbett in His Times, 1990; editor: Jour. of Rutgers U. Libraries, 1975-80; co-editor: A Grammar of the English Language, 1983; contbr. articles to profl. jours. Recipient Henry Browne award for disting. teaching Rutgers U., 1988; Am. Philos. Soc. grantee, 1966, 75 Home: PO Box 426 Ivoryton CT 06442-0426

OSBORNE, LOUISE, publishing executive; Pres. Osborne/Jenks Prodns., Inc., Wethersfield, Conn., 1979—. Home: 21 Whitman Pond Rd Simsbury CT 06070-1532

OSBORNE, MARIE-ANGELA, journalist; b. Detroit, Jan. 20, 1957; d. Angelo Guerino and Domenica Mazzocco; m. John Hampton Osborne, Dec. 10, 1945; children: John Taylor children: Domenique Nicole, Robert Hampton. BA, U. Detroit, 1979. Anchor, reporter WJR Radio-ABC Radio, Detroit, 1994—2004; reporter, anchor WWJ Newsradio 950- CBS Radio, Southfield, Mich., 2004—. Adj. instr. Wayne State U., Detroit, 2000—03. Chmn. Lighthouse Oakland County, Pontiac, Mich., 1992. Recipient Edward R. Murrow award, Radio TV News Dirs. Assn., 1997, 1998, 2000, Clarion award, Women in Comm., 1997, 1998, Headliner award, Atlantic City Press Club, 1998. Mem.: Soc. Profl. Journalists. Office: CBS Radio-WWJ Newsradio 950 26495 American Dr Southfield MI 48034

OSBORNE, RICHARD DE JONGH, mining and metals company executive; b. Bronxville, NY, Mar. 19, 1934; s. Stanley de Jongh and M. Elizabeth (Ide) O.; m. Cheryl Anne Archibald, Dec. 14, 1957 (dec.); children: Leslie Coleman, Lindsay Vogel, Nicholas de J., Stanley de J. AB in Econs., Princeton U., 1956. With Cuno Engring. Corp., Meriden, Conn., 1956-60; fin., planning and mktg. exec. IBM Corp., Armonk, NY, 1960-69; investment adviser Sherman M. Fairchild, NYC, 1969-70; exec. v.p. fin. and bus. devel., dir. Fairchild Camera & Instrument Corp., Mountain View, Calif., 1970-74; v.p. fin. ASARCO Inc. (formerly Am. Smelting & Refining Co.), NYC, 1975-77, exec. v.p., 1977-82, pres., 1982-85, chmn., pres., CEO, 1985-99. Bd. dirs. NACCO Industries, Inc., Tinker Found.; bd. dirs., non-exec. chmn., bd. dirs. Datawatch Corp.; treas., mem. bd. dirs. Ams. Soc. Mem.: Nat. Mining Assn. (hon. dir.), Coun. Fgn. Rels., Econs. Club NY, River Club, Brook Club, Sakonnet Golf Club, John's Island Club. Home and Office: 40 E 94th St Apt 32B New York NY 10128-0759 Personal E-mail: rdejo@att.net.

OSBORNE, ROBERT STEPHEN, automotive executive, lawyer; b. Montreal, Que., Can., Oct. 21, 1954; m. Martha Osborne; children: Tom, Sarah. AB magna cum laude, Harvard U., 1976, JD magna cum laude, 1979. Bar: Ill., 1979. Assoc. Kirkland & Ellis LLP, Chgo., 1979-85, ptnr., 1985—2002, Jenner & Block LLP, Chgo., 2002—, chair corp. practice; group v.p., gen. counsel Gen. Motors Corp., 2006—. Gen. counsel, Lands' End, Inc., Dodgeville, Wis., 1986-95, corp. sec., spl. asst. to bd. dirs., 1995-2002; adj. prof., U. Chgo. Law Sch., 2002-. Bd. dirs. Chgo. Shakespeare Theater, The Nature Conservancy of Alaska. Mem. ABA, Am. Soc. Corp. Secs., Internat. Bar Assn. Avocations: fly fishing, hiking.*

OSBORNE, ROBIN, library and information scientist; BA in Philosophy, U. Calif., Berkeley, 1974; MLS with honors, Columbia U., NYC, 1992. Various positions NY Pub. Libr., 1992—97; adult and outreach svcs. cons. Westchester Libr. Sys., Tarrytown, NY, 1997—. Mem. documentary heritage prog. adv. coun. Met. NY Libr. Coun., 1999—2005. Editor: From Outreach to Equity: Innovative Models of Library Policy and Practice, 2004. Founder Westchester Literacy and Learning Alliance; bd. dirs. Literacy Vols. Westchester County, 1999—2005, Literacy Vols. NY State, 2000—03. Recipient Joseph Lewis Wheeler and Joseph Towne Wheeler award for Leadership, Columbia U. Sch. Libr. Svc., NY Times Libr. award, 2006. Mem.: ALA (chair literacy assembly 2002—05, mem. literacy com. 2003—05, chair adv. com. Office Literacy and Outreach Svcs. 2004—06), REFORMA, Beta Phi Mu (life). Office: Westchester Libr Sys 540 White Plains Rd Ste 200 Tarrytown NY 10591-5110 Office Phone: 914-231-3237. Office Fax: 914-674-4185. E-mail: rosborne@wlsmail.org.

OSBORNE, TOM (THOMAS WILLIAM OSBORNE), college athletic director, former United State Representative from Nebraska; b. Hastings, Nebr., Feb. 22, 1937; m. Nancy Tederman; children: Mike, Ann, Susie. BA in Hist., Hastings Coll., Nebr., 1959; MA in Ednl. Psych., U. Nebr., 1963, PhD in Ednl. Psych., 1965. Flanker Washington Redskins, 1960—61, San Francisco 49ers, 1959; asst. football coach U. Nebr., 1962—67, receivers coach, 1967—71, asst. head coach, 1972, head football coach, 1973-97, prof. emeritus, 1998-2000, athletic dir., 2007—; mem. US Congress from 3rd Nebr. dist., 2001—07, mem. agr. com., mem. edn. and the workforce com., mem. transp. and infrastructure com. Bd. dirs. Corp. Nat. & Community Svc., 2007—. Co-founder Team Mates Mentoring Program. Sgt. in US Army Nat. Guard and USAR, 1960—66. Recipient Amos Alonzo Stagg award, Am. Football Coaches Assn., 2000, Policy Maker of Yr., Assn. Career and Tech. Edn., 2005, Paul "Bear" Bryant Lifetime Achievement award, Nat. Sportscasters & Sportswriters Assn., 2008, Jim Thorpe Lifetime Achievement award, Jim Thorpe Assn., 2000, Tuss McLaughry award, Am. Football Coaches Assn. (AFCA), 2008; named Big Eight Coach of Yr., 1975, 1978, 1980, Bobby Dodds Nat. Coach of Yr., 1978; named to The Coll. Football Hall of Fame, 1999. Mem.: Fellowship Christian Athletes. Republican. Meth. Achievements include coaching the U. Nebr. football team to 25 consecutive bowl games 1973-1977; coached team to NCAA Divsn. IA Nat. Championship, 1994, 1995, 1997. Office: U Nebr Athletics One Memorial Stadium PO Box 880120 Lincoln NE 68588-0120 Office Phone: 202-225-6435, 402-472-3011.*

OSBOURN, JOSEPH A., information technology executive; B in Physics, U. Louisville; MBA, Memphis State U. V.p. info. svcs. Walt Disney World Co., 1989—99; sr. v.p., chief info. officer Kmart Corp., 1999—2000; exec. v.p., worldwide chief info. officer Tech Data Corp., Clearwater, Fla., 2000—. Named one of Named one of Premier 100 IT Leaders, Computerworld, 2007. Office: Tech Data Corp 5350 Tech Data Dr Clearwater FL 33760-3122

OSBOURNE, OZZY (JOHN OSBOURNE), singer; b. Birmingham, Eng., Dec. 3, 1948; m. Thelma Mayfair, 1971 (div. 1981); children: Jessica Starshine, Louis Jon; m. Sharon Arden, July 4, 1982; children: Aimee Rachel, Kelly, Jack. Singer Black Sabbath, 1969—79, solo career, 1980—. Singer: (albums with Black Sabbath) Black Sabbath, 1969, Paranoid, 1970, Master of Reality, 1971, Volume 4, 1972, Sabbath, Bloody Sabbath, 1975, Sabotage, 1975, Technical Ecstasy, 1976, We Sold Our Soul For Rock and Roll, 1976, Never Say Die, 1978, Reunion, 1998, Past Lives, 2002, (solo albums) Blizzard of Ozz, 1980, Diary of a Madman, 1981, Speak of the Devil, 1982, Bark at the Moon, 1983, The Ultimate Sin, 1986, Tribute, 1987, No Rest for the Wicked, 1988, Just Say Ozzy, 1990, No More Tears, 1991, Live & Loud, 1993, Ozzmosis, 1995, Ozzman Cometh, 1997, Down to Earth, 2001, Live at Budokhan, 2002, Essential Ozzy Osbourne, 2003, Under Cover, 2005, Black Rain, 2007; performer: (films) Black Sabbath: Live, 1978, Ozzy Osbourne: Bark at the Moon, 1986, The Decline of Western Civilization Part II: The Metal Years, 1988, Ozzy Osbourne: Don't Blame Me, 1992, Ozzy Osbourne: Live and Loud, 1993, Black Sabbath: The Last Supper, 1999; actor: (films) Trick or Treat, 1986, The Jerky Boys, 1995, Private Parts, 1997, Little Nicky, 2000, (voice only) Moulin Rouge!, 2001,: (TV films) Billy's Shout, 1991; appeared in (TV series) The Frank Skinner Show, 1996, The Osbournes, 2002—05, Battle for Ozzfest, 2004—, Osbournes: Reloaded, 2009—, voice only South Park, 1997. Recipient Grammy award, Best Heavy Metal Performance for I Don't Want to Change the World, 1994; named to Rock and Roll Hall of Fame (as mem. of Black Sabbath), 2006.*

OSBURN, CHARLES BENJAMIN, retired librarian, dean; b. Pitts., May 25, 1939; s. C. Benjamin and Lydia (Harmon) O.; divorced; 1 child, Christopher Bart; m. Sharon Tuffendsam, June 12, 1987; 1 stepchild, Bradley Alan Tuffendsam. BA, Grove City Coll., 1961; MA, Pa. State U., 1963; MS, U. N.C., 1971; PhD, U. Mich., 1978. Instr. French Pa. State U., University Park, 1963-66; asst. prof. U. Wis.-Whitewater, 1966-69; humanities bibliographer U. N.C., Chapel Hill, 1969-74; asst. dir. libraries SUNY-Buffalo, 1974-76; asst. univ. librarian Northwestern U., Evanston, 1976-80; dean, univ. librarian U. Cin., 1980-86; dean libraries U. Ala., Tuscaloosa, 1986—2001, prof. library sci., 1986—2001, dean, prof. emeritus univ. libraries, 2001—. Bd. dirs. Ctr. for Research Libraries, Chgo., SOLINET, Atlanta, Assn. Rsch. Librs., 1987-93; mem. rsch. libr. adv. counc. to Online Computer Library Ctr., Dublin, Ohio; adj. prof. Sch. Libr. and Info. Studies, U. Ala., Tuscaloosa, 2001-. Author: The Social Transcript: Uncovering Library Philosophy, 2009, Academic Research and Library Resources: Changing Patterns in America, 1979 (award ALA 1980); compiler: Research and Reference Guide to French Studies, 2d edit., 1981; mem. editorial bd. Literary Research: A Journal of Scholarly Method and Technique, 1986—; co-editor: (with R. W. Atkinson) Collection Management: A New Treatise, 2 vols., 1991. Mem. ALA, MLA, Assn. Rsch. Librs., Phi Sigma Iota, Beta Phi Mu. Office: Univ Ala Sch Library and Info Studies Tuscaloosa AL 35487-0252 Office Phone: 205-348-1519. Business E-Mail: cosburn@bama.ua.edu.

O'SCANNLAIN, DIARMUID FIONNTAIN, federal judge; b. NYC, Mar. 28, 1937; s. Sean Leo and Moira (Hegarty); m. Maura Nolan, Sept. 7, 1963; children: Sean, Jane, Brendan, Kevin, Megan, Christopher, Anne, Kate. BA, St. John's U., 1957; JD, Harvard U., 1963; LLM, U. Va., 1992; LLD (hon.), U. Notre Dame, 2002, Lewis & Clark Coll., 2003. Bar: Oreg. 1965, NY 1964. Tax atty. Standard Oil Co. (NJ), NYC, 1963—65; oassoc. Davies, Biggs, Strayer, Sotel & Boley, Portland, Oreg., 1965—69; dep. atty. gen. State of Oreg., 1969—71, pub. utility commr., 1971—73; dir. Oreg. Dept. Environ. Quality, 1973—74; sr. ptnr. Ragen, Roberts, O'Scannlain, Robertson & Neill, Portland, 1978—86; judge US Ct. Appeals (9th cir.), San Francisco, 1986—, mem. exec. com., 1988—89, 1993—94; mem. Jud. Coun. 9th Cir., 1991—93. Mem. US Jud. Conf. Com. on Automation and Tech., 1990—; cons. Office of Pres.-elect and mem. Dept. Energy Transition Team (Reagan Transition), Washington, 1980—81; chmn. com. adminstrv. law Oreg. State Bar, 1980—81; chmn. fed. jud. ctrs. adv. com. appellate edn., 2003. Bd. trustees James Madison Meml. Fellowship Found.; mem. coun. of legal advisors Rep. Nat. Com., 1981—83, mem., 1983—86; chmn. Oreg. Rep. Party, 1983—86; del. Rep. Nat. convs., 1976, 1980, chmn. Oreg. del., 1984; nominee US Ho. of Reps., 1st Congl. Dist., 1974; team leader energy task force Pres.'s Pvt. Sector Survey on Cost Control, 1982—83; trustee Jesuit H.S.; bd. visitors U. Oreg. Law Sch., 1988—; mem. citizens adv. bd. Providence Hosp., 1986—92. Maj. USAR, 1955—78. Mem.: ABA (sec. Appellate Judges Conf. 1989—90, exec. com. 1990—, chmn. 1994—95, chmn. jud. divsn. 2001—02), Fed. Judges Assn., Fed. Bar Assn., Multnomah Club. Roman Catholic. Office: US Ct Appeals Pioneer Courthouse 700 SW 6th Ave Ste 313 Portland OR 97204-1396 Home: 700 SW 6th Ave # 313 Portland OR 97204-1396 Office Phone: 503-833-5380. E-mail: Judge_O'Scannlain@ca9.uscourts.gov.*

OSCEOLA, TINA, museum director; married; 2 children. BA in Polit. Sci., Rollins Coll.; MPA, Nova Southeastern U. Pub. info. officer, pub. affairs supr. Collier County Sheriff's Office, Fla.; exec. dir. Tribal Historic Resources Dept., Seminole Tribe of Fla., Hollywood, Fla., Ah-Tah-Thi-Ki Mus., Clewiston, Fla. Office: Ah-Tah-Thi-Ki Mus HC-61, Box 21-A Clewiston FL 33440 Office Phone: 877-902-1113. E-mail: tosceola@semtribe.com.

OSEI, EDWARD, economist, researcher; b. Accra, Ghana; s. Isaac K. and Comfort Kwafo-Mensah Osei. PhD in Agrl. Econs., Iowa State U., Ames, 1994; BSc, U. Ghana, Legon, 1989. Rsch. & tchg. asst. U. Ghana, 1989—90; rsch. asst. Iowa State U., 1990—94, postdoc. rsch. assoc., 1994—95; rsch. economist Tex. Inst. Applied Env. Rsch., Tarleton State Univ., Stephenville, 1996—2000, sr. rsch. economist, 2000—. Rev. panelist USDA CSREES Nat. Rsch. Initiative Program, Washington, 2008. Contbr. articles to profl. jours. State conf. rep. Seventh Day Adventist Ch., Stephenville, Tex., 1998—. Recipient Premium Academic Excellence, Iowa State U., 1990—92. Mem.: Agrl. Applied Econs. Assn., Gamma Sigma Delta. Conservative. Seventh Day Adventist. Achievements include invention of home air circulation & home fire prevention; development of economic simulation model & integrated computer modeling system; research in data disaggregation to generate hypothetical farm distributions and use of statistical clustering to develop and simulate representative farm types. Avocation: farming. Office: Texas Inst Applied Env Research Box T-0410 Tarleton State Univ Stephenville TX 76402 Personal E-mail: edwardosei@hotmail.com. Business E-Mail: osei@tiaer.tarleton.edu.

OSGOOD, CHARLES, news broadcaster, journalist; b. NYC, Jan. 8, 1933; s. Charles Osgood and Mary F. (Wilson) Wood; m. Jean Crafton, Dec. 5, 1973; children: Kathleen, Winston, Anne Elizabeth, Emily Jean, James Edward. BS, Fordham U., 1954; L.H.D. (hon.), St. Bonaventure U., 1977; PhD (hon.), Fordham U.; LLD, St. John's U. Program dir. Sta. WGMS, Washington, 1955—63; gen. mgr. Sta. WHCT, Hartford, Conn., 1963—64; reporter ABC Radio News, 1964—67; anchorman Sta. WCBS, 1967—71; corr. television and radio CBS, NYC, 1971—; anchor CBS News Sunday Morning, 1994—. Author: Nothing Could be Finer Than A Crisis That Is Minor in the Morning, 1979, There's Nothing That I Wouldn't Do If You Would Be My POSSLQ, 1981, Osgood on Speaking, 1988, The Osgood Files, 1991, See You on the Radio, 1999; actor(voice): (films) Horton Hears a Who!, 2008. Recipient Sol Taishoff award for broadcasting excellence, Nat. Press Found., 2005. Mem.: AFTRA. Office: CBS News 524 W 57th St New York NY 10019-2924

OSGOOD, CHRIS, professional hockey player; b. Peace River, Alta., Canada, Nov. 26, 1972; m. Jenna Osgood. Goaltender Detroit Red Wings, 1991—2001, 2005—, NY Islanders, 2001—05. Co-recipient William M. Jennings Trophy, 1996, 2008; named to Sporting News All-Star Team, 1996, Second All-Star Team, NHL, 1996, NHL All-Star Game, 1996—98, 2008. Achievements include being a member of Stanely Cup Champion Detroit Red Wings, 1997, 1998, 2008. Office: c/o Detroit Red Wings Joe Louis Arena 600 Civic Center Dr Detroit MI 48226-4408

OSGOOD, CHRISTOPHER MYKEL, radio sales manager; b. Northampton, Mass., Nov. 8, 1963; s. Robert Mansfield and Susanne (Mykel) Osgood; m. Angela Baxter; 1 child, Robert Marley. BS, Cornell U., 1989. Media rsch. mktg. analyst Vitt Media Internat., NYC, 1988-89; acct. exec. KAOI AM/FM Radio, Maui, Hawaii, 1989-91, KTXH-TV, Houston, 1991-92; dir. advt. Oilers News, Browns News Illustrated, 49ers Report, Cleve., 1992-93; acct. exec. KRBE-FM, Houston, 1993-96, KLOL-FM, Houston, 1996-99; local sales mgr. KUCD-FM, Honolulu, 1999-2001; gen. sales mgr. KLOL-FM, Houston, 2001—03; local sales mgr. WSB-AM, Atlanta, 2003—05, gen. sales mgr., 2005—08; chief oper. officer Pacific Radio Group, Maui, 2008—; chmn. sales adv. com. Radio Advertising Bureau. Chmn. Sales Adv. Com., Radio Advt. Bur.; advanced competitive tng. coord. Radio Divsn. Cox Enterprises. Coach Bear Creek Basketball League, Houston, 1993—94. Mem.: Cornell Soc. Hotelmen. Home: 2605 Moolio Pl Kihei HI 96753 Office: Pacific Radio Group 311 Ano St Kahului HI 96732-1304 Office Phone: 808-877-5566. Business E-Mail: osgood@pacificradiogroup.com.

OSGOOD, NANCY JEAN, medical educator, writer; b. July 6, 1951; d. Jack Kent and Lois Emma (Stober) Luttrell; m. Raymond Clifford Jordan, Jr., Oct. 13, 1984. BA in Sociology and Spanish, Yankton Coll., 1972; MA in Sociology, Drake U., 1974; cert. in gerontology, Syracuse U., 1979; PhD in Sociology, 1979. Rsch. assoc. Syracuse Rsch. Corp., NY, 1975—78; asst. prof. SUNY, Cortland, 1979—80, Med. Coll. Va., Richmond, 1980—92, prof., 1992—. Mem. Nat. Com. on Vital and Health Stats., Washington, 1982—84. Author: Senior Settlers: Social Integration in Retirement Communities, 1982, Suicide in the Elderly: A Practitioner's Guide to Diagnosis and Mental Health Intervention, 1985, Suicide Among the Elderly in Long-Term Care Facilities, 1991; editor: Life after Work: Retirement, Leisure, Recreation and the Elderly, 1982; co-author: Seniors on Stage: The Impact of Applied Theatre on the Elderly, 1985, Suicide and the Elderly: An Annotated Bibliography and Review, 1986; co-editor: Dynamic Leisure Programming with Older Adults, 1987, The Science and Practice of Gerontology: A Multidisciplinary Guide, 1989, Alcoholism and Aging: An Annotated Bibliography and Review, 1995, Treating Alcohol and Drug Abuse in the Elderly, 2002. Selection com. King William HS, Va., 1985; active Va. State Rehab. Bd., Am. Cancer Soc. Recipient acad. scholarship, Yankton Coll., 1969—72, N.Y. State Dept. Mental Hygiene Rsch. fellowship, 1974—75, Nat. Inst. Edn. award, 1975—78, NIMH award, 1977—79, Presdl. Invitation to White House, 1984, 1991; grantee Va. Commonwealth U., 1981—82. Fellow: Gerontol. Soc. Am.; mem.: Internat. Platform Assn., So. Gerontol. Soc., Am. Sociol. Assn., Am. Assn. Suicidology. Avocations: playing piano and clarinet, gourmet cooking, parrots. Home: PO Box 245 Manquin VA 23106-0245 Home Phone: 804-769-4285. Personal E-mail: osgoodn@yahoo.com.

OSGOOD, RICHARD MAGEE, JR., electrical engineering professor, researcher; b. Kansas City, Mo., Dec. 28, 1943; s. Richard Magee and Mary Neff (Russell) O.; m. Alice Rose Dyson, June 25, 1966; children: Richard Magee, III, Nathaniel David, Jennifer Anne BS in Engring., U.S. Mil. Acad., 1965; MS in Physics, Ohio State U., 1968; PhD, MIT, 1973. Rsch. assoc. dept. physics MIT, Cambridge, Mass., 1969-72, rsch. staff Lincoln Lab., 1973-80, project leader Lincoln Lab., 1980-81; assoc. prof. applied physics and elec. engring. Columbia U., NYC, 1981-82, prof., 1982-91, Higgins prof., 1989—. Assoc. dir. Brookhaven Nat. Lab., Upton, NY, 2000—03; dir. Microelectronics Sci. Labs., 1984—90; mem. Army Sci. and Tech. Basic Energy Scis. Adv. Com., Def. Scis.-Advanced Rsch. Projects Agy.; cons. Los Alamos Nat. Lab.; mem. ad hoc com. Air Force Sci. Adv. Bd. Editor: Laser Diagnostics and Photochemical Processing of Semiconductor Devices, 1983; contbr. articles to profl. jours.; patentee in field Served to capt. USAF, 1965-69 Recipient Samuel Burka award USAF Avionics Lab., 1968, Leos Travelling Lectr. award, 1986-87, Disting. Travelling Lectr. APS, R.W. Wood Prize, 1991, Optical Soc. Am.; John Simon Guggenheim fellowship, 1989. Fellow IEEE, Am. Phys. Soc., Optical Soc. Am. (R.W. Wood award, 1991); mem. Am. Chem. Soc., Materials Rsch. Soc. (councillor 1983-86), Optical Device Assn. (Japanese hon. lectr. 1990), Am. Phys. Soc. (travelling lectureship 1992). Office: Columbia U Radiation Lab New York NY 10027

OSGOOD, ROBERT T., JR., architect, strategic planner; b. St. Louis, Sept. 25, 1958; s. Robert T. and Gale Farris (Brandau) Osgood; m. Cheryl Lenor Denler, June 26, 1982; children: Robbie, Chelsea. B cum laude in environ. design, SUNY, Buffalo, 1981; M in Architecture, Ga. Instit. Tech., 1984. Planner Stevens & Wilkinson, Atlanta, 1983—84; sr. rsch. assoc. BOSTI, Buffalo, 1984—86; sr. v.p. HOK, St. Louis, 1986—94; v.p. FLAD, Madison, Wis., 1994—98; sr. v.p. VOA, Columbus, 1999—. Lectr. Washington U., St. Louis, 1989—90, St. Louis, 1992; dir. HOK, 1986—94, FLAD, 1994—98, NBBJ, 1998—99, VOA, 1999—. Contbr. numerous articles to profl. jours. Mem. Downtown St. Louis, Mo., 1993; coach Waunakee Youth Soccer, Madison, 1995—98, BWSA Crew, Columbus, 2000—; vol. Columbus Crew, Columbus, 2000—. Recipient Planning & Design award Famous Footwear HQ, Madison Mag., 1997, Environ. Sustainability award, SC Johnson, 1997, Planning & Design award, SC Johnson HQ Bldg., AIA, 1998, Rsch. and Design awards, Progressive Architecture Jour. Mem.: Internat. Facility Mgmt. Assn., CoreNet Global, Alpha Lambda Delta, Tau Sigma Delta. Avocations: soccer, skiing, running, art, music. Office: VOA Assoc 4449 Easton Way 2nd Fl Columbus OH 43219 Office Phone: 614-934-1117. E-mail: bosgood@voa.com.

OSGOOD, RUSSELL KING, academic administrator; b. Fairborn, Ohio, Oct. 25, 1947; s. Richard M. and Mary Russell Osgood; m. Paula Haley, June 6, 1970; children: Mary, Josiah, Micah, Iain. BA, Yale U., 1969, JD, 1974. Bar: Mass. 1974, U.S. Dist. Ct. Mass. (admitted to) 1976. Assoc. Hill & Barlow, Boston, 1974—78; assoc. prof. Boston U., 1978—80; prof. Cornell U., Ithaca, NY, 1980—88, dean law sch., 1988—98; pres. Grinnell Coll., Iowa, 1998—. Lt. USNR, 1969—71. Mem.: Selden Soc., Stair Soc., Mass. Hist. Soc. Office: Grinnell Coll 1121 Park St Grinnell IA 50112-1640 Office Phone: 641-269-3000. E-mail: osgood@grinnell.edu.

OSGUTHORPE, JOHN DAVID, otolaryngologist, educator; b. Fairbanks, Alaska, 1948; MD, U. Utah, 1973; grad., Med. Ed. in Otolaryngology. Intern UCLA, 1973-74, resident surgery, 1974-75, resident otolaryngology, 1975-78; prof. Med. U. SC, Charleston, SC, 1979—, surg. dir.; otolaryngologist Med. U. Hosp., Charleston, SC. Accreditation coun. Skull Base fellowship U. Zurich. Mem.: HNS, AMA (del. 1998—2005), ACGME (residence rev. comm. 1998—2004, chair, residence rev. comm. 2002—04, bd. mem. 2004—06), Sinus Allergy Health Partnership (bd. dir. 1998—, pres. 2004), Am. Rhinologic Soc. (bd. dir. 1998—2001, editor 1998—2001), Am. Laryngological Assn., Am. Acad. Otolarynologic Allergy (pres. 1995, pres. award 1999, 2003, 2008), Am. Acad. Otolaryngology, Head and Neck Surgery (bd. dirs. 1997—, coord.

continuing edn. 2000—, Disting. Svc. award 1995, 2004, Pres. award 2004). Office: Med Univ SC Dept Otolaryngology 150 Ashley Ave Charleston SC 29401-5803 Office Phone: 843-792-3533.

OSGUTHORPE, RICHARD D., science educator; PhD, U. Mich., Ann Arbor, 2005. Asst. prof. Boise State U., Idaho, 2005—. Office: Boise State Univ 1910 University Dr Boise ID 83725

O'SHAUGHNESSY, JAMES PATRICK, lawyer, consultant; b. Rochester, NY, Mar. 3, 1947; s. John Andrew and Margaret May (Yaxley) O'S.; m. Terry Lee Wood. BS cum laude, Rensselaer Poly. Inst., 1972; JD, Georgetown U., 1977. Bar: Va. 1977, Ohio 1979, Wis. 1987. Assoc. Squire, Sanders & Dempsey, Cleve., 1978-81; ptnr. Hughes & Cassidy, Sumas, Wash., 1981-84; patent counsel Kimberly-Clark Corp., Neenah, Wis., 1984-85; ptnr. Foley & Lardner, Milw., 1986-96; v.p., chief intellectual property counsel Rockwell Internat., Inc., Milw., 1996—2004; ind. cons. Mequon, Wis., 2004—. Founder Innovatech Co., 1996-2000, Lake Street Holdings, LLC 2006-, Donges Bay Group, LLC 2007-; mem. tech. adv. coun. Ideation Internat., Inc., 1999-2004; mem. adv. bd. Licensing Econs. Rev., 1998-2002; co-founder Intellectual Property Bus. Internat., 2002-04; mem. bd. visitors Georgetown U. Sch. Nursing, 1996-2000; bd. dir. Gemstar TV Guide Internat. Inc., 2004-08, comp. com., 2004-08; bd. dir. Macrovision Solutions Corp., 2008-, chair comp. com., 2008-; mem. coun. of advisors Nat. Inst. Play, 2006-; chmn. bd. dirs. ICmty. Svcs., Inc. 2007-; lectr. in field. Contbg. author: Technology Licensing: Corporate Strategies for Maximizing Value, 1996, Profiting From Intellectual Capital: Extracting Value From Innovation, 1998; mem. editl. bd. Am. Criminal Law Rev., 1976-77; contbr. articles to profl. jours. Bd. dirs. Skylight Opera Theatre, 1991-92, Milw. Florentine Opera Co., 1999-2008, pres., 2002-03. With USN, 1964—68, USS Boxer. Recipient Matthew Albert Hunter prize, Rensselaer Poly. Inst., 1972. Mem. Internat. Inst. Conflict Prevention and Resolution (mediation/arbitration panel), Lic. Execs. Soc. (cert. licensing profl.), Am. Intellectual Property Law Assn., Assn. Chief Patent Coun. (emeritus), Innovation Practitioners Network, Disabled Am. Vets., Tau Beta Pi, Alpha Sigma Mu. Avocations: golf, fly fishing, curling, bridge. Home and Office: 5772 Silent Wash Pl Marana AZ 85658 Business E-Mail: jim@jposhaughnessy.com.

O'SHAUGHNESSY, JOYCE ANN, oncologist, director; b. Poughkeepsie, NY, Oct. 3, 1956; d. Joseph and Ann O'Shaughnessy; m. Edward Omeara, Sept. 30, 1989; children: Mark Omeara, Tess Omeara. BS in Biology summa cum laude, Holy Cross Coll., Boston, 1978, MA, 2003; MD cum laude, Yale U. Med. Sch., 1982. Postdoc. fellow, Lab. Tumor Virus Biology Nat. Cancer Inst., 1986—87, sr. investigator, biologics evaluation sect., investigational drug br., therapy evaluation program, 1987—88, spl. asst. dir., 1988—90, sr. investigator, med. breast cancer sect., divsn. cancer treatment, 1990—95; med. oncologist Kentuckiana Med. Oncology Assocs., Louisville, 1995—97, Tex. Oncology, Pa., 1997—; dir., cancer prevention program US Oncology Baylor-Charles A. Sammons Cancer Ctr., Dallas, 2000—. Contbr. articles to numerous sci. jours. Recipient Francis Parker award, Yale Med. Sch., 1982, Santae Crucis award, Holy Cross Coll., Disting. Alumni award, 2003. Mem.: Phi Beta Kappa, Alpha Sigma Nu, Alpha Omega Alpha. Office: Baylor-Sammons Cancer Ctr 3535 Worth St Dallas TX 75246 Office Fax: 214-370-1886. Business E-Mail: joyce.o'shaughnessy@usoncology.com.

O'SHAUGHNESSY, ROBERT T., automotive executive; Sr. mgr. Ernst & Young LLP, 1987—97; asst. controller United Auto Group, Bloomfield Hills, Mich., 1997—99, v.p., controller, 1999—2005, sr. v.p. fin., 2005—07, exec. v.p., CFO, 2007—. Office: Penske Automotive Group 2555 Telegraph Rd Bloomfield Hills MI 48302-0954

O'SHAUGHNESSY, ROSEMARIE ISABELLE RAO, clinical nutritionist; b. NYC, Sept. 25, 1940; d. Dr. John O. and Maria Wellmann (Larranaga) Rao; m. John Michael O'Shaughnessy, 1961 (div. 1976); children: Michelle Marie, Chevonne Eileen, Melany Rose; m. Louis L. Feldman, May 3, 1980 (dec. Nov. 17, 2002). BA, St. Mary's Coll., Notre Dame, Ind., 1961; MS, Union U., LA, 1978; PhD, Donsbach U., LA, 1979; postdoctoral, Union for Experimenting Colls. and Univs., Cin., 1987. Cert. clin. nutritionist, 1991. Pvt. practice clin. nutrition, Orlando, Fla., 1979-92, Kissimmee, Fla., 1992—96; ind. dir. Beauticontrol Cosmetics Inc., Orlando, Fla., 1992-94, dir., 1992—2002, RAO Properties, Kissimmee, Fla., 2000—05; pres. Wonderland Inn Inc., 2000—07, Maris W. RAO Bus. Inc., 2000—. Expert witness for clin. nutritionists and nutritional cons. testimony before state legis. coms. State of Fla., Tallahassee, 1983-88; speaker in field. Interviewee numerous TV and radio programs. Fellow Am. Coun. Applied Clin. Nutrition; mem. Internat. and Am. Assn. Clin. Nutritionists (founder 1987, bd. dirs. 1987-91, co-founder Fla. chpt. 1983, bd. dirs. 1986-91, exec. dir. 1986-90, pres. 1991; founding dir. life), Internat. Acad. Nutrition and Preventive Medicine (bd. dirs. 1987-89), N.Am. Acad. Nutrition and Preventive Medicine. Republican. Roman Catholic. Avocation: public speaking. Home and Office: 8743 The Esplanade Blvd Ste 33 Orlando FL 32836 Office Phone: 407-346-1036. Personal E-mail: rosemarieo33@yahoo.com.

OSHCHAPOVSKY, VALENTIN VLADIMIROVICH, chemist, ecologist; b. Lvov, Ukraine, May 26, 1949; s. Vladimir Vasiliyevich and Polina Ivanovna Oshchapovsky; divorced; 1 child, Igor. Degree, Lvov State U., 1971, candidate of chem. scis., 1982. Engr. Spl. Bur. "Systemotechnika", Lvov, 1971-72; sr. scientist Lvov Poly. Inst., 1972-92; leading engr. Inst. Biochemistry, Lvov, 1992-94, Ukrainian Rsch. Inst. of Polygraphic Industry, Lvov, 1994-99, Lviv Chem Silmash Co., Lvov, 2000—02. Scientist Chem. Inst. of Univ., Magdeburg, Germany, 2000—; docent Lviv State U. Life Safety, Lvov, 2001—; cons. Eurotech Ltd., Haifa, Israel, 2000—; mem. editl. bd. Fire Safety jour., 2003—08; sci. cons. State Branch Assn. Lviv Railway, 2007-. Contbr. articles to profl. jours.; patentee in field. Mem.: Am. Chem. Soc. Avocation: football. Home Phone: (380-32) 272-06 81; Office Phone: (380-32) 233-02-02. Personal E-mail: oschapovsky@yahoo.com.

O'SHEA, ANNA BELLE MARIE, music educator, liturgy administrator; b. Evergreen Park, Ill., Apr. 9, 1956; d. Joseph Bernard and Anna Belle Marie O'Shea. MusB, De Paul U., 1978; diploma in Pastoral Liturgy, St. Joseph's Coll., 2003, MA in Ch. Music and Liturgy, 2004. Pvt. flut instr., Chgo., 1976—; prin. flutist N.W. Ind. Symphony, Munster, Ind., 1977—88; freelance flutist Chgo., 1978—; founder, pres, dir. music Flutes Unlimited, Chgo., 1997—. Mem. music staff Archdiocese Chgo., 2000—, dir. liturgies and music Office for Divine Worship, 2007—. Co-author: The Liturgical Flutist: A Method Book and More, 2005. Mem.: Nat. Flute Assn. (performer), Nat. Assn. Pastoral Musicians (clinician, bd. dirs. ensemble sect. 1999—). Roman Catholic.

O'SHEA, CATHERINE LARGE, marketing and public relations consultant; b. Asheville, NC, Feb. 27, 1944; d. Edwin Kirk Jr. and Mary Mitchell (Westall) Large; m. Roger Dean Lower, Dec. 19, 1970 (dec. Sept. 1977); children: Thaddeus Kirk Lower and David Alexander Lower (twins, dec.); m. Michael Joseph O'Shea, Dec. 29, 1980 (div. 2001); m. Arthur I. Wetstein, Mar. 28, 2007. BA in History magna cum laude, Emory U., 1966. Mktg. staff mem. Time Inc., NYC, 1966-69; mktg. adminstr. Collier-Macmillan Internat., NYC, 1970-71; circulation mgr. Coll. Entrance Exam. Bd., NYC, 1971-73; spl. asst. to pres. Wayne Dressel Assocs. Exec. Search, NYC, 1973-75; freelance writer, editor, pub. rels. Princeton, N.J., 1975-78; dir. constituency rels. Emory U., Atlanta, 1978-80; devel. assoc. U. Del., Newark, 1981-83; asst. to pres. Elizabethtown (Pa.) Coll., 1983-85; assoc. v.p. Beaver Coll., Glenside, Pa., 1985—86; cons. mktg. and pub. rels. Phila., S.C., Ga., 1985—. Lectr. in field. Co-author: 50 Secrets of Highly Successful Cats, 1994 (trans. German edit. Schnurrende Tyrannen by Manfred Sommer, 1996); editor Elizabethtown mag., 1983-85; contbr. articles to nat. mags. and profl. jours. Founder Helping Hands Internat.; founding trustee Newberry Opera House Found.; mem. founding com. Rachel Longstreet Found., Jessye Norman Sch. of Arts. Mem. Mortar Bd., Phi Beta Kappa, Phi Mu.

O'SHEA, DONALD C., physicist, educator, optical engineer; b. Akron, Ohio, Nov. 14, 1938; s. Donald Joseph and Sarah O'S.; m. Helen Rose Spustek, Oct. 20, 1962; children: Kathleen Susan, Sean Stanley, Sheila Sarah, Patrick Donald. BS, U. Akron, 1960; MS, Ohio State U., 1963; PhD in Physics, Johns Hopkins U., 1968. Rsch. fellow McKay Lab., Harvard U., Cambridge, Mass., 1968-70; asst. prof. Ga. Inst. Tech., Atlanta, 1970-75, assoc. prof., 1975-87, prof. physics, 1987—2004, prof. emeritus, 2004—. Author: Elements of Modern Optical Design, 1985; co-author: Introduction to Lasers and Their Applications, 1978; editor Optical Engring., 1998-99, 2001-09; co-author Diffractive Optics, 2004; contbr. some 40 articles to profl. jours. Fellow Internat. Soc. Optical Engring. (sec. 1997, v.p. 1999, pres. 2000), Optical Soc. Am. (Esther Hoffman Beller award 1996). Democrat. Roman Catholic. Achievements include creation of the optics discovery kit for children; 3 patents in optical design. Business E-Mail: doshea@prism.gatech.edu.

O'SHEA, JAMES E., former editor-in-chief; b. St. Louis, 1944; BA, MA, U. Mo. Reporter US Army; fin. editor The Des Moines Register, 1973—76, Washington corr., 1976—79; reporter The Chgo. Tribune, 1979—90, assoc. mng. editor for fgn. & nat. news, 1990—95, dep. mng. editor for news, 1995—2001, mng. editor, 2001—06; exec. v.p., editor LA Times, 2006—08. Bd. gov. Oversea Press Club Am. Author: The Daisy Chain, 1991; co-author (with Charles Madigan): Dangerous Company, 1997. Recipient Disting. Svc. award for Washington Correspondence, Sigma Delta Chi, 1985, 1989, Peter Lisagor award, Pub. Svc. award, AP Mng. Editors, Nat. Edn. Writers award, William Jones award, Chgo. Tribune, 1989. Mem.: Sigma Delta Chi.

O'SHEA, JOYCE BURNETT, English educator; b. Six Mile, SC, Oct. 5, 1935; d. William Flavius and Sibyl Marguerite (Wertz) Burnett; m. Roger Clites, Aug. 28, 1955 (div. 1969); children: Margaret Palmer, Nina, John, Paul; m. Robert Martin O'Shea, Jan. 1, 1971; 1 child, Brian Burnett. BA in English, Catawba Coll., Salisbury, NC, 1963; MA in Am. Lit., Appalachian State U., Boone, NC, 1965; postgrad., Kent State U., Ohio. Instr. English Appalachian State U., Boone, N.C., 1965-66; instr. humanities, asst. prof. Parsons Coll., Fairfield, Iowa, 1966-73; instr. English Greenville (S.C.) Tech. Coll., 1975-83, U. Akron (Ohio), 1983-85, So. Ohio Coll., Akron, 1983-85; dept. head communications skills Stark Tech. Coll., Canton, Ohio, 1990—; tchr. Wharton County Jr. Coll, Richmond, Tex. Advisor humanities adv. bd. So. Ohio Coll., Akron, 1990—. Foster parent Foster Parents Plan, 1983—. Mem. AAUP, Nat. Coun. Tchrs. English, Inverness Capers, Mensa. Unitarian Universalist. Avocations: reading, miniatures, criminology, trivia, murder mysteries. Office: Wharton County Jr Coll FBTC Richmond TX Office Phone: 281-239-1570. Business E-Mail: joyceo@wcjc.edu.

O'SHEA, PATRICK GERARD, engineering educator, department chairman; s. Michael and Josephine O'Shea; m. Miriam Smyth, 1986; 1 child, Ronan. BSc in physics, U. Coll. Cork, 1979; MS in physics, U. Md., Coll. Pk., 1982; PhD in physics, U. Md., 1986. Chief accelerator physicist, beam expt. aboard rocket proj. Los Alamos Nat. Lab, N.Mex., 1986—90, project leader apex free-electron laser, 1990—93; instr. physics Duke U., Durham, NC, 1994—98; instr. engring. U. Md., 1998—, dir., inst. rsch. in electronics and applied physics, 2001—05, chmn. elec. and computer engring., 2005—. Contbr. articles to profl. jours. Fellow: AAAS, IEEE, Am. Phys. Soc.; mem.: Wash. Acad. Scis. Office: Univ Md Dept Elec Engring and Computer Engring College Park MD 20742

OSHEROFF, DOUGLAS DEAN, physics professor, researcher; b. Aberdeen, Wash., Aug. 1, 1945; s. William and Bessie Anne (Ondov) Osheroff; m. Phyllis S.K. Liu, Aug. 14, 1970. BS in Physics, Calif. Inst. Tech., 1967; MS, Cornell U., 1969, PhD in Physics, 1973. Mem. tech. staff Bell Labs., Murray Hill, NJ, 1972—82, head solid state and low temperature physics research dept., 1982—87; prof. Stanford (Calif.) U., 1987—, J.G. Jackson and C.J. Wood prof. physics, 1992—, chair physics, 1993—96, 2001—. Mem. Columbia Accident Investigation Bd., 2003. Recipient Oliver E. Buckley Solid State Physics prize, 1981, Walter J. Gores award, 1991, Nobel prize in Physics, 1996; co-recipient Simon Meml. prize, Brit. Inst. Physics, 1976; fellow John D. and Catherine T. MacArthur prize, 1981. Fellow: Am. Acad. Arts and Scis., Am. Phys. Soc.; mem.: NAS. Achievements include research in properties of matter near absolute zero of temperature; co-discovery of nuclear antiferromagnetic resonance in solid 3He, superfluidity in helium-3. Office: Stanford U Rm 150 Varian Physics Bldg 382 Via Pueblo Mall Stanford CA 94305-4060 Fax: 650-725-6544. E-mail: osheroff@stanford.edu.*

OSHEROFF, NEIL, biochemist, educator; b. Washington, Apr. 23, 1952; s. Milton and Ruthanne Osheroff; m. Cheryl Ann Guyer, Nov. 24, 1985; 1 child, Michael Addison. PhD, Northwestern U., Evanston, Ill., 1979. Prof., biochemistry & medicine Vanderbilt U. Sch. Medicine, Nashville, 1994—, John G. Coniglio chair, biochemistry, 2003—09. Contbr. articles to jours. Rsch. grants, NIH, 1984—2009. Office: Vanderbilt Univ Sch Medicine 2200 Pierce Ave Nashville TN 37232-0146 Office Fax: 615-322-6350. Business E-Mail: neil.osheroff@vanderbilt.edu.

OSHINSKY, DAVID M., history professor, writer; PhD, Brandeis Univ., 1971. Prof. polit., cultural history Rutgers U., New Brunswick, NJ, 1971—2002; George Littlefield Prof. Am. History U. Tex., Austin, 2002—. Co-editor The Oxford Companion to United States History; co-author: American Passages: A History of the United States; author: A Conspiracy So Immense: The World of Joe McCarthy, 1983 (Hardeman Prize as best book about US Congress, NY Times Notable Book), Worse Than Slavery: Parchman Farm and the Ordeal of Jim Crow Justice, 1996 (Robert Kennedy Prize for contbn. to human rights, NY Times Notable Book), Polio: An American Story, 2005 (Pulitzer Prize for History, 2006). Office: Univ Tex Austin David M Oshinsky--GAR 206 1 Univ Station Austin TX 78712 Office Phone: 512-475-7230. Business E-Mail: oshinsky@mail.utexas.edu.

OSHINSKY, JAMES STEVEN, psychologist; b. NYC, Oct. 29, 1951; s. Myron H. and Marilyn (Robinson) O.; m. Candace H. Pinquist, Aug. 19, 1972 (div. 1985); 1 child, Joshua Adam; m. Emily Jane Metcalf, May 27, 1990; children: Breanna Bell, Kira Lani. BA, U. Pa., 1972; PhD, U. Tenn., 1977; postgrad., Adelphi U., 1981; Profl. Cert., Derner Inst. Lic. psychologist, N.Y.; cert. sch. psychologist, N.Y. Vis. asst. prof. psychology Ind. U., Bloomington, 1977-78; asst. prof. Adelphi U., Garden City, N.Y., 1978-81; assoc. psychologist Cen. Islip Psychiat. Ctr., N.Y., 1981-84; sch. psychologist Vision Impaired Program, Nassau BOCES, Wantagh, N.Y., 1984-89, Farmingdale (N.Y.) Pub. Schs., 1989—; pvt. practice Baldwin, N.Y., 1982—. Author: Discovery Journal, 1991; feature writer newsletter Free Spirit News and View on Growing Up, 1991-92, War and Young People, 1991; contbr. articles to profl. jours.; published poet and songwriter; appeared on recordings of storyteller Heather Forest and folkartists Patricia Shih and Janice Buckner. Bd. dirs. Music for People, 1990-91, interim dir., 1997; coord. music retreats with Paul Winter, 1984-89. Mem. APA, Nassau County Psychol. Assn., Pi Kappa Phi. Avocations: music improvisation, camping, vintage baseball.

OSHMAN, GENE JAY, lawyer; b. Wharton, Tex., Jan. 21, 1958; s. Ben J. and Esther B. (Balfour) O.; m. Karen Eve Appel, May 30, 1982; children: Stephen, Katherine. BA summa cum laude, hist., Yale U., 1980, JD, 1983. Bar: Tex. 1984. Law clk. to Hon. M. Joseph Blumenfield US Dist. Ct. Conn., Hartford, 1983-84; assoc. Baker Botts LLP, Houston, 1984-90, ptnr., 1990—. Sr. editor: Yale Law Jour., 1982—83; contbr. articles to profl. jours. Recipient Best Lawyers in America, Woodward White, Inc., 2001—, Best Lawyers, H Tex. mags., 2001—, Tex. Super Lawyer, Tex. Monthly and Law & Politics, 2003—; named Guide to World's Leading Mergers and Acquisitions Lawyers, Exports Guides, 2004—06; named to BTI Client Svcs. All-Star Team for law firms. Mem. Coronado Club, Phi Beta Kappa, Houston Bar Assn., bd. trustees, Houston Ballet(mem., bd. trustees, 2007-) Office: Baker Botts LLP 910 Louisiana St 1 Shell Plaza Houston TX 77002 Office Fax: 713-229-7778. Business E-Mail: gene.oshman@bakerbotts.com.

OSICKA, TERESA D., health economist, consultant; arrived in US, 1998; d. Antoni Osicki and Apolonia Osicka; m. Andrzej Delegacz, Aug. 17, 2003. MA in Econs., U. Warsaw, Warsaw, Poland, 1990, diploma in Health Econs., 1991, U. Tromso, Norway, 1993; MS in Computer Sci., The Cath. U. Am., DC, 2002. Sr. specialist health care Nat. Ctr. Health Sys. Mgmt., Warsaw, 1990—94; coord. health reform project Ministry Health and Social Welfare, Warsaw, 1991—93; chief specialist health care fin. Ministry Fin., Warsaw, 1994—99; database mgr. The Georgetown U., Washington, 1999—, rsch. asst. Med. Ctr., 1999—. Cons. UNESCO, Paris, 2005—, The World Bank, Washington, 2002—; fellow George Wash. U., 1998, Johns Hopkins U., Balt., 1999; lectr. in field. Contbr. articles to profl. jours. Recipient Cum Laude Poster award, Internat. Soc. Optical Engring. Med. Imaging, 2002, Hon. Poster award, 2003. Mem.: Assn. Health Care Mgrs. (v.p. 1991—93). Achievements include research in discrete wavelets transform application to the pulmonary nodules characterization on computer tomography (CT) scans with regard to their ability to discriminate benign and malignant nodules signals. Office: Georgetown U Medical Center 2115 Wisconsin Ave NW Washington DC 20007 Home: 1020 N Quincy ST Apt 1023 Arlington VA 22201-4654 Office Fax: 202-784-3479. Business E-Mail: osicka@isis.imac.georgetown.edu.

OSINSKI, MARTIN HENRY, healthcare consultant; s. Stanley and Shirley (Bobick) Osinski; m. Margie Osinski; children: Ashley, Brett, Justin, Kevin. BBA in Acctg., U. Miami, Coral Gables, Fla., 1975, MBA, 1977. Cert. Accredited Valuation Analyst Nat. Assn. Cert. Valuation Analysts. Grad. asst. U. Miami, Fla., 1975-77; staff acct. Ernst & Ernst, CPA, Miami, 1977-78; asst. buyer, dept. mgr. Burdines Dept. Stores, Miami, 1978-80; buyer menswear Jefferson Ward Dept. Stores, Miami, 1980-82, Richway Dept. Stores, Atlanta, 1982-84; pres. Nat. Health Search, Inc., Miami, 1984-95; chief oper. officer MD Resources, Inc., Miami, 1989-95; prin. Am. Med. Consultants, Inc., Miami, 1996—; pres. Nephrology USA, 2002—. Mem. editl. adv. bd. Nephrology News and Issues, 2004—; contbr. articles to profl. pubs. Bd. dirs. Congregation Bet Breira, 1994-98, 2002-. Mem.: Am. Soc. Nephrology, Nat. Assn. Physician Recruiters (bd. dirs. 1989—96, v.p. 1990—91, pres. 1991—92, ethics com. 2001—, bd. dirs. 2004—, v.p. 2006—, pres. 2008—09, Presdl. award 1991, 2006), Iron Arrow Soc. U. Miami, Mens Club (pres. 1992—94). Office: Am Med Consultants Inc 11625 SW 110th Rd Miami FL 33176-3152 Home Phone: 305-274-9910; Office Phone: 305-271-9225. Personal E-mail: amcmo@bellsouth.net.

OSMAN, LEE R., lawyer; b. 1965; BS in Mech. Engring., Colo. State U., 1988; JD, U. Denver, 1993. Bar: Colo. 1993, registered: US Patent and Trademark Office. Engr. Honeywell, ATMEL Corp.; atty., intellectual property group Holland & Hart, Denver; ptnr. Dorsey & Whitney LLP, Denver, 2000—, and chair, worldwide patent group, 2003—06, head, intellectual property group, 2004—07, chair worldwide patent group, 2007—. Named one of 40 Under 40, Denver Bus. Jour., 2004. Mem.: Pi Tau Sigma. Office: Dorsey & Whitney LLP Ste 4700 Republic Plz Bldg 370 Seventeenth St Denver CO 80202-5647 Office Phone: 303-629-3434. Office Fax: 303-629-3450. Business E-Mail: osman.lee@dorsey.com.

OSMAR, CHRISTINA, psychologist; d. William Kennith Senters and Molly Ann. Fischer, Gregory Allen Fischer (Stepfather); m. John Francis Osmar, July 17, 2004; 1 child, Alexander Bryce. PsyS, MA, Cleve. State U., Ohio, 2004. Sch. psychologist Summit County Ednl. Svc. Ctr., Cuyahoga Falls, Ohio, 2004—07, Moore County Schs., Carthage, NC, 2007—. Office: Moore County Schs PO Box 1180 Carthage NC 28327

OSMENT, HALEY JOEL, actor; b. LA, Apr. 10, 1988; s. Eugene Osment. Actor: (Broadway plays) American Buffalo, 2008; (films) Forrest Gump, 1994, Mixed Nuts, 1994, For Better or Worse, 1995, Bogus, 1996, I'll Remember April, 1999, The Sixth Sense, 1999 (Acad. award nomination, 2000, MTV Movie award for Breakthrough Male Performance, 2000), Pay it Forward, 2000, Artificial Intelligence: AI, 2001, Edges of the Lord, 2001, Secondhand Lions, 2003, Home of the Giants, 2007; (TV films) Lies of the Heart: The Story of Laurie Kellogg, 1994, Last Stand at Saber River, 1997, The Lake, 1998, The Ransom of Red Chief, 1998, Cab to Canada, 1998; (TV series) Thunder Alley, 1994—95, The Jeff Foxworthy Show, 1995—97, Murphy Brown, 1997—98, (voice actor): (films) Beauty and the Beast: The Enchanted Christmas, 1997, Edward Fudwupper Fibbed Big, 2000, Discover Spot, 2000, The Country Bears, 2002, The Hunchback of Notre Dame II, 2002, The Jungle Book 2, 2003, (video games) Kingdom Hearts, 2002, Kingdom Hearts II, 2005, Kingdom Hearts: Chain of Memories, 2007. Office: c/o Meredith Fine Coast to Coast Talent Group 3350 Barham Blvd Los Angeles CA 90068-1404*

OSMOND, DENNIS GORDON, anatomist, researcher, medical educator; b. NYC, Jan. 31, 1930; s. Ernest Gordon and Marjorie Bertha (Milton) O.; m. Anne Welsh, July 30, 1955; children: Roger Gordon, Martin Henry, David Richard. BSc with first class honors, U. Bristol, Eng., 1951, MB, ChB, 1954, DSc, 1975. House surgeon Royal Gwent Hosp., Newport, England, 1954-55; house physician Bristol Royal

Infirmary, 1955; demonstrator, lectr. anatomy U. Bristol, 1957-60, 61-64; instr. anatomy U. Wash., Seattle, 1960-61; assoc. prof. anatomy McGill U., Montreal, Que., Canada, 1965-67, prof., 1967-74, Robert Reford prof. anatomy, 1974-00, chmn. dept. anatomy and cell biology, 1985-95, Robert Reford emeritus prof. anatomy, 2000—. Vis. scientist Walter and Eliza Hall Inst. Med. Research, Melbourne, Australia, 1972-73; hon. sr. research fellow U. Birmingham, Eng., 1979; vis. scientist Basel Inst. Immunology, Switzerland, 1980, 96; Gaylord scholar Okla. Med. Rsch. Found., 1995. Contbr. numerous articles to profl. jours. Served with Royal Army Med. Corps, 1955-57. Fellow Royal Soc. Can.; mem. Am. Assn. Anatomists, Can. Assn. Anatomists, Anat. Soc. Gt. Britain and Ireland, Am., Can. assns. for immunology, Am. Assn. Immunology, Internat. Soc. for Exptl. Hematology, Order of Can. Home: 1380 Revell Dr Manotick ON Canada K4M 1K8 Personal E-mail: dennisosmond@rogers.com.

OSMOND, MARIE, singer; b. Ogden, Utah, Oct. 13, 1959; d. George and Olive O.; m. Stephen Craig, June 26, 1982 (div. 1985); m. Brian Blosil, Oct. 28, 1986 (separated); children: Stephen James, Jessica Marie, Rachel, Michael, Brandon, Brianna, Matthew, Abigail. Student pub. schs., pvt. tutors. Appeared with The Osmond family singing group from age 7, solo act, 1973;(TV co-star): Donny & Marie TV show, 1976-79, Donny & Marie Christmas Spl, 1979, Osmond Family Show, 1979, Osmond Family Christmas Show, 1980, Donny & Marie, 1998; (star TV spl.) Marie, 1981; appeared in TV series Maybe This Time, 1995, video Buster & Chauncey's Silent Night, 1998; (record albums) include (with Donny Osmond): Make the World Go Away, I'm Leaving It All Up To You; songs from their TV Show Goin Coconuts; (solo albums) include: Paper Roses, In My Little Corner of the World, Who's Sorry Now?, This Is The Way That I Feel, There's No Stopping Your Heart, 1985, I Only Wanted You, 1987, All In Love, 1988, Steppin' Stone, 1989, Twenty Five Hits-Special Collection, 1995; (#1 singles) include Meet Me in Montana (Best Country Duo of Yr. award with Dan Seals), 1986, You're Still New to Me, 1986, There's No Stoppin' Your Heart, 1986, I Only Wanted You, 1987, The Best Of, 1990; toured with Bob Hope, Persian Gulf, 1991; (co-author): Fun, Fame, and Family, 1973; Marie Osmond's Guide to Beauty, Health, and Style, 1980; performer Dancing With the Stars, 2007. Recipient (with Donny Osmond) Georgie award for best vocal team Am. Guild Variety Artists, 1978. Mem. Lds Ch.

OSNOS, DAVID MARVIN, lawyer, director; b. Detroit, Jan. 10, 1932; s. Max and Florence (Pollock) O.; m. Glenna DeWitt, Aug. 10, 1956; children: Matthew, Alison AB summa cum laude, Harvard U., 1953, JD cum laude, 1956. Bar: D.C. 1956. Assoc. Arent Fox LLP (formerly Arent, Fox, Kintner, Plotkin & Kahn), Washington, 1956—61, ptnr., 1962—2002, chmn. exec. com., 1978—97, of counsel, 2003—. Bd. dirs. EastGroup Properties, Jackson, Miss., VSE Corp., Alexandria, Va., Washington Wizards Basketball Club, Washington. Trustee Mt. St. Mary's Coll., Emmitsburg, Md., 1981-90; bd. dirs. Greater Washington Jewish Cmty. Found., Rockville, Md., Jewish Cmty. Ctr. Greater Washington, 1964-75. Avocations: tennis, music, enology. Office: Arent Fox 1050 Connecticut Ave NW Ste 600 Washington DC 20036-5339 Office Phone: 202-857-6150. Business E-Mail: osnosd@arentfox.com.

OSOFF, JEFFREY ARLIN, media company executive; b. Everett, Mass., June 5, 1936; s. Meyer and Minerva (Cogan) O. (dec.); m. Arlene Shuman, Sept. 23, 1962 (div. Jan. 1988); children: Judith Robin (dec.), David Eric; m. Donna M. Peyre-Ferry, May 26, 1997. BA, Bowling Green State U., 1958; MS, Columbia U., 1959. Reporter Boston Post, 1954-55, Boston Globe, 1955-64, rewriteman, 1962-63, acting asst. city editor, 1963-64; dir. News Bur. Brandeis U., Waltham, Mass., 1964-67, asst. dir. pub. affairs, 1967-69, dir. pub. affairs, 1969-76; chmn. bd. Jansson, Inc., Waltham, 1976-87; pres., chief exec. officer JAO Enterprises, Ltd., Hudson, Mass., 1987—; chmn. Dorian Enterprises, Ltd., 1992—, D & J Enterprises, Ltd., Hudson, Mass., 1995—; chmn. bd. Concannon's Inc., Marlborough and Wellesley, Mass., 1990—98. Lectr. in journalism and pub. rels. cons. First v.p. Dysautonomia Found., NY, 1965-66, bd. dirs., 1965-76, pres., 1973-74; bd. dirs. New Eng. region Anti-Defamation League. Served with USAF, 1961-62. Recipient citation for outstanding journalistic reporting Mass. N.G., 1961; several awards for high achievement in graphics. Mem. New Eng. Press Assn., Internat. Thermographic Assn., Printing Industries Am., Printing Industries New Eng., Am. Coll. Pub. Rels. Assn., Jewish Pub. Relations Soc. Am., Pub. Rels. Soc. Am., Publicity Club Boston, Sigma Delta Chi, Zeta Beta Tau. Jewish. Home and Office: 3E Autumn Dr Hudson MA 01749-2855 Personal E-mail: josoff@comcast.net.

OSOSANYA, ESTHER TITILAYO, engineering educator; PhD in Elec. Engring., U. DC. Prof. elec. and computer engring. U. DC, Washington, 2001—. Office: Univ DC 4200 Connecticut Ave NW Washington DC 20008 Office Fax: 202-274-6311. Business E-Mail: eososanya@udc.edu.

OSSELLO, KRISTIE, music educator; d. Carmen Holmes; m. John Ossello, Dec. 11, 1991; children: Bailey, Kiley, Jack. BA, U. St. Mary, Leavenworth, Kans., 1992; postgrad., Emporia State U., 2005—. Band dir. Most Pure Heart of Mary Sch., Topeka, 1996—, Hayden H.S., Topeka, 2003—. Musician: (performance) Coleman Hawkins Jazz Festival; composer: (drum line, handbells) Drum Line Features, Handbell Scores. Educator nominator Nat. Youth Leadership Coun., Washington, 2004—07; judge 4-H, Topeka, 1996—98; band mem. Marshall's Civic Band, Topeka, 1997—2006; summer camp tchr. Camp Polycarp, Topeka, 1998—99, Lion's Band, Baldwin City, Kans., 2000—00; dir. parade band St. Patrick's Day Parade, Topeka, 2002—07; judge Battle of the Bands, Topeka, 2004—06; music dir. Most Pure Heart of Mary Ch., Topeka, 1997—2002. Recipient Teachers Make a Difference award, Channel 49 TV Sta., 2001; named Educator of Distinction, Nat. Soc. H.S. Scholars, 2005. Mem.: Cath. Band Dirs. Assn., Am. Guild English Handbell Ringers, Internat. Assn. Jazz Educators, Nat. Assn. Music Educators, Kappa Gamma Pi. Avocations: range shooting, travel, reading, walking, hiking. Personal E-mail: ossellok@haydenhigh.org.

OSSEO-ASARE, KWADWO, engineering educator; Disting. prof. metals sci. and engring. and geo-environ. engring. U. Pa.; Kwadwo Osseo-Asare disting. prof. material sci. and engring. and geo-environ. engring. Pa. State U., University Park. Contbr. articles to profl. jours. Mem.: NAE. Office: Pa State U 208 Steidle Bldg University Park PA 16802-5000 Office Phone: 814-865-4882. Office Fax: 814-863-4718. E-mail: asare@ems.psu.edu.

OSSER, DAVID NEAL, psychiatrist, educator; b. NYC, Aug. 30, 1946; s. Abe A. and Edna (Meisel) Osser; m. Stephanie D. Fleischer; children: Roselin Emily, Daniel Alexander. BA, Amherst Coll., 1968; MD, SUNY, Syracuse, 1972. Intern in psychiatry U. So. Calif., LA, 1972-73; resident in psychiatry Mass. Mental Health Ctr. Harvard U., Boston, 1973-76; pvt. practice Needham, Mass., 1976—; assoc. prof. psychiatry Harvard U. Med. Sch., Boston, 1999—. Lectr. Tufts U. Med. Sch., 1978—, Taunton State Hosp., 1976—, Faulkner Hosp., 1976—, Brockton VA Med. Ctr., 1995—. Author: internet decision support software for psychopharmacology; contbr. to pharmacol. websites, internat. psychopharmacology algorithm project, articles to profl. jours. Recipient Lundbeck Internat. Neuroscience Found. prize, 2004, Journalism award, Kantar Found., 2001, award of excellence in edn., Internat. Psychopharm. Algorithm Project, 2006. Fellow: Am. Psychiat. Assn. (life; disting. mem.); mem.: Internat. Coll. Neuro-psychopharmacologicum, Mass. Psychiat. Soc. (pres. 2001—02), Am. Soc. Clin. Psychopharmacology. Democrat. Jewish. Avocations: classical music, opera, piano, canoeing, hiking. Office: 150 Winding River Rd Needham MA 02492-1025 Office Phone: 781-237-7444.

OSSOFF, ROBERT HENRY, otolaryngologist, surgeon; b. Beverly, Mass., Mar. 25, 1947; s. Michael Max and Eve Joan (Kladky) G.; m. Lynn Spilman, 1984; 2 children: Leslin, Jacob. BA, Bowdoin Coll., Brunswick, Maine, 1969; DMD, Tufts U., Medford, Mass., 1973, MD, 1975; MS in Otolaryngology, Northwestern U., Evanston, Ill., 1981. Diplomate Am. Bd. Otolaryngology. Intern Northwestern Meml. Hosp., Chgo., 1975-76; resident in otolaryngology and maxillofacial surgery Northwestern U. Med. Sch., Chgo., 1976—80, NIH rsch. fellow dept. otolaryngology and maxillofacial surgery, 1977-78, clin. fellow in head and neck surgery, 1980-81; jr. faculty clin. fellow Am. Cancer Soc. Northwestern Med. Sch., Chgo., 1981-84; faculty practice, otolaryngology, head and neck surgery, laryngology and care of profl. voice Northwestern Med. Sch., Chgo., 1981—86, Vanderbilt U. Med. Ctr., Nashville, 1986—, prof., chmn. dept. otolaryngology, 1986—2008, prof., otolaryngology, 2008—; exec. med. dir. Vanderbilt Voice Ctr., 1991—. Attending physician Cook County Hosp., Chgo., 1981—83, cons. physician, 1983—86; attending physician Northwestern Meml. Hosp, Chgo., 1981—86, Children's Meml. Hosp., Chgo., 1981—86; attending physician, chief otolaryngology svc. VA Lakeside Hosp., Chgo., 1982—85; attending physician, head divsn. otolaryngology head and neck surgery Evanston Hosp., 1983—86, chief divsn. otolaryngology, 1983—86; asst. prof. Northwestern U. Dental Sch., Chgo., 1980—86, Northwestern U. Med. Sch., Chgo., 1981—85, assoc. prof., 1985—86; attending surgeon, otolaryngologist-in-chief Vanderbilt U. Hosp., Nashville, 1986—, chief staff, 1995—97; attending surgeon VA Hosp., Nashville, 1986—; Guy M. Maness prof., chmn. dept. otolaryngology Vanderbilt U. Med. Ctr., Nashville, 1986—, assoc. vice chancellor health affairs, 1995—2005; assoc. dir. Vanderbilt Free-Electron Laser Ctr. Med. and Materials Rsch., Nashville, 1992—95; dir. Vanderbilt Bill Wilkerson Ctr. Otolaryngology Communication Scis., Nashville, 1997—. Sr. editor Lasers in Surgery and Medicine, 1987—94, editor-in-chief, 1995—2005, laryngology sect. editor Otolaryngology-Head and Neck Surgery, 2005—, mem. editl. bd. Clin. Laser Monthly, 1984—, Jour. Voice, 1987—, The Laryngoscope, 1988—2003, Jour. of Laser Applications, 1988—2004, Otolaryngology-Head and Neck Surgery, 1988—, mem. editl. adv. bd. Gen. Surgery News, 1990—97, mem. editl. bd. Archives of Otolaryngology, 2006—, assoc. editor Diagnostic and Therapeutic Endoscopy, 1992—2000; co-editor: Complications in Head and Neck Surgery, W.B. Saunders Co., 1993, The Larynx, Lippincott Williams and Wilkins, 2002; contbr. over 160 articles to profl. jours., 60 chpts. in books; editor, co-editor (8 books in field). Bd. dirs. Laser Inst. Am., 1984—90; trustee Midwest Biolaser Inst., Chgo., 1981—86, Leadership Nashville, 1988—89. Recipient Nat. Rsch. Svc. award, NIH, 1977-78; Francis L. Lederer-Norval H. Pierce award, Chgo. Laryngol. and Otol. Soc., 1978, Hon. mem., 1986; Guest of Honor, First European Carbon Dioxide Laser Surgery Coruse and Workshop in Otolaryngology Head and Neck Surgery, Roskilde, Denmark, 1984; named a Prin. Investigator, NIH, 1977-78; Am. Cancer Soc., Ill. Divsn., 1981-82; VA Merit Rev., 1884-85; Nat. Cancer Inst., 1985-88; Office Naval Rsch., 1987-90, 91-94; A. Ward Ford Found., 1989-90. Fellow: ACS (bd. govs. 1996—2002, adv. coun. Otorhinolarygology 1996—2003), Am. Laryngol. Assn. (chmn. rsch. support task force 1994—96, coun. mem. 1996—98, sec. 1998—2003, Daniel C. Baker Jr. lectr. 2001, v.p., pres. elect 2003—04, pres. 2004—05, presdl. citation 2008, Guest of Honor 2002, Presdl. citation 2003, DeRoaldes medal 2004, James Newcomb award 2007), The Triological Soc. (nat. nominating com. 1993, coun. mem. 1996—99, thesis adv. com. 1998—99, v.p. so. sect. 2002—03, coun. mem. 2002—03, 2005—, dir., CME 2005—, Presdl. Citation 2008, Presdl. Citation 2006), Am. Soc. Head and Neck Surgery (coun. mem. 1991—94); mem.: AMA, Soc. Univ. Otolaryngologists Head and Neck Surgeons (coun. mem. 2002—05, pres.-elect 2004—05, pres. 2005—06), Assn. Academic Depts. Otolaryngology Head Neck Surgery (sec.-treas. 1996—98, pres. elect 1998—2000, pres. 2000—02, coun. mem. 2002—04), Am. Laryngol. Voice Rsch. Edn. Found. (bd. dirs. 1996—, sec. 1998—2003), Am. Bd. Otolaryngology (task force for new materials mem. 1985—89, assoc. examiner 1994—97, dir. 1995—2007), Cartesian Soc., Am. Broncho-Esophagological Assn. (coun. mem. 1987—90, treas. 1990—94, pres.-elect 1994—95, pres. 1995—96, Chevalier Jackson award 1997, Guest of Honor 2000), Soc. Head and Neck Surgeons, Am. Soc. Laser Medicine and Surgery (bd. dirs. 1985—88, chmn. program com. 1986—87, pres.-elect 1988—89, pres. 1989—90, nominating com. 1990—91, William B. Mark award 1992, Presdl. citation 2003), Am. Acad. Otolaryngology-Head and Neck Surgery (chmn. laser surgery com. 1983—89, chmn. self instl. package com. 1990—96, bd. dirs. 1992—95, coord. for devel. 2001—06, Cert. of Honor 1984, Disting. Svc. award 1995, Presdl. citation 1999, Disting. Svc. award 2004, Presdl. citation 2005), Am. Acad. Oral Pathology, Am. Acad. Oral Medicine, Sigma Xi, Omicron Kappa Upsilon. Achievements include reestablishment of department of otolaryngology at Vanderbilt University Medical Center in 1986; establishment of the Vanderbilt Voice Center in 1991; establishment of an advanced training laryngology fellowship program at Vanderbilt University Medical Center in 1992. Avocations: boating, skiing, fly fishing, golf, photography. Office Phone: 615-322-6326. Business E-Mail: robert.ossoff@vanderbilt.edu.

OSSTYN, RANDOLPH BEIER, lawyer; b. Royal Oak, Mich., Apr. 24, 1943; s. Alouis and Doris Helen (Finnie) O.; children: Alicia Anne, Neal Randolph; m. Carrie Ann Wood, May 3, 1997. BA, MA, U. Mich.; JD magna cum laude, U. Detroit. Bar: U.S. Supreme Ct. 1980; bd. cert. creditors rights atty. Am. Bd. Cert., 1993. Tchr., dept. head Detroit Bd. Edn., 1969—76; founding ptnr. Osstyn, Ferns & Quinnell, Marquette, Mich., 1979—. Lectr. collection law in Mich., 2002. Treas. Prince of Peach Luth. Ch., Marquette, 1978-81; founding mem. Save the Janzen Com., Marquette, 1983-85; mem ch. council Messiah Luth. Ch., Marquette, 1984-85; bd. dirs. Marquette Mountain Racing Team, 1982-90, pres., 1986-89. Mem.: ABA, Comml. Law League Am., Mich. Bar Assn., Wis. Bar Assn. Democrat. Avocations: skiing, running, bridge. Home: 43 White Oak Dr Marquette MI 49855-9450 Office: Osstyn Ferns & Quinnell 419 W Washington St Ste 500 Marquette MI 49855-4322 Office Phone: 906-228-3650. E-mail: rosstyn@charternet.net.

OSTAR, ALLAN WILLIAM, educational consultant; b. East Orange, NJ, Sept. 4, 1924; s. William and Rose O.; m. Roberta Hutchison, Sept. 10, 1949; children. Cert. engring., U. Denver, 1943; BA, Pa. State U., 1948; postgrad., U. Wis., 1949-55; LL.D., U. No. Colo., 1968, Eastern Ky. U., 1972, Whittier Coll., 1973; L.H.D., U. Maine, 1975; D.Letters, Central Mich. U., 1975; D.P.S., Bowling Green State U., 1975, R.I. Coll., 1983; D.Higher Edn., Morehead State U., 1977; L.H.D., Appalachian State U., 1977, No. Mich. U., 1978, Dickinson State Coll., ND, 1979, Towson State U., 1980, Salem State Coll., 1980, Mont. Coll. Mineral Sci. and Tech., 1983, Ball State U., 1984; LL.D., U. Alaska, 1978, Ill. State U., 1983, Western Mich. U., 1984; D. Polit. Sci., Kyung Hee U., Korea, 1984; L.H.D., Fitchburg State Coll., 1986, Bridgewater State Coll., 1988, No. State Coll., 1988, Harris-Stowe State Coll., 1986; LLD, Edinboro U. Pa., 1987, Loch Haven U., Pa., 1989; LHD, No. Ariz. U., 1990, Shepherd Coll., W.Va., 1992, SUNY, 1993, Lincoln U., Mo., 1995. Dir. nat. pub. relations U.S. Nat. Student Assn., 1948-49; exec. asst. Commonwealth Fund, NYC, 1952-53; asst. to dean extension div. U. Wis., 1949-52, dir. office communications services, 1954-58; dir. Joint Office Instnl. Research, Nat. Assn. State Univs. and Land Grant Colls., Washington, 1958-65; pres. Am. Assn. State Colls. and Univs., Washington, 1965-91, pres. emeritus, 1991—; sr. cons. Acad. Search Consultation Svc., 1991—2005. Adj. prof. edn. Pa. State U., 1991—98; bd. dir. Seabrook Village, 2007—. Co-author: Colleges and Universities for Change, 1987; contbr. chpts. in books. Mem. 42d (Rainbow) div. U.S. Army, 1943-46. Decorated 2 Bronze Stars with V, Combat Infantryman's badge; recipient Centennial award U. Akron, 1970, Fogelsanger award Shippensburg (Pa.) State Coll., 1974, World Peace Through Edn. medal Internat. Assn. U. Pres., 1975, Disting. Achievement award, U. So. Colo., 1979, Chancellor's award U. Wis., 1985, Chancellor's medal CUNY, 1986, Disting. Alumnus award Pa. State U., 1989, svc. award Coun. on Internat. Ednl. Exch., 1990, Chancellor's medal Internat. Svc. U. Ark., Little Rock, 1990, Disting. Pub. Svc. medal Dept. of Def., 1991; Alumni fellow Pa. State U., 1975. Unitarian-Universalist. Home: 404 Sandy Cove Tinton Falls NJ 07753-7745

OSTARLY-ULFERS, LORI ANN, history professor; b. Corpus Christi, Tex., Nov. 29, 1964; d. Adam Raymond and Juliette Anne Ostarly; m. Ron Paul Ulfers, Nov. 19, 1999; children: Angelle Marie Ulfers, Juliette Ann Ulfers, Audrey Jeanmarsi Ulfers, Christian Loraine Ulfers. MA in History, Southeastern La. U., Hammond, 1990. Instr. Southeastern La. U., 1991—. Office: Southeastern La Univ POBox 10895 Hammond LA 70402 Business E-Mail: lostarly@selu.edu.

OSTBERG, HENRY DEAN, marketing executive; b. Bocholt, Germany, July 21, 1928; came to U.S., 1939, naturalized, 1945. s. Fred and Lotte (Hertz) O.; m. Sydelle Burns, Dec. 13, 1987; 1 child, Neal; stepchildren: Elysa Bari, Brent Adam, Ross Jay. LLB, N.Y. Law Sch., 1950; MBA, Ohio State U., 1953, PhD, 1957. Pres. H.D. Ostberg Assocs., NYC, 1950—; assoc. prof. mktg. NYU, 1954—63. Chmn. bd. Admar Group,Inc., 1960; dir. Self-Instructional Devel. Corp., Amherst Group, Porter Industries, Inc.; pres. Eastman Enterprises, Inc. Contbr. articles to profl. jours. Trustee Ostberg Found.; chmn. Givat Haviva Edn. Found. Capt. USAF, 1950—53. Jewish. Personal E-mail: hdousa@earthlink.net.

OSTBY, FREDERICK PAUL, JR., meteorologist, retired government official, science administrator; b. New Haven, Jan. 20, 1930; s. Frederick Paul and Edna Maria (Kruckenberg) O.; m. Joanne Bernice Sorvig, Jan. 1, 1955 (div. 1989); children: Paul, Neil, Karen, Lynn; m. Barbara Richards, Mar. 17, 1989. BS in Meteorology, NYU, 1951, MS in Meteorology, 1960. Cert. Consulting Meteorologist. Meteorologist TWA, NYC, 1953-54, Kansas City, Mo., 1955-56, N.E. Weather Service, Lexington, Mass., 1955, Travelers Weather Service, Hartford, Conn., 1956-60; research scientist Travelers Research Center, Hartford, 1960-70; meteorologist Nat. Weather Service, Silver Spring, Md., 1970-72; dep. dir. Nat. Severe Storms Forecast Center, Dept. Commerce, Kansas City, Mo., 1972-80; dir. Nat. Severe Storms Forecast Center, 1980-96; assoc. Climatological Cons. Corp., 1997—. Severe weather cons. The Weather Channel, 1997—98. Contbr. papers to profl. lit. Air weather officer USAF, 1951—53. Fellow Am. Meteorol. Soc. (council 1977-80, 84-87). Republican. Methodist. Home: 12537 Broadmoor St Overland Park KS 66209-3234 Home Phone: 913-338-4222; Office Phone: 913-338-4222. Personal E-mail: fostby@sbcglobal.net.

OSTBYE, TRULS, medical researcher, educator; b. Norway, Dec. 15, 1954; arrived in U.S., 1999; m. Hemali Kulatilaka, 1984; children: Trevor, Adrian. MD, U. Bergen, 1979; MPH, Harvard U., 1983; PhD, U. Bergen, 2000; MBA, Edinburgh Bus. Sch., 2000. Exec. officer Directorate of Orgn. and Mgmt., Norway, 1981—84; spl. med. officer Nat. Inst. Pub. Health, Norway, 1984—85; lectr. U. Otago, New Zealand, 1985—86; Lalia B. Chase rsch. fellow Dalhousie U., Halifax, N.S., Canada, 1986—88; asst. prof. to prof. U. We. Ont., London, Canada, 1988—99; prof., vice chair rsch. Dept. Cmty. and Family Medicine Duke U., Durham, NC, 2000—; prof. Duke-NUS Grad. Med. Sch., Singapore, 2008—. Contbr. more than 220 articles to profl. jours. Office: Duke U Dept Cmty and Family Medicine DUMC 104006 Durham NC 27710 E-mail: truls.ostbye@duke.edu.

OSTEEN, JOEL, minister; b. Houston, Mar. 5, 1963; s. John and Dodie Osteen; m. Victoria Iloff, 1987; children: Jonathan, Alexandria. Student, Oral Roberts U., 1981—82. Ordained 1992. Prodr., creator John Osteen TV Program, 1982—99; pres., co-owner Sta. KTBU Channel 55, Houston, 1998—; sr. pastor Lakewood Ch., Houston, 1999—. Author: Your Best Life Now: 7 Steps to Living at Your Full Potential, 2004, Become a Better You: 7 Keys to Improving Your Life Every Day, 2007 (Publishers Weekly bestseller). Named one of Barbara Walters 10 Most Fascinating People, 2006. Achievements include ministering to the one of the largest and most diverse congregations in America; weekly television program appears on six cable networks and internationally in over 100 nations; aquired lease for the Compaq Center in Houston to accommodate growing congregation. Office: Lakewood Church PO Box 23297 Houston TX 77228 Office Phone: 713-635-4154. Office Fax: 713-635-4753.

O'STEEN, VAN, lawyer; b. Sweetwater, Tenn., Jan. 10, 1946; s. Bernard Van and Laura Emelyne (Robinson) O'Steen; m. Deborah Ann Elias, May 18, 1974; children: Jonathan Van, Laura Ann. BA, Calif. Western U., 1968; JD cum laude, Ariz. State U., 1972. Bar: Ariz. 1972, cert.: US Dist. Ct. Ariz. 1972, US Ct. Appeals (9th cir.) 1973, US Supreme Ct. 1975. Staff atty. Maricopa Legal Aid Soc., Phoenix, 1972—74; atty. Bates & O'Steen Legal Clinic, Phoenix, 1974—77, O'Steen Legal Clinic, Phoenix, 1977—80; ptnr. Van O'Steen Mktg. Group, Inc., Phoenix, 1985—; mng. ptnr. Van O'Steen and Ptnrs., Phoenix and Tucson, 1980—2004; ptnr. O'Steen & Harrison, Phoenix and Tucson, 2004—. Founding dir. Ariz. Ctr. for Law in the Pub. Interest, 1974—80. With USNR, 1963—69. Mem.: ABA (chmn. spl. com. delivery legal svcs. 1982—85), Assn. Trial Lawyers Am., Am. Legal Clinic Assn. (pres. 1979). Democrat. Office: Ste 400 300 W Clarendon Ave Phoenix AZ 85013-3424 Office Phone: 602-252-8888. Business E-Mail: vosteen@vanosteen.com.

O'STEEN, WENDALL KEITH, anatomist, neurologist, educator; b. Meigs, Ga., July 3, 1928; s. Wellna Hubert and Lillian (Powell) O'S.; m. Sandra Lynn Kraeer, July 30, 1983; children: Lisa Diane, Kerry Keith, Buckley Powell. BA, Emory U., 1948, MS, 1950; PhD, Duke U., 1958. Asst. prof. Emory U. Jr. Coll., Valdosta, Ga., 1948-49; instr. Emory U., Atlanta, 1950-51; prof. Emory U. Sch. Medicine, Atlanta, 1968-77; from asst. prof. to prof. med. br. U. Tex., 1958-67; asst. prof. Wofford Coll., Spartanburg, SC, 1951-53; prof., chmn. dept. neurobiology and anatomy, Bowman Gray Sch. Med. Wake Forest U., Winston-Salem,

NC, 1977-93, prof. emeritus, 1993—. Mem. anatomy com. Nat. Bd. Med. Examiners, Phila., 1982-87. Contbr. over 150 articles to books, nat. and internat. jours. Lt. col. USAR. Recipient Golden Apple teaching award Med. Br. U. Tex., Galveston, 1967, Outstanding Tchr. award Emory U., 1973, Williams Disting. Teaching award Emory U., 1974, award for teaching excellence Bowman Gray Sch. Medicine, Wake Forest U. Mem. Am. Assn. Anatomists (exec. com. 1980-84, v.p. 1990-92), Assn. Anatomy Chairmen (exec. com. 1982-84, pres. 1990-91), So. Soc. Anatomists (pres. 1975-76), Soc. for Neurosci., N.C. Soc. Neurosci. (pres. 1980-81), Western N.C. Soc. Neurosci. (pres. 1987-88), Assn. Rsch. in Vision and Ophthalmology, Alpha Omega Alpha. Republican. Methodist. Avocations: gardening, music. Office: Wake Forest U Bowman Gray Sch Medicine Dept Neurobiology and Anatomy Winston Salem NC 27157-0001 Home Phone: 904-221-1646.

OSTEEN, WILLIAM LINDSAY, SR., federal judge; b. Greensboro, NC, July 15, 1930; BA, Guilford Coll., 1953; LLB, U. N.C., 1956. With Law Office of W.H. McElwee, Jr., North Wilkesboro, NC, 1956-58; pvt. practice Greensboro, N.C., 1958-59; with Booth & Osteen, Greensboro, NC, 1959-69; US atty. (mid. dist.) Tenn. US Dept. Justice, Greensboro, NC, 1969-74; ptnr. Osteen, Adams & Osteen LLP, Greensboro, NC, 1974-91; judge US Dist. Ct. (mid. dist.) N.C., Greensboro, NC, 1991—2006, sr. judge, 2006—. With USAR, 1958-51. Recipient Judge John J. Parker Meml. award, 2008. Fellow Am. Coll. Trial Lawyers; mem. ABA, N.C. State Bar, N.C. Bar Assn. (mem. and chair subcom. N.C. sentencing commn.), U. N.C. Law Alumni Assn., Greensboro Bar Assn. (Disting. Svc. award, 2004) Office: Us District Judge PO Box 21345 Greensboro NC 27420-1345

OSTEEN, WILLIAM LINDSAY, JR., federal judge; b. Greensboro, NC, Aug. 8, 1960; BS, U. NC, 1983, JD, 1987. Bar: NC 1987. Assoc. Osteen, Adams, Tilley & Walker, Greensboro, NC, 1987—91; ptnr. Adams & Osteen, Greensboro, NC, 1991—2007; judge US Dist. Ct. (mid. dist.) NC, Greensboro, NC, 2007—. Office: US Dist Ct Mid Dist of NC 324 W Market St Greensboro NC 27401 Office Phone: 336-332-6090.

OSTELL, JAMES M., library and information scientist, biotechnologist; BS in zoology, MS in zoology, U. Mass.; PhD in molecular biology, Harvard U. Founding mem. and chief info. engring. br., Nat. Ctr. Biotechnology Info. NIH Nat. Libr. Medicine, Bethesda, Md., 1988—. Mem.: Inst. Medicine. Office: Nat Ctr Biotechnology Info US Nat Libr Medicine 8600 Rockville Pike Bethesda MD 20894 E-mail: ostell@ncbi.nlm.nih.gov.*

OSTENDORF, LANCE STEPHEN, lawyer, financial consultant, educator, importer exporter entrepreneur; b. New Orleans, Aug. 16, 1958; 1 child, Christine Marie Ostendorf. BBA in Acctg. and Fin., Loyola U., 1976, JD, 1980. Bar: La. 1980, U.S. Dist. Ct. (ea. dist.) La. 1981, U.S. Dist. Ct. La., U.S. Supreme Ct. 1980, U.S. Dist. Ct. (we. and mid. dists.) La. 1983. Founder GO Entertainment, Inc. L.A., New Orleans,Balt./Washington, L.A./Orange County, San Diego/Riverside, Ostendorf, Tate, Barnett & Wells, PLC, L.A./Orange County, San Diego/Riverside, Houston, Balt., New Orleans. Treas., CFO La. State U. Med. Ctr. Found., New Orleans, 1992—; lectr. Lorman Ednl. Seminars; bd. dirs. La. State U. Med. Ctr. Found., New Orleans, tech. transfer com.; speaker and tchr. Lorman Ednl. Svcs., Inc. Author: Insurance Law; contbr. articles to profl. jours. Mem. ABA, Fed. Bar Assn., Internat. Bar Assn., La. Bar Assn., Metairie Bar Assn., Maritime Law Assn., Comite Maritime Internat., Assn. for Transp. Law, Trucking Industry Def. Assn., Logistics and Policy, Assn. Average Adjusters of U.S., Jefferson Bar Assn., New Orleans Bar Assn., La. Restaurant Assn., Am. Trial Lawyers Assn., La. Bar Assn., Jefferson Bar Assn., Fifth Cir. Bar Assn., Def. Rsch. Inst., La. Trial Lawyers Assn., Law Def. Lawyers Assn., Houston Mariners Club, Southeastern Adm. Law Inst., St. Thomas Moore Club, La. Notary Soc., New Orleans South African Connection, Blue Key Honor Soc. Home: P O Box 88 Houston TX 70001 Office: 650 Poydras Suite 1460 New Orleans LA 70130 Office Phone: 504-527-0700, 713-335-5566. Personal E-mail: lanceostendorf@yahoo.com. Business E-Mail: lance.ostendorf@otbw-law.com, lance@otbn.us.

OSTENDORFF, WILLIAM CHARLES, federal agency administrator, career military officer; b. Shreveport, La., Oct. 22, 1954; s. Thomas Julian and Emilie Anne (Connell) O.; m. Christina Lee Miller, July 16, 1977; children: Rebecca, Chuck, Jeff. BS in Systems Engring., U.S. Naval Acad., 1976; JD with honors, U. Tex., 1984; LLM with distinction, Georgetown U., 1992. Bar: Tex. 1984. Commd. USN, 1976, advanced through grades to comdr., 1991, nuclear submarine officer; nuclear power prog. mgr. Office of Chief Naval Ops., Washington; mem. rsch. staff Inst. for Def. Analyses, 2002—03; counsel House Armed Services Com., 2003—07; prin. dep. adminstr., Nat. Nuc. Security Adminstrn. US Dept. Energy, Washington, 2007—. Mem. ABA, State Bar Assn. Tex., U.S. Naval Acad. Alumni Assn., Order of the Coif. Episcopalian. Avocation: running. Office: US Dept Energy Forrestal Bldg 1000 Independence Ave SW Rm 7A-199 Washington DC 20585*

OSTER, GARY WAYNE, innovation and entrepreneurship educator; b. Newport, RI, Aug. 12, 1956; s. Gordon Wayne and Barbara Jean Oster; m. Priscilla Jean Bartels; children: George Woo, Geneva Lee. BA in English and Polit. Sci., Hope Coll., Holland, Mich., 1978; MS in Librarianship, Western Mich. U., Kalamazoo, 1979; MBA in Sys. Mgmt., Baldwin-Wallace Coll., Berea, Ohio, 1985; MA in Economics, Case Western Res. U., Cleve., 1988; Dr. in Strategic Leadership, Regent U., Va. Beach, 2007. V.p., academic affairs and provost William Tyndale Coll., Farmington Hills, Mich., 2001—04; assoc. dean Regent U. Sch. Undergrad. Studies, 2005—07; assoc. prof. Regent U. Sch. Global Leadership & Entrepreneurship, 2007—. Independent. Home: 713 Churchill Virginia Beach VA 23464 Office: Regent Univ 1000 Regent Univ Dr Virginia Beach VA 23464 Personal E-mail: garyost@gmail.com. Business E-Mail: garyost@regent.edu.

OSTER, LEWIS HENRY, manufacturing executive, industrial engineer, consultant; b. Mitchell, SD, Jan. 18, 1923; s. Peter W. and Lucy (Goetsch) Oster; m. Mary Mills, Aug. 17, 1948; children: David, Lewis, Nancy, Susan. BS in Engring., Iowa State U., 1948; MBA, Syracuse U., 1968. Registered profl. engr., Iowa. Mgr. Maytag Co., Newton, Iowa, 1953—59; sr. staff engr., mgr. Philco-Ford Corp., Phila., 1959—62; mgr. mech. and indsl. engring. Carrier Corp., Syracuse, NY, 1962—75; v.p. Superior Industries Internat., Van Nuys, Calif., 1981—. V.p., gen. mgr. Superior/Ideal, Inc., Oskaloosa, Iowa, 1975—; cons. in field. Author: MTM Application Manual, 1957. Leader Boy Scouts Am., Syracuse, NY, 1965—73; fund chmn. United Fund, Syracuse, 1965—73. Lt. col. USAFR, ETO. Decorated Purple Heart, DFC, Air medal with four oak leaf clusters. Mem.: Am. Inst. Indsl. Engrs. (pres. 1951—53), Ret. Officers Assn., Oskaloosa Country Club, Am. Legion, Elks.

OSTER, MARCIA REBECCA, mental health services professional; b. Birmingham, Ala., Sept. 26, 1942; d. Ralph Wilder and Helen Brocha Davidson; m. Arthur Gerald Oster, Dec. 21, 1972 (div. 1982); 1 child, David Robert. BA, Brandeis U., Waltham; MEd, Tufts U., Medford, 1965. Tchr. Wakefield Sch. Dept., 1965—70, Dade County Sch. Dept., Miami, Fla., 1970—74, Santa Monica YWCA, 1983—86; asst. tchr. Stephen Samuel Wise Synagogue, LA, 1981—82, aast. instr., substitute tchr. Santa Monica, 1982—83; consumer adv. LA County Dept Mental Health, 2004—. Author: (book) The Bunny's Doormat, 1974. Donor Vet. Foreign Wars of US, Kans., 2000—06, Paralyzed Vet. America, Washington, 2008. Mem.: Calif. Network Mental Health Clients, LA County Clint, Svc. Area Adv. Com. Avocations: reading, Scrabble, puzzles, music. Home: 1470 S Robertson Blvd Los Angeles CA 90035-3402

OSTER, ROSE MARIE GUNHILD, foreign language professional, educator; b. Stockholm, Feb. 26, 1934; came to US, 1958; d. Herbert Jonas and Emma Wilhelmina (Johnson) Hageторn; m. Ludwig F. Oster, May 17, 1956; children: Ulrika, Mattias. Fil. mag., U. Stockholm, 1956; PhD, Kiel U., Germany, 1958. Postdoctoral rsch. fellow linguistics Yale U., 1958-60, rsch. fellow Germanic langs., 1960-64, lectr. Swedish, 1964-66; mem. faculty U. Colo., Boulder, 1966-80, assoc. prof. Germanic langs. and lits., 1970-77, prof., 1977-80, chmn. dept., 1972-75, assoc. dean Grad. Sch., 1975-79, assoc. vice chancellor for grad. affairs Grad. Sch., 1979-80; dean for grad. studies and rsch. U. Md., College Park, 1980-83, prof. Germanic langs. and lits., 1980—, acting chair dept., 1997—2001. Mem. Fulbright Nat. Screening Com., Scandinavia, 1973, 83-87, chair, 1986-87; mem. selection com. Scandinavia Internat. Exch. of Scholars, 1982-86; cons. panelist Nat. Endowment for Humanities, 1975—, mem. bd. cons., 1980—; state coord. Am. Coun. on Edn., Colo., 1978-80, Md., 1981-83, dir. dept. leadership program, 1986-91; mem. exec. com. Assn. Grad. Schs., 1980-83; mem. dean's exec. com. African-Am. Inst., 1981-85; interim dir. Washington Sch. Psychiatry, 1994-95; cons. in field. Contbr. articles and revs. to profl. publs. Bd. dirs. Washington Sch. Psychiatry, Am.-Swedish Hist. Mus., Phila., Open Theatre, Washington; mem. nat. fellowship com. Am.-Scandinavian Found., 1997—, bd. trustees, 2001—. Carnegie fellow, 1974; grantee Swedish Govt., 1977, Am. Scandinavian Found., 1997, German Acad. Exch. Svc., 1983; recipient Translation prize Am.-Scandinavian Found., 1997. Mem. NOW, MLA (mem. Del. Assembly 1995—), AAUP, Soc. Advancement Scandinavian Studies (pres. 1979-80), Am. Scandinavian Assn. of Nat. Capital Area (pres. 1983-86, 96—, pres. 2009), Am.-Scandinavian Found., Am. Assn. Higher Edn. Home: 4977 Battery Ln Bethesda MD 20814-4931 Office: U Md Dept Germanic Studies College Park MD 20742-0001 Office Phone: 301-405-4096. Business E-Mail: rmoster@umd.edu.

OSTER, SHARON B., literature and language professor; d. Morris and Jeannine Oster; life ptnr. George Ketsios. PhD in English, U. Calif., LA, 2003. Postdoc. fellow U. Calif., Irvine, 2003—04, vis. lectr., 2004—05; asst. prof. English U. Redlands, Calif., 2005—. Faculty advisor U. Redlands Hillel, 2006—; co-convener, rsch. colloquium Southern Calif. Americanist Group, LA, 2007—. Recipient English Tchg. Excellence award, U. Calif., 2000, Student of Yr. Award, 2001; fellowship, Philip & Ada Siff Ednl. Found. Grad., U. Calif., 2002, Faculty Rsch. grant, U. Redlands, 2007. Mem.: MLA, Henry James Soc., Assn. Jewish Studies.

OSTER, SHARON M., dean, management educator; b. NYC, Sept. 3, 1948; BA, Hofstra Coll., 1970, LittD (hon.), 2001; PhD in Econs., Harvard U., 1974. Tchg. asst. Dept. Econs. Harvard U., 1973—74; asst. prof. Dept. Econs. Yale U., New Haven, 1974—79, assoc. prof., 1979—82, assoc. prof. Sch. Orgn. and Mgmt., 1982—83; prof. econs. and mgmt. Yale U. Sch. Mgmt., New Haven, 1983—94, Frederic D. Wolfe prof. mgmt. and entrepreneurship, 1992—, assoc. dean, 1992—94, dean, 2008—. Bd. dirs. Health Care REIT. Author: Modern Competitive Analysis, 1990, Strategic Management for Nonprofit Organizations, 1995; editor: Management of Nonprofit Organizations, 1994; co-author: Generating and Sustaining Nonprofit Earned Income: A Guide to Successful Enterprise Strategies, 2004; contbr. articles to profl. jours. Bd. mem. Choate Rosemary Hall, Yale U. Press. Office: Yale U Sch Mgmt 135 Prospect St Box 208200 New Haven CT 06520-8200 Office Phone: 203-432-6035. Office Fax: 203-432-5092. E-mail: sharon.oster@yale.edu.*

OSTER, TOM (THOMAS J. OSTER), state official, school system administrator; m. Lori Oster; children: Tiffany, Matt, Adam. BA in Secondary Edn., No. State U., 1984, MEd, 1990. Supt., elem. prin., athletic dir. Avon Sch. Dist.; sec. edn. SD Dept Edn., Pierre, 2008—. Mem. State Aid Task Force for Edn., SD. Mem.: Mitchell Area Supts. Assn., SD Athletic Adminstrs. Assn., Avon Lions Club. Office: SD Dept Edn Office of Sec 700 Governors Dr Pierre SD 57501 Office Phone: 605-773-5669. Office Fax: 605-773-6139. E-mail: tom.oster@state.sd.us.*

OSTERBERG, EDWARD CHARLES, JR., lawyer; b. Honolulu, Jan. 1, 1942; s. Edward Charles and Emily Julia (Preston) O.; m. Susan Rhea Snider, Aug. 26, 1967; 1 child, Edward Charles III. BA, Northwestern U., Evanston, Ill., 1963, JD cum laude, 1966; LLM in Taxation, So. Meth. U., Dallas, 1972. Bar: Tex. 1966, Ill. 1966. Assoc. Vinson & Elkins, Houston, 1967-73, ptnr., 1974—. Reporter Internat. Fiscal Assn., Sydney, Australia, 1978, Barcelona, Spain, 1991. Contbr. articles to profl. publs. Mem. ABA (chmn. taxation com.), Houston Bar Assn. (chmn. taxation sect. 1987), Petroleum Club, Houston Racquet Club. Methodist. Home: 11222 Wilding Ln Houston TX 77024-5308 Office: Vinson & Elkins LLP 1001 Fannin St Ste 3300 Houston TX 77002-6760 Office Phone: 713-758-2192. Business E-Mail: eosterberg@velaw.com.

OSTERGAARD, JONI HAMMERSLA, lawyer; b. Seattle, May 26, 1950; d. William Dudley and Carol Mae (Gillett) Hammersla; m. Gregory Lance Ostergaard, May 22, 1976 (div. 1985); 1 child, Bennett Gillett; m. William Howard Patton, Jan. 1, 1988; 1 child, Morgan Hollis; stepchildren: Colin W., Benjamin C. BS, U. Wash., 1972; MS, Purdue U., 1974; JD, U. Wash., 1980. Bar: Wash. 1980, U.S. Dist. Ct. (we. dist.) Wash. 1980, U.S. Ct. Appeals (9th cir.) 1981, U. S. Ct. Claims 1983. Clin. psychol. intern Yale Med. Sch., 1976-77; law clk. U.S. Ct. Appeals (9th cir.), Seattle, 1980-81; assoc. Roberts & Shefelman, Seattle, 1982-86, ptnr., 1987, Foster Pepper & Shefelman, Seattle, 1988-92; sole practitioner Seattle, 1996—2003; dep. pros. atty. Snohomish County Prosecuting Attys. Office Civil Divsn., Everett, Wash., 2004—. Contbr. articles to profl. jours.; notes and comments editor Wash. Law Rev., 1979-80. Recipient Sophia and Wilbur Albright scholarship U. Wash. Law Sch., 1979-80, law sch. alumni scholarship U. Wash. Law Sch., 1978-79; fellow NIMH. Avocations: gardening, reading. Office: Snohomish County Prosecuting Attys Office Civil Divsn 3000 Rockefeller Ave M/S 504 Everett WA 98201-4046 Home Phone: 425-697-3050; Office Phone: 425-388-6370. Office Fax: 425-388-6333. Business E-Mail: jostergaard@co.snohomish.wa.us.

OSTERGARD, PAUL MICHAEL, foundation executive; b. Akron, Ohio, Apr. 1, 1939; s. Paul and Janette Beryl (Laube) O.; m. Elizabeth K. McCombs, Jan. 1965 (div. Nov. 1971). AB magna cum laude, Case-Western Res. U., 1961; JD, U. Mich., 1964; MPA, Harvard U., 1969; diploma in hispanic studies, U. Madrid, Spain, 1960. Bar: Ohio 1964. Atty. US Steel Corp., Pitts., 1967—69; gen. atty. TWA Inc., NYC, 1969—71; v.p. adminstrn., sec., counsel Pa. Co. (now Penn Ctrl. Corp.), 1971—74, and subs. Buckeye Pipe Line Co., NYC, 1972—74; pub. affairs exec. GE, Fairfield, Conn., 1974—84; pres. GE Found., Fairfield, 1984—90; chmn., CEO, bd. dirs. Citigroup Found., NYC, 1990—99; pres. Com. to Encourage Corp. Philanthropy, NYC, 1999—2001; pres., CEO Jr. Achievement Internat., 2001—04; pres. Hispanic Scholarship Fund, San Francisco, 2006—07. Bd. dirs. Master Card Found., Securities Industry Fin. Markets Found., Hispanic Scholarship Fund; trustee Case Western Res. U. Decorated Bronze Star, Legion of Merit (Vietnam); Univ. scholar, 1957-61; Littauer fellow, 1968-69 Mem. Harvard Club, Wexford Plantation Club, Phi Beta Kappa, Omicron Delta Kappa. Episcopalian. Home: 29 Oxford Dr Hilton Head Island SC 29928

OSTERHOLM, MICHAEL T., epidemiologist, public health service officer; b. 1953; BA in Biology & Polit. Sci., Luther Coll., 1975; MS in Environmental Health, U. Minn., 1976, MPH in Epidemiology, 1978, Ph.D in Environmental Health, 1980. Various positions Minn. Dept. Health, 1975—84, state epidemiologist & chief of acute epidemiology sect., 1984—99; dir. Ctr. Infectious Disease Rsch. & Policy (CIDRAP) U. Minn., Mpls.; prof. U. Minn. Sch. Pub. Health, Mpls. Mem. World Econ. Forum Working Group on Pandemics, 2008—. Author: Living Terrors: What America Needs to Know to Survive the Coming Bioterrorist Catastrophe, 2001; editorial bd. Infection Control & Hosp. Epidemiology, Microbial Drug Resistance; contbr. articles, chapters to books, columns in newspapers, scientific papers. Spl. advisor to sec. US Dept. Health & Human Services, 2001—05, mem. nat. sci. adv. bd. on biosecurity, 2005—; mem. interim mgmt. team Centers for Disease Control (CDC), 2002—03; mem. U. Minn. Acad. Health Center's Acad. of Excellence in Health Rsch., 2008—. Recipient Pump Handle award, Charles C. Shepard Sci. award, Centers for Disease Control (CDC), Harvey W. Wiley medal, FDA, Wade Hampton Frost Leadership award, Am. Pub. Health Assn. (APHA). Fellow: Infectious Diseases Soc. America, Am. Coll. Epidemiology; mem.: Am. Soc. Microbiology (mem. pub. & scientific affairs bd., chmn. pub. health com., mem. task force on biological weapons, mem. task force on antibiotic resistance), Coun. State & Territorial Epidemiologists (past pres.), Inst. Medicine. Office: Ctr Infectious Disease Rsch & Policy MMC 263 Mayo 8263 420 Delaware St SE Minneapolis MN 55455 Office Phone: 612-626-6770, 612-625-3908. Office Fax: 612-626-6783. E-mail: mto@umn.edu.*

OSTERHOUT, RICHARD CADWALLADER, lawyer; b. Abington, Pa., Nov. 16, 1945; s. Robert Edward and Charlotte Leedom (Cadwallader) O.; m. Diane Renee Higgins, Sept. 15, 1982; children: Steven M., Schuyler C., Cody R. BA in History magna cum laude, Pa. State U., U. Pk., 1967; JD, Temple U., Phila., 1974. Bar: Pa. 1974, U.S. Dist. Ct. (ea. dist.) Pa. 1974, U.S. Ct. Appeals (3d cir.) 1984. Assoc. Wood & Floge, Bensalem, Pa., 1974—77; pvt. practice Trevose, Pa., 1978—85, Feasterville, Pa., 1985—. Solicitor Zoning Hearing Bd., Hulmeville, Pa., 1983—. Contbr. articles to publs. of various hist. socs. Mem. Langhorne Borough Planning Commn. (Pa.), 1974; candidate Rep. Nat. Conv., 1984. With U.S. Army, 1968-70. Mem. Pa. Bar Assn., Bucks County Bar Assn., Feasterville Business Assn. (treas. 1985, 86, v.p. 1987), Phi Beta Kappa. Home: 309 Hemlock Ave Bensalem PA 19020-7331 Office: 1744 Bridgetown Pike Bensalem PA 19020-7331

OSTERKAMP, DALENE MAY, psychology educator, artist; b. Davenport, Iowa, Dec. 1, 1932; d. James Hiram and Bernice Grace Simmons; m. Donald Edwin Osterkamp, Feb. 11, 1951 (dec. Sept. 1951). BA, San Jose State U., 1959, MA, 1962; PhD, Saybrook Inst., 1989. Lectr. San Jose (Calif.) State U., 1960—65, U. Santa Barbara (Calif.) Ext., 1970-76; prof. Bakersfield (Calif.) Coll., 1961-87, prof. emerita, 1987—; adj. faculty, counselor Calif. State U., Bakersfield, 1990—95. Gallery dir. Bakersfield Coll., 1964-72. Juried group shows include Berkeley (Calif.) Art, Ctr., 1975, Libr. of Congress, 1961, Seattle Art Mus., 1962; permanent collections include Archives of Nat. Mus. Women in the Arts. Founder Kern Art Edn. Assn., Bakersfield, 1962, Bakersfield Printmakers, 1976. Staff sgt. USAF, 1952-55. Recipient 1st Ann. Svc. to Women award Am. Assn. Women in C.C., 1989. Mem. APA, Assn. for Women in Psychology, Assn. for Humanistic Psychology, Calif. Soc. Printmakers. Home: PO Box 387 Glennville CA 93226-0387 Office: Calif State Univ Stockdale Ave Bakersfield CA 93309

OSTERKAMP, T. E., retired physics professor; s. Joseph and Olivia Osterkamp; m. J. M. Oliver, June 13, 1964; children: T. E., K. M., E. M., J. E. PhD, St. Louis U., 1966. Emeritus prof. physics U. Alaska, Fairbanks, 1997—2009. Com. mem. in fields, 1974—97. With US Army, 1958—59, Ft. Leonard Wood, Mo. Recipient Rsch. Achievement award, Geophysics Inst. U. Alaska, 1983. Mem.: US Permafrost Assn., Internat. Permafrost Assn., Am. Geophys. Union. Personal E-mail: tomeo@yhti.net. Business E-Mail: ffteo@uaf.edu.

OSTERMAN, JOHN CARL, biology professor; b. Cannonsburg, Pa., July 3, 1952; s. George and Alice Jane Osterman; life ptnr. Patricia Louise Herman. PhD, Ind. U. Bloomington, 1979. Asst. prof. U. Nebr. Lincoln, 1983—89, assoc. prof., 1989—. Mem.: Genetics Soc. Am. Achievements include patents for heat labile alkaline phosphatase. Office: Sch Biol Sci Univ Nebr Lincoln Lincoln NE 68588 Office Fax: 402-472-2083. Business E-Mail: josterman@unl.edu.

OSTERMAN, LISA ELLEN, geologist, researcher; b. Cin., July 11, 1953; d. Clifford Paul Osterman and Norma Lee (Bledsoe) Gould; m. Mark Bykowsky, June 18, 1977; children: Marcus Burton, Spencer Paul. BS, U. Dayton, 1975; MS, U. Maine, Orono, 1977; PhD, U. Colo., 1982. Rsch. assoc. Inst. Arctic and Alpine Rsch., Boulder, Colo., 1982-85; postdoctoral fellow Smithsonian Inst., Washington, 1985-86, rsch. collaborator dept. paleobiology, 1986-93; asst. prof. George Washington U., Washington, 1986-93; rsch. assoc. dept. paleobiology Smithsonian Instn., Washington, 1993—; geologist U.S. Geol. Survey, 1996—. Presenter in field. Contbr. articles to profl. jours. Rsch. grantee NSF, 1981, 83, 85, Petroleum Rsch. Fund Am. Chem. Soc., 1989-90. Fellow Cushman Found.; mem. AAAS, Geol. Soc. Am. (J. Hoover Mackin award 1978), Am. Quaternary Assn., Paleontol. Soc. Washington (pres. 1991-92), Am. Women in Sci., Sigma Xi. Achievements include rsch. in polar paleo-oceanography and foraminiferal paleoecology. Home: 4513 Chase Ave Bethesda MD 20814-4635 Office: US Geol Survey 600 Fourth St S Saint Petersburg FL 33701 Office Phone: 727-803-8747. Business E-Mail: osrerman@usgs.gov.

OSTERWEIL, ARA CYBELE, art educator; b. Bklyn., Apr. 9, 1977; d. Allan Bryant and Enid Weisman Osterweil; m. David Joseph Baumflek, Nov. 8, 2008. BA, NY U., 1997, MA, 1999; PhD, U. Calif., Berkeley, 2005. Dir. ednl. programming Jacob Burns Film Ctr., Pleasantville, NY, 2002—06; asst. prof. film studies and art Muhlenberg Coll., Allentown, Pa., 2006—. Dir.: (film) The Tourists; contbr. chapters to books, articles to profl. jour. Recipient Grad. Opportunity award, U. Calif., 1999—2002; Ronald P. Wilmot grant, Bur. Jewish Edn., San Francisco, 2000. Mem.: Soc. Cinema and Media Studies. Liberal. Jewish. Avocations: painting, writing, filmmaking. Home: 120 DaCosta Ave Oceanside NY 11572 Office: Muhlenberg Coll 2400 Chew St Allentown PA 18104 Personal E-mail: aosterweil@hotmail.com.

OSTFIELD, ALAN, professional sports team executive; m. Jennifer Ostfield; children: Benjamin, Hannah. B in Econs., U. Pa.; JD magna cum laude, Boston U., MBA. Atty. Wilmer, Cutler & Pickering, Washington; sr. v.p., gen. counsel San Diego Padres Baseball Club; sr. v.p. bus. & legal affairs Palace Sports & Entertainment/Detroit Pistons, 2000—02, COO, asst. gen. mgr., 2002—. Tchr. sport mgmt. masters prog. U. Mich.; tchr. U. San Diego Sch. Law; bd. dirs. Mich. Sports Hall of Fame; bd. advs. Nat. Sports Law Inst. Contbr. articles to profl. publs. Named one of Forty Under 40, St. & Smith SportsBusiness Jour., 2000, 2001, 2002; named to Forty Under 40 Hall of Fame, St. & Smith, 2002. Office: Detroit Pistons 5 Championship Dr Auburn Hills MI 48326*

OSTLIND, DAN A., retired parasitologist; b. McPherson, Kans., June 19, 1936; s. Harry Dewey and Laura (Bartles) O.; m. Eleanor Ruth Ahlstedt, Oct. 5, 1958; 1 child, Dyanne Dee. MS, Kans. State U., 1962, PhD, 1966. Parasitologist Moorman Mfg. Co., Quincy, Ill., 1966-67; sr. rsch. parasitologist Merck & Co., Rahway, NJ, 1967-69, rsch. fellow, 1969-77, sr. rsch. fellow, 1977-86, sr. investigator, 1986-96. Office Phone: 908-236-9238. Personal E-mail: stanton94@embarqmail.com.

OSTLING, RICHARD NEIL, journalist; b. Endicott, NY, July 14, 1940; s. Acton Eric Sr. and Christine Cathryn (Cumins) O.; m. Joan Elaine Kerns, July 8, 1967(dec. Jan. 11, 2009); children: Margaret Anne, Elizabeth Anne. BA, U. Mich., 1962; MS in Journalism, Northwestern U., 1963; MA in Religion, George Washington U., 1970; LittD (hon.), Gordon Coll., Mass., 1989. Reporter, copyreader Morning News and Evening Jour., Wilmington, Del., 1963-64; asst. news editor Christianity Today mag., Washington, 1965-67, news editor, 1967-69; staff corr. Time mag., NYC, 1969-74, religion writer, 1975-94, sr. corr., 1994-98; broadcaster Report on Religion, CBS Radio, 1979-98; religion corr. Newshour with Jim Lehrer formerly MacNeil/Lehrer Newshour, 1991-98; religion writer, Bible columnist AP, NYC, 1998—2006; freelance, 2006—. Author: Secrecy in the Church, 1974; co-author: Aborting America, 1979, Mormon America, 1999, rev. edit., 2007. Served with USNG, 1964-70. McCormick Found. fellow, 1962-63; recipient Supple, Templeton, Am. Acad. Religion and Wilbur awards for religion writing. Mem. Religion Newswriters Assn. (pres. 1974-76, Lifetime Achievement award 2006), Northwestern U. Alumni Hall of Achievement (charter), Phi Beta Kappa. Mem. Christian Reformed Ch. Home and Office: 280 Hillcrest Rd Ridgewood NJ 07450-2400 Office Phone: 201-445-4795. Personal E-mail: ostlingrn@aol.com.

OSTOJA-STARZEWSKI, MARTIN, engineering scientist, educator; b. Cracow, Poland, Apr. 22, 1954; s. Witold and Anna Wierzbianska; m. Iwona Jasiuk, Dec. 1991; children: Pauline, Michael. Engr., Cracow Technol. U., 1977; M in Engring., McGill U., Montreal, Que., Can., 1980, PhD, 1983. Pres. Quadra Dynamics Inc., Montreal, 1984-85; asst. prof. aeronautics and astronautics Purdue U., West Lafayette, Ind., 1985-90; asst. prof. materials sci. and mechanics Mich. State U., East Lansing, 1990-95; prof. engring. Inst. Paper Sci. and Tech., Atlanta, 1995—. Adj. faculty material sci. engring. Ga. Tech. Co-editor 7 books; contbr. articles to profl. jours. Fellow ASME. Roman Catholic. Avocations: classical music, literature, skiing. Fax: 404-894-4778. E-mail: martin.ostoja@ipst.edu.

OSTRAGER, BARRY ROBERT, lawyer; b. NYC, July 14, 1947; m. Pamela Goodman, Apr. 8, 1972; children: Ann Elizabeth, Katie, Jane, Betty, Michael. BA, City Coll. of CUNY, 1968, MA, 1973; JD, NYU Sch. Law, 1972. Bar: NY 1973, Calif. 1996, US Dist. Ct. (ea. dist.) NY, 1973, US Dist. Ct. (so. dist.) NY, 1973, US Dist. Ct. Conn., 1978, US Dist. Dist. Tex. 1986, US Dist. Ct. (no. dist.) NY 1993, US Ct. Appeals (2nd cir.) 1974, US Ct. Appeals (7th cir.) 1977, US Dist. Ct. (no. dist.) Calif. 1983, US Ct. Appeals (3rd cir.) 1984, US Ct. Appeals (9th cir.) 1985, US Ct. Appeals (4th cir.) 1989, US Ct. Appeals (6th cir.) 1993, US Supreme Ct. 1982, US Dist. Ct. (ctrl. dist.) Calif. 1997, U.S. Ct. Appeals (D.C. cir.) 1997. Judicial clk. to Hon. Arnold Bauman US Dist. Ct. (So. dist.) NY, 1972—73; sr. litig. ptnr., co-head, litig. dept., mem. exec. com. Simpson Thacher & Bartlett, NYC, 1980—. Lectr. on fed. securities and insurance law. Co-author: Modern Reinsurance Law and Practice, 2nd edit., 2000, Handbook on Insurance Coverage Disputes, 13th edit., 2006; contbr. articles to profl. jours. Named one of Top 10 Litigators, Nat. Law Jour., 2003. Mem. Am. Law Inst., Assn. of Bar of City of NY, ABA. Office: Simpson Thacher & Bartlett 26th Fl 425 Lexington Ave New York NY 10017-3954 Address: Simpson Thacher & Bartlett LLP 1999 Avenue of the Stars 29th Fl Los Angeles CA 90067 Office Phone: 212-455-2655. Office Fax: 212-455-2502. Business E-Mail: bostrager@stblaw.com.

OSTRANDER, ROBERT EDWIN, retired United Nations interregional advisor, petroleum company executive; b. Pitts., June 30, 1931; s. Robert Jesse and Elizabeth Raymond (Comstock) O.; m. Margaret Valentina Servello, Dec. 21, 1958; children: Robert Glen, Roseanne. BA, Cornell U., 1953. Cert. petroleum geologist; registered geol. scientist. Area reservoir engr. Mene Grande Oil Co., San Tome, Venezuela, 1956-61; dist. engr. Oasis Oil Co. of Libya, Tripoli, 1962-67; reservoir/petroleum chief engr. Occidental Oil of Libya, Tripoli, 1967-71; divsn. head Iranian Oil Consortium, Ahwaz, Iran, 1972-75; mgr. ops. Ultramar Co. Ltd., Mt. Kisco, NY, 1975-81; v.p. engring. Weeks Petroleum Ltd., Westport, Conn., 1982-85; mng. dir. Reomag Inc., South Salem, NY, 1980—. Cons. World Bank, Washington, 1981—; cons. UN Secretariat, 1994—; advisor to govts. of China, India, others in Asia, Africa, Middle East; lectr. in field. Contbr. articles to profl. jours. Sec. Rep. Com., Town of Lewisboro; chair conservation adv. com. Town of Lewisboro; pres. Ostrander Family Assn.; mem. Rep. Com. Westchester County; past. bd. dirs. Oakridge Condominium Assn., Vista, NY; fellow Herbert F. Johnson Mus. Art, Cornell U., 1999—. 1st lt. US Army, 1953-55. Mem. Am. Assn. Petroleum Geologists, Soc. Petroleum Engrs., Soc. Mil. Engrs., Holland Soc. NY, Phi Kappa Tau. Address: 5715 State Route 89 Romulus NY 14541-9546 Personal E-mail: reomag@rochester.rr.com.

OSTRANDER, THOMAS WILLIAM, retired investment banker; b. Detroit, July 20, 1950; s. Roland J. and Sybil (Swartout) O.; m. Kelli Turner, Aug. 28, 2004; children: John Charles, Elizabeth Ann, Brian Thomas, Evan Jacob, Emily Lauren. BA, U. Mich., 1972; MBA, Harvard Bus. Sch., 1976. CPA., Mich. Staff acct. Ernst & and Whinney, Detroit, 1972-74; sr. acct. Ernst and Whinney, Detroit, 1974, Cleve., 1975; assoc. Kidder, Peabody and Co., NYC, 1976-78, asst. v.p., 1978-80; v.p. Kidder, Peabody and Co., NYC, 1980-86; mng. dir. Kidder, Peabody and Co., NYC, 1986-89, Salomon Bros., Inc., NYC, 1989-97, Salomon Smith Barney, NYC, 1997—2003, Citigroup Global Markets, Inc., NYC, 2003—06, Banc of Am. Securities, NYC, 2006—08. Bd. dirs., Westmoreland Coal Co., 1995-2007; mem. adv. bd. Paton Sch. Accountancy U. Mich., 1984-87,; mem. vis. com. Lit., Sci., and Arts Sch., 1988-90, 95-. Pres. Ballet Hispanico, 1996- Mem. AICPA, Met. Club, Harvard Club, Hasty Pudding Club, Bond Club, Beaver Dam Winter Sports Club, and Theta Delta Chi Home: 18 Pheasant Run Old Westbury NY 11568 Business E-Mail: tomostrander@optonline.net.

OSTRANDER, WILLIS FREDERICK, retired real estate appraiser; b. Berkeley, Calif., Apr. 23, 1926; s. Willis Frederick and Grace Jackson Ostrander; m. Nancy Majors Ostrander, Jan. 2, 1950; children: Margaret Jaffee, Frederick Adam, Daphne Grace Miller, John Ellery. BA, U Calif., 1948. Cert. MAI, SRA Appraisal Inst., 1994, State Certification Real Estate Appraisal State of Calif., 1996. Sales rep. Signal Oil Co. (Chevron), Alemeda, Calif., 1951—62; exec. v.p. Twin Pines Fed., Berkeley, 1962—84; pres. W.F. Ostrander & Assoc., Inc., Berkeley, 1984—2006; ret., 2006. Dir. East Bay chpt. Soc. Real Estate Appraisers, Calif., 1975—76. Contbr. articles to poetry mag.; author: The Hunchback and the Swan, 1978; editor: Blue Unicorn Mag., 1990—. Sec. Fair Housing and Fair Employment, Berkeley, 1965—. With US Merchant Marines, 1944—45. Mem.: Berkeley Breakfast Club, Appraisal Inst. Democrat. Roman Catholic. Home and Office: 2630 Saklan Indian Dr 3 Walnut Creek CA 94595 Personal E-mail: ostrand7@pacbell.net.

OSTRAND-ROSENBERG, SUZANNE, immunology researcher; b. NYC, July 8, 1948; d. Arnold O. and Marianne (Steinberg) Ostrand; m. Robert Charles Rosenberg, July 18, 1971; children: David E., Aron M. AB, Barnard Coll., NYC, 1970; PhD, Caltech, Pasadena, Calif., 1974. Postdoctoral fellow Johns Hopkins U., Balt., 1974-77; asst. prof. U. Md. Balt. County, 1977-81, assoc. prof., 1982-92, prof., 1992—. Mem. study sect. NIH, Bethesda, Md., 1986—. Contbr. articles to sci. jours. Recipient Faculty Rsch. award Am. Cancer Soc., 1983-88; grantee NIH, NSF, Am. Cancer Soc., 1977—. Mem. AAAS, Am. Assn. Immunologists. Achievements include research in immunology, tumor immunology, histocompatibility, and immunogenetics. Office: U Md Baltimore County Dept Biol Scis Baltimore MD 21228

OSTREM, WALTER MARTIN, librarian, educator, consultant; b. Mpls., May 27, 1930; s. Oscar Martin and Helen Therese (Marcio) O.; m. Gertrud Franciska Tunkel, Aug. 6, 1956; children: Thomas, Paul, Francine. BA, U. Minn., 1953, MA, 1958; BS, Mankato State U., 1962, MS, 1964; postgrad., U. Mich., U. Iowa. Serials libr. Agr. Libr. U. Minn., 1958-59; acquisitions libr. Mankato State U., Minn., 1959-66, Eastern Mich. U., 1966-67; dir. media Iowa City Sch., 1967-69; libr. John F. Kennedy Sch., Berlin, 1969-73; disting. profl. libr. St. Paul Schs., 1973-90; libr. Open Sch. St. Pauls Schs., 1990-93; cons. in field. Librarian, educator, consultant; b. Mpls., May 27, 1930; s. Oscar Martin and Helen Therese (Marcio) O.; m. Gertrud Franciska Tunkel, Aug. 6, 1956; children— Thomas, Paul, Francine. B.A., U. Minn., 1953, M.A., 1958; B.S., Mankato State U., 1962, M.S., 1964; postgrad. U. Mich., U. Iowa. Serials librarian Agr. Library U. Minn., 1958-59; acquisitions librarian Mankato State U., Minn., 1959-66, Eastern Mich. U., 1966-67; dir. media Iowa City Sch., 1967-69; librarian John F. Kennedy Sch., Berlin, W.Ger., 1969-73; dist. profl. librarian St. Paul Schs., 1973-90; librarian Open Sch. St. Pauls Schs., 1990-93; cons. in field. Served to 1st lt. U.S. Army, 1954-55. Recipient Ency. Brit. 1st place Sch. Library Media System award, 1969. Mem. Minn. Ednl. Media Orgn., Am. Fedn. Tchrs., M Club, Phi Delta Kappa. Contbr. articles in field. Contbr. articles to profl. jours. Served to 1st lt. U.S. Army, 1954-55. Recipient Ency. Brit. 1st place Sch. Libr. Media System award, 1969. Mem. Minn. Ednl. Media Orgn., Am. Fedn. Tchrs., M Club, Phi Delta Kappa. Home: 5536 Harriet Ave Minneapolis MN 55419-1830 *Personal philosophy: I believe school libraries and school librarians are essential for increasing children's understanding of themselves and their society.*

OSTRENKO, WIT, museum administrator; Pres. Challenger Learning Ctr.; dir. mus. Hillsborough County, 1988—89; pres. Mus. of Sci. & Industry (MOSI), Tampa, Fla., 1989—. Bd. mem. Heartbeat Internat. Mem.: Assn. Sci.-Tech. Ctrs. (pres. bd. dirs. 2005). Office: Mus Sci & Industry 4801 E Fowler Ave Tampa FL 33617 Office Phone: 813-987-6100. E-mail: wostrenko@mosi.org.

OSTRIKER, ALICIA SUSKIN, poet; b. NYC, Nov. 11, 1937; d. David and Beatrice (Linnick) Suskin; m. Jeremiah P. Ostriker, 1958; children: Rebecca, Eve, Gabriel. BA, Brandeis U., 1959; MA, U. Wis., 1961, PhD, 1964. Asst. prof. Rutgers U., New Brunswick, NJ, 1965—68, assoc. prof., 1968—72, prof. English, 1972—2004; mem. faculty MFA program New Eng. Coll. Poetry, Henniker, NH, 2004—. Author: Vision and Verse in William Blake, 1965, Songs, 1969, Once More Out of Darkness, and Other Poems, 1974, A Dream of Springtime, 1979, The Mother/Child Papers, 1980, A Woman Under the Surface: Poems and Prose Poems, 1982, Writing Like a Woman, 1983, The Imaginary Lover, 1986 (William Carlos Williams prize Poetry Soc. Am. 1986), Stealing the Language: The Emergence of Women's Poetry in America, 1986, Green Age, 1989, Feminist Revision and the Bible, 1993, The Nakedness of the Fathers: Biblical Vision and Revisions, 1994, The Crack in Everything, 1996 (Nat. Book award finalist 1996, Paterson Poetry prize 1996, San Francisco State Poetry Ctr. award 1997), The Little Space: Selected and New Poems, 1998 (Nat. Book award finalist 1998), Dancing at the Devil's Party: Essays on Poetry, Politics, and the Erotic, 2000, The Volcano Sequence, 2002, No Heaven, 2005, For The Love of God: The Bible as an Open Book, 2008; editor: William Blake: Complete Poems, 1977. Nat. Coun. on Humanities grantee, 1968; NEA fellow, 1976-77, N.J. Arts Coun. fellow, 1982, Guggenheim Found. fellow, 1984-85, faculty fellow Rutgers Ctr. for Hist. Analysis, 1995-96, Rockefeller Found. fellow, 1982; recipient Strousse Poetry prize Prairie Schooner, 1986, Edward Stanley award Prairie Schooner, 1994, Anna David Rosenberg Poetry award, 1994, Best American Poetry award, 1996, Paterson prize, 1997, San Francisco State Poetry Ctr. award, 1997, Pushcart prize, 1999, Larry Levis prize 2001. E-mail: ostriker@rci.rutgers.edu.

OSTRIKER, JEREMIAH PAUL, astrophysicist, educator; b. NYC, Apr. 13, 1937; s. Martin and Jeanne (Sumpf) Ostriker; m. Alicia Suskin, Dec. 1, 1958; children: Rebecca, Eve; 1 child, Gabriel. AB, Harvard U., 1959; PhD, U. Chgo., 1964, degree (hon.), 1992; postgrad., U. Cambridge, Eng., 1964—65. Rsch. assoc., lectr. astrophysics Princeton U., Princeton, 1965—66, asst. prof., 1966—68, assoc. prof., 1968—71, prof., 1971—, chmn. dept. astronomy, dir. obs., 1979—95, Charles A. Young prof. astronomy, 1982—2002, provost, 1995—2001; Plumian prof. astronomy and exptl. philosophy U. Cambridge, England, 2001—04; dir. Princeton Inst. Computational Sci. and Engring., 2005—. Author: Development of Large-Scale Structure in the Universe, 1991; edit. bd., trustee Princeton U. Press; contbr. articles to profl. jours. Recipient Vainu Bappu Meml. award, Indian Nat. Sci. Acad., 1993, Karl Schwarzschild medal, Astronomische Gesellschaft, 1999, U.S. Nat. medal of Sci., 2000; fellow Alfred P. Sloan, 1970—72; NSF fellow, U. Chgo., 1960—64. Fellow: AAAS; mem.: NAS (counselor 1992—95, bd. govs. 1993—95), Royal Soc. UK (fgn.), Royal Netherlands Acad. Arts and Scis. (fgn.), Am. Acad. Arts and Scis., Am. Philos. Soc., Internat. Astron. Union, Am. Astron. Soc. (councilor 1978—80, Warner prize 1972, Russel prize 1980), Royal Astron. Soc. (assoc. Gold medal 2004), Am. Mus. Natural History (trustee 1997—2006, hon. trustee 2007—). Home: 33 Philip Dr Princeton NJ 08540-5409 Office Phone: 609-258-4267. Business E-Mail: ostriker@princeton.edu.

OSTROFF, DAWN T., broadcast executive; b. Miami, Mar. 31, 1960; m. Mark Ostroff; children: Lane, Michael, Justin, Jonathan. BS, Fla. Internat. U. V.p. devel. Kushner-Locke Co., 1984—89; pres. Michael Jacobs Prodns.; sr. v.p. creative affairs 20th Century Fox; sr. v.p. programming & prodn. Lifetime TV, 1996—99, exec. v.p. entertainment, 1999—2002; pres. entertainment UPN, 2002—05, pres., 2005—06; pres. entertainment The CW, 2006—. Recipient Star award, Am. Women in Radio & TV, 1999; named one of Top 100 in the Cable Industry, Cablefax mag., 2001, Wonder Women of Cable, Ny ch. Women in Cable & Telecommunication/Cablevision mag., 2001, Most Powerful Women in TV, TV Week, 2002, 12 to Watch, 2003, 100 Most Powerful Women in Entertainment, Hollywood Reporter, 2002—06, 2006, 2007. Office: The CW 3300 W Olive Ave Burbank CA 91505 Office Phone: 818-977-2500.*

OSTROM, DON, retired political science professor; b. Chgo., Mar. 9, 1939; s. Irving and Margaret (Hedberg) O.; m. Florence Horan, Jan. 13, 1972; children: Erik, Rebecca, Katherine. BA, St. Olaf Coll., Northfield, Minn., 1960; MA, Washington U., 1970, PhD, 1972. Prof. polit. sci. Gustavus Adolphus Coll., St. Peter, Minn., 1972—2004; state rep. Minn. Ho. of Reps., St. Paul, 1988-96; vis. prof. polit. sci. St. Olaf Coll., Northfield, 2004—08. Co-editor: Perspectives on Minnesota Government and Politics, 1998. Democrat. Home: 2737 Ewing Ave S Minneapolis MN 55416 E-mail: dostrom@gac.edu.

OSTROM, ELINOR, political science professor, researcher; b. LA, Aug. 7, 1933; d. Adrian and Leah (Hopkins) Awan; m. Charles Scott, Aug. 8, 1954 (div. 1961); m. Vincent Ostrom, Nov. 23, 1963. AB with honors, UCLA, 1954, MA, 1962, PhD, 1965; D in Econs. (hon.), U. Zurich, 1999; D (hon.), Inst. Social Studies, The Hague, 2002, Luleå U. Tech., Sweden, 2005, Uppsala U., 2007, Humboldt U., Berlin, 2007; DHL (hon.), U. Mich., Ann Arbor, 2006; PhD (hon.), McGill U., 2008, Norwegian U. Sci. & Tech., 2008. Vis. asst. prof. dept. gov. Ind. U., Bloomington, 1965-66, asst. prof., grad. advisor, dept. gov., 1966-69, assoc. prof. dept. polit. sci., 1969-74, prof. polit. sci., 1974-91, Arthur F. Bentley prof. polit. sci., 1991—, prof., chmn. dept. polit. sci., 1980—84, acting chair dept. polit. sci., 1989—90, co-dir. workshop in polit. theory and policy analysis, 1973—2009, sr. rsch. dir. workshop polit. theory & policy analysis, 2009—, co-dir. Ctr. Study Instns., Population and Environ. Change, 1996—2006, prof. part-time Sch. Pub. and Environ. Affairs; founding dir. Ctr. for Study Instl. Diversity, Ariz. State U., 2007—. Employment interviewer, asst. employee relations mgr., Godfrey L. Cabot, Inc., Boston, 1955-57; personnel analyst III, U. Calif., LA, 1957-61; bd. cons., Internat. Assn. Chiefs Police: Police Discipline Project, 1974-75; adv. bd. Nat. Evaluation Program Law Enforcement Assistance (Adminstrn.), Washington, 1975-76; mem. Nat. Adv. Panel, Nat. Acad. Pub, Adminstrn.; Neighborhood-Oriented Metropolitan Gov., 1975-76, task force on criminal justice rsch. and devel. Nat. Adv. Com. on Criminal Justice Standards and Goals, 1975-76, Nat. Sheriffs Assn.: Study of Contract Law Enforcement, 1975-76; adv. panel Div. Policy Rsch. and Analysis, NSF, Washington, 1977-78, panel on Instl. Develop., 1985; rev. panel Polit. Sci. div. NSF, 1983-84; Interuniversity Consortium for Polit. and Social Rsch. Coun., 1983-85; adv. com. nat. urban policy NAS/NRC, 1985-88, panel on Common Property Resources Mgmt., 1985-86, Scientific Com. on Problems of the Environ., 1995-98; rsch. adv. com. U.S. AID, 1989-91; local gov. rsch. adv. bd., US Adv. Commn. on Intergovernmental Rels., 1985-88; adv. bd., Inst. for Policy Reform, 1993-96; bd. dirs., Beijer Internat. Inst. Ecol. Econs., Royal Swedish Acad. Scis., 1997-; academic adv. bd., Max-Planck-Inst. für Gesellschaftsforschung, 2000-; cons. in field. Co-author: Policing Metropolitan America, 1978, Local Government in the United States, 1988, Institutional Incentives and Sustainable Development: Infrastructure Policies in Perspective, 1993, Rules, Games, and Common-Pool Resources, 1994, The Samaritan's Dilemma, 2005, Seeing the Forest and the Trees, 2005; author: Governing the Commons, 1990, Crafting Institutions for Self-Governing Irrigation Systems, 1992, Understanding Institutional Diversity, 2005; editor: Strategies of Political Inquiry, 1982; co-editor: People and Forests: Communities, Institutions, and Governance, 2000, Protecting the Commons: A Framework for Resource Management in the Americas, 2001, Foundations of Social Capital, 2003, The Commons in the New Millennium: Challenges and Adaptations, 2003, Trust and Reciprocity: Interdisciplinary Lessons from Experimental Research, 2003; mem. editl. bd. Am. Jour. Polit. Sci., Am. Polit. Sci. Review, Criminal Justice Review, Pub. Jour. Theoretical Politics Productivity Review, Publius, Quarterly Jour. Adminstrn., Sage Urban Affairs Ann. Review, Social Sci. Quarterly, Urban Affairs Quarterly, Ecol. Economics; contbr. articles to profl. jours. Grantee NSF, 1974-85, 87—, NIMH, 1977-81, U.S. Dept. Justice, 1978-82, AID, 1984-94, U.S. Geol. Survey, 1987-89, Ford Found., 1991—, FAO, 1992—, MacArthur Found., 1996-; recipient Frank E. Seidman Disting. award in Polit. Economy, 1997, Johan Skytte prize in Polit. Sci., Uppsala University, 1999, Aaron Wildavsky Enduring Contbn. award for Governing the Commons, APSA, Pub. Policy Sect., 2000, John J. Carty award for the Advancement Sci., NAS, 2004, Sustainability Sci. award Ecol. Soc. Am., 2005, James Madison award Am. Polit. Sci. Assn., 2005, Cozzarelli prize Proceeding Nat. Acad. Scis., NAS, 2006, Lifetime Achievement award Atlas Econ. Rsch. Found. 2003, Rumar Lust award Frity Thyssex Found. & Alexander von Humboldt Found., Germany, 2007, William H. Riker prize U. Rochester, 2008, Galbraith award, Am. Agrl. Economics Assn., 2008, Jonathan M. Tisch Prize, Tufts U., 2009, Elazer Disting. Federalism Scholar award APSA, Faleralism & Intergovernmental Rels. Sec., 2009. Fellow AAAS, Am. Acad. Arts and Scis; mem. NAS, Am. Philos. Soc., Assn. for Politics and the Life Scis., Pub. Choice Soc. (pres. 1982-84, co-chair Duncan Black award com. 1986-87, chair Duncan Black award com. 1990, exec. coun. 1982-), Am. Polit. Sci. Assn. (v.p. 1975-76, pres.-elect 1995-96, pres. 1996-97, chmn. several coms. 1978-88, mem. several coms. 1970-2007), Midwest Polit. Sci. Assn. (pres. 1984-85), Internat. Polit. Sci. Assn., Am. Econ. Assn., Internat. Assn. for Study Common Property (pres. 1990-91, program co-chair 2000), Policy Studies Orgn., (nominating com. 1986-87, Miriam Mills award 1996, Thomas R. Dye Svc. award 1997). Democrat. Home: 5883 E Lampkins Ridge Rd Bloomington IN 47401-9726 Office: Ind Univ Workshop in Polit Theory & Policy Analys 513 N Park Ave Bloomington IN 47408-3895 Home Phone: 812-332-9821; Office Phone: 812-855-0441. Office Fax: 812-855-3150. Business E-Mail: ostrom@indiana.edu.

OSTROV, BARBARA E., physician; b. Bklyn., Aug. 6, 1978; SB, MIT, Cambridge, Mass., 1979, SM; MD, SUNY Buffalo Sch. of Medicine, 1983. Cert. in Rheumatology Am. Bd. of Internal Medicine, 1990, in pediat. rheumatology Am. Bd. Pediat., 1994. Clin. asst. prof. Children's Hosp. Phila., 1989—91; asst. prof. to prof., pediat. and medicine Pa. State Hershey Med. Ctr., 1991—, dir., 1994—2004, adminstrv. vice chair, 2006—. Bd. mem. Am. Juvenile Arthritis Orgn., Atlanta, 2001—05; mem., pediatric rheumatology sub bd. Am. Bd. Pediat., Chapel Hill, NC, 2007—, sub bd. mem.; mem., local bd. Ctrl. Pa. Arthritis Found., Harrisburg, 1991. Recipient Distinguished Educator award. Mem.: Am. Acad. Pediat., Am. Coll. Rheumatology. Office: Penn State Hershey Children's Hosp 500 University Dr Hershey PA 17033 Office Fax: 717-531-0135. Business E-Mail: bostrov@psu.edu.

OSTROV, GERALD MARTIN, pharmaceutical executive; b. Bklyn., Oct. 29, 1949; s. Joshua and Harriet (Theaman) O.; m. Aimee Ostrov; children: Betsy, David. BS in Indsl. Engring. and Ops. Rsch., Cornell U.,

1971; MBA, Harvard U., 1973. Product mgr. Proctor & Gamble, Cin., 1973-76; pres. CIBA Consumer Pharm., Ciba-Geigy AG, Edison, NJ, 1985—91; pres. personal products Johnson & Johnson, 1991, group chmn. N.Am. comsumer and personal care, group chmn. worldwide vision care, 1998—2006; chmn., CEO Bausch & Lomb, Inc., 2008—. Bd. dirs. NuLens Ltd. Mem. Proprietary Assn. (bd. dirs. 1987—). Jewish. Avocation: marathon running. Office: Bausch & Lomb Inc One Bausch & Lomb Pl Rochester NY 14604-7201 Office Phone: 585-338-6000. Office Fax: 585-338-6007.*

OSTROV, JEROME, lawyer; b. Boston, Dec. 2, 1942; s. Harold S. and Etta (Resnick) O.; m. Roberta S. Baruch, Sept. 3, 1978; children: Rebecca Ann, Max Abraham, Julia Grace. BSBA cum laude, Boston U., 1964; JD, Union U., 1967; LLM in Taxation, NYU, 1968; MPA, Harvard U., 1980. Bar: NY 1968, DC 1971, Md. 1991. Pvt. practice, Washington, 1983—; law clk. to presiding judge US Tax Ct., 1969-71; pvt. practice Washington, 1971-73; dep. assoc. gen. counsel US EPA, 1973-79; fellow John F. Kennedy Sch. Govt., Harvard U., 1979-80; staff counsel US House of Reps., 1982-83; sr. counsel Kozusko Harris Vetter Wareh LLP, 2007—. Author: (law treatise) Tax and Estate Planning with Real Estate, Partnerships and LLC's, 2d edit., 2007; contbr. articles to profl. jours. Bd. govs. Am. Jewish Com. Mem. ABA. Democrat. Jewish. Avocations: swimming, hiking, skiing, classical music, ballet. Office: Kozusko Harris Vetter Wareh LLP 1666 K St NW Ste 400 Washington DC 20006 Home Phone: 301-571-7339; Office Phone: 202-454-6708. Business E-Mail: jostrov@kozlaw.com.

OSTROVERKHOVA, OKSANA, physicist; arrived in U.S., 1996; d. Grigoriy and Liliya Franchuk; Diploma in Optical Engrng. and Physics, Kiev Shevchenko U., 1996; PhD in Physics, Case Western Res. U., 2001—01. Rschr. Rsch. Inst. UkrAnalyt, Kiev, 1994—96; tchg. asst. Case Western Res. U., Cleve., 1996—97, rsch. asst., 1997—2001; postdoctoral fellow Stanford (Calif.) U., 2001—03; Killam meml. fellow U. Alta., Edmonton, Canada, 2003—04. Referee various sci. jours. in field, 2001—. Recipient Career award, NSF, 2008; grantee Internat. Soros Found. grant for student excellence, 1995; Killam Meml. fellow, Killam Trust, 2002—04, Loshkarev scholarship for student excellence, Kiev Shevchenko U., 1991—96. Achievements include research in nonlinear optics of organic materials; patents for ultrafast spectroscopy and single-molecule microscopy of organic semiconductors.

OSTROVSKII, MIKHAIL IOSIFOVICH, mathematician; b. Kharkov, Ukraine, USSR, Dec. 26, 1960; s. Iosif Vladimirovich and Larisa Semyenovna (Kudina) O.; m. Marina Anatol'evna Likhosherst, Apr. 20, 1991; 1 child, Stanislav Mikhailovich. MSc, Kharkiv U., Ukraine, 1982; PhD, Kharkov Inst. Mcpl. Engrs., 1985. Rsch. fellow Inst. for Low Temperature Physics and Engrng. Ukrainian Acad. Scis., Kharkov, 1985-89; sr. scientist Inst. for Low Temp. Physics and Engirng. Ukrainian Acad. Sci. Contbr. articles to profl. jours. Mem. Kharkov Math. Soc. Office: St Johns Univ 8000 Utopia Parkway Jamaica NY 11439

OSTROW, JAY DONALD, gastroenterology educator, researcher; b. NYC, Jan. 1, 1930; s. Herman and Anne Sylvia (Epstein) O.; m. Judith Fargo, Sept. 9, 1956; children: George Herman, Bruce Donald, Margaret Anne. BS in Chemistry, Yale U., 1950; MD, Harvard U., 1954; M.Sc. in Biochemistry, Univ. Coll., London, 1970. Diplomate Am. Bd. Internal Medicine, Am. Bd. Gastroenterology. Intern Johns Hopkins Hosp., Balt., 1954—55; resident Peter Bent Brigham Hosp., Boston, 1957—58; NIH trainee in gastroenterology, 1958—59; NIH trainee in liver disease Thorndike Meml. Lab. Boston City Hosp., 1959—62; instr. in medicine Harvard U., Boston, 1959—62; asst. prof. medicine Case-Western Res. U., Cleve., 1962—70; assoc. prof. U. Pa., Phila., 1970—76, prof., 1977—78; Sprague prof. medicine Northwestern U., Chgo., 1978—89, prof. medicine, 1989—95, prof. emeritus, 1995—, chief gastroenterology sect., 1978—87; vis. prof. gastroenterology and hepatology dept. Acad. Med. Ctr., U. Amsterdam, Netherlands, 1995—98; affiliated prof. medicine GI/Hepatology divsn. U. Wash., Seattle, 1999—. Med. investigator VA Hosp., Phila., 1973-78, VA Med. Ctr. Lakeside, Chgo., 1990-95. Editor, contbg. author: Bile Pigments and Jaundice, 1986. Asst. scoutmaster Valley Forge coun. Boy Scouts Am., Merion, Pa., 1972-78, asst. scoutmaster N.E. Ill. coun., 1978-81; vestryman St. Matthew's Episcopal Ch., Evanston, Ill., 1979-82, Christ Episcopal Ch., Seattle, 2004-07; treas. Classical Children's Chorale, Evanston, 1982; mem. Sacred Music Chorale, Seattle, 1999-, bd. dirs., sec. and editor, 2002-05, mng. dir., 2005—. Advanced from lt. j.g. to lt. comdr. med. corps. USN, 1955—57, with USNR, 1957—63. Recipient Gastroenterology Rsch. award Beaumont Soc., El Paso, 1979, Sr. Disting. Scientist award Alexander von Humboldt Found., Germany, 1989-90; NIH fellow, 1958-62, grantee, 1962-92; VA grantee, 1970-95. Mem. Am. Assn. Study Liver Diseases (councillor 1983-85, v.p. 1985-86, pres. 1987), Am. Gastroent. Assn. (chmn. exhibit com. 1969-72, mem. undergrad. tchg. project 1972-88), Am. Soc. Clin. Investigation, Am. Physiol. Soc. (asst. editor 1979-84), Internat. Assn. Study Liver, Seattle Audubon Soc. (co-chair membership com. 1999-2004). Avocations: birdwatching, singing. Office: GI/Hepatology Divsn HSB AA 103-F Box 356424 Univ Wash Sch Medicine 1959 NE Pacific St Seattle WA 98195-6424 Office Phone: 206-221-6147. Business E-Mail: jdostrow@medicine.washington.edu.

OSTROW, JOSEPH W., advertising executive; b. NYC, Feb. 22, 1933; s. Meyer H. and Helen (Small) O.; m. Francine Lee Goldberg, Sept. 4, 1955; children: Elizabeth Sara, Peter Mathew, William Nathan. BS in Mktg., NYU, 1955. Researcher W.R. Simmons, NYC, 1954-55; with Young & Rubicam, NYC, 1955-87, sr. v.p., dir. communication planning, 1972-73, exec. v.p., dir. communications services, 1973-87, mem. N.Y. exec. com., U.S.A. bd. dirs.; pres., chief operating officer worldwide Direct Mktg. Group of Cos., 1983-84; exec. v.p., dir. media worldwide Foote, Cone & Belding Co., NYC, 1987-94; pres., CEO Cabletelevision Advt. Bur., NYC, 1994—2003; pres. Ostrow Cons., NYC, 2003. Multichannel Advt. Bur. Internat.; hon. chair bd. dir. Cable Positive; past chmn. Traffic Audit Bur.; dir. Audit Bur. Circulations; bd. dir., past mem. exec. com. Advt. Info. Svc., Advt. Rsch. Found.; lectr. in field. Mem. nat. coun. Boy Scouts Am. Mem. Media Dirs. Coun. (past pres.), Am. Assn. Advt. Agys. (past vice chmn. media policy com.), Internat. Radio and TV Found. (bd. dirs.), Advt. Coun. (bd. dirs.), John Reisenbach Found. (bd. dirs.). E-mail: joe.ostrowconsulting@yahoo.com. *It is important that one continue to set goals that seem unachievable and at the same time live by standards that remain consistently high. The maintenance of integrity and adherence to principles which support it, are especially critical when dealing with consumer commercial persuasion. Anything less would be detrimental to the proper pursuit of both personal and business achievements.*

OSTROW, STUART, theatrical producer, educator, author; b. NYC; m. Ann Elizabeth Gilbert; children: Julie Elizabeth, Katherine Ann, John Stuart. Disting. univ. prof. theater U. Houston. Pres. Stuart Ostrow Found., Inc., Mus. Theater Lab.; founding mem. opera-mus. theatre panel NEA; mem. bd. overseers com. to visit Loeb Drama Ctr. Harvard U. Prodr.: We Take the Town, 1961, The Apple Tree, 1966, 1776, 1969, Scratch, 1971, Pippin, 1972, The Moony Shapiro Songbook, 1981, American Passion, 1983, M. Butterfly, 1988, La Bête, 1991, Face Value, 1993; prodr., dir.: Here's Love, 1963, Swing, 1980; author, producer: Stages, 1978; assoc. dir.; Chicago, 1975; author: A Producer's Broadway Journey, 1999, Thank You Very Much, 2002, Present At the Creation, Leaping in the Dark and Going Against the Grain, 2005, Booklist Top Ten Arts Books, 2006. Mem. Pulitzer Prize Drama Jury; chmn. bd. trustees Inst. for Advanced Study in Musical Theatre. With USAF, 1952—55.

OSTROWSKI, STACEY, athletic trainer, educator; b. Detroit, Dec. 2, 1973; d. Harry and Betty Ostrowski. AAS, Henry Ford C.C., Dearborn, Mich., 1995; BSc in Sports Medicine/Athletic Tng., Ea. Mich. U., Ypsilanti, 1998; M in Kinesiology/Biomechanics, U. Tenn., Knoxville, 2000. Grad. asst. athletic trainer U. Tenn., Knoxville, 1998—2000; asst. athletic trainer/lectr. Lander U., Greenwood, SC, 2000—02; cert. athletic trainer No. Mich. Sports Medicine Ctr., Petoskey, Mich., 2002—. Guest lectr. anatomy and physiology U. Tenn., 1999—2001; guest spkr. sports medicine No. Mich. Sports Medicine, 2002—. Author: (case studies, articles) Jour. Athletic Tng., Am. Coll. Sports Medicine. Mem. Am. Red Cross, 1998—; lectr. cmty. edn. on knee injuries Bay St. Orthop., Cheboygan, Mich., 2003; lectr. cmty. soccer injury prevention Mich. Dept. Cmty. Health, Indian River, 2004; facilitator phys. therapy/sports medicine involvement Spl. Riders Program, Cheboygan, 2004—; lectr. H.S./cmty. on sports medicine and athletic tng., 2005—. Recipient academic excellence citation, Ea. Mich. U., 1997, Dr. Youman Academic scholarship, Knoxville, 2000. Mem.: Mich. Athletic Trainers Soc., Nat. Athletic Trainers Assn. Catholic. Avocations: hiking, bicycling, kayaking, ice hockey. Office: No Mich Sports Medicine 11153 N Straits Hwy Cheboygan MI 49721 Personal E-mail: michiganatc@aol.com.

OSTRUM, ROBERT F., orthopaedic surgeon; b. Phila., Pa., 1955; MD, Temple U., 1980. Cert. Orthopaedic Surgery. Resident, gen. surgery Albert Einstein Med. Ctr., Phila., 1980—81, resident, orthop., 1981—85; fellow, trauma AONA/ Assn. for the Study of Internal Fixation, 1985; assoc. dir. orthop. trauma, dir. trauma rsch. Ohio State Univ., Columbus, asst. prof. orthop. surgery; med. staff Grant Med. Ctr., Columbus, Ohio; dir., orthop. trauma surgery Cooper Bone & Joint Inst., Camden; assoc. prof. Cooper Univ. Hosp., Camden, NJ. Lectr. in field. Contbr. articles to profl. jours. Named Top Doctor, Columbus Mag. Mem.: Orthop. Trauma Assn., Am. Acad. Orthop. Surgery, Am. Bd. Orthop. Surgery. Office: Three Cooper Plz Ste 403 Sells AZ 85634 Address: 401 S Kings Hwy Ste 3A Cherry Hill NJ 08034 Office Phone: 856-342-3159.

OSTRUSZKA, KATHLEEN ZELEK, economics professor; d. John and Josephine Zelek; m. Wayne D. Ostruszka, July 26, 1969; children: Katherine, Leo. BA, De Paul U., Chgo., 1969. Life underwriter CNA Ins. Co., Chgo., 1969—70; customer svc. rep. Pky. Bank and Trust Co., Harwood Heights, Ill., 1970—73; economics instr. Waukesha County Tech. Coll., Pewaukee, Wis., 1982—. Cmty. beautification Willaura W. Homeowners Assoc., Brookfield, Wis., 1998—2008; liturgical participation St. Mary's Visitation Parish, Elm Grove, Wis., 2000—08. Conservative. Roman Catholic. Avocations: gardening, golf. Home: 15670 Mark Dr Brookfield WI 53005 Office: Waukesha County Tech Coll 800 Main St Pewaukee WI 53072 Business E-Mail: kostruszka@wctc.edu.

OSTWALD, MARTIN, retired classicist; b. Dortmund, Germany, Jan. 15, 1922; arrived in U.S., 1946, naturalized, 1956; s. Max and Hedwig (Strauss) Ostwald; m. Lore Ursula Weinberg, Dec. 27, 1948; children: Mark F., David H. BA, U. Toronto, 1946; AM, U. Chgo., 1948; PhD, Columbia U., 1952; D (hon.), Fribourg U., Switzerland, 1995, Dortmund U., Germany, 2001. Instr. classics and humanities Wesleyan U., Middletown, Conn., 1950-51; from lectr. to asst. prof. Greek and Latin Columbia U., 1951-58; mem. faculty Swarthmore Coll., 1958—, prof. classics, 1966-92, prof. emeritus, 1992—; prof. classical studies U. Pa., 1968-92, prof. emeritus, 1992—. Vis. assoc. prof. Princeton (N.J.) U., 1964, mem. Inst. Advanced Study, 1974—75, 1981—82, 1990—91; vis. prof. U. Calif., Berkeley, 1969, Tel-Aviv U., 1996—; vis. fellow Balliol Coll. Oxford (Eng.) U., 1970—71, vis. fellow Wolfson Coll., 1987, 91; dir. fellowships-in-residence classics NEH, 1976—77; dir. d'etudes EHESS, Paris, 1991; mem. Inst. Advanced Studies, Tel Aviv, 1994, 2003. Translator: Nicomachean Ethics (Aristotle), 1962; author: (book) Nomos and the Beginings of the Athenian Democracy, 1969, Autonomia, Its Genesis and Early History, 1982, From Popular Sovereignty to the Sovereignty of Law, 1987, Ananke in Thucydides, 1988, Oligarchia, 2000; author: (with T. G. Rosenmeyer and J. W. Halporn) The Meters of Greek and Latin Poetry, 2d edit., 1980; author: Language & History in Ancient Greek Literature, 2009; mem. editl. bd. Cambridge Ancient History, 1976—94; contbr. articles to profl. jours. Fellow, Am. Coun. Learned Socs., 1965—66, NEH, 1970—71, 1990—91; Fulbright Rsch. fellow, Greece, 1961—62, Guggenheim fellow, 1977—78, Lang. fellow, Swarthmore Coll., 1986—87. Fellow: AAAS; mem.: Soc. Ancient Philosophy, Classical Assn. Atlantic States, Classical Assn. Can., Am. Philol. Assn. (pres. 1986—87), Am. Philos. Soc., Soc. Promotion Hellenic Studies (hon.). Home: 408 Walnut Ln Swarthmore PA 19081-1137 Business E-Mail: mostwal1@swarthmore.edu.

OSTWALD, VENICE ELOISE VARNER, librarian, educator, minister, writer; b. Denver, July 19, 1928; d. Earl Robert and Madeline (Shoemaker) Varner; m. Leonard F. Ostwald (div.). BA, U. Colo., Boulder, 1946; MS, U. Southern Calif., 1954. Libr., tchr. Long Beach Pub. Schs., Calif., 1954—61; asst. prof. U. Oreg., Eugene, 1961—63; dir. libr. & audio-visual Hillsborough Pub. Schs., Calif., 1963—65; adminstrv. asst. to libr. dir. San Jose State U., 1965—67; instrn. specialist-libr. DeAnza Coll., Cupertino, Calif., 1967—87, emeritus, 1987—. Founder, bd. dirs. Singles Svc., Santa Clara, Calif., 1972; co-founder Casa Serena Hosp., San Jose, 1981; pres. Spiritual Edn. Endeavors Publ. Co., 1985—; chmn. bd. SHARE Found., 1985—. Co-author: (book) New Teachings for an Awakening Humanity, 1985, Secret Truths for Young Adults, 1986, Cosmic Revelations Ann Valentin & Virginia Essene, 1987, Descent of the Dove Ann Valentin & Virginia Essene, 1988, New Bodies, New Celss, New Life! Virginia Essene, 1994, You Are Becoming A Galacic Human Virginia Essene & Sheldon Nidle, 1994, The Hathor Material:Messages from an Ascended Civilization, 1996, Energ Blessings from the Stars Virginia Essene & Irving Feurst, 1998, Earth, the Cosmos and You, 1999, Anna, Grandmother of Jesus: A Message of Wisdom and Love, 2002; lyricist (songs) Part of Me, Oasis, Peru, Caliente, Hyano Cucarumba, Esclava. Mem.: Kappa Delta, Beta Phi Mu. Office: SHARE Found 1556 Halford Ave # 288 Santa Clara CA 95051-2661 Home Phone: 408-248-8244; Office Phone: 408-248-8244. Business E-Mail: lovecorps@sharefoundationnetwork.com.

OSUCH, DEBRA K., environmental engineer; b. 1969; married; 3 children. BS in Med. Physics, Oakland U.; MS in Hazardous Waste Mgmt., Wayne State U. Mgr. devel. svcs. Soil Materials Engrs. Inc., Shelby Twp. Named one of 40 Under 40, Crain's Detroit Bus., 2006. Mem.: Comml. Real Estate Women (pres., Detroit Chpt.). Office: Soil Materials Engrs Inc 13019 Pauline Dr Shelby Township MI 48315 Office Phone: 586-731-3100. Office Fax: 586-731-3582.

O'SULLIVAN, DANIEL JOHN, research and development company executive; b. Dublin, Aug. 1, 1954; came to U.S., 1976; s. Daniel and Moya (Emmett) O'S.; m. Patricia Ann Becchina, Aug. 29, 1981; 2 children. BSEE, Coll. Tech., Dublin, 1976; MS in Computer Sci., Poly. Inst. N.Y., 1978. Systems-devel. engr. Acco, Bristol, Conn., 1976-79; sr. project engr. ADT, NYC, 1979-80; mem. tech. staff, cons. AT&T/Bell Labs., Holmdel, N.J., 1980-82, 84-86; elec. engrng. cons. OSI Techs., Aberdeen, N.J., 1982-84; pres., v.p. R & D, prin., researcher, developer Next Generation Info., Morganville, N.J., 1986—; owner IT Systems, Morganville, 1990—. Inventor convenient chair, ceiling hook, video case.

O'SULLIVAN, DANIEL W., chemistry professor; married. PhD, U. RI, Narragansett, 1994. Rsch. assoc. U. Miami, Fla., 1994—97; prof. chemistry dept. US Naval Acad., Annapolis, Md., 1997—. Office: US Naval Academy 572M Holloway Rd Annapolis MD 21402

O'SULLIVAN, DONAL, educator; MA, Bonn U., Germany; PhD, Bonn U.; degree in Habilitation, Cath. U. Eichstaett, Germany. Asst. prof. Calif. State U., Northridge, 2005—08. Office: Calif State Univ Nothridge 18111 Nordhoff St Northridge CA 91330

O'SULLIVAN, EUGENE HENRY, retired advertising executive, management consultant; b. Plainfield, NJ, June 8, 1942; s. Patrick J. and Helen (Callahan) O'S.; m. Tracy O'Sullivan; children: Meredith Heather, Charlie Hiromichi. BBA, U. Notre Dame, 1964. Media buyer Foote Cone Belding, NYC, 1967-68; account exec., mgmt. supr. Group Dtr, NYC; exec. v.p., dir. client svcs. Young & Rubicam, NYC, 1968-84; sr. v.p., group dir. Ogilvy & Mather, NYC, 1984-86, 87; exec. v.p. Hill, Holliday, Boston, 1986-87; exec. v.p., gen. mgr. McCann Erickson, NYC, 1988-90; ret., 1990. Served to lt. (j.g.) USN, 1964-66. Mem. Lotos Club. Democrat. Home: 21 E 10th St New York NY 10003-5923 Office Phone: 212-614-9570. E-mail: eugeneo@earthlink.net.

O'SULLIVAN, JUDITH ROBERTA, lawyer, writer, artist; b. Pitts., Jan. 6, 1942; d. Robert Howard and Mary Olive (O'Donnell) Gallick; m. James Paul O'Sullivan, Feb. 1, 1964; children: Kathryn, James. BA, Carlow Coll., 1963; MA, U. Md., 1969, PhD, 1976; JD, Georgetown U., 1996. Editor Am. Film Inst., Washington, 1974—77; assoc. program coord. Smithsonian Resident Assocs., Washington, 1977—78; dir. instl. devel. Nat. Archives, Washington, 1978—79; exec. dir. Md. State Humanities Coun., Balt., 1979—81, 1982—84, Ctr. for the Book, Libr. of Congress, Washington, 1981—82; dep. asst. dir. Nat. Mus. Am. Art, Washington, 1984—87, acting asst. dir., 1987—89; pres., CEO The Mus. at Stony Brook, NY, 1989—92; exec. dir. Nat. Assn. Women Judges, Washington, 1993; clk. Office Legal Adviser US Dept. State, Washington, 1994—96; trial atty. Atty. Gen.'s honors program US Dept. Justice, 1996—, sr. trial atty. Criminal divsn., Domestic Security sect., 2002—08, civil divsn., 2008—; spl. asst. US atty. US Dist. (ea. dist.) Va., 1998—2002; asst. US atty. US Dist. Ariz., Tucson, 1999—2000. Summer assoc. Piper & Marbury, Balt., 1995; chair Smithsonian Women's Coun., Washington, 1988-89. Author: The Art of the Comic Strip, 1971 (Gen. Excellence award Printing Industry Am.); Workers and Allies, 1975; (with Alan Fern) The Complete Prints of Leonard Baskin, 1984, The Great American Comic Strip, 1991, Suicide in Sea Isle City, 2006, Death and the Jersey Devil, 2007, A Drop of Deadly Ink, 2008, Death of a Cougar, 2009; editor Am. Film Inst. Catalogue: Feature Films, 1961-70, 1974-77; mem. editl. bd. Am. Film Inst. Catalog, 1979-1990. Trustee Child Life Ctr., U. Md., College Pk., 1971-74; chair Smithsonian Women's Coun., 1988-89. Univ. fellow, U. Md., 1967—70, Mus. fellow, 1970—71, Smithsonian fellow, Nat. Collection Fine Arts, Washington, 1972—73. Mem.: Mystery Writers of Am. (exec. bd. Mid-Atlantic br. 2003—), D.C. Bar Assn., Md. Bar Assn. Avocations: landscape painting, mystery writing.

O'SULLIVAN, LYNDA TROUTMAN, lawyer; b. Oil City, Pa., Aug. 30, 1952; d. Perry John and Vivian Dorothy (Schreffler) Troutman; m. P. Kevin O'Sullivan, Dec. 15, 1979; children: John Perry, Michael Patrick. BA, Am. U., 1974; JD, Georgetown U., 1978, postgrad., 1982-83. Bar: D.C. 1978. Ptnr. Perkins Coie, Washington, 1985-92, Fried, Frank, Harris, Shriver & Jacobson, Washington, 1993-97, Miller & Chevalier, Washington, 1997—2004; asst. dep. gen. counsel dispute resolution USAF, 2004—. Mem. adv. bd. Fed. Contracts Report, 1991-97, Govt. Contract Costs, Pricing & Acctg. Report, 1997-99; mem. faculty govt. contracts program George Washington U., 1993-99; lectr. in field. Contbg. author: Cost Reimbursement Contracting, 3d edit., 2005. Fellow Am. Bar Found.; mem. ABA (chair truth in negotiations com. 1991-94, chair acctg., cost and pricing com. 1996-2000, coun. sect. pub. contract law 1993-95). Office: 1777 N Kent St Arlington VA 22209 Business E-Mail: lynda.osullivan@pentagon.af.mil.

O'SULLIVAN, NANCY LOUISE, immunologist, educator; b. Detroit, Feb. 1, 1951; d. Aldwin Wayne and Corlene May Chilson; m. Russell Martin O'Sullivan, May 19, 1973. AS, Schoolcraft Coll., Livonia, Mich., 1979; BS, Wayne State U., Detroit, 1984, PhD, 1991. Cert. med. lab. technician ASCP, 1979. Rsch. assoc. Wayne State U. Sch. Medicine, 1992—96, rsch. asst. prof., 1996—. Mem. Covenant Cmty. Ch., Redford, Mich., 1958—2009. Mem.: Soc. Mucosal Immunology, Creation Rsch. Soc., Am. Assn. Immunologists, Sigma Xi. Avocations: photography, gardening, birdwatching. Home: 25457 Keeler Redford MI 48239 Office: Wayne State Univ Sch Med 540 E Canfield Ave Detroit MI 48201 Office Fax: 313-577-1155. Personal E-mail: nosullivan@twmi.rr.com. Business E-Mail: nosulliv@med.wayne.edu.

O'SULLIVAN, PATRICIA ANN, principal, writer; b. Boston, Apr. 8, 1952; d. Robert Charles and Irene Emily Ritchie; m. Paul Francis O'Sullivan, Jr., June 16, 1974; 1 child, Paul Francis O'Sullivan, III. AS in Early Childhood Edn., Lasell Coll., 1972; BS in Behavioral and Social Scis., U. Md., 1992; postgrad., Bridgewater State Coll., 1994—95; MEd, Framingham State U., 1997. Cert. profl. educator Fla. Dept. Edn., 2001, tchr. Mass. Dept. Edn., 1995, ednl. leadership U. Ctrl. Fla., 2004. Instrnl. asst. Hayfield Elem. Sch., Alexandria, Va., 1988—91; resource tchr. Am. Sch. Bolivia, La Paz, 1992—94; elem. tchr. Internat. Am. Sch. Guatemala, Guatemala City, 1995—99, Sculptor Charter Sch., Titusville, Fla., 1999—2002, asst. prin., 2002—06, prin., 2006—. Internat. Sch. Guatemala rep. Basic Sch., Harrisonburg, Va., 1997—99; mentor tchr. Brevard County Sch. Bd., Viera, Fla., 2000—; Sculptor Sch. rep. Core Knowledge Found., Charlottesville, Va., 2002—; elem. rep. to dirs. adv. coun. Internat. Am. Sch. Guatemala, Guatemala City. Advisor Sculptor Charter Sch. Student Coun., Titusville; adminstrv. team rep. and program director's designee Brevard Innovative Charter Sch., Titusville, 2002. Named Tchr. of Yr., Brevard Innovative Charter, 2000. Mem.: ASCD, Fla. Consortium Charter Schs., Fla. Assn. Sch. Administrs., Nat. Assn. Elem. and Mid. Sch. Administrs., Kapp Delta Pi. Avocations: reading, travel, walking, gardening. Office: Sculptor Charter School 1301 Armstrong Dr Titusville FL 32780 Office Fax: 321-264-9995. Personal E-mail: posullivan1@cfl.rr.com. Business E-Mail: o'sullivanp@brevardschools.org.

O'SULLIVAN, PAUL KEVIN, business executive, management and instructional systems consultant; b. Syracuse, N.Y., May 10, 1938; s. John Hugh and Helen Troy (Smith) O'S.; m. Lynda Troutman; children: Mary Kathleen and Karin Jennifer (twins), John Perry, Michael Patrick. A.B., Dartmouth Coll., 1960. Comm. specialist Gen. Electric Co., Schenectady, N.Y., 1963-66; nat. inst. dir. Gen. Learning Corp., Washington, 1966-67; sr. con. ednl. sys. Aries Corp., McLean, Va., 1967-69; dir. profl. devel. Nat. Audio-Visual Assn., Fairfax, Va., 1969-74; exec. dir. Am. Soc. Tng. and Devel., Madison, Wis., 1974-80; sr. v.p. Sterling Inst., Washington, 1980-87, nat. account mgr. Orgnl. Dynamics, Inc., 1987-94; account exec. Zenger Miller, 1995-96, pres. The O'Sullivan Group, Inc., 1996—; staff dir. Nat. Audio-Visual Inst. for Effective Comm. Ind. U., 1969-74; chief adminstr. Internat. Fedn. Tng. and Devel. Orgns., 1974-80; dir. Internat. Symposia for Tng. Comm. in Switzerland, Australia and Middle East. Producer and dir. films and multi-media presentations; author, editor comm. and tng. courses, textbooks; contbr. articles to profl. jours.; spkr. various profl events. Served to lt. (j.g.), USNR, 1956-63. Recipient Honor medal for Lit. Freedoms Found., 1963; Writers Gold Cup award Gen. Electric, 1966; Resolution for Outstanding Achievement Nat. Audio-Visual Assn., 1974, Pres.'s award for bus. achievement, 1989, 90, 91, 92, 93. Mem. Nat. Soc. for Performance and Instrn. (Presdl. citation 1977), Am. Soc. Assn. Execs. (Grand award for mgmt. achievement 1978), Am. Soc. Tng. and Devel. (hon. life, mem. Training Officers Consortium, Spencer Logan Lifetime Outstanding Contbns. award 2007).

O'SULLIVAN, STEPHANIE L., federal agency administrator; With Office of Naval Intelligence, CIA, 1995—, assoc. dep. dir. sci. & tech., 2003—05, dep. dir. sci. & tech., 2005—. Office: Directorate of Science & Technology CIA Office Dir of National Intelligence Washington DC 20505*

O'SULLIVAN, TERENCE M., labor union administrator; b. San Francisco, July 29, 1955; BBA, Am. U., Washington. Laborer Washington Metrorail, mem. Laborers' Union Local 456; former HS tchr. W.Va.; founder computer svcs. co., 1978; instr. W.Va. Laborers' Training Fund, 1987, adminstr., 1989; mem. local 1353 Laborers Internat. Union N.Am. (LIUNA), Parkersburg, W.Va., 1987, asst. dir. construction, maintenance & svc. trades dept. Clifton, Va., 1993, internat. v.p., 1999, mid-atlantic regional mgr., asst. to pres., LIUNA chief of staff, 1999, gen. pres., 2000—. Bd. dirs. Union Labor Life Ins. Co. (ULLICO), chmn., CEO, 2002—07; bd. dirs. Nat. Coord. Com. Multiemployer Plans; v.p. exec. coun. AFL-CIO, mem. gov. bd. Pres.'s of Bldg. & Construction Trades Dept.; mem. leadership coun. Change to Win. Bd. dirs. America's Agenda: Health Care for All; mem. mgmt. com. Americans for Transp. Mobility; bd. dirs. Apollo Alliance. Office: LIUNA 905 16th St NW Washington DC 20006 Office Phone: 202-737-8320.*

O'SULLIVAN, THOMAS J., lawyer; b. New Haven, Apr. 7, 1940; s. Thomas J. and Marjorie (Hession) O'S.; m. Anita Brady, Aug. 10, 1968; children: Kathleen, Margaret, Mary Tess, Anne Elizabeth. BA in History, Yale U., 1961; LLB, Harvard U., 1966. Bar: Conn. 1966, U.S. Dist. Ct. Conn. 1967, N.Y. 1967, U.S. Dist. Ct. (so. and ea. dists.) N.Y. 1967, U.S. Ct. Appeals (2d cir.) 1971, U.S. Supreme Ct. 1971, U.S. Dist. Ct. (no. dist.) N.Y. 1976, U.S. Ct. Appeals (11th cir.). 2004. Assoc. White & Case, NYC, 1966-74, ptnr., 1974—. 1st lt. U.S. Army, 1961-63. Mem. ABA, N.Y. State Bar Assn., Assn. of Bar of City of N.Y., Internat. Bar Assn. Clubs: Milbrook (Greenwich, Conn.); Yale (N.Y.C.). Home: 56 Hillside Rd Greenwich CT 06830-4835 Office: White & Case Bldg Ll 1155 Avenue of The Americas New York NY 10036-2787

OSVATH, LUDOVIC LAJOS, minister; b. Lupoaia, Romania, July 22, 1938; arrived in US, 1980; s. Lajos and Anna (Feher) O.; m. Jolan Pacso, May 4, 1963; 1 child, Judith. Grad., Inst. Tech., Romania, 1954, Inst. Bus., 1957, Ady Endre Coll., 1978; student, Heritage Bapt. Inst., Cleve., 1986. Ordained to ministry Bapt.Ch., 1955. Preacher Bapt. Ch., Romania, 1955—, mem. coms. Egrespatak, Romania, 1955-65, treas., mem. com. Zalau, Romania, 1965-73; pres. Hungarian Missionary Soc. Inc., Cleve., 1989—. Del. Romanian Bapt. Congress, Bucharest, Romania, 1978; maintenance exec. Sponge, Inc., Cleve., 1985—. Underground rep. Amnesty Internat., Romania, 1977-80; founding mem. Defenders of Religious Freedom and Ideas, Romania, 1978, persecuted and excluded from the country; mem. Internat. Christian Solidarity, Zurich, Switzerland. Mem. Christian Mgmt. Assn., Bocskai Cultural Soc. (sec. 1988—). Office Phone: 440-234-4329.

OSWALD, JAMES MARLIN, education educator, researcher; b. Plainview, Tex., Aug. 17, 1935; s. James Buchanan and Eula Bea (Marlin) O.; m. Dorothy Anne Veigel, Dec. 27, 1956; children: Richard, Ramona, Roberta. BS, West Tex. State Coll., 1957, MA, 1958; EdD, Stanford U., 1970. Tchr., supr. Salt Lake City Pub. Schs., 1958-66; curriculum specialist Am. Insts. Rsch., 1966-68; staff assoc. Nat. Coun. Social Studies, 1968-69; asst. prof. social studies and social sci. edn. Syracuse U., NY, 1969-72; rschr.writer, dir. global cultural studies edn. projects Am. Univs. Field Staff, 1972-75; asst. supt. instrn. East Penn Sch. Dist., Emmaus, Pa., 1975-78; field coord. Pa., Del. and N.J. citizen edn. Rsch. for Better Schs., Phila., 1978-80; instrnl. devel. specialist Cmty. Coll. Phila., 1980-96; energy conservation cons., 1959—. Propr. Energy Cons. and Main Line Stoves, 1972—, Fin. and Retirement Planning Cons., 1980—, Macro/Micro Agro, 1992—, DudeSpa, 2002—; pres. N.Y. State Coun. Social Studies, 1971-72; co-founder, pres. Inst. Plant Based Nutrition, 1996—; nutrition educator, 1997—; career mentor, life coach, 2002—; phys. fitness trainer, martial arts self def. coach, 2002—; model, 1935—; cons. in field. Author: The Monroe Doctrine: Does It Survive?, 1969; Research in Social Studies and Social Science Education, 1972; co-author: Earthship, 1974, Planet Earth, 1976, Our Home, the Earth, 1980, Marco Polo Vegan Cuisine, 1998, Christopher Columbus Vegan Cuisine, 1999, Criteria for Nutritional Guidelines for Century 21, 1999, Ferdinand Magellan Vegan Cuisine, 2000, Commemoration of Heroic Produce Grower Sacrifices, Death and Survival on September 11, 2001, 2001, Garden of Eden Vegan Cuisine, 2003, Astronaut Vegan Cuisine, 2003, New York City Vegan Cuisine, 2003, Philadelphia Vegan Cuisine, 2003; introduced concepts of the snaggle-toothed curriculum, 1959, global cultural studies, 1972, humanself, 1972, zero runoff landscaping, 1959, veganomics, 1998, veganocracy, 1998, veganagro, 1998, microagro, 2003, Plant Kingdom Gourmet, 2003, Green Gourmet, 2006, Hollow Headed Zero Skill Schooling, 2007; editor quar. newsletter Plant Based Nutrition, 1997—; contbr. articles to profl. jours. With U.S. Army, 1957-58, USAR, 1958-68. Recipient Sertoma Svc. to Mankind award, Salt Lake City, 1966; grantee Stanford U., NSF, U.S. Office Edn., Inst. Internat. Studies; Henry Newell fellow Stanford U., 1966-68; Fulbright-Hays SEAsia U. Singapore Study Program fellow, 1967. Mem. Am. Vegan Soc. (life), Vegan Organic Network Horticulture-Agr. (U.K.), Hastings-Halliburton Vegetarian Assn. (Can.), Inst. Nutrition Edn. and Rsch. (bd. advisor), Inst. Plant Based Nutrition, N.Am. Vegetarian Soc. (life), Toronto Vegetarian Assn., Main Line Vegan Soc. (founding pres.), Ctr. for Cancer Edn., Hindu Temple Soc. Am., Internat. Soc. Kirsna Consciousness, Food for Life Internat., Social Sci. Edn. Consortium (emeritus), Tex. Panhandle-Plains Hist. Soc. (life), Utah Hist. Soc. (life), Desc. Founders of Ancient Windsor (life), Windsor Hist. Soc. (life), St. Lawrence County Hist. Soc., Pa. Forestry Assn., Pa. Vegetable Growers Assn., Pa. Nut Growers Assn., NY Fruit and Vegetable Growers Assn., Vegetable Growers Assn. NJ, Phi Delta Kappa (emeritus). Avocation: gardening. Home and Office: 333 Bryn Mawr Ave Bala Cynwyd PA 19004-2606 Office Phone: 610-667-6876.

OSWALD, RUDOLPH A., economist; b. Milw., Aug. 4, 1932; s. Carl J. and Anne O.; m. Mary Louise Hurney BA, Holy Cross Coll., 1954; postgrad. (Fulbright scholar), U. Munich, W. Ger., 1954-55; MS, U. Wis., Madison, 1958; PhD in Econs., Georgetown U., 1965. Research and edn. dir. Internat. Assn. Fire Fighters, Washington, 1959-63; economist research dept. AFL-CIO, Washington, 1963-72, asst. dir. edn. dept., 1975-76, dir. research dept., 1976-96, economist-in-residence George Meany Ctr for Labor Studies, 1996—. Vis. prof. Cornell U., 1997, 99, 2000; rsch. dir. Svc. Employees Internat. Union, Washington, 1972-75, instr. GM-UAW Paid Ednl. Leave program, 2001-02; adj. prof. econs. George Washington U., 1966-75; mem. Fed. Employees Pay Coun., 1970-72, Sec. Navy's Adv. Bd. Edn. and Tng., 1975-78, Nat. Commn. Employment and Unemployment Stats., Fgn. Investment Adv. Com.; mem. adv. coun. Indsl. Labor Rels. Sch., Cornell U., 1981-85, 95-99, Sch. Bus. U. S.C. 1992-98; mem. consumer adv. com. SEC, 1994-98mem. labor rsch. adv. coun. Bur. Labor Stats.; mem. Pres.'s Adv. Com. on Trade, 1984-98; mem adv. com. Ex-Im Bank, 1989-92; cons. Alliance for Ret. Ams., 2004-05. Bd. dirs. Nat. Industries for the Blind, 1965-71, Montgomery County United Way, 2006-09, Rockville Meals Wheels, 2005-09. With US Army, 1956-57. Mem. Indsl. Rels. Rsch. Assn. (past pres.), Nat. Bur. Econ. Rsch. (dir.), Nat. Policy Assn. (dir. 1988-2003), Nat. Coun. on Econ. Edn. (dir. 1976-96). Home: 11804 Devilwood Dr Rockville MD 20854-3407 Personal E-mail: rudyo6@aol.com.

OSWALD, TINA ATKINSON, librarian; b. Titusville, Fla., July 13, 1962; d. Edward Lammon and Patricia Matheson Atkinson; m. Brian Paul Oswald, July 23, 1988; children: Jessica Lammon, Rebecca Irene. BA, Winthrop Coll., Rock Hill, SC, 1984; MLIS, U. SC, Columbia, 1986. Circulation, reference govt. docs. libr. Ala. A&M U., Normal; rsch. libr. Stephen F. Austin State U., Nacogdoches, Tex., 1997—. Contbr. articles to profl. jours. Mem.: ALA, Tex. Libr. Assn. (rrt and ttrt officer, TALL Texans Leadership Devel. Inst. award 1999). Lutheran. Avocations: reading, exercise. Home: 1904 Creekview Bend Nacogdoches TX 75965 Office: Stephen F Austin State Univ PO Box 13055 SFA Sta Nacogdoches TX 75962-3055 Business E-Mail: toswald@sfasu.edu.

OSWALT, ROY EDWARDS, professional baseball player; b. Kosciusko, Miss., Aug. 29, 1977; s. Jean and Billie Joe Oswalt; m. Nichol Oswalt; 2 children. Attended, Holmes CC, Goodman, Miss. Pitcher Houston Astros, 2001—. Mem. US nat. team World Baseball Classic, 2009. Recipient Darryl Kile award, 2003; named Rookie of Yr., Baseball Writers Assn. Am. (BBWAA) Houston chpt., NL Rookie Pitcher of Yr., Sporting News, Nat. League Championship Series MVP, 2005; named to TOPPS All-Rookie team, Nat. League All-Star Team, 2005—07. Achievements include leading the National League in wins (20), 2004. Office: Houston Astros Po Box 288 Houston TX 77001-0288*

OTAL, MONICA D., music educator; d. Frank N and Amapola Otal. MusB, Oberlin Coll. Conservatory of Music, 1975; MusM, Johns Hopkins U., 1977. Music faculty Duke Ellington Sch. of the Arts, Washington, 1977—93; dir. of music Glenmont United Meth. Ch., Silver Spring, Md., 1988—; lectr. in music Morgan State U., Balt., 1993—99; assoc. prof. of music C.C. of Balt. County, Balt., 1999—; artistic dir. Ctrl. Md. Chorale, Laurel, Md., 2001—. Singer washington opera chorus, baltimore opera chorus. Artistic dir. Ctrl. Md. Chorale, Laurel, Md., 2001. Named Outstanding CC Educator of Yr., Essex, Md., 2006; ECISL grantee, C.C. of Balt. County, 2001. Mem.: Coll. Music Soc. (campus rep. 2001), Nat. Assn. of Teachers of Singing, Am. Choral Directors Assn. (chairperson repertoire and stds. com. for 2-yr. colls. 2000). Office: C C Balt County 7201 Rossville Blvd Baltimore MD 21237 Office Phone: 443-840-1726. Personal E-mail: divacoach1@comcast.com. E-mail: motal@ccbcmd.edu.

OTANI, NIELS FUJIO, electrical engineering educator; b. Washington, June 30, 1955; s. Theodore Toshiro and Tomie (Kojima) O. BA with honors, U. Chgo., 1977; PhD, U. Calif., Berkeley, 1986. Postdoctoral assoc. Courant Inst. Math. Sci./NYU, NYC, 1986-87; asst. prof. Sch. Elec. Engring. Cornell U., Ithaca, N.Y., 1988—. Vis. rsch. scientist Lawrence Livermore (Calif.) Nat. Lab., 1989; vis. asst. prof. Wilder Physics Lab., Dartmouth Coll., Hanover, N.H., 1989, 90. Contbr. articles to Astrophys. Jour., Physics of Fluids, Jour. Computational Physics. Recipient NSF Presdl. Young Investigator award, 1991. Mem. AAAS, Am. Geophys. Union, Am. Phys. Soc., Phi Beta Kappa. Office: Sch Elec Engring Cornell Univ Ithaca NY 14853

OTANI, YURIKO L. (CHARKO), retired artist; b. Pasadena, Calif., Mar. 11, 1931; d. Giichi and Shiki Nakamura; m. Herbert Otani, Nov. 24, 1959 (dec.); children: Diana R. Furhmann, Laura M., Glen K., Julia M. Otani Caruso, David E., Robert K. BFA, The Cooper Union Advancement Sci. and Art, 1976. Cert. tchr. Ramapo Coll., N.J. Graphic artist JJ Michaels, Little Ferry, NJ, 1981; art tchr. No. Valley Old Tappan HS, NJ, 1988—93; with prodn. dept. Cmty. Life, Westwood, NJ, 1993—97; graphic artist The Town Jour., Allendale, NJ, 1998, Rockland County Times, NY, 1998—2007. Guest lectr. WWII Japanese-Am. interment at local elem. & HS. Rivervale Pub. Libr., 1993, No. Valley HS, Old Tappan, 1993; contbr. articles to newspapers and profl. jour. WWII internee, Tulare, Calif., Gila, Ariz.; guest lectr. WWII Japanese-Am. internments; contr. essays to local newspapers. Recipient Recognition award, Bergen County, 1991, Point of Light award, Pres. George H.W. Bush, 1991, Low Fund prize, Cooper Union, 1976, Tchrs. Recognition award, Gov. of NJ. Avocations: art, quilting, swimming.

O'TANYI, THEODORE J., JR., retired biology professor; b. Darby, Pa., Oct. 9, 1941; s. Theodore J. and Charlotte M. O'Tanyi; m. Sandra Jones, Oct. 12, 1968; children: Eva Zuvich, Eileen Webb, Frank. BS, Pa. Mil. Coll., Chester, 1963; MS, PhD, Lehigh U., Bethlehem, Pa., 1968. Biology faculty Widener U., Chester, 1968—2007, premed. advisor, 1982—2008, adj. faculty, 2007—, assoc. prof. emeritus dept. biology, 2008—; writer Medtronic Inc., Mpls., 1977, Intellimedia Inc., Blue Bell, Pa., 1997. Physiology faculty Temple U. Sch. Dentistry, Phila., 1964—65, physiology biophysics faculty, 1985—86; biology faculty Lehigh U., 1965—66. Contbr. scientific papers to numerous profl. jours. Pres. Rotary Club Chester, 2008—; mem. Governor's Adv. Coun. Exceptional Citizens, Dover, Del.; chmn. State Adv. Coun. Coordination Svcs. Handicapped, Dover. Postdoc. fellowship, USPHS, NIH, 1968—69. Mem.: AAAS, NE Assn. Advisors Health Professions (pres. 1993—94), Nat. Assn. Advisors Health Professions, Am. Soc. Zoologists, NY Acad. Scis., Rotary Internat. (pres. 2008—), Omicron Delta Kappa, Sigma Xi, Beta Beta Beta, Alpha Psi Omega, Phi Kappa Phi (chpt. pres. 2006—08). Roman Catholic. Home and Office: TOT Ednl Consulting 121 Vernon Woods Glen Mills PA 19342-3312 Business E-Mail: tjotanyi@comcast.net.

OTČENÁŠEK, KAREL, archbishop of Roman Catholic church; b. Ceske Mezirici, Czechoslovakia, Apr. 13, 1920; s. František and Žofie O. Degree in theology, Lateran U., 1945; Doctorate (hon.), Pedagogical U., 1995. Ordained priest, 1945, bishop, 1950. Bishop Internation Communist Prison, 1951-62; dairy laborer, 1962-65; priest Czech borderland, 1965-90; archbishop, 1998; diocesan bishop, 1990-98; now bishop emeritus. Recipient Golden Medallion of Merit of City of Hradec Králové, 1994, Golden Medallion of Honors, Charles U. 1995, Order of T.G. Masaryk, 1995. Home Phone: +420 495 063 638; Office Phone: +420 495 063 611.

OTELLINI, PAUL STEVENS, electronics company executive; b. San Francisco, Oct. 12, 1950; s. David Otellini; m. Sandy Otellini; 2 children. BA in Econs., U. San Francisco, 1972; MBA, U. Calif., Berkeley, 1974. Joined Intel Corp., Santa Clara, Calif., 1974, managed Intel's bus. with IBM Corp., 1980—85, gen. mgr. peripheral components ops., 1985—87, gen. mgr., Folsom Microcomputer Divsn., 1987—89, v.p. operating group, 1988, asst. to pres. (Andrew S. Grove), 1989, gen. mgr., microprocessor products group, 1990, corp. officer, 1991, exec. v.p., sales and mktg., 1992—98, sr. v.p., 1993—96, exec. v.p., 1996—2002, exec. v.p., gen. mgr., architecture group, 1998—2002, pres., COO, 2002—05, pres., CEO, 2005—. Bd. dirs. Intel Corp., 2002—, Google Inc., 2004—. Named one of The 50 Who Matter Now, CNNMoney.com Bus. 2.0, 2006. Office: Intel Corp 2200 Mission College Blvd Santa Clara CA 95052-8119 Office Phone: 408-765-8080. Office Fax: 408-765-9904.*

OTERO, MARIA, federal agency administrator, former international development executive; b. La Paz, Bolivia, Aug. 26, 1950; came to U.S., 1960; d. Jose Rene and Maria Teresa (Bailey) Otero; m. George Richard Fletcher, Aug. 19, 1972 (div. Jan. 1980); m. Joseph Thomas Eldridge, Sept. 5, 1981; children: Justin, Dvid, Ana Marisa. BA in English, U. Md., 1972, MA in English Lit., 1974; MA in Internat. Economics, Johns Hopkins U., 1977; student, London Bus. Sch., 1999. Tchr. asst. U. Md., 1972-74; photographer, children's portraits self employed, Bolivia, 1974-75; program officer The Inter-Am. Found., Va., 1975-78; program dir. Ctr. for Devel. & Population Activities, Washington, 1979-83; economist for Latin Am. U.S. AID/Women in Devel. Office, Washington, 1983-85; dir. for Honduras, Accion Internat., Washington, 1986-89, 92, exec. v.p., 1992-99, pres., CEO, 2000—09; under sec. for democracy & global affairs US Dept. State, Washington, 2009—. Chair bd. dirs. Inter-Am. Found., 1994-99, Bread for the World, Md., 1992-97; bd. dirs. Calmeadow Found., Toronto, 1998—; adj. prof. Johns Hopkins U., 1997—. Editor: The New World of Microenterprise, 1995; author monographs and articles. Mem. del. to Mrs. Clinton's travel to Latin Am., Office of First Lady, Washington, 1996; mem. policy adv. group World Bank, Washington, 1995-99. Mem. Assn. Women in Devel. (founding mem., bd. dirs. 1992-94), D.C. Humanities Cmty. Coun. (founding mem., bd. dirs. 1978-82). Democrat. Methodist. Avocations: reading literature and poetry, photography, sports, gardening. Office: US Dept State Harry S Truman Bldg Rm 7261 2201 C St NW Washington DC 20520*

OTHERSEN, HENRY BIEMANN, JR., surgeon, physician, educator; b. Charleston, SC, Aug. 26, 1930; s. Henry and Lydia Albertine (Smith) Othersen; m. Janelle Lester, Apr. 4, 1959; children: Megan, Mandy, Margaret, Henry Biemann III. BS, Coll. Charleston, 1950; MD, Med. Coll. S.C., 1953. Diplomate Am. Bd. Surgery, Am. Bd. Thoracic Surgery, Am. Bd. Pediatric Surgery. Intern Phila. Gen. Hosp., 1953-54; postgrad. U. Pa., 1956-57; resident in gen. surgery Med. Coll. S.C., Charleston, 1957-62; resident in pediatric surgery Ohio State U. and Columbus Children's Hosp., 1962-64; research fellow Harvard U., Mass. Gen. Hosp., Boston, 1964-65; from asst. prof. to assoc. prof. pediatric surgery Med. U. S.C., Charleston, 1962—72, prof., 1972—, chief pediatric surgery, 1972-98; med. dir. Med. U. S.C. Hosp., 1981-85, Children's Hosp., 1985—2001, med. dir. profl. staff, 1996—2001, physician liaison documentation, 2002—03; acting chief surgery VA Hosp., 2002—04. Editor: The Pediatric Airway; mem. editl. bd. Jour. Pediatric Surgery, Jour. Parenteral and Enteral Nutrition; contbr. articles to profl. jours. Bd. Children's Hosp. Fund; bd. dirs., pres. S.C. divsn. Am. Cancer Soc., 1977—79; bd. dir. SC Safe Kids. With USN, 1954—56, Korea. Fellow: ACS, Am. Acad. Pediat.; mem.: Charleston County Med. Soc. (pres. 1981—83), Am. Trauma Soc., SC Surg. Assn. (pres. 1991—92), Am. Surg. Assn., Brit. Assn. Pediatric Surgeons (overseas coun. 1995—99), Am. Pediatric Surg. Assn. (pres. 1998—99), Alpha Omega Alpha (councilor 1978—93). Republican. Lutheran. Achievements include first academic pediat. surgeon in SC; first to Established divsn. pediat. surgery and children's hosp. Med. U. SC. Avocation: water sports. Home: 3 West St Charleston SC 29401-1929 Home Phone: 843-722-5939. Personal E-mail: jnbothersen@bellsouth.net. *A man ought to do what he thinks is right.*

OTIS, BUD (HAROLD F. OTIS), legislative staff member; Cmty. outreach asst. to Rep. Roscoe Bartlett, US House of Reps., 2001—03, adminstrv. asst., 2003, chief of staff Washington, 2003—. Office: Office of Congressman Roscoe Bartlett 2412 Rayburn House Office Bldg Washington DC 20515-2006 Office Phone: 202-225-2721. Office Fax: 202-225-2193.*

OTIS, CLARENCE, JR., restaurant executive; BA magna cum laude, Williams Coll., 1977; JD, Stanford Univ., 1980. Atty., NY; investment banker First Boston, Kidder Peabody; mng. dir., co-head Mcpl. Securities group Chem. Securities; v.p., treas. Darden Restaurants Inc., Orlando, Fla., 1995-97, sr. v.p. investor rels., treas., 1997-98, sr. v.p. fin., 1998-99, sr. v.p., CFO, 1999—2002, exec. v.p., CFO, 2002, exec. v.p., pres. Smokey Bones div., 2002—04, CEO, 2004—05, chmn., CEO, 2005—. Bd. dir. St. Paul Travelers Ins., VF Corp., Verizon Communications Inc.; mem. Exec. Leadership Council. Trustee Williams Coll.; bd. mem. Enterprise Fla. Inc., Preserve Eatonville Inc. Named to Power 150, Ebony mag., 2008. Mem.: Phi Beta Kappa. Office: Darden Restaurants Inc 5900 Lake Ellenor Dr Orlando FL 32809

OTIS, JACK, social work educator; b. NYC, Feb. 13, 1923; s. Abraham Osipowitz and Esther (Goldberg) O.; children: Elisabeth H., Erich R., Greta M., Marcus H., Alicia. AB, Bklyn. Coll., 1946; MS in Social Work, U. Ill., 1948, MEd, 1955, PhD, 1957. Social worker Jewish Social Svc. Bur. Dade County, 1948-49; Psychiat. social worker Free Synagogue Social Service, NYU, 1949-50; asso. prof. U. Ill., 1950-61; dep. dir. Office Juvenile Delinquency and Youth Devel., Dept. Health, Edn. and Welfare, 1961-65; dean Grad. Sch. Social Work U. Tex., 1965-77, prof. emeritus, 1993—. Cons. to govt., 1961—; presenter Internat. Coun. on Social Welfare, Inter-Univ. Consortium for Internat. Social Devel., Internat. Assn. Schs. Social Work, 1994; dep. dir. Pres.'s Com. Juvenile Delinquency and Youth Crime, 1961-65; spl. cons. for Am. social work edn. and rsch. European Ctr. for Social Welfare Tng. and Rsch., Vienna, Austria, 1976—; Dean Dan Sanders Meml. lectr. U. Ill., 1999. Author:

(with George Barnett) Corporate Society and Education, 1961; contbr. article on child labor to Ency. Social Work, 1995. Bd. overseers Ctr. for Study Violence, Brandeis U., 1966-70; commencement spkr. U. Tex. Sch. Social Work, 2001. With AUS, 1943-46, PTO. Fulbright-Hays rsch.fellow Austria, 1977-78; established annual Dean Jack Otis Social problem and Social Policy Lecture, U. Tex., 2007. Mem. AAUP, Coun. on Social Work Edn. (commn. on accreditation), Philosophy of Edn. Soc., Nat. Assn. Social Workers (chair Calif. Task Force on Child Labor 2001-03), Am. Acad. Polit. and Social Sci., N.Y. Acad. Sci., Johannesburg Child Welfare Soc. (rsch. cons. South Africa chpt. 1990-91), Phi Kappa Phi (pres.). Office Phone: 949-240-9490. *The meaning of my life is whether I have added to the meaning of another's.*

OTIS, JAMES, JR., architect; b. Chgo., July 8, 1931; s. James and Edwina (Love) O.; m. Diane Cleveland, Apr. 9, 1955; children: James III, Julie C., David C. BArch cum laude, Princeton U., 1953; postgrad., U. Chgo., 1955-57. Registered architect, Ill., Ariz., Colo., Ind., Iowa, Wis., N.Mex., Mo. Designer Irvin A. Blietz Co., Wilmette, Ill., 1955-57; pres. Homefinders Constrn. Corp., Wilmette, 1957-59, O & F Constrn. Co., Northbrook, Ill., 1959-61; chmn. bd., chief exec. officer Otis Assocs., Inc., Northbrook, Ill., 1960-89; chmn., CEO Otis Co., 1981—. Bd. dirs. Banco Popular, Chgo., Trout & Grouse, Inc., OCO, Inc., Ranch Ptnrs., LLC, Lane Fin., Inc.; ptnr. Good Otis, LLC. Prin. works include GBC Corp. Hdqrs., Northbrook, Ill., AON Ins. Co. Corp. Hdqrs., Performing Arts Ctr., Northbrook, All State Regional Hdqrs., Skokie, Ill., Zurich Nat. Hdqrs.-Zurich Towers, Schaumburg, Ill. Trustee Evanston Hosp., Ill., 1971-93, Better Govt. Assn., Chgo., Graham Found., 1984-86; vice chmn. bd. trustees Ill. Nature Conservancy, 2008-, North Suburban YMCA, Northbrook, 1990-97; governing mem. Shedd Aquarium; bd. govs. Chgo. Zool. Soc.; mem. adv. bd. Cook County Forest Preserve Dist.; mem. founder's coun. Field Mus., Chgo. Lt. USNR, 1953—55. Mem. AIA, Nat. Coun. Archtl. Registration Bds., Urban Land Inst., Northwestern U. Assocs., Princeton Club (pres. 1971-72), Econ. Club, Commonwealth Club, Chgo. Club, Comml. Club, Glen View Golf Club, Old Elm Club, Coleman Lake Club, Angler's Club. Republican. Episcopalian. Office: Otisco 1450 American Ln Ste 1750 Schaumburg IL 60173-6010 Office Phone: 847-969-9000. Business E-Mail: jotisjr@otiscompany.com.

OTIS, JOHN JAMES, project manager; b. Syracuse, NY, Aug. 5, 1922; s. John Joseph and Anna (Dey) O.; m. Dorothy Fuller Otis, June 21, 1958; children: Mary Eileen Dawn, John Leon. B in Chem. Engring., Syracuse U., 1943, MBA, 1950, postgrad., 1951—55. Registered profl. engr., Ala., Tex. Jr. process engr. GM, Syracuse, 1951-53, prodn. engr., 1954-58, process control engr., 1958-59, process engr., 1960-61; engr., writer GE, Syracuse, 1961-63, configuration control engr. Phila., 1969; assoc. rsch. engr. Boeing Co., Huntsville, Ala., 1963-65; assoc. Planning Rsch. Corp., Huntsville, 1965-67; prin. engr. Brown Engring. Co. subs. Teledyne Co., Huntsville, 1967-69; mech. designer Drever Co., Beth Ayres, Pa., 1970-71; civil engr. U.S. Army Corps Engrs., Mobile, Ala., 1971-74, Galveston, Tex., 1974—2006, supervisory civil engr., 2006—, project mgr., 2007—, gen. engring., 2008. Lector, lay minister Roman Cath. Ch. Served with USNR, 1944-50. Mem. Am. Inst. Indsl. Engrs. (past v.p. Syracuse and Huntsville chpts.), Tex. Soc. Profl. Engrs. (dir. Galveston County chpt. 1976-79, sec.-treas. 1979-80, v.p. 1980-81, pres. 1982-83), Am. Legion, Tau Beta Pi, Phi Kappa Tau, Alpha Chi Sigma, Chi Eta Sigma. Office Phone: 409-766-3157. Business E-Mail: john.j.otis@usace.army.mil.

OTIS, LEE (SARAH) LIBERMAN, lawyer, educator; b. NYC, Aug. 19, 1956; d. James Benjamin and Deen (Freed) L.; m. William Graham Otis, Oct. 24, 1993. BA, Yale U., 1979; JD, U. Chgo., 1983. Bar: N.Y. 1985, D.C. 1994. Law clk. US Ct. Appeals (DC cir.), Washington, 1983-84; spl. asst. to asst. atty. gen., civil div. US Dept. Justice, Washington, 1984-86, dep. assoc. atty. gen., 1986, assoc. dep. atty. gen., 1986; law clk. to Justice Antonin Scalia US Supreme Ct., Washington, 1986-87; asst. prof. law George Mason U., Arlington, Va., 1987-89; assoc. counsel to the Pres. Exec. Office of the Pres., Washington, 1989-92; assoc. Jones, Day, Reavis & Pogue, Washington, 1993-94; chief judiciary coun. US Sen. Spence Abraham, 1995-96; chief counsel subcom. on immigration Com. on the Judiciary, US Senate, 1997-2000; gen. counsel US Dept. Energy, 2001—05; assoc. dep. atty. gen., 2005—07; sr. v.p., dir. faculty div. Federalist Soc. Law and Pub. Policy, 2007—. Adj. prof. law Georgetown Law Sch., 1995, 96, 2008-09. Mem. Federalist Soc. for Law and Pub. Policy (founder). Republican. Jewish. Avocations: sailing, computers. Office Phone: 202-822-8138.

O'TOOLE, AUSTIN MARTIN, lawyer, mediator, arbitrator; b. New Bedford, Mass., Oct. 5, 1935; s. John Brian, Jr. and Helen Veronica O'T.; m. Valerie Sherlock O'Toole; children: Erin Ann, Austin Martin Jr. BBA, Coll. Holy Cross, 1957; JD, Georgetown U., 1963. Bar: NY 1965, DC 1963, Tex. 1975; cert. disting. mediator, Tex. Mediator Credentialing Assn. Law clk. to judge U.S. Ct. Appeals, Washington, 1962-63; assoc. White & Case, NYC, 1963-74; sr. v.p., sr. counsel, sec. Coastal Corp., Houston, 1974—2001. Bd. editors Georgetown Law Jour., 1962-63. Bd. dirs. Nat. Coun. on Alcoholism and Drug Dependency, Inc., 2001—; charter mem., certificated mediator Inst. for Responsible Dispute Resolution, Houston, 2000—; bd. dirs. Houston Marathon Com., 1973—2002, Houston Dispute Resolution Ctr., 2007—. Officer USMC, 1957—60. Mem. ABA, Am. Soc. Corp. Secs. (bd. dirs. 1982-85), State Bar of Tex., Houston Bar Assn. (past chmn. corp. counsel sect. 1979-80, chair ADR sect. 2007-08), Assn. Atty.-Mediators, Tex. Assn. Mediators (bd. dirs. 2007-). Office: 5050 Ambassador WAS Houston TX 77027 Home: 3711 San Fecipe 8H Houston TX 77027 Office Phone: 713-628-3079. Personal E-mail: austinotoole@msn.com.

O'TOOLE, LAURENCE JOSEPH, public administration and policy educator, researcher; b. Syracuse, NY, Dec. 7, 1948; s. Laurence Joseph and Marjorie Rose (Weinheimer) O.; m. Mary Irene Gilroy, June 26, 1971; children: Conor Gilroy O'Toole, Kathleen Easton O'Toole. BS with high honors, Clarkson U., 1970; MPA, Syracuse U., 1972, PhD, 1975. Asst. prof. polit. sci. U. Va., Charlottesville, 1975-79; assoc. prof. polit. sci. Auburn U., Ala., 1979-85, prof. polit. sci., 1985-92, U. Ga., Athens, 1992—, M. Hughes and Robert T. Golembiewski prof. pub. adminstrn., 2000—, head dept. pub. admisntrn. and policy, 2002—08. Vis. rschr. Internat. Inst. Mgmt. Sci. Ctr., Berlin, 1978; prof. comparative sustainability policy studies Ctr. for Clean Tech. and Environ. Policy, Twente U., The Netherlands, 1994—; sr. rsch. assoc. Carl Vinson Inst. of Govt., U. Ga., Athens, 1994-2002; mem., bd. editors Administrn. and Society, Blacksburg, Va., 1995—, Administrv. Theory and Praxis, San Francisco, 1995-2002, Beleidswetenschap Groningen, The Netherlands, 1997—, Evaluation and Program Planning, 2000—, Jour. Pub. Affairs Edn., 2001—, Jour. Pub. Admin. Rsch. Theory, 2005-, Chinese Pub. Admin. Review, 2006-. Author: Institutions, Processes and Outputs for Acidification, 1998; co-author: American Government: Origins, Institutions and Public Policy, 1984, Regulatory Decision Making: The Virginia State Corporation Commission, 1984, Implementation Theory and Practice, 1990, Bureaucracy in a Democratic State, 2006; editor: American Intergovernmental Relations, 1985, 2d rev. edit., 1993, 3d edit., 2000, 4th edit., 2006; co-editor: International Comparative Policy Research, 1992, Networks for Water Policy, 1995, Participation and the Quality of Environmental Decision Making, 1998, Advancing Public Management, 2000, Johns Hopkins Studies in Governance and Public Management, 2001—, Jour. Policy and Mgmt., 2004—, Public Services Performance, 2006; contbr. articles to profl. jours. Recipient outstanding prof. award Ga. Students for Pub. Adminstrn., Athens, 1994, 95; vis. scholar Erasmus U., Rotterdam, The Netherlands, 1989, 94, Calif. U. Wales, 2003. Fellow: Nat. Acad. Pub. Adminstrn.; mem.: ASPA (Burchfield award 1979, Mosher award 1987, Stone award 1999, Levine award 2002, Wholey award 2004, Waldo award 2005), Pub. Mgmt. Rsch. Assn. (bd. dirs. 2001—, pres. 2005—), So. Polit. Sci. Assn., Am. Polit. Sci. Assn. (chair pub. adminstrn. sect. 1985, Gaus award 2009). Home: 190 Avalon Dr Athens GA 30606-3235 Office: Univ Ga Sch Pub and Internat Affairs Dept Pub/Adminstrn Policy/Baldwin Hall Athens GA 30602 E-mail: cmsotool@uga.edu.

O'TOOLE, MICHAEL ANTHONY, academic administrator; b. Phila., Feb. 20, 1950; s. John Joseph O'Toole, Jr. and Louise Mary Kopka; m. Mary Louise Castaldi, Jan. 8, 1977; children: Lara Nicole Castaldi, Daniel Peter Castaldi, Colin Peter Castaldi(dec.). AB magna cum laude, U. of Pa., 1972, MA, 1978; EdM, Columbia U., 1997. Info. specialist US FDA, Rockville, Md., 1974; lectr. Abington Coll., Pa. State U., 1987—; tchr. La Salle Coll. HS, Wyndmoor, Pa., 1974—2000, chmn. Dept. English, 1980—88, dir., curriculum and summer sessions, 1989—2000, v.p., 2000—05; prin. Holy Ghost Prep. Sch., Bensalem, Pa., 2005—. Founder NW Cmty. Scholars Program; reader Ednl. Testing Svc., Princeton, NJ, 1987—94; svc. bd. mem. La Salle Coll. HS, 2000—05; team editor NAIS Leading Edge Award, 2005; v.p. Bicentennial Athletic League, 2007—. Editor: (alumni jour.) Explorer Mag., (profl. newsletter) Klingenstein Newsletter. Lay min. music St. Vincent De Paul Ch., Germantown, Pa., 1995—2001; lay mem. Lasallian Soc. Justice Inst., El Paso, Tex., 2004; bd. dirs. Face to Face, Inc., Phila., 2003—. Recipient President's medal, La Salle Coll. HS, 2005, Klingenstein Ctr. fellowship, Tchrs. Coll., Columbia U., 1994—95, fellowship in Am. Civilization, U. of Pa., 1978—79, Ford Fund scholarship, Ford Motor Co. Fund, 1968—72. Mem.: Nat. Coun. Tchrs. of English, Nat. Assn. Secondary Sch. Prins., Nat. Cath. Edn. Assn., Am. Studies Assn., Penn Club of NY. Independent. Roman Catholic. Avocations: bicycling, piano, music, swimming, writing. Home: 810 Elkins Ave Elkins Park PA 19027 Office: Holy Ghost Prep Sch 2429 Bristol Pike Bensalem PA 19020

O'TOOLE, TARA JEANNE, medical educator, former federal agency administrator; b. Newton, Mass., May 3, 1951; d. Harold J. and Jeanne (Whalen) O'T. BA, Vassar Coll., 1974; MD, George Washington U., 1981; MPH, Johns Hopkins U., 1988. Diplomate Am. Bd. Internal Medicine, Am. Bd. Preventive/Occupational Medicine. Rsch. asst. Sloan-Kettering Cancer Inst., NYC, 1974-77; resident in internal medicine Yale New Haven (Conn.) Hosp., 1981-84; physician Balt. Cmty. Health Ctrs., 1984-87; fellow in occupational medicine Johns Hopkins U., Balt., 1987-89; sr. analyst Office Tech. Assessment, Washington, 1989-93; asst. sec. energy for environ., safety and health US Dept. Energy, Washington, 1993-97; dep. dir. Johns Hopkins U. Ctr. Civilian Biodefense Studies, 1998—2001, dir., 2001—03; prof. medicine U. Pitts., 2003—; CEO Ctr. for Bio Security, U. Pitts. Medical Ctr., 2003—. Chmn. Bd. Fedn. Am. Scientists, 2004—. Democrat. Office: Ctr for Biosecurity The Pier IV Bldg 621 E Pratt St Ste 210 Baltimore MD 21202 Business E-Mail: Totoole@upmc-biosecurity.org.*

O'TOOLE, WILLIAM EDWARD, III, retired computer science and mathematics professor; b. Waynesboro, Pa., May 27, 1942; s. William Edward Jr. and Dora Alberta O'Toole; m. Annette Marie Smith, June 25, 1966 (div. July 15, 1977); m. Catherine Claire Bodin, Dec. 16, 1989; 1 child, Wendy Elizabeth Garilli. BS in Math. Edn., Mt. St. Mary's Coll., 1966; MA in Math., U. Md., 1975. Prof. math. and computer sci. Mt. St. Mary's U., Emmitsburg, Md., 1966—2007; sci. editor and prognosticator Gruber Almanack Co., Hagerstown, Md., 1969—. Computer cons. Nat. Inst. Stds. and Tech., Gaithersburg, 1969—91. Author: (textbook and software) GRASP: A Generic, Realistic Assembler Simulation Program, 1991—. Mem. Balt. Symphony Orch. Com., Frederick, 1970—90. King Ferdinand III Sci. scholar, Diocese of Harrisburg, Pa., 1960—62. Democrat. Roman Catholic. Avocations: travel, classical music, photography, computers and electronics. Personal E-mail: billotoole@hotmail.com.

O'TOOLE, WILLIAM GEORGE, lawyer; b. Chgo., Oct. 25, 1934; s. George P. and Margaret (Battenhouse) O'T.; m. Gail M. McGregor, Aug. 13, 1960; children: Joyce M. Masterton, Paul G., Katherine A. Gorski. BS, U. Detroit, 1956; JD, DePaul U., Chgo., 1961. Bar: Ill. 1961, US Dist. Ct. (no. dist.) Ill. 1962. Assoc. Jaros, Tittle & O'Toole (and predecessor firm), Chgo., 1961-74, ptnr., 1974-90, pres., 1990—. Pres. Ill. State Title Corp. Bd. dirs. De Paul U. Law Sch.; mem. bd. advisors Mercy Hosp.; bd. dirs. Mortgage Bankers of Ill.; bd adv. De Paul U. Law Sch., Mercy Hosp. Mem. ABA, Ill. Bar Assn., Ill. Mortgage Bankers Assn. (bd. dirs.), Chgo. Bar Assn., Southwest Bar Assn. (past pres.), Chgo. Athletic Assn., Abbey Springs Country Club, Ridge Country Club, Union League Club Chgo., Univ. Club Chgo., Elks, K.C., Beta Alpha Psi. Roman Catholic. Office: Jaros Tittle & O'Toole 20 N Clark St Ste 510 Chicago IL 60602-4188 Home: 127 Acacia Cir Unit 407 Indian Head Park IL 60525 Office Phone: 312-750-1000.

OTSUKA, RYO, medical educator; b. Bunkyo-ku, Tokyo, July 16, 1971; married. MD, PhD, Osaka City U., Japan. Postdoc. fellow Columbia Presbyn. Med. Ctr., NYC, 2002—04; clin. asst. prof. Osaka City U., 2004—. Avocation: golf. Office: Osaka City Univ Med Sch 1-4-3 Asahi-machi Abeno-ku Osaka 545-8585 Japan Office Fax: 81-6-6646-6808. Business E-Mail: m2048984@med.osaka-cu.ac.jp.

OTT, DAVID MICHAEL, engineering company executive; b. Glendale, Calif., Feb. 24, 1952; s. Frank Michael and Roberta (Michie) O.; m. Cynthia Dianne Bunce. BSEE, U. Calif., Berkeley, 1974. Electronic engr. Teknekron Inc., Berkeley, 1974-79; chief engr. TCI, Berkeley, 1979-83; div. mgr. Integrated Automation Inc., Alameda, Calif., 1983-87, Litton Indsl. Automation, Alameda, 1987-92; founder, chmn. Picture Elements Inc., Berkeley, 1992—. Inventor method for verifying denomination of currency, method for processing digited images, automatic document image revision. Mem. IEEE, AAAS, Assn. Computing Machinery, Union of Concerned Scientists. Office: Picture Elements Inc 777 Panoramic Way Berkeley CA 94704-2538

OTT, DORIS ANN, librarian; b. Elgin, ND, Sept. 24, 1942; d. Oscar Edward Hirning and Lorraine Wilhelmina Gruebele; m. Richard Donald Ott, Nov. 21, 1998; m. Bennett Gordon Reinke, Sept. 1961 (div.); 1 child, Scott Bennett Reinke; m. James Lee Daugherty, June 1974 (div.). BS, Dickinson State U., 1964; MLS, George Peabody Coll., 1965. Lic. Ind. life tchr. Elem. tchr. Mott Pub. Schs., ND, 1963-64; asst. prof. Dickinson State U., ND, 1965-73; media specialist Minot Pub. Schs., ND, 1973-74; head tech. svcs. Bartholomew County Libr., Columbus, Ind., 1974-75; media specialist Rushville Pub. Schs., Ind., 1975-86; head interlibr. loan ND State Libr., Bismarck, 1986-87, asst. state libr., 1987—2001, state libr., 2001—. Image cons. Beauty For All Seasons, 1984—. Mem. Humane Soc. Mem.: ALA, Mountain Plains Libr. Assn., ND Libr. Assn. Avocation: image consulting. Office: ND State Libr 604 E Boulevard Ave Dept 250 Bismarck ND 58505-0800 Office Phone: 701-328-2492.

OTT, GILBERT RUSSELL, JR., lawyer; b. Bklyn., Apr. 15, 1943; s. Gilbert Russell Sr. and Bettina Rose (Ferrel) O.; m. Lisa S. Weatherford, Apr. 12, 1986; children: Gilbert R. III, Laura Elisabeth. BA, Yale U., 1965; JD, MBA, Columbia U., 1969. Bar: N.Y. 1970. Assoc. Chadbourne, Parke, Whiteside & Wolff, NYC, 1969-72, LeBoeuf, Lamb, Leiby & MacRae, NYC, 1972-78; assoc. gen. counsel Kidder, Peabody & Co., Inc., NYC, 1978-96, asst. sec., 1978-91, asst. v.p., 1978-79, v.p., 1979-86, mng. dir., 1986-91, sr. v.p., sec., 1992-96; v.p. Kidder, Peabody Group Inc., NYC, 1989-96, asst. sec., 1986-96; exec. v.p., gen. counsel, sec. Rodman & Renshaw Capital Group, Inc., Chgo. and NYC, 1996-98; counsel Cadwalader, Wickersham & Taft, NYC, 1998-99; dep. gen. counsel Datek Online Holdings Corp., Jersey City, 1999—2002; chief legal officer instl. divsn. Ameritrade Holding Corp., Jersey City, 2002—05; dep. gen. counsel TD Ameritrade Holding Corp., Jersey City, 2006—. Mem.: Assn. Bar City of N.Y., Univ. Club, Piping Rock Club. Home: 260 Highwood Cir Oyster Bay NY 11771-3205 Office: Harborside Financial Ctr Plz 4A Jersey City NJ 07310 Home Phone: 516-922-4241; Office Phone: 201-369-8559. Business E-Mail: gilbert.ott@tdameritrade.com.

OTT, JOHN HARLOW, museum administrator; b. Ottawa, Ont., Can., Jan. 29, 1944; s. Thomas Gordon and Lois Elizabeth (Wright) O.; m. Lili Reineck, May 20, 1972; children: Jennie Elizabeth, Michael James Hutchins BA, Eastern Bapt. Coll., St. David's, Pa., 1966; MA, SUNY-Oneonta, 1975; postgrad. Mus. Mgmt. Inst., U. Calif., Berkeley, 1987. Curator Hancock Shaker Village, Inc., Pittsfield, Mass., 1970-72, dir., 1972-83; exec. dir. Atlanta Hist. Soc., 1983-91, B&O R.R. Mus., Inc., Balt., 1991-99, The Nat. Heritage Mus., Lexington, Mass., 1999—. Curator Ga. Hist. Soc., Savannah, 1983-87; mem. adv. bd. Concord (Mass.) Mus. Author: Hancock Shaker Village, 1976 Mem. Lexington Tourism Com., 2002—; bd. dirs. Devens Hist. Mus., 2001—03, bd. govs., 2003—; bd. dirs. Merimack Valley Conv. and Visitors Bur., N.E. Document Conservation Ctr., 2005—; pres. Cooperstown Grad. Program Alumni Assn., 2005—. Decorated Bronze Star; named mus. profl. of yr. in Ga., 1991, profl. of yr. Acad. for Travel, Hospitality and Tourism, 1996. Mem. Am. Assn. Mus. (accrediting officer 1982—), Am. Assn. for State and Local History, Mid-Atlantic Mus. Assn., Ga. Soc. Assn. Execs., Nat. Hist. Communal Socs. Assn. (pres. 1983-84), Nat. Soc. Fund Raising Execs. (bd. dirs. Ga. chpt. 1985-91, bd. dirs. Md. chpt. 1993), Am. Antiquarian Soc., Balt. City C. of C. (bd. dirs., past chmn.), Md. Assn. History Mus. (bd. dirs. 1996), Freedom's Way Heritage Assn. (bd. dirs. 2000—, pres. 2007), Lexington C. of C. (chmn. 2002-2004). Republican. Episcopalian. Office: The Nat Heritage Mus 33 Marrett Rd Lexington MA 02421-5703 Office Phone: 781-457-4102. E-mail: jott@monh.org.

OTT, KARL OTTO, nuclear engineer, consultant; b. Hanau, Germany, Dec. 24, 1925; arrived in U.S., 1967, naturalized, 1987; s. Johann Josef and Eva (Bergmann) Ott; m. Gunhild G. Göring, Sept. 18, 1958 (div. 1986); children: Martina, Monika; m. Birgit Fehse, May 1, 1995. BS, J. W. von Goethe U., Frankfurt, Germany, 1948; MS, G. August U., Göttingen, Fed. Republic Germany, 1953, PhD, 1958. Physicist Nuc. Rsch. Ctr., Karlsruhe, Germany, 1958-67, sect. head, 1962-67; prof. Sch. Nuc. Engring. Purdue U., West Lafayette, Ind., 1967-2001, prof. emeritus, 2000—. Cons. Argonne Nat. Lab., 1967—2001. Author: (book) Nuclear Reactor Statics, 1983, 2d edit., 1989, Nuclear Reactor Dynamics, 1985, Chinese edit., 1991. Recipient Disting. Appointment award, Argonne Universities Assn., 1973. Fellow: Am. Nuc. Soc. (Arthur Holly Compton award 1993). Office Phone: 765-494-5739. Personal E-mail: ott132@yahoo.com.

OTT, WALTER RICHARD, information technology executive, writer; b. Bklyn., Jan. 20, 1943; s. Harold Vincent and Mary Elizabeth (Butler) Ott; m. Carla M. Narrett, May 27, 2002; children: Regina Winter Burrell, Christina W. Chiappetta, Walter R. Jr. BS in Ceramic Engring., Va. Poly. Inst. and State U., 1965; MS in Ceramic Engring., U. Ill., 1967; PhD in Ceramic Engring., Rutgers U., 1969; DSc (hon.), Alfred U., 2001. Registered profl. engr., Pa. Process engr. Corning Inc., Buckhannon, W.Va., 1965-66; staff rsch. engr. Champion Spark Plug Co., Detroit, 1969-70; prof. engring. Rutgers U., New Brunswick, NJ, 1970-80; dean, assoc. provost N.Y. State Coll. Ceramics, Alfred, 1980-88; provost, chief acad. officer Alfred U., Alfred, 1988-2000; pres. Predictive Edge, Inc., Punta Gorda, Fla., 1999—; v.p. enrollment mgmt. Caldwell (N.J.) Coll., 2002—04. Rsch. assoc. Atomic Energy Commn.-E.I. duPont de Nemours, Aiken, SC, 1971; cons. Haight & Hofeldt Inc., Chgo., 1984-88, Pillsbury, Mpls., 1977-79, Ctr. for Profl. Advancement, New Brunswick, 1971-79, Hammond Lead Products, Ind., 1970-80; bd. dirs. Victor Insulator Inc., NY, UNIPEG, 1987-88; treas. Alfred Tech. Resources NY; bd. dirs. Grads Found., NYC, 1988-2002. Contbr. articles to profl. jours.; patentee in field. Recipient Ralph Teetor award Soc. Automotive Engrs., 1973, PACE award Nat. Inst. Ceramic Engrs., 1975, Ann. award Ceramic Assn. N.J., 1980; named to Greaves Walker Roll, Keramos, 1991. Fellow Am. Ceramic Soc. (trustee 1980-83, v.p. 1988-89); mem. Ceramic Ednl. Coun. (pres. 1976-77), Ceramic Assn. N.Y. (treas. 1980-88, bd. dirs.), Ceramic Assn. N.J. (bd. dirs. 1974-80), Keramos (pres. 1982-84, Greaves-Walker Roll of Honor 1991), Tau Beta Pi. Avocations: sailing, reading, golf. Home: 2156 Charlotte Amalie Ct Punta Gorda FL 33950 Business E-Mail: ott@predictiveedge.com.

OTT, WAYNE ROBERT, environmental engineer; b. San Mateo, Calif., Feb. 2, 1940; s. Florian Funstan and Evelyn Virginia (Smith) Ott; m. Patricia Faustina Bertuzzi, June 28, 1967 (div. 1983). BA in Econs., Claremont McKenna Coll., Calif., 1962; BSEE, Stanford U., Calif., 1963, MS in Engring., 1965, MA in Comm., 1966, PhD in Environ. Engring., 1971. Commd. lt. USPHS, 1966, advanced through grades to capt., 1986; chief lab. ops. br. U.S. EPA, Washington, 1971—73, sr. systems analyst, 1973—79, sr. rsch. engr., 1981—84, chief air toxics and radiation monitoring rsch. staff, 1984—90; vis. scientist dept. stats. Stanford U., 1979—81, 1990—. Vis. scholar Ctr. for Risk Analysis and dept. stats., civil engring., Stanford U., 1990—93; sr. environ. engr. EPA Atmospheric Rsch. and Exposure Assessment Lab., 1993—95; cons. prof. civil engring. Stanford U., 1995—; dir. field studies Calif. Environ. Tobacco Smoke Study, 1993—95. Author: Environmental Indices: Theory and Practice, 1976, Environmental Statistics and Data Analysis, 1995, Exposure Analysis, 2007; contbr. articles to profl. jours. Decorated Commendation medal USPHS; recipient Nat. Statistician award, EPA, 1995. Mem.: Internat. Soc. Indoor Air Quality and Climate, Air and Waste Mgmt. Assn., Am. Soc. for Quality Control, Am. Statis. Assn., Internat. Soc. Exposure Analysis (v.p. 1989—90, Jerome J. Weselowski Internat. award for career achievement in exposure assessment 1995), Sierra Club, Theater Club, Jazz Club, Kappa Mu Epsilon, Tau Beta Pi, Sigma Xi, Phi Beta Kappa. Democrat. Achievements include development of nationally uniform air pollution index, first total human exposure activity pattern models; research in indoor air pollution, total human exposure to chems., stochastic models of indoor exposure to chems., stochastic models of indoor exposure, motor vehicle exposures, pers monitoring instruments and environ tobacco smoke. Avocations: hiking, photography, model trains, jazz. Home: 1008 Cardiff Ln Redwood City CA 94061-3678 Office: Stanford U Dept Stats Sequoia Hall Stanford CA 94305 Home Phone: 650-364-1430; Office Phone: 650-906-8442. Personal E-mail: wott@mac.com. Business E-Mail: wott1@stanford.edu.

OTTAWAY, DAVID BLACKBURNE, journalist; b. Endicott, NY, Oct. 27, 1939; s. James Haller Sr. and Ruth Blackburne (Hart) O.; m. Marina Seassaro, July 18, 1963; children: Eric, Robin. BA, Harvard U., 1962; MA, Columbia U., 1964, PhD, 1972. Dep. fgn. editor Washington Post, 1971-73, Africa corr., 1974-79, Mid. East corr., 1981-85, nat. security corr., 1985-90, South Africa corr., 1990-92, Ea., So. and Ctrl. South Europe corr., 1992-94, investigative reporter, 1994—2006; fellow Woodrow Wilson Internat. Ctr., 2006—07, sr. scholar, 2007—, Columbia U., Sch Internat. Pub. Affairs Adv. Bds., 2006—. Chmn., pres. Buck Hill Falls Co., Buck Hills, Pa., 1995-98, bd. dirs., 1999-2005. Co-author: (with Marina Ottaway) Algeria - The Politics of a Socialist Revolution, 1965, Ethiopia - Empire in Revolution, 1978, Afrocommunism, 1983; author: Chained Together - Mandela, De Klerk and the Struggle to Remake South Africa, 1993, The King's Messenger: Prince Bandar Bin Sultan And America's Tangleo Relationship With Saudi Arabia, 2008 Pres. NBO Found., 1995-98, 2001-2004, found. treas., Nicholas B. Ottaway, 2004-; trustee Lawrenceville Sch., 1998—. Co-recipient George Polk award for fgn. coverage, 2006. Mem. Harvard Club of Washington. Avocations: skiing, hiking, jogging, tennis. Office: Washington Post 1150 15th St NW Washington DC 20071-0002 Office Phone: 202-334-6537. E-mail: dbottaway@aol.com.

OTTAWAY, JAMES HALLER, JR., newspaper publisher; b. Binghamton, NY, Mar. 24, 1938; s. James Haller and Ruth Blackburne (Hart) O.; m. Mary Warren Hyde, June 16, 1959; children: Alexandra, Christopher, Jay. Grad., Phillips Exeter Acad., 1955; BA, Yale U., 1960; DJournalism (hon.), Suffolk U., Boston, 1970; DBA (hon.), Southeastern Mass. U., 1984. Reporter, mgmt. trainee New-Times, Danbury, Conn., 1960—62, Times Herald-Record, Middletown, NY, 1962—63; editor Pocono Record, Stroudsburg, Pa., 1963—65; publisher New Bedford (Mass.) Standard-Times, 1965—70; pres. Ottaway Newspapers, Inc., Campbell Hall, NY, 1970—85, CEO, 1976—88, chmn. bd., 1979—2003, CEO, 1998—2003; ret. V.p. Dow Jones & Co., 1980-86, sr. v.p., 1986-2003, also bd. dirs.; dir., vice-chmn. AP, 1982-91. Past. v.p. bd. trustees Phillips Exeter Acad.; trustee Am. Sch. Classical Studies at Athens, chmn., 1996-99; trustee, vice-chmn. Storm King Art Ctr., Mountainville, N.Y., World Wildlife Fund USA, 1993-96; trustee Bard Coll., 1996—; chmn. World Press Freedom Com., 1996—; treas. Internat. Commn. Transitional Justice, 2002—; chmn. Words Without Borders, 2004-; past pres., bd. dirs. Arden Hill Hosp. Found., Goshen, N.Y. Mem. Am. Newspaper Pubs. Assn., Am. Soc. Newspaper Editors. Episcopalian. Office: PO Box 401 Campbell Hall NY 10916-0401 Office Phone: 845-294-4902. E-mail: jimottaway837@yahoo.com.

OTTEN, ROBERTA ANN, theater and dance educator, choreographer; MEd, U. Mich., Ann Arbor, 1973. Cert. interplay leader Body Wisdom, Inc., 2000. Tchr. performer, edn. coord. Happendance, Inc., Okemos, Mich., 1982—2002; adj. theatre and dance instr. Lansing CC, Mich., 2000—. Choreographer (drama) The Death of Hector and Ensemble Dance (City Pulse Choreographers award, 2006); perfomer, dir. S'Moves Performance Co., (dance prodn.) Pride and Prejudice, (dramatic prodn.) Sunsets with Shakespeare Theatre Co. Riverwalk Theatre. Mem.: Am. Theatre Movement Educators. Office: Lansing CC 500 N Washington Sq Lansing MI 48901 Business E-Mail: ottenmar@lcc.edu.

OTTENWELLER, ALBERT HENRY, bishop emeritus; b. Stanford, Mont., Apr. 5, 1916; s. Charles and Mary (Hake) O. STL, Cath. U. Am., 1943. Ordained priest Diocese of Toledo, Ohio, 1943; assoc. pastor St. John's Parish, Delphos, Ohio, 1943—59, St. Richard's Parish, Swanton, Ohio, 1959—61; pastor St. Joseph's Parish, Blakeslee, Ohio; pastor, also mission Sacred Heart, Montpelier, Ohio, 1961—62; pastor Our Lady of Mt. Carmel Parish, Bono, Ohio, 1962—68, St. John's Parish, Delphos, 1968—76, St. Michael's Parish, Findlay, Ohio, 1976—77; ordained bishop, 1974; aux. bishop Diocese of Toledo, Ohio, 1974; bishop Diocese of Steubenville, Ohio, 1977—92, bishop emeritus Ohio, 1992—. Chmn. laity com. Nat. Conf. Cath. Bishops, 1978; Mem. Ohio Gov.'s Com. on Migrant Labor, 1955—75; mem. governing bd. Retreats Internat., 1975. Roman Catholic. Office: Chancery Office PO Box 969 422 Washington St Steubenville OH 43952-2159

OTTER, BUTCH (C. L. OTTER, CLEMENT LEROY OTTER), Governor of Idaho, former United States Representative from Idaho; b. Caldwell, Idaho, May 3, 1942; s. Joseph Bernard and Regina Mary (Buser) O.; m. Gay Corinne Simplot, 1964 (div. 1992); children: John Simplot, Carolyn Lee, Kimberly Dawn, Corinne Marie; m. Lori Easley, Aug. 18, 2006 BA in Polit. Sci., Coll. Idaho, 1967; PhD (hon.), Mindanao State U., 1980. Mgr. J.R. Simplot Co., Caldwell, Idaho, 1971-76, asst. to v.p. adminstrn., 1976-78, v.p. adminstrn., 1978-82, internat. pres., 1982—93; mem. Idaho House Reps., 1973—77; lt. gov. State of Idaho, Boise, 1987—2001, gov., 2007—; mem. US Congress from 1st Idaho Dist., 2001—07. Mem. Presdl. Task Force-AID, Washington, 1982—84, U.S. C. of C., Washington, 1983—84; com. mem. invest tech. devel. State Adv. Council, Washington, 1983—84; mem. exec. council Bretton Woods Com., 1984—. With Nat. Guard, 1968—73. Mem. Young Pres.' Orgn., Sales and Mktg. Execs., Idaho Assn. Commerce and Industry, Idaho Agrl. Leadership Council, Idaho Ctr. for Arts, Idaho Internat. Trade Council, Pacific N.W. Waterways Assn., N.W. Food Producers, Ducks Unltd, Safari Club Internat. (life). Clubs: Arid, Hillcrest Country. Lodges: Moose, Elks. Republican. Roman Catholic. Avocations: jogging, music, art collecting, horse training, fishing. Office: Office of Gov PO Box 83720 Boise ID 83720

OTTER, JOHN MARTIN, III, retired television advertising consultant; b. Pottsville, Pa., Nov. 26, 1930; s. John Martin and Ruth A. (Knipe) O.; m. Susan Morgan Eaves, May 21, 1960; children— John Martin, IV, Robert Marshal. BA, Cornell U., 1953. Comml. producer Arlene Frances Home Show, 1953-55; producer Dave Garroway Today Show, 1956-59; dir. spl. programs sales NBC-TV, 1959-61, v.p. nat. sales, 1962-64, v.p. charge sales, 1965-73; cons. sta. WNET-TV, Practising Law Inst., also Dragonwk Prodns., 1973-75; v.p., dir. network programming SSC&B Inc., 1975-78; sr. v.p., dir. network programming SSC&B Lintas Worldwide, NYC, 1978-84; sr. v.p. dir. nat. broadcast McCann-Erickson U.S.A., NYC, 1984-88; sr. v.p. spl. projects McCann-Erickson Worldwide, NYC, 1988; pres. RETTO Internat. Inc., NYC, 1989-94; retired, 1994. Mem.: The Chatham Club, The Landings Yacht Club, The Landings Club. Republican. Episcopalian. Home: Four Seafarer's Cir Savannah GA 31411 Home Phone: 912-598-1791.

OTTERBOURG, ROBERT KENNETH, public relations consultant, writer; b. NYC, Jan. 26, 1930; s. Albert Marcus and Frances (Roset) O.; m. Susan Delman, Apr. 14, 1957; children— Laura Ann, Kenneth Douglas. BA, Colgate U., 1951; MS, Columbia U., 1954. Reporter, editor Fairchild Publs., NYC, 1953-57; editor McGraw-Hill Pub. Co., 1957-59; v.p. pub. rels. Charles Mathieu & Co., 1959-61; pres. pub. rels. Otterbourg & Co., NYC, 1962-69, 71—. Sr. v.p. Daniel J. Edelman, 1970. Author: It's Never Too Late, 1993, Retire and Thrive, 1995, 4th edit., 2006, Switching Careers, 2001; contbr. articles to profl. and consumer jours. Legis. asst. N.Y. State Senate, 1962-64; mem. exec. com. Columbia U. Sch. Journalism, N.Y.C., 1980-93, pres. exec. com., 1985-87; trustee Flat Rock Nature Ctr., pres., 1991-92; trustee Planned Parenthood Bergen County, 1985-88, v.p., 1986-88; trustee Urban League for Bergen County, 1988-93; chmn. Durham County Libr., 1997-99, Exec. Svc. Corps of the Greater Triangle; bd. dirs. Colgate U. Alumni Corp., 1969-73; bd. dirs., pres. Threshold, 2003; pres. Triangle Radio Reading Svc., 2004. 1st lt. USAF, 1951-53. Mem. Columbia U. Grad. Sch. Journalism Alumni Assn. (pres. 1985-87, bd. mem., sr. pharmassist 2008). Democrat. Jewish. Home and Office: 68 Beverly Dr Durham NC 27707-2224 Office Phone: 919-489-9591. Personal E-mail: rkotter@aol.com.

OTTINGER, RICHARD LAWRENCE, dean emeritus, former congressman; b. NYC, Jan. 27, 1929; s. Lawrence and Louise (Lowenstein) O.; children from previous marriage: Ronald, Randall, Lawrence, Jenny Louise; m. June Godfrey. BA, Cornell U., 1950; LLB, Harvard U., 1953. Assoc. Cleary, Gottlieb, Friendly & Hamilton, NYC, 1955-56; ptnr. William J. Kridel, Law Firm, NYC, 1956-60; second staff mem., dir. programs Peace Corps, L.Am., 1961-64; mem. 89th-91st Congresses, 1965-71, 94th-98th Congresses, 1975-85; prof. Pace U. Sch. Law, White Plains, NY, 1985—, dean, 1994—99, dean emeritus, 1999—. Chmn. bd. dirs. Environ. and Energy Study Inst., Washington, Legal Environl. Assistance Found., Tallahasse, Fla.; mem. Congress Westchester County, NY, 1965—71, 1976—85; Dem. candidate US Senate, 1970; chair energy law & climate change speciality group IUCN Commn. Environ. Law. Author: Environmental Costs of Electricity, 1990; co-author: Energy Law and Sustainable Development, 2003; co-author and co-editor The Law of Energy for Sustainable Development, 2005; co-editor Compendium of Laws on Energy for Sustainable Development, 2005; contbr. articles to profl. jours. Contract mgr. Internat. Coop. Adminstrn., 1960-61; organizer Grassroots to Action, 1971-73. Office: Pace U Sch Law 78 N Broadway White Plains NY 10603-3710 Office Phone: 914-422-4121. Business E-Mail: rottinger@law.pace.edu.

OTTINO, JULIO MARIO, engineering educator; b. La Plata, Buenos Aires, Argentina, May 22, 1951; came to U.S., 1976; naturalized, 1990; s. Julio Francisco and Nydia Judit (Zufriategui) O.; m. Alicia I. Löffler, Aug. 20, 1976; children: Jules Alessandro, Bertrand Julien. Diploma in Chem. Engring., U. La Plata, 1974; PhD in Chem. Engring., U. Minn., 1979; exec. program Kellogg Sch. Mgmt., Northwestern U., 1995. Instr. in chem. engring. U. Minn., Mpls., 1978-79; asst. prof. U. Mass., Amherst, 1979-83, adj. prof. polymer sci., 1979-91, assoc. prof. chem. engring., 1983-86, prof., 1986-91; Chevron vis. prof. chem. engring. Calif. Inst. Tech., Pasadena, 1985-86; sr. rsch. fellow Ctr. for Turbulence Rsch. Stanford (Calif.) U., 1989-90; Walter P. Murphy prof. chem. engring. Northwestern U., Evanston, Ill., 1991-2000, chmn. dept. chem. engring., 1992-2000; McCormick Inst. prof., 2000—; George T. Piercy Disting. prof. U. Minn., 1998, adj. prof. mech. engring., 2001—; dir. Northwestern Inst. Complex Sys., 2004—, dean Sch. Engring. and Applied Sci. Cons. to U.S. and European corps.; mem. tech. adv. bd. Dow Chem.; mem. bd. dirs. Coun. Chem. Rsch.; prof. U. Minn.; Reily lectr. Notre Dame U., 2006; lectr. in field. Author: The Kinematics of Mixing: Stretching, Chaos and Transport, 1989; contbr. articles to profl. jours.; assoc. editor Physics Fluids A, 1991—; assoc. editor Am. Inst. Chem. Engring. Jour., 1991-95, assoc. editor., 1995—; one man art exhibit, La Plata, 1974. Recipient Presdl. Young Investigator award NSF, 1984, Alpha Chi Sigma award AIChE, 1994, W.H. Walker award AIChE, 2001, E.W. Thiele award AIChE, Chgo., 2002, named 100 Engrs. Modern Era, Am. Inst. Chem. Engrs., 2008; Univ. fellow U. Mass., 1988, J.S. Guggenheim fellow, 2001; Lacey lectureship, Calif. Inst. Tech., 1994, Danckwerts lectureship Royal Instn., 1999, Robb lectr. Pa. State U., 2002, Reily lectr., U. Notre Dame, 2006. Fellow Am. Phys. Soc. (Fluid Dynamics prize, named Otto Laporte Lectr. 2008); mem. AAAS, NAE, Am. Acad. Arts and Scis., Am. Chem. Soc., Am. Phys. Soc., Am. Soc. Engring. Edn., Sigma Xi (disting. lectr. 1997-99), Coun. for Chem. Rsch.(gov. bd. coun. 1999-2001). Achievements include research in granular dynamics, chaos, complex systems and mixing. Avocations: visual arts, painting. Home: 1092 Crescent Ln Winnetka IL 60093-1501 Office: Northwestern U Dept Chem Engring 2145 Sheridan Rd Evanston IL 60208-0834 Office Phone: 847-491-5221, 847-491-3195. Business E-Mail: jm-ottino@northwestern.edu.

OTTMAN, BOB, insurance company executive; B, Ea. Conn. State U., Willimantic. Cert. flexible compensation instrn. Employers Coun. Flexible Compensation. V.p. Frank Gates USA (formerly Acordia of Dallas); mgmt. position AFLAC Inc., Columbus, Ga., 1999, various leadership positions including v.p. adminstrv. svcs., new bus. & underwriting and new account set-up, sr. v.p. account implementation and mgmt., sr. v.p. claims, AFLAC benefit services & NY adminstrn. Office: AFLAC Inc 1932 Wynnton Rd Columbus GA 31999 Office Phone: 706-323-3431.

OTTO, BYRON LEONARD, retired lawyer, state agency administrator; b. Battle Creek, Mich., Oct. 4, 1940; s. Henry John and Mildred Alice (Wagner) O. BBA, St. Edward's U., 1964, MBA, 1979; JD, U. Tex., 1968. Bar: U.S. Dist. Ct. (we. dist.) 1976. Staff atty. State Welfare Dept., Austin, Tex., 1968-75; sole practice Austin, Tex., 1975-77; assoc. James R. Sloan, Austin, Tex., 1978-79; adminstr. State Comptroller, Austin, Tex., 1980—; ret., 2000. Author articles and monographs. St. Edward's U. scholar, Austin, 1978. Mem. ABA, Tex. Bar. Democrat. Roman Catholic. Home: 4604 S Lamar Blvd Apt C202 Austin TX 78745-1358 Home Phone: 512-899-8268. Personal E-mail: byron3@austin.rr.com.

OTTO, CATHERINE MARY, cardiologist, educator; BA, Reed Coll., Portland, Oreg., 1975; MD, U. Wash. Sch. Medicine, Seattle, 1979. Lic. physician Wash., 1982, cert. Am. Bd. Internal Med., 1982, Am. Bd. Internal Med., Cardiovascular Diseases, 1985. Intern The NY Hosp. Cornell Med. Ctr., NYC, 1979—80, resident, internal medicine, 1980—82; cardiology fellow U. Wash. Sch. Medicine, 1982—85, prof. medicine, 1999—, J. Ward Kennedy-Hamilton endowed prof. cardiology, 2005—; assoc. dir. echocardiography U. Wash. Med. Ctr., 1987, co-dir. adult congenital heart disease clinic, 1992, dir. tng. programs in cardiovasc. disease, 1993—. Editor-in-chief, cardiology sect. Up To Date, Waltham, Mass., 2006—. Author: The Textbook of Clinical Echocardiography, 2004, Valvular Heart Disease, 2004; co-author (with Becky Schwaegler): Echo Review Guide, 2007; co-author: (with Don Oxorn) Atlas of Intraoperative Echocardiography, 2007; editor: The Practice of Clinical Echocardiography, 2007. Mem.: Alpha Omega Alpha. Office: Univ Wash Med Ctr 1959 NE Pacific St Box 356422 Seattle WA 98195-6422 Office Fax: 206-616-4847. Business E-Mail: cmotto@u.washington.edu.

OTTO, CHARLOTTE R., consumer products company executive; b. Duluth, Minn., Aug. 15, 1953; BS, Purdue U., 1974, MS in Mgmt., 1976. With Procter & Gamble, 1976—, from asst. brand mgr. to brand mgr. various products, 1977-83, assoc. advt. mgr. paper products divsn., 1984-87, assoc. advt. mgr. toilet tissue/towels, paper products div., 1987-89, dir. issues mgmt., pub. affairs divsn., 1989-90, dir. pub. rels., pub. affairs divsn., 1990-91; v.p. pub. rels. Procter & Gamble USA, 1991-93; v.p. corp. comms. Procter & Gamble Worldwide, 1993-95, v.p. pub. affairs, 1995-96; sr. v.p. pub. affairs The Procter & Gamble Co., 1996-99, global pub. affairs officer, 1999—2000, global external rels. officer, 2000—. Dir. Royal Bank Fin. Grou, Canada; adv. bd. Jour. Corp. Pub. Rels., The Medill Sch. Journalism, Northwestern Univ. Mem. nat. bd. Boys & Girls Club Am.; mem. YWCA Acad. Career Women of Acheivement; chair (past pres.) Cin. Playhouse in the Park; chair exec. com. Downtown Cin., Inc.; mem. Riverfront Advisors Commn.; v.p. exec. com. Joy Outdoor Edn. Ctr.; trustee Arts & Cultural Coun. Greater Loveland; bd. mem. Am. Red Cross, Cin. Chpt.; bd. selectors, The Jefferson Awards Am. Inst. Pub. Svc.; vice-chmn. exec. com. Greater Cin. C. of C.; bd. mem. The Port of Greater Cin. Devel. Authority, Good Samaritan Hosp., Cin. Fire Mus.; mem. Leadership Cin. - Class XIV. Recipient YWCA Career Woman of Achievement award, 1993, Woman of Distinction award Gt. Rivers Girl Scouts Coun., Inc., 1998, Purdue "Old Master", 1996; recipient Disting. Alumni, Purdue U., Krannert Sch. Mgmt.; named Cincinnatian of the Yr., 2003, Juvenile Diabetes Rsch. Found., Cin. Enquirer Woman of the Yr., 2005; recipient Human Rels. award, Am. Jewish Com., 2004, Matrix award for public rels., NY Women in Comm., 2005. Mem. Ctr. Quality Leadership Founders, Vice Pres.'s Forum, Commonwealth Club, Women's Capital Club, Queen City Club (bd. govs.), Club at Harper's Point, Arthur Page Soc., PR Seminar Com., Kenwood Country Club. Office: Procter & Gamble Co 1 Procter And Gamble Plz Cincinnati OH 45202-3393*

OTTO, DEVIN THEOPHIL, music educator; MusB, U. Idaho, Moscow, 2001; MusM, Ea. Wash. U., Cheney, 2003. Vis. instr. tuba and euphonium U. Idaho, 2005—06; adj. instr. low brass Spokane Falls CC, Wash., 2006—08; asst. dir. bands and instr. tuba euphonium Ea. Wash. U., Cheney, 2003—; artistic dir. Spokane Brit. Brass Band, Wash., 2007—.

OTTO, DONALD R., museum director; b. North Loup, Nebr., Oct. 7, 1943; s. Leonard R. and Lorraine E. (Lindsay) O.; m. Sylvia D. Cook, Aug. 7, 1965; 1 child, Allison Lindsay. BA, Hastings Coll., Nebr., 1967. With Kans.-Nebr. Natural Gas Co., Hastings, 1967-68; exhibits dir. Hastings Mus., 1968-72; asst. dir. Kans. State Hist. Soc., 1972-75; program dir. Ft. Worth Mus. Sci. and History, 1975-77, pres., CEO, 1977—2003; head, exhbn. and prog. devel. Ominples Sci. Mus., Okla. City, 2004, interim dir., 2005, dir., 2005—. Pres. Kans. Mus. Assn., 1974, 75; officer Mountain Plains Mus. Conf., 1976-79, pres., 1977-78; spl. cons. mus. curriculum planning Coll. Liberal Studies, U. Okla., 1980. Mem. adminstrv. bd. 1st Meth. Ch., 1978-80, 81-83, 84-86, 97-98; bd. dirs. Sci. Mus. Exhibit Collaborative, 1983, pres., 1997, Ft. Worth Conv. and Visitors Bur., 1986-97, Internat. Space Theater Consortium, 1981, pres., 1984-86, exec. com., 1991-92; mem. Ft. Worth Cultural Dist. Com., 1979, Ft. Worth Air Power Coun., 1985, Leadership Ft. Worth, 1988, Forum Ft. Worth, 1989; mem. grants com. Cultural Arts Coun. of Houston, 1988-89; mem. adv. couin. Ft. Worth Sr. Citizen Ctrs., 1986-88; trustee Big Bros.-Big Sisters, 1988-89; chmn. Ft. Worth Tourism Coun., 1983. Mem. Am. Assn. Mus. (accreditation on site com. 1974-96), Mt. Plains Mus. Assoc. Bd., 1975-78, pres., 1977, Am. Assn. State and Local History, Am. Assn. Sci. and Tech. Ctrs. (bd. dirs. 1984-88), Assn. Sci. Mus. Dirs., Tex. Assn. Mus. (coun. 1980-82, v.p. 1983-84), Ft. Worth Aviation Heritage Soc. (bd. dirs. 1988), Ft. Worth C. of C. (bd. dirs. 1992-96), Ridglea Country Club, Rotary (Ft. Worth), Ft. Worth Club. Methodist. Office: Omniplex Sci Mus 2100 NE 52nd Oklahoma City OK 73111

OTTO, ELIZABETH HALL, education educator; b. Florence, SC, Aug. 5, 1939; d. William Everette and Elizabeth Hines Hall; m. Willmer Jerome Otto, Nov. 26, 1971; children: Teresa, Michael, John. BA, Winthrop Coll., Rock Hill, SC, 1961; MA, U. N.C., Chapel Hill, 1964. Tchr. Lancaster H.S., SC, 1961—62; instr. Mitchell Coll., Statesville, NC, 1963—65; tchr. Myers Park H.S., Charlotte, 1967—68; instr. Bee County Coll., Beeville, Tex., 1968—72; prof. Fla. C.C., Jacksonville, 1979—. Dept. chair Fla. C.C., 1999—2003. Co-author: (article) Jour. Social Sci., 1990; project dir. (coll. course) Cmty. Econ. Devel., 1983 (2d pl. Joint Coun. Econ. Edn.). Named Outstanding Faculty, Fla. C.C., 1994. Mem.: So. Hist. Assn. Avocations: reading, travel. Home: 3665 Manor Oaks Dr Jacksonville FL 32277 E-mail: eotto@fccj.edu.

OTTO, RANDAL ALLEN, otolaryngologist, educator; b. Sheboygan, Wis., June 17, 1954; MD, U. Mo., 1981. Diplomate Am. Bd. Otolaryngology. Resident in pathology Queens Med. Ctr., Honolulu, 1981-82; resident in otolaryngology U. Mo., Columbia, 1982-87; asst. prof. dept. otolaryngology U. Tex. Health Sci. Ctr., San Antonio, 1989—90, acting chmn. dept. otolaryngology, 1989—90, assoc. prof. with tenure, 1992—97, prof., 1997—, interim chmn., 1999-2001, prof., chmn., 2001—; asst. prof. dept. otolaryngology U. Fla., Gainesville, 1987—89; physician U. Tex. Cancer Therapy & Rsch. Ctr., chief physician, 2008—. Fellow ACS, Am. Acad. Otolaryngology-Head and Neck Surgery, Triologic Soc.; mem. AMA, Am. Soc. for Head and Neck Surgeons, Tex. Med. Assn. Office Phone: 210-567-5662. E-mail: otto@uthscsa.edu.

OTTONI, GUILHERME DE LIMA, computer engineer, researcher; s. Elias Jose Garcia and Maria Lucia Lima Ottoni; m. Desiree Leopoldo da Silva Silva; 1 child, Lucas Leopoldo. BS in Computer Engring., Fundacao U. Fed. do Rio Grande, 1999; MS in Computer Sci., U. Estadual de Campinas, Brazil, 2002; PhD, Princeton U., NJ, 2008. Software engr. Motorola Inc. Eldorado Rsch. Inst., Campinas, 2003; rsch. scientist Intel Corp., Santa Clara, Calif., 2008—. Contbr. articles to profl. jours. Recipient GPA award, Fundacao U. Fed. do Rio Grande, 2000, Wu prize, Princeton U. Sch. Engring. and Applied Sci., 2007, Programming Excellence award, Upsilon Pi Epsilon Honor Soc. Computer Scis., 2001, Best Paper award, Program Com. Internat. Workshop Software and Compilers Embedded Sys., 2003, Academic Merit prize, Dept. Computer Sci., Princeton, 2003—04; finalist Internat. Collegiate Programming Contest, Assn. Computer Machinery, 2000, 2002; nominee Best Paper award, INTL Conf. Microarchitecture, 2005; PhD fellowship, Intel Found., 2007—08, Grad. fellowship, CNPq, 2000—01, CAPES, 2001—02, Princeton U. Sch. Engring. and Applied Sci., 2003—04, Honorific Grad. fellowship, Dept. Computer Sci., Rice U., 2003—07. Mem.: Assn. Computing Machinery.

OTU, HASAN HUSEYIN, medical researcher, educator; b. Bingol, Turkey, Mar. 23, 1974; s. Izzet and Marifet Otu; m. Handan Can, June 28, 2007; children: Ceren Kaplan, Defne. PhD, U. Nebr., Lincoln, 2002. Instr. medicine Harvard Med. Sch., Boston, 2002—, dir. bioinformetics core, 2003—; asst. prof Sabanci U., Istanbul, 2008—. Fellowship, Dubai Harvard Found. Med. Rsch., 2008—, Various Rsch. Grants, NIH, 2002. Mem.: AAAS. Achievements include patents for bioinformatics and genomics. Office: Harvard Med Sch 3 Blackfan Cir CLS Bldg Rm 540 Boston MA 02115 Office Fax: 1 617 735-2509. Business E-Mail: hotu@bidmc.harvard.edu.

OTUNNU, OLARA A., childrens organization official; b. Mucwini (Chua), Northern Uganda, Sept. 1950; Attended, Makerere U., Kampala; LLM, Oxford U., 1978; Fulbright Scholar, Harvard U. Assoc. atty.

Chadbourne and Parke, NY; asst. prof. law Albany Law Sch.; mem. Uganda Nat. Consultative Coun., 1979—80; permanent rep. of Uganda UN, 1980—85; pres. UN Security Coun., 1981; chmn. African Group, 1981; vice pres. Gen. Assembly, 1982—83; chmn. Contact Group on Global Negotiations, 1982—93, Commn. on Human Rights, 1983—84, Gen. Assembly Credientials Com., 1983—84, Drafting Com. of the Ministerial Mtg. of Non-Aligned Countries, 1983; min. Fgn. Affairs of Uganda, 1985—86; vis. fellow Inst. Francais des Relations Internat., 1987—89; vis. prof. Am. U., Paris, 1987—89; pres. Internat. Peace Acad., 1990—97; spl. rep., sec. gen. for children & armed conflict UN, 1998—2005; pres. LBL Found. for Children, NYC, 2006—. Mem. Internat. Task Force on Security Coun. Peace Enforcement; pres. Internat. Peace Acad.; mem. UN Group of Experts on New Concepts of Internat. Security, 1984—85, Commonwealth Group of Experts Study Group on the Security of Small States, 1984—85, Internat. Panel on Mgmt. and Decision-Making in the UN, 1986—87, Group on Rethinking Internat. Governance, 1986—90, Commn. on Global Governance, 1992—95, Carnegie Commn. on Preventing Deadly Conflict, 1994—. Bd. mem. Aspen Inst., Internat. Selection Commn. of the Philadelphia Liberty Medal, Carnegie Endowment for Internat. Peace, Aspen France, Coun. of African Advisors to the World Bank, Internat. Patrons of the Refugee Studies Programme, Oxford U., Aspen Italia; advisory com. Stockholm Internat. Peace Rsch. Inst.; bd. mem. Carnegie Corp. of NY, Hampshire Coll. Recipient Disting. Svc. award, UN Assn. USA in NY, 2001, German Africa prize, 2002, Sydney Peace Prize, 2005, Harvard Law Sch. Assn. award, 2007. Office: LBL Foundation for Children Carnegie Corporation of New York 437 Madison Ave New York NY 10022

OTWELL, RALPH MAURICE, retired newspaper editor; b. Hot Springs, Ark., June 17, 1926; s. Walter Clement and Pearl Oda (Tisdale) O.; m. Janet Barbara Smith, July 18, 1953; children— Brian Thornton, Douglas Keith, David Smith. Student, U. Ark., 1947-48; BS, Northwestern U., 1951; postgrad. (Nieman fellow), Harvard, 1959-60. Reporter, telegraph editor So. Newspapers, Inc., Hot Springs, 1943-44, 47; asst. city editor Chgo. Sun-Times, 1953-59, news editor, 1959-63, asst. mng. editor, 1963-65, asst. to editor, 1965-68, mng. editor, 1968-76, editor, 1976-80, exec. v.p., editor, 1980-84. Mgmt. bd. newspaper div. Field Enterprises, Inc., 1967-84; lectr. Medill Sch. Journalism, Northwestern U., 1955—; charter mem. Nat. News Council, 1973-80; coord. Northwestern Inst. Learning in Retirement, 1992—. Trustee Garrett-Evang. Theol. Sem., 1965-79; Mem. nat. bd. Christian Social Concerns, United Meth. Ch., 1968-72; mem. bd. Community Renewal Soc., 1987-90, Chgo. Reporter, 1987-90, student publs. Northwestern U., 1968-72. Served to 1st lt. AUS, 1944-47, 51-53. Recipient Page One award Chgo. Newspaper Guild, 1964; named Ill. Journalist of Year No. Ill. U., 1974 Mem. Am. Soc. Newspaper Editors (chmn. ethics com. 1976-77), AP Mng. Editors Assn., Soc. Profl. Journalists (dir. 1966-71, sec. 1971-72, v.p. 1972-73, pres. 1973-74), Northwestern U. Alumni Assn. (dir. 1965-68, 91-93, sec. 1993-94, Merit award 1969, Svc. award 1995, chair seminar day com. 2001-2002), Sigma Delta Chi (pres. 1987-89), Kappa Tau Alpha, Econ. Club, Headline Club (pres. Chgo. chpt. 1965-66), Harvard Club Chgo., Chgo. Press Club (dir. 1968-77), Northwestern Club. Home: 34 Knox Cir Evanston IL 60201-1912 Personal E-mail: ralph@otwell.com.

OU, CHAOHUA, academic administrator; EdD, Tex. Tech U., Lubbock, 2008. Grad. rsch. asst. Tex. Tech U., 2002—05; academic profl. instrnl. tech. Ga. Inst. Tech., Atlanta, 2005—. Contbr. articles to profl. jours. Mem.: Assn. Ednl. Comm. and Tech., Am. Ednl. Rsch. Assn., Phi Kappa Phi.

OU, DUAN LI, chemist; b. Canton, China, Oct. 21, 1964; PhD, U. London, 1994. Cert. charter chemist, Royal Soc. Chemistry, 1997. Contbr. articles to profl. jour. Recipient Dow Corning Tech. Achievement award, 1999. Master: RSC. Office: Saint Gobain Performance Plastics 9 Goddard Rd Northborough MA 01532 Business E-Mail: danny.ou@saint-gobain.com.

OU, LO-CHANG, physiology educator; b. Shanghai, Oct. 16, 1930; came to U.S., 1964; m. Cynthia Chin Ou, June 10, 1960; children; Winnie, Edward, Emily, Joseph. BS, Peking U., Beijing, 1954; PhD, Dartmouth Coll., 1971. Tchg. asst., dept. biochemistry Peking U., Beijing, 1954-60, lectr., dept. biochemistry, 1960-62; demonstrator, dept. physiology Hong Kong U., 1962-64; asst. prof. dept. physiology Dartmouth Med. Sch., Hanover, N.H., 1977-80, assoc. prof., 1980-85, rsch. prof., 1985—, prof. emeritus (active), 1998—. NIH rsch. grantee, 1977-94. Mem. Am. Physiol. Soc. Achievements include research on pathophysiology of high altitude. Office: Dartmouth Med Sch Dept Physiology Lebanon NH 03756 Office Phone: 603-650-7729. Business E-Mail: Lo.Chang.Ou@Dartmouth.edu.

OU, SHAN-HWEI, academic administrator, engineering educator; BS, Nat. Cheng Kung U., Tainan, Taiwan, 1968, MS, 1971, PhD, 1977. Asst. rschr. dept. hydraulic and ocean engring. Nat. Cheng Kung U., Tainan City, Taiwan, 1974-75, lectr. dept. hydraulic and ocean engring., 1975-78, assoc. prof. dept. hydraulic and ocean engring., 1978-82, prof. dept. hydraulic and ocean engring., 1982—; pres. Tajen U., Taiwan, 2006—. Chmn. dept. hydraulic and ocean engring. Nat. Cheng Kung U., Tainan, 1986-92, dean coll. engring., 1993-99, v.p., 2001-06; vis. rschr. U. Hawaii, U. Del., 1978-79. Mem. Pub. Construction Commn., 2005—. Fellow: Chinese Inst. Civil & Hydraulic Engring.; mem.: Soc. Theoretical and Applied Mechanics, Inst. Chinese Engrs. (pres. 2005—, 2004—). Office: 20 Weishin Rd Yanpu Hsia Pingtung 907 Taiwan Home Phone: 886-6-2389348; Office Phone: 886-8-7624969. Fax: 886-8-7625045. E-mail: president@mail.tajen.edu.tw.

OUALLINE, VIOLA JACKSON, psychologist, consultant; b. Edna, Tex., Oct. 17, 1927; d. S.R. Jackson and Myrtle Mae Wood; m. Charles M. Oualline Jr., Sept. 3, 1949; children: Stephen, Susan, Shari. BS, U. Houston, 1949; MS, North Tex. State U., 1962, PhD, 1975. Phys. therapist Hermann Hosp., Houston, 1948-49; pvt. practice Austin, Tex., 1949-54; Miller Orthopedic Clinic, Charlotte, N.C., 1956-57; psychologist Dallas Easter Seal Soc., 1963-81, dir. psychology dept., 1981-93; pvt. practice, 1993—. Psychol. cons. Mesquite Ind. Sch. Dist., Tex., 1974—, Duncanville Sch. Dist., Tex., 1974-76, Grand Prarie Ind. Sch. Dist., Tex., 1976-79. Mem. Am. Psychol. Assn., Tex. Psychol. Assn., Dallas Psychol. Assn., Am. Assn. Counseling Devel., Coun. for Exceptional Children, Chi Omega Mother's Club. Baptist. Avocations: reading, bicycle riding. Office: Ste 208 11311 N Central Expy Dallas TX 75243-6729 Office Phone: 214-696-1079.

OUCHI, MASAMI, astronomer; b. Hachioji, Tokyo, Japan, Jan. 21, 1976; s. Tsutomu and Keiko Ouchi; m. Satoko Fukushima. PhD in Astronomy, U. Tokyo, 2003. Postdoc. fellow Space Telescope Sci. Inst., Balt., 2004—07, Carnegie Instn. Washington, Pasadena, Calif., 2007—. Recipient Young Astronomer award, Astron. Soc. Japan, 2008. Mem.: Am. Astron. Soc. Office: Carnegie Inst Washington 813 Santa Barbara St Pasadena CA 91101 Office Fax: 626-795-8136.

OUDENS, GERALD FRANCIS, architect, architectural firm executive; b. Manchester, NH, May 18, 1934; s. John and Louise Esther (Wagner) Oudens; m. Monica Elizabeth Wohlfert, June 16, 1962; children: Elizabeth Marian, Matthew Thomas, Katherine Frances. BA in Architecture cum laude, Yale U., 1956, MArch, 1958. Registered arch., D.C., Md. Intern arch. Koehler & Isaak, Manchester, 1955-58; staff architect Office Surgeon Gen. USAF, Washington, 1958-61; assoc. Metcalf & Assocs., Washington, 1961-69; prin. Oudens, Knoop, Knoop & Sachs Archs., PC, Chevy Chase, Md., 1970—. Vis. critic, thesis advisor dept. architecture Cath. U. Am., 1968—88; mem. adv. com. Acad. Med. Ctr. Study Sch. Architecture Rice U., 1975; mem. ambulatory care adv. panel U.S. VA, 1974—75; mem. adv. panel No. Ind. Health Sys. Agy., 1977—81, AIA Rsch. Corp., 1978, Nat. Inst. Bldg. Scis., 1982—88; mem. design award juries Modern Healthcare Ann. Design Awards, 1992, 2002, 07, Soc. Critical Care Medicine/AACN/AIA ICU Design Awards, 1992—97, Soc. Critical Care Medicine, AACN, AIA ICU Design Awards, 1999—2006, AIA Health Facilities Rev. Jury, 1995; presenter in field. Prin. works include NIH Master Plan, Bethesda, Md., NIH Animal Rsch. Ctr., NIH Rocky Mountain Labs. Master Plan, Hamilton, Mont., Nat. Inst. Aging Gerontol. Rsch. Ctr., Balt., Md., Nat. Cancer Inst. Master Plan, Frederick, Md., Sibley Meml. Hosp., Washington, Washington Hosp. Ctr. Master Plan, Washington Adventist Hosp., Takoma Park, Md., Martha Jefferson Hosp., Charlottesville, Va., Marion (Ind.) Gen. Hosp., Humana Hosp. de Pedregal, Mexico City, Humana Audubon Hosp. and Heart Inst., Louisville, Humana Greensboro (N.C.) Hosp., Centre Universitaire des Scis. de la Sante, Yaounde, Cameroon, Washington Home and Hospice, Cuttington U. Coll., Suakoko, Liberia, Escuela Agricola Panamericana, El Zamorano, FM, Honduras, others; contbr. articles to profl. jours. Recipient Nat. Capital Architecture award, D.C. Coun. Engring. and Archtl. Socs./Washington Acad. Scis., 1961, ICU Design citation, Soc. Critical Care Medicine, 1998. Fellow: AIA (acad. architecture for health 1971—, nat. healthcare policy task force 1993—, mem. adv. com. Am. Collegiate Schs. Architecture coun. archtl. rsch. 1994—, Am. Hosp. Assn. Grad. Fellowship Rev. Panel, Henry Adams award 1958, Honor award Ky. chpt. 1980, Outstanding Leadership and Commitment to Healthcare Design award 1987, Merit award Washington Met. chpt. 1989, Citations for Design Excellence 1988, 1990), Am. Coll. Healthcare Archs. (bd. regents, sec., chmn. membership com.); mem.: Internat. Hosp. Fedn., Am. Hosp. Assn. (mem. faculty continuing edn. insts. 1972—76, adv. panel 1978), Lambda Alpha Internat. Office: Oudens Knoop Knoop & Sachs Archs PC 2 Wisconsin Cir Chevy Chase MD 20815-7003 Office Phone: 301-718-0080. E-mail: goudens@okarch.com.

OUDERKIRK, MASON JAMES, lawyer; b. Des Moines, Feb. 1, 1953; s. Mason George and Florence Astor (Lowe) O.; m. Kari Aune Hormel, May 28, 1983; 1 child, Mason Christopher. BA, Drake U., 1975, JD, 1978. Bar: Iowa 1978, US Dist. Ct. (so. dist.) Iowa 1978, US Dist. Ct. (no. dist.) Iowa 2006, US Ct. Appeals (8th cir.). Assoc. M.G. Ouderkirk Law Office, Indianola, Iowa, 1978-79; ptnr. Ouderkirk Law Firm, Indianola, 1979-96; sr. mem. Ouderkirk, Ouderkirk & Dougherty, P.L.C., Indianola, 1996-98; proprietor Ouderkirk Law Firm, Indianola, Iowa, 1998—; pres. Avanti Realty Co. (formerly Landmark Real Estate, Ltd.), Indianola, 1978—2002, Avanti Builders Co., Indianola, 1991—2002. Mem. Vol. Lawyers Project of Iowa, 1987-93. Mem. Indianola Police Retirement Bd., 1983-88; instr. Eric Heintz Black Belt Acad., 1988-93, Indianola Parks and Recreation Dept., 1988-93; mem. Nominating Commn., Warren County Assoc. Dist. Ct., 1999-05, 2009-; mem. Jud. Nominating Commn. for 5A Jud. Dist. of Iowa, 2002-08. Mem. ABA, Iowa Bar Assn. (pub. rels. com. 1989-94, family law com. 1989-90), Warren County Bar Assn. (sec., treas. 1985-89, v.p. 1989-90, pres. 1990-92), 5th Jud. Dist. Bar Assn. (sec., treas. 1995), Assn. Trial Lawyers Am., Iowa Trial Lawyers Assn. Episcopalian. Avocations: fishing, fitness and weight training, gardening. Home and Office: 108 S Howard St PO Box 156 Indianola IA 50125-0156 Office Phone: 515-961-5315. Office Fax: 515-961-0304. Business E-Mail: olfirm@qwestoffice.net.

OUDSHOORN, MICHAEL JOHN, computer science educator; b. Adelaide, Australia, Feb. 26, 1963; s. Nicolaas Antonius and Gysberta Aleida (Coolen) O.; m. Joanne Fay Bruns, Mar. 7, 1987. BSc, U. Adelaide, 1983, BSc with honors, 1984, PhD, 1992. Tutor U. Adelaide, 1984-89, lectr. computer sci., 1989-92, sr. lectr., 1993—; prof. invité U. Nice, 1992, 95. Cons. Ctr. Computer Systems and Software Engring.; mem. numerous conf. program coms. Author: Ada: A First Course in Programming and Software Engineering, 1991; contbr. articles to profl. jours.; mem. editl. bd. numerous jours. Mem. IEEE, Internat. Soc. Computers and Their Application, Assn. Computing Machinery, Australian Software Engring. Inst., Computer Sci. Assn., Australian Computer Soc. Avocations: photography, skiing, travel, four-wheel driving. Office: Univ of Texas at Brownsville 80 Fort Brown Brownsville TX 78520 Office Fax: 956-882-6604. Business E-Mail: michael.oudshoorn@utb.edu.

OULTON, DONALD PAUL, lawyer; b. Kingston, NY, July 22, 1930; s. Francis Terrance and Anne Agnes (Carrol) Oulton; m. Carol Jane Burke; children: David P., Nancy, Sarah, Carol. AA in Edn., Boston U., 1955, BS in Bus. Adminstrn., 1958; JD, Suffolk U., 1969. Bar: Mass. 1970, US Dist. Ct. Mass. 1973, US Supreme Ct. 1978, US Ct. Appeals (1st cir.) 1980, US Ct. Claims 1980, US Tax Ct. 1980, US Ct. Mil. Appeals 1981, US Ct. Internat. Trade 1984, US Ct. Appeals (Fed. cir.) 1984. Contract negotiator Raytheon Corp., Bedford, Mass., 1959—65; chief negotiator claims Quincy Shipbldg. Divsn., Mass., 1970—72, assoc. divsn. counsel, 1970—72; part-time trial counsel Natick, Mass., 1970—; asst. dist. atty. Middlesex County, Cambridge, Mass., 1972—75; real estate broker Mass. Realtors Assn., Boston, 1972—; contract negotiator Electronic Sys. Divsn. Office of Staff Judge Adv., US Air Force, Hanscom AFB, Mass., 1974—76, chief atty. fgn. mil. sales, 1976—2003; chief Internat. Law Br., 1987—2003; ret. Air Force, 2003. Hearing officer Zoning Bd. Appeals, Natick, 1976; lectr. Western New Eng. Coll. Author: Inquests, 1973, Technology Transfer, 1983, Air Force Trivia, 1985, A Review of Executive Agreements From The Standpoint of Current Case Law, 1999; co-author (with others): Poem In Remembrance of Korea, 1987. Bd. dirs., co-founder Shamrock Soc., Natick, Mass., 1976—; bd. dirs., counsel Little League, Natick, 1972—75, Mass. Korean War Meml. Com., 1988—; tchr. 9th grade, CCD St. James Ch., Wellesley, Mass., 1976—83. Served with inf. US Army, 1951—53, Korea. Recipient US Senate Mil. & Govt. Svc. Honor, 2003; named Outstanding Civilian Atty. of Yr., US Air Force Sys. Command, 1980, US Air Force, Pentagon, 1980, Outstanding Civilian, Air Force Electronic Sys. Divsn., 1983. Mem.: Mass. Police Chiefs Assn., Fed. Bar Assn., Mass. Bar Assn., Middlesex Bar Assn., Air Force Assn., Am. Soc. Internat. Law, Officers Club. Democrat. Roman Catholic. Home: 54 Macarthur Rd Natick MA 01760-2938

OUNDJIAN, PETER, conductor, music director; b. Toronto, Ontario, Canada, 1955; m. Nadine Oundjian; children: Lara, Peter. Grad, Royal Coll. Music, London; studied violin, Julliard Sch., NYC. First violinist Tokyo String Quartet, 1981—95; music dir. Nieuw Sinfonitetta Amsterdam, 1998—2003; artistic dir., prin. condr. Caramoor Internat. Music Festival, Katonah, NY, 1995—; prin. guest condr. Colo. Symphony Orch., 2003—06; music dir. Toronto Symphony Orchestra, 2004—; princ. guest condr., artistic adv. Detroit Symphony Orch., 2006—. Adj. prof. Yale Sch. Music, 1981—; guest condr. San Francisco Symphony, Pitts. Symphony, Detroit Symphony, Houston Symphony, St. Louis Symphony, Nat. Symphony Orch., Cin. Symphony Orch., Konzerthaus, Berlin, City of Birmingham Symphony, NDR Hanover Symphony, Saarbrucken Radio Symphony, Zurich Tonhalle, Chgo. Symphony, LA Philharm.; guest artistic dir., condr. Mozart Festival; guest condr. Grand Teton Festival, 2005, Aspen Festival, 2005, Tanglewood Festivals, 2005. Recipient First prize, Internat. Violin Competition, Vina Del Mar, Chile, 1980, Stoutzker prize, Royal Coll. Music. Office: Toronto Symphony Orch 212 King St W 6th Fl Ste 550 Toronto ON Canada M5H 1K5*

OURISMAN, MANDELL JACK, automotive executive; b. Nov. 10, 1926; m. Mary Martin Stiles, June 1993. Student, U.S. Naval Acad., 1944, Georgetown U., 1947. Chmn., CEO Ourisman Automotive Enterprises, Marlow Heights, Md. Office: Ourisman Automotive Enterprises 4400 Branch Ave Temple Hills MD 20748-1802 Home Phone: 202-667-6696; Office Phone: 301-423-4028. Personal E-mail: mjo@ourismanchevrolet.com.

OURISMAN, MARY M., United States Ambassador to Barbados and the Eastern Caribbean; Attended, NY Sch. Interior Design, Acad. Arts Coll., San Francisco; BS, U. Tex., Austin, 1970. US amb. to Barbados and the Eastern Caribbean US State Dept., Bridgetown, Barbados, 2006—. Bd dirs., mem. decorating com. Blair House; bd. trustees, chmn. nominating com. Washington Nat. Opera; nat. bd. dirs., emeritus trustee, chmn. travel and study tours com. Smithsonian Instn.; bd. trustees, mem. nat. com. performing arts, founding mem. internat. com. Kennedy Ctr.; mem. nat. coun. World Wildlife Fund. Office: 3120 Bridgetown Pl Washington DC 20521-3120*

OURSLER, TARA LINNEHAN, legislative staff member; Dist. dir., Rep. Dutch Ruppersberger US House of Reps., dep. chief of staff, Rep. Dutch Ruppersberger, chief of staff to Rep. Dutch Ruppersberger Washington. Democrat. Office: 2453 Rayburn House Office Bldg Washington DC 20515 Office Phone: 202-225-3061. Office Fax: 202-225-3094.*

OURUSOFF, NICHOLAS, science educator; b. Washington, Mar. 25, 1938; s. Leonide Sergeivich Ourusoff and Katherine Carlisle. AB in Philosophy cum laude, Harvard Coll., Cambridge, Mass., 1959; MS in Computer Sci., U. Colo., Boulder, 1973; IMAS in Computer Sci. & Psychology, N.Mex. State U., Las Cruces, 1997. Programmer, analyst Computer Usage Co., Washington, 1962—71, WHO, Geneva, 1975—79; census data processing advisor UN, Dakar, Senegal, 1980—80, Lisbon, Portugal, 1981—82, data processing advisor, Nat. Statis. Office Malawi Zomba, Malawi, 1982—83; assoc. prof. computer sci. Lander Coll., Greenwood, SC, 1984; instr. computer info. sys. Northern Ariz. U., Coll. Bus. Adminstrn., Flagstaff, 1988—91; asst. prof. computer info. sys. U. Maine, Augusta, 1997—2003; instr. computer sci. and info. tech. Leech Lake Tribal Coll., Cass Lake, Minn., 2006—07. Info. systems cons., Boulder, 1974—75; vis. lectr. Petrozavodsk State U., Russia, 1991—92; vis. lectr. computer info. sci. Western State Coll. Colo., Gunnison, 2004—05. Vol. Move On, Claremont, NH, 2008—, Concord, New London. Fubright Scholar, C.I.E.S., Petrozavodsk State U., 2005—06. Mem.: Assn. Computing Machinery. Home: 65 Seamans Rd New London NH 03257 Personal E-mail: nourusoff@yahoo.com.

OUSTERHOUT, DOUGLAS KENNETH, plastic surgeon; b. Bellaire, Mich., Aug. 30, 1935; s. Kenneth and Naomi Ousterhout; children from previous marriage: Donald, Susan, Oliver, Thomas. Student, U. Colo., 1953—55; DDS, U. Mich., 1961, MD, 1965. Resident gen. surgery U. Med.; resident in plastic surgery Stanford U., Palo Alto, Calif., 1969—72; craniofacial tng. Dr. Tessier, Paris, 1972—73; clin. instr. U. Calif., San Francisco, 1973—86, clin. prof., 1986—. Editor: Aesthetic Contouring of the Craniofacial Skeleton, 1991; author: Cocktails for Two (AKA: Death Gets a Facelift), 1993, A Guide to Feminization Male to Female Transsexual. Capt. US Army, 1966—68. Mem.: French Soc. Maxillofacial Surgeons, French Soc. Plastic, Reconstructive and Aesthetic Surgeons, Pan Pacific Surg. Assn. (pres. 1998—2000), Am. Soc. Maxillofacial Surgeons (pres. 1994—95), Internat. Soc. Craniofacial Surgeons, Am. Assn. Plastic Surgeons, Am. Soc. Plastic Surgeons, Equadorian Soc. Craniofacial Surgery (hon.), Japan Soc. Craniofacial Surgery (hon.). Avocations: piano, sculpting, gardening, travel. Home: 2640 Steiner St San Francisco CA 94115 Office: Ste 150 45 Castro St San Francisco CA 94114 Office Phone: 415-626-2888. E-mail: ousterht@cris.com.

OUTCALT, DAVID LEWIS, academic administrator, mathematics professor, consultant, musician; b. L.A., Jan. 30, 1935; s. Earl Kinyon and Alberta Estes (Ferguson) Outcalt; m. Marcia Lee Beach, July 1, 1956 (dec.); children: Jeffrey David, Kevin Douglas, Gregory Mark, Eric Matthew. BA in Math., Pomona Coll., Claremont, Calif., 1956; MA in Math., Claremont Grad. U., 1958; PhD in Math., Ohio State U., Columbus, 1963; DPub Adminstrn. (hon.), Kyung Hee U., Korea, 1984. Asst. prof. math. Clarement McKenna Coll., 1962-64; from asst. prof. to prof. U. Calif., Santa Barbara, 1964-80, chmn. dept. math., 1969-72, dean instrnl. devel., 1977-80; vice chancellor acad. affairs U. Alaska, Anchorage, 1980-81, prof. math., 1980-86, chancellor, 1981-86; prof. natural and applied sci. U. Wis., Green Bay, 1986-93, Hendrickson prof. econ. devel., 1994-98, chancellor, 1986—93, chancellor emeritus, 1998—. Pres. Mid-Continent Athletic Conf., 1990—91. Author: math. textbooks; contbr. articles to profl. jours. Mem. exec. bd. western Alaska coun. Boy Scouts Am., 1982—86, mem. exec. bd. Bay-Lakes Coun., 1987—97, v.p. exploring, 1988—92, v.p. ops., 1992—93, pres., 1993—94; mem. Anchorage Symphony Bd., 1986, Green Bay Symphony Bd., 1988—97, Weidner Ctr. Presents Bd., 1994—98; peer reviewer NCAA, 1994—99; trustee, v.p., treas. Kauai Internat. Theatre, 1998—2000; trustee Kauai CC Fund, 2000—05, trustee emeritus, 2005—; Stephen minister Long Range Planning Com., 2008—, chair, 2009—; stephen min. Pacific Palisades Presbyn. Ch., 2008—, mem., 2009—; moderator bd. trustees Humana Hosp., Anchorage, 1982—83. Grantee, USAF Office Sci. Rsch., 1964—71, U. Calif., 1975—78, NSF, 1976—79. Mem.: Brown County Indsl. Devel. (pres. bd. dirs. 1994—97), Internat. Assn. Univ. Pres.'s (mem. exec. com. 1988—96, mem. N.Am. coun. exec. com. 1988—2002, newsletter editor 1994—95, mem. internat. com. tech. higher edn. 1996—2002), Math. Assn. Am., Greater Green Bay C. of C. (advance bd. 1987—97, bd. dirs. 1991—94, 1995—97), Rotary (bd. dirs. Kapaa club 1999—2004, pres. 2002—03, chair 2003—05, bd. dirs. Kapaa Found. 2003—05), Sigma Xi. Presbyterian. Home: 1606 Palisades Dr Pacific Palisades CA 90272 Business E-Mail: doutcalt@roadrunner.com.

OUTCALT, KENNETH W., ecologist, researcher; s. Victor A. and Jane L. Outcalt; m. Patricia A. Outcalt, July 12, 1984; children: Michael D. Elliott, Melinda K. Lewis. MS, U. Minn., St. Paul, 1978. Rsch. forester US Forest Svc., Olustee, Fla., 1977—82, rsch. soil scientist Gainesville, Fla., 1983—93, rsch. ecologist Athens, Ga., 1994—2002, supervisory rsch. ecologist, 2002—. State representative Soc. Ecol. Restoration,

Tucson, 2002—06. Coach Girls Softball League, Macclenny, Fla., 1986—88. Sgt. US Army, 1973—74, Ft. Campbell, KY. Recipient Superior Svc. award, US Dept. Agr., 1999, Chief's award, US Forest Svc., 2006; Joint Fire Sci. Program Funding grant, US Dept. Interior, 2000—06. Mem.: Ecol. Soc. Am. Avocations: hiking, canoeing. Office: US Forest Svc 3020 Green St Athens GA 30602

OUTIN, MARY LOUISE, business, multi-cultural history and geneology educator; b. Peak, SC, July 18, 1948; d. Ralph T. Williams and Mary Frances Wicker-Outin, Theopolis Outin (Stepfather). BA in Bus. Adminstrn., Columbia Coll., SC, 1987; MEd, Lesley U., 1999; grad., SC Sch. Real Estate, 1986. Owner MO Businesses, Inc., Columbia, 2000—. Mem.: SC Afro-Am. Hist. and Geneal. Soc., Inc. (co-pub. rels. dir. 1998—2000), Am. Legion Aux. (Unit 219 2000). Avocations: family history research, genealogy, cooking, reading. Office: MO Businesses Inc P O Box 3393 Columbia SC 29230

OUTLAW, WANDA CECELIA, priest; b. Washington, Oct. 17, 1954; d. Augustus King and Mary Lena (Booze) Brown; 1 child, Stephen Thomas Jr. Ordained priest 2002. Tng. mgr. Bur. ATF, Washington, 1989—; leadership, women's retreat leader African-Am. Cath. Congregation, Washington, 1993—, priest, 2002—. Preacher Women Uplifting Women Ministries, Washington, 2003—; designer, trainer LJR Group, Inc., Dallas, 2005—. Author: Woven Baskets on the Baobab Tree, In The Fulfillment. Active socks and sandwiches for the homeless Dynamic Crossroads, Washington, 2005; motivational spkr. Execs. of FEW, Balt., 2003—04. Mem.: NAACP (assoc.), NAFE (assoc.). Office: Imani Temple on Capitol Hill 609-611 Maryland Ave NE Washington DC 20002 Personal E-mail: wanda.outlaw@atf.gov. Business E-Mail: noni.crowmother@verizon.net.

OUTT, HELEN MAY, retired elementary school educator, psychologist; d. Spurgeon Eugene Weir and Edna May Kling; m. Terry Franklin Outt, May 25, 1960; children: Daina, Holly. BS, West Chester U., Pa., 1964, MEd, 1971. Cert. tchr. Ind., 1987, sch. counselor Ind., 1988, psychologist Assn. Masters in Psychology, 1999, lic. mental health counselor Ind., 2000, psychologist Ind., 2002. Tchr. Interboro Sch. Dist., Prospect Pk., Pa., 1966—69; counselor mid. sch. Chester (Pa.) Sch. Dist., 1969—70; tchr. elem. sch. Cin. (Ohio) Sch. Dist., 1974—85; tchr., counselor Indpls. (Ind.) Sch. Dist., 1986—2005, ret., 2005. Actor: (plays) Little Theater. Vol. food and clothing drive Indpls. (Ind.) Pub. Schs., 1986—2005; vol. polls Cin. (Ohio) Rep., 1975. Recipient Above and Beyond Call of Duty award, Indpls. (Ind.) Pub. Schs., 1993. Mem.: NEA (lic. adminstrn. and supr. 1987), Ind. Mental Health Counselors Assn., N.Am. Masters Psychology, Ind. Sch. Counseling Assn., Ind. Counseling Assn., Ind. State Tchrs. Assn., Indpls. (Ind.) Edn. Assn. (dir. region 1986—2000, dir. dist. 1986—2000, bldg. rep. 1986—2005, chmn. profl. devel. com. 1990—98, nat. rep.), Phi Delta Kappa. Republican. Meth. Avocations: photography, making greeting cards.

OUTWATER, JOHN OGDEN, mechanical engineering educator; b. London, Jan. 2, 1923; came to U.S., 1924; s. John Ogden and Nenny (Boe) O.; m. Alice Hooker Davidson, Dec. 13, 1952; children— Anne Hooker, Catherine Boe (Mrs. Carl B. Colby), Alice Brookfield (Mrs. Robert B. Lang), John Ogden III. BS, Princeton U., 1943; MA, Cambridge U., Eng., 1948; PhD, MIT, Cambridge, MA, 1950, Cambridge, Eng., 1976. Registered profl. engr. Research engr. DuPont Co., 1950-52; project engr. Universal Moulded Products, 1952-53; indsl. liaison officer Mass. Inst. Tech., 1954-55; prof. mech. engring. U. Vt., Burlington, 1955—71, chmn., 1955-93, prof. emeritus, 1993—. Leader archaeol. expdns. Wenner-Gren Found., Central Mexico, 1954, Yucatan, 1955, Peru-Bolivia, 1957, Haiti, 1959; cons. non-metallic materials Naval Ordnance Lab., Nat. Acad. Scis., Monsanto Rsch. Corp., Smithsonian Instn., pres. Vt. Inst. Co., Inc. Author: (with others) Engineering Materials, 1959, Esplendor del Mexico Antigua; papers on metal cutting, plastics, archaeology, bones, ski safety, botany. Chmn. Vt. Instrument Co., Inc.; Mem. Vt. Conf. Econ. Growth; vestryman St. Paul's Cathedral, Burlington. Served as officer Brit. Army, 1943-47. Named Vt. Engr. of Year, 1970; grantee USPHS; Timken fellow MIT, 1950 Fellow ASME; mem. ASTM, Holland Soc., Vt. Soc. Engrs., Delta Psi, Tau Beta Pi. Achievements include patents for ski boot tension. Home: 26 Nicklaus Cir South Burlington VT 05403-8015

OUYANG, JUN, electrical engineer, researcher; s. Shi Ouyang and Jinbing Peng; m. Hong Cai, July 31, 2005. PhD, U. Md., College Park, 2000—05. Grad. tchg. asst. Stevens Inst. Tech., Hoboken, NJ, 1999—2000, U. Md., 2000—01, grad. rsch. asst., 2001—05; sr. elec. integration engr. Seagate Tech., Rec. Head Operation, Bloomington, Minn., 2005—. Guest rschr. Nat. Inst. Stds. and Tech., 2004—05; product devel., quality control Seagate Tech., 2005—. Reviewer Jour. Applied Physics; contbr. papers to profl. jours. and pubs. V.p., coord. of entertainment activities Chinese Student and Scholar Assn., U. Md., 2002—03. Recipient Chinese Govt. award outstanding rsch., U. Md., 2005, Significant Alumni Achievement award, A. Clark Engring. Sch., 2006; named Outstanding Grad. Student Employee of Yr., 2005. Mem.: Tsinghu Alumni Assn. Minn. (v.p.), Minerals, Metals & Materials Soc., Am. Soc. Metals, Materials Rsch. Soc., Am. Ceramic Soc. (First and second prizes ceramographic competition 2005). Office: Seagate Tech 7801 Computer Ave S Mailstop: NRW112 Bloomington MN 55435 Office Fax: 952-402-7063. Personal E-mail: jouyang2002@yahoo.com. Business E-Mail: jun.ouyang@seagate.com.

OUYANG, XIAOMEI O., corporate financial executive; d. Zuxi Ouyang and Zongrun Zhang. BA, Stanford U., Palo Alto, Calif., 1995; MBA, Harvard Bus. Sch., Boston, Mass., 2000. Cons. McKinsey & Co., Beijing, Shanghai, Hong Kong, China, 1995—97; investment banker Morgan Stanley, Hong Kong, China, 1997—98; pvt. wealth mgmt. Goldman Sachs, NYC, 1999; interim coo Camouflage Corp., New York, NY, 2000; strategy & ops. dir. Primedia Inc., NYC, 2000—01; cfo Jupiter Partners, New York, NY, 2001—. Bd. mem. Pvt. Equity CFO Assn., NYC, 2002—; dir. of mktg. North Am. Chinese Mgmt. Assn., NYC, 2003—. Mem. Mus. of Modern Art, NYC, 2004. Recipient, Dept. of Economics, Stanford U., 1995; scholar, Harvard Bus. Sch., 1998-2000, Stanford U., 1992-1995. Mem.: N.Am. Chinese Mgmt. Assn. (dir. of mktg. 2003—04), Pvt. Equity CFO Assn., Harvard Bus. Sch. Alumni Assn. Achievements include design of designed and created a fashion line - Fuchsia; completed Milford Triathlon; Founded Stanford Alumni Association China Chapter. Avocations: fashion design, photography, world travel, tennis. Office: International Finance Corporation 2121 Pennsylvania Avenue, NW, F10P-158 Washington DC 20433 Office Phone: 202-458-8248. Office Fax: 212-332-2828, 202-522-0597; Home Fax: 212-712-2591. Personal E-mail: olivia_ouyang@hotmail.com. Business E-Mail: oouyang@jupiterpartners.com, xouyang@ifc.org.

OUYANG, XU, research and development company executive; PhD, Stanford U., Calif., 2001. Cons. PDF Solutions, San Jose, Calif., 2001—05; sr. engr., scientist IBM, Hopewell Junction, NY, 2005—07, R & D mgr., 2007—. Achievements include patents pending for semiconductor manufacturing. Office: IBM 2070 Rt 52 Hopewell Junction NY 12533

OUZTS, DAVID PERRY, church music director, organist; b. Greenville, SC, Nov. 30, 1962; s. Perry Cooper and Sara Owens Ouzts; life ptnr. Joseph Lee Middleton, Oct. 8, 1995. MusB, Furman U., Greenville, SC, 1985; MusM in Organ Performance, Yale U., New Haven, 1987; diploma in sacred music, Yale Inst. Sacred Music, New Haven, 1987; diploma in Anglican studies, Berkeley Divinity Sch., New Haven, 1987; DSM in Sacred Music, Grad. Theol. Found., South Bend, Ind., 2008. Diocesan cert. in musician leadership Standing Commn. on Ch. Music The Episc. Ch. with Va. Theol. Sem., Alexandria. Organist, choirmaster Trinity Episcopal Ch., Huntington, W.Va., 1987—90; dir. of music Congregation B'nai Sholom, Huntington, W.Va., 1988—90; assoc. dir. of music and fine arts St. Luke's United Meth. Ch., Houston, 1990—96; canon musician, liturgist Grace Episcopal Cathedral, Topeka, 1996—2001; dir. music and liturgy Ch. of Holy Communion, Memphis, 2001—. Liturgy and music cons. Episcopal Diocese of W.Va., Charleston, 1988—90; commn. on liturgy and music Episcopal Diocese of Kans., Topeka, 1997—2001; music dir. Memphis Girls Choir, 2002—. Mem. Rotary Club, Huntington, W.Va., 1987—89, Yale Club Greater Kansas City, 1997—2002; exec. com. Greater Kans. City Furman Club, 2000—02; founding mem. Memphis Furman Club, 2003—; mem. Rhodes Coll. Mastersingers Chorale, Memphis, 2006—. Recipient Cmty. Svc. Citation, Mayor of Topeka, 1995; named to Order of Ky. Colonels, Commonwealth of Ky., 1989; Homozel Mickel Daniel Music scholarship, Furman U., 1981-85, Grad. Assistantship in Sacred Music, Yale Inst. of Sacred Music, 1985-87, Grad. Assistantship in Organ, Ind. U., 1990. Mem.: Hymn Soc. in the US and Can., Choristers Guild (exec. bd. Houston chpt. 1992—94), Assn. of Diocesan Liturgy and Music Commns., Am. Recorder Soc., Am. Guild of English Handbell Ringers (exec. bd. Houston chpt. 1993—95), Am. Choral Dirs. Assn., Royal Sch. of Ch. Music, Assn. of Anglican Musicians, Organ Hist. Soc., Am. Guild of Organists (dean W.Va. chpt. 1989—90, exec. bd. Houston chpt. 1993—95, exec. bd. Topeka chpt. 1997—99). Democrat. Episcopalian. Avocations: walking, history, computers, reading. Office: Church of Holy Communion 4645 Walnut Grove Rd Memphis TN 38117-2597 Office Fax: 901-767-7034.

OUZTS, KARL CLAYBOURNE, history educator; b. Elberton, Ga., Sept. 24, 1961; s. Ronald Claybourn and Carl Ann Pass O.; m. Kellie Anne Rutledge, Nov. 29, 1997; children: Brooks Rutledge Farmer, Forbes Claybourne Ouzts, Addison Brantley Ouzts. Graham Jefferson Ouzts, Nackenzie Anne Ouzts. AA, Anderson Coll., 1981; BSEd, U. Ga., 1985; MA in History, West Ga. Coll., 1989; PhD in History, Fla. State U., 1996. Tchg. asst. Fla. State U., Tallahassee, 1992-94; asst. prof. of history Gainesville (Ga.) Coll., 1997-98, Truett-McConnell Coll., Watkinsville, Ga., 1998—2002; prof. history & environ. studies Gainesville State Coll., 2003—. Vis. asst. prof. State U. West Ga., Carrollton, 1995-96. Active Elbert County Hist. Soc., Elberton, Ga., 1986—, Elbert County Bicentennial Com., 1989-90. Mem. So. Hist. Assn., Ga. Assn. Historians, Am. Soc. Environ. History. Independent. Baptist. Address: 437 Dunahoo Rd Winder GA 30680-3741 Business E-Mail: couzts@gsc.edu.

OVADIA, MARC, pediatric cardiologist, educator; b. Chgo., July 10, 1959; s. Jacques and Florence (Reuben) O.; m. Vera Claire Mezvinsky, Aug. 12, 1991. BA with honors, U. Chgo., 1980; MD, U. Ill., Chgo., 1984. Diplomate Am. Bd. Pediat., Am. Bd. Pediat. Cardiology. Resident in pediat. Stanford U., Palo Alto, Calif., 1984-87; fellow in pediat. cardiology Columbia U., NYC, 1987-89; fellow in electrophysiology and pacing NIH, Bethesda, Md., 1989-90; head pediat. electrophysiology and pacing Coll. Medicine U. Ariz. and Steele Meml. Children's Rsch. Ctr., Tucson, 1990-94; asst. prof. pediat. cardiology Coll. Medicine U. Ariz., 1990-94; physician-in-charge electrophysiology North Shore U. Hosp., Manhasset, N.Y., 1994—; asst. prof. Med. Coll. Cornell U., NYC, 1994—; vis. scientist dept. biophysics SUNY, Stony Brook, 1994—. Session chairperson Computers in Cardiology XX, NIH, Bethesda, Md., 1994; mem. sci. adv. com. Heart Rhythym Techs. subs. Eli Lilly, Inc., Temecula, Calif., 1992-94. Contbg. author: Myocardial Viability, 1995; reviewer, contbr. articles to sci. jours. Mem. peer rev. com. study sect. Am. Heart Assn., N.Y., 1994—. James scholar U. Ill., 1980-84; rsch. grantee Ariz. Disease Control Rsch. Commn., Phoenix, 1993-95, EchoCATH, Inc., Princeton, N.J., 1993-95. Fellow Am. Coll. Cardiology, Am. Acad. Pediat.; mem. N.Am. Soc. Pacing and Electrophysiology (diplomate), Biophys. Soc. Achievements include research in anti-inflammatory biomaterials applicable to cardiac pacemakers, in gap junction patch-clamp electrophysiology. Office: Boas-Marks Biomed Rsch Bldg 300 Community Dr Manhasset NY 11030-3801 Home: 1948 Dewes St Glenview IL 60025-4237

OVANESOV, MIKHAIL V., biophysicist, researcher, biomedical engineer; b. Kaluga, Russia, June 8, 1977; s. Vladimir N. Ovanesov and Zoya M. Losovskaya. BS in Biophysics, Moscow Inst. Physics and Tech., 1999, MS in Biophysics, 2000; PhD in Biophysics and Biochemistry, Nat. Rsch. Ctr. Hematology, 2002. Rsch. scientist Nat. Rsch. Ctr. Hematology, Moscow, 2001—03; rsch. fellow ARC, Rockville, Md., 2002—. Office: American Red Cross 15601 Crabbs Branch Way Rockville MD 20855 E-mail: misha@clinlab.ru.

OVECHKIN, ALEXANDER, professional hockey player; b. Moscow, Sept. 17, 1985; s. Mikhail and Tatiana Ovechkin. Left wing Dynamo Moscow (Russian Super League), 2001—05, Washington Capitals, 2005—. Mem. Team Russia, World Junior Championships, 2003—05, Team Russia, World Championships, 2004, 05, Team Russia, World Cup of Hockey, 2004, Team Russia, Olympic Games, Torino, Italy, 2006. Recipient Calder Meml. Trophy, 2006, Art Ross Trophy, 2008, Maurice Richard Trophy, 2008, 2009, Lester B. Pearson Award, 2008, 2009, Hart Meml. Trophy, 2008, 2009; named NHL Rookie of Yr., Sporting News, 2006, NHL Player of Yr., 2008, 2009; named to First All-Star Team, NHL, 2006—09, NHL All-Star Game, 2007, 2008, 2009, All-NHL Team, Sporting News, 2009. Achievements include being a member of gold medal Team Russia, World Junior Championships, 2003; being the first overall draft pick in NHL entry draft, 2004. Office: c/o Washington Capitals MCI Center 601 F St NW Washington DC 20004 also: 627 N Glebe Rd, Ste 850 Arlington VA 22203*

OVENS, DAVID, food service executive, marketing professional; b. Australia; Various mktg. positions Unilever, Kimberly-Clark Corp., Johnson & Johnson; joined Yum! Brands Inc., 2001, chief mktg. officer Yum! Restaurants Internat. Australia, New Zealand, chief mktg. officer Taco Bell Corp. (subs.), 2007—. Named a Power Player, Advt. Age, 2008. Office: Taco Bell Corp 17901 Von Karman Irvine CA 92614 Office Phone: 949-863-4500. Office Fax: 949-863-2252.*

OVERALL, DIANNA, elementary school educator; d. Mildred and Otha Bush; m. Lester Overall, Feb. 1, 1992; 1 child, Jawanza Dianna. BS in Elem. and Early Childhood Edn., U. Mo., St. Louis, 1976. Cert. in acct., Urban League Bus. Sch., 1979. Tchr. Human Devel. Corp., St. Louis, 1977—87; tech. sgt. Mo. Air Nat. Guard, 1983—93; tchr. St. Louis Pub. Schs., 1987—, tutor, 1988—89. Computer and telecom. Lambert Combat Unit. Recipient Tchr. of Yr., Schlafly Found., Adelaide, 2007. Mem.: Caring and Sharing. Office: St Louis Public Schs 801 N 11th St Saint Louis MO 63101 Personal E-mail: doverall1@netzero.net.

OVERALL, THERESA LYNNE, educational technology professor; d. Edsel and Patricia Overall. AB Divisional Scis., Math. and Stats., Hollins U., Roanoke, Va., 1978; MS Computer Edn. and Cognitive Sys., U. North Tex., Denton, 2001, PhD in Ednl. Computing, 2007. Classroom tchr., tech. coord. The Lamplighter Sch., Dallas, 1978—99; rsch. asst. Inst. Integration Tech. into Tchg. and Learning, Denton, Tex., 1999—2006; vis. asst. prof. U. Maine, Farmington, 2007—. Founder, pres. The Logo Opportunity, 1980—. Author: (curriculum guide) TI Logo Curriculum Guide, (manual) On the Road to Silver and Gold-A Leader's Guide to Helping Girls Earn Preliminary Silver and Gold Award Recognitions: Studio 2B Edition; contbr. articles to profl. jours. Vol. Girl Scouts of the USA, Dallas, 1974—2008. Recipient Presdl. award for Excellence in Math. Tchg., The Lamplighter Sch., Dallas, 1990, 1991, Outstanding Vol. award, Girl Scouts Tejas Coun., 1995, Green Angel, 1996, Appreciation Pin, 1998, Honor Pin, 2000, Heart of Gold Award, 2005, Tejas award, 2006; named Outstanding Young Women of Am., 1981, 1984, 1985, Outstanding Student of Yr., Computer Edn. and Cognitive Systems Dept., U. North Tex., 2001, Faculty of Yr., U. of Maine, Farmington, 2007—08; Toulouse Sch. Grad. Studies scholar, U. North Tex., Denton, 1999, Alumnae Dau. scholar, Hollins Coll. Alumnae Assn., 1974, 1975, 1976, 1977. Mem.: So. Info. Tech. and Tchr. Edn., Am. Ednl. Rsch. Assn., Internat. Soc. for Tech. Edn., Nat. Coun. Tchrs. Math., Leadership Richardson, Kaligrafos, The Dallas Calligraphy Soc.

OVERBY, CHARLES L., foundation administrator; m. Andrea Overby; children: Anna, Melissa, Chad. Grad., U. Miss. Reporter, editor, corp. exec. Gannett Co., v.p. news and comm.; press asst. to Sen. John Stennis; chmn. Senate Armed Svcs. Com.; spl. asst. for adminstr. to Gov. Lamar Alexander; pres., CEO Gannett Found., 1989—97; chmn., CEO The Freedom Forum (formerly Gannett Found.), Newseum & Diversity Inst., Arlington, Va., 1997—. Chmn., CEO The Newseum, Washington, The Freedom Forum First Amendment Ctr., Nashville, Arlington, Va.; mem. mgmt. com. Gannett, USA Today; bd. dirs. Com. to Protect Journalists; bd. regents Baylor U.; bd. dirs. Nat. Collegiate Athletic Assn. Found.; found. bd. U. Miss. Recipient Pulitzer Prize. Home: 555 Pennsylvania Ave Nw Washington DC 20001-2114

OVERDAHL, JAMES A., economist; b. 1958; PhD in Econs., Iowa State U., 1984. In-house cons. Strategic Petroleum, Inc., Dallas; sr. fin. analyst SEC, 1989—92; sr. fin. economist Office Comptr. of Currency, US Dept. Treasury, Commodity Futures Trading Commn., chief economist, 2002—07, SEC, 2007—. Lectr. in econs., finance U. Tex., Georgetown U., Johns Hopkins U.; adj. prof. George Wash. U. Co-author: Financial Derivatives, 2003, Understanding Futures Markets, 2003, Futures, Options, and Swaps, 2007; contbr. articles to profl. jours. Office: SEC 100 F St NE Washington DC 20549

OVERGAARD, CORDELL JERSILD, lawyer, rancher, director; b. Chgo., June 1, 1934; s. Kristin and Rose Marie (Jersild) Overgaard; m. Gail A. Gill, Sept. 5, 1959; children: Diane, Karen, Susan. BS with honors, U. Ill., 1957; LLB magna cum laude, Harvard U., 1960. CPA Ill.; bar: Ill. 1960. Assoc. Hopkins & Sutter, Chgo., 1960—67, ptnr., 1967—96, chmn. bus. fin. sect.; chmn., CEO SNG Internet Innovations LLC, 2005—. Dir. mem. exec. com. UPI, Inc., 1982—83; pres. Cmty. Cablevision, Inc., 1980—86, Gore-Overgaard Broadcasting, Inc., 1986—; pres. bd. trustees NorthCare, 1979—81; sec. Family Weekly, Inc., 1976—80; dir. Prudential Health Care Plan, Inc., 1980—89, Cahners Pub. Co., 1970—74; dir., v.p. Small Newspaper Group, Inc., 1981—; prin. mem. Rancho Paso Grande LLC (RanchoPasoGrande-.com); exec. com. mem. Paso Fino Horse Assn., 2005—07. Editor: Harvard Law Rev., 1960. Mem. Ill. Bd. Ethics, 1973—76, chmn., 1976—80. Mem.: Chgo. Bar Assn. (chmn. corp. law com. 1972—73), February Group, Alpha Delta Phi, Beta Alpha Psi, Beta Gamma Sigma. Home: 11310 E Arabian Park Dr Scottsdale AZ 85259-4913

OVERGAARD, WILLARD MICHELE, retired political scientist; b. Montpelier, Idaho, Oct. 16, 1925; s. Elias Nielsen and Myrtle LaVerne (Humphrey) O.; m. Lucia Clare Cochrane, June 14, 1946; children: Eric Willard, Mark Fredrik, Alisa Claire. BA, U. Oreg., 1949; MA, U. Wis., 1955; PhD in Polit. Sci., U. Minn., 1969. Instr., Soviet and internat. affairs Intelligence Sch., U.S. Army, Europe, 1956-62, dir. intelligence rsch. tng. program, 1958-61; asst. prof. internat. affairs George Washington U., 1964-67; sr. staff polit. scientist Ops. Rsch. Inst., U.S. Army Inst. Advanced Studies, Carlisle, Pa., 1967-70; assoc. prof. polit. sci., chmn. dept., dir. Internat. Studies Inst., Westminster Coll., New Wilmington, Pa., 1970-72; prof. polit. sci. and pub. law Boise (Idaho) State U., 1972-94, chmn. dept., 1972-87, acad. dir. M.P.A. degree program, pers. adminstr., mem. humanities coun. interdisciplinary studies in humanities, 1976-87, prof. of pub. law emeritus, 1994—, dir. Taft Inst. Seminars for Pub. Sch. Tchrs., 1985-87, coord. Legal Asst. Program, 1990-95. Mem. comml. panel Am. Arbitration Assn., 1974—; mem. Consortium for Idaho's Future, 1974-75; adv. com. Idaho Statewide Tng. Program Local Govt. Ofcls., 1974-78; adv. group Gov. Idaho Task Force Local Govt., 1977; co-dir. Idaho State Exec. Inst., Office of Gov., 1979-83; grievance hearing officer City of Boise, 1981-85; arbitrator U.S. Postal Svc., 1988-90; cons. in field. Author: The Schematic System of Soviet Totalitarianism, 3 vols, 1961, Legal Norms and Normative Bases for the Progressive Development of International Law as Defined in Soviet Treaty Relations, 1945-64, 1969; co-author: The Communist Bloc in Europe, 1959; editor: Continuity and Change in International Politics, 1972; chief editor: Idaho Jour. Politics, 1974-76. Served with USAAF, 1943-45; with AUS, 1951-54; ret. maj. USAR. Named Disting. Citizen of Idaho, Idaho Statesman, 1979; Fulbright scholar, U. Oslo, 1949—50, Non-resident scholar, U. Wis., 1954—55, Adminstrv. fellow, U. Minn., 1955—56, Rsch. fellow, 1962—64. Mem. ABA (assoc.), Res. Officers Assn. (life), Am. Legion. Home: 2023 S Five Mile Rd Boise ID 83709-2316 Personal E-mail: wgaard@velocitus.net.

OVERHAUSER, ALBERT WARNER, physicist; b. San Diego, Aug. 17, 1925; s. Clarence Albert and Gertrude Irene (Pehrson) Overhauser; m. Margaret Mary Casey, Aug. 25, 1951; children: Teresa, Catherine, Joan, Paul, John, David, Susan, Steven. AB, U. Calif., Berkeley, 1948, PhD, 1951; DSc (hon.), U. Chgo., 1979; LLD (hon.), Simon Fraser U., 1998; DSc (hon.), Purdue U., 2005. Rsch. assoc. U. Ill., 1951—53; asst. prof. physics Cornell U., 1953—56, assoc. prof., 1956—58; supr. solid state physics Ford Motor Co., Dearborn, Mich., 1958—62, mgr. theoret. scis., 1962—69, asst. dir. phys. scis., 1969—72, dir. phys. scis., 1972—73; prof. physics Purdue U., West Lafayette, Ind., 1973—74, Stuart disting. prof. physics, 1974—2004, Stuart disting. prof. emeritus, 2004—. With USNR, 1944—46. Recipient Alexander von Humboldt sr. U.S. scientist award, 1979, Nat. medal of Sci., Pres. of U.S., 1994, Russell Varian prize, European Congress Magnetic Resonance, 2009. Fellow: Am. Acad. Arts and Scis., Am. Phys. Soc. (Oliver E. Buckley Solid State Physics prize 1975); mem.: NAS. Home: 236 Pawnee Dr West Lafayette IN 47906-2115 Office: Purdue U Dept Of Physics West Lafayette IN 47907 Home Phone: 765-463-4662; Office Phone: 765-494-3037. Business E-Mail: awo@purdue.edu.

OVERHOLT, HUGH ROBERT, lawyer, retired military officer; b. Beebe, Ark., Oct. 29, 1933; s. Harold R. and Cuma E. (Hall) O.; m. Laura Annell Arnold, May 5, 1961; children: Sharon, Scott. Student, Coll. of Ozarks, 1951-53; BA, U. Ark., 1955, LL.B., 1957. Bar: Ark. 1957. Commd. 1st lt. U.S. Army, 1957, advanced through grades to maj. gen., 1981; chief Criminal Law Div., JAG Sch., Charlottesville, Va., 1971-73; chief personnel, plans and tng. Office of JAG, U.S. Army, Washington, 1973-75; staff judge adv. XVIII Airborne Corps, Ft. Bragg, NC, 1976-78; spl. asst. for legal and selected policy matters Office of Dep. Asst., 1978-79; asst. judge adv. gen. for mil. law Office of JAG, Washington, 1979-81, asst. judge adv. gen., 1981-85, judge adv. gen, 1985-89; atty. Ward & Smith, New Bern, NC, 1989—. Notes and comment editor Ark. Law Rev, 1956-57. Decorated Army Meritorious Service medal with oak leaf cluster, Army Commendation medal with 2 oak leaf clusters., Legion of Merit, Def. Meritorious Service medal, D.S.M. Mem. ABA, N.C. Bar Assn., Ark. Bar Assn., Assn. U.S. Army, Delta Theta Phi, Omicron Delta Kappa, Sigma Pi. Presbyterian. Office: Ward and Smith 1001 College Ct New Bern NC 28562-4972 Office Phone: 252-672-5400. Business E-Mail: hro@wardandsmith.com.

OVERLIE, MARY G., choreographer, theater educator; b. Terry, Mont, Jan. 15, 1946; d. Olau Richard and Elaine Elizabeth Overlie. Merce canning ham, San Francisco, 1968; Suzunne Linke, Tanz Wochen Wocri, Viennce, Australia, 1989. Founder Danspace, NYC, 1978, Movement Rsch., NYC, 1978, hon. bd. mem., 1998—2008; 1st faculty Exptl. Theater Orgn., NYC, 1978; founder, adminstr. Pre Seasons, Viennce, 1989; arto progerson Exptl. Theatre Wing, NYC, 2006. Mentor, dirs., 1994—2008. Author: I Was a Wild Indian, Six Viewpoints Chapter in Training the American Actor, Six Viewpoints a Re-Evolution of Theater. Avocations: dance, reading, skiing. Office: NYU 721 Broadway New York NY 10003-6807 Personal E-mail: m.overlie02@aol.com.

OVERMAN, ANN CATHLENE, school librarian, educator; b. El Paso, Tex., Nov. 22, 1963; d. Joy and Dan Overman. MA in Christian Edn., Dallas Theol. Sem., 2000. Cert. classroom tchr. State Bd. Edn., 1990, in ESL State Bd. Edn., 2001, libr. State Bd. Edn., 2007. 2nd grade classroom tchr. El Paso ISD, 1990—95; 1st grade classroom tchr. Casa View Bapt. Sch., Dallas, 1997—99; 2nd and 3rd grade tchr. Carrollton-farmers Br. ISD, Tex., 2000—02; 3rd grade tchr. Dallas ISD, 2003—04, 6th grade tchr., 2004—05, libr., 2005—. Internat. missionary First Bapt. Ch. Carrollton, 2000—08. Mem.: Parent Teacher's Assn., SAM'S Club (Tchr. of Yr. award 2001), Kappa Delta Pi. Avocations: travel, reading, scrapbooks, piano. Office: John Ireland Elem 1515 N Jim Miller Dallas TX 75217 Personal E-mail: aovrm@verizon.net. Business E-Mail: aoverman@dallasisd.org.

OVERMAN, DEAN LEE, lawyer, investor, writer; b. Cook County, Ill., Oct. 9, 1943; s. Harold Levon and Violet Elsa (True) O.; m. Linda Jane Olsen, Sept. 6, 1969; children: Elisabeth True, Christiana Hart. BA, Hope Coll., 1965; student, Princeton Sem. and U., 1965-66; JD, U. Calif., Berkeley, 1969; postgrad. in bus., U. Chgo., 1974, U. Calif. Bar: Ill. 1969, D.C. 1977. Assoc. to ptnr. D'Ancona, Pflaum et al., Chgo., 1970-75; White House fellow, asst. to v.p. Nelson Rockefeller, Washington, 1975-76; assoc. dir. Domestic Council The White House, Washington, 1976-77; sr. ptnr., ptnr.-in-charge Winston & Strawn, Washington, 1977—. Cons. White House; spl. counsel to Gov. James Thompson, Springfield, Ill.; faculty in secured financing U. Va. Law Sch., Charlottesville; vice chmn. J.F. Forstmann Co.; chmn. Holland Investment Co.; adj. fellow Ctr. for Strategic and Internat. Studies, 1993-95; vis. scholar, officer Harvard U., 1994-95; Templeton scholar Oxford U., 1999—2005, chmn. adv. bd. First Trust Portfolios, LP Author: Toward a National Policy on State and Local Government Finance, 1976, Effective Writing Techniques, 1980, (with others) Financing Equipment, 1973, Sales and Financing Under the Revised UCC, 1975, A Case Against Accident and Self Organization, 1997, A Case for the Existence of God, 2009, Valuation of a Business, 2000; monthly newspaper column Chgo. Daily Law Bull.; contbr. articles to profl. jours. Commencement spkr. Hope Coll., Holland, Mich., 1978; bd. dirs. Internat. Bus. Inst., White House Fellows Assn., Cmtys. in Schs., Inc.; adv. bd. The Beacon Group; former bd. dirs. U.S. Decathlon Assn. Reginald Heber Smith fellow U. Pa., 1969-70. Mme. Mensa, Intertel, ABA, Ill. Bar Assn., DC Bar Assn., Chgo. Bar Assn., Met. Club (DC), Internat. Soc. Philos. Enquiry, Triple Nine Soc., Burning Tree Club (Bethesda, Md.), Congl. Country Club (Bethesda), Harvard Club of NYC, Macatawa (Mich.) Bay Yacht Club. Office: 4900 Glenbrook Rd NW Washington DC 20016

OVERMAN, LINDA RADER, literature and language professor, writer; b. Hollywood, Calif., Apr. 18, 1951; d. William James Rader and Henriette Balague; m. James Marvyn Overman, June 23, 1978; children: Michael James, Deva Marie. BA, Calif. State U. Northridge, 1997, MA, 2001; MFA, Calif. State U. Chico, 2003. Prof. Calif. State U. Northridge, 2001—. Author: (novel) Letters Between Us (Best Books award, 2008). Mem.: Golden Key, Sigma Tau Delta. Home Fax: 818-906-1029. Personal E-mail: loverman.writes@yahoo.com. Business E-Mail: loverman@csun.edu.

OVERMIER, J. BRUCE, psychology professor; s. James J. Wheelwright and Emma Annette (Carlton) Overmier Jacobson; m. Judith Ann Smith, Aug. 19, 1962; 1 child, Larisa Nicole. BA, Kenyon Coll., 1960; MA, Bowling Green State U., 1962; PhD, U. Pa., 1965; DSc (hon.), Kenyon Coll., 1990, U. Montreal, 2008, U. Bergen, Norway, 2008. Prof. psychology U. Minn., Mpls., 1965—. Mem. adv. bd. NSF, Washington, 1976-79, 86, USPHS, Washington, 1988-92; exec. bd. mem. Internat. Coun. Sci., 2008-; editl. bd. mem. Applied Psychology: Health & Well Being. Co-author: (with others) Animal Learning: Survey and Analysis, 1979; editor: Learning and Motivation, 1973-76, Affect, Conditioning and Cognition, 1985, Animal Research and Human Health, 2001; cons. editor: Jour. Exptl. Psychology, 1971-74, 88-2004; mem. editl. bd. Behavioral Brain Rsch., 1979-84; editl. bd. Review Gen. Psychology; contbr. over 200 chpts. to books and articles to jours. Recipient W. Horsely Gantt medal Pavlovian Soc., 2003, Outstanding Contributions award Minn. Psychol. Assn., 2004, John P. Zubek award U. Manitoba, 2006, award U. Aconcagua, Argentina, 2007; Grantee NIMH/NICHD, 1966-2003, NSF, 1966-83, 87-93; Fulbright Hays scholar, 1980, Scholar of the Coll., U. Minn., 1989-92; Fogarty Ctr. USPHS fellow, 1984, James McKeen Cattell Found. fellow, 1985, Joseph P. Kennedy found. fellow, 1989. Fellow APA (council 1987-97, 2006-pres. divsn. comparative psychology 1991, pres. divsn. experimental psychology 1993, bd. dirs. 1999-2004, pres. divsn. gen. psychology 2003, Disting Svc. award in Begavioral Neurosci. 2002, Neal E. Miller award 2004, Disting. Svc. to Psychol. Sci. award 2005); mem. AAUP (local pres. 1981), Midwestern Psychol. Assn. (council 1984-87, pres. 1987), Psychonomics Soc. (sec.-treas. 1981-83, bd. govs. 1983-88), Internat. Union Psychological Sci. (exec. 1993-2004, pres. 2004-08), Pavlovian Soc. (pres. 1996-97), Delta Kappa Epsilon, Sigma Xi (Disting. Lectr. 1999-2001). Avocation: skiing. Office: Psychology Dept Univ Minn 75 East River Terr Minneapolis MN 55455 Office Phone: 612-625-1835. Office Fax: 612-626-2079. Business E-Mail: psyjbo@umn.edu.

OVERMYER, DANIEL LEE, humanities educator; b. Columbus, Ohio, Aug. 20, 1935; s. Elmer Earl and Bernice Alma (Hesselbart) O.; m. Estella Velazquez, June 19, 1965; children: Rebecca Lynn, Mark Edward. BA, Westmar Coll., LeMars, Iowa, 1957; BD, Evang. Theol. Sem., Naperville, Ill., 1960; MA, U. Chgo., 1966, PhD, 1971. Pastor Evangel. United Brethren Ch., Chgo., 1960-64; asst. prof. dept. religion Oberlin (Ohio) Coll., 1970-73; prof. Asian studies U. B.C., Vancouver, Canada, 1973—2000, acting head religious studies, 1984-85, head Asian studies, 1986-91, prof. emeritus, Asian Studies and Ctr. Chinese Rsch., 2000—. Vis. prof. Princeton (N.J.) U., 1983, U. Heidelberg, Heidelberg, Germany, 1993, Nat. Chengchi U., Taiwan, 2002; prof. Chinese U., Hong Kong, 1996—98; hon. prof. Shanghai Normal U., China, 1997—. Author: Folk Buddhist Religion, 1976, 2005, Religions of China, 1986; author: (with David Jordan) The Flying Phoenix, 1986, 2005; author: Precious Volumes: An Introduction to Chinese Sectarian Scriptures From the Sixteenth and Seventeenth Centuries, 1999; editor: Ethnography in China Today: A Critical Assessment of Methods and Results, 2002, Religion in China Today, 2003; editor spl. issue: The China Quar.; contbr. articles to encys. and profl. jours. Chmn. Sch. Consultative Com., Vancouver, 1976-77; coord. Vancouver Boys Soccer League, 1979-81; adult edn. coord. United Ch. Can., Vancouver, 1981-84; co-chmn. Endowment Lands Regional Park Com., 1987-90; co-chair China and Inner Asia Coun., Assn. Asian Studies, 1992—. With USNR, 1953-61. Recipient Killam faculty rsch. prize U. B.C., 1986, Killiam faculty tchg. prize, 2000; named Alumnus of Yr., U. Chgo. Divinity Sch., 2001; NEH fellow, 1978, 79, China Rsch. fellow, 1981, sr. fellow coun. humanities Princeton U., 1983, Wang Inst. Grad. Studies fellow, 1985-86. Fellow Royal Soc. Can.; mem. Am. Soc. Study Religion, Soc. Study Chinese Religions (pres. 1985-88), Assn. Asian Studies. Democrat. Avocations: photography, swimming, hiking, gardening, birdwatching. Home: 3393 W 26th Ave Vancouver BC Canada V6S 1N4 Office: UBC Ctr Chinese Rsch Vancouver BC Canada V6T 1Z2 E-mail: eodano@shaw.ca.

OVERSTREET, CATHERINE ANN, sales executive; b. Richlands, Va., Dec. 27, 1970; d. Garnet Edward Taylor and Mary Ann Jones, Samuel Powell Jones (Stepfather) and Anita Taylor (Stepmother); m. James Edward Overstreet, Sept. 10, 1995; 1 child, Ashley Ann Taylor. BS in Bus. Adminstrn., Regent Internat. U., Miami, Fla., 2006. Inside sales coord. King Pharms., Bristol, Tenn., 2003—. Mem.: PDMA Alliance. Home: 601 Southview Rd Bristol TN 37620 Office: King Pharmas 501 5th St Bristol TN 37620

OVERSTREET, REGINA NIX, mathematics educator; b. Dawsonville, Ga., Feb. 13, 1946; d. Vernon Stancel and Jewell Fouts Nix; m. James Edward Overstreet, Sr., June 27, 1970; children: Jennifer Overstreet Flacke, James Edward Jr. BS in Edn., U. of Ga., Athens, 1968; MEd, Ga. State U., Atlanta, 1979. Math. tchr. Clayton County Schs., Jonesboro, Ga., 1968—70, Marietta City Schs., Ga., 1970—71, Cobb County Schs., Marietta, 1971—81; adj. math instr. Kennesaw State U., Ga., 1986—99; math. instr. Chattahoochee Tech. Coll., Marietta, 2004—. Pres. bd. of edn. Transfiguration Cath. Ch., Marietta, 1983—84. Named Tchr. of the Yr., Sprayberry H.S. Key Club, 1979. Mem.: Am. Math. Assn. of 2-Yr. Colls., Ga. Assn. for Devel. Edn., Nat. Assn. for Devel. Edn. Roman Catholic. Avocation: tennis. Office: Chattahoochee Tech Coll 980 S Cobb Dr Marietta GA 30060 Office Fax: 770-528-4584; Home Fax: 770-528-4584. Business E-Mail: roverstreet@chattcollege.com.

OVERTON, EDWIN DEAN, retired campus minister, educator; b. Dec. 2, 1939; s. William Edward and Georgia Beryl (Fronk) O. BTh, Midwest Christian Coll., 1963; MA in Religion, Ea. N.Mex. U., 1969, EdS, 1978; postgrad., Fuller Theol. Sem., 1980. Ordained to ministry Christian Ch., 1978. Min. Christian Ch., Englewood, Kans., 1962-63; youth min. 1st Christian Ch., Beaver, Okla., 1963-67; campus min. Cen. Christian Ch., Portales, N.Mex., 1967-68, Christian Campus House, Portales, 1968—2005; acting chmn. religion dept. Ea. N.Mex. U., Portales, 2000, tchr. religion, philosophy, counseling, 1970—2005; ret. Dir. Campus Christian House, 1980-2005; farm and ranch partner, Beaver, Okla., 1963—; guide Beaver HS Cl. 57 Bus Tour, 2008. Editor: (book) The Christian Campus House at Eastern New Mexico University (1968-2005), 2008. State dir. Beaver Jr. C. of C., 1964-65; pres. Beaver H.S. Alumni Assn., 1964-65; elder Cen. Christian Ch., Portales, 1985-88, 90-93; chmn. Beaver County March of Dimes, 1966; neighborhood chmn. Portales March of Dimes, 1997; pres. Portales Tennis Assn., 1977-78. Mem. U.S. Tennis Assn., Am. Assn. Christian Counselors, Ea. N.Mex. U. Faith in Life Com., Lions Club. Republican. Home: 1129 Libra Dr Portales NM 88130-6123 Home Phone: 505-359-0608. E-mail: campusmin@juno.com.

OVERTON, MARCUS LEE, performing arts association administrator, actor, writer; b. Calhoun, Ga., Aug. 13, 1943; s. Marcus Burl, Jr. and Eva Mae (Greene) Overton. BS in Speech and Theatre, Northwestern U., 1965. Actor, tchr. Southeastern Shakespeare Festival, Atlanta, 1965; actor, co. mgr. Eagles Mere Assocs. Repertory Co., Chgo., 1966; prodn. stage mgr. Lyric Opera Chgo., 1966-72; mgr. Ravinia Festival, Highland Park, Ill., 1973-77; performing arts program mgr. Smithsonian Instn., Washington, 1983-92; exec. dir., prod. dir. Spoleto Festival U.S.A., Charleston, SC, 1992-94; program prodr., host Who Do You Know S.C. Pub. Radio, Charleston, 1994-97; instr. theatre and arts mgmt. Coll. Charleston, 1995-97. Adv. panelist Nat. Endowments Arts, 1977—79, DC Commn. Arts and Humanities, 1989, 90, 92; narrator talking books Libr. Congress, Washington, 1982—83; bd. dirs. Performing Arts Assistance Corp., 1992—97; con. in field. Prodr.: Falstaff (LA Philharm.), 1981—82; prodr., host Spoleto Today, S.C. Pub. Radio, 1996—, Supertitles, San Diego Opera, 1999—2003; prodr.: Inside Spoleto, 2001— (Emmy award, 2004). Scholar, Northwestern U., 1961—65. Mem.: La Jolla Music Soc. (artistic adminstr. 2006—07), Actors Alliance San Diego (bd. pres. 2001—02, chmn. 2003—06, announcer XLNC1-FM 2004—). Avocations: travel, prehistoric cave art, motorcycle touring, linguistics, French culture. Address: 5581-A Adobe Falls Rd San Diego CA 92120 Home Phone: 619-286-5581. Personal E-mail: smoketree13@juno.com.

OVERTON, TIM, chemical engineer; BS in Chem. Engring, U. Tex., Austin, 1981. Cert. profl. engr., Tex., 1993. Chief process safety engr. The Dow Chem. Co., Freeport, Tex., 1999—. Office: The Dow Chem Co 2301 N Brazosport Blvd B-101 Freeport TX 77541

OVERTON, WILLIS F., psychology professor; s. Willis and Gladys Overton; m. Carol Groves, July 19, 1991; children: Laura Baller, Leslie Mihok. PhD, Clark U., Worcester, Mass., 1967. Chmn., dept. psychology Temple U., Phila., 2001—07, Thaddeus L. Bolton prof., psychology, 1972—. Pvt. practice, Phila., 1986—2008. Author: (book) Developmental Perspective on Embodiment and Consciousness.; contbr. chapters to books. Pres. South St. Neighborhood Assn., Phila., 1986—93. Sgt. US Marine Corps, 1953—56, Camp LeJeune, NC. Recipient award, City Coun., Phila., 1993. Fellow: APA (assoc. editor, devel. psychology 1978); mem.: Soc. Rsch. Child Devel. (editor 2000—06), Jean Piaget Soc. (pres. 1979—80, bd. dirs.). Home: 978 Swayze Ave Washington Crossing PA 18977 Office: Temple Univ Psychology Dept 1701 N 13th Philadelphia PA 19122 Business E-Mail: overton@temple.edu.

OVERTON-ADKINS, BETTY JEAN, foundation administrator; b. Jacksonville, Fla., Oct. 10, 1949; d. Henry and Miriam (Gordon) Crawford; children from previous marriage: Joseph Alonzo III, Jermaine Lamar; m. Eugene Adkins, Apr. 24, 1992. BA in English, Tenn. State U., 1970, MA in English, 1974; PhD in English, Vanderbilt U., 1980; student Inst. Ednl. Mgmt., Harvard U., 1990. Reporter Race Rels. Reporter Mag., Nashville, 1970-71; tchr. Met. Nashville Sch. System, 1971-72; instr., project dir. Tenn. State U., Nashville, 1972-76; asst. prof. Nashville State Tech. Inst., 1976-78, Fisk U., Nashville, 1978-83; assoc. dean. grad. sch. U. Ark., Little Rock, 1983-85, dean grad. sch., 1985-91; program dir. Kellogg Found., Battle Creek, Mich., 1991—; asst. dir. Kellogg Nat. Fellowship Program, Battle Creek, Mich., 1991-94; coord. higher edn. programs Kellogg Found., Battle Creek, 1994—. Instr. U. Tenn., Nashville, 1976-82; dir. rsch. sponsored programs U. Ark., 1986-88; bd. dirs. Ark. Sci. and Info. Liaison Office, 1984-91. Bd. dirs. Ark. Sci. and Tech. Authority, Little Rock, 1989—, Women's Project, 1986—, Ark. Pub. Policy Panel, 1988-91, No. Bank Women's Adv. Bd., 1988-91, Nashville Panel, 1974-83, Ctrl. Ark. Libr. Sys., 1990-91, Ark. coun. NCCJ, 1990-92, Bread for World, 1990-95; mem. Commn. on Edn. Credits and Credentials, Am. Coun. on Edn., 1989-95; chmn. bi-racial adv. com. Little Rock Sch. Dist., 1987— Fellow Am. Coun. Edn., 1981-82, W.K. Kellogg Found., 1988-93. Mem. Nat. Coun. Tchrs. of English, Coun. Grad. Schs., Coun. So. Grad. Schs., Women Color United Against Domestic Violence (pres.), An. Assn. High Edn., Rotary, Alpha Kappa Alpha. Democrat. Roman Catholic. Office: W K Kellogg Found One Michigan Ave E Battle Creek MI 49017

OVITZ, MICHAEL S., communications executive; b. Chgo., Dec. 14, 1946; m. Judy Reich, 1969; children Christopher, Kimberly, Eric. Grad., UCLA, 1968. With William Morris Agy., 1969—75; pres., bd. dir. Walt Disney Co., Burbank, Calif., 1995-97; co-founder, chmn. Creative Artists Agy., LA, 1975-95; principal Artists Mgmt. Group, 1998—2002; owner, principal CKE Assocs., Beverly Hills, Calif., 1998—. Chmn. exec. bd. dirs. UCLA Hosp. and Med. Ctr.; bd. advisors Sch. Theater, Film and TV UCLA; bd. dirs. Livent, Inc., Gulfstream Aero. Corp., J. Crew Group, Inc., Opsware, Inc., Yankee Candle Corp. Exec. prodr.: Gangs of NY, 2002; exec. prodr.: Timeline, 2003. Trustee Mus. Modern Art, N.Y.C.; bd. govs. Cedars-Sinai Hosp., L.A.; mem. exec. adv. bd. Pediatric AIDS Found.; bd. dir. D.A.R.E. America; nat. bd. advisors, Children's Scholarship Fund. Named one of Top 200 Collectors, ARTnews Mag., 2004—08. Mem. Coun. Fgn. Rels., Zeta Beta Tau. Avocation: art collector. Office: 2601 Colorado Ave Santa Monica CA 90404-3518

OWADA, HISASHI, judge; b. Niigata, Japan, Sept. 18, 1932; s. Takeo and Shizuka (Tamura) Owada; m. Yumiko Egashira, Oct. 7, 1962; children: Masako, Reiko, Setsuko. BA, U. Tokyo, 1955; LLB, Cambridge U., Eng., 1956. Pvt. sec. to Fgn. Min. of Japan, 1971; dir. UN polit. affairs div., 1972-74; dir. treaties div., 1974-76; pvt. sec. to Prime Min. of Japan, Tokyo, 1976-78; min. Japanese Embassy, Washington, 1979-81, Moscow, 1981-84; dir.-gen. treaties bur. and for law of sea Ministry Fgn. Affairs, 1984-87, dep. vice minister, 1987-88; amb., permanent rep. of Japan to OECD, Paris, 1988-89; dep. min. Ministry Fgn. Affairs, Tokyo, 1989-91; vice min. Fgn. Affairs of Japan, Tokyo, 1991-93; advisor Ministry Fgn. Affairs Japan, Tokyo, 1993-94; amb., permanent rep. of Japan to UN, 1994-98; prof. Waseda U., 1999—2003; advisor to Ministry Fgn. Affairs, Tokyo, 1999—2003; pres. Japan Inst. of Internat. Affairs, 1999—2003; sr. advisor to pres. of World Bank, 1999—2003; judge Permanent Ct. Arbitration, 2001—, Internat. Ct. of Justice, The Hague, Netherlands, 2003—. Adj. prof. U. Tokyo, 1963—68; vis. prof. Harvard U., Cambridge, Mass., 1979—81, 1987, 89, 1999—2002; adj. prof. internat. law Columbia U., 1994—98; Inge Rennert disting. vis. prof. NYU Global Law Sch., 1994—; academic adv. Hiroshima U., 2002—; hon. prof. Leiden U., 2006—. Author: Japanese Practice in the Field of International Law, 1984, From Involvement to Engagement, 1994, Diplomacy, 1996, A Treatise on International Relations, 2002. Bd. hon. trust UN Found., Ditchley Found. Mem.: l'Institut de Droit Internat., Internat. Law Assn., Am. Soc. Internat. Law, Japanese Assn. Internat. Law. Avocations: skiing, mountain walking, music. Office: Internat Court of Justice Peace Palace 2517 KJ The Hague Netherlands Office Phone: 31 70302 23 23. Fax: 31 70 302 2409. E-mail: h.owada@icj-cij.org.

OWEISS, IBRAHIM MOHAMED, economist, educator; b. Egypt, Sept. 25, 1931; came to U.S., 1960; s. Mohamed Zaki and Warda (Zeiden) O.; m. Celine M. J. Lesuisse, July 19, 1975; children: Yasmeen, Kareem. B.Com., Alexandria U., Egypt, 1952; MA, U. Minn., 1961, PhD, 1969. Tchr., 1953-55; econ. dir. indsl. projects Cairo, 1958-60; mem. faculty U. Minn., Mpls., 1961-67, Georgetown U., Washington, 1967—2009, prof. econs., 1973-75; mem. faculty Johns Hopkins U., 1971-74; first undersec. state econ. affairs Govt. Egypt, Cairo, 1977; ambassador, 1977-79; chief Egyptian Econ. Mission to U.S., 1977-79; prof. econs. Harvard U., 1997-98. Cons. econs., 1971—; mem. Pres. Coun. on Egyptian-Am. Rels., 1999—; mem. bd. regents Georgetown U., 2003—. Author: Pricing of Oil in World Trade, 1974, The Israeli Economy, 1974; editor: The Dynamics of U.S.-Arab Economic Relations, 1980, Economic Development of Egypt, 1982, Arab Civilization, Challenges and Responses, 1988, Political Economy of Contemporary Egypt, 1990, The Arab Gulf Economies: Challenges and Prospects, 2000, Economics: New Horizons, Shifting the Paradigm, 2001, A View on Islamic Economic Thought, 2003, A Tale of Two Cultures, 2009. Pres. Assn. Egyptian-Am. Scholars, 1984-88; chmn. bd. dirs. Arab-Am. Bus. and Profl. Assn., Howard and Georgeanna Jones Inst. for Reproductive Medicine, 1984-90, Egyptian Am. Cultural Assn., 1975-77, Faith and Hope Project, 1975-77. Officer Egyptian Army, 1955-58. Decorated Egyptian Merit decoration 1st Order, Comdr. Order of St. John, knight Order of Queen of Sheba, grand cordon Order Mohammed Ali Pasha; Ford Found. fellow, 1979-80. Mem.: Univ. Club (N.Y.C.), Cosmos Club (Washington). Muslim. Home: 4017 Glenridge St Kensington MD 20895-3708

OWEN, BERNIECE MARIE, law librarian, director; b. Parker, SD, Sept. 14, 1941; d. Leo Elton Campbell and Ellagonda Helena VanSambeek, Peter Anton DeVaal (Stepfather); m. Carlton McDuffie Owen, Aug. 16, 1965; 1 child, Sophie Owen Rich. BS, U. SD, Vermillion, 1963; MSLS, U. Southern Calif., 1964. Reference libr. Phoenix Pub. Libr., 1964—65; serials cataloger Ariz. State U. Libr., Tempe, 1965—71; acquisitions libr. Crosby Libr. Gonzaga U., Spokane, Wash., 1975—81, cataloging libr. law, 1981—86; tech. svcs. libr. Portland CC Libr., Oreg., 1986—2004, libr. dir., 2004—07; chair Friends of Portland CC Libr., 2008—. Co-owner McDuffie's Old Books, Lake Oswego, Oreg., 1965—2006. Mem. and vol. ARC, Lopez, Wash., 1972—74; founder & coord. Lopez Island Pre-Sch., 1972—73; fund raising chair, united way Portland CC, 1991—93; del. Dem. Party State Conv., Seattle, 1976—76. Mem.: Phi Beta Kappa. Office: Friends Portland CC Libr PO Box 718 Lake Oswego OR 97034-0318 Business E-Mail: berniece.owen@comcast.net.

OWEN, BRADLEY SCOTT, Lieutenant Governor of Washington; b. Tacoma, May 23, 1950; s. Laural Willis; m. Linda Knoll, Jan. 20, 1983; children: Shanie, Dana, Mark, Sherrie, Adam, Royce. Student pub. sch.,

Germany. Mem. Wash. House of Reps., Olympia, 1976-82, Wash. State Senate, Olympia, 1983-96, pres., 1997—; lt. gov. State of Wash., Olympia, 1997—. Chmn. Legis. Com. on Economic Devel.; founder, pres. Strategies for Youth. Mem. Wash. State substance abuse coun., 1997—. Mem. Elks. Democrat. Office: Office Lt Governor 220 Legislative Bldg PO Box 40400 Olympia WA 98504-0400 Office Fax: 360-786-7749. Business E-Mail: ltgov@leg.wa.gov.*

OWEN, CATHY HESSE, nanotechnology company executive; d. Albert and Margaret Hesse; m. Ronald Owen; children: Michelle, Christine. BSBA, San Jose State U., Calif., 1977. Programmer IBM, San Jose, Calif., 1978—80, tech. writing mgr., 1984—87, sr. programming mgr., 1987—95, sr. mktg. manger, 1995—99, programmer Tucson, 1980—84; dir., product mgmt. Cardonet, Inc., Santa Clara, Calif., 1999—2000; pres. hotU, Inc., Honolulu, 2000—04, Nanopoint, Inc., Honolulu, 2004—. Bd. dirs. Nanopoint, Inc., Honolulu, 2005—, hotU, Inc., Honolulu, 2002—04. Recipient Outstanding Tech. Achievement award, IBM, 1984, Outstanding Co. award, World Tech. Network, 2005; Rsch. grant, Hawaii Tech. Devel. Venture, 2005—06. Mem.: Women In Tech. (assoc.), NanoBioNexus (assoc.). Office: Nanopoint Inc 900 Fort Street Mall Ste A20 Honolulu HI 96813 Office Fax: 808-537-4245.

OWEN, CHUCK, composer, music educator; b. Norfolk, Va. Grad., Calif. State U., Northridge; MusB in music edn., U. North Tex. Disting. prof. jazz studies U. South Fla., Tampa, founding dir. Ctr. Jazz Composition; founder, condr. the Jazz Surge, Fla., 1995—. Recipient Pres.'s award for Faculty Excellence, U. South Fla., 2003; fellow John Simon Guggenheim Meml. Found., 2009. Mem.: ASCAP, Internat. Assn. Jazz Edn. (past. nat. composition chmn., past. pres. Fla. state unit). Office: U South Fla Sch Music 4202 E Fowler Ave Tampa FL 33620 Office Phone: 813-989-0880. E-mail: owen@arts.usf.edu.*

OWEN, CLIVE, actor; b. Keresley, Warwickshire, Eng., Oct. 3, 1964; m. Sarah-Jane Fenton, Mar. 6, 1995; children: Hannah, Eve. Various stage roles including: Design for the Living, The Day in the Death of Joe Egg; actor: (films) Vroom, 1988, Close My Eyes, 1991, Century, 1993, The Turnaround, 1994, The Rich Man's Wife, 1996, Bent, 1997, Croupier, 1998, Greenfingers, 2000, Ambush, 2001, Chosen, 2001, Star, 2001, The Follow, 2001, Powder Keg, 2001, Godsford Park, 2001, The Bourne Identity, 2002, Hostage, 2002, Beat the Devil, 2002, Ticker, 2002, I'll Sleep When I'm Dead, 2003, Beyond Borders, 2003, King Arthur, 2004, Closer, 2004 (Golden Globe award for best supporting actor, 2005), Sin City, 2005, Derailed, 2005, The Pink Panther, 2006, Inside Man, 2006, Shoot 'Em Up, 2007, Elizabeth: The Golden Age, 2007, The International, 2009, Duplicity, 2009; (TV films) Precious Bane, 1989, Lorna Doone, 1990, Class of '61, 1993, The Magician, 1993, An Evening with Gary Lineker, 1994, Nobody's Children, 1994, Doomsday Gun, 1994, The Echo, 1998, Second Sight, 1999, Second Sight: Parasomnia, 2000, Second Sight: Kingdom of the Blind, 2000, Second Sight: Hide and Seek, 2000; (TV series) Capital City, 1989—90, Chancer, 1990, Sharman, 1996. Office: c/o 42 West 11400 W Olympic Blvd Los Angeles CA 90064

OWEN, CYNTHIA CAROL, sales executive; b. Ft. Worth, Oct. 16, 1943; d. Charlie Bounds and Bernice Vera (Nunley) Rhoads; m. Franklin Earl Owen, Oct. 20, 1961 (div. Jan. 1987); children: Jeffrey Wayne, Valeria Ann, Carol Darlena, Pamela Kay; m. John Edward White, Jan. 1, 1988 (div. Sept. 1991), m. John Wayne Napier, Nov. 26, 2002. Cert. Keypuncher, Comml. Coll., 1963; student, Tarrant County Jr. Coll., 1974-77; BBA in Mgmt., U. Tex., Arlington, 1981. Keypunch operator Can-Tex. Industries, Mineral-Wells, 1966-67; sec. Electro-Midland Corp., Mineral-Wells, 1967-68; exec. sec. to v.p. sales Pangburn Co., Inc., Ft. Worth, 1972-78; bookkeeper, sec. CB Svc., Ft. Worth, 1978-82; project mgr. Square D Co., Carrollton, Tex., 1982—. Mem.: NAFE, NOW, AAUW. Baptist. Home: 1221 Pine Ridge Rd Roanoke TX 76262 Office: 1650 W Crosby Rd Carrollton TX 75006-6628 Business E-Mail: cindy.owen@us.schneider-electric.com.

OWEN, DUNCAN SHAW, JR., internist, retired educator; b. Fayetteville, NC, Oct. 24, 1935; s. Duncan S. and Mary Gwyn (Hickerson) O.; m. Irene Lacy Rose, Oct. 22, 1966; children: Duncan Shaw III, Robert Burwell, Frances Gwyn. BS in Medicine, U. N.C., 1957, MD, 1960. Diplomate Am. Bd. Internal Medicine (proctor 1977-97). Intern Med. Coll. Va., Richmond, 1960-61; jr. asst. resident in medicine N.C. Meml. Hosp., Chapel Hill, 1961-62; asst. resident in medicine Med. Coll. Va., Richmond, 1964-65, fellow in rheumatic diseases, 1965-66; internal medicine and rheumatology physician Richmond, Va., 1966—; from instr. in medicine to assoc. prof. Med. Coll. Va., Richmond, 1966-78, prof. dept. internal medicine, 1978—; Taliaferro/Scott Disting. prof. internal medicine Med. Coll. Va., Va. Commonwealth U., 1989-2000, emeritus prof., 2000—; dir. residency tng. Med. Coll. Va. Hosp.; dir. rheumatology clinics. Dir. clin. tng. divsn. rheumatology, allergy, immunology, 1975-98, chmn. clin. activities comm., dept. internal medicine, 1970-90; chmn. med. adv. com. Richmond br. Arthritis Found., 1966-75, nat. patient edn. com., 1979-80; med. advisor Social Security Adminstrn., HHS, 1967-2004; co-chmn. arthritis project Va. Regional Med. Program, 1975-76; prodr. Your Health TV series Va. Ednl. TV, 1978-79; prodr. Update in Medicine, Good Morning Virginia TV show, 1980; cons. McGuire VA. Contbr. articles to profl. jours.; assoc. editor: Va. Med., 1978-98; editl. reviewer Jour. AMA, 1979—, Arthritis Rheumatism, 1981-2004, Jour. Rheumatology, 1984—. Mem. usher's guild First Presbyn. Ch., Richmond, Va., 1966-70, deacon, 1974-77, chmn. of diaconate, 1976-77, elder, 1978—, chmn. witness com., 1978-80; co-chmn. physicians statewide capital funds campaign Va. Commn. U., 1986-87; bd. dirs. Mooreland Farms Assn., 1971-73, 77-81, Va. chpt. Arthitis Found., 1970-85; mem. Va. Mus., Richmond Symphony; bd. dirs. Richmond Area Health Care Coalition, 1980-84. Med. officer US Army, 1962—63, Womack Army Hosp., Fort Bragg, NC, post surgeon, asst. divsn. surgeon US Army, 1963—64, Camp Kaiser, Korea. Decorated Army Commendation medal; recipient Gerard B. Lambert award, 1974-75, Disting. Svc. award Arthritis Found., 1971, U. N.C., Chapel Hill, 1999; Nat. Inst. Arthritis and Metabolic Diseases fellow, 1965-66 Fellow ACP (Laureate award 1997), Am. Coll. Rheumatology; mem. AMA (expert on diagnostic and therapeutic tech. assessment program 1990-99), Am. Rheumatism Assn. (exec. com. 1979-80), Richmond Acad. Medicine (pres. 1982, chmn. bd. 1983, parliamentarian 1988-99), Med. Soc. Va. (com. on aging 1980-89, v.p. 1973, 75, del. 1972-99, scholarship com. 1980-89), Richmond Soc. Internal Medicine (bd. dirs. 1971-73), Met. Richmond C. of C. (bd. dirs. 1981-84), Jr. Clin. Club (emeritus), Custis Hunting and Fishing Club, Alpha Omega Alpha Honor Med. Soc. Presbyn. Achievements include development of techniques for arthrocenteses; cellophane tape polarizing microscopic compensator for identifying crystals in joint fluid. Avocations: hunting, fishing, photography, amateur radio. Home: 8910 Brieryle Rd Richmond VA 23229-7704 Personal E-mail: dowen75089@aol.com.

OWEN, EDWARD ROGER JOHN (E. ROGER OWEN), Middle Eastern studies professor, writer; MA, Oxford U., Eng., DPhil, 1964. Dir. Mid. East Ctr. St. Antony's Coll., Oxford U., England, emeritus fellow; A.J. Meyer Prof. Mid. Ea. History Harvard U., Cambridge, Mass., 1993—, dir. Ctr. Mid. Ea. Studies, 1996—99, dir. Contemporary Arab Studies Program, 1995—. Co-author (with Sevket Pamuk): (books) A History of the Middle East Economics in the 20th Century, 1998; author: Cotton and the Egyptian Economy, 1820-1914: A Study in Trade and Development, 1969, The Middle East in the World Economy 1800-1914, 1981, State, Power and Politics in the Making of the Modern Middle East, 1992, 2000, 2004, Lord Cromer: Victorian Imperialist: Edwardian Proconsul, 2004. Fellow: Am. Acad. Arts & Scis. Office: Harvard U Ctr Mid Ea Studies 1430 Massachusetts Ave Cambridge MA 02138

OWEN, ELIZABETH MARIE, art historian, educator; d. James E. and Frances R. Owen. BA, Bryn Mawr Coll., Pa., 1985; MA, MPhil, PhD, Yale U., New Haven, 2005. Instr. East Asian art history U. Colo., Boulder, 2002—05; asst. prof., Asian art history U. Denver, 2005—. Part-time acting instr., head tchg. asst. dept. art history Yale U., New Haven, 1994—2001, rsch. asst. Silk Rd. project, 1997—98; adj. prof. art history So. Conn. State U., New Haven, 1995—2002, U. Conn., Storrs, 2000—02, Waterbury, 2000—01, Stamford, 2000—01; adj. prof., art history St. Joseph U., Hartford, Conn., 2001—01, Ctrl. Conn. State U., New Britain, 2000—01; curatorial asst. Asian art dept. Yale U. Art Gallery, New Haven, 1997—98, Andrew W. Mellon curatorial asst. Asian art dept., 1994—95. Exhibition organizer Across Cultures: Foreign Influences in Asian Art, Yale U. Art Gallery, Selections of Chinese and Japanese Art; contbg. author: Three Thousand Years of Chinese Painting. Mem. alumni schs. com. Yale U.; chmn. alumnae admissions rep. com. Colo., Bryn Mawr Coll., 2006—. Recipient Outstanding Tchg. award, Tchr. of Yr., So. Conn. State U., 2001; fellow Lehman Grant for pre-dissertation rsch., Yale U., 1994, Mellon pre-doctoral fellow, 1996; U. fellow, 1993—97, Fgn. Lang. and Area Studies fellow, U. Pa., 1992—93, Andrew W. Mellon pre-dissertation fellowship, Yale U., 1994, 1995, 1997—98, Summer Travel and Rsch. grantee, 1997, Mellon pre-doctoral fellow, 1998—99, Louise Wallace Hackney fellow, Am. Oriental Soc., 1999—2000, Dissertation Rsch. Supplementary grantee, Yale U., 1998—2000. Mem.: Assn. Asian Studies (Svc. award 2005), Coll. Art Assn., AAUP. Office: U Denver 2121 E Asbury Ave Denver CO 80208 Office Fax: 303-871-4112. Business E-Mail: elizabeth.owen@aya.yale.edu.

OWEN, GUILLERMO, mathematician, educator; b. Bogota, Colombia, May 4, 1938; came to U.S., 1961; s. Gilberto and Cecilia (Salazar); m. Maria Mercedes Londoño, Aug. 26, 1961; children: Maria Christina, Claudia. BS, Fordham U., 1958; PhD, Princeton U., 1962. Asst. prof., assoc. prof. Fordham U., NYC, 1961-69; assoc. prof., prof. Rice U., Houston, 1969-78; prof. U. Andes, Bogota, Colombia, 1978-82, Naval Postgrad. Sch., Monterey, Calif., 1983—. Author: Game Theory, 1982; contbr. articles to profl. jours. Mem. Colombian Acad. Scis., Catalonian Acad. Arts and Scis., Third World Acad. Scis. Avocations: golf, tennis, coin collecting/numismatics. Office: Naval Postgrad Sch Monterey CA 93943 Home: 1333 Jones St Apt 802 San Francisco CA 94109-4112

OWEN, H. MARTYN, retired lawyer; b. Decatur, Ill., Oct. 23, 1929; s. Honore Martyn and Virginia (Hunt) O.; m. Candace Catlin Benjamin, June 21, 1952; children: Leslie W., Peter H., Douglas P. AB, Princeton U., NJ, 1951; LLB, Harvard U., 1954. Bar: Conn. 1954, U.S. Ct. Appeals (2d cir.) 1961, U.S. Dist. Ct. Conn. 1962, U.S. Supreme Ct. 1963, U.S. Dist. Ct. Vt. 1975. Assoc. Shipman & Goodwin, Hartford, Conn., 1958-61, ptnr., 1961-94, of counsel, 1995-96; ret. Mem. Simsbury (Conn.) Zoning Bd. Appeals, 1961-67, Simsbury Zoning Commn., 1967-79; sec. Capitol Region Planning Agy., 1965-66; bd. dirs. Symphony Soc. Greater Hartford, 1967-73; trustee Renbrook Sch., West Hartford, Conn., 1963-72, treas. 1964-68, pres., 1968-72, hon. life trustee, 1972—; trustee Simsbury Free Libr., 1970-84; pres. Hartford Grammar Sch., 1987-98, trustee; corporator Hartford Hosp., 1984-96; vestry St. Alban's Ch., Simsbury, 1988-94; warden, vestry St. Paul's Ch., Brunswick, Maine, 1999-2001. Lt. USNR, 1954-62. Mem. ABA, Conn. Bar Assn., Hartford County Bar Assn., Am. Law Inst., Princeton (NYC) Club, Ivy Club (Princeton, NJ). Democrat. Episcopalian. Home: 80 Matthew Dr Brunswick ME 04011-3275 Personal E-mail: hmowen@gwi.net.

OWEN, HARRISON HOLLINGSWORTH, management consultant; b. Evanston, Ill., Dec. 2, 1935; s. Raymond Smith and Mary Crawford (Siter) Owen; m. Ethelyn Abbot, July 9, 1967; children: Cameron, Amy, Barry, Mary, Harrison Jr. BA, Williams, 1957; BD, Va. Sem., 1960; MA, Vanderbilt U., 1965. Pres. H.H. Owen & Co., Potomac, Md., 1979—. Author: Riding the Tiger, 1992, Millennium Orgn., 1994, Tales from Open Space, 1995, (users guide) Open Space Technology, 2d edit., 1997, Open Space Technology, 3rd edit., 2008, Expanding Our Now, 1997, Growing Our Now, 1997, The Spirit of Leadership, 1999, The Power of Spirit: How Organizations Transform, 2000, The Practice of Peace, 2003, Wave Rider: Leadership For High Performance, 2008. Home and Office: 7808 River Falls Dr Potomac MD 20854-3878 Home Phone: 301-365-2093; Office Phone: 301-365-2093. E-mail: hhowen@verizon.net.

OWEN, HENRY, former ambassador, consultant; b. NYC, Aug. 26, 1920; AB, Harvard U., 1941. Economist Dept. State, Washington, 1946-55, mem. policy planning staff, 1955-62, dep. counselor, vice chmn. policy planning coun., 1962-66, chmn. coun., 1966-69; dir. fgn. policy studies Brookings Instn., 1969-77; personal rep. of Pres. U.S. with rank of ambassador to participate in preparations for summit meetings, 1977-81; sr. adviser Salomon Bros., 1981—2002; co-chmn. Capitol Ptnrs. for Edn., Washington, 2002—. Spl. adv. Pan-European Oil Pipeline Romania-Serbian-Croatia-Slovenia- Italy. Editor: Next Phase of U.S. Foreign Policy, 1971, (with Charles Schultze) Setting National Priorities, 1976. Served to lt. USN, 1942-46. Office: 2946 University Ter NW Washington DC 20016 Office Phone: 202-363-8370. Office Fax: 202-363-3492.

OWEN, JOHN ATKINSON, JR., internist, educator; b. South Boston, Va., Sept. 24, 1924; s. John Atkinson and Mary Helen (Carrington) O.; m. Wanda Earle Reamy, Nov. 29, 1952; children— John Atkinson III, Ryland R. BS, Hampden-Sydney Coll., 1944; MD, U. Va., 1948. Intern Cin. Gen. Hosp., 1948-49; resident, fellow U. Va. Hosp., 1950-52; rsch. fellow Duke Med. Center, 1954-56; asst. prof. medicine Med. Coll. Ga., 1956-58, George Washington U. Med. Sch., 1958-60; mem. faculty U. Va. Sch. Medicine, 1960-96, prof., 1970-96, vice chmn. dept. internal medicine, 1972-74, James M. Moss prof. diabetes, sr. assoc. dean, 1995-96, prof. emeritus, 1997—. Mem. Va. Vol. Formulary Bd.; mem. exec. com. U.S. Pharmacopeia, 1970-75, pres., 1975-80, trustee, 1975-85. Mem. editorial bd.: Jour. Clin. Pharmacology, 1971-84; editor-in-chief: Hosp. Formulary, 1974-83. Served with USNR, 1942-45, 48-50, 52-53; capt. M.C. Res. Recipient Raven award U. Va., 1948; co-recipient Horsley Research prize, 1962, Walter Reed Disting. Achievement award, 1998; laureate ACP, 1998. Mem. AMA, ACP, Am. Fedn. Clin. Rsch., So. Soc. Clin. Investigation, Med. Soc. Va. (pres. 1990-91), Am. Diabetes Assn., Endocrine Soc. Presbyterian. (elder 1965—). Home: 106 Tally Ho Dr Charlottesville VA 22901-2034

OWEN, LARRY GENE, academic administrator, educator, electronics engineer, consultant; b. Pine Bluff, Ark., Oct. 2, 1932; s. Cecil Earl and Helen Marie (Jacks) O.; m. Ruth Myra Newton, Sept. 3, 1953; children: Deborah, Patricia, Larry Gene, Shea. BS in Physics and Math., U. So. Miss., 1967; postgrad., Inst. Tech., 1974-75; MS in Ops. Mgmt., U. Ark., 1987; DPM, Masters Divinity Sch., 2004. Enlisted USAF, 1951, advanced through ranks to master sgt., 1968, electronic technician, 1951-61, comms. supt., 1961-71, ret., 1971; tchr. math. and Physics Southwestern Tech. Inst., Camden, Ark., 1971-72, tchr. electronics, 1972-75; dean tech. engrng.omputer Integrated Mfg. Ctr. So. Ark. U. Tech., Camden, 1988-89, dean, dir. divsn. Computer Integrated Mfg. Ctr., 1989-91, dean, prof., 1991-97, assoc. vice chancellor, 1996-98, dean emeritus, 1996—. Adj. asst. prof. So. Ark. U.; project dir. Ark. Consortium for Mfg. Competitiveness So. Growth Policies Bd., 1988-98; vice chair South Ark. Fiber Optics Coun., 1997. Contbr. articles to profl. jours. Mem. Rep. Task Force; chair Atea Coll. Cons., 1991—. Mem. Instrumentation Soc. Am. (sr.), Am. Assn. Physics Tchrs. Am. Tech. Edn. Assn. (rep. Ark. 1989-91, 95-96, pres. so. region 1992-93, chair Coll. of Cons.), Soc. Mfg. Engrs. (sr., chmn. South Ark. chpt. 1991-92, mem. govs. mfg. network adv. com.), Am. Legion (fin. dir. post 45). Baptist. Home: 306 Lakeside Ave Camden AR 71701-3237

OWEN, LAURI J., lawyer; b. Camp Pendleton, Calif., May 23, 1967; d. Larry H. Owen and Lois L. Allen. BS in Social Scis. summa cum laude, Boise State U., 1998, MA in Comm. summa cum laude, 2001; JD, U. Calif. Boalt Sch. Law, Berkeley, 2006. Cert. peace officers stds. and tng. level III Idaho. Sr. commd. dep. sheriff Ada County Sheriff's Office, Boise, 1990—2003; law clk. Bay Area Legal Aid, San Mateo, Calif., 2005; advocate Internat. Inst. of the East Bay, Oakland, Calif., 2005—06. Presenter workshops on domestic violence; cmty. activist. Contbr. scientific papers to profl. confs. Pres. STOP Domestic Violence U. Calif. Berkeley, Calif., 2004—06; mem. VAWA Task Force, Bay Area, Calif., 2004—06, human Trafficking Task Force, Bay Area, 2006—. Recipient Team award, Ada County Sheriff's Office. Mem.: Alaska Bar Assn., Phi Kappa Phi. Democrat. Office: PO Box 924 Bethel AK 99559

OWEN, MARC E., health products executive; b. Wales; Grad., Oxford U.; MBA, Stanford U., Calif. Sr. ptnr. McKinsey and Co., 1988—2000; pres., CEO MindCrossing, 2000—01; sr. v.p. corp. strategy and bus. devel. McKesson Corp., San Francisco, 2001, exec. v.p. corp. strategy and bus. devel. Office: McKesson Corp One Post St San Francisco CA 94104*

OWEN, MICHAEL, federal agency administrator; m. Anne Bucher; 3 children. BS in History and Polit. Sci., Towson State U., Balt., 1973; grad. Fed. Policy Inst., Harvard U. John F. Kennedy Sch. Govt., Cambridge, Mass., 1987. Staff asst. Balt. City Coun., 1972—73; chief of staff Congresswoman Marjorie Holt, Washington, 1973—85; asst. sec., prin. dep. asst. sec. for installations, logistics and environment US Army, Washington, 1985—94; v.p. Allied Rsch., Vienna, Va., 1994—96; pres. Govtl. Strategies, Inc., Annapolis, Md.; dir., office of worker and cmty. transition Dept. Energy, Washington, dir., office of legacy mgmt., 2003—. Advance rep. The White House, 1981—85; mem. Pres.-elect George Bush's Transition Team, 2000. Support staff, Md. del. Rep. Nat. Convention, 1976, 1980; mem. White House Polit. Liaison Team, Dallas, 1984; campaign mgr. US Rep. Marjorie Holt, 1974—84, County Exec. John Gary, 1994; Md. campaign coord. Reagan-Bush, 1980, 1984; mem. fin. com. US Reps. Robert Ehrlich, Wayne Gilchrest. Office: US Dept Energy Office Legacy Mgmt 1000 Independence Ave SW Washington DC 20585 Office Phone: 202-586-7550. Office Fax: 202-586-1540.

OWEN, MICHAEL LEE, lawyer; b. LA, Aug. 17, 1942; s. Richard M. Owen and Betty Hamilton; m. Espy Bolivar-Owen. AB in Econ. with distinction, Stanford U., Calif., 1964; LLB, Harvard U., Cambridge, Mass., 1967. Bar: Calif., 1968, NY 1968. Assoc. Reid & Priest, NYC, 1967—69; mem. legal dept. Bank of Am. NT&SA, San Francisco, 1969—81; corp. sec. BRE Properties, San Francisco, 1970—75; v.p., assoc. gen. counsel Bank of Am. NT&SA, LA, 1979—81; ptnr., past co-chair L.Am. practice group Paul, Hastings, Janofsky & Walker, LLP, LA, 1981—. Former, vice chmn. adv. bd. Inst. for Internat. and Comparative Law Ctr. Am. and Internat. Law (formerly Southwestern Legal Found.). Contbr. articles to profl. jours. regarding legal issues affecting financing and investment in Latin Amer. Bd. dirs. Constnl. Rights Found. Mem. US-Mex. Law Inst. (mem. adv. bd.). Office: Paul Hastings Janofsky & Walker LLP 515 S Flower St 25th Fl Los Angeles CA 90071-2228 Office Phone: 213-683-6214. Office Fax: 213-627-0705. Business E-Mail: michaelowen@paulhastings.com.

OWEN, MOLLY JACKSON, music educator; b. Corpus Christi, Tex., Nov. 19, 1955; d. James Barton and Mary Elizabeth (Gilbert) Jackson; m. John Brooks Owen, June 6, 1981; 1 child, John Frederick. AA, Del Mar Coll., Corpus Christi, 1976; B Music Edn., Corpus Christi State U., 1978; M Choral Conducting, West Tex. State U., Canyon, 1983. Choir dir. Wynn Scale Jr. HS, Corpus Christi, 1979, Strack Intermediate Sch., Spring, Tex., 1979—81, Rockport-Fulton Mid. Sch., Rockport, Tex., 2000—; office mgr. Steeplechase Pediat. Ctr., Houston, 1986—2000. Clnician various choirs, Tex. Mem. choir St. Peter's Episcopal Ch., Rockport, 2005—. Mem.: Am. Choral Dirs. Assn. (Nat. Student award 1982), Tex. Music Educators Assn. (judge All State process 2000—), Tex. Choral Dirs. Assn. Democrat. Episcopalian. Avocations: reading, gardening, dogs. Home: 121 N Santa Clara Rockport TX 78382 Office: Aransas County Ind Sch Dist 1701 Colorado St Rockport TX 78382

OWEN, PRISCILLA RICHMAN, federal judge, former state supreme court justice; b. Palacios, Tex., Oct. 4, 1954; BA, Baylor U., 1975; JD, Baylor U. Sch. of Law, 1977. Bar: Tex. 1978, US Ct. Appeals (4th, 5th, 8th and 11th cirs.). Law clerk Sheehy, Lovelace & Mayfield, 1976—77; assoc. Andrews, Kurth, Campbell & Jones, 1978—85, ptnr., 1985—94; justice Supreme Ct. Tex., Austin, 1995—2005; judge US Ct. Appeals (5th cir.), New Orleans, 2005—. Liaison to Tex. Legal Svcs. for Poor Spl. Supreme Ct. Tex., Supreme Ct. Adv. Com. on Ct.-Annexed Mediations. Bd. mem. Tex. Hearing & Service Dogs, A.A. White Dispute Resolution Inst.; advisory bd. mem. Federalist Soc. (Houston & Austin Chapter). Named Young Lawyer of Yr., Baylor U., Outstanding Young Alumna. Mem.: ABA, Am. Judicature Soc., Am. Law Inst. Office: US Courthouse 903 San Jacinto Blvd Rm 310 Austin TX 78701-2450*

OWEN, RANDALL P., surgeon, researcher; b. LA, Jan. 16, 1968; s. Timothy and Edie Owen; m. Jane Weber, Aug. 20, 1994; 1 child, Timothy. MD, Columbia U. Coll. Physicians & Surgeons, NYC, 1994. Intern/resident in gen. surgery Albert Einstein Coll. Medicine, Yeshiva U., NYC; surgeon Montefiore Med. Ctr., Bronx, NY, 1999—. Asst. prof. dept. otolaryngology-head and neck surgery Albert Einstein Coll. Medicine. Contbr. articles to profl jours. Grantee MAP Internat. Fellowship, 1994. Achievements include invention of radiofrequency ablation of head and neck tumors. Office: Montefiore Med Ctr 3400 Bainbridge Ave 4th floor Bronx NY 10467 Office Fax: 718-655-5047. E-mail: rowen@montefiore.org.*

OWEN, RAY DAVID, biology professor; b. Genesee, Wis., Oct. 30, 1915; s. Dave and Ida (Hoeft) O.; m. June J. Weissenberg, June 24, 1939; 1 son, David G. BS, Carroll Coll., Wis., 1937, ScD, 1962; PhD, U. Wis., 1941, ScD, 1979, U. of Pacific, 1965, Ohio State U., 2002. Asst. prof. genetics, zoology U. Wis., 1944-47; Gosney fellow Calif. Inst. Tech., Pasadena, 1946-47, assoc. prof. div. biology, 1947-53, prof. biology, 1953-83, also chmn., v.p. for student affairs, dean of students, prof. emeritus, 1983—. Research participant Oak Ridge Nat. Lab., 1957-58; Cons. Oak Ridge Inst. Nuclear Studies; mem. Pres.'s Cancer Panel. Author: (with A.M. Srb) General Genetics, 1952, 2d edit. (with A.M. Srb, R. Edgar), 1965; Contbr. articles to sci. jours. Recipient Gregor Mendel medal Czech Acad. Scis., 1965, Medawar prize The Transplantation Soc., 2000, President's Disting. Achievement award, Am. Soc. Transplantation, 2005. Fellow AAAS; mem. Genetics Soc. Am. (pres., Thomas Hunt Morgan medal 1993), Am. Assn. Immunologists (Excellence in Mentoring award 1999), Am. Soc. Human Genetics, Western Soc. Naturalists, Am. Soc. Zoologists, Am. Genetics Assn., Nat. Acad. Scis., Am. Acad. Arts and Scis., Am. Philos. Soc., Am. Acad. Allergy and Immunology (hon.), Internat. Soc. Animal Genetics (hon.), Sigma Xi. Home: 1583 Rose Villa St Pasadena CA 91106-3524 Office: Calif Inst Tech # 156-29 Pasadena CA 91125-0001 Office Phone: 626-395-4960.

OWEN, ROBERT HUBERT, lawyer, real estate broker; b. Birmingham, Ala., Aug. 3, 1928; s. Robert Clay and Mattie Lou (Hubert) O.; m. Mary Dane Hicks, Mar. 14, 1954; children: Mary Kathryn, Robert Hubert. BS, U. Ala., 1950; JD, Birmingham Sch. Law, 1956. Bar: Ala. 1957, Ga. 1965. Methods and procedures analyst, supr. Ala. Power Co., Birmingham, 1952-58; assoc. Martin, Vogtle, Balch & Bingham, Birmingham, 1958-63; asst. sec. So. Services, Atlanta, 1963-69; sec. Southern Co., Atlanta, 1969-71, sec., asst. treas., 1971-77; exec. v.p., sec., gen. counsel, dir. Proverbs 31 Corp., Atlanta, 1978-81, 90-97; broker Bob Owen Realty, Atlanta, 1990-97; pvt. practice law Marietta, 1978-85; v.p., gen. counsel Hubert Properties, 1985-86. Atlanta area rep. Inst. Basic Life Principles, 1970-80; elder Calvary Bapt. Ch., 1997—. Served to maj. USAF, 1951-52, 61-62. Mem.: Meteoritical Soc., Jasons, Phi Eta Sigma, Beta Gamma Sigma, Omicron Delta Kappa, Delta Chi, Delta Sigma Pi. Home and Office: 6590 Bridgewood Valley Rd NW Sandy Springs GA 30328-2906 Personal E-mail: roberthowen@bellsouth.net.

OWEN, ROBERTS BISHOP, lawyer, arbitrator; b. Boston, Feb. 11, 1926; s. Roberts Bishop and Monica Benedict (Burrell) O.; m. Kathleen Comstock von Schrader, Aug. 27, 1966; children— David Roberts, Lucy Leffingwell, William Atreus. Student, Dartmouth Coll., 1943-44; AB cum laude, Harvard U., 1948, LL.B. cum laude, 1951; Dip.C.L.S., Cambridge U., Eng., 1952. Bar: D.C. 1952, U.S. Ct. Appeals (D.C. cir.) 1953, U.S. Supreme Ct. 1958. Assoc. Covington & Burling, Washington, 1952-60, ptnr., 1960-79, 81—; the legal advisor U.S. Dept. State, Washington, 1979-81. Sr. advisor Sec. of State former Yugoslavia, 1995; arbitrator Fedn. Bosnia and Herzegovina, 1995; mem. Permanent Ct. Arbitration, The Hague, The Netherlands, 1980—86, 1993—98; mem. arbitration panel Internat. Ctr. for Settlement of Investment Disputes, 1995—; chair bd. dirs. Internat. Human Rights Law Group, 1996—99; mem. Claims Resolution Tribunal for Dormant Accounts in Switzerland, 1998—2000; sr. U.S. negotiator U.S.-Can. Pacific Salmon Treaty dispute, 1998; vice chair, sr. claims judge Claims Resolution Tribunal, 2001—02. Served to ensign USN, 1943-46. Fulbright scholar, 1951-52; recipient Disting Honor award Dept. of State, 1981, Sec. of State Disting. Svc. award, 1996, Sec. of Defense's medal for outstanding pub. svc., 1996. Fellow Am. Coll. Trial Lawyers; mem. ABA, Council Fgn. Relations, Am. Soc. Internat. Law (exec. council 1981-85). Clubs: Royal Ocean Racing (London); Metropolitan (Washington). Office: Covington & Burling PO Box 7566 1201 Pennsylvania Ave NW Washington DC 20004 Home Phone: 202-363-1134; Office Phone: 202-662-5254. Business E-mail: rowen@cov.com.

OWEN, SHAUN SONIA, elementary school educator, small business owner, consultant; d. Rose Marie Owen. Degree in Mid. Grades Edn., Augusta State U., Ga., 1995; M in Ednl. Leadership, Troy State U., Augusta, Ga., 2002; Specialist Degree in Ednl. Leadership, Lincoln Meml. U., Cleve., Tenn., 2003. Cert. tchr. Ga. State Dept. Edn., 2000. Tchr. 7th grade Hephzibah Mid. Sch., Ga., 1995—2000; tchr. 6th, 7th, 8th grades Greenbrier Mid. Sch., Evans, Ga., 2000—. Owner Shaun Owen (My Ednl. Co.), Martinez, Ga., 2005—; presenter Ga. Assn. Curriculum and Instrnl. Suprs.' Ann. Conf., Athens, Ga., 2005, Ga. Coun. for Social Studies, Athens, 2005, DeKalb County Sch. Sys., Decatur, Ga., 2005, ASCD Ann. Conf., Chgo., 2006, Mid. Ga. Regional Ednl. Svc. Agy., Macon, 2006, Lowndes Mid. Sch., Valdosta, Ga., 2006, Discovery Educator Network, Atlanta, 2006, and various others; travel team mem. Ga. Dept. Edn. Excellence Recognition, Atlanta, 2006; com. mem. Ga. Gov. Sonny Perdue's Master Tchr. and Academic Coach Implementation Com., Atlanta, 2005—06, Ga. State Sch. Supt. Kathy Cox's Tchr. Adv. Com., Atlanta, 2005—; framework rev. com. mem. Ga. Assessment for the Certification of Educators, Atlanta, 2005—; mem. supt. selection com. Columbia County, 2006—07; mem. social studies framework devel. team, 2007—; adv. bd. leader Ga. Pub. Broadcasting, 2007. Camp counselor for deaf and hard-of-hearing children Camp Julienna, Winder, Ga., 1993—95; vol. Red Cross Disaster Relief Emergency Team, Valdosta, Ga., 1990, Spinal Cord Rehab. Ctr. at Veterans' Hosp., Augusta, 1992, Safe Kids of Augusta, 1998; vol./mentor Girl's Home of Augusta, Augusta, 1998; mistress of ceremonies Lakeside HS Scholarship Pageant, Evans, Ga., 2005. Recipient Sallie Mae First Class Tchr. award, Richmond County Bd. Edn., 1995—96, Tchr. of Quarter, Greenbrier Mid. Sch., 2002—03, Tchr. of Yr., 2003—04, Columbia County Tchr. of Yr., Columbia County Bd. Edn., 2004—05; finalist Top Ten for Ga. Tchr. of Yr., Ga. Dept. Edn. Excellence Recognition, 2006. Mem.: Nat. Mid. Sch. Assn., Nat. Coun. for Social Studies, Ga. Mid. Sch. Assn., Ga. Coun. for Social Studies, Ga. Coun. o Econ. Edn., Alpha Kappa Delta Internat. Sociology Honor Soc., ASCD, PA of Ga. Educators, Ga. Tchr. of Yr. Assn. Achievements include presenting in Canada and Chicago, asked by companies interested in marketing the unique teaching strategies I have developed in my classroom over the past 11 years. Office: Greenbrier Middle Sch 5120 Riverwood Pkwy Evans GA 30809 Home: 1315 HAWKSMOOR WAY Grovetown GA 30813-5866 Office Fax: 706-650-6085. Personal E-mail: shaunowen@comcast.net.

OWEN, THOMAS SUMNER, lawyer; b. Grand Junction, Colo., Nov. 24, 1946; s. Roger W. and Nancy (Burrage) O.; m. Chris L. Owen, July 18, 1981; 1 child, Jessica Ciara. BA, Colo. State U., 1969, MA, 1970; JD, Stanford U., 1974. Bar: Calif., U.S. Dist. Ct. (no. and cen. dists.) Calif., U.S. Ct. Appeals (9th and D.C. cirs.). Assoc. Wilson, Jones, Morton & Lunch, Crescent City, Calif., 1974-77; counsel Del Norte County, Crescent City, 1977-81; judge Jud. Dist. Del Norte County, 1981-82; ptnr. Schafer, Cochran, Follett & Owen, Crescent City, 1983—. Co-author: The Sun as a Municipal Utility Source, 1976. Pres. Del Norte Assn. Cultural Awareness, 1985—; mem. Dem. Cen. Com., 1986—. Woodrow Wilson fellow Stanford U., 1969. Mem.: Del Norte Men's Golf (pres. 1981-82), Rotary (pres. local chpt. 1985-86), Elks. Avocations: golf, writing. Office: Schafer Cochran Follett & Owen 888 4th St Crescent City CA 95531-4011 Home: 195 Sea View Cir Crescent City CA 95531-3252

OWEN, TONY QUINN, investment company executive, horse trainer; b. Oklahoma City, Mar. 19, 1974; s. John Blair Owen and Margaret Ruth Wolford; 1 child, Danielle Kaye. AA in Architecture & Bus. Mhmt., Harrisburg C.C.; BA in Bus. and Fin. Mgmt., Northwestern U.; BA in Bus. Law, Villanova U., 1995. Cert. horse trainer. Gen. ptnr. Real Estate Lease Cons., Harrisburg, Pa., 1991—2002; architect Stonewall Golf Links, Elverson, 1992—94; pres., CEO Aztec Security Group, Carlisle, 1998—, Mystical Hannah Studios, 2005—, Stone Mountain Concrete, 2004—. Fin. advisor Loda Investment Group, Harrisburg, 2000—; equine instr. One Trick Pony, New Cumberland, 2000—02. Author: 26 Week Equitation Classes, 2003, OCD-Pieces of String, 2005, Tranquility Spirit Guides and Angel Guardians. Asst. master counselor/chevaliar Order of DeMolay, Carlisle, 1987—; sec.youth aide panel Office Dist. Atty., Cumberland, 2004. Fellow: Am. Gemological Soc.; mem.: Pa. Guild of Craftsmen, Golf Soc. U.S., PGA Tour Ptnrs. Club. Avocations: horse training, skiing, cliff diving, hot air ballooning, golf. Home: 414 E Main St Rear Mechanicsburg PA 17055-6515 Home Phone: 717-421-6347; Office Phone: 717-557-1293. Personal E-mail: mysticalhannastudios@wildfun.com.

OWEN, WILLIAM FRANKLIN, JR., academic administrator, former research and development company executive; b. Memphis, Nov. 11, 1955; m. Alice Crosby Owen; children: Lauren Leslie, William Franklin III. MD, Tufts U., 1980. Cert. nephrology Am. Bd. Internal Medicine, 1985, internal medicine Am. Bd. Internal Medicine, 1984. Dir. dialysis svcs. Brigham and Women's Hosp., Boston, 1996—99; dir. Duke Inst. Renal Outcomes Rsch. Duke U. Med. Ctr., Durham, NC, 1999—2001; tenured prof. medicine Duke U. Sch. Medicine, Durham, 2001—01, adj. prof. medicine, 2002—; chief scientist Baxter Healthcare Corp., Renal, Deerfield, Ill., 2002—05; chancellor, v.p, health affairs U. Tenn. Health Sci. Ctr., Memphis, 2005—07; pres. U. Medicine and Dentistry NJ, Newark, 2007—. Chmn. internat. med. adv. bd. Nat. Kidney Found. Singapore, 1998; bd. sci. counsilors NIH, Bethesda, Md., 1998—2001; sci. adv. bd. U.S. Renal Data Sys., Bethesda, 2000—01; pres. Renal Physicians Assn., Bethesda, 2001—03; mem. medicare coverage adv. com. Ctrs. for Medicare and Medicaid Svcs., Balt., 2003—. Contbr. articles to profl. jours. Mem. site based com. Hillandale Elem. Sch., Durham, 1999—2000. Grantee, NIH, 1984—; fellow, Robert Wood Johnson Found., 1985—89. Avocation: astronomy. Office: U Medicine and Dentistry NJ Office of Pres 65 Bergen St Newark NJ 07103

OWEN-LEINERT, SUSAN HUFF, voice educator, vocalist; b. Salisbury, NC, Sept. 6, 1958; d. James Bobby Huff and Mildred Clark Huff Simerson; m. Michael Leinert, Mar. 19, 1999. MusB, East Carolina U., 1980; MusM, U. Tex., 1983. Opera singer Freelance, NYC, 1985—95, Staatstheater Kassel, Germany, 1995—99, Staatstheater Darmstadt, Germany, 2000—02, Freelance, Duesseldorf, Germany, 2003—05; asst. prof. voice U. Memphis, 2005—; classical singer opera and concert Memphis, 2005—. Dir. Carolina Opera & Song Acad., Salisbury, NC, 2005—, Met. Opera Nat. Coun. Auditions, Memphis, 2005—, Memphis Opera & Song Acad., 2007—. Singer: Der Ring des Nibelungen, Elektra, Tristan und Isolde, Der Fliegende Hollaender, Discography: Wagner-Die Walkuere, Siegfried, Goetterdaemmerung; author: (ARS prodn.) Treasure Chest of German Lied; composer: (Highwater Classics) Wagner, Strauss, Wagner. Recipient First Pl. award, Met. Opera Nat. Coun., 1990, Opera Am., 1991, Sullivan Grant award, 1991. Mem.: Nat. Assn. of Tchrs. Singing (life). Office: U Memphis Rudi E Scheidt Sch Music Memphis TN 38152 Home: PO Box 11508 Memphis TN 38111-0508 Business E-Mail: susan.owen-leinert@memphis.edu.

OWENS, B. CRAIG, food products executive; BA in Politics, Wash. and Lee U., Lexington, Va.; MA, Tufts U. Fletcher Sch. Law and Diplomacy, Medford, Mass.; MBA, U. Pa. Wharton Sch. Bus., Phila. Gen. mgmt. and sr. fin. positions The Coca-Cola Co., region dir. Coca-Cola HBC, pres., CEO Coca-Cola Enterprise France, contr.; exec. v.p., CFO Delhaize Group, Belgium, 2001—08; sr. v.p., CFO, chief adminstrv. officer Campbell Soup Co., Camden, NJ, 2008—. Office: Campbell Soup Co Campbell Pl Camden NJ 08103 Office Phone: 856-342-4800. Office Fax: 856-342-3878.*

OWENS, BILL (WILLIAM FORRESTER OWENS), investment company executive, former governor; b. Ft. Worth, Tex., Oct. 22, 1950; s. Arthur and June Owens; m. Frances Westbrook, 1975; children: Monica, Mark, Brett. BA, Stephen F. Austin State U., 1973; MPA, U. Tex., 1975. Staff asst. to Senator John Tower US Senate, 1974—75; mgmt. cons. Touche Ross & Co., 1975—77; project mgr. Gates Rubber Co., 1977—79; exec. dir. Colo. Petroleum Assn.; chmn. Aurora Planning Commn., 1979—81; mem. Colo. Ho. Reps. from Dist. 49, 1983-89, chmn. State Affairs Com., 1987—88, chmn. Nat. Conf. State Legis. Energy Com., 1987—88; mem. Colo. State Senate from Dist. 27, 1989-94, mem. State, Vet. & Mil. Affairs Com., 1991—94; treas. State of Colo., 1994-98, gov., 1999—2007; vice chmn. Greenwich Capital Markets, Inc., Greenwich, Conn., 2007—. Chmn. Aurora County Reagan for Pres., 1979-80; mem. White House Commn. Edn., 1987-91; bd. mem. Colo. Com. Concern for Soviet Jews, U. Colo. Sch. Pub. Affairs & Inst. Internat. Edn., Rocky Mt. Region, Colo. Hwy. Users Fedn.; guest host Mike Rosen, Ken Hamblin and Chuck Baker talk shows; lectr. Russia; part-time fellow, Inst. for Pub. Policy Studies U. Denver, 2007-Contbr. more than 50 articles to profl. jours. Mem. Aurora C. of C. Named One of Country's Ten Up-and-Coming leaders Robert Novak. Mem.: Am. Coun. Young Polit. Leaders (nat. bd. mem.), Am.-Israel Friendship League, Family Focus, Pub. Employee Retirement Assn. (bd. mem.), Leadership Denver, Colo. Conservative Union (bd. mem. 1981—), Jaycees. Republican. Catholic. Office: Greenwich Capital Markets Inc 600 Steamboat Rd Greenwich CT 06830

OWENS, CHRISTINE M., delivery service executive; BS, Shippensburg Univ. Joined UPS, Atlanta, 1979, dist. mgr. NE Tex, Metro Chgo., region mgr., 1997—2004, v.p. transp., 2004—05, sr. v.p. comm. & brand mgmt., mem. mgmt. com., 2005—. Mem. Ill. Gov.'s Commn. on Status of Women. Named one of Best Marketers, BtoB Mag., 2008. Office: UPS 55 Glendale Pky Atlanta GA 30328*

OWENS, CHRISTOPHER TAFT, pharmacist, educator; b. Moses Lake, Wash., Sept. 9, 1972; s. Richard R. and Gladys Owens; m. Jessica Abbott, May 24, 1997; children: Noah, Lauren, Ella. PharmD, Idaho State U., Pocatello, 2002. Cert. Bd. Pharm. Specialties, 2005. Assoc. prof. Idaho State U. Coll. Pharmacy, 2007—, chair, dept. pharmacy practice and adminstrv. scis., 2008—. Fellow: Am. Coll. Clin. Pharmacy. Home: 73 Fordham St Pocatello ID 83201 Office: Idaho State Univ 970 South 8th Ave Pocatello ID 83209

OWENS, DANA ELAINE See QUEEN LATIFAH

OWENS, FREDRIC NEWELL, animal nutritionist, educator; b. Hammond, Wis., Sept. 1, 1941; s. Fred Newell and Stella Elvera Owens; m. Christa F. Hanson, Dec. 1983; children: Gwen, Eric, Crystal. Student, Wis. State U., River Falls, 1959-61; BS, U. Minn., 1964, PhD, 1968. Asst. prof. animal sci. U. Ill., Urbana, 1968-74; prof. animal sci. Okla. State U., Stillwater, 1974-86, Regents prof., 1986-90, Regents prof., Sarkeys Disting. prof., 1990—; sr. rschr. Pioneer Hi-Bred Internat., Johnston, Iowa, 1998—. Lectr. Sigma Xi, 1990, numerous other invted lectures; mem. com. on animal nutrition NRC, 1985-88. Contbr. chpts. to 13 books, more than 180 articles to profl. jours.; sect. editor Jour. Animal Sci., 1975-78, editor-in-chief, 1987-90. Recipient Tyler award Okla. State U., 1980, Am. Feed Industry Nutrition Rsch. award, 1986, Elmo Baumann Prof. award Okla. State U., 1990; NSF fellow, 1966-68. Mem. Am. Soc. Animal Soc. (pres. 1992, Morrison award 1996), Am. Inst. Nutrition, Am. Dairy Sci. Assns., Nutrition Soc. Lutheran. Home: 5004 Brookview Dr West Des Moines IA 50265-2733 Office Phone: 515-334-6416. Business E-Mail: fred.owens@pioneer.com.

OWENS, JAMES W. (JIM OWENS), manufacturing executive; b. Elizabeth City, NC, 1946; 3 children. BS in Textile Tech., NC State U., 1968, MS in Textile Tech., 1970, PhD in Economics, 1973. Corp. economist Caterpillar Inc., Peoria, Ill., 1972—75; chief economist Caterpillar Overseas S.A., Geneva, 1975—80; mgmt. positions, Acctg., Product Source Planning Depts. Caterpillar Inc., Peoria, 1980—87, mng. dir., P.T. Natra Raya Indonesia, 1987—90, pres., Solar Turbines Inc., 1990—93, v.p. group svcs. divsn. Peoria, Ill., 1993-94, group pres., 1995—2003, vice chmn., 2003—04, chmn., CEO, 2004—. Bd. dirs. Caterpillar Inc., 2004—, Alcoa Inc., 2005—, FM Global Ins. Co., 2005—, IBM Corp., 2006—; mem. President's Econ. Recovery Advisory Bd., 2009—. Mem. cmty. adv. bd. St. Francis Med. Ctr.; mem. Civic Fedn. Bd., Peoria. Mem.: Conf. Bd. NY (mem. global adv. coun.), Bus. Roundtable, Bus. Coun., Mfg. Coun., Coun. Fgn. Rels. Office: Caterpillar Inc 100 NE Adams St Peoria IL 61629 Office Phone: 309-675-1000. Office Fax: 309-675-1182.*

OWENS, JANA JAE, entertainer; b. Great Falls, Mont., Aug. 30, 1943; d. Jacob G. Meyer and Bette P. (Sprague) Hopper; m. Sidney Greif (div.); children: Matthew N., Sydni C.; m. Buck Owens. Student, Interlochen Music Camp, 1959, Internat. String Congress, 1960, Vienna Acad. Music, 1963—64; BA magna cum laude, MusB magna cum laude, Colo. Womens Coll., 1965. Tchr. music Ontario Pub. Schs., Oreg., 1965—67, Redding Pub. Schs., Calif., 1969—74; entertainer Buck Owens Enterprises, Bakersfield, Calif., 1974—78, Tulsa, 1979—. Concertmistress Boise Philharm., Idaho, 1965—67, Shasta Symphony, Redding, 1969—74; founder Grand Lake Festivals, Inc., Tulsa, 1996—. Rec. artist (violinist, vocalist) Lark Records, 1978—. Avocations: skiing, tennis, swimming. Office: Jana Jae Enterprises Lark Record Prodns Inc PO Box 35726 Tulsa OK 74153-0726 Office Phone: 918-786-8896.

OWENS, LAURA LEWIS, lawyer; b. Atlanta, Sept. 27, 1960; BA cum laude, Furman U., 1982; JD cum laude, U. Ga., 1985. Bar: Ga. 1985. Ptnr. Alston & Bird L.L.P., Atlanta. Mem. editl. bd. Ga. Jour. Internat. and Comparative Law, 1983-85, editor-in-chief, 1984-85; author: Annual Survey of Developments in International Trade Law, 1983. Mem. Atlanta Bar Assn., State Bar of Ga. Office: Alston & Bird 1 Atlantic Ctr 1201 W Peachtree St NW Atlanta GA 30309-3424 Office Phone: 404-881-7363. Office Fax: 404-881-7777. Business E-Mail: lowens@alston.com.

OWENS, MAJOR ROBERT ODELL, former congressman; b. Memphis, June 28, 1936; m. Marie Cuprill; children: Christopher, Geoffrey, Millard, Carlos, Cecilia. BA with high honors in Math., Morehouse Coll., Atlanta, 1956; MLS, Atlanta U., 1957; grad. student, Columbia U. V.p. Met. Coun. Housing, 1964; chair Bklyn. Congress Racial Equality, 1964—66; cmty. coord. Bklyn. Pub. Libr., 1964—66; exec. dir. Brownsville Cmty. Coun., 1966—68; commr. NYC Cmty. Devel. Agy., 1968—73; dir. cmty. media libr. prog. Columbia U., 1973—75; mem. NY State Senate, 1975—82, US Congress from 11th NY dist., 1983—2007, mem. edn. and the workforce com., mem. govt. reform com., ranking minority mem. workforce protections subcommittee, chmn. select edn. and civil rights subcommittee, mem. progressive caucus. Mem. Internat. Commn. on Ways of Implementing Social Policy to Ensure Maximum Pub. Participation and Social Justice for Minorities, The Hague, Netherlands, 1972; keynote speaker White House Conf. on Librs., 1979. Pub. author and lectr. on libr. sci. Chmn. Dem. Ops. Com. Major R. Owens Day named in his honor, City Bklyn., 1971; named one of Most Influential Black Americans, Ebony mag., 2006. Mem.: ALA, NAACP. Democrat. Baptist.

OWENS, MICHAEL HOWARD, otolaryngologist; b. Evanston, Ill., Jan. 15, 1958; MD, U. South Fla., Tampa, 1984. Diplomate Am. Bd. Otolaryngology, 1990. Intern in otolaryngology U. South Fla., 1984—86, resident in gen. surgery and otolaryngology, 1986—90; otolaryngologist Miami Children's Hosp., Bapt. Health South Fla.; clinical asst. prof. U. Miami. Office: Miami Childrens Hosp #204 4675 Ponce De Leon Blvd Coral Gables FL 33146 Office Phone: 305-666-0203. Office Fax: 305-666-0535.

OWENS, PHILLIP CLYDE, biochemist, educator; married. BSc, U. Queensland, 1977, MSc, 1984; PhD, U. Newcastle, Australia, 1986. Sr. rsch. scientist CSIRO Human Nutrition, Adelaide, Australia, 1987—96; sr. lectr. U. Adelaide, 1996—2002; brain pool scientist Chungbuk Nat. U., Cheongju, Republic of Korea, 2004—06; adj. lectr.,natural & health scis. Carroll U., Waukesha, Wis., 2006—08; chemistry lectr. U. Wisconsin, 2008—09. Recipient Commonwealth Tertiary award, Fed. Govt. Commonwealth Australia, 1969; Early Origins Adult Health grant, Nat. Health & Med. Rsch. Coun. Australia, 2002—06. Mem.: Am. Chem. Soc. Achievements include patents for selection of livestock using IGF levels; invention of regulation of cytotrophoblast migration and differentiation. Personal E-mail: phillip_c_owens@yahoo.com.au.

OWENS, ROBERT W., oil industry executive; Bus. Degree, Calif. Poly. State U., 1976; MBA, Northwestern U. From mktg. trainee to dist. mgr. Mobil Oil Corp., 1976—88; corp. planner Amerada Hess, 1988—89, mgr. East Coast Branded mktg. ops., 1989—94; v.p. mktg. and svcs. Ultramar Diamond Shamrock, 1994—97; joined Sunoco, Inc., Phila., 1997, v.p. East Coast mktg., 1997—2000, sr. v.p. mktg., 2000—, v.p. Midwest mktg., 2001—. Office: Sunoco Inc Ten Penn Ctr 1801 Market St Philadelphia PA 19103-1699*

OWENS, ROCHELLE, poet, playwright; b. Bklyn., Apr. 2, 1936; d. Max and Molly (Adler) Bass; m. George Economou, June 17, 1962. Writer-in-residence, Brown U., 1989; tchr. U. Calif. 1982, U. Okla., 1985, 87, 88, U. Southwestern La., 1998, Tex. A&M Univ. Author: (plays) The String Game, 1965, Istanboul, 1965 (Obie award 1966), Futz, 1967, Homo, 1966, Beclch, 1966, Futz and What Came After, 1968, He Wants Shih, 1969, Farmers Almanac, 1969, The Queen of Greece, 1969, Kontraption, 1970, The Karl Marx Play, 1971, O.K. Certaldo, 1975, Emma Instigated Me, 1976, The Widow and the Colonel, 1977, Mountain Rites, 1977, Who Do You Want, Peire Vidal,

1978, Chucky's Hunch, 1981 (Obie award 1982), Who Do You Want, Peire Vidal, 1982, Plays by Rochelle Owens, 2000, (poetry) Not be Essence That Cannot Be, 1961, Salt and Core, 1968, I am the Babe of Joseph Stalin's Daughter, Poems from Joe's Garage, The Joe 82 Creation Poems, The Karl Marx Play & Others, The Joe Chronicles, Part 2, Four Young Lady Poets, 1962, Shemuel, 1979, French Light, 1984, Constructs, 1985, Anthropologists at a Dinner Party, 1985, Who Do You Want Peire Vidal, 1986, W.C. Fields in French Light, 1986, How Much Paint Does the Painting Need, 1988, Black Chalk, 1995, New and Selected Poems: 1961-1996, Rubbed Stones: Poems from 1960-1992, 1994, The Passersby, 1993, Wild River, Poems, 1999, Luca: Discourse on Life and Death, 2001, (radio play) Sweet Potatoes, 1979 (Obie award 1982); The Passerby by Liliane Atlan (translation); (feature film) Futz, 1969 (Obie award); North American Women's Drama From Colonial Times to Present, 2004, Pro Quest, 2005, Penn Sound, 2006, Triptych, 2006, Poems Rochelle Owens New Verse news .com, 2006-09, Solitary Workman, Journey to Purity, 2009; editor: (plays) Spontaneous Combustion (Obie award 1967); recs. include: From a Shaman's Notebook, 1968, The Karl Marx Play, 1974, Totally Corrupt, 1976, Black Box 17, 1979, (play) Three Front, 1990, (radio play) Guerre a'Trois, 1991; reading performances at St. Mark's Poetry Project, Mus. Modern Art, Guggenheim, Whitney Mus., Oxford U., Am. Coll., Paris, Kelly Writer's House, Pa.; host of The Writer's Mind; prodr. radio show, U. Okla.; (video) Oklahoma Too, 1987, How Much Paint Does the Painting Need, Black Chalk, 1995; prodr.: (CD ROM) N.Am. Women's Drama, 2004; reading performance: Am. Coll. Athens, Greece, Am. Consulate Jerusalem Isreal U. de Lyon France, 2009, Contemporary Authors autobiography series vol. 2, Gate Rsch. Co., 1985. Founding mem. N.Y. Theatre Strategy, Women's Theatre Coun. Ford Found. grantee, 1965, Creative Arts Pub. Svc. grantee, 1973, Nat. Endowment for Arts grantee, 1974, Rockefeller Found. grantee, 1974; Yale Sch. Drama fellow, 1968, Guggenheim fellow, 1971; honors N.Y. Drama Critics Cir.; Rockefeller Found. Bellagio resident, 1993; recipient Nomination in poetry Okla. Ctr. for the Book, 1995. Mem. Dramatists Guild, ASCAP. Achievements include being in anthologies. Address: 226 W Rittenhouse Sq Apt 1001 Philadelphia PA 19103 *Creativity and idealism have enabled me to pursue the world of ideas, transforming itself always into art.*

OWENS, STEPHEN ALAN (STEVE OWENS), federal agency administrator, lawyer; b. 1955; m. Karen Owens; children: John, Ben. AB with honors, Brown U., Providence, RI, 1978; JD, Vanderbilt U., Nashville, 1981. Counsel to subcommittee on investigations and oversight US House Sci. & Tech. Com., 1982—84; chief counsel to state dir. to Senator Al Gore US Senate, 1985—88; pvt. practice atty. Phoenix; dir. Ariz. Dept. Environ. Quality, Phoenix, 2003—09; asst. adminstr. for prevention, pesticides, & toxic substances EPA, Washington, 2009—. Mem. EPA Clean Air Act Adv. Com., Phoenix Environ. Quality Commn.; mem. Clean & Diversified Energy Adv. Com. Western Govs. Assn.; mem. Joint Pub. Adv. Com. North Am. Commn. Environ. Cooperation, 1999—2002; pres. Environ. Coun. States, 2008—09. Office: Office Prevention Pesticides and Toxic Substances EPA MC 7101M 1200 Pennsylvania Ave NW Washington DC 20460*

OWENS, STEPHEN THOMAS, lawyer; b. San Jose, Calif., Aug. 2, 1948; s. Thomas Cunnane and Patricia Ann (Howie) O.; m. Joyce Ruckman, June 15, 1970 (div. Dec. 1972); 1 child, Eric Albert; m. Janet Lynn Gattuccio, Aug. 28, 1977; 1 child, Monica Lisa Cali. Diplôme des Etudes Franç, Université de Provence, Aix-en-Provence, France, 1973; BA, San Jose State U., 1974; JD, UCLA, 1978. Bar: Calif. 1978, U.S. Ct. Appeals (9th cir.) 1980, U.S. Dist. Ct. (no, cen., ea. & so. dists.) Calif., U.S. Dist. Ct. (ea. dist.) Ark. Assoc. Graham & James, L.A., 1978-84, ptnr., Squires Sanders & Dempsey L.L.P., L.A. Judge pro tem Mcpl. Ct. L.A. County, 1989—94; bd. dirs. Constitutional Rights Found., 2002—04. Vol. atty. Pub. Counsel, L.A., 1990-95, bd. dirs., 1992-95 Recipient Pro Bono Svc. award State Bar of Calif., 1992, John Minor Wisdom Profl. & Pub. Svc. award ABA, 1993; named a Super Lawyer, Los Angeles Mag., 2004 Mem.: L.A. County Bar Assn. Avocations: sailing, skiing, sea kayaking. Office: Squires Sanders & Dempsey LLP 555 S Flower St 31st Fl Los Angeles CA 90071 Office Phone: 213-624-5134. Office Fax: 213-623-4581. E-mail: sowens@ssd.com.*

OWENS, SUSAN, state supreme court justice; b. Kinston, NC, Aug. 19, 1949; d. Frank and Hazel Owens; children: Sunny Golden, Owen Golden. BA, Duke U., 1971; JD, U. N.C., Chapel Hill, 1975. Bar: Oreg. 1975, Wash. 1976. Judge Dist. Ct., Western Clallam County, 1981—2001; chief judge Quileute Tribe, Lower Elwha S'Klallam Tribe; justice Wash. Supreme Ct., 2001—. Co-founder, chair Rural Cts. Com., 1990; lectr. Jud. Coll., Nat. Coll. Prosecuting Attorneys' Domestic Violence Conf. Co-author: Northwest Tribal Judges Domestic Violence Manual. Mem.: Dist. and Mcpl. Ct. Judges' Assn. (bd. dirs., sec.-treas., v.p., pres.-elect). Avocation: baseball. Office: Wash Supreme Ct PO Box 40929 Olympia WA 98504-0929*

OWENS, SUSAN ELIZABETH, realtor; b. Providence, Nov. 22, 1957; d. Lee Edward and Nancy Elizabeth Norton; children: Michael, Melissa, George Ray III; 1 stepchild, Bobby. Cert. ct. reporter, Reporting Acad. Va., 1993; study real estate, Tidewater CC, Chesapeake, Va., 2001. Sec. capital campaign United Way, Norfolk, Va., 1985—86; med. transcriptionist Humana Hosp. Bayside, Virginia Beach, Va., 1986—90; property mgr. Kamla Condominium Assn., Virginia Beach, 1990—93; ct. reporter Adams, Harris & Martin, Norfolk, 1993—94; office mgr. Slone Chiropractic Clinic, Norfolk, 1994—99, Riddle Assoc. Inc., Chesapeake, Va., 1999—. Pres. So. Bass'n Gal, 1998—2006, Hunter's Creek Property Owners Assn., 2006—07, Va. Bassmasters, Inc., 1997—, sec., 1998—2006, pres., 2007, sec., treas., 2008—; youth coord. Va. Region 7 Bass Fedn. Avocations: bass fishing, bowling, writing. Office: Riddle Assoc Inc Ste 100 530 Woodlake Cir Chesapeake VA 23320 Home Phone: 757-962-1987; Office Phone: 757-523-1900. E-mail: sowens@riddleassociates.com, ladybass96@cox.net.

OWENS, TERRELL ELDORAD, professional football player; b. Alexander City, Ala., Dec. 7, 1973; s. Marilyn Heard; 1 child, Terique. BA in Merchandising, U. Tenn. Chattanooga, 1996. Wide receiver San Francisco 49ers, 1996—2003, Phila. Eagles, 2004—06, Dallas Cowboys, 2006—09, Buffalo Bills, 2009—. Co-author (with Steven Singular): Catch This: Going Deep With the NFL's Sharpest Weapon, 2004; co-author: (with Jason Rosenhaus) T.O., 2006; co-author: (with Courtney Parker) (children's books) Little T Learns to Share, 2006; actor: Under One Roof, 2008. Named First Team All-Pro, NFL, 2000—02, 2004, 2007; named to Nat. Football Conf. Pro-Bowl team, 2000—04, 2007. Achievements include leading the NFL in: receiving yards per game, 2000, receiving touchdowns, 2001, 2002, 2006; setting the NFL record for most receptions in a single game (20), 2000; becoming second all-time in touchdown receptions, 2008. Office: Buffalo Bills One Bills Dr Orchard Park NY 14127*

OWENS, WILLIAM ARTHUR (BILL OWENS), telecommunications industry executive, retired military officer; b. Bismarck, ND, May 8, 1940; s. Earl and Ruth (Arthur) O.; m. Monika Bastian, Sept. 30, 1967; 1 child, Todd. BS in Math., US Naval Acad., 1962; BA, MA in Politics, Philosophy and Econ., U. Oxford, Eng., 1974; MBA, George Washington U., 1976. Registered profl. engr. Commd. ensign USN, 1962, advanced through ranks to admiral, 1996, multiple assignments in nuclear submarines, 1962-77; comdg. officer USS Sam Houston (SSBN609), Honolulu, 1977-80, USS Corpus Christi (SSN705), New London, Conn., 1980-81, Submarine Squadron 4, Charleston, SC, 1984-85, Submarine Group 6, Charleston, SC, 1987-88; dir. office of program appraisal, Dept. of Navy US Dept. Def., Washington, 1988, sr. mil. asst. to sec., 1988—91; comdr. US 6th Fleet, Gaeta, Italy, 1990—91; dep. chief naval ops. for resources, warfare requirements and assessments USN, Washington, 1991—93; vice-chmn. Joint Chiefs of Staff US Dept. Def., Washington, 1993—96; vice chmn., pres., COO Sci. Applications Internat. Corp., 1996-98; joined Teledesic LLC, 1998, vice-chmn., co-CEO, 1999—2003, chmn., CEO, 2003—04; CEO Nortel Networks Corp., Brampton, Ont., Canada, 2004—05, vice-chmn., 2005—. Founder Extend America; bd. dirs. Daimler Chrysler AG, Nortel Networks Corp., 2002—05, Polycom, Inc.; chmn. Intelius LLC; lead dir. EMBARQ. Author: Future of the Maritime Strategy, 1988, High Seas, 1994, Lifting the Fog of War, 2000; contbr. articles on national security. Bd. dirs. Carnegie Corp., Carnegie Found.; mem. Brookings Instn., Fred Hutchinson Cancer Rsch. Ctr., Can. Coun. Chief Execs. Decorated 4 Stars; recipient Intrepid Salute award, Intrepid Foundation, 2004; named 50 Most Powerful People in Networking, Network World, 2004. Mem. Oxford Soc., Coun. Fgn. Rels. Episcopalian. Avocations: golf, skiing.

OWENS, WILLIAM DON, anesthesiology educator; b. St. Louis, Dec. 12, 1939; s. Don and Caroline Wilhemena (Raaf) Owens; m. Patricia Gail Brown, Dec. 12, 1964; children: Pamela, David, Susan. AB, Westminster Coll., 1961; MD, U. Mich., 1965. Diplomate Am. Bd. Anesthesiology. Resident and fellow Mass. Gen. Hosp. and Harvard Med. Sch., Boston, 1969—72; instr. Harvard Med. Sch., Boston, 1972—73; asst. prof. anesthesiology Washington U. Sch. Medicine, St. Louis, 1973—76, assoc. prof., 1976—82, prof., 1982—2004, prof. emeritus, 2004—, chmn. dept., 1982—92. Trustee Barnes Hosp., St. Louis, 1987—89; bd. dirs. Anesthesia Found., 1994—, pres., 1999—; sec.-treas. Am. Bd. Anesthesiology, 1991—94, pres., 1995—96, bd. dirs., 1984—96, Found. Anesthesia Edn. and Rsch., 1990—95, pres., 1994—95; mem. Mo. State Bd. Healing Arts, 2003—04. Assoc. editor Survey of Anesthesiology, 1977—92; contbr. numerous articles to profl. jours. and chpts. to books. Served to lt. comdr. USN, 1966—69. Fellow: Am. Coll. Anesthesiology; mem.: Assn. Univ. Anesthesiologists, Acad. Anesthesiology, Internat. Anesthesia Rsch. Soc., Am. Soc. Anesthesiologists (bd. dirs. 1989—99, 1st v.p. 1995—96, pres. 1997—98, assoc. mem.). Office: Washington U Sch Med Dept Anesthesiology 660 S Euclid Ave Saint Louis MO 63110-1010

OWES, JAUNITA, library director; Grad., Ala. State U., 1972. Dir. Montgomery City-County Pub. Libr., Ala. Mem.: Ala. Libr. Assn. (past pres., nominating chair, named Beta Phi Mu Libr. of Yr. 2005). Office: Montgomery City County Pub Libr PO Box 1950 Montgomery AL 36102 Office Phone: 334-240-4300. Office Fax: 334-240-4977. E-mail: jowes@mccpl.lib.al.us.

OWINGS, MALCOLM WILLIAM, retired management consultant; b. Cin., Feb. 5, 1925; s. William Malcolm and Margaret (Benvie) O.; m. Margie M. Gehiker, Sept. 4, 1948 (dec. June 2000); children: Lynn A., Sandra S., Wendy K., Cheryl M; m. Doris Marie Gorman, Aug. 23, 2002, (dec. Dec, 2008) BS in Bus. Adminstrn., Miami U., Oxford, Ohio, 1950, LL.D., 1976; A.M.P., Harvard U., 1975. With Continental Can Co., 1950-83, corp. v.p., from 1971; v.p., gen. mgr. pub. affairs Continental Packaging Co (Continental Group, Inc.), 1982-83; owner, pres. Owings Assocs., Inc., Pinehurst, NC, 1983-92; ret., 1992. Dir. First Bank, Pinehurst, N.C.; adviser to Am. del. Internat. Tin Coun., 1978-82 Columnist The Pilot, Southern Pines, N.C., 1997-2004. Dean's assoc. exec. in residence Sch. Bus., Miami U., 1973, mem. alumni coun., 1958-65, mem. pres.'s devel. coun., 1965-69, meem. resource devel. bd., 1982; trustee Village of Thiensville, Wis., 1956-59; mem. N.C. Clean, 1985-94, chmn., 1986-93; bd. dirs. Barrington Area Devel. Coun., 1974-79, Sales Mgmt. Execs. Grad. Sch., Am. Soc. Environment, 1976, Keep Am. Beautiful, 1980-81, also chmn., 1990; chmn. Keep N.C. Beautiful Coun., Raleigh, 1988-92, Moore Meml. Hosp. Found., Pinehurse, N.C., 1986-89; mem. Moore Regional Hosp. Scroll Soc., 1991-94, chmn., 1992-93; chmn. Moore County (N.C.) Rep. Party, 1986-88; co-founder Rep. Presdl. Task Force; mem. U.S. Senate Bus. Adv. Bd., 1981-91; commr. Moore County, 1988-96, Youth Svcs., 1993-95; apptd. to N.C. Watershed Protection Adv. Com. by N.C. Environ. Mgmt. Commn., 1990-92; bd. dirs. Pub. Edn. Found., 1994-99, Ptnrs. for Children and Family, 1994-97, Drug-Free Moore County Inc., 1995-98, Dispute Settlement Ctr. of Moore County, 1995-97, Keep Moore County Beautiful, 1997—; mem. Moore County Bd. of Health, 1994-97; pres. Belle Meade Residents Assn., 2000, rep. precinct chairs East Knollwood Precinct, 2009, elected chmn. Moore City Rep. Party, 2009-. Recipient Cert. of Meritorious Svc. Miami U., 1967, Meritorious Svc. award Keep Moore County Beautiful, Inc., 1993-94; named Alumnus of Yr. Miami U., 1970; 1st Am. recipient Order of Apteryx Earth Awareness Found., 1971, Order of Long Leaf Pine. Mem. Ill. C. of C. (bd. dirs. 1976-78), Miami U. Alumni Assn. (nat. pres. 1964-65), Omicron Delta Kappa, Sigma Chi, Delta Sigma Pi Clubs: Pinehurst Country, Country of N.C. (Pinehurst). Home: Belle Mead Retirement Resort 107 Caritas Ct Southern Pines NC 28387-2242 E-mail: mwonings1@ne.rr.com. *The Golden Rule - "treating others as thyself" is not only a cornerstone for success, it is the foundation of personal happiness. However, it is well to remember that none of this is possible without political freedom and the contingent responsibilities that freedom requires.*

OWINGS, VICKIE ANN, librarian; b. Caldwell, Idaho, Apr. 29, 1953; d. A. Henry and Mary Elizabeth (Bellaire) Kinsey; m. Keith A. Owings; children: Nicholas, Christopher, Holly. BS in Elem. Edn., U. Idaho, 1974. Elem. tchr. Hagerman (Idaho) Sch. Dist., 1975-77; 3d grade tchr. Kimberly (Idaho) Sch. Dist., 1978-81, elem. sch. libr., 1981—, tech. mentor, 1995—. Ch. libr. Presbyn. Ch., 1995-97. Master: Instrnl. Tech., ISU; mem.: Delta Kappa Gamma, PEO. Home: 3081 E 3500 N Twin Falls ID 83301-0310 Office: Kimberly Elem Sch 311 Main St S Kimberly ID 83341-2081 Personal E-mail: owingsv@yahoo.com.

OWINO, TOM OBUYA, science educator, researcher; b. Nakuru, Rift Valley, Kenya, Sept. 15, 1961; s. George Lazarus and Esther Odero Owino; children: Sharon Amadi, Arnold Kitaka, Obuyakima, Oude Akama. BSc, U. Nairobi, Kenya, 1985; MSc, U. Alta., Edmonton, Can., 1993; PhD, Pa. State U., State Coll., 1999. Asst. prof. Clemson U., SC, 2000—06, assoc. prof., 2006—. Rsch. asst. Pa. State U., 1994—99; lectr. U. Alta. Contbr. scientific papers (Lund Prof. of Yr., 2000). Choir mem. Connerstone Assembly of God, Anderson, SC. Achievements include research in in-situ determination of electrical conductivity of potting media using time domain reflectometry. Office: Clemson Univ 252 McAdams Hall Clemson SC 29634 Office Fax: 864-656-0338. Business E-Mail: towino@clemson.edu.

OWNBY, DAVID H., theatre company executive; b. 1969; With Ernst & Young, 1992—99; v.p. fin., dir. fin. projects Regal Entertainment Group, Knoxville, Tenn., 1999—2002, sr. v.p. fin., 2002—09, chief acctg. officer, 2006—09, exec. v.p., CFO, treas., 2009—. Office: Regal Entertainment Group 7132 Regal Ln Knoxville TN 37918 Office Phone: 865-922-1123. Office Fax: 865-922-3188.*

OWNBY, DENNIS RANDALL, pediatrician, allergist, educator, researcher; b. Athens, Ohio, July 14, 1948; s. Dillard Ralph and Miriam (Lee) Ownby; m. Helen Louise Engelbrecht, May 24, 1970; children: David Randall, Kathryn Louise. BS, Ohio U., 1969; MD, Med. Coll. Ohio, 1972. Diplomate Am. Bd. Allergy and Immunology (bd. dirs. 1993-98, chair 1998, residency rev. com. 1995-2000), Am. Bd. Pediat., Nat. Bd. Med. Examiners. Intern and resident Duke U. Sch. Medicine, Durham, NC, 1972—74, asst. prof., 1977—80; staff physician Henry Ford Hosp., Detroit, 1980—97, dir. Allergy Rsch. Lab., 1986—97; prof. pediat. Case Western Res. U., Cleve., 1997; prof. pediat. and medicine Med. Coll. Ga., Augusta, 1998—. Clin. asst. prof. pediat. U. Mich., Ann Arbor, 1980—86, clin. assoc. prof. pediat., 1986—95. Contbr. articles to med. jours., chpts. to books. Fellow: Am. Acad. Allergy, Am. Acad. Pediat. Office: Med Coll of Georgia Sect Allergy & Immunology BG-1019 Augusta GA 30912-3790 Home Phone: 706-651-9229; Office Phone: 706-721-3531. Business E-Mail: downby@mcg.edu.

OWNBY, JERRY STEVE, landscape architect, educator; b. Shawnee, Okla., Jan. 25, 1939; s. Hugh H. and N. Lorraine (Hopkins) O.; children by previous marriage: Gregory Steve, Mitchell Hugh; m. Arnola Colson, Dec. 19, 1971; 1 child Steven Cory. BS, Okla. State U., 1961; MS in Landscape Architecture, Kans. State U., 1964, M in Landscape Architecture, 1970. Coun. Landscape Archtl. Registration Bds. cert. and registered landscape architect, Ariz., Mo. Extension landscape architect Kans. State U., Manhattan, 1963-64, instr., 1969-70; landscape architect Beardsley & Talley, Seattle, 1964-65; extension specialist Okla. State U., Stillwater, 1965-69, from asst. prof. to prof. landscape architecture and coordinator landscape architecture, 1970-85; pvt. practice, 1985—. Chmn. Okla. Landscape Architect Registration Bd., 1980-85; mem. 1985 Expert Panel for Uniform Nat. Exam., 1984-85; gov.'s appointee Mo. Coun. Landscape Architects, 1991-97 Designs include Las Laderas residence, 1978 (Merit award 1981), Student Union courtyard Okla. State U., 1981 (Honor award 1983). Chmn. Oklahomans for Landscape Architecture, 1979-80; chmn., vice chmn. Stillwater Park and Recreation Adv. Bd., Okla., 1971-79. Recipient Outstanding Prof. award, Okla. State U. chpt. Alpha Zeta, 1975, Svc. award, Stillwater City Commn., 1980, design awards, Springfield Planning and Zoning Commn., 1988, 1989, 1990, 1999, design award, Springfield Environ. Adv. Bd., 1990, Gov.'s Landscape Design award for Andy Williams's Moon River Theatre, Branson, Mo., 1992, for Charley Pride Theater, Branson, 1995, design award, Watershed Com., 1993, Disting. Alumnus award, dept. horticulture and landscape architecture Okla. State U., 2005; alumni fellow, Kans. State U., 1995, Paul Harris fellow, Rotary Internat., 2006. Fellow Am. Soc. Landscape Architects (v.p. 1983-85, Okla. chpt. Svc. award 1980); mem. Nat. Coun. State Garden Clubs (accredited instr. 1964—), Nat. Coun. of Educators in Landscape Architecture, Mo. Assn. of Landscape Architects, Coun. Landscape Archtl. Registration Bds. (cert.), Phi Kappa Phi, Sigma Lambda Alpha. Republican. Baptist. Avocations: travel, photography, fishing. Home: 234 Sunset Cove # 108 Branson MO 65616-3604 Home Phone: 417-338-8432. E-mail: jsownby@aol.com.

OWSLEY, FREDERICK MARK, plastic surgeon; b. July 29, 1959; BA in Sci., Carroll Coll., Helena, Mont., 1981; MD, St. Louis U. Med. Sch., 1986. Cert. Am. Bd. Plastic Surgery, lic. Idaho. Resident, gen. surgery U. Tex., 1986—92, resident, plastic surgery, 1992—95; private practice Idaho, 1995—; staff mem., med. dir. Northwest Specialty Hosp., Idaho; staff mem. Bonner Gen. Hosp., Kootenai Med. Ctr. Mem.: Soc. Plastic Surgery. Achievements include being the first surgeon to bring free flap reconstruction & tram flap reconstruction of the breast, and endoscopic breast augmentation to Kootenai County. Avocations: camping, fishing, hiking, rides mules. Office: North Idaho Plastic and Reconstructive Surgery 750 N Syringa St Ste 204 Post Falls ID 83854 Office Phone: 208-777-7830, 800-873-3823. Office Fax: 208-777-7850.

OWSLEY, JOHN QUINCY, IV, plastic surgeon, educator; b. Manila, Luzon, Philipines, Oct. 2, 1928; came to US, 1930; s. John Quincy Owsley III and Sara Christine Maxwell; m. Mary Leslie Marriott, Apr. 27, 1957 (div. 1969); children: John Quincy V, Sara Elizabeth; m. Sharon Theresa Anton, Jan. 2, 1971. BA, Vanderbilt U., 1950; MD, Vanderbilt U. Sch. Medicine, 1953. Intern, surgery U. Calif. Med. Ctr., San Francisco, 1953—54, asst. resident in surgery, 1956—58, asst. resident, chief resident plastic surgery, 1959—60, clin. instr. to asst. prof. to assoc. prof., clin. prof. surgery, 1960—80, disting. prof. surgery, 2009—; resident Franklin Hosp., 1958—59; pvt. practice San Francisco, 1960—. Dir. Esthetic Surgery Inst. San Francisco Fellowship, 1989—; vis. prof. Columbia U. Coll. of Physicians and Surgeons, 1989, Divsn. of Plastic Surgery U. Pa., 1993; Donald P. Hause Meml. lectr. U. Calif., Davis Med. Ctr., 1993; guest reviewer Jour. of Plastic and Reconstructive Surgery; founder, dir. ann. aesthetic surgery symposium U. Calif., San Francisco, 1989-2002; past chmn., dept. plastic surgery, Davies Med. Ctr., San Francisco, Calif. Author: Aesthetic Facial Surgery, 1994; contbr. chpts. to books and articles to profl. publs. Fellow ACS; mem. Am. Soc. of Plastic Surgeons (chmn. ethics com. 1973-76, Plastic Surgery Ednl. Found. award for spl. recognition for innovation and excellence in edn., 2003), Am. Soc. for Aesthetic Plastic Surgery (gen. sec. 1975-77), Am. Assn. of Plastic Surgeons, Am. Soc. Plastic and Reconstructive Surgeons (past chmn. ethics com.), Am. Cleft Palate Assn. (pres. 1977-78), Internat. Soc. for Aesthetic Plastic Surgery, Bohemian Club, Pacific Union Club Avocations: sailing, bird hunting, travel. Office: 45 Castro St Ste 111 San Francisco CA 94114 Office Phone: 415-861-8040. Office Fax: 415-861-0626. Business E-Mail: owsley@drjohnowsley.com.

OXENDALE, ROGER A., hospital administrator; m. Diane Oxendale; 3 children. BA, Clarion U., MA in Bus. Adminstrn. Sr. audit mgr. with PricewaterhouseCoopers, Pitts.; sr. fin. exec. Allegheny Health, Edn. and Rsch. Found.; CFO Children's Hosp. Pitts., 1995—2000, exec. v.p., COO, 2000—05, pres., CEO, 2005—. Bd. mem. Pittsburgh Project, Mission Meadows, Coalition for Christian Outreach, Covenant Bible College Found., Lawrenceville Devel. Corp. Office: Children's Hosp of Pitts 3705 Fifth Ave Pittsburgh PA 15213 Office Phone: 412-692-5325.*

OXENHANDLER, NEAL, literature educator, writer; b. St. Louis, Feb. 3, 1926; s. Joseph and Billie (Lutsky) O.; m. Jean Romano (div. May 1976); children: Noelle, Daniel, Alicia; m. Judith I. Josel, Dec. 12, 1979; stepchildren: Rebecca, Marjorie Menza. AB, U. Chgo., 1948; MA, Columbia U., 1951; PhD, Yale U., 1955; MA (hon.), Dartmouth Coll., 1973. Lectr. French St. Louis U., 1951-52; asst. instr. Yale U., New Haven, 1952-54, instr., 1954-57; asst. prof. UCLA, 1957-60, assoc. prof., 1960-65, U. Calif., Santa Cruz, 1965-66, prof., 1966-69, Dartmouth Coll., Hanover, NH, 1969—, Edward Tuck prof., 1987—, chmn. dept. comparative lit., 1980—85, chmn. dept. French and Italian, 1987-91. Dir. NEH Summer Seminar in Comparative Lit., 1981. Author:

Scandal and Parade: Theater of Jean Cocteau, 1957, Aspects of French Literature, 1961, French Literary Criticism: The Basis of Judgment, 1966, Max Jacob and Les Feux de Paris, 1964, (novel) A Change of Gods, 1962, Looking for Heroes in Post-War France, 1996, Rimbaud: the cost of Genius, 2009,adv. editor Film Quar., Berkeley, 1958-91; mem. editl. com. U. Calif. Press, Berkeley, 1966-69; asst. editor French Rev., 1969-73; contbr. articles, revs., poetry and translations to profl. jours. With U.S. Army, 1941-43, ETO, PTO. Decorated Combat Inf. badge; Fulbright scholar, Italy, 1953; Cross-Disciplinary fellow Soc. for Values in Higher Edn., France, 1966, Guggenheim fellow, France, 1962, Inst. for Shipboard Edn., 1995. Mem. MLA (adv. editor proc. 1977-80), Assn. Literary Scholars and Critics, Assn. Hebrew Caths. Democrat. Roman Catholic. Office: Dartmouth Coll Dept French Hanover NH 03755 Home: 700 John Ringling Blvd Apt 1507 Sarasota FL 34236-1554 Office Phone: 941-330-2086. Personal E-mail: nealoxen@aol.com.

OXER, JOHN PAUL DANIELL, civil engineer; b. Atlanta, Sept. 7, 1950; s. Robert B., Sr. and Leila Marie (Hammond) Oxer; m. Catherine Ann Stevens, Jan. 8, 1977. BCE, Ga. Inst. Tech., Atlanta, 1973; postgrad., U. Tex., Arlington, 1982-83. Lic. profl. engr. Ala., Ark., Ariz., Calif., Colo., Conn., Del., Fla., Ga., Hawaii, Idaho, Ill., Ind., Iowa, Kans., Ky., La., Maine, Mich., Minn., Miss., Mo., Mont., Nebr., Nev., NH, NJ, N.Mex., NC, ND, Ohio, Okla., Oreg., SC, SD, Tenn., Tex., Utah, Vt., Va., Wash., W.Va., Wis., Wyo.; diplomate Am. Acad. Environ. Engrs. Project engr. J.S. Ross & Assocs. Inc., Smyrna, Ga., 1973-75, Welker & Assocs. Inc., Marietta, Ga., 1976-78; sr. project. engr. Claude Terry & Assocs., Inc., Atlanta, 1978-79; chief environ. engr. Bernard Johnson Inc. (SE), Atlanta, 1979-80; chief civil engr. region VI Ecology & Environ., Inc., Dallas, 1981-84, S.E. regional mgr. Tallahassee, 1984-88, dir. program devel. Dallas, 1988-91, exec. asst. to the pres., 1991-92, Houston, 1992-97; project dir. ENRON Engring. and Constrn. Co., Houston, 1997-98; dir. internat. devel. Azurix Corp., Houston, 1998-99, v.p. internat. devel., 1999-2000; gen. mgr. nat. accts., dir. Enron Energy Svcs., Houston, 2001; ind. cons. Houston and Atlanta, 2002—04; sr. program dir. PBS&J, Atlanta, 2005—06; mng. dir. McDaniell, Hunter & Prince, Atlanta, 2007—09. Guest lectr. Fla. State U., U. Louisville, Ga. Tech.; mem. Nat. Def. Exec. Res., 1982-2007, Industry Functional Adv. Com. on Stds. for Trade Policy Matters, 1990-2001, Industry Trade Adv. Com., Small Bus., 2004-07. Exec. prodr. video documentary; writer, prodr. video documentary; co-author, dir. video prodn. Indsl. bd. advisors Speed Sci. Sch. U. Louisville, 1991-2006, chmn., 2002; mem. external adv. bd. Sch. Civil/Environ. Engring., Ga. Inst. Tech., 2000—. Named Young Engr. of Yr., Ga. Soc. Profl. Engrs., 1980. Mem. NSPE, ASCE, Am. Pub. Works Assn., Am. Soc. Landscape Archs., Am. Soc. Agrl. Biol. Engrs., Masons. Republican. Office Phone: 770-432-9460. Personal E-mail: jpoxer@charter.net.

OXFORD, HUBERT, III, lawyer; b. Beaumont, Tex., Sept. 25, 1938; s. Hubert Burton and Virginia Mary (Cunningham) O.; m. Cynthia Lynn Culp, Apr. 25, 1987; children: Mary Francelia, Hubert IV, Mary Cunningham, Virginia Barrett, Alaina Danielle, Adriana Victoria, Gabriella Elizabeth. BSME, Tex. A&M U., 1960; LLB, U. Tex., 1963. Bar: Tex., 1963, Mont. 1996, Wyo. 1996, Okla. 1996, DC 1998, Colo. 1998, U.S. Ct. Appeals (5th cir.) 1967, U.S. Dist. Ct. (ea., so., no., we. dists.) Tex., U.S. Supreme Ct. 1975, U.S. Dist. Ct., Okla., Mont., 1996, Wyo., 1996, DC 1998, Colo. 1998. Briefing atty. to U.S. dist. judge Eastern Dist. Tex., Beaumont, 1966; asst. dist. atty. Jefferson County, Tex., 1967; mng. ptnr. firm Beckenstein & Oxford, L.L.P., Beaumont, 1966; gen. counsel Sabine-Neches Navigation Dist., Lower Neches Valley Authority. Mem. Gov. Reorganization Commn. Tex. 70th Legislature, 1987-88, Tex. Oil Spill Commn.; U.S. Commr. Ea. Dist. Tex., 1968-70; mem. Tex. Bd. Registration for Profl. Engrs., 1994-2000. Assoc. editor Tex. Law Rev., 1962-63. Bd. dirs. Ducks Unltd., 1978-86, Gulf Coast Conservation Assn., 1978-86; sec. bd. regents Lamar U., 1978-84, gen. counsel, 1986; mem. Tex. Air Control Bd., 1984-90; chmn. Tex. Clean Air Study Com., 1989. Capt. JAGC, USAF, 1963-66. Fellow Tex. Bar Assn., Internat. Soc. Barristers, ABA.; mem. ATLA, Southeastern Admirality Law Inst., Internat. Assn. Def. Counsel, Tex. Assn. Def. Lawyers, Nat. Bd. Trial Advocacy, Best Lawyers in Am., State Bar Tex. (chmn. CLE com. 1979-81, course dir. admirality and maritime seminar 1991, 96, grievance com. Dist. 3A, dir. Dist. 3 1997-2000), Maritime Law Assn., Jefferson County Bar Assn. (pres. 1987-88, Outstanding Young Lawyer 1972), Def. Rsch. Inst., Beaumont C. of C. (dir. 1978-84), Phi Delta Theta, Tau Beta Pi, Phi Kappa Phi, Phi Delta Phi. Democrat. Roman Catholic. Home: 4810 Calder Rd Beaumont TX 77706 Office: Beckenstein & Oxford LLP 3535 Calder Ave Ste 300 Beaumont TX 77706-5087 Personal E-mail: hubertoxford@benoxford.com.

OXFORD, VAYL, federal agency administrator; Asst. prof. aeronautics USAF Acad., 1982—86; dir. counterproliferation Def. Nuc. Agy., Def. Spl. Weapons Agy., 1993—98; dep. dir. tech. devel. Def. Threat Reduction Agy.; dir. counter proliferation NSC; dir. Office Domestic Nuc. Detection US Dept. Homeland Security, 2005—. With USAF. Office: US Dept Homeland Security 12th & C St SW Washington DC 20024*

OXLEY, JAMES GRIEVE, mathematics professor; b. Sale, Victoria, Australia, Feb. 4, 1953; s. William A. and Dilys C. (Grieve) O.; m. Judith Danute Surkevicius; children: Margaret Catherine, David Grieve (dec.). BSc, U. Tasmania, 1974; MSc, Australian Nat. U., 1975; PhD, U. Oxford, 1978. Lectr., rsch. fellow Australian Nat. U., 1978—82; asst. prof. La. State U., Baton Rouge, 1982—85, assoc. prof., 1985—90, prof., 1990—99, alumni prof., 1999—. Vis. instr. U. N.C., Chapel Hill, 1978; vis. rsch. fellow Merton Coll., Oxford, England, 2005. Author: Matroid Theory, 1992.; mem. editl. bd. Combinatorics, Probability and Computing, Soc. Indsl. and Applied Math. Jour. on Discrete Math., Jour. Combinatorial Theory Series B; reviewer Mathematical Reviews, Zentralblatt für Mathematik; contbr. chpts. to books, articles to profl. jours. Grantee NSF, 1985-87, 89-91, La. Edn. Quality Support Fund, 1987-94, Nat. Security Agy., 1994—, others; Fulbright fellow U. N.C., 1980; named Disting. Rsch. Master of Engring, Sci. and Tech., La. State U., 1999. Mem. Am. Math. Soc., London Math. Soc. Office: La State U Math Dept Baton Rouge LA 70803-4918 Home Phone: 225-769-9106; Office Phone: 225-578-1577. Business E-Mail: oxley@math.lsu.edu.

OXLEY, MARGARET CAROLYN STEWART, elementary school educator; b. Petaluma, Calif., Apr. 1, 1930; d. James Calhoun Stewart and Clara Thornton (Whiting) Bomboy; m. Joseph Hubbard Oxley, Aug. 25, 1951; children: Linda Margaret, Carolyn Blair Oxley Greiner, Joan Claire Oxley Willis, Joseph Stewart, James Harmon, Laura Marie Oxley Brechbill. Student, U. Calif., Berkeley, 1949—51; BS summa cum laude, Ohio State U., 1973, MA, 1984, student, 1985, student, 1988, student, 1992, student, 2003—08. Cert. tchr., Ohio. 2d grade tchr. St. Paul Sch., Westerville, Ohio, 1973—. Mem. editl. bd. Reading Tchr., vol. 47-48, 1993—94, Jour. Children's Lit., 1996—2007; mem. adv. bd. Lang. Arts, 2006—; presenter in field. Co-author: Reading and Writing, Where it All Begins, 1991, Teaching with Children's Books: Path to Literature-Based Instruction, 1995, Adventuring With Books, vol. 12, 2000, vol. 13, 2002, Children's Literature Remembered: Issues, Trends, and Favorite Books, 2004. Active Akita Child Conservation League, Columbus, Ohio, 1968-70. Named Columbus Diocesan Tchr. of Yr., 1988; Phoebe A. Hearst scholar, 1951, Rose Sterheim Meml. scholar, 1951; recipient Mary Karrer award Ohio State U., 1994. Mem. Nat. Coun. Tchrs. English (Notable Children's Books in the Lang. Arts com. 1993-94, chair 1995-96, treas. Children's Literature Assembly bd. dirs. 1996-99, co-chair fall breakfast children's lit. assembly, 2000-03, co-chair excellence in poetry for children com. 2003-06), Internat. Reading Assn. (Exemplary Svc. in Promotion of Literacy award 1991), Ohio Coun. Internat. Reading Assn., Literacy Connection (pres.), Children's Lit. Assembly, Ohio Coun. Tchrs. English Lang. Arts (Outstanding Educator 1990), Phi Kappa Phi, Pi Lambda Theta (hon., Outstanding Work in Literacy Edn. citation 2004, v.p. local chpt.). Democrat. Roman Catholic. Avocations: reading, writing, travel, gardening, working with children. Home: 298 Brevoort Rd Columbus OH 43214-3826

OXLEY, MICHAEL GARVER, lawyer, former United States Representative from Ohio; b. Findlay, Ohio, Feb. 11, 1944; s. George Garver and Marilyn Maxine (Wolfe) Oxley; m. Patricia Ann Pluguez, Nov. 27, 1971; 1 child, Michael Chadd. BA in Govt., Miami U., Oxford, Ohio, 1966; JD, Ohio State U. Coll. Law, 1969. Bar: Ohio 1969, US Supreme Ct. 1986. Agt. FBI, 1969—71; atty. Oxley, Mallone, Fitzgerald & Hollister, 1971—81; mem. Ohio State House of Reps., 1973-81, US Congress from 4th Ohio Dist., 1981—2007; of counsel Baker & Hostetler LLP, Washington, 2007—; non exec. vice-chmn. Nasdaq Stock Market Inc., NYC, 2007—. Recipient Taxpayer's Friend award, Nat. Taxpayers Union, Guardian of Small Bus. award, Nat. Fedn. Ind. Bus., Spirit of Enterprise award, US C. of C., Award for Mfg. Legis. Excellence, Nat. Assn. Mfrs., Jefferson award, Citizens for Sound Economy, Friend of the Farm Bur. award, Nat. Security award, Am. Security Coun. Mem. ABA, Ohio Bar Assn., Findlay Bar Assn., Soc. Former Spl. Agts. FBI, Ohio Farm Bur., Sigma Chi., Rotary, Elks. Republican. Lutheran. Office: Baker & Hostetler LLP Washington Sq Ste 1100 1050 Connecticut Ave NW Washington DC 20036*

OXMAN, THOMAS ELLIOT, psychiatrist; b. Denver, May 15, 1949; s. Albert Charles and Leah (Hurwitz) O.; m. Judy Ann Heldman, May 27, 1971; children: Elliot Warren, Robert Charles, Annaleah H. AB in Philosophy, Dartmouth Coll., 1971; MD, U. Colo., 1975. Diplomate in psychiatry and geriatric psychiatry Am. Bd. Psychiatry and Neurology (mem. test com. 1987-95). Intern Mt. Zion Med. Ctr., San Francisco, 1976; resident in psychiatry Dartmouth Med. Sch., Hanover, N.H., 1979, fellow in consultation/liaison and cancer psychiatry, 1979-80; asst. prof. psychiatry and family medicine U. Cin. Med. Ctr., 1980-83; asst. prof. Dartmouth Med. Sch., Hanover, 1983-87, assoc. prof. psychiatry and family and cmty. medicine, attending, 1987-95, prof., 1995—2007, prof. emeritus, 2007—. Assoc. dir. consultation liaison psychiatry svc. Dartmouth Hitchcock Med. Ctr., Hanover, 1983-90, dir. geriatric psychiatry, 1988—, mem. sci. rev. com. Hitchcock Found., 1988-95; mem. Mental Disorders of Aging rev. group NIMH, 1995-99; med. dir. glencliff Home for the Elderly, NH, 1996-; assoc. chair MacArthur Found. Initiative on Depression in Primary Care, 2000-2007; ptnr. 3CM, LLC, 2006—. Editor Internat. Jour. Psychiatry in Medicine, 1996-2000, Online Abstract Svc. Am. Assoc. Geriatric Psychiatry, 2005-07; contbr. articles to profl. jours Recipient Merrell Resident Rsch. award Dartmouth Med. Sch., 1978; Rufus Choate scholar Dartmouth Coll., 1971; Mental Health Acad. awardee NIMH, 1987-90, Aging, Social Support and Phys. and Emotional Disability grantee, 1990-95; MacArthur Found. and Hartford Found. Depression in Primary Care grantee, 1995—. Dist. fellow Am. Psychiat. Assn. (liaison com. on consultation/liaison psychiatry 1982-88,)bd. dirs. Am. Assn. Geriatric Psychiatry, 2002-2006 (sec.-treas. 2007-09); mem. Phi Beta Kappa. Avocations: running, conservation. Office: Dartmouth Med Sch Dept Psychiatry Lebanon NH 03756 Office Phone: 603-650-2887.

OXNARD, CHARLES ERNEST, anatomist, anthropologist, biologist, educator; b. Durham, Eng., Sept. 9, 1933; arrived in Australia, 1987; s. Charles and Frances Ann (Golightly) O.; m. Eleanor Mary Arthur, Feb. 2, 1959; children: Hugh, David. BSc with 1st class honors, U. Birmingham, Eng., 1955, MB, BChir in Medicine, 1958, PhD, 1962, DSc, 1975. Med. intern Queen Elizabeth Hosp., Birmingham, 1958-59; rsch. fellow U. Birmingham, 1959-62, lectr., 1962-65, sr. lectr., 1965-66, court govs., 1958-66; assoc. prof. anatomy, anthropology and evolutionary biology U. Chgo., 1966—78, prof., 1970-78, gov. biology collegiate div., 1970-78, dean coll., 1973-77; dean grad. sch. U. So. Calif., Los Angeles, 1978-83, univ. rsch. prof. biology and anatomy, 1978-83, univ. prof., prof. anatomy and cell biology, prof. biol. scis., 1983-87; prof. anatomy and human biology U. We. Australia, 1987-98, dir. ctr. for human biology, 1989-99, head div. agr. and sci., 1990-92, prof. emeritus, 1998—, sr. rsch. fellow, 1998—, adj. prof. forensic sci., 2007—; Leverhulme prof. U. Liverpool (U.K.), Univ. Coll., London, 2000—03; hon. prof. U. Hull, England, 2004—, Hull York Med. Sch., 2004—. Rsch. assoc. Field Mus. Natural History, Chgo., 1967; overseas assoc. U. Birmingham, 1968—; Lo Yuk Tong lectr. U. Hong Kong, 1973, 94, 97, 2003, hon. prof., 1978, Chan Shu Tzu lectr., 80, vis. scholar, 95, 96; Octagon lectr. U. Western Australia, 1987; Latta lectr. U. Nebr., Omaha, 1987; Stanley Wilkinson orator, 91; rsch. assoc. L.A. County Natural History Mus., 1984—, George C. Page Mus., LA, 1986; vis. scholar Shaw Coll. Chinese U. of Hong Kong, 1995; bd. dirs. U. Western Australia Press, 1993—95; advisor on human biology World Sci. Pub. Co., 1993—; vis. prof. Northwestern U., Xian, China, 1999, U. York, England, 2003, hon. prof., 2004—, Hull York Med. Sch., 2004—; hon. prof. bioengring. U. Hull, 2004—. Author: Form and Pattern in Human Evolution, 1973, Uniqueness and Diversity in Human Evolution, 1973, Human Fossils: The New Revolution, 1977, The Order of Man, 1983, Humans, Apes, and Chinese Fossils, 1985, Fossils, Teeth and Sex, 1987, Anatomies and Lifestyles, 1990; series editor Recent Advances in Human Biology Series World Sci. Pub., Vol. I, The Origin and Past of Modern Humans, 1995, Vol. 2, Bone Structure and Remodeling, 1995, Vol. 3 The Origins and Past of Modern Humans: Towards Reconciliation, 1998, Vol. 4 The Natural History of the Doucs and Snub-nosed Langurs, 1998, Vol. 7 Morphometrics for the Life Sciences, 2000, Perspectives in Human Biology, Vol. 1 Genes, Ethnicity and Aging, 1995, Vol. 2 Humans in the Australasian Region, 1996, Vol. 3 Human Adaptability: Future Trends and Lessons from Past, 1998, Vol. 4, Is Human Evolution a Closed Chaptr, 1999, Vol. 4, Child Growth, Secular Trends and Continuing Human Evolution, Vol. 4, Dento-Facial Variation in Perspective, 1999, Vol. 5 Towards Consilience, 2000, Dedicatee, Shaping Primate Evolution, 2004, Anatomical Terms and their Derivation, World Sci., 2007, Ghostly Muscles, Wrinkled Brains, Heresies and Holbits, World Sci., 2008; mem. editl. bd. Annals of Human Biology; cons. editor: Am. Jour. Primatology, Jour. Human Biology, Jour. Human Evolution: Australia com. mem. Ency. Britannica, 1991-99; bibliographic referee Britannica On-Line, 1994-99; contbr articles to anat. and anthrop. jours. Mem. Pasteur Found., 1988; bd. dirs. West Australian Inst. for Child Health, 1991-98; mem. electoral bd. Freemantle Hosp., 1991-94. Recipient Book award, Hong Kong Coun., 1984, S.T. Chan Silver medal, U. Hong Kong, 1980, Charles Darwin Lifetime Achievement award, Am. Assn. Phys. Anthropology, 2001, Chancellor's medal, U. Western Australia, 2008; grantee, USPHS, 1960—71, NIH, 1974—87, NSF, 1971—87, Raine Found., 1988—91, Viertel Found., 1993—94, Australian Acad. Sci., 1995, Leverhulme Trust, Eng., 2003—06; Marie Curie Evan Rsch. Tng. grantee, 2005—, Marie Curie Palaeo Rsch. Tng. grantee, 2005—. Fellow N.Y. Acad. Sci., AAAS, So. Calif. Acad. Sci. (bd. dirs. 1985); mem. Chgo. Acad. Soc. (hon. life), Australasian Soc. for Human Biology (pres. 1987-90), Australia and New Zealand Anat. Soc. (pres. 1989-90), Anat. Soc. Gt. Britain and Ireland (councillor 1992-94), Nat. Health and Med. Rsch. Coun. (grantee 1994-97), Australian Rsch. Coun. (grantee 1988—), Med. and Health Infrastructure Fund, Western Australia (grantee 2001-03, Leverhulme Trust Rsch. grant, 2003-06, Marie Curie awards 2005-, BBSRC Rsch. grant, 2007—), Soc. Study Human Biology (treas. 1962-66), Sigma Xi (pres., nat. lectr. 1990), Phi Beta Kappa (pres. chpt.), Phi Kappa Phi (pres., Book award 1984). Office: U Western Australia Nedlands WA 6009 Australia Business E-Mail: coxnard@cyllene.uwa.edu.au.

OXNER, GEORGE DEWEY, JR., lawyer; b. Greenville, SC, Dec. 31, 1933; s. George Dewey and Frances (Ruckman) O.; m. Louise Earle, Sept. 16, 1960; children: Frances, Dewey, Earle. BA, Washington & Lee U., 1956; LLB, U. S.C., 1959. Bar: S.C. 1959, U.S. Dist. Ct. S.C. 1959, U.S. Ct. Appeals (4th cir.) 1959. From assoc. to mng. ptnr. Haynsworth, Marion, McKay & Guerard, Greenville, 1959-98, ptnr., 1998—. Co-chair Chief Justice's Commn. on the Profession. Fellow Am. Coll. Trial Lawyers (state chair 1994), SC Def. Trial Attys. Assn. (pres. 1976), SC Bar Assn. (sec. 1997-98, treas. 1998—), Assn. (sec. 1997-98, treas. 1998-99, pres. elect, 1999-00, pres. 2000-01), Am. Bd. Trial Advs. (pres. 1990-91, pres. SC, 1990-91) Home: 10 Parkins Lake Rd Greenville SC 29607-3668 Office: Haynsworth Sinkler Boyd PA 75 Beattie Pl Greenville SC 29601-2130 Office Phone: 864-240-3208. Business E-Mail: doxner@hsblawfirm.com.

OXTOBY, DAVID WILLIAM, academic administrator, chemistry professor; b. Bryn Mawr, Pa., Oct. 17, 1951; s. John Corning and Jean (Shaffer) O., m. Claire Bennett, Dec. 17, 1977; children: Mary-Christina, John, Laura. BA, Harvard U., Cambridge, Mass., 1972; PhD, U. Calif., Berkeley, 1975; DHL (hon.), Occidental Coll., LA, 2005. Asst. prof. U. Chgo., 1977-82, assoc. prof., 1982-86, prof., 1986—2003, Mellon prof., 1987-92, dir. James Franck Inst., 1992-95, dean phys. scis. divsn., 1995—2003, William Rainey Harper prof., 1996—2003; pres., prof. chemistry Pomona Coll., Claremont, Calif., 2003—. Co-author: Principles of Modern Chemistry, 1986, Chemistry: Science of Change, 1990. Trustee Bryn Mawr Coll., 1989—2009, Tchrs. Acad. Math. and Sci., 1999-03, Toyota Technol. Inst., Chgo., 2002—, The Webb Schs., 2005-09; mem. bd. govs. Argonne Nat. Lab., 1996-02, Astrophys. Rsch. Consortium, 1998-03; mem. bd. overseers Claremont Univ. Consortium, 2003-, Harvard U., 2008-. Recipient Quantrell award U. Chgo., 1986, Alumni award of merit William Penn Charter Sch., 2003; Alfred P. Sloan Found. fellow, 1979, John Simon Guggenheim Found. fellow, 1987; Camille and Henry Dreyfus Found. tchr.-scholar, 1980. Fellow AAAS, Am. Phys. Soc.; mem. Am. Chem. Soc., Am. Assn. Colls. and Univs. (bd. dirs. 2006—, vice chair 2009), Royal Soc. Chemistry (Marlow medal 1983), Phi Beta Kappa. Office: Office of the Pres Pomona Coll 550 N College Ave Claremont CA 91711 Home Phone: 909-624-0931; Office Phone: 909-621-8131.

OYANA, TONNY J., geoscientist, educator; b. Kampala, Uganda, Apr. 20, 1968; arrived in U.S., 2000; s. Jerry Oyana Odongo and Mary Phoebe Oyana; m. Damalie M. Oyana, Feb. 4, 1992; children: Owen Kiredi-Jean, Phoebe Makimoth-Fayola. BS in Biology and Geography, U. Dar-Es-Salam, Tanzania, 1993; MS in Geog. Info. Sys., Environ. Planning, Nat. U. Ireland, Cork, 1996; PhD in Geog. Info. Sys., Geog. Info. Sci., SUNY, Buffalo, 2003. Biology and geography tchr. Jangwani Secondary Sch., Dar-es-Salaam, 1990—91, Kisitu Girls' Sch., Dar-es-Salaam, 1992; tchr., cons. SNV Netherlands Devel. Orgn., Tanzania and Uganda, 1993—94; tchg. asst. dept. geography Makerere U., Kampala, Uganda, 1993—95, lectr. dept. geography, 1996—98; child advocacy officer Nat. Coun. Children, Redd Barna, Norway, 1994; grad. tutor dept. geography U. Coll. Cork, 1995—96; rsch. fellow, project cons. Internat. Ctr. Tropical Agr., Colombia, 1997—98; tchg. asst. dept. geography U. BC, Vancouver, Canada, 1998—99; rsch. asst. dept. geography SUNY, Buffalo, 2000—02, postdoctoral fellow Ctr. Asthma and Environ. Exposure, 2003; assoc. prof. geography info. sys. So. Ill. U., Carbondale, 2003—. Rsch./grad. asst. Nat. Ctr. Geog. Info. and Analysis, Sch. Medicine and Biomed. Scis., Ctr. Asthma and Environ. Exposure, SUNY, 2000—02; dir. rsch. lab. geographic medicine and broad band mapping project; cons. in field. Reviewer: various jours. in field; contbr. articles to profl. publs., chpts. to books. Recipient U. Nairobi Collaborative Rsch. award, Ctr. Devel. Rsch., Denmark, 1995—97, Cross-Border Activities Rsch. award, UN Ctr. Regional Devel., 1995; postgrad. fellow, Dept. Fgn. Affairs, Dublin, Ireland, 1995—96. Mem.: Am. Assn. Geographers, Am. Acad. Sleep Medicine. Office: So Ill U 1000 Farner Carbondale IL 62901

OYEYEMI, OLUSOLA OLAYINKA, lawyer; b. Ile-Ife, Osun, Nigeria, Nov. 1, 1968; U.S., 1999; s. Titus Adewuyi and Christiana Amoke Oyeyemi; children: Oluseyi, Olamide. LLB, Ogun State U., Ago-Iwoye, Nigeria, 1988, Nigerian Law Sch., Lagos, 1989; LLM, U. Pretoria, South Africa, 1999. Bar: Nigeria 1989, Wash. 2002, U.S. Dist. Ct. (no. dist.) Ill. 2002. Jr. counsel Adegbo Yega Awomolo & Co., Ilorin, Nigeria, 1989—92; head chambers Olusola Oyeyemi & Co., Ibadan, Nigeria, 1992—; assoc. Oshiyoye & Co., Southfield, Mich., 2000—02; ptnr. Pntrs. LLC, Chgo., 2002—06, Simmons Cooper LLC, Chgo., 2006—. Legal advisor De Friendship Orgn., Ibadan, 1995—99. Pro bono lawyer Wash. State Bar, 2005; sec. Christ Apostolic Ch., Chgo., 2000—04; vol. Redeemed Christian Ch. of God, Chgo., 2004—. Recipient Pro Bono Work Recognition award, Wash. State Bar, 2005. Mem.: ACLU, ABA, Am. Immigration Lawyers Assn. Mem. Pentecostal Ch. Avocations: reading, sports, travel, driving. Home: 1457 Gordon Ave Calumet City IL 60409 Office Phone: 312-759-7507. Business E-Mail: ooyeyemi@simmonscooper.com.

OYINLADE, A. OLU, sociologist, educator; s. Moses David and Bade (Adejumo) Oyinlade; 1 child, Bisi Bade-Alexandra. BS, U. Ky., Lexington; MS, Ctrl. Mo. State U., Warrensburg; PhD, SD State U., Brookings. Asst. prof. Bristol CC, Fall River, Mass., 1987—90, Northern State U., Aberdeen, ND, 1990—93; asst. prof. to assoc. prof. Nebr. Wesleyan U., Lincoln, Nebr., 1993—2000; prof., indsl. orgnl. sociology U. Nebr., Omaha, 2000—. Dir., honors program No. State U., Aberdeen, SD, 1992—93; state dir. Midwest Sociol. Soc., 1992—93, 2003—05, bd. mem., 2003—05, 1992—93, chair, minority scholars com., 1993—96; chair, ethics com. Gt. Plains Sociol. Assn., 1992—93; alpha kappa delta chpt. adviser U. Nebr., Omaha; undergrad. students adviser U. Nebr., Omaha, Orgnl. Sociology Program. Contbr. articles to profl. jours. Resource cons. Ogoni Refugees Cmty., Lincoln; making recommendations to organization's pres. Save Sub-Sahara Orphans Orgn., Lincoln, 1999—2001; mng. association's affairs Midwest Sociol. Assn., 1992—93, 2003—05. Mem.: The Midwest Sociol. Soc. (bd. mem. 2003—05). Independent. Achievements include research creation of the essential behavioral leadership qualities method of leadership assessment; research in Author and co-author of scientific articles, abstracts, newspaper articles and opinion columns, a text book and study guide. Office: Univ Nebraska Omaha 6001 Dodge St Omaha NE 68182 Office Phone: 402-554-2626. Office Fax: 402-554-3786. Business E-Mail: aoyinlade@mail.unomaha.edu.

OYLER, ANNE, audiologist; Assoc. dir. audiology profl. practices Am. Speech-Language Hearing Assn. Office: 2200 Research Blvd #305 Rockville MD 20850-3289 Office Phone: 301-296-5700. E-mail: aoyler@asha.org.*

OZ, AMOS (AMOS KLAUSNER), writer, educator; b. Jerusalem, 1939; m. Nily Zuckerman; children: Fania, Gallia, Daniel. BA, Hebrew U., Jerusalem, 1965; MA, Oxford U., 1970; D (hon.), Hebrew Union Coll., Western New Eng. Coll., Tel Aviv U. Mem. Kibbutz Hulda, Israel, 1957-86; full prof., Agnon chmn. Hebrew Lit. Ben-Gurion U. Negev, Beer-Sheva, Israel, 1986—. Author-in-residence Hebrew U., Jerusalem, 1975, 90, Boston U., 1987, U. Calif., Berkeley, 1980, Colo. Springs Coll. Am., 1984-85; vis. fellow Oxford U., 1969-70; vis. writer N.Y. State Writers Inst., 1997. Author: (collection) Where the Jackals Howl, 1965, Elsewhere Perhaps, 1966, adapted for stage1982, My Michael, 1968, film version, 1975, Unto Death, 1971, Touch the Water, Touch the Wind, 1973, The Hill of Evil Counsel, 1976 (Brenner prize Lit. 1977), (children's book) Soumchi, 1978, (collection) Under This Blazing Light, 1979, The Slopes of Lebanon, 1981, A Perfect Peace, 1982, In the Land of Israel, 1983, Black Box, 1987 (Prix Femina Etranger 1988), To Know a Woman, 1989, The Third Condition (Fima), 1991, The Silence of Heaven, 1993, Don't Call It Night, 1994, Israel, Palestine & Peace, 1994, Panther in the Basement, 1995, The Story Begins, 1996, The Same Sea, 1998, All Our Hopes: Essays on the Israeli Condition, 1998; short stories; editor: The Seventh Day, (anthology) Stories from the Kibbutz; contbr. 450 articles and essays to profl. jours. and newspapers. Active various groups Israeli Peace Movement, 1967—, Peace Now, 1977—. Served with Israeli Army. Recipient Holon prize for Lit., 1966, B'nai Brith Ann. Lit. award, 1972, Brenner Prize, 1976, Bialik prize, 1986, Wingate prize, 1988, German Friedenspreis Internat. Peace prize, 1992, French Cross of Knight of Légion d'Honneur, Pres. Jacques Chirac, 1997, Israel Prize in Lit., 1998; Am. Israel Cultural Found. fellow. Mem. I.T.I., Internat. PEN Assn., Acad. Hebrew Lang., Am. Acad. Arts & Scis.(fgn. hon.). Office: Ben Gurion U Negev Be'er Sheva Israel

OZ, MEHMET CENGIZ, cardiac surgeon; b. Cleve., June 11, 1960; s. Mustafa and Suna (Atabay) Oz; m. Lisa Oz; children: Daphne, Arabella, Zoe, Oliver. BA magna cum laude, Harvard U., 1982; MD, U. Pa. Sch. Medicine, 1986; MBA, Wharton Bus. Sch., U. Pa., Phila., 1986; doctorate (hon.), Istanbul U. Cert. Am. Bd. Surgery, Am. Bd. Thoracic Surgery. Intern/resident, gen. surgery Columbia-Presbyn. Med. Ctr., NYC, 1986—90, chief resident, gen. surgery, 1990—91, resident, cardiothoracic surgery, 1991—93; attending surgeon NY Presbyn. Hosp./Columbia U. Med. Ctr., 1993—; Irving asst. prof., surgery Columbia U. Coll. Physicians and Surgeons, NYC, 1994—2000, assoc. prof., surgery, 2000—01, prof., surgery, 2001—; dir. Cardiovasc. Inst., Dept. Surgery Columbia U. Med. Ctr., 2001—, vice-chmn., cardiovascular svcs., dept. surgery, 2001—. Bd. dirs. Siga Corp.; med. class chmn. U. Pa. Med. Sch., 1982—83, med. sch. pres., 1984—85; dir., Cardiac Assist Device Program Columbia-Presbyn. Med. Ctr., 1994—2001, founder, Complementary Medicine Program; mem. Thoracic Surgical Workforce Com., 1998. Author: Healing from the Heart: A Leading Surgeon Combines Eastern and Western Traditions to Create the Medicine of the Future, 1998 (Books for a Better Am. award, 1999); co-editor (with Daniel J. Goldstein): Minimally Invasive Cardiac Surgery, 1998 (Voted the best health sci. book, Doody, 2000), Minimally Invasive Cardiac Surgery, 2nd edit., 2004, Cardiac Assist Devices, 2000; co-author (with Michael F. Roizen): YOU: The Owner's Manual: An Insider's Guide to the Body That Will Make You Healthier and Younger, 2005, YOU: The Smart Patient: An Insider's Handbook for Getting the Best Treatment, 2006, YOU: On a Diet- The Owner's Manual for Waist Management, 2006, YOU: Staying Young: The Owner's Manual for Extending Your Warranty, 2007, YOU: Being Beautiful: The Owner's Manual to Inner and Outer Beauty, 2008, (compact disc) YOU: on a Walk, 2007, YOU: Breathing Easy: Meditation and Breathing Techniques to Help You Relax, Refresh and Revitalize, 2008; numerous network news appearances, guest host The Charlie Rose Show, host Second Opinion with Dr. Oz, Discovery Health Channel, Oprah & Friends, XM Satellite Radio, 2006—, health expert Oprah Winfrey Show, Discovery Channel. Recipient Blakemore Rsch. Prize, Columbia U. Coll. Physicians & Surgeons, 1988—91, P & S Club Outstanding House Officer award, 1991, 25th Anniversary Silver award, Bastyr U., 2004; named Turkish-Am. of Yr., Assembly Turkish-Am. Assns., 1996; named a Doctor of Yr., Hippocrates mag.; named one of The Best and Brightest, Esquire mag., Healers of the Millenium, Healthy Living mag., Best Doctors of Yr., NY Mag., Global Leaders of Tomorrow, World Econ. Forum, 1999, the 100 Most Influential People in the World, TIME mag., 2008; named to Castle Connolly Guide. Fellow: ACS, Am. Coll. Cardiology; mem.: Am. Coll. Angiology (mem. scientific coun.), Am. Soc. for Laser Medicine and Surgery (Rsch. award 1991), Internat. Soc. for Optical Engring., Assn. Turkish-Am. Scientists, NY Soc. Thoracic Surgery, NY State Soc. Surgeons, 21st Century Cardiac Surgical Soc., Found. Advancement of Cardiac Therapies (bd. dirs.), Am. Turkish Soc. (bd. dirs.), Global Leader Tomorrow, World Econ. Forums, Am. Soc. Artificial Internal Organs, Am. Heart Assn. (mem. scientific coun.), Turkish-Am. Physicians Assn., Assn. Acad. Surgery, Internat. Soc. for Heart and Lung Transplantation, Am. Bd. Surgery, Am. Bd. Thoracic Surgery, Am. Assn. Thoracic Surgeons. Achievements include patents in field. Office: NY Presbyn Hosp Columbia Med Ctr 177 Fort Washington Ave MHB 7 435 New York NY 10032 Office Phone: 212-342-3520. Office Fax: 212-305-4434. E-mail: mco2@columbia.edu.

ÖZALP, NESRIN, mechanical engineer, research scientist; d. Mehmet Orhan and Aysel Özalp. MS, Ege U., Izmir, Turkey, 1998, Stanford U., San Francisco, 2002; PhD, U. of Wash., Seattle, 2005. Rsch. asst. Stanford U., Mech. Engring. Dept., San Francisco, U. Wash., Mech. Engring. Dept., Seattle; prof. dept. mech. engring. Tex. A&M U. at Qatar. Rep. grad. student Stanford U., San Francisco, 2001—02; sen. mech. engring. dept. Grad. and Profl. Students Senate, 2003—05; bd. mem. pres. rsch. adv. bd. U. Wash., Seattle, 2004—05, com. mem. provost's fund for innovation and redesign; bd. mem. a Wash. State EPA, 2004; vis. prof. dept mech. and process engring. Swiss Fed. Inst. Tech. Contbr. articles to profl. jours. Fellow, Pacific NW Nat. Lab. Mem.: ASME. Office Fax: 90 (232) 388 8562. E-mail: nesrin.ozalp@ege.edu.tr.

OZAN, EROL, engineering educator, researcher; BS in Elec. & Electronics Engring., Mid. East Tech. U., Ankara, Turkey; MS in Physics, U. Istanbul, Turkey; PhD in Engring. Mgmt., Old Dominion U., Norfolk, Va. Grad. asst. Old Dominion U., 1999—2003; asst. prof. East Carolina U., Greenville, 2003—. Office: East Carolina Univ Dept Tech Sys Charlotte NC 28258

OZAWA, MARTHA NAOKO, social work educator; b. Ashikaga, Tochigi, Japan, Sept. 30, 1933; arrived in US, 1963; d. Tokuichi and Fumi (Kawashima) O.; m. May 1959 (div. May 1966). BA in Econs., Aoyama Gakuin U., 1956; MS in Social Work, U. Wis., 1966, PhD in Social Welfare, 1969. Asst. prof. social work Portland State U., Oreg., 1969-70, assoc. prof. social work, 1970-72, 1975-76; assoc. rsch. prof. social work NYU, 1972-75; prof. social work Washington U., St. Louis, 1976-85, Bettie Bofinger Brown prof. social policy, 1985—2003, Bettie Bofinger Brown Disting. prof. social policy, 2003—; dir. Martha N. Ozawa Ctr. Social Policy Studies, 2005—. Author: Income Maintenance and Work Incentives, 1982; editor: Women's Life Cycle: Japan-U.S. Comparison in Income Maintenance, 1989, Women's Life Cycle and Economic Insecurity: Problems and Proposals, 1989; editl. bd. Social Work, Silver Spring, Md., 1972-75, 85-88, New Eng. Jour. Human Svcs., Boston, 1987-95, Ency. of Social Work, Silver Spring, 1974-77, 91-95, 99-2003, Jour. Social Svc. Rsch., 1977-97, Children and Youth Svcs. Rev., 1991—, Social Work Rsch., 1994-97, Jour. Poverty, 1997-2004; co-editor-in-chief Asian Social Work and Policy Rev., 2005—. Grantee Adminstrn. on Aging, Washington, 1979, 84, NIMH, 1990-93. Mem. Nat. Assn. Social Workers (presdl. award 1999), Nat. Acad. Social Ins., Nat. Conf. on Social Welfare (bd. dirs. 1981-87), The Gerontol. Soc. Am., Soc. for Social Work and Rsch., Washington U. Faculty Club (bd. dirs. 1986-91). Avocations: photography, tennis, swimming, gardening. Home: 13018 Tiger Lily Ct Saint Louis MO 63146-4339 Office: PO Box 1196 Saint Louis MO 63130-4899 Office Phone: 314-935-6615. Business E-Mail: ozawa@wustl.edu.

OZAWA, SEIJI, conductor, music director; b. Shenyang, China, Sept. 1, 1935; s. Kaisaku and Sakura Ozawa; m. Kyoko Edo; m. Vera Motoki-Ilyin Ozawa; children: Seira, Yukiyoshi. Student, Toho Sch. Music, Tokyo; studied with Hideo Saito, Eugene Bigot, Herbert Von Karajan, Leonard Bernstein, Charles Munch; MusD (hon.), U. Mass., New Eng. Conservatory Music, Wheaton Coll. Asst. condr. NY Philharm., 1960—64; music dir. Toronto Symphony Orch., 1965—70, San Francisco Symphony Orch., 1969—76, Boston Symphony Orch., 1973—2002, music dir. laureate, 2002—; music dir. Vienna State Opera, 2002—. Music dir. Ravinia Festival, Highland Park, Ill., 1964—71; apptd. artistic adv. Tanglewood Festival, Boston, 1970; music adv. Boston Symphony Orch., 1972—73, condr. Evening at Symphony; music adv. Saito Kinen Festival, Matsumoto, Japan, 1992; mem. internat. tour Dvorak Gala, Prague, 1993, Vienna Philharm. Asia, 1993, 96, 2000, Vienna Philharm. Europe, 1997, 98, 2000; mem. concert tour Berlin Philharm. Salzburg Festival; co-founder, artistic dir. Tokyo Opera Nomori, 2005—. Recipient 1st prize, Internat. Competition Orch. Condrs., 1959, Koussevitzky prize, Tanglewood Music Ctr., 1960, Inouye award for Lifetime Achievement, 1964; named Laureate, Found. du Japan, 1988, Seiji Ozawa Hall for him, Tanglewood Music Ctr., 1994, Music Dir. Laureate, Boston Symphony Orch., 2002, Musician of the Yr., Musical America; named a Chevalier de la Legion d'Honneur, Pres. France Jacques Chirac; conducting fellow, Tanglewood Music Ctr., 1959. Avocations: golf, tennis, skiing. Office: Veroza Japan Co Ltd 2F 6 13 n21 Seijo Setagaya ku Tokyo 157 0066 Japan also: Vienna State Opera 1010 Wien Opernring 2 Austria*

ÖZBAY, HITAY, electrical engineering educator; b. Ankara, Turkey, May 17, 1962; came to U.S., 1987; s. Ömer and Üklü (Hitay) Ö. BSc, Mid. East Tech. U., Ankara, 1985; MEngring., McGill U., Montreal, Que., Can., 1987; PhD, U. Minn., 1989. Trainee Teknim, Ankara, 1983, Aselsan, Ankara, 1984; rsch. asst. McGill U., 1985-87; teaching asst. U. Minn., Mpls., 1987, rsch. asst., 1988-89; asst. prof. U. R.I., Kingston, 1989-90; asst. prof. elec. engring. Ohio State U., Columbus, 1991—. Contbr. articles to sci. jours. Scholar Turkish Sci. and Tech. Rsch. Coun., 1982-85, Turkish Edn. Found., 1985-87; grantee Ohio State U., 1991—, NSF, 1992—. Mem. IEEE, Galatasaray Alumni Assn., Am. Soc. Engring. Edn. Avocations: music, soccer, bridge. Office: Ohio State U Dept Elec Engring 2015 Neil Ave Dept Elec Columbus OH 43210-1210

OZCAN, AYDOGAN, electrical engineer, educator; b. Sinop, Turkey, Sept. 24, 1978; BS in Elec. Engring., Bilkent U., Turkey, 2000; MS in Elec. Engring., Stanford U., Calif., 2002, PhD in Elec. Engring., 2005. Post-doctoral fellow Stanford U., 2005—06; instr. Med. Sch. Harvard U., Boston, 2006—07; prof. elec. engring. dept. UCLA, 2007—. Contbr. articles to profl. jours. Mem.: IEEE, OSA. Achievements include patents pending in field; patents in field; by adding a few off-the-shelf parts (cost less than $50) to a typical Sony Ericsson cell phone, has created LUCAS, which stands for lensless ultra-wide-field cell monitoring array platform based on shadow imaging. It uses a short wavelength blue light to illuminate a sample of liquid blood, saliva or another fluid on a laboratory slide. Office: Elec Engring Dept UCLA Los Angeles CA 90095 Home: 827 Levering Ave Los Angeles CA 90024 Business E-Mail: ozcan@ee.ucla.edu.*

OZCELIK, HAKAN, finance educator; b. Canakkale, Turkey, June 21, 1972; married. Grad. student, Bosphorus U., Istanbul, Turkey, 1998; PhD, U. BC, Vancouver, Can., 2004. Asst. prof. Calif. State U., Sacramento, 2004—. Recipient Citation of Excellence award, 2005. Mem.: Acad. Mgmt. Office: Calif State Univ Sacramento 6000 J St Sacramento CA 95825 Office Fax: (916) 278-5580.

OZDEN, CAGLAR, economist; married; children: Nuray, Nedim. BS, Cornell U., Ithaca, NY, 1992; PhD, Stanford U., Palo Alto, Calif., 1998. Sr. economist World Bank, Washington, 2002—. Co-editor: (book) International Migration, Remittances and the Brain Drain; editor: International Migration, Economic Development and Policy. Office: World Bank 1818 H St NW MC3-303 Washington DC 20433

OZEKI, AKICHIKA, statistician; BS in Elec., Electronic Engring. and Info., Nagoya U., Aichi, Japan, 1998; MS in Ops. Rsch., NC State U., 2000—00. Cert. RedHat JAPAN, 2001, UNIX adminstr. IBM, 2001, in DB2 UDB advisory IBM, 2002, Cisco Sys., Inc, 2003; APEF, 1999. IT engr., server sys. IBM Japan Systems Engring., Chiba, 2000—03, IT specialist, server sys., 2003—04; rschr. U. Wis. Madison, 2004—. Co-author: (computer book) The Complete Partitioning Guide fo IBM eserve pSeries Servers; translator: (book) J. Lahmann, et al. Linux Applications on AIX, A. Farazdel, et. al. Additional AX Security Tools on pSeries. Achievements include invention of algorithm for a rank method. Office: Univ Wis Madison 1300 Univ Ave Madison WI 53706 Business E-Mail: ozeki@wisc.edu.

OZEL, TUGRUL, engineering educator, researcher; b. Izmir, Turkey, Jan. 4, 1967; s. Rafet and Kaya Sadriye Ozel; m. Muge Ozel; children: Doruk children: Pelin. PhD, Ohio State U., 1998. Asst. prof. Cleve. State U., 1998—2001, Rutgers U., Piscataway, NJ, 2002—08, assoc. prof., 2008—. Contbr. articles to profl. jours. Recipient NJ Space Grant Consortium award, 2002; nominee Fraunhofer Bessel Rsch. award, 2006; grantee, Rutgers U. Rsch. Coun., 2005, 2006; NASA summer faculty fellowship, 1999. Mem.: ASME, AAUP, N.Am. Mfg. Rsch. Inst., Soc. Mfg. Engrs. Office: Rutgers U 96 Frelinghuysen Rd Piscataway NJ 08854 Home Phone: 908-304-0357; Office Phone: 732-445-1099. Business E-Mail: ozel@rci.rutgers.edu.

OZER, HOWARD, oncologist, hematologist; s. Ozer; m. Angel Ozer. MD, PhD, Yale U., New Haven, Conn. Lic. physician Mass., 1977, dea Fed., 1977, diplomate Am. Bd. Internal Medicine, 1979, lic. physician NY, 1979, cert. lab director cellular immunology NY State Dept. Health, 1983, lic. physician NC, 1985, Ga., 1994, Pa., 1997, Okla., 2000. Rsch. assoc. divsn. tumor immunology Sidney Farber Cancer Inst., Boston, 1975—79; clin. rsch. fellow, dept. of medicine Peter Bent Brigham Hosp., Boston, 1975—79, Harvard Med. Sch., Boston, 1975—79; cancer rsch. clinician Roswell Pk. Meml. Inst., Buffalo, 1979—83; asst. prof. medicine and microbiology SUNY, Buffalo, 1979—83, dir. tumor immunology lab., 1979—85, tenured assoc. prof. of medicine and microbiology, 1983—85, assoc. rsch. prof. dept. microbiology, immunology, 1983—85; dir. Core Flow Cytometry Facility, Roswell Pk. Meml. Inst., Buffalo, 1984—85; assoc. dir. clin. affairs Lineberger Comprehensive Cancer Ctr., Chapel Hill, NC, 1985—94; dir. hematology, oncology fellowship program U. NC, Chapel Hill, 1985—94, chief divsn. med. oncology, 1985—94, prof. medicine, 1985—94, clin. svc. chief hematology, oncology svc., 1991—94; prof. medicine Emory U. Sch. Medicine, Atlanta, 1994—97, Hahnemann U., Phila., 1997—2000, dir. cancer ctr., 1997—2000, divsn. chief hematology, oncology, 1997—2000; acting divsn. chief pediat. hematology, oncology St. Christopher's Hosp., Phila., 1998—99; dir. cancer ctr. Okla. U., Oklahoma City, 2000—06; prof. medicine Okla. U. Health Scis. Ctr., Oklahoma City, 2000, Eason chair and chief hematology, oncology, 2000—, dir. hematology, oncology fellowship program, 2002—07. Contbr. articles to profl. jours. Mem. steering com. Okla. Comprehensive Cancer Control Plan, 2004—05. Grantee, PPD Devel., 2006-2007, Globeimmune, 2006—, Genentech, 2004—, ECOG, 2004-2007; fellow, Amgen, 2006. Mem.: Network Steering Com. for Implementation of an Okla. Comprehensive Cancer Control Plan, Am. Assn. Cancer Rsch. (assoc.), Am. Soc. Clin. Oncology (assoc.), Am. Soc. Hematology (assoc.), Am. Assn. Immunologists (assoc.), Okla. Soc. Clin. Oncology (assoc.), The Leukemia & Lymphoma Soc., Okla. Chpt. (assoc.; bd. mem. 2003—04), CALGB (assoc.; at-large mem. rep. 2004—0+). Socialist. Office: Okla U Health Scis Ctr 920 Stanton L Young Blvd WP 2080 Oklahoma City OK 73104 Business E-Mail: howard-ozer@ouhsc.edu.

OZERO, BRIAN JOHN, chemical engineer; b. Manitoba, Can., 1932; came to U.S., 1963; s. Daniel and Mary Ozero; m. Ila Atlas, 1985. BS in Chem. Engring., Queens U., Kingston, Ontario, Can., 1954; MS in Chem. Engring., NYU, 1968. Technologist Shell Oil Co., Montreal, Quebec, Can., 1954-60; design engr. Chem. Constrn. Co., London, 1960-63; sr. process engr. Sci. Design Co., NYC, 1963-65, process mgr., 1965-75; tech. dir. Halcon SD Group Inc., NYC, 1976-85; sr. process mgr. Tech. Evaluation and Devel. Assocs., Hoboken, N.J., 1986; pres., prin. cons. Scientech Assocs. Inc., NYC, 1986—. Recognized expert in ethylene oxide/ethylene glycol, VCM, maleic anhydride, propylene oxide; contbr. articles and chpts. to tech. jours. and encyclopedias in field; patentee in field. Vice pres., past pres. Barrier Beach Preservation Assn., Westhampton, N.Y., 1985-88. Mem. Am. Inst. Chem. Engrs., Rotary. Democrat. Roman Catholic. Avocations: reading, tennis, skiing. Home: PO Box 1524 Westhampton Beach NY 11978-7524 Office: Scientech Assoc Inc PO Box 768 Westhampton Beach NY 11978-0768 Office Phone: 631-288-2144. E-mail: ozerowhb@aol.com.

OZGUNER, FUSUN, engineering educator; d. Kazim and Remziye Ergin; m. Umit Ozguner, Mar. 4, 1971; children: Tolga, Ceylan. PhD, U. Ill., Champaign-Urbana, 1975. Prof. Ohio State U. Elec. and Computer Engring. Dept., Columbus, 1991—, dept. chair, 2004—06. Contbr. numerous articles to profl. jours. Grantee, NSF, 2001—03. Mem.: IEEE (sr. mem.). Achievements include research in heterogeneous computing and fault tolerance. Office: Ohio State Univ ECE Dept 2015 Neil Ave Columbus OH 43210 Business E-Mail: ozguner@ece.osu.edu, ozguner.2@osu.edu.

OZGUR, ARZUCAN, computer engineer, researcher; d. Haydar and Rahime Ozgur. BS in Computer Engring., Bogazici U., Istanbul, Turkey, 2002, MS, 2004. Rsch. and tchg. asst. Bogazici U., 2002—06; grad. student rsch. asst. U. Mich., Ann Arbor, 2006—. Business E-Mail: ozgur@umich.edu.

OZICK, CYNTHIA, writer; b. NYC, Apr. 17, 1928; d. William and Celia (Regelson) O.; m. Bernard Hallote, Sept. 7, 1952; 1 child: Rachel Sarah. BA cum laude with honors in English, NYU, 1949; MA, Ohio State U., 1950; LHD (hon.), Yeshiva U., 1984, Hebrew Union Coll., 1984, Williams Coll., 1986, Hunter Coll., 1987, Jewish Theol. Sem. Am., 1988, Adelphi U., 1988, SUNY, 1989, Brandeis U., 1990, Bard Coll., 1991, Spertus Coll., 1991, Skidmore Coll., 1992, Seton Hall U., 1999, Rutgers U., 1999, U. N.C., Asheville, 2000, NYU, 2001, Bar-Ilan U., Israel, 2002, Balt Hebrew U., 2004; LHD (hon.), Georgetown U., 2007. Author: Trust, 1966, reissued, 2004, The Pagan Rabbi and Other Stories, 1971, Bloodshed and Three Novellas, 1976, Levitation: Five Fictions, 1982, Art and Ardor: Essays, 1983, The Cannibal Galaxy, 1983, The Messiah of Stockholm, 1987, Metaphor & Memory: Essays, 1989, The Shawl, 1989, Epodes: First Poems, 1992, What Henry James Knew, and Other Essays on Writers, 1994, Portrait of the Artist as a Bad Character, 1996, The Cynthia Ozick Reader, 1996, Fame & Folly, 1996, The Puttermesser Papers, 1997, Heir to the Glimmering World, 2004, The Din the Head: Essays, 2006, Dictation:A Quartot, 2008, 09, (plays): Blue Light, 1994, The Shawl, 1996; guest editor: Best Am. Essays, 1998, Quarrel & Quandary: Essays, 2000, Collected Stories, 2006; contbr. poetry, criticism, revs., translations, essays and fictions in numerous periodicals and anthologies. Recipient Rea award for short story, 1986, PEN/Spiegel-Diamonstein award for the art of the essay, 1997, Harold Washington Lit. award City of Chgo., 1997, John Cheever award, 1999, Lannan Found. award for fiction, 2000, Koret Found. award for lit. studies, 2001, Nat. Book Critics Circle award for nonfiction, 2001, Mary McCarthy award Bard Coll., 2007, Nat. Humanities medal NEH, 2007, Presdl. medal, Washington, DC, 2007, Maison des ecrivaine Etranger, 2007, PEN/Nabokov Lifetime Achievement award, 2008, PEN/Malamud Lifetime Achievement award, 2008; Guggenheim fellow, 1982, Lucy Martin Donnelly fellow Bryn Mawr Coll., 1992; grantee, Nat. Endowment Arts, 2007. Mem. PEN, Authors League, Am. Acad. Arts and Scis., Am. Acad. Arts and Letters (Mildred and Harold Strauss Living award 1983), Dramatists Guild, Académie Universelle des Cultures (Paris), Phi Beta Kappa. Jewish.

OZKURT, TOLGA ESAT, engineer, researcher; b. Istanbul, Turkey, May 4, 1980; s. Huseyin and Melek Ozkurt. MSc in Computer Sci., Istanbul Tech. U., 2004; PhD, U. Pitts., 2009. Rschr. Inst. Informatics, Istanbul Tech. U., 2002—05, Lab. Computational Neurosci., U. Pitts., 2005—. Dir.: (short film) Alie-nation. Mem.: IEEE (reviewer 2005—). Achievements include research in spatial filtering of brain signals using spherical harmonics. Personal E-mail: tolgaozkurt@gmail.com.

OZMUCUR, SULEYMAN, economics professor, researcher; BA, Bogazici U., Istanbul, 1973; MA in Econ., Manchester U., England, 1974; PhD, Istanbul U., Turkey, 1976. Economist Greater Istanbul Master Plan Bur., 1975—75; lectr. Bogazici U., Istanbul, 1976—79, prof., 1982—2000; asst. prof. Vassar Coll., Poughkeepsie, NY, 1977—82, prof., 1977—82; lectr. U. Pa., Phila., 1997—, rsch. specialist, 2003—05. Contbr. articles to numerous jours. on economics. Recipient Sedat Simavi Vakfi Sosyal Bilimler Odulu, 1987, Arthur H. Cole prize,

2002; finalist Franz Edelman Ops. Rsch. and Mgmt. Sci. Achievement award, 1998; fellow Social Sci. Rsch. Coun. Rsch. Studentship, Manchester U., 1973—74. Office: Univ Pennsylvania 3718 Locust Walk Philadelphia PA 19104 Office Fax: 215-898-4477. Business E-Mail: ozmucur@ssc.upenn.edu.

OZUMBA, BENJAMIN CHUKWUMA, obstetrician, gynecologist, educator; b. Onitsha, Anambra, Nigeria, Mar. 21, 1954; s. Arthur Nwabunwanne and Alice chiebonam (Igebuike) O.; m. Chinelo Obianuju Udokwu, Jan. 29, 1994; children: Benjamin Chukwumdindu, Sarah Onyinyechukwu, Elizabeth Chimfumnanya, Rachel Chidinma. MB, BChir, U. Lagos, Nigeria, 1979; FMCOG, Post Grad. Med. Coll., Nigeria, 1987; MRCOG, Royal Coll. Ob.-Gyn., London, 1993; FICS, Internat. Coll. Surgeons, U.S., 1991; FWACS, W. African Coll. Surgeons, Lagos, Nigeria, 1993. Intern Lagos U. Tchg. Hosp., 1979—80; med. officer Coll. of Edn., Minna, Nigeria, 1980—81; sr. house officer Univ. Nigeria Tchg. Hosp., Enusu, 1981—82, registrar, 1982—83, sr. registrar, 1983—88, sr. lectr./ cons., 1988—93; prof. ob./gyn. U. Nigeria, Nsukka, 1993—, dean faculty med. scis. and dentistry, 2002—04, provost Coll. Medicine, 2004. Chmn. Enugu Med. Soc., 1993-95; coord. Tutorial System Internat., Nigeria, 1993-95; dean medicine U. Nigeria. Editor: Tropical Pediatrics and Child Health, 1999; assoc. editor Orient Jour. Medicine, 1988—, Nigerian Jour. Surgical Scis., 1991—; contbr. articles to profl. jours. V.p. Enugu chpt. Full Gospel Businessmen's Fellowship Internat., 1994-95, chpt. pres., 1997—; chmn. Harvest and Love Feast Com., Chapel of Redemption, Enugu, Nigeria, 1994-95. Takemi fellow Internat. Health Harvard U., 1995-96. Fellow Internat. Coll. Surgeons, W. African Coll. of Surgeons, Nigerian Postgrad. Med. Coll.; mem. AAAS (internat. mem.), Royal Coll. Obstetricians and Gynecologists. Born Again Christian. Achievements include measuring: serum concentrations of alphafetoprotein in mormal pregnancy and in pregnancy induced hypertensions; ivermectin levels in human breast milk. Office: Univ Nigeria Teaching Hosp Dept Ob-gyn Enugu Anambra Nigeria Mailing: 45 Duffield Dr South Orange NJ 07079 Home Phone: 236 42 253496. Personal E-mail: BenOzumba@hotmail.com.

OZZELLO, LAWRENCE MURAL, retired professor of accountancy, consultant; b. Wis., Feb. 28, 1927; s. James Louis and Marie (Church) O.; m. Patricia E. Anderson, Nov. 4, 1950; children— Janice L., David C., Brian W., Lori J. B.S., No. Mich. U., 1949; M.A., U. Mich.--Ann Arbor, 1955; Ph.D., Mich. State U., 1967; postgrad. U. Chgo., U. Wis., U. Mont., 1949-69. Cert. mgmt. acct. tchr. Breitung Twp. Schs., Kingsford, Mich., 1950-51, supr. fin. dept. Kaiser-Frazer Mfg. Co., 1951-53; prin. Mesick Area Schs., Mich., 1953-55; asst. prof. bus. Ferris State U., Big Rapids, Mich., 1955-64; instr. Mich. State U., East Lansing, 1964-66; prof., div. chmn. bus. Lake Superior State U., Sault Ste. Marie, Mich., 1966-71; prof., chmn. dept. accountancy U. Wis., Eau Claire, 1971—94; disting. prof. accounting, 1995-2007; prof. emeritus 2007; sales mgr. Aluminum Co. Am., New Kennington, Pa., 1956-64; cons. various U.S. and Can. Corps. Author: (with others) Principles of Accounting, 1985, NCSA-Ski Manual 1973. Served with USN, 1945-46, USNR 1946-51. PTO. Recipient Excellence in Teaching award U. Wis. Eau Claire, 1985, Excellence award, Sch. Bus. Advisory Coun., 1993, Disting. Svc. award, award, Iron Mountain, Kings Ford, Mich., Rotary Club, 2000. Mem. Am. Acctg. Assn., Inst. Indsl. Accts., Nat. Collegiate Ski Assn. (dir. 1972—92, dir. intercollegiate racing 1978-84; recipient Pres's. award 1978, 79, 80, 83, 84), Beta Gamma Sigma, Beta Alpha Psi, Delta Pi Epsilon. Roman Catholic. Avocation: ski jumping, skiing. Home Phone: 715-832-1514. Business E-Mail: ozzelll@uwec.edu.

OZZIE, RAY (RAYMOND E. OZZIE), computer software company executive; b. Nov. 20, 1955; B in Computer Sci., U. Ill., Urbana-Champaign, 1979. Sys. programmer Protection Mut. Ins. Co., 1972—73; technician dept. nuc. engring. U. Ill., 1974, sys. programmer PLATO project, 1974—79; co-founder Urbana Software Enterprises, 1978—79; with Data Gen. Corp., 1979—81; co-founder Microcosm Corp., 1981; with Software Arts, 1981—82, Lotus Devel., 1983—84; founder, pres. Iris Assocs., 1984—97; founder, chmn., CEO Groove Networks, Inc. (acquired by Microsoft Corp.), Beverly, Mass., 1997—2005; chief tech. officer Microsoft Corp., Redmond, Wash., 2005—06, chief software architect, 2006—. Adv. bd. mem., Live Labs (rsch. partnership between MSN and Microsoft Rsch.) Microsoft Corp., 2006—. Recipient W. Wallace McDowell award, IEEE Computer Soc., 2000; named Person of Yr., PC Mag., 1995, Disting. Alumnus, U. Ill., Urbana-Champaign; named one of Seven "Windows Pioneers", Microsoft Corp., Top Five Developers of the Century, Computer Reseller News, 50 Who Matter Now, CNNMoney.com Bus. 2.0, 2006, 50 Most Important People on the Web, PC World, 2007; named to Computer Mus. Industry Hall of Fame, InfoWorld Hall of Fame. Mem.: NRC (mem. computer sci. and telecom. bd.), World Econ. Forum (gov. IT and telecom., honored as technology pioneer 2001), NAE. Achievements include first to field of collaboration technology; creator, developer Lotus Notes, 1984; instrumental in development of Lotus Symphony, TK!Solver and VisiCalc. Office: Microsoft Corp 1 Microsoft Way Redmond WA 98052-6399*

O'BRIEN, PATRICIA, international organization official; b. Ireland, Feb. 8, 1957; 3 children. Barrister-at-Law, Kings Inns, Dublin, 1978; BA in Legal Sci., Trinity Coll., Dublin, 1978, MA, 1987; LLB, U. Ottawa, Can., 1990. Bar: Ireland 1978, England and Wales 1986. Lawyer Irish Bar, 1979—88, Bar of BC, 1988—89; academic positions U. BC, 1989—92; sr. legal adviser Irish Atty. Gen.; legal counsellor Irish Permanent Representation to the EU, Brussels; legal adviser Dept. Fgn. Affairs, Ireland, 2003—08; under-sec. gen. legal affairs, legal counsel UN, NYC, 2008—. Legal adviser, expert Govt. of Ireland. Fellow: Soc. Advanced Legal Studies, Inst. Advanced Legal Studies, London. Office: c/o UN Hdqs Rm 3427A First Ave at 46th St New York NY 10017 Office Phone: 212-963-6430.

O'CONNOR, KEVIN J., lawyer, former federal agency administrator; BA with honors, U. Notre Dame, 1989; JD with high honors, U. Conn., 1992. Law clerk to the Hon. William H. Timbers s US Ct. Appeals (2nd cir.), 1992—93; litig. assoc. Cahill Gordon & Reindel, NYC, 1993—95; staff atty., sr. counsel Divsn. Enforcement US Securities & Exchange Commn., Washington, 1995—97; corp. counsel Town of West Hartford, Conn., 1999—2001; ptnr. Day, Berry & Howard; US atty. gen. Dist. Conn. US Dept. Justice, 2002—08, assoc. dep. atty. gen. Washington, 2007, chief of staff to atty. gen., 2007, assoc. atty. gen., 2008—09; ptnr. Bracewell & Giuliani LLP, Hartford, Conn., 2009—. Office: Bracewell & Giuliani LLP 225 Asylum St #26 Hartford CT 06103 Office Phone: 860-947-9000.*

PÄÄBO, SVANTE, molecular biologist, biochemist; b. Stockholm, 1955; PhD in Molecular Immunology, Uppsala U., 1986; PhD (hon.), U. Zurich, 1994, U. Helsinki, 2000. Postdoctoral rsch. Inst. Molecular Biology, U. Zurich., 1986—87, U. Calif., Berkeley, 1987—90; rsch. scientist U. California; prof. biology U. Munich, 1990—98; dir. Max Planck Inst. for Evolutionary Anthropology, Leipzig, Germany, 1997—; hon. prof. genetics and evolutionary biology U. Leipzig, 1999—. Guest prof. comparative genomics Uppsala U., Sweden, 2003. Recipient Leibniz prize, Deutsche Forschungsgemeinschaft, 1992, Max Delbruck medal, 1998, Carus medal, 1999, Rudbeck prize, Uppsala, 2000, Leipzig Sci. prize, 2003, Ernst Schering prize, 2003, Louis Jeantet prize for medicine, 2005, Virchow medal, U. Würzburg, Germany, 2005; named an The World's Most Influential People, TIME mag., 2007. Mem.: NAS (fgn. assoc.), Finnish Soc. Arts & Letters, Saxonian Acad. Scis., Deutsche Akademie der Naturforscher Leopoldina, Berlin-Brandenburg Acad. Scis., Royal Swedish Acad. Scis., Academia Europaea. Achievements include pioneering ancient DNA extraction studies. Office: Max Planck Inst Evolutionary Anthrpology Deutscher Platz 6 04103 Leipzig Germany

PAANANEN, VICTOR NILES, language educator; b. Ashtabula, Ohio, Jan. 31, 1938; s. Niles Henry and Anni Margaret (Iloranta) P.; m. Donna Mae Jones, Aug. 15, 1964; children: Karl, Neil. AB magna cum laude, Harvard U., 1960; MA, U. Wis., 1964, PhD, 1967. Instr. English Wofford Coll., Spartanburg, SC, 1962-63; asst. prof. Williams Coll., Williamstown, Mass., 1966-68, Mich. State U., East Lansing, 1968-73, assoc. prof., 1973—82, prof., 1982—2002, asst. dean Grad. Sch., 1977-82, chmn. dept. English, 1986-94, prof. emeritus, 2002—. Vis. prof. Roehampton U., London, 1982, 96, hon. fellow, 92; mem. Harvard Inst. Learning Ret., 2006. Author: William Blake, 1977, 2d edit., 1996, British Marxist Criticism, 2000; contbr. articles to profl. and scholarly jours. Univ. fellow U. Wis., 1962, 63-64, Roehampton Inst. hon. fellow, London, 1992—; Harvard Nat. scholar, 1956-60. Home: 350 Revere Beach Blvd 5-5W Revere MA 02151-4851 E-mail: paananen@msu.edu.

PAASWELL, ROBERT EMIL, civil engineer, educator; b. Red Wing, Minn., Jan. 15, 1937; s. George and Evelyn (Cohen) P.; m. Rosalind Snyder, May 31, 1958; children: Judith Marjorie, George Harold. BA (Ford Found. fellow), Columbia U., 1956, BS, 1957, MS, 1961; PhD, Rutgers U., 1965. Field engring. asst. Spencer White & Prentis, Washington, 1954-56, engr. NYC, 1957-59; rsch. scientist Davidson Lab., NJ, 1964; rsch. fellow Greater London Council, 1971-72; rsch. and teaching asst. Columbia U., 1959-62; asst. prof. civil engring. SUNY, Buffalo, 1964-68; chmn. bd. govs. Urban Studies Coll., 1973-76, assoc. prof., 1968-76, prof. civil engring., 1976-82; dir. Center for Transp. Studies and Research, 1979-82, chmn. dept. environ. design and planning, 1980-82; prof. transp. engring. U. Ill., Chgo., 1982-86, 89-90, dir. Urban Transp. Ctr., 1982-86; exec. dir. Chgo. Transit Authority, 1986—89; dir. Univ. Transp. Rsch. Ctr. CCNY, 1990—, disting. prof., 1991—; dir. CUNY Inst. Urban Systems, 2000—. Faculty-on-leave Dept. Transp., 1976-77, cons., 1981—; v.p. Faculty Tech. Cons., Inc., Midwest Sys. Scis., Inc., 1982-86; dir. Urban Mass Transp. Adminstrn. Summer Faculty Workshop, 1980, 81; cons. transp. planning, energy and soil mechanics; spl. cons. to Congressman T. Dulski, 1973; vis. expert lectr. Jilin U. Tech., Changchun, Peoples Republic of China, 1985, hon. prof. transp., 1986—; bd. dirs. E'Escuto Archs. and Engrs., Chig, Hickling Co., Ottawa, Can., Transic Devel. Corp.; chmn. transp. steering adv. bd. Office of Tech. Assessment for Infrastructure and the Urban Core Project, 1994—; faculty Lincoln Inst. of Land Policy, 1994-95; vis. scholar Tel Aviv U., Israel, 1995—; arbitrator in productivity Met. Transp. Authority, N.Y.C., 1996—; mem. exec. com. Coun. on Transp., 1996—, NSF Ctr. for Infrastructure Sys.; cons. Coun. of North East Govs., 1997—; faculty "Conflict Resolution," NYU, 1998—; mem. exec. com. Inst. for Civil Infrastructure Sys. (NSF), 1998—; chair panel new paradigms in transit Transp. Rsch. Bd., chair panel on risk analysis for informatics, 2006—; bd. dirs. Transit Stds. Consortium, chmn., 2000—; bd. dir. CUNY Sch. Profl. Studies, 2005—, Urban Sustainability Inst., Newman Real Estate Inst., 2008-, York Coll. Charter Inst., 2009-. Author: Problems of the Carless, 1977; contbg. author: Transport and Urban Development, 1995, Panels for Transportation Planning, 1997, Studies in Israel Planning, 1996, Dynamic Networks and Spatial Change, 1999, After the World Trade Center, 2002; editor: Site Traffic Impact Assessment, 1992; contbg. author: Decisions for the Great Lakes, 1982, World Book Encyclopedia, 1992, 93, 94, Transport and Urban Development, 1995, Israel Planning Studies, 1996, 97, Panels for Transportation Planning, 1997, New Contributions to Transportation Analysis in Europe, 1999, Intelligent Transportation Systems in "Moving People, Goods and Information", 2002, Policy Analysis of Transport Networks, 2005; mem. bd. editors Jour. Environ. Systems, 1974—, Transp., 1978—, Jour. Urban Tech., 1992—; contbr. articles to profl. jours. Mem. Buffalo Environ. Mgmt. Commn., 1972-74; mem. Area Com. for Transit, Mayor's Energy Adv. Bd., 1974, Block Grant Rev. Com., City of Buffalo; chmn. com. on transp., mem. rev. adv. bd. Rsch. and Planning Coun. Western N.Y.; mem. transp. com. Chgo. 1992 Worlds Fair; mem. citizens' adv. bd. Chgo. Transit Authority, 1985—; mem. strategic planning com. Regional Transp. Authority, 1985; mem. steering com. Nat. Transit Coop. Rsch. Program, 1991—, Borough pres. (Manhattan) Trans. Adv. Bd., Bronx Ctr. Devel. Project; bd. dirs. Transit Devel. Corp., 1992—; exec. bd. Transp. Coun., 1996—; mem. exec. com. Colin Powell Ctr.; bd. dirs. York Aviation Inst., 2003—; chmn. adv. bd. Cmty. Transp. Devel. Ctr., 2003—; mem. MTA Blue Ribbon Commn. 0n Constrn., 2007—, MTA Blue Ribbon Commn. on Workforce Devel., 2007—, NY State Commn. on Higher Edn., 2007-. Recipient Dept. Transp. award, 1977, Outstanding Alumnus award, Rutgers U., 2003; SUNY faculty fellow, 1965-66, Lifetime Achievement award, Coun. Transp., 2009. Fellow ASCE (past pres. Buffalo sect., chmn. steering com. 1992 splty. conf. traffic impact analysis, chair com. on peer rev. of pub. agys.); mem. AAAS, Transp. Rsch. Bd. (chmn. com. on transp. disadvantaged, mem. exec. com., peer rev. com. nat. transp. ctrs. 1988—), Inst. Transp. Engrs. (transit coun., exec. com., chmn. legis. policy com., rsch. com. surface transp. policy project 1995—), Coun. on Transp. (bd. dirs. 1996—), N.Y. Acad. Scis., Sigma Xi. Avocation: astronomy. Office: CCNY Marshak 917 135th St and Convent Ave New York NY 10031 Business E-Mail: paaswell@utrc2.org.

PAAU, ALAN SHIUKEE, academic administrator, biotechnologist, educator; b. Macau, Dec. 16, 1951; arrived in US, 1971, naturalized, 1985; s. Lokfu and Ping (Li) Paau; m. Florence Hau, Aug. 14, 1978; 1 child. PhD, U. Houston, 1978; MBA, Cardinal Stritch Coll., 1990. Tchg. coord. U. Houston, 1974—78; rsch. assoc U. Wis., Madison, 1978—79, project scientist, 1979—81; scientist, project leader Cetus Madison Corp., Middleton, Wis., 1982—84; sr. scientist, project mgr. Agracetus Corp., Middleton, Wis., 1984—90; project mgr., assoc. W.R. Grace & Co., Columbia, 1991—92; assoc. dir. Biotech. Ctr. Ohio State U., Columbus, 1992—94; exec. dir. Iowa State U. Rsch. Found. Inc., Ames, 1994—98; dir. tech. transfer U. Calif., San Diego, 1998—2006, asst. vice chancellor Tech. Transfer & Intellectual Property Svcs.; vice provost tech. transfer and econ. devel. Cornell U., Ithaca, NY, 2007—, exec. dir. Cornell Ctr. Tech., Enterprise and Commercialization (CCTEC), 2007—. Tech. advisor Chimertech Devel. Corp., 1990—; sci. adv. bd. Human Gene Therapy Rsch. Inst., 1995—97; bd. dirs. Pre-Comp, Inc.; cons. in field. Contbr. articles to prof. jours. Recipient Outstanding Grad. Student award, Am. Soc. Plant Physiologists, 1974. Mem.: AAAS, Assn. Univ. Tech. Mgrs., Licensing Execs. Soc., Am. Soc. Microbiology, Sigma Xi. Roman Catholic. Office: Cornell Ctr Tech, Enterprise, and Commercializa 20 Thornwood Dr, Ste 105 Ithaca NY 14850 Office Phone: 607-257-1081. Office Fax: 607-257-1015. E-mail: ap364@cornell.edu.

PAAUW, SCOTT H., linguist, educator; s. Douglas Seymour and Helen Kathleen Paauw; children: Alan Bima, Cindy Melati. BA, U. Mich., Ann Arbor, 1979; MA, York U., Toronto, Ont., Canada, 2004; PhD, U. Buffalo, 2008. Program dir. AELT Ctr., Jakarta, Indonesia, 1982—2002; vis. lectr. U. Rochester, NY, 2005—. Recipient Excellence Grad. Tchg. award, U. Buffalo, 2007. Mem.: Linguistic Soc. America. Office: Univ Rochester 503 Lattimore Hall Rochester NY 14627

PAAVERUD, MERLAN E., JR., museum director; Site supr. Fort Totten, ND, 1983—87; dep. state hist. preservation officer, dir. preservation divsn. State Hist. Soc. ND, Bismarck, grants and contracts officer, 1987—88, dir.; with Office Inter-govtl. Assistance, 1988—91. Served in USAF, 1969—72. Office: State Hist Soc 612 E Blvd Ave Bismarck ND 58505-0830 Business E-Mail: mpaaverud@nd.gov.

PABISCH, PETER KARL, literature and language professor, humanities educator; b. Vienna, Apr. 17, 1938; came to U.S., 1969; s. Ernst and Gertrude (Engel) P.; m. Patricia Ann Trench, Nov. 25, 1959; 1 child, Angela. MA, U. Ill., 1971, PhD, 1974. Tchr. pub. schs., Vienna, 1959-69; dir. summer children's homes Vienna Social Welfare Sys., Italy, 1964-69; co-dir. German summer sch. U. N.Mex., Albuquerque, 1976—2003, from asst. prof. to assoc. prof., 1972-84, prof. German and European studies, 1984—2004, prof. emeritus, 2004—. Author: Austrian Poet H. C. Artmann, 1978, Modern German Lyrics, 1992, Cultural Study on Vienna on liberal politician: Ruckauf, 2006, also 6 poetry books; editor 11 books on German, Swiss, and Austrian studies and on 250 years of J.W. Goethe, 1982— Pres. Atlantic Bridge on the Camino Real, Inc., 1997—, Austrian-Am. Coun. of N.Mex., Inc., 1999— Decorated Order of Merit 1st Class (Germany), Gt. Order of Merit (Austria); named Best German Tchr., Am. Assn. Tchrs. of German, 1982, Outstanding German Educator, 2005; recipient Recognition award Goethe-Inst. Munich, 1995, poetry award Poetry in the Arts, Tex., 1992, arts award Poetry in the Arts Tex., 1993, Friedestrom prize Internat. Dialect Archives, 2000; Check Point Charlie Found. scholar, 2005. Democrat. Avocations: skiing, scuba diving, playing music, travel, sketching. Home: 417 Jefferson St NE Albuquerque NM 87108-1279 Office: U N Mex German Program Fgn Langs and Lits Albuquerque NM 87131-0001 Business E-Mail: pabisch@unm.edu.

PABON CHARNECO, MILDRED G., territorial supreme court justice; b. San Juan, Nov. 27, 1957; d. Julio Pabon Maldonado and Charneca Aida Villanueva; 3 children. BS with highest honors, Univ. PR, JD, 1983. Bar: PR 1985, US Dist. Ct. PR Dist. 1987. With Bufete Troncoso Fuentes-Agostini; legal adv. Office of Legis. Services, PR Legis., 1989—92, dir. legal div., 1992; dep. dir. & asst. gov. PR Gov. Office of Legis. Affairs, 1992—95; judge PR Cir. Ct. Appeals, 1995—2009; assoc. justice PR Supreme Ct., 2009—. Mailing: Rama Judicial de Puerto Rico PO Box 9022392 San Juan PR 00902-2392 Office Phone: 787-723-6033.*

PACALA, LEON, retired professional society administrator; b. Indpls., May 3, 1926; s. John and Anna (Ferician) P.; m. Janet Lefforge, Dec. 28, 1947 (dec. July 1987); children: Mark, Stephen, James; m. Virginia Strasenburgh, Mar. 10, 1990. AB, Franklin Coll., Ind., 1949; BD, Colgate Rochester Div. Sch., 1952; PhD, Yale U., 1960; LLD (hon.), Nazareth Coll., 1980; LHD (hon.), Franklin Coll., 1987. Ordained to ministry Baptist Ch., 1952. Asst. prof. philosophy and religion DePauw U., 1956-61; participant study religion undergrad. coll. Lilly Found., 1957-59; assoc. prof. religion Bucknell U., 1961-68, prof., 1968-73, chmn. dept., 1961-64, dean, 1962-73; pres. Colgate Rochester (N.Y.) Div. Sch., pres. emeritus, 1995—; also Bexley Hall, Crozer Theol. Sem., 1973-80; exec. dir. Assn. Theol. Schs. in U.S. and Can., 1980-91. Chair, founding mem. World Coun. Theol. Instns., 1986-2002; cons. acad. adminstrn. Beirut Coll. Women, 1972. Author: The Role of ATS in Theological Education, 1980-90, 1998; contbr. articles to profl. jours. Exec. com. Christian Faith in Higher Edn. Projects, 1965-68; trustee Franklin Coll., 1967-73, 98-2002; bd. dirs. Rohesters Jobs, Inc., 1973-80, Union Theol. Sem., N.Y.C., 1999—; trustee Rochester Area Colls., 1973-80; dir. Nat. Housing Ministries, Am. Bapt. Chs., 1976-80; mem. adv. bd. Colgate Rochester Div. Sch., 1997—. With USAAF, 1944-45. Internat. Rotary scholar, Louvain U., Belgium, 1952-53. Mem. Am. Conf. Acad. Deans (exec. com., treas., chmn., presiding officer 1973-74), Am. Assn. Higher Edn., Assn. Am. Colls. (commn. religion higher edn.), Assn. Theol. Schs. (com. accreditation), Am. Bapt. Assn. Sem. Adminstrs. (chmn 1975-80). Home: 56 Woodbury Pl Rochester NY 14618

PACE, CAROL REBECCA, elementary school educator; b. Tokyo, Mar. 9, 1960; d. John Lawrence and Melba Johnson Greene; m. George Swanson Pace, Mar. 12, 1988. AA, Jones County Jr. Coll., Ellisville, Miss., 1980; BA in Edn., U. Miss., Oxford, 1982; MEd, Miss. Coll., Clinton, 1998, degree spcialist in edn., 2008. Lic. educator Miss. Tchr. 1st, 4th, 5th and 6th grades Pine Hills Acad., Gloster, Miss., 1983—85; 4th grade tchr. St. Patrick's Episcopal Day Sch., Zachary, Miss., 1985—86; 5th grade tchr. Vicksburg (Miss.) Mid. Sch., 1986—89; tchr. 1st, 2d and 5th grades Grove St. Elem., Vicksburg, 1989—99; 1st grade tchr. Sherman Ave. Elem., Vicksburg, 1999—2003; instnl. lead tchr. Dana Rd. Elem., Vicksburg, 2003—, AmeriCorps site supr., 2004—. Named Tchr. of yr., Sherman Ave. Elem., 2000—01. Mem.: NEA, Internat. Reading Assn., Nat. Coun. Tchrs. English, Miss. Assn. Educators, Ole Miss Alumni Assn. Republican. Methodist. Avocations: reading, arts and crafts, metal detecting, antiques, jogging. Home: 8023 Oak Ridge Rd Vicksburg MS 39183 Office: Dana Rd Elem 1247 Dana Rd Vicksburg MS 39180 Office Phone: 601-619-2340. Office Fax: 601-619-2343. Personal E-mail: countrygirlorange@yahoo.com. Business E-Mail: bpace@vwsd.k12.ms.us.

PACE, CAROLINA JOLLIFF, communications executive, investor; b. Dallas, Apr. 12, 1938; d. Lindsay Gafford and Carolina (Juden) Jolliff; m. John McIver Pace, Jr., Oct. 7, 1961. Student, Holton-Arms Jr. Coll., 1956—57; BA in Comparative Lit., So. Meth. U., 1960. Promotional advisor, dir. season ticket sales Dallas Theatre Ctr., 1960—61; exec. sec. Dallas Book and Author Luncheon, 1959—63; promotional and instl. cons. Henry Regnery-Reilly & Lee Pub. Co., Chgo., 1962—65; pub. trade rep. various cos.; instl. rep. Don R. Phillips Co., Southea. area, 1965—67; Southwestern rep. Ednl Reading Svc., Inc.-Troll Assocs., Mahwah, NJ, 1967—72; v.p., dir. multimedia divsn. Melton Book Co., Dallas, 1972—79; v.p. mktg. Webster's Internat., Inc., Nashville, 1980—82; pres. Carolina Pace, Inc., 1982—. Mem. adv. bd. Nat. Info. Ctr. of Spl. Edn. Materials; mem. materials rev. panel Nat. Media Ctr. for Materials of Severely-Profoundly Handicapped, 1981; mem. mktg. product rev. bd. LINC Resources, 1982, 83, 84, mktg. task force, 83, adv. bd., 87; reviewer spl. edn. U.S. Dept. Edn., 1975—79, 1985; rev. cons. HHS, 1982, 83, 84, 86; product rev. task force CEC, 1984, 85, 86; cons. Ednl. Cable Consortium, Summit, NJ, 1982—87. Prodr. ednl. videos; contbr. articles to profl. jours. Mem. adv. coun. Grad. Sys. Sch. Libr. and Info. Sci. Found., U. Tex., 1987—; co-vice chair Friends Highland Park Libr., 1989; mem. focus group City Dallas Growth Policy Plan; mem. art and design com. Downtown Ctrs.; active Dallas City Wide Parking Task Force, Ctrl. Transp. Forum Ctrl. Bus. Dist., Union Sta. Art & Design Com., Downtown Transfer Ctrs., Art and Design Com., West End Task Force, Ctrl. Bus. Dist. Task Force, Tex. Parking Assn.; co-founder

Operation TexRec, 1990—91; bd. dirs. Transp. Mgmt. Assn., 1995—; chair Vanpool Use Study, 1995; budget chmn. Dallas County Sesquicentennial com., 1996; mem. adv. bd. Friends of Old Red Courthouse, 1997—, Trinity River Econ. Devel. Bd., 1998—; active Downtown Dallas: Vision 2020, 2001—02; mem. com. Trinity Commons Found., 2002—; active Downtown Dallas Task Force, Ctrl. Bus. Dist., West End, Individual Site Task Force, Dallas. Mem.: DAR (Jane Douglas chpt.), Coun. Exceptional Children (conf. spkr. 1981, dir. exhibitors com., chmn. publ. com. 1979 conf.), Pub. Rels. Soc. Am., Women in Comm., Assn. Spl. Edn. Tech. (nat. dir., v.p. publicity 1980—82), Assn. Ednl. and Comm. Tech., Internat. Comm. Industries Assn., Nat. Audio Visual Assn. (conf. panelist 1979), Downtown Dallas, Ctrl. Dallas Assn. (transp. com. 1996—, planning and greenspace com. 1998—), Dallas Plan (focus com.), Women's Nat. Book Assn., Dallas Founders, Friends of the West End (pres. 1988—), West End Assn. Dallas (chmn. subcom. on traffic and parking 1986—87, com. demographic study 1987—88), Downtown Transp. Mgmt. Assn. (adv. bd., chmn. vanpools subcom. 1995—, econ. devel. com. Trinity project 2000—, citizens adv. com. 2003—), Kimball Art Mus., Dallas So. Meml., Dallas Mus. Art, Dallas Zool. Soc., Dallas West End Hist. Dist. Assn., Tex. Parking Assn., Alpha Delta Pi. Presbyterian. Home: 4524 Lorraine Ave Dallas TX 75205-3613

PACE, CHARLES, library director; m. Wendy Pace; children: David, Emily. BA, U. North Tex., Denton, MLS, 1990. Reference libr. Bklyn. Pub. Libr., Dallas Pub. Libr.; br. mgr. Houston Pub. Libr., Chgo. Pub. Libr.; dir. Fargo Pub. Libr., ND, 2001—06, St. Louis County Libr., 2006—. Named one of the Movers & Shakers, Libr. Jour., 2006. Mem.: ALA, Pub. Libr. Assn. Office: St Louis County Libr 1640 S Lindbergh Blvd Saint Louis MO 63131-3598

PACE, ERIC DWIGHT, retired journalist; b. NYC, Oct. 13, 1936; s. Eric and Eleanor Robertson (Jones) Paepcke; m. Suzanne Monique Wiedel, June 12, 1976 (div. Jan. 1987); children: Christine, Lydia. Grad., Phillips Exeter Acad., 1953; student, U. Heidelberg, Germany, 1955-56; BA magna cum laude, Yale, 1957; MA, Johns Hopkins, 1959. Reporter San Angelo Standard Times and Evening Standard, Tex., 1957—58; mem. staff Life mag., NYC, 1959—61, assigned to Paris, 1961-62; corr. Time mag., Bonn., 1962-63, Hong Kong, 1963-65; mem. staff New York Times, NYC, 1965—2004, assigned to Saigon, 1966, Cairo, 1966—69, Paris, 1969—70, Beirut, 1970—71, Teheran, 1974—77. Author: (novels) Saberlegs, 1970, Any War Will Do, 1973, Nightingale, 1979; contbr. articles to Fgn. Affairs, also others. Served with AUS, 1957. Recipient George Polk Meml. award Overseas Press Club, 1968, Page One award NYC Newspaper Guild, 1968 Mem. Mystery Writers Am., Crime Writers Assn. (Gt. Britain), Am. P.E.N. Clubs: Century (NYC).

PACE, G. MICHAEL, JR., lawyer; b. Roanoke, Va., Mar. 11, 1957; BA, Hampden-Sydney Coll., 1979; JD, Washington & Lee U., 1984. Bar: Va. 1984. Mng. ptnr. Gentry Locke Rakes & Moore LLP, Roanoke, Va. Mem. adv. bd. SunTrust, Roanoke, Va.; bd. mem., chmn. Roanoke Regional C. of C., 2002—04; pres. Roanoke Valley Econ. Devel. Partnership, 2002—04; exec. com. Roanoke Valley Bus. Coun.; chmn. Bus. Leadership Fund; bd. mem. Fifth Planning Dist. Regional Alliance, Va. Western Cmty. Coll. Found.; mem. Roanoke Regional Airport Alliance; bd. trustees Hampden-Sydney Coll.; pres. Hampden-Sydney Coll. Alumni Assn.; trustee Hampden Sydney Coll. Recipient Gold Best Local Lawyer award, The Roanoker Mag., 2004; named one of Legal Elite in field of corp. law, Va. Bus. Mag., 2000—02, Legal Elite in field of real estate/construction, 2003—04, Legal Elite in field of bus., 2005—06, Va. Super Lawyers, 2007, Best lawyers in Am. Mem.: Roanoke Valley Econ. Devl. Partnership (pres. 2002—05), Roanoke Regional C. of C., Va. We. Cmty. Coll. Found. (bd. mem.), Bus. Coun. (chair elect.), Bus. Leadership Fund (chmn.), Va. State Bar (past chmn. real property sect.), Va. Bar Assn. (pres.-elect 2006—07, pres. bd. govs. 2008, chmn. bd. gov.), Roanoke Bar Assn. (pres. 2000—01, Presidents Volunter Svc. award, Silver level 2006). Mailing: Gentry Locke Rakes & Moore PO box 40013 Roanoke VA 24022-0013 Office: Gentry Locke Rakes & Moore 10 Franklin Rd SE Roanoke VA 24011 Office Phone: 540-983-9312. Office Fax: 540-983-9400. E-mail: mike_pace@gentrylocke.com.

PACE, (AUDREY) JOY, theater educator; b. Baytown, Tex., Nov. 19, 1970; d. Harvey Rudolph and Joyce Johnson Pace. BA in Speech Comm. Minor Theatre, Centenary Coll. La., Shreveport, 1993; MFA in Directing, Va. Commonwealth U., Richmond, 1999. Asst. prof. theatre Ky. Wesleyan Coll., Owensboro, Ky., 1999—2004; adj. instr. Va. Commonwealth U., 1996—99, McMurry U., Abilene, Tex., 2004; coord. theatre, dept. performing arts McNeese State U., Lake Charles, La., 2006—. Actor: (production) Doubt, (college campaign theatrical production) The Vagina Monologues; dir.: (play production) Twelfth Night, No Exit. Mem. PFLAG, Abilene, Tex., 2004—06; adv. bd. mem. Rape Crisis Outreach, Lake Charles, La., 2008—; bd. mem. RiverPark Ctr., Owensboro, Ky., 2003—04. Recipient Honor Soc., Phi Kappa Phi, 10. Mem.: Alpha Psi Omega (faculty advisor 2007—). Democrat. Avocations: reading, travel, dog breeding, photography. Office: McNeese Theatre Program MSU Box 92175 Lake Charles LA 70609 Personal E-mail: playjoy@aol.com. Business E-Mail: jpace@mcneese.edu.

PACE, NATHAN LEON, anesthesiologist, educator; b. San Diego, Feb. 28, 1943; s. Joseph Leon and pauline (Clyde) P.; m. Jennifer Anna Geertsen, Jan. 13, 1973; children: Garrett, Ramsey, Andalyn, Marielle, Evany. BS, U. Calif., Berkeley, 1967; MD, U. Calif., San Francisco, 1970. Diplomate Am. Bd. Anesthesiology. Intern Santa Clara Valley Med. Ctr., San Jose, Calif., 1970-71; resident in asesthesiology U. Wash., Seattle, 1971-74; staff anesthesiologist U.S. Army, Ft. Sam Houston, Tex., 1974-76; prof. anesthesiology U. Utah, Salt Lake City, 1976—. Vis. prof. various med. schs. Contbr. articles to profl. jours. 1st tenor Utah Symphony Chorus, Salt Lake City, 1977—. Mem. AMA, Am. Soc. Anesthesiologists, AMA, Soc. Critical Care Medicine, Assn. Univ. Anesthetists, Phi Beta Kappa. Republican. Mem. Lds Ch. Avocations: travel, singing, reading. Home: 2211 Scenic Dr Salt Lake City UT 84109-1430 Office: U Utah Sch Medicine Dept Anesthesiology Salt Lake City UT 84132-0001

PACE, NORMAN R., science educator, microbiologist; b. Washington, Ind., Sept. 20, 1942; BA, Ind. U., 1964; PhD, U. Ill., 1967. From asst. prof. to prof. biophysics and genetics U. Colo. Med. Ctr., 1974-84; prof. biology, then disting. prof. biology and chemistry Ind. U., Bloomington, 1975-97; prof. plant and microbial biology UCLA, Berkeley, 1996—99; prof., dept. molecular, cellular and dev. biology U. Colorado, Boulder, Colo., 1999—. Recipient Abbott-ASM Lifetime Achievement award, Am. Soc. Microbiology, 2007. Fellow AAAS, Am. Acad. Arts & Scis., Nat. Speleol. Soc., Am. Acad. Microbiology (award 1996); mem. Am. Soc. Biol. Chemists. Office: U Colorado Dept of Molecular, Cellular & Dev Bio Boulder CO 80309-0347

PACE, OLE BLY, III, lawyer; b. 1939; AB, Ill. Wesleyan Univ., 1963; JD, Univ. Ill. Coll. of Law, 1966. Bar: 1966, US Dist. Ct., No. and Ctrl. Dist. Ill. Law clerk Appellate Ct. Justice A. J. Scheineman; spl. asst. atty. gen., 1968—80; ptnr. Ward, Murray, Pace & Johnson. Bd. dir. Northwestern Steel & Wire Co., First Nat. Bank, Sterling-Rock Falls, Ill., Mercantile Bank, Sterling-Rock Falls, Ill. Past pres. Sterling C. of C., Sinnissippi Mental Health Ctr. US Army, 1958—60. Named Illinois Super Lawyer, 2005—08; named one of the Best Lawyers in Am., 2003—08. Fellow: Ill. Bar Found.; mem.: ABA, Ill. Cmty. Coll. Attorneys Assn. (bd. mem., vice chair), Ill. Acad. of Lawyers (bd. regents, chancellor), Nat. Assn. of Coll. and Univ. Attorneys, Whiteside County Bar Assn. (past pres.), Ill. State Bar Assn. (bd. gov. 1995—2001, third v.p. 2001, pres. 2004, Bd. of Gov. award 1989), Order of Coif, Phi Delta Phi. Office: Ward Murray Pace & Johnson PC PO Box 400 202 E Fifth St Sterling IL 61081 Office Phone: 812-625-8200. Office Fax: 815-625-8363. Business E-Mail: pace@wmpj.com.

PACE, ORLANDO LAMAR, professional football player; b. Sandusky, Ohio, Nov. 4, 1975; m. Carla Pace; children: Justin, Jalen, Kendall, Landon. Attended, Ohio State U., 1993—97. Offensive tackle St. Louis Rams, 1997—2009, Chgo. Bears, 2009—. Patron Disadvantaged Kids; participant Spearheads Annual Offensive Line Thanksgiving Project, Chesterfield, Mo. Recipient Lombardi award, 1995, 1996, Outland Trophy, 1996; named First Team All-Pro, NFL, 1999, 2001, 2003, All-Nat. Football Conf., 1999—2005; named to The NCAA Football All-Century Team, Sports Illus., 1999, Nat. Football Conf. Pro-Bowl Team, NFL, 1999—2005. Achievements include first to being the first player in college history to win two consecutive Lombardi awards, 1995, 1996; being the overall first pick in NFL Draft, 1997; being a member of Super Bowl XXXIV Champion St. Louis Rams, 2000. Office: Chgo Bears 1000 Football Dr Lake Forest IL 60045*

PACE, PETER, former Chairman of the Joint Chiefs of Staff, management consultant; b. Bklyn., Nov. 5, 1945; m. Lynne Ann Holden; children: Peter Jr., Tiffany Marie. BS, US Naval Acad., 1967; MBA, George Washington U., 1972; student, USMC Command & Staff Coll., 1979; grad., Nat. War Coll., 1986; student in Nat. and Internat. Security, Harvard U. Commd. lt. USMC, 1967, advanced through grades to gen., 2000, ret., 2007; served in 2d Bn., 5th Marines, 1st Marine Divsn., Vietnam, 1968-69; ops. officer, Security Element Marine Aircraft Group 15, 1st Marine Aircraft Wing, Nam Phong, Thailand, 1972, exec. officer, 1972; asst. majors' monitor Hdqs. Marine Corps, Washington, 1973-76; ops. officer, 2nd Bn., 5th Marines, exec. officer, 3rd Bn., & divsn. staff sec. 1st Marine Divsn., Camp Pendleton, Calif., 1976—79; commdg. officer Marine Corps Recruiting Sta., Buffalo, 1980-83, 2nd Bn, 1st Marine Divsn., Pendleton, Calif., 1983—85; chief, ground forces branch Combined/Joint Staff, Seoul, Republic of Korea, 1986-87, exec. officer to asst. chief of staff, 1987—88; commdg. officer Marine Barracks, Washington, 1988—91; chief of staff, 2nd Marine Divsn. USMC, Camp Lejeune, NC, 1991—92, pres. Marine Corps. U., commdg, gen. Marine Corps. Combat Devel. Command Quantico, Va., 1992—94, dep. comdr. Marine forces Somalia, 1992—93, dep. comdr. Joint Task Force, 1993—94; dep. comdr., chief of staff US Forces Japan, 1994—96; dir. ops. (J-3) Joint Staff, Washington, 1996—97; comdt. USMC, Washington, 1997—2000; comdr. US So. Command (USSOUTHCOM), Miami, 2000—01; vice chmn. Joint Chiefs of Staff, US Dept. Def., Washington, 2001—05, chmn., 2005—07; pres., CEO SM&A Strategic Advisors Inc., Newport Beach, Calif., 2008—; operating ptnr. Behrman Capital, NYC & San Francisco, 2008—; chmn. Pelican Products, Inc., 2008—. Bd. dir. SM&A Inc., 2008—, ILC Industries Inc., 2008—, Nephapsis Inc., 2008—; mem. Def. Policy Bd. Advisory Com., 2007—, Fgn. Intelligence Adv. Bd., Washington, 2008—. Decorated Def. DSM, Def. Legion of Merit, Def. Superior Service medal, Def. Meritorious Service medal, Navy Commendation medal, Navy Achievement medal, Combat Action medal; recipient Tongil Medal of Nat. Security, Govt. of South Korea, 2007, Presdl. Medal of Freedom, The White House, 2008. Office: SM&A Strategic Advisors 8th Fl 4695 MacArthur Ct Newport Beach CA 92660*

PACE, STANLEY DAN, lawyer; b. Dayton, Ohio, Dec. 10, 1947; s. Stanley Carter and Elaine (Cutchall) Pace; m. Judy Roehm, Sept. 8, 1973; children: Stanley Carter, Barbara Roehm. BA, Denison U., Granville, Ohio, 1970; JD, Toledo U., Ohio, 1975. Bar: US Dist. Ct. (so. dist.) Ohio 1975, US Dist. Ct. (no. dist.) Ohio 1977, US Ct. Appeals (6th cir.) 1975. Atty. ARMCO Steel Corp., Middletown, Ohio, 1975-77; assoc. Spieth, Bell, McCurdy & Newell, Cleve., 1977-82, dir., 1982—2006, co-mng. dir., 1987—2005; shareholder Ogletree, Deakins, Nash, Smoak & Stewart, P.C., Cleve., 2007—. Bd. dirs. Indsl. Rels. Resh. Assn., Cleve., 1985. Bd. dirs. pres. Judson Retirement Cmty., Cleve., 1985; bd. dirs. Arthritis Found. N.E. Ohio, Cleve., 1984, Western Res. Hist. Soc., 1998. Mem.: ABA, Greater Cleve. Bar Assn., Ohio Bar Assn. (named one of Best Lawyers in America, Chambers America's Leading lawyers Bus.), 50 Club, Laurel Valley Golf Club, Chagrin Valley Hunt Club, Rolling Rock Club, Tavern Club, Pepper Pike Club, The Country Club. Home: 3911-1 Lander Rd Orange Village OH 44022 Office Phone: 216-241-6100. Business E-Mail: dan.pace@odnss.com.

PACE, STEPHEN SHELL, artist, educator; b. Charleston, Mo., Dec. 12, 1918; s. John C. and Ora K. (Reeves) P.; m. Palmina Natalini, Feb. 26, 1949. Student, Inst. Fine Arts, San Miguel, 1945-46, Art Students League, NYC, 1948-49, Grande Chaumiere, Paris, 1950, Inst. D'Arte Statale, Florence, Italy, 1951, Hans Hofmann Sch., NYC, 1951-52; ArtsD (hon.), U. So. Ind., Evansville, 2002, Maine Coll. Art, Portland, 2003. Artist in residence Washington U., 1959; instr. painting Pratt Inst., NYC, 1961-69; artist in residence Des Moines Art Ctr., 1970; vis. artist U. Calif., 1968; asso. prof. Bard Coll., 1969-71, Am. U., 1975-83; artist in residence U. So. Ind., Evansville, 2005. Artist in residence U. So. Ind., Evansville, 2005. One-man shows include Hendler Gallery, 1953, Artists Gallery, 1954, Poindexter Gallery, 1956, 57, Washington U., St. Louis, 1959, Holland-Goldowsky Gallery, Chgo., 1960, Howard Wise Gallery, Cleve., 1960, N.Y., 1960, 61, 63, 64, Dilexi Gallery, San Francisco, 1960, HCE Gallery, 1956-59, 61-63, 66, Dwan Gallery, L.A., 1961, Hayden Gallery, Cambridge, Mass., 1961, Ridley Gallery, Evansville, Ind., 1966, U. Calif., Berkeley, 1968, Graham Gallery, N.Y.C., 1969, Des Moines Art Ctr., 1970, U. Tex., Austin, 1970, Kansas City Art Inst., 1973, A.M. Sachs Gallery, N.Y.C., 1974, 76, 77, 78, 79, 81, 83, 85, Drew U., 1975, Bard Coll., 1975, Am. U., 1976, Roberto Polo Gallery, Washington, 1976, New Harmony (Ind.) Gallery, 1977, Farm Gallery, Far Hill, N.J., 1978, Barbara Fiedler Gallery, Washington, 1980, Chastenet Gallery, Washington, 1981, Katharina Rich Perlow Gallery, N.Y.C., 1987, 89, 91, 94, 97, 98, 00, 02, 04, 06, Vanderwoude-Tananbaum Gallery, N.Y.C., 1991, U. N.C., Greensboro, 1991, Evansville Mus., 1992, Maine Coast Artists, Rockport, 1994-2006, Bates Coll. Mus., Lewiston, Maine, 1994, Union Coll., Schenectady, NY, 1999, A.J. Buecke Gallery, Northeast Harbor, Maine, 2001, Portland (Maine) Mus. Art, 2004, Farnsworth Mus., 2004; exhibited in group shows in U.S., Europe, Japan, Mid. East, India, Burma, Australia, New Zealand, Hawaii, Ctrl. and S.Am.; represented in permanent collections, Whitney Mus., Chrysler Mus., Norfolk, Va., Provincetown (Mass.) Mus., Evansville Mus., U. So. Ill., Carbondale, Michener Found., Walker Art Ctr., U. Calif., CIBA-Geigy Collection, Hallmark Collection, Bundy Art Gallery, U. N.C., Greensboro, Chase Manhattan Bank, Munson-Williams-Procter Inst., Utica, N.Y., Des Moines Art Ctr., Boston Mus. Fine Arts, Met. Mus., N.Y.C., Phillips Collection, Washington, Am. U., Washington, Corcoran Gallery, Washington, Curie Inst., Paris, Hirshhorn Mus., Washington, Bristol Myers Collection, Indpls. Mus., Portland (Maine) Mus., Bowdoin Coll. Mus., Brown U., Providence, Oberlin (Ohio) Coll. Mus, Farnsworth Art Mus., Rockland, Maine, Bates Coll. Mus., Lewiston, Maine, Nat. Mus. Am. Art, Washington, Columbus Mus. Art, Yale U., New Haven, U. of S. Indiana, Evansville, Union Coll., Schenectady, Newark Art Mus., N.J., U. No. Iowa, Cedar Falls, Colby Coll. Mus., Waterville, Maine, Rutgers U. Mus., NB, NJ, New Orleans Mus. Art, NAD, Baruch Coll., N.Y., U. Maine, Orono, U. Denver, Ogunquit (Maine) Mus., Fryeburg (Maine) Acad., Sweet Briar (Va.) Mus., Yeshiva U., NYC Served with AUS, 1941-45, ETO. Recipient Dolian Lorian award for promising Am. painters, 1954, Hallmark award, 1961, Am. Acad. Arts and Letters prize, 2004; grantee Creative Artists Pub. Svc. Program, 1973; Guggenheim fellow, 1980. Mem.: NAD (Benjamin Altman prize 1993, Edwin Palmer Marine prize 2001, William A. Paton prize 2005). Address: 109 Glen Ave Millburn NJ 07041-1715 Office Phone: 212-563-0249.

PACE, THOMAS M., lawyer; b. Mesa, Ariz., Feb. 5, 1952; s. Lemuel Max and Ann (Green) P.; m. Vi Garrett Pace, Jan. 24, 1981; children: Melanie, Brittany. BA, Stanford U., 1973; JD, U. Ariz., 1976. Bar: Ariz.; cert. real estate specialist. Assoc. Martin, Feldhacker & Freidl, Phoenix, 1976-77, Trew & Woodford, Phoenix, 1977-78; ptnr. Hecker, Phillips & Hooker, Tucson, 1978-88; sr. ptnr. O'Connor Cavanagh, Tucson, 1988-95; pvt. practice Law Office of Thomas M. Pace, Tucson, 1995—. Mem. Mayor's Housing Task Force, Tucson, 1993; bd. dirs. Tucson Urban League, 1986-96; chmn. So. Ariz. Homebuilders Polit. Action Com., 1995, 96. Mem. So. Ariz. Homebuilders (tech. com), Stanford Club So. Ariz. Democrat. Office: 1670 E River Rd Ste 124 Tucson AZ 85718-8900 Office Phone: 520-322-5511. Business E-Mail: tom@pacelawaz.com.

PACELLE, WAYNE, animal rights organization administrator; b. Aug. 4, 1965; m. Kirsten Rosenberg. BA in History and Environ. Studies, Yale U., 1987. With anti-hunting group Fund for Animals, 1988—94; with Human Soc. U.S., Washington, 1994—, sr. v.p. comm. and govt. affairs; pres., CEO The Humane Soc. US, Washington, 2004—. Spkr. in field; bd. dirs. Humane USA. Contbr. articles to newspapers. Named one of America's most important animal rights activists, LA Times, 1997. Office: Humane Society US 2100 L St NW Washington DC 20037 Office Phone: 202-452-1100.*

PACH, PETER BARNARD, columnist, editor; b. Bklyn., Aug. 3, 1951; s. Stewart Warner and Constance (Barnard) P.; m. Kathleen Ann Megan, Sept. 7, 1985; children: Nell, Samuel. BA in English, Union Coll., 1973. Reporter Record Jour., Meriden, Conn., 1974-78, Wallingford bur. chief, 1978-83; Middletown bur. chief Hartford Courant, Conn., 1983-84, columnist Conn., 1984-95; mem. editorial bd. Hartford (Conn.) Courant, 1992—, town editls. editor, 2001—06, assoc. editor, 2006—. Vis. instr. Wesleyan U., Middletown, Conn., 1985—2003. Recipient First Bus. and Econ. Reporting award New England Press Ass., 1977. Mem. Dedham County and Polo Club. Avocations: running, skiing, golf, squash, gardening. Home: PO Box 46 Middle Haddam CT 06456-0046 Office: Hartford Courant 285 Broad St Hartford CT 06115-2510

PACHAL, LEAH ZAVIN, minister, writer, interior designer, educator; b. Portland, Oreg., June 21, 1945; d. William Herman and Gail Grebe Zavin; children: Gina Marie, Tasha Noelle, Krista Nicole. BA cum laude, Colo. Womens Coll., 1967; student, Portland State U., 1987, Rhema Bible Coll., 1992. Cert. in tchg. Lewis & Clark Coll., 1970. Tchr., Vienna, 1967—68, Beaverton Sch. Dist., Oreg., 1970—74; asst. chaplain Good Samaritan Hosp., Portland, 1982—85, Meridian Pk. Hosp., Portland, 1985—89; tchr. elem. sch. Tigard, Tualatin Sch. Dist., Oreg., 1992—95; pvt. practice minister, cons. Portland, 1995—; designer decorator DL Property Devel. LLC, Astoria, Oreg., 2007—08. Min., patient adv. Tigard Care Ctr., 1982—86, Emanuel Children's Hosp., Portland, 1982—, Portland Good Samaritan Hosp., 1982—85, Tualatin Meridian Pk. Hosp., 1985—89, Dorenbecher Children's Hosp.; min. North Coast Recovery Outreach, Seaside, Oreg., 2008—; decorator, design cons. D&L Property Devel. LLC, Astoria, Oreg., 2007—. Contbr. articles to newspapers. Vol. hospice, Cannon Beach, Oreg., 1996—2005, Portland, 1996—2005; patient advocate, 2004—06, Providence, 2004—05. Avocations: walking, guitar, singing, interior decorating, writing.

PACHECO-RANSANZ, ARSENIO, language educator, historian, educator; b. Barcelona, Feb. 8, 1932; s. Arsenio Pacheco and Jacoba Ransanz-Alvarez; m. Mercedes Olivella-Sole, Sept. 1, 1956; children: Arsenio-Andrew, David-George. MA, U. Barcelona, 1954, PhD, 1958. Tutor Colegio Mayor Hispanoamericano Fray Junipero Serra, Barcelona, 1954-56; lectr. Hochschüle für Wirtschaft und Sozialwissenschaften, Nurnberg, Germany, 1956; asst. lectr. U. Glasgow, Scotland, 1957-59; lectr. U. St. Andrews, Scotland, 1960-70; vis. prof. U. Pitts., 1966; prof. Hispanic and Italian studies U. B.C., Vancouver, Canada, 1970-97, prof. emeritus, 1997—. Editor: Historia de Xacob Xalabin, 1964, Testament de Bernat Serradell, 1971, Varia fortuna del soldado Pindaro, 1975, Obres de Francesc de la Via, 1997; contbr. articles to profl. jours. Bd. dirs. Can. Fedn. Humanities, 1981-84. Fellow Royal Soc. Can.; mem. Can. Assn. Hispanists (pres. 1978-81), Asociacion Internacional de Hispanists, MLA, Assn. Hispanists Gt. Britain and Ireland, N.Am. Catalan Soc. (v.p. 1984-87, pres. 1987-90), Anglo Catalan Soc., Associacio Internacional de Llengua i Literatura Catalana. Roman Catholic. Office: U BC Dept French Hispanic Ital Vancouver BC Canada V6T 1Z1 Home Phone: 604-263-8106. Business E-Mail: arp@interchange.ubc.ca.

PACHT, ERIC REED, pulmonary and critical care physician; b. Madison, Wis., Mar. 24, 1954; s. Asher Roger and Perle (Landau) P.; m. Karen Sue Dalpiaz, Aug. 7, 1982; children: Ben, Lora. BA summa cum laude, Lawrence U., 1976; MD cum laude, U. Wis., Madison, 1980. Diplomate Nat. Bd. Med. Examiners, Am. Bd. Internal Medicine. Intern, resident Ohio State U. Hosps., 1980-83, fellow in pulmonary and critical care medicine, 1983-86; asst. prof. Ohio State U., 1986-91, assoc. prof., 1991-99; staff phys. Mt. Carmel Med. Ctr. and St. Ann's Hosp., Columbus, Ohio, 1999-01, Licking Meml. Heatlh Profls., Columbus, Ohio, 2001—. Asst. dir. pulmonary and critical care Ohio State U., 1988-96, dir. pulmonary and critical care fellowship tng. program, 1988-99, med. sch. rep. to Am. Fedn. for Clin. Rsch., 1990-94, med. dir. lung transplantation program, 1992-95, dir. clin. rsch., 1993-99. Contbr. articles to profl. jours. Vol. Am. Lung Assn., Columbus, Ohio, Columbus Cancer Clinic. Recipient numerous rsch. awards. Fellow Am. Coll. Chest Physicians; mem. Am. Thoracic Soc., Ohio Thoracic Soc., Am. Fedn. Clin. Rsch., Phi Beta Kappa. Achievements include description of new form of respiratory failure and emphysema in patients with HIV. Home: 1224 Leicester Pl Columbus OH 43235-2181 Office Phone: 740-348-1805. Personal E-mail: EPacht@aol.com.

PACHTER, IRWIN JACOB, pharmaceutical consultant; b. NYC, July 15, 1925; s. Nathan and Ethel Lillian (Thomases) P.; m. Elaine Anna White, Aug. 23, 1953; children: Wendy, Jonathan. BS, UCLA, 1947; MS, U. N.Mex., 1949; PhD, U. So. Calif., 1951; postgrad., U. Ill., 1951-52, Harvard U., 1952-53. Research chemist Ethyl Corp., 1953-55;

asso. research chemist Smith Kline & French, 1955-62, asst. sec. head, 1962; dir. medicinal chemistry Endo Labs., 1962-66; dir. research Endo div. du Pont Co., 1967-70; v.p. research and devel. Bristol Labs. div. Bristol-Myers Co., 1970-82; lectr. Adelphi U., 1963-69. Contbr. articles to profl. jours.; patentee in field Trustee Gordon Research Conf., 1972-75; chmn. medicinal chemistry study group Walter Reed Inst. Research, 1975-77. Served with USN, 1944-46. Mem. Am. Chem. Soc. (chmn. div. medicinal chemistry 1974-76), Pharm. Mfrs. Assn. (chmn. research and devel. sect. 1975-76) Home: 101 Woodberry Ln Fayetteville NY 13066-1745 Personal E-mail: ijpac@aol.com.

PACHTER, LEE M., pediatrician; b. Bklyn., Mar. 12, 1957; s. Harvey Leonard and Rosalind Blau Pachter; married Diedre Reynolds-Pachter; 1 child, Lauren. BA, Franklin and Marshal Coll., 1979; DO, Phila. Coll. Osteo. Medicine, 1983. Diplomate Am. Bd. Osteo. Physicians. Intern Metro. Hosp., Springfield, Pa., 1983-84; resident in pediatrics St. Christopher's Hosp. Children, Phila., 1984-87; fellow in pediatrics Children's Hosp. Phila., 1987-89; from asst. prof. to prof. pediats. and anthropology U. Conn. Sch. Medicine, Farmington, 1989—, head divsn. gen. pediat., 1998—. Trustee The Artists Collective, Hartford, Conn., 1989—. Fellow Am. Acad. Pediatrics, Soc. Applied Anthropology; mem. Am. Anthropol. Assn., Ambulatory Pediat. Assn., Soc. Rsch. and Child Devel., Soc. Applied Anthropology, Soc. for Pediat. Rsch. Personal E-mail: lpachter@comcast.net.

PACHTER, MARC, retired museum director; B summa cum laude, Univ. Calif., Berkeley; postgrad, Harvard Univ. Faculty Harvard Univ.; chief historian Smithsonian's Nat. Portrait Gallery, 1974—90, asst. dir., 1974—90, dep. asst. sec., external affairs, 1990—94, Nat. Portait Gallery dir., 2000—07; acting dir. Smithsonian's Nat. Mus. of Am. History, 2001—02; former counselor to sec. Smithsonian Instn., 1995—2000. Chair Smithsonian's 150th Anniversary; sr. cons. various history documentaries; cons. Internat. Broadcasting; commentator CBS, Voice of Am., C-SPAN. Author/editor (books) Abroad in America: Visitors to the New Nation, Champions of American Sport, Documentary History of the Supreme Court, Telling Lives: The Biographer's Art, A Gallery of Presidents. Fellow Woodrow Wilson, Harvard Univ., five-yr. prize. Home: 3505 30th St NW Washington DC 20008-3251 Office Phone: 202-275-1740. Office Fax: 202-275-1887. Business E-Mail: pachterm@si.edu.

PACI, RUTH A., freelance/self-employed writer; b. West New York, NJ, Mar. 7, 1928; d. Joseph Frederick and Theresa Becker Paci. BA in History and Polit. Sci., Fordham U., Bronx, NY, 1984; MA in Journalism, NYU, 1987. Adminstrv. officer, press officer U.S. Info. Agy., Washington and NYC, 1951—86, dep. dir. Fgn. Press Ctr. NYC, 1985—86; ret., 1986; freelance writer. Author: Down By the River and Under the Cliff, 1994, Dearest Friends, 2004, short stories and essays. V.p., trustee Edgewater Pub. Libr., 1995—; mem., founder Cultural and Hist. Commn. Edgewater, 2000—; hist. preservation advisory bd. Bergen County, 2004. Recipient Cert. of Commendation, Bergen County Bd. Chosen Freeholders, 2003, Hist. Preservation resolution, NJ Gen. Assembly, 2003, Career Achievement award, US Info. Agy., 1986. Roman Catholic. Avocations: travel, gardening, reading. Personal E-mail: ruthwrite123@aol.com.

PACIFICO, ALBERT DOMINICK, cardiovascular surgeon; b. Bklyn., Sept. 24, 1940; s. Dominick Vincent and Amelia Catherine (Jannelli) P.; m. Vicki Lynne Overton, May 16, 1980; children: Albert D., Nicole M., Paul V. BS, St. Johns U., 1960; MD, N.J. Coll. Medicine, 1964. Diplomate Am. Bd. Surgery, Am. Bd. Thoracic Surgery. Med. intern Jersey City Med. Ctr., Seton Gall Coll. Medicine, 1964-65; asst. resident in surgery Mayo Clinic, Rochester, Minn., 1965-67; research fellow in surgery U. Ala., Birmingham, 1967-69, sr. resident, then chief resident surgery, resident in thoracic and cardiovascular surgery, 1968-72, mem. faculty dept. surgery, 1970—2006, prof. surgery, 1978-83, John W. Kirklin prof. cardiovascular surgery, 1983—2006, vice chmn. dept. surgery, 1990, dir. divsn. cardiothoracic surgery, 1984—2006, dir. Congenital Heart Disease Diagnosis and Treatment Ctr., 1985—2006; ret., 2006. Mem. staff gen., thoracic and cardiovascular surgery Univ. Hosp., Birmingham, 1972-2006, VA Hosp., Birmingham, 1972-2006; mem. staff Children's Hosp., Birmingham, 1971-2006, chief gen., thoracic and cardiovascular surgery, 1984-2006. Author: (with others) Pediatric Cardiac Surgery, 1985, Cardiology, 1985, Textbook of Surgery, 13th edit., 1986, The Treatment of Congenital Cardiac Anomalies, 1986, Perspectives in Pediatric Cardiology, 1988, Current Therapy in Cardiothoracic Surgery, 1989, Decision Making in Surgery of the Chest, 1989, Cardiac Surgery: Cyanotic Congential Heart Disease, 1989, Reoperation in Cardiac Surgery, 1989, others; mem. editorial bd. Am. Jour. Cardiology, 1983-2006, Heart and Vessel, 1985-2006, Jour. Cardiac Surgery, 1985-2006; cons. editorial referee Ala. Jour. Med. Scis., 1974-75; contbr. articles to med. jours. Fellow ACS, Am. Coll. Cardiology, Am. Surg. Assn.; mem. AMA, Ala. State Med. Soc., Jefferson County Med. Soc., Am. Heart Assn. (Paul Dudley White Internat. Svc. Citation 1977), Am. Assn. Thoracic Surgery, Soc. Thoracic Surgeons, Am. Surg. Soc., Internat. Coll. Pediatrics, John Kirklin Soc., Congentital Heart Surgeons Soc., Assn. Acad. Surgery, Ala. chpt. Mayo Clinic Alumni Assn., Panamanian Soc. Cardiology (hon.), Peruvian Soc. Thoracic and Cardiovascular Surgery (hon.), Soc. Nat. Inst. Cardiology Mex. (hon.), Cardiac Soc. Australia and New Zealand (corr.), Peruvian Soc. Cardiology (corr.), Alpha Omega Alpha. Republican. Roman Catholic.

PACINO, AL (ALFREDO JAMES PACINO), actor; b. NYC, Apr. 25, 1940; s. Salvatore and Rose Pacino; 1 child (with Jan Tarrant) Julie Marie; children (with Beverly D'Angelo) Anton, Olivia. Student, High Sch. of Performing Arts, Actors Studio. Formerly mail deliverer editorial offices Commentary Mag.; formerly messenger, movie theatre usher, bldg. supt.; co-artistic dir. The Actors Studio, Inc., NYC, 1982-84. Actor: (films) Me, Natalie, 1969, The Panic in Needle Park, 1971, The Godfather, 1972 (Best Actor award Nat. Soc. Film Critics, Acad. award nominee), Scarecrow, 1973, Serpico, 1973 (Golden Globe for best actor), The Godfather, Part II, 1974 (BAFTA award for best actor), Dog Day Afternoon (BAFTA award for best actor), 1975, Bobby Deerfield, 1977, And Justice for All..., 1979, Cruising, 1980, Author! Author!, 1982, Scarface, 1983, Revolution, 1985, Sea of Love, 1989, Dick Tracy, 1990, The Godfather Part III, 1990, Frankie and Johnny, 1991, Glengarry Glen Ross, 1992, Scent of a Woman, 1992 (Acad. award for Best actor, 1992, Golden Globe award for Best Actor), Carlito's Way, 1993, Two Bits, 1995, Heat, 1995, City Hall, 1996, Donnie Brasco, 1997, Devil's Advocate, 1997, Chinese Coffee, 1999, The Insider, 1999, Any Given Sunday, 1999, People I Know, 2002, Simone, 2002, Insomnia, 2002, The Recruit, 2003, Gigli, 2003, The Merchant of Venice, 2004, Two for the Money, 2005, 88 Minutes, 2007, Ocean's Thirteen, 2007, Righteous Kill, 2008; actor, dir.: (films) Chinese Coffee, 2000; actor: (TV miniseries) Angels in America, 2003 (Golden Globe for best actor, Screen Actors Guild Award for best actor, 2004, Emmy award Outstanding Lead Actor in a Miniseries or a Movie, 2004); (short films) The Local Stigmatic, 1990; dir. (documentaries) Looking for Richard, 1996 (Dir. Guild of America award for Best Dir. of Documentary); appeared in a one-act play Off Broadway The Indian Wants the Bronx, opened Astor Pl. Theater on Jan. 17, 1968 (Obie as best actor in Off-Broadway prodn. 1967-68); Does A Tiger Wear A Necktie?, 1969 (Tony award as Best Dramatic Actor in a Supporting Role), The Basic Training of Pavlo Hummel, Boston Repertory Theater, 1972, Camino Real, Richard III, 1973, 79, Jungle of Cities, 1979, The Connection, Hello Out There, Tiger at the Gates, American Buffalo, 1980, Julius Caesar, 1988, Salome, Chinese Coffee, 2000, Circle in the Square, 1992; actor, dir.: (plays) Hughie, 1996 Recipient Lifetime Achievement award Ind. Feature Project Gotham awards, 1996, Cecil B. DeMille Award Hollywood Fgn. Press. Assn., 2001, Am. Cinematheque Lifetime Achievement award, 2006, Lifetime Achievement award, Am. Film Inst., 2007, Marcus Aurelius Lifetime Achievement award, Rome Film Festival, 2008, Internat award, Variety Club, 2008 Office: c/o Rick Nicita Creative Artists Agy 9830 Wilshire Blvd Beverly Hills CA 90212-1804*

PACINO, MARIA ANTONIETA, education educator, department chairman; d. Antonio Augusto Osorio de Carvalho and Maria da Conceicao Ponte (de Carvalho); m. Joe Louis Pacino, Dec. 2, 1974; children: Monique Caroline Morelli, Vanessa Paula Morelli. BA, Ball State U., 1977, MLS, 1981, EdD, 1988. Tchg. credential Ind., 1977. Tchr., libr. Muncie Cmty. Schools, Ind., 1978—90; asst. prof. sec. edn. Ball State U., Muncie, 1990—93; assoc. prof. edn. Azusa Pacific U., Calif., 1993—97, prof., dept. chair, 1997—. Spkr. in field. Contbr. articles to profl. jours., chapters to books. Mem. Human Rels. Commn., Azusa, 1999—2000, Pub. Libr. Commn., Azusa, 2000—03; chair U. Diversity Coun., Azusa, 2004—. Mem.: ASCD, Nat. Assn. Multicultural Edn., Am. Ednl. Rsch. Assn. Roman Catholic. Avocations: reading, opera, music, travel, theater. Office: Azusa Pacific U P O Box 7000 Azusa CA 91702 Office Fax: 626-815-5416. Business E-Mail: mpacino@apu.edu.

PACK, RUSSELL T., retired theoretical chemist; b. Grace, Idaho, Nov. 20, 1937; s. John Terrell and Mardean (Izatt) P.; m. Marion Myrth Hassell, Aug. 21, 1962; children: John R., Nathan H., Allen H., Miriam, Elizabeth, Quinn R., Howard H. BS, Brigham Young U., 1962; PhD, U. Wis., 1967. Postdoctoral fellow U. Minn., Mpls., 1966-67; asst. prof. Brigham Young U., Provo, 1967-71, assoc. prof., 1971-75, adj. prof., 1975-88; staff scientist Los Alamos (N.Mex.) Nat. Lab., 1975-83, fellow, 1983—2008, assoc. grp. leader, 1979-81. Vis. prof. Max Planck Institut, Gottingen, 1981; chmn. Gordon Rsch. Conf., 1982; lectr. in field. Contbr. articles to profl. jours. Named Sr. U.S. Scientist, Alexander Vol Humboldt Found., 1981. Fellow Am. Phys. Soc. (sec.-treas. div. Chem. Physics 1990-93); mem. Am. Chem. Soc., Sigma Xi. Mem. Ch. of Jesus Christ of Latter Day Saints. Home: 240 Kimberly Ln Los Alamos NM 87544-3526

PACK, SANDY (SANDRA LEE PACK), former federal agency administrator; BS, Coll. Notre Dame, 1991. CPA. Dir. treasury Phil Gramm for Pres., Inc., Washington, 1995; dep. dir. treasury Bob Dole for Pres., Inc., Washington, 1996; dir. planning and ops. MicroProse divsn. Spectrum Holobyte, Inc., Hunt Valley, Md., 1994—95; dir. small bus. cons. and acctg. svcs. Ernst & Young, Balt., dir. microcomputer consulting and acctg. svcs. Atlanta; dir. of treasury Bush for Pres., Inc., Bush-Cheney 2000, Inc.; asst. sec. for fin. mgmt., comptr., Dept. Army US Dept. Def., Washington, 2001—04; CFO Bush-Cheney Re-Election Campaign, 2004; asst. sec. for mgmt. US Dept. Treasury, Washington, 2005—06; CFO Rudolph Guiliani Presdl. Exploratory Com., NYC, 2007—. Office: Rudy Giuliani Presdl Com Inc 295 Greenwich St #371 New York NY 10007

PACKARD, JOHN MALLORY, physician, researcher; b. Saranac Lake, NY, Sept. 25, 1920; s. Edward Newman and Mary Bissell (Betts) P.; m. Ann Maurine Schoonover, June 15, 1944; children: Michael David, John Mallory, Ann Maurine, Mary Betts, Charles Edward, Kris Asvananda, Frank Schoonover, Charlotte Mellen. BA, Yale U., 1942; MD, Harvard U., 1945. Diplomate Am. Bd. Internal Medicine. Intern Presbyn. Hosp., NYC, 1945-46; resident in internal medicine Peter Bent Brigham Hosp., Boston, 1948-49; practice medicine specializing in internal medicine and cardiology Pensacola, Fla., 1954-68; prof. medicine, asso. dean Med. Sch. U. Ala., Birmingham, 1968-76; exec. dir. Ala. Regional Med. Program, Birmingham, 1968-73; corp. v.p. med. edn. Bapt. Med. Centers, Birmingham, 1976-92; ret., 1992. Contbr. articles to med. jours. Served with USN, 1946-54. Fellow ACP, Am. Coll. Cardiology, AHA; mem. Jefferson County Med. Soc., Med. Assn. Ala., AMA, Am. Soc. Internal Medicine, Ala. Soc. Internal Medicine (pres. 1981-82), Alpha Omega Alpha. Republican. Episcopalian. Personal E-mail: jmpackard@juno.com.

PACKARD, JOYCE HORNADAY, retired counselor; b. Fordyce, Ark., June 21, 1925; d. John Wesley and Nora (Wright) Hornaday; m. Robert G. Packard, Apr. 15, 1954. BA, Baylor U., 1952, MS, 1957; postgrad., Columbia U., 1966, Baylor U., 1980. Lic. counselor Tex. Office mgr./tchr. Western Union Telegraph Co., Crossett, Ark., 1944-48; asst. dean of women Baylor U., Waco, 1952—54; tchr. Edison High Sch., Stockton, Calif., 1954-55, Clinton (Miss.) High Sch., 1955-56; tchr. Am. history/govt. Richfield High Sch., Waco, 1963-66, counselor, 1966—81, 1982—86; lectr. Baylor U., Waco, 1981-82, supr. practice tchrs., 1986—90. Tchr. English, U. Calif. Team Arlangga U., Sarabaja, Indonesia, 1961-62; tchr. cons. U. Sci., Penang, Malaysia, summer 1976; mem. Internat. Del. Citizen Ambassador, China, 1990. Mem. team Greater Asian Evangelism Team, Taiwan, 1970; bd. dirs. Brazos Forum, Waco, 1989—, pres., 1997; bd. dirs. Waco Historic Found., 1988—, pres., 1995-96; reg. facilitator Tex. Hospitality Course, 1987—; mem., chair Waco Conv. and Visitors Adv. Bd., 1987-2006; mem. Ind. Sch. Dist. Ednl. Bd., 1996—; bd. dirs. Brazos Higher Edn., Brazos Performing Arts; pres. Baptist Southern Deans, 1958-59; mem. Baylor U. Student Life. Adv. Bd., 2006—. Recipient Woman of Achievement award, 1972, Waco Hospitality award Convention and Tourism Adv. Bd., 1990, Pathfinder award Waco YWCA, 1990, Cert. award Vol. Svcs. Waco City Coun., 1991, Leadership Waco C. of C. Alumnus award, 1994, Athena award, 1995, DAR Cmty. Svc. award Elizabeth Gordon Bardley Chpt., 1997, Madison Cooper award cmty. leadership Madison Cooper Found. Trustees, 1999, Woman of Distinction award Bluebonnet Girl Scouts, 2003, Disting. Faculty award Waco Ind. Sch. Dist., 2004. Mem. Greater Waco Beautification Assn., Baylor Round Table (pres. 1988-89), Baylor Alumni Assn. (W.R. White Meritorious Svc. award, 2007, abner V. McCall Svcs. award, 2007), Leadership Waco Alumni Assn., Epsilon Chi (achievement award 1984, pres. 1976-78), Delta Kappa Gamma (achievement award 1984, corres. sec. 1987-89). Baptist. Avocations: cooking, travel. Home: 69 Sugar Creek Pl Woodway TX 76712-3407

PACKARD, ROBERT GOODALE, III, urban planner; b. Denver, Apr. 12, 1951; s. Robert and Mary Ann (Woodward) Packard; m. Jane Ann Collins, Aug. 25, 1973; children: Jessica Nelson, Robert Gregg. BA, Williamette U., 1973; M in Urban and Regional Planning/Cmty. Devel., U. Colo., 1976. Project mgr. Environ. Disciplines, Inc., Portland, 1973—75; asst. dir. planning Portland Pub. Schs., 1976—78; dir. planning Bur. Parks, 1978—79; dir. planning and urban design Zimmer Gunsul Frasca, 1979—81, dir. project devel., 1981—84, mng. ptnr., 1984—. Mem. Mayor's Task Force for Joint Use of Schs., 1979—80, Waterfront Commn., Portland, 1982—83; mem. steering com. Washington Pk. Master Plan, 1980—81; dir., pres. Grant Park Neighborhood Assn., 1981—83. Co-author: The Baker Neighborhood/Denver, 1976; contbr. articles to profl. jours. Pres. New Rose Theatre, 1981—83, Arts Celebration Inc./Artquake, 1986—, Pioneer Square Bd., 1997—98; mem. Archtl. Found. Oreg., 1992; trustee Williamette U., 1994; bd. mem. Regional Arts and Cultural Coun.; mem. crafts bd. Oreg. Sch. Arts; bd. dirs. Washington Pk. Zoo, 1983—86. Recipient Spl. Citation, Nat. Sch. Bds. Assn., 1978, Meritorious Planning Project award, Nat. Am. Planning Assn., 1981, Meritorious Design award, Am. Soc. Landscape Architects, 1981, Honor award, Progressive Arch, 1983. Mem.: AIA (assoc. Architecture Firm award 1991), Young Pres. Assn., Am. Planning Assn. (Meritorious Planning Project award 1980), City Club, Arlington Club, Racquet Club. Office: Zimmer Gunsul Frasca Partnership 320 SW Oak St Ste 500 Portland OR 97204-2737 Home: PO Box 1775 Edwards CO 81632-1775

PACKARD, ROCHELLE SYBIL, retired elementary school educator; b. June 25, 1951; d. Dave Wallace and Jeanette (Goddy) P. BA in Early Childhood Edn., Point Park Coll., 1973; MEd in Elem. Edn., U. Pitts., 1975. Instrnl. II permanent tchg. cert., Pa. Substitute tchr. Pitts. Pub. Bd. Edn., 1973-77, tchr. kindergarten, 1st grade, 2d grade, 1977—92, tchr. kindergarten, 1992—2007; tchr. early childhood dept. Beth Shalom Congregation, Pitts., 2007—. Chair Israel Day Parade, Pitts., 1981; mem. Hadassah, Pitts., 1983—, Pioneer Women, Pitts., 1982—, ORT, Pitts., 1975—. Mem. Pitts. Fedn. Tchrs., Pitts. State Edn. Agy. Democrat. Jewish. Home: 4100 Lydia St Pittsburgh PA 15207-1135 Office: Beth Shalom Congregation Early Childhood Dept 5915 Beacon St Pittsburgh PA 15217 Home Phone: 412-422-0823; Office Phone: 412-421-8857.

PACKARD, RUSSELL CALVERT, deacon; b. Alhambra, Calif., Apr. 10, 1946; s. Homer W. and Ruth Ellen Packard; m. Beverly Albert, Dec. 26, 1966 (div. Dec. 1976); children: Tara, Todd, Brent; m. Gretchen Myers, Feb. 25, 1978 (div. 2006); children: Christine, Jennifer; m. Debra Johnson, July 5, 2008. MD, U. Calif., Irvine, 1971; BS in Religious Studies summa cum laude, St. Leo Coll., 1981. Ordained deacon Roman Cah. Ch., 1981; diplomate Am. Bd. Psychiatry and Neurology. Instr. pastoral counseling Permanent Diaconate Program, 1981-88; pastoral assoc. St. Paul Cath. Ch., Pensacola, Fla., 1984—; psychiat. cons. Diocese of Pensacola-Tallahassee, 1981—. Adj. prof. psychology-psychiatry U. West Fla., 1988—; dir. Headache Mgmt. and Neurology, Pensacola, 1981—; bishop's rep. bd. dirs. Community Health Ctr., 1982-85; mem. Permanent Diaconate Bd., Diocese Pensacola-Tallahassee, 1981-88; chairperson bioethics com. Sacred Heart Hosp., Pensacola, 1988—. Author: Come, Journey with Me, 1984, The Psychiatric Wards, 1984; editor: Psychiatric Aspects Headache, 1989. Comdr. USN, 1970-80. Fellow ACP, Am. Acad. Neurology; mem. Am. Psychiat. Assn., Am. Assn. Study Headache, Escambia County Med. Soc. Republican. Office: East Texas Neurology 3201 S Loop 256 Ste 140 Palestine TX 75801 Office Fax: 903-661-7165. E-mail: rcpneuron@msn.com.

PACKARD, SANDRA PODOLIN, education educator, consultant; b. Buffalo, Sept. 13, 1942; d. Mathew and Ethel (Zolte) P.; m. Martin Packard, Aug. 2, 1964; children: Dawn Esther, Shana Fanny BFA, Syracuse U., 1964; MSEd, Ind. U., 1966, EdD, 1973. Cert. tchr. art K-12, N.Y. Asst. prof. art SUNY-Buffalo, 1972-74; assoc. prof. art Miami U., Oxford, Ohio, 1974-81, spl. asst. to provost, 1979-80, assoc. provost, spl. programs, 1980-81; dean Coll. Edn. Bowling Green State U., Ohio, 1981-85; provost and vice chancellor for acad. affairs U. Tenn., Chattanooga, 1985-92; pres. Oakland U., Rochester, Mich., 1992-95, prof. edn., 1995—, chairperson, dept. ednl. leadership, 2008—09, dir. higher edn. doc. cognate; sr. fellow, dir. tech. in edn. Am. Assn. State Colls. and Univs., 1995; acting dir. PhD program in ednl. leadership Oakland U., 2003—04. Cons. Butler County Health Ctr., Hamilton, Ohio, 1976-78, Univ. of the North, South Africa Project of the Am. Coun. on Edn., 1995; vis. prof. art therapy Simmons Coll., 1979, Mary Mount Coll., Milw., 1981; corp. adv. com. Corp. Detroit Mag., 1994-95. Sr. editor Studies in Art Edn. jour., 1979-81; mem. editl. adv. bd. Jour. Aesthetic Edn., 1984-90; editor: The Leading Edge, 1986; contbr. articles to profl. jours., chpts. to conf. papers Chmn. com. Commn. on Edn. Excellence, Ohio, 1982-83, Tenn. State Peformance Funding Task Force, 1988, Tenn. State Task Force on Minority Tchrs., 1988; reviewer art curriculum NY Bd. Edn., 1985; supt. search com. Chattanooga Pub. Schs., 1987-88; mem. Chattanooga Met. Coun., 1987-88, Chattanooga Ballet Bd., 1986-88, Fund for Excellence in Pub. Edn., 1986-90, Tenn. Aquarium Bd. Advisors, 1989-92, Team Evaluation Ctr. Bd., 1988-90; strategic planning action team Chattanooga City Schs., 1987-88, Siskin Hosp. Bd., 1989-92, Blue Ribbon Task Force Pontiac 2010: A New Reality, City of Pontiac Planning Divsn., 1992—; steering com., cultural action bd. Chattanooga, planning com United Way, 1987; Jewish Fedn. Bd., 1986-91; mem. coun. for policy studies Art Edn. Adv. Bd., 1982-91; ex-officio mem. Meadow Brook Theatre Guild, 1992-95; bd. chair Meadow Brook Performing Arts Co., 1992-95; chair World Cup Soccer Edn. Com./Mich. Host Com. 1993-95; bd. dirs. Ptnrs. for Preferred Future, Rochester Cmty. Schs., 1992-95, Traffic Improvement Assn. Oakland County, 1992-95, Oakland County Bus. Roundtable, 1993-95; Rochester C. of C. host com. chair on edn. World Cup, 1992-95; fin. adv. com. Jewish Fedn. Detroit, 1995-97; bd. dirs. United Way Southeastern Mich., 1992-95: bd. dirs. United Way Oakland County, 1992-95, Pontiac 2010: A New Reality, mayor's transition team city/sch. rels. task force: team evaluation leader Dept. of State Am. U. Bulgaria, 1995; bd. trustees Cohn's & Colitis Found., 1996-97; trustee Nat. Art Edn. Found., 2004—, chair fin. com.; steering com. Nat. Forum Access to Democracy Project, 2004. Am. Coun. on Edn. and Mellon fellow Miami U., 1978-79; recipient Cracking the Glass Ceiling award Pontiac Area Urban League, 1992. Fellow Nat. Art Edn. Assn. (disting.); mem. Nat. Coun. Profs. of Ednl. Adminstrn. (technology com., 2000-03), Am. Assn. Colls. for Tchr. Edn. (com. chair 1982-85), Am. Art Therapy Assn. (registered), Nat. Art Edn. Assn. Women's Caucus (founder, pres. 1976-78, McFee award 1986), Am. Assn. State Colls. and Univs. (com. profl. devel. 1993-95, state rep. 1994-95), Econ. Club Detroit (bd. dirs. 1992-95), Rotary Club, Great Lakes Yacht Club (social chmn. 1996-97, ground chmn., bd. dirs. 1997-98), Phi Delta Kappa (Leadership award 1985), Nat. Assn. Profs. of Edn. Adminstrn. (com. chair 1998-), Great Lakes Yacht Club, 1995 (bd. dir. 1996-1998). Avocation: sailing. Home: 10471 Scout Trail White Lake MI 48386 Office: Oakland U 475 Education Bldg Rochester MI 48309-4423 Business E-Mail: packard@oakland.edu.

PACKARD, SOPHIE S., elementary school educator; b. Anacoco, La., Dec. 15, 1935; d. Willie Cranford and Lorea Grace (Dixon) Snell; m. Hyland D. Packard; children: Lajuan Michelle Packard Chopin, Michael Harry. BA in Elem. Tchg. and Reading, EdS in Elem. Tchg. and Reading, Northwestern State U., Natchitoches, La. Cert. Gesell devel. examiner Gesell Inst. Human Growth and Devel. Tchr./supr. Northwestern State U., Natchitoches. Vol. Lov'n Care Mission, 1996—2006, co-dir., 1997—2006. Recipient Tchr. of the Yr. award, Weaver Elem. Sch., 1984, Dist. Tchr. of Yr. award, Natchitoches, 1985, Outstanding Elem Cooperating Tchr. of Year, Northwestern State U., 1994—95, Disting. Clinician Yr., La. Assn. Tchr. Edn., 1996, Presdl. Point of Light award, Dec. 13, 2000. Mem.: Retired Tchrs. La., Lions Club (pres. 2004—05),

Order of Eastern Star (worthy matron 2003—04, organist 2005, grand rep. to Idaho from La. 2005—), Phi Delta Kappa (past pres.), Delta Gamma Kappa (past pres.). Baptist. Avocations: piano, gardening, handwork.

PACKER, BILLY, former sports announcer; b. Wellsville, NY, Feb. 25, 1940; m. Barbara Packer; 3 children. Graduated, Wake Forest Univ., 1962. Asst. basketball coach Wake Forest Univ., 1965; basketball announcer, ACC conference games Jefferson Pilot Sports, 1972, NBC Sports, 1974—81; basketball announcer, final four announcer CBS Sports, 1981—2008. Co-founder Tour DuPont, Buckler Challenge. Author: (sports books) Hoops, College Basketball's 25 Greatest Teams, History of the Final Four, Why We Win. Recipient NC Sportscaster Yr. award; named to NC Hall of Fame, Wake Forest Hall of Fame, Nat. Basketball Hall of Fame, Nat. Polish Hall of Fame, Nat. Collegiate Basketball Hall of Fame, 2008.*

PACKER, C. SUBAH, physiologist, educator; b. Winnipeg, Manitoba, Canada, Dec. 24, 1954; d. William Clifford and Ellen Mary Packer. BSc in Zoology, U. Man., Sch. Sci., Winnipeg, 1976; PhD, U. Man. Sch. Medicine, Winnipeg, 1986. Postdoc. fellow, Can. Heart Found. Ind. U., Sch. Medicine, Indpls., 1986—88, scientist, 1988—94, asst. prof. physiology, 1994—2001, assoc. prof. physiology, 2001—. Frontiers physiology local outreach team leader Am. Physiol. Soc. & Ind. U. Sch. Medicine, Indpls., 1995—; editl. bd. mem. Open Hypertension Jour., 2008—. Contbr. articles to profl. jours. (M Irené Ferrer award, 2001). Preceptor Indy Project SEED, Indpls., 1994—2009. Recipient Recognition award, Ind. U. Purdue U. Indpls., 2007. Mem.: Am. Chem. Soc. (Recognition award 2003), Am. Lung Assn. (Career Investigator award 1995—98), Am. Physiol. Soc. (team leader 2003—09). Achievements include discovery of rapid contraction—impaired arterial relaxation in hypertension; research in elucidation of various oxygen free radicals including hydrogen peroxide & oxidized low density lipoprotein as arterial muscle contractile agents. Office: Indiana Univ Sch Medicine 635 Barnhill Dr Indianapolis IN 46202-5120

PACKER, JAMES INNELL, theology studies educator, writer; b. Gloucester, Eng., July 22, 1926; BS, MA, DPhil, Oxford U. Corpus Christi Coll., Eng. Ordained priest Ch. of Eng. Greek lang. tchr. Oak Hill Theol. Coll., London, 1948—49; sr. tutor Tyndale Hall, Bristol, 1955—61, prin., 1970—71; warden Latimer House, Oxford, 1961—69; assoc. prin. Trinity Coll., Bristol, 1971—79; Sangwoo Youtong Chee prof. theology Regent Coll., Vancouver, 1979—96; sr. ed. Christianity Today; bd. gov. prof., 1996—. Author: Fundamentalism and the Word of God, 1958, Evangelism and the Sovereignty of God, 1961, Knowing God, 1973, Keep In Step With The Spirit: Finding Fullness In Our Walk With God, 1984, A Quest for Godliness: The Puritan Vision of the Christian Life, 1994, Concise Theology: A Guide to Historic Christian Beliefs, 2001, The Redemption and Restoration of Man in the Thought of Richard Baxter, 2003, Praying, 2006; co-author: Christianity: The True Humanism, 1985, One Faith: The Evangelical Consensus, 2004, Guard Us Guide Us, 2008. Named one of 25 Most Influential Evangelicals in America, Time Mag., 2005. Anglican. Office: Regent Coll 5800 University Blvd Vancouver BC V6T 2E4 Canada Office Phone: (604) 224-3245. Office Fax: (604) 224-3097.

PACKER, JUDITH ANNE, mathematics professor; m. James V. Jesudason, July 3, 1982. MA, Wesleyan U., Middletown, Conn., 1978; PhD, Harvard U., Cambridge, Mass., 1982. NSF postdoc. fellow Math. Scis. Rsch. Inst., Berkeley, Calif., 1982—83; lectr. to sr. lectr.,Dept. Math. Nat. U. Singapore, 1983—89. Mem. Inst. Advanced Study, Princeton, NJ, 1987; asst. prof., assoc. prof.,Dept. Math. U. Colo., Boulder, 1989—92, prof., Dept. Math., 2002—; sr. lectr., assoc. prof., prof., Dept. Math. Nat. U. Singapore, 1992—2001. Co-editor: (mathematics book) A Celebration of the Mathematical Work; contbr. scientific papers to profl. jours. Rsch. grant, NSF, 1990—93, Conf. grant, 2006—08, Std. grant, 2007—. Mem.: Assn. Women Math., Am. Math. Soc., Phi Beta Kappa. Achievements include research in study of twisted group C*-algebras, study of relationship of wavelets to C*-algebras. Avocations: travel, reading.

PACKER, LINDA S., geriatric care manager; b. NYC, July 30, 1941; d. Joseph Wolf Stark and Jean Carson; children: William Joseph, Andrew Landes. BA in English and Psychology, with honors, NYU, 1972. Fellow Am. Psychotherapy Assn.; LCSW Nat. Assn. Social Workers and SUNY Edn. Dept.; cert. Nat. Acad. Cert. Care Mgrs. Rsch. asst. alcoholic rsch. unit Silver Hill Found., 1972—75; intern clin. social worker Prog. Devel. Human Potential, Bishop Ford HS, 1985—86; intern clin. social worker outpatient psychiat. clinic Met. Hosp., 1986—87; psych. social worker NY Svc. Prog. for Older People, 1987—88; sr. cons. Helena Internat., Morristown, NJ, 1988—89; psychiat. social worker Geriatric Psychiat. Inpatient Unit, 1989—92; psychiat. social worker adult psychiat. inpatient unit Mt. Sinai Hosp., NYC, 1992—95; sr. assoc. Fine & Newcombe Assocs., NYC, 1995—99; founder, dir. Prime Life Network, NYC, 2000—. Cons., founder Care Mgrs. Consortium, NYC, 2000—; pvt. practice, 1987—. Mem.: NY State Soc. Clin. Social Work Psychotherapists, Nat. Assn. Social Workers, Nat. Assn. Profl. Geriatric Care Mgrs., East Side Coun. on Aging, Am. Soc. on Aging, Am. Psychotherapy Assn., Am. Geriatric Soc. Avocations: gardening, reading, interior decorating. Office: PrimeLife Network 200 E End Ave #10-I New York NY 10128 Office Phone: 212-534-4412. Business E-Mail: lpacker@nyc.rr.com.

PACKER, MARK BARRY, lawyer, financial consultant, foundation official; b. Phila., Sept. 18, 1944; s. Samuel and Eve (Devine) P.; m. Donna Elizabeth Ferguson (div. 1994); children: Daniel Joshua, Benjamin Dov, David Johannes; m. Helen Margaret (Jones) Klinedinst, July, 1995. AB magna cum laude, Harvard U., 1965, LLB, 1968. Bar: Wash. 1969, Mass. 1971. Assoc. Ziontz, Pirtle & Fulle, Seattle, 1968-70; pvt. practice Bellingham, Wash., 1972—. Bd. dirs., corp. sec. BMJ Holdings (formerly No. Sales Co., Inc.), 1977—; trustee No. Sales Profit Sharing Plan, 1977—; bd. dirs. Whatcom State Bank, 1995-98. Mem. Bellingham Planning and Devel. Commn., 1975—84, chmn., 1977—81, mem. shoreline subcom., 1976—82, capital improvements adv. com., 1999—2001; mem. Bellingham Mcpl. Arts Commn., 1986—91, landmark rev. bd., 1987—91; chmn. Bellingham campaign United Jewish Appeal, 1979—90; trustee, chmn. program com. Bellingham Pub. Sch. Found., 1991—96, Heavy Culture classic lit. group, 1991—, Jewish studies group, 1993—; trustee Kenneth L. Kellar Found., 1995—; mng. trustee Bernard M. & Audrey Jaffe Found.; Torah reader, trustee Frederick S. & Emma Gartner Charitable Trust, 1996—2007; instr. Acad. Lifelong Learning, 2004—; pres. Congregation Eytz Chaim, Bellingham, 1998—2000; bd. dirs. Whatcom Cmty. Coll. Found., 1989—92. Recipient Blood Donor award ARC, 1979, 8-Gallon Pin, 1988, Mayor's Arts award City of Bellingham, 1993. Mem. Wash. State Bar Assn. (sec. real property, probate and trust, com. law examiners 1992-94). Office: PO Box 1151 Bellingham WA 98227-1151 Office Phone: 360-671-7500. Business E-Mail: Packer@nas.com.

PACKER, MYRNA, choreographer, dancer; Co-founder Bridgman/Packer Dance, Valley Cottage, NY, 1978—. Dancer, choreographer (with Art Bridgman) Carried Away, 2000, Point A to Point B (You Can't Get There from Here), 2001, Seductive Reasoning, 2003, Under the Skin, 2005, Memory Bank, 2007. Grantee Nat. Endowment Arts, 2007, New England Found. Arts, 2007; fellow John Simon Guggenheim Meml. Found., 2008; Digital fellow, Dance Theater Workshop, 2005—06, numerous other fellowships and grants. Office: Bridgman/Packer Dance 281 Old Mill Rd Valley Cottage NY 10989 also: c/o Michelle Coe Pentacle 246 W 38th St 8th Fl New York NY 10018 Office Phone: 845-268-9008. E-mail: info@bridgmanpacker.org.*

PACKMAN, AARON IAN, environmental engineer, educator; b. St. Louis, Mo., Sept. 19, 1969; s. Jerrold Barry and Bella Ruth Packman; m. Jennifer Suzanne Grimmer; 1 child, Ariel Rose. BSME, Wash. U., St. Louis, 1991; MS, Calif. Inst. of Tech., Pasadena, 1992, PhD, 1997. Asst. prof. Drexel U., Phila., 1997—2000, Northwestern U., Evanston, Ill., 2000—04, assoc. prof., 2004—. Recipient Career award, NSF, 1999—2004; NDSEG Grad. Fellow, Office of Naval Rsch., 1991—94, Myers Fellow, Wash. U., 1987—91. Achievements include research in stream-subsurface exchange; fine sediment dynamics in streams; multiphase contaminant transport; microbial transport processes. Office: Northwestern U Dept Civil & Environ Engring 2145 Sheridan Rd Evanston IL 60208

PACQUIAO, MANNY (EMMANUEL DAPIDRAN PACQUIAO), boxer; b. Bukidnon, The Philippines, Dec. 17, 1978; Profl. boxer, 1995—. Flyweight champion World Boxing Commn., 1998—99, super featherweight champion, 2008, lightweight champion, 2008—09; super bantamweight champion Internat. Boxing Fedn., 2001—03; light welterweight champion Internat. Boxing Orgn., 2009—. Candidate, South Cotabato constituency House of Reps., Philippines, 2007. Named Fighter of Yr., Boxing Writers Assn. America, 2006, 2008, Ring Mag., 2006, 2008, ESPN, 2006, 2008, World Boxing Hall of Fame, 2007; named one of The World's Most Influential People, TIME mag., 2009. Achievements include a professional boxing record of: 49 wins (37 by knockout), 3 losses and 2 draws. Office: c/o Wild Card Boxing Club 1123 Vine St West Hollywood CA 90038 Office Phone: 323-461-4170.*

PACTER, PAUL ALLAN, accounting standards researcher; b. NYC, Jan. 26, 1943; s. Bernard David and Hilda Libby (Margolies) P. BS, Syracuse U., 1964; PhD, Mich. State U., 1967. C.P.A., N.Y. Asst. prof. N.Y.U., 1967-69; rsch. mgr. KPMG, NYC, 1969-73; exec. dir. Fin. Acctg. Standards Bd., Stamford, Conn., 1973-84; commr. fin. City of Stamford, 1984-90; prof. acctg., MBA program U. Conn., Stamford, 1990-96, adj. prof., 1982-84. Adj. prof. NYU, 1982-84; project cons. Fin. Acctg. Standards Bd., 1990-96; fellow Internat. Acctg. Standards Com., London, 1993-2000, dir., 2003—; bd. dirs. Deloitte Touche Tohmatsu, Hong Kong, 2000—. Consulting editor The Jour. of Accountancy, 1968-73 Chmn. Stamford Commn. on Human Rights, 1977-84, Stamford Film Commn., 1984-90; mem. Charter Revision Commn., Stamford, 1979-80, Gov.'s Tourism Coun., Conn., 1984-90, acctg. adv. coun. U. Conn., 1984-90; pres. N. Stamford Dem. Club, 1983-84, treas., 1987-95; dir. Stamford Coliseum Authority, 1984-90; vice chmn. govtl. acctg. stds. adv. coun., 1984-91; vice chmn. China Beijing Ctr. for Asia-Pacific Fin. and Acctg. Rsch., 2000—; treas. Conn. Tourism Assn., 1987-90, North Stamford Assn., 1993-94; bd. dirs. Stamford Ctr. for the Arts, United Way Stamford, Stamford Theatre Works, Stamford Cmty. Fund, Housing Devel. Fund of Fairfield County. Earhart Found. fellow Mich. State U., 1966-67; U.S. Office of Edn. grantee, 1967 Mem. AICPA, Am. Acctg. Assn. (coun.), N.Y. State Soc. CPA's, Beta Gamma Sigma, Beta Alpha Psi. Jewish. Office: Deloitte Touche Tohmatsu 35/F One Pacific Pl 88 Queensway Hong Kong China Home Phone: +852 2829 7129. Business E-Mail: ppacter@iasb.org.

PADBERG, HARRIET ANN, mathematician, educator; b. St. Louis, Nov. 13, 1922; d. Harry J. and Marie L. (Kilgen) P. AB with honors, Maryville Coll., St. Louis, 1943; MMus, U. Cin., 1949; MA, St. Louis U., 1956, PhD, 1964. Registered music therapist, cert. tchr. math. and music La., Mo. Tchr. elem. math. and music Kenwood Acad., Albany, N.Y., 1944-46; tchr. secondary math. Acad. of Sacred Heart, Cin., 1946-47; instr. math. and music Acad. and Coll. of Sacred Heart, Grand Coteau, La., 1947-48; secondary tchr. music Acad. Sacred Heart, St. Charles, Mo., 1948-50; instr. math. and music Acad. and Coll. Sacred Heart, Grand Coteau, 1950-55, Maryville Coll., St. Louis, 1955-56; tchr. elem. and secondary math. and music Acad. Sacred Heart, St. Louis, 1956-57; asst. prof. Maryville Coll., St. Louis, 1957-64, assoc. prof., 1964-68, prof. math., 1968-92, prof. emeritus, 1992—; music therapist Emmaus Homes, Marthasville, Mo., 1992—. Recipient Alumni Centennial award Maryville Coll., St. Louis, 1986, Deans award Sch. Health Professions, Alumni Recognition Program Maryville U., St. Louis, 2006, Diana award ESA Mo. State Coun., 2006, Humanitarian award ESA Found., 2006; grantee Danforth Found., Colorado Springs, 1970, Tallahassee, 1970, Edn. Devel. Ctr., Mass., 1975, U. Kans., 1980. Mem. Assn. Women in Math., Am. Math. Soc., Math. Assn. Am., Nat. Coun. Tchr. Math., Mo. Acad. Sci., Delta Epsilon Sigma (sec. local chpt. 1962), Pi Mu Epsilon (sec. local chpt. 1958), Sigma Xi. Avocations: computer music, organist, knitting. E-mail: hpadberg@rscj.org.

PADBERG, HELEN SWAN, violinist; b. Shawnee, Okla. d. Frank P. and Birdie B. (Rudell) Swan; m. Frank Padberg, Feb. 6, 1943; children: Frank, Kristen. AA, Stephens Coll., 1938; MusB, U. Okla., 1940; MusM, Northwestern U., 1941; student, Jacques Gordon. Solo performances and concerts, 1932—; mem. faculty string quartet and symphony soloist Stephens Coll., 1937-38; violinist Oklahoma City Symphony Summer Concerts, 1940; soloist Northwestern U. Symphony, 1941; violinist USO Tours World War II, 1941-43; mem. Nat. Orchestral Assn. and Am. Youth Orch., NYC, 1944-46; asst. concertmaster West Suburban Symphony, Chgo., 1947-48; mem. Chgo. Women's Symphony, Chgo. Civic Orch. and chamber music groups, 1947-51; violinist Ark. Piano Trio, 1952-58; concertmaster Ark. Symphony and Little Rock Philharm., 1953-57, Marjorie Lawrence TV Series, 1953-54; pvt. tchr. violin Little Rock, 1953-66; accompanist and performer on piano, harp. Pres. Ark. Med. Soc. Alliance, 1962-63, historian, 1963-94. Co-founder Little Rock Chamber Music Soc., 1954; pres. bd. dirs. Vis. Nurse Assn. of Pulaski County, Ark., 1967-69; bd. dirs. Internat. Visitors Ctr., Chgo., 1988—, Stephens Coll. Alumna Assn. Bd.; elder, trustee Presbyn. Ch.; docent Newberry Libr., Chgo., 1998—. Recipient Holmberg award, Okla. U., Spl. Recognition award, Am. Opera Soc., Chgo. Mem.: Mu Phi Epsilon, Internat. Women Assocs. (pres. 1988—91), Am. Opera Soc. Chgo. (v.p. and program chmn. 1981—82, pres. 1984—87), Am. Opera Soc. (historian 1987—), Am. Fedn. Musicians, Chgo. Harp Soc. (sec. 1979—84), Am. Harp Soc., English Spkg. Union (Chgo. br., bd. govs. 1997—), Musicians' Club of Women (Chgo., bd. dirs.), Women's Athletic Club of Chgo., Aesthetic Club (pres. Little Rock), Pi Beta Phi (pres. Little Rock Alumnae Club), Pi Kappa Lambda. Home: 175 E Delaware Pl Chicago IL 60611-1756

PADDEN, ANTHONY ALOYSIUS, JR., retired federal government official; b. Kearny, NJ, Apr. 3, 1949; s. Anthony Aloysius and Harriet Margaret Padden. PBA, Fairleigh Dickinson U., 1970, MA in Pub. Adminstrn., 1980; postgrad., U. Tenn. Sch. Law, 1970. Employment interviewer N.J. Dept. Labor, Trenton, 1970—76, prin. procedure analyst, 1976—79; nat. procedure coord. Interstate Compendium Employment Svc. Activities Project, Trenton, 1979—80; mgmt. analyst Dept. Justice, Washington, 1980—83; chief clk. ct. U.S. Immigration Ct., Falls Church, Va., 1983—. Adj. faculty Nat. Judicial Coll., Reno, 1998—2003; cons., Dumfries, Va., 1978—. Author: Dept. Labor tech. report, 1980; contbr. and editor: other profl. studies. Presdl. mgmt. intern, 1980, Logan Chambers grantee, Internat. Assn. Pers. in Employment Security, 1979. Mem.: Pi Alpha Alpha (Adminstr. of Yr. 1991).

PADDIO-JOHNSON, EUNICE ALICE, educational administrator; b. Crowley, La., June 25, 1928; d. Henry Paddio and Cecile A. (Chesle) Williams; m. Clarence H. Reed, Sept. 11, 1949 (div. Dec. 1980); children: Deidre, Clarence, Henry, Bertrand, Cecile; m. John D. Johnson, June 23, 1984. BS, Grambling State U., 1949; MA, UCLA, 1960. Tchr., counselor St. Helena Parish Sch. Bd., Greensburg, La., 1949-72, mem. sch. bd. dirs., 1972-73; adminstr. St. Helena Assistance Establishment, 1972-73, Cornell U., Ithaca, NY, from 1973; pres. Martin Luther King Scholarship, Ithaca, from 1983; now dir. St. Helena Parish Head Start, Greensburg. Co-author: The Star, 1964; author: (manual) Creative Career Exploration Programs, 1975, (pamphlet) Genealogy, 1976. Sec., 6th Dist. La. Edn. Assn., Baton Rouge, 1965-68; bd. dirs. Ithaca City Schs., 1973-82. Recipient Black and Gold award Grambling State U., 1973; named Outstanding Citizen, New Orleans, 1973. Mem. Am. Assn. Curriculum Devel., Am. Assn. Ret. Persons, AAUW, Nat. Coun. Negro Women. Democrat. Clubs: Bell de Nuit (pres. Greensburg); Essence (pres. Ithaca 1983—). Lodges: Order of Eastern Star (past assoc. matron 1963-74), Order of Amaranth (grand treas. 1965-74, historian). Personal E-mail: eunicep@juno.com.

PADDISON, STEPHEN JOHN, engineering educator; b. Calgary, Alberta, Can., Feb. 21, 1964; m. Joan Elaine Lewis; children: Kassaundra Mary Anne, Cooper Andrew Thaine. BSc with honors, U. Calgary, 1986, PhD, 1996. Asst. prof. chemistry and materials sci. U. Ala., Huntsville, 2004—07; assoc. prof. chem. and bio molecular engring. U. Tenn., Knoxville, 2007—. Author: (edited book) Device and Materials Modeling of PEM Fue. Office: Univ Tenn 321 Dougherty Engring Bldg Knoxville TN 37996-2200 Office Fax: 865-974-7076. Business E-Mail: spaddison@utk.edu.

PADDOCK, ANTHONY CONAWAY, financial consultant; b. Paris, July 9, 1935; came to U.S., 1940; s. H. Watson and Mildred V. (Decker) P.; m. Wendy E. Brewer, Apr. 24, 1971. AB, Harvard U., 1957, JD, 1960; MBA, Columbia U., 1961. Bar: N.Y. 1961. Assoc. investment bank Merrill Lynch & Co., NYC, 1961-69; v.p. Chase Manhattan Bank, NYC, 1970-78, Standard Rsch. Cons., NYC, 1978-84; mng. dir. Benchmark Valuation Cons., NYC, 1978-84; prin. KPMG Peat Marwick, NYC, 1984-96; mng. dir. Empire Valuation Cons., NYC, 1997—. Adj. prof. NYU, 1979-90. Trustee Sun Capital Advisors Trust, 1998-2007. Mem. Assoc. for Corp. Growth, Inst. Mgmt. Cons. (cert.). Episcopalian. Home: 14 N Chatsworth Ave Larchmont NY 10538-2142 Office: Empire Valuation Cons 350 5th Ave Ste 5513 New York NY 10118-5513 Office Phone: 212-714-0122. Business E-Mail: acpaddock@empireval.com.

PADDOCK, JOHN (ALVIN JOHN PADDOCK), professional sports team executive, former professional hockey coach; b. Oak River, Man., Can., June 9, 1954; m. Jill Paddock; children: Jenny, Sally, Anna, Alyssa. Head coach Maine Mariners, 1983—84, asst. coach, 1984—85; head coach Hershey Bears, 1985—89; asst. gen. mgr. Phila. Flyers, 1989-90, 2009—; head coach Binghamton Rangers, 1990—91, Winnipeg Jets, 1991—95; gen. mgr. Phoenix Coyotes, 1996-97; head coach Hartford Wolf Pack, 1999—2002, Binghamton Senators, 2002—04, co-head coach, 2004—05; asst. coach Ottawa Senators, 2005—07, head coach, 2007—08, Phila. Phantoms (Am. Hockey League), 2008—09. Recipient Louis A.R. Pieri Meml. Award. Office: Philadelphia Flyers Wachovia Ctr 3601 S Broad St Philadelphia PA 19148

PADEGS, ANDRIS, electrical engineer, company executive; b. Riga, Latvia, Mar. 27, 1929; s. Arturs and Vera Padegs; m. Mara Berzins, Aug. 28, 1954; children: Anita Batarags, Gints, Sandra Slokenbergs. BA magna cum laude, Dartmouth Coll., Hanover, NH, 1953, MS with highest distinction, 1954; PhD in Elec. Engring., Carnegie Inst. Tech., Pitts., 1958. Engring. positions Internat. Bus. Machines, Poughkeepsie, NY, 1958—68, mgr. processor architecture, 1968—69, mgr., architecture design & control, 1969—71, program mgr., sys. architecture, 1971—87, program mgr., enterprise systems ctrl. architecture, 1987—92; pres. Infologistik Inc., Poughkeepsie, 1992—2006. Cons. Padegs Consulting, Poughkeepsie, NY, 1992; vice chmn. SWH-Technology, Riga, Latvia, 1994—2000; adv. bd. on computers Republic of Latvia, Riga, Latvia, 1991—. Contbr. more than 25 articles to profl. jours.; author: four U.S. patents. Pres. Latvian Found., Inc., Kalamazoo, 1980—82, Mid-Hudson Latvian Assn., Poughkeepsie, NY, 1972—75; exec. vice chmn. Latvian Cultural Assn. TILTS, Poughkeepsie, NY, 1976—. Recipient Three Star Medal (highest civilian medal granted by Republic of Latvia), Republic of Latvia, 2001. Mem.: IEEE (life), Latvian Acad. Scis. (elected fgn. mem., Grand medal 2004), Assn. Latvian Engrs. (v.p. 1986—92), Sigma Xi. Achievements include one of two authors of original IBM System/360 Principles of Operation; patents in field. Avocations: photography, singing, history. Home: 2 Merry Hill Rd Poughkeepsie NY 12603-3214 Personal E-mail: apadegs@optonline.net.

PADEN, HARRY, municipal official; children: Shahara, Angela. Student, Am. U., 1971-73, Essex County (N.J.) Coll., 1981-83. Dir. social svcs. Unity Freedom Bapt. Ch., Newark, 1989-92; aide to freeholder pres. Essex County, 1992-96; code enforcement officer Township of Irvington, N.J., 1992-94, chief field rep. Office Neighorhood Preservation, 1994-98; CEO HP Inc. Host, prodr. (cable T.V. program) Parent to Parent; contbg. writer Jersey Girl mag.; columnist Irvington Herald. Chmn. Irvington juvenile conf. com. Superior Ct.; v.p., former pres. PTA Irvington H.S.; program coord. Neighborhood Preservation, 1998—; parent coord. Essex County PTA; ednl. liaison mayor of Irvington; aide Irvington West Ward Council; celebrity reader Essex and Hudson County chpts. United Way; deacon, adminstrv. asst. to pastor Unity Freedom Bapt. Ch., Newark; former mem. Irvington Bd. Edn. Named Irvington African Am. Male of Yr., 1994, One of 100 Most Influential in State, City News, 1997; recipient Pinnacle award Being Single mag., 1995, Spl. Civil award Irvington C. of C. Home: 31 Civic Sq W Apt 14 Irvington NJ 07111-2425 Office Phone: 973-580-2496. Personal E-mail: harry_paden@hotmail.com.

PADGETT, GREGORY LEE, lawyer; b. Greenfield, Ind., May 9, 1959; s. William Joseph and Anna Katherine (Hyre) Padgett; m. Ruth Anne Dorworth, June 5, 1982; children: Joshua David, William Joel, Emily Xiao Lei. BA summa cum laude, DePauw U., 1981; JD, Northwestern U., 1984. Bar: Ill., U.S. Dist. Ct. (no. dist.) Ill. 1984, U.S. Ct. Appeals (7th cir.) 1986, Ind. 1988, U.S. Dist. Ct. (no. & so. dists.)

Ind. 1988. Assoc. Kirkland & Ellis, Chgo., 1984-88, Baker & Daniels, Indpls., 1988-92; ptnr. Johnson, Lawhead, Buth & Pope, P.C., Indpls., 1992-2000; of counsel Barnes & Thornburg, Indpls., 2000—04; prin. Padgett Law, Indpls., 2004—. Adj. prof. Butler U., 1989—90. Pres., bd. dirs. Theatre on the Square, Indpls., 1994-95; mem. coun. Hope Evang. Covenant Ch., 1992-96; bd. dirs. Meridian St. Found., 1994-96, Ind. Arts Chorale, 2003-06, Oaks Acad., 2006-. Mem. Ind. State Bar Assn., Indpls. Bar Assn., Christian Legal Soc., Phi Beta Kappa. Avocations: theatre arts, vocal music, hiking, writing. Office: Padgett Law Ste 230 9000 Keystone Crossing Indianapolis IN 46240 Office Phone: 317-218-0316. Business E-Mail: gp@indianaestatelaw.com.

PADGETT, JOHN DAVID, lawyer; b. Norfolk, Va., July 8, 1958; s. Royal Claytor and Phyllis (Hunt) Padgett; m. Lee Ann Hagy. BA with distinction, U. Va., 1980; JD, Washington & Lee U., 1983. Bar: Va. 1983, US Bankruptcy Ct. Ea. Dist. 1983, US Dist. Ct. Ea. Dist. Va. 1983, US Ct. Appeals 4th Cir. 1983. Ptnr. Jett, Berkley, Furr & Padgett (merged with McGuireWoods LLP), Norfolk, Va., 1983—93, McGuire-Woods LLP, Norfolk, Va., 1993—, mng. ptnr. Norfolk office. Escheator City of Norfolk, Va., 1994—2003; gen. counsel Rep. Party of Va. Vice chair Hampton Rd. YMCA, 2005—; chmn. State Coun. of Higher Edn., Va., 1998—2001. Mem. Maritime Law Assn., Southeastern Admiralty Law Inst., Hampton Roads C. of C.(chmn. 2003), Phi Delta Phi., Hampton Roads Fgn. Commerce Club (pres.), Norfolk Rotary Club. Presbyterian. Avocations: baseball, golf, book collecting, politics. Office: McGuireWoods LLP World Trade Ctr Ste 9000 101 W Main St Norfolk VA 23510-1655 Office Phone: 757-640-3779. Office Fax: 757-640-3968. Business E-Mail: jpadgett@mcguirewoods.com.

PADGETT, NANCY WEEKS, retired law librarian, lawyer, consultant; b. Newberry, SC, June 3, 1932; d. Price John and Caroline (Weeks) P.; m. David Lazar, Aug. 6, 1953 (dec. May 19, 2002). BS, Northwestern U., 1953; MLS, U. Md., 1972; JD, Georgetown U., 1977. Bar: D.C. 1977. Asst. law libr. U.S. Ct. Appeals for D.C., Washington, 1972—74, supervisory law libr., 1974—84, circuit libr., 1984—2007. Mem. ALA, D.C. Bar Assn. Home: 5301 Duvall Dr Bethesda MD 20816-1873

PADGETT, WILLIAM JOWAYNE, mathematics professor, researcher; s. Joe J. and Edith A. Padgett; m. Faye S. Padgett; children: Carla Padgett-Clark children: William S. BS, Clemson U., SC; MS, Clemson U., 1968; PhD, Va. Poly. Inst. & State U., Blacksburg, 1971. Asst. prof. to disting. prof. emeritus U. SC., Columbia, 1971—2003; vis. prof. Clemson U., 2003—. Chair, dept. stats. U. SC., 1985—2001. Contbr. articles to profl. jours. Recipient fellow, Am. Statis. Assn., 1982—, Inst. Math. Stats., 1989—; grant, Nsf, Afosr, Aro, 1978—2006. Home: 697 S Glassy Mountain Rd Pickens SC 29671 Office: Univ SC Columbia SC 29208 Business E-Mail: padgett@stat.sc.edu.

PADILLA, ALEXANDRE, economics professor; s. Jose Padilla and Julia Isabel Padilla Garcia. PhD, U. Law, Economics, and Scis., Aix-Marseille, France, 2003. Economics instr. Met. State Coll. Denver, 2002—03, asst. prof. economics, 2004—. Recipient Outstanding Faculty award, Golden Key Internat. Honour Soc., 2007, Don Lavoie Meml. Essay award, Soc. Devel. Austrian Economics, 2000; Doctoral Rsch. fellowship, Ludwig von Mises Inst., 2000—01, Sci. Liberty grant, Charles G. Koch Charitable Found., 2008. Mem.: Western Econ. Assn. Internat., Soc. Devel. Austrian Economics, Am. Econ. Assn., So. Econ. Assn., Assn. Pvt. Enterprise Edn. Office: Met State Coll Denver 1201 5th St Denver CO 80217-3362 Office Fax: 303-556-3966. Business E-Mail: padilale@mscd.edu.

PADILLA, ALFREDO, territorial banking agency administrator; Commr. PR Bur. Fin. Insts., San Juan, 2002—. Office: Office of Commr Financial Instns Fernandez Juncos Sta PO Box 11855 San Juan PR 00910-3855 Office Phone: 787-723-8004. Office Fax: 787-723-4042. E-mail: comisionado@ocif.gobierno.pr.*

PADILLA, ART, finance educator; BS, NC State U., Raleigh; PhD, UNC-Chapel Hill, NC. Prof. to dept. head Coll. Mgmt., NC State U., Raleigh, 2009. Office: NC State Univ Coll Mgmt Box 7229 Raleigh NC 27695

PADILLA, CHRISTOPHER ALAN, lobbyist, former federal agency administrator; b. Kans. City, 1964; BA, Johns Hopkins U., 1986, MA, 1987. Various positions network systems divsn. AT&T Corp., 1987—90, fed. govt. affairs dir. Washington, 1990—96; v.p. internat. pub. affairs Lucent Technologies, 1996—97; dir. internat. trade rels. Eastman Kodak Co., 1997—2002; asst. US Trade Rep. for intergovernmental affairs, pub. liaison Exec. Office of the Pres., Washington, 2002—05; sr. adv. & dep. chief of staff US Dept. State, Washington, 2005—06; asst. sec. for export adminstrn., Bur. Industry & Security US Dept. Commerce, Washington, 2006—07, under sec. for internat. trade, 2007—09; v.p. govtl. programs IBM Corp., Washington, Del., 2009—. Chmn. Bus. Coalition Export Reform, 1993—94; comm. dir., spokesman Bus. Coalition for U.S.-China Trade, 2000, US Trade, 2001—02. Office: IBM Corp 1801 K St NW Washington DC 20006*

PADILLA, JAMES G., paralegal; Degree in Tech. Journalism, Colo. State U., Fort Collins, 1986. Cert. paralegal Colo., 1990. Newpaper journalist, Denver, 1986—89; practice support mgmt. Padilla Trial & Ligit. Supprt, Inc., LA, 1989—. Cons. in field. Mentor Top 100 Law Firms, LA, 1991—2007. Mem.: Internat. Legal Tech. Assn., Religious Tolerance, Election Protection. Independent. Avocations: iaido, Aikido, religious studies. Office: Padilla Trial & Litig Supprt Inc PO Box 93430 City Of Industry CA 91715 Office Phone: 213-675-0597. Personal E-mail: j.padillatrial@me.com.

PADILLA, JAMES JEROME (JIM PADILLA), retired automotive executive; b. Detroit, June 13, 1946; s. David J. and Irene C. (Clos) P.; m. Alice M., Dec. 27, 1968; children: James Jr., Kathryn, Daniel. BSChemE, MS in Engring., U. Detroit, 1969, MA in Econ., 1970. Fuel econ. planning mgr. Ford Motor Co., Dearborn, Mich., 1977-78, engine planning engring. mgr. Detroit, 1979-80, engine controls dept. mgr., 1980-83, exec. engr., powertrain-electronics, 1983-85, chief engr., trim-chassis-elect-emissions, 1985, programs operations mgr., 1990, dir., small cars unit, 1991, exec. dir., engring. and mfg., Jaguar Cars, Ltd., 1992—94, dir., performance luxury vehicle lines, 1994—96, pres., Argentina and Brazil operations, 1996—98, pres. S. Am. operations, group v.p., mfg. and quality, 1999—2001, group v.p., N. Am., 2001—02, exec. v.p. Detroit, 2002, pres. Americas, 2002—04, pres., COO, 2004—06, chmn. worldwide automotive operations, 2004—06. Spl. asst to sec., US Dept. Commerce, 1978-79; bd. dirs. Am. Supplier Inst., Dearborn. Pres. Civic Assn., Canton, Mich., 1972-74, Plymouth (Mich.) Sch. Bd., 1981-84; mem. Plymouth Parish Council, 1980-84, Plymouth Edn. Commn., 1980-85. Served to 2d Lt. USNG, 1970-76. White House fellow U.S. Govt., Washington, 1978-79, fellow, Nat. Acad. Engring., 2001-; rsch. grantee Dow Chem. Co., Detroit, 1968-69; recipient Engr. of the Year, Hispanic Engr. Nat. Achievement Awards Conf., 2000, Ohtli medal from Mexican President Vincente Fox, 2004; named one of 50 Most Important Hispanics in Tech. & Bus., Hispanic Engr. & Info. Tech. mag., 2005. Mem. Soc. Automotive Engrs., Engring. Soc. Detroit. (selection com. U.S. Senate fellows 1982-84, named Outstanding Young Engr. 1980). Roman Catholic.

PADILLA, MARIO RENÉ, literature educator, writer; b. Detroit, Oct. 4, 1949; s. Marcelino Ramos and Nina Consolata (Macioce) P.; children: Francesca, Miguel, Marcello, Gabriella; m. Christine Jasiorkowski; stepchildren: Trevor, Laura. BS, Ohio State U., 1971; MA, Loyola Marymount U., 1987; PhD, U. So. Calif., 1993. Prodn. supr. CBS TV, LA, 1972-78; actor LA, 1980—; prof. English lit. and creative writing, Latin Am. lit. Santa Monica (Calif.) Coll., 1994—. Author: Reaching Back for the Neverendings, 1993, Borges, Faulkner, Hemingway: Young Poets of Prose, 1993 (Fulbright award 1993); composer (ballet) The Harbinger of Evolution, 1980 (ASCAP award 1981), (song) I Found Love, (musical) Hercules on Normandie, 2006, and numerous other songs and ballets; actor including Mario on Falcon Crest, 1981-83, Jimmy Rivera on Hunter, 1991-92, officer Lopez in General Hosp., 2000, Dragnet, 2003 (films) Losin' It, 1983, Star Trek III, 1984. Capt. U.S. Army, 1971-72. Mem. ASCAP, MLA, Screen Actors Guild, Am. Fedn. TV Radio Artists, Actor's Equity. Avocations: Karate, soccer, basketball, coaching children's sports, yoga. Home: 1211 Vienna Way Venice CA 90291-4026 Office Phone: 310-434-4064. Personal E-mail: Padilla_mario@smc.edu.

PADILLA, SUE ANN, librarian; b. Horton, Kans., Dec. 11, 1950; d. Moulder and Elva Mae (Grimes) Oaks; m. John H. Padilla (div.); children: Elizabeth, Matthew. BS in Edn., Kans. State Tchrs. Coll., 1972; MLS, Emporia State U., 1988. Tchr. Our Lady of Guadalupe Sch., Topeka, 1973-75, Topeka Pub. Schs., 1975-88; libr. Ida Long Goodman Meml. Libr., St. John, Kans., 1988—2001, Newton Pub. Libr., Newton, Iowa, 2001—. Contbg. author: Booktalk!3, Booktalk!4, Booktalk!5, The Booktalkers' Companion, Vol. 1, Booktalking the Award Winners, 1993-94, Booktalking the Award Winners: Young Adult Retrospective Volume, Booktalking the Award Winners 3. Bd. dirs. St. John Planning Commn., 1997-2001, St. John Hosp. Dist., 1991-92, St. John Sci. Mus., 1997-2001; chair Cmty. Arts Series, St. John, 1990—. Mem. ALA, Iowa Libr. Assn., Iowa Libr. Adminstrn. and Mgmt. Assn. Forum (pres. 2005), Iowa Librs. of Medium Size (pres. 2007-), Iowa pub. Libr. Forum (pres. 2009-), Emporia State U. Alumni Assn. (bd. dirs. 1991-94), Lions Club (com. chair St. John's club 1990-2001), Kans. Ctr. for the Book (bd. dirs. 1999-2001), Arts Connection (bd. dir. 2001-), Jasper County Concert Assn. (bd. dirs. 2003-), Jasper Libr. Assn. (pres. 2004-). Avocations: travel, antiques, cooking, gardening, reading. Home: 108 E 28th St S Newton IA 50208-2710 Office: Newton Pub Libr 100 N 3rd Ave W Newton IA 50208-0796

PADLAN, EDUARDO AGUSTIN, retired immunologist; b. Manila, Philippines, Aug. 31, 1940; s. Feliciano Macaraeg Padlan and Aida Almeda Agustin; m. Rosemarie Dino, Dec. 10, 1960; children: Josefina Padlan Simpson, Ramon Eduardo, Cristina Padlan Packard, Anna Maria, Cecilia Padlan Mikita. BS, U. of the Philippines, Diliman, Quezon City, 1960; PhD, Johns Hopkins U., Balt., 1968. Asst. prof. U. The Philippines, Quezon City, Philippines, 1968—69, adj. prof., 2002—; rsch. scientist Johns Hopkins U., Balt., 1978—83, rsch. assoc., 1969—71; vis. scientist NIH, Bethesda, Md., 1971—78, rsch. physicist, 1983—2000. Editor: ImmunoMethods vol. 1 no. 2, 1992; co-editor: Current Opinion in Biotechnology vol. 8, 1997; mem. editl. bd.: Molecular Immunology, 1980—99, Receptor, 1990—96, Macromolecular Structures, 1993—97; author: (book) Antibody-Antigen Complexes, 1994; contbr. articles to more than 140 sci. publs. Mem.: Am. Soc. for Biochemistry and Molecular Biology, Am. Assn. Immunologists, Philippine Am. Acad. Sci. and Engring., Nat. Acad. Sci. and Tech. Philippines (corr.). Achievements include patents in field; patents pending in field. Home: 4006 Simms Dr Kensington MD 20895 Office: Univ of the Philippines Velasquez St Diliman Quezon City 1101 Philippines Personal E-mail: edpadlan@aol.com. Business E-Mail: epadlan@upmsi.ph.

PADMANABHAN, BHARANI, neurologist, educator; s. Rajam and Chitra Padmanabhan. MD, Semmelweis U. Medicine, Budapest, Hungary, PhD summa cum laude, 1995. Cert. neurologist Tufts Med. Sch. Neurology Program, 2000, neuroimmunologist Harvard Med. Sch. & Brigham Womens Hosp., Boston, 2003. Dir., multiple sclerosis svc. Angels Neurol. Ctrs., Abington, Mass., 2004—07; faculty neurologist Cambridge Health Alliance, Mass., 2007—, M.S. specialist Everett, Mass., 2007—. Pub. educator, multiple sclerosis, Mass., 2004. Editor: (indsl. design) Dieter Rams, (graphic design) Otl Aicher. Recipient Quality Cir. award, Cambridge Health Alliance, 2008; Multiple Sclerosis fellowship, U. Mass. Meml. Med. Ctr., 2004. Mem.: Am. Acad. Neurology. Hindu. Achievements include first to launch biggest solo multiple sclerosis clinic. Avocations: photography, architecture, music. Office: Cambridge Health Alliance 1493 Cambridge St Cambridge MA 02139 Personal E-mail: scleroplex@earthlink.net.

PADMANABHAN, SANTHOSH, research scientist; s. Padmanabhan Subramani Iyer and Visalakshy Subramanian; m. Kulathumani Lalitha, Feb. 11, 2008. PhD, Alagappa U., Karaikudi, India, 2005. Postdoc. rschr. U. Calif., San Diego, 2009—. Contbr. scientific papers to profl. jours. Fellowship, MPG. Office: Univ California-San Diego 9500 Gilman Dr San Diego CA 92101 Business E-Mail: spadmanabhan@ucsd.edu.

PADMANABHAN, SWAMINATHAN, hematologist, oncologist, researcher; m. Yamini Vasanth; children: Shankar, Sriram. MBBS, MD, Bangalore Med. Coll., India, 1995. Asst. prof. Roswell Pk. Cancer Inst., Buffalo, 2003—08; dir. phase I hematologic malignancies CTRC at UTHSCSA, San Antonio, 2008—. Adv. Leukemia and Lymphoma soc. Recipient Young Investigator award, Am. Soc. Clin. Oncology, 2002; named one of Top Physicians in America, Consumer Research Council, 2007; Translational grant, Am. Cancer Soc., 2007. Mem.: Am. Assn. Advancement Sci. (life). Achievements include research in translational drug development in cancer. Office: 7979 Wurzbach Rd Mail Code 8232 San Antonio TX 78229 Personal E-mail: swami.padmanabhan@gmail.com.

PADNICK, JENNIFER C., lawyer; b. NYC, Jan. 29, 1972; BA in Polit. Sci., U. Ill., 1994; JD, Bklyn. Law Sch., 1997. Bar: NY 1998. Assoc. J.P. Morgan; assoc. atty. Cohen & Perfetto, L.L.P., NYC, founding ptnr. Office: Cohen & Perfetto LLP 444 Madison Ave 5th Fl New York NY 10022 Office Phone: 212-488-1303. Office Fax: 212-813-0767. E-mail: jpadnick@cpllplaw.com.

PADNOS, MARK, library administrator, translator; b. NYC, Sept. 24, 1944; s. Morton and Edna (Nass) P.; m. Alla Lipina, July 8, 1997 (div. 2000). BA, U. Iowa, 1966; MLS, L.I. U., 1978; cert. in advanced librarianship, Columbia U., 1992; MA in Liberal Studies-Translation, CUNY, 1993. Asst. libr. YIVO Inst. for Jewish Rsch., NYC, 1978—80; dir. libr. Anthology Film Archives, NYC, 1980—82; libr. Aviation Week & Space Technology McGraw-Hill, NYC, 1982—84; ref. libr. Bronx C.C., NYC, 1986—89; asst. dir. multimedia ctr. Pratt Inst., Bklyn., 1989—90; reference libr. Fordham U., Bronx, 1991—93; humanities reference libr. grad. sch. CUNY, NYC, 1993—98; coord. pub. svcs. Bronx CC Libr., 1998—, acting chief libr., 2000—02. Rsch. cons. and book reviewer in field. Translator: (German poetry) Contemporary Literature in Translation, 1971, Modern Poetry in Translation, 1973, Romanian Library Bulletin, 1973, Dimension: Contemporary German Arts and Letters, 1994; reviewer American Reference Books Annual, 1991-2007; subject editor German langs. and lit. Resources for College Libraries, 2005—, RCL Resources for College Libraries, 2006, 07, Encyclopedia Judaica, 2d edit., 2007; contbr. articles to profl. publs. Con Edison grantee, 1985. Mem. Am. Libr. Assn., Am. Literary Translators Assn., Poetry Soc. Am., Spl. Libr. Assn. (sec. info. tech. group), Assn. Jewish Libr. Jewish. Avocations: poetry, short fiction, genealogy, weight training. Office: Bronx CC Library Meister Hall W 181st St and Univ Ave Bronx NY 10453 Home Phone: 212-998-2884; Office Phone: 718-289-5440. Business E-Mail: mark.padnos@bcc.cuny.edu.

PADOS, FRANK JOHN, JR., investment company executive; b. Easton, Pa., Feb. 9, 1944; s. Frank John and Mary Helen (Pokrifscak) P.; m. Barbara Janselwitz, July 6, 1968; children— Frank John (dec.), Kelly Ann, Kristin, Matthew John, Kaitlyn. BA cum laude in Econs, Boston Coll., 1966; MBA, U. Pa., 1968. Securities analyst Tchrs. Ins. and Annuity Assn., NYC, 1971-74, investment officer, 1975-77, v.p., 1977-78, sr. v.p., mgr. securities div., 1978-83; mng. dir. Trust Co. of the West, 1983-95; exec. v.p. Desai Capital Mgmt., NYC, 1995—2003; mng. ptnr. Dublin Clark and Co., Greenwich, Conn., 2003—. Bd. dirs. Tulsa Power Sentient Med. & Action Target. Served with U.S. Army, 1969-70. Decorated Bronze Star. Mem. Overlook Hosp. Found. Roman Catholic. Home: 57 Thornley Dr Chatham NJ 07928-1360 Office: 485 W Putnam Ave Greenwich CT 06830 Office Phone: 203-629-2030.

PADOVANI, ROBERTO, communications executive; Degree, U. Padova, Italy; MS in Elec. and Computer Engring., PhD in Elec. and Computer Engring., U. Mass. With M/A-COM Linkabit, 1984—86; from mem. staff to exec. v.p., chief tech. officer QUALCOMM Inc., San Diego, 1986—2002, exec. v.p., 2002—, chief tech. officer, 2002—. Contbr. articles to profl. jours. Mem.: NAE, IEEE (Best Paper award 1991). Achievements include holds over 50 patents on wireless CDMA systems. Office: QUALCOMM Inc 5775 Morehouse Dr San Diego CA 92121

PADOVANO, ANTHONY JOHN, fine arts educator, artist; b. Bklyn., July 19, 1933; s. Pasquale Anthony and Teresa (Pignataro) P.; m. Margaret Padovano, June 6, 1973 (div. 1981); children: Lea, Nicole, Roberto; m. Gerarda Santina Declement, Sept. 15, 1986; children: Francesca, Gina; m. Marie DeBrosse, Oct. 3, 1998; 1 child Perry. BFA, Columbia U., 1957; MA, CUNY, 1980. Instr. U. Conn., Storrs, 1962-64; asst. prof. Columbia U., NYC, 1964-71, Sarah Lawrence Coll., Bronxville, 1972-79; assoc. prof. Kingsborough Community Coll., Bklyn., 1983—. Tchr. U. Conn., Storrs, 1962-64, Columbia U., N.Y.C., 1964-70, Queens Coll., N.Y., 1971-73, Sarah Lawrence Coll., 1974-78, Lacoste, France, summers 1976-78, Kingsborough Coll., 1978-, Parsons Sch. Design, 1978-82, Art Students League, summers 1983, 84; Fulbright fellowship judge UN, N.Y.C., 2001, 02, 03. One-man shows include Lincoln Meml. Gallery, 1954, Columbia U., 1957, Sculptors Studio, 1958, George Lester Gallery, 1962, Ruth White Gallery, 1962, Richard Feigen Gallery, 1964, U. Conn., 1964, Columbia U., 1965, Bertha Schaefer Gallery, 1968, Galerie Simmons Stern, 1968, Graham Gallery, 1972, 75, 79, 81, 82, I.F.A. Gallery, 1976, Alwin Gallery, 1978, Vorpal Gallery, 1986, 88, 90; exhbns. in group shows at Herron Mus. of Art, 1966, Newark Mus., 1969, Inst. Arts and Letters, 1976, Bard Coll, 1979; permanent collections, Newark Mus., Herron Gallery (Ind.), Storm King Art Ctr., Whitney Mus. Am. Art, Grounds for Sculpture, NJ, 2007, Kreelar Mus., Washington, 2007; author: The Process of Sculpture, 1981. Mem.: Audubon Artists (pres. 2002—). Office: Kingsborough CC 2001 Oriental Blvd Brooklyn NY 11235-2333

PADOVANO, ANTHONY THOMAS, theologian, literature educator; b. Harrison, NJ, Sept. 18, 1934; s. Thomas Henry and Mary Rose (Cierzo) P.; m. Theresa Lackamp, 1974; children— Mark, Andrew, Paul, Rosemarie BA magna cum laude, Seton Hall U., 1956; S.T.B. magna cum laude, Pontifical Gregorian U., Rome, Italy, 1958, S.T.L. magna cum laude, 1960; S.T.D. magna cum laude, 1962; Ph.L. magna cum laude, St. Thomas Pontifical Internat. U., Rome, 1962; MA, NYU, 1971; PhD, Fordham U., 1980. Ordained priest Roman Cath. Ch., 1959. Asst. chaplain Med. Center, Jersey City, 1960; asst. St. Paul of the Cross Ch., Jersey City, 1962, St. Catharine Ch., Glen Rock, NJ, 1963; prof. systematic theology Darlington Sem., Mahwah, NJ, 1962-74; founding faculty mem., disting. prof. lit. and philosophy Spiritual Ctr. Ramapo Coll. Padovano Peace Pavilion, NJ, 1971—; adj. prof. theology, religious studies Fordham U., 1973—93. Mem. Archdiocesan Commn. Ecumenical and Interreligious Affairs, 1965, Commn. Instrn. Clergy in Documents Vatican II, 1966; del. dialogue group Luth.-Roman Cath. Theol. Conversations, 1969; del.-at-large senate of priests Archdiocese of Newark; Danforth assoc., 1975—; Cath. pastor Inclusive Cmty. World Coun. Chs., 1986—; lectr. in field, also appearances on radio and TV; parish min. St. Margaret of Scotland, Morristown, NJ. Author: The Cross of Christ, the Measure of the World, 1962, The Estranged God, 1966, Who is Christ, 1967, Belief in Human Life, 1969, American Culture and the Quest for Christ, 1970, Dawn Without Darkness, 1971, Free to be Faithful, 1972, Eden and Easter, 1974, A Case for Worship, 1975, America: Its People, Its Promise, 1975, Presence and Structure, 1975, The Human Journey, 1982, Trilogy, 1982, Contemplation and Compassion, 1984, Winter Rain: A Play, 1985, His Name is John: A Play, 1986, Christmas to Calvary, 1987, Love and Destiny, 1987, Summer Lightening: A Play, 1988, Conscience and Conflict, 1989, Reform and Renewal, 1990, A Celebration of Life, 1990, The Church Today: Belonging and Believing, 1990, Scripture in the Streets, 1992, A Retreat with Thomas Merton, 1996, Hope is a Dialogue, 1998, Resistance and Renewal, 2002, Life Choices, 2004; editor: Centenary Issue Roman Echoes, 1959; editl. bd. The Advocate, 1966-73; contbr. articles to mags., Padovano Papers, personal and profl. papers, Archives, U. Notre Dame. With Padovano Peace Pavilion, Bldg. Spiritual Ctr., Ramapo Coll., Diocese Paterson Ecumenical Commn.; founding pres. Justice and Peace Commn., Diocese of Paterson, active Resigned Priests Com. Mem. Cath. Theol. Soc. Am., Mariological Soc. Am., Nat. Fedn. Priests Couns. (ofcl. rep. to Constl. Conv., Chgo. 1968), Corpus (pres.), Fedn. Christian Ministries, Internat. Fedn. of Married Cath. Priests (v.p. for N.Am.), North Atlantic Fedn. for Renewal Cath. Priesthood (bd. dirs.). Home: 9 Millstone Dr Morris Plains NJ 07950-1536 Office: Sch of Am Internat Studies Ramapo Coll NJ Mahwah NJ 07430 Personal E-mail: tpadovan@optonline.net. *People rather than ideas have been most formative in my life. More accurately, people, as they embodied certain ideas have proved most decisive. There is nothing more persuasive than an idea which becomes so vital that it transforms the person who proclaims it.*

PADULA, FRED DAVID, filmmaker; b. Santa Barbara, Calif., Oct. 25, 1937; s. Fred and Mary (Adams) P.; married; 1 child. BA in Music, San Francisco State U., MA in Art, 1965. Adj. faculty U. Calif., San Francisco Art Inst., San Francisco State U.; artist-in-residence U. Minn., Mpls. Filmmaker: Ephesus, 1965 (1st pl. award San Francisco Internat.

Film Festival, awards N.Y. Film Festival, Chgo. Internat. Film Festival, others), The Artist Speaks, Two Photographers: Wynn Bullock and Imogen Cunningham, Little Jesus (Hippy Hill), Anthology of Boats, David and My Porch, Salmon River Run, El Capitan (awards: Grand Prize Festival Internat. de Film D'Aventure Uecue, La Plagne, France, Grand Prize Film Festival Internat. Montagna Esplorazione, Trento, Italy, Grand Prize Banff Festival of Mountain Films, Can., Grand Prize Mountain Film, Telluride, Colo., Gold medal Festival Internat. du Film Alpine, Les Diablerets, Switzerland; electronic music compositions include: Barking Dogs, Charnet Loops, others; one-man shows (photography) include San Francisco Internat. Airport, San Francisco Mus. Modern Art, Kalamazoo Inst. Arts, DeYoung Mus., San Francisco, San Fernando Valley State Coll., Bakersfield Coll., Wash. State U., West Chester Coll., Valhalla, NY, George Eastman House; represented in permanent collections, Kalamazoo Inst. Arts, State of Calif., George Eastman House, San Francisco Internat. Airport, Crocker Art Mus., Oakland Mus. Art, 1004 Gallery, Port Towsend, Wash., New Horizons Nat. Bank Hdqs., San Rafael, Calif., SUNY/Westchester CC, Valhalla, NY, Grace Mus., Abilene, Tex. Address: PO Box 254 Mill Valley CA 94941-1551

PAE, HOLLY, special education educator; d. Roger and Carol Pae; m. Richard Combes, May 3, 2006. EdD, W.Va. U., Morgantown, 2000. Cert. in spl. edn. W.Va. Assoc. prof. U. SC Upstate, Spartanburg, 2000—. Office: Univ SC Upstate 800 University Way Spartanburg SC 29303 Business E-Mail: hpae@uscupstate.edu.

PAEZ, RICHARD A., federal judge; b. 1947; BA, Brigham Young U., 1969; JD, U. Calif., Berkeley, 1972. Staff atty. Calif. Rural Legal Assistance, Delano, Calif., 1972—74, Western Ctr. on Law and Poverty, 1974—76; sr. counsel Legal Aid Found. of LA, 1976—78, dir. litigation, 1978—79, act. exec. dir., 1980—81; judge LA Mcpl. Ct., 1981—94, superior ct, Los Angeles, 1993—94, US Dist. Ct. (ctrl. dist.) Calif., LA, 1994—2000, US Dist. Ct. (9th cir.), Pasadena, Calif., 2000—. Active Hollywood-Los Feliz Jewish Cmty. Ctr. Mem.: Calif. Jud. Coun., Mex.-Am. Bar Assn. LA County, LA County Bar Assn., Calif. State Bar Assn. Office: US Ct Appeals Richard H Chambers US Courthouse 125 S Grand Ave Rm 204 Pasadena CA 91105-1652*

PAGÁN, GILBERTO, JR., psychologist; b. San Juan, Dec. 30, 1950; Exch. student, SUNY, Albany, 1969-70; BA in Psychology magna cum laude, U. P.R., 1972; MS in Devel. Psychology, Rutgers U., 1974, PhD in Clin. Psychology, 1984. Lic. psychologist, N.J.; cert. sch. psychology. Psychometrician Well Baby Clinic of New Brunswick, N.J., 1972-73; staff psychologist Community Orgn. for Mental Health and Retardation, Inc., Phila., 1976-77; intern in clin. psychology Multimodal Therapy Inst., Kingston, NJ, 1979-80; sch. psychologist New Brunswick Pub. Sch. System, 1980-83; mental health clinician Community Mental Health Ctr. U. Medicine and Dentistry N.J., Piscataway, 1983-93; sch. psychologist Perth Amboy Pub. Sch. Sys., 1993-95; pvt. practice clin. psychology Newark, 1988—; sch. psychologist Jersey City Pub. Sch. Sys., 1995-98, Elizabeth (N.J.) Pub. Sch. Sys., 1998—. Assoc. in psychiatry Univ. of Medicine and Dentistry of N.J., Piscataway, 1988-98; field supr. Rutgers U., New Brunswick, N.J., 1988—; cons. in field to clients including Bloomfield Pub. Sch. System, Div. of Youth and Family Svcs. of State of N.J., Project Head Start, Plainfield, N.J. Columnist San Juan Star, 1990-93, 97-98, El Hispano, Phila., 1977-78; contbr. profl. publs.; presenter in field. Pres. N.J. chpt. Nat. Com. for Puerto Rican Statehood, 1990-95; mem. U.S. Coun. for Puerto Rico Statehood, 2004-. NIMH fellow, 1978-79; predoctoral rsch. fellow Inst. for Rsch. in Human Devel., Divsn. Psychol. Studies of Ednl. Testing Svc., Princeton, N.J., 1974-75; recipient P.R. Psychol. Assn. award, 1972, Puerto Rican Action Bds. Parents Assn. award 1985; inducted into Nat. Honor Soc. in Psychology, 1973. Mem. APA, NEA, N.J. Edn. Assn., N.J. Psychol. Assn., Elizabeth Edn. Assn. Democrat. Roman Catholic. Avocation: swimming. Office: 467 Mount Prospect Ave Newark NJ 07104-2907 Home Phone: 732-324-2322; Office Phone: 973-483-0448.

PAGAN, JOHN RUSTON, law educator; b. Little Rock, Aug. 4, 1951; s. John Frank and Betty (Hardin) P. BA, Coll. of William and Mary, 1973; MLitt, Oxford U., 1975; JD, Harvard U., 1978; DPhil, Oxford U., 1997. Bar: Ark. 1979, Va. 1982, D.C. 1984, N.Y. 1996. Clk. hon. Ozell M. Trask US Ct. of Appeals (9th cir.), Phoenix & San Francisco, 1978—79; from asst. to assoc. prof. Marshall-Whyte Sch. of Law Coll. of William and Mary, Williamsburg, Va., 1979-84; assoc. prof. Sch. of Law U. Ark., Little Rock, 1984-86, prof. Sch. of Law, 1986-95; global prof., dir. (global law sch. prog.) NYU, 1996—97; dean, prof. of law U. Richmond Sch Law, Richmond, Va., 1997—2003, u. prof., 2003—. Author: Anne Orthwoods Bastard: Sex and Law in Early Virginia (Prize in Atlantic History, 2003) Contbr. articles to profl. jours. Ark. state senator, Little Rock, 1991-92; legislator Pulaski County Quorum Ct., Little Rock, 1987-90. Mem. Assn. of Marshall Scholars, Phi Beta Kappa. Democrat. Avocation: historical research. Office: U Richmond Sch Law 28 Westhampton Way Rm 216 Richmond VA 23173 Office Phone: 804-289-8188. Office Fax: 804-289-8992.

PAGAN, KEITH AREATUS, music educator, academic administrator; b. Beggs, Okla., June 7, 1931; s. Areatus and Opal Gail (Facker) P.; m. Betty Lois Wallace; children: Melva Joy, Lisa Lynne, Beryl Kay. B in Music Edn., Bethany Nazarene Coll., 1952; M in Music Edn., Okla. U., 1953; D in Music Edn. with honors, Ind. U., 1970. Asst. prof. music Bethany (Okla.) Nazarene Coll., 1952-53, 55-58; prof. music Pasadena (Calif.) Coll., 1961-76; acad. dean, v.p. acad. affairs Point Loma Nazarene Coll., San Diego, 1976-88, prof. music, chair dept. music., 1989—98. Cons. Sch. for Creative and Performing Arts, San Diego, 1990-99, Chula Vista, Calif., 1992-94; dir. S.W. Music Symposium, San Diego, 1991-; mem. vis. team Western Coll. Assn., Calif., 1977-82. Arranger (choral) To God be the Glory, (brass) Keith A. Pagan Brass Quintet Series, The King Shall Come; mem. editl. bd. Christian Scholars Rev., 1986-2006, EverGreen Morning Music Press. Trustee Christian Scholars Rev., 1994-2008; dir. music Village Ch., Rancho Santa Fe, Calif.; v.p. Calif. Higher Edn. Assn., 1970-71. With U.S. Army, 1953-55. Recipient WHO award Calif. Higher Edn. Assn., 1971, Lawrence Vredevoe Disting. Leadership award 1986, Spl. Svc. to Music award Calif. Music Educators Assn., 1991; winner 4th ann. anthem contest Choral Condrs. Guild; grantee Danforth Found., 1960. Mem. Calif. Coll. and Univ. Faculty Assn. (state pres. 1969-70), Music Tchrs. Assn. Calif. (parliamentarian 1971-73), Western Assn. Schs. and Coll. (accreditation liaison 1976-88). Avocations: travel, photography. Home: 5875 Friars Rd #4316 San Diego CA 92110

PAGANELLI, CHARLES VICTOR, physiologist, educator; b. NYC, Feb. 13, 1929; s. Charles Victor and Mary Paganelli; m. Barbara Harriet Slauson, Sept. 18, 1954; children: William, Kathryn, Peter, Robert, John. AB, Hamilton Coll., Clinton, NY, 1950; MA, Harvard U., Cambridge, Mass., 1952, PhD, 1957. Instr. physiology U. Buffalo, 1958-60, asst. prof., 1960-63; assoc. prof. SUNY, Buffalo, 1963-71, prof. physiology, 1971-97, disting. svc. prof., 1997—. Interim chair SUNY, Buffalo, 1991-98, emeritus, 1998. Editor: Physiological Function in Special Environments, 1990; contbr. articles to profl. jours. Recipient Elliott Coues award Am. Ornithologists Union, 1981, Newman award 1998. Mem.: Am. Physiol. Soc., Gold Humanism Honor Soc., Phi Beta Kappa, Sigma Xi, Alpha Omega Alpha. Office Phone: 716-829-2738. Business E-Mail: cvp@buffalo.edu.

PAGANO, CELESTE ANN, retired realtor, social services coordinator; b. Bridgeport, Conn., Apr. 12, 1950; d. Peter Angelo and Carmella Marie (Carrafiello) P.; m. June Albert, 2008. AAS in Broadcast Journalism, Grahm Jr. Coll., Boston, 1970; BA magna cum laude, Fairfield U., Conn., 1997; MPA, NYU, 2000. Self employed real estate investor, property mgr. Pagano-Albert, 1981—97; coord. cmty. rels., vol., bd. mem. Vol. Ctr. Greater Bridgeport, 1997—99; coord. program and vol. Interfaith Vol. Caregivers, 1999—2000; coord. program Bridgeport Supportive Housing Program, 2000—02; coord. domestic violence Ctr. for Women and Families, 2002—. Guest spkr. on discrimination Conn. Realtors Conv., Hartford, 1987. Mem. adv. bd. Coordinated Assessment and Referral for the Elderly Program, Bridgeport Hosp., 1999; steering com. mem. Caring Connections Program, Cath. Family Svcs., 2000-04. Recipient Outstanding Fair Housing Action award Bridgeport Fair Housing, 1986. Avocations: writing, music, kayaking, travel. Home and Office: 56 Livingston St Bridgeport CT 06605-3303

PAGANO, EDWARD, legislative staff member; b. 1963; Grad., U. Vt.; JD, Fordham U. Staff Senator Patrick Leahy, Washington, 1993—, chief of staff, 2005—; chief counsel Senate Judiciary Com. Office: Office of Senator Patrick Leahy 433 Senate Russell Office Bldg Washington DC 20510-4502 Office Phone: 202-224-4242. E-mail: ed_pagano@leahy.senate.gov.*

PAGANO, ROSARIO, staff scientist; b. Catania, Italy, Aug. 10, 1976; s. Salvatore Pagano and Maria Fichera. PhD, U. Catania, 2004. Cert. profl. engr., U. Catania, 02. Application engr. Philips Semiconductors, Nijmegen, Netherlands, 2005—06; very large scale integration designer NXP Semiconductors, Nijmegen, 2006—08; staff scientist Broadcom Corp., Fort Collins, Colo., 2008—. Contbr. articles to profl. jours. Fellow, Italian Nat. Coun. Rsch., 2003. Mem.: IEEE (assoc.). Achievements include patents for protection for faulted power devices. Office: Broadcom Corporation 2950 E Harmony Rd Ste 270 Fort Collins CO 80528-3429 Business E-Mail: rpagano@broadcom.com.

PAGANO, VINCENT, JR., lawyer; b. Morristown, NJ, Oct. 14, 1950; BS summa cum laude, Lehigh U., 1972; MS in environ. engring., U. Calif. Berkeley, 1973; MS in statistics, Rutgers U., 1976; JD cum laude, Harvard U., 1981. Bar: NY 1980, NJ 1981, lic.: US Dist. Ct., So. Dist. NY. Assoc. Simpson, Thacher & Bartlett LLP, NYC, 1981—86, ptnr., 1986—, mem. exec. com. Mem.: ABA, Assn. Bar City NY. Office: Simpson Thacher & Bartlett LLP 425 Lexington Ave New York NY 10017-3954 Office Phone: 212-455-3125. Office Fax: 212-455-2502. Business E-Mail: vpagano@stblaw.com.

PAGDEN, ANTHONY ROBIN, political science professor, historian, writer; b. Bexhill, Sussex, Eng., May 27, 1945; arrived in US, 1997; s. John Brian and Joan Elizabeth Pagden; m. Chantal Brotherton-Ratcliffe, 1991 (div. 1998); children: Felix Alexander Xavier, Sebastian George Aurelian. BA, U. Oxford, 1972, MA, 1975, DPhil, 1982. Fellow Merton Coll., Oxford, England, 1973-76, The Warburg Inst., London, 1976-79; reader Cambridge U., England, 1980-96; prof. European U. Inst., Florence, Italy, 1982-83; fellow King's Coll., Cambridge, 1985-96; Harry C. Black prof. history Johns Hopkins U., Balt., 1997—2002; disting. prof. polit. sci. and history UCLA, 2002—. Author: The Fall of Natural Man: The American Indian and the Origins of Comparative Ethnology, 1982, Spanish Imperialism and the Political Imagination: Studies in European and Spanish-American Social and Political Theory 1513-1830, 1990, European Encounters with the New World: From Renaissance to Romanticism, 1993, Lords of all the World: Ideologies of Empire in Spain, Britain and France c.1500-c.1800, 1995, Facing Each Other: The World's Perception of Europe and Europe's Perception of the World, 2000, Peoples and Empires: A Short History of European Migration, Exploration, and Conquest, from Greece to the Present, 2001, Imperialisms: Historical and Literary Investigations, 1500-1900, 2004, Worlds at War: The 2,500-Year Struggle Between East and West, 2008; editor: The Languages of Political Theory in Early-Modern Europe, 1987, The Idea of Europe: From Antiquity to the European Union, 2002; co-editor: Colonial Identity in the Atlantic World, 1500-1800, 1987. Grantee Guggenheim Found. Fellowship, 2006. Fellow: Real Acad. de Buenas Letras (corr. fellow), Royal Hist. Soc.; mem.: Athenaeum. Office: UCLA Dept Polit Sci 4289 Bunche Hall Box 951472 Los Angeles CA 90095-1475 Office Phone: 310-825-9984. Office Fax: 310-825-0778. E-mail: pagden@polisci.ucla.edu.

PAGE, ALAN CEDRIC, state supreme court justice; b. Canton, Ohio, Aug. 7, 1945; s. Howard F. and Georgianna (Umbles) P.; m. Diane Sims, June 5, 1973; children: Nina, Georgianna, Justin, Khamsin. BA, U. Notre Dame, 1967; JD, U. Minn., 1978; LLD (hon), U. Notre Dame, 1993, St. John's U., 1994, Westfield State Coll., 1994, Luther Coll., 1995, U. New Haven, 1999; LHD (hon), Winston-Salem State U., 2000, Gustavus Adolphus Coll., 2003, U. Notre Dame, 2004. Bar: Minn. 1979, U.S. Dist. Ct. Minn. 1979, U.S. Supreme Ct. 1988. Defensive tackle Minn. Vikings, Mpls., 1967-78, Chgo. Bears, 1978-81; assoc. Lindquist & Vennum, Mpls., 1979-85; special asst. atty. gen. employment law Minn. Atty. Gen.'s Office, St. Paul, 1985—87, asst. atty. gen., 1987—93; assoc. justice Minn. Supreme Ct., St. Paul, 1993—. Cons. NFL Players Assn., Washington, 1979-84. Commentator Nat. Pub. Radio, 1982-83. Founder Page Edn. Found., 1988. Named NFL All-Pro, 1969-71, 73-75, NFL MVP, 1971, Nat. Football Conf. Defensive Player of the Yr., 1970, NFL Defensive Playyer of the Yr., AP, 1971; named to the Nat. Football Conf. Pro Bowl Team, 1969-77, The NFL Hall of Fame, 1988, Coll. Football Hall of Fame, 1993, Internat. Scholar-Athlete Hall of Fame, 2002; named one of The 10 Outstanding Young Men Americans, U.S. Jaycees, 1981, 50 Greatest Sports Figures from Ohio Sports Illustrated, 1999; recipient NCAA Theodore Roosevelt award, 2004, Disting. Am. award Nat. Football Found. and Coll. Hall Fame, 2005, Honoree Trumpet awards Found., 2007. Mem. ABA, Minn. Bar Assn., Nat. Bar Assn., Hennepin County Bar Assn., Minn. Assn. Black Lawyers, Am. Law Inst. Avocations: running, biking. Office: 423 Minnesota Judicial Ctr 25 Rev Dr Martin Luther King Jr Blvd Saint Paul MN 55155-1500*

PAGE, ALBERT LEE, soil science educator, researcher; b. New Lenox, Ill., Mar. 19, 1927; m. Shirley L. Jessmore, Sept. 14, 1952; children: Nancy, Thomas. BA in Chemistry, U. Calif.-Riverside, 1956; PhD in Soil Sci., U. Calif.-Davis, 1960. Prof. soil sci. U. Calif.-Riverside, 1960—. Dir. Kearney Found., Univ. Calif.-Riverside, program of excellence in energy research Editor: Methods of Soil Analysis, 1983, Utilization of Municipal Wastewater and Sludge on Land, 1983, Heavy Metals in the Environment, 1977 With USN, 1944—52. Recipient Environ. Quality Research award Am. Soc. Agronomy, 1984, Disting. Teaching award U. Calif., Riverside, 1976, Disting. Svc. award USDA, 1991; Fullbright scholar, 1966-67; Guggenheim Meml. Found. fellow, 1966-67 Fellow AAAS, Am. Soc. Agronomy, Soil Sci. Soc. Am.; mem. Internat. Soil Sci. Soc., Western Soil Sci. Soc., Soc. Environ. Geochemistry and Health, Sigma Xi. Home: 5555 Canyon Crest Dr Apt 1F Riverside CA 92507-6443 Office: U Calif Dept Soil & Environ Sci Riverside CA 92521-0001 Home Phone: 951-682-1913; Office Phone: 951-827-3433, 951-787-3433. Business E-Mail: albert.page@ucr.edu.

PAGE, ANTHONY, theater director, film director; b. Bangalore, India, Sept. 21, 1935; Student, U. Oxford. Dir.: (Broadway plays) Inadmissible Evidence, 1965, Heartbreak House, 1983, A Doll's House, 1996 (Tony award for Best Direction of a Play, 1997), Cat on a Hot Tin Roof, 2003, Who's Afraid of Virginia Woolf?, 2005, Waiting for Godot, 2009, (plays) A Patriot for Me, Look Back in Anger, Uncle Vanya, Cowardice, (films) Inadmissible Evidence, 1968, Alpha Beta, 1976, F. Scott Fitzgerald in Hollywood, 1976, I Never Promised You a Rose Garden, 1977, Absolution, 1979, The Lady Vanishes, 1979, Silent Cries, 1993, (TV films) The Patricia Neal Story, 1981, Bill, 1981, Johnny Belinda, 1982, Grace Kelly, 1983, Bill: On His Own, 1983, Murder by Reason of Insanity, 1985, Forbidden, 1985, Second Severe, 1986, Monte Carlo, 1986, Pack of Lies, 1987, Scandal in a Small Town, 1988, Absolute Hell, 1991, Chernobyl: The Final Warning, Human Bomb, 1998, My Zinc Bed, 2008, (TV miniseries) The Nightmare Years, 1990, Middlemarch, 1994. Mem. Dirs. Guild Am.*

PAGE, DAVID C., biologist, educator; MD magna cum laude, Harvard Med. Sch. Mem. Whitehead Inst. for Biomedical Rsch., 1986—, interim dir., 2004—05, dir., 2005—; prof. biology MIT; investigator Howard Hughes Med. Inst. Editor Current Opinion in Genetics and Develop.; assoc. editor Ann. Rev. Human Genetics and Genomics. Recipient Searle Scholar's award, 1989, Amory prize, Am. Acad. Arts and Sciences, 1997, Curt Stern award, Am. Soc. Human Genetics, 2003; MacArthur Found. prize fellowship, 1986. Mem.: NAS, Inst. Medicine. Achievements include mapping and cloning the Y chromosome; publishing the complete sequence of Y chromosome. Office: Whitehead Inst 9 Cambridge Ctr Cambridge MA 02142-1479 Office Phone: 617-258-5203. E-mail: page_admin@wi.mit.edu.*

PAGE, DEBORAH J., accountant; d. Richard T. and Esther J. Thompson; m. Robert E. Page; children: Nolan T.C., Jonathan E. BEE, Union Coll., Schenectady, NY, 1987. Cert. tchr. Ariz., 2005. Capt. USAF, 1987—96; acct., human resources Bisbee Hospitality Group, Ariz., 1996—; math. instr. Cochise Coll., Douglas, Ariz., 1997—2007. Treas. Bisbee Youth Soccer, 2003—08. Office: Bisbee Hospitality Group PO Box BV Bisbee AZ 85603

PAGE, ELLEN, actress; b. Halifax, Canada, Feb. 21, 1987; d. Dennis Page and Martha Philpots. Actress (TV series) Pit Pony, 1999, Rideau Hall, 2002, Trailer Park Boys, 2001—02, ReGenesis, 2004 (Best Performance by an Actress in a Featured Supporting Role in a Dramatic Series, Gemini Awards, 2005), (films) Marion Bridge, 2002 (Outstanding Performance award, Alliance of Canadian Cinema, TV and Radio Artists, 2003), The Wet Season, 2002, Touch & Go, 2003, Love That Boy, 2003, Wilby Wonderland, 2004 (Outstanding Performance by an Actor, Atlantic Film Festival, 2004), Hard Candy, 2005 (Best Actress award, Austin Film Critics Assn., 2007), Mouth to Mouth, 2005, X-Men: The Last Stand, 2006, An American Crime, 2007, Juno, 2007 (Best Actress in a Motion Picture, Comedy or Musical, Satellite Award, 2007, Phoenix Film Critics Soc. award, 2007, Best Breakthrough Performance, Nat. Bd. Review, 2007, Best Actress award, Chgo. Film Critics Assn., 2007, Ind. Spirit award for Best Female Lead, Film Ind., 2008, Best Female Performance, MTV Movie Awards, 2008, Choice Movie Actress: Comedy, Teen Choice Awards, 2008, Choice Movie Breakout Female, Teen Choice Awards, 2008), The Stone Angel, 2007, The Tracey Fragments, 2007 (Best Actress award, Atlantic Film Festival, 2007), Smart People, 2008, (TV films) Homeless to Harvard: The Liz Murray Story, 2003, Going for Broke, 2003, Mrs. Ashboro's Cat, 2003 (Best Performance in a Childrens' or Youth Program or Series, Gemini Awards, 2004). Named Breakthrough Actress of Yr., Hollywood Film Festival, 2007. Office: c/o Gaby Morgerman William Morris Agy 1325 Ave of the Americas New York NY 10019

PAGE, ERIC J., physics professor; b. Ashburnham, Mass., Aug. 16, 1974; PhD, U. Rochester, NY, 2005. Vis. asst. prof. physics Allegheny Coll., Meadville, Pa., 2005—06; asst. prof. physics U. San Diego, 2006—. Office: Univ San Diego 5998 Alcala Pk San Diego CA 92110 Office Fax: 619-260-6874. Business E-Mail: epage@sandiego.edu.

PAGE, ERNEST, retired medical educator; b. Cologne, Germany, May 30, 1927; came to US, 1936, naturalized, 1942. s. Max Ernest and Eleanor (Kohn) P.; m. Eva Veronica Gross, June 5, 1967; 1 son, Thomas J. AB, U. Calif., Berkeley, 1949; MD, U. Calif., San Francisco, 1952. Intern Peter Bent Brigham Hosp., Boston, 1952-53, resident, 1953-54, 57-58; rsch. assoc. Harvard Med. Sch., 1957-65; assoc. prof. medicine and physiology U. Chgo. Med. Sch., 1965-69, prof. physiology & cardiology, 1968—98, prof. emeritus, 1998—. Editor: (jour.) Am. Jour. Physiology: Heart and Circulatory Physiology, 1981—86; editor: (sects.) Handbook of Physiology Vol. I The Heart, 2002. Served with AUS, 1945-46. Established investigator Am. Heart Assn., 1959-65. Mem. Am. Physiol. Soc., Biophys. Soc., Am. Soc. Cell Biology, Soc. Gen. Physiologists, Assn. Am. Physicians. Home: ALFASI 33 APT 7 Jerusalem 92302 Israel Personal E-mail: pageeoa@yahoo.com.

PAGE, FRANK J., music educator; b. Salt Lake City, Feb. 11, 1946; s. William Frank Page and Louise Black; 1 child, Joseph F. PhD in Sociology, U. Utah, Salt Lake City, 2000. Temp. asst. prof. Westminster Coll., Salt Lake City, 2002—04; adj. asst. prof. U. Utah, 2004—, adj. faculty rep., 2007—. Author: (short stories) Dancing at the North Yard Cafe, Stars and Stripes; contbr. articles to encyclopedia. Animal rights activist, Salt Lake City, 1980—2009. Recipient Best Music award, Salt Lake City, Best Adj. Sociology Tchg. award, U. Utah, 2009. Mem.: Pacific Sociologicical Assn., Am. Sociol. Assn., Writers Guild (licentiate). Avocations: camping, hiking. Home: 4649 Wallace Ln Salt Lake City UT 84117 Office: Univ Utah 380 Southern 1530 E Salt Lake City UT 84112 Business E-Mail: frank.page@soc.utah.edu.

PAGE, FRANK S., head of religious order; b. Greensboro, NC, 1952; m. Dayle Page; children: Melissa, Lauren, Allison. BS in Psychology, Gardner Webb Univ.; MDiv., PhD, Southwestern Baptist Theological Seminary. Former pastor Southern Baptist Convention Church (SBC Church) Tex., SBC Church No. Carolina, Warren Baptist SBC Church Ga., Taylor's First SBC Church So. Carolina; pres. So. Baptist Church, 2006—. Office: Southern Baptist Convention 1 Lifeway Plz MSN 146 Nashville TN 37234-1001

PAGE, FREDERICK WEST, retired business consultant; b. East Orange, NJ, Oct. 19, 1932; s. Frederick West and Dorothy (Donham) P.; m. Miriam Lowell Jones, Feb. 14, 1959; children: William, Janet, Thomas, James. AB, Dartmouth Coll., 1954; postgrad., Wharton Grad. Sch. Bus., U. Pa., 1956-57; MBA, NYU, 1960. With Schering Corp. (now Schering-Plough), 1957-91, various mktg. positions, 1957-73, gen. mgr. animal health products, 1973-80, pres. U.S. Animal Health Products Div., 1980-83, v.p. pharm. ops., 1983-91; pres. Bus. Cons. Svcs., 1991—2007; dir. Immune Tech. Inc., 1996-98. With US Army,

1954—56. Mem. Animal Health Inst. (exec. com. 1978-81, chmn. 1979-80) Clubs: Phi Kappa Psi. Republican. Home and Office: 22 Martin Rd West Caldwell NJ 07006-7419

PAGE, GREGORY R., agricultural products and diversified services company executive; b. Bottineau, ND, 1951; m. Cynthia M. Page. BA in Economics, U. ND, 1973. Joined as trainee in Feed divsn., various positions in the US animal nutrition bus. in merchandising, prod. services and admin. Cargill, Inc., Kansas City, Kan.; Fort Worth, Texas; Stockton, Calif.; Minneapolis, 1974—85, head animal nutrition operations in Asia, Cargill Southeast Asia Ltd Singapore, 1985, head poultry processing bus., Sun Valley Thailand Saraburi Province, Thailand, 1989—92, returned to US to work with the U.S. beef operations of Cargills Excel subs. Mpls., 1992, pres. red meat group, 1995—98, corp. v.p., sect. pres., 1998—2000, exec. v.p., 1999—2000, pres., COO, 2000—07, chmn., pres., CEO, 2007—. Bd. dirs. Eaton Corp. Mem.: Am. Meat Inst. (chmn. 2000). Office: Cargill Inc PO Box 9300 Minneapolis MN 55440

PAGE, HARRY ROBERT, business administration educator; b. Milw., Mar. 22, 1915; s. Harry Allen and Lydia (Rosendahl) P.; m. Jeanne Tompkins, Apr. 1, 1945; children: Patricia Jeanne, Margaret Berenice. AB, Mich. State U., 1941; postgrad., U.S. Army Command and Staff Coll., 1945-46, Indsl. Coll. Armed Forces, 1958-59; MBA, Harvard, 1950; PhD, Am. U., 1966. Served from 2d lt. to lt. col. U.S. Army, 1941-46; from lt. col. to col. USAF, 1947-61; exec. officer logistics directorate U.S. Joint Chiefs of Staff, Washington, 1959-61; asst. prof. bus. adminstrn. George Washington U., Washington, 1961-65, assoc. prof., chmn. dept., 1965-69, prof., chmn. dept. bus. adminstrn., 1970-74, assoc. dean, 1975-80, prof. emeritus, 1981—. Cons. advanced study program Brookings Instn., Washington, 1966-70, Ednl. Svcs. Inst., US Postal Svc., 1985-92. Author: Church Budget Development, 1964, An Analysis of the Defense Procurement Program Decision-Making Process, 1966, Public Purchasing and Materials Management, 1980, rev. edit., 1989; co-author: Federal Contributions to Management, 1972. Chmn. task force edn. and tng. Commn. Govt. Procurement, 1972-73; bd. dirs., treas. Coun. Chs., Greater Washington, 1963-68; bd. dirs. Hunter Assocs. Lab., Inc.; deacon Rock Spring Congregational Ch., 1994-97. Decorated Air medal USAF, Purple Heart, Legion of Merit, Commendation medal USAF, U.S. Army. Fellow Nat. Contract Mgmt. Assn.; mem. Acad. mgmt., Nat. Assn. Purchasing Mgmt., Internat. Fedn. Purchasing and Materials Mgmt., Harvard Bus. Sch. Assn., Air Force Assn., Nat. Parks and Conservation Assn. (trustee), Air Force Sgts. Assn. (trustee, chmn. scholarship bd. 1971—), Harvard Bus. Club, Sch. of Wash. Club (dir., pres. 1980-81), Alpha Phi Omega, Lambda Chi Alpha Alpha Kappa Psi, Pi Sigma Alpha, Beta Gamma Sigma. Home: 3612 N Glebe Rd Arlington VA 22207-4317 Home Phone: 703-538-4861.

PAGE, HELEN (LYN) BARD WARD, literature educator; b. Evanston, Ill., Oct. 30, 1947; d. Herschel Wayne and Helen Doris (Davies) Ward; m. Joseph Leon Page, 1986; 1 child, Julia Helen. BA in English magna cum laude, Cornell Coll., Mount Vernon, Iowa, 1968; MA in English Lit., Northwestern U., Evanston, 1971; postgrad., Nat. Louis U., Evanston, 1972—82, U. Ill., Chgo., 1983—87. English tchr. Niles West HS, Skokie, 1969—70; program co-designer Niles Off-Campus Learning Ctr., Skokie, 1970—71, tchr. and program design team, 1971—76; instrnl. supr. Glenbrook North HS, Northbrook, Ill., 1976—80; prof. English Oakton CC, DesPlaines, Ill., 1980—; co-creator ednl. program ASSIST: Additional Student Svcs. Instrnl. Support Team, 1980—81. Part-time instr. English Northwestern U., Evanston, 1987—93, Kendall Coll., 1987—88; coord. Great Books Program Oakton CC, DesPlaines, 2005—; cons. in field; presenter in field. Contbr. articles to profl. jours. Bd. mem., mem.-at-large Experiment in Internat. Living, Chgo., 1969—; active mem., leader, trainer, nat. del. Girl Scouts USA, 1995—2007; mem., choir mem., com. mem. First Congl. Ch. Evanston, 2003—. Recipient Outstanding Tchg. Effectiveness award, Oakton CC, 1982, Presdl. citation, 1986, 1987, award, Nat. Inst. Staff and Orgnl. Devel., 1996, Beamon-Denoyer award, Girl Scouts USA, 2004; finalist Hartstein Tchg. award, Oakton CC, 1987, 2004, Coll. Tchg. award, Northwestern U., 1989; nominee Hartstein Tchg. award, Oakton CC, 2002, 2007. Mem.: Nat. Coun. Tchrs. English, Girl Scouts (life), Phi Beta Kappa. Avocations: volunteer work, music, theater. Office: Oakton CC 1600 E Golf Rd Des Plaines IL 60016 Office Phone: 847-376-7669.

PAGE, JIMMY (JAMES PATRICK PAGE), musician; b. Heston, Eng., Jan. 9, 1944; s. James Page & Patricia Elizabeth Gaffikin P.; one child, Scarlet Lilith Eleida (with Charlotte Martin); m. Patricia Ecker, 1986 (div. 1995); 1 child, James Patrick; m. Jimena Gomez-Paratcha; children: Asher, Sophia-Jade, Jana Guitarist Neil Christian & the Crusaders, Carter-Lewis & The Southerners, Mickey Finn, The Yardbirds, 1966-68, Led Zeppelin, 1968-80, The Firm, 1984—86. Guitarist (albums with The Yardbirds) Little Games, 1967, (albums with Led Zeppelin) Led Zeppelin, 1968, Led Zeppelin II, 1969, Led Zeppelin III, 1970, Led Zeppelin IV, 1971, House of the Holy, 1973, Physical Graffiti, 1975, The Song Remain the Same, 1976, Presence, 1976, In Through the Out Door, 1979, Coda, 1982, Remasters, 1990, BBC Sessions, 1997, Early Days: The Best Of Led Zeppelin Volume One, 2000, Latter Days: The Best Of Led Zeppelin Volume Two, 2002, How the West Was Won, 2003, Mothership, 2007, (albums with The Honeydrippers) The Honeydrippers: Volume One, 1984, (albums with Roy Harper) Whatever Happened to Jugula?, 1985, (albums with The Firm) Firm, 1985, Mean Business, 1986, (albums with David Coverdale) Coverdale/Page, 1993, (albums with Robert Plant) No Quarter: Jimmy Page and Robert Plant Unledded, 1994, Walking into Clarksdale, 1998, (albums with The Black Crowes) Live at the Greek, 2000, (solo albums) Outrider, 1988; composer: (soundtracks) Death Wish II, 1982; performer: (concert films) The Song Remains the Same, 1976, Unledded, 1994; appeared in (documentaries) It Might Get Loud, 2009. Active in Action for Brazil's Children Trust, 1998—. Recipient Polar Music prize, Royal Swedish Acad. Music, 2006; co-recipient Grammy Award for Best Hard Rock Performance, 1999, Lifetime Achievement award, Grammy Awards, 2005; named London's Greatest Guitarist, Total Guitar mag., 2001; named an Officer of the Most Excellent Order of the British Empire (OBE), Her Majesty Queen Elizabeth II, 2005; named to Rock & Roll Hall of Fame (as mem. of The Yardbirds, 1992, as mem. of Led Zeppelin, 1995), United Kingdom Music Hall of Fame (as mem. of Led Zeppelin), 2006. Was highly sought after as a studio sessions guitarist during the early part of his career; his guitar playing appears in recordings by such acts as Sonny Boy Williamson, John Mayall's Bluesbreakes, The Who, The Rolling Stones The Kinks, The Jeff Beck Group, Joe Cocker & Al Stewart. Office: 46 Kensington Ct St London W8 5DP England

PAGE, JOHN MARTIN, JR., economist; b. Pitts., Nov. 16, 1949; s. John Martin Page and Lola Frances Robinson; m. Elisabeth Jeanne Rice, June 27, 1998; 1 child, Matthew James. BA, Stanford U., 1971; PhD, U. Oxford, 1974. Dir. poverty reduction The World Bank, Washington, 2000—04, chief economist mid. east and north Africa, 1993—2000, chief economist Africa region, 2004—08, Brookings Instn., Washington, 2008—. Chair inter-agency task force enabling environment econ. and social devel. UN, NYC, 1996—97, mem. millenium task force econ. and social devel., 2004—05; dir. Africa Econ. Rsch. Consortium, Nairobi, Kenya, 2004—; chair investment com. Phi Beta Kappa Found., Washington. Author: (books) Small Manufacturing Enterprises, 1987, The East Asian Miracle, 1993; editor: Africa at a Turning Point? World Bank, 2008; contbr. articles to profl. jours. Lt. comdr. USN, 1974—77, USS Kansas City. Am. Rhodes Scholar, The Rhodes Trust, 1971—74. Fellow: Econ. Rsch. Forum Arab Countries; mem.: Phi Beta Kappa. Independent. Protestant Christian. Achievements include research in in the fields of economic development and trade and industrial policy in developing economies. Avocations: writing, golf. Home: 10817 Hidden Trail Ct Potomac MD 20854 Office: The Brookings Instn 1775 Mas Ave Washington DC 20036 Office Phone: 202-741-6569. Home Fax: 301-365-1683.

PAGE, KELLY ANDREW, physics professor; BS in Physics, Ill. State U., Normal, 1991; MS in Astrophysics, Mich. State U., Lansing, 1995; PhD in Physics, U. Wyo., Laramie, Wyo, 2005. Asst. prof. Harper Coll., Palatine, Ill., 2002—.

PAGE, KENNETH R., lawyer; b. Rockville Centre, NY, May 20, 1946; s. Charles Herbert and Dorothy Emma (Koster) P.; m. Nancy McNeer Cummings, Oct. 27, 1973; children: Katherine Spessard Page, Taylor Benton Page; m. Deborah Ann Donovan, Feb. 14, 1998 AB cum laude, with distinction in Govt., Dartmouth Coll., 1968; JD, Cornell U., 1971. Bar: N.Y. 1972, U.S. Dist. Ct. (so. dist.) N.Y., U.S. Ct. Appeals (2d cir.) 1975, U.S. Tax Ct. 2000. Assoc. Cadwalader, Wickersham & Taft, NYC, 1971-80; ptnr. Cole & Deitz, NYC, 1980-83, Coudert Bros., NYC, 1983—2005, head Trusts & Estates practice; ptnr. Baker & McKenzie, NYC, 2005—06, Hughes Hubbard & Reed LLP, NYC, 2006—. Trustee Family Dynamics, N.Y.C., 1976-86, Mus. Am. Folk Art, N.Y.C., 1976-86, Isaac H. Tuttle Fund., N.Y.C., 1980—; bd. trustees Estate and Property of Diocesan Conv., N.Y.C., 1987-93, 94-2000, 01—. Mem. ABA, N.Y. State Bar. Assn., Order St. John, Pilgrims US, Union Club. Avocations: skiing, tennis, fishing, art. Office: Hughes Hubbard and Reed LLP 1114 Ave of the Americas New York NY 10036-7710 Office Phone: 212-837-6440. Business E-Mail: pagek@hugheshubbard.com.

PAGE, LARRY (LAWRENCE E. PAGE), information technology executive; b. Ann Arbor, Mich., Mar. 26, 1973; s. Carl Victor and Gloria Page; m. Lucy Southworth, Dec. 8, 2007. BS in Computer Engring., U. Mich., 1995; student, Stanford U. Co-founder Google, Inc., Mountain View, Calif., 1998, CEO, 1998—2001, pres. products, 2001—. Spkr. in field; spkr. World Econ. Forum; bd. dirs. Google, Inc., 1998—. Mem. nat. adv. com. U. Mich. Coll. Engring., Ann Arbor, Mich.; bd. trustee X Prize, 2005—. Recipient Engring. Grad. award, U. Mich. Alumni Soc., Golden Plate award, Acad. Achievement, 2004, Bus. Leader of Yr. for Google, Inc., Sci. Am. 50, 2005; co-recipient (with Sergey Brin) Marconi prize, 2004; named Innovator of Yr., R&D Mag., 2002; named a Global Leader for Tomorrow, World Econ. Forum, 2002, Young Innovator Who Will Create the Future, MIT Tech. Rev. Mag.; named one of Persons of Week (with Sergey Brin), ABC World News Tonight, 2004, World's 100 Most Influential People, TIME mag., 2005, Forbes Richest Americans, 2006, 50 Who Matter Now, CNNMoney.com Bus. 2.0, 2006, 2007, World's Richest People, Forbes Mag., 2006, 2007, 2008, 50 Most Important People on the Web, PC World, 2007, 25 Most Powerful People in Bus., Fortune Mag., 2007. Mem.: NAE, Eta Kappa Nu. Office: 1600 Amphitheatre PKWY #41 Mountain View CA 94043-1351 Office Phone: 650-623-4000. Office Fax: 650-618-1499.

PAGE, LARRY KEITH, neurosurgeon, educator; b. Rayville, La., July 7, 1933; s. Ardie Lee and Edris Estelle (Chaney) P.; m. Joan Marie Doherty, Aug. 27, 1960; children: Matthew, Elizabeth, Jennifer. BS, La. State U., 1955, MD, 1958. Diplomate: Am. Bd. Neurol. Surgery. Intern Grad. Hosp., U. Pa., Phila., 1958-59; resident Children's Hosp. and Peter Bent Brigham Hosp., Boston, 1962-66; assoc. neurosurgeon Children's Hosp., assoc. surgeon Peter Bent Brigham Hosp., 1966-71; cons. Beverly Hosp., Mass., Robert Breck Brigham Hosp., Boston, Pondville Hosp., Boston, West Roxbury VA Hosp., Boston VA Hosp.; clin. instr. neurosurgery Harvard U., Boston, 1966-71; prof., vice chmn. dept. neurosurgery U. Miami, Fla., 1971-95, prof. emeritus Fla., 1995—, chief div. pediatric neurosurgery Fla., 1971-95; neurosurgeon VA Hosp., Miami, 1971-88, Jackson Meml. Hosp., Miami, 1971-95, dir. neurosurgery, 1994-95; chief neurosurgery Mt. Sinai Hosp., Miami, 1990-94. Chmn. CSF Shunt Standard Com. for ASTM, ISO, AANS & CNS, 1974-86, cons. neurosurg. FDA, 1976-79, NASA, 1979-80 Mem. editorial bds., contbr. articles to profl. jours. Served to lt. USN, 1959-62. Mem. ACS, Am. Acad. Pediatrics, Am. Assn. Neurol. Surgeons, Internat. Soc. Pediatric Neurosurgery, Am. Soc. Pediatric Neurosurgery, Congress Neurol. Surgeons, Fellowship of Acad. Neurosurgeons, Internat. Neurosurg. Forum, Royal Soc. Medicine, Soc. for Rsch. in Hydrocephalus and Spina Bifida, New Eng. Neurosurg. Soc., Fla. Neurosurg. Soc. (pres. 1989-90), Mass. Med. Soc., Dade County Med. Assn., Internat. Palm Soc., Alpha Omega Alpha. Roman Catholic. Home and Office: 13845 SW 73rd Ct Miami FL 33158-1213

PAGE, LESLIE ANDREW, retired consumer products company executive; b. Mpls., June 5, 1924; s. Henry R. and Amelia Kathryn (Steinmetz) Page; m. DeEtte Abernethy Griswold, July 6, 1952 (div. Sept. 1975); children: Randolph, Michael, Kathryn, Caroline; m. Mary Ellen Decker, Nov. 26, 1976. BA, U. Minn., 1949; MA, U. Calif., Berkeley, 1953, PhD, 1956. Asst. microbiologist, lectr. U. Calif., Davis, 1956-61; cons. San Diego Zoological Soc. Zoo Hosp., 1957-60; microbiologist, research leader Nat. Animal Disease Ctr., USDA, Ames, Iowa, 1961-79; specialist in Chlamydial nomenclature and disease; med. text cons. Bay St. Louis, Miss., 1979-85; founder, pres., chmn. bd. Steri-Derm Corp., San Marcos, Calif., 1987—2005. Cons. McCormick Distilling Co., Weston, Mo., 1994—95. Editor: Jour. Wildlife Diseases, 1965—68, Wildlife Diseases, 1976; contbr. chpts. to textbooks, articles to profl. jours. Pres. Garden Island Cmty. Assn., Bay St. Louis, Miss., 1980—81; chief commr. East Hancock Fire Protection Dist., Bay St. Louis, 1982—83; treas. Woodridge Escondido Property Owners Assn., 1986—88; pres. Westminster Men's Group, Westminster Presbyn. Ch., Escondido, Calif., 2002. With 89th inf. divsn US Army, 1943—46, US. Fellow: Am. Acad. Microbiology; mem.: Am. Soc. Microbiology, Wildlife Disease Assn. (life; pres. 1972—73, Disting. Svc. award 1980), Les Familles Pagé d'Amérique, Sigma Xi, Phi Zeta (hon.). Achievements include patent for Liquid Antiseptic Composition. Home: 2209 SE Pine Gate Cir Blue Springs MO 64014 Personal E-mail: lapage1234@hotmail.com.

PAGE, PATRICIA (PATTY) NEWTON, real estate broker, real estate company executive; b. Nashville, Tenn., May 16, 1963; d. James Kelton and Alice (Clement) Cuff; m. James T. Baxter. Grad., Realtor Inst., 1999. Cert. affiliate broker North Ctrl. Inst., 1993, accredited credit buyer rep. Nat. Assn. Realtors, 2001, lic. real estate broker, cert. residential specialist. Sr. customer svc. rep. Comdata Corp., Brentwood, Tenn., 1981—92; realtor Century 21 ABC, Clarksville, Tenn., 1993—94, Lakeland Properties, Dover, Tenn., 1994—96; designated realtor Cherry Properties, Dover, Tenn., 1996—2003; owner, broker Patty Page Properties, LLC, 2004—. Mem.: Nat. Assn. Realtors (coun. residential specialist 2002). Methodist. Avocations: continued education, travel. Office Phone: 931-232-5082. Personal E-mail: PattyPage2000@aol.com.

PAGE, RANDALL, state official; b. Mt. Vernon, Ohio, Feb. 18, 1967; s. James and Nancy Page; m. Melissa Rohrman, Feb. 16, 1991; children: Julie Anne, Jason Ryan. BS, Bob Jones U., Greenville, 1990. Dir. of pub. events Office of the Gov., Columbia, SC, 1995—99; exec. v.p. Jordan and McCallum Co., Greenville, SC, 1999—2001; legislative affairs dir. Office of the Lt. Gov., Columbia, SC, 2001—03, chief of staff, 2003—04; campaign mgr. Beasley for Senate, Columbia, SC, 2004; pres. South Carolinians for Responsible Govt., Columbia, 2005—; sr. assoc. Richard Quinn & Assocs., Columbia, SC, 2004—05. Bd. dirs. Insights, Greenville, SC, 1994—2001; adv. bd. LifeEd, Greenville, SC, 2000—, Eagle Mil. Acad., Summerville, SC, 2006—; exec. bd. SC Citizens for Life, Columbia, 2001—. Cons. George W. Bush for Pres., Columbia, SC, 2000; fourth dist. chmn. SC Rep. Party, Columbia, 2001—03; mem. Lexington County Rep. Exec. Com., 2007—; bd. dirs. Kennerly Rd. Bapt. Ch., Irmo, SC, 2003—06, 2008—, chmn., 2004—06, 2008—; mem. exec. bd. Greenville County Libr. Sys., SC, 1999—2001; bd. dirs. Palmetto Family Coun., 2006—. Recipient Order of the Palmetto, Gov. David M. Beasley, SC., 1998, Hon. Order of Ky. Colonels, Gov. Paul Patton, Ky., 2003, Disting. Svc. award, Bob Jones U. Alumni Assn., 2006. Republican. Baptist. Avocation: swimming. Office: South Carolinians for Responsible Govt 3020 Devine St Columbia SC 29205 Office Fax: 803-212-1052. Personal E-mail: govpage@sc.rr.com. Business E-Mail: randy@scrgov.org.

PAGE, REX L, computer scientist, educator, software consultant; b. Wichita, OK, Feb. 4, 1944; s. Warren Rector Page, Mildred Irene Page; m. Lucy Garcia Garcia Lopez; m. Beverly Jane Brown (div. Mar. 15, 1991); children: Peter Nicholas, Kathleen Alanna, Cammie Jane. AB, Stanford University, Stanford, CA, 1962—66; PhD, University of California at San Diego, La Jolla, CA, 1966—70. Professor of Computer Science University of Oklahoma, Norman, OK, 1993—2002; Senior Member of Technical Staff Eclipse International, Mountain View, CA. Software Architect Amoco, Houston, 1982—93; Professor of Computer Science Colorado State University, Fort Collins, CO, 1970—82. Author: (book) Fortran for Humans, 1974, Using Basic, 1980, Symbolic Computing with Lisp and Prolog, 1986. Office: University of Oklahoma 200 Felgar Street - EL120 Norman OK 73019 Home Phone: 405-329-6182; Office Phone: 405-325-5408.

PAGE, RICHARD LEIGHTON, cardiologist, medical educator, researcher; b. San Diego, Mar. 8, 1958; s. Ellis Batten and Elizabeth Latimer (Thaxton) P.; m. Jean Reynolds, Oct. 12, 1985; children: Franklin Reynolds, Gillian Grace, Edward Batten. BS in Zoology magna cum laude, Duke U., 1980, MD, 1984. Diplomate Nat. Bd. Med. Examiners, Am. Bd. Internal Medicine, subspecialties cardiovascular disease and clin. cardiac electrophysiology; lic. physician, Tex. Rsch. fellow in pharmacology Columbia Presbyn. Med. Ctr., 1982-83; intern dept. medicine Mass. Gen. Hosp., Boston, 1984-85, resident dept. medicine, 1985-87; cardiology fellow clin. electrophysiology Duke U. Med. Ctr., Durham, N.C., 1987-89, clin. cardiology fellow, 1989, lectr. medicine divsn. cardiology, 1989-90, assoc. in medicine, 1990, asst. prof., dir. clin. electrophysiology lab., 1990-92; asst. prof. medicine U. Tex. Southwestern Med. Ctr., Dallas, 1992-95, assoc. prof., 1995-2001, prof., 2001—02; prof. and head cardiology U. Wash. Sch. Medicine, Seattle, 2002—, Robert A. Bruce endowed chair in cardiovascular rsch., 2002—. Dir. sect. clin. electrophysiology U. Tex. Southwestern Med. Ctr., Dallas, 1992; dir. clin. electrophysiology lab., arrhythmia and pacemaker svc., Parkland Meml. Hosp., Dallas, 1992; holder Dallas Heart Ball Chair in Cardiac Arrhythmia Rsch., 1997; dir. Stanley J. Sarnoff Endowment for Rsch. in Cardiovasc. Sci., Inc., Bethesda, Md., 1990, co-chmn., 1992; Dallas Heart Ball chair in Cardiac Arrhythmia Rsch., 1997. Mem. editl. bd. Cardiac Chronicle, 1993, Am. Heart Jour., 1998—, Am. Jour. Cardiology, 1999—; author: (with others) Manual of Clinical Problems in Cardiology, 5th edit., 1995; contbr. articles to profl. jours., chpt. to book. Sarnoff Endowment fellow, 1982, Sarnoff scholar, 1987. Fellow Stanley J. Sarnoff Soc., Am. Heart Assn., Am. Coll. Cardiology; mem. N.Am. Soc. Pacing and Electrophysiology, Tex. Med. Assn., Dallas County Med. Soc., North Tex. Electrophysiology Soc. (trustee), Sigma Xi, Alpha Omega Alpha. Episcopalian. Avocations: tennis, sailing, gardening. Address: 7214 94th Ave SE Mercer Island WA 98040-5826 Office: U Wash Med Ctr Box 356422 1959 NE Pacific Seattle WA 98195*

PAGE, ROBERT EUGENE, JR., biology professor; b. Bakersfield, Calif., Nov. 12, 1949; PhD in Entomology, U. Calif., Davis, 1980. Mem. faculty dept. entomology Ohio State U., 1986—89, U. Calif., Davis, 1989—91, prof., 1991—2004, prof. emeritus, 2004; found. prof., founding dir. Ariz. State U. Sch. Life Scis., 2004—. Chair dept. entomology U. Calif., Davis, 1999—2004. Contbr. articles to profl. jours., chapters to books; co-editor: Genetics of Social Evolution, 1988; co-author: Queen Rearing and Bee Breeding, 1998. 1st lt. US Army, 1969—72, capt. USAR, 1973—76. Recipient Alexander von Humboldt Sr. Scientist award, German Govt.; named highest cited rschr., ISI. Fellow: AAAS, Am. Acad. Arts & Scis.; mem.: Genetics Soc. Am., Soc. for Study of Evolution, Animal Behavioral Soc., Internat. Union for Study of Social Insects, Brazilian Acad. Sci. (frgn. mem.), Sigma Xi. Office: Ariz State U Sch Life Sci PO Box 874501 Tempe AZ 85287 Business E-Mail: Robert.Page@asu.edu.

PAGE, ROBERT HENRY, retired engineering educator, researcher; b. Phila., Nov. 5, 1927; s. Ernest Fraser and Marguerite (MacFarland) P.; m. Lola Marie Griffin, Nov. 12, 1948; children: Lola Linda, Patricia Jean, William Ernest, Nancy Lee, Martin Fraser. BS in Mech. Engring, Ohio U., 1949; MS, U. Ill., 1951, PhD, 1955. Instr., research assoc. U. Ill., 1949-55; research engr. fluid dynamics Esso Research & Engring. Co., 1955-57; vis. lectr. Stevens Inst. Tech., 1956-57, dir. fluid dynamics lab., prof. mech. engring., 1957-61; prof. mech. engring., chmn. dept. mech., indsl. and aerospace engring. Rutgers-The State U., 1961-76, prof., research cons., 1976-79; dean engring. Tex. A&M U., 1979-83, Forsyth prof., 1983-93, prof. emeritus mech. engring., 1994—; ret., 1994. Spl. research base pressure and heat transfer, wake flow and flow separation. Contbr. over 250 articles to profl. publs.; inventor impingement nozzles. Served with AUS, 1945-47, Pacific Theatre of Operations. Recipient Western Electric Fund award Am. Soc. Engring Edn., 1968, Lindback Found. award, 1969, Disting. Alumnus award U. Ill., 1971; Disting. Svc. award, 1973, Life Quality Engring. award, 1974, James Harry Potter Gold medal, 1983, Ohio U. medal, 1983, Ruhr medal, Ruhr U., Germany, 2006; named hon. prof. Ruhr U., Buchum, Fed. Republic Germany, 1984; named to Acad. Disting. Grads., Ohio U., 2001, Hall of Fame, Ctrl. H.S., Phila., 2002. Fellow AAAS, AIAA, ABET, Am. Astron. Soc. (chmn. nat. space engring. com. 1969-70, 72-76), Am. Soc. Engring. Edn. (Centennial medal 1993); mem. ASME (hon. mem. award 1988), Am. Phys. Soc., Pan Am. Acad. Engring. (charter). Home: 1905 Comal Cir College Station TX 77840-4818

PAGE, ROBERT WESLEY, engineering and construction company executive, federal official; b. Dallas, Jan. 22, 1927; s. Arch Cleo and Zelma (Tyler) P.; m. Nancy Ann Eaton, Sept. 17, 1952; children: Robert W. Jr., David, Mark, Margaret. BS in Archtl. Engring., Tex. A&M U., 1950. Asst. prof. Am. Univ., Beirut, 1952-54; project mgr. Aramco, The Hague and Saudi Arabia, 1954-56; dir. constrn. and devel. Internat. Coll., Beirut, N.Y.C., 1956-58; internat. mgr. Bechtel Co., NYC, 1958-64; v.p. Rockresorts Co., NYC, 1964-71; pres., chief exec. officer George A. Fuller Co., NYC, from 1971; corp. v.p. Northrop Corp., NYC, from 1971; pres., chief exec. officer Rust Engring. Co., Birmingham, Ala., 1976-81, Kellogg Rust Inc., Houston, 1981-85, chmn., chief exec. officer, dir., 1985-86; pres., chief exec. officer PM Co., Houston, 1986; asst. sec. U.S. Dept. of Army, Washington, 1987-90; chmn. Panama Canal Commn., 1989-90; exec. v.p. McDermott Internat., Washington, 1990—; sr. lectr. MIT, 1993; chmn. Pegasus Cons., Inc., Cambridge, Mass., 1996—; vice-chmn. Indevo Group, 2001—. Adj. prof. Georgetown U., Am. U.; bd. dirs. I.C.F./Kaiser Internat.; bd. dirs. Thormatrix, Inc., San Jose, Calif. Trustee Internat. Coll. Beirut; mem. Pres.'s Coun., U. Ala.; bd. dirs. Coll. Football Hall of Fame. With USNR, 1944-46, PTO. Trustee Am. U. in Cairo; trustee Wortham Theatre Ctr., Houston, Internat. Coll. Beirut; mem. Pres.'s Council, U. Ala.; mem. adv. bd. John E. Gray Inst., Lamar U.; bd. dirs. Coll. Football Hall of Fame. Served with USNR, 1944-46, PTO. Recipient Distinguished Scholar, MIT. Mem. ASME, ASCE, Rolling Rock Club (Ligoner, Pa.), Internat. Club (Washington), Army-Navy Club (Washington), Georgetown Club (Washington), Sakonnet Country Club (Little Compton, R.I.), Cosmos Club, Tau Beta Pi. Home: 3025 P St NW Washington DC 20007-3054 Office: 1850 K St NW Ste 950 Washington DC 20006-2213

PAGE, ROGER ALLAN, retired psychology professor; s. Nicholas Andrew and Norlee Francis Page; m. Trudy Kay Page; 1 child, Sean Allan. BS, Mich. State U., Lansing, 1969; MA, Ohio State U., 1973, PhD, 1975. Prof. Ohio State U., 1993—2008. Pres. divsn. psychol. hypnosis APA, DC, 2001—02. Contbr. articles to numerous profl. jours. Fellowship, APA, 2006. Mem.: Ohio State U. Retirees Assn. Office: Ohio State Univ 4240 Campus Dr Lima OH 45804 Personal E-mail: page.6@osu.edu.

PAGE, ROY CHRISTOPHER, periodontist, scientist, educator; b. Campobello, SC, Feb. 7, 1932; s. Milton and Anny Mae (Eubanks) P. BA, Berea Coll., 1953; DDS, U. Md., 1957; PhD, U. Wash., 1967; ScD (hon.), Loyola U., Chgo., 1983. Cert. in periodontics. Pvt. practice periodontics, Seattle, 1963-98; asst. prof. U. Wash. Schs. Medicine and Dentistry, Seattle, 1967-70, prof., 1974—2002, Disting. prof. dentistry, 1996-98, dir. Ctr. Research in Oral Biology, 1976-96; dir. grad. edn. U. Wash. Sch. Dentistry, 1976-80, dir. rsch. Seattle, 1976-94, dir. Regional Clin. Dental Rsch. Ctr., 1990—2008, assoc. dean rsch., 1994-2000, prof. emeritus, 2003—. Vis. scientist MRC Labs., London, 1971-72; cons., lectr. in field; fellow Pierre Fauchard Acad. Author: Periodontal Disease, 1977, 2d edit., 1990, Periodontitis in Man and Other Animals, 1982. Recipient Gold Medal award U. Md., 1957; recipient Career Devel. award NIH, 1967-72, Disting. Alumnus award U. Wash. Sch. Dentistry, 2000. Fellow Internat. Coll. Dentists, Am. Coll. Dentists, Am. Acad. Periodontology (Gies award 1982, fellowship award 1989, spl. citation 1998); mem. ADA (Norton Rose award for clin. rsch. 1998), Am. Assn. Dental Rsch. (pres. 1982-83, disting. scientist award 2001), Am. Soc. Exptl. Pathology, Internat. Assn. Dental Rsch. (pres. 1987, basic periodontal rsch. award 1977). Home: 5583 171st Ave SE Bellevue WA 98006-5503 Office Phone: 206-543-5599. E-mail: roypage@u.washington.edu.

PAGE, SALLY JACQUELYN, university official, management educator; b. Saginaw, Mich., 1943; d. William Henry and Doris Effie (Knippel) P. BA, U. Iowa, 1965; MBA, So. Ill. U., 1973. Copy editor C.V. Mosby Co., St. Louis, 1965-69; editl. cons. Editl. Assocs., Edwardsville, Ill., 1969-70; rsch. adminstr. So. Ill. U., 1970-74, asst. to pres., affirmative action officer, 1974-77; officer of instn. U. ND, Grand Forks, 1977—, lectr. mgmt., 1978—. Polit. comentator Sta. KFJM, Nat. Public Radio affiliate, 1981-90; mem. mayor's com. Employment of People With Disabilities, 1980-97. Contbr. articles to profl. jours. Chmn. ND Equal Opportunity Affirmative Action Officers, 1987-2003; chmn. NDUS Diversity Coun.; pres. Pine to Prairie coun. Girl Scouts US, 1980-85; mem. employment com. Ill. Commn. on Status of Women, 1976-77; mem. Bicentennial Com., Edwardsville, 1976, Bikeway Task Force, Edwardsville, 1975-77, Greater Grand Forks Bus. Leadership Network, ND; bd. dirs. Grand Forks Homes, 1985—2003, pres., 1996-2001; mem. found. bd. Valley Meml. Homes, 2005-, vice chair, 2007; mem. Civil Svc. Rev. Task Force, Grand Forks, 1982, civil svc. commr., 1983-98, chmn., 1984, 86, 88, 92, 96; ruling elder 1st Presbyn.; mem. Grand Forks Mayor's Adv. Cabinet, 1998-2000. Mem. AAUW (dir. Ill. 1975-77), PEO, Coll. and Univ. Pers. Assn. (rsch. and publs. bd. 1982-84), Soc. Human Resource Mgmt., Am. Assn. Affirmative Action, ADA Coords. Democrat. Presbyterian. Home: 3121 Cherry St Grand Forks ND 58201-7461 Office: U ND Grand Forks ND 58202 Business E-Mail: SallyPage@mail.und.nodak.edu.

PAGE, SCOTT E., social sciences educator; b. Hastings, Mich., Mar. 21, 1963; s. Raymond and Marilyn Page; m. Jenna Bednar, Mar. 30, 1986; children: Orrie, Cooper. BA, U. Mich., Ann Arbor, 1985; MA, U. Wis., Madison, 1988; PhD, Northwestern U., Evanston, 1993. Prof. U. Mich., 2000—. Author: (book) The Difference: How the Power of Diversity Creates Better Groups, Firms, Schools, and Societies.

PAGE, WILLIAM J., criminal justice educator; b. May 22, 1951; AA in Police Sci., Harrisburg Area CC, Pa., 1974; BS in Law Enforcement, York Coll. of Pa., 1974; postgrad., Pa. State U., 1992—99; attending, 2009. Cert. vocat II tchr. criminal justice Pa. Dept. Edn. Patrol officer Lower Allen Twp., Camp Hill, Pa., 1976—92; criminal justice instr. Cumberland-Perry AVTS, Mechanicsburg, Pa., 1992—. Mem.: Cumberland Perry Tchrs. Edn. Assn. (v.p. 1997—98, pres. 1998—2000), NEA, Pa. State Edn. Assn. Home and Office: Cumberland Perry AVTS 110 Old Willow Mill Rd Mechanicsburg PA 17055

PAGE, WILLIS, conductor; b. Rochester, NY, Sept. 18, 1918; Grad. with distinction, Eastman Sch. Music, Rochester., 1939. Mem. Rochester Philharm., 1937-40, Rochester Civic, 1939-40; prof. conducting Eastman Sch. Music, 1967-69; prof. conducting, dir. orchestral activities Drake U., Des Moines, 1969-71. Guest condr. Sony concerts, Chiba, Japan, 1992. Mem. Boston Symphony Orch., 1940-55; prin. bass Boston Pops, 1947-55; condr. Cecilia Soc. Boston, 1952-54, New Orchestral Soc. Boston; assoc. condr. Buffalo Philharm., 1955-59; music dir./condr. Nashville Symphony Orch., 1959-67; music dir. Linwood Music Sch., 1955-59; 1st condr. Yomiuri Nippon Symphony, Tokyo, 1962-63; condr. Des Moines Symphony, 1969-71, Jacksonville (Fla.) Symphony Orch., 1971-83; founder, condr. St. John's River City Band, 1985-86; guest condr. Boston Pops, Toronto, Rochester Civic, Eastman-Rochester, Denver, Muncie, Jerusalem, St. Louis, Colorado Springs, Memphis, Hartford orchs., Yomiuri Nippon Symphony, 1988, 92; founding condr., exec. dir. First Coast Pops Orch., 1989; condr. all-state orchs. of N.Y., Iowa, Ky., Tenn., Fla., also regional festivals; condr. 13 L.P. recordings including Symphony of the Air (Roger Williams soloist), Boston Festival Orch., Cook Labs., Nashville Symphony, Symphony of the Air. Sgt. 95th inf. divsn. U.S. Army, 1943-45. Decorated Bronze Star; recipient Ford Found. European travel award, 1967. Address: 1567 Flanders Rd 302 Jacksonville FL 32207 Home Phone: 904-737-7191. Personal E-mail: wpage11@comcast.net.

PAGEL, PAUL STANLEY, cardiac anesthesiologist; b. Madison, Wis., Dec. 6, 1957; s. Gerald Gordon and Mary Ellen (Young) P.; m. Judith A. May, Sept. 13, 1996. BS, Carroll Coll., 1979; MD, Med. Coll. Wis., 1986, MS, 1991, PhD, 1994. Cert. Am. Bd. Anesthesiology, 1991, Nat. Bd. Echocardiography, 1998. Intern in medicine St. Josephs Hosp., Milw., 1986-87; anesthesiology resident Med. Coll. Wis., Milw., 1987-90, fellow in anesthesiology rsch., 1990—93, instr. cardiac anesthesiology, 1990—93, asst. prof., 1994—96, assoc. prof., 1996—99, prof. and dir. cardiac anesthesia, 1999—. Assoc. examiner Am. Bd. Anesthesiology, 2000—; sr. editor ABA/ASA Written Exam., 2005—. Contbr. articles to profl. jours.; editl. bd. Anesthesiology, Jour. of Cardiothoracic and Vascular Anesthesia, Anesth Analg Faculty 1000 Medicine. Disting. Alumnus award, Carroll Coll., 2004; rsch. Anesthesiology fellow Med. Coll. Wis., 1992-93, Rsch. fellow NIH, 1990-92. Fellow: European Soc. Cardiology, Am. Soc. Echocardiography, Am. Heart Assn., Am. Coll. Chest Physicians, Am. Coll. Cardiology. Office: Zablocki VA Med Ctr 5000 W National Ave Milwaukee WI 53295 Office Phone: 414-384-2000 Ext. 42417. Office Fax: 414-384-2939. Business E-Mail: pspagel@mcw.edu.

PAGELS, ELAINE HIESEY, theology studies educator, writer; b. Palo Alto, Calif. d. William McKinley and Louise Sophia (van Druten) Hiesey; m. Heinz R. Pagels, June 7, 1969 (dec. July 1988); children: Sarah Marie, David van Druten. BA, Stanford U., 1964, MA, 1965; PhD, Harvard U., 1970. Asst. prof. history religion Barnard Coll., Columbia, 1970—74, from assoc. prof. to prof., chair dept. religion, 1974—82; Harrington Spear Paine prof. religion Princeton U., 1982—. Author: The Johannine Gospel in Gnostic Exegesis, 1973, The Gnostic Paul, 1975, The Gnostic Gospels, 1979 (Nat. Book award and Nat. Book Critics Cir. award), Adam, Eve and The Serpent, 1988, Beyond Belief: The Secret Gospel of Thomas, 2003, Reading Judas: The Gospel of Judas and the Shaping of Christianity, 2007. Grantee, NEH, 1973; Mellon fellow, Aspen Inst. Humanistic Studies, 1974, Hazen fellow, 1975, Rockefeller fellow, 1978—79, Guggenheim fellow, 1979—80, MacArthur prize fellow, 1981—87. Mem.: Am. Acad. Religion., Soc. Bibl. Lit., Bibl. Theologians Club. Episcopalian.

PAGES-RANGEL, ROXANA, language educator; b. San Juan, Aug. 8, 1961; d. Fernando A. Pages-Morales and Rosario L. Rangel-Fernandez Paniagua; m. Luis I. Fernandez-Cifuentes, July 10, 1995; children: Diego L. Fernandez-Pages, Camila E. Fernandez-Pages. PhD, Harvard U., Cambridge, Mass., 1994. Assoc. prof. Bentley U., Waltham, Mass., 1993—. Author: (book) Del dominio público: itinerarios de la carta privada, 1997. Office: Bentley Univ Forest St Waltham MA 02154

PAGET, JOEL HATHAWAY, lawyer; b. Seattle, Mar. 21, 1945; s. John Bucher and Ruth (Hathaway) P.; children: Dene' Marie, Jeremy Hathaway. BA, Seattle Pacific U., 1967; JD, U. Wash., 1970. Bar: Wash. 1970, U.S. Dist. Ct. (we. dist.) Wash. 1971, U.S. Ct. Appeals (9th cir.) 1971, U.S. Supreme Ct. 1973, U.S. Tax Ct. 1972. Law clk. Wash. Ct. Appeals, Seattle, 1970-71; ptnr. Ryan, Swanson & Cleveland PLLC, Seattle, 1971—. Lectr. bus. law Seattle Pacific U., 1972-81. Contbr. articles to profl. jours. Trustee Seattle Pacific U., 1972-2005, mem. alumni exec. bd., 1969—; sec.-treas. Christian Legal Soc. Puget Sound, Seattle, 1969-90; chmn. Seattle-King County Drug Commn., 1972-78; dir. Seattle Pacific Found., 1979—; bd. dirs. Seattle Pacific Credit Union, 1975-79; mem. Adv. Com. for Drug Abuse, Seattle, 1976-79; bd. dirs. Sammamish Bible Camp Assn., Seattle, 1974-77. Mem. Wash. State Bar Assn. (chmn. sect. taxation 1986-87, mem. bd. bar examiners 1982-84), Am. Immigration Lawyers Assn. (chmn. Wash. chpt. 1984-85, mem. bd. govs. 1984-85), Harbor Club. Republican. Avocations: golf, swimming. Office: Ryan Swanson & Cleveland PLLC 1201 3rd Ave Ste 3400 Seattle WA 98101-3034 Home: 2600 Second Ave Seattle WA 98121 Office Phone: 206-464-4224. Business E-Mail: paget@ryanlaw.com.

PAGET, JOHN ARTHUR, mechanical engineer; b. Ft, Frances, Ont., Can., Sept. 15, 1922; s. John and Ethel (Bishop) Paget; m. Vicenta Herrera Nunez, Dec. 16, 1963 (dec. Sept. 2004); children: Cynthia Ellen, Kevin Arthur, Keith William. B in Applied Sci., Toronto, 1946. Chief draftsman Gutta Percha & Rubber, Ltd., Toronto, Ont., 1946—49, Viceroy Mfg. Co., Toronto, 1949—52; supr., design engr. C.D. Howe Co. Ltd., Montreal, Que., Canada, 1952—58; sr. staff engr. Gen. Atomic, Inc., La Jolla, Calif., 1959—81; ret., 1981. Mem.: Brit. Nuc. Energy Soc., Inst. Mech. Engrs., Soc. History Tech., ASME. Achievements include patents in field. Home: 3183 Magellan St San Diego CA 92154-1515 Home Phone: 619-423-6723.

PAGLIA, CAMILLE, writer, humanities educator; b. Endicott, NY, 1947; d. Pasquale John and Lydia (Colapietro) P. BA in English summa cum laude with highest honors, SUNY, Binghamton, 1968; MPhil, Yale U., 1971, PhD in English, 1974. Mem. faculty Bennington (Vt.) Coll., 1972-80; vis. lectr. Wesleyan U., 1980, Yale U., New Haven, 1980-84; asst. prof. humanities Phila. Coll. Performing Arts U. Arts, 1984—86, assoc. prof. humanities, 1987—91, prof. humanities, 1991—2000; Univ. prof. humanities and media studies U. Arts, Phila., 2000—. Spkr. in field. Author: Sexual Personae: Art and Decadence from Nefertiti to Emily Dickinson, 1990, Sex, Art, and American Culture, 1992, Vamps and Tramps: New Essays, 1994, Alfred Hitchcock's "The Birds", 1998, Break, Blow, Burn: Camille Paglia Reads Forty-Three of the World's Best Poems, 2005; columnist: Salon.com, 1995—2001, 2007—; contbg. editor: Interview Magazine, 2001—. Mailing: Univ of the Arts 320 S Broad St Philadelphia PA 19102-4994 Office Phone: 215-717-6265.

PAGLIARO, HAROLD EMIL, language educator; b. NYC, June 19, 1925; s. Harry E. and Linda (Ricci) P.; m. Judith Marie Egan, Sept. 16, 1966; children: Blake, Robert, Susanna, John. AB, Columbia U., 1947, MA, 1948, PhD, 1961. Instr. English, Columbia U., NYC, 1956-60, asst. prof., 1961-63, faculty fellow, 1962, dir. honors sch. gen. studies, 1962-64; asst. prof. Swarthmore (Pa.) Coll., 1964-65, asso. prof., 1966-69, prof., 1970—, Alexander Griswold Cummins prof. English lit., 1982—, chmn. dept. English lit., 1970-74, 86-91, provost, 1974-79, Alexander Griswold Cummins prof. emeritus English, provost emeritus, 1992—; mem. sr. common room St. Edmund Hall, Oxford (Eng.) U., 1973-74, 79-80; assoc. Columbia U. Seminar 18th Century European Culture, 1982—, Harold E. Pagliaro Scholarship Fund, Columbia U., 1963; sr. rsch. scholar Swarthmore Coll., 2003—. Author: Selfhood and Redemption in Blakes's "Songs", 1987, Naked Heart: A Soldier's Journey to the Front, 1996, Henry Fielding: A Literary Life, 1997, Relations Between the Sexes in the Plays of George Bernard Shaw, 2004; editor: Fielding's Journal of a Voyage to Lisbon, 1963, Major English Writers of the Eighteenth Century, 1969, Studies in Eighteenth Century Culture, Vol. 2, 1972, Vol. 3, 1973, Vol. 4, 1974; contbr. articles to profl. jours. Mem. coll. evaluation bd. Middle States Assn., 1966—. Served with AUS, 1943-45. Decorated Purple Heart, Combat Infantryman badge, Bronze Star; NEH sr. fellow, 1983-84; George Becker fellow, 1988-89. Mem. MLA, Am. Soc. for Eighteenth-Century Studies (editor Proc. 1971-75), Am. Soc. Eighteenth-Century Studies (mem. publs. com. 1974-76) Home: 536 Ogden Ave Swarthmore PA 19081-1129 Office: Swarthmore Coll Dept English Literature 500 College Ave Swarthmore PA 19081 Office Phone: 610-328-8085. Business E-Mail: hpaglia1@swarthmore.edu.

PAGLIARO, JAMES DOMENIC, lawyer; b. Phila., Aug. 18, 1951; s. Domenic A. and Nancy I. (D'Amore) P.; m. Susan B. Boag, Aug. 25, 1973; children: Jamie C., Justin A. BA cum laude, LaSalle U., 1973; JD, Dickinson Law Sch., 1976. Bar: Pa. 1976, U.S. Dist. Ct. (ea. dist.) Pa. 1977, U.S. Ct. Appeals (3d, 4th, 8th, 9th and 10th cirs.) 1989, U.S. Supreme Ct. 1989. Regional atty. Gov. of Pa., Phila., 1976-79; sr. trial atty. office regional solicitor U.S. Dept. Labor, Phila., 1979-85; assoc. Morgan, Lewis & Bockius, LLP, Phila., 1985-88, ptnr. litigation, 1988—, mng. ptnr. litigation sect., 1999—2009, Morgan & Ptnr. Client Rels., 2009—. Chmn. Home & Sch. Bd. Norwood Acad., Chestnut Hill, Pa., 1983-87; guide, Phila. Mus. Art, 2003-. Fellow Am. Coll. Trial Lawyers; mem. ABA, Pa. Bar Assn. (speaker continuing legal edn. 1987—), Phila. Bar Assn., Woolsach Honors Soc. Office: Morgan Lewis & Bockius LLP 1701 Market St Philadelphia PA 19103-2903 Home Phone: 215-517-6747; Office Phone: 215-963-5668. Business E-Mail: jpagliaro@morganlewis.com.

PAGNANI, MICHAEL JOSEPH, orthopaedic surgeon; b. Endicott, NY, Apr. 23, 1961; s. Bruno and Patricia Ann Connors P.; m. Kelly Jackson, May 14, 1988; children: Sarah, Connor. MD, Vanderbilt U., 1987. Diplomate Am. Bd. Orthopaedic Surgery. Intern Baylor U., Dallas, 1987-88; resident in orthop. surgery The Hosp. for Spl. Surgery-Cornell U., NYC, 1988-92, fellow in sports medicine, 1992-93; pvt. practice The Lipscomb Clinic, Nashville, 1993, Nashville Knee & Shoulder, Nashville; attending orthop. surgeon Centennial Med. Ctr., Nashville, 1993—, St. Thomas Hosp., Nashville, 1993—; clin. asst. prof., orthop., rehabilitation Vanderbilt U., Nashville, 1993—. Bd. dir. Nashville Sports Coun., 1997-2002; asst. orthop. cons. St. John's U., 1992-93; orthop. cons. Tenn. Technological U., 1993-94, Nashville Xpress Baseball Team, 1994, Chgo. White Sox Baseball Orgn., 1995-97, Pitts. Pirates Baseball Orgn., 1998-2003, Miami Dolphins, 2001-; team physician NY Pub. Sch. Athletic League, 1988-92, numerous Nashville area high schools, 1993-, Elite Runner, Country Music Marathon, 2000-2003; orthop. team physician, Nashville Sounds Baseball team, 1994-2003; asst. team physician, NY Giants Football team, 1992-93, NY Mets, 1992-93; med. cons. Ohio Valley Conf. Basketball Tournament, 1994-2000, NCAA Sectional Basketball Tournament, 2000; med. staff mem. US Open Tennis Championships, 1989-92; US Figure Skating Championships, 1997; head team physician, Nashville Kats arena football team, 1997-2002, Tenn. State Univ., 1993-, Nashville Predators Hockey team, 1998-. Cons. Am. Journal of Sports Medicine, Journal of Bone and Joint Surgery. Named Tenn. Sports Medicine Person of Yr., Tenn. Athletic Trainers' Soc., 2004. Fellow, Am. Acad. Orthop. Surgeons, mem. Am. Orthop. Soc. Sports Medicine (rsch. com., 1997-), Nat. Hockey League Team Physicians' Soc., Arthroscopy Assn. N. Am., Nashville Acad. Medicine, Tenn. Med. Assn., Am. Shoulder and Elbow Surgeons. Office: Nashville Knee And Shoulder Center Pllc 345 23rd Ave N Ste 301 Nashville TN 37203-1513 Office Phone: 615-329-2520. Office Fax: 615-329-3530.

PAGNI, ALBERT FRANK, lawyer; b. Reno, Jan. 28, 1935; s. Bruno and Daisy Rose (Recami) Pagni; m. Nancy Lynne Thomas, Aug. 12, 1961; children: Elisa, Michelle, Melissa, Michael. AB, U. Nev., 1961; JD, U. Calif., 1964. Bar: Nev. 1964. Assoc. Vargas, Dillon, Bartlett & Dixon, Reno, 1965—70; ptnr. Vargas & Bartlett and Jones Vargas, Reno, 1970—. Adv. bd. 9th Cir. Ct., 2001—, chmn. adv. bd., 2006—07; ct.-apptd. arbitrator; dist. ct. judge pro tem. Mem. Nev. Dist. Appeal Bd.; mem. hospice coun. St. Mary's Hosp.; mem. adminstrv. coun. U. Nev., 1974—81; treas. U. Nev. Legis. Commn., 1973—74, pres., 1975; bd. dirs. Better Bus. Bur. With US Army, 1955—57. Recipient Outstanding Alumni award, U. Nev., 1978; named Mountain States Super Lawyer; named one of Best Lawyers in Am. Master: Am. Inns Ct.; fellow: Am. Bd. Trial Advocates (mem. nat. bd. 1991—2007), Nev. Law Found. (trustee, vice chair), Am. Coll. Barristers, Am. Coll. Trial Lawyers (state chair); mem.: ATLA, ABA, State Bar Nev. (bd. govs. 1976—87, v.p. 1984—85, pres.-elect 1985—86, pres. 1986—87, mediator, arbitrator 1990), Am. Judicature Assn., Assn. Def. Counsel Calif. and Nev. (state chmn. 1983—85), Def. Rsch. Inst., Nev. Trial Lawyers Assn., Washoe County Bar Assn., Am. Softball Found. (bd. dirs.), Wolf Club, Order of the Coif. Office: 12th Fl 100 W Liberty St Fl 12 Reno NV 89501-1962 Office Phone: 775-786-5000.

PAGNI, PATRICK JOHN, mechanical engineering science educator, safety engineer, researcher; b. Chgo., Nov. 28, 1942; s. Frank and Helen P.; m. Carol DeSantis, Dec. 26, 1970 (div. Jan. 2000); children: Christina Marie, Catherine Ann, Patrick John Jr; m. Feriel Palmer, Mar. 21, 2003. B in Aeronautical Engring. magna cum laude, U. Detroit, 1965; SM, MIT, 1967, ME, 1969, PhD, 1970. Registered profl. mechanical engr., Calif., fire protection engr., Calif. Rsch. asst. MIT, Cambridge, 1965-70; asst. prof. dept. mech. engring. U. Calif., Berkeley, 1970-76, assoc. prof., 1976-81, prof., 1981—2003, prof. emeritus, 2003—, vice chmn. grad. study, 1986-89; acting assoc. dean Coll. Engring. U. Calif., 1990; assoc. faculty scientist Lawrence Berkeley Lab., 1976—. Vis. scientist Factory Mut. Research Corp., Norwood, Mass., 1980; cons. on fire safety sci. various orgns., 1972—; affiliate prof. fire protection engring. dept. Worcester Poly. Inst., 2000-03; vis. rsch. scholar U. Ulster, No. Ireland, 2000-03. Editor: Fire Science for Fire Safety, 1984, Fire Safety Science--Procs. of the First Internat. Symposium, 1986, Procs. of the Second Internat. Symposium, 1989; contbr. articles to profl. jours. Grantee NSF, NASA, Nat. Bur. Standards, Nat. Inst. Standards and Tech., U.S. Forest Svc., 1971—; Applied Mechanics fellow Harvard U., 1974, 77; Pullman Found. scholar, 1960. Mem. ASME (life), Am. Phys. Soc. (life), Combustion Inst., Soc. Fire Protection Engrs. (hon., Bono award for best paper 1999), Internat. Assn. Fire Safety Sci. (life mem., exec. com.), Tau Beta Pi, Pi Tau Sigma, Alpha Sigma Nu Democrat. Roman Catholic. Home: 1901 Ascot Dr Moraga CA 94556-1412 Office: U Calif Coll Engring Mech Engring Dept Berkeley CA 94720-1740 Office Phone: 925-376-4288. Business E-Mail: pjpagni@me.berkeley.edu.

PAGON, ROBERTA ANDERSON, pediatrician, educator; b. Boston, Oct. 4, 1945; d. Donald Grigg and Erna Louise (Goettsch) Anderson; m. Garrett Dunn Pagon Jr., July 1, 1967; children: Katharine Blye, Garrett Dunn III, Alyssa Grigg, Alexander Goettsch. BA, Stanford U., 1967; MD, Harvard U., 1972. Diplomate Am. Bd. Pediat., Am. Bd. Med. Genetics. Pediatric intern U. Wash. Affiliated Hosp., Seattle, 1972-73, resident in pediat., 1973-75; fellow in med. genetics U. Wash. Sch. Medicine, Seattle, 1976-79, asst. prof. pediat., 1979-84, assoc. prof., 1984-92, prof., 1992—. Prin. investigator, editor in chief GeneTests (www.genetests.org), Seattle, 1992—; pres. Am. Bd. Med. Genetics, 2002, 03; bd. sci. counselors Nat. Human Genome Rsch. Inst., NIH, 2000—04. Sponsor N.W. region U.S. Pony Club, 1985-94. Mem. Am. Soc. Human Genetics (bd. dirs. 2005-2007, Excellence award in Edn. 2006), March of Dimes (Col. Harland Sanders Lifetime Achievement award 2009), Am. Coll. Med. Genetics, Western Soc. Pediat. Rsch., Phi Beta Kappa. Avocations: hiking, backpacking, horseback riding. Office: Gene Tests 9725 Third Ave NE Ste 602 Seattle WA 98115 Office Phone: 206-221-4674. Business E-Mail: bpagon@u.washington.edu.

PAGONIS, WILLIAM GUS, retired army general; b. Charleroi, Pa., Apr. 30, 1941; s. Constantinos V. and Jennie (Kontos) P.; m. Cheryl Elaine Miller, June 14, 1964; children: Gust, Robert. BS, Pa. State U., 1964, MBA in Bus. Logistics, 1970; D in Pub. Svc. (hon.), Washington Jefferson Coll., 1997. Commd. 2d lt. U.S. Army, 1964, advanced through grades to lt. gen., 1991; comdr. 1097th Transp. Co., Vietnam, 1968; div. transp. officer, then exec. officer 2d bn., 501st inf., 101st Airborne Div., Vietnam, 1970-71; pers. staff officer U.S. Army Mil. Pers. Ctr., Alexandria, Va., 1973-75; staff officer Office Chief of Legis. Liaison, Washington, 1975-76; comdr. 10th transp. bn. 7th Transp. Group, Ft. Eustis, Va., 1977-78; chief of staff 193d Inf. Brigade, Panama, 1980-81, comdr. Logistics Support Command, 1981-82; comdr. Div. Support Command, 4th Inf. Div., Ft. Carson, Colo., 1982-85; dir. transp., energy and troop support Office Dep. Chief of Staff for Logistics, Washington, 1989-90; comdg. gen. 22d Support Command, Dhahran, Saudi Arabia, 1990-91, 1990-92, 21st Support Command Europe, Germany, 1992-93; lt. gen., ret. U.S. Army, 1993; exec. v.p. logistics Sears & Roebuck Co., Hoffman Estates, Ill., 1993—. Author: Moving Mountains (Logistics Leadership and Management of the Gulf War), (one of top 30 best bus. books of 1992, top leadership book 1992 Soundview Exec. Book Summaries, 1992), 1992. Decorated D.S.M., Silver Star, Legion of Merit with oak leaf cluster, Bronze Star with 3 oak leaf clusters, Air medal with 2 oak leaf clusters, Meritorious Svc. medal with 4 oak leaf clusters, King Abdul Aziz 2d Class award Chief of Staff, Saudi Arabian Army, 1991, Kuwait Liberation medal Chief of Staff, Kuwait Army, 1992; recipient Merit and Honor award Govt. of Greece, 1991, Joseph C. Scheleen award Am. Soc. Transp. and Logistics, 1991, Man of Yr. award Modern Materials Handling, 1991, Grad. Man of Yr. award Alpha Chi Rho, 1991, AHEPA Man of Yr., 1992, Disting. Alumni award Pa. State U., 1994; named Hellenic Man of Yr., 1992; Pa. State U. fellow, 1992. Home: 202 Smalstig Rd Evans City PA 16033 Office: C&G Ranch LLC 202 Smalstig Rd Evans City PA 16033 Office Phone: 724-789-7680. Business E-Mail: pagonisg@genco.com.

PAGTER, CARL RICHARD, lawyer; b. Balt., Feb. 13, 1934; s. Charles Ralph and Mina (Amelung) P.; m. Judith Elaine Cox, May 6, 1978; 1 child by previous marriage: Corbin Christopher. AA, Diablo Valley Coll., 1953; BA, San Jose State U., 1955; LLB, U. Calif., Berkeley, 1964. Bar: Calif. 1965, D.C. 1977, U.S. Supreme Ct. 1976. Law clk. Kaiser Industries Corp., Oakland, Calif., 1963-64, counsel, 1964-70, assoc. counsel Washington, 1970-73, counsel Oakland, Calif., 1973-75, dir. govt. affairs Washington, 1975-76; v.p., sec., gen. counsel Kaiser Cement Corp., Oakland, Calif., 1976-88, cons., gen. counsel San Ramon, 1988-98, cons., 1998—. Author: (with A. Dundes) Urban Folklore from the Paperwork Empire, 1975, More Urban Folklore from the Paperwork Empire, 1987, Never Try to Teach a Pig to Sing, 1991, Sometimes the Dragon Wins, 1996, Why Don't Sheep Shrink When It Rains, 2000. Trustee Internat. Bluegrass Music Mus., Owensboro, Ky.; bd. mem., treasurer Bluegrass Music Found., Nashville. With USNR, 1957—61, to comdr. USNR, 1978. Mem. Calif. Bar, Am. Folklore Soc., Calif. Folklore Soc., Calif. Bluegrass Assn. (founder, chmn. bd. emeritus), Mariners Square Athletic Club. Republican. Home and Office: 17 Julianne Ct Walnut Creek CA 94595-2610

PAHL, JON F., religious studies educator; children: Justin Lucas, Nathan John, Rheanne Marie. PhD, U. Chgo., 1990. Assoc. prof. theology Valparaiso U., Ind., 1988—2000; prof. history Christianity Northern Am. Luth. Theol. Sem., Phila., 2000—; vis. prof. religion Temple U., Phila., 2004—, Princeton U., NJ, 2006—08. Actor: (film) Malls 'R' Us; contbr. to monographs. Dir. Luth. Settlement House, Phila., 2005—. Lutheran. Avocations: saxophone, sports. Home: 713 Pine Ridge Rd Media PA 19063 Office: Lutheran Theological Sem 7301 Germantown Ave Phila PA 19119-1794 Home Fax: 610-627-5877. Business E-Mail: jpahl@ltsp.edu.

PAHL SCHUETTE, ELFRIEDE, pediatric transplant cardiologist; d. Adam and Rosalia Pahl; m. Michael Allen Schuette, Sept. 9, 1989. MD, Northwestern U. Med. Sch., Chgo., 1983. Diplomate in pediat. cardiology Am. Bd. Pediat., 1988. Med. dir., heart transplantation Children's Meml. Hosp., Chgo., 1994—; prof. pediat. Feinberg Northwestern Sch. Medicine, Chgo., 2001—. Contbr. articles to med. jours. Fellow: Am. Acad. Pediat., Am. Coll. Cardiology; mem.: Internat. Soc. Heart and Lung Transplantation, Am. Transplant Soc., Am. Heart Assn., Pediatric Heart Transplant Study (sec. 2008—, treas. 2008—). Avocations: piano, travel, bicycling. Office: Children's Memorial Hosp 2300 Children's Pl Chicago IL 60614

PAHUJA, MADHURI (PAHUJAA), scientist, educator; d. Ved Prakash and Sneh Lata Pahuja. BS in Pharmacology, Stony Brook U., NY, 2005; MS in Cell & Moecular Medicine, U. Medicine & Dentistry NJ, Stratford, 2007. Rsch. scientist Cancer Inst. NJ, New Brunswick; prof. Middlesex County Coll., Edison, NJ, Raritan Valley CC, North Branch, NJ; rsch. scientist Johnson & Johnson, Skillman, NJ, NJ Inst. Successful Aging; rsch. tchg. specialist, cancer rsch. study U. Medicine & Dentistry NJ; clin. rsch. extern Stony Brook U. V.p., mentor Prospective Physicians Assn., Stratford; mentor, rep., pres. Pharmacology Soc., Stony Brook; editor & writer Undergrad. Pharmacology Newsletter, Stony Brook; writer The Statesman, Stony Brook; sec. Premed Soc., Stony Brook, Club OM, Stony Brook. Contbr. scientific papers to profl. publs. Recipient PRIDE award, Stony Brook U.; fellowship. Home Phone: 551-206-5665. Personal E-mail: madhuripahujaa@gmail.com.

PAI, BALAKRISHNA S., research scientist; s. Satchithananda V. and Padmavathy S. Pai; m. Rekha Prabhu, Apr. 22, 1984; 1 child, Rohith B. BS in Zoology, Kerala U., 1971, MS in Zoology, 1973; PhD, Indian Inst. Sci., 1979. Rsch. scientist Yale U. Sch. Medicine, New Haven, 1992—97; sr. rsch. scientist Vets. Affairs Med. Ctr., Decatur, Ga., 1998—2004; cons., advisor Internat. Program on Molecular Markers and Anticancer Drug Study, 2004. Panelist, faculty, invitee citizen amb. program Indo-US Tech Transfer, Kidwai Meml. Inst. of Oncology, Bangalore, Karnataka, India, 1985—88; adj. faculty Mercer U., Atlanta, 2006—; vis. scientist, affiliate Georgia Inst. Tech., Atlanta, 2008—. Contbr. over 40 articles to profl. jours. Vol. Conn. Food Bank, New Haven Schools Fund, Salvation Army, New Haven, Atlanta, 1992—2005, United Way. Recipient 1st prize in English Essay competition, Maharaja's Coll., India, 1970, Sealy Meml. award (B.S.), Bhaskaran Nair Gold medal, Dr. N.G. Kurup Meml. gold medal (M.S), Kreala U., India, 1971-1973, U. Union Gold medal for securing 1st rank in M.S, Kerala U., India, 1973, Invitation to study cancers in China and USSR, People to People Internat., 1986-1987; grantee, NIH, 1999—2001; fellow, 1979—83; scholar UGC Jr. Rschr., CSIR Sr. rschr. and ICMR (supernumerary cadre), UGC, CSIR and ICMR, 1977, 1978 and 1986, Kerala U., 1971—73. Mem.: Am. Assn. Pharm. Scientists, Am. Assn. for Cancer Rsch. (active mem. 1985—2005). Achievements include patents for clevudine, a breakthrough drug for HBV, in phase III clinical trials in the US and approved for clinical use by the Korean Food and Drug Administration; sterol-modified oligonucleotide duplexes having anti-cancer activity; L-nucleosides for the treatment of Epstein- Barr virus; L-nucleosides with various applications; hydoxymethyl modified nucleosides for anti-HBV therapy. Personal E-mail: pairb2000@yahoo.com.

PAI, KALPANA, economics professor; PhD, U. Tex., Dallas, 2004. Asst. prof. econs. & fin. Tex. Wesleyan U., Ft. Worth, 2005—. Office: Texas Wesleyan Univ 1201 Wesleyan St Fort Worth TX 76105

PAI, SATISH UPENDRA, publishing executive; b. Udupi, Karnataka, India, Nov. 26, 1941; s. Upendra Anantha and Parvathi Pai; m. Sandhya Satish, July 19, 1970; children: Nandana, Gautham. Dir. Manipal Press Ltd., 1960—; mng. dir. Manipal Media Network Ltd., 1989—. Editor Udayavani Daily, 1970, Tushara Mo., 1973, Roopathra Mo., 1976, Taranga Weekly, 1983. Mem. Graphic Arts Tech. Found., IFRA, Fellow Inst. Printing. Avocations: stamp collecting/philately, photography, travel. Home: 38 Anant Nagar Manipal 576104 India Office: Manipal Media Network Ltd Udayavani Bld, Press Corner Manipal 576104 India Business E-Mail: satishpai@manipalmedia.com.

PAIDOUSSIS, MICHAEL PANDELI, mechanical engineering educator; b. Nicosia, Cyprus, Aug. 20, 1935; emigrated to Can., 1953, naturalized, 1976; s. Pandelis Aristeidis and Parthenope (Leptou) P. B in Engring., McGill U., 1958; PhD in Engring., U. Cambridge, 1963. Overseas fellow Gen. Electric Co., Erith, Kent, England, 1958-60; rsch. officer Atomic Energy of Can., Chalk River, Ont., 1963-67; with McGill U., Montreal, 1967—, prof., dept. mech. engring., 1976—, chmn., 1977-86, Thomas Workman prof., 1986—2000, Thomas Workman emeritus prof., 2000—. Cons. and rschr. in field. Author: 2 books; editor: Jour. Fluids and Structures; contbr. articles and books in field. Pres. Hellenic-Can. Solidarity Com. for Cyprus, 1974-80, Com. Pan-Can. de Solidarite pour Chypre, 1978-83; hon. consul gen. Republic of Cyprus, Montreal, 1983—. Recipient Brit. Assn. medal for high distinction in mech. engring., 1958, George Stephenson prize Inst. Mech. Engrs., 1976, commemorative medal for 125th ann. of Confederation of Can., 1993, medal Can. Congress Applied Mechs., 1995. Fellow Instn. Mech. Engrs., ASME (Fluids Engring. award 1999), Can. Soc. Mech. Engring., Royal Soc. Can., Am. Acad. Mechanics, Can. Acad. Engring., Am. Acad. Mechanics (pres. 2005); mem. Internat. Assn. Hydraulic Rsch., Internat. Assn. Structural Mechanics in Reactor Tech., Order Engrs. Que. Home: 2930 Edouard Montpetit #PH2 Montreal PQ Canada H3T 1J7 Office: 817 Ouest Rue Sherbrooke Montreal PQ Canada H3A 2K6 Home Phone: 514-735-7233; Office Phone: 514-398-6294. Business E-Mail: mary.fiorilli@mcgill.ca.

PAIER, ADOLF ARTHUR, management consultant; b. Branford, Conn., Oct. 27, 1938; s. Adolf Arthur and Margaret Mary (Almond) P.; m. Geraldine Shnakis, Sept. 17, 1966; children: Nathaniel Jason, Andrew Joseph, Alena Catherine. AA, Quinnipiac Coll., 1958; BS in Econs., U. Pa., 1960. Audit mgr. Touche Ross & Co., Phila., 1960-67; pres., dir. Safeguard Scientifics, Inc., Wayne, Pa., 1967-92; chmn., CEO Healthworks Alliance, Inc., King of Prussia, Pa., 1992—2005; pres., CEO Novus Corp., Radnor, Pa., 1992—. Bd. dirs. Deltapaper, Levittown, Pa., Analytical Graphics, Exton, Pa., Probaris Techs., Inc., Phila. Bd. dirs., treas. Univ. of Arts, Phila. bd. dirs. Lincoln Ctr. Family and Youth, Audubon, Pa. Mem. World Pres. Orgn., Phila. Country Club (bd. govs.). Office: Novus Corp 5 Radnor Corp Ctr 100 Matsonford Rd Ste 520 Radnor PA 19087-4526

PAIGE, DAVID MARTIN, pediatrician, educator; m. Nancy Ellen Kramer, Aug. 27, 1959; children: Tara Rachel, Daniel Frederick. MD, NYU, 1964; MPhil, Johns Hopkins U., Balt., 1969. Prof. Johns Hopkins U., 1969—. Cons. multiple, various cities, Md., Govt., NGO. Editor: (textbook) Clinical Nutrition, Manual Of Clinical Nutrition. Supporter Pub. Justice Ctr., Balt., 1998; bd. mem. Everyman Theater, Balt.; exec. com. mem. Balt. Opera Co., 2003—08; award com. Mar. Dimes, NY; supporter Easter Seals, Silver Spring, DC. Recipient Pediat. And Maternal And Child Health award, NY Med. Coll., 1994, Sampson Green Hunger award, Md. Food Com., 1990, Agnes Higgins award, Mar. Dimes, 1996, 1997, Leadership award, Nat. Assn. Wic Dirs., 1997, Child Advocacy award, Am. Acad. Pediat., Md., 2008, Wic Program Devel. award, State Md., 2007, Pub. Health Program award, Morgan State U., 2004; named Pub. Health Hero, State Md., 1998; grant, HHS, USDA, Md., MCHS, NIH Found. Achievements include research in determinants of breastfeeding. Avocation: skiing. Office: Johns Hopkins Univ 615 N Wolfe St Baltimore MD 21205 Business E-Mail: dpaige@jhsph.edu.

PAIGE, DOROTHY BILLIARD, consultant-academic coach; d. Webb Billiard and Doretha Billiard-Johnson; 1 child, Rochelle Denise Paige-Jones. AA in Polit. Sci., LA Harbor Jr. Coll., Wilmington, Calif., 1978; BA in Polit. Sci., Calif. State U. Dominguez Hills, Carson, 1979, MA in Pub. Adminstrn., 1981. Tchr. Calif. Commn. on Tchg., 1982, cert. Bilingual Edn. Calif. Commn. on Tchg., 2002. History tchr. Compton Unified Sch. Dist., Calif., 1979—2002, resource tchr., program coord., 2002—05; edn. cons. Paige-Schwartz & Assoc., Inc., Carson, Calif., 2005—07; cons.-academic coach CUSD, 2007—08. Prof. staff devel. workshop presenter Sigma Gamma Rho Sorority, 2007. Christian edn. dir., fin. dir. Mt. Pilgrim Missionary Bapt. Ch., Compton, 1987—95. Recipient Woman of Yr. award Compton br., Nat. Assn. U. Women, 2007. Mem.: Compton Edn. Assn. (CTA pres. 1982—, segment dir. mid. sch. 1997—99). Democrat. Baptist. Avocations: reading, surfing the net, travel. Home: 21621 Villa Pacifica Cir Carson CA 90745 Office: Paige-Schwartz & Assoc Inc 21621 Villa Pacifica Cir Carson CA 90745 Office Phone: 310-427-0279; Home Fax: 310-427-0279. Personal E-mail: dotpaige47@aol.com.

PAIGE, GLENN DURLAND, political scientist, educator; b. Brockton, Mass., June 28, 1929; s. Lester Norman and Rita Irene (Marshall) P.; m. Betty Gail Grenier, Jan. 2, 1949 (div.); children: Gail, Jan, Donn, Sean, Sharon, Van; m. Glenda Hatsuko Naito, Sept. 1, 1973. Grad., Phillips Exeter Acad., 1947; AB, Princeton U., 1955; MA, Harvard U., 1957; Ph. D., Northwestern U., 1959; PhD (hon.), Soka U., 1992. Asst. prof. pub. adminstrn. Seoul Nat. U., 1959-61; asst. to assoc. prof. politics Princeton U., 1961-67; prof. polit. sci. U. Hawaii, Honolulu, 1967-92, prof. emeritus, 1992—. Author: The Korean Decision, 1968, The Scientific Study of Political Leadership, 1977, To Nonviolent Political Science, 1993, Nonkilling Global Political Science, 2002. Program chmn. Hawaii Gov.'s Conf. on Yr. 2000, 1970; faculty UN Univ. Internat. Leadership Acad., 1997; pres. Non-profit Ctr. for Global Nonviolence, 1994—2008; convenor First Global Nonkilling Leadership Forum, 2007. With U.S. Army, 1948-52, chair governing coun. Ctr. Global Nonkilling, 2009. Decorated Commendation medal; recipient Seikyo Culture prize, 1982, Dr. G. Ramachandran award for internat. understanding, 1986, Anuvrat award for internat. peace, 1987, Jai Tulsi Anuvrat award, 1995, Hawaii Lifetime Peacemaker award Ch. of the Crossroads, Honolulu, 2005, Peace Day award Hawaii, 2008; named Woodrow Wilson nat. fellow, 1955-56, Princeton U. Class of 1955 award, 1987, 3rd Gandhi Meml. lectr., New Delhi, 1990. Mem. Internat. Polit. Sci. Assn., Am. Polit. Sci. Assn. (Disting. Career award organized sect. ecol. and transformational politics 2004), Phi Beta Kappa. Home: 3653 Tantalus Dr Honolulu HI 96822-5033 Office Phone: 808-536-7442. E-mail: cgnv@hawaii.rr.com.

PAIGE, HILLIARD WEGNER, corporate executive, consultant; b. Hartford, Conn., Oct. 2, 1919; s. Joseph Wegner and Ruth (Hill) P.; m. Dorothea Magner, Dec. 8, 1945; children: Elizabeth, Deborah, Hilliard, Jr. BSME, Worcester Poly. Inst., 1941, D (hon.) of Engring., 1971. Sr. v.p. for aerospace and computer ops. GE, NYC, 1941—71; pres. Gen. Dynamics, St. Louis, 1971—73; CML Satellite Bus. Sys., Inc., Washington, 1973—76; vice-chmn. bd. Internat. Energy Assocs., Ltd., Washington, 1976—85; chmn. bd. H.A. Knott, Ltd., Silver Spring, Md., 1984—89. Vice-chmn. The Atlantic Coun. of U.S., 1987—, Gallager Marine Systems, Inc., 1993—. Patentee in field; contbr. articles to profl. jours. Mem. Def. Sci. Bd. U.S. Dept. Def., Washington, 1973-78; trustee Worcester Poly. Inst., Mass., 1974—. Recipient Pub. Service award NASA, 1969, Space Reconncissance Pioneer award NRO, 2008, Order of Merit Italy, 1970, Engr. of Year award Greater Phila. Engring Council, 1960 Fellow AIAA (founding dir.), Explorers Club (nat.); mem. NAE. Clubs: Metropolitan, Chevy Chase (Washington); Conquistadores del Cielo. Republican. Congregationalist. Avocations: skiing, tennis, scuba diving, golf. Home and Office: 5834 Williamsburg Landing Dr Williamsburg VA 23185 Office Phone: 757-220-8709.

PAIGE, KATHLEEN K., naval officer; b. Schenectady, NY, Aug. 31, 1948; m. David Tuma. BS, U. N.H., 1970; MS, Naval Postgrad. Sch., 1976; grad., Def. Sys. Mgmt. Coll.; grad. program for execs., Cornell U. Commd. USN, advanced through grades to rear admiral; acquisition mgr. Navy's Std. Embedded Computer Resource Office; AEGIS C3 warfare officer USN; baseline mgr. combat sys. divsn. AEGIS Shipbuilding Program; chief engr. Naval Surface Warfare Ctr., Port Hueneme; tech. dir. AEGIS Program Office; comdr. Naval Surface Warefare Ctr., Arlington, Va., 1996-98, admiral, 1998—. Decorated Legion of Merit. Office: Naval Sea Systems Command SE#1100 1333 Isaac Hull Ave Washington DC 20376-1100

PAIGE, PAUL, retired music educator; b. Boston, July 4, 1934; married; 3 children. AA, North Park U.; MM, Northwestern U.; BM, PhD, Boston U. Chmn. music dept. Ricker Coll., Cazenovia Coll., Marymount Coll.; prof. emeritus Grand Canyon U. Justice court mediator. Mem. Music Tchrs. Nat. Assn., Music Educators Nat. Conf., Coll. Music Soc., Am. Choral Dirs. Assn., Am. Guild Organists, Ariz. State Music Tchrs. Assn. (pres. 1992-95, Tchr. of Yr. 2000). Avocation: travel.

PAIGE, RODERICK RAYNOR, educational consultant, former United States Secretary of Education; b. Monticello, Miss., June 17, 1933; div., one child. BS, Jackson State U., 1955; MS, Ind. U., 1964, PhD, 1969. Head football coach Utica Jr. Coll., 1957—67, Jackson St. U., 1962—69; dean Coll. Edn. Tex. So. U., 1984—94, developer Ctr. Excellence in Urban Edn.; supt. Houston Ind. Sch. Dist., 1994—2000; sec. US Dept. Edn., Washington, 2001—05; co-founder, chmn. Chartwell Edn. Group LLC, NYC, 2005—; cons. on edn. matters News Corp., 2008—. Trustee, officer bd. edn. Houston Ind. Sch. Dist., 1989—94, pres.; active Edn. Commn. States, Coun. Great City Schs.; mem. rev. com. Tex. Edn. Agy., State Bd. Edn. Task Force on H.S. Edn.; chair youth employment issues subcom. Nat. Commn. Employment Policy US Dept. Labor; bd. dirs. News Corp., 2006—08. Co-author: A Declaration of Beliefs and Visions. Mem. NAACP; mem. adv. bd. Tex. Commerce Bank, Am. Leadership Forum. Recipient Harold W. McGraw, Jr. Prize in Edn., 2000; named Supt. of the Yr., Nat. Assn. Black Sch. Educators, 2000, Nat. Supt. Yr., Am. Assn. Sch. Adminstr., 2001. Mem. review coms. Tex. Edn. Agy., State Bd. Edn. Task Force H.S. Edn.; chair, Youth Employment Issues Nat. Com. Employment Policy U.S. Dept. Labor subcom.; mem. Nat. Assn. Advancement Colored People, Edn. Com. States, Coun. Great City Schs.(recipient Richard R. Green award for Outstanding Urban Educator, 1999). Republican. Office: Chartwell Education Group LLC Empre State Bldg Ste 7506 New York NY 10118 E-mail: paige@chartwelleducation.com.

PAIGE, VIVIAN JO-ANN, accountant; b. Memphis, May 7, 1960; d. Charles Thomas and Mary Elizabeth (Manning) P. BS, Old Dominion U., 1981, MBA, 1994. CPA, Va. With IRS, Norfolk, Va., 1980-85; pres. Individual Returns Svcs. Inc., Norfolk, 1991-95; prin. Vivian J. Paige, CPA, P.C., 1986—; adj. instr. acctg. Old Dominion U., 2000—, mem. adv. coun., dept. acctg., 2000—. Bd. dirs. St. Columba Ecumenical Ministries, Inc., 1989-93, v.p. bd. dirs., 1990-91, pres. bd. dirs., 1992-93, Neighborhood Network steering com.; mem. Real Estate Bd. Equalization, 1999-2005, sec., 1999-2001, pres., 2002-05; co-founder Norfolk United Facing Race, bd. dirs., 2001-04. With USAR, 1979-81. Mem. AICPA, NAFE, AAUW, NAACP, LWV, Urban Leauge, Va. Soc. CPAs. Avocations: music, singing, computers. Business E-Mail: vivian@vjpcpa.com.

PAIGE, WAYNE LEO, visual arts educator, artist; b. Chgo., Mar. 5, 1944; s. Henry and Lucille Mabel Paige; 1 child, Matthew. BFA in Painting, U. Ill., Champaign/Urbana, 1968; MFA in Painting, The George Washington U., Washington, DC, 1971. Lic. tchr. Va. Drafting and art tchr. Eastern HS, Washington, 1971—95; drafting instr. Md. Drafting Inst., Langley Pk., 1979—90; constrn. tech. tchr. Potomac HS, Dumfries, Va., 1995—96; visual arts instr. and chairperson Notre Dame Acad., Middleburg, Va., 1996—; adj. prof. art Lord Fairfax CC, Warrenton, Va., 2007—. Exhibited in group shows at Corcoran Gallery Art, Washington, DC, 1980, Anderson Art Gallery, Richmond, 1983, Strathmore Art Ctr., Bethesda, 1986, Danville Mus. Art, Va., 1990, Western Mich. U., Kalamazoo, 1990, Md. Coll. Art and Design, Silver Spring, 1998, Katzen Art Ctr., Washington, DC, 2006, 20 one man shows. Recipient Print and Drawing award, Va. Commn. Arts, 1989, Best in Show award, Arts Coun. Fairfax County, 1994. Mem.: Tchr. Inst. Contemporary Art, Mid. St. Gallery (Washington, Va.), Wash. Tchrs. Union. Office: Notre Dame Acad 35321 Notre Dame Ln Middleburg VA 20117 Home: 5406 Connecticut Ave NW #506 Washington DC 20015 Office Phone: 540-687-5581. Personal E-mail: paigeart@waynepaige.com.

PAIK, HO JUNG, physics professor; b. Seoul, Republic of Korea, Mar. 25, 1944; s. In Kee Paik and Young Pal Choi; m. Minja Koh Paik, Sept. 6, 1969; children: Ellen Trina Jeong, Terri Wren. BS, Seoul Nat. U., 1966; PhD, Stanford U., Calif., 1968—74. Rsch. assoc. Stanford U., 1974—78; asst. prof. physics U. Md., College Park, 1978—83, assoc. prof. physics, 1983—89, prof., 1989—. Disting. vis. scientist Jet Propulsion Lab., Pasadena, Calif., 2004—. Grantee Sloan fellowship, Sloan Found., 1981—83. Fellow: Am. Phys. Soc.; mem.: Assn. Korean Physicists Am. (pres. 2005—). Achievements include development of superconducting gravity gradiometer; research in precision tests of the laws of gravity. Office: Univ Md Dept Physics College Park MD 20742 Office Fax: 301-405-6087. Business E-Mail: hpaik@umd.edu.

PAIK, JOHN KEE, structural engineer; b. Seoul; came to U.S., 1955; s. Nam Suk and Kyong Ock (Yun) P.; m. Aine Fenoula Ievers, Feb. 20, 1970; 1 child, Brian Ievers Paik. BSCE, So. Meth. U., 1961; PhD, NYU, 1975. Lic. profl. engr. N.Y., N.J., Conn., Pa., Md., Mass., Vt., Ga., Fla., N.C. Chief engr. T.Y. Lin and Assocs., NYC, 1960-67; chief structural engr. Soros Assocs., NYC, 1967-68; sr. project engr. Stauffer Chem. Co., Dobbs Ferry, N.Y., 1975-77; prin., founder Paik and Assocs., Westchester County, N.Y., 1977—; chmn., founder The Future Home Tech. Inc., Port Jervis, N.Y., 1986—; chmn., pres. J.K.P. Constrn. Co. Inc., Mohegan Lake, N.Y., 1989—. Adj. assoc. prof. Grad. Sch. Engring. Manhattan Coll., Bronx, 1985; lectr. Grad. Sch. Engring. Polytech. U., Bklyn., 1973-85, Cooper Union, N.Y.C., 1972. Mem. ASCE, NSPE, Am. Inst. Steel Constrn., Prestressed Concrete Inst., N.Y Acad. Scis., Am. Concrete Inst., Post Tensioning Inst., Constrn. Specifications Inst., Am. Arbitration Assn. (dispute arbitrator, constrn.), So. Meth. U. Alumni Club (pres. 1964), Chi Epsilon. Republican. Methodist. Achievements include the design of over 200 million sq. feet of comml., residential, indsl. and instnl. structures including several highrise bldgs. over 40 stories in N.Y.C. and White Plains, N.Y. Personal E-mail: jpaik@tampabay.rr.com.

PAIKEDAY, THOMAS M., lexicographer, linguistic consultant; arrived in U.S., 1962, arrived in Can., 1964; m. Mary Kurien Kizhakethottam, Jan. 4, 1967; children: Anthony, Anne-Marie. LPH, Coll. of Jesuits, 1955; BA with 1st class honors, Madras Christian Coll., 1958; MA, U. Madras, 1960; postgrad, Boston Coll., 1962—63, U. Mich., 1963—64; PhD, Cosmopolitan U., 2006. Lectr. English St. Joseph's Coll., Tiruchy, Madras, India, 1958—59, Ramjas Coll., Delhi, India, 1960—61; copy editor Statesman, New Delhi, 1961—62; asst. lexicographer W.J. Gage Ltd., Toronto, Ont., Canada, 1964—66; editor Ont. Min. Edn., Toronto, 1966—67; head lexicography divsn. Holt, Rinehart & Winston, Toronto, 1967—73; chief lexicographer Lexicography, Inc., Brampton, Ont., Canada, 1973—. Cons. Collier-Macmillan Can., Toronto, 1980-81, Can. advisor Collins Publs., Glasgow, Scotland, 1981-82. Chief editor Winston Interm. Dictionary, 1969, Compact Dictionary of Canadian English, 1970, Winston Canadian Dictionary, elem. edit., 1975, New York Times Everyday Dictionary, 1982, The Penguin Canadian Dictionary, 1990, The User's Webster, 2000; author: The Native Speaker is Dead!, 1985; contbr. articles to profl. jours. Mem. Dictionary Soc. N.Am., MLA, Am. Dialect Soc., Am. Name Soc. Roman Catholic. Avocations: computer applications in lexicography, tennis, swimming. Office: Lexicography Inc 83 Sunny Meadow Blvd Brampton ON Canada L6R 1Z3 Office Phone: 905-790-7076. Personal E-mail: thomaspaikeday@yahoo.ca.

PAIN, GEORGE H., lawyer; b. Corry, Pa., Nov. 18, 1950; BA, BS cum laude, Bucknell U., 1973; JD cum laude, U. Conn., 1977; LLM, NYU, 1988. Bar: Conn. 1977, U.S. Dist. Ct. Conn. 1981, NY 1986, U.S. Dist. Ct. NY (We dist.) 1986, Ill. 1988. Assoc. Holland & Twachtman, Glastonbury, Conn., 1977—78; sr. counsel Environ. Law Inst., Washington, 1978—80; assoc. counsel Olin Chem. Group, Stamford, Conn., 1980—85; with Jaeckle, Fleischmann & Mugel, 1985—86; of counsel Olin Corp., Clayton, Mo., 1986—88, sr. counsel, 1988—91, chief counsel, 1991—94, dep. gen. counsel, 1995—96, v.p., gen. counsel, sec., 2002—. Primex Technologies, Inc., St. Petersburg, Fla., 1997—2000; v.p., gen. counsel, asst. sec. Gen. Dynamics Ordinance and Tactical Systems Inc., St. Petersburg, Fla., 2001—02. Adj. prof. law Stetson U., 2001—02. Mem. editl. adv. bd.: Environmental Law Reporter, 1982—91. Mem.: ABA, Am. Corp. Counsel Assn., Ill. State Bar Assn. Office: Olin Corp Legal Dept 190 Carondelet Plz Ste 1530 Clayton MO 63105 E-mail: ghpain@olin.com.

PAINCHAUD, PHILLIP ANDRE, metrologist; b. Somerville, Mass., Apr. 24, 1919; s. Phillip Andre Painchaud and Gertrude Marie Shanley; m. Josephine Daisy Wandschneider, Dec. 18, 1943 (dec. Feb. 1988); children: Phillip A. III, Denise Michele, Valerie Yvonne; m. Arlene Roberts Painchaud, July 12, 1992 (dec. Dec. 1999). Student, MIT and U. Ill., 1943, RI State Coll., 1938-41; BS in Engring., Pacific States U., 1947. Lic. profl. engr., Calif. Gen. supr. metrology Northrop Corp., Anaheim, Calif., 1948-65; dir. corp. stds. E-H Rsch. Labs., Oakland, Calif., 1965-70; sr. scientist Alcon Labs., Ft. Worth, 1970-71; dir. mktg. Metron Corp., Upland, Calif., 1971-72, 78-79; cons. Painchaud Cons., Brea, Calif., 1970—. Vice-chair Calif. Profl. Metrology Com., Sacramento, 1965—74; chair Gov.'s Commn. Metrology, Sacramento, 1967—68; mem. metrology adv. bd. Calif. State Poly. U., San Luis Obispo, 1970—76; chair Woodington award selection com. Meas. Sci. Conf., 2008. Columnist The Std., 1993— Mem. curriculum bd. Calif. State U.-Dominguez Hills, Carson, 1998—. With U.S. Signal Corps, 1942-45. Laureate Woodington award Meas. Sci. Conf. Inc., 1996; disting. vis. scholar Butler County C.C., 1996. Fellow Precision Measurements Assn. (co-founder 1958, exec. dir. 1980-89, life, pres. 1963-64), IEEE (life, sr. mem.); mem. Internat. Soc. Weighing and Measurements (life, sr. mem., gov. precision measurement divsn. 1997-99), Instrument Soc. Am. (life, sr. mem., dir. met. divsn. 1966-70), Am. Soc. for Quality (sr. mem., Max J. Unis award for lifetime achievement in measurement sci., measurement quality divsn. 2006), ENG Club San Francisco. Avocations: computer operations, photography. Home and Office: 1110 W Dorothy Dr Brea CA 92821-2017 Office Phone: 714-529-6604. Office Fax: 714-529-1109. E-mail: painchaud4@cs.com.

PAINE, ALAN, poet; b. Panama City, Fla., Nov. 30, 1956; s. Charles Russell and Edna Pearl (Pierce) Williams. Student, U. Nev., Las Vegas, 1978—80, Taft Coll., Calif., 1975—77. Adj. prof. S. Nev. CC, Las Vegas, 1996—99; pres. Diogenes Prodns., Las Vegas, 2000—. Prodr., dir., actor: (plays) What Happens to a Dream Deferred; author: (screenplays) Clear Skies on Tuesday, Shadow Chasers, The Love Child, What Kind of Fool, (book) Ode to Madonna and Other Poems, 1991, numerous poems; actor: (plays) Raisin in the Sun, Don't Bother Me, I can't Cope, No Place to be Somebody; (films) No Not One. Counselor S. Nev. Suicide Prevention Ctr., Las Vegas, 1992. Recipient Golden Poet award, World Poetry, Inc., 1991, 1992, cert. of spl. recognition, Watermark Press, award of merit, Verses, cert. of honor, Hidden Springs Rev., Critics Choice award, Nat. Libr. Poetry, 1996, Editors Choice award, Poetry website, 2005. Personal E-mail: alankpaine@yahoo.com.

PAINE, STEVEN L., state official, school system administrator; m. Jackie Paine; 4 children. Grad., Fairmont State Coll.; MS in Ednl. Adminstrn., W.Va. U., PhD in Ednl. Leadership. Tchr. Harrison, Upshur and Morgan Counties, W.Va.; curriculum dir.; asst. prin.; prin.; county supt. Morgan County; dep. state supt. schs. W.Va. Dept. Edn., 2003—05, state supt. schs., 2005—. Recipient Milken Family Found. Nat. Educator Award. Office: WVa Dept Edn 1900 Kanawha Blvd E Charleston WV 25305 E-mail: dvermill@access.k12.wv.us.*

PAINE, WALTER CABOT, journalist, consultant; b. Brookline, Mass., May 9, 1923; s. Richard Cushing and Ellen Eliot Paine; m. Ethel Landon Penzel, Dec. 1948 (div. Aug. 14, 1958); children: Michael, Christopher, Piera; m. Eleanor Cole Meyer, Aug. 27, 1959 (div. June 16, 1970); children: Alita, Benjamin; m. Barbara Ann Moyer, June 10, 1995. Student, St. John's Coll., Annapolis, Md., 1942—43; AB cum laude, Harvard U., 1949; postgrad., Columbia U., 1951. Cert. scuba diver, lic. capt. USCG, 1985. Assoc. editor Balt. Sunpapers, 1951—53; editor-in-chief, pub. Valley News, West Lebanon, NH, 1956—80. Pres. Keene (N.H.) Pub. Co., 1955—80; dir. Chelsea Green Pub., White River Junction, Vt., 1995—; cons. Montshire Mus. Sci., Norwich, Vt., 1990—, founder, chmn., 1974—90. Trustee U. Vt., Burlington, 1963—71. Sgt. USAF, 1943—46. Recipient Granite State award for outstanding pub. svc., N.H. State Univ. Sys., 1991. Avocations: ocean racing, marine research, music, poetry. Home: PO Box 90 213 Palmer Rd Enfield Center NH 03749 Office: Montshire Mus Sci 1 Montshire Rd Norwich VT 05055 E-mail: verve@gwi.net.

PAINE-CLEMES, BUNNY LEE, humanities educator; d. Harry Murray and Gloria Celeste Paine; m. Jack Lee Clemes, Aug. 8, 1998. BEd, U. Tex., Austin, 1967; MA, PhD, U. Houston, Tex., 1980. English & latin tchr. Aldine HS, Houston, 1967—71; tchg. fellow U. Houston, 1971—76; humanities instr. Houston CC, 1975—91; humanities tchr. Meml. Hall HS, Houston, 1975—76; adj. english instr. Various Colls., San Francisco, 1991—93; prof. liberal arts Cal State Maritime, Vallejo, Calif., 1993—. Dir. creative writing Houston CC, 1980—91, editor award-winning lit. mag., 1983—91; dir. assessment Cal State Maritime, Vallejo, Calif., 1998—2005, faculty senate chair, 1999—2001, dir. faculty devel., 2004—07. Author: (mythic story) Kirshna's Rasa dance, Parabola, (poem) In Vienna. Buffalo Press 3, Song for my Hari, (novels) A Winter's Day, Meltdown, Melana of Malagon; contbr. articles to profl. jours. & paper presentation. Commr. Vallejo Culture & Arts Commn., 1994—2001; founder & facilitator Vallejo Writers' Group, 1996—2003; pres. & sec. Vallejo Arts Found., 1998—2000; meditation group leader Ananda & Radhakrishna Fellowship, Houston, 1981—91. Recipient, Fish Award Com., 2003, Bedicheck award, Houston CC, 1988; named Disting. Woman of Yr., Soroptimists Club Vallejo, 1998. Mem.: AAUP, Calif. Faculty Assn., Inst. Noetic Scis. Liberal. Avocations: writing, reading, movies. Office: Cal State Maritime 200 Maritime Acad Dr Vallejo CA 94590 Office Fax: 707-654-1110. Business E-Mail: bclemes@csum.edu.

PAINTER, JACK TIMBERLAKE, civil engineer; b. Kincaid, W.Va., July 23, 1930; s. Troy Earl and Nannie Bell (Proffit) P. BSCE, W.Va. U., 1950, MSCE, 1955. Instr. civil engring. W.Va. U., 1950-51, 53-55; mem. faculty La. Tech U., Ruston, 1955—; prof. civil engring. La. Tech. U., 1962-92; Alumni Found. prof. La. Tech U., 1977-78; prof. emeritus La. Tech. U., 1992—. Vis. lectr. Manhattan Coll., Coll. Forestry, SUNY, Syracuse, Cornell U., U. Wis., 1954-60 Nat. pres. Circus Fans Assn. Am., 1967; lic. layreader Episcopal Ch. With USNR, 1951-52, comdr. res., 1966-90. Recipient Mech. Engring. program Outstanding Svc. award, 2008; named Man of Year Omicron Delta Kappa, 1972, Jack T. Painter Scholarship in his honor, 1998, The Jack T. Painter Professorship in Engring. in his honor, 2003, Super Computer Painter, 2008; Faculty fellow NSF, 1958—59. Fellow Nat. ASCE (life, 11 Outstanding Prof. award 1969-90), La. Tech. ASCE; mem. La. Engring. Soc. (Charles M. Kerr Pub. Rels. award 1990), Am. Soc. Engring. Edn., Tau Beta Pi (Outstanding Prof. award 1963, 68, 74, 78), Chi Epsilon (Nat. Excellent Tchg. award 1985). Address: 101 Biel Lane New Bern NC 28562

PAINTER, JANE A., medical educator; AS Data Processing, Ind. U., Ft Wayne, 1972; BS, Ind. U., Indianapolis, 1978; MHS Occupl. Therapy, U. Fla., Gainesville, 1980; EdD, NC State U., Raleigh, 1994. Cert. matter balance master trainer Portland MA, 2008. Assoc. prof. East Carolina U., Greenville, NC, 1988—; dir., occupl. therapy West Fla. Regional Hosp., Pensacola, 1980—86. Lead person fall prevention Eastern N C Fall Prevention Coalition, Greenville, 2001—08. Achievements include research in fall prevention and intervention in older adults. Home: 115 Galahad Dr Greenville NC 27858 Office: East Carolina Univ 3305 F Health Scis Bldg Greenville NC 27858 Business E-Mail: painterj@ecu.edu.

PAINTER, JOHN HOYT, engineer; b. Winfield, Kans., Mar. 27, 1934; s. John Paul and Marjorie Marietta (Slack) P.; m. Joy Lou Vaughan, June 7, 1955; children: John Mark, Paul Burton, William Vaughan, Joy Lynn. BS, U. Ill., 1961, MS, 1962; postgrad., Coll. William and Mary, 1967—69; PhD, So. Meth. U., 1972. Apollo comm. engr., tchr. astronauts Manned Spacecraft Ctr. NASA, Houston, 1962—65; sr. engr. Motorola Govt. Electronics divsn., Scottsdale, Ariz., 1965—67; rsch. engr. NASA Langley Rsch. Ctr., Hampton, Va., 1967—74; assoc. prof. elec. engring. Tex. A&M U., College Station, 1974—79, prof. elec. engring., 1979—, prof. computer sci., 1989—, prof. aerospace engring., 1999—. Pres. ALTAIR Corp. cons., College Station, 1980—; tchr. Christian eschatology seminars; adj. instr. Nat. Emergency Response and Rescue Training Ctr., 2003-. Author: The Church Visited, 2002; patentee digital signal processing and fuzzy logic. With USAF, 1953—58, Navigator. Recipient Recognition cert. NASA, 1975; GE Found. fellow, 1962. Mem.: IEEE (life). Avocation: radio operating. Office: Tex A&M U Dept Aero Engring College Station TX 77843-3141 Business E-Mail: painter@tamu.edu.

PAINTER, MATT, men's college basketball coach; b. Muncie, Ind., Aug. 27, 1970; m. Jerri Painter; children: Maggie, Brayden, Emma. BA, Purdue U., West Lafayette, Ind., 1994; MS, Ea. Ill. U., Charleston, 1998. Asst. coach Wash. & Jefferson Coll. Presidents, 1993—94, Barton Coll. Bulldogs, 1994—95, Ea. Ill. U. Panthers, 1995—98, So. Ill. U. Salukis, 1998—2003, head basketball coach, 2003—04; assoc. head coach Purdue U. Boilermakers, 2004—05, head basketball coach, 2005—. Named Coach of Yr., Mo. Valley Conf., 2004, Big Ten Conf., 2008; finalist Naismith Coach of Yr., 2008; nominee Henry Iba Coach of Yr., US Basketball Writers Assn., 2008. Office: Purdue Univ Men's Basketball Mackey Arena Rm 31 900 N University St West Lafayette IN 47907*

PAINTER, RICHARD WILLIAM, lawyer, educator; b. Phila., Oct. 3, 1961; s. William Hall and Marion (Homer) Painter; m. Karen Lindsley; children: Elizabeth Homer, William Hall II, Anne Symmes. BA, Harvard Coll., 1984; JD, Yale U., 1987. Bar: NY 1989, US Dist. Ct. (so. dist.) NY, Conn. 1990, US Dist. Ct. Conn., US Supreme Ct. Clk. Judge John T. Noonan, Jr. US Ct. Appeals, San Francisco, 1987—88; assoc. Sullivan & Cromwell, NYC, 1988-91, Finn Dixon & Herling, Stamford, Conn., 1991-93; asst. prof. U. Oreg. Sch Law, Eugene, 1993-97, dir. law and enterpreneurship ctr., 1994-97; prof. law U. Ill., Champaign, 1998—2005, Guy Raymond and Mildred Van Voorhis Jones prof., 2003—05; S. Walter Richey prof. corp. law U. Minn., Mpls., 2005—; assoc. counsel to pres. (head of ethics office) The White House, 2005—07. Vis. prof. law Boston U., 1997, Cornell U., Ithaca, NY, 1997—98, Warren Knowles; vis. prof. govt. ethics U. Wis, 2001; vis. prof. U. Bielefeld, Germany, 1999, 2000, 01; vis. prof. law U. Mich., Ann Arbor, 2002; vis. scholar Humboldt U., Berlin, 2000, Harvard U. Ctr. European Studies, 2003—04. Co-author: Professional and Personal Responsibilities of the Lawyer, 1997, 2nd edit, 2001, Securities Litigation and Enforcement, 2003, Getting the Government America Deserves: How Ethics Reform Can Make a Difference, 2009; contbr. articles to profl. jours. Mem.: ABA, Am. Law Inst., Cosmos Club (Washington). Republican. Episcopalian. Avocation: classical music. Home: 7128 Mark Terrace Drive Minneapolis MN 55439 Home Phone: 612-216-5117.

PAINTER, THEOPHILUS SHICKEL, JR., internist, allergist; b. Austin, Tex., Apr. 29, 1924; s. Theophilus Shickel and Anna Parkey (Thomas) P.; m. Dorothy Bulkley, July 11, 1957; children: Dana Parkey, Amy Hur, Theophilus III. BA, U. Tex., 1944, MD, 1947. Diplomate Am. Bd. Internal Medicine, Am. Bd. Allergy and Immunology. Rotating intern Univ. Hosp., U. Mich., Ann Arbor, 1947-48, resident in internal medicine, 1948-51, fellow, jr. clin. instr., 1956-58; pvt. practice, Austin, Tex., 1958—. Capt. USAF, 1951-53. Fellow ACP, Am. Coll. Allergy and Immunology, Am. Acad. Allergy and Immunology. Avocations: fishing, carving, hunting, painting. Home: 3222 Tarryhollow Dr Austin TX 78703-1639 Office: 800 W 34th St Ste 201 Austin TX 78705-1146 Office Phone: 512-454-5821. Personal E-mail: tspainterjr@gmail.com.

PAINTER, WILLIAM HALL, law educator; b. Pitts., May 2, 1927; s. John Littleton Dawson and Eleanor Cramer (Hall); m. Marion Symmes Homer, July 9, 1955; children: Richard William, Edward Homer. AB, Princeton U., 1950; JD, Harvard U., 1954. Bar: N.Y. 1955. Assoc. Debevoise, Plimpton & McLean, NYC, 1954-58; teaching fellow Harvard U.Law Sch., Cambridge, Mass., 1958-59; prof. Villanova U. Law Sch., Phila., 1959-65; vis. prof. U. Mich. Law Sch., Ann Arbor, 1965; prof. U. Mo., Kansas City, 1965-71; spl. counsel, dir. study securities industry U.S. Ho. Reps., Washington, 1971-72; prof. U. Ill. Coll. Law, Champaign, 1972-81, Albert E. Jenner Jr. prof., 1981-87; Theodore Rinehart prof. of business law George Washington U., Washington, 1987—97, emeritus, 1997—. Author: Federal Regulation of Insider Trading, 1968, Corporate and Tax Aspects of Closely Held Corporations, 1971, 2d edit., 1981, Problems and Materials in Business Planning, 1975, 3d edit., 1994, The Federal Securities Code and Corporate Disclosure, 1979, Painter on Close Corporations, 1991; contbr. articles to legal publs. Mem. Ill. Bus. Corp. Act Revision Com., 1981-83. Mem. ABA (fed. securities commn. sect. corp., banking and bus. law, chmn. subcom. on legis. 1974-81), Assn. Am. Law Schs. (chmn. sect. bus. assn. 1976), Am. Law Inst., Phi Beta Kappa. Home: 6652 32d St NW Washington DC 20015 Personal E-mail: wpainterw@aol.com.

PAINTON, RUSSELL ELLIOTT, retired lawyer, mechanical engineer; b. Port Arthur, Tex., Dec. 5, 1940; s. Clifford Elliott and Edith Virginia (McCutcheon) P.; m. Elizabeth Ann Mullins, July 2, 1965 (div. Dec. 1977); 1 child, Todd Elliott; m. Mary Lynn Weber, May 9, 1981. BS in Mech. Engring., U. Tex.-Austin, 1963, JD, 1972. Registered profl. engr., Tex., 1972. Engr. Gulf States Utilities, Beaumont, Tex., 1963-66, Tracor, Inc., Austin, Tex., 1966-70, corp. counsel, 1973-83, v.p., gen. counsel, 1983-98, v.p., gen. counsel, corp. sec., 1991-98; atty. Brown, Maroney, Rose, Baker & Barber, Austin, 1972-73, Childs, Fortenbach, Beck & Guyton, Houston, 1973; corp. sec. Westmark Systems, Inc., Austin, 1990-91; sole practitioner, 1998—2005; ret., 2006. Gen. counsel Paramount Theatre for Performing Arts, 1977-83, 2d vice chmn., 1978-80, 1st vice chmn., 1980-82, chmn. bd., 1982-84, retiring chmn., 1984-85; mem. Centex chpt. ARC; mem. adv. bd. Austin Sci. Acad., 1985-88, 93-95; mem. adv. coun. Austin Transp., 1985-88; bd. dirs. Tex. Industries for the Blind and Handicapped, 1988-95, vice chmn., 1990-91; bd. dirs. Aransas County Ind. Sch. Dist. Found., 2002—, Key Allegro Homeowners Assn., 2002—, pres. 2004-06, dir., 2007. Named Boss of Yr., Austin Legal Secs. Assn., 1981. Mem.: ABA, Am. Electronics Assn. (chmn. Austin coun. 1985—86), Better Bus. Bur. (arbitrator 1983—), Nat. Chamber Litigation Ctr., Tex. Bar Assn. (treas. corp. counsel sect. 1982—83), Houston Yacht Club, Order Blue Gavel, Austin Yacht Club (race comdr. 1968—69, treas. 1970—71, sec. 1972, 1975, vice commodore 1980, commodore 1981, fleet comdr. 1986), Delta Theta Phi. Republican. Episcopalian. Personal E-mail: sailor44@swbell.net.

PAIRO, PRESTON ABERCROMBIE, JR., lawyer; b. June 5, 1927; s. Preston Abercrombie and Blossom Winona (Pritchett) P.; 1 child, Preston Abercrombie III. AA, U. Balt., 1948; JD, 1951. Bar: Md. 1951. Legal investigator Office of City Solicitor, Balt., 1947-50; mem. Md. Ho. Dels., 1950-54; asst. states atty. State of Md., Balt., 1954-58; atty. Liquor Bd. City of Balt., 1958-60; savs. and loan atty., 1960—90. Mem. Md. Criminal Def. Bar (bd. dirs., past pres.), Assn. Trial Lawyers Am., Md. Bar Assn., Howard County Bar Assn. Democrat. Episcopalian. Club: Ellicott City Optimists (pres. 1968). Lodges: Ben Franklin, Masons, Shriners, Jesters. Home: 9032 Overhill Dr Ellicott City MD 21042-5221 Office: Pairo & Pairo 9050 Frederick Dr # A Ellicott City MD 21042-4014 Home Phone: 410-465-2300; Office Phone: 410-461-1800. Personal E-mail: papjr@verizon.net. Business E-Mail: pairo@pairo.com.

PAIS, CLAUDETTE RACHEL, former horse breeder, political consultant; b. Timmins, Ont., Can., Aug. 11, 1941; arrived in US, 1962, naturalized, 1975; d. Patrick Xavier and Jeannette Marie (Labelle) Bigras; m. Alfred Frank Pais, May 5, 1965; children: Louise, Frank. Student, U. Toronto, 1956—61, UCLA, 1981. Co-owner Pais Properties, Santa Monica, Calif., 1965—; founding pres. Golden Bear Raceway, Sacramento, 1975—76, Standardbred Owners Calif., Santa Monica, 1977—78; dir., organizer stockholder rels. Hollywood Pk. Inc., Inglewood, Calif., 1978—82; mem. Calif. Horse Racing Bd. Com. & Subcom. Off-Track Wagering Calif., 1975—. Mem. citizens adv. com., Santa Monica, 1976; commr. Pks. & Recreation, Santa Monica, 1977—79; dir., sec. Girls Club Santa Monica Bay Area Inc., 1978—80; assoc. Pepperdine U., 1980—; bd. dirs. Santa Monica Coll. Assos., 1982—; vol., cons. polit. campaigns; mem. adv. coun. U. Ariz. Race Track Industry Program; assoc. mem. com. off-track wagering Calif. Horse Racing Bd., 1983—. Recipient award, Santa Monica, 1977, 1979; named Ky. Col. Mem.: Nat. Cowboy Hall Fame, Santa Monica Club. Republican. Home: 70655 Sunny Ln Rancho Mirage CA 92270-2340 Fax: 760-318-4231. Personal E-mail: claudette.pais@verizon.net.

PAISLEY, BRAD, musician; b. Glen Dale, West Virigina, Oct. 28, 1972; m. Kimberly Williams, Mar. 15, 2003; children: William Huckleberry, Jasper Warren. Grad., Belmont U., 1995. Musician: (albums) Who Needs Pictures, 1999, Part II, 2001, Mud On The Tires, 2003, Time Well Wasted, 2005 (Album of Yr., Acad. Country Music Awards, Country Music Assn. Awards, 2006), A Brad Paisley Christmas, 2006, 5th Gear, 2007, Play, 2008, (songs) He Didn't Have to Be, 1999 (Song of Yr., Single of Yr. & Video of Yr., Country Music Assn., 2000), I'm Gonna Miss Her, 2001 (Song of Yr., Single of Yr. & Video of Yr., Country Music Assn., 2002, Grammy award for Best Male Country Vocal Performance, 2003), Celebrity, 2003 (Song of Yr., Single of Yr. & Video of Yr., Country Music Assn., 2003), Online, 2007 (Music Video of Yr., Country Music Assn., 2007, Comedy Video of Yr., Country Music TV, 2008, Video of Yr., Acad. Country Music, 2008), Throttleneck, 2007 (Grammy award, Best Country Instrumental Performance, 2008), Letter to Me, 2007 (Grammy award for Best Male Country Vocal Performance, 2009), Cluster Pluck (Grammy award for Best Country Instrumental Performance, 2009), (with Chely Wright) Hard to be a Husband, Hard to be a Wife (Vocal Event of Yr., Country Music Assn., 2001), (with Alison Krauss) Whiskey Lullaby, 2003 (Video of Yr. & Event of Yr., Country Music Assn., 2004, Video of Yr. & Event of Yr., Acad. Country Music, 2005, Collaborative Video of Yr., Country Music TV, 2005), (with Dolly Parton) When I Get Where I'm Going, 2005

(Inspiring Video of Yr., Country Music TV, Video of Yr. & Vocal Event of Yr., Acad. Country Music, Musical Event of Yr., Country Music Assn., 2006), (with Andy Griffith) Waitin' on a Woman (Country Music Assn. award for Music Video of Yr., 2008, Video of Yr., Acad. Country Music, 2009), (with Keith Urban) Start a Band (Vocal Event of Yr., Acad. Country Music, 2009). Founder The Brad Paisley Foundation, 2001—. Recipient Male Vocalist of Yr. award, Country Music Assn., 2000—03, 2007, Country Music Assoc., 2008, Best New Artist award, Grammy Awards, 2001, Top Male Vocalist award, Acad. Country Music, 2007, 2008, 2009, Favorite Male Country Artist, Am. Music Awards, 2008. Office: c/o William Morris Agy 1600 Division St Ste 300 Nashville TN 37203-2755*

PAISLEY, JOHN, psychologist; MS, Mankato State U., 1979. Cert. sch.psychology U. WI - Stout, 1990. Sch. psychologist Centennial Sch. Dist., Cir. Pines, Minn., 1991—. Office: Centennial Sch Dist 4757 N Rd Circle Pines MN 55014 Business E-Mail: jpaisley@isd12.org.

PAIZIS, ANDREW, economist, educator; s. Orestis and Amalia Paizis. BBA in Economics cum laude, Baruch Coll., NY, 1987; MA in Economics, Queens Coll., NYC, 1990; MPhil, City U., NY, 1992, PhD, 1997. Adj. asst. prof., economics dept. Queens Coll., 1990—, summer chmn., economics dept., 1993—94, 1997; rsch. economist NYS Gov.'s Office Econ. Affairs, 1998—2006; adj. asst. prof., economics dept. NYU, 2007—09, clin. assoc. prof. economics dept., 2009—. Recipient Pres. award, Queens Coll., 1997. Office: NYU Economics Dept 19 W 4th St 6th Fl New York NY 10012

PAJAK, DAVID JOSEPH, lawyer, consultant; b. Buffalo, June 19, 1956; s. William H. and Theresa A. (Granato) P.; m. Peggy J. Fisher, Aug. 1, 1981; children: Andrew J., Karl W. BA, State Coll. Buffalo, 1978; JD, U. Buffalo, 1982. Bar: NY 1983, US Dist. Ct. (we. dist.) NY, 1991. Social svcs. counsel Genesee County Dept. Social Svcs., Batavia, NY, 1984-93; pvt. practice Corfu, NY, 1983—93, Amherst, 1993—2006, Alden, NY, 2006—; town justice Town of Pembroke, NY, 1994—2005; with Genesee County Attys. Office, 2001—04. Mem. legis. com. NY Fed. on Child Abuse and Neglect, Albany, 1986—99, bd. dirs., 1987—89; cons. NY Pub. Welfare Assn., Inc., Albany, 1987—92; pres. Social Svcs. Attys. Assn. NY State, 1990—91; instr. Bill Adam's Martial Arts & Fitness Ctr., Buffalo, 1999—2002, Klassic Karate Studios, 1990—98, Filipino Karate Acad., 1989—90. Contbr. articles to profl. jours. Mem.: Genesee County Bar Assn., Erie County Bar Assn., NY State Bar Assn. (chair com. on lawyer referral svcs. 2004—08). Republican. Avocations: Karate, martial arts. Home: 17 E Main St Corfu NY 14036-9665 Office: 13179 Broadway Ste 2 Alden NY 14004 Home Phone: 585-599-3890; Office Phone: 716-630-0400. Business E-Mail: dave@pajakpersonalinjury.com.

PAK, HYUNG WOONG, community advocate; b. Ham-Hoong, Korea, Nov. 6, 1932; came to U.S., 1955, naturalized, 1968; s. Kyung-Koo and Myung-Sook (Lee) P.; m. Diana Lee Stenen Woodruff, 1975; children: Jonathan Tong-Hee, Michelle Hyun-Mi Lee. AB, U. Chgo., 1958. Editor and publisher Chgo. Rev., 1958-63, cons., 1963-65; assoc. editor Ency. Britannica Press, Chgo., 1963-64, sr. editor social scis. and humanities, 1964-66; edn1. dir. Bantam Books, Inc., NYC, 1966-69; gen. mgr. sch. dept. Appleton-Century-Crofts/New Century, NYC, 1970-72; v.p., editorial dir. D. Van Nostrand Co., NYC, 1972-74, pres., 1974-76, Chatham Sq. Press, NYC, 1976-83; pub. Urizen Books, Inc., NYC, 1978-81; exec. v.p. Bus. Software Mag., Palo Alto, Calif., 1983-84; pub., editor Asian High-Tech. Report, 1984-90; exec. dir. The Philip Jaisohn Meml. Found., Inc., Phila., 1990-99; pres. Asian Cmty. Devel. Corp., 2000—. Fellow Hoover Instn., Stanford, Calif., 1984-85. Author: The Pacific Rim, 1990; columnist The Phila. Bus. Rev., 1993-99. Mem. Bd. Sch. Dist. Cheltenham Twp., Pa., 1987-94; mem. Asian task force Phila. Sch. Dist., 1988-95; co-chmn. bus. adv. com. Montgomery County, Pa., 1991-93; del. Citizens' Assembly for a Greater Phila., 1991-95; chmn. Pan Asian Assn. Greater Phila., 1992-96, trustee 1996-, mem. bd. fellowship commn., 1992-95; bd. dirs. Brandywine Art Ctr., 1995-99, vice chair, 1998-99; Pa. del. The White Ho. Conf. on Aging, 1995; trustee Abington Meml. Hosp. Found., 1995-2000; mem. cmty. adv. com. Keystone Mercy Health Plan, 1998-2002; bd. dirs. Nat. Conf. Cmty. and Justice, 2000-02. Mem. ACLU (life), AHA (mem. comms. com. 1998-2000, mem. Phila. All-Am. city host com. 1998-99), Phila. Mus. Art. Home: 1015 Sharpless Rd Elkins Park PA 19027-3040 also: PO Box 7101 Elkins Park PA 19027-0101 Office Phone: 267-254-4234. Personal E-mail: hwpak1@gmail.com.

PAK, JOHN, plastic surgeon; m. Jeehyun Lee, Aug. 27, 2002; children: Emilee Clare, Cate Minnah. MD, Boston U. Sch. Medicine, PhD, 2000. Cert. Bd. Ophthalmolgy, 2006. Oculoplastic surgeon Wheaton Eye Clin., Wheaton, Ill., 2006—. Office: Wheaton Eye Clin 2015 N Main St Wheaton IL 60187 Business E-Mail: jpak@wheatoneye.com.

PAK, SE RI, professional golfer; b. Daejeon, Korea, Sept. 28, 1977; Professional golfer LPGA Tour, 1997—. Mem. KLPGA, 1996, 97. Recipient Rolex Rookie of Yr. award, South Korea Order of Merit, 1998, Vare trophy, 2003; named Player of Yr. Golf Writers Assn. Am., 1998; named to World Golf Hall of Fame, 2007. Achievements include winning 24 LPGA events including four Grand Slam titles; winning the LPGA championship in 1998, 2002, 2006; winning the US Open 1998; winning the du Maurier Classic 2001; winning the Jamie Farr Owens Corning Classic five times, 1998, 99, 2001, 03, 07; being the first woman in 58 years to make cut in men's golf tournament, SBS Super Tournament on Korean tour (finished 10th overall); qualifying for the LPGA Hall of Fame, 2004; being the youngest player ever to be inducted into the World Golf Hall of Fame, 2007. Address: LPGA 100 International Golf Dr Daytona Beach FL 32124-1082 Office Phone: 386-274-6200. Office Fax: 386-274-1099.

PAKBAZNIA, EHSAN, electrical engineer; b. Ahvaz, Khouzestan, Iran, July 28, 1978; s. Khosrow Pakbaznia and Tahereh Hazrat Beki. BS, Sharif U. Tech., Tehran, Iran, 2001; MS, U. Tehran, 2003; PhD student, U. Southern Calif., LA, 2004—. Contbr. articles to profl. jours. Recipient State Govt. award, 1996; nominee Best Paper award, 43rd Design Automation Conf., 2006, Internat. Symposium Quality Electronic Design, 2009. Mem.: IEEE. Achievements include patents for charge recycling in multi-thereshold complementary metal—oxide—semiconductor circuits; design of tri-modal power switch for power gating in complementary metal—oxide—semiconductor and multi-modal power gating structures; development of finger print classification algorithm. Avocations: swimming, skiing, travel. Office: Univ Southern Calif 3740 McClintock Ave EEB214 Los Angeles CA 90089 Personal E-mail: ehsan.pakbaznia@gmail.com. Business E-Mail: pakbazni@usc.edu.

PAKENHAM, ROSALIE MULLER WRIGHT, magazine and newspaper editor; b. Newark, June 20, 1942; d. Charles and Angela (Fortunato) Muller; m. Lynn Wright, Jan. 13, 1962; children: James Anthony Meador, Geoffrey Shepard; m. E. Michael Pakenham, Sept. 29, 2001. BA in English, Temple U., 1965. Mng. editor Suburban Life mag., Orange, NJ, 1960-62; assoc. editor Phila. mag., 1962-64, mng. editor, 1969-73; founding editor Womensports mag., San Mateo, Calif., 1973-75; editor scene sect. San Francisco Examiner, 1975-77; exec. editor New West mag., San Francisco and Beverly Hills, Calif., 1977-81; features and Sunday editor San Francisco Chronicle, 1981-87, asst. mng. editor features, 1987-96; v.p. and editor-in-chief Sunset Mag, Menlo Park, Calif., 1996—2001. Editl. cons., 2002—; tchr. mag. writing U. Calif., Berkeley, 1975—76; participant pub. procs. course Stanford U., 1977—79; chmn. mag. judges at conf. Coun. Advancement and Support of Edn., 1980, judge, 84, Nat. Mag. Awards, 1998, 99, 2005. Contbr. numerous mag. articles, critiques, revs., Compton's Ency. Mem.: Internat. Assn. Culinary Profls., Am. Soc. Mag. Editors (nat. mag. awards judge, 1998, 99, 2005), Am. Newspaper Pubs. Assn. (Chronicle minority recruiter 1987—94, pub. task force on minorities in newspaper bus. 1988—89), Am. Assn. Sunday and Feature Editors (treas. 1984, sec. 1985, 1st v.p. 1986, pres. 1987, Hall of Fame 1999), Washington D.C. Women's Forum, Women's Forum West (bd. dirs. 1993—, sec. 1994), Internat. Women's Forum. Office Phone: 717-292-6969. Personal E-mail: RosalieMPakenham@aol.com. *Keep a sharp eye out for talent, recognize it and reward it, and everyone profits.*

PAKHOMOV, ALEXANDER ALEXANDROVICH, information scientist, consultant; b. Saint-Petersburg, Leningrad, Russia, Jan. 3, 1948; s. Alexander Ivanovich Pakhomov and Maria Alexandrovna Pakhomova; m. Lidia Khadzimurzaevna Butaeva, Dec. 5, 1981; 1 child, Andrey Alexandrovich. BS, MS in Physics, St. Petersburg State U., Russia, 1972, PhD in Physics and Math, 1975; MS in Electronics and Comm. Engring., Naval Acad. Russia, St. Petersburg, 1983, DSc in Engring. Cert. geophysics rsch. sic. Higher Attestation Bd., Coun. Ministers, Russia, 1979, prof. Ministry Gen. and Profl. Edn., Russia, 1998. Jr. rsch. scientist Sci. Rsch. Inst. Physics Saint-Petersburg State U., Russia, 1975—76; sr. rsch. scientist State Sci. Rsch. Inst. Nav. and Hydrography, Saint-Petersburg, 1976—81; prof., sr. rsch. scientist Naval Acad., Saint-Petersburg, 1983—98; dir. of sci. Ripas, Llc, 1998—2001; prin. scientist Gen. Sensing Sys., LLC, Ardsley, NY, 2001—. Mem. young scientists coun. St. Petersburg U., Russia, 1972—76; chmn. young scientists com. Naval Rsch. Instns., 1977—81; pres. St. Petersburg Young Sci. Club, 1980—84; dep. chmn. specialized coun. for Dr. degrees Naval Acad., St. Petersburg, Russia, 1990—2000, mem. specialized methodology coun., 1991—2000, mem. academic coun., 1992—2000. Contbr. 173 scientific papers to profl. pubs. Recipient Golden Medal, Dept. of Edn., USSR, 1966, Dept. of Def., USSR, 1983. Mem.: Peter the Great Acad. Scis. and Arts (corr.). Russian Orthodox Church. Achievements include research in processing geophysical fields, pattern recognition and design of automated electronic safety and environment control systems; patents for 5 US patents related to defense and security issues; perimeter system for detecting intruders. Avocations: piano playing, tennis, theatre. Personal E-mail: alexpakh@optonline.net.

PAKTER, JEAN, maternal and child health consultant; b. NYC, Jan. 1, 1911; d. David and Lillian (Kunitz) P.; m. Arnold L. Bachman, Sept. 17, 1939 (dec. Dec. 1992); children: Ellen Bachman Mendelson, Donald M. Bachman. BS, NYU, 1931, MD, 1934; MPH, Columbia U., 1955. Diplomate Am. Bd. Pediat. Intern Mt. Sinai Hosp., NYC, 1934-36, resident in pediat., 1937-39; pvt. practice, NYC, 1939-43; dir. Bur. Dept. Health, Maternity, Newborn and Family Planning, NYC, 1950-82; cons., lectr. maternity, child health Columbia U. Sch. Pub. Health, NYC, 1984—, dep. dir. maternal and child health program, 1984-94, lectr. maternity, child health, 1970—. Contbr. numerous articles to profl. med. jours. Advisor March of Dimes, N.Y.C., 1975—. Recipient Fund for City of N.Y. Pub. Svc. award, 1974, Jacobi medal Mt. Sinai Hosp., 1975, N.Y. State Med. Soc. award, 2006. Fellow APHA (Martha May Eliot award 1990), Am. Acad. Pediatrics, N.Y. Acad. Medicine (trustee 1979-83), N.Y. Obstet. Soc. (assoc.); mem. Pub. Health Assn. N.Y.C. (bd. dirs. 1992-96, The Haven Emerson award 2006), Women's City Club, Alpha Omega Alpha. Avocations: concerts, opera, theater, reading. Home: 1175 Park Ave New York NY 10128-1211

PAKULA, HANNAH, writer; b. Omaha, July 23, 1933; d. Mayer Louis and Gertrude (Marks) Cohn; m. Robert L. Boorstin, Dec. 31, 1953 (dec. May 1969); children: Anna, Robert O., Louis C.; m. Alan J. Pakula, Feb. 17, 1973 (dec. Nov. 1998). Student, Wellesley Coll., 1951-53, Sorbonne, 1953-54; BA, So. Meth. U., 1956. Author: Historic Biography of Queen Marie of Romania, The Last Romantic, 1985, Historic Biography of Empress Frederick of Germany, An Uncommon Women, 1995, The Last Empress. Madame Chiang Kai-Shek, 2009. Recipient Eleanor Roosevelt Val-Kill medal for human rights, 1999. Mem.: Coun. Fgn. Rels., PEN (freedom to write com.), Century Club. Democrat. Jewish. E-mail: hcpathome@aol.com.

PAL, LENARD, physicist; b. Gyoma, Hungary, Nov. 7, 1925; s. Imre and Erzsebet (Varga) P.; m. Angela Danoci, 1963; 1 child. Student, Budapest U., Moscow U. Dept. head Ctr. Rsch. Inst. for Physics, Budapest, Hungary, 1953-56, dep. dir., 1956-69, dir., 1970-71, 75, dir. gen., 1975-77; prof. nuc. physics Eotvos Lorand U., Budapest, Hungary, 1961—77, 1989—95. Pres. State Office Tech. Devel., 1978-80, 84-85, Nat. Atomic Energy Commn., 1978-80, 84-85; mem. Sci. Policy com. Council of Ministers, 1978-85; sec. Central Com. of the Hungarian Socialist Worker's Party, 1985-88. Contbr. articles to profl. jours. Recipient Gold medal Order Labour, 1956, 68, Kossuth prize, 1962, Meml. medal 25th Anniversary of the Liberation, 1970, Kurcsatov Meomry medal, USSR, 1970, Gold medal Hungarian Acad. Scis., 1975, Red Banner Order of Labor, USSR, 1975, medal Eotvos Lorand Phys. Soc., 1975, Red Banner Order of Work, 1985. Mem. Hungarian Acad. Sci. (gen. sec. 1980-84, pres. Intercosmos Coun. 1980-84, Wigner medal 2001), Acad. Scis. USSR, Russian Acad. Scis., Acad. Sci. German Democratic Republic, Acad. Scis. Czechoslovakia, Leibniz-Sozietat e.V. Home: II Széher 21/a H-1021 Budapest Hungary

PAL, PRATAPADITYA, curator; b. Bangladesh, Sept. 1, 1935; came to U.S., 1967; s. Gopesh Chandra and Bidyut Kana (Dam) P.; m. Chitralekha Bose, Apr. 20, 1968; children: Shalmali, Lopamudra. MA, U. Calcutta, 1958, DPhil, 1962; PhD (UK Commonwealth Scholar), U. Cambridge, 1965. Rsch. assoc. Am. Acad. Benares, India, 1966—67; keeper Indian collections Mus. Fine Arts, Boston, 1967—69; sr. curator Indian and Southeast Asian art Los Angeles County Mus. Art, 1970—95, acting dir., 1979; vis. curator Indian and S.E. Asian art Art Inst. Chgo., 1995—2003; rsch. fellow Norton Simon Mus., Pasadena, Calif., 1995—2005. Gen. editor Marg Publs., Mumbai, 1993-; adj. prof. fine arts U. So. Calif., 1971-89; vis. prof. U. Calif., Santa Barbara, 1980, Irvine, 1994-95; Sir George Birdwood Meml. lectr., The Royal Asiatic Soc., London, 1973; William Cohn lectr. Oxford U., 1983; Catherine Mead meml. lectr. Pierpont Morgan Libr., NYC, 1986; Ananda K. Coomaraswamy meml. lectr. Prince of Wales Mus., Bombay, 1987; D.J. Sibley prehistoric art lectr. U. Tex., Austin, 1989; Anthony Gardner meml. lectr. Victoria and Albert Mus., London, 1993, keynote spkr. 1st Internat. Conf. on Tibetan Art, 1994; spkr. Chgo. Arts Festival, 2002, Aspen Ideas Festival, 2008; mem. commr.'s art adv. panel IRS, Washington, 1986-96. Author: Vaisnava Iconology in Nepal, 1970, The Arts of Nepal, vol. 1, 1974, vol. 2, 1979, The Sensuous Immortals, 1977, The Ideal Image: Gupta Sculptures and its Influence, 1978, The Classical Tradition in Rajput Painting, 1978, Elephants and Ivories, 1981, A Buddhist Paradise: Murals of Alchi, 1982, Art of Tibet, 1983, Tibetan Painting, 1984, Art of Nepal, 1985, From Merchants to Emperors, 1986, Indian Sculpture, vol. 1, 1986, Icons of Piety, Images of Whimsey, 1987, Indian Sculpture, vol. 2, 1988, Buddhist Book Illuminations, 1988, Romance of the Taj Mahal, 1989, Art of the Himalayas, 1991, Pleasure Gardens of the Mind, 1993; Indian Painting, vol. 1, 1993, The Peaceful Liberators: Jain Art from India, 1994, A Collecting Odyssey, 1997, Divine Images, Human Visions, 1997, Tibet Change and Tradition, 1997, Desire and Devotion, 2001, Himalayas: An Aesthetic Adventure, 2003, Asian Art in the Norton Simon Museum, vols. 1 and 2, 2003, vol. 3, 2004; Painted Poems, 2004, Durga: Avenging Goddess Nurturing Mother, 2005, The Arts of Kashmir, 2007; Sindh: Past Glory Present Nostalgia, 2008, Goddess Durga: The Power & the Gelooy, 2009. Khaira Rsch. Scholar, Kolkata U. 1959-62, Commonwealth Scholar, UK, 1962-65, John D. Rockefeller III Fund fellow, 1964, 69, fellow NEA, 1974; Getty scholar, 1995-96; recipient Padma Shri award, India, 2009, U. Gold medal, 1959. Fellow Asia Soc. (Bombay, hon.); mem. Asiatic Soc. (Calcutta, B.C. Law gold medal 1993, R.P. Chanda Centenary medal, 2003), Indian Art Histry Congress (pres. 2009)

PAL, RAKTIM, technology consultant; b. Calcutta, Apr. 12, 1970; s. Chittaranjan and Juthika Pal; m. Sagnika Sen. B Tech. with honors, Indian Inst. Tech., Kharagpur, India, 1992; MSCE, Purdue U., 1995, MS in Indsl. Engring., 1996, PhD, 1999. Mgmt. trainee, engr. Engrs. India Ltd., New Delhi, 1992-93; rsch. asst. Purdue U., West Lafayette, Ind., 1993-99; cons. i2 Techs., 1999—. Contbr. articles to peer reviewed profl. jours.; author reports in field. Awards Inst. Transp. Engrs., 1998, Indian Inst. of Tech., Kharagpur, 1992, Govt. of India, 1988. Mem. ASCE (mem. com. on advanced techs., urban transp. divsn.), Inst. Ops. Rsch. and Mgmt. Scis., Decision Scis. Inst., Inst. Transp. Engrs., Chi Epsilon, Omega Rho, Sigma Xi. E-mail: raktim_pal@yahoo.com.

PAL, UDAY B., engineering educator, consultant; PhD, Pa. State U., U. Pk., 1984. Tchr. Boston U., 1998—, cons., 1998—, 2006—08, divsn. head, materials sci. and engring., 2008—. Recipient Tech. award, Metal. and Materials Transactions, 2003. Mem.: Materials Rsch. Soc. (prinicipal editor, jour. materials rsch. 2001—). Office: Boston Univ 15 Saint Mary's St Brookline MA 02446 Office Fax: 617-353-5548. Business E-Mail: upal@bu.edu.

PALACIOS, CONNY, language educator, writer; d. Abel Flores and Miriam Rayo; m. Edgar Palacios, May 1, 1971; children: Naraya, Edgar Joseé, Isaac. BA, St. Thomas U., Miami, Fla., 1984; PhD, U. Miami, Coral Gables, 1995. Asst. prof. Whitworth Coll., Spokane, Wash., 1997—2000, Southeast Mo. State U., Cape Girardeau, 2000—04; assoc. prof. Anderson U., SC, 2004—. Inventor: En Carne Viva, 1994. Recipient Plaque, Ctr. Nicaraguense Escritores, 2005. Mem. Inst. Cultural Rubén Darío, Am. Assn. Tchrs. of Spanish and Portugese, Inc. Avocations: creative writing, reading. Home: 2011 Woodside Ave Anderson SC 29625 Business E-Mail: cpalacios@andersonuniversity.edu.

PALACIOS-FEST, MANUEL ROBERTO, geologist, paleoecologist; s. Manuel Ricardo Palacios-Luna and Germania Victoria Fest-Salmerón; m. Martha Isabel Tenorio; children: Rodrigo Palacios-Tenorio, Jania Elizabeth Palacios-Tenorio. PhD in Geoscis., U. Ariz., Tucson, 1994. Cert. biologist Labor Secretariat Mex., 1975. Owner, pres. Terra Nostra Earth Scis. Rsch., Tucson, 1990—; staff geologist Statis. Rsch., Inc., Tucson, 2003—07. Post doctoral rschr. U. Ariz., 1997—99. Author: (poetry) Prosas Vulgares. Mem. Fundación Méx., Tucson, 2000—07. Fellow, Banco de México, 1988-1991, Leo S. Rowe Found., Pan-American Fund, 1989-1990, Am. Mus. of Natural History Theodore Roosevelt Meml. Fund, 1989-1990; scholar, Fulbright Found., 2005—. Mem.: Sociedad Mexicana de Paleontología (assoc.), Soc. Am. Archaeology (assoc. Best Profl. Poster award 2002), Geol. Soc. Am. (assoc.). Achievements include research in a mathematical model to calculate temperatures of lakes no longer extant; design of a freeze corer for collecting modern lake deposits up to one meter thick. Avocations: jogging, reading, travel, music, theater. Office: Terra Nostra Earth Scis Rsch PO Box 37195 Tucson AZ 85740-7195 Office Fax: 520-878-9432. E-mail: mrpalacios@tnesr.com.

PALADINO, ALBERT EDWARD, venture capitalist; b. NYC, Aug. 4, 1932; s. Albert E. and Jennie (Fiato) Paladino; m. Dorothy M. Hayes (div. June 1979); children: Thomas A., Robert E., Catherine J., Paul F.; m. Susan Flynn, June 11, 1983. BS in Ceramic Engring., Alfred U., 1954, MS in Ceramic Engring., 1956; ScD in Materials Sci., MIT, 1962. Registered profl. engr., Mass. Staff mem. rsch. divsn. Raytheon Co., Waltham, Mass., 1955-59, mgr. materials and crystal growth lab., 1962-69, mgr. materials and techniques group microwave & power tube divsn., 1969-72, mgr. electronics materials group, 1972-75; program mgr. materials Office of Tech. Assessment US Congress, Washington, 1975-78; asst. dir. tel. ops. tech. ctr. GTE Labs., Waltham, 1978-79; dep. dir. Office Energy Programs US Dept. Commerce, Nat. Inst. Stds. and Tech., Washington, 1979-81; mng. ptnr. Advanced Tech. Ventures, Boston, 1981-98. Bd. dir. TranSwitch Corp., 1988—; chmn. Telaxis Comm. Corp., South Deerfield, Mass., 1988—2003, Electro-Scan Corp., Billerica, Mass., 1990—95, Onex Comm. Corp., 1999—2001, RF Micro Devices, Greensboro, NC, 1992—2009, Paladino & Co., 2002—; telecom. bd. adv. Prism Ventures, 1997—2006, Early Stage Enterprises, 1997—2006; bd. advisers Battelle Ventures, 2004—. Contbr. articles to profl. jours. Pres. West Needham Civic Assn., Mass., 1967—69; mem. Needham Town Meeting, 1973—74, Boston Harbor Angels, 2007—; trustee Alfred U., 1991—. Fellow: Am. Ceramic Soc. (chmn. basic sci. divsn. 1968—69, chmn. New Eng. sect. 1969—70, Disting. New Eng. Ceramic award). Achievements include patents in field. Avocations: painting, music, physical fitness, hiking, reading.

PALADINO, STEVEN, health products executive; b. 1957; BBA, Bernard Baruch Coll. CPA. Acct. BDO Seidman; controller Henry Schein Inc., 1987—90, v.p. & treas., 1990—92, dir., 1992—, sr. v.p. & CFO, 1993—2000, exec. v.p. & CFO, 2000—. Mem.: NY State Soc. CPA's, Inst. Mgmt. Acct., Am. Inst. CPA's. Office: 135 Duryea Rd Melville NY 11747 Office Phone: 631-843-5500. Office Fax: 631-843-5658.*

PALAHNIUK, CHARLES MICHAEL See PALAHNIUK, CHUCK

PALAHNIUK, CHUCK (CHARLES MICHAEL PALAHNIUK), writer, journalist; b. Pasco, Wash., Feb. 21, 1962; s. Fred and Carol Palahniuk. BA, U. Oreg. Sch. Journalism, 1986. Former intern NPR sta. KLCC, Eugene, Oreg.; diesel mechanic Freightliner Inc., Portland, Oreg. Author: (fiction) Fight Club, 1996 (Pacific Northwest Booksellers Assn. award, 1997, Oregon Book award for best novel, 1997), Survivor, 1999, Invisible Monsters, 1999, Choke, 2001, Lullaby, 2002 (Pacific Northwest Booksellers Assn. award, 2003), Diary, 2003, Haunted, 2005, Rant, 2007, Snuff, 2008, Pygmy, 2009 (Publishers Weekly bestseller, NY Times bestseller), (non-fiction) Fugitives and Refugees: A Walk in

Portland, Oregon, 2003, Stranger Than Fiction: True Stories, 2004, (novels adapted to film) Fight Club, 1999, Choke, 2008. Mem.: Cacophony Soc. Office: c/o Doubleday Divsn Random House Inc 1745 Broadway New York NY 10019*

PALAMARA, SHERRY A., psychologist; b. Detroit, Sept. 21, 1962; d. Ronald Dominic and Margot Cathrine Palamara. BA in Psychology cum laude, St. Leo Coll., Fla., 1984; MS, Butler U., 1987, Carlos Albizu U., 2000, D in Psychology, 2000. Lic. massage therapist 1991. Behavior specialist Behavior Therapy and Learning Ctr., Long Beach, Calif., 1988—89; program coord. Geriatric Residentail Treatment Sys., Miami, Fla., 1989—95; addictions therapist Families in Transition, Miami, 2002—03, child devel. specialist, 2003—06; pvt. practice clin. and neuro psychology Miami Beach, Fla., 2005—. Counselor Exceptional Children's Found., LA, 1988—89; adj. faculty Miami-Dade Coll., 1999—, Fla. Internat. U., Miami, 2001—; clin. and neuropsychologist Dr.'s and Assocs., Doral, Fla., 2006—. Contbr. articles to profl. jours. Counselor Exceptional Childrens Found., LA, 1988—89. Mem.: APA. Achievements include research in infant massage, trauma, addictions, motivation, employee relations. Avocations: meditation, running, swimming, writing. Office: 407 Lincoln Rd Ste 6L Miami Beach FL 33139 Office Phone: 305-450-1470. Office Fax: 305-271-1633. Personal E-mail: shpalamara@aol.com.

PALANIAPPAN, KANNAPPAN, engineering educator; s. P. L. Kannappan and K. N. Renganayaki; m. Sala Manian, Aug. 23, 1983; children: Kanna, Anand children: Nila. PhD, U. Ill., Urbana-Champaign, 1990. Tech. staff Can. Ministry Environment, AES, Toronto, Ont., Canada, 1978; asst. engr. Ont. Hydro, Tiverton, 1978; assoc. engr. Bell Can. Enterprises, Ottawa, Ont., 1979—80; asst. engr. Preussen Elektra, Landesbergen, Germany, 1981; grad. asst. U. Ill., Urbana-Champaign, 1986—90; mem. tech. staff Bell No. Rsch., Montreal, Ont., Canada, 1986; sr. rsch. scientist Univ Space Rsch. Assn., NASA, Greenbelt, Md., 1991—95; vis. asst. rsch. prof. U. Md., Coll. Pk., Md., 1995—96; sr. scientist SSAI, Mesoscale Atmospheric Processes Br., NASA, Greenbelt, Md., 1995—97; assoc. prof. U. Mo., Columbia, 1997—. Summer faculty fellow USAF, Rome, 2007—08; welliver summer faculty fellowship Boeing, St. Louis, 2004—04. Author: (teaching) Teaching excellence at Univ. of Missouri (William T. Kemper fellowship, 2002), (exhibition) Pioneering contributions to scientific visualization of petabyte archives (NASA Pub. Svc. medal, 2001); contbr. invention (NASA Tech. Commercialization Office and Fed. Lab. Consortium award of Merit, 1998), exhibition (NASA Rsch. and Edn. Network Cert. of Appreciation, 1998), software management leadership (NASA Mesoscale Dynamics and Precipitation Br. Outstanding Achievement award, 1993). Trustee Shanthi Mandir, Columbia, Mo. Mem.: IEEE, ACM. Achievements include research in early vision software and hardware for object detection and tracking; quantifying deformable motion in growth and motility; massively parallel semi-fluid motion analysis; visualization and analysis testbed system for EOS global assimilated datasets and satellite data. Avocations: running, travel, fantasy basketball. Office: Univ Mo Columbia 329 Engring Bldg West Columbia MO 65211 Office Fax: 573-882-8318. Business E-Mail: palaniappank@missouri.edu.

PALANISAMY, PRAKASH, research assistant; b. Coimbatore, India, May 31, 1980; s. Palanisamy Subramaniam and Jayammal Palanisamy. MS in Engring., Indian Inst. Sci., Bangalore, 2004; PhD, U. Va., Charlottesville, 2008. Project asst. Indian Inst. Sci., 2004—05; rsch. asst. U. Ctrl. Fla., Orlando, 2005—08, U. Va., 2008—. Sec., mrs-ucf chpt. U. Ctrl. Fla., 2005—08; sec., materials rsch. soc. (mrs) - uva chpt. U. Va., 2008—. Contbr. to scientific paper (Fla. chpt. Am. Vacuum Soc. and Microscopy, 2007), to peer reviewer pub. (Jour. Alloys and Compounds - Elsevier, Jour. Crystal Growth - Elsevier, 2007). Sponcer Orphanages, Bangalore, India, 2002—08. Recipient Gold medal, SN-GIT, 1999, All India Rank (AIR) - 20, GATE - Ministry of Human Resource Dept. - Govt. of India; scholar, Ministry of Human Resource Dept. (Govt. of India), 2002. Mem.: Materials Rsch. Soc. (assoc.; charlottesville 2008). Achievements include first to Biosurfactant mediated nanoparticle synthesis; research in Micron scale actuator fabrication; Expertise in electron microscopy. Home: 124 Shamrock Rd Charlottesville VA 22903 Office: Dept of Materials Sci and Engring 395 McCormick Rd Charlottesville VA 22904 Office Fax: 434-982-5660. Business E-Mail: pp3n@virginia.edu.

PALANISWAMY, CHANDRASEKAR, surgeon, researcher; b. Coimbatore, Tamil Nadu, India, Dec. 18, 1980; s. Palanisamy Gounder Palaniswamy and Venkatachala Goonder Kaliammal; m. Dhana Rekha Selvaraj, June 17, 2007. MBBS, Madras Med. Coll., India, 2004; MD, All India Inst. Med. Scis., New Delhi, 2007. Diplomate Ednl. Commn. Fgn. Med. Grads., 2006. Contbr. articles to profl. jours. Recipient GV James award, Madras Med. Coll., 2000, Gold medal Pediat., 2003, Gold medal Dermatology, 2003; named to Best Intern, NY Med. Coll., 2008. Mem.: ACP. Hindu. Achievements include research in epidemiology of coronary artery disease; atrial fibrillation in diabetes; QRS-T angle in prediction of coronary disease. Avocations: travel, music, cooking. Home: 70 Virginia Rd Apt 7E White Plains NY 10603 Office: Westchester Med Ctr 95 Grasslands Rd PMB 503 Valhalla NY 10595 Personal E-mail: drpchandrasekar@gmail.com.

PALANS, LLOYD ALEX, lawyer; b. St. Louis, Aug. 6, 1946; s. Hyman Robert and Mae (Sherman) P.; m. Deborah Regn, Aug. 5, 1972; children: Emily Rebecca, Samantha Jane. BS, Tulane U., 1968; JD, U. Mo., 1972. Bar: Mo. 1972, US Dist. Ct. (ea. and we. dists.) Mo. 1972, US Ct. Appeals (8th cir.) 1972, US Ct. Appeals (5th cir.) 1974, US Supreme Ct. 1975, US Ct. Appeals (9th cir.) 1992. Ptnr. Kramer, Chused, Kramer, Shostak & Kohn, St. Louis, 1972-77, Blumenfeld, Marx & Tureen, P.C., St. Louis, 1978-81, Gallop, Johnson & Neuman, St. Louis, 1981-90, Bryan Cave, LLP, St. Louis, 1990—. Adj. prof. Washington U. Sch. Law, St. Louis, 1989—. Bd. dirs. St. Louis Chpt. ARC, 1987—, St. Louis Chpt. Leukemia Soc., 1988—, Combined Health Appeal Greater St. Louis, 1988—, Combined Health Appeal of Am., 1990. Fellow Am. Coll. Bankruptcy; mem. ABA, Mo. Bar, St. Louis Met. Bar Assn. Office: Bryan Cave LLP 1 Metro Sq 211 N Broadway Saint Louis MO 63102-2733 Office Phone: 314-259-2301.

PALATNICK, FRANK SIDNEY, educational consultant; b. Bklyn., Oct. 13, 1951; s. Abraham (dec. 1998) and Miriam Palatnick. Pres. & founder Inst. for Global Edn. Adminstrn., Scottsdale; dir. Global Edn./Adminstrn. & Higher Edn. (IAED); pres. Global_Ed.Conversations Edn. Cons.; edn./adminstrn. amb. People to People, 2003; prodr. Higher Edn. (TV broadcast/Webcast); keynote spkr. Global Edn. Adminstrn. Conf., Rajahstan, India, 2008, World Edn. Conf., Burj Al Arab, Jumeirah, Dubai, 2007, Global Leadership Conf., 2007, Siberia Acad. for Pub. Adminstrn., Russia, Internat. Edn. Adminstrn. Conf., Washington, 2007, Coll. Bd. of Trustees Conf., Phoenix, 2007, Nat. Inst. on the Assesment of Experiential Learning, Princeton U., 2007; participant Coll. Improvement Conf., U. Ohio, Columbus, 2006, Coll. Exec. Summit, Hampton U., Va., 2006; keynote spkr. Nassau Acad. Law, 2003. Cert. in spl. edn. law Nat. Bus. Inst., 2004, sch. bd. specialist NY State Sch. Bd. Assn., 2005, internat. edn. credentials examiner/evaluator for undergrad. and grad. programs WES, 2007, facilitator sch. leadership stds. ETS. Paralegal Albert Grant Esq., Woodbridge, NJ, 1994—96; chief paralegal Oyster Bay Paralegal Assocs., Muttontown, NY, 1996-99; sr. assoc. Foresight Inst., Palo Alto, Calif., 2000-01; chief paralegal Glen Cove Paralegal Svcs., NY, 2001—02; accreditation examiner Distance Edn. and Tng. Coun., Washington, 2002—. Mem. Presdl. Adv. Com. on Fed. Pay, Washington, 1981-82, Nassau County Task Force Office Mgmt. and Budget, Mineola, NY, 2002; substitute attendance tchr. Wyandanch Sch. Dist., LI, 1997; substitute tchr. BOCES Nassau City, Greenlawn and Plainview, NY, 2000; chief cons. LI Degree Consulting Svc., Uniondale, NY, 2005; spkr., presenter in field. Although qualified in agrl., arts and humanities, bus. and econ. devel., edn., health and medicine, law, diplomacy, science and technology, and in the spirit of globalization, he has embarked on a mission of exchanging ideas on edn. adminstrn. as an amb. through People to People Amb. Programs chaired by Pres. George Bush to countries like China. Attended conf. and gave speech in Sydney with ednl. dels. from around the world, as well as Amman, Jordan, Moscow, Cairo. He is also involved with various other national think tanks i.e. Ctr. for Edn. Policy and Rand. He is co-authoring a book on alternative edn. to be published this year. He was a great lecturer at LI U. C W Post as well as other instns. Through his "Degrees Ahead" he is helping learners with attaining degrees and career devel. as well as giving seminars in portfolio devel. UN advisor, dir. Global Edn. Adminstrn. and Higher Edn. Adminstrn. (IAED), 2006. Assoc. editor: Nassau Lawyer, 2001-; asst. editor: The Flying Lady, 2000-02; contbg. editor: Jour. Cardinal Points, 2002. Mem. US Power Squadron, USCG Aux.; active People to People Ambs. Programs; poll taker Nassau County Dem. Com., Mineola. Named Outstanding Intellectual of the 21st Century; life fellow, Internat. Hall of Fame, Lifetime Achievement, Internat. Order of Merit, Order of Internat. Fellowship, v.p. recognition bd. of World Congress of Arts, Scis., and Comm., Internat. Medal of Honor, Laureate of DaVinci Diamond, Life Patronage; nominated Nobel Peace prize, Norway, 2008; nominee NYC Liberty Lifetime Achievement medal, 2005; named to Wall of Tolerance, Civil Rights Mem. Ctr., Ala., 2005; recipient Letter of Appreciation Mayor of Glen Cove, 2001, Letter of Accomplishment Supt. of Schs., Mineola, 2003, Letter of Acknowledgement for expertise in career devel. Cornell U., 2005, Letter of Acknowledgement for expertise in edn. adminstrn. Dir.-Gen. IAED, 2006. Mem. ASCD (cert. assessment edn. adminstrn.), ABA (individual right and responsibilities com., internat. law com., judiciary com.), Am. Assn. for Adult and Continuing Edn., Assn. for Continuing Higher Edn., Edn. Writers Assn., Am. Coun. on Edn. (alumnus course evaluator tng.), NY State Bar Assn., Nat. Career Devel. Assn. (alumnus career devel. facilitator tng.), Nat. Assn. Secondary Sch. Prins., Nat. Assn. for Edn. Young Children, Coun. Adult & Experiential Learning (alumnus), Nat. Inst. Assessment Experiential Learning (alumnus), Am. Soc. Notaries, LI Paralegal Assn., Am. Mgmt. Assn. Suffolk County Bar Assn. (ednl. law com., family law com., real estate com.), Nassau County Bar Assn. (publs. com., ednl. law com., com. on coms., civil rights law com., med. legal com., cmty. and pub. rels. com., county clerks office com.), Foresight Inst. (sr.), Mensa, Amnesty Internat. Avocations: stamp collecting/philately, coin collecting/numismatics.

PALAZOTTO, ANTHONY N., aerospace engineering educator; b. Bklyn., Dec. 15, 1934; s. Andrew Anthony and Marie Palazotto; m. Helen Potosnak, June 11, 1960; children: Gary, Jane, Daniel, Terri, Christine, Loren, Sandra, Tracy. BCE, NYU, 1955, PhD in Engring., 1968; MCE, Bklyn. Poly. U., 1961. Registered profl. engr., Ohio. Pvt. practice, 1955—68; prof. mech. engring. U. Bridgeport, Conn., 1968—75; prof. aerospace engring. Air Force Inst. Tech., Wright-Patterson AFB, Ohio, 1975—. Author: Nonlinear Shell Analysis, 1992. Recipient Best Paper award, Aerospace Jour., 2004. Fellow: ASCE, AIAA, Am. Acad. Mechanics. Office: Air Force Inst Technology Dept of Aerospace Engineering Wright Patterson AFB OH 45433

PALAZZO, ROBERT PAUL, lawyer, accountant; s. Joseph Francis and Mickey Palazzo; m. Vivianne Palazzo. BA in Econs., UCLA, 1973; MBA, JD, U. So. Calif., 1976; postgrad., U. Oxford, Eng., 1979. CPA Calif., Nev., Colo.; bar: Calif. 1976, US Dist. Ct. (so. dist.) Calif. 1977, US Tax Ct. 1977, US Ct. Appeals (9th cir.) 1978, US Supreme Ct. 1980. Assoc. Graham & James, LA, 1976-78; ptnr. Rader, Cornwall, Kessler & Palazzo CPAs, LA, 1978-81, Palazzo & Kessler, LA, 1978-81; pvt. practice LA, Darwin, Calif., 1981—. Judge pro tem LA Mcpl. Ct., 1982—2000, L.A. Superior Ct., 2001—; alumni advisor UCLA, 1977—81, adv. and scholarship com., 1978—81; lectr. U. Oxford, 1979, U. So. Calif., LA, 1986, Calif. Poly. Inst., Pomona, 1997; profl. adv. com. West L.A. Coll., 1993—96; session chair Medieval and Renaissance Conf. Ariz. State U., 2000—01, 2003; bd. dirs. Cons. Am. Oil. Co., Fin. Sys. Internat. Inc.; part-time faculty Moorpark Coll., Calif., 2004—; spkr. in field. Author: Inyo County Post Offices and Postmasters 1866-1966, 2007; hist. cons. A&E Civil War Jour., (films) Death Valley Memories, hist. and archival cons. Echoes Through Death Valley, Chasing the Rainbow, hist. cons. (TV series) A&E Biography, Guns of Infamy, archival cons., hist. cons., prodr. Haunted History, Echoes Through Time Death Valley; editor: Gun Report; prodr.: (films) L.A. Bounty, the 20 Mule Team of Death Valley; (TV series) Magnificent Failures, 20th Century Infamous Guns; featured (TV series) Tales of the Gun, 1998—2000, Collector's Cafe, 2007; contbr. articles to profl. jours.; author: (book) Darwin, California, Death Valley, INYO Country Post Offices & Postmasters, 1866—1966. Treas. Italian Am. Civic Coalition; chmn. dist. bd. dirs. Darwin Cmty. Svcs., 1990—92; mem. ethics bd. Universal Autograph Collectors Club; founder Ohio History Flight Mus.; bd. dirs. Calif. Cancer Found., LA, 1978—85, pres., 1979—80; bd. dirs. Friends William S. Hart Pk. and Mus., 1990—93, v.p. mus. rels. Mem.: NARAS, S.E. Ohio Oil and Gas Assn., Nat. Italian Am. Bar Assn., Century City Bar Assn. (vice-chmn. estate planning, trust and probate com. 1979—80), Italian Am. Lawyers Assn. (bd. govs. 1980—, 1st v.p. 1984—88), LA County Bar Assn. (arbitration com., fee dispute resolution program), Medieval Assn. of the Pacific, Universal Autograph Collectors Club (mem. ethics bd., registered dealer review bd., registered authenticator We. Americana), So. Calif. Autograph Soc. (v.p.), Death Valley History Assn. (life), Western Writers Assn., English Westerners Soc., Am. Numismatic Assn. (dist. rep. Carson City 1981—82, L.A. 1982—83), Medieval Acad. Am. (conf. session chair 2001—02), Mensa, Ariz. Ctr. Medieval Renaissance Studies Conf. (chair 2000—01, 2003), Wig and Pen Club (London), Zeta Phi Eta, Phi Alpha Delta, Pi Gamma Mu, Beta Alpha Psi (pres. 1972), Omicron Delta Epsilon. also: 230 S Main St Darwin CA 93522 Office Phone: 805-777-7223.

PALDUS, JOSEF, mathematics professor; b. Bzi, Czech Republic, Nov. 25, 1935; arrived in Can., 1968; s. Josef and Ludmila (Danicek) P.; m. Eva Zdena Bajer, Jan. 26, 1961; 1 dau., Barbara Alice. MSc, Charles U., Prague, 1958, DSc, 1995; PhD, Czechoslovak Acad. Sci., Prague, 1961; Drhc, Comenius U., Bratsilava, Slovakia, 2006, U. Louis Pasteur, Strasbourg, France, 2008. Research scientist Czechoslovak Acad. Scis., Prague, 1961-62, 64-68; postdoctoral fellow NRC, Ottawa, Canada, 1962-64; assoc. prof. applied math. U. Waterloo, Ont., Canada, 1968-75, prof. Ont., 1975-2001, disting. prof. emeritus Ont., 2001—; assoc. dir. Fields Inst., 1992-95. Vis. prof. U. Rheims, 1973, U. Louis Pasteur, Strasbourg, France, 1975-76, 82-83, Cath. U., Nijmegen, Holland, 1981, Technion, Haifa, Israel, 1983, Max Planck Inst. for Astrophysics, Munich, Germany, 1997, 98, 99, 2005; vis. scientist NRC, Ottawa, 1966-68, Free U. Berlin, 1981; adj. prof. chemistry U. Fla., Gainesville, 1984—; fellow Inst. for Advanced Study, Berlin, 1986-87. Mem. editl. bd. Comtex Sci., 1981-83, Advances in Quantum Chemistry, 1986, Jour. Chem. Physics, 1987-89, Can. Jour. Chemistry, 1994-96, Internat. Jour. Quantum Chemistry, 1996; mem. adv. editl. bd. Internat. Jour. Quantum Chemistry, 1977-88, Theoretica Chimica Acta, 1988-94, Jour. Math. Chemistry, 1989; contbr. numerous articles to profl. jours., chpts. to books. Recipient prize Chemistry divsn., Czechoslovak Acad. Scis., 1962, 1967, J. Heyrovsky Gold medal, Czechoslovak Acad. Sci., 1992, Gold medal Faculty of Math and Physics, Comenius U., Slovakia, 1994, Alexander von Humboldt Sr. Scientist award, 1996, Charles U. Gold medal, Prague, Czech Republic, 2005, De Scientia et Humanitate Optime Meritis medal, Czech Republic Acad. of Sci., 2007, PATRIA prize, Unipetrol Framework Project Ceska Hlava, Prague, 2008; Killam Rsch. fellow, 1987—89, Fields Inst. for Rsch. in Math. Scis. fellow, 2002. Fellow Royal Soc. Can.; mem. Internat. Acad. Quantum Molecular Sci., Internat. Soc. Theoretical Chem. Physics (bd. dirs.), European Acad. Scis., Arts and Letters (corr.), Czech Learned Soc. (hon.), Am. Inst. Physics, NY Acad. Scis., Applied Math. Soc. Can. Roman Catholic. Avocations: music, history. Office: U Waterloo Dept Applied Math 200 University Ave W Waterloo ON Canada N2L 3G1 Home Phone: 519-746-4435; Office Phone: 519-888-4567 ext. 36267. Business E-Mail: paldus@uwaterloo.ca.

PALECEK, MICHAEL R., information technology manager; b. Milw., Feb. 9, 1975; s. Michael H. Palecek and Kimberly S. Karas. Student, U. Phoenix, Brookfield, Wis., 2004—. Cert. profl. Microsoft, 2001. Network adminstr. iNET Computers, Inc., Waukesha, Wis., 2001—05; bus. systems mgr. Quick Cable, Franksville, Wis., 2005—. Author: (web site) Quick Cable Home Page. With US Army, 1993—2000. Decorated Army Commendation medal with 2 oak leaf clusters US Army, Good Conduct medal. Roman Catholic. Avocation: golf. Office: Quick Cable 3700 Quick Dr Franksville WI 53126 Personal E-mail: mpalecek@wi.rr.com. Business E-Mail: mpalecek@quickcable.com.

PALERM, CESAR C., electrical engineer, researcher; s. Maria Vera Palerm Ferri. BSEE, ITESO U., Guadalajara, Mexico; MSc in Math., Rensselaer Poly. Inst., Troy, NY, MSEE, PhD in Engring. Sci. Cert. profl. engr., Dept. Edn., Mex., 1994. Postdoc. rsch. fellow U. Calif., Santa Barbara, 2004—07; prin. scientist Medtronic Diabetes, Northridge, Calif., 2007—. Guest lectr. U. Girona, Catalonia, Spain; adj. asst. prof. Rensselaer Poly. Inst.; guest investigator Sansum Diabetes Rsch. Inst., Santa Barbara, 2004—07. Contbr. scientific papers. Asst. scoutmaster Boy Scouts America, Defreetsville, NY, 1996—2004. Recipient Eagle Scout award, Boy Scouts America, 1985, Outstanding Staff award, Am. Sch. Found. Guadalajara, 1988, Academic Excellence award, ITESO U., 1992; Grad. fellowship, Consejo Nat. Ciencia Tech., Mex., 1994—98. Mem.: IEEE (chair joint chpt. control sys. and engring. medicine and biology soc. 2006—07, computer soc. chpt. 1993, sr. mem. 2005), Am. Diabetes Assn., Sigma Xi, Phalanx: Rensselaer's Sr. Leadership Soc. Office: Medtronic Diabetes 18000 Devonshire St Northridge CA 91325

PALERMO, ANTHONY ROBERT, lawyer; s. Anthony C. and Mary (Palvino) P.; m. Mary Ann Coyne, Jan. 2, 1960; children: Mark Henry, Christopher Coyne, Peter Stuart, Elisabeth Megan McCarthy, Julie Coyne Lawther, Gregg Anthony. BA, U. Mich., 1951; JD, Georgetown U., 1956. Bar: DC 1956, NY 1957, U.S. Supreme Ct. 1961. Trial atty. U.S. Dept. Justice, Washington, 1956-58, asst. U.S. atty. NYC, 1958-60, asst. U.S. atty. in charge Rochester, NY, 1960-61; ptnr. Brennan, Centner, Palermo & Blauvelt, Rochester, 1962-81, Harter, Secrest & Emery, Rochester, 1981-94, Hodgson, Russ, Andrews, Woods & Goodyear, LLP, Rochester, 1994-97, of counsel, 1998, Woods Oviatt Gilman LLP, Rochester, 1999—. Note editor Georgetown Law Jour., 1956. Bd. dirs. McQuaid Jesuit H.S., Rochester, 1978-84, St. Ann's Home, Rochester, 1974-2001; bd. dirs., sec. St. Ann's Found., Rochester, 1989-2001; trustee, charter chmn. Clients' Security Fund N.Y. (now Lawyer's Fund for Client Protection), 1981-90; chmn. Govs. Jud. Screening Com. 4th Jud. Dept., mem. statewide com., 1987-89; chair magistrate selection com. U.S. Dist. Ct. (we. dist.) N.Y., 1995, 98; mem. N.Y. Chief Judge's Commn. on Jud. Salaries, 1997-2000; mem. N.Y. Office Ct. Adminstrn. Commn. on Fiduciary Appointments, 2000-06. With US Army, 1951—54. Fellow Am. Bar Found., N.Y. State Bar Found. (bd. dirs. 1978-91), Am. Coll. Trial Lawyers; mem. ABA (ho. dels. 1980-98, 2004—, state del. 1982-85, bd. govs. 1985-88, 1989-93, sec. 1990-93), N.Y. State Bar Assn. (pres. 1979-80, ho. dels. 1973-75, 77—), Monroe County Bar Assn. (pres. 1973, Rodenbeck award, 1998), Oak Hill Country Club. Roman Catholic. Home: 38 Huntington Meadow Rochester NY 14625-1813 Home Phone: 585-381-8847; Office Phone: 585-987-2882. Business E-Mail: apalermo@woodsoviatt.com.

PALERMO, GREGORY SEBASTIAN, architect; b. Westfield, NY, Oct. 28, 1946; s. Sebastian and Frances Joan (Ciminella) P.;m. Olivia Madison; children: Mark Sebastian, Christopher Anthony. BArch, Carnegie Mellon U., 1969; MArch in Urban Design, Wash. U., 1976. Registered architect, Mo., Calif., N.Y., Iowa. Architect PGAV Inc., St. Louis, 1976-79; sr. v.p. HOK, Inc., St. Louis, 1980-87; sr. assoc. Mackey Assocs., St. Louis, 1987-89; v.p., prin. Stone Marraccini Patterson, St. Louis, 1989-91. Affiliate asst. prof. Washington U. Sch. Arch., 1984-90; vis. assoc. prof. Iowa State U. Dept. Arch., 1992-95, assoc. prof., 1995-2001, prof., 2001—, undergrad. program coord., 1996-98, assoc. chair undergrad. program, 1999—; chair Des Moines Archtl. Adv. Com., 1996-97; mem. Des Moines Gateway Planning Com., 1996. Mem. editl. bd. Iowa Architect mag., 1992—, assoc. ed., 1995—; mem. editl. bd. Jour. Archtl. Edn., 2001-04. Mem. Light Rail Transit Rev. Com., 1985, St. Louis Mayoral Task Force, 1986; exec/coun. Arts in Transit Com., St. Louis, 1987—; chmn. design rev. com.,St. Louis Metrolink Transit System, 1989-91; chair Nat. AIA Edn. Task Force, 1990; mem. Leadership St. Louis, 1990-91, Archtl. Adv. Commn. city of Des Moines, 1992-2000. Fellow AIA (bd. dirs., nat. v.p., pres. St. Louis chpt. 1984, pres. Iowa chpt. 2004, Iowa Edn. award, 2007); mem. Nat. Archtl. Accreditation Bd (pres. 1993-94), Assoc. Coll. Sch. Architecture (bd. dirs., Disting. Prof., 2008), Iowa State Faculty Senate (pres. 2006-07) Home: 2048 Pinehurst Dr Ames IA 50010-4561

PALERMO, JOSEPH ANTHONY, history professor; b. San Jose, Calif., Jan. 27, 1959; s. Joseph Nick and Lorayne Mary Palermo; m. Jannette LeeAnn Dayton, June 3, 2006; children: Gianna Isabella, Dante Joseph, Palesa Bianca, Marco Blake; m. Kerry Elizabeth Maloney, July 23, 1979 (div. Mar. 10, 1989). AA, West Valley CC, Saratoga, Calif., 1981; BA, U. Calif., Santa Cruz, 1984; MA, PhD, Cornell U., Ithaca, NY, 1998. Cert. in cmty. tchg. credential State of Calif., 1987. Adj. prof. Colgate U., Hamilton, NY, 1999—2001; assoc. prof. Am. history Calif. State U., Sacramento, 2002—. Vis. adj. prof. U. Calif., Santa Cruz; vis. asst. prof. Cornell U., Ithaca, NY, 2003—05; writer Huffington Post, LA, 2006—. Author: (book) In His Own Right: The Political Odyssey of

Senator Robert F. Kennedy, 2001, Robert F. Kennedy and the Death of American Idealism, 2008. Mem.: Orgn. Am. Historians. Independent. Avocation: drums. Office: Calif State Univ Sacramento 6000 J St Sacramento CA 95819

PALESE, PETER M., biology professor; s. Kurt and Elisabeth Palese; m. Mady L. Loecker, Aug. 1, 1970; children: Michael A., Caren Palese Venturi. PhD, U. Vienna, 1969. Prof. & chair, dept. microbiology Mt. Sinai Sch. Medicine, NYC, 1987—. Mem. Nat. Acad. Scis., German Acad. Scis., Austrian Acad. Scis. Contbr. scientific papers. Recipient Robert Koch prize, Koch Com., Berlin. Office: Mt Sinai Sch Medicine 1 Gustave Levy Pl New York NY 10029 Office Fax: 212-722-3634. Business E-Mail: peter.palese@mssm.edu.

PALESTRANT, DANIEL, Internet company executive; BS in Biology, Johns Hopkins U., 1992—96; MD in Medicine, Duke U., 1996—2003. Trained Beth Israel-Deaconess Hosp., Boston; designer, founder, mgr. CIGNA Internet Based Universal Resource; founder Azygos, Inc., 1999—2001; dir. health care BioNetrix (now BNX Systems); founder, CEO Sermo, Inc., Cambridge, Mass., 2006—. Office: Sermo Inc 215 First St Cambridge MA 02142

PALESTRO, CHRISTOPHER J., physician; m. Lynnette V. Stevens, May 24, 1985; children: Christopher J., Sarah Alice, Alexander Steven, Lissette Halle, Vincent Giancarlo. MD, Universidad Autonoma de Guadalajara, Mex., 1975. Diplomate Am. Bd. Nuc. Medicine, 1982. Chief nuc. medicine Norwalk Hosp., Conn., 1982—85; nuc. medicine physician Mt. Sinai Med. Ctr., NYC, 1985—92; chief nuc. medicine LI Jewish Med. Ctr., New Hyde Park, 1992—2007, North Shore U. Hosp., Manhassett, NY, 2006—07; chief nuc. medicine and molecular imaging North Shore LI Jewish Health Sys., 2007—. Prof. nuc. medicine and radiology Albert Einstein Coll. Medicine, Bronx, NY, 1996—; chmn. Am. Bd. Nuc. Medicine, 2006; mem. residency rev. com. for nuc. medicine Accreditation Coun. Grad. Med. Edn., 2007—; mem. editl. bd. Quar. Jour. Nuc. Medicine and Molecular Imaging. Assoc. editor: Radiology; contbr. articles to profl. jours. including Jour. Nuc. Medicine, Radiology, RadioGraphics. Fellow: Am. Coll. Nuc. Physicians; mem.: NY Acad. Medicine, Internat. Skeletal Soc., Radiol. Soc. N.Am., Soc. Nuc. Medicine. Office: Long Island Jewish Med Ctr 270-05 76th Ave New Hyde Park NY 11040 Business E-Mail: palestro@lij.edu.

PALEVSKY, MAX, industrialist, director; b. Chgo., July 24, 1924; s. Isadore and Sarah (Greenblatt) P.; children: Nicholas, Madeleine, Alexander, Jonathan, Matthew. Ph.B., BS, U. Chgo., 1948; postgrad., U. Calif.-Berkeley, U. Chgo., UCLA, 1951-52. Mathematician Computer div. Bendix Corp., LA, 1952—56; v.p., gen. mgr., dir. Packard Bell Electronics, LA, 1957—61; pres., chmn. bd. Sci. Data Systems; chmn. bd. Xerox Data Systems, Inc., El Segundo, Calif., 1961-72; dir. Xerox Corp., 1969-72, chmn. exec. com. of bd., 1969-72. Bd. dirs. Intel Corp., Santa Clara, Calif., Komag, Inc., Milpitas, Calif. Organized George McGovern's campaign for Pres. of US, 1972; organized and ran Tom Bradley's campaign for Mayor of LA, 1973; mem. Folger com. Folger Shakespeare Libr., Washington, 1977—; mem. Dem. Adv. Com., 1968—; bd. dirs. ACLU, Constl. Rights Found.; trustee The Inst. for Advanced Study, Princeton U., 1988—. With USAAF, 1943-46. Office: 924 Westwood Blvd Ste 700 Los Angeles CA 90024-2928 Personal E-mail: palevsky@mindspring.com.

PALEVSKY, PAUL MARC, nephrologist, educator; b. NYC, Dec. 29, 1957; s. Gerald and Estelle (Moore) P.; m. Sharon Renee Roseman, Sept. 4, 1983; children: Hilary Ilana, Jason Michael. BS, Northestern U., 1979, MD, 1981. Diplomate Am. Bd. Internal Medicine, Am. Bd. Internal Medicine (Nephrology). Intern, resident Internal Medicine Hosp., U. Pa., Phila., 1981-84; fellow nephrology U. Pa., Phila., 1984-88, rsch. assoc., 1988-89; asst. prof. U. Pitts. Med. Sch., 1989-95, assoc. prof., 1995—2001, prof., 2001—. Chief Hemodialysis unit VA Pitts. Health Care Sys., 1989—2003, chief renal sect., 1993—; pres. ESRD Network, 2008-, chair MRB ESRD network 1997-2007. Contbr. articles to profl. jours. Fellow ACP, ACCP, Am. Soc. Nephrology; mem. Internat. Soc. Nephrology, Am. Soc. Nephrology, Am. Heart Assn. (Coun. on Kidney in Cardiovasc. Disease), Nat. Kidney Found., Renal Physicians Assn., Alpha Omega Alpha. Home: 109 Bell Farm Ests Sewickley PA 15143-8367 Office: VA Pitts Health Care Sys University Dr Divsn Pittsburgh PA 15240 Office Phone: 412-360-3932. E-mail: palevsky@pitt.edu.

PALEY, EILEEN Y., city councilwoman, lawyer; b. 1963; BA in Psychology, Ohio State U.; JD, Capital U. Law Sch., Columbus, Ohio. Bar: Ohio 1988, US Dist. Ct. (so. dist.), Ohio 1988. Commr. Columbus Civil Svc. Commn.; atty. Peden, Paley & Assoc. Co., L.P.A., Columbus; councilwoman Columbus City Coun., 2009—, chair judiciary & court adminstrn. com., utilities com. V.p. Dynamic Leadership, Inc.; bd. dirs. Nat. Coun. Jewish Women, The Neighborhood House. Office: Columbus City Coun 90 W Broad St Columbus OH 43215 also: Peden Paley & Assoc Co LPA 5969 E Livingston Ave Ste 200 Columbus OH 43215*

PALEY, GERALD LARRY, lawyer; b. Albany, NY, Sept. 11, 1939; s. Arthur and Mary (Peckner) P.; m. Joyce R., June 25, 1961 (div. June 1985); children: Jonathan, Eric, Suzanne; m. Sheryl Gae, Aug. 14, 1985. BA, Union Coll., 1961; JD with distinction, Cornell U., 1964. Bar: N.Y. 1964. Assoc. Nixon, Hargrave, Devans & Doyle, Rochester, NY, 1964-69; assoc. solicitor Dept. Labor, Washington, 1969-71; ptnr. Nixon, Hargrave, Devans & Doyle, Rochester, 1971-87, Phillips, Lytle, Hitchcock, Blaine & Huber, Rochester, 1987—. Author: Handbook of Federal Labor Relations Laws, 1981, Understand Employee Regulations, 1984. Mem. ABA. Republican. Jewish. Office: Phillips Lytle Hitchcock et al 1400 First Federal Plz Rochester NY 14614-1981 Office Phone: 585-238-2008. Personal E-mail: gpaley@phillipstytle.com.

PALFENIER, DAVID, food products executive; BBA, Ea. Wash. U., Cheney. Sales and mktg. assoc. Proctor & Gamble; dir. mktg., Famous Brands Chiquita Brands Internat., Cin., 1990—91, v.p. mktg., John Morell, 1990—91; mktg. and mgmt. positions including v.p. mktg. and gen. mgr. immediate consumption bus. Frito Lay Corp., Plano, Tex., 1991—2004; sr. v.p. mktg. frozen foods divsn. ConAgra Foods, Inc., 2004—05, gen. mgr. frozen foods divsn., 2005, pres. frozen foods divsn., pres. grocery foods, 2006—. Office: Conagra Foods 8101 E Kaiser Blvd Ste 160 Anaheim CA 92808-2256 Office Phone: 402-595-6000.

PALFREY, THOMAS ROSSMAN, economics professor, political science professor; b. Lafayette, Ind., Oct. 11, 1953; s. Thomas Rossman and Emily Skillings Palfrey; m. Cheryl Craig, July 9, 1976; 1 child, Rossman Craig. BA in Polit. Sci. magna cum laude, U. Mich., 1975, MA in Polit. Sci., 1976; PhD, Calif. Inst. Tech., 1981. Prof. politics and econs. Princeton U., NJ, 2004—06; prof. econs. and polit. economy Carnegie Mellon U., Pasadena, Pa., 1980—; prof. econs. and polit. sci. Calif. Inst. Tech., Pasadena, 1986—2005, Flintridge Found. prof. econs. and poliitcal sci., 2006—. Author: (book) Bayesian Implementation, 1993, Voting: What is, What Could Be, 2001; editor: Laboratory Research in Political Economy, 1991, Experimental Foundations of Political Science, 1993; contbr. over 100 scholarly articles to profl. jours. Dir. Caltech-MIT Voting Tech. Project, Pasadena, 2000—02. Fellow, Ctr. Advanced Study Behavioral Scis., 1986—87; grant, NSF, 1982—. Fellow: Am. Acad. Arts and Scis., Econometric Soc.; mem.: Pub. Choice Soc., Am. Econ. Assn., Game Theory Soc., Econ. Sci. Assn. (pres., v.p., exec. bd. 1988—99). Avocations: classical guitar, tennis, hiking. Office: Calif Inst Tech Mail Code 228-77 (HSS) Pasadena CA 91125

PALIA, ASPY PHIROZE, marketing educator, researcher, consultant; b. Bombay, Nov. 27, 1944; arrived in US, 1973; s. Phiroze E. and Homai P. (Irani) P. BSME, U. Bangalore, 1966; MBA, U. Hawaii at Manoa, 1976; DBA, Kent State U., 1985. Sales engr. Larsen & Toubro Ltd., 1966—72, export sales engr., 1972—73; tchg. fellow Coll. Bus. Adminstrn. Kent State U., 1977—80, instr. Coll. Bus. Adminstrn., 1982—84; asst. prof. Coll. Bus. Adminstrn. U. Hawaii, Manoa, 1984—89, assoc. prof., 1990—95, prof., 1996—2005, prof. Shidler Coll. Bus., 2006—, pres. faculty coun., 1995—96; senator U. Hawaii Manoa Faculty Congress, 1996—98, 2007—; sr. fellow dept. mktg. Nat. U. Singapore, 1998—99, vis. sr. fellow dept. mktg., 2000—02. Vis. prof. Coll. Mgmt. Nat. Sun Yat-sen U., Kaohsiung, Taiwan, 1992, Chulalongkorn U., Bangkok, 1992, 93, 97, 2003, 2005—06, U. Otago, New Zealand, 1995, Adminstrv. Staff Coll. India, Hyderabad, 1992, Indian Inst. Mgmt., Ahmedabad, 2000, Asian Inst. Tech., Bangkok, 2001; mem. U. Hawaii, Manoa Ctr. Teaching Excellence Faculty Adv. Group, 1991; mem. mktg. plan adv. com. U. Hawaii, 1994, mem. honors and awards com., 1990—91, pres. faculty coun., 1995—96, mem. faculty adv. com. on acad. freedom, 1997; vis. scholar faculty bus. adminstrn. Nat. U. Singapore, 1991, Mktg. Inst. Singapore Exec. Devel. Seminars, 1991, 1994—95, 1997, Hong Kong Inst. Mktg. Exec. Devel. Seminar, 1996, Kathmandu Coll. Mgmt. Exec. Devel. Workshop, 2000; sr. fellow dept. mktg. faculty of bus. adminstrn. Nat. U. Singapore, 1998—99, vis. prof., 2000, 01, 02; affiliate faculty Japan Am. Inst. Mgmt. Sci., Honolulu, 1989—; vis. prof. Grad. Sch. Internat. Mgmt., Internat. U. Japan, Uhrasa, Yamato-machi, 1991, U. Internat. Bus. and Econs., Beijing, 1991, U. Kebangsaan Malaysia, Bangi-Selangor, Kuala Lumpur, Malaysia, 1991, 92, Mt. Carmel Inst. Mgmt., Bangalore, India, 1997, Vietnam Nat. U., Hanoi Sch Bus., 2002, Singapore Mgmt. U., 2003, 04; condr., leader exec. devel. workshop on strategic market planning Boston Network, Bangkok, 2003; lectr., cons., presenter in field. Editor: (with Dennis A. Rondinelli) Project Planning and Implementation in Developing Countries, 1976; assoc. editor e-Services Quar., 1999—; contbr. articles to profl. jours. including Indsl. Mktg. Mgmt., Internat. Bus. Jour., Asia-Pacific Jour. Mgmt., Internat. Mktg. Rev., European Jour. Mktg., Fgn. Trade Rev., Internat. Rev. Econs. & Bus., others; chpts. to books; developer various mktg. decision support systems and decision-making tools for use in strategic market planning and in marketing simulations. Program rev. com. Pacific and Asian Mgmt. Inst., Acad. Internat. Bus., Assn. Bus. Simulation and Exptl. Learning, others; bd. examiners Nat. U. Singapore Sch. Postgrad. Mgmt. Studies, 1991; external examiner Bd. Grad. Studies, Nat. U. Singapore, 2001-2002; adv. bd. Soc. Coll. of Bus. Adminstrn. Alumni and Friends Exec. Com., 1991-93, Salvation Army Residential Treatment Facilities for Children and Youth Adv. Coun., 1989-96, vice chair, 1987-89; chair Salvation Army Family Treatment Svcs. Adv. Coun., 1997-98; mem. Salvation Army Honolulu Adv. Bd., 1997-98; treas., bd. dirs. Kings Gate Home-owners Assn., 1994-96; bd. advisors Ctr. for Nat. Competitiveness Inst. Indsl. Policy Studies, Korea, 1998—. Univ. fellow Kent State U., 1983; East-West Ctr. scholar East-West Ctr., 1973-75; Ednl. Improvement Fund grantee, 1989, Instrl. Travel and Devel. Fund grantee Office Faculty Devel. and Acad. Support, 1991, 95, joint rsch. grants U. Kebangsaan Malaysia, Nat. U. Singapore, U. So. Queensland, Australia, U. Otago, New Zealand, Lingnan Coll., Hong Kong; recipient Internat. Agreements Fund award Office Internat. Programs and Svcs., 1990-92, ORA travel award U. Rsch. Coun., 1986, 88-89, 91-92, 94-98. Mem. Am. Mktg. Assn. (academia editor Honolulu chpt. 1986-87), Acad. Internat. Bus. (chair Pacific Basin Region 1995, chair Pacific Basin chpt. 1996-2002, co-chair Asia Pacific Conf. 1997), Pacific Asian Consortium for Internat. Bus. Edn. and Rsch., Assn. for Bus. Simulation and Exptl. Learning, Pan-Pacific Bus. Assn. (charter), Mortar Bd. (Outstanding Educator award 1993, Mentor award 1995), East-West Ctr. Alumni Assn. U.S. (v.p. Hawaii chpt. 1987-89, ad campaign com. 1987-88), Beta Gamma Sigma (faculty advisor, sec.-treas. Alpha of Hawaii chpt. 1990—, Outstanding Svc. award 1992-93, Bd. Govs. Commitment to Excellence award 1997, Prof. of Yr. award 2003), Mu Kappa Tau, Pi Sigma Epsilon. Avocations: music, photography, swimming, reading, hiking. Home: 2724 Kahoaloha Ln # 1605 Honolulu HI 96826-3337 Office: U Hawaii Dept Mktg 2404 Malie Way Honolulu HI 96822-2223 Office Phone: 808-956-8642. Business E-Mail: aspy@hawaii.edu.

PALII, LARISA P., language educator; b. Frumusica, Soroca, Romania, May 18, 1925; d. Petru Ion and Domnica A. (Kalinowski) Tomacinschi; m. Petru Eftimie Palii, Feb. 3, 1949; children: Corneliu, Arcadie, Lucia, Sergiu. Student, Mihail Sturdza Coll. Edn., Iasi, Romania, 1937—44, Coll. Edn., Soroca, Moldova, 1947, Inst. Edn., Chisinau, Moldova, 1949; BS, Inst. Edn., Balti, 1954. Tchr. french lang. Frumusica HS, Floresti, Moldova, 1945—89, tchr. drawing painting, 1987—90, tchr. romanian lang., 1989—95. Prodr.: (radio broadcasts) Radio broadcasts on French culture and history, local radiostation, Audio shows of French songs and poetry on the local radiostation involving a broad participation of students from Frumusica High Sch., Floresti, Moldova. Decorated Golden Jubliee medal Republic Moldova, Labor Vet. medal; recipient Badge Outstanding Person Pub. Edn. award, 1957; named one of Best Tchr. award, Frumusica High Sch., 1956—57, 1969—70. Mem.: Environ. Protection Soc. Moldova., Hist. Monuments Protection Soc., Bibliophile Soc., Assn. Tchrs. French. Avocations: literature, art, ballroom dancing, music, gardening. Home: Frumusica Floresti Soroca County MD-5020 Moldova Personal E-mail: petruemail@gmail.com.

PALII, SERGIU PETRU, chemist, researcher; b. Moldova, Aug. 5, 1962; s. Petru Eftimie and Larisa P. (Tomacinschi) Palii; m. Stela Simona Sciuca, Aug. 29, 1987; 1 child, Miorel-Lucian. PhD, Inst. Chemistry, Acad. Scis. of Republic of Moldova, Chisinau, Physico-Chemistry Inst. of Ukrainian Acad. Scis., Odessa, 1991. Head mass spectrometry group, rsch. scientist in lab. of coord. chemistry Inst. of Chemistry, Acad. Scis. of Republic of Moldova, Chisinau, 1991—98; postdoctoral rsch. assoc. dept. chemistry U. Fla., Gainesville, 1999—2005, rsch. assoc. dept. medicine, 2006, sr. chemist biomed. mass spectrometry lab., gen. clin. rsch. ctr., 2007—. Joint faculty dept. chemistry Moldova State U., Chisinau, 1991—96; mem. organizing com. Conf. on Phys. Methods in Coordination and Supramolecular Chemistry, Chisinau, 1993—99. Actor: (movie) Miorita (Telefilm-Chisinau, Moldova), 1987, In Memoriam: Mihai Eminescu (TV Moldova), 1989; author: (series of essays) Historical Architecture and Monuments of Chisinau City (Essay of Yr., Moldavian Soc. Arch., 1990); contbg. author: Chisinau Encyclopedia (Museum, Chisinau), 1997; contbr. chpts. to books and articles to profl. jours. Recipient Young Scientists prize, Moldavian Nat. Coun. for Sci. Achievement, 1992, Internat. Sci. Exch. award, Natural Scis. and Engring. Rsch. Coun. Can., 1993, award, French Acad. Scis., 1996, Young Scientists prize, Acad. Scis. Moldova, 1997, Recognition cert. and medal, Rsch. and New Techs. Eureka, Belgium, 1999; co-recipient Scientia Europaea prize, French Acad. Scis. & Rhone-Poulenc Found., 1999; grantee Vis. fellow, United Kingdom's Royal Soc., 1996; Rsch. grant, Internat. Sci. Found., 1993. Mem.: Acad. Scis. Rep. Moldova (coun. Young Scientists vice chmn. 1992—97), U. Fla. Alumni Assn., Romanian Inst. Genealogy and Heraldry, Am. Chem. Soc., Internat. Mass Spectrometry Soc., Am. Soc. for Mass Spectrometry, Internat. Union of Pure and Applied Chemistry, Scientia Europaea. Achievements include research in Gas Phase Chemistry of Organometallic, Macrocyclic, Polynuclear and Supramolecular Species; patents in field. Business E-Mail: palii@ufl.edu.

PALILEO, HAZEL VALENCIA, videographer; b. Pila, Laguna, Philippines, May 22, 1951; came to US, 1971, naturalized citizen, 1979; naturalized Can. Citizen, 2007. d. Lauro Gomez and Edna (Valencia) P. BFA in Photography and Media, Wright State U., 1976; student, DeVry Inst. Tech., 1995-97; diploma, Applied Multimedia Tng. Ctrs., 1998; cert. web designer, U. Calgary, 2002. Lab. tech. Valdhere Films, Inc., Dayton, Ohio, 1973-76; news photographer Sta. WDTN-TV, Dayton, 1977-79; videographer Sta. WKEF-TV News, Dayton, 1979-86, chief videographer, 1983-86; videographer, still photographer Wycliffe Bible Translators, Calgary, Alta., Can., 1986-92, co-mgr. media prodns. dept., 1990-92; video mgr., media coord. Cornerstone Comms., Calgary, 1992-94; photographer, videographer and multi media specialist freelance, Calgary, 1994—; media technician U. Calgary, 1998—. Videographer (TV news) Haviland Ave. Fire, 1984 (Emmy 1984). Recipient Best Video award Nat. Cath. Stewardship Conf., 1993. Avocations: reading, photography, travel, walking. Office: Univ Calgary 2500 University Dr NW Calgary Calgary AB T2N 1N4 Canada Business E-Mail: palileo@ucalgary.ca.

PALIN, SARAH HEATH, former Governor of Alaska; b. Sandpoint, Idaho, Feb. 11, 1964; d. Chuck and Sally Heath; m. Todd Mitchell Palin, Aug. 29, 1988; children: Bristol, Piper, Track, Willow, Trig Paxon. BS in Journalism, U. Idaho, 1987. Mem. city council City of Wasila, Alaska, 1992—96, mayor, 1996—2002; chair Alaska Oil & Gas Conservation Commn., 2003—04; gov. State of Alaska, Juneau, 2006—09; Rep. vice-presdl. nominee, 2008. Mem. Alaska Resource Devel. Coun., Interstate Oil & Gas Compact Commn. Pres. Alaska Conf. Mayors; mem. steering com. Youth Ct.; bd. mem. Alaska Mcpl. League, Valley Hosp. Assn. Recipient Person of Yr. award, Am. Pub. Works Assn. (Alaska chpt.), Top 40 Under 40 award, Alaska State Chamber; named Miss Wasila, 1984; named one of The Ten Most Fascinating People of 2008, Barbara Walters, The World's Most Influential People, TIME mag., 2009. Mem.: Alaska Miner's Assn., Alaska Outdoor Coun., NRA (life), Rotary (hon.), Sigma Beta Delta. Republican. Achievements include being the youngest person and the first woman to hold the office of governor of Alaska, 2006. Avocations: hunting, fishing, running, history.*

PALIS, JAMES, pediatrician; MD, U. Rochester, NY, 1981. Cert. Am. Bd. Pediat., Am. Bd. Pediatric Hematology Oncology. Faculty, dept. pediat. U. Rochester, 1988—. Contbr. scientific papers. Mem.: Internat. Soc. Exptl. Hematology (editl. bd. mem.), Internat. Soc. Stem Cell Rsch., Am. Soc. Hematology. Office: Univ Rochester 601 Elmwood Ave Rochester NY 14642 Office Fax: 585-276-0232. Business E-Mail: james_palis@urmc.rochester.edu.

PALISI, ANTHONY THOMAS, psychologist, educator; b. Rahway, NJ, Mar. 8, 1930; s. Anthony Francis and Marianne Catherine (Picone) P.; m. Dyane Cassidy, Apr. 19, 1954; children: Jane, Anthony Francis II, Phyllis, Damian-Marie. BS, Seton Hall U., 1951, MA, 1958; EdD, Temple U., 1973. Cert. secondary tchr., elem. prin., psychologist, rehab. counselor, N.J.; mem. Nat. Register Health Care Profls. in Psychology. Tchr., coach pub. schs., Rahway, 1953-60; sports editor Rahway News-Record, 1950-60; prin. elem. pub. sch. Franklin Twp., NJ, 1960-65; asst. prof. edn. Seton Hall U., 1965-73, assoc. prof., 1974-77, prof., 1977-82, acting grad. dean, 1976-77, dir., 1969-80, indsl. cons. group dynamics, 1967-97; pvt. practice psychology, 1977; dir. cons. divsn. FormTech Graphics, Inc., 1997—. Adj. faculty Brookdale C.C., 2005—, Prevention, Inc. Contbr. articles and short stories to profl. jours. and popular periodicals. Mem. Rahway Bd. Edn. 1961-62; trustee Rahway Libr., 1961-68, pres. 1967-68. Recipient award N.J. Sportswriters' Assn., 1953. Mem. APA, ACA, Am. Mgmt. Assn. (co-author video tng. program), N.J. Psychol. Assn., Assn. for Specialists in Group Work (mem. rsch. com. 1980-82), N.Y. Acad. Scis., Nat. Acad. Counselors and Family Therapists (chmn., exec. dir. 1988-93, co-editor Family Letter 1985-93), Nat. Register of Health Svc. Providers in Psychology, Am. Coll. Counselors., Clin. Hypnosis Soc. NJ. Roman Catholic. Office Phone: 732-223-5379. Business E-Mail: atpalisi@optonline.net.

PALIWAL, AABHAS VASANT, engineering educator, consultant; s. Vasant Vithal and Jayshree Vasant Paliwal; m. Shailu Shelat. BS in Electronics Engring., Telecom., U. Mumbai, 1997; MS in Computer Engring., Rutgers U., NJ, 2002, PhD in Mgmt., Info. Tech., 2007, MBA, 2007. Rschr. CIMIC, Rutgers U., Newark, 2002—; sr. tech. cons. Mindlance Life Scis., Edison, NJ, 2008—. Contbr. chapters to books, articles to profl. jours. Mem.: IEEE, ACM, Beta Gamma Sigma. Business E-Mail: aabhas@cimic.rutgers.edu.

PALIWAL, BHASKER, mechanical engineer, researcher; b. India; PhD, Johns Hopkins U., Balt., 2008. Engr., R & D LG Electronics, Noida, UP, India, 2002—03; rsch. asst. Johns Hopkins U., 2003—08, postdoctoral fellow, 2008, Sandia Nat. Labs., Albuquerque, 2008—. Contbr. articles to profl. jours. (Invited submission). Grant, NSF Summer Inst. nanomechanics and materials, 2007, Johns Hopkins U., 2003—08. Mem.: Minerals, Metals & Materials Soc., Am. Phys. Soc., ASME, Am. Ceramic Soc.

PALIWAL, DINESH C., electronics executive; married; 2 children. BS, St. Johns Coll., Agra, India; MS, MBA, Miami Univ., Ohio. Engring. & mgmt. positions with Ballarpur Industries, Yamunanagar, India, AccuRay Corp., Columbus, Ohio, Combustion Engring., Singapore & Melbourne, Australia; engring. & mgmt. positions through dir. Asia Pacific mktg. & sales ABB Ltd., 1985—94, v.p. industries Beijing, 1994—2001, pres. process industries Zurich, Switzerland, 2001—02, pres. automation tech. worldwide Norwalk, Conn., 2002—04; chmn., CEO ABB No. Am., 2004—06; pres. global markets & tech. ABB Group, Zurich, Switzerland, 2006—07; vice-chmn., pres., CEO Harman Internat. Industries Inc., Washington, 2007—08, chmn., CEO, 2008—. Econ. adv. to Gov. Guangdong Province, China; bd. dir. Embarq Corp., U.S. India Bus. Council; chmn. Nat. Fgn. Trade Council; mem. U.S. Bus. Roundtable; past dir. U.S. China Bus. Council. Dir. Internat. Swimming Hall of Fame. Office: Harman Internat Industries Ste 1010 1101 Pennsylvania Ave NW Washington DC 20004

PALKOVIC, MICHAEL W., broadcast executive; With Times Mirror Cable TV, DIRECTV Group, El Segundo, Calif., 1996—, sr. v.p., CFO US bus., 2001—04, exec. v.p., CFO US bus., 2004—, exec. v.p., CFO, 2005—07, exec. v.p. ops., 2007—. Office: DIRECTV Group 2230 E Imperial Hwy El Segundo CA 90245 Office Phone: 310-964-5000.

PALL, ELLEN JANE, writer; b. NYC, Mar. 28, 1952; d. David B. and Josephine H. (Blatt) P.; m. Richard Holmes Dicker, July 12, 1986; 1 child, Benjamin. BA, U. Calif., Santa Barbara, 1973. Freelance writer for several jours., 1987—. Staff assoc. Bread Loaf Writers Conf., Middlebury, Vt., 1986; instr. UCLA-Ext., 1980-83; adj. asst. prof. Fordham U./Coll. at Lincoln Ctr., N.Y.C., 1990-93. Author (under pen name Fiona Hill): The Trellised Lane, The Wedding Portrait, The Practical Heart, Love in a Major Key, Sweet's Folly, The Autumn Rose, The Love Child, The Stanbroke Girls, 1981, The Country Gentleman, 1987; author: (as Ellen Pall) Back East, 1983, Among the Ginzburgs, 1996, Corpse de Ballet, 2001, Slightly Abridged, 2003; contbr. articles to N.Y.Times Mag., N.Y. Times Arts & Leisure, New Yorker mag., Chgo. Tribune, Washington Post; book reviewer. Shane Stevens fellow, Bread Loaf Writer's Conf., Vt., 1983. Mem. Am. PEN (freedom to write com.). Office: care Mary Evans Inc 242 E 5th St New York NY 10003-8501 Business E-Mail: ellen@ellenpall.com.

PALL, GURDEEP SINGH, computer software company executive; Grad., Birla Inst. Tech., India; MS in Computer Sci., U. Oreg., 1989. Software design engr. Microsoft Corp., Redmond, Wash., 1990, gen. mgr. Windows networking, 2001, gen. mgr. Windows real-time comm. efforts, 2002, corp. v.p. unified comm. group, 2005—. Co-recipient Innovation of Yr. award, PC Magazine, 1996; named one of the 15 Innovators & Influencers Who Will Make A Difference in 2008, Info. Week. Office: Microsoft Corp One Microsoft Way Redmond WA 98052-6399*

PALLADINO, CHRISTOPHER JAMES, social studies educator; b. Phila. married. BS, Phila. Bibl. U., Langhorne Manor, Pa., 1994; MEd, U. Va., Charlottesville, 2002. History tchr. Lynchburg City Sch., Va., 1999—2006; asst. prof. Phila. Bibl. U., 2006—. Recipient Neighborhood Champion award, Bank America, 2005; named Tchr. of Yr., Lynchburg City Sch., 2004—05. Office: Phila Bibl Univ 200 Manor Ave Langhorne PA 19047 Business E-Mail: cpalladino@pbu.edu.

PALLADINO-CRAIG, ALLYS, museum director, educator; b. Pontiac, Mich., Mar. 23, 1947; d. Stephan Vincent and Mary (Anderson) Palladino; m. Malcolm Arnold Craig, Aug. 20, 1967; children— Ansel, Reed, Nicholas. BA in English, Fla. State U., 1967; grad., U. Toronto, Ont., Can., 1969; MFA, Fla. State U., 1978, PhD in Humanities, 1996. Editorial asst. project U. Va. Press, Charlottesville, 1970-76; instr. English Inst. Franco Americain, Rennes, France, 1974; adj. instr. Fla. State U., Tallahassee, 1978-79, dir. Four Arts Ctr., 1979-82, dir. U. Mus. of Fine Arts, 1982—, prof. mus. studies. Mem. grad faculty Mus. Studies Cert. Program Fla. State U. Curator, contbg. editor: Nocturnes and Nightmares, Monochrome/Polychrome, Chroma, High Roads & Low Roads-Anthems, Dirges, Myths; contbg. editor: Body Language; guest curator, author: Mark Messersmith: New Mythologies; curator, editor Albert Paley--Sculpture, Drawings, Graphics and Decorative Arts, Trevor Bell: A British Painter in America, and Trial by Fire: Contemporary Glass; curator, author: The Abridged Walmsley--Selections from the Career of William Aubrey Walmsley, co-curator, contbg. author: Terrestrial Forces; author: Jack Nichelson: Micro-Theatres, Alexa Kleinbard: Talking Leaves, Jake Fernandez--Ethereal Journeyman, Jim Roche-Sense of Place; editor: Athanor I-XXVII, 1980—. Individual artist fellow Fla. Arts Coun., 1979 Mem. Am. Assn. Mus., Fla. Art Mus. Dirs. Assn. (sec. 1989-91), Phi Beta Kappa. Democrat. Avocation: antiques. Home: 1410 Grape St Tallahassee FL 32303-5636 Office: Fla State U Mus of Fine Arts 250 Fine Arts Bldg Tallahassee FL 32306-1140 Home Phone: 850-224-4188. Business E-Mail: apalladinocraig@fsu.edu.

PALLAPA, GAUTHAM, webmaster; s. Venkataram Pallapa and Bharathi Kuppaswamy; m. Rama Sallangulla, Mar. 12, 2006. BE in Elec. and Electronics, RV Coll. Engring., Bangalore, Karnataka, 2000; MTech in Computer Sci. and Engring., Jawaharlal Nehru U., New Delhi, 2003; attending in Computer Sci. and Engring., U. Tex., Arlington, 2004—. Lectr. computer sci. and engring. MS Ramaiah Inst. Tech., Bangalore, 2003—04; asst. prof. info. tech. Padre Conceicao Coll. Engring., Verna, Goa, India, 2004; network and web adminstr. CReWMaN, U. Tex., 2005—; lab coord. Dept. CSE, U. Tex., 2005—07, instr., 2007—, webmaster, 2008. Rsch. asst. Indian Inst. Sci., Bangalore, 2004; grad intern Cisco Sys. Inc., Richardson, Tex., 2008; founding mem. Orgn. Computer and Info. Tech. Engrs., Goa, India. Contbr. articles to profl. pubs. Vol. and fundraiser HelpAge India, Bangalore, 1992—93. Mem.: IEEE. Achievements include research in wireless Ad Hoc networks, autonomic computing, ubiquitous and assisted computing.

PALLASCH, MAGDALENA HELENA (MRS. BERNHARD MICHAEL PALLASCH), artist; b. Chgo., Sept. 6, 1908; d. Frank and Anna (Meier) Fixari; m. Bernhard Pallasch, Nov. 26, 1931 (dec. Nov. 1977); children: Bernhard Michael, Diana Pallasch Miller Student, Art Inst. Chgo., Chgo. Acad. Fine Arts, 1922-26, Am. Acad. Fine Arts, 1926-30; studied with Joseph Allworthy, 1935-38; student, U. Chgo., 1960; doctorate (hon.), 1985. Contbr. two murals and ten life size figures for Woman's World Fair, Chgo., 1928, Century of Progress Exhbn., Chgo., 1933-34; portrait artist, subjects include Cardinal Cody, Chgo., 1980—, Cardinal Francis George, Chgo., 1998, Carlotta Ames, Boston, Mrs. Timothy Kingston, Arlington Heights, Ill., Dr. Neal Coleman, Hinsdale, Ill., Catherine Eardley Murphy, Lake Forest, Ill., Anita Mangels, Sao Paulo, Brazil, Canon Regis Barwig, Oshkosh, Wis., 2000, Dr. Dale King Phelps, Pittsford, NY, Laurel Cummings, Palm Beach Fla.,2001, Barbara and Robert Pendergast, Lake Forest, Ill., Mara Pallasch, Chgo., 2003, Lois Kay Simanton, Northfield Ill., 2004, Bernhard Anthony Miller, Chgo., 2004; mural St. Mary of the Lake Ch., Chgo., 1987; exhbn. at Montifiori Estate, 1992, 93, 94, Hinsdale Art Ctr., 1995, 96, 97; represented in pvt. and pub. collections Loyola U., Chgo., Barat Coll., Lake Forest, Ill., Internat. Coll. Surgeons, Chgo., Med. Library, Columbus Hosp and others.h Recipient first award for still life Arts Club, NYC, 1960, First award Nat. League Am. Pen Women, 1972, 1st place and best of show State Exhibit, Springfield, Ill., 1973, 1st award Chgo. Woman's Club, 1978, hon. mention for portrait Italian Cultural Ctr., hon. alumna award Loyola U., Chgo., 1983, award of excellence for portrait of author Gail Brook Burket, Wheaton Hist. Mus., 1987, Gold Medal of Honor for disting. lifelong achievements, 1987, award of honor for portrait of sculptor Lisa Gengler, 1989, medallion from Archduke Markus Habsburg of Austria, 2003, first award for still life Vanderpoel Gallery, 2005, Best Classic Art award Vanderpoel Gallery, 2006; named Dame Commandeur with Starbust, 1997, with second Starburst, 2003, Sovereign Mil. Order Temple of Jerusalem, 1995 Mem. Presentation Ball Aux.; mem. President's Club, Loyola U., also mem. women's bd. Nat. League Am. Pen Women (v.p. Chgo. br. 1966-68, art chmn. 1978-80, Margaret Dingle Meml. award 1979), Mcpl. Art League Chgo., Nat. Soc. Arts and Letters (art chmn. chgo. chpt. 1982—, apptd. nat. chmn. 1997—), Friends of Austria, Friends of D'Arcy Gallery of Medieval and Renaissance Art., Ill. Cath. Women Club (gov. 1979-), Cuneo Mus. (Vernon Hills, Ill.). Home and Office: 723 W Junior Ter Chicago IL 60613-1512

PALLER, AMY S., pediatric dermatologist, educator; b. Cleve., Dec. 14, 1952; BA in Biology, Brown U., 1974, MS in Genetics, 1974; MD, Stanford U., 1978. Diplomate Am. Bd. Pediatrics, Am. Bd. Dermatology. Resident in pediatrics Northwestern U./Children's Meml. Hosp., Chgo., 1978-81; resident, chief resident in dermatology Northwestern U., 1981-83; NIH postdoctoral fellow in dermatology U. N.C. Sch. Medicine, Chapel Hill, 1983-84; asst. prof. Rush-Presbyn.-St. Luke's Med. Ctr., Chgo., 1984—88; head divsn. dermatology Children's Meml. Hosp., 1988—2004; prof. pediats. and dermatology Northwestern U. Med. Sch., 1996—, chair dermatology dept., 2004—. Affiliate physician dept. pediatrics Evanston (Ill.) Hosp., 1989—; med. adj. staff Northwestern Meml. Hosp., Chgo., 1989—; mem. Lurie Cancer Ctr., Northwestern U. Med. Sch., 1992. Mem. editl. bd. Jour. Am. Acad. Dermatology, 1991-, asst. editor, 1993-2008; mem. editl. bd. Cutis, 1992—, Current Opinion in Dermatology, 1993—, Advances in Dermatology, 1995—, Exptl. Dermatology, 1996—, Current Opinion in Women's Health, 1998—, Dermatology Insights, 2000—, Pediat. Devel. Pathology, 2001—; assoc. editor Jour. Invest Dermatology, 2002—; contbr. articles to profl. jours. Named among Top Chgo. Drs., Chgo. mag., 1993, 97, 99, 01, 03, 05, 07, 09; recipient numerous grants in field. Fellow Am. Acad. Dermatology (bd. dirs. 2000-2004), Am. Acad. Pediat.; mem. Soc. for Pediat. Dermatology (sec.-treas. 1993-2003, pres. 2004-2005), Soc. for Investigative Dermatology (bd. dirs. 1999-2004, pres. 2007-2008), Dermatology Found. (bd. trustees), Am. Bd. Dermatology (dir. 2006-), Phi Beta Kappa, Sigma Xi. Office: Children's Meml Hosp 2300 N Childrens Plz Chicago IL 60614-3394

PALLI, SUBBA REDDY, scientist, professor; b. Tyajumpudi, Andhrapradesh, India, Nov. 15, 1959; s. Venkata Reddy and Varahalu Palli; m. Usha Rekha Muppidi, May 10, 1987; children: Rohith, Roshan. PhD, U. of Western Ont., Canada, 1984—88. Group leader Rohm and Haas Co., Sprinh House, Pa., 1999—2002; prof. U. Ky., Lexington, 2002—. Rsch. scientist Canadian Forest Svc., Sault Ste. Marie, Ont., Canada, 1992—98. Achievements include research in published 100 peer reviewed journal articles, co-invetor on two issued patents and 15 applications. Presented over 200 talks at international meetings. Office: Univ of Kentucky S221 AgrlScience North Lexington KY 40546 Home: 2236 Lovell Ct Lexington KY 40513 Office Fax: 859-223-1120; Home Fax: 859-223-1120. Business E-Mail: rpalli@uky.edu.

PALLMEYER, REBECCA RUTH, judge; b. Tokyo, Sept. 13, 1954; arrived in U.S., 1957; d. Paul Henry and Ruth (Schrieber) Pallmeyer; m. Dan P. McAdams, Aug. 20, 1977; 2 children. BA, Valparaiso U., Ind., 1976; JD, U. Ill., Chgo., 1979. Bar: Ill. 1980, U.S. Ct. Appeals (7th cir.) 1980, U.S. Ct. Appeals (11th and 5th cir.) 1982. Judge clk. Minn. Supreme Ct., St. Paul, 1979-80; assoc. Hopkins and Sutter, Chgo., 1980-85; judge, administrv. law Ill. Human Rights Commn., Chgo., 1985-91; magistrate judge U.S. Dist. Ct. (No. Dist.), Chgo., 1991-98, dist. judge, 1998—. Mem. jud. resources com. Jud. Conf. U.S., 1994—2000. Nat. adv. coun. Christ Coll., Valparaiso U., 2001—; bd. dirs. Augustana Ctr., 1990—91; mem. vis. com. U. Chgo. Div. Sch., 2006—. Recipient Profl. Achievement award, Chgo.-Kent Coll. of Law, 2002, Alumni Achievement award, Valparaiso U., 2002, President's Award for Disting. Svc., N.W. Suburban Bar Assn., 2003. Mem.: FBA (bd. mgrs. Chgo. chpt. 1995—2004), Intellectual Property Law Assoc. Chgo., Alliance Women Chgo. Bar Assn. (exec. bd. 2007—), Chgo. Bar Assn. (chair devel. law com. 1992—93, bd. mgrs. 2004—06, David C. Hilliard award 1990—91), Fed. Magistrate Judges Assn. (bd. dirs. 1994—97), Womens Bar Assn. Ill. (bd. mgrs. 1995—98), Valparaiso U. Alumni Assn. (bd. dirs. 1992—94). Lutheran. Avocations: choral music, sewing, running. Office: US Dist Ct 219 S Dearborn St Ste 2178 Chicago IL 60604-1877

PALLONE, FRANK, JR., United States Representative from New Jersey, lawyer; b. Long Branch, NJ, Oct. 30, 1951; m. Sarah Hospodor; 3 children. BA cum laude in Hist. and French, Middlebury Coll., Vt., 1973; MA in Internat. Rels., Tufts U. Sch. Law and Diplomacy, Mass., 1974; JD, Rutgers U. Sch. Law, NJ, 1978. Bar: Fla., NJ, NY, Pa. Coastal law specialist NJ Marine Adv. Svc., 1980—81; asst. prof. sea grant ext. prog. Cook Coll.-Rutgers U., NJ, 1980—81; counsel Monmouth County Protective Svcs. for the Elderly, NJ; instr. Monmouth County Cmty. Coll.; maritime atty. NYC, 1982—84; mem. City Council, Long Branch, NJ, 1982-88, NJ Senate, 1984-88, US Congress from 6th NJ dist., 1988—, mem. energy and commerce com., natural resources com., chmn. health subcommittee. Co-chair Congl. caucus on Armenian issues US Congress, founder Congl. caucus on India and Indian Am., chair Dem. caucus task force on health and medicare. Recipient Cancer Advocacy award, Cancer Inst. NJ, 1998, Internat. Yr. of Ocean award, Clean Ocean Action, 1998; named Consumer Hero, Consumer Fedn. Am., 1997, Legislator of Yr., NJ Acad. Ophthalmology, 1998, Outstanding Legislator of Yr., VFW, 1999. Democrat. Roman Catholic. Address: 504 Broadway Ste 118 Long Branch NJ 07740-5951 Office: US House Reps 237 Cannon House Office Bldg Washington DC 20515-3006 Office Phone: 202-225-4671. Office Fax: 202-225-9665.*

PALLONI, ALBERTO BRUNO, social sciences educator; b. Valparaiso, Chile, Apr. 29, 1949; s. Franco Angelo Palloni and Carolina Caterina Garofalo; m. Lora Patricia Jordan; 1 child, Giordano Enrico. PhD, U.Wash., Seattle, 1977. Cert. in stats. & economics CIENES, 1973. T. Edwin young prof. population & internat. studies U. Wisconsin-Madison, 1980—2007; bd. trustees,prof. Northwestern U., Evanston, 2007—. Guggeheim fellow, Guggenheim found., 1992. Mem.: Am. Acad. Arts & Scis., Population Assn. Am. (pres. 1996—97). Achievements include development of techniques for estimating mortality. Office: Inst Policy Rsch 2040 Sheridan Ave Evanston IL 60208-4100 Office Fax: 847-491-9916. Business E-Mail: a-palloni@northwestern.edu.

PALLOTTA, JOHANNA ANTONIA (JOHANNA STEPHEN), endocrinologist, educator; b. Boston, May 7, 1937; d. John and Antonia (Lanni) P.; m. Michael John Stephen, Aug. 13, 1966; children: Jacqueline, Antonia, Michael, Andrew. BS in Chemistry magna cum laude, Boston Coll., 1958; MD, N.Y. Med. Coll., 1962. Diplomate Am. Bds. Internal Medicine, Endocrinology and Metabolism; lic., Mass., Calif. Intern St. Elizabeth's Hosp., Boston, 1962-63; resident in medicine N.Y. Med. Coll. Metro. Hosp., NYC, 1963-64; resident in medicine, fellow radioisotope svc. VA Hosp., Bronx, 1964—66; fellow metabolism and endocrinology Yale U. Sch. Medicine, New Haven, 1966-67; instr. medicine Harvard Med. Sch., Boston, 1967-69, Beth Israel Deaconess Hosp. Harvard Med. Sch., 1969-70; asst. prof. medicine Harvard Med. Sch., 1970—2003, assoc. prof. medicine, 2004—. Tutor med. scis. Harvard Med. Sch., 1972-73; dir. endocrinology clinic Beth Israel Deaconess Hosp., Boston, 1967—, dir. radioimmunoassay lab., 1972-83, clin. cons., 1984—, asst. in medicine, 1967-69, assoc. in medicine, 1969-70, asst. physician, 1970-79, assoc. physician, 1979-87, sr. physician, 1987—, dir. clin. rsch. ctr. core radioimmunoassay lab., 1984-93; cons. staff Mount Auburn Hosp., Cambridge, 1974-90; mem. numerous other coms., 1969—. Rschr. in field; contbr. articles to profl. jours. Recipient S. Robert Stone Harvard Med. Sch.-BIDMC tchg. award, 1998; named Carl Shapiro scholar, BIDMC-Harvard Med. Sch., 2000—. Fellow: ACP, Am. Assn. Clin. Endocrinologists; mem.: Am. Fedn. Clin. Rsch., Am. Thyroid Assn., Endocrine Soc., Harvard Aesculapian Club, Alpha Omega Alpha. Roman Catholic. Home: 16 Fresh Pond Ln Cambridge MA 02138-4616 Office: Beth Israel Hosp Harvard Med Sch 330 Brookline Ave Boston MA 02215-5491 Home Phone: 617-868-1494; Office Phone: 617-667-4016. Business E-Mail: jpallott@bidmc.harvard.edu.

PALLOZOLA, CHRISTINE, not-for-profit executive; b. St. Louis, Mar. 28, 1952; BS, U. Mo., 1974. Purchasing and sales mgmt. computer industry, Mo., 1984-92; exec. dir. Cahokia Mounds Mus. Soc., Collinsville, Ill., 1993—2001, dir. spl. events, mktg. Arts and Edn. Coun., 2001—04; exec. dir. Am. Acad. Comm. Healthcare, St. Louis, 2004—. Sec. Businesspersons Between Jobs, St. Louis, 1998—2004. Mem.: Assn. Fundraising Profls. Home: 150 Burtonwood Ballwin MO 63011

PALM, GREGORY K., lawyer, diversified financial services company executive; b. Binghamton, NY, Sept. 25, 1948; m. Susan Palm; children: Jennifer, Katherine, Eleanor, James. SB, MIT, 1970; MBA, JD, Harvard U., 1974. Bar: N.Y. 1977, DC 1978. Law clk. to Hon. Henry J. Friendly US Ct. Appeals (2nd Cir.), 1974—75; law clk. to Justice Lewis F. Powell US Supreme Ct., 1975—76; assoc. Sullivan & Cromwell LLP, 1976—82, ptnr., 1982—92; gen. counsel, co-head, legal dept. Goldman Sachs LP, NYC, 1992—99; exec. v.p., gen. counsel, co-head of legal dept. Goldman Sachs Group, Inc., NYC, 1992—. Mem. Harvard Law Rev. Mem.: Am. Law Inst., DC Bar. Office: Goldman Sachs Group Inc Legal Dept 37th Fl 1 New York Plz New York NY 10004 Office Phone: 212-902-1000. Office Fax: 212-902-3876.*

PALM, JESSANA, biology professor; b. Concord, NH, May 11, 1970; d. Jan Roland and Marsha Ellen Palm. MSc in Environ. Studies Conservation Biology, Antioch New Eng. Grad. Sch., Keene, NH, 2003. Assoc. prof. biology and chemistry CC Sys. NH, Concord, 2003—. Bioblitz vol. Nature Conservancy, Concord, 2001, invasive species monitoring vol., 05; mus. vol. Little Nature Mus., Hopkinton, NH, 2005; Wetland bird survey vol. Audubon Soc. NH, Concord, 2006. Sec. Field Dreams Equestrian Ctr., Chichester, NH, 2006—08. Green Party. Avocations: horseback riding, hiking, birdwatching, painting, photography. Office: CC NH 31 College Dr Concord NH 03301

PALMA, ANNABEL, city councilwoman; 1 child. CNA cert., Bx. Cmty. Coll., 1991; degree in bus. adminstr., Monroe Coll. Cert. nursing asst. St. Vincent de Paul Sr. Residence, Bronx, NY, 1991—95; labor union organizer & trainer Local 1199 SEIU, 1999—2003; city councilwoman Dist. 18 NY City Coun., 2004—. Chmn. Drug Abuse subcommittee NY City Coun. Democrat. Office: 1041 Castle Hill Ave Bronx NY 10472 Office Phone: 718-792-1140. Office Fax: 718-931-0235. Business E-Mail: palma@council.nyc.ny.us.*

PALMATIER, MALCOLM ARTHUR, editor, consultant; b. Kalamazoo, Nov. 11, 1922; s. Karl Ernest and Cecile Caroline (Chase) Palmatier; m. Mary Elizabeth Summerfield, June 16, 1948 (dec. Oct. 1982); children: Barnabus, Timothy K., Duncan M.; m. Marie-Anne Suzanne van Werveke, Jan. 12, 1985. BS in Math., Western Mich. U., 1945; MA in English, UCLA, 1947; MA in Econs., U. So. Calif., 1971. Instr. English Pomona Coll., Claremont, Calif., 1949-51; editor Naval Ordnance Test Sta., Pasadena, Calif., 1951-54; head editl. unit Rocketdyne, LA, 1954-55; editor RAND Corp., Santa Monica, Calif., 1955-87, cons. editor, 1987—. Instr. English UCLA, 1950; participant Internat. Conf. Corp. Citizenship, Wilton Park, England, 2002. Mng. editor, cons. editor: Studies in Comparative Communism, 1968—80; co-editor: Perspectives in Economics, 1971; contbr. chapters to books, book revs. and articles to profl. jours. Chmn. bd. dirs. New Start, LA, 1982—84. With USNR, 1943—45. Mem.: Jonathan Club. Avocations: music, travel. Home: 516 Avondale Ave Los Angeles CA 90049-4804 Office: 1776 Main St Santa Monica CA 90407-2138 Personal E-mail: Malcolm27@earthlink.net.

PALME, DERYCK A., lawyer; b. NYC, Nov. 21, 1956; BA, Syracuse U., 1978; JD, U. Mich., 1982. Bar: NY 1984. Ptnr., bus., fin. restructuring dept. Cadwalader, Wickersham & Taft LLP, co-head fin. restructing dept., mem. mgmt. com. & co-chair. Adj. prof. law NY Law Sch.; mem. Bureau Nat. Affairs Adv. Bd., Bankruptcy Law Reporter. Coauthor: Restructuring: The Search for Value in a Troubled Enterprise, 1993, History of Bankruptcy Law in the Second Circuit, 1995, The PRC Enterprise Bankruptcy Law- The Poeples Work in Progress, 2008. Bd. dirs. Boys & Girls Harbor, Inc., Insol Internat., Greater NY Couns. Boy Scouts Am., Maplewood Village Alliance, Syracuse U., Cleveland Clinic Found., Coalition Consumer Bankruptcy Debtor Edn. Named one of Am. Top Black Attys., Black Enterprise, 2003. Fellow: Am. Coll. Bankruptcy; mem.: ABA, NY State Bar Assn. Office: Cadwalader Wickersham & Taft LLP One World Financial Ctr New York NY 10281 Office Phone: 212-504-6000. Office Fax: 212-504-6666. Business E-Mail: deryck.palmer@cwt.com.

PALMEIRO, RAFAEL CORRALES, former professional baseball player; b. Havana, Cuba, Sept. 24, 1964; Degree in Comml. Art, Miss. State U. Baseball player Chgo. Cubs, 1986-88, Tex. Rangers, 1988—93, 1999—2003, Balt. Orioles, 1994-98, 2004—05. Named Nat. League All-Star Team, 1988, Am. League All-Star Team, 1991, 1998, 1999; recipient Gold Glove award, 1997-1999; led Am. League in runs (124), 1993; hit 500th career home run, May 10, 2003; had his 3,000th career hit, July 15, 2005

PALMER, ANN THERESE DARIN, lawyer; b. Detroit, Apr. 25, 1951; d. Americo and Theresa (Del Favero) Darin; m. Robert Towne Palmer, Nov. 9, 1974; children: Justin Darin, Christian Darin. BA, U. Notre Dame, 1973, MBA, 1975; JD, Loyola U., Chgo., 1978. Bar: Ill. 1978, U.S. Supreme Ct. 1981. Intern Wall Street Jour., Detroit, 1974; freelancer Time Inc. Fin. Publs., Chgo., 1975—77; extern, Midwest regional solicitor U.S. Dept. Labor, 1976—78; tax atty. Esmark Inc., 1978; counsel Chgo. United, 1978—81; ind. contractor Legal Tax Rsch., 1981—89; fin. and legal news contbr. Chgo. Tribune, 1991—; fin. & legal news contbr. Bus. Week, 1991—2009; fin. and legal news contbr. Automotive News, 1993—97, Crain's Chgo. Bus., 1994—2000; contbg. editor Registered Rep, 2002—. Mem.: Village Club (Bloomfield Hills, Mich.), Glen View Club (Golf, Ill.). Home: 1570 Christina Ln Lake Forest IL 60045

PALMER, ANTHONY J., health products executive; BS in Mktg., Monash U., Melbourne, Australia, 1986; MBA, Internat. Mgmt. Inst., Geneva, 1989. Bus. devel. mgr. PA Consulting Group, 1986—91; sr. cons. LEK Partnership, 1991—92; mktg. mgr. Mars Confectionery, Australia, 1992—95, CSR Refined Sugars, Australia, 1995—96; mktg. and gen. mgmt. positions Minute Maid divsn. Coca-Cola Co., 1996—2000, region dir. Australia; pres. natural, frozen and warehouse club businesses Kellogg Co., mng. dir. UK; sr. v.p., chief mktg. officer Kimberly-Clark Corp., Dallas, 2006—. Office: Kimberly-Clark Corp PO Box 619100 Dallas TX 75261-9100

PALMER, ARNOLD DANIEL, professional golfer; b. Youngstown, Pa., Sept. 10, 1929; s. Milfred Jerome and Doris M. Palmer; m. Winnie Walzer, Dec. 20, 1954 (dec. Nov. 1999); children: Peggy Palmer Wears, Amy Palmer Saunders; m. Kathleen Gawthrop, Jan. 26, 2005. Student, Wake Forest Coll., LLD, 1970. Profl. golfer, 1954—; businessman, entrepreneur, 1960—. Nat. spokesman Sears Can., Rolex, Golf Digest, Callaway Golf, Encore Bank, Cessna, Ketel One, Administaff, Spectrum Brands, Ez-Go, Jacobsen, Pennington Seed, Luna Vineyards, Starkey Labs., Lamkin Corp., Golf Channel, Wyndham Hotels, Starkey Labs., Lawkiu Corp. Author: Arnold Palmer's Golf Book, 1961, Portrait of a Professional Golfer, 1964, My Game and Yours, 1965, rev. edit., 1983, Situation Golf, 1970, Go for Broke, 1973, Arnold Palmer's Best 54 Holes of Golf, 1977, Arnold Palmer's Complete Book of Putting, 1986, Play Great Golf, 1987, (with Thomas Hauser) A Personal Journey, 1994, (with James Dodson) Arnold Palmer, A Golfer's Life, 1999, Playing by the Rules, 2002, Arnold Palmer, Memories, Stories, and Memorabilia, 2004. Served USCG, 1951—54. Recipient Bob Jones award U.S. Golf Assn., William D. Richardson award Golf Writers Assn. Am., Herb Graffis award Nat. Golf Found., Presdl. Medal of Freedom, 2004, Byron Nelson prize Salesmanship Club, 2009; named Sportsman of Yr. Sports Illustrated mag., 1960, Player of Yr. Profl. Golfers Assn., 1960, 62, AP Athlete of Decade, 1969, others; Profl. Golfers Assn. Tour Money Leader, 1958, 60, 62, 63; named one of The Most Influential People in the World of Sports Bus. Week, 2007; named to World Golf Hall of Fame, Profl. Golfers Assn. Hall of Fame. Mem. Latrobe (Pa.) Country Club, Laurel Valley Golf Club, Rolling Rock Club (Ligonier, Pa.), Bay Hill Club, Duquesne Club (Pitts.). Winner of over 90 major golf tournaments since 1955, including Masters Championship, 1958, 60, 62, 64, U.S. Open, 1960, U.S. Amateur, 1954, Brit. Open, 1961, 62. Home and Office: PO Box 52 Youngstown PA 15696-0052 Office Phone: 724-537-7751.

PALMER, BEVERLY BLAZEY, psychologist, educator; b. Cleve., Nov. 22, 1945; d. Lawrence E. and Mildred M. Blazey; m. Richard C. Palmer, June 24, 1967; 1 child, Ryan Richard. PhD in Counseling Psychology, Ohio State U., 1972. Lic. clin. psychologist, Calif. Adminstrv. assoc. Ohio State U., Columbus, 1969—70; rsch. psychologist Health Svcs. Rsch. Ctr. UCLA, 1971—77; commr. pub. health L.A. County, 1978—81; pvt. practice Torrance, Calif., 1985—; prof. psychology Calif. State U., Dominguez Hills, 1973—2006; faculty Saybrook Grad. Sch. and Rsch. Ctr., 2005—. Author: Interpersonal Skills for Helping Professionals Online Course, 2001, 04, reviewer manuscripts for numerous textbook pubs; contbr. articles to profl. jours. Recipient Proclamation, County of L.A., 1972, 1981, Outstanding Prof. award, Calif. State U., 1995; Fulbright scholar, Borneo, 2001, Fulbright Sr. scholar, Malaysia, 2004—05, Fulbright scholar, Barbados, 2005. Mem. APA. Office: Calif State U Dominguez Hills Dept Psychology Carson CA 90747-0001 Office Phone: 310-373-6691 ext. 2.

PALMER, BRIAN EUGENE, retired lawyer; b. Mpls., May 16, 1948; s. Eugene Philip and Virginia Breeze (Rolfshus) P.; m. Julia Washburn Morrison, Dec. 29, 1972; 1 child, Julia Hunter. AB, Brown U., 1970; JD, William Mitchell Coll. of Law, 1974. Bar: Minn. 1974, U.S. Dist. Ct. Minn. 1975, U.S. Dist. Ct. (ea. dist.) Wis. 2001, U.S. Ct. Appeals (8th cir.) 1980, U.S. Ct. Fed. Claims 1984, U.S. Supreme Ct. 1980. Asst. pub. defender Hennepin County Pub. Defender, Mpls., 1974-78; assoc. Dorsey & Whitney LLP, Mpls., 1978-82, ptnr., 1983—2004, of counsel, 2005—06, ret., 2006. Home: 1190 Lyman Ave Wayzata MN 55391-9671 Office Phone: 612-340-2797. E-mail: palmer.brian@dorsey.com.

PALMER, CARSON, professional football player; b. Fresno, Calif., Dec. 27, 1979; s. Bill and Danna Palmer; m. Shaelyn Fernandes, July 5, 2003. BA in Pub. Policy, U. So. Calif., 2002. Quarterback Cin. Bengals, 2003—. Co-founder Carson Palmer Found., 2004—. Recipient Heisman Meml. Trophy, Heisman Trophy Trust, 2002; named Pro Bowl MVP, NFL, 2007; named to Am. Football Conf. Pro Bowl Team, 2005—06. Achievements include being the first overall selection in the 2003 NFL Draft; leading the NFL in touchdown passes (32), 2005. Office: c/o Cincinnati Bengals 1 Paul Brown Stadium Dr Cincinnati OH 45202*

PALMER, CHRISTINE (CLELIA ROSE VENDITTI), opera singer, musician; b. Hartford, Conn., Apr. 2, 1919; d. John and Immacolata (Morcaldo) Venditti; m. Arthur J. Whitlock, Feb. 25, 1953. Student, Mt. Holyoke Coll., 1942; RN with honors, Hartford Hosp. Sch. Nursing, 1941. Artist-in-residence El Centro Coll., Dallas, 1966-71. Pvt. vocal instr.-coach, Gifted With Absolute Pitch, pianist by Ear; voice adjudicator San Francisco Opera Co., 1969-72, Tex. Music Tchrs. Assn., 1964-75, lectr. S.M. Chartocks' Gilbert and Sullivan Co.; leading opera pianist NYC Club Opera, Chgo., San Francisco, San Carlo, other cities, 1944-62, NY Town Hall Concert, 1951. Soloist with symphony orchs. maj. US Cities, 1948-62; ch. soloist Marble Collegiate Ch., Holy Trinity Ch., NYC; coast-to-coast concert tour, 1948; numerous lead appearances with St. Louis MUNY Opera, Indpls. Starlight Theatre, Lambertville Music Circus; soloist Holiday on Ice, 1949-50, NY Borscht Cir.; TV performer, including Home Show on NBC, Telephone Hour on NBC, Holiday Hotel; performer various supper clubs, N.Y.C., Atlanta, Bermuda, Catskills, others, including Number One Fifth Avenue, The Embers, The Carriage Club, Viennese Lantern. Hon. mem. women's bd. Dallas Opera Assn.; mem. adv. bd. Tex. Opera News; mem. Tex. Music Tchrs. Cert. Bd., Collegiate Chorale, Don Craig Singers, The Vikings; mem. women's bd., Dallas Bapt. Univ. Oliver Ditson scholar, 1942; recipient Phi Xi Delta prize in Italian, 1937; named Victor Herbert Girl, ASCAP; Spl. Recognition Gold book of Dallas Soc. Mem. Nat. Assn. Tchrs. of Singing (pres. Dallas chpt. 1972-74), Nat. Fedn. Music Clubs, Tex. Fedn. Music Clubs, Dallas Fedn. Music Clubs (pres. 1972-74), Dallas Symphony League, Dallas Music Tchrs. Assn. (pres. 1971-72, Tchr. of Yr. 1974), Thesaurus Book Club (pres. 1990-91, 97-98), Friday Forum (Dallas, bd. dirs.), Dallas Women's C. of C., Eagle Forum, Pub. Affairs Luncheon Club, Dallas Fedn. Music Club, Pro Am., Wednesday Morning Choral Club, Dallas Knife and Fork Club, Prestoncrest Rep. Club. Presbyterian. Home: 6232 Pemberton Dr Dallas TX 75230-4036

PALMER, CHRISTOPHER E., lawyer; BA cum laude, St. John's U., Minn., 1982; JD magna cum laude, Georgetown Univ., 1986. Bar: Minn. 1986, DC 1988. Ct. law clerk Ct. Appeals for DC Cir.; ptnr. Shea & Gardner (merged with Goodwin Procter LLP); ptnr.,chair, bus. law dept. Goodwin Procter LLP, Washington, 2004—. Articles editor Georgetown Law Jour. Office: Goodwin Procter LLP 901 New York Ave NW Washington DC 20001 Office Phone: 202-346-4253. Office Fax: 202-346-4444. Business E-Mail: cpalmer@goodwinprocter.com.

PALMER, DAVE RICHARD, retired military officer, academic administrator; b. Ada, Okla., May 31, 1934; s. David Furman and Lorena Marie (Clardy) P.; m. LuDelia Clemmer, Apr. 13, 1957; children: Allison, J. Kersten. BS, U.S. Military Acad., 1956; MA in History, Duke U., 1966; postgrad., Army War Coll., 1972-73; PhD (hon.), Duke U., 1990. Commd. U.S. Army, 1956, advanced through grades to lt. gen.; mem. faculty dept. history U.S. Mil. Acad., 1966-69; mem. staff (Pentagon), 1973-76, Joint Chiefs of Staff, 1979-81; comdr. Baumholder Mil. Community, W. Ger., 1981-83; dep. comdt. Command and Gen. Staff Coll., Ft. Leavenworth, Kans., 1983-85; comdg. gen. 1st Armored Div., W.Ger., 1985-86; supt. U.S. Mil. Acad., 1986-91, ret., 1991; pres. Walden U., 1995-99; CEO Walden Corp., 1999-2000. Author: The River and the Rock, 1969, The Way of the Fox, 1975, Summons of the Trumpet, 1978, 1794-America, Its Army, and The Birth of the Nation, 1994, First in War, 2000, Provide for the Common Defense, 2001, Washington and Arnold, 2006. Bd. dirs. Walden U., 1992-2001. Decorated Legion of Merit (3); Bronze Star (2), D.S.M.(2); named Disting. Grad., U.S. Mil. Acad., 2005. Mem. Assn. U.S. Army, Armor Assn., Mil. History, Soc. Cin. Office Phone: 254-933-0554. Personal E-mail: davepalmer@clearwire.net.

PALMER, DAVID GILBERT, lawyer; b. Lakewood, NJ, Jan. 10, 1945; s. Robert Dayton and Lois (Gilbert) P.; m. Susan Edmundson Walsh, Aug. 17, 1968; children: Jonathan, Megan. AB, Johns Hopkins U., 1967; JD, U. Colo., 1970. Bar: Colo. 1970, U.S. Dist. Ct. Colo. 1970, U.S. Ct. Appeals (9th and 10th cirs.) 1970, U.S. Supreme Ct. 1970. Ptnr., mng. ptnr., chmn. litig. dept Holland & Hart, Denver, 1970-87; ptnr., mng. ptnr. Gibson, Dunn & Crutcher, Denver, 1987-97; mng. ptnr. Zevnik, Horton, Palmer, Denver, 1997-2001; mng. shareholder Greenberg Traurig LLP, Denver, 2001—. Chmn. N.W. region Am. Heart Assn., Dallas, 1986—, bd. dirs., 1986—, sec., 1990—, nat. chmn., 1992-93; pres., bd. dirs. Colo. Heart Assn., Denver, 1974; bd. dirs. C.H. Kempe Nat. Ctr. for Prevention of Child Abuse, Denver, 1984-90, pres., 1989-90; bd. dirs. Goodwill Industries, Denver, 1981-84, Metro Denver Econ. Devel. Corp., 2004—; mem. coun. of advisors U. Colo. Med. Sch., 2004—. Mem. ABA, Colo. Bar Assn., Denver Law Club, Univ. Club of Denver (pres. 2004-05), Mile High Club. Office: Greenberg Traurig Tabor Ctr 1200 17th St Ste 2400 Denver CO 80202 Office Phone: 303-572-6539. Office Fax: 303-572-6540. Business E-Mail: palmerdg@gtlaw.com.

PALMER, DAVID KEITH, otolaryngologist; s. Merlin and Elna Palmer; m. Elizabeth Palmer; children: Aimee Palmer Stewart, Erin Palmer Morley, David M., Matt, Whitney. BS magna cum laude, U. Utah, Salt Lake City, 1978; MD, Med. Coll. Pa., Phila., 1986. Diplomate Am. Bd. Otolaryngology; RN Utah, 1978. Intern Penn. State U. Hershey Med., resident; clin. instr. Penn. State U., Hershey, 1991—92; chief otolaryngology St. Mark's Hosp., Salt Lake City, 1995—; adj. clin. prof. U. Utah Sch. Medicine, Salt Lake City, 2001—. Instr. Mormon Tabernacle Choir, Salt Lake City, 2001—. Singer: Mormon Tabernacle Choir (Nat. Medal Arts, 05). Voluntary missionary svc. LDS Ch., Sao Paolo, Brazil, 1972—74, bishop Hershey, Pa., 1989—92. 1st lt. US Army, 1978—83. Scholar, Harvard U., 1982; Delmore scholar, Med. Coll. Pa., 1986. Fellow: Am. Acad. Otolaryngic Allergy (chmn., patient and profl. rels. 2005—, bd. dirs. 1996—), Am. Acad. Otolaryngology Head and Neck Surgery; mem.: AMA (life). Office: ENT Specialists 4000 S 700 E #10 Salt Lake City UT 84107 Office Fax: 801-261-8609.

PALMER, DAVID SCOTT, political scientist, educator; b. Boston, July 16, 1937; s. Walter S. and Jean (Stuart) P.; m. Sarah Crawford, 1966 (dec. Nov. 1985); children: Walter Scott, Henry Crawford, Asa MacAdam; m. Diane Nagel, 1998. BA in Internat. Rels. cum laude, Dartmouth Coll., 1959; MA in Hispanic Am. Studies, Stanford U., 1962; PhD in Comparative Govt., Cornell U., 1973. Vol. leader Peace Corps, Peru, 1962-64; asst. dean freshmen, asst. to dir. admissions Dartmouth Coll., Hanover, NH, 1964-68; from instr. to asst. prof. dept. govt. Bowdoin Coll., 1972-76; professorial lectr. Sch. Advanced Internat. Studies Johns Hopkins U., Washington, 1977-88; assoc. dean for programs Fgn. Svc. Inst., Dept. State, 1984-88, chair Latin Am. and Caribbean studies, 1976-88; prof. polit. sci. Boston U., 1988—, prof. internat. rels., 1990—, assoc. chair undergrad. studies internat. rels. dept., 1997-99, chair dept. polit. sci., 1998-2001, dir. Latin Am. studies program, 1991—94, 2004—05, 2009—. Vis. lectr. Princeton U., 1978—79, Georgetown U., 1985; vis. prof. U. Salamanca, Spain, 1997—; vis. scholar Inter-Am. Dialogue, 2001—02. Author: Peru: The Authoritarian Tradition, 1980, (with Kevin Middlebrook) Military Government and Political Development: Lessons from Peru, 1975 (with Robert Wesson and others) The Latin American Military Institution, 1985; editor, contbr.: Shining Path of Peru, 1992, 2d edit., 1994, U.S. Relations with Latin America during the Clinton Years, 2006; contbr. chpts. to books, articles and revs. to profl. jours. Bd. visitors Tucker Found., Dartmouth Coll., 2005—; mem. Fulbright nat. screening com., 2005—09. Recipient Meritorious Honor award U.S. Dept. of State, 1981; Daniel Webster nat. scholar, 1955-59; Edward John Noble Found. leadership grantee 1959-62; Fulbright fellow, 1998. Mem. Latin Am. Studies Assn. (exec. com. 1983-86), New Eng. Coun. Latin Am. Studies (exec. com. 1989-98, 2000—, pres. 1993-94), Phi Beta Delta, Phi Kappa Phi, Sigma Delta Pi. Home: 69 Waverley St Belmont MA 02478-1958 Office: Boston U 152 Bay State Rd Boston MA 02215-1501 Office Phone: 617-353-9388. Business E-Mail: dspalmer@bu.edu.

PALMER, DEBORAH JEAN, lawyer; b. Williston, ND, Oct. 25, 1947; d. Everett Edwin and Doris Irene (Harberg) P.; m. Kenneth L. Rich, Mar. 29, 1980; children: Andrew, Stephanie. BA, Carleton Coll., 1969; JD cum laude, Northwestern U., 1973. Bar: Minn. 1973, U.S. Dist. Ct. Minn. 1973, U.S. Ct. Appeals (8th cir.) 1975, U.S. Supreme Ct. 1978, U.S. Ct. Appeals (11th cir.) 1999. Econ. analyst Harris Trust & Savs. Bank, Chgo., 1969-70; assoc. Robins, Kaplan, Miller & Ciresi LLP, Mpls., 1973-79, ptnr., 1979—2001. Trustee Carleton Coll., 1984-88; mem. bd. religious edn. Plymouth Congl. Ch., 1992-95; bd. dirs. Mpls. YWCA, 1996-99; mem. Dist. Minn. Civil Justice Reform Act Adv. Group, 1990-93; bd. dirs. RKM&C Found. Edn., Pub. Health & Social Justice, 1999-, St. Paul Chamber Orchestra, 2002-, Jeremiah Program, 2005-, Inst. New Am., 2004-07. Mem. ABA, Minn. Bar Assn., Minn. Women Lawyers Assn. (sec. 1976-78), Minn. Fed. Bar Assn. (chpt. bd. dirs. 1996-98), Hennepin County Bar Assn., Hennepin County Bar Found. (bd. dirs. 1978-81), Carleton Coll. Alumni Assn. (bd. dirs. 1978-82, sec. 1980-82), Women's Assn. of Minn. Orch. (bd. dirs. 1980-85, treas. 1981-83). Home: 1787 Colfax Ave S Minneapolis MN 55403-3008 E-mail: djpalmer@rkmc.com.

PALMER, DENISE E., publishing executive; b. Seymour, Ind., Feb. 12, 1957; m. Gregory G. Palmer. BA, U. Dayton, 1977; MS in Mgmt., Northwestern U., 1984. CPA. Sr. auditor Coopers & Lybrand, Dayton, Ohio, 1977—80; corp. auditor Tribune, 1980—86, planning analyst, 1983—86, mgr. planning, 1986—88; dir. fin. WGN Radio, Chgo., 1988—93, sta. mgr., 1993; dir. fin. Chgo. Tribune, Chgo., 1994—95, v.p. fin. & adminstrn., 1996—97, v.p. fin. strategy & fin., 1996—98, v.p. devel., strategy, fin., 1998—2000; pres., CEO CLTV, Oakbrook, Ill., 2000—02; pres., pub., CEO Balt. Sun, 2002—06; pres., pub. Tampa Tribune, 2006—. Bd. mem. Greater Baltimore Com., 2003—, Econ. Alliance of Greater Baltimore, 2003—, Md. Bus. Roundtable for Edn., 2003—; bd. visitors U. Md. Baltimore County, 2003—; mem. adv. bd. U. Dayton; mem. Northwestern U. Coun. of 100 Women; mem. bus. sch. adv. bd. U. Dayton. Named one of Maryland's Top 100 Women, 2005. Mem.: Inland Press Assn. Office: Tampa Tribune 200 S Parker St Tampa FL 33606 Mailing: Tampa Tribune PO Box 191 Tampa FL 33601 Office Phone: 813-259-7711.

PALMER, DOUGLAS HAROLD, Mayor, Trenton, New Jersey; b. Trenton, NJ, Oct. 19, 1951; s. George H. and Dorothy (Vaughn) P. BS in Bus. Mgmt., Hampton U., 1973. With C.V. Hill Co., Trenton; civil svc. worker N.J. Dept. Motor Vehicles, Trenton; dir. Community Schs. Trenton; asst. dir. Trenton Bd. Edn., dir. purchasing; small bus. owner Trenton; mayor City of Trenton, 1990—. Bd. dirs. ARC, Urban League Met. Trenton, Forum Project, Rider Coll. Ednl. Opportunity Fund Program, We, Inc., Carver Ctr., NAACP, treas.; freeholder Dem. Party Mercer County, 1981-91; mgr. West End Little League, Trenton, 1965-75, treas., 1975—. Named Outstanding Young Man Am., Del. Valley United Way Bd.; recipient Fai Ho Cha award Omega Psi Phi; recipient City Livability award, US Conf. of Mayors, Twenty Year Alumnus award, Hampton U., Spirit of St. Francis award, St. Francis Hosp., Equal Justice medal, Legal Svcs. NJ, State of Israel Peace medal award, 1993, Tending the Garden State, Cmty. Develop. Leadership award, Worldworks Found. NJ, 1993. Baptist. Office: 319 E State St Trenton NJ 08608-1809 Office Phone: 609-989-3030. Office Fax: 609-989-3939. E-mail: mayorsoffice@trentonnj.org.*

PALMER, DOUGLAS S., JR., lawyer; b. Peoria, Ill., Mar. 15, 1945; AB cum laude, Yale U., 1966; JD cum laude, Harvard U., 1969. Bar: Wash. 1969. Mem. Foster Pepper & Shefelman PLLC, Seattle, 1975—2002, Hillis Clark Martin & Peterson, P.S., Seattle, 2002—. Office: Hillis Clark Martin & Peterson PS 1221 Second Ave Ste 500 Seattle WA 98101-2925 Office Phone: 206-623-1745.

PALMER, EDWARD L., psychologist, educator, writer; b. Hagerstown, Md., Aug. 11, 1938; s. Ralph Leon and Eva Irene (Brandenburg) P.; children: Edward Lee, Jennifer Lynn. BA, Gettysburg Coll., 1960; BD, Luth. Theol. Sem., Gettysburg, 1964; MS, Ohio U., 1967, PhD, 1970. Asst. prof. Western Md. Coll., Westminster, 1968-70, Davidson Coll., NC, 1970-77, assoc. prof. NC, 1977-86, chair, 1985—99, prof. NC, 1986—, Watson prof. NC, 1991—, Watson prof. chair, 2009—. Guest rschr. Harvard U., Cambridge, Mass., 1977; vis. scholar UCLA, 1984, UNC Chapel Hill, 1991, U. Exeter, 2000, U. Ala., 2005; cons. Council on Children, Media, Merchandising, 1978-79, 1st Union Bank Corp., Charlotte, N.C., 1975-79; NSF proposal reviewer, 1978—. Editl. reviewer Jour. Broadcasting and Electronic Media, 1978—, editl. bd. Media Psychology; editor: Children and the Faces of TV, 1980, Faces of Televisual Media, 2003; author: Children in the Cradle of TV, 1987; contbr. to Wiley Ency. of Psychology, 1984, 2002, Lawrence Erlbaum Assocs., 1991, Sage Pub., 1993-96; author jour. articles and book chpts. Sec. Mecklenburg Child Devel. Assn., Davidson and Cornelius, N.C., 1974-78; bd. mem. pub. radio Sta. WDAV, 1970-90, Telecomms. task force Rutgers U., 1981. Recipient Thomas Jefferson Tchg. award Robert Earl McConnell Found., 1993, Deptl. Psychology in Svc. award, 2007. Mem. APA, Am. Psychol. Soc., Assn. Heads Depts. Psychology (chair 1994-96), Am. Psychol. Assn. (task force on advt. and children 2001-03), Southeastern Psychol. Assn., Southeastern Soc. Social Psychologists, Phi Beta Kappa (pres. Davidson chpt. 1985-86). Avocations: sunrise and sunset walks, poetry, bird watching, music composition and performance, hiking. Office: Davidson Coll PO Box 7007 Davidson NC 28035-7007 Office Phone: 704-894-2882. E-mail: edpalmer@davidson.edu.

PALMER, FORREST CHARLES, librarian, educator; b. Burlington, Wis., Oct. 17, 1924; s. Forrest Blaire and Marie Florence (Rubach) P.; m. Lois Mae Davis, June 12, 1946; children: Forrest Charles Jr., Beth Elaine, Janet Lorrayne. Student, U. Pitts., 1943-44; BA, Valparaiso U., 1948; BS in Libr. Sci., George Peabody Coll., 1949, MS in Libr. Sci., 1953. Head catalog dept. Janesville (Wis.) Pub. Library, 1949-50; serials cataloger N.C. State U., Raleigh, 1950-51, head serials dept., 1951-55; dir. libraries Miss. State U., State College, 1955-62; librarian, head dept. library sci. James Madison U., Harrisonburg, Va., 1962-70, head librarian, 1970-74, prof. library sci., documents librarian, 1973-89, ret., 1989, prof. emeritus, 1990—, faculty senate, 1982-86, faculty marshall, 1983-85, treas. senate, 1985-86. Mem. libr. com. Va. Higher Edn. Study Commn.; sec. joint law libr. com. Laird L. Conrad Meml. Law Libr., Harrisonburg, 1974-89; adv. com. Va. Coun. Higher Edn.; Madison Coll. rep. libr. affairs Va. U. Ctr Editor: Virginia Librarian, 1963-65. Contbr. articles to profl. publs. Mem. edn. com. Starkville (Miss.) Youth Ctr., 1956; chmn. adv. bd. YMCA, State College, Miss., 1957-59; vice-chmn. Rep. city com., Harrisonburg, 1979-81; mem. land use adv. com. Ctrl. Shenandoah Planning Dist. Commn., 1979; mem. Bd. Zoning Appeals, Harrisonburg, 1981-91, vice chmn., 1983-85, chmn., 1985-91; ruling elder Presbyn. Ch. U.S., clk. of session; mem. task force on maintenance Synod of Mid-Atlantic, Presbyn. Ch., Massanetta Springs, 1991; mem. Ft. Delaware Soc., 1992, life mem., 1995—; mem. LaPorte County Hist. Steam Soc., Inc., 1996—; mem. Massanetta Springs Heritage Soc., 1997—; mem. Peabody Pioneers, Vanderbilt U., 2003—. With Signal Corps AUS, PTO, 1943-46; vol. Keister Elem. Sch., Harrisonburg, Va., 1992—. Recipient Outstanding Libr. Sci. student award, George Peabody Coll.,1949, Golden Triangle award YMCA. Mem. ALA (liaison com. Library Instrn. Round Table 1978-80, com. on instrn. in use of libraries 1977-79, mem. Govt. Documents Round Table 1983-89), Southeastern Library Assn. (chmn. coll. sect. 1960-62, treas., mem. exec. bd. 1975-76, budget com. 1974-80, hdqrts. liason com., 1987-91), Miss. Library Assn. (chmn. standards and planning com. 1958-59, chmn. coll. sect. 1959-60), Va. Library Assn. (activities com. 1962-65, chmn. publs. com. 1963-65, 1st v.p. 1968, pres. 1969-70), WWII Meml. Soc. (charter), Pi Gamma Mu, Alpha Beta Alpha (adviser 1962-70), Beta Phi Mu. Republican. Presbyterian. Home: 60 E Weaver Ave Harrisonburg VA 22801-3041 *Long-lasting and meaningful contributions to society are those made out of consideration for others, not those where another individual is harmed.*

PALMER, IRENE SABELBERG, retired dean, nursing educator, genealogist; b. Franklin, NJ, May 28, 1923; d. John Joseph and May (Heiser) Sabelberg. BS, N.J. State Tchrs. Coll., 1945; diploma, Jersey City Med. Center Sch. Nursing, 1945; MA, NYU, 1951, PhD, 1963. Edn. dir. Diploma Schs. Nursing NJ and Mass, 1948—52; ednl. dir. Glenn Dale Hosp. and DC Dept. Pub. Health, Md., 1956, dir. nursing svc. and edn., 1956—61; assoc. clin. prof. nursing Georgetown U., Washington, 1960—61; USPHS trainee, 1961—62; assoc. chief nursing svc. for rsch. VA Hosp., San Francisco, 1963—64; rsch. nurse cons. divsn. nursing HEW and USPHS Nursing Rsch. Field Ctr., San Francisco, 1964—66; asst. dean and assoc. prof. nursing U. Colo. Sch. Nursing, Denver, 1966—68; dean, prof. nursing Boston U. Sch. Nursing, 1968—74; founding dean, prof. nursing Hahn Sch. Nursing U. San Diego, 1974—91, prof. emeritus, 1991—; dean emeritus Hahn Sch. Nursing, U. San Diego, 1988—. Lectr. Classical Alliance of Western States, Uskudar, Turkey, 1994, Italy, 95. Editor: Nursing Clinics of North America, 1970; contbr. articles to profl. jours. Served to capt. Nurse Corps US Army, 1953—56. Recipient Excellence in Nursing Scholarship award, Orgn. nurse Execs., 1993; Internat. Nightingale scholar, Nat. Health Svc. fellow. Fellow: Am. Acad. Nursing, Nat. League Nursing (bd. visitors 1977—87); mem.: ANA, German Rsch. Assn. (pres. 1995), Am. Assn. Colls. Nursing (hon.), Am. Assn. History Nursing, Boston U. Nursing Archives, Sigma Theta Tau (Leadership award Zeta Mu chpt. 1986, Excellence in Nursing award 1991).

PALMER, JAMES DANIEL, information technology educator; b. Washington, Mar. 8, 1930; s. Martin Lyle and Sarah Elizabeth (Hall) P.; m. Margret Kupka, June 21, 1952; children: Stephen Robert, Daniel Lee, John Keith. AA, Fullerton Jr. Coll., 1953; BS (Alumni scholar), U. Calif., Berkeley, 1955, MS, 1957; PhD, U. Okla., 1963; DPS (hon.), Regis Coll., Denver, 1977. Chief engr. Motor vehicle and Illumination Lab. U. Calif., Berkeley, 1955-57; assoc. prof. U. Okla., Norman, 1957-63, prof., 1963-66, asst. to dir. Rsch. Inst., 1960-63, cons. Rsch. Inst., 1966-69, dir. Sch. Elec. Engring., 1963-66, dir. Systems Rsch. Center, 1964-66; dean sci. and engring., prof. elec. engring. Union Coll., Schenectady, 1966-71; pres. Met. State Coll., Denver, 1971-78; rsch. and spl. programs adminstr. Dept. Transp., Washington, 1978-79; v.p., gen. mgr. rsch. and devel. div. Mech. Tech., Inc., Latham, NY, 1979-82; exec. v.p. J.J. Henry Co., Inc., Moorestown, NJ, 1982-85; BDM internat. prof. info. tech. George Mason U., Fairfax, Va., 1985-95, prof. emeritus, 1995—; software cons., 1995—. Bd. dirs. J.J. Henry Co., Inc.; cons. Sym Mgmt. Co., Boston, Higher Edn. Exec. Assocs., Denver, PERI, Princeton; adj. prof. U. Colo. Co-author: (with A.P. Sage) Software Systems Engineering, (with Aseltine, Beam and Sage) Introduction to Computer Systems, Analysis, Design and Application. Bd. dirs., exec. v.p. adv. com. U.S.A. Vols. for Internat. Tech. Assistance, 1967-83, exec. v.p., 1970-71, chmn. exec. com.; trustee, vice chmn. Nat. Commn. on Coop. Edn.; mem. exec. policy bd. Alaska Natural Gas Pipeline, 1978-79; trustee Auraria Higher Edn. Program, Denver; mem. Fulbright fellow Selection Com., Colo.; bd. mgrs., mem. exec. com. Hudson-Mohawk Assn. Colls. and Univs., trustee, chmn. bd., 1970-71; adv. com. USCG Acad., 1972-82, chmn. adv. com., 1979-82; mem. Colo. Gov.'s Sci. and Tech. Adv. Coun.; pres. Denver Cath. Cmty. Svcs. Bd.; mem. Archdiocesan Cath. Charities and Cmty. Svcs.; bd. dirs. U. Okla. Rsch. Inst.; chair bd. dirs. Tri-City Vols. Inc., 2004—; mem. adv. com. Mile-Hi Red Cross; mem. Tri-City Vols., chair. With USMC, 1950-51. Recipient U.S. Coast Guard medal, 1983; named James D. Palmer scholarship in his honor, George Mason U., 2002; Centennial scholar, Case-Western Res., 1981. Fellow IEEE (exec. and adminstrv. coms., v.p. long-range planning and finance, chmn. com. on large scale systems, Joseph E. Wahl Outstanding Career Achievement award 1993, Millennium medal 2000); mem. Systems, Man and Cybernetics Soc. (pres., Outstanding Contbns. award 1981), alumni assns. U. Calif. and U. Okla., Inst. Internat. Edn. (bd. dir. Rocky Mt. sect.), Soc. Naval Architects and Marine Engrs., Am. Soc. Engring. Edn., Am. Mil. Engrs., N.Y. Acad. Sci., Navy League, Sigma Xi, Eta Kappa Nu, Pi Mu Epsilon, Alpha Gamma Sigma. Home: 860 Cashew Way Fremont CA 94536-2646 Office: George Mason U Sch of Info Tech & Engring Fairfax VA 22030 Personal E-mail: jdpalmer@ix.netcom.com.

PALMER, JAMES F., aerospace transportation executive; BS, Southeast Mo. State, 1971. Sr. v.p., CFO McDonnell Douglas Corp., 1995—97; pres., Boeing Shared Services Group The Boeing Co., 1997—2000, sr. v.p.; pres. Boeing Capital Corp., 2000—04; exec. v.p., CFO Visteon Corp., 2004—07; corp. v.p., CFO Northrop Grumman Corp., LA, 2007—. Office: Northrop Grumman Corp 1840 Century Park E Los Angeles CA 90067-2199 Office Phone: 734-710-2020.*

PALMER, JEFFREY BRUCE, physiatrist, researcher; b. NYC; s. Walter and Barbara Norma (Doctor) P.; m. Sara Sarnoff, July 5, 1975; children: Joshua Henry, Noah Gabriel. BA, NYU, 1976, MD, 1980; M in Rehab. Medicine, U. Wash., 1983. Diplomate Am. Bd. Phys. Medicine & Rehab., Am. Bd. Electrodiagnostic Medicine. Resident U. Wash., Seattle, 1980-83; asst. prof. Johns Hopkins U., Balt., 1983-92, assoc. prof., 1992—; assoc. Harvard U., Cambridge, Mass., 1990—94. Mem. editorial bd. Arch. Phys. Medicine Rehab., 1994-95, 2001-; guest editor Physical Medicine and Rehabilitation Clinics of America, 2008; editorial adv. bd. Dysphagia, 1986—; mem. editorial bd. Jour. Thermology, 1989—; contbr. (co-author) Spinal Cord Injury: A Guide for Living, Eds. 1 and 2; contbr. (chpt.) Normal and Abnormal Swallowing, 1991, 2003; Rehabilitation Medicine: Principles and Practice (Ed. 3 and 4), 1998 and 2005; Encyclopedia of Disabililty, 2005; Essentials of Physical Medicine and Rehabilitation (Eds. 1 and 2), 2002 and 2008; Physical Medicine and Rehabilitation, 2007; Physical Medicine and Rehabilitation Secrets (Ed. 3), 2008; Stroke Recovery and Rehabilitation, 2009. NIH grantee, 1987-2008. Fellow Am. Acda. Phys. Medicine and Rehab., Am. Assn. Electrodiagnostic Medicine; mem. Assn. Acad. Psychiatrists, Phi Beta Kappa. Office: Johns Hopkins U 600 N Wolfe St Phipps 160 Baltimore MD 21239 Office Phone: 410-502-2446. Office Fax: 410-502-2420. Business E-Mail: jpalmer@jhmi.edu.*

PALMER, JOHN BERNARD, III, lawyer; b. Ft. Wayne, Ind., May 18, 1952; s. John Bernard and Dorothy Alma (Lauer) P. BA, Mich. State U., 1974; JD, U. Mich., 1977. Bar: Ill. 1977, US Dist. Ct. (no. dist.) Ill. 1977, US Ct. Appeals 2002, US Tax Ct. 1979, US Ct. Claims 2001. Assoc. Mayer Brown & Platt, Chgo., 1977-80, Hopkins & Sutter, Chgo., 1980-83, ptnr., 1983-2001, Foley & Lardner LLP, Chgo., 2001—, chmn. taxation practice group. Adj. prof. Ill. Inst. Tech.- Kent Coll. of Law, Chgo., 1984—. Mem. ABA (tax sect.). Office: Foley & Lardner LLP 321 N Clark St Chicago IL 60610 Office Phone: 312-832-4575. Business E-Mail: jpalmer@foley.com.

PALMER, JOHN DERRY, physiology educator; b. Chgo., May 26, 1932; s. John and Florence (Eley) P.; m. Carla Bianchi, Sept. 15, 1960; 1 child, John Charles. BA, Lake Forest Coll., 1957; MS, Northwestern U., 1959, PhD, 1962. Asst. prof. U. Ill., Chgo., 1961-63; fellow NSF, U. Bristol, Eng., 1963-64; prof., dept. chmn. NYU, 1964-74; prof. U. Mass., Amherst, 1974—, dept. chmn., 1974-80. Edit. bd. Marine Behavior and Physiology, 1988—, Chronobiology Internat., 1986—; author: Textbook of Modern Biology, 1968, The Biological Clock: Two Views, 1970, Biological Clocks in Marine Organisms: The Control of Physiological and Behavioral Tidal Rhythms, 1974, An Introduction to Biological Rhythms, 1976, (with others) Biological Rhythms and Living Clocks, 1977, Human Biological Rhythms, 1983, The Biological Rhythms and Clocks of Intertidal Animals, 1995, The Living Clock, 2000, The Biological Clock, 2003; contbr. articles to profl. jours. With U.S. Army, 1953-55. Fellow AAAS, Explorers Club; mem. Internat. Soc. of Chronobiology, Nat. Assn. of Scholars, Marine Biol. Lab., Phi Beta Kappa, Sigma Xi (pres., v.p., treas. N.Y. chpt., Disting. Rschr. award 1968). Avocation: trout and saltwater fishing. Office: U Mass Dept Biology 611 North Pleasant St Amherst MA 01003 Home: 98 January Hill Rd Amherst MA 01002 Office Phone: 413-545-4400. Business E-Mail: ftodd@bio.umass.edu.

PALMER, KEKE (LAUREN KEYANA PALMER), actress; b. Harvey, Ill., Aug. 26, 1993; Actor: (films) Barbershop 2: Back in Business, 2004, Akeelah and the Bee, 2006 (Actress in a Motion Picture, NAACP Image Awards, 2007), Madea's Family Reunion, 2006, The Longshots, 2008; (TV films) The Wool Cap, 2004, Keke & Jamal, 2005, Knights of the South Bronx, 2005, Jump In!, 2007; guest appearances (TV series) Cold Case, 2004, Strong Medicine, 2004, Second Time Around, 2005, ER, 2005, Law & Order: Special Victims Unit, 2005. Office: c/o Coast To Coast 3350 Barham Blvd Los Angeles CA 90068

PALMER, KENT FRIEDLEY, physics professor; b. Chgo., Sept. 26, 1941; s. Wilson Gerard and Evelyn Abbie Palmer; m. Marna Lee Warner, June 15, 1968; children: Dain Ryan, Shera Lynn. BS, Ohio State U., Columbus, 1964; PhD, 1972. Rsch. scientist Mead Corp., Chillicothe, Ohio, 1963—64; academic counselor The Ohio State U., 1971—72; postdoc. fellow Kans. State U., Manhattan, 1972—74; vis. asst. prof. U. Ky., Lexington, 1976; prof. physics Westminster Coll., Fulton, Mo., 1976—. Summer faculty rsch. assoc. USAF Arnold Engring. & Devel. Ctr., Tullahoma, Tenn., 1976, cons., 1978—94; summer rsch. assoc. Kans. State U., 1977, Energy Measurements Divsn. EG & G, Las Vegas, Nev., 1984, U. Nev., 1985. Elder First Presbyn. Ch., Fulton, 1986—2008. Recipient Governor's Excellence Tchg. award, Westminster Coll., 2002. Mem.: Am. Assn. Physics Tchrs., Optical Soc. Am., Omicron Delta Kappa, Sigma Pi Sigma. Avocations: travel, camping, hiking, astronomy. Home: 9 Country Club Dr Fulton MO 65251-2330 Office: Westminster Coll 501 Westminster Ave Fulton MO 65251-1299 Business E-Mail: kent.palmer@westminster-mo.edu.

PALMER, LARRY GARLAND, music educator, writer, musician; b. Warren, Ohio, Nov. 13, 1938; s. Gerald Leroy and Esther Garland Palmer. MusB, Oberlin Coll., Ohio, 1960; MusM, Eastman Sch. Music, 1961, MusD, 1963. Head Dept. Fine Arts St. Paul's Coll., Lawrenceville, Va., 1963—65; prof. music Norfolk (Va.) State U., 1965—70; prof. harpsichord and organ So. Meth. U., Dallas, 1970—. Author: Hugo Distler and his Church Music, 1967, Harpsichord in America: A 20th-Century Revival, 1989, paperback edit., 1993, Letters from Salzburg: A Music Student in Europe 1958-1959, 2006; contbg. author: The New Grove Dictionary of Music, The Grove Dictionary of Opera; musician: The Harpsichord Now and Then, 1975, Organ Works of Hugo Distler, 1978, Dedication Recital, Fisk Organ opus 101, 1993, Larry Palmer /Harpsichord/ Bach, 1994, Harpsichord Recital, 1997, Music of Rudy Davenport, 1999, Dos Prados: Larry Palmer Plays the 1762 Oldovini Organ in the Meadows Museum, SMU, 2001, Hommages: Music for Harpsichord, 2008; harpsichord editor: The Diapason, 1969—. Mem.: Am. Guild Organists (dean Norfolk chpt. 1968—70, dean Dallas chpt. 1977—79), Southeastern Hist. Keyboard Soc. (pres. 2004—08). Avocations: reading, cooking. Office: Southern Methodist University Meadows School of the Arts Dallas TX 75275 E-mail: lpalmer@smu.edu.

PALMER, LARRY LEON, foundation administrator, former ambassador; b. Augusta, Ga. BA, Emory U., 1970; MEd in African History, Tex. So. U., 1973; EdD in Higher Edn., Ind. U., Bloomington, 1978. Vol. Peace Corps., Liberua, West Africa, 1971—73; joined Foreign Svc., 1982; vice consul Dominican Republic, 1982—84; personnel officer Montevideo, Uruguay and Asuncion, Paraguay, 1984—86; staff asst. to asst. sec. African Affairs US Dept. State, 1986—87, counselor for adminstrn. Freetown, Sierra Leone, 1987—89, personnel officer Seoul, Republic of Korea, 1991—94, counselor for adminstrn. Dominican Republic, 1994—98, dep. chief of mission to chargé d'affaires Quito, Ecuador, 1999—2002, US amb. to Honduras Tegucigalpa, 2002—05; pres. Inter-Am. Found., Arlington, Va., 2005—. Asst. dir. fin. aid U. Va., Charlottesville, 1973—74; prof. hist. Cuttington Coll., Suakoko, Liberia, 1974—76, Wake Forest U., Winston Salem, NC, 1978—81; Pearson fellow, asst. to pres. U. Tex., El Paso, 1989—91. Office: Inter-Am Found 901 N Stuart St, 10 Fl Arlington VA 22203 Office Phone: 703-306-4301. E-mail: lpalmer@iaf.gov.

PALMER, LOUIS THOMAS, pathologist; b. Omaha, Dec. 12, 1937; s. Harry Calvin and Helen Irene (Hansen) P.; m. Rosario Garcia, Dec. 28, 1977; children: Ria Charrise, Ryan Christopher. BS, Wash. State U., 1960; MS, Kans. State U., 1965; PhD, U. Minn., 1968. Cert. profl. plant pathologist; cert. pest control operator, Fla. Plant pathologist Rockefeller Found., Mex. and India, 1968-71; extension plant pathologist U. Nebr., Lincoln, 1971-75; plant pathologist Internat. Rice Rsch. Inst., Sukamandi, Indonesia, 1975-79; dir. United Fruit Co., La Lima, Honduras, 1979-81; field devel. biologist E.I. duPont de Nemours, Campinas, Brazil, 1982-85, mgr. Madera, Calif., 1985-88; cons. Checchi & Co., Dhaka, Bangladesh, 1988-91; plant pathologist Harris Moran Seed Co., Ruskin, Fla., 1992—94, Pioneer Vegetable Genetics, Ruskin, Fla., 1995—96; pres., owner Tropical Foliage Inc., Wimauma, Fla., 1997—2007. Part-time faculty U. Fla., Plant City, 2003—07; adj. prof. Fla. So. Coll., Lakeland, 2004—. Contbr. articles to profl. jours. Mem. Cubscout and Boy Scout Leadership, 1983—. Carl Raymond Grey scholar Union Pacific R.R., 1955, Carl J. Erickson scholar Benton County, Washington, 1956. Mem.: Am. Legion (2nd vice comdr. Brandon post 2002—). Roman Catholic. Avocation: photography. Home: 1343 Monte Lake Dr Valrico FL 33596-8109

PALMER, MARILYN JOAN, English composition educator; b. Mahoning County, Ohio, Mar. 3, 1933; d. Rudolph George and Marian Eleanor Wynn; m. Richard Palmer, Nov. 10, 1956 (dec. 1987); children: Ricky, Larry, Kevin. Phys. therapy cert., UCLA, 1954, BS, 1955; MA in Philosophy, Ohio State U., 1969; PhD, U. Okla., 1996. Phys. therapist Neil Ave. Sch. for Handicapped, Columbus, Ohio, 1968-69; instr. philosophy Ohio State U., Columbus, 1969; instr. English Youngstown (Ohio) State U., 1970-71; writer, editor The Economy Co., ednl. publs., Oklahoma City, 1977-81; grad. asst. in English U. Okla., Norman, 1981-87, lectr. in English, 1988-90, tech. writing instr. ind. studies, 1988-97. Free-lance editing and cons.; cons. for on-line CD-ROM to accompany a textbook, 2002. Author: Technical Writing for Science, Business and Industry, 1988, An Enthymeme as a Platform for Understanding Audience Values, 1997; editor: Kindergarten Keys Teacher's Guidebook, 1982, author parochial supplement, 1982. Fund-raiser Easter Seal Soc., 1965-68; den mother coord. Boy Scouts Am., 1966, 67. Dept. Energy grantee, 1976. Mem. AAUP, Am. Phys. Therapy Assn., Soc. for Women in Philosophy, Alpha Xi Delta (nat. editor Quill 1984-86). Office Phone: 405-447-6495. Personal E-mail: doclynn@cox.net.

PALMER, MICHAEL A., history professor; b. Phila., Pa., Dec. 31, 1951; s. Howard V. and Florence J. Palmer; m. Carol J. Roop; children: Ryan M., Lisa A. BA, Temple U., Phila., 1973, PhD, 1981. Historian Naval Hist. Ctr., Washington, 1983—89, asst. br. head, 1989—91; prof. and chair Dept. Geography, Greenville, 1997—99; asst. prof. Dept. History, Greenville, 1991—95, assoc. prof., 1995—99, prof. and interim chair, 1999—2007, Dept. English, Greenville, 2007—09. Author: (history) The Last Crusade: Americanism and the Islamic Reformation, Command at Sea: Naval Command and Control since the 16th Century, Lee Moves North: Robert E. Lee on the Offensive, Guardians of the Gulf: A History of America's Expanding Role in the Persian Gulf, 1833-1992, On Course to Desert Storm: The U.S. Navy and the Persian Gulf, Origins of the Maritime Strategy: American Naval Strategy in the First Postwar Decade, Stoddert's War: Naval Operations during the Quasi-War with France, 1798-1801, (novel) The War That Never Was, Arctic Strike. Decorated Meritorious Civilian Svc. medal Dept. Navy; recipient 1988 Samuel Eliot Morison award, Naval Order United State, 1988, Hon. Mention, John Lyman Book award, North Am. Soc. Oceanic History, 1987, Cold War Essay Contest First prize, VMI: John A. Adams Ctr. Mil. History and Strategic Analysis, 2008; named Book of Yr., Am. Revolution Round Table of NY, 1988. Mem.: US Naval Inst., Soc. Mil. History (Moncado Prize 1997). Roman Catholic. Avocation: computers. Home: 1411 Cadenza Ct Greenville NC 27858 Office: East Carolina Univ 2201 Bate Bldg Greenville NC 27858 Business E-Mail: palmerm@ecu.edu.

PALMER, PAMELA MURRILL, educator; b. Jacksonville, NC, Apr. 21, 1967; d. Roosevelt Dean Lee and Dorsay Ann Mitchell; m. Alan Wade Palmer, Feb. 19, 2000; 1 child, Joshua Alan. BA, Winston-Salem State U., NC, 1990; MS, NC A&T State U., Greensboro, 1996; cert. in nonprofit mgmt., Duke U. Cmty. and econ. devel. specialist NC A&T State U., 1995—97; prof. High Point U., NC, 1998—. Dir. Nonprofit Leadership Enhancement Program, High Point U., 2005—. Mem., com. leader Love and Faith Christian Fellowship, Greensboro, 2003; sec. United Way of Greater High Point, 2006—; mem. exec. com. Am. Friends Svc. Com.-SERO, Atlanta, 2003; mem. Guilford County Mental Health Bd., Greensboro, 2004. Recipient Outstanding Faculty award, High Point U. Evening Degree Program, 2004, 2005; named Minority Bus. Advocate, High Point C. of C., 2005; grantee Nonprofit Leadership Enhancement Program, Hayden-Harman Found. and High Point U., 2006—. Home: 307 Jackson St Jamestown NC 27282 Office: High Point U 833 Montlieu Ave Campus Box 3471 High Point NC 27262 Home Fax: 336-454-9009. E-mail: pmurrill@highpoint.edu.

PALMER, PAMELA PIERCE, anesthesiologist; b. Tucson, Ariz., Jan. 25, 1963; d. Edwin Patterson and Patricia Anne Pierce; life ptnr. Thomas John Musci; 1 child, Paloma Elizabeth. BS in Elec. Engring., U. Ariz., Tucson, 1985; MD, Stanford U., Palo Alto, Calif., 1992; PhD. Diplomate Am. Bd. Anesthesiology, 1998, in pain mgmt. Am. Bd. Anesthesiology. Co-founder,cons. Omeros Med. Sys., Inc., Seattle, 1994—; dir., UCSF pain mgmt. ctr. U. Calif., San Francisco, 1999—2005; dir. UCSF Pain Ctr., 2005—; co-founder,chief med. officer AcelRx Pharmaceuticals, Redwood City, 2005—. Recipient Top Anesthesiologists, Consumers' Rsch. Coun. Am., 2007, 2008; named to, 2006, Best Dr., Best Doctors Am., Inc., 2006. Achievements include patents for irrigation solutions to decrease pain and inflammation during surgery; patents pending for novel sublingual drug formulations for acute pain management and procedural sedation. Office: AcelRx Pharmaceuticals 575 Chesapeake Dr Redwood City CA 94063 Business E-Mail: ppalmer@acelrx.com.

PALMER, PHILIP EDWARD STEPHEN, radiologist; b. London, Apr. 26, 1921; MBBS, U. London, 1944, DMR, 1946, DMRT, 1947; MD (hon.), U. Tirgu Mures, Romania, 2004. Intern, then resident Westminster Hosp.; cons. radiologist West Cornwall (Eng.) Hosp. Group, 1947-54; sr. govt. radiologist Matabeleland, Rhodesia-Zimbabwe, 1954-64; prof. radiology U. Cape Town, South Africa, 1964-68; prof. U. Pa., 1968-70; prof. diagnostic radiology and vet. radiology U. Calif., Davis, 1970—. Dir. Bd. World Health Imaging; WHO cons. in field. Author: The Imaging of Tropical Diseases, 1980 and 2nd edit.: 2000; contbr. 200plus articles to profl. publs. Recipient German Röentgen award, 1993, 1st Béclère medal Internat. Soc. Radiology, 1996, 1st Antoine Béclère lectr. Internat. Soc. Radiology, 1996, Presdl. award Radiol. Soc. N.Am., 2000. Fellow Calif. Radiol. Assn., Royal Coll. Physicians (Edinburgh), Royal Coll. Radiologists (Eng.), Romanian Soc. Radiol. and Nuclear Med.; mem. Brit. Inst. Radiology, Brit. Med. Assn., Calif. Med. Assn., Internat. Skeletal Soc., Assn. Univ. Radiologists, Radiol. Soc. N.Am. (Spl. Pres.'s award 2000), Kenya Radiol. Soc., South African Coll. Medicine, Egyptian Soc. Radiology and Nuclear Medicine, Yugoslav Assn. for Ultrasound, West African Assn. Radiologists. Address: 821 Miller Dr Davis CA 95616-3622

PALMER, RAQUEL VARGAS, private equity firm executive; BA in Polit. Sci., Stanford U., 1994. Investment banker Kidder, Peabody & Co., NYC, 1994; ptnr. Keilin & Co., NYC, 1994—97, KPS Capital Partners, LP, NYC, 1997—. Bd. dirs. Hephaestus Holdings, Inc./Jernberg Industries, Inc., Chgo., United Road Services, Inc., Mich., Bristol Compressors Internat., Inc., Bristol, Va., Global Brass and Copper, Inc., East Alton, Ill.; chmn. Attends Healthcare, Inc., Greenville, NC, Cloyes Gear and Products, Inc., Ft. Smith, Ark. Office: KPS Capital Partners LP 31st Fl 485 Lexington Ave New York NY 10017 Office Phone: 212-338-5115. Office Fax: 646-307-7115. E-mail: rpalmer@kpsfund.com.*

PALMER, RICHARD N., state supreme court justice; b. Hartford, Conn., May 27, 1950; BA, Trinity Coll., 1972; JD with high honors, U. Conn., 1977. Bar: Conn. 1977, U.S. Dist. Ct. Conn. 1978, D.C. 1980, U.S. Ct. Appeals (2d cir.) 1981. Law clk. to Hon. Jon O. Newman U.S. Ct. Appeals (2d cir.), 1977—78; assoc. Shipman & Goodwin, 1978—80; asst. U.S. atty. Office U.S. Atty. Conn., 1980—83, 1987—90, U.S. atty., 1991, chief state's atty., 1991—93; ptnr. Chatigny and Palmer, 1984—86; assoc. justice Conn. Supreme Ct., Hartford, 1993—. Mem. Phi Beta Kappa. Office: Connecticut Supreme Ct 231 Capitol Ave Hartford CT 06106-1548 Office Phone: 860-757-2115.*

PALMER, RICHARD WARE, retired lawyer; b. Boston, Oct. 20, 1919; s. George Ware and Ruth French (Judkins) P.; m. Nancy Fernald Shaw, July 8, 1950; children: Richard Ware Jr., John Wentworth, Anne Fernald. AB, Harvard U., 1942, JD, 1948. Bar: N.Y. 1950, Pa. 1959. Sec., dir. N.Am. Mfg. Co., Natick, Mass., 1946-48; assoc. Burlingham, Veeder, Clark & Hupper, Burlingham, Hupper & Kennedy, NYC, 1949-57; ptnr. Rawle & Henderson, Phila., 1958-79; co-founder, ptnr. Palmer, Biezup & Henderson, Phila., 1979—97, of counsel, 1998—2004; ret., 2004. Sec. Underwater Technics, Inc., Camden, NJ, 1967-85; adv. on admiralty law to U.S. del. Inter-Govtl. Maritime Consultative Orgn., London, 1967, U.S. del. 30th-34th internat. confs.; mem. U.S. Shipping Coord. Com., Washington legal sub com., 1967—; titular mem. Comité Maritime Internat.; v.p., sec., bd. dirs. Phila. Belt Line R.R., Mather (Bermuda) Ltd. Editor: Maritime Law Reporter. Mem., permanent adv. bd. Tulane Admiralty Law Inst., Tulane U. Law Sch., New Orleans, 1975—2009; trustee Seamen's Ch. Inst., Phila., 1967—2001, pres., 1972—84; mem. exec. com. Harvard Law Sch. Assn., Phila., 1986—2005; bd. dirs. Havrford (Pa.) Civic Assn., 1972—85, pres., 1976—79; consul for Denmark State of Pa., 1980—91, consul emeritus, 1992—. Lt. comdr. USNR, 1942—46. Fellow World Acad. Art and Sci. (treas. 1988-2002); mem. ABA (former chmn. stdg. com. on admiralty and maritime law 1978-79), N.Y.C. Bar Assn., Phila. Bar Assn., Maritime Law Assn. U.S.(chmn. limitation liability com. 1977-83, 2d v.p. 1984-86, 1st v.p. 1986-88, pres. 1988-90, immediate past pres. 1990-92), Assn. Average Adjusters USA and Gt. Britain, Port of Phila. Maritime Soc., Consul Assn. Phila., Colonial Soc. Pa. (treas. 2003-05, bd. govs. 2005-08, counselor 2007-08), Danish Order of Dannebrog, Merion Cricket Club, Phila. Club, Rittenhouse Club, Geneal. Soc. Pa. (bd. dirs. 1997-2002, v.p. 2003-04, bd. dirs. 2005-08, counsel 2007-08), Harvard Club NYC and Phila. (exec. com. 1983-86, 94-97). Episcopalian. Home: 432 Montgomery Ave Haverford PA 19041-1527 Home Phone: 610-649-3130. Home Fax: 610-649-7824.

PALMER, ROBERT BAYLIS, librarian; b. Rockville Centre, NY, Apr. 5, 1938; s. John Frederick and Marion (Baylis) P.; divorced; 1 child, Michele Palmer Fracasso. AB, Kenyon Coll., Gambier, Ohio, 1960; MS in L.S, Simmons Coll., Boston, 1965; MA in English, Middlebury Coll.,

Vt., 1965. Tchr. Brooks Sch., North Andover, Mass., 1960-65, libr., 1961-65; acting libr. Columbia Coll., 1965-66; asst. to dir. libraries Columbia U., 1965-67; dir. Barnard Coll. Libr., 1967-81. Fulbright lectr. Tribhuvan U. Library, Kathmandu, Nepal, 1972-73, Kathmandu, 1980; vol. lectr. USIS, library cons., Asia, 1976; Fulbright lectr. Wuhan, Peoples Republic China, 1984-85; library cons., advisor, Peoples Republic China, 1986-87, Zanzibar, Tanzania, 1988; lectr., cons. Kenya, Ethiopia, Zimbabwe, 1988; English lang. escort officer US Dept. State, 1989—2009. Mem. ALA. Address: 190 Riverside Dr New York NY 10024-1008 *Success in life is greatly enhanced by inheritance but not necessarily the inheritance of material riches. The inheritance of a happy, stable, secure upbringing by loving parents is more valuable.*

PALMER, ROBERT LESLIE, lawyer; b. Porterville, Calif., Apr. 10, 1957; s. Harrison Rowe and Margaret Elizabeth (Witty) P.; m. Huisuk Kim, Feb. 1, 1986; 1 child, Aaron Rowe. BA, Tulane U., 1979; JD, Georgetown U., 1982. Bar: D.C. 1982, U.S. Ct. Mil. Appeals 1985, Tex. 1987, Ala. 1987, U.S. Dist. Ct. (no. dist.) Ala. 1987, U.S. Ct. Appeals (11th cir.) 1987, U.S. Supreme Ct. 2005, U.S. Dist. Ct. (mid. dist.) Ala. 2006; registered lobbyist, Ala. Assoc. Lewis Martin Burnett & Dunkle, P.C., Birmingham, Ala., 1987-89, Lewis and Martin, Birmingham, Ala., 1989-90, Martin, Drummond and Woosley, Birmingham, 1990-91, bd. dirs., 1991-92, Martin, Drummond, Woosley and Palmer, Birmingham, 1992-95; staff atty. Environ. Litig. Group, P.C., Birmingham, 1995—2005, shareholder, 2005—. Ala. del. 6th Joint Conf. between Korea and S.E. U.S., Kyongju, Republic of Korea, 1991, 7th Joint Conf., Atlanta, 1992; founder, dir., pres. Ala. Legal Reform Found.; asst. scoutmaster Boy Scouts Am., 2003—08; bd. dirs. Jimmie Hale Mission, 2005—, chmn. elect, 2008-. Capt. JAGC, U.S. Army, 1983-87, USAR, 1987-91. Recipient commendation Republic of Korea Ministry of Justice, 1984, Champion Justice award Ala. Assn. Justice, 2007, Access Justice award Pub. Justice Found., Washington, 2008. Mem. VFW (life mem.), AAJ, Ala. Assn. for Justice (exec.com., sustaining mem.), Tex. Trial Lawyers Assn., Christian Legal Soc. (pres. Birmingham chpt. 2007-09), Phi Beta Kappa, Omicron Delta Kappa. Independent. Baptist. Office: Environ Litig Group PC 3529 7th Ave S Birmingham AL 35222-3210 Home: 351 Highland View Dr Birmingham AL 35242 Office Phone: 205-328-9200. Business E-Mail: bob@elglaw.com.

PALMER, ROBERT TOWNE, lawyer, bank executive; b. Chgo., May 25, 1947; s. Adrian Bernhardt and Gladys (Towne) P.; m. Ann Therese Darin, Nov. 9, 1974; children: Justin Darin, Christian Darin. BA, Colgate U., 1969; JD, U. Notre Dame, 1974. Bar: Ill. 1974, DC 1978, US Supreme Ct. 1978. Law clk. to Hon. Walter V. Schaefer Ill. Supreme Ct., 1974-75; assoc. McDermott, Will & Emery, Chgo., 1975-81, ptnr., 1982-86, Chadwell & Keyser, Ltd., Chgo., 1987—88, Connelly, Mustes, Palmer & Schroeder, Chgo., 1988-89; of counsel Garfield & Merel Ltd., Chgo., 1990-2000. Adj. faculty Chgo. Kent Law Sch., 1975—77, Loyola U., 1976—78; adv. com. Fed. Home Loan Mortgage Corp., 1988—89; bd. dirs. Ctrl. Fed. Savs. & Loan Assn. of Chgo., chmn., COO, 2000—; dir. Chgo. Assn. Fin. Insts., 2001—03, sec., 2002—03; mem. Chgo. Crime Commn., 2001—, dir., 2002—; alderman City of Lake Forest, Ill., 2008—. Contbr. articles to legal jours. and textbooks. Mem. ABA, Ill. State Bar Assn. (Lincoln award 1983), Chgo. Bar Assn., Chgo. Club, Dairymen's Country Club, Lambda Alpha. Office: Central Fed Savs 1601 W Belmont Ave Chicago IL 60657-3044 Personal E-mail: rpalmer916@aol.com.

PALMER, RONALD R, history professor; b. Cohose, NY, July 15, 1961; m. Annmarie Tweedy Palmer; children: Michael Daniel, Jordan David, Alexander John Curtis, Joshua Christopher Curtis. PhD, U. SC., Columbia, 1998. Mrs US Cenus Bur., Albany, 1989—91; prof. Jefferson Cmty Coll, Watertown, NY, 1991—. Contbr. articles to profl. jours. Office: Jefferson Cmty Coll 1220 Coffeen St Watertown NY 13601 Personal E-mail: rpalmer@sunyjefferson.edu.

PALMER, ROSS HOWARD, veterinarian, educator; BS, Kans. State U., Manhattan, 1982, DVM, 1984; MS in Physiology, U. Ga., Athens, 1989. Diplomate Am. Coll. Vet. Surgeons, 1989. Intern, medicine & surgery Animal Med. Ctr., NYC, 1984—85; resident, surgery U. Ga., 1985—88; asst. prof., orthopedics Tex. A&M U. Vet Med Ctr, Coll. Sta., Tex., 1988—91; staff surgeon Santa Cruz Vet. Hosp. Splty. Svcs., Calif., 1991—97; owner & dir. Vet. Surg. Group Monterey Bay, Aptos, Calif., 1997—2004; assoc. prof., orthop. surgery, Vet. Med. Ctr. Colo. State U., Fort Collins, 2004—, affiliate faculty Sch. Bioengring. Contbr. scientific papers (Best Clin. Rsch. Paper award, 2007). Mem.: External Skeletal Fixation Rsch. & Educators Group (founder 1991), Assn. Vet. Orthopedic Rsch. & Edn., AO Vet., Vet. Orthop. Soc. Office: Colo St Univ Vet Med Ctr 300 West Drake Rd Fort Collins CO 80523 Business E-Mail: ross.palmer@colostate.edu.

PALMER, RUSSELL EUGENE, investment company executive, retired dean; b. Jackson, Mich., Aug. 13, 1934; s. Russell E. and Margarite M. (Briles) P.; m. Priscilla G. Palmer; children: Bradley Carl, Stephen Russell, Russell Eugene, III, Karen Jean. BA with honors, Mich. State U., 1956; D in Comml. Sci. (hon.), Drexel U., 1980; MA (hon.), U. Pa., 1984; PhD (hon.), Chulalongkorn U., 1988, Free U. Brussels, 1989, York Coll., 1989. With Touche Ross & Co., NYC, 1956-83, mng. ptnr., CEO, 1972-82, also bd. dirs., exec. coms.; mng. dir., CEO Touche Ross Internat., 1974-83; dean, Reliance prof. mgmt. and pvt. enterprise Wharton Sch. U. Pa., 1983-90, CEO. Bd. trustees Main Line Health, Nat. Constitution Ctr.; bd. dirs. Smithsonian. Mem. Pres.'s Mgmt. Improvement Coun., 1979—80; mem. adv. bd. Salvation Army, past mem. nat. adv. bd.; former mem. adv. coun. Women's Way; bd. dirs. UN Assn. U.S.A.; former mem. adv. panel Comptr. Gen. U.S.; former chmn. bd trustees U. Pa. Health Care Sys.; trustee Acctg. Hall of Fame U. Pa.; bd. dirs. Joint Coun. Econ. Edn., 1978—83, United Fund Greater N.Y., 1980—83; mem. Bus.Com. Arts, 1977—83; bd. dirs. SEI Ctr. for Advanced Studies in Mgmt.; former mem. adv. coun. Sch. Internat. and Pub. Affairs Columbia U., Grad. Sch. Bus. Stanford U.; mem. assocs. coun. Bus. Sch. Oxford U.; mem. U.S. Sec. Labor's Commn. on Workforce Quality and Labor Market Efficiency; pres. Fin. Acctg. Found., 1979—82; pub. mem. Hudson Inst. Recipient Gavin Meml. award Beta Theta Pi, 1956, Disting. Community Svc. award Brandeis U., 1974, Outstanding Bus. Alumnus award Mich. State U., 1978, Humanitarian award Fedn. Jewish Philanthropies, 1979, Disting. Aux. Svc. award Salvation Army, 1979, LEAD Bus. award, 1984, Good Scout award Phila. coun. Boy Scouts Am., 1987, Oxford Cup Beta Theta Pi, 2005, Disting. Alumni award Mich. State U., 2008. Mem. Merion Cricket Club, Union League Club. Presbyterian. Office: The Palmer Group 3600 Market St Ste 530 Philadelphia PA 19104-2649 Office Phone: 215-243-2590. Business E-Mail: rpalmer@palmer-group.com.

PALMER, STEPHEN E., psychology professor; s. Elwood Marshall and Frances E. Palmer; life ptnr. Paul W. Harris; children: Emily A., Nathan W. BA, Princeton U., NJ, 1970; PhD, U. Calif. San Diego, La Jolla, 1975. Prof. psychology and cognitive sci. maj., dir. U. Calif., Berkeley, 1974—. Editor Jour. Cognitive Psychology, 1986—90; dir. Inst. Cognitive Studies, Berkeley, 1990—2000. Author: (textbook) Vision Science: Photons to Phenomenology. Fellow: APA, Am. Psychol. Soc.; mem.: Soc. Exptl. Psychologists, Psychonomic Soc. (chair, exec. com. 2001—02, chair, publs. com. 2000—02). Office: Univ Calif Berkeley Psychology Dept Berkeley CA 94720-1650 Office Phone: 510-642-7135.

PALMER, VENRICE ROMITO, lawyer, educator; b. Springfield, Mass., Jan. 11, 1952; s. Venrice Wellesley and Mildred Adlay (Foster) P. Higher diploma, U. Besançon, France, 1973; AB maxima cum laude, King's Coll., Wilkes-Barre, Pa., 1974; JD, Harvard U., 1977. Bar: N.Y. 1978, U.S. Dist. Ct. (so. and ea. dists.) N.Y. 1979, Ill. 1986, Calif. 1997. Spl. asst. atty. gen. Office N.Y. Atty. Gen., NYC, 1977-79; staff atty. SEC, NYC, 1979-82, br. chief, 1982-83, spl. trial counsel, 1983-85, acting asst. regional adminstr., 1984-85; sr. counsel Sears, Roebuck and Co., Hoffman Estates, Ill., 1985-97, Bank of Am., San Francisco, 1997-99; counsel McCutchen, Doyle, Brown & Enersen, LLP, San Francisco, 1999—2002; of counsel Bingham McCutchen LLP, San Francisco, 2002—07; pvt. practice San Francisco, 2007—. Guest lectr. St. John's U. Bus. Sch., N.Y.C., 1984; lectr. Practicing Law Inst., N.Y.C., 1995—, Glasser LegalWorks, Little Falls, N.J., 1997—, Am. Soc. Corp. Secs., 1997-99, Nat. Bus. Inst., Eau Claire, Wis., 2000—. Contbr. articles to various law publs. Recipient cert. of appreciation N.Y. State Bar Assn., 1978, Benaglia award King's Coll., 1974. Mem.: ABA, Calif. State Bar Assn. (mem. fin. instns. com. 2000—03), Alpha Mu Gamma, Delta Epsilon Sigma. Avocations: opera, ballet, reading. Home and Office: 1200 Gough St Apt 7A San Francisco CA 94109-6616 E-mail: steveintel@aol.com.

PALMER, WILLIAM JOSEPH, accountant; b. Lansing, Mich., Sept. 3, 1934; s. Joseph Flammin Lacchia and Henrietta (Yagerman) P.; m. Judith Pollock, Aug. 20, 1960 (div. Nov. 1980); children: William W., Kathryn E., Leslie A., Emily J.; m. Kathleen Francis Booth, June 30, 1990; stepchildren: Blair T. Manwell, Lindsay H. Manwell. BS, U. Calif., Berkeley, 1963. CPA. With Coopers & Lybrand, 1963—80, mng. ptnr. Sacramento, 1976—80; ptnr. Arthur Young & Co., San Francisco, 1980—89, Ernst & Young, San Francisco, 1989—94; prof. U. Calif., Berkeley, 1994—. Bd. dirs. Dutra Group; chair constrn. industry group Coopers & Lybrand, 1973-80, Arthur Young, 1980-89, Ernst & Young, 1989-94; guest lectr. Engring. Sch. Stanford U., 1976; lectr. Golden Gate Coll., 1975. Author: Businessman's Guide to Constuction, 1981, Construction Management Book, 1984, Construction Accounting and Financial Management, 5th edit., 1994, Construction Litigation-Representing The Contractor, 1992, Construction Insurance, Bonding and Risk Management, 1996. Bd. dirs. Sacramento Met. YMCA, 1976-82, KXPR, Sacramento 1976-85, V.p., 1979-82; bd. dirs. Sacramento Symphony Found., 1977-80; asst. state fin. chmn. Calif. Reagan for Pres., 1980. Lt. USN naval aviator, 1953-59. Mem. AICPA (vice chmn. com. constrn. industry 1975-81), Nat. Assn. Accts. (pres. Oakland/East Bay chpt. 1972, Man of Yr. 1968), Calif. Soc. CPAs, Assn. Gen. Contractors Calif. (bd. dirs. 1971-74), World Trade Club, Del Paso Country Club, Sutter Club, Lambda Chi Alpha. Roman Catholic. Avocations: antique boats, golf, book collecting, pipe collecting. Home: PO Box 60405 Sacramento CA 95860-0405 Personal E-mail: kathpalm@hotmail.com.

PALMETER, N. DAVID, lawyer; b. Elmira, NY, Jan. 29, 1938; s. Neal Henry and Elizabeth Jane (McHale) P.; m. Mary Lee Morken, 1964 (div. 1979); m. Mary Faith Tanney, Jan. 15, 1983; children: Stephen Michael, John David, Elizabeth Jane, James Martin. AB, Syracuse U., 1960; JD, U. Chgo., 1963. Bar: N.Y. 1963, D.C. 1969. Trial atty. U.S. Dept. Justice, Washington, 1966-68; assoc. Daniels & Houlihan, Washington, 1969-73, ptnr., 1973-75, Daniels, Houlihan & Palmeter, Washington, 1975-84, Mudge, Rose, Guthrie, Alexander & Ferdon, Washington, 1984-95, Graham & James, Washington, 1995-98, Powell, Goldstein, Frazer and Murphy, 1998—2002, Sidley Austin, 2002—06, sr. counsel, 2006—. Author: The World Trade Organization as a Legal System, 2003; co-author: Dispute Settlement in the World Trade Organization, 1999, 2d edit., 2004; contbr. articles to profl. publs. Mem. ABA, Internat. Bar Assn. (chmn. internat. trade and customs law com. 1989-93, liaison to World Trade Orgn. 1994-96), N.Y. State Bar Assn., D.C. Bar Assn., Washington Fgn. Law Soc. (pres. 1992-93), Am. Soc. Internat. Law, Can. Coun. on Internat. Law, Brit. Inst. Internat. and Comparative Law. Home: 2804 29th St NW Washington DC 20008-4112 Office Phone: 202-736-8861. Personal E-mail: dpalmeter@sidley.com.

PALMIERI, DORA ANN, retired language educator; b. Monmouth, Ill., Dec. 31, 1943; d. John and Ruth Douffas; m. Ronald Naedele, Feb. 3, 1966 (dec. Sept. 30, 1966); children: Ronnann, Joey; m. Frank William Palmieri, Jan. 2004. BA in English, Milligan Coll., 1966; MA in English, E. Tenn. State U., 1974; postgrad. in Adult Edn., U. NC, Charlotte, 1985. Cert. tchr. Miss., Tenn., N.C., Md., Fla. Editor/asst. editor Courier And Gateway Newspapers, Suitland, Md., 1966—69; English tchr. Long Beach (Miss.) HS, 1969—74, Garinger HS Night Program, Charlotte, NC, 1974—76; curriculum specialist, English instr. Ctrl. Piedmont CC, Charlotte, 1976—81; mgr. tng. and devel. Control Data Corp. and Comml. Credit Corp., Charlotte, Balt., 1980—87; program designer, rschr. Rutledge Coll. Sys., Charlotte, 1987—88; assoc. prof. Daytona Beach (Fla.) CC, 1990—2005. Lead tchr. adult HS English Daytona Beach CC, 1998—2005. Co-author: Ecology: The Living World, 1996; author: English All Around Us, vols. 1-4, 1999—2003, We Call Him Puddles, 2007. Vol. Resources for Women, 2006—; singles' lay min. South Daytona Christian Ch., 1990—2001; Sunday sch. tchr. Women's Ministry; ptnr. Jeremiah Missions. Named Lay Person Of The Yr., Kiwanis Port Orange And South Daytona, 1996. Mem.: Fla. Assn. CCs, Nat. Coun. Tchrs. English. Republican. Mem. Christian Ch. (Disciples Of Christ). Avocations: photography, theater, writing, crafts, movies. Personal E-mail: hollyhilla@hotmail.com.

PALMIERI, FREDERICK WILLIAM, structural engineer; s. Mario and Maria Palmieri; m. Judy Anna Drystek, Dec. 22, 1973; children: Corey, Caroline. BS, MS, Stanford U., 1961; PhD, Madison U., 2003. Chief structures space sys. divsn. AVCO, Lowell, Mass., 1965—68; head basic loads Lockheed Missiles and Space Sys., Sunnyvale, Calif., 1957—65; dir. Palmieri Co., Phila., 1968—73; sect. head advanced rsch. and devel. Hughes Aircraft Co., Fullerton, Calif., 1973—74; cons. structural dynamics Palmieri Cons. Co., Anaheim Hills, Calif., 1974—92; dir. Marwais Internat., S.A., Luxembourg, 1992—94; pres. Pacific Consol. Co., Inc., Las Vegas, Nev., 1994—. Mem.: ASME, Soc. Exptl. Mech. Democrat. Roman Catholic. Avocation: golf. Office: Pacific Consol Co Inc 4300 Meadows Ln Ste 136 Las Vegas NV 89107 Home: 4302 Callahan Ave Las Vegas NV 89120 Home Phone: 310-640-2515. Office Fax: 702-433-5450. E-mail: fredpalmieri@hotmail.com.

PALMIERI, VICTOR HENRY, lawyer, director, investment advisor; b. Chgo., Feb. 16, 1930; s. Mario and Maria (Losacco) P.; children: Matthew B., John W.; m. Cathryn Connors, July 6, 1990. AB in History, Stanford U., 1951, JD, 1954. Bar: Calif. 1954. Assoc. O'Melveny & Myers, LA, 1955-59; exec. v.p. Janss Investment Corp., LA, 1959-63, pres., 1963-68; chmn. Pa. Co. and its subs. Great S.W. Corp., 1969-77; chmn. bd. Palmieri Co., NYC, 1969—. Chmn. PHL Corp., Inc. (formerly Baldwin-Unitaed Inc.), Phila., 1983—87; trustee, CEO Colo. Ute Electric Assn., Inc., 1990—92; spl. dep. rehabilitator Confedn. Life Ins. Co., 1994—98; dep. rehabilitator, CEO Mut. Benefit Life Ins. Co., 1991—94; pres., CEO MBL Life Assurance Corp., 1994—95; chmn. AlixPalmieri Assocs., 1997—99; bd. dirs. Mullin Cons., Inc., vice chmn., 2002—06; bd. dir. M Fin. Holdings Inc., M Benefit Solutions, M Fin. Investment Advisors, LA Universal Pre-Sch. Ambassador-at-large, coord. refugee affairs US Dept. State, 1979—81; chmn. Am. Learning Corp., 1970—85; dep. exec. dir. Nat. Adv. Commn. on Civil Disorders, 1967—68; mem. Coun. on Fgn. Rels.; trustee Rockefeller Found., 1979—89; pres. bd. dis. Lincoln Ctr. Theater, 1985—89; chmn. Overseas Devel. Coun., 1985—91; bd. trustees The Police Found., 1996—2002. Office: MullinTBG 2029 Century Park E 37th Fl Los Angeles CA 90067 Business E-Mail: victor.palmieri@mullintbg.com.

PALMINTERI, CHAZZ, actor; b. Bronx, NY, May 15, 1952; m. Gianna Ranaudo, June 6, 1992; children: Gabriella Rose, Dante Lorenzo. Actor: (theatre) The Guy in the Truck, 1982, Broadway, 1983, The King's Men, 22 Years, The Flatbush Faithful, 1985, A Bronx Tale, 2008; actor, actor: (TV films) Peter Gunn, 1990, Boss of Bosses, 2001; (TV series) Kojak, 2005; (films) Oscar, 1991, Bullets Over Broadway, 1994 (Academy award nomination best supporting actor, 1994), The Perez Family, 1994, The Usual Suspects, 1995, Jade, 1995, Faithful, 1996, Diabolique, 1996, Mulholland Falls, 1996, Scar City, 1998, Hurly Burly, 1998, Cadaveri eccellenti, 1998, Company Man, 1999, Analyze This, 1999, (voice) Stuart Little, 1999, Poolhall Junkies, 2002, Just Like Mona, 2003, One Last Ride, 2003, Noel, 2004, In the Mix, 2005, (voice) Hoodwinked, 2005, A Guide to Recognizing Your Saints, 1996, Running Scared, 2006, Push, 2006, Little Man, 2006, (voice) Arthur et les Minimoys, 2006, Body Armour, 2007, The Dukes, 2007, Yonkers Joe, 2008, Jolene, 2008; playwright, actor (theatre) A Bronx Tale, 1989, screenwriter, actor (films), 1993; actor, prodr.: (films) Dante and the Debutante, 2006. Office: c/o Neighborhood Films Inc PO Box 622 Bedford NY 10506

PALMISANO, SAMUEL J., information technology executive; b. Balt., July 29, 1951; m. Gaier Notman; 4 children. BA in History, Johns Hopkins U., 1973. Joined IBM Corp., Balt., 1973, various sales, mktg. and prod. devel. positions, 1973—89, exec. asst. to CEO John F. Akers, 1989; sr. mng. dir. ops. IBM Japan, 1991; pres., CEO Integrated Systems Solutions Corp., IBM subs., 1993—96; sr. v.p., group exec. IBM Personal Systems Group, 1997, IBM Global Svcs., 1998, IBM Enterprise Systems Group, 1999; pres., COO IBM Corp., White Plains, NY, 2000—02, pres., CEO, 2002—03, chmn., pres., CEO, 2003—. Bd. dirs. IBM, 2000—, ExxonMobil Corp., 2006—. Trustee Johns Hopkins U. Recipient Disting. Alumni award, Johns Hopkins U., 2003. Avocations: golf, history, jogging, skiing. Office: IBM Corp 1 New Orchard Rd Armonk NY 10504-1722*

PALMORE, JOHN STANLEY, JR., retired lawyer; b. Ancon, C.Z., Aug. 6, 1917; s. John Stanley and Antoinette Louise (Gonzalez) P.; m. Eleanor Anderson, July 31, 1938 (dec. 1980); 1 child, John Worsham (dec.); m. Carol Pate, Jan. 1, 1982. Student, Western Ky. State Coll., 1934-36; LL.B. cum laude, U. Louisville, 1939. Bar: Ky. 1938. Practice law, Henderson, 1939-42, 47-59; judge Ct. Appeals Ky. (name changed to Supreme Ct. Ky. 1975), 1959-82, chief justice, 1966, 73, 77-82; practice law Frankfort, Ky., 1983-84; ptnr. Palmore & Sheffer, Henderson, 1984-86; sr. counsel Jackson & Kelly, Lexington, Ky., 1986-92; ret., 1992. City pros. atty., Henderson, 1949-53, city atty., 1953-55; commonwealth's atty. 5th Circuit Ct. Dist. Ky., 1955-59 Served to lt. USNR, 1942-46, 51-52. Mem. VFW, Ky. Bar Assn., Am. Legion, Ky. Hist. Soc., Frankfort Country Club, Lexington Club, Frankfort Rotary Club (pres. 1993-94), Masons, Shriners, Elks, Phi Alpha Delta. Episcopalian (past vestryman, sr. warden). Home: 2310 Peaks Mill Rd Frankfort KY 40601-9437

PALMORE, RICK (RODERICK A. PALMORE), consumer products company executive, lawyer; b. Pitts., Feb. 14, 1952; s. Jefferson and Sophie (Spencer) Palmore; m. Lynne Avril Janifer, June 3, 1978; children: Jordan, Adam. BA in Econs., Yale U., 1974; JD, U. Chgo., 1977. Bar: Pa. 1977, Ill. 1982. Assoc. atty. Berkman, Ruslander, Pohl, Lieber & Engel, Pitts., 1977-79; asst. US atty. (no. dist.) Ill. US Dept. Justice, Chgo., 1979-82; assoc. atty. Wildman, Harrold, Allen & Dixon, Chgo., 1982-86, ptnr., 1986-93, Sonnenschein, Nath & Rosenthal, Chgo., 1993-96; v.p., dep. gen. counsel Sara Lee Corp., Chgo., 1996-99, sr. v.p., gen. counsel, sec., 1999—2004, exec. v.p., gen. counsel, sec., 2004—08; exec. v.p., gen. counsel, chief compliance & risk mgmt. officer Gen. Mills, Inc., Mpls., 2008—. Commr. Oak Park Plan Commn., 1988—, chair, 1994—; lectr. Youth Motivation Prog. Chgo. Coun. Commerce & Industry, 1989—; chair Oak Pk. Pub. Art Adv. Com., 2002—; bd. dirs. Pub. Interest Law Initiative, Legal Assistance Found. Chgo., Chgo. Bd. Options Exch., 2002—, Nuveen Investments, 2003—, United Way Met. Chgo., 2003-07; trustee Chgo. Symphony Orch., 2006—. Recipient ACC Excellence in Corp. Practice award, 2003, MCCA Employers of Choice award, ACC Diversity award, 2005, Equal Justice Works Acales of Justice award, 2005, ABA Spirit of Excellence award, 2006, Corp. Exemplar award Nat. Legal Aid & Defender Assn., 2007; named to Outstanding African-Am. Businessmen Dollars & Sense mag., Chgo., 1991; named one of 50 Most Influential Gen. Counsels Inside Counsel, 2006, 50 Most Influential Minority Lawyers in America Nat. Law Jour, 2008. Mem. ABA (minority ptnrs. conf. 1991—), Nat. Bar Assn., Cook County Bar Assn., Chgo. Bar Assn. (bd. dirs. 1992-94, co-chmn. minority clerkshop prog. 1991-92), Chgo. Com. on Minorities in Law Firms (bd. dirs. 1990-92), Chgo. Bar Found. (bd. dirs. 1993-94). Mem. Trinity United Ch. Of Christ. Avocations: running, biking, tennis, reading. Office: General Mills Inc 1 General Mills Blvd Minneapolis MN 55426*

PALMQUIST, MARK L., energy and food products executive; Grad., Gustavus Adolphus Coll., St. Peter, Minn., 1979; student, U. Minn. Grain buyer Harvest States, Inver Grove Heights, Minn., 1979, v.p., dir. grain mktg. divsn., 1990-93, sr. v.p., 1993; exec. v.p., COO Ag. Bus. CHS Inc. (merger of Cenex and Harvest States), Inver Grove Heights, Minn., 2005—. Bd. dirs. Agriliance LLC, Ventura Foods, LLC, InTrade, Nat. Coop. Refinery Assn., Schnitzer Steel Industries, Inc., Portland, Oreg. Office: CHS Inc PO Box 64089 Saint Paul MN 55164-0089 Office Phone: 651-355-6000.*

PALMQUIST, WENDY JEAN, psychology professor; b. Syracuse, NY, Nov. 21, 1948; d. Martin Lee and Carol Ann Palmquist; life ptnr. Celia Jewel Gibbs. BA, Pomona Coll., Claremont, Calif., 1970; PhD, Cornell U., Ithaca, NY, 1977. Instr. U. Manitoba, Winnipeg, Canada, 1975—76; asst. prof. SUNY, Brockport, 1976—81; prof. Plymouth State U., NH, 1981—. First yr. seminar coord. Plymouth State U., 2003—, dir. frost faculty ctr. for learning & tchg. excellence, 2005—. Bd. mem. Lakes Region Mental Health, Laconia, NH, 1984—94, NH Humane Soc., Laconia, 1998—2004, 2006—. Recipient James Hogan award, Plymouth State U., 1991, Meritorious Svc. award, Lakes Region Mental Health, 1994, Disting. Tchg. award, Plymouth State U., 2006, Theo Kalikow award, 2006, Excellence award, 2007. Mem.: Soc. Rsch. Adolescence, Soc. Rsch. Child Devel., Assn. Psychol. Sci., Am. Psychology Assn. Office: Plymouth State Univ Dept Psychology Msc 31 Plymouth NH 03264 Business E-Mail: palm@mail.plymouth.edu.

PALMS, JOHN MICHAEL, academic administrator, physicist; b. Rijswijk, The Netherlands, June 6, 1935; naturalized, 1956; s. Peter Joannes and Mimi Adele (DeYong) P.; m. Norma Lee Cannon, June 2, 1958; children: John Michael, Danielle Maria, Lee Cannon. BS in Physics, The Citadel, 1958, DSc (hon.), 1980; MS in Physics, Emory U., 1959; PhD, U. N.Mex., 1966. Commd. 2d lt. USAF, 1958, retired capt. Res., 1970; lectr. physics dept. U. N.Mex., 1959-60; instr. physics dept. USAF Acad., 1961-62; staff mem. Western Electric Sandia Lab., 1961-62, U. Calif. Los Alamos Sci. Lab., 1962-66, Oak Ridge Nat. Lab., 1966; asst. prof. Emory U., Atlanta, 1966-69, assoc. prof., 1969-73, chmn., assoc. prof. dept. physics, asso. prof. radiology dept. Med. Sch., 1973-74, prof., chmn. dept. physics, 1969-74, dean Coll. Arts. and Scis., 1974-80, acting chmn. dept. math. and computer sci., 1976-77, v.p. arts and scis., acting chmn. dept. anthropology, 1979-80, acting dean Emory Coll., 1979-80, acting dir. Emory U. Computing Ctr., 1980-82, v.p. acad. affairs, 1982-88, interim dean Grad. Sch., 1985-86, Charles Howard Candler prof. nuclear, radiation and environ. physics, 1988-90; pres., prof. physics Ga. State U., Atlanta, 1989-91, U. S.C., Columbia, 1991—92. Chmn. bd. Assurant Inc., 2003-, Inst. for Def. Analyses; bd. dirs. Fortis, Inc., N.Y.C., Exelon Corp., Chgo., NCAA, Simcom Internat. Holdings, Inc., Atlanta, Computer Task Group, Assurant, 1990-; adv. com. Oak Ridge Nat. Lab., 1985-89; mem. nat. nuclear accrediting bd. Inst. Nuclear Power Ops., 1985-91, mem. nat. adv. coun., 1997-2001; mem. panel for semicondr. detectors NAS/NRC, 1963-74; cons. Acad. Natural Scis., Phila., Hughes, Inc., Santa Barbara, Calif., Tennelec, Inc., Three Mile Island Environ. Study, TRW Space Sys. Divsn., L.A., Ga. Dept. Human Resources, Nat. Cancer Inst.; mem. high tech. task force Atlanta C. of C. Contbr. articles on nuclear, atomic, med. and environ. physics to profl. jours. Mem. adv. bd. The Citadel, Oak Ridge Nat. Lab.; mem. exec. bd. Atlanta Area Coun. Boy Scouts of Am., 1989-90; mem. cmty. rels. bd. U.S. Penitentiary, Atlanta; trustee, chmn. Inst. Def. Analyses, Wesleyan Coll., 1984-89, Pace Acad., 1984-89, St. Joseph's Hosp., Atlanta, 1987-89, Ga. Rsch. Alliance, 1988-89; mem. S.C. Univs. Edn. Found., Devel. Found. and Rsch. Found., S.C. Rsch. Inst. Bds.; bd. dirs. Civic-Atlanta Partnership Bus. and Edn., Inc., 1988-90, United Way; chair Rhodes scholar selection com., 1987, S.C., 1995-99; bd. dirs. Nat. Merit Scholarship Corp. Mem. AAAS, Am. Phys. Soc., Am. Assn. Physics Tchrs., IEEE (Nuclear Sci. Group), Am. Nuclear Soc., Am. Coun. Edn., Coun. Provosts and Acad. V.P.s, Am. Conf. Acad. Deans, Soc. Nuclear Medicine, Health Physics Soc., Greater Columbia C. of C. (bd. dirs.), Rotary, Columbia C. of C., Phi Beta Kappa, Sigma Xi, Phi Kappa Phi, Omicron Delta Kappa, Sigma Pi Sigma. Home and Office: Pres U SCO Osborne Bldg Columbia SC 29208-0001

PALMS, ROGER CURTIS, writer, educator, minister; b. Detroit, Sept. 13, 1936; s. Nelson Curtis and Winifred Jessie (Bennett) P.; m. Andrea Sisson, Aug. 22, 1959; children: Grant Curtis, Andrea Jane BA, Wayne State U., 1958; B.D., Eastern Baptist Sem., Phila, 1961, M.Div., 1971, D.D., 1977; MA, Mich. State U., 1971. Ordained to ministry Am. Bapt. Chs., 1961. Pastor Ronceverte Bapt. Ch., W.Va., 1961-64; pastor 1st Bapt. Ch., Highland Park, NJ, 1964-67; chaplain Am. Bapt. Student Found., Mich. State U., East Lansing, 1967-73; assoc. editor Decision mag. Billy Graham Evang. Assn., Mpls., 1973-76, editor, 1976-98. Lectr. in field. Author: Enjoying the Closeness of God, 1989, Let God Help You Choose, 1989, An Unexpected Hope, 1998, Effective Magazine Writing, 2000, Your Best Years, 2003, others; newspaper columnist Trustee No. Bapt. Theol. Sem., 1973— Mem. Evang. Press Assn. (pres. 1991-93). Baptist. Personal E-mail: rcpalms@aol.com. *Investing in people's spiritual lives, giving time and counsel, will bring multiplied results for generations. It is one of the most far-reaching ways I can put faith to work.*

PALOIAN, JOHN R., printing company executive; Joined R.R. Donnolley & Sons Co., 1986, sr. v.p., gen. mgr. Mag. Publishing Svcs., group pres., Global Print Solutions Chgo., 2004—07, COO, 2007—. Office: RR Donnelley & Sons Co 111 S Wacker Dr Chicago IL 60606-4301*

PALOMO, JUAN MARTIN, dental educator, director, orthodontist; s. Jorge Alberto and Maria Cristina Sere de Palomo; m. Leena Bahl, Oct. 8; 1 child, Veda Caroline. MSD, Case Western Res. U., Cleve., DDS, 1997. Cert. orthodontics Case Western Res. U., 1997, diplomate Am. Bd. Orthodontics, 2008. Clinic dir. Case Western Res. U., 1998—2003, tenured assoc. prof., 2007—, program dir., orthodontics, 2008; dir. Craniofacial Imaging Ctr., Cleve., 2005—. Contbr. numerous sci. articles & chpts. Recipient Rsch. award, Am. Assn. Orthodontists Found., 1999, 2001, 2006, Am. Soc. Anesthesiologists, 2006—07. Office: Case Western Res Univ 10900 Euclid Ave Cleveland OH 44106 Office Fax: 216-368-3204. Business E-Mail: palomo@case.edu.

PALPANAS, THEMIS, engineering educator, consultant; BSc, Nat. Tech. U. Athens, Greece, 1996; MSc, U. Toronto, Can., 1998, PhD, 2002. Cert. elec. and computer engr., Greece, 1996. Rschr. IBM T.J. Watson Rsch. Ctr., Hawthorne, NY, 2004—06; prof. U. Trento, Povo, TN, Italy, 2007—. Office: DISI-UNITN via Sommarive 14 Povo TN 38100 Italy

PALS, TONY MITCHEL, public relations executive, director; b. Belmond, Iowa, Feb. 11, 1970; s. Pamela and Randall Frohling (Stepfather); m. Traci Kiesling, May 18, 2007. BA in Journalism, Drake U., Des Moines, 1992; MA in Communication, U. Pa., Phila., 1995. Field organizer Iowa Dem. Party, Sioux City, 1992; staff reporter Des Moines Register, 1992—93; sr. media rels. coord. Coun. Advancement Support Edn., Washington, 1995—97; dir. pub. info. Nat. Assn. Ind. Coll. & U., Washington, 1997—. Mem.: Pub. Rels. Soc. Am., Nat. Press Club, Sigma Phi Epsilon. Episcopalian. Avocations: travel, photography, scuba diving, hiking. Office: Nat Assn Independent Coll & Univ 1025 Conn Ave NW #700 Washington DC 20036 Business E-Mail: tony@naicu.edu.

PALSHO, DOROTHEA COCCOLI, information services executive; b. Phila., June 9, 1947; d. John Charles and Dorothy Lucille (Decker) Coccoli; m. Edward Robert Palsho; children: Christopher, Ryan, and Erica (stepchild). BS, Villanova Univ., 1976; MBA, Temple Univ., 1977. V.p. info. svc. Dow Jones and Co., Princeton, NJ, 1977-97, pres. bus. info. svc., 1995-97, v.p. interactive pub. NYC, 1997—2002, v.p. electronic pub., 2000—02, v.p. stragetic mktg., 2002—. Named to Class of Women Achievers, YWCA Acad. of Women Achievers, 1985. Avocation: sports. Office: Dow Jones and Co Inc 200 Liberty St New York NY 10281

PALTER, ROBERT MONROE, humanities educator; b. NYC, June 19, 1924; s. Meyer and Mildred (Gilder) Palter; m. Ruth Rappeport, July 15, 1945 (div. 1953); 1 child, Alex D. Cielo; m. Toni Ann Inman, Apr. 5, 1955 (div. 1977); children: Geoffrey Meyer, Jennifer Thorn, Nicholas Trask, Adam Finch; m. Annette B. Weiner, May 21, 1979 (div. 1982). AB, Columbia U., 1943; PhD, U. Chgo., 1952. From instr. to assoc. prof. phys. scis. and philosophy U. Chgo., 1949-64; prof. philosophy and history U. Tex., Austin, 1964-82; Dana prof. history of sci. Trinity Coll., Hartford, Conn., 1983-91, prof. emeritus, 1991—. Author: (book) Whitehead's Philosophy of Science, 1960, The Duchess of Malfi's Apricots and Other Literary Fruits, 2002; editor: Toward Modern Science, 1961, The Annus Mirabilis of Sir Isaac Newton, 1971. With US Army, 1944—46. Mem.: Phi Beta Kappa. Personal E-mail: rmpalterss@sbcglobal.net.

PALTROW, GWYNETH, actress; b. LA, Sept. 28, 1972; d. Bruce Paltrow and Blythe Danner; m. Chris Martin, Dec. 5, 2003; children: Apple Blythe Alison Martin, Moses Bruce Anthony Martin. Student, U. Calif. Santa Barbara. Grad. Spence Sch., NYC, 1990. Spokesmodel Estee Lauder; designer ZOEtee's Loves Gwyneth, 2009—. Actress (films) Shout, 1991, Hook, 1991, Malice, 1993, Flesh and Bone, 1993, Mrs. Parker and the Vicious Circle, 1994, Jefferson in Paris, 1995, Se7en, 1995, Moonlight and Valentino, 1995, Hard Eight, 1996, The Pallbearer, 1996, Emma, 1996, Out of the Past (voice), 1998, Great Expectations, 1998, Sliding Doors, 1998, Hush, 1998, A Perfect Murder, 1998, Shakespeare in Love, 1998 (Acad. Award for Best Actress, 1998, Golden Globe award for Best Actress, 1998), The Talented Mr. Ripley, 1999, The Intern, 2000, Duets, 2000, Bounce, 2000, The Anniversary Party, 2001, The Royal Tenenbaums, 2001, Shallow Hal, 2001, Possession, 2002, View From the Top, 2003, Sylvia, 2003, Sky Captain and the World of Tomorrow, 2004, Proof, 2005, Infamous, 2006, Love and Other Disasters, 2006, Running with Scissors, 2006, The Good Night, 2007, Iron Man, 2008, Two Lovers, 2008, (TV films) Cruel Doubt, 1992, Deadly Relations, 1993, appearances in theatre Picnic, The Adventures of Huck Finn, Sweet Bye and Bye, The Seagull, Proof, host (TV series) Spain...On the Road Again, 2008. Named one of The 100 Most Powerful Celebrities, Forbes.com, 2008. Mem.: SAG. also: Screen Actors Guild 5757 Wilshire Blvd Los Angeles CA 90036-3635*

PALUMBO, ANTHONY HOWARD, lawyer; b. Brookhaven, Sept. 14, 1970; s. Anthony and Diane Gail Palumbo; m. Tracy Lynne Karsch, Apr. 27, 2002; 1 child, Ryan Anthony. JD, St. John's U., Flushing, NY, 1998. Bar: US Dist. Ct. (ea. dist.) 2006, Appellate Divsn., Second Dept., NY 1999. Asst. dist. atty. Suffolk County Dist. Atty.'s Office, Riverhead, NY, 1998—2002, asst. dist. atty., trial supr., 2002—04; ptnr. Goggins & Palumbo, Mattituck, NY, 2004—. Pres. New Suffolk Thoroughbreds, Mattituck, NY, 2005—. Office: Goggins & Palumbo 13105 Main Rd PO Box 65 Mattituck NY 11952 Business E-Mail: tony@gogginsandpalumbo.com.

PALUMBO, BENJAMIN LEWIS, public relations executive, consultant; b. Boston, Mar. 4, 1937; s. Guido Americo and Stella Marie (Lombardo) P.; m. Magdalene Julia Palinczar, Nov. 18, 1961; children: Matthew, Jason, Guy. BA, Rutgers U., 1959, MA, 1961. Adminstrv. asst. to Gov. Richard J. Hughes, NJ, 1963-65; dir. rsch. NJ Dem. Com., Trenton, 1965-66; asst. to commr. NJ Dept. Transp., Trenton, 1966-70; asst. dean Woodrow Wilson Sch., Princeton U., NJ, 1970—71; adminstrv. asst. to Senator Harrison Williams, US Senate, Washington, 1971-73, staff dir. US Ho. Dem. caucus, 1975-77, Ho. subcom. on govt. activities and transp., 1977-78; nat. campaign dir. Bentsen for Pres., Washington, 1973-75; dir. fed. govt. rels. Phillip Morris, Inc., Washington, 1978-83; chmn., CEO Palumbo & Cerrell, Inc., Washington, 1983—; bd. dirs. Copyright Alliance. Bd. dirs., past pres. Nyumbani Child of God Hospice and Orphanage; treas., bd. dirs. John Mott Found. Mem.: NJ State Soc., Am. League Lobbyists, Nat. Dem. Club, Rutgers Club Washington, Nat. Press Club. Democrat. Roman Catholic. Office: 401 9th St NW Ste 770 Washington DC 20004 Office Phone: 202-737-4181. Office Fax: 202-879-9340. Business E-Mail: bpalumbo@covad.net.

PALUMBO, JAMES FREDRICK, finance company executive; b. Everett, Mass., Nov. 30, 1950; s. Bruno James and Lillian Elizabeth (Picardi) P.; m. Nancy Laurie Richards, July 24, 1976; children: Elizabeth Richards, Andrew Reid, Alexander Thomas. BA, Lake Forest Coll., Ill., 1973; MBA, Washington U., St. Louis, 1975. Market surveillance analyst Nat. Assn. of Securities Dealers, Washington, 1975-76, asst. treas., 1976-78; regional rep. Student Loan Mktg. Assn., Washington, 1978-79, mgr., 1979-81, dir., 1981-82, asst. v.p., 1982-83, v.p., 1983-87; sr. v.p. Connie Lee Mgmt. Svcs. Corp., Coll. Constrn. Loan Ins. Assn., Washington, 1987-95; with N.Y. Life Ins. Co., NYC, 1995—2000, N.Y. Life Securities Inc., NYC, 1995—2000; prin. Treasury Investment Svcs., Reston, Va., 2000—03; mng. dir. TransCapital Group, Reston, 2000—03, sr. mng. dir., 2003—04; v.p. RyanLabs Fund Mgmt. LLC, 2003—; registered broker Bedminster Fin. Group, 2003—; prin. TransGlobal Capital LLC, 2004—06, Dynamic Capital Ptnrs. LLC, 2006—08; pres. Comml. Funding Group LLC, Great Falls, Va., 2006—. Participant Govt.-Univ.-Industry Rsch. Roundtable, Washington, 1986; chmn. Palumbo Properties L.L.C.; chmn. Capital Holdings Ltd., Great Falls, Va. Actor popular and children's theater, 1973-76. Chmn. sports announcers com. D.C. Spl. Olympics, Washington, 1986, 87, D.C. Regional Counsel, Lake Forest Coll., Washington, 1976-80; mem. Elliott Soc. membership com. Washington U., 1986—, Great Falls (Va.) Hist. Soc., Great Falls Citizens Assn., 1996—; bd. govs. Lake Forest Coll., 1978-82, trustee, 1992-99; trustee Abruzzo and Molise Heritage Soc., 2002-03. Mem.: CFA Soc. Washington, Nat. Assn. Ins. and Fin. Advisors, CFA Inst., Great Falls Swim and Tennis Club (bd. dirs. 1988—91), Alpha Psi Omega. Avocations: polo, horseback riding, painting. Office: Comml Funding Group 11710 Plz America Dr Ste 2000 Reston VA 20190 Home Phone: 703-759-6467.

PALUSCI, VINCENT JOHN, physician, researcher; b. Camden, NJ, June 24, 1958; s. John and Dorothy Irene (Laskowski) P.; m. Roslyn Sara Scheiber, Sept. 11, 1983; children: John Vincent, Katherine Rebecca. BA, U. Pa., 1980; MD, Univ. Medicine and Dentistry N.J., 1984; MS in Epidemiology, Mich. State U., 2002. Diplomate Am. Bd. Pediats. Resident pediats. NYU, Bellevue Hosp., NYC, 1984—87; pvt. practice Huntington, NY, 1987—93; asst. prof. Mich. State U. Coll. Human Medicine, 1995—2001, assoc. prof., 2001—05; dir. child protection team DeVos Children's Hosp., Grand Rapids, Mich., 1995—2005; Helppie prof. pediats. Wayne State U. Sch. Medicine; dir. child protection ctr. Chidren's Hosp. Mich., Detroit, 2005—07; prof. NYU Sch. Medicine, 2008—. Mem. Am. Acad. Pediats., Am. Profl. Soc. on Abuse of Children (bd. dirs. 2008-). Office: Frances Loeb Child Protection & Devel Ctr 462 First Ave New York NY 10016 Office Phone: 212-562-6073.

PALVINO, JACK ANTHONY, retired broadcasting executive; b. Rochester, NY, May 28, 1934; s. John Charles and Mary Aurelia P.; m. Joyce Ann Vilkaitis, Oct. 8, 1960; children: John Charles, Jill Marie, Jason Allen. BS, St. John Fisher Coll., 1955. Broadcaster, program dir. Sta. WGVA, Geneva, N.Y., 1958-60; radio personality Sta. WBBF, Rochester, N.Y., 1958-78; pres. Sports and Spls. TV, 1970-73; co-owner, exec. v.p. Lincoln Group Ltd., 1978-98; gen. mgr. Stas. WHAM, WVOR, WHTK, WPXY, Rochester, 1978-98; ret., 1998. Chmn. bd. trustees St. John Fisher Coll. Served with U.S. Army, 1957-58. Mem. St. John Fisher Alumni Assn., Nat. Assn. Broadcaster, Rochester Radio Broadcasters Assn. (pres. 1987-97), N.Y. State Broadcasters Assn., Rochester C. of C. Clubs: University, Rochester Press Radio (pres. 1974), Rotary. Roman Catholic. Home: 780 Beach Ave Rochester NY 14612-2028

PAMBUCCIAN, STEFAN E., cytologist, educator; s. Krikor G. and Sona Pambuccian; m. Corina A. Pavel, Dec. 25, 1985; 1 child, Felix S. MD, U. Bucharest Med. Sch., Romania, 1983. Diplomate in anatomic and clin. pathology Am. Bd. Pathology, 1994, cert. in cytopathology 1996. Asst. prof. U. Minn., Mpls., 1996—2003, dir., cytopathology, 1996—2008, assoc. prof., 2003—08, prof., 2008—. Contbr. scientific papers. Recipient Outstanding Tchr. of Yr. award, U. Minn., 2004. Mem.: Am. Soc. Cytopathology. Office: Univ Minn 420 Delaware St SE Minneapolis MN 55455 Office Fax: 612-273-1142. Business E-Mail: pambu001@umn.edu.

PAMIES, RUBENS JOHN, dean; s. George and Lillian Pamies. MD, SUNY at Buffalo, Sch. of Medicine, 1982—86. AAMC Health Services Reseaarch Institute ACP, 2004, diplomate Nat. Bd. Examiners, Am. Bd. Internal Medicine. Dir. and founder of minority affairs U. of South Fla. Coll. of Medicine, 1994; vice chancellor for academic affairs U. of Nebr. Med. Ctr., 2004—; program dir. Mt. Sinai Med. Ctr., Cleve., 1994—94; assoc. dean for academic programs and student affairs Case Western Res. U. Sch. of Medicine, Cleve., 1994—2000; chmn. and prof. Meharry Med. Coll., Nashville, 2000—03; prof. of medicine Vanderbilt U. Sch. of Medicine, Nashville, 2001—03; chief of svc. Met. Nashville Gen. Hosp., 2000—03; prof. of internal medicine U. of Nebr. Med. Ctr., 2004—, dean of grad. studies, 2004—. Author: (text book) Multicultural Medicine And Health Disparities. Mem. Va.-Nebr. Alliance, Richmond, Va., 2004, Joslyn Art Mus., Omaha, 2004. Grant, Nat. Heart, Lung, & Blood Inst., 2002, scholarship, Case Western Res. U. SOM, 2000—. Mem.: ACP, AMA, Assn. of Am. Med. Colleges, Internat. Soc. of Hypertension in Blacks, Assn. of Academic Minority Physicians. Achievements include research in early clinical exposure and its effect in performance in the third year clearkship. Office: Univ of Nebr Med Ctr 987810 Nebraska Med Ctr Omaha NE 68198-7810 Office Fax: 402-559-7845. Personal E-mail: rpamies@unmc.edu.

PAMPLIN, ROBERT BOISSEAU, JR., manufacturing company executive, minister, writer; b. Augusta, Ga., Aug. 3, 1941; s. Robert Boisseau and Mary Katherine (Reese) P.; m. Marilyn Joan Hooper; children: Amy Louise, Anne Boisseau. Student, Va. Poly. Inst., 1960-62, BSBA, 1964, BS in Acctg., 1965, BS in Econs., 1966; BS (hon.), Va. Tech., 2001; LHD (hon.), Va. Poly. Inst., 1995, Pacific U., 2001; DHL (hon.), Va. Poly. Inst., 1995; MBA, U. Portland, 1968, LLD (hon.), 1972, MEd, 1975; MA, Western Conservative Bapt. Sem. (name now Western Sem.), 1978, DMin, 1982, D (hon.) of Sacred Letter, 1991, MA, 2000; PhD, Calif. Coast U.; DHL (hon.), Warner Pacific Coll., 1988; LLD (hon.), Western Baptist Coll., 1989, George Fox U., 2005; cert. in wholesale mgmt., Ohio State U., 1970; cert. labor mgmt., U. Portland, 1982; cert. in advanced mgmt., U. Hawaii, 1975; DD (hon.), Judson Baptist Coll., 1984; DBA (hon.), Marquis Giuseppe Scicluna Internat. U. Found., 1986; LittD (hon.), Va. Tech. U., 1987, LHD (hon.), BS (hon.) in Bus. Adminstrn., 2001; LHD (hon.), Western Seminary, 1991; DD, Western Evang. Sem., 1994; DBA (hon.), U. S.C., 1996; D Pub. Svc., DHL (hon.), U. Puget Sound, Pacific U., 1999, 2001. Pres., CEO R.B. pamplin Corp., Portland, Oreg., 1964—. Chmn. bd., CEO Columbia Empire Farms Inc., Lake Oswego, Oreg., 1976—, Pamplin Comms.; chmn. bd., CEO Mt. Vernon Mills Inc.,; pres., CEO Ross Island Sand & Gravel; lectr. bus. adminstrn. Lewis and Clark Coll., 1968-69; adj. asst. prof. bus. adminstrn., U. Portland, 1973-76; pastor Christ Cmty. Ch., Lake Oswego; lectr. in bus. adminstrn. and econs. U. Costa Rica, 1968, Va. Tech. Found., 1986; chmn. bd. dirs. Christian Supplly Ctrs. Inc.; prof. with tenure U. Portland, 1999. Author: Everything is Just great, 1985, The Gift, 1986, Another Virginian: A Study of the Life and Beliefs of Robert Boisseau Pamplin, 1986; author: (with others) A Portrait of Colorado, 1976, Three in One, 1974, The Storybook Primer on Managing, 1974, One Who Believed, Vol. I, 1988, vol. II, 1991, Climbing the Centuries, 1993, Heritage the Making of an American Family, 1994, American Heroes, 1995, Prelude to Surrender, 1995, Alaska Gold, 1998, Robert Reese, 1998; editor: Oreg. Mus. Sci. and Industry Press, 1973; trustee Oreg. Mus. Sci. and Industry Press, 1971, 1974—; editor: Portrait of Oregon, 1973; editor: (with others) Oregon Underfoot, 1975. Trustee Lewis and Clark Coll., 1989—, chmn. bd. trustees, 1988-96, life trustee 1996-; hon. life pres. Western Conservative Bapt. Sem.; chmn. regents Western Sem., 1994; mem. nat. adv. coun. on vocat. Edn., 1975—; mem. Western Interstate Com. on Higher Edn., 1981-84; co-chmn. Va. Tech. $50 Million Campaign for Excellence, 1984-87, Va. Tech. Found., 1986—, Va.-Oreg. State Scholarship Commn., 1974—, chmn. 1976-78; mem. Portland dist. adv. coun. SBA, 1973-77; mem. rewards rev. com., City of Portland, 1973-78, chmn., 1973-78; bd. regents U. Portland, 1971-79, chmn. bd., 1975-79, regent emeritus, 1979—; trustee Oreg. Episc. Schs., 1979, Linfield Coll., U. Puget Sound, 1989—; dr. pub. svc., U. Puget Sound, 1999; chmn. bd. trustees Portland Art Mus., 2003-05. Recipient Disting. Alumnus award, Lewis and Clark Coll., 1974, ROTC Disting. Svc. award, USAF, 1974, bronze medal, Albert Einstein Acad., 1986, Disting. Leadership medal, Freedoms Found., Disting. Bus. Alumnus award, U. Portland, 1990, Nat. Caring award, Caring Inst., 1991, Pride of Portland award, Portland Lions Club, Hero Athlete award, 1994, Herman Lay Entrepreneurship award, 1995, Thomas Jefferson award, Oreg. Hist. Soc., 1998, Aubrey R. Watzek award, Lewis and Clark Coll., 1998, Leadership award, Portland Living Mag., 1998, Unique Contbns. to Comms. award, Portland Advt. Fedn., 2001, Oliver Wendell Holmes, Jr. award for Civil War Preservationalist of Yr., 2001, Govs. Arts award, 2001, Legacy award, Civil War Preservation Trust, 2003, Gov.'s Gold award as Oregonian of Achievement, 2003, Corp. Citizenship award, Woodrow Wilson Internat. Ctr. for Scholars, 2005, Nat. Vol. Outstanding Svc. award, Vol. Am., 2006; named Outstanding Philanthropist of Yr. award, Nat. Soc. Fund Raising Execs., 1997, Western Conservative Bapt. Sem. Lay Inst. for Leadership, Edn. Devel. and Rsch. named for R.B. Pamplin Jr., 1988, Textile World's Top 10, 1999, Portland First Citizen, Portland Met. Assn. Realtors, 1999, Parents of Yr., Juvenile Diabetes Found., 2001, Entrepreneur of Yr., Oreg. Entrepreneur Forum, 2001, Va. Tech. Coll. Bus. Adminstrn. renamed R.B. Pamplin Coll. Bus. Adminstrn. in his honor, U. Portland Sch. Bus. renamed Dr. Robert B. Pamplin, Jr. in his honor, Civil War Preservationalist of Yr., Civil War Preservation Trust, 2003, Nat. Vol. of Yr., Vols. of Am., 2006; named one of 20 Most Influential Execs. Past 20 Yrs., Bus. Jour. Mem. Acad. Mgmt., Delta Epsilon Sigma, Beta Gamma Sigma, Sigma Phi Epsilon, Waverley Country Club (pres. 2003-04), Arlington, Multnomah Athletic Clulb, Capitol Hill Club, Greenville Country Club, Poinsett Club, Eldorado Country Club, Thunderbird Country Club, Rotary. Republican. Episcopalian. Office: RB Pamplin Corp Inc Ste 2400 805 SW Broadway Portland OR 97205-3341

PAN, BAOCHENG, biophysicist, researcher; PhD, Ohio State U., Columbus, 1998. Postdoc. assoc. Yale U., New Haven, 2003—. Mem.: ACA. Achievements include research in crystal structures of protein and nucleic acids and their interaction mechanisms. Office: Yale Univ Bass Ctr Rm 421 266 Whitney Ave New Haven CT 06520 Personal E-mail: baocheng.pan@gmail.com. Business E-Mail: baocheng.pan@yale.edu.

PAN, CHAI-FU, engineering educator; b. Loshon, Szechwan, China, Sept. 8, 1936; arrived in US, 1960; s. I-Chen Pan, Shih-Liang Shih; m. Maria Chia-Yao Shih, Aug. 18, 1962; children: Lawrence, Mariette. BS in Chem. Engring., Nat. Taiwan U., 1956; PhD in Phys. Chemistry, U.

Kans., Lawrence, 1966. Assoc. prof. Ala. State U., Montgomery, 1966—71, prof., 1971—91, prof. emeritus, 1991—. Contbr. numerous articles to profl. jours. Recipient Rsch. award, Ala. State U., 1985; grantee MISIP grantee, NSF, 1985. Fellow: Am. Inst. Chemists; mem.: Am. Chem. Soc. (referee), Phi Lambda Upsilon. Achievements include development of Pan equations; research in methods to study hydrophilic and hydrophobic phenomena in electrolyte solutions. Avocations: reading, writing, gardening, photography. Home: 2420 Wentworth Dr Montgomery AL 36106 Personal E-mail: ppan@charter.net.

PAN, ERNIAN, engineering educator, researcher; b. Xiantao, Hubei, China, Feb. 10, 1955; arrived in USA, 1989, naturalized, 1995; s. Xishan Pan and Peizhi Lei; m. Judy Chen, Nov. 22, 1983; 1 child, Rui. PhD in Civil Engring., Geophys., U. Colo., Boulder, 1993. Project mgr. Optimal Coop., Cary, NC, 1998—2002; assoc. prof. engring. U. Akron, Ohio, 2002—08, prof. engring. and applied math. Mem.: ASCE, ASME. Achievements include patents pending for super-fast algorithm for the prediction of surface response of multi-layered half-spaces. Office: Univ Akron ASEC Bldg Coll Engring Akron OH 44325 Home: 1060 Bull Creek Ln Macedonia OH 44056 Office Fax: 330-972-6020.

PAN, FLORENCE Y., judge; b. NYC, 1966; m. Max Stier; 2 children. BA summa cum laude, U. Pa., 1988; JD, Stanford U., 1993. Law clk. to Hon. Michael Mukasey US Dist. Ct. (so. dist.) NY, 1993—94; law clk. to Hon. Ralph Winter US Ct. Appeals (2nd Cir.), 1994—95; Bristol fellow, Office Solicitor Gen. US Dept. Justice, 1995—96, with appellate section criminal divsn.; sr. adviser to under sec. for domestic finance US Dept. Treasury; prosecutor US Atty. Office US Attorney's Office, US Dept. Justice, DC, 1999—2009, dep. chief appellate divsn., 2007—09; assoc. judge DC Superior Ct., 2009—. Adj. prof. criminal procedure Am. U. Washington Coll. Law. Office: DC Superior Ct Moultrie Courthouse 500 Indiana Ave Washington DC 20001 Office Phone: 202-879-1880.*

PAN, HUI-LIN, medical educator; married. MD, Tongji Med. U., Wuhan, China, 1991. Prof. U. Tex., Houston, 2006—. Office: Univ Tex Anderson Cancer Ctr 1515 Holcombe Blvd Houston TX 77030

PAN, JOSHUA JIH, architect; b. Tientsin, Hopei, China, July 10, 1942; s. Eber D.H. and Hazel (Wu) P.; m. Bonnie Sun, July 12, 1969; children: Bertha, Bernice. BS in Architecture, Cheng Kung U., 1963; BArch, Rice U., 1966; MS in Architecture, Columbia U., 1967. Registered architect, N.Y., N.J., Tex., Republic of China. Designer Philip Johnson and Richard Foster, NYC, 1967-68; project architect Davis, Brody and Assocs., NYC, 1968-72; assoc. Collins Uhl Hoisington Anderson, Princeton, NJ, 1972-76; ptnr. Fei Cheng, Pan and Assocs., Taipei, Republic of China, 1976-80; prin. J.J. Pan and Ptnrs. Architects & Planners, Taipei, 1981—. Chmn. bd. dirs. Horizon Design Corp., 1988—; adj. prof. Taiwan U. Sci. and Tech., 1994—. Archtl. projects over 100 pub. in domestic and internat. profl. mags. and books (numerous nat. and interna. design awards). Named Outstanding Architect, Republic of China. Fellow AIA, Archtl. Inst. Republic of China (bd. dirs. 1983-85); mem. Taipei Inst. Architects (bd. dirs. 1983-85), Nat. Ctrl. Bur. Standard (reviewing com. 1984—), Chinese Inst. Urban Design (pres. 2001-03), Tau Sigma Delta. Avocations: music, photography. Office: J J Pan & Ptnrs 21 Alley 12 Ln 118 Ren Ai Rd Sect 3 Taipei 106 Taiwan Office Phone: 886-2-2701-2617.

PAN, JUNFENG, application developer, researcher; b. China, 1979; BS (hon.), Sun Yat Sen (Zhongshan) U., Guangzhou, China, 2003; PhD, Hong Kong U. Sci. and Tech., 2007. Rsch. asst. Hong Kong U. Sci. and Tech., 2004—07; vis. scholar MIT, Cambridge, 2007; software engr. Google Inc., Mt. View, Calif., 2007—. Program com. mem. Internat. Conf. Advances Comp. Human Interaction, 2008. Author: (book) Programming in PHP; contbr. scientific papers to profl. publs. Recipient First prize, Higher Edn. Divsn. Ministry Edn. Nat. Math. Contest, 2001. Mem.: IEEE (program com. mem. 2007, reviewer, Best Paper award 2006), Assn. Computing Machinery (Creativity award 2005, Precision award 2005, Performance award 2005). Office: Google Inc 1600 Amphitheatre Pkwy Mountain View CA 94043

PAN, LIANG RU, physicist, researcher; b. Szechuan, China, Apr. 24, 1917; arrived in U.S., 1947; s. Min Gau Pan and Yun Dou Chong; m. Zhong De Ding, Apr. 10, 1934; children: Luanne, Feng. BS, Nat. Southwest U., China, 1943; MS, Va. Polytech. Inst., 1950; PhD, Cornell U., 1956. Assoc. prof. Chinese Acad. Sci., Beijing, 1956—78; assoc. editor The Chinese Jour. Mechanics, Beijing, 1957—60; prof. Chinese Acad. Sci., Beijing, 1978—. Vis. sr. scientist Blackett Lab. Imperial Coll., London, 1986; vis. sr. scientist Lab. Plasma Studies Cornell U., Ithaca, NY, 1987. Contbr. articles to profl. jours. Recipient award, Beijing (China) Sci. and Tech. Assn., 1986, State Dept., China, 1993. Mem.: N.Y. Acad. Scis., Beijing (China) Soc. Plasma Sci. and Tech. (founder 1978—, vice chmn. 1978—85). Avocations: exercise, bridge, travel, television. Home Phone: 212-369-4088.

PAN, LONG, chemist; s. Jiaxin Pan and Xiuhua Chen; m. Shun Liang; 1 child, Yue. PhD, U. Sci. & Tech. China, Hefei, 2000. Sr. rsch. scientist Colgate Palmolive Co., Piscataway, NJ, 2006—08, tech. assoc., 2008—. Asst. rsch. prof. Rutgers U., Piscataway, 2005—06. Author: (book) Synthesis of New Compounds; contbr. chapters to books, articles to profl. pubs. Mem.: North East Corridor Zeolite Assn. (First Pl. Presentation award). Office: Colgate Palmolive Co 909 River Rd Piscataway NJ 08855

PAN, QING, statistician, educator; d. Erling Pan and Xiaoyang Zhang; m. John Charles Bult, Apr. 1, 2008. PhD, U. Mich., Ann Arbor, 2007. Rsch. asst. Kidney Epidemiology and Costs Ctr., Ann Arbor, Mich., 2003—07; asst. prof. stats. dept. GWU, Washington, 2007—, rsch. scientist, biostats. ctr., 2008—. Mem.: Am. Statis. Assn. Office: Stats Dept GWU 2140 Pennsylvania Ave NW Washington DC 20052 Office Fax: 202-994-6917. Business E-Mail: qpan@gwu.edu.

PAN, QISHENG, urban planner, educator; PhD, U. SC, LA, 2003. Assoc. prof., interim chair Tex. So. U., Houston, 2003—.

PAN, XIAOQING, materials scientist, educator; b. Shuyang, Jiangsu, China, July 31, 1961; s. Yanfang and Zhihua Hwang Pan; m. Hong Zheng, May 24, 1989; children: Sussy, Katharine. PhD, U. Saarlandes, Saarbruecken, Germany, 1991. Rsch. assoc. U. Saarlandes, 1987—91; postdoc. fellow Max-Planck Inst. fuer Metallforschung, Stuttgart, Germany, 1991—96; assoc. prof. U. Mich., Ann Arbor, 1996—2004, prof., 2004—. Dir., divsn. functional materials and nanodevices Ningbo Inst. Materials Technologies and Engring. Chinese Acad. Sci., Jiejiang, 2007—; cons. Toyota Motor Engring. & Mfg. N.Am. Inc., Ann Arbor, 2008—. Contbr. scientific papers (NSF Career award, 1999). Recipient Outstanding Young Investigator award, Chinese Natural Sci. Found., 2004; named Chang-Jiang Chair Prof., China Ministration Edn., 2008. Mem.: Am. Phys. Soc., Am. Ceramic Soc., Materials Rsch. Soc. Achievements include research in interfaces of advanced materials. Home: 2347 Timbercrest Ct Ann Arbor MI 48105 Office: Univ Mich 2300 Hayward Ann Arbor MI 48109 Office Fax: 734-763-4788. Business E-Mail: panx@umich.edu.

PAN, YA-HUI LAURIE, toxicologist, director; m. Larry Swales. BS in Biology & Chemistry, Bethel Coll., N.Newton, Kans., 1983—87; PhD in Toxicology, U. Kans. Med. Ctr., Kans. City, 1987—92. Diplomate of American Board of Toxicology Am. Bd. of Toxicology/North Carolina, 1996. Human safety toxicologist Proctor & Gamble, Co., Hunt Valley, Md., 1992—94; sr. scientist product safety Mary Kay, Inc., Dallas, 1994—95, group leader product safety, 1995—2000, mgr. product safety, 2000—05; dir. regulatory affairs Sally Beauty Holdings, Inc., Denton, Tex., 2006—. Chmn. safety & regulatory toxicology com. Cosmetic, Toiletry & Fragrance Assn., DC, 2002—04. Mem.: Am. Contact Dermatitis Soc. (assoc.), Am. Acad. Dermatology (assoc.), Soc. Toxicology (assoc.).

PAN, YI, computer science educator; b. Wujiang, Jiangsu, China, May 12, 1960; came to U.S., 1987; s. Jun and Xiuzhen (Fei) P.; m. Hong Miao, Aug. 4, 1986; children: Marissa, Anna. BEng, Tsinghua U., Beijing, 1982, MEng, 1984; MSc, U. Pitts., 1988, PhD in Computer Sci., 1991. Rsch. asst. Tsinghua U., 1982-86; tchg. asst. U. Pitts., 1987-89, tchg. fellow, 1989—91; asst. prof. computer sci. U. Dayton, Ohio, 1991-96, assoc. prof. Ohio, 1996-2000; assoc. prof. computer sci. Ga. State U., Atlanta, 2000—, now chair computer sci. Director of Graduate Studies in Computer Science University of Dayton, Dayton, 1998—2000. Contbr. articles to profl. jours. Recipient Rsch. Opportunity award NSF, 1995, Investment Competition Fund award Ohio Bd. Regents, 1996, World Acad. Scis. Achievement award, 2002; Mellon Found. fellow 1990, Summer Rsch. fellow U. Dayton Rsch. Coun., 2000, Air Force Office for Sci. Rsch., JSPS fellow, 1998. Mem.: IEEE (sr.; Secretary of the IEEE Computer Society Dayton Chapter 1996—97, BIBE Outstanding Achievement award 2007, IEEE Computer Soc. Disting. Visitor Program Spkr. 2000). Home: 615 Summer Breeze Ter Alpharetta GA 30005-6431 Office: Ga State U Computer Sci Dept 34 Peachtree St Ste 1450 Atlanta GA 30303 Office Phone: 404-413-5719. E-mail: pan@cs.gsu.edu.

PAN, YUDE, forest ecologist; d. Yongjun Pan and Tianran Chang; 1 child, Margaret Manshu Shih. BS, Oceanography U. China, Qingdao, 1982; MSc, Grad. Sch. Chinese Acad. Scis., Beijing, 1984; PhD, SUNY, Syracuse, 1993. Rsch. assoc. Marine Biol. Lab., Woods Hole, Mass., 1996—97, postdoc. rsch. assoc., 1994—96; rsch. scientist USDA Forest Svc., Newtown Square, Pa., 1997—. Summer rsch. asst. Columbia U., NYC, 1996; vis. rsch. fellow Darmouth Coll., Hanover, NH, 1996—97; vis. rsch. scholar Princeton U., NJ, 2009; pres. Sino-Ecologist Club Overseas, 2000—02; adj. prof. U. Toledo, 2001—07; adj. fellow U. Pa., Phil., 2005—; editl. bd. mem. Open Forest Sci. Jour., Bentham Sci. Pubs., Oak Park, Ill., 2007—; assoc. editor-in-chief Acta Ecologica Sinica Elsevier, Beijing, 2009—. Author scientific research articles. Recipient Natural Sci. award, Chinese Acad. Scis., 1990, Merit award, USDA Forest Svc., 2001—04, 2006, 2008; Jessie Smith Noyes Found. Rsch. fellowship, Dartmouth Coll., 1986—87, grant, NASA, 2001—. Mem.: Am. Geophys. Union, Ecol. Soc. America (chair Asian ecology sect. 2008—). Office: US Forest Svc 11 Campus Blvd Newtown Square PA 19073

PAN, ZHUO-HUA, science educator; s. Yongjian Pan and Xianyu Zhao; m. Ya Li, Oct. 1, 1984; children: Ruoquan Lily, Henry Siyong. BS, U. Sci. & Tech. China, Hefei, 1982; MS, Inst. Biophysics, Chinese Academic Sci., Beijing, 1984; PhD, SUNY, Buffalo, 1990. Instr. Children's Hosp. and Harvard Med. Sch., Boston, 1991—97, Brigham & Women's Hosp. and Harvard Med. Sch., Boston, 1997—98, asst. prof., 1998—99, Wayne State U., Detroit, 1999—2003, assoc. prof., 2003—07, prof., 2007—. Recipient Faculty Rsch. Excellence award, Wayne State U. Sch. Medicine, 2001, Career Devel. Chair award, Wayne State U., 2004, Bd. Governors Faculty Recognition award, 2007; Multiple grants, NIH, 1995, grant, Hope vision, 2006. Mem.: Am. Soc. Gene Therapy, Assn. Rsch. Vision and Ophthalmology Am., Soc. Neurosci. Achievements include research in proof the principle of a novel strategy for treatment of blinding retinal degenerative diseases. Office: Wayne State Univ 540 E Canfield Ave Detroit MI 48201 Business E-Mail: zhpan@med.wayne.edu.

PANA, ELISABETA, finance educator; d. Alexandru and Ileana. PhD, U. New Orleans. Asst. prof. IWU, Bloomington, Ill., 2004. Recipient Hocevar Toussaint, UNO. Office: Ill Wesleyan Univ 205 Beecher Bloomington IL 61701

PANAGIDES, JOHN, pharmacologist; b. NYC, Aug. 15, 1944; s. Chris and Sophie (Marmar) P.; m. Kathleen Ann Heimann, July 9, 1967; children: Christopher, Melissa, Adrienne. BS, CCNY, 1966; MS, U. N.C., 1968; PhD, SUNY, Buffalo, 1972. Rsch. assoc. Rockefeller U., NYC, 1972-73; sr. scientist Lederle Labs., Pearl River, NY, 1973-83; sr. clin. monitor Ayerst Labs., NYC, 1983-87; dir. clin. projects, CNS Organon Pharms. USA Inc., 1987-99, sr. dir. clin. projects, CNS, 1999—. Contbr. articles to profl. jours. NDEA Title IV fellow, Chapel Hill, 1966-68. Mem. AAAS, Am. Soc. Pharmacology and Exptl. Therapeutics, Am. Coll. Neuropsychopharmacology, N.Y. Acad. Scis. Achievements include development of haemophilus influenza vaccine, 23-valent pneumococcal vaccine, fenbufen, lodine, cotazym, cotazym-S, zymase, remeron and asenapine. Home: 7 Catawba Dr West Nyack NY 10994-2304 Office: Organon Pharms USA Inc 56 Livingston Ave Roseland NJ 07068 E-mail: j.panagides@organonusa.com.

PANAGOS, STEVEN GREGORY, investment banker; b. Royal Oak, Mich., Nov. 18, 1961; BS in Acctg., U. Mich., 1983. CPA; cert. insolvency reorganization acct. Sr. acct. KMG Main Hurdman, Stamford, Conn., 1984-86; corp. contr. Van Wagner Communcations Inc., NYC, 1986-88; mng. dir., nat. practice leader Kroll Zolfo Cooper LLC, NYC, 1988—2008; pres., COO Krispy Kreme Doughnuts Inc., 2005—06; founder Panagos Katz Situational Investing, 2008—09; mng. dir., vice chmn. recapitalization & restructuring group Moelis & Co., NYC, 2009—. Office: Moelis & Co 245 Park Ave 32nd Fl New York NY 10167 Office Phone: 217-407-6770. Business E-Mail: steve.panagos@moelis.com.

PANARESE, WILLIAM C., civil engineer; b. Framingham, Mass., Mar. 6, 1929; s. Angelo and Stephanie (Di Profio) P. BSCE, Purdue U., 1952. Structural research engr. Assn. Am. Railroads, Chgo., 1952-55; with Portland Cement Assn., Chgo. and Skokie, Ill., 1957-76, 80-94, mgr. concrete tech. sect., 1973-76, assoc. mgr. bldg. constrn. sect., 1980-83, mgr. bldg. tech. dept., 1983-86, mgr. constrn. info. services dept., 1987-94. Author, editor: Concrete Floors on Ground, 1983, Transporting and Handling Concrete, 1987, The Homeowner's Guide to Building with Concrete, Brick and Stone, 1988, Cement Mason's Guide, 1990, Concrete Masonry Handbook for Architects, Engineers, Builders, 1991, 2008, Fiber Reinforced Concrete, 1991, High Strength Concrete, 1994, Design and Control of Concrete Mixtures, 1988, 2002, Performance of Architectural Concrete Panels in the PCA Outdoor Display, 2004, Environmental Performance of Concrete, 2005, Concrete Floors and Moisture, 2005, Specifier's Guide to Durable Concrete, 2005, Concrete Finisher's Guide, 2006, Mass Concrete for Buildings and Bridges, 2007, author, editor: other bldg. guides and handbooks; editor: Concrete Constrn. mag., 1976—80, Concrete Tech. Today newsletter, 1980—94. Served with C.E. U.S. Army, 1955-57. Fellow Am. Concrete Inst. (coms. 302 on constrn. of concrete floors and slabs, 332 on residential concrete work, chmn. 332 1984-88), Chi Epsilon. Roman Catholic. Avocations: music, walking, tennis, skiing, writing. Home and Office: 1625 Glenview Rd Unit 304 Glenview IL 60025-2973 Office Phone: 847-729-5885. Personal E-mail: wmpanarese@aol.com.

PANAYIOTIS, ZAVOS MICHAEL, retired medical educator; BA, MS, EdS, U. Minn., Twin Cities, PhD, 1974. Prof. U. Ky., Lexington, 1978—2001, Andrology Inst. America, Lexington, 2001—08. Pres. & CEO ZDL Inc., Lexington, 1991—2008; dir., gen. mgr. and cons. Contbr. articles to profl. jours. Recipient Disting. Rschr. and Inventor award, 2006. Mem.: ASA (advisor bd. mem. 1999—2008, Disting. Svc. award 2001), MEFS, ASRM (Greek Fertility Soc. Disting. Rschr. award 2001). Achievements include discovery of semen preparation technology. Home: PO Box 23777 Lexington KY 40523 Office: 181 Southland Dr Lexington KY 40503 Home Fax: 859-278-6906. Personal E-mail: zavos@zavos.org.

PANCHAGNULA, MAHESH, engineering educator; PhD, Purdue U. Rsch. assoc. Lehigh U., Bethlehem, Pa., 2004—05; asst. prof. Tenn. Tech U., Cookeville, 2005—. Recipient Ann. Sigma Xi award, Sigma Xi chpt., TTU, 2008. Achievements include research in discovered fundamental physics related to hysteresis. Office: Tenn Technol Univ 115 E 10th St Cookeville TN 38505 Office Fax: 931-372-6340.

PANCHANATHAN, SETHURAMAN, computer science educator; BSc in Physics, Madras U., India, 1981; BE in Electronics and Comm. Engring., Indian Inst. Sci., Bangalore, 1984; MTech in Elec. Engring., Indian Inst. Sci., 1986; PhD in Elec. Engring., Ottawa U., Can., 1989. Assoc. prof. elec. engring. U. Ottawa, adj. prof. dept. elec. engring., 1997—; prof. computer sci. and engring. Ariz. State U., Tempe, affiliate prof. elec. engring., 1998—2007, chmn., dept. computer sci. & engring., 2001—08, dir., Sch. Computing & Informatics, 2001—, dir., Rsch. Ctr. Cognitive Ubiquitous Computing, dep. v.p. rsch. & economic affairs, 2006—08. Adj. prof. Sch. Info. Tech. and Engring. U. Ottawa; hon. vis. prof. U. NSW, Sydney, Australia; co-chair IS&T/SPIE Digital Video Compression-Algorithms and Techs. '96 and Multimedia Hardware Architectures '97 Confs., San Jose, Calif.; symposium chair Electronic Imaging '98, San Jose, chair Multimedia Hardware Architectures '98 conf., 13th IASTED Internat. Conf. Internat & Multimedia Sys. & Applications, 2009, 3rd Internat. Conf. on Body Area Networks, 2008, HVEI Embedded Processors Multimedia & Communication, 2005; co-chair Multimedia Storage and Archiving Systems III conf., Photonics East; co-chair Media Processors '99, Multimedia Storage and Archiving Systems IV conf.; program com. mem. several confs., invited panel mem. spl. sessions. Contbr. over 300 articles to profl. jours. and conf. procs.; guest editor spl. issue Can. Jour. Elec. and Computer Engring., 2-part spl. issue Jour. Visual Comm. and Image Representation. Fellow IEEE, Canadian Acad. Engring., SPIE, Soc. Photo-Optical Instrumentation Engrs., IEEE (sr.; tutorials chair Internat. Conf. on Multimedia Systems '97; guest editor 2-part spl. issue IEEE Trans. Circuits and Systems for Video Tech. 1998; editor-in-chief, Multimedia Mag., 2006-), Profl. Engrs. Ont., European Assn. Signal Processing. Office: Ariz State Univ VP Rsch & Economic Affairs PO Box 87 7205 Tempe AZ 85287-7205

PANCHAPAKESAN, SUBRAHMANIAN, mathematics professor; b. Chennai, Tamilnadu, India, Aug. 27, 1933; s. P. N. and Visalakshi Subrahmanian. MA, Madras U., 1955; M in Stats., Indian Statis. Inst., Kolkata, India, 1962; PhD, Purdue U., West Lafayette, Ind., 1969. Lectr., math. Islamiah Coll., Vaniyambadi, Tamilnadu, 1955—60; staff, data processing ctr. Indian Statis. Inst., West Bengal, 1965; vis. asst. prof., stats. dept. Purdue U., Ind., 1969—70; asst. prof., math dept. Southern Ill. U., Carbondale, 1970—74, assoc. prof., 1974—80, prof., 1980—98, prof. emeritus, 1998—. Vis. expert Inst. Math., Acad. Sinica, Taipei, Taiwan, 1980; reviewer Math. Reviews, 1971—; assoc. editor Jour. Statis. Planning & Inference, 1984—2000; mem. internat. editl. bd. Comm. Stats., 1985—94; mem., editl. bd. Am. Jour. Math. & Mgmt. Scis., 1993—; assoc. editor Comm. Stats. Theory & Methods, 2001—, Comm. Stats. Simulation & Computation, 2001—; exch. scholar Cheng Shui U., Kaohsiung, Taiwan, 2006. Joint author (book) Multiple Decision Procedures, 1979 (Thomas L. Saaty award (Am. Jour. Math. & Mgmt. Scis.), 2002); contbr. articles to profl. jours. Mem.: Internat. Statis. Inst., Inst. Math. Stats., Am. Statis. Assn. Home: 411 Creek Point Ln Arlington TX 76002-3331 Office: Southern Ill Univ Carbondale IL 62901

PANCHAWAGH, HRISHIKESH VIJAYKUMAR, mechanical engineer, researcher; m. Shweta Dhapare. BSc in Engring., Pune U., Maharashtra, India, 1998; MS, U. Colo., Boulder, 2001, PhD, 2005. Mems design engr. InLight Comm., Fremont, Calif., 2001, U. Colo., 2002—05; mems rsch. scientist Eastman Kodak Co., Rochester, NY, 2006—.

PANCHYK, RICHARD ROBERT, writer; b. Elmhurst, NY, Mar. 30, 1970; s. Robert and Katherine Panchyk; m. Caren Prommersberger, June 11, 1994; children: Matthew, Elizabeth. BA in Anthropology, Adelphi U., Garden City, NY, 1992; MA in Anthropology, U. Mass., Amherst, 1994, postgrad. in anthropology, 1996. Inst. U. Mass., Mass., 1994—95. Author (with Matthys Levy): Engineering the City, 2000; author: Archaeology for Kids, 2001; author: (foreword by Senator John McCain) World War II for Kids, 2002 (Notable Book, Children's Lit. Coun., Nat. Tchrs. Social Studies, 2003, 10 Most Popular Student-Selected Books award, Hong Kong, 2006); author: (foreword by Mr. Imagination) American Folk Art for Kids, 2004; author: (foreword by Buzz Aldrin) Galileo for Kids, 2005; author: (foreword by Senator John Kerry, afterword by James Baker III) Our Supreme Court, 2006; author: (foreword by Senator Edward Kennedy) Franklin Delano Roosevelt for Kids, 2007; author: A History of Westbury, Long Island, 2007, Forgotten Tales of Long Island, 2008; author: (foreword by Nassau County Executive Thomas Suozzi) 101 Glimpses of Long Island's North Shore, 2008; author: German New York City, 2008, Keys to American History, 2009; author: (foreword by Edward Cardinal Egan) Catholic New York City, 2009; author: (foreword by Suffolk County Executive Steve Levy) 101 Glimpses of the South Fork, 2009; editor: Handbook of Amherst, 2007; contbr. (ency.) Americans at War, 2004, contbr. American Countercultures, 2008, The Encyclopedia of North American Colonial Conflicts to 1775, 2008. Mem.: Author's Guild. Democrat. Episcopalian. Avocations: book collecting, antiques, genealogy, tennis. Personal E-mail: panchyk@yahoo.com.

PANCZENKO, RUSSELL, museum director; b. Frille, Fed. Republic Germany, Mar. 23, 1947; came to U.S., 1950; s. Stanislaw Panczenko and Jaroslawa (Lysaniuk) Horiatshun; m. Paula McCarthy, Mar. 14,

1980. BA, Fairfield U., Conn., 1969; Dr. Lettere, Università degli Studi di Firenze, Florence, Italy, 1979. Tchr. Latin Notre Dame High Sch., Bridgeport, Conn., 1969-71; asst. dir. Williams Coll. Mus. Art, Williamstown, Mass., 1980-84; dir. Chazen Mus. Art (formerly Elvehjem Mus. Art), Madison, Wis., 1984—. Bd. dirs. Upper Midwest Conservation Assn., Mpls., 1986—, Wis. Citizens for Arts Inc., Madison, 1986—. Fellow NEH, 1984. Mem. Assn. Art Mus. Dirs., Coll. Art Assn., Am. Assn. Mus., Wis. Fedn. Mus., Midwest Mus. Assn. Lodges: Rotary. Home: 160 N Prospect Ave Madison WI 53705-4073 Office: Chazen Mus Art 800 University Ave Madison WI 53706-1414 Office Phone: 608-263-2842. E-mail: rpanczenko@chazen.wisc.edu.

PANDE, PRAKASH NARAIN, cardiologist, educator, consultant; b. Basti, UP, India, Jan. 1, 1942; came to U.S., 1971; s. Bhawnath and Chandra (Misra) P.; m. Lora Joann Kargina, June 19, 1974; children: Jennifer, Robby. BSc, Lucknow U., India, 1958, MBBS, 1964, MD in Internal Medicine, 1968. Diplomate Am. Bd. Internal Medicine, Am. Bd. Cardiovascular Diseases. Rotating house officer Associated Hosps. Med. Coll. (India) Kanpur, 1964-66, resident med. officer, 1966-67; sr. house officer Bury and Rosendale Hosp., Eng., 1969-71; resident in medicine Rochester (N.Y.) Gen. Hosp., 1971-73; trainee in cardiology U. Rochester, 1973-75; cons. cardiology, attending physician Rochester (N.Y.) Gen. Hosp., 1975-98, dir. cardiac catheterization labs., 1982-90, head cardiology unit, 1990-97; from clin. asst. prof. medicine to clin. prof. U. Rochester, 1980-97, adj. prof., 1998—99; prof. clin. medicine, cardiology Ind. U. Sch. Medicine, Indpls., 1998—. Cardiologist Krannert Inst. Cardiology, Indpls.; hon. chmn. Physicians' Adv. Bd. Nat. Rep. Congl. com., 2003-04; dir. Johnson Meml. Homecare, 1998-2003, chair credentials com., 2001-2004; dir., continuing med. edn. for physicians, Johnson Meml. Hosp., 1999-2004; chmn. dept. medicine, 2003-2004, dir. cardiology and cardiac rehab., 2003-06. Editor Clarian Cardiology newsletter, 1998-2003. Fellow Sr. rsch. fellow, Coun. Scientific and Indsl. Rsch., 1968. Fellow ACP, Am. Heart Assn. (coun. clin. cardiology 1990), Am. Coll. Cardiology (Ind. councilor 1994, 1996), Soc. Cardiac Angiography and Interventions (sr.), Coun. Geriatric Cardiology. Office: Krannert Inst Cardiology 1800 Capitol Indianapolis IN 46202-4832 Business E-Mail: ppande@iupui.edu.

PANDEY, DEEPAK K., physicist; s. Narsingh and Kalawati Pandey. PhD, Purdue U., West Lafayette, Ind., 2009. Project asst. Indian Inst. Sci., Bangalore, India, 2002—03; tchg. asst. Purdue U., 2003—. Contbr. scientific papers. Organizer Village Cricket Club, West Lafayette, 2003—, Asha for Edn., Purdue Grad. Student Govt., Indian Grad. Student Assn., Purdue, Purdue Fin. Club. Mem.: Am. Phys. Soc., Am. Assn. Physics Tchrs. (Outstanding Tchg. award 2007).

PANDEY, GIRDHAR KUMAR, molecular biologist; b. Almora, Utter Paradesh, India, Feb. 15, 1972; arrived in US, 2000; s. Kishan Chand and Kamala Devi Pandey; m. Amita Tyagi, Dec. 3, 1997; children: Daksh, Aryan. BSc in Biochemistry, Jawaharlal Nehru U., New Delhi, 1992; MSc in Biotech., U. Delhi South Campus, 1994; PhD in Life Scis., Plant Molecular Biology and Biotech., Jawaharlal Nehru U., 1999. Postdoctoral fellow U. Calif., Berkeley, 2000—06; lead scientist Delmonte Fresh Produce Co., Richmond, Calif., 2006—08; assoc. prof. plant molecular biology and genetic engring. dept. U. Delhi, New Delhi, 2008—. Contbr. articles to profl. jours. Moderator, vol. Sch. and Edn. Bd., El Cerrito, Calif., 2004—06. Grantee, NSF, 2003; fellow, Dept. Bio-Tech., India, 1992, Coun. Sci. and Indsl. Rsch., India, 1994, USDA, 1998, Indo-Srilankan Rsch. Com., 1999. Mem.: NY Acad. Sci., Calif. Acad. Sci., Am. Soc. Plant Biologist. Independent. Hindu. Achievements include two patents for developing strees tolerant plants. Avocations: reading, writing, gardening, cricket, golf. Home: 6426 Waldo Ave Apt 5 El Cerrito CA 94530 Office: Dept Plant Molecular Biology Univ Delhi South Campus New Delhi 110021 India Personal E-mail: giridhar98@gmail.com.

PANDEY, RAMESH CHANDRA, chemist, chemicals executive; b. Naugaon, Uttarakhand, India, Nov. 5, 1938; arrived in US, 1967; s. Gauri Dutt and Jivanti Pandey. BSc, U. Allahabad, India, 1958; MSc, U. Gorakhpur, India, 1960; PhD, U. Poona, India, 1965. Jr. rsch. fellow CSIR Nat. Chem. Lab., Poona, 1960-64, rsch. officer, 1965-67, scientist organic divsn., 1970-72; rsch. assoc. dept. chemistry U. Ill., Urbana, 1967-70, vis. scientist, 1972-77; sr. scientist fermentation program Nat. Cancer Inst. Frederick (Md.) Cancer Rsch. Facility, 1977-82, head chem. sect., 1982-83; sr. scientist Abbott Labs., North Chicago, Ill., 1983-84; pres. Xechem, Inc., Melrose Pk., Ill., 1984-90, pres., CEO, dir. tech. devel. New Brunswick, NJ, 1990—2003; chmn., CEO, pres. Xechem Internat. Inc., 1994—2004, chmn., CEO, 2004—07; chmn., CEO, pres. Xetapharm Inc., 1996—2007; chmn. Pres. G.D. Pandey Ayurvedic U., 2001—. Cons. Washington U. Sch. Medicine, St. Louis, 1976-85, LyphoMed, Inc., Melrose Park, 1984-85; vis. prof. Waksman Inst. Rutgers U., Piscataway, NJ, 1984-86; mem. life sci. adv. bd. NJTC, 1999—; mem. statewide adv. com. bd. mgrs. NJ Agrl. Exptl. Sta., Rutgers State U. NJ in Biotechnology, 2002—; founder G.D. Padney Ayurvedic U., New Brunswick, NJ. Mem. editl. bd. Internat. Jour. Antibiotics, 1986—07; patentee graft thin layer chromatography; several US and internat. patents for the isolation and purification of antibiotics and anticancer agents. Mem. Middlesex County (NJ) Work Force Investment Bd., 1999-2005; mem. adv. com. for sci. transfer and sci. tech. program Middlesex County Coll., Edison, NJ, 1999-2001. Recipient P. Ray Meml. award, Indian Chem. Soc., 2006, Lifetime Achievement award, Pres. HE Rt. Sir. A. Jugnauth, Mauritius, 2009; named Readers Choice CEO of Yr., CBS Marketwatch.com, 2006. Fellow Am. Inst. Chemists, Royal Soc. Tropical Medicine & Hygine; mem. Am. Chem. Soc., Am. Soc. Microbiology, Am. Soc. Mass Spectrometry, Am. Assn. Cancer Rsch., Am. Soc. Hosp. Pharmacists, Am. Soc. Pharmacognosy, Soc. Indsl. Microbiology, NY Acad. Scis., Indian Sci. Congress Assn., Am. Acad. Ayurvedic Medicine (founder, exec. trustee), Rotary Club (Paul Harris fellow 1996—, pres. New Brunswick club 1999-2000, Named Readers Choice CEO of Yr. CBSMarketwatch.com, 2006). Office: PO Box 5965 New Brunswick NJ 08903-5965 Office Phone: 732-317-8124. Business E-Mail: ramesh@gdpau.com.

PANDIAN, SHANTHA G., psychiatrist; b. Bklyn., Dec. 19, 1972; d. Dorairaj Sivajothi and Sugirtha Rose Pandian; m. Juan Francisco Rodriguez, Apr. 24, 1998; children: Christopher Rodriguez, Ethan Rodriguez. MBBS, Kasturba Med. Coll., India, 1995. Cert. MD Tenn., Fla., diplomate psychiatry Am. Bd. Psychiatry Neurology. Psychiatry residency E. Tenn. State U., Johnson City, 1997—2001; assoc. chief mental health clin., outpatient psychiatrist James H. Quillen Vets. Admntrn. Med. Ctr., Mt. Home, Tenn., 2001—; asst. prof. psychiatry E. Tenn. State U., 2001—. Chair psychiatry and neurology section Southern Med. Assn., Ala., 2003—. Mem.: Southern Med. Assn. (chair 2003—). Meth. Avocations: reading, exercise, cooking. Office: James H Quillen Vets Adminstrn Med Clinic PO Box 4000 Johnson City TN 37604 Office Phone: 423-926-1171.

PANDIT, SUDHAKAR MADHAVRAO, engineering educator; arrived in U.S., 1968; s. Madhavrao Dhondopant and Ramabai P.; m. Maneesha Sudhakar Mangala Nulkar, May 12, 1966; children: Milind, Devavrat. MS in Indsl. Engring., Pa. State U., 1970; MS in Statistics, U. Wis., 1972, PhD in Mech. Engring., 1973. Trainee engr. Kirloskar Oil Engines Ltd., Pune, India, 1961-62; engr. East Asiatic Co., Bombay, India, 1962; asst. engr. Heavy Engring. Corp., Ranchi, India, 1962-68; teaching asst. Pa. State U., State College, 1968-70; rsch. asst. U. Wis., Madison, 1970-73, lectr., 1973-76; prof. Mich. Technol. U., Houghton, 1976—. Faculty rep. Nat. Tech. U., Mpls., 1991—; ASA/NSF/NIST sr. rsch. fellow, 1993-94. Author: Time Series and System Analysis with Applications, 1983, Modal and Spectrum Analysis: Data Dependent Systems in State Space, 1991; contbr. articles to profl. jours. Recipient faculty rsch. award Mich. Technol. U., 1994; honored by Mich. Assn. Governing Bds. State Univs., 1995. Fellow: ASME, Soc. Mfg. Engrs. Achievements include developed a new philosophy and methodology of system analysis, prediction and control called data dependent systems. Home: 22218 Ridge Rd Houghton MI 49931-9801 Office: Mich Technol U ME-EM Dept 1400 Townsend Dr Houghton MI 49931-1200 Office Phone: 906-487-2153. Business E-Mail: pand@mtu.edu.

PANDIT, VIKRAM SHANKAR, diversified financial services company executive; b. Bombay, Jan. 14, 1957; s. Shankur B. and Shailaja Pandit; m. Swati V. Pandit; children: Maya, Rahul. BS in Electric Engring., Columbia U., 1976, MS in Electric Engring., 1977; MBA, Columbia Bus. Sch., 1980, PhD in Finance, 1986. Prof. fin. Ind. U., Bloomington, 1980—83; joined Morgan Stanley, 1983, mng. dir., head US equity syndicate, 1990—94, head worldwide instl. equities divsn., 1994—96, mng. dir., head instl. equities divsn., 1997—2000, pres., CEO instl. securities & investment banking divsn., 2000—05; co-founder, CEO Old Lane Capital Mgmt. LLC, 2005—07; chmn., CEO Citi Alternative Investments (CAI), 2007; chmn. CEO Citi Instl. Clients Group, 2007; CEO Citigroup Inc., 2007—. Bd. dirs. NASDAQ, 2000—03, Citigroup Inc., 2007—. Bd. trustees Columbia U., 2003—, Trinity Sch.; bd. overseers Columbia Bus. Sch.; founder Maina Found. for Raising Breast Cancer Awareness. Named one of The Top 25 Market Movers, US News & World Report, 2009. Hindu. Office: Citigroup Inc 399 Park Ave New York NY 10043 E-mail: vikram.pandit@citi.com.*

PANDOLFI, FRANCES, health facility administrator; b. NYC, Sept. 7, 1944; d. Frank Pandolfi and Rose McGinn; m. Edmund Lewiska Menelik Bobbitt, May 19, 1973. BA, Vassar Coll., 1965; MPA, NYU, 1990. Health planner N.Y.C. Dept. City Planning, 1965-74; planner West Midlands County Coun., Birmingham, Eng., 1974-81, dir. recreation and tourism planning, 1981-85, dir. strategic planning, 1985-86; dep. dir. housing coord. N.Y.C. Mayor's Office, 1987-89; dir. nurses housing N.Y.C. Health & Hosps. Corp., 1989-92, exec. asst. to v.p., 1992-94, asst. v.p., 1994-97; chief of staff N.Y.C. Health and Hosps. Corp., 1998-2001, chief info. officer, 2001—. Dir. Women in Housing and Fin., N.Y.C., 1990-96. Mem.: Am. Soc. Pub. Adminstrn. Office: NYC Health & Hosps Corp 125 Worth St New York NY 10013-4006 Office Phone: 212-788-3437. Business E-Mail: pandolff@nychhc.org.

PANDO ZAYAS, LEOPOLDO A., physicist; b. Havana, Cuba; children: Mariaida X. Pando Girard, Aldo L. Pando Girard. PhD in Physics and Math., Moscow State U., 1998. Assoc. prof. U. Mich., Ann Arbor. Mem. Inst. Advanced Study, Princeton, NJ, 2002—03. Contbr. articles to profl. jours. Office Phone: 734-764-5236. Business E-Mail: lpandoz@umich.edu.

PANDYA, JYOTSNA, biotechnologist; d. Ram Vijoy and Kanchan Singh; m. Utpal Pandya, Feb. 4, 2001. PhD, Post Grad. Inst. Med. Edn. & Rsch., Chandigarh, 2000; MS in Biotech., Devi Ahilya Vishwavidyalaya, Indore, India, 1993. Postdoc. fellow U. Tex. Med. Br., Galveston, Tex., 2000—08, faculty, 2009—. Fellowship, Dept. Biotechnology, India, 1991—93, Jr. & Sr. Rsch. fellowships, U. Grants Commn., India, 1995—2000, grant, NIH, 2005—07.

PANDYA, UTPAL, microbiologist; s. Kumudrai Purshottam and Leela Pandya; m. Jyotsna Singh, Feb. 4, 2001; 1 child, Aarini. BSc, Lucknow Christian Coll., Lucknow U., India, 1985; MSc in Chemistry, Lucknow U., 1987; PhD, Kanpur U., India, 1993. Cert. biol. & chem. safety program UTMB, Galveston, Tex., 2009, UTMB, Galveston, Tex., 2005, basic radiation safety UTMB, Galveston, Tex., 1998. Jr. rsch. fellow Ctrl. Drug Rsch. Inst., Lucknow, Uttar Pradesh, 1988—90, sr. rsch. fellow, 1990—93, rsch. assoc., 1993—97; postdoct. fellow U. Tex. Med. Br., Galveston, Tex., 1997—2001, post doctoral fellow, Dept. Microbiology & Immunology, 2001—08, rsch. scientist, Dept. Microbiology & Immunology, 2008—. Contbr. scientific papers to profl. jours. (NASA Group Achievement award, 2008). Rsch. Assoc. fellowship, CSIR, New Delhi, 1994—97. Mem.: AAAS, Am. Soc. Mass Spectrometry, Internat. Soc. Infectious Diseases, Indian Soc. Parasitology, Am. Soc. Microbiology. Avocations: cricket, gardening, travel. Home: 321Magnolia Estates Dr League City TX 77573 Home Fax: 1-866-886-8814. Personal E-mail: utpalpandya@yahoo.com.

PANEK, WILLIAM DOMINICK, systems engineer executive; b. Perth Amboy, NJ, Jan. 14, 1970; s. Richard William Panek and Marjaree Marie Mayne; m. Crystal Marie Pellerin, Feb. 11, 1995; children: Paige children: Alexandria. Assoc. degree, Computer Learning Ctr., 1994. MCSE Microsoft, 1997, Microsoft, 2001, cert. trainer Microsoft, 1997, database adminstr. Microsoft, 2000, network assoc. Cisco Corp., 2000. Microsoft cert. instr. The Associates, Shrewsbury, Mass., 1997—98; pres. Stellacon Corp, Farmington, NH, 1998—. Cons. MicroScript, Danvers, Mass., 1994—2000. Firefighter/EMT; spl. advisor to the chmn. Bus. Adv. Coun., Washington, 2002—03. E4 USAF, 1988—92, Spain. Recipient NH Businessman Yr., Bus. Adv. Coun., 2003. Mem.: AOPA (corr.), NRA (assoc.). R-Conservative. Roman Catholic. Avocations: flying, hunting, scuba diving. Home and Office: Stellacon Corp 18 Polliwog Ln Farmington NH 03835

PANERIO, ROBERT MAJOR, SR., music educator, composer; b. Roslyn, Wash., June 28, 1929; s. Major Annible and Margaret Beatrice (Hunter) Panerio; m. Charlotte Ruth Klein, June 10, 1950; children: Deborah Jo, Robert Major Jr. BA in Edn., Ctrl. Wash. U., 1953, BA, 1953, MusM in Edn., 1958; postgrad., Eastman Sch. Music, 1963. Supr. instrumental music Moses Lake (Wash.) Pub. Sch., 1953—62; head arts and humanities Big Bend Coll., Moses Lake, 1962—63; prof. music Ctrl. Wash. U., Ellensburg, 1963—91. Composer: Marauders, Nocturne, Ensenada, Concert March, Passacaglia, Pastorale, Two Contemporary Songs for Children, The Beepers' March, Theme for Band, Concert Suite for Bank, Brassology, Quartal Quartet, Dark Blue, Beguine for Orchestra, Softly. Recipient Am. Bandmasters Composition award, 1975, Disting. Alumni award, Coll. Arts & Humanities Ctrl. Wash. U., 1953, 2009; named Disting. Univ. Prof., Ctrl. Wash. U., 1982; named to Wash. Music Educators Hall of Fame, 1998. Mem.: Am. Soc. Composers, Authors and Publishers, Music Educators Nat. Conf. (adj. clinician). Home: 8204 51st Street Ct W University Place WA 98467-1904

PANES, JACK SAMUEL, publishing executive; b. NYC, Apr. 6, 1925; s. Max S. and Sophie (Levine) P.; m. Pearl Shaine, Dec. 25, 1949; children— Stephanie Jill, Michael Jonathan. BA, Bklyn. Coll., 1947; MS in Journalism, Northwestern U., 1949. Editor, pub. The Howe Service, Inc., NYC, 1949-54; founder, pub. Publs. for Industry, NYC, 1955—, Panes Publs., Inc., NYC, 1959—; owner Drug Products Display Service Advt. Co., NYC, 1955—, Supplies for Industry Co., NYC, 1956—; pres. Senap Devel. Corp., Great Neck, N.Y., 1972—. Pres. Russell Woods Civic Assn., Great Neck. Served with inf. AUS, 1942-45, ETO. Decorated Silver Star medal, Bronze Star medal. Mem. 94th Infantry Divsn. Assn. (pres.), Deadline Club, Sigma Delta Chi. Home: 21 Russell Woods Rd Great Neck NY 11021-4644 Office: Panes Publications Inc Great Neck NY 11021 Home Phone: 516-487-0991.

PANETTA, JOSEPH DANIEL, biotechnologist, director; b. Syracuse, NY, Mar. 1, 1954; s. Salvatore and Josephine Mary (Sbardella) P.; m. Karin Ann Hoffman, Oct. 21, 1978; children: Lauren Marie, Christopher Daniel. BS, LeMoyne Coll., 1976; MPH, U. Pitts., 1979. Environ. protection specialist EPA, Washington, 1979-82, sr. policy analyst, 1982-84; project leader Schering Corp./NorAm Chem Co., Wilmington, Del., 1984-85; mgr. regulatory affairs agrchems. divsn. Pennwalt Corp., Phila., 1985-88; mgr. corp. regulatory affairs Mycogen Corp., San Diego, 1988-90, dir. corp. regulatory affairs and quality assurance, 1990-92, dir. corp. regulatory, environ. affairs San Diego, 1992-97, v.p. govt. and pub. affair, 1998-99; pres., CEO BIOCOM, San Diego, 1999—. Bd. dirs. Gene Therapy Sys., San Diego (Calif.) Econ. Devel. Corp., eStudy Site; chmn. agr. and environment subcom. Internat. Bioindustry Forum; guest lectr. biotech. U. Calif., San Diego, and Calif. Western Law Sch.; advisor bd. on agr. NAS; mem. San Diego Pub. Utilities Adv. Commn., 2002—06; adv. Com. Calif. Food Biotech., 2002-2004, U. Calif. Sch. Pharm. Sci., San Diego, Calif., 2003—; mem. adv. coun. Keck Grad. Inst., 2003—07; vice chmn. Coun. State Biotech Assocs., 2002—04, chmn. Coun. State Biotechnology Assn., 2004-06, Calif. Biotechnology Found., 2006-. Columnist San Diego Daily Transcript, 1999—2003; contbr. articles to profl. jours. Mem. Rep. State Com. Del., 1987; bd. dirs., chmn San Diego Work Force Partnership, 2008; mem. exec. com. Calif. Cmty. Colls. Econ. Devel. Network; mem. adv. bd. UCSD-Connect; bd. dirs. San Diego C. of C.; commissioner San Diego City Pub. Utilities commn., 2002—06. Mem. Am. Crop Protection Assn. (chmn. com. biotech.), Nat. Agrl. Chems. Assn. (mem. registrations com. 1986-89), Biotech. Industy Orgn. (mem. food and agr. steering com., chmn. bipesticides com., internat. affairs com.), Calif. Indsl. Biotech. Assn. (mem. agrl. affairs com.), Am. Chem. Soc. (mem. agrl. div.), Am. Seed Trade Assn. (chmn. steering com. biotech.), Gov.'s Biotech. Coun. (Calif.), San Diego C. of C. (mem. pub. policy com.), San Diego Workforce Partnership (mem. youth coun.), CA Comn. Econ. Devl.(biotech. adv. com, 2008-) Roman Catholic. Avocations: yachting, skiing, classical piano. Home: 5459 Shannon Ridge Ln San Diego CA 92130-4808 Office: BIOCOM San Diego 4501 Executive Dr San Diego CA 92121-3025 Home Phone: 858-481-5336. E-mail: jpanetta@biocom.org.

PANETTA, LEON EDWARD, CIA Director, United States Representative from California; b. Monterey, Calif., June 28, 1938; s. Carmelo and Carmelina Panetta; m. Sylvia Marie Varni, July 14, 1962; children: Christopher, Carmelo, James. BA magna cum laude, U. Santa Clara, Calif., 1960, LL.B., JD, 1963. Bar: Calif. bar 1965, US Supreme Ct. 1965, US Dist. Ct. (no. dist.) Calif. 1965, US Ct. Appeals 1965. Legis. asst. to Senator Thomas Kuchel US Senate, Washington, 1966-69; dir. Office Civil Rights US Dept. Health Edn. & Welfare, Washington, 1969-70; exec. asst. to mayor NYC, 1970-71; ptnr. Panetta, Thompson & Panetta, Monterey, 1971-76; mem. US Congress from 17th Calif. dist., 1976—93, mem. adminstrn. com., 1976—84, chmn. budget com., 1989—92, chmn. select com. hunger; dir. Office Mgmt. & Budget Exec. Office of the Pres., Washington, 1993-94; chief of staff to Pres. The White House, Washington, 1994-97; founder, co-dir. Leon & Sylvia Panetta Inst. Pub. Policy, Calif. State U., Monterey Bay, Seaside, Calif., 1998—2009; dir. CIA, 2009—. Mem. Iraq Study Group, 2006. Co-author: Bring Us Together, 1971. Counsel NAACP, 1971-76; mem. bd. trustees U. Santa Clara Law Sch., Nat. Marine Sanctuary Found., 2005-, Monterey Bay Aquarium; founder Monterey Coll. Law; mem. Monterey County Dem. Cen. Com., 1972-74; v.p. Carmel Valley Little League, 1974-75; spl. advisor to chancellor, Calif. State U.; presdl. prof. pub. policy Santa Clara U., chmn. com. rev. bd. dirs., co-chair corp. governance and listing stds. com. bd. dirs., Calif. Forward Leadership Coun., Fleishman-Hillard's Internat. Adv. Bd.; mem. nat. rev. bd. US Conf. Cath. Bishops; mem. U. Calif. Santa Cruz Found., 2005-; chmn. nat. bd. advisors Ctr. Nat. Policy, 2005-, Pew Ocean Commn., DCO-chair Joint Ocean Commn. Initiative; former mem. Task Force on Immigration and America's Future, 2005-; bd. dirs. Blue Shield Calif., 2005-, Public Policy Inst., Calif., former IDT, 2005-, Zenith, 2005-, Connetics, 2005-, Bread for the World, 2005, Close Up, 2005-, co-chmn. Com. Responsible Fed. Budget; mem. external adv. bd. BP America First lt. US Army, 1964—66. Recipient Army Commendation medal, 1966, Lincoln award NEA, 1970, A. Philip Randolph award, 1971, Disting. Svc. award NAACP, 1972, Bread for World award, 1978, 80, 82, 91, Nat. Hospice Orgn. award, 1984, Golden Plow award Am. Farm Bur. Fedn., 1988, 91, Pres.'s award Am. Coun. on Tchr. of Fgn. Langs., 1991, Coastal and Ocean Mgmt. award Coastal Zone Found., 1991, Food Rsch. and Action Ctr. award, 1991, Disting. Pub. Svc. medal Ctr. Study Presidency, 1995, Peter Burnett award disting pub. svc., 1993, Spl. Achievement award Nat. Italian Am. Found., 1997, John H. Chafee Coastal Stewardship award, 2001, Spl. Achievement award Santa Clara U. Sch. Law, 2002, Julius A. Stratton award coastal leadership, 2003, Coastal Stewarship award Aquarium of the Pacific, 2006, Lifetime Achievement award Nat. Marine Sanctuary Found., 2006, Paul Peck Presdl. award Smithsonian Instn. Nat. Portrait Gallery, 2006, City Yr. Lifetime of Svc. award, 2007; named Lawyer of Yr., Law Sch. U. Santa Clara, 1970. Mem.: Calif. Bar Assn. Roman Catholic. Office: CIA Office of the Director Washington DC 20515*

PANETTA, MICHAEL, Shadow Representative to US Congress from DC; b. July 14, 1971; m. Cady Panetta; 1 child. BA, Am. U., 1993, MA in Polit. Sci., 1994. Dep. task leader internet devel. Advanced Tech. Sys., 1998—2000; cons. Issue Dynamics Inc., 2000—03; asst. v.p. emerging media and pub. affairs Grassroots Enterprise, Washington, 2003—. DC shadow rep. to US Congress, 2007—. Exec. dir., treas. X-PAC. Office: 1101 17th St NW, Ste 1350 Washington DC 20036 also: John A Wilson Bldg 1350 Pennsylvania Ave, NW Washington DC 20004 Office Phone: 202-727-7891, 202-783-5910.*

PANETTIERE, HAYDEN, actress; b. Palisades, NY, Aug. 21, 1989; d. Skip and Lesley Panettiere. Spokesperson SaveTheWhalesAgain.org. Actor: (TV series) One Life to Live, 1994—97, Guiding Light, 1996—2000, Ally McBeal, 2002, Malcolm in the Middle, 2003—05, Heroes, 2006— (Choice TV Actress: Drama, Teen Choice Awards, 2007, Choice TV Actress: Action Adventure, Teen Choice Awards, 2008, 2009); (TV miniseries) A Will of Their Own, 1998; (TV films) How Do You Spell God?, 1996, Too Rich: The Secret Life of Doris Duke, 1999, If You Believe, 1999, Chestnut Hill, 2001, Normal, 2003, Tiger Cruise, 2004, Lies My Mother Told Me, 2005; (films) The Object of My Affection, 1998, (voice only) A Bug's LIfe, 1998, Message in a Bottle, 1999, (voice only) Dinosaur, 2000, Remember the Titans, 2000, The Affair of the Necklace, 2001, Joe Somebody, 2001, Raising Helen, 2004, The Dust Factory, 2004, Racing Stripes, 2005, Ice Princess, 2005, Mr. Gibb, 2006, The Architect, 2006, Bring It On: All or Nothing, 2006,

Shanghai Kiss, 2007, Fireflies in the Garden, 2008, I Love You, Beth Cooper, 2009, The Cove, 2009, (TV appearances) Aliens in the Family, 1996, Touched by an Angel, 1999, Fillmore!, 2004, Law & Order: Special Victims Unit, 2001, 2005, Commander in Chief, 2006, Skater Boys, 2006, Robot Chicken, 2007. Recipient Gretchen Wyler award, Humane Society of the US, 2008. Office: NBC-TV 30 Rockefeller Plz New York NY 10112*

PANG, JING, engineering educator; Asst. prof. Calif. State U., Sacramento, 2003—. Asst. prof. Calif. State U., Sacramento, Sacramento, 2003—. Contbr. articles to profl. jours. (Best Paper award, 2008). Office: Calif State Univ 6000 J St Sacramento CA 95819

PANG, LAP-YIN, molecular biologist; PhD, Chinese U. Hong Kong. Sr. rsch. fellow NIH, Bethesda, Md., 2005—08, biologist, 2008—. Achievements include patents for malarial vaccine formulation. Office: Nat Insts Health 49 Convent Dr Rm 2C08 MSC 4429 Bethesda MD 20892-4429

PANG, WEI CHIANG, civil engineer, educator; married. BSc in Civil Engring., Mich. Technol. U., Houghton, MSc, PhD, 2005. Postdoc. rschr. Tex. A&M U., Coll. Sta., 2005—08, rsch. scientist, 2005—08; asst. prof. civil engring. Clemson U., SC, 2008—. Mem.: ASCE. Office: Clemson Univ Dept Civil Engring 312 Lowry Hall Clemson SC 29634-0911 Business E-Mail: wpang@clemson.edu.

PANGLE, THOMAS LEE, political scientist; b. Gouverneur, NY, Nov. 29, 1944; AB with distinction, Cornell U., Ithaca, NY, 1966; PhD in Polit. Sci., U. Chgo., 1972. Lectr., asst. to assoc. prof. Yale U., New Haven, 1971—79; fellow, Victoria Coll. U. Toronto, Canada, 1979—84, apptd. to grad. sch. with tenure, 1979, assoc. prof. polit. sci., 1979—83, prof. polit. sci., 1983—2001, fellow, St. Michael's Coll., 1985—2004, univ. prof. in polit. sci., 2001—04; Joe R. Long chair in democratic studies, dept. govt. U. Tex. at Austin, 2004—. Mem. exec. coun. Am. Polit. Sci. Assn. Author: Montesquieu's Philosophy of Liberalism, 1973, The Spirit of Modern Republicanism: The Moral Vision of the American Founders and the Philosophy of Locke, 1988, The Ennobling of Democracy: The Challenge of the Postmodern Age, 1992, (with Lorraine Pangle) The Learning of Liberty: The Educational Ideas of the American Founders, 1993, (with Peter Ahrensdorf) Justice Among Nations: On the Moral Basis of Power and Peace, 1999, Political Philosophy and the God of Abraham, 2003, Leo Strauss: An Introduction, 2006; editor: The Rebirth of Classical Political Rationalism: An Introduction to the Thought of Leo Strauss, 1989, The Roots of Political Philosophy: Ten Forgotten Socratic Dialogues, 1987; polit. theory editor The Ency. of Democracy, 4 vols., 1995; gen. editor The Agora Editions; sr. adv. editor Books in Canada: The Canadian Review of Books, 1995-98; mem. editl. bd. Polit. Rsch. Quar. and Polis, Jour. the Soc. the Study of Greek Polit. Thought; contbr. numerous articles to various jours. Recipient Robert Foster Cherry award, 1992; NEH fellow, 1975-76, 1985-86, 1993, 2001-02; Guggenheim fellow, 1981-82; Connaught fellow, 1994; Siemens fellow, 1997-98; Killam fellow, 2002-04. Fellow: Royal Soc. Can.; mem.: Phi Beta Kappa. Office: Univ Tex at Austin Dept Govt 1 University Sta A1800 Austin TX 78712-0119 Office Phone: 512-232-1529. Office Fax: 512-471-1061. Business E-Mail: tpangle@austin.utexas.edu.

PANGRACE, RUTH A., history professor; b. Lakewood, Ohio, Aug. 10, 1951; d. Paul and Martha Bomba; m. John Bomba, Aug. 4, 1973; children: Martin, Meredith, Nathan. BA, Cleve. State, MEd, 1990. Cert. in ruth pangrace Ohio Dept. Edn. Gifted and talented tchr. Lakewood City Schs., Ohio, 2001—. Adj. instr. Cleve. State U., 1998—2006. Actor(historical reenactor): (dramatic portrayals of woman) Women in History. Democrat. Lutheran. Avocations: sailing, art. Home: 20035 Frazier Rocky River OH 44116 Office: Lakewood City Schs 16601 Madison Ave Lakewood OH 44107

PANIAGUA, DAVID, physician; b. Alajuela, Costa Rica, Sept. 13, 1963; s. Ismael and Nidia (Lopez) P.; m. Elizabeth Gonzalez, Nov. 22, 1986; children: David, Liza Mariel. MD summa cum laude, U. Costa Rica, 1986. Rural physician, Costa Rica, 1987-91; attending in cardiology Costa Rica CCSS, 1991; fellow in cardiology Mt. Sinai Med. Ctr., Miami, Fla., 1996—. Contbr. articles to profl. jours. Mem. ACP, Am. Coll. Cardiology, Am. Coll. Chest Physicians. Roman Catholic. Office: 6620 Main St, Ste 1225 Houston TX 77030 E-mail: davidpaniag@pol.net.

PANICCIA, PATRICIA LYNN, journalist, writer, lawyer, educator; b. Glendale, Calif., Sept. 19, 1952; d. Valentino and Mary (Napoleon) P.; m. Jeffrey McDowell Mailes, Oct. 5, 1985; children: Alana Christine, Malia Noel. BA in Comm., U. Hawaii, 1977; JD, Pepperdine U., 1981. Bar: Hawaii 1981, Calif. 1982, U.S. Dist. Ct. Hawaii 1981. Extern law clk. hon. Samuel P. King U.S. Dist. Ct., Honolulu, 1980; reporter, anchor woman Sta. KEYT-TV, Santa Barbara, Calif., 1983-84; reporter Sta. KCOP-TV, LA, 1984-88; reporter CNN, LA, 1989-93. Adj. prof. comm. law Pepperdine Sch. Law, 1987, gender & the law, 1994—, adj. prof.; profl. surfer, 1977-81. Author: Worksmarts for Women: The Essential Sex Discrimination Survival Guide, 2000. Recipient Clarion award Women in Comm., Inc., 1988. Mem. ABA (chair of law and media com. young lawyers divsn. 1987-88, nat. conf. com. lawyers and reps. of media 1987-91), Calif. State Bar (mem. com. on fair trial and free press 1983-84, pub. affairs com. 1985-87), Hawaii Bar Assn., Phi Delta Phi (historian 1980-81). Office: PO Box 881 La Canada CA 91012-0881

PANICEK, DAVID, radiologist; b. Johnson City, NY, Oct. 7, 1954; MD, Cornell U., 1980. Cert. diagnostic radiology 1984. Intern Lenox Hill Hosp., NYC, 1980—81; resident NY Hosp. Cornell Med. Ctr., NYC, 1981—84; radiologist U. Hosp., Syracuse, NY, 1984—88; asst. prof. radiology SUNY Health Sci. Ctr., Syracuse, 1984—88, Cornell U. Med. Coll., 1988—93; radiologist Meml. Sloan-Kettering, NYC, 1988—; assoc. prof. radiology Cornell U. Med. Coll., 1993—98, prof. radiology, 1999—; vice chair, Clin. Affairs, Radiology Meml. Sloan-Kettering, NYC. Fellow: Am. Coll. Radiology; mem.: Am. Roentgen Ray Soc., Radiological Soc. N.Am., Internat. Skeletal Soc. Office: Meml Sloan-Kettering Cancer Ctr 1275 York Ave New York NY 10021-6007

PANICHAS, GEORGE ANDREW, language educator, critic, editor; b. Springfield, Mass., May 21, 1930; s. Andrew and Fotini (Dracouli) Panichas. BA, Am. Internat. Coll., Springfield, Mass., 1951, LittD (hon.), 1984; AM, Trinity Coll., Conn., 1952; PhD, Nottingham U., Eng., 1962. Instr., English and comparative lit. U. Md., College Park, 1962-63, asst. prof., 1963-66, assoc. prof., 1966-68, prof., 1968-92. Co-chmn. Conf. Irving Babbitt: Fifty Years Later, 1983; mem. Richard M. Weaver fellowship awards com., 1984—88, Ingersoll Prizes Jury Panel, 1986. Author: Adventure in Consciousness: The Meaning of D. H. Lawrence's Religious Quest, 1964, Epicurus, 1967, The Reverent Discipline: Essays in Literary Criticism and Culture, 1974, The Burden of Vision: Dostoevsky's Spiritual Art, 1977, The Courage of Judgment: Essays in Criticism, Culture and Society, 1982, The Critic as Conservator: Essays in Literature, Society, and Culture, 1992, The Critical Legacy of Irving Babbitt: An Appreciation, 1999, Growing Wings to Overcome Gravity: Criticism as the Pursuit of Virtue, 1999, Joseph Conrad: His Moral Vision, 2005, Restoring the Meaning of Conservatism, 2008; editor (with G. R. Hibbard and A. Rodway): Renaissance and Modern Essays: Presented to Vivian de Sola Pinto in Celebration of His Seventieth Birthday, 1966; editor: Mansions of the Spirit: Essays in Literature and Religion, 1967, Promise of Greatness: The War of 1914-1918, 1968, The Politics of Twentieth-Century Novelists, 1971, The Simone Weil Reader, 1977, Irving Babbitt: Representative Writings, 1981, Modern Age: The First Twenty-Five Years. A Selection, 1988, In Continuity: The Last Essays of Austin Warren, 1996, The Essential Russell Kirk. Selected Essays, 2007; editor: (with C. G. Ryn) Irving Babbitt in Our Time, 1986; editl. advisor Modern Age: A Quar. Rev., 1971—77; assoc. editor: Modern Age: A Quar. Rev., 1978—83; editor, 1984—2007; adv. bd. Continuity: A Jour. of History, 1984—88, Humanitas, 1993—, Culture and Cultivation, 2009—; contbr. articles and revs. to profl. jours. Mem. Acad. Bd. Nat. Humanities Inst., 1985—; trustee Found. Faith in Search of Understanding, 1987. Recipient Henry Regnery award, 2003; grantee, Earhart Found., 1982. Fellow: Royal Soc. Arts (Eng.). Eastern Orthodox. Home and Office: PO Box Ab College Park MD 20741-3025 Office Phone: 301-779-6894. *In a profane age of unrest and breakdown, it is not enough for the critic to be purely and simply critical. He must work to conserve what is timeless, time-tested, time-honored. He must fight for causes he believes in, even if they appear to be lost causes. The critic's burden of responsibility is also his vision of order.*

PANICKAR, PRAVEEN, aeronautical engineer, researcher; s. Rama Govinda and Sulekha Panickar. PhD, Ill. Inst. Tech., Chgo., 2008. Rsch. asst. Ill. Inst. Tech., 2001—08; rsch. scientist Combustion Rsch. and Flow Tech. Inc., Pipersville, Pa., 2008, University City, Miss., 2008—. Contbr. articles to profl. jours. Mem.: AIAA. Office: Craft Tech NCPA Univ Miss 1 Coliseum Dr University MS 38677

PANIELLO, RANDAL C., otolaryngologist, educator; b. Panama City, Fla., July 18, 1958; s. Raymond J. and Katherine B. Paniello; m. Jane G. Vojtech, May 18, 1985; children: Andrew R., Allyson C. BS in Biology with honors, U. Ill., Urbana, 1979, BS in Chemistry, 1979, MS in Immunochemistry, 1980; MD, U. of Ill., Chicago, 1980—84; MBA, Wash. U., St. Louis, Mo., 1999, BS in Aerospace Engring., 2007, attending in Earth & Planetary Scis., 2007—. Cert. in otolaryngology Am. Bd. Otolaryngology, 1991, Amer. Bd. Facial Plastic & Reconstructive Surg., 1992. Assoc. prof. otolaryngology Wash. U. Sch. Medicine, 1990—; chief otolaryngology St. Louis Va. Med. Ctr., 1990—. Avocations: flying, scuba diving, travel.

PANISH, BRIAN JOSEPH, lawyer; b. LA, Apr. 19, 1958; s. Howard Raymond and Mary Patricia (Murphy) P. Student, Calif. State U., 1980; JD cum laude, Southwestern Sch. Law, 1984. Bar: Calif. 1984, U.S. Dist. Ct. (no., ea. and cen. dists.) Tex. 1984. Assoc. Engstrom, Lipscomb & Lack, LA, 1984-86, Greene, Broillet, Taylor & Wheeler and predecessor firm, LA, 1987—93, ptnr., 1993—2005, Panish, Shea & Boyle, LLP, LA, 2005—. Recipient American Jurisprudence Awards in Evidence, Wills and Trusts, Legal Ethics and Sales and Secured Transactions, Fresno State Scholar Athlete Award, 1980, Athletics Directors Award, 1980; named Trial Lawyer of the Yr., Trial Lawyers for Pub. Justice; named one of 100 Most Influential Lawyers, Nat. Law Jour., 2006. Mem. L.A. County Bar Assn., Am. Bar Assn., Assn. Trial Lawyers Am., Calif. Trial Lawyers Assn., L.A. Trial Lawyers Assn., Consumer Attorneys Assn. of Calif. (Bd. Govs.), Internat. Soc. of Barristers, Consumer Attorneys Assn. of L.A., Am. Bd. of Trial Advocates, Western Trial Lawyers Assn., Trial Lawyers for Pub. Justice, Eighth Street Lawyers, Am. Bd. Advocates, Inner Circle Advocates, Santa Monica Leaders Club. Home: 2527 3rd St Santa Monica CA 90405-3604 Office: Panish, Shea & Boyle, LLP 11111 Santa Monica Blvd Suite 700 Los Angeles CA 90025 Office Phone: 310-477-1700. Personal E-mail: panish@psblaw.com. Business E-Mail: panish@psandb.com.

PANISH, MORTON B., retired physical chemist; b. NYC, Apr. 8, 1929; s. Isidore and Fanny (Glasser) P.; m. Evelyn Wally Chaim, Aug. 20, 1951; children: Steven, Paul, Deborah. Student, Bklyn. Coll., 1946-48; BS in Chemistry, Denver U., 1950; MS in Chemistry, Mich. State U., 1951, PhD in Phys. Chemistry, 1954. Chemist Oak Ridge (Tenn.) Nat. Lab., 1954-57; mem. tech. staff RAD div. AVCO Corp., Wilmington, Mass., 1957-61, sect. chief, 1961-64; mem. tech. staff Bell Telephone Labs. (now Bell Labs.), Murray Hill, NJ, 1964-69, dept. head, 1969-86, disting. mem. tech. staff, 1986-92; cons., 1992—2003. Mem. com. on microgravity rsch. NRC, 1991-96, mem. com. on future of space sci. rsch. priorities, 1994-95, space studies bd., 1996-98; mem. com. on human rights NAS, 1996-02. Co-author: Heterostructure Lasers, 1978, Gas Source Molecular Beam Epitaxy, 1993; contbr. numerous articles to profl. jours.; patentee in field. Mem. dean's adv. bd. Coll. Natural Sci., Mich. State U., 1990-95. Recipient Electrochem Soc. Electronics Divsn. award, 1972, Solid state medal, 1979, C&C Found. prize, Japan, 1986, Internat. Crystal Growth award Am. Assn. Crystal Growth, 1990, John Bardeen award The Minerals, Metals and Materials Soc., 1994, The Kyoto prize, 2001. Fellow IEEE (Morris N. Liebmann Meml. award 1991), Am. Phys. Soc.; mem. Nat. Acad. Engring., Nat. Acad. Scis. Avocation: photography. Home and Office: 52 Baldwin Rd Freeport ME 04032 Personal E-mail: mort@att.net.

PANITZ, DANIEL R., inventor, scientist, composer, psychologist, minister; b. Bklyn., May 1, 1945; s. Daniel Panitz and Lilian Victor. BA in Psychology, Rutgers U., 1968; MA in Psychology, New Sch., 1972; PhD Candidate, NYU, 1975; PhD in Pastoral Counselling, Eagle Ministries, 2006. Chief psychologist NY State Narcotic Addiction Control Commn., 1970—79; psychologist NY State Alcoholism, 1980—89; dir. Human Svcs., 1990—2004, Eagle Ministeries, 2005; project dir. Hope Internat. Ministeries, 2004—05; founder Green World Crete Inc. Gen. Mgr.; exec. global mgr. Green World Crete Inc., 2007—. Mem. editl. bd.: Am. Jour. Family Therapy, 1990—; composer (album): Songs Carried on Angel's Wings, 2001, River, 2002; author: Other Side of Sun, 2001. Recipient Eleanor Roosevelt award, Congl. Honor, 2002; named Humanitarian of Yr., Hero 911, 2001, First Response, 911 Katrina Pakistan. Mem.: Internat. Soc. Arts Scis. Avocation: writing. Office: 3840 W Hillsboro Blvd Deerfield Beach FL 33442 Office Phone: 5619298384. Personal E-mail: danielinvestments@hotmail.com.

PANITZ, LAWRENCE, physician; b. Apr. 30, 1928; s. Max and Gussie (Gorenstein) Panitz; m. Adrienne Ruth Luke, June 20, 1965; children: Jennifer, Michael. BA, NYU, 1962; MD, Upstate Med. U., Syracuse, 1966. Diplomate Am. Bd. Family Practice. Intern St. Joseph's Hosp., Syracuse, NY, 1966—67; pvt. practice gen. medicine Elmsford, NY, 1967—90, Hawthorne, NY, 1968—. Affiliated with Docs Physicians Beth Israel Med. Ctr., NYC, Shrub Oak, NY, Hartsdale, NY, Larchmont, NY, Yonkers, NY, Thornwood, NY, Crestwood, NY, New City, West Haverstraw, NY; mem. staff New Rochelle Hosp., NY, St. Agnes Hosp., White Plains, NY, Westchester County Med. Ctr., Valhalla, NY, N.Y. Dobbs Ferry Hosp., Beth Israel Hosp. Med. Ctr., NYC, Sound Shore Med. Ctr., Phelps Meml. Hosp., Sleepy Hollow, NY, dep. dir. dept. family practice, North Tarrytown, NY; dir. Elmsford Med. Ctr.; police surgeon, Tarrytown, North Tarrytown, Sleepy Hollow, Elmsford, Town of Greenburgh; med. dir. Margaret Chapman Sch. Exceptional Child, Hawthorne; med. dir., prin. rschr. Clin. Tech. Assoc., Elmsford, CNS Bioservices, Pleasantville, NY; physician Westchester County Correctional Health Dept., Valhalla; sch. physician, Elmsford; cons., expert witness Vogel & Rosenberg, NYC, Britcher, Leone & Roth, LLC, Glen Rock, NJ; cons. on malpractice litig. for law firms. With US Army, 1946—48, with US Army, 1982—88, lt. col. Med. Corps USAR. Fellow: AMA, Am. Acad. Family Physicians; mem.: Westchester Acad. Medicine, Westchester County Med. Soc., Med. Soc. State NY, Jewish War Vets., Masons, Shriners. Jewish. Home and Office: Riveredge 3 David Ln Yonkers NY 10701-1122 Office: 132 S Central Ave Elmsford NY 10523 Home Phone: 914-968-6033; Office Phone: 914-968-6135. E-mail: lp711md@aol.com.

PANKAU, BARBARA ROPES, lawyer; b. Miami, Apr. 4, 1951; d. Paul Chapman Ropes and Inga Ropes Roberts; m. Stephen Lamarr Pankau, May 1, 1976 (dec. Feb. 2001); children: Jonathan Lamarr, Emmy Ingrid; m. Jonathan L. Alpert, Dec. 4, 2003. Student, Sorbonne, Paris, 1970—71; BA cum laude, Tufts U., 1972; JD cum laude, U. Fla., 1975. Cert.: Fla. Bar (health law), bar: US Dist. Ct. (ctrl. dist.), US Ct. Appeals (11th cir.) 1981, US Ct. Appeals (5th cir.) 1976, US Claims Ct. 1979, US Supreme Ct. 1979. Legal writing instr. U. Fla. Coll. Law, Gainesville, 1975; assoc., litig. practice Trenam, Simmons, Kempker, Scharf, Brakin, Frye & O'Neill, Tampa, Fla., 1975—79; shareholder Carlton, Fields, Warrd, Emmanuel, Smith & Cutler, P.A., Tampa, 1979—89, Stearns Weaver Miller Alhadeff & Shierson, P.A., Tampa, 1989—90; lawyer Law Offices Barbara R. Pankau, P.A., Tampa, 1990—94; ptnr. Honigman, Miller, Schwartz and Cohn, Tampa, 1994—97, Shumaker, Loop & Kendrick, L.L.P., Tampa, 1997—2008; gen. counsel Universal Healthcare, St. Petersburg, Russia, 2008—, Pankau Law Firm P.A., 2008—. Lectr. in field of health law. Contbr. articles to profl. jours.; guest editor: health law issue, Fla. Bar Jour., 1998. Past dir. Hospice of Fla. Suncoast; past adv. bd. Burdines; adv. bd. trustees Humana Women's Hosp. Tampa, 1983—93; chmn. Tufts Alumni Admissions Program, Ctrl. Fla., 1986—92; moderator, adv. bd. trustees Humana Hosp., St. Petersburg, Fla., 1990—91, trustee, 1988—91; vice chmn., bd. counselors U. Tampa, 1982—83; adv. bd. Suncoast AIDS Network, 1990—91; adv. com. Tampa Tribune/Health Care Guide, 1989—91. Recipient numerous svc. awards, various profl. assns., svc. distinction awards, Tampa C. of C., Jr. League of Tampa, Big Bros./Big Sisters, others; named an Outstanding Lawyer of Am., 2003. Mem.: ABA (gov. bd. health law forum 1989—92, mem.health law forum, adminstrv. law and regulatory practice, bus. law), Fla. Bar Assn. (chmn. health law com., mem. exec. coun. health law sect. 1988—2003), Athena Soc., Fla. Bar (cert. com. health law sect. 1994—96, mem. health law, admninstrv. law, and bus. law sects.), Suncoast Healthcare Execs., Am. Health Lawyers Assn., Hillsborough County Bar Assn., Fla. Acad. Healthcare Attys. Office: Shumaker Loop & Kendrick LLP Bank of Am Plz Ste 2800 101 E Kennedy Blvd Tampa FL 33602 Office Phone: 813-227-2321, 813-238-1667. Personal E-mail: bpankau@aol.com, brpankau@hotmail.com.

PANKE, HELMUT, retired automotive executive; b. Storkow, Germany, Aug. 31, 1946; PhD in Physics, U. Munich, 1976. Tchr. U. Munich, 1976—78; with Swiss Inst. Nuclear Rsch., 1976—78, McKinsey & Co., Dusseldorf, Germany, 1978—82; from various positions to head N. American operations BMW AG, Munich, 1982—93, head N. American operations, 1993—96, mem. bd. mgmt. for Human Resources and Info. Technol., 1996—99, mem. bd. mgmt. for fin., 1999—2002, chmn. bd. mgmt., 2002—06. Bd. dirs. UBS AG, Switzerland, Microsoft Corp., 2003—; supr. bd. mem. Bayer AG; adv. bd. Global Strategic Equities Fund, Dubai Internat. Capital LLC. Office: Microsoft Bd Directors 1 Microsoft Way Redmond WA 98052*

PANKEN, PETER MICHAEL, lawyer; b. NYC, Dec. 30, 1936; s. Harold Ira and Sylvia Rita (Haimes) P.; m. Beverly Muriel Goldner, June 19, 1960; children: Aaron, Melinda. BA cum laude, Haverford Coll., 1957; LLB magna cum laude, Harvard U., 1962. Bar: N.Y. 1962, U.S. Dist. Ct. SD and ED N.Y. 1962, U.S. Ct. Appeals (2d cir.) 1969, (3d cir.) 1988, (10th cir.) 1989, (7th cir.) 2003, U.S. Supreme Ct. 1989. Assoc. Paul Weiss Rifkind Wharton Garrison, NYC, 1962-66, Poletti Freiden Prashker Feldman & Gartner, NYC, 1966-67, Parker Chapin Flattau & Klimpl, NYC, 1967-72, ptnr., 1973-99, Epstein Becker & Green PC, NYC, 1999—; chair employment and labor law dept. Parker Chapin Flattau & Klimpl, NYC, 1986-99. Editor: Harvard Law Rev., 1961-62; author: A State-by-State Survey of the Law of Religion in the Workplace, 2001; contbg.: Employment Law Desk Book for Human Resources Professionals; editor-in-chief ALIABA Resource Materials: Employment and Labor Law; mem. bd. editors The Practical Litigator; contbr. articles to profl. jours. Pres., bd. dirs. Fedn. of Handicapped, N.Y.C., 1984-92; bd. dirs. Fedcap Rehab. Svcs., 1993—; pres. metro N.Y. chpt. Soc. for Human Resource Mgmt., 1990-92, gen. counsel, 1993-2003. Mem. ABA (labor and employment sect., com. on NLRB law, contbg. editor The Developing Labor Law), NY State Bar Assn. (labor and employment law sect., continuing legal edn. com.), Am. Law Inst.-ABA (chmn. employment and labor law programs), Am. Law Inst. (com. on restatement of agy. and restatement of employment law), Soc. for Human Resource Mgmt. (com. on employment practices 1990-99). Office: Epstein Becker & Green PC 250 Park Ave Ste 1200 New York NY 10177-1211 Office Phone: 212-351-4840. Business E-Mail: ppanken@ebglaw.com.

PANKEY, GEORGE ATKINSON, internist, educator, researcher; b. Shreveport, La., Aug. 11, 1933; s. George Edward and Annabel (Atkinson) P.; m. Patricia Ann Carreras, Sept. 22, 1972; children: Susan Margaret, Stephen Charles, Laura Atkinson, Edward Atkinson. Student, La. Poly. Inst., 1950-51; BS, Tulane U., 1954, MD, 1957; MS, U. Minn., 1961. Diplomate Am. Bd. Internal Medicine, Am. Bd. Infectious Disease. Intern U. Minn. Hosps., 1957-58, resident in internal medicine, 1958-60, Mpls. VA Hosp., Mpls. Gen. Hosp., 1960-61; asst. vis. physician Charity Hosp. La., New Orleans, 1961-62, vis. physician, 1962-75, sr. vis. physician, 1975-95; ptnr. Ochsner Clinic, New Orleans, 1968—99; head sect. infectious diseases Ochsner Clinic Found., 1972—94, dir. infectious disease training program, 1972—94, dir. infectious disease rsch., 1999—; instr. dept. medicine, div. infectious diseases Tulane U. Sch. Medicine, New Orleans, 1961-63, clin. instr., 1963-65, clin. asst. prof. medicine, 1965-68, clin. assoc. prof., 1968-73, clin. prof., 1973—. Dir., founder Century Nat. Bank, New Orleans; medicine test com. Nat. Bd. Med. Examiners, 1979-83; infectious diseases adv. bd. Hoffman-LaRoche, 1982-92; dir. Nat. Found. Infectious Diseases, 2004—. Author: A Manual of Antimicrobial Therapy, 1969; co-author: (with Charles W. Gross and Michael G. Mendelsohn) Contemporary Diagnosis and Management of Sinusitis, 1997, 4th edit., 2004; (with Julia Garcia-Diaz and Layne O. Gentry) Contemporary Diagnosis and Management of Diabetic Foot Infections, 2006; editor: Infectious Diseases Digest, 1983-95, So. Med. Assn. Program for Infectious Diseases Dial-Access, 1983-92, Ochsner Clinic Reports on Serious Hosp. Infections, 1985-2005, Ochsner Clinic Reports on Geriatric Infectious Diseases, 1990-93, Ochsner Clinic Reports on the Mgmt. of Sepsis, 1991-93, Infectious Disease Clinics of N.Am., 1994; co-editor: (with Geoffrey A. Kalish) Outpatient Antimicrobial Therapy - Recent Advances, 1989; contbg. editor: Antimicrobial Therapy Guide, 18th edit., 2006; mem. editl. bd. Patient Care, 1969-75, Today in Medicine, 1990, Nat. Infectious Disease Info. Network, 1983, Compendium Continuing Edn. in Dentistry, 1984-2004, Quinolones Bull., 1985-93, Ochsner Jour., 1999-2003, Infectious Disease News, 2001—; contbr. articles to profl. jours. Dir. Camp Fire Inc.; Pres. New Orleans Young Republican Club, 1969-71; adv. bd. Angie Nall Sch. Hosp., Beaumont, Tex.; trustee Nall Found. for Children, Beaumont. Recipient cert. merit Am. Acad. Gen. Practice, 1969, 70, 2002. Master ACP-ASIM (laureate award La. chpt. 1997); fellow Am. Coll. Preventive Medicine, Infectious Disease Soc. Am. (Clinician award 1996), Am. Coll. Chest Physicians, Royal Soc. Medicine; mem. Am. Soc. of Transplantation, Assn. Contamination Control (chpt. pres. 1968-70), Am. Fedn. Med. Rsch., So. Med. Assn. (certificate of award 1970), Am. Soc. Internal Medicine (del. ann. meeting 1971-72), Am. Soc. Microbiology, Am. Thoracic Soc., New Orleans Acad. Internal Medicine (pres. 1977-78, 96-97), AMA, Aerospace Med. Assn., Am. Soc. Tropical Medicine and Hygiene, Am. Venereal Disease Assn., Am. Soc. Parasitologists, Internat. Travel Medicine Soc., La. Soc. Internal Medicine (pres. 1972-73), La. Med. Soc., La. Thoracic Soc. (chmn. program com. 1968, governing council 1976-80), Surg. Infection Soc., Immunocompromised Host Soc., Musser Burch Soc., Orleans Parish Med. Soc., N.Y. Acad. Scis., Pan Am. Med. Assn. (diplomate mem. sect. internal medicine 1971, sect. pres. infectious diseases and virology 1978-85), SAR, Huguenot Soc. Founders Manakin in Colony of Va., Aviation Med. Examiner, Federal Air Surgeon(inf. dis cons.), Masons (32 deg), Shriners. Home: 5910 Prytania St New Orleans LA 70115-4348 Office: Ochsner Clinic Found 1514 Jefferson Hwy New Orleans LA 70121-2483 Office Phone: 504-842-4006. Personal E-mail: gpankey@ochsner.org.

PANKOV, GRADIMIR KRUNISLAV, performing company executive; b. Skopje, Macedonia, Yugoslavia, Oct. 25, 1938; s. Krunislav Ivan Pankov and Dragica Isak (Mihajlovska); m. Margret Maria Kaufmann, Dec. 30, 1980. Baccalaureat, Josip Broz Tito Gymnasium, Skopje, 1956; diploma, State Conservatory of Dance & Music, Skopje, 1957. Dancer Nat. Theatre Macedonia, Skopje, 1956-63; guest artist Nat. Theatres, Belgrade, Zagreb, Sarajevo, 1963-67; soloist City Theatres, Nuremberg, Karlsruhe, Wuppertal, Fed. Republic Germany, Theater Am Gärtnerplatz, Munich, 1967-74, Nat. Theatre, Mannheim, Fed. Republic Germany, 1974-76; ballet master City Theatre, Dortmund, 1976-80; artistic dir., tchr. Netherlands Dance Theatre Jr. Co., The Hague, 1980-81; artistic dir. Nat. Ballet of Finland, Helsinki, 1981-84; artistic dir., tchr. Cullberg Ballet, Stockholm, 1984-88; artistic dir. Ballet du Grand Theatre, Geneva, 1988-96, Les Grands Ballets Canadiens de Montreal, 2000—. Dancer (ballets) Mercutio in Romeo and Juliet, 1963, title role in Petrushka, 1965, title role in Pulcinella, 1971, The Faun in Afternoon of a Faun, 1975, choreographer (Operas) Eugene Onegin, 1977, Carmen, 1978, Don Giovanni, 1978. Office: Les Grands Ballets Canadiens de Montreal 4816, rue Rivard Montreal PQ H2J 2N6 Canada*

PANNABECKER, RACHEL K., museum director, social sciences educator; BA, Bluffton Coll., 1971; PhD in Textiles and Clothing, Ohio State U., 1986. Asst. prof. social sci. Bethel Coll., North Newton, Kans., dir. Kauffman Mus. Contbr. articles to profl. jours. Mem.: Internat. Quilt Study Ctr. (assoc. fellow), Costume Soc. Am., Am. Assn. Mus., Am. Assn. State and Local History (Merit award 2006), Kansas Mus. Assn. (chair instl. grants com.). Office: Bethel Coll 300 E 27th St North Newton KS 67117 Office Phone: 316-283-1612. E-mail: rpannabe@bethelks.edu.

PANNELL, THIERRY EDGARD, engineer, information technology manager; s. Frank James Pannell and Emiliene Eugenie Omont. AAS, Brookdale C.C., 1989; BS, So. Ill. U., 1991; MS, Regis U., 2003. Lic. gen. radio operator, with radar endorsement, FCC, 1991, cert. broadcast engr., Soc. of Broadcast Engrs., 1991, sr. electronics technician, ETA/Iowa State U., 1990, cert. electronics technician, ISCET, 1991. Electronics mechanic U.S. Navy, Colts Neck, NJ, 1983—88; electronics technician U.S. Marine Corps, Cherry Point, NC, 1988—90, U.S. Army Yuma Proving Ground, Yuma, Ariz., 1990—93; grad. tchg., rsch. asst. Ill. State U., Normal, Ill., 1993—94; electromagnetic test technician Delco Electronics, Kokomo, Ind., 1995; electromagnetic interference, electromagnetic compatability technician Ford Motor Co., Dearborn, Mich., 1996—98; sr. electro-mechnical technician Barry Controls, Brighton, Mass., 1998; assoc. electro-magnetic interference compatibility engr. Sundstrand Aerospace, Rockford, Ill., 1998—2000; hardware engr. Rockwell Automation, Mayfield Heights, Ohio, 2000; info. tech. analyst Caterpillar, Inc., Lafayette, Ind., 2004; train controls sys. engr. GE Rail, Erie, Pa., 2004—06; EMI sys. engr. Ingenium Technologies, Rockford, Ill., 2006—08; elec. engr. Goodrich Pump & Engine Control Sys., Inc., West Hartford, Conn., 2009—. Cons. 24 Hour Club, Kokomo, Ind., 1999—2003, ClearView Windows, Hastings, Nebr., 2004, Brian's Lawn Svc., Kokomo, Ind., 2006—, Jewel Machine Inc., Harvard, Ill. Specialist 5th class US Army, 1978—81. Mem.: IEEE, Assn. Computing Machinery, Internat. Soc. Profl. Electronics Technicians (assoc.). Achievements include development of computer applications. Home: 1701 E Empire St Ste 360 #140 Bloomington IL 61704

PANNIER, ANGELA KAYE, science educator; d. Richard E. and Debra K. Wild; m. Tyler N. Pannier, June 16, 2001; 1 child, Lillian K. BS, U. Nebr.-Lincoln, 2001, MS, 2002; PhD, Northwestern U., Evanston, Ill., 2007. Grad. rsch. asst. U. Nebr.-Lincoln, 2001—02, Northwestern U., Evanston, Ill., 2003—07; asst. prof. U. of Nebr.-Lincoln, 2007—. Grad. Rsch. fellowship, NSF, 2001. Mem.: AAAS, AIChE. Achievements include research in exploring extracellular and intracellular factors that influence nonviral gene delivery for tissue engineering applications. Office: Univ Nebraska-Lincoln 231 Chase Hall Lincoln NE 68583-0726

PANNKE-SMITH, PEGGY, president; b. Chgo., Oct. 26; d. Victor E. and Leona (O'Leary) Stich; m. Craig D. Smith, July 18, 1998; children from previous marriage: Thomas Scott, David Savonne, Heidi Mireille, Peter. V.p. long term care ins. Sales & Seminars, Des Plaines, 1986-90; pres., founder Nat. Consumer Oriented Agy., Des Plaines, 1990—. Cons. on long-term care ins. The Travelers, Tchrs. Inc. & Annuity Assocs., others; spkr. Exec. Enterprises, NYC, 1988—93. Columnist Sr. News, Vital Times, Daily Herald, Sr. Connection, Sr. Marketplace News, Prime Time for Seniors, Pioneer Press, Boulder Daily Camera, Longmont Times-Call, Aurora Sun, Mature Times Lifestyles, 50 Plus Marketplace. Sponsor Ill. Alliance for Aging, Chgo., 1990—, Ill. Assn. Homes for Aging, 1990-91; bd. govs. St. Matthew Luth. Home, Park Ridge, Ill., 1993-95. Recipient Spkrs. awards Health Ins. Assn. Am., Washington, 1990, Ret. Officers Assn., Glenview, Ill., 1991, 93, Nat. Assn. Sr. Living Industries, Denver, 1992, Exec. Enterprises, NYC, 1993, Gov.'s Conf. on Aging, Chgo., 1996, Golden Harvest Long Term Care award Ret. Officers Assn., 2001, Nat. awards UNUM, 2001, AIG 2002, Conseco, 2000, Allianz, 2002, Mut. of Omaha, 2003, Presidents Club, Lincoln Benefit. Mem.: Internat. Soc. for Retirement Planning, Am. Soc. on Aging, Mature Am., Nat. Coun. on Aging (ad hoc com.), Ctr. for Applied Gerontology, Nat. Assn. Long Term Care Profl., Nat. Assn. Sr. Living Industries, Friends of the Colo. Trail, Colo. Mountain Club, Boulder C. of C., Park Ridge C. of C., Kiwanis (bd. dir. Park Ridge 1992—98, pres. 1996—97, Boulder publicity chair 2006—, bd. dirs. 2009—), Am. Mensa (program dir. in Ill. 1983—85, Colo. chpt. 1999—, pres. Boulder chpt. 2003—, regional vice chairperson 2007—, bd. dirs. 2007—, leadership devel. chair 2009—). Avocations: showshoeing, travel, sketching wildflowers, hiking, trekking the Colorado Trail. Address: 310 Busse Hwy #305 Park Ridge IL 60068 Office Phone: 800-554-1996. E-mail: rvc7@us.mensa.org, ncoa.pps@sbcglobal.net.

PANNUTI, THOMAS GREGORY, aerospace scientist, educator; BS, Rensselaer Poly. Inst., Troy, NY, 1994; MS, U. N.Mex, Albuquerque, 2000; PhD, U. N.Mex, 2000. Postdoc. assoc. MIT, Cambridge, 2000—03; postdoc. scholar Calif. Inst. Tech., Pasadena, 2003—06; asst. prof. space sci. Morehead State U., Ky., 2006—. Mem.: Sigma Xi, Sigma Pi Sigma, Internat. Astronomy Union, Astron. Soc. Pacific, Am. Astron. Soc.

PANOPOULOS, NICK ANTONIOS, retired speech and drama educator; b. Dafnona, Greece, Nov. 20, 1952; arrived in US, 1957; s. Antonios N. and Maria P. Panopoulos; m. Linda L. Panopoulos; children: Jeannine Marie, Elizabeth Ann. BA, U. Wyo., Laramie, 1975, MEd, 1979. Instr. drama and speech Laramie County CC, Cheyenne, Wyo., 1976—86; drama and speech tchr. Cheyenne Ctrl. High, 1987—2007; adj. communication instr. Laramie County Cmty. Coll., 2004—; asst. speech & debate coach Cherry Creek HS, Greenwood Village, Colo., 2007—. Vol. Cheyenne Frontier Days, 1987—. Named Wyo. 4A Coach of Season, 2005, 2007; named one of Outstanding Young Men. of Am., Jaycees, 1980, 1982, 1983, 1985, 1987. Mem.: Nat. Forensics League, Kiwanis (2nd. v.p., Outstanding Educator of Yr. 2002), Phi Delta Kappa. Greek Orthodox. Home: 7227 Tumbleweed Dr Cheyenne WY 82009 Office: Laramie County Cmty Coll 1400 E Coll Dr Cheyenne WY 82007

PANOS, TAS, information technology executive, lawyer; BA, U. Nev., Las Vegas; JD, U. San Diego Sch. Law. Pvt. practice, Calif., 1985—2002; litigation, labor & employment group counsel Affiliated Computer Svcs. Inc., sr. v.p. & group counsel, 2002—08, exec. v.p. & gen. counsel, 2008—. Adj. prof. U. San Diego Sch. Law. Office: 2828 N Haskell Dallas TX 75204 Office Phone: 214-841-6111. E-mail: info@acs-inc.com.*

PANOVSKI, NAUM, theater director; married. PhD, U. Tex., Dallas, 1991. Dir. MFA in theatre RI Coll., Providence, 2005—. Dir.: (theatre) Hamlet. Business E-Mail: naum@naumpanovsw.net.

PANSINI, JILL ANNE, medical/surgical nurse, consultant; b. Pompton Plains, NJ, June 14, 1965; d. Charles Carmen and Joyce Martha (Hagen) Cullari; m. David Anthony Pansini, May 5, 1991; children: Stephanie Rianne, Sloane Marie, Madison Taylor. AAS, Bergen C.C., 1986; BSN (hon.), Pace U., 1989; cert. in Legal Nurse Consulting (hon.), Fairleigh Dickenson U., 1998. Lic. practical nurse, N.J., 1987, RN N.J., 1988. Staff nurse The Valley Hosp., Ridgewood, NJ, 1986—91; nurse mgr. surg. ICU Clara Maass Med. Ctr., Belleville, NJ, 1991—94; nurse mgr. Post Anesthesia Care Unit St. Barnabas Med. Ctr., Livingston, NJ, 1994—97, perioperative clin. coord., 1997—99; pre-operative staff and charge nurse St. Barnabas Ambulatory Care Ctr., Livingston, 1999—. Tchr. religious edn. St. William the Abbot, Howell, NJ, 2004. Mem.: Am. Assn. Legal Nurse Cons. (assoc.), Sigma Theta Tau (assoc.). Office: 200 S Orange Ave Livingston NJ 07039 Personal E-mail: jillpansini@optonline.net.

PANSINI, MICHAEL SAMUEL, financial analyst, tax specialist; b. Molfetta, Italy, July 12, 1928; arrived in U.S., 1935; s. Ralph and Isabel (Cirilli) P.; m. Anna D'Angelo, June 5, 1949 (div. 1970); children: Elizabeth, Valerie, Michael; m. Elizabeth Bischoff, Oct. 3, 1970 (div. Feb. 1992); 1 child, Elissa Michelle. BS, NYU, 1950, MBA, 1952, LLM, 1960; LLD, Fordham U., 1956. Bar: NY 1956, US Tax Ct. Tax mgr. Pfizer Corp., NYC, 1951-64; asst. treas. Hooker Chem. Corp., NYC, 1964-69; treas., dir. United Indsl. Corp., NYC, 1969-72; sr. v.p., gen. counsel Beker Industries Corp., Greenwich, Conn., 1972-87; pres., dir. Panmer, Inc., 1987—; tax, fin. cons., 1988—; v.p., corp. counsel Champion Energy Corp. and affiliates, 1991-93, Champion Holdings Co. and affiliates, 1993-96. V.p., chmn. various coms. Tax Exec. Inst., NYC, 1963-72; pres., dir. Fed. Tax Forum, Inc., NYC, 1961-72; dir. Intelligent Bus. Communications Corp. Commr., vice chmn. Econ. Devel. Commn., Stamford, Conn., 1994—; mem. Rep. Town Com. 19th Dist., Stamford, 1993—; bd. dirs. Stamford Sr. Ctr., 2000—06, treas., 2007—08; bd. dirs., treas. Women's Bus. Devel. Ctr., Inc., 2003—06, chmn. audit com, 2007—; bd. dirs., treas. Food Bank of Lower Fairfield County, 2004—06. Mem.: Sr. Men's Assn. Stamford (bd. dirs., 2d v.p. 2005—06, 1st v.p. 2007—08, pres. 2008—), North Stamford Assn. (bd. dirs. 1999—2005, v.p. 2000, pres. 2001). Republican. Home and Office: 76 Lawrence Hill Rd Stamford CT 06903-2120 Home Phone: 203-329-8073.

PANT, RAVI, research scientist; m. Himani Joshi. PhD, U. Ariz., Tucson, 2008. Rsch. scientist U. Sydney, 2008—. Contbr. articles to profl. jours. publs. Mem.: Optical Soc. Am. Office: Coll Optical Scis 1630 East University Boulevard Tucson AZ 85721

PANTALEO, LEA, biology professor; b. Harvard, Ill., Sept. 16, 1979; d. Edward and Eileen Anderson; m. Christopher Pantaleo, Dec. 18, 2004; 1 child, Malin. MS in Human Anat. Scis., Northern Ill. U., Dekalb, 2005. Faculty Rock Valley Coll., Rockford, Ill., 2006—. Office: Rock Valley Coll 3301 N Mulford Rd Rockford IL 61114 Business E-Mail: lpantaleo@ednet.rvc.cc.il.us.

PANTALEO, PETER S., lawyer; BA, U. Wis., 1971; JD with honors, U. ND, 1976. Bar: Pa. 1976, ND 1977, DC 1989. Atty. Verner Liipfert Bernhard McPherson and Hand; ptnr. Piper Rudnick, Washington, 2002—04; ptnr., chair labor and employment law practice group DLA Piper Rudnick Gray Cary LLP, Washington, 2005—. Editor-in-chief ND Law Rev., lectr.; contbr. articles to profl. jours. Mem.: ABA, Inst. of Directors, London. Office: DLA Piper Rudnick Gray Cary LLP 1200 Nineteenth St NW Washington DC 20036-2412 Office Phone: 202-861-3956. Office Fax: 202-223-2085. Business E-Mail: peter.pantaleo@dlapiper.com.

PANTANO, ALESSANDRA, mathematics professor; b. Italy; MS, Univ. Tor Vergata, Rome, 1999; MA, Princeton Univ., 2001, PhD, 2004. H. C. Wang asst. prof. math. Cornell Univ., 2004—. Achievements include being one of 18 top mathematicians and computer scientists (Atlas of Lie Groups Project) from the US to successfully map E8, one of the largest and most complicated structures in mathematics.

PANTELIDES, SOKRATES THEODORE, research scientist; b. Limassol, Cyprus, Nov. 20, 1948; s. Theodore and Katerina (Sokratous) P.; m. Mimi Lisbeth Hardtke, Aug. 13, 1972; children: Kate Lisbeth, Natasha Lisa. BS in Physics with highest honors, Northern Ill. U., 1969; MS in Physics, U. Ill., 1970, PhD in Physics, 1973. Rsch. staff mem. rsch. divsn. IBM, Yorktown Heights, N.Y., 1975-94, mgr., 1984-86, sr. mgr., 1986-89, program dir., 1990-91, tech. asst. to v.p. for sci. and tech. Armonk, N.Y., 1989-90; McMinn prof. physics Vanderbilt U., Nashville, 1994—, chair dept. phys. & astro., 1995—97. Disting. vis. scientist Oak Ridge Nat. Lab., 1995—; chmn. four maj. internat. tech. confs. Editor 9 tech. books; mem. editorial bd. Comments in Condensed Matter Physics, 1984-92, Ency. of Applied Physics, 1989-1992; contbr. 350 articles to tech. publs. Trustee Bd. Edn., Yorktown, N.Y., 1986-92. With Cyprus Army, 1966-67. Fellow Am. Physical Soc. (exec. bd. materials physics group 1986-89, chmn. com. on application of physics, 1989-90), IEEE, AAAS, Materials Rsch. Soc., Electrochem. Soc. Home: 4566 Peytonsville Rd Franklin TN 37064-7611 Office: Vanderbilt U Dept Physics & Astronomy Nashville TN 37235

PANTELL, ROBERT HOWARD, pediatrician, educator; b. NYC, Oct. 6, 1945; s. Milton and Rose (Rappaport) P.; m. Marcia Ruth Snell, Oct. 30, 1971 (div. 1980); m. Maureen Theresa Shannon, Aug. 29, 1982; children: Matthew Shannon, Gregory Michael, Megan Elizabeth. BA, Columbia U., 1965; MD, Boston U., 1969. Cert. in pediat. Am. Bd. Med. Specialties, 1974. Intern in pediat. NC Meml. Hosp., Chapel Hill, resident in pediat., 1969-72; fellow in health svcs. rsch., behavioral pediat. Stanford U.; pediatrician, med. dir. Cmty. Health Clinics, Nampa, Idaho, 1972-74; Robert Wood Johnson Found. clin. scholar Stanford (Calif.) U., 1974-77; asst. prof. med. U. SC, Charleston, 1977-80; prof., dir. divsn. gen. pediat. U. Calif.-San Francisco, 1980—. Cons. for fed. and pvt. founds. Author: Taking Care of Your Child, 1977, 8th edit., trans. to Japanese, 1982, Spanish, 1983, Italian, 1990, Chinese, 2007, (Book of Yr. award Am. Med. Writers Assn. 1978); author, editor: Parents' Pharmacy, 1982, Pediatrics: A Study Guide, 1987, The Common Sympton Guide, 1977, 7th edit., 2009; contbr. articles to profl. publs. Grantee HHS, David and Lucile Packard Found., Nat. Ctr. Health Svcs. Rsch., Investigator award Am. Assn. Med. Colleges, 1986. Fellow Am. Acad. Pediat.; mem. Ambulatory Pediatric Assn. (bd. dirs. 1988, Tchg. award Cmty. Program, 1998), Am. Pediat. Soc. Office: Divsn Gen Pediact U Calif Box 0503 3333 California St Ste 245 San Francisco CA 94118 Home: 11 Piedmont St San Francisco CA 94117 Office Phone: 415-476-4349. Office Fax: 415-476-6106. Business E-Mail: pantellr@peds.ucsf.edu.

PANTER, NICOLE OLIVIERI, film educator, writer, film critic; d. Pasquale Olivieri (Stepfather) and Evelyn Beldner Olivieri Cirillo; m. Gary Brad Panter, July 23, 1978 (div. Dec. 1, 1989). BA, UCLA, 1976; studied with Peggy Feury and William Traylor, Loft Studio, 1981—85. Faculty Calif. Inst. of Arts, Valencia, 1995—; prof. Coll. Santa Fe, 2005—09. Sr. lectr. Am. Film Inst., LA, 1998—2005; bd. mem. Big Sky Documentary Film Festival, Missoula, Mont., 2002—03. Author: (book) Mr. Right On; author, reader: spoken word recordings The Story Lady, Drinking from Puddles, author, critic: film Missoula Independent, editor, writer: anthology Unnatural Disasters: Recent Writings from the Golden State; actor, writer: The Pee Wee Herman Show; contbr. numerous pieces to lit. jours. Workshop leader The Heart Project, LA, 1997, 1999; adv. bd. Mojave Desert Land Trust, Twentynine Palms, Calif., 2005—; founder Bohemian Women's Polit. Alliance, LA, 1990—93. Avocations: land use issues, photography, travel, history, art. Office: 71524 Samarkand Dr Twentynine Palms CA 92277 Personal E-mail: npanter@csf.edu.

PANTHAKI, ZUBIN JAL, medical educator, plastic surgeon; b. Bombay, Feb. 26, 1968; arrived in U.S., 2000; s. Jal Minocher Panthaki and Nergish Nanabhoy Sethna; m. Dimple Panthaki. B in Engring., McGill U., Montreal, Quebec, 1991, MD, 1995. Diplomate Am. Bd. Plastic Surgeons, cert. for hand surgery Am. Bd. Plastic Surgeons, lic. N.H., Fla. Resident in surgery McGill U., Montreal, 1995—2000; microsurgery and hand surgery fellow Buncke Clinic, San Francisco, 2000—01; assoc. prof. plastic surgery U. Miami, Fla., 2001—, program dir. plastic surgery, 2005—. Cons. Miami Children's Hosp., Jackson Meml. Hosp., 2001—, U. Miami Hosps., Miami Vets. Hosp., chief hand surgery, plastic surgery; cons. West Palm Beach Vets. Hosp.; editor Chief Plastic Surgery @ Miami Vets. Hosp., Plastic Surgery Hyperguide, 2009—. Editor: Jour. Craniofacial Surgery, 2004—. Vol. Interplast, 2003—; trustee Stanstead Coll., 2007—. Capt. mil. engrs., 1987—2000, Can. Fellow: Royal Coll. Surgeons; mem.: Am. Soc. Surgery Hand, Am. Soc., Miami Soc. Plastic Surgeons (pres. 2007—), Fellow Am. Coll. Surgeons, Fla. Soc. Plastic Surgeons, Nat. Bd. Med. Examiners, Am. Soc. Plastic Surgeons. Avocation: computers. Office: Univ Miami Jackson Meml 1611 NW 12th Ave ET-3019 Miami FL 33136 Home: 6002 SW 58th St South Miami FL 33143 Home Phone: 305-531-0601; Office Phone: 305-585-5285. Office Fax: 305-324-7384. Business E-Mail: zpanthaki@med.miami.edu.

PANTOLIANO, JOE, actor; b. Hoboken, NJ, Sept. 12, 1951; s. Dominic and Mary Pantoliano; m. Morga Kester, 1979 (div. 1985); 3 children; m. Nancy Sheppard, Feb. 18, 1994; 1 child. Actor: (stage prodns.) Brothers, 1982, Orphans, 1983, One Flew Over the Cuckoo's Nest, Italian American Reconciliation, The Death Star, Visions of Kerouac, (feature films) The Godfather Part II, 1974, The Idol Maker, 1980, Monsignor, 1982, Risky Business, 1983, Eddie and the Cruisers, 1983, The Mean Season, 1985, Goonies, 1985, Running Scared, 1986, The In Crowd, 1987, The Squeeze, 1987, Scenes from the Goldmine, 1987, Amazon Women on the Moon, 1987, La Bamba, 1987, Empire of the Sun, 1987, Midnight Run, 1988, Downtown, 1990, The Last of the Finest, 1990, Short Time, 1990, Zandalee, 1991, Used People, 1992, Three of Hearts, 1993, The Fugitive, 1993, Baby's Day Out, 1994, Calendar Girl, 1994, Steal Big, Steal Little, 1995, Bad Boys, 1995, Bound, 1996, Top of the World, 1997, Self Storage, 1997, Tinseltown, 1997 (also assoc. prodr.), The Tax Man, 1998, U.S. Marshals, 1998, The Life Before This, 1999, Black and White, 1999, Tinseltown, 1999, The Matrix, 1999, Ready to Rumble, 2000, Memento, 2000, Silver Man, 2000, (voice) Cats & Dogs, 2001, The Adventures of Pluto Nash, 2002, A Piece of My Heart, 2002, Daredevil, 2003, Bad Boys II, 2003, 5-25-77, 2003, Second Best, 2004 (also prodr.), A Piece of My Heart, 2004, (voice) Racing Stripes, 2005, The Check Up, 2005, The Moguls, 2005, (voice) The Easter Egg Adventure, 2005, Larry the Cable Guy: Health Inspector, 2006; (TV movies) More Than Friends, 1978, Alcatraz: The Whole Shocking Story, 1980, Destination: America, 1987, El Diablo, 1990, One Special Victory, 1991, Through the Eyes of a Killer, 1992, (voice) Olive, the Other Reindeer, 1999, (TV mini-series) From Here to Eternity, 1979, Robert Kennedy and His Times, 1985, (TV spl.) Mr. Roberts, 1984 (TV Series) Free Country, 1978, The Fanelli Boys, 1990-91, Sugar Hill, 1999, The Sopranos, 2001-02 (Emmy award best sup. actor drama, 2003), Dr. Vegas, 2004-05; writer, dir. (films) Just Like Mona, 2003; TV appearances include Tales From the Crypt, Amazing Stories, L.A. Law, The Hitchhiker, NYPD Blue, Arlis$, Hill Street Blues, The Hitchhiker, Highlander, The Marshal. Avocations: skiing, jogging, shopping. Office: UTA care Lisa Hellerman 9560 Wilshire Blvd Fl 5 Beverly Hills CA 90212-2401

PANTOS, WILLIAM PANTAZES, mechanical engineer, consultant; b. Ann Arbor, Mich., May 15, 1957; s. William Van and Lillian William (Skinner) P. BS in Mech. Engring., Northwestern U., 1979; MS in Mech. Engring., San Diego State U., 1991. Registered profl. engr., Calif. Owner

Signs & Symbols, Niles, Ill., 1975-80; engr. Hughes Aircraft, El Segundo, Calif., 1980-83, Gen. Dynamics, San Diego, 1983-85; staff engr. TRW, San Diego, 1985-90; pres. Tekton Industries, Escondido, Calif., 1990—. Patentee animal lift and transport apparatus. NROTC scholar USN, 1975. Mem. ASME, NSPE, Alpha Delta Phi. (pres. 1978). Greek Orthodox. Achievements include patents for force adjustable toilet seat lifting and lowering device. Personal E-mail: williampantos@gmail.com.

PANTUSO, VINCENT JOSEPH, food service consultant; b. Charleston, W.Va., Aug. 13, 1940; s. Fortunato F. Pantuso and Josephine Malcom (Ginestra) Pantuso Messer; m. Carol Barber, Dec. 10, 1964 (div. 1976); children: Lisa, Barbara, Tina; m. Nancy Josephine Chellman, Sept. 30, 1978 (div. 1995). Student, Drexel U.; BSBA, St. Joseph's U., 1968; postgrad., Rollins Coll., 1984-85. Asst. mgr. Marriott Hotels, Inc., Bethesda, Md., 1962-64; v.p. sales mktg. ARA Services, Inc., Phila., 1964-72; sr. v.p. Interstate United Corp., Chgo., 1972-84; pres. V.J. Pantuso Services, Inc., Orlando, Fla., 1984—, New Vista Services, Inc., 1988-97. Mem. Nat. Assn. Concessionaires (bd. dirs. 1982—, pres. 1989-91, chmn. 1991-94, Master Concessionaire, Chgo. 1985), Nat. Assn. Food Equipment Mfrs. (doctorate 1989). Republican. Episcopalian. Avocation: fishing. Home: Apt 5 120 Monarch Cir Casselberry FL 32730-2718 Office Phone: 321-397-1670. Business E-Mail: vpantuso@mckinleyinsurance.com.

PANUSKA, JOSEPH ALLAN, retired academic administrator; b. Balt., July 3, 1927; s. Joseph William and Barbara Agnes (Preller) P. BS, Loyola Coll., Balt., 1948; PhD, St. Louis U., 1958; STL, Woodstock Coll., 1961; D of Health (hon.), Trnava U., Slovakia, 1997; LLD (hon.), U. Scranton, 1974; LHD (hon.), Marywood Coll., 1992; LLD (hon.), Alvernia Coll., 2007. Joined S.J., 1948; ordained priest Roman Cath. Ch., 1960. Instr. dept. physiology Emory U. Sch. Medicine, 1962-63; asst. prof. biology Georgetown U., 1963-66, assoc. prof., 1966-72, prof., 1973; provincial, bd. dirs. Jesuit Conf. Md. Province (S.J.), 1973-79; acad. v.p., dean faculties, prof. biology Boston Coll., 1979-82; pres. U. Scranton, Pa., 1982-98, pres. emeritus, 1998—2004; rector Jesuit Ctr., 1988—2003; pres. emeritus, 2004—. Mem. Pa. Commn. Ind. Colls. and Univs., 1982-98, mem. exec. com., treas., 1987-91, vice chmn., 1988-89, chmn., 1990-91; mem. Pres.'s Commn., NCAA, 1989-90; spiritual dir. Scranton Ctrl. City Ministerium, bd. dirs., 2003—. Mem. editl. bd. Crybiology, 1968-88, editor-in-chief, 1971-74; contbr. chpts. to books, articles to sci. rsch. jours. Mem. corp. Am. Found. Biol. Rsch., 1967-85, pres. bd. dirs., 1974-79, v.p., 1979-83; trustee Loyola Coll., 1979-85, St. Joseph's U., 1979-84, U. Scranton, 1970-73, 1982-98, St. Peter's Coll., 1971-72, Woodstock Coll., 1973-76, Fordham U., 1982-88, Cambridge Ctr. for Social Studies, 1973-79 (pres. 1973-79), Corp. Roman Cath. Clergymen, 1973-79 (pres. 1973-79); rector Jesuit Cmty. at Georgetown U., 1970-73; bd. dirs. United Way Pa., 1985-87, Scranton Prep. Sch., 1984-90, Scranton Area Found., 1997-98, John Carroll U., 1992-98, Nat. Inst. Environ. Renewal, 1992-98, Woodstock Theol. Ctr., Washington, 1998-2001, St. Joseph's Prep. Sch., Phila., 1998-2001, Alvernia Coll., 2001-07, Ctrl. Scranton (Pa.) Ministerium, 2004—; chmn. Pa. Commn. for Ind. Colls. and Univs., 1990-91; bd. visitors Panuska Coll. Profl. Studies, U. Scranton, 1998-; pres. emeritus, spiritual dir. and advancement Campus Ministry. NIH postdoctoral fellow, 1962-63; recipient Danforth Found. Harbison prize for disting. tchg., 1969, B'nai B'rith Americanism award, 1997, recipient from 2001, Michelini award Outstanding Svc. to Higher Edn. AICUP (Assoc. Ind. Coll. and U. Pa.), 2001; vis. fellow St. Edmunds Coll., Cambridge U., 1969; college named J.A. Panuska Coll. of Profl. Studies, Univ. at Scranton, Interfaith Person of Yr. Scranton Ctrl. City Ministerium, 2004. Mem. Assn. Jesuit Colls. and Univs. (bd. dirs. 1982-98, treas. 1993-96), Pa. Assn. Colls. and Univs. (exec. com., adv. com. to State Bd. Edn. 1990-91). Home and Office: La Colombiere Residence 5704 Roland Ave Baltimore MD 21210 Home Phone: 410-532-1425; Office Phone: 443-451-1651. Personal E-mail: panuskaja@hotmail.com. *In order to be happy in a leadership role and to succeed in it, I have to possess a sense of coherence with my life values. I also need to recognize that my own activity makes a real difference in the empowerment of others so that there is a multiplier effect which extends me beyond my own person and activity.*

PANUTHOS, PETER J., federal judge; b. NY, 1943; BS, Bernard Baruch Sch. Bus., CUNY; diploma, Bryant Coll., Providence, RI, 1966; JD, Suffolk U. Law Sch., Boston, 1969; LLM in Taxation, Boston U. Sch. Law, 1972. Bar: DC, admitted to: Supreme Jud. Ct., Mass., US Supreme Ct. Trial atty., asst. dist. counsel Boston Office of Chief Counsel, IRS, 1970—83; spl. trial judge US Tax Ct., 1983—92, chief spl. trial judge, 1992—. Adj. prof. Bentley Coll., Boston, Cath. U. America, Columbus Sch. Law, David A. Clarke Sch. Law, U. DC; mem. law rev. Suffolk U. Law Sch. Mem.: ABA, Inns of Ct., Fed. Bar Assn. Office: US Tax Ct 400 2nd St NW Washington DC 20217 Office Phone: 202-521-4707.*

PANWAR, SHIVENDRA SINGH, education educator, researcher; b. Delhi, India, Dec. 15, 1959; came to U.S., 1981; s. Surendra Singh and Lakshmi (Singh) P.; m. Shruti Kumari, Apr. 8, 1988. B Tech., Indian Inst. Tech., Kanpur, India, 1981; MS, U. Mass., 1983, PhD, 1986. Tchr., rsch. asst. U. Mass., Amherst, 1981-85; asst. prof. Poly. U., Bklyn., 1985-90; assoc. prof. Poly U., Bklyn., 1990—2003, prof., 2003—. Vis. scientist IBM Rsch., Yorktown Heights, N.Y., 1987; spl. cons. AT&T Bell Labs., Holmdel, N.J., 1988; dir. N.Y. State Ctr for Adv. Tech. in Telecom., 1996—. Co-author TCP/IP Essentials: A Lab Based Approach, 2004; contbr. articles to profl. jours. Recipient Rsch. Initiation award NSF, Washington, 1989 Mem. IEEE (sr., tech. com. computer comms., Leonard G. Abraham prize 2004), Sigma Xi, Tau Beta Pi. Hindu. Office: Polytechnic Inst NY Univ Six Metrotech Ctr Brooklyn NY 11201-2907

PANY, KURT JOSEPH, finance educator, consultant; b. St. Louis, Mar. 31, 1946; s. Joseph Francis and Ruth Elizabeth (Westerman) P.; m. Darlene Dee Zabish, June 3, 1971; children: Jeffrey, Michael. BSBA, U. Ariz., 1968; MBA in Mgmt., U. Minn., 1971; PhD in Accountancy, U. Ill., 1977. CPA, Ariz., cert. fraud examiner. Staff auditor Arthur Andersen & Co., Mpls., 1968-69, Touche Ross & Co., Phoenix, 1971-73; teaching asst. U. Minn., Mpls., 1969-71; teaching asst. auditing and acctg. U. Ill., Urbana, 1972-76; asst. prof. acctg. Ariz. State U., Tempe, 1977-81, assoc. prof., 1981-85, Arthur Andersen/Don Dupont prof. acctg., 1985-91. Mem. acctg. and auditing standards com. State of Ariz., Phoenix, 1989—; reviewer Jour. Acctg. and Pub. Policy, 1983—. Contbg. author: CPA Exam. Rev., 1983—; co-author: Principles of Auditing, 1988—, Auditing, 1993—; co-editor Auditing: A Jour. Practice and Theory, 1984-88; mem. editl. bd. Advances in Acctg., 1982—, Jour. Acctg. Edn., 1983—; reviewer Acctg. Rev., 1984—, ad hoc editor, 1989—; contbr. numerous articles to profl. jours. Active various child-related orgns. Peat, Marwick, Mitchell & Co. Found. grantee, 1985. Fellow AICPA (auditing stds. divsn. 1989-90, acctg. lit. selection com. 1989-90, acctg. lit. awards com. 1979-83, mem. auditing stds. bd. 1995—); mem. Am. Acctg. Assn. (tech. program com. 1980-81, chairperson Western region auditing sect. 1981-83, acctg. lit. nominating com. 1982-84, 88-89, acctg. lit. selection com. 1989-90, dir. auditing stds., chmn. auditing stds. com. 1989-90), Ariz. Soc. CPA's (auditing stds. com. 1978-81, ethics com. 1981-84). Avocation: baseball. Address: 7445 S Rita Ln Tempe AZ 85283-4792 Office: Ariz State U Sch Accountancy Tempe AZ 85287 Business E-Mail: kpany@cox.net, kurt.pany@asu.edu.

PANZARELLO, MELISSA, costume designer, educator; d. Edward Panzarello and Karen Sutton; m. Eric Koger, Sept. 26, 2002; 1 child, Kitty Koger. BA in Comm., U. Southern Ind., Evansville, 1999; MFA in Theatre, Fla. State U., Tallahassee, 2002. Asst. prof. costume design NC A&T State U., Greensboro, NC, 2003—04, Longwood U., Farmville, Va., 2006—. Costume designer (theatrical prodn.) Ears on a Beatle, I Do! I Do!, Dracula, Ubu Roi; dir.: Crimes of the Heart. Mem. Stepping Stones, Farmville, 2008—. Mem.: US Inst. Theatre Tech. Office: Longwood Univ 201 High St Farmville VA 23909 Business E-Mail: panzarelloms@longwood.edu.

PANZER, MARY CAROLINE, historian, museum curator; b. Flint, Mich., May 29, 1955; d. Milton and Caroline Alice (Weis) P. BA, Yale U.; MA, Columbia U., 1980; PhD, Boston U., 1990. Asst. prof. U. Kans., Lawrence, 1989-91; curator photographs Spencer Mus. Art, Lawrence, 1989-91; asst. dir. SMART Mus. Art U. Chgo., 1991; curator photographs Nat. Portrait Gallery Smithsonian Instn., Washington, 1992-2000; ind. historian NYC, 2000—; adj. faculty NYU, 2002—, Hunter Coll., CUNY, 2003. Author: Philadelphia Naturalistic Photography, 1982, Rudolf Eickemeyer, Jr. and the Art of the Camera, 1986, Mathew Brady and the Image of History, 1997, Halsman: A Retrospective, 1998, Brady 55, 2001, Hine 55, 2002 Separate, But Equal, 2002, Nickolas Muray and Miguel Corarrubias, 2004, Things as They Are: Photojournalism in Context Since 1955, 2005 (winner Infinity award, 2006); contbg. editor Am. Photo, 2002. Mem. Am. Studies Assn., Coll. Art Assn., Oracle, Mid-Atlantic Radical Historians Orgn., Orgn. Am. Historians.

PAO, CHIA-VEN, mathematics professor; b. Ho-hsien, China, Aug. 10, 1933; s. Chuan-S. and Shyu-Xi Pao; m. Mei-Shan K. Pao; children: Gene S., Bing S., Phillip S. BS, Nat. Taiwan U., 1959; M, Kans. State U., 1962; PhD, U. Pitts., 1968. Engr. Westinghouse Elec. Co., Pitts., 1962—67; tchg. asst. U. Pitts., 1967—68, rsch. assoc., 1968—69, asst. prof., assoc. prof., 1969—79; prof. N.C. State U., Raleigh, 1979—2002, prof. emeritus, 2002—. Pres. Cen-Condo Corp., Raleigh, 1984—89; chmn. Cen Karlay Ptnrship., Raleigh, 1986—93. Contbr. over 150 articles to profl. jours. Mem.: Fedn. Nonlinear Analysis. Avocations: music, ballroom dancing, travel, reading. Office: NC State U Dept Math Box 8205 Raleigh NC 27695 Office Phone: 919-513-2112. Business E-Mail: cvpao@math.ncsu.edu.

PAO, LINCOLN K., oncologist, educator; s. James and Sandra Pao; 1 child, Sophia. MD, Johns Hopkins, Baltimore. Diplomate Am. Bd. Radiology, 1995. Asst. prof. Cornell U., NYC, 2004—, Columbia U., NYC, 2004—. Chmn., radiation oncology NY Roentgen Soc., NYC, 2005—06; bd. advisors Am. Cancer Soc., NYC, 2004—; councilor Am. Coll. Radiology, NYC, 2007—; chmn. radiation oncology NY State Radiol. Soc., NYC, 2008—. Bd. mem., arts com. Redeemer Presbyn., NYC, 2006. Mem.: Am. Soc. Therapeutic Radiology & Oncology. Personal E-mail: radcare@yahoo.com.

PAO, YEN-CHING, engineering educator, consultant; m. Rosaline Shao-Ann Pao. BSChemE, Nat. Taiwan U., Taipei, 1956; MME, U. UT, Sal Lake City, 1959, MA in Math., 1961; PhD, Cornell U., Ithaca, NY, 1965. Sci. programer, engr. Boeing, Seattle, 1961—63; draftsman EIMCO, Salt Lake City, 1961—65; prof. engring. U. Nebr., Lincoln, 1966—. Design engr. Garrett Corp., LA, 1965—66. Author books; contbr. scientific papers to profl. jours. Recipient ATT Teaching award, U. Nebr., Award, US Dept. Energy; Rsch. grant, NIH, NSF. Fellow: Sigma Xi, Am. Soc. Mech. Engrs. Home: 1711 Buckingham Dr Lincoln NE 68506 Personal E-mail: ycp3836@msn.com.

PAOLETTA, MARK R. A., lawyer; b. 1962; BA, Duquesne U., 1984; JD, Georgetown U., 1987. Bar: DC, US Supreme Ct. Asst. counsel to the Pres. Exec. Office of the Pres., Washington, 1990-93; ptnr. O'Connor & Hannan, Washington, 1993, Keck, Mahin & Cate, Washington, Dickstein Shapiro LLP, Washington, 2007—; counsel oversight and investigations subcommittee, House Com. on Energy & Commerce, 1996—97, chief counsel, 1997—2007. Office: Dickstein Shapiro LLP 1825 Eye St NW Washington DC 20006-5403 Office Phone: 202-420-3447.

PAOLINI, GILBERTO, literature educator; b. L'Aquila, Italy; naturalized citizen, 1954; s. John and Assunta Angela P.; m. Claire Jacqueline Landro; children: Angela Janet, John Frank. BA, U. Buffalo, 1957, MA, 1959; postgrad., Middlebury Coll., summer 1960, 61; PhD, U. Minn., 1965. Lectr. Spanish Rosary Hill Coll., Buffalo, 1957-58; instr. Italian and Latin lit. U. Mass., Amherst, 1958-60; instr. Spanish and Italian Syracuse U., 1962-65, asst. prof., 1965-67; assoc. prof. Spanish lit. Tulane U., New Orleans, 1967-76, prof. comparative lit., 1976—, dir. Tulane scholars and honors program, 1981-83, chmn. colloquia dept., 1981-83. Originator Spanish Culture Week, New Orleans, 1977, 79; chmn. adv. com. Jambalaya program Nat. Endowment Humanities, New Orleans, 1975-80; Spanish essay reader Ednl. Testing Svc., Princeton, 1979-85; founder, gen. chmn. La. Conf. on Hispanic Langs. and Lits., 1981, 83, 85, 87, 89, 93, 95, 97, 99. Author: Bartolome Soler: novelista: Procedimientos estilísticos, 1963; An Aspect of Spiritualistic Naturalism in the Novel of B.P. Galdos: Charity, 1969, La Vita Transecolare nel Contado Aquilano, 2003, Complesso Monastico St. Maria Agraiano Sec. X-XXI, 2007; mem. editl. bd.: Forum Italicum, 1967-71, Critica Hispanica, 1979—, Discurso Literario, 1985—, Letras Peninsulares, 1987—, Ojáncano, 1994—; assoc. editor: South Central MLA Bull, 1978-80; editor: La Chispa: Selected Procs., 1981-99, Papers on Romance Literary Relations, 1983; cons. editor South Central Rec., 1988-99; contbr. articles to profl. jours. With AUS, 1952-54, USAF, 1954-57. Recipient Disting. Service award Sociedad Espanola, 1979, Knight Cross of Order of Isabel the Catholic, 1984; subject of Festscrift Studies in Honor of Gilberto Paolini, 1996. Mem. MLA, AAUP, Am. Assn. Tchrs. Spanish and Portuguese (chmn. pub. rels. com. 1981-86, pres. La. chpt. 1979-81, 88-89), Am. Assn. Tchrs. Italian, Am. Assn. Advancement Humanities, Soc. for Lit. and Sci., Asociacion Internacional de Hispanistas, Southeastern Am. Soc. 18th Century Studies (exec. v.p.), Assn. Internat. Galdosistas, Soc. Literatura Española del Siglo XIX, Phi Sigma Iota, Sigma Delta Pi (v.p. for S.W. 1989-92). Office: Tulane Univ 304 Newcomb Hall New Orleans LA 70118 Business E-Mail: gpaolini@tulane.edu.

PAOLINO, RAY, theater director; s. Vincenzo and Assunta Paolino; m. Patricia McCarthy, Sept. 12, 1981; children: Sean Patrick, Julia Raffaella. BFA, U. RI, Kinston, 1974; MFA, Ind. U., Bloomington, 1988. Assoc. prof. U. Okla., Norman, 1988—98; dir. theatre U. Ga., Athens, 1998—. Actor(dir.): (theatre performances) Who's Afraid of Virginia Woolf?.

PAOLUCCI, ANNE ATTURA, playwright, poet, literature educator, educational consultant; b. Rome; d. Joseph and Lucy (Guidoni) Attura; m. Henry Paolucci(dec.). BA, Barnard Coll; MA, Columbia U., PhD, 1963; D (hon.), Lehman Coll., CUNY, 1995. Mem. faculty English dept. Brearley Sch., NYC, 1957—59; asst. prof. English and comparative lit. CCNY, 1959—69; univ. rsch. prof. St. John's U., Jamaica, NY, 1969—97, acting head dept. English, 1973—74, chmn. dept. English, 1982—91, dir. doctor of arts degree program in English, 1982—97; ednl. cons.; editl. cons. Bagehot Coun. Fulbright lectr. in Am. drama U. Naples, Italy, 1965-67; spl. lectr. U. Urbino, summers 1965-67, U. Bari, 1967, univs. Bari, Bologna, Catania, Messina, Palermo, Milan, Pisa, 1965-67; disting. adj. vis. prof. Queens Coll., CUNY; bd. dir. World Centre for Shakespeare Studies, Globe project, London; spl. guest Yugoslavia Ministry of Culture, 1972; rep. U.S. at Internat. Poetry Festival, Yugoslavia, 1981; founder, exec. dir. Coun. on Nat. Lits., 1974—; mem. exec. com. Conf. Editors Learned Jour.-MLA, 1975—85; del. to Fgn. Lang. Jours., 1977—85; mem. adv. bd. Commn. on Tech. and Cultural Transformation, UNESCO, 1978—80; vis. fellow Humanities Rsch. Centre, Australian Nat. U., 1979; rep. U.S. woman playwright Inter-Am. Women Writers Congress, Ottawa, Ont., Can., 1978; organizer, chmn. profl. symposia, meetings; TV appearances; hostess Mag. in Focus, Channel 31, N.Y.C., 1971-73; mem. N.Am. Adv. Coun. Shakespeare Globe Theatre Ctr., 1981—; mem. Nat. Grad. Fellows Program Fellowship Bd., 1985—87; mem. Nat. Garibaldi Centennial Com., 1981; trustee Edn. Scholarship, Grants Com. of NIAF, 1990-94; guest spkr. with E. Albee Ohio No. State U., 1990; Apptd. by Pres. Reagan to Nat. Coun. on Humanities, 1986-1993; One of the 10 top Women in Bus. in Queens, 2003. Author (with H. Paolucci): Hegel On Tragedy, 1962, new edition, 2001, From Tension to Tonic: The Plays of Edward Albee, 1972, new edit., 2000, Pirandello's Theater: The Recovery of the Modern Stage for Dramatic Art, 1974, 2d edit. 2002, (auto biography) Escape and Return, The Search for Identity: A Cultural Journey, 2008, The Plays and Fiction of Luigi Pirandello: Selected Essays, 2009; editor: Henry Paolucci: Selected Writings on Literature and the Arts; Sci. and Astronomy; Law, Govt., and Pol. Sci., 1999, Dante's Gallery of Rogues, 2001; author: Do Me a Favor (and other short stories), 2001 (nominated for the Pulitzer Prize), Poems Written for Sbek's Mummies, Marie Menken, and Other Important Persons, Places, and Things, 1977, Eight Short Stories, 1977, Sepia Tones, 1985, 2nd edit., 1986, In Wolf's Clothing, 2004, (a mystery novel) Slow Dance to Samarra, 2007, Rev. National Literature Selected Esseys of Anne Paolucci, Henry Paolucci, 1970-2005; plays include: Minions of the Race (Medieval and Renaissance Conf. of Western Mich. U. Drama award 1972), video version, 2002, Cipango!, 1985, pub. as book, 1985, 86, videotape excerpts, 1986, revision, 1990; performed NYC and Washington, 1987-88; The Actor in Search of His Mask, 1987, Italian translation and prodn., Genoa, 1987, The Short Season, Naples, 1967, Cubiculo, NY, 1973, German translation, Vienna, 1996, mini-prodn. of Minions of the Race, The Players, 1999, video prodn. 2002, In the Green Room (play), 1999, Three Short Plays, 1995; editor Dino Bigongiari: Backgrounds to the Divine Comedys; editor with introduction: Readings in the Divine Comedy, 2006; poems Riding the Mast Where It Swings, 1980, In the Green Room (orig. play), 1999; Gorbachev in Concert, 1991, Queensboro Bridge (and other Poems), 1995 (Pulitzer prize nominee 1995-96), Terminal Degrees, 1997; contbr. numerous articles, rev. to profl. jour.; editor, author intro. to: Dante's Influence on Am. Writers, 1977; gen. editor tape-cassette series China, 1977, 78; founder Coun. on Nat. Lit.; gen. editor series Rev. Nat. Lit., 1970-2000, CNL/Quar. World Report, 1974-76, semi-ann., 1977-84, ann., 1985-2000; full-length TV tape of play Cipango! and ednl. TV with original music by Henry Paolucci, 1990, screenplay, Admiral of the Ocean Sea, Columbus, 2009; grant Queens Pub. TV for 48 Min Videotape of award-winning play, Minions of the Race, 2003, About Thomas More, Thomas Cromwell, and Cardinal Thomas Wolsey, 2003-04; featured in PBS psl. Italian-Americans II: A Beautiful Song, 1998; translations of Selected Poems by Giacomo Leopardi (with Thomas Bergin), 2004 (Italian Ministry Fgn. Affairs prize 2005), The Woman in Dante's "Divine Comedy" and Spenser's "Faerie Quene", 2005. Pres. Reagan appointee Nat. Grad. Fellows Program Fellowship Bd., 1985—86, Nat. Coun. Humanities, 1986—, Ann. award FIERI, 1990; bd. dirs. Am. Soc. Italian Legions of Merit, chmn. cultural com., 1990—; bd. dirs. Italian Heritage and Culture City-wide com., 1986—; pres. Columbus: Countdown 1992 Fedn.; mem. Gov. Cuomo's Heritage Legacy Project for Schs., 1989—; trustee CUNY, 1996—, chairwoman bd. trustees, 1997—99; mem. adv. com. on edn. N.Y. State Senate, 1996—. Decorated cavaliere Italian Republic, commendatore Order of Merit (Italy); named one of 10 Outstanding Italian Ams. in Washington, awarded medal by Amb. Rinaldo Petrignani, 1986; recipient Notable Rating for Mags. in Focus series N.Y. Times, 1972, Woman of Yr. award Dr. Herman Henry Scholarship Found., 1973, Amita award, 1970, award Women's Press Club N.Y., 1974, Gold medal for Quincentenary Can. trustee NIAF, 1990, ann. awards Consortium of Italian-Am. Assns., 1991, Am.-Italian Hist. Assn., 1991, 1st Columbus award Cath. Charities, 1991, Leone di San Marco award Italian Heritage Coun. of Bronx and Westchester Counties, 1992, Children of Columbus award Order of Sons of Italy in Am., 1993, 1st Nat. Elena Cornaro award Order of Sons of Italy, 1993, Golden Lion award, 1997, Can.'s Gold medal Christopher Columbus Can. Commn., 1992, Ann. award Am. Italian Cultural Roundtable, 1997, Am. Italian Tchrs. Lifetime Achievement award, 1997, Italian-Am. Legislator's award, Albany, 1997, N.Y. State Italian-Am. Legis. Lifetime Achievement award, 1997, Columbus Citizens Fedn. Ann. award, 1997, Italian Welfare League award, 1998, Queens Coun. on Arts award, 1998, N.Y. State Conservative Party Bronx com. award, 1998, Woman of Distinction award Kingsborough C.C./CUNY, 1999, Woman of Distinction award N.Y. State Senate, 2000, prize Italian Ministry Fgn. Affairs, 2005; named one of "Ten Top Queens Women in Bus.", 2003; Fulbright scholar U. Rome, 1951-52; Columbia U. Woodbridge hon. fellow, 1961-62; Am. Coun. Learned Socs. grantee Internat. Pirandello Congress, Agrigento, Italy, 1978; Woodbridge fellow Dept. English and Comparitive Literature, Columbia U., 1961. Mem. Internat. Shakespeare Assn., Shakespeare Assn. Am., Renaissance Soc. Am., Internat. Comparative Lit. Assn., Am. Comparative Lit. Assn., MLA, Am. PEN, Hegel Soc. Am., Dante Soc. Am. (v.p. 1976-77), Am. Found. Italian Arts and Letters (founder, pres.), Pirandello Soc. (pres. 1978-85, 1990-2001), Am. Soc. Italian Legions of Merit (bd. dir. 1990-93). Achievements include pioneering work in multi-comparative literary studies. *My own first practical premise has been to organize every task (even routine chores) so that there is always time and energy for whatever important projects come up. There is enough room in the day for doing a number of things— and for creating "space" every so often to do one's own special work (writing fiction or poetry or plays, in my case). Organization is all-important; but perhaps the basic premise in intellectual things is organic growth, letting "in" those things that are meaningful because they already suggest an intrinsic pattern. In my case, I discovered long after the projects and books themselves had taken shape and had been published, that I had been tending for a number of years more and more exclusively toward drama and dramatic criticism and theory. Well, that, obviously, was my own potential "law" organizing from within my various interests. One must continue to allow for new interests to revitalize those already familiar.*

PAOLUCCI, UMBERTO, computer software company executive; b. Ravenna, Italy; M in Elec. Engring., Bologna U., Italy, DHC (hon.) in Info. Tech. and Bus. Stats. Prof. High Tech. Sch., Italy; systems analyst Hewlett-Packard Co.; various mgmt. pos. Gen. Automation; gen. mgr. in charge of establishing and running Italian subs. Microsoft Corp., Redmond, Wash., 1985, regional dir. So. European region, corp. v.p. Europe, Middle East and Asia (EMEA) region, 1998—, sr. chmn., 2003—. Named Cavaliere del Lavoro, 2002. Mem.: Confcommercio (v.p. innovation 2004). Office: Microsoft Corp One Microsoft Way Redmond WA 98052-6399*

PAONE, PETER, artist; b. Phila., Oct. 2, 1936; s. George and Angelina (Vitrella) P.; m. Alma Alabilikian, 1976. BA, Phila. Mus. Coll. Art, 1958. Head graphics dept. Fleisher Art Meml., 1959—62; instr. Phila. Mus. Coll. Art, 1959—66, Positano Art Sch., Italy, 1961; tchr. Pa. Acad. Fine Arts, 1978—, chmn. graphics dept., 1978; instr. Pratt Inst. One-man shows include Grippi Gallery, 1959—61, Phila. Print Club, 1961—64, Ft. Worth Mus., 1963, Clydie Jessop Gallery, London, 1968, David Gallery, Houston, 1970—72, Kennedy Gallery, NYC, 1970—72, Robinson Gallery, Houston, 1978—79, Hooks Epstein Gallery, 1978, 1980—83, Pa. Acad. Fine Arts, 1983, Phila. Print Club, 1983, Hooks Epstein Gallery, 1985, 1987—88, 1990, Rider Coll., NJ, 1991, Ryder Coll., Pa., 1991, Merlin Verlag, Hamburg, Germany, 1996, Dresden, Germany, 1996, Pascal Robinson Gallery, Houston, 2000, exhibited in group shows at Poets, Phila. Mus. Art, 1960—61, Contemporary Am., 1961, Lehigh U., Pa., 1962, Bklyn. Mus., 1962, Poets, Phila. Mus. Art, 1963, Paris Biennial, 1963, Dallas Mus., 1964, Otis Art Inst., LA, 1964, Syracuse U., NY, 1964, La Escuela Nacional, Mexico City, 1967, Vanderbilt U., 1967, NY World's Fair Exhbn., Pakistan, 1967, 176 Anniv. Nat. Acad. Design, NYC, 2001, Poets, Nat. Acad. of Design Mus., 2003, Jersey City Mus., 2004, James A. Michener Mus., Doylestown, Pa., 2004, Lancaster Mus., 2006, Represented in permanent collections Libr. Congress, Washington, DC, Phila. Mus. Art, NY Mus. Modern Art, Princeton Libr., Phila. Libr., Gen. Mills, Phila. Print Club, Rosenwald Collection, Carl Sandburg Meml. Libr., Syracuse U., Ft. Worth Mus., Victoria and Albert Mus., Brit. Mus., Art Inst. Chgo., Yale U., Nat. Portrait Gallery, Washington, Okla. Mus. Art, Oklahoma City. Recipient award of merit Phila. Print Club, 1983, Painting prize Nat. Acad., 1997; Tiffany Found. grantee, 1962, 64; John Simon Guggenheim fellow, 1965-66; grantee Penn Council for the Arts, 1985, Nat. Portrait Gallery, Washington. Mem. NAD. Home: 1027 W Westview St Philadelphia PA 19119-3718 Personal E-mail: ppaone@aol.com. *Somewhere between the world of realism and surrealism, there is a world that deals with the reality of relationships, favoring the substance of the imagination rather than the substance of everyday vision. Objects that seemingly have no real relationship to each other in their existence are juxtaposed in the life of the artist. They have touched each other and have become part of the vision, and in turn have become his iconography. There is no urgency in this vision. The private reality has always been there and always will be. The viewer is allowed to question his knowledge of it, and in doing so, he often is uneasy and bewildered before the assemblage. This, at first, implies fantasy; this is not true. Instead, this is a reconstruction of reality, not an escape from it.*

PAPA, MARK GARY, oil and gas industry executive; b. Monroeville, Pa., Sept. 16, 1946; s. Mark W. Papa and Jean Feiler; m. Susan Berryman, Dec. 21, 1970; 1 child, Christine. BS in Petroleum Engring., U. Pitts., 1968; MBA in Econs./Fin., U. Houston, 1980. Registered profl. engr., Tex. Various petroleum engring., supervisory & engring. positions Conoco, Inc., various locations, 1968-81; divsn. prodn. coord. Belco Petroleum, Houston, 1981-82, mgr. ops., 1982-83; v.p. drilling and prodn. Belnorth, Houston, 1983-84, sr. v.p. drilling and prodn., 1984-85; sr. v.p. ops. Enron Oil & Gas, Houston, 1986—94, pres. N.Am. ops., 1994—98, pres., 1996—99, COO, 1997—98, CEO, 1998—99; chmn., CEO EOG Resources, 1999—. Bd. dir. Oil States Internat., Magellan Midstream Partners; chmn. U.S. Oil & Gas Assn. Mem. Soc. Petroleum Engrs., Am. Assn. Petroleum Geologists, Natural Gas Supply Assn., Tex. Ind. Prodrs. Royalty Orgn. Avocation: tennis. Office: EOG Resources 333 Clay St PO Box 4362 Houston TX 77002

PAPA, VINCENT T., insurance company executive; b. NYC, Dec. 11, 1946; s. Frank R. and Carmela (Farruggia) P.; m. Karen Ann Conroy, July 4, 1969; children: Kimberly, Jennifer, Kristen. AA, Nassau C.C., 1967; BBA, Hofstra U., 1969. CPA, N.Y. Staff acct. Arthur Andersen & Co., NYC, 1969-72; comptr. Finserv Corp., NYC, 1972-80; sr. v.p. Orion Capital Corp., NYC, 1980-99; chmn. bd. dirs. Wm. H. McGee & Co. Inc., NYC, 1995-99; CEO NYMAGIC Inc., 1999. Mem. AICPAs, Am. Mgmt. Assn. (mem. ins. and risk mgmt. coun.), N.Y. State Soc. CPAs.

PAPACHRISTOU, COSTAS JOHN, physicist, researcher; b. Athens, July 16, 1957; s. John C. and Katherine (Luckmas) Papachristou. BS in Physics, U. Athens, 1981; PhD, Brigham Young U., 1987. Postdoctoral assoc. Brigham Young U., Provo, Utah, 1987—88; faculty Ctr. Naval Edn. for Petty Officers, Athens, 1988—89; faculty dept. physics Naval Acad. Greece, Piraeus, 1989—. Course dir. Athens Inst. Tech., 1989-93, 96—. Contbr. articles to profl. jours. John E. Anderson scholar Brigham Young U., 1981-87. Mem. N.Y. Acad. Scis., Sigma Xi, Phi Kappa Phi. Avocations: music, poetry. Office: Naval Acad Greece Dept Physics 18539 Piraeus Greece Office Phone: 30-210-4581616. Business E-Mail: papachristou@snd.edu.gr.

PAPADAKIS, EMMANUEL PHILIPPOS, physicist, consultant; b. NYC, Dec. 25, 1934; s. Philippos E. and Helen (Eastman) P.; m. Stella Christopher, Sept. 4, 1960; children: Susan H., Philip E., Christopher E., Nicholas E. BS in Physics, MIT, 1956, PhD in Physics, 1962; M.M. in Mgmt, U. Mich., 1979. Mem. tech. staff Bell Telephone Labs., Allentown, Pa., 1962-69; dept. head Panametrics, Inc., Waltham, Mass., 1969-73; prin. staff engr. Ford Motor Co., Detroit, 1973-75, supr., 1975-87; ptnr. E&S Antiques, 1978—; pres. Quality Sys. Concepts Inc., 1991—; assoc. dir. Ctr. for Nondestructive Evaluation, Iowa State U., Ames, 1988-95. Adj. prof. Northeastern U. ext., Waltham, 1970-73, elec. engring. and computer engring. Iowa State U., 1988-95; cons. quality, NDT, TQM, ISO-9000, acoustics and ultrasonic testing sys., 1969-73, 88—. Contbr. numerous articles on electronics, ultrasonics, acoustics, nondestructive testing and quality to profl. jours.; tech. editor Materials Evaluation, 1988—; reviewer various jours. in physics, testing materials and sci. instrumentation; guest editor for Academic Press, 1995-2000; reviewer proposals to various govtl. agencies; patentee in field; author: Financial Justification of Nondestructive Testing- Cost of Quality in Manufacturing, 2007. Fellow: IEEE, Am. Soc. Nondestructive Testing (Mehl honor lectr. 1979, Tutorial award 1993, Mentoring award 2007, Meritorious Svc. award 2009), Acoustical Soc. Am. (Biennial award 1968); mem.: ASTM, Am. Phys. Soc., Sigma Xi. Achievements include developing method and instrument for measuring ultrasonic velocity, method for bonding thin slabs to substrates, instrument for sheet metal texture determination, method using DSSS in ultrasonic flaw detection, method to calculate effect of quality on profitability quantitatively, new economic field of nanoeconomics. Office: QSC Inc 379 Diem Woods Dr New Holland PA 17557-8800 Home Phone: 717-355-2142. Personal E-mail: epp34@comcast.net.

PAPADAKIS, PANAGIOTIS AGAMEMNON, corporate financial executive; b. Athens, Greece, Mar. 29, 1935; s. Agamemnon Ioannou and Anna Karyatis (Kyriakopoulou) P.; m. Alexandra Argyropoulou, July 12, 1959. Student, U. Athens, 1953-57. Registered rep., Del., Athens, Greece, Zurich, Switzerland, Chgo., NY, DC, 50 other countries. Pub., owner newspaper Peristeri, Athens, 1953-64; owner, gen. dir. printing house, advt. office, ins. agy., Athens, 1953-64; leader Nat. Radical Party Youth, Athens, 1958-59; founder, gen. dir. Servis Advt., Athens, 1963-78, Book-Servis, Athens, 1974-78; pres. Investments Promotions and Assocs. of Chgo., Athens, 1979-85; chmn. Internat. Investments World Co. Inc., Athens and Zurich, 1985—, Internat. Bus. Co. Inc., Internat. Comml. Co. Inc., Athens and Zurich, 1985—, Papadakis Internat. Fin. Co. Inc., Guarantor Co. Inc., Athens and Zurich, 1992—, Internat. Banker Fin. Co. Inc., Athens and Zurich, 1992—. Chmn. Internat. Pap Financing and Investment Group, Vaduz Liechtenstein and US, Konekt Financing Investment Group AG; chmn., pres. 30 companies in several countries. Author, editor: Historical Biography of President Karamanlis, 1974-77; author: Why the Revolution of 21 April 1967 Happened, 1968; author numerous articles in Recently Humanity '93, Human Rights. Mem. Democracy Party, Christian Orthodox Ch. Mem. Internat. C. of C., Assn. Bus. Leaders Inc., London Diplomatic Acad., Comml. and Indsl. Chamber Athens, Greece. Mem. New Democracy Party. Christian Orthodox. Office: Internat Invest World Co Inc PO Box 140 88 115 10 Athens Greece also: Bahnhofstrasse 52 8001 Zurich Switzerland also: 24 Pontou St Ilisia 115 28 Athens Greece Office Phone: 302107795444. Personal E-mail: papadaki@hol.gr. Business E-Mail: papgroup@otenet.gr.

PAPADAKOS, NICHOLAS PETER, retired state supreme court justice; b. Hoboken, NJ, Jan. 24, 1925; s. Petros and Olga (Christopoulou) P.; m. Roula Sakellariou, 1950; children: Peter, James, Thomas BA, Dickinson Coll., 1949; LLB, Columbus Law Sch., Washington, 1952. Bar: DC 1952, Pa. 1957, US Supreme Ct. 1975. Atty. Dept. Labor, Washington, 1950-55; office mgr. Pa. Dept. Labor, McKeesport, 1955-57; pvt. practice McKeesport, Pa., 1957-75; judge Ct. of Common Pleas, Pitts., 1976-84; justice Pa. Supreme Ct., 1984-95. Solicitor Versailles Sch. Dist., McKeesport, Pa., 1964-65, Port Vue Borough, Pa., 1969-75, City of McKeesport, 1974-75; instr. in bus. law Pa. State U.-McKeesport, 1960-75; mem. nat. panel arbitrators Am. Arbitration Assn., 1986. Trustee Hellenic Coll./Holy Cross Greek Orthodox Sch. of Theology; mem. charter rev. com. Greek Orthodox Archdiocese Am.; del. World Coun. Hellenes Abroad; Laic chmn. Greek Orthodox Diocese of Pitts.; past mem., past chmn. U.S. Selective Service Bd., McKeesport, Pa., early 1970s; bd. dirs. Mendelssohn Choir, Pitts. Sgt. A.C., U.S. Army, 1943-46; PTO Recipient Ellis Island Medal of Honor, Gold medallion Chapel Four Chaplains Dept. Pa. Mil. Order Purple Heart, 2003. Mem. Pa. State Trial Judges Conf., Greek-Am. Progressive Assn., Am. Hellenic Ednl. Progressive Assn., Tall Cedars Club, Optimists Club, Lions, Elks, Masons. Democrat.

PAPADEMOS, LUCAS, bank executive; BS in Physics, MIT, 1970, MSEE, 1972, PhD in Econs., 1977. Rsch. asst. MIT, 1973—75; lectr., econs. Columbia U., NYC, 1975—77, asst. and assoc. prof., econs., 1977—84; sr. economist Fed. Reserve Bank, Boston, 1980; prof., econs. U. Athens, Greece, 1988—; econ. counsellor Bank of Greece, Athens, 1985—93, dep. gov., 1993—94, gov., 1994—2002; v.p. European Ctrl. Bank, Frankfurt, Germany, 2002—. Vis. prof. Athens Sch. Economics & Bus., 1984—85. Contbr. articles to numerous profl. jours. Mem. Coun. Econ. Experts, Greece, 1985—88, 1991—94; mem. sci. coun. Greek Ctr. European Studies, 1988—89; mem. Bid Com the Olympic Games, Athens, 2004; chmn. adv. bd. Hellenic Obs. at the European Inst. London Sch. Econs., 1998—; mem. Padoa Schioppa Com., 1986—87, Angelopoulos Com., 1989—90, Trilateral Commn., 1998—; mem. monetary com. European Communities, 1985—88, 1990; mem. com. of alternates European Communities Ctrl. Bank Govs., 1985—93, chmn., 1989; mem. bd. dirs. Ctr. Planning and Econ. Rsch., 1987—88; chmn. monetary policy sub-com. European Communities Ctrl. Bank Govs. and Coun. the European Monetary Inst., 1992—94; mem. coun. European Monetary Inst., 1994—98; gov. Internat. Monetary Fund, Greece, 1994—2002; mem. gen. coun. European Ctrl. Bank, 1999—, mem. gov. coun., 2001—; chmn. Govs. Club, 2001—02.

PAPADIMITRIOU, DIMITRI BASIL, economist, educator, academic administrator; b. Thessaloniki, Greece, June 9, 1946; s. Basil John and Ellen (Takas) P.; m. Rania Antonopoulos. BA, Columbia U., 1970; PhD, New Sch. for Social Rsch., 1986. V.p., asst. sec. ITT Life Ins. Co. NY, NYC, 1970-73; exec. v.p., sec., treas. William Penn Life Ins. Co. NY, NYC, 1973-78, also dir.; exec. v.p., provost Bard Coll., 1978—, Jerome Levy prof. econs., 1978—; exec. dir. Bard Ctr., 1980—; pres. Levy Econs. Inst., 1988—; disting. scholar Shanghai Acad. Social Scis., 2002. Adj. lectr. econs. New Sch., 1975-76; fellow Ctr. for Advanced Econ. Studies, 1983; Wye fellow Aspen Inst.; bd. dirs. William Penn Life Ins. Co. NY; bd. govs. Levy Econs. Inst., 1986—; mem. subcoun. capital allocation Competitiveness Policy Coun., 1998-2000; mem., vice-chmn. Congrl. Commn. to Rev. the Trade Deficit, 2000-02; mem. adv. com. Women's World Banking; radio econs. commentator Sta. WAMC, NPR, PRI, Money Radio, Marketplace. Author: Employment Policy Community Development and the Underclass, 1997, Employment Policy: Theory and Practice, 1998; co-author: Community Development Banking, 1993, A Path to Community Development, 1993, An Alternative in Small Business Finance, 1994, Monetary Policy Uncovered: The Federal Reserve's Experiment with Unobservables, 1994, Targeting Inflation: The Effects of Monetary Policy on the CPI and Its Housing Component, 1996, The Fed Should Lower Interest Rates More, 1998, What to Do With the Surplus, 1998, How Can We Provide for the Baby Boomers in their Old Age?, 1999, Can Social Security Be Saved, 1999, Fiscal Policy for the Coming Recession, 2001, Is Personal Debt Sustainable?, 2002, Understanding Deflation: Treating the Disease not the Symptom, 2003, Is Deficit-Financed Growth Limited? Policies and Prospects in An Election Year, 2004, How Fragile is the US Economy?, 2005, The United States and Her Creditors: Can the Symbiosis Last?, 2005, Are Housing Prices Household Debt and Growth Sustainable?, 2006, Can the Growth in the US Current Account Deficit be Sustained?, 2006, Can Global Imbalances Continue? Policies for the US Economy, 2006, The US Economy, 2007, Cracks in the Foundations of Growth, 207, Perspectives on Aging, 2007; editor, contbr. Profits, Deficits and Instability, 1992, Aspects of Distribution of Wealth and Income, 1994, Stability in the Financial System, 1996, Modernizing Financial Systems, 2000, Employment Policies: Theories and Evidence, 2001, Induced Investment and Business Cycles, 2004, The Distributional Effects of Government Spending and Taxation, 2006, Government Expenditures to the Elderly, 2007; co-editor, contbr.: Poverty and Prosperity in the USA in the Late Twentieth Century, 1993, Financial Conditions and Macroeconomic Performance, 1992; bd. editors Challenge, Rev. of Income and Wealth; book reviewer Econ. Jour., Ea. Econ. Jour. Trustee, treas. Am. Symphony Orch. Mem. Am. Econ. Assn., Royal Econ. Soc., Am. Fin. Assn., Econ. Club NY, The Bretton Woods Com., European Econ. Assn., Eastern Econ. Assn., Econ. Sci. Chamber of Greece, Assn. for Evolutionary Econs. Home and Office: Bard Coll Annandale On Hudson NY 12504-5000

PAPADIMITRIOU, PANAYIOTIS D., electrical engineer; BSc in Physics, U. Patras, Greece, 1995, MSc in Electronics, 1997; PhD in Elec. Engring., Tex. A&M U., Coll. Sta., 2004. Sr. rsch. engr. Nokia Rsch. Ctr., Dallas, 2000—06; IPR specialist Nokia, Mountain View, Calif., 2007—. Author: (book) Code Design Based on Metric-Spectrum and Applications; contbr. articles to profl. publs. Mem.: IEEE. Achievements include patents in field.

PAPADONIKOLAKIS, ANASTASIOS, orthopedist, surgeon; s. Ioanna Pentarakis and Petros Rouggeri (Stepfather). MD, Ioannina, Greece, 1999, PhD, 2003. Diplomate NC, 2005. Resident Wake Forest Med. Ctr., Dept Orthopaedic Surgery, Winston Salem, NC, 2005—. With Greek Mil., 2003—04. Recipient Gold award, Wake Forest U., Dept. Surg. Sci., 2004; fellow, Wake Forest Med. Ctr., Dept Orthopaedic Surgery, 2004—05. Mem.: NC Med. Bd. (licentiate). Achievements include research in distal radius fractures, 3D joint kinematics (first study to prove rotational instability of the knee during walking after anterior cruciate ligament disruption-American Journal of Sports Medicine). Personal E-mail: papadonik@hotmail.com.

PAPADOPOULOS, GREGORY MICHAEL, information technology executive; b. Oakland, Calif., Apr. 30, 1958; s. Michael Nicholas and Imogen (Sherman) Papadopoulos; m. Elizabeth Ann Woellner, Nov. 26, 1982; children: Michael Gregory, Kathryn Elizabeth. BA in Systems Sci., U. Calif., San Diego, 1979; MS in Elec. Engring. and Computer Sci., MIT, Cambridge, 1983; PhD in Elec. Engring., MIT, 1988. Programmer Scripps Instn. Oceanography, La Jolla, Calif., 1977—79; devel. engr. Hewlett-Packard, Inc., San Diego, 1979—81; sr. rsch. scientist Honeywell, Inc., Mpls., 1981—84; co-founder, chief systems arch. PictureTel Corp., Danvers, Mass., 1984—86; co-founder, chief tech. officer A.I. Archs., Inc., Cambridge, 1985—88; project mgr. MIT Lab. Computer Sci., 1988—90; asst. prof. elec. engring. and computer sci. MIT, 1990—93, assoc. prof., 1993—95; sr. arch. Thinking Machines Corp., Cambridge, 1993—94; chief scientist server sys. engring. Sun Microsystems Computer Co. (now Sun Microsystems Inc.), Santa Clara, Calif., 1994—95, bd. dirs., 1994—, chief tech. officer enterprise servers and storage group, 1995—96, v.p. tech. and advanced devel., chief tech. officer, 1996—98, v.p., chief tech. officer, 1998—2000, sr. v.p., chief tech. officer, 2000—02, exec. v.p. R & D, chief tech. officer, 2002—. Rsch. fellow Charles Stark Draper Labs., Cambridge, 1981—83; dir. Ergo, Inc., 1989—90; co-founder Exa Corp.; vis. prof. elec. engring. and computer sci. MIT, 2002—03; mem. Pres.'s Bd. Sci. and Innovation U. Calif.; tech. advisor BP Alien Techs. Contbr. articles to profl. jours. Mem. Meml. chpt. Am. Field Svc., Houston, 1975—76; bd. trustees Anita Borg. Inst. Women and Tech. Recipient Spl. Distinction award, Forensic League, 1976, Presdl. Young Investigators award, NSF; U. Calif. Regents scholar, 1978. Mem.: AAAS, Search Extraterrestrial Intelligence (chmn. bd.), Sigma Xi, Phi Beta Kappa. Republican. Avocations: bicycling, soccer, diving. Office: Sun Microsystems 4150 Network Cir Santa Clara CA 95054 Office Phone: 650-960-1300. Office Fax: 408-276-3804.

PAPADOPOULOS, PETER JOSEPH, theater educator, playwright; b. Cin., Mar. 28, 1969; s. Peter Antis Papadopoulos and Josephine Ann Marchetti. BA, Trinity Coll., Hartford, Conn., 1991; MFA, RI Coll. Trinity Repertory, Providence, 1999. Cert. Nat. Theater Inst., Waterford, Conn., 1990. Author: (stage play) Lost Love, In the Cool Cool Cool (Finalist, Actors Theatre Louisville Heideman award, 2006), last love (co-winner, Algonquin Prodns. Project Footlight, 2006). Recipient Frank Whitlock Playwriting award, Trinity Coll., 1989, 1990. Mem.: Actors' Equity Assn., Dramatists Guild, Phi Beta Kappa. Office: Ind State Univ Theater Dept 540 N 7th St Terre Haute IN 47809 Personal E-mail: peter@peterpop.com. Business E-Mail: ppapadopoul@indstate.edu.

PAPAGEORGIOU, CHRIS, economist; b. Nicosia, Cyprus, June 8, 1968; s. Evripides and Helen Papageorgiou; m. Keiko Antoku; children: Celine, Sofia. PhD, U. Pitts., 1997. Prof. La. State U., Baton Rouge; economist Internat. Monetary Fund, Washington, 2006—. Editor: Jour. Macroeconomics. Office: Internat Monetary Fund 700 19th St NW Washington DC 20015 Office Fax: 202-589-7503. Business E-Mail: cpapageorgiou@imf.org.

PAPAGEORGIOU, JOHN CONSTANTINE, management science educator; b. Kallithea, Greece, Nov. 22, 1935; came to U.S., 1969, naturalized, 1975; m. Thalia Christidou, 1969; children: Constantine, Elena, Demetrios, Antigone. B.Sc., Athens Sch. Econs. Bus. Scis., Greece, 1957; diploma tech. sci., U. Manchester, Eng., 1963, PhD in Mgmt. Scis, 1965. Lectr. Athens Sch. Econs. and Bus. Scis.; also postgrad. Inst. Bus. Adminstrn., Athens, 1966-68; asst. prof. Faculty Adminstrv. Studies, York U., Toronto, Ont., Can., 1968-69; asst. prof. mgmt. Wayne State U., 1969-71; assoc. prof. mgmt. scis. St. Louis U., 1971-72; vis. prof. ops. rsch. Athens Sch. Econs. and Bus. Scis., 1972-73; assoc. prof. ops. analysis U. Toledo, 1974-76; assoc. prof. mgmt. sci. and coord. Coll. Profl. Studies, U. Mass., Boston, 1976-78, prof., coord., 1978-80; prof. mgmt. scis. dept. Coll. Mgmt. U. Mass., 1980—2002, chmn. mgmt. scis. dept., 1980-85; assoc. dean Coll. Mgmt. U. Mass., 1995. Head dept. econ. research Agrl. Bank Greece, 1966-67; ops. analyst Esso-Pappas Indsl. Co., Greece, 1967-68; spl. adv. Center Planning and Econ. Research, Greece, 1972-73; cons. in field; condr. seminars. Author: Introduction to Operations Research (in Greek), 1973, Fundamentals of Operations Research, 1973, Management Science and Environmental Problems, 1980; co-author: Data on the Greek Economy, 1966; assoc. editor technos: Ops. Mgmt. Newsletter; spl. issues editor: Interfaces; guest editor: Internat. Jour. Tech. Mgmt.; mem. editorial bd. Jour. Managerial Issues, Southwestern Bus. Rev.; editor: TIMS COLIME Newsletter; contbr. articles to profl. jours. 2d lt. Greek Army, 1958—60. Greek Govt. scholar, 1962-65; NATO postdoctoral fellow, 1965; Air Force Office Sci. Research fellow, summer 1980. Fellow AAAS; mem. INFORMS (1985 nat. meeting program com., 1994 joint nat. meeting program chmn., chmn. nat. meeting com. 1985, faculty-in-residence com., coll. officer, chpt. officer, activities com.), Am. Inst. Decision Scis. (nat. innovative edn. com. 1981, programs and meetings com. 1983, Fulbright Sr. Specialist, 2001-07). Address: 14 Putney Rd Wellesley MA 02481-5315 Business E-Mail: john.papageorgiou@umb.edu. *Our achievements are a function of our goals. I usually set ambitious but achievable goals and I try to achieve them through hard work, and persistence. I believe that there is always room for improvement in the status-quo and that a continuous search for improvements is the major factor for continuous progress.*

PAPAKONSTANTINO, STACY, language educator; b. San Francisco, Feb. 27, 1967; d. Demetrios and Eugenia (Yiallely) P. AA, City. Coll. of San Francisco, 1987; BA in English Lit., San Francisco State U., 1989, MA in English Lang. Studies, 1991. Cert. in tchg. composition and postsecondary reading. English, ESL tutor City Coll. of San Francisco, 1986-87, instr. of English, 1991—; Greek instr. Holy Trinity Sch., 1988-90; program dir. Inst. Reading Devel., Novato, Calif., 2004; supr. Barnes and Noble Booksellers, Colma, Calif., 2004—; SAT scorer Pearson, Iowa, 2006—. Chair student grade and file rev. com., City Coll. of San Francisco, 1996-98, resource mem. student success com., 1997-98, mem. student complaint com., 1997-98, mem.

composition/lit./reading com., 1996-98. Mem. Nat. Coun. Tchrs. of English. Democrat. Orthodox. Avocations: reading, movies and plays, helping needy people, spiritual worship, exercise. Home: 48 Westpark Dr Daly City CA 94015-1055 Office: Barnes & Noble Booksellers 280 Metro Mall Colma CA 94014 Personal E-mail: spapak@hotmail.com.

PAPALIA, DIANE ELLEN, humanities educator; b. Englewood, NJ, Apr. 26, 1947; d. Edward Peter and Madeline (Borrin) P.; 1 child, Anna Victoria Finlay. AB, Vassar Coll., 1968; MS, W.Va. U., 1970, PhD, 1971. Asst. prof. child and family studies U. Wis., Madison, 1971-75, assoc. prof., 1975-78, prof., 1978-87, coord. child and family studies, 1977-79. Adj. prof. psychology in pediatrics U. Pa. Sch. Medicine, 1987-89. Author (with Sally W. Olds and Ruth D. Feldman): A Child's World: Infancy Through Adolescence, 1975, 11th edit., 2008, Human Development, 1978, 10th edit., 2007; author: (with Harvey Sterns, Cameron J. Camp & Ruth D. Feldman) Adult Development and Aging, 1996, 3rd edit., 2007; author: (with Dana Gross and Ruth D. Feldman) Child Development: A Topical Approach, 2003; co-author: Psychology, 1985, 2d edit., 1988; contbr. articles to profl. jours. NSF fellow, 1971, Am. Coun. on Edn. fellow, 1979-80; U. Wis. grantee. Fellow: Gerontol. Soc.; mem.: APA, Nat. Coun. Family Rels., Soc. Rsch. in Child Devel., Am. Psychol. Soc., Author's Guild, Psi Chi. Home: Apt 6D 253 W 73d St New York NY 10023 Office Phone: 212-724-4244. Personal E-mail: depapalia@aol.com.

PAPANEK, GUSTAV FRITZ, economist, educator; b. Vienna, July 12, 1926; s. Ernst and Helen Papanek; m. Hanna Kaiser, June 13, 1947; children: Thomas H., Joanne R. Papanek Orlando. BA in Agrl. Econs, Cornell U., 1947; MA in Econs, Harvard U., 1949, PhD, 1951. Economist, dep. dir. program planning for Asia, tech. coop. adminstrn. Dept. State, 1951-53; from econ. adv. to dir. adv. group to planning commn. Harvard U., Pakistan, 1954-58, from dep. dir. to dir. devel. adv. svc. Cambridge, Mass., 1958—70, dir. adv. group to planning commn. Indonesia, 1970—73; prof. econs. Boston U., 1974-92, prof. emeritus, 1992—, chmn. dept., 1974-83, interim dir., 1977-80, dir. Ctr. Asian Devel. Studies, 1983-90, dir. Asian program, 1991-92; pres. Boston Inst. Developing Econs., Ltd. (BIDE), 1987—; dir., cons. team devel. studies to planning commn. Govt. of Indonesia, 1987—89; dir. policy adv. team to Federated States of Micronesia, 1995—2002. Cons. Govt. of Indonesia, 1998—2007, Govt. of Liberia, 2006—07; co-dir. pro-poor growth study U.S. AID, 2002—03; cons. in field. Author: (book) Pakistan's Development: Social Goals and Private Incentives, 1967, The Indonesian Economy, 1980, Development Strategy, Growth Equity and the Political Process in Southern Asia, 1986; co-author: Decision Making for Economic Development, 1971, The Indian Economy, 1988, others; contbr. articles to profl. jours. With US Army, 1944—46. Grantee, Ford Found., AID, World Bank, UN Devel. Program, UN Univ., HEW, Asian Devel. Bank. Mem.: Pakistan Econ. Assn., Assn. Asian Studies (pres. New Eng. conf. 1975—77), Assn. Comparative Econ. Studies (pres. 1982), Soc. Internat. Devel. (past mem. exec. com.), Am. Agrl. Econs. Assn., Am. Econs. Assn. Home and Office: 2 Mason St Lexington MA 02421-6315 Home Phone: 781-862-4549; Office Phone: 781-862-7776. E-mail: papanek@bide.com.

PAPANICOLAOU, ANDREW C., neuroscientist, educator; b. Sikyon, Greece, July 8, 1950; U.S. s. Constantinos A. and Photeini C. Papanicolaou; m. Nora Kapouralis, Nov. 21, 1950; children: Constantinos, Anastasia. Student, U. Athens, 1968—70; BS, Xavier U., 1972, MA, 1974; PhD, So. Ill. U., 1978. Asst. prof. U. Tex., Galveston, 1980—86, assoc. prof., 1986—90, prof. neurosurgery, 1990—93; prof., dir. divsn. clin. neurosci. U. Tex., Houston Med. Sch., 1993—. Dir. Vivian L. Smith advanced studies Inst. Internat. Neuropsychol. Soc., Houston, Xylocastro, Greece. Author: Emotion: A Reconsideration of the Somatic Theory, 1989; editor: Bergson and Modern Thought: Towards A Unified Science, 1987; author: Fundamentals of Functional Brain Imaging, 1998, Plato: 4 Critique of Pragmatism (in Greek), 2002; co-author: The Amnesias: A Clinical Textbook of Memory Disorders, 2006. Grantee, NIH, 1999—, 2000—, NSF, 2001—. Mem.: APA, AAAS, Soc. Psychophysiological Rsch., NY Acad. Sciences, Internat. Neuropsychological Soc., Hellenic Psychological Assn., Am. Soc. Neurophysiological Monitoring. Office: Univ Tex Houston Med Sch 1333 Moursund Ste H114 Houston TX 77030*

PAPANTONI KAZAKOS, TITSA, engineering educator; b. Piraeus, Greece, Mar. 28, 1945; d. Athanasios Papantonis and Eleni Papantoni; 1 child, Effie Kazakos. BS, Nat. Tech. U. Athens, Greece, 1968; MS, Princeton U., NJ, 1970; PhD, U. Southern Calif., LA, 1973. Lic. profl., Greece, 1968, Tex., Calif., 1973. Prof. U. Ala., Tuscaloosa, 1995—2000, U. Colo. Denver, 2000—. Asst. prof. Rice U., Huston, 1973—77; mem., tech. staff Bell Labs., Holmdel, NJ, 1977—78; prof. U. Conn., Storrs, 1978—86, U. Va., Charlottesville, 1986—93, U. Ottawa, Canada, 1993—94. Author: (book) Detection and Estimation; contbr. scientific papers. Advisor, devel. of minority sch. Fishing Sch., Washington, 1997—99. Fellow: IEEE. Achievements include development of algorithm deployed by AT&T for ISDN. Office: Univ Colo Denver PO Box 173364 Denver CO 80217

PAPANTONIO, MIKE (JAMES MICHAEL PAPANTONIO), lawyer, talk radio host; b. Oct. 24, 1953; married; 1 child. Grad., U. Fla.; JD, Samford U. Cumberland Sch. Law, Birmingham, Ala. Bar: Fla. 1982, US Dist. Ct. (mid. dist.), Fla. 1983. Sr. ptnr. Levin, Papantonio, Thomas, Mitchell, Echsner & Proctor, P.A., Pensacola, Fla., 1983—; co-host weekly radio program Ring of Fire, Air America Radio, 2004—. Founder legal edn. orgn. Mass Torts Made Perfect, Pensacola, 1983. Author: In Search of Atticus Finch, A Motivational Book for Lawyers, 1996, Clarence Darrow, the Journeyman: Lessons for the Modern Lawyer, 1997, Resurrecting Aesop: Fables Lawyers Should Remember, 2000; contbr. articles to profl jours. Co-founder Emerald Coastkeepers, Inc., 1998. Fellow: Internat. Acad. Trial Lawyers, Internat. Soc. Barristers; mem.: Acad. Fla. Trial Lawyers, Southern Trial Lawyers Assn., Am. Trial Lawyers Assn., Am. Bd. Trial Advocates. Office: Levin, Papantonio, Thomas, Mitchell, Echsner & Proctor 316 South Baylen St Ste 600 Pensacola FL 32502 Office Phone: 850-435-7001. Office Fax: 850-435-7020.*

PAPAPOLYMEROU, JOHN, engineering educator; b. Athens, Greece; married. PhD, U. Mich., 1999. Asst. prof., dept. elect., comm. engr. U. Ariz., Tucson, 1999—2001; asst. prof. Ga. Tech., Sch. of Elect. Comm. Engring., Atlanta, 2001—. Recipient Best Paper award, 3rd Internat. Conf. Microwave Millimeter-Wave Tech., 2002, Career award, NSF, 2002. Mem.: IEEE, Am. Soc. Engring. Edn. Office: Ga Tech Sch Elect Comm Engring 777 Atlantic Dr Atlanta GA 30332-0250 E-mail: papapol@ece.gatech.edu.

PAPARELLA, LEON RALPH, psychotherapist, consultant; b. Providence, Dec. 31, 1944; s. Ralph A. and Eleanor Paparella; m. Jacqueline Z. Anderson, Sept. 19, 1987 (div. Aug. 5, 1993). BA, RI Coll., Providence, 1967; MSW, Howard U., Washington, 1969; cert. in group psychotherapy, Washington Sch. Psychiatry, 1972. Lic. psychotherapist Md., Washington, Va. Social worker Cmty. Mental Health Ctr., Washington, 1969—72; psychotherapist Inst. Marriage and Family Rels., Annandale, 1972—74, Va. Cmty. Mental Health Ctr., Fairfax, 1974—78, Treatment Ctr. Washington Sch. Psychiatry, 1977—90; pvt. practice Washington, 1973—. Mem. faculty Washington Sch. Psychiatry, 1974—; cons. Walter Reed Army Hosp., 1984—; support group specialist Parkinson Found. Nat. Capital Area, Washington, 1999—; dean Nat. Group Psychotherapy Inst., 2004—06; presenter in field. Recipient appreciation, Washingotn Sch. Psychiatry, 1994, Social Work commendation, Walter Reed Army Hosp., 1997; named Social Work Mentor of the Yr., 2002. Mem.: NASW, Mid-Atlantic Group Psychotherapy Assn., Nat. Registry Certified Group Psychotherapists, Am. Group Psychotherapy Assn. Avocations: singing, sports. Personal E-mail: leonpaparella@comast.net.

PAPAS, IRENE KALANDROS, English language educator, poet, writer; AA with highest honors, Balt. C.C.; BA magna cum laude, Goucher Coll., 1968; MA in English Lang. and Lit., U. Md., 1974, postgrad., 1980—. Lic. theology profl. Tchr./tutor various schs., Balt., 1965—; tchr. theology U. Md. Free Univ., College Park, 1979—; author/pub. Ledger Publs., Silver Spring, Md., 1982—; TV producer Arts and Humanities Prodns., Silver Spring, 1991—. Lectr. in English, philosophy, Montgomery Coll., Goucher Coll.; instr. English Composition, World Literature, U. Md., College Park, 1968—; adj. faculty various colls.; White House duty, 1997—. Author: Irene's Ledger Songs of Deliverance, 1982, Irene's Ledger Song at Sabbatyon, 1986, Small Meditations, Leaves for Healing, 1996; prodr./dir. tv. progs. Election judge, Montgomery County (Md.) Suprs. Bd. of Elections, 90's; tutor in literacy, 1989, 90. Recipient First Prize Arts and Culture Category Smithsonian Inst., 1991; honored 6th Annual Awards Ceremony Montgomery Community, 1991. Mem. AAUP, Internat. Platform Assn., Nat. Poetry Assn., Phi Beta Kappa. Democrat. Greek Orthodox. Avocations: art/iconography, calligraphy, music, needlepoint. Office: PO Box 10303 Silver Spring MD 20914-0303

PAPATHANASIOU, THANASIS D., chemical engineer, educator; b. Larissa, Greece, Aug. 6, 1961; came to U.S., 1997; s. Dimitrios and Lina (Themeli) P. BSc in Engring., Nat. Tech. Athens, Greece, 1985; MSc, U. Calgary, Can., 1987; PhD, McGill U., Montreal, 1991. Postdoctoral fellow Los Alamos Nat. Lab., 1991-92; lectr. Imperial Coll., London, 1992-97; assoc. prof. U. S.C., Columbia, S.C., 1997—. Editor: Flow-Induced alignment in Composites, 1997. Grantee Dept. of Energy, 1998, Dept. of Def., 1999. Mem. ASME, AIChE, Soc. Rheology, Am. Soc. Chem. Engrs. Office: U SC Dept Chem Engring Columbia SC 29208-0001 E-mail: papathan@engr.sc.edu.

PAPATHOMAS, GEORGIA NIKOLAKOPOULOU, technology executive; b. Kato Achaia, Greece, Sept. 11, 1950; d. Andreas and Corina (Fotopoulou) Nikolakopoulos; m. Thomas Vergil Papathomas, Aug. 15, 1976; children: Lia Natassa, Alexander Vergil. BS in Engring. Sci., Columbia U., 1973, MS in Engring. Sci., 1974, PhD in Engring. Sci., 1978; cert. in bus. devel., U. Pa., 1994; cert. in strategic mktg., Harvard U., 1995. Mem. tech. staff Bell Labs., Murray Hill, NJ, 1978-84, supr. Whippany, NJ, 1984-90, program mgr., 1990-93; dir. strategy AT&T, Morristown, NJ, 1993-96, dir. ops. Bedminster, NJ, 1996—2002; v.p. network solutions Lucent Tech., 1998—2002; v.p. info. tech. Pfizer, 2003—. Sloan Found. rsch. fellow, N.Y.C., 1974. Mem. ASCE, Soc. Women Engrs., Sigma Xi. Business E-Mail: georgia.papathomas@pfizer.com.

PAPAY, LAURI LOUISE, mathematics professor; d. Wilbert DiAgostino and Dorothy Maguire; 1 child, Sean. MS in Math., San Jose State U., Calif., 1996. Lectr. Santa Clara U., Calif., 1999—. Mem.: MAA. Democrat. Office: Santa Clara Univ El Camino Real Santa Clara CA 95053 Business E-Mail: lpapay@scu.edu.

PAPAY, LAWRENCE T., management consultant, retired engineer; b. Weehawken, NJ, Oct. 3, 1936; s. Joseph Adam and Elizabeth Ethel (Corse) P.; m. Carol Diana Hornby, Dec. 31, 1960; children: Lisa, Gregory, Diane. BS, Fordham U., 1958; MS, MIT, 1965, DSc, 1969. Registered profl. engr., Calif. Sr. shift supr. MIT, Cambridge, 1965-68; rsch. fellow Euraton Rsch. Ctr., Ispra, Italy, 1968-70; dir. rsch. So. Calif. Edison, Rosemead, 1970-78, gen. supt., 1978-79, v.p., 1980-83, sr. v.p., 1983-92; sector v.p. for integrated solutions SAIC; CEO, prin. PQR, LLC. Pres., bd. dirs. So. States Realty, Rosemead, 1981—. Mem. energy rsch. adv. bd. U.S. Dept. Energy, 1984-90; chmn. Planning Commn., City of Arcadia, Calif., 1986—; bd. dirs. San Gabriel Valley Coun. Boy Scouts Am., Pasadena, Calif., 1985—, San Gabriel Region United Way, Arcadia, 1988—. Lt. USN, 1959-63. NATO postdoctoral fellow U.S. Govt., 1968; Euraton fellow European Econ. Community, 1969; recipient Extraordinary Pub. Service award, U.S. Dept. Energy, 1988. Mem. NAE(councillor 2004-), Am. Nuclear Soc.; fellow World Tech. Network. Republican. Roman Catholic. Avocations: skiing, bicycling, tennis.

PAPAZIAN, DENNIS RICHARD, retired historian, educator, commentator; b. Augusta, Ga., Dec. 15, 1931; s. Nahabed Charles and Armanouhe Marie (Pehlevanian) P.; m. Mary Arshagouni. BA, Wayne State U., 1954; MA, U. Mich., 1958; NDG, Moscow State U., 1962; PhD, U. Mich., 1966. Head dept. social and behavioral scis. U. Mich., Dearborn, 1966-69, head div. lit., sci. and the arts, 1969-73, assoc. dean acad. affairs, 1973-74, dir. grad. studies, 1979-85, prof. history, dir. Armenian Rsch. Ctr., 1985—2006, prof., dir. emeritus, 2006—; dir. Armenian Assembly Am., Washington, 1975-79. Fellow Ctr. for Russian and East-European Studies, U. Mich., Ann Arbor, 1982-92; chmn. bd. dirs. Mich. Ethnic Heritage Studies Ctr., U. Mich., 1987-92. Author: St. John's Armenian Church, 1974; editor: The Armenian Church, 1983, Out of Turkey, 1994; editor Jour. of Soc. Armenian Studies, 1994—. Bd. dirs. Armenian Apostolic Soc., Southfield, Mich., 1968-78; chmn. bd. dirs. Alex Manoogian Found., Taylor, Mich., 1969-77; mem. evaluation team Ind. Schs. Assn. Ctrl. States, Chgo., 1985; polit. commentator WXYZ-TV, ABC, Detroit, Southfield, 1984—, WWJ-Radio, Detroit, 1984—; bd. dirs. Southeastern Mich. chpt. ARC, 1988-98, chmn. internat. svcs. com., 1988-98, disaster and mil. family svcs. com., 1988-98; mem. NJ Commn. on Holocaust Edn., 2005—. Scholar/diplomat U.S. Dept. State, Washington, 1976; grantee NEH, Washington, 1977, AID, Washington, 1978. Mem. AAUP (chpt. pres. 1962-65), Nat. Assn. Armenian Studies and Rsch. (bd. dirs. 1961-91), Nat. Ethnic Studies Assn. (bd. dirs. 1976-85), Am. Hist. Assn., Soc. Armenian Studies (pres. exec. com. 1988-91, 97—, sec./treas. exec. com. 1991-97), Am. Assn. Advancement of Slavic Studies, Am. Acad. Polit. Sci., Armenian Students Assn. (Arthur S. Dadian Armenian Heritage award 1993), Knights of Vartan (mid-atlantic interlodge chmn., 2007-08). Armenian Orthodox. Avocations: reading, travel. Home: 9 Blueberry Dr Woodcliff Lake NJ 07677 Office: U Mich 4901 Evergreen Rd Dearborn MI 48128-1491 Office Phone: 313-593-5181. Business E-Mail: papazian@umich.edu.

PAPE, GLENN MICHAEL, lawyer, retired financial planner; b. Aug. 20, 1954; s. Gilbert Thomas and Janine Elizabeth (Beheyt) P.; m. Nancy Ann Vaske, Apr. 7, 1979 (div. 2006); children: Katherine Jo, Courtney Johanna. BA in Classics, U. Chgo., 1978, MBA, 1981; JD, DePaul U., 1979. Cert. fin. planner, Ill., 1979, CPA Ill., 1979, Calif., 2005; CLU Ill., 1979; bar: Ill. 1979; cert. investment mgmt. analyst Investment Mgmt. Cons. Assn., 1998. Cons. tax divsn. No. Trust Co., Chgo., 1980-81, fin. planner, 1981-82; fin. counselor Continental Ill. Nat. Bank, Chgo., 1982—84; tax mgr. Arthur Andersen & Co., Chgo., 1984-88; v.p., ptnr. Fin. Related Svcs., Ayco Co., L.P., Albany, NY, 1988-96; ptnr., nat. svc. leader broad market fin. planning svcs. Ernst & Young, Chgo., 1996—2005, west zone fin. svcs. leader San Francisco, 2003—06. Developer Money in Motion Fin. Edn. System; mem. bd. govs. Cert. Fin. Planning Standards, 2000-05; chair bd. of stds. Cert. Fin. Planning, 2005. Active Five Hosp. Homebound Elderly Program, Chgo., 1981; treas. Chamber Music Coun., Chgo., 1982. Mem. AICPA (accredited pers. fin. specialist), Nat. Spkrs. Assn. (cert.) Home and Office: 207 Mendocino Way Redwood City CA 94065 Office Phone: 408-390-6814. Personal E-mail: glenn_pape@hotmail.com.

PAPE, STUART M., lawyer; b. Paterson, NJ, Dec. 24, 1948; BA, U. Va., 1970, JD, 1973. Bar: Va. 1973, DC 1980, US Ct. Appeals (6th cir.) 1975, US Supreme Ct. 1976. Law clk. to Hon. Leonard Braman Superior Ct. DC, 1973-74; exec. asst. to commr. FDA, 1979; mng. ptnr., Food & Drug Law, Legis. Affairs practices, mem. exec. com. & mgmt. com. Patton Boggs LLP, Washington. Contbr. articles to profl. jours. Mem. ABA (com. food and drug law, sect. adminstrv. law 1973-2006), Va. State Bar, DC Bar. Office: Patton Boggs LLP 2550 M St NW Washington DC 20037-1350 Office Phone: 202-457-5240. Office Fax: 202-457-6315. Business E-Mail: spape@pattonboggs.com.

PAPE, WILLIAM JAMES, II, newspaper publisher; b. Waterbury, Conn., Aug. 14, 1931; s. William B. and Helen (Cronan) P.; m. Patricia Moran, Oct. 15, 1959; children: William B. II, Andrew J. BS, U.S. Naval Acad., 1953; MBA, Harvard U., 1959; LHD (hon.), Teikyo Post U., 1991. Commd. ensign USN, 1953, advanced through grades to lt., 1955, resigned, 1957; asst. treas. Ea. Color Printing Co., Waterbury, 1959-63, pres., treas. Avon, Conn., 1977-87; v.p., asst. treas. Am.-Republican Inc., Waterbury, 1963-64, asst. publisher, comptroller, v.p., treas., 1964-72, pres., 1972—, treas., 1972-98; pub. Republican-Am., 1972—, editor, 1988—; also bd. dirs.; v.p., asst. treas. & dir. Paper Delivery, Inc., 1972—. Bd. dirs. Platt Bros., 1977-2009. Bd. dirs. Conn. Coun. Freedom of Info., 1968-88, Conn. Bus. and Industry Assn., 1980-83, Naugatuck Valley Devel. Corp., Regional Action Coun., Waterbury, 1991; bd. dirs. Conn. Citizens for Jud. Modernization, pres., 1973-75; bd. dirs. Waterbury YMCA, 1970-78, trustee, 1972-2001, chmn. trustees, 1976-85; trustee Northeast Utilities, 1974-2001, Greater Waterbury Health Network Inc., 1993-95; mem. Conn. Pub. Expenditure Coun. Inc., 1974-77, dir. Conn. policy and econ. coun., 1994-2000; trustee Teikyo Post U., 1976-96; grants com. Waterbury Found., 1980-87; pub. affairs com. Waterbury Hosp., 1984-90, past trustee; incorporator Conn. Found. for Open Govt. Inc.; active Conn. Legislature Commn. to Study Modernization and Unification of Cts., 1973-75, Citizens for Better Govt. Through Reorganization, 1977. Mem. Am. Judicature Soc. (assoc. dir. 1975-76), New England Newspaper Assn. (Conn. bd. govs. 1983-87), Conn. Bar Assn. (task force conflict of interest 1979), Conn. Daily Newspaper Assn. (pres. 1970, exec. com. 1971-91), Waterbury C. of C. (exec. com., v.p. 1975, chmn. 1977-79, dir. 1964-2001, vice-chmn. transp. 1981-2001), Navy League U.S. (comms. bd. 1982), Waterbury Club, Madison Beach Club, Highfield, Liverpool Nautical Rsch. Soc., Am. Legion, Vet. Foreign Wars. Republican. Roman Catholic. Avocations: sailing, firearms, walking, carpentry. Home: Old Sherman Hill Rd Woodbury CT 06798 Office: Republic Amer PO Box 2090 389 Meadow St Waterbury CT 06722-2090 E-mail: wjpape@rep-am.com.

PAPELBON, JON(ATHAN) (ROBERT), professional baseball player; b. Baton Rouge, Nov. 23, 1980; s. John and Sheila Papelbon; m. Ashley Jeffries. Student, Miss. State U. Pitcher Boston Red Sox, 2005—. Spokesman Hood Red Sox Kids Nation, 2007. Recipient Closer of Yr. award, MLB.com, 2007, Delivery Man of Yr. award, Maj. League Baseball, 2007; named to Am. League All-Star Team, 2006—09. Achievements include holding record for most Saves thrown by a rookie pitcher in his first month, 2006. Mailing: c/o Boston Red Sox Fenway Pk 4 Yawkey Way Boston MA 02215-3496*

PAPER, LEWIS J., lawyer, educator; b. Newark, Oct. 13, 1946; s. Sidney and Dorothy (Nieman) P.; m. Jan Clachko, Sept. 4, 1972; children: Lindsay, Brett. BA, U. Mich., 1968; LLM, Harvard U., 1971; JD, Georgetown U., 1972. Bar: D.C. 1971, Md. 1984. Fellow Inst. Pub. Interest Representation Georgetown U. Law Sch., Washington, 1971-72; staff atty. Citizens Comms. Ctr., 1972—73; legis. counsel to Sen. Gaylord Nelson U.S. Senate, 1973—75; assoc. atty. Lowenstein, Sandler, Brochin, Kohl & Fisher, Newark, 1975—78; asst. gen. counsel FCC, Washington, 1978—79, assoc. gen. counsel, 1979—81; ptnr. Grove Engelberg & Gross, 1981—86, Keck, Mahin & Cate, 1986—95, Dickstein, Shapiro, LLP (formerly Dickstein, Shapiro, Morin & Oshinsky LLP), 1995—. Adj. prof. law Georgetown U. Law Sch., Washington, 1983-86. Author: John F. Kennedy: The Promise and the Performance, 1975, 79, Brandeis: An Intimate Biography, 1983, Empire: William S. Paley and the Making of CBS, 1987, Deadly Risks, 2008, Perfect: Don Larsen's Miraculous World Series Game and the Men Who Made It Happen, 2009; contbr. articles to newspapers, mags., and profl. jours. Office: Disckstein Shapiro LLP 1825 Eye St NW Washington DC 20006 Office Phone: 202-420-2265. Business E-Mail: paperl@dicksteinshapiro.com.

PAPERMASTER, MARK D., computer company executive; b. 1961; m. Kathy Papermaster. BS in Elec. Engring., U. Tex.; MS in Elec. Engring., U. Vt., 1988. With IBM Corp., 1983—2008, v.p. microprocessor & systems tech. devel., v.p. blade devel. unit; sr. v.p. devices hardware engring. Apple Inc., Cupertino, Calif., 2008—. Office: Apple Inc Hdqs 1 Infinite Loop Cupertino CA 95014 Office Phone: 408-996-1010. Office Fax: 408-974-2113.*

PAPERNIK, JOEL IRA, lawyer; b. NYC, May 4, 1944; s. Herman and Ida (Titefsky) Papernik; m. Barbara Ann Barker, July 28, 1972; children: Deborah, Ilana. BA, Yale U., New Haven, Conn., 1965; JD cum laude, Columbia U., NYC, 1968. Bar: NY 1969. Assoc. Shea & Gould, NYC, 1968—76, ptnr., 1976—91; ptnr., chmn. corp. and securities dept., mem. mgmt. com. Squadron, Ellenoff, Plesent & Sheinfeld, NYC, 1991—2000; ptnr., mem. opinion and policy com. Mintz, Levin, Cohn, Ferris, Glovsky and Popeo P.C., NYC, 2000—. Lectr. various panels. With 11th Spl. Forces USAR, 1967—73. Mem.: ABA (sect. corp. law), Negotiated Acquisitions Com., Tri-Bar Opinion Com., Assn. Bar City NY (securities regulation com. 1992—95, chmn., lectr., corp. law com.), NY State Bar Assn. (lectr. various panels, securities law com.), NY Biotech. Assn. (bd. dirs. 2005—), Yale Club. Office: Mintz Levin Cohn Ferris Glovsky and Popeo PC 666 3rd Ave New York NY 10017-4011 Office Phone: 212-692-6774. Business E-Mail: jpapernik@mintz.com.

PAPIC, MILORAD, electrical engineer, researcher; b. Priboj, Serbia-Monteneg, Yugoslavia, Mar. 21, 1948; s. Mika and Ilinka Papic; m. Gordana Mirkovic, Nov. 9, 1974; children: Vladimir, Nikola. BSc, U. Sarajevo, Bosnia & Herzegovina, 1972, DSc, 1980; MSc, U. Zagreb, 1977. Cert. engr., Idaho, 1997, Bosnia & Herzegovina, 1977. Tchg. asst. U. Sarajevo, 1972—76, lectr., 1976—80, rschr., 1980—84, asst. prof., 1984—88, assoc. prof., 1988—94; owner, cons. Energy Tech. Internat.,

Twin Falls, Idaho, 1994—96; planning engr. Idaho Power Co., Boise, 1996—. Contbr. articles to profl. jours. (Best paper award, 1986). Mem. NAMI, Boise, 2004—08; translator Refugee Ctr., Twin Falls, 1994—98; pres. Boise Tennis Club, 2004—05; founding mem. STELEKS - U. Sarajevo, 1968—94. Postdoc. fellowship, European Cmty. DG XII, 1989—90. Achievements include research in reliability of electric power systems. Office: Idaho Power Co 1221 W Idaho St Boise ID 83702 Personal E-mail: mi_pa2@yahoo.com.

PAPISOV, MIKHAIL I., chemist; s. Ivan M. Papisov and Valeria I. Naidich; m. Elena A. Tokareva, Aug. 23, 1986; children: Vera M., Eugenia M. MS in Chemistry, Moscow State U., 1982; PhD in Biochemistry and Biology, Inst. Exptl. Cardiology, Moscow, 1988. Rsch. scientist Nat. Cardiology Rsch. Ctr., Moscow, 1988—91; assoc. chemist Mass. Gen. Hosp., Boston. Sci. founder, cons. Mersana Therapeutics, Cambridge, Mass., 2002—. Recipient Outstanding Pharm. Paper, Controlled Release Soc., 1995; grantee Several Rsch. grants, U.S. Govt., The Whitaker Found., Pharm. Industry, 1996—2006. Mem.: Controlled Release Soc., Am. Chem. Soc. Achievements include U.S. and foreign patents in the areas of pharmacology and biomaterials. Home: PO Box 441 Winchester MA 01890 Office: Mass General Hosp 55 Fruit St Boston MA 02114-2696

PAPITTO, RALPH RAYMOND, manufacturing executive; b. Providence, Nov. 1, 1926; s. John and Maria (David) P.; m. Norma J. Ewart, June 10, 1943 (div.); children: Andrea (Mrs. Harry Crump), Aurelia (Mrs. William Young), David John; m. Barbara Auger, Apr. 1982. BS in Finance, Bryant Coll., Providence, 1947, DSc Bus. Adminstrn. (hon.), 1987; student, Boston U. Law Sch., 1948-49; DSc Bus. Adminstrn. (hon.), Roger Williams Coll., 1985; LLD (hon.), New Eng. Inst. Tech., 1985, Suffolk U., 1986, New England Inst. Tech. With Arthur Andersen & Co. and Ernst & Ernst, Providence, 1948-51; exec. v.p. fin. Ritz Products, Inc., Providence, 1951-55; founder, pres., chmn., dir. Glass-Tite Industries, Inc., Providence, 1956-63, chmn. bd., 1963—, also bd. dirs.; founder, chief exec. officer, pres., chmn. Nortek Inc., Providence, 1967-90, bd. dirs.; Chair and CEO AFC Cable Systems, Inc., Providence, 1993—. Bd. dirs. Hi-G, Inc. Fin. dir. Town of Johnston, R.I., 1955-59; trustee Roger Williams U., Bristol, R.I., chmn. bd. trustees, 1972-2007; bd. dirs. Meeting St. Sch. Retarded; mem. Gov.'s Blue Ribbon Commn., Roger Williams Hosp.; mem. Aurora Civic Assn. Named Man Yr. in R.I., R.I. C. of C., 1961. Mem. Alpine Country Club (pres. 1966-68, 92—), Jockey Club, Surf Club, LaGorce Country Club (Fla.). Office: AFC Cable Systems Inc 1020 Park Ave Ste 108 Cranston RI 02910 Home Phone: 401-828-5751; Office Phone: 401-453-2000, 401-275-1925. Fax: 401-453-2009, 401-828-0613.

PAPOIU, ALEXANDRU DRAGOS PETRU, medical researcher, chemist; s. Dumitru (Dorin) and Lizica Papoiu; m. Anca Parghel, 2004. BS, Poly. U. Bucharest, 1996; MD, Carol Davila U. Medicine and Pharmacy, Bucharest, 1996; PhD, Rutgers U., 2004. Rschr. Nat. Inst. Electrochemistry, Bucharest, 1996—98; grad. fellow U. Medicine and Dentistry N.J., Piscataway, 1998—2004; rsch. assoc. NYU, NYC, 1999—2000; postdoctoral fellow N.Y. Med. Coll., Valhalla, 2004—. Contbr. articles to profl. jours. Recipient Young Investigator award, Robert Wood Johnson Med. Sch., 2002, 2003; fellow Grad. fellow, Rutgers U., NIH, 1998—2004. Mem.: N.Y. Acad. Scis., Electrochem. Soc. Achievements include patents pending for fullerene derivatives that modulate the activity of nitric oxide synthase. Personal E-mail: alp29@yahoo.com.

PAPOULIAS, KAROLOS, President of the Republic of Greece; b. Ioannina, Greece, 1929; s. Gregorios Papoulias; m. Maria Panou; 3 children. Student, U. Athens, U. Munich, U. Cologne. M.P., Greece, 1977—; dep. minister fgn. affairs Republic of Greece, 1981-85, minister fgn. affairs, 1985-89, alt. minister fgn. affairs, 1984-85, alt. minister nat. def., 1990, pres., 2005—. Founding mem. Panhellenic Socialist Movement, Greece, 1974, mem. exec. bur., 1995—, political secretariat, 1995—. Contbr. articles to profl. jour. Chmn. National Sports Assn., Greece, 1985—. Achievements include former track and field and volley ball champion. Office: Office of the President Odos Vas Georgiou 7 106 74 Athens Greece

PAPP, LASZLO GEORGE, retired architect; b. Debrecen, Hungary, Apr. 28, 1929; arrived in USA, 1956; m. Judith Liptak, Apr. 12, 1952 (dec. 2005); children: Andrea, Laszlo-Mark(dec.). Archtl. Engr., Poly. U. Budapest, 1955; MArch, Pratt Inst., 1960; D of Liberal Arts, Tech. U. Budapest, 1998. Designer Harrison & Abramovitz, Architects, NYC, 1958—63; ptnr. Whiteside & Papp, Architects, White Plains, NY, 1963—67; pres. Papp Architects, P.C., White Plains, 1967—96, chmn., 1996—2005; exec. dir. Urban Redevel. Commn., Stamford, Conn., 2001—05. Adj. prof. U. Debrecen, Hungary, 1999—2007; chmn. Planning and Zoning Commn., New Canaan, Conn., 2004—. Mem. Pres.'s Adv. Com. on Pvt. Sector Initiatives, 1980-85; mem. adv. com. Westchester C.C., 1971-75, Iona Coll., New Rochelle, N.Y., 1982-87, Norwalk State Tech. Coll., 1983-95; v.p. Clearview Sch., 1985-89, pres., 1990-91, bd. dirs. 2007—; mem. Town Coun. New Canaan, Conn., 1993-99; chmn. Planning and Zoning Commn., New Canaan, 2004—. Fellow AIA (reg. dir. 1983-85); mem. Internat. Union Architects (rep. habitat com. 1986-90), N.Y. State Assn. Architects (v.p. 1977-80, pres. 1981), Am.-Hungarian Engrs. Assn. (bd. dirs. 1978-90), Am. Coun. World Fedn. Hungarians (pres. 1993-97, regional pres. 1996-2000), Hungarian Univ. Assn. (pres. 1958-60), Westchester County C. of C. (bd. dirs. 1968-71, vice chmn. bd. for area devel. 1983-89, chmn. bd. dirs. 1989-90), Am.-Hungarian C. of C. (charter 1989—). Home: 1197 Valley Rd New Canaan CT 06840-2428

PAPPACHRISTOU, JENNIFER, psychologist; PhD in Psychologist, Yeshiva U., Bronx, NY. Sch. psychologist Cresskill Bd. Edn., NJ, 1994—. Home: 66 Rugen Dr Harrington Park NJ 07640 Office: Cresskill Board of Education 1 Lincoln Dr Cresskill NJ 07626

PAPPAJOHN, JOHN G., venture capitalist; b. St. Luke's, Greece, July 31, 1928; s. George and Maria (Zanios) P.; m. Mary; children Ann Vassiliou. BSc, U. Iowa, 1952. Owner Pappajohn Ins. Agy., Mason City, Iowa, 1953-59; pres., founder Guardsman Life Investors, Inc., Des Moines, 1962-69; co-founder, v.p. Guardsman Life Ins. Co., West Des Moines, Iowa, 1962-69; pres. Equity Dynamics Inc., Des Moines, 1969—, Pappajohn Capital Resources, Inc., Des Moines, 1969—. Bd. dirs. United Systems Tech., Dallas, Optimumcare Corp., La Jolla, Calif., Galagen, Inc., BioCryst, Inc., Neose Pharms., Drug Screening Systems. Horatio Alger Assn., Leadership 100. Trustee Anatolia Coll., Thessalonia, Greece, 1988, Pine Manor Coll., Boston, 1990, U. Iowa Found., Iowa City, 1990; mem. adv. bd. Kennedy Ctr. for Performing Arts, Washington, 1986, 90; philanthropic causes with wife: John Pappajohn Bus. Bldg., Univ. Iowa Sch., Pappajohn Pavilion, Univ. Iowa Hosp. and Clinics, John and Mary Pappajohn Clin. Cancer Ctr.; founder, John and Mary Pappajohn Scholarship Fund, 1997; organizer, financer John Pappajohn Entrepreneurial Ctrs. at five different univs. and colls. in the state of Iowa; funder, NIACC Pappajohn Bus. Bldg., Mason City, Iowa, 2001; active mem. Nat. Com. of the Performing Arts; mem. trustee coun., collectors com., Nat. Gallery Art, Washington, DC.; dir. Hirshhorn Mus., Washington, DC; mem. nat. com., Whitney Mus., NYC; hon. trustee, Des Moines Art Ctr., Iowa; bd. visitors Univ. Iowa; mem. Greek Orthodox Archdiocese Exec. Com., 2001-04; coun. mem. Greek Orthodox Archdiocese of Am.; associated with JF Kennedy Ctr. for Performing Arts, Washington, D.C., former mem. advisory bd. Recipient Spl. Achievement award Big Bros., 1972, Big Bro. of Yr. award, 1974, Oscar D. Schmidt Iowa Bus. Leadership award, U. Iowa Coll. Bus., 1993, Horatio Alger award, Horatio Alger Assn., 1995, Brotherhood award, Iowa Region Nat. Conf. of Christian and Jews, 1997, Beta Gamma Sigma Mediallion for Entrepreneur of Yr., 1997, Hellenic Hertiage Achievement award, 1997, Meredith Willson Heritage award, 1998, Ellis Island Medal of Honor, 2000, Greek Orthodox Archon award, 2000, Univ. Iowa Homecoming Honored Guest, 2002; Finkbine award, U. Iowa Bus. Sch., 2004; named Iowa Bus. Leader of Yr., 1993; named to Iowa Hall of Fame, 1996, Central Iowa Bus. Hall of Achievement, 1999; named one of Top 200 Collectors, ARTnews Mag., 2004-08. Mem. U. Iowa Alumni Assn. (pres.' club), Des Moines Club, Embassy Club, Univ. Club, Order AHEPA, Masons, Shriners, Phi Gamma Delta. Republican. Greek Orthodox. Avocations: Collector of Modern and Contemporary Art, wines, philanthropy. Office: Pappajohn Capital Resources 2116 Financial Ctr Des Moines IA 50309-3908 Address: John Pappajohn Entrepreneurial Ctr Curris Bus Bldg Stes 5 & 264 U Northern Iowa Cedar Falls IA 50614-0130

PAPPALARDO, A. JOHN, former prosecutor, lawyer; b. Nashua, NH, Dec. 15, 1948; BA in Govt., Bowdoin Coll., 1971; JD, Suffolk Univ., 1974. Asst. dist. atty. Off. of Dist. Atty., Norfolk County, 1975—78; Chief, Public Integrity Unit Off. of Atty. Gen., Commonwealth of Mass., 1981, deputy chief counsel,spl. commn., 1978—81; asst. US atty. Dept. Justice, 1981—86, Chief, Public Corruption Unit, US Attys. Off., 1986—87; dep. atty. gen., chief criminal bur. Office Atty. Gen., Commonwealth of Mass., Boston, 1987—89; 1st asst. US atty, Dist. of Mass. Dept. Justice, 1989—92, U.S. atty. Boston, 1992—93; now co-mng. shareholder Greenberg Traurig LLP, Boston. Roman Catholic. Office: Greenberg Traurig LLP One International Place Boston MA 02110 Office Phone: 617-310-6072. Office Fax: 617-310-6001. Business E-Mail: pappalardoj@gtlaw.com.

PAPPALARDO, ROSA GLORIA, secondary school educator; b. Bklyn., Mar. 10, 1932; d. Angelo Charles and Rose (Paternostro) Borgia; m. Leonard Thomas Pappalardo, Apr. 16, 1955; children: Marianne, Leonard, Charles, Roseanne. BS, NYU, 1952, MA, 1953; postgrad., Seton Hall U., 1980-81, Rutgers U., 1984. Cert. supr. of art K-12, N.J., N.Y. Art edn. tchr. Islip (N.Y.) Bd. Edn., 1953—54, Herricks (N.Y.) Bd. Edn., 1954-57, 61-62; tchr. spl. edn. Passaic Assn. for Mentally Retarded, Passaic, NJ, 1958—60; supr. art/home edn. Randolph (N.J.) Twp. Schs., 1962—95; adj. prof. Jersey City State Coll., 1971—98, N.J. State U., Trenton, 2002—03, Jersey City State U., 2002—. Art cons.; editor GAINS Leadership Curriculum, Jersey City U.; presenter in field. Co-author art and math. curricula for Randolph Twp. Schs. K-12; contbr. chpt. to books Organizer, host children's art exhibits Cmty. Children's Mus., Dover, NJ, 2007. Recipient numerous svc. awards, recognition awards, awards for art edn. and art adminstrn. Fellow: Art Educators N.J. (Disting., pres.); mem.: NABA (pres.), Art Adminstrs. N.J. (pres.), N.J. Art Educators, Arts Coun. of Morris Area (planning com. 2002, Chinese, U.S. and Croatia exhibits in NYC galleries), Kiwanis, Delta Zeta (pres.), Phi Delta Kappa. Republican. Roman Catholic. Avocations: swimming, visual arts. Home: 312 Mountain Way Morris Plains NJ 07950-1910 Office: 73 Evans Ln Lake Placid NY 12946-1605 E-mail: lenpgloria@optonline.net.

PAPPAS, ALCESTE THETIS, consulting company executive, educator; b. Dix Hills, NY, May 5, 1945; d. Costas Ernest and Thetis (Hero) P.; m. Sylvan V. Endich, Sept. 13, 1987. AB, U. Calif.-Berkeley, 1967, PhD, 1978; EdM, Harvard U., 1969. Cert. guidance counselor, Mass., secondary sch. tchr., Mass. Dir. student-young alumni affairs Calif. Alumni Assn., Berkeley, 1969-71; dir. residential programs U. Calif., Berkeley, 1971-73, dir. housing and childcare, 1973-79; sr. cons., mgr. Peat, Marwick, Mitchell & Co., NYC, 1979-80, 80-82, sr. mgr., 1982-84; ptnr. in charge edn., other instns. KPMG, NYC, 1984-93; pres., CEO Pappas Cons. Group, Inc., Greenwich, Conn., 1992—. Spkr. in field. Author: Reengineering Your Non-Profit Organization: A Guide to Strategic Transformation, 1996; contbr. articles to profl. jours., author monographs. Mem. Merola Opera Bd., San Francisco, 1978-80, Calif. Alumni Council, 1976-79; bd. overseers Regents Coll., 1986-89; bd. dirs., mem. fin. com. Hellenic Coll. and Holy Cross Sch. Theology, Brookline, Mass., 1983-87, Seabury Western Theol. Sem., Evanston, Ill., 1983-89; bd. dirs. N.Y. Chiropractic Coll., 1986-88, Com. on Econ. Devel., 1986-88, Greek Orthodox Archdiocese Council, N.Y.C., 1985-89; bd. dirs., vice chmn. St. Basil Acad., 1983-87; bd. dirs., mem. exec. com. YWCA, N.Y.C., 1985-90, Catalyst, 1988-90; chairperson capital campaign com. U. Calif., Berkeley, exec. v.p. exec. coun. Coll. Letters and Sci.; trustee Clark U., 1993-95, U. Calif. Found., 1993-99; bd. dirs. Nat. Coun. for Rsch. on Women, 1996-98; mem. adv. bd. Grad. Sch. Edn. U. Calif., Berkeley, 2005—. Named mem. Acad. Women Achievers, YWCA, N.Y.C., 1984; recipient award Nat. Mgmt. Assn., 1997. Mem. Mid. States Assn. Schs. and Colls. (bd. dirs., fin. com. 1984-89, planning com. 1988-89), Order of the Ky. Colonels, Mortar Bd., Pi Lambda Theta, Prytanean. Avocations: opera, gourmet cooking, travel, photography. Office: 1 Stamford Landing Ste 116 Stamford CT 06902 Office Phone: 203-357-7058. Personal E-mail: pappas01@aol.com.

PAPPAS, ATHINA, pediatrician, educator; b. Detroit, May 30, 1970; MD, Wayne State U. Sch. Medicine, Detroit, 1998. Diplomate Am. Bd. Pediat., 2001. Asst. prof. pediat. Wayne State U., 2004—, prin. investigator, 2005—08. Recipient Critical Care Medicine award, Children's Hosp. Mich., 2000, Sanford N. Cohen award, 2001, Tchg. award, Wayne State U., 2008; named one of America's Top pediatricians, Consumers Rsch. Coun. Am., 2006—08. Mem.: AAP Sect. Young Physicians, AAP Sect. Perinatal Pediat., Am. Acad. Pediat. Achievements include discovery of predictive value of amplitude integrated EEG in neonatal ECMO, outcome of the high risk infant. Office: Childrens Hosp Mich 3901 Beaubien Detroit MI 48201 Business E-Mail: apappas@med.wayne.edu.

PAPPAS, CHARLES NICHOLAS, III, dentist, educator; b. Phila., Jan. 14, 1936; s. Charles Nicholas, Jr. and Marie (Pero) Pappas; m. Edith Basedow, Aug. 24, 1974. Student, U. Colo., 1953—55; DDS, Northwestern U., 1959. Assoc. practice dentistry, South Weymouth, Mass., 1962; pvt. practice dentistry Weymouth Heights, Mass., 1962—65; public health dentist Dept. Health and Hosps., Boston, 1965—70; assoc. practice Weymouth, 1965—68, Brookline, Mass., 1969; practicing clin. dentist Harvard U., 1970—71, clin. instr. operative dentistry, 1967—71; clin. rsch. asst. Forsyth Dental Ctr., 1972; asst. prof. restorative dentistry U. Pa., 1972—83; dentist Dept. Pub. Health, City of Phila., 1984—. Clin. instr. Tufts U., 1965. Author: The Life and Times of G.V. Black, 1983, (pamphlet) Self-Control of Tooth Decay, 1967; contbr. articles to profl. publs. Program, fund-raising chmn. Phillips Brooks Club Boston Trinity Ch., 1965—66. Capt. AUS, 1960—62. Recipient Earle Banks Hoyt award for excellence in tchg., 1980. Mem.: AAAS, ADA, Christian Dental Soc., NY Acad. Scis., Pa. Assn. Dental Surgeons, Mass. Dental Soc., Philadelphia County Dental Soc., Harvard Odontological Soc., Yale Libr. Assocs., U.S. Submarine Vets WWII (assoc. Cert. of Appreciation 1982), Goethe Soc. New Eng., English-Speaking Union, 4001 Lit. Union (founder, faculty advisor), New Haven Colony Hist. Soc., Hist. Soc. Pa., Ill. State Hist. Soc., G.V. Black Soc., Northwestern U. of Delaware Valley Club (pres. 1978), Xi Psi Phi, Lambda Chi Alpha. Home: 5723 Charles St Philadelphia PA 19135-3806 Office: City of Phila Dist Health Ctr # 10 Dental Clinic 2230 Cottman Ave Philadelphia PA 19149

PAPPAS, DENNIS G., otolaryngologist; m. Kellie Pappas. MD, U. Ala., Birmingham, 1988. Diplomate Am. Otolaryngology Bd., 1995. Physician, pres. Pappas Ear Clinic, Birmingham, 1996—. Contbr. articles to profl. jour. Bd. mem. Outpatient Care Ctr., Birmingham, 1999—. Neurotology fellowship, Ear Found., 1995. Fellow: Am. Otologic Soc. Office: Pappas Ear Clinic 2937 7th Ave S Birmingham AL 35233

PAPPAS, EDWARD HARVEY, lawyer; b. Midland, Mich., Nov. 24, 1947; s. Charles and Sydell (Sheinberg) P.; m. Laurie Weston, Aug. 6, 1972; children: Gregory Alan, Steven Michael. BBA, U. Mich., 1969, JD, 1973. Bar: Mich. 1973, U.S. Dist. Ct. (ea. dist.) Mich. 1973, U.S. Dist. Ct. (we. dist.) Mich. 1980, U.S. Ct. Appeals (6th cir.) 1983, U.S. Supreme Ct. 1983, U.S. Ct. Appeals (3d cir.) 1994, U.S. Ct. Appeals (1st cir.) 2002. Ptnr. firm Dickinson & Wright, P.L.L.C., Detroit and Bloomfield Hi, Mich., 1973—; pres. State Bar Mich., 2008—09. Mediator Oakland County Cir. Ct., Pontiac, Mich., 1983—; hearing panelist Mich. Atty. Discipline Bd., Detroit, 1983—, chmn., 1987—; mem. bus. tort subcom. Mich. Supreme Ct. Com. Std. Jury Instrns., 1992-94; bd. commrs. State Bar Mich., 1999-, v.p., 2006-. Trustee Oakland Community Coll., Mich., 1982-90, Oakland-Livingston Legal Aid, 1982-90, v.p., 1982-85, pres., 1985-87; trustee, adv. bd. Mich. Regional Anti-Defamation League of B'nai B'rith, Detroit, 1983-90; planning commr. Village of Franklin, Mich., 1987-91, chmn. 1989-91, councilman, 1991-92, chmn. charter com., 1993-94; chmn. State Bar Mich. Long Range Planning com.; pres.-elect Oakland County Bar Assn., 1996-97, pres., 1997-98, chmn. Jud. Selection Task Force, 1997; bd. dirs. Franklin Found., 1989-92; trustee The Oakland Medication Ctr., 1992-96; treas. State Bar of Mich., 2004-05. Master Oakland County Bar Assn. Inn of Ct.; fellow Mich. State Bar Found., Oakland Bar-Adams Pratt Found., ABA Found., Am. Coll. Civil Trial Mediators; mem. ABA, Fed. Bar Assn., State Bar Mich. (co-chmn. nat. moot ct. competition com. 1974, 76, com. on legal aid, chmn. standing com. on atty. grievances 1989-92, comml. litig. com., civil procedure com. 1992-94, bd. commrs. 1999—, treas. 2004-05, sec. 2005-06, v.p. 2006-07, pres. 2008-09), Oakland County Bar Assn. (vice-chmn. CLE com., chmn. CLE com. 1985-86, mediation com. 1989-90, chmn. mediation com. 1990-91, bd. dirs. 1990-98, chmn. select com. Oakland County cir. ct. settlement week 1991, chmn. strategic planning com. 1992-93, editor Laches monthly mag. 1986-88, co-chair task force to improve justice systems in Oakland County 1993—, pres.-elect, bd. dirs. 1996-97, pres. 1997-98), Am. Judicature Soc., Mich. Def. Trial Lawyers, Def. Rsch. and Trial Lawyers Assn. (com. practice and procedure), B'nai B'rith Barristers. Office Phone: 248-433-7228. Business E-Mail: epappas@dickinsonwright.com.

PAPPAS, EFFIE VAMIS, language educator, finance educator, writer, poet, artist; b. Cleve., Dec. 26, 1924; d. James Jacob and Helen Joy (Nicholson) Vamis; m. Leonard G. Pappas, Nov. 3, 1945; children: Karen Pappas Morabito, Leonard J., Ellen Pappas Daniels, David James. BBA, Western Res. U., 1948; MA in Edn., Case Western Res. U., 1964, postgrad., 1964—68; MA in English Lit., Cleve. State U., 1986; postgrad., Ind. U. Pa., 1979—86. Cert. elem. and secondary tchr. Ohio. Tchr. elem. schs., Ohio, 1963-70; office mgr. Cleve. State U., 1970-72, adminstr. pub. rels., 1972-73; med. adminstr. Brecksville VA Hosp., Ohio, 1974-78; lectr. English, econs./bus. mgmt., math., comm., composition Cuyahoga CC, Cleve., 1978-92. Tchg. asst. Case Western Res. U., 1979—80; lectr. bus. comm. Cleve. State U., 1980; participant in sci. and cultural exch. dels. Am. Inst. Chemists, China, 1984, Russia, 89. Feature writer: The Voice, 1970—78, editor, writer: Cleve. State U. newsletter and mag., 1970—73. Cub scout leader Boy Scouts Am., Brecksville, 1960; mem. local coun. PTA, 1965—70; sec. St. Paul's Coun., 1990—91; mem. membership com. St. Paul Ladies Philoptohos, 1990—; active Women's Equity Action League, 1995—2003; mem. Greater Cleve. Learning Project; Sunday sch. tchr., mem. choir Brecksville United Ch. of Christ, 1975—76, mem. bd. missions, 1966—67, mem. membership com., 1993; mem. planning com. edn. Case Western Res. U.; mem. 75th Anniversary steering com. Cleve. Coll. Recipient Editor's Choice award for outstanding achievement in poetry, Nat. Libr. Poetry, 1995, 2000; grantee, Cuyahoga CC, 1982. Mem.: AARP, AAUW (del. meetings, legis. chair 1993—94, co-chair Cleve. br. 1994, 1996—97, legis. chair 1997—98), NAFE, NAE (life named to Nat. Women's Hall Fame), Ohio Edn. Assn. (rep. assembly Columbus 1994, 1999—2001, 2002—03), N.E. Ohio Edn. Assn. (licentiate), Nat. Mus. Women in Arts (hon. roll. mem.). Avocations: travel, art, legal studies, theater, correspondence with national and international friends. Home: 8681 Brecksville Rd Brecksville OH 44141-1912

PAPPAS, ERIC CHARLES, director; b. NYC, Mar. 10, 1950; s. Robert Lester and Betty Pappas; children: Jesse, Angelea. BS in Econ. Theory, Wagner Coll., NYC, 1972; MA in English, Va. Tech., 1987, EdD in English Edn., 1990. Furniture designer, furniture maker, Ithaca, NY, 1973—81; composer, singer Blacksburg, Va., 1979—85; dir., founder Va. Dept. Corrections Sch., Floyd, 1980—82; lit. instr. Va. Tech., Blacksburg, 1985—93; founder, dir. Va. Tech. Engring. Ctr., Blacksburg, 1993—2003; founder, dir. Inst. Higher Order Thinking James Madison U., Harrisonburg, Va., 2003—. Cons., spkr. in field. Songwriter, singer (record album) All Your Heart, 1983, founder (academic jour.) Cutting Ed, 2001—; contbr. articles to engring. jours.; editor: Managing Quality and Productivity, 1988; author: A Rural Community Organizer's Manual, 1988. Founding organizer Ithaca (NY) Farmer's Market, 1973—78; cmty. organizer Coalition of Am. Electric Consumers, Va., 1980—82; chair Va. Tech. Commn. on Outreach, Blacksburg, 2001—03. Named Artist of Mo., Swamp Records, 2003; grantee, Honeywell Internat., 1994—2002, State Coun. of Higher Edn., Richmond, Va., 1997. Mem.: AAUP, Am. Soc. Engring. Edn., Phi Kappa Phi (pres. Va. Tech. chpt. 1990—92). Office: James Madison U ISAT 117 MSC 4102 Harrisonburg VA 22807 Office Phone: 540-568-1694. Office Fax: 540-568-2761. E-mail: pappasec@jmu.edu, epappas@cisat.jmu.edu.

PAPPAS, GEORGE DEMETRIOS, retired anatomist, cell biologist, educator; b. Portland, Maine, Nov. 26, 1926; s. James and Anna (Dracopoulos) Pappatheodoros; m. Bernice Levine, Jan. 14, 1952; children: Zoe Alexandra, Clio Nicollette. BA, Bowdoin Coll., Brunswick, Maine, 1947; MS, Ohio State U., Columbus, 1948, PhD, 1952; DSc (hon.), U. Athens, Greece, 1988. Vis. investigator Rockefeller Inst., NYC, 1952-54; assoc. in anatomy Coll. Physicians and Surgeons, Columbia U., NYC, 1956-57, asst. prof. anatomy, 1957-63, assoc. prof., 1963-66; prof. anatomy Albert Einstein Coll. Medicine, Yeshiva U., NYC, 1967-77, prof. neurosci., 1974-77, vis. prof. neurosci., 1977-97; prof., head dept. anatomy and cell biology U. Ill. Coll. Medicine, Chgo.,

1977-96, prof. cell biology and psychiatry, 1996—2008. Trustee Marine Biol. Lab., Woods Hole, Mass., 1975-81. Author: (with others) The Structure of the Eye, 1961, Growth and Maturation of the Brain, vol. IV, 1964, Nerve as a Tissue, 1966, The Thalmus, 1966, Pathology of the Nervous System, vol. 1, 1968, Structure and Function of Synapses, 1972, Methodological Approaches to the Study of Brain Maturation and Its Abnormalities, 1974, Advances in Neurology, vol.12, 1975, The Nervous System, vol. 1 The Basic Neurosciences, 1975, Cellular and Molecular Basis of Synaptic Transmission, 1988; contbr. over 250 articles to profl. jours.; former mem. editl. bd. Anatomical Record, Biol. Bull., Brain Rsch., Jour. Neurocytology, Microstructure, Neurol. Rsch. Arthritis and Rheumatism Found. fellow, 1954-56; recipient Career Devel. award Columbia U., 1964-66; Rsch. grant NIH. Fellow AAAS, NY Acad. Scis., Inst. Medicine Chgo.; mem. Am. Soc. Cell Biology (pres. 1974-75), Am. Assn. Anatomists (chmn. pub. policy com. 1981-82, Henry Gray award 2003), Assn. Anatomy Chmn. (exec. com. 1978-80, pres. 1981-82), Electron Microscopy Soc. Am. (program chmn. 1984-85), NY Soc. Electron Microscopy (pres. 1967-68), Soc. for Neurosci. (pres. Chgo. chpt. 1985-86), Harvey Soc., Internat. Brain Rsch. Orgn., Cajal Club, Sigma Xi. Achievements include patents for method inducing analgesia by implantation of cells releasing neuroactive substances. Mailing: 1015 Sawmill River Rd Bedford Hills NY 10507 Personal E-mail: agedp2@yahoo.com.

PAPPAS, JAMES PETE, university administrator; b. Price, Utah, June 30, 1939; s. Pete S. and Dia P. (Metrakis) P.; m. Peggy Ann Kunz, Aug. 30, 1964; children: C. Jennifer, Peter T. AS in Psychology, Coll. Eastern Utah, 1959; BA in Psychology, U. Utah, 1961; MS in Counseling Psychology, Ohio U., 1964; PhD in Clin. Psychology, Purdue U., 1968; cert. in Mgmt., Stanford U., 1979; cert. in adminstrn., Harvard U., 1985. Asst. dir. counseling ctr. U. Utah, Salt Lake City, 1969-72, dir. ctr. for acad. advising, assoc. dean liberal edn., 1975-78, assoc. dean divsn. of continuing edn., 1978-87; prof. ednl. psychology and liberal studies U. Okla., Norman, 1987—, v.p. for univ. outreach; dean Coll. of Continuing Edn., 1994-00, Coll. of Liberal Studies, 2000—. Author: (book) Windows of Opportunity: Preparing University Based Residential Continuing Education for the Twenty-First Century, 1992, The University's Role in Economic Development: From Research to Outreach, 1997; co-author: (workbook) Promotional Techniques, 1987. Mem. Norman Econ. Devel. Coalition, 1996—; state chmn. Utah Endowment for Humanities, 1985-88; pres. Norman Arts and Humanities Coun., 1994-95. Recipient St. Paul award Greek Orthodox Ch. of N. Am., Denver, 1990, Christopher Outstanding Leadership and Bittner Svc. awards U. Continuing Edn. Assn.; inductee Internat. Adult and Continuing Edn. Hall of Fame, 1997. Mem. Am. Assn. Counseling and Devel. (nat. senator 1975-77), Assn. Acad. Affairs Adminstr. (bd. dirs. 1977-78), Adult Edn. Assn. Utah (bd. dirs. 1979-82), Univ. Continuing Edn. Assn. (pres. 1996-97, Julius M. Nolte award 2006), Nat. Assn. State Univs. and Land Grant Colls. (bd. dirs. 1994-97), Assn. Grad. Liberal Studies Programs (bd. dirs. 2000—), Assn. Continuing Higher Edn. (exec. v.p. 2008-). Avocations: reading, community service, writing, sports, travel. Office: Coll Continuing Edn 1700 Asp Ave Rm 111 Norman OK 73072-6407 Office Phone: 405-325-6361. Business E-Mail: jpappae@ok.edu.

PAPPAS, LEAH AGLAIA, foundation administrator, political organization worker, secondary school educator; b. Ogden, Utah, Mar. 23, 1936; d. George Thomas and Maria (Harames) P. BA, Coll. St. Mary of the Wasatch, 1959. Tchr. Bishop Gorman High Sch., Las Vegas, Nev., 1959-64; with Dist. Atty.'s staff, Las Vegas, 1972-75; tchr. Weber State Coll., Las Vegas, 1985. Civic worker various orgns., including Opera Guild, Heart Fund, City of Hope, March of Dimes, also groups for prevention of blindness, sr. citizens' groups, others, Ogden and Las Vegas, 1955—; cons. numerous polit. campaigns, Ogden, Las Vegas and Boston, L.A., John F. Kennedy campaign, 1959; alt. del. Chgo. Nat. Conv.; vol. Senator Robert Kennedy Campaign, 1968; supr. Senator Edward M. Kennedy Campaign, Boston, 1970, 76, Presdl. Campaign, 1980; campaign worker Gov. Jerry Brown, L.A., 1978, office mgr., Reagan-Bush campaign, 1984, Pres. Bill Clinton, 1992, 96, Presdl. campaign Hillary Clinton, 2008. Greek Orthodox. Home: 1323 Marilyn Dr Ogden UT 84403-0424 E-mail: Leahap@msn.com.

PAPPAS, MARGENE, retired music educator; d. Eugene Wallace and Marietta Joan Kirkwood; m. Peter Michael Pappas, Dec. 30, 1973. BS, U. Ill., Champaign-Urbana, 1969, MS, 1973. Tchr. Oswego Dist. 308, Ill., 1969—2006; band dir. Oswego Cmty. Band, 1994—2006; ret., 2006. Guest conductor Ill. All-State Band, 2001. Contbr. articles to NBA Jour. Recipient Studs Terkel Humanitarian award, Village of Oswego, 2002, Sudler Legion of Honor, John Philip Sousa Found., 2003, John P. Paynter Lifetime Achievement award, Quinlan and Fabish Music Co., 2006; named to Hall of Fame, Phi Beta Mu, Ill. Chpt., 2003. Mem.: Bands of Am. (adv. bd. 2001—), Ill. Music Edn. Assn., Am. Sch. Band Dirs. Assn., Nat. Band Assn. (bd. dirs. 2000—06). Achievements include directing the HS Wind Symphony performance at 2004 IMEA All-State; directing Oswego HS Marching Band in the 2005 Tournament of Roses; Margene Pappas Day named in her honor Village of Oswego, May 28, 2006. Avocations: travel, reading, music, hiking, cross stitch. Home: 2469 Lakeside Dr Aurora IL 60504 Office Phone: 312-501-4610. E-mail: tntohsband@aol.com.

PAPPAS, MARJORIE L., library studies educator; b. Adrian, Mich., Oct. 4, 1938; d. Raymond C. Spielman and Adalene E. Dickey, Alfred Dickey (Stepfather); children: David J, Mark J. BS, U. Toledo, 1961; MEd, Miami U., Oxford, Ohio, 1977, PhD, 1987. Sch. libr. Watts Mid. Sch., Centerville, Ohio, 1970—78; dir. tech. and librs. Troy (Ohio) City Schs., 1978—85; asst. prof. Wright State U., Dayton, Ohio, 1986—95; assoc. prof. U. No. Iowa, Cedar Falls, 1995—98, vis. prof. online, 1998—2001; assoc. prof. Ea. Ky. U., Richmond, 2001—04; adj. prof. Mansfield U., Mansfield, Pa., 2004—05; assoc. prof. sch. libr. and Dept. Info. Tech. Mansfield (Pa.) U., 2005—, chmn. sch. libr. and Dept. Info. Tech., 2005; freelance writer, cons. Danville, Ky., 2005—; virtual instr. profl. devel. studies Sch. Libr, Communication Studies, Rutgers U., New Brunswick, NJ, part-time instr. profl. devel. studies. Pres., cons. C L Assocs., Inc., Danville, Ky., 1999—2000. Author: (information process model) Pathways to Knowledge, 1997, Searching Electronic Resources, 1998, Pathways to Knowledge and Inquiry Learning, 1998; contbr. articles to profl. jours. Recipient Edgar Dale award, Assn. Ednl. Comm. and Tech., 1995. Mem.: ALA, Ky. Sch. Media Assn., Am. Assn. Sch. Librs. (regional dir. 1993—96), Ohio Ednl. Libr. Media Assn. (life award of merit 2001), Delta Kappa Gamma. Home: 426 Cloverdale Dr Danville KY 40422 Business E-Mail: marjorie.pappas@gmail.com.

PAPPAS, MICHAEL, payroll consultant; b. NYC, Sept. 10, 1940; s. Michael Papadopoulos and Despina (Vrioni) Kokindo; m. Eileen McGovern, Jan. 25, 1969. BBA in Acctg. and Data Processing, Pace U., NYC, 1973. Mgr. acctg. E.F. Hutton, NYC, 1972-75, bus. unit mgr., 1976-77; mgr. payroll and commn. acctg. Drexel Burnham Lambert, NYC, 1977-81, v.p., project mgr., 1981-83, v.p., mgr. gen. acctg., 1983-85, v.p., mgr. fin. info. systems, 1985-86, v.p., govt. reporting coord., 1986-89; dir. compensation Gruntal & Co., Inc., NYC, 1989-2000; v.p. Donaldson, Lufkin, Jenrette, NYC, 2000—01; Credit Suisse First Boston, 2001—02; cons. MP Cons. Svc., 2002—. Sgt. U.S. Army, 1963-65. Mem. Am. Payroll Assn. (N.Y. Met. chpt. pres. 1998-2001), Securities Industry Assn. (tech. tax com. 1986-88), Hellenic Am. Bankers Assn. (bd. dirs. 1991-92, v.p. 1992-94, pres. 1995-98, treas. 1998-2002). Greek Orthodox. Avocations: golf, bowling, collecting award winning movies. Personal E-mail: m.p.consulting@comcast.net.

PAPPAS, SANDRA LEE, state legislator; b. Hibbing, Minn., June 15, 1949; m. Neal Gosman, 1976; 3 children. Attended, U. Minn., 1967—69; BA, Met. State U., 1986; MPA, John F. Kennedy Sch. Govt., Harvard U., 1994. Mem. Minn. House of Reps., St. Paul, 1984-90; mem. Dist. 65 Minn. State Senate, St. Paul, 1990—. Part-time coll. instr. Mem. Dem. Farmer Labor Party. Jewish. Office: Minn State Senate Capitol Bldg Room 120 75 Rev Dr Martin Luther King Jr Blvd Saint Paul MN 55155-1606 Home: 66 East 9th St #2605 Saint Paul MN 55101 Office Phone: 651-296-1802. Fax: 651-227-5816; Office Fax: 651-296-4135. E-mail: sen.sandra.pappas@senate.mn.*

PAPPAS-SPEAIRS, NINA, financial planner, educator; d. Steve E. and Martha (Hicks) Kalfas; m. Harry J. Pappas, 1951 (div.); children: John J., Nicholas S., Vivian E. Pappas Unger, Mark A., Carol A. Pappas Siegel; m. Mitchell F. Speairs, 1992 (dec. 2001). BS, U. Cin., 1950; MA, Northwestern U., Evanston, Ill., 1957; PhD, U. Ill., Champaign, 1978. Faculty St. Mary's H.S., Chgo., Sch. Dist. 102, LaGrange, Ill., U. Ill., Chgo., 1969-79, U. Tex., Arlington, 1979-82, Tex. Wesleyan Coll., Ft. Worth, 1982-83; realtor Merrill Lynch Realty, Ft. Worth, 1983-84; fin. planner Cigna Corp., Irving, Tex., 1984-90; pvt. practice fin. planning and investments, Ft. Worth, 1990—. Organizer, condr. 1st U.S. Olympic Acad., Chgo., 1977; collaborator Internat. Olympic Acad., Olympia, Greece, 1977, guest lectr., 77, 78; chief of mission to Greece U.S. Olympic Com., 1977; guest lectr. Nat. Olympic Acad. Republic of China, 1982. Author: History and Development of the International Olympic Academy: 1927-1977, 1978; editor: Perspectives of the Olympic Games, 1979; also articles. Vice chair edn. coun. U.S. Olympic Com., 1977—85; sch. bd. Dist. 107, LaGrange, Ill., 1971—74. Recipient Silver Medal Internat. Olympic Acad., Olympia, Greece, 1981. Mem. Lecture Found., Symphony League, Opera Guild (pres. 1982-83), Ft. Worth Woman's Club, Women's Wednesday Club (pres. 2003-04), River Crest Country Club, Ft. Worth Boat Club, Ridglea Rejebian Club, Carousel Club. Republican. Greek Orthodox. Avocations: reading, sailing, dance.

PAPPERT, JERRY (GERALD J. PAPPERT), lawyer, former state attorney general; m. Ellen Pappert; 2 children. Grad. with honors, Villanova U., 1985; JD, Notre Dame U., 1988. Atty. Duane, Morris and Heckscher, Phila., 1988—96; first deputy atty. gen. State of Pa., Harrisburg, Pa., 1996—2003, acting atty. gen., 2003—04, atty. gen., 2004—05; ptnr. Ballard, Spahr, Andrews & Ingersoll LLP, Phila., 2005—08; exec. v.p., gen. counsel Cephalon Inc., Frazer, Pa., 2008—. Office: Cephalon Inc 41 Moores Rd Frazer PA 19355

PAPROCKI, THOMAS JOHN, bishop, lawyer; b. Chgo., Aug. 5, 1952; s. John Henry and Veronica Mary (Bonat) P. BA, Loyola U., Chgo., 1974; student Spanish lang. study, Middlebury Coll., 1976, student Italian lang. study, 1987; MDiv, St. Mary of the Lake Sem., 1978; student Spanish lang. study, Instituto Cuannahuac, 1978; Licentiate in Sacred Theology, St. Mary of the Lake Sem., 1979; JD, DePaul U., 1981; JCD, Gregorian U., Rome, 1991; student Polish lang. study, Cath. U. Lublin, Poland, 1989, Jagiellonian U., Cracow, Poland, 2000. Bar: Ill. 1981, U.S. Dist. Ct. (no. dist.) Ill. 1981, U.S. Supreme Ct. 1994. Ordained priest Archdiocese of Chgo., 1978, vice-chancellor, 1985-92, chancellor, 1992-2000, titular bishop Vulturara, aux. bishop Chgo., episc. vicar, Vicariate IV, 2003—, canonical affairs com., 2003—, archbishop's liaison health and hosp. affairs, 2005—, chmn. region VII, 2006; assoc. pastor St. Michael Ch., Chgo., 1978-83; pres. Chgo. Legal Clinic, 1981-87, 91—; exec. dir. South Chgo. Legal Clinic, 1981-85, bd. dirs., 1987—; adminstr. St. Joseph Ch., Chgo., 1983-86; adj. faculty Loyola U. Law, 1999—; pastor St. Constance Parish, 2001—03; with canonical affairs com. US Conf. Cath. Bishops, 2003—; v.p. Ill. Cath. Health Care Assn., 2005—. Senator Presbyteral senate Archdiocese of Chgo., 1985-87, mem. Presbyteral coun., 1992-2000, mem. Cardinal's cabinet, 1992-2000, sec. coll. consultors, 1992-2000; chmn. incardination com., 1991-2000, chmn. policy devel. com., 1998-2000, chmn. Fgn. Priests Initiative, 1998-2000; asst. to the Gen. Sec., Vatican Synod of Bishops, Spl. Assembly for Am., Rome, 1997, cardinal's del. to profl. rev. bd., 1991-2003, chmn. profl. conduct adminstrv. com., 1991-2002; bd. dirs. Cath. Conf. Ill., 1985-87. Mem. editl. adv. bd. Chgo. Cath. Newspaper, 1984-85; contbr. articles to profl. jours. Bd. dirs. United Neighborhood Orgn., Chgo., 1982-85, S.E. Community Youth Svc. Bd., Chgo., 1985, Ctr. for Neighborhood Tech., Chgo., 1986-87, Chgo. Area Found. for Legal Svcs., 1994-2002; active Chgo. Cmty. Trust Com. on Children, Youth and Families, 1991-2002, Ill. Family Violence Coordinating Coun., 1994—. Recipient Humanitarian award Polish Am. Congress, 1997, Alumni award for Outstanding Pub. Svc., DePaul Coll. of Law, 2001; named Man of Yr., Nat. Advs., 1999. Fellow Leadership Greater Chgo.; mem. Ill. Bar Assn., Chgo. Bar Assn. (bd. mgrs. 1999-2001, Maurice Weigle award 1985), Advs. Soc. (award of merit 1996), Cath. Lawyers Guild (Cath. Lawyer of Yr. award 2003), Canon Law Soc. Am., Polish Am. Leadership Initiative (bd. dirs. 2001—), Polish Am. Assn. (bd. dirs. 1998—), The Chgo. Jr. Assn. Commerce and Industry (Ten Outstanding Young Citizens award 1986), Union League Club of Chgo., Pi Sigma Alpha, DePaul U. Alumni Assn. Roman Catholic. Avocations: hockey, running, reading. Office: Aux Bishop of Chgo 1400 S Austin Blvd Cicero IL 60804 Office Phone: 708-329-4040. Business E-Mail: tpaprocki@archchicago.org.

PAPROSKY, WAYNE G., orthopedist; BA in Physiology, Univ. Western Canada, London, On., 1972; MD, McMaster Univ. Sch. Med., Hamilton, On., 1975. Cert. Am. Bd. Orthopaedic Surgeons, 1982, Am. Acad. Orthopaedic Surgeons, 1985, Am. Coll. Surgeons, 1986. Staff Edwards Hosp., Naperville, Ill., Ctrl. Dupage Hosp., Winfield, Ill., Rush Presbyterian-St. Luke's Med. Ctr., Chgo. Assoc. prof., adult joint reconstruction Rush Presbyn.-St. Luke's Med. Ctr., Chgo. Mem.: The Hip Soc., Ontario Med. Assn., Mid-America Orthopaedic Assn., Ill. State Med. Soc., Ill. Orthopaedic Soc., Dupage Co. Med. Soc., Can. Orthopaedic Soc., Can. Med. Soc., Assn. Arthritic Hip and Knee Surgery, Am. Med. Soc., Am. Acad. Orthopaedic Surgeons. Office: Rush Presbyn St Lukes 1653 W Congress Pkwy Chicago IL 60612 Office Phone: 630-339-2227.*

PAPS, BETTY LOU, nursing educator; b. Chrisman, Ill., Nov. 17, 1937; d. Robert Bertram Bonwell and Katherine Carol (Hess) Buchanan; m. Peter George Paps, Apr. 22, 1989 (dec.); children: Jill Stuebe Thompson, Nena Carol Mihailovic. RN, Lakeview Hosp. Sch. Nursing, 1958; BSN, U. Ill., Chgo., 1965; MSN, DePaul U., 1970; PhD, LaSalle U., 1998. Nurse educator Danville Jr. Coll., Ill., 1963-65, Chgo. Pub. Schs., 1966-68, Mt. Sinai Hosp. Sch. Nursing, Chgo., 1970; prof. nursing Kennedy King Coll., Chgo., 1970—96; chief nurse 63d Aeromedical Evacuation Squadron, 1980—92, troop comdr. Persian Gulf War, 1991; evaluator Nat. League Nursing, 1994—98. Col. USAFR, 1974—94. Decorated Commendation award, Air medal, Meritorious Svc. award, Southeast Asia award, Kuwait Liberation medal, Chief Nurse's badge, Chief Flight Nurse award, Nat. Def. medal. Mem.: VFW, Air Force Assn., Res. Officers Assn., Aerospace Med. Assn., Mil. and Hospitallar Order of St. Lazarus of Jerusalem (Dame, Silver medal), Am. Legion, Order of The Eastern Star. Personal E-mail: bpaps@aol.com.

PAPUCHIS, MATTHEW J., communications executive, journalist; b. Wash., DC, June 10, 1980; s. John Charles and Ruth Marie Papuchis; m. Kristie Lynne Gishen, Apr. 24, 2004. BS in Mass. Comm., Towson U., Md., 2003. Sr. comm. specialist Sodexho, Inc., Gaithersburg, Md., 2003—07; comm. mgr. Marriott Internat., Inc., DC, 2007—. Freelance journalist Balt. Sun, 2003—. Comm. coun. mem. Montgomery Village Found., Md., 2006. Recipient Spirit of Sodexho award, Region II Mark of Excellence award, Soc. Profl. Journalists. Mem.: Toastmasters Internat. (chpt. sec. 2006), Internat. Assn. Bus. Communicators (Silver Inkwell award 2005, Silver Quill award 2005). Office: Marriott Internat Inc One Marriott Dr Washington DC 20058 Personal E-mail: mjpapuchis@msn.com.

PAPY, CHARLES C., III, lawyer; b. Miami, Fla., Feb. 16, 1952; s. Charles C. and June (Marlow) Papy; m. Anne Lang, Aug. 6, 1977; children: Jennifer, Ryan, Alyson, Douglas. BBA, U. Miami, 1974, JD, 1977. Bar: Fla., US Dist. Ct. So. Dist. Fla. Atty. Papy Poole & Weissenborn, Miami, 1977-83; ptnr. Papy Weissenborn & Papy, Miami, 1983-92, Eckert, Seamans, Cherin & Mellott, Miami, 1992—98, Duane Morris LLP, Miami, 1999—, mng. ptnr. Miami office. Bd. mem. Am. Red Cross, Dade County; appointee Jud. Nominating Com., Miami, 1986—90, Health Fin. Com., Dade County, Miami. Presbyterian. Avocations: fishing, hunting, sports. Office: Duane Morris LLP Ste 3400 200 S Biscayne Blvd Miami FL 33131-2318 Office Phone: 305-960-2222. Office Fax: 305-397-1905. Business E-Mail: ccpapy@duanemorris.com.*

PAQUETTE, JACK KENNETH, management consultant, author, historian; b. Toledo, Ohio, Aug. 14, 1925; s. Hector J. and Nellie (McCormick) P.; m. Jane Russell, Sept. 13, 1947; children: Jan Eriksen, Mark Russell, Mary Beth, John Eric. Student, Baldwin-Wallace Coll., 1943-44, Marquette U., 1944; BA, Ohio State U., 1949, MA, 1951; postgrad., Wayne State U., 1966. Editor monthly pub. Bur. Motor Vehicles, Ohio, 1947-49; asst. city editor, copy editor Ohio State Jour., 1949-51; copywriter Owens-Ill., Inc., Toledo, 1951-53, copy chief mktg. dept., 1953-55, asst. advt. mgr. mktg. dept., 1955-59; advt. mgr. Owens-Ill., Inc. (Libbey div.), 1959-61; mgr. advt. and sales promotion Owens-Ill., Inc. (Libbey products), 1961-64, mgr. customer mktg. services glass container div., 1964-67, dir. corporate orgn. planning, 1967-69, v.p. adminstrv. div., dir. corp. relations, 1969-70, corporate v.p., dir. corp. relations, 1970-80, corp. v.p., asst. to chmn. bd., 1980-84, cons., 1984-86; pres. Paquette Enterprises, 1984—; owner The Trumpeting Angel, antiques, 1985—. Mem. adv. bd. Cresset Chem. Co., 1987—. Author: A History of Owens-Illinois Inc., (1818-1984), 1985, The Glassmakers, 1994, Blowpipes, 2002, A Boy's Journey Through the Great Depression, 2005. Bd. dirs. Toledo YMCA, 1970-74, Vis. Nurse Svc., 1970-73, Children's Svcs., Lucas County, 1973-80, Toledo coun. Boy Scouts Am., trustee, v.p. fin., 1978-84; trustee Owens Tech. Coll. Found, 1978-81; mem. Advt. Club Toledo, 1951-75, trustee, 1960-62; hon. bd. dirs. Greater Toledo area chpt. ARC, 1970—; mem. adv. bd. Mercy Hosp., Toledo, 1981-84, Mary's Adult Day Care Ctr., 1989-93, St. Anthony's Children's Ctr., 1993, Mid-Coast Hosp., Brunswick, Maine, 1998—; mem. pub. rels. com. Cath. U. Am., 1979-82; chmn. U.S. Savs. Bonds, Lucas County, 1977-79; trustee Bowling Green State U. Found., 1976-83, pres., 1980-82; mem. Nat. Commn. on a Free and Responsible Press, 1980-83; v.p. trustee, Toledo Repertoire Theatre, 1984-88; trustee Crosby Gardens, 1983-89, chmn. 1987-88; trustee Toledo Bot. Gardens, 1989-90, chmn. emeritus and hon. lifetime trustee, 1990—; mem. pres.'s coun. Toledo Mus. Art, Bowling Green State U.; trustee Riverside Hosp. Found., 1984-94, chmn. 1986-89; mem. Juvenile Justice Adv. Bd., 1986-87; advisor R.B. Hayes Presdl. Ctr., 1990-92. With USNR, 1943-46, PTO. Recipient Gold Key award Pub. Rel. News, 1970, Silver Anvil award Pub. Rel. Soc., 1971, 72; named to Toledo Clean Hall of Fame, 1983. Mem. Soc. Profl. Journalists (co-founder Columbus and Toledo chpts.), Ohio Mfrs. Assn. (v.p., trustee 1969-84), Keep Am. Beautiful, Inc. (nat. chmn., exec. com., 1978-84, chmn. emeritus, mem. nat. adv. coun. 1984—), Bus. Com. for the Arts (corp. liaison 1980-84), U.S. C. of C. (cons. affairs com. 1980-84), Western Lake Erie Hist. Soc. (life, trustee 1998-2003), USN Armed Guard Assn., Sampson WWII Navy Vets. Assn., OSU Alumni Assn. (life), Maine Maritime Mus., Toy Soldier Collectors of Am. Soc., Toledo Glass Club, Fostoria Glass Club, Toledo Press Club (founding trustee), Toledo Club, Torch Club (pres.-elect), Rotary (Paul Harris fellow), U.S. Navy League, Am. Legion (Toledo post), Pi Sigma Alpha. Home and Office: 2355 Parliament Sq Toledo OH 43617-1256

PAQUETTE, WILLIAM ARTHUR, historian, educator; b. Lawrence, Mass., Aug. 6, 1947; s. Arthur Conrad Paquette and Dorothy Lucille Root; m. Sylvia Lois Kreps, June 14, 1969 (div. 1987). BA, Grove City Coll., Pa., 1969; MA, Duquesne U., Pitts., 1971; PhD, Emory U., Atlanta, 1994. Tchr. Acad. Holy Cross, Kensington, Md., 1972—75, chmn. dept. social sci., 1973—75; from adj. prof. to prof. history Tidewater C.C., Portsmouth, Va., 1975—94, prof., 1994—. Grad. tchg. asst. Duquesne U., Pitts., 1969—71; adj. prof. history Old Dominion U., Norfolk, Va., 1975—78, Spelman Coll., Atlanta, 1983—84, adj. prof., 1989—90; adj. prof. history Ga. Perimeter, Atlanta, 1983—84; adj. prof. edn. Emory U., Atlanta, 1989—90; project historian NEH, 1979—82, 1995—96, 2000—02; reviewer ETS, 1995—2002; chmn. chancellor's prefix review com. Va. CC. Sys., Richmond, 1998—2000; nat. editor history Merlot Project, 2000—; mem. adv. bd. history digital project Nat. Humanities Alliance, 2000—, Gale Group Pubs., 2003—, ProQuest Pubs., 2004—, Prentice-Hall, 2004—, Houghton Mifflin, 2005—; cons. in field; grants reviewer Dept. Edn., 2004—; edn. reviewer Nat. Gallery of Art, 2004—. Author: U.S. Colored Troops from Lower Tidewater in the Civil War, 1992, Encyclopedia of African-American Civil Rights, 1992, Ready Reference: Censorship, 1997, Great Events from History, North America Series, 1997, The War of 1812: An Encyclopedia, 1998, Dictionary of World Biography: 20th Century, 1999, Biographical Encyclopedia of Twentieth Century World Leaders, 1999, Encyclopedia of the U.S. Supreme Court, 2000, Encyclopedia of America's Historic Sites, 2000, Putting the World into World History textbooks, Teaching History, 2001, Great Events: 1900-2001, 2002, World Education Encyclopedia, 2002, World Press Encyclopedia, 2003, A Taste of Merlot: The Multimedia Resources for Historians and Others, Perspectives, 2003; co-author: Instructor's Guide to the Teaching of American History, 1979, Readings in Black and White, 1982, Suffolk: A Pictorial History, 1987, Dictionary of World Biography: Renaissance, 1998, Encyclopedia of North America, 1998, Teaching History, A Journal of Methods, 2001; photographer Fashion Doll Wardrobe, 2002, Suffolk: A Celebration of History, 2006, Instructor's Manual, Western Civilization, 2007; contbr. articles to profl. jours.; author: Great Events From History Modern Scandals, 2005, City As Living Organism: The Case Study Of Bolivar NY, 2008. Mem. adv. bd. US Com. World Food Day, 1999—; commr. Mus. Fine Arts, Portsmouth, Va., 1997—2002; mem. adv. bd. Ba. Fest. of the Book, 1998—2004; adv. bd. H-NET, 2005. Grantee Am. Cities and Pub. Spaces, NEH, 2005—09, Alamo, John Adams, 2007, Transcendentalists, 2008, Nat. Lyceum Rutherford B. Hayes, 2009; fellow, NEH, 1985; Gilder-Lehrman fellow, U. Va., 2005, Landmark grants, NEH Inst., 2007—08, Grad. fellowship, Brown U., 2008, Lyceum Movement, the Gilded Age. Mem.: Va. Political Scientists, History of Edn. Soc., Comparative and Internat. Edn. Soc., US Capitol Hist. Soc., Internat. Standing Conf. History Edn., Am. Ednl. Rsch. Assn., Am. Coun. Quebec Studies, Cmty. Coll. Humanities Assn. (v.p. 1991—93, bd. dirs. 1993—97, Disting. Svc. award 1997, Merlot award Tchg. Distinctive Use & Devel. of Online Materials 2008), Orgn. Am. Historians (com. cmty. coll. 2002—, chmn. 2004—05), Am. Hist. Assn. (Nancy Roelker Mentorship com. 1997—2000, chmn. 1999—2000, joint com. adj. 2000—04), Mayflower Soc. Va. (asst. historian 1992—93, historian 1993—98, dep. gov. 2004—07, gov. 2007—, GSMD Edn. chair 2008—). Avocations: stamp collecting/philately, photography, travel, genealogy. Office: Tidewater CC 7000 Coll Dr Portsmouth VA 23703 Home: 13565 Filly Ct Gainesville VA 20155 Office Phone: 757-822-2386. Business E-Mail: wpaquette@tcc.edu.

PAQUIN, ANNA HELENE, actress; b. Winnipeg, MB Canada, July 24, 1982; d. Brian and Mary Paquin. Actor: (films) The Piano, 1993 (Academy Award best supporting actress, 1993, Golden Globe nomination best supporting actress, 1993, Best Supporting Actress LA Film Critics Assn., 1993, Best Supporting Actor - Female Film Critics Cir. of Australia Awards, 1994), Jane Eyre, 1995, Fly Away Home, 1996, Amistad, 1997, A Walk on the Moon, 1988, Hurly-burly, 1998, Begin the Beguine, 1998, Sleepless Beauty, 1998, A Walk on the Moon, 1999, She's All That, 1999, X-Men, 2000, Almost Famous, 2000 (Best Ensemble Cast Performance Online Film Critics Soc., 2001), Finding Forrester, 2000, Buffalo Soldiers, 2001, Darkness, 2002, 25th Hour, 2002, X2: X-Men United, 2003, Steamboy, 2004, The Squid and the Whale, 2005 (Best Ensemble Cast Gotham Awards, 2005), X-Men: The Last Stand, 2006, Blue State, 2007, Trick 'r Treat, 2008; (TV films) Member of the Wedding, 1997, Hercules (voice only), 1988, All the Rage, 1999, (voice) Joan of Arc, 2005, Bury My Heart at Wounded Knee, 2007; (plays) After Ashley, 2005; (TV series) True Blood, 2008— (Best Performance by an Actress in a TV Series - Drama, Golden Globe award, Hollywood Fgn. Press Assn., 2009). Avocations: rugby, running, piano, singing, skiing, knitting, reading. Office: Double Happy Talent c/o Gail Cowan PO Box 9585 Wellington New Zealand also: c/o William Morris Agy One William Morris Pl Beverly Hills CA 90212*

PAQUIN, EDWARD H., JR., state legislator, not-for-profit developer; b. Bennington, Vt., Feb. 12, 1953; s. Edward H. Sr. and Alice Marie P.; m. Patricia LaRose, July 4, 1981 (div. Dec. 2005); 1 child, Katherine Marie BA, U. Vt., 1975. Various positions including silversmith and factory worker; builder; rep. Vt. Gen. Assembly, Montpelier, 1991—2002; exec. dir. Vt. Protection and Advocacy, Inc., Montpelier, 2002—. Dir. summer camp for low-income rural children CAMP!; bd. dirs. Vt. Ctr. Ind. Living. Recipient Victory award Nat. Rehab. Hosp., 1991. Democrat. Baptist. Home: PO Box 219 Fairfax VT 05454-0219 Office: Vt Protection and Advocacy Inc 141 Main St Ste 7 Montpelier VT 05602

PAQUIN, THOMAS CHRISTOPHER, lawyer; b. Quincy, Mass., Feb. 12, 1947; s. Henry Frederick and Rita Marie (St. Louis) P.; m. Jean Jacqueline O'Neill, Aug. 5, 1972; children: Martha, Edward. BS in Acctg., Bentley Coll., 1969; JD, U. Notre Dame, 1974. Bar: Mass. 1974, U.S. Dist. Ct. Mass. 1976. Tax atty. Coopers and Lybrand, Boston, 1974-76; assoc. Cargill, Masterman & Cahill, 1976, Wilson, Curran & Malkasian, Wellesley, 1976-77; ptnr. Bianchi and Paquin, Hyannis, 1977-98; shareholder, dir. Quirk and Chamberlain, P.C., Yarmouthport, 1998—2001; of counsel Quirk, Chamberlain & Marsh, P.C., 2002—04; pvt. practice Barnstable, Mass., 2004—; pub. adminstr. Barnstable County, 2006—. Bd. dirs., chmn. nominating com. Elder Svcs. Cape Cod and Islands, Inc., Dennis, Mass., 1986-91; bd. dirs., corporator Vis. Nurse Assn. Cape Cod Found., Inc., Dennis, 1988-97; pres. Life Svcs. Inc., 1991-95; bd. dirs. Woodside Cemetery Corp., 1998—, pres., 1999—; corporator Yarmouth Port Libr., 2009-. Mem. Bass River Golf Commn., trustee Yarmouth, Mass., 1980-83, chmn., 1982-83; chmn. Yarmouth Golf Course Bldg. Com., 1985-89; mem. hearing com. bd. Bar Overseers of the Supreme Jud. Ct., 1989-95, 2008-; bd. dirs. Project Coach, Inc., 1990-97, Arts Found. Cape Cod, 2006—, treas. 2008-; conciliator Barnstable Superior Ct., 1992—, Barstable Dist. Ct., 2000—; trustee, asst. treas. Cape Symphony Orch., 1999-2004, chmn. fin. com., 2003-04. Fellow Mass. Bar Found.; mem. ABA, Mass. Bar Assn. (del. 1986-87, mem. com. on bicentennial U.S. Constn. 1986-88, fee arbitration bd. 1985-86, chmn. spkrs. and writers subcom. 1986-88), Barnstable County Bar Assn. (chmn. seminar com. 1979-83, mem. exec. com. 1981-84, v.p. 1984-86, pres. 1986-87), Estate Planning Coun. Cape Cod (exec. com. 1985-98, sec. 1991-93, pres.-elect 1993-95, pres. 1995-97), Mass. Conveyancers Assn., Mid-Cape Men's Club (v.p. 1992, pres. 1993), Cummaquid Golf Club (dir. 2003-07). Office: PO Box 1145 3010 Main St Barnstable MA 02630-1145 Home Phone: 508-362-4588; Office Phone: 508-375-9004. Personal E-mail: thomaspaquin@verizon.net.

PARADA, LUIS FERNANDO, science educator; b. Santa Fe de Bogota, Colombia, July 18, 1954; came to the U.S., 1993; s. Alfonso and Clara Parada. BS, U. Wis., 1979; PhD, MIT, 1985. Postdoctoral fellow Pasteur Inst., Paris, 1985-87; group leader Nat. Cancer Inst., Frederick, Md., 1988-91, sect. chief ABL, 1991-94; prof., dir. Ctr. Devel. Biology U. Tex. Southwestern Med. Ctr., Dallas, 1994—, Dana and Richard C. Strauss disting. chmn. in devel. biology, 1994—, dir. Kent Waldrep Ctr. for Basic Rsch. on Nerve Growth, 1997—, Southwestern Bell disting. chair in basic neurosci. rsch., 1998—; prof. Amer. Cancer Soc., 2003. Mem. sci. adv. bd. Rett Syndrome Found., N.Y., 1999—, Christopher Reeve paralysis Found., N.Y.C., 1996—; mem. sci. adv. coun. Damon Runyan-Walter Winchell Cancer Fund., N.Y.C., 1998—, Nat. Neurofibromatosis Found., N.Y.C., 1997—; chmn. bd. sci. counselors Nat. Inst. Neurol. Disorders and Stroke, Bethesda, Md., 1999—; mem. bd. sci. counselors Nat. Cancer Inst., Bethesda, 1995-99; rschr. in field. Patentee in field. Peter A. Steck Memorial ward, Soc. for Neuro-Oncology, 2000 Fellow Am. Acad. Arts & Scis.; mem. AAAS, Inst. Medicine, Soc. for Neuroscience, Amer. Assn. for Cancer Rsch, Soc. for Devel. Biology. Office: U Tex Southwestern Med Ctr 5323 Harry Hines Blvd Dallas TX 75390-9133*

PARADIES, MICHELE A., biology professor; PhD, Thomas Jefferson Coll. Grad. Studies, Phila., 1993. Asst. prof. SUNY Orange, Middletown, 2000—. Mem.: Am. Assn. Anatomists, NABT. Avocation: gardening. Office: SUNY Orange 115 South St Middletown NY 10940 Business E-Mail: michele.paradies@sunyorange.edu.

PARADIS, ROGER, history & folklore professor, researcher; b. Ft. Kent, Maine, Sept. 19, 1935; s. Fred Joseph Paradis and Mary Soucy; m. Roseanne Levesque, Sept. 23, 1961; children: Elaine Ruth, Sonya Marie, Daniel Roger, Marc Gregory. BS, U. Maine, 1957; MEd, U. Maine, Orono, 1959, MA in History, 1965, postgrad. in History, 1966—68. Tchr. Acadia Sch, Madawaska, Maine, 1957—58, Cunningham Sch., Presque Isle, Maine, 1959—60, Cmty. HS, Ft. Kent, 1960—66; prof. history U. Maine, Ft. Kent, 1968—. Feature art lectr.-at-large United Pres Internat., 1968—; cons. The History Channel, Nat. Geog. Mag.; folklore instr. Laval U., Que., Canada. Author: (books) History of the Madawasa Training School, 1878-64 Brons Mag. U. Mass., 1964, Gilbert O. Roy. Paintre Populaire, 1979, 1975, 1998, (reference book) Papers of Prudent L. Mercure, 1998, Madawaska Hist. Soc., 1998, folklore; contbr. 17 articles to profl. jours.;, singer folksongs; presenter Inst. Folklore Com. Culture com. Club Français, Madawaska, 2006. Sgt. US Nat. Guard, 1954—64, Ft. Kent. Recipient Rsch. Recognition award, Adrienne Clarkson, Can. Chancellor, 2003. Mem.: Soc. Historique Acadienne, Assn. Can. Folklore, Madawaska Hist. Soc. Democrat. Roman Catholic. Achievements include research in folklore and tales. Avocations: fishing, camping, canoeing, gardening. Home: PO Box 72 Fort Kent Mills ME 04744 Home Phone: 207-834-5957; Office Phone: 207-834-7501. Business E-Mail: rparadis@maine.edu.

PARADISE, LOUIS VINCENT, education educator, dean; b. Scranton, Pa., Apr. 19, 1946; s. Louis Benjamin and Lucille P.; children: Christopher, Gabrielle,Victoria. BS, Pa. State U., 1968; MS, Bucknell U., 1974; PhD, U. Va., 1976. Lic. psychologist, profl. counselor; cert. sch. psychologist. Assoc. prof. Cath. U. Am., Washington, 1976-83; prof. edn., chmn. edn. leadership U. New Orleans, 1983-90, dean Coll. Edn., 1990-92, univ. vice chancellor, provost, 1992-94, exec. vice chancellor, provost, 1994—2003, prof. Dept. Ednl. Leadership, Counseling, and Found., 2003—. Author: Ethics in Counseling and Psychotherapy, 1979, Questioning: Skills for the Helping Process, 1979, Counseling in Community College, 1982. 1st lt. U.S. Army, 1968-72. DuPont scholar U. Va., 1974. Mem. APA, ACA (ethics com. 1986-89), Am. Edn. Rsch. Assn., So. Assn. Counselor Edn. (chmn. ethics com. 1988-89), Acad. Counseling Psychology, Chi Sigma Iota (founding chpt. pres. 1985-87). Roman Catholic. Avocations: running, bicycling, music. Office: U New Orleans Dept Ednl Leadership Counseling & Found New Orleans LA 70148-0001 Office Phone: 504-280-6026. Business E-Mail: louis.paradise@uno.edu.

PARAMESWARAN, RAJU, accountant; b. Aymanam, India, Oct. 5, 1955; s. Raghunatha Iyer and Rajalakshmi Raghunathan; m. Ramaa Ramharith, June 3, 1981; children: Arjun children: Arun. BSc, U. Kerala, India, 1972—75. Chartered acct., Inst. Chartered Accts. India, 1979, CPA Botswana Inst. Accts., 1990. Chmn. Moores Rowland, Gaborone, Botswana, 1981—; dir. Drawtech Pty, Ltd., Lobatse, Botswana, 1995—2005; founder, dir. Flotek, Lobatse, 1999—, Budgetax, Ft. Myers, Fla., 2003—, Capri-Budgetax, Chennai, India, 2003—. Contbr. articles to profl. jours. Chmn. BOCCIM-Lobatse Bus. Coun., Lobatse, 2004—05. Mem.: Rotary Club Lobatse (pres. 1993—94, Paul Harris Fellow 2004).

PARAMESWARAN, RUPA, software security developer; BE, Bangalore U., India, 2000; PhD, Ga. Inst. Tech., Atlanta, 2006. Software developer Oracle, Redwood City, Calif., 2006—. Course instr. Ga. Inst. Tech., Atlanta, 2005—06, grad. rsch. asst. Contbr. articles to profl. jour. Office: Oracle 500 Oracle Pky Redwood City CA 94065

PARAN, MARK LLOYD, retired lawyer; b. Cleve., Feb. 1, 1953; s. Edward Walter and Margaret Gertrude (Ebert) P. AB in Sociology cum laude, Harvard U., 1977, JD, 1980. Bar: Ill. 1980, Mass. 1986, Tex. 1993. Assoc. Wilson & McIlvaine, Chgo., 1980-83, Lurie Sklar & Simon, Ltd., Chgo., 1983-85, Sullivan & Worcester, Boston, 1985-92; pvt. practice Boston, 1992, Euless, Tex., 1992—2002. Mem. ABA, State Bar Tex. Avocations: tornado hunting, severe thunderstorms, photography. Home and Office: 1050 W Ash Ln Apt 1015 Euless TX 76039-2171 Office Phone: 817-684-0725. Personal E-mail: f6tornado@tx.rr.com.

PARASCANDOLA, JOHN LOUIS, science historian; b. NYC, July 14, 1941; s. Louis Salvatore and Ann (Guido) P.; m. Elisa Castellon, June 1, 1963 (div. Dec. 1983); children: Mark, Adam; m. Randee Chapkin, Apr 24, 2004. BS, Bklyn. Coll., 1963; MS, PhD, U. Wis., 1968. Macy postdoc. rsch. fellow in history of medicine/biol. sci. Harvard U., 1968-69; asst. prof. history of pharmacy and history of sci. U. Wis., Madison, 1969-73, assoc. prof., 1973-80, prof., 1980-83; chief history of medicine divsn. Nat. Libr. of Medicine, Bethesda, Md., 1983-92; historian Pub. Hlth. Svc., 1992—2004; adj. faculty U. Md., Coll. Pk., 2003—. Author: The Development of American Pharmacology: John J. Abel and the Shaping of a Discipline, 1992; contbr. articles on history of biomed. sci. to profl. jours. Recipient Edward Kremers award, 1980, George Urdang medal, 1994; grantee NSF, 1971-76, Am. Acad. Arts and Scis., 1977-81, NIH, 1979-83. Mem. APHA, Internat. Acad. History of Pharmacy, Am. Inst. History of Pharmacy (dir.1973-81, chmn. coun. 1989—2007), Am. Assn. History of Medicine (pres. 2007-09), History of Sci.Soc., Am. Hist. Soc., Am. Chem. Soc. Home Phone: 301-984-2527; Office Phone: 301-346-3760. Personal E-mail: parascandola@verizon.net.

PARASHAR, NEETI, physics professor, researcher; d. Dayanand and Santosh Parashar; m. Sudhir Malik, July 7, 1995; children: Priya Malik, Prateek Malik. PhD, U. Delhi, 1995. Postdoc. rsch. assoc. Northeastern U., Boston, 1997—2002; assoc. prof. physics Purdue U. Calumet, Hammond, Ind., 2005—. Recipient Outstanding Faculty Scholar award; Rsch. grant, NSF, 2004. Office: Purdue Univ Calumet 2200 169th St Hammond IN 46323 Business E-Mail: neeti@fnal.gov.

PARASURAMAN, RAJA, psychology professor; b. New Delhi, Aug. 2, 1950; s. Tayamukulam Seshaier Parasuraman and Rukmani Iyer; life ptnr. Carryl Baldwin; children: Rachna, Shanta. BSc, Imperial Coll., London, 1972; PhD, Aston U., Birmingham, 1976. Prof. Cath. U. America, Washington, 1982—2004, George Mason U., Fairfax, Va., 2004—. Cons. Cognitive Sci. Lab, Falls Church, Va., 2004. Fellow: APA, AAAS, Internat. Ergonomics Assn.; mem.: NAS, NRC, Soc. Neurosci., Human Factors and Ergonomics Soc. (Paul M. Fitts Edn. award 2006, Franklin V. Taylor award 2004). Avocations: travel, music, art. Office: George Mason Univ 4400 University Dr MS 3F5 Fairfax VA 22030 Business E-Mail: rparasur@gmu.edu.

PARASURAMAN, RAVI KUMAR, nephrologist; b. Karnataka, India, Dec. 10, 1958; s. Parasuraman and Pattammal; m. Sathya Ramanujam, Feb. 4, 1987; 1 child, Emmanuel Kumar. MD, U. Bangalore, India, 1982. Lic. Am. Bd. Internal Medicine, 1996. Sr. staff, transplant nephrologist Henry Ford Hosp., Detroit, 1998—, med. dir. kidney and pancreas transplant program, 2002—; assoc. prof. medicine Wayne State U., Detroit, 2006—. Contbr. articles to profl. jours. Mem.: Royal Coll. Physicians. Office Fax: 313-916-2554. Business E-Mail: rparasu1@hfhs.org.

PARAVANO, DINO, artist; b. Rome, Nov. 9, 1935; arrived in US, 1992; s. Domenico and Gemma Paravano; m. Maria Grazia Malinverni, Jan. 25, 1964; children: Daniela Maria, Paolo Carlo, Domenico. Co-owner The Sandton Gallery, Johannesburg, 1970—73; owner Kempel's Gallery, Pretoria, South Africa, 1973—75; owner studio Johannesburg, 1956—75, Sandton, 1976—93, Tucson, 1992—. Exhibitions include Pride's Proud Family, Witte Mus., San Antonio (Elliot Lipskin award for representational painting, Soc. Animal Artists, NYC, 1996), Cheetah with Cubs (Soc. Animal Artist's award of excellence, NYC, 1990, Hiram Blauvelt Art Museum Purchase award, 2007), North of San Francisco (Master of Wildlife Artist award, Birds in Art, Leigh Yawkey Woodson Art Mus., Wausau, Wis., 1993), exhibited in group shows at Night Games (Second Place award on wild cat art, Frsno, LA, 2001), Big Rock (First Place landscape category award, Artist's Mag. Competition, Cin., 2005). Mem.: Pastel Soc. Am., Soc. Animal Artists. Roman Catholic. Avocation: trap and skeet shooting (won over 30 interclub and nat. trophies). Office Phone: 520-749-0197. Home Fax: 520-749-0197. Personal E-mail: dinoparavano@msn.com.

PARAZYNSKI, SCOTT E., astronaut; b. Little Rock, Ark., July 28, 1961; m. Gail Marie Vozzella; 2 children. BS in Biology, Stanford U., 1983, MD with honors, 1989. Intern Brigham and Women's Hosp., 1990; resident in emergency medicine Denver; astronaut NASA, Houston, 1992—, crew rep. for extravehicular activity, Astronaut Office Mission Devel. Br., crew rep. for space shuttle, space station, dep. Astronaut Office ISS Br. Author numerous publs. in the field of space physiology. Team coach for the Philippines Olympic Winter Games, Calgary, Canada, 1988. Recipient Predoctoral Tng. award in cancer biology, NIH, 1983, NASA-Ames Cert. of Recognition, 1990, Space Station Team Excellence award, 1996, NASA Exceptional Svc. medal, 1988, 1999, NASA Space Flight medal, 1994, 1997, 1998, 2001, NASA Disting. Svc. medal, 2002, Ellis Island Family Heritage award in Technology, Statue of Liberty-Ellis Island Found., Inc., 2005. Fellow: Aerospace Med. Assn.; mem.: Aircraft Owners and Pilots Assn., Exptl. Aircraft Assn., Assn. Space Explorers, Wilderness Med. Soc. (Rsch. award 1991), Am. Soc. Gravitational and Space Biology, Am. Alpine Club. Achievements include logged over 2,000 flight hours in a variety of aircraft; logged over 1.019 hours in space; 20 hours EVA; crew mem. STS-66 Atmospheric Laboratory for Applications and Science-3 (ATLAS-3)(1994), STS-86 Atlantis (1997), STS-95 Discovery (1998) and STS-100 Endeavour (2001); mission specialist reassigned from mission STS-118 to STS-120 to Internat. Space Station, 2006; mission specialist, lead spacewalker (EV1) that delivers Node 2 connecting module to the International Space Station for STS-120 Discovery Mission to International Space Station, 2007; competed on the US Development Luge Team and was ranked amoung the top 10 competitors in the nation during the 1988 Olympic Trials; served as an Olympic Team Coach for the Phillippines during the 1988 Olympic Winter Games in Calgary, Canada. Avocations: mountain climbing, rock climbing, flying, scuba diving, skiing, woodworking, nature photography. Office: Astronaut Office/CB NASA Johnson Space Ctr Houston TX 77058

PARCELLS, BILL (DUANE CHARLES PARCELLS), professional sports team executive, retired professional football coach; b. Englewood, NJ, Aug. 22, 1941; s. Charles and Ida (Naclerio) Parcells; m. Judith Parcells, 1962 (div. Jan. 16, 2002); children: Suzy, Jill, Dallas. BA, Wichita State U., 1964. Asst. coach Hastings Coll., Nebr., 1964, Wichita State U., Kans., 1965, US Mil. Acad., West Point, NY, 1966—69, Fla. State U., Tallahassee, 1970—72, Vanderbilt U., Nashville, 1973—74, Tex. Tech U., Lubbock, 1975—77; head coach USAF Acad., Colorado Springs, Colo., 1978—79; linebackers coach New England Patriots, 1980—81; defensive coord. NY Giants, 1979—80, defensive coord., linebackers coach, 1981—82, head coach, 1983—91, New England Patriots, 1993—97; NY Jets, 1997—2000, chief football ops., 2000—01; head coach Dallas Cowboys, 2003—07; studio analyst NBC Sports, 1991—92, NFL Pregame Show, ESPN, 2002, Monday Night Countdown, ESPN, 2007—; radio co-host ESPN radio, 2007; v.p. football ops. Miami Dolphins, 2007—. Co-author (with Jeff Coplon): Finding a Way to Win: The Principles of Leadership, Teamwork and Motivation, 1995; co-author: (with Will McDonough) The Final Season: My Last Year as Head Coach in the NFL, 2000. Named NFL Coach of Yr., Sporting News, 1986, UPI, 1986, 1994, AP, 1986, 1994, Maxwell Football Club, 1994, Pro Football Weekly, 1994, 1996; named to NFL 1990s All-Decade Team. Achievements include coaching the NY Giants to two Super Bowl Championships, 1986, 1990. Office: Miami Dolphins 7500 SW 30th St Davie FL 33314

PARCHER, L. PETER, lawyer; b. Bklyn., Apr. 30, 1937; BA, Hofstra U., 1958; LLB, St. Johns U., 1961. Bar: NY 1962, US Ct. Appeals, 2d Cir., US Dist. Ct., So. Dist. NY 1964, US Dist. Ct., Ea. Dist. NY 1964. Founding ptnr. Parcher, Hayes & Snyder; spl. sr. ptnr. Manatt, Phelps & Phillips, LLP, NYC. Named one of 3000 Leading Lawyers in Am., Lawdragon Mag., 2006, Entertainment Power Lawyers Top 100 - Outside Counsel, Hollywood Reporter, ESQ., 2007; named to Best Lawyers in Am., 2005—08. Fellow: Internat. Acad. Trial Lawyers, Am. Coll. Trial Lawyers. Office: Manatt Phelps & Phillips LLP 7 Times Sq New York NY 10036 Office Phone: 212-790-4520. Office Fax: 212-790-4545. Business E-Mail: pparcher@manatt.com.

PARDAVI-HORVATH, MARTHA MARIA, engineering educator, researcher; b. Budapest, Hungary, Feb. 1940; came to the U.S., 1985; d. Elek and Katalin (Sattelberger) Horvath; m. Ferenc Pardavi, July 7, 1967; 1 child, Martha Pardavi. MSc in Physics, Moscow State U., Moscow, 1967; PhD in Physics, Hungarian Acad. Scis., 1985, Roland Eotvos U., Budapest, Hungary, 1988. Jr. rsch. assoc. Hungarian Acad. Scis., 1967—69, rsch. assoc., 1969—74, rsch. group head Magnetic Crystal Growth and Characterization, 1977—81, dep. head dept. crystal tech., 1981—85, sr. rsch. assoc. Ctrl. Rsch. Inst. Physics, 1988—89; postdoctoral fellow Ohio State U., 1985—86; prof. engrng. and applied sci., dept. elec. and computer engrng. George Washington U., Washington, 1989—2006, assoc. dean, 2006—. Vis. prof. NRC, Rome, 1989, U. Calif., San Diego, 1999, Inst. Applied Magnetism, Madrid. Co-author: 6 books; contbr. more than 170 articles to profl. jours. Mem.: AAAS, IEEE (magnetic soc., edn. com., publ. com., v.p.), Internat. Symmetry Assn. (bd. dirs.), Am. Inst. Physics, Sigma Xi. Avocations: classical music, fine arts. Office: George Washington U Dept ECE Washington DC 20052-0001 Home Phone: 301-230-2577. Business E-Mail: mpardavi@gwu.edu.

PARDEE, ARTHUR BECK, biochemist, educator; b. Chgo., July 13, 1921; s. Charles A. and Elizabeth B. (Beck) Pardee; m. Ruth Sager (dec.); m. Ann Goodman; children: Michael, Richard, Thomas. BS, U. Calif., Berkeley, 1942; MS, Calif. Inst. Tech., 1943, PhD, 1947; D (hon.), U. Paris, 1993. Merck postdoctoral fellow U. Wis., 1947—49; mem. faculty U. Calif., Berkeley, 1949—61, assoc. prof., 1957—61; NSF fellow Pasteur Inst., 1957—58; prof. biology, chmn. dept. biochem. scis. Princeton (NJ) U., 1961—67, prof. biochemistry, 1961—75, Donner prof. sci., 1966; prof. Dana Farber Cancer Inst. and biochem. pharmacology dept. Harvard Med. Sch., Boston, 1975—. Co-author: Experiments in Biochemical Research Techniques, 1957; editor: Biochemica et Biophysica Acta, 1962—68; contbr. over 500 articles to publs. Mem. rsch. adv. coun. Am. Cancer Soc., 1967—71; trustee Cold Spring Harbor Lab. Quantitative Biology, 1963—69. Recipient Young Biochemists travel award, NSF, 1952, Krebs medal, Fedn. European Biochem. Socs., 1973, Rosenstiel award, Brandeis U., 1975, 3M award, Fedn. Am. Socs., Exptl. Biology, 1980, CIIT prize, 1993, Disting. Alumnus award, Calif. Inst. Tech., 1999; named Princess Takamatu lectr., 1990, hon. faculty mem., Nanjing U., 1999; fellow, Internat. Inst. for Advanced Studies, 1999. Fellow: AAAS; mem.: NAS (editl. bd.

proc. 1971—73, com. on scis. and pub. policy 1973—76), Chem. Industry Inst. Toxicology (Founders award, Boehringer-Mannheim award 1998), Ludwig Inst. Cancer Rsch. (sci. com. 1988—), Japanese Biochem. Soc., Am. Philos. Soc., Am. Soc. Microbiologists, Am. Assn. Cancer Rsch. (pres. 1985—86), Am. Soc. Biol. Chemists (treas. 1964—70, pres. 1980—81), Am. Chem. Soc. (Paul Lewis award 1960). Office: 44 Binney St Boston MA 02115-6013 Office Phone: 617-632-3372. Business E-Mail: arthur_pardee@dfci.harvard.edu.

PARDEE, JEFFREY CLARK, county government official; b. NYC, May 14, 1944; s. Jack Howard II and Florence (Brennan) P.; m. Mary Anna Weil, Dec. 23, 1966; children: Brennan James, Kennedy Clark. BBA, Eastern Mich. U., 1968; MBA in Fin., U. Detroit, 1971; postgrad., Nova U., 1975-81. Cert. pub. fin. officer. Fin. analyst Sterling Axle Plant div. Ford Motor Co., Sterling Heights, Mich., 1968-73; budget dir. Genesee County, Flint, Mich., 1973-76, Oakland County, Pontiac, Mich., 1976-95, dep. dir. mgmt. and budget, 1996-99, dir. mgmt. and budget, 1999—. Treas. Flint-Genesee Corp. for Econ. Growth, 1978-81; pres. Genesee County Econ. Devel. Corp., Flint, 1982-84; bd. dirs. Forward Devel. Corp; chmn. bd. dirs. Communications Services Network, Inc.; adj. prof. pub. budgeting U. Mich., Flint, 1984-85. Editor Statewide News-Mich. Rental Housing Assn. Newsletter, 1985-95. Merit counselor Boy Scouts Am., Grand Blanc, Mich., 1982—, dist. com. chmn. Tall Pines Coun., 1998-2001; councilman City of Grand Blanc, 1985—; treas. Crime Watch Assn., Grand Blanc, 1985—, Genesee County Met. Alliance, Flint, 1986-91; bd. dirs. Flint-Genesee Revolving Loan Fund, 1980-90; treas. Partnership Saginaw Bay Watershed, 1987-2001, Grand Blanc Vision 2020, 1998—; pres. Mich. Mcpl. Fin. Officers Assn., 1995-96; mem. GFOA Mgmt. Budget Com., 1998—; mem. City Coun., Grand Blanc, Mich., 1985--. Recipient Fin. Officer award CFO Mag., 2000. Mem. Govt. Fin. Officers Assn. U.S. and Can. (review com. 1984—, Disting. Budget Presentation award, Excellence in Fin. Reporting award), Am. Soc. Pub. Adminstrs., G.M.I. Mgmt. and Engring. Inst. (adv. bd. 1984-87). Republican. Mem. Lds Ch. Avocations: racquetball, auto racing. Home: 11390 Grand Oak Dr Grand Blanc MI 48439-1219 Office: Oakland County Dept Mgmt & Budget 1200 N Telegraph Rd Pontiac MI 48341-0407 E-mail: pardeej@co.oakland.mi.us.

PARDEE, MARGARET ROSS, violinist, violist, educator; b. Valdosta, Ga., May 10, 1920; d. William Augustus and Frances Ross (Burton) P.; m. Daniel Rogers Butterly, July 4, 1944. Diploma, Juilliard Sch. Music, 1940, grad. diploma, 1942; diploma, Juilliard Grad. Sch., 1945. Instr. violin and viola Manhattanville Coll. Sacred Heart, NYC, 1942-54, Juilliard Sch., NYC, 1942, Meadowmount Sch. Music, Westport, NY, 1956-84, 88-92, Bowdoin Coll. Music Festival and Sch., Maine, summer 1987. Mem. faculty Estherwood Sch. and Summr Festival, 1984-86, Killington (Vt.) Music Festival, 1993—, Mannes Sch. Music, 1996—; concert master Gt. Neck (L.I., N.Y.) Symphony, 1954-85; adj. assoc. prof. Aaron Copeland Sch. Music, Queens Coll., CUNY, Flushing, 1978—, Adelphi U., Garden City, N.Y., 1979-83; adj. prof. SUNY, Purchase, 1980-93; vis. prof. Simon Bolivar Youth Orch. and Conservatory, Caracas and Barquisimeto, Venezuela, 1988, 89, Conservatorio Orch. Nat. Juvenil, Caracas, 1988, 89; mem. jury for internat. competitions; guest artist profl. 1st Internat. Festival for Young Violinists, Caracas, 1988; guest vis. prof. Orch. Filarmonica Nat. y Mcpl. Sinfonica Caracas, 1992, 97. Debut N.Y. Town Hall, 1952; toured U.S. as soloist and in chamber music groups; soloed with symphony orchs., Miss., N.J., D.C., N.Y. Bd. dirs. Meadowmount Sch. Music. Recipient Andres Bello award Venezuela Min. Edn., 1993. Mem. Soc. for Strings (dir. 1965-92), Assoc. Music Tchrs. League N.Y. (cert.), N.Y. State Music Tchrs. Assn. (cert., citation 1989), Music Tchrs. Nat. Assn., Am. String Tchrs. Assn. (citation for exceptional leadership 1990), Am. Fedn. Musicians, Viola Rsch. Soc. Office: care Juilliard Sch Lincoln Ctr Plz New York NY 10023

PARDEE, OTWAY O'MEARA, computer scientist, educator; b. Seattle, June 26, 1920; s. Otway and Mary Gertrude (O'Meara) Pardee; m. Marilynn Lowrie, Aug. 9, 1946; children: Irene, Loraine, Suzanne. BS in Elec. Engring., U. Wash., 1941; PhD in Elec. Engring., Stanford U., 1948. Instr. math. Syracuse U., NY, 1948-52, asst. to assoc. prof. NY, 1952-69, dir. Computing Ctr. NY, 1962-69, prof. computer sci. NY, 1969-86, prof. emeritus, 1986—. With USNR, 1944—46. Mem.: IEEE, AAUP (pres. Syracuse U. chpt. 1960), Am. Phys. Soc., Math. Assn. Am., Am. Math. Soc., Assn. Computing Machinery (chmn. Syracuse chpt. 1963), Tau Beta Pi, Sigma Xi. Avocations: camping, photography. Home: 843 Maryland Ave Syracuse NY 13210-2502 Office: Syracuse U Ctr for Sci and Tech Ste 2-175 Syracuse NY 13244-0001 Personal E-mail: rpardee1@twcny.rr.com. Business E-Mail: oopardee@syr.edu.

PARDEN, ROBERT JAMES, engineering educator, management consultant; b. Mason City, Iowa, Apr. 17, 1922; s. James Ambrose and Mary Ellen (Fahey) P.; m. Elizabeth Jane Taylor, June 15, 1955; children: Patricia Gale, James A., John R., Nancy Ann. BS in Mech. Engring, State U. Iowa, 1947, MS, 1951, PhD, 1953. Reg. profl. engr. Iowa, Calif.; lic. gen. contractor Calif. Indsl. engr. LaCrosse Rubber Mills, 1947-50; asso. dir. Iowa Mgmt. Course, 1951-53; asso. prof. indsl. engring. Ill. Inst. Tech., 1953-54; prof. engring. mgmt. Santa Clara U., 1955—, dean Sch. Engring., 1955-82; prin. Saratoga Cons. Group (Calif.), 1982—. Mem. Sec. Navy's Survey Bd. Grad. Edn., 1964 Mem. Saratoga Planning Commn., 1959-61. Served to 1st lt., Q.M.C. AUS, 1943-46. Named to Silicon Valley Engring. Hall of Fame Silicon Valley Engring. Coun., 1993. Mem. ASME (chmn. Santa Clara Valley sect. 1958), Am. Soc. Engring. Edn. (chmn. Pacific N.W. sect. 1960), Am. Inst. Indsl. Engrs. (edn. chmn. 1958-63, dir. ASEE-ECPD affairs 1963-68), Nat. Soc. Profl. Engrs., Engrs. Council Profl. Devel. (dir. 1964-65, 66-69), Soc. Advancement Mgmt., ASEM, Sigma Xi, Tau Beta Pi. Roman Catholic. Home: 19832 Bonnie Ridge Way Saratoga CA 95070-5010 Office: Santa Clara U Sch Engring Santa Clara CA 95053-0001 Business E-Mail: rparden@scu.edu.

PARDES, HERBERT, health facility executive, psychiatrist, educator; b. Bronx, NY, July 7, 1934; s. Louis and Frances (Bergman) P.; m. Juidith Ellen Silber, June 9, 1957; children: Stephen, Lawrence, James. BS, Rutgers U., 1956; MD, SUNY-Downstate Med. Center, Bklyn., 1960; DSc (hon.), SUNY, 1990. Straight med. intern Kings County Hosp., 1960-61, intern & resident in psychiatry Bklyn., 1961-62, 64-66; asst. prof. psychiatry Downstate Med. Ctr., Bklyn., 1968-72, prof., chmn. dept., 1972-75; dir. psychiat. svcs. Kings County Hosp., Bklyn., 1972-75; prof., chmn. dept. psychiatry U. Colo. Med. Sch., 1975-78; dir. psychiat. svcs. Colo. Psychiat. Hosp., Denver, 1975-78; dir. NIMH, Rockville, Md., 1978-84; asst. surgeon gen. USPHS, 1978-84; prof. psychiatry Columbia U., NYC, 1984—, chmn. dept., 1984; dir. Psychiat. Svc. Presbyn. Hosp. (now Columbia Presbyn. Center of NY Presbyn. Hosp.), NYC, 1984-89; dir. NY State Psychiatric Inst., 1984—89; v.p. for health scis., dean faculty medicine Columbia U., NYC, 1989—99; pres., CEO NY-Presbyn. Hosp. and Healthcare Systems, NYC, 2000—. Bd. trustees Healthcare Leadership Coun.; bd. dirs. Value Line, Inc., 2000—. Contbr. articles to med. jours. Pres. sci. bd. Alliance for Rsch. on Schizophrenia and Depression. Capt. M.C., AUS, 1972-74. Named Ann. Hon. Lectr. Downstate Med. Ctr. Alumni Assn., 1972; recipient Alumni Achievement medal, 1980, William Menniner award ACP, 1992, Dorothy Dix award Mental Illness Fedn., 1992, Vester Mark award, 1994, Salmon award, 1996. Mem. Assn. Am. Med. Colls. (chair 1995-96), Am. Psychiat. Assn. (v.p. 1986-88, pres. 1989-90, Disting. Svc. award 1993), Inst. Medicine, Am. Psychoanalytic Assn., Coun. of Deans (adminstrv. bd., chair-elect 1993-94, chair 1994-95), Assoc. Med. Schs. NY (pres. 1995-2000), Phi Beta Kappa, Alpha Omega Alpha. Office: NY Presbyn Hosp Pres and CEOs Office 177 Ft Washington Ave New York NY 10032 also: NY Presbyn Hosp 525 E 68th St New York NY 10021 Office Phone: 212-305-8000. Business E-Mail: pardesh@nyp.org.*

PARDIECK, ROGER L., lawyer; b. Seymour, Ind., Mar. 1, 1937; s. Martin W. and Lorna (Wente) P.; m. Mary Ann Pardieck; children: Amy, Andrew, Melissa, Duncan. AB, Ind. U., 1959, LLB, 1963; student, Internat. Grad. Sch., Stockholm, 1960. Bar: Ind. 1963, US Dist. Ct. (so. dist.) Ind. 1964, US Ct. Appeals (7th cir.) 1965; diplomate Am. Bd. Trial Advocates. Ptnr. Montgomery, Elsner and Pardieck, 1965-84; prin. Pardieck Law Firm, Seymour, Ind., 1985—. Faculty Nat. Inst. Trial Advocacy, Ind.; lectr. in field. Contbr. articles to profl. jours. Fellow Internat. Acad. Trial Lawyers, Am. Coll. Trial Lawyers, Ind. Trial Lawyers Assn. (bd. dirs. 1969—, pres. 1975), Ind. Coll. Trial Lawyers, Roscoe Pound Found., Ind. Bar Assn.; mem. FBA, ATLA (bd. govs. 1985-88), Ind. State Bar Assn. (bd. govs. 1980-82), Inst. for Injury Reduction (bd. dirs. 1992-95), Nat. Bd. Trial Advocacy, Safety Attys. Fedn. (bd. dirs. 1993-95), Internat. Soc. Primerus Law Firms (bd. dirs. 1995-2004), Am. Bd. Trial Advocates, Trial Lawyers Pub. Justice (Ind. coord. 1991-, bd. dirs. 2005-), Am. Judicature Soc., Inner Cir. Advocates Office: 100 N Chestnut St PO Box 608 Seymour IN 47274-0608 Office Phone: 812-523-8686. Business E-Mail: rlp@pardiecklaw.com.

PARDINGTON, MARY ELIZABETH, elementary school educator; d. John and Elizabeth Curell; m. David Charles Pardington, July 9, 1993; children: Catherine, Sarah, Veronica, Mary Kate. BS in Elem. Edn., Oakland U., Rochester, Mich., 1987, MA in Curriculum, Instrn., and Leadership, 1991. Continuing tchg. cert. Dept. Edn. Mich., 1991. Elem. tchr. Birmingham (Mich.) Pub. Schs., 1987—. Mem. accreditation team Mich. Accreditation Program, 1990—91; co-head tchr. Beverly Elem. Sch., Beverly Hills, Mich., 1995—, svc. squad leader, 1995—. V.p. Concerned Catholics Shelby Twp., Mich., 1993—, catechism tchr., 1995—; soprano soloist Assumption Grotto Choir, Detroit, 1992—, asst. choir dir., 1994—; dir., prodr. Coffee Ho. Fundraiser, Detroit, 1999—2002. Recipient Workplace Excellence award, Birmingham Pub. Schs., 2002, 2003, award, Friends of Different Learners, 2005; Paul Douglas Tchr. scholar, US Congress, 1986—87, Performance grantee, Birmingham Pub. Schs., 1988. Mem.: NSTA. Republican. Roman Catholic. Avocations: music, old movies, logic puzzles. Office: Beverly Elementary School Beverly Hills MI 48025

PARDO, JANETTE M., archivist, librarian; b. Passaic, NJ, May 22, 1970; d. Jesus and Gladys Pardo. BA, Rutgers U., Newark, 1992, MLS, 2001. Libr. Wayne Pub. Libr., NJ, 1995—. Archival cons. Caucus Archival Projects Evaluation Svc., Trenton, NJ, 2001—. Mem.: ALA, Assn. Documentary Editors, Romance Writers Am., Mid-Atlantic Regional Archival Conf. Democrat. Roman Catholic. Avocation: writing. Office: Wayne Pub Libr 461 Valley Rd Wayne NJ 07470 Personal E-mail: jpardo22@yahoo.com.

PARDUE, A. MICHAEL, retired plastic and reconstructive surgeon; b. Nashville, June 23, 1931; s. Andrew Peyton and Ruby (Fly) P. BS, Sewanee U. of the South, 1953; MD, U. Tenn., 1957. Resident in gen. surgery Pittsfield (Mass.) Affiliated Hosps., 1966; resident in plastic surgery N.Y. Hosp./Cornell Med. Ctr., 1968; plastic surgeon A. Michael Pardue, M.D., Thousand Oaks, Calif., 1968-98; ret., 1995. Lt. comdr. USN, 1956-62. Fellow ACS; mem. Am. Soc. Plastic Surgeons, Am. Soc. Aesthetic Plastic Surgery, Calif. Soc. Plastic Surgeons. Episcopalian. Avocations: fly fishing, skiing, golf, horses, African safaris. Home: 3217 Augusta Dr Bozeman MT 59715-8792

PARDUE, MARY-LOU, biology professor; b. Lexington, Ky., Sept. 15, 1933; d. Louis Arthur and Mary Allie (Marshall) P. BS, William and Mary Coll., 1955; MS, U. Tenn., 1959; PhD, Yale U., 1970; DSc (hon.), Bard Coll., 1985, U. Edinburgh, Scotland, 2008. Postdoctoral fellow Inst. Animal Genetics, Edinburgh, Scotland, 1970—72; assoc. prof. biology MIT, Cambridge, 1972—80, prof., 1980—, Boris Magasanik prof. biology, 1995—. Summer course organizer Cold Spring Harbor Lab., NY, 1971—80; mem. rev. com. NIH, 1974—78, 1980—84, nat. adv. gen. med. scis. coun., 1984—86; sci. adv. com. Wistar Inst., Phila., 1976—2004; mem. health and environ. rsch. adv. com. U.S. Dept. Energy, 1987—94; bd. trustees Associated Univs., Inc., 1995—97; mem. Burroughs Wellcome Adv. Com. on Career Awards in Biomed. Scis., 1996—2000, bd. dirs., 2002—08; chair Inst. of Medicine Com. on Biol. Basis of Sex and Gender Differences, 1999—2001. Mem. editl. bd.: profl. jours.; contbr. articles to profl. jours. Mem. rev. com. Am. Cancer Soc., 1990-93, Howard Hughes Med. Inst. Adv. Bd., 1993-2000. Recipient Esther Langer award Langer Cancer Rsch. Found., 1977, Lucius Wilbur Cross medal Yale Grad. Sch., 1989; grantee NIH, NSF, Am. Cancer Soc. Fellow AAAS, MA Acad. Sci., NAS (chmn. genetics sect. 1991-94, coun. 1995-98), Am. Acad. Arts and Sci. (coun. mem. 1992-96); mem. NRC (bd. on biology 1989-95), Genetics Soc. Am. (pres. 1982-83), Am. Soc. Cell Biology (coun. 1977-80, pres. 1985-86), Phi Beta Kappa, Phi Kappa Phi, Sigma Xi. Office: MIT Dept Biology 68-670 77 Massachusetts Ave Dept 68-670 Cambridge MA 02139-4307 Office Phone: 617-253-6741. Business E-Mail: mlpardue@mit.edu.

PARDUN, THOMAS E., telecommunications industry executive; BBA in Economics, Mktg., U. Iowa. Various mgmt. positions IBM; pres., ctrl. group Sprint; pres., Asia-Pacific MediaOne Internat., 1996—2000; chmn. Western Digital Corp., 2000—01, 2007—. Bd. dirs. Occam Networks, Inc., MegaPath Networks, Inc., Western Digital Corp., 1993—, CalAmp Corp., 2006—. Office: Western Digital Corp 20511 Lake Forest Dr Lake Forest CA 92630-7741 Office Phone: 949-672-7000.*

PARE, LAURA, neurosurgeon, educator; d. David Pare; married; children: Julian Delfino, Chiara Delfino. BA, Reed Coll., Portland,Oreg., 1981; MD, U. Chgo., Ill., 1985. Diplomate in neurosurgery Am. Bd. Neurol. Surgeons, 1999. Assoc. prof. U. Calif., Irvine, 2002—. Recipient Roland P. Mackie award, Am. Acad. Neurology, 1984, Donaghie Prize, New Eng. Neurosurg. Soc., 1991. Fellow: RCS; mem.: Congress Neurol. Surgeons. Office: Univ Calif Irvine 101 The City Dr Orange CA 92868

PAREDES, JAMES ANTHONY, anthropologist; b. NYC, Sept. 29, 1939; s. Antonio Paredes Piñeiro and Mildred Olene (Brown) P.; m. Anna Hamilton, Nov. 25, 1959 (div. 1984); children: J. Anthony Jr., Anna Teresa P. Lesinski, Sara Caroline P. Campbell; m. Elizabeth Dixon Purdum, Aug. 10, 1985 (div. 1994): 1 stepchild, David Joseph Plante; m. Alleen Dimitroff Deutsch, July 24, 2003. BA, Oglethorpe U., 1961; MA, U. N.Mex., 1964, PhD, 1969. Rsch. coord. Upper Miss. Mental Health Ctr., Bemidji, Minn., 1964-67; asst. prof., acting dir. Am. Ind. Studies Bemidji State Coll., 1967-68; community devel. specialist U. Minn. Agrl. Extension Svc., Bemidji, 1967-68; asst. prof. dept. anthropology Fla. State U., Tallahassee, 1969-74, assoc. prof., 1974-78, prof., 1979-99, emeritus prof., 1999—, chmn. dept., 1974-77, 84-90; chief ethnography and Indian affairs S.E. regional office Nat. Park Service, Atlanta, 1999—2006. Adj. prof. dept. anthropology U. Fla., Gainesville, 1979-2004; cons. Nat. Marine Fisheries Svc., Galveston, Tex., 1987-88, Bur. Indian Affairs, Washington, 1985, 92, Fed. Recognition Panel, Assn. on Am. Indian Affairs, N.Y.C., 1987-88. Author: Indios de los Estados Unidos Anglosajones, 1992; editor: Anishinabe: Six Studies of Modern Chippewa, 1980, Indians of the Southeastern United States in the Late 20th Century, 1992; co-editor: Classics of Practicing Anthropology: 1978-1998, 2000; co-editor: Anthropologists and Indians in the New South, 2001; series editor: Contemporary American Indian Studies; author or co-author numerous articles, chpts. in books, revs. Mem. Sci. and Statis. Com., Gulf of Mex. Fishery Mgmt. Coun., Tampa, Fla., 1978-88. Recipient svc. award Poarch Creek Indians, 1990, Woodrow Wilson Found. fellow U. N.Mex., 1961-62; Nat. Inst. Mental Health predoctoral fellow U. N.Mex., 1968-69; Rockefeller Ctr. for Study of So. Culture and Religion fellow, Fla. State U., 1978. Fellow: Soc. for Applied Anthropology (assoc. editor 1983—88, pres. 1993—95), Am. Anthrop. Assn. (exec. bd. 2004—07); mem.: Assn. Sr. Anthropologists (pres. 2008—), Fla. Acad. Scis. (sect. chair 1984—85), So. Anthrop. Soc. (pres. 1988—89), Sigma Xi (Fla. State U. chpt. pres. 1977—78). Democrat. Avocation: walking. Personal E-mail: janthonyparedes@bellsouth.net.

PAREDES, TROY ALLAN, commissioner, law educator; b. Feb. 21, 1971; s. Smiley and Hollie Paredes; m. Laura Paredes. AB in Econs., with honors, U. Calif., Berkeley, 1992; JD, Yale Law Sch., New Haven, 1996. Bar: (Calif.). Assoc. corp. dept. O'Melveny & Myers LLP, LA, San Francisco, 1996—99; assoc. corp., energy, natural resources dept. Steptoe & Johnson LLP, LA, 1999—2000; assoc. corp. securities grp. Irell & Manella LLP, LA, 2000—01; assoc. prof. Wash. U. Sch. Law, St. Louis, 2001—05, prof., 2005—08; commr. SEC, Washington, 2008—. Reporting simplification task force AICPA, 2004—07; visiting prof. UCLA Sch. Law, 2005, Georgetown U. Law Ctr., Washington, 2006, Wash. U. Olin Bus. Sch., 2007—; mem. Mo. Securities Adv. Com., 2007—; museum com. SEC Hist. Soc., 2007—. Co-author (with Louis Loss & Joel Seligman) multi-volume securities regulation treatise; contbr. articles to profl. jours. Rsch. grant, Boeing Ctr. Tech., Info. & Mgmt., 2005, Microsoft Corp., 2005. Mem.: Federalist Soc., Hispanic Nat. Bar Assn., Am. Law Econs. Assn. Office: SEC 100 F St NE Washington DC 20549

PAREENE, ALEX E., blog editor; b. July 23, 1985; Attended, NYU. Guest editor Gawker Media, 2004—06, blogger, 2007—; co-editor Wonkette.com, 2006, editor, 2006—07. Office: Gawker Media 210 Elizabeth St 4th Fl New York NY 10012 Business E-Mail: alexp@gawker.com.*

PAREKH, DIPEN, medical educator; m. Amruta Parekh. MD, U. Poona, India, 1991. Diplomate U. Poona, 1991. Asst. prof. UT Health Sci. Ctr., San Antonio, 2006—07, assoc. prof., 1997—. Office: UT Health Sci Ctr 7703 Floyd Curl MC 7845 San Antonio TX 78229 Business E-Mail: parekhd@uthscsa.edu.

PARENT, ANGELE, research scientist; d. Jean-Baptiste Parent and Therese Rioux; m. Gopal Thinakaran, May 17, 1998; children: Abigael Abirami Thinakaran, Daphne Devika Thinakaran, Cedric Chandran Thinakaran. PhD, U. Montreal, Canada, 1990. Postdoc. fellow U. McGill, Montreal, Quebec, Canada, 1990—93, Jonhs Hopkins U., Balt., 1993—97; vis. assoc. NIH, Rockville, Md., 1997—99; rsch. asst. prof. U. Chgo., 1999—2005, rsch. assoc. prof., 2005—. IIRG-02-3952, Alzheimer's Assn., 2003—05, IIRG-06-26148, 2006—09, 1R01 Ns055223, NIH-NINDS, 2007—. Office: Univ Chgo 924 East 57th St Chicago IL 60637

PARENT, ANNETTE RICHARDS, freelance writer, artist; b. Elizabeth, NJ, May 5, 1924; d. Edward Carrington Mayo and Elizabeth Veech (Coan) Richards; m. Hiram Lincoln Parent, Mar. 23, 1957; children: Laurence Edward, Anne Mayo Parent Fischer Pasqual. BA, Swarthmore Coll., 1946; postgrad., U. Ariz., Western N.Mex. U. Nat. lit. sec. Woman's Internat. League for Peace and Freedom, Phila., 1946-48; free lance writer various, 1948—. Contbr. poems to ann. anthologies Intermountain Friendly Rev., 1990, 91, 92; contbr. non-fiction articles to numerous publs.; painter, photographer, poet, book reviewer, presenter elderhostel commencement addresses, talks about Quakerism to coll. classes and Presbyn. youth groups; slide talks on Russia; editor: The Troglodyte at Carlsbad Caverns Nat. Park, 1966-80. Mem. search com. for Western N.Mex. U. mus. dir., 1987; co-founder Youth Coun. Against Conscription, Phila., 1946-48; organizer Westtown (Pa.) Sch. peace team, 1940-42; mem. Nat. Coun. Fellowship of Reconciliation, N.Y.C., 1941-46; former mem. safety com. Carlsbad Caverns Nat. Park; charter mem., officer A Christian Ministry in the Nat. Parks, Carlsbad Caverns Nat. Park, N.Mex., 1970-80, centennial com., 1975; founder, leader of Peace Team, Westtown Sch., 1940-42. Winner N.C. Wyeth 1st in Art award Westtown Sch., 1942, Alumni Assn. 1st in Art award 1942; recipient awards in juried and non-juried art shows Carlsbad Area Art Assn., N.Mex., Grant County Art Guild, Black Range Artists Inc., Best of Show award for The Great American Litterbug, Annual N. Mex. State Exhbition, NLAPW, 2005. Mem. AAUW, Nat. League Am. Pen Women (in dual categories of art and letters, v.p., sec., treas., winner non-fiction nat. contest 1955), Soc. Southwestern Authors, Grant County Art Guild, Black Range Artists Inc. (v.p. 1991), Nat. Audubon Soc. (publicity chmn. Southwestern N.Mex. coun. del. 1987-92); mem. many nat. environ., peace, and civil rights organizations. Mem. Religious Soc. of Friends. Avocations: hiking, sewing, piano, swimming, reading, bridge. Home and Office: Apt A478 2645 E Southern Ave Tempe AZ 85282-7512

PARENT, ELIZABETH SCHIRO, costume designer, educator; b. New Orleans, Apr. 9, 1942; d. Elizabeth Jane Grossimon and Roman Michael Schiro; m. Beauregard Jean Parent, Aug. 18, 1962; children: Lisa Angele Hickey, Christine Michel Smith, Colette Andree Raphel. MFA, Tulane U., New Orleans, 1994. Costume designer Free Lance Artist, New Orleans, 1980—2008.

PARENT, LOUISE MARIE, lawyer, corporate financial executive; b. San Francisco, Aug. 28, 1950; d. Jules D. and Mary Louise (Bartholomew) P.; m. John P. Casaly, Jan. 5, 1980. AB, Smith Coll., 1972; JD, Georgetown U., 1975. Bar: N.Y. 1976, U.S. Dist. Ct. (so. dist.) N.Y. 1976. Assoc. Donovan Leisure, NYC, 1975-77; various positions, then gen. counsel Am. Express Info. Svcs. Corp., NYC, 1977-92; dep. gen. counsel Am. Express Co., NYC, 1992-93, exec. v.p., gen. counsel, 1993—. Bd. dirs. A Better Chance Inc., Cooke Ctr. for Learning and Devel., Nat. Womens Law Ctr; trustee Smith Coll.; mem. adv. bd. Studio in a Sch. Mem. ABA (com. depts. corp. law), NYC Bar Assn., N.Y. State Bar Assn., Coun. on Fgn. Rels. Home: 1170 5th Ave New York NY 10029-6527 Office: Am Express Co Am Express Tower World Fin Ctr New York NY 10285-0001 Office Phone: 212-640-2000.*

PARENT, MARY CAMPBELL, film company executive; b. 1965; Agt. trainee ICM; dir. develop. to v.p. prodn. New Line Cinema, 1994—97; sr. v.p. prodn. Universal Pictures, Universal City, Calif., 1997—2000, exec. v.p. prodn., 2000—01, co-pres. prodn., 2001—03, vice chmn., worldwide prodn., 2003—05, prodr., 2006—08; chairperson worldwide motion picture group Metro-Goldwyn-Mayer Inc., L.A., 2008—, mem. Office of CEO, 2009—. Exec. prodr.: (films) Set It Off, 1996, Trial and Error, 1997, Pleasantville, 1998, The Kingdom, 2007; prodr.: You, Me and Dupree, 2006, Welcome Home, Roscoe Jenkins, 2008; prodn. mgr.: Dangerous Ground, 1997. Named one of The 100 Most Powerful Women in Entertainment, Hollywood Reporter, 2004, 50 Women to Watch, The Wall St. Jour., 2008. Office: Metro-Goldwyn-Mayer Inc 10250 Constellation Blvd Los Angeles CA 90067*

PARENT, RODOLPHE JEAN, retired Canadian air force officer, pilot; b. Thurso, Que., Can., June 16, 1937; s. Eugène Jean and Eliane Marie (Raby) P.; m. Michelle Marie Masse, Aug. 10, 1963; children: Stéphane, Nathalie, Cynthia Student, Coll. Militaire Royal de St-Jean, 1958-61; B.Sc., Royal Mil. Coll. Can., Kingston, Ont., 1963. Commd. Royal Can. Air Force, 1958; advanced through grades to brig.-gen., 1984; joined 425 Squadron for ops. on CF-101 aircraft Bagotville, Que., 1964-69; worked for Directorate of Recruiting and Selection at Nat. Def. Hdqrs., Ottawa, Ont., Canada, 1969-71; chief of ops. 433 Tactical Fighter Squadron, Bagotville, 1972-75, Can. Forces Base Bagotville, 1975-76; comdg. officer 433 Tactical Fighter Squadron, 1976-80; asst. dir. personnel careers Nat. Def. Hdqrs., Ottawa, 1980-81; base comdr. Can. Forces Base Lahr, Federal Republic Germany, 1981-83; commandant Coll. Militaire Royal de Saint-Jean, Que., 1983-86; dir. gen. personnel careers other ranks Nat. Def. Hdqrs., Ottawa, 1986-89; def. attaché Paris, 1989-92; ret., 1992. Decorated Order of Mil. Merit, Order of St. John of Jerusalem Roman Catholic. Avocations: hockey, tennis, windsurfing. E-mail: rudy.michelle@rogers.com.

PARENTE, ROBERT BRUCE, electrical engineer, consultant; b. Sept. 10, 1936; s. Almerico Elmer and Royda (Boyd) P.; m. Rozalinda Thelma Saturnio, May 28, 1977; children: Jennifer Dee, Jessica Dale, Jacquelyn Dawn. BSEE, MIT, 1959, MS in Engring., 1959, EE, 1961, PhD, 1966. Registered profl. engr., Calif. Instr. elec. engring. MIT, Cambridge, 1959-65; asst. prof. engring. UCLA, 1965-70; mgr. electric power sys. Sys. Devel. Corp., Santa Monica, Calif., 1970-72, dir. planning, 1973-75, dep. dir. energy devel., 1975-76; sr. cons. Theodore Barry & Assocs., LA, 1976-78; propr. Parente & Assocs., mgmt. cons., LA, 1978—. Expert witness before utility commns.; cons. to U.S. and fgn. electric power cos. Author: Electric Power Pools, 1983; contbr. articles to profl. jours.; patentee in field. Res. lt. sheriff L.A. County Sheriff's Dept., 1970—. Mem. IEEE, Inst. Mgmt. Scis., Ops. Rsch. Soc. Am., Sigma Xi, Tau Beta Pi, Eta Kappa Nu, Hex-Alpha, Theta Chi. Office: 2715 Angelo Dr Los Angeles CA 90077-2142 Office Phone: 310-271-4248.

PARENTE, WILLIAM JOSEPH, political science professor; b. Chgo., July 7, 1937; s. Salvatore S. and Genevieve (Rooney) P.; m. Diane Alpern, Nov. 30, 1963; children: Elizabeth, Margaret, William Joseph, Caroline, Rebecca, Catherine, Abigail, Christopher, Natalya. AB cum laude, Xavier U., Ohio, 1961; PhD (Woodrow Wilson fellow, Woodrow Wilson dissertation fellow), Georgetown U., 1970. Woodrow Wilson intern Wilberforce (Ohio) U., 1965-66; asst. prof., chmn. polit. sci. dept. Antioch Coll., 1966-69, assoc. dean faculty, 1969-70; dean Coll. Arts and Scis., U. Scranton, Pa., 1970-85, assoc. prof. polit. sci., 1970-73, prof., 1973—; Fulbright scholar Chulalongkorn U., Bangkok, Thailand, 1985-86, Inst. for Policy Studies, Washington, 1986-87. Mem. nat. Fulbright screening com. for East Asia, Southeast Asia; mem. adv. com. Inst. Internat. Edn.; cons. on world affairs to Peace Corps. Author articles in field. Fellow Inst. Acad. Deans, 1971, Inst. Ednl. Mgmt., Harvard Bus. Sch., 1972, Fulbright fellow, Korea, 1974, Indonesia, 1978, Germany, 1980, Thailand, 1985-86, fellow NEH Seminar, U. Va., 1976, Harvard U., 1985, Columbia U., 1988, George Mason U., Va., 1990, UCLA, 1991, U. Mich., 1992, William and Mary, 1993, U. Iowa, 1994, U. Accra, Ghana, 1996; scholar-diplomat program State Dept., 1970, 73; vis. scholar in humanities NYU, 1989; named Tchr. of Yr., U. Scranton, 2006. Fellow Union Experimenting Colls. and Univs., Inst. for Policy Studies, Soc. for Religion in Higher Edn.; mem. Am. Polit. Sci. Assn., Assn. Jesuit Colls. and Univs. (chmn. conf. on internat. edn. 1981-85), Alpha Sigma Nu (nat. sec.-treas. 1979-82, nat. pres. 1983-85), Pi Sigma Alpha, Eta Sigma Phi, Alpha Sigma Lambda, Tau Kappa Alpha, Phi Alpha Theta. Roman Catholic. Office: U Scranton Coll Arts & Sciences Scranton PA 18510 Home: 5 Watres Dr Scranton PA 18505 Office Phone: 570-941-7644. Business E-Mail: parentew1@scranton.edu.

PARESKY, DAVID S., travel company executive; b. Boston, Sept. 27, 1938; s. Paul and Ada (Rudnick) P.; m. Linda Kotzen, Aug. 18, 1963; children: Pamela, Laura, Mark. BA, Williams Coll., 1960; JD, Harvard U., 1963, MBA, 1965. Bar: Mass. Pres., chmn. bd. Crimson Travel Svc., Inc., Cambridge, Mass., 1965-89; pres., CEO, chmn. bd. Thomas Cook Travel, Cambridge, Mass., 1989-94. Mem. Bd. Higher Edn., Boston, 1980; trustee New Eng. Med. Ctr., 1982-83; mem. Bd. Regents of Higher Edn., Boston, 1980-86. Mem. Young Pres. Orgn. (chmn. New Eng. chpt. 1985), Chief Execs. Orgn., Phi Beta Kappa, Fisher Island Club (bd. dirs. 1998-01).

PARET, PETER, historian; b. Berlin, Apr. 13, 1924; s. Hans and Suzanne Aimée (Cassirer) P.; m. Isabel Harris, Sept. 23, 1961; children: Suzanne Aimée, Paul Louis Michel. BA, U. Calif., Berkeley, 1949; PhD, U. London, 1960, DLitt, 1992; LittD (hon.), U. S.C., 1995; HHD (hon.), Coll. of Wooster, 1996; PhD (hon.), Humboldt U., 2007. Resident tutor, delegacy of extramural studies Oxford U., 1959-60; research assoc. Center of Internat. Studies, Princeton U., 1960-62, 63; vis. asst. prof. U. Calif., Davis, 1962-63, assoc. prof., 1963-66, prof., 1966-69; prof. history Stanford U., 1969-77, Raymond A. Spruance prof. internat. history, 1977-86; Andrew W. Mellon Prof. in humanities Inst. Advanced Study, Princeton, N.J., 1986-97, Andrew W. Mellon Prof. in humanities emeritus, 1997—. Mem. Inst. for Advanced Study, Princeton, 1966-67; fellow Ctr. for Advanced Study in Behavioral Scis., Stanford, Calif., 1968-69; vis. fellow London Sch. Econs., 1972-73; NEH fellow, 1979-80; sr. fellow Hoover Instn., Stanford U., 1988-93; Lees Knowles lectr. military history Cambridge U., 2008, guest curator, Princeton U. Art Mus., 2009 Author: (with John Shy) Guerrillas in the 1960's, 1962, French Revolutionary Warfare from Indochina to Algeria, 1964, Yorck and the Era of Prussian Reform, 1966, Clausewitz and the State, 1976, rev. edit. 2007; The Berlin Secession, 1980, Art as History, 1988, (with Beth Irwin Lewis and Paul Paret) Persuasive Images, 1992, Understanding War, 1992, Imagined Battles, 1997, German Encounters with Modernism, 1840-1945, 2000, An Artist against the Third Reich: Ernst Barlach, 1933-1938, 2003, The Cognitive Challenge of War, 2009; editor, translator: (with Michael Howard) On War (C. v. Clausewitz), 1976, (with Daniel Moran) Historical and Political Writings (C. v. Clausewitz), 1992; editor: Frederick the Great, 1968, Frederick the Great: A Historical Profile, 1972, Sisyphus or the Limits of Education, 1973, The Age of German Liberation, 1977, Berliner Secession, 1981, Makers of Modern Strategy, 1986, (with Ekkehard Mai) Sammler, Stifter & Museen, 1993. Served with inf. U.S. Army, 1943-46. Decorated Officer's Cross, Order of Merit, Germany. Fellow AAAS, Leo Baeck Inst., London Sch. Econs. (hon.); mem. Am. Philos. Soc. (Jefferson medal), Hist. Kom zu Berlin, Soc. for Mil. History (Samuel Eliot Morison and Moncado prizes), Clausewitz Gesellschaft (hon.). Office: Sch Hist Studies Inst Advanced Study Princeton NJ 08540 Office Phone: 609-734-8344. Business E-Mail: paret@ias.edu.

PARETS, PAUL L., music educator; b. Bangor, Maine, Apr. 29, 1942; s. J. P. and Berneta L. Parets; children: Timothy E. VanderGraaff, Meredith Anne. B of Music Edn., Cen. Mich. U., 1965; postgrad., U. Mich., 1980—83, U. Md., 1980—83. Cert. tchr. Del. Band dir. Sacred Heart H.S., Mt. Pleasant, Mich., 1965—66, Croswell (Mich.)-Lexington H.S., 1966—76; band dir., politics/govt. educator Alexis I. duPont H.S., Greenville, Del., 1976—. Mem. city coun. City of Delaware City, 1998—2006; assoc. mem. Rep. Nat. Com. Recipient Order of the 1st State, Gov. Michael Castle, 1987; named Del. Tchr. of Yr., State of Del., 1987; named to 50 Who Make a Difference, SBO Mag., 2003, 2004. Mem.: Music Educators Nat. Conf. (state pres. 1984—86, Disting. Music Educator award 1988). Anglican. Avocations: astronomy, travel. Home: PO Box 711 Delaware City DE 19706 Office: Alexis I duPont H S 50 Hillside Rd Greenville DE 19807

PARHAM, BETTY ELY, credit bureau executive; b. Drumright, Okla., Aug. 14, 1928; d. Wayne Albert and Edith May (Ledgerwood) Bingamon; m. Richard D. Ely, Dec. 22, 1946 (dec. Jan. 1971); children: Richard Wayne, Stephen Wyatt; m. Capt. Billy S. Parham, Mar. 10, 1991 (dec. Sept. 2007). BS, East Cen. U., Ada, Okla., 1962, M Teaching, 1965. Office mgr. Louiis M. Long, Loans, Ada, 1946-78; owner Credit Bur. Ada, 1956—, mgr., 1978—. Mem. Soc. Cert. Credit Bur. Execs., Assoc. Credit Burs. Okla. (bd. dirs. 1980—, pres. 1990), AAUW (cert. of achievement 1989), Ada Bus. and Profl. Women (chmn. YC, Pres.'s award 1991), Toastmasters (pres. Ada 1984, Presdl. Excellence award 1984), Kiwanis (bd. dirs. Ada 1990-92). Democrat. Avocations: boating, travel, reading. Home: PO Box 506 Ada OK 74821-0506

PARHAM, PETER ROBERTSON, geologist; b. Raleigh, NC, June 9, 1960; s. Francis Taylor and Miriam Powell Parham; children: Granville Robertson, Sarah Emily, Thomas Burke. BA, Beloit Coll., Wis., 1986; MS, East Carolina U., Greenville, NC, 2003, PhD, 2008. Ranch mgr. Mont. State U. Agr. Field Sta., Havre, 1993—2002. Contbr. articles to profl. rsch. jours. Lance cpl. USMC, 1979—83, Camp Lajeune, NC, reconnaissance marine, 1979—83. Mem.: Am. Soc. Petroleum Geologists, Geol. Soc. America. Avocations: hunting, fishing, canoeing, camping, diving. Home: 1301 W Ragsdale Rd Greenville NC 27858 Office: East Carolina Univ Geology Dept Greenville NC 27858 Personal E-mail: prparham@hotmail.com. Business E-Mail: prp0609@ecu.edu.

PARHAM, THOMAS DAVID, education educator; b. Chgo., Sept. 6, 1963; s. Thomas David and Marion Cordice Parham. BS, U.S. Naval Acad., Annapolis, 1985; MA, Regent U., Va. Beach, 1992, PhD, 1995. Cert. Surface Warfare Officer U.S. Navy, 1988. Commd. officer U.S. Navy, Washington, 1985—92; writers' prodn. asst. Family Prodns., Inc., Va. Beach, 1993—94; supr. pub. Viacom Consumer Products, Hollywood, 1995—96; writers' asst. CBS Prodns., Salt Lake City, 1996—97, Paramount Pictures, Hollywood, 1997—99; asst. prof. Biola U., La Mirada, Calif., 1999—2002; assoc. prof. Azusa (Calif.) Pacific U., 2002—. Tech. cons. Paramount Pictures, Hollywood, 1999—2002; adv. bd. Act One, Inc., Hollywood, 2000—. Author: (play) Inside Out, Steeple Chasers; dir.: (play) The Skin of Our Teeth, Dinner with Friends; contbr. book; author: (TV episode) Big Brother Jake, 1994, JAG, 1998; exec. prodr.: (student film) Giver Her Away. Planning com. Reel Spirituality, Pasadena, Calif., 2002; writer-in-residence Lake Ave. Ch., Pasadena, Calif., 1996—2005. Lt. USN, 1985—92. Mem.: Popular Culture Assn., Nat. Comm. Assn., Comic-Con Internat., Writers Guild of Am. Independent. Southern Baptist. Avocations: comic books, singing, swimming, travel, weightlifting. Office: Azusa Pacific Univ/Theater-Film-TV 901 E Alosta Ave Azusa CA 91702 Office Fax: 626-815-2045. Business E-Mail: tparham@apu.edu.

PARHAM-HOPSON, DEBORAH, health programs administrator; BSN, U. Cin., 1977; MS in Pub. Health, U. NC, 1979, PhD in Pub. Health, 1990. Rear adm. USPHS Commd. Corps.; dep. assoc. adminstr. Health Resources and Svcs. Adminstrn., HIV/AIDS Bur., HHS, 2000—02, acting assoc. adminstr., 2002, assoc. adminstr., 2002—. Office: US Dept Health and Human Svcs Health Resources Svcs Adminstrn 5600 Fishers Ln Rm 7-05 Rockville MD 20857 Office Phone: 301-443-1993. Business E-Mail: dparham@hrsa.gov.

PARHI, KESHAB KUMAR, electrical and computer engineering educator; b. Balasore, Orissa, India, June 15, 1959; came to U.S., 1983; B Tech., Indian Inst. Tech., Kharagpur, 1982; MSEE, U. Pa., 1984; PhD, U. Calif., Berkeley, 1988. Tchg. and rsch. asst. U. Pa., Phila., 1983—84; postgrad. rschr. U. Calif., Berkeley, 1984—88; mem. tech. staff T.J. Watson Rsch. Ctrs. IBM, Yorktown Heights, NY, 1986, AT&T Bell Labs., Holmdel, NJ, 1987; asst. prof. U. Minn., Mpls., 1988—92, assoc. prof., 1992—95, prof., 1995—, Edgar F. Johnson prof., 1997—; Disting. McKnight U. prof., 2000—, dir. grad. studies, 2008—. Sr. prin. scientist Broadcom Corp., Irvine, Calif., 2000-01, tech. dir. DSP Sys., 2002; vis. rschr. NEC Computer Comm. Lab., Kawasaki, Japan, 1992, 96-97; cons. AT&T Bell Labs., 1987, US West Sci. and Techs., Boulder, Colo., 1989, Medtronic Corp., Mpls., 2006-07. Author: (text book) VLSI Digital Signal Processing Systems, 1999; Editor: Jour. VLSI Signal Processing, 1993—; contbr. articles to profl. jours Recipient NSF Young Investigator award, 1992, Eliahu Jury award U. Calif., Berkeley, 1987, Demetri Angelakos award U. Calif., Berkeley, 1987, Frederick Emmons Terman award Am. Soc. Engring. Edn., 2004; IBM grad. fellow, 1987-88, Regents fellow U. Calif., 1986-87 Fellow IEEE (Browder J. Thompson Meml. Prize Paper award 1991, W.R.G. Baker prize 2001, Kiyo Tomiyasu Tech. Field award 2003), Cirs. and Sys. Soc. (bd. govs. 2005-07, Guillemin-Cauer award 1993, Darlington award 1994, Golden Jubilee medal 1999, Disting. lectr. 1994-99, Design Automation Conf. Best Paper award 1996, assoc. editor trans. on cirs. and sys. 1990-91, editor-in-chief 2004-05, assoc. editor trans. on cirs. and sys. part II 1995-97, 2002-03, trans. on VLSI sys. 1997-98), Signal Processing Soc. (assoc. editor trans. on signal processing 1993-95, signal processing letters 1997-99, signal processing mag. 2003-04, signal processing soc. paper award 1991). Avocations: swimming, gardening, hiking, travel. Office: U Minn Dept Elec/Computer Engring 200 Union St SE Minneapolis MN 55455-0154 Office Phone: 612-624-4116. Business E-Mail: parhi@umn.edu.

PARIDA, LAXMI, research scientist, educator; PhD, NYU, NYC, 1998. Rsch. scientist IBM TJ Watson, Yorktown Heights, NY, 1998—; vis. prof. NYU, 2003—. Author: (book) Purba: Feasts From the East, Pattern Discovery in Bioinformatics: Theory & Algorithms. Achievements include patents for related to biological systems; founded Argentine Tango community. Business E-Mail: parida@cs.nyu.edu.

PARIENTE, BARBARA J., state supreme court justice; b. NYC, Dec. 24, 1948; m. Frederick A. Hazouri; children: David, Leslie, Josh. Grad. with highest honors, Boston U., 1970; JD with highest honors, George Washington U., 1973. Bar: Fla. 1973; cert. civil trial lawyer Fla. Bar; cert. Nat. Bd. Trial Advocacy. Law clk. to hon. Norman C. Roettger, Jr. US Dist. Ct. (so. dist.) Fla., 1973-75; assoc. Cone Wagner and Nugent, 1975—77, ptnr., 1977—83, Pariente & Silber, P.A., 1983; pvt. practice, 1983—2001; judge US Ct. of Appeals (4th dist.), 1993-97; justice Fla. Supreme Ct., Tallahassee, 1997—, chief justice, 2004—06, liaison, task force on treatment-based drug cts., 1999—2004, chair, steering com. families and children in cts., 2002—04, faculty mem., Justice Tchg. Inst. Participant Twenty-First Century Justice Conf.; mem. Jud. Cir. Grievance Com., 1989-92, chair, 1990-92; appointee gov.'s adv. com. character edn., 1999; second v.p. Conf. of Justices, 2005-06; mem. 15th jud. cir. nominating commn.; mem. nat. judges adv. com. balanced and restorative justice project, Dept. of Justice; bd. dirs. Fla. Bar Found., Legal Aid Soc., Palm Beach County Bar Assn.; conf. organizer in field; spkr. in field. Contbr. articles to profl. jours. in field. Mentor Take Stock in Children, 1992-2003, Communities in Schs.; mentoring program mem. Cities in Schs., 1993; mem. Palm Beach County Commn. on Status of Women; program vol. judge Palm Beach County Youth Ct. Recipient Disting. Svc. to Arts award Palm Beach County Bar Assn., 1987, Civil Litig. Pro Bono award Legal Aid Soc., 1993, Lifetime Achievement award Palm Beach County Jewish Fedn., 1998, Disting. Jud. Svc. award Fla. Coun. Crime and Delinquency, 2000, Breaking the Glass Ceiling award Jewish Mus. Fla., 2002, Good Govt. award Palm Beach County LWV, 2005, Lifetime Achievement award Fla. Assn. Sch. Social Workers, 2005, Disting. Alumni award George Washington U., 2006, Jurist of Yr. award Fla. Chpt. Am. Acad. Matrimonial Lawyers, 2006, award Fla. Assn. Women Lawyers, Palm Beach Chapter, 2007, Lifetime Achivement award Fla. Justice Assn., 2007, Fla. Women's Hall Of Fame Governor Charlie Crist, 2008. Master Am. Inns of Ct. (Palm Beach County chpt.); mem. ABA (mem. coalition for justice com. 2000-03, Law Day Speech award 1998), Nat. Assn. Women Judges, Am. Inns of Ct. (founding mem. Palm Beach County chpt.), Acad. Fla. Trial Lawyers (bd. dirs., chair spkr.'s bur. program 1984-87, outreach com. 1991-92, co-chair workhorse seminar 1991-92), Assn. Trial Lawyers Am. (vice chair profl. rsch. and devel. dept. 1980-82, chair comml. litig. sect. 1984-85, women's trial lawyer caucus 1986-87, mem. ethics com. 1989-90, conv. planning com. 1992-93), Fla. Assn. Women Lawyers (Lifelong Dedication award 2000), Fla. Bar Assn. (civil rules com. 1981-87, commn. legal needs of children 2000-02, Family Law Visionary award 2004, William M. Hoeveler Jud. Professionalism award 2004, Hugh S. Glickstein Child Adv. of Yr. award 2005), Order of Coif. Office: State Supreme Ct of Florida 500 S Duval St Tallahassee FL 32399-1925 Business E-Mail: supremecourt@flcourts.org.*

PARIKH, CHIRAG R., physician scientist; b. Ahmedabad, Gujarat, India, Sept. 13, 1973; arrived in US, 1996; s. Rohit R. and Kirtida R. Parikh. MD, Seth GS Med. Coll. & KEM Hosp., Bombay, 1996; PhD, U. Colo., 2003. Diplomate Am. Bd. Internal Medicine, Am. Bd. Nephrology. Resident internal medicine Nassau U. Med. Ctr., NY, 1996—99; fellow nephrology U. Colo. Health Scis. Ctr., Denver, 1999—2001, clin. instr., 2001—02, asst. prof., 2002—. Contbr. chapters to books, articles to profl. jours. Office: Univ Colo HealthScisCtr Box C-281 4200 E Ninth Ave Denver CO 80262

PARIKH, JAY R., radiologist; s. Rajendra Somalal and Minaxi Rajendra Parikh; m. Niyati Parikh, July 5, 1992; children: Viraj, Miti. MD, U. Ottawa, Ontario, Can., 1990. Cert. physician exec. Am. Coll. of Physician Execs., 2005. Med. dir. Women's Diagnostic Imaging Ctr., Seattle, 2001—. Pres. Nat. Consortium of Breast Ctrs., Warsaw, 2005—07; cons., sci. adv. panel Hologic, Bedford, Mass.; med. advisor Confirma, Kirkland, Wash., 2005—. Contbr. articles to profl. jours. Troop com. pack 624 Boy Scouts Am., Seattle, 2005—06. Named Honorary Texan, Gov. Tex., 2006; Leadership Conf. scholar, WSMA, 2004. Fellow: Am. Coll. Physician Execs., Soc. Breast Imaging, Am. Coll. Radiology (clin. image rev., nat. mammography accreditation program 2005—, clin. image rev. nat. breast ultrasound accreditation program 2006—), Royal Coll. Physicians and Surgeons Can. (licentiate); mem.: Wash. State Med. Assn. (trustee 2004—), Pacific NW Radiol. Soc. (pres. 2007—08), Hawaii Breast Soc. (hon.; life), Alaska State Soc. Radiol. Technologists (hon.), Ariz. State Soc. Radiol. Technologists (life), Am. Assn. Radiologists of Indian Origin (life), Hawaii Radiol. Soc. (hon.), Western Wash. Mammography Soc. (hon.), Wash. State Radiol. Soc. (pres. 2004—06), Radiol. Soc. N.Am., Am. Roentgen Ray Soc., King County Med. Soc., Am. Coll. Physician Execs. Office: Women's Diagnostic Imaging Center 1221 Madison St Seattle WA 98104 Office Fax: 206-215-3909. Business E-Mail: jay.parikh@swedish.org.

PARIKH, PRITI P., food scientist; b. Surat, Gujarat, India, Nov. 15, 1979; d. Kishorkumar S. and Ranjan K. Shastri; m. Pratik J. Parikh, July 8, 2003; 1 child, Shiven P. PhD, Va. Poly. Inst. and State U., Blacksburg, 2007. Product exec. Span Diagnostics Ltd., Udhna, Gujarat, India, 2002—03; grad. rsch., tchg. asst. Va. Poly. Inst. and State U., 2005—07; product devel. scientist Life Therapeutics, Clarkston, Ga., 2007—. Summer trainee Span Diagnostics Ltd., Udhna, 2002. Contbr. articles to profl. jours. Recipient Excellence award, Dept. Food Sci. and Tech., Va. Tech., 2007. Mem.: Internat. Assn. Food Protection, Inst. Food Technologists, Gamma Sigma Delta. Home: 2465 Lake Pk Dr Apt Q Smyrna GA 30080 Business E-Mail: priti@vt.edu.

PARIKH, RAHUL KEDAR, physician; MD, Tufts U. Sch. Medicine, Boston, 1999. Diplomate Am. Bd. Pediat., 2002. Attending physician Permanente Med. Group, Walnut Creek, Calif., 2003—, DSA chief patient edn., 2006—. Fellow: Am. Acad. Pediat.

PARINS, ROBERT JAMES, professional football team executive, judge; b. Green Bay, Wis., Aug. 23, 1918; s. Frank and Nettie (Denissen) P.; m. Elizabeth L. Carroll, Feb. 8, 1941; children: Claire, Andrée, Richard, Teresa, Lu Ann. BA, U. Wis., 1940, LLB, 1942. Bar: Wis. Supreme Ct. 1942. Pvt. practice, Green Bay, Wis., 1942-68; dist. atty. Brown County, Wis., 1949-50, cir. judge Wis., 1968-82, res. judge Wis., 1982—; pres. Green Bay Packers, Inc., 1982-90, chmn. bd., 1990-92; hon. chmn. bd., 1992-94. Mem.: Wis. State Bar Assn. Roman Catholic.

PARIS, ELIZABETH CREWSON, federal judge; b. Altus, Okla., Jan. 14, 1958; d. Joel and Judy Crewson; BS, U. Tulsa, Okla., 1980, JD, 1987; LLM in Taxation, U. Denver, 1993. Bar: Okla. Supreme St., US Dist. Ct. (Okla. dist.) 1988, US Tax Ct., US Ct. Fed. Claims, US Ct. Appeals (10th circuit) 1993, Colo. Supreme Ct. 1994. Legal intern Boys Nichols & Cates, Tulsa, Okla., 1985—88; assoc. McCormick Andrew & Clark, Tulsa, Okla., 1988—90; sr. assoc. LaSorsa Weiber & Miles, Tulsa, Okla., 1990—92; tax atty. Brumley Bishop & Paris, Tulsa, Okla., 1992—; sr. assoc. McKenna & Cuneo LLP, Denver, 1994—; ptnr. Reinhart, Boerner, Van Deuren, Norris & Rieselbach, Denver, 1998—; tax counsel US Senate Fin. Com., 2000—08; judge US Tax Ct., 2008—. Adj. prof. Georgetown U. Law Ctr. Editor (Colo. Bar Assn.): Trust and Estates Notes, Tax Sec. Newsletter; contbr. articles to law jours., chapters to books. Recipient American Jurisprudence award in Real

Estate, Distinguished Alumni award, U. Tulsa Coll. Law. Mem.: ABA (mem. real property probate and trust sec., vice chair entity selection com., condemnation com., former vice chair taxation sec. com., agrl. com.), Colo. Bar Assn., Okla. Bar Assn., Phi Alpha Theta, Pi Sigma Alpha. Office: US Tax Court 400 Second St NW Washington DC 20217*

PARIS, LEE ANNE HAGEWOOD, academic librarian; b. Gallatin, Tenn., July 30, 1971; d. Mark Douglas Hagewood and Carolyn Ruth Lee; m. Tobin Leroy Paris, July 31, 1993; children: Bethany Anne, Trenton Lee. BA, Vanderbilt U., Nashville, TN, 1992; MLIS, U. Okla., Norman, 1994; PhD, U. NC, Chapel Hill, 1998. Asst. prof. libr. sci. Okla. Christian U., 1998—. Bible class tchr. Edmond Ch. Christ, Okla., 1998—2008, mission trip Nicaragua, 2006—08, mission trip Brazil, 1999—2003. Scholarship, Nat. Merit Scholarship Corp., 1988—89. Mem.: Christian Coll. Librarians, Beta Phi Mu, Phi Beta Kappa. Mem. Ch. Of Christ. Avocations: reading, travel, cooking. Office: Okla Christian Univ PO Box 11000 Oklahoma City OK 73136-1100

PARIS, MARGARET G., librarian; d. James W. and Jennie G. George; m. Michael L. Paris, Sept. 15, 1979; children: Matthew A., Mandy L., Marshall L. BA in Elem. Edn. and Libr. Sci., Northwestern State U., La., 1982. Elem. tchr. Moss Bluff Elem., Lake Charles, La., 2000—07, sch. libr., 2007—. Ch. planter N.Am. Mission Bd., Grand Lake, La., 2008. Grantee, Drew Found., 2005, South Ctrl. Bell, 2007. Mem.: Calcasieu Paris Reading Coun. (sec. 2008). Office: Moss Bluff Elem 215 School St Lake Charles LA 70611 Business E-Mail: margaret.paris@cpsb.org.

PARIS, MARGARET L., dean, law educator; BA with distinction, Northwestern U., 1981, JD, 1985. Bar: Ill., US Supreme Ct., US Ct. Appeals (6th cir.), US Ct. Appeals (7th cir.), US Dist. Ct. (no. dist.) Ill., US Dist. Ct. (no. dist.) Ind., US Dist. Ct. (ea. dist.) Mich. Law clk. for Judge Joel Flaum US Ct. Appeals (7th cir.); atty. criminal law Cotsirilos, Tighe & Streicker Ltd., Chgo.; prof. law U. Oreg. Sch. Law, 1992—, assoc. dean academic affairs, Elmer Sahlstrom sr. fellow, interim dean, 2005—06, Philip H. Knight dean, 2006—. Contbr. articles to law jours. Recipient Orlando John Hollis Faculty Tchg. Award, U. Oreg. Mem.: ABA. Office: U Oreg Sch Law 1515 Agate St Eugene OR 97403-1221 Office Phone: 541-346-3836.*

PARIS, NORMA JEAN, psychologist, educational consultant; b. Muskogee, Okla., Jan. 15, 1937; d. Howard Charles and Eleanor Ruth Lewis; m. Barney McKinley Paris, Jr., Feb. 17, 1957; children: Donna Katherine Paris Willis, Cynthia Elizabeth Paris Bickham, Barney McKinley Paris III(dec.). BA summa cum laude, La. State U., Baton Rough, 1975, psychologist, 1985, MEd, 1977, PhD, 1997; Edn. Specialist in Counseling, La. Tech. U., Ruston, 1980. Tchr. Bossier Parish Sch. Bd., Bossier City, La., 1975—84, sch. psychologist, 1984—87, Caddo Parish Sch. Bd., Shreveport, 1987—2001; spl. lectr. Centenary Coll. La., Shreveport, 2001—06; psychoednl. cons., 2008—. Psychol. advisor Compassionate Friends, Shreveport, 1981—92; cons. Children's Advocacy Ctr. Task Force, Shreveport, 1996—98; spkr. Oxford Round Table, England, 2005, England, 06; presenter in field. Bd. mem. Juvenile Justice Bd. Dirs., Shreveport, 1996—2000; exec. bd. mem. Caddo-Bossier Mental Health Assn. Bd. Dirs., Shreveport, 1996—2000. Mem.: La. Sch. Psychologists Assn. (exec. bd. mem. 2001—, La. Sch. Psychologist of Yr. 2001), Assn. Tchr. Educators, Internat. Reading Assn., Mensa. Republican. Baptist. Avocations: bridge, puzzles, water aerobics, travel. Home: 4406 Curtis Loop Bossier City LA 71112 Personal E-mail: parisn@bellsouth.net.

PARIS-DE MONTE, ILEANA M., assistant principal; d. Alfredo Paris and Margarita Badilla; m. Roland Wyler; children: Adriana M. De Monte, Leonard Alfredo De Monte. BA in Journalism, Calif. State U., Northridge, 1979, Bilingual Tchg. Credential, 1993, M Ednl. Adminstrn., 2005. Cert. adminstr. Calif., nat. bd. cert. tchr. 2001. Media release officer Bank of Am., LA, 1980; elem. sch. tchr. Serrania Ave. Elem. Sch., LA Unified Sch. Dist., Woodland Hills, Calif., 1988—2002; asst. prin. Napa St. Elem. Sch., Northridge, 2002—. Master tchr. Pepperdine U., Nat. U., LA, 1992—2002; instr. Nw Tchr. Acad., LA Unified Sch. Dist., 2001—02. Elem. tchr. liaison Taft Complex, LA Unified Sch. Dist., Woodland Hills, Calif., 1997—99. Named Tchr. of Yr., 1998. Mem.: ASCD. Personal E-mail: idemon1@lausd.net.

PARISE, ZACH, professional hockey player; b. Mpls., July 28, 1984; s. Jean-Paul and Donna Parise. Attended, U. ND, 2002—04. Left wing NJ Devils, 2005—. Named MVP, NHL YoungStars Game, 2007; named to West First All-Am. Team, NCAA, 2004, NHL YoungStars Game, 2007, NHL All-Star Game, 2009, All-NHL Team, Sporting News, 2009, Second All-Star Team, NHL, 2009. Office: NJ Devils Prudential Ctr 165 Mulberry St Newark NJ 07102*

PARISER, DAVID MICHAEL, dermatologist, educator; b. Norfolk, Va., Sept. 8, 1946; s. Harry and Alice Pariser; m. Carol Odessky, Mar. 25, 1975; children: Michael Steven, Jana Robin. MD, Med. Coll. Va., Richmond, 1972. Cert. Am. Bd. Dermatology, 1977, Va. State Bd. Med. Examiners, Nat. Bd. Med. Examiners, Am. Bd. Pathology, spl. competence in dermatopathology. Intern Med. Coll. Va., Richmond; resident Univ. Miami Sch. Medicine/Jackson Meml. Med. Ctr., 1973—76; prof., dept. dermatology Ea. Va. Med. Sch., Norfolk, 1995—; sr. physician Pariser Dermatology Specialists, Ltd., Norfolk, Va. Spkr. in field. Contbr. articles to profl. jours.; review coms. of several peer-reviewed jours., mem. editl. bds. of several peer-reviewed jours. Pres. Ea. Va. Dermatology Found., Norfolk, 2001—07, bd. dirs., Sentara Health Mgmt., Dermatology Services, Inc., Nat. Psoriasis Found. Recipient Gold Triangle award, Am. Acad. Dermatology, 2007. Fellow: Am. Soc. for Laser Medicine and Surgery, Am. Soc. for Dermatologic Surgery, Am. Acad. Dermatology (secretary-treasurer 2003—06, pres. elect 2008—, bd. dirs., Gold Triangle award for outstanding dedication to isotretinoin awareness initiatives 2002, (9) Continuing Med. Edn. award, (4) Presdl. Citations); mem.: Med. Soc. Va., Am. Soc. for Dermatologic Surgery, AMA (Physician's Recognition award 2004), Internat. Hyperhidrosis Soc. (pres., founding mem., bd. dirs. 2003—). Office: Ea Va Med Sch Pariser Dermatology SpecialistsLtd 601 Medical Tower Norfolk VA 23507 Office Fax: 757-625-6940.

PARISH, J. MICHAEL, lawyer, mutual fund executive, writer; b. Decatur, Ill., Nov. 9, 1943; s. John Mitchell and Gladys Margaret (Daulton) P.; m. Susan Lee Sgarlat, July 24, 1976 (div.); m. Ellen R. Harnett, Dec. 3, 1991; children: Margaret Ruth, William Walter. AB cum laude, Princeton U., 1965; LLB, Yale U., 1968. Assoc. LeBoeuf Lamb et al, NYC, 1968-73, ptnr., 1974-89, Winthrop Stimson Putnam & Roberts, NYC, 1989-95, Thelen, Reid & Priest, NYC, 1995—2002, Wolf, Block, Schorr & Solis-Cohen, NYC, 2002—03. Chmn. bd. dirs. Forum Funds, Portland, Maine, Core Trust. Contbr. stories and poetry to mags. Dir. PBS Am. Poetry Project, 1985-90; coord. Yale Law Sch. Clinton Election com.; class sec. Princeton Class of 1965; trustee Hackensack Riverkeeper. Univ. scholar Princeton U., 1965, Nat. scholar Yale U., 1968. Avocation: creative writing. Home: 236 David Hooper Pl Westwood NJ 07675-1910 Home Phone: 917-328-0402; Office Phone: 201-634-0812. Personal E-mail: mparish@alumni.princeton.edu.

PARISH, JAMES MICHAEL, medical educator; BS in Biology with honors, U. Ill., 1974; MD, U. Ill., Chgo., 1978. Diplomate Am. Bd. Internal Medicine, Am. Bd. Pulmonary Medicine. Resident internal medicine Mayo Clinic, 1978—81, fellow pulmonary medicine, 1981—84; pulmonary and critical care specialist Sharp Meml. Hosp., San Diego, 1984—87; cons., Assoc. Prof. Mayo Clinic Coll. Medicine, Scottsdale, Ariz., 1987—; chair Divsn. Pulmonary Medicine, Mayo Clinic, Ariz.; bd. dir. Nat. Assn. Med. Direction Respiratory Care. Fellow: ACP, Am. Acad. Sleep Medicine, Am. Coll. Chest Physicians; mem.: AMA, Am. Thoracic Soc. Achievements include research in sleep disorders. Office: Mayo Clinic 13400 Shea Blvd Scottsdale AZ 85259

PARISH, JAMES ROBERT, writer, cinema historian; b. Cambridge, Mass., Apr. 21, 1944; s. Fred Arthur and Ann Lois (Magilevy) P. BA, U. Pa., 1964, LLB, 1967. Pres. Entertainment Copyright Rsch.Co. Inc., NYC, 1967-68; film reporter, reviewer, interviewer Variety, Motion Picture Daily, 1968-69; entertainment publicist Harold Rand & Co., 1969-70; free-lance writer, publicist, film book cons., film reviewer, novelist, 1970—; acquisition editor Renaissance Books, 1996-99. Author: (with P. Michael) The Emmy Awards: A Pictorial History, 1970, The Fox Girls, 1971, The Great Movie Series, 1971 (with A.H. Marill) The Cinema of Edward G. Robinson, 1972, The Slapstick Queens, 1972, The Paramount Pretties, 1972, (with R. Bowers) The MGM Stock Company, 1973, Actors TV Credits, 1950-72, 73, Good Dames, 1973, (with M.R. Pitts) The Great Spy Pictures, 1973, The RKO Gals, 1973, (with S. Whitney), The George Raft File, 1973, (with M.R. Pitts) Film Directors: A Guide to Their American Pictures, 1974, Hollywood's Great Love Teams, 1974, (with S. Whitney) Vincent Price Unmasked, 1974, The Great Movie Heroes, 1975, (with D. Stanke), The Glamour Girls, 1975, The Debonairs, 1975, (with L. DeCarl) Hollywood Players: The Forties, 1975, (with J. Ano) Liza! (The Liza Minnelli Story), 1975, (with M.R. Pitts) The Great Gangster Pictures, 1975, The Elvis Presley Scrapbook, 1975, (with W. Leonard) Hollywood Players: The Thirties, 1976, (with D. Stanke) The All Americans, 1976, Film Directors: A Guide for Western Europe, 1976, Great Child Stars, 1976, The Jeanette MacDonald Story, 1976, (with D. Stanke) The Leading Ladies, 1977, (with M.R. Pitts) The Great Science Fiction Pictures, 1977, Film Actors Guide: Western Europe, 1977, The Elvis Presley Scrapbook (update), 1977, (with M. Trost) Actors TV Credits: Supplement One, 1977, (with M.R. Pitts) Hollywood on Hollywood, 1978, (with R. Braff et al.) Hollywood Character Actors, 1978, (with G. Mank and D. Stanke) The Hollywood Beauties, 1978, (with W. Leonard) The Funsters, 1979, (with D. Stanke) The Forties Gals, 1980, (with G. Mank) The Hollywood Reliables, 1980, The Great American Movies Book, 1980, (with G. Mank) The Best of MGM, 1981, (with M.R. Pitts) The Great Spy Pictures II, 1986, (with M.R. Pitts) The Great Gangster Pictures II, 1987, (with M.R. Pitts) The Great Western Pictures II, 1988, Black Action Pictures from Hollywood, 1989, (with M.R. Pitts) The Great Science Fiction Pictures II, 1990, (with V. Terrace) Complete Actors TV Credits, 1990, (with M.R. Pitts) Hollywood Songsters, 1990, updated edit., 2002, The Great Cop Pictures, 1990, Prison Pictures from Hollywood, 1991, (with M.R. Pitts) Hollywood's Great Musicals, 1992, (with D. Stanke) Hollywood Baby Boomers, 1992, Prostitution in Hollywood Film, 1992, The Hollywood Death Book, 1992; Let's Talk: America's Favorite Talk Show Hosts, 1993, Gays and Lesbians in Mainstream Cinema, 1993, Hollywood's Celebrity Death Book, updated and expanded, 1994, Ghosts and Angels on the Hollywood Screen, 1995, Today's Black Hollywood, 1995, Pirates and Seafaring Swashbucklers, 1995, The Great Child Stars, 1996, The Unofficial "Murder She Wrote" Casebook, 1997, Rosie: Rosie O'Donnell's Biography, 1997, updated edit., 1998, Whoopi Goldberg: From Poverty to Mega Stardom, 1997, updated edit., 1999, Jason Biggs, 2000, The Hollywood Book of Death, 2001, Gus Van Sant, 2001, Hollywood Bad Boys, 2002, Jet Li, 2002, The Encyclopeida of Ethnic Groups in Hollywood, 2002, Hollywood Divas, 2002, The Hollywood Book of Love, 2003, Whitney Houston, 2003, Steven Spielberg, 2004, The Hollywood Book of Scandals, 2004, Tom Hanks, 2004, Stephen King, 2004, Halle Berry, 2004, Twyla Tharp, 2005, Denzel Washington, 2005, Stan Lee, 2005, Katie Couric, 2005, Katharine Hepburn: The Untold Story, 2005, Jim Henson, 2006, Gloria Estefan, 2006, Fiasco: A History of Hollywood's Iconic Flops, 2006, The Hollywood Book of Breakups, 2006, (with Allan Taylor) Career Opportunities in Writing, 2006, (with Allan Taylor) Career Opportunities in Television and Cable, 2006, It's Good to Be the King: The Serious Funny Life of Mel Brooks, 2007, (with Allan Taylor) Career Opportunities in the Internet, Video Games, and Multimedia, 2007, The Hollywood Book of Extravagance, 2007, (with Allan Taylor) Career Opportunities in Energy Indistry, 2008, Career Opportunities in Library and Information Science, 2009; assoc. editor: The American Movies Reference Book, 1969, TV Movies, 1969, The Great American Movie Book, 1980. Mem. Phi Beta Kappa. Avocations: docent, reading, writing. Address: 4338 Gentry Ave Unit 1 Studio City CA 91604-1764 Personal E-mail: jrparish@sbcglobal.net. *To succeed in one's ambitions requires an unyielding avoidance of other people's skepticisms.*

PARISH, RICHARD LEE, engineer, consultant; b. Kansas City, Mo., May 31, 1945; s. Charles Lee and Ruth (Duncan) P.; m. Patricia Ann Erickson, June 2, 1968; children: Christie Lynn White, Kerry Anne Parish-Philp. BS in Agrl. Engring., U. Mo., 1967, MS in Agrl. Engring., 1968, PhD, 1970. Registered profl. engr., Ohio. Asst., then assoc. prof. engring. Univ. Ark., Fayetteville, 1969-74; mgr. mech. research and devel. O.M. Scott & Sons Co., Marysville, Ohio, 1974-83; assoc. prof., then prof. La. State U., Baton Rouge, 1983-97; prof. Hammond Rsch. Sta., 1995—2008, resident coord. Coastal area rsch. sta., 2005—08. Cons. in equipment patents, equipment safety, product liability, personal injury, design and evaluation; expert witness testimony in agrl. and hort. equipment, patents, 1984—. Contbr. over 120 articles to profl. jours.; patentee in field. Bd. dirs. Agrl. Devel. Found. Recipient Quality award, ITT, 1979, Doyle Chambers award for excellence in rsch., La. State U. Agrl. Ctr., 2001; NSF fellow, 1967—69. Mem. Am. Soc. Agrl. Engrs. (chmn. agrl. chem. application com. 1982-83, chmn. power and machinery divsn. program com. 1986-87, chmn. cultural practices equipment com. 1994-95, chmn. fruit and vegetable prodn. engring. com. 1999-2001), Am. Soc. Hort. Sci. Republican. Baptist. Avocations: old tractors, gardening, woodwork, bicycling. Home: 21135 Highway 16 Amite LA 70422-4733 Office: Richard L Parish PE LLC 21135 Hwy 16 Amite LA 70422 Office Phone: 985-748-7019. Business E-Mail: parish@agmachineryengr.com.

PARISH, ROY CLAYTON, medical researcher; b. Jacksonville, Fla., Sept. 17, 1945; s. Roy Clayton and Edna (Jones) P. AA, Pensacola Jr. Coll., 1964; BS in Pharmacy, U. Fla., 1967, PharmD, 1985. Diplomate Am. Bd. Clin. Pharmacology; cert. Pharmacotherapy specialist BCPS, 1997. Pvt. practice, 1967-74; assoc. dir. pharmacy svcs. Santa Rosa Hosp., Milton, Fla., 1974-83; fellow adult medicine Gainesville (Fla.) VA Med. Ctr., 1985-86; asst. prof. U. Ga., Athens, 1986-93; cons. clin. pharmacologist Ctrl. State Hosp., Milledgeville, Ga., 1988-94; asst. prof. Sch. Medicine La. State U., Shreveport, 1994-07; assoc. prof. Coll. of Pharmacy, N.E. La. U., Shreveport, La., 1997—2004; prof. Coll. Pharmacy South U. Savench, 2004—06; prof. scott endowed chair, 2006—. Assoc. clin. pharmacologist Pediatric Pharmacology Rsch. Unit, Shreveport, 1994-97. Mem. editl. bd. Annals of Pharmacotherapy, Cin., 1987—; contbr. articles to profl. publs. Gratis faculty LSU Sch. of Medicine, 1997—2004, adj. faculty Lsu Sch. Medicine, 2006-. Mem. Am. Coll. Clin. Pharmacy, Am. Coll. Clin. Pharmacology, Sigma Xi, Am. Soc. Clin. Pharmacology Therapeutics. Achievements include research showing that smokeless tobacco does not affect the metabolism of theophylline, smokeless tobacco does not affect serum alpha-1 acid glycoprotein, high-fat meals do not affect volume of distribution of theophylline. Home: 615 Longleaf Rd Shreveport LA 71106-1225 Office: Coll Pharmacy Shrevepoch Campus 1725 Claiborre Ave Shreveport LA 71103

PARISH, THOMAS SCANLAN, psychology professor; b. Oak Pk., Ill., Jan. 24, 1944; s. Robert S. and Florence Catherine (Fleming) P.; children: Robert V., Kimberly E., David G., Thomas P., Kathryn E., Lydia E.; m. Joycelyn G. Parish, Dec. 29, 2000. BA, No. Ill. U., 1968; MA, Ill. State U., 1969; PhD, U. Ill., 1972. Cert. reality therapy Inst. Reality Therapy, LA, 1980. Instr. psychology Parkland Coll., Champaign, Ill., 1971-72; asst. prof. Okla. State U., Stillwater, 1972-76; assoc. prof. Kans. State U., Manhattan, 1976-80, prof., 1980—2005, asst. to dean of edn., 1992-97; assoc. dir. ARIOS-Kan., 1994-96. Rsch. coord. for Midwest Desegration Asst. Ct., 1994-96; regional dir. Excel Comm., 1997-98; assoc. prof. Upper Iowa U., Fayette, 2001-07. Assoc. editor Jour. of Social Studies Rsch., 1994-98; cons. editor Jour. Genetic Psychology, 1984—, Internat. Jour. Reality Therapy, 1992-2003, 2006-07, The Genetic, Social and General Psychology Monographs, 1984-2003; contbr. articles to profl. jours. Bd. dirs. Friendship Tutoring Program, Manhattan, 1982-91, Stillwater Awareness Coun., 1973-74; co-founder, bd. dirs. Youth Alternatives, Inc., Champaign, 1971-72; pres. Mid-Western Edn. Rsch. Assn., 1998-99, life mem. Fellow Am. Psychol. Soc.; mem. APA, Assn. Reality Therapists, Soc. Rsch. in Child Devel., Phi Delta Kappa, Phi Kappa Phi. Achievements include research in discerning the possible impact of parent loss on children and youth; ways to motivate one's self and others. Avocation: dance. Home Phone: 785-862-1379. Personal E-mail: parishthomas@yahoo.com.

PARISH, WILLIAM HENRY, lawyer; b. Oakland, Calif., July 28, 1954; s. Harry and Elaine Katherine (Triplett) P.; m. Kathryn Annette, Aug. 14, 1976; children: Michael Erik, Jennifer Christine, Melissa Ann. AA, Hartnell Coll., 1974; BA, Calif. State U., 1977; JD, U. Pacific, 1980. Bar: Calif. 1980, U.S. Dist. Ct. (ea. dist.) Calif. 1980, U.S. Ct. Appeals (9th cir.) 1980, U.S. Supreme Ct. 1990. Assoc. Cavalero, Bray, Geiger & Rudquist, Stockton, Calif., 1980-82, ptnr., 1982-87, Bray, Geiger, Rudquist, Nuss & Parish, Stockton, 1987; prin. Law Offices of William H. Parish, Stockton, 1987—96, Parish & Nelson, A Profl. Corp., Stockton, 1997—2002, Parish & Small, A Profl. Corp., Stockton, 2003—. Bd. dirs. Cmty. Bus. Bank. Dir. Cmty. Bus. Bank, 2005—. Mem. ABA (litigation sect. 1980—), Am. Bd. Trial Advs., Order of Coif, Am. Heart Assn., San Joaquin County (bd. dirs. 2001—, pres. 2002—). Office: Parish & Small Profl Corp 1919 Grand Canal Blvd Ste A-5 Stockton CA 95207

PARISI, ANGELA I., chemist; b. Jersey City, Apr. 8, 1953; d. Biagio and Mary G. Parisi; m. James Menoutis, July 3, 1976; children: William J. Menoutis, Mary E. Menoutis, Stephen J. Menoutis, Jonathan A. Menoutis. BS in Biology, NJ City U., Jersey City, 1976, BS in Chemistry, 1976. Chemist Colgate Palmolive Co., Jersey City, 1974—80; sr. rsch. chemist LONZA, Fair Lawn, NJ, 1980—88; v.p. Analab, Edison, NJ, 1988—92; mgr. analytical svcs. CycleChem, Elizabeth, NJ, 1992—93; sr. v.p. Quantex Labs., Edison, 1993—. Advisor and vol. Somerset County 4 H - Rutgers Coop. Ext., 1997—2007; deacon & elder Faith Fellowship Ministries, Sayreville, NJ, 2000—08. Recipient Outstanding Svc. award, Somerset County 4 H - Rutgers Coop. Ext. Bridgewater, NJ, 2007. Mem.: Am. Inst. Chemists, AOAC Internat., Am. Chem. Soc. Office: Quantex Labs 22 Distribution Blvd Edison NJ 08817

PARISI, CHERYL LYNN, art educator; b. Hackensack, NJ, Aug. 26, 1955; d. Elza A. and Constance Leah (Sculley) Sockey; m. Albert J. Parisi, Apr. 18, 1981; 1 child, Christopher Thomas. BA, Fairleigh Dickinson U., 1977; MA in Art Edn., Columbia U., NYC, 2005. Cert. tchr., N.J. Piano instr., Bergen County, N.J., 1972-79; art tchr. Meml. Sch., South Hackensack, N.J., 1979-80, Hackensack Mid. Sch., 1980-84, Nellie K. Parker Sch., Hackensack, 1984—. Exhibited in group shows at The Jacob Javits Conv. Ctr., N.Y.C., 1990, The Designer Craftsmen's Gallery, New Brunswick, N.J., 1993, Gloucester County Coll., Sewell, N.J., 1993, Johnson and Johnson Corp., Titusville, N.J., 1993, Arts Coun. Princeton, N.J., 1993, Montclair State U., Upper Montclair, N.J., 1992, 94, Old Cultural Ctr. juried Small Works Show, Demarest, N.J. 2004, Macy Gallery, T.C., Columbia U., 2004, Art Ctr. No. NJ, 2006, James Howe Gallery, Kean U., Union, N.J., 2005; mem. panel for selection of educators for the NEH seminar Am. and Brit. Children's Lit., Princeton, 1999; author, co-dir. children's musical Claude Monet: A Bridge to the Past, 1999. Recipient Art Educator Achievement award Fantasy Fund Inc. at the Cathedral of St. John the Divine, N.Y.C., 1992, Anthony Guadadiello Svc. award Art Educators of N.J., 2007, NJ Governors award Arts Edn., 2008; grantee Hackensack Edn. Found., 1991; grantee Hackensack Small Grants Program, 2003, Hackensack Rotary Club, Art Educators of N.J., 2004, Target Corp., 2004, 2009; NEH fellow Princeton U., 1991. Mem. Art Educators N.J. (chairperson 1993 Yr. of the Am. Craft 1991-93, publicity 50th anniversary conf. 1990; pres. Bergen County chpt. 1984-86, Achievement award 1989), Nat. Art Edn. Assn. Achievements include selected as participant in the National Endowment for the Humanities Landmarks of American History and Culture Workshop, Mississippi, 2009. Avocation: reading. Home: 167 Godwin Ave Wyckoff NJ 07481-2004 Office: Nellie K Parker Elem Sch 261 Maple Hill Dr Hackensack NJ 07601-1497

PARISI, LEAH EVANS, dean, nursing educator, lawyer; d. Leslie Malcom and Elizabeth Stoughton Evans; m. Alfonso Parisi, Oct. 6, 1990; stepchildren: Anne Marie, Joseph, Nancy, Paula; m. Ronald Katz (div.). BSN, Ohio State U., Columbus, 1962; MA in Healthcare Adminstrn., Lindenwood Coll., LA, 1975; EdD in Instl. Mgmt., Pepperdine U., LA, 1982; JD, Loyola Law Sch., LA, 1985. Bar: Calif. 1985; RN Ohio, 1962, N.Y., 1967, Tex., 1967, Ontario, Can., 1989, S.C., 1999, Calif., 1973, CRNA, Am. Assn. Nurse Anesthetists, 1965. Nurse anesthetist cardiac surgery Cleve. Clinic, Cleve., 1960—67, Baylor Coll. Medicine, Houston, 1967—73; dir. nurse anesthesia program Martin Luther King Gen. Hosp., LA, 1973—74, UCLA Sch. Medicine, 1973—85; attorney med. malpractice and staff privileges law Rushfeld Shelley & Drake, 1985—88; prof. sch. nursing Faculty Health Scis. McMaster U., Hamilton, Ontario, Canada, 1989—99; instr. legal asst. and paralegal program Tech. Coll. Lowcountry, Beaufort, SC, 2000—, dean bus. tech., 2000—06. Adj. assoc. prof. dept. anesthesiology UCLA Sch. Medicine, 1974—85; ednl. cons. and sr. on- site visitor Am. Assn. Nurse Anesthetists, Chgo., 1975—85; prof. sch. nursing Faculty Health Scis. McMaster U., Hamilton, Ontario, 1989—99; invited vis. faculty U. Nebr., Lincoln, Henry Ford Hosp. U. Detroit, U. So. Calif., LA; invited participant McMaster U. Faculty Health Scis. Program Academic Leaders, Hamilton, Ontario; dir. Hummingbird Enterprises, Hilton Head, SC. Contbr. to conf. proceedings, chapters to books, scientific papers, articles to profl. jours. Bd. mem St. Josephs Villa, Hamilton, Ontario,

1992—99. Recipient Helen Lamb award Educator of Yr., Am. Assn. Nurse Anesthetists, 1984, Alumni Assn. Ann. award, Ohio State U, Nurse Anesthesia Program, 1985, Faculty Tchg. Excellence award, McMaster U. students, 1999, hon. mention Ann. Grad. Student Supr. award, McMaster U. Mem.: ABA. Achievements include established first graduate level program in nurse anesthesia U.S. Office Phone: 843-525-8278. Business E-Mail: lparisi@tcl.edu.

PARISI, VALERIE MARIE, dean, medical educator; b. Bklyn., 1952; m. Gary Strong. BS in Biology, Brown U., 1972, MD, 1975; MPH, U. Calif. Sch. Pub. Health, 1980; MBA, U. NC, 2004. Lic. Calif., 1979, Tex., 1984, NY, 1994, NC, 1998, diplomate Nat. Bd. Med. Examiners, 1976, Am. Bd. Ob-gyn., 1981, Am. Bd. Ob-gyn. Divsn. Maternal-Fetal Medicine, 1987. NIH rsch. fellow, Dept. Chemistry and Physics Brown U., Providence, 1970, Noyes Found. rsch. fellow, Dept. Sociology & Divsn. Reproductive Biology and Medicine, 1971; Noyes Found. rsch. fellow, Dept. Ob-gyn. Women and Infants Hosp. RI, Providence, 1972; intern in categorical gen. surgery Brown U. Affiliated Hospitals, RI Hosp., Providence, 1975—76; resident in ob-gyn. Women and Infants Hosp. of RI, Providence, 1976—79; fellow divsn. maternal-fetal medicine, Dept. Ob-gyn. U. Colo. Health Sci. Ctr., Denver, 1982—83, U. Wis. Ctr. for Health Sciences, Madison, 1983—84; instr. Dept. Human Growth and Reproduction Brown U., 1976—79; lectr., divsn. maternal child health U. Calif. Sch. Pub. Health, Berkeley, 1980—81; clin. instr. Dept. Ob-gyn. and Reproductive Sciences, U. Calif., San Francisco, 1980—81, clin. asst. prof., 1981—82; asst. prof. Dept. Ob-gyn. U. Colo. Health Sci. Ctr., Denver, 1982—83, U. Wis. Health Sci. Ctr., Madison, 1983—84; asst. prof. Dept. Ob-gyn. and Reproductive Sciences U. Texas Med. Sch., Houston, 1984—89, assoc. prof. Dept. Ob-gyn. and Reproductive Sciences, 1989—94, dir. divsn. maternal-fetal medicine, 1984—94, asst. prof. Dept. Pediatrics, 1987—89, assoc. prof. Dept. Pediatrics, 1989—94, co-dir. maternal-fetal medicine fellowship program, 1987—94; vis. prof. divsn. neonatology Dept. Pediatrics U. Cin. Med. Ctr., 1991—92; prof. & chair Dept. Ob-gyn. and Reproductive Medicine U. Med. Ctr. at Stony Brook, NY, 1994—97; Robert A. Ross prof. & chair Dept Ob-gyn. U. NC, Chapel Hill, 1997—2004, residency program dir. Dept. Ob-gyn., 1999—2004, rsch. fellow Cecil G. Sheps Ctr. for Health Sciences Rsch., 2003—; dean medicine U. Tex. Med. Branch, Galveston, 2004—06, chief acad. officer, v.p. acad. program adminstrn. and services, 2004—06, adv., 2006; vice dean hosp. relations and clinical affairs, sr. advisor to chmn. CEO, U. Physician Group Wayne State U. Sch. Medicine, Detroit, 2007—, prof. dept. obstetrics and gynecology, 2007—. Attending staff Providence Neighborhood Health Centers, RI, 1977—79; dir. Ob-gyn. Services Bristol County Cmty. Med. Ctr., RI, 1977—79; dir. gynecological services Brown U. Student Health Services, 1978—79; consulting staff Letterman Army Med. Ctr., Presidio of San Francisco, 1979—82; attending staff Kaiser Found. Hosp., Oakland, Calif., 1980, San Francisco, 1980—82; clin. staff Moffitt Hosp. U. Calif. San Francisco Med. Ctr., 1980—82; med. dir. Ambulatory Care Ctr. Dept. Ob-gyn. U. Colo. Health Sci. Ctr., Denver, 1982—83; attending staff Madison Gen. Hosp., Wis., 1983—84, U. Wis. Clin. Sciences Ctr., Madison, 1983—84; consulting staff St. Mary's Med. Ctr., Madison, Wis., 1983—84; attending staff Hermann Hosp., Houston, 1984—94, dir. Maternal-Fetal Spl. Care Unit, 1985—92, obstetrical dir. labor and delivery, 1987—88, Houston, 1992—94, med. dir. Family Ctr., 1992—94; consulting staff St. Joseph's Hosp., Houston, 1987—94, Meml. Southwest Hosp., Houston, 1990—94; active staff Lyndon Baines Johnson Hosp., Houston, 1990—94; ob-gyn. chief U. Hosp., Stony Brook, NY, 1994—97; consulting staff Southampton Hosp., NY, 1995—97, St. Charles Hosp., Port Jefferson, NY, 1996—97; obstetrician-gynecologist-in-chief NC Women's Hosp., Chapel Hill, 1997—2004; attending staff Dept. Ob-gyn REX Hosp., 2002—04. Bd. dirs. Am. Bd. Family Practice, 1999—2004; fin. and investment com., nominating com. Am. Bd. Med. Specialties, 2004; basic examiner Am. Bd. Obstetrics and Gynecology, 1990—, maternal and fetal medicine examiner, 1992—, divsn. maternal and fetal medicine, 1996—2002, bd. dirs. and divsn. chief maternal and fetal medicine, 1998—2002, exec. com., 1999—2002, fin. com., 2004—09, sec., treas., 2009—; mem. Coun. on Residency Edn. in Ob-gyn., 1995—2000; bd. dirs. Planned Parenthood of Suffolk County, 1994—97; exec. bd. Western Perinatal Collaborative Group, 1986—92, chair membership com., 1986—88, vice pres. & pres.-elect, 1988—90, pres., 1990—92. Fellow: Am. Gynecologic and Obstetrical Soc. (nominating com. 1992, fellowship com. 1992—95), Am. Assn. Advancement Sci.; mem.: Tex. Perinatal Assn., Tex. Med. Found., Tex. Med. Assn., Tex. Assn. Obstetricians and Gynecologists, Soc. for Study of Reproduction, Soc. Obstetric Anesthesia and Perinatology (bd. dirs. 1995—99), Soc. for Maternal Fetal Medicine (bd. dirs. 1989—92, scientific program chair 1993, pres.-elect 1993—94, pres. 1994—95), Soc. Gynecological Investigation, Perinatal Rsch. Soc. (exec. coun. 1993—95), NY Obstetrical Soc., Internat. Soc. for Study of Hypertension in Pregnancy, Houston Gynecological and Obstetrical Soc., Harris County Med. Soc., Assn. Reproductive Health Professionals, Assn. Professors of Gynecology and Obstetrics, Am. Med. Women's Assn., AMA, Am. Coll. Obstetricians and Gynecologists (patient edn. com. 1989—91, scientific program com. 1993, edn. commn. 1995—97), Sigma Xi.*

PARISIER, CARLOS, lawyer, economist; b. Buenos Aires, Oct. 21, 1930; m. Alicia Parisier, Nov. 25, 1965; children: Martin, Jacqueline. BA, Colegio Nacional de Buenos Aires, 1948; LLB cum laude, U. Buenos Aires, 1954. Bar: Argentina, 1954, Uruguay, 1955, Spain, 1985. Sr. ptnr. Estudio Parisier, Buenos Aires, 1954—2004; pres. Hermitage Hotel S.A., Mar del Plata, Argentina, 1958-75; founder Fundacion Pro Justitia, Buenos Aires, 1980. Film producer, 1963—. Author: La nueva ley argentina en materia de convenciones de trabajo, 1955; contbr. articles on corp. and bankruptcy law to legal publs. Recipient motion picture award, Acapulco, Mexico, 1963. Mem. ABA, Buenos Aires Bar Assn., Uruguay Bar Assn., Madrid Bar Assn., Argentine Inst. Comml. Law, Comml. Bank Lawyers Argentina. Office: Maipu No 1252 Fl 10 1006 Buenos Aires Argentina Home Phone: 54-11-4814-3132; Office Phone: 54-11-5779-7777.

PARIZEK, ELDON JOSEPH, geologist, educator, dean; b. Iowa City, Apr. 30, 1920; s. William Joseph and Libbie S. P.; m. Mildred Marie Burger, Aug. 9, 1944; children: Richard, Marianne, Elizabeth, Amy. BS, U. Iowa, 1942, MS, 1946, PhD, 1949. Instr. U. Iowa, 1947-49; asst. prof. geology U. Ga., 1949-54, asso. prof., 1954-56, U. Kansas City, 1956-63; prof. U. Mo., Kansas City, 1963—, chmn. dept. geoscis., 1968-78; dean U. Mo. (Coll. Arts and Scis.), 1979-86. Served with USN, 1942-45. Fellow Geol. Soc. Am.; mem. AAUP, Assn. Mo. Geologists, AAAS, Sigma Xi. Roman Catholic. Achievements include research, numerous publs. on mass wasting, slope failure, underground space, geology of West Mo. Home: 6913 W 100th Shawnee Mission KS 66212 Office: 5100 Rockhill Rd Kansas City MO 64110-2481

PARK, BARBARA LYNNE, writer; b. Mt. Holly, NJ, Apr. 27, 1947; d. Doris and Brooke Tidswell; m. Richard A. Park, 1969; children: Steven, David. Attended, Rider Coll., 1965—67; BS, U. Alabama, 1969. Author: (children's books) Don't Make Me Smile, 1981, Operation: Dump the Chump, 1982 (Tennessee Children's Choice Book award, 1986), Skinnybones, 1982, Beanpole, 1983, Buddies, 1985 (Parents' Choice award, 1985), Kid in the Red Jacket, 1987 (Library of Congress Book of the Yr., 1987), Almost Starring Skinnybones, 1988, Mother Got Married: and Other Disasters, 1989, Rosie Swanson, 1991, Junie B. Jones and the Stupid Smelly Bus, 1992, Junie B. Jones and Her Big Fat Mouth, 1993, Junie B. Jones and a Little Monkey Business, 1993, Junie B. Jones and Some Sneaky Peeky Spying, 1994, Mick Harte Was Here, 1995, Junie B. Jones and the Yucky Blucky Fruitcake, 1995, B. Jones Loves Handsome Warren, 1996, Junie B. Jones and that Meanie Jim's Birthday, 1996, Junie B. Jones Loves Handsome Warren, 1996, Junie B. Jones has a Monster Under Her Bed, 1997, Junie B. Jones is Not a Crook, 1997, Junie B. Jones is a Party Animal, 1997, Junie B. Jones is a Beauty Shop Guy, 1998, Psst! It's Me...the Bogeyman, 1998;: Junie B. Jones Smells Something Fishy, 1998, Junie B. Jones is Almost a Flower Girl, 1999, Junie B. Jones and the Mushy Gushy Valentine, 1999, Junie B. Jones has a Peep in her Pocket, 2000, Junie B. Jones is Captain Field Day, 2001, Junie B. Jones is a Graduation Girl, 2001, Junie B. Jones: First Grader, 2001, Junie B., First Grader: Boss of Lunch, 2002, Junie B., First Grader: Toothless Wonder, 2002, Top Secret, Personal Beeswax: A Journal by Junie B., 2003, Junie B., First Grader: Cheater Pants, 2003, Junie B., First Grader: One-Man Band, 2003, Junie B., 1st Grader: Shipwrecked, 2004, Junie B., First Grader: Boo...and I MEAN it!, 2004, Junie B., First Grader: Jingle Bells, Batman Smells! (p.s. so does May), 2005, Junie B., First Grader: Aloha-ha-ha!, 2006, Junie B., First Grader: Dumb Bunny, 2007. Recipient Young Hoosier award, 1985, Milner award, 1986. Office: c/o Random House 1745 Broadway New York NY 10019

PARK, BYUNGKYU (BRIAN PARK), engineering educator; b. Daegu, Republic Of Korea, Feb. 24, 1970; s. Hee-Bong Park and Soon-Hee Jung; m. Yejin Yim; 1 child, Adrian J. PhD, Tex. A&M U., Coll. Station, 1998. Rsch. asst. Tex. Transp. Inst., Coll. Station, 1995—98; rsch. fellow Nat. Inst. Statis. Scis., Rsch. Triangle Pk., NC, 1998—2001; asst. prof. U. Va., Charlottesville, 2004—, rsch. asst. prof., 2001—04. Vis. rschr. Seoul Devel. Inst., 1995—95, TNO, Delft, Netherlands, 2008—08. Contbr. articles to profl. jours. V.p. ASCE Blue Ridge Br., Charlottesville, 2006—07. Recipient C.V. Wootan award, Coun. U. Transp. Ctrs., 1998, Jack H. Dillard Outstanding Paper award, Va. Transp. Rsch. Coun., 2004. Mem.: IEEE, ASCE (Tchg. fellow 2004), TRB Statis. Com., TRB Traffic Signal Sys. Com. Achievements include patents pending for sustainable transportation system. Office: Univ Va Civil Engring dept 351 McCormick Rd Charlottesville VA 22904-4742 Business E-Mail: bpark@virginia.edu.

PARK, CHAE GYU, immunologist, educator; b. Pusan, Republic Of Korea, Sept. 12, 1968; s. Hyun Kyong Park and Jung Hwan Sung; m. Sun Seung An, Dec. 18, 1999; children: Jong Eun Sylvia, Jong Won Benjamin. BSc magna cum laude, Seoul Nat. U., Republic Of Korea, 1990; MSc, Wichita State U., Kans., 1992; PhD, Rockefeller U., NYC, 1996. Rsch. assoc. Rockefeller U., 2001—07, rsch. asst. prof., 2007—. Sgt. Republic of Korea Army, 1997—98, Republic of Korea Armed Forces Ctrl. Med. Rsch. Inst. Decorated Citation for Excellence Republic of Korea Armed Forces Med. Command; recipient Internat. Immunology Outstanding Merit award, Editl. Bd. and Editor-in-Chief Internat. Immunology, 2004. Mem.: Harvey Soc. Achievements include patents pending for OLLAS epitope tag and anti-OLLAS tag monoclonal antibody. Home: 504 E 63rd St #19L New York NY 10065 Office: Rockefeller Univ 1230 York Ave New York NY 10065 Office Fax: 212-327-8875. Personal E-mail: chaegyu@gmail.com. Business E-Mail: parkc@mail.rockefeller.edu.

PARK, CHAN HO, professional baseball player; b. Kongju, South Korea, June 30, 1973; Grad., Hanyang U., South Korea. Pitcher LA Dodgers, 1994—2001, 2008, Tex. Rangers, 2002—05, San Diego Padres, 2005—06, NY Mets, 2007, Phila. Phillies, 2009—. Pitcher, Korean nat. team World Baseball Classic, 2006. Named to Nat. League All-Star Team, Maj. League Baseball, 2001, All-Tourney Team, World Baseball Classic, 2006. Achievements include becoming the first South Korean pitcher in Major League Baseball history to reach 100 career wins. Office: Phila Phillies Citizens Bank Pk One Citizens Bank Way Philadelphia PA 19148 Office Phone: (619) 795-5000.*

PARK, CHAN HYUNG, cell biologist, physician; b. Seoul, Korea, Aug. 16, 1936; s. Chung Suh and Yoon Sook Yuh; m. Mary Hyungrok Kim, Apr. 16, 1966; 1 child, Christopher Myungwoo. MD, Seoul Nat. U., 1962, MS, 1964; PhD, U. Toronto, 1972. Diplomate in internal medicine and med. oncology Am. Bd. Internal Medicine. Asst. prof. U. Kans. Med. Ctr., 1974—80, assoc. prof., 1980—86, prof., 1986—89; prof., chief divsn. oncology/hematology, dept. internal med. Tex. Tech U. Health Scis. Ctr., 1989—94; dir. Cancer Ctr. Samsung Med. Ctr., Seoul, 1994—2001, head divsn. hematology/oncology dept. medicine, 1994—99; sr. rsch. scientist Ctr. for Improvement of Human Functioning Internat., Inc., Wichita, Kans., 2001—; prof. medicine Sungkyn-Kwan U. Med. Sch., 1997—2001, prof. emeritis, 2007—. Cancer ctr. cons. 2001; adv. com. Samsung Cancer Ctr., 2006—. Transl. novel from German to Korean; mem. editl. bd. Jour. Nutrition, Growth and Cancer, 1986-87; mem. editl. bd. Internat. Jour. Hematology, 1999—; contbr. articles to biomed and sci. jours. Recipient Rsch. Career Devel. award USPHS, NIH, 1979-84. Fellow: ACP; mem.: Am. Soc. Hematology, Internat. Soc. Exptl. Hematology, Am. Soc. Clin. Oncology, Am. Assn. Cancer Rsch. Home: 611 S 291 ST Federal Way WA 98003 Office: The Ctr for the Improvement Human Functioning Internat Inc 3100 N Hillside Wichita KS 67219 Personal E-mail: park.chanh@gmail.com.

PARK, CHAN-MO, academic administrator, educator; BS, Soeul Nat. U., 1958; MS, U. Md., College Park, 1964, PhD, 1969, LittD (hon.), 2001. Asst. prof. Dept. Computer Sci. U. Md., College Park, 1969—72; assoc. prof. Korea Advanced Inst. of Sci. & Tech., 1973—76; sr. rsch. scientist Nat. Biomedical Rsch. Found., Georgetown U., 1976—79; assoc. prof. computer sci. Cath. U. of Am., 1979—82, prof., chmn. computer sci., 1982—89; prof. Dept. Computer Sci. & Engring. Pohang U. Sci. and Tech., 1990—, chmn., 1990—94, dean Grad. Sch. Info. Tech., 1991—94, dir. Ctr. for Advanced Software Tech., 1994—97, dean, 2000—02, acting pres., 2002—03, pres., 2003—. Vis. prof. computer info. sys. Boston U. Overseas Programs, 1985—86; adj. prof. Northeastern U., Shenyang, China, 1994—, Yabian U. of Sci. and Tech., 1996—; vis. prof. U. Md. Asian Div., 1997—98; adj. prof. Shenyang Bohai Coll., 1999—. Recipient Dong-Baek Nat. Medal of Honor, Republic of Korea, 1986, Blue Stripes Order of Svc. Merit Medal, 2005, James E. Donan Meml. Tchr. of Yr., Cath. U. of Am., 1987. Fellow: Korean Acad. Sci. and Tech.; mem.: IEEE, Info. Tech. Forum for Unification (pres. 2000—04), Korea Computer Graphics Soc. (pres. 1996—97), Korea Simulation Soc. (pres. 1991—92), Korea Info. Sci. Soc. (pres. 1993), Korean Scientists and Engrs. Assn. in Am. (pres. 1984—85, 1988—90), Soc. for Computer Simulation, Assn. for Computing Machinery. Office: Pohang U Sci and Tech San 31 Hyoja Dong Pohang 790-784 Republic of Korea Office Phone: +82-54-279-2701. Office Fax: +82-54-279-2020. Business E-Mail: parkcm@postech.ac.kr.

PARK, CHULHWAN, chemical engineering educator, researcher; b. KyungSangBuk Province, Republic Of Korea, Oct. 26, 1974; m. Yeonsook Lee; children: Ganghee, Juhee. BS, Kwangwoon U., Seoul, Republic of Korea, 1997; MS, Kwnagwoon U., Seoul, Republic of Korea, 1999; PhD, Korea U., Seoul, 2003. Postdoctoral rschr. U. Cambridge, England, 2003—04; sr. rschr. Korea Inst. Indsl. Tech., ChonAn, 2003—07; prof. Kwangwoon U., Seoul, 2007—. Quality mgr. test and cert. Test Biodegradable Plastics. Composer preparation nat. tech. roadmap in eco-friendly process Korean Ministry Sci. and Tech., Seoul, 2001—02. Recipient DIN Certco, Germany, 2002, Excellent Paper award, Korea Inst. Indsl. Tech., 2003, Outstanding Poster Presentation award, 7th Asia-Pacific Biochemical Engring. Conf., 2005. Achievements include development of bioprocess for renewable energy, pollution prevention methodology for cleaner production, wastewater treatment/bioremediation process; research in succinic acid production by continuous fermentation process using Mannheimia succiniciproducens; continuous production of lactosucrose by immobilized Strerigmatomyces elviae mutant; biodegradation and biosorptin for decolorization of synthetic dyes by Funalia troggi; bioremediation of 2, 4, 6-Trinitrotoluene contaminated soil in slurry and column reactors; decolorization of disperse and reactive dye solutions using ferric chloride; decolorization of dye solutions by a membrane bioreactor (MBR) using white-rot fungi; comparison of disperse and reactive dye removals by chemical coagulation and fenton oxidation; decolorization of three acid dyes by enzymes from fungal strains; water recycling from desalination and purification process of reactive dye manufacturing industry by combined membrane filtration; upgrading of anaerobic digestion by incorporating two different hydrolysis processes; flux optimization using genetic algorithms in membrane bioreactor; decolorization of acid black 52 by fungal immobilization; production of penicillic acid by Aspergillus sclerotiorum CGF; pilot scale treatment of textile wastewater by combined process (fluidized biofilm process-chemical coagulation-electrochemical oxidation; decolorization of disperse and reactive dyes by continuous electrocoagulation process; COD reduction and decolorization of textile effluent using combined process; effect of various pretreatments for enhanced anaerobic digestion of waste activated sludge; effect of Cl-based chemical coagulants on electrochemical oxidation of textile wastewater; patents for strain for polyvinyl alcohol treatment and a method for biological treatment of textile wastewater; method for enhanced anaerobic digestion of waste activated sludge; reaction system for biodegradable tests of polymeric plastic materials; dye synthesis making method for a distillation underreduced pressure; A method on manufatcturing of synthesis gas from papersludge; continuous upflow electrolysis reactor; method for treatment of sewage and wastewater; method on synthesis of organic-inorganic hybrid nanoporous anion-exchange resins for the treatment of wastewater contaminated by perchlorate. Office: Kwangwoon Univ Dept Chem Engring Wolgye-Dong Nowon-Gu Seoul 139-701 Republic of Korea Business E-Mail: chpark@kw.ac.kr.

PARK, CYNTHIA, sociology educator, consultant; b. Schenectady, NY, Feb. 7, 1925; d. Robert Hiram and Miriam Elizabeth (Nelson) Park; m. Robert Wentworth Christy (div.). BA, New Sch. Social Rsch., 1959; MS in Secondary Social Studies, Yeshiva U., 1961; MA in Sociology, Hunter Coll., CUNY, 1969; postgrad., New Sch. U., 1970—75. Permanent lic. secondary social studies NYC and NY State. Tchr. hs sci. and social studies NY Bd. Edn., NYC, 1961, tchr. hs social studies Brandeis HS, 1962—66; tchr. Nassau CC, LI, NY, 1970; instr. sociology Bloomfield Coll., NJ, 1967—70, Quinnipiac Coll., New Haven, 1971—73, U. New Haven, West Haven, Conn., 1973—75; ind. cons. NYC, 1975—. Cons. Paulo Mesdag Gruppe Rec. Yale U. Archives; owner 98 1/2 McDougal St., NYC, 1951; dir. Coop Gallery, NYC, 1960—65, Westerly Gallery, NYC. Prodr.: (mus. recs.) Music of Finland. Local campaign worker Lexington Dem. Club, NYC, 1963—67. Recipient Fulbright grant to Finland, 1959—60, grants in field. Mem.: Soc. Ethnomusicology, Ind. U., Am. Sociol. Assn., Violoncello Soc., Am. Fedn. Musicians. Democrat. Episcopalian. Avocations: art, violincello, singing. Home: 965 Lexington Ave New York NY 10021

PARK, DAEYOUNG, engineer, researcher; b. Seoul, Republic of Korea, Mar. 30, 1975; arrived in US, 2007; s. Jeong-Gi Park and Eunhee Yoon; m. Joo Yeon Choi, Feb. 18, 2006. BS, Seoul Nat. U., 1998, MS, 2000, PhD in Elec. Engring. and Computer Sci., 2004. Sr. engr. Samsung Electronics, Suwon, Republic of Korea, 2004—07; rsch. scholar U. So. Calif., LA, 2007—. Contbr. scientific papers to tech. jours. Recipient Tech. Paper award, Samsung, 2005. Office: Univ Southern Calif Sch Engineering 3740 McClintock Ave EEB 506 Los Angeles CA 90089 Personal E-mail: dpark@ieee.org.

PARK, DANIEL SANG-WON, research scientist; s. Min Kyun and Soon Jin Park; m. Se Young Han, May 29, 1995; children: Ye Eun, Sarah Ha-Eun. BS, Sung Kyun Kwan U., Seoul, 1990; ME, Sung Kyun Kwan U., 1993; MS, La. State U., Baton Rouge, 2001; PHD, U. Tex., Dallas, 2004. Grad. tchg. asst. La. State U., Baton Rouge, 1998—2000, grad. rsch. asst., 2000—01, postdoc. rschr., 2004—06, postdoc. rsch. assoc., 2006—; grad. rsch. asst. U. Tex., Dallas, 2001—04, postdoc. rschr., 2004—04. Contbr. to numerous profl. jours. Pres. Korean Student Assn. U. Tex., Dallas, 2002—03; v.p. Baton Rouge Sch. Korean Lang., 1997—98. Excellence Rsch. Fellowship, U. Tex., 2002—04. Mem.: IEEE (Best Student Paper award 2006). Democrat. Presbyterian. Achievements include patents for methods of reproduction of micromold inserts; modular microfluidic devices.

PARK, DAVID ALLEN, physicist, researcher; b. NYC, Oct. 13, 1919; s. Edwin Avery and Frances (Paine) P.; m. Clara Justine Claiborne, Aug. 18, 1945; children: Katharine, Rachel, Paul, Jessica. AB, Harvard, 1941; PhD, U. Mich., 1950. Instr. Williams Coll., 1941-44; ops. research on radar countermeasures Harvard U. and Eng., 1944-45; instr. U. Mich., 1950; mem. Inst. Advanced Study, Princeton, 1950-51; mem. faculty Williams Coll., 1952-88, prof. physics, 1960-88, emeritus, 1988—; sr. vis. Cambridge (Eng.) U., 1962-63; vis. lectr. U. Ceylon, 1955-56, 72, Mass. Inst. Tech., 1966; vis. prof. U. N.C., 1964. Author: Quantum Theory, 1964, 3d edit., 1991, Contemporary Physics, 1964, Strong Interactions, 1966, Classical Dynamics and Its Quantum Analogues, 1979, 2d edit., 1990, The Image of Eternity, 1980, (with P.J. Davis) No Way, 1987, The How and the Why, 1988, The Fire Within the Eye, 1997, The Grand Contraption, 2005. Fellow Am. Phys. Soc.; mem. Internat. Soc. for Study Time (pres. 1973-76). Office: Williams Coll Dept Physics Williamstown MA 01267 Business E-Mail: dpark@williams.edu.

PARK, EUI-SOO, dermatologist, consultant; b. Daegu, Republic of Korea, Feb. 16, 1953; s. Nam-Ho Park and Sung-Hyea Kim; m. Hyea-Myung Cho, Jan. 18, 1977; children: Sung-Eun, So-Eun, Sung-Min. MD, Kyungpook Nat. U., Daegu, Korea, 1978, MA, 1982, PhD, 1985. Lic. Korean Med. Bd. Medicine, 1978, Korean Bd. Dermatology, 1983. Instr. sch. medicine Keimyung U., Daegu, 1983—87, asst. prof. sch. medicine, 1988—91, assoc. prof. sch. medicine, 1992—94; fellow dermatology U. Toronto, 1992; dir. Bosung Skin & Laser Clinic, Daegu, 1995—96, Dr. Park's Skin & Laser Clinic, Daegu, 1997—. Med. cons. sch. medicine Keimyung U., 2000—04. Contbr. articles to profl. jours. Elder The Presbyn. Ch., Daegu, 2002—07. Maj. Korean Army,

1986—88. Fellow: Am. Acad. Dermatology; mem.: Korean Assn. Practitioners Dermatology (chmn. 2001—02, mem. com. 2005—), Soc. Investigative Dermatology. Achievements include research in effects of UVB-inducible cytokines on melanoma growth; serum testosterone levels on leprosy patients; serum angiotensin converting enzyme levels on leprosy; expression of epidermal growth factor receptor in malignant epidermal tumors; mutant p53 protein expression squamous cell carcinoma. Avocations: travel, tennis, mountain climbing. Home: 101-402 Dalim E Pyunhan Sesang Apt Suseong-dong 4-ga Suseong-gu Daegu 706926 Republic of Korea Office: Skin & Laser Clinic Ste 402 1431-4 Dowon-Dong Dalseo-gu Daegu 704380 Republic of Korea Office Phone: 82-53-637-7477. Office Fax: 82-53-636-2123; Home Fax: 82-53-636-2123. Personal E-mail: pes7977@hanmail.net.

PARK, EUNSUNG, scientist, education educator; s. Jaewoo Park and Youngjin Lee; m. Eunkyung Park; children: Soyeon, Changyeon. BS, Ohio State U., 1987, MS, 1990; PhD, Alfred U., 1997. Rsch. assoc. Ohio State U., Columbus, Ohio, 1987—90; rsch. engr. Edison Rsch. Inst., Columbus, 1990—93; tchg. assoc. Alfred U., Alfred, NY, 1994—97; sr. rsch. scientist X-ray Therapeutics, St. Paul, 1998—99; sr. scientist Medtronic AVE, Santa Rosa, Calif., 2000—02; prin. scientist Medtronic, Inc., Mpls., 2002—. Adv. Korea Small and Medium Bus. Adminstrn., Seoul, 2001—04; pres. Korean Group of Am. Ceramic Soc., Ohio, 2001—03; guest prof. Yonsei U., Seoul, 2005. Recipient Best Grad. Spkr., Materials Rsch. Soc., 1997, Invited Presentation, Gordon Rsch. Conf., 2003. Mem.: NY Acad. Sci. Achievements include patents in field. Office: Medtronic Inc LT 240 710 Medtronic Pkwy Minneapolis MN 55432 E-mail: eunsung.park@medtronic.com.

PARK, EUN-YOUNG, medical educator; b. Daegu, Gyeongsangbuk-do, Republic of Korea, Dec. 19, 1968; d. Su-Kyu Park and Ki-Yeon Nam. MD, Hanyang U., Seoul, 1993, PhD, 2000. Instr. Hallym U. Coll. Medicine, Chuncheon, Gangwon-do, Republic of Korea, 2002—04, asst. prof., 2004—05; pediatrician Mizmedi Hosp., Seoul, 2006—08, Seoul Red Cross Hosp., 2008—. Contbr. articles to profl. jours. Mem.: Korean Pediat. Assn. Personal E-mail: neonatol@hanmail.net.

PARK, HYUN, lawyer, utilities executive; BA summa cum laude, Columbia U., NYC; MA, Oxford U.; JD cum laude, Harvard U., 1989. Ptnr. Latham & Watkins, LA, NYC, Hong Kong; sr. v.p., gen. counsel, sec. Sithe Energies Inc., 1998—2005; v.p., gen. counsel Allegheny Energy Inc., Greensburg, Pa., 2005—06; sr. v.p., gen. counsel PG&E Corp., San Francisco, 2006—. Office: PG&E Corp Ste 2400 One Market Spear Tower San Francisco CA 94105-1126 Office Phone: 415-367-7070. Office Fax: 415-267-7268.*

PARK, HYUNG CHUL, electronics engineer, educator; b. Daegu, Republic of Korea, Jan. 16, 1974; s. Jong Woo Park and Ok Lan Seo; m. Yeun Yee Ha, Nov. 27, 1999; 1 child, Yun Jeong. BS, Korea Advanced Inst. Sci. and Tech., Daejeon, Republic of Korea, 1996, MS, 1998, PhD, 2003. Sr. rsch. engr. Hynix Semiconductor Inc., Seoul, Republic of Korea, 2003—05; lectr. Hanbat Nat. U., Daejeon, 2005—07, asst. prof., 2007—. Vis. rschr. U. Calif., Davis, 2000—01; tech. advisor Phychips Inc., Daejeon, Republic of Korea, 2005—. Contbr. articles to profl. jours. Pvt. second class Army, 2000, Republic of Korea. Mem.: IEEE, Inst. Electronics Engrs. Korea. Achievements include research in modulation/demodulation algorithms; VLSI for wireless communication; interface between MODEM and RF transceiver; digital calibration for RF transceiver. Avocation: swimming. Home: 203-101 Youlmae Apt Jijok-Dong Yuseong Daejeon 350-770 Republic of Korea Office: Hanbat Nat Univ San 16-1 Duckmyoung-Dong Yuseong-Gu Daejeon 305-719 Republic of Korea Office Fax: +82-42-821-1595. Business E-Mail: hcpark@hanbat.ac.kr, chori@dimple.kaist.ac.kr.

PARK, IN SUH, internist, educator; b. Seoul, South Korea, May 27, 1937; s. Jun Keun Park and Jung Won Kim; m. Soon Doe Park, Mar. 27, 1967. MD, Yonsei U., Seoul, 1962, M in Med. Sci., 1967; PhD, Yonsei U. Coll. of Medicine, Seoul, 1978. Intern, resident Severance Hosp., Seoul, 1962—66; prof. Yonsei U. Coll. Medicine, 1970—, prof. emeritus, 2002—; prof. medicine, dir. digestive disease ctr. Myungi Hosp. Kwandong U., Republic of Korea. Fellow Med. Cancer Inst. Hosp., Tokyo, 1972; vis. prof. Tech. U. Munchen, Germany, 1991; chief gastroenterology Yonsei U. Med. Ctr., Seoul, 1991—97; dir. Inst. Gastroent. Yonsei U., Seoul, 1992—97. Author: (book) Gastritis, 1998; contbr. articles to profl. jours. Maj. Korean Air Force, 1967—69. Recipient Acad. award, Korean Soc. Internal Medicine, 1977, 1989. Fellow: Am. Gastroenterological Assn.; mem.: Korean Assn. Internal Medicine (v.p. 1999—2000), Nat. Acad. Medicine Korea, Korean Coll. H.pylori Rsch. (pres. 1999), Korean Soc. Gastrointestinal Motility (pres. 1997—99), Korean Soc. Gastroenterology (pres. 1998—99, Acad. award 2000), Korean Soc. Gastrointestinal Endoscopy (pres. 1993—94), Am. Gastroenterology Assn. Office: Myungji Hosp Kwandong U 697-24 Hwajunng-Dong Dukyang-Ku Kyonggi 412-270 Republic of Korea Business E-Mail: ispark@kd.ac.kr.

PARK, IN-SEOP, orthopedist, researcher; b. Seoul, Republic Of Korea, Mar. 24, 1964; s. Sang-Soon Park and Ok-Lim Yoon; m. Gi-Un Kim, Apr. 26, 1992; children: U-Jin, U-mi. Attended, Seoul Nat. U., 1984—90; M in Medicine, Gangwon Nat. U., 2006. Diplomate Seoul Nat. Med. U., 1990. Internship Nat. Med. Ctr., Seoul, 1991, resident, 1992—95; gen. orthopaedic dr. Yong-Dong Hosp., Jeonbuk, Republic of Korea, 1995—2002; arthroscopist, orthopaedic dept. Gangnam Hosp., Yongin-si, Gyeonggi-do, Republic of Korea, 2002—. Rschr. Severance Joint & Arthroscopy Rsch. Inst., Seoul, 2001—. Contbr. articles to profl. jours. Recipient Douglas W. Jackson award, Severance Joint & Arthroscopy Rsch. Inst., 2004. Office Phone: 82 31 300 0110, 82 31 300 0106. Business E-Mail: kju0115@naver.com.

PARK, INYONG, science educator; married. PhD, Stony Brook U., NY, 2000. Postdoc. rschr. Tex. A&m U., Coll. Sta., 2000—02, Ohio State U., Columbus, 2002—04, lectr., 2004—06, Longwood U., Farmville, Va., 2006—07; asst. prof. U. Ark., Pine Bluff, 2007—08; assoc. prof. Philander Smith Coll., Little Rock, 2008—. Deacon Disciples' Ch., Little Rock, 2007.

PARK, JEONG-HEON, electronics engineer, researcher; b. Chunyang, Kyungsangbuk-Do, Republic Of Korea, Aug. 20, 1974; s. Jinoh Park and Suja Jeong; m. Eunsang Lee; children: Hyewon, Jiwon. BS, Seoul Nat. U., Republic of Korea, 1997, MS, 1999, Carnegie Mellon U., Pittsburgh, 2009. Cert. green belt, Samsung Electronics, 2004. Sr. engr. Samsung Electronics, Suwon, Kyunggi-Do, Republic of Korea, 1999—; rschr. Carnegie Mellon U., 2005—. Recipient Best Paper award, Samsung Electronics, 2003; fellow, 2005—09. Mem.: IEEE. Achievements include research in Co Pt multilayer based magnetic tunnel junctions using perpendicular magnetic anisotropy, spin-transfer induced switching in nano-magnetoresistive devices; patents for method for isolating self-aligned contact pads, CMP slurry for forming aluminum film, methods of fabricating thin ferroelectric layers and capacitors; development of SEC Al CMP slurry & post CMP cleaning solution. Office: Carnegie Mellon Univ 5000 Forbes Ave Pittsburgh PA 15213 Business E-Mail: jaman@cmu.edu.

PARK, JIN GYU, research scientist; b. Yeongju, Gyeongsang, Republic Of Korea, Mar. 5, 1975; s. Seong Koo Park and Chun Hong Kang; m. Taekyoung Lee; 1 child, Bryan Sangwoo. PhD, Seoul Nat. U., 2003. Postdoc. assoc. Fla. State U., Tallahassee, 2003—08, rsch. scientist, 2008—. Achievements include research in carbon nanotube characterization & its application. Office: FL State Univ 2525 Pottsdamer St Tallahassee FL 32310

PARK, JOHN, Internet company executive; b. Seoul, South Korea, 1970; arrived in US, 1973; married; 2 children. BS in Info. Sys., NYU, 1993, BS in Mgmt., 1993. With NY WEB, Prodigy, Ameritrade; developer iWON.com; group v.p. product mgmt. MyWay.com; exec. v.p., gen. mgr. toolbars and portals Mindspark Interactive Network, White Plains, NY, 2005—08, CEO, 2008—. Avocation: snowboarding. Office: Mindspark Interactive Network 1 N Lexington Ave 9th Fl White Plains NY 10601*

PARK, JOHN K., neurosurgeon; MD, Harvard Med. Sch., Boston, PhD, 1992. Cert. neurol. surgery ABNS, 2001. Head, surg. and molecular neuro-oncology NINDS NIH, Bethesda, Md., 2002—.

PARK, JOON BU, biomedical engineer, researcher, educator; b. Pusan, Republic of Korea, June 20, 1944; arrived in U.S., 1964; s. Sung Sub and Jung Ju (Kim) P.; m. Hyonsook Yoo, Apr. 15, 2000; children: Misun, Yoon Ho, Yoon Il, Lajong. Student, Seoul Nat. U., 1962—64; BS, Boston U., 1967; MS, MIT, 1969; PhD, U. Utah, 1972. NIH postdoctoral fellow U. Wash., Seattle, 1972—73; vis. asst. prof. U. Ill., Urbana, 1973—76; asst. prof., assoc. prof. Clemson U., SC, 1976—81; prof. Tulane U., New Orleans, 1981—83; prof. biomed. engring. U. Iowa, Iowa City, 1983—. Advisor, cons. FDA, Rockville, Md., 1980—. Author: Biomaterials: An Introduction, 1979, 3rd edit., 2007, Biomaterials Science and Engineering, 1984, Biomaterials: Principles and Applications, 2002, Bioceramics: Properties, Characterizations and Applications, Springer, NY, 2008; contbr. articles to profl. jours. Fellow Am. Inst. Med. and Biol. Engring.; mem. Soc. for Biomaterials (founding mem.), Biomed. Engring. Soc., Orthop. Rsch. Soc., NY Acad. Scis. Achievements include patents in field. Home: 1810 Country Club Dr Coralville IA 52241-1183 Office: Univ Iowa Dept Biomed Engring Iowa City IA 52242 Office Phone: 319-335-5636.

PARK, KOOHYUN, industrial engineer, professor; b. Incheon, Republic of Korea, Mar. 19, 1957; s. Jaeha Park and Pilgu Chung; m. Miran Lee; children: Chanyoung, Keonyoung. BS, Seoul Nat. U., Republic of Korea, 1980; MS, Korea Advanced Inst. Sci. and Tech., Seoul, 1982; PhD with honors, U. Wis., Madison, 1989. Instr. Dong-A U., Busan, Republic of Korea, 1982—85; rsch. asst. U. Wis., Madison, 1986—89; sr. rschr. Electronics and Telecommunication Rsch. Inst., Daejeon, Republic of Korea, 1990—91; prof. Hongik U., Seoul, 1991—, assoc. dean grad. sch., 2003—06. Vis. rschr. Electronics and Telecomm. Rsch. Inst., Daejeon, 1998, U. Wis., 2006—07. Author: (book) Semidefinite Programming: Theory, Algorithm and Applications, Management Science: Spreadsheet Modeling and Solver Applications; contbr. articles to profl. jours. Mem.: Korean Telecommunication Mgmt. Rsch. Soc. (mem. com. gen. bus.), Korea Soc. Simulation (editor jour. 2000—04), Korean Inst. Indsl. Engrs. (editor jour. 2001—02), Korean Ops. Rsch. and Mgmt. Sci. Soc. (editor jour. 1996—98, chmn. com. 2000), Sigma Xi. Presbyterian. Office: Hongik U Dept Indsl and Info Engring 72-1 Sangsu-dong Mapo-gu Seoul 121-791 Republic of Korea Home: 2060 N High St Apt 206 Columbus OH 43201-1155 Business E-Mail: khpark@hongik.ac.kr.

PARK, KWANG WOO, financial planner, educator; b. Seoul, Republic of Korea, Mar. 23, 1966; permanent resident, 2007; s. Man Yong Park and Sun Ae Kang; m. Seung Hyun Yoo, Feb. 5, 1967; children: Jee Yoon Claire, Joseph Yoon Jay. PhD, Claremont Grad. U., Calif., 2001. Cert. fin. planner CFP Bd. Stds. Asst. vis. prof. Claremont Grad. U., Calif., 2002—03; assoc. prof. Minn. State U., Mankato, 2003—. Fin. planner Sunset Fin. Svcs., Mankato, Minn., 2006—07. Contbr. articles to profl. jours. Faculty Rsch. grant, Minn. State U., 2005, 2007. Mem.: Fin. Planning Assn., We. Econ. Assn., Am. Econ. Assn. Achievements include research in financial planning and economic growth. Home: 504 Ledlie Ln Mankato MN 56001 Office: Minn State U 150 Morris Hall Mankato MN 56001 Home Fax: 508-535-0310. Business E-Mail: parkk@mnsu.edu.

PARK, LEE (LEE PARKLEE), artist; b. Seoul, Republic of Korea; s. Chung-Kun Park and Mil-Hwa Kim; m. Chai Kyung Lim, June 3, 1994. MA, Fla. State U., 1986. Prof. associated academician dept. arts Vinzaglio, Italy, 2002—. Group shows include Shinpara Gallery, LA, Up-Stairs Gallery, LA, Beverly Plz. Hotel, Pacific Mus., Pasadena, Calif., Barnsdall Art Gallery, Hollywood, Calif., Brand XXII The Assn. of Brand Art Ctr., Glendale, Calif., Asia Invitation Art Exhibn., Sejong Cultural Ctr., Seoul, la Peintre Moderne Coreend '93, Paris, Korea-Japan Interchange Exhbn., Tokyo, 1994, Downtown Lives '96 Art Exhbn., LA, City Hall of Paris, 4, Biennale Internat. de Paris, 1994, Musee d'Art Moderne de la Commanderie d'Unet, Paris, 1994, Bridgeport (NY) U., 1995, San Bernardino County Mus., 1995, Kong-Ja Culture Art Exhbn., China, 1995, His Majesty the King's 50th Anniversary Art Exhbn., Thailand, 1996, 1st Venice Ann. Internat. Open Art Exbhn., Venice, 1998, 1st Internat. Biennial Contemporary Art, Perugia, Italy, 1998, Heukyong-gangsung Internat. Art Exhbn., China, 1998, Ting Shao-Kuang Fine Art Ctr., Beverly Hills, Articulture Gallery, Hermosa Beach, Calif., 1998, '99 World Peace Art Exhbn., Sejong Cultural Ctr., Seoul, 1999, The Millennium Art Collection, 2000, Invitational Art Exhbn. Jin-Jiang Gen. Assn. Gallery, Philipines, 2001, Galerie Michelangelo, Las Vegas, 2002, Reasons to Love the Earth, Den Haag, Netherlands, 2002; 2 person shows include Cosmos Gallery, Honolulu, The City of LA Cultural Affairs Dept.; solo exhibits include Modern Art Gallery, LA, Olympic Gallery, LA, Sun Space Gallery, LA, Gallery Nuevo, Pusan, Republic of Korea, Westside Jewish Cmty. Ctr., LA, World Festival of Art Exhbn., Slovenia, Caesars Palace Hotel Michelangelo, Las Vegas, Nev., 49th Toyo Calligraphy Art Assn., Tokyo, Eloge du Petit Fermat Dans L'Art D'Aujourd' Hui, Paris, Singapore, Korea Art Exhbn., Ngee Annual Cultural Ctr., Rubicon Gallery, LA, 2007, LA Mcpl. Art Gallery, Hollywood, 2007, Rancho Palos Verdes Art Ctr., LA, 2007, Luoyang Mus. Art Invitational Exhbn., China, 2007, Bunam Gallery, Seoul, Republic of Korea, 2008, See and Sea Gallery, Pusan, Republic of Korea, 2008, Asia Expo, LA Convention Ctr., West Hall "A", 2008, Metro Art Gallery Internat. Exhibition, 2008, Korea Internat. Art Expo., 2008, The 26th Korea New Art Festival, 2008; publ. artwork in American References, Art of California mag., Artweek mag., The Biweekly Art Jour., Seoul, Artprint mag., Washington, Art Exposure mag., Calif., Ency. of Living Artists mag., Calif., Art 2000, Seoul, Mag. for World Art & Culture Vergil Quarterly, Seoul, 2004, Art Diary Internat. 1998—, Milan, Italy, Internat. Encyclopaedic Dictionary Modern and Contemporary Art, Ferrara, Italy, 2002-08, Dictionary Internat. Biography Ctr., Cambridge, Eng. (Top 100 artists 2005), Portraits d'Artistes (Regards), France, 2008. Recipient Bronze award Art of Calif., 1993, Gold award Art Addiction, Stockholm, 1997. Avocations: collecting stamps and antiques, music, jogging, playing tennis, reading. Home: 1935 S La Salle Ave Apt 31 Los Angeles CA 90018-1627 E-mail: park@b17.com.

PARK, LEE CRANDALL, psychiatrist, physician; b. Washington, July 15, 1926; s. Lee I. and Alice (Crandall) P.; m. Barbara Ann Merrick, July 1, 1953; children: Thomas Joseph, Jeffrey Rawson; m. Mary Woodfill Banerjee, Apr. 27, 1985; stepchildren: Stephen K., Scott K. Grad., Putney Prep. Sch., Vt.; BS in Zoology, Yale U., 1948; MD, Johns Hopkins U., 1952. Diplomate Nat. Bd. Med. Examiners, Am. Bd. Psychiatry and Neurology. Intern medicine Johns Hopkins Hosp., Osler Clinic, Balt., 1952-53; resident psychiatry USN Hosp., Oakland, Calif., 1953-54, Henry Phipps Psychiat. Clinic, Johns Hopkins Hosp., Balt., 1955-59, asst. psychiatrist, 1955-59, staff psychiatrist, 1959—, staff dept. medicine, 1970—, hon. staff dept. medicine, 1991—, dir. psychiat. outpatient svcs. and community psychiatry program, 1972-74, asst. dir. clin. svcs. dept. psychiatry, 1973-74, mem. departmental coun., 1974-76. Fellow psychiatry Johns Hopkins U., 1955-59, faculty in psychiatry, 1959—, assoc. prof., 1971—, physician charge psychiat. svcs. student health svc., 1961-73; vis. psychiatrist Balt. City Hosp., 1960-61; co-prin., prin. investigator NIMH Psychopharmacology Rsch. Br. Outpatient Study of Drug-Set Interaction, 1960-68, co-dir. (with Eugene Meyer) Time-Limited Psychotherapy Rsch. Grant, 1969-73; pvt. practice psychiatry, 1964—; cons. Met. Balt. Assn. Mental Health, 1961-63, Bur. Disability Ins., Social Security Adminstrn., 1964-81; attending staff Seton Psychiat. Inst., 1966-73, exec. bd., 1970-73; staff Sheppard and Enoch Pratt Hosp., 1974—. Co-author: A Primer on Mental Disorders: A Guide for Educators, Families and Students, 2001; contbr. articles and chpts. to profl. jours. and books. Served to lt. M.C., USNR, 1953-55, div. psychiatrist 1st Marine Div., Korea with Letter of Appreciation from Commanding Officer "Outstanding Performance of Duty. Commn." staff psychiatrist USN Hosp., Camp Pendelton, Calif., 1954-55; mem. Md. Interdisciplinary Coun. for Children and Adolescents, 1978-98, treas., 1980-87. Fellow: AAAS, Am. Psychiat. Assn. (mem. assembly 1983—93, Psychiat. Rsch. Network 1994—2002, Disting. life fellow); mem.: AAUP, AMA, Johns Hopkins Med. and Surg. Assn., Balt. County Med. Assn., Balt. City Med. Soc., Med. and Chirurg. Faculty Md., Group Therapy Network, N.Y. Acad. Scis., Soc. Psychotherapy Rsch., Md. Psychiat. Soc. (pres. 1978—79), Md. Assn. Pvt. Practicing Psychiatrists, Am. Assn. Pvt. Practicing Psychiatrists, Am. Coll. Neuropsychopharmacology, Am. Soc. Adolescent Psychiatry, Internat. Soc. Study Personality Disorders, Am. Psychosomatic Soc., Md. Found. Psychiatry (bd. dirs. 1995—2003, pres. 2000—03), Nat. Assn. Scholars, St. George's Soc., Avery Assn., Denison Soc., Crandall Assn., Van Kouwenhoven-Conover Assn., Van Voorhees Assn., Parke Soc., Nat. Soc. Sons and Daus. of Pilgrims (gov. State of Md. 2006—08), Gen. Soc. War 1812 (pres. State of Md. 2004—06, v.p. gen. 2006—08, asst. surgeon gen. 2008—), Nat. Huguenot Soc. (surgeon gen. 2005—08), Descendants Mexican War Vets, Sons Union Vets. Civil War, SAR (surgeon State of Md. 2006—, surgeon gen. 2009—), Gen. Soc. Colonial Wars, S.R. (bd. mgrs. State of Md. 2006—08), Yale Club NYC, Farmington Country Club (Va.), Met. Club (Washington), Johns Hopkins Club (Md.), Chevy Chase Country Club (Md.), Phi Beta Pi. Republican. Episcopalian. Achievements include research in borderline and narcissistic conditions; long-term effects of childhood emotional abuse and neglect; psychotherapy; interrelationships of psychotherapy and pharmacotherapy; genesis and nature of social, personal and emotional intelligence. Home: 308 Tunbridge Rd Baltimore MD 21212-3803 Office: 1205 York Rd Ste 35 Lutherville Timonium MD 21093-6268 Office Phone: 410-321-1276. E-mail: lpark3@jhmi.edu.

PARK, LELAND MADISON, retired librarian; b. Alexandria, La., Oct. 21, 1941; s. Arthur Harris and Jane Rebecca (Leland) P. Student, McCallie Sch., 1957—59; AB, Davidson Coll., 1963; MLS, Emory U., 1964; postgrad., Simmons Coll., 1968; AdvM in Libr. Sci., Fla. State U., 1973, PhD, 1974. Reference libr. Pub. Libr. of Charlotte and Mecklenburg County, NC, 1964-65; head reference and student pers. Davidson (N.C.) Coll. Libr., 1967-70, asst. dir., 1970-75, dir., 1975—2006. Cons. coll. cons. network So. Assn. Colls and Schs.; vis. lectr. Emory U., summer 1972; temporary instr. Fla. State U., 1973; libr. cons.; conf. spkr.; chmn. state adv. com. Libr. Svcs. and Constrn. Act, 1975-79; mem. N.C. State Libr. Commn., 1983-85, 87-92, chmn., 1989-92; mem. Davidson (N.C.) Town Appearance Commn., 1986-93, design rev. bd. 98-, Hist. Preservation Commn., 1994-96; mem. editl. bd. CHOICE, 2003-06. Editor Southeastern Librarian, 1976-78; acad. sect. editor N.C. Libraries, 1972-77; contbr. articles to profl. jours. Mem. Wake County Citizens for Better Librs., N.C., 1965-67; sec. com. libr. affairs Piedmont U. Ctr., 1969-70, chmn., 1970-72; mem. nat. bd. cons. NEH, 1976-2006; clk. mission com. St. Alban's Episcopal Mission, Davidson, N.C., 1969-72, layreader, 1970-75, treas., 1975-86; bd. dirs. statewide computer libr. resource network NC-LIVE, 1997—2006. Recipient H.W. Wilson Libr. periodical award, 1979, Alumni Achievement award The McCallie Sch., 1989, Order of Long Leaf Pine presented by N.C. Gov. James G. Martin, 1993. Mem. ALA, Southeastern Libr. Assn. (chmn. coll. and univ. sect. 1976-78, exec. bd. 1976-78), N.C. Libr. Assn. (2d v.p. 1975-77, 1st v.p. 1981-83, pres. 1983-85), Metrolina Libr. Assn. (pres. 1969-71), Mecklenburg County Libr. Assn. (treas. 1969-70), Soc. of Cin. (2d v.p. Ga. Soc. 1982-83), SAR, Mil. Order World Wars, Raleigh Jaycees (chmn. libr. com. 1965-67), Res. Officer Assn., SCV, Soc. Colonial Wars, S.C. Huguenot Soc., Rotary, Beta Phi Mu, Sigma Nu, Omicron Delta Kappa, Davidson Coll. (bd. visitors). Home: PO Box 777 235 Ney Circle Davidson NC 28036-0777 E-mail: lepark@aol.com.

PARK, MARY WOODFILL, information consultant, librarian, writer; b. Nevada, Mo., Nov. 20, 1944; d. John Prossor and Elizabeth (Devine) Woodfill; m. Salil Kumar Banerjee, Dec. 29, 1967 (div. 1983); children: Stephen Kumar, Scott Kumar; m. Lee Crandall Park, Apr. 27, 1985; stepchildren: Thomas Joseph, Jeffrey Rawson. BA, Marywood Coll., 1966; postgrad., Johns Hopkins U., 1983, Goucher Coll., 1986. Asst. to dir. U. Pa. Librs., Phila., 1968-69; investment libr. Del. Funds, Phila., 1969-71; investment officer Investment Counselors Md., Balt., 1980-84, 1st Nat. Bank Md., Balt., 1984-85; founder Info. Consultancy, Balt., 1985—. Lectr. Loyola Coll., Balt., 1991-92, Cath. U., 1993. Author: InfoThink—Practical Strategies for Using Information in Business, 1998; editor, contbr. to profl. publs. Vol. Internat. Visitors' Ctr., Balt., 1979-80, 91; del. White House Conf. on Librs.; v.p. bd. dirs. Friends of Goucher Libr., 1988-90; mem. industry applications com. Info. Tech. Bd., State of Md., 1993-96; mem. info. tech. com. of the Tech. Coun., Greater Balt. Com., 1993-98. Named One of Md.'s Top 100 Women, Warfield's Bus. Publn., 1996. Mem.: DAR, Yale Club NYC, Star-Spangled Banner Flag House Assn. (bd. dirs. 2007—), Huguenot Soc. Md. (bd. dirs. 2003—), Nat. Huguenot Soc., Md. Found. for Psychiatry (bd. dirs. 1998—2005), Assn. Ind. Info. Profls., Info. Futures Inst., Spl. Librs. Assn. (pres. Md. chpt. 1991—92), Nat. Soc. Colonial Dames Am., Md. (bd. dirs. 2008—), Daus. of Colonial Wars, Colonial Dames Am. (bd. dirs. chpt. III 2007—08), Soc. Daughters Holland Dames, Descendants of Ancient and Honorable Families of New Netherland (directress gen. 2008—), Nat. Soc. Daus. Am. Colonists (Md. state regent

2006—08), Nat. Soc. of the Sons and Daus. of the Pilgrims, Nat. Soc. Colonial Dames XVII Century, Nat. Soc. of U.S. Daus. of 1812, Nat. Soc. Dames Ct. Honor, Nat. Inst. Geneal. Rsch. Alumnae Assn., Three Arts Club Homeland, Hamilton St. Club (bd. dirs. 1989—92). Episcopalian. Office: The Information Consultancy 308 Tunbridge Rd Baltimore MD 21212-3803 Business E-Mail: mwpark@informationconsultancy.com.

PARK, MICHAEL S., computer software company executive; married; 3 children. BA, U. Rochester; MBA, Harvard U. Sales and brand mgmt. Procter & Gamble; gen. mgr. Siebel Sys., Inc.; exec. Hire.com; sr. v.p. product mktg. SAP AG; joined Microsoft Corp., Redmond, Wash., 2005, corp. v.p. US small and mid-market solutions & ptnrs. group, corp. v.p. Microsoft bus. solutions sales, mktg. and ops., 2009—. Avocations: golf, tennis, bicycling. Office: Microsoft Corp One Microsoft Way Redmond WA 98052-6399*

PARK, MINSEO, physicist, educator; b. Seoul, Republic of Korea, July 28, 1968; arrived in US, 1991; s. Seungryul and Jungia (You) Park; m. Soohyun Baik; children: Michelle, Joshua. BS in Ceramic Engring., Yonsei U., 1991; MS in Materials Sci., Engring., Iowa State U., 1994; PhD in Materials Sci., Engring., NC State U., 1998. Rsch. asst. prof. NC State U., Raleigh, 2001—03; asst. prof. Auburn (Ala.) U., 2003—. Mem.: Materials Rsch. Soc., Am. Phys. Soc. Office: Auburn U Dept Physics 303 Allison Lab Auburn AL 36849 E-mail: park@physics.auburn.edu.

PARK, MOON SUH, otolaryngologist; b. Seoul, Republic of Korea, Feb. 25, 1954; s. Geun Ju Park and So Yon Eum; m. Hye Ki Han, Dec. 17, 1979; children: Eun Jung, Jun Woo. BS, Kyung Hee U., 1978, MS, 1982, DSc, 1989. Cert. Korean Bd. Otolaryngology, 1983. Resident Kyung Hee Univ. Hosp., Seoul, 1979-82; instr. Hallym U., Seoul, 1983-86, asst. prof., 1986-91; vis. prof. Bonn U., Germany, 1986-87; from assoc. prof. to prof. Hallym U., 1987—2002; dir. Dain ENT Clinic, Republic of Korea, 2002—04, Park's ENT Clinic, 2005—06; prof. Kyung Hee U., Republic of Korea, 2006—. Chmn. dept Ear Nose and Throat Choonchun Sacred Heart Hosp., Hallym U., Republic of Korea, 1987—88, Hangang Sacred Heart Hosp., Hallym U., Seoul, 1989—2001; chmn. resident training com. Hallym Med. Ctr., Seoul, 1999—2001; chmn. Ear Nose and Throat Ctr. East-West Neo Med. Ctr., Kyung Hee U., Seoul, 2006—. Author: Otorhinolaryngology- Head & Neck Surgery, 1995, Principles and Practices of Hearing Aids, 1998, Otorhinolaryngology - Head & Neck Surgery, 2002. Scholar Alexander von Humboldt Found., Bonn, Germany, 1986. Mem. Internat. Soc. Audiology, NY Acad. Scis., Am. Otolaryngol Soc., Politzer Soc. (Active Fellow), Korean Audiol. Soc. (councilor 1996-2001), Korean Otol. Soc. (councilor 1997-2001, dir. 2007—). Avocations: travel, swimming. Home: 13-102 Hyundai Apt Abgujung-dong Gangnam-ku Seoul 135 787 Republic of Korea Personal E-mail: pmsuh@yahoo.co.kr.

PARK, MYUNG KUN, medical educator; b. Suhung, Hwanghae, Republic of Korea, Sept. 30, 1934; arrived in U.S., 1962; s. Jung-Jin and Sonnyu (Lee) Park; m. Issun Kim, Jan. 21, 1967; children: Douglas Yongwoon, Christopher Yongchul, Warren Yongsun. Diploma, Seoul Nat. U., Republic of Korea, 1956, MD, 1960. Intern Vassar Brothers Hosp., Poughkeepsie, NY, 1962—63; pediat. resident Georgetown U., Washington, 1963—64; chief resident Univ. Hosp., Morgantown, W.Va., 1964—65; pediat. cardiology fellow U. Washington, Seattle, 1965—68; asst. prof. U. Kans. Coll. Medicine, Kansas City, 1973-76; assoc. prof. U. Tex. Med. Sch., San Antonio, 1976-83, prof., 1983—2003, prof. emeritus, 2003—; prof., chmn. pediat. Arabian Gulf U. Med. Coll., Bahrain, 1995-98. Author: (book) How to Read Pediatric ECG, 1982, 3d rev. edit., 1992, Pediatric Cardiology for Practitioners, 1984, 4th rev. edit., 2002, The Pediatric Cardiology Handbook, 1991, 3d rev. edit., 2002; contbr. articles to profl. jours. Postdoctoral fellow, NIH, 1965—68, Rsch. fellow, 1971—73, Rsch. grantee, Maternal and Child Health Bur., 1991—95. Fellow: Am. Acad. Pediat., Am. Coll. Cardiology; mem.: Am. Assn. Pharmacology Therapy, Soc. Pediatric Rsch. Personal E-mail: drmpark@satx.rr.com.

PARK, MYUNG SEOK, finance educator; s. Jung Park and Ko Lee; m. Youngsook Na, Nov. 4, 1955; children: Kristie, Michael. PhD, Purdue U., West Lafayette, Ind., 1999. Asst. prof. Ball State U., Munci, Ind., 1998—99, San Francisco State U., 1999—2004, Va. Commonwealth U., Richmond, 2004—08, assoc. prof., 2008—. Assoc. dir. US-Korea Bus. Inst., San Francisco, 1999—2004; editl. bd. mem. Jour. Fin. and Acctg., 2003—. Contbr. articles to profl. publs. Big Ten Acctg. Doctoral Consortium fellow, Purdue U., 1997, Summer Rsch. grant, San Francisco State U., 2000, Sch. Bus., Va. Commonwealth U., 2005—08, Rsch. grant, PricewaterhouseCoopers, 2008. Mem.: Am. Acctg. Assn. (mem. info. systems sect. 2001—, mem. fin. acctg. and reporting sect. 1999—), Va. Commonwealth U. (faculty senate 2007—, Deloitte-FSA Faculty Consortium fellow 2007).

PARK, MYUNGKARK, president, publisher, physicist; b. Kangwon Do, Republic of Korea, July 24, 1950; came to U.S., 1977; m. Hyunmi Suh, July 17, 1977; children: Brian. BS, Seoul Nat. U., Republic of Korea, 1972; MS, Wayne State U., 1979; PhD candidate, Wash. State U., 1979—83; PhD student, Kent State U., 1983—85, U. Cin., 1985—87, Southern Ohio Coll., 1987—88. Cert. presdl. inaugural 2009. Teaching asst. Seoul Nat. U., 1974-76; tchr. physics Jeonnong Girl's Mid. Sch., 1976-77; teaching and rsch. asst. Wayne State U., Detroit, 1977-79; tchg. and rsch. asst. Wash. State U., Pullman, 1979-83, Kent (Ohio) State U., 1983-85, U. Cin., 1985-87; pres., owner Prompter Publs., Cin., 1988-90, Seoul, 1990—. Author and editor several books and jours.; contbr. over 750 articles to profl. jours. and 1000 rsch. notebooks. 1st lt. Republic of Korea Army, 1972-74. Nat. scholar, 1962-68, 70-72, Hamchoon scholar, 1968-70, tchg./rsch. asst. scholar, 1977-87, Am. Vacuum Soc. scholar, 1989, The Knoller Physics-Chemistry scholar 1977-78; faculty fellow Wayne State U., 1977-79; recipient Salute Greatness award 2009; named Gt. Minds of 21st Century 2005, Man of Yr., 2005, Outstanding Intellectuals of 21st Century, 2006. Mem. AAAS, APS, Am. Math. Soc., Korean Phys. Soc., Am. Vacuum Soc., Phi Theta Kappa, Pi Sigma Alpha, Nat. Geog. Soc. Home: PO Box 167 Chongnyangni Tongdaemoon-gu Seoul 130-650 Republic of Korea

PARK, OH-SOO, finance educator, electronics executive; b. Dec. 24, 1952; BA in bus. admin., Seoul Nat. U., 1975, MBA, 1977; PhD, Pa. State U., 1986. Prof. Seoul Nat. U., 1988—; vis. prof. Stanford U., 1995—96; v.p. for planning and coord. Seoul Nat. U., 2001—02, dean, Sch. Bus., 2003—05. Ind. dir. Korean Air, 2000—; mem., bd. dirs. Samsung Electronics, Ltd., 2006—. Mem.: Korean Acad. Leadership (pres. 2003—04), Korean Acad. Mgmt. (pres. 2002—03), Korean Assn. Pers. Admin., Korean Assn. Bus. Admin. (pres. 2008—). Office: Seoul Nat Univ Coll of Bus Admin San 56-1 Shinlim-dong Gwanak-gu Seoul 151-742 Republic of Korea Business E-Mail: ospark@snu.ac.kr.

PARK, PHIL W., legislative staff member; Legis. dir. to George V. Voinovich US Senate, Washington, chief of staff, 2007—. Office: Office of Senator George Voinovich 524 Senate Hart Office Bldg Washington DC 20510-3504 Office Phone: 202-224-3353. E-mail: phil_park@voinovich.senate.gov.*

PARK, RICHARD A., ecologist; b. Sedalia, Mo., Dec. 20, 1938; m. Darlene R. Park; children: Holly, Leigh. BS, La. State U., Baton Rouge; MS, U. Wis., Madison, PhD, 1966. Prof. Rensselaer Poly. Inst., Troy, NY, 1966—85; coord. inst. projects Holcomb Rsch., Inst. Butler U., Indpls., 1985—91; vis. prof. Sch. Pub. & Environ. Affairs, Ind. U., Bloomington, 1991—93; sr. environ. modeller Abt Assocs., Inc., Bethesda, Md., 1993—95; pres. Eco Modeling, Diamondhead, Miss., 1995—. V.p. Internat. Soc. Ecol. Modelling; councilor Internat. Assn. Landscape Ecology. Sr. warden St. Thomas Episcopal Ch., Diamondhead, 2007—. Mem.: Soc. Environ. Toxicology & Chemistry, Ecol. Soc. America, Am. Chem. Soc. Office: Eco Modeling 5522 Alakoko Pl Diamondhead MS 39525

PARK, ROY HAMPTON, JR., advertising executive; b. NC, 1938; s. Roy Hampton and Dorothy Goodwin (Dent) P.; m. Elizabeth Tetlow Parham; children: Elizabeth P. Fowler, Roy H. III. BA in Journalism, U. NC, Chapel Hill, 1961; MBA, Cornell U., Ithaca, NY, 1963. Sr. acct. exec., rev. bd. exec., advt. planning dir., J. Walter Thompson Co., NYC and Miami, 1963-70; v.p. mktg. and account mgmt. Kincaid Advt. Agency divsn. First Union Nat. Bank Corp., Charlotte, NC, 1970-71; v.p. Park Outdoor Advt., Ithaca, NY, 1971—75, v.p., gen. mgr., 1981—84; v.p. advt. and promotion Park Broadcasting Inc., Ithaca, 1976-81; dir., 1993-95; mng. editor Park Comm. Newsletter, Ithaca, 1976-81; mng. dir. Agrl. Rsch. Advt. Agy., Ithaca, 1976-81; pres., CEO, dir. Park Outdoor Advt. of NY Inc., 1984—; pres. Outdoor Advt. Coun. NY Inc., 1986—91, chmn., dir., 1992—95; dir., sr. v.p. RHP Inc., 1994-96, RHP Properties Inc., 1994-96. Mem. region I planning bd. Inst. Outdoor Advt., 1984—86. Dir. Boyce Thompson Inst. for Plant Rsch. Inc., 1995-, dir., vice chmn. 2002-07, dir. co-vice chmn., 2008-; trustee, v.p. Park Found. Inc., 1995-2002; pres., chmn. Triad Found., Inc., 2003—; founding mem. alumni exec. com. Cornell U., 1984-88, trustee, 1999-2007, trustee emeritus, 2007—; presdl. councillor, 2007-; mem. adv. coun. Johnson Grad. Sch. Mgmt., 1996—, named to Johnson Hall Hon., 1999—; bd. advisors U. NC Sch. Journalism and Mass Comm., 1994—; chmn. Ithaca Assembly Cotillion, 1979-81; dir. pub. rels. Tompkins County Conf. and Tourist Coun., 1976; exec. com. Tompkins County Rep. Fin. Com., 1983-84; chmn. fin. com. MacNeil for Assembly, 1984-86, co-chmn. 1978-82; bd. dir. Tompkins County Coun. Arts, 1976; chmn. pub. rels. com. United Way Tompkins County, 1973-74, loaned publicity exec., 1977; bd. chmn., publicity dr. Jr. Olympics, 1973-74; dir. pub. rels. United Fund Raleigh, NC, 1971; fin. com. Spl. Children's Ctr., 1979. Recipient Disting. Alumnus award, U. NC, 2005. Mem. Tompkins County C. of C. (chmn. sign ordinance com., 1975-76, chmn. legis. action com. 1976, acting chmn. nominating com. 1976, pub. rels. coun. 1976, Project of Yr. award 1974, Recognition award 1975), Charlotte C. of C. (pub. rels. com. 1970-71), Boque Banks Beach Preservation Assn., Ithaca Yacht Club, Ithaca Country Club, Boca Bay Pass Club, Gasparilla Inn and Club. Office: Park Outdoor Advt PO Box 4680 Ithaca NY 14852-4680 Office Phone: 607-257-1477. Business E-Mail: roy.park@parkoutdoor.com.

PARK, SANG-DAI, molecular biologist, educator; b. Kimhae, Kyungnam, Korea, Aug. 20, 1937; s. Dong-Jo and Nam-Ji (Kang) P.; m. Kyungza Ryu, Dec. 20, 1969; 1 child, Kyung-Ryul. BS, Seoul Nat. U., 1960, MS, 1962; PhD, St. John's U., NYC, 1974. Instr. Seoul Nat. U., 1967-72, asst. prof., 1972-77, assoc. prof., 1977-82, prof. molecular biology, 1982—2002, prof. emeritus, 2002—, dir. Inst. for Molecular Biology and Genetics, 1985-89, dean rsch. affairs, 1991-95. Vis. prof. U. Calif., San Francisco, 1977-78; mem. Presdl. Commn. Sci. and Tech., Korea, 1989-90; hon. v.p. 17th and 18th Internat. Congress Genetics, Birmingham/Beijing, 1993-98; chmn. Korean Rsch. Coun. Fundamental Sci. and Tech., 2003— Contbr. articles to profl. jours.; adv. bd. Jour. Biochemistry, Tokyo, 1994-97, Cytotech., London, 1987—. With Korean Army, 1962-63. Recipient Korea Sci. award (presdl.) Korea Sci./Engring. Found., 1987, Korea Nat. Acad. Sci. award, 1998. Fellow Korean Acad. Sci. and Tech., Third World Acad. Scis.; mem. Korean Soc. for Molecular Biology (pres. 1991-92), Asian Soc. Toxicology (v.p. 1994-97), Internat. Vaccine Inst. (spl. advisor 2001—); mem. Korean Nat. Acad. Scis. Avocation: hiking. Home: Banpo-4-dong Seocho-ku 45-13 Daelim Villa B-103 Seoul 137-802 Republic of Korea Office: Internat Vaccine Inst c/o Seoul Nat U San 4-8 Bongcheon-7-dong Seoul 151-818 Republic of Korea Office Phone: (82-2) 881-1301. Personal E-mail: sdpark@ivi.int. E-mail: sdpark@snu.ac.kr.

PARK, SOOHONG, electrical engineer, researcher; b. Seoul, Republic Of Korea, Sept. 15, 1972; s. Kwangsoo Park and Jungsik Min; m. Seunghye Jung, Jan. 8, 2000; children: Yeeun, Joonsun. AB in Electronics, Dankook U., Seoul, 1999. Prin. engr. OPICOM Inc., Seoul, 1999—2002; sr. rschr. Samsung Electronics, Suwon, Gyeonggi-do, Republic of Korea, 2002—. Contbr. articles to profl. jours. Mem. Gwangiu Migrant Shelter, 2002—04. With Korean Army, 1994—95. Recipient Best Paper award, Digital Media R&D Ctr. Samsung Electronics, 2006. Achievements include patents in field; patents pending for. Avocations: reading, tennis. Office: Samsung Electronics 416 Maetan-3dong Gyeonggi-do Suwon 443-742 Republic of Korea Home: Kyeongan dong Haetae Apt 101-1504 Gyeonnggi Gwanggu 464 010 Republic of Korea Office Fax: 82-31-200-3195. Personal E-mail: soohongp@gmail.com. Business E-Mail: soohong.park@samsung.com.

PARK, SUNG, engineering educator, consultant; b. Seoul, Republic of Korea, Aug. 19, 1963; s. Keun Bae Park and Jai Yeon Choi; m. Woo Mee Lee, July 18, 1963; children: Jai Young, Jai Hee. BS in Ceramic Engring., Yonsei U., Seoul, 1986; MS in Materials Sci. and Engring., Korea Advanced Inst. Sci. and Tech., Seoul, 1987, PhD in Materials Sci. and Engring., 1990. Post-doctoral rschr. Korea Advanced Inst. Sci. and Tech., 1990—91; head materials rsch. 1st lab. Samyoung Electronics Co., Sungnam, Kyunggi-do, Republic of Korea, 1991—93; asst. prof. Myongji U., Yongin, Kyunggi-do, 1993—97, assoc. prof., 1997—2002, prof., 2002—. Expert advisor Ministry Commerce, Industry and Energy, Seoul, 1999—; cons. Small and Medium Bus. Adminstrn., Suwon, Kyunggi-do, Republic of Korea, 1998—; expert advisor Ministry Sci. and Tech., Seoul, 2002—03; cons. Korea FDA, Seoul, 2003—. Author: (book) Nanomaterials; contbr. articles to profl. jours. Outside dir. BK Sys., Seoul, 1997—99, Basentech, Seoul, 2000—01, Daejin Semiconductor Co., Daejeon, 2002—03, Patech Engring. Co., Asan, 2003—05. Mem.: Soc. Info. Display, Materials Rsch. Soc., Korean Inst. Elec. Engrs., Korean Inst. Elec. and Electronic Material Engrs., Korean Ceramic Soc. Presbyterian. Achievements include research in A.C. powder electroluminescence materials and devices; synthesis of oxide nanopowders by solution combustion method; development of ZnO and ZnGa2O4 phosphors; photocatalytic ZnO and TiO2 nanopowders; patents for a method for preparing ZnO nanopowders; A.C. powder electroluminescence device and method for making the same. Avocations: movies, bicycling, travel. Office: Myongji Univ 38-2 San Namdong Cheoinku Yongin 449-728 Republic of Korea Office Fax: 82-31-330-6457. Business E-Mail: spark@mju.ac.kr.

PARK, SUNG MIN, finance educator; s. Kum Hwan Park and Ki Nan Lee; m. Young Eun Lee, July 12, 2003. MA, Yonsei U., Seoul, 1997; M.I.A, Columbia U., NY, 2002; PhD, U. Ga., Athens, 2007. Asst. prof. U. Nev., Las Vegas, 2007—. Recipient Morris W. H. Collins award. Office: Univ Nevada Las Vegas 4505 S Maryland Pky Box 456026 Las Vegas NV 89154-6026 Business E-Mail: sungmin.park@unlv.edu.

PARK, SUNG-JIN, chemist, educator; arrived in US, 1999, permanent resident; s. Choon Kyung Park and Sin Jul Kim; m. Seung Hee Kim, 1999; children: Ji Soo, Ji On. BS in Chemistry, Myongji U., 1993, MS in Chemistry, 1995, PhD in Chemistry, 1999. Lectr. Myongji U., 1995—97; postdoctoral rsch. U. Ill., Urbana, 1999—2001, rsch. cons., 2001—04; prof., rschr. Ajou U., Republic of Korea, 2001—04; co-founder Eden Pk. Illumination Inc., Champaign, Ill., 2007—, v.p., 2007—. Vis. prof. U. Ill., 2004—07, adj. prof, 2007—; reviewer various profl. jours.; inventor in field. Contbr. articles to profl. jours. Recipient Innovation Discovery award, U. Ill., 2009. Mem.: IEEE (corr.), Am. Phys. Soc., Electrochemical Soc., Soc. for Info. Display, Directed Energy Profl. Soc. (corr.), Sigma Xi. Presbyterian. Achievements include research in microcavity plasma phenomena and applications; development of microcavity devices for various applications including microlaser, lightings, microchemical reactors and plasma display; patents in field; patents pending in field. Office: Univ Illinois 1406 W Green St Urbana IL 61801 Office Phone: 217-333-6686, 217-403-1866. Office Fax: 217-244-7097. Business E-Mail: sjinpark@illinois.edu.

PARK, SUNG-YEON, communications educator; b. Busan, Republic of Korea, Jan. 3, 1973; d. Si-Hwa Park and Hong-Ja Kim; m. Gi Woong Yun, June 7, 1998; children: Miriam Park Yun, Tony Park Yun. BA, Korea U., Seoul, 1995, MA, 1997; PhD, U. Wis.-Madison, 2003. Asst. prof. Bowling Green State U., Ohio, 2005—. Editl. rev. bd. mem. Jour. Communication Rsch., 2008—. Contbr. scientific papers to profl. jours. (Top Paper award, Info. Sys. Divsn., 2002, Top Paper award, Intergroup Communication Interest Group ICA Conf., 2009). Mem.: Assn. Edn. Journalism & Mass Communication, Internat. Communication Assn. Office: Bowling Green State Univ 302 W Hall Bowling Green OH 43403 Office Fax: 419-372-0202. Business E-Mail: sunpark@bgsu.edu.

PARK, THOMAS JOSEPH, biology researcher, educator; b. Balt., June 8, 1958; s. Lee Crandall and Barbara Ann (Merrick) P.; m. Stephanie Suzanne Reynolds, June 22, 1985; 1 child, Nicholas Timothy. BA in Psychology, Johns Hopkins U., 1982; MSc in Exptl. Psychology, U. Md., 1984, PhD in Exptl. Psychology, 1988. Postdoctoral fellow Inst. Cellular and Molecular Embryology, Paris, 1989; postdoctoral rsch. assoc. dept. zoology U. Tex., 1989—94; faculty dept. biol. scis. U. Ill., Chgo., 1994, prof. dept. biol. scis., 2000—09. Contbr. articles and chpts. to profl. jours. and books. Grantee NIMH, 1986-88, Nat. Ctr. Sci. Rsch., Paris, 1989, NIH, 1989-90, 1997-2003, Nat. Orgn. Hearing Rsch., 1996-97, NSF, 2008-; Alexander von Humboldt Rsch. fellowship, Zool. Inst., U. Munich, 1993-94, Max Planck Inst. Neurobiology, Munich, 2001-02. Mem. AAAS, Soc. Neurosci., Assn. Rsch. in Otolaryngology. Achievements include research in neurobiology of sensory information processing and sensorimotor integration. Office: Univ Ill Chgo Dept Biol Sci Neurobiology Group 840 W Taylor St Chicago IL 60607 Business E-Mail: tpark@uic.edu.

PARK, WILLIAM ANTHONY (TONY PARK), lawyer; b. Blackfoot, Idaho, June 4, 1934; s. William Clair and Thelma Edelweiss (Shear) P.; m. Elizabeth Taylor, Aug. 26, 1961 (div.); children: Susan E., W. Adam, Patricia A.; m. Gail Chaloupka, Aug. 6, 1983. AA, Boise Jr. Coll., 1954; BA, U. Idaho, 1958; JD, U. Idaho, 1963. Bar: Idaho 1963. Sole practice, Boise, Idaho, 1963-70, 82-83; atty. gen. State of Idaho, 1971-75; ptnr. Park & Meuleman, Boise, 1975-81, Park & Burkett, Boise, 1983-84, Martin, Chapman, Park & Burkett, Boise, 1984-90, Park, Costello & Burkett, Boise, 1990-93, Park, Redford, Thomas & Burkett, Boise, 1994-97, Park, Thomas, Burkett & Williams, Boise, 1997-99; of counsel Huntley Park (formerly Huntley, Park, Thomas, Burkett, Olsen & Williams), Boise, 1999—2008, Thomas Williams & Pk., 2008—. Chmn. Idaho Bicentennial Commn., 1971—77; bd. dirs. ACLU, Idaho, 1996—2000, pres. Idaho, 1997—99, Am. Lung Assn., 1991, 1995, 2002—04; chmn. Idaho State Dem. Party, 1998—99; bd. dirs. Radio Free Europe/Radio Liberty, Inc., 1977—82, Am. Lung Assn., Idaho, 1978—90, 1976—96, Am. Lung Assn. Northwest, 1999—2009. With US Army, 1956—58. Recipient Disting. Svc. award. Home: 706 Warm Springs Ave Boise ID 83712-6420 Office: PO Box 1776 Boise ID 83701-1776 Office Phone: 208-345-7800. Personal E-mail: tonypark34@msn.com. Business E-Mail: tpark@twplegal.com.

PARK, WILLIAM H(ERRON), financial services executive; b. Monongahela, Pa., Sept. 19, 1947; s. William M. and Marjorie (Herron) Park; m. Mary Cornell, June 25, 1977; children: William H., Douglas C. BS in Indsl. Engring. with distinction, Cornell U., 1969, MBA, 1970. Engr. True Temper Corp., Geneva, Ohio, 1970-72; with Price Waterhouse & Co., Boston, 1972-82; exec. v.p., CFO United Asset Mgmt. Corp., Boston, 1982—2001; v.p. The UAM Funds, 1982—2001; pres., CEO Prizm Capital Mgmt., 2001—05; CEO Structured Capital Ptnrs., 2005; vice chmn. Comml. Indsl. Fin. Corp., 2006—. Bd. dirs. No. Light Asset Mgmt.; bd. trustees Eaton Vance Group of Mut. Funds, 2003—; chair Audit Com., 2008—. Treas., trustee Tower Sch. in Marblehead, 1982—92; trustee Proctor Acad., 1998—2006; bd. dirs. Nat. Com. to Preserve Social Security and Medicare, 1997—2005, chmn., 2000—03; bd. dirs. Chautauqua Found., Inc., 1992—2005. Home: 3 Fort Sewall Ter Marblehead MA 01945-3505 Office: Charlesbank Capital Ptnrs 200 Clarendon St 54th Fl Boston MA 02116 Personal E-mail: parkwilliam@comcast.net. Business E-Mail: wpark@cifc.com.

PARK, WILLIAM WYNNEWOOD, law educator; b. Phila., July 2, 1947; s. Oliver William and Christine (Lindes) Park. BA, Yale U., 1969; JD, Columbia U., 1972; MA, Cambridge U., 1975. Bar: Mass. 1972, DC 1980. Law practice, Paris, 1972-79; prof. law Boston U., 1979—, dir. Ctr. Banking Law Studies, 1990—93. Pres. London Ct. Internat. Arbitration; vis. prof. U. Dijon, France, 1983—84, U. Hong Kong, 1990, U. Auckland, 2007, U. Geneva, 2008; arbitrator Claims Resolution Tribunal Dormant Accts., Switzerland, 1998—2002, Internat. Commn. Holocaust Era Ins. Claims, London, ICSID Roster of Arbitrators, 2008. Author: International Chamber of Commerce Arbitration, 3d edit., 2000, International Forum Selection, 1995, International Commercial Arbitration, 1997, Arbitration in Banking and Finance, 1998, Income Tax Treaty Arbitration, 2004, Arbitration of International Business Disputes, 2006; gen. editor: Arbitration Internat.; contbr. articles to profl. jours. Trustee Mass. Bible Soc.; sr. warden King's Chapel, Boston. Fellow, Selwyn Coll., Cambridge, Eng., 1975—77. Fellow: Coll. Comml. Arbitrators, Chartered Inst. Arbitrators (U.K.); mem.: ABA (chmn. internat. dispute resolution com.). Home: 36 King St Cohasset MA 02025-1304 Office: Boston Univ Law Sch 765 Commonwealth Ave Boston MA 02215-1401 Office Phone: 617-353-3149.

PARK, WON CHAN, mechanical engineer; b. Taegu, Republic Of Korea, Nov. 12, 1972; s. Young Kwang Park and Dong Yeon Jung; m. Kyung Hee Lee; children: Sejeong, Bradley Jin. PhD, U. Mich., Ann Arbor, 2008. Rsch. engr. GM Daewoo Automotive Tech., Incheon, Republic of Korea, 1998—, LS Cable, Anyang, Kyunggido, Republic of Korea, 2000—03; sr. thermal engr. Hybrid Design Svcs., Troy, Mich. Mem.: Combustion Inst. Home: 3745 Green Brier Blvd 212A Ann Arbor MI 48105 Office: Hybrid Design Svcs Inc 2479 Elliott Ave Troy MI 48083 Office Fax: 313-586-0610. Personal E-mail: park.wonchan@gmail.com. Business E-Mail: wcpark@hybriddesignservices.com.

PARK, WON KUK, foundation administrator; b. Bukchang Dong, Chung-Ku, Korea, Mar. 24, 1929; s. Jun Seop and Kum Sun (Song) P. BA in Economics, Sungkyunkwan U., Seoul, Korea, 1957; MA in Economics, Am. U., 1960; PhD in Economics, Kyunghee U., Seoul, Korea, 1975; PhD (hon.), Caldwell Coll., 1997. Asst. prof. Duksung Women's U., Seoul, Republic of Korea, 1961-63, assoc. prof., 1965-67, v.p., 1965-70, prof., 1967-77, pres., 1970-77, chmn. bd. trustees Duksung Sch. Found., 1979—2001; v.p. Korean Pvt. Ednl. Found., Seoul, Republic of Korea, 1987-90, Korean Assn. for Univ. Found., Seoul, Republic of Korea, 1987-92. Dir. Korean Pvt. Ednl. Found., Seoul, 1978—, Korean Assn. for Univ. Found., 1987—. Chmn. bd. trustees Jungam Found. of Culture in Korea, 2002—. Recipient Choon Kang award, Republic of Korea, 1995. Mem. Korean Sect. World Edn. Fellowship (v.p. 1987—), The Seoul Ctrl. Club of Good Will.

PARK, WON-HEE, mechanical engineer, researcher; b. Seoul, Dec. 13, 1975; s. Dong-Gu Park and Kyung-Hee Lee; m. Soon-Ja Choi. B, Chung-Ang U., Seoul, 1998, M, 2000, PhD, 2004. Cert. gen. machine engr., Human Resource Devel. Svc. Korea, constrn. machine engr., Human Resource Devel. Svc. Korea. Sr. rschr. Korea R.R. Rsch. Inst., Uiwang, Gyeonggi-do, Republic of Korea, 2004—. Contbr. articles to profl. jours. Mem.: Korean Soc. Combustion, Korea Soc. Aero. and Space Scis., Korea Soc. Rlwy., Korean Soc. Mech. Engr. Avocation: swimming. Office: Korea RR Rsch Inst 360-1 Woulam-Dong Gyeonggi Uiwang 437-757 Republic of Korea Home: 1301-104 Dongmun Goodmorning Hill Apt Annyeong-dong Hwasung-si Gyeonggi-do 445-721 Republic of Korea Home Phone: 82-70-8291-1951. Office Fax: 82-31-460-5319. Business E-Mail: whpark@krri.re.kr.

PARK, YIKYUNG, epidemiologist, oncologist; Staff scientist Nat. Cancer Inst. Office: NCI Public Inquiries Office 6116 Executive Blvd Room 3036A Bethesda MD 20892-8322 E-mail: parkyik@mail.nih.gov.*

PARK, YONG HUN SAM, engineering company executive; b. Taegu, Kyungpook, Republic Of Korea, July 17, 1972; s. Jongki Park and Soonok Kim; m. Mihwa Lee, May 1, 1999; children: Uria Yeajin, Andrew Samuel. BS, Kyungpook Nat. U., Taegu, 1999; MS, Tex. A&M U., Coll. Sta., 2003, PhD, 2007. Mech. engr. Pyeonghwa Automotive Co. Ltd., Taegu, 1998—99; rsch. asst. Tex. A&M U., 2001—03, 2004—05, tchg. asst., 2003—04; fuel cell engr. Arbin Instruments, Coll. Sta., 2005—08, fuel cell project leader, 2008—. Contbr. articles to profl. jours. Vol. Taegu Rehab. Ctr., 1996—97. Sgt. 3rd Divsn. Army, 1994—96, Republic of Korea. Decorated Leadership award 3rd Divsn., Army; named Empolyee of Yr., Arbin Instruments, 2006. Mem.: ASME, Electrochemisty Soc., Soc. Automotive Engrs. Achievements include research in water transport in polymer electrolyte memebrane fuel cell; development of hydrogen recycling systems; design of module to monitor water balances. Office: Arbin Instruments 762 Peach Creek Cut Off Rd College Station TX 77845 Office Fax: 979-690-2761. E-mail: park00@gmail.com, ysampark@gmail.com.

PARK, YOUNG H., dean; b. Kyung-Buk, Korea, Aug. 5, 1937; s. Won K. Park and Tae S. Lee; m. Jong-Hwa Park, Oct. 20, 1967; children: Grace, David. BD, Presbyn. Gen. Assembly Theol. Seminary, 1961; BA in English Lit., Kyung Hee U., Seoul, 1963; BD, Covenant Theol. Sem., St. Louis, 1967, M in Theology, 1968; MA in Bibl. Lit., St. Louis U., 1973; PhD in Theology, Calif. Grad. Sch. Theol., 1978. Lic. Midwestern Presbyn., 1970. Minister First Presbyn. Ch., St. Louis, 1970—83; prof. New Testament Chongshin U., Seoul, 1983—86, pres., 1986—92; dean grad. sch. Midwest Theol. U., St. Louis, 1992—93, acad. dean, 2002—; pres. Taeshin Christian U., Taegu, Republic of Korea, 1994—2002. Author: Exegetical Principles of N.T., 1988, A Study of Christological Titles, 1990. Avocations: classical music, reading, walking, travel. Home: 1322 Creve Coeur Mill Saint Louis MO 63146 Personal E-mail: younghpark@sbcglobal.net.

PÁRKÁNYI, CYRIL, chemistry educator, research scientist; b. Prague, Czechoslovakia, Sept. 11, 1933; came to U.S., 1965; s. Ivan and Olga (Petrik) P.; m. Marie Hřebíček, Jan. 16, 1960; 1 child, Michael Peter. B.S. equivalent Charles U., Prague, 1954, M.S. with honors, 1956, Dr. rerum natur., 1966; Ph.D., Czechoslovak Acad. Scis., Prague, 1962. Phys. and analytical chemist Research and Control Inst. Food Industry, Prague, 1955-56; research scientist Inst. Phys. Chemistry, Czechoslovak Acad. Scis., Prague, 1960-65, sr. research scientist, 1967-68; assoc. prof. chemistry U. Tex.-El Paso, 1969-71, prof., 1971-88, chmn., 1982-88; prof., chmn. dept. chemistry Fla. Atlantic U., Boca Raton, 1989-94, prof., 1995—; vis. prof. Rijksuniversiteit te Leiden, Netherlands, 1965, Calif. Inst. Tech., Pasadena, 1965-67, 68-69, U. d'Aix-Marseille, France, 1974, 77, 86, 95, U. Kuwait, 1976, Rijksuniversiteit te Groningen, Netherlands, 1978, Univ. des Scis. et Techniques de Lille 1, Villeneuve d'Ascq, France, 1980, 81, 82, U. Denis Diderot-Paris 7, Paris, 1995, U. Ulm (Germany), 1997; lectr. in field. Contbr. articles to profl. jours. Recipient Czechoslovak Acad. Scis. Rsch. award, 1963, Faculty Research award U. Tex.-El Paso, 1980, Disting. Achievement in Teaching award, 1982; Outstanding Tchr. award Amoco Found., 1982, Acad. Excellence award, 1985, medal U. Qatar, Doha, Qatar, 1993, U. Cairo, 2000, Prof. Excellence Program award 1998. Fellow AAAS; mem. Am. Chem. Soc., Inter-Am. Photochem. Soc., Internat. Soc. Quantum Biology, Am. Soc. Photobiology, European Acad. Scis., Arts and Humanities (corr.), Sigma Xi, Phi Kappa Phi. Catholic (Byzantine rite). Achievements include research on physical properties of aromatic and heteroaromatic compounds. Home: 245 NW 69th St Boca Raton FL 33487-2390 Office: Fla Atlantic U Dept Chemistry & Biochemistry PO Box 3091 Boca Raton FL 33431-0991 Office Phone: 561-297-3391. Business E-Mail: parkanyi@fau.edu.

PARKE, DAVID ALAN, lawyer; b. Marlboro, Mass., May 23, 1953; s. Richard Alan Parke and Barbara Ann Morse; m. Patrice Ann Meacham, Aug. 5, 1955; 1 child, Geoffrey David. BA, U. Pa., Phila., 1975; JD, Georgetown U., Washington, 1979. Bar: Mass. 1980. Ptnr. Bulkley, Richardson and Gelinas LLP, Springfield, Mass., 1980—. Bd. dirs. Safety Coun. Western New England, Inc., Springfield, 2004—, Affiliated C. of C. Greater Springfield, Inc., 2006—. Author: Forming a Massachusetts Corporation Under Chapter 156D, 2005; contbg. author: Doing Business in States Other Than State of Incorporation, 2006; co-author: The Massachusetts Corp. Legal Aspects Orgn. and Ops., 2007. Mem. fin. com. Town of Wilbraham, Mass., 2005—. Mem.: MCLE Bus. Comm. Adv. Com., Diocese Springfield Catholic Sch. Bd. Office: Bulkley Richardson and Gelinas LLP 1500 Main St Springfield MA 01115 Office Phone: 413-272-6257.

PARKE, DAVID WILKIN, II, ophthalmologist, educator, health facility administrator; b. Columbus, Ohio, May 19, 1951; s. David William Parke and Eunice Joyce Erikson; m. Julie Diane Thorne, Sept. 15, 1975; children: David W. III, Laura Thorne, Lindsey Diane. AB, Stanford U., 1973; MD, Baylor Coll. Medicine, 1977. Diplomate Am. Bd. Ophthalmology. Resident in internal medicine Baylor Coll. Medicine, Houston, 1977-78, resident in ophthalmology, 1978-81, fellow in med. retina, 1981-82, asst. prof., 1983-90, assoc. prof., 1990-92; fellow diseases and surgery of the retina and vitreous Med. Coll. of Wis., 1982-83; prof., chair dept. ophthalmology U. Okla., Oklahoma City, 1992—; pres., CEO McGee Eye Inst., Oklahoma City, 1992—. Chmn., bd. dirs. Medem, Inc., 2004—; vice chair Ophthalmic Mut. Ins. Co., 2005—. Active Okla. Econ. Devel. Found., 1992, Okla. Health Ctr. Found., 1992—; trustee Presbyn. Health Found., 1995-2006, Casady Sch., 1997-2004, vice chair, 1999-2004; mng. dir. Stephenson Laser Ctr., 1996—; bd. mgrs. Okla. Health Alliance, 1995-97; dir. Oklahoma City C. of C. Fellow: Am. Acad. Ophthalmology (assoc. sec. 1983—92, trustee 2000—, sr. sec. for ophthalmic practice 2002—, pres. 2007—08, Honor award 1980, Sr. Honor award 1998); mem.: Am. Soc. Ret. Specialists, Retina Soc., Assn. Univ. Profs. Ophthalmology (trustee 1997—2003, pres. 2001—02), Greater Oklahoma City C. of C. (bd. dirs. 1998—99, 2004—), Alpha Omega Alpha. Office: Dean A McGee Eye Institute 608 Stanton L Young Blvd Oklahoma City OK 73104-5065 E-mail: david-parke@ouhsc.edu.

PARKE, ROSS DUKE, psychology professor; b. Huntsville, Ont., Can., Dec. 17, 1938; BA, U. Toronto, 1962, MA, 1963; PhD, U. Waterloo, 1965. From asst. to prof. psychology dept. U. Wis., Madison, 1965-71; chief social devel. sect. Fels Rsch. Inst., Yellow Springs, Ohio, 1971-75; prof. psychology U. Ill., Champaign-Urbana, 1975-90, U. Calif., Riverside, 1990—, dir. Ctr. for Family Studies, 1992—, disting. prof. psychology, 1998—2008, disting. prof. emeritus, 2008—. Author: Fathers, 1981, Fatherhood, 1996; co-author Child Psychology, 7th edit., 2008, Throwaway Dads, 1999; editor Jour. Family Psychology, 1998-2003; assoc. editor Child Devel. 1973-77, editor Devel. Psychology, 1987-92; co-editor Family-Peer Relationships, 1992, Children in Time and Place, 1993; contbr. over 250 articles to profl. jours., chpts. to books. Grantee Office Child Devel., 1978-80, NICHD, 1980-90, 94-97, 99-2008, NSF, 1990-95, Spencer Found., 1991, 2003, NIMH, 1997-2008. Fellow APA (pres. divsn. devel. psychology 1991, G. Stanley Hall award divsn. devel. psychol. 1995); mem. Soc. for Rsch. in Child Devel. (exec. com. 1978-83, pres. 2001-03, SRCD Dist. Sci. Contbn. Child Devel. award, 2009). Office: U Calif Riverside Dept Psychology Riverside CA 92521-0001 Office Phone: 951-827-4144. Business E-Mail: ross.parke@ucr.edu.

PARKER, ALAN JOHN, veterinary neurologist, educator, researcher; b. Portsmouth, Eng., Oct. 28, 1944; arrived in U.S., 1969, naturalized, 2002; s. William Barton and Emily (Begley) P.; m. Heather Margaret Nicholson, Oct. 30, 1971; children: Alyxander John, Robert William. BSc with honors, Bristol U., 1966, BVSc with honors, 1968; MS, U. Ill., 1973, PhD, 1976. Diplomate Am. Coll. Vet. Internal Medicine-Neurology, European Coll. Vet. Neurology. Intern Vet. Coll., U. Calif.-Davis, 1969—70; instr. vet. clin. medicine U. Ill., Urbana, 1970—71, 1972—76, asst. prof., 1976—77, assoc. prof., 1977—82, prof., 1982—2000, prof. emeritus, 2001—. Cons. pharm. cos., seminar presenter; cons. in neurology Berwyn Vet. Hosp., Chgo., 1973—2009, Lake Shore Animal Hosp., Chgo., 1978-03. Contbr. numerous articles to sci. jours., chpts. to books. Active Boy Scouts Am., Champaign, Ill., 1982—; active Presbyn. Ch., Monticello, Ill., 1979-2006. Recipient Vigil Honor and Founder's award Order of the Arrow, Silver Beaver award Boy Scouts Am.; sci. grantee various orgns., 1972-2000. Mem. AVMA, RCVS, Brit. Vet. Assn. Republican. Home Phone: 217-352-2225.

PARKER, ALICE, composer; b. Boston, Dec. 16, 1925; d. Gordon and Mary (Stuart) P.; widowed; children: David, Timothy, Katharine, Mary, Elizabeth. BA, Smith Coll., Northampton, Mass., 1947; MS, Juilliard Sch., NYC, 1949; MusD (hon.), Hamilton U., 1979, Macalester Coll., St. Paul, 1989, Bluffton Coll., Ohio, 1991, Westminster Choir Coll., Princeton, NJ, 1996, Shenandoah U., Winchester, Va., 2007. Arranger Robert Shaw Chorale, NYC, 1948-66; artistic dir. Melodious Accord, NYC, 1985—. Tchr., workshop leader Westminster Choir Coll., Princeton, N.J., summers, 1972-98; McDonald chair Emory U., 2003. Composer 4 operas, 41 cantatas, 8 song cycles and numerous anthems and suites. Recipient composer's award ASCAP, 1968—, AGO Disting. Composer of the Yr., 2000, Barlow Endowment, 1992, spl. award Nat. Endowment Arts, 1976, Gottschalk award Pioneer Valley Symphony, 2003, Lifetime Achievement award Choral Arts New Eng., 2004. Fellow Hymn Soc., Hymn Soc. Am. (conf. composer in residence, 2006); mem. Am. Choral Dirs. Assn. (ea. disvn. conf. dedicated in her honor 2006), Am. Condrs. Guild, Chorus Am. (Founders award 1994), Am. Music ctr., Sigma Alpha Iota. Office: Melodious Accord Inc Park West Sta PO Box 20801 New York NY 10025-1523 Personal E-mail: alice@aliceparker.com.

PARKER, BARRINGTON D., JR., federal judge; b. Washington, Aug. 21, 1944; BA, Yale U., 1965, JD, 1969. Bar: NY 1971. Law clk. to Hon. Aubrey E. Robinson, US Dist. Ct. for DC, Washington, 1969-70; assoc. Sullivan & Cromwell, NYC, 1970-77; ptnr. Parker Auspitz Neesemann & Delehanty, P.C., NYC, 1977-87, Morrison & Foerster, NYC, 1987-94; judge US Dist. Ct. (so. dist.) NY, White Plains, 1994—2001, US Ct. Appeals (2nd cir.), NY, 2001—. Bd. dirs., v.p. NAACP Legal Def. and Educational Fund, Inc., 1980—; com. on grievances, com. on civil discovery US Dist. Ct. (so. dist.) NY, 1983—; com. on pre-trial phase civil cases US Ct. Appeals (2nd cir.) 1983—. Trustee Governance Inst., Greenwich Acad., South Africa Legal Svcs. and Legal Edn. Project, Inc.; successor trustte an mem. Yale Corp. Mem. ABA, Fed. Bar Coun., Assn. Bar City NY (com. on the judiciary 1978-82, exec. com. 1982-86, nominating com. 1987), Coun. on Fgn. Rels. Office: US Courthouse 300 Quarropas St Rm 633 White Plains NY 10601-4150 also: Thurogood Marshall US Courthouse 40 Foley Square New York NY 10007 Home: 40 Foley Sq Ste 1702 New York NY 10007-1504*

PARKER, BOBBY DOUGLAS, radio broadcaster, photographer, educator; b. Anthony, Kans., Feb. 12, 1935; s. Luther Joseph and Inez Beatrice (Lawrence) Parker; m. Nelda Arlene Parker, Aug. 23, 1958; children: Steven Douglas, Gregory Allen, Kirby Lynn. Attended, Kans. State U., Manhattan, 1953—56; B in Music Edn., Wichita State U., 1960, M in Music Edn., 1964; grad. with spl. honors, Modern Sch. Photography, NYC, 1981; grad., NY Inst. Profl. Photography, 1982; student, Nikon Sch. Photography, 1980. Cert. specialists in edn. U. Colo., 1975, tchr. kANS., lic. in 3d class radio Kans., Colo. Photographer student portraits small studio Brooks Inst. Photography, Santa Barbara, Calif., 1982; tchr. elem. & sr. HS vocal music Moscow Pub. Schs., Kans., 1960—64; jr. & sr. HS vocal music Sublette Pub. Schs., Kans., 1966—73; salesman, announcer Sta.-KLEY, Wellington, Kans., 1966—73; tchr. vocal music Jefferson County Pub. Sch., Colo., 1973—93, instr. photography, dark-room tech., 1981—; owner, photographer Universal Creations, Arvada, Colo., 1979—; tour guide Coors Brewery, 1958—75; dir. ch. choirs First United Meth. Ch., Wellington, 1958—75; choir dir. Sumner County Cmty. Chorus, Kans., 1966—73; dir. prize-winning music groups contests. Mem.: NEA, Photographers Soc. America, Wedding Photographers Internat. (Hon. award 1981—82), Profl. Photographers America (2 Nat. Merit award), Am. Choral Dirs. Assn., Music Educators Nat. Conf., Colo. Tchrs. Assn., Shriners (Denver), Masons (Wellington), Phi Mu Alpha, Phi Delta Kappa. Democrat. Home: 9157 W 101st Ave Broomfield CO 80021-3869 Personal E-mail: bobby1406@comcast.net.

PARKER, BONITA M., civil rights organization executive; b. Jan. 23, 1968; married; 2 children. Degree in Fin., DePaul U. Several positions with Urban Fin. Services, Am. Bankers Assn.; intern Northern Trust Co., second v.p.; co-owner Skills For Life Tng. Co.; dir., Investments and Econ. Empowerment Salem Bapt. Ch., Chgo.; COO Rainbow/Push Coalition, Chgo. Fin. specialist USAR. Mem.: Nat. Assn. County Officials. Office: RainbowPush Coaltion 930 E 50th St Chicago IL 60615-2702 Home Phone: 708-331-5473; Office Phone: 773-551-8661. Personal E-mail: bp5225@aol.com.

PARKER, BRENT MERSHON, retired medical educator, internist, cardiologist; b. St. Louis, July 3, 1927; s. William Bahlmann and Florence (Mershon) P.; m. Martha Shelton, Aug. 1, 1953; children: Martha Parker Burgess, Elizabeth, Margaret. MD cum laude, Wash. U., St. Louis, 1952. Diplomate Am. Bd. Internal Medicine. Intern and asst. resident N.Y. Hosp.-Cornell, NYC, 1952-54; asst. resident, fellow Barnes Hosp., Wash. U., St. Louis, 1954-57; cardiology sect. chief VA Hosp., U. Oreg., Portland, 1957-59; asst. prof. to assoc. prof., co-dir. cardiovascular div., chief adult cardiac catherization Wash. U. Sch. Medicine, St. Louis, 1959-73; prof. medicine U. Mo., Columbia, 1973-89, prof. emeritus, 1989-94, chief of staff, assoc. dean, 1976-82, chief of cardiology, 1983-89. Mem. colloquium faculty Merck, Sharp and Dohme, West Point, Pa., 1980-86. Author or co-author 58 papers in referred jours., 6 book chpts., teaching papers, others. Bd. dirs. St. Louis Heart Assn., 1962-73, v.p. 1972-73; bd. dirs. Mo. Heart Assn., 1965-75, pres. 1970-71. Served with USN, 1945-46. Recipient Arthur Strauss award St. Louis Heart Assn., 1973, 3 teaching awards U. Mo. Sch. Medicine, 1974, 75, 86, Preventive Cardiology Acad. award, Nat. Heart Lung and Blood Inst., 1982-87, Alumni Achievement award Washington Univ. Sch. Medicine, 1992; Brent Mershon Parker professorship estab. in honor U. Mo., 1989. Fellow ACP, Am. Coll. Cardiology (Mo., Kans. council rep. 1973-77), Clin. Cardiology Soc. Am. Heart Assn.; mem. Am. Fedn. Clin. Research, Cen. Soc. for Clin. Research, Alpha Omega Alpha, Sigma Xi. Episcopalian. Avocations: choral singing, jogging, camping, back packing.

PARKER, CANDACE NICOLE, professional basketball player; b. St. Louis, Apr. 19, 1986; d. Larry and Sara Parker; m. Shelden Williams, Nov. 13, 2008; 1 child, Lailaa Nicole Williams. B in Sports Mgmt., Psychology, U. Tenn., 2008. Forward, center, guard U. Tenn. Lady Volunteers, 2005—08, LA Sparks, 2008—. Mem. USA Basketball Women's Sr. Nat. Team, Beijing, 2008. Recipient John R. Wooden award, 2007, 2008, Sports award, Honda, 2007, Wade Trophy, 2007, ESPY award, Best Female Athlete, ESPN, 2008, ESPY award, Best Female Coll. Athlete, 2008, Gold medal, women's basketball, Beijing Olympic Games, 2008; named Tournament MVP, Southeastern Conf., 2006, Freshman of Yr., 2006, Rookie of Yr., 2006, Freshman of Week, 2006, Player of Week, 2006, 2007, Player of Yr., 2007, US Basketball Writers Assn., 2007, Lady Vol Athlete of Week, U. Tenn., 2006, Lady Vol Athlete of Month, 2006, Most Outstanding Player, NCAA Women's Basketball Tournament, 2007; named a Kodak All-Am., 2006; named to, 2007, NCAA Cleve. Regional All-Regional Team, 2006, All-Southeastern Conf. First Team, 2006, 2007, All-Southeastern Conf. Freshman Team, 2006, Second Team All-Am., AP, 2006, 1st Team All-Am., 2007, John R. Wooden All-Am., 2007. Achievements include being a member of the NCAA Women's Basketball Championship winning University of Tennessee Lady Volunteers, 2007, 2008; being the first overall pick in the WNBA draft, 2008. Office: LA Sparks 1111 S Figueroa St Ste 3100 Los Angeles CA 90001

PARKER, CLEA EDWARD, retired university president; b. Talisheek, La., Apr. 2, 1927; s. William A. and Lutritia (Davis) P.; m. Peggy Ann Faciane, June 21, 1953; children: Brian, Stephen, Karen, Robin. BA, Southeastern La. U., 1948; M.Ed., La. State U., 1952, Ed.D., 1965. Coach, tchr. Rugby Acad., New Orleans, 1948-50; tchr., prin., supr. instr., dir. curriculum and instrn. St. Tammany Parish Sch. Bd., 1950-67; prof. edn., head dept. student teaching Nicholls State Coll., Thibodaux, La., 1967-68; acting pres. Southeastern La. U., Hammond, 1968, pres., 1968-80, pres. emeritus, 1980—86. Liaison La. State Dept. Edn., Higher Edn. and Bds. for Edn. in La., 1986; vis. lectr. La. State U. at NC, 1965-69; past pres. St. Tammany Parish Tchrs. Assn., La. Assn. Supervision and Curriculum Devel.; past pres. elementary dept. La. Tchrs. Assn.; chmn. Pres.'s Coun. La. Bd. Edn., 1972-73; v.p. Conf. La. Colls. and Univs., 1973-74, pres., 1974-75; pres. elect Gulf South Conf., 1974-75, pres., 1975-76; mem. Steering Com. on Curriculum Devel. and Revision for Career Edn. for State La., 1973; mem. adv. council for State Plan for Career Edn., 1973 Mem. planning com. Gov.'s Conf. on Aging, 1976; v.p. chpt. 15 La. Good Samaritans, 1987-88; bd. dirs. Assn. for Retarded Citizens, pres.-elect, 1981; mem. Zemurray Park Recreation Commn., Hammond, 1992-95; chmn. bd. dirs. Lallie Kemp Meml. Hosp., 1993-94; bd. dirs. Lallie Kemp Med. Ctr., 1994—, chmn., 1994-95. With USCGR, 1945, 93-94. Named Hon. State Farmer La., 1970, Disting. Alumnus of Yr., Southeastern La. U. Alumni Assn., 1977, 91, 92; inductee La. Spl. Olympics Hall of Fame, 1998. Mem. Am. Assn. State Colls. and Univs. (com. on nat. svc. 1972-73, task force on aging 1975-76, 78-79, nominating com. 1977—, state Rep. for La. 1979—, com. agr. renewable resources and rural devel. 1979-80, Svc. to Edn. award 1980), Hammond C. of C., La. Assn. for Sch. Execs., Ozone Ramblers Camping Club (pres. 1988), KC (lectr. 1982, 85, 90-91, chancellor 1983-84, 87—, dep. grand knight 1995-96), Rotary (bd. dirs. Hammond, internat. svc. dir. 1972), Phi Delta Kappa, Kappa Delta Pi. Home: 10 Golden Dr Hammond LA 70401-1010 Personal E-mail: ceparker10@bellsouth.net.

PARKER, DAN, human resources executive; B, U. Ga., 1969, M, 1971; grad., Brewton-Parker Coll. Sr. mgmt. positions Samsonite Corp., Aladdin Industries; v.p., mng. dir. Atlanta office A.T. Kearney; ptnr. Baker-Parker Exec. Search; pres. Parker Exec. Search, Atlanta. Former vice chmn., bd. dirs. Amrop Hever Group; spkr. in field. Trustee Brewton-Parker Coll. Named Alumni of Yr., Brewton-Parker Coll. Mem.: Am. Soc. Personnel Adminstrn. (past nat. v.p., mem. exec. bd.), Assn. Exec. Search Cons., Rotary Internat. (Paul Harris fellow). Office: Parker Exec Search Five Concourse Pkwy Ste 2440 Atlanta GA 30328 Office Phone: 770-804-1996 ext. 104. Office Fax: 770-804-1917. Business E-Mail: dparker@parkersearch.com.

PARKER, DAN J., political organization administrator; b. Braintree, Mass. married; 2 children. BA in Govt., George Mason U., Fairfax, Va. Chmn. Ind. Dem. Party, Indpls., 2004—. Mem. Dem. Nat. Com. Democrat. Office: Ind Dem Party Ste 200 One North Capitol Indianapolis IN 46204 Office Phone: 317-231-7100. Office Fax: 317-231-7129. E-mail: dparker@indems.org.*

PARKER, DAVID MILLER, history professor, retired advertising executive; b. Bklyn., Oct. 10, 1949; AB magna cum laude, Cornell U., Ithaca, NY, 1971; MA, Stanford U., Calif., 1972; PhD, Claremont Grad. U., Calif., 2003. Media planner Young & Rubicam, NYC, 1972—74, Ted Bates, NYC, 1974—76; sr. media planner John F. Murray Advt., NYC, 1976—77; media planning supr. N.W. Ayer, NYC, 1977—80, Doyle Dane Bernbach West, LA, 1980—82; assoc. media dir. Young & Rubicam, Dentsu, LA, 1982—83; media planning officer Bank of Am., San Francisco, 1983—87; media dir. Font & Vaamonde, Grey Hispanic, NYC, 1988—90, media cons. LA, 1990—94; lectr., history Calif. State U., Channel Islands, 2003—04, lectr., Am. studies Fullerton, 2004; lectr., history San Diego State U., 2005, Calif. State U., Northridge, 2005—, LA Pierce Coll., Woodland Hills, Calif., 2007—. Contbr. articles to profl. jours. Vol. Hollywood-Sunset Free Clinic, LA, 1991—93, LA Gay and Lesbian Ctr., 1992—94, Project Open Hand, San Francisco, 2004—05. Mem.: Nat. Social Sci. Assn., LA Coll. Faculty Guild, Calif. Faculty Assn., Southwestern Hist. Assn., Orgn. Am. Historians, Am. Studies Assn., Book Club Calif., Phi Alpha Theta, Internat. Honor Soc. History. Office: Calif State Univ 18111 Nordhoff St Northridge CA 91330-8250

PARKER, DONALD FRED, dean, human resources specialist, educator; b. Oilton, Okla., Nov. 7, 1934; s. Robert Fred Parker and Georgia Marie (Culley) Meek; m. Jo Ellen Dunfee, Apr. 6, 1963; children: Margaret Elizabeth, Emily Lyle. BA in Sociology, U. Okla., 1957; MS in Personnel Adminstrn., George Washington U., 1966; PhD in Human Resource Mgmt., Cornell U., 1974. Commd. ensign USN, 1957, advanced through grades to capt., 1977, staff officer with chief naval ops. Washington, 1969-71, comdg. officer, exec. officer, Patrol Squadron Ten Brunswick, Maine, 1974-76, prof. Naval War Coll. Newport, RI, 1976-78, comdg. officer Navy Personnel Research & Devel. Ctr. San Diego, 1978-80, ret., 1980; asst. prof. Grad. Sch. Bus., U. Mich., Ann Arbor, 1980-84; prof., dean Coll. Commerce and Industry U. Wyo., Laramie, 1984-91; Sara Hart Kimball dean bus., prof. human resources mgmt. Oreg. State U., Corvallis, 1991—2001, dean emeritus, 2003—; lectr. Student Leadership Forum; vis. prof. St. Georges U., 2007—08. Advisor US West Wyo. State Bd. Advisors, Cheyenne, 1986-91; ex-officio dir. Wyo. Indsl. Devel. Corp., Casper, 1987; vis. prof. Acad. Internat. Econ. Affairs, Hsinchu, Taiwan, 1986-91, St. George's U., 2007, 08. Author numerous articles, book chpts., case studies. Mem. Acad. of Mgmt. (human resource mgmt. divsn. dir. 1983-85), Midwest Assn. Deans and Dept. Chairs in Bus. (pres.), Western Assn. Collegiate Schs. Bus. (bd. dirs., pres. 1999), Phi Kappa Phi, Beta Gamma Sigma (pres. 1998-2000, past pres. 2000—02). Avocations: skiing, hiking.

PARKER, DOUG (WILLIAM DOUGLAS PARKER, W. DOUGLAS PARKER), air transportation executive; m. Gwen Parker; 3 children. BA in Econ., Albion Coll., 1984; MBA, Vanderbilt U., 1986. Various fin. mgmt. positions Am. Airlines, 1986—91; v.p., fin. planning and analysis, v.p., asst. treas. Northwest Airlines; sr. v.p., CFO Am. West Holdings, 1995—99, exec. v.p., corp. group, 1999—2000, pres., COO, 2000—01, chmn., pres., CEO, 2001—05; interim pres. US Airways Group Inc., Tempe, Ariz., 2005, chmn., CEO, 2005—. Recipient Disting. Alumnus award, Vanderbilt U. Owen Grad. Sch. Mgmt., 2004. Methodist. Office: US Airways 111 W Rio Salado Pkwy Tempe AZ 85281*

PARKER, ELIZABETH RINDSKOPF, dean, law educator; b. Detroit, Dec. 2, 1943; d. Arthur C. and Kathryn G. (Rodgers) Roediger; m. Peter E. Rindskopf, May 25, 1968; 1 child; m. Robert Parker. BA in Philosophy cum laude, U. Mich., 1964, JD, 1968. Bar: Ga. 1968, U.S. Dist. Ct. (no. dist.) Ga. 1969, U.S. Ct. Appeals (5th cir.) 1970, U.S. Supreme Ct. 1971, U.S. Ct. Appeals (6th cir.) 1972, U.S. Ct. Appeals (3rd cir.) 1974, U.S. Ct. Appeals (4th cir.) 1977, U.S. Ct. Appeals (9th cir.) 1978, D.C. 1979. Reginald Heber Smith fellow, mng. atty. Emory Legal Svcs., Atlanta, 1968-71; ptnr. Moore, Alexander & Rindskopf, Atlanta, 1971-74; dir. New Haven Legal Assistance Assn., Inc., 1974-76; dep. dir. Lawyers Com. Civil Rights Under Law, Washington, 1978-78; ptnr. Cohen, Vitt & Annand, Alexandria, Va., 1978-79; acting asst. dir. mergers and joint ventures, dep. asst. dir. health care Bur. of Competition, Fed. Trade Commn., 1979-81; of counsel Surrey & Morse, Washington, 1981-84; gen. counsel Nat. Security Agy., Washington, 1984-89; prin. dep. office of the legal adviser US Dept. State, Washington, 1989-90; gen. counsel CIA, Washington, 1990-95; of counsel Bryan Cave, LLP, 1995—99; gen. counsel U. Wis. Sys., 1999—2002; dean, prof. law U. Pacific McGeorge Sch. Law, Sacramento, 2002—. Cooperating atty. NAACP Legal Def. and Edn. Fund, Inc., 1971-74; trustee Monterey Inst. Internat. Studies. Contbr. articles to profl. jours. Mem. ABA (standing com. law and nat. security, counsel sect. internat. law and politics, adv. bd. Ctr. and Eastern European Law Initiative), Coun. Fgn. Rels, NAS (com. on sci. comm. and nat. security, com. on a new govt.-univ. partnership on sci. and security). Office: Univ of Pacific McGeorge Sch Law 3200 Fifth Ave Sacramento CA 95817 Office Phone: 916-739-7151. E-mail: elizabeth@pacific.edu.*

PARKER, ELLIS D., retired military officer; b. Adams, Tenn., Nov. 1, 1932; s. Ellis A. and Lorene P.; m. Judy C. Matthews, Dec. 24, 1952; children: Donald S., Phillip R., David B. BS in Psychology, U. Nebr., 1972; MPA, Shippensburg U., 1979; LLD (hon.), Miles U., 1989. Rated aviator FAA. Commd. 2d lt. U.S. Army, 1957, advanced through ranks to lt. gen., 1992, aviation officer, comdr. 17th aviation brigade Republic of Korea, 1978-80; dir. requirements army staff Pentagon, Washington, 1980-83; asst. divsn. comdr. 101st airborne divsn. U.S. Army, Ft. Campbell, Ky., 1983-84, commdg. gen. Army Aviation Ctr. Sch. Ft. Rucker, Ala., 1984-89; dir. army staff Pentagon, Washington, 1989-92; bd. dirs. Can. Aviation Electronics, 1993—2008, chmn., CEO Can., 1993—2001, chmn. govt. security com., 2001—08; co-chmn., bd. dirs. Doss Aviation. Bd. dirs. Doss Aviation, Colorado Springs; chmn., bd. dirs. Hammer Constrn. Co., Samson, Ala.; bd. dirs. Aereus Internat., Enterprise, Ala. Contbr. articles to profl. jour. Chmn. Fort Rucker Mus. Found., 1995—; adv. bd. Troy U., Dotham, 1992—2002; chair retiree coun. for chief of staff U.S. Army, 1993-99; co-chair Dept. of Def. Retiree Coun., 1994-99. Decorated D.S.M. with oak leaf cluster, D.F.C., Legion of Merit, Bronze Star with two oak leaf clusters, Meritorious Svc. medals, 23 Air medals; named to Hall of Honor Bd. by Gov. Ala., 1993-. Mem.: C. of C., Army Assn. Am., Enterprise C. of C. (chmn bd. dirs. 1993—95), Assn. U.S. Army (mem. exec. com. Ft. Rucker chpt. 1994, named to Army Aviation Hall of Fame 1994), Ret. Officers Assn. (bd. mem.), Army Aviation Assn. Am. (pres., Order of St. Michel, Gold 1992), Enterprise Rotary Club (Paul Harris fellow). Republican. Avocations: flying, hunting, fishing, volunteering in community. Home and Office: 128 Deer Run Strut Enterprise AL 36330-7812

PARKER, ELLIS JACKSON, III, lawyer, broadcaster; b. Haleyville, Ala., Oct. 2, 1931; s. Ellis J. and Elizabeth (Funderburg) P.; m. Nancy Elizabeth Bealer; children: Francis Hill, Ellis Stuart. At, U.S. Mil. Acad., West Point, NY, 1953—57; AB, U. Ala., University, 1958, LLB, 1960, JD, 1961; diploma, Droit Compare, Luxembourg, 1959; cert., Acad. Internat. Law, Hague, Netherlands, 1960. Bar: Ala. 1960, U.S. Tax Ct. 1960, U.S. Supreme Ct. 1966, U.S. Ct. Appeals D.C. 1972, Md. Ct. Appeals 1973, U.S. Ct. Claims 1977. Legis. atty. IRS, Washington, 1961—62; chief of staff to U.S. Congressman Grant Ala., 1963—64; pvt. practice Birmingham, Ala., 1964—84; spl. advisor to Pres. Richard Nixon White House, Washington, 1968—69, transitional staff; v.p., counsel Birmingham Broadcasting Co., 1964—83; ptnr. Taylor, Smith & Parker Law Office, Upper Marlboro, Md., 1970—86; prin., owner Ellis J. Parker, Law Office, Washington, 1986—. V.p., sec. Constrn. Components Corp., Upper Marlboro, Md., 1968-72; pres. Washington-Ala. News Reports, Washington, 1980-01, Parker Real Estate, Birmingham, Bealer-Parker, LLC, Washington; chmn. bd. Blackbelt Broadcasting Co., Selma, Ala., 1986-2000; founding mem. Women's Nat. Bank, Washington; CEO Birmingham Broadcasting Co.; ptnr. Linden Radio Joint Venture, Faunsdale, Ala., 1969-89; pres., bd. dirs. 17th St LLC, N.B. Devel. Co. LLC, Washington, 2006, Hartford E. Bealer Devel. Corp., Washington. Mem. Presdl. Inaugural Com., inaugural protocol officer V.p. Agnew, 1968; mem. steering com. Rep. Party, Balt., 1972; chmn. bd. trustees Prince George's Hist. and Cultural Trust, Upper Marlboro, 1974; chmn. bd. advisors Prince George's Equestrian Ctr., Upper Marlboro, 1980; founder, pres. bd. dirs, Hospice of Prince George's County, Upper Marlboro, 1982; mem. Upper Marlboro Devel. Com. Mem. IEEE, ABA, FCC Bar Assn., Fed. Bar Assn., Inter-Am. Bar Assn., Ala. Bar Assn., Md. Bar Assn., D.C. Bar Assn., Nat. Assn. Broadcasters, Ala. Broadcasters Assn., Balt. Coun. Fgn. Affairs, Assn. Grads. U.S. Mil. Acad., Chevy Chase Club, Md. Club, St. Andrews Soc., Met. Club, Ala. Alumni Assn., Scabbard and Blade (chmn. nat. alumni coun. 1986-2006), Pi Kappa Alpha, Sigma Delta Kappa., Palm Beach Iheatic Guild, Mayford Yatch Club. Home: Chateau Rambouillet 2165 Ibis Island Palm Beach FL 33480 Personal E-mail: eparker124@aol.com.

PARKER, EUGENE NEWMAN, retired physicist, educator; b. Houghton, Mich., June 10, 1927; s. Glenn H. and Helen (MacNair) Parker; m. Niesje Meuter, 1954; children: Joyce, Eric. BS, Mich. State U., East Lansing, 1948, DSc (hon.), 1975; PhD, Calif. Inst. Tech., Pasadena, 1951; DHC in Physics and Math. (hon.), U. Utrecht, The Netherlands, 1986; DHC in Theoretical Physics (hon.), U. Oslo, 1991. Instr. math. and astronomy U. Utah, 1951—53, asst. prof. physics, 1953—55; mem. faculty physics U. Chgo., 1955—95, prof. dept. physics, 1962—95, prof. dept. astronomy and astrophysics, 1967—95, prof. emeritus, 1995—. Author: Interplanetary Dynamical Processes, 1963, Cosmical Magnetic Fields, 1979, Spontaneous Current Sheets in Magnetic Fields, 1994, Conversations on Electric and Magnetic Fields in the Cosmos, 2007. Recipient Space Sci. award, AIAA, 1964, Chapman medal, Royal Astron. Soc., 1979, Gold medal, 1992, Disting. Alumni award, Calif. Inst. Tech., 1980, Karl Schwarzschild award, Astronomische Gesselschaft, 1990, Bruce medal, Astron. Soc. Pacific, 1997, medal, Assn. Internat. Devel. Nice (France) Obs., 1997, Kyoto prize, Inamori Found., 2003, Maxwell prize, plasma physics divsn., Am. Phys. Soc., 2003. Mem.: NAS (H. K. Arctowski award 1969, US Nat. medal of Sci. 1989), Norwegian Acad. Sci. and Letters, Am. Geophys. Union (John Adam Fleming award 1968, William Bowie medal 1990), Am. Astron. Soc. (Henry Norris Russell lectr. 1969, George Ellery Hale award 1978). Achievements include development of theory of the origin of the dipole magnetic field of Earth; prediction and theory of the solar wind and heliosphere; theoretical basis for the X-ray emission from the Sun and stars. Home: 1006 Gardner Rd Flossmoor IL 60422 E-mail: parker@oddjob.uchicago.edu.

PARKER, EVA ANNETTE, retired librarian; b. North Island, Calif., Nov. 27, 1950; d. R.L. and Eva Mae (Helm) Peters; m. Darrell Dwight Parker, Nov. 9, 1970; children: Geoff, Jenny. BS, Okla. Christian Coll., 1974; MEd, Southwestern Okla. State U., 1984. Cert. libr. media specialist. Tchr. Summer Safari program Oklahoma City Zoo, 1973; libr., tchr. Leedey (Okla.) Pub. Sch., 1983-87; prof. Draughon Tng. Inst., Wichita Falls, Tex., 1988-89; tchr. Region IX Edn. Svc. Ctr., Wichita Falls, 1990; libr. media specialist Vernon (Tex.) Mid. Sch., 1990—2003; libr. Burgess Elem. Sch., Wichita Falls, Tex., 2004—09; tchr. art and sci. Vernon Kids Kollege, 1999—; organisor, edn issues Cmty GED Classes, 2009—. Tutor Vernon Intermediate Sch., 1993—; del. alt. to NEA, Leedey, 1987; storm spotter for City of Grandfield, Okla. Contbg. author: What America's Teachers Wish Parents Knew, 1993; contbr. article to profl. jour. Tchr. Bible sch. Ch. of Christ, Iowa Park, Tex., 1987-93, Grandfield, Okla., 1994—; vol. ARC, Wichita Falls, 1987-93; coach bowling Spl. Olympics, 1992-93; coach track and field Spl. Olympics, Vernon, 1993—; bd. mem. Harvest Playhouse; spl. olympics coach. Libr. improvement grantee Okla. State Dept. Edn., Leedey, 1984, Sch.-to-Work grantee, 1996-2001, IDEA grantee Wichita Falls ISD, 2006, 07-08, Lowe's Toolbox Edn. grant, 2007-08. Mem. Tex. Libr. Assn., Assn. Tex. Profl. Educators, P.E.O. (pres. Okla. orgn.). Avocations: rock collecting, painting, calligraphy, reading, music. Home: 1303 W 1st St Grandfield OK 73546 Office: Fowler Elem Sch 5100 Ridgecrest Wichita Falls TX 76310 Home Phone: 580-479-5422; Office Phone: 940-716-2850, 940-720-3052. Personal E-mail: annettep_1@yahoo.com.

PARKER, EVERETT CARLTON, clergyman; b. Chgo., Jan. 17, 1913; s. Harry Everett and Lillian (Stern) P.; m. Geneva M. Jones, May 5, 1939; children: Ruth A. (Mrs. Peter Weiss), Eunice L. (Mrs. George Kolczun, Jr.), Truman E. AB, U. Chgo., 1935; BD magna cum laude, Chgo. Theol. Sem., 1943, Blatchford fellow, 1944-45, DD, 1964, Catawba Coll., Salisbury, NC, 1958; L.H.D., Fordham U., 1978, Tougaloo Coll., 1987; LLD, Coll. St. Elizabeth, 2000. Pastor Waveland Ave. Congl. Christian Ch., 1943; asst. pub. service and war program mgr. NBC, 1943-45; founder-dir. Protestant Radio Commn., 1945-50; lectr. communication Yale Div. Sch., 1946-58, dir. communications research project, 1950-54; dir. Office Communication United Ch. Christ, 1954-83; sr. research assoc., adj. prof. Fordham U., 1983—2008; founder citizen movement to protect minority rights in media, 1963—. Chmn. broadcasting and film commn. Nat. Coun. Chs., 1969-72, gen. bd., 1966-72; chmn. Study Commn. on Theology, Edn. and Electronic Media, 1985-87; funder Found. for Minority Interests in Media, 1985—, treas., 1985-08. Producer-dir.: nat. TV programs including series Off to Adventure, 1956, Tangled World, 1965; originator: series Six American Families, PBS-TV, 1977; Author: Religious Radio, 1948, Film Use in the Church, 1953, The Television-Radio Audience and Religion, 1955, Religious Television, 1961, (with others) Television, Radio, Film for Churchmen, 1969, Fiber Optics to the Home: The Changing Future of Cable, TV and The Telephone, 1989, Social Responsibility of Television in the United States, 1994. Recipient Human Relations award Am. Jewish Com., 1966, Faith and Freedom award Religious Heritage Found., 1966, 77, Alfred I. DuPont-Columbia U. award pub. service in broadcasting, 1969; Roman Cath. Broadcasters Gabriel award pub. service, 1970; Lincoln U. award significant contbn. human relations, 1971; Racial Justice award Com. for Racial Justice, United Ch. Christ, 1973; Ch. Leadership award Coun. for Christian Social Action, 1973; Public Svc. award Black Citizens for a Fair Media, 1979, Pioneer award World Assn. for Christian Comm., 1988, award for Ecumenical Leadership Nat. Coun. Chs., 2000, Ellul award Media Ecology Assn., 2004 Mem.: Star (NYC). Home: 11 Midland Ave White Plains NY 10606-2828 Personal E-mail: ecparker92@msn.com.

PARKER, FAYE C., elementary school educator; b. Madisonville, Ky., Sept. 5, 1954; d. Willis Owen and Mary Agnes (Hill) P. BS, Murray State U., Ky., 1976, MEd, 1980, Rank I in elem. edn., 1982. Cert. elem. tchr., Ky. Tchr. Hopkins County Bd. Edn., Madisonville, 1976—94; extended sch. coord. Jesse Stuart Sch., Madisonville, 1976—2007, tchr., 1994—. Leader Hopkins County Sch. Sys. Fellow Ky. Edn. Reform Act; named Hopkins County Tchr. of Yr., 1985, 92. Mem. Assn. Childhood Edn. (treas., past local and state pres.), Ky. Reading Assn., Ky. Sci. Tchrs. Assn., Ky. Math. Tchrs. Assn., Hopkins County Edn. Assn., Delta Kappa Gamma. Home: 531 Brown Ln Madisonville KY 42431-1161 Office: Jesse Stuart Sch 1710 Anton Rd Madisonville KY 42431-8514 Home Phone: 270-821-6064; Office Phone: 270-825-6033. Personal E-mail: parker531@newwavecomm.net. E-mail: faye.parker@hopkins.kyschools.us.

PARKER, GERALD M., osteopath, researcher; b. Olean, NY, Nov. 20, 1943; s. Richard and Kathleen (Manwaring) P.; m. Linda Kay Stuart, Dec. 28, 1968; children: Kimberly, Gerald, Cassandra, Kevin. BA, Western Wash. U., 1965; DO, Kirksville Coll. Osteopathy & Surgery, 1969. Intern Art Centre Hosp., Detroit, 1969-70; ptnr. Doctor's Clinic, Amarillo, Tex., 1970. Dir. S.W. Inst. Preventive Medicine, Amarillo, 1978—, Hyperbaric Oxygen Ctr., Amarillo, 1979—; appeared on That's Incredible TV show, 1982. Contbr. articles to profl. jours. Pres. S.W. Amarillo Little Dribblers Assn., 1979—; coach Girls Nat. Champion Basketball Teams, 1981, 83-87, 89. Named Physician of Yr., Nat. Rep. Com. Physician Adv. Bd., 2003. Fellow Am. Acad. Med. Preventics; mem. S.W. Acad. Preventive Medicine (pres. 1980—), Am. Osteo. Assn. Methodist. Avocation: athletics. Office: Doctors Clinic 4714 S Western St Amarillo TX 79109-5950 Office Phone: 806-355-8263.

PARKER, H. LAWRENCE, retired investor, rancher, investment banker; b. Portchester, NY, June 16, 1926; s. Raeburn H. and Alice (Lawrence) P.; m. Eleanor Sage, Mar. 3, 1951 (div. 1967); children: Katherine, Richard, Michael, Douglas (dec.); m. Regine Hawes, Nov. 15, 1994. BA, Yale U., 1949. With Morgan Stanley & Co., NYC, 1950—, ptnr., 1959-75, mng. dir., 1975-83, adv. dir., 1984—; pres. Morgan Stanley Can. Ltd., 1976-79, chmn., 1979-84, ret. Mem. adv. bd. on edn. and tng. Sec. Navy, 1985-87; dir. Jupiter (Fla.) Med. Ctr. Found., vice chmn., 2002—. Trustee Green Mountain Valley Sch., Waitsfield, Vt., 1981-91. Served with USMC, 1944-46. Mem. Investment Bankers Assn. Am. (bd. govs. 1966-70, pres. 1969), Nat. Assn. Securities Dealers (gov. 1981-84), Sublette County Hist. Soc. (trustee 1987-91), Blind Brook Club, Augusta (Ga.) Nat. Golf Club, Jupiter (Fla.) Island Club, Seminole Golf Club, Ekwanok Country Club. Home: One Angas Trail Hobe Sound FL 33455 Home Phone: 772-546-3818; Office Phone: 212-762-8865. E-mail: thepard@aol.com.

PARKER, H. WORTH, medical association administrator; MD, UNC, Chapel Hill, NC, 1975. Diplomate pulmonary internist Am Bd. Internal Medicine, 1984. Dir. grad. med. edn. Dartmouth Hitchcock Med. Ctr., Lebanon, NH, 1996—2008; dir. DHMC Dept. Medicine NH Cystic Fibrosis Ctr., Lebanon, 2003—. Chair instl. rev. com. Accreditation Coun. Grad. Med. Edn., Chgo., 2005—08. Recipient Robert Kerr Disting. Svc. award, NH. Lung Assn., 2006. Avocations: tennis, hiking, golf, hunting. Office: Dartmouth-Hitchcock Med Ctr 1 Med Ctr Dr Norwich VT 05055

PARKER, HARRY LEE, retired army officer, academic administrator; b. Birmingham, Ala., Feb. 20, 1944; s. Guy Milburn and Grace (Lee) P.; m. Sheri Lynn Pogue (div. Oct. 1973); children: John Lee, Suzanne Grace, Stephen Scott; m. Melanie Louise Cox, Apr. 20, 1979; 1 child, Christopher Robert. BA, Miss. State U., 1966; MS, Johns Hopkins U., 1980; postgrad., U.S. Army Command & Staff Coll, 1982. Commd. 2d lt. U.S. Army, 1966, advanced through grades to lt. col., 1967; maintenance officer 85th Maintenance Bn., Hanau, Germany, 1967—69; commanding officer 143d Engr. Co. and A Co. 34th Engr. Bn., Long Binh, Vietnam, 1969—70; chief plans and ops. divsn. Dir. Logistics, Ft. Rucker, Ala., 1971—73; supply and maintenance officer 97th Signal Bn. NATO, Mannehim, Germany, 1973—76; asst. materiel officer 8th Maintenance Bn., Grossalheim, Germany, 1977; tng. evaluator HQ 1st US Army, Ft. Meade, Md., 1978—81; logistics coord. Cuban Task Force, Ft. Indiantown Gap, Pa., 1980; project officer Dept. Def., Project Office Mobile Electric Power, Washington, 1982—85; exec. officer 193d Support Bn., Ft. Clayton, Panama, 1986—87; chief divsn. maintenance U.S. Army South, Ft. Corozol, Panama, 1987—88; prof. mil. Sci. Army ROTC Miss. State U., Starkville, 1988—90; ops. officer 101st area support group, Guardian City, Saudia Arabia, logistics officer, 1st Corps Support Command, XVIII Airborne Corps., Damman, Saudi Arabia, 1990—91; career/coop. edn. counselor Ctrl. Fla. C.C., Ocala, 1992—95; educator Seminole County Pub. Sch. Sys., Fla., 2000—02; asst. dir. office of vets. svcs. U. Ctrl. Fla., Orlando, 2003—, asst. registrar, 2004—. Elder Presbyn. Ch. Decorated Bronze Star with oak leaf cluster, Meritorious Svc. medal with two oak leaf clusters, Army Commendation medal with four oak leaf clusters. Mem. Mil. Officers Assn. Am. (life), Am. Legion, VFW(life) Presbyterian. Avocations: woodworking, scuba diving, boating, computers. Home: 5 Briggs Pond Way Sharon MA 02067-3009 Office Phone: 407-314-2753. Personal E-mail: hleepark@comcast.net.

PARKER, HENRY GRIFFITH, III, insurance executive; b. Plainfield, NJ, Oct. 27, 1926; s. Henry Griffith and Ruth Martin (Van Auken) P.; m. Audrey Lansing Turner, May 11, 1957; children: Henry Griffith, IV, Elizabeth Wright. AB, Princeton U., 1948; postgrad., U. Pa. Sch. Law. With Chubb & Son, Inc., 1949-97, v.p., 1968-70, sr. v.p., dir., 1971-92, mng. dir., 1986-92; cons. to chmn., 1992-97; v.p. Fed. Ins. Co., 1968-73, sr. v.p., 1973-91; v.p. Vigilant Ins. Co., 1966-91, mgr. internat. div., 1967-84; chmn. Parker Assocs., Madison, NJ, 1997—. Adv. bd. Firemark Global Ins. Fund II, L.P., 1997-2005, bd. dirs. Alliance Assurance Co. Am., NYC, Sun Ins. Office Am. Inc., NYC; mem. industry sector adv. com. on svcs. US Dept. Commerce, Washington; bd. dirs. Nat. Fgn. Trade Coun., chmn. declarations com., 1974-81, chmn. ins. com., 1976-81; chmn. internat. policy com. US C. of C., 1970-73; chmn. US del. XII-XIII-XX-XXII-XXII Hemispheric Ins. Conf., Chile, 1969, Paraguay, 1987, Panama, 1985, Buenos Aires, 1989; chmn. Internat. Ins. Adv. Coun., Washington, 1970-73, 85-90, chmn. Internat. Com. Am. Ins. Assn., 1991-93; mem. NJ Commn. on Internat. Trade, 1986—; chmn. bus. adv. com. bus. coun. UN, 1988—; mem. adv. bd. Liaison Office Peoples Ins. Co. China, 1986-94. Appeared on numerous TV and radio programs; contbr. articles to profl. jours. Chmn. bd. Overlook Hosp., Summit, NJ, 1973-80; trustee Drew U., Madison, 1974—. Lt. (j.g.) USNR, 1944-46. Recipient Internat. Ins. award US C. of C., 1981, Disting. Service award Internat. Ins. Council, 1988. Mem. Nat. Assn. Ins. Commrs. (chmn. internat. adv. com.), Am. Ins. Assn. (chmn. internat. com.), Downtown Assn. Club (NYC), Princeton Club (NYC),

River Club (NYC), Devon Yacht Club, Morris County (NJ) Golf Club, Hillsboro Club (Fla.), Psi Upsilon. Republican. Episcopalian. Office: Parker Assocs 38 East Ln Madison NJ 07940-2652

PARKER, HENRY HERBIN, humanities educator; s. Ben and Ray Parker; m. Marilyn Irene Crist, July 2, 1987; children: Alicia Erica Maya, Shauna Kay Crist. BA in English, magna cum laude, U. St. Thomas, St. Paul, 1956; MA in English, U. Minn., Mpls., 1958; PhD, U. Ill., Champaign-Urbana, 1977. Cert. hypnotherapist Ameriican Bd. Hypnotherapy, 2006. Prof. U. No. Iowa, Cedar Falls, 1965—90; prin., owner Parker Acad., Waterloo, Iowa, 1970—82, Parker Reading Co., Chgo., 1979—85; prof. modern fgn. language dept. U. No. Iowa, 1985—90; prof. dept. psychology and philosophy U. Tenn., Martin, 1990—95, dir. African Am. studies, 1995—, Cunningham disting. prof., 1998—2007. Nat. dir. curriculum operation push-excel Rev. Jesse Jackson, Chgo., 1979—80; pub. Parker Tribune Newspaper, Waterloo, Iowa, 1974—80; spkr. in field. Prodr.: (TV series) The Hank Parker Show, 1972—77; author (with Marilyn Crist): (book) Teaching Minorities to Play the Corporate Language Game, 1995, Apollo vs. Dionysus: A Philosophy to Increase College Success by 85%, 2001. Mem. com. ethnic, race and gender fairness Tenn. Supreme Ct., Nashville, 1995—98; bd. dirs. Gov. Bredesen's First Families, Nashville, 2004—07. Recipient George Washington Carver award, Simpson Coll., Iowa, 1977, Cert. of Appreciation, Tenn. Supreme Ct., 2000; fellow, Ford Found., 1969, Danforth Assoc., 1975. Mem.: African Am. Leadership Assn. (pres. 1995—2000). Avocations: hypnosis, classical music. Home: 139 Glenwood Dr Martin TN 38237 Office: Univ Tenn Martin 322 Humanities Martin TN 38237 Office Fax: 731-588-0388. Business E-Mail: hparker@utm.edu.

PARKER, IAN, science educator; m. Anne Tournay, June 30, 1985. PhD, U. London, 1973. Prof. U. Calif., Irvine, 1984—. Fellow, Royal Soc., London, 2008. Office: Univ Calif Irvine 1217 McGaugh Hall Irvine CA 92697

PARKER, IRA H., Internet company executive, lawyer; b. NYC, 1956; m. Jill Parker; children: David, Gregory. BA, Bklyn. Coll., City U. NY, 1978; JD, Emory U. Sch. Law, Atlanta, 1981. Asst. gen. counsel, litig. and policy FDIC, 1989—92, dep. gen. counsel, Resolution Trust Corp., 1992—93; ptnr. Alston & Bird, Washington, 1993—97; v.p., dep. gen. counsel GTE Corp., 1997—2000; v.p., gen. counsel Genuity Inc., 1997—2000, sr. v.p., gen. counsel, sec., 2000—03, pres., CEO, 2003; v.p., gen. counsel, corp. sec., chief compliance officer Polaroid Corp., 2004—06; exec. v.p. bus. develop., gen. counsel AOL LLC, Dulles, Va., 2006—. Office: AOL LLC 22000 AOL Way Dulles VA 20166 Office Phone: 703-265-1000. Office Fax: 703-433-7263.*

PARKER, JACK, men's college hockey coach; b. Somerville, Mass., Mar. 11, 1945; m. Jacqueline Gibson; children: Allison, Jacqueline. Grad., Boston U., 1968, LittD (hon.), 1997. Coach Medford HS Hockey Team; asst. coach Boston U. Terriers, 1969—72, head coach, 1973—. Head coach US Nat. Jr. Team, IIHF World Jr. Championships, 1996; former mem. NCAA Ice Hockey Com. Recipient Spencer Penrose Meml. Trophy, NCAA, 1975, 1978, 1978, Disting. Alum Award, Boston U., 1992; named New Eng. Coach of Yr., 1978, 1984, 1986, Hockey East Coach of Yr., 1986, 1992, 2000, 2005, 2006; named to Boston U. Athletic Hall of Fame, 1994, Beanpot Hall of Fame, 1995. Mem.: Am. Hockey Coaches Assn. (past pres.). Achievements include being the coach of NCAA National Championship Team, Boston University, 1978, 1995, 2009; being the Boston University Terrier's All-Time Winningest Coach. Office: Boston U Agganis Arena 925 Commonwealth Ave Boston MA 02215-1204*

PARKER, JAMES AUBREY, federal judge; b. Houston, Jan. 8, 1937; s. Lewis Almeron and Emily Helen (Stuessy) P.; m. Florence Fisher, Aug. 26, 1960; children: Roger Alan, Pamela Elizabeth. BA, Rice U., 1959; LLB, U. Tex., 1962. Bar: Tex. 1962, N.Mex. 1963. With Modrall, Sperling, Roehl, Harris & Sisk, Albuquerque, 1962-87; judge U.S. Dist. Ct. N.Mex., Albuquerque, 1987—2000, chief judge, 2000—03. Mem. Standing Comm. on Rules of Practice and Procedures of U.S. Cts., 1993-99, N.Mex. Commn. on Professionalism, 1986-2004; bd. vis. U. N.Mex. Law Sch., 1996-2004; bd. dirs. Fed. Jud. Ctr., 2004-2007. Articles editor Tex. Law Rev., 1961-62. Mem. Fed. Judges Assn., Am. Judicature Soc., Am. Bd. Trial Advocates, N.Mex. Bar Assn. (Outstanding Judge award 1994), Albuquerque Bar Assn. (Outstanding Judge award 1993, 00), Law Dragon 500 Leading Judges in Am. 2006, Nat. Assn. Criminal Def. Lawyers (Courageous Judiciary award 2001), Order of Coif, Chancellors, Phi Delta Phi. Avocations: ranching, fly fishing, skiing. Office: US Dist Ct 421 Gold S W 6th Fl Albuquerque NM 87102-2277 Mailing: PO Box 669 Albuquerque NM 87103 Office Phone: 505-348-2220. Office Fax: 505-348-2225. Business E-Mail: jparker@nmcourt.fed.us.

PARKER, JAMES FRANCIS, former air transportation executive, lawyer; b. San Antonio, Jan. 1, 1947; s. Raymond Francis and Libbie Olivia (Dusek) P.; m. Patricia Elaine Lorang, May 15, 1971; children: James, Jennifer. BA with hons., U. Tex., 1969, JD with hons., 1971. Bar: Tex., U.S. Dist. Ct. (ea., we., so. no. dists.) Tex., U.S. Ct. Appeals (5th and 11th cirs.), U.S. Supreme Ct. Law clk. to presiding judge U.S. Dist. Ct., Austin, Tex., 1972-76; asst. atty. gen. State of Tex., Austin, 1976-79; atty. Oppenheimer, Rosenberg, Kelleher & Wheatley, San Antonio, 1979-86; v.p., gen. counsel SW Airlines Co., Dallas, 1986—2001, vice chmn., CEO, 2001—04. Mem. ABA, Tex. Bar Assn. Democrat. Lutheran.

PARKER, JAMES JOHN, engineer, marketing professional; s. John J. and Marjorie (Grohmann) P.; m. Mary P. Nash, Oct. 21, 1972; children: Elizabeth Ann Parker Fahey, John James, Patricia Mary. BSEE, Marquette U., Milw., 1971; BSBA, Elmhurst Coll., Ill., 1982; MBA, U. Chgo., 1987. Student engr. Motorola Consumer Products, Franklin Park, Ill., 1968—70, engring. assoc., 1972—74; co-op engr. Warwick Electronics, Niles, 1971—72; sr. engr. R&D Quasar Electronics, Inc., Franklin Park, 1974—76; sr. project engr. Motorola Data Products, Carol Stream, 1978—79, Zenith Electronics Co., Glenview, 1979—82, mgr. market rsch., 1982—85, mgr. sect., 1985—86, mgr. program, 1988—95; mgr. displays Zenith Data Sys./Groupe Bull, Buffalo Grove, 1995—96; v.p. mktg. AVC Tech, Niles, 1996—97; mgr. product Visiontek, Gurnee, 1997; dir. product planning Telular, Inc., Vernon Hills, 1997—98; mgr. product mktg. Motorola BCS/SBNS, Schiller Park, 1998—2001; sr. cons. Pro-Team Cons., Palatine, 2001—03; dir. tech. Graphic Solutions Internat., Burr Ridge, Ill., 2003—06; sr. cons. Pro-Team Consulting, Palatine, Ill. Faculty Wright Jr. Coll., Chgo., 1975-80. Mem. editl. bd. Electronic Products Mag., 1976-77; contbr. to conf. and forums. Adviser Jr. Achievement, Chgo., 1972-78; treas. Immaculate Conception Parish Christian Svc. Commn., 1988-91; vol. Pub. Action to Deliver Shelter, 1987-2000; alderman 5th ward Elmhurst, 1993-2005; vice-chmn. fin. com. City of Elmhurst, 1995-2003, chmn. pub. works and bldg. com., 2003-05, vice-chmn. telecom. and tech. adv. group, 1997. Mem. IEEE Midcon. (vice-chmn. pub. rels. 1979, chmn. spl. exhibits 1981, vice-chmn. spl. exhibits 1983), Hon. Order Ky. Cols., Internat. Microelectronics and Packaging Soc., Tech. Assn. Graphic Arts, Delta Mu Delta (hon.) Roman Catholic. Avocations: ham radio, flying. Home: 421 Berkley Ave Elmhurst IL 60126-3706 Personal E-mail: jimparker@ameritech.net.

PARKER, JANET, language educator; BA, Wittenberg U., Springfield, Ohio, 1971; MA, U. Md., Coll. Pk., 1975. Fgn. lang. resource tchr. Montgomery County Pub. Schs., Bethesda, Md., 1997—2000, world lang. grant specialist, 2000—; instr. fgn. lang. edn. Coll. William & Mary, Williamsburg, Va., 2000—; coord., internat. baccalaureate primary yr. program James River Elem. Sch., Williamsburg, 2005—. Business E-Mail: jdpark@wm.edu.

PARKER, JEANETTE, psychology professor; married. PhD, Capella U., Mpls., 2005. Asst. prof., psychology Campbellsville U., Ky., 1997—. Recipient Academic Excellence Tchg. award, Campbellsville U., 2005. Office: Campbellsville Univ 1 Univ Dr Campbellsville KY 42718

PARKER, JEFF D., operations research specialist; s. Richard Bordeau and Jeanne Jaccard Parker; m. Nancy C. Belkov; children: Laila Belkov, Andrea Belkov. PhD, U. Wis., Madison, 1980. Software engr. Agile Networks, Boxborough, Mass., 1990—95; rsch. advisor Harvard U., Cambridge, Mass., 2008—. Home: 67 Lewis St Newton MA 02458

PARKER, JEFFREY SCOTT, law educator; b. Alexandria, Va., Sept. 6, 1952; s. Clarence Franklin and Mary Florence (Partlow) P. B in Indsl. Engring., Ga. Inst. Tech., 1975; JD, U. Va., 1978. Bar: N.Y. 1979, U.S. Dist. Ct. (ea. and so. dists.) N.Y. 1979, U.S. Ct. Appeals (3d cir.) 1981, U.S. Ct. Appeals (2d cir.) 1984, U.S. Supreme Ct. 1984, U.S. Ct. Appeals (fed. cir.) 1985, U.S. Ct. Appeals (4th cir.) 1992, U.S. Ct. Appeals (D.C. cir.) 1997. Assoc. Sullivan & Cromwell, NYC, 1978-86, Sacks Montgomery, NYC, 1986-87; dep. chief counsel U.S. Sentencing Commn., Washington, 1987-88; of counsel Sacks Montgomery, NYC, 1988-90; assoc. prof. law George Mason U Sch. Law, Arlington, Va., 1990-94; prof. George Mason U. Sch. Law, Arlington, Va., 1994—, assoc. dean acad. affairs, 1994-96. Cons. counsel U.S. Sentencing Commn., Washington, 1988-89. Contbr. articles to law revs.; mem. editorial bd. Va. Law Rev., 1976-78. Mem. ABA, Assn. of Bar of City of N.Y., N.Y. State Bar Assn., Am. Law and Econs. Assn., Am. Econs. Assn., Am. Judicature Soc. Office: George Mason U Sch of Law 3401 Fairfax Dr Arlington VA 22201-4411 E-mail: jparke3@gmu.edu.

PARKER, JEFFREY SCOTT, systems engineer, researcher; s. Richard Emmett and Bonnie Jean Parker; married. BA, Whitman Coll., Walla Walla, Wash., 2001; MS, U. Colo., Boulder, 2003, PhD, 2007. Spacecraft sys. engr. Jet Propulsion Lab., Pasadena, Calif., 2008—. Rschr. U. Colo., Boulder, 2007—. Mem.: Am. Inst. Aeronautics. Achievements include research in low energy trajectories between the earth and the moon. Avocations: mountain climbing, astronomy, travel. Office: Jet Propulsion Lab 4800 Oak Grove Dr Pasadena CA 91109 Personal E-mail: parkerjs@gmail.com.

PARKER, JOEL L., nursing administrator; d. Hattie Louise Williams and Joe Williams Jr.; children: Dannett Jenkins, Jewel. BS in Nursing, Tex. Christian U., Ft. Worth, 1977; MS in Human Resources, Golden Gate U., San Francisco, 1990; MS in Nursing Informatics, U. Md., Balt., 1999. Cert. operating room nurse, project mgmt. profl., in med. informatics. Relief charge nurse Surg. Intensive Care Unit Vets. Adminstrn. Hosp., Dallas, 1983—87; operating room staff nurse St. Joseph's Hosp., Ft. Worth, 1987—88; charge nurse Ear, Nose, Throat & Eye Surg. Svcs. Naval Hosp., Camp Lejeune, NC, 1988—91, charge nurse Post Anesthesia Care Unit & Gen. Surgery Svc. Okinawa, Japan, 1991—94; clin. coord., operating room Nat. Naval Med. Ctr., Bethesda, Md., 1994—97, dept. head Ambulatory Procedure Unit, 2005—06, asst. dir. profl. edn., 2006—; dept. head, oper. room Naval Hosp., Jacksonville, Fla., 1999—2003; dep. dir. program integrations Resources Info. Tech. Office, Falls Church, Va., 2003—04; dir. Centralized Credentials Quality Assurance Sys., Falls Church, Va., 2004—05. Vol. Habitat for Humanity, Jacksonville, IM Sultzbacher Children's Home; pres. ushers bd. First Bapt. Ch. of Mandarin, Jacksonville. Comdr. 2nd Fleet Surg. Svc. Group USN, 2003—05, Iraq. Decorated Navy/Marine Corps Achievement medal, Naval Officers Disting. Svc. award, Navy and Marine Corps Overseas Svc. ribbon, Global War on Terrorism Expeditionary medal, Navy Fleet Marine Force ribbon, Joint Meritorious Unit award, Navy Unit Commendation, Meritorious Unit Commendation, Nat. Def. Svc. medal; recipient Helping Hands award for cmty. svc., Alpha Kappa Alpha, 2002. Mem.: Wash. Area Navy Nurse Corps Coun., Assn. Operating Room Nurses, Nat. Naval Med. Ctr. Nurses Assn., Nat. Naval Officers Assn. (life; pres. 1995—97, Disting. Svc. award 1996), Sigma Theta Tau. Democrat. Baptist. Avocation: running. Personal E-mail: texjop@yahoo.com.

PARKER, JOHN CARLYLE, retired librarian and archivist, editor; b. Ogden, Utah, Oct. 14, 1931; s. Levi and Marietta (Parkinson) P.; m. Janet C. Greene, May 31, 1956; children: Denise, Nathan, Bret. BA, Brigham Young U., 1957; MLS, U. Calif., Berkeley, 1958. Cert. jr. coll. life credential, Calif. Spl. svcs. libr. Humboldt State U., 1958-60; cataloger, reference libr. Ch. Coll. Hawaii, 1960-62, acting libr., 1962-63; head Pub. svcs. Calif. State U. Libr., Stanislaus, 1963-68, head pub. svcs., asst. libr. dir., 1968-83, 84-90, acting libr. dir., 1983-84, univ. archivist, 1990-94, libr. and univ. archivist emeritus, 1994—. S ctr. reference svc. for genealogists and geneal. rsch. for genealogists, 1966-98; cons. Bailey's Moving and Storage Co., Allied Van Lines, Bountiful, Utah, 1983-85, Gale Rsch. Co., Detroit, 1986, 92, E & J Gallo Winery, Modesto, Calif., 1990; editor Marietta Pub. Co., 1985—. Author: Library Service for Genealogists, 1981, Going to Salt Lake City to Do Family History Research, 3d rev. and expanded edit., 1996; compiler numerous books, including Directory of Archivist and Librarian Genealogical Instructors, 2d edit., 1990, Rhode Island Biographical and Genealogical Sketch Index, 1991; contbr. articles and book revs. to profl. jours. Founder, vol. libr. Modesto Family History Ctr., 1968-90, Turlock (Calif.) Family History Ctr., 1990-97; chmn. Stanislaus County United Way campaign Calif. State U., Stanislaus Campus, 1980-81; sec. bd. dirs. Turlock Centennial Found., 1971-75; pres. Turlock Cmty. Concert Bd., 1973-75; trustee Turlock Libr., 1969-70; merit badge counselor Yosemite coun. Boy Scouts Am., 1973—. With U.S. Army, 1953-55. Fellow Utah Geneal. Assn., 1984. Mem. ALA (chmn. genealogy com. 1989-92, award reference and adult svcs. divsn., history sect.-Geneal. Pub. Co. award 1994), AAUP, Nat. Geneal. Soc. (award of merit 1984), Calif. Libr. Assn. (pres. Redwood dist. 1959-60, state coll. libns. divsn. 1969, chmn. geneal. librs. round table 1994, 96-97), Calif. State Geneal. Alliance (historian 1991—), Stanislaus County Hist. Soc. (v.p., program chmn. 1972-73), Geneal. Soc. Stanislaus County (founding mem. 1968-70, 1980-, hon.), Turlock Hist. Soc. Democrat. Me. LDS Ch. Avocations: birding, travel, singing solos and in choirs. Home: 2115 N Denair Ave Turlock CA 95382-1821

PARKER, JOHN HOWARD, educator; b. Jackson, Tenn., Feb. 23, 1946; m. Jill Roberson Parker; children: John Robert, Sharon Elizabeth. PhD, U. Tenn., Knoxville. Faculty Freed-hardeman U., Henderson, Tenn.; prof. Lipscomb U., Nashville, 1982—2008. Author: (non-fiction) Abide With Me: A Photographic Journey Through The Great British Hymns. Home: 829 Glenn Leven Dr Nashville TN 37204 Office: Lipscomb Univ University Oe Nashville TN 37204 Business E-Mail: john.parker@lipcomb.edu.

PARKER, JOHN R., JR., food products executive, lawyer; b. Anderson, S.C., 1951; BA, Univ. Ga.; JD, Univ. NC, 1973. Bar: Ga., US Ct. Appeals, 11th Cir. Atty. Coca-Cola Co., 1987—92; v.p., gen. counsel The Coca-Cola Bottling Co. of N.Y., 1992—95; counsel for Nordic and No. Eurasia Divsn. The Coca-Cola Co., 1995; gen. counsel. European group Coca-Cola Enterprises, 1996—99, sr. v.p., gen. counsel, 1999—2004, v.p., gen. mgr. west ctrl. region, 2004—05, sr. v.p. strategic initiatives, 2005—08, sr. v.p., gen. counsel, 2008—. Editor (articles): UNC Law Rev. Mem.: State Bar Ga., ABA, Order of the Coif. Office: Coca-Cola Enterprises 2500 Windy Ridge Pkwy Atlanta GA 30339*

PARKER, KAREN F., sociology educator; b. Monroe, NC, Apr. 6, 1967; d. Judy Draughon and Sammy Frank Parker; m. Aaron D. Griffin, Nov. 15, 1997. BA in Sociology, U. N.C., Wilmington, 1989; MS, N.C. State U., 1992, PhD, 1996. Asst. prof. sociology U. Fla., Gainesville, 1996—2001, assoc. prof. sociology, 2002—. Contbr. chpts. to books and articles to profl. jours. Mem. Am. Sociol. Assn., Am. Soc. Criminology, So. Sociol. Soc., Homicide Rsch. Working Group. Office: Univ Fla Criminology & Law Box 115950 Gainesville FL 32611-5950 Office Phone: 353-392-1025. Office Fax: 352-392-5065. E-mail: karenp@ufl.edu.

PARKER, KATHY P., dean, nursing educator; ADN, We. Ky. U., Bowling Green, 1970; BSN, Columbia U., NYC, 1973; MN, Emory U., Atlanta, 1977; PhD in Family and Cmty. Nursing, Ga. State U., Atlanta, 1990. Diplomate Am. Bd. Sleep Medicine, 2001; RN Ga., 1974, cert. adult nurse practitioner, Am. Nurses Credentialing Ctr., 1981, clin. nurse specialist, Am. Nurses Credentialing Ctr., 1982, in med./surg. nursing, Am. Nurses Credentialing Ctr., 1982; in French U. Paris Coll. Sorbonne, 1974. Staff nurse, charge nurse Columbia Presbyn. Med. Ctr., NYC, 1970—73; staff nurse Ga. Meml. Hosp., Atlanta, 1973—74; instr., advanced med./surg. nursing Ga. Bapt. Hosp. Sch. Nursing, Atlanta, 1974—76; head nurse, dialysis unit VA Med. Ctr., Atlanta, 1977—79; ops. officer, nurse practitioner nephrology Veterans Affairs Med. Ctr., Atlanta, 1979—87, clin. nurse specialist, nurse practitioner nephrology, 1989—93; rsch. asst. Ga. State U. Sch. Nursing, Atlanta, 1987—89; rsch. assoc. Emory U. Nell Woodruff Sch. Nursing, Atlanta, 1987—88, clin. track assoc. prof., 1989—93, assoc. prof., 1993—2003, tenured, 1998, prof., 2000—08, Edith F. Honeycutt endowed chair, 2003—08; nurse practitioner, Sleep Disorders Ctr. Emory U., Atlanta, 1993—2008, co-dir. Emory sleep program, dept. neurology, 2006—08; prof., dean U. Rochester Sch. Nursing, NY, 2008—. Cons. in field; vis. prof. U. Pitts. Renal Divsn. Contbr. articles to profl. jours. Recipient Disting. Alumni in Nursing award, Emory U., 2000; named Grad. Clin. Preceptor of Yr., Ga. State U., 1982; fellow, Woodruff Leadership Acad., 2003. Fellow: Am. Acad. Nursing, Am. Acad. Sleep Medicine; mem.: ANA, Am. Acad. Nurse Practitioners, Sleep Rsch. Soc., Am. Nephrology Nurses Assn. (Nephrology Nurse Rschr. award 2000), Ga. Nurses Assn., Sigma Theta Tau. Office: Univ Rochester Med Ctr Sch Nursing 601 Elmwood Ave Rochester NY 14627 Office Phone: 585-275-8902. Business E-Mail: kathy_parker@urmc.rochester.edu.*

PARKER, KEVIN JAMES, electrical engineer, educator, professor; BS in Engring. Sci. summa cum laude, SUNY, Buffalo, 1976; MSEE, MIT, 1978, PhD, 1981. Rsch. assoc. lab. for med. ultrasound MIT, Cambridge, 1977-81; asst. prof. dept. elec. engring. U. Rochester, NY, 1981-85, assoc. prof., 1985-91, assoc. prof. dept. radiology, 1989-91, prof., 1992—, chair, 1992-98, dean sch. engring. & applied scis., 1998—2008, William F. May Prof. Engring., 2005—. Com. mem. Internat. Symposium Ultrasound Imaging, 1989—; dir. Rochester Ctr. Biomedical Ultrasound, 1990—2006. Mem. editl. bd. Ultras. Med. Biology, 1989—; contbr. articles to profl. jours. Recipient Ultrasound Medicine and Biology prize, World Fed., 1991, Outstanding Innovation award, Eastman Kodak Co., 1991; named IBM Supercomputing Contest finalist, 1989; fellow, NIH, 1979; Lilly Tchg. fellow, 1982. Fellow: IEEE, Am. Inst. Ultrasound Medicine (ethics com. 1987—90, stds. com. 1990—93, bd. govs. 1996—99, Joseph P. Holmes Pioneer award 1999); mem.: Acoustical Soc. Achievements include patents in field of 13 patents, liscenced by several companies in field of engring. Office: Univ of Rochester Dept Elec and Computer Engring Hopeman Bldg Rm 203 Rochester NY 14627

PARKER, LEE BRYAN, retired physician; b. Dermott, Ark., May 10, 1929; s. Lee Bryan and Viola Lee Parker; m. Beverly Edith Brosell, Dec. 23, 1951; children: Susan Leigh Brewer, Elizabeth Ann Beecher, Steven Lee, Edith Lynn Hegwood. BS, U. Ark., Fayetteville, 1950; MD, U. Ark., Little Rock, 1954. Lic. physician Ark., 1954. Intern Crawford Long Hosp., Atlanta, 1954—55; pvt. practice Dermott, 1957—59, McGehee, Ark., 1959—67; gen. practice Doctor's Bldg., Fayetteville, Ark., 1967—74; dir. U. Ark. Med. Scis., Area Health Edn. Ctr. NW, Fayetteville, 1974—96; ret., 1996. Chief med. staff S.t Mary's Hosp., Dermott, 1964—65, McGehee Desha Hosp., Ark., 1965—67, Fayetteville City Hosp., 1975—76, Wash. Regional Med. Ctr., Fayetteville, 1980—81; vis. prof. Kaohsiung Med. U., Taiwan, 1986; bd. dirs. Ark. Regional Med. Program, Little Rock, 1967—70, Butterfield Trail Village, Fayetteville, 2001—06; dir. continuing med. edn. U. Ark. Sch. Medicine, Little Rock, 1970—74, adj. prof., 1996—; adv. bd. U. Ark. Sch. Medicine, Area Health Edn. Ctr. NW, Fayetteville, 2004—. Sec. Wash. County Med. Soc., Fayetteville, 1973—74. Capt. USAF, 1955—57. Recipient Disting. Svc. award, McGehee Jaycees, 1963, Distinguised Svc. award, U. Ark. for Med. Scis. Coll. Medicine, 1992, Founders Soc. award, U. Ark. for Med. Scis., 1996, Eagle award, Wash. Regional Med. Found., 1999, Diamond Soc. award, Ark. Cmty. Found., 2004, Doyne Soc. award, U. Ctrl. Ark., 2004, Legacy Soc. award, U. Ark. for Med. Scis., 2005. Mem.: Ark. Acad. Family Physicians (life; bd. dirs. 1962—67, chmn. continuing edn. com. 1971—89, pres. 1982—83, alt. del. 1984—89, Family Dr. of Yr. 1993), Ark. Med. Soc. (life; councilor 4th dist. 1965—67, jour. editor 1993). Independent. Methodist. Avocations: hunting, fishing, golf, gardening. Office: Univ Ark Med Sci 2907 E Joyce Fayetteville AR 72703

PARKER, LISA FREDERICK, music educator, Dalcroze specialist; b. NYC, Sept. 17, 1934; d. Karl Telford and Anne (Moore) Frederick; m. Dec. 24, 1966 (div. May, 1979); children: Eden Elizabeth, Wendy Margaret. BA cum laude, Smith Coll., 1956; M of Music in Conducting, New Eng. Conservatory, 1962; Diplôme, Inst. Jacque Dalcroze, Geneva, 1965. Instr. eurythmics, solfége New Eng. Conservatory, Boston, 1959-71; conductor NEC Youth Singers, Boston, 1965-71; dir. Dalcroze Program, Belmont (Mass.) Music Sch, 1970-77; chair Dalcroze dept. Longy Sch. of Music, Cambridge, 1977—. Mem. guest faculty Inst. Jaques Dalcroze, at internat. conf., 1974—; presenter at workshops internationally; tchr., 1999—; founder Boston Ctr. Osteophonie. Author: (children's skit) Curious George Goes to Music School, 1993—; contbr. articles to profl. jours. Recipient George Seamon award Excellence in Tchg., 2003. Mem. Dalcroze Soc. Am. (pres. 1972-75, editor jour.

1975-81), Nat. Music Tchrs. Assn., Dalcroze Soc. Can. Democrat. Episcopalian. Avocations: gardening, french language, travel, reading, chamber music. Office: Longy Sch of Music 1 Follen St Cambridge MA 02138-3599

PARKER, LYNDA CHRISTINE RYLANDER, secondary school educator; b. Bremerton, Wash., Apr. 21, 1949; d. Richard Algot and Marian Ethelyn (Peterson) Rylander; m. Joseph Hiram Parker, Feb. 7, 1981; 1 child, Joseph Hiram IV. BA in English, Sociology, Pacific Luth. U., 1971, MA in Ednl. Administrn., 1981, prin.'s credential, 1982, postgrad. Tchr. lang. arts Cen. Kitsap Schs., Silverdale, Wash., 1971-74; tchr. English gifted Okanagan Schs., Kelowna, B.C., Can., 1974-78; tchr. lang. arts gifted Federal Way (Wash.) Schs., 1978-86; tchr. lang. arts, remedial reading, humanities gifted Bethel Sch. Dist., Spanaway, Wash., 1986—. Counselor Okanagan Sch. Dist., Kelowna, 1974-78; advisor Ski Club, Cheerleaders, Svc. Club, Pep Club, Kitsap Schs., Silverdale, 1971-74, Cheerleaders, Pep Club, Svc. Club, Ski Club, annual, newspaper, class advisor, Okanagan Sch. Dist., Kelowna, 1974-78, newspaper, Cheerleaders, Bethel Schs., Spanaway, 1986—; multi-media, at-risk program, gifted program, video prodns., journalism, 1996-; presenter of workshops for parents, tchrs., adminstrs., 1988—. Named Christa McAuliffe Outstanding Tchr. of Yr. State of Wash., 1988, Walmart Tchr. of Yr., 2004, Bethel Sch. Dist. Tchr. of Yr., 2008; recipient Supts. Superior Svc. award, Beyhel Schs., 2007. Mem. NEA, ASCD, NAFE, Nat. Assn. Secondary Sch. Prins., Wash. Edn. Assn., Wash. Assn. Secondary Sch. Prins., Bethel Educators Assn. Republican. Lutheran. Avocations: piano, skiing, body building. Home: 1721 169th Street Ct S Spanaway WA 98387-9141 Personal E-mail: stefanlay@msn.com. E-mail: lparker@bethdsd.org.

PARKER, LYNDA MICHELE, psychiatrist; b. Sept. 28, 1947; d. Albert Francis and Dorothy Thomasina (Herriott) P. BA, C. W. Post Coll., 1968; MA, NYU, 1970; MD, Cornell U., 1974; postgrad., N.Y. Psychoanalytic Inst., 1977-82. Diplomate Am. Coll. Forensic Examiners. Intern N.Y. Hosp., NYC, 1975; resident in psychiatry Payne Whitney Clinic, NYC, 1975-78; psychiatrist-in-charge day program Cabrini Med. Ctr., NYC, 1978-79, attending psychiatrist, supr. psychiatry residents, 1978-96, supr. long-term psychotherapy, 1980-82; attending psychiatrist N.Y. Hosp., Cornell Med. Ctr., 1979-96; practice medicine specializing in psychiatry NYC, 1979-96; from instr. psychiatry to asst. prof. Cornell U. Med. Coll., 1979-96; instr. psychiatry N.Y. Med. Coll., 1978-96; assoc. prof., regional chair dept. psychiatry Tex. Tech. U. Health Scis. Ctr., Amarillo, 1996-99, No. region dir. correctional mental health scis., 1999—2002, clin. dir. PAMIO, 1999—2002; pvt. practice, 2002—. Assoc. prof. pharmacy practice in psychiatry Tex. Tech U. Sch. Pharmacy, 1996-99; psychiat. cons. Bldg. Service 32BJ Health Fund, 1983-89, Inwood House, N.Y.C., 1983-86, Time-Life Inc., 1986-96, Ind. Med. Examiners, 1986-96, Epilepsy Inst., 1986-87, asst. med. dir., 1987-88, med. dir., 1988; ind. med. examiner Rep. Health Care Rev. Sys. Mem. adv. bd. St. Bartholomew Community Presch., N.Y.C., 1990-96. Martin Luther King Jr. scholar, NYU, 1968—70. Mem.: AAUW, Tex. Med. Assn., Tex. Soc. for Psychiat. Physicians, Am. Womens Med. Assn., Am. Psychiat. Assn. Episcopalian. Office: 909 Scenic Meadow Cv Georgetown TX 78626-6371 Home Phone: 806-356-8824; Office Phone: 806-457-9200. Personal E-mail: LyParker@aol.com.

PARKER, LYNETTE, elementary school educator, secondary school educator; d. Henry and Rosilyn Parker. BA in Tech. Writing, Calif. State U., Long Beach, 1995; MA, NYU, NYC, 2003; MSc, U. No. Colo., Greeley, 2005. Tchr. Compton Unified Sch. Dist., Calif., 1995—2001; grad. asst., tutor Metro Ctr. Urban Edn., NY, 2002—03; grad. asst., rsch. cons. U. No. Colo., 2004—05; tchr. New Haven Unified, Union City, Calif., 2005—06, Hayward Unified Sch. Dist., Calif., 2006—. Grantee, U. No. Colo., 2005; fellow, U. Calif., LA, 1999, NY U., 2001—03; scholar, U. No. Colo., 2004—05. Mem.: Soc. Profl. Journalism. Personal E-mail: lp450@nyu.edu.

PARKER, MARIETTA, prosecutor; Asst. U.S. atty. US Dept. Justice, Kansas City, Mo., interim US atty. (we. dist.) Mo., 1993—, acting US atty. Dist. Kans. Witchita, 2008—. Office: US Attys Office 1200 Epic Ctr 301 N Main Wichita KS 67202 Office Phone: 316-269-6481.*

PARKER, MARK G., apparel executive; b. Poughkeepsie, NY; BS in Polit. Sci., Pa. State U., 1977. With Nike, Inc., 1979—, designer, devel. mgr. Exeter, NH, 1979—80, mgr. advanced product design, 1980—81, dir. design concepts & engring. Beaverton, Oreg., 1981—82, dir. footwear design, 1982—83, mgr. footware mktg., 1983—85, head, spl. design project teams, 1985—87, divsn. v.p. footware rsch., design and devel., 1987—88, corp. v.p. rsch. design & devel., 1988—93, v.p. consumer product mktg., 1993—98, v.p., gen. mgr. global footware, 1998—2001, pres. Nike Brand, 2001—06, pres., CEO, 2006—. Named one of The Most Influential People in the World of Sports, Bus. Week, 2007, 2008. Avocations: running, rock climbing, mountain biking, sailing, kayaking, drawing, painting, collecting art. Office: Nike Inc One Bowerman Dr Beaverton OR 97005-6453 Office Phone: 503-671-6453.

PARKER, MARY-LOUISE, actress; b. Ft. Jackson, SC, Aug. 2, 1964; 1 child, William Atticus. Attended, Bard Coll. Actress: (plays) Hay Fever, 1987, The Miser, 1988, The Art of Success, 1989, The Importance of Being Earnest, 1989, Prelude to a Kiss, Broadway, 1990-91 (Theatre World award, Clarence Derwent Award, Tony nomination, 1990), Babylon Gardens, 1991, How I Learned to Drive, 1997 (Lucille Lortel Award for outstanding actress, OBIE Award, 1997), Proof, Broadway (Tony award for best actress in a play, 2001), Dead Man's Cell Phone, 2008, Hedda Gabler, 2009; (films) Signs of Life, 1989, Longtime Companion, 1990, Grand Canyon, 1991, Fried Green Tomatoes, 1991, Mr. Wonderful, 1993, Naked in New York, 1994, The Client, 1994, Bullets Over Broadway, 1994, Boys on the Side, 1995, A Portrait of a Lady, 1996, Reckless, 1995, Murder in Mind, 1997, The Maker, 1997, Let the Devil Wear Black, 1998, Goodbye, Lover, 1998, Five Senses, 1999, Pipe Dream, 2002, Red Dragan, 2002, The Best Thief in the World, 2004, Saved!, 2004, Romance & Cigarettes, 2005, The Assassination of Jesse James by the Coward Robert Ford, 2007, The Spiderwick Chronicles, 2008; (TV movies) Too Young the Hero, 1988, A Place for Annie, 1994, Sugartime, 1995, Legalese, 1998, Saint Maybe, 1998, The Simple Life of Noah Dearborn, 1999, Cupid & Cate, 2000, Master Spy: The Robert Hanssen Story, 2002, Miracle Run, 2004, Vinegar Hill, 2005, The Robber Bride, 2007; (TV miniseries) Angels in America, 2003 (Golden Globe for best supporting actress 2004, Emmy award, Outstanding Supporting Actress in a Miniseries or a Movie, 2004); (TV series) Ryan's Hope, 1975, West Wing, 2001-05,(Emmy nomination, 2002), Weeds, 2005- (Best Performance by an Actress in a TV Series-Musical or Comedy, Hollywood Fgn. Press Assn. (Golden Globe award), 2006. Named one of Top 25 Entertainers of Yr., Entertainment Weekly, 2007. Office: William Morris Agy care Scott Henderson 151 S El Camino Dr Beverly Hills CA 90212-2775*

PARKER, MAURICE S., United States Ambassador to Swaziland; b. Calif. B, U. Calif., Berkeley; M, San Francisco State U. Fgn. svc. assignments US Dept. State, Guyana, Colombia, Scotland, Nigeria, prin. officer Barcelona, Ciudad Juarez, Mexico, dir. office employee rels. and fgn. svc. assignments, Bur. Human Resources Washington, US amb. to the Kingdom of Swaziland Mbabane, 2007—; dir. consular and internat. programs The White House Homeland Security Coun., Washington. Office: DOS Amb 2350 Mbabane Pl Washington DC 20521-2350*

PARKER, MEL, editor; b. NYC, Feb. 11, 1949; s. David Parker and Mollie (Kantorowicz) Lederman; m. Diane Nancy Goldberg, June 27, 1971; children: Emily, David. AB, Rutgers U., 1971; AM in English, NYU, 1973. Editl. rschr. Esquire Mag., NYC, 1973; grad. asst. NYU Dept. English, 1974-77; adj. lectr. CUNY, 1977-78; editor Leisure Books, NYC, 1978-81; sr. editor Playboy Paperbacks, NYC, 1981-82, Berkley Pub. Group, NYC, 1982-85, exec. editor, 1985-86, editor-in-chief, 1986-87; v.p. editor-in-chief Warner Paperbacks, 1987-90, pub., 1990-96; sr. v.p. Warner Books, NYC, 1996-98, sr. v.p., editor-in-chief Book-of-the-Month Club, 1999-2000; sr. v.p., editl. dir. Bookspan, 2000—03; pres. Mel Parker Books, LLC, 2004—. Co-chair exec. pub. com. United Jewish Appeal Fedn.; mem. faculty Stanford Pub. Course, 1997-98. Mem. Jerusalem Book Fair Com., 1997-99. Mem. Assn. Am. Publs. (chmn. trade exec. com. 1997-99), Book Table, Pub. Lunch Club (sec.-treas. 2000-01, v.p. 2001-02, pres. 2002-03). Office Phone: 718-788-0080. Business E-Mail: mel@melparkerbooks.com.

PARKER, MELISSA BERNICE, advertising executive; d. Marzine Parker, Sr. and Moretha Parker. BS in Agrl. Econs., U. Calif., Davis, 1995; MBA, Calif. State U., Hayward, 2000. Cert. notary pub. Calif., lic. Realtor Calif., property mgmt. Calif. Apt. Assn. Property mgr. M & M Parker & Assocs., Oakland, 1991—; banking officer Citibank F.S.B., San Francisco, 1995—96; sr. claims rep. Farmers Ins. Exch., Pleasanton, Calif., 1996—2000, Richmond, Calif., 1996—2000; applied materials Human Resources Exec. Program, Santa Clara, Calif., 2000; advt. exec. SBC Calif., Oakland, 2001—04, Valley Yellow Pages, Hayward, Calif., 2004—05, Hilltop Learning Corp., 2004—, Jack London Square Realty, Inc., 2005—. Photo journal dvd, Celebrations Article Oakland Tribune Marzine & Moretha Parker Sr. Co-chair Taylor Meml. United Meth. Ch. Ann. Woman's Day; with Marilyn Hickey Ministries; mem. U. Calif.-Davis. Mem.: NAFE. Office: 311 Oak St Ste 116 Oakland CA 94607 Personal E-mail: parkermel@aol.com, melissabparker@yahoo.com. Business E-Mail: melissa.parker@jacklondonrealty.com, mellisabparker@gmail.com.

PARKER, OLIVIA, photographer; b. Boston, June 10, 1941; d. Harvey Perley and Barbara Ellen (Churchill) Hood; m. John Otis Parker, Apr. 4, 1964; children: John Otis, Helen Elizabeth. BA, Wellesley Coll., 1963. Tchr. photog. workshops, 1975—. Photographer, 1969—; author: (monographs) Signs of Life, 1978, Under the Looking Glass, 1983, Weighing the Planets, 1987; portfolios of black and white photographs Ephemera, 1977, Lost Objects, 1980; one-woman shows include Vision Gallery, Boston, 1976, 1977, 1979, 1982, 1983, 1986, 1987, Friends of Photography, Carmel, Calif., 1979, 1981, Marcuse Pfeifer, N.Y.C., 1980, 1983, George Eastman House, Rochester, N.Y., 1981, Art Inst. Chgo., 1982, Photo Gallery Internat., Tokyo, 1983, 1984, 1987, Fotografie Forum Gallery, Frankfurt, Germany, 1985, Lieberman and Saul, N.Y.C., 1988, Mus. Photgraphic Arts, San Diego, 1988, Photographers' Gallery, London, 1990, Brent Sikkema, N.Y.C., 1990, 1991, Parco, Tokyo, 1991, ICAC/Weston, 1992, Vision, San Francisco, 1993, Robert Klein, Boston, 1993, 1996, 1999, 2005, 2009, Wooster Gardens, N.Y.C., 1996, (with Jerry Uelsmann) Isabella Stewart Gardner Mus., Boston, 1997, Huntington (W.Va.) Mus. of Art, 2000, Lancaster (Pa.) Mus. of Art, 2000, Toledo (Ohio) Art Mus., 2002, Visual Arts Ctr. Coll. of Santa Fe, 2003, Edelman Gallery, Chgo., 2004, exhibited in group shows at Mus. Fine Arts, Boston, 1978, 1992, 1993, 1996, 1999, Chgo. Art Inst., 1978, Internat. Ctr. Photography, N.Y.C., 1985, 1987, Fogg Art Mus. Harvard U., 1989, Aldrich Mus. Contemporary Art, 2004, Represented in permanent collections Mus. Modern Art, N.Y.C., Art Inst. Chgo., Boston Mus. Fine Arts, Victoria and Albert Mus., London, TV documentary, Africans in America, 1998. Trustee Art Inst. Boston, 1992—99; bd. dirs. MacDowell Colony, 1988—, Photographic Resource Ctr., 2008—. Recipient Wellesley College Alumnae Achievement award, 1996; Artists Found. fellow, 1978. Mem.: Soc. for Photog. Edn., Chilton Club. Office: Robert Klein 4th Fl 38 Newbury St Fl 4 Boston MA 02116-3210 E-mail: glasslight@mac.com. *I am interested in the way people think about the unknown. New ideas form, the old are shattered, and sometimes old ideas pop up among the new like graffiti on a wall. All is uncertainty and change, but optimists and bingo players are on the look out for moments of perfect knowledge and perfect cards.*

PARKER, PHYLLIS R., secondary school educator; b. Liberty, Tex., Feb. 9, 1947; d. Mark H. and Mary Jane (Stallworth) Richards; m. J. David Parker, Nov. 27, 1970; children: Anson D., J. Nealin, Laura A. BA, Baylor U., Waco, Tex., 1970; M of Pub. Affairs, U. Tex., Austin, 1976. Cert. tchr. Va. Daycare dir. Waco Home and Family Ctr., 1971; tchr., trainer Tex. Dept. Pub. Welfare, Austin, 1972—73, supr. contract devel., 1973; triage Emergency Rm. Group Health Hosp., Seattle, 1980—82; tchr. geography, art Rockbridge County HS, Lexington, Va., 1993—98, tchr. world history, 1998—; intern US Rep. Barbara Jordan, Washington, 1975. Child welfare caseworker Mo. Dept. Pub. Welfare, Jefferson City, 1967—69; dir. summer camp Iraqi Youth on Leadership and Democracy USAID/ACDI-VOCA, 2009. Author: Brazil and the Quiet Intervention, 1979. Coord. Geography Awareness Week Va. chpt. Nat. Geographic Soc., 1994; bd. dirs. Rockbridge Assn. for Retarded Citizens, 1986—93. Recipient Excellence in Tchg. award, US State Dept./Am. Coun. for Intermediate Edn., 2000, award, SAR, 2001; named Brit. Univs. Summer Scholar, Oxford U., 2007; fellow, Armonk Found., Germany, 1996, Keizai Koho Ctr., Japan, 1998, Korea Soc., 2002. Mem.: NEA, Va. Geographic Alliance. Avocations: painting, quilting, travel. Home: 22 Hillcrest Ln Lexington VA 24450 Office: Rockbridge County High Sch 143 Greenhouse Rd Lexington VA 24450 Office Phone: 540-463-5555. Business E-Mail: phyllis_parker@rockbridge.k12.va.us.

PARKER, PIPPIN, playwright, theater director; b. Athens, Ohio, Oct. 12, 1960; m. Kim Soden, Sept. 18, 1998; 1 child, Julius. Chair, dept. grad. playwrighting New Sch. Drama, New Sch. U., NYC, 2005—. Co-founder Naked Angels Theater Co., NYC, former artistic dir. Dir.(dramaturge): (play) Betrayed (Lucille Lortel Award, 2008). Elected coun. mem. Writers Guild Am., East, NYC, 2007—. Office: New Sch Drama 151 Bank St New York NY 10014 Business E-Mail: parkerp@newschool.edu.

PARKER, R. JOSEPH, lawyer; b. St. Louis, June 29, 1944; s. George Joseph and Ann Rosalie Parker; m. Theresa Gaynor, Aug. 26, 1967; children: Christa Michele, Kevin Blake. AB, Georgetown U., 1966; JD, Boston Coll., 1969. Bar: Ohio 1969. Law clk. to judge U.S. Ct. Appeals (6th Cir.), Akron, Ohio, 1969-70; assoc. Taft, Stettinius & Hollister, Cin., 1970-78, ptnr. Arbitrator Am. Arbitration Assn., Cin., 1980—; faculty Nat. Inst. for Trial Advocacy, 1990—; faculty advanced trial advocacy program IRS, 1993. Editor Law Rev. Ann. Survey Mass. Law, 1967-69; contbg. author: Fed. Civil Procedure Before Trial-6th Circuit. Bd. dirs. West End Health Ctr., Inc., Cin., 1972-76, Legal Aid Soc. Cin., 1982-85; chmn. bd. dirs. Vol. Lawyers for Poor Found., Cin., 1986-88; master Am. Inn of Court, 1984—. Fellow Am. Coll. Trial Lawyers; mem. Ohio State Bar Assn., Cin. Bar Assn., Cin. Country Club, Order of Coif. Democrat. Roman Catholic. Office: 425 Walnut St Ste 1800 Cincinnati OH 45202-3759 E-mail: parker18002000@yahoo.com.

PARKER, RICHARD DAVIES, law educator; b. Boston, Apr. 3, 1945; BA, Swarthmore Coll., 1967; JD, Harvard U., 1970. Bar: Mass. 1973. Law clk. to Judge J. Skelly Wright US Ct. Appeals (DC cir.), 1970—71; law clk. to Assoc. Justice Potter Stewart US Supreme Ct., 1971—72; atty. Children's Def. Fund., Cambridge, Mass., 1973—74; asst. prof. law Harvard Law Sch., 1974—79, prof., 1979—98, Paul W. Williams prof. criminal justice, 1998—. Author: The People Rule: A Constitutional Populist Manifesto, 1994. Office: Harvard Law Sch 1563 Massachusetts Ave Cambridge MA 02138 Office Phone: 617-495-7925. Office Fax: 617-496-4913. Business E-Mail: parker@law.harvard.edu.

PARKER, RICHARD WILSON, lawyer, retired rail transportation executive; b. Cleve., June 14, 1943; s. Edgar Gael and Pauline (Wilson) P.; m. Helen Margaret Shober, Jan. 3, 1998; children from previous marriage: Brian Jeffrey, Lauren Michelle, Lisa Christine. BA in Econs. cum laude, U. Redlands, 1965; JD cum laude, Northwestern U., 1968. Bar: Ohio 1968, Va. 1974. Assoc. Arter & Hadden, Cleve., 1968—71; asst. gen. atty. Norfolk & Western Ry. Co., Cleve. and Roanoke, Va., 1971-74, asst. gen. solicitor Roanoke, 1974-78, gen. atty., 1978-84, Norfolk So. Corp., 1985-88, sr. gen. atty., 1988-93, asst. v.p. real estate, 1993-99, v.p. properties, 1999-2000, v.p. real estate, 2000—03. Mem. ABA, Va. State Bar, Norfolk-Portsmouth Bar Assn. Presbyterian. Office: 3 Commercial Pl Norfolk VA 23510-2108

PARKER, ROBERT BROWN, writer; b. Springfield, Mass., Sept. 17, 1932; s. Carroll Snow and Mary Pauline (Murphy) Parker; m. Joan Hall, Aug. 26, 1956; children: David, Daniel. BA, Colby Coll., Waterville, Maine, 1954; MA in English Lit., Boston U., 1957, PhD in English Lit., 1971; LittD (hon.), Northeastern U., 1987. Various bus./advt. positions, NYC, Boston, 1956-62; lectr. Boston U., 1962-64; mem. faculty Lowell State Coll., Mass., 1964-66, Bridgewater State Coll., Mass., 1966-68; asst. prof. English Northeastern U., Boston, 1968-73, assoc. prof., 1973-76, prof., 1976-79; co-founder Pearl Prodns., Boston. Lectr. Suffolk U., Boston, 1965—66. Author: (novels) (Spenser series) The Godwulf Manuscript, 1973, God Save the Child, 1974, Mortal Stakes, 1975, Promised Land, 1976 (Edgar award for Best Novel, 1977), The Judas Goat, 1978, Looking for Rachel Wallace, 1980, Early Autumn, 1980, A Savage Place, 1981, Ceremony, 1982, The Widening Gyre, 1983, Valediction, 1984, A Catskill Eagle, 1985, Taming a Sea Horse, 1986, Pale Kings and Princes, 1987, Crimson Joy, 1988, Playmates, 1989, Stardust, 1990, Pastime, 1991, Double Deuce, 1992, Paper Doll, 1993, Walking Shadow, 1994, Thin Air, 1995, Chance, 1996, Small Vices, 1997, Sudden Mischief, 1998, Hush Money, 1999, Hugger Mugger, 2000, Potshot, 2001, Widow's Walk, 2002, Back Story, 2003, Bad Business, 2004, Cold Service, 2005, School Days, 2005, Hundred-Dollar Baby, 2006, Now and Then, 2007, Rough Weather, 2008, (Jesse Stone series) Night Passage, 1997, Trouble in Paradise, 1998, Death In Paradise, 2001, Stone Cold: A Jesse Stone Novel, 2003, Sea Change, 2006, High Profile, 2007, Stranger In Paradise, 2008, Night and Day, 2009, (Sunny Randall series) Family Honor, 1999, Perish Twice, 2000, Shrink Rap, 2002, Melancholy Baby, 2004, Blue Screen, 2006, Spare Change, 2007, (Philip Marlowe series) Poodle Springs, 1989, Perchance to Dream, 1991, (Everitt Hitch Westerns) Appaloosa, 2006, Resolution, 2008, (fiction) Wilderness, 1979, Love and Glory, 1980, All Our Yesterdays, 1994, Gunman's Rhapsody, 2001, Double Play, 2004, Edenville Owls, 2007, The Boxer and the Spy, 2008, (non-fiction) Sports Illustrated Training with Weights, 1974, Three Weeks in Spring, 1982, A Year At The Races, 1990, Spenser's Boston, 1994. Served with US Army, Korea. Recipient Gumshoe Lifetime Achievement award, 2008. Mem.: Writers Guild of America (Grand Master award 2002). Avocations: jogging, weightlifting. Office: care Putnam Publicity 375 Hudson St New York NY 10014*

PARKER, ROBERT M., JR., (BOB PARKER), wine critic, writer; b. Balt., July 23, 1947; m. Patricia Parker; 1 child, Maia. BA in History, U. Md., College Park; JD, U. Md., Balt., 1973. From sr. atty. to asst. gen. counsel Farm Credit Banks of Balt., 1973—84; founder, writer, pub. The Wine Advocate (formerly The Baltimore-Washington Wine Advocate), Parkton, Md., 1978—. Author Bordeaux, 1985 (Glenfiddich Award, 1986, Goldene Feder, 1993, Moët Hennessy Wine and Vine Comm. Award, 1993), 2nd edit., 1991 (Internat. Assn. of Cooking Profls. Award, 1992), 3rd edit., 1998, 4th edit., 2003, Parker's Wine Buyer's Guide, 1987, 2nd edit., 1989, 3rd edit., 1993, 4th edit., 1995, 5th edit., 1999, 6th edit., 2002, The Wines of the Rhone Valley and Provence, 1987 (Tastemaker's Award, 1989, Wine Guild's Wine Book of Yr. Award, 1989), Burgundy, 1990 (Moët Hennessy Wine and Vine Comm. Award, 1993), The Wines of the Rhone Valley, 1997, The World's Greatest Wine Estates: A Modern Perspective, 2005, contbg. editor Food and Wine Mag., contbr. The Field, wine critic L'Express mag., columnist BusinessWeek, 2006—. Named Marylander of Yr., Loyola Coll., 1992, Chevalier, Ordre Nat. du Merite, 1993, Légion d'honneur, 1999, Officer, 2005, Hon. Citizen of Châteauneuf-du-Pape, 1995, Wine and Spirits Profl. of 1997, James Beard Found., 1998, Comdr., Italy's Nat. Order of Merit, 2002. Office: The Wine Advocate PO Box 311 Monkton MD 21111 Office Phone: 410-329-6477. Office Fax: 410-357-4504. E-mail: wineadvocate@erobertparker.com.

PARKER, RONALD DEAN, environmental engineer; b. Waterloo, Iowa, Feb. 7, 1948; s. Lyle Robert and Ruth Eitemiller Parker; m. Renee Marie Smith, May 20, 1995; children: Benjamin William Nitti, Priya Narayan, Lauren Nadine Nitti. BS in Engring. Ops., Iowa State U., Ames, 1971, BS in Biology, 1971, MS in Civil & Environ. Engring., 1978; PhD in Watershed Hydrology, U. Ariz., Tucson, 1991. Environ. engr. Peace Corps., Yaounde, Cameroon, 1972—74, Trans Century Corp., Gaborone, Botswana, 1980—82, UN WHO, Male, Maldives, 1983—85, Jakarta, Indonesia, 1985—86, UN FAO, Rome, 2001—02; sr. environ. engr. US EPA, Washington, 1991—. Mem.: Am. Chem. Soc., Internat. Union Pure and Applied Chemistry, Chi Epsilon. Office Phone: 703-305-5505.

PARKER, SARAH ELIZABETH, state supreme court chief justice; b. Charlotte, NC, Aug. 23, 1942; d. Augustus and Zola Elizabeth (Smith) Parker. AB, U. NC, 1964, JD, 1969; LHD (hon.), Queens Coll., 1998. Bar: NC 1969, US Dist. Ct. (mid., ea. and we. dists.) NC. Vol. US Peace Corps, Ankara, Turkey, 1964-66; pvt. practice Charlotte, 1969-84; judge NC Ct. Appeals, Raleigh, 1985—92; assoc. justice Supreme Ct. NC, Raleigh, 1993—2005, chief justice, 2006—. Bd. visitors U. NC, Chapel Hill, 1993—97; pres. Mecklenburg County Dem. Women, Charlotte, 1973; NC ct. commr., 1999—; bd. dirs. YWCA, Charlotte, 1982—85. Recipient Woman of Achievement award, Nat. Fedn. Women's Clubs, 1997, Disting. Woman of NC award, 1997, Humanitarian award, NC Assn. Black County Officials, 2003; named Judge of Yr., NC Women Attorneys Assn., 2002. Mem.: ABA, Women Attys. Assn. (Gwyneth David Pub. Svc. award 1986), NC Internat. Women's Forum, Wake

County Bar Assn., NC Bar Assn. (v.p. 1987—88), Mecklenburg County Bar (sec.-treas. 1982—84), Inst. Jud. Adminstrn. Episcopalian. Office: NC Supreme Ct PO Box 1841 Raleigh NC 27602-1841*

PARKER, SARAH JESSICA, actress; b. Nelsonville, Ohio, Mar. 25, 1965; m. Matthew Broderick May 19, 1997; children: James Wilkie Broderick, Marion Loretta Elwell Broderick, Tabitha Hodge Broderick Launched fragrance Lovely perfume, 2005; designer, clothing line Bitten, 2007—. Actress: (theatre) The Innocents, 1976, The Sound of Music, 1977, Annie, 1978, The War Brides, 1981, The Death of a Miner, 1982, To Gillian on Her 37th Birthday, 1983, 84, Terry Neal's Future, 1986, The Heidi Chronicles, 1989, How to Succeed in Business Without Really Trying, 1996, Once Upon a Mattress, 1996, (films) Rich Kids, 1979, Somewhere Tomorrow, 1983, Firstborn, 1984, Footloose, 1984, Girls Just Want to Have Fun, 1985, Flight of the Navigator, 1986, L.A. Story, 1991, Honeymoon in Vegas, 1992, Hocus Pocus, 1993, Striking Distance, 1993, Ed Wood, 1994, Miami Rhapsody, 1995, If Lucy Fell, 1996, Mars Attacks!, 1996, The First Wives Club, 1996, Extreme Measures, 1996, 'Til There Was You, 1997, The Substance of Fire, 1996, (voice) A Life Apart: Hasidism in America, 1997, Isn't She Great, 1999, Dudley Do-Right, 1999, State and Main, 2000, Life Without Dick, 2001, Strangers with Candy, 2005, The Family Stone, 2005, Failure to Launch, 2006, Spinning Into Butter, 2007, Smart People, 2008, Sex and the City: The Movie, 2008; (TV movies) My Body, My Child, 1982, Going for the Gold: The Bill Johnson Story, 1985, A Year in the Life, 1986, The Room Upstairs, 1987, Dadah Is Death, 1988, The Ryan White Story, 1989, Twist of Fate, 1989, In the Best Interest of the Children, 1992, The Sunshine Boys, 1995, Sex and the Matrix, 2000, (TV series) Square Pegs, 1982-83, A Year in the Life, 1987-88, Equal Justice, 1990-91, Sex and the City, 1998-2004 (Best Supporting Actress Golden Globe award 1999, 2000, 01, 02, 04, Emmy nominee for Outstanding Lead Actress 1999-2002, Outstanding Performance by Female Actor in Comedy Series award 2001, Emmy award Outstanding Lead Actress in a Comedy Series, 2004), (TV pilots) The Alan King Show, 1986; guest appearances The Ben Stiller Show, 1992, The Larry Sanders Show, 1992, (video) Sesame Beginnings: Moving Together, 2007; co-exec. prodr. Sex and the City. Nat. amb. US Fund for UNICEF. Recipient, Am. Civil Liberties Union award, 1995, Vanguard award, ShoWest, 2008; named one of The 50 Most Powerful Women in NYC, NY Post, 2008, The 100 Most Powerful Celebrities, Forbes.com, 2008. Office: c/o Creative Artists Agy care Jane Berliner 9830 Wilshire Blvd Beverly Hills CA 90212-1804

PARKER, SASHA SMILKA, medical educator, nurse, consultant; b. Neustadt, Holstein, Germany, Nov. 3, 1947; arrived in US, 1952; d. Blagoje Blazo and Sofia Soka Dragic; life ptnr. Richard A. Polemeni; 1 child, Peter Joseph. Student, Ind. U., 1978; AS in Nursing, Broward CC, 1982. Lic. massage therapist Fla., cert. electrologist Fla.; RN Fla.; cert. facial specialist Fla. Asst. surg. adminstr. Am. Med. Inst. Surgery, Ft. Lauderdale, Fla., 1988—89; surg. adminstr. Eye Care & Surgery Ctr., Ft. Lauderdale, 1989—91; clin. supr. Spl. Care Home Health, 1991—97; pres., CEO Gem Homecare Svcs., Inc., Ft. Lauderdale, 1997—2005, Eclectic Skin Inst., LLC, Ft. Lauderdale, 1998—2003; pres., CEO, CFO Esthetic Skin Inst., Inc., 2003—. Cons. Innovative Health Svcs., Inc., Ft. Lauderdale, 1997—; faculty spa mgmt. and hospitality program U. Calif., Irvine, Calif. Vol. Women in Distress, Ft. Lauderdale, Adult Congregate Living Assn., Ft. Lauderdale. Recipient Spotlight Entrepreneur award, Nursing Spectrum, 2004; named Ultimate Nurse, Ultimate Nurses, Inc., 2004, Businesswoman of Yr., Nat. Rep. Congl. Com., Inc., 2004, 2005, 2006. Mem.: Am. Massage Therapy Assn., Nat. Bus. Adv. Coun., Fla. Electrology Assn., Fla. Nurses Assn., Assn. Med. Esthetic Nurses (pres., founder 2004). Avocations: dancing, travel, music, cooking. Office: Esthetic Skin Inst Inc 1120 S Fed Hwy Ste 4 Fort Lauderdale FL 33316 Office Fax: 954-463-4459. Personal E-mail: sashas@bellsouth.net.

PARKER, SCOTT BENSON, legislative staff member; b. Fairfax County, Va., Apr. 27, 1973; Grad., Brigham Young U. State legis. intern Utah House of Reps.; polit. dir. Utah Rep. Party, exec. dir.; campaign mgr. Office of Rob Bishop for Congress; adminstrv. asst. for Rob Bishop, US House of Reps., Washington, chief of staff, 2003—. Mormon. Avocations: sports, travel. Office: Office of Congressman Rob Bishop 123 Cannon House Office Bldg Washington DC 20515 Office Phone: 202-225-0453. E-mail: scott.parker@mail.house.gov.*

PARKER, STEPHEN G., linguist, consultant; b. Indpls., Oct. 23, 1958; s. Raymond Parker and Jeanne Ravaux; m. Monica V. Fajardo. AB, Ind. U., Bloomington, 1980; MA, U. Tex., Arlington, 1988; PhD, U. Mass., Amherst, 2002. Linguistic cons. Wycliffe Bible Translators, Huntington Beach, Calif., 1981—, Summer Inst. Linguistics, Huntington Beach, 1981—. Contbr. articles to numerous profl. jours. Doc. Dissertation Improvement grant, NSF, 2000. Home: 7500 W Camp Wisdom Rd Dallas TX 75236 Office Phone: 972-708-7692. Personal E-mail: steve-monica_parker@sil.org.

PARKER, TAMMY A., economics professor; m. Michael E. Parker, Nov. 27, 1999. PhD, Southern Ill. U., Carbondale. Prof. economics U. La., Monroe, 1997—. Office: Univ of La at Monroe 700 Univ Ave Monroe LA 71209 Business E-Mail: tparker@ulm.edu.

PARKER, THERESA ANN BOGGS, records manager, retired special education educator, retired music educator; b. Spencer, W.Va., Jan. 16, 1947; d. Harry Clay and Betty Jean (Richards) Boggs; m. Larry Glen Parker, Apr. 29, 1967; children: Carey Ann, Jill Renee, Timothy Preston, Jeremy David, Leanna Michelle. AA in Secretarial Studies, Glenville State Coll., 1967, BA in Music Edn., 1970; MA in Spl. Edn., Coll. Grad. Studies, 1991; EdS in Ednl. Leadership, W.Va. Grad. Coll., 1996. Cert. tchr. Pvt. practice piano tchr., Spencer, 1967—; sub. tchr. Roane County Schs., Spencer, 1970—71, tchr. spl. edn., 1987—2001, tchr. music K-8, 2001—02, tchr. spl. edn., 2002—06, tchr. music K-8, 2006—07, educator team mem.-parent/educator resource ctr., 1989—2002; sub. tchr. Marietta City Schs., Ohio, 1986; adminstr. Sand Hill Day Care Ctr., Reno, Ohio, 1986—87; founding mem. Roane County Cmmty. Band, 1999—; records mgr. Boggs Natural Car Co., Spencer, W.Va., 2008—. Spl. edn. rep. W.Va. Dept. Edn., Charleston, 1995-98; dir. Safetytown Roane County, Spencer, 1989-93. Author: (with others) Selected Teaching Models Integrated with West Virginia's Academic Model for Gifted Education, 1991; poet with works appearing in Echoes of Yesteryear, America at the Millennium, 2000, Enlightened Shadows, Miracles of Nature, Best Poems and Poets of 2001, The Road That Never Ends, Internat. Libr. Poetry. Chmn. Cub Scout Pack Boy Scouts Am., Reno, 1983-87, dist. trainer, Parkersburg, W.Va., 1986-87, chmn. Boy Scout Troop, Spencer, 1987-91; Roane County rep. to Clay Ctr. for Arts Charleston, 2005—; organizer First Bapt. Ch. Diabetes Sup. Group, 1995-98. Safetytown grantee W.Va. Dept. Edn., Roane County, 1989, grantee W.Va. Edn. Fund, Roane County, 1992, W.Va. Edn. Fund, Clover Sch., 1992, Diabetes Support Group grantee Benedium Found., Roane and Calhoun/Jackson Counties, 1995, Youth and Edn. grantee Tri-County Partnership, Inc., 1998, W.Va. Humanities Coun., 2000-01, 05, The Edn. Alliance, 2004, 05, Exceptional Tchg. Techniques award RESA V, 2005; named Tchr. of Yr. Spencer Middle Sch., 1999-2000. Mem. MENC, ASCD, W.Va. Profl. Educators, Blue Grass Riding Club, Lions (program chmn., pres. 1997-98, dist. Leo chmn. 1998-00, dist. Flag Day/Peace Poster contest 2000-2001), Roane Arts and Humanities Coun. (charter, pres. 2000—), W.Va. Celtic Soc., Cultural Diversity Soc. Democrat. Baptist. Avocations: reading, sewing, playing piano. Home: 5754 Charleston Rd Walton WV 25286 Office: Roane County Schs 102 Chapman Ave Spencer WV 25276

PARKER, TINA M., lawyer; b. Sheffield, Ala., Oct. 10, 1970; d. Jerry W. and Sue R. Miller. BS in English, U. N.Ala., Florence, 1989—93; JD, Birmingham U., Ala., 1998—2001. Bar: Ala. 2001, US Dist. Ct. (no., mid. and so. dists.), Ala. 2001. Owner, dir. Kid Safari, Inc., Muscle Shoals, Ala., 1995—96; atty. Carr Allison, Florence, 2002—05, Alvis & Willingham, LLP, Birmingham, 2005—06; mng. shareholder Berry-Parker Law Group, PC, Florence, 2006—. Contbr. to profl. jours. Cmty. edn. com. Ala. State Bar, Montgomery, 2004—. Mem.: ATLA (assoc.), Ala. Def. Lawyers Assn. R-Liberal. Baptist. Avocations: music, art, travel. Office: Tina M Parker PC 406 S Cedar St Florence AL 35630 Office Fax: 256-766-3124, 256-766-0459. Business E-Mail: tina@tplawgroup.com.

PARKER, TOM, state supreme court justice, lawyer; b. Montgomery, Ala., Aug. 19, 1951; s. Tom Parker and Gloria Parker Pennington; m. Dottie James. BA, Dartmouth Coll., 1973; JD, Vanderbilt U., 1978; attended, U. Sao Paulo Sch. of Law, Brazil. Prtnr. Parker & Kotouc; asst. atty. gen. State of Ala.; legal adviser, to Chief Justice Ala. Supreme Ct.; dep. administrative dir., gen. counsel Ala. Ct. System, 2001—03; assoc. justice Ala. Supreme Ct., 2004—. Former special projects mgr. Found. for Moral Law. Founding exec. dir. Ala. Family Alliance (now Alabama Policy Institute), Ala. Family Advocates. Grantee Rotary Internat. Fellowship, U. São Paulo Sch of Law, Brazil. Office: Ala Supreme Ct 300 Dexter Ave Montgomery AL 36104-3741*

PARKER, TONY (WILLIAM ANTHONY PARKER II), professional basketball player; b. Bruges, Belgium, May 17, 1982; s. Tony Parker and Pamela Firestone; m. Eva Longoria, July 7, 2007. Degree in Econ., Nat. Inst. Physical Edn., Paris. Guard San Antonio Spurs, 2001—. Mem. French Sr. Nat. Basketball Team, 2001—. Singer: (albums) Top of the Game, 2007. Recipient Bronze medal, European Championships, 2005; named Champion of French Champions, L'Equipe, 2003, Chevalier, French Legion of Honor, 2007, NBA Finals MVP, 2007; named to All-Rookie First Team, NBA, 2002, Western Conf. All-Star Team, 2006, 2007, 2009. Achievements include member of NBA Championship winning San Antonio Spurs, 2003, 2005, 2007. Office: San Antonio Spurs One SBC Ctr San Antonio TX 78219*

PARKER, TOWANA D., entrepreneur, director; d. John Richard Martin and Bernice Eason; m. Towana D. Parker, Sept. 25, 1976; children: Tanaya S., Yoshaundala S., Edmond II M., Gabriel T. Child Evangelism Metro Child Evangelism, 1985. Entrpreneur Special-T Uniform & Embroidery, Detroit, 1995—; pres. Ladies of Destiny and Purpose Internat., 1997—; exec. dir. Destiny and Purpose Cmty. Outreach, 1999—. TV host Public Report Host. Contbr. articles to profl. jours. Master puppeteer Kings Kids Puppet Ministry, Detroit, 1986—2004; mem. Detroit Exch. Club, 2004—. Grantee, Detroit Empowerment Zone Devel. Corp., 2002-2004, City of Detroit Neighborhood Opportunity Fund, 2004-2005. Office Fax: 313-533-1932; Home Fax: 313-535-8810. Personal E-mail: ladyteedp@aol.com. Business E-Mail: dapco7outreach@aol.com. E-mail: dapcol@sbcglobal.net.

PARKER, WALTER BRUCE, arctic research specialist, consultant; b. Spokane, Wash., Aug. 11, 1926; s. Bruce Velorus and Lucille Kathryn (Chessman) P.; m. Patricia Isabelle Ertman, Jan. 28, 1946; children: Sandra Wassilie, Patrick B., Jeffrey K., Douglas S., Lisa M. BA in History, U. Alaska, Fairbanks, 1964; DSc, U. Alaska, Anchorage, 1998. Air traffic controller FAA, 1946-64, evaluation officer Anchorage, 1964-66, analyst Washington, 1966-68, planner Anchorage, 1968-70; sr. planner Fed. Field Com. for Alaska, Anchorage, 1970-71; rsch. assoc. U. Alaska, Anchorage, 1971-74; commr. Alaska Dept. Hwys., Juneau, 1974-76; chmn. Alaska Fed./State Land Use Planning Commn., 1976-79; disting. practioner in residence U. Alaska, Anchorage, 1979-80; chmn. Alaska Oil Spill Commn., Anchorage, 1989-90; pres., cons. transp. and telecom. sys. Parker Assocs., Inc., Anchorage, 1971—; commr. U.S. Arctic Rsch. Commn., Anchorage, 1995—2001. Sr. fellow Inst. of the North, 2000—; mem. marine bd., com. on advances in pilotage and navigation NRC, 1991-94, North Pacific rsch. bd., 2000-04, Oil Spill Recovery Inst. bd., 1999-2004; chmn. Alaska Hazardous Substance Spill Coun., 1991-95; chmn. Arctic Coun. Circumpolar Infrastructure Task Force, 2000—. Author: Alaska and The Law of the Sea, 1974, Alaska People's and Alaska Lands, 1977; contbr. reports to profl. publs. Chmn. Alaska Conservation Soc., Anchorage, 1969-71, Alaska Humanties Forum, Anchorage, 1987-93, Anchorage Parks and Recreation Coun., 1971-74; active Alaska Bd. Fish and Game, Juneau, 1971-74; chmn. Prince William Sound Sci. Ctr., 1996-2004, chmn.; assemblyman Anchorage Borough, 1971-74. With USN, 1944-46. Mem. Am. Soc. Pub. Adminstrn. (chmn. Alaska chpt. 1971-73). Democrat. Avocations: skiing, dog mushing and breeding, gardening. Home: 3724 Campbell Airstrip Rd Anchorage AK 99504-4422 Office Phone: 907-343-2444. E-mail: wbparker@gci.net.

PARKER, WAYNE, JR., insurance company executive; m. Lisa Archer; 4 children. BA in Econs., Auburn U.; MA in Internat. Mgmt., Am. Grad. Sch. Internat. Mgmt. With Export Import Bank, Washington, Internat. Found., Washington; joined Hilb, Rogal and Hamilton, 1998; v.p. Insurance Office of America (IOA), 2003—. Bd. mem. Lincoln Village Preservation Corp., Devel. Coun. of Huntsville Hosp. Found. Republican. Presbyterian. Office: PO Box 16132 Huntsville AL 35802 Office Phone: 256-694-9100. E-mail: wayneparker08@gmail.com.*

PARKER, WILLIAM, education educator; b. Savannah, Ga., May 23, 1965; s. William Robert and Carolyn Parker; m. Maria Susanne Meza-Keuthen, Aug. 4, 1989. PhD, U. Nebr., 1992. Asst. prof. Duke U. Med. Ctr., Durham, NC, 1993—. Co-author: more than 90 sci. articles. Grantee, NIH. Mem.: Fedn. Am. Socs. for Exptl. Biology, Protein Soc., Sigma Xi Sci. Rsch. Soc., AAAS, Am. Soc. Transplant Surgeons, Am. Chem. Soc. Achievements include discovery of new model for host-bacterial interactions in the gut, the apparent function of the cecal appendix in humans and a variety of other mammals; new model for evaluation of the hygiene hypothesis; evidence for universal protein folding mechanism proposed by Valery Lim; new member of the family of antibodies that includes isohemagglutinins. Home: 1023 Wells St Durham NC 27707 Office: Duke Univ Med Ctr DUMC Box 2605 Durham NC 27710 Business E-Mail: bparker@duke.edu.

PARKER, WILLIAM HOWARD, obstetrician-gynecologist; b. NYC, 1948; BA, Rutgers U., 1970; MD, SUNY Downstate Med. Sch., 1974. Diplomate Am. Bd. Ob-Gyn; cert. Accreditation Coun. Gynecologic Endoscopy. Intern U. Calif.-San Diego Med. Ctr., 1974-75, resident in ob-gyn., 1975-78; tchg. faculty Houston Laser Inst., Tex., 1988—93; asst. clin. prof. UCLA Sch. Medicine, Calif., 1979—91, assoc. clin. prof. Calif., 1992—95, clin. prof. Calif., 1995—; vice-chmn., obstetrics and gynecology Santa Monica-UCLA Med. Ctr., Calif., 1985—91, chmn., gynecologic laser/pelviscopy subcommittee Calif., 1988—96, chmn., interdisciplinary advanced tech. com. Calif., 1990—96, chmn. dept. obstetrics and gynecology Calif., 1992—99, mem. exec. med. bd. Calif., 1992—99; vice-chmn., obstetrics and gynecology St. John's Hosp. and Health Ctr., Santa Monica, Calif., 2003—04, chmn., dept. obstetrics and gynecology, 2004—05, mem. med. exec. com., 2004—05; pvt. practice ob-gyn. Santa Monica, Calif., 1978—. Supervisong attending physician, Santa Monica Rape Treatment Ctr., 1990-2007; scientific program chmn., Global Congress of Gynecologic Endoscopy, 1999; med. cons. OBGYN.net; cons. Nat. Women's Health Resource Ctr., Women's Health Adv. Coun., Found. for Informed Med. Decision Making -Fibroids, Abdominal Bleeding-Benign Uterine Conditions, Women's Health and Hysterectomy Project, The Rand Corp., 1997; lectr. in field. Ad hoc reviewer Jour. Am. Assn. Gynecologic Laparoscopists, 1993—95, mem. editl. bd., 1995—96; editor: Jour. Am. Assn. Gynecologic Laparoscopists, 1997—2003; mem. editl. adv. bd. OB/GYN and Endoscopy News, 1995—96, ad hoc reviewer Obstetrics and Gynecology, 1992—, Jour. Gynecologic Techniques, 1994—, New England Jour. Medicine, 1996—, Fertility and Sterility, 1997—, reviewer Jour. Gynecologic Techniques & Am. Jour. Obstetrics and Gynecology, mem. editl. bd. Jour. Minimally Invasive Gynecology, 2003—05; editor: Jour. Minimally Invasive Gynecology, 2006—; author: A Gynecologist's Second Opinion: The Questions and Answers You Need to Take Charge of Your Health, 1996, A Gynecologist's Second Opinion: The Questions and Answers You Need to Take Charge of Your Health, 2nd edit., 2003; co-author (with Amy Rosenman): The Incontinence Solution: Answers for Women of All Ages, 2002; featured guest spkr. Lifetime Med. Network, Laparoscopic Ovarian Surgery, 1991, med. editor Lifetime Med. Network, Gynecologic Surgical Procedures, 1993. Named one of Best Doctors in Am.; named to Top Doctor's Book. Fellow ACOG; mem. AMA, Calif. Med. Assn., L.A. County Med. Assn., Am. Assn. Gynecological Laparoscopists (adv. bd. mem. 1994-95, bd. trustee, 1995-96, sec.-treas., 1998, v.p., 1999, pres. 2000), LES Angles Ob-Gyn Soc., 2009. Address: 1450 10th St Ste 404 Santa Monica CA 90401 Office Phone: 310-451-8144.

PARKERSON, GEORGE ROBERT, JR., medical educator; s. George Robert and Nettie Sue Parkerson; m. Mary McCowen, June 4, 1949 (dec. 2006); children: Sue, George Robert III, Ann Jones, Lyn Carpenter. MD, Duke U. Sch. Medicine, Durham, NC, 1953; MPH in Epidemiology, U. NC Sch. Pub. Health, Chapel Hill, 1977. Diplomate Am. Bd. Family Practice, 1984. Pvt. practice, Winder, Ga., 1955—73; dir. family practice residency program Med. Ctr. Ctrl. Ga., Macon, 1973—74. Asst. prof. family practice Med. Coll. Ga., Augusta, 1973—74; asst. prof. cmty. family medicine Duke U. Sch. Medicine, Durham, NC, 1974—80, assoc. prof. cmty. family medicine, 1980—88, chmn., 1985—94, prof., 1988—; adj. asst. prof. U. NC Sch. Pub. Health, 1978—83, adj. assoc. prof., 1983—89, adj. prof., 1989—; chmn. Instl. Rev. Bd. Clin. Investigations, Duke U. Health Sys., Durham, NC, 2000—. Contbr. scientific papers. Seaman first class USN, 1945—46, Bainbridge, Newport, Boston, destroyer duty on USS Robert L. Wilson. Mem.: North Am. Primary Care Rsch. Group, NC Acad. Family Physicians, Soc. Teachers Family Medicine, Am. Acad. Family Physicians (life). Office: Duke Univ Med Ctr Durham NC 27710

PARKES, JACQUELINE DALE, marketing executive; b. 1966; d. James C. and Margaret Parkes; m. Brian Dean Hendrix, Apr. 13, 1996. BA in English, Mount St. Mary's Coll., Emmitsburg, Md. Mktg. dir. Henson Muppets, Maj. League Baseball, NYC, 1995—2000, sr. dir. mktg., 2000—02, v.p., adv. mktg., 2002—04, sr. v.p., adv. mktg., 2004—08, sr. v.p., chief mktg. officer, 2008—. Mem. Maj. League Baseball in 21st Century. Named one of Forty under 40, Crain's NY Bus., 2004. Office: Maj League Baseball 245 Pk Ave 31st Fl New York NY 10167 Office Phone: 212-931-7800. Office Fax: 212-949-8636.*

PARKES, WALTER F., film company executive; b. Bakersfield, Calif. m. Laurie MacDonald; 2 children. AB in Anthropology, Yale U.; student, Grad. Sch. Comm., Stanford U. Pres. Amblin Entertainment, 1994; co-head, dir. motion pictures Dreamworks Pictures, 1995—. Prodr., dir.: (films) The California Reich, 1975 (nominated Acad. Award, spl. citation Cannes Film Festival); prodr.: Volunteers, 1985, True Believer, 1987, Awakenings, 1990 (nominated best picture, 1990), Men in Black, 1997, The Peace Maker, 1997, Gladiator, 2000, Artificial Intelligence, 2001; prodr.: (films) The Time Machine, 2002; prodr.: (films) Minority Report, 2002, Men in Black II, 2002, Road to Perdition, 2002, The Tuxedo, 2002, The Ring, 2002, Catch Me If You Can, 2002, The Terminal, 2004, Lemony Snicket's A Series of Unfortunate Events, 2004, The Ring Two, 2005, The Island, 2005, Just Like Heaven, 2005, The Legend of Zorro, 2005; prodr.: (films) The Lookout, 2007; exec. prodr.: (TV series) Birdland, 1994, Men in Black: The Series, 1997; (films) Littler Giants, 1994, Twister, 1996, The Trigger Effect, 1996, Amistad, 1997, Deep Impact, 1998, Small Soldiers, 1998, Mask of Zorro, 1998; writer: WarGames, 1983 (nominated best original screenplay, 1983); prodr., writer: (films) Sneakers, 1992 (nominated Acad. Award, spl. citation Cannes Film Festival). Named one of 50 Most Powerful People in Hollywood, Premiere mag., 2004—05. Office: DreamWorks SKG 1000 Flower St Glendale CA 91201 Office Phone: 818-733-7000. Office Fax: 818-695-7574.

PARKEY, ROBERT WAYNE, radiology and nuclear medicine educator, research radiologist; b. Dallas, July 17, 1938; s. Jack and Gloria Alfreda (Perry) P.; m. Nancy June Knox, Aug. 9, 1958; children: Wendell Wade, Robert Todd, Amy Elizabeth. BS in Physics, U. Tex., 1960; MD, S.W. Med. Sch., U. Tex., Dallas, 1965. Diplomate Am. Bd. Radiology, Am. Bd. Nuclear Medicine. Intern St. Paul Hosp., Dallas, 1965-66; resident in radiology U. Tex. Health Sci. Ctr., Dallas, 1966-69, asst. prof. radiology, 1970-74, assoc. prof., 1974-77, prof., chmn. dept. radiology, 1977—, Effie and Wofford Cain Disting. chair in diagnostic imaging, 1994—. Chief nuc. medicine Parkland Meml. Hosp., Dallas, 1974-79, chief dept. radiology, 1977—. Contbr. numerous chpts., articles and abstracts to profl. publs. Served as catp. M.C., Army N.G., 1965-72. NIH fellow Nat. Inst. Gen. Med. Sci., U. Mo., Columbia, 1969-70; Nat. Acad. Scis.-NRC scholar in radiol. rsch. James Picker Found., 1971-74. Fellow Am. Coll. Cardiology, Am. Coll. Radiology; mem. Am. Coll. Nuclear Physicians (charter, ho. of dels. 1974—), Coun. on Cardiovascular Radiology of Am. Heart Assn., AMA, Assn. Univ. Radiologists, Dallas County Med. Assn., Dallas Ft. Worth Radiol. Soc., Radiol. Soc. N.Am., Soc. Chmn. of Acad. Radiology Depts., Soc. Nuclear Medicine (acad. coun.), Tex. Med. Assn., Tex. Radiol. Soc., Sigma Xi, Alpha Omega Alpha. Achievements include Achievements include academic research on nuclear cardiology, development of new imaging technologies, medical education. Avocations: gardening, golf, tennis. Office: U Tex Southwestern Med Ctr Dept Radiology 5323 Harry Hines Blvd Dallas TX 75390-8896

PARKHURST, JACK LEE, theater educator; s. C.L. Lee and June Lee Parkhurst; children: Megan Lee Curtis, Shannon Lynn Conley. MFA in Directing, U. Nebr., Lincoln, 1987. Prof. Mo. State U., Springfield, Nebr. Wesleyan U., Lincoln, 1999—. Home: 5741 Culwells Rd Lincoln NE 68516

PARKHURST, TED A., publishing executive; b. Cadillac, Mich., Dec. 27, 1947; s. Ted Archie and Rose Mary (Flemming) Parkhurst; m. Elizabeth Smith, June 27, 1981; 1 child, Lucy Rose. Student, Harding U., Searcy, Ark.; BA in Hist., U. Ark., Little Rock, 1970. Pers. mgr. C. Finkbeiner, Inc., Little Rock, 1970-77; writer Little Rock, 1977-79; cons. writer Little Rock Sch. Dist., 1979-80; pres., founder August House Pubs., Inc., Little Rock, 1979—2006, Parkhurst Bros. Pubs., Inc., Little Rock, 2007—. Author: (children's lit.) What Giants Eat, 1979, The Get-Even Fairy, 1981; editor: A Fruitbowl of Rhinos, 1979. Active Vols. in Pub. Schs., Little Rock, 1982—; bd. dirs. Univ. Hist. Inst., Little Rock, 1988—96, v.p., 1991—92, pres., 1992—96; chair coun. on ministries 1st United Meth. Ch., Little Rock, 1988—89, chair bd. stewards, 1989—90. Recipient Disting. Svc. award, U. Ark. Coll. Arts, Humanities & Social Scis. Mem.: South Ctrl. Booksellers Assn. (v.p. 1991—93, bd. dirs.), SE Booksellers Assn. (bd. dirs. 1988—90), Pubs. Assn. of South (bd. dirs. 1985—86, v.p. 1986—87, pres. 1987—88, v.p. 1996—97). Avocations: reading, movies, watercolor. Office: Parkhurst Bros Pubs Inc 415 N McKinley St Ste 280J Little Rock AR 72205 Office Phone: 501-663-3551.*

PARKIN, FERN AGNES MARVEL, medical/surgical nurse, educator; b. Pocatello, Idaho, Nov. 22, 1931; d. Clarence J. and May Agnes Cuppett; m. Jesse James Marvel, Apr. 16, 1948 (div. Aug. 28, 1973); children: Alexa Ann Adams, Marco Lewis Marvel, Jill Lynn Osburn; m. William Heber Parkin, Jan. 4, 1991. AA, LA Harbor Coll., Wilmington, Calif., 1967; B in Vocat. Edn., Calif. State U., Long Beach, 1978. RN Calif., Idaho, Ariz., Wyoming, Wash., cert. adult cardiopulmonary resuscitation, Calif., coronary care. Staff nurse, clinic nurse Kaiser Found. Hosp., Harbor City, Calif., 1964—65, 1967—69; charge nurse Bishop Randal Hosp., Lander, Wyo., 1970, Needles Hosp., Calif., 1971, Icelandic Rest Home, Blaine, Wash., 1971—, Shuksans Nursing Home, Bellingham, Wash., 1971—72; nursing instr. LA Unified Sch. Dist., 1973—78; charge nurse Pacific Hosp., Long Beach, Calif., 1972—74; acting head nurse L.A. Harbor Gen. Hosp., Torrance, Calif., 1974—76; LVN nurse instr. YWCA Job Corp, LA, 1976—77; intensive care and coronary care nurse Profl. Nurses Bur., Long Beach, Calif., 1971—77; psychiatric facilitation instr. Atascadero State Hosp., Calif., 1979; dir. staff devel. Paso Robles Convalescent, Calif., 1987—88; welfare missionary Church of Jesus Christ of LDS, Ormoc, Cebu, Bohol, Philippines, 1988—90; charge nurse Twin Cities Convalescent Ctr., Templeton, Calif., 1990—92. Painted portraits, Pres. Aquina, Pres. Ronald Regan. Counselor relief soc. Ch. Jesus Christ LDS, Wilmington, 1973, mem. choir Pocatello, Idaho, 1969; pres. PTA, Idaho, 1962—63. Mem.: Alpha Gamma Sigma. Democrat. Mem. Lds Ch. Avocations: painting, writing, reading. Home: 200 N PO Box 220667 Centerfield UT 84622 Home Phone: 435-528-3529.

PARKIN, GERARD FRANCIS RALPH, chemistry educator, researcher; b. Middlesbrough, Cleveland, Eng., Feb. 15, 1959; s. Ralph and Clementine (Gill) P.; m. Rita K. Upmacis. BA with honors, Oxford U., Eng., 1981, MA, 1984, PhD, 1985. NATO/SERC (U.K.) postdoctoral rsch. fellow Calif. Inst. Tech., 1985-88; asst. prof. Columbia U., NYC, 1988-91, assoc. prof., 1991-94; prof., chmn. chemistry dept., 1994—; chmn. dept. chemistry, 1999—2002. Contbr. numerous articles to profl. jours. Recipient Camille and Henry Dreyfus Tchr.-Scholar award, 1991, award in pure chemistry Am. Chem. Soc., 1994, Corday Morgan medal Royal Soc. Chemistry, 1995, Organometallic Chemistry award, Am. Chem. Soc., 2004, 2008; A.P. Sloan rsch. fellow; NSF Presdl. faculty fellow, 1992—. Roman Catholic. Achievements include discovery that bond stretch isomerism in an artifact. Office: Columbia U 116th St And Broadway New York NY 10027

PARKIN, STUART STEPHEN PAPWORTH, materials scientist, physicist; IBM fellow IBM Almaden Rsch. Ctr., San Jose, Calif., 1983—. Recipient Internat. prize for new materials Am. Phys. Soc., 1994, C.V. Boys prize Inst. Physics, London, 1991, Inaugural Outstanding Young Investigator award Materials Rsch. Soc., 1991, Europhysics prize Hewlett-Packard, 1997, Indsl. Applications of Physics prize Am. Inst. Physics, 1999-2000, Humbboldt award, 2005; named Innovator of Yr., R&D Mag., 2001. Fellow AAAS, NAS, IEEE (Daniel Noble award, 2008, Disting. Lecturer award, 2008), Am. Phys. Soc., Royal Soc. London, Inst. Physics (London), MRS. Office: IBM Almaden Rsch Ctr 650 Harry Rd San Jose CA 95120-6099 Office Phone: 408-927-2390. E-mail: parkin@almaden.ibm.com.

PARKINS, FREDERICK MILTON, dental educator, dean; b. Princeton, NJ, Sept. 8, 1935; s. William Milton and Phyllis Virginia (Plyler) P.; m. Carolyn V. Rude; children: Bradford, Christopher, Eric. Student, Carleton Coll., 1953-56; D.D.S., U. Pa., 1960; MSD. in Pedodontics, U. N.C., Chapel Hill, 1965; PhD in Physiology, 1969. Instr. pedodontics U. N.C., 1965-67; asst. prof. pedodontics U. Pa., 1967-68, dir. Dental Aux. Utilization program, chmn. pedodontics, 1968-69; assoc. prof., head pedodontics U. Iowa, Iowa City, 1969-72, prof., head pedodontics, 1972-75; asst. dean acad. affairs U. Iowa (Coll. Dentistry), 1974-75, asso. dean acad. affairs, 1975-79, dir. continuing edn., 1975-77; prof. pedodontics, dean Sch. Dentistry, U. Louisville, 1979-85, prof. pediatric dentistry, 1985—2003, prof. pediatric dentistry emeritus, 2003—. Mem. Hillenbrand Fellowship adv. com. Am. Fund Dental Health, 1980-85; cons. Div. Dental Health USPHS, 1969-72; dental cons., med. staff Children's Hosp. Phila., 1968-71; med. staff Kosair Children's Hosp. Louisville, 1983—; cons., mem. pedodontic adv. com. Council Dental Edn., 1974-80, chmn. pedodontic adv. com., 1978-80, cons. council on legislation, 1978-79; dental cons. Aux. Utilization VA, 1968-69; cons. Bur. Health Resources Devel., 1974-76, Dept. Army, 1980-, numerous others Assoc. editor Jour. Preventive Dentistry, 1973-79, mem. editl. bd., 1980-83; editl. reviewer Jour. Pediatrics, 1969-, Jour. Dental Edn, 1978-, Jour. AMA, 1979-; assoc. editor Jour. Clin. Preventive Dentistry, 1979-84; mem. editl. bd. Jour. Clin. Laser Medicine and Surgery, 1999-; contbr. chpts. to textbooks, articles to profl. publs. Bd. govs. Youth Performing Arts Coun., Louisville-Jefferson County Sch. Dist., 1980-89, pres., 1986-88; bd. govs. Regional Cancer Ctr., U. Louisville, 1979-84, Univ. Hosp., 1979-84; mem. human studies com. U. Louisville, 1988-90. Robert Wood Johnson Congl. fellow Inst. of Medicine, 1977-78; USPHS postdoctoral fellow, 1963-67; NIH grantee, 1971-75; Recipient Earle Banks Hoyt Teaching award, 1969 Fellow AAAS, Am. Acad. Pediat. Dentistry (chmn. rsch. com. 1972-73, Ann. Rsch. award 1968, chmn. advanced edn. com. 1974-75, chmn. dental care programs com. 1978-80); mem. ADA, Am. Coll. Dentistry, Am. Soc. Dentistry for Children (exec. bd. Iowa unit 1969-75, award com. 1973-76, edn. com. 1974-77, chmn. rsch. adv. com. 1973-76), Biophys. Soc., Internat. Assn. Dental Rsch., N.Y. Acad. Dentistry, Ky. Dental Assn. (exec. bd. 1979-84), Am. Assn. Dental Schs. (coun. deans 1979-85, chmn. pedodontics sect. 1976, chmn. continuing edn. sect. 1979, legis. com. 1978-83), Louisville Dental Alumni Assn. (bd. govs. 1979-84), Am. Assn. Dental Rsch. (nat. affairs com. 1978-85), Acad. Laser Dentistry (co-chmn. rsch. and edn. 1997, chair 1998-2003, bd. dirs. 1997-2003, cert. com., T.H. Maiman award for excellence in dental laser rsch.), U.S. Power Squadron (bd. govs. 1987-93, sec. 1989, adminstrv. officer 1990, exec. officer 1991, comdr. 1992), Aircraft Owners and Pilots Assn., Omicron Kappa Upsilon (pres. Wa. chpt. 1991-92), Rotary. Unitarian Universalist. Home: 6424 Marina Dr Prospect KY 40059-8846 Office: U Louisville Sch Dentistry Dept Orth and Pediatric Dentistry Rm 240N Louisville KY 40292 Office Phone: 502-228-3389. Business E-Mail: fmpark01@louisville.edu.

PARKINSON, BRADFORD WELLS, astronautical engineer, educator; b. Madison, Wis., Feb. 16, 1935; s. Herbert and Metta Tisdale (Smith) P.; m. Virginia Pinkham Wier, Nov. 26, 1977; children: Leslie, Bradford II, Eric, Ian, Bruce, Jared Bradford. BS, U.S. Naval Acad., 1957; MS, MIT, 1961; PhD, Stanford U., 1966; grad. (disting.), USAF Command and Staff Coll., 1969, Naval War Coll., 1972. Commd. 2d lt. USAF, 1957, advanced through grades to col., 1972; divsn. chief AF Test Pilot Sch., 1966-68; chair dept. astronautics and computer sci. USAF Acad., 1969-71; dir. engring. ABRES, 1972; program mgr. NAVSTAR GPS, 1972-78; ret. USAF, 1978; prof. mech. engring. Colo. State U., Ft. Collins, 1978-79; v.p. advanced engring. Rockwell Internat., Downey, Calif., 1979-80; gen. mgr., v.p. Intermetrics, Inc., Cambridge, Mass., 1980-84; prof. emeritus, assoc. dir. gravity probe-B Stanford (Calif.) U., 1984—; CEO, pres. Trimble Navigation Ltd., 1998-99. Chair adv. coun. JPL NASA; dir. Trimble Navigation Ltd., Sunnyvale, Calif., NTV, Cambridge; past chair bd. dirs. Aerospace Corp., El Segundo, Calif. Decorated Def. Superior Svc. medal, AF Commendation medal with oak leaf cluster, Meritorius Svc. medal, Presdl. Unit citation, Bronze Star, Legion of Merit, Air medal with oak leaf cluster; recipient Pub. Svc. award, Disting. Pub. Svc. award, NASA, 1984, Thurlow award Inst. Navigation, 1986, Burka award, 1987, Kepler award, 1991, Aerospace Contbn. to Soc. award, 1991, Goddard medal, von Karman Lectureship AIAA, 1996, Magellan Premium, Am. Philos. Soc., 1997, Gold medal Space Tech. Hall of Fame of U.S. Space Found., 1998, Williams Space medal Soc. Logistics Engrs., 1996, ASME medal, 2004; named to National Inventors Hall of Fame, 2004. Fellow AIAA, Royal Inst. Navigation (Gold medal 1983), Inst. Navigation, IEEE (Kirchner award 1986, Pioneer award 1994, Sperry award 1999, Simon Remo medal); mem. AAS, NAE (councillor, Charles Stark Draper Prize, 2003), Internat. Acad. Astronautics, Sigma Xi, Tau Beta Pi. Avocations: hiking, skiing, sailing. Office: Stanford U 4085 Mail Code Stanford CA 94305 Home: 2360 Camino Edna San Luis Obispo CA 93401

PARKINSON, JAMES THOMAS, III, investment consultant; b. Richmond, Va., July 10, 1940; s. James Thomas and Elizabeth (Hopkins) P.; m. Molly O. Owens, June 16, 1962 (div. June 1998); children: James Thomas, Glenn Walser; m. Caroline Smith Pyle, Oct. 10, 1998. BA, U. Va., 1962; MBA, U. Pa., 1964. Trainee Chem. Bank, NYC, 1964—66; assoc., corp. fin. dept. Blyth & Co., Inc., NYC, 1968—69; v.p., corp. fin. dept. Clark Dodge & Co., Inc., NYC, 1969—72; pvt. practice investment mgmt. NYC, 1972—85, Va., 1987—; v.p. Pleasantville Advisors, Inc., NYC, 1986—87. Instr. corp. fin. Ind. U., 1966-68; bd. dirs. Bowles Fluidics Corp. Sr. warden Ch. of Holy Trinity, NYC, 1978-79; trustee Am. Bible Soc., 1980—, vice chair bd. trustees, 2006-; trustee Funds, Episcopal Diocese of Va., 2000-06, 2008-, Diocesan Missionary Soc., 2006—, Mus. Bibl. Art, NYC, 2005-06. With AUS, 1966-68. Mem. Univ. Club (N.Y.C.), Va. Country Club. Republican. Episcopalian. Home and Office: PO Box 2247 Middleburg VA 20118-2247

PARKINSON, MARK VINCENT, Governor of Kansas; b. Wichita, Kans., June 24, 1957; s. Henry Filson and Barbara Ann (Gilbert) Horton; m. Stacy Abbott Parkinson, Mar. 7, 1983; children: Alex Atticus, Sam Filson, Kit Harlan. BA in Edn., Wichita State U., 1980; JD, Kans. U., 1984. Assoc. Payne and Jones Law Firm, Olathe, Kans., 1984-86; ptnr. Parkinson, Foth & Reynolds, Lenexa, Kans., 1986—96; mem. Kans. House Reps., 1990-92, Kans. State Senate, 1993-97; chmn. Kans. Rep. Party, 1999—2003; lt. gov. State of Kans., Topeka, 2007—09, gov., 2009—. Mem. ABA, Johnson County Bar Found. (pres. 1993—), Kans. Bar Assn. Democrat. Avocations: travel, running, movies. Office: Office of the Governor State Capitol 2nd Fl Topeka KS 66612 Office Phone: 785-296-3232. Office Fax: 785-296-7973.*

PARKINSON, REBECCA, music educator; d. Albert Monson and Melba Mae Parkinson. MusB, Utah State U., Logan, 1986. Tchr. Brigham Young U.-Idaho, Rexburg, Idaho, 1987—. Mem.: Am. Guild Organists.

PARKINSON, ROBERT L., JR., medical products executive, health facility administrator; BBA, MBA, Loyola U., Chgo. With Abbott Labs., Abbott Park, Ill., 1976, v.p. European ops., 1990-93, sr. v.p. chem. and agrl. products, 1993-95, pres. internat. divsn., 1995-98, bd. dirs., 1998, pres., COO, 1999-2001; dean Loyola U. Chgo.'s Sch. of Bus. Adminstrn. and Grad. Sch. of Bus., 2002—04; chmn., pres., CEO Baxter Internat., Inc., 2004—. Chmn. Geneva (Switzerland) Proteomics, 2001; bd. trustees Healthcare Leadership Coun. Bd. dirs. Northwestern Mem. Hosp., Northwestern Mem. Found. Office: Baxter Internat Inc One Baxter Pkwy Deerfield IL 60015 Office Phone: 847-948-2000.*

PARKINSON, WILLIAM CHARLES, physics professor, researcher; b. Jarvis, Ont., Can., Feb. 11, 1918; came to U.S., 1925, naturalized, 1941; s. Charles Franklin and Euphemia Alice (Johnston) P.; m. Martha Bennett Capron, Aug. 2, 1944; children: Martha Reed, William Reid. BSE, U. Mich., 1940, MS, 1941, PhD, 1948. Physicist Applied Physics Lab., Johns Hopkins U., 1942-46, OSRD, 1943-44; mem. faculty U. Mich., 1947—, prof. physics, 1958-88, prof. emeritus physics, 1988—, dir. cyclotron lab., 1962-77; mem. subcom. nuclear structure NRC, 1959-68; mem. nuclear physics sub panel mgmt. and costs nuclear program, 1969-70; adv. panel physics NSF, 1966-69. Cons. grad. sci. facilities, 1968, chmn. postdoctoral fellowship evaluation panel, 1969, cons. to govt. and industry, 1955— Quondam mem. Trinity Coll., Cambridge, Eng. Recipient Ordnance Devel. award Navy Dept., 1946; Fulbright research scholar Cavendish Lab., Cambridge U., 1952-53 Fellow Am. Phys. Soc.; mem. N.Y. Acad. Scis., Biophys. Soc., Grad. "M" Club (awarded hon. "M" 1991), Flounders Water Polo, Sigma Xi, Phi Kappa Phi, Kappa Kappa Psi. Achievements include invention of automatic judging and timing for swim meets, fast neutron spectroscopy using cyclotrons; development of high resolution nuclear spectroscopy with cyclotrons. Home: 1600 Sheridan Dr Ann Arbor MI 48104-4052 Office: Univ Mich Dept Physics Ann Arbor MI 48109 Office Phone: 734-764-3458. Business E-Mail: wcpark@umich.edu.

PARKINSON, WILLIAM WOODALL, theater educator; b. Salt Lake City, Aug. 18, 1948; BS, U. Utah, Salt Lake City, 1972. Prof., dept. theater U. Utah, 1974—2008. Office: Univ Utah Theater Dept Salt Lake City UT 84112

PARKS, A. LAURISTON, lawyer; b. Providence, July 18, 1935; s. Albert Lauriston and Dorothy Isabel (Arnold) Parks; m. Martha Ann Anderson, Jan. 12, 1961; children: Amy Woodward, George Webster, Reed Anderson. BA, Kent State U., 1958; JD, U. Chgo., 1961. Bar: R.I. 1962, U.S. Dist. Ct. R.I. 1963, U.S. Ct. Appeals (1st cir.) 1966, U.S. Supreme Ct. 1980. Assoc. Hanson, Curran, Parks & Whitman, Providence, 1961-65, ptnr., 1966-2000. Town solicitor No. Kingstown, RI, 1978—80, RI, 1997—2006, Jamestown, 1999—2000, 2003—07. Fellow: Am. Coll. Trial Lawyers; mem.: ABA, R.I. Bar Assn., Maritime Law Assn., Wickford Yacht Club, Saunderstown Yacht Club. Republican. Episcopalian. Office: 53 Narragansett Ave Jamestown RI 02835 Home: 14 Church Ln North Kingstown RI 02852-5004 Office Phone: 401-423-8900. E-mail: alp@alparks.net.

PARKS, ARVA MOORE, historian; b. Miami, Fla., Jan. 19, 1939; d. Jack and Anne (Parker) Moore; m. Robert Lyle Parks, Aug. 19, 1959 (div. May 1986); children: Jacqueline Carey, Robert Downing, Gregory Moore; m. Robert Howard McCabe, June 20, 1992. Student, Fla. State U., 1956-58; BA, U. Fla., 1960; MA in History, U. Miami, Coral Gables, 1971; LLD (hon.), Barry U., 1996. Tchr. Rolling Crest Jr. H.S., West Hyattsville, Md., 1960-63, Miami Edison Sr. H.S., Fla., 1963-64; grad. asst. U. Miami, Coral Gables, 1964-65; tchr. Everglades Sch. for Girls, Miami, 1965-66; cons., 1966-70; free-lance rsch. historian Miami, 1970-86; adj. prof. U. Miami, Coral Gables, 1986-87; pres. Arva Parks & Co., Miami, 1986—. Cons. thematic and interpretive rsch. and design Harry S. Truman Little White House, Key West, Fla., 1989-91; pres. Centennial Press, 1991—. Author: Miami the Magic City, 1981, rev. edit., 1991, 2008, The Forgotten Frontier, 1977 (rev. edit. 2004), Harry Truman and the Little White House in Key West, 1991, Miami: Then and Now, 1992, The Pathway to Greatness, 2001; co-author: (with Gregory M. Bush) Miami: The American Crossroad, 1996, (with Carolyn Klepser) Miami Then & Now, 2002, George Merrick's Coral Gables, 2006; exhbn. include Coral Gables Mus., 2007-; editor Tequesta Jour. Hist. Soc. Fla., 1986-95; writer: (film) Our Miami: The Magic City, 1994. Bd. advs., Nat. Trust Hist. Preservation, 1984-93, chmn. so. region, 1990-91, Fed. Adv. Coun. Hist. Preservation, 1995-2003; trustee Miami-Dade Coll., 1984-90, U. Miami, 1994—; bd. dirs. Louis Wolfson Media History Ctr., Miami, 1985-90, Orange Bowl Com., 1989—, Bapt. Health Systems of Miami, Inc., 1992—2008, Dade Found., 1997-2004, Drs. Hosp. Bd., 2004—08; cmty. adv. Dade Heritage Trust, Miami, 1988-97, mem. Bi-Racial Tri-Ethnic Adv. Bd., Miami, 1984-99, New World Sch. Arts (exec. com.), Miami, 1986-90, Bok Sanctuary Bd., 2005—, City of Coral Gables Mus. Bd., 2005-; chmn. Vizcaya Trust, 1998-2004, pres. Fla. Forum, 2003-05; chair City of Miami Planning Adv. Bd., 2005—09. Recipient Historic Preservation award AIA, 1993, Outstanding Women of History award Cuban Am. Women's Club, 1992, Women Helping Women award Soroptimists, 1992, Am. History award DAR, 1987, Pathfinder's award Women's Com. 100, 1985, Outstanding Citizen award Coral Gables C. of C., 1983, Outstanding Preservationist award Dade Heritage Trust, 1983, Good Faith award Black Archives and Rsch. Found., 1981, Mus. of Sci. award, 1981, Cmty. Headliner award Women in Comm., 1980, Humanitarian award Urban League Guild, 1980, award City of Coral Gables Hist. Preservation Bd., 1978, Women of Impact award Cmty. Coalition for Women's History, 1996, Cmty. Star award Family Counseling Svcs. of Greater Miami, 1996, Edward T. Foote Alumnae of Distinction award U. Miami, 2002, Henriette Harris award Dade Heritage Trust, 2004, George Merrich award, Coral Gables Chamber Commerce, 2008; named to Alumni Hall of Fame Dade County Pub. Schs., 1985, Fla. Women's Hall of Fame, 1986, one of Women Who Made a Difference YWCA, 1988, City Miami Women's Hall Fame, 1996, Woman of Distinction award Soroptimist Internat. of Ams., Woman of Distinction award Girl Scouts Am., 1996, Alumni Women Distinction U. Fla., 1997, Tebeau prize Fla. Hist. Soc. for Am. Crossroad, 1997, Theodore Gibson Unity award, 1999, Vizcayans Cultural Millennium award, 1999, Miami Herald Spirit of Excellence award, 1999, George Merrick Scirity Excellence award, Coral Salites C. of C., 2008, Joseph R. Narot Cmty. Svc. award, 2003, Olympian award Olympia Theater at Gusman Ctr., 2006, Julia Tuttle award Commn. on the Status of Women, City of Miami, 2006, Carolina O. Rossetter Outstanding Woman Fla. History, Fla. Historical Soc., 2008, Historian Of Year, Miami Woman's Club, 2009, Chmn. award, Red Cross Rosiland R. Luduig, 2009, Historic Pres. Carl Weinhard Lifetime Achievement award, 2009. Mem. Internat. Women's Forum (found. pres., 2001-05, pres. Fla. chpt. 2003-05, bd. dirs. Fla. chpt. 2005-), Jr. League. Democrat. Methodist. Avocation: photography. Home and Office: 1601 S Miami Ave Miami FL 33129-1103 Office Phone: 305-854-8087. Personal E-mail: arvamiami@bellsouth.net.

PARKS, BERNARD, councilman; s. Earl W. Parks; m. Bobbie Parks; children: Felicia, Michelle, Trudy, Bernard Jr. BS, Pepperdine U.; MPA, U. Southern Calif. Police officer LA Police Dept., police chief, 1997—2002; councilman, Dist. 8 LA City Coun., 2003—. Coach Baldwin Hills Youth Football. NAACP (life); Challengers Boys & Girls Club; LA Urban League; Brotherhood Crusade; Civil Rights Walk of Fame, Atlanta, Ga. Office: 200 N Spring St Rm 460 Los Angeles CA 90012 Office Phone: 213-473-7008. Office Fax: 213-485-7683. E-mail: councilmember.parks@lacity.org.*

PARKS, BETH, physics professor; b. Huntsville, Ala., May 28, 1966; PhD, U. Calif., Berkeley, 1995. Postdoc. rschr. MIT, Cambridge, 1995—97; asst. prof. physics Colgate U., Hamilton, NY, 1997—2003, assoc. prof. physics, 2003—. Office: Colgate Univ Physics Dept 13 Oak Dr Hamilton NY 13346

PARKS, D. GENE, gynecologist; b. Vinita, Okla., Mar. 12, 1946; s. Norman Fred and Esther Viola Parks; m. Jane Marie Guth, Dec. 24, 1985; children: John Norman, Jaclyn Ann. BS, Okla. State U., Stillwater, 1968; MD, U. Okla., 1972. Cert. physician State Calif., 1973. Physician, ob-gyn. Marina Womens Med. Group, Marina del Rey, Calif., 1976—; med. expert cons. Med. Bd. Calif., 1981—; med. dir. vol. Westside Family Health Ctr., Santa Monica, Calif., 1985—; asst. clin. prof., dept. ob-gyn. UCLA, Westwood, 1981—, v.p., dept. ob-gyn. clin. faculty assn., 1989—. Contbr. chapters to books. Mem. Westside Family Health Ctr., Santa Monica, Calif., 1996—2006. Recipient Resident Rsch. award, La. Ob-Gyn. Soc., 1974, Cmty. Vol. Svc. award, Westside Family Health Ctr., 2002. Fellow: Am. Coll. Ob-Gyn. Office: Marina Womens Med Group 4560 Admiralty Way #303 Marina Del Rey CA 90292 Office Fax: 310-827-4420. E-mail: drgeneparks@aol.com.

PARKS, DONALD LEE, mechanical engineer, human factors engineer; b. Delphos, Kans., Feb. 23, 1931; s. George Delbert and Erma Josephine (Boucek) P.; m. Bessie Lou Schur, Dec. 24, 1952; children: Elizabeth Parks Anderson, Patricia Parks-Holbrook, Donna, Charles, Sandra Parks-Bennett. Student, Kans. Wesleyan U., 1948-50; BSME, BSBA, Kans. State U., 1957, MS in Psychology, 1959. Cert. profl. ergonomist. Elem. tchr., 1950-51; with Kans. State U. Placement Svc., 1957—59; human factors engr., sys. engr. Boeing Co., Seattle, 1959-90, sr. specialist engr., 1972-74, sr. engring. supr., 1974-90; pres. D-Square Assocs. Engring. Cons., 1990-95, Venture Worlds, 1995—. Adj. lectr. UCLA Engring. Extension, 1989—; cons., lectr. in field; participant workshops on guidelines in profl. areas, NATO, NSF, Nat. Acad. Sci., NRC. Author Mystery Codes From Ancient Times, 2007; authored over 80 documents, 5 articles in profl. publs., 8 book chpts. Mem. Derby (Kans.) Planning Commn., 1961-62, chmn., 1962; del. King County (Wash.) Rep. Conv., 1972. With AUS, 1952-54. Mem. ASME, APA, Human Factors Soc. (Puget Sound Pres.'s award 1969), Elks. Presbyterian. Home: 6232 127th Ave SE Bellevue WA 98006-3943

PARKS, FREDRICK SCOTT, systems engineer; b. Phoenix, Ariz., Jan. 7, 1961; s. David Walker and Carrie Ellen (Abbott) P.; m. Kimberly Louise Kubeja, May 8, 1993. BS, Rensselaer Poly. Inst., 1982, MS, 1984. Rsch. material physicist DSM, Geleen, The Netherlands, 1982; sr. engr. analyst Anser Inc., Arlington, Va., 1983-93; sr. systems engr. Lockheed Missiles and Space Co., Inc., Sunnyvale, Calif., 1993-96; assoc. systems engr. Steven Myers & Assocs, Newport Beach, Calif., 1996—. Contbr. articles to profl. jours. Emergency Planning Coun. ARC, Arlington, 1985-92. Mem. AIAA, Internat. Coun. Systems Engring., Am. Def. Preparedness Assn. Achievements include development of first detailed system architecture to enable multi-shot theater missile defense doctrine, development of Integrated Theater High Altitude Area Defense system architecture, lead system integrator for ground-based missile defense battle management, command, control and communication. Office: 4695 Macarthur Ct Fl 8 Newport Beach CA 92660-1882

PARKS, HAROLD RAYMOND, mathematician, educator; b. Wilmington, Del., May 22, 1949; s. Lytle Raymond Jr. and Marjorie Ruth (Chambers) P.; m. Paula Sue Beaulieu, Aug. 21, 1971 (div. 1984); children: Paul Raymond, David Austin; m. Susan Irene Taylor, June 6, 1985; 1 stepchild, Kathryn McLaughlin. AB, Dartmouth Coll., 1971; PhD, Princeton U., 1974. Tamarkin instr. Brown U., Providence, 1974-77; asst. prof. Oreg. State U., Corvallis, 1977-82, assoc. prof., 1982-89, prof. math., 1989—, chmn. dept. math., 2001—04. Vis. assoc. prof. Ind. U., Bloomington, 1982-83. Author: Explicit Determination of Area Minimizing Hypersurfaces, vol. II, 1986; (with Steven G. Krantz) A Primer of Real Analytic Functions, 1992, 2d edit., 2002; (with G. Musser, R. Burton, W. Siebler) Mathematics in Life, Society and the World, 1997, 2d edit., 2000; (with Steven G. Krantz) The Geometry of Domains in Space, 1999; (with Krantz) The Implicit Function Theorem: History, Theory, and Applications, 2002, (with G. Musser, L. Trimpe, V. Maurer, R. Maurer) A Mathematical View of Our World, 2007, (with Steven G. Krantz) Geometric Integretion Theory, 2008; contbr. articles to profl. jours. Cubmaster Oregon Trail Coun. Boy Scouts Am., 1990-92. Grantee, NSF, 1971—74. Mem. Am. Math. Soc., Math. Assn. Am., Soc. Indsl. and Applied Math., Phi Beta Kappa. Mem. Soc. Of Friends. Home: 33194 Dorset Ln Philomath OR 97370-9555 Office: Oreg State U Dept Math Corvallis OR 97331-4605 Home Phone: 541-929-6822; Office Phone: 541-737-5166. Business E-Mail: parks@math.orst.edu.

PARKS, J. MANLY, lawyer; b. Balt., Nov. 21, 1969; s. Floyd Lavinius and Lanetta Jane (Wolfe) Parks. BA cum laude, Colgate U., 1991; JD, Coll. William and Mary, 1994. Bar: Md. 1995, Pa. 1995, NY, US Dist. Ct. (ea. dist.) Pa. 1996, US Dist. Ct., Md. 1996, Supreme Ct. Pa., Md. Ct. Appeals, NY Ct. Appeals, US Ct. Appeals (2nd, 3rd, 4th cirs.), US Dist. Ct. (ctrl. dist.) Ill., US Dist. Ct. (ea. dist.) Mich. Law clk. to Hon. Donald W. VanArtsdalen US Dist. Ct. (ea. dist.) Pa., Phila., 1994—95; assoc. Duane Morris LLP, Phila., 1996—2002, ptnr., 2003—. Contbr. articles to law jours. Chmn. Cmty. Arts Ctr. Capital Campaign, Wallingford, Pa., 2008—. Avocations: fishing, golf, rowing, hiking. Office: Duane Morris LLP 30 S 17th St Philadelphia PA 19103-4196 Office Phone: 215-979-1342. Office Fax: 215-689-3682. E-mail: JMParks@duanemorris.com.*

PARKS, J. MICHAEL, data processing executive; b. Independence, Mo., Dec. 29, 1950; s. Emory C. and Lorene (Belt) P.; m. Maureen C. Weston; children: Christopher Michael, Daniel John. BS in Edn., U. Kans., 1973. Sales rep. Ingersoll-Rand Corp., Kansas City, Mo., 1973-75; sales rep., then sr. v.p. First Data Resources/Am. Express Info. Svcs. Co., Omaha, San Francisco, Boston, Atlanta, 1976-88; chief exec. officer Call Interactive (joint venture of Am. Express Info. Svcs. Corp. and AT&T), Omaha, 1989—93; pres. First Data Resources, 1993—94; chmn., pres., CEO Alliance Data Systems, Dallas, 1997—2006, chmn., CEO, 2006—. Bd. dirs. Commerce Bank Omaha, Data Transmission Network Inc., Am. Express Info. Svcs. Corp., WATS Mktg. of Am. Inc. Chief YMCA Indian Guide Program, Omaha, 1988-89; Cub Scouts den leader local chpt. Boy Scouts Am., Omaha, 1989—. Methodist. Avocations: golf, tennis, camping. Office: Alliance Data 17655 Waterview Pkwy Dallas TX 75252

PARKS, JAMES WILLIAM, II, public facilities executive, lawyer; b. Wabash, Ind., July 30, 1956; s. James William and Joyce Arlene (Lillibridge) P.; m. Neil Ann Armstrong, Aug. 21, 1982; children: Elizabeth Joyce, Helen Frances, James William III. BS, Ball State U., 1978; JD, U. Miami, 1981. Bar: La. 1981, U.S. Dist. Ct. (ea. dist.) La. 1981, U.S. Ct. Appeals (5th and 11th cirs.) 1981. Fla. 1982, U.S. Dist. Ct. (mid. dist. La.) 1982. Atty. Jones, Walker, Waechter, Poitevent, Carrere et al., New Orleans, 1981-83, Foley & Judell, New Orleans, 1983-88, McCollister & McCleary, pc, Baton Rouge, 1988-95; pres., CEO La. Pub. Facilities Authority, Baton Rouge, 1995—. Mem. AICPA, Nat. Assn. Bond Lawyers, La. State Bar Assn., Fla. Bar Assn., Assn. for Gifted and Talented Students, Baton Rouge (treas. 1994-96, pres.-elect 1996-97, pres. 1997-98), Soc. La. CPA (govt. acctg. and auditing com. 1994-95), Nat. Assn. Higher Edn. Facilities Authorities (bd. dirs. 1996-2001, v.p. 1997-99, pres. 1999-2001), Nat. Coun. Health Facilities Fin. Authorities (bd. dirs. 2004—, treas. 2004-06), Coun. of Devel. Fin. Agys. (bd. dirs. 2002—, treas. 2008-), La. Assistive Tech. Access Network (bd. dirs. 2001-07, chmn. 2004—06), La. Pub. Health Inst. (bd. dirs. 2005—), Nat. Assn. Health and Ednl. Facilities Fin. Authorities (bd. dirs. 2006-08, treas. 2008-). Avocations: travel, computers. Home: 5966 Tennyson Dr Baton Rouge LA 70817-2933 Office: La Pub Facilities Authority 2237 S Acadian Thruway Ste 650 Baton Rouge LA 70808-2380 Office Phone: 225-923-0020. Personal E-mail: jameswparks2@hotmail.com. Business E-Mail: parks@lpfa.com.

PARKS, JEAN ANNE, retired acute care nurse; b. Grand Rapids, Mich., Aug. 3, 1940; d. Edwin Charles and Ruth Katherine (Skellenger) Paepke; m. Charles Wilbur Parks, Nov. 24, 1961; children: Charles Edwin, Catherine Ann, Michael Allan. Diploma in Nursing with highest honors, Blodgett Meml. Hosp., 1961; BS summa cum laude in Health Studies, Western Mich. U., 1987; MA magna cum laude in Health and Humanities, Mich. State U., 1994. RN. Staff nurse Blodgett Meml. Hosp., Grand Rapids, 1961—62; nurse Ctrl. Mich. Cmty. Hosp., Mt. Pleasant, 1962—64; med.-surg. staff Blodgett Meml. Hosp., 1964—70, part-time staff, 1979—2003; part-time Medicaid evaluator for Kent County, Mich. Dept. Pub. Health, Lansing, 1987—88. Mem. Grand Rapids Symphony Chorus, 1987—2003. Baptist. Avocations: travel, music (toured with chorus to several countries).

PARKS, JOE BENJAMIN, entrepreneur visionary, state legislator; b. McAlester, Okla., Dec. 17, 1915; s. James Allen and Mary Florence (Youngblood) P.; m. Florence M. Evans, Oct. 25, 1941; children: Anne, Kathryn. BS in Pub. Adminstrn., Okla. State U., 1939. Divsn. dir. U.S. VA, Washington, 1946—56; spl. asst., cons. U.S. GSA, Washington, 1957—58; mgr. dist. EDP divsn. RCA Corp., Washington, 1959—65; mgr. Ea. region Dashew Bus. Machines, Arlington, Va., 1966—68; assoc. adminstr. social and rehab. svc. U.S. Dept. HEW, Washington, 1969—73; dir. mktg. govs. sys. divsn. Booz, Allen & Hamilton, Washington, 1974—75; ptnr. Forbes & Parks, Dover, NH, 1976—2002; pres. PatPar, Inc., 1990—; mem. N.H. State Legislature, Concord, 1984—92, chmn. joint com. on elderly affairs, 1987—92, mem. com. on health, human svcs. and elderly, 1983—90; chmn. subcom. mileage and electronic roll call, 1989—90; vice chmn. legis. adminstrn. com., 1990—91; mem. appropriations com., 1991—92; propr. Portsmouth Athenaenum, Portsmouth, NH, 1992—. Corporator Wentworth Douglas Hosp., Dover, 1980-89; pres. Berr Par, Inc., 1994—. Columnist Nat. Antiques Rev., 1975-77, Boston Globe N.H. Weekly 1987-88, Foster's Daily Democrat (Dover, N.H.), 1988-90; freelance writer, 1990—. Vice-chmn. NH State Rep. Com., 1987-88; chmn. Strafford County, NH, Reps., 1988; Strafford County campaign mgr. George W. Bush for Pres., 1999-2000; bd. dirs. Coastal Maine Bot. Garden, 2001-05, Rockingham Bot. Garden, 2005-06, Ageless Dreamer, 2007-08. Decorated Bronze Star; recipient Lawmakers award for disting. environ. svc. Sierra Club, 1990, NH State award New England Wildflower Soc., 1998; named Norris Cotton Rep. of Yr., 1993; Paul Harris fellow Rotary Internat. Found., 1998. Mem. Am. Rhododendron Soc. (pres. Mass. chpt. 1995-96, Bronze medal 1992, 2003, Silver medal, 2006, Dover NH Pk. renamed Joe B. Parks River Walk Gardens, 2007—). Congregationalist. Avocation: plant breeding. Home and Office: Parkwood Farm 195 Long Hill Rd Dover NH 03820-6108

PARKS, JOHN SCOTT, pediatric endocrinologist; b. Washington, Oct. 14, 1939; s. John Louis and Mary Dean (Scott) P.; m. Georgia Bigley, May 7, 1959, (dec.) Sept 25, 2008; children: Stephanie Dean, Paige Wallace Parks Adams, John Thurston. AB in Am. Studies magna cum laude, Amherst Coll., 1961; MD, U. Pa., 1966, PhD in Biochemistry, 1971. Diplomate Nat. Bd. Med. Examiners, Am. Bd. Pediat. Intern in pediat. Children's Hosp. Phila., 1967-68, resident in pediat., 1968-69; clin. assoc. endocrinology br. Nat. Cancer Inst. NIH, Bethesda, Md., 1969-71; endocrinology fellow Children's Hosp. Phila., 1971-73; from instr. pediat. to assoc. prof. pediat. U. Pa., 1971-83; asst. physician, asst. endocrinologist Children's Hosp. Phila., 1972-74, assoc. physician, assoc. dir. endocrinology, 1974-80, assoc. endocrinologist, 1974-82, dir. hypothyroidism program, 1978-81, sr. physician, dir. adolescent medicine, 1980-82; prof. pediat. Emory U., Atlanta, 1982—, assoc. prof. biochemistry, 1983—, dir. divsn. pediat. endocrinology and diabetes, 1982—; pediat. endocrinologist Henrietta Egleston Hosp., 1982—, Grady Meml. Hosp., 1982—. Lectr. in field. Author books; contbg. author over 50 book chpts.; contbr. over 65 articles to profl. jours. Bd. dirs. Spruce Hill Cmty. Assn., 1967-69, Hill Top Prep. Sch., 1977-81. Recipient fellowship NIH, 1963-64, 66-67, 75-80, GM Nat. scholarship, 1957-61, Ford Found. fellowship, 1960-61, Am. Cancer Soc. fellow, 1962-63, Morton McCutcheon award, 1963, Merck award, 1966, numerous rsch. awards, 1964—. Mem. Am. Pediat. Soc., Endocrine Soc. (organizing com. 1990), Soc. for Pediat. Rsch., Coll. Physicians and Surgeons of Phila., Lawson Wilkins Pediat. Endocrine Soc. (program com. chair 1983-87, bd. dirs. 1990-93, pres. 1996-97), Spinx Soc., Scarab Soc., Phi Beta Kappa, Psi Upsilon. Office: Emory U Sch Medicine Dept Pediat 2015 Uppergate Dr NE Atlanta GA 30322 Office Phone: 404-778-2400. Office Fax: 404-727-9834. Business E-Mail: jparks@emory.edu.

PARKS, LINDA S., lawyer; b. Oneida, NY, Aug. 19, 1957; BA summa cum laude, Washburn U., 1979, JD cum laude, 1983. Bar: Kans. 1983, Kans. Supreme Ct., US Ct. Appeals (10th Cir.), US Dist. Ct. (Dist. Kans.). Ptnr. Hite Fanning & Honeyman LLP, Wichita, Kans. Bd. mem. YWCA. Fellow: ABA (Kans. Bar Assn. del. 1999—2005); mem.: Kans. Bar Found. (trustee 2000—02), Am. Bar Found., Nat. Assn. Women Bar Assoc. (bd. mem. 2005—), Wichita Women Attys. Assn., Kans. Women Attys. Assn. (pres. 1994—96), Kans. Bar Assn. (mem. bd. gov. 1999—, chair law related edn. com. 2000—02, exec. com. 2000—, v.p. 2005—06, pres.-elect 2006—07, pres. 2007—08), Wichita Bar Assn. Office: Hite Fanning & Honeyman LLP Ste 950 100 N Broadway Wichita KS 67202-2209 Office Phone: 316-265-7741. Office Fax: 316-267-7803. E-mail: parks@hitefanning.com.

PARKS, LLOYD LEE, oil industry executive; b. Kiefer, Okla., Dec. 9, 1929; s. Homer Harrison and Avis Pearl (Motes) P.; m. Mary Ellen Scott, Aug. 20, 1948; children: Connie Jo, Karyn Ann, Rebecca Lee. Student, Okla. State U., 1948-50, Tulsa U., 1950-51, Harvard U. Bus. Sch., 1965. Acct. Deep Rock Oil Corp., 1951-54; chief acct. Blackwell Oil & Gas Co., Tulsa, 1954-60, sec. treas., 1960-62; v.p., controller Amax Oil & Gas Inc., Houston, 1962-67, pres., CEO, 1968—92; v.p. Amax, Inc., 1975-92; pvt. practice oil and gas and real estate imvestment Salado, Tex., 1992—. Served with AUS, 1946-48, 50-51. Mem.: Lions Club. Republican. Office: PO Box 1021 Salado TX 76571-1021 Personal E-mail: llparks9@aol.com. *Work hard, work smart and believe in yourself. You can and will be successful; if you want to be.*

PARKS, MICHAEL CHRISTOPHER, journalist, educator; b. Detroit, Nov. 17, 1943; s. Robert James and Rosalind (Smith) P.; m. Linda Katherine Durocher, Dec. 26, 1964; children: Danielle Anne (dec.), Christopher, Matthew. AB, U. Windsor, Ont., Can., 1965. Reporter Detroit News, 1962-65; corr. Time-Life News Service, NYC, 1965-66; asst. city editor Suffolk Sun, Long Island, NY, 1966-68; polit. reporter, foreign corr. The Balt. Sun, Saigon, Singapore, Moscow, Cairo, Hong Kong, Peking, 1968-80; fgn. corr. L.A. Times, L.A., Peking, Johannesburg, Moscow, Jerusalem, 1980-95, dpty. fgn. editor, 1995-96, mng. editor, 1996-97, editor, 1997-2000, v.p., 1996-97, sr. v.p., 1997-98, exec. v.p., 1998-2000; v.p. Times Mirror Co., 1998-2000; prof. Annenberg Sch. Comm. U. So. Calif., LA, 2000—02, dir. Annenberg Sch. Journalism, 2002—08, prof. journalism and internat. rels., 2002—. Disting. fellow Pacific Coun. Internat. Policy, 2000-02, dir. 1998-2008; dir. L.A. Jewish Jour., 2004-. Recipient Pulitzer prize, 1987. Mem. Am. Soc. Newspaper Editors, Pacific Coun. Internat. Policy, Soc. Profl. Journalists, Athenaeum (Pasadena, Calif.), Coun. on Fgn. Rels., Nat. Coun. US-China Rels., Reuters Inst. Study Journalism, Oxford U. (adv. bd. mem.), Nat. Press Club. Office: Annenberg Sch U So Calif Los Angeles CA 90089-7725 Office Phone: 213-243-5324. E-mail: mparks@usc.edu.

PARKS, MICHAEL E., art educator, department chairman; b. Dec. 2, 1949; BA, Anderson Coll., Ind., 1973; MA, Ball State U., Muncie, Ind., 1979, EdD, 1985. Tchr. art Frankton Elem. and Jr. H.S., Ind., 1973—79; fellow Ball State U., 1979—81; prof. Buffalo State Coll., 1981—, chmn. dept. art, 1981—. Author: The Art Teacher's Desktop Reference, 1994. Mem.: Nat. Art Edn. Assn. (v.p. 2001—03, Outstanding Svc. award 2003), NY State Art Tchrs. Assn. (life; pres. 1990—91). Office: Buffalo State Coll 1300 Elmwood Ave Buffalo NY 14222 Home: 155 Dorchester Rd Buffalo NY 14213

PARKS, MICHAEL JAMES, editor; b. Spokane, Wash., June 3, 1944; s. Floyd Lewis and Marie (McHugh) Parks; m. Janet K. Holter, Aug. 12, 1967; children: Michael J., Gregory F., Sarah M. BA, Seattle U., 1966. Reporter The Seattle Times, 1966—74, fin. editor, 1974—77; pub., editor Marple's Pacific N.W. Letter, Seattle, 1977—. Bd. govs. Seattle U. Alumni Assn.; trustee Seattle Rotary Svc. Found. Fellow, Am. Press Inst., N.Y.C., 1973. Mem.: Rotary. Roman Catholic. Avocations: opera, reading, swimming, walking. Office: Marples NW Letter Ste 200 117 W Mercer St Seattle WA 98119-3960 Personal E-mail: michaeljparks@gmail.com. E-mail: info@marples.com.

PARKS, PATRICIA JEAN, lawyer; b. Portland, Oreg., Apr. 2, 1945; d. Robert and Marion (Crosby) Parks; m. David F. Jurca, Oct. 17, 1971 (div. 1976). BA in History, Stanford U., 1967; JD, U. Pa., Phila., 1970. Bar: N.Y. 1971, Wash. 1974. Assoc. Milbank, Tweed, Hadley & McCoy, NYC, 1970-73, Shidler, McBroom, Gates & Lucas, Seattle, 1974-81, ptnr., 1981-90, Preston, Thorgrimson, Shidler, Gates & Ellis, Seattle, 1990-93; pvt. practice Seattle, 1993-99; spl. counsel Karr Tuttle Campbell, Seattle, 1999—2007. Active Vashon Allied Arts; former bd. dirs. Seattle chpt. Western Pension and Benefits Conf. Mem.: ABA, Pension Roundtable, Seattle-King County Bar Assn., Wash. Women Tax, Wash. State Bar Assn. (past chair gift and estate tax com.), Wash. Native Plant Soc., Wash. Athletic Club. Avocations: kayaking, hiking, contra dancing, birdwatching. Personal E-mail: parkspat@comcast.net.

PARKS, PAUL JOSEPH, curator, educator; b. Queens, NY, June 27, 1953; s. Seymour and Irene Parks; m. Caroline Weaver, July 20, 1986; 1 child, Simeon Terrill. MFA, Syracuse U., NY, 1978. Curator, photography Everson Mus., Syracuse, 1977—78; instr. Syracuse U., 1977—78, Network for Learning, NYC, 1981—83; curator, lectr. Parks & Stock, Ltd., Lansing, NY, 1983—; dir. St. Marks Gallery, NYC, 1984—86; prof. art history Tompkins Cortland CC, Dryden, NY, 2006—, SUNY, Cortland, 2007—. Curator (exhibitions) One Tree: Many Branches, Beyond the Desert, Documenting The Diaspora. Co-chair Temple Beth El Arts Com., Ithaca, NY, 1998—. Avocations: canoeing, poetry, fishing, cross country skiing. Home: 95 Drake Rd Lansing NY 14882 Office: SUNY Cortland Dowd Fine Arts Ctr PO Box 2000 Cortland NY 13045 Personal E-mail: pks@twcny.rr.com. Business E-Mail: parksp@cortland.edu.

PARKS, ROBERT MYERS, appliance manufacturing company executive; b. Nevada, Mo., July 18, 1927; s. Cecil R. and Marcella (Myers) P.; m. Audrey Lenora Jones, June 18, 1955; children: John Robert, Janet M. Parks Huston. BS, U. Mo., 1949; MBA, Harvard U., 1952. Asst. dept. mgr. Jewett & Sherman Co., Kansas City, Mo., 1949-50; staff cons. Harbridge House, Inc., Boston, 1952; v.p. Electronic Splty. Co., Inc., Los Angeles, 1952-57; founder, chmn. bd. Parks Products, Inc., Hollywood, Calif., 1957—; pres. Generalist Industries, Inc., Hollywood, 1960-73. Chmn. bd. Shaver Corp. Am., LA, 1965—; lectr. mktg. UCLA Extension divsn., 1960-61. Contbr. articles to profl. jours.; patentee in field. Active YMCA; bd. dirs. Hollywood Presbyn. Med. Center Found., Presbyn. Homes Found.; mem. dean's adv. council U. Mo. Bus. Sch., mayor's task force on L.A. River Cahuenga Pass Coalition. With USNR, 1944-45. Named in his honor Grad. Bus. Sch., U. Mo. Mem. Sales and Marketing Execs. Assn., C. of C., Navy League, World Affairs Coun., Calif. Caballeros, Rangers, Vaqueros del Desierto, Los Caballeros, Rancheros Visitadores, E Clampus Vitus, Delta Sigma Pi, Sigma Chi. Clubs: Mason (Shriner), LA Breakfast, Braemar Country, Saddle and Sirloin. Presbyterian. Home: 7421 Woodrow Wilson Dr Los Angeles CA 90046-1322 Office: 3611 Cahuenga Blvd Hollywood CA 90068-1205 Office Phone: 323-876-5454.

PARKS, SHANNON LYNN ISOVITSCH, civil engineer; d. Donald L. and Judy A. Isovitsch; m. Michael L. Parks, Apr. 19, 2008. BS in Civil Engring., Pa. State U., University Park, PA, 1997; MS in Civil & Env. Eng., Carnegie Mellon U., Pitts., 2005, PhD., 2008. Cert. professional engineer, Pa. Sr. engr. Alcoa Inc., Alcoa Center, Pa., 2008—, Hatch Mott MacDonald, Pittsburgh, 2000—05. Office: Alcoa Tech Ctr 100 Tech Dr New Kensington PA 15069 Business E-Mail: shannon.parks@alcoa.com.

PARKYN, JOHN WILLIAM, editor, writer, columnist; b. London, Dec. 7, 1931; came to U.S., 1967; citizen, 1973; s. James R. and Eva M. (Dix) P.; m. Sybil (Judy) Hetherington; 1 child, Elaine. Student, Dulwich Coll., 1943-48. Staff writer Bus. Mag., London, 1954-56; writer-editor Amalgamated Press, London, 1956-58; features editor Woman's Illustrated mag., London, 1958-60; staff writer Internat. Pub. Corp., London, 1960-61; editor Westward mag. Daily News Ltd., London, 1961-64; assoc. editor Daily Telegraph mag., London, 1964-66; features editor King mag. Europress, Ltd., London, 1966-67; assoc. editor Tropic mag. Miami Herald, 1967-69; editor Tropic mag., 1969-77; editor Calif. Today mag. San Jose Mercury News, Calif., 1977-83; editor Sunshine: The Mag. of South Fla. Sun-Sentinel Co. (subs. Tribune Co.), Ft. Lauderdale, Fla., 1983-96; columnist S. Fla. Sun-Sentinel, 1997—2005; exec. editor, sr. writer Vero Beach Mag., Fla., 1998—; columnist, feature writer City & Shore mag., 2000—05. Cons. Het Parool newspaper, Amsterdam, 1965. Contbr. numerous articles to Am. and European mags. Chmn. Sunday Mag. Editors Conf., Louisville, 1973. With RAF, 1950-52. Recipient Outstanding Use of Editl. Color award Editor & Pub. mag., 1974, 75, 77, Nat. Headliner award, 1976, 79; named Editor Best Weekly Mag. in State Fla. Press Club, 1985-93, 95. Personal E-mail: johnparkyn@aol.com.

PARLAMIS, MICHAEL FRANK, civil engineer, construction executive; b. Bklyn., May 29, 1940; s. Frank Michael and Phyllis (Burnago) P.; m. Marguerite Koskinas, Aug. 21, 1966; children: Franklin, Christine, Alexander. BSCE, MIT, 1962, BS in Indsl. Mgmt., 1962; MSCE, Stanford U., 1963. Registered profl. engr., NY. Engr. Port Authority of NY and NJ, 1963—64; asst. to chief engr. George A. Fuller Co., NYC, 1964-67; pres. Frank Parlamis Inc., Bklyn., 1968—, Parlamis Bros. Inc., Bklyn., 1968—, Hermes Constrn. Corp., Bklyn., 1968—; ptnr. City Path LLC, City Jam LLC, 128 MAC LLC, 128 MAPP LLC, 29 Prime Numbers, LLC. Author: CPM/PERT As Basis for Management Information Systems in Building Construction, 1966, Regulation of Building Construction in the City of New York, 1967, Greece and the Panama Canal, 1988. Chmn. expansion program Greek Orthodox Cathedral St. John the Theologian, Tenafly, NJ, 1978—; mem. Leadership 100 of Greek Orthodox Ch.; Archon of Ecomenical Patriarcate, Greek Orthodox Ch., regional commdr. State of NJ; mem. ednl. coun. MIT, William Barton Rogers Soc.; trustee Frank Parlamis Sr. Citizens Ctr., Jamaica, NY, Space Camp Turkey, Izmir; founder Michael F. Parlamis endowed fellowships, MIT, St. John the Theologian Peace Meml. Gymnasium; exec. dir. St. John the Theologian World Peace Inst.; founding trustee New Hagia Sophia, Hagia Eirene 250 Charitable Trust. Recipient Ellis Island medal of honor, 2002, Gold Key award for best engineered restaurant in USA, Internat. Hotel, Motel an Restaurant Show, 1992. Mem. Am. Hellenic Progressive Assn., Bklyn. Tech. Rsch. Found. (life), Tau Beta Pi, Chi Epsilon, Am. Turkish Soc. Republican. Avocations: engineering and religious history, peace advocacy, ecumenical religious activities. Home: 128 Downey Dr Tenafly NJ 07670-3006 Office: 328 Atlantic Ave Brooklyn NY 11201-5804 Office Phone: 718-875-6744. Business E-Mail: parlamis@alum.mit.edu.

PARLANGE, JEAN-YVES, environmental engineer, educator; PhD, Brown U., 1962. Asst. prof. Yale U., Dept. Engring. and Applied Sci., 1964—69, assoc. prof., 1969—72; assoc. scientist Conn. Agr. Exp. Station, 1968—71, mathematician, 1971—77; prof. Coll. Forest Resources, U. Wash., 1977—78; prof. applied math. Environ. Scis., Griffith U., 1978—85; prof. biological and environ. engring. Cornell U., 1985—. Vis. prof. U. Grenoble, 1981—82; prof. hydrology Flinders U., 1993—94. Contbr. articles to profl. jours. Recipient Minta Martin Nat. Award, 1962, AGU Horton Award, 1997; Fulbright Grant, 1958. Mem.:

NAE, Soil Science Soc. Am., Am. Geophysical Union, Sigma Xi. Office: Cornell U Biological and Environ Engring 228 Riley-Robb Hall Ithaca NY 14853-5701 Office Phone: 607-255-2476. Office Fax: 607-255-4080. Business E-Mail: jp58@cornell.edu.

PARLEE, MARY BROWN, psychology educator; b. Oak Park, Ill., Feb. 11, 1943; d. Grant Sylvester Brown and Esther (Bonter) de Neufville; 1 child, Elizabeth. BA, Harvard U., 1965; PhD, MIT, 1969. Asst. prof. Wellesley Coll., Mass., 1969-72; fellow Bunting Inst. of Radcliffe Coll., Cambridge, Mass., 1972-74; fellow lab. social psychiatry Harvard U., Boston, 1974-75; assoc. prof. Barnard Coll. of Columbia U., NYC, 1975-78; dir. ctr. for study women and soc. CUNY, 1979-84, prof. psychology grad. ctr., 1984-93; vis. prof. MIT, 1993—99, vis. lectr., 2000—. Contbr. articles to profl. jours. Vol. St. Ignatius, NYC, 1987-88. NIH grantee, 1975-78, 79-82; recipient Publ. award Assn. for Women in Psychology, 1978. Fellow APA (pres. divsn. psychology of women 1983-84); mem. Harvard Club NYC, Radcliffe Club NY (bd. dirs. 1989), Radcliffe Club Boston. Catholic. Office: MIT 46-2004 Cambridge MA 02139 Business E-Mail: mbparlee@alum.mit.edu.

PARLIER, GREG H., military officer, analyst, engineer, educator, researcher; b. San Luis Obispo, Calif., May 10, 1952; s. Merton B. and Kathleen F. Parlier; m. Judy D. Olson, Aug. 30, 1975; children: Jamie Lynn, Timothy Scott, Steven Hugh. BS, U.S. Mil. Acad., 1974; MS, Naval Postgrad. Sch., 1983; MA, Georgetown U., 1988; postgrad., USMC Command and Staff Coll., 1988—89, U. Va., 1992, U.S. Army War Coll., 1995—96; PhD, Wesleyan U., 2004. Registered profl. engr., Va.; master parachutist, army strategist, battle staff officer, cert. strategy and innovation MIT, 2005, mgmt. and leadership MIT, 2006, tech. and ops. MIT, 2008. Vulcan and redeye platoon leader 3-4 ADAR, 82d Airborne Divsn., Ft. Bragg, NC, 1975—76; exec. officer Battery C, 3-4 ADAR, 82d Airborne Divsn., 1976—77, Battery C, 2-71 ADA, 31st ADA Brigade, Republic of Korea, 1977; battery comdr. Battery D, 3-4 ADAR, 82d Airborne Divsn., 1979—81; asst. prof. dept. engring. U.S. Mil. Acad., West Point, NY, 1983—86; chief officer plans U.S. Army Mil. Pers. Ctr., Alexandria, Va., 1986—88, 3-4 ADAR ops. officer, 1989—90, exec. officer, 1990—91; G-3 air def. element XVIII Airborne Corps, Ft. Bragg, 1991—92; bn. comdr. 5-2 ADAR, 69th ADA Brigade, V Corps, Crailsheim and Bamberg, Germany, 1992—94; chief resource plans and analysis divsn. Office of the Chief of Staff U.S. Army, Washington, 1996—98; dir. program analysis and evaluation U.S. Army Recruiting Command, Ft. Knox, Ky., 1998—2002; dir. for transformation U.S. Army Aviation and Missile Command, Redstone Arsenal, Ala., 2002—03; sr. rsch. scientist U. Ala., Huntsville, 2003—05; def. analyst Inst. Def. Analyses, 2004—; sr. sys. analyst Sci. Applications Internat. Corp., 2005—; v.p. strategic planning Rsch., Sys., and Analytical Engring., Inc., 2005—07. Pres. Ops. Rsch. Soc. Ala., 2005. Sr. tactical comdr. McKee Barracks, Crailsheim, 1993; vice chmn. Bamberg (Germany) Scholarship Com., 1993—94; mentor Georgetown U. ROTC, Washington, 1996—98. Col. US Army, 1997. Decorated Bronze Star U.S. Army, Legion of Merit; recipient German Efficiency Badge (Gold), Bundeswehr (German Army), 1999, 2001, plaque of appreciation, Korean Nat. Assembly, 1978, Can. Parachutist Badge, Can. Forces, 1977, USMC CSC Disting. Grad. and Gen. Clifton B. Cates award, 1989, Jim and Rafer Johnson Outstanding Athlete Award, Kingsburg H.S. Faculty and Coaches, 1970; named Dept. of the Army Rsch. Analyst of Yr., 1987; Nat. Def. Fellow, MIT, 1994—95. Mem.: Mil. Ops. Rsch. Soc. (Grad. Rsch. award 1983), Inst. Ops. Rsch. and Mgmt. Scis. (Edelman Laureate 2006), 82nd Airborne Divsn. Assn. (life), Sigma Xi. Avocations: reading, classical music, sports. Home: 255 Avian Ln Madison AL 35758-6863 Home Phone: 256-325-1974. Personal E-mail: gparlier@knology.net.

PARMELEE, ARTHUR HAWLEY, JR., pediatric medical educator; b. Chgo., Oct. 29, 1917; s. Arthur Hawley and Ruth Frances (Brown) P.; m. Jean Kern Rheinfrank, Nov. 11, 1939; children: Arthur Hawley III, Ann (Mrs. John C. Minahan Jr.), Timothy, Ruth Ellen. BS, U. Chgo., 1940, MD, 1943. Diplomate Am. Bd. Pediatrics (examiner 1966—). Intern U.S. Naval Hosp., Bethesda, Md., 1943-44; extern Yale Inst. Child Devel., 1947, New Haven Hosp., 1947-48, L.A. Children's Hosp., 1948-49; mem. faculty UCLA Med. Sch., 1951—, prof. pediat., 1967-88, prof. emeritus, 1988, dir. divsn. child devel., 1964-88; mem. Brain Rsch. Inst., 1966-88, Mental Retardation Rsch. Ctr., 1970-88. Rsch. prof. pediat. U. Göttingen, Germany, 1967-68; mem. com. child devel. rsch. and pub. policy NRC, 1977-81; cons. Nat. Inst. Child Health and Human Devel., 1963-70, Holy Family Adoption Svc., 1949-80. Author articles, chpts. in books. Trustee Los Angeles Children's Mus., 1979. Served with USN, 1943-47. Recipient C. Anderson Aldrich award in child devel., 1975; Commonwealth fellow Centre de Recherches Biologiques Neonatales, Clinique Obstetricale Baudelocque, Paris, 1959-60; fellow Ctr. Advanced Study in Behavioral Scis., Stanford U., 1984-85; hon. lectr. Soc. for Developmental and Behavioral Pediat., 1996. Mem. AMA, Am. Pediat. Soc., Soc. Pediat. Rsch., Western Soc. Pediat. Rsch., Am. Acad. Pediat. (chmn. com. sect. child devel. 1966), Assn. Ambulatory Pediat. (mem. coun. 1966-69), Soc. Rsch. in Child Devel. (pres. 1983-85, Disting. Sci. Contbns. to Child Devel. award 1993), Assn. Psychophysiol. Study of Sleep, Los Angeles County Med. Soc., Phi Beta Kappa. Home: 764 Iliff St Pacific Palisades CA 90272-3927 Office: Univ Calif Dept Pediatrics Los Angeles CA 90024 Home Phone: 310-454-2618.

PARMELEE, JOHN H., communications educator; b. Washington, July 23, 1970; s. Foster Parmelee and Mary L. Becker; m. Amy L. Moulden, Dec. 15, 2001; 1 child, Scott Evan. BS, James Madison U., Harrisonburg, Va., 1992; MS, Columbia U. Grad. Sch. Journalism, NYC, 1993; PhD, U. Fla., Gainesville, 2001. Reporter Kiplinger's Personal Fin. Mag., Washington, 1994—97, Congl. Quar., Washington, 1997—98; assoc. prof. comm. U. North Fla., Jacksonville, 2001—. Author: (book) Meet the Candidate Videos: Analyzing Presidential Primary Campaign Videocassettes, If you're Clueless about Financial Planning and Want to Know More; contbr. articles to profl. jours. Recipient Outstanding scholar, Fla. Comm. Assn., 2006. Mem.: Internat. Comm. Assn. Office: Univ N Fla Dept Comm 1 UNF Dr Jacksonville FL 32224 Business E-Mail: jparmele@unf.edu.

PARMENTER, KELLI DENISE, middle school educator, small business owner; b. Dallas, Feb. 10, 1963; d. Ted M. and Grace M. Porter; m. Ernest Eugene Parmenter, Jr., July 26, 1986; children: Joshua Shane, Clint Martin. MusB in Edn., Baylor U., Waco, Tex., 1986; MEd, Tex. A&M, Commerce, 1994. Tchr. elem. music, mid. sch. choir Mesquite Ind. Sch. Dist., Tex., 1986—. Owner Kelli's Angels Animal Sitters, Mesquite, Tex., 2002—. Recipient Featured Tchr. award, Mesquite Daily News, 1993. Mem.: Mesquite Edn. Assn. (com. mem. 2006—), Tex. Music Educators Assn. (assoc.). Baptist. Avocations: reading, gardening, travel, horseback riding. Personal E-mail: kellisangels@sbcglobal.net.

PARMESE, GABRIEL J., corporate financial executive; s. James and Martha (Phillips) Parmese; m. Ann C. Mullen, Oct. 20, 2000; children: Norah, Jimmy. BSc in Commerce and Fin., Rider U.; MBA, N.H. Coll., 1987. V.p. fin., corp. contr. Art Tech., Cambridge, Mass., 2001—04; CFO SynQor Inc., Boxboro, Mass., 2004—. Corp. contr. Applix, Westbrough, Mass., 2000—01. Active homeless shelter activities and abuse programs, 1993—2005. Mem.: Fed. Executives Inst. (assoc.). Conservative. Achievements include public reporting, turn around and operational efficiency expert for US based companies. Office: SynQor Inc 155 Swanson Rd Boxboro MA 01719 Business E-Mail: gabrielparmese@synqor.com.

PARMET, HARRIET ABBEY L., literature educator; b. Phila., July 22, 1928; d. Jacob and Belle Cecil (Popolow) Leibowitz; m. Sidney B. Parmet, June 7, 1950; children: Howard B., Jonathan L. AB, Temple U., 1950, MS, 1960; B in Hebrew Lit., Gratz Coll., 1979; PhD in English, Lehigh U. Cert. secondary edn. tchr., Pa. Tchr. Hebrew Temple U., Phila., 1946-50, Beth Israel, Phila., 1946-51; tchr. English and social studies Gillespie Jr. High Sch., Phila., 1950-55; tchr. Hebrew and Jewish history Temple Beth El, Allentown, Pa., 1964-77; tchr. Hebrew and Israeli lit. Lehigh U., Bethlehem, Pa., 1976—95; prof. emeritus, 1995. Hillel co-advisor, mem. exec. bd. Lehigh U., 1976—; lectr. Judiac topics. Author: The Terror of Our Days: Four Am. Poets Respond to the Holocaust, 2001; contbr. articles to profl. jours. Vice pres. Temple Beth El Sisterhood, Allentown, 1973-75; mem. exec. bd. Jewish Family Svc., Allentown, 1988—; bd. dirs. Women's Profl. Jewish Fedn., Allentown, 1973-75. Coolodge Colloquim fellow, 1986, Givat Haviva Rsch. fellow, 1987; named Outstanding Alumna Gratz Coll. Centenial Celebration. Mem. Women's Studies Consortium, Lehigh Valley Assn. Ind. Colls. (chairperson), Am. Jewish Congress (pres. Allentown chpt. 1970), Assn. Jewish Studies, Nat. Assn. Hebrew Profs., Temple U. Alumni Assn. (Disting. Alumni award 1995), Gratz Coll. Alumni Assn., Hadassah (life). Home: 1118 N 28th St Allentown PA 18104-2908 Office: Lehigh U Modern Lang Dept Maginnes Hall # 9 Bethlehem PA 18015-3206 Home Phone: 610-433-2484; Office Phone: 610-758-3090. Business E-Mail: hlpo@lehigh.edu.

PARMET, HERBERT SAMUEL, historian, writer; b. NYC, Sept. 28, 1929; s. Isaac and Fanny (Scharf) P.; m. Joan Kronish, Sept. 12, 1948; 1 child, Wendy. BS, SUNY, Oswego, 1951; MA, Queens Coll., 1957; postgrad., Columbia U., 1958-62. Prof. history Grad. Sch. CUNY, 1968-95, disting. prof. history, 1983-95, prof. emeritus, 1995—. Cons. ABC-TV, N.Y.C., 1983, KERA-TV, Dallas, 1986-91, WGBH-TV, Boston, 1988-91, 2007. Author: Aaron Burr: Portrait of an Ambitious Man, 1967, Never Again: President Runs for a Third Term, 1968, Eisenhower and the American Crusades, 1972, The Democrats, 1976, Jack: The Struggles of John F. Kennedy, 1980, JFK: The Presidency of John F. Kennedy, 1983, Richard Nixon and His America, 1990, George Bush: The Life of a Lone Star Yankee, 1997, Presidential Power: From the New Deal to the New Right, 2001, Richard Nixon: An American Enigma, 2007. Cpl. U.S. Army, 1952-54. Grantee, NEH, 1987. Fellow Soc. Am. Historians; mem. Am. Hist. Assn., Orgn. Am. Historians, Authors Guild. Avocation: photography. Home: 36 Marsten Ln Hillsdale NY 12529-5816 Personal E-mail: hparmet@fairpoint.net. Business E-Mail: hparmet@taconic.net.

PARMET, ROBERT DAVID, historian, educator; b. NYC, Dec. 11, 1938; s. Isaac and Fanny (Scharf) Parmet; 1 child, Andrew Charles. BA, CCNY, 1960; MA, Columbia U., 1961, PhD, 1966. Fellow CCNY, 1960-62, lectr., 1962-65; asst. prof. Newark State Coll., Union, NJ, 1965-67, CUNY, Jamaica, NY, 1967-70, assoc. prof., 1971-77, chmn. dept. history, 1972-75, prof., 1978—. Author: Labor and Immigration in Industrial America, 1981, rev. edit., 1986, The Master of Seventh Avenue: David Dubinsky and the American Labor Movement, 2005; co-author: American Nativism 1830-1860, 1971, rev. edit., 1979; contbr. articles to encys., profl. jours. Fellow, Woodrow Wilson Nat. Found., 1960, CUNY, 1994. Mem.: Labor and Working Class History Assn., Immigration History Soc., Am. Jewish Hist. Assn., So. Hist. Assn., N.Y. Labor Hist. Assn. (mem. exec. bd. 1990—), Conn. Hist. Soc., Acad. Polit. Sci., Orgn. Am. Historians, Am. Hist. Assn., Phi Alpha Theta. Democrat. Jewish. Avocations: photography, travel, musical theater, baseball. Home: 1 Highland Pl Great Neck NY 11020 Office: York Coll CUNY 94-20 Guy R Brewer Blvd Jamaica NY 11451 Office Phone: 718-262-2644. Business E-Mail: parmet@york.cuny.edu.

PARMLEY, RICHARD TURNER, pediatric hematologist, oncologist; b. Madison, Wis., Sept. 10, 1949; BA, U. Va., 1970; MD, Med. U. S.C., 1973. Diplomate in pediatrics and in pediatric hematology/oncology Am. Bd. Pediatrics; diplomate in hematopathology Am. Bd. Pathology. Intern Med. U. S.C., Charleston, S.C., 1973, resident in pediats., 1974-75; fellow in pediat. hematology-oncology St. Jude Children's Rsch. Hosp., Memphis, 1976-77, U. Ala., Birmingham, 1977; clin. fellow in med. oncology bone marrow transplant svc. Fred Hutchinson Cancer Rsch. Ctr., Seattle, 1986; dir. electron microscopy and histology unit inst. dental rsch. U. Ala., Birmingham, 1978-83, assoc. scientist Comprehensive Cancer Cancert Ctr., 1978-83, asst. prof. pediats. and pathology, 1978-82, assoc. prof. pediats., 1982-83; assoc. prof. pediats. and pathology U. Tex. Health Sci. Ctr., 1983-88, prof. pediats., 1988-94; dir. divsn. pediat. hematology/oncology Carolinas Med. Ctr., Charlotte, NC, 1994—2000; clin. prof. pediat. U. NC, Chapel Hill, 1994—2000; mem. med. staff Spartanburg Reg. Med. Ctr., SC, 2000—07; clin. prof. pediat. Med. Univ. SC, Charleston, 2000—07; pediat. hematologist-oncologist Nemours Children's Clinic, Pensacola, Fla., 2007—; clin. prof. Fla. State U., 2007—. Mem. Am. Soc. Pediatric Hematology/Oncology, Am. Acad. Pediat., Am. Pediatric Soc., Soc. Pediatric Rsch., Alpha Omega Alpha. Office Phone: 850-505-4790. Personal E-mail: rparmley@nemours.org.

PARNAS-SIMPSON, MARIANNA, chorus director, singer; arrived in U.S., 1990, naturalized, 1996; d. Abram and Yeva Parnas; m. Robert Louis Simpson, May 29, 1994; 1 child from previous marriage, Faina Goldstein. BA in Choral Conducting and Music Edn., Coll. Music Leningrad N.A. Rimsky-Korsakov State Conservatory, St. Petersburg, Russia, 1978; MusM in Choral Conducting and Music Edn., Leningrad N.A. Rimsky-Korsakov State Conservatory, St. Petersburg, Russia, 1983. Dir. children's chorus studio Pioneer Ho. State Ednl. Inst., St. Petersburg, Russia, 1980—89; asst. dir. and vocal instr. Houston Children's Chorus, 1994—99; chorus dir. and music appreciation instr. Parker Elem. Sch., 1999—; chorus dir. Revels Houston. Condr. region 23 treble choir Tex. Music Educators Assn., Houston, 2002; clinician in music appreciation Nat. Suzuki Piano Workshop, Texas City, 2005, 06; clinician and adjudicator Children's Music Festival, Houston, 2006. Performer: Tex. Music Educators Assn. Conv., 2003, 2005. Recipient First pl., Nat. Children's Chorus Competition, Russia, 1988, Nat. Grammy award, Parker Music Acad., Houston, 2002; named Tchr. of Yr., Parker Elem. Sch., 2004—05. Mem.: Am. Choral Dir. Assn., Tex. Choral Dir. Assn., Tex. Music Educators Assn. Avocations: Russian folk songs, travel, reading. Office: Parker Elem Sch 10626 Atwell Dr Houston TX 77076 Office Phone: 713-726-3634. Office Fax: 713-726-3660. Business E-Mail: msimpso1@houstonisd.org.

PARNELL, CHARLES L., speechwriter; b. Myrtis, La., Feb. 13, 1938; s. Forrest L. and Dorothy D. (Jones) P. BA, Rice U., 1960; M Bus. and Pub. Adminstrn., Southeastern U., 1977. Commd. ens. USN, 1960, advanced through grades to comdr., 1975, ret., 1987; speechwriter Mead Data Cen., Dayton, Ohio, 1987-89, Nationwide Ins. Co., Columbus, Ohio, 1989-90; exec. speechwriter Miller Brewing Co., Milw., 1990-96; speechwriter, Milw., 1996-98; exec. speechwriter, Dallas, 1998—. Contbr. articles to profl. jours.; frequently quoted in leading speech-related publs.; speeches used as models in 8 college level textbooks in U.S. and Can. Mem. U.S. Naval Inst., Mil. Officers Assn., World Future Soc. Avocations: reading, writing, travel. Home and Office: 1311 Brittany Ln Mansfield TX 76063-4013

PARNELL, FRANCIS WILLIAM, JR., otolaryngologist; b. Woonsocket, RI, May 22, 1940; s. Francis W. and Dorothy V. (Lalor) P.; m. Diana DeAngelis, Feb. 27, 1965; children: Cheryl Lynn, John Francis, Kathleen Diana, Alison Anne, Thomas William. Student, Coll. Holy Cross, 1957-58; AB, Clark U., 1961; MD, Georgetown U., 1965. Diplomate: Nat. Bd. Med. Examiners, Am. Bd. Otolaryngology. Intern Univ. Hosps., Madison, Wis., 1965-66, resident in gen. surgery, 1966-67, otolaryngology, 1967-70; pvt. practice medicine specializing in otolaryngology San Rafael, Calif., 1972-75, Greenbrae, Calif., 1978—2000; chmn., pres., CEO Parnell Pharms., Larkspur, Calif., 1982—. Cons. corp. med. affairs, 1978-82; corp. med. dir. Becton, Dickinson & Co., Rutherford, N.J., 1976-78; clin. instr. U. Calif. at San Francisco, 1972-75, asst. clin. prof., 1975-76; Alt. del., U.S. Del. 27th World Health Assembly WHO, Geneva, 1974. Contbr. articles to profl. jours. Candidate Calif. State Assembly, 1988; bd. dirs. Marin Coalition, 1980-96, 97-01, chmn., 1986-87; trustee Ross (Calif.) Sch. Dist., 1981-89; mem. governing bd. Marin Cmty. Coll. Dist., 1995-03, pres., 1999-00, 02-03; dir. Coll. Marin Found., 2004-, pres., 2006-. Maj. M.C. AUS, 1970-72, lt. col. M.C., USAR, 1985-93. Fellow ACS (gov. 1988-94), Am. Acad. Otolaryngology. Home: PO Box 998 Ross CA 94957-0998 Office: 1100 S Eliseo Dr Greenbrae CA 94904-2017 Office Phone: 415-256-1800.

PARNELL, SEAN, Governor of Alaska, former state legislator; b. Hanford, Calif., Nov. 19, 1962; m. Sandy Parnell; children: Grace, Rachel. BBA, Pacific Luth. U., 1984; JD, U. Puget Sound, 1987. Comml. atty., 1987—; pvt. bus. owner, 1991—2000; mem. Alaska State House of Representatives, 1992—96, Alaska State Senate, 1996—2000, co-chair fin. com., mem. resources com., legis. budget and audit com.; ptnr. Patton Boggs, LLP, Anchorage; lt. gov. State of Alaska, Juneau, Alaska, 2007—09, gov., 2009—. Vol. mentor for H.S. youth groups and orgns., 1988-91; mem. Telecom. Info. Coun., Energy Coun., Western Legis. Timber Task Force, Bayshore-Klatt Cmty. Coun., Uniform Code Revision Commn.; dissenting mem. Long Range Fin. Planning Commn. Mem. Nat. Fedn. Ind. Bus. Republican. Avocations: teaching and coaching high school youth, running, reading, softball. Office: Office of the Governor PO Box 110001 Juneau AK 99811 Office Phone: 907-465-3500. Office Fax: 907-465-3532.*

PARNELL, THOMAS ALFRED, physicist; b. Lumberton, NC, Nov. 24, 1931; s. Johnathan Alfred and Lula Beale (Lashley) P.; m. Elizabeth G. Brite, June 4, 1955; children: Marc Thomas, Gina Ann. BS in Physics, U. N.C., 1954, MS in Physics, 1962, PhD in Physics, 1965. Rsch. adj., dept. physics U. N.C., Chapel Hill, 1962-65; ops. analyst U.S. Air Force Europe, Wiesbaden, W. Ger., 1965-66; asst. prof. physics Marshall U., Huntington, W.Va., 1966-67; physicist NASA-Marshall Space Flight Center, Huntsville, Ala., 1968—99, chief astrophysics br., 1969-98; prin. rsch. scientist, dir. high energy photonics lab U. Ala., Huntsville, 1999—. Mem. editorial bd. Radiation Measurements; contbr. articles to profl. jours. Served to capt. USNR, 1954-91. Recipient Exceptional Sci. Achievement medal, Outstanding Leadership medal NASA, U.S. Antarctic Svc. medal. Mem. Am. Phys. Soc. Home: 907 Corinth Cir SE Huntsville AL 35801-2064 Office Phone: 256-961-7845. Business E-Mail: tom.parnell@msfc.nasa.gov.

PARNEROS, DEMOS, retail executive; Gen. mgr. Staples, Inc., Framingham, Mass., 1987, various positions in human resources, mktg., merchandising and store ops., v.p. ops., 1996—99, sr. v.p. ops., 1999—2002, pres. US stores, 2002—. Office: Staples Inc 500 Staples Dr Framingham MA 01702

PARNES, STUART L., museum director; b. Mass. m. Sue Ellen Thompson. Degree in Art History, Middlebury Coll. Various positions through dir. exhbns. Mystic Seaport, Conn., 1973—2000; exec. dir. Conn. River Mus., Essex, 2000—06; pres. Chesapeake Bay Maritime Mus., 2006—. Sec. gen. Internat. Congress of Maritime Mus. Mem.: Conn. Humanities Coun. (bd. dirs.), Coun. Am. Maritime Mus. (bd. dirs.), New Eng. Mus. Assn. (bd. dirs.), Nat. Assn. Mus. Exhbn. (bd. dirs.). Office: Chesapeake Bay Maritime Mus 213 N Talbot St Saint Michaels MD 21663 Office Phone: 410-745-2916. Office Fax: 410-745-6088. Business E-Mail: sparnes@cbmm.org.

PARNESS, IRA ALLEN, pediatric cardiologist; BA, Touro Coll., 1975; MD, SUNY, Bklyn., 1979. Diplomate Am. Bd. Pediat., Am. Bd. Pediat. Cardiology. Intern then resident in pediat. Brookdale Hosp. Med. Ctr., Bklyn., 1979—81, chief resident pediat., 1981-82; fellow pediat. cardiology Children's Hosp., Boston, 1982-85; asst. cardiology Children's Hosp. Boston, 1985-89, med. dir. heart transplant, 1986-92, assoc. cardiology, 1990-92; assoc. prof. divsn. pediat. cardiology Mt. Sinai Med. Ctr., NYC, 1992—, dir. pediat. echo. lab., 1992-2000, dir. divsn. pediat. cardiology, 1998—. Mem. Am. Heart Assn., Am. Acad. Pediat., Am. Coll. Cardiology, Soc. Pediat. Echocardiography, Am. Soc. Echocardiography. Office: Mt Sinai Med Ctr Box 1201 1 Gustave Levy Pl New York NY 10029 Office Phone: 212-241-6640.

PARNESS, JEROME, medical educator; s. Philip and Matilda Parness; m. Smadar Lerner Parness, Jan. 24, 1978; children: Elior Bat-Dor, Daniel Yitzhak, Ariele Maor, Noam Ezra Naftali. BA, Yeshiva Univer-sity, 1971; MSc, Hebrew U. Jerusalem, Israel, 1975; PhD, Sue golding Grad. Divsn., Albert Einstein Coll. Medicine, Yeshiva, 1982; MD, Albert Einstein Coll. Medicine Yeshiva U., Bronx, NY, 1985. Diplomate Am. Bd. Anesthesiology, 1991. Internship Bronx Mcpl. Hosp. Ctr., 1985—86; resident Hosp. U. Pa., Phila., 1986—89; fellow Children's Hosp. Phila., Phila., 1989—89; vis. prof. U. Pitts. Sch. Medicine, Pitts., 2005—; asst. prof. Robert Wood Johnson Med. Sch., U. of Medicin & Dentistry NJ, New Brunswick, NJ, 1989—96, assoc. prof., 1996—2005. Mem., bd. dirs. Congregation Ohr Torah, Edison, 2004—05; mem., bd. dirs. & edn. com. Congregation Poale Zedeck, Pitts., 2007—08; mem-,founder Moshe Aaron Yeshiva H.S., South River, NJ, 1993—2005; hotline cons. Malignant Hyperthermia Assn. US, Sherburne, NY, 2004—08; mem., rsch. com. Soc. Pediatric Anesthesia, Richmond, Va., 1999—2008. Recipient Anesthesiology Young Investigator award, Found. Anesthesia Edn. & Rsch., 1995—97; Albert Cass Traveling fellowship, Rockefeller U., 1984, Internat. Exch. fellowship, Ben-Gurion U., 1985. Mem.: AAAS, Soc. Pediatric Anesthesia, Am. Soc. Anesthesiologists, Biophysical Soc., Alpha Omega Alpha. Achievements include discovery of drug dantrolene works in controlling skeletal muscle calcium fluxes. Office: Children's Hosp Pitts 3705 Fifth Ave Pittsburgh PA 15213 Business E-Mail: parnessj@upmc.edu.

PARR, CAROLYN MILLER, arbitrator, retired federal judge; b. Palatka, Fla., Apr. 17, 1937; d. Arthur Charles and Audrey Ellen (Dunklin) Miller; m. Jerry Studstill Parr, Oct. 12, 1959; children: Kimberly Parr, Jennifer Parr Turek, Patricia Parr Smith. BA, Stetson U., 1959; MA, Vanderbilt U., 1960; JD, Georgetown U., 1977; LLD (hon.), Stetson U., 1986. Bar: Md. 1977, U.S. Tax Ct. 1977, D.C. 1979, U.S. Supreme Ct. 1983. Gen. trial atty. IRS, Washington, 1977-81, sr. trial atty. office of chief counsel, 1982; spl. counsel to asst. atty. gen. tax divsn. US Dept. Justice, Washington, 1982-85; judge US Tax Ct., Washington, 1985-2000, sr. judge, 2001—02; founder, abitrator/mediator: tax & comml. disputes Beyond Dispute Associates, Washington, 2002—. Nat. Def. fellow Vanderbilt U., 1959-60; fellow Georgetown U., 1975-76; recipient Spl. Achievement award, US Dept. Treasury, 1979; named a Disting. Alumnus, Stetson U., 1992 Mem. ABA, Md. Bar Assn., Nat. Assn. Women Judges, D.C. Bar Assn. Office: Beyond Dispute Associates 1750 K St NW Ste 350 Washington DC 20006 Office Phone: 202-359-6141. E-mail: carolynparr@beyonddispute.com.

PARR, GRANT VAN SICLEN, surgeon; b. NYC, Dec. 30, 1942; s. Ferdinand Van Siclen and Helene H. P.; m. Helen Mushat Frye, July 1, 1967; children: Kathleen Gage, Helen Johnston. AB with honors, Wesleyan U., 1965; MD, Cornell U., 1969. Diplomate Am. Bd. Thoracic Surgery, Am. Bd. Surgery. Intern, resident U. Hosps. of Cleve., 1969-71; resident in surgery U. Ala. Hosps., Birmingham, 1971-74, chief resident in surgery, 1974-75, resident in cardiovascular and thoracic surgery, 1975-77; practice medicine specializing in thoracic surgery Hershey, Pa., 1978-82; mem. staff Presbyn.-U. Pa. Med. Ctr., Phila., 1982-88, chief div. Thoracic surgery, 1984-88, acting chmn. Dept. Surgery, 1988, chief cardiovascular surgery, 1984-88; asst. prof. cardiothoracic surgery M.S. Hershey Med. Center, Hershey, Pa., 1987-88; chief cardiovascular surgery Morristown (N.J.) Meml. Hosp., 1988-97, co-chmn. dept. cardiovasc. scis., 1997—2004, chmn. dept. cardiovasc. medicine, 2004—06, med. dir. Cardiac Svc. Line, 2004—; asst. prof. Pa. State U., 1978-82; clin. assoc. prof. surgery U. Pa., 1982-89; assoc. prof. clin. surgery Columbia U., 1992—; physician in chief Gagnon Heart Hosp., 2007—. Chief cardiovasc. surgery Overlook Hosp., 1988—, Morristown Meml. Hosp., 1988—98; chmn. cardiovasc. surgery Atlantic Health Sys., 1998—, trustee, 1998—, med. dir. cardiac svcs., 2004—; vice chair Morris Township Parks and Recreation Found., 2005—; bd. mem. Homeless Solutions Inc., 2007—, Morristown Meml. Health Found., 2008—. Contbr. articles to profl. jours. Fellow Am. Coll. Cardiology, ACS, Am. Coll. Chest Physicians, Phila. Coll. Physicians, Royal Soc. Medicine; mem. AMA, Internat. Cardiovascular Soc., Assn. of Acad. Surgeons, Am. Assn. Thoracic Surgery, County Med. Soc., Soc. Thoracic Surgeons, Soc. Critical Care Medicine Pa., Thoracic Surg. Soc., John W. Kirklin Soc., Morris County Med. Sch., N.J. Soc. Thoracic Surgery, N.Y. Soc. Thoracic Surgery, Morris County Golf Club, NYU Club, Beaverkill Trout Club (pres., 2005). Office: 100 Madison Ave Morristown NJ 07960-6136 Office Phone: 973-971-7300, 973-971-5597.

PARR, JAMES ALLAN, literature professor; b. Ritchie County, W.Va., Oct. 7, 1936; s. James William and Virginia Alice (Bragg) P.; m. Franciszka Duda, May 4, 1957 (div. 1967): 1 child, Jacqueline; m. Carmen Salazar, Aug. 19, 1968 (div. 1980); m. Patricia Catherine Brinck, June 28, 1985. BA, Ohio U., 1959, MA, 1961; PhD, U. Pitts., 1967. Prof., chmn. Murray (Ky.) State U., 1964-70; prof. U. So. Calif., Los Angeles, 1970-90, U. Calif., Riverside, 1990—. Dir. Nat. Def. Edn. Act Inst., summers, 1966, 67, 69. Author: Don Quixote: An Anatomy of Subversive Discourse, 1988, Confrontaciones calladas, 1990, After Its Kind: Approaches to the Comedia, 1991, Don Quixote, Don Juan and Related Subjects, 2004, Don Quixote: A Touchstone for Literary Criticism, 2005; editor: Critical Essays on Juan Ruiz de Alarcon, 1972, El Burlador de Sevilla, 1991, On Cervantes: Essays for L.A. Murillo, 1991, Don Quixote, 1998; editor jour. Bull. of the Comediantes, 1973-98 Recipient Phi Beta Kappa award, Ohio U., 1960, Mellon fellowships, U. Pitts., 1961-63, Del Amo fellowship, U. So. Calif., Los Angeles, 1977, 84, 89, Fulbright, 1991. Mem. MLA, Am. Assn. Tchrs. of Spanish and Portuguese (pres.), Cervantes Soc. Am. (pres.). Avocation: travel. Home: 421 Elmwood Dr Pasadena CA 91105-1358 Office Phone: 951-827-1210.

PARR, JANET SMYTH, finance educator; d. Earl and Lillian Momi Smyth. BBA, Sam Houston State U., Huntsville, Tex., 1974. Letter of credit issuer, negotiator Allied Bank Tex., Houston, 1976—81; mgr. letters of credit Western Bank, Houston, 1981—86; trade fin. specialist, asst. cashier Bank America Internat., Houston, 1987; prof. dept. bus., fin. and legal studies Houston CC, 1987—, faculty mentor student mentor program, 2007—. Faculty rep. Adv. Com., Dept. Bus., Fin. and Legal Studies, Houston, 1987—. Leader Cub Scouts America, Houston, 1993—96, Vacation Bible Sch., First Bapt. Ch., Houston, 1994—2008, dir., 2007—08; leader, girls in action program First Bapt. Ch., 2007—08. Achievements include development of selling bank products and services course curriculum and implementation of departmental student job success tracking system. Business E-Mail: janet.parr@hccs.edu.

PARR, ROBERT GHORMLEY, chemistry professor; b. Chgo., Sept. 22, 1921; s. Leland Wilbur and Grace (Ghormley) P.; m. Jane Bolstad, May 28, 1944; children: Steven Robert, Jeanne Karen, Carol Jane. AB magna cum laude with high honors in Chemistry, Brown U., 1942; PhD in Phys. Chemistry, U. Minn., 1947; D (hon.), U. Leuven, 1986, Jagiellonian U., 1996. Asst. prof. chemistry U. Minn., 1947-48; mem. faculty Carnegie Inst. Tech., 1948-62, prof. chemistry, 1957-62, Johns Hopkins U., 1962-74, chmn. dept., 1969-72; William R. Kenan, Jr. prof. theoretical chemistry U. N.C., Chapel Hill, 1974-90, Wassily Hoeffding prof. chem. physics, 1990—. Vis. prof. chemistry, mem. Ctr. Advanced Study, U. Ill., 1962; disting. vis. prof. SUNY, Buffalo, Pa. State U., 1967; vis. prof. Japan Soc. Promotion Sci., 1968, 79, U. Haifa, 1977, Free U., Berlin, 1977, Duke U., 1996-97; Firth prof. U. Sheffield, 1976; Coochbehar prof. Indian Assn. Cultivation of Sci., 1990; Sandoval Vallarta prof. UAM-Iztapalapa, 1992; chmn. com. postdoctoral fellowships in chemistry NAS-NRC, 1961-63; chmn. panel theoretical chemistry Westheimer com. survey chemistry NAS, 1964; mem. coun. Gordon Rsch. Conf., 1974-76; mem. Commn. on Human Resources, NRC, 1979-82; mem. coun. Inst. for Molecular Sci., Okazaki, Japan, 1986-88; bd. trustees Inst. for Fundamental Chemistry, Kyoto, Japan, 1988—. Author: Quantum Theory of Molecular Electronic Structure, 1963, Density-Functional Theory of Atoms and Molecules, 1989, also numerous articles.; Assoc. editor: Jour. Chem. Physics, 1956-58, Chem. Revs, 1961-63, Jour. Phys. Chemistry, 1963-67, 77-79, Am. Chem. Soc. Monographs, 1966-71, Theoretica Chimica Acta, 1966-69, 92-96; Chinese Chem. Letters, 1998—; bd. editors: Jour. Am. Chem. Soc, 1969-77; adv. editorial bd.: Internat. Jour. Quantum Chemistry, 1967—, Chem. Physics Letters, 1967-79. Recipient Outstanding Achievement award U. Minn., 1968, N.C. Disting. Chemist award, 1982; fellow U. Chgo., 1949; research asso., 1957; Fulbright scholar U. Cambridge, Eng., 1953-54; Guggenheim fellow, 1953-54; NSF sr. postdoctoral fellow U. Oxford (Eng.) and Commonwealth Sci. and Indsl. Research Orgn., Melbourne, Australia, 1967-68; Sloan fellow, 1956-60, N.C. award in sci., 1999, North Carolina Govs. Alumni Sci. award, 1999. Fellow AAAS, Am. Phys. Soc. (chmn. divsn. chem. physics 1963-64); mem. NAS (award in chem. scis., 2004), AAUP, Am. Chem. Soc. (chmn. divsn. phys. chemistry 1978, Irving Langmuir award in chem. physics 1994, theoritical chemistry award 2009), Am. Acad. Arts and Sci., Indian Nat. Sci. Acad., Internat. Acad. Quantum Molecular Sci. (pres. 1991-97), Phi Beta Kappa, Sigma Xi, Phi Lambda Upsilon, Pi Mu Epsilon. Home: 701 Kenmore Rd Chapel Hill NC 27514-2019 Office: U NC Dept Chemistry Chapel Hill NC 27599-3290 Business E-Mail: rgparr@email.unc.edu.

PARR, VIRGINIA HELEN, retired librarian; b. Mansfield, Ohio, May 23, 1937; d. Bernard Franklin and Frances Cole (Downes) P.; m. Marvin E. Lickey, June 14, 1959 (div. 1972); children: Sarah Elizabeth, David Andrew, Rachel Alison; m. Laurence E. Steadman, Nov. 27, 1993 (div. 2007). AB, Oberlin Coll., 1959; AM, U. Mich., 1961; MLS, U. Oreg., 1973. English and social studies tchr. Whittier Jr. High Sch., Livonia, Mich., 1961-64; libr. U. Oreg. Libr., Eugene, 1973-79, head edn. and psychology, 1979-80, acting asst. univ. libr. for pub. svcs., 1980-82; head reference, rsch. and instrn. svcs. U. Cin., 1982-89, reference libr., bibliographer, 1989—2002, ret., 2002—. Chair, mem. budget com. Eugene Sch., 1976-79. Founding editor: Behavioral and Social Scis. Libr., 1978; contbr. articles to profl. jours. Bd. dirs. Eugene Jr. Symphony Assn., 1979-82; mem. adv. bd. various mental health groups, Eugene, 1971-79. Mem. Assn. Coll. and Rsch. Librs. of ALA (various offices edn. and behavioral sci. sect. 1977-86, numerous coms. reference and adult svcs. divsn. 1981-92), Beta Phi Mu, Pi Lambda Theta. Democrat. Avocations: reading, classical music, travel. Home: 5532 S Shore Dr 12F Chicago IL 60637-1990 E-mail: v_parr@sbcglobal.net.

PARRA, RAUL O., urologist, educator; s. Raul F. and Olena Parra; married; 3 children. MD, U. Seville, Spain, 1980. Diplomate Bd. Urology. Chmn. urology St. Louis U., 1989—99, Mayo Clinic, Jacksonville, Fla., 1995—2002; dir. urologic cancer surgery Oreg. Health and Sci. U., Portland, 2002—04; chmn. urology Cooper Health Sys., Robert Wood Johnson Sch. Medicine, Camden, NJ, 2004—. Author med. papers, book chpts., and textbooks. Office: Cooper Urology 3 Cooper Plz Camden NJ 08103 Home Phone: 856-424-0192; Office Phone: 856-963-3577. Business E-Mail: parra-raul@cooperhealth.edu.

PARRA, RO (ROSENDO G. PARRA), former computer company executive; b. Ecuador, Nov. 12, 1959; m. Cheryl L. Parra; 4 children. BA in Mktg., U. Md., 1982. Various sales, mgmt. positions, bus. prod. divsn. Tandy Corp.; various sales, gen. mgmt. positions GRiD Sys. Corp.; v.p. Dell USA, 1993—94; group v.p. sales, mktg. & services Dell Inc., 1994—97, v.p. pub. & Americas internat., 1997—98, sr. v.p. Americas pub. & Americas internat., 1998—2001, sr. v.p., gen. mgr. Americas, 2002—06, sr. v.p., worldwide home & small bus. group, 2006—07. Bd. dirs. Dell Inc., 2004—07. Named one of Most Important Hispanics in Tech., Bus., Hispanic Engineer and Info. Tech. mag., 2005.

PARRA-ARANGUREN, GONZALO, judge; b. Caracas, Venezuela, Dec. 5, 1928; Degree in Juridical and Polit. studies, Ctrl. U. Venezuela, 1950; degree, Inter-Am. Law Inst., NYU; LLD, Ludwig-Maximilians U., Munich. Prof. Ctrl. U. Venezuela, Caracas, 1956—96, Andrés Bello Cath. U., Caracas, 1957—96; judge 2d Ct. of 1st Instance Fed. Dist. and State of Miranda, Caracas, 1958-71; 1st assoc. judge Chamber of Cassation Supreme Ct. of Justice, Caracas, 1988-92, alt. judge, 1992—96; judge Internat. Ct. of Justice, The Hague, Netherlands, 1996—. Mem. legal adv. com. Ministry Fgn. Affairs, 1984—96, Nat. Congress, 1990—96; nat. grp. mem. Venezuela Permanent Ct. of Arbitration, The Hague, 1985—; Venezuelan rep. sessions of Hague Conf. on Pvt. Internat. Law. Author: (books) Die Regel "Locus Regit Actum" und die Fromen der Testamente, 1955, La Nacionalidad Venezolana Originaria, vols. I and II, 1964, La Constitucion de 1830 y los Venzolanos por Naturalizacion, 1969, La Influencia del Matrimonio sobre la Nacionalidad de la Mujer en la Legislacion Venzolana, 1983, Ensayos de Derecho Procesal Civil Internacional, 1986, Estudios de Derecho Mercantil Internacional, 1998, El Régimen de los Bienes en el Matrimonio en el Derecho Internacional Privado Venezolano, 2007, others. Mem.: Inst. Internat. Law, Acad. Polit. & Social Scis. Caracas (pres. 1993—95). Office: Internat Ct of Justice Peace Palace 2517 KJ The Hague Netherlands Business E-Mail: mail@icj-cij.org.

PARRA-DAVILA, EDUARDO, surgeon, educator; arrived in US, 1992; s. Alfonso Parra and Enma del Socorro Davila; m. Thaisabel Grisolia, May 23, 2003. MD, Universidad de los Andes, Merida, 1988. Gen. surgeon Jackson Meml. Hosp., U. Miami Miller Sch. Medicine, Fla., 1998; colorectal surgeon Colon and Rectal Clinic U. Tex., 1999; minimally invasive surgery fellow Tex. Endosurgery Inst., San Antonio, 2000; clin. asst. prof. surgery U. Miami Miller Sch. Medicine, 2001—03; staff colorectal and gen. surgeon VA Hosp., Miami, 2001—03, chief surgery, 2003; asst. prof. biomedical sci. U. Miami Miller Sch. Medicine, Fla. Atlantic U., Boca Raton, Fla., 2004—; dir. minimally invasive surgery program Boca Raton Cmty. Hosp., Fla., 2004—, co-dir. Abdominal Wall Reconstruction Ctr., 2006—07. Fellow: ACS (licentiate), Am. Soc. Colon and Rectal Surgeons (licentiate). Office: Surgical Assocs Palm Beach County 670 Glades Rd Ste 300 Boca Raton FL 33431 Home: 808 Rosa St Celebration FL 34747-4806 Personal E-mail: parra11@bellsouth.net.

PARRAGUIRRE, RONALD DAVID, state supreme court justice; b. Reno, July 8, 1959; s. Paul Charles and Iris Mae (Bleick) P.; m. Leslie, 2 children. BBA, San Diego State U., 1982; JD, U. San Diego, 1985. Bar: Pa. 1986, Nev. 1986, D.C. 1987. Legis. asst. U.S. Senator Paul Laxalt, Washington, 1985-86; counsel subcom. on criminal law, judiciary com. U.S. Senate, Washington, 1986-87; lawyer Parraguirre & Parraguirre, Las Vegas, Nev., 1987-91; mcpl. ct. judge Dept. 6 City of Las Vegas, 1991-99; dist. ct. judge Eighth Jud. Dist. Ct., Clark County, Nev., 1999—2004; justice Nev. Supreme Ct., 2004—. Mem. Nev. State-Federal Jud. Council, Nev. Supreme Ct. State Ct. Funding Com.; former mem. Nev. Supreme Ct. Jud. Election Practices Com. Mem. ABA, ATLA, Am. Judges Assn., Nev. Judges Assn., Nev. State Bar Assn. (mem. multi-jurisdictional task force com.), Clark County Bar Assn. (former exec. bd. mem.) Republican. Lutheran. Avocations: skiing, racquetball, hunting, fishing. Office: Nev Supreme Court 201 S Carson St Carson City NV 89701-4702*

PARRAMORE, BARBARA MITCHELL, education educator; b. Guilford County, NC, Aug. 29, 1932; d. Samuel Spencer and Nellie Gray (Glosson) Mitchell; m. Lyman Griffis Worthington, Dec. 23, 1956 (div. 1961); m. Thomas Custis Parramore, Jan. 22, 1966 (dec. Jan. 2004); children: Lisa Gray, Lynn Stuart. AB, U. N.C., Greensboro, 1954; MEd, N.C. State U., 1959; EdD, Duke U., 1968. Counselor, thcr. Raleigh City Schs., 1954-59, sch. prin., 1959-65; prof. dept. of curriculum and instrn. N.C. State U., 1970-96, prof. emeritus, 1996—. Acad. specialist Office Internat. Edn., U.S. Info. Svcs., sec. sch. initative program, The Philippines, 1987. Author: The People of North Carolina, 1972, 3rd edit. 1983. Japan Inst. Social and Econ. Affairs fellow, 1980; N.C. AAUW award for juvenile lit., 1973, Holladay medal for excellence N.C. State U., 1994. Mem. ASCD, N.C. ASCD (pres. 1994-96), N.C. Coun. for Social Studies (pres. 1985-87), Assn. Tchr. Educators, Delta Kappa Gamma, Kappa Delta Pi. Home: 5012 Tanglewood Dr Raleigh NC 27612-3135

PARRAN, RICHARD B., JR., telecommunications industry executive; BS in Mech. Engring., Duke U.; MBA, U. Chgo. Mgmt. positions Centel Corp.; gen. mgr., bus. svcs. telecom. bus. Paragon Cable; joined ADC Telecom. Inc., 1995, v.p., bus. devel., mergers & acquisitions, divestitures & venture capital investment activities, 2001—05, interim leader, profl. svcs. bus. unit, 2005—06, pres., profl. svcs. bus. unit, 2006—09, v.p. & pres., network solutions, 2009—. Bd. dirs. ADC Found. Office: ADC Telecommunications Inc 13625 Technology Dr Minneapolis MN 55440 Office Phone: 952-938-8080. Office Fax: 952-917-1717.*

PARR-CORRETJER, POLLY, singer, music educator; b. Sheffield, Eng., Jan. 9, 1951; arrived in U.S., 1981; d. Stanley and Edith Mary (Charlton) Parr; m. Carlos Ramon Corretjer, Dec. 16, 1978; 1 child, Richard Spencer. Assoc. in Singing and Piano, Royal No. Coll. Music, Manchester, Eng., 1972, Assoc. in Performing, 1973; grad., Royal Schs. Music, 1973; AA in Music and Gen. Studies, Prince Georges C.C., 1991. Featured soloist Cruise Ships, 1973—78; faculty Levine Sch. Music, Washington, 2002—04. Soprano soloist, dir. children's music Universalist Nat. Meml. Ch., Washington, 1989—96; asst. music dir., condr. Interact Theatre, Washington, 2001; guest coach for accompanists Washington Bible Coll., Greenbelt, Md.; fine arts vocal judge Grace Christian Sch., Bowie, 1998—2002; pvt. practice vocalist tchr., Bowie, Md., 1978—; piano & vocal judge Anne Arundel Music Tchrs. Assn. Spring Solo Festival, 2009. Mem.: Music Tchrs. Nat. Assn., Md. State Music Tchrs. Assn. Avocations: sewing, reading, travel. Home: 13201 Idlewild Dr Bowie MD 20715

PARRETT, JANELLE SWILLEY, secondary school educator; b. Meridian, Miss., Nov. 20, 1922; d. Edgar Rowan and Ada Swilley; m. Leslie Loring Parrett (dec. Nov. 2004); children: Ann Loring, John Edward. BS, La. State U., Baton Rouge, 1945; MA, Ohio State U., Columbus, 1949; elem. conversion, Ind. U., South Bend, 1964. Cert. tchr. La., Ohio. Instr. Ohio State U., 1945—49; tchr. elem. Plymouth Cmty. Schs., Ind., 1960—63, tchr. phys. edn. mid. sch., 1963—72, tchr. phys. edn., coach H.S., 1972—75. Vol. Fla Hosp. Heartland, 2000—01; group leader Covenant Presbyn. Ch. Summer Bibha Sch., asst. recreational leader, arts & carfts asst., kitchen asst.; chmn. food pantry for needy Covenant Presbyn. Ch. Women's Ministries, 2006—07. Mem.: AAHPERD, Ind. Alliance for Health, Phys. Edn. and Recreation (sec. 1963, v.p. 1964—66, chmn. Girls and Women's Sports divsn. 1969), St. Joseph Valley Golf Assn. (v.p. 1999, pres. 2001), Sun'n Lake Golf and Country Club (v.p. 1999—2000, pres. 1999—2000, study com. mem.). Republican. Presbyterian. Avocations: reading, bridge, swimming, golf. Home: 5710 Hampton Woods Blvd Sebring FL 33872 Personal E-mail: janelleparrett@comcast.net.

PARRETTE, LESLIE JACKSON, lawyer; b. Mt Pleasant, Mo., Aug. 25, 1961; s. Leslie Jackson and Janet Parrette. AB, Harvard Coll., 1983; JD, Harvard Law Sch., 1986. Assoc. Hale & Dorr, Boston, 1986-89, Watson Ess Marshall & Enggas, Kansas City, Mo., 1989-91, Bryan Cave, Kansas City, Mo., 1991-92; ptnr. Blackwell Sanders Peper Martin, Kansas City, Mo., 1992-2000; gen. coun., sr. v.p., corp. sec. Aquila Inc., Kansas City, Mo., 2000—05; corp. sec., gen. counsel Novelis Inc., 2005—09; sr. v.p. legal affairs Wesco Internat., Pitts., 2009—. Mem. Sister City Commn. of Kansas City, Mo., 1999—; bd. dirs. Am. Jazz Mus., 2002—03. Office: Wesco Internat 225 W Station Sq Dr Pittsburgh PA 15219*

PARRICK, GERALD HATHAWAY, communications and marketing executive; b. Cushing, Okla., Oct. 27, 1924; s. Gerald H. and Phyllis A. (Sheppard) B.; m. Gail V. Straney, Dec. 5, 1984; children: Gerald Hathaway III, Candace Anne. BJ, U. Mo., 1948. Creative account exec. George Knox & Assoc., Oklahoma City, 1948-51; account exec. Batten, Barton, Durstine & Osborn, San Francisco, 1952-60; account dir. McCann-Erickson, LA, 1960-67, v.p. Portland, Oreg., 1967-72; dir. comm. Pacific Power Co., Portland, 1972-77, spl. asst. to chmn. bd., 1977-79; pres. Entreepublic Comm., West Linn, Oreg., 1979—, Bailey/Parrick, Inc., Portland, 1981-84, Parrick/Milpacher, Inc., Portland, 1984-85, The Laugh Clinic, Inc., Portland, 1984-90, K-KOR, Inc., 1990-93. Author: A 20th Century Miracle, 1981, Touched by a Miracle, 1997. Mem. Oreg. Advt. Rev. Bd., 1974-75. Capt. AUS, 1943-45, 51-52, ETO. Named Oreg. Advt. Man of Yr., Oreg. Advt. Club, 1971. Mem. Am. Advt. Fedn. (chmn. edn. western region 1973-74), Portland Advt. Fedn. (pres. 1974-75), Toastmasters (pres. 1966-67) (Encino, Calif.), Kappa Tau Alpha. Home: 17185 Carlson Ct Lake Oswego OR 97034-5802 Home Phone: 503-675-3716. Personal E-mail: jergail@aol.com.

PARRILLO, JOSEPH EDISON, JR., allergist, immunologist, cardiologist; b. Paterson, NJ, Jan. 5, 1947; MD, Cornell U., 1972. Diplomate Am. Bd. Allergy and Immunology, Am. Bd. Internal Medicine, Am. Bd. Cardiology. From intern to resident in medicine Mass. Gen. Hosp., Boston, 1972-74, fellow in cardiology, 1978-80; resident in medicine N.Y. Hosp.-Cornell Med. Ctr., NYC, 1977-78; resident in allergy & immunology and infectious disease Clin. Ctr. Nat. Inst. Allergy and Immunology Disease, Bethesda, Md., 1974-77; med. staff Rush-Presbyn.-St. Lukes Med. Ctr., Chgo.; chief divsn. cardiology and critical care medicine Rush Heart Inst.; dir., chief medicine Cooper Heart Inst.; Edward Viner chmn. Dept. Med. Cooper U. Hosp.; and prof. medicine UMDNJ-RWJMS at Camden. Mem. Am. Coll. Cardiology, Am. Fedn. Clin. Rsch., Am. Heart Assn., Am. Soc. Clin. Investigation, Assoc. Am. Phys., Am. Coll. Critical Care Medicine, Am. Coll. Chest Physicians, Soc. Critical Care Medicine, Alpha Omega Alpha. Office: Cooper Univ Hosp Dorrance Bldg 3d Fl One Cooper Plaza Camden NJ 08103 Office Phone: 856-968-8349. Business E-Mail: Parrillo-Joseph@cooperhealth.edu.

PARRIS, NINA GUMPERT, curator, writer, researcher, photographer; b. Berlin, Sept. 11, 1927; came to U.S., 1937, naturalized, 1944; d. Martin and Charlotte (Blaschko) Gumpert; m. Arthur Parris, Feb. 13, 1949 (div. 1974); children: Carl Joseph, Thomas Martin. BA, Bryn Mawr Coll., 1968; MA, U. Pa., 1969, PhD, 1979. Tchg. fellow U. Mich., Ann Arbor, 1969-70; lectr. Phila. Coll. Art, 1970-71; rsch. asst. Phila. Mus. Art, 1970-71; curator, lectr. U. Vt. Robert Hall Fleming Mus., Burlington, 1971-79; chief curator Columbia Mus., SC, 1979-89, 2003—; resident faculty visual arts Vt. Coll. Norwich U., 1991—2003; chair visual arts Burlington Coll., 1996-99, Union Inst. Author: Prints, Paintings and Drawings in Collection of Robert Hall Fleming Mus., 1979 (exhbn. catalog) Through a Master Printer, 1985, The South Carolina Collection of the Columbia Museum, 1987; columnist State newspaper, Columbia, 1984-88; solo shows at Meteor Gallery, Columbia, 1993, Living Learning Ctr., U. Vt., 1994, St. Michael's Coll. McCarthy Arts Ctr., 1995, Colburn Gallery, U. Vt., 1996; group shows at Westbeth Gallery, N.Y.C., 1993, Thomas Waterman Wood Gallery, Vt., 1994, 96, 2001, 02, Firehouse Gallery, Burlington, 1996, Box Car Exhbn., Burlington, 1996, 98, Soho 20 Gallery, N.Y.C., 1996, 97, 98, Flynn Dog Gallery, 2003. Bd. dirs. Photography Coop., Montpelier, Vt.,

1977-79, Chittenden Arts Coun., Burlington, 1976-78. Woodrow Wilson fellow, 1968, Univ. fellow Ford Found., 1968-72; grantee NEA, NEH, S.C. Com. Humanities, Vt. Coun. Arts. Mem. Am. Assn. Museums (pres. curator's com. 1985-87, v.p. 1983-85). Personal E-mail: nina.parris85@gmail.com.

PARRISH, ALISSA RENEE, nursing educator; b. Murray, Ky., Sept. 29, 1979; d. Terry and Cynthia Rice; m. Jonathan Parrish, June 5, 1999; children: Emilee Faith, Gavin Blaine. MSN, U. Phoenix, 2007; BSN, Murray State U., 1997—2002. RN Henry County Med. Ctr., Paris, Tenn., 2002—; asst. prof. nursing U. Tenn. Martin, 2007—. Mem.: Assn. Womens's Health and Neonatal Nurses. Home: 100 Dixie Village Ln Paris TN 38242 Office: Univ Tenn Martin Dept Nursing 141B Gooch Hall Martin TN 38238 Office Fax: 731-881-7939. Business E-Mail: aparrish@utm.edu.

PARRISH, CARL E., liberal arts professor, director; b. Cuthbert, Ga., Jan. 21, 1945; s. Carl Edward and Frances Allen Parrish; m. Sarah Carter, Dec. 22, 1966 (div. Dec. 1976); 1 child, Rebecca Carter. AB cum laude, Harvard U., 1967; MA, Emory U., Atlanta, 1972. Head liberal arts dept. Atlanta Coll. of Art, 1997—2006; prof. liberal arts Savannah Coll. Art and Design, Atlanta, 2006—. Rschr. Helike (Greece) Archeol. Project, 2004. Author: (plays) Jimmy!, 1993. Head protocol Alex. Coliseum, Internat. Olympic Com., Atlanta, 1996; vol. Caretta Rsch. Project for sea turtle preservation, 2003, 2005. Study grantee, Atlanta Coll. Art, Harvard U., 2000, Rsch. grantee, Atlanta Coll. Art, Oxford U., Eng., 2001, Atlanta Coll. Art, Sorbonne, 2002, del., Social Justice and Ednl. Equity, 2008. Mem.: Harvard Club Hong Kong, Ednl. Equity and Social Justice (China) (people del. 2008), Archeol. Inst. Am., Nat. Assn. Schs. Art and Design, Caretta Rsch Project (vol. sea turtle preservation), Coll. Art Assn. (mem. diversity com.), Harvard Club of N.Y.C., Harvard Faculty Club, Harvard Club of Ga. (scholarship com. 1992—95, v.p. membership 1994—96). Avocation: bridge.

PARRISH, CHARLES S., lawyer, oil industry executive; BA in History with honors, U. Va.; JD, U. Houston Law Sch. Pvt. practice, Houston and San Antonio; v.p., asst. gen. counsel, sec. Tesoro Corp., San Antonio, 1994—2005, 2005—06, sr. v.p., gen. counsel, sec., 2006—, exec. v.p., gen. counsel & sec., 2009. Mem.: ABA, State Bar Tex. Office: Tesoro Corp 19100 Ridgewood Pky San Antonio TX 78259 Office Phone: 210-626-6000. Office Fax: 210-745-4494. Business E-Mail: charles.s.parrish@tsocorp.com.

PARRISH, D. MICHAEL, manufacturing executive; BSCE, U. Toledo, Ohio, 1975. Engr. Vulcraft divsn. Nucor Corp., St. Joe, Ind., 1975-81, engring. mgr. Vulcraft divsn. Brigham City, Utah, 1981-86, prodn. mgr. Vulcraft divsn. Ft. Payne, Ala., 1986-89, gen. mgr. Vulcraft divsn. Brigham City, 1989-91, gen. mgr. steel divsn. Jewett, Tex., 1991-95, Hickman, Ark., 1995-90, v.p. Charlotte, NC, 1990-98, exec. v.p. steel products, 1998—. Office: Nucor Corp 1915 Rexford Rd Charlotte NC 28211 Office Phone: 704-366-7000. Office Fax: 704-362-4208.

PARRISH, DAVID WALKER, JR., retired legal publishing company executive; b. Bristol, Tenn., Feb. 8, 1923; BA, Emory and Henry Coll., 1948, LLD, 1978; BS, US Mcht. Marine Acad., 1950; LLB, U. Va., Charlottesville, 1951. Pres. The Michie Co., Charlottesville, Va., 1969-89, vice chmn., 1989-96. Named to Sports Hall of Fame, Emory & Henry Coll. Mem.: ABA, Va. Bar Assn.

PARRISH, DENISE KAY, regulatory accountant; b. Garden City, Mich., May 20, 1954; d. Lewis William and Carol Ruby (Doederlein) P.; m. Michael Joseph Krause, Oct. 10, 1986 (div. Apr. 1992); m. Joseph Rickie Walsh, Oct. 2000. BA in Acctg., Mich. State U., 1976. Analyst Mich. Pub. Svc. Commn., Lansing, 1977-81; sr. fin. analyst Colo. Pub. Utilities Commn., Denver, 1981-85; chief rate analyst Ariz. Residential Utilities Consumer Office, Phoenix, 1985—86, Ariz. Corps. Commn., Phoenix, 1986-91; mgr. rates and pricing Wyo. Pub. Svc. Commn., Cheyenne, 1991—2003, dep. adminstr. office of consumer advocate, 2003—. Faculty mem. Inst. Pub. Utilities Mich. State U.; seminar instr. in field; presenter in field. Mem. ch. coun. local Luth. Ch., 1999—2001, chmn. long range planning com., 2005. Mem. Nat. Assn. Regulatory Utility Commrs. (chair SEC/FASB Task Force 1992-98, vice chmn. 1997-2000, mem. oversight com. on joint telecomm. audits 1991-92, 96-2001, chmn. acctg. subcom. 2000-03, subcom. internat. rels. 2005-, chmn. internat. rels. 2008—). Lutheran. Avocations: reading, travel, gardening. Office: Wyo Office Consumer Advocate 2515 Warren Ave Ste 304 Cheyenne WY 82001-3113 Home Phone: 307-632-5606; Office Phone: 307-777-5743. Business E-Mail: dparri@state.wy.us.

PARRISH, EDGAR L., financial services executive; b. Washington, Apr. 11, 1948; s. Frank Jennings Parrish and Lorene (Lomax) Parrish.; m. Katherine Ellen MacLachlan; children: Robert Alexander Wilson, Stephen Edgar MacLachlan. BS in Commerce, U. Va., 1970. Cert. fin. planner, investment mgmt. analyst. Sr. v.p. Wheat, First Securities, Inc., Washington, 1971—79; v.p. Merrill Lynch, Pierce, Fenner & Smith, Inc., Washington, 1979—82, Phila., 1982—85; mem. chmns. club Merrill Lynch, Pierce, Fenner & Smith, 1983—84; sr. v.p., fin. cons. Shearson Lehman Bros., Inc., Phila., 1985—87, Washington, 1987—93, mem. chmn.'s coun., 1987—92, mem. dirs. coun., 1986; sr. v.p. investments, Parrish Consulting Group UBS Fin. Svcs., Inc., Washington, 1993—2004, mem. Pacesetter Coun., 1994—2003, managed account cons., 1998—99, sr. managed account cons., 2000—04, Parrish Consulting Group, Merrill Lynch, 1st v.p. investments, wealth mgmt. advisor, 2004—, mem. pres. club, 2004, mem. chmns. club, 2005—07. Pres. HESCO Corp., Manassas, Va., 1989—2007, also chmn. bd. dirs.; arbitrator FINRA. Mem. Adv. Bd. McIntire Sch. Commerce U. Va., 2002—; past chmn. investment com. Nat. Presbyn. Sch., Washington. Capt. USAFR, 1970-76. Mem. U. Va. Alumni Assn. (life), Investment Mgmt. Cons. Assn., Fin. Planning Assn. Reserve Officers Assn. (life), Rotunda Soc., Kenwood Country Club Episcopalian. Home: 4502 Wetherill Rd Bethesda MD 20816-1813 Office Phone: 202-659-7532.

PARRISH, EDWARD ALTON, JR., electrical and computer engineering educator, academic administrator; b. Newport News, Va., Jan. 7, 1937; s. Edward Alton and Molly Wren (Vaughn) Parrish; m. Shirley Maxine Johnson, Oct. 26, 1963; children: Troy Alton, Gregory Sinton. BEE, U. Va., 1964, MEE, 1966, DScEE, 1968. Registered Tenn., Va. Group leader Amerad Corp., Charlottesville, Va., 1961—64; asst. prof. elec. engring. U. Va., Charlottesville, 1968—71, assoc. prof. elec. engring., 1971—77, prof. elec. engring., 1977—86, chmn. dept. elec. engring., 1978—86; dean, centennial prof. electrical engring. Vanderbilt U., Nashville, 1987—95; pres., prof. elec. and computer engring. Worcester Poly. U., 1995—2004, pres. emeritus, 2004—. Cons. U.S. Army, Charlottesville, Va., 1971—77, ORS, Inc., Princeton, NJ, 1973—74, Sperry Marine Systems, Charlottesville, 1975—76, Hajime Industries Ltd., Tokyo, 1978—84. Contbr. articles to profl. jours. With USAF, 1954—58. Grantee numerous rsch. grants. Fellow: IEEE (bd. dirs. 1990—91, v.p. ednl. activities 1992—93, engring. accreditation commn. 1989—96, exec. com. 1991—96, officer 1993—96, chmn. elect 1994—95, chmn. 1995—96, past chmn. 1996—97, editor-in-chief IEEE Computer 1995—98), ABET (bd. dirs. 2000—); mem.: IEEE Computer Soc. (sec. 1997, v.p. 1978—81, pres. 1988), Tau Beta Pi, Eta Kappa Nu, Sigma Xi. Baptist. Avocations: music, woodworking. E-mail: eap@wpi.edu.

PARRISH, JILL NIEDERHAUSER, state supreme court justice; BA, Weber State U., 1982; JD, Yale U., 1985. Bar: Utah 1985, 10th Cir. Ct. Appeals 1987, U.S. Supreme Ct. 2000. Clk. Hon. David K. Winder U.S. Dist. Ct., Utah, 1985; atty. Parr, Wadddoups, Brown, Gee & Loveless, Salt Lake City, 1986—90, shareholder, 1990—95; asst. U.S. atty. Civil Divsn. U.S. Dist. Ct., Utah, 1995—2003; justice Utah Supreme Ct., Salt Lake City, 2003—, mem. tech. com., judicial performance evaluation com., 2003—. Supr. Fin. Litigation Unit U.S. Attys. Office. Mem.: Fed. Bar Assn. (pres.). Office: Utah Supreme Ct PO Box 140210 Salt Lake City UT 84114-0210*

PARRISH, JOHN EDWARD, state appellate judge; b. Lebanon, Mo., June 10, 1940; s. Folie and Thelma (Osborn) P.; m. Claudia Barbee, Sept. 1, 1962; 1 child, Mark Everett. BBA, U. Mo., 1962, JD, 1965. Acct. Arthur Andersen & Co., St. Louis, 1965-66; ptnr. Phillips & Parrish, Camdenton, Mo., 1968-73; prosecuting atty. Camden County, Camdenton, 1969-73; circuit judge State of Mo., Camdenton, 1973-1990, judge Mo. Ct. Appeals (southern dist.), 1990-; mem. State Adv. Group on Juvenile Justice, Jefferson City, Mo., 1981—; Bd. dirs. Lake Regional Health Sys., Osage Beach, Mo., 1977—, pres. 1983-85, 1991-93, 1999-2001. Capt. U.S. Army, 1966-68. Mem. Mo. Bar Assn., Mo. Jud. Conf. (exec. coun. 1980-87, 92-94). Mem. Methodist Ch. Office: MO Ct Appeals 300 Hammons Pky Springfield MO 65806

PARRISH, OVERTON BURGIN, JR., pharmaceutical corporation executive; b. Cin., May 26, 1933; s. Overton Burgin and Geneva Opal (Shinn) P. BS, Lawrence U., 1955; MBA, U. Chgo., 1959. With Pfizer Inc., 1959-74; salesman Pfizer Labs., Chgo., 1959-62, asst. mktg. product mgr. NYC, 1962-63, product mgr., 1964-66, group product mgr., 1966-67, mktg. mgr., 1967-68, v.p. mktg., 1969-70, v.p., dir. ops., 1970-71; exec. v.p. domestic pharm. div. Pfizer Pharms., 1971-72; exec. v.p., dir. Pfizer Internat. Divsn., 1972-74; pres., chief operating officer G.D. Searle Internat., Skokie, Ill., 1974-75, pres., chief exec. officer, 1975-77; pres. Worldwide Pharm./Consumer Products Group, 1977-86; pres., chief exec. officer Phoenix Health Care, Chgo., 1987—; chmn., CEO, bd. dirs. Wis. Pharmiacal Co., Inc., 1990-96; co-chmn. Inhalon Pharms., 1991-95, also bd. dirs.; chmn. ViatiCare Fin. Svcs. LLC, 1993—, also bd. dirs.; chmn., CEO, bd. dirs. The Female Health Co., 1996—. Bd. dirs., chair Abiant Inc.; dir. Pharms. Inc., 2007—. Author: The Future Pharmaceutical Marketing; International Drug Pricing, 1971. Trustee Mktg. Sci. Inst.; trustee Food and Drug Law Inst., 1979-86, Lawrence U., 1983-87, 98—. Served to 1st lt. USAF, 1955-57. Mem. Beta Gamma Sigma, Phi Kappa Tau.

PARRISH, STEVEN C., tobacco company executive; BA in Polit. Sci., U. Mo., 1972, JD, 1975. Joined Philip Morris Cos., 1990, sr. v.p. external affairs, gen. counsel, 1992—94, sr. v.p. worldwide regulatory affairs, 1994—95; sr. v.p. corp. affairs Altria Group, Inc., NYC, 1995—. Vice chmn. bd. dirs. Safe Horizon; bd. dirs. Stamford Symphony Orch. Office: Alteria Corporate Services INC 615 Maury ST Richmond VA 23224-4121

PARRISH, THOMAS KIRKPATRICK, III, marketing consultant; b. Richmond, Va., May 18, 1930; s. Thomas Kirkpatrick and Sally Cary (Friend) P.; divorced: children: Linn Cary, Wayne Elizabeth, Susan Scott, Thomas Kirkpatrick IV. AB, Princeton U., 1952. Product mgr. Vick Chem. Co., NYC, 1955-58; v.p. Benton & Bowles Advt. Agy., NYC, 1958-65; pres. Am. Chicle Co. div. Warner-Lambert Co., Morris Plains, NJ, 1965-70, Life Savers Inc. div. Squibb Corp., NYC, 1970-73, Lanvin-Charles of Ritz Inc. subs. Squibb Corp., NYC, 1974-76; dir. parent co. Squibb Corp., 1974-77; group dir. new bus. devel. Gillette Co., Boston, 1977-78; exec. v.p. SSC & B, Inc., NYC, 1978-81; sr. assoc. Am. Cons. Corp., 1982-86; prin. The Parrish Co., NYC, 1986—. Mem. N.Y. State Republican Com., 1962-63; bd. dirs. YMCA Ctr. for Internat. Mgmt. Studies, N.Y.C., 1970-85. Served to lt., jr. grade USN, 1952-55. Home: 231 Elsinore St Apt 7 Concord MA 01742 Home Phone: 978-254-5069.

PARR-JOHNSTON, ELIZABETH, economist, consultant; d. Ferdinand Van Siclen and Helene H. Parr; m. David E. Bond, Dec. 28, 1962 (div. July 1975); children: Peter V.S., Kristina Aline; m. Archibald F. Johnston, Mar. 6, 1982; children: James, Heather, Alexandra, Margaret. BA, Wellesley Coll., 1961; MA, Yale U., 1962, PhD, 1973; postgrad., Harvard U., 1986; DLitt, U. NB, 2004. Various positions Govt. of Can., Ottawa, Ont., Canada, 1973-76, INCO Ltd., Toronto, 1976-79; chief of staff, sr. policy advisor Ministry of Employment and Immigration, Govt. of Can., 1979-80; various positions Shell Can. Ltd., Calgary, Alta., Canada, 1980-90; pres. Parr-Johnston & Assocs., Calgary, 1990-91; pres., vice-chancellor Mt. St. Vincent U., Halifax, Nova Scotia, N.S., Canada, 1991-96, The U. New Brunswick, Fredericton, Canada, 1996—2002; pres. Parr Johnston Econ. and Policy Cons., Chester Basin, N.S., Canada, 2002—. Instr. U. We. Ont., London, 1964—67, U. B.C., Vancouver, 1967—71; vis. scholar Wesleyan U., Middletown, Conn., 1971—72; acad. rsch. assoc. Carleton U., Ottawa, 1972—73; bd. dirs. Emera Ltd., Bank of Nova Scotia, Social Rsch. Demonstration Corp., Can. Millennium Scholarships Found.; chair Coun. Can. Acads.; spkr. and presenter in field; chair IRDC. Mem. editl. bd. Can. Econ. Jour., 1980—83; contbr. articles to profl. jours. Planning chmn. John Howard Soc., 1980—84; mem. policy adv. com. C.D. Howe, 1980—85; mem. Ont. Econ. Coun., 1981—84, 2005—06; bd. dirs. Dellcrest Home, 1980—84, Calgary S.W. Fed. Riding Assn., 1985—91, The Learning Ctr., Calgary, 1989—91, Halifax United Way, 1991—92, North/South Inst., 1992—96, Can. Unity Coun., 1993—2005, Vol. Planning N.S., 1992—93, Nova Scotia Power, 1993—2007, Social Sci. Human Rsch. Coun., 1995—98, FPI Ltd., 1996—2001, Empire Co., 1994—2002, Atlantic Inst. Market Studies, 2002—06, Sustainable Devel. Tech. Found., 2002—07, Symphony Nova Scotia, 2003—06, Nat. Theatre Sch. Recipient C. M. (Order Can.), Canada 125 medal, Queen's Jubilee medal; Hon. Woodrow Wilson fellow, 1962. Mem. Assn. Atlantic Univs. (chair 1994-96), Assn. Univs. and Colls. in Can. (bd. dirs., mem. exec. com. 1994-96), Women in Acad. Adminstrn. (adv. bd. 1991-96), Calgary Coun. Advanced Tech. (exec. 1990-91), Can. Econs. Assn., Inst. Pub. Adminstrn. Can., Sr. Women Acad. Adminstrs. Can., Assn. Commonwealth Univs. (former mem. exec. com.), Order of Can., Phi Beta Kappa. Anglican. Avocations: golf, travel. Home: PO Box 219 Chester Basin NS Canada B0J 1K0

PARRON, DELORES L., retired federal agency administrator; b. Red Bank, NJ, Jan. 14, 1944; d. James W. and Ruth Pitts Parron; m. Sherman L. Ragland. BA, Georgian Ct. Coll., 1966; MSW, Cath. U., 1968, PhD, 1977. Psychiat. social worker Hillcrest Children's Ctr., Washington, 1969—71; asst. prof. dept. psychiatry Howard U. Coll. Medicine, Washington, 1971—78; social sci. analyst Pres. Commn. on Mental Health, Washington, 1977—78; sr. program officer Inst. Medicine, NAS, Washington, 1978—83; assoc. dir. Nat. Inst. Mental Health, Rockville, Md., 1983—99; dep. asst. sec. for planning and evaluation U.S. Dept. Health and Human Svcs., Washington, 1999—2001; sci. advisor for capacity devel. Nat. Inst. Health, Bethesda, Md., 2001—07. Trustee Georgian Ct. Coll., Lakewood, NJ, 1996—2001, Ctr. for the Advancement Health, Washington, 1995—2001. Recipient Disting. Alumnae award, Cath. U. Am., 1993, George Ct. U. Fellow: Nat. Acad. Pub. Adminstrn.; mem.: Am. Psychological Assn. (award 2008).

PARROQUIN, RACHEL RIVERS, language educator; b. Indpls., Aug. 15, 1962; d. Clarence Charles and Margaret Michael Rivers; m. Eduardo Francisco Parroquin, Nov. 29, 1986; children: Marc Eduard, Elisabeth Marie, John Charles. BA in Spanish, 1985, BS in Elem. Edn., 1985; MEd, Valparaiso U., Ind., 1990; EdD, Loyola U., Chgo., 2008. Primary tchr., English as fgn. lang. Colegio Americano de Puebla, Mexico, 1985—86; tchr. Kouts Elem. Sch., Ind., 1986—89, Immanuel Luth. Sch., Valparaiso, 1991—93; ESL instr. Interlink Lang. Ctr., Valparaiso, 1996—2000; lectr. Spanish Valparaiso U., 2000—. Translating & interpreting Porter County Interlocal Spl. Edn. Coop., Valparaiso, 2008—, Med. & Ednl. Svc. Learning Trips Costa Rica, Nicaragua, 2009; translator Alzheimer's Assn., Chgo., 2003, Indsl. Steel Corp., Gary, Ind., 2001, Interlink Lang. Ctr., Valparaiso. Contbr. to conference presentations. Grant, Valparaiso U., 2002, 2003, 2004, 2007—08, VUAA Faculty Devel. Grant, Valparaiso U. Alumni Assn., 2007. Office: Valparaiso Univ 1800 Chapel Dr Valparaiso IN 46383 Office Fax: 219-464-6952. Business E-Mail: rachel.parroquin@valpo.edu.

PARROTT, DENNIS BEECHER, retired insurance industry executive; b. St. Louis, June 13, 1929; s. Maurice Ray and Mai Ledgerwood (Beecher) P.; m. Vivian Cleveland Miller, Mar. 24, 1952; children: Constance Beecher, Dennis Beecher, Anne Cleveland. BS in Econs., Fla. State U., Tallahassee, 1954; postgrad., Princeton U., NJ, 1964; MBA, Pepperdine U., Malibu, Calif., 1982. With Prudential Ins. Co. Am., 1954-74, v.p. group mktg. LA, 1971-74; sr. v.p. Frank B. Hall Cons. Co., LA, 1974—83; v.p. Johnson & Higgins, LA, 1983-95; exec. v.p. Arthur J. Gallagher & Co., LA, 1995-98; ret., 1998. Spkr. in field. Chmn. Weekend with the Stars Telethon, 1976-80; chmn. bd. dirs. United Cerebral Palsy/Spastic Children's Found., LA County, 1979-82, chmn. bd. govs., 1982-83; bd. dirs. Nat. United Cerebral Palsy Assn., 1977-82, pres., 1977-79; bd. dirs. LA Emergency Task Force, 1992; mem. cmty. adv. coun. Birmingham High Sch., Van Nuys, Calif., 1982-85; sect. chmn. United Way, LA, 1983-84; bd. dirs. The Betty Clooney Found. for Brain Injured, 1986-88; mem. com. to fund an endowed chair in cardiology at Cedars-Sinai Med. Ctr., 1986-88; adv. coun. Family Health Program, Inc., 1986-88; bd. deacons Bel Air Presbyn. Ch., 1990-92, chmn., 1991-92, elder, 1993-96; mem. adv. coun. Blue Cross Calif., 1996-98; chmn. Danny Arnold Meml. Golf Classic at Riviera Country Club benefitting John Wayne Cancer Inst., 1997. 1st lt. AUS, 1951-53. Named Tournament Champion, Sunkist Invitational Golf Tournament, 1995. Mem. Am. Soc. CLUs, Internat. Found. Employee Benefits, Mchts. and Mfrs. Assns. 44th Ann. Mgmt. Conf. (chmn. 1986), Employee Benefits Planning Assn. So. Calif., LA Club, Woodland Hills Country Club, Jonathan Club (LA). Republican. Presbyterian. Home: 17023 Encino Hills Dr Encino CA 91436-4009 Personal E-mail: CallParrott@aol.com.

PARROTT, JEFFREY KEITH, linguist, researcher; b. 1974; s. Keith and Wanda Parrott; m. Klara Hobza, 2002. BA in Applied Linguistics, Portland State U., Oreg., 1998; PhD in Linguistics, Georgetown U., Wash., 2007. Vis. lectr. sociolinguistics Univ. Cyprus, Dept. English Studies, Nicosia, 2007; postdoc. rschr. LANCHART Ctr., Univ. Copenhagen, 2008—. Office: LANCHART Ctr Univ Copenhagen Njalsgade 136 275 Copenhagen 2300 Denmark Business E-Mail: jeffreyp@hum.ku.dk.

PARROTT, NEVA, language educator; d. Frank and Marian Walker; m. Tom Parrott. MA, Wichita State U., Kans., 1977. Bilingual sec. J. A. Chalkley Elem. Sch., Chesterfield, Va., 2006—; adj. prof. Spanish John Tyler CC, Richmond, Va., 2007—. Office: John Tyler CC 800 Charter Colony Pky Midlothian VA 23114-4383

PARRY, DALE D., publisher, editor; BS in Journalism cum laude, Ball State U., Muncie, Ind., 1981. Feature writer Richmond (Ind.) Palladium-Item, 1981-84, Cin. Enquirer, 1984-86; editor Today section The Dallas Morning News, 1987-90; assignment editor The Way We Live sect. Detroit Free Press, 1990-92, dep. features editor, 1992-94, features editor, 1993-96, asst. mng. editor, 1997-2000, dep. mng. editor, 2001—06; pub. Signature Media, Detroit, 2007—. Mem. Am. Assn. Sun. and Feature Editors. Office: Signature Media 615 W Lafayette Blvd Detroit MI 48226

PARRY, DAVID C., engineering executive; BSc in Chemistry, U. Manchester, Eng., 1974, MSc in Chemistry, 1975, PhD in Chemistry, 1977. With Ill. Tool Works (ITW), Glenview, Ill., 1994—, gen. mgr. Devon Plexus and ITW Devcon, v.p., gen. mgr. Performance Polymers, 2001—04, pres. Performance Polymers, 2004—06, exec. v.p. polymers and fluids, 2006—. Office: Ill Tool Works 3600 W Lake Ave Glenview IL 60026-1215 Office Phone: 847-657-4575. Office Fax: 847-657-4392.*

PARRY, JANET, retired health facility administrator; b. Salt Lake City, Nov. 5, 1943; d. Nathaniel Edmunds Parry and Dortha Nell (Harris) Parry-Miller. BSN, U. Utah, Salt Lake City, 1966. RN Calif. Pres. Med. Mgmt. Cons., Anaheim, Calif., 1970—91; v.p. Parry Devel. Co., Anaheim, 1971—91; property mgr. Parry Profl. Bldg., Anaheim, 1981—95; founding ptnr. Med. Billing Specialist, Anaheim, 1991, PPP Med. Practice Sales, Anaheim, 1995; sales assoc. P & F Investment Property Mgmt., Anaheim, 1994, Boydston Realty, Anaheim, 1994—95; ret., 1995. Pres., chmn. bd. dirs. Anaheim Meml. Hosp. Contbr. articles to profl. publs. V.p. Aspen Hollow Homeowners Assn., 2003—05, pres., 2007—; mem. Caritas Chorale of Sun Valley, 2001—, pres., 2005—06, co-chmn. benefit dinner com., 2003—04, bd. dirs., 2003—07, v.p., 2004—05; asst. dir. Promise Christmas Chorale, 2001—02; mem. St. Luke's Hosp. Aux., Sun Valley, 2000—01; bd. dirs. Anaheim Meml. Hosp. Found., 1987—96, v.p., 1991—96, chmn. bd. dirs., 1994; mem. Anaheim Bd. Realtors, 1987—97; mem., bd. dirs., treas. Tustin Main St. Chorus, 1991—94; mem. med. adv. bd. So. Calif. Coll. Med. and Dental Assts., 1972—85; mem. citizen's adv. com. Anaheim Hills Hosp., 1982—84; mem. Anaheim Sister City Com. to Mito, Japan, 1985; exec. prodr. Miss Anaheim Pageant, 1983—84; mem. Anaheim Halloween Festival Com., 1983; treas. Tu Casa Condo. Assn., Carlsbad, Calif., 1976—77; mem. Mormon Tabernacle Choir, Salt Lake City, 1966—68; bd. dirs. U. Utah Coll. Nursing, 2001—03, Am. Heart Assn., 1993—95. Recipient Annie Accolade award, Women's Divsn. Anaheim C. of C., 1984, Women of Achievement award, YWCA, Orange, Calif., 1985. Home: PO Box 3299 Ketchum ID 83340

PARRY, LANCE AARON, publishing executive; b. Allentown, Pa., Sept. 4, 1947; s. Harwood Clayton Bachman and Iola Mary (Johnson) P.; m. Virginia Eleanor Ford, Apr. 24, 1971; children: Halloran Lee, Christine Ford. BS in English Edn., Kutztown U., 1969; MS in

Journalism, W.Va. U., 2003. With Call-Chronicle Newspapers, Allentown, 1970-81, mng. editor, 1979-81; asst. news editor The Phila. Inquirer, 1981-82, systems editor, 1982-84, night news editor, 1984-86, news editor daily edit., 1986-87, news editor Sunday edit., 1987-89, sr. editor/systems and tech., 1989-93, page design dir., 1993-94, features news editor, 1994-96, news editor Sunday edit., 1996-98, features news editor, 1998—2004, news editor, 2005, sr. news editor, 2005—. Recipient 1st Place award for front page design Pa. Newspaper Pubs. Assn./Pa. Soc. Newspaper Editors, 1985, 87, 88, Disting. Alumnus award Kutztown U., 1992; Sigma Delta Chi scholar, 1969. Mem. Soc. Profl. Journalists, Pen and Pencil Club. Democrat. Presbyterian. Home: 16 Salisbury Ln Malvern PA 19355-2836 Office: The Phila Inquirer 400 N Broad St Philadelphia PA 19130-4099

PARRY, MICHAEL, not-for-profit fundraiser, singer, actor; b. Cleve., Sept. 15, 1957; s. George and Eleanor Parry. MusB in Edn., Baldwin-Wallace Coll., Berea, Ohio, 1981. Cert. fundraising exec. 2005. Devel. dir. Svcs. for Ind. Living, Cleve., 1990—95, Hitchcock Ctr. for Women, Cleve., 1995—97; dir. planned giving Salvation Army of NE Ohio, Cleve., 1997—99; sr. mgr., corp. and found. support ARC, Cleve., 1999—. Actor: (solo dramatic presentation) PAUL - Apostle of Christ; singer: (concert soloist) REQUIEM of Giuseppe Verdi, Five Mystical Songs, others. Adv. bd. Found. Ctr., Cleve., 2005—07; v.p., treas. Mary Ministries Found., Westlake, Ohio, 2002—07; sec. Cedarwood Townhouse Assn. #1, Westlake, 2005—07. Recipient Spirit of Excellence award, ARC Greater Cleve. Chpt., 2006; named Bd. Mem. of Yr., Mary Ministries Found., 2005. Mem.: Assn. Fundraising Profls. (v.p. 2005—07, v.p. Greater Cleve. chpt. 2005—, Fundraising Exec. of Yr. 2006). Avocations: art, architecture, antiques. Office: Am Red Cross 3747 Euclid Ave Cleveland OH 44115 Office Fax: 216-431-3663. Business E-Mail: parrym@redcross-cleveland.org.

PARRY, WILLIAM DEWITT, lawyer and speech-language pathologist, speech pathology/audiology services professional; b. Hartford, Conn., June 4, 1941; s. William Brown and Mary Elizabeth (Caton) p.; m. Andrea Hannah Lewis, June 30, 1973 (div.); children: Sara, Jessica. BA, U. Mass., 1963; JD, U. Pa., 1966; MA, Temple U., 2009. Cert: speech-lang. pathologist; bar: NJ 1987, Pa. 1967, US Dist. Ct. (ea. dist.) Pa. 1974, US Ct. Appeals (3d cir.) 1980, US Ct. Appeals (9th cir.) 1998, US Supreme Ct. 1980. Assoc. Shapiro, Cook & Bressler, Phila., 1966-67; asst. dir. ABA joint com on continuing legal edn. Am. Law Inst., Phila., 1967-73; assoc. Lowenschuss Assocs., Phila., 1973-85; of counsel Weiss, Golden & Pierson, Phila., 1985-88; pvt. practice Phila., 1988; ptnr. Rubin, Quinn, Moss & Patterson, Phila., 1989-93; pvt. practice Phila., 1993—. Lectr. in field. Author: Understanding and Controlling Stuttering: A Comprehensive New Approach Based on the Valsalva Hypothesis, 1994, 2000; editor U. Pa. Law Rev., 1964-66, The Practical Lawyer, 1967-73. Founder Phila. area chpt. Nat. Stuttering Project, 1985; bd. dirs. Nat. Stuttering Assn., 1996-2002; trustee Unitarian Soc. Germantown, Phila., 1983-86. Mem.: ABA, Pa. Trial Lawyers Assn., Phila. Bar Assn., Pa. Bar Assn. Democrat. Avocations: acting, writing. Home: 520 Baird Rd Merion Station PA 19066-1302 Office: 1608 Walnut St Ste 900 Philadelphia PA 19103-5451 Home Phone: 610-664-5139; Office Phone: 215-735-3500. Personal E-mail: wdparry@aol.com.

PARSA, CAMERON FARROKH, ophthalmologist, educator; b. Bklyn., July 23, 1962; s. Khosrov and Eftekharsadat Parsa. MD, Health Sci. Ctr., SUNY, Bklyn., 1991. Diplomate Am. Bd. Ophthalmology, 1999. Asst. prof. ophthalmology Johns Hopkins Hosp., Balt., 2000—. Home: 2 West Univ Parkway Apt # 405 Baltimore MD 21218 Office: Johns Hopkins Hosp 600 North Wolfe St Baltimore MD 21287-9028 Office Fax: 410-955-0809. Business E-Mail: cparsa@jhmi.edu.

PARSA, FEREYDOUN DON, plastic surgeon; b. Tehran, Iran, May 20, 1942; came to U.S., 1970; s. Issa and Zahra (Bismark) P.; m. Touri Akhlaghi, June 17, 1972; children: Natalie, Alan, Sean. MD, Lausanne U., Switzerland, 1969. Diplomate Am. Bd. Plastic Surgery. Chief of plastic surgery, prof. surgery U. Hawaii, Honolulu, 1981—. Contbr. articles to profl. jours. Mem. AMA, Am. Soc. Plastic Surgeons, Hawaii Med. Assn. Avocation: painting. Office: U Hawaii Sch Med Surgery 1329 Lusitana St 807 Honolulu HI 96813-2421 Personal E-mail: hawaiiplasticsurgery@yahoo.com.

PARSHALL, BRIAN J., mathematician, educator; b. Penn Yan, NY, Oct. 28, 1945; s. Wellington and Lucille Parshall; m. Karen Hunger, Aug. 8, 1978. PhD, Yale U., New Haven, 1972. Whyburn prof. math. U. Va., Charlottesville, 1972—; prof. math. U. Ill., Champaign-Urbana, 1987—89. Contbr. scientific papers to rsch. jours. Sgt. US Army, 1970—72, Penagon. Mem.: Am. Math. Soc. Achievements include first to notion of a quasi-hereditary algebra; research in theory of support varieties for restricted Lie algebras; theory of generic cohomology for algebraic groups. Office: Univ Va Dept Math PO Box 400137 Charlottesville VA 22904-4137 Business E-Mail: bjp8w@virginia.edu.

PARSHALL, GEORGE WILLIAM, chemist, researcher; b. Hackensack, Minn., Sept. 19, 1929; s. George Clarence and Frances (Virnig) Parshall; m. Naomi B. Simpson, Oct. 9, 1954; children: William, Jonathan, David; m. Anna Mae Buhl, Oct. 28, 2006. BS, U. Minn., 1951; PhD, U. Ill., 1954. Rsch. chemist E.I. duPont de Nemours & Co., Wilmington, Del., 1954—65, rsch. supr., 1965—79, dir. chem. sci., 1979—92, cons., 1992—2004, mem. com. on environ. mgmt. techs., 1994—97; mem. chem. stockpile disposal com. NRC, Washington, 1992—98, mem. non-stockpile com., 1998—99, 2001—06, mem. chem. weapons adv. com., 2004—08, mem. coop. threat reduction com., 2008—09. Bd. chem. sci. NRC, Washington, 1983—86; Reilly lectr. Notre Dame U., 1980; Ipatieff lectr. Northwestern U., 1994; mem. sci. adv. bd. Phoenix S&T, 2002—. Author: (book) Homogeneous Catalysis, 1980, Homogeneous Catalysis, 2d rev. edit., 1992; editor: Inorganic Syntheses, 1974, Jour. Molecular Catalysis, 1977—80. Recipient Ballar Inorganic Chemistry medal, U. Ill., 1976, Alumni Achievement award, 2005. Mem.: NAS, Am. Acad. Arts Scis., Am. Chem. Soc. (award in inorganic chemistry 1983, award leadership in chem. rsch. mgmt. 1989), Inst. Chemists (Chem. Pioneer award 1992, Gold medal award 1995), Guild Episcopal Scholars (treas. 1994—99). Episcopalian. Home: Apt 714 2401 Pennsylvania Ave Wilmington DE 19806 Home Phone: 302-658-2066. Personal E-mail: parshallgw@aol.com.

PARSHALL, GERALD, journalist; b. St. Paul, Apr. 24, 1941; s. William Elmer and Evelyn (Steckling) P.; m. Sandra Grant, Dec. 20, 1970. BA, U. Minn., 1963; MA, U. Mich., 1964; grad. fellow, U. Chgo., 1966-67. Reporter York (Pa.) Gazette and Daily, 1968, Balt. Evening Sun, 1968-71; Capitol Hill staff U.S. News & World Report, Washington, 1971-77, sr. editor, 1977-79, asst. mng. editor, 1979-90, sr. writer, 1990-99, contbg. editor, 1999—2004. Mem. Exec. Com. of Periodical Corrs., U.S. Congress, 1974-80, chmn., 1979-80 Served to 1st lt. U.S. Army, 1964-66. Recipient Front Page award Washington-Balt. Newspaper Guild, 1971, Silver Gavel award ABA, 1983 Home: 1004 Congress Ln Mc Lean VA 22101-2116 Personal E-mail: gparshall@verizon.net.

PARSKY, BARBARA J., utilities executive; BA, Rollins Coll., Winter Park, Fla. Various mgmt. positions in mktg. and strategic comm. GE, mgr. corp. advt.; gen. mgr. Porter Novelli, LA, ptnr.; prin., owner consulting bus.; v.p. corp. comm. Edison Internat., Rosemead, Calif., 2002—07, sr. v.p. corp. comm., 2007—, sr. v.p. corp. comm. So. Calif. Edison subs., 2007—. Office: Edison Internat 2244 Walnut Grove Ave Rosemead CA 91770-3714

PARSKY, GERALD LAWRENCE, lawyer; b. West Hartford, Conn., Oct. 18, 1942; s. Isadore and Nettie (Sanders) P.; m. Susan Haas, June 26, 1966; children: Laura, David; m. Robin Cleary, Jan. 27, 1980. AB, Princeton U., 1964; JD, U. Va., 1968. Bar: N.Y. 1969, D.C. 1974, Calif. 1983. Assoc. Mudge Rose Guthrie & Alexander, NYC, 1968-71; spl. asst. to under sec. U.S. Treasury Dept., Washington, 1971-73, exec. asst. to dep. sec. Fed. Energy Office, 1973-74, asst. sec. internat. affairs, 1974-77; sr. ptnr. Gibson, Dunn & Crutcher, LA, 1977-90; of counsel Gibson, Dunn & Crutcher, 1990-92; chmn. Aurora Capital Ptnrs., 1990—. Bd. dirs. James A. Baker III Inst. Pub. Policy. Trustee George Bush Presdl. Libr. Found., 1993—, Ronald Reagan Presdl. Found., 1995—; bd. dirs. Music Ctr. Found., 1998—. Recipient Alexander Hamilton award U.S. Treasury, 1976, Woodrow Wilson award, 2000. Mem. ABA, Coun. Fgn. Rels., N.Y. Princeton Club, Calif. Club, Racquet Club N.Y., Rolling Rock Club, Rancho Santa Fe Golf Club. Office: Aurora Capital Group 10877 Wilshire Blvd Ste 2100 Los Angeles CA 90024-4376

PARSLEY, BRANTLEY HAMILTON, librarian; b. Oct. 15, 1927; s. Clarence Elroy and Florence Sally (Barnes) P.; m. Loyce Marie Franklin, Apr. 18, 1951; children: Linda Marie, Brantley Hamilton; m. Bettye Abercrombie, 1996. AA, Balt. Jr. Coll., 1950; BA, U. Md., 1952; BD, New Orleans Bapt. Theol. Sem., 1955, MRE, 1958; M in Librarianship, Emory U., 1965. Ordained to ministry Bapt. Ch., 1956. Pastor Calvary Bapt. Ch., Albany, Oreg., 1955-57; libr. asst. New Orleans Pub. Libr., 1958-61; supt. night circulation and stacks Theology Libr., Emory U., 1961-65; dir. libr. Campbellsville (Ky.) Coll., 1965-82; dir. Genealogy Workshop, Ch. History Writing Workshop. Dir.: (radio broadcast series) Kentucky Authors, 1976, Study of Black Literature, 1978; coll. page editor Ala. Libr., 1985-87. Bd. dirs. Taylor County Comty. Concerts, Mobile (Ala.) Coll., 1982-93; pres. Cen. Ky. Arts Series, 1975-78; dir. Sch. Merger Workshop, 1976; sec. ACTS of Mobile, bd. dirs., 1985-88; mem. Ala. Sch. Libr. Task Force, 1990-93; mem. bd. dirs. Habitat for Humanity, 1993-99, west covenant adv. coun., mem. family selection com. constrn. crew; outreach vol., team leader, workshop trainer Widowed Persons Svcs., 1993; pres. Widowed Persons Svcs. of Greater Mobile, 2007; mem. Helpline Mobile, 1994-2007; mem. adv. coun. Ret. Sr. Vol. Program; tchr. Adult Men's Sunday Sch.; hospice chaplain Mobile Infirmary, 1998—. Recipient Sch. award Am. Legion, 1947. Mem. ALA, Southeastern Libr. Assn., Ky. Libr. Assn. (chmn. coll. and rsch. sect. 1970-71, sec. treas. edn. sect. 1972-73), Ala. Libr. Assn. (chmn. project com. coll., univ. and spl. libr. divsn.), Bay Area Libr. Assn. (pres.-elect 1984), Ala. Assn. Coll. and Rsch. Librs. (chmn. 1986-87), Coun. Ind. Ky. Colls. (chmn. 1970-75), Taylor County Hist. Soc. (dir. 1970), Taylor County Bapt. Assn. (dir. tng. 1968-70), Taylor County Bapt. Sunday Sch. Assn. (supt. 1968-70). Home: 808 Montfort Rd E Mobile AL 36608-3576 Home Phone: 251-342-7530. Personal E-mail: hamilton_53@bellsouth.net.

PARSLEY, RONALD LEE, paleontology educator; b. Madison, Wis., July 14, 1937; s. Palo and Gertrude E. (Heidel) P.; m. Shirley Ann Michel, May 9, 1986; children: Rodney A., Andrew A. AB, UCLA, 1960; MS, U. Cin., 1962, PhD, 1969. Asst. prof. dept. geology Tulane U., New Orleans, 1966-71, assoc. prof., 1971-79, prof., 1979—, chmn. dept. geology, 1971-74. Exchange scientist NAS, Prague, Czechoslovakia, 1981, 83, 86, 89, 92. Recipient Sediments on Mars award NASA, 1972, grant NSF, 2002-03,05 Mem. AAAS, Geol. Soc. Am., Palaeontol. Soc., Paleontol. Rsch. Instn., Palaeontol. Assn., Sigma Xi. Achievements include research into systematics, functional morphology, paleontology, and mode and tempo of evolution of primitive Echinodermata. Home: 1329 Papworth Ave Metairie LA 70005-1748 Office: Tulane Univ Dept Earth & Environ Scis New Orleans LA 70118 Business E-Mail: parsley@tulane.edu.

PARSONNET, JULIE, medical educator; d. Victor and Mia Parsonnet; m. Anthony James Alfrey, Jan. 17, 1992; 1 child, Lauren Siena Alfrey. AB, Harvard U., Cambridge, Mass., 1979; MD, Cornell U., NYC, 1983. Cert. internal medicine ABIM, 1986, infectious diseases 1988, lic. physician Calif., 1989. Sr. assoc. dean, med. edn. Stanford U., Calif., 2001—06, prof., 2005—. Contbr. more than 100 sci. papers. Lt. comdr. US Pub. Health Svc., 1987—89, Ctrs. Disease Ctrl., Atlanta. Decorated Fgn. Svc. award USPHS, Unit Commendation, Achievement award; recipient Henry J. Kaiser award, Stanford U., 2002, 2004, George DeForest Barnett Professorship award, 2005; named to Hall of Fame, Leon G. Smith Infectious Diseases Inst., 2000. Fellow: Infectious Diseases Soc. America; mem.: Am. Fedn. Clin. Rsch., Soc. Epidemiologic Rsch., Alpha Omega Alpha, Phi Beta Kappa, Am. Soc. Clin. Investigation. Achievements include discovery of helicobacter pylori in causing diseases of GI tract. Office: Stanford Univ Sch Medicine Grant Bldg Rm S125 Stanford CA 94305 Business E-Mail: parsonnt@stanford.edu.

PARSONS, A. CRISTINA, economics professor; b. Lajes do Pico, Azores, Portugal, July 19, 1967; d. Elvino S. and Donna A. Cunha (Stepmother); m. Donald O. Parsons, May 17, 1997; 1 child, Madalena. PhD, Ohio State U., Columbus, 1997. Asst. prof., economics Fairfield U., Conn., 1997—2000; asst. prof. economics Trinity U., Washington, 2000—06, chair, 2000—06, assoc. dean, coll. arts and sci., 2006—07, assoc. prof., economics, 2006—. Office: 125 Mich Ave NE Washington DC 20017 Business E-Mail: parsonsc@trinitydc.edu.

PARSONS, ALEXANDRA CLARE, literature and language educator; b. London, Sept. 3, 1975; arrived in U.S., 1976; d. Andrew and Carol Parsons. BA in English cum laude, Wellesley Coll., 1997; MA, Columbia U., Tchrs. Coll., 2001. Permanent tchg. cert. NY, 2001. TV rsch. analyst Katz Media, Seltel, Inc., NYC, 1997—98; broadcast assoc. CBS News Prodns., NYC, 1998—99; media rels. publicity coord. ABC News, NYC, 1999; asst. kindergarten tchr. Marymount Sch., NYC, 1999—2000; English tchr. The Nightingale-Bamford Sch., NYC, 2001—. Scholar, Japan Fulbright Meml. Fund, 2005. Mem.: Nat. Coun. Tchrs. English, Assn. Tchrs. Ind. Sch., Kappa Delta Pi.

PARSONS, BOB (ROBERT R. PARSONS), entrepreneur, domain register and web host company executive; b. Balt., Md., 1950; BS in Acctg., U. Balt., 1975. CPA. Founder Parsons Technology (sold to Intuit, Inc.), 1984—96; founder, CEO The Go Daddy Group, Inc., Scottsdale, Ariz., 1997—. Rifleman USMC, 1969, Vietnam War. Decorated Combat Action Ribbon, Vietnamese Cross of Gallantry, Purple Heart Medal; recipient Ed Denison Bus. Leader of the Yr., Ariz. Governor's 2005 Innovation Celebration, 2005. Office: The Go Daddy Group Inc 14455 N Hayden Rd Ste 219 Scottsdale AZ 85260-6947 Office Phone: 480-505-8800. Office Fax: 480-505-8844.

PARSONS, CHARLES ALLAN, JR., lawyer; b. Mpls., July 16, 1943; s. Charles Allan and Grace Adelaide (Covert) P.; m. JoAnne Ruth Russell, Oct. 16, 1965; children: Charles, Daniel, Nancy. BS, U. Minn., 1965, JD cum laude, 1972. Bar: Minn. 1972, U.S. Dist. Ct. Minn. 1972, U.S. Supreme Ct. 1995. Ptnr. Moss & Barnett, P.A., 1972—. Bd. dirs. Legal Advice Clinics Ltd., Mpls., 1975-93, Legal Aid Soc. Mpls., 1999-2004, first v.p., 2000-02, pres., 2002-04; bd. dirs. Mid-Minn. Legal Assistance, 2001-04; chair steering com. S.E. Asian Legal Assistance Project, Mpls., 1988-93. Capt. USMCR, 1968—69, Vietnam. Named Vol. Atty. of Yr., Legal Advice Clinics, Ltd., Mpls., 1990, Top 100 Super Lawyers in Minn., 2004, 05, 06, 07, 08, 09, Best Lawyer Am. Real Estate, 2008, Chambers USA. Fellow Am. Coll. Mortgage Attys., Am. Coll. Real Estate Lawyers, Minn. State Bar Assn. (co-chair legis. com. real property sect. 1986-06, coun. mem. 1986-06, chair real property sect. 1993-94), Hennepin County Bar Assn. (chair real property sect. 1988-89, Van Valkenburg award for pub. svc. 2002); mem. ABA, Minn. Leaders Real Estate. Roman Catholic. Avocations: reading, walking, biking, hiking. Office: Moss & Barnett PA 4800 Wells Fargo Ctr 90 S 7th Minneapolis MN 55402-4129 Office Phone: 612-877-5276. Business E-Mail: parsonsc@moss-barnett.com.

PARSONS, DONALD FRANCIS, judge; b. Phila., June 28, 1948; BSEE cum laude, Lehigh U., 1970, MA, 1972; JD, Georgetown U., 1977. Bar: Del. 1977. Law clk. to Hon. James L. Latchum U.S. Dist. Ct. Del., 1977-79; ptnr. Morris, Nichols, Arsht & Tunnell, Wilmington, Del., 1979—2003; vice chancellor Del. Ct. of Chancery, Wilmington, 2003—. Case and note editor Georgetown Law Jour., 1976-77. Mem. ABA, Am. Intellectual Property Law Assn., Intellectual Property Owners Assn., Del. Bar Assn. (pres. 1999-2000), Am. Coll. Bus. Ct. Judges (dir. 2006—08, pres. 2009-). Office: NCC Courthouse 500 N King St Wilmington DE 19801-3734 Office Phone: 302-255-0509. Business E-Mail: donald.parsons@state.de.us.

PARSONS, DONALD JAMES, retired bishop; b. Phila., Mar. 28, 1922; s. Earl and Helen (Drabble) P.; m. Mary Russell, Sept. 17, 1955; children— Mary, Rebecca, Bradford. BA, Temple U., 1943; MDiv, Phila. Div. Sch., 1946, ThD, 1951, DD (hon.), 1964; postgrad., U. Nottingham, Eng., 1968; DCL, Nashotah House, wIS., 1973. Ordained priest Episcopal Ch., 1946, consecrated bishop, 1973; curate Immanual Ch., Wilmington, Del., 1946-49; rector St. Peter's Ch., Smyrna, Del., 1949-50; prof. N.T. Nashotah House, 1950-73, pres., dean, 1963-73, Ramsey prof. ascetical theology, 2000—; bishop Diocese of Quincy, Ill., 1973-88. Author: A Life-time Road to God, 1966, In Time with Jesus, 1973, Holy Eucharist: Rite Two, 1976. Episcopalian. Home: 6901 N Galena Rd Apt 111 Peoria IL 61614-3158

PARSONS, EDWIN SPENCER, clergyman, educator; b. Brockton, Mass., Feb. 16, 1919; s. Edwin Webber and Ethel Faunce (Marsh) P.; m. Tai Shigaki, Sept. 22, 2007, Eleanor Millard, Nov. 3, 1944 (dec.); children: William Spencer, Ellen, James Millard, Bradford Delano. AB, Denison U., Granville, Ohio, 1941, DD, 1967; BD, Andover Newton Theol. Sch., 1945; DD, Kalamazoo Coll., Mich, 1966; LHD, Chgo. Coll. Osteo. Medicine, 1978. Ordained to ministry Am. Baptist Ch., 1944; asst. minister First Bapt. Ch., Newton Centre, Mass., 1945-47; exec. dir. Bapt. Student Found., Inc., Cambridge, Mass., 1947-59; pastor Hyde Park Union Ch., Chgo., 1959-65; assoc. prof. ethics U. Chgo. Div. Sch., 1965-78, prof., 1978-81; dir. ministerial field edn., 1977-79; asst. to dean, 1981-88; dean Rockefeller Meml. Chapel, 1965-79; v.p., dir. New Eng. office Health Resources Ltd., Kansas City, Mo., 1979-89; ret. Cons. dept. ch. and soc. Am. Bapt. Chs. of Mass., 1979-86, also editor Mass. Bapt. News, 1983-85; chmn. strategy and action com., bd. dirs. Mass. Coun. Chs., 1983-85; adj. prof. Andover Newton Theol. Sch., 1981-85 Author: The Christian Yes or No, 1964; contbr. chapters to books. Pres. Coun. Hyde Park-Kenwood Chs. and Synagogues, 1963; chmn. Abortion Rights Assn. Ill., 1974-79; founder, chmn. Ill. Religious Coalition for Abortion Rights, 1975, Ill. Clergy Consultation Svcs. on Problem Pregnancies, Chgo. Clergy Consultation Svcs., 1969-73; bd. dirs., chmn. clergy adv. com. Planned Parenthood Assn., Chgo., 1977-79; bd. dirs. Hyde Park YMCA, Facing History and Ourselves Nat. Found., 1983-87; bd. govs. Internat. House, Chgo., 1969-79; trustee Packard Manse (Mass.), Bapt. Theol. Union, U. Chgo., 1960-70, 81-96, hon. trustee, 1996—; pres., bd. mgrs. Ministers and Missionaries Benefit Bd., 1975-81; mem. policy coun. Religious Coalition for Abortion Rights of Mass., 1980-86; sec., treas. Bolton Inst. for Sustainable Future, 1983-87; mem. gen. bd., mem. exec. com., mem. commn. on Christian unity Am. Bapt. Chs., 1963-72, 74-81; bd. dirs. Planned Parenthood League of Mass., 1984-92. Democrat. Baptist. Home: 65 Briarwood Cir Apt 410 Worcester MA 01606-1254

PARSONS, ERIC E., insurance company executive; Degree, Lewis & Clark Coll., Northwestern U. V.p. Standard Ins. Co., pres. mortgage and real estate subs.; sr. v.p., CFO, then COO StanCorp Fin. Group/Standard Ins. Co., Portland, Oreg.; pres., CEO StanCorp Fin. Group, Portland, Oreg., 2003—04, chmn., pres., CEO, 2004—08, chmn., CEO, 2008—. Vice-chmn. Oreg. Health & Sci. Univ. Found.; chmn. OSHU Cancer Inst. Council; trustee Oreg. Zoo Found.; bd. dirs. Oreg. Bus. Council, Portland Opera, Portland Art Mus. Fellow: Life Mgmt. Inst. Office: StanCorp Fin Group Inc 1100 SW 6th Ave Portland OR 97204

PARSONS, ESTELLE, actress, director, theater producer; b. Lynn, Mass., Nov. 20, 1927; d. Eben and Elinor (Mattson) P.; m. Richard Gehman, Dec. 19, 1953 (div. Aug. 1958); children: Martha and Abbie (twins); m. Peter L. Zimroth, Jan. 2, 1983; 1 child, Abraham. BA in Polit. Sci., Conn. Coll. Women, 1949; student, Boston U. Law Sch., 1949-50; DFA (hon.), Conn. Coll., 2005. Stage appearances include Happy Hunting, 1957, Whoop Up, 1958, Beg, Borrow or Steal, 1960, Threepenny Opera, 1960, Mrs. Dally Has a Lover, 1962, Ready When You Are C.B, 1964, Malcolm, 1965, Seven Descents of Myrtle, 1968, And Miss Reardon Drinks a Little, 1971, Mert and Phil, 1974, The Norman Conquests, 1975-76, Ladies of the Alamo, 1977, Miss Margarida's Way, 1977-78, The Pirates of Penzance, 1981, The Shadow Box, 1994; adapted, dir., performer Orgasmo Adulto Escapes from the Zoo, 1983, The Unguided Missile, Baba Goya, 1989, Shimada, 1992, Grace & Glorie, 1996, The Last of the Thorntons, 2000-01, Morning's At Seven, 2002, The Bay at Nice, 2004, Harold & Maude, 2005, (Broadway) August: Osage County, 2008; film appearances include Bonnie and Clyde, 1966 (Acad. award), Rachel, Rachel, 1967, I Never Sang for My Father, 1969, Dick Tracy, 1990, Boys On The Side, 1995, Looking for Richard, 1996, That Darn Cat, 1997; TV appearances include Roseanne, 1990—98, NBC Today, 1951-56; artistic dir. NY Shakespeare Festival Players, 1986, Actors' Studio, 1997-2003; dir. (Broadway play) Salome, the Reading, 2003. Recipient Theatre World award, 1962-63, Obie award, 1964, Motion Picture Acad. Arts and Scis. award, 1967, Medal of Honor, Conn. Coll., 1969; named Dr. of Fine Arts, Conn. Coll., 2005; named to Theatre Hall of Fame, 2004. Home: 924 West End Ave Apt T5 New York NY 10025-3543 *It's in attempting all, that one succeeds.**

PARSONS, GAIL PAT, history professor; d. Armon Lee and Frances Wilson Jones. PhD, U. Calif., San Francisco, 1984. Assoc. prof. Gordon Coll., Barnesville, Ga., 2002—. Contbr. articles. Office: Gordon Coll 419 College Dr Barnesville GA 30204 Business E-Mail: gparsons@gdn.edu.

PARSONS, GARY M., broadcast executive; m. Kathy. B in Engring., Clemson U.; MBA, U. So. Carolina, 1977. With Bellsouth; prin. Telecom USA, 1984—90; with MCI Comm. Corp., 1990—96, CEO, MCImetro Inc., exec. v.p. telecommunications; joined Motient Corp., 1996, CEO, pres., chmn., 1998—2002; chmn., CEO Mobile Satellite Ventures LP; CEO XM Satellite Radio, chmn., 1997—. Office: XM Satellite Radio 1500 Eckington Pl NE Washington DC 20002 Office Phone: 202-380-4000. Office Fax: 202-380-4500.

PARSONS, IVY, art educator, sculptor, digital and multi media artist; b. Balt., Mar. 3, 1955; d. Joseph H. and Geneva Mae (Tabor) P. BFA cum laude, Md. Inst. Coll. of Art, 1977; MFA magna cum laude in Sculpture, Va. Commonwealth U., 1980; postgrad., Skowhegan Sch. Paint/Sculpture, 1980; MFA magna cum laude in Imaging and Digital Arts, U. Md., Balt., 2007. Artist-in-residence Bklyn. Museum, 1980-81, MacDowell Colony, Peterborough, N.H., 1981, Provincetown (Mass.) Fine Arts Work Ctr., 1981-82, Sculpture Space, Utica, N.Y., 1989, ArtPark, Lewiston, N.Y., 1991, Va. Ctr. Creative Arts, Sweet Briar, 1995—96, 1999, 2004, Tyrone Guthrie Ctr., County Monoghan, Ireland, summer 1997, Hungarian Multicultural Ctr., Budapest, summer 1997; gallery dir. Catonsville C.C. Balt., 1998-99; mem. faculty Md. Inst. Coll. Arts, 1998—. Mem. studio artist selection panel School #33 Art Ctr., Mayor's Com. Art and Culture, Balt., 1987-93; lectr., panelist South Eastern Coll. Art Conf., Georgetown U., Washington, 1995, Md. Inst. Coll. of Art, Balt., Munson-Williams Proctor Inst. Art Museum, Utica, 1995; Alfred and Trafford Klots resident Rochefort En Terre, France, 1999, Polar Circuit Residency, Rovaneimi, Finland, 2000. Exhibits include The Corcoran Gallery of Art, Washington, 1996, The Tyrone Guthrie Ctr., Ireland, 1997, New House Ctr. for Contemporary Art, Snug Harbor Cultural Ctr., S.I., N.Y., 1995-96, Munson-Williams Proctor Inst. Art Museum, 1995, Artist Space, N.Y.C., 1994, Chateau Rochefort-en-terre, 1999, 2003, U. Md., Balt. County, 2007. Fulbright-Hays fellow, Washington, 1982-83, NEA fellow, 1983, Soros Open Soc. Inst. Balt. Cmty., 2008-09; grantee Pollack Krasner Found., N.Y.C., 1987, 99, Adolph and Esther Gottlieb Found., N.Y.C., 1994, Md. State Arts Coun., 1986, 87, 89, 91, 96.; Arts Vantage grant, Md. State Arts Coun., 2008, Cultural Expansions grant, 2007-08, Md. Inst. Coll. Arts, 2008, 09. Fellow Mid-Atlantic Arts Found., Ruth Chenven Found., Soros Open Soc. Inst., 2008-, Balt. Cmty. fellowship, Barbara Deming Meml. Fund, Alpha Delta Kappa. Office Phone: 410-327-3051. Business E-Mail: iparso1@mica.edu. E-mail: iparso1@gl.umbc.edu.

PARSONS, JEFFREY ROBINSON, anthropologist, educator; b. Washington, Oct. 9, 1939; s. Merton Stanley and Elisabeth (Oldenburg) P.; m. Mary Thomson Hrones, Apr. 27, 1968; 1 child, Apphia Hrones. BS, Pa. State U., 1961; PhD, U. Mich., 1966. Asst. prof. anthropology U. Mich., Ann Arbor, 1966-71, assoc. prof., 1971-76, prof., 1976—2006, dir. mus. anthropology, 1983-86, emeritus prof., 2006—. Vis. prof. Universidad Nacional Autonoma de Mexico, 1987; vis. prof. Universidad Buenos Aires, 1994, Univ. Nac de Catamarca, Argentina, 1996, Univ. Nac de Tucuman, Argentina, 1996, Univ. Mayor de San Andres, Bolivia, 1999. Author: Prehistoric Settlement Patterns in the Texcoco Region, Mexico, 1971; (with William T. Sanders and Robert Santley) The Basin of Mexico: The Cultural Ecology of a Civilization, 1979; (with E. Brumfiel) Prehispanic Settlement Patterns in the Southern Valley of Mexico, 1982; (with M. Parsons) Chinampa Agriculture and Aztec Urbanization in the Valley of Mexico, 1985; (with Mary H. Parsons) Maguey Utilization in Highland Central Mexico, 1990; The Production and Consumption of Salt During Postclassic Times in the Valley of Mexico, 1994; (with E. Brumfiel and M. Hodge) The Developmental Implications of Earlier Dates for Early Aztec in the Basin of Mexico, 1996; (with C. Hastings and R. Matos) Rebuilding the State in Highland Peru, 1997; A Regional Perspective on Inca Impact in the Sierra Central, Peru, 1998; (with C. Hastings and R. Matos) Prehispanic Settlement Patterns in the Upper Mantaro-Tarma Drainage, Peru, 2000; The Last Saltmakers of Nexquipayac, Mexico, 2001; (with Luis Morett) Recursos acuaticos en la subsistancia Azteca, 2004; The Last Pescadores of Chimalhuacan, Mexico, 2006, Prehaspanic Settlement Patterns in the Northwestern Valley of Mexico, 2008. Rsch. grantee NSF, 1967, 70, 72-73, 75-76, 81, Nat. Geog. Soc., 1984, 86, 88, 2003. Mem. Am. Anthrop. Assn. (Alfred V. Kidder award 1998), Soc. Am. Archaeology, AAAS, Inst. Andean Rsch., Inst. Andean Studies, Sociedad Mexicana de Antropologia, Sociedad Argentina de Antropologia. Office: Museum of Anthropology U Mich Ann Arbor MI 48109 Business E-Mail: jpar@umich.edu.

PARSONS, LEONARD JON, marketing educator, consultant; b. Pitts., Sept. 1, 1942; s. Leonard J. and Marion Jane (Williams) P.; m. Julia Grieve, Jan. 23, 1965; children: Lorelei, Leonard Jon Jr. BSChemE, MIT, 1964; MS in Indsl. Adminstrn., Purdue U., 1965, PhD in Indsl. Adminstrn., 1968. Asst. prof. Ind. U., Bloomington, 1968-70; assoc. prof. Claremont (Calif.) Grad. Sch., 1970-77; prof. marketing Ga. Inst. Tech., 1977—. Vis. scholar MIT, Cambridge, fall 1973; Fulbright-Hays sr. scholar Cath. U. Leuven, Belgium, spring 1977; vis. prof. INSEAD, France, fall 1984, Norwegian Sch. Mktg., Oslo, fall 1989, UCLA, spring 1990, Advt. Edn. Found., Anheuser Busch, St. Louis, summer 1993, CREER/FUCAM, Belgium, Fall 1995; mem. rsch. and test devel. com. Grad. Mgmt. Admissions Coun., 1988-90. Author: Using Microcomputers in Marketing, 1986; co-author: Marketing Management, 7th edit., 2000, Market Response Models, 2d edit., 2001, others; edtl. bd. Jour. Mktg. Rsch., 1970-80, 83-85, Jour. Bus. Rsch., 1973-79, Jour. Mktg., 1978-80; assoc. editor: Decision Scis., 1976-79; mktg. dept. editor: Mgmt. Sci., 1980-82; contbr. numerous chpts. to books, articles to profl. jours. Recipient first prize rsch. design contest Am. Mktg. Assn., 1971-72. Mem. Am. Mktg. Assn. (mem. adv. bd. mktg. rsch. spl. interest group 1998), Am. Statis. Assn. (chmn. stats. in mktg. sect. 1995), European Mktg. Acad. (mem. exec. com. 1981-84), Theta Delta Chi, Beta Gamma Sigma, Phi Kappa Phi. Office: Ga Inst Tech Coll Mgmt Atlanta GA 30308-0520 Office Phone: 404-894-4381. Business E-Mail: len.parsons@mgt.gatech.edu.

PARSONS, MICHAEL GENE, engineering educator; b. Eugene, Oreg., Oct. 17, 1941; s. Winfield Scott and Elizabeth Agnes Parsons; m. Sandra Armstrong, June 11, 1970; children: Jared Michael, Beth Armstrong. BSE in Naval Architecture and Marine Engring., U. Mich., Ann Arbor, 1963; MME, Cath. U. America, Washington, 1969; PhD in Applied Mechanics, Stanford U., Palo Alto, Calif., 1972. Asst. project officer, surface ships Bur. Ships US Navy Code 08 AEC, Washington, 1963—65, fluid sys. engr., 1965—69; asst. prof., naval architecture and marine engring. U. Mich., 1972—77, assoc. prof., naval architecture and marine engring., 1977—82, chair, dept. naval architecture and marine engring., 1981—91, prof., naval architecture and marine engring., 1982—2008, dir., mich. sea grant coll. program, 1987—92, assoc. dean, undergrad. edn. coll. engring., 1991—96, Arthur F. Thurnau prof., 1997—2008, prof. emeritus, naval architecture and marine engring., 2008—, Arthur F. Thurnau prof. emeritus, 2008—. Contbr. numerous articles and sci. papers to profl. jours. (Vice Adm. Cochrane award, 1985, Spring Meeting award, 1988, Vice Adm. Cochrane Best Paper award, 2002, Joseph H. Linnard prize, 2008). Chair Coun. Sea Grant Dirs., Washington, 1991. Lt. USN, 1963—69, Washington. Recipient Nat. award, Am. Soc. Mil. Engrs., 1962, Rosenblatt-Michigan award, Dept. Naval Architecture and Marine Engrs. U. Mich., 1997. Fellow: Soc. Naval Archs. and Marine Engrs. (v.p. 1990—93, 1998—2001, William H. Webb medal 2003); mem.: US Naval Inst., Am. Soc. Naval Engrs., Scabbard and Blade Honor Soc., Quarterdeck Honor Soc. (hon. commodore 2007), Phi Kappa Phi Honor Soc., Tau Beta Pi Honor Soc., Phi Eta Sigma Honor Soc. Independent. Achievements include patents for ballast free ship system. Office: Univ Mich 2600 Draper Rd Ann Arbor MI 48109-2145 Business E-Mail: parsons@umich.edu.

PARSONS, RICHARD DEAN (DICK PARSONS), diversified financial services company executive, former multimedia company executive; b. NYC, Apr. 4, 1948; s. Lorenzo Locklair and Isabelle (Judd) Parsons; m. Laura Ann Bush, Aug. 30, 1968; children: Gregory, Leslie, Rebecca. Student, U. Hawaii, 1968; JD, U. Ala. Law Sch., 1971; LLD (hon.), Adelphi U., 1990, Medgar Evers Coll., NYC, 1991; LHD (hon.), U. Hawaii, 2003. Bar: NY 1972. Asst. counsel to Gov. State of NY, Albany, 1971-73, 1st asst. counsel to Gov., 1973-74; dep. counsel to V.P. The White House, Washington, 1975, gen. counsel, assoc. dir. Domestic Policy Coun., 1975-77; ptnr. Patterson, Belknap, Webb & Tyler, NYC, 1979—88; pres., COO Dime Savs. Bank NY, NYC, 1988-90, chmn., CEO, 1990-94; pres. Time Warner Inc., NYC, 1995—99; co-COO AOL Time Warner, Inc., NYC, 1999—2002; CEO Time Warner Inc., NYC, 2002—07, chmn., 2003—08, Citigroup Inc., NYC, 2009—. Bd. dirs. Time Warner Inc., 1991-, Citigroup Inc., 1996-, The Estee Lauder Companies Inc., 1999-; bd. trustees, Rockefeller Brothers Fund. Mem. Presdl. Drug Task Force; mayor-elect transition coun., head, 1993; chmn. Wildcat Svc. Orgn., NYC Econ. Devel. Corp.; bd. dir. NY Zool. Soc., Am. TV & Comm. Inc., Colonial Williamsburg Found., Com. to Encourage Corp. Philanthropy, Mus. Modern Art; trustee Howard U., Met. Mus. Art. Recipient Disting. Alumnus award, U. Hawaii, 2003, Pub. Svc. award, Ad Coun., 2007; named one of The Most Influential Black Americans, Ebony mag., 2006. Apollo Theatre Found. (chmn.).*

PARSONS, RICHARD HUGO, lawyer; b. Okla., June 9, 1936; s. Alfred Richard and Veronica Cecilia (Hugo) Parsons; m. Catherine Ann Logan; children: Karen Ann (Parsons) Voss, Anne Logan (Parsons) Muren, Alfred Richard Parsons II. BA, Bradley U., Peoria, Ill., 1958; JD, Wash. & Lee, Lexington, Va., 1961; Cert., Harvard Law Sch. Bar: Ill., DC. Asst. sec. Chgo. Title and Trust, 1961—68; pvt. practice Peoria, Ill., 1968—95; fed. pub. defender Ctrl. Dist. of Ill., Peoria, 1995—. Commr./trial judge Ill. Ct. of Claims, Springfield, Ill., 1975—95; pres. Ill. Assn. of Criminal Def. Lawyers, 1994, Clarence Darrow Inn of the Am. Inns of Ct., Peoria, Ill.; chmn. ABA Criminal Justice Sect. Amicus Curiae Com., 2000—03; dir. Peoria County Bar Assn., Peoria, Ill. Author: Possible Issues for Review in Criminal Appeals, 2d edit., Warrants and Motions to Suppress: Inst. CLE Fed. Criminal Practice; editor: (newsletter) The Back Bencher. Founder, pres., grand marshall City of Peoria St. Patrick's Day Parade, Peoria, Ill., 1981; screening com. mem. Ill. Capital Litigation Trial Bar, 2004—06; del. Dem. Nat. Conv., 1972; pres. Ancient Order of Hibernians, Peoria, Ill., 1981; precinct committeeman Dem. Precinct Committeeman, Peoria, Ill.; lector Sacred Heart Ch., Peoria. Mem.: Ill. Assn. Criminal Def. Lawyers (pres. 1994—95, Lawyer of the Yr. 2000), Nat. Assn. Criminal Def. Lawyers (life), KC (3d degree knight), Union League Club Chgo., Mt. Hawley Country Club, Sigma Phi Epsilon. Democrat. Avocations: tennis, golf, literature, crossword puzzles. Office: Federal Public Defender 401 Main Street - Suite 1500 Peoria IL 61602 Office Phone: 309-671-7891.

PARSONS, TERENCE DWIGHT, linguist, educator; b. 1939; BS in Physics, Univ. Rochester; PhD, Stanford Univ., 1966. Faculty Univ. Pitts., Univ. Calif., Berkeley, Univ. Ill-Chgo. Cir., Univ. Mass., Amherst; prof. philosophy, dean of humanities Univ. Calif., Irvine; disting. prof. philosophy, linguistics UCLA. Fellow: Am. Acad. Arts & Scis. Office: Dept Philosophy UCLA Los Angeles CA 90095-1451 Office Phone: 310-825-4641. Business E-Mail: tparsons@ucla.edu.

PARSONS, VINSON ADAIR, retired computer company executive; b. Frankfort, Ky., Oct. 22, 1932; s. Richard Adair and Nina (Mefford) P.; m. Elizabeth Ann Peltier, June 2, 1956. AS, Mitchell Coll., 1959; BS, U. Conn., 1960; Advanced Mgmt. Program cert., Harvard U., 1985. Auditor, Price Waterhouse & Co. (C.P.A.s), Hartford, Conn., 1960-65; controller Pervel Industries Inc., Plainfield, Conn., 1965-70; v.p., controller Akzo Am. Inc., Asheville, NC, 1970-71, 73-83, v.p., chief fin. officer, 1983-86, System Software Assocs. Inc., Chgo., 1986-89, also bd. dirs.; ret., 1990. Bd. dirs. Am. Tape Co., BRIntec Co., Control Tech. Corp. Elected commr. Town of Weaverville Bd. Commrs., 1994-2000. With USN, 1953-57. Mem. Am. Mgmt. Assn., Fin. Execs. Inst., Inst. Mgmt. Accts. (pres. local chpt. 1969-70) Clubs: Asheville Country; University (N.Y.C.); Reems Creek Golf. Personal E-mail: ssn571@charter.net.

PARSONS, WILLIAM JONATHAN, cardiologist; b. Apr. 3, 1955; married; 3 children. BA, Dartmouth Coll., 1977, MD, 1980. Diplomate Am. Bd. Internal Medicine, Am. Bd. Cardiovascular Diseases, Am. Bd. Nuclear Cardiology, Nat. Bd. Echocardiography. Resident in internal medicine Strong Meml. Hosp. U. Rochester (N.Y.), 1983-85; cardiology fellow Duke U. Med. Ctr., Durham, 1985-88, asst. prof., 1988-91; asst. prof. medicine Southwestern Med. Ctr. U. Tex., Dallas, 1991-93; attending cardiologist Baylor U. Med. Ctr., Dallas, 1993—2001, Rex Hosp., Raleigh, NC, 2001—. Contbr. articles to profl. jours. Gen. med. officer USPHS-IHS, 1981-83. Fellow Am. Coll. Physicians, Am. Coll. Cardiology, Am. Soc. Echocardiography, Am. Soc. Nuc. Cardiology. Office: Carolina Cardiology Cons 3324 Six Forks Rd Raleigh NC 27609 Home Phone: 919-845-6743; Office Phone: 919-781-7772. Personal E-mail: wjpdnp@aol.com.

PARTAIN, GREGORY L., composer, educator; b. Seattle, June 26, 1960; s. Leland C. and Diane Marie Partain; m. Carolyn Renee Dupont, June 1, 1996; children: Julianne Renee Norman, Daniel Dwayne Norman, Elise Dupont. BM, U. Wash., Seattle, 1982; MM, DMA, U. Tex., Austin, 1994. Prof. Bingham Award Tchg. Excellence, 1996. Musician: (piano CDs) Gregory Partain, vols. I and II, (cappella work) Requiem (Commd. Composer, Ky. MTA, 2005). Bd. mem. Ky. MTA, Lexington, 1992—2008, Bluegrass Area MTA, Lexington, 1991—2008. Named Ky. Col., Ky. Govs. Scholars Program, 2001—08. Liberal. Avocation: long-distance running. Office: Transylvania Univ 300 N Broadway Lexington KY 40508 Business E-Mail: gpartain@transy.edu.

PARTAN, DANIEL GORDON, lawyer, educator; s. Toivo Antero and Lempi Sivia (Adamson) P.; m. Doris Liepmann, June 8, 1957; children: Andrew Stewart, Matthew Alexander, Sarah Ruth, Iliana Maria, Juan Carlos. AB, Cornell U., 1955; LLB, Harvard U., 1958, LLM, 1961. Bar: Mass. 1959. Rsch. assoc. Harvard Law Sch., 1961, Rule of Law Ctr., Duke U. Law Sch., 1962-65; assoc. prof. U. N.D., 1964-65; assoc. prof. law Boston U., 1965-68, prof., 1968—, London Inst., 2003, 2006, 2008. NAFTA dispute settlement roster and binat. dispute panel U.S.-Can. Free Trade Agreement; dispute settlement panel roster World Trade Orgn.; sr. specialist roster U.S. Fulbright Commn.; cons. Dept. State, UN Devel. Program, Am. Acad. Arts and Sci.; pres., chmn. Bd. dirs. UN Assn. Greater Boston, 1969-71, 76-77; chmn. Brookline Selectmen's Com. on Harvard Energy Plant, 1976—; vis. scholar Harvard Law Sch., 1977-78; vis. fellow Cambridge (Eng.) U., 1972; vis. prof. Peking U., Beijing, 2000, 05; Fulbright prof. Tsinghua U. Law Sch., Beijing, 2003-04; vis. prof. Xiamen U. Law Sch., China, 2006, 07, Fulbright disting. lectr. Xiamch U. Law Sch. China, 2009- Author: Population in the United Nations System, 1973, Documentary Study of the Politicization of UNESCO, 2 vols., 1975, The International Law Process, 1992, Documents Supplement to the International Law Process, 1999; co-author: Legal Problems of International Administration, 1968, The United States and the International Labor Organization, 1980; co-editor: Corporate Disclosure of Environmental Risks: U.S. and European Law, 1990; contbr. chpts. to books, articles to profl. jours. Past elected mem. town meeting, Brookline, Mass.; appointed chair Brookline Selectmen's Harvard Energy Plant Com. Mem. ABA (amicus brief com. sect. internat. law and practice), Bretton Woods Com., Commn. to Study the Orgn. Peace, Am. Law Inst., Acad. Coun. UN System, Am. Soc. Internat. Law, Internat. Law Assn., European Communities Studies Assn., UN Assn., Coalition for a Strong UN, Trade Law Consultative Group, Boston Area Tchrs. Internat. Law (convenor). Office: 765 Commonwealth Ave Boston MA 02215-1401 Business E-Mail: partan@bu.edu.

PARTANEN, CARL RICHARD, biology professor; b. Portland, Oreg., Nov. 23, 1921; s. Emil and Ellen (Engstrom) P.; m. Jane Nelson, June 24, 1961; children: Karen, Kirsten, Richard (dec.) Student, Multnomah Jr. Coll., 1946-48; BA, Lewis and Clark Coll., 1950; MA, Harvard, 1951, PhD, 1954. Am. Cancer Soc. postdoctoral research fellow Columbia, 1954-55, Harvard, 1955-57; research asso. Childrens Cancer Research Found., Boston, 1957-61; asso. prof. biology U. Pitts., 1961-64, prof. biology, 1964-86, chmn. biology, 1964-70, prof. emeritus, 1987—; Research fellow U. Edinburgh, Scotland, 1971-72, U. Nottingham, Eng., 1978-79. Contbr. articles to profl. jours. Served with AUS, 1942-45, ETO. Recipient Distinguished Achievement award Lewis and Clark Coll., 1968 Mem. AAAS, Bot. Soc. Am., Soc. for Devel. Biology, Soc. for In Vitro Biology. Home: 1112 Farragut St Pittsburgh PA 15206-1746 Office: U Pitts Dept Biol Scis Pittsburgh PA 15260 Personal E-mail: cpartanen@comcast.net.

PARTEN, PRISCILLA M., medical and psychiatric social worker, educator; b. Lowell, Mass., Dec. 7, 1944; d. Ralph Bailey and Margaret Lillian (McDonagh) Newton; m. Samuel L. Parten, June 27, 1965; children: Delora Parten Power, Edward Bailey, Ethan Rogers. BA, Northeastern U., 1968; MSW, Adelphi U., Burlington, Vt., 1987. Lic. ind. clin. social worker, Mass., NH, LCSW, Maine; bd. cert. diplomate NASW. Family support coord. Easter Seal Early Intervention, Derry, NH, 1988-91; med. and psychiat. social worker Salem (NH) Vis. Nurses, 1992-96; home sch. coord. Timberlane Regional Sch. Dist., Plaistow, NH, 1992—; dir. Priscilla M. Parten, MSW, ACSW, BCD, Londonderry, NH, 1992—. Spkr., author, presenter in field, interviewed on Nat. Pub. TV. Bd. dirs. Norwich U. Parents' Assn., 1st v.p., 1999—2001. Recipient commendation Pres.'s Com. on Mental Retardation, 1968. Mem. NASW, Nutfield Exch. Club (bd. dirs. 1994-96). Democrat. Congregationalist. Avocations: skiing, photography, crocheting, gardening, snorkeling. Office: 50 Nashua Rd Ste 214 Londonderry NH 03053-3444 E-mail: senatchie@hotmail.com.

PARTENSKII, MICHAEL B., science educator, researcher; s. Boris M. and Rakhil I. Partensky; m. Ludmila K. Kolmakova; children: Boris M. Partensky, Jane Partensky, Peretz D. Partensky. PhD, Ural Poly. U., Sverdlovsk. Russia, 1974. Assoc. prof. Ural Acad. Forestry, Sverdlovsk, 1979—89; rsch. fellow Brandeis U., Waltham, Mass., 1990—; adj. faculty Bransdeis, Rabb Sch., Waltham, 2002—. Author: (ednl. book) The Physics Teacher; contbr. more than 100 sci. papres to profl. jours. Mem.: AAPT, Am. Biophys. Soc. Office: Brandeis Univ 415 South St Waltham MA 02454 Personal E-mail: partensky@gmail.com. Business E-Mail: moshep@brandeis.edu.

PARTER, SEYMOUR VICTOR, computer science and mathematics educator; b. Chgo., June 9, 1927; s. Peter and Tillie (Dekovetzky) P.; m. Ruth Ghitman, Oct. 9, 1957; children: Paul Jeffry, David William. BS, Ill. Inst. Tech., 1949, MS, 1951; PhD, N.Y.U., 1958. Staff mem. Los Alamos Sci. Lab., 1951-57; instr. math. Mass. Inst. Tech., 1957-58; asst. prof. math. Ind. U., 1958-60, Cornell U., 1960-62; vis. asst. prof. computer sci. Stanford, 1962-63; asso. prof. computer sci. and math. U. Wis., Madison, 1963-65, prof., 1965—, chmn. computer sci. dept., 1968-70. Mem. NRC adv. com. on math. to Office Naval Research, 1970-72; mem. adv. com. on computing to pres. Stanford, 1969-72; mem. ICASE Sci. Council, 1981-87 Contbr. articles to profl. jours. Mem. Math. Assn. Am., Soc. Indsl. and Applied Math. (vis. lectr. 1969-72, mem. council 1978-80, mng. editor Jour. Numerical Analysis 1977-80, pres. 1981-82), Bd. Math. Scis. (chmn. 1984-86). Home: 5 S Rock Rd Madison WI 53705-4634 E-mail: parter@cs.wisc.edu.

PARTH, FRANK R., consulting company executive, educator; b. Eichendorf, Germany, Aug. 26, 1949; came to US, 1952. s. Frank and Erna (Framelsberger) P.; m. Jane Hoppe, Dec. 27, 1974 (div. Jan. 1985); children: Katherine, Frank. BS in Physics, Creighton U., 1972; MS in Physics, U. Wyo., 1978; MS in Sys. Mgmt., U. So. Calif., LA, 1986; MBA, Peter Drucker Inst., 2000. Design engr. Tex. Instruments, Dallas, 1978-81; asst. tech. dir. Martin-Marietta Space Sys., Long Beach, Calif., 1981-92; pres. InterVolve Mgmt. Sys., Mission Viejo, Calif., 1993-95; dir. sys. engring. Experian, Orange, Calif., 1995-97; mgr. Deloitte & Touche, Santa Ana, Calif., 1997-98; practice mgr. Keane, Inc., Long Beach, 1998-99; v.p. devel. Overstock Market (e-commerce), 2000—01; pres. Project Auditors, LLC, 2001—. Faculty U. So. Calif. Inst. Safety and Sys. Mgmt., LA, 1993-97, U. Calif. Irvine, 1996—, Claremont Grad. U., 2000—; vis. prof. Am. U. Sharjah, United Arab Emirates; Internat. spkr. in field. Author: Introduction to IT Project Management, 2006; contbr. articles to profl. jours. Bd. dirs. Orange County Search and Rescue, Calif., 1989-2002, OC Project Mgmt. Inst., 1996-2004 v.p. membership, 2003, v.p. profl. devel., 2004; constitutional rev. officer Mensa, 1993—. Recipient Disting. Contbn. award, PMI, 2009. Mem. Internat. Coun. Sys. Engring., Mensa Internat. (pres. Orange County chpt. 1993), Project Mgmt. Inst. (Spkr.'s award 1998). Avocations: sailing, skiing, wine. Home: 21901 Palanca Mission Viejo CA 92692-1012 Office: PO Box 80688 Rancho Santa Margarita CA 92688-0688 Home Phone: 949-452-0579; Office Phone: 800-545-1340. Business E-Mail: Fparth@projectauditors.com.

PARTHASARATHY, SAIRAM, pulmonologist; MD, Madras Med. Coll., Chennai, 1989. Staff physician SAVAHCS, Tucson, 2004—05, chief pulmonary & critical care, 2005—07, chief rsch., 2007—08. Contbr. scientific papers. Office: Southern Ariz Va HealthCare System 3601 S Sixth Ave Mail Stop 0-151 Tucson AZ 85721 Office Fax: 520-629-1801. Personal E-mail: sparthamd@yahoo.com.

PARTHASARATHY, SANJAY, computer software company executive; BS in Mech. Engring., Anna U., Madras, India; MS in Engring., MIT, MS in Mgmt. Product mgr. Windows multimedia group Microsoft Corp., Redmond, Wash., 1990, product unit mgr. internet security products, regional dir. South Asia Region, gen. mgr. worldwide customer sys., corp. v.p. strategy & bus. devel. group, corp. v.p. developer and platform evangelism group (D&PE), corp. v.p. startup bus. accelerator, 2008—. Office: Microsoft Corp One Microsoft Way Redmond WA 98052-6399*

PARTHASARATHY, TRIPLICANE ASURI, materials scientist; b. Chennai, India, Apr. 17, 1954; s. Triplicane Asuri Gopalakrishnan and Vathsala Krishnan; m. Shubha Parthasarathy, June 2, 1986; 1 child, Sriya. BTech, Indian Inst. Tech., Chennai, 1976; MS, Ohio State U., 1982, PhD, 1983. Devel. engr. Welding Rsch. Inst., Tiruchirapalli, India, 1977-80; asst. prof. materials sci. U. Ill., Urbana-Champaign, 1984-89; rsch. scientist UES, Inc., Dayton, Ohio, 1988-90, sr. scientist, 1990-98, prin. scientist, 1998—. Mem. rev. panel, NSF, 2000. Recipient Best Paper award, NASA Glenn Rsch. Ctr., Cleve., 1996. Mem. Am. Ceramic Soc. (assoc. editor jour. 1997—). Avocations: indian classical music, physical fitness, philosophy. Home: 2493 Christalee Dr Beavercreek OH 45434 Office: UES Inc 4401 Dayton-Xenia Rd Dayton OH 45432 E-mail: Triplicane.Parthasarathy@afrl.af.mil.

PARTHASARATHY, VINOD, manufacturing engineer, consultant; b. Bombay, Aug. 17, 1979; arrived in U.S., 2001; s. Gopalan and Vedha Parthasarathy. B in Engring. (hon.), U. E. London, 2000; MBA, Harvard U., 2005. Project engr. Ford Motor Co., London, 1999, Dormer Tools, Sheffield, England, 1999—2001; product engr. Freudenberg-Nok, Laconia, NH, 2001—04, sys. mgr., 2005—. Mng. ptnr. Digitized Artisan, Perth, Australia, 2005—. Contbr. articles to profl. jours. Vol. Red Cross, London, 1997—2000, Rep. Party, Concord, 2004—. Recipient Six Sigma Black Belt award, Freudenberg-Nok, 2005. Mem.: IEEE (chartered). Republican. Hinduism. Achievements include patents for drill detection transducer. Avocations: skydiving, writing, travel, surfing.

PARTHEMORE, JACQUELINE GAIL, internist, educator, hospital administrator; b. Harrisburg, Pa., Dec. 21, 1940; d. Philip Mark and Emily (Buvit) Parthemore; m. Alan Morton Blank, Jan. 7, 1967; children: Stephen Eliot, Laura Elise. BA, Wellesley Coll., 1962; MD, Cornell U., 1966. Diplomate Am. Bd. Internal Medicine. Resident in internal medicine N.Y. Hosp./Cornell U., 1966-69; fellow in endocrinology Scripps Clinic and Rsch. Found., La Jolla, Calif., 1969-72; rsch. ednl. assoc. VA Hosp., San Diego, 1974-78; staff physician VA San Diego Health Care Sys., 1978-79, asst. chief, med. svc., 1979-83, acting chief, med. svc., 1980-81, chief of staff, 1984—2009; asst. prof. medicine U. Calif. Sch. Medicine, San Diego, 1974-80, assoc. prof. medicine, 1980—85, prof. medicine, assoc. dean, 1985—2009. Mem. nat. rsch. resources coun. NIH, Bethesda, Md., 1990—94; mem. Blue Ribbon Panel Acad. Affiliations, 2007—09. Contbr. chapters to books, articles to profl. jours. Mem. adv. bd. San Diego Opera, 1993—2009; mem. Roundtable and Channel 10 Focus Group, San Diego Millennium Project, 1999; v.p. bd. dirs. San Diego Vets. Med. Rsch. Found., 1989—2009. Recipient Bullock's 1st Annual Portfolio award, 1985, San Diego Pres.'s Coun. Woman of Yr. award, 1985, YWCA Tribute to Women in Industry award, 1987, San Diego Women Who Mean Bus. award, 1999, Excellence in Leadership award Am. Hosp. Assn., 2002, Local Legend award AMWA/Nat. Libr. Medicine, 2005. Fellow ACP (gov. 2005-09, mem. edn. com. 2006-09, vice-chair edn. com. 2008-09), Am. Assn. Clin. Endocrinologists; mem. Endocrine Soc., Nat. Assn. VA Chiefs Staff/Physician Execs. (pres. 1989-91), Assn. Am. Med. Colls. (mem. steering group chief med. officers, 2005—09), Wellesley Coll. Alumnae Assn. (1st v.p. 1992-95), San Diego Wellesley Club (pres. 1997-99), San Diego Herb Soc. (co-pres. 2003-04), Nat. Assn. VA Rsch. and Ednl. Fedn. (bd. mem., 2003—09), Vets. Med. Rsch. Found. (v.p. 1989-2009). Avocations: gardening, reading, sailing, cooking, travel. Office: VA San Diego Healthcare Sys 3350 La Jolla Village Dr San Diego CA 92161-0002 Home Phone: 858-756-2917; Office Phone: 858-552-7419. Business E-Mail: jparthemore@ucsd.edu.

PARTHIER, BENNO, biologist; b. Holleben, Germany, Aug. 21, 1932; s. Hermann and Helene (Bielig) P.; m. Christiane Luecke, Aug. 19, 1968; children: Juliane, Christoph, Dorothea. Diploma in Biology, U. Halle, Germany, 1958, D of Natural Scis., 1961, D of Habilitation, 1967. Rsch. asst. U. Halle, 1958-61, docent, 1962-66; dept. head Acad. Scis. German Dem. Rep., Halle, 1967-90, prof. biology, 1975; dir. Fed. State Inst. Plant Biochemistry, Halle, 1990-97; prof. U. Halle, 1993. V.p. Deutsche Akademie Naturforsch Leopoldina, Halle, 1987-90, pres., 1990-2003; chmn. sci. commn. Sci. Coun., Koeln, Germany, 1991-97. Author: Die Leopoldina, 1994; editor (encyclopedia) Plant Physiology, 1982; editor Biochemie Physiol. Pflanzen jour., 1971. Mem. Saechsische Akad. Wissensch., Bayerische Akad. Wissensch., Academia Europaea, Berlin Akad. Wissenschaft. Avocation: gardening. Home: Am Birkenwaeldchen 12 D-06120 Halle Germany Office: Deutsche Akad der Naturforsch Leopoldina Emil Abderhalden Str 37 D-06108 Halle Germany Office Phone: 0049-345-4723915. Business E-Mail: parthier@leopoldina-halle.de.

PARTIE, DAVID JOHN, language educator; b. Detroit, Apr. 14, 1944; s. William Richey and Arlene Esther Partie; m. Janice Sue Stanage, June 14, 1975; 1 child, Elizabeth Catherine. BA, U. of Redlands, 1966; postgrad., U. Heidelberg, Germany, 1967—68; MA, UCLA, 1971; MDiv, Talbot Theol. Sem., 1978; MA, U. of So. Calif., 1982, PhD, 1988. C.C. Instr. Credential in German Calif. Cmty. Colleges, 1974, Cert. of Completion, World Travel Counselor Tng. Program Automobile Club of So. Calif., 1981, Apollo Travel Services Tng. Cert. United Airlines, 1982, Qualification Cert. as an ESL Tchr. for Speakers of Japanese Japanese Cross Cultural Ctr./ LA, Calif., 1984, sys. direct access tng. program cert. Ea. Airlines, 88. Tchg. asst. in German UCLA, 1968—70; instr. in German, French, Spanish and English LA Bapt. Coll., Newhall, Calif., 1969—73; instr. in German Santa Monica City Coll., 1974—77; instr. in German and French Biola Coll., La Mirada, Calif., 1974—78; instr. in French and Spanish Baymonte H.S., Santa Cruz, Calif., 1978—79; tchg. asst. in freshman writing U. of So. Calif., 1979—82; tour counselor/world travel agt. Automobile Club of So. Calif., LA, 1979—82; account exec. Agnew Tech-Tran, Woodland Hills, Calif., 1982—84; instr. in ESL and German Berlitz Sch. of Langs., Pasadena, 1984—85; prof. English and modern langs. Liberty U., Lynchburg, Va., 1985—2007; PACE instr. USS Mesa Verde US Navy, 2008. Chmn. dept. of modern langs. Liberty U., 1985—93, co-chair Writer's Conf., 1999, mem., adv. bd. for the ctr. for global ministries, 2001—, moderator of the faculty senate, 2002—03, chair, faculty senate exec. com., poetry editor Lamplight, 2003—, mem. pres.' com. on faculty devel. and welfare, 2004—, mem. modern langs. com. dept. English, 2004—; adj. prof. English Ctrl. Va. CC, Lynchburg, 1997—; presenter in field. Author: The Poet's Domain; actor: (films) The Gathering, 1998, Pilgrim's Progress, 2006, The Great Sacrifice of Jefferson Davis, 2007; (plays) U. Redlands, 1963—66, Cmty. Theater, Coll. Theater (outstanding contbn. to theater at Sweet Briar Coll., 1999, 2000), Morgan Theatre, 1967, Biola Coll., 1976, U. So. Calif., 1980, Lynchburg Fine Arts Ctr., 1990—2004, Sweet Briar Coll., 1999—2000, Civil War Seminar, 2004, 2007; guest poet: TV series Joe Campbell Show, 1991, All the Arts, 1996, Words and Music, 1997, Riverviews, 2006, Focus on the Phrase, 2006, radio guest author: Literary Pages of the Air, 1986; contbr. poems to mags. and jours. (Hon. Mention, Poet's Choice Award, vol. 13 of The Poet's Domain, 1997), acad. papers presented at numerous conf. Roving reader Lynchburg Pub. Schools, 1995—96; tchr. of creative writing Lynchburg Parks and Recreation Dept., 1995—95; forensics judge Va. Orgn. of German Students, Lynchburg, 1997—97; crisis counselor Centinella Valley Hotline, 1977—78, Suicide Prevention Ctr., LA, 1985, Life Aid, 1988—89; mem. com. readers judging poems Maier Mus. of Art, 2005; counselor Crisis Line Ctrl. Virginia, 2008—; mem. Lynchburg Rep. City Com., Lynchburg, 1988—2000; del. to state polit. conventions Rep. Party, Richmond, Va., 1988—96; legis. liaison to Va. state del. Joyce Crouch Va. Soc. for Human Life, Lynchburg, 1991—92; mem., mission selection com. Heritage Bapt. Ch., Lynchburg, 1991—98, 2002—04; student poetry contest judge Poetry Soc. of Va., Williamsburg, 1996—96. Recipient William Ward Bass award, Talbot Theol. Seminary, 1978, First Pl. In The Serious Poem Category, Lynchburg Poetry Festival, 1987, 1991, 1994, 2000, Karma Deane Ogden Prize for Poetry, Poetry Soc. of Va., 1991, Brodie Herndon Meml. Prize for Poetry, 1997, Carleton Drewry Meml. Prize for Poetry, 2000, J. Franklin Dew award, Poetry Soc. Va., 2008; Chancellor's Tchg. fellow, UCLA, 1966—70, Walter Loewy fellow for Grad. Study Abroad, U. of Heidelberg, 1967-68. Mem.: Poetry Soc. of Va. (assoc.; regional v.p. 2002—06, 2009—), Assn. for the Interdisciplinary Study of the Arts (assoc.), F. Scott Fitzgerald Soc. (assoc.), MLA (assoc.), Alpha Mu Gamma (life). Avocations: travel, athletics, church work, drama, book collecting. Office: Ctrl Virginia CC 3506 Wards Rd Lynchburg VA 24503 Office Phone: 434-832-7657. Personal E-mail: daveword444@yahoo.com.

PARTLETT, DAVID F., dean, law educator; b. 1947; LLB, Sydney U., 1970; LLM, Mich. U., 1972-74; SJD, U. Va., 1980. Bar: New South Wales 1971, Australian Cap. Terr. 1978. Vis. asst. prof. U. Ala., 1972-73; legis. officer Australia Atty. Gen.'s Office, 1974—75; dir, rsch. Australian Law Reform Commn., 1975—78; lectr. Australian Nat. U., 1978-80, sr. lectr., 1980-87, assoc. dean, 1982—85; vis. prof. Vanderbilt U., Nashville, 1987-88, prof. law, 1988-2000, acting dean, 1996-97; v.p., dean, prof. Sch. Law Washington & Lee U., Lexington, Va., 2000—06; dean Emory U. Sch. Law, Atlanta, 2006—. Sparkman Dist. vis. prof. Ala. U., 1986-87. Office: Emory University School of Law G546 Gambrell Hall 1301 Clifton Rd Atlanta GA 30322 Business E-Mail: david.partlett@law.emory.edu.*

PARTNOY, RONALD ALLEN, lawyer; b. Norwalk, Conn., Dec. 23, 1933; s. Maurice and Ethel Marguerite (Roselle) P.; m. Diane Catherine Keenan, Sept. 18, 1965. BA, Yale U., 1956; LL.B., Harvard U., 1961; LL.M., Boston U., 1965. Bar: Mass. 1962, Conn. 1966. Atty. Liberty Mut. Ins. Co., Boston, 1961-65; assoc. counsel Remington Arms Co., Bridgeport, Conn., 1965-70, gen. counsel, 1970-88, sec., 1983-93; sr. counsel DuPont Co., Wilmington, Del., 1985—95. Served to capt. USNR, 1956-85. Mem.: ABA, Naval Res. Assn. (nat. exec. com. 1981—85, 1997—99, nat. v.p. 1997—99, nat. exec. com. 2001—03, nat. v.p. 2001—03, 3d dist. pres.), U.S. Navy League (pres. Bridgeport coun. 1975—77, Conn. pres. 1977—80, v.p. Empire region 1980—85, nat. dir.), Am. Judicature Soc., Sporting Arms and Ammunition Mfrs. Inst. (chmn. legis. and legal affairs com. 1971—86), Assn. of Yale Alumni (del. 1997—2000), Yale Club of N.Y.C., Harvard Club of Phila., Harvard Club of Boston, Chancery Club. Home: 10 Longwood Dr Apt 122 Westwood MA 02090

PARTON, DOLLY, singer, composer, actress; b. Sevier County, Tenn., Jan. 19, 1946; d. Robert Lee and Avie Lee (Owens) P.; m. Carl Dean, May 30, 1966. D in Humane & Musical Letters (hon.), U. Tenn., Knoxville, 2009. Country music singer, rec. artist, composer, actress, radio and TV personality. Entrepreneur, owner entertainment park Dollywood, established 1985. Radio appearances include Grand Ole Opry, WSM Radio, Nashville, Cass Walker program, Knoxville; TV appearances include Porter Wagoner Show, from 1967, Cass Walker program, Bill Anderson Show, Wilburn Bros. Show, Barbara Mandrell Show; rec. artist, Mercury, Monument, RCA, CBS record cos.; albums include Here You Come Again (Grammy award 1978), Real Love, 1985, Just the Way I Am, 1986, Portrait, 1986, Think About Love, 1986, Trio (with Emmylou Harris, Linda Ronstadt) (Grammy award 1988), 1987, Heartbreaker, Great Balls of Fire, Rainbow, 1988, White Limozeen, 1989, Home for Christmas, 1990, Eagle When She Flies, 1991, Slow Dancing with the Moon, 1993 (Grammy nomination, Best Country Vocal Collaboration for Romeo (with Tanya Tucker, Billy Ray Cyrus, Kathy Mattea, Pam Tillis, & Mary-Chapin Carpenter), (with Tammy Wynette and Loretta Lynn) Honky Tonk Angels, 1994, The Essential Dolly Parton, 1995, Just the Way I Am, 1996, Super Hits, 1996, (with others) I Will Always Love You & Other Greatest Hits, 1996, Hungry Again, 1998, Trio II, 1998, Grass is Blue, 1999 (Grammy award for best bluegrass album), Best of the Best-Porter & Doll, 1999, Halos and Horns, 2002, For God and Country, 2003, Makin' Believe, 2003, Live and Well, 2004, Those Were the Days, 2005, Backwoods Barbie, 2008; appears on song "Creepin' In" with Norah Jones, 2004; composer numerous songs including Nine to Five (Grammy award 1981, Acad. award nominee and Golden Globe award nominee 1981); Film appearances include Nine to Five, 1980, The Best Little Whorehouse in Texas, 1982, Rhinestone, 1984, Steel Magnolias, 1989, Straight Talk, 1991, Frank McKlusky, C.I., 2002, (TV films) A Smoky Mountain Christmas, 1986, Wild Texas Wind, 1991, Unlikely Angel, 1996, Blue Valley Songbird, 1999; (TV series) Heavens to Betsy, 1994, Mindin My Own Business, 1996, Reba, 2005, Hannah Montana, 2006-07; Author: Dolly, 1994; music and lyrics (Broadway plays) 9 to 5, 2009. Recipient (with Porter Wagoner) Vocal Group of Yr. award, 1968, Vocal Duo of Yr. award All Country Music Assn., 1970, 71, Nashville Metronome award, 1979, Am. Music award for best duo performance (with Kenny Rogers), 1984, Grammy awards for best female country vocalist, 1978, 81, for best country song, 1981, for best country vocal performance with group, 1987, People's Choice award, 1980, 88, Nat. Medal of Arts Nat. Endowment for the Arts, 2005, Kennedy Ctr. Honor, John F. Kennedy Ctr. for Performing Arts, 2006; co-recipient (with Emmylou Harris and Linda Ronstadt) Acad. Country Music award for album of the yr., 1987, (with Brad Paisley) Most Inspiring Video of Yr. for When I Get Where I'm Going, CMT Awards (Country Music TV), 2006, Video of Yr. and Vocal Event of Yr., Acad. Country Music award, 2006; Cliffie Stone Pioneer award, Acad. Country Music, 2008, Jim Reeves Internat. award, 2009; named Female Vocalist of Yr., 1975, 76, Country Star of Yr., Sullivan Prodns., 1977, Entertainer of Yr., Country Music Assn., 1978, Female Vocalist of Yr., Acad. Country Music, 1980; Dolly Parton Day proclaimed, Sevier County, Tenn., designated Oct. 7, 1967, Los Angeles, Sept. 20, 1979; named to Small Town of Am. Hall of Fame, 1988, East Tenn. Hall of Fame, 1988. Address: RCA 6 W 57th St New York NY 10019-3901 Office: Dollywood Co 1020 Dollywood Ln Pigeon Forge TN 37863-4101

PARTON, LANCE A., pediatrician, educator; s. Earl B. and Jean V. Parton; m. Patricia A. Galvin-Parton, July 15, 1978; children: Kristen P., Lisa M., Brian L. MD, NY Med. Coll., Valhalla, 1980. Diplomate Am. Bd. Pediat., 1985, Am. Bd. Pediatrics-Neonatology, 1991. Attending neonatologist Maria Fareri Children's Hosp. Westchester Med. Ctr., Valhalla, NY, 1999; prof. pediat. NY Med. Coll., 2007—. Assoc. dir. Regional Neonatal ICU MFCH WMC, Valhalla, 2004—. Contbr. scientific papers. Pres. Suffolk Pediatric Soc., NY, 1997—99; chmn. Am. Acad. Pediat., NYC, 2002; coun. Eastern. Soc. Pediatric Rsch., 2004. Mem.: Am. Acad. Pediat., Am. Thoracic Soc. Achievements include research in Genetic foundations of BPD. Office: Maria Fareri Children's Hosp 95 Grasslands Rd Valhalla NY 10595 Office Fax: 914-493-1005. Business E-Mail: lanceaparton@yahoo.com.

PARTON-STANARD, SUSAN, music educator, voice educator, musician; b. Alton, Ill. d. Raymond Hays and Dorothy J. (Kaus) Parton; 1 child, Raymond Harris Stanard. MusB in Voice, Opera, Jacksonville U., 1979, MA in Tchg. Music Edn., 1988. Adj. prof. music Jacksonville U., Fla., 1983—95; orch., choral dir. Mayport Jr. HS, Atlantic Beach, Fla., 1985—87; prof. music Fla. CC, Jacksonville, 1999—2002; assoc. prof. music Lewis & Clark CC, Godfrey, Ill., 2002—, dept. chair, 2002—. Operatic, concert artist, 1980—; dir. worship, music Isle Faith United Meth. Ch., Jacksonville, 1995—2002; co-dir. choral, vocal edn. Douglas Anderson Sch. Arts, Jacksonville; dir. choral activities, vocal studies, dir. music 12th St. Presbyn. Ch., Alton, Ill., 2004—07; dir. music Godfrey First United Meth. Ch., 2007—; organist St. Paul United Meth. Ch., Jacksonville; lectr. in field; vocal coach. Singer, musician: Verdi Requiem, Mozart Requiem, Handel's Messiah; singer: (Operas) Carmen, Cavalleria Rusticana, Tosca, Don Giovanni, Tannhauser. Recipient First Pl. winner, Met. Opera Auditions, Fla. Ea. Regional, 1981—82, Outstanding Tchr. of Yr., Mayport Jr. HS, 1985—86, Excellence Tchg. award, Emerson Electric, 2007—08; named Outstanding Artist of Yr., NJ State Opera, 1981, Outstanding Artist N.E. Fla., Cummer Gallery Art, 1982, Woman of Distinction, YWCA, 2009. Fellow: United Meth. Musician in Music Worship Arts; mem.: Ill. Bd. Higher Edn. Music (adv. com. mem.), Ill. Bd. Higher Edn. Assoc. Fine Arts (steering com. mem.), Ill. CC Bd., Am. Guild Organists, Music Tchrs. Nat. Assn., Music Educators Nat. Conf., Am. Choral Dirs. Assn., Nat. Assn. Tchrs. Singing. Avocations: antiques, Depression glass. Office: Lewis Clark Cmty Coll Music Dept 5800 Godfrey Rd Godfrey IL 62035 Home: PO Box 5371 Godfrey IL 62035 Office Phone: 618-468-4732.

PARTOVI, M. HOSSEIN, physics professor, department chairman; PhD, Mass. Inst. Tech., Cambridge, 1969. Prof., physics & astronomy dept. Calif. State U., Sacramento, 1985—, chair, physics & astronomy dept., 1985—; chair, physics dept. Sharif U. Tech., Tehran, Iran, 1969—76, prof., physics dept., 1969—76; vis. scientist Stanford Linear Accelerator Ctr., Stanford U., Palo Alto, Calif., 1981—83. Contbr. articles to profl. jours. Mem. Columbia U., NYC, 2000, contbr., 2000. Recipient Outstanding Tchg. award, Calif. State U., 1993; named one of Outstanding Prof., 1996. Mem.: Am. Assn. Physics Tchrs., Anacapa Soc. (founder 2008—, bd. mem. 2008—), Am. Phys. Soc., Soc. Physics Students (life). Office: Physics & Astronomy Dept CSUS 6000 J St Sacramento CA 95819-6041

PARTOYAN, GARO ARAKEL, lawyer; b. Toledo, Dec. 6, 1936; s. Garo and Vartoohi Partoyan; m. Beverly Meadows Partoyan; children: Garo Linck, Elizabeth Margaret, Martin Joseph. BS in Chem. Engring., Northwestern U., 1959; JD, U. Mich., 1962; LLM, NYU, 1964. Bar: N.Y. 1963, U.S. Dist. Cts. (so. dist.) N.Y. 1964, U.S. Ct. Claims 1966, U.S. Ct. Appeals (2nd cir.) 1966, U.S. Dist. Ct. (ea. dist.) N.Y. 1968. Ptnr. Curtis, Morris & Safford, NYC, 1962-76; gen. counsel mktg. and tech. Mars, Inc., McLean, Va., 1976-98; pres. Mgmt. of Intellectual Property, Inc., Sarasota, Fla., 1998—. Mem. Dobbs Ferry (N.Y.) Bd. Edn., 1972-76, pres., 1975-76; chmn. Fairfax Citizens Group, Fairfax County, Va., 1988-90. Mem. ABA, Licensing Execs. Soc., Am. Intellectual Property Law Assn., N.Y. Intellectual Property Law Assn., Internat. Trademark Assn. (pres. 1990-91, bd. dirs. 1983-2006), Intellectual Property Owners (bd. dirs. 1992-99), Armenian Bar Assn. Avocations: sailing, curling, croquet. Office: 419 MacEwen Dr Osprey FL 34229 Home Phone: 941-918-0720; Office Phone: 941-918-0595. Fax: 941-918-0678. E-mail: partoyanga@aol.com.

PARTRIDGE, BRUCE JAMES, lawyer, educator, writer, parliamentarian; b. Syracuse, NY, June 4, 1926; arrived in Can., 1969; s. Bert James and Lida Marion (Rice) P.; m. Mary Janice Smith, June 13, 1948 (dec. 1986); children: Heather Leigh, Eric James, Brian Lloyd, Bonnie Joyce; m. May S. Archer, May 28, 1988; stepchildren: Sheila Archer, Laurel Archer. AB cum laude, Oberlin Coll., Ohio, 1946; LLB, Blackstone Coll., Chgo., 1950, JD, 1952; LLB, U. B.C., 1974. Bar: B.C. 1976, N.W.T. 1980. Rsch. physicist Am. Gas Assn., Cleve., 1946-48; bus. mgr. Cazenovia (N.Y.) Coll., 1948—51; bus. mgr., purchasing agt., asst. treas. Rochester Inst. Tech., NY, 1953—58; bus. adminstr. Baldwin-Wallace Coll., Berea, Ohio, 1951-53; v.p. bus. and mgmt. U. Del., Newark, 1958-63; v.p. adminstrn. Johns Hopkins U., Balt., 1963-69; pres. U. Victoria, B.C., Can., 1969-72; assoc. Clark, Wilson & Co., Vancouver, B.C., Can., 1975-78; successively solicitor, mng. solicitor, gen. solicitor, v.p. law and gen. counsel, sec. Cominco Ltd., Vancouver, 1978-88; exec. dir. Baker & McKenzie, Hong Kong, 1988-90; v.p. Pacific Creations, Inc., 1990-92; faculty Camosun Coll., 1992-99. Author: Management in Canada: The Competitive Challenges, 2000; co-author: College and University Business Administration, 1968; chmn. editl. com. Purchasing for Higher Education, 1962; contbr. numerous articles to profl. jours. Chmn. commn. on adminstrv. affairs Am. Coun. on Edn., Washington, 1966-69; mem. Pres.'s Com. on Employment of Handicapped, Washington, 1967-69; mem. adv. coun. Ctr. for Resource Studies, Queen's U., 1983-88; bd. dirs. L'Arche in the Americas, 1984-88; mem. adv. coun. Westwater Rsch. Ctr., U. B.C., 1982-88. Mem. Assn. Can. Gen. Counsel, Def. Rsch. Inst. (product liability com.), Am. Inst. Parliamentarians, Nat. Assn. Parliamentarians. Fair Vote Can. Unitarian Universalist. Office Phone: 250 722-3081. Business E-Mail: brucepart@telus.net.

PARTRIDGE, LOREN WAYNE, art historian, educator; b. Raton, N.Mex., Apr. 11, 1936; s. Don F. and Ruth (Isaacson) P.; widowed; children: Wendy, Amy; married. BA in English Lit., Yale U., 1958; cert. in L.Am. lit., U. Buenos Aires, 1959; diploma in Russian, U.S. Army Lang. Sch., Monterey, Calif., 1961; MA in Fine Arts, Harvard U., 1965, PhD in Fine Arts, 1969. Tchg. fellow Harvard U., Cambridge, Mass., 1964-66; lectr. U. Calif., Berkeley, 1968, acting asst. prof., 1969-70, asst. prof., 1970-76, assoc. prof., 1976-80, prof., 1980—, chmn. Dept. Art History, 1978—87, 1990—93, 1999, chmn. Dept. Art Practice, 2002—03, 2004—08. Resident in art history Am. Acad. in Rome, 1985; reviewer Art Bull, 1972, 78, 80, 83, Renaissance Quar., 1984, 87, 90, 99, Design Book Rev., 1987, Master Drawings, 1987, Am. Hist. Rev., 1993, Apollo, 1996. Author: John Galen Howard and the Berkeley Campus: Beaux-Arts Architecture in the Athens of the West, 1978, Caprarola, Palazzo Farnese, 1988, (with Randolph Starn) A Renaissance Likeness: Art and Culture in Raphael's Julius II, 1980, (with Randolph Starn) Arts of Power: Three Halls of State in Italy 1300-1600, 1992, The Art of Renaissance Rome, 1400-1600, 1996, Michelangelo: The Sistine Chapel Ceiling, Rome, 1996, Michelangelo Last Judgement: A Glorious Restoration, 1997; contbr. author: Ency. of Italian Renaissance, 1981, Internat. Dictionary Art and Artists, 1990, Dictionary of Art, 1996; contbr. articles to profl. jours. With U.S. Army, 1960-63. Scholar Yale U., 1955-58, Harvard U., 1964-66; Fulbright fellow, 1958-59, 75, Am. Acad. in Rome fellow, 1966-68, Kress fellow Inst. for Advanced Studies, 1974-75, U. Calif., 1972, 77, 82, 85, 93-94, 99-2000, 2003-04, Guggenheim fellow, 1981-92; grantee Kress Found., 1968-69, 71-72, Getty. sr. rsch. grantee, 1988-89. Office: U Calif Dept Art History 620 416 Doe Libr Berkeley CA 94720-6020 Office Phone: 510-643-6301. Business E-Mail: lpart@berkeley.edu.

PARTRIDGE, MARK VAN BUREN, lawyer, author, professional speaker, educator, mediator; b. Rochester, Minn., Oct. 16, 1954; s. John V.B. and Constance (Brainerd) P.; m. Mary Roberta Moffitt, Apr. 30, 1983; children: Caitlin, Lindsay, Christopher. BA, U. Nebr., 1978; JD, Harvard U., 1981. Bar: Ill. 1981, U.S. Dist. Ct. (no. dist.) Ill. 1981, U.S. Dist. Ct. (ea. dist.) Mich. 1983, U.S. Ct. Appeals (1st. cir) 2003, U.S. Ct. Appeals (4th cir.) 1986, U.S. Ct. Appeals (7th cir.), 1992, U.S. Ct. Appeals (5th cir.) 1993, U.S. Ct. Appeals (3rd cir.) 1998. Assoc. Pattishall, McAuliffe, Newbury, Hilliard & Geraldson, LLP, Chgo., 1981-88, ptnr., 1988—, exec. com., 2003—. Adj. prof. John Marshall Law Sch., Chgo., 1987—;arbitrator and mediator Am. Arbitration Assoc., 2007-, Cook County Mandatory Arbitration Program, 1989-2003; v.p. Harvard Legal Aid Bur., 1980-81; mediator no. dist. Ill. Voluntary Mediation Program, 1997—; panelist World Intellectual Property Orgn., Domain Name Dispute Resolution Svc., 1999—; neutral Nat. Arbitration Forum, Intellectual Property Mediation and Arbitration Panel, 2004—; mediator Internat. Trademark Assn. Panel of Neutrals, 2005—; bd. adv. N.W. Law Sch., Jour. Tech. and Intellectual Property. Author, Guilding Rights Trademarks, Copyright and the Internet, iUniverse, 2003, Alternate Dispute Resolution: An Essential Competency for Lawyers, 2009; Contbr. articles to profl. jours.; mem. editl. bd. The Trademark Reporter, 1994-97; adv. bd. IP Litigator, 1995—. Vol. Chgo. Vol. Legal Svcs., 1983—. Fellow Am. Intellectual Property Law Assn. (com. chmn. 1989-91, 96-98, bd. dirs. 1998-2001); mem. ABA (com. chmn. 1989-91, 94-99, rep. 2006—), Am. Bar Found. Internat. Trademark Assn. (com. vice chmn. 1996), World Intellectual Property Orgn. (experts panel internet domain name process 1998-99), Intellectual Property Law Assn. Chgo. (com. chmn. 1993-96), Brand Names Ednl. Found. (moot ct. regional chmn. 1994-96, nat. vice-chmn. 1997-98, nat. chmn. 1998-99), Nat. Spkrs. Assn. (Ill. chpt. pres. 2007), Legal Club (v.p. 1998, pres. 1999), Lawyers Club Chgo. (pres. 2000, bd. dirs. 2000-01), Execs. Club, Union League Club, Harvard Club Chgo., Vistage Internat., Bagatelle Club. Avocations: writing, music, genealogy, travel, internet. Office: Pattishall McAuliffe Newbury Hilliard & Geraldson LLP 311 S Wacker Dr Ste 5000 Chicago IL 60606-6631 Office Phone: 312-554-8000. Business E-Mail: mpartridge@pattishall.com.

PARTRIDGE, SCOTT FRANCIS, lawyer; JD, Georgetown U., 1974. Patent examiner US Patent and Trademark Office, 1969—71, internat. and legis. specialist Office of Legis. and Internat. Affairs, 1972—74; asst. dep. gen. counsel, sect. dir. US Presdl. Clemency Bd., 1975; sr. ptnr., head intellectual property dept. Baker Botts LLP, Houston. Exec. sec. US Side Joint Working Group on Intellectual Property for US/USSR Agreements on Sci. Cooperation, 1973, 74; adj. prof. Georgetown U. Law Ctr. Mem.: ABA (me.-at-large bd. govs. for sect. sci. and tech. law 2007—, mem. fin. com. 2007—, bd. liaison to sect. intellectual property law 2007—, bd. liaison to commn. on IOLTA 2007—, bd. liaison to com. on continuing legal edn. 2007—, house dels. 2001—). Office: Baker Botts LLP One Shell Plz 910 Louisiana St Houston TX 77002-4995 Office Phone: 713-229-1569. Office Fax: 713-229-7769. E-mail: scott.partridge@bakerbotts.com.

PARTRIDGE, WILLIAM FRANKLIN, JR., lawyer; b. Newberry, SC, July 16, 1945; s. William F. and Clara (Eskridge) P.; m. Ilene S. Stewart, Aug. 16, 1969; children: Allison, William F. BA in History, The Citadel, 1967; JD, U. S.C., 1970. Bar: S.C. 1970, U.S. Ct. Claims 1971, U.S. Ct. Mil. Appeals 1971, U.S. Tax Ct. 1971, U.S. Supreme Ct. 1973, U.S. Dist. Ct. S.C. 1980. Instr. internat. law Chapman Coll., 1973-74; pub. issue com. S.C. Bar, 1982-83. Lt. Col. USAFR. Mem. Newberry Bar Assn. (pres. 1982-83), Palmetto Club, County of Newberry Club, Cotillion Club, Assn. Citadel Mens Club, Masons, Phi Delta Phi. Democrat. Methodist. Home: 2029 Harrington St Newberry SC 29108-3055 Office: 1201 Boyce St Newberry SC 29108-2705 Office Phone: 803-276-5968.

PARUCHURI, JITHENDRA KUMAR, signal processing researcher; s. Suresh Babu and Vijaya Lakshmi Paruchuri. BS in Tech., JNT U., Hyderabad, India, 2005; MS, U. Ky., Lexington, 2008, attending, 2007—. Rschr. U. Ky., Lexington, 2005—. Contbr. articles to jours. Recipient Gold medal, Lions club, Narsapur, 2001. Mem.: IEEE. Achievements include patents pending for privacy preservarion using video data hiding; development of privacy protected video surveillance system; video copy detection system for media hosting sites. Home: 183 Transcript Ave Apt 11 Lexington KY 40508 Office: Ctr Visualization & Virtual Envir 1 Quality St Ste 865 Lexington KY 40507 Home Phone: 859-327-2854. Personal E-mail: jk.paruchuri@gmail.com. Business E-Mail: jkparu0@engr.uky.edu.

PARVEEN, ZAHIDA, medical educator, researcher; married. PhD, Drexel U., Phila., 1994. Asst. prof. medicine Thomas Jefferson U., Phila., 2007—. Contbr. scientific papers to profl. publs. Grantee, NIH, 2006—. Achievements include research in gene therapy. Office: Thomas Jefferson Univ 1020 Locust St Philadelphia PA 19107

PARVEN, SCOTT, lawyer, lobbyist; m. Cari Parven; 3 children. BA, Vassar Coll.; JD, U. Va. Atty. Fed. Policy Group, Mayer Brown; head internat. policy Aetna, global policy chief, chief of staff to chmn. Aetna Internat.; founder, pres. Parven Pomper Strategies, Washington. Office: Parven Pomper Strategies Inc 1155 21st St NW, Ste 202 Washington DC 20036 Office Phone: 202-351-6820. Office Fax: 202-233-9805.*

PARVIZI, JAVAD, orthopedist, educator; s. Mahmood Parvizi and Sedigheh Eskandarion; m. Fariba Kasemkhani, June 8, 1997; children: Niosha, Cyrus. MB in Surgery, U. Sheffield, 1991; MS in Orthop., Mayo Found., Rochester, Minn., 1999; MD, Pa. Cert. in advanced trauma life support Newcastle, 1993, diplomate Am. Bd. Orthop. Surgery, 2005, cert. in microvascular reconstrn. Course Mayo Clinic, Rochester, 1999, Advanced Pediatric Life Support (APLS) London, UK, 1995. Internship gen. surgery & orthops. U. Sheffield Sch. Medicine, 1991—92; residency gen. surgery & orthops. U. Newcastle, England, 1991—95; rsch. fellowship molecular biology, dept. orthops. Mayo Clinic, Rochester, 1995—97, residency orthop. surgery, 1997—2002; fellowship adult reconstrn. Hip Soc.-Muller Found., Berne, Switzerland, 2002—03; asst. prof., dept. orthops. surgery Jefferson Med. Coll., Thomas Jefferson U., Phila., 2003—08, prof., dept. orthop. surgery, 2008—; dir., clin. rsch. divsn. Rothman Inst., Phila., 2003—. Bd. dirs. Muller Found. North America, 2006; com. blood mgmt. mem. Thomas Jefferson Hosp., 2005; bd. dirs. Orthop. Overseas, 2004—08; grant reviewer Furlong Charitable Rsch. Found., England, 2008, Health Rsch. Coun., New Zealand, 2008, Musculoskeletal Transplant Found., 2008, NSF, 2008. Contbr. chapters to books. Recipient Multipurpose Rsch. award, Mid-America Orthop. Assn., 2000, Frank Stinchfield award, Am. Hip Soc., 1999, 2003, 2004, Young Investigator award, IAMA, 2001, award, Marmor Arthritis Found. Award, 2002, Infectious Soc. North America, 2002, Mark Coventry, 2002, Minn. Orthop. Assn., 2002, Asia Pacific Orthop. Assn., 2008, Vernon Nickel award, Orthop. Rehab. Assn., 2004, Clinician Scientist award, Orthop. Rsch. & Edn. Found., 2004, Disting. Basic Sci. Rsch. award, MSIS, 2004, J.R.Neff award, Musculoskeletal Transplant Found., 2007. Fellow: Royal Coll. Surgeons Eng.; mem.: AMA, Mid-America Orthop. Assn., Eastern Orthop. Soc., Interurban Orthop. Soc., Orthop. Rsch. Soc., Am. Bd. Orthop. Surgeons, Am. Assn. Hip & Knee Surgeons, Am. Acad. Orthop. Surgeons, Phila. Orthop. Soc., Pa. Orthop. Soc., Brit. Med. Assn., Brit. Orthop. Rsch. Soc., Brit. Orthop. Assn., Health Vol. Overseas, A-O Alumni Assn., Hip Soc. (Otto Aufrant award 2009). Office: Rothman Inst 925 Chestnut St Philadelphia PA 19107 Office Phone: 267-339-3617.

PASAHOW, LYNN HAROLD, lawyer; s. Samuel and Cecelia (Newman) P.; m. Leslie Aileen Cobb, June 11, 1969; 1 child, Michael Alexander. AB, Stanford U., 1969; JD, U. Calif., Berkeley, 1972. Bar: Calif. 1972, U.S. Ct. Appeals (9th cir.) 1972, U.S. Dist. Ct. (no. dist.) Calif. 1973, U.S. Dist. Ct. (ctrl. dist.) Calif. 1974, U.S. Supreme Ct. 1976, U.S. Dist. Ct. (ea. dist.) Calif. 1977, U.S. Ct. Appeals (fed. cir.) 1990. Law clk. judge US Dist. Ct. (no. dist.) Calif., San Francisco, 1972—73; with McCutchen, Doyle, Brown & Enersen, 1973—2001; ptnr. Fenwick & West LLP, Mountain View, Calif., 2001—. Co-author: Civil Discovery and Mandatory Disclosure: A Guide to Effective Practice, 1994, Federal Judicial Center Patent Case Management Judicial Guide, 2009; author: Pretrial and Settlement Conferences in Federal Court, 1983; contbr. articles to profl. jours. Bd. dirs. Bay Area Biosci. Ctr. Mem. ABA, Calif. Bar Assn. Democrat. Office: Fenwick & West LLP Silicon Valley Ctr 801 California St Mountain View CA 94041 Office Phone: 650-335-7225. Business E-Mail: lpasahow@fenwick.com. *Notable cases include: Amazon.com v. BarnesandNoble.com, duPont vs. Cetus PCR patent litigation, Elan Pharmaceutical transgenic mouse litigation, Iomega Zip Disk litigation, University of California & Abbott Laboration FISH litigation.*

PASCAL, AMY BETH, film company executive; b. LA, Mar. 1958; d. Tony and Barbara Pascal; m. Bernard Weinraub, Aug. 9, 1997; 1 adopted child, Anthony. BA in Internat. Rels., UCLA. With Kestral Films; v.p. prodn. 20th Century Fox, 1986—87, Columbia Pictures, 1987—89, exec. v.p. prodn., 1987—94; pres. prodn. Turner Pictures, 1994—96; pres. Columbia Pictures, Culver City, Calif., 1996-99, chmn., 1999—2002; vice chmn. Sony Pictures Entertainment, Culver City, Calif., 2002—06, co-chmn., 2006—; chmn. Sony Pictures Entertainment Motion Picture Group, Culver City, Calif., 2003—. Bd. trustees Rand Corp. Bd. trustees AFI; mem. UCLA Sch. Theater, Film & Television. Named one of 50 Most Powerful People in Hollywood, Premiere mag., 2004—06, 100 Most Powerful Women in Entertainment, Hollywood Reporter, 2004—07, 100 Most Powerful Women, Forbes mag., 2005—09, 50 Most Powerful Women in Bus., Fortune mag., 2006, 2007, 50 Smartest People in Hollywood, Entertainment Weekly, 2007. Office: Sony Pictures Entertainment 10202 Washington Blvd Culver City CA 90232*

PASCAL, C(ECIL) BENNETT, classics educator; b. Chgo., May 4, 1926; s. Jack and Goldie (Zeff) P.; m. Ilene Joy Shulman, Feb. 1, 1959; 1 child, Keith Irwin. BA, UCLA, 1949, MA, 1950, Harvard U., 1953, PhD, 1956. Instr. U. Ill., Champaign, 1955-56, Cornell U., Ithaca, NY, 1957-60; asst. prof., then assoc. prof. U. Oreg., Eugene, 1960-75, prof. classics, 1975-96, prof. emeritus, 1996—, head dept., various years - 1965-85. Author: Cults of Cisalpine Gaul, 1964; contbr. articles to profl. jours. Active Eugene Bicycle Com., 1971-83. Wwith USN, 1944-46. Traveling fellow, Italy, Harvard U., 1956-57, Fulbright-Hays fellow, Rome, 1967-68. Mem. Am. Philol. Assn., Classical Assn. Pacific N.W. (pres. 1965-66), AAUP, Archeol. Inst. of Am. (past pres., sec. Eugene Soc.) Democrat. Jewish. Avocations: skiing, fly fishing, novel writing. Home: 330 Fulvue Dr Eugene OR 97405-2788 Office: U Oreg Dept Classics Eugene OR 97403 Business E-Mail: cbpasc@uoregon.edu.

PASCAL, ROGER, lawyer; b. Chgo., Mar. 16, 1941; s. Samuel A. and Harriet E. (Hartman) P.; m. Martha Hecht, June 16, 1963; children: Deborah, Diane, David AB with distinction, U. Mich, 1962; JD cum laude, Harvard U., 1965. Bar: Ill. 1965, US Dist. Ct. (no. dist. Ill.) 1965, US Ct. Appeals (7th cir.) 1969, US Supreme Ct. 1976, Wis. 1985, US Ct. Appeals (2nd, 6th, 9th and 10th cirs.) 1986. Lic. pilot, FAA, 1977, instrument rating, 1979. Assoc. Schiff Hardin, LLP, Chgo., 1965-71, ptnr., 1972—. Adj. prof. law Northwestern U. Law Sch., 1994—; bd. dirs. Evanston Cmty. Defender; instr. Nat. Inst. for Trial Advocacy, 1989-2006. Bd. dirs., mem. exec. com. Chgo. Law Enforcement Study Grp., 1975-80, pres., 1978-80; pres. Harvard Law Soc. Ill., 1976-78; bd. dirs. ACLU of Ill., 1984—, gen. counsel, 1986—. Recipient Roger Baldwin Lifetime Achievement award, 2003. Fellow Am. Bar Found.; mem. ABA (antitrust, intellectual property, and litig. sects.), Pub. Interest Law Initiative (bd. dirs. 1989—, v.p. 1995-97, pres. 1997-98), Fund for Justice (v.p., bd. dirs. 1986-97), Chgo. Coun. Lawyers (bd. dirs. 1970-74, 80-84, 2004—), Chgo. Legal Assistance Found. (bd. dirs. 1985-88), Chgo. Bar Found.(recipient Edward Lewis II Pro Bono Svc. award, 2003), Univ. Club, Met. Club, Phi Beta Kappa. Avocation: flying. Office: Schiff Hardin LLP 6600 Sears Tower Chicago IL 60606-6473

PASCAL, TRACEY MICHELE, software engineer, director; d. Harold Saunders and Dinah Lee Pascal. BBA, Tex. Tech U., Lubbock, 1986. Lic. nursing home adminstr. Tex., 1986. Adminstr. ARA Living Ctrs., Weatherford, Tex., 1986—87, Beverly Enterprises, Van, Tex., 1987—88; CFO Center Nursing Homes, Inc, Corsicana, Tex., 1988—90; sr. software engr./tech. lead Sprint, Irving, Tex., 1990—. Employee trainer and mentor Sprint, Irving, Tex., 2002—06. Author: (manual) Sprint Operatons for Offshore Employees, (training manual) How to Complete and Fix Production Codes, (flash cards) Sprint History Past and Present; contbr. articles to profl. jours. Mem.: Project Mgmt. Inst., Am. Acad. Med. Adminstrs., Nat. Soc. DAR, Golden Key, Pi Beta Phi. Home: 1200 Fuller Wiser Rd Apt 1217 Euless TX 76039-3099 Personal E-mail: valinese@aol.com.

PASCALE, DANIEL RICHARD, lawyer; b. Racine, Wis., Mar. 22, 1940; s. Domenic and Fannie Colette (Julian) P.; m. Mary Sara McDonald, June 28, 1986; 1 child, Alexander. AB cum laude, Harvard U., 1962; JD, U. Chgo., 1965. Bar: Ill. 1966, U.S. Ct. Appeals (7th cir.) 1967, U.S. Dist. Ct. (no. dist.) Ill. 1969, U.S. Supreme Ct. 1972. Asst. corp. counsel City of Chgo., 1966-72, chief appellate atty., 1972-79, 1st dep. corp. counsel, 1979-84; assoc. Rudnick & Wolfe, Chgo., 1984-87, ptnr., 1987-90; judge Circuit Ct. of Cook County, Ill., 1990-94, 96-98; adminstrv. dir. Adminstrv. Office of Ill. Cts., Chgo., 1995-96; sr. corp. atty. Dean Foods Co., 1999—2002; instr. Northeastern Ill. U., 2004—05. Counsel to the chmn. com. on fin. Chgo. City Coun., 2005—. Bd. dirs. DeKoven Found., Racine, 1986—, The Church Home/Montgomery Pl., 1998-2007; adv. bd. Art Resources in Teaching, Chgo., 1987-94; v.p. Episcopal Homes Mgmt., Inc., Milw., 1988-94. Mem. Ill. Bar Assn., Chgo. Bar Assn., Chgo. Bar Assn. Independent. Episcopalian.

PASCARELLA, PERRY JAMES, editor, writer; b. Bradford, Pa., Apr. 11, 1934; s. James and Lucille Margaret (Monti) P.; m. Carol Ruth Taylor, May 4, 1957; children: Cynthia, Elizabeth. AB, Kenyon Coll., 1956; Coll. William and Mary, William and Mary Coll., 1957; postgrad., George Washington U., 1958. Credit reporter Dun & Bradstreet, Cleve., 1956, 60; from asst. editor to mng. editor Steel mag., Cleve., 1961-69; mng. editor Industry Week mag., Cleve., 1970-71, exec. editor, 1971-86, editor-in-chief, 1986-89; v.p. editorial Penton Pub. Inc., 1989-96. Lectr. in field. Author: Technology-Fire in a Dark World, 1979, Humanagement in the Future Corporation, 1981, The New Achievers, 1984, The Purpose-Driven Organization, 1989, The Ten Commandments of the Workplace, 1996, Leveraging People and Profit, 1998, Christ-Centered Leadership, 1999; co-author: Optimistic Outlooks, 1982, Creating a Global Agenda, 1984, Leadership in a New Era, 1994, The New Bottom Line, 1996. Lt. comdr. USNR, 1957-60. Recipient Disting. Service award Kenyon Coll., 1975, 81, Am. Bus. Press Crain award, 1992; Carnegie scholar, 1952-56 Mem. World Future Soc., U. Akron Inst. for Future Studies (bd. advisors). Presbyterian (elder). Home: 694 Coronado Cir Avon Lake OH 44012

PASCH, ALAN, philosopher, educator; b. Cleve., Dec. 1, 1925; s. P. Jerome and Esther (Broverman) P.; m. Eleanor Kudlich Berna, Dec. 27, 1950; 1 child, Rachel. BA, U. Mich., 1949; MA, New Sch. Social Research, 1952; PhD, Princeton U., 1955; Bamford fellow, 1955-56. Instr. philosophy Ohio State U., 1956-59, asst. prof., 1959-60; assoc. prof. philosophy U. Md., College Park, 1960-67, prof., 1967-97, prof. emeritus, 1997—. Founding editor Faculty Voice, U. Md., 1986. Author: Experience and the Analytic, 1958; contbr. articles, revs. Served with AUS, 1944-46, PTO. Mem. Am. Philos. Assn. (exec. dir. 1969-72, sec.-treas. Eastern div. 1965-68), Metaphys. Soc. Am., Washington Philosophy Club (pres. 1978-79), Washington Rare Book Group. Office: Dept Philosophy Univ Md College Park MD 20742 Business E-Mail: pasch@umd.edu.

PASCH, JAMES ROY, consultant, military employee; b. Bangkok, Oct. 2, 1960; s. Robert Edward and Carol Jean Pasch; m. Leslie Elaine McGee, Nov. 12, 1983; children: Eric Allen, Lindsay Elaine, Ryan Travis. BS in Bus. Adminstrn., US Naval Acad., Annapolis, Md., 1983; MS in Military Studies, USMC Command & Staff Coll., Quantico, Va., 1999; Cert. in Performance-based Svc. Contracting, George Wash. U., 2005, PhD in Orgn. and Mgmt., 2008. Cert. info. warfare specialist USN, 1995, gen. mech. engrng. specialist USN, 1992, in nat. security studies USN, 1999, in sr. leader devel. program E.Carolina U., 2005, in performance-based svc. contracting George Wash. U., 2005. Officer USN, Norfolk, Va., 1983—99; gunnery officer, adminstrv. officer, and navigating officer USS Conolly (DD-979), Norfolk, 1984—86; aide and flag lt. to comdr. Naval Base Norfolk, 1986—88; weapons dept. head USS Lawrence (DDG-4), Norfolk, 1988—90; combat sys. dept. head USS Bainbridge (CGN-25), Norfolk, 1990—92; electronic warfare officer Surface Warfare Devel. Grp., Norfolk, 1992—95; damage control asst. USS Wasp (LHD-1), Norfolk, 1995—97; exec. officer USS Estocin (FFG-15), Norfolk, 1997—98; chief info. mgr. US Joint Forces Command, Norfolk, 1999—. Cons. in program mgmt. US Joint Forces Command, Norfolk, 1999—. V.p. PTA, Va. Beach, 2000—07. Surface warfare officer USN, 1983—2003, Norfolk. Decorated Achievement medal USN, Commendation medal, Mil. Outstanding Vol. Svc. medal, Nat. Def. Svc. medal US Joint Forces Command; recipient Tng. & Readiness medal, Assn. Old Crows, 1993, Gold Cert. Achievement award, 1994, Joint Meritorious Unit award, US Joint Forces Command, 2000—01, Exemplary Performance award, 2004—06. Mem.: IEEE, Soc. Info. Mgmt., Assn. Computing Machinery, MIS Quar., Mil. Officer Assn. Am. (life), Am. Legion (life), VFW (life). Republican. Roman Catholic. Avocations: camping, jogging. Home: 1405 Edgartown Ct Virginia Beach VA 23456-5408 Office: US Joint Forces Command 1562 Mitscher Ave Norfolk VA 23551 Office Fax: 757-836-9109. Personal E-mail: james.pasch@verizon.net. Business E-Mail: james.pasch@jfcom.mil.

PASCHE, BORIS CLAUDE ROGER, physician; b. Lausanne, Vaud, Switzerland, Aug. 5, 1961; came to U.S., 1989; Rene Charles Edouard and Marina (Guidetti) P. MD, Karolinska Inst., Stockholm, 1986, U. Lausanne, Switzerland, 1987; PhD, Karolinska Inst., Stockholm, 1989. Cert. diplomate, Am. Bd. of Internal Med. 1994, diplomate, Am. Bd. of Medical Oncology 1997, 2008, diplomate, Am. Bd. of Hematology 1999, lic. New York State Med. Lic. 1995, Illinois Med. Lic. 2001, Ala., 2008. Clin. trial dir. Symtonic S.A., Renens, Switzerland, 1983-86, chief sci. officer, 1986—; pres. Symtonic U.S., NYC, 1992-96; rsch. fellow in cardiovascular medicine Harvard Med. Sch., Boston, 1989-92; intern in medicine N.Y. Hosp. Meml. Sloan-Kettering Cancer Ctr., Cornell U. Med. Ctr., NYC, 1992-93, resident in medicine N.Y. Hosp., 1993-94; fellow in hematology-oncology Meml. Sloan-Kettering Cancer Ctr., NYC, 1994—2000; att. phys. Northwestern Meml. Hosp., Chgo., 2001—08; dir. cancer genetics program Robert H. Lurie Comprehensive Cancer Ctr., 2002—08; assoc. prof. medicine Feinberg Sch. Medicine, Northwestern U.; dir., divsn. hematology/oncology U. Ala. Comprehensive Cancer Ctr., 2008—, assoc. dir. for translational rsch., 2008—; founder & mem. Thera Bionic LLC, Chgo., 2007—. Asst. in medicine Clinique Bon Port, Montreux, Switzerland, 1988—2000; asst. physician Meml. Sloan-Kettering Cancer Ctr., Cornell U. Med. Ctr., NYC, 1993—2000; asst. prof. medicine Feinberg Sch. Medicine. Northwestern U., 2000—05, assoc. prof. medicine, 2006—08; co-leader cancer genes and molecular targeting program Robert H. Lurie Comprehensive Cancer Ctr., 2006—07; founder, mem. TheraBionic LLC, Chgo., 2007; prof. medicine U. Ala., Birmingham, 2008—, assoc. dir. translation sci., dir., div hematology/oncology; Martha Ann & David L. May chair in cancer rsch.; leader, cancer gene and molecular targeting program Robert H. Lurie Comprehensive Cancer Ctr., 2008. Inventor (with others): chimeric molecule with plaminogen activator activity and affinity for atherosclerotic plaques, method and system for applying low energy emission therapy; author: (books) Non-thrombogenic Properties of Artificial and Biological surfaces, Medecine Homeopathique Moderne; contbg. editor to Jour. Am. Med. Assn.; editor Jour. Exptl. and Clin. Cancer Rsch.; contbr. articles to profl. jours. and chpt. to book. With Swiss Med. Corps., 1980. Recipient Swiss Academic Soc. fellowship, 1983, Lausanne Academic Soc. Rsch. fellowship, 1984-86, Swedish Bd. for Tech. Devel. Rsch. fellowship, 1986-89; Physician Scientist award Nat. Cancer Inst.; Ohio State Human Cancer Genetics Program Commemorative medal, 2005. Fellow of the Am. Coll. Physicians (assoc.), mem. AAAS, AMA, Nat. Inst. Electromed. Info., Bioelectromagnetics Soc., European Bioelectromagnetics Soc., Internat. Soc. on Thrombosis and Haemostasis (Young Scientist Merit award 1989, Young Investigator Merit award 1991) Am. Soc. Hematology, Am. Soc. Clinical Oncology, Am. Assn. Cancer Rsch., Am. Soc. Human Genetics, Am. Fedn. for Clin. Rsch. (Trainee Investigator award 1992), Am. Soc. Clin. Investigation (elect 2007), Cancer Genetics Panel of the National Comprehensive Cancer Network, Cancer Genetics Study Sec., NIH (ad hoc mem.). Achievements include invention of electronic system for influencing cellular functions. Avocations: skiing, windsurfing, classical music, fine arts. Home: 415 East North Water St Apt 1406 Chicago IL 60611 Office: Univ Ala Div Hematology Oncology 1802 6th Ave S NP 2566 Birmingham AL 35294 Office Phone: 205-934-9591. Business E-Mail: bons.pasche@ccc.uab.edu.

PASCHETTO, JOHN J., lawyer; b. Long Branch, NJ, Sept. 18, 1959; s. Edward and Elizabeth McCue Paschetto; m. Katherine Anne Dobrosky, Feb. 20, 1982. BA, Rutgers U., 1981; MA, U. Del., 1988; JD, Harvard U., 1998. Bar: Del. 1998, U.S. Dist. Ct. Del. 1999. Ptnr. Young Conaway Stargatt & Taylor, LLP, Wilmington, Del., 1998—. Contbr. chapters to books. Mem.: ABA, Del. State Bar Assn., Harvard Law Sch. Assn. Del. (treas. 1998—). Office: Young Conaway Stargatt & Taylor LLP 1000 West St Wilmington DE 19801 Office Phone: 302-571-6608. Business E-Mail: jpaschetto@ycst.com.

PASCHKE, DONALD VERNON, music educator; b. Menominee, Mich., Oct. 22, 1929; s. Leo Carl Ferdinand and Augusta O. (Fritz) P.; m. Helen Inez Burton, Feb. 17, 1951; children: David Vernon, Celeste Eileen. MusB in Voice, U. Ill., 1957, BS in Choral Music Edn., 1957, MusM in Voice, 1958; D Mus. Arts, U. Colo., 1972. Instr. music Berea (Ky.) Coll., 1958-62; asst. prof. music Eastern N.Mex. U., Portales, 1962-71, assoc. prof., 1971-76, prof., 1976-94; prof. emeritus, 1994. Translator, editor: A Complete Treatise on the Art of Singing, Part Two (Manuel Garcia II), 1975; Part One, 1984. Songleader Portales Christian Breakfast, 1976-2008, pres. 1975-76, 90-91, v.p. 1974-75, 89-90; chancel choir dir. 1st Presbyn. Ch., Clovis, N.Mex., 1976-95; with U.S. Army, 1951-53; interim choir dir. 1st United Meth. Ch., Clovis, 2007-08. Mem. Nat. Assn. Tchrs. Singing (lt. gov. N.Mex. 1968-72, v.p. Gt. Plains chpt. 1972-74, chpt. pres. 1974-78), Am. Legion, Pi Kappa Lambda, Phi Kappa Phi. Republican. Presbyterian. Avocations: photography, do-it-yourself projects. Home: 228 Kansas Dr Portales NM 88130-7121

PASCIUTO, JOSEPH DORIA, priest; b. Bklyn., June 27, 1945; s. Carmine Michael Pasciuto, Rose Marie (Doria) Pasciuto. BA, St. John's U., 1968, MBA, 1981; MDiv, Immaculate Conception Sem., Huntington, NY, 1991; MA in Theology, Immaculate Conception Sem., 1999; theol. studies, Pontifical N.Am. Coll., Vatican City, 2003. Ordination Roman Cath. Diocese Bklyn., 1991. CFO Local 371 AFSCME, NYC, 1981—84; mgr. pers./labor rels Child Welfare Adminstrn., NYC, 1984—87; vicar Our Lady Help of Christians, Bklyn., 1991—99, Our Lady of Hope, Queens, NY, 1999—2000, St. Brendan, Bklyn., 2000—03; adminstr. Holy Cross Roman Cath. Ch., Bklyn., 2003—. Chaplain Boy Scouts Am., Bklyn., 2000—, Internat. Firefighters Assn., NYC, 2001. Mem.: KC (chaplain 1995—, 4th degree L.I. Assembly 2001), Montauk Club. Democrat. Avocations: music, reading, cooking. Home: 451 Abingdon Ave Staten Island NY 10308

PASCO, ALLAN HUMPHREY, literature educator; s. Ray Edwin and Bernedine May (Humphrey) P.; m. Dallas Marlene Christiansen, Dec. 29, 1960; children: Schuyler, Teague, Brandt, Chandar. BA, Whitman Coll., Walla Walla, Wash., 1960; MA, Northwestern U., 1961; PhD, U. Mich., 1968. Asst. prof. French U. Chgo., 1967-73; assoc. prof. French Purdue U., West Lafayette, Ind., 1973-79, prof. French, 1979-89; Hall disting. prof. 19th century lit. U. Kans., Lawrence, 1989—. Vis. prof. French UCLA, 1979; mem. editl. bd. Purdue U. Press, 1975-78; mem. bd. visitors U.S. Army War Coll. Author: The Color Keys, 1976, Novel Configurations, 1987, 2d edit., 1994, Balzacian Montage, 1991, Allusion: A Lit. Graft, 1994, reprinted, 2002, Sick Heroes: French Society and Lit. in the Romantic Age, 1997, Nouvelles francaises du dix-neuvieme siecle, 2006, Revolutionary Love, 2009; editor: Purdue U. Monographs, 1977—, Summa, 1990—, Frenc Rev., 1989—, Nineteenth-Century French Studies, 1995—, EMF: Studies in Early Modern France, Lingua Romana; co-editor: The Play of Terror in 19th Century France, 1996; contbr. articles to profl. jours. and volumes. With US Army, 1961-63. Recipient Cramer Teaching award, U. Kans., 1996, 1999, 2000-02, 2006, Outstanding Civilian Svc. award, 2006; Chancellor's Outstanding Mentor award, 2004; Ctr. for Humanistic Studies fellow Purdue U., 1985, Lilly Libr. summer rsch. fellow, 1976, various rsch. fellow, 1969-88, Hall Ctr. Humanities fellow, U. Kans., 1996. Mem. MLA, Assn. Am. Tchr. of French, Am. Soc. 18th Century Studies, Phi Sigma Iota, Phi Kappa Phi. Lutheran. Office: 1445 Jayhawk Blvd Rm 2044 Lawrence KS 66044-7590 Office Phone: 913-796-9936. Business E-Mail: apasco@ku.edu.

PASCOE, B. LYNN, international organization official, former ambassador; b. Mo., July 7, 1943; m. Diane Pascoe; 2 children. BA, U. Kans.; MA, Columbia U. Spl. asst. to dep. sec. state US Dept. State, dep. exec. sec., Am. dep. chief of mission Beijing China, prin. dep. asst. sec. East Asian and Pacific Bur.; dir. Am. Inst. Taiwan, Taipei, 1993—96; US spl. negotiator, Nagorno-Karabakh & regional conflicts, US co-chair, Orgn. Security & Cooperation in Europe's Minsk Group US Dept. State, 1997—98, US amb. to Malaysia Kuala Lampur, 1999—2001, dep. asst. sec. Bur. European and Eurasian Affairs Washington, 2001—04, US amb. to Indonesia Jakarta, 2004—07; under-sec. gen. polit. affairs UN, NYC, 2007—. Fluent in Mandarin Chinese. Office: UN Dept Political Affairs Room S-3755A New York NY 10017

PASCOE, JOHN M., pediatrician, educator; s. John E. and Jean Dolores Pascoe; m. Kathryn R. Kiehl, June 15, 1974; children: David Earl, Elizabeth Jean, John Erich. MD, U. Mich., Ann Arbor, 1971; MPH, U. NC, Chapel Hill, 1979. Diplomate Am. Bd. Pediat., 1980. Asst. prof. pediat. Mich. State U., East Lansing, 1982—88, U. Wis Madison, 1988—94, prof. pediat, 1994—2000, Wright State U. Boonshoft Sch. Medicine, Dayton, Ohio. Mem., Nat. Steering com. Agy. Healthcare Rsch. Quality, Nat. Practice Based Rsch. Network's Resource Ctr., Bethesda, Md.; mem. Nat. Program com. Head Srart Nat. Rsch. Conf., Washington, 1992—; mem. Nat. Exec. Com., Washington, 1997—2002. Contbr. articles to profl. jours. (Rsch. Writing award, 2007). Dir. comm. Academic Ambulatory Pediat., 1990—93. Maj. USAF, 1974—76, KI Sawyer AFB, Mich. Recipient Primary Care Tng. award, Divsn. Medicine and Dentistry, Bur. Health Profession, HHS, 1990—. Mem.: Am. Public Health Assn., Am. Pediat. Soc., Soc. Pediat. Rsch., Am. Acad. Pediat. (mem., Wis. chpt. exec. com. 1988—2000), Academic Ambulatory Pediat. Assn. Lutheran. Avocations: reading, gardening, running. Office: Children's Med Ctr Dayton One Children's Plz Dayton OH 45404

PASCOE, PATRICIA HILL, former state legislator; b. Sparta, Wis., June 1, 1935; d. Fred Kirk and Edith (Kilpatrick) Hill; m. D. Monte Pascoe, Aug. 3, 1957; children: Sarah, Edward, William. BA, U. Colo., 1957; MA, U. Denver, 1968, PhD, 1982. Tchr. Sequoia Union H.S. Dist., Redwood City, Calif. and Hayward (Calif.) Union H.S. Dist., 1957-60; instr. Met. State Coll., Denver, 1969-75, Denver U., 1975-77, 81, rsch. asst. bur. ednl. rsch., 1981-82; tchr. Kent Denver Country Day Sch., Englewood, Colo., 1982-84; freelance writer Denver, 1985—; mem. Colo. Senate, Dist. 32, Denver, 1989—93, Colo. Senate, Dist. 34, Denver, 1995—2003; chair minority caucus Colo. Senate, Denver, 1996-2000, chair policy and planning com., 2001, chair edn. com., 2002. Commr. Edn. Commn. of the States, Denver, 1975-82, 01-05. Contbr. articles to numerous publs. and jours. Bd. dirs. Samaritan House, 1990-94, Cystic Fibrosis Found., 1989-93, 2007—, chmn. legis. com.; pres. East HS Parent Tchr. and Student Assn., Denver, 1984-85; mem. Moore Budget Adv. Com., Denver, 1966-72; legis. chmn. alumni bd. U. Colo., Boulder, 1987-89; del. Dem. Nat. Conv., San Francisco, 1984, NYC, 1992; mem. Denver Woman's Press Club, 1986—, pres., 2005-06, Colo. Arts Coalition, 1988-97, Conflict Ctr. Bd., 2003-05; bd. dirs. Opera Colo., 1996-02; mem. bd. ACLU Colo., 2003-09, chair legis. com. Mem. Soc. Profl. Journalists, Common Cause (bd. dirs. Denver chpt. 1986-88), Denver Lions Found. (bd. mem., Westminster choir bd.), Lions Club (dir. 2003-05), Phi Beta Kappa. Democrat. Presbyterian.

PASCOTTO, ALVARO, lawyer; b. Rome, Mar. 8, 1949; came to U.S., 1984; s. Antonio and Anna Ludovica (Habig) P.; m. Linda Haldan, July 20, 1985. JD, U. Rome, 1973. Bar: Italy 1976, Calif. 1987, U.S. Dist. Ct. (cen. dist.) Calif. 1987, U.S. Ct. Appeals (9th cir.) 1987. Ptnr. Studio Legale Pascotto, Rome, 1976-86, Pascotto, Gallavotti & Gardner, LA and Rome, 1986-90, Pascotto & Gallavotti, LA, 1990—; of counsel Irell & Manella LLP, LA, 1994—2003, Morrison & Foerster, LLP, LA, 2003. Ofcl. counsel Consulate Gen. Italy, L.A., 1987—. Mem. ABA, Calif. Bar Assn., Italian-Am. Bar Assn., Am. Mgmt. Assn., Consiglio dell'Ordine Degli Avvocati e Procuratori di Roma. Clubs: Circolo del Golf (Rome); Malibu (Calif.) Racquet Club, Regency Club (L.A.), L.A. Country Club, Calif. Club. Home: 6116 Merritt Dr Malibu CA 90265-3847 Office: 555 W 5th St Ste 3500 Los Angeles CA 90013 Office Phone: 213-892-5635. Office Fax: 213-892-5637. Business E-Mail: apascotto@mofo.com.

PASCRELL, WILLIAM J., JR., United States Representative from New Jersey; b. Paterson, NJ, Jan. 25, 1937; s. William J. Sr. and Roffie (Loffredo) Pascrell; m. Elsie Marie Botto; children: William III, David, Glenn. BA in Journalism, Fordham U., NY, 1959, MA in Philos., 1961; postgraduate student, Fairleigh Dickinson U. Tchr. Jr. HS, Clifton, NJ, 1962, Paramus HS, NJ, 1962-74; adj. prof. Fairleigh Dickinson U., Madison, NJ, 1964—69; ophthalmic technician Seymour Pollack Opticians, 1968—74; adult sch. tchr. Dwight Morrow HS, Englewood, NJ, 1969-70; dir. Dept. Pub. Works, Paterson, NJ, 1974-77, Dept. Policy, Planning and Devel., Paterson, NJ, 1979—87; mem. Paterson Planning Bd., NJ, 1975—77; pres. Bd. Edn., Paterson, NJ, 1979—82; mem. NJ Gen. Assembly, 1987—90; mayor Paterson, NJ, 1990—96; mem. US Congress from 8th NJ dist., 1997—. Co-chair Congl. Brain Injury Task Force US Congress, mem. ways and means and homeland security com. Bd. dirs. Passaic County Cmty. Coll., 1973-79, Boys Club, 1975-; campaign coord. Robert A. Roe for Gov., NJ, 1977; regional coord. James Florio for Gov., Hudson County, NJ, 1981; active County Chairmen for Sen. Frank Lautenberg, NJ, 1982; chmn. Passaic County Democrats, NJ, 1982-1990. Enlisted US Army, 1961—62, sgt. USAR, 1962—67. Recipient Congl. Recognition award, Internat. Assn. Fire Fighters, 2001; named Man of Yr., Mother Cabrini Soc., 1979, Fedn. Italian Socs., 1981, Unico Passaic County, 1982, Am. Legion John Raad Post, 1983, Passaic County Young Democrats, 1983. Mem.: Pat Mone Assn., Charles Alfano Assn., Riverside Vets., KC, Fordham U. Alumni Assn., Am. Cancer Soc., Italian-Am. Fedn., Paterson Taxpayers Assn., Elks. Democrat. Roman Catholic. Office: US House Reps 2464 Rayburn House Office Bldg Washington DC 20515-3008 Office Phone: 202-225-5751. Office Fax: 202-225-5782.*

PASCUAL, CARLOS ENRIQUE, United States Ambassador to Mexico; b. Cuba, 1958; BA in Internat. Rels., Stanford U., 1980; MA in Pub. Policy, Harvard U., 1982. With USAID, South Africa, Mozambique, Washington, project devel. officer Sudan, 1983—92, dir., Office of Program Analysis and Coordinatoin for New Ind. States Task Force, 1994—94, dep. asst. adminstr. for Europe and New Ind. States, 1994—95; dir. for Russian, Ukrainian and Eurasian Affairs Nat. Security Coun., 1995—98, spl. asst. to Pres., sr. dir. for Russia, 1998—2000; US amb. to Ukraine US Dept. State, Kiev, 2000—03, coordinator for U.S. assistance to Europe and Eurasia, 2003—04, dir. Office of Reconstruction & Stabilization, 2004—06, US amb. to Mexico Mexico City, 2009—; v.p., dir. fgn. policy studies The Brookings Instn., Washington, 2006—09. Office: US Embassy 8700 Mexico City Pl Washington DC 20521*

PASETTI, LOUIS OSCAR, retired dentist; b. Tampa, Fla., Dec. 27, 1916; s. Joseph G. and Carmen (Gonzalez) P.; m. Mary Mendez, Jan. 11, 1942; children: Louis M., Arleen Pasetti Mariotti. BS, U. Fla., 1937; DDS, Emory U., 1941; postgrad., U. Pa., 1978. Capt. U.S. Army, 1942—46; pvt. practice Tampa, Fla., 1947—2002; ret., 2002. Contbr. articles on Differential Diagnosis of Dental Pain. Past. pres. Tampa Civitan Club, 1953; past lt. gov. Civitan Clubs of Tampa, 1962; past dep. gov. Civitan Internat., Fla., 1964; fin. officer Am. Legion Post 248. Named Fla. Dentist of the Yr., Fla. Acad. Gen. Dentistry, 1983; recipient meritorious Svc. award Fla. Acad. Gen. Dentistry, 1989, Disting. Svc. award, 1985, finalist Nat. Competetion Humanterian award. Fellow Acad. Gen. Dentistry (Lifetime Achievement award 2004), Am. Coll. Dentists, Internat. Coll. Dentists, Acad. Dentistry Internat.; mem. ADA, Fla. Dental Assn., Fla. Acad. Gen. Dentistry (pres. 1981, Lifetime Achievement award 1996, mem. emeritus 2002), Tampa Bay Acad. Gen. Dentistry (pres. 1977-78), Elks, Round Table of Civic Clubs of Tampa (sec. 1953), Palma Ceia Golf and Country Club. Democrat. Roman Catholic. Avocations: photography, orchid culture. Home: 10023 Hampton Pl Tampa FL 33618-4227

PASHGIAN, M. HELEN, artist; b. Pasadena, Calif., Nov. 7, 1934; d. Aram John and Margaret (Howell) P. BA, Pomona Coll., 1956; student, Columbia U., 1957; MA in Fine Arts, Boston Univ., 1958. Art instr. Harvard-Newton Program Occidental Coll., 1977-78; artist in residence Calif. Inst. Tech., 1970-71. Grants panelist Calif. Arts Coun., Sacramento, 1993. One-woman shows include Rex Evans Gallery, LA, 1965, 67, Occidental Coll., 1967, Kornblee Gallery, NYC, 1969-72, U. Calif., Irvine, 1975, U. Calif. Santa Barbara, 1976, Stella Polaries Gallery, LA, 1981-82, Kaufman Galleries, Houston, 1982, Modernism Gallery, San Francisco, 1983, Works Gallery, Long Beach, Costa Mesa, Calif., 1986-92, Malka Gallery, LA, 1997, Patricia Faure Gallery, LA, 2006, Charlotte Jackson Fine Art, Santa Fe, 2009; exhibited in group shows at Pasadena Art Mus., 1965, Carson Pirie Scott, Chgo., 1965, Calif. Palace of Legion of Honor, San Francisco, 1967, Esther Bear Gallery, Santa Barbara, 1967, 69, Lytton Ctr. of the Visual Arts, LA, 1968, Salt Lake Art Inst., Salt Lake City, 1968, Mus. Contemporary Crafts, 1969, Second Flint (Mich.) Invitational, 1969, Milw. Art Ctr., 1969, U.S.I.S. Mus., NYC, Mus. Contemporary Art, Chgo., 1970, Studio Merconi, Milan, 1970, Calif. Inst. Tech., Baxter Art Galley, 1971, 1980, Calif. Innovations, Palm Springs Dessert Mus., 1981, Calif. Internat. Arts Found. Mus. Modern Art, Paris, 1982, LA Artists in Seoul, Donsangbang Gallery, 1982, An Artistic Conversation, 1931-82, Poland, USA, Ulster Mus., Belfast, Ireland, 1983, Madison Art Ctr., Wis., 1994, Calif. State U., Fullerton, 1995, Oakland Mus., Calif., 1995, Molly Barnes Gallery, LA, Calif., 2000, Pasadena Mus. Calif. Art, 2002, Norton Simon Mus., Pasadena, Calif., 2006; represented in pub. collections at River Forest State Bank, Ill., Atlantic Richfield Co., Dallas, Frederic Weisman Collection, L., Security Pacific Bank, LA, Singapore, Andrew Dickson White Mus. Art, Cornell U., Ithaca, NY, LA County Mus. Art, Santa Barbara Art Mus., Laguna Beach Mus. Art, Orange County Mus. Art, Portland Art Mus., Oreg., Palm Springs Art Mus., Calif. Trustee, Pomona Coll, Claremont, Calif., 1987—; parade judge Tournament of Roses Centennial Parade, Pasadena, 1987; bd. dirs. LA Master Chorale, 1992—, Ojai Music Festival, 2004— NEA grantee, 1986. Home: 731 S Grand Ave Pasadena CA 91105-2424

PASI, GEETA, diplomat; BA, Duke U., Durham, NC; M in French Studies, NYU. Instl. fin. market rschr., NYC; with US Fgn. Svc. US Dept. State, 1988—, assignments in Cameroon, Romania, Ghana and India, mem. Sec. of State's advance team Washington, desk officer for Afghanistan, 2001—03, dep. prin. officer Am. Consulate Gen. Frankfurt, Germany, US charge d'affaires to Bangladesh. Office: US Embassy 3120 Dhaka Pl Washington DC 20521-3120

PASICH, KIRK ALAN, lawyer; b. La Jolla, Calif., May 26, 1955; s. Chris Nick and Iva Mae (Tormey) P.; m. Pamela Mary Woods, July 30, 1983; children: Christopher Thomas, Kelly Elizabeth, Connor Woods. BA in Polit. Sci., UCLA, 1977; JD, Loyola Law Sch., LA, 1980. Bar: Calif. 1980, U.S. Dist. Ct. (no., so., ea. and cen. dists.) Calif. 1981, Mich. (ea. dist.) 1997, Tex. (ea. dist.) 2001, U.S. Ct. Appeals (9th cir.) 1981, U.S. Ct. Appeals (1st cir.) 1992. Assoc. Paul, Hastings, Janofsky & Walker, LA, 1980-88, ptnr., 1988-89, Troop Steuber Pasich Reddick & Tobey, LLP, 1989-2000, Howrey Simon Arnold & White LLP, 2001—03, Pasich & Kornfeld LLP, 2003—05, Dickstein Shapiro LLP, 2005—. Author: Casualty and Liability Insurance, 1990, 2000, 03; co-author: Officers and Directors: Liabilities and Protections, 1996, 2000, 03, The Year 2000 and Beyond: Liability and Insurance for Computer Code Problems, 2000; contbg. editor: West's California Litigation Forms: Civil Procedure Before Trial, 2000; co-author, co-editor: ABA Manual for Complex Insurance Coverage Litigation, 1999, 2000, 04; entertainment law columnist, ins. law columnist L.A. and San Francisco Daily Jour., 1989—; contbr. articles to profl. jours. Active bd. dirs. Nat. Acad. Jazz, L.A., 1988-89, chmn. bd. dirs. Woody Herman Found., L.A., 1989-92, Constnl. Rights Found., 2000; active L.A. City Atty's. Task Force for Econ. Recovery, 1992-93. Named to Calif's. Legal Dream Team as 1 of state's top 25 litigators, Calif. Law Bus., 1992; named one of the nation's top 45 lawyers under age 45, Am. Lawyer, 1995, market leader for policyholder representation in California, Chambers Am. Leading Bus. Lawyers, 2003-07; named one of 500 Leading Lawyers in Am., Lawdragon, 2005, 06, Nation's Top 12 Leading Policyholder Lawyer, Chambers USA, 2007, 08. Mem. ABA (mem. Task Force on Complex Insurance Coverage Litigation), Risk & Insurance Mgmt. Soc., Def. Rsch. Inst. Democrat. Avocations: reading, music, basketball. Office: Dickstein Shapiro LLP 2049 Century Park East Ste 700 Los Angeles CA 90067 Home Phone: 310-476-2329; Office Phone: 310-772-8305. Business E-Mail: pasichk@dicksteinshapiro.com.

PASIK-DUNCAN, BOZENNA JANINA, mathematics professor, researcher; b. Radom, Warsaw, Poland, June 30, 1947; d. Janina and Antoni Pasik; m. Tyrone Edward Duncan, May 21, 1983; 1 child, Dominique Duncan. MS, Warsaw U., 1970, PhD, 1978, D, 1986. Asst. prof. Warsaw Sch. Econ., 1970—84; instr. U. Kans., Lawrence, 1984—87, asst. prof., 1987—89, assoc. prof., 1989—93, prof. math., 1993—. Lectr. Warsaw Tech. U., 1973—75. Contbr. scientific papers to profl. jours. Membeer of the bd. of governors IEEE Control Systems Soc., Piscataway, NJ, 1996—2002. Recipient Excellence in Rsch. and Tchg., Ministry of Higher Edn. and Sci., 1975; fellow, IREX, 1982—83; Rsch. grant, NSF, 1987—. Mem.: AAUW, IEEE (v.p. 1999, bd. govs. 1996, medal 2000, Dist. Mem. award 2000, fellow 2001), Internat. Stats. Inst., Soc. Indsl. and Applied Math., Bernoulli Soc., Am. Math. Soc., Polish Math. Soc., Assn. Women in Math. (L. Hay award 2004), Math. Assn. Am. Achievements include research in stochastic adaptive control of continous time systems. Avocations: travel, music, poetry. Home: 1208 Schwarz Rd Lawrence KS 66049 Office: Univ Kans Dept Math Lawrence KS 66045 Office Fax: 785-864-5255. Business E-Mail: bozenna@math.ku.edu.

PASINETTI, NINA DENTON, dance educator, artistic director, choreographer; b. Charleston, W.Va., July 27, 1943; d. Oliver Berman and Lelia Bernice Lyons Denton; m. Thomas Patrick Pasinetti, Mar. 10, 2000; stepchildren: Thomas Jr., Terri Brannan. BS, U. Charleston, W.Va.; MA, Ohio U., Athens. Grad. asst. math. tchr. Ohio U., 1965—66; math. tchr. Glouster HS, Ohio, 1968; math. and theater tchr. George Washington HS, Charleston, 1968—99, choreographer, dir. musicals, 1968—; choreographer Charleston Light Opera Guild, 1971—, artistic dir., 1983—; choreographer Kanawha Players, Charleston, 1968, 1969, 1974, W.Va. State Coll. Fine Arts, Institute, 1969, 1970; theater adjudicator W.Va. State Thespian Festival, 2000—. Tchr., dir. dance studio YWCA, Charleston, 1970—82; choreographer, dir. Jenny Wiley Profl. Music Theatre, Prestonsburg, Ky., 1983—85; dir., founder George Washington Dance Co., 1968—83, Appalachian Youth Jazz Ballet Co., 1983—93; owner, tchr. Ballet and Mus. Theatre Dance Arts Inc., Charleston, 1983—93; dir. Charleston Theatre Festival, 2000—03. Choreographer W.Va. dance festivals, 1976—93. Pres. Dance W.Va., 1981—85; program com. mem. Clay Ctr. Arts, Charleston, 2004—; v.p., dance chair Festivall Charleston, 2004—. Recipient recognition at Gov.'s Arts Awards, Gov. of W.Va., 2006; named Outstanding Individual Artist, Mayor's Arts Awards, 1996, East Bank HS Alumnus of Yr., Charleston, 1999. Avocations: movies, antiques, travel, theater. Home: 1603 Clark Rd Charleston WV 25314 Personal E-mail: pasinettindrudi@aol.com.

PASINETTI, PIER MARIA, author; b. Venice, Italy, June 24, 1913; came to U.S., 1946, naturalized, 1952; s. Carlo and Maria (Ciardi) P. Dottore in Lettere, U. Padua, Italy, 1935; PhD in Comparative Lit., Yale U., 1949. Fellow La. State U., 1935-36, U. Calif. at Berkeley, 1936-37; lectr. U. Stockholm, 1942-46; prof. Italian and comparative lit. UCLA, 1949—. Author: L'ira di Dio, 1942, Venetian Red, 1960, The Smile on the Face of the Lion, 1965, From the Academy Bridge, 1970, Suddenly Tomorrow, 1971, Dall' Estrema America, 1975, Il Centro, 1979, Dorsoduro, 1983, Life for Art's Sake: Studies in the Literary Myth of the Romantic Artist, 1985, Melodramma, 1993, Piccole Veneziane Complicate, 1996, Astolfo, 1999; also articles, revs., film scripts. Recipient Fiction award Nat. Inst. Arts and Letters, 1965, Prix Écureuil Li. Etrangère, 1996. Mem. Authors Guild. Clubs: Elizabethan Yale. Office: 1259 Dorsoduro Venice Italy 30123 Home: 11307 Andasol Ave Granada Hills CA 91344-3402

PASK, SCOTT, set designer; Grad., Yale Sch. Drama. Broadway: Cabaret, 1998, Urinetown (Lucille Lortel nom.), 2001, Amour, 2002, Take Me Out, 2003, Little Shop of Horrors (Touring Broadway award, best prodn. design, 2005), La Cage aux Folles, 2004, Pillowman, (Tony award, best scenic design, 2005) Sweet Charity, 2005, The Wedding Singer, 2006, Fame Becomes Me, 2006, The Lieutenant of Inishmore, 2006, The Coast of Utopia, 2006-07 (Outer Critics Cir. award outstanding set design, 2007, Drama Desk award outstanding set design of a play, 2007, Tony award best scenic design of play, 2007), The Vertical Hour, 2006, The Ritz, 2007, November, 2008, Cry-Baby, 2008, Les Liaisons Dangereuses, 2008 (Drama Desk award for Oustanding Set Design, 2008), Pal Joey, 2008; in London: On an Average Day, Tales from Hollywood, Albert Herring, Pillowman; also appeared at Almeida Theatre, Royal Nat. Theatre, Donmar Warehouse, Opera North, Atlantic Theater Co., The Pub. Theatre, Roundabout Theatre, Yale Rep., South Coast Rep., Ctr. Stage, Williamstown, NY Theatre Workshop, Classic

Stage Co., Playwrights Horizons, Chgo. Opera Theater, Bklyn. Acad. Music. Recipient Lucille Lortel award, 1999, Henry Hewes award, Am. Theater Wing, 1999, Bessie award, 2001. Office: 4 Times Sq #15 New York NY 10036-6518

PASKAWICZ, JEANNE FRANCES, pain specialist; b. Phila., Mar. 3, 1954; d. Alex and Lillian (Pyluck) P. BSc, Phila. Coll. Pharmacy; MA, Villanova U., 1973; postgrad., St. Joseph U., 1979; PhD, Kensington U., 1984. Mem. anesthesiology staff Einstein Med. Ctr., Phila., 1990-94, Temple U. Hosp., 1994—; mem. detox./rehab. staff Presbyn. Med. Ctr., Phila., 1984—; house officer Tenet Hosps., Elkins Park, Pa., 1990—; mem. psychiatry staff Hahnemann U. Hosp., Phila., 1984-90; hostage negotiator Office of Mental Health, Phila., 1984-90; mem. surgery/anesthesiology staff Mt. Sinai Hosp., Phila., 1989-91. Bd. dirs. Phila. Coll. Pharmacy, St. Joseph U. Mem. NAFE, Am. Pain Soc., Lambda Kappa Sigma.

PASKELL, LINDA RUTH, art educator, photojournalist; b. Suffern, NY, Apr. 26, 1959; d. Jack Robert Paskell and Elaine Anderson; children: Jacob Steven Miller, Josef Vernon Miller. BFA, Arcadia U., Glenside, Pa., 1981, MEd, 1991. Art tchr. Open Door Christian Acad., Ft. Washington, Pa., 1981—, Phila.-Mont. Christian Acad., Dresher, Pa., 1986—96; photographer Peek-A-View Photography, Gleside, 1997—; adj. prof. edn. Phila. Bibl. U., Langhorne, Pa., 1998—; art educator nursing homes 3 ACTS Retirement Cmtys., Springhouse, Pa., Southampton, Pa., Normandy Farms, Pa. Photo journalist The Color of Poverty, Ecuador, Peru, Guatemala, Mexico, Ghana, Uganda, 2006—, artist (exhbn.) African Am. Mus. Phila. Avocation: photography.

PASKETT, ELECTRA, epidemiologist, oncologist, educator; PhD in Epidemiology, U. Wash. Prof. cancer rsch. divsn. epidemiology Ohio U. Sch. Pub. Health, assoc. dir. population sciences; co-program leader cancer control program Ohio U. Comprehensive Cancer Ctr.; dir. diversity enhancement program James Cancer Hosp.; chmn. cancer ctrl. & health outcomes com. Cancer & Leukemia Group B. Fellow: Am. Assn. Advancement Sci.; mem.: Am. Soc. Preventive Oncology (pres. elect). Office: Ohio State University Comprehensive Cancer Center 320 W 10th Ave Columbus OH 43210 Office Phone: 614-293-3917. Office Fax: 614-293-5611. E-mail: cansrp@gwumc.edu.*

PASKINS, JANET LYNN, psychology professor, educational consultant; d. Melvin L. and Cherryl Nadine Cannon; married, Mar. 21, 1986; children: Derek Ryan Nevins, Deren Ross Nevins. EdB, Ball State U., Muncie, Ind., 1970, MEd, 1972, MA in Counseling Psychology, 1983; postgrad., U. S. Fla., Tampa, 2000—. Pvt. practice psychotherapist, Anderson, Ind., 1983—84, Clearwater, Fla., 1984—98; coord. workplace devel. and placement ctr. coord. PHCC, New Port Richey, Fla., 1995—99; prof. psychology and sociology Pasco Hernando CC, Brooksville, Fla., 1999—. Cons. Internat. Sch. Connection, Tampa, Fla., 1998—. Bus. devel. bd., New Port Richey, Fla., 1996—2000. Recipient Excellence in Curriculum and Instruction award, Fla. Assn. CC, 1998, Exemplary Initiatives award, Nat. Coun. Instl. Adminstrs., 1999, Sylva Thompson Leadership award, 1999, Nat. Tech. Prep award, 1999, Workforce Devel. award, Rotary, 2000; Curriculum Devel. grantee, Dept. of Edn., 1996. Mem.: APA (assoc.). Avocations: travel, tennis.

PASLEY, ANTHONY J., history professor; b. Omaha, June 1, 1979; s. Dennis Pasley and Diane Biniewicz; m. Catherine J. Warren, July 23, 2005; 1 child, Joseph William Warren-Pasley. MA, U. Nebr., Omaha, 2004. Exec. dir. Wash. County Hist. Assn., Fort Calhoun, Nebr., 2006—08; history instr. U. Nebr., Omaha, 2008—. Contbr. to profl. jours. Mem.: Black Elk - Neihardt Pk. Assn. (ex-officio mem. 2006—08). Office: Univ of Nebr at Omaha 6001 Dodge St Omaha NE 68182 Business E-Mail: apasley@mail.unomaha.edu.

PASNICU, CORNEL, mathematician, educator; b. Bucharest, Romania, Sept. 6, 1953; arrived in U.S., 1992; s. Tanasa Pasnicu, Xenia Adina Pasnicu; m. Adina Melania Truta; 1 child, Nastasia Laura. BA, U. Bucharest, 1976, MS, 1977, PhD, 1987. Rsch. fellow INCREST (IMAR), Bucharest, Romania, 1980—91; vis. scholar U. Copenhagen, 1991—91; vis. assoc. prof. U. Toronto, Ont., Canada, 1992—92; assoc. prof. U. P.R., San Juan, 1992—97, full prof., 1997—. Mem. operator algebras/operator theory panel NSF, Arlington, Va., 2002. Contbr. articles to profl. jours. Recipient S. Stoilov prize, Romanian Acad., 1988; grantee, NSF, 1994—96, 1996—2000, 2001—, Army Rsch. Office, 2000—. Mem.: Am. Math. Soc. Avocations: reading, music, sports. Office: Univ of Puerto Rico Dept of Mathematics PO Box 23355 San Juan PR 00931 E-mail: cpasnicu@gmail.com.

PASOUR, KATHERINE MEADOR, dean, educator; b. Winston-Salem, NC, June 7, 1953; d. James Ratliffe and Elizabeth Mitchell Meador; m. Robert Gerard Pasour, Dec. 17, 1988; children: Mark Alexander Chambers, Katie Leigh. MA, Appalachian State U., Boone, NC, 1977; PhD, U. NC, Greensboro, 1996. Tchr. Rockingham County Schs., Eden, NC, 1979—96; prof. Lenoir-Rhyne U., Hickory, NC, 1997—, dean, Coll. Health Scis., 2008—. Choir dir., author, Christmas Programs Bethlehem United Meth. Ch., Reidsville, NC, leader, Administrative Coun., Sunday sch. tchr., 1985—2008. Recipient Svc. Award, NC Alliance for Athletics, Health, Phys. Edn., Recreation and Dance, 2004. Mem.: NC Alliance (jour. editor 1997—2006, Svc. award 2004, Honor award 2006), Am. Alliance, Delta Kappa Gamma Internat. (pres. Alpha Delta Chpt. 1996—98). Methodist. Avocations: gardening, writing, horseback riding. Office: Lenoir-Rhyne Univ Box 7356 Hickory NC 28603

PASQUARIELLO, PATRICK S., JR., pediatrician; b. Phila., Mar. 29, 1930; MD, Jefferson Med. Coll., 1956. Cert. in pediat. Am. Bd. Pediat., 1963. Intern St. Joseph's Hosp., Phila., 1956—57; resident in pediat. Children's Hosp. of Phila., 1961—63, acting chief divsn., 1997—2000, dir. diagnostic ctr., dir. spina bifida program; prof. U. Pa. Sch. Medicine. Co-investigator Spina Bifida Rsch. Resource. Office: Childrens Hosp Phila Diagnostic Ctr 34th St and Civic Ctr Blvd Philadelphia PA 19104 also: Joseph Stokes Jr Rsch Inst Childrens Hosp Phila 1120 Wood Bldg Philadelphia PA 19104 Office Phone: 215-590-4020, 215-590-1760.

PASQUIER, JOËL, music educator; b. Montmorency, France, Sept. 25, 1943; arrived in Can., 1967; s. Jean and Raymonde (Gourdin) P.; m. Anne Vachon, Nov. 28, 1970; 1 child, Ariane. Grad. in piano and chamber music, Conservatoire Nat. Superieur de Musique, Paris, 1962. Prof. Conservatoire de Musique de St. Germain-en-Laye, France, 1964-65; grad. asst. Sch. Music, Ind. U., Bloomington, 1965-67; tchr. piano U. Laval, Quebec, Canada, 1967—2003, dir., 1988-91. Recording artist ATMA Records. Appeared as solo pianist concert halls, radio, TV, with chamber and symphony orchs. in France, U.S., Can., The Netherlands. Fulbright scholar Ind. U., 1965. Mem. Que. Yacht Club. Personal E-mail: orion_556@hotmail.com.

PASS, CAROLYN JOAN, dermatologist; b. Balt., May 14, 1941; d. Isidore Earl and Rhea (Koplowitz) P.; m. Richard Malcolm Susel, June 23, 1963; children: Steven, Gary. BS, U. Md., 1962, MD, 1966. Diplomate Am. Bd. Dermatology. Rotating intern USPHS Hosp., Balt., 1966-67; med. resident St. Agnes Hosp., Balt., 1967-68; dermatology resident and fellow U. Md. Sch. Medicine Hosps., 1968-71; pvt. practice specializing in dermatology Balt. and Ellicott City, Md., 1971—. Mem. staff St. Agnes Hosp.; vol. dermatology clinics U. Md., St. Agnes hosps.; asst. clin. prof. dermatology U. Md. Sch. Medicine, 1978—; mem. exec. com. adv. bd. Nat. Program in Dermatology, 1975. Mem. AMA, Med. and Chirurgical Soc. State Md. (del.), Balt. City Med. Soc. (del 1974, pub. rels. com., 1992-94, alternate del. 1994—), Am. Women's Med. Assn., Am. Acad. Dermatology (award exhibit 1970), Soc. Investigative Dermatology, Md. Dermatology Soc. (sec.-treas. 1974-76, pres. 1976-77), U. Md. Sch. Medicine Alumnae Assn. (bd. dirs. 1987—), Woodholme Country Club, Country Garden Club. Jewish. Avocations: gourmet cooking, gardening, art, golf. Office: Pine Heights Med Ctr 1001 Pine Heights Ave Ste 301 Baltimore MD 21229-5285

PASS, CHARLOTTE LOUISE, literature educator, consultant; b. Oneonta, Ala., Sept. 2, 1966; d. James Arnold and Betty Jo Pass. Cert. English Edn. Ala., 1998, ESL Ala., 2005. Acad. tutor, supr. U. Ala. Athletic Dept., Tuscaloosa, 1986—93; English/journalism tchr. Tuscaloosa Acad., 1989—91; grad. tchg. asst. U. Ala., Tuscaloosa, 1988—91, grad. instr., 2002—; English/music appreciation tchr. Hillcrest HS, Tuscaloosa, 1998—2001; home sch. tchr. Victory Christian Sch., Tuscaloosa, 2002—04. Literacy cons. Eastwood Mid. Sch., Ala., 2003—; presenter and cons. in field. Mem.: Am. Assn. Applied Linguistics (assoc.), Am. Ednl. Rsch. Assn. (assoc.), Mid-South Ednl. Ednl. Rsch. Assn. (assoc.), Tchrs. of English to Speakers of Other Languages (assoc.), Internat. Reading Assn. (assoc.), Nat. Reading Conf. (assoc.), Nat. Coun. Tchrs. of English (assoc.), Assn. Tchr. Educators (assoc.), ASCD (assoc.), Ala. Reading Assn. (assoc.), Ala. Coun. Tchrs. of English (assoc.), ASPCA, Amnesty Internat., Peta, Nat. Humane Soc., Phi Delta Kappa (assoc.), Phi Kappa Phi (life). Independent. Episcopalian. Avocations: reading, piano, singing. Home: 1022 Fairfax Dr Tuscaloosa AL 35406 Office: Univ Ala PO Box 870232 204 Graves Hall Tuscaloosa AL 35487

PASS, ROBERT, pediatrician; BS in chemistry, U. Ala., 1969, MD, 1973. Intern and resident in pediat. Stanford U. Med. Ctr., 1973—76; fellow in pediatric infectious diseases U. Ala., Birmingham, 1976—79, faculty in pediat., 1979—, prof. pediat. and microbiology. Fellow: Infectious Diseases Soc. America; mem.: Am. Soc. Virology, Am. Soc. Microbiology, Am. Pediatric Soc., Soc. Pediatric Rsch., Alpha Omega Alpha, Phi Beta Kappa. Office: Childrens Harbor Bldg 309 1530 3rd Ave S Birmingham AL 35294-0011 Office Phone: 205-934-2441, 205-996-4104. Office Fax: 205-934-2370. E-mail: rpass@peds.uab.edu.*

PASSANO, E. MAGRUDER, JR., management consultant; b. Balt., Oct. 2, 1942; s. Edward M. and Mildred P. (Nelson) P.; m. Helen C. Marikle, Sept. 4, 1971; children: Catherine, Tammy, Sarah. BS, Johns Hopkins U., 1967, MA, 1969. With Waverly Inc., Balt., 1965-98, salesman, 1970-73, v.p., 1973-75, v.p. adminstrn., sec., 1975-90, vice chmn., sec., 1990-98; pres., CEO One Waverly LLC, Balt., 1998—. Chmn. Passano Found., Balt., 1982—, mem. adv. coun. Wawerly Mgmt. LLC, 2007-; pres. Am. Lung Assn., Md., 1982-84; mem. exec. com. Vol. Coun. Equal Opportunity, Balt., 1978-2002, chmn., 1995-2002; bd. dirs. Combined Health Appeal Am., 1994-97; pres. (CHA) Combined Health Agys., Md., 1985-87, chmn. exec. com., 1987-95; pres. 12:30 Club Balt., 1981-83; mem. exec. com. Balt. City Life Mus., 1982-93, v.p. 1987-93; trustee emeritus, 1993-98; mem. adv. coun. Johns Hopkins U. Sch. Profl. Studies in Bus. and Edn., 1984—, mem. John Hopkins U. Sch. Edn. Nat. Adv. Coun., 2008, exec. chair alumni chpt., 1986-89, chair edn. cmty. devel. iniative, 1995—2006; mem. Md. Gov.'s Commn. on High Blood Pressure and Related Cardiovascular Risk Factors, 1986-2002; bd. govs. Md. New Directions, Inc., 1987-94; bd. dirs., mem. exec. com. YMCA Ctrl. Md., 1988-96; treas., bd. dirs., chmn. edn. com. Pride of Balt., 1990—; bd. dirs. Ind. Coll. Fund Md., 1994—; mem. bd. visitors Towson State U., 1994—2006, chmn. 1997-2001, mem. deans adv. coun. & bd. visitors Sch. Medicine U. Md., 1995—; co-chair campaign planning com. U. Md. Sch. Medicine, 2008-, mem. planning com., bd. vis. Md. Bus. Responsive Govt., 1994-2002. With USN, 1963-65 Recipient Prince Hall Bicentennial award Masons, 1975; citations Mayor of Balt., 1976, City of Balt., 1977, Vol. of Yr. award for outstanding svc. to CICHA, 1984-85, Presdl. award for outstanding svc. to Am. Lung Assn. Md., 1985, Outstanding Vol., 1988, Disting. Svc. award Soc. Profl. Journalists, 1987, Outstanding Svc. award Am. Heart Assn., 1988, Outstanding Vol. Svc. award Balt. Assn. Retarded Citizens, 1990, Vol. of Yr./Outstanding Leadership and Dedication award Combined Health Agys., 1991-92, Outstanding Family of the Century, Am. Lung Assn. Md., 2003, Outstanding Bd. Mem., Ind. Coll. Fund Md., 2004. Mem. Purchasing Mgmt. Assn. Md. (chmn. com. 1968-70), Balt. Jaycees (v.p. 1974-76, internat. senator 1975), Greater Balt. Minority Purchasing Coun. (Svc. award 1978), Soc. Colonial Wars (chpt. gov. 1989-91), Johns Hopkins U. Alumni Assn. (pres. Balt. 1984-86, Univ. Heritage award 1987). Democrat. Episcopalian. Home: 3925 Linkwood Rd Baltimore MD 21210-3001 Office: One Waverly LLC 1122 Kenilworth Dr Ste 115 Towson MD 21204-2142 E-mail: macpassano@verizon.net.

PASSER, JULIETTE MAYABELLE, lawyer; b. USSR; MusB, Manhattan Sch. Music, 1981, MA in Music Edn., 1984; postgrad., NYU, 1985-86, Columbia U., 1988-89; JD cum laude, Yeshiva U., 1990. Bar: N.Y. 1990. Solist, music dir. mus. theater cos. in U.S. and Europe, 1977-87; dir. admissions and pub. rels. St. Sergius Sch., NYC, 1981-83; tchg. asst. edn. dept. NYU, NYC, 1985-86; assoc. Debevoise & Plimpton, NYC, 1990-94, Patterson, Belknap, Webb & Tyler, LLP, NYC, 1994-96; pres., gen. counsel Internat. Project Devel. Group, LLC, NYC, 1996—. Adj. lectr. Hunter Coll. CUNY, and Hunter Coll. H.S., 1981-82; tchg. asst., substitute lectr. Manhattan Sch. Music, N.Y.C., 1981-83; judge numerous music competitions, including Bklyn. Acad. Music, 1985, 86. Contbr. numerous articles to law and other publs.; performer, dir. musicals, including Camelot, Sound of Music, Fantasticks, Grease, West Side Story, Show Boat, Little Night Music, Carousel, King and I, and Jesus Christ Superstar; spl. guest 3d Internat. Festival Contemporary Music, Leningrad, USSR, 1988. Bd. dirs. Coun. for Trade and Econ. Cooperation, U.S.-Uzbekistan Coun., St. Petersburg Found. Scholar Jewish Found. for Edn. Women, 1977-78, Manhattan Sch. Music. Mem. Internat. Law Soc., N.Y. State Bar Assn., Bar Assn. City N.Y., Women in Internat. Trade, Coun. on Fgn. Rels. Office: Internat Project Devel Group 730 5th Ave 9 flr New York NY 10019 Office Phone: 212-541-3909. Fax: 212-541-2486.

PASSERINI, FILIPPO, information technology executive; b. Rome; PhD in Statistics & Operating Rsch., Univ. Rome. Series of info. mgmt. roles Procter & Gamble Co., U.K., Greece, Italy, Latin Am., Turkey, pres., global bus. svcs., chief info. officer, 2003—. Bd. govs. EPCglobal Inc., Lawrenceville, NJ. Named one of Premier 100 IT Leaders, Computerworld, 2007; named to Outsourcing Hall of Fame, Internat. Assn. Outsourcing Profls., 2006. Office: Chief Info Officer Procter & Gamble Co 1 P&G Plz Cincinnati OH 45202 Office Phone: 513-983-1100. Office Fax: 513-983-4381.*

PASSET, JOANNE ELLEN, history professor, writer; d. Norman Frank and Almeda Harrison Passet. BA, Bluffton Coll., Ohio, 1975; MA in History, Bowling Green State U., Ohio, 1979; MLS, Ind. U., Bloomington, 1980, PhD in Libr. & Info. Sci., 1988; PhD in US History, U. Wis., Madison, 1999. Elem. sch. tchr. Bath Local Sch. Sys., Lima, Ohio, 1975—77; reference libr. Ind. U., 1982—88, asst. prof. libr. & info. sci., 1990—94, UCLA, 1988—90; dir. librs. and assoc. prof. history Bluffton U., Ohio, 1998—2000; assoc. prof. libr. & info. sci. Dominican U., River Forest, Ill., 2000—01; prof. history Ind. U. East, Richmond, 2001—. Author: (nonfiction book) Cultural Crusaders: Women Librarians in the American West, Aspirations and Mentoring in an Academic Environment, Sex Radials and the Quest for Women's Equality, (biography) Sex Variant Woman: The Life of Jeannette Howard Foster. Recipient Trustees Tchg. award, Ind. U., 2004, Martin Luther King Jr. Multicultural and Diversity Enhancement Award, Ind. U. East, 2004. Mem.: ALA, Soc. History Authorship, Reading, and Pub., Ind. Hist. Soc., Orgn. Am. Historians. Independent. Avocations: knitting, travel. Office: IN Univ E 2325 Chester Blvd Richmond IN 47374 Business E-Mail: jpasset@indiana.edu.

PASSEY, GEORGE EDWARD, psychologist, educator; b. Stratford, Conn., Sept. 28, 1920; s. Henry Richard and Elizabeth (Angus) P.; m. Algie Aldridge Ashe, Nov. 18, 1950; children— Richard Ashe, Elizabeth Aldridge, Mary Louise. BS, Springfield Coll., 1942; MA, Clark U., 1947; PhD, Tulane U., 1950. Asst. prof. U. Ala., Tuscaloosa, 1952-55, assoc. prof., 1955-56, 57-59, prof., 1959-63, prof. psychology, chmn. div. social and behavioral scis. Birmingham, 1967-73, prof. engring., 1969-84, Disting. Service prof. psychology, 1984-85, Disting Service prof. emeritus, 1985—; dean U. Ala. (Sch. Social and Behavioral Scis.), Birmingham, 1973—84. Research scientist Lockheed Ga. Co., Marietta, Ga., 1956-57, 63-65, cons., 1965-67; prof. Ga. Inst. Tech., 1965-67 Served with USNR, 1942-46, PTO; with USAF, 1951-52, lt. col. USAF, 1980 Fellow Am. Psychol. Assn.; mem. So. Soc. for Philosophy and Psychology, Southeastern Psychol. Assn., Ala. Psychol. Assn., Sigma Xi. Home: 400 University Pk Dr Apt G15 Birmingham AL 35209-6787 E-mail: gpassey3299@charter.net. *Whatever success I have enjoyed ought to be attributed to the attempt I have made to carry out the admonitions of my parents to make choices only after having appraised the alternatives in terms of their consequences, to weigh ethical considerations above all others, never to demand of others what one is unwilling to give of himself, and to work untiringly for those causes to which one is committed.*

PASSLEY, JOSEF ANTONIO, psychologist, educator, writer; b. Kingston, Jamaica, Oct. 22, 1974; s. Harold Arnold and Yvonne Claire Passley; m. Staci Latreese Manago, July 29, 2005. AS, Lancaster Bible Coll., 1995, BS, 1996; MA, Towson U., Md., 1999; PhD, Walden U., 2004. Licensed Clinical Professional Counselor Md., 2004. Mental health worker Sheppard and Enoch Pratt Hosp., Towson, 1996—99, spl. edn. tchr., 1999—2000; child adolescent therapist Johns Hopkins Bayview Med. Ctr., Balt., 2000—05, sr. child, adolescent therapist Baltimore, Md., 2005—09; psychotherapist Cedar Ridge Counseling Ctr., Eldersburg, Md., 2005—08; owner, psychotherapist, cons. Passley Consulting & Psychol. Svcs., 2008—. Radio guest WOLB Radio, Lanham, Md., 2004—08; cons. Johns Hopkins Hosp., Balt., 2005—08; adj. prof. Lancaster Bible Coll., Pa., 2004—, U. Balt., 2005—; assoc. prof. Ctrl. Mich. U., 2006—; faculty assoc. Johns Hopkins U., 2006—, 2006—. Co-author: (tng. manual) Keeping Families Strong: A Clinic Based Intervention, Single Parenting in the 21st Century and Beyond; author (books), 2006, From Depression to Aggression: Understanding the Violent World of Urban Males, 2008. Recipient Psi Chi Nat. Honor Soc., Walden U., 2000, Outstanding Clinician award, Johns Hopkins Bayview Med. Ctr., 2003, Employee Excellence award, 2003. Mem.: Media Psychology (assoc.), Soc. Child and Adolescent Psychology (assoc.), Am. Assn. Christian Counselors (assoc.), APA (assoc.). Avocations: reading, travel. Office: Johns Hopkins Bayview Med Ctr 4940 Eastern Ave Baltimore MD 21224 Business E-Mail: jasphd1@yahoo.com.

PASSLOF, PAT, artist, educator; b. Brunswick, Ga. m. Milton Resnick. Student, Queens Coll., Flushing, 1946—48, Black Mountain Coll., NC, 1948, Willem de Kooning, 1948—50; BFA, Cranbrook Coll., Bloomfield Hills, Mich., 1951. Prof. art Coll. of Staten Island, CUNY, 1972—. One-woman shows include Elizabeth Harris Gallery, 1993, 1996, 1998, 2000, 2002, 2005, exhibitions include 184 Annual Exhibit of Contemp Amer. Ar Nat Acad, 2009, The Shape of Imagination:Women of Black Mtn College, 2008—09, Black Mtn Museum & Arts Center Ashville, NC, Club Without Walls Butler's Fine Art, Eadt Hampton, 2008—09, 184th Annual Exhbn. Contemporary Am. Nat. Acad., 2009, The Shape of Imagination: Women of Black Mtn Coll., Black Mtn Coll. Mus. Arts Ctr., Asheville, NC, 2008—09, Club Without Walls, Butlers Fine Art, East Hampton, 2008—09; contbr.: di Suvero Peace Tower, Whitney Biennial, 2006. Fellow John Simon Guggenheim Meml. Found., 1999-2000; recipient award of Merit for painting, Am. Acad. of Arts and Letters, 2000, Purchase award Hassam, Speicher, Betts and Symons Fund of the Am. Acad., 2000, award for achievement in the arts Coun. on Arts and Humanities for S.I., 2001. Mem.: Nat. Acad. (Edwin P. Palmer award 2006). Address: c/o Elizabeth Harris Gallery 529 W 20th St 6E New York NY 10011

PASSMAN, PAMELA S., computer software company executive; b. NYC, Aug. 11, 1961; m. Frederick Guinee; children: Emily, Sarah. BA, Lafayette Coll., 1983; JD, U. Va., 1987. Bar: Va. & DC 1987. Articles editor Va. Jour. Internat. Law, 1985—87; with Covington & Burling, Washington, 1987—91, 1994—96, Nagashima & Ohno, Tokyo, 1991—93; spl. counsel Office of Polit. & Econ. Rsch., Itochu Corp., 1993; assoc. gen. counsel Microsoft Corp. Law & Corp. Affairs Dept., Tokyo, 1996—2002, dep. gen. counsel, v.p. Redmond, Wash., 2002—. Mem. Coun. Fgn. Rels. Mem. bd. Bus. for Social Responsibility, Seattle Art Mus., Nat. Bur. Asian Rsch., 2004—, Pacific Coun. Internat. Policy. Fellow Thomas J. Watson Found., 1983—84. Mem.: Info. Tech. Industry Council (exec. com.). Office: Microsoft Corp Law & Corp Affairs Dept 1 Microsoft Way Redmond WA 98052-6399 Office Phone: 425-882-8080. Office Fax: 425-936-7329.*

PASSOA, STEVEN C., entomologist; BS, Cornell U., Ithaca, NY, 1978; MS, U. Fla., Gainesville, 1984; PhD, U. Ill., Urbana, 1990. Eastern region domestic identifier USDA, APHIS, PPQ, Reynoldsburg, Ohio, 1990—94, nat. lepidoptera specialist Columbus, Ohio, 1995—. Recipient, USDA, APHIS, PPQ, 1994, 1999—2001, 2003—04, 2008. Office: Usda Aphis Ppq 4700 River Rd Riverdale MD 20737

PASSON, RICHARD HENRY, retired academic administrator, language educator; b. Hazleton, Pa., Aug. 18, 1939; s. Henry Richard and Grace Miriam (Bernstein) P.; m. Margaret Rose Ferdinand, Aug. 14, 1965; children— Michael, Rebecca, Christopher. BA (Bishop Hafey scholar), King's Coll., Pa., 1961; MA, U. Notre Dame, 1963, PhD (NDEA fellow), 1965. From instr. to prof. English U. Scranton, 1964-73, chmn. English dept., 1970-73, fgn. student adviser, 1965-67; dean Coll. Arts and Scis., Creighton U., Omaha, 1973-77; acad. v.p. St. Joseph's U., Phila., 1977-84; provost U. Scranton, Pa., 1984-2000, prof. English

Pa., 2000—02, Pa., 2004—09; interim acad. v.p. St. Joseph's U., Phila., 2002—04. Contbr. articles profl. jours. Recipient grant Nat. Assn. Fgn. Students, 1966 Mem. MLA, Am. Assn. Higher Edn., Am. Assn. Acad. Deans, Nat. Coun. Tchrs. English. Democrat. Roman Catholic. Office: U Scranton 402 Brennan Hall Scranton PA 18510 Home Phone: 570-586-1880; Office Phone: 570-941-4327. Business E-Mail: passonr1@scranton.edu.

PASSONNO STOTT, NICOLE, astronaut; b. Albany, NY; BS in Aeronautical Engring., Embry-Riddle Aeronautical U., 1987; MS in Engring. Mgmt., U. Ctrl. Fla., 1992. Structural design engr. Pratt and Whitney Govt. Engines, West Palm Beach, Fla.; ops. engr., Orbiter Processing Facility NASA Kennedy Space Ctr., Fla., 1988, detailed to the Dir. of Shuttle Processing, 1988, lead for joint AMES/Kennedy Space Ctr. software project to develop intelligent scheduling tools, 1988, mem., Space Station Hardware Integration Office, NASA project lead for the Internat. Space Station truss elements under construction at the Boeing Space Station facility. Huntington Beach, Calif.; several positions, vehicle ops engr. NASA convoy comdr.; shuttle flow dir. for Endeavour and orbiter project engr. for Columbia. NASA Shuttle Processing; mem., NASA Aircraft Ops. Divsn., serving as a Flight Simulation Engineer (FSE) on the Shuttle Training Aircraft (STA) NASA Johnson Space Ctr., 1998; mission specialist, astronaut NASA, 2000—. Tech. duties in the Astronaut Office Station Ops. Br. NASA; support astronaut for the Expedition 10 crew and as an ISS CAPCOM; crew mem. on the NEEMO 9 mission (NASA Extreme Environment Mission Ops.), 2006; mem., ISS Expeditions 20 and 21 crews; mem. of mission to International Space Station with the crew of STS-128, 09. Recipient Aircraft Ops. Divsn., Newt Myers Team Spirit award, Kennedy Space Ctr. Pub. Affairs Cert. Appreciation for Svc., NASA Exceptional Achievement medal, NASA Cert. Commendation, NASA Performance award, NASA On-the-Spot award, Lockheed Cert. Appreciation. Avocations: flying, snow skiing, scuba diving, woodworking, painting, gardening. Office: Lyndon B Johnson Space Ctr Astronaut Office 2101 NASA Pwy Houston TX 77058*

PASSOS, MARIA DE LOURDES, psychological researcher; b. Rio de Janeiro; married. PhD in Exptl. Psychology, U. São Paulo, Brazil. Prof. U. Fed. Rio de Janeiro, 1985—2000; rsch. scholar U. Mass. Med. Sch. Shriver Ctr., Waltham, 2007—08. Author: Bloomfield e Skinner: Língua e Comportamento Verbal, 2004, Linguistic Sources of Skinner's Verbal Behavior, 2006, The Influence of Bloomfield's Linguistics on Skinner, 2007, Bloomfield and Skinner: Speech-Community, Functions of Language and Scientific Activity, 2007. Mem.: Assn. Behavior Analysis.

PASSTY, JEANETTE NYDA MENDELSSOHN, literature and language professor, writer, editor; b. LA, Jan. 19, 1947; d. Walter Isaac and Mollie Sarah Nyda; m. Gregory Bohdan Passty, June 18, 1976; children: Benjamin and Jocelyn. AA, L.A. Valley Coll., 1966; BA, UCLA, 1968; MA, U. So. Calif., 1974, PhD, 1982. Cert. CC instr., Calif. Tchg. asst., lectr., assoc. dir. Freshman English program U. So. Calif., 1971—78; vis. scholar English dept. Tex. State U., San Marcos, 1982—83; lectr. English dept. U. Tex., Austin, 1983—85; vis. asst. prof., adj. assoc. prof. Tex. Luth. U., Seguin, 1983, 1985—87; from instr. to asst. prof. St. Philip's Coll., San Antonio, 1988—92, assoc. prof., 1992—. Lectr. UCLA, U. Tex., Austin, Western Mich. U., U. Louisville, Salisbury State U., Morehead State U., Tex. Tech. U., U. Wales, Bangor; humanities book reviewer CHOICE (ALA Jour.), 1985—86; manuscript reviewer Fairleigh Dickinson U. Press, 1991—; editl. cons. CONNECTIONS: Online Distance Learning Faculty Forum, 2002—; coll. English cons. Scholar Strategies Korean Program. Author: Eros and Androgyny: The Legacy of Rose Macaulay, 1988, The Lion Tells Her Story: A Biography of the Honorable N.P. Brooks Hinton, 1998, Bringing Denis Home: The Hero from Hope, Kansas, 2001; annotator: Alice Crawford's Paradise Pursued, 1995; contbr. articles to encyclopedia, profl. and lit. jours.; guest Sta. KSPL Radio in Touch With, 1989; appearance Sta. KENS-TV, 1992; Channel 12 Morehead, KY, 1998; CNN, 1995, Roadside (entr'acte with G.S. Bailey), 2000, Ossie Davis Libr., 2009; contbr. chapters to book. Mem. Nat. Abortion Rights Action League, Environment Tex., Greenpeace, Environ. Def. Fund, The Nature Conservancy, NOW, Sierra Club, Handgun Control, Orgn. Internat. Conf. on the Holocaust, San Antonio, 2000. Recipient Elizabeth K. Pleasants Tchg. award, U. So. Calif., 1974, letters of appreciation, Lord Bonham-Carter, 1987, HRH Princess Margaret, 1989—90, Oustanding Acad. Book award, ALA, 1989, Women Honoring Women award, Am. Assn. Women in C.C.s, 1997, Katherine Anne Porter Lit. prize, 1999, NISOD Internat. Conf. on Tchg. and Leadership Excellence Award, 2003, St. Philip's Coll. Tchg. Excellence award, 2003—04; named to Alamo Colls. Women's Hall of Fame, 2009. Mem. AAUW, MLA, Nat. Coun. Tchrs. English, South Ctrl. Soc. 18th Century Studies, Victorians Inst., Virginia Woolf Soc. Avocations: Tae Kwon Do, travel. Office: Saint Philip's Coll 1801 Martin Luther King Dr San Antonio TX 78203-2098 Home Phone: 512-396-5968; Office Phone: 210-486-2377. Business E-Mail: jpassty@mail.ccd.edu.

PASSUT, CHRISTINE DIANA, special education educator; b. Fairfax, Va., Dec. 9, 1974; d. Robert Charles and Barbara Ann Passut. BA in Psychology, Roanoke Coll., Salem, Va., 1997; M in Spl. Edn., Marymount U., Arlington, Va., 2002. Lic. tchr. learning disabled/emotionally disabled Va. Dept. Edn., 2002. Lead tchr. for four and five yr. olds Child Time Child Care Ctr., Faifax, 1997—98; pub. health tng. asst. Fairfax County Pub. Schs. - Langley HS, McLean, Va., 1998—99, instrnl. asst. for students with autism, 1999—2000, tchr. for students with autism; tchr. for students with autism and mild mental retardation Fairfax County Pub. Schs. - Annandale HS, Va., 2003—. Support tchr. Tech. Outreach Program, Annandale HS, 2004, co-sponsor B-Buddies club, 2005—, co-sponsor B-Buddies. Mem.: Sierra Club, World Wildlife Fedn., Fairfax Edn. Assn., Endometriosis Assn., Eddie's Club, Gardening Club Am. (life), Cooking Club Am. (life). Lutheran. Avocations: reading, gardening, cooking, playing with my dogs. Office: Annandale HS 4700 Medford Dr Annandale VA 22003 Business E-Mail: cpassut@fcps.edu.

PASSWATER, BARBARA GAYHART, real estate broker; b. Phila., July 10, 1945; d. Clarence Leonard and Margaret Jamison; m. Richard Albert Passwater, June 2, 1964; children: Richard Alan, Michael Eric. AA, Goldey-Beacom Coll., 1963; BA, Salisbury State U., 1981. Notary pub., Md. Sec. DuPont, Wilmington, Del., 1963-65, Nuclear-Chgo., Silver Spring, Md., 1965-67; office mgr. Montgomery County Sch. System, Wheaton, Md., 1977-79; adminstrv. asst. Solgar Nutritional Rsch. Ctr., Berlin, Md., 1979-94, asst. to v.p. R&D, 1995—2001; assoc. broker Prudential-Groff Realty, Berlin, Md., 1983-87, ReMax, Inc., Berlin, Md., 1987-88; broker, mgr., developers rep. River Run Sales Ctr., Berlin, Md., 1988-96; broker Solgar Realty LLC, Berlin, Md., 1997—98, CAMBR Realty LLC, Berlin, 1998—. Treas. Ocean Pines (Md.) Vol. Fire Dept. Aux., 1981—84, emergency med. tech., 1983—95, life mem., 1996—; sec. Ocean Pines Fire Dept., 1990—95; mem. Citizens Rev. Bd., Snow Hill, Md., 1984—2008; state bd. del. Child Protection Sys., 2002; bd. dirs. Worcester Gold, 2002—; mem. Worcester County Panel on Child Abuse and Neglect, 2002—; Worcester County organizer Rainbows, 2003—04; mem. com. Worcester County YMCA, 2005; Sunday sch. tchr. Cmty. Ch. of Ocean Pines, 1999—2005, co-chair nuture and edn. com., 2001—05. Named Woman of the Yr., Worcester County Commn. for Women, 2006—. Mem. Coastal Assn. Realtors of Md., Inc., Women's Coun. Realtors, Worcester County Commn. Women, Friends Worcester County Commn. Women, Mcguffy Com., Beta Sigma Phi, Phi Kappa Phi. Avocations: photography, golf. Office: CAMBR Realty LLC 11017 Manklin Meadows Ln Berlin MD 21811-9340 Office Phone: 410-208-9006. Business E-Mail: cambr@dmv.com.

PASSWATER, RICHARD ALBERT, biochemist, author; b. Wilmington, Del., Oct. 13, 1937; s. Stanley Leroy and Mabel Rosetta (King) P.; m. Barbara Sarah Gayhart, June 2, 1964; children: Richard Alan, Michael Eric. BS, U. Del., 1959; PhD, Bernadean U., 1976. Cert. firefighter. Supr. instrumental analysis lab. Allied Chem. Corp., Marcus Hook, Pa., 1959-64; tech. svcs. rep. F&M Sci. Corp., Avondale, Pa., 1965; dir. applications lab. Am. Instrument Co., Silver Spring, Md., 1965-77; dir. Am. Gen. Enterprises, Minn.; former daily broadcaster Sta. WMCA, NYC, 1980-88, Sta. WRNG, Atlanta, 1982-85; rsch. dir. Solgar Nutritional Rsch. Ctr., Berlin, Md., 1978—2001. Corp. v.p. Solgar Co., Inc., 2002-; v.p. R & D Solgar Vitamin & Herb Co. Inc.; mem. health, edn., rsch. coun. adv. bd. ICCC, NGO, UN, 2003—; chmn. Worcester County Emergency Planning Com., 1995-96; bd. dirs. Worcester Meml. Hosp., Atlantic Gen. Hosp., River Run Assn.; pres. 1989-92, Subaqueous Exploration and Archeology Ltd.; apptd. Md. State One Md. Com. and the Eastern Shore Econ. Task Force, Md. Gov. Glendenning, 1999, 2000. Author: Guide to Fluorescence Literature, vol. 1, 1967, vol. 2, 1970, vol. 3, 1974, Supernutrition, 1975, Supernutrition for Health Hearts, 1977, Super Calorie, Carbohydrate Counter, 1978, Cancer and Its Nutritional Therapies, 1978, 83, 93, The Easy No-Flab Diet, 1979, Selenium as Food and Medicine, 1980, The Slendernow Diet, 1982, (with Dr. E. Cranton), Trace Elements, Hair Analysis and Nutrition, 1983, The New Supernutrition, 1991, The Longevity Factor, 1993, Cancer Prevention and Nutritional Therapy, 1993, (with Ben Friedrich and Hans Kugler) Heart Health, 1994, Pycnogenol: The Super Protector Nutrient, 1994, Lipoic Acid: The Metabolic Antioxidant, 1995, numerous others; contbg. author: Fire Protection Guide to Hazardous Materials, 1991; editor Fluorescence News, 1966-77, Jour. Applied Health Scis., 1982-83; mem. editl. bd. Nutritional Perspectives, 1978-96, The Body Forum, 1979-80, Jour. Holistic Medicine, 1981-88, VIM Newsletter, 1979—99; contbg. Firehouse Mag., 1988-94, Jour. Applied Nutritrion; contbr. over 500 health articles to mags.; co-editor booklet series Your Good Health; sci. adv. and columnist Whole Foods mag.; patentee in field. Bd. dirs. Sci. Documentation Ctr., Dunfermline, Eng.; Am. Found. Firefighter Health and Safety; chief Ocean Pines Vol. Fire Dept., 1984-93; active Emergency Med. Tech.; adviser Nat. Inst. Nutrition Edn.; past adv. bd. Stephen Decatur High Sch., Worcester County Dept. Edn. Cubmaster, 1975-79. Named Citizen of Yr. Ocean Pines, Md., 1987; recipient 5th Ann. Achievement award, 1989, VFW Cert. of Commendation, 1988, Industry award Nat. Inst. Nutritional Edn., 1991, Pres.'s award Nat. Nutritional Foods Assn., 1999, 2008, James Lind Scientific Achievement award, 2004, James Peter Zarger Free Press award, 2004; named to Delmarva Fireman's Hall of Fame, 1993. Fellow Internat. Acad. Preventive Medicine, Am. Inst. Chemists; mem. ASTM, AAAS, Am. Chem. Soc., Gerontology Soc., Am. Geriatric Soc., Am. Aging Assn., Internat. Found. Preventive Medicine (v.p.), Internat. Union Pure and Applied Chemistry, Royal Soc. Chemistry (London), Internat. Acad. Holistic Health and Medicine, Capital Chem. Soc., Nutrition Today Soc., Am. Acad. Applid Health Sci. (pres., bd. dirs.), Internat. Found. Preventive Medicine (v.p., dir.), Inst. Nutritional Rsch., N.Y. Acad. Scis., Nat. Fire Protection Assn. (cert. firefighter level III, com. on properties of hazardous chemicals), Pi Kappa Alpha. Office: 11017 Manklin Meadows Ln Berlin MD 21811-9340

PASSY, CHARLES, writer; b. NYC, Jan. 9, 1964; s. Victor and Beverly (Green) P.; m. Leslie M. Olsen, Dec. 15, 1989; two children: Jacob E., Emma F. BA, Columbia U., 1985. Assoc. Jay K. Hoffman and Assocs., NYC, 1983-87; sr. editor, mng. editor Ovation Mag., NYC, 1988-89; editor Classical Mag., NYC, 1989-91; editor-in-chief Musical Am. Pub., NYC, 1991-92; staff writer The Palm Beach Post, West Palm Beach, Fla., 1992—. Announcer, prodr. WNYC FM, N.Y., 1984-85; entertainment stringer N.Y. Newsday, 1987-92. Author (with others): New Voices: Selected University and College Prize Winning Poems, 1989, The New Grove Dictionary of Jazz, 1988, The New Grove Dictionary of American Music, 1986, The New Grove Dictionary of Music and Musicians, 2d edit., 2001; editor: The Letters of Virgil Thomson, 1988; contbr. numerous articles to publs. in field, columns in newspapers, articles to various newspapers and mags. Recipient Poetry award Acad. Am. Poets Columbia U., 1985, Criticism & Writing awards Soc. Profl. Journalists, 1995, 97, 99, 2001, 03, 05, Fla. Press Club, 1993, 2004, Fla. Soc. Newspaper Editors, 1993, 2001, Cox Newspapers, 2001, Am. Assn. Sunday and Feature Editors, 2002, 05, award Mo. Lifestyle Journalism, 2005, Assn. Food Journalists, 2008; fellow Knight Ctr. for Specialized Journalism, 1993. Home: 180 Bent Tree Dr Palm Beach Gardens FL 33418-3597 Office: Palm Beach Newspapers Inc 2751 S Dixie Hwy West Palm Beach FL 33405-1298 Office Phone: 561-820-4589. Personal E-mail: chazpbg@aol.com. Business E-Mail: charles_passy@pbpost.com.

PAST, KAY CUDE, language educator; b. Beeville, Tex., Nov. 28, 1945; d. William Leslie and Mary Nancy (Chesnutt) Cude; m. Alvin W. Past, Nov. 2, 1968; children: Mariana Francesca, Elena Margarita. BA, U. Tex., Austin, 1968, MA, 1975. Cert. secondary tchr. Tex., 1968. Spanish instr. A. C. Jones HS, Beeville, Tex., 1991—2000, Coastal Bend Coll., Beeville, 2000—. Pres. Beeville Concert Assn., 1995—2008; bd. mem. Beeville Vineyard, 2000—08; hand bell choir mem. St. Philip's Ch., Beeville, 1987—2008. Mem.: Tex. Fgn. Lang. Tchrs. Assn. Democrat. Episcopalian. Avocations: reading, gardening, piano, travel. Home: 842 Gill Ranch Rd Beeville TX 78102 Office: Coastal Bend Coll 3800 Charco Rd Beeville TX 78102 Business E-Mail: kaypast@coastalbend.edu.

PASTAN, IRA HARRY, medical researcher; b. Winthrop, Mass., June 1, 1931; s. Jacob and Miriam (Ceder) P.; m. Linda Olenik, June 14, 1953; children— Stephen, Peter, Rachel BS, Tufts U., 1953, MD, 1957. Med. house officer Yale U. New Haven Hosp., 1957-59; clin. assoc. Nat. Inst. Arthritis and Metabolic Disease, NIH, Bethesda, Md., 1959-61, sr. investigator sect. on endocrine biochemistry, clin. endocrinology br., 1963-69; postdoctoral fellow Lab. of Cellular Physiology Nat Heart and Lung Inst., NIH, Bethesda, Md., 1961-62; head molecular biology sect. endocrinology br. Ctr. Cancer Rsch., Nat. Cancer Inst., NIH, Bethesda, Md., 1969-70, chief lab. molecular biology, 1970—. Author: An Atlas of Immunofluorescence, 1985; author, editor: Endocytosis, 1985; contbr. articles to profl. jours. Recipient Van Meter prize Am. Thyroid Assn., 1971, Superior Service award Dept. HEW and NIH, 1973, Meritorious Service medal USPHS, NIH, Nat. Cancer Inst., 1983, Disting. Service medal, 1985 Mem. AAAS, Am. Soc. Clin. Investigation, Am. Soc. Biol. Chemists, Am. Soc. for Microbiology, Am. Soc. for Cell Biology, Peripatetic Club, Nat. Acad. Scis., Clin. Immunology Soc., Am. Assn. Physicians, Am. Acad. Arts and Scis., Molecular Medicine Soc., Alpha Omega Alpha. Office: Ctr Cancer Rsch Lab Molecular Biology 37 Convent Dr Bldg 37 Rm 5106 Bethesda MD 20892 Office Phone: 301-496-4797. Office Fax: 301-402-1344. E-mail: pastani@mail.nih.gov.*

PASTERNAC, ANDRÉ, cardiologist, educator; b. Toulouse, France, July 22, 1937; came to Can., 1971, naturalized, 1978. s. Jacques and Règine P. Adv. math., Lyceé Henri IV, Paris, 1956; BA in Polit. Sci., Toulouse U., 1963, MD Med. Sch., 1968; grad. in Mgmt. Program, Columbia U., 2000. Cert. Ins. and Disability Assessment U. Montreal, 2002. Intern Toulouse Univ. Hosp., 1962-63, resident, 1963-64, Edouard-Herriot Hosp., Lyon, France, 1965-66; Fulbright scholar in cardiology Harvard U., 1968-71; research fellow Peter Bent Brigham Hosp., Boston, 1968-69; Milton fellow Children's Hosp., Boston, 1969-71; fellow in cardiology Toronto (Ont., Can.) U., 1971-72; staff cardiologist Montreal (Que., Can.) Heart Inst., 1972—; asst. prof. medicine U. Montreal, 1972-78, clin. assoc. prof., 1978—, clin. prof. medicine, 1994—. Vis. lectr. U. Liège (Belgium), 1977, U. Madrid, 1977, U. Warsaw, 1979, 83; cons. Harley St. Clinic, Cromwell Hosp., Wellington Hosp., London; vis. assoc. prof. McGill U., Montreal, 1975-76; medico-legal and ins. expert U. Montreal, 2002. Contbr. articles to profl. jours. Bd. dirs. Heart-Brain Rsch. Found. Inc., NYC, Cardiostat Inc., Montreal, Cardiostat USA Inc., West Palm Beach, Fla. Am. Field Svc. grantee, Oreg., 1954-55. Mem. French Cardiac Soc., European Soc. Cardiology, Canadian Cardiovasc. Soc., Am. Coll. Cardiology, Am. Heart Assn., Internat. Soc. Heart Rsch., Am. Fedn. Clin. Rsch., NY Acad. Scis. Research in stress-related myocardial ischemia and dysfunction, mitral valve prolapse, cardiovascular drugs, cardiomyopathies, catecholamines, neuroendocrine control of the heart, stress and the heart, prevention of cardiovascular disease. Home: Port Royal 1455 Sherbrooke St W # 703 Montreal PQ Canada H3G 1L2 Office: Montreal Heart Inst 5000 Belanger E Montreal PQ Canada H1T 1C8 Office Phone: 561-644-3999. Personal E-mail: apasternac@aol.com. Business E-Mail: andre.pasternac@sympatico.ca.

PASTERNACK, ROBERT FRANCIS, chemistry professor; b. NYC, Sept. 20, 1936; 2 children. BA, Cornell U., 1957, PhD in Chemistry, 1962. Research assoc. in chemistry U. Ill., Champaign, 1962-63; from asst. to prof. chemistry Ithaca Coll., NY, 1963-66, Charles A. Dana Endowed prof. chemistry NY, 1976-82; Edmund Allen prof. chemistry Swarthmore Coll., Pa., 1984—. Invited speaker seminars, colls., univs., nat., internat. meetings, confs. including Bioinorganic Chem., Italy, Portugal, Gordon Rsch. Confs., Spanish Royal Soc. Chem., many others; lectr. series Nankai U., China, U. Messina, Italy; mem. adv. com. Rsch. Corp.; mem. sci. & art com. Franklin Inst.; co-organizer, chmn. workshop on rsch. at undergrad. instn. NSF, mem. undergrad. curriculm chem.; vis. prof., vis. rschr. U Messina, U. Paris, Nakai, Rome, King's Coll., London, Fritz Haber Inst., Berlin, Doshisha U., Kyoto; co-developer A Unified Lab. Program; initiator, chmn. C.P. Snow Lectr. Series. Author, co-author more than 100 sci. publs. Mem. com. on sci. and the arts Franklin Inst., 1992-98. Grantee NSF, 1965-66, 69-72, 77-78, 83-84, 86-94, 95-03, Petroleum Rsch. Fund, 1967-74, 86-88, NIH, 1971-82, 85-89, 2001-05, Monsanto Corp., 1986-92, Rsch. Corp., 1974-75, 78-79, 84-85, Danforth Assocs., 1978-84, Camille and Henry Dreyfus Found., 1981, 95, NATO, 1979, 88-89, 95-96; recipient Camille and Henry Dreyfus Tchg./Scholar award, 1987-89, NSF Manpower Improvement award, King's Coll., U. London, 1977-78, Commemorative medal for sci. contbns. U. Catania, 1994, Excellence in Tchg. award, Am. Chem. Soc., Phila. Section, 2005, Conspicuous Sci. Achievement Through Rsch. award, Am. Chem. Soc., 2005; NSF sci. faculty fellow U. Rome, 1968-70. Mem. AAAS, Am. Inst. Chemists (Hon. Scroll award 1998), Am. Chem. Soc. (award for rsch. at an undergrad. instn. 2001, Excellence award 2005, award conspicuous sci. achievement through rsch. 2005), NY Acad. Sci., Sigma Xi. Office: Swarthmore Coll Dept Chemistry Swarthmore PA 19081 Office Phone: 610-328-8559. Business E-Mail: rpaster1@swarthmore.edu.

PASTERNACK, STEFAN ALAN, psychiatrist, psychoanalyst; b. Jersey City, Nov. 5, 1939; BA, Cornell U., 1961; MD, Georgetown U., 1965. Diplomate in psychiatry Am. Bd. Neurology and Psychiatry; lic. physician, D.C., Md. Resident in psychiatry U. Cin. Gen. Hosp., 1966-69; psychiat. cons. North Cmty. Mental Health Ctr., Washington, 1971-97; asst. prof. psychiatry Georgetown U. Sch. Medicine, Washington, 1971-79, assoc. clin. prof. psychiatry, 1979-86, clin. prof. psychiatry, 1986—, co-dir. advanced studies prog. in psychiatry/psychoanalysis, 1995—; clin. prof. biomed. sci. Fla. Atlantic U., 2007—; tchg. analyst Fla. Psychoanalytic Inst., 2008—. Pvt. practice psychiatry and psychoanalysis, Washington, 1978-2005; Fla., 2005; faculty, Fla. Psychoanalytic Inst., 2006; clin. prof. psychiatry, Fla. Atlantic U., 2007. Editor: Violence and Victims, 1975; contbr. articles to profl. jours. Bd. dirs. Nat. Capital Med. Found., Washington, 1973-76, Forum for Psychoanalytic Study of Film, Washington, 1989—, vol. clin. prof. psychiatry U. Miami Miller Sch. Medicine, 2007-. Lt. comdr. USN, 1969-71. Mem.: Fla. Psychiat. Soc., Washington Psychiat. Soc. (mem. coun. 1987—99), Am. Psychoanalytic Assn., Am. Psychiat. Assn. (disting. life fellow), Cosmos Club. Avocations: motorboating and yachting, piano, writing. Home: 6924 Balboa Island Ct Delray Beach FL 33446-5641 Office: 4800 N Federal Hwy Ste E-102 Boca Raton FL 33431 Office Phone: 561-706-9584. Personal E-mail: sp39@aol.com.

PASTERNAK, JILL MARGOT, radio producer, host, musician, educator; b. Newark, Mar. 9, 1934; d. Albert Aaron and Dorothy Vera Bengelsdorf; children from previous marriage: Amy Lydia Pasternak Hendry, William. BS in Harp, Juilliard Sch. Music, NYC, 1955; MA in Pub. Media, Montclair State U., NJ, 1981. Radio broadcasting lic. FCC. Freelance musician, prin. harp Little Orch. Soc. NY, NYC, 1954—56; prin. harp Radio City Music Hall, NYC, 1955—56, 1960—63, 1977—79; prin. harp, soloist Halifax Symphony Orch., NS, Canada, 1956—57, Orlando Symphony Orch., Fla., 1960—63; prin. harp Kennett Symphony Orch., Kennett Square, Pa., 1991—2001; classical host WMHT-FM, Schenectady, NY, 1984—87, WFLN-FM, Phila., 1987—97, WRTI-FM, Phila., 1997—, exec. prodr., 1997—. Asst. to pres. Nonesuch Records, NYC, 1977—79; mgr. tng. & devel. Exxon, East Millstone, NJ, 1979—84; coord. MD/PhD program Thomas Jefferson U., Phila., 1987—96; lectr. Arcadia U., Phila., 2003—05, Jewish Cmty. Ctrs., Phila., 2003—. Freelance music, prin. harp: albums Broadway shows recs., editl. asst.: Hi-Fi/Stereo Rev. Mag., 1960—62, lit. editl. asst.: New World Records, 1975—77, prodr., host: WRTI-FM, 1997—. Bd. dirs. Strings for Schs., Phila., 1999—2002, Alliance Franscaise, 2006—08. Recipient Sarah award, Assn. Women in Comm., 1999, Svc. award, Darlington Arts Ctr., 2004, Judges Merit award, Crossover, Pa. Assn. Broadcasters, 2005—07; Fulbright scholar, Ecole Normale de Musique, 1956—57. Mem.: Musicians Union, Mu Phi Epsilon. Avocations: travel, dance. Office: WRTI FM Temple Pub Radio 1509 Cecil B Moore Ave Philadelphia PA 19121 Office Phone: 215-204-8405.

PASTIDES, HARRIS, academic administrator; m. Patricia Moore, Aug. 27, 1980; children: Katharine, Andrew. BS in Biological Scis., U. Albany, 1975; MPH, Yale U., PhD in Epidemiology. Sr. Fulbright rsch. fellow U. Athens, Greece, 1987—88; prof. epidemiology, chmn. Dept.

Biostatistics and Epidemiology U. Mass., Amherst; dean Arnold Sch. Pub. Health U. SC, Columbia, 1998—2003, v.p. rsch. and health scis., exec. dir. rsch. found., 2003—08, pres., 2008—. Cons., advisor WHO, 1994, 95. Author: Foundations of Cancer Epidemiology; contbr. articles to profl. jours. Office: U SC Office of Pres Columbia SC 29208 Office Phone: 803-777-5458. Office Fax: 803-777-5457. E-mail: pastides@sc.edu, president@sc.edu.*

PASTIN, MARK JOSEPH, health science association administrator, educator; b. Ellwood City, Pa., July 6, 1949; s. Joseph and Patricia Jean (Camenite) Pastin; m. Joanne Marie Reagle, May 30, 1970 (div. Mar. 1982); m. Carrie Patricia Class, Dec. 22, 1984 (div. June 1990); m. Christina M. Brecto, June 15, 1991. BA summa cum laude, U. Pitts., 1970; MA, Harvard U., 1972, PhD, 1973. Asst. prof. Ind. U., Bloomington, 1973-78, assoc. prof., 1978-80; founder, bd. Compliance Resource Group, Inc., 1983—; chmn., CEO, pres. Coun. Ethical Orgns., Alexandria, Va., 1986—; prof. mgmt., dir. Ariz. State U., Tempe, 1988-92, prof. emeritus, 1996—; chair Health Ethics Trust, 1995—. Dir. Learned Nicholson, Ltd., 1990-91; bd. Japan Am. Soc. Phoenix, Found. for Ethical Orgns.; cons. GTE, Interim Healthcare, 1997-2000, U.S. Dept. Edn., 2002, Tex. Instruments, MicroAge Computers, Med-Tronic, Blood Sys., Inc., Opus Corp., GTE, NyNex, Am. Express Bank, Kaiko Bussan Co., Japan, Arex Co., Japan, Century Audit Co., U.S. Dept. Edn., Japan, Scottsdale Meml. Hosp., Cosanti Found., Lincoln Electric Co., Tenet Healthcare, The Williams Co.; vis. faculty Harvard U., 1980; presenter Australian Inst. Mgmt., Nippon Tel. & Tel., Hong Kong Commn. Against Corruption, 1984, Young Pres.'s Orgn. Internat. U., 1990, Nat. Assn. Indsl. & Office Parks, 1990, ABA, 1991, Govt. of Brazil, 1991; columnist Jour. Clin. Medicine. Author: Hard Problems of Management, 1986 (Book of Yr. Armed Forces Mil. Comtrs. 1986, Japanese edit. 1994), The Hotline Handbook, 1996, Planning Forum, 1992; editor: Public-Private Sector Ethics, 1979; mem. editl. bd. Report on Medicare Compliance; pub. Pastin Report on Best Compliance Practices, 1998—, Columnist jours. clin. medicine; Guerin Lect. on Philanthropy, 1996. Founding bd. mem. Tempe Leadership, 1985-89; bd. mem. Ctr. for Behavioral Health, Phoenix, 1986-89, Tempe YMCA, 1986—, Valley Leadership Alumni Assn., 1989-92; mem. Clean Air Com., Phoenix, 1987-90. Nat. Sci. Found. fellow, Cambridge, Mass., 1971-73; Nat. Endowment for the Humanities fellow, 1975; Exxon Edn. Found. grant, 1982-83. Mem.: Am. Assn. Physician Specialists (exec. com.), Found. Ethical Orgns. (chmn. 1988, pres.), Am. Soc. Assn. Execs. (presenter 1987—97), Harvard Club D.C., Phi Beta Kappa, Golden Key. Avocations: golf, running. Office: 214 S Payne St Alexandria VA 22314-3530 Home: 7205 Regent Dr Alexandria VA 22307-2044 Office Phone: 703-683-7916. Personal E-mail: councile@aol.com.

PASTNER, JOSH, men's college basketball coach; s. Hal Pastner. B in Family Studies, U. Ariz., Tucson, 1998, M in Tchg. and Tchg. Edn., 1999. Video & recruiting coord., adminstrv. asst. U. Ariz. Wildcats, 2001—02, asst. coach, 2002—08, U. Memphis Tigers, 2008—09, head basketball coach, 2009—. Head coach Houston Hoops, AAU, 1999—2000. Active Boys and Girls Clubs, Tucson, Boy Scouts America, Leukemia and Lymphoma Soc., Naval Spl. Warfare Found., Spl. Olympics. Named to 40 Under 40, Tucson Bus. Edge, 2007. Achievements include member of the NCAA Men's Basketball National Championship winning University of Arizona Wildcats, 1997. Office: Univ Memphis Athletics Dept 570 Normal Athletic Office Bldg Rm 230 Memphis TN 38152*

PASTOR, EDWARD, United States Representative from Arizona; b. Claypool, Ariz., June 28, 1943; m. Verma Mendez; children: Yvonne, Laura. BA in chemistry, Ariz. State U., 1966, JD, 1974. Former chem. teacher N. High Sch.; former dep. dir. Guadalupe Org., Inc.; mem. Maricopa County Bd. Suprs., Phoenix, 1976-91, U.S. Congress from 4th Ariz. dist. (formerly 2nd), Washington, 1991—; mem. appropriations com., steering & policy com. Mem. Arts Caucus, Biotechnology Caucus, Border Caucus, Congressional Caucus on Women's Issues, Congressional Children's Caucus. Democrat. Office: US Ho Reps 2465 Rayburn Ho Office Bldg Washington DC 20515-0304*

PASTOR, RICHARD WALTER, research chemist; b. Oceanside, NY, June 21, 1951; s. William Henry and Alma Dolores (Strachy) P.; m. Dale Melanie Seecof, June 21, 1981; children: William Abraham, Joseph Mark. BA, Hamilton Coll., 1973; MS, Syracuse U., 1977; PhD, Harvard U., 1984. Sr. staff fellow Ctr. for Biology Evaluation & Rsch., FDA, Bethesda, Md., 1984-90, rsch. chemist, 1990—. Adj. prof. Am. U., Washington, 1991—. Contbr. articles to profl. jours. Achievements include development of structural and dynamic microscopic model of lipid bilayers; development of stochastic dynamic computer simulation methods. Home: 12 Infield Ct N Potomac MD 20854-5506 Office: CBER/FDA Biophysics Lab 1401 Rockville Pike Rockville MD 20852-1428

PASTOR, STEPHEN DANIEL, chemistry professor, researcher, consultant; b. New Brunswick, NJ, Feb. 15, 1947; s. Stephen and Irene (Bors) P.; m. Joan Ordemann, Apr. 3, 1971 (div. 1979); 1 child, Melanie; m. Joanne Behrens, July 13, 1985 (div. 1990). BA in Chemistry, Rutgers U., 1969, MS in Chemistry, 1978, PhD in Chemistry, 1983. Chemist Nat. Starch and Chem. Corp., Bridgewater, NJ, 1972—79; rsch. group leader CIBA-Geigy Corp., Ardsley, NY, 1979—84, rsch. mgr., 1985—87; group leader Ctrl. Rsch. Labs. CIBA-Geigy Ag. Basel, Switzerland, 1987—89, rsch. fellow Ardsley, 1989—90, rsch. mgr., 1990—97, sr. rsch. fellow, 1997—2003; cons. Mayhill, N.Mex., 2003—. Asst. adj. prof. Pace U., Pleasantville, NY, 1984—, assoc. adj. prof., 1989-93, adj. prof., 1994—. Contbr. articles to profl. jours. 1st lt. US Army, 1969—71, Vietnam. Sr. Rsch. Fellow, Ciba Specialty Chemicals Corp., 1998—2003. Mem.: Am. Chem. Soc. (Westchester sect. Disting. Scientist award 1977). Achievements include research on organophosphorous and organosulfur chemistry, conformational analysis, germanium chemistry, organometallic chemistry, asymmetric synthesis, homogeneous catalysis, hypercoordinated compounds, spectroscopy, astronomy. Home: PO Box 6 Mayhill NM 88339-0195 E-mail: astro3d@pvtnetworks.net.

PASTOREK, PAUL G., state official, school system administrator, lawyer; b. Anchorage, Alaska, June 27, 1954; m. Kathy Pastorek; children: Ryan, Jeffery, Kaitlin. BA, Loyola U., 1976, JD, 1979. Bar: La. 1979. Former ptnr. Adams and Reese, New Orleans; gen. counsel NASA, Washington, 2002—04; ptnr., spl. bus. svcs. Adams & Reese, LLP, New Orleans, 2004—07; supt. of edn. State of La., Baton Rouge, 2007—. Served La. State Bd. Elem. and Secondary Edn., 1996—2004, pres., 2000—04; mem. various state bds. and commns. Chair, coun. exec. com. New Orleans Regional C. of C. area. Mem.: La. State Bar Assn. Office: La Dept Edn Office of Supt PO Box 94064 Baton Rouge LA 70804-9064 Office Phone: 877-453-2721. Office Fax: 225-342-0193. E-mail: paulpastorek@la.gov.*

PASTORES, STEPHEN M., internist; b. NYC, Sept. 5, 1958; s. Jovito Camara and Annie McCarthy Pastores; m. Maria Teresa Desancho; children: Steven Michael, Monica Cristina. MD, Lyceum Northwestern Coll. Medicine, Philippines, 1982. Diplomate Am. Bd. Internal Medicine, Am. Bd. Pulmonary Disease, Am. Bd. Critical Care Medicine. Resident Met. Hosp. Ctr., 1989; attending critical care physician Montefiore Med. Ctr., Bronx, NY, 1993—96; dir. emergency svcs. Dept. VA Med. Ctr., Bronx, 1996—99, asst. dir. surg. ICU, 1996—99; attending critical care physician Meml. Sloan-Kettering Cancer Ctr., NYC, 1999—, dir. critical care rsch. and critical care fellowship program; prof. medicine and anesthesiology Weill Med. Coll. Cornell U., NYC, 2001—. Editor: (book) ICU Bedside Technology, 2000; contbr. articles to profl. jours. Fellow: ACP (2000-Present), Am. Coll. of Critical Care Medicine, Am. Coll. Chest Physicians (1997-Present). Office: Meml Sloan-Kettering Cancer Ctr 1275 York Ave M-210C New York NY 10021 Business E-Mail: pastores@mskcc.org.

PASTRANA, BELINDA, science educator, researcher; b. Bronx, NY, Nov. 21, 1963; d. Hector Pastrana and Olinda De Leon; m. Robert Rios, June 23, 1990; children: Roberto Andres Rios, Ricardo Daniel Rios. BS, U. PR, Humacao, 1987; MS, Rutgers U., NJ, 1992, PhD, 1995. Asst. prof. U. PR, 1996—99, assoc. prof., 1999—2003, prof., 2003—. Study sect. com. mem. NIH-CSR, Bethesda, Md., 2005—06. Contbr. articles to profl. sci. jours. Recipient Henry Dreyfus Tchr. award, Henry and Camile Dreyfus Found., 2008; Faculty scholar, Mayo Clinic and Found., 1997—98, Minority Biomedical Rsch. grant, Nat. Inst. Health, 1984—95, Rsch. grant, 1999—2006. Mem.: AAAS, Protein Soc., Biophysical Soc., Am. Soc. Cell Biologist, Am. Chem. Soc. (regional treas. 1999—2000). Achievements include patents pending for determination of protein, peptide or peptoid aggregation, atability and viability. Office: Univ Puerto Rico PO Box 9019 Mayaguez PR 00681-9019 Office Fax: 787-265-3849. Business E-Mail: belinda@hpcf.upr.edu.

PASTRANA, RONALD RAY, theology studies educator, earth and space science educator, department chairman, psychotherapist, retired school system administrator; b. NYC, Sept. 5, 1939; s. Anthony and Mildred Pastrana; m. Josephine Pastrana; children: Christine, Therese. BA in History/Sci. Edn., Queens Coll., 1963; advanced sci. cert., Pace U., NYC, 1964-68; MS in Counseling Edn., St. John's U., 1967; diploma, US Acad. of Health Sci., 1975, US Army Command and Gen. Staff Coll., 1979; D Ministry, Sch. Bible Theology Sem., 1996, ThD, 2000. Ordained min. Pentecostal Assemblies of God of Am.; diplomate Am. Bd. of Psychotherapy; cert. life support sys. in internat. space NOAA, NASA. Tchr. sci. Marie Curie Jr. HS, Bayside, NY, 1963-68; guidance counselor Half Hollow Hills HS, Dix Hills, NY, 1969-71, Walt Whitman HS, Huntington Station, NY, 1968-69, coord. occupl. svcs., 1971-74; guidance coord. Dutchess County Bd. Coop. Ednl. Svcs. Tech. Edn. Ctr., Poughkeepsie, NY, 1974-86; asst. prin., supr. sci. and math. Career and Tech. Inst. and Tech. Shop Programs, Poughkeepsie, 1986-96; asst. dir. Reach Out Sch. of Ministry, Hyde Park, NY, 1996—; prof. Bibl. theology Sch. Bible Theology Sem., San Jacinto, Calif., 1999—. Ednl. cons. NY State Edn. Dept., Albany, 1975-83, Armed Forces Vocat. Testing Group, Dept. of Def., Washington, 1975-77; cert. educator Lunar Edn. Project, NASA, 1986-87, Asteroids, Lunar Rocks, Meteorites Edn. Projects, 1999—; earth and space sci. cons., 1998; pub. Reach Out Ministries; rschr. NASA Astronauts and Space Program. Author: Career Guidance in the Classroom, 1974, A Curriculum Guide to the Study of the Seven Dispensations and Eight Covenants, 1996, Dispensational Theology, 1997, Pentecostal Doctrine and Theology, 1998, Student Guide to the Seven Dispensations and Eignt Covenants, 1999, The Greek Fathers of the Early Christian Church, 2000, The Latin Fathers of the Early Christian Church, 2000, The Reformers of the Christian Church, 2001, Reach Out Ministries. Lt. col. USAR, ret. 1992. NSF Sci. Geology, Biochemistry, Biology, Genetics, Cell Physiology, Physics, Astronomy and Advanced Biol. Lab. Techniques Study grantee, 1964-68, grantee NASA and Nat. Ocean. and Atmos. Adminstrn., 1999; recipient Recognition award outstanding cultural and hist. achievement Town of Hyde Pk., 1987, Recognition award outstanding performance guidance and counseling Dutchess County Counseling Assn., 1990, Dutchess Counselor of Yr. award Dutchess County Counseling Assn., 1995, Commemorative Recognition award NASA Space Project and Jason Space Project Wappingers Ctrl. Sch. Dist., 2001, NASA medallion NASA Hdqrs., Washington, 2005; decorated Joint Svc. Commendation medal, Army achievement medal, Selective Svc. Meritorious medal, Army Res. Components Achievement medal, Nat. Def. Svc. medal, NY State medal Meritorious Svc., Meritorious Svc. award for civilian svc. USN, 2000. Mem. Am. Counselors Assn., Am. Mental Health Counselors Assn., Nat. Career Devel. Assn., Am. Assn. Christian Counselors, Am. Psychotherapy Assn., Planetary Soc., Nat. Space Soc., NY Acad. Scis., NY State Assn. Counseling and Devel., Sch. Adminstrs. Assn. NY State, Dutchess County Counseling Assn. (exec. bd. 1989-96), Sci. Tchrs. Assn. NY State, Assn. US Army Meteorite Collection and Rsch., Phi Delta Kappa, Nat. Tech. Honor Soc. (founder career and tech. ctr. chpt.). Avocations: rock and mineral collecting, exercise, canoeing, hiking. Home: 24 Meadow Dr Red Hook NY 12571-1200

PASTRICK, HAROLD LEE, aeronautical engineer; b. Ambridge, Pa., June 28, 1936; s. Samuel and Mary (Makara) P.; m. Vivienne Lee Nusser Heinricher, June 3, 1961; children: Tracy Lee, Gregory Harold, Michael Joseph Samuel. BSEE, Carnegie-Mellon U., 1958; postgrad., Rutgers U., 1959-61, CCNY, 1961-63, U. Ala. Huntsville, 1964-66, 68-73; student, MIT, summers 1961-63; MS in Aeronautics & Astronautics, Stanford U., 1967, engr. in Aeronautics & Astronautics, 1972; PhD in Engring., Calif. Western U., 1977. Registered prof. engr., Ala. Metallurgical engring. aide Jones & Laughlin Steel Corp., Aliquippa, Pa., 1955-56; asst. engr., designer Am. Bridge Divsn., U.S. Steel Corp., Ambridge, 1957; electronics engr. Avionics Divsn., U.S. Army Signal R&D Labs., Ft. Monmouth, N.J., 1958-63; aerospace engr., Inertial Systems Team Missile R&D Labs., Redstone Arsenal, Ala., 1963-64; tech. dir. Army Inertial Guidance & Tech. Ctr., Redstone Arsenal, 1964-66; project engr. Inertial Guidance Br., Redstone Arsenal, 1967-71; rsch. aerospace engr. Guidance & Control Br., Redstone Arsenal, 1971-73; group leader Terminal Homing Missile Analysis, Redstone Arsenal, 1973-79; staff specialist, asst. to dir., land warfare Office of Under Sec. Def., Rsch. and Engring., Washington, 1979-80; chief, guidance and control analysis U.S. Army Missile Command, Redstone Arsenal, Ala., 1980-81; v.p. engring. Control Dynamics Co., Huntsville, 1981-83; asst. v.p., engring. analysis divsn. Sci. Applications Internat. Corp., Huntsville, 1983-86; v.p. theater missile def. and system analysis operation, 1986-91; corp. v.p., gen. mgr. SRS Technologies, Huntsville, 1991—2004; CEO, Pastrick Engring. and Mgmt. Cons., 2005—. Acting pres. and COO SRS Techs., 1994, mem. corp. exec. mgmt. com., 1991-2004, mem. profit sharing and 401(k) com., 1993-2004; lectr. Sch. of Sci. and Engring., U. Ala., Huntsville, 1967-83; lectr. dept. continuing edn. George Washington U., 1985-87; engring. seminar dir. Applied Tech. Inst., Frankfurt, Germany, 1984, Singapore, 1986; tech. tng. dir. Tech. Tng. Corp., Tel Aviv, 1988; lectr. Advanced Tech. Internat., Ltd., London, 1985; guidance and control cons. various labs Dept. of Def., Washington, 1971-2001; lectr., rsch. advisor Southeastern Inst. Tech., Huntsville, 1978-84; lectr., seminar leader Guidance and Control Technologies, U.S., Europe, Asia, Mex., 1980-94. Contbr. over 120 articles to profl. jours. Chmn. combined fed. campaign ARDEC United Way, Redstone Arsenal, 1976; mem. Huntsville Econ. Devel. Com., 1994; chmn. indsl. contbns. Armed Forces Week C. of C. Huntsville-Madison County, 1993—96, 1999, vice chmn. mil. affairs. com., 1994—95, chmn. mil. affairs com., 1996; program chmn. tech. and bus. symposium and exhbn. Huntsville, 1994—95; gen. chmn., 1995—96; chmn. adv. com., 1997—98; founding trustee Ala. Constn. Village Found., 2001—; mem. All-Peoples Meml. for All Vets., Madison County, 2001—; mem. elec. and computer engring. adv. bd. The Citadel, Charleston, SC, 2001—; pres. St. Michael's Orthodox Ch., 2002—; pathfinder chmn., mem. exec. cabinet Huntsville Madison County (Ala.) United Way, 2005—07; pres. Greek Orthodox Ch., 1967, 1973, chmn. planning com., 1993—2000. Capt. US Army, 1958—64. Recipient Eminent Engr. Disting. Tau Beta Pi, 1998. Fellow: AIAA (assoc.; vice-chmn. Huntsville chpt. 1979, guest editor Jour. Guidance and Control 1981, missile tech. com. 1989—91); mem.: Ala. Acad. Sci. (vice chmn. 1978—79, engring. chmn. 1979—81), Inst. Navigation, Assn. U.S. Army, IEEE (sr.; chpt. program chmn. 1972—73), Soc. Computer Simulation, Am. Def. Preparedness Assn. (vice-chmn. Huntsville chpt. 1974—75), Huntsville Assn. Tech. Socs. (adv. com. 1997—98, pres. 1998—99, chmn.), Redstone Golf Club, Greenwhyche Club (v.p. 1979), Heritage Club, Rotary (sec. 1994—95, pres.-elect. 1995—96, pres. 1996—97, asst. gov. dist. 6860 1997—2000, dist. task force dir. 2000—01), Greater Huntsville Rotary Found. (dir. internat. svc. 1992—94, CEO 1998—2000). Achievements include pioneering hardware in the loop simulations for testing laser semi-active guided missiles. Avocations: golf, weightlifting, choral music, reading, running. Home and Office: Patrick Engring and Mgmt Cons 2624 Trailway Rd SE Huntsville AL 35801-1474 Office: SRS Technologies 500 Discovery Dr NW Huntsville AL 35806-2810 Office Phone: 256-509-6700. Personal E-mail: hpastrick@bellsouth.net.

PASUKINIS, CHERYL RENEE, elementary school educator; b. Danville, Pa., Feb. 10, 1960; d. William Wayde and Janet Marie (Thomas) Beishline; m. William Albert Pasukinis, Dec. 14, 1985; children: William Beishline, Joseph Albert, Benjamin Thomas, Stanislaus Edward. BS in Elem. Edn., Bloomsburg U., Pa., 1983, MEd, 1985. Cert. reading specialist Bloomsburg U., profl. tchg. cert. Bloomsburg U., cert. tutor Laubach Literacy Action. Title I reading specialist So. Columbia Sch. Dist., Catawissa, Pa., 1983—84; remedial reading specialist, math instr., gifted instr. Cen. Susquehanna Intermediate Unit, Montandon, Pa., 1985; title I reading, remedial reading specialist Milton Area Sch. Dist., Pa., 1985—2003, lang. arts instr. 6th grade mid. sch., 2003—04; title I reading, Reading is Fundamental coord. Berwick Area Sch. Dist., Pa., 2004—. Fed. programs monitor Pa. Dept. Edn.'s Divsn. of Fed. Programs, Harrisburg, 1988—94; cooperating tchr. for grad. assts. and student tchrs. Milton Area Sch. Dist.; tchr. edn. course rev. com. Pa. Power and Light, Berwick; mem. instrnl. support team Milton Area Sch. Dist., 1996—2004, tchr. trainer, 1996—2004, peer coaching mentor model; mem. reading conf. planning com. Bloomsburg U.; mem. parent and child planning conf. com. Bloomsburg U. and Cen. Susquehanna Intermediat Unit #16, Bloomsburg; intergenerational program coord. Milton Elem. Sch., 1999—2004; ARC cmty. project coord. Milton Area Sch. Dist., 2003—04; mem. planning com., early childhood com., kindergarten transition conf. planning com., early childhood conf. planning com., presch. rep. Columbia County Early Childhood Conf., 2006—. Mem. elem. by-laws com. Benton Elem. Parent Tchr. Assn.; asst. coach Am. Youth Soccer Orgn., Benton; actor Bloomsburg U. Cmty. Theater Group, soloist; mem. Columbia County Covered Bridge Soc.; mem. com. Cmtys. that Career; stake seminar supr. Ch. of Jesus Christ of Latter-Day Saints, Ch. Ednl. Sys., Williamsport, Pa., 2005—; stake primary 1st counselor Ch. of Jesus Christ of Latter-Day Saints, Williamsport, 1998—2005, primary 1st counselor Berwick Ward, music chairperson, dir. Berwick Ward choir. Recipient music scholarship, Bloomsburg U., Preschooler R.E.A.D.Y. Kits grant, Berwick Health and Wellness Found., Vocal Music award, Benton Area Sch. Dist. Chorus, Gift of Time Tribute award, Am. Family Inst., 1996, 1997. Mem.: Internat. Reading Assn., Pa. State Edn. Assn. (assoc.), Berwick Area Edn. Assn. (assoc.), Pa. Assn. of Fed. Programs Coords. (life), Women's Relief Soc. (life). Home: 439 State Rte 239 Benton PA 17814 Office: Berwick Area Sch Dist 500 Line St Berwick PA 18603 Office Fax: 570-759-6439. Business E-Mail: cpasukinis@berwicksd.org.

PASUPATHY, RAGHU, engineering educator; b. Chennai, India, July 23, 1973; s. Pasupathy Venugopal and Sunitha Susarla. PhD, Purdue U., West Lafayette, Ind., 2005. Asst. prof. Va. Tech, Blacksburg, 2005—. Office: Virginia Tech 250 Durham Hall Blacksburg VA 24061

PASUPULETI, VENUMADHAV, information technology executive; s. Srinivas Rao and Rama Kumari P.; m. Marilyn L. Miller, May 7, 1992; 1 child, Teja. Grad., Bur. of Data Processing Sys., Hyderabad, 1985; student, Wright State U., 1988-92. Info. tech. cons., 1984-93; mgr. Info. Horizons, Parsippany, NJ, 1993-95; exec. v.p. Globe Tech. Exch., Dayton, Ohio, 1995; COB/CEO, owner Megasoft, Dayton, 1995—. Pres. Indian Student Assn. Wright State U., Dayton, 1989-92; vol. India Literacy Project, Dayton, 1990-95, Ohio India Project, Dayton, 1990-95, Project Outreach, Dayton, 1999—, Day of Caring, Dayton, 1990-95. Mem. IEEE, Assn. for Computing Machinery, Math. Assn. of Am. Office: Megasoft PO Box 340591 Beavercreek OH 45434-0591 Office Phone: 530-323-6370. Business E-Mail: ceo@megasoft.us.

PATAKI, ANDREW, bishop emeritus; b. Palmerton, Pa., Aug. 30, 1927; Attended, St. Vincent Coll., St. Procopious Coll., Lisle, Ill., Sts. Cyril and Methodius, Byzantine Cath. Sem., Gregorian U., Rome. Ordained priest Eparchy of Passaic (Ruthenian), NJ, 1952, aux bishop, 1983—84, bishop NJ, 1996—2007, bishop emeritus, 2007—; ordained bishop, 1983; bishop Eparchy of Parma (Ruthenian), Ohio, 1984—96. Roman Catholic. Home: 445 Lackawanna Ave West Paterson NJ 07424-2969

PATAKI, GEORGE ELMER, lawyer, former governor; b. Peekskill, NY, June 24, 1945; s. Louis P. Pataki and Margaret (Lagana) P.; m. Elizabeth (Libby) Rowland, 1973; children: Emily, Teddy, Allison, George Owen. BA, Yale U., 1967; JD, Columbia U. Sch. Law, 1970. Mayor City of Peekskill, NY, 1981—84; mem. NY State Assembly, 1985-92, NY State Senate from dist. 37, 1993—95; assoc. Dewey, Ballantine, Bushby, Palmer & Wood LLP, 1970-74; ptnr. Plunckett & Jaffe, P.C., NYC, White Plains, Albany and Peekskill, 1974-89; co-proprietor Pataki Farm, Peekskill, NY; gov. State of NY, Albany, NY, 1995—2007; counsel Chadbourne & Parke LLP, NYC, 2007—. Co-author (with Daniel Paisner): Pataki: An Autobiography, 1998. Advanceman Friends of Rockefeller Team, 1970; upstate campaign coord. Com. to Elect Gov. Wilson, 1974; mem. Peekskill Rep. City Com., 1974—, chmn. 1977-83; mem. N.Y. State Rep. Com., 1980-85. Republican. Office: Chadbourne & Parke LLP 30 Rockefeller Plz New York NY 10112 E-mail: gpataki@chadbourne.com.

PATAKY, PAUL ERIC, ophthalmologist; b. Phila., May 19, 1945; s. Andrew and Helen (Koffler) P.; Meryl Corinne, Lisa Ann. BS, Trinity Coll., 1966; MD, Pa. State U., 1971. Diplomate Am. Bd. Ophthalmology. Resident ophthalmology Mass. Eye and Ear Infirmary, Boston, 1972-76; asst. in ophthalmology Harvard Med. Sch., Boston, 1976-79; ophthalmologist Dedham (Mass.) Med. Assocs., 1976-79, Paul E. Pataky M.D. P.A., Boynton Beach, Fla., 1979—. Chmn. dept. surgery Bethesda Meml. Hosp., Boynton Beach, 1988-89; pres. med. staff, 1990-91, chmn. credentials chmn., 1992-93, chmn. surg. care com.,

1993-97. Named South Fla. Super Drs., 2009; named one of One of Am.'s Top Ophthalmologists, Consumer Rsch. Coun. Am., 2004—09. Fellow: Am. Acad. Ophthalmology; mem.: AMA, Pan-Am. Assn. Ophthalmology. Avocations: travel, fine art, bicycling. Office: 2623 S Seacrest Blvd Ste 102 Boynton Beach FL 33435-7531 Home Phone: 561-381-4486; Office Phone: 561-734-5056.

PATAY, ZOLTÁN, radiologist, educator; b. Budapest, Hungary, Apr. 12, 1957; s. Pál Patay and Klára Mózes; m. Lívia Villányi, Oct. 15, 1983; children: Eszter Anna, Farkas Adam. MD, Semmelweis Med. Sch., Budapest, Hungary, 1982; PhD, Hungarian Acad. Scis., Budapest, 1996. Cert. bd. in neurology Postgrad. Med. Sch., Budapest, 1987, bd. in radiology & neuroradiology U. Louis Pasteur, Strasbourg, France, 1992, European Bd. Neuroradiology, 2007. Resident neurology St. Stephen Hosp., Budapest, 1982—84, Ctrl. Mil. Hosp., Budapest, 1984—87, resident radiology, 1987—89, Pasteur Hosp., Colmar, France, 1989—92; asst. prof. Erasmus Hosp., Free U. Brussels, 1992—94; chief, dept. neuroradiology Ctrl. Mil. Hosp., Budapest, 1994—97; cons. King Faisal Specialist Hosp. & Rsch. Ctr., Riyadh, Saudi Arabia, 1997—2001, chief, sect. neuroradiology, 2001—07; prof. U. Tenn. Health Sci. Ctr., Coll. Medicine, Memphis, 2007—; chief, sect. neuroradiology St. Jude Children's Rsch. Hosp., Memphis, 2007—. Recipient Ziedes des Plantes prize, European Soc. Neuroradiology, 1994. Mem.: Hungarian Soc. Neuroradiology, Internat. Soc. Magnetic Resonance Medicine, Am. Soc. Functional Neuroradiology, Am. Soc. of Neuroradiology. Office: St Jude Children's Rsch Hosp 262 Danny Thomas Pl Memphis TN 38105 Office Fax: 901-595-3962. Business E-Mail: zoltan.patay@stjude.org.

PATCHEN, JEFFREY HART, museum director, music educator; b. Syracuse, NY, Apr. 28, 1954; s. Hart C. and Virginia (Chase) P.; m. Cheryl Elizabeth Patchen, June 2, 1984. MusB, Ithaca Coll., 1976, MusM, 1981; DME, Ind. Univ., 1986. Lic. tchr. (life), N.Y. Dir. bands East Syracuse-Minoa High Sch., 1976-82; assoc. instr. Ind. U., Bloomington, 1982-84; state music/arts supr. Ind. Dept. Edn., Indpls.; assoc. prof. music edn., Lyndhurst chair of excellence in arts edn. Univ. Tenn., Chattanooga; sr. prog. officer Getty Edn. Inst. for the Arts, LA, 1996—99; pres., CEO Children's Mus. of Indpls., Ind., 1999—. Bd. dirs. Very Spl. Arts, Ind. Contbr. articles to profl. jours. Grantee Ind. U., 1985, NEA, 1987, Ind. Arts Commn., 1987, Ind. Commn. Humanities, 1988. Mem. Assn. Children's Museums, Nat. Network for Educational Development, Nat. Council State Suprs. Music, Music Educators Nat. Conf., Ind. Music Educators Assn., Nat. Art Educators Assn., Art Edn. Assn. of Ind. Office: Children's Museum Indpls 3000 N Meridian St Indianapolis IN 46208-4716

PATCHETT, ARTHUR ALLAN, medicinal chemist, retired pharmaceutical executive; b. Middletown, NY, May 28, 1929; s. Arthur Allan and Anna Gertrude (Vossler) P.; m. Lois Rhoda Mc Neil, Aug. 18, 1962; Thomas John, Steven Edward. BA, Princeton U., 1951; PhD, Harvard U., 1955; DSc (hon.), Bloomfield Coll., 2001. Rsch. assoc. NIH, Bethesda, Md., 1955-57; rsch. chemist Merck Rsch. Labs., Rahway, NJ, 1957-62, dir. synthetic chem. rsch., 1962-69, sr. dir. synthetic chem. rsch., 1969-71, sr. dir. new lead discovery, 1971-76, exec. dir. new lead discovery, 1976-88, v.p. exploratory chemistry, 1988-95, v.p. medicinal chemistry, 1995-2000, cons., 2000—. Contbr. over 180 papers to profl. jours., sci. confs. Recipient Discoverers award, Pharm. Mfrs. Assn., 1992, Smissman Bristol-Myers Squibb award, 2001, NAS award for Chemistry in Svc. to Soc., 2007; named to, N.J. Inventors Hall of Fame, N.J. Inst. Tech., 1990. Fellow AAAS; mem. Am. Chem. Soc. (chmn. div. medicinal chemistry 1971, E.B. Hershberg Important Discoveries in Medicinally Active Substances award 1993, Alfred Burger award in medicinal chemistry 2002, Nat. Acad. Sci. award for chemistry in svc. to soc. 2007). Achievements include 180 U.S. patents (co-holder); co-inventor antihypertensive drug Vasotec; key contbr. to discovery of cholesterol lowering drug Mevacor.

PATCHETT, P. JONATHAN, science educator; b. Grantham, Eng., Nov. 18, 1951; s. Peter Garry and Brenda Patchett; m. Kaye Patchett, Sept. 4, 1976; 1 child, Nicholas David. BA, U. Oxford, Eng., 1973; PhD, U. Edinburgh, 1976. Scientist Max Planck Inst. Chemistry, Mainz, Germany, 1981—84; prof. U. Ariz., Tucson, 1984—. Named ISI Highly Cited Rschr., Thomson Pubs., 2002—; grant, Rsch. Corp., 1985—87, Rsch. grant, NASA, 1986—90, NSF, 1986—2008. Fellow: Am. Geophys. Union, Geol. Soc. America; mem.: Geo-Chem. Soc. (F.W. Clarke medal 1982). Office: Univ Ariz Dept Geosci Tucson AZ 85721 Office Phone: 520-621-2070. Business E-Mail: patchett@email.arizona.edu.

PATCHIN, REBECCA J., anesthesiologist, educator, administrator; b. Detroit, Dec. 8, 1949; d. Robert Ira and Doris J. (Hubert) P.; m. Carl W. Anderson, 1988 (dec.) ASN, Pacific Union Coll., 1969; BSN, Walla Walla Coll., 1971; MD, Loma Linda U., 1989. Diplomate in anesthesiology and pain mgmt. Am. Bd. Anesthesiology. Resident internal medicine Loma Linda U. Med. Ctr., Calif., 1989-90, resident anesthesiology Calif., 1990-93, fellow pain mgmt. Dept. Anesthesiology Calif., 1993-94, asst. prof. anesthesiology, 1994—; assoc. med. dir. Ctr. for Pain Mgmt., Loma Linda, 1995—; pvt. practice Riverside, Calif. Appointed to Joint Commn. on Accreditation od Healthcare Organizations' Standards and Surveys Coms., 2006; mem. Accreditation Coun. Grad. Med. Edn. (mem. liaison com. med. edn., co-chair 2001-2002); presenter in field. Contbr. abstracts to profl. jours. Mem. AMA (mem. credentials com. 1986-, mem. bd. nominations and awards com. 1988-89, chair, Med. Liability Task Force, del. ho. of dels. 1990-99, mem. reference com. 1994-, mem. coun. on med. edn. 1996-2003, chair, 2002-03, mem. bd. trustee 2003-, sec. 2006-07, liasion polit. action com., mem. young physician sect., chair, membership com., bd. audit, mem. orgn. and ops. com., chair-elect 2008-), Internat. Anesthesiology Rsch. Soc., Internat. Assn. for Study of Pain, Am. Soc. Anesthesiology, Am. Pain Soc., Am. Soc. Regional Anesthesia, Am. Acad. Pain Medicine, Calif. Soc. Anesthesiology (del. resident component 1991-93, mem. com. on young physicians 1994—96, chair com. on young physicians 1996—), Calif. Med. Assn. (mem. reference com. 1988, trustee 1991-93, mem. com. on health professions and licensure 1992-, chair com. on health professions and licensure 1993-96, mem. coun. on legislation 1995-96, chair coun. on legislation, liaison com. on specialty bds., bd. dir.), So. Calif. Cancer Pain Initiative, Riverside County Med. Assn. (sec.-treas 2002, pres. 2004), San Bernardino County Med. Soc. Avocation: sailing. Home Phone: 951-780-8121; Office Phone: 951-413-0200. E-mail: rebpatchin@aol.com.*

PATE, ALEXS DELANEY, writer, educator; b. Phila. s. Alexander Pate and Lois Williams; m. SooJin Link, Aug. 12, 2004; children: Sxela Kiboon, Gyanni, Chekesha; life ptnr. Carolyn Thompson; 1 child, Alexs Thompson. Vp Human Resources Network, Phila., 1976—81; mgr. strategy elements City Venture Corp., Mpls., 1981—85; pres. ADP Comm., Mpls., 1985—90; prof. Macalester Coll., St. Paul, 1992—97, U. Minn., Mpls., 1997—. Author: (novel) Losing Absalom (Named Best First Novel Black Caucus ALA, 1994), Finding Makeba, The Multicultiboho Sideshow (Minn. Book award, 2000), Amistad, West of Rehobeth, In the Heart of the Beat: The Poetry of Rap. Sgt. USN, 1968—72. Achievements include patents for displaying information on a gate system. Office: Univ Minn 808 Social Scis Bldg 267 19th Ave S Minneapolis MN 55455 Business E-Mail: patex003@umn.edu.

PATE, ANDREW LIDDEN, JR., religious organization administrator; b. Humble, Tex., Apr. 8, 1935; s. Andrew Lidden and Gale Marie Carpenter Pate; m. Carol Dean Walker, Aug. 2, 1997; children: Andrew Lidden III, Gale Marie, Martha Lokey Pate Mooney. Attended, Tex. State U., San Marcos, 1954, Rice U., Houston, TX, 1954; BA, U. Tex., Austin, 1957; MDiv, Emory U., Atlanta, 1959; ThD, Pacific Sch. Religion, Berkeley, Calif., 1968. Cert. in ordination United Meth. Ch., Ga., 1959, in ordination standing transferred Christian Ch., Iowa, 1985. Assoc. pastor St. John United Meth. Ch., Augusta, Ga., 1959—61; pastor Young Meml. United Meth. Ch., Thomson, Ga., 1964—66; dir. admissions, asst. prof. Oxford Coll. Emory U, Ga., 1966—78; dir. admissions Centenary Coll., Shreveport, La., 1978—80; sr. pastor 1st United Meth. Ch., Blanco, Tex., 1982—84, Schulenburg, Tex., 1980—82, transitional min., 2001—04, 1st Christian Ch., Bryan, Tex., 1997—2000, sr. pastor Orange, Tex., 2008—, Ctrl. Christian Ch., Galveston, Tex., 1991—94; dean admissions Iowa Wesleyan Coll., Mt. Pleasant, 1984—85. Transitional min. Coll. Hills Christian Ch., San Angelo, Tex., 2000—01, Oaks Christian Ch., Houston, 2007—08; bus. mgr. 1st Presbyn. Ch., Bryan, 2005—07. Contbr. articles to profl. publs., columns in newspapers. Dir. Telethon, Augusta, 1960; mem. Rotary Internat., Covington, Ga., 1976—78, Lions Internat., Schulenburg, Tex., 1980—82; pres., mem. Ministerial Assn., Burlington, Iowa, 1985—91, Blanco, Tex., 1982—84; sr. pastor 1st Christian Ch., Burlington, Iowa, 1985—2001; higher edn. com. mem. Articulation Com., Ga., 1975—78. Recipient Nat., Best Admissions Hand Out award, Paper Co., 1979, Editl. and Humor Columns award, South Tex. Small Town Publs., 2007; named to Dean's List, U. Tex. Austin, 1956—57. Home: 1312 Essex Green College Station TX 77845-9355 Personal E-mail: andrewpatejr@aol.com.

PATE, MICHAEL LYNN, lawyer; b. Ft. Worth, July 9, 1951; s. J.B. and Mary Anna (Hable) P.; m. Barbara Ann Linch, May 28, 1977. AA, Schreiner Coll., 1971; BS, Tex. Wesleyan Coll., 1973; JD, U. Tex., 1975. Bar: Tex. 1976, DC 1983, US Tax Ct. 1986, US Supreme Ct. 1987. Adminstrv. asst. to Senator Sherman, counsel natural resources com. Tex. Senate, 1976-77; adminstrv. asst. to Lt. Gov. Bill Hobby, Austin, Tex., 1977-79; legis. asst. Senator Bentsen, Washington, 1979-81, legis. dir., 1981-86; ptnr., head Washington office Bracewell & Giuliani LLP, Washington, 1986—. Trustee Schreiner U. Mem. ABA, Tex. Bar Assn., DC Bar Assn. Democrat. Methodist. Avocations: basketball, tennis, golf. Office: Bracewell & Giuliani LLP 2000 K St NW Ste 500 Washington DC 20006-1872 Office Phone: 202-828-5841. Business E-Mail: michael.pate@bgllp.com.

PATE, PAUL DANNY, mayor; b. Ottumwa, Iowa, May 1, 1958; s. Paul Devern and Velma Marie (McConnell) P.; m. Jane Ann Wacker, July 15, 1978; children: Jennifer Ann, Paul Daniel III, Amber Lynn. AA in Bus., Kirkwood Coll., 1978; cert. fin. mgmt. program, U. Pa., 1990. Exec. dir. Jr. Achievement, Cedar Rapids, Iowa, 1978-82; pres. PM Systems Corp., Cedar Rapids, 1982—; senator Iowa State Senate, Des Moines, 1989-93; Sec. of State of Iowa, 1994-98; mayor City of Cedar Rapids, 2002—06. Chmn. Iowa Young Reps., Des Moines, 1989-93, Recipient Guardian Small Bus. award Nat. Fedn. Independent Bus., 1990; named Young Entrepreneur of Yr. U.S. Small Bus. Adminstrn., Iowa, 1988, Alumnus of Yr. Kirkwood Coll., Cedar Rapids, 1990. Republican. Methodist. Avocation: water-skiing. Home: 6801 Bowman Ln NE Cedar Rapids IA 52402-1575 Office: Pate Group 3285 3rd Ave Marion IA 52302-3928

PATE, R. HEWITT (ROBERT HEWITT PATE III), lawyer, oil industry executive; b. Ft. Sill, Okla., June 14, 1962; s. Robert and Ellen Pate; m. Lindsey Haines, Aug. 2, 1986; 2 children. BA, U. NC, 1984; JD, U. Va., 1987. Bar: Va. 1989, DC 2000, bar: Brussels 2006. Law clk. for Hon. J. Harvie Wilkinson, US Ct. Appeals (4th cir.), Charlottesville, Va., 1987—88; law clk. for Justice Lewis F. Powell, Jr., US Supreme Ct., Washington, 1988—89, law clk. for Justice Anthony M. Kennedy, 1989—90; assoc. Hunton & Williams, Richmond, Va., 1990—95, ptnr., 1995—2000; dep. asst. atty. gen., Antitrust Divsn. US Dept. Justice, Washington, 2001—03, asst. atty. gen., 2003—05; ptnr. Hunton & Williams, Richmond, Va., 2005—09; v.p., gen. counsel Chevron Corp., San Ramon, Calif., 2009—. Mem. Commn. on Future of Higher Edn. in Va., Richmond, 1994—95, Governor's Commn. on Self-Determination and Federalism, Richmond, 1994—96; Ewald disting. vis. prof. U. Va. Sch. Law, Charlottesville, Va., 1999; chmn. competition com. working party 3 Orgn. for Econ. Cooperation and Devel., Paris, 2003—05; chair internat. working group US Atty. General's Task Force on Intellectual Property, Washington, 2004—04. Contbr. numerous articles to legal jours. Gen. counsel Children's Mus. Richmond, 1996—2000; bd. gov. St. Catherine's Sch., 2006—; bd. dir. John Marshall Found., 2007—. Mem.: ABA, Fourth Circuit Jud. Conf. Republican. Office: Chevron Corp 6001 Bollinger Canyon Rd San Ramon CA 94583*

PATE, ROBERT HEWITT, JR., retired counselor educator; b. Abingdon, Va., Apr. 5, 1938; s. Robert Hewitt and Esther Frances (Kirk) P.; m. Ellen O'Neal Pope, Dec. 11, 1960; children: Robert Hewitt III, Mary Ellen Pate Barton. AB, Davidson Coll., 1960; MEd, U. Va., 1965; PhD, U. N.C., 1968. Lic. prof. counselor, Va. Marketer Sinclair Refining Co., Abingdon, Va., 1960-61, 63-64; counselor St. Andrews Presbyn. Coll., Laurinburg, NC, 1965-66; counselor educator U. Va., 1968—2008, interim dean, 1994-95, assoc. dean, 1995—2007, prof. edn., emeritus, William Clay Parrish Jr. prof. edn., 2003—08. Mem. adj. faculty Fed. Exec. Inst., Charlottesville, 1978—. Author: Being A Counselor, 1983. 1st lt. U.S. Army 1961-63. Mem. ACA, Va. Counselors Assn. (pres. 1983-84), Nat. Bd. Cert. Counselors (chair 1996-97), Raven Soc. Avocation: reading. Home: 552 Dryden Pl Charlottesville VA 22903-4666 Office: Curry Sch Dean's Office 405 Emmet St S PO Box 400260 Charlottesville VA 22904-4260

PATE, STEPHEN PATRICK, lawyer; b. Beaumont, Tex., May 6, 1958; s. Gordon Ralph and Shirley Jean (Riley) P.; m. Jean Janssen; 1 child, Teddy. BA, Vanderbilt U., 1980, JD, 1983. Bar: Tex. 1984, U.S. Dist. Ct. (ea. dist.) Tex. 1984, U.S. Dist. Ct. (so. dist.) Tex. 1985. Law clk. to judge Joe J. Fisher U.S. Dist. Ct. Tex., Beaumont, 1983-84; ptnr. Fulbright & Jaworski, Houston. Contbr. articles to profl. jours. Fellow Houston Bar Found., Tex. Bar Found.; mem. Fedn. Defense and Corp. Counsel (v.p., chair, property ins. sect., 2003-05, John Applemon award, 2004), Tex. Bar Assn., Tex. Young Lawyers Assn. (bd. dirs. 1992-94), Houston Young Lawyers Assn. (bd. dirs. 1990-92, sec. 1992-93, chmn. professionalism com., mem. sunset rev. com. 1990), Am. Bd. Trial Advocates, Sons of the Republic Tex., SAR (pres. Paul Carrington chpt. 2001-02), Soc. Colonial Wars, Manitoba Master Angler, Billfish Found. (Top Angler 1993), Knight of Momus, The Briar Club, Phi Beta Kappa. Republican. Roman Catholic. Avocations: hunting, fishing. Home: 2740 Arbuckle St Houston TX 77005-3932 Office: Fulbright & Jaworski 1301 Mckinney St Houston TX 77010-3031 E-mail: spate@fulbright.com.

PATE, WILLIAM PATRICK, city manager; b. Duplin County, NC, July 30, 1962; s. William Atlas and Bonny Lou (O'Leary) P.; m. Sandra Martin, Aug. 17, 1985; children: William Glenn, Andrew Patrick. BA in Polit. Sci. and Religion, U. N.C., 1984, MPA, 1986. Budget and evaluation analyst intern City of Winston-Salem, NC, 1985-86, budget and evaluation analyst NC, 1986-87, lead budget and evaluation analyst NC, 1987; budget and rsch. mgr. City of Greensboro, NC, 1987-90, budget and evaluation dir. NC, 1990-99; asst. city mgr. City of High Point, NC, 1999—. Inst. of Govt. intern N.C. Office Coastal Mgmt., Raleigh, N.C., 1984; rsch. asst. U. N.C., Chapel Hill, 1984-85. Mem. Chmns. Soc. United Way of High Point, 1998—; mem. Leadership Greensboro, 1993-99, Leadership High Point, 2000—; elder, clk. session Faith Presbyn. Ch., Greensboro; mem. Salem Presbyn. World Ministries Cluster, 1997-99; chair staff parish rels. team Covenant Ch., 2005-07, adminstrn. bd., 2005-07, pres. SW Guilford HS Baseball Booster Club, 2008-. Recipient Disting. Svc. award Alpha Phi Omega, 1984. Mem. Internat. City Mgrs. Assn., Am. Soc. Pub. Adminstrn. (pres. Piedmont Triad chpt. 1994), Gov. Fin. Officers Assn. U.S. and Can. (exec. bd. 1998-2004, nat. com. on govtl. budgeting and mgmt. 1993-98, nat. com. on debt and fiscal policy 1998-2001, pres. 2002-03, Disting. Budget Presentation award reviewer, Disting. Budget Presentation award 1992-98), N.C. Local Govt. Budget Assn. (bd. dirs. 1990-92, 95, 1st v.p. 1992-93, pres. 1993-94), N.C. City/County Mgrs. Assn., U. N.C. MPA Alumni Assn. (program chmn. 1992, pres-elect 1993, pres. 1994, Scholarship award 1985), U. N.C. Gen. Alumni Assn. (bd. dirs. 1994-95, v.p. 2006-07, pres. 2008-), Kiwanis Club (v.p. 2006—). Methodist. Home: 4509 Calabria Ct High Point NC 27265-9595 Office: City of High Point PO Box 230 High Point NC 27261-0230 E-mail: pat.pate@highpointnc.gov.

PATÉ-CORNELL, MARIE-ELISABETH LUCIENNE, engineering educator; b. Dakar, Senegal, Aug. 17, 1948; (parents Am. citizens); d. Edouard Pierre Lucien and Madeleine (Tournissa) Paté; m. C. Allin Cornell, Jan. 3, 1981 (dec.); children: Phillip, Ariane. BS in Math. and Physics, 1968; MS in Engrng., Inst. Polytechnique de Grenoble, France, 1970; MS in Ops. Rsch., Stanford U., Calif., 1972; PhD in Engrng.-Econ. Sys., Stanford U., 1978. EIT Inst. Polytechnique de Grenoble, 1971. Asst. prof. civil engrng. MIT, 1978-81; asst. prof. indsl. engrng. Stanford U., 1981-84, assoc. prof. indsl. engrng., 1984-91, prof. indsl. engrng., 1991—99, chmn. dept. indsl. engrng., 1997-99, Burt & Deedee McMurtry prof., chmn. dept. mgmt. sci. and engrng., 1999—. Cons. SRI Internat., 1993, Electric Power Rsch. Inst., 1995, Atty. Gen. of N.Mex., 1995, Swiss Re, 2002, Boeing, 2003—; mem. Marine Bd. NRC, 1995—97; mem. adv. coun. NASA, 1995—98; mem. Army Sci. Bd., 1995—97, Air Force Sci. Bd., 1998—2002, Calif. Coun. Sci. & Tech., 2000—, Fgn. Intelligence Adv. Bd., Washington, 2001—; chmn. bd. advs. Naval-Postgrad. Sch., 2004—06. Contbr. articles to profl. jours. Fellow: Inst. Mgmt. Scis.; mem.: Nat. Acad. Engrng. (councilor 2001—), Ops. Rsch. Soc. of America, Soc. Risk Analysis (councilor 1985—86, pres. 1995). Avocations: tennis, swimming, chess, music. Home: 110 Coquito Way Menlo Park CA 94028-7404 Office: Stanford U Dept Mgmt Sci and Engrng Stanford CA 94305 E-mail: mep@leland.stanford.edu.*

PATEL, AJAY, finance educator; m. Aparna Patel; 2 children. BS, St. Joseph's Coll., India; MBA, U. Balt.; PhD, U. Ga. Faculty appointments U. Mo., Bentley Coll.; faculty mem. Babcock Grad. Sch. Mgmt., Wake Forest U., 1993, Babcock rsch. prof. fin., 2001—08, interim dean, 2003—04, dean, 2004—08, GMAC chair in fin., 2008—, prof., 2008—. Office: Babcock Grad Sch Mgmt Wake Forest U PO Box 7659 Winston Salem NC 27109-7659 Home Phone: 336-760-2862; Office Phone: 336-758-5575. E-mail: ajay.patel@mba.wfu.edu.*

PATEL, ALPA V., epidemiologist, director; PhD, U. So. Calif. Keck Sch. Medicine, LA, 2003. Sr. epidemiologist Am. Cancer Soc., Atlanta, 2003—06, dir., 2006—.

PATEL, AMIT N., surgeon, researcher; b. Dallas, Dec. 8, 1972; s. Nilkanth and Manjula Patel. BS, Youngstown State U., 1993, MS in Immunology, 1994; MD, Case Western Res. U., 1998. Surgery resident Baylor U. Med. Ctr., Dallas, thoracic and cardiovasc. surgery rsch. fellow, dir. cardiac surgery rsch., 2002—03; cardiothoracic surgery fellow U. Pitts. Med. Ctr.; clin. rsch. fellow dept. thoracic and cardiovasc. surgery Cleve. Clinic Found.; dir. cardiac cell therapy U. Pitts. Med. Ctr., McGowan Inst. of Regenerative Medicien; assoc. prof. surgery U. Utah Sch. Medicine, 2008—. National principal investigator Phase II Impact-DCM clinical trial Aastrom Biosciences Inc. Author (with Dr. Urschel Jr.): Atlas of Thoracic Surgery 2nd ed.; author: (with Dr. F. Benetti) Atlas of Off Pump Cardiac Surgery; contbr. articles to profl. jours. Recipient First Pl. - Paravertebral Blocks in Thoracic Surgery, Inst. Surg. Pain Mgmt.; named Best Resident in Am., Am. Assn. Physicians Indian Origin. Mem.: ACS (Best Overall Presentation award 2001, 2002, 2003, 2005), Soc. Thoracic Surgeons, Internat. Soc. Minimally Invasive Cardiac Surgery. Achievements include patents for Patel Minimally Invasive Cardiac Retractor; first to first surgeon to perform epicardial defibrillation for postoperative atrial fibrillation in America; first Surgeon to implant human stem cells in the heart in America. Office: U Utah Cardiovascular Ctr 50 N Medical Dr Salt Lake City UT 84132 Personal E-mail: anpatel72@hotmail.com.*

PATEL, BHARAT, financial executive; b. Wednesbury, West Midlands, Eng., Oct. 29, 1965; came to U.S., 1981; s. Maganbhai and Shantaben Patel; m. Naynitaben Bharatbhai, Feb. 14, 1990; children: Pritesh, Kunal. AS, Heald Bus. Coll., San Francisco; BS, Golden Gate U. Chmn. bd. dirs. API San Francisco, 1993—; CEO Patelco Investments, Brit. V.I., 1990—. Contbr. articles to profl. publs. Law enforcement cadet Calif. Peace League Activities, San Francisco, 1986; mem. coun. Calif. Dem. Assn., Modesto, 1998. Recipient award Internat. Fedn. for Bus., 1987, Amateur Athletic Assn., Eng., 1998. Mem. Golden Gate Hotel Assn. (bd. dirs. 1989-94). Avocations: travel, reading, playing cricket, movies, teaching. Office: 1255 Post St (Suite 849) San Francisco CA 94109

PATEL, CHANDRA KUMAR NARANBHAI, communications executive, educator, entrepreneur, researcher; b. Baramati, India, July 2, 1938; came to U.S., 1958, naturalized, 1970; s. Naranbhai Chaturbhai and Maniben P.; m. Shela Dixit, Aug. 20, 1961; children: Neela, Meena. BS in Engrng., Poona U., 1958; MS, Stanford U., 1959, PhD, 1961. Mem. tech. staff Bell Telephone Labs., Murray Hill, NJ, 1961-93, head infrared physics and electronics rsch. dept., 1967-70, dir. electronics rsch. dept., 1970-76, dir. phys. rsch. lab., 1976-81, exec. dir. rsch. physics and acad. affairs div., 1981-87, exec. dir. rsch., materials sci., engrng. and acad. affairs div., 1987-93; trustee Aerospace Corp., LA, 1979-88; vice chancellor rsch. UCLA, 1993-2000, prof. dept. physics and astronomy, dept. chemistry, 2000—, prof. dept. elec. engrng., 2000—; chmn., CEO Pranalytica, Inc., Santa Monica, Calif., 2001—. Mem. governing bd. NRC, 1990-91; bd. dirs. Newport Corp.; chmn. bd. Calif. Accuwave Corp., 1994-98; founder, chmn. bd. Pranalytica, Inc., Santa Monica, Calif.; co-founder Photuris, Inc. Contbr. articles to tech. jours. Chmn. Calif. Biomed. Found., 1994-2000; mem. exec. bd. Calif. Healthcare Inst., 1995-2000; mem. LA Regional Tech. Alliance, 1997-

2003. Recipient Ballantine medal Franklin Inst., 1968, Nat. Sci. medal 1996, Coblentz award Am. Chem. Soc., 1974, Honor award Assn. Indians in Am., 1975, Founders prize Tex. Instruments Found., 1978, award N.Y. sect. Soc. Applied Spectroscopy, 1982, Schawlow medal Laser Inst. Am., 1984, Thomas Alva Edison Sci. award N.J. Gov., 1987, William T. Ennor Manufacturing Technology award ASME, 1995, Nat. Medal of Sci., Pres. of US, 1996. Fellow AAAS, IEEE (Lamme medal 1976, medal of honor 1989, Millennium medal 2000), Am. Acad. Arts and Scis., Am. Phys. Soc. (coun. 1987-91, exec. com. 1987-90, George E. Pake prize 1988, pres. 1995), Optical Soc. Am. (Adolph Lomb medal 1966, Townes medal 1982, Ives medal 1989, Lifetime Achievement award Def. and Security Symposium 2006), Indian Nat. Sci. Acad. (fng.); mem. NAS (coun. 1988-91, exec. com. 1989-91), NAE (Zworykin award 1976), Def. and Security Symposium (Lifetime Achievement award 2006), Gynecol. Laser Surgery Soc. (hon.), Am. Soc. for Laser Medicine and Surgery (hon.), Third World Acad. Scis. (assoc.), Calif. Biomed. Found. (pres. 1994-00), Calif. Healthcare Inst. (exec. com. 1995-00), Fedn. Am. Scientists (bd. dirs. 2002-), Internat. Photoacoustic and Photothermal Assn. (prize 2007), Sigma Xi (pres. 1994-96). Achievements include invention of many lasers including the Carbon Dioxide laser. Office: Pranalytica Inc 1101 Colorado Ave Santa Monica CA 90401 Business E-Mail: patel@pranalytica.com.

PATEL, DEV, actor; b. Harrow, London, Eng., Apr. 23, 1990; s. Raj and Anita Patel. Actor: (TV series) Skins, 2007—08; (films) Slumdog Millionaire, 2008 (Best Actor, Black Reel Awards, 2008, Most Promising Newcomer, Brit. Ind. Film Awards, 2008, Most Promising Performer, Chgo. Film Critics Assn., 2008, Best Breakthrough Performance - Male, Nat. Bd. Review, 2008, Outstanding Performance by a Cast in a Motion Picture, SAG, 2009, Best Young Actor/Actress (Under 21), Broadcast Film Critics Assn., 2009). Office: c/o Curtis Brown Group Ltd Haymarket House 28-29 Haymarket London SW1Y 4SP England

PATEL, MULCHAND SHAMBHUBHAI, biochemist, researcher; b. Sipor, India, Sept. 9, 1939; came to U.S., 1965; s. Shambhubhai J. and Puriben (Patel) P.; m. Kankuben M. Patel; children: Sumitra, Yashomati, Mayank. BS, Gujarat U., 1961; MS, U. Baroda, 1964; PhD, U. Ill., 1968. Asst. prof. pediat. rsch. Sch. Medicine Temple U., Phila., 1970-72, rsch. asst. prof. medicine, 1972-75, rsch. asst. prof. biochemistry, 1970-75, rsch. assoc. prof. biochem. medicine, 1975-78; assoc. prof. biochemistry Sch. Medicine Case Western Res. U., Cleve., 1978-86, prof., 1986-93; prof., chmn. biochemistry SUNY, Buffalo, 1993-98, assoc. dean biomed. rsch. edn., 1999—, prof., 1999—2004, UB disting. prof., 2004—, disting. prof., 2008—. Mem. NIH biochem. study sect. 2, 1984-88; mem. editl. bd. Jour. Biol. Chem., 1991-97, 99-2004, 06-. Contbr. articles to profl. jours. Recipient gold medal in biochemistry U. Baroda, 1973, Fulbright Rsch. Scholar award to India, 1987; prin. investigator, rsch. grantee NIH. Mem. Am. Soc. for Biochemistry and Molecular Biology, Am. Soc. Nutritional Scis. Office: SUNY-Dept Biochemistry Sch Medicine 140 Farber Hall 3435 Main St Buffalo NY 14214-3001 Office Phone: 716-829-3074. Business E-Mail: mspatel@buffalo.edu.

PATEL, NIKETA, medical researcher; PhD, USF. Scientist Jah Va, Tampa, Fla., 1995—; rsch. investigato. Achievements include discovery of gene regulation.

PATEL, NILDEEP MUKUNDRAY, mechanical engineer, researcher; b. Uttarsanda, India, May 3, 1980; s. Mukundray Purushottamdas and Nalini Mukundray Patel. BSME with honors, Sardar Vallabhbhai Insitute Tech., Gujarat, India, 2001; PhD in Space Robotics, U. Surrey, Guildford, Eng., 2005. Trainee mech. engr. Sayaji Iron and Engring. Co. Ltd., Baroda, Gujarat, 2001; lectr. Kingston U., Surrey, England, 2003—04; systems engr., tech. cons. European Space Agy. and U. Surrey Contract, Guildford, Surrey, 2004—06; rsch. officer Cranfield & Airbus intiative Cranfield U., Bedfordshire, England. Mobility systems expert European Space Agy., Surrey Space Ctr. Astrium Ltd., Guildford, 2004—05. Manuscript reviewer ASME Jour. Mech. Design; contbr. articles to profl. jours. Recipient Best Rsch. Poster award, Kingston U., 2003; grantee, Tchg. Co. Scheme and Kingston U., 2002—04, European Space Agy., 2002, Surrey Space Ctr., 2004—05. Mem.: ASME, AIAA (assoc.), UK Students for Edn. and Devel. Space (assoc.). Hindu. Achievements include research in locomotion systems for autonomous planetary rovers; first to rover chassis performance evaluation tool; design of baseline rover design for European Space Agency's 2011 mission to Mars. Avocations: music, movies, cricket, reading. Home: 1520 Anchor's Way Salisbury MD 21801 Office: Cranfield Univ NSRI SIISORE Bedfordshire MK43 4DT England Home Fax: 00442084072652. Personal E-mail: nildeep.patel@gmail.com. Business E-Mail: n.patel@cranfield.ac.uk.

PATEL, PARESH, application developer; married. PhD, Miss. State U., Starkville, 2005. Mech. engr. Makson Engring., Surendranagar, Gujarat, India, 1998—99; rsch. asst. Kettering U., Flint, Mich., 2000—01, Miss. State U., 2002—05; mem. tech. staff MSC Software Corp., Santa Ana, Calif., 2005—. Named to Rsch. Asst. of yr. award, Miss. State U., 2005. Mem.: Sandia Nat. Lab's Internat. Meshing Roundtable, AIAA, ASME. Office: MSC Software Corp 2 MacArthur Pl Santa Ana CA 92707 Office Fax: 866-372-4703. Business E-Mail: paresh.patel@mscsoftware.com.

PATEL, PRAGNA, epidemiologist; b. NYC, Sept. 20, 1971; d. Ashvin D. and Jaya A. Patel. BA, SUNY, Binghamton, 1992; MD, SUNY HSC, Bklyn., 1998; MPH, Harvard U., Boston, 2002. Diplomate Am. Bd. Internal Medicine, 2001, cert. HIV specialist Am. Acad. HIV Medicine, 2007. Med. epidemiologist Ctrs. Disease Control and Prevention, Atlanta, 2002—. Contbr. scientific papers to profl. jours. Comdr. USPHS, 2002—08, Atlanta. Decorated Achievement medal USPHS. Mem.: Infectious Disease Soc. America. Achievements include research in incidence of non-AIDS malignancies among HIV-infected persons; screening for acute HIV infection. Home: 827 Inman Village Pky NE Atlanta GA 30307 Office: Ctrs Disease Control & Prevention 1600 Clifton Rd MS-E46 Atlanta GA 30333

PATEL, SANJAY, pulmonologist, educator; AB in Mathematics, Princeton U.; MD, Harvard Med. Sch. Resident U. Pa. Hosp; fellow in pulmonary & critical care Harvard U.; former instr. Harvard Med. Sch.; clinical staff divsn. sleep Brigham & Women's Hosp.; staff divsn pulmonary, critical are & sleep medicine Beth Israel Deaconess Med. Ctr.; prof. divsn. clinical epidemiology Case Western Reserve U., asst. prof. divsn. pulmonary, critical care & sleep medicine, 2005—. Mem.: Am. Acad. Sleep Medicine, Am. Thoracic Soc., Am. Coll. Chest Physicians, Mass. Med. Soc. Office: 11100 Euclid Ave Ste WRM5067 Cleveland OH 44106*

PATEL, SUNIT, telecommunications industry executive; Treas. MFS Comm., Inc., 1994—97, MCI WorldCom, 1997—2000; CFO, cofounder Looking Glass Networks, Inc., 2000—03; group v.p., CFO Level 3 Comm., Inc., Broomfield, Colo., 2003—. Office: Level 3 Comm 1025 Eldorado Blvd Broomfield CO 80021

PATEL, UPTAL DINESH, nephrologist, researcher; BA, U. Calif. San Diego, 1993; MD, U. Calif. San Francisco, 1997. Diplomate Am. Bd. Internal Medicine, 2001, Diplomate, Subspecialty in Nephrology Am. Bd. Internal Medicine, 2005, Diplomate Am. Bd. Pediat., 2001, Diplomate, Subspecialty in Pediat. Nephrology Am. Bd. Pediat., 2005. Robert Wood Johnson clin. scholar U. Mich., Ann Arbor, 2003—05; asst. prof. medicine and pediat. Duke U., Sch. Medicine, Durham, NC, 2005—. Mem. editl. bd.: Jour. Am. Soc. Nephrology, 2007—, Clinical Medicine: Cardiology, 2007—. Rsch. Career Devel. award, NIH, 2006—.

PATEL, VIKAS, orthopedist, educator; MD, Wash. U., St. Louis, 1997. Diplomate Am. Bd. Orthop. Surgeons, Colo., 2006. Asst. prof. U. Colo. Denver, Aurora, 2005—, assoc. prof., 2009—. Recipient Best Basic Sci. award, John H. Moe, 2004. Mem.: AO N.Am., Western Orthop. Assn., Scoliosis Rsch. Soc., Colo. Med. Soc., Acad. Orthop. Spine Surgery, N. Am. Spine Soc. Office: Univ Colo Denver 12631 E 17th Ave Aurora CO 80045 Office Phone: 303-724-2969.

PATEL, VIMLA L., research scientist; b. Nadi, Fiji Islands; d. Harvovind Mavji and Kantaben Lodhia; m. Yogesh C Patel (dec.); children: Sunil, Camille. BSc, Otago U., New Zealand, 1976; MA, McGill U., Montreal, 1980, MA, 1990, PhD, 1982; DSc (hon.), U. Victoria, B.C., Can., 1990. Prof. psychology and medicine McGill U., Montreal, 1991—2000, asst. prof. medicine and psychology, assoc. prof. medicine and psychology, 1997—2000; prof. psychiatry and biomed. informatics Columbia U., NYC, 2000—07, adj. prof. psychology and edn., 2000—; prof., vice-chair dept. biomed. informatics Ariz. State U., Phoenix, 2007—, dir. med. edn. rsch. Coll. Medicine, 2007—, ctr. decision making and cognities dir., 2007—; prof. basic med. scis. U. Ariz. Coll. Medicine, Phoenix, 2007—. Dir. med. edn. McGill U., Montreal, 1993—2000, dir. cognitive sci. ctr., 1993—97; dir., lab. of decision making and cognition Columbia U., 2000—07; vis. scholar Stanford U., Palo Alto, Calif., 1999—2000; vis. prof. Universty of Tex., Houston, 1998—99. Contbr. articles to profl. jours. Recipient Woman of Sci. award, Rsch. Coun., Sweden, 1994. Fellow: N.Y. Acad. Sci.; mem.: Acad. of Humanities and Social Sci. of Can., Royal Soc. Can., Am. Med. Informatics Assn. (assoc.), Cogniitve Sci. Soc. (assoc.), Psychonomics Socoety (assoc.), Am. Ednl. Rsch. Assn. (corr.), Am. Coll. Med. Informatics. Office: Ariz State U 425 N Fifth St Phoenix AZ 85004 Business E-Mail: vimla@asu.edu.

PATEL, VIRENDRA CHATURBHAI, mechanical engineer, educator; b. Mombasa, Kenya, Nov. 9, 1938; arrived in US, 1969, naturalized, 1975; s. Chaturbhai S. and Kantaben N. (Rai) Patel; m. Manjula Patel, May 29, 1966; children: Sanjay, Bindiya. BSc with honors, Imperial Coll., London, 1962; PhD, Cambridge U., Eng., 1965; Dr. honoris causa, Tech. U. Civil Engring., Bucharest, Romania, 1994. Sr. asst. in rsch. Cambridge U., 1965-69; vis. prof. Indian Inst. Tech., Kharagpur, 1966; cons. Lockheed Ga. Co., Marietta, 1969-70; from mem. faculty to disting. prof. U. Iowa, Iowa City, 1971—90, disting. prof., 1990—, Edwin B. Green chair in hydraulics, 2000—; rsch. engr. Iowa Inst. Hydraulic Rsch., 1971—, dir., 1994—2004, hon. prof. Dharamsinh Desai Inst. Tech., 2002—, dir. Ctr. Computer Aided Design, 2003—05. Mem. Iowa Gov. Sci. Adv. Coun., 1977—83; mem. resistance com. Internat. Towing Tank Conf., 1978—87; vis. prof. U. Karlsruhe, Germany, 1980—81, Ecole Nationale Superieure de Mechanique, Nantes, France, 1984, Nantes, 96; jubilee prof. Chalmers Inst. Tech., Goteborg, Sweden, 1988; dir. Ctr. for Computer Aided Design, 2003—; cons. in field. Author: (book) Three Dimensional Turbulent Boundary Layers, 1972; contbr. articles to profl. jours.; assoc. editor: AIAA Jour., 1987—90. V.p. internat. com. Anoopam Mission, Mogri, India. Recipient Sr. Scientist award, Alexander von Humboldt Found., 1980, 1993. Fellow: ASME (Fluids Engring. award 1997), AIAA (assoc.); mem.: Soc. Naval Archtl. Marine Engrs., Am. Soc. Engring. Edn., Pi Tau Sigma, Sigma Xi. Home: 60 Kennedy Pkwy Iowa City IA 52246-2780 Office: IIHR Hyrdoscience and Engring U Iowa 302 Hydraulics Laboratory Iowa City IA 52242-1585 Office Phone: 202-280-9897. Business E-Mail: v-c-patel@uiowa.edu.

PATERNO, JOE (JOSEPH VINCENT PATERNO), college football coach; b. Bklyn., Dec. 21, 1926; s. Angelo Lafayette and Florence (de LaSalle) P.; m. Suzanne Pohland, May 12, 1962; children: Diana Lynne, Mary Kathryn, David, Joseph Vincent, George Scott. BA, Brown U., Providence, 1950, LLD, 1975. Asst. football coach Pa. State U., 1950-66, head coach, 1966—. Co-author: (with Bernard Asbell): The Paterno Principle, 1989; Paterno: By the Book, 1991, (with Brice Durbin) Portrait of an Athlete, 1991, (with Bob Reade) Coaching Football Successfully, 1993, (with Mickey Bergstein) Penn State Sports Stories and More, 2000, (with L. Budd Thalman) Quotable Joe: Words of Wisdom by and About Joe Paterno, 2001 Served with AUS, 1945-46. Recipient Coach of Yr. award Am. Football Coaches Assn, 1968, 1978, 1982, 1986, 2005, Walter Camp Coach of Yr. award, Walter Camp Football Found., 1972, 1994, 2005, Paul "Bear" Bryant award, Nat. Sportscasters & Sportswriters Assn., 1978, 1982, 1986, Bobbie Dodd Coach of Yr. award, 1981, 2005, Amos Alonzo Stagg award, Am. Football Coaches Assn., 2002, The Home Depot Coach of Yr. award, 2005, Gold Medal, Nat. Football Fedn. awards, 2006; named Coach of Yr. Washington Touchdown Club, 1973, 1986; Sportsman of Yr., Sports Illus., 1986, Big Ten Coach of Yr. Sporting News, 2008; inducted into Coll. Football Hall of Fame, 2006. Mem. Am. Football Coaches Assn. Achievements include head coach of the NCAA National Championship winning Pennsylvania State University Nittany Lions, 1982, 1986. Office: Pa State U Lasch Football Bldg University Park PA 16802-7101*

PATERSON, BASIL ALEXANDER, lawyer; b. NYC, Apr. 27, 1926; s. Leonard J. and Evangeline (Rondon) P.; m. Portia Hairston, 1953; children: Daniel, David. BS, St. John's Coll., 1948; JD, St. John's U., 1951. Bar: N.Y. 1952. Ptnr. Paterson, Michael, Dinkins and Jones, NYC, 1956—77, Meyer, Suozzi, English & Klein, P.C., Garden City, NY, 1983—; mem. N.Y. State Senate, 1965-70; dep. mayor for labor rels. City of N.Y., 1978; sec. of state State of N.Y., 1979-82. Pres. Inst. Mediation and Conflict Resolution, 1971-77; chmn. 2d Jud. Screening Com., 1985-95; assoc. chmn. N.Y. State Sentencing Guidelines Com.; commr. Port Authority N.Y. and N.J., 1989-95; mem. commn. to promote confidence in judicial elections, 2003-. Bd. dirs. St. Benedict's Day Nursery, 1999—; vice chmn. Dem. Nat. Com., 1972-78, mem., 1972-78; chmn. Nat. Grid Found., 2003—. Recipient Eagleton Inst. Politics award, Disting. Svc. award Guardians Assn. N.Y. Police Dept., City Club N.Y. award, Black Expo award, Excellence medal St. John's U., Kibbe award CUNY, Citizens Union Civic leadership award, ABA, Lawyers & Problem Solve award. Roman Catholic. Office: Meyer Suozzi English Klein Pc PO Box 9194 Garden City NY 11530-9194

PATERSON, CRAIG, philosopher, researcher; b. Glasgow, Scotland, Dec. 20, 1965; arrived in US, 1997, permanent resident, 2008; s. James Allan and Evelyn Rita (Jackson) Paterson. BA in Social Sci., with honors, Glasgow Caledonian U., Scotland, 1987; MA, U. York, Eng., 1990; Dip.Lib. Librarianship with distinction, Robert Gordon U., Scotland, 1990; LLB with distinction, U. Edinburgh, Scotland, 1997; PhD in Ethics, St. Louis U., 2000. Faculty Providence Coll., 2000—03; cons. bioethicist BioEthicWorld, Topanga, Calif., 2004—. Librarian U. Coll. North Wales, Bangor, Wales, 1990—93; legal indexer, bibliographer Faculty of Advocates, Edinburgh, 1993—95; part time faculty St. Louis U., 1998—2000. Author: (book) Assisted Suicide and Euthanasia: A Natural Law Ethics Approach, Analytical Thomism: Traditions in Dialogue; contbr. articles to profl. jours. Mem. gen. coun. U. Edinburgh, 1997—; benefactor Saint Louis U., 2001—; supporter Soc. Authors, 2007—, Soldiers, Sailors, Airmen and Families Assn., 2008—, Zimbabwe a National Emergency, 2009—. Fellow: Royal Soc. Tropical Medicine and Hygiene, Royal Soc. Health, Royal Asiatic Soc. Great Britain and Ireland, Linnean Soc. London, Royal Anthrop. Inst. Great Britain and Ireland, Royal Soc. Medicine, Royal Soc. Arts, Royal Numismatic Soc.; mem.: NY Acad. Sci., Royal Inst. Great Britain, Royal Inst. Philosophy (assoc.), Am. Philosophical Assn. (assoc.), Am. Acad. Religion, UK Coll. Tchrs., Phi Sigma Tau, Alpha Epsilon Delta (hon.). Anglican. Avocations: history, coin collecting/numismatics, theater, travel, classical music. Business E-Mail: cpaterson65@aol.com.

PATERSON, DAVID ALEXANDER, Governor of New York, former state legislator; b. Bklyn., May 20, 1954; s. Basil and Portia (Hairston) P.; m. Michelle Paige, 1992; children: Ashley Dennis, Alexander Basil BA in History, Columbia U., NYC, 1977; JD, Hofstra U., 1983. Mediator Inst. Mediation and Conflict Resolution, NYC, 1975; legal asst. Mcpl. Credit Union, NYC, 1976-78; asst. grants officer Bronx CC, NY, 1981; dir. Housing Preservation Dept. Fair Housing Office, 1982; asst. criminal law Queens Dist. Atty.'s Office, NY, 1983-85; mem. NY State Senate from Dist. 30, 1985—2006, dep. minority leader, 1985—2002, minority leader, 2002—06; lt. gov. State of NY, Albany, 2007—08, gov., 2008—. Adj. prof. Columbia U. Sch. Internat. and Pub. Affaris; mem. adv. coun. Lower Manhattan Devel. Corp.; bd. dirs. Mil-Gar Home Care Service, NY. Contbr. articles to profl. jours. Fundraising chmn. George McGoverns Presdl. Campaign, NY, 1972, Herman Badillo's Mayoral Campaign, NY, 1973, Black Citizens for Fair Media, NY, 1976, Manhattan Borough Pres. David Dinkins, NY, 1985; mem. Martin Luther King Dem. Club, NY, 1977—, Jewish Guild for the Blind, NY, 1986; mem. bd. trustees Am. Found. for Blind; bd. dirs. Achilles Track Club; mem. fed. steering com. African Burial Ground. Recipient Cmty. Svc. award N.H. Hairston Clan, 1984, Achievement award Courtsman A.A., Inc., 1986, Spl. award Profl. Archaeologists NYC, 1993, Migel award Am. Found. for Blind, 1996; named Senator of Yr., NY State NOW, 1989; named to Power 150 Ebony mag., 2008. Mem. NAACP (bd. dirs. Mid-Manhattan br. 1981—), NY State Bar Assn. on Minorities, Macon B, Allen Black Bar Assn., Met. Com. of 100 (legal advisor 1979—). Democrat. Achievements include becoming the first non-white legislative leader in New York's history, 2002; being elected New York's first African-American and first legally blind lieutenant governor, 2006. Avocations: basketball, theater, baseball, history. Office: Office of Gov State Capitol Albany NY 12224

PATERSON, DAVID J., paper company executive; b. Washington, Aug. 15, 1954; BS, Cornell U., 1976; MBA, U. Mich., 1978. Mktg. analyst Continental Forest Industries, 1978—79, supr. fibre supply, 1979—80, shift foreman, 1980—82, mgr. quality control, 1982—83; sales mgr. containerboard S.W. Forest Industries, 1983—87; export sales mgr. containerboard Ga.-Pacific Corp., Atlanta, 1987—88, dir. export pulp sales, 1988—92, dir. pulp sales & mktg., 1992—94, v.p. sales & mktg. pulp & bleached bd., 1994—95, v.p. market pulp and recycling ops., 1995—96, v.p. market pulp, 1996—2000, v.p. electronic commerce, 2000, sr. v.p. comm. papers, 2000—01, pres. paper, 2001, pres. paper & bleached bd., 2001, exec. v.p. pulp & paperboard, 2001—03, exec. v.p., pres. bldg. products, 2003—06; pres., CEO Bowater Inc., Greenville, SC, 2006, chmn., pres., CEO, 2007; pres., CEO AbitibiBowater Inc., Montreal, Canada, 2007—. Bd. mem. Rsch. Atlanta, Inc.; mem. ISAC12 U.S. Dept. Commerce. Mem.: Japan-Am. Soc. Ga. Office: AbitibiBowater Inc 1155 Metcalfe St Montreal PQ H3B 5H2 Canada Office Phone: 864-271-7733. Office Fax: 864-282-9482.

PATERSON, ELEANOR COHEN, language educator, director; d. Philip and Anne Cohen; m. Anthony Ralph Paterson, Nov. 23, 1963; children: Robert Anthony, David Carl. BFA, Mass. Coll. Art, Boston, 1961; PhD, SUNY, Buffalo, 1989. Cert. art tchr. Mass. Bd. Edn., 1965, art and elem. edn. tchr. NYSED, 1985, in English lang. proficiency SUNY, 1987. Art tchr., cons. Boston Bd. Ed., 1961—68; art tchr./ cons. Pub. Schs., Boston, 1965—68; extensive tchr. State Coll. Bridgewater, 1965—; preparation program Studio Work Painting, 1968—81; substitute tchr. Buffalo, 1980—81, Buffalo Public Sch., 1981—89; dir. bilingual program Erie CC, 1989—2006, adj. asst. prof. ESL and Spanish, 1991—2007, dir. ESL student support ctr., 2006—. Project facilitator Hispanic Americans NEH, Buffalo, 1995—96; project dir., Perkins Multilingual Lab. Erie Cmty. Coll., 2005—07, project dir., advisor EOP, ESL summer inst., 2006—07, project dir., adult literacy grant. Exhibitions include African Violets, Albright Knox, 1987; contbr. articles to profl. jours. including SABE jour. (1990). Founding mem. Latino Br. Buffalo Host Lions Club, 2006—08; 2d v.p. Western NY Hispanics and Friends Civic Assn., Buffalo, 2003—07; sec. Hispanic Alliance, Buffalo, 2007—08; com. mem. Erie County Dem. Com., Buffalo; mem. City of Buffalo Bd. Ethics, 2002—08; corr. sec. Hispanic Women's League, Inc., Buffalo, 2006—08; exec. mem. Hispanics United of Buffalo, 2007—08. Recipient Pres. award, Erie CC, 1993, Dedicated Svc. award, Hispanic Women's League, Inc., 1997, Chancellor's award, NY State Edn. Dept., 1998; grantee Travel grant, Nat. Assn. Fgn. Student Advisors Internat. Educators, 1995; fellow Fed. Tchr. Tng. fellow, NYU, 1981—83, Rsch. Master Program in Bilingual Edn., SUNY, 1981—83, Fed. Doctoral Program, Rschr. Evaluation Billingual Edn., 1983—89, Rsch. in Bilingual Edn. fellow, NY State Edn. Dept., 1985—87. Mem.: Nat. Assn. Foreign Student Advisors, Nat. Assn. Bilingual Edn., NY Assn. Bilingual Edn. (corr.), Nr. East and West Side Task Force (chair edn. com. 2006—08). D-Liberal. Achievements include research in subjective and objective determinants of code-switching between Spanish and English in Puerto Rico. Avocations: painting, travel. Home: 530 Norwood Ave Buffalo NY 14222 Office: Erie CC 121 Ellicott St Buffalo NY 14203 Office Phone: 716-851-1049. Business E-Mail: patersonec@ecc.edu.

PATERSON, KATHERINE WOMELDORF, writer; b. Huaiyin, China, Oct. 31, 1932; came to U.S., 1940; d. George Raymond and Mary Elizabeth (Goetchius) Womeldorf; m. John Barstow Paterson, July 14, 1962; children: Elizabeth Polin, John Barstow, David Lord, Mary Katherine Nah-he-sah-pe-che-a. AB, King Coll., Bristol, Tenn., 1954; post grad., Kobe Sch. Japanese Lang., 1957-60; MA, Presbyn. Sch. Christian Edn., 1957; MRE, Union Theol. Sem., 1962; LittD. (hon.), King Coll., Bristol, Tenn., 1978; LHD (hon.), Otterbein Coll., 1979; LittD (hon.), St. Mary's of the Woods, 1981; LittD, Washington and Lee U., 1982; LittD (hon.), U. Md., 1982, Shenandoah Coll., 1982, LHD, Washington and Lee U, 1982; LHD (hon.), Norwich U., 1990, Mount St. Vincent U., Halifax, NS, Can., 1994; LittD, Hope Coll., 1997; DLitt (hon.), Prebyn. Coll., 2002. Tchr. Lovettsville Elem. Sch., Va., 1954-55; missionary Presbyn. Ch., Japan, 1957-61; master sacred studies and English Pennington Sch. for Boys, NJ, 1963-65. Author: The Sign of the Chrysanthemum, 1973, Of Nightingales That Weep, 1974, The Master Puppeteer, 1976, Bridge to Terabithia, 1977, The Great Gilly Hopkins, 1978, Angels and Other Strangers, 1979, Jacob Have I Loved, 1980,

Rebels of the Heavenly Kingdom, 1983, Come Sing, Jimmy Jo, 1985, (with John Paterson) Consider the Lilies, 1986, Park's Quest, 1988, The Tale of the Mandarin Ducks, 1990, The Smallest Cow in the World, 1991, Lyddie, 1991, The King's Equal, 1992, Who Am I?, 1992, Flip-Flop Girl, 1994, A Midnight Clear: Stories for the Christmas Season, 1995, A Sense of Wonder, 1995, The Angel and the Donkey, 1996, Jip: His Story, 1996, Marvin's Best Christmas Present Ever, 1997, (with John Paterson) Images of God, 1998, Parzival, 1998, Celia and the Sweet, Sweet Water, 1998, Preacher's Boy, 1999, The Wide-Awake Princess, 2000, The Field of the Dogs, 2001, Marvin One Too Many, 2001, The Invisible Child, 2002, The Same Stuff as Stars, 2002, (with John Paterson) Blueberries for the Queen, 2004, Bread & Roses, Too, 2006, The Light of the World, 2008; translator: The Crane Wife, 1981, The Tongue-Cut Sparrow, 1987. V.p. Nat. Children's Book and Literacy Alliance. US nominee for Hans Christian Andersen award, 1979, 89, 97, 98; recipient Nat. Book award, 1977, 79, Newbery medal, 1978, 91, Newbery honor, 1979, New Eng. Book award New Eng. Booksellers Assn., 1982, Union medal Union Theol. Sem., 1992, Scott O'Dell award for hist. fiction, 1997, May Hill Arbuthnot Lectr. award, 1997, Lion award NY Pub. Libr., 1998, Literary Light award Boston Pub. Libr., 2000, Living Legend award Libr. of Congress, 2000, Jefferson cup Va. Libr. Assn., 2000, Vt. Gov.'s award for excellence in arts, 2001, Astrid Lindgren Meml. award Swedish Govt., 2006, Christopher award, 2007, NHK Newstadt award, 2007. Mem. Authors Guild, Children's Book Guild Washington, Everybody Wins (James and Elizabeth Jeffords award, 2007). Democrat. Office: Clarion Books 215 Park Ave S New York NY 10003-1603

PATERSON, PAUL CHARLES, retired private investigator, security consultant; b. Bethlehem, Pa., Dec. 31, 1927; s. Thomas and Ida (Weiss) P.; m. Estelle Marie Nabors; children: Linda Ann, Thomas Scott, Terry Maurice Leard. Grad., Inst. Applied Sci., Chgo., 1950. Jr. credit analyst Bethlehem Steel Corp., Pa., 1947-50; inspector claim spec., claim dir., field supr. Equifax Svcs., Inc., Allentown, Pa., 1953-61, field claim supr. St. Louis, 1961-63, regional claims mgr. Phila., 1963-71, spl. claim sales, sales exec.-claims Atlanta, 1971-89; pvt. investigator, pres. Paterson Investigations, Inc., Douglasville, Ga., 1989-2001. Editor CFE newsletter The Ga. Examiner, 1994-95. With U.S. Army, 1950-53. Mem. VFW, Am. Legion, Life, Accident and Health Claims Assn. Phila. (life, pres. 1969-70), Mktg. Ins. Claims Assn. (life, v.p. 1985—, pres. 1989-90), So. Loss Assn., Nat. WWII Meml. Assn. (charter), Atlanta Claims Assn., Ga. Assn. Profl. Pvt. Investigators (chair ethics com. 1999, treas. 2000), Assn. Cert. Fraud Examiners (cert., past pres. Ga. chpt. 1990, 93, bd. dirs. 1991-92, faculty 1995-96, bd. regents 1996, Disting. Achievement award 1994, 95, Regent Emeritus, life mem.), Criminal Investigation Divsn. Agts. Assn. Inc., Ga. Sheriffs' Assn., Ga. Claims Assn., Ga. Fire Investigators Assn., Ret. Mil. Police Assn. (assoc.), Am. Legion, Chapel Hills Golf Club. Republican. Avocations: golf, music, swimming, physical conditioning. Home: 5235 Stilesboro Rd NW 215 Kennesaw GA 30152-3968 E-mail: paulpaterson@earthlink.net.

PATERSON, RICHARD DENIS, corporate financial executive; b. Ottawa, Ont., Can., Oct. 13, 1942; m. Antoinette Paterson; children: Christopher, Russell, Kathlyn, Victoria, Connor. B in Commerce, Concordia U., Montreal, Que., Can., 1964. Auditor Coopers & Lybrand, Montreal, 1964-67; acct. Genstar Corp., Montreal, 1967-69; dir. fin. and adminstrn. Indussa Corp. (subs. Genstar Corp.), NYC, 1969-73; v.p., comptroller Genstar Corp., Montreal and San Francisco, 1973-83, sr. v.p., CFO San Francisco, 1983-87; exec. v.p. Genstar Investment Corp., San Francisco, 1987-95; mng. dir. Genstar Capital LP, San Francisco, 1996—. Bd. dirs. Installs Inc., Am. Pacific Enterprises, Inc., Propex Fabrics, Inc., Woods Equipment Co. Mem. Order Chartered Accts. Que. Office: Genstar Capital LP Four Embarcadero Ctr Ste 1900 San Francisco CA 94111-4191 E-mail: rpaterson@gencap.com.

PATERSON, ROBERT E., retail executive; b. Kearny, NJ, 1926; s. Robert McKinley and Ethel Paterson; m. Eileen Josephine Connolly; children: Carol, Robert, Richard, Donald, Jeffrey, Joan. MBA, Columbia U., 1971. Sr. v.p. fin., treas. The Sperry & Hutchinson Co., Inc., NYC, 1952-87, also bd. dirs. Bd. dirs. Govt. Obligations Fund, 1986—87. Mem. Borough Coun., 1991—98, 2002—04, coun. pres., 1995—98, 2002. With US Army, 1944—45, PTO.

PATES, RICHARD EDMUND, bishop; b. St. Paul, Minn., Feb. 14, 1943; BA in Philosophy and Latin, St. Paul Sem., Minn., 1965; attended, North Am. Coll., Rome; lic. in Sacred Theology, Gregorian U., Rome. Ordained priest Archdiocese of St. Paul and Mpls., 1968; assoc. pastor Ch. Blessed Sacrament, St. Paul, 1967—70; vocation dir. Archdiocese of St. Paul and Mpls., 1970—74, sec. to archbishop Leo C. Byrne, 1973—75, vice chancellor, 1973—75, vicar for seminaries; sec. to apostolic del. Washington, 1975—81; rev. monsignor, 1979; rector St. John Vianney Sem., St. Paul, 1981—87; chaplain Serra Club of Midway, St. Paul, 1981—90; pastor Ch. St. Kevin, Mpls., 1990, Ch. Resurrection, Mpls., 1990, Ch. Our Lady of Peace, Mpls., 1991—98, Ch. St. Ambrose, Woodbury, 1998—2001; ordained bishop, 2001; aux. bishop Archdiocese of St. Paul and Mpls., 2001—08; bishop Diocese of Des Moines, Iowa, 2008—. Moderator Mpls. Deaneries Coun. Cath. Women, 1990—98. Roman Catholic. Office: Diocese of Des Moines 601 Grand Ave Des Moines IA 50309 Office Phone: 515-237-5039. Office Fax: 515-237-5071.

PATHAK, SANJEEV, psychiatrist, researcher; b. Shimla, Himachal Pradesh, India; MD, All India Inst. Med. Sci., 1993. Diplomate Am. Bd. of Psychiatry and Neurology. Resident in psychiatry U. Cin., 1996—99, fellowship in child and adolescent psychiatry, 1999—2001; asst. prof. psychiatry and neurology Cin. Children's Hosp., U. Cin. Coll. Medicine, Cin., 2001—. Contbr. articles to profl. jours. Achievements include research in pediatric mood disorders. Office: Cin Children's Hosp 3333 Burnet Ave D-3014 Cincinnati OH 45229 E-mail: sanjeev-pathak@cchmc.org.

PATHAK, SIDDHARTHA, materials scientist; s. Arup Kumar and Sangita Pathak. BTech, Nat. Inst. Tech., Warangal, India, 2003; PhD, Drexel U., Phila., 2003—. Postdoc. rschr. EMPA-Swiss Fed. Labrs. Materials Testing and Rsch., Thun, Switzerland, 2008—. Contbr. scientific papers to profl. jours. Recipient Dean award, Drexel U. Rsch. Day Poster Competition, 2004, Arthur E. Focke LeaderShape award, 2006; CINT User Proposal grant, Los Alamos Nat. Lab., 2007. Mem.: AAAS, Materials Rsch. Soc., Am. Soc. Bone and Mineral Rsch. (Young Investigator Travel grant 2007), Sigma Xi, Sci. Rsch. Soc. (Grants-in-Aid 2006). Home Fax: 215-895-6760. Personal E-mail: siddharthapathak@gmail.com. Business E-Mail: sp324@drexel.edu.

PATHAN, NUZHAT, medical researcher; b. Mumbai, Apr. 6, 1966; d. Ishaq and Mumtaz Pathan; m. Hitesh Brahmbhatt, Sept. 2, 1998; 1 child, Anika Brahmbhatt. PhD, Purdue U., Ind, 1996. Post-doc. rsch. fellow Burnham Inst., San Diego, 1997—2000; sr. scientist Biogen Idec Inc, San Diego, 2000—. Contbr. to research paper. Vol. Torrey Hills Sch., San Diego, 2006—08. Postdoc. Rsch. Fellowship, Leukemia and Lymphoma Soc., 1998—2000. Achievements include discovery of application of a novel monoclonal antibody for the treatment of chronic lymphocytic leukemia. Office: Biogen Idec 5200 Research Pl San Diego CA 92122 Business E-Mail: nuzhat.pathan@biogenidec.com.

PATHELA, PREETI, research scientist, educator; b. Queens, NY, Oct. 14; d. Jagdish Kumar and Kamal Pathela. DPH, Johns Hopkins Bloomberg Sch. Pub. Health, Balt., 2003. Epidemiologist Ga. Divsn. Pub. Health, Atlanta, 1996—98; rsch. scientist NYC Dept. Health and Mental Hygiene, NYC, 2003—; adj. instr. Mt. Sinai Sch. Medicine, NYC, 2005—. Contbr. articles to profl. jours.

PATIENCE, GREGORY SCOTT, chemical engineer, educator; b. Victoria, BC, Can., Aug. 19, 1961; s. Danny Alexander Patience and Margaret Puczko; m. Nadine Aboussouan; children: Paul Alexander, Christian Alexander, Nicolas Alexander, Brendan Alexander. BSc, U.Calgary, Alta., Canada, 1983; MSc, U. Calgary, Alta., Canada, 1987; PhD, Ecole Polytechnique de Montreal, Que., Can., 1990. Rsch. engr. DuPont Chems., Wilmington, Del., 1990—94; sr. engr. Lycra/Terathane DuPont, Gijon, Asturias, Spain, 1996—2000, rsch. assoc. apparel and textile scis. Meyrin, Geneva, Switzerland, 2000—04; prof. Agregé Ecole Polytech., Montreal, 2004—. Scholar, NSERC, Can. Govt., 1987—90, Alta./Can. Energy Resources Rsch. Fund, Govt. of Alta., 1983, Home Oil Co. Ltd., 1986, Ecole Polytechnique de Montreal, 1987—90, Bourse d'Etude Superieures Fonds, Govt. Que., 1987—90. Achievements include patents for new reactor type based on membrane technology and fluidization technology - Membrane Reactor; catalyst process; research in gas-solid hydrodynamic model; laminar entry length model for non-Newtonian fluids; laminar start-up time for fluids in pipes; design of fundamental principle related to scaling up a chemical process - scale-up factors; development of kinetic model to describe partial oxidation catalysis.

PATIERNO, ALYCIA LYNN, school psychologist; b. Youngstown, Ohio, May 16, 1971; d. Dominic Muto and Anna Marie Rockhold; m. Vito Patierno; children: Vito Anthony, Marco Joseph. EdM, Kent State U., Ohio, EdS, 1996; BS in Applied Sci. Psychology, MEd. Lic. psychologist NC Dept. Pub. Instrn. Psychologist Youngstown City Schs., 2000—08, Wake County Pub. Schs., Raleigh, NC, 2008—. Team capt. Am. Cancer Soc. Mem.: Ohio Sch. Psychologist Assn. Avocations: travel, running. Office: Wake County Pub Schs 307 S Main St Rolesville NC 27571 E-mail: apatierno@wcpss.net.

PATIL, NAVEEN, preventive medicine physician; b. Virajpet, Ark., India, Mar. 17, 1972; s. Venkatesh and Meera Patil; m. Sowmya Naveen Prakash, Jan. 10, 2002; 1 child, Khushi. MD, Jss Med. Coll., Mysore, India, 1996; MHSA, U. Ark., Little Rock, 2001, MA, 2005; MD in Internal Medicine, U. Ark. Med. Scis., Little rock, 2008, MD in Infectious Diseases, 2009. Med. officer Rmv Hosp., Bangalore, Karnataka, India, 1996—99; adminstrv. fellow Ark. Childrens Hosp., Little Rock, 2001—02. Mem.: AMA, ACP, Sigma Phi Omega, Alpha Epsilon Lambda, Phi Kappa Phi, Kaplan Med. Honors Soc., Nat. Scholars Honor Soc. Home: 12 Alton Ln Little Rock AR 72211 Office: Univ Ark Med Scis 4301 W Markham St Little Rock AR 72205 Personal E-mail: drnaveen72@hotmail.com. Business E-Mail: npatil@uams.edu.

PATIL, PARAG G., neurosurgeon, educator; s. Ganapati P. and Lalita G. Patil. MD, PhD, Johns Hopkins U. Asst. prof. U. Mich., Ann Arbor, 2005—. Office: Univ Mich 1500 E Medical Center Dr SPC 5338 Ann Arbor MI 48109-5338

PATIL, SHIVAPUTRA A., research scientist; s. Appanna S. and Sharavva A. Patil; m. Renukadevi Patil, June 11, 2003; children: Shrivatsa S., Shriteja S. PhD, Karnatak U. Dharwad, India, 1998. Postdoc. U. Tenn., Memphis, 2003—05, staff rsch. assoc., 2005—. Adj. faculty chemistry Memphis U., 2006—07. Mem.: Am. Chem. Soc. Achievements include research in design and synthesis of anti-cancer, anti-hiv and anti-hypertensive drugs. Home: 141 N Manassa Apt 3A Memphis TN 38105 Office: Univ Tenn 847 Monroe Ave Rm 327 Memphis TN 38163 Office Fax: 901-448-6828. Personal E-mail: shivaputrap@yahoo.com. Business E-Mail: spatil3@utmem.edu.

PATINKIN, TERRY ALLAN, physician; b. Oak Park, Ill., Feb. 1, 1950; s. Lester D. and Marcella Jaqueline (Steynburg) P.; m. Sandra Lee Friedman, Apr. 21, 1985; children: Jonathan, Zachary. BS, U. Ill., 1971; MD, U. Calif., San Francisco, 1975; MPH in Health Care Mgmt., Harvard U., 1996. Diplomate Am. Bd. Emergency Medicine, Am. Bd. Family Medicine; cert. physician exec. Intern, resident in family practice U. Calif. San Francisco/Natividad Med. Ctr., Salinas, Calif., 1975-78, assoc. dir. family medicine residency program, 1978-90; dir. emergency dept. Natividad Med. Ctr., Salinas, 1985-91, dir. continuing med. edn., 1978-91, dir. undergrad. edn., 1978-90, emergency physician, 1979-91, Sturdy Meml. Hosp., Attleboro, Mass., 1991-94; dir., chmn. emergency dept. Roger Williams Hosp., Providence, 1994-99, Landmark Med. Ctr., Woonsocket, RI, 2000—02; med. dir. urgent care East Boston Neighborhood Health Ctr., 2002—. Asst. clin. prof. U. Calif., San Francisco, 1981-88, assoc. clin. prof., 1988-91; clin. asst. prof. Stanford U., 1990-93; asst. clin. prof. Brown U., Providence, 1995—, Boston U., 1999—. Fellow Am. Coll. Emergency Physicians; mem. Am. Coll. Physician Execs., Mass. Coll. Emergency Physicians, Mass. Med. Soc., U. Ill. Alumni Assn. (life), U. Calif. San Francisco Alumni Faculty Assn. Office: 10 Gove St East Boston MA 02128 Home Phone: 617-332-3752; Office Phone: 617-568-4639. Business E-Mail: patinkit@ebnhc.org.

PATINO, DOUGLAS XAVIER, academic foundation and government agency administrator; b. Calexico, Calif., Apr. 11, 1939; s. Jose Luis and Maria Teresa (Seymour) P.; m. Barbel Wilma Hoyer, Aug. 13, 1970; 1 child, Viktor Xavier. AA, Imperial Valley Coll., 1960; BA, Calif. State U., San Diego, 1962, MA, 1966; PhD, U.S. Internat. U., 1972. Deputy dir. Sacramento Concilio, Inc., Calif., 1968-69; v.p. student affairs U. So. Colo., Pueblo, 1973-75; dep. dir. for planning and rev. svc. br. to dir. Calif. Employment Devel. Dept., dir.; sec. Calif. Health & Welfare Agy., 1975-83; dir. Ariz. Dept. of Econ. Security, Phoenix, 1983-87; pres., chief exec. officer Marin Community Found., Larkspur, Calif., 1987-91; vice chancellor Calif. State U. Sys., Long Beach, 1993—2002; prof. social welfare Calif. State U., LA, 1998—2004. Commr. W.T. Grand Found., 1986—88, Enterprize for the Ams., Washington, 1994—; trustee C.S. Mott Found., Flint, Mich., 1995—, Calif. Wellness Found., Woodland Hills, 1997—; chmn., treas. Hispanics in Philanthropy, 1993—2002. Mem. Sec. of U.S. Dept. of Labor Task Force, Ariz., 1985-86, Staff Adv. Com. of the Human Resource Com., Nat. Gov. Assn., Washington, 1983-86; bd. dirs. Calif. Leadershp, Santa Cruz, Calif., 1985-95, No. Calif. Grantmakers, 1990-91, Ariz. Assn. Bus., 1984; chair U.S. Savs. Bond Dr. for State of Calif., 1982; trustee Nat. Hispanic U., Oakland, Calif., 1987-90, Hispanic Community Fund, San Francisco, 1989-95, bd. dirs. Calif. Sch. Profl. Psychology, 1989-94, Coun. on Found., Washington, 1990-96, Found. Ctr., N.Y., 1993; pres. Calif. State U. Found. Recipient Monty Disting. Alumni award San Diego State U., 1997, Simon Bolivar award Hispanic Cmty. Found. and Bay Area United Way, 1996, Azteca award Human Devel. Corp., 1991, Leadership award Nat. Concilors Am. and United Way of Bay Area, 1990, Disting. Performance award Nat. Alliance of Bus., Washington, 1985, Superior Svc. Mgmt. award Am. Soc. Pub. Adminstrn., 1985, Humanitarian award Los Padrinos, Inc., 1981, Small and Minority Bus. award for the State of Calif. 1982, Disting. Alumni award Calif. Jr. CC Assn., Sacramento, 1982, Silver Spur award Nat. Fedn. Charros in Guadalajaro, Jalisco, Mex., 1974, Calif. Cmty. Svc. award Former Gov. Ronald Reagan, Sacramento, 1973; named to 100 Most Influential Hispanics, Hispanic Bus., 1995, 1997, 1999; named one of 100 Most Influential Latinos, Latino Leaders Mag., 2005-07. Mem. Am. Pub. Welfare Assn. (bd. dirs., Leadership award 1987), Assn. Black Found. Execs. (dir. 2003-07), Rotary, 1987-93.

PATINO-BRANDFON, SYLVIA, retired psychologist; d. Alfonso and Zenobia Moeller Patino; children: Andrea, Thea. AB in English, U. N.Mex., 1956; MS in English, Wis. U., 1958; student, Tavistock Inst., London, 1970—71; MA in Child Study, Tufts U., 1975; PhD in Psychology, Boston Coll., 1980; student in Psychopharmacology, Internat. Coll. Prescribing Psychologists, 1995—97. Lic. psychologist Mass., 1981. Intern psychotherapy Judge Baker Guidance Ctr., Boston, 1972—74; intern McLean Hosp., Belmont, Mass., 1979—80, post doctoral fellow, 1980—81; pvt. practice Quincy and Taunton, Mass., 1982—99; ret., 1999. Spkr. in field. Author: (newsletter) ADHD and Other Behavior Problems, 1994—98. Mem. com. superior cts. Ariz. Supreme Ct., 2004—, mem. jud. performance rev. commn., 2004—, bd. overseeing reporters, 2004; mem. Ariz. Commn. Jud. Conduct, 2007—. Fellow: APA (life).

PATINO-GOMEZ, CARLOS, hydrologist; s. Carlos Patino and Aurea Gomez; m. Silvia Santiago-Cordero, May 10, 1997; 1 child, Carlos Emmanuel Patino-Santiago. PhD, U. Tex., Austin, 2008. Rschr. Mexican Inst. Water Tech., Jiutepec, Morelos, 1994—2001, cons., 2002—07, dep. coord., 2008—; rsch. asst. U. Tex., 2002—08. Cons. Internat. Boundary & Water Commn., El Paso, Tex., 2003—06, US Geol. Survey, Austin, 2005—06, Inst. de Investigaciones Científicas Avanzadas y Svcs. de Alta Tech. de Panama, Ciudad del Saber, 2006—07, Assn. Nat. de Alcantarillados, San Salvador, El Salvador, 2007—08. Contbr. articles to profl. jours. Mem.: U. Coun. Water Resources, Mexican Hydraulic Assn. Office: Mexican Inst Water Tech Paseo Cuauhnahuac 8532 Jiutepec Morelos 62550 Mexico Business E-Mail: carlos_patino@tlaloc.imta.mx.

PATMON, WILLIAM WESLEY, III, lawyer; b. Lincoln Park, Mich., Jan. 11, 1965; s. William Wesley Patmon II and Joyce Jordan; m. Teela Patmon, Jan. 30, 1985; children: William IV, Alexandria, Daniel, Kayla. BA, U. Mich., Ann Arbor, 1989; JD, Ohio State U., Columbus, 1993. Bar: Ohio 1993, U.S. Ct. Appeals (6th cir.) 1994, U.S. Dist. Ct. (no. and so. dists.) Ohio 1994, U.S. Supreme Ct. 2004, US Supreme Ct. 2005. Jud. law clk. US Dist. Judge James Graham, Columbus, 1994—96; pvt. practice Columbus. Del. Sixth Cir., 2002. Deacon First Ch. God, Columbus, 2004—. Recipient, Leadership Columbus award, 1999, Bus. First 40 Under Forty award. Mem.: Million Dollar Adv. Forum. Avocations: golf, reading. Office: 4100 Regent St Ste U Columbus OH 43219-6190 Office Fax: 614-470-9930; Home Fax: 614-470-9930. Business E-Mail: wpatmon@patmonlaw.com.

PATMORE, KIMBERLY S., financial services executive; BBA, U. Toledo. CPA Colo. With Ernst & Young, 1981—92; named contr. First Data Corp., Greenwood Village, Colo., 1992, exec. v.p., CFO, 2000—08. Mem. Colo. Econ. Futures Panel. Recipient CFO Excellence Award, CFO Mag., 2000, "Best Workplaces" Award, 2001, Woman of Distinction Award, Girl Scouts, 2001, Outstanding Woman in Bus. Award, Denver Bus. Jour., 2005. Mem.: AICPA, Colo. Soc. CPAs.

PATNAIK, ANIL KUMAR, engineering educator, researcher; s. Balagangadhar and Lakshmi B. Patnaik; m. Asha Lata Ashalata Rajamohanty, May 13, 1993; children: Shyam, Sachin. BSc in Engring., Regional Engring. Coll., Rourkela, India, 1983; MTech in Structures, Indian Inst. Tech., Kanpur, 1988; PhD in Structures, U. Calgary, Can., 1993. Engr. Engrs. India Ltd., New Delhi, 1983—87, sr. structural engr., 1989—89; tchg. and rsch. asst. Indian Inst. Tech., Kanpur, 1987—88, U. Calgary, 1989—93; sr. structural engr. Worley Ltd., Perth, Western Australia, Australia, 1993—95; lectr./asst. prof. Curtin U. Tech., Perth, 1996—2000; sr. structural engr. Clough Engring. (Offshore Divsn.), Perth, 2000—01; asst. prof. S.D. Sch. Mines and Tech., Rapid City, 2001—. Contbr. articles to profl. jours. Recipient Best Student Paper award, Can. Soc. for Civil Engring., 1991, Martin P. Korn award, Precast/Prestressed Concrete Inst., Chgo., 1994; Titular fellow, Assn. Commonwealth Univs., London, 1999. Mem.: Coll. Structural Engrs. Australia, Nat. Profl. Engrs. Register Australia (registered profl. engr. 1997), Can. Soc. for Civil Engring., Instn. Engrs. Australia (registered profl. engr. 1997), Am. Concrete Inst. Office: SD Sch Mines and Tech 501E Saint Joseph St Rapid City SD 57701-3995 E-mail: anil.patnaik@sdsmt.edu.

PATNAUDE, WILLIAM EUGENE, architect; b. Sanger, Calif., Sept. 24, 1937; s. Eugene Joseph Patnaude and Vera Mae (Giles) Patnaude Fagan; m. Mary Esther Simerly, Aug. 22, 1971 (div. 1987); children: Nathaniel, Matthew BArch, U. Calif., Berkeley, 1961; postgrad., Calif. State U., Fresno, 1968-72. Registered arch., Calif., Wash., Idaho, Nev., Colo., Utah, Ariz., Mont., Nebr. Draftsman, arch. Robert Stevens Assoc., Santa Cruz, Calif., 1963-66; arch. Llewelyn Davies, Weeks & Ptnrs., London, 1966, Allen Y. Lew, Fresno, Calif., 1967-69, assoc., 1969-74; v.p., arch. Lew & Patnaude, Inc., Fresno, Calif., 1978-84, pres., 1985—. Instr. Calif. State U., Fresno, 1968-81 Constn. arbitrator Am. Arbitration Assn., 1976-96; chair ctrl. area plan citizen's adv. com. City of Fresno, 1991-93, chair gen. plan update com., 1994-97; bd. dirs. Fresno Arts Ctr., 1971-74, Fresno County Alliance for the Arts, 1986-88, 91-94. With USNR, 1961-63. Recipient Merit award Calif. Hist. Preservation Conf., Orange County, 1983, Excellence award Woodwork Inst. Calif., 1982, Recognition cert. City Fresno, 2004, Calif. State Assembly commendation City Fresno, 2004. Fellow AIA (nat. dir. 1983-85, pres. Calif. Coun. 1982, San Joaquin chpt. 1978, Awards of Excellence, 1972-95); mem. Constrn. Specifications Inst. (pres. Fresno chpt. 1977). Democrat. Avocations: photography, fine wines. Home: 4190 N Van Ness Blvd Fresno CA 93704-4213 Office: Lew & Patnaude Inc 1050 S St Fresno CA 93721-1497 Personal E-mail: wp@lewpatnaude.com. Business E-Mail: billp@csufresno.edu.

PATON WALSH, JILL, writer; b. London, Apr. 29, 1937; d. John Llewelyn and Patricia (Dubern) Buss; m. Antony Edmund Paton Walsh, Aug. 5, 1961; Children: Edmund, Margaret, Clare. Author: Hengest's Tale, 1966, The Dolphin Crossing, 1967, Fireweed, 1969, (World Book Festival award 1970), Wordhoard, 1969, Goldengrove 1972, Farewell Great King, 1972, Toolmaker, 1973, The Dawnstone, 1973, The Emperor's Winding Sheet, 1974 (Whitbread prize 1974), The Huffler, 1975, The Island Sunrise: Preshistoric Culture in the British Isles, 1975, Unleaving, 1976 (Boston Globe, Horn Book award 1976), Children of the Fox: Crossing to Salamis, 1977, The Walls of Athens, 1978, Persian Gold, 1978, A Chance Child, 1978, The Green Book, 1981, Babylon, 1982, Parcell of Patterns, 1983 (Universe prize 1984), Lost and Found, 1984, Gaffer Samson's Luck, 1984 (Smarties Grand prix 1984), Lapsing,

1985, A School for Lovers, 1989, Birdy and the Ghosties, 1990, "Grace", 1991, Matthew and the Sea Singers, 1992, When Grandma Came, 1992, The Wydham Case, 1993, Knowledge of Angels, 1994, A Piece of Justice, 1995, Connie Came to Play, 1995, Thomas and the Tinners, 1995, The Serpentine Cave, 1997, When I Was Little Like You, 1997, (with Dorothy L. Sayers) Thrones, Dominations, 1998, A Desert in Bohemia, 2000, (with Dorothy L. Sayers) A Presumption of Death, 2002, Debts of Dishonor, 2006, The Bad Quarto, 2007. Fellow Royal Soc. of Lit. (CBE award 1996). Address: care David Higham Assocs 5-8 Lower John St Golden Sq London W1R 3PE England

PATRA, AMLAN KUMAR, animal scientist, educator; b. Dewanchak, West Bengal, India, June 13, 1975; s. Badal Chandra and Soudamini Patra; m. Jyotisna Saxena, Feb. 15, 2008. BS in Vet. Sci. and Animal Husbandry, West Bengal U. Animal and Fishery. Scis., Kolkata, West Bengal, 1999; MS in Animal Nutrition, Indian Vet. Rsch. Inst. Izatnagar, UP, 2001, PhD in Animal Nutrition, 2004. Vis. rsch. fellow Am. Goat Rsch. Inst., Langston, Okla., 2004—06; sr. rsch. fellow Indian Vet. Rsch. Inst. Izatnagar, 2006—07; lectr. West Bengal U. Animal and Fishery Scis., 2007—. Contbr. articles to profl. jours. Recipient Dr. Gouri Ganguly Meml. award, Indian Sci. Congress Assn., 2009; Nat. Merit scholarship, Govt. India, 1994—99, Jr. Rsch. fellowship, Indian Coun. Agrl. Rsch., 1999—2001, Sr. fellowship, Inidan Vet. Rsch. Inst., 2001—, Travel grant, Ministry of Agr. Govt. New Zealand, 2007, Internat. Travel grant, Dept. Sci. and Tech. Govt. India, 2008. Mem.: Animal Nutrition Soc. India, Indian Sci. Congress, Animal Nutrition Assn. India. Office: WB Univ Animal & Fishery Scis 37 K B Sarani Kolkata West Bengal 700037 India Personal E-mail: patra_amlan@yahoo.com.

PATRA, PRIYADARSAN, architectural engineer; s. Harihar and Padma Patra; m. Anu Patra; children: Ashutosh, Adarsh. BE, Indian Inst. Sci., Bangalore; MS, U. Mass., Amherst; PhD, U. Tex. Austin, 2005. Sr. validation arch. Digital Enterprise Group, Hillsboro, Oreg., 2008—; intel rsch. scientist Microprocessor Tech. Labs; sr. mem., rsch. staff Strategic CAD Labs; chair, bd. directors Sustainable Econ. & Ednl. Devel. Soc. Contbr. scientific papers to numerous scholarly papers. Sec. The Orissa Soc. Americas, Wash.; dir. Mahakali Spiritual Soc.; founder Sustainable Econ. & Ednl. Devel. Soc.; vice chair IEEE. Recipient Trail Blazer award, Intel, Intel Quality award, Divisional Recognition award, Design & Test Tech., Intel; named one of Disting. Young Leader of the Yr., Orissa Soc. Americas. Mem.: IEEE. Achievements include design of High-end, flagship processors at Intel & rapid SIngle Flux Quantum circuits with SUNY collaboration; patents pending for validation technology; invention of delay-insensitive quantum circuits & generalized posynomial optimization methods; Established and lead organizations for grassroots and sustainable development; Taught, as a volunteer coach and speaker, at middle-school to University levels. Avocation: travel.

PATRE, PARAG, research scientist; PhD student, U. Fla., Gainesville, 2005—. Grad. engr. trainee, devel. engr. Larsen & Toubro Ltd., Mumbai, 2004—05; rsch. assoc. U. Fla., 2005—. Recipient Indian Nat. Physics Olympiad Gold Medallist, 2000, Cert. Merit, Maharashtra State Edn. Bd., 2000, Internat. Student Academic award, U. Fla., 2008. Mem.: IEEE. Achievements include research in the area of nonlinear robust adaptive control and robotics. Avocations: travel, reading, music, art. Office: Univ Fla Dept MAE MAE-A 319 Gainesville FL 32611

PATRIC, JASON, actor; b. June 17, 1966; s. Jason and Linda Gleason Miller. Actor: (films) include The Lost Boys, 1987, The Beast, 1988, After Dark, My Sweet, 1990, Denial Loon, 1991, Rush, 1991, Geronimo-An American Legend, 1993, The Journey of August King, 1995, Sleepers, 1996, Incognito, 1997, Speed 2, 1997, Friends and Neighbors, 1998, 3 Days of Rain, 2000, Narc, 2002, The Alamo, 2004, Downloading Nancy, 2008;(TV movies) Toughlove, 1985. Office: United Talent Agy care David Schiff 9560 Wilshire Blvd Ste 500 Beverly Hills CA 90212-2427*

PATRICIA, MATHES-BURNETT G., education educator; b. Dallas, Sept. 27, 1961; d. Donald Hoover and Patricia Golden Mathes; m. John Ward Burnett; children: Ashley Hilton Burnett, John Anthony Burnett, Julianna Nicole Burnett. EdB, Baylor U., Waco, Tex., 1984; MEd, U. Houston, Tex., 1987; PhD, Vanderbilt U., Nashville, 1992. Cert. tchr. Bd. Edn., Tex., 1984. Tchr. Katy Ind. Sch. Dist., Tex., 1984—89; rsch. asst. prof. Peabody Coll. Vanderbilt U., 1992—95; asst. prof. spl. edn. Fla. State U., Tallahassee, 1995—99; tex. instruments chair reading So. Meth. U., Dallas, 2003—, prof. tchg. and learning, 2003. Dir. SMU Inst. Reading Rsch., Dallas, 2003—. Contbr. articles to profl. jours. Bd. mem. Nat. Inst. Literacy (George W. Bush), 2006. Recipient Palmer O. Johnson Meml. award, Am. Ednl. Rsch. Assn., 1997, Samuel A. Kirk award, Coun. Exceptional Children, 1999, Disting. Early Rschr. Career award, 2001, Albert J. Harris award, Internat. Reading Assn., 2006; grantee grant, Inst. Ednl. Scis., 2004—; Predoc. fellowship, Nat. Inst. Child Health and Human Devel., 1988—93, Interpretive scholarship, Am. Ednl. Rsch. Assn., 2002, English Lang. Learning and Literacy Acquisition grant, Inst. Ednl. Scis., 2004—, Maximizing Literacy Learning grant, 2005—, Continuous Monitoring Early Reading Skills grant, Today Found., 2007—. Achievements include research in proven treatment to prevent dyslexia in young children. Office: Southern Methodist Univ PO Box 750381 Dallas TX 75275-0381 Office Fax: 214-768-8700. Personal E-mail: patriciaburnett@tx.rr.com. Business E-Mail: pmathes@smu.edu.

PATRICIA, PITRE AGNES, media specialist; b. Galliano, La., Jan. 12, 1960; d. James Anthony and Marie Lefort Pitre. BA in Secondary Social Studies Edn., Nicholls State U., Thibodaux, La., 1991, MEd in Curriculum and Instrn., 1994; degree, U. New Orleans, New Orleans, 1998. Elem. tchr. Galliano Elem., La., 1991—92; jr. high tchr. Larose Cut Off Jr. HS, La., 1992—97; HS media specialist South Lafourche HS, Galliano, 1998—2000, Hahnville HS, Boutte, La., 2000—. Mem.: LLA, Phi Delta Kappan. Office: 200 Tiger Dr Boutte LA 70039 Personal E-mail: ppitre@mobiletel.com. Business E-Mail: ppitre@stcharles.k12.la.us.

PATRICK, CHARLES WILLIAM, JR., lawyer; b. Monroe, NC, Oct. 9, 1954; s. Charles William and Louise (Nisbet) P.; m. Celeste Hunt, June 5, 1976; children: Laura Elizabeth, Charles William III. BA magna cum laude, Furman U., 1976; JD, U. SC, 1979. Bar: S.C. 1979, U.S. Dist. Ct. S.C. 1981, U.S. Ct. Appeals (11th cir.) 1981, U.S. Ct. Appeals (10th cir.) 1983, U.S. Ct. Appeals (4th cir.) 1986. Law clk. to presiding judge 9th Cir. Ct. State of S.C., Charleston, 1979—80; assoc. Ness, Motley, Loadholt, Richardson and Poole and predecessor firm Blatt and Fales, Charleston, 1980—2002, 1980—84; ptnr. Ness, Motley, Loadholt, Richardson & Poole & Predecessor firm Blatt & Fales, Charleston, 1984—2009, Richardson, Patrick, Westbrook & Brickman, LLC, Charleston, 2002—. Exec. editor S.C. Law Review, 1978; contbr. articles to profl. jours. Mem. ABA, Assn. Trial Lawyers Am., S.C. Assn. Trial Lawyers, Trial Lawyers for Pub. Justice, Phi Beta Kappa. Democrat. Presbyterian. Avocations: boating, skiing, jogging. Home: 38 Church St Charleston SC 29401-2742 Office: Richardson Patrick Westbrook & Brickman LLC PO Box 879 174 East Bay St Charleston SC 29402-0879 Home Phone: 843-853-8601; Office Phone: 843-727-6500. Business E-Mail: cpatrick@rpwb.com.

PATRICK, CONNIE L., federal agency administrator; m. John Patrick; 4 children. BA in Criminal Justice, U. Ctrl. Fla.; Grad., FBI Nat. Acad., Fla. Criminal Justice Exec. Inst., Fed. Exec. Inst. Dep. Sheriff's Office Brevard County, 1976—81; various positions including spl. agent, spl. agent supr., asst. spl. agent in charge of Tampa reg. ops. bur., dir. Fla. Criminal Justice Inst. Fla. Dept. Law Enforcement, 1981—95, dir. divsn. human resources & training, 1995—96; dir. gen. training Fed. Law Enforcement Training Ctr., 1996—98, assoc. dir. planning & resources, 1998—2001, assoc. dir. planning & workforce devel., 2001—02, dir., 2002—. Recipient Presdl. Meritorious Rank award, 2001. Office: Fed Law Enforcement Training Ctr 1131 Chapel Crossing Rd Brunswick GA 31524*

PATRICK, DAN, sportscaster; b. May 15, 1957; married; 2 children. BA in Broadcasting, U. Dayton, 1979. Morning sports and news reporter WTUE Radio, Dayton, Ohio, 1979-81; weekend sports anchor, reporter WDTN-TV, Dayton, Ohio, 1981-83, CNN, 1983-89; sports dir. WKLS, Atlanta, 1987-91; anchor, reporter SportsCenter ESPN, Bristol, Conn., 1989—2007; reporter weekday sports KSEG, Sacramento, 1991, Laser 103, Milw., 1989-91, WLVQ-AM, Columbus, 1989-91; host The Dan Patrick Show (ESPN Radio), 1999—2007, The Dan Patrick Show (syndicated), 2007—; sr. writer Sports Illus., 2007—; co-host NBC Sports, Football Night in America, 2008—. Guest host ABC Good Morning America, 1996. Author: Outtakes, 2000; actor: The Definite Maybe, 1997, Arli$$, 1998, BASEketball, 1998, The Waterboy, 1998, Clerks, 2000, Clone High, 2002, The Longest Yard, 2005, Benchwarmers, 2006, I Now Pronounce You Larry and Chuck, 2007. Recipient CableACE award, 1997, Disting. Alumni award, U. Dayton, 1997, Sports Emmy award for studio host, 1998; named Nat. Sportscaster of Yr., Nat. Sportscasters and Sportswriters Assn., 2000. Office: c/o The Content Factory 875 N Michigan Ave Ste 3522 Chicago IL 60611 also: c/o Sports Illus Time & Life Bldg New York NY 10020-4049 Office Phone: 312-751-8638. Office Fax: 312-951-1373.

PATRICK, DANICA SUE, race car driver; b. Beloit, Wis., Mar. 25, 1982; d. T.J. and Bev Patrick; m. Paul Edward Hospenthal, Nov. 19, 2005. Race car driver Indy Racing League Rahal Letterman Racing, 2005—06, Andretti Green Racing, 2007—. 4th pl. Indy Japan 300 Twin Ring Motegi, 2005, 1st pl. Indy Japan 300, 08; 4th pl. Indpls. 500 Indpls. Motor Speedway, 2005; 4th pl. Firestone Indy 200 Nashville Superspeedway, 2006, 3rd pl. Firestone Indy 200, 07; 4th pl. ABC Supply Co. A.J. Foyt 225 Milw. Mile, 2006; 3rd pl. Bombardier Learjet 550 Tex. Motor Speedway, 2007; 2nd pl. Detroit Indy Grand Prix Raceway on Belle Isle, 2007. Co-author (with Laura Morton): Danica: Crossing the Line, 2006. Named Rookie of Yr., Indy 500, 2005, Indy Racing League, 2005; named one of Most Influential People in the World of Sports, Bus. Week, 2008. Roman Catholic. Achievements include being the first female driver to win pole position at the Toyota Atlantic, Portland, 2004; being the fourth woman ever to qualify for the Indianapolis 500, 2005; becoming the first female driver in the Indy Racing League's history to place first, 2008. Mailing: c/o Andretti Green Racing 7615 Zionsville Rd Indianapolis IN 46268

PATRICK, DEVAL LAURDINE, Governor of Massachusetts, lawyer; b. Chgo., July 31, 1956; s. Laurdine Kenneth and Emily Mae (Wintersmith) Patrick; m. Diane Louise Bemus, May 5, 1984; children: Sarah Baker, Katherine Wintersmith. AB cum laude, Harvard Coll., 1978, JD, 1982; JD (hon.), DC Law Sch., 1994, Morris Brown Coll., 1996, Curry Coll., 1997, Clark U., 1999, New Eng. Sch. Law, 1999, Suffolk U., 2000, Northeastern U., 2002; LLD (hon.), Tufts U., 2009. Bar: Calif. 1983, DC 1985, Mass. 1987, US Dist. Ct. Mass. 1987, US Dist. Ct. (ctrl. dist.) Calif. 1983, US Ct. Appeals (1st and 5th cirs.) 1984, US Ct. Appeals (9th and 11th cirs.) 1984, US Supreme Ct. 1988. Law clk. to Hon. Stephen Reinhardt US Ct. Appeals (9th cir.), LA, 1982-83; asst. counsel NAACP Legal Def. Fund, NYC, 1983-86; assoc. Hill & Barlow, Boston, 1986—90; ptnr. Hill & Barlow LLP, Boston, 1990—94; asst. atty. gen. civil rights divsn. US Dept. Justice, Washington, 1994-97; ptnr. Day, Berry & Howard LLP, Boston, 1997-99; v.p., gen. counsel Texaco Inc., White Plains, NY, 1999-2001; exec. v.p., gen. counsel, mem. exec. com. The Coca-Cola Co., Atlanta, 2001—04, corp. sec., 2002—04; gov. Commonwealth of Mass., Boston, 2007—. Herman Phleger disting. vis. prof. Stanford Law Sch., 1997; lectr. Boston Coll. Sch. Law, 1997, Harvard Law Sch., 1998; mem. various corp. bd. dirs.; bd. overseers Harvard U., 1998-2003; dir. UAL Corp., 1997-2001, Reebok Internat. Ltd., 2001-05, Coca-Cola Enterprises Inc., 2001-04, ACC Capital Holdings (Ameriquest), 2004-06 Dir., mem. exec. com., chmn. New Eng. steering com. NAACP Legal Def. and Edn. Fund., Inc., 1991-94, vice chmn. Mass. Jud. Nominating Coun., 1991-93; trustee, mem. exec. com. Milton Acad., 1985-97; overseer WGBH, 1993-94; trustee Nathan Cummings Found., 1998-2000, Ford Found., 2000-05 Recipient George Leisure award Harvard Law Sch., 1981; Rockefeller Traveling fellow, 1978; named to Power 150 Ebony mag., 2008. Mem. ABA (numerous bds. and coms.), Mass. Bar Assn., Mass. Black Lawyers Assn., Boston Bar Assn. (coun. mem. 1993), Harvard Alumni Assn. (dir. 1993-96). Democrat. Avocations: squash, cooking, gardening. Office: Deval Patrick Committee 55 Court St Ste 310 Boston MA 02108-2104

PATRICK, DICK (RICHARD M. PATRICK), professional sports team executive; b. Victoria, BC, Can., Oct. 20, 1946; married; 3 children. BA, Dartmouth Coll.; JD, Am. U. Joined Washington Capitals, 1982, exec. v.p., pres, gov., 1992—; ptnr. Lincoln Holdings LLC, 1999—. Office: Washington Capitals MCI Center 601 F St NW Washington DC 20004-1605

PATRICK, H. HUNTER, retired judge, lawyer; b. Gasville, Ark., Aug. 19, 1939; s. H. Hunter Sr. and Nelle Frances (Robinson) P.; m. Charlotte Anne Wilson, July 9, 1966; children: Michael Hunter, Colleen Annette. BA, U. Wyo., 1961, JD, 1966. Bar: Wyo. 1966, U.S. Dist. Ct. Wyo. 1966, Colo. 1967, U.S. Supreme Ct. 1975. Mcpl. judge City of Powell, 1967-68; sole practice law Powell, 1966-88; atty. City of Powell, 1969-88; justice of the peace County of Park, Wyo., 1971-88; bus. law instr. Northwest C.C., Powell, 1968-98; dist. judge State of Wyo. 5th Jud. Dist., 1988—2006; drug ct. judge Park County, Wyo., 2001—06; ret, 2006; sole practice law Powell, 2006—. Mem. Wyo. Dist. Judges Conf., sec.-treas., 1993-94, vice chair, 1994-95, chair, 1995-96. Editor: Bench Book for Judges of Courts of Limited Jurisdiction in the State of Wyoming, 1980-90; author: (nonfiction essay) Visualize-Verbalize, 2007, 2008. Dir. cts. Wyo. Girls State, Powell, 1982—85, 1989—99, 2005—; mem. Wyo. Commn. Jud. Conduct and Ethics, 1997—2003; judge, chair mgmt. com. Park County Drug Ct., 2001—06; adv. bd. NW Coll. Nursing Program, 2007—08; elder, deacon, moderator of deacons Powell Presbyn. Ch., 1997; bd. dirs. Heart Mountain Vol. Med. Clinic, 2007—09. Recipient Wyo. Crime Victim Compensation Commn. Judicial award, 1995, Wyo. Criminal Justice Assn. Svc. award, 2005. Fellow Am. Bar Found. (life), Wyo. Jud. Adv. Coun.; mem. ABA (Wyo. state del. to ho. of dels. 1994-2001, Wyo. del. jud. adminstrn. divsn., exec. com. nat. conf. trial ct. judges representing Wyo., Colo., Kans., Nebr., N.Mex. 1996-2000, bd. govs. 2001-04, Pub. Svc. award for ct.-sponsored Law Day programs 1990, 92, standing com. judges adv. com. on ethics in profession 2004-07), Wyo. Bar Assn. (Cmty. Svc. award 1999, Ann. Pub. Svc. award 1999), Colo. Bar Assn., Park County Bar Assn. (sec. 1969-70, pres. 1970-71), Wyo. Assn. Cts. Ltd. Jurisdiction (pres. 1973-80), Wyo. Dist. Judges Conf. (chair 1996), Am. Judicature Soc. (mem. jud. adv. coun.). Avocations: photography, travel, fishing, reading, writing. Home: PO Box 941 Powell WY 82435-0941 Personal E-mail: hpatrick@bresnan.net.

PATRICK, HUGH TALBOT, economist, educator; b. Goldsboro, NC, Feb. 22, 1930; s. Talbot and Paula (Miller) P.; children: Stephen, Matthew, Catherine. BA, Yale U., 1951; MA in Far Eastern Studies, U. Mich., 1955, MA in Econs., 1957, PhD in Econs., 1960; MA (hon.), Yale U., 1968; PhD (hon.), Lingnan U., 2000. Econ. analyst U. S. Govt., 1951-52; lectr. econs. U. Mich., 1958-60; asst. prof. econs. Yale U., New Haven, 1960-64, assoc. prof., 1964-68, prof. Far Eastern econs., 1968-84; dir. Yale U. Econ. Growth Ctr., 1976-79, 80-83; R.D. Calkins prof. internat. bus. Columbia U., NYC, 1984—2001, prof. emeritus, 2001—. Vis. prof. U. Bombay, 1961-62; mem. Japan-U.S. Econ. Rels. Group, 1978-81, U.S. Com. for Pacific Econ. Coop.; dir. Ctr. on Japanese Econ. and Bus., Columbia U., 1986—. Editor: Japanese Industrialization and Its Social Consequences, 1976, Japanese High Technology Industries-Lessons and Limitations of Industrial Policy, 1986; contbr. chpt. and co-editor (with Henry Rosovsky): Asia's New Giant-How the Japanese Economy Works, 1976, (with Masahiko Aoki): The Japanese Main Bank System: Its Relevance for Developing and Transforming Economies, 1994, (with Takatoshi Ito and David Weinstein) Reviving Japan's Economy: Problems and Prescriptions, 2005; co-editor (with Larry Meissner): Pacific Basin Industries in Distress: Structural Adjustment and Trade Policy in Nine Industrialized Economies, 1991 (Masayoshi Ohira Meml. prize 1992), (with Yung Chul Park) The Financial Development of Japan, Korea and Taiwan: Growth, Repression and Liberalization, 1994, (with Takeo Hoshi) Crisis and Change in the Japanese Financial System, 2000. Ford Found. fellow 1957-58; grantee Am. Coun. Learned Socs., 1962; Guggenheim fellow, 1964-65; Fulbright rsch. prof., 1964-65; Fulbright-Hays NDEA fellow, 1968-69; Assn. Asian Studies Disting. lectr., 1977. Mem. Japan Soc. (dir. 1973-79, 81-2000), Social Sci. Rsch. Coun. (dir., chmn. 1985-88), Pacific Trade and Devel. Confs. (chmn. 1985-2005), Coun. Fgn. Rels. Democrat. Office: Columbia U 320 Uris Hall 3022 Broadway New York NY 10027-6945 Office Phone: 212-854-3497. Business E-Mail: htp1@columbia.edu.

PATRICK, JAMES DUVALL, JR., lawyer; b. Griffin, Ga., Dec. 28, 1947; s. James Duvall and Marion Wilson P. BS in Indsl. Mgmt., Ga. Inst. Tech., 1970; JD, U. Ga., 1973. Bar: Ga. 1973, U.S. Dist. Ct. (mid. dist.) Ga. 1973, U.S. Dist. Ct. (so. dist.) Ga. 1983, U.S. Ct. Appeals (5th cir.) 1974, U.S. Ct. Appeals (11th cir.) 1981, U.S. Tax Ct. 1985, U.S. Supreme Ct., 1977. Assoc. Cartledge, Cartledge & Posey, Columbus, Ga., 1973-74; ptnr. Falkenstrom, Hawkins & Patrick, Columbus, 1975, Falkenstrom & Patrick, Columbus, 1975-77; sole practice Columbus, 1977—. Instr. bus. law Chattahoochee Valley C.C., Phenix City, Ala., 1975-77; instr. paralegal course Columbus Coll., 1979, 84; del. U.S./China Joint Session on Trade, Investment, and Econ. Law, Beijing, 1987, Moscow Conf. on Law and Bilateral Econ. Rels., Moscow, 1990; U.S. del. U.S./Cuba Law Initiative, Havana, 2000. Mem. Hist. Columbus Found., Mayor's Comn. for the Handicapped, 1987-88; local organizer, worker Joe Frank Harris for Gov. Campaign, Columbus, 1982; bd. dirs. Columbus Symphony Orch., 1988-94. Fellow Am. Bar Found.; mem. ATLA, ABA (fellow found.), Am. Judicature Soc., State Bar Ga., Fed. Bar Assn., Ga. Trial Lawyers Assn., Columbus Lawyers Club, Columbus Kappa Alpha Alumni Assn. (sec.), Civitan (bd. dirs. 1975-77), Country Club of Columbus, Georgian Club (Atlanta), Buckhead Club, Chattahouchee River Club, Phi Delta Phi, Kappa Alpha. Methodist. Office: PO Box 2745 Columbus GA 31902-2745

PATRICK, JOHN, secondary school educator; b. Enfield, Middlesex, England, Nov. 11, 1945; s. John T. and Joyce M. Patrick; m. Sherry L. Johnson; children: Thomas E., Wendy M. Golden. BS, Southern Ill. U., Edwardsville, 1972. Tchr. Newman HS, Ill., 1971—73, Cape Girardeau Jr. HS, 1973—2002, Jackson Alternative Sch., Mo., 2002—. With US Army, 1966—68, Vietnam. Office: Jackson Sr HS 315 S Missouri St Jackson MO

PATRICK, NANCY J., special education educator, researcher; m. William A. Patrick, July 12, 1975; children: Craig, Scott, Blair. BA, Tex. A & I U., Corpus Christi, 1977; MEd, U. North Fla., Jacksonville, 1981; PhD, Pa. State U., Univ. Pk., 1992. Cert. spl. edn. tchr. State Fla., 1981, spl. educator Pa. Dept. Edn., 1985, sch. psychologist 1989, lic. Pa. Psychologist Lic. Bd., 1992. Sch. psychologist Ctrl. Dauphin Sch. Dist., Harrisburg, Pa., 1992—2000, supr. spl. edn., 2000—02, autism cons., 2000—04; assoc. prof. spl. edn. Messiah Coll., Grantham, Pa., 2002—. Co-author: (book) Hints And Tips For Helping Children With Autism Spectrum Disorders.; author: Autisme Wegwijzer: Doeltreffende Oplissingen Voor Alledaagse Problemen; co-author: Homespun Remedies: Strategies in the Home and Community for Children with Autism Spectrum and Other Developmental Disabilities. Dir. Harrisburg Christian Sch., Pa., 2007—09, Connections Ministry, Harrisburg, Pa., 2008—09. Mem.: APA, Pa. Psychol. Assn., Pa. Coll. Tchr. Assn., Coun. Exceptional Children, Kappa Delta Pi. Achievements include development of wireless enabled remote co-presence for the cognitively & behaviorally challenged. Home: 134 Stirrup Ln Harrisburg PA 17112 Office: Messiah Coll One College Ave Grantham PA 17027 Business E-Mail: npatrick@messiah.edu.

PATRICK, PAULINE MARGARET, secondary school educator; b. Mpls., Oct. 18, 1949; d. Melvin H. and Margaret P. (Calvelage) Boone; m. Mark H. Patrick, Dec. 18, 1971; children: Lance, Megan. BS, U. Mankato, 1971; MEd, St. Mary's Coll., Winona, Minn., 1993; MA (hon.), Minnetonka U., 1990. Cert. tchr., Minn. Tchr. Edina (Minn.) Sch., 1972-79, Minnetonka (Minn.) Schs., 1986—. Adj. prof. U. St. Thomas, St. Paul, 1989—, mem. T.E.A.C.H., 1991—. Recipient Apple award Ashland Oil Co., 1989. Mem. ASCd, Nat. Coun. Tchrs. English, Nat. Coun. Tchrs. Social Studies. Office Phone: 952-401-5000. E-mail: pelly.patrick@minnetonka.k12.mn.us.

PATRICK, ROBERT, playwright; b. Kilgore, Tex., Sept. 27, 1937; s. Robert and Beulah (Goodson) O'Connor. Author numerous plays produced off-off Broadway, off-Broadway, Broadway, also abroad including Robert Patrick's Cheep Theatricks (23 plays), 1972, Simultaneous Transmissions, 1973, Play-By-Play, 1975, The Golden Circle, 1975, Kennedy's Children, 1975, Let Me Tell It To You, Dr. Paroo, 1976, One Man, One Woman (6 plays), 1978, T-Shirts, 1979, Mutual Benefit Life, 1980, Mercy Drop and Other Plays (5 plays), 1980, My Cup Ranneth Over, 1984, Big Sweet, 1985, Untold Decades (7 plays), 1988, Drowned Out, 1990, Connie, 1991, Michaelangelo's Models, 1994, Bread Alone, 1994, The Trial of Socrates, 1994, Evan on Earth, 1995, Hollywood at Sunset, 2004, Pouf Positive (CD), 1996; author: (novels) Temple Slave, 1986, Echo, 1990, (book on CD) Film Moi, 2003, (films) Resident Alien, 1990, The O Boys Documentary, 1999; teleplays include: High Tide, 1994, Robin's Hoods, 1995, Ghost Story, 1997, (essay) Film Moi, 1999, Caffe Cino Picture Pages, 2006; contbr. poems, articles, stories to profl. jours. Rockefeller grantee, 1974, N.Y. State CAPS grantee, 1975; recipient Show Bus. Best Playwright award 1968-69, Glasgow Citizens' Theatre Best World Playwright award, 1974, Omni-Act One award, 1975, Robbie award, 1976, Founders award Internat. Thespians Soc., 1980, Blue is for Boys weekends in Manhattan, 1983, 86, Lifetime Achievement award for Gay Playwriting Robert Chesley Found., 1996, West Hollywood Rainbow Key award, 2008. Home and Office: 1837 N Alexandria Ave Apt 211 Los Angeles CA 90027-4068 Office Phone: 323-423-4330, 323-310-1469. Personal E-mail: rbrtptrck@aol.com. *No object or action has any meaning except that given to it by a writer. Writers create the consciousness of humanity, which in turn creates our world. Writers write the world.*

PATRICK, RUTH (MRS. RUTH HODGE VAN DUSEN), botany educator, curator; b. Topeka; d. Frank and Myrtle (Jetmore) Patrick; m. Charles (IV) Hodge, July 10, 1931; 1 child, Charles (V). BS, Coker Coll., 1929; MS, U. Va., 1931, PhD, 1934; LLD (hon.), Coker Coll., 1971; LHD (hon.), Chestnut Hill Coll, 1974; DSc (hon.), Beaver Coll., 1970, PMC Colls., 1971, Phila. Coll. Pharmacy and Sci., 1973, Wilkes Coll., 1974, Cedar Crest Coll., 1974, U. New Haven, 1975, Hood Coll., 1975, Med. Coll. Pa., 1975, Drexel U., 1975, Swarthmore Coll., 1975, Bucknell U., 1976, Rensselaer Poly. Inst., 1976, St. Lawrence U., 1978, U. Mass., 1980, Princeton U., 1980, Lehigh U., 1983, U. Pa., 1984, Temple U., 1985, Emory U., 1986, Wake Forest U., 1986, U. S.C., 1989, Clemson, 1989, Glassboro State Coll., 1992. Assoc. curator microscopy dept. Acad. Natural Scis., Phila., 1939-47; curator Leidy Micros. Soc., 1937-47, curator limnology dept., 1947—, chmn. limnology dept., 1947-73; occupant Francis Boyer Research Chair Acad. Natural Scis., Phila., 1973—, chmn. bd. trustees, 1973-76, hon. chmn. bd. trustees, 1976—; lectr. U. Pa., 1950-70, adj. prof., 1970—; guest Fellow of Saybrook Yale, 1975. Participant Am. Philos Soc. limnology expdn. to Mexico, 1947; leader Catherwood Found. expdn. to Peru and Brazil, 1955; del. gen. assembly Internat. Union Biol. Scis., Bergen, Norway, 1947; bd. dirs. E.I. Du Pont, Pa. Power and Light Co.; chmn. algae com. Smithsonian Oceanographic Sorting Ctr., 1963—68; mem. panel on water blooms Pres. Sci. Adv. Com., 1966; mem. panel on water resources and water pollution Gov.'s Sci. Adv. Com., 1966; mem. nat. tech. adv. com. on water quality requirements for fish and other aquatic life and wildlife Dept. Interior, 1967—68; mem. citizen's adv. coun. Pa. Dept. Environ. Resources, 1971—73; mem. hazardous materials adv. com. EPA, 1971—74, exec. adv. com., 1974—79; chmn. com.'s panel on ecology, 1974—76; mem. Pa. Gov.'s Sci. Adv. Coun., 1972; mem. exec. adv. com. nat. power survey FPC, 1972—75; mem. coun. Smithsonian Instn., 1973—; mem. Phila. Adv. Coun., 1973—76; mem. energy R&D adv. coun. Pres.s Emergy Policy Office, 1973—74; mem. adv. coun. Renewable Nat. Resources Found., 1973—76, Elecric Power Rsch. Found., 1973—77; mem. adv. com. for rsch. NSF, 1973—74; mem. gen. adv. com. ERDA, 1975—77; mem. adv. bd. Sec. Energy, 1975—89; mem. com. on human resources NRC, 1975—76; trustee Biological Abstracts, 1974—76; mem. adv. coun. dept. biology Princeton U., 1975—80; mem. com. on sci. and arts Franklin Inst., 1978—; mem. univ. coun. com. Yale Sch. Forestry and Environ. Studies, 1978—80; mem. sci. adv. coun. World Wildlife Fund-US, 1978—80; trustee Aquarium Soc., Phila., 1951—58, Henry Found.; bd. dirs. Wissahickon Valley Watershed Assn.; bd. govs. Nature Conservancy; bd. mgrs. Wistar Inst. Anatomy and Biology. Author: (series of volumes) Rivers of the United States Vol. 1, 1994, Rivers of the United States Vol. 2, 1997, Chemical and Physical Characteristics Vol. 3, 1995, Rivers of Atlantic and Eastern Gulf Drainage Vol. 4, The Mississipi River and Major Tributaries; co-author (with C.W. Reimer): Diatoms of the United States Vol. 1, 1966, Vol. II, Part 1, 1975; co-author: (with others) (books) Ground Water Contamination in the United States, 1983, 2nd edit.; co-author: (with others) (book) Surface Water Quality: Have the Laws Been Successful?, 1992; mem. editorial bd.with C. W. Reimer: sci. jours. Science, 1974—76, mem. editorial bd.: sci. jours. American Naturalist; contbr. articles over 150 to profl. jours. Recipient Disting. Dau. of Pa. award, 1952, Richard Hopper Day Meml. medal, Acad. Nat. Scis., 1969, Gimbel Phila. award, 1969, Gold medal, YWCA, 1970, Lewis L. Dollinger Pure Environment award, Franklin inst., 1970, Pa. award for excellence in sci. and tech., 1970, Eminent Ecologist award, Ecol Soc. Am., 1972, Phila. award, 1973, Gold medal, Pa. State Fish and Game Protective Assn., 1974, Internat. John and Alice Tyler Ecology award, 1975, Gold meda;, Phila. Soc. for Promoting Agr., 1975, Pub. Svc. award, U.S. Dept. Interior, 1975, Iben award, Am. Water Resources Assn., 1976, Outstanding Alumna award, Coker Coll., 1977, Francis K. Hutchinson medal, Garden Club of Am., 1977, Golden medal, Royal Zool. Soc., Antwerp, 1978, Green World award, N.Y. Bot. Garden, 1979, Hugo Black award, U. Ala., 1979, Sci award, Gov. Pa., 1988, Founders award, Soc. Environ. Toxicology and Chemistry, 1982, Environ. Regeneration award, Rene DuBois Ctr., 1985, Disting. Citizen award, Pa., 1989, Excellence award, N. Am. Benthological Soc., 1993, Benjamin Franklin medal, Am. Philosophical Soc., 1993, U.S. medal of svc., Pres. Bill Clinton, 1996, Nat. medal for sci., 1997, Nat. Wetlands award, 2000, Sci. Edn. Ctr. named in her honor, U. S.C., 1989. Fellow: AAAS (com. environ. alternatives 1973—74); mem.: Internat. Phycol. Soc., Am. Inst. Biol. Scis., Ecol. Soc. Am., Am. Soc. Naturalists (pres. 1975—76), Am. Soc. Limnology and Oceanography (Lifetime Achievement award 1996), Am. Soc. Plant Taxonomy, Internat. Soc. Plant Taxonomists, Internat. Limnological Soc., Phycol Soc. Am. (pres. 1954), Bot. Soc. Am. (mem. Darbarker prize com. 1956, Merit award 1971), Am. Acad. Arts and Scis., Assn. Metro. Sewage Agys. (Environ. award 1995), Am. Philos. Soc. (Benjamin Franklin Outstanding Sci. Achievement award 1993), Nat. Acad. Engring. (com.environ. engr. study explicit criteria for power plant siting 1973), Nat. Acad. Scis. (chmn. panel com. on pollution 1966, mem.environ. measures panel com. remote sensing earth resources survey 1973—74, mem. nominating com. 1973—75, mem. com. sci. and public policy 1973—77), Water Pollution Control Fedn. (hon.), Soc. Study Evolution, Sigma Xi. Presbyterian. Office: Acad Natural Scis 19th at Benjamin Franklin Pkwy Philadelphia PA 19103 Office Phone: 215-299-1098. Business E-Mail: Patrick@acnatsci.org.

PATRICK, STEPHEN C., consumer products company executive; Mgr. Price Waterhouse; mgmt. positions through v.p., corp. contr. and v.p. fin. Colgate - L.Am. Colgate-Palmolive Co., NYC, 1982—96, CFO, 1996—. V.p. Fin. Acctg. Found.; bd. dirs. Arrow Electronics, 2003—. Office: Colgate-Palmolive Co 300 Park Ave New York NY 10022-7499 Office Fax: 212-310-3284.

PATRICK, SUSAN D., educational association administrator, former federal agency administrator; B in English, Colo. Coll.; M in Comm. Mgmt., U. So. Calif. Dir. distance learning campus Old Dominion U.; coord. Digital State Survey 2002 State of Ariz.; dep. dir. Office Edn. Tech. US Dept. Edn., Washington, dir. Office Edn. Tech., 2004—05; pres., CEO North American Coun. for Online Learning (NACOL), Vienna, Va., 2005—. Office: NACOL 1934 Old Gallows Rd, Ste 350 Vienna VA 22182-4040 Office Phone: 703-752-6216. Office Fax: 703-752-6201. E-mail: spatrick@nacol.org.

PATRICK, VICTOR PHILLIP, lawyer, manufacturing executive; b. Lake Forest, Ill., Jan. 7, 1958; s. Rodger Ralph Patrick and Phyllis Elaine Bachler; m. Elizabeth Fletcher, Aug. 9, 1985; children: Kathryn Elaine, Stephen James, Diane Elizabeth, Marie Christine, Thomas Grant, John Wallace, Daniel Victor, Emily Frances. AB in Politics magna cum laude, Princeton U., 1982; JD cum laude, Harvard U., 1985. Bar: DC 1986, NY 1986, U.S. Ct. Appeals (10th cir.) 1986. Law clk. U.S. Ct. Appeals 10th Cir., Denver, 1985-86; assoc. Cleary, Gottlieb, Steen & Hamilton, Washington, 1986-88, 92-94, Brussels, 1988—91; from asst. gen. counsel to v.p., sec. and dep. gen. counsel Honeywell Internat. Inc. (formerly AlliedSignal Inc.), Morristown, NJ, 1994—97, 1999—2002, Torrance, Calif., 1997—99; sr. v.p., gen. counsel, sec. Walter Industries, Inc., Tampa, Fla., 2002—06, vice chmn., gen. counsel, 2006—. Pres. Tampa Fla. Stake; mem. bd. BS Gulf Ridge Coun. Mem. ABA. Republican. Lds Ch. Business E-Mail: vpatrick@walterind.com.

PATRICOF, ALAN JOEL, venture capitalist; b. NYC, Oct. 22, 1934; s. Martin and Dorine (Glass) Patricof; m. Susan Patricof; children: Jonathan, James, Mark. BS in Fin., Ohio State U., 1955; MBA, Columbia U., 1957. Various positions Naess & Thomas, NYC, 1957-58, Lambert & Co., NYC, 1958-60; asst. v.p. to v.p. Ctrl. Nat. Corp., NYC, 1960-68; asst. to chmn. N.W. Industries, NYC, 1968-70; co-founder, chmn. Apax Ptnrs., Inc. (formerly Alan Patricof Assocs.), NYC, 1969—2001; dir. Boston Properties, Inc., 1997—; founder, mng. dir. Greycroft Ptnrs., L.P., 2006—. Bd. dirs. Harman Internat. Industries, Inc., Datascope, Inc., Quantronics Corp., Cellular Comm., Inc.; founder, former chmn. bd. NY mag.; chmn. pvt. equity grp. Global Corp. Governance Forum; bd. mem. NY Small Bus. Venture Fund; mem. NY adminstrv. com. Fleet Nat. Bank. Trustee NY Sci. and Tech. Found.; bd. trustees Columbia U. Grad. Sch. Bus. Served in US Army, 1958, served in US Army, 1961—62. Mem. NY Acad. Scis. (former mem. bd. govs., former treas.). Clubs: Friars. Democrat. Office: Apax Ptnrs LP 153 E 53rd St 53rd Fl New York NY 10022*

PATRIE, CHERYL CHRISTINE, elementary school educator; b. Dobbs Ferry, NY, June 8, 1947; d. Edward F. and Antoinette C. (Patrie) P. BA in Edn., U. Fla., 1969; MS in Edn., U. Miami, 1979. Cert. assoc. master tchr., Fla. Tchr. Marion County Sch. Bd., Ocala, Fla., 1970, Dade County Sch. Bd., Miami, 1973—. Mem. faculty coun. Lorah Park Elem. Sch., Miami, 1979-89, 1991—95, career lab. cons., 1983-85, human growth and devel. cons., 1983—87, phys. fitness co-chmn., 1984-90, chair dept., 1993—, coord. quality instrn. incentives program, 1984-89, faculty adv. com., 1990-; mem. Dade County Elem. Sch. Day Task Force, 1987-88. Mem. United Tchrs. Dade (bldg. union steward 1979-89, mem. crisis in inner city task force 1984-85, mem. sch. adv. com., 1987—, Disting. Svc. award 1984). Office: Lorah Park Elem 5160 NW 31st Ave Miami FL 33142-3439 Home: 555 NE 15th St #28-I Miami FL 33132-1406 Office Phone: 305-633-1424.

PATRIKIS, ERNEST T., lawyer; b. Lynn, Mass., Dec. 1, 1943; s. Theodore A. and Ethel (Stasinopolous) Patrikis; m. Emily Herrick Trueblood, Mar. 18, 1972. BA in Econs. with honors, U. Mass., Amherst, 1965; JD, Cornell U., Ithaca, 1968. Bar: N.Y. 1969. Exec. v.p., gen. counsel Fed. Res. Bank N.Y., NYC, 1968—95, 1st v.p., 1995—98; spl. adv. to chmn. Am. Internat. Group Inc., NYC, 1998—2000, sr. v.p., gen. coun., 1998—2006; ptnr. Pillsbury Winthrop Shaw Pittman LLP, NYC, 2006—08, White & Case LLP, NYC, 2008—; head fin. svc. & regulatory practice Pillsbury Winthrop Shaw Pittman LLP, NYC, 2006—. Dep. gen. counsel Fed. Open Market Com., 1988—95, alternative mem., 1995—98; bd. dirs. Atlantic Legal Found. Contbr. articles to legal jours. Mem.: ABA (subcom. gen. banking matters 1986), Internat. Bar Assn. (coun. fgn. rels., com. internat. monetary law), Internat. Inst. Conflict Prevention & Resolution (mem. banking and fin. svc. com.), Internat. Law Assn. (monetary law com. 1990—), Fed. Bar Assn. (banking law exec. com. 2006—), Internat. Swaps and Derivatives Assn. (dir. 1999—2006), Coun. Fgn. Rels., N.Y. State Bar Assn. (banking law com. 1986—, chmn. com. internat. banking, securities and fin. transaction 1987—91, vice chmn. internat. practice sect. 1991—2003, derivatives and structured products com. 2006—), Assn. Bar City N.Y. (banking law com. 1982—84, 1990—, ins. com. 2000—03, corp. law com. 2003, European law com. 2004—06, futures regulations com. 1986-89 2007—, Joint Yr. 2000 Coun.). Office: White & Case LLP 1155 Ave of the Americas New York NY 10036-2787 Home Phone: 212-677-5178; Office Phone: 212-819-7903. Personal E-mail: erniepatrikis@yahoo.com. Business E-Mail: ernest.patrikis@whitecase.com.

PATRIZIO, PASQUALE, reproductive endocrinologist, andrologist, and infertility specialist; b. Torre Annunziata, Napoli, Italy, Jan. 31, 1959; came to U.S., 1988; s. Vincent and Assunta Patrizio; m. Teri Susan Ord, Aug. 27, 1993; children: Alessandra, Vincent. MD summa cum laude, U. Naples, Italy, 1983. Diplomate of residency in ob-gyn., Italy; lic. physician, Calif., U.K., Italy; cert. Edn. Coun. for Fgn. Med. Grads. Intern in medicine and surgery U. Naples, 1983-84, resident in ob-gyn., 1983-87; postgrad. fellow in andrology U. Pisa, Italy, 1987-90; rsch. fellow in reproductive endocrinology and infertility U. Calif.-Irvine, Orange, 1989-93, resident in ob-gyn., 1993-94, clin. instr. in reproductive endocrinology and infertility dept. ob-gyn., 1994-95, asst. prof. ob-gyn., 1995-96; dir. male infertility svc. Reproductive Endocrinology Fertility Ctr., San Antonio, 1996—; asst. prof. ob-gyn., dir. male infertility U. Pa., Phila., 1996—. Sr. house officer ob-gyn. Victoria Hosp. and Forth Park Hosp., Kirkcaldy, Fife, Scotland, 1986; sr. house officer ob-gyn. Royal Gwent Hosp., Newport, South Wales, 1987; one of pioneers of epididymal sperm aspiration technique for treatment of infertile males; discovered relationship between gene mutations and male infertility; presenter in field. Contbr. chpts. to books, articles to med. jours. Recipient 1st prize for best rsch. paper Wyeth-Ayerst Labs., 1992; co-recipient Practicing Physician award Pacific Coast Fertility Soc., 1989, 92, 94, TAP Poster award Am. Fertility Soc., 1992; ACOG/Mead Johnson clin. fellow, 1992-93; Meml. Health Svcs. grantee, 1994-95. Fellow ACOG (jr.); mem. AMA, Am. Fertility Soc. (co-winner poster presentation 45th ann. meeting 1989), Am. Soc. Andrology, European Soc. Human Reprodn., Italian Soc. Fertility and Sterility (hon.), Italian Soc. Ob-Gyn., Italian Soc. Andrology, Royal Coll. Ob-Gyn. (Eng.), Soc. for Study of Reprodn. Achievements include pioneering in development of epididymal sperm aspiration technique for treatment of infertile males; discovery of relationship between genetic mutations and male infertility. Office: Yale U Fertility Ctr 150 Sargent Drive New Haven CT 06511

PATRON, JUNE EILEEN, retired federal agency administrator; b. NYC, May 15, 1943; d. Irving B. and Mollie Patron. BA in Govt. with honors, Clark U., Worcester, Mass., 1965; MA, Am. U., 1967. Mgmt. intern U.S. Dept. Labor, 1966—67, various manpower adminstrn. budget and planning positions, 1967—71, chief welfare reform policy and legis. support group, 1971—72, chief spl. projects staff policy and planning group, office the under sec., 1972—73, spl. asst. to the dep. asst. sec. labor-mgmt. services, 1974—75, spl. asst. to the solicitor of labor, 1976, dir. Black Lung benefits program, 1976-79, asst. adminstr. pension and welfare benefit programs, 1979-84, assoc. dir. pension and welfare benefit programs, 1984-88, dir. pension and welfare benefit program svcs., 1988-95; ret., 1995. Mem. Sr. Exec. Svc.; ind. contractor, mgmt. cons., 1997—2003. Vol. Van Ness Neighbor Network, 2003—; vol. alumni and parent admissions program Clark U., 1998—; vol. US Presdl. Inauguration, 2009. Recipient various awards, Dept. Labor. Mem.: Sr. Execs. Assn., Nat. Active and Ret. Fed. Employees. Avocations: travel, photography. Home: 3001 Veazey Ter NW Washington DC 20008-5405 Personal E-mail: jpdcny@aol.com.

PATTANAYAK, DEVA NARAYAN, engineering company executive; b. Banki, Orissa, India, Nov. 15, 1948; s. Purna Chandra and Kamalini Patnaik; m. Anuradha Rout; children: Siddhartha, Vikram. PhD, U. Rochester, NY, 1973. Physicist GE Corp. R & D, Niskayuna, NY, 1984—98; dir. Vishay Siliconix, Santa Clara, Calif., 2001—. Adj. prof. U. Pa., Phila., 1996—2001. Contbr. scientific papers. Vol. Orissa Soc. Am., NJ, 1982. Recipient Mayurbhanja Gold medal, Ravenshaw Coll., Utkal U., 1966. Mem.: IEEE (pres., local eds chpt. 1986—87), OSA. Achievements include patents for semiconductor & optics. Avocation: curling. Home: 19123 Brookhaven Dr Saratoga CA 95070 Office: Vishay Siliconix 2201 Laurelwood Rd Santa Clara CA 95054 Personal E-mail: deva_pattanayak@yahoo.com. Business E-Mail: deva.pattanayak@vishay.com.

PATTEN, BERNARD MICHAEL, neurologist, writer, educator; b. NYC, Mar. 23, 1941; s. Bernard M. and Olga (Vaccaro) P.; m. Ethel Doudine, June 18, 1964; children: Allegra, Craig. AB summa cum laude, Columbia Coll., 1962; MD, Columbia U., 1966. Med. intern N.Y. Hosp. Cornell Med. Ctr., NYC, 1966-67; resident neurologist Columbia Presbyn. Med. Ctr., NYC, 1967-69, chief resident neurologist, 1969-70; assoc. prof. neurology Baylor Coll. Medicine, Houston, 1973-95; ret., 1995. Asst. chief med. neurology NIH, Bethesda, Md., 1970-73; mem. med. bd. Nat. Myasthenia Gravis Found., 1973—, Nat. AmyoTrophic Lateral Sclerosis Found., 1982—, Nat. Myositis Assn., 1995—; invited faculty Rice U., 1999—; faculty Women's INst. Houston. Author: One or Two Things I Remember About Her, 1999, Tristan and Iseult: Modern Version, 2000, Investment Pearls for Modern Times Expressed in Meter and in Rhymes, 2000, The Great Cotzias, 2001, Ascent to Heaven, 2001, Quia Imperfectum, 2001, Truth, Knowledge or Bull: How to Tell the Difference, 2004, The Blood of a Million Christs, 2004, Cruising Around the World on the Queen Elizabeth 2, 2006, The Logic of Alice: Clear Thinking in Wonderland; contbr. articles to profl. jours. With USPHS, 1970-73. Rsch. grantee NIH, pvt. founds., nat. health orgns. Fellow ACP, Royal Coll. Physicians, Tex. Neurol. Soc. Achievements include discovery (with others) of L-Dopa for Parkinson's disease; pioneered use of immune suppression for myasthenia gravis, diagnosis and treatment of medical and neurologcal complications of breast implants. Home: 1019 Baronridge Dr Seabrook TX 77586-4001 Office Phone: 713-252-1306. Personal E-mail: dadpatten@aol.com.

PATTEN, BETSEY LELAND, state legislator; b. Newton, Mass., Apr. 26, 1945; m. Richard C. Patten (dec.); 1 child. Student, Kings Coll. With publ. dept. Raytheon Co., 1978—84; rec. sec. Planning and Zoning Bds. of Moultonborough, 1985—91; state rep. N.H. Ho. Reps., former chmn. mcpl. and county govt. com. Former chmn. Joint Legis. Com. on Adminstrv. Rules; chmn. Assessing Standards Bd., Carroll County Rep. Com., 1996—. Home: 46 Patten Hill Rd Moultonborough NH 03254 Office Phone: 603-271-3317. E-mail: blpatten@worldpath.net.

PATTEN, DUNCAN THEUNISSEN, ecologist educator; b. Detroit, Oct. 13, 1934; s. Marc T. and Doris (Miller) P.; m. Eva Chittenden, July 27, 1957; children: Michael, Marc, Robin, Scott. BA, Amherst Coll., 1956; MS, U. Mass., Amherst, 1959; PhD, Duke U., 1962. Asst. prof. ecology Va. Poly. Inst., Blacksburg, 1962-65, Ariz. State U., Tempe, 1965-67, assoc. prof., 1967-73, prof., 1973-95, prof. emeritus, 1995—, dir. ctr. environ. studies, 1980-95. Rsch. prof. Mont. State U., 1995—. Contbr. articles to profl. jours. Fellow AAAS, Ariz.-Nev. Acad. Sci.; mem. Ecol. Soc. Am. (bus. mgr. 1979-95), Brit. Ecol. Soc., Soc. Range Mgmt., Am. Inst. Biol. Scis., Soc. Wetland Scientists (pres. 1996-97), Am. Water Resource Assn., Am. Geophys. Union, Sigma Xi Office: Mont State U Land Resources and Environ Scis Box 173120 Bozeman MT 59717-3120 Office Phone: 406-994-2784. Business E-Mail: dtpatten@montana.edu.

PATTEN, LANNY RAY, gas industry executive; b. St. Joseph, Mo., July 31, 1934; s. E.L. and Sarah Catherine (Langner) P.; m. Ann Rogers Hall, Oct. 26, 1957; children: David, John, Jeffrey, Mark. BS in Engring., Iowa State U., 1956; AMP, Harvard U., 1976. Net sr. v.p. gases and equipment Air Products and Chems., Inc., Allentown, Pa., 1960—90; pres., COO Airgas Inc., Radnor, Pa., 1990-91; founder CylServ, Inc., West Conshohocken, Pa., 1992—. Chmn. Lehigh U. Parents Assn., Bethlehem, Pa., 1977—90. Officer USAF, 1957—60. Recipient PACE award for Engring. Achievement Iowa State U., 1990, Friend of Lehigh award, 1991. Mem.: SAR (Phila. chpt. pres. 2006—07, Pa. state pres. 2008—), NSSAR (ex-com. mem. 2008—), Allentown C. of C. (exec. bd. dirs. 1978—82), Internat. Oxygen Mfg. Assn., Compressed Gas Assn. (exec. bd. dirs. 1977—91), Pa. Soc. SAR (pres. 2008—), Pa. Soc. SR (sec. 2007—, bd. dirs.), Union League of Phila., Phila. Country Club, Kappa Sigma (Alumni Hall of Fame). Republican. Episcopalian. Avocations: baseball, golf, history. Home: 1306 Club House Rd Gladwyne PA 19035-1006

PATTEN, ROBERT LOWRY, language educator; b. Oklahoma City, Apr. 26, 1939; s. Charles H. and Helen (Lowry) P.; m. Faith L. Harris, June 12, 1960 (div. 1974); children: Jocelyn S., Christina S. BA, Swarthmore Coll., 1960; MA, Princeton U., 1963, PhD, 1965. Lectr. Bryn Mawr (Pa.) Coll., 1964-66, asst. prof. English, 1966-69; asst. prof. Rice U., Houston, 1969-71, assoc. prof., 1971-76, prof. English, 1976-96, chair, dept. of English, 1991-92, master Grad. House, 1992-95, Lynette S. Autrey prof. humanities, 1996—. Pres. PEN S.W., Houston, 1989—92. Author: Charles Dickens and His Publishers, 1978, George Cruikshank's Life, Times and Art, vol. 1, 1992, vol. 2, 1996 (best biography of the decade Guardian); editor: (book by Charles Dickens) Pickwick Papers, 1972, George Cruikshank: A Revaluation, 1974, 2d edit., 1992, (with John O. Jordan) Literature in the Marketplace, 1995, (with John Bowen) Palgrave Advances in Charles Dickens Studies, 2005; editor SEL: Studies in English Lit., 1978-84, 90—06, pub. & exec. editor, 2009-. Bd. dirs. Cultural Arts Coun., Houston, 1979-80, Tex. Com. for the Humanities, 1979-80; pres., bd. dirs. Houston Ctr. for the Humanities, 1976-84; v.p. Houston Philosophical Soc., 2007-08, pres., 2008-09. NEH fellow, 1968-69, 77-78, 87-88; Guggenheim fellow, 1980-81; Nat. Humanities Ctr. fellow, 1987-88; Nat. Gallery of Art Assoc., 1988-89. Mem. AAUP (pres. Rice Chpt. 2009), MLA (chair, Victoria Divsn. 2008), PEN Am. Ctr., Dickens Fellowship, Dickens Soc., Soc. for the History of Authorship, Reading and Pub. (bd. dirs. 1992-2003, treas. 1997-2003, v.p. 2003-05, pres. 2005—09), Coun. Editors of Learned Jours., Phi Beta Kappa (pres. Beta chpt. Tex. 1991-94, 97-2002, 07-08, bd. dirs. Houston chpt. 1997-2000, adv. dir. 2000-03, senator 2002-03, Couper scholar, 2004-06). Episcopalian. Avocations: travel, classical music. Office: Rice U Dept English MS 30 PO Box 1892 Houston TX 77251-1892 Home Phone: 713-524-1485; Office Phone: 713-348-4697. Business E-Mail: patten@rice.edu.

PATTEN, RONALD JAMES, university dean; b. Iron Mountain, Mich., July 17, 1935; s. Rudolph Joseph and Cecelia (Fuse) Pataconi; m. Shirley Ann Bierman, Sept. 5, 1959; children: Christine Marie, Cheryl Ann, Charlene Denise. BA, Mich. State U., East Lansing, 1957, MA, 1959; PhD, U. Ala., Tuscaloosa, 1963. Acct. Price Waterhouse & Co., Detroit, 1958; instr. No. Ill. U., 1959-60; asst. prof. U. Colo., 1963-65; assoc. prof. Va. Poly. Inst. and State U., 1965-67, prof., 1967-73, head dept. accounting, 1966-73; dir. research Financial Accounting Standards Bd., Conn., 1973-74; dean Sch. Bus. Adminstrn., U. Conn., Storrs, 1974-88; chief of party-Eastern Caribbean Arthur D. Little Internat., 1988-89; dean Coll. Commerce and Kellstadt Grad. Sch. Bus. De Paul U., Chgo., 1989-99; dean Ritsumeikan Asia Pacific U. Grad. Sch. Mgmt., Beppu, Japan, 2003—06. Individual investors adv. com. NY Stock Exch., 1993—98; cons. in field. Contbr. chapters to books, articles to profl. jours. Bd. dirs. US com. UNICEF, Chgo., 1996—99. Recipient Nat. Quartermaster award Nat. Quartermaster, Assn., 1956; Earhart Found. fellow, 1962-63. Mem. AICPA, Am. Acctg. Assn., Inst. Mgmt. Accts., Acad. Internat. Bus. (Internat. Dean of Yr. award 1987), Internat. Assn. for Acctg. Edn. and Rsch., Ill. Coun. Econ. Edn. (Chgo., trustee 1989-2006, chmn. bd. trustees 1997-2000), Pacioli Soc., Internat. Trade and Fin. Assn., dir. 1998-2000, Heidelberg Club Internat., Scabbard and Blade, Golden Key, Beta Gamma Sigma (mem. bd. govs. 1975-90, nat. sec.-treas. 1980-82, nat. v.p. 1982-84, nat. pres. 1984-86), Beta Alpha Psi (bd. dirs. 1992-94), Delta Sigma Pi, World Assn. for Case Method Rsch. and Application, Adv Bd., 1998-, Phi Kappa Phi, Delta Mu Delta. Avocations: hiking, golf, travel, singing, barbershop quartets. Home and Office: PO Box 190 Newfield ME 04056

PATTEN, THOMAS HENRY, JR., retired educator, personnel director; b. Cambridge, Mass., Mar. 24, 1929; s. Thomas Henry and Lydia Mildred (Lindgren) Patten. AB, Brown U., 1953; MS, Cornell U., 1955, PhD, 1959. Dir. program planning Ford Motor Co., Dearborn, Mich., 1957-65; prof. mgmt. and sociology U. Detroit, 1965-67; prof. orgnl. behavior and personnel mgmt. Sch. Labor and Indsl. Relations, Mich. State U., E. Lansing, 1967-84; prof. mgmt. and human resources Calif. State Poly. U., Pomona, 1984—2003, prof. emeritus, 2003—07; ret., 2007. Cons. in field. Author: The Foreman: The Forgotten Man of Management, 1968, Manpower Planning and the Development of Human Resources, 1971, OD-Emerging Dimensions and Concepts, 1973, A Bibliography of Compensation Planning and Administration, 1960-1974, 2d rev. edit., 1981, 3d rev. edit., 1987, Pay: Employee Compensation and Incentive Plans, 1977, Classics of Personnel Management, 1979, Organizational Development Through Teambuilding, 1981, A Manager's Guide to Performance Appraisal, 1982, Fair Pay: The Managerial Challenge of Comparable Job Worth and Job Evaluation, 1988, Exercises for Developing Human Resources Management Skills, 1996. With USMC, 1946—51. Mem. ASTD (chmn. orgn. devel. div. 1972), Indsl. Rels. Rsch. Assn. (chpt. pres. 1970-71), Am. Sociol. Assn., Internat. Pers. Mgmt. Assn., Internat. Indsl. Rels. Assn., Inst. Applied Behavioral Sci., Am. Compensation Assn. Home: 407 Mossy Ct Lincoln CA 95648-8158 Home Phone: 916-408-2026. *Human values come first.*

PATTENAUDE, RICHARD LOUIS, academic administrator, educator; b. Seattle, Feb. 22, 1946; s. Joseph Arthur and Alice June (Vrooman) P.; m. Michele Arlen Stevenson, May 31, 1975; children: Lauren, Lisa, Dylan, Joshua. BA with honors in Econs., San Jose State U., 1968; PhD in Polit. Sci., U. Colo., 1974. Asst. to assoc. prof. Drake U., Des Moines, 1974-80, assoc. dean liberal arts, 1976-80; asst. v.p. acad. affairs SUNY-Binghamton, 1980-82, assoc. v.p., 1982-86; v.p. acad. affairs; prof. polit. sci. Ctrl. Conn. State U., New Britain, 1986-91; pres., prof. polit. sci. U. So. Maine, Portland, 1991—2007; chancellor U. Maine Sys., 2007—. Cons. in field; panelist, presenter various nat. higher edn. meetings. Contbr. numerous articles to profl. jours., chpts. to books in field. Commr. Occupational and Licensing Commn., Iowa, 1978-80; mem. Gov.'s Com. Efficiency, 1979; mem. adv. coun. planning dept. City of Binghamton, 1984-1986; bd. dirs. Broome County United Way, 1985, Greater Hartford Red Cross, 1991-93, Mercy Hosp., Portland, 1992-94, Portland Symphony Orch., Maine Devel. Found., 1991-97, Maine Sci. & Tech. Found., 1992-98, Portland Mus. Art, 1993-99, Pmt. Symphony 1998-, Lee Altomalls, 2000—, Maine Med. Ctr., 2002-05, Maine Health, 2005—, Inst. Civic Leadership, 1992-94, Greater Portland United Way, 1998-2002. With U.S. Army, 1969-71, Vietnam. Fanny W. Ames scholar, 1965; Title II fellow, 1970. Mem. Assn. Instl. Rsch. and Planning Officers (v.p. 1983-84, pres. 1984-85), Am. Assn. State Colls. and Univs. (state rep. 1995—, bd. dirs. 1999—2003), Greater Portland C. of C. Office: U Maine System 16 Central St Bangor ME 04401 Business E-Mail: pattenaude@maine.edu.

PATTERSON, AMANDA MARGARET, music educator; b. Luxemburg, Wis., May 15, 1931; d. Alois Milton Arendt and Martha Anastacia Dorner-Arendt; m. Neil A. Patterson (dec.); children: Debra Lee, Patrick Neil, Dean Michael, Jane Marie Mlenar. Student, Milw. State Tchrs. Coll., 1949—53. Tchr. music Walworth County, Elkhorn, Wis., 1953—56; tchr. Milw. Music City, 1956—57; tchr. instrumental music City of Milw., 1956—68; tchr. music Greendale, 1968—2006. Musician Anita McKnights All Women Orch., Milw., 1970—81, West Allis Adult Band, Wis., 1972—80. Pres. Wis. State Podiatry Aux. Soc., Milw., 1972—73, Greendale PTA, Wis., 1968—69, active, 1968—85; chmn. Ballet Co. Friends, Milw., 1973—76; pres. Greendale VFW Aux., Wis., 1980—82, 4th Dist. VFW Aux., Milw., 1992—93; bd. dirs. Milw. Ballet Co., 1973. Mem.: VFW (pres. auxiliary Greendale chp. 2004—), Am. Legion. Roman Catholic. Home: 5342 Lakeview Dr Greendale WI 53129-1928 Personal E-mail: amandamp515@aol.com.

PATTERSON, ANNA, information technology executive; b. Chgo., 1973; m. Tom Costello; 4 children. PhD in Computer Sci., U. Ill., Urbana-Champaign. Rsch. scientist Stanford U.; arch., technical lead Google Inc., 2004—06; co-founder, pres., v.p. engring. Cuil, Inc., Menlo Park, Calif., 2006—. Designer, writer 12 billion page search engine Recall; arch. search index TeraGoogle, 2006. Achievements include design of a search engine index of 30 billion pages using information from the Internet Archive at Archive.org. Office: Cuil Inc 66 Willow Pl Menlo Park CA 94025 Office Fax: 650-325-1701, 650-325-1702.

PATTERSON, ANNE WOODS, United States Ambassador to Pakistan; b. Ft. Smith, Ark., 1949; m. David R. Patterson; children: Edward, Andrew. BA in Econs., Wellesley Coll., Mass.; grad. student, U. NC. With US Fgn. Svc., 1973—, econ. officer Ecuador, 1974-77, desk officer Nicaragua, analyst for C.Am., trade specialist Canada, econ. counselor Riyadh, Saudi Arabia, 1984-88, polit. counselor US Mission to UN Geneva, dir. Office Andean Affairs, 1991-93, dep. asst. sec. C.Am. and the Caribbean, 1993-95, prin. dep. asst. sec. for inter-Am. affairs, 1995—97, US amb. to El Salvador San Salvador, 1997—2000, US amb. to Colombia Bogota, 2000—03; dep. insp. gen. US Dept. State, Washington, 2003—04, asst. sec. Bur. Internat. Narcotics and Law Enforcement Affairs, 2005—07, US amb. to Pakistan Islamabad, 2007—; dep. permanent US rep. UN, NYC, 2004—05, acting permanent US rep., 2005. Recipient Superior Honor award, US Dept. State, 1981, 88 Meritorious Honor award, 1977, 83, Presdl. award, 1993; Order of the Congress, Congress of Colombia, Order of Boyaca, Govt. Colombia, Order of Jose Matias Delgado, Govt. El Salvador. Office: DOS Amb 8100 Islamabad Pl Washington DC 20521-8100*

PATTERSON, AUBREY BURNS, JR., banker; b. Grenada, Miss., Sept. 25, 1942; s. Aubrey Burns and Elizabeth (Staten) P.; m. Ruby Kathryn Clegg, Dec. 12, 1964; children: Aubrey B. III, Clayton H., Jennifer L. BBA, U. Miss., 1964; MBA, Mich. State U., 1969. With Bancorp South (formerly Bank of Miss.), Tupelo, 1972—, pres., 1983—90, chmn., chief exec. officer, 1990—. Chmn., CEO Bancorp-South, Inc. Former chmn. bd. dirs. Salvation Army, Tupelo; bd. dirs. Cmty. Devel. Found., chmn. bd., 1994-95; bd. dirs. Columbia Theol. Sem., Decatur, Ga., Fin. Svs. Roundtable, Presbyn. Ch. U.S.A. Found., New Covenant Trust Co.; former chmn. CREATE, Inc.; bd. dirs. Miss. Econ. Coun., Jackson, 1986—, chmn., 1994; chmn. bd. dirs. North Miss. Health Svcs. Inc., 1987—, also exec. com.; bd. dirs. Miss. Partnership Econ. Devel.; bd. dir. Furniture Brands Internat. and Miss. Instns. Higher Learning; moderator St. Andrews Presbytery Presbyn. Ch. USA; chmn., bd. dirs. U. Miss. Found.; laureate Miss. Bus. Hall of Fame; bd. dirs. Journal Pub. Co.; mem. exec. com. Miss. Pub. Edn. Forum. Capt. USAF, 1965-72. Decorated Air Force Commendation medal, Meritorious Svc. medal, Nat. Def. Svc. medal. Mem. ABA (govt. rels. coun.), Am. Bankers Assn. (chmn. 2002-2003), U. Miss. Hall of Fame, Miss. Bankers Assn. (pres. 1995—), Soc. Internat. Bus. Fellows, Conf. of State Bank Supr., Bankers Adv. Coun. (chmn.), Tupelo Country Club, Univ. Club, Kiwanis (pres. Tupelo 1987), Beta Gamma Sigma, Beta Alpha Psi, bd. dirs. Furniture Brand Internat. and Miss. Power Co., bd. trustees Miss. instns. Higher Learning. Presbyterian. Office: BancorpSouth PO Box 789 Tupelo MS 38802-0789

PATTERSON, CARLY, singer, former Olympic gymnast; b. Baton Rouge, Feb. 4, 1988; d. Ricky and Natalie. Mem. TOPS Nat. Team, 1996, 1997, US Nat. Gymnastics Team, 2000—06; gymnast Team USA, Athens Olympic Games, 2004; singer Musicmind Records, 2008—. Contestant Celebrity Duets, 2006. Singer: Back to the Beginning, 2007. Achievements include member of US World Championships Gold medal team, 2003; winning silver medal, all-around, World Championships, 2003; won Visa Am. Cup Championship by winning all four events, 2004; winning gold medal, all-around, Athens Olympic games, 2004; member of US Women's Silver medal Gymnastics team, Athens Olympic games, 2004. Office: c/o MusicMind Records Chicago IL 60607 Office Phone: 312-733-2424. Office Fax: 312-733-2425.

PATTERSON, CHRISTOPHER NIDA, lawyer; b. Washington Courthouse, Ohio, Apr. 17, 1960; s. Donis Dean and JoAnne (Nida) O.; m. Vicky Patterson; children: Travis, Kirsten. BA, Clemson U., 1982; JD, Nova U., 1985. Bar: Fla. 1985, U.S. Dist. Ct. (mid. dist.) Fla. 1985, U.S. Ct. Mil. Rev. 1986, U.S. Ct. Appeals Armed Forces 1987, U.S. Dist. Ct. (ea. dist.) Va. 1987, U.S. Supreme Ct. 1989, U.S. Ct. Appeals (11th cir.) 1992, U.S. Dist. Ct. (no. dist.) Fla. 1992, U.S. Dist. Ct. (so. dist.) Tex. 1995; cert. criminal trial specialist Fla. Bar., 1995, cert. criminal trial advocate Nat. Bd. Trial Advocacy, 1995.; cert. dependency mediator, family law mediator, county ct. mediator, arbitrator. Pros. Fla. State Attys. Office, Orlando, Fla., 1985; spl. asst. U.S. Atty. U.S. Dist. Ct. (ea. dist.) Va., 1987-90; pvt. practice, 1991—. Adj. prof. law Gulf Coast CC, 1994—95; mem. Fla. Supreme Ct. Mediators Qualifications Bd.; family law mediator Fla. Supreme Ct., dependency law mediator, county ct. mediator, mem. mediators qualifications bd.; mediator County Ct.; on-air legal analyst Nex Media-WYOO-FM. Author: Queen's Pawn, 1996, Treasure Trove, 1997, Krysha, 2006; contbr. Nat. DAR Mag., Fla. Defender mag, Ct. TV Chancellor St. Thomas Episcopal Ch.; bd. dirs. Bay County Teen Ct., Inc., Gulf Coast, Girs Inc. Svc. Orgn., Widowed Persons Svc., The Unlimited Path, Inc. With judge advocate gen. corps U.S. Army, 1986—91. Recipient U.S. Army Chief of Staff award for legal excellence, 1989, Guardian ad litem commendation, Fla. Supreme Ct., 1999. Mem. ABA, FBA, SAR, NACDL (life), Am. Coll. Barristers, Fla. Assn. Criminal Def. Lawyers, Acad. Fla. Trial Lawyers, Assn. Fed. Def. Attys., Fla. Acad. Profl. Mediators, Fla. Bar Spkrs. Bur. (criminal law sect., del. 11th cir. jud. conf. 1999, Pro Bono Svc. award, nominee Jefferson award for pub. svc. 1999), Bay County Bar Assn., The Ret. Officers' Assn., Christian Legal Soc., Am. Legion, Fellowship of Christian Athletes, Nat. Triathlon Fedn., Soc. Colonial Wars, Mil. Order Fgn. Wars, Rotary Internat. (past pres., Paul Harris fellow). Episcopalian. Avocations: athletics, travel, writing. Office: 111 Moonlight Dr Panama City FL 32413 Office Phone: 850-872-0226, 850-233-9119. Business E-Mail: pattersonlaw@knology.net.

PATTERSON, DEB, women's college basketball coach; Grad., Rockford Coll., 1979. Coach Hononegah HS, Ill., 1982—86; asst. coach No. Ill. U., 1986—87, asst. coach, recruiting coord., 1987—91, Vanderbilt U., 1992-96; asst. coach So. Ill. U., 1991-92; head coach Kans. State U., 1996—. Asst. coach World U. Games, 1997, World Championships, 1998, Jr. World Championship Qualifying Team, 2000; asst. coach Women's Sr. Nat. Team USA Invitational Tournament of Champions, 1997. Named Women's Coll. Basketball Coach of Yr., Kans. Basketball Coaches Assn., 1997, 2008, Coach of Yr., ESPN The Mag., 2002, Big 12 Conf., 2002, 2008, Dist. V Coach of Yr., Women's Basketball Coaches Assn., 2002, 2003, 2008, Big 12 Coach of Yr., San Antonio Express News, 2002, Austin-Am. Statesman, 2002, Dallas Morning News, 2002, 2008, Waco Tribune, 2008, Kans. City Star, 2008; named to Rockford Coll. Hall of Fame; finalist Nat. Coach of Yr., Women's Basketball Coaches Assn., 2002, 2003, 2008, AP, 2008, Naismith Nat. Coach of Yr., 2002, 2003, 2008. Achievements include leading Kansas State to Women's National Invitational Tournament Championship as head coach, 2006. Office: Kansas State Univ Womens Basketball 1800 College Ave Manhattan KS 66502-3308 Office Phone: 785-532-6970. E-mail: dlpip@k-state.edu.*

PATTERSON, DENNIS M., bank executive; Grad., Ga. Inst. Tech., Atlanta, 1971. Corp. exec. v.p. corp. sales adminstrn., mem. mgmt. com. SunTrust Banks, Inc. Mem. adv. bd. Ga. Inst. Tech. Coll. Mgmt. Named to Acad. Disting. Alumni, Ga. Inst. Tech. Coll. Mgmt., 2006. Office: SunTrust Banks Inc PO Box 4418 Atlanta GA 30302-4418 Office Phone: 404-588-7711. Office Fax: 404-827-6173.

PATTERSON, DONALD ROSS, lawyer, educator; b. Sept. 9, 1939; s. Sam Ashley and Marguerite (Robinson) P.; m. Peggy Ann Schulte, May 1, 1965; children: D. Ross, Jerome Ashley, Gretchen Anne. BS, Tex. Tech U., 1961; JD, U. Tex., 1964; LLM, So. Meth. U., 1972. Bar: Tex. 1964, U.S. Ct. Claims 1970, U.S. Ct. Customs and Patent Appeals 1970, U.S. Ct. Mil. Appeals 1970, U.S. Supreme Ct. 1970, U.S. Dist. Ct. (ea. dist.) Tex. 1982, U.S. Ct. Appeals (5th cir.) 1991, U.S. Ct. Appeals (D.C. cir.) 1994; bd. cert. in immigration and naturalization law, Tex. Commd. lt. (j.g.) USN, 1964, advanced through grades to lt. comdr., 1969; asst. officer in charge Naval Petroleum Res., Bakersfield, Calif., 1970-72; staff judge adv. Kenitra, Morocco, 1972-76; officer in charge Naval Legal Svcs. Office, Whidbey Island, Wash., 1976-79; head mil. Justice divsn., Subic Bay, The Philippines, 1979-81; ret. USN, 1982; pvt. practice Tyler, Tex., 1982—. Former instr. U. Md., Chapman Coll., U. LaVerne, Tyler Jr. Coll., Jarvis Christian Coll., U. Tex., Tyler. Mem. East Tex. Estate Planning Coun. Mem. Coll. of State Bar of Tex., Tex. Bar Assn., Smith County Bar Assn., Am. Immigration Lawyers Assn., Masons, Rotary (past pres.), Shriners, Toastmasters (past pres.), Phi Delta Phi. Republican. Baptist. Home: 703 Wellington St Tyler TX 75703-4666 Office: 777 S Broadway Ave Ste 106 Tyler TX 75701-1648 Office Phone: 903-592-8186. Business E-Mail: oneworldtogether@sbcglobal.net.

PATTERSON, DOUGLAS MACLENNAN, finance educator; b. Jan. 16, 1945; s. Thomas and Ruth (MacLennan) P.; m. Sara Louise Lucas; children: Cara Beth, John Douglas BSEE, U. Wis., 1968, MBA, 1972, PhD, 1978. Elec. engr. Westinghouse Electric, Balt., 1968—71; asst. prof. U. Mich., Ann Arbor, 1976—80, Va. Tech., Blacksburg, 1980—86, assoc. prof., 1986—98, prof., 1998—. Vis. prof. U. Calif., Santa Barbara, 1989; vis. scholar U. Tex., Austin, 1994; dir. PhD program fin. Va. Tech., 1991—95; invited spl. spkr. Statis. Inference and Non-Linear Dynamics in Time Series conf., Bressanone, Italy, 2005; presenter, spkr. in field; dir. program on free markets Pampin Coll. Bus., 2007—; vis. scholar U. Calif., Santa Barbara, 2008. Co-author: A Nonlinear Times Series Workshop: A Tool Kit for Detecting and Identifying Nonlinear Serial Dependence; contbr. articles to profl. jours Mem. ad hoc com. Detroit Area Hosp. Assn., 1978-79 Recipient Tchg. Excellence award Va. Tech., 1983; U. Mich. fellow, 1979; USN grantee, 1984, 85, 90 Mem. Am. Fin. Assn., Am. Econ. Assn., Fin. Mgmt. Assn., Beta Gamma Sigma. Methodist. Home: 702 Crestwood Dr Blacksburg VA 24060-6006 Office: Va Poly Inst Dept Finance 0221 Blacksburg VA 24061

PATTERSON, ELAINE WILCOX, art educator; b. Newburgh, NY, Nov. 16, 1948; d. William Thomas and Julia B. Wilcox; m. Russell Saunders Patterson, Dec. 23, 1974; children: John Russell, Heath Tyler. BA English Art, Delta State Univ., 1970. Nat. bd. cert. tchr. 2004. Mutual funds liaison Merrill Lynch, Memphis, 1969—71; flight attendant Delta Airlines, Memphis, 1971—74; adminstr. asst. Pikeville Coll./Tchr. Corps, Pikeville, Ky., 1974—79; art tchr. East Jr. HS, Gaffney, SC, 1981—86, W.C. Friday Jr. HS, Dallas, NC, 1986—93; missionary Honduras Bapt. Med. Dental Mission, Tegucigalpa, Honduras, 1992—99; tchr. Forestview HS, Gastonia, NC, 1999—. Presenter NC Art Educators Assn., 2002—. Various local and state level exhbns., 1999—. Sun. sch. tchr. East Bapt. Ch., Gastonia, NC, 1999—, choir mem., 1999—, banner ministry dir., 1999—. Named Outstanding Young Woman of the Yr., Tchr. of Yr., W.C. Friday Jr. HS, 1992. So. Bapt. Office: Forestview HS 5545 Union Rd Gastonia NC 28056

PATTERSON, ELIZABETH C., choir director; b. Lakeland, Fla., Mar. 1, 1938; d. Jewell King Patterson and Loreta Marie Woodruff; m. Richard Pugsley; children: Richard Pugsley, Wendy Saran. B, 1960; MusM, Milliken U., 1962; postgrad., Cambridge U., Eng. Dir. Gloriae Dei Cantores, Orleans, Mass., 1988—. CEO Paraclete Press, Brewster, Mass., 1983—90, cons., 1990—. Co-author: (book) The Sound Eternal, 1987. Prioress Cmty. of Jesus Inc., 1990—. Mem.: NARAS, Am. Choral Dirs. Assn. Avocations: needlepoint, knitting, painting, sewing. Office: Gloriae Dei Cantores PO Box 2831 11 Bayview Dr Orleans MA 02653

PATTERSON, ELIZABETH JOHNSTON, Former United States Representative, South Carolina; b. Columbia, SC, Nov. 18, 1939; d. Olin DeWitt and Gladys (Atkinson) Johnston; m. Dwight Fleming Patterson, Jr., Apr. 15, 1967; children: Dwight Fleming, Olin DeWitt, Catherine Leigh. BA, Columbia Coll., 1961; postgrad. in polit. sci., U. S.C., 1961, 62, 64; LLD (hon.), Columbia Coll., 1987; D Pub. Svc. (hon.), Converse Coll., 1989, M in Liberal Arts, 1999; LLD (hon.), Wofford Coll., 1999. Pub. affairs officer Peace Corps, Washington, 1962-64, VISTA, OEO, Washington, 1965-66; D Pub. Svc. Head Start and VISTA, OEO, Columbia, 1966-67; tri-county dir. Head Start, Piedmont Community Actions, Spartanburg, SC, 1967-68; mem. Spartanburg County Coun., 1975-76, S.C. State Senate, 1979-86, 100th-102nd Congresses from 4th S.C. dist., 1987-93; dir. continuing edn., converse II program Converse Coll., 1993—2003; ret. Adj. prof. Spartanburg Meth. Coll., 1993—2001. Trustee Wofford Coll., 1978—90, Columbia Coll., 1991—2003, Spartanburg Meth. Coll., 2004—; pres. Spartanburg Dem. Women, 1968; v.p. Spartanburg County Dem. party, 1968—70, sec., 1970—75, pres., 2004—08; bd. dirs. S.C. Ind. Colls. and Univs., 1995—99, Charles Lea Ctr., 1978, Spartanburg Coun. on Aging; chmn., bd. dirs. Bethlehem Cmty. Ctr., 1998—, Gen. Conf. United Meth. Ch. and Southeastern Jurisdictional Conf., U.M.A., 2008. Mem.: Bus. and Profl. Women's Club, Alpha Kappa Gamma. Democrat. Methodist.

PATTERSON, EUGENE CORBETT, retired editor, publishing executive; b. Valdosta, Ga., Oct. 15, 1923; s. William C. and Annabel (Corbett) P.; m. Mary Sue Carter, Aug. 19, 1950; 1 child, Mary Patterson Fausch. Student, North Ga. Coll., Dahlonega, 1940-42; AB in Journalism, U. Ga., 1943; LL.D., Tusculum Coll., 1965, Harvard U., 1969, Duke U., 1978, Stetson U., 1984, Ind. U., 1990; Litt.D., Emory U., 1966, Oglethorpe Coll., 1966, Tuskegee U., 1966, Roanoke Coll., 1968, Mercer U., 1968, Eckerd Coll., 1977, U. South Fla., 1986, Dillard U., 1992, Colby Coll., 1994, North Ga. Coll. & State U., 1999. Reporter Temple (Tex.) Daily Telegram and Macon (Ga.) Telegraph, 1947-48; mgr. for S.C. United Press, 1948-49, N.Y. night bur. mgr. NYC, 1949-53, mgr. London bur., also chief corr. U.K., 1953-56; v.p., exec. editor Atlanta Journal-Constitution, 1956-60; editor Atlanta Constitution, 1960-68; mng. editor Washington Post, 1968-71; prof. polit. sci. Duke U., 1971-72; editor, pres. St. Petersburg (Fla.) Times, 1972-84, chmn., chief exec. officer, 1978-88, editor emeritus, 1988—; editor, pres. Congl. Quar., Washington, 1972-86, chmn., chief exec. officer, 1978-88. Chmn. bd., chief exec. officer Fla. Trend mag., 1980-88, Ga. Trend mag., 1984-88, Ariz. Trend mag., 1986-88, Governing mag., 1987-88, Modern Graphic Arts, Inc., 1978-88, Poynter Inst. Media Studies, 1978-88, Poynter Fund, 1978-88. Author: The Changing South of Gene Patterson, 2002, Patton's Unsung Armor of the Ardennes, 2008. Vice chmn. U.S. Civil Rights Commn., 1964-68; mem. Pulitzer Prize Bd., 1973-84; trustee ASNE Found., 1981-84, U. Ga. Found., 1982-88, North Ga. Coll. Found., 1991-93, Am. Press Inst., Reston, Va., 1983-88, Duke U., 1988-94, Fla. Bar Found., 1992-93, LeRoy Collins Ctr. for Pub. Policy, 1990-93. Decorated Silver Star, Bronze Star with oak leaf cluster in 10th Armored Divsn., Gen. Patton's 3rd Army; recipient Pulitzer prize for editl. writing Columbia U., 1967, William Allen White Nat. Citation award U. Kans., 1980, Elijah Parish Lovejoy award Colby Coll., 1994; inducted into Fla. Newspaper Hall of Fame Fla. Press Assn., 1997, named a Great Floridian Fla. Gov. and Sec. State, 2009. Fellow Soc. Profl. Journalists; mem. Am. Soc. Newspaper Editors (pres. 1977-78), St. Petersburg Yacht Club. Home: Snell Isle 1967 Brightwaters Blvd NE Saint Petersburg FL 33704-3007 Personal E-mail: ecp1015@aol.com.

PATTERSON, GARY, college football coach; b. Larned, Kans., Feb. 13, 1960; m. Kelsey Patterson; children: Josh, Cade, Blake. BS in Phys. Edn., Kans. State, 1983; MEd, Tenn. Tech., 1984. Grad. asst. Kans. State U., 1982; linebackers coach Tenn. Tech. U., 1983—84, U. Calif.-Davis, 1986, Pitts. State U., Kans., 1988; defensive coord. Cal Lutheran, 1987, Sonoma State U., Calif., 1989—91; coach Oreg. Lightning Bolts, 1992; secondary coach Utah State U., 1992—94, US Naval Acad., 1995; defensive coord., safeties coach U. N.Mex., 1996—97, Tex. Christian U., 1998—2000, head football coach, 2000—. Named Coach of Yr.,

Conf. USA, 2002, Mountain West Conf., 2005; finalist Eddie Robinson Nat. Coach of Yr. award, 2003, Bobby Dodd Nat. Coach of Yr. award, 2003. Office: TCU Athletics PO Box 297600 Fort Worth TX 76129*

PATTERSON, GORDON M., history professor; b. Springfield, Mo., Aug. 18, 1948; s. Maurice E. and Molly O. Patterson; m. Joy L. Bacon, Aug. 28, 1972; 1 child, Ben G. BS, Northwestern U., Evanston, Ill., 1970; PhD, UCLA, 1974. Lectr. European Divsn. U. Md., Heidelberg, Germany, 1974—81; prof. history Fla. Inst. Tech., Melbourne. Vis. scholar Ctr. Vector Biology, Rutgers U., NJ. Author: (book) The Mosquito Wars, The Mosquito Crusades, Florida Institute of Technology: A College History. Mem.: Dante Soc., Am. Mosquito Control Assn. Home: 315 Barton Ave Melbourne FL 32901 Office: Fla Inst Tech 150 W University Blvd Melbourne FL 32901 Personal E-mail: gordonmpatterson@gmail.com.

PATTERSON, JAMES (JIM), economist, writer; b. Ft. Belvoir, Va., Jan. 1, 1955; s. James G. and Helen L. Patterson; m. Sheryl Rene Alexander (div.); children: James H., Alexandra Baker. BS in Econs., Auburn U., 1977, MS in Econs., 1980. Economist Dept. Agrl. Econs., Auburn, Ala., 1978—80; sys. analyst Ind. Employment Security Divsn., Indpls., 1981—84; elected GOP precinct committeeman, 1983; economist /statistician U.S. Dept. of Commerce, 1984—87; sr. economist USDA, 1987—92, diplomat/fgn. svc. officer, 1992—98; freelance writer, 1999—; elected adv. neighborhood commr., 2000. Prof. econs. Grad. Sch., USDA, 1989—91; adj. prof. econs. No. Va. C.C., Woodbridge, 1987; instr., cons. mktg. Fairfax County Adult Edn. Dept., Va., 1985—87. Author: (newspaper column) Washington Scene, 1995; contbr. articles to mags. Mem. Fed. GLOBE; mem. nat. adv. com. Lillian Gish Theater, Bowling Green State U.; coord. USDA AIDS Walk, Wash., 1994. Recipient Spl. Svc. award, US Dept. Commerce, 1986, Productivity award, 1987, Performance award, 1989, Presdl. Point of Light award, USDA, 1992, certs. from, EEO award; named one of Outstanding Young Men of Am., 1989. Mem.: GLAAD, Nat. Book Critics Cir., Nat. Lesbian & Gay Journalist Assn., Integrity, William J. Clinton Found., Gerald R. Ford Found., Am. Foreign Svc. Assn., Nat. Gay & Lesbian Task Force, Rock & Roll Hall Fame & Mus., Alpha Zeta (sec., treas., VP 1988—92). Episcopalian. Achievements include being profiled in New York Times, Wall Street Journal, The Washington Times, American Writer and The Foreign Service Journal. Avocations: travel, writing, reading. Home: 766 Harrison St San Francisco CA 94107

PATTERSON, JAMES, telecommunications industry executive; m. Martha Patterson; 1 child, Jimmy. BA in Econs., Davidson Coll., NC; MBA, U. Va.; student in Brit. lit. and econ. history, Cambridge U., Eng. Cons. Andersen Consulting; various leadership roles Sprint Nextel Corp., 1994—2003, head, wholesale, access and carrier markets group, 2003—05, v.p. cable solutions, 2005—08, acting pres. cable joint venture, 2007—, pres. wholesale services, 2008—. Named one of 100 Most Influential Industry Execs., Cable Fax Daily, 2007. Avocations: running, skiing, horticulture. Office: Sprint Nextel Corp 6200 Sprint Pky Overland Park KS 66251*

PATTERSON, JAMES BRENDAN, JR., writer; b. Newburgh, NY, Mar. 22, 1947; s. Charles H. and Isabelle (Morris) Patterson. BA, Manhattan Coll., 1969; MA, Vanderbilt U., 1970. With J. Walter Thompson Co., NYC, 1971—96; chmn. J. Walter Thompson U.S., 1990—96. Author: (novels) The Thomas Berryman Number, 1976 (Edgar Allen Poe award Mystery Writers Am.), Season of the Machete, 1977, Virgin, 1980, The Midnight Club, 1988, Hide & Seek, 1996, Miracle on the 17th green, 1996, See How They Run, 1997, When the Wind Blows, 1998, Black Friday, 2000, Cradle & All, 2000, Suzanne's Diary for Nicholas, 2001, The Beach House, 2002, The Jester, 2003, The Lake House, 2003, Sam's Letters To Jennifer, 2004, Honeymoon, 2005, Lifeguard, 2005, Beach Road, 2006, Judge & Jury, 2006, The Quickie, 2007 (Publishers Weekly bestseller), You've Been Warned, 2007 (Publishers Weekly bestseller), Sundays at Tiffany's, 2008, Sail, 2008 (Publishers Weekly bestseller), Swimsuit, 2009 (Publishers Weekly bestseller), (Alex Cross series) Along Came a Spider, 1992, Kiss the Girls, 1995, Jack & Jill, 1996, Cat and Mouse, 1997, Pop! Goes the Weasel, 1999, Roses are Red, 2000, Violets are Blue, 2001, Four Blind Mice, 2002, The Big Bad Wolf, 2003, London Bridges, 2004, Mary, Mary, 2005, Cross, 2006, Double Cross, 2007 (#1 Publishers Weekly bestseller), Cross Country, 2008 (#1 Publishers Weekly bestseller), Alex Cross's Trial, 2009, (Women's Murder Club series) 1st to Die, 2001, 2nd Chance, 2002, 3rd Degree, 2004, 4th of July, 2005, The 5th Horsemen, 2006, The 6th Target, 2007, 7th Heaven, 2008 (Publishers Weekly bestseller), 8th Confession, 2009 (Publishers Weekly bestseller), (Michael Bennett series) Step on a Crack, 2007 (Publishers Weekly bestseller), Run for Your Life, 2009; co-author (with Hal Friedman): (non-fiction) Against Medical Advice: One Family's Struggle with an Agonizing Medical Mystery, 2008 (#1 Publishers Weekly bestseller); author: (children's books) SantaKid, 2004, The Angel Experiment, 2005, School's Out-Forever, 2006, Saving the World and other Extreme Sports, 2007, The Final Warning, 2008. Recipient 6 Clio awards, 1983, Effie award, 1983; named one of The 100 Most Powerful Celebrities, Forbes.com, 2008. Mem.: Phi Beta Kappa. Mailing: c/o Author Mail Hachette Book Group USA 237 Park Ave New York NY 10017*

PATTERSON, JAMES RANDOLPH, physician; b. Lancaster, Pa., Jan. 30, 1942; m. Linda Lewis Patterson, Nov. 22, 1969. AB, U. Pa., 1964; MD, Columbia U., 1968. Diplomate Nat. Bd. Med. Examiners, Am. Bd. Internal Medicine, Subsplty. of Pulmonary Disease. Pulmonary and critical care specialist The Oreg. Clinic, Portland, 1975—; clin. prof. medicine Oreg. Health Scis. U., Portland, 1978—. Mem. Am. Bd. Internal Medicine, Phila., 1995—, sec.-treas., 2002-; trustee Collins Med. Trust, Portland, Oreg., 1992—, chair subsplty. bd. pulmonary disease, 1998-2002. Contbr. numerous articles to profl. jours. Recipient Class of 1964 award U. Pa., Van Loan award Am. Lung Assn. Oreg., 1990, Meritorious Achievement award Oreg. Health Scis. U., 1991; named Class Pres. Coll. Physicians and Surgeons of Columbia U., 1968, Tchr. of Yr. Providence Med. Ctr., Portland, Oreg., 1976, Internist of Yr., 1983, Best Doctors in Am., 1992—, Consumers Guide to Top Doctors, 2002-. Mem. AMA, Am. Thoracic Soc. (Clinician Tchr. of Yr. 2009), Am. Coll. Chest Physicians, Oreg. Lung Assn., North Pacific Soc. of Internal Medicine, Pacific Interurban Clin. Club, Multnomah County Med. Soc., Oreg. Med. Assn., Oreg. Soc. Critical Care Medicine. Office: The Oregon Clinic 1111 NE 99th St Ste 200N Portland OR 97220 Office Phone: 503-963-3030. Business E-Mail: jpatterson@orclinic.com.

PATTERSON, JAN EVANS, epidemiologist, educator; b. Ft. Worth, May 13, 1956; d. C. Wayne and Zona (Horn) Evans; m. Thomas F. Patterson, June 22, 1985. BA, Hardin-Simmons U., 1978; MD, U. Tex., 1982. Diplomate Am. Bd. Internal Medicine, Am. Bd. Infectious Diseases. Asst. prof. medicine and lab. medicine Yale U. Sch. Medicine, New Haven, 1988-92; assoc. prof. medicine and pathology Health Sci. Ctr. U. Tex., San Antonio, 1993—99, prof. medicine and pathology, assoc. chair medicine, 1999—2005, prof. medicine and pathology, vice chair medicine, 2005—06, prof. medicine and pathology, interim chair medicine, 2006—07, prof. medicine pathology, 2008—, dir. Ctr. Patient Safety & Health Policy, 2008—; chief med. svc. South Tex. Vets. Healthcare Sys., 2004—06, 2008—. Hosp. epidemiologist Univ. Health Sys., San Antonio, 1993-2005, Audie Murphy Meml. Vets. Hosp., San Antonio, 1993-95, S. Tex. Vets. Healthcare System, San Antonio and Kerrville, 1995-2005. Contbr. articles to profl. jours. Fellow ACP, Infectious Disease Soc. Am.; mem. Soc. Hosp. Epidemiologists, Am. Soc. Tropical Medicine and Hygiene, Exec. Leadership in Academic Medicine, Alpha Omega Alpha Office: Health Sci Ctr U Tex Divsn Infectious Diseases 7703 Floyd Curl Dr San Antonio TX 78284-6200 Office Phone: 210-567-4810. Business E-Mail: pattersonj@uthscsa.edu.

PATTERSON, JOHN DE LA ROCHE, JR., lawyer; b. Schenectady, NY, July 8, 1941; s. John de la Roche Sr. and Jane C. (Clay) P.; m. Michele F. Demarest, Nov. 28, 1987; children: Daniel C., Sara R., Amy C. BA, Johns Hopkins U., 1963; LLB, Harvard U., 1966. Bar: Mass. 1968. Vol. Peace Corps, Chad, 1966-67; assoc. Foley Hoag LLP, Boston, 1967-73, ptnr., 1974—, mem. exec. com., 1989-97. Chmn. Kodaly Ctr. Am. Inc., Newton, Mass., 1977-87. Mem. ABA, Boston Bar Assn. Democrat. Avocations: sailing, tennis, travel, reading. Office: Foley Hoag LLP 155 Seaport Blvd Boston MA 02210- Office Phone: 617-832-1144. Business E-Mail: jpatterson@FoleyHoag.com.

PATTERSON, JOHN MALCOLM, judge, former Governor of Alabama; b. Goldville, Ala., Sept. 27, 1921; s. Albert Love and Agnes Louise (Benson) P.; m. Florentine M. Sawyers, Oct. 17, 1975; children: Albert L., Barbara Louise. JD, U. Ala., 1949. Bar: Ala. 1949. Practiced in, Phenix City, 1949-51, 53-55; atty. gen., securities commr. State of Ala., 1955-59, gov., 1959-63; practice law Montgomery, Ala., 1963-84; judge Ala. Ct. Criminal Appeals, 1984-97, part-time judge, 1997—2002. Chief judge Ct. of the Judiciary, 1989-97; cattle farmer. Bd. editors: Ala. Law Review, 1948-49. Served to maj., F.A. AUS, 1940-45; maj. 1951-53. Nominated one of 10 outstanding young men of US, 1956, one of four outstanding young men of Ala. Jr. C. of C. Mem. ABA, Ala. Bar Assn., VFW, Am. Legion. Farrar Order of Jurisprudence, Ala. Acad. Honor, Alpha Tau Omega, Phi Alpha Delta, Sigma Delta Kappa, Phi Eta Sigma, Omicron Delta Kappa.

PATTERSON, JOSEPH REDWINE, retired lawyer; b. Corsicana, Tex., Apr. 16, 1927; s. Joseph Isham and Caroline Anderson (White) P.; m. Ann Louise Cumber, Mar. 9, 1956; children— Joseph Redwine, Amy Cumber. BA in Philosophy, So. Methodist U., 1948, MA in Govt, 1951, JD, 1954. Bar: Tex. 1954. Asst. dist. atty., Dallas County, 1955-56; assoc. gen. counsel Traders and Gen. Ins. Co., Dallas, 1957; ptnr. PLS Properties (real estate), Dallas, 1971—99; ptnr. firm Patterson, Lamberty & Robinson, Dallas, 1971—2002; ret., 2002. Contbr. legal jours. Founding dir. Dallas chpt. Action on Smoking and Health. With USN, 1945-46. Fellow Tex. Bar Found., Dallas Bar Found.; mem. ABA, Tex. Bar Assn., Dallas Bar Assn., Cross Country Club Dallas USA Triathlon. Democrat. Home: 6131 Meadow Rd Dallas TX 75230-5058

PATTERSON, LAURIE J., science educator; d. John Edwin and Leona Burns Patterson; m. Philip Furia, Aug. 5, 1995; 1 child, Olivia Leona Patterson Furia. ALA, U. Minn., 1982; BA, 1985, MEd, 1996; EdD, Nova Southeastern U., Fort Lauderdale Fla., 2005. Contbr. articles to profl. jours., scientific papers. Bd. sec. DREAMS Wilmington, NC, 1996—97. Math. Sci. Partnership grant, Dept. of Edn./NC State Bd. Edn., 2007—. Dfl.

PATTERSON, LEE, language educator; s. George Stuart and Marguerite Bushnell Patterson; children: Anne Candler, Thomas Willing, Charles Philip. BA, Yale U., New Haven, 1962, PhD, 1968. Asst. prof. U. Toronto, Ontario, 1967—79; prof. Johns Hopkins U., Baltimore, 1979—86, Duke U., Durham, NC, 1986—94; F. W. Hilles prof. English Yale U., 1994—. Author: (book) Negotiating the Past: The Historical Understanding of Medieval Literature, Chaucer and the Subject of History (Christian Gauss prize, 1992), Temporal Circumstances. Campaign mgr. New Dem. Party, Toronto, Ontario, Canada, 1971—77. Fellow: Medieval Acad. Am. (CARA Tchg. award 2006); mem.: Phi Beta Kappa (Christian Gauss prize 1992). Democrat. Avocations: golf, bicycling. Home: 2516 Ridge Rd North Haven CT 06473 Office: Yale Univ 63 High St New Haven CT 06520 Business E-Mail: lee.patterson@yale.edu.

PATTERSON, MARK AINSLEY, federal official; b. Albany, NY, Dec. 15, 1961; s. Raymond Coughtry and Barbara Ann Patterson. m. Jennifer Sue Leete, Sept. 6, 2003 BA, SUNY, Albany, 1984; JD, Cath. U., 1990. Bar: D.C. 1995, Pa. 1990, U.S. Supreme Ct. 1997. Spl. asst. to Senator Daniel Patrick Moynihan, Washington, 1985-88, legis. dir. to, 1993-95; ptnr. Fox Bennett & Turner, Washington, 1990-93; minority staff dir., chief counsel Senate Fin. Com. US Senate, Washington, 1995-99, staff dir., Senate Democratic Leadership Com., 1999, policy dir. to Senator Tom Daschle; v.p. govt. rels. Goldman Sachs Group & Co., 2005—08; chief of staff US Dept. Treasury, Washington, 2009—. Democrat. Office: US Dept Treasury 1500 Pennsylvania Ave NW Rm 3330 Washington DC 20220*

PATTERSON, OSCAR, III, retired academic administrator; b. July 25, 1945; s. Oscar Jr. and Frances (Killian) P.; m. Kathy E. Gibson, June 6, 1966 (div. Apr. 1979); 1 child, Elizabeth Anne Patterson Cassel; m. Julie Ann Holmes, Dec. 28, 1990. BA, Pfeiffer U., Misenheimer, NC, 1967; MFA, U. Ga., Athens, 1973; PhD, U. Tenn., 1982. Asst. prof. architecture and fine arts Auburn (Ala.) U., 1972-75; chairperson BFA in Theatre program Western Carolina U., Cullowhee, NC, 1975-79; dir. telecom. U. NC, Pembroke, NC, 1984—98; chair comm. and visual arts U. North Fla., Jacksonville, Fla., 1998—2006, prof. comm., 2006—07; ret., 2007. Juvenile probation officer Cleveland Ct. Sys., Shelby, NC, 1967-68; gen. mgr., news dir. WNCP-TV, NC, 1984-98. Contbr. articles to profl. jours.; host pub. tv program, 1989-98. Served US Army, 1968-75, Vietnam. Mem. AEJMC, Soc. Profl. Journalists, Phi Kappa Phi. Republican. Avocations: historical reenactment, beach exploration. Personal E-mail: opatters@comcast.net.

PATTERSON, PHILIP EDWARD, engineering educator; b. Gary, Ind., Oct. 24, 1957; s. Willie Edward and Barbara Jean Patterson; m. Jacqueline Gayle Ragland, July 27, 1985; children: Krista LeeAnne, Brittany Kathleen. PhD, U. Ga., Athens, 2006. Area mgr.; tool constrn. coord. GM, Kalamazoo, 1982—86; lab mgr. So. Poly. State U., Marietta, Ga., 1994—98. Chmn deacon bd. Zion Bapt. Ch., Marietta, 2006—08. Grants, U. Sys. Ga., 2000—02. Mem.: Kappa Delta Pl (assoc.; none). Independent. Baptist. Home: 1508 Rockcrest Way Marietta GA 30062 Office: Southern Poly State Univ 1100 S Marietta Pky Marietta GA 30060 Office Fax: 678-915-7223. Business E-Mail: ppatters@spsu.edu.

PATTERSON, P(ICKENS) ANDREW, lawyer; b. Cotton Plant, Ark., Aug. 1, 1944; s. Pickens Andrew and Willie Mae (Miller) Patterson; m. Gloria Neltine Peebles, Nov. 25, 1967; children: Pickens Andrew, Staci Elizabeth. BA, Fisk U., 1965; JD, Harvard U., 1968. Bar: Ga. 1969, NC 1978, US Dist. Ct. (no. dist.) Ga. 1969, US Dist. Ct. (mid. dist.) NC 1978, US Ct. Appeals (11th cir.) 1983. V.p. Urban East Housing Consl., Atlanta, 1968—69; mng. atty. Atlanta Legal Aid, 1968—70; sr. ptnr. Patterson, Parks, Jackson & Howell, Atlanta, 1970—77; atty. adviser HUD, Greensboro, NC, 1977—81; exec. v.p. Arrington, Patterson & Thomas, P.C., Atlanta, 1982—; ptnr. Thomas, Kennedy, Sampson & Patterson, 1985—. Pres. Atlanta Legal Aid Soc., 1976, Ctrl. Carolina Legal Svcs., Greensboro, 1980; chair State Bd. Bar Examiners. Co-author pamphlet. Active Atlanta Charter Study Commn., 1972; bd. dirs. Louisville Presbyn. Theol. Sem., 1983—86, Heritage Fund, Atlanta Med. Assn., 2006; trustee Fisk U., Nashville. Recipient Key to City Atlanta, 1972, Plaque awards, Atlanta Legal Aid Soc., 1977, Ctrl. Carolina Legal Svcs., 1981, Spl. Achievement award, Office Gen. Counsel, HUD, 1980. Mem.: Gate City Bar Assn., Atlanta Bar Assn., NC Bar Assn., State Bar Ga., Nat. Bar Assn., Sigma Pi Phi, Alpha Phi Alpha. Democrat. Methodist. Home: 3905 Somerled Trl Atlanta GA 30349-2035 Office: 3355 Main St College Park GA 30331 Home Phone: 404-763-1521; Office Phone: 404-688-4503. Business E-Mail: pa.patterson@tksp.com.

PATTERSON, REMINGTON PERRIGO, retired English language educator; b. Nice, France, Dec. 16, 1926; s. Howard Ashman and Elizabeth Mary (Perrigo) P.; m. Eleanor Duane Lloyd, Sept. 6, 1957; children: Burns, Sarah. BA, Yale U., 1950, MA, 1953, PhD, 1957. Instr. English Hill Sch., 1950-51; instr. English Barnard Coll., Columbia U., NYC, 1955-58, asst. prof., 1958-64, assoc. prof., 1964-73, prof., 1973—94, acting dean faculty, 1975-77, chmn. dept. English, 1982-85, ret., 1994. V.p. Axe-Houghton Found. Served with AUS, 1945-46, ETO. Recipient Fulbright award, 1961-62 Mem. Malone Soc., MLA Democrat. Episcopalian. Home: 280 Riverside Dr New York NY 10025-9010

PATTERSON, RICHARD MYRON, retired lawyer, editor, writer; b. Indpls., Dec. 21, 1934; m. Wynonia Yvonne Burch, July 26, 1958; children: Michael Richard, Steven Charles. BA, U. Indpls., 1960; JD, Ind. U., Indpls., 1964. Bar: Ind. 1964, US Dist. Ct. (so. dist.) Ind. 1964. Assoc. Nisenbaum & Brown, Indpls., 1961—65; staff atty. Blue Cross & Blue Shield of Ind., Indpls., 1965—69; v.p. editl. Allen Smith Co., Indpls., 1969—85; sr. exec. editor Michie Co., Charlottesville, Va., 1986—88; ret., 1988. Editor: Def. Law Jour., Lawyers' Medical Cyclopedia, Drugs in Litigation, Harney's Medical Malpractice, 1988—; contbr. articles to profl. jours. Home Fax: 317-329-6883. Personal E-mail: rpatter188@aol.com.

PATTERSON, RICHARD NORTH, writer, lawyer; b. Berkeley, Calif., Feb. 22, 1947; s. Richard Wallace and Marjorie Frances (North) P.; children: Shannon Heath, Brooke North, Katherine Amber, Adam Chandler, Chase Kenyon. BA History, Ohio Wesleyan U., 1968; JD, Case Western Reserve, 1971. Bar: Ohio, 1971, D.C., 1973, Ala., 1975, Calif., 1984. Asst. atty. gen. State of Ohio, 1971-73; with divsn. enforcement SEC, Washington, 1973-75, San Francisco, 1878-81; assoc. atty. Berkowitz, Lefkovits & Patrick, Birmingham, Ala., 1975-77, ptnr., 1978; assoc. McCutchen, Doyle, Brown & Enersen, San Francisco, 1985-87, ptnr., 1987-93, of counsel, 1993-94. Author: The Lasko Tangent, 1979, The Outside Man, 1981, Escape the Night, 1983, Private Screening, 1985, Degree of Guilt, 1993, Eyes of a Child, 1995, The Final Judgement, 1995, Silent Witness, 1997, No Safe Place, 1998, Dark Lady, 1999, Protect and Defend, 2000, Balance of Power, 2003, Conviction, 2005, Exile, 2007, The Race, 2007., Eclipse, 2009, The Spire, 2009. Chmn. Common Cause, 2006—07; bd. mem. Ohio Wesleyan U., 1996—2001, Brady Campaign Nat. Partnership for Women and Families, 2000—05. Recipient Edgar Allan Poe award for best 1st novel, Mystery Writers Am., 1979, Grand Prix de Literateur Policiere, 1995, Pres.'s award for Disting. Alumni, Case Western Res. U., 1997, Maggie award, Planned Parenthood, 2001, Disting. Achievement Citation award, Ohio Wesleyan U., 2008; named Man of Yr., WWRAP, 2001.

PATTERSON, ROBERT PORTER, JR., federal judge; b. NYC, July 11, 1923; s. Robert Porter and Margaret (Winchester) P.; m. Bevin C. Daly, Sept. 15, 1956; children: Anne, Robert, Margaret, Paul, Katherine. AB, Harvard U., 1947; LLB, Columbia U., 1950. Bar: N.Y. 1951, D.C. 1966. Law clk. Donovan, Leisure, Newton & Lumbard, NYC, 1950-51; asst. counsel N.Y. State Crime Commn. Waterfront Investigation, 1952-53; asst. U.S. atty. Chief of Narcotics Prosecutions and Investigations, 1953-56; asst. counsel Senate Banking and Currency Com., 1954; assoc. Patterson, Belknap, Webb & Tyler, NYC, 1956-60, ptnr., 1960-88; judge U.S. Dist. Ct. (So. Dist.), NY, 1988—98, sr. judge NY, 1998—. Counsel to minority select com. pursuant to house resolution no. 1, Washington, 1967; mem. Senator's Jud. Screening Panel, 1974-88, Gov.'s Jud. Screening Panel, 1975-82, Gov.'s Sentencing Com., 1978-79. Contbr. articles to profl. jours. Chmn. Wm. T. Grant Found., 1974-94, Prisoners' Legal Services N.Y., 1976-88; dir. Legal Aid Soc., 1961-88, pres., 1967-71; chmn. Nat. Citizens for Eisenhower, 1959-60, Scranton for Pres., N.Y. State, 1964; bd. mgrs. Havens Relief Fund Soc., 1994—, Millbrook Sch., 1966-78, Vera Inst. Justice, 1981-99, New Sch. for Social Rsch., 1986-94, George C. Marshall Found., 1987-93; mem. exec. com. Lawyers Com. for Civil Rights Under Law, 1968-88; mem. Goldman Panel for Attica Disturbance, 1972, Temporary Commn. on State Ct. System, 1971-73, Rockefeller U. Council, 1986-88, exec. com. N.Y. Vietnam Vets. Meml. Commn., 1982-85, Mayor's Police Adv. Com., 1985-87. Served to capt. USAAF, 1942-46. Decorated D.F.C. with cluster, Air medal with clusters. Mem. ABA (ho. of dels. 1976-80), N.Y. State Bar Assn. (pres. 1978-79), Assn. Bar City N.Y. (v.p. 1974-75), N.Y. County Lawyers Assn., Am. Law Inst., Am. Judicature Soc. (bd. dirs. 1979). Republican. Episcopalian. Home: Fair Oaks Farm 1657 Route 9D Cold Spring NY 10516-3543 Office: US Dist Ct So Dist NY US Court House 500 Pearl St New York NY 10007-1316

PATTERSON, RONALD R(OY), management consultant; b. Baton Rouge, Mar. 4, 1942; BS, U. Houston, 1965; MS, Trinity U., San Antonio, 1973. Asst. adminstr. U. Tex. Med. Br., Galveston, 1972-75; asst. v.p. Hosp. Affiliates Internat., Nashville, 1975-81; chief oper. officer Affiliated Hosp. Systems, Houston, 1981-82; sr. v.p. Republic Health Corp., Dallas, 1982-88; pres. Miller Patterson Inc., Plano, Tex., 1988-89; ind. healthcare mgmt. cons. Plano, 1989-90; sr. v.p. Harris Meth. Health System, Ft. Worth, 1990-91; exec. v.p., COO Champion Healthcare Corp., Houston, 1991-96; exec. v.p., pres. healthcare ops. Paracelsus Healthcare Corp., Houston, 1996-99; pres. R. Patterson Assocs., 1996—; sr. v.p. Signature Hosp. Corp., Houston, 2007—08. Bd. dirs. Tarrant County Hosp. Dist., 2002—05, sec., 2002—05; bd. chair Metrowest Health Plan, 2002—04, Tex. Health Facilities Devel. Corp., 2002—05. Fellow Am. Coll. Healthcare Execs. (life), Tex. Hosp. Assn. (vice-chmn. multi-hosp. constituency 1987), Fedn. Am. Health Sys. (bd. govs. 1996-99, bd. dirs., sec. 1997-99). Home and Office: 2020 Cedar Ridge Dr Keller TX 76248 Office Phone: 817-692-5132.

PATTERSON, SAMUEL C., retired political science professor; b. Omaha, Nov. 29, 1931; s. Robert Foster and Garnet Marie (Jorgensen) P.; m. Suzanne Louise Dean, June 21, 1956; children— Polly Ann, Dean Foster, Grier Edmund. BA, U. S.D., 1953; MS, U. Wis., 1956, PhD, 1959. Asst. prof. polit. sci. Okla. State U., Stillwater, 1959-61; asst. prof. U. Iowa, Iowa City, 1961-64, assoc. prof., 1964-67, prof., 1967-85, Roy J. Carver prof., 1985-86; prof. Ohio State U., Columbus, 1986-98, prof. emeritus, 1998—; ret., 1998. Vis. prof. U. Wis., 1962, U. Okla., 1966-78, U. Essex, Colchester, Eng., 1969-70, U. S.D., 2001. Co-author: (with others) Representatives and Represented, 1975, A More Perfect Union,

4th edit., 1989, The Legislative Process in the United States, 4th edit., 1986, Comparing Legislatures, 1979, Great Theatre: The American Congress in the 1990, 1998; editor: American Legislative Behavior, 1968; co-editor: Comparative Legislative Behavior: Frontiers of Research, 1972, Handbook of Legislative Research, 1985, Political Leadership in Democratic Societies, 1991, Parliaments in the Modern World, 1994, Senates: Bicameralism in the Contemporary World, 1999; editor Am. Jour. Polit. Sci., 1970-73; co-editor Legis. Studies Quar., 1981-85; mng. editor Am. Polit. Sci. Rev., 1985-91. Served with U.S. Army, 1953-55 Recipient Disting. Scholar award Ohio State U., 1990; fellow Social Sci. Rsch. Coun., 1961, 67, Guggenheim, 1984-85; vis. fellow Brookings Instn., 1984-85, Ctr. Advanced Study in Behavioral Scis., 1993-94; Fulbright Bologna chair, 1995. Mem. Am. Polit. Sci. Assn. (Frank J. Goodnow award, 2000), Midwest Polit. Sci. Assn. (pres. 1980-81), Phi Beta Kappa, Phi Kappa Phi, Pi Sigma Alpha. Home Phone: 239-395-2784. Personal E-mail: patpat851@embarqmail.com.

PATTERSON, SCOTT DAVID, lawyer; b. Phila., Feb. 15, 1954; s. Walter Blake Jr. and Rosemary Jeanne P.; m. Susan Patricia Brestrup, June 27, 1981; children: Julia Connell, Amanda Macaulay. AB magna cum laude, Princeton U., 1974; JD cum laude, Harvard U., 1977. Bar: Pa. 1977, US Ct. Appeals (3d cir.) 1977, US Dist. Ct. (ea. dist.) Pa. 1977, US Dist. Ct. (mid. dist.) Pa. 1988, US Ct. Appeals (4th cir.) 1989. Assoc. Saul, Ewing, Remick & Saul, Phila., 1977-85, ptnr., 1985, Saul, Ewing, Wayne, Pa. Panelist. Pa. Bar Inst. tech. Mem. Healthcare Information Mgmt. Sys. Soc. Mem. ABA, Pa. Bar Assn., Assn. of U Tech. Mgrs. Avocations: computers, photography, hiking, piano, genealogy. Office: Saul Ewing 1200 Liberty Ridge Dr Ste 200 Wayne PA 19087 Office Phone: 610-251-5089. Office Fax: 610-408-4407.

PATTERSON, STEPHEN M., psychology professor; b. Eugene, Oreg., Feb. 2, 1960; s. Peter V. and Alice L. Patterson; m. Cornelia A. Farrell, Sept. 8, 2007. PhD, Uniformed Svcs. U. Health Scis., Bethesda, 1993. Rsch. asst. prof. U. Tenn., Memphis, 1995—98; assoc. prof. Ohio U., Athens, 1998—. Maj. USAF, 1980—2002. Office: Ohio Univ 200 Porter Hall Athens OH 45701 Office Fax: 740-594-0579. Business E-Mail: patterss@ohio.edu.

PATTERSON, STEVE, former professional sports team executive; b. Beaver Dam, Wis., Sept. 21, 1957; BBA with honors, U. Tex., 1980, JD, 1984. Bar: Tex. 1984. Gen. mgr., profl. basketball team counsel Houston Rockets, NBA, 1984-89, profl. basketball mktg. exec. group ticket sales, mgr., bus. ops. exec., gen. mgr., 1989-94; pres. profl. hockey team Houston Aeros, 1994-97; pres. Arena Oper. Co., Houston, 1995-99; exec. v.p. Houston NFL Holdings, 1997—2003; pres. Portland Trail Blazers, NBA, Oreg., 2003—07, gen. mgr., 2006—07; pres. Pro Sports Consulting, 2007—. Home Phone: 503-699-8003; Office Phone: 503-680-3500. Personal E-mail: stevewpatterson@gmail.com. Business E-Mail: spatterson@prosportsconsulting.net.

PATTERSON, STEVEN EARL, chemistry professor, researcher; b. Decatur, Ga., Jan. 5, 1963; s. James Ralph and Beverly Patterson. BS, Ga. State U., Atlanta, 1991; PhD, Ga. State U., 1995. Posdoctoral fellow U. Notre Dame, 1997; vis. rsch. scholar Ga. Combichem Ctr., Atlanta, 1998—2000; sr. scientist Pharmasset, Inc., Tucker, Ga., 2000—04; assoc. dir., assoc. prof. chemistry Ctr. for Drug Design, U. Minn., Mpls., 2004—. Contbr. chapters to books, articles to profl. jours. Grantee Rsch. grants, NIH-NIAID, 2000—01, Rsch. grant, 2001—04, Rsch. grants, 2003—04, Rsch. grant, Minn. Partnership for Genomics and Biotechnology, 2005—08, NIH-NINDS, 2006—, Minn. Academic Health Ctr., 2008—; Bayer fellowship, Bayer Corp., 1996—98. Mem.: Internat. Soc. Nucleosides, Nucleotides and Nucleic Acids, Am. Chem. Soc. Bpatist. Achievements include patents for nucleotide derivatives and mycophenolic acid derivatives as antiviral agents for treatment of flaviviridae infections and abnormal cellular proliferation; Novel anti-HIV agents and preparation therof; patents pending for anti-giardia agents; synthesis of benzamide riboside and derivatives. Avocations: bicycling, trap, skeet and clay shooting, fly fishing. Office: Univ Minn Ctr for Drug Design 516 Delaware St MMC204 7-216 PW Bldg Minneapolis MN 55455

PATTERSON, W. MORGAN, college president; b. New Orleans, Oct. 1, 1925; s. E. Palmer and Jess Margaret (Wood) P.; m. Ernestine North, June 10, 1948; children— W. Morgan, II, Jay North BA, Stetson U., 1950, D.D. (hon.), 1979; M.Div., New Orleans Baptist Theol. Sem., 1953, Th.D., 1956; postdoctoral, Oxford U., 1965-66, 72-73. Prof. ch. history New Orleans Bapt. Theol. Sem., 1956-59; prof. ch. history, David T. Porter prof. ch. history, dir. grad. studies So. Baptist Theol. Sem., Louisville, 1959-76; dean acad. affairs Golden Gate Bapt. Theol. Sem., Mill Valley, Calif., 1976-84; pres. Georgetown Coll., Ky., 1984-91; asst. to pres. Coll. of Ozarks, Mo., 1994—. Vis. prof. Midwestern Bapt. Theol. Sem., Kansas City, Mo., La. Coll., Pineville, 1991—92, Golden Gate Bapt. Theol. Sem., Mill Valley, Calif., 1992—94, 1997, 2003—05, Okla. Bapt. U., 1997, Fla. Bapt. Theol. Coll., 1998—99, New Orleans Bapt. Sem., 1995—96, 1999—2000; vis. scholar Campbellsville U., Ky., 2000—03, 2006, 2007—09; chmn. hist. commn. So. Bapt. Conv., Nashville, 1969—72; honored guest 2d Vatican Coun., Rome, 1965. Author: Baptist Successionism: A Critical View, 1969; co-editor: Professor in the Pulpit, 1963; contbr., editor: Ency. Southern Baptists; book rev. editor Review and Expositor, 1965-70 Served as flight officer USAF, 1943-46 Recipient Disting. Alumnus award Stetson U., 1992, Disting. Svc. award for outstanding contbn. to Bapt. history Hist. Commn., So. Bapt. Conv., 1993; Am. Assn. Theol. Schs. fellow, 1965-66. Mem. Am. Soc. Ch. History, So. Bapt. Hist. Soc. (pres. 1979-80), William H. Whitsitt Bapt. Heritage Soc., Commn. on Bapt. Heritage of Bapt. World Alliance. Avocations: travel, stamp collecting/philately, collecting books. Home: 7 Pierce Dr Novato CA 94947-4450

PATTERSON, WILLIAM BROWN, retired dean, history professor; b. Charlotte, NC, Apr. 8, 1930; s. William Brown and Eleanor Selden (Miller) P.; m. Evelyn Byrd Hawkins, Nov. 27, 1959; children: William Brown Patterson, Evelyn Byrd Donatelli, Lucy Patterson Murray, Emily Patterson Higgs. BA, U. South, 1952; MA, Harvard U., 1954, PhD, 1966, cert. ednl. mgmt., 1982; BA, Oxford U., Eng., 1955, MA, 1959; MDiv, Episc. Div. Sch., Cambridge, Mass., 1958. Ordained to ministry Episcopal Ch. as deacon, 1958, as priest, 1959. Asst. prof. history Davidson (N.C.) Coll., 1963-66, assoc. prof., 1966-76, prof. history, 1976-80, U. of South, Sewanee, Tenn., 1980—2005, dean Coll. Arts and Scis., 1980-91; Francis S. Houghteling prof. hist., 2001. Author: (with others) Discord, Dialogue, and Concord, 1977, This Sacred History: Anglican Reflections for John Booty, 1990, Richard Hooker and The Construction of Christian Community, 1997, King James VI and I and the Reunion of Christendom, 1997, A Companion to Richard Hooker, 2008, Sewanee Perspectives on the History of the University of the South, 2008; mem. bd. editors St. Luke's Jour. Theology, Sewanee, 1982-90; contbr. numerous articles to profl. jours. Trustee U. South, 1968-71; mem. internat. adv. com. U. Buckingham, Eng., 1977-93; pres. So. Coll. and Univ. Union; organizer Associated Colls. of South, 1988-89. Danforth Found. grad. fellow, 1952, Mellon Appalachian fellow U. Va., 1992-93, rsch. fellow NEH, 1967, Folger Shakespeare Libr., Washington, 1975, Inst. for Rsch. in Humanities, U. Wis., Madison, 1976, Newberry Libr., Chgo., 1979; Rhodes scholar, 1953. Mem. Am. Hist. Assn., Am. Soc. Ch. History (Albert C. Outler prize for best book in ecumenical ch. history 1999), N.Am. Conf. on Brit. Studies, Eccles. History Soc. Eng., Royal Hist. Soc. Eng., So. Hist. Assn., Soc. for Values in Higher Edn., Episcopal Div. Sch. Alumni/ae Assn. (mem. exec. com. 1984-87), Phi Beta Kappa, Beta Theta Pi. Avocations: gardening, tennis. Home: 195 N Carolina Ave Sewanee TN 37375-2040 Business E-Mail: bpatters@sewanee.edu.

PATTERSON, WILLIAM J., investment company executive; BA, Harvard Univ.; MBA, Stanford Univ.; graduate studies, Australian Nat. Univ. Fin. analyst Goldman Sachs, 1985—87; investment mgmt. positions through mng. dir. SPO Partners, Mill Valley, Calif., 1989—; chmn. Calpine Corp., Houston, 2009—. Chmn. Calif. Acad. Sciences; chmn. investment com. Marin Cmty. Found.; vice chmn. Stanford Bus. Sch. Trust. Henry Crown fellow, Aspen Inst., 2004. Mailing: Calpine Corp Bd Directors Ste 1000 717 Texas Ave Houston TX 77002*

PATTERSON, WILLIAM S., lawyer; b. Kings Mountain, NC, July 16, 1947; BA, Wake Forest U., 1969; JD with honors, U. N.C., 1973. Bar: N.C. 1973. Staff atty. interpretive divsn. Office Chief Counsel U.S. Dept. Treasury, 1973-75, staff atty. tax ct. litigation divsn., 1975-77; mng. ptnr. Raleigh office Hunton & Williams LLP, NC. Office: Hunton & Williams 1 Hanover Sq Ste 1400 421 Fayetteville St Raleigh NC 27601 Office Phone: 919-899-3022. Office Fax: 919-833-3233. Business E-Mail: bpatterson@hunton.com.

PATTESON, CHARLES LYNN, musician, retired music educator; b. Dallas, Mar. 20, 1923; s. James Nelson and Eula Lee (Jolly) P.; children: Lisa Ann Patteson Kennedy, Charles Lynn Jr. BA, Tex. Christian U., 1948. Band dir. Poly. High Sch., Ft. Worth, 1948-50, Handley High Sch., Ft. Worth, 1948-50; owner TV store Ft. Worth, 1951-61; band dir. McLean Mid. Sch., Ft. Worth, 1961—84; leader Charlie Patteson Dance Orch., Ft. Worth, 1950—. Composer (band) March 200, 1974; (orch.) Two Minute Waltz, 1976, Fantasy, 1991, Paris In June, October in London, November in Rome, Starlight Waltz, Opus in Eb, Dreamer's Waltz, Stardust Waltz, Meadowbrook Waltz, Swinging at the Starlight, Ft. Worth Symphony Orchestra, others. With USAF, 1943-46. Recipient ten 1st place Concert Competition award (dir. McLean Middle Sch. Band), Ft. Worth., 1974-84. Mem. Am. Fedn. Musicians, Musician's Fed. Credit Union (life, v.p.), Lions, Elks, Masons, Shriners (50 yr. mem., 1st chair clarinet in band 1950-91). Republican. Avocations: water-skiing, recording, music arranging. Home: 5101 Westhaven Dr Fort Worth TX 76132-2036 E-mail: clpatteson@aol.com.

PATTI, MARCO GIUSEPPE, surgeon, educator; b. Catania, Italy, Apr. 15, 1956; came to U.S., 1983; s. Francesco P. and Ada (Travali) P.; m. Verna C. Gibbs, Nov. 30, 1985; 1 child, Verna Ada. MD, U. Catania, 1981. Resident in gen. surgery U. Calif., San Francisco, 1986—93, dir. swallowing ctr., assoc. prof. surgery, 1994—. Fellow ACS, Assn. Acad. Surgery, Internat. Soc. Diseases of Esophagus, San Francisco Surg. Soc., Italian Surg. Assn., Esophageal Club. Avocations: classical music, swimming, languages, travel. Office: Univ Calif San Francisco 533 Parnassus Ave Rm C-341 San Francisco CA 94142-0890 Office Phone: 415-363-2161. E-mail: pattim@surgery.ucsf.edu.

PATTILLO, GARY A., beverage distribution executive; b. Newport Beach, Calif., Dec. 11, 1969; s. J. Lee Pattillo and Janice E. Beach; m. Charlene E. Pattillo, June 26, 1999; children: Naliyah R. children: Alex L., Kyla N. BS in Criminal Justice Adminstrn., San Diego State U., 1993. Account mgr. Mesa Distbg. Co., Inc., San Diego, 1999—2005, dist. mgr., 2005—. Recipient Top Sales award, Mesa Distbg. Co., 2001, 2002. Mem.: Am. Mensa. Green Party. Avocations: home Internet business, travel, computers, Kakuro puzzles.

PATTINSON, ROBERT (ROBERT THOMAS-PATTINSON), actor; b. London, May 13, 1986; Actor: (films) Vanity Fair, 2004, Harry Potter and the Goblet of Fire, 2005, Harry Potter and the Order of the Phoenix, 2007, The Summer House, 2008, How to Be, 2008 (Best Actor award Strasbourg Film Festival, 2008), Little Ashes, 2008, Twilight, 2008 (Breakthrough Performance - Male, MTV Movie Awards, 2009, Best Fight, MTV Movie Awards, 2009, Best Kiss, MTV Movie Awards, 2009, Choice Movie Actor: Drama, Teen Choice Awards, 2009, Choice Movie Liplock, Teen Choice Awards, 2009, Choice Movie Rumble, Teen Choice Awards, 2009); (TV films) Ring of the Nibelungs, 2004, The Haunted Airman, 2006, The Bad Mother's Handbook, 2007. Recipient New Hollywood award, Hollywood Film Festival, 2008, Choice Male Hottie, Teen Choice Awards, 2008. Avocations: guitar, piano, skiing, soccer, snowboarding. Office: c/o Curtis Brown Group Ltd Haymarket House 5th Fl 28-29 Haymarket London SW1Y 4SP England*

PATTIS, S. WILLIAM, publishing executive; b. Chgo., July 3, 1925; s. William Robert and Rose (Quint) P.; m. Bette Z. Levin, July 16, 1950; children: Mark Robert, Robin Quint Himovitz. BS, U. Ill., 1949; postgrad., Northwestern U., 1949-50. Exec. v.p., pub. United Bus. Publs., 1949-59; chmn., CEO 3M/Pattis, 1959-88; pres. NTC Pub. Group, Lincolnwood, Ill., 1961-96, Next Chapter Holdings, L.P., Highland Park, Ill., 1996—; dir. P-B Comm., Winnetka, Ill., 1978-98; vice-chmn. Profl. Media Group, Norwalk, Conn., 1999—2008. Bd. dirs. 1st Colonial/Highwood; mem. book and libr. com. USIA, Washington, 1986—89, chmn., 1989—93; mem. exec. com. Pub. Hall of Fame, 1987—2000; chmn. U.S.-USSR Bilateral Media Confs., Washington and Moscow, 1990—91. Author: Opportunities in Advertising Careers, 1984, 1988, 1995, Opportunities in Magazine Publishing Careers, 1992, 2001, VGM Career Planing, 1988, Careers in Advertising, 1996, 2d edit, 2002, 3d edit., 2003, 4th edit., 2004; co-author: Opportunities in Publishing Careers, 1995, 2001. Mem. Pres.'s Coun. Youth Opportunity, 1968-70; bd. dirs. Photography Youth Found., 1968-70, Expt. in Internat. Living, 1970, Inst. Human Creativity, 1983—, Fund for Am.'s Libraries, 1996-99; vice chmn. bd. dirs. Annenberg Ctr. for Health Scis., 1991—, vice chmn., 1996-99; trustee Eisenhower Med. Ctr., Rancho Mirage, Calif., 1989—, exec. com. mem., 1996—, chmn. investment com., 2000-03; trustee Am. Coun. Tchrs. Russian, 1992-96; bd. dirs. Nat. Security Edn. Act, Washington, 1993-94, Knapp Sch. Entrepreneurship, Ill. Inst. Tech., 2005-; bd. dirs. resource bd. Coll Comm. U. Ill., 2006-; lord of manor, Kirkbride, Eng., 1989—. Recipient Human Rels. award Am. Jewish Com., 1971, Paul Simon award Ctrl. States Conf. on Tchg. Fgn. Langs., 1992. Mem. Standard Club (Chgo.), Club Internat. (Chgo.), Northmoor Country Club (Highland Park, Ill.), Tamarisk Country Club (Rancho Mirage). Office: Next Chpt Holdings Port Clinton Sq 600 Central Ave Highland Park IL 60035-3211 Home (Winter): 70843 Tamarisk La Rancho Mirage CA 92270 Office Phone: 847-432-8700. Personal E-mail: billpattis@aol.com. Business E-Mail: bpattis@nextchapterholdings.com.

PATTON, ALTON DEWITT, electrical engineering consultant; b. Corpus Christi, Tex., Feb. 1, 1935; s. Alton G. and Civilia Louise (Taylor) P.; m. Nancy Jo Elder, Mar. 1, 1959; children: Elizabeth, Carolyn. BEE, U. Tex., 1957; MEE, U. Pitts., 1961; PhD in Elec. Engring., Tex. A&M U., 1972. Registered profl. engr., Tex. Engr. Westinghouse Electric Corp., Pitts., 1957-65; prof. elec. engring. dept. Tex. A&M U., College Station, 1965-79, 82-2000, head elec. engring. dept., 1992-96, Brockett prof., 1986, Dresser prof., 1987, dir. Electric Power Inst., 1976-79, 85-92, prof. emeritus, 2005—; rsch. fellow Tex. Engring. Expt. Sta., College Station, 1985, dir. Ctr. for Space Power, 1987-92; pres. Associated Power Analysts Inc., College Station, 1973—. Mem. panel for assessment of NIST Elec. and Electronics Engring. Lab., 1995-2000, NRS, ind. mem., bd. dirs. Electric Reliability Coun. Tex., Inc. and Tex. Regional Entity Contbr. articles to elec. engring. jours. Fellow IEEE (life, tech. com., Prize Paper award 1975, 94, Richard Harold Kaufmann award 2000); mem. NSPE. Republican. Presbyterian. Avocations: fishing, hunting, photography, stamp and coin collecting. Home: 8411 Spring Crk College Station TX 77845-4608 Office: Associated Power Analysts Inc 303 Anderson St College Station TX 77840-3114 Home Phone: 979-693-1918; Office Phone: 979-696-0010. Business E-Mail: adpatton@suddenlink.net. E-mail: adewittpatton@msn.com.

PATTON, ANTWAN ANDRE (BIG BOI), rap artist, singer; b. Savannah, Ga., Feb. 1, 1975; children: Jordan Alexus, Bamboo. Performer Outkast, 1992—. Singer: (albums) Southernplayalisticadillacmuzik, 1994, ATLiens, 1996, Aquemini, 1998, Stankonia, 2000 (Grammy awards: Best Rap Album, 2001, Best Rap Performance By A Duo Or Group for song "Ms Jackson", 2001), Big Boi and Dre Present...Outkast, 2001 (Grammy award: (with Killer Mike) Best Rap Performance By A Duo Or Group for song "The Whole World", 2002), Speakerboxxx/The Love Below, 2003 (Grammy awards: Album Of The Yr., 2003, Best Urban/Alternative Performance for song "Hey Ya!", 2003, Best Rap Album, 2003, Am. Music Awards Favorite Album-Rap/Hip-Hop, 2004), Idlewild, 2006; actor: (films) ATL, 2006, Idlewild, 2006; performer: (with Atlanta Ballet) Big, 2008. Recipient Best New Rap Group of Yr., Source award, 1995, Favorite Band, Duo or Group-Pop or Rock, Am. Music Awards, 2004, Favorite Band, Duo or Group-Rap/Hip-Hop, 2004, Duo/Group Artist of Yr., Billboard Music Awards, 2004, Billboard 200 Duo/Group Album Artist of Yr., 2004, Hot 100 Duo/Group of Yr., 2004, R&B/Hip-Hop Duo/Group of Yr., 2004, Digital Track of Yr., 2004. Address: Arista Records Inc 8750 Wilshire Blvd Beverly Hills CA 90211-2713

PATTON, BRUCE M., law educator, management consultant; b. Terre Haute, Ind., Oct. 14, 1956; s. William Eugene and Carol Ann P.; m. Diana McLain Smith, Oct. 21, 1994. AB, Harvard U., 1977, JD, 1984. Bar: Mass. Co-founder, assoc. dir. Harvard Negotiation Project, Cambridge, Mass., 1979-84, dep. dir., 1984—; co-founder, assoc. dir. Program on Negotiation at Harvard Law Sch., Cambridge, Mass., 1983—2002; co-founder, ptnr. Vantage Partners, LLC, Cambridge, 1997—. Co-founder, prin. Conflict Mgmt. Inc., Cambridge, 1984—; co-founder, dir. Conflict Mgmt. Group, Cambridge, 1984-2000; Thaddeus R. Beal lectr. Harvard Law Sch., Cambridge, 1985-99. Co-author: The Mainstream of Alegbra and Trigonometry, 2d edit., 1980, Getting To Yes, 2d edit., 1991, Difficult Conversations, 1999; contbr. articles to profl. jours. Fellow: Coll. of Trial Mediators (hon.). Avocations: squash, hiking, tennis, skiing. Office: Harvard Negotiation Project Pound Hall 524 Harvard Law Sch Cambridge MA 02138 also: Vantage Ptnrs Brighton Landing W Ste 350 10 Guest St Boston MA 02135 Home Phone: 781-642-1211; Office Phone: 617-354-6090. E-mail: bpatton@post.harvard.edu.

PATTON, CARL VERNON, retired academic administrator; b. Coral Gables, Fla., Oct. 22, 1944; s. Carl V. and Helen Eleanor (Benkert) Patton; m. Gretchen West, July 29, 1967. BS in Cmty. Planning, U. Cin., 1967; MS in Urban Planning, U. Ill.-Urbana, 1969, MS in Pub. Adminstrn., 1970; MS in Pub. Policy, U. Calif.-Berkeley, 1975, PhD in Pub. Policy, 1976. From instr. to prof. U. Ill., 1968—83, dir. Bur. of Urban and Regional Planning Rsch., 1977—79, prof., chmn. dept., 1979—83; prof., dean Sch. Architecture and Urban Planning U. Wis., Milw., 1983—89; v.p. acad. affairs, prof. polit. sci., geography and urban planning U. Toledo, 1989—92; pres. Ga. State U., Atlanta, 1992—2008. Author: Academia in Transition, 1979; co-author: The Metropolitan Midwest, 1985; co-author: (with David Sawicki) Basic Methods of Policy Analysis and Planning, 1986, rev. 2d edit., 1993 Chinese translations, 2001, 2002; co-author: (with Kathleen Reed) Guide to Graduate Education in Urban and Regional Planning, 1986, 1988; editor: Spontaneous Shelter: International Perspectives and Prospects, 1988; co-editor (with G. William Page): Quick Answers to Quantitative Problems: A Pocket Primer, 1991; assoc. editor: Jour. of Planning Edn. and Rsch., 1983—87, editl. bd.: Habitat International, 1993—99, Intertrade and Investment (formerly Atlanta Internat. Mag.), 1993—2000; contbr. articles to profl. jours. Fellow U. Ill. Ctr. Advanced Studies, 1973—74; chmn. Cmty. Devel. Commn., Urbana, 1978—82; mem. Civic Design Ctr., Milw., 1983—87, City Milw. Art Commn., 1988—89, Toledo Vision, 1989—92, City Toledo Bd. Cmty. Rels., 1990—92, Ga. Rsch. Alliance, Atlanta Convention Vis. Bur., 1995—2005, Woodruff Art Ctr., 1996—2006, Fulton-Dekalb Hosp. Authority, 2008—, DBA Grady Meml. Hosp., 2008—, Fox Theatre, Ga. Coun. Econ. Edn., Atlanta Neighborhood Devel. Partnership; chair Centennial Olympic Park Area Inc., 1998—2000, Grady (Hosp.) Healthcare, Inc., 1998—2000, Atlanta Reg. Coun., 1998—, Ctrl. Atlanta Progress, 2000—03; co-chair Atlanta Belt Line Task Force, 2004—05; bd. dirs., chair The Atlanta Downtown Partnership, 1997—2000. Fellow, NIMH, 1973—75. Fellow: Am. Inst. Cert. Planners; mem.: Met. Atlanta C. of C., Assn. Collegiate Schs. of Planning (v.p. 1985—87, pres. 1989—91), Am. Planning Assn. Avocations: racquetball, gardening, travel. Office Phone: 404-413-1300. Business E-Mail: cpatton@gsu.edu.

PATTON, DIANA LEE WILKOC, artist, educator, illustrator; b. New Rochelle, NY, June 28, 1940; d. August E. and Meta Diane (Neuburg) Wilkoc; m. Gardner C. Patton, Aug. 10, 1963; children: Michael, Talryn, Shawn. AB cum laude, Brown U., 1962; postgrad., Pan-Am. Art Inst., 1962-63. Svc. mgr. Lord and Taylor, NYC, 1962-63; tchr. adult edn., Mountain Lakes, NJ, 1972-74, Somerville, NJ, 1978-82, Jointure for Cmty. Adult Edn., 1982—. Artist in watercolors, pen and ink and acrylics; writer, illustrator of children's books; card designer; instr. in field; developer art appreciation courses for children and adults; toymaker, 1973-76. Exhibited N.E. US, Perth, Australia, 1977, spl. bicentennial exhibit, Trenton, NJ, 1976, Rutgers U., 1980, Brookdale Coll., 1982, Camden County Coll., 9186, Moris County Coll., 1988, Bergen Mus. Arts and Scis., 1987-88, 90-91, Princeton Med. Ctr., 1993-94, 96, Madison Gallery--Morristown Hosp., 2001, 03, 05, Salmagundi Club, NYC, 2002, Gallery Capital Health Mercer, 2005, 08, Children's Book, writing & illustrating programs for the classroom; one-woman show SAA Pluckemin Galleries, 1998; represented in pvt. and pub. collections in US, Australia, NZ, Germany, Luxembourg, Japan, Eng.; designer ofcl. poster NJ Festival Ballooning, 1990, Arc Challenge Races, 1993-94, Capital Health Sys. Hosp., Trenton, NJ 2004, 07. Recipient Bronze medal in watercolor Nat. Mystic (Conn.) Outdoor Art Festival, 1977, Mayor's purchase prize Franklin Twp., 1976, Tri-State Watercolor award Somerset County Coll., 1978, Best in Show award Raritan Valley Art Assn., 1978, 94, award Garden State Watercolor Soc., 1979, 84-85, 1st, 2d and Best in Show award Somerset and Westfield Art Assns. shows, 1st place for profl. watercolor Plainfield Tri-State Arts Festival, 1983,

85, 87, 96, 2001, N.E. Art Festival, Caldwell Coll., 1990, 95, Tewksbury award, 1990, 2d place in watercolor Internat. Miniature Art Show, Washington, 1983, Best in Show and Grumbacher award Caldwell State show, 1984, 1st place Carrier Clinic Tri-State, 1984, Grumbacher Bronze award, 1984, Grumbacher silver award, 1985, 88, 94, watercolor award Artists League Ctrl. NJ Show, Cornelious Lowe Mus., 1986, Winsor-Newton award Am. Artists Proleague, 1987, Robert Simmons award, 1989, Basking Ridge Environ. Ctr. award, 1994, Best in Show award NJ State Juried, Piscataway, 1988, 2d place NJ Miniature Art Soc., 1989, 1st Pro award Raritan Valley, 1992-93, 1st mixed media award Basking Ridge Environ. Ctr., 1994, award Essex Watercolor Club, 1999, Grumbacher Gold award Essex Watercolor Club, 2000, 1st Pro award Bridgewater Arts, 2001, 03; artist-in-residence grantee Middlesex Librs., 1983-92, watercolor demonstrator, 1983—; TV appearances State of Arts-NJ, 1986, Midday (spl. art shows), 1986, TKR, 1995; 3rd Pl. Internat. Childrens Book Contest, ABC Book competition, 2007; Elisha Benjamin scholar Brown U., 1960. Mem. Garden State Watercolor Soc. (writer, editor 1994—), Miniature Art Soc., Washington, NJ Watercolor Soc., AAUW (life, various offices 1963-73), Art Assn. Raritan Valley (pres. 1980-82, writer, editor newsletter 1993—), Art Assn. Somerset, Art Assn. North Haven (Maine), Essex Watercolor Club, Am. Artists Profl. League Nat., Soc. Children's Book Writers and Illustrators, Hunterdon County Children's Book Writers & Illustrators Group, Bee Sharps Square Dance Club. Presbyterian. Home: 497 Stony Brook Dr Bridgewater NJ 08807-1945 Personal E-mail: diana@dianapatton.com.

PATTON, GREGORY KENNETH, management educator; b. Sheridan, Wyo., Dec. 20, 1960; s. Philip Kenneth and Martha Jane Patton; children: Christopher Kenneth, Gentina Leigh. BA, Northwestern Coll., Orange City, Iowa, 1984; MBA, U. S.D., Vermillion, 1993; PhD, U. Iowa, Iowa City, 2002. Rsch. asst. bus. rsch. bur. U. S.D., Vermillion, 1992—93; instr. econs. Buena Vista Coll., Storm Lake, Iowa, 1993—95; grad. tchg./rsch. asst. U. Iowa, Iowa City, 1995—2000; asst. prof. mgmt. U. N.D., Grand Forks, 2000—. Retail store mgmt. Duckwall-ALCO Stores, Inc., Abilene, Kans., 1984—92; adj. instr. Northwestern Coll., Orange City, Iowa, 1993—95, Western Iowa Tech. CC, Sioux City, Iowa, 1994—95. Contbr. articles to profl. jours. Second v.p. Kiwanis, Alliance, Nebr., 1989—92; com. mem. parish health ministries Bethel Luth. Ch., Grand Forks, ND, 2004. Recipient Superior Instrn. and Noteworthy Devotion to the Advancement of Students, Quo Vadis Chpt. of Mortar Bd., 2003; named Vol. of Yr., YMCA of Alliance, Nebr., 1992, Outstanding Student Orgn. Advisor, 2006, Nat. award excellence in advising, Mortar Bd., 2006; Rsch. grantee, Small Bus. Devel. Ctr. ND, 2003—04. Mem.: APA, Soc. Indsl. and Orgnl. Psychology, Acad. Mgmt. (assoc. Scholarly Achievement award (Human Resources divsn.) 2002), Golden Key, Beta Gamma Sigma. Avocations: running, architecture. Office: Univ ND Box 8377 Grand Forks ND 58202 Business E-Mail: gregory_patton@und.nodak.edu.

PATTON, JACK THOMAS, family practice physician; b. Rogers, Ark., Feb. 18, 1941; s. Jack Marcus and Jewell Selah (Pense) P.; m. Lynette Anne Carr, Sept. 2, 1960; children: Robert, John, Mark, Christopher. BA in History, Calif. State U., Long Beach, 1963; MA in History, Calif. State U., Fresno, 1993; MD in Medicine, U. So. Calif., 1967; MA in Bibl. Studies, Mennonite Brethren Bib. Sem., Fresno, Calif., 1980. Cert. Bd. Med. Examiners, Calif., Hawaii. Intern Tripler Army Med. Ctr., Honolulu, 1967-68; resident in gen. practice Walson Army Hosp., Ft. Dix, NJ, 1968-70; med. supt. Nazarene Hosp., Papua New Guinea, 1973-80; chmn. family practice dept. Sharp Rees-Stealy, San Diego, 1981-86; chmn. occupational medicine Kaiser Permanent, Fresno, 1986-87; assoc. med. dir. Sharp Rees-Stealy, San Diego, 1987-92; med. dir. Summer Inst. Linguistics, Papua New Guinea, 1993-94; with family practice dept. Sharp Rees-Stealy Med. Group, San Diego, 1994-97, Northwest Med. Group, Fresno, Calif., 1997—2007; chmn. dept. family practice St. Agnes Med. Ctr., 2002—05, family medicine cons. Sanger, Calif., 2007—. Family practice residency liaison Tripler Army Med. Ctr., Honolulu, 1972-73; chief medicine, dep. commr. Schofield Army Med. Clinics, Wahiawa, Hawaii, 1970-72; lectr. Calif. State U., Fresno, 1978-79, Pt. Loma Nazarene Coll., 1982-85, San Jose Christian Coll., 1997-2003; v.p. Patton Industries, Inc., 2005—. Mem. med. sch. support Salerni Collegium, U. So. Calif. Sch. Medicine, 1967-85; lectr. Ch.-Mission Inst., Mennonite Brethren Bib. Sem., 1984-92; sec. S.E. Asian task force Mennonite Brethren Ch. Fresno, 1990-93. Maj. U.S. Army, 1966-73. Mackenzie scholar U. So. Calif. Sch. Medicine, 1966-67; decorated Meritorious Svc. medal. Fellow Am. Acad. Family Physicians; mem. Am. Bd. Family Practice (diplomate), Calif. Acad. Family Physicians, Royal Soc. Medicine (assoc., London). Avocations: history, travel, hiking. Home: 847 Rosewood Ave Sanger CA 93657-5400 Office: 831 Rosewood Ave Sanger CA 93657-5400 Office Phone: 559-875-9791. E-mail: dr_jack@verizon.net.

PATTON, JOSEPH DONALD, JR., management consultant; b. Washington, Pa., Jan. 4, 1938; s. Joseph Donald and Priscilla Ann (Johnson) P.; m. Susan Oertel, June 3, 1967; children: Jennifer Ann, Joseph Donald III (dec.). BS in Phys. Scis. and Math. Edn., Pa. State U., 1959; MBA in Mktg., U. Rochester, NY, 1974. Registered profl. quality engr., Calif.; cert. profl. logistician; cert. quality engr.; cert. reliabilty engr. Tchr. Aschaffenburg (W.Germany) Am. Sch., 1963-64; with Xerox Corp., Rochester, 1964-75, mgr. field engring., 1975—93; CEO Patton Cons., Inc., Rochester, NY, 1976—93, Hilton Head, SC, 1993—. Chmn., Mgmt. Metrics Svcs., Inc., 1996-2001; mem. adj. faculty Rochester Inst. Tech., SUNY, Geneseo. Author 8 textbooks; contbr. over 200 articles to profl. jours. Capt. U.S. Army, 1959-63. Recipient Leadership and Svc. award, Pa. State U. Coll. Edn., 1999, Lifetime Achievement award, Svc. Industry Assn., 2007. Fellow Am. Soc. Quality (reliability and maintainablity tech. award 1982), Internat. Soc. Logistics (SOLE Armitage medal 1980, 82, 97); mem. Instrument Soc. Am. (sr.), Assn. Svcs. Internat. (AFSMI publs. award 1981, Pres.'s Club 2005), Nat. Assn. Svc. Mgrs. (life cert. svc. exec.). Republican. Presbyterian (elder). Office: Patton Consultants Inc 36 Blue Heron Pt Hilton Head Island SC 29926-1209 Office Phone: 843-384-6232. Personal E-mail: JDPatton@aol.com.

PATTON, LAUREN L., dentist, researcher; AB, Dartmouth Coll., Hanover, NH, 1980; DDS, U. NC Sch. Dentistry, Chapel Hill, 1986. Diplomate Am. Bd. Oral Medicine, 1991, Am. Bd. Spl. Care Dentistry, 2004. Gen. practice dentistry resident NC Meml. Hosp., Chapel Hill, 1986—88; clin. dental staff fellow Nat. Inst. Dental Rsch., Bethesda, Md., 1988—90; asst. prof. U. NC Sch. Dentistry, 1990—97, assoc. prof., 1997—2004, prof., 2004—, chair dept. dental ecology, 2008—. Chair dept. dentistry U. NC Hosps., Chapel Hill, 1992—97, gen. practice dentistry residency program dir., 2002—. Grant, NIH, 1994—, Ctrs. Disease Control, 1999—2002. Fellow: RCS (Edinburgh), Am. Assn. Hosp. Dentists, Spl. Care Dentistry (vice chair, chair coun. fellowship 1994—99); mem.: ADA (cons. 1995—), Am. and Internat. Assn. Dental Rsch., Am. Acad. Oral Medicine (dir., treas. 2004—). Office: Univ NC Sch Dentistry CB 7450 Dental Ecology Chapel Hill NC 27599-7450

PATTON, MARILYN DILWORTH, english and literature educator; d. David Edgar and Betty Barker Dilworth; m. Gary Alan Patton, Sept. 27, 1969; children: Sonya Elizabeth Drottar, Philips Dilworth. PhD, U. Calif., Santa Cruz, 1989. Instr. Stanford U., Calif., 1988—89; vis. asst. prof. U. Calif., 1989—91; prof. De Anza Coll., Cupertino, Calif., 2007—. Co-chair Alliance Children, Santa Cruz, 1998—2009; active Friendly Woman, Santa Cruz, 1979—81. Recipient Disting. Educator, De Anza Coll., 2007; grantee, NEH, 1988. Democrat. Soc. Of Friends. Avocations: snorkeling, hiking. Office: De Anza Coll 21250 Stevens Creek Blvd Cupertino CA 95014 Business E-Mail: pattonmarilyn@deanza.edu.

PATTON, MARY RITCHIE, retired pediatric nurse practitioner, consultant; b. Lexington, Ky., Oct. 23, 1942; d. Robert L. Ritchie and Lucille Hisle, John P. Moores (Stepfather); m. John Logan Patton, Aug. 1, 1964; children: Angela Lynn, Stephanie Anne. RN, Ky. Bapt. Hosp. Sch. Nursing, 1964; PNP, Mass. Gen. Hosp. Harvard U., 1972; BSc, St. Joseph Coll., 1986. RN Ky. Bd. Nursing, 1964, lic. PNP, Nat. PNP Assn., 1980. Nurse mgr. James C. Ramsey Med. Care, Frankfort, Ky., 1969—71; PNP Hugh C. Williams Med. Ctr., Carrolton, 1972—74, Wedco Dist. Health Dept., Paris, Ky., 1977—80, maternal and child health nursing dir., 1980—84; nurse cons. Ky. Dept. Health Svcs., Frankfort, 1984—90, perinatal coord., 1990—92; ret., 1992. Adv. com. mem. Ky. Perinatal Assn., Lexington, 1990—92. Adv. com. mem. Ky. Mar. of Dimes, Lexington, 1990—92; vol. disaster svcs. ARC, Lexington, 1992—2005; bd. mem. First Bapt. Ch., Lexington, 1980—94; missionary Ky. Bapt. Assn., Louisville, 1984, 2000; adv. bd. mem. Elkhorn Bapt. Assn., Lexington, 2002—03. Recipient Partnership Evangelism award, Fgn. Mission Bd. of So. Bapt. Conv., 1992, Disaster Svc. award, ARC, 1994, Hours of Svc. award, 1994, 1995. Mem.: Scott County Humane Soc., Georgetown Coll. Women's Assn., Scott County Woman's Club, Rose Rebekka Lodge. Independent-Republican. Christian. Avocations: quilting, travel, reading. Home: 124 E Clinton St Georgetown KY 40324

PATTON, REBECCA M., nursing administrator; BSN, Kent State U.; MSN, Case Western Res. U. RN, CNOR. Clin. instr. Frances Payne Bolton Sch. Nursing, Case Western Res. U.; dir. nursing, dir. surgical services, dir. ambulatory ops. U. Hospitals Health System; dir. perioperative services EMH Regional Healthcare System, Elyria, Ohio. Recipient Cmty. Involved Polit. Action award, Sigma Theta Tau, Delta Xi chapt., Kent State U., 2000. Mem.: ANA (bd. dirs. 1994—98, treas. 1998—2002, del. 2003—05, pres. 2006—), Ohio Nurses Assn. (first v.p. 1990—92, fin. com. 2003—05, del. 2005—06, Dorothy E. Cornelius Leadership Congress award 1999). Office: ANA Ste 400 8515 Georgia Ave Silver Spring MD 20910*

PATTON, SHARON F., retired museum director; BA, Roosevelt U., 1966; MA, U. Ill., 1969; PhD in Art History, Northwestern U., 1980. Mem. faculty U. Houston, 1976—79, U. Md., 1979—85; dir. art galleries Montclair State Coll., NJ, 1986—87; chief curator Studio Mus., NYC, 1988—91; assoc. prof. art history U. Mich., Ann Arbor, 1991—98, dir. Ctr. for Afroamerican and African Studies, 1996—98; dir. Allen Meml. Art Mus. Oberlin Coll., 1998—2003; mem. adv. bd. Nat. Mus. African Art, Washington, 2000—08, dir., 2003—08. Author: Memory and the Metaphor, the Art of Romare Bearden, 1991, African-American Art, 1998 (Choice Outstanding Book of Yr. award); contbr. articles to publs. in field. Mem. Rapid Transit Pub. Art Commn., Cleve., ArtTable, Cleve.; mem. visual arts jury Cleve. Arts Prize, 2000—02; mem. African Am. adv. coun. and Acquisition adv. com. Cleve. Art Mus. Mem.: ArtTable, Assn. Art Mus. Dirs., Am. Assn. Museums. Office: Nat Mus African Art Smithsonian Instn MRC 708 PO Box 37012 Washington DC 20013-7012

PATTON, STUART, biochemist, educator; b. Ebenezer, NY, Nov. 2, 1920; s. George and Ina (Neher) P.; m. Colleen Cecelia Lavelle, May 17, 1945; children: John, Richard, Gail, Thomas, Mary Catherine, Patricia, Joseph. BS, Pa. State U., 1943; MS, Ohio State U., 1947, PhD, 1948. Chemist Borden Co., 1943-44; rsch. fellow Ohio State U., Columbus, 1946-48; faculty Pa. State U., University Park, 1949-80, prof., 1959-80, Evan Pugh rsch. prof. agr., 1966-80; adj. prof. neuroscis. Sch. Medicine U. Calif., San Diego, 1981—99; ret., 1999. Vis. scientist Scripps Instn. Oceanography; cons. in field. Author: (with Robert Jenness) Principles of Dairy Chemistry, 1959; (with Robert G. Jensen) Biomedical Aspects of Lactation, 1975; Milk: Its Remarkable Contribution to Human Health and Well-Being, 2004. Lt. (j.g.) USNR, 1944-46. Recipient Borden award chemistry milk Am. Chem. Soc., 1957, Agrl. and Food Chemistry award, 1975, Alexander von Humboldt sr. scientist award, 1981, Macy-Gyorgy award Internat. Soc. for Rsch. on Human Milk and Lactation, 1997, Distinguished Alumnus award, Pa. State U., 2002, Distinguished Svc. award Am. Dairy Sci. Assn., 1999, fellow Pa. State Alumni Assn., 2001. Fellow Am. Dairy Sci. Assn.; mem. Am. Chem. Soc., Am. Soc. Biochemistry and Molecular Biology, Am. Soc. Cell Biology. Home and Office: 6208 Avenida Cresta La Jolla CA 92037-6510

PATTON, THOMAS EARL, lawyer; b. Nov. 25, 1940; s. Thomas E. and Alice F. (Rodarmel) P.; m. Patricia Mann, Aug. 12, 1965 (dec.); m. Barbara Wood, Sept. 21, 1974 (div. 2005); 1 child, David Earl; m. Yogi Yogan, 2006. AB, Cath. U. Am., 1962, JD summa cum laude, 1965. Bar: NY 1966, DC 1966, Va. 1982. Assoc. Sullivan & Cromwell, NYC, 1965-69; mem. Williams Connolly & Califano, Washington, 1970-75; asst. gen. counsel US Dept. Energy, Washington, 1977-78; ptnr. Schnader, Harrison, Segal & Lewis, Washington, 1979-94. Disting. lectr. Cath. U. Am., 1970-90, 95—, bd. regents; nat. arbitrator Am. Arbitration Assn.; bd. dirs. Elcotel, Inc., IXI, Inc., Vanguard Found. Author: Securities Litigation, 1989, Federal Procedure Casebook, 1990; contbr. articles to profl. jours.; editor in chief Cath. U. Am. Law Rev. Mem. Washington World Affairs Coun., 1980—. Mem. ABA, DC Bar (founder and chair litigation sect.), Cosmos Club. Roman Catholic. Office: Tighe Patton Armstrong Teasdale 1747 Pennsylvania Ave NW Washington DC 20006-4688 Office Phone: 202-454-2840. Business E-Mail: tpatton@tighepatton.com.

PATTON-NEWELL, JANET LAVELLE, minister; b. Sharon, Pa., Jan. 15, 1965; d. Henry Elbert and Flora Lee Newby; m. Derrick Lamount Newell, June 17, 2000; children: Flora Evette Harris, Kellen Dauntae Newby, Kent Michael Patton, Kaston Moneke Patton, Grace Newell. Diploma in Bible studies, Full Bible Inst. Farrell, Pa., 2002; HHD, diploma in biblical studies, NCI Bible Coll. and Sch. Prophets, 2005; cert., Cambria County Prison Tng. Acad., Pa. Lic. ordained World Missions Ministerial Assn., minister Ranha Outreach Internat. Orders clk. Mercer County Domestic Rels., (Child Support Bur.), Mercer, Pa., 1996—98; youth and young adult activities coord. Americorp Vista, (Mercer County Housing Authority), Sharon, Pa., 1998—99; evangelist New and Living Way Apostolic Ch. of Jesus Christ, Farrell, Pa., 1998—2000; overseer Paramount Ctr. for Learning, Farrell, Pa.; pastor Rivers Living Water Outreach Ministry, Farrell, Pa., 2000—01, Wind in the Word Worship Ctr., Farrell, Pa., 2001—. Correction officer Mercer County Prison. Author: (self help) You are a Woman of Excellence, 2001, You are a Man of Excellence, 2001, Our Weapons are not Carnal, 2001; The Three Dimensions of the Prophetic, 2005. Mem. E.R.A.S.E. Anti Drug Coalition, Farrell, 1999, Wheels To Work, (Prince of Peace), Farrell, Pa., 1999; dir. New and Living Way Edn. Dept., Farrell, 1998—2000, Wind in the Word Outreach Ministry Edn. Dept., Farrell, 2001—05; mem. Walking in Black History, Erie, Pa., 1999. E-5 US Army, 1987—2001, Fort Bragg, N. Carolina and Ansbach, Germany. Recipient Appreciation cert., Anointed Call to Singleness, 1999, Wind in the Word Worship Ctr., 2002, 2003, 2004, Congratulations cert., New and Living Way Apostolic Ch. Jesus Christ, 2000. Mem.: Women In Truth Fellowship, Women Speakers, Prophetic Women, Women N Power. Democrat. Apostolic. Avocations: computers, writing. Business E-Mail: dr.janetl.newell@windintheword.com.

PATTY, CLAIBOURNE WATKINS, JR., lawyer; b. Cleve., Feb. 19, 1934; s. Claibourne Watkins and Eleanor (Todd) P.; m. Barbara Benton, May 4, 1968; children— Claibourne Watkins III, William Jordan. BA, U. of South, 1955; JD, U. Ark., 1961. Bar: Ark. 1961. Law clk. U.S. dist. judge, Ft. Smith, 1961-63; pvt. practice Little Rock, 1963-68; asst. ins. commr. State of Ark., 1968-69; trust officer Union Nat. Bank of Little Rock, 1969-77; asst. dean U. Ark. Sch. Law, Little Rock; also exec. dir. Ark. Inst. for Continuing Legal Edn., 1977-86; law clk. 2d Div. Chancery Ct., Pulaski County, 1986-89; of counsel Gruber Law Firm, North Little Rock, 1989-2001; prin. Patty Law Firm, North Little Rock, 2001—. Lectr. law Ark. Sch. Law, 1965; bd. dirs., chmn. Pulaski County Legal Aid Bur., 1966—69; mem. com. on civil practice Ark. Supreme Ct., 1998—2004. Bd. dirs., pres. Family Svc. Agy. of Ctrl. Ark., 1976—81, 1986—93, 1999—2004, 2009—, Good Shepherd Ecumenical Retirement Ctr., 1975—2002; mem. Ark. adv. com. U.S. Commn. on Civil Rights, 1985—89; bd. dirs. Am. Diabetes Assn., Ark. Affil., 1996—2005, Ark. Gerontol. Soc., 1996—. With AUS, 1955—57. Mem.: Phi Alpha Delta, Beta Theta Pi. Office: Patty Law Firm 315 N Broadway St North Little Rock AR 72114-5379 Home Phone: 501-663-0604; Office Phone: 501-375-5061. Personal E-mail: clairgpm@swbell.net.

PATTYN, SUE, publishing executive; b. Sept. 1, 1958; Pub. The Nat. Infectious Disease Directory, 1994—2006. Home: 1658 Saint St SE Palm Bay FL 32909 Business E-Mail: sue@paradisesoundarts.com.

PATURIS, E(MMANUEL) MICHAEL, lawyer; b. Akron, Ohio; s. Michael George and Sophia (Manos) P.; m. Mary Ann Toompas, Febr. 28, 1965. BS, U. N.C., 1954, JD with honors, 1959. Bar: NC 1959, DC 1969, Va. 1973; CPA. Acct., Charlotte and Wilmington, N.C., 1960-63; assoc. Poyner, Geraghty, Hartsfield & Townsend, Raleigh, N.C., 1963-64; atty. advisor Chief Counsel's Office, Washington, 1964-66, sr. trial atty. Richmond, Va., 1966-69; ptnr. Reasoner, Davis & Vinson, Washington, 1969-78; sole practitioner Alexandria, 1978—. Acctg. lectr. U. N.C., Chapel Hill, 1959-60; acctg., econs. lectr. N.C. State U., Raleigh, 1963-64; business law lectr. George Mason U., Fairfax County, Va., 1978-79. Mem. bd. editors U. N.C. Law Rev. With U.S. Army, 1954-56. Recipient U. N.C. Law Sch. Block award, 1959. Mem.: Washington Golf and Country Club, Beta Gamma Sigma, Phi Beta Kappa. Home: 6326 Stoneham Ln Mc Lean VA 22101-2345 Office: Law Offices of E Michael Paturis 431 N Lee St Alexandria VA 22314-2301 Office Phone: 703-836-2501.

PATWA, HUNED S., neurology educator; b. Godhra, India, July 26, 1966; s. Saifuddin and Mehfuza Patwa; m. Zehra Patwa, July 1995. BS in Biology, Carnegie Mellon U., 1988; MD, NYU, 1992. Intern Beth Israel Hosp., NYC, 1992—93; resident in neurology Sch. Medicine Yale U., New Haven, 1993—96, clin. instr., 1996—97, asst. prof. dept. neurology, 1997—2004, assoc. prof., 2004—; chief Neurology Svc. Va. Ct. Healthcare Sys., West Heaven, 2007—. Dir. neurology clerkship Yale U., dir. clin. neurosci. physician assoc. program; chief neurology svc. VA Conn. Healthcare Sys., 2007—. Mem. Am. Acad. Neurology, Am. Assn. Electrodiagnostic Medicine. Office: Yale U Sch Medicine Dept Neurology PO Box 208018 New Haven CT 06520-8018

PATZEK, TADEUSZ W., petroleum engineer, educator; m. Joanna Patzek; 1 child, Lucas. PhD, Silesian Tech. U., Gliwice, Poland, 1980. Prof. U. Calif., Berkeley, 1990—2008; prof., chmn. Petroleum & Geosys. Dept., Austin, Tex., 2008—. Sr. rschr. Shell Devel., Houston, 1983—90. Office: Univ Tes Austin CPE 2502 Austin TX 78712

PAUDEL, KALPANA S., pharmacist, educator; b. Kathmandu, Nepal; married. Registered Nepal Pharmacy Coun. Lectr. Inst. Medicine, Tribhuvan U., Kathmandu, 2000—03; postdoctoral scholar U. Ky., Lexington, 2003—05, rsch. assoc., 2005—06, asst. prof rsch., 2006—. Contbr. chapters to books, articles to profl. jours. Recipient Cert. Appreciation, US Pharmacopoeia, 2002, Cert. Acknowledgement, Grad. Pharmacists' Assn., Nepal, 2002; Colombo Plan scholar, Govt. Singapore, 1988. Mem.: Internat. Cannabinoid Rsch. Soc., Controlled Release Soc., Am. Assn. Pharm. Scientists, Nepal Pharm. Assn. (life), Grad. Pharmacists Assn. (Nepal) (life).

PAUKEN, THOMAS WEIR, venture capital executive, mediator; b. Victoria, Tex., Jan. 11, 1944; s. Thomas N. and Patricia (Weir) P.; m. Ida Ayala; children: Thomas II, Michelle, Angela, Elizabeth, Daniel, Victoria, Monica. AB in Polit. Sci., Georgetown U., 1965, postgrad., 1966-67; JD, So. Meth. U., 1973. Bar: Tex., 1975. White House staff asst., dep. dir. White Ho. fellows, Washington, 1970-71; pvt. practice atty. Dallas, 1974-80; dir. ACTION, Washington, 1981-85; pres. Sta. KRZI-Radio, Waco, Tex., 1985-86; v.p., corp. counsel Garvon, Inc., Dallas, 1986-91; pres. TWP, Inc., Dallas, 1991—. Bd. dirs. TOR Minerals, Inc. Author: The Thirty Years War - The Politics of the 60s Generation, 1994. Mem. Reagan transition team Counsel's Office, Washington, 1980-81; Tex. Rep. State chmn., 1994-97; chmn. Gov.'s Tex. Task Force on Appraisal Reform, 2006-07, chmn Tex. Workforce Commn., 2008-. With US Army, 1967—70. Recipient Drug Edn. Leadership award PRIDE, 1985, Dir.'s award U.S. Office of Personnel Mgmt., 1985; Weaver fellow 1965. Mem. State Bar Tex., VFW (life). Roman Catholic. Avocation: reading. Office Phone: 214-378-9340. Business E-Mail: twpauken@sbcglobal.net.

PAUL, ALIDA RUTH, retired arts and crafts educator; b. San Antonio, May 30, 1953; d. Richard Irving and Anne Louise (Holman) Paul. B.S. in Edn., Southwest Tex. State U., 1975; M.Ed., U. Houston, 1984. Cert. tchr., Tex. Tchr. art and crafts Houston Ind. Sch. Dist., 1975—2006. Republican. Episcopalian. Home: 16830 Grampin Dr Houston TX 77084-1945

PAUL, ARA GARO, university dean; b. New Castle, Pa., Mar. 1, 1929; s. John Hagop and Mary (Injejikian) P.; m. Shirley Elaine Waterman, Dec. 21, 1962; children: John Bartlett, Richard Goyan. BS in Pharmacy, Idaho State U., 1950; MS, U. Conn., 1953, PhD in Pharmacognosy, 1956. Cons. plant physiology Argonne Nat. Lab., Ill., 1955; asst. prof. pharmacognosy Butler U., Indpls., 1956-57; faculty U. Mich., Ann Arbor, 1957—, prof. pharmacognosy, 1969—; dean U. Mich. Coll. Pharmacy, 1975-96, dean emeritus, Hans W. Vahlteich prof. pharmacognosy, 2001—04, prof. emeritus, 2005—. Vis. prof. microbiology Tokyo U., 1965-66; mem. vis. chemistry faculty U. Calif., Berkeley, 1972-73; del. U.S. Pharmacopeial Conv., 1980, 90; scholar-in-residence Am. Assn. Colls. Pharmacy, 1996; bd. grants Am. Found. Pharm. Edn., 1997—, chmn., 1999, 2007-, co-chmn. endowment com., 2002—, bd.

dirs., 2003—; mem. organizing com. Millennial World Congress Pharm. Scis., 1996-2000; mem. FIP Found., 2000—05, chmn. bd. trustees, 2001—05. Contbr. articles to profl. jours. Recipient Outstanding Tchr. award Coll. Pharmacy, U. Mich., 1969, Outstanding Alumnus award Idaho State U., 1976, Profl. Achievement award Coll. Pharmacy, Idaho State U., 1990; G. Pfeiffer Meml. fellow Am. Found. Pharm. Edn., 1965-66, Disting. Svc. Profile award Am. Found Pharm. Edn., 1992; fellow Eli Lily Found., 1951-53, Am. Found. Pharm. Edn., 1954-56, NIH, 1972-73. Fellow AAAS; mem. Am. Pharm. Assn., Am. Soc. Pharmacognosy, Acad. Pharm. Scis., Am. Assn. Colls. Pharmacy, Am. Assn. Pharm. Scientists, Phi Lambda Upsilon, Sigma Xi, Phi Delta Chi, Phi Sigma Kappa, Rho Chi. Home: 1415 Brooklyn Ave Ann Arbor MI 48104-4496 Office: U Mich Coll Pharmacy Ann Arbor MI 48109-1065 Office Phone: 734-763-4267. Business E-Mail: arapaul@umich.edu.

PAUL, ARTHUR, artist, illustrator, graphics designer; b. Chgo., Jan. 18, 1925; m. Beatrice Miller, Dec. 24, 1949 (div. 1973); children: William Warren, Fredric; m. Suzanne Seed, Mar. 8, 1975; 1 stepdaughter, Nina. Student, Inst. Design, 1947-51. Vice-pres., art dir. HMH Pub. Co., Playboy, Chgo., 1953-82; also sr. art dir., corp. art dir. Playboy mag.; pres. Art Paul Design; freelance artist Chgo., 1984—. Lectr. in field. Freelance illustrator, designer, 1951-53; designer 1st issue: Playboy mag, 1953, Playboy Rabbit symbol, 1953; one-man shows include Etc. Gallery, 1949, 500D Gallery, 1965, U. Ill., 1965, Visual Identity Chgo., 1991, Chgo. Cultural Ctr., 1997-98; organizer, exhibitor: traveling exhbn. Beyond Illustration-The Art of Playboy; museums, Europe, Asia, U.S., 1971-73, Can., 1976-77; author: Vision-Art Paul, 1983, Art of Playboy, 1986, Sex Appeal, 2000; designer PBS-TV title Sence of Humor for humorous feature film presentations on American Playhouse; prodn. design cons. (PBS-TV movie) Who Am I This Time?; featured in Contemporary Master Works, 1991, Print mag., 2000, Graphis mag., 2004, Picturing Text, 2004. Trustee Chgo. Mus. Contemporary Art, 1970-86; apptd. trustee by Gov. of Ill. to Ill. Summer Sch. of Arts, 1987—. With USAAF, 1943-46. Recipient numerous art awards, including Outstanding Achievement in Trademark Design for Playboy Mag. award Soc. Typographic Arts, 1970, Gold medal for exhbn. Beyond Illustration City of Milan, 1971, Polycube award Art Dirs. Club Phila., 1975, Art Direction Mag. award, 1975, Top Midwest Mktg. award Playboy TV Subscription Ad, 1979, 82, Gold medal for Chgo. Film Festival poster Art Dirs. Club N.Y., 1980, Profl. Achievement award IIT Inst. Design Alumni Assn., 1983, Herb Lubecin Lifetime Achievement award Soc. Publ. Designers, 2006; Art Inst. scholar, 1943; named to Art Dirs. Hall of Fame, 1986. Mem. Alliance Graphique Internat., AIGA (fellow, 2008-). *Design is more than a sense of order for me. It is beauty and common sense. To draw, to paint and to look at art is in the fabric of my life. I enjoy working with ideas and seeing them develop into a reality, after which I am fortunate enough to learn whether they have performed as intended.*

PAUL, BIPUL C., senior research scientist; s. Dasarathi and Sephali Paul; m. Manjulika Saha, Jan. 19, 2001. MTech, U. Calcutta, India, 1993—95; PhD, Indian Inst. Sci., Bangalore, 1996—99. Design engr. Alliance Semiconductor, Bangalore, 1999; rsch. assoc. Purdue U., W.Lafayette, Ind., 2000—05; sr. rsch. scientist Toshiba Am. Rsch. Inc., San Jose, Calif., 2005—; vis. scientist Stanford U., Calif., 2005—. Editor: IET Digital Technologies on Computers, 2007—, Jour. Low Power Electronics, 2007—. Sr. Rsch. fellow, Coun. Sci. & Indsl. Rsch., Govt. India, 1995. Mem.: IEEE (sr.; Best Paper award 2006), Giga Scale Silicon Rsch., Assn. Computing Machinary. Achievements include invention of device design for ultra-low power subthreshold circuit operation; design of robust circuit design techniques in the nanoscale regime; research in state-of-the-art memory design; patents pending for high performance circuit design; modeling of nanoscale device such as carbon nanotubes and nanowires for high performance circuit applications. Personal E-mail: bipul_paul@hotmail.com.

PAUL, CAROL ANN, retired academic administrator, biology educator; b. Brockton, Mass., Dec. 17, 1936; d. Joseph W. and Mary M. (DeMeulenaer) Bjork; m. Robert D. Paul, Dec. 21, 1957; children: Christine, Dana, Stephanie, Robert. BS, U. Mass., 1958; MAT, R.I. Coll., 1968, Brown U., 1970; EdD, Boston U., 1978. Tchr. biology Attleboro (Mass.) High Sch., 1965-68; asst. dean., mem. faculty biology North Shore Community Coll., Beverly, Mass., 1969-78; master planner N.J. Dept. for Higher Edn., Trenton, 1978-80; assoc. v.p. Fairleigh Dickinson U., Rutherford, N.J., 1980-86; v.p. acad. affairs Suffolk Community Coll., Selden, N.Y., 1986-94, prof. biology, 1994-98; ret., 1998. Faculty devel. cons. various colls., 1979-98, title III evaluator, 1985-98. Author: (lab. manual and workbook) Minicourses and Labs for Biological Science, 1972 (rev. edit., 1975); (with others) Strategies and Attitudes, 1986; book reviewer, 1973-77, 94-98. V.p. LWV, Beverly, 1970—74, Cranford, NJ, 1982—83; alumni rep. Brown U., 1972—92; mem. Cape Cod Area LWV, 2001—03; mem. bd. dirs. YMCA of Cape Cod, 2004—07, bd. dirs., clk. of bd., 1998—2003. Commonwealth Mass. scholar, 1954-58; recipient Acad. Yr. award NSF, 1968-69, Proclamation for Leadership award Suffolk County Exec., 1989. Mem.: AAUW, AAWCC, AAHE, Nat. Coun. for Staff (nat. exec. bd. 1979—80), Profls. and Orgn. Developers (planning com. 1977—79), Brown Alumni Club of Cape Cod (sec. 2001—04, bd. dirs. 2001—07), Pi Lambda Theta, Phi Theta Kappa. Roman Catholic. Avocation: swimming. Home Phone: 508-660-1461. Personal E-mail: artrdpaul@verizon.net.

PAUL, CHRIS, professional basketball player; b. Winston-Salem, NC, May 6, 1985; Attended, Wake Forrest Univ., NC, 2002—05. Guard New Orleans Hornets, 2005—. Mem. US Men's Sr. Nat. Basketball Team, Beijing, 2008. Recipient ESPY award, Best Breakthrough, ESPN, 2006, Gold medal, men's basketball, Beijing Olympic Games, 2008; named Rookie of Yr., Atlantic Coast Conf., 2003—04, Player of Yr., 2004—05, Rookie of Yr., NBA, 2006; named to All-Rookie First Team, 2006, Western Conf. All-Star Team, 2008, 2009, All-Defensive First Team, 2008, All-NBA First Team, 2008. Achievements include setting the NBA record for steals in consecutive regular-season games (106), 2008; leading the NBA in: assists, 2008, 2009; steals, 2009. Office: New Orleans Hornets 1250 Poydras St Fl 19 New Orleans LA 70113*

PAUL, EDWARD MARK, psychiatrist, educator; s. Bernard and Gertrude Paul; m. Caryl Oris; children: Sarah, Harry. AB, Harvard U., Cambridge, Mass., 1978, MA; MD, Columbia Physicians & Surgeons, NYC, 1982. Cert. psychiatrist ABPN, 1987. Private practice, alcoholism unit bellevue, 1986—2008; lectr., 2008—. Clin. asst prof. NYU med. sch., 1991—2008; fellow substance abuse NY Hosp., 1986—87. Mem.: APA, AAAP, ASAM, Phi Beta Kappa Alpha Chpt. Avocations: ballroom dancing, bicycling, writing. Office: Edward M Paul MD 155 e 31st 25 J New York NY 10016 Office Phone: 212-447-5712. Office Fax: 212-447-1331. Business E-Mail: epaul417@gmail.com.

PAUL, EVE W., retired lawyer; b. NYC, June 16, 1930; d. Leo I. and Tamara (Sogolow) Weinschenker; m. Robert David Paul, Apr. 9, 1952; children: Jeremy Ralph, Sarah Elizabeth. BA, Cornell U., 1950; JD, Columbia U., 1952. Bar: N.Y. 1952, Conn. 1960, U.S. Ct. Appeals (2nd cir.) 1975, U.S. Supreme Ct. 1977. Assoc. Botein, Hays, Sklar & Herzberg, NYC, 1952-54; pvt. practice Stamford, Conn., 1960-70; staff atty. Legal Aid Soc., NYC, 1970-71; assoc. Greenbaum, Wolff & Ernst, NYC, 1972-78; v.p. legal affairs Planned Parenthood Fedn. Am., NYC, 1979—91, v.p., gen. counsel, 1991—2003; ret., 2003. Bd. dirs. Ctr. Advancement of Women, Inc. Contbr. articles to profl. jours Trustee Cornell U., Ithaca, N.Y., 1979-84; mem. Stamford (Conn.) Planning Bd., 1967-70; bd. dirs. Stamford LWV, 1960-62. Harlan Fiske Stone scholar Columbia Law Sch., 1952. Mem.: ABA, Fairfield County Bar Assn., Assn. Bar of City of N.Y., Conn. Bar Assn., Phi Kappa Phi, Phi Beta Kappa. Personal E-mail: evewpaul@aol.com. *The ability to plan the number and timing of my children has made it possible for me to enjoy career, marriage and family.*

PAUL, GARY WAYNE, music educator; b. Tulsa, July 15, 1954; s. Bill and Ellen Ada Paul; m. Bonnie Jean McIntosh, May 22, 1981; children: Jeanette Ellen, Marisa Nicole. BA in Edn., East Ctrl. U., 1977. Dir. bands Joliet H.S., Mont., 1987—88, Yale H.S., Okla., 1988—91, Hominy H.S., 1991—93, Wetumka H.S., 1993—96, Pocola H.S., 1996—99, Chelsea H.S., 1999—2003, Inola H.S., 2003—. Chair Mid-East Honor Band, Glenpool, Okla., 2000; adjudicator Northeastern A&M Coll. Contest, Miami, 1992; mem. staff ARk. Tech. U. Band Camp, Russellville, 1996—99. Mem. Tulsa Cmty. Band, 2001—. Mem.: Music Edn. Nat. Conf., Okla. Music Educators Assn., Okla. Bandmasters Assn. Democrat. Avocations: tennis, golf, camping. Home: 107 E 9th Pl S Claremore OK 74017 Office: Inola High Sch Inola OK 74036 Home Phone: 918-342-8923; Office Phone: 918-543-3122. E-mail: gpaul3@cox.net.

PAUL, GERALD D., electronics executive; D in Physics, Tech. U. Munich. Asst. to mgr. capacitor plant Draloric Electronic GmbH, Selb, Germany, 1978; from prodn. mgr. to mng. dir. Vishay Intertechnology, Malvern, Pa., 1987-94, pres. electronic components Europe, 1994-96, COO, 1996—2006, pres., 1998—, CEO, 2004—. Office: Vishay Intertechnology 63 Lancaster Ave Malvern PA 19355

PAUL, GORDON LEE, behavioral scientist, psychologist; b. Marshalltown, Iowa, Sept. 2, 1935; s. Leon Dale and Ione Hickman (Perry) P.; m. Joan Marie Wyatt, Dec. 24, 1954; children: Dennis Leon, Dana Lee, Joni Lynn. Student, Marshalltown Community Coll., 1953-54, San Diego City Coll., 1955-57; BA, U. Iowa, 1960; MA, U. Ill., 1962, PhD, 1964. Social sci. analyst VA Hosp., Danville, Ill., 1962; counseling psychologist U. Ill., Urbana, 1963; clin. psychologist VA Hosp., Palo Alto, Calif., 1964-65; pvt. practice clin. psychology, 1964-65; asst. prof. psychology U. Ill., Champaign-Urbana, 1965-67, assoc. prof., 1967-70, prof., 1970-80; Cullen disting. prof. psychology U. Houston, 1980—; pvt. practice psychology Champaign, 1965-80, Houston, 1980—. Psychotherapy rsch. cons., Palo Alto, 1964-65; cons. Ill. Dept. Mental Health, 1965-73, 78-82, NIMH, 1968-78; adviser Ont. (Can.) Mental Health Found., 1968-69, NSF, 1968-69, Can. Coun., 1969-75, VA, 1972, 80—, APA, 1970—, UCLA/VA Med. Ctr./Camarillo Schizophrenia Rsch. Ctr., 1978-93, Alliance for Mentally Ill, 1980—. Author: Insight vs. Desensitization in Psychotherapy, An Experiment in Anxiety Reduction, 1966, Anxiety and Clinical Problems, 1973, Psychosocial Treatment of Chronic Mental Patients, 1977, Assessment in Residential Treatment Settings, Part 1, 1986, Observational Assessment Instrumentation for Service and Research, Part 2, 1987, Part 3, 1988; mem. editl. bd. Behavior Therapy, 1969-75, Behavior Therapy and Exptl. Psychiatry, 1969—, Schizophrenia Bull., 1971-99, Jour. Abnormal Psychology, 1972-76, Jour. Behavioral Residential Treatment, 1983—96, Jour. Psychopathology and Behavioral Assessment, 1985—; cons. editor Jour. Applied Behavior Analysis, 1966-77, 81—, Psychol. Bull., 1967—, Jour. Abnormal Psychology, 1970-72, 76—, Psychosomatic Medicine, 1971-77, Psychophysiology, 1971—77, Archives Gen. Psychiatry, 1973-74, Behavior Therapy, 1976-87, Profl. Psychologist, 1977-87, Psychiat. Svcs. (formerly Hosp. Cmty. Psychiatry), 1980—, Biobehavioral Revs., 1980-84, Jour. Cmty. Psychology, 1983, Am. Psychologist, 1983—, Brit. Jour. Clin. Psychology, 1985-87, Jour. Nervous and Mental Disease, 1992, Current Directions in Psychol. Sci., 1992—; contbr. articles to profl. jours. Served with USN, 1954-58. Recipient Creative Talent award Am. Inst. Rsch., 1964, Teaching award U. Ill., 1968, 75; rsch. award Mental Health Assn., 1985; listed one of 327 Best Mental Health Experts in Nation, Good Housekeeping, 1994; NIMH fellow, 1963-64. Fellow APA (corr. com. 1965-70, pres. sect. III div. 12 1972-73, exec. coun. div. 12 1974-77, Disting. Scientist award sect. III, div. 12 1977, Disting. Sci. Contbns. to Clin. Psychology award Soc. Clin. Psychology divsn. 12 1999), recipient Trail Blazer award for lifetime achievment in schizophrenia and serious mental illness Assoc. for Cognitive and Behavioral Therapy, 2007 Am. Psychol. Soc., Assn. Clin. Psychosocial Rsch., Am. Assn. Applied and Preventive Psychology; mem. Midwestern Psychol. Assn., Tex. Psychol. Assn., Houston Psychol. Assn., Assn. for Advancement Psychology, Phi Beta Kappa, Chi Gamma Iota. Achievements include being subject of NIMH sci. report monograph, 1981: Treating and Assessing the Chronically Mentally Ill: The Pioneering Research of Gordon L. Paul. Office: U Houston Dept Psychology 126 Heyne Bldg Houston TX 77204-5022 Home: 3402 Parkside Dr Pearland TX 77584 Home Phone: 281-692-9543; Office Phone: 713-743-8564. Business E-Mail: gpaul@uh.edu.

PAUL, HERBERT MORTON, lawyer, accountant, educator; b. NYC; s. Julius and Gussie Paul; m. Judith Paul; children: Leslie Beth, Andrea Lynn. BBA, Baruch Coll.; MBA, LLM, NYU; JD, Harvard U. Ptnr. Touche Ross & Co. (predecessor Deloitte Touche), NYC, assoc. nat. NY dir. tax, NY dir. taxes; mng. ptnr. Herbert Paul, P.C., NYC, 1983—. Prof. taxation, trustee NYU. Author: Ordinary and Necessary Expenses; editor: Taxation of Banks; adv. tax editor The Practical Acct.; mem. adv. bd. Financial and Estate Planning, Tax Shelter Insider, Financial Planning Strategist, Tax Shelter Litigation Report; bd. dirs. Partnership Strategist, The Business Strategist; cons. Profl. Practice Mgmt. Mag.; mem. panel The Hot Line; advisor The Partnership Letter, The Wealth Formula; cons. The Insider's Report for Physicians; mem. tax bd. Business Profit Digest; cons. editor physician's Tax Advisor; bd. fin. cons. Tax Strategies for Physicians; tax and bus. advisor Prentice Hall; contbg. editor. Jour. of Accountancy; mem. editl. bd. Family Bus. Advisor. Life trustee NYU, mem. bd. overseers Grad. Sch. Bus.; mem. com. on trusts and estates Rockefeller U.; trustee Alvin Alley Am. Dance Theatre; bd. trustee Assoc. Y's of N.Y.; mem. accts. divsn. Fedn. Philanthropies; mem. adv. bd. Family Bus. Advisor. Mem. ABA, Inst. Fed. Taxation (adv. com. chmn.), Internat. Inst. on Tax and Bus. Planning (adv. bd.), Assn. Bar City NY, NYU Tax Soc. (pres.), Bur. Nat. Affairs-Tax Mgmt. (adv. com. on exec. compensation), Am. Inst. CPAs (com. on corp. taxation), Tax Study Group, N.Y. County Lawyers Assn., NY State Soc. CPAs Dir. (chmn. tax div. com. on fed. taxation, gen. tax com., furtherance com., com. on rels. with IRS, bd. dirs.), Nat. Assn. Accts., Assn. of Bar of City of NY, Accts. Club of Am., Pension Club, Nat. Assn. Estate Planners (bd. dirs.), NY Estate Planning Coun. (bd. dirs.), NY C. of C. (tax com.), Grad. Sch. Bus. of NYU Alumni Assn. (pres.), NYU Alumni Assn. (pres.), Grad. Sch. Bus. NYU (bd. overseers), Wall St. Club, City Athletic Club (NYC), Seawane Club. Office: Herbert Paul PC 450 7th Ave Ste 3000 New York NY 10123 Office Phone: 212-752-3700.

PAUL, JAMES CAVERLY NEWLIN, law educator, retired dean; b. Chestnut Hill, Pa., Apr. 30, 1926; s. William Allen Butler and Adelaide Sims (Newlin) P.; m. Margaret Morris Clausen, June 25, 1948; children: Nicholas Newlin, Martha Morris, Adelaide Sims. BA, Princeton U., 1948; JD, U. Pa., 1951. Bar: Pa. 1952. Legal sec. to Chief Justice US, 1951-53; asst. prof. U. NC, 1953-55; asst. dir. Inst. Govt., U. NC, 1953-55; prof. law, dir. Inst. Legal Research, U. Pa., 1955—67; prof. law, dean and founder of faculty of law Haile Selassie U., Ethiopia, 1962—67, v.p. acad. affairs, 1967-69; exec. v.p. Ednl. and World Affairs, NYC, 1969-70; dean Sch. Law, Rutgers U., Newark, 1970-74, prof. law, 1970-96, Newhouse scholar in law, 1984-88, William J. Brennan prof., 1988-96; exec. sec., trustee Internat. Ctr. for Law in Devel., NYC, 1974—. Founding mem., sec.-treas. Internat. Third World Legal Studies Assn., NYC, 1980—96; adj. prof. Columbia U., 1973—95; cons. US Peace Corps, 1961—62, Constl. Commn. Transitional Govt. of Ethiopia, 1992—95, UN Devel. Programme, 1994—96, 2005; commr. Internat. Eritrean-Ethiopian Claims Commn., The Hague, 2001—; chmn. Fund for Assistance to Legal Edn. in Ethiopia and Eritrea, 2006—. Author: Rift in the Democracy, 1951, The School Segregation Decision, 1954, (with others) Federal Censorship, 1961, Ethiopian Constitutional Development, 1969, Lawyers in the Third World, 1981, The International Context of Rural Poverty in the Third World, 1986, Incorporating Human Rights Into the World Summit for Social Development, 1995; editor-in-chief U. Pa. Law Rev., 1950-51. Candidate for US Congress from 9th Dist. Pa., 1958; del. Dem. Nat. Conv., 1960. Served with USNR (Amphibious forces), 1943-46, PTO. Recipient Spl. medal for distinguished service to the devel. of law and univ. edn. in Ethiopia, Emperor Haile Sellassie 1st, 1969; Eisenhower Exch. fellow, Africa, 1960. Mem. ABA, NJ Bar Assn., Pa. Bar Assn., Am. Soc. Internat. Law, Internat. Third World Legal Studies Assn. (sec.-treas. 1980-96), Orgn. Am. Historians, Am. Law and History Assn., Order of Coif, Princeton Club (NYC). Home: 1352 Chancellor Pt Trappe MD 21673-1540 *My life in law and teaching about law gives satisfaction because it enables me to direct my energies towards thinking about social justice, individual dignity, and the possibilities of attaining more of the conditions enabling these ideals. But that satisfaction is tempered by constant realization of my own frailities and the failure everywhere of people, particularly those most fortunately endowed, to be guided by principled thinking.*

PAUL, JEREMY RALPH, dean, law educator; b. NYC, July 22, 1956; s. Robert D. and Eve (Weinschenker) P.; m. Laurel Ann Leff, Aug. 29, 1981; 2 children. AB, Princeton U., 1978; JD, Harvard U., 1981. Bar: N.Y.C. 1982. Law clk. to presiding judge U.S. Ct. Appeals (2d cir.), NYC, 1982-83; instr. U. Miami, Coral Gables, Fla., 1981-82, asst. prof. law, 1983-87, assoc. prof. law, 1987-92; assoc. dean for rsch. U. Conn. Sch. Law, Hartford, 1992—2007, Thomas F. Gallivan prof. real property law, 2002—, dean, 2007—. Asst. to the pres. Travelers Group, 1993-94; vis. prof. law Boston Coll. Law Sch., 1997-98. Democrat. Office: Univ Conn Sch Law Chase Hall 103 65 Elizabeth St Hartford CT 06105-2290 Office Phone: 860-570-5127. Business E-Mail: jepaul@law.uconn.edu.*

PAUL, KENNETH, newspaper editor; b. NYC, June 7, 1948; s. Samuel D. and Rose (Markoff) P.; m. Sevara Jeleva, Dec. 5, 1993; 1 child, Kathryn Hannah. BA in English, Dartmouth Coll., Hanover, NH, 1969; spl. diploma in social studies, Oxford U., Eng., 1973. Tchr. Concord HS, NH, 1969-71; dep. European editor LA Times/Washington Post News Svc., London, 1972-73; reporter, news editor Riverside Press Enterprise, Calif., 1973-76; specialists editor, copy editor, asst. nat. and day nat. editor Newsday, NY, 1976—87; mng. editor NY Observer, NYC, 1987-91; editor The Litchfield County Times, New Milford, Conn., 1993—2002, Housatonic Pubs., New Milford, 2001—02; editor-in-chief Manhattan Media, NYC, 2002—04; day editor The NY Sun, NYC, 2004—05; staff editor New York Times, 2005—. Business E-Mail: kenpaul@nytimes.com.

PAUL, KETEMA NNAMDI, neuroscientist, educator; b. Washington, Aug. 31, 1971; s. Kojo Nnamdi and Pamela Kai Paul; m. Diane Asha Hawkins, Aug. 14, 1999; children: Naiima Kailyn, Nazira Sana, Hasan William. BS, Howard U., Washington, 1994; PhD, Ga. State U., Atlanta, 2003. Rsch. fellow Northwestern U., Evanston, Ill., 2003—06; asst. prof. Morehouse Sch. Medicine, Atlanta, 2006—. Contbr. scientific papers. Environ. activist Clean Water Action, Washington, 1994—95; cmty. organizer Evanston Civic Assn., Evanston, 2004—06. Recipient Predoc. Nat. Rsch. Svc. award, NIH, NINDS, 2000—03, Neurobiology Behavior award, Ga. State U., 2003; Postdoc. Sci. Rsch. fellowship, United Negro Coll. Fund-Merck Sci. Initiative, 2004—06, Investigator-Initiated grant, Merck & Co. Inc., 2006—07, Ednl. grant, Takeda Pharms., 2006—07, Faculty Rsch. fellowship, Am. Coll. Neuropsychopharmaclogy, 2006—08, Venture grant, NSF Ctr. Behavioral Neuroscience, 2007—08. Mem.: AAAS, Sleep Rsch. Soc., Soc. Rsch Biol. Rhythms, Soc. Neurosci. Achievements include research in study of the genes, molecules, and hormones that influence sleep and wakefulness. Avocations: music, aerobics. Office: Morehouse Sch Medicine 720 Westview Dr SW Atlanta GA 30349 Office Fax: 404-752-1041. Business E-Mail: kpaul@msm.edu.

PAUL, MALCOLM DAVID, plastic and reconstructive surgeon; b. Balt., Nov. 8, 1943; s. William and Rose (Friedman) P.; m. Pamela Sisk Paul, May 15, 1981; children: Stephen, Scott, Jacquie, Matthew. BS, U. Md., 1965; MD, U. Md., Balt., 1969. Cert. Am. Bd. Platic Surgery, 1976. Intern Mt. Sinai Hosp., NYC, 1969-70, resident, 1970-71, George Washington U., Washington, 1971-75; practice medicine specializing in plastic surgery Fountain Valley, Calif., 1975—. Asst. clin. prof. to assoc. prof. clin. surgery, divsn. plastic surgery U. Calif., Irvine, 1976-; bd. dirs. CAP-MPT; adv. bd. mem., med. spa advisor Cosmetic Surgery Exposition Group; mem. adv. bd. Cosmetic Enhancement Expo. Named to Best Doctors in America, Orange County Top Doctors, Guide to Top Doctors. Mem. Am. Soc. Plastic and Reconstructive Surgery, Am. Soc. Aesthetic Plastic Surgery, Inc. (past pres., chmn. bd. trustees), Am. Bd. Plastic Surgery (past dir.), Orange County Soc. Plastic Surgeons, Inc. (past pres.), Am. Assn. Plastic Surgeons, Am. Soc. Plastic Surgery, Inc.(bd. trustee, 2009), Aesthetic Surgery Edn. and Rsch. Found., Internat. Soc. Aesthetic Plastic Surgery (past US Nat. sec.), Calif. Soc. Plastic Surgeons Republican. Jewish. Office: 1401 Avocado Ave Ste 810 Newport Beach CA 92660-8708 Office Phone: 949-760-5047.

PAUL, MARGARET LEE, psychologist; d. Jess David and Lee Woo Yeung Paul; children: Ryan Hughes, Evan Hughes. BS in Psychology, Kans. State U., Manhattan, 1977; degree in Edn. Specialist, Kans. U., Lawrence, 1980. Pupil pers. svcs. Calif. State Dept. Edn., 1989, spl. srvs. tchg. credential Kans., 1980, nationally cert. sch. psychologist NASP, 1989. Tchr. Living Learning Sch., Manhattan, Kans., 1977—78, support staff, 1977—78; rsch. analyst Kans. State Dept., Divsn. Mental Health, Social and Rehab. Svcs., Topeka, 1977—77; rsch. asst. Kans. U. Learning Disabilities Rsch. Inst., Lawrence, Kans., 1978—79; sch. psychologist Atchison Jefferson Ednl. Coop., Oskaloosa, Kans., 1980—89, San Bernardino City Schs., Calif., 1989—. Author: (poetry) Roadkill Haiku. Shepherd, ch. leader Redlands United Ch. Christ, Calif.,

2005—. Mem.: NASP, Calif. Assn. Sch. Psychologists, Psy Chi. Conservative. Avocations: travel, reading, scuba diving, computers, history. Office: San Bernardino City Schs 777 North F St San Bernardino CA 92410

PAUL, NORMAN LEO, psychiatrist, educator; b. Buffalo, July 5, 1926; s. Samuel Joseph and Tannie (Goncharsky) P.; m. Betty Ann Byfield, June 6, 1951 (dec. May 1994); children: Marilyn, David Alexander; m. Janet Athos, Aug. 16, 2002. MD, U. Buffalo, 1948. Fellow pharmacology U. Cin. Coll. Medicine, Ohio, 1949-50; resident psychiatry Mass. Mental Health Ctr., Boston, 1952-55; fellow child psychiatry James Jackson Putnam Children's Ctr., Boston, 1957-59, Mass. Gen. Hosp., Boston, 1958-59; chief psychiatrist Day Hosp. Mass. Mental Health Ctr., Boston, 1960-64; dir. conjoint family therapy Boston State Hosp., 1964-65, cons. in family psychiatry, 1965-70; assoc. clin. prof. dept. neurology Boston U. Sch. Medicine, 1977—. Cons. Mental Health Ctr., Alaska Native Hosp., Anchorage, 1967-68; cons. family psychiatry Boston VA Hosp., 1967-71, Mass. Soc. for the Prevention of Cruelty to Children, Boston, 1993—; vis. family therapist St. George's Med. Sch., London, 1996-97; lectr. in psychiatry Harvard Med. Sch., Boston, 1976-2003; faculty assoc. Mgmt. Analysis Corp., Cambridge, Mass., 1979-82; presenter Internat. Conf. on Telemedicine and Telecare, London, 1996 Family therapist: (tv documentary) PBS-Trouble in the Family, 1965 (George Foster Peabody award 1965); co-author A Marital Puzzle, 1977, 86, German edit., 1987, French edit., 1995, Chinese edit., 1997, contbr. articles to profl. jours. Sponsor Mass. Orgn. to Repeal Abortion Laws, Boston, 1965-70; chair Audio Unit of Child Devel. and Mass Media, White House Conf. on Children and Youth, Washington, 1970; bd. trustees Cambridge (Mass.) Coll., 1977-89; bd. dirs. Let's Face It, 1990—, Ctr. for Family Connections, 1998—2002. Capt. USAF, 1950-52. Recipient Edward A. Strecker, M.D. award for young psychiatrist of yr., 1966, Cert. of Merit, Mass. Coun. on Family Life, Boston, 1967, Cert. of Commendation, Mass. Assn. for Mental Health, Boston, 1967, Disting. Achievement award Soc. for Family Therapy and Rsch., Boston, 1973, Lifetime Achievement award Mass. Assn. for Marriage and Family Therapy, 1998, Disting. Svc. award Physician Health Svcs., 1998. Fellow Royal Soc. Medicine, Am. Psychiat. Assn. (life); mem. Am. Assn. Marriage and Family Therapy (bd. dirs. 1983-86), Am. Family Therapy Assn. (v.p. 1982-83, Disting. Contbn. award 1984), Assn. for Rsch. in Nervous and Mental Disorders, Group for the Advancement Psychiatry (chair com. on the family 1982-84). Avocations: study of codes, travel. Office Phone: 978-369-3754. Personal E-mail: nlpaul@aol.com.

PAUL, OUIDA FAY, music educator; b. Deatsville, Ala., Jan. 18, 1911; d. Elza Bland and Martha Eleanor (Hinton) P. AB in Math. and English, Huntingdon Coll., 1930, BS in Music Edn., 1933; MA in Music and Music Edn., Columbia U., 1943, EdD in Music and Music Edn., 1957; postgrad., U. Ill., 1968; studied oil painting, Gloria Foss Sch. of Art, 1978—83. Tchr. math., English and music pub. schs., Ala., 1930—42; tchr. math. Sacred Heart Convent Sch., NYC, 1942-43; tchr. h.s. choral music Kingsport, Tenn., 1943-45; instr., asst. prof. music edn. Greensboro (N.C.) Coll., 1945-49; asst. prof. U. Fla., Gainesville, 1949-61, U. Hawaii, Honolulu, 1961-68; tchr. musicology and voice Leeward C.C., Pearl City, Hawaii, 1968-77; pvt. tchr. voice, Honolulu, 1977-95, Gainesville, 1996—. Choir dir. 1st Presbyn. Ch., Gainesville, 1950-61, Protestant Chapel, USN, Honolulu, 1962-68, Cmty. Ch., Honolulu, 1969-78, Wesley United Meth. Ch., Honolulu, 1978-94; contralto soloist various chs., 1950-94; adjudicator solo and choral auditions and festivals, 1945-94; tchr. adults with singing problems, 1950-. One-woman art shows include Honolulu Cmty. Theatre, 1980, 84, First United Meth. Ch., 1980; group shows with Honolulu Artists, others; permanent collections René Malmezac, Tahiti; contbr. articles to profl. jours. Cons. to com. on edn. Hawaii Gov.'s Commn. on Status of Women, 1965; English lang. tutor Hawaii Literacy, Inc., Honolulu, 1978-95. Recipient Alumni Achievement award, Huntingdon Coll. Alumnae Assn., 1998. Mem. Music Educators Nat. Conf. (1st v.p. Hawaii 1969-70), Am. Choral Dirs. Assn. (Hawaii chmn. 1963-66), Nat. Assn. Tchrs. Singing, Altrusa (pres. Gainesville 1960-61, past pres. Honolulu), Delta Kappa Gamma (pres. Hawaii Theta chpt. 1963-64, past state music chmn., named one of Makers of Destiny Hawaiian Style 2002.). Methodist. Avocation: painting. Home: 7950 NW 27th Blvd Apt 8 Gainesville FL 32606-8694

PAUL, PAMELA MIA, concert pianist; b. NYC, Nov. 9, 1949; d. Charles F. Paul; m. Richard John Dufallo, June 19, 1988. BM, Juilliard Sch. of Music, 1970, MM, 1972, DMA, 1976. Prof. U. North Tex., 1987—. Debuted Vienna Symphony; appeared with Vienna ORF Orch., Orchestre de la Suisse Romande, RTE Orch., Dublin, Berlin Stadtskapelle, Stuttgart Chamber Orch., Dutch Radio Symphony, Krakow Philharm., Orchestre Philharm. de Monte Carlo, N.Y. Philharm., Detroit, St. Louis, Pitts. and Houston Symphonies, others. Office: Univ North Tex College of Music Denton TX 76203

PAUL, RICHARD WRIGHT, lawyer; b. Washington, May 23, 1953; s. Robert Henry Jr. and Betty (Carey) P.; m. Paula Ann Coolsaet, July 25, 1981; children: Richard Haven, Timothy Carey, Brian Davis. AB magna cum laude, Dartmouth Coll., 1975; JD, Boston Coll., 1978. Bar: Mich. 1978, U.S. Dist. Ct. (ea. dist.) Mich. 1978, U.S. Ct. Appeals (6th cir.) 1982, U.S. Supreme Ct. 1989, U.S. Dist. Ct. (we. dist.) Mich. 1991. Assoc. Dickinson, Wright, Moon, Van Dusen & Freeman, Detroit, 1978-85, ptnr., 1985—. Case evaluator Wayne County Cir. Ct., Oakland County Cir. Ct.; mediator Mich. State Ct. Adminstrv. Office. Co-author, Barbarians At The Gate: Daubert Two Years Later, 1995; contbr. articles to profl. publs. Trustee Bloomfield Village Assn., Birmingham, Mich., 2001-04, sec., 2003-04, bd. dirs; mem. Little League, Birmingham, 2000-07, treas. 2005-07; treas. Seaholm Baseball Boosters, 2005—, v.p., 2006, pres., 2007—08. Mem. ABA, State Bar of Mich. (treas. litig. sect. 1998-99, sec. litig. sect. 1999-2000, chmn. elect litig. sect. 2000-01, chairperson litigation sect. 2001-02, mem. representative assembly 2004—), Fed. Bar Assn., Def. Rsch. Inst., Detroit Met. Bar Assn., Mich. Def. Trial Counsel, Dartmouth Lawyers Assn., Oakland County Bar Assn., Assn. Def. Trial Counsel, Alumni Coun. Dartmouth Coll., Dartmouth Detroit Club (pres. 1980—); fellow Oakland County Bar Found. Avocations: tennis, bicycling. Office Phone: 248-433-7200. Business E-Mail: rpaul@dickinsonwright.com.

PAUL, ROBERT ARTHUR, steel company executive; b. NYC, Oct. 28, 1937; s. Isadore and Ruth (Goldstein) P.; m. Donna Rae Berkman, July 29, 1962; children: Laurence Edward, Stephen Eric, Karen Rachel. AB, Cornell U., 1959; JD, Harvard U., 1962, MBA, 1964. With Ampco-Pitts. Corp. (formerly Screw & Bolt Corp. Am.), 1964—, v.p., 1969-71, treas., 1973-79, exec. v.p., 1972-79, pres., COO, 1979-94, pres., CEO, 1994—2004, dir., 1969—, chmn., CEO, 2004—. Pres., bd. dirs. Louis Berkman Co.; bd. dirs. ECHO Real Estate Svs.; gen. ptnr. Romar Trading Co.; instr. Grad. Sch. Indsl. Adminstrn. Carnegie Mellon U., 1966-69; trustee emeritus Cornell U.; bd. dirs. Pitts. br. Fed. Res. Bank Cleve. Trustee H.L. and Louis Berkman Found., U. Pitts. Med. Ctr. Sys., Jewish Healthcare Found., U. Pitts.; trustee, pres. Fair Oaks Found. Mem. ABA, Mass. Bar Assn., Harvard Club (NY), Pitts. Athletic Club, Duquesne Club, Laurel Valley Golf Club, Fox Chapel Golf Club. Republican. Jewish. Office: Ampco-Pitts Corp 600 Grant St Pittsburgh PA 15219-2702 Office Phone: 412-456-4400. Personal E-mail: rpaul@ampcopgh.com.

PAUL, ROBERT CAREY, lawyer; b. Washington, May 7, 1950; s. Robert Henry and Betty Jane (Carey) Paul. AB, Dartmouth Coll., 1972; JD, Georgetown U., 1978. Assoc. Milbank, Tweed, Hadley & McCloy, NYC, 1978—85; ptnr. Dechert Price & Rhoads, NYC, 1986—89, Kelley Drye & Warren, Brussels, 1989—93; counsel Rockefeller & Co., Inc., NYC, 1995—2003; cons. NYC, 2003—05; corp. coun. Rockefeller Group Internat., Inc., 2005—; v.p. Rockefeller Group Tech. Solutions, Inc., 2005—, corp. coun., 2005—, chief adminstrv. officer, 2007—. Editor-in-chief Real Property Probate and Trust Jour., 2001—06. Mem.: ABA (real property, probate and trust law sect. coun. 2006—), Am. Coll. Real Estate Lawyers. Home: 310 E 46th St Apt 19E New York NY 10017-3029 Office: 1221 Ave of the Americas New York NY 10020 Office Phone: 212-282-2650. Business E-Mail: rpaul@rockgrp.com.

PAUL, ROLAND ARTHUR, lawyer; b. Memphis, Jan. 19, 1937; s. Rol and Hattye (Mincer) P.; m. Barbara Schlesinger, June 10, 1962; children: Deborah Lynn, Arthur Eliot. BA summa cum laude, Yale U., 1958; LL.B. magna cum laude, Harvard U., 1961. Bar: N.Y. 1962, Mich. 1978, Conn. 1989. Law clk. to judge U.S. Ct. Appeals, 1961-62; fgn. affairs officer, spl. asst. to gen. counsel Dept. Def., 1962-64; assoc. firm Cravath, Swaine & Moore, NYC, 1964-69; counsel fgn. relations subcom. security commitments U.S. Senate, 1969-71; assoc. firm Simpson Thacher Bartlett, NYC, 1971-73; v.p., gen. counsel Howmet Corp., Greenwich, Conn., 1976-2000, Howmet Internat. Inc., 1997-2000; v.p., gen. counsel, dir. Pechiney Corp., Greenwich, Conn., 1984-95; counsel Day, Berry & Howard, Stamford, Conn., 2000—03, Ivey, Barnum & O'Mara, Greenwich, 2003—. Author: American Military Commitments Abroad. Mem. ABA, Coun. Fgn. Rels. Home: 8 Ellery Ln Westport CT 06880-5202 Office: 170 Mason St Greenwich CT 06832 Office Phone: 203-862-7740.

PAUL, RONALD ERNEST, United States Representative from Texas; b. Pitts., Aug. 20, 1935; m. Carol Paul; 5 children. BA in Biology, Gettysburg Coll., Pa., 1957; MD, Duke U. Med. Ctr., Durham, NC, 1961. Intern, resident Henry Ford Hosp., Detroit, 1961, 1962; ob-gyn. tng. U. Pitts., 1965—68; physician pvt. practice Brazoria County, Tex., 1968; mem. US Congress from 14th Tex. dist., 1976—77, 1979—85, 1997—, mem. internat. rels. com., mem. joint econ. com., mem. fin. svcs. com., vice chmn. oversight and investigations subcommittee. Author: Gold, Peace and Prosperity, 1981, The Case for Gold, 1982, Challenge to Liberty, 1990, A Republic, If You Can Keep It, 2000, Pillars of Prosperity, 2007, A Foreign Policy of Freedom: Peace, Commerce, and Honest Friendship, 2007, The Revolution: A Manifesto, 2008 (NY Times bestseller). Libertarian nominee 1988 Presdl. Election; Republican candidate 2008 Presdl. Election, 2007—08. Flight surgeon USAF, 1963—65, flight surgeon US Air N.G., 1965—68. Recipient Taxpayer's Best Friend award Nat. Taxpayers Union, Mises Inst. Groseclose Prize and Leadership award, Leadership award Coalition for Peace Through Strength, Disting. Svc. award Am. Constl. Action, Torch Freedom award Young Conservatives Tex., Guardian Freedom award Young Am. Freedom. Republican. Baptist. Office: US House Reps 203 Cannon House Office Bldg Washington DC 20515-4314 Office Phone: 202-225-2831.*

PAUL, RONALD NEALE, management consultant; b. Chgo., July 22, 1934; s. David Edward and Frances (Kusel) P.; m. Nona Maria Moore, Dec. 27, 1964 (div. Oct. 1981); children: Lisa, Karen, Brenda; m. Georgeann Elizabeth Lapkoff, Apr. 10, 1982. BS in Indsl. Engring., Northwestern U., 1957, MBA, 1958. Asst. to pres. Victor Comptometer Co., Chgo., 1958-64; cons. Corplan, Chgo., 1964-66; pres. Technomic Inc., Chgo., 1966—. Mng. ptnr. L/P Ptnrs., Chgo., 1978-84; bd. dirs. Summit Restaurants, Salt Lake City, 1990-96. Co-author: The 101 Best Performing Companies in America, 1986, Winning the Chain Restaurant Game, 1994. Mem. Am. Mktg. Assn., Am. Mgmt. Assn., Planners Forum, Pres.'s Assn., Beta Gamma Sigma. Avocations: reading, racquetball. Office: Technomic Inc 300 S Riverside Plz Ste 1200 Chicago IL 60606-6613 Office Phone: 312-876-0004. Business E-Mail: rpaul@technomic.com.

PAUL, STEPHEN HOWARD, lawyer; b. Indpls., June 28, 1947; s. Alfred and Sophia (Nahmias) P.; m. Deborah Lynn Dorman, Jan. 22, 1969; children: Gabriel, Jonathan. AB, Ind. U., 1969, JD, 1972. Bar: Ind. 1972, US Dist. Ct. (so. dist.) Ind. 1972. Assoc. Baker & Daniels, Indpls., 1972-78, ptnr., 1979—, chmn. mgmt. com., 2004. Mem. bd. visitors Ind. U. Sch. Law, Bloomington, adj. prof. Editor in chief Ind. U. Law Jour., 1971. Pres. Belle Meade Neighborhood Assn., Indpls., 1974-78; v.p., counsel Brentwood Neighborhood Assn., Carmel, Ind., 1985-88, pres., 1988-91. Mem. ABA (state and local tax com. 1985—, sports and entertainment law com.), Am. Property Tax Counsel (founding mem.), Counselors to Real Estate, Ind. State Bar Assn., Order of Coif. Office: Baker & Daniels 300 N Meridian St Ste 2700 Indianapolis IN 46204-1782 Office Phone: 317-237-0300. Business E-Mail: stephen.paul@bakerd.com.

PAUL, STEVEN M., pharmaceutical executive; BA magna cum laude in Biology and Psychology, Tulane U., New Orleans, 1972, MS in Anatomy and Neuroanatomy, 1975, MD, 1975. Intern neurology Charity Hosp., New Orleans; resident psychiatry, instr. dept. psychiatry U. Chgo. Pritzker Sch. Medicine; prof. psychiatry Tulane U. Sch. Medicine; chief clin. neuroscience br., chief preclinical studies sect. NIH NIMH, Bethesda, sci. dir. intramural rsch. program; v.p. ctrl. nervous sys. discovery and decision phase med. rsch. Lilly Rsch. Labs. Eli Lilly and Co., Indpls., 1993—96, v.p. therapeutic area discovery rsch. and clin. investigation Lilly Rsch. Labs., 1996—98, group v.p. therapeutic area discovery rsch. and clin. investigation Lilly Rsch. Labs., 1998, exec. v.p. sci. and tech., pres. Lilly Rsch. Labs., 2003—, mem. corp. policy and strategy, ops. coms., mem. sr. mgmt. coun. Chmn. exec. bd. Pharm. Rsch. and Mfrs. Am. Sci. and Regulatory Com.; bd. mem. Biotechnology Industry Orgn. Contbr. articles to profl. jours., chapters to books. Bd. dirs. Lilly Found., Found. of NIH, Butler U., Indpls., Indpls. Zoological Soc. Recipient A.E. Bennett award, Soc. Biol. Psychiatry, Foundations' Fund prize for Rsch., Am. Psychiat. Assn., Disting. Svc. medal, US; named Chief Sci. Officer of Yr., 2005. Mem.: NAS Inst. Medicine, Tulane Scholars and Fellows, Alpha Omega Alpha Med. Soc., Phi Beta Kappa, Sigma Xi, Alpha Epsilon Delta, Phi Eta Sigma. Office: Eli Lilly and Co Lilly Corp Ctr Indianapolis IN 46285 Office Phone: 317-276-2000.

PAUL, WILLIAM, physicist, researcher; b. Deskford, Scotland, Mar. 31, 1926; came to U.S., 1952; s. William and Jean (Watson) P.; m. Barbara Anderson Forbes, Mar. 28, 1952; children: David, Fiona. MA, Aberdeen U., Scotland, 1946; PhD, Aberdeen U., 1951; A.M. (hon.), Harvard U., 1960; D Honoris Causa, Paris, 1994. Asst. lectr., then lectr. Aberdeen U., 1946-52; mem. faculty Harvard U., 1953—, Gordon McKay prof. applied physics, 1963-91, Mallinckrodt prof. applied physics, 1991—2000, prof. physics, 1980-2000, Mallinckrodt rsch. prof. applied physics, 2000—04, rsch. prof. physics, 2000—04, Mallinckrodt prof. applied physics emeritus, prof. physics emeritus, 2004—. Professeur associé U. Paris, 1966-67; cons. solid state physics, 1954—; Ripon prof., Calcutta, 1984 Author: Handbook on Semiconductors: Band Theory and Transport Properties, 1982; co-editor: Solids Under Pressure, 1963, Amorphous and Liquid Semiconductors, 1980, Physics of Semiconductor Materials and Applications, 1986, High Pressure in Semiconductor Physics, Vols. 1 and 2, 1998. Carnegie fellow, 1952-53; Guggenheim fellow, 1959-60; Humboldt awardee, 1990; fellow Clare Hall Cambridge U., 1974-75. Fellow Am. Phys. Soc., Brit. Inst. Physics, N.Y. Acad. Scis., Royal Soc. Edinburgh Home: 57 Dartmouth Ct Bedford MA 01730 Office: Harvard U Pierce Hall Cambridge MA 02138 Home Phone: 781-275-6787. Business E-Mail: paul@seas.harvard.edu.

PAUL, WILLIAM DEWITT, JR., retired art educator, collector, artist; b. Wadley, Ga., Sept. 26, 1934; s. William DeWitt and Sonoma Elizabeth (Tinley) Paul; m. Dorothy Hefling Paul, Sept. 2, 1962; children: Sarah Elizabeth, Barbara Susan, Dorothy Ann. Student, Emory U., Atlanta, summer 1952, U. Rome, summer 1953, Ga. State Univ., Atlanta, 1953—; BFA, Atlanta Coll. Art, 1955; AB, U. Ga., Athens, 1958, MFA, 1959. Instr. art and art history Park Coll., Parkville, Mo., 1960-61; dir. exhbns., instr. art history Kansas City Art Inst., 1959-64, curator study collections, asst. prof. art, 1964-65; coordinator basic courses dept. art, asst. prof. art U. Ga., Athens, 1965-67; curator Ga. Mus. Art, assoc. prof. art, 1967-69, dir., asso. prof., 1969-80, prof., 1997—2002, gen. Sandy Beaver tchr. prof., 2000—02, prof. emeritus, 2002—. Lectr. Boston, LA, New Orleans, San Antonio, Memphis, Birmingham; chmn. visual arts rev. panel Ga. Council for Arts and Humanities, 1976-77; v.p. Arts Festival Atlanta, 1982, 84, 85, trustee, 1982-93; guest artist Arts Festival Atlanta, 1987; mem. parents council Randolph-Macon Woman's Coll., Lynchburg, Va., 1986-87. Exhibited in one man shows at Ga. Mus. Art, 1959, Atlanta Art Assn., 1959, Unitarian Gallery, Kansas City, 1960, Palmer Gallery, Kansas City, 1965, Heath Gallery, Atlanta, 1976, Hunter Mus. Art, Chattanooga, 1976, Forum Gallery, NYC, 1977, Madison, Ga., Morgan Cultural Ctr., 1980, Columbus, Ga., Mus. Arts and Scis., 1980, Macon, Ga., Mus. Arts and Sci., 1980, Banks Haley Gallery, Albany, Ga., 1980, Augusta Richmond County, Ga., Mus., 1980, Heath Gallery 1982, Moon Gallery, Berry Coll., Rome, Ga., 1983, Bathhouse Gallery, Atlanta, 1987, MIA Gallery, Seattle, 1988, Valencia CC, Orlando, Fla., 1991, Gasperi Gallery, New Orleans, 1993, Contemporary Arts Ctr., New Orleans, 1994, Lyndon House Art Ctr., Athens, Ga., 2005, Averitt Art Ctr., Statesboro, Ga., 2006, Splitbeard Gallery, Athens, 2008; numerous site-specific installations, 1986-97; exhibited group shows, New Arts Gallery, Atlanta, 1961, Kansas City Art Inst., 1960-64, Park Coll., 1960, Mulvane Art Ctr., Topeka, 1965, Palazzo Venezia, Rome, 1984, Elaine Benson Gallery, Bridgehampton, LI, NY, 1986, Dulin Gallery Art, Knoxville, Tenn., 1986, 1987 Atlanta Biennale, Nexus Contemporary Art Ctr., Atlanta, Valencia CC, Orlando, 1988, Greg Kucera Gallery, Seattle, 1992, King Plow Arts Ctr., Atlanta, 1994, Leslie-Lohman Found., NYC, 1995, Mus. Fine Arts, Tallahassee, 1996, Art Ctr., Miami Beach, Fla., 1997, Lebanon Valley Coll., Annville, Pa., 1998, others; represented in permanent collections Gen. Mills, Inc., Mpls., Hallmark Cards, Kansas City, Little Rock Arts Ctr., Ga. Mus. Art, U. Ga., The Kinsey Inst., Ind. U., Calif. State U., Tom of Finland Found. Ford Found. faculty enrichment grantee, 1978; recipient numerous awards for paintings. Mem. Am. Fedn. Arts (trustee 1969-81), Coll. Art Assn., Am. Assn. Museums (coun. 1981), Lovis Corinth Meml. Found., Ga. Alliance Arts Edn. (dir. 1975-77), Phi Kappa Phi. Home: 150 Bar H Ct Athens GA 30605-4702 Office: 4900 Barnett Shoals Rd Athens GA 30605 Home Phone: 706-548-4816; Office Phone: 706-613-2312.

PAUL, WILLIAM ERWIN, immunologist; b. Bklyn., June 12, 1936; s. Jack and Sylvia (Gleicher) Paul; m. Marilyn Heller, Dec. 25, 1958; children: Jonathan M. Carmel, Matthew E. BA summa cum laude, Bklyn. Coll., 1956; MD cum laude, SUNY, Bklyn., 1960, DSc (hon.), 1991; PhD (hon.), Hebrew U., Jerusalem, 2003, Med. U. Cluj-Napoca, Romania, 2003, Nat. U. Athens, Greece, 2007; Laurea hon. causa, U. Rome, 2005. Intern, asst. resident Mass. Meml. Hosp., Boston Med. Ctr., 1960—62; clin. assoc. Nat. Cancer Inst., NIH, Bethesda, Md., 1962—64; post doctoral fellow, instr. NYU Sch. Medicine, NYC, 1964—68; prin. investigator lab. immunology Nat. Inst. Allergy and Infectious Diseases, NIH, Bethesda, Md., 1968—70, chief lab. immunology, 1970—; dir. office of AIDS rsch. NIH, Bethesda, Md., assoc. dir. AIDS rsch., 1994—97, disting. investigator, 2007—. Awards jury mem. Albert Lasker Med. Rsch. Awards Program, 1993—; chmn. selection com. Irene Diamond Fund Professorship in Immunology, 1997—2005; Sackler sr. prof. Tel Aviv U., Israel; chair sci. adv. bd. Lupus Rsch. Inst.; mem. Novartis Sci. Bd., 2001—05; adj. prof. U. Pa., 2002—; governing dir. Am. Found. for AIDS Rsch., 2002—05, mem. program adv. bd., 2006—; chair visiting com. assessment of basic biomed. rsch. Israel Acad. Sci. and Humanities, 2007; mem. sci. adv. bd. Trudeau Inst. Adv. editor Jour. Exptl. Medicine, 1974—2006; editor: Ann. Rev. Immunology, Volumes 1-28, 1983—, Fundamental Immunology, 1st - 6th edits., 1984—, Immunity, 2003—06; assoc. editor Cell, 1985—96, transmitting editor Internat. Immunology, 1989—96, corr. editor Procs. Royal Soc. Series B, 1989—93, mem. editl. bd. Molecular Biology of Cell, 1990—93; contbg. editor: Procs. NAS U.S.A., 1992—94; mem. editl. bd. Procs. NAS U.S.A., 2004—; contbr. numerous articles to sci. journals. With USPHS, 1962—64, with USPHS, 1975—96. Recipient Founders' prize, Tex. Instruments Found., 1979, Alumni medal, SUNY Downstate Med. Ctr., 1981, DSM, USPHS, 1985, Life Sci. Award, 3M, 1988, Tovi Comet - Wallerstein prize, CAIR Inst., Bar Ilan U., 1992, 6th ann. Excellence Award in Immunologic Rsch., Duke U., 1993, Alumni Honors, Bklyn. Coll., 1994, Abbott Labs. Award in Clin. and Diagnostic Immunology, Am. Acad. Microbiology, 1998, Lifetime Achievement award, Am. Assn. Immunologists, 2002, Sci. Achievement in award, The Irvington Inst., 2002, Rsch. in Action award, Treatment Action Group, 2003, Scientific Leadership award, Lupus Found., 2005, Hon. Lifetime Achievement award, Internat. Cytokine Soc., 2007. Fellow: Am. Acad. Arts and Sci.; mem.: NAS, Am Assn. Immunologists (pres. 1986—87, Lifetime Achievement award 2002, Mex Delebruck medal 2008), Assn. Am. Physicians, Scandinavian Soc. Immunology (hon.), Am. Soc. Clin. Investigation (pres. 1980—81), Inst. Medicine NAS. Achievements include discovery of interleukin-4 and demonstration of its central role in allergic inflammatory responses; determination of mechanisms of Th2 differentiation. Office: NIH Bldg 10 Rm 11n311 Bethesda MD 20892-1982 Office Phone: 301-496-5046. Business E-Mail: wpaul@niaid.nih.gov.

PAUL, WILLIAM GEORGE, lawyer; b. Pauls Valley, Okla., Nov. 25, 1930; s. Homer and Helen (Lafferty) P.; m. Barbara Elaine Brite, Sept. 27, 1963; children: George Lynn, Alison Elise, Laura Elaine, William Stephen. BA, U. Okla., 1952, LL.B., 1956. Bar: Okla. bar 1956. Pvt. practice law, Norman, 1956; ptnr. Oklahoma City, 1957-84; with Crowe & Dunlevy, 1962-84, 96—; sr. v.p., gen. counsel Phillips Petroleum Co., Bartlesville, Okla., 1984-95; ptnr. Crowe & Dunlevy, Oklahoma City, 1996—. Assoc. prof. law Oklahoma City U., 1964-68; adv. bd. Martindale Hubbell, 1990—. Author: (with Earl Sneed) Vernon's Oklahoma Practice, 1965. Bd. dirs. Nat. Ctr. for State Cts., 1993-99, Am. Bar Endowment, 1986—, Bank 2, 2005-; trustee Nat. Constitution Ctr., 2000—. 1st lt. USMCR, 1952-54. Named Outstanding Young Man Oklahoma City, 1965, Outstanding Young Oklahoman, 1966, Okla. Hall of Fame, 2003. Fellow Am. Bar Found. (chmn. 1991), Am. Coll. Trial Lawyers; mem. ABA (bd. govs. 1995—, pres. 1999), Okla. Bar Assn. (pres. 1976), Oklahoma County Bar Assn. (past pres.), Okla Lottery Commn., Nat. Conf. Bar Pres. (pres. 1986), U. Okla. Alumni Assn. (pres. 1973), Order of Coif, Phi Beta Kappa, Phi Delta Phi, Delta Sigma Rho. Democrat. Presbyterian. Home: 13017 Burnt Oak Rd Oklahoma City OK 73120-8919 Office: Crowe & Dunlevy 20 N Broadway Ave Ste 1800 Oklahoma City OK 73102-8273 Office Phone: 405-239-6676.

PAUL, WILLIAM MCCANN, lawyer; b. Cambridge, Mass., Feb. 9, 1951; s. Kenneth William and Mary Jean (Lamson) P.; m. Janet Anne Forest, Feb. 25, 1984; children: Emily L'Engle, Andrew Angwin, Elizabeth Seton. Student, U. Freiburg, Fed. Republic of Germany, 1971-72; BA, Johns Hopkins U., 1973; JD, U. Mich., 1977. Bar: D.C. 1978, U.S. Dist. Ct. D.C. 1978, U.S. Ct. Claims 1984, U.S. Ct. Appeals (4th cir.) 1980, U.S. Ct. Appeals (fed. cir.) 1983, U.S. Tax Ct. 1990. Law clk. to judge U.S. Ct. Appeals (5th cir.), Austin, Tex., 1977-78; assoc. Covington & Burling, Washington, 1978-87, ptnr., 1987-88, 89—; dep. tax legis. counsel U.S. Treasury Dept., 1988-89. Mem. ABA (asst. sec. tax sect. 1995-97, sec. 1997-99, coun. mem. 1999-2002, vice chair govt. rels. 2005-07), D.C. Bar Assn., Am. Law Inst., Am. Coll. Tax Counsel, Order of Coif. Presbyterian. Home: 5604 Chevy Chase Pkwy NW Washington DC 20015-2520 Office: Covington & Burling PO Box 7566 1201 Pennsylvania Ave NW Washington DC 20004-2401 E-mail: wpaul@cov.com.

PAUL, WILLIAM S., city health department administrator; b. Chgo. m. Tonya Paul; 3 children. BS, Stanford Univ.; MD, MPH, Univ. Ill. Cert. internal med. & infectious diseases. Positions through dep. commr. & chief med. officer Chgo. Dept. Pub. Health, 1992—2007; dir. health Metro. Bd. Health Nashville/Davidson County, 2007—. Office: Metro Bd Health 311 23d Ave Nashville TN 37203 Office Phone: 615-340-5622. Office Fax: 615-340-2131.*

PAULEY, BARBARA ANNE, author, educator; b. Nashville, Jan. 12, 1925; d. William Moncrief and Lucile Elizabeth (Dies) Cotton; m. Robert Reinhold Pauley, June 22, 1946; children: Lucinda T., Nicholas Andrew, Robert Reinhold, John Adams. Student Wellesley Coll., 1942. Editorial asst. Ideal Pub. Co., N.Y.C., 1965-70; founder, dir. North Shore Writers' Assn., Wenham, Mass., 1975—. Author: (novels) Blook Kin, 1972; Voices Long Hushed, 1976. Pres., Friends of the Library, Wenham, 1979-81. Republican. Methodist. Home: 1120 Durham Rd Madison CT 06443 Home Phone: 203-421-8664.

PAULEY, BRUCE FREDERICK, retired history professor; b. Lincoln, Nebr., Nov. 4, 1937; s. Carroll Righter and Blanche Marie (Hulsebus) P.; m. Marianne Barbara Utz, Dec. 21, 1963; children: Mark Allan, Glenn Hamilton. BA, Grinnell Coll., 1959; MA, U. Nebr., 1961; PhD, U. Rochester, 1966. Instr. history Coll. of Wooster, Ohio, 1964-65, U. Nebr., Lincoln, 1965-66; asst. prof. history U. Wyo., Laramie, 1966-71; from assoc. prof. to prof. history U. Ctrl. Fla., Orlando, 1971—2006, chmn. faculty senate, 1978-79, prof. emeritus, 2006. Vis. prof. history U. Nebr., Lincoln, 2002, 06; cons., expert witness war crimes divsn. Can. Justice Dept., 1998-99. Author: The Habsburg Legacy, 1867-1939, 1972, Hahnenschwanz und Hakenkreuz: Steirischer Heimatschutz und österreichischer Nationalsozialismus, 1918-1934, 1972, Hitler and the Forgotten Nazis: A History of Austrian National Socialism, 1981, Der Weg in den Nationalsozialismus: Ursprünge und Entwicklung in Österreich, 1988, From Prejudice to Persecution: A History of Austrian Anti-Semitism, 1992 (Charles Smith prize So. Hist. Assn. best book European history, 1992, best book Austrian studies Austrian Cultural Inst., 1993), Eine Geschichte des österreichischen Antisemitismus: Von der Ausgrenzung zur Auslöschung, 1993, Hitler, Stalin and Mussolini: Totalitarianism in the Twentieth Century, 1997, 2d edit., 2003, 3rd edit., 2009. Chmn. parents' adv. com. Oviedo (Fla.) High Sch., 1981-82. Named Disting. Alumnus, U. Nebr., Lincoln, 1996; Fulbright fellow, 1963-64, rsch. fellow NEH, 1972, 87, Lifetime Achievement award, U. Nebr., Lincoln, 2005. Mem.: Am. Hist. Assn., Soc. Austrian and Habsburg Historians, German Studies Assn. (exec. com. 1986—89). Avocations: traveling to historical sites, photography, golf. Business E-Mail: bpauley@pegasus.cc.ucf.edu.

PAULEY, EDWARD E., museum administrator; b. Huntington, W.Va. BFA, Marshall U.; MFA in painting, Ohio U. Dir. edn. Huntington Mus. Art, W.Va.; exec. dir. Black Mountain-Swannanoa Ctr. for Arts, NC, Cultural Ctr. Fine Arts, Parkersburg, W.Va.; pres., CEO Plains Art Mus., Fargo, ND, 2003—. Tchr. Marshall U., Huntington, U. NC, Asheville. Office: Plains Art Mus 704 1st Ave N Fargo ND 58102 E-mail: epauley@plainsart.org.

PAULEY, SHIRLEY STEWART, religious organization executive; b. Boston, Sept. 13, 1938; d. Charles Norris and Nellie Consuelo (Yorke) Stewart; m. Edward Haven Pauley, May 29, 1964; children: David Stewart, Deborah Jeanne. BA, Gordon Coll., 1960; postgrad., Ariz. State U., 1961, Boston U., 1963. Sec., receptionist Atwell Co., Boston, summer 1956; sec., typist Kelley Girl, Boston, 1956-60; asst. office mgr. Radiator Chem. Corp., Scottsdale, Ariz., 1960-62; sec., clerical worker GM, Westwood, Mass., 1962-64; v.p. Truth Alive Ministries, Dallas, 1995—. Spkr. At Large, Boston, 1956-60; Sunday sch. tchr. Blaney Meml. Bapt. Ch., Boston, 1956-60; choir dir. Sherwood Bapt. Ch., Phoenix, 1961-62, co-youth dir., 1961; co-youth dir. Blaney Meml. Ch., Boston, 1964-66; messenger Bapt. Gen. Conv. Tex., Ft. Worth, 1996; leader bible study Prestonwood Bapt. Ch., Dallas, 2006—; v.p. Truth Alive Ministries, 1996—. Republican. Avocations: photography, reading, music. Office: Truth Alive Ministries PO Box 794945 Dallas TX 75379-4945 Personal E-mail: sspauley@att.net.

PAULIKAS, GEORGE ALGIS, retired physicist; b. Pagegiai, Lithuania, May 14, 1936; came to U.S., 1949, naturalized, 1955; s. George and Olga (Pacas) P.; m. Joan Marie Gross, Sept. 7, 1957; 1 child, Nancy Marie. BS in Engring. Physics, U. Ill., Chgo. and Urbana, 1957, MS (univ. fellow 1957-58), 1958; PhD in Physics (NSF fellow 1958-61), U. Calif., Berkeley, 1961. With Aerospace Corp., El Segundo, Calif., 1961-98; ret., head space particles and fields dept., 1968, dir. space scis. lab., 1968-81, v.p. labs., 1981-85, sr. v.p. devel., 1985-89, sr. v.p. programs, 1989-94, exec. v.p., 1992-98, ret. cons. emp., 1998—. Mem. various ad hoc coms. NAS, 1970—, ann., 1984—2008; mem. adv. coun. geophysics U. Calif., 1973—75, exec. com. space scis. lab., 1978—81; mem. sci. adv. bd. USAF, 1975—82, 1991—95; mem. def. space tech. com. NRC, 1987—92; mem. NAS/NRC Space Studies Bd., 1999—2006, vice chair, 2003—06; cons. in field. Author papers in field; asso. editor: Jour. Geophys. Research, 1972-75. Trustee Calif. Sci. Ctr., 1994-2000, Boy Scouts Am., L.A., 1996-2000. Recipient Aerospace Corp. Trustees Disting. Achievement award, 1980, Meritorious Civilian Svc. award USAF, 1982, 95, U. Ill. Alumni Disting. Engring. award, 1992, Nat. Reconnaissance Office Gold Medal, 1998; named U. Ill. (Navy Pier) Hall of Fame, 1996. Fellow AIAA (chmn. tech. com. space sci. and astronomy 1976-77), Am. Phys. Soc.; mem. Am. Geophys. Union, Sigma Xi. Home: 1537 Addison Rd Palos Verdes Estates CA 90274 Office Phone: 310-336-7076. E-mail: george.a.paulikas@aero.org.

PAULIN, AMY RUTH, civic activist, consultant, state legislator; b. Bklyn., Nov. 29, 1955; d. Ben and Alice Lois (Roth) P.; m. Ira Schuman, May 25, 1980; children: Beth, Sarah, Joseph. BA, SUNY, Albany, 1977, MA, 1978. Instr. SUNY, Albany, 1978, Queens (N.Y.) House of Detention, 1979; fundraiser United Jewish Appeal Fedn., NYC, 1979-83; dir. devel. Altro Health & Rehab., Bronx, N.Y., 1983-86; fundraising cons. NYC, 1986-88; pres. LWV, Scarsdale, N.Y., 1990-92, Westchester, N.Y., 1992-95; trustee Scarsdale (N.Y.) Village, 1995-99; exec. dir. My Sisters' Place, 1999—2000; mem. Dist. 88 NY State Assembly, 2000—. Mem. adv. coun. Family Ct.; co-chair woman Westchester Womens Agenda, Westchester Dept. Social Svcs.; mem. adv. com. Fund for Women & Girls; bd. dirs. Mid. Sch. PTA, 1995-97, Westchester Coalition for Legal Abortion, Scarsdale Open Soc. Assn., 1992-95, United Jewish Appeal Fedn. Scarsdale Women's Campaign; v.p. Westchester Children's Assn.; troop leader Girl Scouts U.S., 1992-96; mem. Town Club Edn. Com., 1983-89; mem. Scarsdale Bowl com., 1992-95, chair, 1994-95; mem. Scarsdale Japanese Festival, 1992-93; mem. Westchester Women's Equality Day, 1987-92; mem. nominating com. Heathcote Neighborhood Assn., 1991-92; bd. advisors Westchester County Found., 1994—; mem. Scarsdale Village Youth Bd., 1992-95; mem. U.S. legislators task force on families at risk Westchester County Bd., 1994—; mem. Updating Voting Equipment Com., 1994; mem. Tobacco Free Westchester, 1993-95, chair 1995—; co-chair Parent Tchr. Coun. Sch. Budget Study, 1991-94; planning chair Kids Base Bd., 1992-95, dir. 1992-94 chair parking and traffic subcom. Village Downtown Devel. Com., 1994-95; mem. Westchester Commn. Campaign Fin. Reform, Westchester Commn. Child Abuse, 1996-87; exec. com. Westchester Mcpl. Officals. Assn., 1996-97; adv. com. Jr. League, 1996-99. Named Westchester County Woman of Yr., 1995, Bridge Fund award, 1998, Women's Health Network Ann. award, 1999. Mem. LWV (bd. dirs. women and children's issues Westchester chpt., dir. social policy NY state), State Communities Aid Assn. (econ. securities com.), NY State Pub. Health Assn. (bd. dirs. Lower Hudson Valley chpt.), NY State Coalition Choice, New Yorkers Against Gun Violence (bd. dirs.). Democrat. Jewish. Avocations: swimming, dance. Home: 12 Burgess Rd Scarsdale NY 10583-4410 Office: Dist Office 700 White Plains Rd Ste 252 Scarsdale NY 10583 also: Capitol Office Legislative Office Bldg Albany NY 12248 Office Phone: 518-455-5585, 914-723-1115. E-mail: paulina@assembly.state.ny.us.*

PAULISON, ROBERT DAVID, former federal agency administrator; b. Miami, 1947; m. Kathy Paulison. BA, Fla. Atlantic U.; postgrad., Harvard U. Rescue firefighter, lt., battalion comdr., dist. chief ops., divsn. chief, asst. chief, deputy dir. adminstrn. Miami-Dade Fire Rescue Dept., chief, 1992—2001; adminstr. US Fire Adminstrn. US Dept. Homeland Security, Emmitsburg, Md., 2001—03, dir. preparedness divsn. Emergency Preparedness & Response Directorate (FEMA) Washington, 2003—05, acting under sec. of emergency preparedness & response, 2005—06, acting under sec. for Fed. Emergency Mgmt. (FEMA dir.), 2005—06; adminstr., Fed. Emergency Mgmt. (FEMA dir.) US Dept Homeland Security, Washington, 2006—09. Pres. Internat. Assn. Fire Chiefs, 1996—97. Recipient Motorola Mason Lankford Fire Svc. Leadership award, Congl. Fire Svc. Inst., 2004, Leroy Collins Disting. Alumni award; named Fire Chief of the Year, State of Fla., 1993; named to The Miami-Dade Community Coll. Hall of Fame.*

PAULISSEN, JAMES PETER, retired pediatrician, county official; b. Chgo., Aug. 14, 1928; s. Joseph Edward and Louise Catherine (Muno) P.; m. Lorraine Antoinette Polly, Sept. 11, 1954; children: Linda, Steven, Mark, Daniel. Student, Loyola U., 1946-49, MD cum laude, 1953; MPH, Johns Hopkins U., 1966. Diplomate Am. Bd. Pediat. Intern Milw. County Hosp., 1953-54; resident Milw. Children's Hosp., 1957-58; practice medicine specializing in pediats. Wauwatosa Children's Clinic, Wis., 1959-65; pediat. fellow Johns Hopkins U., 1965—66; chief Bur. Maternal and Child Health Ill. Dept. Pub. Health, Springfield, 1966-70, chief Divsn. Family Health, 1970-76; exec. dir. DuPage County Health Dept., Wheaton, Ill., 1976-93. Bd. dirs., mem. exec. com. Suburban Cook-DuPage Health Sys. Agy., Oak Park, Ill., 1976-82; bd. dirs., past pres. Comprehensive Health Coun. Met. Chgo., 1977-87; dir. Sr. Home Sharing, Inc., Wheaton, 1981-83; mem. Ill. Commn. on Children, 1971-85, vice chmn., 1983-85; chmn. Ill. Perinatal Adv. Com., 1981-84, mem., 1981-92; mem. Ill. Sch. Health Adv. Com., 1982-93, Gov.'s Adv. Coun. on Devel. Disabilities, 1973-76, Ill. Med. Determinations Bd., 1985-93; vice chmn. Ill. Pub. Health Advisors, 1988-91; mem. adv. bd. divsn. Svcs. Crippled Children U. Ill., 1986-94; trustee DuPage County Med. Found., 1976-82, 86-92, 1999-2006, treas. 2002-06; bd. dirs. DuPage Cmty. Clinic, 1993-2008, Cmty. Nursing Svc. of DuPage, 1993-99, vice chair, 1997-99; mem. cmty. health com. Ctrl. DuPage Health Sys., 1993-98; del. White House Conf. for Children, 1970. Capt. USAF, 1954-56. Recipient Dir.'s award for Sustained Excellence Ill. Dept. Pub. Health, 1988, Ill. Pediatrician of Yr. award, 1992, Humanitarian award DuPage County Health Planning Coun., 1994. Fellow Am. Acad. Pediats. (exec. com. Ill. chpt. 1978-81, sec. 1988-92), APHA, Am. Coll. Preventive Medicine; mem. Ill. Pub. Health Assn. (pres. 1977-78, Disting. Svc. award 1983), Ill. Assn. Maternal and Child Health (pres. 1975-76). Avocation: model building. Home: 28w660 Hawthorne Ln West Chicago IL 60185-2472

PAULK, DAVID MITCHELL, II, religious studies educator; b. Valdosta, Ga., Apr. 12, 1974; s. David Mitchell and Alice Carolyn Paulk; m. Kelly Nidole Foutz, June 15, 1996; children: David Mitchell III, Emily Grace, Catherine Hope. MA in History, Valdosta State U., Ga., 1997, MPA, 2003; MDiv, Southeastern Bapt. Theol. Sem., Wake Forest, NC, 2000. Pastor Benevolence Bapt. Ch., Valdosta, Ga., 1992—2008; history and religion instr. North Fla. CC, Madison, 2007—08. Home: 6142 White Ln Valdosta GA 31601 Office: 325 NW Turner Davis Dr Madison FL 32340 Business E-Mail: paulkd@online.nfcc.edu.

PAULL, RICHARD ALLEN, geologist, educator; b. Madison, Wis., May 20, 1930; s. Ethra Harold and Martha (Schaller) P.; m. Rachel Kay Krebs, Mar. 6, 1954; children: Kay Marie, Lynn Ellen, Judith Ann. BS, U. Wis., 1952, MS, 1953, PhD, 1957. Party chief Pan Am. Petroleum Co., 1955-57; research group leader Jersey Prodn. Research Co., 1957-62; mem. faculty U. Wis.-Milw., 1962-97, chmn. dept. geol. scis., 1962-66, prof., 1966-97, prof. emeritus, 1997—. Cons. in field, 1966— Author books, papers in field. Co-exec. sec. NAGT/USGS/AASG-Coop. Summer Field Tng. Program, 1994-99. Served with USAF, 1953-55. Recipient Amoco Disting. Tchg. award, 1975 Fellow Geol. Soc. Am. (chmn. ann. meeting 1970, tech. program com. 1970, 77, membership com. 1977-80, chmn. 1980); mem. Am. Assn. Petroleum Geologists (chmn. sci. fair award com. 1980, membership com. 1981-87, vis. petroleum geologists com. 1982-87, pub. affairs com. 1982-85), Soc. Econ. Paleontologists and Mineralogists, Nat. Assn. Geology Tchrs. (v.p. 1976-77, pres. 1977-78), Am. Geol. Inst. (governing bd. 1977-79, sec. and exec. com. 1986-88. Home: 1657 W Canal Ct Littleton CO 80120-4515 Personal E-mail: rocdox@comcast.net.

PAULOSE, RACHEL KUNJUMMEN, federal agency administrator, former prosecutor; b. Kerala, India, Mar. 12, 1973; d. Joseph and Rachel Paulose. BA, U. Minn., 1994; JD, Yale Law Sch., 1997. Law clk. to Hon. James B. Loken US Ct. Appeals (8th Cir.), 1997—98; trial atty. Civil Rights Divsn. US Dept. Justice, Washington, 1998—99, asst. US atty. Dist. Minn. Mpls., 1999—2002; atty. Williams & Connolly LLP, Washington; atty Dorsey & Whitney LLP, Mpls.; sr. counsel to atty. gen. US Dept. Justice, Washington, 2006, interim US atty. Dist. Minn. Mpls., 2006, US atty., 2006—07, counselor to acting asst. atty. gen. for legal policy Washington, 2007—. Mem.: Nat. Asian-Am. Bar Assn. (bd. mem.), Fed. Bar Assn. (bd. mem.). Office: US Dept Justice Rm 4234 Main Justice Bldg 950 Pennsylvania Ave NW Washington DC 20530

PAULRAJ, ANTONY, management consultant, educator; s. Chellappa Thathuvarayar Swamy and Sugantha Bai Madavadas; m. Leena A. Paulraj, Jan. 19, 2000; children: Austin Emmanuel, Evelyn Maria. D in Bus. Adminstrn., Cleve. State U., 2001. Asst. prof. U. North Fla., Jacksonville, 2005—; sr. cons. TekSys Inc., Columbus, Ohio. Recipient Best paper award, Jour. Purchasing and Supply Mgmt., 2007, numerous grants and awards. Mem.: Decision Scis. Inst.

PAULS, DAVID, human geneticist, researcher; b. Corn, Okla., Aug. 5, 1944; s. Peter B. and Helen (Funk) P.; m. Grace Marie Dick, Aug. 27, 1966; children: Scott, Jonathan. BA, Fresno Pacific Coll., 1966; PhD, U. Minn., 1972. Prof. genetics Fresno (Calif.) Pacific Coll., 1971-77; postdoctoral fellow U. Iowa, Iowa City, 1977-79; prof. Child Study Ctr. Yale U., New Haven, Conn., 1983—. Contbr. articles to profl. jours. Recipient Rsch. Scientist Devel. award NIMH, Washington, 1984—. Mem. AAAS, Am. Soc. Human Genetics, Soc. Rsch. in Child Devel., Behavior Genetics Assn. Office: Yale U Child Study Ctr 230 S Frontage Rd New Haven CT 06519-1124

PAULS, THOMAS ALBERT, astrophysicist, educator; b. Paterson, N.J., Jan. 17, 1944; s. Albert and Alyson (Blackshaw) P.; m. Eleanor Pelta, Nov. 1987. A.B., Gettysburg Coll., 1965; M.S., W.Va. U., 1967; M.A., Ind. U., 1970; Ph.D., N.Mex. State U., 1974. Staff scientist Max Planck Inst. for Radio Astronomy, Bonn, W.Ger., 1972-79; asst. prof. physics U. Cologne, West Germany, 1979-86; staff Naval Research Lab., Washington, 1986—. Contbr. articles to profl. jours. Grantee German Sci. Found., U. Cologne, 1981-84, NASA, 1989. Fellow Internat. Astron. Union, Am. Astron. Soc., Royal Astron. Soc.; mem. AAAS, N.Y. Acad. Sci. Office: Code 4130 Naval Research Lab Washington DC 20375-0001

PAULSEN, BRIAN OLIVER, art educator, artist; b. Seattle, Mar. 29, 1941; m. Dianne C. Coulter, Sept. 1963; children: Geoffrey E., Erica L. Knudsvig. BA, U. Wash., 1963; MFA, Wash. State U., 1966. Asst. prof. Chico (Calif.) State Coll., 1966—71; sessional instr. U. Calgary, Canada, 1971—73; prof. U. ND, Grand Forks, 1973—2007, Chester Fritz disting. prof., 1990; ret. Vis. artist 12 venues; juror nat. art exhbns. 86 one-man shows, more than 1000 group exhbns., more than 200 invitational exhibits. Artist fellowship award, Nat. Endowment Arts, Washington, 1981—82. Mem.: Nat. Acad. Design. Avocations: photography, biking. Business E-Mail: brian.paulsen@und.nodak.edu.

PAULSEN, ERIK, United States Representative from Minnesota, former state legislator; b. Bakersfield, Calif., May 14, 1965; s. Gerald and Janet (Lindfors) Paulsen; m. Kelly Spowls, 1989; children: Cassie, Briana, Tayler, Liesl. BA in Math., St. Olaf Coll., Northfield, Minn., 1987. Mktg. mgr. CVN Co., 1987—89; staff mem., field dir. US senator Rudy Baschwitz, Minn., 1989—90; legis. asst. to US Congressman Jim Ramstad, Washington, 1991—93, state dir. 3rd. dist. Minn., 1994; mem. dist. Minn. Ho. Reps. from Dist. 42B, 1995—2009, majority leader, 2003—06; bus. analyst Target Corp., Minn.; mem. US Congress from 3rd Minn. Dist., 2009—. Trustee Mpls. Inst. of Arts; bd. dirs. A Better Chance Found., Eden Prairie, Minn., Southdale YMCA. Mem.: Eden Prairie C. of C. Republican. Lutheran. Office: US Congress 126 Cannon House Office Bldg Washington DC 20515-2303 also: Dist Office 250 Prairie Ctr Dr Ste 230 Eden Prairie MN 55344 Office Phone: 202-225-2871, 952-405-8510. Office Fax: 202-225-6351, 952-405-8514.*

PAULSEN, RUTH ANN, French and Spanish language educator; b. Cosby, Mo., Dec. 9, 1940; d. Ernest Raymond and Ollie Hasque (Clouse) Thornton; m. Reuben Ray Paulsen, June 15, 1962 (div. 1982); children: Terrill Kent, Jeffrey Alan. AA, St. Joseph's Jr. Coll., Mo., 1960; BS in Edn., N.W. Mo. State U., 1962; MA, Baker U., 1985; postgrad., U. de Dijon, France, 1982, U. de l'Ouest, 1988-92. Cert. tchr. French and Spanish 7-12. Tchr. French, Spanish Highland Park High Sch., Topeka, 1962-68, Cen. N. Jr. High Sch., Kansas City, Mo., 1968-70; adult edn. instr. French Johnson County Community Coll., Overland Park, Kans., 1971-73; tchr. French, Spanish Cen. S. Jr. High Sch., Kansas City, 1974-77; tchr. French Ctr. Sr. HS, Kansas City, 1977—95, chair fgn. lang. dept., 1980—86, 1993—95; tchr. French and Spanish Blue Valley North HS, Overland Park, Kans., 1996—2002. Lectr. French, U. Mo., Kansas City, 1987-95; life mem. Mo. PTA. Author, photographer: (slide and video units with script) France at a Glance, 1989; co-editor: (book) Introduction to Language, 1976. Cub scout den mother Boy Scouts Am., 1969-74; sec. Brookridge Homes Assn., 1980-84. Grantee NDEA, 1964, 65, Rockefeller Found., Angers, France, 1988; Alliance Française scholar, Paris, 1983. Mem. NEA (life), NOW, Am. Coun. Teaching Fgn. Langs., Am. Assn. Tchrs. French, Alliance Française (bd. dirs. 1991-93, scholar Paris 1983), Fgn. Lang. Assn. Mo., Kans. Fgn. Lang. Assn. (sec. 1989—), Mo. Edn. Assn., Cen. Edn. Assn. (pres. 1988-89, chief negotiator 1989-90), Planned Parenthood, Phi Theta Kappa, Alpha Delta Kappa. Democrat. Baptist. Avocations: photography, travel. Home: 10932 Rosehill Rd Overland Park KS 66210-1178 Personal E-mail: rpaulsen@aol.com.

PAULSEN, SERENUS GLEN, retired architect, educator; b. Spooner, Wis., July 27, 1917; s. Serenus Justin and Edna Anne (Dalton) P.; m. Virginia C. Habel, Jan. 26, 1944; children: Thomas J., Nancy Lee (Mrs. John Marshall). Student, U. Ill., 1938-42; B.Arch. cum laude, U. Pa., 1947; Diploma in Architecture and City Planning, Royal Acad. Art, Stockholm, 1948. With Carroll, Grisdale & Van Alan (Architects), Phila., 1946-47, Eero Saarinen & Assos., Bloomfield Hills, Mich., 1949-51, 53-57; chief designer Reisner & Urbahn (Architects), NYC, 1951-52; archtl. coordinator Knoll Assos., NYC, 1952-53; prin. Glen Paulsen Assos., Birmingham, Mich., 1958-69; prin., v.p. Tarapata-MacMahon-Paulsen Assos., Inc. (Architects), Bloomfield Hills, 1969-77; pres. Cranbrook Acad. Art, head dept. architecture, 1966-70; prof., chmn. Masters Program in Architecture U. Mich., 1976-78, Emil Lorch prof. architecture, 1982-85, prof. emeritus, 1985—. Mem. Nat. Com. on Urban Planning and Design, 1971-72; archtl. commn. U. Wash., Seattle, 1968-76 (Recipient 3d prize Bi-Nat. Competition for Design Rainbow Center Plaza, Niagara Falls, N.Y. 1972). Gov. emeritus Cranbrook Acad. Art. Served with C.E. USAAF, 1942-46. life gov. Cranbrook Acad. Art, 2005. Fellow AIA (honor awards Detroit chpt. for Shapero Hall of Pharmacy 1965, Our Shepherd Lutheran Ch. 1966, Ford Life Sci. Bldg. 1967, Birney Elementary Sch., Detroit 1971, Fed. Bldg., Ann Arbor, Mich. 1978, gold medal for 1980 Detroit chpt.); mem. Mich. Soc. Architects, (Robert F. Hastings award 1985).

PAULSEN, VIVIAN, editor; b. Salt Lake City, May 10, 1942; d. Paul Herman and Martha Oline (Blattmann) P. BA, Brigham Young U., 1964, postgrad., 1965, U. Grenoble, France, 1966. Cert. tchr., Utah. Tchr. French Granite Sch. Dist., Salt Lake City, 1966-67; assoc. editor New Era mag., Salt Lake City, 1970-82; mng. editor Friend mag., Salt Lake City, 1982—. Am. Field Service scholar, 1959; grad. fellow Brigham Young U., 1964-66 Republican. Mem. Ch. of Jesus Christ of Latter-day Saints Office: The Friend 50 E North Temple # F23 Salt Lake City UT 84150-0002

PAULSON, ANDREW, publishing executive, Internet company executive; b. New Haven, Conn., 1958; Developer of various news, bus. & entertainment magazines, Moscow, 1993—98; founder, publisher Afisha Publishing House (Afisha Mag., Bolshoi Gorod Mag., MIR), Moscow, 1998—2006; founder, pres. SUP, Moscow, 2006—. Office: SUP 16th Fl Smolensky Passage 3 Smolenskaya Sq 121099 Moscow Russia

PAULSON, ARCHIE MILLER, geophysicist, educator; b. Rumbi, Indonesia, Dec. 25, 1970; s. Clifford Walter and Sharon Grace Paulson; m. Barbara Rodriguez Guridi. PhD in Phyisics, U. Colo., Boulder, 2006. Rsch. assoc. geophysics U. Calif., Berkeley, 2006—07; rsch. assoc. U. Colo., Colo., 2007—. Office: Univ Colo Dept Physics 390 UCB Univ Colo Boulder CO 80309

PAULSON, BELDEN HENRY, political scientist, educator; s. Henry Thomas and Evelina (Belden) P.; m. Louise D. Hill, Jan. 9, 1954; children: Eric, Steven AB, Oberlin Coll., 1950; MA, U. Chgo., 1955, PhD, 1962. With Italian svc. mission, Naples, 1950—53; organizer Homeless European Land Program, Sardinia, 1957—59; with UN High Commn. Refugees, Rome, 1960—61; mem. faculty U. Wis., Milw., 1962—; prof. polit. sci. U. Wis. ext., 1969—; founder and chmn. Ctr. Urban Cmty. Devel., 1967—90; co-founder and pres. High Wind Assn. for Modeling Cmty. for Sustainable Living, 1980—; pres. Plymouth Inst., 1995—98. Hon. rsch. prof. Internat. Tech. and Economy Inst, Inst. for Sci. of Scis., Shanghai, China, 1990—; mem. edn. task force Pres.'s Coun. on Sustainable Devel., 1995-98; co-founder Global Learning Ctr., 1998-2004 Author: The Searchers, 1966, Odyssey of a Practical Visionary; also articles Served with USNR, 1945-46 Findhorn Found. fellow; grantee Social Sci. Rsch. Coun., 1967-68; recipient Lifetime Disting. Achievement award Oberlin Coll., 2004 Mem.: World Future Soc. Home: W7122 County Rd U Plymouth WI 53073-4538 Office: U Wis Dept Urban Cmty Devel 161 W Wisconsin Ave Fl 6 Milwaukee WI 53203-2602 Office Phone: 414-224-3280. E-mail: paulson@dotnet.com.

PAULSON, BERNARD ARTHUR, oil industry executive, consultant; b. Lakeview, Mich., July 12, 1928; s. Arthur Bernard and Genevieve Talbard (Bushley) P.; m. Joan Lee Curtiss, Dec. 4, 1954; children: James, Joseph (dec.), Ann, Thomas (dec.), Bernadette, Patricia, Steven. BS in Chem. Engring., Mich. State U.-East Lansing, 1949. Registered profl. engr., Tex. Process engr. Mid-West Refineries Inc., Alma, Mich., 1949-57; plant mgr. Kerr-McGee Corp., Cleve. and Wynnewood, Okla., 1957-66; v.p. Coastal States Petrochemical, Corpus Christi, Tex., 1966-71, Koch Industries Inc., St. Paul and Wichita, 1971-88, cons. Corpus Christi, Tex., 1988-94; pres. Koch Refining Co., Wichita, 1981-88; chmn. The Automation Group Inc.; chmn., CEO The Inspection Group Inc. CEO Tor Minerals Internat., 1997, also bd. dirs; dir. Orion Refining Corp., 1999—. Chmn., pres. Cleve. Area Hosp. Corp., 1962; bd. govs. Water Devel. Bd. Tex. Region 10 Water JCom.; pres. Corpus Christi Bd. Trade; commr. Port of Corpus Christi Authority, vice chmn., 1997; bd. dirs. Ada Wilson Hosp. Found., Driscoll Hosp. Found., Coastal Bend Cmty. Found., Del Mar Coll. Found., Tex. A&M U. Corpus Christi Found., Art Mus. South Tex. 1st lt. USAF, 1955—57. Recipient Claud R. Erickson Disting. Alumnus award Mich. State U., 1994. Mem.: AIChE (fuels and petrochem. award 1989), Bd. Trade, Refining Am. Petroleum Inst., Nat. Petroleum Refiners Assn., Corpus Christi Town Club, Elks. Home and Office: Tor Minerals 4350 Ocean Dr #405 Corpus Christi TX 78412

PAULSON, HANK (HENRY MERRITT PAULSON JR.), former United States Secretary of the Treasury; b. Palm Beach, Fla., Mar. 28, 1946; s. Henry Merritt and Marianna (Gallaeur) Paulson; m. Wendy Judge, Sept. 6, 1969; children: Henry Merritt III, Amanda Clark. BA in English, Dartmouth Coll., 1968; MBA, Harvard U., 1970; Degree (hon.), Hamilton Coll., 2008. Staff asst. to the asst. sec. (comptr.) US Dept. Def., Washington, 1970-72; staff asst. to Domestic Policy Coun. The White House, Washington, 1972-73; assoc. Goldman Sachs & Co., Chgo., 1974-77, v.p., 1977-82, ptnr., 1982—88, ptnr. in charge investment banking services Midwest region, 1983—88, mng. ptnr., 1988—90, co-head investment banking divsn. NYC, 1990—94, pres., COO, 1994—98, co-CEO, 1998—99; chmn., CEO The Goldman Sachs Group, Inc., NYC, 1999—2006; sec. US Dept. Treasury, Washington, 2006—09; Disting. vis. scholar, fellow Bernard Schwartz Forum on Constructive Capitalism Paul H. Nitze Sch. Advanced Internat. Studies, Johns Hopkins U., Washington, 2009—. Mem. exec. com. NYC Investment Fund. Named Outstanding Coll. Lineman, Divsn. I, New Eng. Football Coaches, 1967; named to 1st team All-Ivy, All New Eng., All-East; NCAA Scholar Athlete, 1967. Republican. Mem. Christian Science Ch. Avocations: skiing, fishing, canoeing, tennis, birdwatching.*

PAULSON, JAMES MARVIN, retired engineering educator; b. Wausau, Wis., Jan. 1, 1923; s. Gustav Victor and Susanna (Dracy) P.; m. Marjorie Beulah Burton, May 11, 1946; children— Vicki Rae, Michael James. BS in Civil Engring, The Citadel, 1947; MS in Civil Engring, Ill. Inst. Tech., 1949; PhD, U. Mich., 1958. Registered profl. engr., Mich. Draftsman Wausau Iron Works, 1946; engr. Charles Whitney Cons. Engr., Milw., 1948-49; faculty Wayne State U., Detroit, 1949—, prof., 1961-85, chmn. dept. civil engring., 1967-72, assoc. dean Coll. Engring., 1973-83, prof. emeritus, 1985—; ret., 1985. V.p. Civil Engrs., Inc., 1954—; cons. in field. Served with AUS, 1943; Served with USMCR, 1943-46. Mem. ASCE (life), Mich. Soc. Profl. Engrs. (life), Am. Soc. for Engring. Edn., Sigma Xi, Tau Beta Pi, Chi Epsilon. Presbyterian. Home: 1017 Holly Dr Seymour IN 47274

PAULSON, JEROME AVROM, pediatrician; b. Balt., July 31, 1949; s. Robert R. and Edna (Brenner) P.; m. Susan Miller, 1973 (div. 1986); m. Gwen Victor Gampel, July 2, 1989. BS in Biochemistry, U. Md., 1971; MD, Duke U., 1974. Diplomate Am. Bd. Pediatrics, Nat. Bd. Med. Examiners. Resident in pediatrics Johns Hopkins Hosp., Balt., 1974-76, Sinai Hosp., Balt., 1976-77, fellow in ambulatory pediatrics, 1977-78; asst. prof. pediatrics Case Western Res. U., Cleve., 1978-86; dir. sci. rsch. and pub. policy devel. Joseph P. Kennedy Jr. Found., Washington, 1986-87; dir. pediatrics Regional Inst. for Children and Adolescents, Rockville, Md., 1987-89; clin. assoc. prof. pediatrics Georgetown U., Washington, 1987—; exec. dir. Research!America, Alexandria, Va., 1989-90; assoc. prof. medicine (formerly healthcare scis.) George Washington U., Washington, 1990—2002, assoc. prof. pediats., 1991—, fellow Ctr. Health Policy Rsch., 1991—98, assoc. prof. prevention and cmty. health, 1997—, assoc. rsch. prof. environ. and occupl. health, 2003—; co-dir. Mid-Atlantic Ctr. for Children's Health and the Environment George Washington U. Med. Ctr., 2000—; med. dir. Nat. Global Affairs, Children's Health Adv. Inst., 2008—. Mem. conf. on methodology and std. definitions for childhood injury rsch. Nat. Inst. Children & Human Devel., 1989; health adv. com. Congressman James Moran, 8th Congl. Dist., Va., 1992—94; mem. benefits working group Nat. Drinking Water Adv. Coun. EPA, 1989—99; adv. Health Pages, 1994—97; spl. asst. to dir. Nat. Ctr. for Environ. Health, Ctrs. for Disease Control, Washington, 1999—2001; Soros advocacy fellow Children's Environ. Health Network, 2000—02; bd. dirs. Crative Glass Ctr. Am. Author: Pediatrics: Review for New National Boards, 2000; editor Pediat. Clinics N.Am., 2001, 07; contbr. articles to profl. jours., chpts. to books. Profl. adv. bd. Nat. Safety Town Ctr., Cleve., 1981-85; bd. dirs., pres. James Renwick Alliance, Washington, 1986-93, 95-98; bd. dirs. Jewish Social Svcs. Agy Greater Washington, 2002—08, chmn. No. Va. com., 2002—08, adv. com. mem. Child Health Protect, USEPA, 2007-. Recipient Cert. for Ednl. and Pub. Policy Activity, Ohio State Senate/Ho. of Reps., 1985; Robert Wood Johnson Health Policy fellow, 1985-86, Soros Advocacy fellowship 2000-02. Fellow Am. Acad. Pediat. (mem. com. environ. health 2007—); mem. Acad. Pediatric Assn. Jewish. Avocation: collecting contemporary american crafts. Office: Children's Health Adv Inst 2233 WI Ave NW Washington DC 20007 Home Phone: 703-461-7683; Office Phone: 202-471-4891. Business E-Mail: jpaulson@cnmc.org.

PAULSON, JOHN ALFRED, hedge fund manager; b. NYC, Dec. 14, 1955; s. Alfred and Jacqueline Suzanne (Boklan) Paulson. BS in Fin., summa cum laude, NYU, 1978; MBA with high distinction, Harvard Bus. Sch., 1980. Cons. Boston Cons. Group, 1980-82; assoc. Odyssey Partners, NYC, 1982-84; mng. dir. mergers & acquisitions Bear Stearns Companies, Inc., 1984—88; gen. ptnr. Gruss Ptnrs. LP, 1988—92; founder, pres., portfolio manager Paulson & Co. Inc., 1995—. Author: Reference Book on Investment Banking, 1980. Named one of The 400 Richest Americans, Forbes mag.; Baker scholar, 1980. Mem.: Le Club, West Side Tennis Club, Harvard Club. Republican. Office: Paulson & Co Inc 590 Madison Ave, 29 Fl New York NY 10022 Office Phone: 212-956-2221. Office Fax: 212-977-9505.*

PAULSON, KENNETH ALAN, foundation administrator, former editor-in-chief; b. Chgo., Dec. 3, 1953; s. Knut Norman and Helen Elizabeth (Beardsley) P.; m. Peggy Jean Foot, June 12, 1976; children: Carrie Ann, David. BA in Journalism, U. Mo., 1975; JD, U. Ill., 1978; PhD (hon.), Am. U., 2008. Bar: Ill., 1978, Fla. 1979. Reporter, bur. chief Fort Myers News-Press, Fla., 1978—80; metro editor to mng. editor Courier-News, Bridgewater, NJ, 1980—84; founding staff member USA Today, McLean, Va., 1982; editor Green Bay Press-Gazette, Wis., 1985—86; spl. asst./chief of staff to chmn. Gannett Co., 1986—88; exec. editor Florida Today, Brevard County, 1988—92; exec. editor, v.p. news Gannett Suburban Newspapers, White Plains, NY, 1992—96; exec. dir. 1st Amendment Ctr. Vanderbilt U., Nashville, 1997—2004; sr. v.p., exec. dir. Freedom Forum, Arlington, Va., 1997—2004; sr. v.p., editor USA Today, McLean, Va., 2004—09; editor USAToday.com, 2004—09; pres., COO Freedom Forum, Newseum & Diversity Institute, Washington, 2009—. Adj. prof. Vanderbilt U. Law Sch.; host TV show Speaking Freely; trustee Freedom Forum Bd; juror, Pulitzer Prize awards, 2007. Recipient Al Neuharth award for Excellence in the Media, 2007, Lifetime Svc. award, Am. Press Inst., API Lifetime Svc. award; Fellow Soc. Profl. Journalists, 2007. Office: Freedom Forum 555 Pennsylvania Ave NW Washington DC 20001 Office Phone: 202-292-6100.*

PAULSON, MICHAEL GEORGE, foreign language educator; b. Pitts., Sept. 27, 1945; s. Michael G. Sr. and Ruth Francis (Davis) P.; m. Tamara Alvarez-Detrell, Mar. 18, 1972. BS in French and Spanish, Kutztown U., 1967; MA in French, Fla. State U., 1968, PhD in French and Spanish, 1973. Asst. prof. S.D. State U., Brookings, 1973-76; lectr. U. Ctrl. Ark., Conway, 1976-85, U. Ark., Little Rock, 1980-85; adj. prof. Northampton C.C., Bethlehem, Pa., 1985-86; asst. prof. Muhlenberg Coll., Allentown, Pa., 1986-87; assoc. prof. Kutztown (Pa.) U., 1987-93, prof. fgn. lang., 1993—. Editor Peter Lang Pub., N.Y.C., 1987—. Author: The Fallen Crown, 1980, Facets of a Princess, 1998; translator: Madame de la Fayette, 1995. With U.S. Army, 1969-70. NDEA fellow Fla. State U., 1968-69, 71-72. Mem. South Ctrl. MLA (Rsch. award 1980), Mountain Interstate Fgn. Lang. Assn., Am. Assn. Tchrs. of French (chpt. pres. 1973-76), Am. Assn. Tchrs. of Spanish. Home: Apt 2835 1717 N Bayshore Dr Miami FL 33132-1164

PAULSON, PAUL JOSEPH, advertising executive; b. White Plains, NY, Sept. 25, 1932; s. Paul and Ann (Loughlin) P.; m. Kathryn P. Keeler, June 30, 1962; children: Thomas, Mark, Kathryn, John, Clifford. BSBA, Ohio State U., 1954; MBA, U. Pa., 1959. With Compton Advt. Inc., NYC, 1959-78, mgmt. supr., 1965-78, sr. v.p., 1968-78, also dir.; pres., dir. Doyle Dane Bernbach Inc., NYC, 1978-83; pres., chief exec. officer Isidore & Paulson, Inc., NYC, 1983-93; chmn., pres., CEO Paulson & Co. Mktg. Svcs., Greenwich, 1993—. Chmn. Mktg. Exec. Networking Group, 2000—03; mem. Ohio State U. Alumni Adv. Coun., 1982—; pres. coun. mem. Ohio State U., 1993—. Author: Fundamentals of Consumer Goods Marketing, 1966. Founder, chmn. Christmas for Underprivileged Children, N.Y.C., 1963—. Served to lt. (j.g.) USNR, 1955-58, MTO, ETO. Recipient Commendation letter, MTO, 1957. Mem. Wharton Grad. Bus. Sch. Alumni Assn. (pres. N.Y.C. club 1963-65, dir. 1972—), Ohio State U. Alumni Assn., Wharton Grad. Bus. Sch., Milbrook Owners Assn. (pres.). Clubs: N.Y. (dir.), Milbrook, Sigma Chi. Roman Catholic. Home: 45 W Brother Dr Greenwich CT 06830-6726 Office Phone: 203-629-3347. Personal E-mail: pjpmrktg@verizon.net, pjpmrktg@ortonline.net. E-mail: pjpmrktg@aol.com.

PAULSON, RAYMOND ARNOLD, science engineering executive; b. Eagle Rock, Calif., Dec. 29, 1921; s. Arnold Edwin and Clara (Martin) P.; m. Beverly Doris, Sept. 21, 1941; children: Larry, Jerry, Celeste. JD, Calif. Coll. Law, 1966; postgrad., Citrus Coll., Nat. U., U. S.C. Law instr. U.S. Armed Forces Inst.; dir., mgr. nat. maj. mfr., prodr. first tactical army missile The Corporal, 1959; sales mgr., asst. dir. So. Calif. Credit. Bur.; engr., designer radiation and chem. evaluation test labs. USAF; dir., mgr. electro-mech. bus.; founder Calif. Coll. Law; pres. chmn. bd. Paulson Internat. Corp., 1971-90, ret., hon. chmn., 1990—; pres. World Trust Agy. (div. Paulson Devel. Corp.); founder Paulson Products Co.; sole proprietor Paulson Co.; established pvt. trust Paulson Trust; established Guatemala Pvt. Sector Country Trust Fund. Devel., instr. exec. leadership tng. program dept. adult edn. Baldwin Pk. Schs.; founder Paulson Zero Emission Energy Rsch. and Devel. Found. Talent locator, stage mgr. "I Love Lucy Show"; designer, assoc. dir. World Internat. Air and Space Show, 1995, Sky Harbor and McCarron Airports, Hdqs. World Air and Space Tours; assoc. designer thermal battery and developer 1st semi-perpetual electric vehicle; pioneered color telecasting; 1st color stage mgr. with Carlton Winkler-Ed Wynn on Union Pacific show Sta. CBS-TV; joint originator USMC Christmas program for underprivileged kids Toys for Tots; surveyor, designer congress-approved U.S. Canal, Brownsville, Tex., Nat. City, San Diego; designer Direct Fly by Wire Flight Control Sys.; mfr. 1st all composite single engine bullet proof two place jet spacecraft in world Mach 3 Plus; designer, developer VAC-PAC All Purpose Shipping Container for ship, rail and truck; designer, prodr. semi-perpetual self-contained charging sys. for electric vehicle battery sources, containers and vehicles too way sea level water way; designed concept for US Canal congress-approved Gulfo-Pacific Canal, Mex.; designer-mfr. pacemaker cs. for MedTronics Leadership tng. dir. Boy Scouts Am., Monte Vista dist.; founding mem. Air-Space Mus. Smithsonian Instn., 1994. B-29 radar navaigator pilot USAAF, 1944—45, WWII,Handicap USAF Vet-Resan AF, Hiroshima Atomic Bombing and Nagaski. Decorated Air Medal and Battle Stars with presdl. citation; recipient Merit award, div. rsch. and sci. guidance LA County Supt. Schs. Mem. TV Acad. Arts and Sci. (co-originator, life assoc.). Achievements include designing and developing the first hybrid-electric jet with semi-perpetual electric charging; development of semi petual charging chip and truth cell; all electric space jet with semi petual charging system design. Office: Paulson Co Internat World Trust Agy PO Box 4369 Covina CA 91723-4369 Office Fax: 626-332-4346.

PAULSON, RICHARD JOHN, obstetrician, gynecologist, educator; b. Prague, Czech Republic, Feb. 2, 1955; came to U.S., 1966, naturalized citizen, 1972. m. Lorraine M. Cummings, Oct. 11, 1987; children: Jessica, Jennifer, Philip, Erika, Josef. BS in Physics magna cum laude, UCLA, 1976, MD, 1980; MS, U. So. Calif., 1998. Diplomate Am. Bd. Ob-Gyn., Reproductive Endocrinology and Infertility. Rotating intern Harbor-UCLA Med. Ctr., Torrance, 1980-81, resident in ob-gyn., 1981-84; clin. rsch. fellow dept. ob-gyn. Los Angeles County/U. So. Calif. Med. Ctr., LA, 1984-86, mem. staff, 1984—; clin. instr. ob-gyn. Sch. Medicine U. So. Calif., LA, 1984-86, asst. prof., 1986-91, assoc. prof., 1991-96, prof. clin. ob-gyn., 1996—; affiliate staff mem. Calif. Med. Ctr., LA, 1986—; staff mem. L.A. Clin. & U. So. Calif. Med. Ctr., 1986—, dir. clin. infertility program, 1986—; chief divsn. reproductive endocrinology and infertility Keck Sch. Medicine U. So. Calif., LA, 1996—; med. dir. U. So. Calif. Fertility. Vis. prof. in vitro fertilization lecture series Clinica Kennedy, Guayaquil, Ecuador, 1980; presenter at numerous profl. confs., symposia and grand rounds. Co-editor Infertility, Contraception and Reproductive Endocrinology, 4th edit., 1996; contbr. chpt. to Management of Common Problems in Obstetrics and Gynecology, 2nd. edit., 1988, 3rd edit., 1994, Infertility, Contraception and Reproductive Endocrinology, 1991; co-author several book chpts.; co-author (lay book) Rewinding Your Biological Clock: Motherhood Late in Life, 1998; technical reviewer for Infertility for Dummies, 2007; contbr. or co-contbr. several articles to sci. jours.; mem. editl. bd. Jour. of Assisted Reprodn. and Genetics, Jour. Soc. for Gynecologic Investigation; mem. ad hoc editl. bd. Fertility and Sterility, Am. Jour. Ob-Gyn., Jour. of AMA, Contraception, Am. Jour Reproductive Immunology, others. Co-recipient Wyeth award 1985, recipient, 1989; co-recipient Serono award, 1991, 92, 93, Poster award 1994, Excellence in Tchg. award-Keck Sch. Medicine U. So. Calif., Assn. Professors of Gynecology and Obstetrics, 2004; rsch. grantee Ortho Pharm. Corp., 1986-87, Tap Pharmas., 1989-91, Irvine Sci., 1990-91, Syntex, 1990-92, Serono, 1992-93; named one of Best Doctors in America, 1994-, America's Top Doctors, 2002-; named Best Doctors for Women, 1997. Fellow ACOG (mem. PROLOG task force for reproductive endocrinology 1993), L.A. Obstetrical and Gynecologic Soc.(bd. dirs.); mem. Pacific Coast Fertility Soc. (bd. dirs. 1992, past pres.), Am. Fertility Soc., Am. Fertility Assn. (bd. mem., Howard and Georgeanna Jones Lifetime Achievement award, 2005), Soc. Reproductive Surgeons, Soc. for Assisted Reproductive Tech., Soc. Reproductive Endocrinologists, Soc. for Reproductive Endocrinology and Infertility (past pres.), Am. Soc. Reproductive Medicine (past bd. mem.), Soc. for Gynecologic Investigation, Endocrine Soc. Office: USC Fertility 1127 Wilshire Blvd Ste 1400 & 1410 Los Angeles CA 90017*

PAULSTON, CHRISTINA BRATT, linguistics educator; b. Stockholm, Dec. 30, 1932; arrived in US, 1951; d. Lennart and Elsa Bratt; m. Rolland G. Paulston, July 26, 1963 (dec. Jan. 2006); children: Christopher-Rolland, Ian Rollandsson. BA, Carleton Coll., 1953; MA in English and Comparative Lit., U. Minn., 1955; Ed.D., Columbia U., 1966. Cert. tchr., Minn. Tchr. Clara City and Pine Island High Schs., Minn., 1955-60, Am. Sch. of Tangier, Morocco, 1960-62, Katrineholm Allmanna Laroverk, Katrineholm, Sweden, 1962-63, East Asian Library, Columbia U., NYC, 1963-64; asst. instr. Tchrs. Coll., Columbia U., 1964-66; instr. U. Punjab, Chandigarh, India, summer 1966, Pontificia Universidad Catolica Del Peru, Lima, 1966-67; cons. Instituto Linguistico de Verano, Lima, 1967-68; asst. prof. linguistics U. Pitts., 1969-75, prof., 1975-99, prof. emerita, tchg. pro bono, 1999—, asst. dir. English Lang. Inst., 1969-70, dir. English Lang. Inst., 1970-97, acting dir. Lang. Acquistion Inst., fall 1971, acting chmn. dept. gen. linguistics, 1974-75, chmn., 1975-89. Apptd. internat. advisor in sociolinguistics to Summer Inst. of Linguistics, 1997. Author numerous books and articles on linguistics. Recipient research award Am. Ednl. Research Assn., 1980; Fulbright-Hays grantee, Uruguay, 1985. Mem. Assn. Tchrs. English to Speakers of Other Langs. (2d v.p., conv., chmn. 1972, exec. com. 1972-75, rsch. com. 1973-75, 78-80, chmn. 1973-75, 1st v.p. 1975, pres. 1976), Linguistics Soc. Am. (com. linguistics and pub. interest 1973-77), Internat. Assn. Tchrs. of English as a Fgn. Lang., Am. Coun. on Tchg. of Fgn. Langs., MLA (exec. com. lang. and soc. 1975-76), Ctr. Applied Linguistics (trustee 1976-81, exec. com. 1980, publs. com. 1981, rsch. com. 1981). Democrat. Episcopalian. Office: U Pitts Linguistics Pittsburgh PA 15260 Office Phone: 412-624-5900.

PAULU, FRANCES BROWN, retired international center administrator; b. Hastings, Minn., June 22, 1920; d. Thomas Andrew and Florence Ida (Tuttle) Brown; m. Burton Paulu, June 29, 1942; children: Sarah Leith Paulu Boittin, Nancy Jean Paulu Hyde, Thomas Scott. BA magna cum laude, U. Minn., 1940. Case worker Family Welfare Assn., Mpls., 1943—45; interviewer County Health and Welfare Coun., Mpls., 1963; sch. social worker Project Head Start, Mpls., 1966; program dir. Minn. Internat. Ctr., Mpls., 1970—72, exec. dir., 1972—89; mem. tourism adv. com. City of Mpls., 1976—83; mem. adv. coun. Minn. World Trade Ctr., 1984—86. Pres. UN Rally, 1970—72; chmn. Mpls. Charter Commn., 1972—74; dir. Minn. World Trade Week, 1977—81; del. Nat. Coun. World Affairs, Taipei-Manila, 1988; coord. Voices from Around the World, 1996—2000; bd. dirs. Urban Coalition of Mpls., 1967—70; sec. Becketwood Coop., 2001—04; mgmt. team Minn. Awareness Project, 1982—89; participant Intercultural Comm. Project Japan, 1974; dir. Elder Learning Inst., 1995—2000. Fellow, U. Min. Sch. Social Work, 1942—44; DeWitt Jennings Payne scholar, 1939—40. Mem.: LWV (pres. Mpls. chpt. 1967—69), Nat. Coun. Internat. Visitors (mem. exec. com. 1975—81, sec. 1976—77, v.p. 1977—78, leader fact-finding team N. Africa, Mid. East, India 1978, conf. chair 1989), Alliance Française (bd. dirs. 1991—94), People to People Internat. (Disting. Membership award 1987), UN Assn. Minn. (mem. adv. coun. 1979—92, sec. 1994—96, mem. adv. coun. 1996—2004), U. Minn. Women's Club (pres. 1992—94), Phi Beta Kappa, Lambda Alpha Psi, Alpha Omicron Pi. Home: 4300 W River Pkwy Apt 444 Minneapolis MN 55406-3681

PAULUIS, OLIVIER, science educator; b. Deep River, Ontario, Canada, Nov. 4, 1972; s. Gerard Pauluis and Therese Cangh Van. PhD, Princeton U., 2000. Rsch. assoc. Princeton U., NJ, 2002—04; asst. prof. NYU, 2004—08. Grant, NSF, 2005—. Office: NYU 251 Mercer St New York NY 10012

PAULUS, DIANE, performing company executive, theater director; b. 1966; m. Randy Weiner; 2 children. BA, Harvard U., 1987; MFA, Columbia U. Sch. Arts. Artistic dir. Am. Repertory Theatre, Cambridge, Mass., 2008—. Tchr. Barnard Coll./Columbia U., Yale Sch. Drama. Creator, dir.: (plays) The Donkey Show, 1999; dir.: Running Man, 1998 (Obie award, Pulitzer prize finalist), Brutal Imagination, 2001, Eli's Comin, 2001 (Obie award), Swimming with Watermelons, 2002, The Karaoke Show, 2003, The Golden Mickeys, 2005, Best of Both Worlds, 2005, A Dream Play, 2006, .22 Caliber, 2006, Another Country, 2007, 40th Anniversary Concert of Hair, 2007, Fashion 47, 2007, Turandot: Rumble for the Ring, 2007, Hair, 2008, Kiss Me, Kate, 2008, Lost Highway, 2008; (Broadway plays) Hair, 2009 (Drama Desk award for Outstanding Revival of a Musical, 2009, Tony award for Best Revival of a Musical, 2009); (Operas) Orfeo, 2000, Cosi Fan Tutte, 2002, Turn of the Screw, 2003, L'Incoronazione di Poppea, 2004, Le Nozze di Figaro, 2005, Il Ritorno d'Ulisse in Patria, 2007, Don Giovanni, 2008. Peter Ivers vis. artist fellowship, Harvard U., Directing fellowship, Drama League. Mem.: Phi Beta Kappa. Office: c/o Joyce Ketay Gersh Agy 41 Madison Ave 33rd Fl New York NY 10010 also: Am Repertory Theatre Harvard U 64 Brattle St Cambridge MA 02138 E-mail: diane@dianepaulus.net.*

PAULUS, EUGENIA, chemistry professor; b. Oreg. married, 1999; 2 children. BS, Bangalore U., MS in Chemistry; PhD in Chemistry, Bharathidasan U. Prof. chemistry North Hennepin CC, Brooklyn Park, Minn., 2000—; prof. organic chemistry U. Minn. Recipient US Professors of Yr. Award for Outstanding CC Prof., Carnegie Found. for Advancement of Tchg. and Coun. for Advancement and Support of Edn., 2008. Office: North Hennepin CC 7411 85th Ave N Brooklyn Park MN 55445*

PAULY, JENNIFER L., director, graphics designer; BS in Mass Comm., Advt., St. Cloud State U., 1992; MS in Print Media, Rochester Inst. Tech., 2007. Chair dept.-comml. art Fla. Met. U., Tampa, 1996—2002; program mgr. design studies S.W. Fla. Coll., Tampa, 2002—06; dept. chair Internat. Acad. Design & Technology, 2006—. Graphic designer, owner JP Creations, Brandon, Fla., 1996—; sch. adv. Ad Illusions; assoc. AIGA. Adj. faculty quarter Fla. Met. U., 1997; vol. Designer One Child's Dream, Driving For Donors; catalog designer Lowry Pk. Zoo Ednl. Dept., Tampa, 2002—03; vol. designer Am. Heart Assn., St. Petersburg, Fla., 2003, Driving for Donors/One Child's Dream Campaign. Scholar, Gen. Mills, 1987-1990. Mem.: AIGA (assoc.), Nat. Assn. Photoshop Profls. (assoc.), Am. Advt. Fedn. (assoc.), Tampa Bay Advt. Fedn. (assoc.), Ad 2 Tampa Bay (assoc.), Jr. League Tampa (assoc.), Creative Club Tampa Bay (assoc.; membership chair 1996—2000). Office: International Acad Design & Technology 5104 Eisenbhower Blvd Tampa FL 33634 Personal E-mail: j.pcreations@verizon.net.

PAULY, JOHN EDWARD, retired anatomist; b. Elgin, Ill., Sept. 17, 1927; s. Edward John and Gladys (Myhre) P.; m. Margaret Mary Oberle(dec.), Sept. 3, 1949; children: Stephen John (dec.), Susan Elizabeth, Kathleen Anne, Mark Edward; m. Dola S. Thompson, Jan. 7, 2006. BS, Northwestern U., 1950; MS, Loyola U., Chgo., 1952, PhD, 1955. Grad. asst. gross anatomy Stritch Sch. Medicine, Loyola U., 1953-54; rsch. asst. anatomy Chgo. Med. Sch., 1952-54, rsch. instr., 1954-55, instr. in gross anatomy, 1955-57, assoc. in gross anatomy, 1957-59, asst. prof. anatomy, 1959-63, asst. to pres., 1960-62; assoc. prof. anatomy Tulane U. Sch. Medicine, 1963-67; prof., head dept. anatomy U. Ark. for Med. Scis., Little Rock, 1967-83, prof., head dept. physiology and biophysics, 1978-80, vice chancellor for acad. affairs and sponsored rsch., 1983-92, assoc. dean Grad. Sch., 1983-92, prof. anatomy, 1967—95, prof. emeritus, 1995—. Flight instr. Ctrl. Flying Svc., Little Rock, 1997—2002; tech. adviser Ency. Brit. Films, 1956; mem. safety and occupl. health study sect. Nat. Inst. Occupl. Safety and Health, Ctr. for Disease Control, 1975—79; vis. prof. faculty medicine Kuwait U., 1993, 94; vis. prof. anatomy U. Nev., 1996; chief of staff Ark. wing Civil Air Patrol, 2002—05. Author: (with Hans Elias) Human Microanatomy, 1960, 3d edit. 1966, (with Elias and E. Robert Burns) Histology and Human Microanatomy, 1978; editor: (with Lawrence E. Scheving and Franz Halberg) Chronobiology, 1974, (with Heinz von Mayersbach and Lawrence E. Scheving) Biological Rhythms in Structure and Function, 1981, The American Association of Anatomists, 1888-1987. Essays on the History of Anatomy in America and a Report on the Membership-Past and Present, 1987, (with Lawrence E. Scheving) Advances in Chronobiology, 1987, (with Dora K. Hayes and Russel J. Reiter) Chronobiology: Its Role in Clinical Medicine, General Biology and Agriculture, 1990; editor Am. Jour. Anatomy, 1980-92; co-mng. editor Advances in Anatomy, Embryology and Cell Biology, 1980-95; mem. adv. editl. bd. Internat. Jour. Chronobiology, 1973-83; contbr. articles to profl. jours. Chief of staff, mission pilot, instr. pilot and check pilot Ark. Wing Civil Air Patrol, 2002—05. With USNR, 1945—47. Recipient merit certificates AMA, 1953, 59; Bronze award Ill. Med. Soc., 1959; Lederle Med. Faculty award, 1966, Coll Medicine Hall of Fame, U. Ark. medical Sci., 2007. Fellow AAAS, Am. Assn. Anatomists (sec.-treas. 1972-80, pres. 1982-83, Centennial award 1987, Henry Gray award 1995); mem. So. Soc. Anatomists (pres. 1971-72), Assn. Anatomy Chmn. (sec.-treas. 1969-71), Am. Physiol. Soc., Internat. Soc. Chronobiology, Pan-Am. Assn. Anatomy, Internat. Soc. Electrophysiol. Kinesiology, Internat. Soc. Steriology, Consejo Nacional de Profesores de Ciencias Morfologicas (hon.), Quiet Birdmen, Sigma Xi, Sigma Alpha Epsilon. Roman Catholic. Home Phone: 501-224-1461. Personal E-mail: flydoc1@comcast.net.

PAULY, REBECCA MEHL, foreign languages educator; b. Ashland, Ohio, Aug. 30, 1942; d. Robert T. and Blanche Virginia (Scott) Mehl; m. Thomas H. Pauly, July 15, 1967 (div. Sept. 1981); 1 child, Jeffrey Thomas; m. Glenn P. Bentley, Mar. 5, 1985. BA cum laude, Smith Coll., Northampton, Mass., 1963; MA in French, U. Calif., Berkeley, 1966; D Modern Langs., Middlebury Coll., 1984. With dir.'s office St. Francis Hotel, San Francisco, 1963-64; with Dillingham Corp., San Francisco, 1964-65; head French dept. Castilleja Sch., Palo Alto, Calif., 1966-67; with French dept. Anna Head Sch., Oakland, Calif., 1967-70, Tower Hill Sch., Wilmington, Del., 1982; with edn. div. Winterthur (Del.) Mus., 1972-81; instr. French and Italian U. Del., Newark, 1982-84, asst. prof. French and Italian, 1984-87, West Chester (Pa.) U., 1987-92, assoc. prof. French and Italian, 1992—96, prof., 1996—. Mem. editl. bd. Lit./Film Quar. Salisbury, Md., 1990—, Coll. Lit., West Chester, 1990—; author: (videos) La Civilisation Francophone, 2001, L'Italia Alfresco, 2002; (books) The Transparent Illusion, 1993, 2003, Le Berceau et la Bibliothèque, 1989; contbr. articles to profl. jours. Regional coord. Am. Cancer Soc., Chester County, 1975-77. Mem. Am. Assn. Tchrs. French, Am. Assn. Tchrs. Italian, Lit./Film Assn. (nat. v.p. 1989-91, pres. 1995-97), Smith Coll. Club of Del., Am. Soc. Eighteenth-Century Studies. Avocations: sports, photography, design. Office: West Chester U Dept Langs & Cultures 109 Main Hl West Chester PA 19383-0001

PAUSA, CLEMENTS EDWARD, electronics company executive; b. South Gate, Calif., Oct. 18, 1930; s. Oscar Clements and Kathleen Patricia (O'Toole) P.; m. Janice Mary Hanson, Jan. 22, 1955; children: Geoffrey Clements, Ronald Edward. Student, UCLA, 1948-50; BS, U. Calif., Berkeley, 1953, MS, 1954, cert. in bus., 1960. Product mgr. Fairchild Semiconductor Corp., 1959-62, mgr. plant, 1962-64; gen. mgr. Fairchild Hong Kong Ltd., 1964-67, dir. plant group, 1967-68; dir. internat. mfg. Nat. Semiconductor Corp., Santa Clara, Calif., 1968-70, gen. mgr. Far East ops., 1970-73, v.p. internat. mfg., 1973-86, corp. v.p. internat. mfg., 1986-90, corp. v.p. internat. mfg. emeritus, 1991—. Dir. Price Waterhouse Coopers STS; v.p. ops. Power Integrations, Inc., 1997-99; bd. dirs. 8 subs. cos., 2 J.V. cos. Mem. internat. adv. bd. U. Santa Clara, 1984—. Capt. USNR, 1952-81. Mem. Naval Res. Assn., Res. Officer's Assn., Sons in Retirement, Calif. Alumni Assn., Delta Chi Alumni Assn. (v.p., pres. 1978-86). Republican. Roman Catholic. Office: Ste 1600 10 Almaden Blvd San Jose CA 95113 Office Phone: 408-817-5738. E-mail: clements.e.pausa@us.pwc.com.

PAVALON, EUGENE IRVING, lawyer; b. Chgo., Jan. 5, 1933; m. Lois M. Frenzel, Jan. 15, 1961; children: Betsy, Bruce, Lynn. BSL, Northwestern U., 1954, JD, 1956. Bar: Ill. 1956. Sr. ptnr. Pavalon, Gifford & Laatsch, Chgo., 1970—. Adj. prof. Northwestern U. Sch. Law; mem. com. discovery rules Ill. Supreme Ct., 1981—, Ill. Judicial Conf.; lectr., mem. faculty various law schs. Author: Human Rights and Health Care Law, 1980, Your Medical Rights, 1990; contbr. articles to profl. jours., chpts. in books. Mem. bd. overseers Inst. Civil Justice, Rand Corp., 1993-99; mem. vis. com. Northwestern U. Law Sch., 1990-96. Capt. USAF, 1956-59. Fellow Am. Coll. Trial Lawyers, Internat. Soc. Barristers, Internat. Acad. Trial Lawyers, Am. Bd. Trial Advs., Inner Cir. Advs., Roscoe Pound Found. (life mem., pres. 1988-90); mem. ABA, Chgo. Bar Assn. (bd. mgrs. 1978-79), Ill. Bar Assn., Ill. State Bar Assn., Ill. Trial Lawyers Assn. (pres. 1980-81, Lifetime Achievement award 1996), Trial Lawyers for Pub. Justice (founding mem., v.p. 1991-92, pres.-elect 1992-93, pres. 1993-94, Champion of Justice award 2000), ATLA (parliamentarian 1983-84, sec. 1984-85, v.p. 1985-86, pres.-elect 1986-87, pres. 1987, pres., bd. trustees, Endowment Fund 2003-05, Champion of Justice award 2003), Am. Bd. Profl. Liability Attys. (diplomate), Laureate, Ill. Acad. Lawyers, Std. Club, Union League Club. Home: 1540 N Lake Shore Dr Chicago IL 60610-6684 Office: Pavalon Gifford et al 2 N La Salle St Chicago IL 60602-3702 Home Phone: 312-280-2331; Office Phone: 312-419-7400. Business E-Mail: pavalon@pglmlaw.com.

PAVAN, TURAGA, research scientist; s. Mohan Vsr and Radha Turaga. BTech, Indian Inst. Tech., Guwahati, India, 2004; PhD, U. Md., Coll. Pk., 2009. Rsch. fellow Ctr. Automation Rsch., Coll. Pk., 2004—; intern IBM Almaden Rsch. Ctr., San Jose, Calif., Mitsubishi Electric Rsch. Labs, Cambridge, Mass. Contbr. chapters to books (IBM Emerging Leader in Multimedia, 2008). Mem.: IEEE, AAAI. Hindu. Avocations: swimming, gardening, cooking.

PAVANI, SRI RAMA PRASANNA, research scientist; s. Satyanarayana and Valli Satyam Pavani. BS in Engring., Govt. Coll. Tech., Coimbatore, India, 2003; MS, U. Colo., Boulder, 2006, PhD student, 2005—. Sr. mem., tech. staff D. E. Shaw & Co., Hyderabad, India, 2003—05; rsch. scholar Nat. U. Singapore, 2005. Rsch. intern CDM Optics Inc., Boulder, 2006; vis. rschr. Stanford U., Calif., 2008. Bd. mem. Environ. Ctr., CU Boulder, 2005—06. Recipient Outstanding Rsch. Paper award, Optical Soc. America, 2008, Best Poster award, CPIA, 2006, Gold medal, Govt. Coll. Tech., India, 1999—2003. Achievements include invention of a quantitative phase microscopy technique that uses structured illumination; a high-efficiency phase mask that generates a double-helix beam; research in localized and tracked microparticles with nanometer scale accuracies in 3D.

PAVARINI, PETER ALFRED, lawyer; b. NYC, Feb. 21, 1952; s. Alfred S. and Anne M. (Pertusi) Pavarini; m. Colleen A. Wulf, Apr. 12, 1980. BA summa cum laude, SUNY-Albany, 1973; JD, Boston Coll., 1977. Bar: Mass. 1977, D.C. 1979, Ohio 1981, NC 2008. Aide N.Y. State Office of Gen. Svcs., Albany, 1973—74; rsch. asst. Boston Coll., 1975—76; intern Office of Mass. Atty. Gen., Boston, 1976—77; atty. HHS, Washington, 1977—81; assoc. Murphey Young & Smith, Columbus, 1981—85, ptnr., 1986—88, Squire, Sanders & Dempsey, Columbus, 1988—90. Lectr. Capital U. Law Sch., 1993—95, Fisher Sch. Bus., 2004—; chmn. adv. bd. Ohio Health Law Insider; editor-in-chief Health Law Jour. of Ohio, 1989—95. Editor: U.S. Health Care Law and Rules. Trustee Friends of the Homeless, 1991—94, Goodwill Columbus, 2003—. Recipient Congressman's medal of Merit, 1970, Gen. Counsel's award, HEW, 1979. Fellow: Am. Acad. Hosp. Attys.; mem.: ABA (Health Law sect.), Ohio Bar Assn. (chmn. 1991—93), Am. Health Lawyers Assn. (bd. dirs.). Avocations: music, skiing, bicycling, songwriting. Home Phone: 740-548-5508; Office Phone: 614-462-5016. Business E-Mail: peter.pavarini@szd.com.

PAVEL, D. MICHAEL, art educator; s. Donald and Anne Pavel. BA, U. Puget Sound, Tacoma, Wash., 1981; EdM, Ariz. State U., Tempe, 1987, PhD, 1991. Prof. Wash. State U., Pullman, 1994—. Lead author of highly regarded book entitled Am. Indian and Alaska Native Student's Guide to Coll. Success. Recipient Faculty Diversity award, Wash. State U., 2007; named Educator of Yr., Wash. State Indian Edn. Assn., 2007; finalist Buffett Indigenous Leadership award, Ecotrust, 2007. Home: 2129 Daves Ave Moscow ID 83843 Office: Wash State Univ PO Box 642136 Pullman WA 99164-2136 Business E-Mail: mpavel@wsu.edu.

PAVELICH, JUDITH, retired secondary school educator; b. Bklyn., July 10, 1924; d. Abraham and Anna (Chaikin) Goldstein; m. Martin Pavelich, Dec. 5, 1948; children: Alyce, Susan, Sharon. BA, Moravian Coll., 1954; MA, Lehigh U., 1961; postgrad., Pa. State U., Mainland Inst., Marywood Coll. Tchr. spl. edn., Bethlehem, Pa., 1961—62; counselor Northampton Area Jr. H.S., Pa., 1962—. Coord., sec. Big Bros. and Sisters Northampton Area; mem. cataract support group, treas. Israel Cancer Rsch. Fund; bd. dirs. Lehigh Social Svc. Exch.; vol. Lehigh Valley Ecumenical Soup Kitchen; vol. coord. Reibman for Congress Campaign, Reibman for Judge Campaign; campaign coord. Alan Black for Judge; aide leisure group B'rith Sholom Synagogue; mem. friendship cir. Jewish Cmty. Ctr. With WAVES USNR, 1943—48. Mem.: NEA, Am. Sch. Assn., Pa. Sch. Counselors Assn. (unit rep.), Lehigh Valley Guidance Assn. (sec.), Pa. Educators Assn., Northampton Area Educators Assn., Pa. Pers. and Guidance Assn., Am. Pers. and Guidance Assn. Home: 2235 W Highland St Allentown PA 18104-3631

PAVELKA, ELAINE BLANCHE, mathematics professor; b. Chgo. d. Frank Joseph and Mildred Bohumila (Seidl) P. BA, MS, Northwestern U.; PhD, U. Ill. With Northwestern U. Aerial Measurements lab., Evanston, Ill.; tchr. Leyden Cmty. H.S., Franklin Park, Ill.; prof. math. Morton Coll., Cicero, Ill. Invited prof. Internat. Congress on Math. Edn., Karlsruhe, Germany, 1976. RecipientSci. Talent award Westinghouse Electric Co. Mem. Am. Edn. Rsch. Assn., Am. Math. Assn. 2-Yr. Colls., Am. Math. Soc., Assn. Women in Math., Can. Soc. History and Philosophy of Math., Ill. Coun. Tchrs. Math., Ill. Math. Assn. C.C., Math. Assn. Am. Math. Action Group, Ga. Ctr. Study and Tchg. and Learning Math., Nat. Coun. Tchrs. Math., Sch. Sci. and Math. Assn., Northwestern U. Alumni Assn., U. Ill. Alumni Assn., Am. Mensa Ltd., Intertel, Sigma Delta Epsilon, Pi Mu Epsilon. Home: PO Box 7312 Westchester IL 60154-7312

PAVELKO, CHRISTINA ALISON, biology teaching assistant; b. Odessa, Tex., Feb. 21, 1985; d. Philip Jacob and Mabel Ellen Pavelko. BS in Biology, U. Colo., Denver, 2009, BA in Psychology, 2009. Cert. phlebotomist 2008. Biology tchg. asst. U. Colo., 2007—; mentor Aurora Lights Saturday Acad. AHEC, Colo., 2009—. Vol. Beth Nahamah Hospice, Aurora, 2007—. Mem.: Golden Key Internat. Honour Soc., Psi Chi. Personal E-mail: christina.pavelko@ucdenver.edu.

PAVER, ROBERT L., lawyer; b. St. Petersburg, Fla., May 1956; BA, U. Fla., Gainesville, 1978; JD, Stetson U. Coll. Law, Gulfport, Fla., 1981. Bar: Fla. 1981, US Fed. Ct. 1982, US Supreme Ct. 1985. Adj. law prof. Stetson U., 1985—; atty. Holland & Knight, St. Petersburg, Fla., 1994—97; gen. counsel, corp. sec. Jabil Circuit Inc., St. Petersburg, Fla., 1997—. Pres. Pinellas County Criminal Def. Lawyers, 1987—88. Recipient Victor D. Wehle Trial Practice award. Office: Jabil Circuit Inc 10560 Dr Martin Luther King Jr St N Saint Petersburg FL 33716 Office Phone: 727-577-9749. Office Fax: 727-579-8529.

PAVEZA, GREGORY J., dean; b. Chgo., Sept. 21, 1947; s. Louis and Joan Paveza; m. Sulie Greendale, Sept. 9, 1979. BA, Lewis U., Joliet, Ill., 1969; MSW, U. Hawaii - Manoa, Honolulu, 1973; PhD, U. Ill., Chgo., 1981—86. Cert. master's social worker clin. & macro lic. Mich., 2007. Dir., ctr. long term mental health evaluation Dept. Veterans Affairs Med. Ctr., Ann Arbor, Mich., 1991—94; assoc. prof. U. South Fla., Tampa, 1994—2001, prof., 2001—07, interim assoc. v.p. Lakeland, Fla., 2004—05, dir., divsn. arts & scis., 2004—06, interim campus assoc., dean, 2006—07; dean, sch. health & human svcs. So. Conn. State U., New Haven, 2007. Contbr. articles to profl. jours., chapters to books. Mem. 13th Judical Circuit Elder Ct. Task Force, Tampa, 1999—2000, Agy. Aging South Ctrl. Conn., New Haven, 2008, NAS Com., Washington, 2000—01, NAS Panel Elder Abuse, Washington, 2001—02. Grant, Nat. Inst. Aging, 1997—2001, fellowship, Am. Coun. Edn., 2003—04. Mem.: NASW (bd. mem. 2008). Avocation: swimming. Home: 56 Knoll Rd Hamden CT 06518 Office: Southern Conn State Univ 501 Crescent St New Haven CT 06515 Home Phone: 203-891-7788; Office Phone: 203-392-7015. Office Fax: 203-392-8067; Home Fax: 866-593-7348. Personal E-mail: drgjp@comcast.net. Business E-Mail: pavezag1@southernct.edu.

PAVLAKIS, MARTHA, medical association administrator, researcher; m. Erik Brynjolfsson, Oct. 7, 1990; children: Ari Eriksson, Xander Eriksson, Luke Eriksson. MD, SUNY, Buffalo Sch. Medicine, 1998. Cert. in internal medicine Am. Bd. Internal Medicine, 1991, in nephrology 1994. Med. dir., kidney and pancreas transplantation Beth Israel Deaconess Med. Ctr., Boston, 1999—. Office: Beth Israel Deaconess Med Ctr 110 Francis St 7th fl Boston MA 02215

PAVLAKOS, ELLEN TSATIRI, sculptor; b. Athens, May 25, 1936; d. Andrew and Katherine (Fliskanopoulou) Tsatiri; m. Andrew George Pavlakos, Nov. 2, 1952; children: James, John Andrew. Student, Arsakeion, Athens, 1952, Norton Sch. Art, West Palm Beach, Fla., 1975-79, Nat. Acad. Design, NYC, 1980-81. Solo shows include Brevard Art Mus., 1981, Hess Galleries, Allentown, Pa., 1983, Cultural Ctr. Athens, Greece, 1990, 5th Ave. Art Gallery, Melbourne, Fla., 1994, 98; group shows include Le Salon des Nations, Paris, 1984, Nat. Exhbn. of Contemporary Realism in Art, Springfield, Mass., 1984, Springville Mus. Art, Utah, 1985, Capitol Gallery, Fla. Dept. Cultural Affairs, Tallahassee, 1988, Outstanding Am. Women Artists Invitational, Sarasota, 1993, Chamber of fine Arts and Min. of Edn. and Civilization Symposium, Nicosia, Cyprus, 1994, Mus. of Art and Sci., Melbourne, 1996, Appleton Mus. Art, Ocala, Fla., 1997, Sculpture '97, Thessaloniki, Greece, 1997, Dunedin (Fla.) Fine Arts Ctr., 1998, Orlando City Hall Gallery, 1998, 621 Gallary, Tallahassee, Fla., 1999, (two person show) Lee County Alliance of the Arts, Fort Myers, Fla., 1999, La. State U., Shreveport, 2000, Mt. Dora (Fla.) Art Ctr., 2000, U. Fla. Arts Ctr., Gainesville, 2001, DeLand (Fla.) Mus. Art, 2001, Oceola Art Ctr., Kissimmee, 2002, Visual Arts Ctr. of NW Fla., Panama City, Fla., 2002, Brevard Mus. of Arts and Sci., Melbourne, Fla., 2002, Gadsen Arts Ctr., Lake Wales, Fla., 2004, Atlantic Ctr. for the Arts at Harris, 2004, Seminol Com. Coll., Sanford, Fla., 2004, Lake Wales Art Ctr., Fla., 2004, South Fla. Coll. Mus. Art, Avon Park, 2005, Albany Mus., Ga., 2006, Turner Ctr. Arts, Valdosta, Ga., 2006, The Deland Mus. Art, Fla., 2007, Melbourne Internat. Airport, Fla., 2007; Thomas Ctr. Gallaries, 2008, Juried Exhbns. Gainsville, Fla., Tampa Internat. Airport, 2009; bronze sculpture commd. The Harry T. Moore Monument, Titusville Social Svcs. Ctr., 1985, wall relief Knowledge, Brevard Libr., 1993, bronze sculpture Mother Earth, Penakotheke, Athens, 1990, painting Interlude, Penakotheke, Mus. Athens, Hydrostone sculpture The Flame Keeper, Kennedy Space Ctr., Fla., 1992, Stephen Girard relief Girard Coll., Phila., 1999, Welcoming Christ, bronze sculpture, Holy Name of Jesus CH., Fla., 2004, Mother and Child, bronze sculpture, Holmes Med. Ctr., Melbourne, Fla., Scaling the Charzts, Internat. Bus. Pk., Heathzow, Fla. Recipient best of Show award Brevard Art Mus., 1980; grantee Brevard County Art in Pub. Places, 1990, 93. Mem. Acad. Artists Assn. (elected mem.), Medalic Sculpture Assn., Chamber of Visual Arts in Greece (elected mem.), Ten Women in Art., Internat. Fedn. Medal FIDEM. Greek Orthodox. Avocations: art collecting, gardening. Studio: 331 Coral Way W Indialantic FL 32903-4401 Office Phone: 321-773-5046. Personal E-mail: pavlakosstudio@cfl.rr.com.

PAVLICK, ANNA CATHERINE, oncologist, hematologist; b. Passaic, NJ, July 25, 1962; d. Donald Stephen and Patricia Ann Pavlick. BS, Fairfield U., 1984; MS, Fairleigh Dickinson U., 1990; DO, UMDNJ, 1990. Resident UMDNJ/Hackensack Med. Ctr., 1990-93; hematology/oncology fellow Meml. Sloan-Kettering Cancer Ctr., NYC, 1993—96; asst. prof. medicine, dir. clin. oncology UMDNJ, Newark, 1996—99; asst. prof. medicine NYU Kaplan Comprehensive Cancer Ctr. (now Langone Med. Ctr.), NYC, 1999—. Mem. NYU Med. Oncology Associates. Office: Clin Cancer Ctr 9 0936 160 E 34th St New York NY 10016 Office Phone: 212-731-5431.*

PAVLIK, KELLY (ROBERT), boxer; b. Youngstown, Ohio, Apr. 4, 1982; s. Michael Pavlik, Sr. and Debbie Pavlik; 1 child, Sydney. Grad. in Computer Graphics, Mahoning County Joint Vocat. Sch., 2000. Profl. boxer, 2000—. Winner vacant title vs. Fulgencio Zuniga by tech. knockout, middleweight divsn. N.Am. Boxing Fedn., 2005, winner title def. vs. Bronco McKart by tech. knockout, middleweight divsn., 06, winner title def. vs. Jose Luis Zertuche by knockout, middleweight divsn., 07; winner world title eliminator vs. Edison Miranda by tech. knockout, middleweight divsn. World Boxing Coun., 2007, winner world title vs. Jermain Taylor by tech. knockout, middleweight divsn., 07, winner world title def. vs. Gary Lockett by tech. knockout, middleweight divsn., 08; winner world title vs. Jermain Taylor by tech. knockout, middleweight divsn. World Boxing Orgn., 2007, winner world title def. vs. Gary Lockett by tech. knockout, middleweight divsn., 08. Named Fighter of Yr., Boxing Times, 2007, SportsIllustrated.com, 2007. Achievements include being the reigning World Boxing Council and World Boxing Organization's Middleweight Champion, 2007. Mailing: Southside Boxing Club 3311 Eerie St Youngstown OH 44507

PAVLISH, CATHERINE ANN, language educator, writer; d. Theodore Joseph and Dorothy Mae Pavlish; m. Gregory A. Carpenter, July 22, 1991; children: Skylar Pavlish Carpenter, Aurora Pavlish Carpenter. BA, Calif. State U., Long Beach, 1985, MA, 1989; PhD, U. North Dakota, Grand Forks, 1998. Cert. secondary tchg. Calif. State U. Long Beach, 1986. Academic advisor, supr. Calif. State U., Long Beach, 1987—92; instr. English Palomar C.C., Vista, Calif., 1999—2001, Mira Costa C.C., Oceanside, Calif., 2000—01, Oreg. Coast C.C., Newport, 2004—. Editor, advisor Waves Literary Program, Newport, 2004—; mem. bd. Writers on the Edge, Newport, 2005—, Internat. Baccalaureate Program, Newport, 2006—. Author: (screenplays) Enough, 2004, Out of the Darkness: An Anthology of Women's Poetry Against Women, 2004, (poetry) A Certain Uncertainty, 2006. Activist anti-poverty programs; advocate human and civil rights, women's rights, consumer rights/protection. Mem.: Am. Fedn. Tchrs., Am. Assn. U. Women, Modern Lang. Assn. Office: Oreg Coast CC 332 SW Coast Hwy Newport OR 97365 Office Phone: 541-574-7129. Business E-Mail: cpavlish@occc.cc.or.us.

PAVLOCK, BARBARA R., literature and language professor; d. August and Esther Pavlock. BA, Barnard Coll.; MA, Yale U.; PhD, Cornell U. Vis. asst. prof. U. Calif., 1977—79; asst. prof. Santa Clara U., Calif., 1979—86; vis. asst. prof. Bowdoin Coll., Brunswick, 1986—88, Emory U., Atlanta, 1988—89; asst. to assoc. prof. Lehigh U., Bethlehem, 1989—. Contbr. articles to profl. jours.; author: Eros, Emitation and the Epic Tradition, The Images of the poet in Ovids Meta Morphoses. Summer Inst. fellow, NEH, 1983, Tchg. and Grad. fellowships, Cornell U., 1973—76. Mem.: Classical Assn. Atlantic States (sec. 2008), Am. Philol Assn. (com. mem. classical tradition 2000—02, chair 2002), Phi Beta Kappa. Office: Lehigh Univ 35 Sayre Dr Bethlehem PA 18015 Business E-Mail: bp01@lehigh.edu.

PAVLOV, VLADIMIR GRIGORIEVICH, language educator; b. Yuzhno-Sakhalinsk, Sakhalin, Russia, Jan. 11, 1958; s. Grigory Pavlovich Pavlov and Maria Georgievna Pavlova; m. Elena Valentinovna Stetsenko; children: Gregory, Anna Pavlova. BA summa cum laude, Azerbaijan U. Langs., Baku, 1980, MA, 1980; MEd, Rutgers U., New Brunswick, NJ, 1996; PhD, Odessa State U., Ukraine, 1985. Lexicographer Azerbaijan U. Langs., 1977—80; asst. to assoc. prof. Simferopol State U., Crimea, Ukraine, 1982—89, English dept. chair, 1989—99; sr. linguist Solv Tech., Mpls., 2001—02; asst. prof. U. Wis., River Falls, 2004—. Translator: Classical Painting Video Workshop Series. Freedom Support Act fellowship, US Congress, 1995, Fellowship, Ministry of Higher Edn., Russia, 1987. Mem.: TESOL, MLA. Office: Univ Wis River Falls 410 S St River Falls WI 54022 Business E-Mail: vladimir.pavlov@uwrf.edu.

PAVLOVA, ANNA, finance educator; d. V. Pavlov and N. Pavlova; m. Dimitri Vayanos, Sept. 3, 2005; 1 child, Evan Vayanos. PhD, U. Pa., Phila., 2000. Asst. prof. fin. MIT, Cambridge, 2000—05; prof. fin. London Bus. Sch., 2005—. Affiliate CEPR, London, 2005—08. Home and Office: London Bus Sch Regents Pk London NW1 4SA England Business E-Mail: apavlova@london.edu.

PAVLOVSKA, ANASTASSIA, physicist, researcher; b. Sofia, Bulgaria; m. Ernst Georg Bauer; 1 child, Peter Conrad Pavlovski. PhD, Bulgarian Acad. Scis., Sofia. Sci. collaborator Inst. Phys. Chemistry, Bulgarian Acad. Scis., 1965—83; rsch. assoc. Inst. Physics, Tech. U., Clausthal-Zellerfeld, Germany, 1983—96; academic assoc. Ariz. State U., Tempe, 1996—. Business E-Mail: pavlovska@asu.edu.

PAVLOW, SHARA TOURSH, professor, medical administrator; b. Miami, Fla., June 21, 1950; d. June R. (Toursh) P. BA, U. Miami, 1972; MA, U. N.C., 1975; PhD, U. Miami, 2004. Reg. Emergency Med. Technician, Fla. Staff writer The Miami Herald, 1971-72; info. officer The N.C. Meml. Hosp., Chapel Hill, N.C., 1972-73; pub. info. dir. Heart Assn. of Greater Miami, 1973-74; sr. health planner Health Systems Agy. South Fla., Miami, 1974-78; asst. adminstr. Jackson Meml. Hosp., Miami, 1978-81; dir. clin. affairs Sch. of Medicine, U. Miami, 1981-87; chief operating officer Healthcare Mgmt. Enterprises, Inc., Miami, 1988-91; pres. Healthcraft Assocs., Inc., Miami, 1991—2000; exec. dir. Dist. 11 Cmty. Health Purchasing Alliance, Miami, 1984—86, Dewey Knight Helath Ctr., Inc., Miami, 1997-99; dir. cmty. & conversation corps, faculty mem. Fla. Atlantic U., Sch. Cômmunication & Multimedia Studies. Cons. South Fla. Emergency Med. Svcs. Coun., 1979-80, HEW, Washington, 1975-76, Assn. Am. Med. Colls., Implications of Medicare Prospective Payment System, 1983; mem. adj. faculty Fla. Internat. U., 1975-79, St. Thomas U., 1987, U. Miami Sch. Comm.; coord. advanced trauma life support U. Miami Sch. Medicine, 1980-81. Mem. devel. com. and Jimmy Carter work project and constrn. team Habitat for Humanity Greater Miami; bd. dirs. Sta. WLRN pub. radio, TV stas., 1988—. Mem. Sierra Club (nat. outings leader). Avocations: backpacking, aerobics, jogging, reading. Home: 7765 SW 86th St # F2-310 Miami FL 33143-7290 E-mail: SharaPavlow@aol.com.

PAVONE, SHIRLEY A., b. Bridgeport, Conn., Aug. 12, 1948; d. Carmelo and Maria Rosemary (Pietad) Pavone. PhD in Health Psychology, Union Inst., 2001. Psychiat. aide Fairfield Hills Hosp., Newtown, Conn., 1968—76, rehab.counselor, 1976—86. Guest lectr., trainer, addiction cons., Easton, 1976—. Recipient Honorable Mention, Internat. Photograhy Assn., 1981. Mem.: APA. Independent. Roman Catholic. Avocations: photography, bicycling, Karate. Home Phone: 203-261-3670; Office Phone: 860-262-6356. Office Fax: 860-262-6496. Personal E-mail: phd2003@aol.com. Business E-Mail: shirley.pavone@po.state.ct.us.

PAVONY, WILLIAM H., financial and management consultant; s. Harry and Mollie (Leibel) Pavony; m. Geraldine Rice; 1 child, Sheryl. BBA cum laude, Hofstra U., 1960. CPA, NY. Mgr. Arthur Andersen & Co. Inc., NYC, 1960-73; group sr. v.p. Purolator Svcs. Inc., New Hyde Park, NY, 1973-75; v.p., contr. Purolator Inc., Piscataway, NJ, 1975-78; sr. v.p. Zale Corp., Dallas, 1978-85; sr. v.p. fin., chief fin. officer Alexander's Inc., NYC, 1985-88, exec. v.p., chief fin officer, 1988-89; exec. v.p. adminstrn. The Kobacker Co., Columbus, Ohio, 1989-93; also bd. dirs.; exec. v.p. Arthur Rutenberg Homes, Clearwater, Fla., 1993-94; CFO Color Tile, Inc., Ft. Worth, 1994-95; pres. Pavony Assocs., Corona Del Mar, Calif., 1995-99, Newport Coast, Calif., 1999, 2001—; exec. bus. cons. The Netplex Group, Newport Coast, Calif., 1999-2001; pres. Pavony Assocs., Newport Coast, 2001—. Treas., bd. dirs. Tex. Vis. Nurses Assn., Dallas, 1984-85. Mem AICPA, Fin. Execs. Internat. (past bd. dirs. North Tex. chpt., sec. Columbus chpts.), N.Y. Soc. CPAs. Home: 5 Adriana Newport Coast CA 92657-1224 Home Phone: 949-376-1613; Office Phone: 949-497-8026. Personal E-mail: Bpavony@aol.com.

PAVSEK, DANIEL ALLAN, banker, educator; b. Cleve., Jan. 18, 1945; s. Daniel L. and Helen A. (Femec) P. AB, Maryknoll Coll., Glen Ellyn, Ill., 1966; MA, Maryknoll Sch. Theology, Ossining, NY, 1971, Cleve. State U., 1972; PhD, Case Western Res. U., 1981; MS, George Washington U., 2000. Pres. Coun. Richmond Heights, Ohio, 1972-75; lectr. econs. Cleve. State U., 1972-75; asst. prof. Baldwin-Wallace Coll., Berea, Ohio, 1975-81; v.p., economist Ameritrust Co., Cleve., 1981-91; dean, prof. econs. Harry F. Byrd Jr. Sch. Bus. Shenandoah U., Winchester, Va., 1992-99, Durell prof. money and banking H.F. Byrd Jr. Sch. Bus., 1999—2007, prof. emeritus, econs., 2007—. Adj. prof. bus. adminstrn. Baldwin-Wallace Coll., Berea, Ohio, 1981-91 Mem. Am. Econ. Assn., Nat. Assn. Bus. Econs. Democrat. Home: 21343 Sawyer Sq Ashburn VA 20147-4728 E-mail: dpavsek@dkdp.net.

PAVUK, ALEXANDER, history professor; s. Thomas and Lubov Pavuk. AB, Colgate U., Hamilton, NY, 1994; MA, U. Md., Balt., 1998; PhD, U. Del., Newark, 2009. Vis. prof. St. Joseph's U., Phila., 2008—. Contbr. articles to profl. jours. E. Lyman Stewart fellowship, U. Del., 1999—2004, Hurst fellowship, Am. U., 1998. Mem.: Soc. Ch. History, History Sci. Soc., Am. Hist. Assn., Phi Alpha Theta. Achievements include research in dissertation on science and religion. Office: St Joseph's Univ 5600 City Ave Philadelphia PA 19131 Business E-Mail: apavuk@sju.edu.

PAWASKAR, MANJIRI D., medical researcher; M in Pharm. Adminstrn., U. Houston, Tex., 2004; PhD in Pharmacy Adminstrn., Ohio State U., Columbus, 2008. Cert. pharmacist Maharashtra, 2002. Tchg. assoc. U. Houston, 2003—04; rsch. analyst Abt Assoc., Lexington, Mass., 2005; rsch. assoc. Ohio State U., 2005—06; rschr. Glaxo Smith Kline, Rsch. Triangle Pk., NC, 2007; rsch. scientist health Eli Lilly & Co., Indpls, 2008—. Cons. Novo Nordisk, NJ, 2005—07; rsch. cons. Sanofi Aventis, NJ, 2006—07. Contbr. articles to med. jours. (Impaired Vision Rsch. award, 2004). Fellowship, Ohio State U., 2005—07. Mem.: APHA, Am. Pharm. Assn., Internat. Soc. Pharmacoeconomics & Outcomes Rsch., Am. Diabetes Assn., Rho Chi. Achievements include research in identified disparities in the quality of care, medication use behavior, healthcare resource use and costs in diabetes. Home: 629 Bridge Crossing Pl Apt H Indianapolis IN 46227 Office: Eli Lilly & Co 1555 S Harding St Indianapolis IN 46221 Personal E-mail: manjiri.pawaskar@gmail.com.

PAWEL, NANCY EMMA RAY, oil industry executive, educator, artist; b. Boston, Feb. 14, 1928; d. Carlon Weston and Anna Urban Ray; m. Thomas Ernst Pawel, Sept. 1, 1951 (dec.); children: Margaret Pawel Moore, Elizabeth Thompson, Charlotte Ray Pawel(dec.). BA, Wellesley Coll., Mass., 1949; MA, U. Incarnate Word, San Antonio, Tex., 1989. Lab. asst. Med. Sch. Tufts Coll., Boston, 1949—51; biochemist Sch. Aviation Medicine, Tex., 1952—55; instr. U. The Incarnate Word, 1968—99; pres. Concord Oil Co., San Antonio, 2004—. Adj. faculty S.W. Sch. Art and Craft, San Antonio, 2000—; mem. art adv. com. U. Tex., San Antonio, 1990—95; bd. dirs. San Antonio (Tex.) Art League Mus. Prin. works include Wall Natatorium, U. Incarnate Word, Sleeping Beauty's Castle Garden for Blind, San Antonio (Tex.) Botanic Garden, Towers of San Antonio (Tex.) Children's Mus., Ctrl. Gateway, St. Mary's Hall, San Antonio, exhibitions include Taipei, Taiwan, 1998. Recipient Lynn Ford Craftsman award, San Antonio (Tex.) Conservation Soc., 2002; named Outstanding Woman in Art, San Antonio (Tex.) Express News, 1970, Artist of Yr., San Antonio (Tex.) Art League, 1977. Home: 123 Geneseo Rd San Antonio TX 78209 Office: Concord Oil Co Houston St 1500 Frost Bank Tower San Antonio TX 78205 Office Phone: 210-224-4455. E-mail: Nerpawel@aol.com.

PAWLENTY, TIMOTHY JAMES, Governor of Minnesota; b. South St. Paul, Minn., Nov. 27, 1960; m. Mary Elizabeth Anderson, 1987; children: Anna, Mara BA, U. Minn., 1983; JD, U. Minn.Law Sch., 1986. Chmn. Eagan Planning Commn., 1988-89; mem. Minn. Ho. of Reps. from Dist. 38, St. Paul, 1993—2002, majority leader, 1999—2002; gov. State of Minn., St. Paul, 2003—. Active Eagan city coun., 1990-92. Fannie Gilbertson Coll. scholar. Republican. Lutheran. Office: Office of the Gov 130 State Capitol 75 Rev Dr Martin Luther King Jr Blvd Saint Paul MN 55155 Office Phone: 651-296-3391. Office Fax: 651-296-2089. E-mail: tim.pawlenty@state.mn.us.

PAWLEY, RAY L., retired zoological park administrator, curator, conservationist; b. Midland, Mich., Nov. 7, 1935; s. Lynn Richard and Alice Marie (Skelton) P.; m. Ethel Marie Condon, Feb. 19, 1955 (div. 1974); children: Ray Allyn, Shanna Sue, Cynthia Ann, Dawn Marie, Brandon Earl, Dareen Joy; m. Hedda P. Saltz, Mar. 16, 1997. Student, Mich. State U., 1954—57. Asst. curator, lectr. Black Hills Reptile Gardens, Rapid City, SD, 1952—53; owner, adminstr. Reptile Exhibit, St. Ignace, Mich., 1957—59; animal coord. Don Meier Prodns. Marlin Perkin's Wild Kingdom, Chgo., 1960—62; zoologist Lincoln Park Zool. Gardens, Chgo., 1960—64; curator Brookfield Zoo, Ill., 1964—97; ret., 1997. Formerly assoc. dept. zoology Field Mus. Natural History, Chgo.; curator assoc. Moscow Zoopark; internat. zoo and conservation cons., Russia, Latvia, Mex., Kenya, China, Ecuador, Galapagos Islands; past instr. herpetology Field Mus., Coll. of DuPage, Triton Coll.; assoc. zoologist Moscow Zool. Pk., Russia; info. resource for fed. and state wildlife agys.; lectr., cons. in field. Contbr. over 100 articles to profl. jours. and popular mags.; co-creator with Hedda P. Saltz money bench Chgo. Children's Mus. Past v.p. Ill. Endangered Species Protection Bd., Springfield; liaison Endangered Species Tech. Adv. Com., Springfield. Mem. Am. Zoo Assn. (3 Outstanding Svc. awards), Chgo. Acad. Scis. (life), Chgo. Herpetological Soc. (life), Nat. Herpetological Alliance (past pres.), Mensa. Achievements include development of several new live animal exibit concepts; research in fossil urolite identification; rattlesnake hibernation physiology; discovery and documentation of parthenogenisis in snakes; discovery and documentation of Goliath frog calls; designed and built air-powered water craft prototype for island biological surveys in lakes Huron and Michigan. Avocations: hiking, archaeology, art, paleontology. Home and Office: PO Box 12 Hondo NM 88336 Business E-Mail: raypawley@pvtnetworks.net.

PAWLICZKO, GEORGE IHOR, academic administrator; b. Rochester, NY, Oct. 26, 1950; s. Roman and Irene Olha (Zubryckyj) P.; m. Ann Maria Lencyk, June 10, 1978. BA, St. John Fisher Coll., 1972; MA, Fordham U., 1974, MBA, 1986, PhD, 1989. Admissions counselor Fordham U., Bronx, N.Y., 1977-78, asst. dean Grad. Sch. of Bus. NYC, 1978-81; asst. to pres., dir. mgmt. info. systems Marymount Coll., Tarrytown, N.Y., 1981-82; exec. dir. N.Y. Inst. Credit, NYC, 1982-94, The Global Inst. Fin. and Banking (formerly Am. Inst. Banking Greater N.Y.), NYC, 1994—. Trustee St. Andrew's Ch., Hamptonburgh, N.Y., 1986-2002; bd. trustees St. Basil Coll., Stamford, Conn., 2006-. Mem. Shevchenko Scientific Soc., Beta Gamma Sigma, Phi Alpha Theta. Office: The Global Inst Fin and Banking 80 Maiden Ln New York NY 10038-4811 Office Phone: 212-480-3200.

PAWLIK, KURT F., psychologist, social science educator; b. Vienna, Mar. 16, 1934; PhD, U. Vienna, 1959. Scientific asst. U. Vienna, 1956-60, 62-65; rsch. assoc. U. Ill., Urbana, 1960-62; acting prof. psychology U. Graz, Austria, 1965-66; prof. psychology U. Hamburg, Germany, 1966—. Pres. Criminology Sci. Coun., Coun. Europe, France, 1978-92, Internat. Social Sci. Coun., Paris, 1998—; sec. gen., pres. Internat. Union Psychol. Sci., Montreal, Man., Can., 1992-96. Contbr. over 175 articles to profl. jours. and books. Mem. J. Jungius Soc. Sci. (pres. 2000—). Office: U Hamburg Von-Melle-Park 11 D-20146 Hamburg Germany E-mail: pawlik@uni-hamburg.de.

PAWLITSCHEK, DONALD PAUL, management consultant; b. Heron Lake, Minn., Aug. 5, 1941; s. Paul P. and Marion (Erickson) Pawlitschek; m. Korrine Kunerth, Oct. 9, 1965; children: Andrew, Jennifer, Heidi, Sarah, Benjamin. Student, Southwest Tech. Inst., 1960, Mankato State Coll., 1965—66. Farmer, Heron Lake, 1967—73; pres. Dundee Steel, Inc., 1973—75, Alpha Prime, Inc., Heron Lake, 1975—80, Prime Ventures, Inc., Lake Crystal, Minn., 1980—. Bd. dirs. Am. Search and Referral Co. With US Army, 1960. Mem.: Am. Entrepreneurs Assn., Nat. Assn. Fin. Cons., Elks, Am. Legion. Conservative. Roman Catholic. Achievements include patents for livestock flooring. Home and Office: Prime Ventures Inc 1801 499th Ave Lake Crystal MN 56055-9700

PAWSON, ANTHONY J., molecular biologist; b. Maidstone, Eng., Oct. 18, 1952; BA in Biochemistry, Cambridge U., 1973; PhD in Molecular Biology, London U., 1976. Postdoc. rsch. fellow U. Calif., Berkeley, 1976—80; asst. prof. dept. microbiology U. Brit. Columbia, Vancouver, Canada, 1981—85; sr. scientist Nat. Cancer Inst. Can., 1985—88, Terry Fox cancer rsch. scientist, 1988—99; assoc. prof. dept. med. genetics U. Toronto, Canada, 1985—88, prof. dept. med. genetics & microbiology, 1989—, sr. fellow Massey Coll., 2003—; sr. investigator Samuel Lunenefeld Rsch. Inst., Mount Sinai Hosp., Toronto, 1985—, Apotex chair molecular oncology, 1991, head rsch. molecular biology & cancer, 1994—, dir. rsch., 2002—06. Mem. sci. adv. bd. Inst. Molecular & Cell Biology, Singapore, 1998—2004, Jane Coffin Childs Meml. Fund Med. Rsch., 1997—2004, MGH Cancer Ctr., 1999—, Argonex Discovery Inc., 1999—; mem. sci. planning com. Nat. Human Genome Rsch. Inst., 1997—98; mem. sci. review bd. Howard Hughes Med. Inst., 1997—2000; mem. med. adv. bd. Gairdner Found., 1998—; mem. adv. bd. Ariad Pharm. Inc., 1992—97. Mem. editl. bd.: Trends in Genetics, Oncogene, Molecular & Cellular Biology, Cell Growth & Differentiation, Chemistry & Biology, Current Opinion in Cell Biology, Developmental Cell, Molecular Biology of the Cell, European Jour. Biochemistry; editor: Jour. Cellular Physiology, Progress in Biophysics & Molecular Biology. Decorated Officer Order of Can.; recipient Gairdner Found. Internat. award, 1994, Robert L. Noble prize, Nat. Cancer. Inst. Can., 1995, George Drummond Meml. award, U. Alberta, 1995, John Colter award, U. Calgary, 1996, Boehringer Mannheim prize, Can. Soc. Biochemistry & Molecular & Cellular Biology, 1997, Disting. Sci. award, Med. Rsch. Coun., 1998, Dr. H.P. Heineken prize for biochemistry/biophysics, Royal Netherlands Acad. Arts & Scis., 1998, Henry Friesen award, Can. Soc. Clin. Investigation, 1998, Pezcoller Internat. award for cancer rsch., Am. Assn. Cancer Rsch./Pezcoller Found., 1998, J. Allyn Taylor Internat. prize in medicine, U. Western Ont., 2000, Killam prize for health scis., 2000, Michael Smith prize in health rsch., 2002, Prix Galien, Can., 2002, Ernst W. Bertner Meml. award, MD Anderson Cancer Ctr., 2004, Louisa Gross Horwitz prize, 2004, Disting. Investigator award, Can. Inst. Health Rsch., 2004, Poulsson medal, Norwegian Soc. Pharmacology & Toxicology, 2004, Louisa Gross Horwitz prize, Columbia U., 2004, Wolf prize in medicine, Jerusalem, 2005, Daniel Nathans Meml. award, Van Andel Rsch. Inst., 2005, Wolf Found. prize in medicine, Israel, 2005, Howard Taylor Ricketts award, U. Chgo., 2007, Kyoto prize for lifetime achievement in basic scis., Inamori Found., 2008; internat. rsch. scholar, Howard Hughes Med. Inst., 1991—2001. Fellow: Am. Acad. Microbiology, Royal Soc. Can. (Flavelle medal 1998), Royal Soc. London (Royal medal 2005); mem.: NAS (assoc.), EMBO (assoc.; mem. editl. bd.), Japanese Biochem. Soc. (hon.), Am. Acad. Arts & Scis. (hon.; fgn.). Office: Mt Sinai Hosp 600 University Ave Rm 1084 Toronto ON Canada M5G 1X5 Mailing: Samuel Lunenfeld Rsch Inst Mt Sinai Hosp 600 Univ Ave Rm 1084 Toronto ON M5G 1X5 Canada Office Phone: 416-586-4800 ext. 8262. Office Fax: 416-586-8869. E-mail: pawson@lunenfeld.ca.

PAXON, BILL (L. WILLIAM PAXON), lobbyist, former congressman; b. Buffalo, Apr. 29, 1954; s. Leon W. and Mary P. (Sellers) P.; m. Susan Molinari, July 3, 1994; children: Susan Ruby, Katherine Mary. BA, Canisius Coll., 1977; PhD (hon.), Daeman Coll., Roberts Wesleyan Coll., Canisius Coll. Mem. Erie County Legis., NY, 1978-82, NY State Assembly, 1983-89, US Congress from 31st (now 27th) NY dist., 1989-98; chair Nat. Rep. Congrl. Com., mem. com. on commerce; sr. advisor Akin, Gump, Strauss, Hauer & Feld, Washington, 1999—. Named one of 50 Top Lobbyists, Washingtonian mag., 2007. Roman Catholic. Office: Akin Gump Strauss Hauer & Feld Ste 400 1333 New Hampshire Ave NW Washington DC 20036-1564 Office Phone: 202-887-4297. E-mail: bpaxon@akingump.com.*

PAXSON, CHRISTINA HULL, dean, economics and public affairs professor; b. 1960; BA with High Honors, Swarthmore Coll., 1982; MA, Columbia U., 1985, PhD, 1987. Lectr. Princeton U., 1986—87, asst. prof. econs. and pub. affairs, 1987—94, faculty rsch. assoc. Office of Population Rsch., 1993—, assoc. prof., 1994—97, prof., 1997—2007, faculty chair MBA program, Woodrow Wilson Sch., 1997—99, founding dir. Ctr. Health and Wellbeing, 2000—, assoc. chair Dept. Econs., 2005—08, dir. Adel Mahmoud Global Health Scholars Program and Lecture Series in Global Health, 2007—, Hughes-Rogers prof. economics & pub. affairs, 2007—, chair Dept. Economics, 2008—09, dean Woodrow Wilson Sch. Pub. and Internat. Affairs, 2009—. Jr. rsch. fellow Inst. for Policy Reform, 1993; rsch. assoc. Nat. Bur. of Econ. Rsch., 1995—; vis. prof. Wharton Sch., U. Pa., 1999; mem. social environment study group Longitudinal Cohort Study of Environ. Effects on Child Health and Devel., 2001—04; mem. MacArthur Found. Rsch. Network on Socioeconomic Status and Health, 2002—04; bd. dirs. Ctr. Health Care Strategies, 2002—; sr. fellow Bur. for Rsch. and Econ. Analysis of Devel. (BREAD), 2005—. Sr. editor The Future of Children, 2004—; contbr. articles to profl. jours. Mem.: Phi Beta Kappa. Office: Woodrow Wilson Sch Princeton U 424 Robertson Hall Princeton NJ 08544 Office Phone: 609-258-4800. Office Fax: 609-258-1418. E-mail: cpaxson@princeton.edu.*

PAXSON, JOHN, professional sports team executive, retired professional basketball player; b. Dayton, Ohio, Sept. 29, 1960; s. Jim Paxson; m. Carolyn Paxson; children: Ryan, Drew. Grad., U. Notre Dame, 1983. Guard San Antonio Spurs, 1983—85, Chgo. Bulls, 1985—94, radio and TV color analyst, asst. coach, 1995—96, exec. v.p. basketball ops., 2003—. Achievements include winning NBA Championships as a member of the Bulls, 1991, 92, 93. Office: Chgo Bulls United Ctr 1901 W Madison St Chicago IL 60612-2459*

PAXTON, BILL, actor, film director; b. Ft. Worth, May 17, 1955; s. John Lane and Mary Lou (Gray) P; m. Louise Newbury, 1987, children: James, Lydia Student, NYU; studies with Stella Adler, Vincent Chase. Actor: (films) Crazy Mama, 1975, Stripes, 1981, Taking Tiger MOuntain, 1983, The Lords of Discipline, 1983, Night Warning, 1983, Streets of Fire, 1983, Mortuary, 1983, Impulse, 1983, Terminator, 1984, Weird Science, 1985, Commando, 1985, Aliens, 1985 (Saturn award Acad. of Sci. Fiction, Fantasy, and Horror Films 1986), Near Dark, 1986, Pass the Ammo, 1987, Slipstream, 1989, Next of Kin, 1989, Back to Back, 1990,

Brain Dead, 1990, The Last of the Finest, 1990, Navy Seals, 1990, Predator 2, 1990, The Dark Backward, 1991, One False Move, 1992, The Vagrant, 1992, Trespass, 1992, Future Shock, 1993, Indian Summer, 1993, Boxing Helena, 1993, Tombstone, 1993, True Lies, 1994, Apollo 13, 1995, Twister, 1995, Evening Star, 1996, The Last Supper, 1996, Titanic, 1997, A Simple Plan, 1998, Mighty Joe Young, 1998, U-571, 2000, Vertical Limit, 2000, Spy Kids 2: Island of Lost Dreams, 2002, Resistance, 2003, Spy Kids 3-D: Game Over, 2003, Ghosts of the Abyss, 2003, Club Dread, 2004, Thunderbirds, 2004, Haven, 2004; actor, dir. (films) Frailty, 2001, dir. only, The Greatest Game Ever Played, 2005; actor, prodr. (films) Traveler, 1997; actor, dir., prodr., writer, (theatrical short) Fish Heads, 1982 (Spl. Award Melbourne Film Festival 1982); actor (TV movies) Deadly Lessons, 1983, An Early Frost, 1985, Frank and Jesse, 1994, A Bright Shining Lie, 1998; actor (TV mini-series) The Atlanta Child Murders, 1985, Fresno, 1986; actor (TV series) The Six O'Clock Follies, 1980, Big Love, 2006-; (TV appearances) The Hitch-Hiker, 1986, Miami Vice, 1986, Tales From the Crypt, 1993, Frasier (voice only), 2003; (theatrical short) Fish Heads, 1982 (Spl. Award Melbourne Film Festival 1982); prodr., co-author (theatrical short) Scoop, 1983. Mem. Screen Actors Guild. Office: c/o Endeavor Agency 9601 Wilshire Blvd, 3rd Fl Beverly Hills CA 90212

PAXTON, FREDERICK S., history professor; b. Detroit, July 18, 1951; s. Frederick E. and Genevieve M. (Beaudin) Paxton; m. Sylvia J. Malizia, Aug. 29, 1975; children: Giselda J. Beaudin, Justin P. Beaudin. PhD, U. Calif., Berkeley, 1985. Brigida Pacchiani Ardenghi prof. history Conn. Coll., New London, 2001—, dean, internat. studies, 2001—05. Author: Christianizing Death: The Creation of a Ritual Process in Early Medieval Europe, Anchoress and Abbess in Ninth-Century Saxony: The Lives of Liutbirga of Wendhausen and Hathumoda of Gandersheim. Co-chair Coalition to Save the Ft. Trumbull Neighborhood, New London, 1999—2005. Fellowship, NEH, 2006—07, Rsch. fellowship, J. William Fulbright Found. Rome, 1993, Faculty fellowship, Andrew W. Mellon Found., 1989—90, Charlotte W. Newcombe fellowship, Woodrow Wilson Nat. Found., 1983—84. Mem.: Am. Hist. Assn., Medieval Acad. America (book rev. editor 2006—). Office: Conn Coll 270 Mohegan Ave New London CT 06320 Business E-Mail: fredpaxton@conncoll.edu.

PAXTON, J. WILLENE, retired academic administrator; b. Birmingham, Ala., Oct. 30, 1930; d. Will and Elizabeth (Davis) P. AB, Birmingham So. Coll., Ala., 1950; MA, Mich. State U., East Lansing, 1951; EdD, Ind. U., Bloomington, 1971; postgrad., U. Tex., Austin, 1965. Dormitory dir. Tex. Tech U., Lubbock, 1951-53; dir. univ. ctr. and housing SUNY, Fredonia, 1953-56, assoc. dean of students, 1956-57; asst. dean of women U. N.Mex., Albuquerque, 1957-63; dean of women East Tenn. State U., Johnson City, 1963-68, 70-78, dir. Counseling Ctr., 1978-93, initiated Paxton lectureship for learning and leadership, 2007. Tng. dir. CONTACT Teleministries, Tenn., 1984-92, chmn. bd. dirs., 1986, 95. Chmn. social concerns Munsey United Meth. Ch., 1989-92, sec. adminstrv. bd., 1980-84, vice chair, 1993, chair, 1994, coun. on ministries, 1980-94, chair stewardship campaign, 1995, chair promotion and publicity subcom. bldg. campaign, 1996-2001, chair scholarship com., 1997-2004, lay leader, 2001-04, sec. staff parish rels. com., 2001-2004, nominations com., 2001-04, sec. ch. coun., 2003-06, mem. SEND team, Circle tchr., 2000-06; visitor for Mended Hearts, 2000—; recording sec. United Meth. Women, 2005—, corr. sec., 2004; mem. Philip D. Cooper Meml. Rsch. Trust Fund Inc., 2006—. U.S. Ednl. Profl. Devel. Act grantee, 1968-69; chosen One of Ten in Tenn. as Cmty. Quarterback Nat. Football League Tenn. Titans, 2004. Mem.: Watauga Pers. and Guild Assn. (pres.-elect 1967—68, chair ETEA guidance divsn. 1968), Tenn. Assn. Women Deans Counselors (pres. 1966—68), Tenn. Coll. Pers. Assn. (legis. chair 1974), Am. Coll. Pers. Assn. (media com., newsletter editor com. XVI 1977—79), East Tenn. State U. Retirees Assn. (bd. dirs. 1993—2000, program chair 1994—95, pres. 1995—96, chair com. to compile Tales of the Univ. 1999—2005, sec. 2000, bd. dirs. 2003—06, bd.dir. 2009—), Asbury Retirement Ctrs. Tenn. and Va. (bd. dirs., policy com. 1991—96, nomination com. 1994—96, chair 1995—96, fin. com. 1996), Gen. Federated Women's Club Monday Club (co-chair edn. dept. 2005—06, chair internat. affairs dept. 2007—08, pres. 2008—), Gen. Federated Woman's Club Monday Club Aux. (corr. sec. 1979—80, pres. 1980—81, 1988—89, v.p. 1993—99, pres. 1995—96, 1999—2000), Univ. Women's Club (pres. 1994—96), Delta Kappa Gamma Soc. Internat. (chpt. pres. 1972—74, state rec. sec. 1975—77, state v.p. 1977—79, chair state nominating com. 1979—81, internat. rsch. com. 1982—84, chair state ad hoc com. to study feasibility exec. sec. 1987—89, internat. exec. bd., state pres. 1989—91, internat. chair rules com. 1992, internat. constn. com. 1992—94, state pers. com. 1995—97, chair 1997—99, archives com. 1999—2001, pers. com. 2001—03, awards com. 2003—05, area dir. 2005—07, mem., Xi state com. to devel. memory book 75th anniversary, Tenn. 2009—, State Achievement award 1987). Avocations: reading, bridge, travel, needlecrafts. Personal E-mail: willenepj@charter.net.

PAXTON, JAY L., lawyer; b. Ft. Worth, Dec. 24, 1947; s. Carl C. Paxton and Mildred F. Shepherd; m. Carolyn P. Paxton, June 21, 1969; 1 child, Laura. BA, U. Calif., Berkeley, 1970, JD, 1973. Bar: Calif. 1973. Spl. asst. to chancellor U. Calif., 1973-74; ptnr., mng. ptnr. Bianchi, Paxton, Engel, Keegin & Sherwood, San Rafael, Calif., 1974—90; mem., mng. dir. Ellman, Burke, Hoffman & Johnson, San Francisco, 1990—. Bd. dirs., v.p. Internat. House, U. Calif., Berkeley, 1974—, mem. exec. com. Fisher Ctr. for Real Estate and Urban Econs., 2004—; trustee U. Calif. Berkeley Found., 1997—, Marin Cmty. Found., 2005—; mem., chair exec. com. San Francisco Dist. Coun., Urban Land Inst., 1976-; bd. dirs. Bay Area Coun., 1996—. Mem. ABA, Calif. Bar Assn., Urban Land Inst., Lambda Alpha. Office: Ellman Burke Hoffman Johnson 601 California St Ste 1900 San Francisco CA 94108-2824 Office Phone: 415-777-2727. Business E-Mail: jpaxton@ellman-burke.com.

PAXTON, PAMELA, social sciences educator; b. Winston-Salem, NC, Apr. 17, 1970; d. William and Ann Paxton; m. Paul Von Hippel, June 24, 2000. BA, U. Mich., Ann Arbor, 1992; PhD, U. NC, Chapel Hill, 1998. Prof. Ohio State U., Columbus, 1998—. Cons. US Agy. Internat. Devel., Washington, 2003—07. Author: (book) Women, Politics, and Power: A Global Perspective; contbr. articles to profl. jours. Deacon Blvd. Presbyn. Ch., Columbus, 2004—08. Recipient Carrie Chapman Catt prize, Catt Ctr. Women and Politics, 2006; Rsch. fellowship, U. NC, 1997—98. Mem.: Am. Polit. Sci. Assn., Am. Sociol. Assn., Phi Beta Kappa, Alpha Chi Omega. Presbyterian. Avocations: gardening, travel. Office: Ohio State Univ 1885 Neil Ave Columbus OH 43210-1222

PAXTON, ROBERT OWEN, historian, educator; b. Lexington, Va., June 15, 1932; s. Matthew W. and Nell B. (Owen) P.; m. Sarah Plimpton, Dec. 9, 1983 BA, Washington and Lee U., 1954, LittD (hon.), 1974; BA, Oxford U., Eng., 1956, MA, 1961; PhD, Harvard U., 1963; DHL (hon.), SUNY, Stony Brook, 1994; DL (hon.), U. Caen, France, 1994; DL (hon.), U. Lyon, France, 2003. Instr. history U. Calif., Berkeley, 1961-63, asst. prof., 1963-67; asso. prof. SUNY, Stony Brook, 1967-69; prof. history Columbia U., 1969—, chmn. dept., 1980-82, dir. Inst. on West Europe, 1991-95. Author: Parades and Politics at Vichy, 1966, Vichy France: Old Guard and New Order, 1940-44, 1972, 2d edit., 2001, Europe in the Twentieth Century, 1975, 4th edit., 2001, French Peasant Fascism, 1997, Anatomy of Fascism, 2004; co-author: Vichy France and the Jews, 1981, 2d edit., 1995; co-editor: De Gaulle and the U.S., 1995. Served with USNR, 1956-58. Decorated office Legion D' Honnem comdr. Ordre National des Arts et des Lettres (France), officer Ordre Nat. du Mérite (France); recipient Scholarly Distinction award Am. Hist. Soc., 1998; Rhodes scholar, 1954-56; Am. Coun. Learned Socs. fellow, 1974-75; Rockefeller Found. fellow, 1978-79; German Marshall Fund fellow, 1986. Fellow Am. Acad. Arts and Letters; mem. Am. Philos. Soc., Linnaean Soc. NY (pres. 1978-80), Century Assn. Home: 460 Riverside Dr Apt 72 New York NY 10027-6801 Office: Columbia U Dept History New York NY 10027 Business E-Mail: rop1@columbia.edu.

PAXTON, TOM, songwriter, entertainer, author; b. Chgo., Oct. 31, 1937; s. George Burton and Esther Hildegard (Peterson) P.; m. Margaret Ann Cummings, Aug. 5, 1963; children: Jennifer Ann, Katherine Claire. BFA, U. Okla., 1959. Rec. artist with Elektra, Flying Fish, Hogeye, Reprise, Vanguard, Mountain Railroad, Pax Records, Sugar Hill, 1962—; owner Pax Records. Albums include Car Full of Songs, Ramblin' Boy, 1964, Ain't That News, 1965, Outward Bound, 1966, Morning Again, 1968, The Things I Notice Now, 1969, Number 6, 1970, The Complete Tom Paxton, 1971, How Come the Sun, 1971, Peace Will Come, 1972, New Songs for Old Friends, 1973, Something in My Life, 1975, New Songs from the Briar Patch, 1977, Heroes, 1978, I Can't Help but Wonder Where I'm Bound, Up and Up, 1980, Politics: Live, The Paxton Report, 1980, One Million Lawyers...and Other Disasters, 1986, The Marvelous Toy and Other Gallimaufry, 1987, Fun Animal Songs, Fun Food Songs, Even a Gray Day, And Loving You, 1987, Politics, 1989, The Authentic Guitar of Tom Paxton Song Book, 1989, It Ain't Easy, 1991, Suzy is a Rocker, 1992, Peanut Butter Pie, 1992, A Child's Christmas, 1992, Wearing the Time, 1994, Goin' to the Zoo, 1997, I've Got a Yo-Yo, 1997, A Car Full of Songs, 1997, Live in Concert, 1998, Fun Animal Songs, 1999, Fun Food Songs, 1999, Live from Mountain Stage, 2001, Under American Skies, 2001, Your Shoes, My Shoes, 2002, Looking for the Moon, 2002, Best of Friends, 2004, Live in the UK, 2004, Live at McCabe's Guitar Shop, 2006, Comedians & Angels, 2008; (video) Folk City 25th Anniversary Concert, Folked Again: Best of Mountain Music, Freedom is a Constant Struggle, Greatest Folk Singers of the 60's, Put On Your Green Shoes, Silverwolf Homeless Project, Storytellers- Singers and Songwriters, Tribute to Woody Gutherie, Troubadours of the Folk Era, vol. 2, Walt Disney Records Presents: Dog Songs, What's That I Hear?: The Songs of Phil Ochs, Where Have All the...Pete Seeger; author: Jennifer's Rabbit, 1988, Belling The Cat, 1990, Englebert the Elephant, 1990, Aesop's Fables Retold in Verse, 1988, Androcles and The Lion, 1991, Birds of a Feather, 1992, The Animals' Lullaby, 1993, Where's the Baby, 1993, The Story of Santa Claus, 1995, The Story of the Tooth Fairy, 1996, The Marvelous Toy, 1996, Goin' to the Zoo, 1996, Engelbert Joins the Circus, 1997. Bd. dirs. Kerrville Polk Festival, 1990. Recipient Lifetime Achievement award Swannanoa Gathering, Warren Wilson Coll., NC, 1996, Lifetime Achievement award for Songwriting, BBC Radio 2 Folk Awards, 2005, Lifetime Achievement award, N.Am. Folk Music & Dance Alliance, 2006; named to Kerrville Folk Festival Hall of Fame, 1996. Mem. ASCAP (Lifetime Achievement award in Folk Music, 2002), AFTRA, Am. Fedn. Musicians, Screen Actors Guild. Office: Fleming Artists 543 N Main St Ann Arbor MI 48104-1026 E-mail: contact@flemingartists.com.

PAYE, JEAN-CLAUDE, lawyer; b. Longué, Aug. 26, 1934; s. Lucien and Suzanne (Guignard) Paye; m. Laurence Jeanneney, 1963; 4 children. Student, Inst. Etudes Politiques, Ecole Nat. Admin. Head pvt. office Mayor of Constantine, 1961-62; sec. Embassy Algiers, 1962-63; with Ministry of Fgn. Affairs, 1963-65; spl. advisor Office Sec. of State for Sci. Rsch., 1965, Office Min. Social Affairs, 1966; head pvt. office M. Barre V.p. Commn. European Communities, 1967-73; counsellor Bonn Embassy, Bonn, 1973-74; dep. head Office Min. Fgn. Affairs, 1974-76; counsellor Prime Min. Raymond Barre, 1976-79; sec. gen. Interministerial Com. for European Economic Coop., 1977-79; dir. econ. and fin. affairs Min. for External Rels., 1979-84; sec. gen. OECD, 1984-96; state counselor Govt. of France, 1996-2000; assoc. GLN, Paris, 2001—09. Bd. dirs. Renault. Pres. Found. for Polit. Innovation, 2005—09. Decorated chevalier Légion d'honneur, comdr. Order Nat du Mèrite. Home Phone: 33(0) 1 45 49 20 30. Business E-Mail: jcl.paye@free.fr.

PAYERHIN, MAREK, political scientist, educator; BA, Jagiellonian U., Krakow, 1984; diploma in Internat. Affairs, Johns Hopkins U., Sch. Advanced Internat. Studies, Bologna, Italy, 1982; MA, U. Conn., Storrs, 1988, PhD, 1996. Vis. asst. prof. Quinnipiac U., Hamden, Conn., 1996—97; adj. prof. U. Conn., Storrs, 1997—98; asst. prof. Alma Coll., Mich., 1998—2005; assoc. prof. Lynchburg Coll., Va., 2005—. Program chair Va. Polit. Sci. Assn., Lynchburg, 2007—08; bd. editors Politics, Culture and Socialization Jour., 2007—. Author: (book) Kajakiem na Nordkapp ; contbr. articles to profl. jours. Dir. Alma Ctr. Ednl. Simulations, Mich., 2001—05. Named Orgn. Advisor of Yr., Lynchburg Coll., 2008; Venture grant, Mich. Campus Compact, 2001—03, grant, Ctr. Russian & Eastern European Studies, U. Mich., 2003, 2005, Future of Edn. grant, MEEMIC Found. Future Edn., 2003, grant, Alma Coll. Mem.: Polish Inst. Arts & Scis. America, Am. Polit. Sci. Assn. Achievements include first to circumnavigate North Cape (Norway) in a sailing kayak. Avocations: kayaking, sailing, travel.

PAYETTE, JULIE, astronaut, electrical engineer, computer engineer; b. Montréal, Oct. 20, 1963; married; 2 children. BEE, McGill U, Montreal, 1986; M in Applied Sci. and Computer Engring., U. Toronto, 1990; degree (hon.), Queen's U., 1999, U. Ottawa, 1999, Simon Fraser U., 2000, U. Laval, 2000, U. Regina, 2001, Royal Roads U., 2001, U. Toronto, 2001, U. Victoria, 2002, Nipissing U., 2002, McGill U., 2003, Mt. Saint Vincent U., 2004, McMaster U., 2004, U. Lethbridge, 2005, Mt. Allison U., 2005, U. Alberta, 2006. bd. dirs. Internat. Bd. Dirs. UWC Colls.; mem. coun. Natural Sciences and Engring. Rsch. Coun. Can. (NSERC)/CRSNG. Sys. engr. IBM Canada, 1986—88; rsch. asst. U. Toronto, 1988—90; vis. scientist IBM Rsch. Lab., Zurich, Switzerland, 1991; rsch. engr. Bell-Northern Rsch./Nortel, Montreal, Canada, 1992; astronaut. engr. Can. Space Agy., St. Hubert, Canada, 1992—, chief astronaut, 2000—07; crew liaison officer NASA, Russia, completed initial astronaut tng., 1998. Crew mem. STS-96 Mission (Discovery), 1999, STS-127 Mission (Endeavour), 2009; assigned to represent the Astronaut Corps at the European and Russian Space Agencies, 1999—2002; spacecraft communicator CAPCOM, Mission Control Ctr., Houston, 2003; lead CAPCOM STS-121 Mission, 2006. Recipient Young Engr. Achievement award Canadian Coun. Profl. Engrs., 1994., Chevalier de l'Ordre de la Pléiade de la francophonie, 2001, Order national du Québec, 2002. Fellow Can. Acad. Engring.;mem. Amies d'Affaires Montreal, l' Ordre Ingénieurs Quebec. Avocations: running, skiing, racquet sports, scuba diving. Office: John H Chapman Space Centre Can Space Agy 6767 route de l'Aéroport Saint Hubert PQ J3Y 8Y9 Canada*

PAYMENT, KENNETH ARNOLD, lawyer; b. Aug. 6, 1941; s. Arnold F. and Eleanor J. (Kinsey) Payment; m. Jane A. Conrad, Aug. 16, 1996; children: Simone, Elise, Ryan. BS, Union Coll., 1963; LLB, Cornell U., 1966. Bar: NY 66, U.S. Dist. Ct. (we. dist.) NY 67, U.S. Ct. Appeals (2d cir.) 68, U.S. Supreme Ct. 89. Assoc. Wiser, Shaw, Freeman, Van Graafeiland, Harter & Secrest, Rochester, 1966—75; ptnr. Harter, Secrest & Emery, Rochester, 1975—. Instr. Rochester Inst. Tech., 1969, U. Rochester, 1970, Cornell U. Law Sch., Ithaca, NY, 1971—72. Mem.: ABA, Best Lawyers in Am. (bus. litigation 1989—, antitrust 2003), Rochester C. of C., Monroe County Bar Assn. (trustee), NY State Bar Assn. (chmn. constrn. and suretyship divsn. 1978), Cornell Club. Home: 268 Harmon Rd Churchville NY 14428-9518 Office: Harter Secrest & Emery 1600 Bausch & Lomb Place Rochester NY 14604-2006 Home Phone: 585-538-6025; Office Phone: 585-231-1227.

PAYNE, BARBARA ANN, artist, educator; b. Marionville, Mo., Jan. 14, 1938; d. Lewis Michel and Velma Etta Rapp; m. Kenneth L. Payne, Nov. 25, 1956 (dec.); children: Kevin James, Kendra Lynne, Keli Song. AA, Fort Scott Cmty. Jr. Coll., Kans., 1965—67; BS in Edn., Kans. State Coll., Pittsburg, 1967—69. Tchr. Dept. Def. Schs., Yokosuka, Japan, 1969—72, Seoul, Republic of Korea, 1972—74, Spangdahlem, Germany, 1974—75, Bitburg, Germany, 1975—76, West Berlin, 1976—83, Doddea, ret., 1984; artist. art instr. Bonn, Königswinter, Germany, 1983—88; artist Würzburg, Germany, 1988—2001, Brussels, Erps Kwerps, 2001—02. Contbr. articles to profl. jours.; one-woman shows include Galerie Fasanenstrasse 71, Berlin, 1983, Am. Embassy Club, Bonn, Germany, 1986, Mobau Wittemann, Aegidienberg, Germany, 1986, Spar-und Darlenhskasse, Aegidienberg, 1987, Stadtbücherei (City Libr.), Bonn-Dottendorf, Germany, 1988, Mehrzweckhalle, Unterpleichfeld, Germany, 1989, 1990, 1991, 1992, 1993, 1994, 1995, 1996, 2001, Kultur Stüble, Höchberg, Germany, 1991, 1992, Hotel Rebstock, Würzburg, Germany, 1993, Firme Volk, Am Markt, 1994, Farewell to Europe exhbn. Erps Kwerps, Brussels, 2002, exhibited in group shows at Berlin Am. Art Guild, West Berlin, Germany and Berlin Am. Cmtys. inside West Berlin, 1977—83, Bildungscentrum des Deutschen Beamtenbundes, Königswinter, Germany, 1986, Akademie Führungskraefte Deutsche Post, Bad Honnef, Germany, 1987, Alte Kirche, Waldbüttelbrunn, Germany, 1990, 1993. Mem. Berlin Am. Art Guild, 1977—83, pres., 1981—82. Mem.: AAUW, Nat. Mus. Women in the Arts. Avocations: piano, antiques, poetry, art.

PAYNE, DANIEL HAROLD (HAROLD PAYNE), real estate developer, small business owner; b. Caddo Mills, Tex., Feb. 12, 1921; s. Flavy Malone and Sally Ella Payne; m. Wanda Louise Lyday, Aug. 3, 1941; 1 child, Kyle Steven. At, Tex. A&M, Commerce, 1940—41; grad., Tex. Real Estate Sch., Dallas, 1971. Sales J.C. Penney, Greenville, Tex., 1940—41, A&P Grocery, Greenville, 1940—41; office and credit mgr. Firestone Tire Co., Ft. Worth, 1941—42; office mgr. Guy F. Atkinson Co., Denison, 1942—43; co-owner Payne Bros. Super Markets, 1945—55; owner Payne's Famous Furniture Village, Caddo Mills, Tex., 1955—90, Payne Magnavox Ctr., Garland, Tex., 1960—61, Harold Payne Land Sales & Devel., Caddo Mills, Tex., 1970—. Adv. bd. Tex. Retail Grocery Assn., Dallas, 1951—55; bd. mem. State Nat. Bank, Caddo Mills, 1972—99; adv. mem. Tex. Retail Furniture Assn., Dallas, 1967—88. Contbr. articles to trade periodicals. Pres. Lions Club Internat., Caddo Mills, Tex., 1955—56; treas. Hunt County Fair Bd., Greenville, 1966—, publicity chmn., 1966—87; public spkr. civic, military and ch. groups in Tex. and Okla., 1963—83; elder Faith Bible Ch., Caddo Mills, Tex.; bd. mem. and publicity chmn. Sky Ranch Christian Youth Camp, Van, 1962—63; founding mem. 390th Bomb Group Meml. Mus., Tucson. 2d lt. USAF, 1942—45. Recipient Advt. award, Tex. Furniture Assn., 1969, Nat. Sales award, Nat. Furniture Assn., 1976, numerous manufacturers' sales awards. Mem.: Hunt County Freedom Forum (chmn. 1957—63, chmn. of bd. 1959—81), Masons (32 degree 1973). Republican. Avocation: sports. Office Phone: 903-527-3149.

PAYNE, DAVID EMER, university administrator; b. Salt Lake City, Mar. 29, 1944; s. John W. and Sara (Harris) P.; m. Grettle Haglund, Mar. 16, 1973; children: Sara, John, Samuel, Daniel, James, David. BS, Brigham Young U., Provo, Utah, 1968; MS, U. N.C., 1970, PhD, 1972. Asst. prof. U. Iowa, Iowa City, 1972-76; assoc. prof. U. N.D., Grand Forks, 1976-80, prof., 1980-81; fellow Am. Coun. Edn., New Orleans, 1981-82; dean social sci. S.E. Mo. State U., Cape Girardeau, 1982-88; v.p. acad. affairs Sangamon State U., Springfield, Ill., 1988-89, Emporia (Kans.) State U., 1989-96, Sam Houston State U., Huntsville, Tex., 1997—2000, provost, 2000—. Vis. prof. U. Iceland, Reykjavik, 1974-75. Contbr. articles to profl. jours. Dist. commr. Boy Scouts Am. Am. Coun. Edn. fellow, 1981-82, Bush Found. sr. fellow, 1982. Mem. Lds Ch. Office: Sam Houston State U Huntsville TX 77340 Home: 4 Rushing Oak Ct Huntsville TX 77320 Office Phone: 936-294-1001. Business E-Mail: payne@shsu.edu.

PAYNE, DAVID L., bank executive; b. 1956; Chmn., pres., CEO Westamerica Bancorporation; gen. mgr. Gibson Publishing Co., Gibson Radio and Publishing Co., Vallejo, Calif. Office: Westamerica Bancorp 1108 5th Ave San Rafael CA 94901-2916

PAYNE, DON J., theology studies educator, consultant; b. Springfield, Mo., June 24; s. Danny and Frances Payne; m. Sharon Stroup, May 28; children: Danielle, Donald, Robert. PhD, U. Manchester, Eng., 2003. Assoc. pastor Southern Gables Ch., Littleton, Colo., 1991—98; assoc. dean, asst. prof. theology and ministry Denver Sem., Littleton, Colo., 1998—. Trainer, cons. Mentoring Group, Grass Valley, Calif., 2007—. Author: (book) The Theology of the Christian Life in J.I. Packer's Thought. Exec. dir. Internat. Christian Mentoring Network, Littleton, 2006—09. Avocations: reading, hunting. Personal E-mail: djslpayne@msn.com.

PAYNE, DONALD MILFORD, United States Representative from New Jersey; b. Newark, July 16, 1934; s. William Evander and Norma (Garrett) Payne; m. Hazel Johnson, June 18, 1958 (dec. 1963); children: Donald Milford, Wanda. BA in Social Studies, Seton Hall U., NJ, 1957; grad. student, Springfield Coll., Mass.; D (hon.), Chgo. State U., Drew U., Essex County Coll., William Paterson U. Tchr. South Side High Sch., Newark, 1957, Robert Treat Jr. High Sch., Newark, 1957—59, Pulaski Elementary Sch., Passaic, NJ, 1959—64; exec. Prudential Ins. Co., 1964—69; v.p. Urban Data Systems, Inc., 1969; mem. Essex County Bd. Chosen Freeholders, 1972—78, Newark Mcpl. Coun., 1982—88, US Congress from 10th NJ Dist., 1989—. Mem. edn. and labor com. US Congress, mem. fgn. affairs com., chmn. subcommittee on Africa and Global Health, mem Dem. whip orgn. Nat. pres. YMCA, 1970—73, chmn. world refugee and rehab. com., 1973—81; bd. dirs. Nat. Endowment Democracy, TransAfrica, Discovery Channel Global Edn. Fund, Congl. Award Found., Enterprise Works, Boys and Girls Club Newark, Newark Day Ctr., Fighting Back Initiative, Newark YMCA; mem. US Com. for UNICEF; mem. congl. del. UN, 2003, 2005. Recipient Leadership award, Hudson County Urban League, NJ, 2003, Visionaries for Africa award, Africa Soc., 2004, Humanitarian Svc. award, Isaac Hayes Found., 2004, Bishop John T. Walker Disting. Humanitarian Svc. award, Africare, 2004; named one of Most Influential Black Americans,

Ebony mag., 2006, People to Watch, Sunday Star Ledger, 2007; named to Power 150, Ebony mag., 2008. Mem.: NAACP (life), Nat. Coun. Negro Women. Democrat. Baptist. Office: US House Reps 2209 Rayburn House Office Bldg Washington DC 20515-0001 Office Phone: 202-225-3436. Office Fax: 202-225-4160.*

PAYNE, GARELD GENE, vocal music educator, medical transcriptionist; b. Colony, Okla., Aug. 27, 1931; s. Eugene A. and Agnes D. (Chastain) P.; children: Gareld, S. Raymond, Lynn Dita, Jana Lee. MusB, Oklahoma City U., 1965; MusM in Edn., North Tex. State U. (name change to U. North Tex.), 1969; ednl. specialist, Pitts. State U., 1989; EdD, Okla. State U., 2007. Ind. organist, pianist numerous nightclubs, nationwide, 1956-64; instr. vocal, instrumental music Muenster Ind. Sch. Dist., Tex., 1965-69; tchr. vocal music Dallas Ind. Sch. Dist., 1966-74, Carrizo Springs Ind. Sch. Dist., Tex., 1976-79, Coffeyville Unified Sch. Dist., Kans., 1979-91; tchr. elem. vocal music Oklahoma City Pub. Schs., 1996—. Rec. artist (album) Evening With Gareld, 1984; composer publ. anthems. With USAF, 1950—53. Scholar Oklahoma City U., 1949. Mem. Am. Fedn. Musicians, NEA, Am. Orff-Schulwerk Assn., Am. Recorder Soc., Am. Theater Organ Soc., Am. Guild Organists, Kodaly Educators, Phi Mu Alpha Sinfonia Frat., Phi Delta Kappa. Republican. Methodist. Avocations: astrology, oil and water color painting, cooking, reading, computers. Home: 3643 NW 15th St Oklahoma City OK 73107-4423 Personal E-mail: pgareld_osu@brightok.net.

PAYNE, GEORGE FREDERICK, academic administrator; b. Summerville, SC, Jan. 29, 1941; s. Fred N. and Lota (Griffith) Payne; m. Kay Martin, June 23, 1963; children: John F., Mark C., Janet E. Student, Ga. Inst. Tech., 1959-60, U.S. Naval Acad., 1960-62; BS, U. S.C., 1963, MA, 1966, MRE, Luth. Theol. Sem., 1968; postgrad., U. Ga., 1969-71; LLD (hon.), Lincoln Meml. U., 1988. Cert. fund raising exec. 2000. From instr. to asst. prof. Ga. So. Coll., Statesboro, 1966-78; dir. admission Brewton-Parker Coll., Mt. Vernon, Ga., 1978-80; v.p. devel. North Greenville Coll., Tigerville, SC, 1980-86; pres. Limestone Coll., Gaffney, SC, 1986-91, dir. various grants, 1976-91; spl. agt., registered rep. Prudential Fin. Svcs., 1991-92; dir. ITT Tech. Inst., Greenville, SC, 1992-95; exec. dir. Inst. Adv. Greenville Tech. Coll., 1996—2006; cons. Greenville Tech. Found., 2007—; exec. dir. GTF McAlister LLC, 2003—, GTF Student Housing LLC, 2004—, Brashier Charter LLC, 2007—, Greenville County Coun., Dist. 28. Author: An Introduction to the Principles of Geography: Facts, Skills, Concepts, and Models, 1973; contbr. articles to profl. jours. Active Leadership Greer, SC, 1980—81, regent, 1982—84; active AACTion Consortium, 1980—82, Leadership Greenville, 1982—83; bd. dirs. Greenville County unit Am. Cancer Soc., 1985—86; advisor Cherokee County Arts Coun., 1986—91; trustee Rolling Green Village Continuing Care Ret. Cmty., 1996—2006, sec., 1998, 2003; trustee Baptist Found. S.C., 2001—05, 2007—, Oakwood Sch., Va., 2002—; bd. dirs. Greenville Redevel. Authority, 2005—06, chair adminstrn. com., 2006. With USN, 1960—62. Recipient Disting. Svc. award, Brewton-Parker Coll., 1980, North Greenville Coll., 1986. Mem.: Coun. Advancement Support Edn. (Circle of Excellence award for ednl. fund-raising 2001, 2004), Assn. Fund-Raising Profls. (cert. fund-raising exec.), Greater Greer C. of C. (bd. dirs. 1981—84), Rotary. Baptist. Avocation: reading. Office: Greenville Tech Found McAlister Ste E-11 225 S Pleasantburg Dr Greenville SC 29607 Office Phone: 864-884-8899. Business E-Mail: Fred.Payne@GvlTec.edu. E-mail: fpayne@greenvillecounty.org.

PAYNE, HARRY MORSE, JR., architect; b. Norwood, Mass., Nov. 3, 1922; s. Harry Morse and Edna May (Beardsley) P.; m. Helen Marion Beasley, Aug. 29, 1946; children: Harry Morse, Thomas Beasley, Amelia Morse. Student, Boston Archtl. Center, 1946—49, MIT, 1949—50. Draftsman William G. Upham, Norwood, 1946-47; designer William Riseman Assos., Boston, 1947-49, Harry J. Korslund, Norwood, 1949-51, William Hoskins Brown, Boston, 1951-52; designer, prin. dir. The Architects Collaborative, Cambridge, Mass., 1952-86, pres., 1975-77, emeritus, 1986—, Boston Archtl. Center, 1963-65, 71-73; asst. prof. Harvard U. Grad. Sch. Design, 1954-63. Prin. works include U.S. Embassy, Athens, Greece, U. Baghdad, Iraq, Temple Israel, Boston, Quincy Sch., Boston, Nauset Regional H.S., Cape Cod, Mass.; author: The Survey System of the Old Colony, 1985, Name Change--Paine to Payne, 1992, Cape Cod Land Strategy, 1994, New England 17th Century Land Strategy, 1997, America's Stonehenge As Architecture, 1998, Payne Paine Family—England and Cape Cod, 1999, The Ordering of Towns: Massachusetts Bay Colony 17th Century Land Strategy, 2002. Served with USN, 1943-46. Recipient Cascieri Lectureship in Humanities medal, Boston Archtl. Ctr., 2002, Selfless Labor award, BAC Com., 2007. Fellow AIA; mem. Soc. Archtl. Historians, N.E. Antiquities Rsch. Assn., Boston Soc. Architects, Mass. State Assn. Architects, New Eng. Hist. and Geneal. Soc., The Colonial Soc. Mass., Mass. Soc. Genealogists (pres. 1986-88), Lincoln Hist. Soc. (pres. 1990-92). Home: 303 Winthrop Terr Bedford MA 01730

PAYNE, JAMES EARL, economics professor, dean; b. Willimantic, Conn., Jan. 1, 1963; s. James Earl and Carol (LeClaire) P. BA, Berea Coll., Ky., 1985; MS, Fla. State U., Tallahassee, 1987, PhD in Econs., 1989. Vis. asst. prof. U. So. Miss., Hattiesburg, 1988-89; asst. prof. econs. Oakland U., Rochester, Mich., 1989-92; asst. prof. Dept. Accounting, Fin., and Info. Sys., Coll. Bus. and Tech., Ea. Ky. U., Richmond, 1992—94, assoc. prof., 1994—2001, prof., 2001—03, rsch. assoc. Ctr. Econ. Devel., Entrepreneurship adn Tech., 2000—03; chair Dept. Econs. Ill. State U., 2003—, interim dean Coll. of Arts and Scis., 2009—. Fulbright rsch. scholar and sr. specialist Inst. Econs., Zagreb, Croatia. Bd. editors Jour. Econs. and Fin., 1990-94; contbr. articles to profl. jours. Mem. Am. Econ. Assn., Midwest Econ. Assn., Omicron Delta Epsilon, Phi Kappa Phi, Pi Gamma Mu. Avocations: running, bicycling, basketball. Home: 1601 Cutter Ct Normal IL 61761-4818 Office: Dept Econs Ill State U 4100 Coll of Arts & Sci Normal IL 61790-4200 Office Phone: 309-438-8588. E-mail: jepayne@ilstu.edu.*

PAYNE, JOHN KENNETH, acadmic administrator; b. Jacksonville, NC, Apr. 30, 1961; s. John Kenneth and Barbara Mae (McKee) P.; m. Dayle Ann Mary DeForge, July 5, 1986. BA in European History, U. N.C., 1983; MLS, U. S.C., 1987. Tech. svcs. libr. Mars Hill (N.C.) Coll., 1987-90, dir. libr. svcs., 1990-93, dean learning resources, 1993—. Chmn. bd. dirs. Mountain Coll. Libr. Network, Asheville, N.C. 1989—; mem. com. on tech. N.C. Ctr. for Ind. Higher Edn., Raleigh, 1994—, mem. adv. com. on automation and networking, 1988-90; mem. resolutions com. Gov.'s Conf. on Libr. and Info. Svcs., Raleigh, 1990; chmn. del. selection com. Regional Conf. on Libr. and Info. Svcs., Franklin, N.C., 1990. Mem. ALA, N.C. Libr. Assn. (exec. bd. dirs. coll. and univ. sect. 1989-93, mem. libr. adminstrn. and mgmt. sect.). Democrat. Unitarian Universalist. Avocations: alternative music, computers, dungeons and dragons, science fiction, whitewater rafting. Office: Mars Hill Coll Harris Media Ctr Mars Hill NC 28754

PAYNE, JOHN ROSS, archivist, educator, library and information scientist; b. Clarksville, Tex., Dec. 4, 1941; BA, Tex. Christian U., 1963; MLS, North Tex. State U., 1967. Successively acting dir., asst. to dir., assoc. libr. for acquisitions, assoc. libr. for ops., rsch. assoc. Harry Ransom Humanities Rsch. Ctr. U. Tex., Austin, 1969—85, prof. Grad. Sch. Libr. and Info. Sci., 1988—89, 1991—92, tchr. course in rare books and lit. manuscripts; dir. Payne Assocs., 1979—. Rare books and hist. archives appraiser. Author: A Bibliography of W. H. Hudson, 1977, Modern British Fiction: An Exhibit, 1972; co-author: (with Elizabeth Johnson) Katherine Mansfield: An Exhibit, 1973, (with Adrian Goldstone) A Bibliographical Catalogue of John Steinbeck, 1975; contbr. articles to profl. jours. Lilly fellow Ind. U., 1967-68. Mem. Manuscripts Soc., Tex. Libr. Assn., Tex. State Hist. Assn., Book Club of Tex., Tex. and Southwestern Collectors' Assn. Address: 2309 Camino Alto Austin TX 78746-2404 Office Phone: 512-328-4535. Business E-Mail: payne@payne-associates.com.

PAYNE, JOHNNY F., minister; s. Floyd and Audrey L. (Gregory) Payne. AA in Indsl. Security/Criminal Justice, CC Air Force, 1989; BA in Bible and Theology, Appalachian Bible Coll., Bradley, W.Va., 1997; postgrad., Liberty Bapt. Theol. Sem., Lynchburg, Va., 2006—. Ordained to ministry Stanford Rd. Bapt. Ch., 1997. Dept. leader Riverdale Bapt. Ch., Malboro, Md., 1989—91; youth pastor Faith Bapt. Ch., Enterprise, W.Va., 1991—93; asst. pastor Stanaford Rd. Bapt. Ch., Beckley, W.Va., 1993—97; evangelist, preacher Appalachian Bible Coll., Bradley, 1993—97, Can You Reach My Friend Ministries, 1997—2001; pastor Lac Du Flambeau Bible Bapt. Ch., Wis., 2000—01; asst. pastor Berean Bapt. Ch., Fairmont, W.Va., 2001—02; guest preacher W.Va., Ky., Va., 2002—03; tchr., guest preacher Integrity Christian Sch., Kingwood, W.Va., 2003—04; preacher W.Va., Ky., 2004—. Guest preacher, Wis., Ill., Minn., 2001. Mem. Civil Air Patrol; Sunday sch. asst. tchr., deacon Norris City Bapt. Ch., Ill., 1980—82; chapel guide, Bible study tchr. Lackland AFB, Tex., 1982—83; asst. tchr. Calvary Bapt. Ch., Anchorage, 1983—85; Sunday sch. tchr. Emmanuel Bapt. Ch., Netherlands, 1985—87; deacon Emmanuel Baptist Ch., Netherlands; evangelist Ind. Bapt. Ch., Clinton, Md., 1985—89; Bible study tchr. Andrew AFB, Md., 1985—89. With USAF, 1983—89. Decorated Joint Svc. Commendation medal, Commendation medal USAF, Two Good Conduct medals; recipient various letter and certs. of appreciation, Disabled Am. Vets., Am. Vet., Dept. Vet. Affairs Med. Ctr., others; named Hosp. Svc. Coordinator of the Yr., W.Va. Disabled Am. Vets. Republican. Office: 916 W Pike St Apt 708 Clarksburg WV 26301

PAYNE, LADELL, retired academic administrator; b. Birmingham, Ala., Dec. 6, 1933; s. Clyde Ladell and Martha Gerusia (McBrayer) P.; m. Mary Jean Taylor, Aug. 23, 1954; children: Lisa, Jennifer BA with honors, Samford U., 1955; MA in English, La. State U., 1956; PhD in English, Stanford U., 1966; LittD, Samford U., 1996; DHL, Randolph-Macon Coll., 1998. From instr. to prof. English, chmn. dept. lit. and presdl. asst. Claremont McKenna Coll., Calif., 1960-79; pres. Randolph-Macon Coll., Ashland, Va., 1979-97, prof. emeritus, 1997—, pres. emeritus, 1998—. Fulbright lectr. U. Vienna, Austria, 1971-72; nat. cons. Ctr. for Study So. Culture, U. Miss., Oxford, 1980—; adminstrv. assoc. Am. Coun. on Edn., Washington, 1979, mem. nat. panel, commn. on women in higher edn., 1981-97; founding mem. pres.'s commn. Nat. Collegiate Athletic Assn., 1984-97. Author: Thomas Wolfe, 1969, Black Novelists and the Southern Literary Tradition, 1981; contbr. articles on William Faulkner, Robert Penn Warren, Thomas Wolfe, and Ellen Glasgow to profl. jours. Mem. Va. bd. dirs. NCCJ, 1980-92, chmn. Va. region, Richmond, 1982-85; trustee, mem. exec. com. The Collegiate Schs., Richmond, 1986-89; bd. dirs. Music in the Mountains, Nevada City, Calif., 2000-02, Congregational Homes: Mt. San Antonio Gardens, Pomona, Calif., 2007—. NEH fellow, 1973. Mem. Nat. Assn. Ind. Colls. and Univs. (bd. dirs. 1990-93), Coun. on Postsecondary Accreditation (bd. dirs. 1991-93), Pi Kappa Phi, Phi Beta Kappa. Methodist. Avocation: classical music.

PAYNE, LEWIS FRANKLIN, JR., (L.F. PAYNE), management consultant, former congressman; b. Amherst, Va., July 9, 1945; m. Susan King; children: Graham, Hunter, Sara, Anna. BA in Civil Engring., Va. Mil. Inst., 1967; MBA, Darden Sch. Bus., U. Va., 1973. Lic. Engr. Chesapeake Potomac Tele. Co., 1969—71; planning devel. mgr. Wintergreen Devel., Inc., 1973—76, pres., 1976—85, chmn. bd., 1985—88; mem. US Congress from 5th Va. dist., Washington, 1988—97; pres. McGuireWoods Cons., Washington DC, 1997—. Mem. House Pub. Works Transp. Com., Veteran Affairs Com., House Budget Com., House Ways Means Com., Dem. Leadership Coun., Conservative Dem. Forum, Young Pres. Orgn., Urban Land Inst.; bd. visitors U. Virginia; bd. mem. UVA Found., Piedmont Cmty. Coll. Found.; oper. bd. U. Virginia Med. Ctr.; bd. dirs. George C. Marshall Found., Virginia Nature Conservancy, VMI Found., Patrick Henry Boys & Girls Found.; pres. Nelson County Cmty. Devel. Found.; prof. U. Va. Dept. Govt. Foreign Affairs, 2000—03; guest lectr. Darden Bus. Sch., U. Va., 1995—. Trustee Rockfish Presbyterian Ch., Nellysford, Va. First lt. US Army, 1967—69. Recipient Spirit of Enterprise award, US Chamber Congress, Guardian of Small Bus. award, Nat. Fedn. Ind. Bus., Eagle of Freedom award, Am. Security Coun. Found., Friend of Farm Bureau award, Am. Farm Bureau. Mem.: Tau Beta Pi Engring. Soc. (hon.). Democrat. Presbyterian. Office: McQuireWoods Cons Wash Sq 1050 Conn Ave NW Ste 1200 Washington DC 20036

PAYNE, MARGARET ANNE, lawyer; b. Aug. 10, 1947; d. John Hilliard and Margaret Mary (Naughton) P. Student, Trinity Coll., Washington, 1965-66; BA magna cum laude, U. Cin., 1969; JD, Harvard U., 1972; LLM in Taxation, NYU, 1976. Bar: N.Y. 1975, U.S. Dist. Ct. (so. dist.) N.Y. 1975, Calif. 1979, U.S. Dist. Ct. (so. dist.) Calif. 1979. Assoc. Mudge, Rose, Guthrie, and Alexander, NYC, 1972-75, Davis, Polk and Wardwell, NYC, 1976-78, Seltzer, Caplan, Wilkins and McMahon, San Diego, 1978-79, Higgs, Fletcher and Mack, San Diego, 1980-82, ptnr., 1983-90, of counsel, 1991—. Adj. prof. grad. tax program U. San Diego Sch. Law, 1979-89, Calif. Western Sch. Law, San Diego, 1980-82; judge pro tem Mcpl. Ct., San Diego Jud. Dist., 1983, 92. Bd. dirs. Artist Chamber Ensemble, Inc., 1983-86, Libr. Assn. La Jolla, Calif., 1983-86, San Diego County Crimestoppers, Inc., 1993-95, San Diego Crime Commn., 1994-95, St. Augustine's H.S., 1994-95, San Diego Hist. Soc., 1993-95. Mem. ABA, Calif. State Bar Assn., San Diego County Bar Assn., Mortar Bd., Guidon Soc., Charter 100, Phi Beta Kappa. Office: Higgs Fletcher & Mack 401 W A St Ste 2600 San Diego CA 92101-7913 Office Phone: 619-595-4292.

PAYNE, MARY LIBBY, retired judge; b. Gulfport, Miss., Mar. 27, 1932; d. Reece O. and Emily Augusta (Cook) Bickerstaff; m. Bobby R. Payne; children: Reece Allen, Glenn Russell. Student, Miss. U. for Women, 1950-52; BA in Polit. Sci. with distinction, U. Miss., 1954, LLB, 1955. Bar: Miss. 1955. Ptnr. Bickerstaff & Bickerstaff, Gulfport, 1955-56; sec. Guaranty Title Co., Jackson, Miss., 1957; assoc. Henley, Jones, & Henley, Jackson, Miss., 1958-61; freelance rschr. Pearl, Miss., 1961-63; solo practitioner Brandon, Miss., 1963-68; exec. dir. Miss. Judiciary Commn., Jackson, 1968-70; chief drafting & rsch. Miss. Ho. Reps., Jackson, 1970-72; asst. atty. gen. State Atty. Gen. Office, Jackson, 1972-75; founding dean, assoc. prof. Sch. Law Miss. Coll., Jackson, 1975-78, prof., 1978-94, scholar in residence, prof. emerita, 2003—; judge Miss. Ct. Appeals, Jackson, 1995—2001; ret., 2001. Mem. bd. disting. alumnae Miss. U. Women, 1988—2000. Contbr. articles to profl. jours. Founder, bd. dirs. Christian Conciliation Svc., Jackson, 1983-93; bd. dirs. Exchange Club's Child Abuse Prevention Ctr. of Jackson, 1999-2001; counsel Christian Action Com. Rankin Bapt. Assn., Pearl, 1968-92; advisor Covenant Ministerial Fellowship, 1995-2002. Recipient Book of Golden Deeds award, Pearl Exch. Club, 1989, Excellence medallion, Miss. U. Women, 1990, Woman of Yr. award, Miss. Assn. Women Higher Edn., 1989, Power of One award, Miss. Govs. Conf., 1996, Disting. Jurist award, Miss. State U., 2004, Lifetime Achievement award, Miss. Bar, 2005; named Miss. Coll. Lawyer of Yr., Miss. Coll. Sch. Law Alumni Assn., 1998, Outstanding Woman Lawyer, Miss. Women Lawyers Assn., 1999, Susie Blue Buchanan award, Women in Profession Com. of Miss. Bar, 2000. Fellow Am. Bar Found.; mem. Miss. Bar Found., Christian Legal Soc. (nat. bd. dirs. 1992-2001, Skeeter Ellis Svc. to Law Students award 1999, Lifetime Achievement award 2002). Baptist. Avocations: public speaking, travel, needlepoint, sewing, reading.

PAYNE, MICHAEL CORDELL, medical researcher; b. Cleve., July 14, 1974; s. Ida Ruth Payne; m. Tori Vales, Aug. 12, 2000; children: Jaylan Lamont, Alexis Nichole. BS, John Carroll U., University Heights, Ohio, 1999, MS, 2001. Machine gun team leader USMCR, Akron, Ohio, 1992—98; rsch. ops. mgr. Nat. Prion Disease Pathology Surveillance Ctr., Case Western Res. U. Sch. Medicine, Cleve., 2001—. Dir. Cleve. Heights Youth Football Assn., 2008—09. With USMC Ress., 1998, Akron. Rsch. scholarship, Ohio Bd. Reagents Minority. Democrat. Baptist. Avocations: sports, photography. Office: Case Western Res Univ 2085 Adelbert Rd Cleveland OH 44106 Business E-Mail: mcp9@case.edu.

PAYNE, MICHAEL DAVID, English language educator; b. Dallas, Jan. 17, 1941; s. Fred G. Payne and Jocie Marie (Kirkham) Lundberg; children: Jeffrey, Jennifer, Albert, Edward. Student, U. Calif.-Berkeley, 1958-59, 61; BA, So. Oreg. Coll., 1962; PhD, U. Oreg., 1969. Tchr. English, Medford (Oreg.) Sr. High Sch., 1962-63; instr. English, U. Oreg., Eugene, 1963-69; asst. prof. to prof. English, Bucknell U., Lewisburg, Pa., 1969—2007, chmn. dept. history, 1980-82, chmn. dept. English, 1982-88, 92-94, chair faculty, 2000—04, Presdl. prof., 1982-86, John P. Crozer prof. English lit., 1986—2006, prof. emeritus, 2007—; dir. Bucknell Univ. Press, 1972-76; assoc. editor Bucknell Rev., 1970-85, editor, 1985-88. Author: Irony in Shakespeare's Roman Plays, 1974, Reading Theory, 1993, Reading Knowledge, 1997; editor: Contemporary Essays on Style, 1969, Shakespeare: Contemporary Critical Approaches, 1979, Text, Interpretation, Theory, 1985, Self, Sign and Symbol, 1986, Perspective, 1986, Criticism, History and Intertextuality, 1987, New Interpretations of American Literature, 1987, The Senses of Stanley Cavell, 1988, Dictionary of Cultural and Critical Theory, 1996, Renaissance Literature: An Anthology, 2003, Life.after.theory, 2003, The Greenblatt Reader, 2005; gen. editor Bucknell Lectures in Lit. Theory, 1990-95. Recipient Lindback award for disting. teaching, 1976, Disting. Svc. award CEA, 1988, Profl. Achievement award, 1993; Folger Shakespeare Libr. fellow, 1973, NEH fellow, 1974, Bucknell Alumni fellow, 1978-79. Mem.: MLA, Children's Lit. Assn., Coll. English Assn., Inst. Romance Studies (U. London), Johnson Soc. London, Phi Beta Kappa (hon.). Home: 24 S Water St Lewisburg PA 17837-1562 Office Phone: 570-577-3020. E-mail: payne@bucknell.edu.

PAYNE, ROGER LEE, geographer; b. Winston-Salem, NC, Oct. 26, 1946; s. Irvin Lee and Gladys Odel (Binkley) P.; m. Sara Lucinda Parker, Aug. 16, 1970 (div. Feb. 1992); 1 child, Jennifer Nicole; m. Anne F. Remen, June 11, 1995. BA, East Carolina U., 1969, MA, 1972. Geographer, chief geog. names U.S. Geol. Survey, Reston, Va., 1974—2006; instr. geography and history Pan Am. Inst./U.S. Geog. Survey, 1989—; exec. sec. U.S. Bd. Names, U.S. Geol. Survey, Washington, 1990—2006, emeritus, 2006—. Instr. East Caroline U., Greenville, N.C., 1969-71, George Washington U., Washington, 1977-90, George Mason U., Fairfax, Va., 1979-83, 1998—2003, Benjamin Franklin U., Washington, 1985-87, Old Dominion U., 2005—; del. UN, N.Y.C., 1987—2006, instr., 1995—; mem. scientist exch. Geol. Survey, Beijing, 1989; instr. Nat. Black Colls., Howard U., 1985; book reviewer AAAS, 1975—; mem. Antarctica Sci. Field Program, 1999-2000; cons. in field. Author: Urban Development in South Africa, 1972, Place Names of Outer Banks, 1985, Manuals on Auto Names, 1987, 89, 97; coord., editor: (book series) National Gazetter U.S., 1982—; contbr. articles to profl. jours. Chmn. E. Carolina Blood Dr., Greenville, 1969. Lt. USAF, 1970-72. Recipient Guy Buzzard award Gamma Theta Upsilon, 1970; Superior Svc. award Geol. Survey, 1988, Outstanding Achievement award, 1985, 86, 88, 97, 2004. Fellow Explorers Club; mem. Assn. Am. Geographers (various coms. 1969-95, pres. mid-Atlantic divsn. 1981-82, treas., sec.), Am. Name Soc. (pres. 1989), Am. Nat. Std. Inst. (rep. 1986-2001), Cosmos Club (cons. 1986—, manuscript reviewer 1975—). Achievements include Mount Payne, Antarctica, named in his honor. Avocation: hiking. Home: 1462 Gleasons Landing Dr Saint Helena Island SC 29920 Office: US Geol Survey 523 National Ctr 12201 Sunrise Valley Dr Reston VA 20192-0523 Business E-Mail: rpayne@usgs.gov.

PAYNE, ROY STEVEN, lawyer; b. New Orleans, Aug. 30, 1952; s. Fred J. and Dorothy Julia (Peck) P.; m. Laureen Fuller, Sept. 8, 1973; children: Julie Elizabeth, Kelly Kathryn, Alex Steven, Michael Lawrence. BA with distinction, U. Va., 1974; JD, La. State U., 1977; LLM, Harvard U., 1980. Bar: La. 1977, US Dist. Ct. (we. dist.) La. 1980, US Ct. Appeals (5th cir.) 1980, US Supreme Ct. 1983. Law clk. to judge U.S. Dist. Ct., Shreveport, La., 1977-79; assoc. Blanchard, Walker, O'Quin & Roberts, Shreveport, 1980-83, ptnr., 1984-87; U.S. Magistrate judge We. Dist. La., Shreveport, 1987—2005; pvt. practice Shreveport, 2005—. Instr. New Eng. Sch. Law, Boston, 1979-80. Contbr. articles to profl. jours. Chmn. Northwest La. Legal Svcs. Assn., Shreveport, 1984-85; pres. Shreveport Bar Found., 2003-06. Mem. 5th Cir. Bar Assn., 5th Cir. Jud. Coun. (magistrate judges com. 1992-2000), La. State Bar Assn. (editl. bd. Forum jour., 1983-87, legal aid com.), Fed. Magistrate Judges Assn. (circuit dir. 2003-05), Shreveport Bar Assn. (pres. -elect 2009), La. Assn. Def. Counsel (bd. dirs. 1987), Harry V. Booth Am. Inn of Ct. (pres. elect 1994-95, pres. 1996-98), Order of Coif, Rotary, Phi Kappa Phi, Phi Delta Phi. Republican. Methodist. Home: 12494 Harts Island Rd Shreveport LA 71115-8505 Office: Gregorio Gregory & Payne 7600 Fern Ave Bldg 700 Shreveport LA 71105 Home Phone: 318-798-0814; Office Phone: 318-865-8680. Office Fax: 318-865-8565.

PAYNE, SIDNEY STEWART, retired archbishop; b. Fogo, Nfld., Can., June 6, 1932; m. Selma Carlson, 1962; children: Carla Ann, Christopher Stewart, Robert Clement, Angela Marie Louise. BA, Meml. U., St. John's, Nfld., 1958; lic. of theology, Queen's Coll., St. John's, 1958; BDiv, Gen. Synod, 1968; DDiv (hon.), King's Coll., Halifax, NS, Can., 1981. Ordained priest Anglican Ch., 1958, bishop, 1978, archbishop, 1990. Deacon Mission of Happy Valley, Goose Bay, Labrador, Nfld., Canada, 1957-65; rector Parish of Bay Roberts, Nfld., Canada, 1965-70, Parish of St. Anthony, 1970-78; bishop Diocese of Western Nfld., 1978-90, archbishop of Western Nfld. and Met. Eccles. Province of Can., 1990-97; ret., 1997. Pres. Diocesan Synod, chmn. exec. com., mem. ex-officio diocesan coms.; pres. Provincial Synod, Provincial Coun.; chair Provincial House of Bishops; mem. long range planning com., ministry com., mem. nat. exec. coun. Partners in World Mission, Stewardship and Fin. Devel. Com.; mem. Anglican/Roman Cath. Bishops' Dialogue, Can.; active Provincial and Nat. House of Bishops. Mem. Internat. Grenfell Assn. (past bd. dirs.). Anglican. Avocations: reading, walking, gardening, cross country skiing. E-mail: sspayne@nf.sympatico.ca.

PAYNE, STANLEY E., mathematics professor; b. Chgo., Sept. 26, 1939; s. Don Ivan Payne and Agnes Eileen Craven - Payne; life ptnr. Angelika Adamic; m. Shirley Ann Ellison, Aug. 22, 1961 (div. Sept. 26, 1983); children: Tanya Marie Ker, Rahn Kenneth, Brian Curtis, Brett Ivan. MS in Math., Fla. State U., Tallahassee, 1963, PhD in Math., 1966. Prof. math. Miami U., Oxford, Ohio, 1966—84, U. Colo., Denver, 1984—. Contbr. articles to profl. jours. Mem.: Inst. Combinatorics and Its Applications, Am. Math. Soc. (life). Achievements include discovery of new examples of ovals and generalised quadrangles. Office: U Colo at Denver CB 170 POBox 173364 Denver CO 80217-3364 Office Fax: 303-556-8550. Business E-Mail: stanpayne@mac.com.

PAYNE, TIMOTHY D., information technology executive; b. Oct. 25, 1958; BS, Univ. Calif., Santa Barbara, 1981. Pres., CEO Openware Technologies Inc., 1994—97; pres., COO Modis Inc., 1997—2000; pres., CEO MPS (Modis Profl. Services) Group Inc., Jacksonville, Fla., 2001—. Bd. dir. ITFlorida.com Inc. Office: MPS Group Inc 1 Independent Dr Jacksonville FL 32202

PAYNE, TYSON ELLIOTT, JR., retired insurance executive; b. Dallas, May 25, 1927; s. Tyson Elliott and Winnie Claris (Denman) P.; m. Billie Jane Spears, Aug. 28, 1948; children: David Tyson, Sally Jane. B.J., U. Tex., 1949. CLU, ChFC. Sports editor Lufkin (Tex.) News, 1949-51, Tyler (Tex.) Courier Times, 1951-53; with Am. Nat. Ins. Co., Galveston, Tex., 1953-88, v.p. health ins. ops. St. Louis, 1965-1970, v.p. mktg. Galveston, 1970-86; pvt. practice ins. agt. Austin, Tex., 1987-88; exec. v. p., dir. Sch. of Ins. & Fin. Svcs. at U. Houston, 1988-92; ret., 1992. Elder Presbyn. Ch. With USNR, 1945-46. Home: 8110 Cardin Dr Austin TX 78759-8704 Office Phone: 512-502-1903. Personal E-mail: tpaynejr1927@sbcglobal.net.

PAYNE, URSULA OCTAVIA, choreographer, educator; b. Charlotte, NC, Aug. 11, 1969; d. James Oliver and Octavia Clark Payne. BA in Dance, Slippery Rock U., Pa., 1992; MFA in Dance, Ohio State U., 1995. Cert. movement analyst Laban Bartenieff Inst. Movement Studies, N.Y., 1996. Tchr. Slippery Rock (Pa.) U., 1995—. Cons., panelist Dance Advance, Phila., 2003—; faculty Am. Dance Festival, Durham, NC, 2002—. Recipient President's Internat. Initiative award, Slippery Rock (Pa.) U., 2001, Young Alumni award, 2005; named one of Top 25 to Watch, Dance Mag.; fellow, Pa. Coun. of the Arts, 2004, 2006. Mem.: Delta Sigma Theta. Democrat. Avocations: travel, theater. Home: 1707 Highland Ave New Castle PA 16105 Office: Slippery Rock University of Pennsylvania Morrow Field House Slippery Rock PA 16057 Office Fax: 724-738-4524. Business E-Mail: ursula.payne@sru.edu.

PAYNE, VELMA L., application developer; d. Earvin A. and Harriet L. Payne. MSc in Computer Info. Sys., Robert Morris U., Pitts., 1996, MBA, 1997; attending in Biomed. Informatics, U. Pitts., 2004—. Computer programmer U. Pitts., 2005—.

PAYNE, WENDY M., federal agency administrator; BS in Commerce, U. Va. CPA NC; cert. Govt. Fin. Mgr. Auditor and expert witness for pub. staff NC Utilities Commn.; with Naval Facilities Engring. Command, Potomac Electric Power Co., Fed. Acctg. Standards Adv. Bd., 1991—, exec. dir. Mem.: Assn. Govt. Accountants, Am. Inst. CPA. Office: Fed Acctg Standards Adv Bd 441 G St NW Ste 6814 Washington DC 20548 Office Phone: 202-512-7350. Business E-Mail: PayneW@fasab.gov.*

PAYNE, WILLIAM ALBERT, JR., agronomist, educator; b. Indpls., Dec. 17, 1958; s. William and Aline Payne; married, June 30, 1984; children: Will, Matt, Ken. BA in Chemistry, Wabash Coll., 1981; MS in Soil Sci., Tex. A&M U., 1986, PhD in Soil Sci., 1990. Vol. Peace Corps, Mauritania, 1981-84; rsch. asst. Tex. A&M U., College Sta., 1984-90, postdoctoral rschr., 1990-91, assoc. prof. crop physiology Bushland, 2000—05, prof. crop physiology, 2005—; prin. scientist ICRISAT, Niger, 1991-97; asst. prof. agronomy Oreg. State U., Pendleton, 1997-2000. Assoc. editor: Agronomy Jour., 1998-; contbr. articles to profl. jours. Fellow AAAS, Am. Soc. Agronomy (chair internat. divsn. 1997-98); mem. Soil Sci. Soc. Am., Crop Sci. Soc. Am., Sigma Xi. Democrat. Achievements include work on crop water use and water-use efficiency. Office: Tex A&M U Sys Tex Agrl Exptl Sta 2301 Experiment Sta Rd Bushland TX 79012 Office Phone: 806-354-5801. Business E-Mail: w-payne@tamu.edu.

PAYNE, WILLIAM BRUCE, lawyer, director; b. Tulsa, Apr. 18, 1943; s. Marvin Ream and Audrey Arlene (Jones) P.; m. Suzanne Cooper, June 4, 1966; children: Allison, Stephanie. BS, U. Okla., 1965, JD, 1968. Bar: Minn. 1968, U.S. Dist. Ct. Minn. 1968, U.S. Ct. Appeals (8th cir.) 1968. With Dorsey & Whitney LLP, Mpls., 1968—, ptnr., 1992—2007. 1st lt. USAR, 1968—74. Mem. ABA, Minn. Bar Assn. Office: Dorsey & Whitney LLP 50 S 6th St Minneapolis MN 55402-1498 Office Phone: 612-340-2722. Office Fax: 612-340-2868. Business E-Mail: payne.bill@dorsey.com.

PAYNE, WILLIAM PORTER (BILLY PAYNE), investment company executive; b. Oct. 13, 1947; m. Martha Payne; 2 children. BA in Polit. Sci., U. Ga., 1969, JD, 1973. Atty. pvt. practice, 1973—88; pres. Olympic Organizing Com.; pres., CEO Atlanta Com. Olympic Games, 1991—97; vice chmn. NationsBank Corp., 1997—98, Bank of America, WebMD, Inc., 1998—; chmn. Orchestrate.com Premiere Techs., Inc., Atlanta, 1998—; investment banker Gleacher Ptnrs. LLC, Atlanta, 2006—; founding mem., pres. CEO Centennial Holding Co. LLC, Atlanta; chmn. Augusta Nat. Golf Club, Atlanta, 2006—. Bd. dirs. Jefferson Pilot Corp., 1993-, Cousins Properties, 1996-, Anheuser-Busch Companies Inc., 1997-, Lincoln Nat. Corp., 2006- Recipient Timmie award, Touchdown Club, Washington DC, 1990, Theodore Roosevelt awrd, NCAA, 1997, Disting. Svc. award, Martin Luther King Jr. Ctr Non-Violent Social Change, Bobby Jones award, Atlanta Area Coun. Boy Scouts America, Disting. Cmty. Svc. award, Atlanta Urban League, 11 Alive Cmty. Svc. Gov.'s award, Olympic Order in Gold; named Georgian of Yr.; named one of Top 100 Individuals in the Am. South during the 20th Century; named to Ga. Hall of Fame. Mem.: Phi Delta Theta. Office: 3050 Peachtree Rd NW Ste 475 Atlanta GA 30305 Office Phone: 404-262-3900. Office Fax: 404-262-3912.

PAYNE-JACKSON, ARVILLA CHAPIN, linguist, anthropologist, consultant; d. John Payne and Virginia Durrant; m. Roy Jackson, Oct. 24, 1990; children: Meagan Price, Michael Price. PhD, U. Pa., Phila., 1976. Prof. Howard U., DC, 1976—. Cons. various fed., state & non-profit orgns., DC, 1987—. Prodr., scriptwriter (documentary) African Roots to American Roots: A Story of Folk Medicine in America. Evaluator Comprehensive Child Devel. Program, dept. families, youth & children, DC, 1990—96, Youth Svcs. Am., DC, 1995—96, Early Head Start, dept. family, youth & children, DC, 1995—2000, Office Nat. Drug Control Policy, DC, 1997—98, US Dept. Labor, DC, 2000—04, Innovation Ctr., DC, 2001—02, Jubilee Enterprise, Inc., DC, 1992; cons. The Morris Arboretum, U. Pa., 1995; evaluator Ctr. Youth Devel. & Policy Rsch., DC, 1995, Marshall Heights Cmty. Orgn., DC, 1999—2001, HIV/Aids Rapid Assesment, HHS, DC, 2006; mem. nat. task force Reaching Out to Others Together, DC, 2007; elder & outreach com. Southminster Presbyn. Ch., Ft. Wash., Md.; bd. mem. One Ministries, DC, 1979—81, Solutions VII, Inc., DC, 2001—04, Ozziddi, DC, 2007. Recipient Outstanding Undergrad. Tchr. award, Amoco, 1990—91, Cert. Appreciation award, Edward C. Mazique Parent Child Ctr., 1999, US Surgeon Gen., 2000; grantee Planning grant, NSF, 1989—90, Rsch. grant, US AID, 1991—92, 1995—97, Tchg. Ethnographic Methods Faculty grant, Consortium Univs., 1993—94, Academic V.P.'s Faculty Rsch. Support grant, Howard U., 1995—99, Rsch. grant, NSF, 1997—98, Prince William Forest Pk. Oral History grant, US Nat. Pk. Svc., 1998—2000, Corp. Nat. Svc. grant, U. NC, 2000—01, Svc. Learning grants, Howard U., 2001—03, Prince William Forest Pk. Oral History grant, US Nat. Pk. Svc., 2004—06, Academic Excellence grant, Howard U., 2005—06; fellow Tchg. fellowship, Am. U., 1968—69; Rsch. fellowship, 1969—70, Tchg. fellowship, U. Pa., 1970—72, Rsch. fellowship, 1972—76, NSF, 1989, Sasakawa fellowship, Tokoyo Found., 2002, Cameroon Christian Women's fellowship. Fellow: Soc. Applied Anthropology; mem.: Wash. Assn. Profl. Anthropologists, Soc. Woman Geographers (exec. coun. 1990—93), Soc. Pidgin and Creole Linguistics, Soc. Caribbean Linguistics, Mid. Atlantic Coun. Latin Am. Studies (pres., v.p., exec. coun. 1990—96), Soc. Med. Anthropology, Am. Anthrop. Assn. Avocations: crocheting, travel, singing, swimming, walking. Office: Howard Univ Dept Sociology & Anthropology Douglass Hall 2441 6th St NW Rm 207 Washington DC 20059 Office Fax: 202-806-4893; Home Fax: 240-493-6448. Business E-Mail: apayne-jackson@howard.edu.

PAYRI, JOEL, pharmaceutical marketing executive; b. Sidi-Bel-Abbes, Algeria, Nov. 29, 1961; s. Rene and Marie P. DVM, Nat. Vet. Sch., Toulouse, France, 1985, diploma of anatomo-pathology, 1988; diploma of med. stats., U. Paris VI, 1989; MBA, INSEAD, Fontainebleau, France, 1991. Pvt. vet. practice, St. Gaudens, France, 1985-86; study dir. Searle Rsch. and Devel., Sophia Antipolis, France, 1986-87; head exptl. cardiology Rhone Poulenc Sante, Vitry sur Seine, France, 1988-90; mktg. mgr. Pharmuka-Rhone Poulenc, Paris, 1991-92; worldwide product mgr. Taxotere Rhone Poulenc Rorer, Paris, 1992-96; internat. mktg. dir. GlaxoSmithkline, London, 1996—2001; v.p. internat. Biogen Idec, Paris, 2001—06; v.p. Johnson & Johnson, Paris, 2006—. Surg. asst. Nat. Vet. Sch., Toulouse, 1984-85; pres. new mgmt. team Rhone Poulenc Sante, Paris, 1989-91; interviewer INSEAD MBA cands. Biogen Idec, Paris, 1995-2006. Author: Telemetry and Gastric pH Measurements, 1985 (gold medal 1985); contbr. to websites and pubs. for Internat. Herpes Alliance. Capt. French Army, 1987-90, Paris. Grantee Ministry Agr., 1985. Mem. Am. Social Health Assn., Infectious Disease Soc. Am. Office: Johnson and Johnson 1 rue Camille Desmoulins 92787 Paris France Fax: 33-147-217535. Business E-Mail: jpayri@jnjfr.jnj.com.

PAYSON, MARTIN F., lawyer; b. Bklyn., Dec. 25, 1940; m. Rhoda Shapiro, Oct. 8, 1961; children: Jacqueline, Marla. BBA, CCNY, 1961; JD, Bklyn. Law Sch., 1966. Bar: N.Y. 1967, Pa. 1989, U.S. Ct. Appeals (1st cir.) 1971, U.S. Ct. Appeals (2d and 3d cirs.) 1968, U.S. Ct. Appeals (4th cir.) 1969, U.S. Supreme Ct. 1970. Gen. ptnr. Jackson Lewis L.L.P. (formerly Jackson, Lewis, Schnitzler & Krupman), White Plains, NY, 1967—. Lectr. in field. Contbr. articles to various publs. With U.S. Army, 1961-62. Mem. N.Y. State Bar Assn. (labor and employee rels. sects.), Soc. for Human Resource Mgmt. Avocations: photography, bicycling, model railroading, gardening. Office: Jackson Lewis LLP One N Broadway White Plains NY 10601 Home Phone: 914-319-5914; Office Phone: 914-328-0404. Business E-Mail: paysonm@jacksonlewis.com.

PAYSON, MARTIN SAUL, mathematics educator; b. NYC, May 18, 1945; s. Harry and Beatrice Clare (Garber) P.; m. Joan Patricia Thompson, Sept. 11, 1969 (div. 1983); 1 child, Susan Elizabeth; m. Ilene Debbie Gellman, Apr. 10, 1983; 1 child, Howard Jeffrey. BA in Philosophy, Monmouth Coll., 1969; MS in Elem. Edn., CUNY, 1975. Tchr. math. Frederick Douglass Intermediate Sch., NYC, 1970-84, John Philip Sousa Jr. H.S., Bronx, NY, 1984—91, leader math. team, 1990—91; tchr. math. Michael Angelo Mid. Sch., Bronx, 1991—, Pub. Sch. #89, Bronx, 1998—2002; ret., 2002. Asst. head philosophy dept. Monmouth (Ill.) Coll., 1968-69. N.Y. State Edn. Dept. Regents scholar, 1963. Mem. Assn. Math. Tchrds. N.Y. State, Nat. Coun. Tchrs. Math., United Fedn. Tchrs. N.Y.C. Avocations: sports, camping, fishing, gardening, duplicate bridge. Home: 42 Chief Nimham Dr Carmel NY 10512-3624 Office: Michael Angelo Mid Sch 2545 Gunther Ave Bronx NY 10469-6105

PAYTON, GARY DWAYNE, sportscaster, retired professional basketball player; b. Oakland, Calif., July 23, 1968; m. Monique Payton; children: Raquel, Gary Dwayne, Julian. Grad., Oreg. State U., 1990. Drafted NBA, 1990; guard Seattle Supersonics, 1990—2003, Milwaukee Bucks, 2003, LA Lakers, 2003—04, Boston Celtics, 2004—05, Miami Heat, 2005—07; ret., 2007; studio analyst NBA TV, 2008—. Author: (novels) Confidence Counts, 1999. Founder Gary Payton Foundation, 1996—. Recipient Gold Medal, Atlanta Olympic Games, 1996, Sydney Olympic Games, 2000; named NBA All-Star, 1994—98, 2000—01, NBA Defensive Player of the Year, 1996; named to All-Am. 1st team, The Sporting News, 1990, NBA All-Def. 1st team, 1994—2001, All-NBA 1st team, 1998, 2000, All-NBA 2nd team, 1995—97, 1999. Office: NBA TV c/o NBA Media Ventures LLC 450 Harmon Meadow Blvd Secaucus NJ 07094

PAYTON, JOHN, legal association administrator, lawyer; b. Dec. 27, 1946; m. Gay McDougall, 1991. BA, Pomona Coll., 1973; JD, Harvard U., 1977. Bar: Calif. 1977, DC 1979. Law clk. to Hon. Cecil F. Poole US Dist. Ct., No. Dist. Calif., 1977—78; corp. counsel D.C., 1991—94; gen. litigator Wilmer, Cutler & Pickering LLP, 1978—91, ptnr., complex comml., civil rights Washington, 1994—2008, head, litig. dept., 1998—2000; pres., dir.-counsel NAACP Legal Def. & Ednl. Fund, Inc., NYC, 2008—. Vis. prof. Harvard Law Sch.; James Nabrit, Jr. vis. prof. constitutional law. Georgetown Law Ctr. Comments editor Harvard Civil Rights, Civil Liberties Law Review. Named one of Am.'s Top Black Lawyers, Black Enterprise mag., 2003, Top Lawyers in DC, Washingtonian mag., 2004, 50 Most Influential Minority Lawyers in America, Nat. Law Jour., 2008; named to Power 150, Ebony mag., 2008. Fellow: Am. Bar Found.; mem.: ABA (mem. House of Delegates 2000—02, mem. sec. on individual rights and responsibilities, mem. commn. of immigration policy), DC Pub. Defender Svc. (vice chair), Internat. Human Rights Law Group, Nat. Lawyers' Com. for Civil Rights Under Law (bd. mem., co-chair), Washington Lawyers' Com. for Civil Rights and Urban Affairs (bd. mem., co-chair), Am. Law Inst., DC Bar (pres. 2001—02). Office: NAACP Legal Def & Ednl Fund Inc 99 Hudson St Ste 1600 New York NY 10013*

PAYTON, SEAN (PATRICK SEAN PAYTON), professional football coach; b. San Mateo, Calif., Dec. 29, 1963; m. Beth Payton; children: Meghan, Connor Thomas. BS in Comm., U. Ea. Ill., 1987. Quarterback Arena Football League Chgo. Bruisers, 1987, Chgo. Bears, 1987; grad. asst. San Diego State U., 1988—89, running backs coach, 1992—93; offensive coach Ind. State U., 1990—91; quarterbacks coach, co-offensive coord. Miami U., Ohio, 1994—95; quarterbacks coach U. Ill., 1996, Phila. Eagles, 1997—98, NY Giants, 1999—2000, offensive coord., 2000—03; quarterbacks coach Dallas Cowboys, 2003, asst. head coach, offensive coord., 2004—05; head coach New Orleans Saints, 2006—. Named NFL Coach Yr., AP, 2006; named to U. Ea. Ill. Hall of Fame, 2000. Office: New Orleans Saints 5800 Airline Dr Metairie LA 70003*

PAYTON-WRIGHT, PAMELA, actress; b. Pitts., Nov. 1, 1941; d. Gordon Edgar and Eleanor Ruth (McKinley) Payton Wright; m. David Arthur Butler, May 8, 1978 (div. 1989); 1 child, Oliver Dickon Hedley. Grad., St. Mary's Jr. Coll., 1961; BA, Birmingham So. Coll., 1963; postgrad., Royal Acad. Dramatic Arts, London, 1963-65. Actress (Broadway plays) The Show-Off, 1968, Exit the King, 1968, The Cherry Orchard, 1968, Jimmy Shine, 1969, The Crucible, 1972, Mourning Becomes Electra, 1972, All Over Town, 1975, The Glass Menagerie, 1976, Romeo and Juliet, 1977, A Streetcar Named Desire, 1988, Night of the Iguana, 1988, M. Butterfly, 1988—90, Something Unspoken, 1995, Long Day's Journey Into Night, 2003, (off-Broadway) The Effect of Gamma Rays on Man-In-The Wood Marigolds, 1970—71, Jesse and the Bandit Queen, 1975, The Seagull, 1980, Don Juan, 1982, Hamlet, 1982, Mrs. Warren's Profession, 1992, The Replacement, 1995, Richard III, 'Til the Rapture Comes, 1998, What You Get and What You Expect, 2000, Fifth of July, 2003, Duet, 2004, The Day Emily Married, 2004, Indian Blood, 2006, Some Americans Abroad, 2008, Cape Disappointment, 2008, Vieux Carre, 2009, (plays) Skin of Our Teeth, 1972, Aimee, 1973, Othello, Troilus and Cressida, As You Like It, 1976, Lunch Girls, 1977, Summerfolk, 1978, The Greeks, 1982, The Misanthrope, 1982, Tobacco Road, 1984, Passion, 1984—85, Cat on a Hot Tin Roof, 1985, Little Eyolf, 1985, On the Verge, 1986, Our Town, 1987, The Road to Mecca, 1990, Picnic, 1991, The Way of the World, 1991, Quartermaine's Terms, 1993, Misalliance, 1993, Six Degrees of Separation, 1993, Ghosts, 1994, Sea Gull, 1994, The Rivals, 1996, Touch of the Poet, 1996, Glass Menagerie, 1997, Voir Dire, 1997, She Stoops to Conquer, 1997, Blithe Spirits, 1998, Transit of Venus, 1998, Sweet Bird of Youth, 1999, A Fair Country, 2000, Philadelphia Story, 2001, Seascape, 2002, Outward Bound, 2002, Hay Fever, 2005, Equus, 2005, The Learned Ladies of Park Avenue, (films) At the Dark End of the Street, 1980, Going in Style, 1981, Starlight, 1985, My Little Girl, 1985, Ironweed, 1987, The Freshman, 1989, In Dreams, 1999, Saving Face, 2004, Learned Ladies Park Avenue, 2005, Indoor Blood, 2005, Richard III, 2007, Arsenic & Old Lace, 2007, The Natch Maker, 2008, After Life, 2008. Recipient Fulbright award, 1963, Spl. medal, Edmund Gray prize for high comedy, Herbert Beerbohm Tree citation, Royal Acad. Dramatic Art, 1963—65, Obie award, 1970, 1975, 1976, Clarence Derwent award, Variety Critics' Poll citation, 1970, Drama Desk award, 1972, Best Actress citation, Dallas Theater Critics' Forum, 1994, Balt., 1997, Dean Goodman award, 1999, Joseph Jefferson award, 1996; nominee Emmy, 1972, Lucille Lortel, 2003; Fox Grant fellow, 1999. Mem.: Screen Actors Guild, AFTRA, Actors Equity Assn. Episcopalian. Office: Bauman & Assocs 1650 Broadwar Ste 1410 New York NY 10019

PAZ, GEORGE, health products executive; b. St. Louis, Aug. 27, 1955; s. Geronimo and Collen May (Hart) P.; m. Georgene Marie Wade, July 27, 1974; children: Stacy, Kelly, Rebecca. BSBA, U. Mo., St. Louis, 1982. CPA, Mo. Jr. acct. Gen. Am., St. Louis, 1980-82, sr. acct., 1982-83, acctg. adminstr., 1983-85, tax planning analyst, 1985-87, dir. tax planning, 1987; ptnr. Coopers & Lybrand, 1988—93, 1996—98; exec. v.p., CFO Life Ptnrs. Group, 1993—95; sr. v.p., CFO Express Scripts Inc., St. Louis, 1998—2003, pres., 2003—, bd. dirs., 2004—, CEO, 2005—, chmn., 2006—. Bd. dirs. Gen. Am. Employees Fed. Credit Union, 1985. Fellow Life Office Mgmt. Assn.; mem. AICPA, Mo. Soc. CPA, Pharm. Care Mgmt. Assn. Lutheran. Avocations: golf, running, softball. Office: Express Scripts Inc 13900 Riverport Dr Maryland Heights MO 63043 Office Phone: 314-770-1666. Office Fax: 314-702-7037.*

PAZ, HAROLD LOUIS, hospital administrator, internist, educator; b. NYC, Jan. 3, 1955; BA in Biology and Psychology, U. Rochester, 1977, MD, 1982; MS in Life Sci. Engring., Tufts U., 1979. Diplomate subspecialty in pulmonary medicine Am. Bd. Internal Medicine. Intern in internal medicine Northwestern U. Med. Ctr., Chgo., 1982—83, resident in internal medicine, 1983—85, chief med. resident, 1985—86; instr. clin. medicine Northwestern U., Chgo., 1985—86; fellow in pulmonary and critical care Johns Hopkins U., Balt., 1986—88, fellow in environ. health scis., 1986—88; asst. prof. medicine Hahnemann U., Phila., 1988—92, asst. prof. anesthesia, 1989—92, assoc. dean grad. med. edn., 1992—94, assoc. prof. medicine, 1992—94, dir. med. ICU, 1988—94, assoc. hosp. med. dir., 1992—94, dir. Ctr. for Clin. Outcomes, 1992—94; med. dir., assoc. dean for clin. affairs U. Medicine and Dentistry NJ Robert Wood Johnson Med. Sch., New Brunswick, 1994—95, assoc. prof. medicine, 1994—2003, dean, 1995—2006, CEO, 1995—2006, prof. medicine, 2003—06; CEO Penn State Milton S. Hershey Med. Ctr., 2006—; dean Penn State Coll. of Medicine, 2006—, sr. V.P. Health Affairs, 2006—. Editor: Jour. Undergrad. Rsch., 1976, Med. Staff News newsletter, 1992—94; cons.: Annals Internal Medicine, Clin. Immunology and Immunopathology, Chest, Intensive Care Medicine, Physician Execs., NY State Med. Jour., mem. editl. bd.: Jour. Disease Mgmt. and Clin. Outcomes, 1996—, Chest, 1998—2003. Recipient Disting. Svc. award, Motolinsky Rsch. Found., 1998, Cmty. Leaders of Distinction award, County C. of C., 1999, Sir William Osler Humanitarian award, 2005, Hon. Alumni award, UMDNJ-Robert Wood Johnson Med. Sch. Alumni Assn., 2005, Alumni Merit award, Northeastern U. Alumni Assn., 2007; named to Gold Humanism Honor Soc., 2005; Eudowood fellow, Johns Hopkins U., 1987—88, U. Rochester scholar, 1979. Fellow: ACP, Am. Coll. Chest Physicians; mem.: AMA, Laennec Soc. (pres. 1994—95), Philip Drinker Soc. for Critical Care (pres. 1992—94), Am. Thoracic Soc. Office: Penn State Hershey Med Ctr 500 University Dr Hershey PA 17033 Office Phone: 717-531-8323.

PAZ, MARCELO, literature and language professor; b. Buenos Aires, Feb. 16, 1961; s. Cristoforo de Jesus and Stella Maris Paz; m. Elizabeth Anne Wing; children: Luca Santiago, Paloma Leah. MA, U. Cin., Ohio, 1988, PhD, 1996. Lic. in abogacia procuracion U. Buenos Aires, 1986. Lectr. Notre Dame de Namur U., Belmont, Calif., 1996—99; asst. prof. U. Evansville, Ind., 1999—2001; assoc. prof. Calif. State U., East Bay, Hayward, Calif., 2001—. Editl. bd. mem. Cin. Romance Rev., Cin., 2000—04; peer rev. com. mem. Brujula: Revista Intedisciplinaria Sobre Estudios Latinoamericanos, Davis, Calif.; spanish reader Ednl. Testing Services, 2003—. Contbr. articles to profl. jours. Mem.: Latin Am. Studies Assn. Home: 2362 Cedar St Berkeley CA 94708 Office: CA State Univ E Bay 25800Carlos Bee Boulevard Hayward CA 94542-3038 Office Fax: 510-885-7797.

PAZAK, JOHN STEPHEN, bishop; b. Gary, Ind., Aug. 13, 1946; Ordained priest Congregation of the Most Holy Redeemer, 1972; ordained bishop, 2001; bishop Eparchy Saints Cyril and Methodius of Toronto (Slovakian), 2001—. Roman Catholic. Office: Eparch for the Byzantine Rite Slovaks in Can 223 Carlton Rd Unionville ON L3R 3M2 Canada

PAZDON, MELISSA JOANN, school psychologist; b. Rochester, NH, Apr. 20, 1974; d. John Joseph and Denise Joan Pazdon; m. Jeff William Symes, Sept. 8, 2007. Magna Cum Laude, Granite State Coll., 2006; MS in Edn., Southern NH U., 2008. Rehabilitative asst. North Hampton Sch., 2004—06; sch. psychologist Pittsfield Sch. Dist., NH, 2008—. Musician: (vocalist) Pazdon & Symes. Office: Pittsfield Sch Dist 34 Bow St Pittsfield NH 03263

PAZ-FILHO, GILBERTO JORGE, endocrinologist; b. Curitiba, Parana, Brazil, June 9, 1977; s. Gilberto and Mirian Paz. MD, U. Fed. do Parana, Curitiba, 2001. Cert. master in internal medicine UFPR, 2006. Postdoc. rsch. fellowship dept. psychiatry Ctr. Pharmacogenomics, U. Miami, 2006—. Recipient Travel award, Latin Am. Thyroid Soc., 2005, Internat. Soc. Endocrinology, 2008. Mem.: AAAS, Brazilian Soc. Endocrinology, Endocrine Soc. Achievements include research in radioiodine treatment triggers security alarms,recombinant human TSH use in differentiated thyroid cancer,effects of leptin replacement on risk factors for cardiovascular disease in genetically leptin-deficient subjects. Personal E-mail: g.paz@uol.com.br.

PAZNOKAS, LYNDA SYLVIA, elementary school educator; b. Portland, Oreg., Feb. 19, 1950; d. Marley Elmo and Undine Sylvia (Crockard) Sims. BA, Wash. State U., Pullman, 1972; MS, Portland State U., Oreg., 1975; EdD, Oreg. State U., Corvallis, 1984. Cert. tchr. Oreg. Tchr. 5th grade, outdoor sch. specialist Clover Park Sch. Dist. 400, Tacoma, 1971-72; tchr. 6th grade, outdoor sch. specialist Hillsboro Elem. Dist. 7, Oreg., 1972-78, Bend-La Pine Sch. Dist., Oreg., 1978-82, elem. curriculum specialist Oreg., 1983-85, tchr. 4th grade gifted and talented Oreg., 1985-90; grad. teaching asst. Oreg. State U., Corvallis, 1982-84; asst. prof., assoc. prof. No. Ariz. U., 1990-99, chair instnl. leadership, 1997-98; Boeing disting. prof. sci. edn. Wash. State U., Pullman, 1999—2008, assoc. dean sch. and cmty. collaboration, 2006—08, prof. emeritus, 2008—. Ednl. cons., tchr. workshops, 1973—; presenter workshop Soviet-Am. Joint Conf., Moscow State U., 1991, Meeting of Children's Culture Promoters, Guadalajara, Mex., 1994, internat. conf. Sci., Tech. and Math. Edn. for Human Devel., UNESCO, Panaji, India, 2001, Nishinomiya Joint Rsch. Conf., Japan, 2001, internat. workshop Promoting Sci. and Tech. Literacy Through Sci. Toys & Out-of-Sch. Sci. Activities, Pattaya, Thailand, 2005, Scientifically Literate Students as World Citizens, Singapore, 2006, World Environ. Edn. Congress, Durban, South Africa, 2007, Internat. Workshop Innovative Sci. Tchg., Guilin, China, 2007, regional coord., E3 Washington, State Environ. Planning Process, others; faculty Ariz. Journey Schs. for Math. and Sci. Tchg. Improvement; coord. Odyssey of the Mind, Bend, 1985-89, tchr. mentor program for 1st yr. tchrs., Beaverton, Oreg., 1982-83; reviewer Sci. Books and Films AAAS, 1992-2006; presenter Social Edn. Assn. of Australia, 1997, Nat. State Tchrs. of Yr., Guam, 2005; steering com. Wash. LASER (Leadership and Assistance for Sci. Edn. Reform), 2002—, mem. sci. drafting team sci. curriculum instrnl. frameworks; mem. Nat. Ecol. Obs. Network Design Consortium. Author: Pathways of America: Lewis and Clark, 1993, Pathways of America: The Oregon Trail, 1993, Pathways of America: The California Gold Rush Trail, 1994, Pathways of America: The Santa Fe Trail, 1995, Fifty States, 1997, U.S. Presidents, 1997, U.S. Map Skills, 1997, Human body, 1998, National Parks and Other Park Service Sites, 1999, Our National Parks, 1999, Pathways of America: The California Mission Trail, 2000, Circling the World: Festivals and Celebrations, 2000, Endangered Species, 2001; mem. adv. bd. (jour.) Sci. and Children; contbr. articles to profl. jours.; reviewer Turkish Jour. Sci. Edn. Vol., leader, bd. dirs. Girl Scouts US, 1957—; elder First Presbyn. Ch., Bend, 1980—; vol. hist. interpretation High Desert Mus., Bend, 1987-91; docent Mus. No. Ariz.; pres. bd. dirs. The Arboretum at Flagstaff; former sec. and v.p. bd. dirs. Palouse Discovery Sci. Ctr. (pres. bd. dirs.); past pres. Arboretum bd.; mem. Ptnrs. Achieving Leadership in Sci., Wash., DC, Leadership and Assistance for Sci. Edn. Reform, Wash., DC. Recipient Excellence in Teaching award Bend Found., 1985-86, 86-87; named Tchr. Yr. Oreg. Dept. Edn., 1982, Higher Edn. Tchr. Yr., Wash. Sci. Tchrs. Assn. (WSTA), 2003; Celebration Teaching grantee Geraldine Rockefeller Dodge Found., 1989, 90, 91, 92, 93, 94, 95, EPA grantee, 1997-99, 2006-, Eisenhower Math and Sci. Edn. Act grantee, 1997, 99, Grand Canyon Assn. grantee, 1996, 97, 98; commd. Ky. Col., 1993, US Fish & Wildlife grant, Pre svc. Tchrs. & Wash. Colls. & U., 2006. Mem. NEA, Internat. Coun. Assns. Sci. Edn. (chair pre-secondary and informal sci. edn. of the exec. com. 2004—08, editor Stepping Into Sci. Internat. Quar. jour. 2004—08, jour/ advisor), Nat. Coun. Tchrs. Math., NSTA (past mem. nat. supervision com., internat. com., mem. sci. and children bd.), Nat. State Tchrs. of Yr. (nat. pres. 1988-90), Nat. Assn. Rsch. in Sci. Tchg., Oreg. Coun. Tchrs. Math. (bd. dirs. 1981-82), Oreg. Coun. Tchrs. English (bd. dirs. 1981-82), Ariz. Reading Assn. (bd. dirs.), Nat. Coun. for Social Studies, Coun. for Elem. Sci. Internat. (bd. dirs. 1995-98, 99—2003, chair informal edn. com.), Internat. Reading Assn., Oreg.-Calif. Trails Assn., Nat. Sci. Edn. Leadership Assn., Assn. for Sci. Tchr. Edn., Sch. Sci. and Math. Assn. (publs. com.), Nat. Assn. for Rsch. in Sci. Tchg., Assn. for Sci. Edn., Wash. Sci. Tchrs. Assn. (higher edn. rep. bd. dirs. 2004—, co-chair WSTA-Wash. Orgn. for Reading Devel. Joint Conf., 2006, conf. chair, 2009, EPA grant 2008-09, PEEP EPA grant, 2006-08), N.W. Oreg.-Calif. Trails Assn., Lewis and Clark Trail Heritage Found., PEO (past corr. sec.), Delta Kappa Gamma (1st v.p.), Phi Delta Kappa (found. rep. 1991-92, v.p. programs 1992-93, historian 1993-94, v.p. membership 1994-95), Golden Key Hon., Pi Lambda Theta, Phi Kappa Phi, Kappa Delta Pi (chpt. counselor, mem. spkrs. bur., nat. Web com., sci. specialist), others. Avocations: cross country skiing, photography, hiking, researching immigrant trails, gardening. Home: 101 Enman-Kincaid Rd Pullman WA 99163

PEABODY, ARLENE L. HOWLAND BAYAR, retired enterostomal therapy nurse; b. Deposit, NY, June 26, 1931; d. Burt and Olive (Oralls) Howland; m. Atilla C. Bayar, Dec. 8, 1956 (div.); m. Norman R. Peabody, Feb. 1, 1975 (dec.); children: Tildy Anne Bayar Sparrow, Carol A. Digilio; m. Robert A. Ehlers, Feb. 15, 2003. Diploma, Ridley's Sec. Sch., Binghamton, NY, 1949, Binghamton Sch. Practical Nursing, 1970, Harrisburg Hosp. Sch. Enterostomal Therapy, Pa., 1971; AAS, Empire State Coll., Saratoga Springs, NY, 1985; BS in Edn., SUNY, Oneonta, 1990. RN, N.Y.; cert. therapeutic touch practitioner, natural force healing practitioner, enterostomal nurse. Sec. pres.'s office Cornell U., Ithaca, NY, 1949—55; exec. sec. Rudolph Lang, Office Execs. Assn. N.Y. and Prestige Expositions Inc., NYC, 1955—69; enterostomal therapy nurse M.I. Bassett Hosp., Cooperstown, NY, 1972—89; pvt. practice enterostomal therapy nurse Oneonta, NY, 1989—2002. Spkr. in field. Vol. Am. Cancer Soc., 1972-2002, Catskill Area Hospice, 1990-02, Glimmerglass Opera, 1975-2002; bd. dirs. Del. Heritage Inc., 1996-2002; trustee Unitarian Universalist Soc.; active Storytelling Ctr. of Oneonta, Oneonta Concert Assn., Oneonta Contradance. Mem. AARP (bd. dirs. 1986-2002), N.Y. State Hist. Assn., Delaware County Hist. Soc., Wound Ostomy and Continence Nurses Soc., United Ostomy Assn. (N.Y. state field svcs. rep.), Order Ea. Star. Avocations: heirloom quilting, traditional folk music, coutourier clothing, costuming, dance. Home: 13511 Pebblebrook Dr Houston TX 77079-6023 Home Phone: 713-467-7191.

PEABODY, DOSSY, performing arts educator, actor; d. George Cabot and Nancy Kunhardt Lodge; children: Abigail, Charles. BA, Harvard U., Cambridge, 1974. Actor Gloucester Stage Co., Mass., 1980—88; acting faculty - dept. performing arts Emerson Coll., Boston, 1999—2008. Actor: The Widow's Blind Date (Elliot Norton Critics award for Outstanding Actress, 1990). Recipient Outstanding Tchr. award, Emerson Coll., Boston, 2008. Personal E-mail: dossypeabody@gmail.com.

PEABODY, LAURA S., lawyer, insurance company executive; b. 1958; m. Robert Peabody, 1986. BA, SUNY, Binghamton; JD, Boston U. Sr. v.p., gen. counsel Harvard Pilgrim Health Care, Wellesley, Mass. Mem. New England Chpt. Bd. US Found. for UNICEF, 2005—. Mem.: Mass. Women's Bar Found. Office: Harvard Pilgrim Health Care 93 Worcester St Wellesley Hills MA 02481 E-mail: laura_peabody@hphc.org.*

PEACE, BERNIE KINZEL, art educator, artist; b. Williamsburg, Ky., Oct. 20, 1933; s. Edgar and Ida M. (Miller) P.; m. Sylvia A. Hitchcock, Dec. 19, 1956; children: Anthony P., Tracy A. Peace-Gantzer. AB in Art, Berea Coll., 1954; MFA in Painting, Ind. U., 1957. Prof. art West Liberty (W.Va.) State Coll., 1960-95, prof. emeritus, 1995—. Invitee arts and letters series Gov.'s Mansion, 1993. One-man shows include Oglebay Inst., Wheeling, W.Va., 1963, Washington & Jefferson Coll., Washington, Pa., 1968, Huntington (W.Va.) Galleries, 1969, W.Va. U., Morgantown, 1971, Weirton (W.Va.) Community Ctr., 1973, N.E. Mo. State U., Kirksville, 1987, Mus. Fine Arts, Oak Ridge, Tenn., 1988, The Art Store, Charleston, W.Va., 1992; group shows include Ky. State Fair, Louisville, 1960, Upper Ohio Valley Art Show, Wheeling, 1961, Grove City (Pa.) Coll. Invitational, 1962, 63, Bethany (W.Va.) Coll. Art Exhbn., 1963, 68, Steubenville (Ohio) Art Assn. Ann. Exhibit, 1964, 65, 69, 88, 91, Mint Mus. Art., Charlotte, N.C., 1967, 70, 71, Butler Inst. Am. Art, Youngstown, Ohio, 1967, Charleston (W.Va.) Art Gallery, 1970, 71, 72, 74, 77, Westmoreland County Mus. Art, Greensburg, Pa., 1970, 71, 74, Purdue U., 1972, New Orleans Mus. Art, 1973, Richard Hackett Galleries, Parkersville, W.Va., 1974, Pitts. Watercolor Soc., 1974, 75, The Country Studio, Hadley, Pa., 1976, 3-Rivers Arts Festival, Pitts., 1976, Upshur County Ctr. Creative Arts, Buckhannon, W.Va., 1976, Erie Art Ctr., 1977, Wayne County Arts Coun., Ceredo, W.Va., 1978, Delf Norona Mus., Moundsville, W.Va., 1979, Stifel Fine Arts Ctr., Wheeling, W.Va., 1979-80, 83-85, 88-89, 91-93, Gallery G, Pitts., 1979, 42d Ann. Exhbn. Contemporary Am. Paintings, Palm Beach, 1980, Nat. Competitive Exhbn. Painting and Sculpture, 1981, Owensboro (Ky.) Mus. Art, 1982, Art Store Gallery, Charleston, 1984, 90-93, Cultural Ctr., Charleston, 1985, 87, 89, 93, W.Va. State Coll., 1986, 87, Washington & Jefferson Coll., Washington, Pa., 1991, Sunrise Mus. Downtown, Charleston, 1991, USX Bldg. Lobby Tower, Pitts., 1992, 93, State Capitol Bldg., Charleston, 1993, West Liberty State Coll., 1995, 2002, 2005 (Purchase award, 2002, Cert. Excellence, 2005), Wheeling Area Photography Club, 2003, 2004, (Fine Arts award, 2003, 2004). With U.S. Army, 1957-60. Recipient numerous awards including 1st prize Steubenville Art Assn., 1965, Grumbacher Medal of Merit, 1989, 92, Albert and Jane Wilson Meml. award, 1993, Best of Show award Upper Ohio Valley Art Show, Wheeling, 1967, 82, award State W.Va. Permanent Collection, 1972, Judges' Choice award Bethany Coll. Fall Ann., 1976, Best of Show award, 1991, award of Excellence Allied Artists of W.Va., 1990. Mem. Allied Artists of W.Va., Silver Eye Ctr. Photography. Avocations: backgammon, walking. Home: 1214 Washington Farms Wheeling WV 26003

PEACE, H. W., II, small business owner, retired oil industry executive; b. Clinton, Okla., May 21, 1935; s. Herman Wilbern and Bernice (Mitchell) P.; m. Norma June Williams; children: Hugh William, Susannah Lee. BS in Geology, U. Okla., 1959, MS in Geology, 1964; postgrad., U. S.W. La., 1968. Jr. geologist Union Oil Co. Calif., Houston, 1964-65, area geologist Lafayette, La., 1965-70, geologist dist. exploration Oklahoma City, 1970-77, mgr. Rocky Mountain exploration Casper, Wyo., 1977-80; mgr. divsn. exploration Cotton Petroleum Corp., Tulsa, 1980-83; v.p. exploration Hadson Petroleum Corp., Oklahoma City, 1983-85, exec. v.p., COO, 1985-88, also bd. dirs.; exec. v.p., COO Mosswood Oil and Gas Co., Oklahoma City, 1985-88, Anadarko Supply Co., Oklahoma City, 1986-88, also bd. dirs.; mng. ptnr. EXAD, Oklahoma City, 1988-91, owner, 2006—; pres., CEO, dir. Panhandle Royalty Co., Oklahoma City, 1991—2006; pres., CEO Wood Oil Co. subs. Panhandle Royalty Co., 2001—06. Mgmt. com. PLC Energy Data, LLC, 1994—2001; bd. dirs. OIL Law Recs. Corp., chmn. bd. dirs., 2006—; bd. dir. Farmers Royalty Co., 2009—, Energy Lib. Online, 2008—. Dir. sch. geology adv. com. U. Okla., Norman, 1984—, vice chmn. 1988-89, chmn. 1989-90, 2006-, exec. com. 1990—. Lt. USN 1959-63, capt. USNR, 1963-82, ret. list 1995. Mem. Am. Assn. Petroleum Geology (rep. del. or alt. 1984—), Soc. Exploration Geophysicists, Soc. Econ. Paleontologists and Mineralogists, Petroleum Assn. Wyo. (v.p. 1979-80), Tulsa Geol. Soc., Oklahoma City Geol. Soc. (chmn. profl. affairs 1976-77, rep. to mid. continent sec. 2007—), Naval Res. Assn., Cherokee Hills Homeowners Assn. (pres. 1971-73), Fieldstone Homeowners Assn. (pres. 1983), Navy League, Okla. Corp. Commn. (royalty adv. com. 1998—), Okla. Nat. Royalty Owners (assoc.)(bd. dirs. 2006—, pres, 2007—), Rotary. Republican. Avocations: golf, swimming, hiking. Office: EXAD Bradley Sq Ste 22 2932 NW 122d St Oklahoma City OK 73120

PEACHER, GEORGIANA MELICENT, poet, educator; b. Syracuse, NY, Nov. 13, 1919; d. William Catlett and Georgiana (Ruckman) P. BS, Syracuse U., 1941, MS, 1943; PhD, Northwestern U., 1946; MFA, Vt. Coll., 1996. Fellow Northwestern U., 1943-45; dir. speech therapy Neuro-Phys. Rehab. Clinic, Phila., 1946-47; prof. speech pathology and psychology Temple U. Med. Sch., Phila., 1948-67; dir. speech therapy N.Y. Hosp., Cornell U., NYC, 1953-56; ind. rschr. various cities, Russia, Eng., Scotland, 1967-75, C.G. Jung Inst., Zürich, Switzerland, 1975-76; prof. speech and psychology John Jay Coll. CUNY, 1976-90; prof. emerita John Jay Coll. CUNY, 1990—; pres. Pearl Shedding Press, Brunswick, Maine, 1990—. Exhibitor AMA, 1960, Am. Speech and Hearing Assn., 1961. Author: How to Improve Your Speaking Voice, 1966, Folio One: Mesmerists, 1971, Folio Two: Trance Duet, 1972, Folio Three: Thin Wind, 1972, Mary Stuart's Ravishment Descending Time, 1976, Folio Four: Thunder Wonder, 1983, Speak to Win, 1985, The Skryabin Mysterium, 2004, (plays) Hatshepsut, 1982, (poetry) Elizabeth of Mariana, 1992 (Eva LeFevre French-form award); exhibitions include Pa. Acad. Fine Arts, 1961, Portland Mus. of Art, 2001, Maine Coll. Art, 2002, Thornton Oaks, 2004, Bowdoin Coll., 2004, U. So. Maine, 2005, Portland Pub. Libr., 2006, Maine Coll. Art, 2007, Thornton Oaks, 2008; contbr. articles to profl. jours. Grantee for performance of Indira India, CUNY, 1988-89, Pharoah Hatshepsut, 1981. Fellow: Am. Speech Hearing Lang. Assn.; mem.: AAAS, APA, Am. Soc. Clin. Hypnosis, Dramatists Guild, Baxter Soc. (sec. 1991—93, pres. 1996—97). Democrat. Avocations: painting, sculpting, book design. Home and Office: 25 Thornton Way Apt 125 Brunswick ME 04011-3282

PEACHEY, LEE DEBORDE, biology professor; b. Rochester, NY, Apr. 14, 1932; s. Clarence Henry and Eunice (DeBorde) P.; m. Helen Pauline Fuchs, June 7, 1958; children: Michael Stephen, Sarah Elizabeth Keating, Anne Palmer Lorenz. BS, Lehigh U., 1953; postgrad., U. Rochester, 1953-56; PhD (Leitz fellow), Rockefeller U., 1959; MA (hon.), U. Pa., 1971. Research asso. Rockefeller U., 1959-60; asst. prof. zoology Columbia U., 1960-63, asso. prof., 1963-65; asso. prof. biochemistry and biophysics U. Pa., Phila., 1965-70, prof. biology, 1970-2000, prof. emeritus, 2000—; adj. prof. molecular, cellular and developmental biology U. Colo., 1969-84; mem. molecular biology study sect. NIH, 1969-73. Internat. vis. prof. Ministry Edn., Sci. and Culture Gunma (Japan) U. Med. Sch., Maebashi, 1992-95; biomed. rsch. tech. rev. com. NIH, 1994-2000; mem. Mayor's Sci. and Tech. Adv. Coun., Phila., 1972-80; chmn. Gordon Rsch. Conf. on Muscle, 1983; ext. evaluation com. Nat. Inst. Physiol. Sci., Okazaki, Japan, 1997; cons. Leica Microsystems, 2002—. Editor: Third and Fourth Conferences on Cellular Dynamics, N.Y. Acad. Scis., 1967, First and Second Confs. on Cellular Dynamics, 1968, Am. Physiol. Soc. Handbook on Skeletal Muscle, 1983; mem. editl. bd. Tissue and Cell, 1969—, Jour. Cell Biology, 1970-73, Pitman Series in Cellular and Development Biology, 1977-2000, Microscopy Rsch. and Technique, 1982-93, Advances in Optical and Electron Microscopy, 1983—, Neuroimage, 1991—95, Jour. Microscopy, 1992-96, Bioimages, 1993—; contbr. articles to profl. jours. Trustee Keith R. Porter Endowment for Cell Biology, Merion Station, Pa., 1981—2004 Guggenheim and Fulbright-Hays fellow, 1967-68, Overseas fellow Churchill Coll., Cambridge, Eng., 1967-68, Fogarty Sr. Internat. fellow, 1979-80, hon. rsch. fellow U. Coll., London, 1979-80; Royal Soc. (London) guest rsch. fellow, Cambridge, 1986; grantee NSF, 1960-72, NIH, 1973-2002, Muscular Dystrophy Assn. Am., Inc. 1973-91. Fellow AAAS, Electron Microscopy Soc. Am. (council 1975-78, pres. 1982), Am. Soc. Cell Biology (program chmn. 1965, coun. 1966-69), Biophys. Soc. (program chmn. 1976, coun. 1976-80, exec. com. 1976-82, pres. 1981-82), Internat. Union Pure and Applied Biophysics (coun. 1978-84, v.p. 1984-87, pres. 1987-90, chmn. commn. on cell and membrane biophysics 1981-84, hon. v.p. 1990-93), Physiol. Soc. (Eng.).; mem. Internat. Soc. Stereology (internat. stereology software com. 1982-94), Soc. Gen. Physiologists. Achievements include research in mechanisms of muscle cell contraction; development of methods in light and electron microscopy; development of computer graphic methods for three-dimensional image analysis and reconstruction. Home: 524 Revere Rd Merion Station PA 19066-1033 Office: U Pa Dept Biology Philadelphia PA 19104-6018 Home Phone: 610-664-0478; Office Phone: 215-898-5788. Business E-Mail: lpeachey@sas.upenn.edu.

PEACOCK, A(LVIN) WARD, textile company executive; b. Durham, NC, June 17, 1929; s. Erle Ewart and Vera Louise (Ward) P.; m. Barbara Sheppard White, July 2, 1955; children: Alvin Ward, Stephen White, Nancy Lay. BS in Commerce, U. N.C., 1950; MBA, Harvard U., 1952. Asst. to v.p. Erwin Mills, Inc., Durham, 1953-55, sec., 1957-62, sec.-treas., 1962-64; v.p. Dixie Yarns, Inc., Chattanooga, 1964-76, sr. v.p., 1976-81, Springs Industries, Fort Mill, SC, 1981-86, exec. v.p., 1986-92. Bd. dirs. Palmetto Seed Capital Corp.; regional dir. First Wachovia Corp., Charlotte, N.C., 1988-92. Trustee Holston Conf. Colls., Tenn., 1968-79, Sci. Mus. Charlotte, 1990-94; bd. dirs. Chattanooga Meml. Hosp., 1979-81, Charlotte Symphony, 1990-94, Greater Carolinas chpt. ARC, 1988-94; dir. Allied Arts Fund, 1978-81, Metrolina Food Bank, 1994-2003; mem. Chattanooga Wastewater Regulation Bd., 1978-81. 1st lt. USAF, 1955-57. Mem. Tenn. Mfrs. Assn. (chmn. bd. dirs. 1980-81), Chattanooga Mfrs. Assn. (pres. 1968-69), Am. Textile Mfrs. Inst., Univ. Club, River Hills Club, Phi Beta Kappa, Alpha Kappa Psi, Sigma Nu. Republican. Methodist. Home: 3800 Shamrock Dr Charlotte NC 28215

PEACOCK, DAVID A., brewery company executive; BA in Journalism, Kansas U., 1990; MBA, Washington U., St. Louis. Joined Anheuser-Busch Cos., Inc., St. Louis, 1992, various bus. ops., wholesaler rels., sales promotion and strategic planning positions, dir. ops. pres. office, 2002—04, v.p. adminstrn., 2004—06, v.p. bus./fin. ops., 2006, v.p. bus. ops., 2006—07, v.p. mktg., 2007—08, pres., 2008—. Mem. Anheuser-Busch Strategy Com. Named a Power Player, Advt. Age, 2008. Office: Anheuser Busch Cos Inc Hdqs One Busch Place Saint Louis MO 63118 Business E-Mail: dave.peacock@anheuser-busch.com.*

PEACOCK, ERLE EWART, JR., surgeon, lawyer, educator; b. Durham, NC, Sept. 10, 1926; s. Erle Ewart and Vera Louise (Ward) P.; m. Mary Louise Lowrey, Apr. 17, 1954; children: James Lowrey, Susan Louise, Virginia Gayle. Cert. in Medicine, U. N.C., 1947, BS, 1990, JD, 1999; MD, Harvard U., 1949. Bar: N.C. 1993. Intern, asst. resident surgery Roosevelt Hosp., NYC, 1949-51; from asst. resident gen. surgery U. N.C. Hosps., Chapel Hill, 1953-54, chief resident gen. surgery, 1954-55; resident in plastic surgery Barnes Hosp., St. Louis, 1955-56; mem. faculty dept. surgery U. N.C., Chapel Hill, 1956-69, prof. surgery, head divsn. plastic surgery, 1965-69; prof., chmn. dept. surgery U. Ariz., Tucson, 1969-77; prof. surgery Tulane U., New Orleans, 1977-82; pvt. practice surgery Chapel Hill, 1982-93; vis. prof. surgery U. Va., Charlottesville, 1988-97; clin. prof. surgery U. N.C., Chapel Hill, 1996—. Chief hand surgery Valley Forge Army Hosp., Phoenixville, Pa., 1951-53. Author: Wound Repair, 1977, 3d edit., 1982; assoc. editor: Am. Jour. Surgery, 1967—, Surgery Yearbook, 1970-89, Plastic and Reconstructive Surgery, 1972-78; asst. editor: Jour. Surg. Rsch., 1970-76. Served with U.S. Navy, 1945-46; served to capt. M.C. U.S. Army, 1951-53. Recipient Yandell medal Louisville Surg. Soc., 1972, McGraw medal Detroit Surg. Soc., 1973, Disting. Svc. award U. N.C., 1979, Jacob Markowitz award Acad. Surg. Rsch., 1993, Lifetime Achievement award Wound Healing Soc., 1994. Mem. AAAS, ACS, ABA, Womack Sur. Soc. (pres. 1979-80), Soc. U. Surgeons (treas. 1965-68), Plastic Surgery Rsch. Coun. (pres. 1966), Am. Surg. Assn., Am. Bd. Plastic Surgery (pres. 1976), Am. Bd. Gen. Surgery, Am. Assn. Plastic Surgeons (Clinician of Yr. 1985), Am. Soc. Surgery Hand, Internat. Soc. Surgeons, So. Surg. Assn., Am. Coll. Legal Medicine, Rotary, Alpha Omega Alpha. Republican. Methodist. Home and Office: 645 Rock Creek Rd Chapel Hill NC 27514-6714 Home Phone: 919-967-0347. E-mail: eepeacockmd@aol.com.

PEACOCK, GEORGE ROWATT, retired life insurance company executive; b. Lakeland, Fla., Aug. 27, 1923; s. Robert and Annie Keane (Rowatt) P.; m. Virginia Jenkins, June 7, 1952; 1 child, Robert George. BA, U. Fla., 1948, postgrad., 1948-49, U. N.C., 1949-50, 51, Ind. U., summers 1966, 67. With Equitable Life Assurance Soc. U.S., 1952-88, v.p., head real estate dept. NYC, 1974-77, sr. v.p., head equities sector, 1977-80, sr. v.p., head real estate sector, 1980-84; chmn., chief exec. Equitable Real Estate Investment Mgmt., Inc., 1984-88; pres., chief exec. officer Carluke Inc., 1988—2002. Past pres. Planters Redevel. Corp., St. Louis, 1984-87; trustee Equitable Life Mortgage & Realty

Investors, 1981-83; emeritus mem. adv. bd. govs. Wharton Real Estate Ctr., U. Pa., 1985—. Author papers in field. Trustee Urban Land Inst., 1982-88; bd. dirs. Urban Land Found., 1994-99; bd. govs. Ctrl. Atlanta Progress, 1984-86. With USAAF, 1942-45, with USAF, 1950-51. Decorated Purple Heart. Mem. Am. Soc. Real Estate Counselors, Urban Land Inst., Am. Inst. Real Estate Appraisers, Real Estate Bd. N.Y. (past gov.), Phi Beta Kappa, Phi Kappa Phi, Phi Gamma Delta. Democrat. Office: GR Peacock PO Box 420979 Atlanta GA 30342

PEACOCK, JOAN SUNITA, literature and language professor; d. John Samuel and Josephine Nirmala Peacock; m. Matthew Issac Onega, Oct. 6, 2007; 1 child, Rachel Anjali Brown. Assoc. prof. English Slippery Rock U., Pa., 1996—, co-advisor internations club, 1999—. Contbr. articles to profl. jours. Sunday sch. tchr., lay reader Ctr. Presbyn. Ch., Slippery Rock, 1998—2009. Mem.: Phi Kappa Phi (pres. elect 2008—09). Office: Slippery Rock Univ 312 J Spotts World Culture Bldg Slippery Rock PA 16057 Office Fax: 724-738-4829.

PEACOCK, MARY WILLA, magazine editor, consultant; b. Evanston, Ill., Oct. 23, 1942; d. William Gilbert and Mary Willa (Young) P. BA, Vassar Coll., 1964. Assoc. lit. editor Harper's Bazaar mag., NYC, 1964-69; staff editor Innovation mag., NYC, 1969-70; editor in chief, co-founder Rags mag., NYC, San Francisco, 1970-71; co-founder, features editor Ms. mag., NYC, 1971-77; pub., pres. Rags mag., NYC, 1977-80; sr. editor Village Voice, NYC, 1980-85, style editor, 1985-89; editor-in-chief Model mag., NYC, 1989—, editorial cons., 1991—; fashion dir. Lear's Mag., NYC, 1992-93; dep. editor In Style Mag., 1993-94, Mirabella mag., 1994-95; pvt. practice, 1995—2002; internat. editor InStyle, 2002—06. Cons. in field. Contbr. articles to popular mags.

PEACOCK, MOLLY, poet, educator, writer; b. June 30, 1947; d. Edward Frank and Pauline Ruth (Wright) P. BA magna cum laude, Harpur Coll., Binghamton, NY, 1969; MA with hons., Johns Hopkins U., 1977. Adminstr., lectr. in english SUNY, Binghamton, 1970-76; instr. english Friends Sem., NYC, 1981-92; poet-in-residence Bucknell U., 1993-94, Cathedral St. John the Divine, 2000—04; mem. grad. faculty Spalding U., 2001—. Author: And Live Apart, 1980, Raw Heaven, 1984, Take Heart, 1989, Original Love, 1995, Paradise, Piece by Piece, 1998, How To Read A Poem and Start A Poetry Circle, 1999, The Private I: Privacy in A Public World, 2001, Cornucopia: New and Selected Poems, 2002, The Shimmering Verge: A One-Woman Show in Poems, 2003, The Second Blush, 2008; contbg. writer House and Garden mag., 1996-2001; contbr. poems to The New Yorker, The New Republic, The Nation, articles to O, the Oprah Mag., Elle, N.Y. Mag. Named Tennessee Williams Playwright in Residence, Sewanee U., 2006, Elliston poet U. Cin., 2006; Danforth Found. fellow, 1970, Yaddo fellow, 1980, 82, 89, Ingram Merrill Found. fellow 1981, 86, Lila Wallace/Woodrow Wilson fellow 1994, 95, 96, 2001; grantee Creative Artists Pub. Svc. Program, 1977, N.Y. Found. for Arts, 1985, NEA, 1991; Regents scholar U. Calif., Riverside, 1998, Leon Levy Biography fellowship CUNY Grad. Ctr., 2008-09. Mem. PEN, Poetry Soc. Am. (governing bd. 1988—, pres. emeritus). Home: 109 Front St E #1041 Toronto ON M5A 4P7 Canada Office Phone: 212-677-3535. Personal E-mail: molly@mollypeacock.org.

PEACOCK, PENNE KORTH, ambassador; b. Hattiesburg, Miss., Nov. 3, 1942; m. Fritz-Alan Korth, Dec. 15, 1965 (div. 1997); children: Fritz-Alan Jr., Maria Korth Chieffalo, James Frederick; m. Andrew Peacock, Sept. 21, 2002. Student, U. Tex., 1960—64. Sr. Washington assoc., client liaison and rep. trust and estate div. Sotheby's, 1986-89; amb. to Mauritius, Port Louis, 1989-92; pres. Firestone and Korth Ltd., Washington, 1993-97; commr. US Adv. Commn. Pub. Diplomacy, 1997—. Bd. dir. Chevy Chase Bank, 1993—2009; rep. Sotheby's Internat., 1997—; adv. com. Sydney Cancer Ctr., 2003—; adv. bd. mem. Harry Ransom Ctr., U. Tex., 2008—. Sr. advisor Ptnrs. in Performance Internat., 2005—; co-chmn. Am. Bicentennial Presdl. Inauguration, Washington, 1988—99; mem. adv. bd. Washington Ballet, 2002—; bd. dirs. Hillwood Mus. and Gardens; counselor Meridian Internat. Ctr.; bd. dirs. Coun. of Am. Ambs., 1994—. Mem.: Assn. for Diplomatic Studies and Tng. (bd. dir. 1996—2002). Office: 3604 Mt Bonnell Rd Austin TX 78731

PEAKE, JAMES BENJAMIN, former United States Secretary of Veterans Affairs, retired military officer; b. St. Louis, June 18, 1944; m. Janice M. Peake; children: Kimberly, Thomas. BS, U.S. Mil. Acad., 1966; MD, Cornell U., 1972; grad., U.S. Army War Coll., 1988. Commd. 2nd lt. inf. US Army, 1972, advanced through grades to lt. gen., 1995, ret., 2004; gen. surgery resident Brooke Army Med. Ctr., Ft. Sam Houston, asst. chief cardiothoracic surgery; staff gen. surgeon, chief gen. surgery clinic DeWitt Army Hosp., Ft. Belvoir, Va.; dep. comdr. for clin. svcs. Tripler Army Med. Ctr., Honolulu; comdr. 18th Med. Command and 121st Evacuation Hosp. US Army, Seoul, Republic of Korea, dep. dir., profl. svcs. chief, cons. Office Surgeon Gen., commdg. gen. 44th Med. Brigade/Corps Surgeon XVIII Airborne Ft. Bragg, NC; commdg. gen. Madigan Army Med. Ctr./N.W. Health Svc. Support Activity, Tacoma; dep. comdr. US Army Med. Command, 1996-97; installation comdr. US Army, Ft. Sam Houston, 1996; comdr. US Army Med. Dept. Ctr. & Sch., 1996-2000, US Army Med. Command, Ft. Sam Houston, Tex., 2000—04; surgeon gen. US Army, 2000—04; exec. v.p., COO Project HOPE, 2004—06; chief med. officer, COO QTC Mgmt. Inc., 2006—07; sec. US Dept. Veterans Affairs, Washington, 2007—09. Presenter in field. Contbr. articles to profl. jours. Decorated Order of Mil. Med. Merit, Silver Star, Def. Superior Svc. medal, Legion of Merit with three oak leaf clusters, Bronze Star with V device and oak leaf cluster, Purple Heart with oak leaf cluster, Meritorious Svc. medal with two oak leaf clusters, Air medal, Joint Svc. Commendation medal, Army Commendation medal with V device and oak leaf cluster, Humanitarian Svc. medal, Armed Forces Expeditionary medal, Joint Meritorious Unit award with oak leaf cluster. Fellow ACS, Soc. Thoracic Surgeons, Am. Coll. Cardiology; mem. Korean Med. Assn. (hon.), Assn. Mil. Surgeons U.S., Soc. Med. Cons. of the Armed Forces. Republican.*

PEAKE, RYAN, musician; b. Can., Mar. 1, 1973; m. Treanna Peake; children: Dax, Adair. Lead guitarist Nickelback, 1995—; signed to Roadrunner Records, NYC. Musician: (albums) Curb, 1996, The State, 2000, Silver Side Up, 2001 (Juno award for Best Album, 2002), The Long Road, 2003, All the Right Reasons, 2005 (Juno award for Best Rock Album, 2006, Favorite Rock Album, Am. Music Awards, 2006, Billboard Rock Album of Yr., 2006), Dark Horse, 2008, (songs) How Your Remind Me (Juno award for Best Single, 2002, Billboard Top 100 Single & Track, Top Hot 40 Track, Top Hot 100 Airplay Track, 2002). Recipient Best New Group award, Juno Awards, 2001, Best Group award, 2002, 2006, Songwriters of Yr. award, 2003, Group of Yr., Billboard Music Awards, 2006, Hot 100 Group of Yr., 2006, World's Best Rock Group, World Music Awards, 2007, Best-Selling Canadian Artist, 2007, Favorite Group, People's Choice Awards, 2007, Favorite Rock Group, Am. Music Awards, 2007; named Top Hot 100 Singles Artist, Billboard, 2002. Office: c/o Bryan Coleman Union Entertainment Group 1323 Newbury Rd Ste 104 Thousand Oaks CA 91320 also: c/o Ron Burman Roadrunner Records 902 Broadway New York NY 10010

PEAPPLES, GEORGE ALAN, retired automotive executive; b. Benton Harbor, Mich., Nov. 6, 1940; s. Arthur L. and Kathleen C. (Peters) Peapples; m. Rebecca Dean Sowers, June 27, 1962; children: Lucia Christine, Sarah Bouton. BA in Econs., U. Mich., 1962, MBA in Fin., 1963. Fin. analyst GM Corp., Detroit, 1964-68, fin. analyst treas. office NYC, 1968—72, dir. capital analysis and investment, 1972—73, asst. divsn. comptr. Delco Moraine divsn. Dayton, Ohio, 1973-75, asst. treas. bank rels. Detroit, 1975-77, asst. comptr., 1980-82; v.p., fin. mgr. GM Can. Ltd., Oshawa, Ont., 1982-84; group dir. strategic bus. planning Chevrolet-Pontiac-Can. group GM Corp., Warren, Mich., 1984-86; v.p. GM Corp., pres., gen. mgr. GM Can. Ltd., Oshawa, 1986-94; v.p. pub. policy GM Corp., Washington, 1994-99; ret., 2000; asst. sec. of Navy US Dept. Def., 1977-80. Bd. dirs. The Ark. Recipient Disting. Pub. Svc. award, Washington, 1980. Personal E-mail: gapeapples@aol.com.

PEAR, CHARLES E., JR., lawyer; b. Macon, Ga., June 18, 1950; s. Charles Edward and Barbara Jane P.; children: Jennifer Sue, Charles Edward III, Stephanie Sue. BA, U. Hawaii, 1972; JD, U. Calif., Berkeley, 1975. Bar: Hawaii 1976, Fla. 1977, Colo. 1994, U.S. Ct. of Appeals (9th cir.). Assoc. Rush, Moore, Craven, Sutton, Morry & Beh, Honolulu, 1976-77, of counsel, 1987-90; assoc., ptnr. Carlsmith & Dwyer, Honolulu, 1977-82; ptnr. Burke, Sakai, McPheeters, Bordner & Gilardy, Honolulu, 1983-87; vis. prof. law and computers U. British Columbia, 1990-93; of counsel Holland & Hart, Denver, 1993-96; counsel, ptnr. McCorriston, Miller, Mukai, MacKinnon, Honolulu, 1996—. Mem. Hawaii Real Estate Commn. com. on condominium and resort real estate legis., 1978-79; spl. counsel to consumer protection com. Hawaii State Ho. of Reps., 1981-82; chair real property and fin. svcs. sect. Hawaii State Bar Assn., ABA; lectr. in field. Editor-in-Chief Hawaii Conveyance Manual II, 1987; editor Hawaii Commercial Real Estate Manual, 1988; bd. editors Hawaii Inst. of Continuing Legal Edn.; co-author: Nat. Assn. of Real Estate Licensing Law Officials and Nat. Timesharing Coun. Model Timesharing Act, 1981-82; contbr. chpts. to books. Named one of Ams. Leading Bus. Lawyers, Chambers USA, 2004—09, Best Lawyers in Am., 2005—09. Mem. ABA.

PEARCE, ALAN S., lawyer; BS, Lehigh U., 1963; LLB, NYU, 1966. Bar: NY 1966. Ptnr. Bryan Cave LLP, NYC, mem. operating group, 2002—05. With IRS, US Treasury Dept., 1966—67. Mem.: ABA (com. on Partnerships & Unincorporated Bus. Orgns. 1977—), NY State Bar Assn., Assn. of the Bar of the City of New York. Office: Bryan Cave LLP 1290 Ave of the Americas New York NY 10104 Office Phone: 212-541-2111. Office Fax: 212-541-1411. E-mail: aspearce@bryancave.com.

PEARCE, AMY R, psychology professor; b. Conway, Ark. married. PhD, Australian Nat. U., Canberra, ACT. Cert. Sci. Communication CPAS. Math. tchr. Escuela Bilingue Honduras, Comayagua, 2000—01; assoc. prof. psychology Ark. State U., Jonesboro, 2001—. Office: AR State Univ 114 Cooley Dr Jonesboro AR 72401 Office Phone: 870-972-3064.

PEARCE, DONALD JOSLIN, retired librarian; b. Southampton, Eng., May 31, 1924; came to US, 1949, naturalized, 1952; s. Alfred Ernest and Constance May (Jeffrey) P.; m. June Inez Bond, Dec. 7, 1946; children: Kristin, Kim. Student, Sch. Oriental and African Studies, U. London, 1942-43; AB, George Washington U., 1953; MS in L.S, Cath. U. Am., 1954. Part-time libr. asst. U.S. Dept. Agr., 1949-54; student asst. George Washington U. Libr., 1950-53; circulation libr. Denison U., 1954-56; staff Ohio State U. Libr., 1956-59, asst. acquisition libr., 1958-59; head libr., asst. prof. U. ND, 1959-69, chief bibliographer, 1969-73, asst. dir. libraries, 1973-75, asst. prof. Oriental philosophy, 1969-75; libr. dir., asst. prof. philosophy U. Minn., Duluth, 1975-88, ret., 1988. Chmn. staff orgn. round table Ohio Libr. Assn., 1958-59 Served with Brit. Army, 1943-47. Mem. ALA, ND Libr. Assn. (pres. 1965-67), Minn. Libr. Assn. (sec. 1978-80, v.p. 1985, pres. 1986), Assn. Coll. Reference Librarians, Mountain Plains Libr. Assn. (v.p. 1968-69), Buddhist Assn., Phi Beta Kappa, Beta Phi Mu. Home: 70 E St Marie St Apt 127 Duluth MN 55803 Personal E-mail: dpearce2310@inbox.com.

PEARCE, DONALD W., music educator; b. Seattle, July 19, 1959; s. William B. and Patricia G. Pearce; m. Lynette S. Karber; children: Nicole P., Jacob W., Matthew J. BA in Secondary Music Edn., Eastern Wash. U., Cheney, 1983. Music tchr. Blaine Sch. Dist., Wash., 1980—83, Bainbridge Island Sch. Dist., Wash., 1987—2001, Christ King Acad., Poulsbo, Wash., 1997—2001, King's West Sch., Chico, Wash., 2001—07, Omak Sch. Dist., Wash., 2007—. Office: Omak Sch Dist PO Box 833 Omak WA 98841 Personal E-mail: don@donpearce.net. Business E-Mail: dpearce@omaksd.wednet.edu.

PEARCE, DRUE, federal official, former state legislator; b. Fairfield, Ill., Apr. 2, 1951; d. H. Phil and Julia Detroy (Bannister) P.; m. Michael F.G. Williams; 1 child, Tate Hanna Pearce-Williams. BA in Biol. Scis., Ind. U., 1973; MPA, Harvard U., 1984; cert. exec. program Darden Sch. Bus., U. Va., 1989. Sch. tchr., Clark County, Ind., 1973-74; curator of edn. Louisville Zoo, 1974—76; dir. Summerscene, Louisville, 1976—77; asst. v.p., br. mgr. Alaska Nat. Bank of the North, 1977-82; legis. aide to Rep. John Ringstad Alaska Ho. of Reps., Juneau, 1983, mem., 1984-88, minority whip, 1987—88; mem. Alaska Senate, 1989—2001, chmn. com. oil and gas, mem. exec. com. energy coun., 1989-90, chmn. com. labor and commerce, mem. exec. coms. western state conf., coun. state govts., energy coun., 1991-92, co-chmn. senate fin., chmn. energy coun., vice chmn. com. energy, nat. coun. state govts., 1993-94, mem. select com. legis. ethics and legis. coun., pres. senate, mem. exec. com. energy coun., vice chmn. senate coms. resources and rules, 1995-96, co-chmn. com. senate fin., mem. exec. com. energy coun., vice chmn. com. senate judiciary, 1997—98; sr. adv. to sec. for Alaska affairs US Dept. Interior, 2001—; fed. coord. for Alaskan Natural Gas Transp. Projects Fed. Energy Regulatory Commn., 2006—. Senate pres., 1995-96, 1999-2000, senate rules chmn., 2001; ptnr. Cloverland N., Anchorage, 1993—; resources cons. Arctic Slope Regional Corp., Anchorage, 1987-91, 95-96; sr. adv. Sec. Interior for Alaska Affairs, 2001-. Former bd. dirs. Alaska Women's Aid in Crisis, Anchorage Econ. Devel. Coun., Alaska Aerospace Devel. Corp., Alaska Spl. Olympics, Gov.'s Bd. Mem. DAR, Commonwealth North, Resource Devel. Coun., Alaska Miners Assn., Alaska Fedn. Rep. Women, Aircraft Owners & Pilots Assn., U.S. Trotting Assn. Republican.

PEARCE, ELI M., chemistry professor, academic administrator; b. Bklyn., May 1, 1929; s. Samuel and Sarah (Reitzen) Perlmutter; m. Maxine I. Horowitz, Feb. 21, 1951 (div. 1978); children:Russell Gane, Debra Nore; m. Judith Handler, May 29, 1980. BS, Bklyn. Coll., 1949; MS, NYU, 1951; PhD, Poly. Inst. Bklyn, 1958. Research chemist NYU-Bellevue Med. Ctr., NYC, 1949-53, DuPont, Wilmington, Del., 1958-62; sec. mgr. J.T. Baker, Phillipsburg, N.J., 1962-68; tech. supr. Allied Corp., Morristown, N.J., 1968-72, research cons., 1972-73; dir. Dreyfus Lab. Research Triangle Inst., Research Triangle Park, N.C., 1973-74; prof. polymer chemistry and chem. engring. Poly. Inst. N.Y., Bklyn., 1974—, dir. Polymer Research Inst., 1981-96, Univ. prof., 1990-99, head dept. chemistry, 1976-82, dean arts and scis., 1982-90, univ. rsch. prof., 1999—; u. rsch. prof., 1999—2008, Poly. Inst. NYU, 2008—. Cons. AMP, Inc., Harrisburg, Pa., Arco, Newton Square, Pa., Colgate, Piscataway, N.J., Dupont, Richmond, Va., Texaco, Beacon, N.Y. Co-author: Laboratory Experiments in Polymer Synthesis and Characterization, 1982, High Performance Thermosets; editor: Macromolecular Synthesis, Vol. 1, 1982; co-editor: Fiber Chemistry, 1983, Contemporary Topics in Polymer Science, vol. 2, 1977, Flame Retardance of Polymeric Materials, vols. 1-3, Jour. Polymer Sci.; mem. editl. bd. Ency. Materials Sci., 1983; contbr. over 250 articles on polymers to profl. jours. Bd. dir. Petroleum Research Fund, 1982-84; bd. dir. Nat. Materials Adv. Bd., 1975-77. Served with U.S. Army, 1953-55. Recipient Edn. Service award Plastics Inst. Am., 1973; recipient Disting. Faculty citation Poly. Inst. N.Y., 1980, Disting. Alumnus citation, 1997, Paul J. Flory Polymer Edn. award, 1992, Kaufman Lectr. award Ramapo Coll., 1992, Gold Medal award N.Y. Inst. Chemists, 1992, Reed-Lignin Lectr. award U. Wis., 1987, Oscar Foster award Chemistry Tchrs. Club, 2000, Giullio Natta 100th Birthday medal Italian Chem. Soc., 2003, Herman F. Mark award Austrian Inst. Chemistry and Tech., 2006. Fellow AAAS, AIS,Am. Inst. Chemists, N.Am. Thermal Analysis Soc., N.Y. Acad. Scis. (chmn. polymer sect. 1972-73), Soc. Plastics Engrs. (Internat. Edn. award 1988); mem. Academia GioENIA, Sicily (hon.), Am. Chem. Soc. (councilor 1978—, chmn. polymer divsn. 1980, coun. policy com. on coms., chmn. com. sci., bd. dir., pres. 2002, exec. com. edn. 2004—, Henry Hill award 2002), Nat. Orgn. Black Chemists and Chem. Engrs. (hon.), Acad. Scis. Catania (hon.), Sigma Xi Home: 2 Fifth Ave New York NY 10011 Office: Polytechnic Inst NYU Polymer Rsch Inst 6 Metrotech Ctr Brooklyn NY 11201-3840 Office Phone: 718-260-3030. Business E-Mail: epearce@poly.edu.

PEARCE, ELIZABETH NIEWOEHNER, endocrinologist, researcher; arrived in U.S., 1968; d. Dennis Erwin and Catherine Beattie Niewoehner; m. Richard A. Pearce, May 24, 1997; children: Alexander, Ian. BA, Harvard U., Cambridge, Mass., 1990; student, Bryn Mawr Coll., 1991—92; MD, Harvard U., 1997; MSc in Epidemiology, Boston U., Mass., 2004. Diplomate internal medicine, endocrinology, diabetes and metabolism. Intern internal medicine Beth Israel Deaconess Med. Ctr., Boston, 1997—98, resident internal medicine, 1998—2000; from fellow in endocrinology to asst. prof. medicine Med. Ctr. Boston (Mass.) U., 2000—04, assoc. prof. medicine Med. Ctr., 2009—. Mem. editl. bd. Thyroid, Endocrine Practice, & Jour. Clin. Endocrinology & Metabolism. Contbr. chapters to books, articles to profl. jours. Recipient K-23 Mentored Career award, NIH, 2003; grantee Pfizer Scholars in Endocrine, 2002. Mem.: Internat. Coun. Control Iodine Deficiency Disorders (bd. dirs. 2009—), Mass. Med. Soc., Am. Thyroid Assn. (chair pub. health com. 2008—), Endocrine Soc. Avocation: singing. Office: Boston Med Ctr Evans 201 88 E Newton St Boston MA 02118 Business E-Mail: elizabeth.pearce@bmc.org.

PEARCE, GEORGE HAMILTON, archbishop emeritus; b. Boston, Jan. 9, 1921; s. George Hamilton and Marie Louise (Duval) P. BA, Marist Coll. and Sem., Framingham, Mass., 1943. Ordained priest Soc. of Mary, 1947; tchr. Marist Coll. & Sem., Bedford, Mass., 1947-48, St. Mary's High Sch., Van Buren, Maine, 1948-49; missionary Roman Catholic Vicariate of Samoa, 1949-67; ordained bishop, 1956; vicar apostolic Roman Catholic Vicariate of Samoa, 1956-66; bishop Diocese of Apia, Am. Samoa, Saint Helena, 1966-67; archbishop Archdiocese of Suva, Fiji, 1967-76; pres. Episcopal Conf. of the Pacific, 1969-71; apostolic adminstr. Diocese of Agana, Guam, 1969; staff mem. Bethany House of Intercession, Hastings-on-Hudson, NY, 1977-83; asst. to bishop Diocese of Providence, RI, 1983—. Roman Catholic. Home: 30 Fenner St Providence RI 02903-3603

PEARCE, GREGORY, botanist; b. Ketchikan, Alaska, Feb. 22, 1953; s. Allen Childress and Gladys McClain Pearce; m. Beverly Maule, June 26, 1994; children: Sean McCartney, Kenneth, Kelsey McCartney, Bradley. BS in Biochemistry, Wash. State U., Pullman, 1975, MS in Animal Nutrition, 1981. Sr. sci. rschr. Wash. State U., 1975—. Achievements include discovery of peptide hormones in plants. Office: Washington State Univ Clark Hall Rm 425 Pullman WA 99164-6340 Business E-Mail: pearce@wsu.edu.

PEARCE, HARRY JONATHAN, lawyer, manufacturing executive; b. Bismarck, ND, Aug. 20, 1942; s. William R. and Jean Katherine (Murray) P.; m. Katherine B. Bruk, June 19, 1967; children: Shannon Pearce Baker, Susan J., Harry M. BS, USAF Acad., Colorado Springs, Colo., 1964; JD, Northwestern U., 1967; Degree in Engring. (hon.), Rose-Hulman Inst. Tech., 1997; LLD (hon.), Northwestern U., 1998. Bar: N.D. 1967, Mich. 1986. Mcpl. judge City of Bismarck, 1970-76, U.S. magistrate, 1970-76, police commr., 1976-80; sr. ptnr. Pearce & Durick, Bismarck, 1970-85; assoc. gen. counsel GM, Detroit, 1985-87, v.p., gen. counsel, 1987-92, exec. v.p., gen. counsel, 1992-94, exec. v.p., 1994-95, vice chmn., 1996—2001; chmn. Hughes Electronics, El Segundo, Calif., 2001—03; non exec. chmn. Nortel Networks Corp., Brampton, Ont., Canada, 2005—. Bd. dirs. GM Corp., Hughes Electronics Corp., GM Acceptance Corp., Delphi Automotive Sys. Corp., Alliance of Automobile Mfrs. of Am., Marriott Internat. Inc., Econ. Strategy Inst., Theodore Roosevelt Medora Found., MDU Resources Group, Inc., Nat. Def. U. Found., Detroit Investment Fund, bd. dirs. Nortel Networks Corp., 2005-2009 Mem. law bd. Sch. Law, Northwestern U.; mem. bd. visitors U.S. Air Force Acad.; chmn. Product Liability Adv. Coun. Found.; founding mem. minority counsel demonstration program Commn. on Opportunities for Minorities in the Profession, ABA; chmn. The Sabre Soc., USAF Acad.; trustee Howard U., U.S. Coun. for Internat. Bus., New Detroit, Inc.; mem. The Mentor's Group Forum for U.S.-European Union Legal-Econ. Affairs, The Conf. Bd., Network of Employers for Traffic Safety's Leadership Coun., Pres.'s Coun. on Sustainable Devel., World Bus. Coun. for Sustainable Devel., World Economic Forum Coun. Innovative Leaders in Globalization. Capt. USAF, 1964-70. Named Michiganian of Yr., The Detroit News, 1997; Hardy scholar Northwestern U., Chgo., 1964-67, recipient Alumni Merit award, 1991. Fellow Am. Coll. Trial Lawyers, Internat. Soc. Barristers; mem. Am. Law Inst. Avocations: amateur radio, woodworking, sailing. Office: Bowman and Brooke LLP 50 W Big Beaver Rd Ste 600 Troy MI 48084

PEARCE, JAY THOMAS, history educator; s. Bill Mack and Bernita Ann Pearce; m. Colleen Melette Westbrook, May 25, 1990; 1 child, Morgan Nicole. BA, Tex. Tech U., Lubbock, 1986, MA, 1990; PhD, U. Tex., Arlington, 2000. Prof. Dallas County CC Dist., 1990—2001, Black Hawk Coll., Moline, Ill., 2001—. Contbr. articles to profl. jour. Faculty advisor BHC Democrats, Moline, 2001—08. Mem.: Am. Polit. Sci. Assn., Am. Hist. Assn. Liberal. Roman Catholic. Avocations: reading, computers. Home: 3680 2nd St Ct East Moline IL 61244 Office: Black Hawk Coll 6600 34th Ave Moline IL 61265-5899 Business E-Mail: pearcej@bhc.edu.

PEARCE, PAUL FRANCIS, retired electronics executive, aerospace engineer; b. Boston, Sept. 17, 1928; s. George Hamilton and Marie Louise (Duval) P.; m. Gilda Troisi, Apr. 11, 1953; children: Janet, Theresa, Diane. BSEE (Edwards scholar), MIT, 1950, MSEE, 1952; postgrad. (Hughes fellow), U. Southern Calif., 1958-59; postgrad. in Mgmt., Inst. Mgmt. Northwestern U., 1966. Project engr. Trans-Sonics, Inc., Burlington, Mass., 1952-55; sect. head application engring., strategic systems Hughes Aircraft Co., Culver City, Calif., 1955-59; with Lockheed Electronics Co., Plainfield, NJ, 1959-67, gen. mgr. div. mil. systems, 1964-65, v.p., gen. mgr., 1965-67; v.p., div. mgr. Tele-Dynamics div. AMBAC Industries, Inc., Ft. Washington, Pa, 1967-74; group v.p. comml. and aerospace electronics group AMBAC Industries, Inc., Carle Place, NY, 1973-80; pres. James G. Biddle Co., Blue Bell, Pa., 1980-93, ret. Bd. dirs. AVO Internat. Ltd., 1987-91. Mem. Armed Forces Communications and Electronics Assn. (pres. 1969-71), Inst. Nav., Delaware Valley Mfrs. Assn. (sr. vice chmn. 1987-89, chmn. 1990-92), Greater Phila. C. of C., Ft. Washington Indsl. Park Mgmt. Assn. (gov. 1973-74), Sigma Xi. Clubs: Mfrs'. Golf and Country (Oreland, Pa.) (handicap chmn. 1987-90), St. David's Golf Club (Wayne, Pa.). Personal E-mail: pfpearce@att.net.

PEARCE, RONALD, retired cosmetic company executive; b. Apr. 29, 1920; s. Fernley Charles and Medora Kate (Lissenden) P.; m. Olive Stacey, Apr. 4, 1942; children: David Fernley, Jane Ryding Robertson. Cambridge matriculation, Lindisfarne Coll., Ruabon, North Wales, UK, 1937. Chief cashier Westminster Bank, Croydon, Eng., 1947-48; comml. officer Brit. Consulate, Dallas, 1949-52; v.p. World Gift Co., Dallas, 1953-63, Nelson Electronics, Dallas, 1963-68; stockbroker Walston & Co., Dallas, 1968-73; dir. purchasing Mary Kay Cosmetics, Inc., Dallas, 1973-85; pres. Global Water Techs., Inc., 1992-95; chmn. bd. Alpha Aqua, 1996—, Concha Holdings LTD, 2002—. Chmn. bd. Dallas Lighthouse for the Blind, 1987. Flight lt. RAF, 1940—46. Republican. Episcopalian. Home: 5550 Harvest Hill Rd Ste W283 Dallas TX 75230-6417 Office Phone: 214-363-9064.

PEARCE, STEVE (STEVAN EDWARD PEARCE), former United States Representative from New Mexico; b. Lamesa, Tex., Aug. 24, 1947; m. Cynthia Pearce. BBA in Econs., N.Mex. State U., Las Cruces, 1970; MBA, Ea. N.Mex. U., Portales, 1991. Owner-operator crop dusting flying svc., Blytheville, Ark., 1975—78; chief pilot, check pilot Marshall Aviation, 1978—81; chief pilot RUNCO, Inc.; co-owner, operator Lea Fishing Tools, Inc., 1989—2002; mem. N.Mex. State House Reps., 1997—2000, chmn. Rep. Caucus; mem. US Congress from 2nd N.Mex. Dist., 2003—09. Mem. fin. svcs. com. US Congress, dep. ranking mem. subcommittee on housing and cmty. opportunity, mem. natural resources com., ranking mem. subcommittee on energy and mineral resources, asst. Rep. whip. Pilot USAF, 1970—76, Philippines. Decorated DFC, Air medal; co-recipient VIVA award, Assn. Commerce and Industry, 2001; named an Outstanding Legislator, N.Mex. Tech. Showcase. Republican. Baptist.

PEARL, HELEN ZALKAN, lawyer; b. Washington, Sept. 12, 1938; d. George and Harriet (Libman) Zalkan; m. Jason E. Pearl, June 27, 1959; children: Gary M., Esther H., Lawrence J. BA with honors, Vassar Coll., Poughkeepsie, NY, 1959; JD, U. Conn., Storrs, 1978. Bar: Conn. 1978, U.S. Dist. Ct. Conn. 1978. Mkt. rsch. analyst Landers, Frary & Clark, New Britain, Conn., 1960-61, managerial statistician, 1961-62; real estate salesperson Denuzze Co., New Britain, 1966-70; property mgr. self-employed New Britain, 1970-75; legal asst. Atty. Gen. Office, State of Conn., Hartford, 1978; assoc. Weber & Marshall, New Britain, 1978-83, ptnr., 1983-99, Weber & Carrier, New Britain, 1999—. Hearing officer Commn. on Human Rights and Opportunities, State of Conn., 1980—98; spl. master Conn. Jud. Dept., 1986—. New Britain rep. to Ctrl. Conn. Regional Planning Agy., 1973-75, 1984-2008, chmn., 1990-92; active New Britain Bd. Fin. and Taxation, 1973-77, Conn. State Ethics Commn., 2004-05; co-v.p. Vassar Class, 2004-08; vice chair Conn. Citizens Ethics Adv. Bd., 2005; founder, mem. Conn. Permanent Commn. on Status of Women, 1975-82, bd. dirs. Human Resources Agy., 2001—, sec., 2009-, others. Recipient Book award for torts, Am. Jurisprudence, 1976, Women in Leadership award, YWCA of New Britain, 1988, Vet. Feminists Am. award, 2005. Mem. AAUW (pres. 1970-72), Acad. Women Leaders, Conn. Bar Assn., New Britain Bar Assn., LWV (Conn. specialist 1987-2004, local pres. 1995-97, co-pres. 2003—, by-laws co-chair 2008-), Hartford Vassar Club (sec. 2006—), Phi Beta Kappa. Democrat. Jewish. Avocations: travel, theater, reading, cooking. Home: 206 Hickory Hill Rd New Britain CT 06052-1010 Office: Weber & Carrier 24 Cedar St New Britain CT 06052-1302 Home Phone: 860-224-0740; Office Phone: 860-225-9463. Personal E-mail: hzpearl@msn.com. Business E-Mail: hpearl@webercarrier.com.

PEARL, JUDEA, computer scientist, educator; b. Tel-Aviv, Sept. 4, 1936; U.S. citizen; m. Ruth Pearl; 3 children. BSc, Israel Inst. Tech., 1960; MSc, Newark Coll. Engring., 1961; PhD in Elec. Engring., Poly. Inst. Bklyn., 1965. Rsch. engr. Dental Sch., NYU, 1960-61; mem. tech. staff RCA Rsch. Labs., 1961-65; dir. advanced memory devices Electronic Memories, Inc., Calif., 1966-69; prof. Sch. of Engring./Dept. Computer Scis. UCLA, 1969—; co-founder, pres. Daniel Pearl Found., 2002—. Instr. Newark Coll. Engring., 1961; cons. Rand Corp., 1972, Integrated Sci. Corp., 1975, Hughes Aircraft, 1989.; dir. Cognitive Sys. Lab., UCLA. Author: Heuristics: Intelligent Search Strategies for Computer Problem Solving, 1984, Probabilistic Reasoning in Intelligent Systems: Networks of Plausible Inference, 1988, Casuality: Models, Reasoning, Inference, 2000. Recipient: Outstanding Achievement award RCA Labs., 1965, Rsch. Excellence award, Allen Newell award, Lakatos award in Philosophy Sci., Internat. Joint Confs. on Artificial Intelligence, 1999, Benjamin Franklin medal in computer and cognitive sci., Franklin Inst., 2008; co-recipient: Purpose prize, Civic Ventures, 2006. Fellow IEEE, ACM, Am. Assn. Artificial Intelligence (Classical Paper award 2000, Lakatos award 2001), Acad. Engring. (Allen Newell award, 2003), NAE; corr. mem. Spanish Acad. Engring. Office: UCLA Dept Computer Sci 4532 Boelter Hl Los Angeles CA 90095-0001

PEARL, LAURENCE DICKSON, retired federal government executive; b. Phila., Mar. 2, 1934; s. Simon and Dorothy (Lichtig) P.; m. Ruth Switzer, Dec. 22, 1959 (div. Apr. 1972); children: Natasha, Lisa Talbott, Thomas Simon; m. Anne Womeldorf, Dec. 20, 1972. AB, Antioch Coll., 1955; postgrad., Harvard U., 1955-56; LLB, Yale U., 1959. Bar: D.C. 1959, U.S. Supreme Ct. 1983. Assoc. Trammell, Rand & Nathan, Washington, 1960-61; rsch. assoc. George Washington U., Washington, 1961; atty., advisor HUD, Washington, 1961-67, exec. asst. to gen. counsel, 1967-69, spl. asst. to asst. sec. for equal opportunity, 1969-72, dir. program standards and data analysis, 1972-74, dir. program compliance, 1974-86, dir. program standards and evaluation, 1986-98; ret., 1998. Pres. Capitol Hill Restoration Soc., Washington, 1990-92. Ford Found. fellow, 1955-56. Mem. Am. Bar Assn., Sr. Execs. Assn. (pres. HUD chpt. 1990-91). Avocations: music, gardening, cross country skiing.

PEARL, MARY CORLISS, wildlife conservationist; b. NYC, July 5, 1950; d. George Carleton and Margaret Lyon (Scheuer) Pearl; m. Don Jay Melnick, Oct. 3, 1981; children: Meredith, Seth. BA, Yale U., 1972, MPhil, 1976, PhD, 1982; DSc (hon.), Marist Coll., 2006. Dir. corp. devel. World Wildlife Fund, NYC, 1983-85, head NY office, 1984-85; adminstr. conservation progs. Wildlife Conservation Soc., NYC, 1985-87, asst. dir., 1988—; exec. dir., pres. Wildlife Trust (formerly Wildlife Preservation Trust Internat.); vis. scholar dept. biol. sci. Stanford U., 1987-88; assoc. dir. Ctr. Environ. Rsch. and Conservation Columbia U. Co-founder Consortium for Conservation Medicine, 1997; adj. rschr. Columbia U., NYC. Editl. adv. Wildlife Conservation mag., 1988; editor: Conservation for the 21st Century, 1989, Conservation Medicine: Ecosystem Health in Practice, 2002; co-editor: Conservation for the 21st Century; columnist Discover Magazine, 2006—; contbr. articles to profl. jour. Founding mem. Cons. in Higher Edn. Group of the Rainforest Alliance, NYC, 1988; trustee Gomez Found., NYC, 1985—; founder Calvin Hill Daycare Ctr., New Haven, 1970. Recipient David Lapham award, Yale U., 1971. Mem.: AAAS, Internat. Ecol. Rsch. (Brazil), Ecohealth Soc., Soc. for Conservation Biology (bd. gov. 1990—93), Internat. Union for Conservation of Nature (primate specialist group species survival commn.), Internat. Women's Forum, Cosmos Club. Avocations: squash, birdwatching, reading, history. Office: Wildlife Trust 460 West 34th St 17th Floor New York NY 10001 Office Phone: 212-380-4460. Personal E-mail: marypearl@aol.com. E-mail: pearl@wildlifetrust.org.

PEARL, RICHARD H., surgeon; b. NYC, Sept. 1, 1944; m. Lauretta M. Pearl, Aug. 4, 1990; children: Emily L., Amanda P. Geneva. MD, Wright Stae U. Coll. Medicine, Dayton, Ohio, 1980. American Board of Surgery Gen. and Pediatric surgey, 1989. Col. Inf. US Army, 1966—76, Med. US Army, 1976—94; chief, pediatric surgery Walter Reed Army Med. Ctr., Wahington, 1988—94; chief, gen. surgery divsn. Hosp. Sick Children, Toronto, Ontario, Canada, 1994—98; chief Surgeon Children's Hosp. Ill., Peoria, 1998—. Contbr. articles to profl. jours., chapters to books. Decorated Legion of Merit US Army; recipient Bronze Star 3, Air medal, 1964—94. Fellow: ACS, Royal Coll. Physicians & Surgeons (Can.), Am. Acad. Pediat.; mem.: Children's Hosp. Ill. Office: Children's Hosp Ill 420 NE Glen Oak Dr Ste 201 Peoria IL 61603 Office Fax: 309-655-3948. Business E-Mail: rhpearl@uic.edu.

PEARLMAN, BRUCE ALLEN, research scientist; b. Feb. 18, 1949; s. Jack Pearlman and Betty Ethyl Yarrows. BA, Harvard Coll., 1971; PhD, Columbia Univ., 1976. Scientist Upjohn Co., Kalamazoo, 1979—80, rsch. scientist, 1980—83, sr. rsch. scientist, 1983—91; sr. scientist Pharmacia & Upjohn, Inc., Kalamazoo, 1991—99, disting. scientist vi, 1999—2001; sr. fellow Pharmacia Corp., Kalamazoo, 2001—03; sr. rsch. fellow Pfizer, Inc., 2004—06; disting. fellow Schering-Plough Rsch. Inst., 2006—. Contbr. articles to sci. jours. Achievements include 17 US patents. Office: Schering-Plough Rsch Inst 1011 Morris Ave U-3-2 2100 Union NJ 07083 Office Phone: 908-820-6106. Business E-Mail: bruce.pearlman@spcorp.com.

PEARLMAN, DAVID SAMUEL, allergist; b. Syracuse, NY, Jan. 20, 1934; s. Benjamin Norman and Sylvia Rene (Karp) P.; m. Doris Ann Greenberg, Apr. 16, 1966; children: Michael, Melanie. Student, Cornell U., 1951-54; MD, SUNY, Syracuse, 1958. Diplomate Am. Bd. Allergy and Immunology (dir. 1973-78). Intern, then asst. resident in pediatrics Univ. Hosps., Cleve., 1958-60; chief resident in pediatrics U. Colo. Med. Center, Denver, 1960-61, mem. faculty, 1962—, clin. prof. pediatrics, 1978—, dir. pediatric allergy tng. program, 1964-66, co-dir., 1966-73; practice medicine specializing in allergy Denver, 1972—. Assoc. Colo. Allergy and Asthma Clinic, 1972—; acting chief dept. pediatric allergy Nat. Jewish Hosp. and Rsch. Ctr., 1972-73, sr. staff physician pediatrics allergy, 1973-92; mem. allergy and infectious disease tng. grant com. NIH, 1970-72. Contbr. articles to med. jours. Served to maj. M.C. AUS, 1967-69. U. Colo. Med. Ctr. fellow, 1961-62, NIH fellow, 1963-66, 69-72; recipient Disting. Clinician award Am. Acad. Allergy, Asthma, and Immunology, 1999. Fellow Am. Acad. Pediatrics (chmn. sect. on allergy and Clin. Immunology, 1992-94, Bret Ratner award 1998), Am. Acad. Allergy, Asthma and Immunology (exec. com. 1978-81), Am. Coll. Allergy, Asthma and Immunology (Disting. Svvc. award 1999); mem. AAAS, Am. Soc. Cert. Allergists, Am. Thoracic Soc., Am. Coll. Chest Physicians, Colo. Allergy Soc., Joint Council Allergy and Immunology (bd. dirs. 1985-92, pres. 1988-90), Colo. Med. Soc., Denver Med. Soc., Adams-Aurora County Med. Soc., Friends of Chamber Music (dir. 1965-81). Jewish. Address: 6029 E Prentice Pl Englewood CO 80111-1415 Office: Colo Allergy & Asthma Ctrs PC 125 Rampart St Ste 150 Denver CO 80230-6405 Home Phone: 303-778-2635; Office Phone: 720-858-7510. E-mail: ds.pearlman@coloradoallergy.com.

PEARLMAN, ELLEN LOIS, writer, filmmaker, critic, curator; b. Bklyn., May 22, 1952; d. Sol and Norma (Fischel) P. BA, Hofstra U., 1974, Ed magna cum laude; postgrad., 1977, Sch. of Mus. Fine Arts, Boston, Internat. Ctr. Photography. Asst. to Oleg Grabar dept. fine arts Harvard U., Cambridge, Mass., 1980; transcription editor Allen Ginsberg, 1990; writer Tricycle Mag., 1991 (UTNE award 1992, 93); adj. faculty mem. Columbia U., prof. CTA program, MAP program digital design Columbia U., 1996; prof. New Sch. U., Parsons Sch. Design; writers residency Banff Ctr., 2004-. Editor-at-large Bklyn. Rail, 2001—, Andy Warhol Found. Pub. Grant, 2007 (UTNE award 2002, 03, 04); Tibetan Sacred Dance Inner Traditions, 2002. Grantee Am. Inst. Indian Studies, Harvard Med. Sch., 1981; non-fiction scholar Breadloaf Writers Conf., 1994; fellow Vt. Studio Ctr., 1997, Pres.'s fellow, 2003, 05, 07; Banff Mountain Ctr. grantee, 2003, writers grantee Great River Arts Inst., Patzluaro, Mex., 2001; Asian Cultural Coun. grantee Writers Residency, Banff Mountain Ctr., Can., 2004, Art Writer grant Andy Warhol Found., 2006, Prince Claus Trust, 2009; Mongol award Red Gate Internat. Residency, China Photographers Assn., 2007, Taiwanese Internat. Photographer Symposium, 2008, Timeout Beijing, 2008, Yuanfen Gallery, Beijing, Art Panel Juror Siggraph Asia, 2009. Buddhist. Avocations: travel, meditation, martial arts (Ninja black belt). Office: 302 Bedford Ave Ste 345 Brooklyn NY 11211

PEARLMAN, JERRY KENT, electronics company executive; b. Des Moines, Mar. 27, 1939; s. Leo R. Pearlman; married; children: Gregory, Neal. BA cum laude, Princeton U., 1960; MBA, Harvard U., 1962. With Ford Motor Co., 1962-70; v.p. fin. dir. Behring Corp., 1970-71; from contr. to chmn. Zenith Electronics Corp., Glenview, Ill., 1971-95. Bd. dirs. Smurfit-Stone Container Corp., Nanophase Techs., Northshore U. Health Sys. Office: 225 Barton Ave Palm Beach FL 33480 Office Phone: 561-655-5209. E-mail: jpearl@northwestern.edu.

PEARLMAN, JUSTIN D., medical educator; s. Lester S. and Amalia C. Pearlman; 1 child, David A. AB Magna cum Laude, Harvard, Cambridge, Mass., 1975; MD, UCHC, Farmington, Conn., 1980; ME, U. Va., Charlottesville, 1985, PhD in Applied Scis., 1986; attending (hon.), Dartmouth, Hanover, NH, 2001—. Diplomate Am. Bd. Internal Medicine; lic. Calif., 1981, Mass., 1986. Instr. Harvard MIT Health Sci Tech, 1989—90, Harvard Med. Sch., 1988—90, asst. prof., 1990—93, assoc. prof., 1993—2001; prof. medicine Dartmouth, 2002—; adj prof. engring. Thayer Sch. Engring., Hanover, 2002—. Instr. MIT, Cambridge, 1989-90, assoc. staff, 1990-92; dir. Mass. Gen. Hosp., Boston, 1987-92, clin. asst., 1988-92; dir. magnetic resonance imaging Beth Israel Hosp., Boston, 1992—. Peer reviewer; lectr. in field; contbr. chpts. in books and articles to profl. jours. Grantee NIH, 1988-93, Am. Heart Assn., 1994, N.Y. Cardiac Ctr., 1996, Whitaker Found., 1993-96, Hewlett-Packard, Sterling Drug, Sun Computers and Microsystems, Silicon Graphics Instruments, Inc. Mem. ACP, Am. Coll. Cardiology, Am. Fedn. Clin. Rschrs., Soc. Magnetic Resonance in Medicine (program com.), Soc. for Magnetic Resonance in Imaging, N.Am. Soc. for Cardiac Imaging, Radiologic Soc. N.Am. Achievements include patents for imaging apparatus and method with compensation for object motion, multivariate cardiac monitor, MRI imaging method; design of electronic medical record and social network system; invention of myocardial tagging, intensity projection angiography. Home: 25 Goddard Cir Brookline MA 02445 Personal E-mail: jdpmd@verizon.net.

PEARLMAN, MICHELLE, retail executive; B, Stanford Univ.; MBA, Univ. Chgo. Various mgmt. positions Procter & Gamble Co., 1993—2000; assoc prin. McKinsey & Co., 2000—04; exec. v.p. ATC Direct Ann Taylor Stores Corp., 2004—08; sr. v.p., pres. jewelry Sears Holdings Corp., Hoffman Estates, Ill., 2008—. Office: Sears Holdings Corp 3333 Beverly Rd Hoffman Estates IL 60179*

PEARLMAN, RONALD ALAN, lawyer, educator; b. Hamilton, Ohio, July 10, 1940; AB with honors, Northwestern U., 1962, JD cum laude, 1965; LL.M. in Taxation, Georgetown U., 1967. Bar: D.C. 1991, U.S. Tax Ct. 1969, U.S. Supreme Ct. 1968. Atty. office chief counsel IRS, Washington, 1965—69; assoc. Thompson Coburn, St. Louis, 1969—70, ptnr., 1970—83; dep. asst. sec. for tax policy Dept. Treasury, Washington, 1983—84, asst. sec. tax policy, 1984—85; ptnr. Bryan, Cave, McPheeters & McRoberts (now Bryan Cave), St. Louis, 1986—88; chief of staff joint com. on taxation U.S. Congress, Washington, 1988—90; ptnr. Covington & Burling, Washington, 1991—2000; prof. Georgetown U. Law Ctr., Washington, 1999—. Ind. trustee Eaton Vance Mut. Funds, 2003—; chair Compliance Reports and Regulatory Matters Com., 2008—; vis. prof. Georgetown U. Law Ctr., Washington, 1998, Harvard U. Law Sch., Cambridge, Mass., 2002; adj. prof. Sch. Law Wash. U., St. Louis, 1972—83; vis. instr. Sch. Law U. Va., Charlottesville, 1995—98; mem. BNA Tax Mgmt. Adv. Bd., 1986—88, 1993—; participant ednl. seminars; bd. trustees Eaton Vance Enhanced Equity Income Fund, 2004—. Mem. bd. editors Northwestern U. Law Rev.; contbr. articles to various publs. Trustee Am. Tax Policy Inst., 1998—2006, pres., 2003—04. Fellow Am. Coll. Tax Counsel; mem. ABA (vice chair govt. rels. 1997-99, chair govt. rels. com. 1996-97, mem. coun., tax sect. 1986-88), Am. Law Inst. (tax adv. group, cons. pass-through entities project and tax integration project), Order of Coif. Office: Eaton Vance Enhanced Equity Income Fund The Eaton Vance Bldg 255 State St Boston MA 02109 Home Phone: 202-342-2335; Office Phone: 202-662-9882, 617-482-8260. Business E-Mail: pearlman@law.georgetown.edu.*

PEARLMAN, SAMUEL SEGEL, lawyer, educator; b. Pitts., May 28, 1942; s. Merle Maurice and Bernice Florence (Segel) P.; m. Cathy Schwartz, Aug. 16, 1964; children: Linda P. Kraner, Caren E. AB, U. Pa., 1963, LLB magna cum laude, 1966. Bar: Pa. 1966, Ohio 1967, U.S. Ct. Appeals (3d cir.) 1967. Law clk. U.S. Dist. Ct. for Ea. Dist. Pa., Phila., 1966-67; assoc. Burke, Haber & Berick, Cleve., 1967-72, prin., 1973-86, Berick, Pearlman & Mills, Cleve., 1986-99; ptnr. Squire, Sanders & Dempsey L.L.P., Cleve., 2000—08; of counsel Singerman Mills, Desberg Kauntz, Beachwood, Ohio, 2009—. Lectr. law Case Western Res. U. Sch. Law, 1978-82; mem. registration com. Ohio Div. Securities, 1979-89; adv. dir. Midland Title Security, Inc.; trustee Realty ReFund Trust, N.Y. Stock Exch., 1990-98. Author: Cases, Forms and Materials for Modern Real Estate Transactions, 1978, 82. Mem. ABA, Ohio Bar Assn., Cleve. Met. Bar Assn. (chmn. securities law sect. 1985-86), Order of Coif. Republican. Jewish. Office: Singerman Mills Desberg Kauntz Beachwood OH 44122 Office Phone: 216-292-5807.

PEARLMAN, STEVEN JAY, otolaryngologist, surgeon, educator; b. NYC, 1956; BA (magna cum laude with high honors) in Biology, Brandeis U., 1978; MD, Mt. Sinai Sch. Medicine, 1982. Cert. Am. Bd. Otolaryngology-Head and Neck Surgery, 1987, Am. Bd. Facial Plastic and Reconstructive Surgery. Resident gen. surgery Mt. Sinai Med. Ctr., NYC, 1982-83, resident otolaryngology-head and neck surgery, 1983-87; fellow facial plastic surgery St. Luke's Roosevelt Hosp., NYC, 1987-88, otolaryngologist, assoc. dir., head and neck surgery, now dir., facial plastic surg. divsn.; attending surgeon Lenox Hill Hosp., NY, Manhattan Eye Ear and Throat Hosp., NY; private practice NYC. Asst. prof. clin. otolaryngology, Columbia U. Hosp. Ctr. of Physicians and Surgeons, clin. assoc. prof.; tchr. facial plastic surgery to residents, Columbia U. Med. Sch. and NY Eye and Ear Infirmary. Contbr. to numerous medical and sci. publs., to chpts. in books.; appeared on nat. and local television talk and news programs (including CNN, WABC, Eyewitness News, Good Day NY, The Food Network, Fox-Channel 5, Montel Williams Show, E! and performed "live" face lift on CNBC's "The Real Story".), frequently quoted in Allure, Elle, Harper's Bazaar, Marie-Claire, W, Fitness Plus, Cosmopolitan, In Style, More, YM, NY Mag., Redbook, NY Times, Daily News, Chicago Tribune and Newsday. Pro bono surgeon Face to Face; pro bono facial reconstructive surgeon Nat. Domestic Violence Project. Named an Top 12 Plastic Surgeons in NYC, NY Mag., 2002. Mem. AMA, Am. Acad. Otolaryngology-Head and Neck Surgeons, Am. Acad. Facial Plastic and Reconstructive Surgery (past eastern region v.p. and nat. com. chmn., pres. 2004-05), NY State Med. Soc., NY Facial Plastic Surgery Soc. (founder, 1993 and past pres.). Office: 521 Park Ave New York NY 10021-8140 Office Phone: 212-262-4444, 212-223-8300. Office Fax: 212-644-8655, 212-523-6364.

PEARLSON, GODFREY DAVID, psychiatrist, researcher, educator; b. Sunderland, England, Jan. 30, 1950; came to U.S., 1975; s. Elias and Blanche (Book) P.; m. Judith G. Sirote. MA, Columbia U., 1975; MD, Newcastle on Tyne, England, 1974. Intern Newcastle-on-Tyne RVI, Newcastle, Eng., 1974; resident in psychiatry Johns Hopkins U., Balt., 1976-79, dir. psychiatry neuroimaging, 1989—, prof. mental hygiene, psychiatry, 1987—. Recipient Ziskin-Somerfeld Rsch. award Soc. Biol. Psychiatry, 1996; fellow Am. Psychopathological Assn., 1987. Fellow Am. Psychiat. Assn. Office: Johns Hopkins Hosp Meyer 3 166 600 N Wolfe St Baltimore MD 21287-0005

PEARLSTEIN, TOBY, retired librarian, archivist; b. Revere, Mass., Jan. 19, 1952; d. Charles Simon and Rita (Swerling) Pearlstein. BA, U. Mass., 1973; MA, U. N.H., Dover, 1975; MLS, Simmons Coll., Boston, 1977, DA, 1987. Curator Archives Commonwealth of Mass., Boston, 1978—80; head libr./ tech. svcs. Ctrl. Transp. Planning Staff, Boston, 1980—83; chief libr. & archivist Mass. Dept. Transp., Boston, 1983—93; dir. global info. svcs. Bain & Co., Boston, 1993—2008; ret., 2007. Recipient Pride in Performance award, Commonwealth of Mass., 1992. Fellow: Spl. Libraries Assn. (chmn. transp. divsn. 1987, bus. & fin. divsn. 2007, Hall of Fame 2008); mem.: Assn. Records Mgrs. & Adminstrs. (bd. dirs. 1987—88, v.p. Boston chpt. 1988—89, mem. of Yr. 1989). Democrat. Jewish. Avocation: reading.

PEARLSTINE, NORMAN, communications executive, consultant, former editor; b. Phila., Oct. 4, 1942; s. Raymond and Gladys (Cohen) Pearlstine; m. Jane Boon. BA, Haverford Coll., 1964; LLB, U. Pa., 1967. Staff reporter Wall Street Jour., Dallas, 1968—73, Detroit, 1968—73, LA, 1968—73, Tokyo bur. chief, 1973—76; mng. editor Asian Wall Street Jour., Hong Kong, 1976—78; exec. editor Forbes Mag., LA, 1978—80; nat. news editor Wall Street Jour., NYC, 1980—82; editor, pub. Wall Street Jour./Europe, Brussels, 1982—83; mng. editor, v.p.

Wall Street Jour., NYC, 1983—91, exec. editor, 1991—92; pres., CEO Friday Holdings, L.P., NYC, 1993—94; editor-in-chief Time Inc., NYC, 1995—2005; sr. adv. Time Warner Inc., NYC, 2006; sr. adv. to telecom & media team The Carlyle Group, NYC, 2006—08; chief content officer Bloomberg L.P., NYC, 2008—. Author: Off the Record: The Press, the Government, and the War Over Anonymous Sources, 2007. Pres. Atsuko Chiba Found.; bd. councilors USC Annenberg Sch. Comm.; pres. adv. bd. Neiman Found. at Harvard U.; mem. adv. bd. CUNY Grad. Sch. Journalism, Arthur F. Burns Fellowship Program; bd. dir. The Carnegie Corp., The Arthur F. Burns Fellowship Program, Com. to Protect Journalists, 2004—, Internat. Ctr. for Journalists, The Berlin Sch. of Creative Leadership Steinbeis U.; trustee NY Hist. Soc., 1985—2005, chmn., 1989—93; pres. Am. Acad. in Berlin, 2006—. Recipient Editor of Yr. award, Nat. Press Found., 1989, Lifetime Achievement award, ASME, 2005, Loeb Lifetime Achievement award for disting. bus. and fin. journalism, 2000; named to, Mag. Editors Hall of Fame, 2005. Mem.: ABA, Am. Acad. Arts and Scis., Japan Soc., Coun. Fgn. Rels., D.C. Bar Assn., Tribeca Film Inst. (bd. dirs.). Office: Bloomberg LP 731 Lexington Ave New York NY 10022*

PEARMAN, RAVEN-SYMONÉ CHRISTINA See SYMONE, RAVEN

PEARSALL, GEORGE WILBUR, materials scientist, mechanical engineer, consultant; b. Brentwood, NY, July 13, 1933; s. Milo Dickerson and Margaret Elizabeth (White) P.; m. Patricia Louise Stevens, Oct. 11, 1962 (dec.) B. Metall. Engring., Rensselaer Poly. Inst., 1955; Sc.D. (Am. Soc. Metals fellow), MIT, 1961. Registered profl. engr., NC. Rsch. engr. Dow Chem. Co., Midland, Mich., 1955-57; rsch. asst. MIT, 1959-60, asst. prof. metallurgy, 1960-64; assoc. prof. mech. engring. Duke U., 1964-66, prof., 1966-81, prof. mech. engring. and materials sci., 1981—2001, prof. pub. policy studies, 1982—2001, acting dean Sch. Engring., 1969-71, dean, 1971-74, 82-83, prof. emeritus, 2001—. Trustee Triangle Univ. Ctr. for Advanced Studies, 1976-92, chmn. exec. com., 1983-88; dir. Duke-IBM Product Safety Inst., 1979-90. Author: (with W.G. Moffatt and J. Wulff) The Structure and Properties of Materials, 1964; mem. editl. bd. Jour. Products Liability, 1977-92, Jour. Products and Toxics Liability, 1993-96, Proceedings of the IEEE, 1994-96; contbr. articles to profl. jour. Served with AUS, 1957. Mem. ASME (Triodyne Safety Award 2001), Am. Soc. Metals (life), Phi Lambda Upsilon, Tau Beta Pi, Pi Tau Sigma. Home: 2941 Welcome Dr Durham NC 27705-5555 Office Phone: 919-660-5344. Personal E-mail: page1212@msn.com. Business E-Mail: pearsall@duke.edu.

PEARSALL, JOHN WESLEY, lawyer; b. Richmond, Va., Aug. 21, 1914; BS, Randolph-Macon Coll., 1935; LLB, U. Richmond, 1941. Bar: Va. 1940. Assoc. McGuire, Riely & Eggleston, Richmond, 1941-50; ptnr. McGuire, Eggleston, Bocock & Woods, Richmond, 1950-53; gen. counsel Va.-Carolina Chem. Corp., Richmond, 1953-56; pvt. practice Richmond, 1956-60; ptnr. McCaul, Grigsby & Pearsall, Richmond, 1960-86, Pearsall & Pearsall, 1986—2008; dir. Estes Express Lines, 1972—. Chpt. chmn. ARC, Chesterfield County, Va., 1944-49, campaign chmn., 1949, campaign chmn. Richmond, Henrico, and Chesterfield, Va., 1950, nat. vice chmn. fund dr., 1956, nat. gov., 1953-55; mem. budget com. Richmond Area Cmty. Chest, 1946-47, mem. exec. com., 1947-55, trustee, 1946-50, campaign chmn., 1951, pres., 1955, United Giver's Fund, 1970; v.p. Children's Aid Soc., Richmond, 1950-55, trustee, 1948-55; active Boy Scouts Am., 1953-56; mem. exec. com. Randolph-Macon Coll., 1958-76, chmn. long range plan com., 1960-76, trustee, 1955-76, mem. alumni bd., 1994-99, trustee emeritus, 2006; mem. Chesterfield County Welfare Bd., 1951-55; trustee Sheltering Arms Hosp., Richmond, 1949-80; dir. Jr. Achievement, 1975-81; vestryman St. Stephens Ch., 1967-70, ch. bearer, 1986-87; mem. exec. com. Hist. Richmond Found. (1965-70), Falls of James adv. bd., 1979-08, Chesterfield Hist. Soc., 1985-95. Served to lt. j.g. USNR, 1944-46. Mem. ABA, Va. Bar Assn., Richmond Bar Assn., Chesterfield County Bar Assn. (pres. 1963-64), Am. Judicature Soc., Va. State Bar Council (chmn. judicial ethics com. 1970-71), Am. Archaeol. Soc. (local chpt., pres. 1976), Phi Beta Kappa (pres. Richmond area chpt. 1976-77), Jr. C. of C. (Disting. Svc. award 1948, state pres. 1948-49), Omicron Delta Kappa, Lambda Chi Alpha. Office: Ellen Glasgow House 1 W Main St Richmond VA 23220-5623 Home: 1550 Westbrook Ct Apt 6205 Richmond VA 23227-3356 Home Phone: 804-200-1189; Office Phone: 804-644-5491. Personal E-mail: jwpearsall@comcast.net.

PEARSALL, OTIS PRATT, retired lawyer; b. Bklyn., Apr. 25, 1932; s. Willard Hall and Marilla Houghton (Pratt) P.; m. Nancy Jeanne Boden, July 7, 1956; 1 child, Melissa Mather. BA, Yale U., 1953, LL.B., 1956. Assoc. Hughes, Hubbard, Blair & Reed, NYC, 1956-59, 60-63; asst. U.S. atty. US Atty.'s Office So. Dist. NY, 1959-60; ptnr. Hughes Hubbard & Reed, NYC, 1964-91, Arnold & Porter, NYC, 1991—2002; ret., 2002. Mem. Art Commn. of the City of N.Y., 2001—; dir. Bridgehampton (N.Y.) Assocs., Inc., 1973—, pres., 2004—. Bd. dirs. Mcpl. Art Soc. NY, NYC, 1967-74, v.p., 1973-74; trustee Soc. for Preservation of L.I. Antiquities, Setauket, NY, 1969-77, Bklyn. Mus., 1986-92, 93—, mem. adv. bd., 1992-93; bd. dirs. LI Hist. Soc., Bklyn., 1971-82; mem. historic city com., NYC, 1987-88; trustee The Green-Wood Cemetery, Bklyn., 1992—; dir. NY Preservation Archive Project, 2003-. Recipient Green Star award Environ. Action Coalition, Inc., 1989, Landmark Lion award NY Hist. Dists. Coun., 1993, Lucy G. Moses Preservation Leadership award, NY Landmarks Conservancy, 2000, Forsythia award Bklyn. Botanic Garden, 2007. Fellow Am. Coll. Trial Lawyers; mem. Bklyn. Heights Assn. (gov., adv. com. 1960-), mem. ABA, Bridgehampton Club (pres. 1989-91), India House Club, Calif. Club, Univ. Club, Phi Beta Kappa. Republican. Congregationalist. Avocation: historic building restoration. Home: 157 Willow St Brooklyn NY 11201-2201

PEARSALL, SAMUEL HAFF, III, ecologist, geographer, foundation administrator; b. Nashville, Sept. 2, 1949; s. Sam H. Jr. and Margaret Isabelle (Ikard) P.; m. Patricia Davenport, July 1973 (div. 1978); 1 child, Rachel Claire; m. Linda Louise Parrish, Sept. 4, 1982; 1 child, Paul Samuel. BS, U. Tenn., 1942; M of Prof. Studies, Cornell U., 1982; PhD, U. Hawaii, 1993. Exec. dir. Coastal Resources Ctr., Bar Harbor, Maine, 1975-77; program dir. Natural Areas and Natural Heritage Survey Tenn. Dept. Conservation, Nashville, 1978-81, dir. Ecol. Svcs. divsn., 1982-85; dir. Pacific Sci. The Nature Conservancy, Honolulu, 1989-91, dir. sci. and stewardship Durham, NC, 1992-99, dir. sci. and Roanoke River Project, 2000—07, dir. sci. and climate change adaptation, 2007—08; southeast regional mgr. land, water and wildlife Environ. Def. Fund, Raleigh, NC. Adj. faculty U. NC, 1993—, Nicholas Sch. Environment Duke U., 1999—, founder Pacific Sci. program Nature Conservancy, 1989, founding mem. conservation com., 1994-96, Ecoregions working group, 1996-97; mem. So. Blue Ridge Ecoregional Planning Team, 1996-97; leader Mid-Atlantic Coastal Plain Ecoregional Planning Team, 1997—; founding mem. Ga.-Pacific/Nature Conservancy Roanoke Ecosys. Partnership, 1995-97; sci. and tech. adv. com. Albermarle-Pamlico Nat. Estuari Program, 2004-05; adv. com. coastal elevations and sea level rise US EPA, 2007-; mem. Nat. Park Svc. Cape Hatteras Regulatory Negotiation Com., 2007-08. Author: Terrestrial Coastal Environments and Tourism in Western Samoa, 1993, Managing for Future Change on the Albemarle Sound, 2005, Adapting Coastal Lowlands to Rising Seas, 2005; (with others) Wildlife Conservation Evaluation Methods in U.S., 1985; contbr. articles to profl. jours. Bd. dirs. Tenn. Environ. Coun., Nashville, 1980-85, Natural Areas Assn., Rockford, Ill., 1984-87, Bend, Oreg., 97-2000, treas., 1999-2000; counselor Conservation Trust for N.C., 1993-98; founder Tenn. Protection Planning Com.; student fellow East-West Ctr., 1985-90. Recipient Hodgson award Assn. Am. Geographers, 1988, Wiens award U. Hawaii, 1993, Conservation by Design award Nature Conservancy, 2003. Achievements include research in nature conservation, adaptive ecosystem management and landscape ecology in Western Samoa and North Carolina, coastal climate change and sea level rise in North Carolina; co-author FERC Lic. Settlement among Dominion Generation, Inc. and stakeholders at Lake Gaston and Roanoke Rapids dams. Home: 1307 Chaney Rd Raleigh NC 27606-2736 Office: 4000 Westchase Blvd #510 Raleigh NC 27607 Home Phone: 919-859-6297; Office Phone: 919-881-2938. Business E-Mail: spearsall@edf.org.

PEARSE, DAMIEN D., neuroscientist, consultant; b. Brisbane, Queensland, Australia, May 15, 1975; s. Ian J. and DiAnne K. Pearse; m. Munsu Lee, Dec. 18, 1999. BSc with honors, Griffith U., Brisbane, 1996, MEd, PhD, Griffith U., Brisbane, 1999. Asst. prof. U. Miami Sch. Medicine, Fla., 2004—. Contbr. articles to profl. jours. Recipient Erica Nader award for Outstanding Work in Spinal Cord Injury Rsch., 2005; grantee, Christopher Reeve Found., 2005—06, Bryon Riesch Paralysis Found., 2005, Hollfelder Found., 2002—04, Craig H. Neilsen Found., 2006; fellow, Christopher Reeve Paralysis Found. Consortium, 2000—04. Mem.: AAAS, Am. Pain Soc., Internat. Assn. for Study of Pain, Am. Soc. Neural Transplantation Repair, Internat. Soc. Neuroimmunology, Am. Soc. Gene Therapy, Nat. Neurotrauma Soc., Soc. Neuroscience, Am. Spinal Injury Assn. Achievements include discovery of cyclic AMP and cell implantation for spinal cord injury repair; chondroitinase ABC and cell implantation for spinal cord injury repair. Office: Univ Miami Sch Medicine 1095 NW 14th Terr Miami FL 33136 Office Fax: 305-243-3923. Business E-Mail: dpearse@miamiproject.med.miami.edu.

PEARSE, WARREN HARLAND, obstetrician, gynecologist, medical association administrator; b. Detroit, Sept. 28, 1927; s. Harry Albridge and Frances (Wressell) P.; m. Jacqueline Anne Langan, June 15, 1950; children: Kathryn, Susan, Laurie, Martha. BS, Mich. State U., 1948; M.B., MD, Northwestern U., 1950. Intern. Univ. Hosp., Ann Arbor, Mich., 1950-51; resident obstetrics and gynecology, 1951-53, 55-56; practice medicine specializing obstetrics and gynecology Detroit, 1956-58; mem. faculty U. Nebr. Med. Ctr., Omaha, 1959-71, Found. prof., chmn. dept. obstetrics and gynecology, 1962-71, asst. dean, 1963-71, mem. residency rev. com. obstetrics and gynecology, 1968-93; dean Med. Coll. Va., Richmond, Va., 1971-75; exec. dir. Am. Coll. Obstetrics and Gynecology, 1975-93; cons., 1993—; editor Women's Health Issues, Washington, 1993—. Author: (with V.L. Seltzer) Primary Health Care for Women, 1999; contbr. chpts., articles tech. lit. Served from 1st lt. to capt. AUS, 1953-55. Mem. Am. Coll. Obstetrics and Gynecology (dist. sec., treas. 1964-68, vice chmn. 1968-71), Am. Gynecology Soc., Soc. Gynecology Investigation, Assn. Profs. Gynecology and Obstetrics (sec., treas. 1969—), Alpha Omega Alpha. Home: #5005 10450 Lottsford Rd Bowie MD 20721-3301

PEARSON, CHERYL A., dentist; Grad. cum laude, Miami Dale CC, 1974; DMD with high distinction, U. Ky., 1981. Dental asst., 1970; resident Tufts U., Boston; pvt. practice cosmetic dentistry Pearson, Justice & Coffman, Lexington, Ky. Official dentist Miss Ky. Pageant. Mem.: Blue Grass Dental Soc. (chmn. sci. session), Ky. Acad. Cosmetic Dentistry (co-founder), Am. Acad. Cosmetic Dentistry. Office: Pearson, Justice & Coffman 3285 Blazer Parkway, Ste 200 Lexington KY 40509 Office Phone: 859-543-0700. Office Fax: 859-543-1078.

PEARSON, CHRISTINA H., public relations executive, former federal agency administrator; b. 1973; BA in English Lit., Hamilton Coll., Clinton, NY, 1995. Dep. comm. dir. fin. com. US Senate, 1995—99; dir. media rels. Policy Impact Comm., 1999—2000; sr. assoc. dir. media rels. Am. Hosp. Assn., Inc., 2000—02; dir. comm. Office Pub. Health & Sci. US Dept. Health & Human Services (HHS), 2002—03, dir. media rels., 2003—05, dep. asst. sec. for pub. affairs (media), 2005—07, asst. sec. for pub. affairs, 2008—09; sr. v.p. Fleishman-Hillard Internat. Communications, 2009—. Office: Fleishman-Hillard Internat Communications 1615 L St NE Ste 1000 Washington DC 20036 Office Phone: 202-659-0330. Office Fax: 202-296-6119.*

PEARSON, DAVID PETRI, chemist; b. Oct. 24, 1926; s. Brewer Petri and Laura Alvine (Johnson) P.; m. Patricia Margaret Cowan, June 4, 1949; children: Kathryn A., James P., Rebecca L., Kristine R., Judith G. BA in Chemistry, Reed Coll., 1949; MS in Phys. Chemistry, Oreg. State U., 1953; PhD in Phys. Chemistry, U. So. Calif., 1960. Rsch. chemist Phillips Petroleum Co. (AEC), Idaho Falls, Idaho, 1957-62, Bartlesville, Okla., 1962-69; lectr. in chemistry Portland State U., 1969-71; asst. prof. chemistry So. Oreg. State Coll., Ashland, 1971-72; rsch. assoc. Oreg. Grad. Ctr., Beaverton, 1972-74; sr. chemist Portland Gen. Electric Co., 1975-87, ret., 1987. Patentee in field. Cpl. USAAF, 1946-47. Mem. Am. Chem. Soc. (treas. Portland sect. 1979-82, chmn. 1983). Clubs: Am. Alpine, Idaho Alpine (sec. Idaho Falls 1961, pres. 1962), Sigma Xi. Republican. Presbyterian. Home: 6324 SW Radcliffe St Portland OR 97219-5749 Personal E-mail: pdpearson49@comcast.net.

PEARSON, FRED ROSS, healthcare educator, consultant; s. Ross Walter and Eila Pearson; m. Joleen J Lueck, May 27, 1967; children: Camile J Hjorten, Cordell J, Calisa J. PhD, U. Tenn., Knoxville, 1978. Pub. health rschr. educator Minn. State Govt., St. Paul, 1979—85; prof. Brigham Young U. Idaho, Rexburg, 1985—. Dir. Project HELP, Mpls., 1978—79. Contbr. chapters to books. Bishop Ch. Jesus Christ Latter-Day Saints, Rexburg, Idaho, 1995—2002. Pub. Health Svc. grant, USPHS, 1969—70. Conservative. Avocations: backpacking, camping, travel. Office: Brigham Young Univ Idaho 525 Center Rexburg ID 83460

PEARSON, GRETCHEN ELAINE, college librarian; b. Boone, Feb. 26, 1950; d. LeRoy A. and Beverley A. Pearson; m. Carmen Joseph Giunta, Sept. 25, 1993. MLS, U. Iowa, 1982. Reference and bibliographic instrn. libr. U. Wis., Platteville, 1982—86; sr. reference libr. U. Ill., Chgo., 1986—89; pub. svcs. libr. Le Moyne Coll., Syracuse, NY, 1989—. Cons., plagiarism, cheating, & copyright, 1999—. Contbr. chapters to books. Ch. coun. Good Shepherd Luth. Ch., Fayetteville, NY, 2008. Recipient Honor Soc. award, Theta Alpha Kappa, 2000. Mem.: ALA. Liberal. Lutheran. Avocation: travel. Home: 4827 Cavalry Green Dr Manlius NY 13104 Office: Le Moyne Coll 1419 Salt Springs Rd Syracuse NY 13214 Business E-Mail: pearson@lemoyne.edu.

PEARSON, JOHN WILLIAM, cardiologist; b. Apr. 25, 1950; MD, Univ. Missouri Columbia Sch. Med., 1976. Cert. Am. Bd. Internal Med., 1979, Am. Bd. Internal Med., Cardiovascular Disease, 1981. Intern Univ. Iowa Hosp. & Clinics, 1976—77, resident in cardiology, 1977—79; fellow in cardiology Med. Coll. Va., Richmond, 1976—81; attending physician Ctrl. Suffolk Hosp., Riverhead, NY; cardiologist East End Cardiology PC, Riverhead, NY, 1994—. Office: East End Cardiology PC 1279 E Main St Riverhead NY 11901 Office Phone: 631-727-2100. Office Fax: 631-727-2646.

PEARSON, JOHN YEARDLEY, JR., lawyer; b. Norfolk, Va., July 23, 1942; BA, Washington & Lee U., 1964; JD, U. Va., 1971. Bar: Va. 1971. Atty. Willcox & Savage P.C., Norfolk. Mem editl. bd.: Va. Law Rev., 1969—71. Fellow Am. Coll. Trial Lawyers; mem. ABA (litig. sect.), Internat. Assn. Def. Counsel, Order of Coif. Office: Willcox & Savage PC 1800 Bank of America Ctr Norfolk VA 23510-2197 Office Phone: 757-628-5503. Business E-Mail: jpearson@wilsav.com.

PEARSON, LON, Spanish educator, translator; b. Murray, Utah, Feb. 13, 1939; s. Milo Willard and Gulli Victoria (Peterson) P.; m. Janet Stepan, Oct. 7, 1961; children: Russell, Stephanie Pearson O'Bryant, Robert, Richard, Sharon Pearson Fletcher. BA, U. Utah, 1966; MA, UCLA, 1969, PhD, 1973. Tchg. fellow U. Utah, Salt Lake City, 1965-66; assoc. instr. UCLA, 1969-70; from asst. prof. to prof. U. Mo., Rolla, 1970-91; prof. U. Nebr., Kearney, 1991—2007, chair, 1991-96; vis. rschr. Dept. Spanish and Portuguese Brigham Young U., 2007—09. Translator Am. Bee Jour., Hamilton, Ill., 1970-95; fgn. lang. cons. Mo. Dept. Edn., Jefferson City, 1973-79; co-dir. Christian Tech. Project in Panama, Rolla, 1978-85; cons. Advanced Placement Reader, Ednl. Testing Svc., Princeton, N.J., 1979-86; soccer coach U. Mo., Rolla, 1979-85; vis. prof. Brigham Young U., Provo, Utah, 1982-83; del. MLA, N.Y.C., 1982-84; interpreter/liaison to Honduran Army, Mo. N.G., Yoro, Honduras, 1985-86; prof. Fed. U. Piaui, Teresina, Brazil, 1999; cons. Invision Project, Nebr. Dept. Edn., Lincoln, 2000-01. Author: Nicomedes Guzmán: Proletarian Author in Chile's Literary Generation of 1938, 1976; editor, pub. Mo. Fgn. Lang. Jour., 1973-78; translator (tchr.'s manual) Bienvenidos a la Vida de Empleo, 1991; editor Chasqui: Jour. Latin Am. Lit., 1993—; contbr. over 100 articles to profl. jours. Organizer, ofcl. Rolla Area Soccer Orgn., 1984-87; ofcl., coach US Soccer Fedn., Nat. Intercollegiate Soccer Ofcls. Assn., Rolla and American Fork, Utah; mem. Optimists Club, Rolla, 1980-85; publicity, fundraiser Def. Marriage Act, Kearney, 2000; bishop LDS Ch., Rolla, 1986-91, Kearney, 2000-04; vol. LDS Missionary, Mexico, 1959-61, 2004-05, Chile, 2009-2010. With U.S. Army N.G., 1961-62, ret., 1999. Nat. Def. Edn. Act fellow, UCLA, 1966-69, Nat. Endowment for Humanities fellow, Johns Hopkins U., 1975-76; recipient Rsch. Svcs. Coun. award to Chile, U. Nebr., 1996, 98, 99, 2000. Mem. Phi Kappa Phi (U. Mo.-Rolla chpt. pres., permanent sec. 1974-80, Meritorious Svc. award 1981). Avocations: church organist, photographer. Personal E-mail: pearsonlon@unk.edu.

PEARSON, LYNDA ANN, music educator; b. Washington, June 1, 1950; d. Frederick Joseph and Nancy Lee Pearson. AA in Music Edn., Luther Rice Coll., Alexandria, Va., 1971, BA in Music Edn., 1973; M in Music Edn., Cath. U. America, Washington, 1977. Substitute tchr. Alexandria City Pub. Schs., 1973—77, vocal music tchr., 1977—. Adjudicator Bland Music Competition, Alexandria, 1985. Singer Fairlington Presbyn. Ch. Choir, Alexandria, 1984. Recipient Good Apple award, Children Together, Alexandria, 2004. Mem.: NEA, Alexandria Edn. Assn., Va. Edn. Assn., Music Educators Nat. Conf., Va. Music Educators Assn. (Dist. 10 rep. 2006—). Baptist. Avocations: counted cross stitch, rubber stamping. Home: 1018 Beverley Dr Alexandria VA 22302-2420 Office: Lyles Crouch Traditional Acad 530 S Saint Asaph St Alexandria VA 22314 Office Phone: 703-706-4430. Office Fax: 703-684-0252. Personal E-mail: misslap@aol.com. Business E-Mail: lpearson@acps.k12.va.us.

PEARSON, MELISSA BERRY, literature and language educator; b. Ft. Jackson, SC, Aug. 25, 1965; d. Charles F. and Hester M. Berry; children: Justin Wayne, Jordan Charles. BA in Liberal Arts-English, Comm., U. Ill., Urbana-Champaign, 1997, MA in English, 2000; attending in English-Rhetoric and Composition, U. SC, Columbia, 2004—. Asst. prof. English Claflin U., Orangeburg, SC, 2005—; interim dir. Jonathan Jasper Wright Inst. Study Southern African Am. History, Culture and Policy, Orangeburg, 2007—. Exec. dir. SC Coun. African Am. Studies, Columbia, 2005—08. Contbr. monograph. Founding bd. mem. SC Coll. Summit, Columbia, 2006—08. Faculty Devel. fellowship, UNCF-Mellon, 2008—. Mem.: Nat. Coun. Tchrs. English. Democrat. Office: Jonathan Jasper Wright Inst 400 Magnolia St Orangeburg SC 29115 Office Fax: 803-535-5892. Personal E-mail: pearson_melissa@bellsouth.net. Business E-Mail: mpearson@claflin.edu.

PEARSON, NATHAN WILLIAMS, communications and investment executive; b. Sewickley, Pa., Aug. 1, 1951; s. Nathan Williams Sr. and Kathleen Patricia (McMurtry) P.; m. Jane Ruth Wallace, Oct. 12, 1985; children: Nathan McMurtry, Howe Quinn, Henry Wallace. BA and MA in Music, Conn. Wesleyan U., 1974; MBA, Columbia U., NYC, 1982. Pvt. practice cons., NYC and Washington, 1974-82; with McKinsey & Co., NYC and LA, 1982-88, CEO; exec. v.p., chief fin. officer, mng. prin., sec., treas. Broadcasting Ptnrs., Inc., NYC, 1988-95; chmn. Broadcasting Ptnrs., LLC, Rye, NY, 1995—2008; pres., CEO and chmn. RadioWave.com Inc., Chgo., 1999—2001; mng. dir. Gallup Hill, LLC, Rye, NY, 2002—. Vice chmn. No. Light Comms., Reykjavik, 1995-2003; mng. dir. Commonwealth Holdings, Inc., NYC, 1996-99; operating affiliate McCown DeLeeuw & Co., NYC, 1997-99; ptnr. Windale Group, 2004-; bd. dirs. 1105 Media Inc., 2006-, Archway Broadcasting Group, 2004-07, WMI Inc., Westport, Conn., 2007-, Las Vegas TV Ptnrs., LLC, 2005-08, Tranzact, Inc., Fort Lee, NJ, 2007; chmn. Adina, Inc., 2007—08; lectr. Harvard U., Dept. Economics, 2005-. Author: Goin' to Kansas City, 1987; producer LP records, TV and radio programs; contbr. articles to profl. jours. Sec., bd. dirs. CityLore, Inc., NYC, 1986—, pres., 1990-92; pres. Young Audiences/NYC, 1995-96; bd. dirs. Young Audiences, 1986—, Rye Nature Ctr., 2004—, The Osborn, 2005—, Young Audiences, Inc., 1995-, pres., 2008-. Mem. Soc. for Ethnomusicology, Am. Folklore Soc., Wadawanuck Club, Nat. Assn. Broadcasting, Manursing Island Club, Hillsboro Club, Rolling Rock Club, Apawamis Club, Beta Gamma Sigma. Avocations: boardsailing, river running, hiking. Home: 3 Holly Ln Rye NY 10580-3953 Office: Gallup Hill LLC Rye NY 10580 Office Phone: 914-643-3278. Personal E-mail: bpearson@gmail.com. Business E-Mail: bpearson@galluphill.com.

PEARSON, PATRICIA ANNETTE, history professor; d. William Clarence Bradley and Eva Mae McCord-Bradley; m. Rickie Leon Pearson, June 15, 1951; children: Ardis Meredith, Remick Cole. PhD, U. Ky., Lexington, 1984. Instr. Tenn. State U., Nashville, 1972—77; prof. history Ky. State U., Frankfort, 1984—. Poll worker City Frankfort, 1989—2003. Named Disting. Prof., Ky. State U., 1998. Mem.: Alpha Kappa Alpha (epistelus 2008—09). Liberal. Roman Catholic.

PEARSON, PAUL DAVID, lawyer, arbitrator, mediator; b. Boston, Jan. 22, 1940; s. Bernard J. and Ruth (Bayla); children: David Todd, Lisa Kari, Grant M. BA, Bucknell U., 1961; LLB, U. Pa., 1964. Bar: Mass. 1966, N.Y. 1987. Staff atty., tech. assoc. lab. cmty. psychiatry dept. Med. Sch. Harvard U., Boston, 1966—68; assoc. Snyder Tepper & Berlin,

Boston, 1969—71, ptnr., 1971—77; ptnr., chmn. family law dept. Hill & Barlow, 1977—87; ptnr. chmn. family law dept. Hodgson, Russ, LLP, Buffalo, 1987—96; of counsel Sullivan Oliverio & Gioia, Buffalo, 1996—2006; with Law Offices Kevin A. Ricotta, 2006—08, Keith B. Schulefand, 2008—; panel mediator West Dist. Fed. Ct. NY, 2009—. Lectr. Mass. CLE, New Eng. Law Inst., 1975-1987, dept. psychiatry SUNY Sch. Medicine, Buffalo, 1989—; instr. law and mental health Boston Psychoanalytic Soc. and Inst., 1975-87; lectr. law, mental health, alternative dispute resolution Contbr. articles to profl. jour. and interdisciplinary publs Founding mem. Alliance for Dispute Resolution, 1996, Buffalo Collaborative Law Coun., 2002; bd. dir. Jewish Cmty. Ctr. Greater Buffalo, 1991-96, Am. Jewish Com. Buffalo, pres., 1995-97, nat. bd. govs., 1997-2008; bd. dir. Arts Coun. Buffalo and Erie County, 1992-99; legal coord. Parent Edn. and Custody Effectiveness program N.Y. 8th jud. dist.; pres., trustee, legal counsel Wayland (Mass.) Townhouse; trustee Family Counseling Svc. (region West); mem., chmn., clk. Wayland Zoning Bd. Appeals, 1970-80; v.p., counsel Arts Wayland Found., 1982-87; vis. fellow Woodrow Wilson Found., 1985-87, Mass. Gov. Spl. Commn. on Divorce, 1985-87. Capt. Mil. Police Corps USAR. Fellow Am. Acad. Matrimonial Lawyers (cert., pres., bd. mgr. Mass); mem. ABA (chair ADR family com.), Mass. Bar Assn. (chmn. family law sect.), Assn. Conflict Resolution (advanced practitioner), N.Y. State Coun. on Divorce Mediation, Assn. Family and Conciliation Ct., Boston Bar Assn. (family law com., legis. chmn.), N.Y. Bar Assn. (family law ADR sect.), Erie County Bar Assn. (chair ADR com. 1992-96, family law com., judiciary com.), NY Mag.'s (Top Lawyers 2007-09). Office: 1301 N Forest Rd Ste 2 Williamsville NY 14221 Office Phone: 716-632-2728. Office Fax: 716-565-1575. Personal E-mail: pdp@pdpesq.com.

PEARSON, PAUL HOLDING, insurance company executive; b. Worcester, Mass., Feb. 14, 1940; s. Malcolm D. and Myra L. (Holding) P.; m. Judith N. Howe, July 13, 1958 (div. June 1974); children: Scott D., Todd E.; m. Anne Beck, July 26, 1974. BA in Bus. and Econs., U. Maine, 1961. C.L.U., 1971. Jr. life underwriter State Mut. Am., Worcester, 1961-63, life underwriter, 1963-67, sr. life underwriter, 1967-69; dir. life underwriting Security Mut. Life Ins. Co., Binghamton, NY, 1969, 2d v.p. underwriting, 1970, v.p., 1971-75, sr. v.p. ins. services div., 1975-79, exec. v.p., 1979-81, pres., 1981-96, chief exec. officer, 1987-97; chmn. Security Mutual Life Ins. Co. of N.Y., Binghamton, 1996-97. Chmn., CEO, bd. dirs. SML Properties corp., Binghamton, Security Equity Life Ins. Co., Binghamton, 1987-93; vice chmn. Generalife, 1997-99. Trustee, treas. Lourdes Meml. Hosp., Binghamton, 1978-92; mem. SUNY Found., Binghamton, 1982-89; trustee, chmn. fin. com. Elmira Coll., 1983-87; bd. dirs. Broome C.C. Found., 1982-91, pres. 1985-86; pres. New Industries for Broome, Binghamton, 1985-95, N.Y. State Bus. Devel. Coun., 1987-96; bd. dirs. Valley Devel. Found., 1987-91, Bus. Coun. N.Y., 1988-97, Am. Coun. Life Ins., 1990-96; bd. dirs., treas. Fiddlesticks C.C., 2002-05. Mem. Assn. for Advanced Life Underwriting, Nat. Assn. Life Underwriters, Broome County C. of C. (bd. dirs. 1980-88, chmn. 1986), Binghamton C/C Live Wire Club, Fiddlesticks Country Club (bd. dirs., treas. 2002-05). Office Phone: 239-768-0162. Personal E-mail: phapearson@aol.com.

PEARSON, REBECCA E., lawyer; b. Balt., Jan. 14, 1964; AB, Duke Univ., 1985; JD, Univ. NC, Chapel Hill, 1989; LLM in Govt. Procurement with highest honors, George Washington Univ., 1996. Bar: Fla. 1989, DC 2000. Assoc. Venable LLP, Washington, ptnr., govt. contract litig., 2004—. Articles editor NC Jour. Internat. Law and Comml. Regulation, 1988—89, student editor-in-chief ABA Public Contract Law Jour., 1995—96; contbr. articles to profl. journals. With USAF, 1989—99. Mem.: ABA. Office: Venable LLP 575 Seventh St NW Washington DC 20004 Office Phone: 202-344-8183. Office Fax: 202-344-8300. Business E-Mail: repearson@venable.com.

PEARSON, RICHARD JOSEPH, archaeologist, educator; b. Kitchener, Ont., Can., May 2, 1938; s. John Cecil and Henrietta Anne Pearson; m. Kazue Miyazaki, Dec. 12, 1964; 1 child, Sarina Riye. BA in Anthropology with honours, U. Toronto, 1960; PhD, Yale U., 1966. Asst. prof., then assoc. prof. archaeology U. Hawaii, 1966-71; mem. faculty U. B.C., Vancouver, 1971-2000. Sr. rsch. advisor Sainsbury Inst. Japanese Arts and Cultures, 2007. Author: The Archaeology of the Ryukyu Islands, 1969, Higashi Ajia no Kodai Shakai to Kokogaku, 1984, Windows on the Japanese Past, Studies in Archaeology and Prehistory, 1986, Ancient Japan, 1992; contbr. articles to profl. jours. Guggenheim fellow.

PEARSON, ROBERT LAWRENCE, executive recruiter; b. Chgo., Apr. 19, 1939; s. Jonas Peter and Caroline Margaret (Reilly) P.; m. Norma Eloise Dale, April 27, 1963; children: Jill C., Keith D. BSEE, Mich. State U., 1961; MS magna cum laude, MIT, 1963. Cons. McKinsey and Co., Inc., Chgo., 1964-68; v.p. Raymond James and Assoc., St. Petersburg, Fla., 1968-70; pres. Pearson Wade and Co., Inc., Ft. Lauderdale, Fla., 1970-71, Pearson, Inc., Racine, Wis., 1971-81; exec. dir. Russell Reynolds Assoc., Inc., Dallas, 1981-83; mng. dir. Lamalie Assoc., Inc., Dallas, 1984-89, chmn., 1989-94; pres. Lamalie Amrop Internat., Dallas, 1994-98, chmn., CEO, 1994—99; CEO Pearson Ptnrs. Internat., Inc., 1999—; mem., bd. dirs. Tatum CFO Inc., 1999—2003; mem. bd. dirs. Pentagon Techs. Inc., 2000—, Baird Capital Ptnrs. Inc., 2000—. Mem. fund raising com. Dallas Mus. of Art, 1983-85; mem. Dallas Mus. Natural History, 1985—, bd. dirs., 1988-90; mem. YMCA, Dallas; patron Ronald McDonald House of Dallas; speech writer Gov.'s Campaign, Chgo., 1968. Contbr. articles to profl. jours. Mem. MIT Enterprise Forum, Dallas C. of C., Phi Delta Theta (pres. 1959-61), Tower Club (Dallas), MIT (Dallas, pres. 1993-96), Gilda's Club North Tex. (founding sponsor), Dallas Nat. Golf Club, Broadmoor Golf Club. Episcopalian. Avocations: squash, jogging, deep sea fishing, hunting, marathon running. Office: Pearson Ptnrs Internat Inc Ste 1200 8080 N Central Expy Dallas TX 75206 Home: Apt 9D 3510 Turtle Creek Blvd Dallas TX 75219 Office Phone: 214-292-4130. Business E-Mail: rpear@pearsonpartners.intl.com.

PEARSON, ROGER, organization executive; b. London, Aug. 21, 1927; s. Edwin and Beatrice May (Woodbine) P.; m. Marion Primrose Simms, June 3, 1959; children: Edwin, Sigrid, Emma, Rupert BS with honors, U. London, 1951, MS, 1954, PhD, 1969. Chmn. Pakistan Tea Assn., 1963-64; mng. dir. Octavius Steel & Co. of Pakistan Ltd., Chittagong, East Pakistan, 1959-65; chmn. Plummer Bros., Ltd., Chittagong, East Pakistan, 1959-65, Chittagong Warehouses, Ltd., Chittagong, East Pakistan, 1960-65; chmn. dept. sociology and anthropology Queens Coll., Charlotte, NC, 1970-71; chmn. dept. anthropology U. So. Miss., Hattiesburg, 1971-74; dean acad. affairs, dir. research Mont. Coll. Mineral Sci. Tech., Butte, 1974-75; exec. dir. Council for Econ. and Social Studies, Washington, 1975—. Author: Eastern Interlude, 1954, Introduction to Anthropology, 1978, Anthropological Glossary, 1985, Race, Intelligence and Bias in Academe, 1991, Shockley on Eugenics and Race, 1992, Heredity and Humanity, 1996, Cultural Anthropology, 2002; editor: Ecology and Evolution, 1982, (jour.) Social Polit. and Econ. Studies, 1976—. Trustee, Benjamin Franklin U., Washington, 1984-87. Served to lt. Brit. Indian Army, 1945-48. Office: Coun Econ and Social Studies 1133 13th St NW Washington DC 20005-4203

PEARSON, ROGER LEE, library director; b. Galesburg, Ill., Dec. 7, 1940; s. Clifford Emmanuel and Lillian Louise (Fisher) P. BA, Knox Coll., 1963; MA in Sociology, U. Nebr.-Omaha, 1968; MA in Library Sci., Rosary Coll., 1974. Vol. U.S. Peace Corps, Brazil, 1964-66; extension service supr. Brown County Libr., Green Bay, Wis., 1974-75; system adminstr. Nicolet Libr. System, Green Bay, 1976-77; exec. dir. South Central Libr. System, Madison, Wis., 1977-81; dir. Corpus Christi Pub. Librs., Tex., 1981-84, Naperville (Ill.) Pub. Librs., 1984-95, Sonoma County Libr., Santa Rosa, Calif., 1996-2001; interim dir. Spokane (Wash.) Pub. Libr., 2001; interim libr. dir. Coll. of Marin, Kentfield, Calif., 2002; interim dist. libr. Dixon (Calif.) Pub. Libr., 2002—03; interim dir. Kans. City (Mo.) Pub. Libr., 2004—05, Sonoma County Libr., Santa Rosa, 2005, Berkeley Pub. Libr., Calif., 2006; interim county libr. Yolo County Libr., Calif., 2008; interim county libr. Colusa County Libr., Calif., 2008. Lectr. Grad. Sch. Libr. and Info. Sci., Dominican U., River Forest, Ill., 1991-95. Mem. ALA, Train Riders Assn. Calif., Calif. Libr. Assn., Wine Libr. Assocs. Sonoma County. Avocations: power walking, travel research, train travel.

PEARSON, ROY LAING, business administration educator; b. Victoria, Hong Kong, Oct. 18, 1939; s. Roy Ross and Martha Ann L.; m. Louise Elliott Johns, June 11, 1960; 1 child, Cynthia Laing. BS in Commerce, U. Va., 1961, PhD in Econs., 1968. Asst. prof. U. Ark. Sch. Bus. Adminstrn., Fayetteville, 1964-68; assoc. prof. Centenary Coll. La., Shreveport, 1968-71; assoc. prof. bus. adminstrn. Coll. William and Mary, Williamsburg, Va., 1971-76, prof. bus. adminstrn., 1976-87, dir. Bur. Bus. Rsch., 1985-98, Chancellor prof. bus. adminstrn., 1987—2005, prof. emeritus, 2005. V.p. Wessex Group, Inc., Williamsburg, Va., 1979—; sec.-treas. McKinley Land Co., Inc., Williamsburg, 1969-2001. Editor, author: (newsletter) Virginia Business Report, Virginia Outlook, 1984-99. Bd. dirs. Williamsburg Community Hosp., 1985-90; gov.'s adv. bd. economists Commonwealth of Va., Richmond, 1984-98, 2002-; mem. trust fund adv. com. Va. Employment Comm., 1984—. NSF fellow, 1963. Mem. Va. Assn. Economists (pres. 1990-91, bd. dirs. 1985-91, disting. fellow 1998), Assn. for Univ. Bus. and Econ. Rsch. (bd. dirs. 1991-92, v.p. 1992-94, pres. 1994-95, hon. mem. 1999—), Nat. Assn. Bus. Economists, Internat. Inst. Forecasters (bd. dirs. 2001-2004), Nat. Bus. and Economics Soc. (v.p. 2004-) Avocations: scuba diving, underwater photography, science fiction. Home and Office: 4400 Chickasaw Ct Williamsburg VA 23188-8020 Business E-Mail: roy.pearson@mason.wm.edu.

PEARSON, SCOTT ROBERTS, retired economics professor; b. Madison, Wis., Mar. 13, 1938; s. Carlyle Roberts and Edith Hope (Smith) P.; m. Sandra Carol Anderson, Sept. 12, 1962; children: Sarah Roberts, Elizabeth Hovden. BS, U. Wis., Madison, 1961; MA, Johns Hopkins U., 1965; PhD, Harvard U., 1969. Asst. prof. Stanford U., Calif., 1968-74, assoc. prof., 1974-80; assoc. dir. Food Rsch. Inst., 1977-84, dir., 1992-96, prof. food econs., 1980—2002; ret., 2002. Cons. AID, World Bank, Washington, 1965—; staff economist Commn. Internat. Trade, Washington, 1970-71. Author: Petroleum and the Nigerian Economy, 1970; (with others) Commodity Exports and African Economic Development, 1974, (with others) Rice in West Africa, Policy and Economics, 1981, (with others) Food Policy Analysis, 1983, (with others) The Cassava Economy of Java, 1984, (with others) Portuguese Agriculture in Transition, 1987, (with Eric Monke) The Policy Analysis Matrix, 1989, (with others) Rice Policy in Indonesia, 1991, (with others) Structural Change and Small-Farm Agriculture in Northwest Portugal, 1993, (with others) Agricultural Policy in Kenya, 1995, (with others) Small Farm Agriculture in Southern Europe, 1998, (with others) Applications of the Policy Analysis Matrix in Indonesian Agriculture, 2004. Mem. Am. Agrl. Econs. Assn., Am. Econ. Asn. E-mail: pearson@stanford.edu.

PEARSON, SELA, poet, speaker; b. Bklyn., Aug. 10, 1952; d. Thomas Turner and Thelma (Brown) Razor; children: Nassar (dec.), Anwar, Jonathan BS, St. Joseph's Coll., Bklyn., 1988; MBA in Healthcare Mgmt., U. Phoenix, 2006; D in Naturopathic Medicine, Washington, 2009. LPN, cert. holistic health cons., 2008. Psychiat., pediat. nurse Syosset Hosp., NY, 1974—78; sales agent Combined Life Ins. Co. N.Y., Albany, 1978—80; med., surg. nurse Bapt. Med. Ctr., Bklyn., 1980—86; nurse counselor Riker's Island Prison Hosp., Queens, NY, 1986—88; clinic nurse St. Christopher Ottilie, Queens, 1988—90; mgr. intensive case AIDS Ctr. Queens County, 1990—92; quality assurance, utilization rev. nurse Vanderbilt U. Med. Ctr., Nashville, 1992—94; program dir. Boys and Girls Club, Franklin, Tenn., 1994—95; spkr., writer, nurse Akanke Creations, Brentwood, Tenn., 1996—; ind. health contractor Clayton County Crisis Unit, 1997—98; nurse Phoenix Program FHC of Nashville, 1998—99; nurse Murci Homes, 1999—. Cons. Murphy Alternative Ctr., Nashville, 1996, Serendipity House, Nashville, 1996, Family and Ednl. Adv. Assocs., Inc., Nashville, 1996, Growing In Grace Leadership Sch., Nashville, 1996; storyteller, presenter poetry recitals; ind. contractor Crisis Group Home, Riverdale, Ga.; faculty mem. Antara Ctr., 2004. Author: Success is a State of Mind, 2008, New York Poetry Foundation Anthology, 1986, Beyond the Stars, 1995 (Editors Choice 1995), Sela's Sounds of Silence, 1995, A Soulful Journey, 2000; performer (video) A Soulful Journey, 1995, The Magic of Peace, 1996, Our Voices, 1996; author numerous poems; contbr. articles to profl. jours., mags Vol. Williamson County Libr., Franklin, 1995—, Boys and Girls Club, Franklin, 1996—, TPAC; bd. dirs. Nashville Peace Action, 1996—; mem. New Gospel Singers Choir, 1995—, Ambassador of Poetry, 2006; storytelling del. to South Africa People to People Amb. Programs, invited Women in Soc. rep., Egypt, 2000—; mem. Coun. for the Written Word. Recipient Vol. Svc. award Berksheire Nursing Ctr., West Babylon, N.Y., 1977, Mayor's award for svc. in cmty. in arts, 2001; incluson of poem Faith to Wm. Kings Regl. Art Ctr., 1999, Cmty. Svc. award Edith Taylor Langster, Ho. of Reps., 54th Dist., 2003, Outstanding Student award (UOP), 2007, Student Commencement Speaker, UOP, 2007. Mem. Nat. Spkrs. Assn., Brentwood Early Risers Toastmasters (v.p. membership 1996—, various awards), Tenn. Writers Alliance, Harpeth Storytelling Group, Nat. Storytelling Assn., Internat. Soc. Poets (Poets Choice award 1995, Internat. Poet of Merit award 1995), Tenn. Writers Group Franklin, Tenn. Assn. Perpetuation Preservation Storytelling, Ga. Writers Group, Creative Artists Tenn., Tenn. Spkrs. Assn., Women Vision Enhancing Network (cert., dir. pub. rels.), Cherokee Wolf Clan (tribal coun.), Leadership mem. Interplay. Avocations: piano playing, travel, reading. Address: PO Box 111341 Nashville TN 37222-1341 Office Phone: 615-365-3187. Personal E-mail: selapearson@bellsouth.net. Business E-Mail: sela@akankecreations.com.

PEARSON, THOMAS ARTHUR, epidemiologist, educator; b. Berlin, Wis., Oct. 21, 1950; married; 2 children. BA, Johns Hopkins U., 1973, MD, MPH, Johns Hopkins U., 1976, PhD in Epidemiology, 1983; MA (hon.), U. Umeå, 2002. Fellow in cardiology Johns Hopkins Sch. Medicine, Balt., 1981-83, from asst. prof. to assoc. prof. medicine, epidemiology, 1983-88; prof. epidemiology Columbia U., 1988-97, prof. medicine, 1995-97, prof. medicine, Jane Forbes Clark chair in health rsch. NYC, 1995-97; dir. Mary Imogene Bassett Rsch. Inst., 1988-97; Kaiser prof. epidemiology, cmty. and preventive medicine U. Rochester, NY, 1997—, sr. assoc. dean for clin. rsch., 2002—. Mem. clin. applications and prevention commn. NIH, 1987—91, chmn., 1990; dir. Rochester Prevention Rsch. Ctr., 2004—; bd. dirs. World Heart Fedn. Co-editor: Scandinavian Jour. Pub. Health, 2000—. Mem. ACP, Am. Heart Assn. (nat. rsch. com. 1987-92, coun. epidemiology 1987—, vice chmn. 1994-95, chmn. 1996-98), Am. Fedn. Clin. Rsch., Am. Coll. Epidemiology, Am. Coll. Preventive Medicine, Am. Coll. Cardiology (prevention com.), Soc. Epidemiol. Rsch. (rsch. prize 1978). Achievements include research in the etiology and pathogenesis of atherosclerosis. Office: U Rochester Sch Medicine Dept Cmty Preventive Med 601 Elmwood Ave Box 644 Rochester NY 14642-0001 Office Phone: 585-275-2191.*

PEARSON, WALTER DONALD, editor, columnist; b. Pittsfield, Mass., Feb. 5, 1916; s. Edgar C. and Edna (Scott) P.; divorced; children: Florence, Donald, Sharon; m. Elsa Swanson (dec.); 1 child, Richard Scott. Student, Dartmouth Coll., 1941-43. Advt. salesman, 1935-41; securities broker Charles A. Day Co., Boston, 1947-55; founder, owner, mgr. First New Eng. Securities Co., Inc., Southbridge, Mass., 1955-71; now owner, editor Pearson Investment Letter, Dover, Fla.; ptnr. Pearson Capital Inc.; fin. columnist World Intelligence Rev., CDL Report, Nationalist Times; free-lance columnist various publications; fin. advisor, investment mgr. Author: Investing for the Millions, 1990, Bridge Made Easy, 1995 With inf. U.S. Army, 1943-45, ETO. Decorated Bronze star, Croix de Guerre (France), Combat Infantry badge. Home: 1628 White Arrow Dr Dover FL 33527-5741 Office Phone: 813-659-2560. Personal E-mail: PearsonCap@aol.com.

PEARSON, WILLIAM RAYMOND, biochemist, educator; s. Raymond and Ann Pearson; m. Sarah McNeil Corse, Oct. 8, 2005; children: Robert Murray Corse Harder, Elizabeth Ann, Robert Murray Corse Harder children: Jennifer Maria, Jennifer Maria; m. Sonia Helen White, June 21, 1980 (div. Dec. 30, 2004). BS, U. Ill., Urbana, 1971; PhD, Calif. Inst. Tech., Pasadena, 1977. Postdoc. fellow Calif. Inst. Tech., Corona del Mar, 1977—78, Johns Hopkins Sch. Medicine, Balt., 1978—83; prof. biochemistry U. Va. Sch. Medicine, Charlottesville, 1983—. Fellow: AAAS. Office: U Va Box 800733 Dept Biochem Mol Gen Charlottesville VA 22908 Business E-Mail: wrp@virginia.edu.

PEARSON, W(ILLIAM) ROBERT, former federal agency administrator, former ambassador; b. Bells, Tenn., June 28, 1943; s. Marion Robert and Louise (Wilson) P.; m. Margaret Coplin, June 20, 1975; 1 child, Matthew. BA, Vanderbilt U., 1965; LLB, U.Va., 1968. Vice consul U.S. Consulate Gen., Auckland, New Zealand, 1976-78; staff asst./Conf. Asia Bur. US Dept. State, Washington, 1978-79, Chinese lang. tng. officer Washington and Taiwan, 1979-81; polit. officer US Embassy, Beijing, 1981-83; dep. dir. Ops. Ctr. US Dept. State, Washington, 1983-85; dep. exec. sec. NSC, Washington, 1985-87; dept. asst. sec. gen. NATO, Brussels, 1987-90; dep. exec. sec. US Dept. State, Washington, 1990-91, exec. sec., 1991—93; dep. permanent rep. to US mission NATO, 1993—97; dep. chief mission US Embassy, France, 1997—2000; US amb. to Turkey US Dept. State, Ankara, 2000—03, dir. gen. US Fgn. Svc. Washington, 2003—06, dir. human resources, 2003—06. Mem. Internat. Inst. of Strategic Studies.

PEARSON, WILLIAM S., epidemiologist; PhD, U. SC., Columbia, 2004. Health scientist Nat. Ctr. Health Stats., Hyattsville, Md., 2004—06; epidemiologist Ctrs. Disease Control and Prevention, Atlanta, 2006—. Achievements include research in health services research and epidemiology.

PEART, DAVID ROSS, biology professor; b. Southport, Queensland, Australia, Nov. 16, 1949; BSc, U. Queensland, Brisbane, Australia, 1969; PhD, U. Calif., Davis, 1982. Math. tchr. Australian Capital Ter. Dept Edn., Canberra, Australian Capital Ter., 1970—72; programmer & sys. analyst Australian Fed. Govt., Canberra, 1973—75; vis. asst. prof. Dartmouth Coll., Hanover, NH, 1983—83, asst. prof. biol. sciences, 1986—92, assoc. prof., 1992—98, prof. biol. scis., 1993—; vis. asst. prof. SUNY, Stony Brook, NY, 1983—84. Mem. bd. dirs. Sustainability Inst., Hartland, Vt., 1996—2001, Hartland, 2007—09, chair, bd. dirs., 2002—06. Mem. Hanover Conservation Coun., 2002—06, pres., 2007—08. Office: Dartmouth Col Gilman Hall Hanover NH 03755

PEART, SANDRA JOAN, dean; b. Stratford, Canada, Apr. 4, 1959; d. Donald MacLean and Beverley Joan Peart; m. Craig Warren Heinicke, June 4, 1988; children: Nathan Casey Heinicke-Peart, Matthew Warren Heinicke-Peart. BA, U. Toronto, Ont., Can., 1982, PhD, 1989. Asst. prof. Coll. William and Mary, Williamsburg, Va., 1989—91; prof. econs. Baldwin-Wallace Coll., Berea, Ohio, 1991—2007; dean Jepson sch. leadership studies U. Richmond, Va., 2007—. Vis. scholar Ctr. Study of Pub. Choice George Mason U., Fairfax, Va., 2004—05, dir. Summer Inst. Ctr. Study of Pub. Choice, 2004—. Co-author (with David Levy): The Vanity of the Philosopher: From Equality to Hierarchy in Post-Classical Economics, 2005, The Street Porter and the Philosopher Conversations on Analytical Egalitarianism, 2008; contbr. articles to profl. jours. Fellow, Am. Coun. Edn., 2005—06. Mem.: History Econs. Soc. (exec. com. 2000—05, pres. 2007—, Best Dissertation award 1990). Achievements include research in the transition from egalitarian thinking to notions of race and hierarchy in economics; the role of sympathy in economics and social science; the role of the expert in social science. Office: Jepson Sch Leadership Studies Univ Richmond Richmond VA 23173 Office Phone: 804-287-6086. Personal E-mail: sandrajpeart@gmail.com. Business E-Mail: speart@richmond.edu.

PEASE, DAVID GORDON, artist, educator; b. Bloomington, Ill., June 2, 1932; s. Gordon A. and June (Stephens) P.; m. Julie Jensen, Mar. 29, 1956; children: Lisa Kay, Kerry Susan. BS, U. Wis., 1954, MS, 1955, M.F.A., 1958. Instr. audio visual ctr. Mich. State U., 1958-60; mem. faculty Tyler Sch. Art, Temple U., Phila., 1960-83, prof., 1970-83, chmn. painting dept., 1968-77, dean, 1977-83; prof. of painting Yale U. Sch. Art, New Haven, 1983-2000, Street prof., dean emeritus, 2000—, dean, 1983-96, dir. grad. studies/painting, 1997-2000. Vis. faculty mem. Yale U. Summer Sch. Music and Art, 1970-72, Ohio State U., spring 2001. One-man shows include Baylor U., 1972, U. Wis., 1972, Pa. Acad. Fine Arts, 1977, Terry Dintenfass Inc., N.Y.C., 1969, 71, 76, Phila. Art Alliance, 1961, 70, Vassar Coll., 1999, Ohio State U., 2001; group exhbns. include Carnegie Internat., Pitts., 1961, Corcoran Biennial, Washington, 1961, 63, Whitney Annual, N.Y.C., 1963; represented in permanent collections Whitney Mus. Am. Art, Phila. Mus. Art, Pa. Acad. Fine Arts, Des Moines Art Center, Pa. State U., U. Wis., Temple U., Hallmark Cards Inc., Columbia Pictures, Yale U. Art Gallery, others. Trustee Louis Comfort Tiffany Found., 1988-97, 98—; bd. trustees Lyme Acad. Coll. Fine Arts, 1999-2007. With U.S. Army, 1955-57. Recipient William A. Clark award Corcoran Biennial, 1963, Lindbeck Found. Disting. Teaching award, 1968, Disting. Alumni award U. Wis., 1991; Guggenheim Found. fellow, 1965-66; Tiffany Found. grantee, 1975-76 Mem. Assn. Ind. Colls. Art and Design (trustee 1992-96). Home: 95 Thankful Stow Rd Guilford CT 06437-2529 Personal E-mail: david.pease@yale.edu.

PEASE, DONALD EUGENE, humanities educator, department chairman; s. Donald Eugene and Marie Theresa Pease; m. Patricia Ann Mckee, June 7, 1985. PhD, U. Chgo., 1973. Avalon chair humanities Dartmouth Coll., Hanover, NH, 1995—, founding dir. futures Am. studies, 1996—, chair masters liberal studies, 1999—. Author: (book) Visionary Compacts: American Renaissance Writings in Cultural Context (Mark Ingaham Best Book prize, 1987, Guggenheim fellowship, 1990), Unacknowledged Legislators: State fantasies from the Persian Gulf War tobarrack Obama; editor: Cultures of US Imperialism, Revisionist Interventions into the Canon, American Renaissance Reconsidered, Futures of American Studies. Bd. govs. Clinton Inst. Am. Studies, Dublin, 2005—08. Tchg. fellowship, NEH, 1990, 1993. Achievements include research in 19thc. American literature, literary theory, transnational American studies. Home: 14 Woban Rd Canaan NH 03741 Office: Dartmouth Coll HB 6032 Hanover NH O3755 Office Fax: 603-646-3590. Business E-Mail: donald.pease@dartmouth.edu.

PEASE, EDWARD A., former congressman; b. Terre Haute, Ind., May 22, 1951; BA with distinction, Ind. U., 1973, JD cum laude, 1977; postgrad. in English, Ind. State U. Past city atty. City of Brazil, Ind.; past gen. counsel Ind. State U., v.p. univ. advancement, 1993; past ptnr. Thomas Thomas & Pease; senator Ind. Gen. Assembly, 1980-92, past chmn. senate jud. com., past chmn. Ind. commn. trial cts., past chmn. Ind. code revision commn.; mem. U.S. Congress from 7th Ind. dist., 1997—2001, mem. jud. com., mem. transp. and infrastructure com.; sr. v.p. Rolls-Royce N.Am. Past mem. adv. coun. on nat. coun. Boy Scouts Am., chmn. com. Nat. Order of Arrow; bd. trustees Nature Conservancy. Recipient numerous awards Boy Scouts Am. Mem. Nat. Interfraternity Conf. (past nat. pres.), Pi Kappa Alpha (nat. dir. alumni affairs, chpt. advisor, nat. pres., pres. ednl. found.). Republican. Office Phone: 703-621-2797.

PEASE, WILLIAM STOESS, physiatrist, educator; b. Cin., Jan. 7, 1955; s. Burton Reiman and Elizabeth Stoess Pease; m. Margaret E. Ginn, Dec. 29, 1979; children: James Burton, Katherine Elizabeth. MD, U. Cin., 1977—81. Lic. dr. Am. Bd. Phys. Medicine & Rehab., 1985, Am. Bd. Electrodiagnostic Medicine, 1989. Resident phys. medicine and rehab. Ohio State U. Med. Ctr., 1981—84; faculty Ohio State U. Coll. Medicine, Columbus, 1984—94, prof., dept. chair, 1994—. Bd. dir. Am. Bd. Electrodiagnostic Medicine, Rochester, Minn., 2003—. Assoc. editor: medical textbook Johnson's Practical Electromyography, 2006; assoc. editor Am. Jour. Phys. Medicine & Rehab., Phila., 2005—; contbr. chapters to books. Bd. mem. St. Joseph Montessori Sch., Columbus, 1999—2001. Recipient Faculty Tchg. award, Ohio State U. Coll. Medicine, 2005, Disting. Clinician award, Am. Acad. Phys. Medicine & Rehab., 2006. Fellow: Am. Assn. Neuromuscular & Electrodiagnostic Medicine, Assn. Academic Physiatrists, Am. Acad. Phys. Medicine & Rehab.; mem.: AMA (alt. del., ho. delegates 2004—), Tau Beta Pi (life), Beta Theta Pi (pres. 1976—76). Meth. Office: Ohio State Univ Med Ctr 480 Medical Center Dr Columbus OH 43210

PEASLEE, ROBERT LEON, metallurgical engineer, consultant; b. Milw., Jan. 4, 1917; m. Betty Kirby Peaslee, Jan. 4, 1941 (dec.); children: Bonnie Jean, Robert Leon Peaslee II. ChE, U. Cin., 1940. V.p. Wall Colmonoy Corporaation, Madison Heights, Mich., 1952—2003; cons. to wall colmonoy corp. Wall Colmonoy Corp., Madison Heights, Mich., 2003—. Dir. Wall Colmonoy Corp., Mont., 1952—95; v.p., dir. Wall Colmonoy Can. Ltd., Montreal, Canada, Wall Gases Inc, Morrisville, Pa., Wall Colmonoy Ltd. (GB), Pontardawe, Swansea. Fellow: Am. Welding Soc. (life); mem.: ASME (life), Am. Chem. Soc. (life), ASM Internat. (life). R-Consevative. Baptist. Achievements include patents for 2, 588.566 Electrolytic Process for Stripping Copper (AC); 3, 275, 240 Spray Apparatus (US); 3, 809, 553 Metal Foil-Making Process (US); 3, 809, 556 Metal-Foil Making Proess; 1, 448, 008 Process for Making Sintered Metal Foils (GB); 506, 364 Spray Aparatus (JP); 2, 833, 030 Brazing Method (Lithium Atmosphere) (US); 2, 833, 030 Method of Joining Metal Parts with Flexible Composit Joining Material (US); 3, 188, 203 Brazing Alloy (US); 3, 275, 240 Spray Apparatus (US); 2, 588, 566 Electrolytic Process for Stripping Copper (US); 2, 800, 711 Brazing Method (Lithium Atmosphere) (US); Method of Joining Metal Parts eith Flexable Joining Material (US); 3.188.203 Brazing Alloy (Ni-Cr-P) (US). Home: 217 Linden Royal Oak MI 48073 Office: Wall Colmonoy Corp 30261 Stephenson Hwy Madison Heights MI 48071

PEAT, RANDALL DEAN, military analyst, retired military officer; b. Chgo., July 6, 1935; s. Thomas R. and Lulu M. (Ray) P.; m. Joyce Enid Hunter, Sept. 15, 1956; children: Brian James, Sondra Lee Peat Gadell BS in Journalism, Medill Sch. Journalism Northwestern U., Evanston, Ill., 1956, MS in Journalism Mgmt., 1957. Commd. officer U.S. Air Force, 1957, advanced through ranks to maj. gen.; pilot, instr. Strategic Air Command, Westover AFB and Clinton-Sherman, Okla., 1958-66; asst. air attache Am. Embassy, Djakarta, Indonesia, 1967; pilot Pacific Command Airborne Command Post, Hickam AFB, Hawaii, 1968-70; staff officer 7th Air Force, Saigon, Vietnam, 1971, Hdqrs. U.S. Air Force, Pentagon, DC, 1972-75, SHAPE, Belgium, 1976-79, Hdqrs. U.S. Air Force, Pentagon, DC, 1980-81; dep. dir. plans Office Joint Chief of Staff, Pentagon, DC, 1982-84; asst. chief of staff ops. Supreme Hdqrs. Allied Powers Europe, Belgium, 1984-87; chief of staff Strategic Air Command, Offutt AFB, Nebr., 1987-89; v.p. R&D Assocs., Europe, 1989—2002. Bd. dirs. Santa Fe Farmer's Market. Decorated Air medal, Bronze Star, Meritorious Service medal, Def. Superior Service medal, Def. Disting. Service medal; Republic of Vietnam Cross of Gallantry with Palm, Republic of Vietnam Campaign medal Mem. Daedalians (vice flight capt. 1976), Air Force Assn., Arroyo Hondo Neighborhood Assn. (pres.), Pi Alpha Mu Avocations: cooking, hiking, painting, british mystery writers.

PEAVY, JAKE (JACOB EDWARD PEAVY), professional baseball player; b. Mobile, Ala., May 31, 1981; m. Katie Peavy; children: Jacob Edward II, Wyatt. Pitcher San Diego Padres, 2002—09, Chgo. White Sox, 2009—. Mem. US nat. team World Baseball Classic, 2006, 09. Recipient Pitching Triple Crown, 2007, Nat. League Cy Young award, 2007, Bullet Rogan Legacy award, Negro Leagues Baseball Mus., 2008, Clyde McCullough award, San Diego Padres, 2007; named to Nat. League All-Star Team, 2005, 2007. Achievements include leading the National League in earned-run average (2.27) in 2004 and strikeouts (216) in 2005. Office: Chgo White Sox 333 W 35th St Chicago IL 60616*

PEAVY, THOMAS OSTINE, psychology professor, retired special education educator; b. Milledgeville, Ga., July 4, 1946; EdD, Miss. State U. Lic. profl. counselor, Ga., 2006; cert. traumatologist green cross project Fla. State U., 2000. With USNR, 1978-98, sr. chief petty officer Hosp. Corps USNR, 1998, ret., 1998; aux. vice flotille comdr., 2007-08; spl. edn. tchr. West Ctrl. Ga. Regional Hosp., 1980-87, ret., 2000; mem. aux. USCG, 2000-, Flotilla comdr., 2001-03. adj. asst. prof. Troy U., 1997-. Author: Directory of Adult Education Services-Milledgeville, Baldwin County, Ga., 1978, Prevalence of Post Traumatic Stress Disorder in US Navy Vietnam Veterans. Chmn., Muscogee Area Literacy Assn., Columbus, 1984-86, Birmingham Theol. Sem., 2006. With USN, 1963-67, with res., 1978—, 2d lt co. comdr. Ga. State Def. Force, 2004-06. Disaster Response generalist FEMA, 2005-. Mem. Vietnam Vets. Am., Am. Acad. Experts in Traumatic Stress, Nat. Alliance Mentally Ill, Fleet Res. Assn. Republican. Presbyterian. Home: 4888 Midland Springs Dr Columbus GA 31909-2154 Personal E-mail: drtop@aol.com.

PEAY, J.H. BINFORD, III, career military officer; b. Richmond, Va., May 10, 1940; m. Pamela Jane Pritchett; children: James, Ryan. BS, Va. Mil. Inst., 1962; MA, George Washington U., 1975; grad., U.S. Army Command and Gen. Staff Coll., U.S. Army War Coll. Commd. 2d lt. US Army, 1962, advanced through grades to gen., 1993, commd. gen., 101st Airborne Divsn., 1989—91, vice chief staff Washington, 1993; comdr. in chief US Ctrl. Command, MacDill AFB, Fla., 1994-97; ret., 1997; chmn. bd. Allied Def. Group, 2001—; supt. Va. Mil. Inst., 2003—. Served in Viet Nam, 1967-68, 71-72, Desert Storm, 1991. Decorated Def. D.S.M., Silver Star, Legion of Merit with oak leaf cluster, Army D.S.M. with three oak leaf clusters, Def. D.S.S.M., Purple Heart, Bronze Star medal with three oak leaf clusters. Home: 412 VMI Parade Lexington VA 24450-2115 Office: Va Military Inst Supt Office 201 Smith Hall Lexington VA 24450 Office Phone: 540-464-7311.

PECA, MICHAEL, professional hockey player; b. Toronto, Ont., Can., Mar. 26, 1974; m. Kristin Peca; children: Trevor, Emily. Center Vancouver Canucks, 1993—95, Buffalo Sabres, 1995—2000, NY Islanders, 2001—05, Edmonton Oilers, 2005—06, Toronto Maple Leafs, 2006—07, Columbus Blue Jackets, 2007—. Mem. Team Can., Olympic Games, Salt Lake City, 2002. Recipient Frank J. Selke Trophy, 1997, 2002. Achievements include being a member of gold medal Team Canada, World Junior Championships, 1994; being a member of gold medal Canadian Hockey team, Salt Lake City Olympic Games, 2002. Office: Columbus Blue Jackets Nationwide Arena 200 W Nationwide Blvd Columbus OH 43215

PECANO, DONALD CARL, automotive manufacturing executive; b. LA, Dec. 2, 1948; s. Domenick Lawrence and Carlotta Noble (Martello) P.; m. Sandra Ann Tuminello, Apr. 26, 1969; children: Julia Ann, Melissa Ann, Donald Carl. BS in Acctg, Pa. State U., 1970; MBA in Mktg., Youngstown State U., 1981. CPA, Pa.; cert. CMA, CFM. Contr. Atlas Guard Svc. subs. SERVISCO, East Orange, NJ, 1974-76; asst. to pres. SERVISCO, Hillside, NJ, 1976-77; v.p. fin. Columbus Svcs., Inc. subs. SERVISCO, New Castle, Pa., 1977-82; dir. fin. East Mfg. Corp. and subs. cos., 1982-88, v.p. fin. and adminstrn., 1988-99, also mem. exec. com., exec. v.p., CFO, 1999—; v.p. fin. Intermodal Techs. Inc., 1991—. Bd. dirs. Intermodal Techs. Inc. Weatherhead fellow Case Western Res. U., 1995. Republican. Roman Catholic. Office: 1871 State Route 44 Randolph OH 44265 *Placing the best interests of the company ahead of your own is ultimately in your own best interest.*

PECEN, RECAYI REG, engineering educator; b. Bayburt, 1965; s. Hanefi and Cemile Pecen; m. Oznur Pecen, 1991; children: Furkan, Fatih. MS in Control & Computer Engring., Istanbul Tech. U., Turkey, 1990; MEE, U. Colo., Boulder, US, 1993; PhD in Elec. Engring., U. Wyo., Laramie, US, 1997. Asst. prof. elec. engring. SD State U., Brookings, 1997—98; assoc. prof. & program coord. U. Northern Iowa, Cedar Falls, 1998—. Exec. dir. Iowa Dialog Ctr., Des Moines, 2004. Summer fellowships, UNI Grad. Sch. Mem.: Am. Soc. Engring. Edn. (energy conversion & conservation divsn. mem. 2008), Tau Beta Pi-Nat. Engring. (Wyoming chpt. mem.). Achievements include research in design and development of wind-solar hybrid renewable energy systems. Avocations: swimming, travel. Home: 1008 Warwick Dr Cedar Falls IA 50613 Office: Univ Northern Iowa 2900 Campus St Ind Tech Dept ITC 39 Cedar Falls IA 50614-0178 Office Fax: 319-273-5818. Business E-Mail: pecen@uni.edu.

PECHAN, MICHAEL JOSEPH, physics professor, researcher; b. Avoca, Wis., Jan. 13, 1950; s. Joseph Edward and Opal Elaine Pechan; m. Kathleen Ruth Finch, Nov. 4, 1978; children: Sarah Elaine, Jessica Mae, Hannah Ruth. BS in Physics and Math., U. Wis., Platteville, 1971; PhD in Physics, Iowa State U., Ames, 1977. Instr. physics Iowa State U., 1978—81; prof. physics Miami U., Oxford, Ohio, 1981—, chair physics, 2001—; vis. scientist Argonne Nat. Lab, Ill., 1983—86, U. Ill., Urbana, 1983—84, U. Calif. San Diego, LaJolla, 1992—93. Presenter (over 100 confs.); contbr. articles to profl. publs. Magnetic Materials Rsch. grant, US Dept. Energy, 1986—. Mem.: Am. Sci. Affiliation, Sigma Xi, Am. Phys. Soc. (grants 2007—). Office: Dept Physics Miami Univ Oxford OH 45056 Business E-Mail: pechanmj@muohio.edu.

PECHEN, ALEXANDER, theoretical physicist, researcher; b. Moscow, Jan. 26, 1979; s. Nikolay Anatolevich and Galina Nikolaevna (Boikova) Pechen. MS in Physics, Lomonosov Moscow State U., 2001; PhD in Math. Physics, Steklov Math. Inst., Russian Acad. Sci., Moscow, 2004. Rsch. assoc. Princeton U., NJ, 2005—. Contbr. articles to profl. jours. Organizer Internat. Conf. Math. Physics & Applications, Samara, Russia, 2008. Grants, INTAS, 2002—03, NATO-CNR, 2003, Russian Found. Fundamental Investigations, 2002—. Mem.: NY Acad. Scis. Russian Orthodox. Achievements include specializing in theoretical and mathematical physics, quantum dynamics, quantum control, open quantum systems. Office: Chemistry Dept Princeton U Princeton NJ 08544 Personal E-mail: apechen@gmail.com. Business E-Mail: apechen@princeton.edu.

PECK, ABRAHAM, editor, media consultant, educator; b. NYC, Jan. 18, 1945; s. Jacob and Lottie (Bell) Peckolick; m. Suzanne Wexler, Mar. 19, 1977; children: Douglas Benjamin, Robert Wexler. BA, NYU, 1965; postgrad., CUNY, 1965-67; cert. in advanced exec. program, Northwestern U., 1997. Engaged in cmty. organizing and tutoring, 1962-64; with NYC Welfare Dept., 1965—67; free-lance writer, 1967—; writer, organizer Chgo. Action Youth Internat. Party, 1968; editor Chgo. Seed, 1968-70; treas. Seed Pub., Inc., 1968-70; mem. coordinating com. Underground Press Syndicate, 1969; assoc. editor Rolling Stone mag., San Francisco, 1975-76, contbg. editor, 1976-2001; feature writer Chgo. Daily News, 1977-78; with features dept. Chgo. Sun-Times, 1978-81; from asst. prof. to prof. Northwestern U., Evanston, Ill., 1981—2001, Sills prof. journalism, 2001—06, Helen Gurley Brown prof. journalism, 2006—08, prof. emeritus svc., 2008—, chair mag. dept., 1981—2006, dir. mag. programs Media Mgmt. Ctr., 2002—, chair journalism and cross-media storytelling, 2006—08, dir., bus. to bus. communication, 2008—. Editor, co-founder Sidetracks, alt. newspaper supplement, Chgo. Daily News, 1977—78; critic at large Sta. WBBM, 1979—82; mem. exec. com. mag. divsn. Assn. Edn. Journalism and Mass Communication, 1987—89, 1992—96, 2003—04, pres., 1994—95; mem. adv. bd. Academe mag., AAUP, 1990—2000, Heartland Jour., 1990—2002, Technos, 1992—; editl. co-auditor Advanstar Comm., 1999—; mem. adv. bd. Chgo. chpt. Asian Am. Journalists Assn., 2002—08; chair ethics subcom. Am. Bus. Media, 2002; cons., lectr. in field. Editor: Dancing Madness, 1976; author: Uncovering the Sixties: The Life and Times of the Underground Press, 1985, 1991; contbg. editor: Satisfaction Mag., 2005—06, consulting editor, contbr.: The Sixties, 1977; contbr. chapters to books. With US Army, 1967. Recipient Lifetime Achievement award, Am. Soc. Bus. Publ. Editors, 2008; named Mag. Divsn. Educator of Yr., Assn. Edn. Journalism and Mass Comm., 2003—04; named to Hall of Fame, Chgo. Journalism, 2006. Home and Office: Northwestern Univ Medill Sch Journalism 1110 Via Bolzano Santa Barbara CA 93111 Office Phone: 805-681-1102. Business E-Mail: a.peck@northwestern.edu.

PECK, ABRAHAM JOSEPH, historian; b. Landsberg, Fed. Republic of Germany, May 4, 1946; came to U.S., 1949. s. Shalom W. and Anna (Koltun) P.; m. Jean Marcus, June 21, 1969; children: Abby, Joel. BA, Am. U., 1968, MA, 1970; PhD, U. East Anglia, Eng., 1977; postgrad., U. Hamburg, Fed. Republic Germany, 1973-74. Adminstrv. dir. Am. Jewish Archives, Cin., 1976—; exec. dir. Holocaust Mus., Houston, 1997—; dir. academic coun. U. South Marrl, 2001—. Lectr. in Judaic studies U. Cin., 1980—; mem. internat. adv. bd. Internat. Ctr. for Holocaust Studies, 1986—; mem. adv. bd. Nat. Cath. Inst. for Holocaust Studies, 1988—; founding mem. Greater Cin. Interfaith Holocaust Found., 1986—. Author: Radicals and Reactionaries, 1978; editor Jews and Christians After the Holocaust, 1982, The Holocaust and History, 1998; co-editor Am. Rabbinate: A Century of Continuity and Change 1883-1983, 1985, Studies in the American Jewish Experience II, 1984, Queen City Refuge: An Oral History of Cincinnati's Jewish Refugees from Nazism, 1989, Sephardim in the Americas: Studies in Culture and History, 1993; editor: The German-Jewish Legacy in America: From Bildung to the Bill of Rights, 1989, Selected Documents of World Jewish Congress, 1936-50, 2 vols., 1991, Holocaust and History, 1998, Marie's Jewish Heritage, 2007; contbr. articles to profl. jours. Spl. advisor U.S. Holocaust Meml. Coun., Washington, 1982-86; bd. dirs. Am. Jewish Com., Cin., 1978-84, Anti-Defamation League of Ohio, Ind. and Ken., Columbus, 1982-86, Jewish Community Rels. Coun., Cin., 1980-86; mem. Am. Hist. Found., Orgn. Am. Historians. Fullbright Found. fellow, 1973-74; Ohio Program in the Humanities grantee, 1980, 83, 85. Mem. Assn. Jewish Studies, Soc. Scholarly Pub., Soc. Am. Archivists, Internat. P.E.N. Centre of German-Speaking Writers Abroad. Avocations: travel, raising dogs. Office Phone: 207-780-5331. Business E-Mail: apeck@usm.maine.edu.

PECK, ART, retail executive; Grad., Occidental Coll., LA; MBA, Harvard Bus. Sch. Fin. and mktg. position Avery Denison, Pasadena, Calif.; sr. v.p. Boston Consulting Group, 1982—2005, dir., 1988—2005; exec. v.p. strategy and ops. Gap, Inc., San Francisco, 2005—, acting pres. Gap Outlet, 2008—, pres. Gap Outlet, 2008—. Office: Gap Inc 2 Folsom St San Francisco CA 94105 Office Phone: 650-952-4400.*

PECK, ARTHUR JOHN, JR., retired manufacturing executive, lawyer; b. Trenton, NJ, Mar. 2, 1940; s. Arthur John and Mary Ellen (Kelly) P.; m. Susan Williams Lodge, July 18, 1970; children: David A., Margaret E. BA in Hist., Yale U., 1962; LLB, Washington & Lee U., 1968. Admissions officer Lawrenceville Sch., NJ, 1962-65; atty. Shearman & Sterling, NYC, 1968-72; asst., assoc. counsel Corning (N.Y.), Inc., 1972-81, asst. sec., 1981—88, sec., v.p., 1988—2000, sr. v.p., 2000-01; ret., 2001. Sec. Teddington Co., Ltd., 1989-2001, Corning Inc. Found. 1981-01, Corning Europe, Inc., 1989-97, Corning Inc., 1988-2001, Corning Internat. Corp., 1991-2001; dir., Corning Inc. Fgn. Sales Corp., 1992-01, Corning Enterprises, Inc., 1974-97; asst. sec. Market St. Restoration Corp., 1974-01, Corning Mus. of Glass, 1981-98, sec., 1998-2001; trustee Rockwell Mus., sec., 1983-01, v.p., 2001—, pres. 2007-; trustee, sec. Corning Classic Charities, Inc., 1977-; bd. dirs. Guthrie Healthcare Sys., 1995-, vice chmn., 2005-; bd. dirs. Kinship Family and Youth Svcs., Inc., 1979-91, bd. dir. Guthrie Health, 2004-; trustee Elmira-Corning Cmty. Found., 2005-, pres. 2007—. Personal E-mail: jpeck@stny.rr.com.

PECK, BERNARD SIDNEY, lawyer; b. Bridgeport, Conn., July 26, 1915; s. James and Sadie Peck; m. Marjorie Eloise Dean, Apr. 10, 1943; children: Daniel Dean, Constance Lynn. BA, Yale U., 1936, LLB, 1939. Bar: Conn. 1939, Fla. 1979, N.Y. 1982. Pvt. practice, Bridgeport, 1939-84; ptnr. Goldstein and Peck, 1946-84, Peck & Peck, Naples, Fla., 1983-87, 97—, Porter, Wright, Morris & Arthur, Naples, 1987-90, Peck, Peck & Volpe, Naples, 1990-92, Peck, Volpe & Sullivan, Naples, 1992-94, Peck & Faga, Naples, 1994-97; judge Mcpl. Ct., Westport, Conn., 1951-55; ptnr. Peck & Peck, 1997—. Moderator town meeting, Westport, 1950—51; pres. Westport YMCA, 1957, trustee, 1964—84; pres. endowment bd. YMCA, Naples, 1987—88; mem. Westport Rep. Town Com., 1951—79. Capt. US Army, 1942—46. Fellow: Internat. Acad. Trial Lawyers, Am. Coll. Trial Lawyers; mem.: ABA, Collier County Bar Assn., Royal Poinciana Golf Club (bd. dirs. 1983—90, pres. 1987—89), Park Meadows Country Club (Park City, Utah), Yale Club SW Fla. (trustee 1985—), Phi Beta Kappa. Office: Peck & Peck 5801 Pelican Bay Blvd Ste 103 Naples FL 34108-2709 Home: Apt 702 4151 Gulf Shore Blvd N Naples FL 34103-2296 Office Phone: 239-566-3600.

PECK, CHARLES EDWARD, retired construction and mortgage executive; b. Newark, Dec. 1, 1925; s. Hubert Raymond and Helen (White) P.; m. Delphine Murphy, Oct. 15, 1949; children: Margaret Peck Iovino, Charles Edward, Katherine Peck Koustmer, Perry Anne Peck Flanagan. Grad., Phillips Acad., 1943; student, MIT, 1944; BS, U. Pa., 1949; PhD in Pub. Svc. (hon.), Univ. Md. Univ. Coll., 1995. With Owens-Corning Fiberglas Corp., 1949-81, from sales mgr. home bldg. products to exec. v.p. Toledo, 1975-81; co-chmn. The Ryland Group, Columbia, Md., 1981-82, chmn., CEO, 1982-91; dir. The Delaware Group of Funds, 1991-2000; sec. Enterprise Homes, Inc., 1992-2000, New Homes by Enterprise, Inc., 2000-01; ret., 2001. Statutory vis. com. U.S. Nat. Bur. Standards, 1972-77; adv. com. Fed. Nat. Mortgage Assn., 1977-78, 85-86; vis. com. MIT-Harvard Joint Ctr. for Urban Studies; chmn. Prodrs. Adv. Forum, 1977-81; mem. nat. adv. bd. Way Sta., 2004-08. Vis. com. Harvard U. Grad. Sch. Design, 1981-86; chmn. Howard County United Way Campaign, Md., 1987; chmn. Cmty. Partnerships, 1991-94; bd. dirs. Nat. Inst. for Urban Wildlife, 1986-90, United Way Ctrl. Md., 1987-91, Howard County Gen. Hosp., 1988-94, NAHB Rsch. Found., 1989-92, Alliance to End Childhood Lead Poisoning, 1990-93, Meml. Hosp. Found., 2004—; adv. bd. U. Md. Engring. Sch., 1990-2003, Continuing Edn. Johns Hopkins U., 1988-91; policy adv. bd. Harvard Joint Ctr. Housing Studies, 1984-94; chancellor's adv. com. U. Md. Sys., 1988-2001, chmn., 1988-99; chmn. U. Md. Found., 1990-94, bd. dirs., 1990—; bd. visitors U. Md. Ctr. Environ. Sci., 2001—; exec. fellow Kennedy Sch., Harvard U., 1990-92; chmn. Affordable Housing Initiative, Columbia, Md., 1990-92; bd. overseers U. Md., College Park, 1994-97; bd. visitors Sch. Law U. Md., Balt., 1996-2004; vis. com. U. Md. Univ. Coll., 1997—; bd. dirs. Ctr. for Grant Devel., 1994-98, Victory '94 com. Md. State Rep. party, chmn. election inquiry funding com., 1994-95; chmn. Children of Separation and Divorce Ctr., 1995-2000; pres. adv. coun. Washington Coll., Chestertown, Md., 1997-2005, chmn., 2000-05; mem. Commn. on Future, Howard C.C. bd. visitors, 1999-2002; mem. Howard County Delta Project; pres. Peck Family Found., 1992—; co-chmn. Smart Growth Forum, 2001; bd. dirs. Columbia Festival of Arts, Md., 1988-91, 2002-03; active Marylanders for Coll. Opportunity, 2005-06; psychiatry adv. bd. mem. Johns Hopkins Med. Inst., 1994-2009, co-chair psychiat. adv. bd., 2005-07. 2nd lt. US Army, Air Force Navigator, 1944-46. Mem. U.S. C. of C. (bd. dirs. 1975-81), Ohio C. of C. (bd. dirs. 1975-81), Depression and Related Affective Disorders Assn. (pres. 1986-89, bd.

dirs. 1986-2000, pres. 1993-94), Ctr. Club, Phi Gamma Delta. Home and Office: 6855 Pea Neck Rd Saint Michaels MD 21663-2725 Office Phone: 410-745-3205. Personal E-mail: tpeck123@toad.net, peck123@mac.com.

PECK, DAVID BLACKMAN, electrical engineer; b. Whitewater, Wis. s. Clarence Neil and Jean Briese (Blackman) P. BSEE, San Diego State U., 1976. Engrng. specialist Litton Systems, Woodland Hills, Calif., 1977-89; engr., proprietor Cockpit Devices, Edgerton, Wis., 1989—. Mem. NSPE, IEEE. Avocations: private pilot, jazz trumpeter. Home and Office: Cockpit Devices 913 Bliven Rd Edgerton WI 53534-9543 Personal E-mail: davidbpeck@yahoo.com.

PECK, DIANNE KAWECKI, architect; b. Jersey City, June 13, 1945; d. Thaddeus Walter and Harriet Ann (Zlotkowski) Kawecki; m. Gerald Paul Peck, Sept. 1, 1968; children: Samantha Gillian Gildersleeve, Alexis Hilary. BArch, Carnegie-Mellon U., 1968. Architect P.O.D. R&D, 1968, Kohler-Daniels & Assocs., Vienna, Va., 1969-71, Beery-Rio & Assocs., Annandale, Va., 1971-73; ptnr. Peck & Peck Architects, Occoquan, Va., 1973-74, Peck Peck & Williams, Occoquan, Va., 1974-81; corp. officer Peck Peck & Assocs., Inc., Woodbridge, Va., 1981—. CEO interior design group Peck Peck & Assocs., 1988—; mem. archtl. rev. bd. Prince William County, 1998—, chair 2000-2005, mem., 2005—. Work pub. in Am. Architecture, 1985. V.p. Vocat. Edn. Found., 1976; chmn. architects and engrs. United Way, Indsl. Devel. Authority of Prince William, 1976, vice chair, 1977, mem. 1975-79, chmn. Prince William County Arch-Rev. Bd., 2001-04, mem., 2004—; mem. Health Sys. Agy. of No. Va., commendations 1977, Washington Profl. Women's Coop.; developed rsch. project Architecture for Adolescents, 1987-88; mem. inaugural class Leadership Am., 1988, Leadership Greater Washington, D.C. Coun. Metrication, 1992—, D.C. Hist. Preservation League, Rep. Nat. Com. Recipient commendation Prince William Bd. Suprs., 1976, State of Art award for Contel Hdqrs. design, 1985, Best Middle Sch. award Coun. of Ednl. Facilities Planners Internat., 1989, Creativity award Masonry Inst. Md., 1990, First award, 1990, Detailing award, 1990, Govt. Workplace award for renovations of Dept. of Labor Bldg., 1990, Creative Use of Materials award Inst. of Bus. Designers, 1991, 1st award Brick Inst. Md., 1993, award Brick Inst. Va., 1994, Bull Elephant award Prince William County Young Reps., 1995, Detailing & Craftsmanship award Washington Builder's Congress, 1998, Pres.'s citation AIA, Atlanta, 2005, Excellence in Design award, Environ. Design and Constrn. Mag., 2006, Presdl. award AIA; Archtl. Design Competition winner Vis. Pavillion Bur. Engraving and Printing, 2002; named Best Instl. Project Nat. Comml. Builders Coun.; subject of PBS spl.: A Success in Howard Co. Mem. Soc. Am. Mil. Engrs., Prince William C. of C. (bd. dirs.), Soroptimist Club. Roman Catholic. Research on inner-city rehab., adolescents and the ednl. environ. Office: 2050 Old Bridge Rd Woodbridge VA 22192-2447 Office Phone: 703-690-3121 ext. 142. Personal E-mail: dpeck@peckpeck.com.

PECK, DOUGLAS CATON, dean, educator; b. Sturgis, Mich., Feb. 12, 1945; s. Herman Darwin and Volga Marceille Peck; m. Anna Kay Abraham, Aug. 23, 1969. BSChemE, Tri-State U., Angola, Ind., 1967; BA, U. Akron, 1972, MA, 1979, MS in Edn., 1997, PhD, 1993; grad., Ohio Statewide Leadership Acad. Cert. computing profl. Inst. for Certification of Computing Profls., 1990. R & d mgmt. trainee The Goodyear Tire & Rubber Co., Akron, Ohio, 1967—68, staff compunder, tire devel. divsn., 1968—70, tech. services engr., plant 2 tire prodn., 1970—72, programmer/analyst, product performance and field engring., 1972—74, engring. analyst, task force on radial passenger tire uniformity, 1974—80, systems analyst, tire devel. info. systems, 1980—82, systems analyst, tech. computer ops., 1982—91, sr. program designer, computer tng., computer applications analyst, exec. compensation and succession planning, 1996—97; vis. asst. prof. of sociology U. Akron, 1998—2000, adj. asst. prof. of sociology, 2000—01; dir. - evening, weekend and summer programs Ashland U., Ashland, Ohio, 2001—03; dean - gen. studies and pub. svc. technologies Stark State Coll. Tech., Canton, Ohio, 1993—. Cons. on statis. analysis, data utilization, and orgnl. analysis. Exhibition, Oculis Sinistris; author: (book review) The Journal of Higher Education (Shaping the College Curriculum: Academic Plans in Action), musician university band and summer symphony; drawings, Old and Young / Noble and Commonplace - Portraits in Color Pencil, sculptures in steel and plaster, Sharp and Pointy / Soft and Rounded, metalworking, Metamorphosis: Ancient, Early Scientific and Advanced Scientific Views of Matter; contbr. articles and papers to jours., confs. Team mem. Summit Edn. Initiative, Akron, Ohio, 2000; mem. - career tech. adv. com.: career paths for the tchg. profession Perry H.S., Massillon, Ohio; judge Canton Artists' League, Canton, Ohio; pres. Hampton Ridge Homeowners' Assn., Akron, Ohio; adv. bd. Akron Chpt. of the Arthritis Found., Akron, Ohio, 1994—98, Dept. Chem. and Bioprocess Engring., Trine U., Angola, Ind.; trustee Tau Kappa Epsilon, Beta-Rho Chpt., Akron, Ohio, The Arthritis Found. of NE Ohio, Cleveland, Ohio, 1989—95; grant reader - fund for the improvement of postsec. edn. US Dept. of Edn.; grant reviewer (small bus. innovation program) NSF; peer reviewer Social Sci. Computer Rev. - NC State U., NC; merit reviewer (course, curriculum, and lab. improvement program) The NSF, Washington; co-chair, curriculum reviewer social sci. transfer and articulation guide project Ohio Bd. of Regents, Columbus, Ohio, 2004—05; steering com. mem. Stark County Coll. Tech Prep Consortium, Canton, Ohio; mem. - tchr. acad. adv. com. Wash. H.S., Massillon, Ohio; facilitator ARC - Akron Chpt., Akron, Ohio; area dir. coord. for united way campaign The Goodyear Tire & Rubber Co., Impact Coun. United Way Stork County; vol. Home at Last Animal Rescue, Akron, Ohio, 1998—2004. Recipient Cert. of Faculty Appreciation, Interfraternity Coun./Panhellenic Coun., The U. of Akron; scholar Trustees' scholar, Bd. of Trustees, Tri-State U., 1967. Mem.: Am. Sociol. Assn., Am. Tech. Edn. Assn., Am. Conf. of Academic Deans (assoc.), Tau Beta Sigma, Kappa Delta Pi, Phi Alpha Theta, Alpha Kappa Delta, Omicron Delta Kappa, Golden Key (hon.). Avocations: playing saxophone and flute, reading. Home: 370 Goodhue Dr Akron OH 44313 Office: Stark State College of Tech 6200 Frank Ave NW Canton OH 44720-7299 Office Fax: 330-494-0571. Personal E-mail: dpeck1@neo.rr.com. Business E-Mail: dpeck@starkstate.edu.

PECK, DOUGLAS EDWARD, lawyer; b. Bloomington, Ill., Apr. 15, 1961; s. Richard Ray and Sarah Josephine (Wilhoit) P.; m. Martha Elaine Jones. BA, U. N.C., 1983, JD, 1986. Bar: NC 1986, Tenn. 1987, US Dist. Ct. (ea. dist.) Tenn. 1987, US Ct. Appeals (6th cir.) 1991, US Tax Ct. 1990. Shareholder Shumacker Witt Gaither & Whitaker, P.C., Chattanooga, 1986—2006; of counsel Spoars Moore, Robinos & Williams, P.C., Chattanooga, 2007—. Editor N.C. Law Rev., 1985-86.

PECK, ELLIE ENRIQUEZ, retired state administrator; b. Sacramento, Oct. 21, 1932; d. Rafael Enriquez and Eloisa Garcia Rivera; m. Raymond Charles Peck, Sept. 5, 1959; children: Reginaldo, Enrico, Francisca Guerrero, Teresa, Linda, Margaret, Raymond Charles, Christina. Student polit. sci., Sacramento State U., 1974. Tng. svcs. coord. Calif. Divsn. Hwys., Sacramento, 1963-67, tech. and mgmt. cons., 1968-78; expert examiner Calif. Pers. Bd., Sacramento, 1976-78; tng. cons. Calif. Pers. Devel. Ctr., Sacramento, 1978; spl. cons. Calif. Commn. on Fair Employment and Housing, Sacramento, 1978; cmty. svcs. rep. U.S. Bur. of Census, No. Calif. counties, 1978-80; project dir. Golden State Sr. Discount Program, 1980-83; dir. spl. programs Calif. Lt. Gov., 1983-90; ret., 1990; pvt. cons. Sacramento, 1990—. Project dir. SSI/QMB Outreach Project, 1993-94; cons., project dir. nat. sr. health issues summit Congress Calif. Srs. Edn. and Rsch. Fund, 1995; project dir. various post-White House Conf. on Aging seminars and roundtables, 1995-97; coord. Calif. Sr. Legis., 1995-97, 2000-05; exec. dir. SMART Coalition Calif., 1997-2004. Mem. editl. adv. bd. Latino Jour. Mag., 1996—2002. Campaign workshop dir. Chicano/Latino Youth Leadership Conf., 1982—; chmn. ethnic minority task force sacramento, sierra Am. Diabetes Assn., 1988—90; steering com. Calif. Self-Esteem Minority Task Force, 1990—93; v.p. Comision Femenil Nacional, Inc., 1987—90; del. Dem. Nat. Conv., 1976, White House Conf. Aging, 1995; mem. exec. bd. Calif. Dem. Ctrl. Com., 1977—95, mem., 1997—2001; bd. dirs. Sacramento/Sierra Am. Diabetes Assn., 1989—90; trustee Stanford Settlement Inc., Sacramento, 1975—79; bd. dirs. Sacramento Emergency Housing Ctr., 1974—77, Sacramento Cmty. Svcs. Planning Coun., 1987—90, Calif. Advs. for Nursing Home Reform, 1990—96, v.p., 1994—96; bd. dirs. Calif. Human Devel. Corp., 1995—2003. Recipient Outstanding Cmty. Svc. award, Comunicaciones Unidos de Norte Atzian, 1975, 1977, Vol. Svc. award, Calif. Human Devel. Corp., 1998, Outstanding Svc. award, Chicano/Hispanic Dem. Caucus, 1979, Vol. Svc. award, Calif. Human Devel. Corp., 1981, Outstanding Advocate award, Calif. Sr. Legis., 1988—89, Meritorious Svc. to Hispanic Cmty. award, Comite Patriotico, 1989, Cert. Recognition, Sacramento County Human Rights Commn., 1991, Tish Sommers award, Older Women's League/Joint Resolution Calif. Legislature, 1993, Latino Eagle award in govt., 1994, Mentor Yr. award, Latina Leadership Network, 2002, Outstanding Vol. Svs. Throughout Yrs. award, Calif. Sr. Legislature, 2003, Outstanding Vol. award, CLYLP, 2005; named Outstanding Advocate on Aging Issues, Calif. State Senate, 1998, Dem. Yr., Sacramento County Dem. Com., 1987. Mem. Hispanic C. of C., Older Women's League, Nat. Coun. Silver Haired Legislators, Nat. Coun. La Raza Home and Office: 101 Simmons Way Folsom CA 95630

PECK, GARNET EDWARD, pharmacist, educator; b. Windsor, Ont., Can., Feb. 4, 1930; s. William Crozier and Dorothy (Marentette) P.; m. Mary Ellen Hoffman, Aug. 24, 1957; children: Monique Elizabeth, Denise Anne, Philip Warren, John Edward. BS in Pharmacy with Distinction, Ohio No. U., 1957; MS in Indsl. Pharmacy, Purdue U., 1959, PhD, 1962. Sr. scientist Mead Johnson Research Center, 1962-65, group leader, 1965-67; assoc. prof. indsl. and phys. pharmacy Purdue U., West Lafayette, 1967—73, prof., 1973—2003, dir. indsl. pharmacy lab., 1975—, assoc. dept. head, 1989-96, prof. emeritus, 2003—. Cons. in field. Contbr. articles to profl. jours. Mem. West Lafayette Mayor's Advisory Com. on Community Devel., 1973-; mem. West Lafayette Citizen's Safety Com., 1974-81; mem. West Lafayette Park Bd., 1981-, pres., 1983-96. Served with U.S. Army, 1951-53. Recipient Lederle Faculty award Purdue U., 1976 Fellow APHA, AAAS, Am. Inst. Chem., Am. Assn. Pharm. Scientists; mem. Am. Chem. Soc., Acad. Rsch. and Sci. (Sidney Riegelman award 1994), Am. Assn. Colls. Pharmacy, Cath. Acad. Sci. (founding mem.), KC, Knight of Holy Sepulchre, Sigma Xi, Rho Chi, Phi Lambda Upsilon, Phi Kappa Phi, Phi Sigma Lambda, Phi Lambda Sigma. Roman Catholic. Office: Purdue U Sch Pharmacy & Pharm Scis Dept Industrial & Physical Pharm West Lafayette IN 47907 Office Phone: 765-494-1400. Business E-Mail: gepeck@pharmacy.purdue.edu.

PECK, JEFFREY JAY, lawyer, lobbyist; b. Rochester, NY, Nov. 2, 1957; s. Sidney and Ruth (Baldwin) P.; m. Lisa K. Vigdor, Aug. 8, 1982. AB in Polit. Sci., Duke U., 1979; JD, U. Chgo., 1982. Bar: D.C. 1982, U.S. Dist. Ct. D.C. 1984, U.S. Ct. Appeals (D.C. cir.) 1986. Law clk. to presiding judge US Dist. Ct (no. dist.) Ill., Chgo., 1982-83; assoc. Seifman, Semo, Slevin & Marcus, Washington, 1983-85, Venable, Baetjer, Howard & Civiletti, Washington, 1986-87; spl. counsel Senate Judicary Com., Washington, 1987; gen. counsel Senate Judiciary Com., Washington, 1988-90, staff dir., 1991-92; mng. dir. govt. and regulatory affairs Andersen Worldwide, Washington, 1993—2000; ptnr. Johnson, Madigan, Peck, Boland & Stewart, Inc., Washington, 2001—, chmn. Mem. D.C. Bar Assn., Phi Beta Kappa. Office: Johnson, Madigan, Peck, Boland & Stewart, Inc 1300 Connecticut Ave, NW, 6th Fl Washington DC 20036 Office Phone: 202-775-8116. Office Fax: 202-223-0358.*

PECK, LEONARD WARREN, JR., lawyer; b. El Paso, Tex., June 3, 1948; s. Leonard Warren and Perry Elizabeth (Lewis) Peck; m. Johanna Lee Blaschke, July 23, 1976; 1 child, Margaret Elizabeth. AB, Harvard U., 1970; JD, U. Tex., 1973; PhD, Sam Houston State U., 2004. Bar: Tex. 1973, US Dist. Ct. (so. dist.) Tex. 1980, US Dist. Ct. (ea. dist.) Tex. 1980, US Dist. Ct. (we. dist.) Tex. 1980, US Dist. Ct. (no. dist.) Tex. 1984, US Ct. Appeals (11th cir.) 1981, US Supreme Ct. 1980. Analyst Tex. Gov.'s Office, Austin, 1974—75; cons. Atty. Gen. Tex. Office, Austin, 1976—80, asst. atty. gen., 1981; dir. R & D Tex. Dept. Corrections, Huntsville, Tex., 1981—82, legal counsel, 1982—2002; asst. prof. Tex. A&M U., Texarkana, Tex., 2006—. Trustee Tri-County MHMR Svcs., 1985—2005; pres. Ind. Communities Inc., 2004—. Home: PO Box 6106 Texarkana TX 75505-6106 Home Phone: 903-223-3011. Business E-Mail: leonard.peck@tamut.edu.

PECK, LESLIE, dancer, educator; d. John Bradley and Doris Lucille Peck; 1 child, Anya Elizabeth Schwender. Prin. dancer Ballet Internat., London, 1977, Pacific NW Ballet, Seattle, 1978—81; ballet mistress, tchr. Richmond Ballet, Va., 1981—96; assoc. prof. Ind. U., Bloomington, 1997—2002, Southern Meth. U., Dallas, 2005—; asst. prof. U. Calif., Irvine, 2002—05.

PECK, MARYLY VANLEER, retired academic administrator, chemical engineer; b. Washington, June 29, 1930; d. Blake Ragsdale and Ella Lillian (Wall) VanLeer; m. Jordan B. Peck, Jr., June 15, 1951; children: Jordan B. III, Blake VanLeer, James Tarleton VanLeer, Virginia Ellaine.; m. 2d, Walter G. Ebert, Sept. 3, 1983 (dec. June 1990); m. 3d Edwin L. Carey, Apr. 13, 1991. Student, Ga. Inst. Tech., 1948, 55-58, Duke U., 1947-48; B.Ch.E., Vanderbilt U., 1951; MSE., U. Fla., 1955, PhD, 1963. Chem. engr. Naval Research Lab., Washington, 1951-52; chem. engr. Med. Field Research Lab., Camp LeJeune, NC, 1952; asso. research and instr. U. Fla., Gainesville, 1953-55; chem. engr., research asso. Ga. Tech. Expt. Sta., Atlanta, 1956-58; lectr. Ga. State Coll., Atlanta, 1957-58; lectr. math. East Carolina Extension, Camp Lejeune, 1959; sr. research engr. Rocketdyne div. N.Am. Aviation Co., 1961-63; self-employed as lectr., 1963; assoc. prof. Campbell Coll., Buie's Creek, NC, 1963-66, prof., 1966; acad. dir. St. John's Episcopal Sch., Upper Tumon, Guam, 1966-68; chmn., prof. phys. scis. U. Guam, Agana, 1968-73, dean Coll. Bus. and Applied Tech., 1973-74, dean Community Career Coll., 1974-77; pres. Cochise Coll., Douglas, Ariz., 1977-78; systems planning analyst Urban Pathfinders, Inc., Balt., 1978-79; dean undergrad. studies U. Md. Univ. Coll., College Park, 1979-82; pres. Polk Community Coll., Winter Haven, Fla., 1982-97, pres. emeritus, 1997—; headmaster All Saints' Acad., 1997-99. Cons. in field. Founder, pres. Guam Acad. Found., 1972-77; bd. dirs. Cochise Coll. Found., 1977-78; charter bd. dirs. Turnaround Inc., 1987-91, chmn. 1990-93; bd. dirs. United Way Ctrl. Fla., 1986-95, vice-chmn., 1992, chair elect, 1993, chmn. 1994; founding mem. Prince George's Ednl. TV Cable Coalition; mem. Prince George's Cable TV Ednl. Adv. Group, 1980-82, Polk County Coun. Econ. Edn., 1982; sec. Polk C.C. Found., 1982-97; mem. Polk County Coord. Coun. Vocat. Edn., 1982-91, PRIDE Adv. Coun.; vice-chmn. Fla. Job Tng. Coord. Coun., 1983-87, Fla. Edn. Fund Bd., 1988-93; active Girls Inc. Bd., 1992—, pres., 2000-2001, hon. mem., 2005; trustee All Sts.'s Acad. 1994-2002; trustee Vanguard Sch., 2001—06, mem. Fdn. Bd., 2001—06; bd. dirs. Theater Winter Haven, 2000—, chair, 2002-03. Recipient She Knows Where She's Going award Girls Inc. of Winter Haven, 1995, Cmty. Svc. award Jr. League Winter Haven, 2002, Disting. Citizen award Lake Region dist. Gulf Ridge coun. Boy Scouts Am., 2005, NDAR Cmty. Svc. award, 2005, Vanderbilt Disting. Alumna award, 2008; named Disting. Alumnus U. Fla., 1992, Woman of Distinction Girls Scouts, 1994, Woman of Distinction, 1997; fellow NSF, 1961-63; named to Fla. Women Hall of Fame, 2007, PCC Sports Hall of Fame, 2008. Fellow Soc. Women Engrs. (nat. v.p. 1962-63); mem. AAUW, AIChE, DAR (Cmty. Svc. award 2005), Am. Chem. Soc., NSPE, Am. Assn. for Higher Edn., Am. Assn. Cmty. and Jr. Colls., Am. Assn. Univ. Adminstrs., Rotary of Winter Haven (hon., sec. 1999-2000, pres.-elect 2003-04, centennial pres. 2004-05, hon. mem 2005), Rotary of Palm Beach Gardens, Sigma Xi, Tau Beta Pi, Chi Omicron Gamma, Phi Kappa Phi, Delta Kappa Gamma. Episcopalian. Home: 5390 Woodland Lakes Dr 206 Palm Beach Gardens FL 33418-3959 E-mail: marylypeck@bellsouth.net.

PECK, MERTON JOSEPH, economist, educator; b. Cleve., Dec. 17, 1925; s. Kenneth Richard and Charlotte (Hart) P.; m. Mary McClure Bosworth, June 13, 1949 (dec. Aug. 2004); children: Richard, Katherine, Sarah, David. AB, Oberlin Coll., 1949; AM, Harvard U., 1951, PhD, 1954; AM (hon.), Yale U., 1963. Teaching fellow, instr. econs. Harvard U., Boston, 1951-55, asst., then assoc. prof. bus. adminstrn., 1956-61; asst. prof. econs. U. Mich., Ann Arbor, 1955-56; dir. systems analysis Office Sec. Def., Washington, 1961-63; prof. econs. Yale U., New Haven, 1963—81, chmn. dept., 1968—74, 1977—84, acting dean sch. of orgn. and mgmt., 1986—88, Thomas DeWitt Cuyler prof., 1981—, prof. emeritus, 2002. Mem. Council Econ. Advisers, Exec. Office of Pres., 1968-69; cons. in field, 1954— Author: (with others) The Economics of Competition in the Transportation Industries, 1959, Competition in the Aluminum Industry, 1945-58, 1961, (with F. Scherer) The Weapons Aquisition Process, An Economic Analysis, 1962, (with others) Technological Change, Economic Growth and Public Policy, 1967, Federal Regulation of Television, 1973; editor The World Aluminum Industry in a Changing Energy Era, 1988; co-editor: What Is To Be Done? Proposals for the Soviet Transition to the Market, 1991, Competitiveness, The Impact of Public Policy, 1992; contbr. (with others) articles to profl. jours. With AUS, 1944-46. Mem. AAUP, Am. Econ. Assn., Lawn Club. Home: 5000 SW 25th Blvd # 3109 Gainesville FL 32608

PECK, NAN J., academic administrator; b. Ill. MS, Ill. State U., Normal, 1981. Coord. Ctr. for Excellence in Tchg. and Learning, Annandale, Va., 1983—. Tng. coord. Northern Va. Hotline, Arlington, Va., 1982—96. Office: Northern Virginia CC 8333 Little River Turnpike Annandale VA 22003 Business E-Mail: npeck@nvcc.edu.

PECK, RICHARD WAYNE, writer; b. Decatur, Ill., Apr. 5, 1934; s. Wayne Morris and Virginia (Gray) P. Student, Exeter U., Eng., 1954-55; BA, DePauw U., 1956; MA, So. Ill. U., 1959; DHL, DePauw U., 1999. Mem. faculty Sch. Edn., Hunter Coll., 1965-71. Lectr. in field; adj. prof. libr. sci. La. State U., 1996—. Author: books for adolescents, including Are You in the House Alone?, 1977 (Edgar Allen Poe award 1977), Father Figure, 1978, Secrets of the Shopping Mall, 1979, Remembering the Good Times, 1986, Never Met, 1989, Anonymously Yours, 1991, Strays Like Us, 1998, A Long Way from Chicago, 1999 (Newbery silver medal, Nat. Book Award finalist), Those Summer Girls I: A Year Down Yonder, 2000 (Newbery award), Fair Weather, 2001, The River Between Us, 2003; (Blossom Culp series) The Ghost Belonged to Me, 1975, Ghosts I Have Been, 1987, Blossom Culp and the Sleep of Death, 1994, Dreadful Future of Blossom Culp, 2001, The Teacher's Funeral: A Comedy in Three Parts, 2004; (poetry anthology) Sounds and Silences, 1970; (novels for adults) New York Time; Contbr. articles on architecture and local history to NY Times. Asst. dir. Council Basic Edn., Washington, 1969-70. Served with U.S. Army, 1956-58. Recipient Nat. Prize for Young People's Lit., ALA, 1990, Newbery Gold medal, 2000, Nat. Humanities medal, 2001; fellow English-Speaking Union fellow, Jesus Coll., Oxford (Eng.) U., 1973. Mem. Authors Guild, Authors League, Delta Chi. Republican. Methodist.

PECK, ROBERT MCCRACKEN, naturalist, historian, writer; b. Phila., Dec. 15, 1952; s. Frederick William Gunster and Matilda (McCracken) P. BA in Art History, Princeton U., 1974; MA, U. Del., 1976. Dir. Pocono Lake (Pa.) Preserve Nature Ctr., 1971, 72; asst. to dir. Natural History Mus. Acad. Natural Scis., Phila., 1976-77, spl. asst. to pres., 1977-82, acting v.p. Nat. History Mus., 1982-83, fellow, 1983—, curator Art and Artifacts, 2000—, editor sci. publs., 2001—03, libr., 2003—07, Sr. fellow, 2003—; tech. dir. Bartram Heritage Study U.S. Dept. Interior and Bartram Trail Conf., Atlanta and Montgomery, Ala., 1977-78. Cons. BBC, Eng., 1987-92; bd. dirs. Longwood Gardens Phila. Conservationists, Natural Lands Trust, Phila., Libr. Co. of Phila., Phila. City Inst.; mng. editor Frontiers, 1979-82, editor Proceedings of The Acad. of Natural Scis., 2001-04; lectr. in field. Author: A Celebration of Birds: The Life and Art of Louis Agassiz Fuertes, 1982, Headhunters and Hummingbirds: An Expedition Into Ecuador, 1987, Wild Birds of America: The Art of Basil Ede, 1991, Land of the Eagle: A Natural History of North America, 1991, German edit., 1992; author: (with others) John James Audubon in the West: The Last Expedition, 2000, William Bartram's Travels, 1980, John Cassin's Illustrations of the Birds of California, Texas, Oregon, British and Russian America, 1991, All In The Bones: A Biography of Benjamin Waterhouse Hawkins, 2008; author: (forward) The Birds of America by John James Audubon, 1985; editor: Bartram Heritage Report, 1978; author (with others), editor: Philadelphia Wildfowl Exposition Catalog, 1979; contbr. chpts. to books, articles to mags. and newspapers including The New York Times. Recipient Richard Hopper Day Meml. award Acad. Natural Scis. of Phila., 1991, Wyck-Strickland award for contbns. to cultural life of Phila., 2003; Eleanor Garvey fellow in printing and graphic arts Houghton Libr., Harvard U., 1995; Yale Ctr. for Brit. Art fellow, 1997. Fellow Royal Geog. Soc., Explorers Club (various coms. 1983—, Explorers award 1988); mem. Soc. History of Natural History, Sigma Xi. Achievements include discovery of new species of frog, Eleutherodactylus pecki; research in status of invasive African Desert Locust in the West Indies; the Orinoco River and its tributaries, botanical, entomological, ichthyological, herpetological and malacological specimens for the Smithsonian Institution and the Academy of Natural Sciences; 19th century exploration. Office: Acad Natural Scis 1900 Benjamin Franklin Pkwy Philadelphia PA 19103-1195 Office Phone: 215-299-1138. Business E-Mail: peck@ansp.org.

PECK, ROBERT STEPHEN, lawyer, educator; b. Bklyn., Dec. 11, 1953; s. Irwin and Edith Rose (Welt) P.; m. Terre Garcia; 1 child, Zachary Madison. BA in Polit. Sci., George Washington U., 1975; JD, Cleve.-Marshall Law Sch., 1978; postgrad., NYU, 1978; LLM, Yale U.,

1990. Bar: N.Y. 1979, U.S. Dist. Ct. (so. and ea. dists.) N.Y. 1979, D.C. 1989, U.S. Ct. Appeals (9th and 11th cirs.) 2004, U.S. Ct. Appeals (2d cir.) 2006, U.S. Supreme Ct. 2002. Congl. aide U.S. Ho. of Reps., Washington, 1972-74; divsn. dir. Automated Correspondence, Washington, 1974-75; law clk. to presiding justice Cleve. Mcpl. Ct., 1976; editor Matthew Bender & Co., NYC, 1977-78; legal dir. Pub. Edn. Assn., NYC, 1978-82; staff dir. ABA, Chgo., 1982-87, Washington, 1987-89; jud. fellow U.S. Supreme Ct., 1990-91; legis. counsel ACLU, 1991-95; adj. prof. Am. U., Washington, 1991—, George Washington U., Washington, 2000—; dir. legal affairs Assn. Trial Lawyers Am., 1995-98, sr. dir. legal affairs, 1998—2003; pres. Ctr. for Constl. Litigation, 2001—. Legal advisor Freedom to Read Found., Chgo., 1986-2002, exec. com. bd. trustees, 1987-90, 93-97, pres., 1988-90, v.p., trustee, 1993-97; bd. dirs. Nat. Constl. Ctr., 1990-93; bd. overseers RAND Inst. Civil Justice, 2001—; mem. lawyers com. Nat. Ctr. for State Cts., 2002—, bd. dirs., 2005—; lectr. on constl. law, legal ethics. Author: We the People, 1987, The Bill of Rights and the Politics of Interpretation, 1991, Libraries, the First Amendment and Cyberspace, 1999; co-author: Speaking and Writing Truth, 1985; editor: Understanding the Law, 1983, Blessings of Liberty, 1986, To Govern A Changing Society, 1990; contbr. articles to profl. jours. Mem. N.Y. State Edn. Adv. Bd., Albany, N.Y., 1979-81; bd. dirs. Nat. Com. on Pub. Edn. and Religious Liberty, 1995-97, Ams. for Religious Liberty, 1995-2000, Citizens for Constitution, 1997—; nat. chair Lawyers for Librs., 1996-2002; chair legal adv. com. Nat. Ctr. for Sci. Edn., 1996-2000; mem. first amendment adv. coun. Media Inst., 1996—. NEH grantee 1983, 85. Mem.: ABA (chmn. pub. election law com. 1983—85, 1987—90, vice chmn. access to justice com. 1997—98, program chmn. consumer and personal rights litigation com. 1997—2000, chmn. 1998—99, chmn. first amendment com. 1999—2005, chmn. appellate adv. com. 2001—02, chmn. com. Am. Law Inst. and Uniform Laws 2002—03, spl. advisor Commn. on 21st Century Judiciary 2002—03, governing coun. tort, trial and ins. law sect. 2003—06, chmn. 20/20 vision task force 2004—06, mem. Commn. Am. Jury 2005—06, chmn. task force disaster relief 2005—07, chmn. emerging issues com. 2008—09, chmn. task forces plaintiffs involvement 2008—09), Ctr. Professionalism U. SC Law Sch. (mem. adv. com. 2009—), Am. Law Inst., US Supreme Ct. Fellows Alumni Assn. (pres. 2004—06). Democrat. Jewish. Avocations: tennis, music, travel. Office: Ctr Constl Litigation 777 6th St NW Washington DC 02001 Home Phone: 703-690-6006; Office Phone: 202-944-2874. Business E-Mail: robert.peck@cclfirm.com.

PECK, SHELDON, orthodontist, educator, dental anthropologist; b. NYC, Sept. 12, 1941; s. Max A. and Sylvia Peck; m. Leena Kataja, Apr. 20, 1986; children: Mark Alvar, Anya Elizabeth. BS, U. NC, Chapel Hill, 1963, DDS, 1966; MSc in Dentistry, Boston U., 1968. Pvt. practice orthodontics Doctors Peck, Peck and Savusalo, Boston, Newton, 1968—; asst. prof. Boston U., 1971—75, adj. prof., 1976—80; asst. prof. Harvard U., Boston, 1992—99, assoc. prof., 1999—2006, clin. prof. devel. biology, 2007—. Exec. sec. The Angle Soc., 1995—2009. Author: Rembrandt Drawings: Twenty-Five Years in the Peck Collection, 2003; co-author: Fresh Woods and Pastures New: Seventeenth-Century Dutch Landscape Drawings from the Peck Collection, 1999; editor: The World of Edward Hartley Angle, MD, DDS, His Letters, Accounts and Patents, 2007; assoc. editor: The Angle Orthodontist, 1997—. Adv. bd. mem. Met. Mus. Art, NYC, Mus. Fine Arts, Boston, Ackland Art Mus., Chapel Hill, NC, Harvard U. Art Museums, Cambridge, Mass. Mem.: St. Botolph Club (gov. 2005), Omicron Kappa Upsilon, Phi Beta Kappa, Alpha Chi Sigma, Phi Eta Sigma. Achievements include discovery of genetic linkage in dental anomaly patterns; research in radiographic and graphic-stroke analysis of old artworks; orofacial morphogenetic fields; dental anthropology. Office: 1400 Centre St Newton Center MA 02459

PECK, WILLIAM HENRY, curator, archaeologist, educator; b. Savannah, Ga., Oct. 2, 1932; s. William Henry Peck and Mildred (Bass) Peck Tuten; m. Ann Amelia Keller, Feb. 2, 1957 (dec. 1965); children: Alice Ann, Sarah Louise; m. Elsie Holmes, July 8, 1967; 1 child, William Henry IV. Student, Ohio State U., 1950-53; BFA, Wayne State U., 1960, MA, 1961. Jr.curator Detroit Inst. Arts, 1960-62, asst. curator, 1962-64, assoc. curator, 1964-68, curator ancient art, 1968—2004, acting chief curator, 1984-88, sr. curator, 1988—2004; lectr. art history Coll. Creative Studies, 2004—. Lectr. art history Cranbrook Acad. Art, Bloomfield Hills, Mich., 1963-65; vis. lectr. U. Mich., Ann Arbor, 1970, U. Mich., Dearborn, 2005—; adj. prof. art history Wayne State U., Detroit, 1966—; excavations in Egypt, Mendes, 1964-66, Precinct of Mut, Karnak, 1978—; adj. faculty art history Coll. Creative Studies, Detroit, 2004—, U. Mich., Dearborn, 2005—; sessional instr. U. Windsor, Ont., 2006; guest curator Ark. Arts Ctr., 2008-09. Author: Drawings from Ancient Egypt, 1978, The Detroit Institute of Arts: A Brief History, 1991, Splendors of Ancient Egypt, 1978; co-author: Ancient Egypt: Discovering its Splendors, 1978, Mummies, Diseases and Ancient Cultures, 1980, Arts and Humanities Through the Ages: Ancient Greece and Rome, 2005; contbr. articles to profl. publs. With U.S. Army, 1953-55. Recipient award in the arts Wayne State U., 1985; Ford Motor Co. travel grantee, 1962; Am. Rsch. Ctr. Egypt fellow, 1971; Smithsonian Instn. travel grantee, 1975. Mem. Archaeol. Inst. Am., Am. Rsch. Ctr. Egypt, Internat. Assn. Egyptologists, Soc. Study Egyptian Antiquities, Assn. Study Travel in Egypt and the Near East, Am. Assn. Mus., Oriental Inst.-U. Chgo. Democrat. Episcopalian. Avocations: oragami, early music performance, collecting T.E. Lawrence material. Office: 1901 Orleans Detroit MI 48207-2718 Personal E-mail: whpeck@yahoo.com.

PECKENPAUGH, ROBERT EARL, investment advisor; b. Potomac, Ill., July 17, 1926; s. Hilery and Zella (Stodgel) P.; m. Margaret J. Dixon, Sept. 21, 1945; children: Nancy Lynn, Carol Sue, David Robert, Daniel Mark, Jeanne Beth, Douglas John. Student, Ind. U., 1946—47; BS, Northwestern U., 1949, MBA with distinction, 1952. Chartered fin. analyst. With First Nat. Bank Chgo., 1949—52; pres. Security Suprs., Inc., Chgo., 1952—73; v.p. Chgo. Title & Trust Co., 1973—77; pres. Hotchkiss & Peckenpaugh, Inc., Chgo., 1977—84; v.p. Morgan Stanley Asset Mgmt. Inc., Chgo., 1984—86, Morgan Stanley & Co., Inc., Chgo., 1986—91; pres. Peckenpaugh Asset Mgmt. Inc., Chgo., 1991—2006; sr. v.p. Whitnell & Co., Oak Brook, 2006—. Chmn., Evang. Covenant Ch. of Hinsdale, Ill., 1981-84. Served with USN, 1944-46. Mem. CFA Soc. Chgo. (pres. 1963-64), Hinsdale Golf Club. Home: 429 S County Line Rd Hinsdale IL 60521-4724 Office: Whitnell & Co 701 Harger Rd Oak Brook IL 60523

PECKER, JEAN-CLAUDE, astronomer, educator, author; b. Reims, Marne, France, May 10, 1923; s. Victor Noel and Nelly Catherine (Herrmann) P.; m. Charlotte Wimel, Sept. 14, 1947 (div. 1964); children: Martine Kemeny, Daniel, Laure; m. Anne-Marie A. Vormser, Dec. 14, 1974 (dec. Nov. 2002). Student Lycée de Bordeaux, U. Grenoble and Paris; Agrégr. des Scis. Physiques, Ecole Normale Superieure, Paris, 1946; DSc, CNRS, Paris, 1950. Rsch. asst. CNRS, 1946-52; assoc. prof. U. Clermont-Ferrand, 1952-55; assoc. astronomer Paris Obs., 1955-62, astronomer, 1962-65; dir. Nice Obs., 1962-69; prof. Coll. de France, Paris, 1963-88; dir. Inst. Astrophysics, Paris, 1972-79; sec. gen. Astron. Internat. Union, Nice, 1964-67; chmn. Nat. Com. for Sci. and Tech. Culture, 1985-87; chmn. adv. com. Mus. LaVillette, Paris, 1983-85; v.p. commn. nt. UNESCO, 1991-95. Author (with P. Couderc and E. Schatzman): L'astronomie au jour le jour, 1954; author: (with E. Schatzman) Astrophysique générale, 1959; author: Le ciel, 1959, L'astronomie expérimentale, 1969, Les laboratoires spatiaux, 1969, Papa, dis-moi: L'astronomie, qu'est-ce que c'est?, 1971; editor: L'astronomie nouvelle, 1971, Clefs pour l'Astronomie, 1981; author: Sous l'Etoile Soleil, 1984; editor: Astronomie Flammarion, 1985, L'avenir du Soleil, 1990; author: le Promeneur du ciel, 1992; editor: le Soleil est une étoile, 1992; co-author, co-editor: Le débat sur le paranormal, 1997, The Mars Effect, 1997, Remembering Edith A. Müller, 1998, Understanding the Heavens, 2001, L'Univers exploré à peu expliqué, 2003, Photographie Astronomique, 2003, co-author, co-editor with S. Dumont: Lalandiana I, 2007. Sec.-gén. Human Rights Com., Acad. Scis., Paris, 1978-81. With French Army, 1944-45, France. Decorated comdr. Palmes académiques; comdr. Légion d'honneur, Grand'Croix Ordre Nat. du Mérite; recipient prix Forthuny, Inst. de France; médaille d'Argent, CNRS, 1956; mèdaille Janssen, Astron. Soc. France, 1967; prix Jean Perrin, Soc. Française de Physique, 1973, prix Lodén, Soc. Astron. Uppsala, 1997; others. Mem. Acad. Scis. (Paris), Acad. Royal Scis. (Brussels), European Acad. Scis., Fine Arts and Humanities, Internat. Acad. Humanism (sec. 1989—), Acad. Europaea (coun. mem., v.p. 1989-92), Soc. Philomathique (Paris) Club. Office: Collège de France Annexe 3 rue d'Ulm 75231 Paris Cedex France Office Phone: 33 (0)144271695.

PECKHAM, ELLEN, artist, poet; b. Rochester, NY, Sept. 28, 1938; d. Walter Fredrick and Florence Albertina (Schmanke) Stoepel; m. Anson Wheeler Peckham, Sept. 10, 1976 (dec.). Co-founder Atelier AE. Exhibitions include Art Internat., NYC, 1998, Boston Printmakers, 1999—, Katonah Mus., NY, 1999—, Collage/Assemblage Soc., NYC, 2000—02, Matrix Internat., Sacramento, 2000, Lakeland CC, Hudson, Ohio, 2000, Brand Libr. and Art Ctr., Glendale, Calif., 2001—, Springfield Art Mus., Mo., 2001, Stocker Ctr., Elyria, Ohio, 2001, U. Richmond, Va., 2002, NW Arts Coun./Ill. Arts Coun., Woodstock, 2002, Sothebeys, NY, 2002, Pacific States Biennial, Hilo, Hawaii, 2002, No. Ariz. U., Flagstaff, 2002, Multisensory Hera Gallery, Warwick, RI, 2003, Warwick, 2004, Zimmerli Mus., Rutgers U., NJ, 2004, Taller Boricua, NY, 2005, NY Soc. Etchers, 2005, Winter Print Salon, NYC, 2005, Albuquerque Art Alliance Gallery, 2005, Bright Hills Art Ctr., NY, 2006, Whitney Artworks, Portland, Maine, 2006—, Emory and Henry Coll., Emory, Va., 2006—, Ctr. for Contemporary Printmaking, Norwalk, Conn., 2006—, Loyola University of Chicago, 2008, 7th Lessedra World Art Print Annual, Sofia, Bulgaria, 2008, one-woman shows include Instituto Cultural Peruano Norte Americano, Lima, Peru, 2009; author (poetry): Continuing Traditions, Doubly Gifted Artists, 1999, Fire, 2005, 2006, Alehouse, 2006, Rattle, 2006, Christian Science Monitor, 2008, Poem: Revised, 2008, Ticket Stubs, 2007, Phoenix I, 2007, Phoenix II, 2008; author: Asahi Haikuist Network, 2009; appeared on (TV show) Printmaking Today, Italy, 2008, Morehead U., Ky., 2008, Appeared on Chelsea: The New Soho?, Continuing Tradition: Doubly Gifted Artists, Alternative Gallery Spaces, Poet to Poet; archives, Harry Ransom Ctr. for the Humanities, Austin, Tex., Dedalo Art Ctr., Italy, Museo Castelo Castigiione. Finalist for solo exhibition, Centro per le arte contemporanee, Dedalo, Italy, 2009. Mem.: PEN, Collage and Assemblage Soc., NY Soc. Etchers, AEVentures Found. (founder), Poetry Soc. of Am., The Players Club (NYC). Avocations: gardening, theater, travel. Office Phone: 212-243-4991. Business E-Mail: peckham@atelierae.com.

PECKHAM, EUGENE ELIOT, judge, lawyer; b. Stamford, Conn., Aug. 11, 1940; s. Joseph E. and Margaret (Nabors) P.; m. Judith Alice Chamberlain, Dec. 19, 1964; children: Margaret, Joseph, Elizabeth. BA with honors, Wesleyan U., Middletown, Conn., 1962; JD, Harvard U., 1965. Bar: N.Y. 1965, Fla. 1981, U.S. Tax Ct. 1974, U.S. Ct. Appeals (2d cir.) 1975, U.S. Dist. Ct. (no. dist.) N.Y. 1965. Assoc. Hinman, Howard & Kattell, Binghamton, N.Y., 1965-72, ptnr., 1972-2000; surrogate judge Broome County, N.Y., 2001—; acting justice N.Y. Supreme Ct. (6th jud. dist.), 2003—; mem. guardianship adv. com Chief adminstrv. judge, 2008—. Instr. Broome C.C., Binghamton, 1968-69, Am. Coll. Life Underwriters, Bryn Mawr, Pa., 1969-70, Am. Coll. Property and Casualty Underwriters, Bryn Mawr, 1970-71; adj. lectr. SUNY, Binghamton, 1972-77, adj. asst. prof., 1977-81, adj. assoc. prof., 1981-87, adj. prof. acctg., 1987—2003; vis. lectr. Cornell U., Ithaca, N.Y., 1978, adj. prof., 1984. Author: Warren's Heaton Surrogate's Courts, Federal and New York Estate Taxes, vol., revised, 1988, 89, Bender's Federal Tax Service " Income Taxation of Estates & Trusts", 1989; mem. bd. editors Warren's Heaton on Surrogate Courts, 2001-; contbr. articles to profl. jours. Peace Corps vol. tchr. Santa Maria U., Arequipa, Peru, 1966-67, treas. Joint Legis. Adv. Com. on Estates, Powers and Trusts Law and The Surrogates Ct. Procedure Act, 1990—; pres. Binghamton Girls Club, N.Y., 1974-76, bd. dirs., 1970-77; chmn. bd. Binghamton Boys and Girls Club, 1977, trustee, 1987-2000, chmn. bd. trustees, 1996-2000; bd. dirs. A. Lindsay and Olive B. O'Connor Found., 1982—, Dr. G. Clifford and Florence B. Decker Found., 1984-2001; bd. dirs. Comty. Found. South Ctrl. N.Y., 1996-2002; mem. trust fund. com. Broome County United Way, N.Y., 1979-94; pres. SUNY Found., Binghamton, 1977-79, bd. dirs., 1975-82; bd. dirs. Estate Planning Coun. So. Tier, 1983-87, treas., 1983, sec., 1984, v.p., 1985, pres., 1986; bd. dirs. Samaritan Counselling Ctr. So. Tier, Inc., 1982-87, v.p., 1986, pres., 1987; co-chmn. sta. WSKG-TV auction, 1983; treas. Roberson Ctr. Arts & Scis., 1980, bd. dirs., 1977-80, 87-95; bd. dirs. Twin Tier Home Health, Inc., 1990-97, v.p., 1991-93, pres., 1993-95; chmn. Broome County Cmty. Ambassador Project, 1970-71; mem. Broome Bd. Ethics, 1985-89, chair, 1999-2000; mem. Broome County Arena Bd., 1987-89; deacon 1st Presbyn. Ch., Binghamton, 1971-74, moderator, 1974, elder, 1975-78, 87-90, trustee, 1980-83, 92-95; exec. com. Broome County Rep. Com., 1980-83, vice chmn., 96-2000, co-chmn. fin. com., 1982-83; pres. Broome County Young Rep. Club, 1969-70. Recipient SUNY-Binghamton Alumni Recognition award, 1984. Fellow Am. Coll. Trust and Estate Coun.; mem. N.Y. State Bar Assn. (exec. com. trusts and estates sect. 1980-84, 86-92, treas. 1986, sec. 1987, chmn. elect 1988, chmn. 1989, tax sect. 1972-2000, chmn. spl. commn. on alt. sources funding legal svcs. 1976-78, action unit 6 1984-86, ethics com. 1979-82, bd. editors N.Y. State Bar Jour. 1998—2007, v.p. 1999-2002, ho. dels. 1990-94, 95-2002), Fedn. Bar Assns. 6th Jud. Dist. (pres. 1984-85), Broome County Bar Assn. (chmn. prepaid legal ins. com. 1976-80, ethics com. 1981-87, chmn. jud. rating com. 1988-90). Home: 1 Stonecrest Ct Binghamton NY 13903 Office: Broome County Surrogate Ct PO Box 1766 Binghamton NY 13902-1766 Office Phone: 607-778-2118.

PECKHAM, JOHN MUNROE, III, investment executive, author, lecturer; b. Abington, Mass., July 25, 1933; s. John Munroe and Mildred P.; m. Ann M. Murphy, Apr. 30, 1995; children: Lisa, Holly, John M. IV. AB, Tufts U., 1955; postgrad., Columbia U., 1962—. Pres. Peckham Boston Adv. Co., 1964—; pres., chmn. Boston Hall Corp., Boston, 1987—; pres. Boston Hall Pub. Co., 1988—; founder, exec. dir. Real Estate Cyberspace Soc., 1996—. Founder Realtors Concerned for Realtors, Chgo., 1986—; mem. bd. advisors Kids Stop, Boston, 1988-89; bd. dirs. Am. Fedn. for Children and Youth, L.A., 1988-89. Lt. comdr. USN, 1956-62. Mem. Nat. Assn. Realtors (v.p.), Realtors Nat. Mktg. Inst. (v.p. 1988), Internat. Fedn. Realtors, Inst. Real Estate Mgmt., Ten Club (pres. Boston chpt. 1974-79), Friends of Bill W. Republican. Baptist. Avocations: bicycling, swimming, cribbage, speaking, reading. Office: Real Estate Cyberspace Soc 4 Longfellow Pl Ste 2003 Boston MA 02114-2817

PECKHAM, THOMAS ELWOOD, lawyer; b. Arlington, Mass., Apr. 25, 1947; s. Alford S. and Janet (Gates) P.; m. Ellen A. Petersen, July 16, 1994; children: Samuel, Anne, Tavish, Duncan. BA, Brown U., 1969; JD, Boston U., 1972, LLM, 1976. Bar: Mass. 1972, U.S. Ct. Claims, U.S. Tax Ct. 1979, U.S. Supreme Ct. 1979, U.S. Dist. Ct. Mass., U.S. Ct. Appeals (1st cir.) 1982. Assoc. Goodwin, Procter & Hoar, Boston, 1976-83; ptnr. Segal, Moran, Feinberg, Peckham & Lobel, Boston, 1983-85; mng. ptnr. Peckham, Lobel, Casey, Prince & Tye LLP, Boston, 1985-99; ptnr. Bingham McCutchen LLP, Boston, 1999—, chmn. estate planning practice group. Adj. prof. grad. tax program Boston U., 2007—. Contbr. articles to profl. publ. including Fun & Games with Split Interest Gifts, ALI-ABA Jour., others; lectr. in field. Pres. Friends of the Marblehead (Mass.) Pub. Schs. Inc., 1994-97, mem. adv. bd., 1997—. Fellow Am. Coll. Trust and Estate Counsel; mem. ABA, Mass Bar Assn., Boston Bar Assn., Boston Estate Planning Coun., Boston Probate and Trust Forum. Office: Bingham McCutchen LLP 1 Federal St Boston MA 02110 Home Phone: 617-306-9644; Office Phone: 617-951-8954. Office Fax: 617-345-5094. Business E-Mail: tom.peckham@bingham.com.

PECKOLICK, ALAN, painter, graphics designer, photographer; b. NYC, Oct. 3, 1940; s. Charles and Belle (Binenbaum) P.; m. Jessica Margot Weber, June 3, 1984. AAS, Pratt Inst., Bklyn., 1968. Art dir. McCann-Erickson, 1964-68; graphic designer Herb Lubalin, 1968-72; v.p., creative dir. Lubalin, Smith, Carnase, Inc., NYC, 1972-74, LCS & P Design Group, Inc., NYC, 1974-76; pres. Lubalin Peckolick Assoc., NYC, 1976-81, Pushpin, Lubalin, Peckolick, NYC, 1981-86, Peckolick and Ptnrs., NYC, 1986-89; design dir. Addison Design Cons., NYC, 1989-91; chmn. Peckolick Inc., NYC, 1991—; painter, 2000—. Bd. adv. Designworld mag., Victoria, Australia, 1983—, Herb Lubalin Study Ctr., NYC; lectr. Pratt Inst., Parsons Sch. Design, Sch. Visual Arts, others. Co-author, designer Herb Lubalin Graphic Designer, 1986; exhibitions include Sony Gallery, Tokyo, 1989, one-man shows include Gallery 468, N.Y.C., 2000, Agora Gallery, 2002, Lucky St. Gallery, Key West, Fla., 2001, 2003, 2004, 2007, Salamagundi Club Invitational, 2002, Gallery 468, N.Y.C., 2002, Agora Gallery, 2003, Photo Dist. Gallery, 2004, Fales Libr. at NYU, 2005, Cosa Gallery, London, 2004, Atlantic Gallery, N.Y.C., 2006, 2007, 2008, Hermes Gallery, 2006, Artspace Gallery, NYC, 2007, 2008, Gallery on the Green, Pawling, NY, 2007. Bd. dirs. Glaucoma Found., 1993, Whale Conservation Inst., 1994. Recipient awards AIGA, Art Directors Club awards. Mem. N.Y. Art Dirs. Club (6 gold medals, over 50 awards), N.Y. Type Dirs. Club (bd. dirs.), Alliance Graphique Internationale, Art Dirs.Club Bergen (Norway) (hon.). Avocations: collecting art and prints, cooking, travel, photography, antique Corvettes. Home: 30 E 10th St New York NY 10003-6202 Personal E-mail: alanart@verizon.net.

PECORA, ANDREW LOUIS, hematologist, oncologist; b. Newark, 1957; B magna cum laude, Seton Hall U.; MD, U. Medicine and Dentistry NJ, 1983. Diplomate Am. Bd. Internal Medicine, Am. Bd. Hematology, Am. Bd. Med. Oncology. Intern NY Hosp.-Cornell Med. Ctr., NYC, 1983—84, resident in internal medicine, 1984—86; fellow in hematology and oncology Meml. Sloan Kettering Cancer Ctr., NYC; asst. dir. adult stem cell/bone marrow transplantation program Hackensack U. Med. Ctr., NJ, 1990—93, chief, program dir., 1993—, dir. stem cell collection and storage svc., 1993—, chmn., 1999—, chmn., dir. Cancer Ctr., 2001—. Prof. medicine U. Medicine and Dentistry NJ Med. Sch.; chmn. & CEO program cell therapy, chmn. techs., chmn. amosayte. Named one of Top Drs. in America for cancer, 2005—08, Top Drs. in America, NY Met. Area, NJ, 2003—08. Office: The Cancer Ctr Hackensack U Med Ctr 20 Prospect Ave Ste 400 Hackensack NJ 07601-1962

PECORA, DAVID VICTOR, retired surgeon; b. Yonkers, NY, Oct. 2, 1916; s. Cavaliere Michael and Tulia (Muzi) Pecora; m. Dorothy Edith Beavers, July 22, 1944; children: Ann Charlene Diamond, Michele. BA, Columbia U., 1937; MD, Yale U., 1941. Diplomate Am. Bd. Gen. Surgery, Am. Bd. Thoracic Surgery. Intern Lakeside Hosp., Western Res. U., Cleve., 1941-42; grad. fellow in surgery NY Med. Coll., NYC, 1946-47; asst. resident in surgery Sch. Medicine, Yale U., New Haven, 1947-49, resident surgeon in thoracic surgery Uncas-on-Thames, Conn., 1949-51; chief thoracic surgery, chief second surg. svc. VA Hosp., Providence, 1951-54, McGuire VA Hosp., Richmond, Va., 1967-72; prin. thoracic surgeon Ray Brook State Tb Hosp., NY, 1954-65; chief surgery Sunmount VA Hosp., Tupper Lake, NY, 1964-65, VA Hosp., Altoona, Pa., 1965—67; chief surg. svc. VA Ctr., Wilmington, Del., 1972-82; pvt. practice in thoracic, vascular and gen. surgery Newark, Del.; mem. staff Med. Ctr. Del., Wilmington, Cmty. Hosp., Chester, Pa., Crozer-Chester Hosp., Pa., Union Hosp., Elkton, Pa., Riverside Hosp., Wilmington; ret., 1995. Instr. in surgery Boston U., 1953-54; clin. assoc. prof. in surgery SUNY, Syracuse, NY, 1961-70; asst. prof. surgery Med. Coll. Va., Richmond, 1967-70, assoc. prof. surgery, 1970-72; prof. surgery Thomas Jefferson U., Phila., 1972—; adj. prof. surgery Hahnemann U., Phila., 1988—; supv. tng. surg. residents numerous hosps. Mem. editl. bd. Del. Med. Jour.; author: Memoir: Between the Raindrops, 1998; contbr. over 130 articles to sci. jours. Capt. med. corps U.S. Army, 1942-46. Fellow ACS (instr. advanved trauma life support); mem. AMA, IEEE, Am. Assn. for Thoracic Surgery, Am. Coll. Chest Physicians, Am. Thoracic Soc., Am. Soc. Microbiology, Am. Med. Writers Assn., Am. Lung Assn. (ea. sect.), Royal Soc. Medicine, Pa. Assn. Thoracic Surgery, Del. Valley Vascular Soc., Md. State Med. Assn., Del. State Med. Assn., Del. Acad. Medicine, Va. Thoracic Soc., New Castle County Med. Assn., Phila. Acad. Surgery, Phila. Coll. Physicians, So. Thoracic Surg. Assn., Soc. Thoracic Surgeons (founder), Soc. Laparoendoscopic Surgeons, Soc. Neurovascular Surgery, Upstate NY Soc. Thoracic Surgery (past pres.), Saranac Lake Med. Soc. (past pres.).

PECORA, LOUIS MICHAEL, physicist; b. Hazleton, Pa., July 31, 1947; s. Michael Angelo and Helen; m. Judith Diane (Miller), Aug. 28, 1976; children: Michael Andrew, Daniel Louis, Anna Ruth. BS in Physics, Wilkes Coll., Pa., 1969; PhD in Solid State Sci., Syracuse U., NY, 1977. Teaching asst. Purdue U., West Lafayette, Ind., 1969-71; foreman Hazleton (Pa.) Weaving Co., 1971-72; rsch. asst. Syracuse (N.Y.) U., 1972-77; NRC postdoc. fellow Naval Rsch. Lab., Washington, 1977—79, rsch. physicist, 1979—. Editor CHAOS, Am. Inst. Physics, NY, 2001-2008, Internat. Jour. Bifurcations and Chaos, World Sci., Singapore, 2002-, Chaos and Fractals Letters, Rome, 2002-; organizer, Exptl. Chaos Conf., various moves around the world. Author: Applied Chaos, 1993; editor: 1st Experimental Chaos Conference, 1992, Nonlinear Dynamicsin Circuits, 1995; contbr. articles to profl. jours. Recipient Physics award Wilkes Coll., 1969, NRL Tech. Achievement award Naval Rsch. Lab., 1989. Fellow: Am. Inst. Physics; mem. AAAS, Am. Phys. Soc., Sigma Chi, Sigma Xi (Pure Sci. award, 1995). Achievements include synchronization of chaotic systems; patents filed in field for Pseudoperiodic Driving, cascading synchronized chaotic systems and tracking unstable states. Office: Naval Rsch Lab Code # 6341 Washington DC 20011

PECORA, VINCENT PITT, English educator; b. Balt., Sept. 7, 1953; s. Pitt and Delores (Kowalski) P.; m. Karen A. McCauley, June 13, 1992; children: Ava, Olivia. BA, Brown U., 1975; PhD, Columbia U., 1983. Asst. prof. U. Ark., Fayetteville, 1984-85, U. Calif., LA, 1985-90, assoc. prof., 1990-95, prof., dir. Ctr. for Modern and Contemporary Studies, 1995—, dir. Humanities Consortium, 1998—. Author: Self and Form in Modern Narrative, 1989, Households of the Soul, 1997. Office: U Calif 405 Hilgard Ave Los Angeles CA 90095-9000

PEDDICORD, ROLAND DALE, lawyer; b. Van Meter, Iowa, Mar. 29, 1936; s. Clifford Elwood and Juanitas Irene (Brittain) P.; m. Teri Linn O'Dell; children: Erin Sue, Robert Sean. BSBA with honors, Drake U., 1961, JD with honors, 1962. Bar: Iowa 1962; cert. civil trial specialist Nat. Bd. Trial Advs.; cert. mediator Am. Acad. ADR Attys., 2000. Asst. atty. gen. State of Iowa, 1962-63; assoc. Steward, Crouch & Hopkins, Des Moines, 1962-65; ptnr. Peddicord, Wharton, Spencer, Hook, Barron & Wegman LLP, Des Moines, 1965—. Lectr. in law Drake U., 1962-68; lectr. law Coll. Osteo. Medicine, Des Moines, 1965-72. Editor and chief Drake Law Rev., 1961-62 Past mem. nat. bd. dirs., nat. coun. YMCA of U.S.A., past vice chmn. nat. bd.; bd. dirs., past chmn. Greater Des Moines YMCA, 1968-89. With USMC, 1954-57. Mem. ABA, AAJ (Top 100 Trial Lawyers), Iowa Bar Assn., Polk County Bar Assn., Iowa Assn. for Justice, Iowa Acad. Trial Lawyers, Am. Bd. Trial Advs. (mem. nat. bd., past pres. Iowa chpt.), Am. Acad. ADR Attys. (past pres.), Verdict Club, Million Dollar Advs. Forum. Republican. Methodist. Office: 405 6th Ave Ste 700 Des Moines IA 50309-2415 also: Peddicord Wharton Spencer Hook Barron & Wegman LLP 405 6th Ave Ste 700 Des Moines IA 50309 Office Phone: 515-243-2100.

PEDDIE, RICHARD A., professional sports team executive; b. Windsor, Ont., Can. m. Colleen McAnoy, 2005. Grad., U. Windsor, Ont., 1970, D (hon.), 2001. With Colgate-Palmolive, 1970—73, Gen. Foods, 1973—83, pres. Hostess Foods, 1983—85; pres., CEO Pillsbury Can., 1985—89, Stadium Corp. Ont. (Skydome), 1989; with The Palestra Grp., Toronto), 1993—96; pres., COO NetStar Comm. (formerly Labatt Comm.); pres. Toronto Raptors, 1996—98; pres., CEO, alt. NBA/NHL gov. Maple Leaf Sports & Entertainment Ltd. (owns NHL Toronto Maple Leafs, NBA Toronto Raptors and Maj. League Soccer Toronto FC), Toronto, 1998—, bd. dirs., 2003—. Recipient North Am. Facility Mgr. of Yr., 1992, Donald B. McCaskill award for Mktg. Excellence in Can. Office: Maple Leaf Sports & Entertainment Ltd 40 Bay St Ste 400 Toronto ON M5J 2X2 Canada*

PEDEN, ERIC KEVIN, thoracic surgeon, educator; s. Donald Charles and Karen Kay Peden; m. Angela Prince, Oct. 8, 1994; children: Morgan, Taylor. MD, UT Southwestern Med. Sch., Dallas, 1993. Cert. surgeon Am. Bd. Surgeon, 2000, vascular surgeon Am. Bd. Vascular Surgery, 2002. Clin. instr. U. Tex. Health Sci. Ctr., Houston, 1999—2000; asst. prof. Baylor Coll. Medicine, Houston, 2004—07, Meth. Cardiovasc. Surgery Assocs., Houston, 2007—, divsn. chief, 2008—. Physician, Houston, 2000; attending tchr. Baylor Coll. Medicine Vascular Surgery Fellows, 2005—07; spkr. Meth., Houston, 2009—. Contbr. articles to jours. Recipient Disting. Surgeon award, AORN, 2008, Fistula First Champion Surgeon award, Renal Network, 2007. Business E-Mail: ekpeden@tmhs.org.

PEDEN, KEITH J., human resources specialist; b. Mich., May 1950; BA, Western Mich. U.; MA, Ea. Mich. U. Human resources staff Honeywell, Prime Computer; dir. worldwide compensation, benefits and human resources info. systems Lotus Devel. Corp.; v.p., head human resources Alexander & Alexander Consulting, Boston; dir. benefits, compensation, human resources mgmt. systems Raytheon Co., Lexington, Mass., 1993—97, v.p., dep. dir. human resources initiatives, 1997—2001, sr. v.p. human resources, 2001—.

PEDERSEN, ARLENE, web design company executive; b. 1974; Creative dir., owner Pedersen Design Grp. Involved with Tanque Verde Sch. Dist.; mem. Leukemia and Lymphoma Soc. Team in Tng.; mentor Nike Women's Marathon. Named one of 40 Under 40, Tucson Bus. Edge, 2006. Office: Pedersen Design Group 12622 E Calle Tatita Tucson AZ 85749-8115 Office Phone: 520-270-7863. Office Fax: 520-270-7957.

PEDERSEN, DARHL MAX, psychology professor; b. Orem, Utah, Oct. 12, 1935; s. Max Barlow and Edith (Aiken) P.; 1 child, Clark. BS, Brigham Young U., 1957, MS, 1958; PhD, U. Ill., 1962. From asst. prof. psychology to prof. Brigham Young U., Provo, Utah, 1962—71, prof., 1971—, chmn. Dept. Psychology, 1967—77. Postdoctoral assoc. Ames Research Ctr., NASA, Moffett Field, Calif., 1969-70. Author: Psychological Tests and Measurements, 1965, Essentials for Understanding Statistics, 1978, Environmental Psychology, 1978, Learning Statistics, 1988; contbr. over 100 papers to profl. jours. V.p. Provo Coun. Boy Scouts Am., 1978-81, coun. commr., 1981-86. NSF fellow, 1962; recipient Creative Talent award Am. Inst. Rsch., 1962. Mem. Soc. for Sci. Study of Religion, Sigma Xi (ann. lecture 1973), Phi Kappa Phi, Psi Chi. Republican. Mem. Lds Ch. Avocation: outdoor activities. Home: 1815 N 1550 E Provo UT 84604-5709 Home Phone: 801-377-8965. Personal E-mail: darhlpedersen@gmail.com.

PEDERSEN, DARLENE DELCOURT, publishing executive, writer, psychotherapist; b. Westbrook, ME; 1 child, Jorgen David. BSN, U. Conn., 1967; postgrad., U. B.C., 1974-75; MSN, U. Penn., 1996—97. RN bd. cert. clinical specialist, advanced practice registered nurse, bd. cert. in adult psychiatric and mental health nursing, Am. Nurses Credentialing Ctr. Various nursing positions, psychiat. cmty. health, 1967-79; assoc. editor JB Lippincott Co., Phila., 1979-84; sr. acquisition editor WB Saunders Co., Phila., 1984-88, v.p., editor in chief, 1988-91, sr. v.p., editorial dir. books divsn., liaison to London office, 1991-95; domestic and internat. pub. cons. Phila., 1995—; psychotherapist pvt. practice, 1997—. Team leader Northwestern Human Svcs. Delaware County, 1998—99; dir. PsychOptions, 2000—; v.p. content ops. MedCases, Phila., 2000—03; exec. editor Thomson Physicians World, 2003—04; dir. content devel. FA Davis Co., Phila., 2004—. Author: Canadian Nurse, 1976, PsychNotes, 2005, 2nd Ed., 2007, Pocket Psych Drugs, 2009; contbg. editor: (book) Basic Nursing Skills, 1977; acquisition editor: book Saunders Manual of Medical Practice, Comprehensive Cytopathology; contbr. chapters to books. Recipient Book of the Year award (for PsychNotes), Am. Jour. Nursing, 2005. Mem.: ANA, Internat. Soc. Traumatic Stress Studies, U.S. Dressage Fedn., Inc., Am. Orthopsychiat. Assn., Internat. Platform Assn., Assn. Profl. Comm. Cons., Manuscript Soc., Forum Exec. Women, Internat. Soc. Psychiat. Mental Health Nurses, Med. Mktg. Assn., Assn. Am. Pubs., Med. Mktg. Assn., Am. Med. Writers Assn., Am. Med. Pubs. Assn., Am. Psychiat. Nurses Assn., Am. Group Psychotherapy Assn., Emily's List, U. Club Penn., Sigma Theta Tau (Xi chpt.). Avocations: autograph and art collection, travel, music, reading, movies. Office: FA Davis Co 1915 Arch St Philadelphia PA 19103 Office Phone: 215-568-2074. Business E-Mail: ddp@fadavis.com.

PEDERSEN, JAMIE D., state legislator, lawyer; b. Puyallup, Wash., Sept. 9, 1968; s. Douglas Kirk and Audrey Mary (Draheim) P. BA summa cum laude, Yale U., 1990, JD, 1994. Bar: Wash. 1994. Law clk. Hon. Stephen F. Williams US Ct. Appeals, DC Cir.; of counsel K & L Gates, Seattle; co-chair nat. bd. dirs Lambda Legal Defense & Edn. Fund, Inc., 2003—05; mem. Dist. 43 Wash. House Reps., 2007—. Outside gen. counsel McKinstry Co., Pacific Med. Ctr., Parametrix, Inc., Wash. Rsch. Found. Pres. Yale Russian Chorus, New Haven, 1992-94. Recipient Charles G. Albom prize Yale Law Sch., 1994; Nat. Merit scholar, 1986. Mem. Phi Beta Kappa. Democrat. Lutheran. Avocations: swimming, flute. Office: K&L Gates Ste 2900 925 Fourth Ave Seattle WA 98104-1158 also: 318 O'Brien Bldg PO Box 40600 Olympia WA 98504-0600 Office Phone: 206-370-7987, 360-786-7826. Office Fax: 206-370-6152. E-mail: jamiep@prestongates.com.*

PEDERSEN, KAREN SUE, electrical engineer; b. Indianola, Iowa, Apr. 27, 1942; d. Donald Cecil and Dorothy Darlene (Frazier) Kading; m. Wendell Dean Pedersen, May 6, 1961; children: Debra Ann Pedersen Schwickerath, Michael Dean. AA in Math., Grand View Coll., Des Moines, 1975; BSEE, Iowa State U., 2007; MBA in Econ., Bentley Coll., Waltham, Mass., 1989. Registered profl. engr., Iowa, Mass., Ill. Engr. Iowa Power & Light Co., Des Moines, 1978—80, rate engr., 1980—84; sr. rsch. engr. Boston Edison Co., Boston, 1984—87, sr. engr., 1987—94, prin. rsch. analyst, 1994—98; sr. engr. MidAmerican Energy Co., Davenport, Iowa, 1998—2006; prin. Pedersen Power Solutions, Davenport, 2006—. Ops. chmn. Old South Ch., Boston, 1989-98. Recipient Disting. Svc. award, Iowa Engring. Soc., 2004. Mem. IEEE (chmn. Iowa ctrl. sect. 1983-84, sec. Iowa-Ill. sect. 2003), NSPE (v.p. 1999-2000, v.p. North Ctrl. region 2001-03, Outstanding Svc. award), Mass. Soc. Profl. Engrs. (pres. 1992-93), Eta Kappa Nu. Independent. Congregationalist. Avocations: golf, gardening. Home: 2222 Linwood Dr Cedar Falls IA 50613 Office Phone: 563-340-2139. Business E-Mail: kspedersen@pedersenpowersolutions.com.

PEDERSEN, KNUD GEORGE, retired economics professor, academic administrator; b. Three Creeks, Alta., Can., June 13, 1931; s. Hjalmar Neilsen and Anna (Jensen) P.; m. Joan Elaine Vanderwarker, Aug. 15, 1953 (dec. 1988); children: Greg, Lisa; m. Penny Ann Jones, Dec. 31, 1988. Diploma in Edn., Provincial Normal Sch., 1952; BA, U. B.C., 1959; MA, U. Wash., 1964; PhD, U. Chgo., 1969; LLD (hon.), McMaster U., 1996; DLitt (hon.), Emily Carr Inst. of Art and Design, 2003, Fraser Valley U. Coll., 2007; LLD (hon.), Simon Fraser U., 2003, U. No. BC, 2005. Asst. prof. econs. of edn. U. Toronto; asst. prof. econs. of edn., assoc. dir. U. Chgo., 1970-72; dean, assoc. prof., then prof. U. Victoria, B.C., 1972-75, acad. v.p., prof., 1975-79; pres., vice-chancellor, prof. Simon Fraser U., Vancouver, B.C., 1979-83, U. B.C., Vancouver, 1983-85; pres., vice-chancellor U. Western Ont., London, Can., 1985-94, prof. econs. of edn., 1985-96; interim pres. U. No. B.C., 1995; founding pres., vice-chancellor Royal Roads U., 1995-96; chancellor U. No. B.C., 1998—2004; vice chmn. bd. govs. Emily Carr Inst. Art and Design, 2004—05, chmn. bd. govs., 2005—. Bd. dirs. Assn. Univs. and Colls., Canada, 1979—84, chmn., Canada, 1989—91; bd. dirs. Vancouver Bd. Trade, 1983—85; pres. Can. Club Vancouver, 1983—84; mem. coun. trustees Inst. for Rsch. on Pub. Policy, Ottawa, Ont., Canada, 1983—89; chmn. Coun. Ont. Univs., 1989—91. Author: The Itinerant Schoolmaster, 1972; contbr. chpts. to books, numerous articles to profl. jours. Chmn. B.C. (Can.) Region Can. Cystic Fibrosis Found.; mem. Min. Advanced Edn. Adv. Com. Decorated officer Order of Can., Order of Ont., Order of B.C.; recipient 125th Anniversary of Confedn. of Can. medal, Queen's Jubilee medal; fellow Ford Found., 1965-68, Can. Coll. Tchrs., 1977, Royal Soc. for Encouragement of Arts, 1984; also 11 major scholarships. Mem. Semiahmoo Golf and Country Club, Loomis Trail Golf and Country Club. Avocations: golf, fishing, gardening, cooking, art. Personal E-mail: pgpedersen@telus.net.

PEDERSEN, LEE G., chemistry professor; b. Oklahoma City, June 15, 1938; s. Leonard Melnot Pedersen and Naomi Shinn; m. Barbara L. Pedersen; children: Lars, Kurt. B in Chemistry, U. Tulsa, 1961; PhD in Chemistry, U. Ark., 1965. From asst. prof. to prof. chemistry U. N.C., Chapel Hill, 1967—, now M.A. Smith prof. chemistry. Cons. NIEHS, Research Triangle Park, N.C., 1985—. Author: Problems in Quantum Chemistry and Physics, 1974. NSF fellow, Columbia U., N.Y.C., 1965-66, NIH fellow Harvard U., Boston, 1966-67. Office: Dept Chemistry U NC Chapel Hill CB 3290 Chapel Hill NC 27599 Home Phone: 919-929-3301; Office Phone: 919-962-1578.

PEDERSEN, PAUL BODHOLDT, psychologist, educator; b. Ringsted, Iowa, May 19, 1936; BA in History and Philosophy, U. Minn., 1958, MA in Am. Studies, 1959; ThM, Luth. Sch. Theology, Chgo., 1962; MA in Ednl. Psychology, U. Minn., 1966; PhD in Asian Studies, Claremont Grad. U., Calif., 1968. Asst. prof. dept. psychoednl. studies, psychologist U. Minn., Mpls., 1971-75; sr. fellow Culture Learning Inst. East-West Ctr., Honolulu, 1975-76, sr. fellow coord., 1975-76; assoc. prof. dept. psychoednl. studies, psychologist U. Minn., 1975-79, higher edn. coord., 1976-77; sr. fellow Culture Learning Inst. East-West Ctr., 1979-81; prof., chmn. dept. counselor edn. Syracuse (N.Y.) U., 1982-90, prof. edn. dept. counseling and human svcs., 1989—95, adj. prof. dept. internat. rels., 1993—95, prof. emeritus, 2000—; prof. counseling edn. U. Ala., Birmingham, 1996-2001. Vis. lectr. Nommensen U., Medan, Sumatra, Indonesia, 1962—65, U. Malaya, 1969—71; vis. prof. dept. psychology U. Hawaii, 1978—81, 2000—; spkr. in field. Author numerous books, chpts. in books, articles to profl. jours.; mem. editl. bd. Am. Jour. Multicultural Counseling and Devel.; editl. advisor Jour. Profl. Psychology, Jour. Simulation and Games, Internat. Jour. Intercultural Rels. Sr. Fulbright fellow Nat. Taiwan U., Taipei, 1999-2000. Mem. APA, Am. Assn. Counseling and Devel. Internat. (mem. rels. com., editl. bd. Jour. Counseling and Devel., editor Internationally Speaking newsletter, mentor media com.), Internat. Assn. for Cross Cultural Psychology, Internat. Coun. Psychologists, Soc. Intercultural Tng. and Rsch. (exec. com., program chairperson 1977, chairperson Pacific Com. 1977, pres. 1978-80, editl. bd. Jour. Intercultural Rels.). Home: 1330 Ala Moana Blvd Apt 1306 Honolulu HI 96814-4221 Home Phone: 808-721-1568; Office Phone: 808-589-2662.

PEDERSEN, PEER, lawyer; BS, U. Ill., 1947, JD, 1948. Bar: Ill. 1949. Assoc. Arrington & Healy; founding ptnr. Pedersen & Houpt, 1957—. Bd. dirs. Delray Farms, Inc., Home Access Health Corp., Martin Brower Co., Spraying Systems Co., Tempel Steel Co., Tennis Corp. Am. Pres. Robert R. McCormick Boys and Girls Club; bd. dirs. Boys and Girls Club Chgo., Children's Meml. Hosp., Children's Meml. Found., Rehabilitation Inst. Chgo., Lyric Opera Chgo., U. Ill. Law Sch. Served USN, WWII. Mem.: ABA, Ill. State Bar Assn., Chgo. Bar Assn., Law Club. Office: Pedersen & Houpt 161 N Clark Ste 3100 Chicago IL 60601-3242

PEDERSEN, RICHARD FOOTE, diplomat, academic administrator; b. Miami, Ariz., Feb. 21, 1925; s. Ralph Martin and Gertrude May (Foote) P.; m. Nelda Newell Napier, May 9, 1953; children: Paige Elizabeth, Jonathan Foote, Kendra Gayle. BA summa cum laude, Coll. of Pacific, 1946; MA, Stanford U., 1947; PhD, Harvard U., 1950; LLD (hon.), George Williams Coll., 1964, U. of Pacific, 1966; DHL (hon.), Am. U., Cairo, 1997. Teaching fellow, tutor Harvard U., Cambridge, Mass., 1949-50; with UN econ. and social affairs Dept. State, Washington, 1950-53; adviser econ. and social affairs U.S. Mission to UN, NYC, 1953—55, adviser polit. and security affairs, 1956-59, sr. advisor polit. and security affairs, 1959-64, minister, counselor, 1964-66, ambassador, sr. adviser to U.S. rep., 1966-67; ambassador, dep. U.S. rep. UN Security Coun., NYC, 1967—69; counselor Dept. State, 1969-73; ambassador to Hungary, 1973-75; sr. v.p. internat. U.S. Trust Co., 1975-78; pres. Am. U., Cairo, 1978-90; dir. internat. programs Calif. Poly Pomona U., 1990-95. Mem. adv. bd. Nat. Coun. U.S.-Arab Rels., 1985—; trustee Consortium for Internat. Devel., 1990—95; mem. adv. bd. Ctr. Near Eastern Studies UCLA, 1996—99; adv. bd. Sch. Internat. Studies, U. Pacific, 1997—. Mem. Nat. Coun. YMCAs, 1961-73; bd. dirs. Ctr. for Civic Edn., 1995—, Physicians for Peace, 1988-90; mem. Fulbright bd., Egypt, 1980-82, adv. bd. Fulbright Cultural Enrichment Program, So. Calif., 1991—2001. With US Army, 1943—45, ETO. Recipient Sumner Peace prize Harvard U., 1950, Outstanding Alumnus award U. Pacific, 1962, Order of Sacred Treasure, Gold and Silver Star, Govt. of Japan, 1987; named One of 10 Outstanding Young Men, U.S. Jr. C. of C., 1956; awarded Order of Scis. and Arts, first class Govt. of Egypt, 1990. Mem. Coun. Fgn. Rels., Am. Soc. Internat. Law, L.A. World Affairs Coun., Am. Fgn. Svc. Assn., Mid. East Inst., Oriental Inst., UN Assn. Am., Internat. Assn. Univ. Pres., Pacific Coun. Internat. Policy, Asia Soc. Clubs: Harvard (N.Y.); Cosmos (Washington). Democrat. Congregationalist. Avocations: swimming, tennis, egyptology, local history. Home: 2 Tanager Ln Greenport NY 11944 Business E-Mail: rfpdrsn@earthlink.net.

PEDERSEN, THOMAS SUNN, physics professor; b. Roskilde, Denmark; PhD in Physics, MIT, Cambridge, 2000. Postdoc. assoc. Columbia U., NYC, 2000, asst. prof., 2000—05, assoc. prof., 2005—. Recipient Faculty Early Career Devel. Program award, NSF, 2005—, Plasma Physics Jr. Faculty Devel. Program award, OFES, US Dept. Energy, 2002—05; High Beta Tokamak Rsch. grant, 2005—, grant, NSF and DOE, 2003—. Achievements include research in lowest aspect ratio and simplest stellarator in world.

PEDERSEN, WESLEY NIELS M., public relations and public affairs counselor; b. South Sioux City, Nebr., July 10, 1922; s. Peder Westergaard and Marie Gertrude (Sorensen) P.; m. Angeline Kathryn Vavra, Oct. 17, 1948; 1 son, Eric Wesley. Student, Tri-State Coll., Sioux City, Iowa, 1940-41; BA summa cum laude, Upper Iowa U., Fayette; postgrad. in Russian, George Washington U., 1958—59. Editor, writer Sioux City Jour., 1941-50; corr. N.Y. Times, Life, Time, Fortune, 1948-50; editor Dept. State, 1950—52, fgn. svc. officer Hong Kong, 1960-63; fgn. affairs columnist, roving corr., counselor summit meetings and fgn. ministers confs. USIA, 1952—60, chief, worldwide spl. publs. and graphics programs, 1963-69; chief Office Spl. Projects, Washington, 1969-78, Office Spl. Projects, Internat. Comm. Agy., 1978-79; v.p. Fraser Assocs., pub. rels., Washington, 1979-80; dir. comm. and pub. rels. Pub. Affairs Coun., Washington, 1980—2006; prin. Wes Pedersen Comms., 2006—. Lectr. creative comm. Upper Iowa U., 1975; chmn., Europe, Ambassadorial Internat. Affairs Seminar, Fgn. Svc. Inst., 1975; lectr. internat. pub. rels. Pub. Rels. Inst., Am. U., 1976; lectr. bus. and mgmt. divsn. NYU, 1976-78; cons. pub. rels., editl. and design; del. founding sessions 1st Amendment Congress, Phila. and Williamsburg, Va., 1980, exec. com., 1980; columnist O'Dwyer Pub. Relations Newsletter, 2008-. Columnist: (as Paul L. Ford) The World Today, 1952-60; (as Benjamin E. West) Behind the Curtain, 1952-60; White House Report, 1966-69 (as Wesley Pedersen), Washington Report-Pub. Rels. Jour., 1980-85; author: Mr. President: Lyndon B. Johnson, 1964, Legacy of a President: The Memorable Words of John F. Kennedy, 1964, Journey to the Pacific, 1965, decision '68', How Am. Elect Their Pres., Mr. President: Richard M. Nixon, 1969, Pres. Nixon in Europe, 1969, American Heroes of Asian Wars, 1969; co-author: Effective Government Public Affairs, 1981; editor: The Imam's Story, 1961, Escape at Midnight and Other Stories (Pearl S. Buck), 1962, Exodus From China (Harry Redl), 1962, Macao, 1962, The Dividing Line (Arturo Gonzalez), 1962, China's Men of Letters (K.E. Priestley), 1963, Children of China (Pearl S. Buck and Margaret Wylie), 1963, Destination the Moon (William Howard), 1964, Man on the Moon, 1964, Nine From Little Rock, 1964, We Shall Overcome, 1964, To the Moon and Beyond, 1965, Bounty From the Land, 1965, Workers Paradise Lost (Eugene Lyons), 1967, The Americans and the Arts (Howard Taubman), 1969, The Dance in America (Agnes de Mille), 1969, Getting the Most From Grassroots Public Affairs Programs, 1980, Computer Applications in Public Affairs, 1984, Cost-Effective Management for Today's Public Affairs, 1984, Making Community Relations Pay Off: Tools and Strategies, 1988, Winning at the Grassroots: How to Succeed in the Legislative Arena by Mobilizing Employees and Other Allies, 1989, Leveraging State Government Relations, 1990, Managing the Business-Employee PAC, 1992, Adding Value to the Public Affairs Function, 1994, Winning at the Grassroots (with Tony Kramer), 2000, Managing the Corporate Political Action Committee, 2001; Pub. Affairs Rev. Mag., 1980-86, 2000-05, Impact newsletter Columist O'Dwyer Pub. Rels. Newsletter, 2008-; on nat. and internat. pub. affairs, 1980-2006; contbr. to The Commissar, 1972, Informing the People: A Public Affairs Handbook, 1981, The Practice of Public Relations, 1984, 2d edit., 2003, Legislative Careers: Why and How We Should Study Them, 1999, Encyclopedia of Public Relations, 2004, Corporate Public Affairs: Interacting with Interest Groups, Media, and Government, 2006, Implausible Deniabilities, 2007; mem. editl. bd. Pub. Rels. Quar., 1975—, Washington editor, Pub. Rels. Quar., 1998—, Fgn. Svc. Jour., 1975-81; mem. editl. adv. bd. Pub. Rels. News, 1991-98, contbg. editor Pub. Affairs News Mag., London, 2004—; author scripts Uncle Walter's Doghouse radio show, 1938; contbr. articles to profl. jours. Founding chmn. bd. dirs. Nat. Inst. for Govt. Pub. Info. Rsch., Am. U., 1977-80. Served with Air Corps, US Army, 1943-46. Recipient 3 awards A.P. Mng. Editors Assn., Iowa, 1948-49, Meritorious Svc. award USIA, 1963, Superior Svc. award USIA, 1964, Presdl. commendation, 1964, 70, 1st prize Fed. Editors Assn., 1970, 74-75, Agy. Dir.'s citation USIA, 1965, 74, 78, Soc. Tech. Comm., 1974-76, Gold award Internat. Newsletter Conf., 1982, Silver award, 1985, Eddi award for design excellence Editor's Workshop, 1983, Gold Circle award Am. Soc. Assn. Execs., 1983-89, 97-2000, Ten Cool award Am. Soc. Assn. Execs., 2001, Editors' Forum award, 1988-90, 94-96, Assn. Trends award, 1989-2005, Lifetime Great Assn. Communicator award, Assn. Trends, 1999, Best of Century Comm. award, Assn. Trends, 2001, spl. citation Assn. Trends, 2001, 07, PR Week 2008, Silver award 2004, 05, Gold award, 2004, Excellence award, 2006, Grand prize Internat. Ann. Report Conf., 1989, Gold award 1997, Comm. Concepts awards, 1989-2006, Grand Comm. Concepts awards, 1992, 95, 2000, 02, 04-06, MerComm awards, 1990-2000, Nat. Media Conf. award, 1989-90, Internat. Acad. Comm. Arts and Scis. award, 1994-98, 2000, Grand prize, 1995, awards Printing and Graphic Assn., 1987, 91, 96-97, 2000, Excell award Soc. of Nat. Assn. Publishers, 2000, Judges' award 2000; named Most Outstanding Info. Officer in

Exec. Br. Govt. Info. Orgn., 1975, Ky. Col. and Adm. Nebr. Navy, 1984. Mem. DAV, Am. Fgn. Svc. Assn., Am. Legion, Internat. Assn. Bus. Communicators (Communicator of Yr. Washington chpt. 1978, various awards 1973, 76-78, 84, 90, 94-2004, Winners' Circle awards dist. III 1996-2003), Nat. Assn. Govt. Communicators (pres. 1978-79, Communicator of Yr. 1977, Disting. Svc. award 1978), Pub. Rels. Soc. Am. (mem. Counselor's Acad. 1980—, chmn. 1st Amendment task force 1980-81, hall of fame steering com. mem., 2008-2009, co-recipient Thoth award 1980-81, 94, twin Thoth awards 1995-97, 2003, Thoth awards 1998-2003, Bronze Anvil award 2000, named to Hall of Fame 2005), Am. Soc. Profl. Communicators (Colonial award 2002, Masters award 2004), World Affairs Coun., Soc. Profl. Journalists, The Acad. Polit. Sci. Episcopalian. Office: Wes Pedersen Comms and Pub Rels 4701 Willard Ave Ste 1007 Chevy Chase MD 20815-4622 Office Phone: 301-718-9191. Personal E-mail: wesped@comcast.net, editorwes@hotmail.com. *Keenness of mind and an abundance of luck, it is said, are the key ingredients of personal success. The truth be told, however, I've performed only one act of brilliance in my lifetime: the selection of my parents. But I've had an enormous amount of good fortune, a fact manifestly clear to anyone who has ever met my wife, my son and my granddaughters. They, thank goodness, chose me.*

PEDERSEN, WILLIAM FRANCIS, lawyer; b. NYC, Apr. 4, 1943; s. William F. and Priscilla S. (Auchincloss) P.; m. Ellen L. Frost, Feb. 2, 1974; children: Mark Francis, Claire Ellen. BA, Harvard U., 1965, LLB, 1968. Bar: Mass. 1969, D.C. 1978. Assoc. Ropes & Gray, Boston, 1969-72; staff atty. EPA, Washington, 1972-75, dep. gen. counsel, then assoc. gen. counsel, 1976-85; staff counsel Senate Com. on Govt. Ops., Washington, 1975-76; lectr. Harvard Law Sch., 1985-86; of counsel Perkins Coie, Washington, 1987—89, ptnr., 1989-94, Shaw, Pittman, Potts & Trowbridge, Washington, 1994-2001; pvt. practice Washington, 2001—. Vis. prof. Law Sch., U. Mich., 1997-98. Contbr. articles to profl. jours. Mem. ABA (standing com. on environ. law 1987-89). Republican. Episcopalian. Office: William F Pedersen PLLC Ste 1350 1615 L St NW Washington DC 20036 Office Phone: 202-296-8884. Business E-Mail: bill.pedersen@billpedersen.com.

PEDERSON, GORDON ROY, retired state legislator, military officer; b. Gayville, SD, Aug. 8, 1927; s. Roy E. and Gladys F. (Masker) P.; m. Betty L. Ballard, Mar. 8, 1955; children: James D., Carol A. Pederson Niemann, Nancy G. Pederson Holub, Gary W. Student, Yankton Coll., 1948-50, Fla. State U., 1963; advanced course, Infantry Sch., 1958-59. Drafted U.S. Army, 1945-47, commd. 2nd lt., 1952, advanced through grades to lt. col., 1967, served CONUS World War II, platoon leader 17th infantry regiment, 7th infantry divsn. Korea, 1953-54, served Korean War, 1950-54, rifle co. commdr. 10th mountain divsn. Germany, 1955-58, instr., dir. instrn. U.S. Army Jungle Warfare Tng. Ctr. Ft. Sherman, Canal Zone, 1961-63, comdr. post, 1963-64, 1st brig., 1st infantry divsn. Vietnam, 1965—66, dir. tng. hdqs. G3, Ft. Leonard Wood, 1966—68; advisor Ministry of Nat. Def., Rep. China on Taiwan, 1969-70; retired U.S. Army, 1970; operator Elkton Restaurant Post, 1971—78; rep. SD Ho. Reps., Pierre, 1977—99, 2001—09, SD State Reps., 1977—98, 2000—08; operator Dairy Queen, Wall, SD, 1990-95. Chmn. transp. com. S.D. Ho. Reps., 1979-93, vice chair state affairs com., 1994-98, vice chair commerce com., 1998, chmn. budget audit com., 2001-2002, chmn. transp. com., 2002—; exec. bd. Legis. Rsch. Coun., 2002—08. Del. S.D. Rep. Conv., 1974-78, 80, 82, 84, 87-98, 2002-04, 06, 08; del. Nat. Rep. Conv., 1976, 80, 84, 88, 92, 96, 2000, 04, 08; bd. dirs. Legis. Rsch. Coun., 1988, 90, 92, 96, 98, 2001-02, 05-08, vice chair, 2004-06. Decorated Bronze Star, Medal of Merit, U.S. Presdl. Unit Citation, Rep. Korea Presdl. Unit Citation, Rep. Vietnam Presdl. Unit Citation, Combat Infantry Badge with Star, Legion of Merit, Air Medal with 2 Oak Leaf Clusters, Army Accomodation medal with 2 oak leaf clusters, Cross of Gallantry with Palm, Republic Vietnam. Mem. VFW, DAV, Am. Legion, Retired Officers Assn., Wall C. of C., Internat. Lions Club, Black Hills. Lutheran. Home: PO Box 312 116 W 7th St Wall SD 57790 Home Phone: 605-279-2610.

PEDERSON, LINDA L., music educator; b. Battineau, ND, Apr. 7, 1948; d. Hjalmer and Louise Nordmark; children: Michael, Jeffrey, Sonja. BS in Elem. Edn. and Music Edn., Minot State U., ND, 1970. Music tchr. Valley Sch. Dist., Gilcrest, Colo., 1979—89; mgr. Longmont Country Gen. Store, 1989—93; coord. learning ctr. Loveland HS, 1993—94; asst. mgr. Ben Franklin, 1994—95; clk. Estes Park 5 & 10, 1995—96, Pizza Hut, 1995—96, Safeway, 1995—97; with Estes Park YMCA, 1995—97; music tchr. Newburg United Sch., ND, 1997—; owner Pederson Properties. Pres. Jayceettes, Kenmare, 1973—75; mem. Young Reps., Minot, 1969—70. Recipient Golden Apple award, Newburg Cmty., 1998—99; named Ourstanding Young Educator, Kenmare Jaycees, ND, 1975—76. Mem.: NEA, Am. Choral Dirs. Assn., Band Dirs. Assn., Clin. Dirs. Assn., Sigma Alpha Iota, Delta Epsilon Phi. Avocations: sewing, reading, walking, gardening.

PEDERSON, SALLY J., former lieutenant governor; b. Muscatine, Iowa, Jan. 13, 1951; d. Gerald and Wineva Pederson; m. James A. Autry, Feb. 6, 1982; children: Rick, Jim Jr., Ronald. Grad., Iowa State U., 1973. With Meredith Corp., 1973-84; sr. food editor Better Homes & Gardens mag.; lt. gov. State of Iowa, Des Moines, 1999—2007. Pres. Polk County Health Svcs.; bast bd. trustees Nat. Alliance for Autism Rsch.; pres. bd. trustees Autism Soc. Iowa; founding pres. The Homestead Living and Learning Ctr. for Adults with Autism; past cmty. bd. svcs. includes Des Moines Cmty. Playhouse, Very Spl. Arts Iowa, YWCA Aliber Child Care Ctr., YMCA Ctr. Br.; parent rep. Heartland AEA Autism Steering Com.; mem. Iowa State Spl. Edn. Adv. Bd; bd. dirs. Blank Children's Hosp., Mid-Iowa Health Found.; gov.'s appointee State Spl. Edn. Adv. Panel. Democrat.

PEDERSON, WILLIAM CHRISTOPHER, plastic surgeon; b. Texas City, Tex., July 15, 1952; s. Alton Curtis and Lucy Vernor (Windham) P.; m. Cynthia Lea Anderson, June 17, 1978; children: Liv, Anton, Candice. BA, U. Tex., 1974, MD, 1978. Hand fellow U. Louisville, 1984; rsch. fellow Duke U. Med. Ctr., Durham, N.C., 1985; microsurgery rsch. fellow St. Vincent's Hosp., Melbourne, 1986; asst. prof. plastic surgery Duke U. Med. Ctr., Durham, 1087-89; chief of plastic surgery U. Tex. Health Sci. Ctr., San Antonio, 1989—; intern, resident surgery U. Tex., San Antonio, 1978—83, resident plastic surgery, 1983—85; pres. Am. Soc. Reconstructive Microsurgery, 2005—06. Contbr. articles to profl. jours. Fellow ACS (assoc.); mem. Am. Soc. Plastic and Reconstructive Surgery, Am. Assn. Hand Surgery, Am. Soc. Reconstructive Microsurgery.

PEDESCLEAUX-MUCKLE, GAIL, retired business analyst, writer, consultant, model; b. Cleve., June 20, 1949; d. Alfonso Pedescleaux and Belle Pinkard Pedescleaux; m. Kirk Muckle, Oct. 24, 1997; 1 stepchild, Christopher Corey Muckle. BA in English Lit., Ctrl. Mich. U., 1971. Cert. youth devel. arts Rutgers U., 2006, tchr. tng. program YogaFit Kids, 2007. Acct. asst. Travelers Ins. Co., Southfield, Mich., 1972—79, underwriter Garden City, NY, 1979—81, Commerce and Industry, NYC, 1981—83; sr. underwriter Firemans' Fund, NYC, 1983—85; bus. analyst Am. Internat. Group, NYC, 1985—94, sr. quality assurance analyst Livingston, NJ, 1994—2000, sr. bus. analyst Parsippany, NJ, 2000—04; ret., 2004. Cons. in field; patient rep. JFK Family Practice, 2005—; coord. creative arts programs, 2006. Author: (anthology) America at the Millennium, 2000 (Editor's Choice, 2000), Poetry's Elite: The Best Poets of 2000, 2001 (Editor's Choice, 2001), Throwing Stardust, 2003 (Editor's Choice, 2003), Celebrating Poetry, 2003, Theatre of the Mind, 2003, The Best Poems and Poets of 2003, 2003, Colours of the Heart, 2004, Twilight Musings, 2005 (Editors Choice award, 2005). Mem. DAV: Comdr.'s Club, 1993—, Nat. Multiple Sclerosis Soc., 1994—, Nat. Trust, 1993—, Am. Mus. Natural History, 1996—, Nat. Civil Rights Mus., 2002—, So. Poverty Law Ctr., 2002—, Susan G. Komen Breast Cancer Found., 2003; patient rep. JFK Family Medicine, 2005—, Women Helping Women, 2006—. Mem.: Acad. Am. Poets, N.Y.C. Ballet Guild, Nat. Mus. Women in the Arts, Met. Mus. Art. Avocations: jazzercise, photography, theater, writing children's stories and poetry, gardening. Home: 54 Rainford Rd Edison NJ 08820-2903 Personal E-mail: pedymuck@msn.com.

PEDIGO, JUSTIN B., audiology services professional, media consultant; b. Springfield, Mo., Feb. 6, 1981; s. Randy and Teresa Pedigo; m. Ashlynne M. Jones, Oct. 12, 2003; 1 child, Brayden. EdM, SW Bapt. U., Bolivar, Mo., 2006. Dir., media svcs. Ozarks Tech. CC, Springfield, 2002—; pres., CEO Oneway Prodn. LLC, Rogersville, Mo., 2005—. Sound engr. 2nd Bapt. Ch., Springfield, 2002—. Recipient Excellence Edn. award, Ozarks Tech. CC, 2007. Office: Ozarks Tech CC 1001 E Chestnut Expy Springfield MO 65742 Business E-Mail: pedigoj@otc.edu.

PEDLEY, JOHN GRIFFITHS, archaeologist, educator; b. Burnley, Eng., July 19, 1931; arrived in U.S., 1959, naturalized, 2002; s. George and Anne (Whitaker) Pedley; m. Mary Grace Sponberg, Aug. 30, 1969. BA, Cambridge U., Eng., 1953, MA, 1959; postgrad. (Norton fellow), Am. Sch. Classical Studies, Greece, 1963-64; PhD, Harvard U., 1965. Loeb rsch. fellow in classical archaeology Harvard U., Cambridge, Mass., 1969-70; asst. prof. classical archaeology and Greek U. Mich., Ann Arbor, 1965-68, assoc. prof., 1968-74, acting chmn. dept. classical studies, 1971-72, 75-76; dir. Kelsey Mus. Archaeology, 1973-86, prof., 1974—2002, prof. emeritus, 2002—. Guest scholar J. Paul Getty Mus.; mem. staff excavations, Sardis, Turkey, 1962—64, Pylos, Greece, 1964; co-dir. excavations, Apollonia, Libya, 1966—68; field dir. Corpus Ancient Mosaics, Tunisia, 1972—73; co-prin. investigator excavations, Carthage, North Africa, 1975—79; dir. excavations, Paestum, Italy, 1982—85, Paestum, 1993, Paestum, 95; vis. scholar UCLA, 1989; resident in archaeology Am. Acad., Rome, 1990. Author: (book) Sardis in the Age of Croesus, 1968, Sardis in the Age of Croesus, reprint, 1999, Ancient Literary Sources on Sardis, 1972, Greek Sculpture of the Archaic Period: The Island Workshops, 1976, Paestum: Greeks and Romans in Southern Italy, 1990, Greek Art and Archaeology, 1992, Greek Art and Archaeology, 3d edit., 2002, Greek Art and Archaeology, 4th edit., 2007, Sanctuaries and the Sacred in the Ancient Greek World, 2005; co-author: Apollonia, the Port of Cyrene, 1977, The Sanctuary of Santa Venera at Paestum, Vol. 1, 1993, Corpus des Mosaiques de Tunisie, Vol. III, 1996; editor: New Light on Ancient Carthage, 1980; co-editor: Studies Presented to GMA Hanfmann, 1971. Grantee, Am. Philol. Soc., 1979, Nat. Endowment Arts Mus., 1974, 1977, 1979, 1980, NEH, 1967, 1975, 1983, 1984; fellow Am. Coun. Learned Socs., 1972—73, NEH, 1986. Home: 1720 Morton Ave Ann Arbor MI 48104-4522 Office: Dept Classical Studies Univ Mich Ann Arbor MI 48109 E-mail: jpedley@umich.edu.

PEDLEY, TIMOTHY ASBURY, IV, neurologist, educator, researcher; b. Phoenix, Aug. 31, 1943; s. Timothy Asbury Pedley III and Mary Adele (Newcomer) Melis; m. Barbara S. Koppel, Mar. 17, 1984. BA, Pomona Coll., 1965; MD, Yale U., 1969. Cert. neurology, electroencephalography, clin. neurophysiology; diplomate Am. Bd. Psychiatry and Neurology. Intern Stanford U. Hosp., 1969-70, resident in neurology, 1970—73, postdoctoral fellow, 1973-75; asst. prof. neurology Stanford U., 1975-79; from assoc. prof. neurology to prof., vice chmn. Columbia U., 1979-98, Henry and Lucy Moses prof., chmn. neurology, 1998—; neurologist-in-chief Columbia U. Med. Ctr., NYC, 1998—. Dir. comprehensive epilepsy ctr. Columbia U. Med. Ctr., 1983-97. profl. adv. bd. Epilepsy Found Am., 1984-98, chmn. profl. adv. bd., 1985-87, pres. bd. dirs., 1991-93, chmn. 1993-95. mem. rev. com. NIH Nat. Inst. Neurol. and Chronic Diseases and Strokes, 1985-89, chmn., 1988-89, mem. Nat. Advisory Neurological Disorders & Stroke Coun. (NINDS/NIH), 2007-; various adv. coms. NIH/NINDS, 1990-98; vis. fellow in exptl. neurology Inst. Psychiatry, London, 1978-79; mem. merit rev. bd. neurobiology rsch., VA, 1992-96, chmn., 1995-96; vis. prof. various univs., U.S. and abroad. Editor-in-chief: Epilepsia, 1993—2001; contbr. articles to profl. jours. Fellow AAAS, 2000, N.Y. Acad. Medicine; Recipient various honors and awards. Fellow Am. Acad. Neurology (bd. trustees 2001—, sec., 2003-07), Am. Electroencephalographic Soc. (pres. 1989-90, bd. dirs. 1981-85), Royal Soc. Medicine; mem. Am. Neurol. Assn. (coun. 1992-94, treas. 1995-98, 1st v.p. 2003-04, pres. 2007-09), Am. Epilepsy Soc. (treas. 1980-83, pres. 1991-92), Soc. Neurosci., Internat. League Against Epilepsy (exec. com. 1994-02), Inst. Med. Nat. Acad. Sci., Vidonian Club, Yale Club, N.Y. Med. Surg. Soc., Shenorock Shore Club, Alpha Omega Alpha. Office: The Neurological Inst 710 W 168th St New York NY 10032-2603 Office Phone: 212-305-6489. Office Fax: 212-305-6978. Business E-Mail: tap2@columbia.edu.

PEDLOSKY, JOSEPH, geophysicist, educator; b. Paterson, NJ, Apr. 7, 1938; s. David and Lillian (Levit) P.; m. Holly Smith, June 1, 1974; children— Anne E. Schulman (stepdau.), Dove Helena. BS, MS, M.I.T., 1960, PhD, 1963. Asst. prof. dept. math. M.I.T., Cambridge, 1964-67, asso. prof., 1967-68; asso. prof. dept. geophys. scis. U. Chgo., 1968-72, prof., 1972-79; sr. scientist, Doherty prof. phys. oceanography Woods Hole (Mass.) Oceanographic Inst., 1979—. Author: Geophysical Fluid Dynamics, 1979, 2d. edit., 1987; contbr. articles to profl. jours. Recipient Meisinger award Am. Meteorol. Soc., 1971; Sloan fellow, 1967-68; Guggenheim fellow, 1977-78; NSF grantee, 1968—. Fellow Am. Meteorol. Soc., Am. Geophysics Union; mem. Nat. Acad. Scis. Home: 24 Meltiah Rd Falmouth MA 02540-1844

PEDOWITZ, ROBERT ALAN, orthopaedic surgeon, researcher; b. NYC, Aug. 1, 1959; s. Irving and Beverly Pedowitz; m. Loraine Pedowitz, Sept. 28, 1986; children: Rachel, Jason. BS in Psychobiology, UCLA, 1981; MD, U. Calif., San Diego, 1985; PhD, U. Gothenburg, Sweden, 1991. Diplomate Am. Bd. Orthop. Surgery. Resident, orthop. surgery U. Calif., San Diego, 1985—92; fellow, sports medicine Duke U., Durham, NC; faculty, dept. orthopaedics U. Calif., San Diego, 1992—, chief sports medicine, 1998—2006, residency dir., dept. orthop., 2001; co-dir. San Diego Arthroscopy and Sports Medicine Fellowship, San Diego, 2001—06; chmn., dept. orthop. surgery Univ. S. Fla. Coll. Medicine, Tampa, 2007—. Cons. Orthop. Mfg. Cos., 1995—2003; internat. adv. bd. Doha Orthop. and Sports Medicine Hosp., Qatar. Author; contbr. articles to profl. jours. Named a San Diego Top Doctor, 2005—06. Fellow: Am. Acad. Orthop. Surgeons; mem.: Orthop. Rsch. Soc., Arthroscopy Assn. N.Am., Am. Orthop. Soc. Sports Medicine, Am. Orthop. Assn. Avocations: golf, travel, skiing. Office: Orthop and Sports Medicine 3500 E Fletcher Ave Ste 511 MDC 106 Tampa FL 33613 Business E-Mail: pedowitz@health.usf.edu.

PEDROIA, DUSTIN LUIS, professional baseball player; b. Woodland, Calif., Aug. 17, 1983; m. Kelli Pedroia, Nov. 11, 2006. Attended, Ariz. State U. Second baseman Boston Red Sox, 2006—. Mem. US nat. team World Baseball Classic, 2009. Recipient Gold Glove award, Maj. League Baseball, 2008, Silver Slugger award, 2008; named Red Sox Minor League Offensive Player of Yr., 2005, Am. League Rookie of Yr., Maj. League Baseball, 2007, Am. League MVP, 2008; named to Am. League All-Star Team, 2008, 2009. Achievements include member of the World Series Championship winning Boston Red Sox, 2007; leading the American League in; runs, hits, doubles, 2008. Avocations: movies, video games, sports. Mailing: c/o Boston Red Sox Fenway Pk 4 Yawkey Way Boston MA 02215 Office Phone: 617-267-9440.*

PEDROW, BRENDA M., retired language educator; b. NYC, Aug. 31, 1942; d. Howard and Stella Stevenson; m. Donald P Pedrow, Aug. 25, 1962; 1 child, Brian D; 1 child, Bradley D. BA in history, Millersville U., 1980. Tutor Millersville U., Millersville, Pa., 1978—80; tchr. Adult Sch. for Cuban Refugees, Lebanon, Pa., 1980, Linden Hall Sch. for Girls, Lititz, Pa., 1981—82; tutor Conestoga Valley Sch. Dist., Lancaster, Pa., 1984—87; tchr. Lancaster Sch., 1985; ESL tchr. Am. Home Life Internat., Lancaster, Pa., 1989; tchr. Manheim Twp. Sch. Dist., Lancaster, 1986—2000; ret. Bd. mem. Lancaster Lit. Coun., 1980—86. Rschr. Interfaith Rels. Lancaster County Human Rels. Commn., 1972; org. fundraiser Lancaster Cmy. Action Program, 1976; founder First Internat. Club, Manheim Twp. H.S. Recipient Cert. Appreciation, Adult Edn. Cuban Refugees, 1980, Exceptional Svc. award, Boy Scouts Am., 1971, Cmty. Svc. award, Cmty. Action Program, 1980. Mem.: Pa. Assn. Sch. Retirees, Nat. Edn. Assn. Avocations: exercise, travel, reading. Home: 6121 Geneva Dr East Petersburg PA 17520

PEEBLES, ALLENE KAY, retired manufactured housing company executive; b. Waukegan, Ill., Feb. 9, 1938; d. Allan Laverne and Kathryn Bernice (McGill) Sedlmayr; m. William Ross Peebles, July 9, 1960; children: Ross William, Robb Allan, Raymond John, Renda Kay (Mrs. Christopher Sivak). BS with high honors, U. Wis., 1960, MS, 1967; grad., Realtors Inst., 1968. Cert. home economist. Tchr. Horicon (Wis.) High Sch., 1960-61, Oconomowoc (Wis.) High Sch., 1961-67; freelance writer, 1967-70; v.p. Luxury Homes, Inc., Watertown, Wis., 1970-93, Land Devel. Plus Devel. Inc., Watertown, 1970—; co-developer Hidden Meadows Condominium Community, Watertown, 1976-96; gen. ptnr. W and A Elderly Housing Ltd. Partnership, Watertown, 1988—; pres. Housing Am., Inc., Watertown, 1991—2003. Gen. ptnr. Sunrise Housing Ltd., 1990—; builder new and rehab low-income housing, 1983-2003 Active Wis. Gov.'s Conf. on Family, 1980, long range planning team, 1996—2003; dist. membership chmn. Boy Scouts Am., 1984—90; chmn. Ams. Abroad Am. Field Svc., Oconomowoc, 1982—87; del. Wis. Rep. Conv., 1997—; chmn. adminstrv. bd. United Meth. Ch., Oconomowoc, 1974—77, 1996—99, lay leader, 2000—03, pres. United Meth. Women, 2002—06, chmn. family ministry Wis. Conf.; chmn. all programs, 2008—09; del. Wis. conf. United Meth. Ch., 2000—03. Recipient Dist. award of Merit Potawatomi Area coun. Boy Scouts Am., 1986; named Woman of Yr., United Meth. Women, 2003. Mem.: AAUW (pres. Oconomowoc br. 1981—83, pres. Oconomowoc 1983—85, officer's bd. 1984—93, fin. advisor 1995—2002, Rsch. grants, Name grant 2009), NAFE, Wis. Assn. Family and Consumer Scis. (state bd. 1999—, state housing chmn. 2000—02), Met. Builders Assn. Greater Milw., Internat. Fedn. Home Economists (USA internat. del. 1997—), Wis. Manufactured Housing Assn. (bd. dirs. 1979—90, chmn. bd. 1985—88, Mem. of Yr. award 1986), Wis. Builders Assn., Waukesha Bd. Realtors, Wis. Assn. Realtors, Am. Assn. Family and Consumer Scis., Nat. Assn. Realtors, Wis. Home Economists in Bus. (state chmn. 1987—88, internat. rep. 1998—2000, Home Economist in Bus. of Yr. 1987), Internat. Profl. and Bus. Women, Nat. Assn. Home Builders, Nat. Home Economists in Bus. (internat. com. 1985—87, regional U.S. advisor 1990—92), Wis. Home Econs. Assn. (parliamentarian 1988—90), Am. Home Econs. Assn., Phi Lambda Theta, Kappa Omicron Nu, Phi Upsilon Omicron, Phi Kappa Phi. Republican. Avocation: writing. Home: 37788 Mapleton Rd Oconomowoc WI 53066

PEEBLES, CHRISTOPHER SPALDING, anthropologist, educator, academic administrator; b. Clearwater, Fla., May 26, 1939; s. Frederick Thomas and Corinne deGarmendia (Stephens) P.; m. Laura Ann Wisen, Oct. 6, 1993. AB, U. Chgo., 1963; PhD, U. Calif., Santa Barbara, 1974. Asst. prof. U. Windsor, Ont., Canada, 1970-74; asst. curator U. Mich., Ann Arbor, 1974-81; prof. prehistory U. Amsterdam, Netherlands, 1981-82; prof. Ind. U., Bloomington, 1983—, dean acad. computing, assoc. v.p., 1992—2005, dean emeritus, assoc. v.p. emeritus. Author: Excavations at Moundville, 1974, Representations in Archaeology, 1992. With USAF, 1956-60. Mem. Cosmos Club. Avocation: flying. Office: Ind U Glenn A Black Lab 423 N Fess Bloomington IN 47408-3800 Business E-Mail: peebles@indiana.edu.

PEEBLES, LUCRETIA NEAL DRANE, education educator; b. Atlanta, Mar. 16, 1950; d. Dudley Drane and Annie Pearl (Neal) Lewis; divorced; 1 child, Julian Timothy. BA, Pitzer Coll., 1971; MA, Claremont Grad. Sch., 1973, PhD, 1985. Special edn. tchr. Marshall Jr. High Sch., Pomona, Calif., 1971-74; high sch. tchr. Pomona High Sch., 1974-84; adminstr. Lorbeer Jr. High Sch., Diamond Bar, Calif., 1984-91; prin. Chapparal Mid. Sch., Moorpark, Calif., 1991-92, South Valley Jr. High Sch., Gilroy, Calif., 1992—95; asst. prof. edn. Spelman Coll., Atlanta, 1995—97; asst. prof. Coll. Edn., U. Denver, 1997—2003; assaoc. prof. edn. St. Mary's Coll. Calif., 2003—05, Loyola Marymount U., LA, 2005—07, Calif. Dept. Edn., 2008—; rsch. and evaluation cons. Policy and Evaluation Divsn. Co-dir. pre-freshman program, Claremont (Calif.) Coll., 1974; dir. pre-freshman program, Claremont Coll., 1975; cons., Claremont, 1983—. Author: Negative Attendance Behavior: The Role of the School, 1985, Teaching Children Proactive Responses to Media Violence, 1996, Validating Children: A Collaborative Model, 1996, The Challenge of Leadership in Charter Schools, 2000, Charter School Equity Issues: Focus on Minority and At-Risk Students, 2000, Millennial Challenges for Educational Leadership: Revisiting Issues of Diversity, 2000. Active Funds Distbn. Bd,-Food for All, 1987—, Funds Distbn. Task Force-Food for All, 1986; mem. Adolescent Pregnancy Childwatch Task Force. Named Outstanding Young Career Woman Upland Bus. and Profl. Women's Club, 1978-79; Stanford U. Sch. Edn. MESA fellow, 1983, NSF fellow Stanford U., 1981, Calif. Tchrs. Assn. fellow, 1979, Claremont Grad. Sch. fellow, 1977-79, fellow Calif. Edn. Policy Fellowship Program, 1989-90; recipient Woman of Achievement award YWCA of West Edn., 1991. Mem. Assn. Calif. Sch. Adminstrs. (Minigrant award 1988), Assn. for Supervision and Curriculum Devel., Nat. Assn. Secondary Sch. Principals, Pi Lambda Theta. Democrat. Am. Baptist. Home: 39370 Civic Center Dr Apt 531 Fremont CA 94538-6736 Office Phone: 916-322-3074. E-mail: 1peebles@ca.rr.com.

PEEBLES, LYNDA, chemistry professor; PhD in Phys. Chemistry, U. North Tex., Denton, 2002. Lectr. Tex. Woman's U., Denton, 2002—. Mem.: Am. Chem. Soc.

PEEBLES, PEYTON ZIMMERMANN, JR., retired electrical engineer, educator; b. Columbus, Ga., Sept. 10, 1934; s. Peyton Zimmermann Peebles Sr. and Maida Erlene Dials; m. Barbara Ann Suydam,

Sept. 6, 1969; children: Peyton Zimmermann III, Edward Arlen. BSEE, Evansville Coll., 1957; MSEE, Drexel Inst., 1963; PhD, U. Pa., 1967. Design engr. RCA, Moorestown, NJ, 1958-64, systems engr., 1966-69; prof. U. Tenn., Knoxville, 1969-75, 76-81; vis. prof. U. Hawaii, Honolulu, 1975-76; prof. U. Fla., Gainesville, 1981-84, 90-96, assoc. chmn., 1984-90, prof. emeritus, 1996—. Cons. in field. Author: Communication System Principles, 1976, Probability, Random Variables and Random Signal Principles, 1980, 4th edit., 2001, Digital Communication Systems, 1987; prin. author: Principles of Electrical Engineering, 1991, Radar Principles, 1998; contbr. articles to profl. jours.; patentee in field, artist:(painting)(oil portrate)for numerous commns. Capt. USAFR, 1957-61. David Sarnoff fellow, 1964-66. Fellow IEEE (life); mem. Sigma Xi, Eta Kappa Nu, Tau Beta Pi, Sigma Pi Sigma, Phi Beta Chi. Methodist. Avocations: fishing, painting, woodworking. Home Phone: 352-375-3764. Personal E-mail: peytonpeebles@cox.net.

PEEBLES, R. DONAHUE, real estate company executive; b. Washington, Mar. 2, 1960; m. Katrina Peebles; children: Donahue III, Choe. Attended, Rutgers U.; D in Hospitality Mgmt. (hon.), Johnson & Wales U. Real estate agent/appraiser, Washington, 1979—83; appt. mem. DC Bd. Equalization and Rev., 1983, chmn., 1984—88; founder RDP Corp., 1983, RDP Assessment Appeals Svcs., Inc., Washington, 1988; founder, chmn., CEO Peebles Corp. (formerly Peebles Atlantic Devel. Corp.), 1997—. Spkr. in field. Author: The Peebles Principles, Tales and Tactics from an Entrepreneur's Life of Winning Deals, Succeeding in Business and Creating a Fortune from Scratch, 2007, The Peebles Path to Real Estate Wealth, 2008; featured in NY Times, Washington Post, Forbes, Wall St. Jour., Black Enterprise, Ebony and others; appeared on: CNBC, CNN, ABC, Fin. Network and others. Named Black Enterprise Co. of Yr., 2004; named to Power 150, Ebony mag., 2008. Achievements include development of the first 5-star Black-owned convention hotel (Royal Palm Crowne Plaza Hotel) in American history, 2002. Office: Peebles Corp 550 Biltmore Way Ste 970 Coral Gables FL 33134 Office Phone: 305-442-4342. Office Fax: 305-442-4345.

PEEBLES, ROBERT M., tobacco company executive; CPA. Acct. Ernst & Young LLP; fin. mgmt. positions CSX Corp., asst. contr., 1997—2000, Pittston Co., 2000—01; cons. Gabriel Group, 2001—03; contr. Universal Corp., Richmond, Va., 2003—. Mem. Controllers' Exec. Roundtable Va. Commonwealth Univ. Office: Universal Corp 1501 N Hamilton St Richmond VA 23230 Mailing: Universal Corp PO Box 25099 Richmond VA 23260 Office Phone: 804-359-9311. Office Fax: 804-254-3582.

PEEK, JEFFREY M., finance company executive; b. 1947; BA in Internat. Affairs, Princeton U., 1969; MBA, Harvard Bus. Sch., 1972. With Merrill Lynch, 1983—2002; exec. v.p. Merrill Lynch & Co., Inc., 1997—2001; pres. Merrill Lynch Investment Managers, 1997—2001; vice chmn. Credit Suisse First Boston LLC, 2002—03; pres., COO CIT Group Inc., Livingston, NJ, 2003—04, pres., CEO, 2004—05, chmn., CEO, 2005—. Bd. dirs. CIT Group, 2003—, Freddie Mac, 2006—07; treas. NYC Ballet; chmn. advisory coun. Bendheim Ctr. for Fin.; bd. trustees Teachers Coll, Columbia U. Office: CIT Group 1 CIT Dr Livingston NJ 07039

PEEK, PAMELA, language educator; PhD in Comparative Lit., U. SC, Columbia, 1984. Vis. prof. Spanish Bapt. Coll., Charleston, SC, 1987—94; dir. & coord., Spanish study abroad program, Spain Charleston Southern U., 1992—2001, asst. prof. Spanish, 1994—99, assoc. prof. Spanish, 1999—2002, chair, dept. lang. & visual arts, 2000—, dir. & coord., Spanish study abroad program, Mex., 2001—, prof. Spanish, 2002—. Translator: (dramatic reading from el trato de argel) Passo e Mezzo Freiburger Renaissance Ensemble; contbr. articles to profl. jours. Recipient Excellence Tchg. award, Charleston Southern U., 2000; finalist SC Gov. award, SCCHE, 2000. Mem.: SC Coun. Langs. (chmn. 1999—2002), SC Fgn. Lang. Tchrs. Exec. Coun., SC Fgn. Lang. Tchrs. Assn. (pres. 1995—96), Sigma Delta Pi (tau nu chpt. advisor 1993—). Office: Charleston Southern Univ PO Box 118087 Charleston SC 29423 Business E-Mail: ppeek@csuniv.edu.

PEEL, HARRIS, retired small business owner; b. Decatur, Ill., Nov. 14, 1923; s. Wilbur David Peel and Ruth Harris; m. Margaret Backus, Oct. 11, 1946 (dec. Nov. 1990); children: Susan Harris, Jane Peel Fuller, David Harris. BS, Columbia U., 1950; MS, George Washington U., 1967. Editor War Dept., Frankfurt, Germany, 1946; writer Holiday Mag., Europe, 1947-48; fgn. svc. officer U.S. Dept. State and USIA, various locations, 1950-74; owner Peel Gallery Fine Art, Danby, Vt., 1976—2005. Author: (book) History of 254th Infantry Regiment, 1945. Advisor on psychol. warfare U.S. Army and USN, Ft. Bragg, N.C., 1971-74. Cpl. U.S. Army, 1943-45. Decorated Bronze star with oak leaf cluster U.S. Army, 1945, Disting. Civilian Svc. medal U.S. Army; 4-yr. scholar Chgo. Tribune, 1941. Mem. Vt. Assn. Galleries (pres. 1978-98), Overseas Press Club. Avocation: astronomy. Home: 1 Peel Rd Danby VT 05739 Office: Peel Gallery Peel Rd Danby VT 05739 E-mail: hpeel@vermontel.net.

PEEL, KENNETH L., federal agency administrator; BA, UCLA. Mem. Sec. of State's Policy Planning Staff The White House; dir. internat. environ., energy and risk regulation affairs Nat. Security Coun.; dep. asst. sec. internat. devel., fin. and debt US Dept. Treasury, US dir. European Bank for Reconstruction and Devel., 2008—. Office: Office of Internat Affairs US Dept Treasury 1500 Pennsylvania Ave NW Washington DC 20220*

PEELE, PAMELA BONIFAY, economics educator; b. Pensacola, Fla., 1953; d. Jack Edward Bonifay; m. James Peele, Nov., 1974. BA magna cum laude, Roanoke Coll., Salem, Va., 1989; MA, Va. Tech., Blacksburg, Va., 1990, PhD, 1994. Technologist VA Med. Ctr., Gainesville, Fla., 1974-75, technologist EEG Salem, Va., 1975-87; prof. health econs. U. Pitts., 1994—. Mem. Omega Delta. Office: U Pitts 130 DeSoto St Pittsburgh PA 15216 Office Fax: 412-624-3146.

PEELER, STUART THORNE, oil industry executive, consultant; b. Los Angeles, Oct. 28, 1929; s. Joseph David and Elizabeth Fiske (Boggess) P.; m. Sylvia Frances Townley, Nov. 5, 1985. BA, Stanford U., 1950, JD, 1953. Bar: Calif. 1953. Ptnr. Musick, Peeler & Garrett, LA, 1958-73; with Santa Fe Internat. Corp., Orange, Calif., 1973-81, v.p., sec., assoc. gen. counsel, 1973-74, sr. v.p., gen. counsel, dir., 1975-81; vice-chmn. bd., chmn. exec. com. Supron Energy Corp., 1978-82; chmn. bd., CEO Statex Petroleum, Inc., 1982-89; chmn., pres., CEO Putumayo Prodn. Co., Tucson, 1989—. Bd. dirs. Chieftain Internat. Inc. Trustee J. Paul Getty Trust, 1963-99; mem. U.S. Tuna Team, 1957-67, capt., 1966. Served with U.S. Army, 1953-55. Decorated Army Commendation medal. Mem. AIME, State Bar Calif., Am. Judicature Soc., Theta Chi, Phi Delta Phi, Skyline Country Club. Republican. Congregationalist. Office: PO Box 35852 Tucson AZ 85740-5852 Office Phone: 520-575-0709. Office Fax: 520-544-0632.

PEEPLES, JACK ALLEN, electrical engineer, educator; b. Flint, Mich., Aug. 26, 1959; s. Jack Anthony and Betty Irene Peeples; m. Susan Gale Ritchey, Aug. 25, 2007. BSEE, Purdue U., West Lafayette, Ind., 1981; MA in Economics, Wayne St. U., Detroit, 1989; AGS in Emergency Medicine summa cum laude, Oakland CC, Bloomfield Hills, Mich., 2000. EIT Ind., 1981, cert. emergency med. technician, Mich., 1999. Elec. engr. Sverdrup & Parcel Inc., St. Louis, 1981—85; sr. elec. engr. Gen. Motors Pontiac Lab., Mich., 1985—2002; adj. instr. Oakland CC, 2001—, Baker Coll., Auburn Hills, Mich., 2004—, Mott CC, Flint, 2004—, Washtenaw CC, Ann Arborq, Mich., 2004—, ITT Ednl. Svcs. Inc., Canton, Mich., 2004—. Instr. ARC, Bloomfield Hills, 2001—; election chairperson City of Framington Hills, Mich., 2000—; chairperson, supervisory com. Chief Pontiac Fed. Credit Union, 1988—91. Mem.: Mich. Tutorial Assn., Phi Theta Kappa, Phi Eta Sigma. Avocations: jogging, bicycling, antiques. Personal E-mail: econman77@yahoo.com.

PEEPLES, MARY ANNE BAUMANN, science educator; b. Binghamton, NY, July 2, 1941; d. Emmanuel Patrick and Ella Lucille (Woods) Baumann; m. Horace Timothy Peeples, Aug. 21, 1993; children: Charles David Steinkuehler, Ayne Elizabeth Ray. BS in Edn., Ctrl. Mo. State U., Warrensburg, 1962, MS in Edn., 1969. Cert. Tchr. Mo. Bd. Edn., Kans. Bd. Edn., N.C. Bd. Edn. Sci. tchr., N. Kansas City, Mo., 1962—64, Immaculata HS, Leavenworth, Kans., 1964—72, Easton, Kans., 1972—73, Topeka Pub. Schs., 1973—79, Cumberland County Schs., Fayetteville, NC, 1979—2003; ret., 2003; adj. chemistry tchr. Fayetteville Tech. CC, 1983—. Med. transcriber, radiology Highsmith-Rainey Meml. Hosp., Fayetteville, 1983—97; med. transcriber, orthopedics Cape Fear Orthopaedics, Fayetteville, 1998—2001. With USAR, 1974—80. Recipient NSF award, Tex. A&M, Emporia (Kans.) Coll., 1965, 1972, Citizen Soldier award, 89th ARCOM, USAR, Wichita, Kans., 1977; grantee Merit fellowship-chemistry, Shell Oil Co., Stanford U., 1966. Mem.: DAR (state corr. sec. 2005—06, chpt. regent, state chmn., DAR Mag., state officer), Pastoral Coun. (sec. 2008—), Cumberland County Rep. Women's Club (past sec.), Woman's Club of Fayetteville (v.p. 2005—07, pres. 2007—09). Republican.

PEEPLES, WILLIAM DEWEY, JR., mathematics professor; b. Bessemer, Ala., Apr. 19, 1928; s. William Dewey and Thelma Jeannette (Chastain) P.; m. Katie Ray Blackerby, Aug. 30, 1956; children: Mary Jeannette, William Dewey III, Gerald Lewis, Stephen Ray. BS, Samford U., 1947; MS, U. Wis., 1949; PhD, U. Ga., 1951. Rsch. mathematician Ballistics Rsch. Lab., Aberdeen, Md., summer 1951; mem. faculty Samford U., Birmingham, Ala., 1951-56, prof. math., 1959-95, head dept., 1967-95; prof. emeritus, 1995; mem. faculty Auburn U., 1956-59. Cons. Hayes Internat. Corp. Co-author: Modern Mathematics for Business Students, 1969, Finite Mathematics, 1974, Modern Mathematics with Applications to Business and the Social Sciences, 4th edit, 1986, Finite Mathematics with Applications to Business and the Social Sciences, 1981, 2d edit., 1987; Contbr. articles to profl. publs. Served to 1st lt. AUS, 1954-56. Mem. Am. Math. Soc., Math. Assn. Am., Nat. Council Tchrs. Math., Ala. Coll. Tchrs. Math. (pres. 1969), Sigma Xi, Pi Mu Epsilon, Phi Kappa Phi (pres. 1977), Lambda Chi Alpha. Baptist (deacon, chmn. 1986). Club: Mason (Shriner). Home: 419 Poinciana Dr Birmingham AL 35209-4129 E-mail: wdpeeples@peoplepc.com.

PEER, LARRY HOWARD, literature educator; b. Ogden, Utah, Jan. 2, 1942; s. Howard Harvey and Edna Celina (Baron) P.; m. Janet Priday; 9 children. BA, Brigham Young U., 1963, MA, 1965; PhD, U. Md., 1969. From asst. to assoc. prof. U. Ga., Athens, 1968-75; assoc. prof. Brigham Young U., Provo, Utah, 1975-78, prof., 1978—. Acting head dept. comparative lit. U. Ga., Athens, 1973-74, Brigham Young U., Provo, 1978-81; pres. Western Regional Honors Coun., 1978-79; exec. dir. Am. Conf. on Romanticism, 1992—. Author: Beyond Haworth, 1984, The Reasonable Romantic, 1986, The Romantic Manifesto, 1988. Mem. MLA, Am. Comparative Lit. Assn. (exec. officer 1988-94), Am. Soc. for Aesthetics, Rocky Mountain Soc. for Aesthetics (pres. 1986-87), Internat. Byron Soc., Internat. Brontë Soc. Mem. Lds Ch. Avocation: travel. Office: Brigham Young U Comparative Lit Dept Provo UT 84602

PEERCY, PAUL STUART, engineering educator; s. Robert L. and Ernest (Bell) P.; m. Catherine B. Christen, July 17, 1965; children: Michael, Mark. BS in physics, Berea Coll., 1961; MS in physics, U. Wis., Madison, 1963, PhD in physics, 1966. Postdoctoral fellow Bell Labs., Murray Hill, NJ, 1966-68; mem. tech. staff Sandia Nat. Labs., Albuquerque, 1968-76, divsn. supr., 1976-82, mgr. ion-solid rsch. dept., 1982-86, mgr. compound semicondr. and device rsch. dept., 1986-91, dir. microelectronics and photonics, 1991-95; pres. SEMI/SEMATECH, 1995—99; dean Coll. Engring. U. Wis., Madison, 1999—, prof. dept. materials sci. and engring., 1999—. Mem. solid state sciences com. NRC, Washington, 1989-91; mem. external adv. bd. U. Ill. elec. engring. dept.; mem. microelectronics sci. bd. Jet Propulsion Lab., Calif. Inst. Tech., Pasadena, Calif., 1992—; mem. indsl. adv. coun. U. Ariz. Coll. Engring., Tucson, 1992—; mem. external rev. bd. Carnegie Mellon Rsch. Inst., Pitts., 1992-97; mem. Roadmap Coordinating Group for the Nat. Tech. Roadmap for Semiconductors Semiconductor Industry Assn., 1994; mem. policy bd. NSF Engring. Rsch. Ctr. in Semiconductor Environment and Safety, 1997-99, Nat. Nanofabrication Users Network, 1998-; chair U. Wis. Tech. Enterprise Coop., 1999-; mem Wis. Tech. and Entrepreneurship Coun., 2000-; bd. dirs. Meriter Hosp. and Health Services, Madison, Wis., 2000-, Mason-Wells, Milw., 2003-. Editor 3 books; prin. editor: Jour. Materials Rsch., 1986-91; contbr. more than 175 articles to profl. jours. Recipient Sandia Award for Excellence, Woody award for Exceptional Svc., Materials Rsch. Soc. Fellow IEEE, AAAS (councilor, 1998-, Am. Phys. Soc. (chair divsn. material physics 1994, councilor 1998—, mem. exec. com. 1999—2000); mem. NAE, The Minerals, Metall., and Materials Soc. (chair electronics materials com. 1991-92), Materials Rsch. Soc. (v.p. 1987, councilor and mem. exec. com., 2001-; Woody Award for Exceptional Svc.), Phi Kappa Phi, Sigma Pi, Tau Peta Pi (disting. mem.); Nat. Acad. Engineers. Achievements include 2 patents in field. Office: U Wis 2610 Engring Hall 1415 Engineering Dr Madison WI 53706-1691 Home Phone: 608-833-0370; Office Phone: 608-262-3482.

PEERSON, MICHAEL B., pharmacist, director; s. Andrew S. and Freda G. Peerson; m. Jeanette Cagle, July 7, 1984; children: Andrea K., LeAnna M. BS in Pharmacy, Southwestern Okla. State U., Weatherford, 1988. Registered pharmacist Tex., Wash., Alaska. Asst. pharmacy mgr. Walmart Stores Inc., Tyler, Tex., 1988—92, pharmacy mgr. Palestine, Tex., 1992—94, dist. mgr. pharmacy ops. Bentonville, Ark., 1994—96, regional mgr. pharmacy ops., 1996—2005, dir., talent acquisitions health & wellness, 2005—08, sr. dir., talent acquisitions, 2008—. Mem.: Tex. Fedn. Drug Stores, Am. Pharm. Assn., Nat. Pharm. Assn., Nat. Assn. Chain Drug Stores (pharmacy edn. adv. coun. mem. 2005—08). Conservative. Avocations: scuba diving, archery, boating, hiking, bowling. Home: 9556 Preservation Dr Rogers AR 72758 Office: Walmart Stores Inc 702 SW 8th St Bentonville AR 72716-0195 Personal E-mail: mbpeers@cox.net. Business E-Mail: mike.peerson@wal-mart.com.

PEET, AMANDA, actress; b. NYC, Jan. 11, 1972; d. Charles and Penny Peet; m. David Benioff, Sept. 30, 2006; 1 child, Frances Pen. BA in History, Columbia U., 1994. Actor: (films) Animal Room, 1995, Winterlude, 1996, She's the One, 1996, Virginity, 1996, Grind, 1997, Touch Me, 1997, One Fine Day, 1996, Sax and Violins, 1997, 1999, 1998, Southie, 1998, Playing by Heart, 1998, Origin of the Species, 1998, Simply Irresistible, 1999, Jump, 1999, Two Ninas, 1999, Body Shots, 1999, Isn't She Great?, 2000, The Whole Nine Yards, 2000, Takedown, 2000, Whipped, 2000, Saving Silverman, 2001, High Crimes, 2002, Changing Lanes, 2002, Igby Goes Down, 2002, Whatever We Do, 2003, Identity, 2003, Something's Gotta Give, 2003, The Whole Ten Yards, 2004, Melinda and Melinda, 2004, A Lot Like Love, 2005, Syriana, 2005, Griffin and Phoenix, 2006, The Ex, 2007, Martian Child, 2007, The X-Files: I Want to Believe, 2008, What Doesn't Kill You, 2008; (TV films) Ellen Foster, 1997, Date Squad, 2001; (TV series) Central Park West, 1995—96, Jack & Jill, 1999—2001, Partners, 1999, Studio 60 on the Sunset Strip, 2006—07, (TV appearances) Law & Order, 1995, The Single Guy, 1996, Spin City, 1997, Seinfeld, 1997; (plays) Whale Music, Winter Lies, 27 Sketches: Fear and Misery in the Third Reich, The Country Club, This Is How It Goes, 2005, Escape: 6 Ways to Get Away, 2005, Barefoot in the Park, 2006. Office: The Gersh Agy Ste 201 232 N Canon Dr Beverly Hills CA 90210

PEET, CHARLES D, JR., lawyer; b. NYC, Sept. 3, 1935; s. Charles D and Margaret Louise (Sherman) P.; children: Alisa, Amanda. BA, Yale U., 1957; JD, Harvard U., 1960. Bar: N.Y. 1962. Assoc. Milbank, Tweed, Hadley & McCloy, NYC, 1960-68, ptnr., 1969-98; of counsel Freshfields Bruckhaus Deringer US LLP (and predecessor firm), NYC, 1998—. Mem. Assn. Bar N.Y.C. Office: Freshfields Bruckhaus Deringer US LLP 520 Madison Ave Fl 34 New York NY 10022-4213 Office Phone: 212-277-4000. Business E-Mail: charles.peet@freshfields.com.

PEET, PHYLLIS IRENE, art historian, women's studies educator; b. Winnipeg, Man., Can., Mar. 3, 1943; came to the U.S., 1948; d. Harold Parsons and Gladys Mae (Riley) Harrison; m. Thomas Peter Richman, June 14, 1963 (div. 1969); m. Charles Francis Peet, Sept. 9, 1972. BA in Art, Calif. State U., Northridge, 1972; MA in Art History, U. Calif., LA, 1976, PhD in Art History, 1987. Sec. L.A. County Supr. Kenneth Hahn, 1960-68; assoc. in art history L.A. County Mus. Art, 1974-75; asst. dir., curator Grunwald Ctr. for the Graphic Arts, U. Calif., LA, 1975-78; Am. art scholar High Mus. Art, Atlanta, 1984-90; instr. women's studies Monterey (Calif.) Peninsula Coll., 1986—; founding dir., instr. women's programs/women's studies Re-entry and Multicultural Resource Ctr. Monterey Peninsula Coll., Calif., 1989—2007, prof. emeritus, 2007—. Dirs.' adv. com. Art Mus. Santa Cruz County, 1981-84, 89-94; vis. lectr. Calif. State U., Fresno, 1984; program coord. conf. Inst. for Hist. Study, San Francisco, 1987; lectr. bd. studies in art U. Calif. Santa Cruz, 1991-95; coord. Monterey County Women's Multicultural Conf., 1993-2007. Author Eight Over Eighty, 2008; co-curator, editor, compiler: (book and exhbn.) The American Personality: The Artist Illustrator of Life in the United States, 1860-1930, 1976; author, curator: (book and exhbn.) American Women of the Etching Revival, 1988; co-author: American Paintings in the High Museum of Art, 1994, Eight in Their 80s, 2008; contbr. articles to profl. jours. including Am. Nat. Biography, Fitzroy Dict. of Women Artists, 1997, Dict. Literary Biography, 1998. Vol., activist Dem. Party, L.A., 1960-66, Peace and Freedom Party, L.A., 1967-71; vol. Dem. Party Candidates, Santa Cruz, Calif., 1979-96, Santa Cruz Action Network, 1980-85; mem. nominating com. Girl Scouts of Am., Monterey Bay, 1991-93. Rockefeller Found. fellow UCLA, 1978-80, Dickson grantee U. Calif. LA, 1981-82; recipient Women Helping Women award Soroptimists, Monterey and Carmel, Calif., 1991, 95, Allen Griffin for Excellence in Edn. award Cmty. Found. Monterey County, 1993, Quality of Life award Econ. Devel. Corp., Monterey, 1994, Excellence in Edn. award Monterey Peninsula Coll. Found., 2004-07; named Tchr. of Yr., Tchrs. of Tomorrow, 2004. Mem.: NAACP, ACLU, AAUW, NOW, Coll. Art Assn., UN Assn., Western Assn. Women Historians, Inst. for Hist. Study, Nat. Women's Studies Assn., Planned Parenthood, Monterey Bay Women's Caucus for Art (founder, bd. dirs. 1988—93), Women's Internat. League for Peace and Freedom. Avocations: print collecting, photography. Office: Womens Programs Monterey Peninsula Coll 980 Fremont St Monterey CA 93940-4704 Personal E-mail: ppeetcat@comcast.net. Business E-Mail: ppeet@mpc.edu.

PEETZ, KAREN BRETHERICK, bank executive; b. Sept. 15, 1955; m. David; 2 children. BS, Pa. State. U., 1977; MS, Johns Hopkins U. Various client services, sales, credit and risk mgmt. positions JP Morgan Chase (formerly Chase Manhattan Bank and Chemical Bank); sales mgr. global trust services then head global client mgmt. Chase Manhattan Bank, NYC, sr. v.p., bus. mgr. global trust services London; sr. v.p., divsn. head domestic corp. trust bus. The Bank of NY, 1998, head global payments services group, head corp. trust, 2003—06, sr. exec. v.p., 2006—07; CEO global corp. trust The Bank of NY Mellon, 2007—08, CEO issuer, treas., broker-dealer and hedge fund svcs., 2008—, mem. exec. com., chairperson Women's Initiatives Network, mem. diversity coun. Mem. Women's Leadership Initiative Pa. State U.; bd. trustees Brooklyn Acad. Music; steering com. Women United in Philanthropy United Way NYC. Named one of 25 Women to Watch, US Banker, 2006, 2007, 25 Most Powerful Women in Banking, 2008. Mem.: Women's Bond Club. Office: The Bank of NY Mellon One Wall St 10th Fl New York NY 10286*

PEETZ, RALF M., chemistry professor; m. Faiza Maza; children: Vincent H., Frederick L. Vordiplom, Martin Luther U. Halle-Wittenberg, Saale, Germany, 1995; MS, U. Hamburg, Germany, 1997, Dr. rer. nat., 2000. Vis. scientist Inst. Polymer Sci., Akron, Ohio; asst. prof. CUNY, CSI & Doctoral Faculty, Staten Island, 2003—08, assoc. prof. Co-dir. Ctr. Engineered Polymeric Materials, Staten Island, NY, 2004—. Contbr. articles to sci. profl. jours. Recipient Presentation awards, Various Judges, 1997; grant, CUNY, 2003—, NY Star, 2004—. Mem.: NSF (grant 2004—07), AAAS, Am. Chem. Soc. Business E-Mail: peetz@mail.csi.cuny.edu.

PEFANIS, HARRY N., oil industry executive; b. Buffalo, 1957; Grad., U. Okla., 1979. Exec. v.p. Plains All American Pipeline LP, Houston, 1998, pres., COO, 1999—. Office: Plains All American Pipline LP 333 Clay St Ste 1600 Houston TX 77002*

PEFFER, RODNEY GENE, philosopher, educator; b. Battle Creek, Iowa, Sept. 20, 1952; s. Harold Eugene and Delores Arlene Peffer; 1 child, David Alexander Ray. BA, Iowa State U., Ames, 1975; MA, U. Ariz., Tucson, 1978, PhD, 1983. Adj. prof. San Jose State U., Calif., 1980—86; prof. U. San Diego, 1986—. Vis. scholar philosophy dept. U. Ariz., 1993; session organizer XIX World Congress Philosophy, Moscow, 1993, XX World Congress Philosophy, Boston, 1998, XXI World Congress Philosophy, Istanbul, Turkey, 2003, XXII World Congress Philosophy, Seoul, Republic of Korea, 2008; co-organizer Mini-Conf. Global Justice & Cosmopolitanism, Pasadena, Calif., 2003; vis. prof. St. Clare's Coll., Oxford, 2003. Author: (book) Marxism, Morality, and Social Justice; musician: (music concert) Voz Alta Art Gallery; contbr. articles to profl. jours., lit. jours. Steering com. mem. San Diego Friends

Cuba, 1995—2009; pres. San Diego-Cuba Sister City Assn., 2001—05; assoc. mem. Ctr. Global Justice Ctr. Para La Justicia Global, San Miguel de Allende, Mexico, 2006—09. Recipient U. Professorship award, U. San Diego, 1999, Disting. Alumni award, Iowa State U., 2007. Mem.: AAUP, Internat. Devel. Ethics Assn., Soc. Philos. Study Marxism, North Am. Soc. Social Philosophy (pacific divsn. co-organizer 1995—99), Radical Philosophy Assn., Am. Philos. Assn., Phi Beta Kappa. Green Party. Avocations: music, writing, poetry. Office: Dept Philosophy Univ San Diego 5998 Acala Pk San Diego CA 92110 Office Fax: 619-260-7950. Business E-Mail: peffer@sandiego.edu.

PEFLEY, NORMAN GORDON, bank executive; b. Eugene, Oreg., Dec. 15, 1955; s. Gordon Vergne Pefley and Jean Pefley (Lee) Hawley; m. Emma Ginete Lacuesta, July 5, 1986. BA, U. Calif., Davis, 1977; MA, Johns Hopkins U., 1979; MBA, U. Chgo., 1981; MA, Golden Gate U., 2001. CFA, CPHQ. Rsch. analyst Chgo. Bd. Options Exch., 1981-83; sr. fin. analyst Bank of Am., San Francisco, 1983-89, v.p., 1989-99. Referee Jour. Futures Markets, N.Y.C., 1984-87. Mem.: ASTD, Nat. Assn. Healthcare Quality, The Security Analysts of San Francisco, Internat. Soc. Performance Improvement, CFA Inst., Toastmasters Internat., Omicron Delta Epsilon, Delta Phi Alpha, Phi Beta Kappa. Avocation: languages.

PEGALIS, STEVEN E., lawyer; b. NYC, Apr. 12, 1942; BA, Queens Coll. of City of NY, 1962; LLB, NY Law Sch., 1965, JD, 1979. Bar: NY 1966, Pa. 1992, US Ct. Appeals (2nd cir.) 1969, US Dist. Ct. (ea. dist. NY) 1969. Founding ptnr. Pegalis & Erickson, LLC, Lake Success, NY, 1972—. Adj. prof. med. malpractice NY Law Sch. Author: American Law of Medical Malpractice (3rd edit.); bd. editors: Cancer Litigation published by NY Law Jour. Pub. Co. Bd. dirs. NY Law Sch. Named one of Top 10 Trial Lawyers in Am., Nat. Law Jour., 2005. Mem.: Am. Assn. Justice, ABA, Am. Soc. Law and Medicine, Am. Coll. Medicine (assoc. in law), Assn. Trial Lawyers Am., NY State Trial Lawyers Assn., Nassau County Bar Assn., Queens County Bar Assn., Assn. Bar City of NY. Office: Pegalis & Erickson 1 Hollow Ln Ste 107 New Hyde Park NY 11042 Office Phone: 516-684-2900. Office Fax: 516-684-2939. Business E-Mail: spegalis@pegalisanderickson.com.

PEGELS, C. CARL, management consultant, educator; b. Barendrecth, Holland, The Netherlands, Feb. 26, 1933; came to U.S., 1962, naturalized, 1968; s. Bertus and Adriana Maria (Denotter) P.; children: Janice Joy, Kevin Carl. BS in Mech. Engring., Detroit Inst. Tech., 1961; MS, Purdue U., 1963, PhD in Mgmt., 1966. Prodn. engr. Ford Motor, Windsor, Can., 1955-62; instr. Purdue U., W. Lafayette, Ind., 1962-66; prof. SUNY, Buffalo, 1966—. V.p. Ctr. Mgmt. Sys., Buffalo, 1978—91. Author: Basic for Business, 1973, Health Care & Elderly, 1980, Japan vs The West, 1984, Q.C. in Health Care, 1985, Decision Support Systems for Production and Operations Management, 1986, Management and Industry in China, 1987, Strategic Management for Hospitals and Health Care Corporations, 1987, Health Care and the Older Citizen, 1988, Decision Support Systems for Management Science/Operations Research, 1989, Strategic Information Systems, 1993, Total Quality management, 1995, Strategies and Tools for the Learning Company, 1998, Proven Solutions for Reducing Health Care Costs, 2003; Proven Solutions for Improving Supply Chain Management, 2005. Krannert fellow, 1966; Krannert scholar Purdue U., 1963. Mem. Acad. of Mgmt., Prodn. and Ops. Mgmt. Soc., Am. Inst. Decision Scis. Avocation: running. Home: 150 Arielle Ct Apt D Buffalo NY 14221-1969 Office: Sch of Mgmt SUNY at Buffalo Buffalo NY 14260-0001 Personal E-mail: cpegels@yahoo.com. Business E-Mail: cpegels@buffalo.edu.

PEGG, MARK GREGORY, historian, educator; b. Port Macquarie, NSW, Australia, Aug. 26, 1963; s. Veronica Aileen (Née Lacy) Seckold. BA with honors, U. Sydney, 1986; PhD, Princeton U., NJ, 1997. Asst. prof. History Dept. Wash. U., St. Louis, 1998—2003, assoc. prof., 2004—. Author: (book) The Corruption of Angels: The Great Inquisition of 1245-1246, A Most Holy War: The Albigensian Crusade and the Battle for Christendom. New Directions fellowship, Andrew W. Mellon Found., 2005—08. Office: Wash Univ History Dept Campus Box 1062 One Brookings Dr Saint Louis MO 63130

PEGIS, ANTON GEORGE, retired language educator; b. Milw., Feb. 21, 1920; s. George Anton and Eugenia (Stathas) Pegis; m. Harriet Louise Stevens, June 1, 1949; children: Stefani Elizabeth, Penelope Eugenia. AB, We. State Coll. Colo., 1949; MA, Denver U., 1951, PhD, 1956. Jr. engr. North Shore Gas Co., Waukegan, Ill., 1946—47; instr. Ft. Lewis Coll., 1952—53; process control technician Gates Rubber Co., Denver, 1953—54; prof. English Colo. Sch. Mines, Golden, 1954—82, asst. to pres., 1964—68, v.p. devel., 1968—73, v.p. external affairs, 1973—74, prof. emeritus, 1982—. Cons. Office Mineral Reports U.S. Bur. Mines, Washington, Civil Svc. Commn., San Francisco, 1974—94, Regional Tng. Ctr. Office Pers. Mgmt., Denver, 1983. Author: Social Theory in the Novels of Ford Madox Ford, 1956, An Intensive Course in English for Foreign Engineering Students, 1957, Humanism and the Practical Order, 1964, Excellence and the Odyssean Philosophy, 1965, Platonism in the Renaissance Lyric, 1965, Education for Leadership, 1966, Totality in Engineering Education, 1968, Course Recommendations for the Resource Engineer, 1968, Encroachment of Competing Land Uses on Mineral Development, 1976. Chmn. United Way Fund; sec. Colo. Sch. Mines Found.; pres. Roland Valley Civic Assn., 1974—75. With US Army, 1940—46, maj. AUS Ret. Recipient Outstanding Prof. award, Colo. Sch. Mines, 1976, Amoco Found. awards; named Disting. Sgt., 121st Field Arty. Rgt., 1988, Outstanding Prof., Tau Beta Pi, 1963, Hon. Col., 115th Engring. Rgt., 1988. Mem.: MLA, Am. Soc. Engring. Edn. (chmn. Rocky Mountain sect.), Am. Alumni Coun. (chmn. dist. VII 1971—72), Golden C. of C. (pres. 1968), Blue Key, Alpha Psi Omega, Theta Chi. Home: 415 Scenic Ct Golden CO 80401-2533 Home Phone: 303-279-2080.

PEGMAN, ANDREW J., literature and language professor; b. Willoughby, Ohio, Nov. 6, 1976; s. Edwin Paul and Cynthia Jean Pegman. BA, John Carroll U., University Heights, Ohio; MA in English, Cleve. State U., Ohio. Cert. in coll. tchg. Kent State U., 2009. Asst. prof. English Cuyahoga CC, Eastern Campus, Highland Hills, Ohio, 2005—, writing ctr. coord., 2007—. Staff writer SUN Newspapers, Beachwood, Ohio, 2001—02. Author: (book review) The Pedestal Magazine. Recipient Dean's award of Excellence, Eastern Campus, 2007, Disting. Exec. Com. Svc. award, CCC AAUP, 2009, Campus Pres. Citation award, Writing Ctr., 2009.

PEGO, MARGARET M., utilities executive; BA in Bus. Adminstrn., William Paterson Coll., Wayne, NJ; MBA in Mgmt. and Labor Rels., Seton Hall U., South Orange, NJ; grad. Human Resources Exec. Program, U. Mich., Ann Arbor. Cert. sr. human resources profl. Various mgmt. positions in human resources PSEG, 1974; v.p. human resources PSEG Svcs. Corp., sr. v.p. human resources, chief human resources officer, 2006—. Mem. EEI Chief Human Resources Execs. Policy Com., NY/NJ Industry Liaison Group; mem. human resources policy com. Am. Gas Assn.; mem. Coun. Human Resources Execs. Conf. Bd. Adv. Coun. Human Resources Mgmt.; bd. trustees Am. Conf. Diversity, Boys and Girls Club Concert for Kids Com. Mem.: Soc. Human Resources Mgmt. Office: PSEG Svcs Corp PO Box 570 Newark NJ 07101 Office Phone: 973-430-7000.

PEHLKE, ROBERT DONALD, materials and metallurgical engineering educator; b. Ferndale, Mich., Feb. 11, 1933; s. Robert William and Florence Jennie (McLaren) P.; m. Julie Anne Kehoe, June 2, 1956; children: Robert Donald, Elizabeth Anne, David Richard. BS in Engring, U. Mich., 1955; S.M., Mass. Inst. Tech., 1958, Sc.D., 1960; postgrad., Tech. Inst., Aachen, Ger., 1956-57. Registered profl. engr., Mich. Mem. faculty U. Mich., 1960—, prof. materials sci. and engring., 1968—2002, prof. emeritus materials sci. and engring., 2003—, chmn. dept., 1973-84. Cons. to metall. industry; vis. prof. Tohoku U., Sendai, Japan, 1994; Campbell Meml. lectr., 2001. Author: Unit Processes of Extractive Metallurgy, 1973; editor, contbr. more than 300 articles to profl. jours. Mem. Eagle Scout, BSA, 1949; pres. Ann Arbor Amateur Hockey Assn., 1977-79. NSF fellow, 1955-56; Fulbright fellow, 1956-57 Fellow Am. Soc. Metals (tech. divsn. bd. 1982-84, sec. metals acad. com. 1977), Minerals, Metals and Materials Soc. of AIME (Gold Medal award extractive metallurgy divsn. 1976), Alpha Sigma Mu (disting. life, pres. 1977-78); mem. Iron and Steel Soc. of AIST (Disting. life mem., chmn. process tech. divsn. 1976-77, dir. 1976-79, Howe meml. lectr. 1980), Germany, London, Japan Socs. Iron and Steel, Am. Foundry Soc., Am. Soc. Engring. Edn., Sigma Xi, Tau Beta Pi. Office: U Mich Materials Sci & Engring Dow Bldg 2300 Hayward St Rm 2006 Ann Arbor MI 48109-2136 Home: 26991 Wyndhorst Ct Bonita Springs FL 34134 Office Phone: 734-764-7489. Business E-Mail: rdpehlke@umich.edu.

PEI, I.M. (IEOH MING PEI), architect; b. Canton, China, Apr. 26, 1917; arrived in US, 1935, naturalized, 1954; s. Tsu Yee Pei and Lien Kwun Chwong; m. Eileen Loo, June 20, 1942; children: Ting Chung, Chien Chung, Li Chung, Liane. BArch, MIT, Cambridge, 1940; MArch, Harvard U., 1946; DFA (hon.), U. Pa., 1970, Rensselaer Poly. Inst., 1978, Carnegie Mellon U., 1980, U. Mass., 1980, Brown U., 1980, NYU, 1980, Dartmouth Coll., 1991, Northeastern U., Harvard U., U. Rochester; LLD (hon.), Chinese U., Hong Kong, 1970, Pace U.; LHD (hon.), Columbia U., NYC, 1980, U. Colo., 1982, U. Rochester, 1982, U. Hong Kong, 1990, Am. U., Paris, 1990. Arch., NYC, 1939—42; with Nat. Def. Rsch. Com., 1943—45; asst. prof. Harvard Grad. Sch. Design, 1945—48; dir. archtl. divsn. Webb & Knapp, Inc., 1948—55; founding ptnr. Pei Cobb Freed & Ptnrs. (formerly I.M. Pei & Ptnrs., I.M. Pei & Assocs.), NYC, 1955—90; ind. arch. NYC, 1990—. Prin. works include Mile High Ctr., Denver, Nat. Ctr. Atmospheric Rsch., Boulder, Colo., Dallas City Hall, John Fitzgerald Kennedy Libr., Boston, Can. Imperial Bank Commerce Complex, Toronto, Overseas Chinese Banking Corp. Ctr., Singapore, Dreyfus Chemistry Bldg., MIT, East-West Ctr. U. Hawaii, Honolulu, Mellon Art Ctr. and Choate Rosemary Hall Sci. Ctr., Wallingford, Conn., Univ. Plz., NYU, Johnson Mus. Art Cornell U., Ithaca, NY, Washington Sq. East, Phila., Everson Mus. Art, Syracuse, NY, Nat. Gallery Art, East Bldg., Washington, Wilmington Tower, Raffles City, Singapore, West Wing Mus. Fine Arts, Boston, expansion and modernization of Louvre Mus., Paris, Morton H. Meyerson Symphony Ctr., Dallas, MIT Arts and Media Ctr., Jacob K. Javits Conv. Ctr., NYC, Fragrant Hill Hotel, Beijing, Tex. Commerce Tower, Houston, Bank of China, Hong Kong, Creative Artists Agy., Beverly Hills, Calif., Guggenheim Pavilion, Mount Sinai Med. Ctr., NYC, Rock n' Roll Hall of Fame and Mus., Cleve., Mus. Modern Art, Athens, Greece, Miho Mus. of Art, Shiga, Japan, Bilbao Estuary Project, Spain, Four Seasons Hotel, NYC, planning projects include, SW Washington Redevelopment Plan, Govt. Ctr. Redevelopment Plan, Boston, Oklahoma City Downtown Redevelopment Plan, Bedford Stuyvesant Super Block, Bklyn., master plan Columbia U. Mem. Nat. Coun. Humanities, 1966—70, Nat. Coun. on Arts, 1981—84. Recipient Thomas Jefferson Meml. medal for Architecture, 1976, gold medal for architecture, AAAL, 1979, Nat. Arts Club Gold medal of honor, 1981, Mayor's award of Honor for Art and Culture, NYC, 1981, La Grande Medaille D'or L'Académie d'Architecture, 1981, Pritzker Architecture prize, 1983, Medal of Liberty, 1986, Medal of French Legion of Honor, 1988, Nat. Medal of Art, 1988, Praemium Imperiale, Japan Art Assn., 1989, UCLA Gold medal, 1990, Colbert Found. first award for excellence, 1991, Excellence 2000 award, 1991, Freedom medal, 1993, Thomas Jefferson medal for Disting. Achievement in the Arts, Humanities or Social Scis., Am. Philos. Soc., 2001, Legion of Honor, France, 2006, Oreint und Okzident Preis, Erwin Wickert Found., 2006; fellow MIT traveling, 1940, Wheelwright, Harvard U., 1951. Fellow: AIA (Medal of Honor NY chpt. 1963, Gold Medal 1979), ASID (hon.); mem.: NAD, Urban Design Coun., Royal Inst. Brit. Archs., Am. Acad. and Inst. Arts and Letters (chancellor 1978—80), Am. Acad. Arts and Scis., Nat. Inst. Arts and Letters (Arnold Brunner award 1961).

PEI, YI, electronics engineer, researcher; s. Qishui Pei and Yefeng Wu. BS, Peking U., Beijing, 2004; BS in Economics, Peking U., 2004; MSc, PhD, U. Calif., Santa Barbara, 2005. Rsch. asst., dept. electronics Peking U., 2002—04; rsch. asst., Dept. elec. and computer engring. U. Calif., 2004—. Achievements include research in device design and develop high speed AlGan and GaN HEMT. Home: Sueno Rd 6759 A Goleta CA 93117 Office: Univ Calif Santa Barbara UCSB Santa Barbara CA 93106

PEIFFER, JERRI ANN, lab administrator, educator; d. George Howard and Sarah Louise Morgan; m. Randy Micheal Peiffer, June 18, 1983; children: Meaghen Elizibeth, Ethan Taylor, Katherine Laurel. MS, Ga. State U., Atlanta, 1981. Biology tchr. DeKalb County Sch., Decatur, Ga., 1976—83, Pasco County Sch., Dade City, Fla., 1983—84, Gwinnett County Sch., Lawrenceville, Ga., 2002—03; adj. biology instr. Ga. Perimeter Coll., Clarkston, 1990—2007, biology lab supr., instr., 2007—. Leader Girl Scouts America, Grayson, Ga., 2006—07; sunday sch. tchr. Southern Bapt., Snellville, Ga., 1997—2008. Mem.: Ga. Sci. Tchrs. Assn. Office: Ga Perimeter Coll 555 N Indian Creek Dr Clarkston GA 30021 Office Fax: 678-891-3747. Business E-Mail: jerri.peiffer@gpc.edu.

PEIPERL, ADAM, sculptor, photographer; b. Sosnowiec, Poland, June 4, 1935; arrived in US, 1953, naturalized, 1958; s. Jacob and Fanny (Alster) P.; m. Martha Rose Dorf, June 15, 1958; children: Maury, Laurence, Linda. Grad., Cours Complementaire Gen, Paris, 1952; BS in Chemistry, George Washington U., 1957; postgrad., Pa. State U., 1959. Cons. in Russian sci. lit. Libr. Congress, Washington, 1959-61, 66-67; chemist Nat. Bur. Standards, Washington, 1961-63; sci. translator Am. Inst. Physics, NYC, 1973-94, Plenum Pub., 1993-98. One-man shows include Balt. Mus. Art, 1969, Pa. Acad. Fine Arts, 1969, Marlborough Gerson Gallery, NYC, 1969, Smithsonian Mus. History and Tech., 1972, Phila. Art Alliance, 1978; group shows include Washington Gallery Modern Art, 1968, Corcoran Gallery Art, 1968, Kent State U., McKay Art Inst., San Antonio, 1969, NASA Manned Spacecraft, Houston, 1970-71, Nat. Mus. Am. Art, 1972-82, Meml. Art Gallery, U. Rochester, 1978, Art of the Sixties, Fred Jones Jr. Mus. of Art, U. Okla., 2002, Radicals and Conservatives: Abstraction 1945 to the Present, Pa. Acad. Fine Arts, 2004, Refract, Reflect, Project: Light Works from the Collection, Hirshhorn Mus. and Sculpture Garden, 2007; Sixth Fl. Mus., Dealey Plaza, 1960, Film Pres.-elect Kennedy, 2008, represented in permanent collections Kreeger Mus., Pa. Acad. Fine Arts, Mus. Boijmans-Van Beuningen, Fred Jones Jr. Mus. Art, U. Okla., Hirshhorn Mus. and Sculpture Garden; with choreographer Maida Rust Withers on UTAH, Spirit Place Spirit Planet, 1996, multimedia dance theater commd. Lincoln Ctr. Out-of-Doors., Denise Vale collaboration involving projections of sculpture video, U. Okla., 2003, Adam Peiperl papers, 1968-2007, Smithsonian Archives Am. Art, 2008, Guide to Adam Peiperl Collection, 2000-2003, Gelman Libr., George Washington U. Home: 1135 Loxford Ter Silver Spring MD 20901-1130

PEIRCE, BONNIE, librarian; MS Internat. Mgmt., Thunderbird, 1993; MLIS, Simmons Coll., 2003. Former bookstore mgr.; head of children's svcs. Dover Town Libr., Mass. Co-founder & chief tech. officer TheBestKidsBooksite.com; continuing edn. instr. Simmons Grad. Sch. Libr. & Info. Sci., Boston. Co-author (blogs) Library Goddesses. Named one of the Movers & Shakers, Libr. Jour., 2007. Mem.: Mass. Libr. Assn. Office: Dover Town Libr 56 Dedham St PO Box 669 Dover MA 02030 Office Phone: 508-785-8117. Personal E-mail: bonnie@thebestkidsbooksite.com. Business E-Mail: bpeirce@minlib.net.

PEIRCE, DWIGHT A(LEXANDER), JR., music educator; s. Dwight Alexander and Helen Frances (Shockley) Peirce. BMus, Cin. Coll. Conservatory, 1969, MusM, 1972. Asst. prof. Howard Payne U., Brownwood, Tex., 1977—81; lectr. in accompaniment Lamar U., Beaumont, Tex., 1982—. Lectr. in field; pianist Beaumont Symphony Orch., Tex., 1982—90; organist Wesley United Meth. Ch., Beaumont, 1983—, Temple Emanuel, 2001—. Performer: Oh How I Love Dwight Pierce, 1998, 2000, 2007. Rehearsal pianist, organist Beaumont Interfaith Choir, 1988—2003; rehearsal pianist Beaumont Civic Opera, 1984—2000. Recipient Svc. award, Delta Omicron, Lamar U., 1989, Orpheus award, Phi Mu Alpha Sinfonia, Lamar U., 1996, Arts award for outstanding achievement, S.E. Tex. Arts Coun., 1998. Mem.: Tex. Music Educators Assn., Am. Guild Organists (dean Beaumont chpt. 1999—2008). Methodist. Avocations: opera, photography, films, collecting records, reading. Office: Lamar U PO Box 10044 Beaumont TX 77710 Office Phone: 409-880-8076.

PEIRCE, GEORGIA WILSON, public relations executive; b. Newton, Mass., Jan. 6, 1960; d. Norris Ridgeway and Anne (McCusker) P. BA, Duke U., 1982. Intern to Speaker of Ho. of Reps., Washington, 1981; prin. PR etc., Quincy, Mass., 1987-94; dir. media rels. and info. sys. The Mass. Gen. Hosp., Boston, 1994—2004, dir. comm. patient care svcs., 2004—. Cons. Mass. Group Insur. Commn., 1985. Contbr. articles to profl. jours. Cmty. rels. com. Vis. Nurse Assn./Hospice of South Shore; bd. dirs. Ctr. for Nursing Advocacy; com. to elect Mondale-Ferraro, Mass., coord. speakers bur., 1984; charitable trust com. Maj. John F. Regan; com. mem. City of Quincy Recycling Com.; del. Mass. Dem. Conv., 1982, 83; v.p. South Shore Ad Club, 1990-91, mem.-at-large, 1991-92; active Nat. Patient Safety Leadership Adv. Bd., 2005-07. Recipient 9th Wave awards 1989, 1st pl. in Pub. Rels. award, 1989, Merit award, 1992, Bell Ringer award, News Release Regional, 2000, Cirsis Mgmt. and Print Feature, 2001, Bell Ringer award for graphic identity, 2007, Bell Ringer award for ann. report, 2007, Svc. Publicity and Print Feature award, 2006, Golden Lamp award Ctr. for Nursing, 2005, Nat. Patient Safety Leadership fellow, 2005—, Media award Am. Acad. Nursing, 2006, Non-profit Pub. Rels. award, 2006; Bell Ringer award Ann. Report, 2008, 09, Aster award 2009. Mem. NAFE, Patient Safety Leadership, Small Bus. Assn. New Eng., Women's Golf Assn. Mass., Publicity Club New Eng. (v.p. media rels. 1989, Merit Bell Ringer award 2000, 01), Rotary Internat., Eastward Ho! Country Club Chatham (club champion 1977-81, 83, 91, 93, bd. gov. 2003-). Democrat. Roman Catholic. Avocation: golf (many awards including state titles). Office: Mass Gen Hosp Patient Care Svcs Fruit St Bulfinch STET Boston MA 02114 Home Phone: 617-388-9867; Office Phone: 617-724-9865. Business E-Mail: gwpeirce@partners.org.

PEIRCE, KAREN PATRICIA, education educator; b. Providence, July 12, 1971; d. Raymond Fales and Patricia Kay Peirce. ABH, Rollins Coll., Winter Park, Fla., 1993; MA, Carnegie Mellon U., Pitts., 1997; PhD, U. Ariz., Tucson, 2006. Peer writing cons. Rollins Coll. Writing Ctr., Winter Park, Fla., 1990—93; Fulbright English tchg. asst. Korean Am. Edn. Commn., Ulsan, 1993—94; pub. rels. asst. Embassy of the Republic of Korea, Washington, 1995—96; rsch. asst. Carnegie Mellon U., Pitts., 1996—97; English instr. The Sawyer Sch., Warwick, RI, 1997—98; upper divsn. English tchr. Berkeley Prep. Sch., Tampa, Fla., 1998—2001; grad. assoc. tchg. U. Ariz., Tucson, 2001—06; asst. prof. English U.S. Mil. Acad., West Point, NY, 2006—. Mem.: MLA, Coun. Writing Program Adminstrs., Coll. English Assn., Rhetoric Soc. Am., Internat. Writing Ctr. Assn., Conf. on Coll. Composition and Comm., Nat. Coun. Tchrs. English. Home: 281 Hudson St Ste 2 Cornwall On Hudson NY 12520-1039

PEIRCE, NEAL R., journalist; b. Phila., Jan. 5, 1932; s. J. Trevor and Miriam deS. (Litchfield) P.; m. Barbara von dem Bach-Zelewski, Apr. 18, 1959; children: Celia, Andrea, Trevor. BA, Princeton U., 1954; postgrad., Harvard U., 1957-58. Polit. editor Congl. Quar., 1960-69; co-founder, contbg. editor Nat. Jour., Washington, 1969-97. Cons. and commentator elections CBS News, 1962, 67-76, NBC News, 1964-66; lectr. in field; syndicated newspaper columnist Washington Post Writers Group; chmn. The Citistates Group; mem. faculty Salzburg (Austria) Seminar, 1980, 84, 97; 1st Weinberg prof. Princeton U.'s Woodrow Wilson Sch. Pub. and Internat. Affairs, 1992. Author: The People's President, 1968, 2d edit., 1981, The Megastates of America, 1972, The Pacific States of America, 1972, The Mountain States of America, 1972, The Great Plains States America, 1973, The Deep South States of America, 1974, The Border South States, 1975, The New England States, 1976, The Mid-Atlantic States of America, 1977, The Great Lakes States of America, 1980, The Book of America: Inside Fifty States Today, 1983, Citistates: How Urban America Can Prosper in A Competitive World, 1993, Breakthroughs: Recreating The American City, 1993; Corrective Capitalism, 1987, Century of the City: No Time to Lose, Rookefeller Found, 2008; editor Peirce Report series on 26 regions' Citistate futures starting with Phoenix Republic and Gazette, 1987; including New England Futures Project, 2005-06. Founder, chmn. S.W. Neighborhood Assembly, Washington, 1963-65; mem. exec. com. Nat. Civic League, 1990-95; trustee German Marshall Fund U.S., 1987-97. With CIC, U.S. Army, 1954-57. Fellow Woodrow Wilson Internat. Center Scholars, 1971-74 Fellow Nat. Acad. Pub. Adminstrn.; mem. Newfound Lake Region Assn. (v.p. 1989-92), Phi Beta Kappa. Episcopalian. Home and Office: 610 G St SW Washington DC 20024-2440 Home Phone: 202-554-8191. Business E-Mail: npeirce@citistates.com.

PEIRSOL, AARON, Olympic swimmer; b. Irvine, Calif., July 23, 1983; s. Tim Hartig and Wela Peirsol. Grad. in govt., U. Tex., 2006. Club swimmer Longhorn Aquatics, Tex.; mem. US Olympic Swim Team Olympic Games, Sydney, 2000, Athens, Greece, 2004, Beijing, 2008. Recipient Silver medal, 200m backstroke, Sydney Olympic Games, 2000, Gold medal, 100m, 200m backstroke, 400m medley relay, Athens Olympic Games, 2004, Gold medal, 100m backstroke, 400m medley relay; Silver medal, 200m backstroke, Beijing Olympic Games, 2008, Gold medal, 100m, 200m backstroke, 400m medley relay; Silver medal 800m medley relay, World Championships, 2003, Gold medal, 100m, 200m backstroke, 400m medley relay, 2005, Gold medal, 100m backstroke; Silver medal, 200m backstroke, 2007, Gold medal, 100m, 200m backstroke, 400m medley relay, Pan Pacific Championships, 2006; named Swimmer of Yr., NCAA, 2003, Male Athlete of Yr., USA Swimming, 2005. Achievements include becoming the youngest American (age 15) to break two minutes in 200m backstroke, 1998; winning National Titles in: 100m backstroke (5), 200m backstroke (6), 2000-06; setting the world record in the 100m backstroke, 2008; being a member of the world record breaking 4x100m medley relay team, 2008. Office: c/o USA Swimming One Olympic Plz Colorado Springs CO 80909

PEISER, ROBERT ALAN, turnaround executive; b. NYC, Apr. 17, 1948; s. Donald Edward and Natalie (Phillips) Peiser; m. Nancy McCormick; children: Karyn, Brian, Craig, Scott. BA, U. Pa., 1969; MBA, Harvard U., 1972. Dir. corp. fin. TWA, NYC, 1972-77, sr. v.p. fin., CFO, 1983-86, exec. v.p. fin., CFO, 1994-96; treas. Hertz Corp., NYC, 1977-80; staff v.p., treas. ops. RCA Corp., NYC, 1980-81; v.p., treas. Trans World Corp., NYC, 1981-83; sr. v.p., CFO ALC Comm. Corp., Birmingham, Mich., 1986-88; sr. v.p. fin., CFO Borman's Inc., Detroit, 1988-89; pres., CEO Orange-Co. Ic., Bartow, Fla., 1989-92; with BBK, Ltd., Southfield, Mich., 1992-94; vice chmn., CEO FoxMeyer Drug Co., Carrollton, Tex., 1996; pres., CEO Western Pacific Airlines, Colorado Springs, Colo., 1996-98; chmn. CVSI, Inc., Bedford, Mass., 1998-99; chmn., CEO Vitality Beverages, Tampa, Fla., 1999—2002; pres., CEO Imperial Sugar Co., Sugar Land, Tex., 2002—08; CEO Omniflight Helicopters, Inc., Addison, Tex., 2008—. Bd. dirs. Solutia, Inc., Omniflight Helicopters, Inc., America's Power Sports Precision Ptnrs., Team, Inc., 2006—. Bd. dirs. Houston Symphony. Mem.: Nat. Assn. Corp. Dirs. (chmn. Tex. Tricities chpt.), Jerehy Country Club (Park City, Utah), Lakeside Country Club (Houston). Office: Omniflight Helicopters Inc 16415 Addison Rd Addison TX 75001*

PEITHMAN, ROSCOE EDWARD, physicist, educator; b. Hoyleton, Ill., Feb. 26, 1913; s. Edward Henry Peithman and Sarah Jane Smith; m. Laura Jane Davenport, Apr. 3, 1936 (dec. Oct. 13, 1987); children: Ann Davenport, Stephen Edward. BS, So. Ill. U., 1935; MS, U. of Ill., 1939; EdD, Oreg. State U., 1955. Tchr. various HS, Ill., 1935—42; prof. of physics Humboldt State U., Arcata, Calif., 1946—77, chmn. divsn. of phys. scis., 1960—69, dean Sch. Scis., 1969—70, emeritus prof. of physics, 1977—. Academic senator Calif. State U. Sys., Calif., 1963—66. Lt. comdr. USNR, 1942—73. Fellow: Am. Men and Women of Sci. (life); mem.: Am. Assn. of Physics Tchrs. Avocation: amateur radio. Home: 2704 Sunny Grove Ave Mckinleyville CA 95519-7912 Personal E-mail: w6bme@suddenlink.net.

PEITSCHER, JUDITH, elementary school educator; d. Charles Ellsworth and Dorothy Mae Peitscher; children: Peter Lane Morrison, Jacqueline Anna Haddad, Jennifer Everett Gervasi, Justine VanZandt Morrison. BS in Secondary Edn., U. Vt., Burlington, 1967, MA in History, 1975. Cert. secondary English and social studies level II Vt. Mid. sch. tchr. Hinesburg Cmty. Sch., Vt., 1980—2002; mus. educator Shelburne Mus., Vt., 2004—; adj. instr. Champlain Coll., Burlington, Vt., 2005—. Recipient 1st Richard Whittemore History prize, Ethan Allen Homestead, 1999; grantee Model Integrated Arts Unit, Gold Fever, Flynn Theatre, 1999; Bread Loaf Sch. fellowship, DeWitt Wallace-Reader's Digest, 1994, Writing fellowship, Nat. Writing Project, Vt., 1996.

PEIXOTO NETO, JOSE ULYSSES, internist, researcher; b. Crato, Ceará, Brazil, Aug. 29, 1930; s. Adérito de Aquino Silva and Adelite Alencar Peixoto; m. Maria Isolda Teles Cartaxo, May 23, 1958; children: Jose Ulysses Peixoto Filho, Eunice Ulysséia Peixoto Maia, Jorge André Cartaxo Peixoto. 1st degree, State Coll. Goias, Brazil, 1942, postgrad., 1942-49; 2d degree, St. John Coll., Fortaleza, Brazil, 1949; postgrad., Fed. U., Recife, Brazil, 1955; Laurel, Cearense Med. Ctr., 1994. Med. resident St. Michael Hosp., Rio de Janeiro, 1956; intern St. Anthony Hosp., Iguatú, Ceará, 1957; founder Social Providence, Crato, Ceará, 1958-64; attendent St. Frances Hosp., Crato, 1958-69; founder St. Michael Hosp., Crato, 1967-93, pres., dir., 1983-93, internist, researcher, 1993—; founder Faculty of Law, Crato, 1977-78. Lectr. faculty of medicine The Fed. U. of Ceará, 1976—. Recipient Good Svc. award Lyons Club, 1992, Laurel Cearense Med. Ctr., 1994, Cert. Merit Health Care Profls. Juazeiro North Profl. Health Assn., 1998, Gold Medal of Profl. Merit, Ceara Estate Regional Coun. Medicine, 1999, Plaque of profl. merit Cariri sect. Coun. of Ceara, 2002, Diploma of Ethical Profl. Merit Fed. Medicine Coun., 2006, Jubilee of Gold, Diploma of Fifty Yrs. as Med. Doctor, Medice Meml. Pernam Buco, 2006. Fellow Brazilian Med. Assn. (specialist); mem. AAAS, ACP, Brazilian Soc. Clin. Medicine (specialist), NY Acad. Sci. Roman Catholic. Avocations: reading, walking, movies, farming.

PEKAR, STEPHEN F., geologist, paleontologist, oceanographer; b. NYC, Jan. 28, 1959; s. Martin and Joanne E. (Lewis) Pekar; m. Anahi Viladrich, May 26, 1964. BA, Queens Coll., 1986; MS in Geology, Rutgers U., 1995, PhD, 1999. Cert. NY, 1986. Petroleum cons. Chevron Overseas Petroleum Inc., San Ramon, Calif., 1996—97, 1998, 1999; rsch. asst. Rutgers U., New Brunswick, NJ, 1997, postdoctoral rsch. scientist, 1999-2000; staff scientist Ocean View Borehole, NJ, 1999; sedimentologist, onsite scientist Bethany Beach Borehole, Del., 2000; rsch. scientist Lamont-Doherty Earth Obs., Columbia U., Palisades, NY, 2000—03, adj. asst. rsch. scientist, 2003—; asst. prof. Sch. Earth and Environ. Scis., Queens Coll., Flushing, NY, 2003—. Contbr. articles to profl. jours. Mem.: AAAS, Soc. Sedimentary Geology, Cushman Found. Foraminiferal Rsch., Am. Geophys. Union, Am. Assn. Petroleum Geologists, Geol. Soc. Am. Office: Queens Coll Sch Earth and Environ Scis 65-30 Kissena Blvd Flushing NY 11367 also: Lamont-Doherty Earth Obs Columbia U Palisades NY 10964 Office Phone: 845-365-8362, 718-997-3305. E-mail: pekar@ldeo.columbia.edu, spekar@qcl.qc.edu.

PEKAREK, THOMAS, substitute teacher; b. Cleve., Nov. 2, 1948; Degree in philosophy, Borromeo Coll., Ohio. Operator Internet devel. services bus.; substitute tchr. Candidate Ohio 19th Congl. Dist., 1982, Ohio House of Reps., 1996, Ohio State Senate, 1998, Cuyahoga County Commr. Served with USN, 1967—71, reservist USNR, 1987—89. Republican. Mailing: 123 E 156th St #1006 Cleveland OH 44110 Office Phone: 216-812-0489.

PEKARSKY, MELVIN HIRSCH, artist; b. Chgo., Sept. 18, 1934; s. Abe and Inda (Levin) P. Student, Sch. of Art Inst., Chgo., 1951-52; BA, Northwestern U., 1955, MA, 1956. Faculty Northwestern U., 1955-56; faculty Kendall Coll., 1960-67, chmn. art dept., 1965-67; asst. dean Sch. Visual Arts, NYC, 1967-68, assoc. dean, 1968-69; grad. faculty NYU, 1970-71; assoc. prof. art SUNY, Stony Brook, 1975-84, prof. art, 1984—, chmn. dept., 1977-78, 84-89, dir. MFA and studio programs, 1990—2003. Chmn. SUNY, 2005—07, prof. emeritus, vis. prof., 2009—. One-man shows include Gimpel and Weitzenhoffer, N.Y.C., 1974, Lehigh U., 1975, Ball State U. Gallery, Muncie, Ind., 1975, G.W. Einstein Co., Inc., N.Y.C., 1975, 77, 78, 80, 81, 82, 84, 86, 88, 91, 95, 97, Hull Gallery, Washington, 1978, Centro Colombo-Americano, Bogotá, Colombia, 1980, 112 Greene St. Gallery, N.Y.C., 1980, 82, Marianne Deson Gallery, Chgo., 1987, Butler Inst. Am. Art, Youngstown, Ohio, 1990, The Mus. at Stony Brook, 1993, Nev. Mus. Art, Reno, 2001, Nielsen Gallery, Boston, 2002-03, Van Deb Editions, 2007, Gallery North Setauket NY, 2009, Dowling Coll., Anthony Giordano Gallery, Oakdale, NY, 2009, Staller Ctr. Arts, Stony Brook U., 2009; group shows include Chgo. Art Inst., 1966, Whitney Mus., N.Y.C., 1971, Bklyn. Mus., 1974, Cleve. Mus., 1978, Cooper-Hewitt Mus., 1971, Mus. Modern Art Corp., Lending and Adv. Svc. Exhbns., Kuznetsky-Most Galleries, Moscow, 1989, NAD, N.Y.C., 1990, Fogg Mus. Art/Harvard U., 2000, 06, Am. Acad. Arts and Letters, N.Y.C., 2001, Nielsen Gallery, Boston, 2001, 02, 03, 04, 05, 07, NAD, 2008, public murals commns., Houston and Crosby Sts., N.Y.C., 1972, Lafayette and Bleecker Sts., N.Y.C., 1969, Nat. Acad. Design, NYC, 2008; represented in permanent collections, Cleve. Mus., Fogg Mus. Art, Harvard U., Indpls. Mus., Nev. Museum of Art, Roswell Mus. Art, N.Mex., Westinghouse Corp., Corcoran Gallery Art, Yale U., Notre Dame U., AT&T, Chase Manhattan Bank, Fidelity Corp., Zimmerli Mus., Rutgers Univ., other pub. and corp. collections, also pvt. collections Founding mem., v.p., bd. dirs. City Walls, 1969-77. Served with Combat Engrs. AUS, 1957-59. Recipient grants in public art through City Walls Kaplan Fund, 1969, City Walls Bernhard Found., 1971, City Walls N.Y. State Council on Arts, 1970, City Walls Nat. Endowment for the Arts, 1971 Mem. Coll. Art Assn., Pub. Art Fund. Home: PO Box 1575 Stony Brook NY 11790-0875 Office: SUNY Art Dept Stony Brook NY 11794-5400 Office Phone: 631-689-9586. Personal E-mail: pekarsky@aol.com. Business E-Mail: mpekarsky@ms.cc.sunysb.edu.

PEKOSKE, DAVID PETER, career military officer; b. 1955; BS in Ocean Engring., US Coast Guard Acad.; MPA, Columbia U., 1989; MBA, MIT, 1997. Commissioned USCG, 1977, advanced through grades to vice admiral, 2008, comdr. Coast Guard Group/Marine Safety Office, Long Island Sound New Haven, 1999—2001, exec. asst. to comdt. Washington, 2001—04, comdr. First Coast Guard Dist./Marine Defense Command One Boston, 2004—06, asst. comdt. for ops. Washington, 2006—08, comdr. Pacific Area, comdr. Defense Force West Alameda, Calif., 2008—09, vice comdt., 2009—. Bd. trustees US Coast Guard Acad., 2006—08. Decorated Coast Guard Disting. Svc. Medal, Legion Merit, Meritorious Svc. Medal, Coast Guard Commendation Medal, Coast Guard Achievement Medal, Commandant's Letter of Commendation. Office: US Coast Guard Headquarters US Dept Homeland Security 2100 2d St SW Washington DC 20593 Office Phone: 510-437-3522. Office Fax: 510-437-3774.*

PELANDA, RAYMOND VICTOR, college administrator; b. Alliance, Ohio, Feb. 25, 1928; s. Gaetano Mario and Adele (Perotti) P.; m. Katherine Rose, Apr. 25, 1953; children— Raymond Paul, Kevin Lee, Melanie Anne, Kenneth Blaine. B.S.Ed., Kent State U., 1952; M.B.A., 1962. High sch. tchr., Canton, Ohio, 1952-66; asst. dir. Trumbull campus Kent State U., Ohio, 1966-69, coordinator retail ops. regional campuses, 1969-70, coordinator bus. affairs regional campuses, 1970-75, bus. mgr. regional campuses, 1974-79; bus. and fin. officer, treas. Northeastern Ohio Univs. Coll. Medicine, Roostown, 1979—85, ret., 1985; asst. prof. acctg. Kent State U., 1967-79; discussion leader Inst. Civic Edn., Akron U., 1980-82. Mem. bd. edn. Cath. Diocese of Youngstown, Ohio, 1975-81, pres., 1979-81; mem. Ohio Bishops Adv. Com., 1981—. Served with USN, 1946-48. Mem. Phi Delta Kappa, Phi Beta Phi, Theta Chi; fellow Paul Harris. Republican. Lodges: Rotary (treas. 1980-82) (Ravenna, Ohio, Canton, Ohio, Rotary, 1985-); Elks. Avocations: outdoor sports; golf; swimming; jogging. Home: 915 24th St NE Canton OH 44714-1905

PELANDER, JOHN, state supreme court justice; BA cum laude, Wittenberg U., Springfield, Ohio, 1973; JD with high distinction, U. Ariz., Tucson, 1976; LLM in Jud. Process, U. Va., 1998. Cert.: (specialist in personal injury and wrongful death). Laws clk. to Honorable Richard H. Chambers US Ct. Appeals (9th cir.), 1976—77; shareholder Slutes, Sakrison, Grant & Pelander, PC, 1977—95; judge Ariz. Ct. Appeals (divsn. 2), Tucson, 1995—2009; justice Ariz. State Supreme Ct., Phoenix, 2009—. Faculty mem. Ariz. Coll. Trial Lawyers; mem. Ariz. Commn. Jud. Performance Rev., past chmn. jud. ethics. adv. commn. Exec. editor: Ariz. Law Rev. Mem.: Am. Bd. Trial Advocates (assoc.), Order of Coif. Office: Ariz Supreme Ct 1501 W Washington Phoenix AZ 85001-3231*

PELAVIN, SOL HERBERT, research company executive; b. Detroit, Dec. 16, 1941; s. Norman J. and Alice A. Pelavin; m. Diane Christine Blakemore, Aug. 14, 1966; 2 children. BA in Math., U. Chgo., 1965, MAT in Math., 1969; MS in Stats., Stanford U., 1974, PhD candidate in mathematical models of edn. research, 1975. Tchr. pub. schs., 1965-70. teaching rsch. asst. Stanford (Calif.) U., 1972-74; cons. Rand Corp., Santa Monica, Calif., 1975; policy analyst SRI Internat., Menlo Park, Calif., 1975-78; exec. officer NTS Research Corp., Durham, N.C., 1978-82; pres. Pelavin Assocs., Inc., Washington, 1982-94; exec. v.p., COO Am. Inst. Rsch., 1994-2001, pres., CEO, 2001-; dir. Data Analysis and Tech. Support Ctr., Washington, 1989-93, Policy Analysis Support Ctr., Washington, 1993—; expert witness to U.S. Congress, 1977, 79, Cabinet briefing, 1983; cons. Frank, Bernstein, Conway and Goldman, Balt., 1980-81; dir. Ednl. Analysis Ctr., Washington, 1982-85. Author: (with P. Barker) A Study of the Generalizability of the Results of Standardized Achievement Tests, 1976, (with J.L. David) Research on the Effectiveness of Compensatory Education Programs: A Reanalysis of Data, 1977, (with others) Federal Expenditures for the Education of Children and Youth With Special Needs, 1981, (with D.C. Pelavin) An Evaluation of the Fund for the Improvement of Postsecondary Education, 1981, 83, (with others) Evaluation of the Commodity Supplemental Food Program, 1982, An Evaluation of the Bilingual Education Evaluation, Dissemination and Assessment Centers, 1984, A Study of a Year-Round School Program, 1978, Teacher Preparation: A Review of State Certification Requirements, 1984, Analysis of the National Availability of Mathematics and Science Teachers, 1983, Minority Participation in Higher Education, 1988, Changing the Odds, 1990, others; contbr. articles to profl. jours. NSF fellow U. Chgo., 1968-69; Cuneo fellow Stanford U., 1973. Mem. Am. Ednl. Research Assn., Am. Psychol. Assn. Democrat. Jewish. Office: American Inst Rsch 1000 Thomas Jefferson Washington DC 20007-3500 Home Phone: 301-299-6681; Office Phone: 202-403-5000. Business E-Mail: spelavin@air.org.

PELHAM, JUDITH, health system administrator; b. Bristol, Conn., July 23, 1945; d. Marvin Curtis and Muriel (Chodos) Pelham; m. Jon N. Coffee, Dec. 30, 1992; children: Rachel Welch, Molly, Edward. BA, Smith Coll., 1967; MPA, Harvard U., 1975. Various govt. postions, 1968-72; prin. analyst Urban Systems, Cambridge, Mass., 1972-73; dir. devel. & planning Roxbury Dental & Med. Group, Boston, 1975-76; asst. to dir. for gen. medicine and ambulatory care Peter B. Brigham Hosp., Boston, 1976-77, asst. dir. ambulatory care, 1977-79; asst. v.p. Brigham & Women's Hosp., Boston, 1980-81; dir. planning and mktg. Seton Med. Ctr., Austin, Tex., 1980-82, pres., 1982-92, CEO, 1987-92; pres., CEO Daughters of Charity Health Svcs., Austin, 1987-92, Mercy Health Svcs., Farmington Hills, Mich., 1993—2000, Trinity Health (merger of Mercy Health Svcs. and Holy Cross Health Sys.), Novi, Mich., 2000—04, pres. emeritus, 2005—. Bd. dirs. Amgen, 1995—, Cath. CEO Healthcare Connection, 1998—2004, Eclipsys Corp., 2009—; cons. Robert W. Johnson Found., 1979—80; mem. mgmt. bd. Inst. for Diversity in Health Mgmt., 1994—97; chair Coalition for Non-Profit Healthcare, 1997—2000, exec. com., 1997—2002; mem. Healthcare Rsch. and Devel. Inst., 1998—2005, bd., 2003—05; mem. adv. com. RAND Health Compare Strategic Policy, 2005—; mem. strategic adv. bd. Shattuck Hammond, 2005—; mem. strategic adv. com. for comprehensive assessment of reform efforts RAND Corp., 2006—. Contbr. articles to profl. jours. Trustee A. Shivers Radiation Therapy Ctr., Austin, 1982—92, Marywood Maternity and Adoption Agy., 1982—86; bd. dirs. Quality of Life Found., Austin, 1985, Austin Rape Crisis Ctr., adv. bd. mem., 1986—88; bd. dirs., trustee League House, 1992—93, Seton Fund, 1982—93, Greater Detroit Area Health Coun.; mem. Gov.'s Job Tng. Coordinating Coun., 1983—85; mem. adv. coun. U. Tex. Social Work Found., 1983—85; charter mem. Leadership Tex., Austin, 1983—93; trustee Smith Coll. Recipient Leadership award, YWCA Austin, 1986, CEO IT Achievement award, Modern Healthcare, Healthcare Info. Mgmt. Sys. Soc., 2004; named one of Detroit's 100 Most Influential Women, Crain's Detroit Bus., 1997, 2002. Fellow: Am. Hosp. Assn., Am. Coll. Healthcare Execs. (bd. dirs. 1987—95); mem.: Cath. Health Assn. (sec., treas. 1982—95, com. on govt. rels. 1984—91, chair fin. com. 1992—95, bd. dirs. 1987—95), Tex. Conf. Health Facilities (bd. dirs. 1985—89, pres. 1988), Austin Area Rsch. Orgn., Tex. Hosp. Assn. (various couns. 1982—87).*

PELINI, BO, college football coach; b. Youngstown, Ohio, Dec. 13, 1967; m. Mary Pat Pelini; children: Patrick, Kate, Caralyn. B Bus. Mktg., Ohio State U., 1990. Grad. asst. Iowa U., 1991; quarterbacks coach Cardinal Mooney HS, 1993; defensive backs coach San Francisco 49ers, 1994—96; linebackers coach New England Patriots, 1997—99, Green Bay Packers, 2000—02; defensive coord., interim coach U. Nebr., 2003, head coach, 2008—; co-defensive coord., def. backs coach Okla. U., 2004; defensive coord. La. State U., 2005—07. Mailing: U Nebr Nebr Football Office One Meml Stadium PO Box 880125 Lincoln NE 68588

PELL, ANTHONY DOUGLAS, financial management company executive; b. Washington, July 2, 1938; s. Robert Thompson and Thecla Caroline (Barker) P.; m. Katharine Murphey, Sept. 27, 1962; children— Theodore, Katharine. AB, Princeton U., 1960; JD with honors, George Washington U., 1976. Bar: NY 1966, Washington 1966. Atty. firm Coudert Bros., NYC, 1966-68, firm Cadwalader, Wickersham & Taft, NYC, 1968-72; v.p. The Boston Co., 1972-75, sr. v.p. fin. strategies, 1975-80; pres., dir. Pell, Rudman & Co., Inc., pres., dir. Union Wharf Securities, 1980—; gen. ptnr. Opportunity Fund; dir. Power Secure, Inc., The Computer Mus., Rochdale Investment Mgmt.; pres., dir. Pelican Investment Mgmt.; dir., treas. Ft. Ticonderoga, NY; dir. Strawberry Bank Mus.; trustee, treas. Hist. New Eng. Mem. Weston Planning Bd., Mass. 1976-83, chmn., 1980-81. Served to lt. USN, 1960-64. Unitarian. Mem: Brookline Country Club Mass., Ausable Club NY. Home: 2 Willow Rd Weston MA 02493-2413 Office: One Liberty Sq Ste 1200 Boston MA 02110-3407 Office Phone: 617-757-8700. Business E-Mail: adp@pelicanim.com.

PELL, ARTHUR ROBERT, human resources specialist, consultant, writer; b. NYC, Jan. 22, 1920; s. Harry and Rae (Meyers) P.; m. Erica Frost, May 19, 1946; children— Douglas, Hilary. AB, NYU, 1939, MA, 1944; PhD, Calif. Coast U., 1977; diploma, Cornell U., 1943. Personnel dir. Eagle-Electric Mfg. Co., Long Island City, NY, 1946-50, North Atlantic Constructors, NYC, 1950-53; v.p. Harper Assos., Inc., NYC, 1953-75; cons. Human Resources Mgmt., Hempstead, NY, 1975—2004; writer, editor Hartsdale, NY, 2004—. Adj. assoc. prof. mgmt. NYU Sch. Continuing Edn., 1962-84, St. John's U. Coll. Bus. Adminstrn., 1971-76; lectr. Baruch Sch. Bus. and Pub. Adminstrn. Coll. City N.Y., 1948-67. Author: (with W.B. Patterson) Fire Officer's Guide to Leadership, rev. edit., 1963, Placing Salesmen, 1963, Placing Executives, 1964, Police Leadership, 1967, How to Get the Job You Want After 40, 1967, Recruiting and Selecting Personnel, 1969, (with M. Harper) Starting and Managing an Employment Agency, 1970, Recruiting, Training and Motivating Volunteer Workers, 1972, Be a Better Employment Interviewer, 1972, rev. edits., 1978, 86, 94, The College Graduate Guide to Job Finding, 1973; (with Wilma Rogalin) Women's Guide to Executive Positions, 1975; (with Albert Furbay) College Student's Guide to Career Planning, 1975; (with Dale Carnegie Assocs.) Managing Through People, 1975, rev. edits., 1978, 1987, Choosing a College Major: Business, 1978, Enrich Your Life: The Dale Carnegie Way, 1979, The Part Time Job Book, 1984, Making the Most of Medicare, 1987, rev. edit., 1990; (with George Sadek) Resumes for Engineers, 1982, Resumes for Computer Professionals, 1984, How to Sell Yourself on an Interview, 1982, The Job Finder's Kit, 1989, Getting the Most from Your People, 1990, Diagnosing Your Doctor, 1991, The Supervisor's Infobank, 1994, The Complete Idiot's Guide to Managing People, 1995, 3d edit., 2003, The Pocket Idiot's Guide to One Minute Management, 1999, The Complete Idiot's Guide to Team Building, 1999, The Complete Idiot's Guide to Recruiting The Right Stuff, 2000, The Complete's Idiot Guide to Human Resources Management, 2001, (with Franklin C. Ashby) Embracing Excellence, 2001; editl. cons. for revision Dale Carnegie's How to Win Friends and Influence People, 1981; author syndicated feature The Human Side; editor: Dale Carnegie's: Public Speaking for Success, 2004, Napoleon Hill's: Think and Grow Rich, 2005; contbr. articles to profl. jours. With AUS, 1942-46. Home and Office: 400 High Point Dr Apt 101 Hartsdale NY 10530-1125 Office Phone: 914-949-1382. Personal E-mail: arpell22@optonline.net.

PELL, ELLIOTT LOUIS, lawyer; b. Bklyn., Aug. 19, 1950; s. Walter and Shirley Ruth Pell; m. Vera Meredith Outland, May 28, 1995; children: Adam David, Kathryn Rachel. BS, Syracuse U., NY, 1972; JD, Bklyn. Law Sch., 1975; LLM, NYC, NYC, 1977. Bar: NJ 1976, NY 1980. Law clk. to Hon. Alan Handler NJ Supreme Ct., Flemington, 1976—77; law clk. to Hon. Joseph Halpern NJ. Appellate Divsn., Somerville; prin. Elliott Louis Pell, PA, Bridgewater, NJ; of counsel Price, Meese, Shulman & D'Arminio, Woodcliff Lake, NJ. Adj. prof. law Bklyn Law Sch., 1981—90. Author: Criminal Defense Techniques-Insanity Defense; Search and Seizure. Home: 378 Valley Rd Watchung NJ 07069 Office: Price Meese Shulman & D'Arminio 50 Tice Blvd Woodcliff Lake NJ 07069

PELL, JONATHAN LAURENCE, performing company executive; b. Memphis, Oct. 20, 1949; s. Burton Marshall and Eleanor (Leopold) P. BA, U. So. Calif., 1971. Interior designer Gene Morse Assocs., Wichita, Kans., 1971-77; mgr. Internat. Artists Mgmt., NYC, 1977-79, Robert Lombardo Assocs., NYC, 1979-80; TV producer Sta. WNET, NYC, 1980-83; dir. publicity John Curry Skating Co., NYC, 1983; prodr. Jerome Kern Centennary Gala Town Hall, NYC, 1984; dir. artistic adminstrn. Dallas Opera, 1984—2009, dir. artistic, 2009—. Vocal competition judge Met. Opera Nat. Coun. Auditions, Pavarotti Competition, Bidu Sayao Internat. Competition, Brazil, Ottavio Ziino Internat. Competition, Rome, Patronesses of the Opera Competition, Miami, Fla.,

George London Awards, Ctr. for Contemporary Opera, Jensen Found. Competition, Dallas Opera Guild, Denver Lyric Opera Guild, Ft. Worth Opera, Marguerite McCammon Competition, San Antonio Opera Guild, Shreveport Opera, Richard Tucker Award, others; tchr. master classes for young singers Opera Am., Nat. Opera Assn., Can. Opera Co., S.W. Chpt. NATS, Performing Arts Assistance Corp., U. North Tex., Internat. Sch. Performing Arts, Amarillo Opera, So. Meth. U.; host Dallas Opera Radio Hour, WRR, 1994—97; guest Inside the Dallas Opera, WRR, 2004—; lectr. on opera Crystal Cruises. Bd. dirs., chmn. nat. auditions com., mem. award selection com. Richard Tucker Music Found., 1996-2009; former mem. adv. bd. Awards Recognizing Individual Artistry; former advisor to singer svcs. com. Opera Am. Named Singer of Yr. Office: Dallas Opera Campbell Ctr I LBI-11 8350 N Central Expy Ste 210 Dallas TX 75206-1601 Office Phone: 214-443-1086. Business E-Mail: jonathan@dallasopera.org.

PELL, SIDNEY, epidemiologist; b. NYC, Dec. 13, 1922; m. Lola May, July 2, 1950. MBA, CCNY, 1952; PhD, U. Pitts., 1956. Biostatistician E.I. Du Pont de Nemours and Co., Wilmington, Del., 1955-76, mgr. epidemiology sect., 1976-82, sr. cons., 1982-85; epidemiology cons. Wilmington, 1985—. Epidemiology cons. Del. Divsn. Pub. Health, Dover, 1986-95. Contbr. articles to New Eng. Jour. Medicine, Jour. Occupational Medicine, Jour. AMA. With U.S. Army, 1943-45, ETO. Recipient Merit in Authorship Hon. Mention, Inds. Med. Assn., 1959. Fellow Am. Coll. Epidemiology, Am. Heart Assn., Am. Pub. Health Assn., Delta Omega. Home: 1416 Emory Rd Wilmington DE 19803-5120 E-mail: pell104@aol.com.

PELLA, MILTON ORVILLE, science educator; b. Wilmot, Wis., Feb. 13, 1914; s. Charles August and Ida Marie (Pagel) P.; m. Germaine Marie Reich, Dec. 9, 1944. B.E., Milw. State Tchrs. Coll., 1936; MS, U. Wis., 1940, PhD, 1948. Tchr. sci. and math. Wyler Mil. Acad., 1937-38; tchr. elementary sch. Delavan Pub. Schs., 1938-39; tchr. sci. U. Wis. High Sch., 1939-42; prof. sci. edn. U. Wis., Madison, 1946-80, prof. emeritus, 1980—; With Fgn. Ednl. Service, 1959—81. Author: Physical Science for Progress, 3d edit, 1970, Science Horizons— The Biological World, (with Branley and Urban), 1965-70. Served with AUS, 1942-46. Fellow AAAS; mem. Ctrl. Assn. Sci. and Math. (pres. 1955), Nat. Assn. for Rsch. in Sci. Tchg. (pres. 1966), Nat. Sci. Tchrs. Assn. (dir. 1950, 60), Masons. Home: 6175 Mineral Point Rd Rm 328 Madison WI 53705

PELLEGRIN, MARIE-LAURE, process engineer; Process engr. US-Filter, Kans. City, Kans., 2001—05; MBR practice leader HDR, Tampa, Fla., 2005—.

PELLEGRINO, EDMUND DANIEL, internist, educator, retired academic administrator; b. Newark, June 22, 1920; s. Michael J. and Marie (Catone) Pellegrino; m. Clementine Coakley, Nov. 17, 1944; children: Thomas, Virginia, Michael, Andrea, Alice, Leah. BS, St. John's U., 1941, DSc (hon.), 1971; MD, NYU, 1944; 39 hon. degrees. Diplomate Am. Bd. Internal Medicine. Intern Bellevue Hosp., NYC, 1944—45, asst. resident medicine, 1948—49; resident medicine Goldwater Meml. Hosp., NYC, 1945—46; fellow medicine NYU, 1949—50; supervising Tb physician Homer Folks Hosp., Oneonta, NY, 1950—53; dir. internal medicine Hunterdon Med. Center, Flemington, NJ, 1953—59, med. dir., 1955—59; prof., chmn. dept. medicine U. Ky. Med. Center, 1959—66; prof. medicine SUNY, Stony Brook, 1966—72, v.p. for health scis., dir. Health Scis. Center, 1968—73, dean Sch. Medicine, 1968—72; v.p. health affairs U. Tenn. System; chancellor U. Tenn. Med. Units, Memphis, 1973—75; prof. med. Yale U., New Haven, 1975—78; pres. Yale-New Haven Med. Center, 1975—78, Cath. U. Am., Washington, 1978—82, prof. philosophy and biology, 1978—82; John Carroll prof. medicine and med. ethics Georgetown U., Washington, 1982—; dir. Kennedy Inst. Ethics, Washington, 1983—88; dir. Ctr. for Advanced Study Ethics Georgetown U., Washington, 1988—94, dir. Ctr. for Clin. Bioethics, 1991—, acting chief Divsn. Gen. Internal Medicine, 1993—94, chief Gen. Internal Medicine, 1995. Founding editor: Jour. Medicine and Philosophy, 1983—. Chmn. Pres.'s Coun. on Bioethics, Washington, 2005—. With USAF, 1946—48. Master: ACP; fellow: N.Y. Acad. Medicine; mem.: Inst. Medicine NAS, AMA, Am. Clin. and Climatol. Assn., Assn. Am. Physicians (chmn. pres. coun. 2005—). Office: Georgetown U Ctr for Clin Bioethics Washington DC 20007

PELLEGRINO, PETER, retired surgeon; b. Camden, NJ, July 7, 1934; s. Peter and Alice (Alchin) Pellegrino; m. Barbara Ann Holden, June 18, 1960; children: Peter Scott, Kathleen Ann, Lisa Marie. AB in Psychology, Franklin & Marshall Coll., Lancaster, Pa., 1960; MD, Hahnemann Med. Coll., Phila., 1960. Diplomate Am. Bd. Surgery. Intern Hahnemann Hosp., Phila., 1960—61, surg. resident, 1961—62, 1965—67, 1968, attending surgeon, 1969—2006; chief dept. surgery Kessler Hosp., Hammonton, NJ, 1969—2006. Assoc. prof. surgery Hahnemann Hosp., Phila., 2003—06. Capt. US Army, 1962—65. Fellow: ACS; mem.: N.J. Med. Soc., Hahnemann Alumni Assn. (1st v.p. 1984). Republican. Office Phone: 856-767-8980.

PELLEN, RITA M., associate dean; b. Phila., Jan. 18, 1950; d. Harold and Esther Shalitt Markus; m. Alain T. Pellen, Nov. 16, 1975; children: Michael Emile, Jessica Suzanne. MLS, U. Pitts. Sch. Info. Scis., Pa., 1972. Tech. libr. Army Materials Mechanics Rsch. Ctr., Watertown, Mass., 1972—75; chief, documentation svc. Comex Seal, Marseille, France, 1976—77; info. specialist Perry Oceanog., Inc., Riviera Beach, 1977—80; sci./engring. reference libr. Fla. Atlantic U. Libr., 1981—86, asst. head, reference dept., 1986—88, asst. dir. pub. svcs., 1988—97, assoc. dean libraries, 1997—. Contbr. articles to profl. jours.; co-editor: (book) Libraries Within Their Institutions: Creative Collaborations, Innovations in Sci.and Tech. Librs., Cooperative Efforts in Libraries, Joint-Use Libraries, Adapting to E-Books, Dealing with Natural Disasters in Libraries, Current Practices in Public Library Service, Google Scholar and More: New Google Applications and Tools for Libraries and Library Users, Googlization of Libraries, Libraries and Google, Evolving Internet Reference Resources, Internet Reference Support for Distance Learners, Libraries Beyond Their Institutions: Partnerships That Work. Mem.: ALA, Libr. Leadership Mgmt. Assn., Assn. Coll. Rsch. Libraries, Toastmasters Internat., Phi Kappa Phi, Beta Phi Mu. Office: Fla Atlantic Univ Libr 777 Glades Rd Boca Raton FL 33431 Office Fax: 561-297-2189. Business E-Mail: pellen@fau.edu.

PELLETIER, ELISE M., Director Health Economics & Outcames Reaserch; BA, Middlebury Coll., Vt.; MS, Harvard U., Boston. Mgr. reimbursement and outcomes planning Boston Sci. Corp., Natick, Mass., 2001—06; dir. health economics and outcomes rsch. IMS Health, Watertown, Mass. Mem.: ISPOR. Personal E-mail: epelletier@us.imshealth.com.

PELLETIER, KENNETH R., behavioral physician, educator, author; b. Nashua, NH, Apr. 27, 1946; s. Roger Norman and Lucy Barbara (Leonetti) P.; m. Elizabeth Anne Berryhill, Oct. 28, 1980. BA in Psychology, U. Calif., Berkeley, 1969, PhD in Clin. Psychology, 1974; MD (hon.), Ministry of Health Sri Lanka, 1985. Lic. clin. psychologist, Calif. Assoc. clin. prof., dept. medicine and dept. psychiatry Univ. Calif., Sch. of Medicine, San Francisco, 1974-90; clin. assoc. prof. Stanford Ctr. for Disease Prevention Stanford U. Sch. Medicine, Calif., 1990—, dir. Stanford Corp. health program Calif., 1990—, dir. complementary and alt. medicine program, 1997—. V.p. Healthtrac, Inc., Menlo Park, Calif. 1995—; vice-chmn. Rite Aid/PCS, clin. adv. com.; sr. clin. assoc. Johnson & Johnson Health Mgmt. Inc., New Brunswick, N.J., Santa Monica, Calif., 1985-95; advisor U.S. Dept. Health and Human Svcs.; bd. Nat. Resource Ctr. on Worksite Health Promotion, Blue Shield, The Can. Ministry of Health, WHO; bd. dirs. HealthNet (FHS), Am. Inst. of Stress, Social Venture Network, Healthtrac Found., Found. for Integrative Medicine. Co-author: Consciousness: East and West, 1976; author: Mind as Healer, Mind as Slayer, 1977, rev. edit., 1992, Toward a Science of Consciousness, 1978, Holistic Medicine: From Stress to Optimum Health, 1979, Longevity: Fulfilling Our Biological Potential, 1981, rev. edit., 1991, Healthy People in Unhealthy Places: Stress and Fitness at Work, 1984, Sound Mind, Sound Body: A New Model for Lifelong Health, 1995; mem. editl. bd. Med. Self-Care Mag., Am. Jour. Health Promotion, Integrative Medicine; contbr. numerous articles to profl. jours. Named Woodrow Wilson fellow Woodrow Wilson Found., 1970, USPHS Svc. fellow, 1973-74. Fellow Soc. Behavioral Medicine; mem. AAAS, APA, CPA, Washington Bus. Group on Health, Am. Heart Assn. Achievements include research in behavioral medicine, health promotion, disease prevention and clinical/cost outcomes. Office: U Arizona Schl of Medicine PO Box 245153 Tucson AZ 85724-5153 Business E-Mail: drkrp@deptofmed.arizona.edu.

PELLETIER, MARSHA LYNN, secondary school educator, poet; b. Mt. Pleasant, Mich., July 29, 1950; d. Eugene Russell and Mary Ellen (Edde) Mingle; m. Arthur Joseph Pelletier, May 19, 1973; 1 child, John Frederick. BS in Home Econs. and Edn., Kans. State U., 1971, MS in Edn. Guidance and Counseling, 1972. Lic. real estate broker N.H. Conf. coord., guidance counselor Kans. State U., Manhattan, 1971-73; tchr. home econs. Franklin (Mass.) HS, 1974, Exeter (N.H.) HS, 1974-75, Barrington (N.H.) Mid. Sch., 1975-81, Pentucket Regional Jr. HS, West Newbury, Mass., 1981-82; realtor assoc. Century 21 Ocean and Norword Realty, Portsmouth, NH, 1983-86; tchr. interior design, cons. U. N.H., Durham, 1986-87; tchr. family and consumer sci. Dover (N.H.) Mid. Sch., 1983—2001; tchr. Dover HS, 2001—; mem. legis. adminstrn. com. N.H. Ho. of Reps., Concord, 1992—94, 1996—2002; ind. real estate broker Dover, 1986-2000. Bd. dirs. N.H. State Profl. Bd. Stds., 1999—2004; assessor Nat. Bd. Profl. Tchg. Stds., 2001; tchr. assessor Nat. Tchrs. Bd. Cert., 2002—. Author: Portsmouth Unabridge: New Poems for an Old City, 2002, Arriving at the Crossroads, 2003, Exeter, New Hampshire: Where the River Meets the Tide, 2005; costume dir. & designer: Guys and Dolls, 2004; actor: (plays) Factory on Fire, 2006; contbr. poems to books. Bd. dirs. Dover Adult Learning Ctr., 1995—98; mem. Health Task Force, Dover, Concord, 1993—94, Cornerstone Dancers, Dover Friends of Pub. Libr., 1996—, bd. supt. adv. com., 2001—06, poetry judge, 2003—, bd. principal's adv. com., 2004—; mem. faculty coun. Dover H.S., 2004—; featured poet and tchr. poetry seminar Madbury Pub. Libr., 2008; trustee St. John's Meth. Ch., 1995—97, 2009—, fin. com., 2009. Recipient Best Poets award, Internat. Soc. Poetry, 2000, 2001, 2002, 2004; named to Nat. Honor Roll for Outstanding Am. Tchrs., 2006. Mem.: NEA (local pres., negotiator, v.p., membership chair, mem. leadership exec. com., bldg. rep. 1979—, N.H. del. to nat. conv.), Poetry Soc. NH, Seacoast Writers Assn., Nat. Coalition Consumer Econ., Alpha Delta Kappa (v.p., historian, altruistic chmn. 1984—89). Democrat. Avocations: gardening, aerobics, poetry, sewing, cooking. Home: 94 Back River Rd Dover NH 03820-4411

PELLETIER, SHO-MEI, musician, educator; b. Tucson, July 25, 1952; d. Harold W. and Mary Pelletier; m. Dwight E. Shambley, Aug. 12, 1979; children: Aaron Joshua Pelletier-Shambley, Alexis Jessica Pelletier-Shambley. Student, No. Ariz. U., 1965—66, Ariz. State U., 1965—66; MusB in Violin, Ind. U., 1974; student with, Josef Gingold, 1970—75, Ivan Galamian, 1969—75, Sally Thomas, 1969, Sydney Harth, 1967, Angel Reyes, 1968, Dr. Frank Spinosa, 1965—70, Dr. Harold W. Pelletier, 1966. Asst. prin. violinist Dallas Symphony Orch., assoc. prin. violinist, 1975—, solo violinist, 1993, 1995; assoc. prin. violinist Santa Fe Opera, Santa Fe, 1973—98; prin. violinist Dallas Chamber Orch., 1975—92, Dallas Bach Soc., 1975—95. Mem. youth edn. svc. quintet Dallas Symphony Orch., 1978—, charter tchr. Young Strings Minority Scholarship program, 1988; part-time tchr. Booker T. Washington Arts Magnet HS, Dallas, 1982—85. Musician (solo violinist): Sun Valley Music Festival, 1966—67, Interlochen, 1968, Meadowmount, 1969, Walden Ensemble, 1975—, New Arensky Piano Trio, 1975—, Anton A Piano Trio, 1975—, Kodaly Duo, 1975—, Voices Change Ensemble, 1975—, Haydn's Double Concerto for Violin & Harpischord, 1993, The Arensky Violin Concerto in Am. with Dallas Symphony Orchestra as Violin Concerto Soloist, 1995; author: (book) The Simple Dictionary for Classical Musicians, 2000. Charter mem. Nat. Mus. Women Art, Washington; mem. Klanwatch So. Poverty Law Ctr. Recipient awards, Plano Art Soc., 1980—, Richardson Art Soc., 1980—; named concertmaster, Ariz. All-State Orch., 1968, 1969, Outstanding Young Women of Am., 1982. Mem.: Nat. Geog. Soc. Avocations: painting, drawing, photography. Home: 9648 Whitehurst Dr Dallas TX 75243 Office: Dallas Symphony Orch 2301 Flora St Dallas TX 75201-2497 Office Phone: 214-871-4000. Personal E-mail: dwightshambley@sbcglobal.net.

PELLETT, DAVID, physics professor; s. Chester Earl and Dorothea Dice Pellett; m. Anne Holmes Pellett, Mar. 29, 1967; 1 child, Braden Holmes. AB in Physics, U. Kans., Lawrence, 1960, AB in Math., 1960, MA in Physics, 1962; PhD in Physics, U. Mich., Ann Arbor, 1966. Asst. rsch. assoc. U. Mich., 1966—67; asst. prof. physics U. Calif., Davis, 1968—74, assoc. prof. physics, 1974—80, prof. physics, 1981—. Sec. treas. SLAC-LBL User's Orgn., Stanford, Calif., 1981—82, chair, 1981—82; tracking rep. US CMS Mgmt. Bd., Batavia, Ill., 1995—96. Contbr. scientific papers. Mem.: AAAS, Am. Phys. Soc. Achievements include research in led US group proposing CMS forward pixel detector.

PELLETT, JON MICHAEL, lawyer; b. Orlando, Fla., Nov. 16, 1961; s. Milton Francis and Jean Ellen (Avery) P.; m. Karen Walker, July 21, 1984 (div. Sept. 1990). BS in Biology, U. Ctrl. Fla., Orlando, 1984, BS in Stats., 1985; JD, Fla. State U., 1993. Bar: Fla. 1995. Legal trainee Dept. Bus. and Profl. Regulation, Tallahassee, 1993-95; staff atty. Agy. for Health Care Adminstrn., Tallahassee, 1995-96; assoc. Freeman, Hunter & Malloy, Tampa, Fla., 1996-2000, Barr, Murman, Tonelli et al, Tampa, 2000—. Vol. guardian ad litem Guardian ad Litem Program, Tallahassee, 1991-95; mem. Coun. for Licensure Enforcement and Regulation, 2003—; bd. dirs. Suncoast Healthcare Execs., Tampa, Fla., 2003-06. Bd. dirs. Friends of Arboretum, Orlando, 1998—2003, Sun Coast Healthcare Execs., Tampa, Fla., 2004—06, treas., 2004—06. Mem. ABA, AAJ, Hillsborough County Bar Assn. Avocations: racquetball, beach volleyball. Office: Barr Murman Tonelli Et Al 201 E Kennedy Blvd Ste 1750 Tampa FL 33602-5829 Office Phone: 813-223-3951.

PELLEYMOUNTER, MARY ANN, research scientist; b. Osage, Iowa, Sept. 25, 1954; d. Richard Paul and Dorothy (Weber) P. BS, Marquette U., 1977; PhD, U. Colo., 1985. Rsch. scientist Abbott Labs., Abbott Park, Ill., 1988-89; asst. prof. Oberlin (Ohio) Coll., 1989-91; rsch. scientist Amgen, Inc., Thousand Oaks, Calif., 1991—. Contbr. articles to profl. jours. Recipient Nat. Rsch. Svc. award Nat. Inst. Aging, 1987, grant NIMH, 1991. Mem. AAAS, Soc. for Neuroscience. Home: 303 Weston Ln New Hope PA 18938-1088

PELLI, CESAR, architect; b. Tucuman, Argentina, Oct. 12, 1926; arrived in US, 1952, naturalized, 1964; s. Victor V. and Teresa S. Pelli; children: Denis G., Rafael A. BArch cum laude, U. Tucuman, 1949; MS in Architecture, U. Ill., 1954. Assoc. Eero Saarinen & Assocs., 1954-64, Daniel, Mann, Johnson & Mendenhall, 1964-68, Gruen Assocs. Inc., LA, 1968-77, Pelli Clarke Pelli Arch. (formerly Cesar Pelli & Assocs.), New Haven, 1977—; dean Yale U. Sch. Architecture, New Haven, 1977-84. Works include Pacific Design Ctr. and Expansion, LA (Honor award So. Calif. chpt. AIA 1976), US Embassy, Tokyo, Mus. Modern Art Expansion, NYC, World Fin. Ctr. and Winter Garden, NYC (Bard award 1992), Cleve. Clinic (Honor award AIA 1986), Herring Hall, Rice U., Houston (Honor award AIA 1986), Carnegie Hall Tower, NYC (Honor award AIA 1994, Design award AIA/Conn. 1991), Boyer Ctr. Molecular Medicine Yale U. (Design award AIA/Conn. 1991), Bank of Am. Corp. Ctr., Charlotte, One Can. Sq., London, NTT Corp. Hdqrs., Tokyo (Design award AIA/Conn. 1997), Terminal B/C Reagan Washington Nat. Airport (Design award AIA/Conn. 1998, NE Design award 1999, Design for Transp. award 2000), Aronoff Ctr. for the Arts, Cin. (USITT Honor award 1996, Design award AIA/CIN 1996, Design award AIA/Conn. 1997), Petronas Towers, Kuala Lumpur, Malaysia (Design award AIA/Conn. 1999, NE Design award 2000, Honor award AIA 2000), Frances Lehman Loeb Art Ctr. Vassar Coll., Poughkeepsie, NY (Design award AIA/Conn. 1996), Internat. Fin. Ctr., Hong Kong, Nat. Mus. of Art, Osaka, Japan (Design award AIA/Conn. 2005), Overture Ctr., Madison, Cira Ctr., Phila.(Am. Architecture award 2006), The Solaire, NY (LEED Gold), Carnival Ctr. Performing Arts, Fla., Mpls. Ctrl. Libr. (AIA/Conn. award, 2006), Bloomberg Tower, NYC (Urban Land Inst. award for excellence, 2005), Orange County Performing Arts Ctr., Costa Mesa, Calif. (AIA/Conn. award, 2007), Bank of Okla. Ctr., Tulsa, Conn. Sci. Ctr., Hartford, Torre de Cristal, Madrid, Torre Libertad, Mexico City, South Sta. Air Rights Devel., Boston, Torre Iberdrola, Bilbao, Paradise St. Devel. & One Park West, Liverpool, Eng., Gran Torre Costanera, Santiago, Chile, Project CityCtr. Hotel and Casino, Las Vegas, Torre Puerto Triana, Seville, Spain, Winnipeg Airport Terminal, Nat. Children's Mus., Wash., DC, Repsol YPF Hdqs., Buenos Aires, Transby Terminal & Tower, San Francisco; editor Yale Seminars on Architecture, 1981-82; author Observations for Young Architects, 1999 Recipient Aga Khan award, Aga Khan Trust for Culture, 2004. Fellow AIA (Firm award 1989, named to top ten list of living Am. archs. 1991, Gold medal 1995); mem. NAD (Arnold M. Brunner Meml. prize 1978), Am. Acad. Arts and Letters (academician), Internat. Acad. Architecture (academician). Office: Pelli Clarke Pelli Archs 1056 Chapel St New Haven CT 06510-2402 Office Phone: 203-777-2515. Office Fax: 203-787-2856.

PELOFSKY, JOEL, lawyer; b. June 23, 1937; s. Louis J. and Naomi (Hecht) Pelofsky; m. Brenda L. Greenblatt, June 19, 1960; children: Mark, Lisa, Carl. AB, Harvard U., 1959; LLB, Harvard Law Sch., 1962. Bar: Mo. 62, U.S. Dist. Ct. (we. dist.) Mo. 62, U.S. Ct. Appeals (8th cir.) 68, U.S. Ct. Appeals (10th cir.) 70. Law clk. to judge U.S. Dist. Ct. (we. dist.) Mo., 1962—63; mem. Miniace & Pelofsky, Kansas City, Mo., 1965—80; asst. pros. atty. Jackson County, Mo., 1967—71; mem. Kansas City (Mo.) City Coun., 1971—79; judge U.S. Bankruptcy Ct. Western Dist. Mo., Kansas City, 1980—85; ptnr. Shughart, Thomson & Kilroy P.C., Kansas City, 1986—95; U.S. Trustee Ark., Mo., Nebr., 1995—2003; of counsel Spencer, Fane, Britt and Browne, LLP, Kansas City, Mo., 2003—. Intermittent lectr. in law U. Mo. Bd. dirs., mem. exec. com. Truman Med. Ctr., Kansas City, Mo., pres. bd., 1988—90, chmn. bd., 1990—92; pres., trustee JVS, 2000—04; mem. Kansas City (Mo.) Sch. Bd., 2002—. Lt. US Army, 1963—65. Mem.: ABA, Am. Coll. Bankruptcy, Kansas City Met. Bar Assn., Mo. Bar. Office: 1000 Walnut Ste 1400 Kansas City MO 64106-2140 Office Phone: 816-292-8189. E-mail: jpelofsky@spencerfane.com.

PELOSI, NANCY PATRICIA, United States Representative from California; b. Balt., Mar. 26, 1940; d. Thomas J. D'Alesandro Jr. and Annunciata M. Lombardi; m. Paul Pelosi, 1963; children: Nancy Corinne, Christine, Jacqueline, Paul, Alexandra. AB in Polit. Sci., Trinity Coll., 1962. Chair No. Calif. Dem. Party, 1977—81; chmn. Calif. State Dem. Com., 1981—83; committeewoman Dem. Nat. Com., 1976, 1980, 1984; fin. chmn. Dem. Senatorial Campaign Com., 1987; mem. US Congress from 5th Calif. Dist., 1987-93, 1987—; asst. minority leader (minority whip), 2002—03; minority leader, 2003—07; spkr. of the House, 2007—. Co-author (with Amy Hill Hearth): Know Your Power: A Message to America's Daughters, 2008. Recipient Pub. Svc. award, Fedn. Am. Societies for Experimental Biology, 1997, Congl. Svc. award, Am. Coun. for Voluntary Internat. Action, 1999, Alan Cranston Peace award, Global Security Inst., 2003, Legacy award, Cesar E. Chavez Found., 2003, Nat. Legis. award, League of United Latin Am. Citizens, 2004, Golden Plate award, Acad. Achievement, 2006; named Barbara Walters Most Fascinating Person of 2006; named one of The 100 Most Powerful Women, Forbes mag., 2005—09, The World's Most Influential People, TIME mag., 2007, America's Best Leaders, US News & World Report, 2007, The 50 Most Powerful People in DC, GQ mag., 2007, The Global Elite, Newsweek mag., 2008. Democrat. Achievements include being the first woman in US history to be elected Speaker of the House, 2006. Office: US Congress 2371 Rayburn Ho Office Bldg Washington DC 20515-0508 also: 450 Golden Gate Ave 14th Fl San Francisco CA 94102*

PELOSO, JOHN FRANCIS XAVIER, lawyer; b. NYC, Oct. 7, 1934; s. Rocco C. and Victoria P.; m. Elizabeth Byrne Peloso, Oct. 7, 1961; children: Alycia, John, Matthew. BA, Fordham U., 1956, LLB, 1960. Bar: NY 1960, US Dist. Ct. (so. dist.) NY 1962, US Ct. Appeals (2nd cir.) 1967, US Supreme Ct. 1968. Law clk. to judge U.S. Dist. Ct. (so. dist.) N.Y., 1960-61; asst. U.S. Atty. U.S. Atty.'s Office, NYC, 1961-65; assoc. Carter Ledyard & Milburn, NYC, 1965-70; chief trial counsel NYRO-SEC, NYC, 1970-75; ptnr. to chmn. Sage Gray Todd & Sims, NYC, 1975-87; ptnr. to mng. ptnr. Morgan, Lewis & Bockius, LLP, NYC, 1987—99, sr. counsel, 2000—07; consultant, 2008—. Adj. prof. law Fordham Law Sch., 2000—; spkr. in field. Contbr. articles to profl. jours. Capt., inf. USAR, 1956—64. Mem. ABA (sect. corp., banking and bus. law, com. fed. regulation securities 1975—, com. bus. and corp. litig., chair subcom. securities litig. 1993-99, litig. co-chmn. com. securities 1983-87, com. on liaison with jud. 1987-88, coun. 1989-91, co-chmn. com. trial evidence 1994-95, co-chmn. task force on the ind. lawyer 1995-99), Assn. Bar of City of NY (arbitration com. 1970-73, fed. legis. com. 1975-78, fed. cts. com. 1982-86), Fin. Industry Regulatory Authority, Nat. Adjudicatory Coun. Office: Morgan Lewis & Bockius LLP 101 Park Ave Fl 44 New York NY 10178-0060 Home Phone: 203-454-4630; Office Phone: 212-309-6240. Business E-Mail: jpeloso@morganlewis.com.

PELOTTE, DONALD EDMOND, bishop; b. Waterville, Maine, Apr. 13, 1945; s. Norris Albert and Margaret Yvonne (LaBrie) P. AA, Eymard Sem. and Jr. Coll., Hyde Park, NY, 1965; BA, John Carroll U., 1969; MA, Fordham U., 1971, PhD, 1975. Ordained priest Congregation of the Blessed Sacrament, 1972; provincial superior Blessed Sacrament, Cleve., from 1978; ordained bishop, 1986; coadjutor bishop Diocese of Gallup, N.Mex., 1986-90, bishop N.Mex., 1990—. Nat. bd. dirs. Maj. Superiors of Men, Silver Spring, Md., 1981-86, Tekakwitha Conf., Great Falls, Mont., 1981—. Author: John Courtney Murray: Theologian in Conflict, 1976. 1st native Am. bishop. Mem. Cath. Theol. Soc. Am., Am. Cath. Hist. Soc. Roman Catholic.

PELTO, GRETEL H., nutritional anthropologist, educator; b. Mpls., May 6, 1940; d. Isaac L. and Deana (Harris) Hoffman; m. Pertti J. Pelto, July 27, 1968 (div. Dec. 1995); children: Jonathan, Dunja, Ari; m. Jean-Pierre Habicht, June 13, 1997. Student, Bennington Coll., Vt., 1957—60; BA, U. Minn., Mpls., 1963, MA, 1967, PhD, 1970; DSc (hon.), U. Helsinki, Finland, 1996. Clin. assoc. U. Conn. Sch. Medicine, Farmington, 1970-74; asst. prof. anthropology U. Conn., Storrs, 1974-77, prof. nutritional scis., 1977-92, prof. emerita, 1992—; scientist, child health divsn. WHO, Geneva, 1992-98; prof. nutritional scis. Cornell U., Ithaca, NY, 1998—2006, vis. prof., 2006, grad. prof., 2007—; disting. adj. prof. Inst. Nat. Salud Publica, Cuernavaca, Mexico. Mem. adv. bd. divsn. diarrheal disease control WHO, 1987-92; mem. adv. bd. subcom. on maternal and infant nutrition NAS, Washington, 1980-83; cons. UN U., Washington and Tokyo, 1985, Population Coun., NYC, 1980-82; hon. prof. investigator in Sci. and Medicine, Nat. Pub. Inst. Solud, Mexico, 2007-. Co-author: Anthropological Research, 1978, Community Assessment of Natural Food rces of Vitamin A; co-editor: Nutritional Anthropology, 2000; symposium editor: Jour. Nutrition, 2006; mem. editl. bd. Ecology of Food and Nutrition, Maternal and Child Nutrition, Human Orgn. Bd. dirs. Parent-Child Rsch. Ctr. for Eastern Conn., 1974-79; mem. task force Hartford Area Health Edn. Ctr., Conn., 1980-82; mem. adv. com. Travelers Ctr. on Aging, Hartford, 1988-89. Fulbright grantee, 1984; hon. rsch. fellow U. Birmingham, Eng., 1994-97; U.S. AID rsch. grantee, Mex., 1982-87. Fellow Soc. for Applied Anthropology (Malinowski award 2007), Am. Soc. for Nutrition (mem. long range planning com. 2001-05, coun. mem. 2004-05, councilor 2004—06, symposium editor 2006), Soc. for Internat. Nutritional Rsch. (bd. dirs. 1989-92); mem. Coun. on Nutritional Anthropology (pres. 1982-84, v.p. 1998-2000), Soc. for Med. Anthropology (bd. dirs. 1980-82). Avocations: photography, cooking. Home: 129 Eastlake Rd Ithaca NY 14850-9700 Office: Cornell U Div Nutritional Sci MVR 3M1 Ithaca NY 14853 Home Phone: 607-272-3262; Office Phone: 607-272-3262. Business E-Mail: gp32@cornell.edu.

PELTON, ELOIS BLEIDT, retired physical education educator; b. Corpus Christi, Tex., Apr. 3, 1939; d. Hodge Lester and Valena (Lee) Bleidt; m. Scott Horton Pelton, July 23, 1961 (div. June 1967); 1 child, Shawn Scott. BS in Edn., U. Ark., 1961; MS in Edn., U. Central Ark., 1967; EdD, Northwestern State U. La., 1972. Phys. edn. tchr. East Side Jr. HS, Little Rock, 1963-65, Searcy Jr. HS, Ark., 1965-68; prof. phys. edn. Ctrl. Mo. State U., Warrensburg, 1968—2000, prof. emeritus, 2000—. Phys. edn. curriculum cons. Ctrl. Mo. State U., Warrensburg, 1965—2000. Mem. Park Bd., City of Warrensburg. Mem. AAHPER and Dance (nat. del. 1988—), Mo. Asns. Health, Phys. Edn., Recreation and Dance (pres. 1989, presidential award 1987). Avocations: exercise, golf, tennis, reading. Home: 39 Letrista Dr Hot Springs AR 71909-6603 Personal E-mail: ebpelton@sbcglobal.net.

PELTON, MARGARET MARIE MILLER, retired art educator, academic administrator, artist; b. Charlotte, NC, Nov. 5, 1934; d. William Andrew Miller and Helen Cook Miller Margolin; m. Donald Wesley Pelton Jr.; children: Donald W. III, Charles F. BS, U. Miami, 1956; MS, Fla. State U., 1957; EdD in Coll. Adminstrn., Southeastern Nova U., 1979. Art tchr. Miami Dade Pub. Sch., Fla., 1957—70; art instr. Kendall Campus, Miami-Dade Coll., Fla., 1970—79, dept. chair, 1971—79, assoc. dean humanities, Rank prof., 1979—86; founder, vice provost New world Sch. Arts, 1987—96; ret., 1996. Bd. mem. Fla. Very Spl. ART, 1986—96; founder Louis Wolfsou II Fla. Moving Image Archive, Miami, 1986—96, pres., 1986—, v.p., 1996—. Exhibitions include Miami Water Color Soc., Spring Exhbn., 1999, 2001, 2002, 2003 (Outstanding award), Miami Water Color Soc., Fall Exhbn., 2001 (Peoples Choice award), Macon County Fair, Franklin, NC, 2000, Watercolor Soc. NC, Western Regional Show, Asheville, 2001, Watercolor Soc. NC, New Bern, 2003, Macon County Fair, Franklin, NC, 2001, Bet Breira Gallery, 2002 (First award), Fla. Profl. Art Guild, 2003 (Second award), Bascon Louise Gallery, Highlands, NC, 2003, Art League Highlands, 2003, one-woman shows include Kendall Campus Gallery, Miami-Dade Cmty. Coll., 2002, Richmond Cottage Deering Estate, Miami, 2006, two-person exhibition, Highlands, NC, 2006, 55 other exhbns. Mem. Dade Commn. Status of Women, Fla., 1983—86; bd. mem. Dade Heritage Trust, Fla., 1995—2001. Recipient Fla. Art Educator of Yr. award, Fla. Art Edn. Assn., 1989, Fla. Endowment award, Humanities Bd., 1984—89. Mem.: DAR (regent Coral Gables chpt. 2006—08, Jacksonville chpt. 2008—), Soc. US Daughters War 1812, Jacksonville Fine Arts Forum, Jacksonville Watercolor Soc., Nat. Soc. Colonial Dames XVII Century (Jacksonville) (Hanna Dustin chpt. 2005—), United Dau. 1812 (Jacksonville) (patriots chpt. 2008), Miami Watercolor Soc. (trustee), Macon County Art Assn., NC Watercolor Soc., Fla. Watercolor Soc., United Daus. Confederacy. Republican. Presbyterian. Home (Winter): 1326 Riverplace Dr Jacksonville FL 32223

PELTON, RUSSELL MEREDITH, lawyer; b. Chgo., May 14, 1938; BA, DePauw U., 1960; JD, U. Chgo., 1963. Bar: Ill. 1963, U.S. Supreme Ct. 1979. Assoc. Peterson, Ross, Schloerb & Seidel, Chgo., 1966—72, ptnr., 1972-90, Oppenheimer, Wolff & Donnelly, Chgo., 1990-2000, Chgo. mng. ptnr., 1992-95, 98-2000; ptnr. Ross & Hardies, Chgo., 2000—03, McGuireWoods LLP, Chgo., 2003—07. Co-founder, gen. counsel Chgo. Opportunities Industrialization Ctr., 1969—83; gen. counsel Delta Dental Plan Ill., 1979—96, Am. Assn. Neurol. Surgeons, 1983—2007; bd. dirs. First United Life Ins. Co., 1979—82. Pres. Wilmette Jaycees, 1970; chmn. Wilmette Sch. Bd. Caucus, 1970-71; Wilmette Dist. 39 Bd. Edn., 1972-80; bd. dirs. Wilmette United Way, 1980-86, campaign chmn., 1983-85, pres., 1985-86; Wilmette Zoning Bd. Appeals, 1989-2000, chmn., 1990-2000. Served to capt. USAF, 1963-66. Mem.: ABA, Mid-Am. Club (bd. govs. 2006—), Am. Soc. Med. Assn. Counsel, Am. Health Lawyer Assn., Soc. Trial Lawyers, Chgo. Bar Assn., Ill. Bar Assn., Ill. State Dental Soc. (hon.), Plaza Club (chair 2003—06). Office: 77 W Wacker Dr Ste 4100 Chicago IL 60601-1815 Home Phone: 847-251-8480; Office Phone: 312-750-8652. Business E-Mail: rpelton@mcguirewoodsemeritus.com.

PELTZ, CISSIE JEAN, art gallery director, cartoonist; d. Morton Dunbar Liebshutz and Myrtle Jewel Friedman; m. Richard Walter Peltz, Jan. 1, 1953 (dec. Feb. 21, 1975); 1 child, David Lee. BA, U. Chgo., 1947. Freelance cartoonist Milw. Jour., 1975—77, Chgo. Tribune, 1948—68, Today's Health, Chgo., 1959—71, Cosmopolitan mag., NYC, 1950—85, Look Mag., NYC, 1950—85, N.Y. Times, NYC, 1950—85, Saturday Rev., NYC, 1950—85, Chgo. Mag., 1950—85, Great Books Found., Chgo., 1950—85; owner, dir. Peltz Gallery, Milw., 1989—. Illustrator: book Everyday Speech, 1949, Laugh Your Way to Work, 1977, illustrator: booklets, advt. filmstrips. Named Communicator of Yr., Univ. Chgo., 1963. Mem.: Milw. Art Mus. Contemporary Art Soc., Mil. Art Mus. Print Forum (v.p., pres. 1987—89, bd. dirs. 1989—2002), Milw. Art Dealers Assn. Democrat. Avocations: collecting art, theater, movies. Office: Peltz Gallery 1119 E Knapp St Milwaukee WI 53202 Office Phone: 414-223-4278. E-mail: peltzgallery@sbcglobal.net.

PELTZ, NELSON A., investment company executive; b. NYC, June 24, 1942; s. Maurice Herbert and Claire (Wechsler) P.; m. Claudia H. Peltz, 1980, 8 children; two children by previous marriage. Student, U. Pa., 1962. With A. Peltz & Sons, Inc., NYC, 1963-70; pres., CEO APS Food Systems, Inc., NYC, 1970-72, Flagstaff Corp., NYC, 1972-78, Coffee-Mat Corp. (merged with Flagstaff Corp.), Kenilworth, NJ, 1975-76; chmn. bd., CEO Triangle Industries, Inc., NYC, 1983—88, Avery Inc., 1989—93, Triarc Companies, Inc., 1993—2007; CEO, founding ptnr. Trian Fund Mgmt., L.P., 2005—. Chmn. bd. NPM Group, Inc.; bd. dirs., Encore Capital Group, Inc., 2003-, H. J. Heinz Co., 2006-; gen. ptnr. Brook Fund. Trustee U.S. Olympic Ski Team, 1975—. Named one of Forbes Richest Americans, 2006. Mem. Young Pres.'s Orgn., Madison Sq. Garden Club, Old Oaks Country Club, City Athletic Club. Office: Trian Fund Mgmt LP 280 Park Ave #41 New York NY 10017-1217*

PELTZMAN, SAM, economics professor; b. Bklyn., Jan. 24, 1940; s. Benjamin Raphael and Ceil (Heller) P.; m. Nancy Virginia Bradney, Sept. 7, 1952; children: Shira Malka, Talya Rose. BBA, CCNY, 1960; PhD, U. Chgo., 1965. Prof. econs. UCLA, 1964-73; sr. staff economist Coun. Econ. Advisers, Washington, 1970-71; prof. econs. grad. sch. bus. U. Chgo., 1973-87, Sears, Roebuck prof., 1987-2001, dir. George J. Stigler Ctr. Study of Economy and the State, 1992—2005, Ralph and Dorothy Keller disting. svc. prof., 2001—05, Ralph and Dorothy Keller prof. emeritus, 2005—. Vis. fellow Inst. for Advanced Study Hebrew U., Jerusalem, 1978; dir. CMP Industries LLC, 1995—; mem. coun. acad. advisers Am. Enterprise Inst., 1995—. Author: Political Participation and Government Regulation, 1998; co-author: Public Policy Toward Mergers, 1967; editor Jour. Law and Econs.; contbr. articles to profl. jours. Mem. Am. Econ. Assn., Mt. Pelerin Soc. Jewish. Office: U Chgo Booth Sch Bus 5807 S Woodlawn Ave Chicago IL 60637-1620 Home Phone: 773-752-4246; Office Phone: 773-702-7457. Business E-Mail: samp@uchicago.edu.

PELURA, JAMES, III, veterinarian, political organization administrator; b. Woodbury, NJ, May 22, 1948; m. Marianne Knight, July 14, 1973; children: Anthony, Jennifer, Kathryn, Mary. BS in Animal Sciences, U. Md., Coll. Park, 1973—75; MS, Purdue U., Lafayette, Ind., 1975—77; DVM, Purdue U., 1977—81. Lab. technician, tumor immunology lab Litton Bionetics, Kensington, Md., 1971—73; lab. technician, non-ruminant nutrition lab Beltsville Agrl. Rsch. Ctr., USDA, Beltsville, Md., 1973—75; internship, residency Reisterstown Vet. Ctr., Md., 1981—83; owner Davidsonville Vet. Clinic, Md., 1983—; lectr. Anne Arundel Cmty. Coll., 2000—01; chmn. Md. Rep. Party, 2006—. Adv. State Bd. Horse Stable Inspections, 1985—92; vet. adv. Soc. Prevention of Cruelty to Animals, Anne Arundel County; mem. Rep. State Ctrl. Com. Anne Arundel County, 2000—; trustee Md. Agrl. Land Preservation Found., 2003; Md. state chmn. Bush/Cheney '04, Inc., 2004; dir. Ehrlich for Md., 2006. Assoc. mem. Rep. Women of Anne Arundel County, 2000—; tres. parish coun. Our Lady of Sorrows Cath. Ch., West River, Md., 1985—87; sch. bd. mem. St. Mary's Schools, Annapolis, Md., 1987—90; mem. bd. dirs. Pets on Wheels, 2006; weekly guest reader Eastport Elem. Sch., Annapolis, 2003—. Served USAF, 1971. Recipient Unsung Hero award, Md. Rep. Ctr. Com., Anne Arundel County, 2001, Dick Hug award, Anne Arundel County Rep. Party, 2004; named Man of Yr., Md. Rep. Party, 2004. Mem.: Anne Arundel County Vet. Med. Assn., Md. Assn. Equine Practitioners, Md. Vet. Med. Assn. (mem. ad hoc com., fin. oversight 2001, mem. pub. rels. com., mem. profl. affairs com., mem. bd. dirs. equine practice 2006), Am. Acad. Vet. Nutrition, Am. Assn. Equine Practitioners, AVMA. Republican. Home and Office: Davidsonville Vet Clinic Endless Call Farm 3725 Tanglewood Ln Davidsonville MD 21035-2408 Office: Md Rep Party 15 West St Annapolis MD 21401 Office Phone: 410-956-5733, 410-263-2125. Personal E-mail: Joelura@verizon.net. Business E-Mail: DrPelura@verizon.net, chairman@mdgop.org.*

PELUSO, JOHN, lawyer, insurance company executive; b. 1947; BA in English, St. John's U.; MBA in Mktg., Bernard Baruch Coll. (CUNY); JD, St. John's U. Law Sch. Bar: N.Y., 1987. Mgr. advt. & sales promotion Guardian Life Ins. Co. of Am., 1974—83, legal asst., 1983—87, asst. counsel, 1987—89, counsel, 1989—96, second v.p., ins. ops. counsel, 1994—96, v.p. & assoc. gen. counsel, 1996—97, v.p. & gen. counsel, 1997—. Mem. ABA. Office: Guardian Life Ins Co of Am 7 Hanover Sq New York NY 10004-2616

PELUSO, MICHELLE, Internet and travel company executive; b. Middletown, NY, Oct. 2, 1971; BS in Fin. & Multinational Mgmt., U. Pa. Wharton Sch. Bus., 1993; MS in Economics, Philosophy & Politics, Pembroke Coll., Oxford U. Mgmt. cons., case leader Boston Consulting Group, NYC, 1995—98; White House Fellow, sr. adv. to sec. US Dept. Labor, 1998—99; founder, CEO Site59.com (acquired by Travelocity), NYC, 1999—2002; sr. v.p. product strategy & distribution Travelocity, 2002, COO, 2003, pres., CEO, 2003—; exec. v.p. Sabre Holdings. Founder A New Generation for Peace. Recipient Thoroun scholarship, Ernst and Young Entrepreneur of the Year award, 2002, Spl. Achievement Award in Bus., Nat. Italian Am. Found., 2005; named Technol. Person of the Year, Travel Agent mag., 2001; named one of 50 Women to Watch, Wall Street Jour., 2004; named to Fast 50, Fast Co. mag., 2004. Office: Travelocity 3150 Sabre Dr Southlake TX 76092

PELYPENKO, ELIZABETH, lawyer; b. Chgo., Dec. 17, 1961; d. Mykola and Lydia Pelypenko; m. Arthur Italo, May 31, 1997; 1 child, Valentino Italo. BA Polit. Sci., Northwestern U., Evanston, Ill., 1984; JD, U.Ga., Athens, Ga., 1988. Atty. Pelypenko Law Firm, P.C., Atlanta, 1992—. Lectr. in field. Editor: Calendar Call mag., Verdict mag.; contbr. articles to profl. jours. Named Pre-eminent Lawyer, Martindale-Hubbell Registry, 2005—06; named a Ga. Super Lawyer, Atlanta Mag., 2005. Fellow: Litig. Counsel Am., Melvin Belli Soc., Knights of the Bar; mem.: ABA, ATLA, MENSA, So. Trial Lawyers Assn., Roscoe Pound Inst., State Bar of Ga., Ga. Trial Lawyers Assn. (chair CLE com. 2004—), Million Dollar Advs. Forum, Ga. Assn. Women Lawyers, Athletic Club NE Fencing, Lawyers Club of Atlanta. Independent. Avocation: fencing. Office: Pelypenko Law Firm PC 100 Galleria Pkwy Ste 1320 Atlanta GA 30339 Business E-Mail: ep@pelypenkolawfirm.com.

PELZ, CAROL E., library director, consultant; d. Mildred and William Elliott (Stepfather). BA, Ind. U., Bloomington, 1974, MS in Libr. Sci., 1976. Dir. Batesville Pub. Libr., Ind., 1974—77, Jefferson County Pub. Libr., Madison, Ind., 1978—80; mgr. audiovisual and fine arts Allen County Pub. Libr., Fort Wayne, Ind., 1980—83; mgr. audiovisual svcs. Columbus Met. Pub. Libr., Ohio, 1984—86, coord. adult svcs., 1986—87; dir. Grandview Heights Pub. Libr., Columbus, 1987—; cons. Pelz Libr. Group, Columbus, 1999—. Exec. dir. Ctrl. Ohio Libr. Consortium, Lithopolis, 1995—; libr. svcs. and tech. act adv. com. State Libr. Ohio, Columbus, 1998—2006; mng. dir. Mid Ohio Libr. Digital Initiative, Columbus, 2006—. Named one of Top Ten US Librs., Hennen Consulting Group Libr. Jour., 2004, 2007; Photohio.Org Formation grant, Inst. Mus. and Libr. Svcs., Ohio State Libr., 2001—, Digital Initiative grant, 2006—. Mem.: Ohio Libr. Coun. Office: Pelz Libr Group PO Box 159 Galloway OH 43119

PELZ, DWIGHT, political organization administrator; b. Seattle, 1951; BA in Gen. Studies, U. Mich., 1974. Cmty. organizer; exec. dir. Wash. Fair Share, Light Brigade; mem. Dist. 37 Wash. State Senate, 1990—97, chmn. edn. com., labor & commerce com.; mem., South Seattle dist. King County Coun., Wash., 1997—2005; mem. Sound Transit Bd., Wash.; chmn. Wash. State Democrats, Seattle, 2006—. Democrat. Office: Wash State Democrats Broderick Bldg 615 2nd Ave Ste 580 Seattle WA 98104 Office Phone: 206-583-0664. Office Fax: 206-583-0301.*

PEMBERTON, ALAN A., lawyer; b. Nov. 4, 1952; BA with honors, U. Chgo., 1974; MA in English Lit., U. Mich., 1977, JD cum laude, 1981. Ptnr. Covington & Burling, Washington, chair Govt. Contracts Practice Group, mng. ptnr. legal pers., vice chmn. pub. svc. com. Adj. prof. law Georgetown U. Law Ctr., Washington. Co-author: Obtaining Adequate Compensation for Delay, 1999, 2d edit., 2006. Bd. dirs. Indigent Civil Litig. Fund, Inc., Covington & Burling Public Sch. Project. Recipient USATF Champion, Master's Marathan, Age Group Winner, Boston Marathan, 2009. Mem.: US Dist. Ct. DC (pro se litig. com.). Avocation: running. Office: Covington & Burling 1201 Pennsylvania Ave NW Washington DC 20004-2401 Office Phone: 202-662-5642. Office Fax: 202-662-6291. Business E-Mail: apemberton@cov.com.

PEMBERTON, BARBARA BUTLER, religious studies educator; d. William Bradley Butler and Elizabeth Ann McGee; m. James Beck Pemberton, Jr., Dec. 7, 1974; children: William Patrick, John David, Michael Beck. BA, U. Miss., Oxford, 1973; MA, Southwestern Bapt. Theol. Sem., Ft. Worth, 1996; PhD, Baylor U., Waco, Tex., 2000. Asst. prof. Christian missions Ouachita Bapt. U., Arkadelphia, Ark., 2001—. Sponsor Chi Rho Phi, Arkadelphia, 2002—, Pruet Sisterhood, Arkadelphia, 2006—; fellow Inst. Ch. and Theology, New Orleans Bapt. Theol. Sem., New Orleans; presenter, spkr. in field. Named Most Inspirational Prof., Ouachita Bapt. U., 2001—02. Fellow: Inst. Ch. and Theology; mem.: Soc. Bibl. Lit., Am. Acad. Religion, Evang. Theol. Soc. Office: Ouachita Bapt U 410 Ouachita street Arkadelphia AR 71998 Business E-Mail: pembertonb@obu.edu.

PENA, CARLOS FELIPE, professional baseball player; b. Santo Domingo, Dominican Republic, May 17, 1978; m. Pamela Pena. Attended, Wright State U., Ohio, 1996, Northeastern U., Mass. First baseman Oakland Athletics, 2002, Detroit Tigers, 2002—05, Boston Red Socks, 2006, Tampa Bay Rays (formerly Devil Rays), 2007—. Recipient Silver Slugger award, 2007, Gold Glove award, 2008; named Am. League Comeback Player of Yr., 2007; named to Am. League All-Star Team, Maj. League Baseball, 2009. Achievements include tying the record for longest hitting streak by and American League rookie in 2002 with 12 games; hitting the longest homerun in Comerica Park history, an estimated 461 feet in 2005. Mailing: c/o Tampa Bay Rays Tropicana Field One Tropicana Dr Saint Petersburg FL 33705 Office Phone: 727-825-3137.*

PEÑA, JUAN JOSÉ, retired interpreter; b. Hagerman, N.Mex., Dec. 13, 1945; s. Rosa Peña; m. Petra Cervantes, Dec. 22, 1974 (div. 1982); children: Federico Ezequiel, Margarita María Blea. BA, N.Mex. Highlands U., 1968, MA, 1972, postgrad. With Albert Garcia Gen. Contr., Las Vegas, N.Mex., 1955-67; tchg. asst. N.Mex. Highlands U., Las Vegas, Nev., 1971-72, prof. Spanish, Chicano studies, 1972-78; teaching asst. U. N.Mex., Albuquerque, 1978-79; attendant N.Mex. State Mental Hosp., Las Vegas, Nev., 1982-83; staff and supervisory interpreter US Dist. Ct. N.Mex., Albquerque, N.Mex., 1983—2005; ret., 2005. Head Raza Unida del to PLO in Lebanon, 1981, head negotiator with Iranians for release of 2 Chicanos and 1 Indian; supr ct. interpreters and reporters sect. US Dist. Ct. N.Mex.; co-chmn. Cuatro-Centennial Com., Inc.; mem. exec. com. N.Mex. Human Rights Coalition. Author: (poetry) Angustias y Remembranzas; contbr. articles to profl. jour.; playwright: Canto a La Raza, 1978. Pres. Dads Against Discrimination, Albuquerque, 1993—; chmn. bd. trustees No. N.Mex. Legal Svc., Las Vegas, 1972-81; exec. com. Ind. Socialist Parties of Latin Am.; exec. commn. N.Mex. Human Rights Coalition; vice chmn. Barelas Cmty. Devel. Corp.; Barelas rep. Hist. Neighborhoods Alliance; cmty. coun. on equity Albuquerque Pub. Sch.; active N.Mex. Cmty. Loan Fund; bd. dir. Albuquerque Downtown Action Team, N.Mex. Land Grant Forum; textbook rev. commn. N.Mex. Dept. Edn., bilingual edn. adv. com.; commr. N.Mex. Textbook Selection Commn., 2001—; nat. sec. Am. GI Forum of US, 2000-01, 03-04, state comdr., 2006-07; v.p. Cmty. Enrichment Svc. Orgn., Inc.; bd. trustees, Nat. Hispanic Cultural Ctr. N.Mex., 2003—; vice-chmn., Hispano Round Table N.Mex., 1999-2003, chmn. 2003-04, 2007, co-exec. vice-pres., 2007; v.p. Cmty. Enrichment Svcs. Orgn., Inc.; bd. dir., bd. trustees Nat. Hispanic Cultural Ctr. N.Mex., v.p. 2005-06, U. N.Mex. Coll. Edu. Advancement Coun.; adv. com. U. N.Mex Coll. Edn.; chmn. N.Mex. Voter Registration Project; bd. dir. Albuquerque Downtown Action Team. Decorated Bronze Star; recipient Human Rights award City of Albuquerque Human Rights Bd., N.Mex. State Coun. Profile of Courage award Vietnam Vets. Am., 1995, N.Mex. Nat. Guard Cinco de Mayo award, 1995, Hispanics for U N.Mex. Achievement award, 1999, Human Rights award Albuquerque Human Rights Bd., 2000. Mem. N.Mex. Translator and Interpreters Assn. (pres. 1984-86), Nat. Assn. Judiciary Interpreters (sec. 1986-88), Nat. Partido Raza Unida (pres. 1976-81), N.Mex. Partido Raza Unida (pres. 1972-75, 77-78), Vietnam Vets. Am. (vice chmn. chpt. 1993—), Vietnam Vets. N.Mex., U. N.Mex. Sch. Ed. Adv. comm. mem., Nat. Assn. Chicano Studies (founding mem.), N.Mex. Chicano Studies Assn. (pres. 1972-78), Barelas Neighborhood Assn. (pres.), Hist. Neighborhoods Assn., Barelas Cmty. Devel. Corp. (rep., chmn. bd. 2006-07), Phi Sigma Iota. Democrat. Roman Catholic. Avocations: weightlifting, swimming, ice skating, hiking, camping. Home: 1115 9th St SW Albuquerque NM 87102-4027 Office: US Dist Ct Dist NMex 333 Lomas Blvd NW Albuquerque NM 87102-2272 Office Phone: 505-220-9139. Personal E-mail: jpena71@comcast.net, jjp3000@aol.com.

PEÑA, MICHAEL ANTHONY, actor; b. Chgo., Jan. 13, 1976; Actor: (films) Running Free, 1994, My Fellow Americans, 1996, Boogie Boy, 1998, La Cucaracha, 1998, Bellyfruit, 1999, Gone in Sixty Seconds, 2000, United States of Leland, 2003, Love Object, 2003, The Calcium Kid, 2004, Crash, 2004 (ALMA award for Outstanding Actor in a motion picture, 2006), Million Dollar Baby, 2004, Little Athens, 2005, Sueño, 2005, Fifty Pills, 2006, Babel, 2006, World Trade Center, 2006, Shooter, 2007, Lions for Lambs, 2007, The Lucky Ones, 2008, Observe and Report, 2009, (TV films) Semper Fi, 2001, Untitled David Diamond/David Weissman Project, 2005, Walkout, 2006, (TV appearances) The Sentinel, 1998, Moesha, 1998, Profiler, 1999, Felicity,

1999-2000, The District, 2000, Roswell, 2001, Men, Women and Dogs, 2001, American Family 2002, Andy Richter Controls the Universe, 2002, Twilight Zone, 2003, ER, 2003, NYPD Blue, 1997, 2004, CSI, 2005, The Shield, 2005. Mailing: c/o Innovative Artists Talent & Lit Agy 1505 Tenth St Santa Monica CA 90401

PENA, MODESTA CELEDONIA, retired principal; b. San Diego, Tex., Mar. 3, 1929; d. Encarnacion E. and Teofila (Garcia) P. BA, Tex. State Coll. for Women, 1950, MA, 1953. Cert. sch. supr., prin., supt., Tex. Tchr. English San Diego H.S., 1950-76; asst. supt. curriculum and instrn. San Diego Ind. Sch. Dist., 1976-80; gifted edn. resource tchr. William Adams Jr. H.S., Alice, Tex., 1980-83, asst. prin. for instrn., 1983-88; ret., 1988. Faculty Bee County Coll., 1975-76. V.p. San Diego PTA, 1963; charter mem. Duval County Hist. Commn., 1975—; reporter Duval Co. Hist. Com., 1988—; chmn. Com. to Establish Local Pub. Libr., 1993; trustee Duval County-San Diego Pub. Libr., pres., 1993-98, mem., 1999-2004, ex officio mem., 2005—, dir. Duval County literacy program, 1994—; cmty. rep. site-based dist. mgmt. com. San Diego Ind. Sch. Dist., 1995-97. Newspaper Fund Inc. fellow, 1964; recipient Adolfo Arguijo Day award, 1990; named Outstanding Sr. of Duval County, Grayfest, 1992; named to San Diego Hall of Honor, 1995. Mem. Tex. State Tchrs. Assn. (local unit rec. sec. 1952-53, 63-64, 1st v.p. 1957-58, 66-67, pres. 1961), Delta Kappa Gamma (rec. sec. chpt. 1972-74, 1st v.p. 1974-76, pres. 1976-78, chpt. parliamentarian 1984-88, 2003-08, state com. constn./bylaws 1979-81, state com. Eula Lee Carter Meml. Fund, 1987-89, area coord., 1989-1991, state com. pers. 1991-93, state rec. sec. 1993-95, state com. nominations 1995-97, chmn. 1997-99, state conv. chair 1999-2000, state com. necrology 2001-03, state com. ceremonies 2003-05, State convent cons., 2008-09., Chpt. Achievement award 1985, Internat. Golden Gift award 1994, State Achievement award 1996, Internat. Mem. in Print award 2002), Phi Delta Kappa (treas. chpt. 1978-79, rec. sec. chpt. 1983-84). Home: PO Box 353 306 W Gravis Ave San Diego TX 78384-2604

PENA, RAYMUNDO JOSEPH, bishop; b. Corpus Christi, Tex., Feb. 19, 1934; s. Cosme A. and Elisa (Ramon) P. DD, Assumption Sem., San Antonio, 1957. Ordained priest Roman Cath. Ch., 1957. Ordained priest Diocese of Corpus Christi, Tex., 1957; asst. pastor St. Peter's Ch., Laredo, Tex., 1957—60, St. Joseph's-Our Lady of Fatima, Alamo, Tex., 1960—63, Sacred Heart, Mathis, Tex., 1963—67, Christ the King and Our Lady of Pillar Parishes, Corpus Christi, 1967—69; pastor Our Lady of Guadalupe Parish, Corpus Christi, 1969—76; v.p. Corpus Christi Diocesan Senate of Priests, 1970—76; ordained bishop, 1976; aux. bishop Archdiocese of San Antonio, 1976—80; bishop Diocese of El Paso, 1980—95, Diocese of Brownsville, Tex., 1995—. Mem. secretariat Prep. Synod of Bishops for Am., 1996—97; Synodal Father Synod of Bishops for Am., 1995. Mem.: US Conf. Cath. Bishops (chmn. bishops' com. for Hispanic affairs 1987—90, bishops' com. for ch. in L.Am. 1994—97, 2000). Roman Catholic. Home: 741 Bowie Alamo TX 78516 Office: PO Box 2279 Brownsville TX 78522-2279 Office Phone: 956-542-2501. Business E-Mail: rjpena@cdob.org.

PENA, RICHARD, lawyer; b. San Antonio, Feb. 13, 1948; s. Merced and Rebecca (Trejo) P.; m. Carolyn Sarah Malley, May 25, 1979; 1 stepchild, Jason Charles Schubert. BA, U. Tex., 1970, JD, 1976. Bar: Tex. 1976, Colo. 1986. Atty. Law Offices of Richard Pena, Austin, Tex., 1976—. Instr. bus. law St. Edwards U., Austin, 1983, Austin CC, 1981-82; broker Tex. Real Estate Commn., 1980—; sports editor Austin Light, 1982. Bd. dirs. Ctr. for Battered Women, Austin, 1979-82, Austin Assn. Retarded Citizens, 1980-82; chmn. Austin Travis County Mental Health/Mental Retardation Pub. Responsibility Com., 1979-84; chmn. pvt. facilities monitoring com. Austin Assn. Retarded Citizens, 1981; bd. dirs. Boys Club of Austin, 1987-88; chair Homeless Task Force Austin, 1999—. Named one of Outstanding Young Men of Am., 1982. Fellow Tex. Bar Found. (sustaining life; trustee 1994, sec., treas. 1994, vice-chmn. 1995, chmn. 1996); mem. ABA (house dels., nominating com. 1998—, immigration bono com. 2000—, chair 2004-07, vice chair credentials com. 2001, state del. 2002-07, bd. govs. 2007—), Am. Bar Found. (bd. dirs. 2000, fellows officer 2003-04, chair 2004-05, vice pres. 2006), Nat. Conf. Bar Pres. (exec. com. 2001-03), State Bar Tex. (bd. dirs. Dist. 9 1991-94, exec. com. 1992—, chmn. minority representation com. 1991-92, chair James Watson Inn 1997-98, pres. 1998-99, chmn. profl. devel. com. 1991-92, policy manual com. 1993, fed. jud. appts. com. 1984-86, opportunities for minorities in the profession com. 1990-91, mem. advt. rev. com., pres.-elect 1997, pres. 1998-99), Travis County Bar Assn. (trustee lawyer referral svc. 1984-85, bd. dirs. 1986-88, sec. 1988, pres. 1990-91, chmn. jud. screening com. 1987, chmn. 1988-89, ins. com. 1988, 89, chmn. law day banquet com. 1988-89, lawyer referrel svc. com. 1983-84, trustee 1984-86, membership com. 1989), Capitol Area Mex. Am. Lawyers (pres. 1985, Outstanding Hispanic Lawyer Austin 1989), Legal Aid Soc. Ctrl. Tex. (bd. dirs. 1984), Austin Young Lawyers Assn., Tex. Trial Lawyers Assn., Austin C. of C. (Leadership Austin 1985-86). Democrat. Office: Law Offices of Richard Pena 2028 E Ben White Ste 220 Austin TX 78741 Office Phone: 512-327-6884. Business E-Mail: richard@rpenalaw.com.

PEÑA, TONY (ANTONIO FRANCISCO PEÑA), professional baseball coach, retired professional baseball player; b. Monte Cristi, Dominican Republic, June 4, 1957; m. Amaris Peña; children: Tony Peña, Jr., Jennifer Amaris, Francisco Antonio. Catcher Pitts. Pirates, 1980-86, St. Louis Cardinals, 1987—89, Boston Red Sox, 1990—93, Cleve. Indians, 1994—96, Chgo. White Sox, 1997, Houston Astros, 1997; coord., Dominican ops. Chgo. White Sox, 1998; mgr. New Orleans Triple-A, 1999—2001, Kans. City Royals, 2002—05; bench coach Houston Astros, 2002; first base coach NY Yankees, 2005—08, bench coach, 2008—. Recipient Golden Glove award, 1983, 1984, 1985, 1991; named Am. League Mgr. of Yr., 2003; named to Nat. League All-Star Team, 1982, 1984, 1985, 1986, 1989. Office: NY Yankees Yankee Stadium One E 161st St Bronx NY 10451*

PENBERTHY, STANLEY JOSIAH, JR., publisher; b. Des Moines, Sept. 3, 1921; s. Stanley Josiah and Beatrice Ann (Voith) P.; m. Dorothea Oehmke, July 7, 1945; 1 child, Robert Bruce. Student, Drake U., 1940—43. Engaged in broadcasting WJR, Detroit, 1941—56; freelance radio, TV, motion picture, actor, narrator, 1956—95. V.p. Fed. I-D Equipment Corp., Dearborn, Mich., 1951-62; pres. Publishers, Inc., Detroit, 1976-99. Author, prodr., narrator nat. radio series These Were Our Presidents, 1975; contbr. Mich. Sesquintennial hist. articles; author: Living Under Cover, Episodes of Life and other Relatives, Cottage Industry, The Photographs of William A. Roeser: A Talent Unfulfilled, From the Golden Tower of the Fisher Building. Past mem. bd. dirs. Sleeping Bear Dunes Citizens Coun., Traverse City, Mich., 1968-72, Cass Park Area Devel. Corp., City of Detroit, 1989; pres. Heritage Village Condominium Assn.; trustee Detroit Masonic Temple Assn.; mem. Founders Soc. Detroit Inst. Arts. Mem. AFTRA (past dir.), Adcraft Club Detroit, Detroit Execs. Assn. (dir.), Am. Film Inst., Detroit Prodrs. Assn., Broadcast Pioneers, Screen Actors Guild, Masons (33rd degree), Alpha Tau Omega (past alumni pres.). Home: 35560 Heritage Ln Farmington MI 48335-3136

PENCE, IRA WILSON, JR., engineering executive, researcher; b. Pontiac, Mich., June 18, 1939; s. Ira Wilson and Fern Elizabeth (Fraser) P.; m. JoAnna Springer, Sept. 5, 1959; children: Ira W. III, Teresa Ann, Deidre Lynn. BS, U. Mich., 1962, MSEE, 1964, PhD, 1970. Rsch. engr. Willow Run Labs., Ypsilanti, Mich., 1960-67, Dow Lab., Ann Arbor, Mich., 1967-70, GE, Schenectady, NY, 1970-80, engring. mgr. Charlottesville, Va., 1980-83; v.p. engring. Unimation, Inc., Danbury, Conn., 1983-87; dir. MHRC Ga. Inst. Tech., Atlanta, 1987-97, dir., pres. Intelligent Integrated Info. Sys., 1999—. Cons. Superior Motor, Hartford, 1987—89; bd. dirs. Wesley Found.; mem. adv. coun. Westinghouse, Pitts., 1983—87; treas. Wesley Comm. Ctrs., Inc., 1999—2007; exec. pres. Intelligent Integrated Info. Sys., 1999—2008; dir. 21iii.com, 2000—. Editor: Progress in Material Handling and Logistics, 1988; Material Handling for 90's, 1990. Trustee United Meth. Ch., 1988—, Camp Wesley, Inc. 1998— (treas. 2003-); cons. West Africa Theol. Sem., 2008-. Recipient New Product of Yr. award Innovation Today, 1985. Mem. IEEE (sr., sect. chmn. 1978), ASME (Materials Handling Engring. divsn. chair 1994). Republican. Methodist. Avocations: cabinet making, golf. Office Phone: 770-435-3183. Office Fax: 770-435-0493. Business E-Mail: ipence@isye.gatech.edu.

PENCE, JEAN VIRGINIA (JEAN PENCE), retired real estate broker; d. William Roscoe and Sophie Cottrell; m. Robert Albert Pence, June 14, 1947; children: Marjorie Pence Tuinstra, Robert J. Grad., Realtors Inst., Ill. Assn. Realtors. Cert. in real estate Central YMCA Coll., 1976. Sales assoc. William Knight Co., Realtors, LaGrange, Ill., 1962—70, sales mgr., 1970—76; pres. Pence & Co., Realtors, LaGrange, 1976—86; freelance writer Sun City Center, Fla., 1999—. Chmn. LaGrange Go-Getters Com. Channel 11 WTTG, Chgo., 1973—74. Author: (genealogy) The Cottrell Adventure With the Wright Connection, (novel) The Apprentice Angel, short stories. Sec. bd. deacons St. Andrew Presbyn. Ch., Sun City Center, 2003—05. Mem.: DAR (vice regent Clearwater chpt. 1984—86), Women's Coun. Realtors (pres. West suburban chpt. 1979—81), DuPage Bd. Realtors, LaGrange Bd. Realtors (sec.-treas. 1973—75, dir. multiple listing service 1978, chmn. profl. standards com. 1985—86), Nat. Assn. Realtors, Coterie (pres. 1982—83), LaGrange Park Woman's (sec. 1967—68), Pierre Chastain Family Assn. (press chmn. 1998—2001).

PENCE, KRIS, political science professor; Asst. prof. polit. sci. Ind. Wesleyan U., Marion, 2004—.

PENCE, MIKE (MICHAEL RICHARD PENCE), United States Representative from Indiana; b. Columbus, Ind., June 7, 1959; m. Karen Pence, June 8, 1985; 3 children. BA in History, Hanover Coll., 1981; JD, Ind. U. Sch. Law, 1986. Atty., 1986—91; pres. Ind. Policy Rev. Found., 1991; mem. US Congress from 2nd Ind. Dist., 2001—03, US Congress from 6th Ind. Dist., 2003—, US House Fgn. Affairs Com., US House Commn. on Security & Cooperation in Europe; chmn. US House Republican Study Com., 2005—07, US House Republican Conf., 2009—. Host (radio shows) The Mike Pence Show, 1992—99. Republican. Office: US Congress 1431 Longworth House Office Bldg Washington DC 20515 also: 1134 Meridian Plz Anderson IN 46016 Office Phone: 202-225-3021. Office Fax: 202-225-3382.*

PENCE, RAY, social studies educator; b. Peoria, Ill., Aug. 14, 1963; s. Ray Pence, Jr. and Selma Schneider; life ptnr. Ayako Mizumura. BA, U. Wyo., Laramie, 1992; MA, Miami U., Oxford, Ohio, 1996; PhD, U. Kans., Lawrence, 2005. Grad. tchg. instr. Miami U., 1994—96, lectr., 1996—97; grad. tchg. instr. U. Kans., 1997—2004, tutor, athletic corp., 1998—, lectr., 2006—. Contbr. articles to profl. jours. Vol. Obama For Am., Chgo., 2007—08, Douglas County Dem. Party, Lawrence, 2007—08. Recipient Excellence In Undergrad. Tchg. award, Ctr. Tchg. Excellence, U. Kans., 2008. Mem.: Soc. Disability Studies, Am. Studies Assn. Democrat. Home: 711 Rockledge Rd 6n Lawrence KS 66049 Office: Univ Kans 1440 Jayhawk Blvd Lawrence KS 66049

PENCE, STEPHEN BEVILLE, lawyer, former lieutenant governor; b. Louisville, Dec. 22, 1953; m. Ruth Ann Cox; 5 children. BS, Ea. Ky. U., 1976, MBA, 1978, LLD (hon.), 2004; JD, U. Ky., 1981. Asst. atty. gen. State of Ky., 1981—82; assoc. Taustine & Post, 1987—88, Borowitz & Goldsmith, 1988—90; ptnr. Sheffer & Hoffman, 1995—96, Pedley, Zielke, Gordinier and Pence, Louisville, 1996—2001; US atty. (we. dist.) Ky. US Dept. Justice, 2001—03; lt. gov State of Ky., Frankfort, 2003—07; ptnr. Dinsmore & Shohl LLP, Louisville, 2007—. With JAGC US Army, 1982—87. Recipient Ky Bar Assn.'s Outstanding Lawyer award, 1993; named an Outstanding Alumnus, Ea. Ky. U., 2004. Republican. Office: Dinsmore & Shohl LLP 500 W Jefferson St Ste #1400 Louisville KY 40202 E-mail: steve.pence@dinslaw.com.*

PENCOLA, ANNAMARIA REGINA, elementary school educator; d. Patrick Andrew and Regina Burnette Pencola. BS, Longwood Coll., Farmville, Va., 1977—81, MS, 1988. Lic. elem. edn. K-3 and mid. sch. 4-8 tchr. Va., 1981. Sch. leadership team Smithfield Mid. Sch., 2004—05; treas. Isle of Wight Edn. Assn., Va., 2003—06; chair dept. history Westside Elem. Sch., Va., 2006—07, team leader, 2006—08, sch. leadership team, 2007—08. Music director (original musical) A Crack in the Sidewalk; editor: (newsletter) The Real Smithfield Jaycees Newsletter (Best in State- 1st Pl., 1990). Vol. various polit. campaigns; Smithfield Jaycees, 1988—94; choir dir. Good Shepherd Cath. Ch., Smithfield, 2005—. Mem.: Nat. Edn. Assn., Va. Edn. Assn., Isle of Wight Edn. Assn., Women of the Moose, Chi Sigma Iota. Episcopalian/Roman Catholic. Avocations: gardening, animals, music, interior decorating.

PENCZNER, MARIUS, media company executive; m. Nancy Penczner. Keyboardist Black Oak Arkansas; co-owner, pres. Penczner Prodns., Inc., Potomac, Md., 1983—; writer, prodr. TV spots Tenn. Gov. Don Sundquist, 1984; prodr. country music videos Ardent Studios; mem. media consulting team Pres. Bill Clinton's reelection race, 1996; ad dir. Al Gore's presdl. bid, 2000, John Edwards presdl. campaign, 2003, mem. media consulting team, 2007; with Penn Schoen & Berland, 2004. Dir., writer (films) I Was a Zombie for the FBI, 1982. Democrat. Office: Penczner Prodns Inc 11800 Gregerscroft Rd Potomac MD 20854-2143 Office Phone: 301-217-0015.*

PENDARVIS, EDWINA DAWN, retired gifted and talented educator; b. Weeksbury, Ky., Sept. 22, 1944; d. Edward Martin Burgess and Mary Annette Johnson; m. Laurence Edward Pendarvis, May 17, 1966 (div.); children: Damon, Rosemary Penelope Avery. BA in English, U. South Fla., Tampa, 1966, MA in Gifted Edn., 1971; PhD in Edn., U. Ky., Lexington, 1979. Unit dir. Bur. Edn. Exceptional Children, Frankfort, Ky., 1974—79; prof. Marshall U., Huntington, W.Va., 1979—2006. Author: Raft Tide and Railroad; co-author: The Rural School Principalship, Abilities of Gifted Children, Teaching Gifted Children. Mem., officer Barnett Child Care Ctr., Huntington, 1985—2006. Recipient Outstanding Svc. award, W.Va. Assn. Gifted & Talented, 1993; John Deaver Drinko fellowship, Marshall U., 2002. Mem.: Appalachian Studies Assn. Socialist. Avocations: drawing, martial arts.

PENDER, MARTHA HELEN, retired dramatic soprano; b. Abilene, Tex., Nov. 8, 1927; d. Herman Arthur and Mary (Paxton) Pender. MusB, North Tex. State U., studied with Mary McCormic, 1949; MusM, U. Tex., 1970; pvt. studies, Rome, 1950—67. Voice tchr. and artist-in-resident Ind. U., 1967—68, Tex. Tech U., Lubbock, 1968—73, soprano with faculty quartet, 1970—73; pvt. practice in studio, 1973—97. Organizer reopening Paramount Theater, Abilene, 1981, organizer concert series, 1981—83. Opera debut with world famous tenor Beniamino Gigli: Cavalleria Rusticana, 1953, soprano: numerous concert recs. and roles in Trovatore, Norma, AIDA, Nabucco, Tosca, 1953—67, Lady MacBeth, Glyndebourne, Eng., 1964, Requiem, Tex. Tech. U., 1970—73; prodr.: (Operas) La Boheme, Carmen, Daughter of the Regiment, The Mikado, H.M.S. Pinafore, 1981—94; performer: (Operas) Paramount Theater and State Tex. Sesquicentennial, 1986, Abilene Civic Center. Organizer reopening Paramount Theater, Abilene, Tex., 1981, organizer concert series, 1981—83. Recipient Patron of Arts award, Abilene Cultural Affairs Coun., 1989, Disting. Svc. award, Harmony Club, Federated Music Club, 2002. Mem.: Nat. Assn. Tchrs. Singing (life), Abilene Opera Assn. (founder, first pres.), Alpha Psi Omega (life), Sigma Alpha Iota (life). Home: 1209 Musken Rd Apt H Abilene TX 79601

PENDERECKI, KRZYSZTOF, composer, conductor; b. Debica, Poland, Nov. 23, 1933; s. Tadeusz and Zofia P.; m. Elzbieta Solecka; children: Lukasz, Dominique. Grad., State Acad. Music, Krakow, 1958; student, Arthur Malawski and Stanislaw Wiechowicz; Dr. honoris causa, U. Rochester, St. Olaf Coll., Northfield, Minn., Cath U., Leuven, Belgium, U. Bordeaux, France, Georgetown U., Belgrade U., Madrid U., Spain, Adam Mickiewicz U., Warsaw U., Poland, 1993, U. Catolica Argentina, Buenos Aires, 1994, Acad. Music, Cracow, 1994, Acad. Music, Warsaw, 1994, U. Glasgow, 1995, Beijing Conservatory, 1998, U. Pitts., 1999; Dr., Yale U., 2003. Prof. composition Krakow State Sch. Music, 1959-65, Folkwang Hochschule für Musik, Essen, Fed. Republic Germany, 1966-68; composer-in-residence Sch. Music, Yale U., alternate years; guest condr. London Symphony Orch., Polish Radio Orch., Berlin Philharm. Orch. Composer: Psalms of David for chorus and percussion, 1958, Emanations for 2 string orchs., 1959, Strophes for soprano, narrator and 10 instruments, 1959, Dimensions of time and silence, 1959-61, Anaklasis, 1959-60, Threnody for the Victims of Hiroshima, 1960, Psalmus for tape, 1961, Polymorphia, 1961; Fluorescences, 1961, Stabat Mater, 1962, Canon, 1962, Sonata for cello and orch., 1964, St. Luke Passion, 1965, De Natura Sonoris I, 1966, Dies Irae, 1967, Capriccio for violin and orch., 1967, Capriccio for cello Solo, 1968; opera The Devils of Loudun, 1968-69; Utrenja for double chorus, soloists and orch., 1969-71, Cosmogony, 1970, Utrenja II-Resurrection, 1971, Actions for jazz ensemble, 1971, Partita for harpsichord, 4 solo instruments and orch., 1971-72, Cello Concerto, 1967-72; for double chorus, soloists and orchestra Ecloga VIII for 6 male voices, 1972; Symphony 1, 1972-73, Canticum Canticorum Salomonis for 16 voices and chamber orch., 1970-73, Magnificat, 1973-74, When Jacob Awoke for orch., 1974, Violin Concerto, 1976-77, Paradise Lost (rappresentazione), 1976-78, (Christmas) Symphony No. 2, 1980, Te Deum, 1979-80, Lacrimosa, 1980, Agnus Dei for a cappella chorus, 1981, Cello Concerto No. 2, 1982, Requiem, 1983, Concerto per Viola, 1983, Polish Requiem, 1983-84, The Black Mask, 1986, Der Unterbrochene Gedanke, 1987, Adagio, 1989, Ubu Rex, 1991, Sinfonietta for orchestra, 1990-91, Symphony No. 5 for orchestra, 1991-92, Partita for orchestra, rev. edit., 1991, Flute concerto, 1992-93, Quartet for Clarinet and String Trio, 1993, Divertimento per Cello solo, 1994, Violin Concerto No. 2, 1992-95, Agnus Dei, 1995, Symphony No. 3, Seven Gates of Jerusalem, 1997, Hymn to St. Daniel, 1997, Hymn to St. Adalbert, 1997, Credo, 1998, Sonata No. 2 for violin and piano, 2000, Sextet for violin, viola, piano, clarinet, and french horn, 2000, Concerto Grosso per Tre Celli, 2001; Piano Concerto Resurrection, 2002, Large for Cello and Orchestra, 2005, Symphony No. 8 (Lieder der Verganglichiect), 2005, also other works; prin. guest condr. NDR Symphony Orch., Hamburg, and MDR Symphony Orch., Leipzig; artistic dir. Casals Festival, PR. Recipient 1st prize for Strophes Polish Composers Assn., 1959, UNESCO award, Fitelberg prize and Polish Ministry Culture award all for Threnody, 1960, Krakow composition prize for Canon, 1961, grand prize State N. Rhine-Westphalia for St. Luke Passion, 1966, Pax prize Poland, 1966, Jurzykowski prize Polish Inst. Arts and Scis., 1966, Sibelius award, 1967, Prix d'Italia, 1967-68, Polish 1st Class State award, 1968, Gottfried von Herder prize, 1977, prix Arthur Honegger, 1978, Sibelius prize Wihouri Found., 1983, Wolf prize in arts (music) Wolf Found., Israel, 1987, 3 Grammy awards, Gamma prize Acad. Rec. Arts and Scis., 1988, Manuel de Falla Gold medal Accademia de Bellas Artes, Granada, 1989, Das Grosse Verdienstkreuz des Verdienstordens der Bundesrepublik Deutschland, 1990, 2 Grammy nominations, 1992, Grawermeyer Music award, 1992, Österreichische Ehrenzeichen für Wissenschaft und Kunst, 1994, 2 Primetime Emmy awards, 1995, 96, Crystall award, Davos, 1997, 2 Grammy awards, 1999, Musikpreis Duisburg, 1999, Cannes Classical award Composer of Yr., 2000, Principe de Asturias, 2001; grantee several founds., govts., insts. Mem. AAAL (hon.), Royal Acad. Mus. London (hon.), Nat. Acad. of Santa Cecilia (Rome) (hon.), Royal Swedish Acad. Music, Acad. of Kuenste West Berlin (extraord. mem.), Nat. Acad. of Bellas Artes (Buenos Aires) (corr.), Internat. Acad. Philosophy and Art (Berne), Nat. Acad. Scis., Belles-lettres et Arts (Bordeaux), Acad. Scientiarium et Artium Europaea (Salzburg), L'Ordre de Saint Georges de Bourgogne (officer, Brussels), Am. Acad. Arts and Letters, Bay. Acad. des Schönen Künste. Achievements include creating original notational system allowing aleatory freedom for performer within sects. of precise duration. Home: ul Cisowa 22 30229 Cracow Poland also: Am Daubhaus 6 D 55276 Oppenheim Germany Address: Akademia Muzyczna ul SW Tomasza 43 Cracow 31-027 Peter Island Fax: 49-6133/92 63 56.

PENDERGAST, JOHN JOSEPH, III, lawyer; b. Lewiston, Maine, Jan. 29, 1936; s. John Joseph and Grace (McCarty) P.; m. Joan Shaw Cole, June 14, 1958; children: John Joseph IV, Timothy S., Terrence B., Mary R., Michael C., Joan M. BA, Yale U., 1957, LLB, 1960. Bar: R.I. 1961, U.S. Dist. Ct. R.I. 1961, U.S. Ct. Appeals (1st cir.) 1963. Assoc. Hinckley, Allen & Snyder, Providence, 1960-66, ptnr., chmn. labor dept., 1966—2002; instr. U. R.I., Kingston, 1984-88; ret., 2002. Adj. prof. law Providence Coll., 1984—86, Roger Williams Law Sch., 1998—; arbitrator labor panels Am. Arbitration Assn. and Fed. Mediation & Conciliation Svc., 2003—. Author: (with others) The Developing Labor Law, 2d edit., 1983, Labor and Employment Arbitration, 1988, NLRA Law and Practice, 1992. Mem. Cath. Charities panel Diocese of Providence, 1976-94; bd. dirs. Smith Hill Ctr., Providence, 1978-93; v.p. Providence Boys Clubs, 1970-72, bd. dirs., 1990—2000, sec., 1996—2000. Mem. ABA (labor law sect.), Am. Coll. Hosp. Attys., Indsl. Rels. Rsch. Assn., R.I. Bar Assn., Sakonnet Yacht Club, Yale Club of R.I. (Providence). Avocations: antiques, fly fishing. Home and Office: 21 Elmhurst Ave Providence RI 02908

PENDERGRAFT, DAVID, lean six sigma consultant; s. Ray Daniel and Sue Pendergraft; m. Wendy Alexander, Nov. 16, 1991; children: Kelsey, Aidan. BS in Math., USAF Acad., Colorado Springs, Colorado, 1987; MS in Mgmt. Sci., U. Dayton, Ohio, 1992. 2nd lt. USAF, 1987, advanced through grades to capt., 1999; exec. Accenture, Reston, Va.,

1999—; advanced through grades to maj. USAFR, 2001. Decorated Meritorious Svc. medal USAF, Nat. Def. Svc. medal, Air Force Commendation medal, Air Force Achievement medal. Achievements include patents for security checkpoint simulation, mobile security unit; patents pending for effective security scheduler, business relationship prospector. Office: Accenture 11951 Freedom Dr Reston VA 20190 Personal E-mail: david.r.pendergraft@accenture.com.

PENDERGRAST, MARK H., writer; b. Atlanta, Oct. 1, 1948; s. John Brittain and Nan Schwab Pendergrast; m. Betty Molnar, Jan. 20, 1991. BA, Harvard Coll., Cambridge, Mass., 1969; MLS, Simmons Coll., Boston, 1975. English tchr., Mass., 1969—72; elem. sch. tchr. Vt., 1972—74; academic libr. Trinity Coll., Burlington, Vt., 1981—91; writer Essex Junction, Vt., 1991—. Bd. dirs. Nat. Ctr. Reason and Justice, Boston, 2002—. Author: (non-fiction book) Victims of Memory, Uncommon Grounds, Mirror Mirror, For God, Country and Coca-Cola (NYT Notable Book of Yr., 1993). Mem.: Soc. Environ. Journalists, League Vt. Writers, Nat. Assn. Sci. Writers. Avocations: singing, hiking, reading, travel, guitar. Personal E-mail: markp@nasw.org.

PENDLETON, FLORENCE HOWARD, former shadow senator; b. Columbus, Ga., Jan. 1928; d. John Milton and Elease Brooks Howard; m. Oscar Henry Pendleton, 1943; children: Oscar Henry Jr., Howard Thompson. BS, Howard U., 1949, MS, 1957. Tchr. Columbus Pub. Sch., Ga., 1951—55; instr. Morgan State Coll., Balt., 1957—58; tchr. DC Pub. Sch., Washington, 1958—70, asst. prin., 1970—80, prin., 1980—93; ret., 1993; chmn. Ward Five Dem. Com., Washington, 1979—82; mem. DC Dem. State Party, Washington, 1979—90; DC shadow senator to U.S. Congress, 1995—2006. Alt. delegate Dem. Nat. Convention, NYC, 1980; commr. Ward Five C07 Advisory Neighborhood Com. Clerk Berean Baptist Ch., 1965—94, clerk emeritus, 1994—. Named Disting. Citizen, Washington, 1980, Outstanding Cmty. Leader Ward Five, Berean Baptist Ch., 1981. Mem.: South St. And Affiliate Streets Block Club (pres. 1975—), Bloomingdale's Civic Assn. (edn. chmn. 1978—80), Ctr. City Cmty. Corp. (mem. chmn. exec. com. 1976—79). Democrat. Home Phone: 202-232-2010; Office Phone: 202-727-8099. Office Fax: 202-483-6301.

PENDLETON, MARY CATHERINE, retired foreign service officer; b. Louisville, June 15, 1940; d. Joseph S. and Katherine R. (Toebbe) Pendleton. BA, Spalding Coll., 1962; MA, Ind. U., 1969; cert., Nat. Def. U., 1990; D (hon.), U. N. Testemitanu, Moldova, 1994. Cert. secondary tchr. Ky. Tchr. Presentation Acad., Louisville, 1962-66; vol. Peace Corps, Tunis, Tunisia, 1966-68; employment counselor Ky. Dept. for Human Resources, Louisville, 1969-75; gen. svcs. Am. Embassy, Khartoum, Sudan, 1975-77, counsular officer Manila, 1978-79, adminstrv. officer Bangui, Central African Republic, 1979-82, Lusaka, Zambia, 1982-84; post mgmt. officer Dept. of State Bur. European and Can. Affairs, Washington, 1984-87; adminstrv. counselor Am. Embassy, Bucharest, Romania, 1987-89; dir. adminstrv. tng. divsn. Fgn. Svc. Inst., Arlington, Va., 1990-92; ambassador Am. Embassy, Chisinau, Moldova, 1992-95, adminstrv. counselor Brussels, 1995-98; consul gen. U.S. Consulate Gen., Montreal, 1998-2001; mgmt. counselor Am. Embassy, Cairo, 2001—04; diplomat in residence U. Memphis, 2004—05; ret., 2005. Bd. dirs. Cairo Am. Coll., 2001—04; vol. instr. Presdl. Classroom, 2006—; bd. dirs. Am. Sch. Bucharest, 1987—89. Named to, Hon. Order Ky. Cols., 1988. Democrat. Roman Catholic. Avocation: outdoor activities. Home: 1946 N Cleveland St Arlington VA 22201 Personal E-mail: pendletonmc@gmail.com.

PENDLETON, MILES STEVENS, JR., diplomat; b. Montclair, NJ, Mar. 22, 1939; s. Miles Stevens and Lucille (Bond) P.; m. Elisabeth Morgan, Aug. 13, 1967; children: Constance Morrow, Nathaniel Palmer. BA magna cum laude, Yale U., 1961; MPA, Harvard U., 1967; diploma, Nat. War Coll., 1980. Tchr. Ghana Secondary Sch., Koforidua, 1962-63, Adisadel Coll., Cape Coast, Ghana, 1963-64; vice consul Am. Embassy, Tel Aviv, 1968-70, polit. and econ. officer Bujumbura, Burundi, 1970-72; watch officer Ops. Ctr. Dept. State, Washington, 1972-73, staff officer Secretariat Staff, 1973-74, spl. asst. to Dep. Sec. of State Office Dep. Sec., 1974-76, dep. dir. Office of No. European Affairs, 1980-82, dir. Office of Israel and Arab-Israel Affairs, 1982-83, exec. asst. to under sec. of state for polit. affairs, 1983-85, dir. Office of Ecology and Terrestrial Conservation, 1995-97; polit. officer U.S. Mission to NATO, Brussels, 1976-79; min.-counselor for polit. affairs Am. Embassy, London, 1985-89, min., counselor for polit. affairs Paris, 1989-93; prof. strategy Indsl. Coll. Armed Forces Nat. Def. U., Washington, 1993-95. Mem. Am. Fgn. Svc. Assn., North Haven (Maine) Yacht Club, Met. Club (Washington), Phi Beta Kappa. Avocations: sailing, reading. Home: 3410 Lowell St NW Washington DC 20016-5023 Office Phone: 202-363-2601. E-mail: milespendelton@hotmail.com.

PENDLETON, ROBERT GRUBB, pharmacologist; b. Kansas City, Mo., Apr. 24, 1939; AA, Kansas City Jr. Coll., 1959; AB in Chemistry, U. Mo., 1961; PhD in Pharmacology, U. Kans., 1966. Sr. scientist SmithKline and French, Phila., 1966-67, assoc. sr. investigator, 1967-69, sr. investigator, 1969-74, asst. dir., 1974-79, assoc. dir., 1977-80, dir. pharmacology, 1980-81; dir. gastroenterology Merck, West Point, 1981-86; dir. pharmacology Rorer Ctrl. Rsch., King of Prussia, 1986-90, Sepracor, Marlborough, Mass., 1991—96; assoc. prof. Temple U., Phila., 1993—; lectr. Thomas Jefferson U., 1997—2006, CCP, 1991—. Lab. sci. cons. Office Surgeon Gen., U.S. Army, Washington, 1989—96, Ft. Detrick, Md., 1996—99. Col. US Army. Decorated Legion of Merit. Mem.: Soc. Armed Forces Med. Lab. Scientist, Am. Chem. Soc., Am. Soc. Pharmacology and Exptl. Therapeutics, Sigma Xi, Phi Beta Kappa. Achievements include discovery of new drugs to activate dopamine receptors in CNS and kidney; PNMT inhibitors, new drugs to inhibit epinephrine biosynthesis in adrenal gland and CNS; new drugs to block histamine receptors insurmountably including Pepcid; tricyclic antidepressant DMI acts in CNS to decrease gastric acid secretion; roles of CCK in gut; research in pharmacology of chiral molecules including Xopenex and in transgenic Drosophila models of Parkinson's disease and neurodevelopment. Avocation: ballroom dancing. Home and Office: 1312 Sumneytown Pike Lower Gwynedd PA 19002-1303 Office Phone: 215-654-5022. Personal E-mail: robertpendleton@comcast.net.

PENDLEY, WILLIAM TYLER, military officer, educator; b. Paris, Ky., June 21, 1936; s. Louis Tyler and Virginia Lorene (Poplin) P.; m. Anne Carroll Cooke, Dec. 13, 1958; children: Stephen Tyler, Robert Randolph, Lisa Carroll, Leslie Brooks. BS in Engring., U.S. Naval Acad., 1958; MA, Am. U., Washington, 1965. Commd. ensign USN, 1958, advanced through grades to rear adm., 1983; comdg. officer Patrol Squadron 45, Jacksonville, Fla., 1975-76; ops. officer Patrol Wing 11, U.S. Atlantic Fleet, Jacksonville, 1976-78, comdr., 1979-81; exec. sec. for joint chief of staff matters Chief Naval Ops., Washington, 1978-79, planner for joint chief of staff matters, 1981-82, dir. plans policy and strategy divsn., 1985-86; exec. asst. to comdr. in chief U.S. Pacific Fleet, Pearl Harbor, Hawaii, 1982-83; comdr. patrol wings U.S. Atlantic Fleet, Brunswick, Maine, 1983-85; commdr. Naval Forces Korea, Seoul, 1986-89; sr. mem. UN Mil. Armistice Commn., 1986-89; dir. strategic plans and policy USCINCPAC, Camp H. M. Smith, Hawaii, 1989-91; dep. asst. sec. def. for East Asia and Pacific affairs Dept. Def., Washington, 1992-93; prof. internat. rels. Air War Coll., Maxwell AFB, Ala., 1993-98. Lectr. and cons., 1998—; fellow Georgetown U. Leadership Seminar, Washington, 1985. Co-author: Nuclear Coexistence, 1994; contbr. articles to profl. jours. Decorated Def. D.S.M. with oak leaf cluster, Legion of Merit with 4 gold stars; named hon. Ky. Col., 1975; recipient Def. medal for disting. pub. svc., 1993. Mem. Phi Kappa Phi, Pi Gamma Mu. Methodist. Avocations: golf, travel. Home: 10 Walden Ln Bluffton SC 29909 Office Phone: 843-705-2334. E-mail: pendleyw@yahoo.com.

PENDYALA, RAM MOHAN, civil engineering educator; b. Aguadilla, P.R., Nov. 14, 1966; s. Balarama Rao and Prabhavati (Narra) P.; m. Neeraja Amirineni, May 6, 1992; 1 child, Neel Akash. B Tech. Civil Engring., Indian Inst. Tech., Madras, 1988; MSCE, U. Calif., Davis, 1990, PhD in Civil Engring., 1992. Registered profl. engr., Fla. Assoc. instr. U. Calif., Davis, 1988-91, rsch. engr., 1988-92; asst. prof. civil engring. U. S.W. La., Lafayette, 1992-94, U. South Fla., Tampa, 1994—. Rschr. Resource Decision Cons., Inc., San Francisco, 1991—. Contbr. articles to profl. jours. Recipient several scholarships and awards. Mem. ASCE (mem. com.), Inst. Transp. Engrs., Transp. Rsch. Bd. (mem. com. 1990—). Avocations: tennis, reading, movies. Office: U South Fla ENB 118 4202 E Fowler Ave Tampa FL 33620-8000

PENDYALA, RAMARAO, chemist, educator; b. Guntur, Andhra Pradesh, India, Aug. 1, 1964; s. Hanumaiah and Ramulamma Pendyala; m. Sri Latha Devi Miriampalli; children: Chandra Jvss, Sindhura Rupa. BS, Andhra U., Waltair, India, 1984, M of Pharmacy, 1991; B of Pharmacy, Gulbarga U., India, 1988; PhD, Osmania U., Hyderabad, India, 1998. Registered pharmacist. Exec. R&D NATCO Pharma Ltd., Hyderabad, 1998—99, scientist R&D, 1999—2001, dep. mgr. R&D, 2001—02, mgr. R&D, 2002—03; scientist UPM Pharms., Balt., 2004—08. Rsch. guide for PhD Jawaharlal Nehru Tech. U., Hyderabad, 1999—; dissertation guide for MPharm Annamalai U., India, 2000—03; examiner Gulbarga U., India, 1991—96; lectr. in pharmacy Vutkoor Laxmaiah, India, 1991—94. Contbr. articles to profl. jours., 20 rsch. papers in various internat. and nat. jours. Ency. Pharm. Tech. Social worker Nat. Cadet Course, Guntur, 1982—84. Sr. rsch. fellow, Coun. Sci. and Indsl. Rsch., 1994. Fellow: Instn. Chemists; mem.: Indian Pharm. Assn. (life; mem. sci. com. 2000). Achievements include 12 patents, India and abroad. Avocations: chess, reading, music. Personal E-mail: Pendyala_ramarao@hotmail.com.

PENELLA, ROBERT JOSEPH, ancient language educator; b. Feb. 16, 1947; s. Domenic M. and Filomena R. Penella; m. Sara Schatzel Penella, May 1, 1968; 1 child, Martha Penella Busemeyer. AB, Boston Coll., Chestnut Hill, 1967; MA, Harvard U., Cambridge, Mass., 1969, PhD, 1971. Asst. prof. classics Fordham U., Bronx, NY, 1971—78, assoc. prof. classics, 1978—91, prof. classics, 1991—. Regional editor Classical Jour., 1985—89; editl. bd. mem New Eng. Classical Jour., 2007—. Author: (book) The Letters of Apollonius of Tyana: A Critical Text with Prolegomena, Translation and Commentary, 1979, Greek Philosophers and Sophists in the Fourth Century A.D.: Studies in Eunapius of Sardis, 1990; translator: The Private Orations of Themistius, 2000, Man and the Word: The Orations of Himerius, 2007. With USAR, 1968—74. Recipient Bowdoin Grad. Prize, Harvard, 1969; Woodrow Wilson fellow, 1967—68, grant, Loeb Classical Libr. Found., 1978, fellowship, Nat. Endowment, 1993, John Simon Guggenheim Meml. Found., 2002. Mem.: Classical Assn. Atlantic States, Am. Philological Assn. Unitarian Universalist. Office: Fordham Univ Dept Classics 441 East Fordham Rd Bronx NY 10458 Office Phone: 718-817-3137. Office Fax: 718-817-0875. Business E-Mail: rpenella@fordham.edu.

PENFIELD, PAUL LIVINGSTONE, JR., electrical engineering educator; b. Detroit, May 28, 1933; s. Paul Livingstone and Charlotte Wentworth (Gilman) P.; m. Martha Elise Dieterle, Aug. 24, 1956 (dec. Apr. 1988); children: David Wesley, Patricia Jane, Michael Baldwin; m. Barbara Jean Buehrig Lory, July 22, 1989. BA, Amherst Coll., 1955; ScD, MIT, 1960. Asst. prof. elec. engring. MIT, Cambridge, 1960-64, assoc. prof., 1964-69, prof., 1969—2005, head dept. elec. engring. and computer sci., 1989-99. Author: Frequency-Power Formulas, 1960, MARTHA User's Manual, 1971; co-author: Varactor Applications, 1962, Electrodynamics of Moving Media, 1967, Tellegen's Theorem and Electrical Networks, 1970. Sr. postdoctoral fellow NSF, 1966-67. Fellow IEEE (chmn. Boston sect. 1971-72, Darlington award 1985, Centennial medal 1984, Golden Jubilee award 1999); mem. Nat. Acad. Engring., Am. Phys. Soc., Assn. for Computing Machinery, Audio Engring. Soc., Sigma Xi. Avocation: field identification of ferns and fern hybrids. Office: MIT Dept EECS Cambridge MA 02139

PENFOLD, LINDA MARGARET, reproductive physiologist, researcher; b. Folkestone, Eng., Dec. 24, 1962; d. Maurice and Stephanie Evelyn Rose Penfold. BSc (hon.), U. of Hull, North Humberside, 1985; PhD in Cell Biology, U. Coll. London and London Zool. Soc., 1993; postgrad., Zool. Soc. London, 1989—93. Lic. med. lab. sci. officer Med. Lab. Sci. Officer Bd. Lab. technician Chelsea Hosp. for Women, London, 1985—86; rsch. technician Zool. Soc. of London, 1988—89; postdoctoral fellow USDA, Beltsville, Md., 1993—95, Smithsonian's Nat. Zoo, Conservation and Rsch. Ctr., Front Royal, Va., 1995—97; rsch. coord. White Oak Conservation Ctr., Yulee, Fla., 1997—. Contbr. reference book Cryobanking the genetic resource. Recipient Wain Trust award, Wellcome Trust, 1992; grantee, Morris Animal Found., 1998. Mem.: Am. Zoo and Aquarium Assn. (reproductive advisor antelope taxonomic adv. group 1998—, mem. reproductive adv. group steering com. 2002—03, com. mem. contraceptive adv. group 2000—, Conservation Endowment Fund 1998), Soc. for the Study of Reproduction. Roman Catholic. Achievements include research in Investigation of hormonal control of reproduction in antelope species. Avocations: travel, dance.

PENG, LIANG-CHUAN, mechanical engineer; b. Taiwan, Feb. 6, 1936; came to U.S., 1965, naturalized, 1973; s. Mu-Sui and Wang-Su (Yang) P.; m. Wen-Fong Kao, Nov. 18, 1962; children: Tsen-Loong, Tsen-Hsin, Lina, Linda. Diploma, Taipei Inst. Tech., 1960; MS, Kans. State U., 1967. Registered profl. engr., Tex., Calif. Project engr. Taiwan Power Co., 1965—66; asst. engr. Carlson & Sweatt, NYC, 1966—67, Pioneer Engrs., Chgo., 1967—68; mech. engr. Bechtel, San Francisco, 1969—71; sr. specialist Nuc. Svcs. Co., San Jose, Calif., 1971—75; sr. engr. Brown & Root, Houston, 1975; stress engr. Foster Wheeler, Houston, 1976; staff engr. AAA Technologists, Houston, 1977; prin. engr. M.W. Kellogg, Houston, 1978—82; pres., owner Peng Engring., Houston, 1982—. Instr. U. Houston; condr. piping tech. seminars. Author: Pipe Stress Engineering; developer: (computer programs) SIMFLEX. Chmn. South Bay Area Formosan Assn., 1974, No. Calif. Formosan Fedn., 1975. Mem. ASME Buddhist. Home: 3010 Manila Ln Houston TX 77043-1312 Business E-Mail: lcpeng@pipestress.com.

PENG, SYD S., mining engineer, educator; arrived in US, 1965; Diploma in Mining Engring., Taiwan; M, SD Sch. Mines; PhD in Mining Engring., Stanford U., Calif., 1970. Mining engr. Twin Cities Rsch. Ctr. US Bur. Mines, 1970—74; asst. prof. mining engring. W.Va. U., Morgantown, 1974—78, chmn. dept. mining engring., 1978—2006, dir. Longwall Mining and Ground Control Rsch. Ctr., 1985—, Charles T. Holland disting. prof., 1987—, Charles E. Lawall chair mining engring. Morgantown, 2006—. Contbr. articles to sci. jours.; author: Coal Mine Ground Control, 1978, Longwall Mining, 1984, Surface Subsidence Engring., 1992. Recipient Instn. Overseas Medal award, Instn. Mining Engrs., UK, 1992, Howard N. Eavenson award, Soc. Mining, Metallurgy and Exploration, 1999, Donald S. Kingery Meml. award, Pitts. Coal Mining Inst. Am., 2001, Erskine Ramsey Medal award, AIME, 2002, Medal for Excellence, Inst. Materials, Minerals and Mining, UK, 2004, R & D 100 award, R & D Mag., 2004, 2005, 2006. Mem.: NAE. Achievements include patents in field. Office: Dept Mining Engring PO Box 6070 365 Mineral Resources Bldg Morgantown WV 26506-6070 Office Phone: 304-293-7680 ext. 3301. E-mail: sspeng@mail.wvu.edu.

PENG, TAO, systems engineer; m. Ning Qiu; 1 child, Alexandra. PhD, U. Md., Coll. Pk., 2006. Faculty rsch. asst. U. Md., 2005—07; imaging sys. engr. Confero Solutions Inc., King of Prussia, Pa., 2008—. Contbr. scientific papers to profl. jours. (Best Paper award, 2006). Mem.: ASME. Achievements include development of 3-D shape measurement using adaptive digital projection patterns.

PENG, YUSHENG, social sciences educator; b. Luoyang, China, 1962; PhD, UCLA, 1993. Asst. and assoc. prof. Chinese U. Hong Kong, 1994—2005; assoc. prof. CUNY Grad. Ctr., NYC, 2005—, Bklyn. Coll. Assoc. editor Modern China, Thousand Oaks, Calif. Contbr. articles to profl. jours. on sociology. Mem.: Acad. Mgmt., Am. Sociol. Assn. Office: Bklyn Coll Economics 2900 Bedford Ave Brooklyn NY 11210 Personal E-mail: yushengpeng@yahoo.com. Business E-Mail: ypeng@brooklyn.cuny.edu.

PENG CHEN, HSIU-HUI, music educator; b. Kaosiung, Taiwan, Jan. 12, 1957; arrived in U.S., 1993; d. San-Jen Chen and Jin-Ju Shi; m. Chin-Yuan Perng, Sept. 13, 1981; children: Wei Perng, Powell Perng. BA, Nat. Cheng-Chi U., Taiwan, 1979. Pvt. piano tchr., Taipei, Taiwan, 1975—83; choir dir., piano accompanist Acctg. Dept. Cheng-Chi U., Taipei, 1976—78; piano tchr. Palo Alto, Calif., 1984—89; pvt. piano tchr. Ann Arbor (Mich.) Piano Tchr. Guild, 1994—. Mem.: Am. Coll. Musicians, Mich. Music Tchrs. Assn., Nat. Guild Piano Tchrs., Music Tchrs. Nat. Assn. (chmn. Students Achievement Test Day N.E. Ctr. Sr. Finals 2003—). Home: 2515 Whitetail Run Ct Ann Arbor MI 48105

PENG-CHI, PENG, metallurgical engineer; b. Taipei, Taiwan, Jan. 19, 1973; s. Peng Tso-Hua and Peng Huang Jui-Chiao; m. Wu Jin-Sang, Oct. 23, 2003. MD, Nat. Pingtung U., Taiwan, 1998; PhD, Nat. Ctrl. U., Taiwan, 2008. Cert. radiographic testing level III Nondestructive Testing Soc. Taiwan, 2006, piping insp. Am. Petroleum Inst., Wash., 2006, pressure vessel insp. Am. Petroleum Inst., Wash., 2007, radiation protection pers. Exec. Yuan Republic of China, 2007, testing lab. dir. Taiwan Accreditation Found., Taiwan, 2007, visual testing level II Am. Nondestructive Testing Soc., Ohio, 2008, insp. Am. Welding Soc., Fla., 2008. Engr. Unilux Corp., Lux Group, Taiwan, 2000—02; with E & C Engring. Corp., CTCI Group, 2002—06; group leader, dept. metall. Dragon Steel Corp., China Steel Group, 2005—. Trainer Am. Petroleum Inst., Taiwan, 2008; asst. prof. Chaoyang U., 2009. Contbr. scientific papers. Recipient Paper award, Chinese Soc. Structural Engring., Taiwan, 2008, Excellence Employees award, Dragon Steel Corp., China Steel Group, 2008. Mem.: Nondestructive Testing Soc. Taiwan (trainer 2005—), Am. Welding Soc., Chinese Inst. Engrs. (outstanding youth award 2008). Avocations: reading, hiking. Office: Dragonsteel Corp 100 Lung Chang Rd Lung Jing Village Taichung Hsien 434 Taiwan

PENHOET, EDWARD E., retired foundation administrator, former biochemicals company executive, former dean; b. Oakland, Calif., Dec. 11, 1940; AB in Biology, Stanford U., 1963; PhD in Biochem., U. Wash., 1968. Prof. biochem. U. Calif., Berkeley, 1971—81; co-founder, CEO Chiron Corp., 1981—98; dean Sch. Pub. Health U. Calif., Berkeley, 1998—2002, dean emeritus, 2002—; sr. dir., Sci. & Higher Education Gordon and Betty Moore Found., 2002—04, pres., 2004—08, bd. trustees. Bd. dirs., sr. adv. to CEO Chiron Corp. Recipient Outstanding Philanthropist award, Assn. of Fundraising Professionals, No. Calif. Entrepreneur of the Yr. award, Ernst & Young and Inc. Mag. Mem.: Am. Soc. of Biological Chemists, Nat. Acad. of Sci., Inst. Medicine. Office: Chiron Corp 4560 Horton St Emeryville CA 94608-2900 also: Gordon and Betty Moore Found Presidio of San Francisco 1661 Page Mill Rd Palo Alto CA 94304-1209

PENHOLLOW, TINA MARIE, health science researcher, educator; b. Dunkirk, NY, Sept. 24, 1980; d. Duane Wesley and Christine Ann Penhollow. BS, SUNY Coll. Fredonia, 2001; MS, U. West Fla., Pensacola, 2003; PhD, U. Ark., Fayetteville, 2006. Cert. Health Edn. Specialist Nat. Commn. Health Edn. Credentialing, Inc. Grad. tchg. and rsch. asst. U. West Fla., 2001—03; health educator women infants and children program Escambia County Health Dept., 2002—03; doctoral acad. fellow and sr. grad. asst. U. Ark., Fayetteville, 2003—06; asst. prof. health promotion Fla. Atlantic U., Davie, 2006—. Presenter in field. Author: Aging and Sexuality: A Study of Active Older Adults, 2007—; contbr. scientific papers, articles to nat. and internat. periodicals, in profl. jours. Recipient Outstanding Doctoral Student in Health Sci. award, U. Ark., 2005; scholar, Western Divsn. Credit Union NY, 1997—98; Pace Grad. scholar, U. West Fla., 2001—03. Mem.: AAHPERD, Soc. Sci. Study of Sexuality, Am. Assn. Health Edn. (Horizon Award 2007). Achievements include youngest PhD graduate from the University of Arkansas's program in Health Science. Office: Florida Atlantic Univ Dept Exercise Sci & Health Promotion 777 Glades Rd FH 11-25B Boca Raton FL 33431 Office Phone: 561-297-2643. Business E-Mail: tpenholl@fau.edu.

PENICK, ANGELA LUCAS, elementary school educator; b. Roanoke Rapids, NC, Sept. 7, 1950; d. George Alexander and Carrie Louise (Hinson) Lucas; m. Charles Inglesby Penick, Jr. (div.); m. Burges Urguhart IV, Jan. 2006; 1 child, Carrie Hayes. AA, Marjorie Hebster Jr. Coll., Washington, 1970; BA in Edn., U. N.C., Chapel Hill, 1972. Cert. tchr. phys. edn., health, presch. handicap. Accounts payable clk. Boddie-Noell Ent., Rocky Mount, NC, 1973—75; tchr. Rocky Mount City Schs., 1975—80; admissions counselor N.C. Wesleyan Coll., 1980—81; drop-out counselor Nash C.C., 1981—85; social worker Britthaven Nursing Home, Nags Head, 1988—89; early childhood interventionist Halifax County Mental Health Ctr., Poanoke Rapids, 1989—99, Edgecombe-Nash Mental Health Ctr., Rocky Mount, 1989—99; tchr. Nash-Rocky Mount Schs., 1999—. Chmn. Good Shepherd Day Sch., Rocky Mount, 2000—02; mem. Tar River Orch. & Chorus League, Rocky Mount, 2004—05, 2008—; vol. Episc. Ch. Women, Am. Cancer Soc., March of Dimes; hosp. vol. Unwealthy Health Sys., 2008—; meals on wheels vol. Rocky Mount, 2008—; leader Bible Study Fellowship, Rocky Mount, 2004—05; mem. vestry Ch. of the Good Shepherd, Rocky Mount, 1999—2002, mem. search com., 2003—04, mem. youth coun.; vestryman Ch. Good Shepherd, Rocky Mt., 2009—; bd. dirs., sec. My Sister's House, Rocky Mount, SC, 1995—98. Mem.: Women's Tennis League, U.S. Tennis Assn., Benvenue Country Club (mem., tennis team

2008—09). Republican. Episcopalian. Avocations: tennis, gardening, drawing, weight training, jogging. Office: Nash-Rocky Mount Schools 930 Eastern Ave Nashville NC 27856 Office Phone: 252-937-5622. E-mail: anjo950@aol.com.

PENICK, ANN CLARISSE, minister, counselor; b. Woodstock, Ill., Feb. 17, 1951; d. Preston Edwin and Marjorie Jane Yeoman; m. John William Schoenberger (div.); m. James Lal Penick, Jr., Aug. 9, 1986; stepchildren: Michael Andrew, Katherine Leona. BA in History, No. Ill. U., DeKalb, 1977; MA in History, Loyola U., Chgo., 1987; MA in Counseling, U. Ala., Birmingham, 1995; MA in Pastoral Ministry, Boston Coll., 2008. Cert. minister Diocese Birmingham, Ala., 1993; lic. counselor S.C., 1997, cert. Nat. Bd. Certified Counselors, 1999, lic. mental health counselor Mass., 2006. Adj. faculty Birmingham So. Coll., 1988—91; chaplain intern Bon Secours St. Francis Hosp., Charleston, 1996—97; minister Cath. Campus Diocese Charleston, Coll. of Charleston, SC, 1997—2000; pastoral assoc. St. Ann U. Parish, Archdiocese Boston, 2000—02, cath. chaplain Tufts U., 2002—08. Adj. faculty Nat. U., Chgo., 1988; coord. sexual abuse awareness Archdiocese Boston, 2002—08, facilitator marriage preparation, 2002—08. Contbr. articles to profl. jours. Aid worker Polish Refugee Camp, Vienna, 1982; spokesperson Nat. Night Out, Charleston, 1996; pres. inaugural com. Dem. Party, 2009; vol. Dem. Nat. Com., Boston, 2004; vol. pastoral counselor Hospice Charleston, 1995—98. Named Advisor of Yr., Emerson Coll., 2001. Mem.: Nat. Assn. Coll. and U. Chaplains, Assn. for Spiritual, Ethical and Religious Values in Counseling, Mass. Mental Health Counselors Assn., Cath. Campus Ministry Assn., Am. Counseling Assn. (bd. dir. 2001—04, Svc. award 2004). Democrat. Roman Cath. Avocations: dance, guitar, singing. Office: Coll S Md LaPlata Campus Advisement & Career Svc 8730 Mitchell Rd La Plata MD 20646-0910 Office Phone: 301-934-7577. Personal E-mail: annpenick@hotmail.com.

PENICK, ELIZABETH C., psychologist; b. New Orleans, July 17, 1934; d. Rawley M. Penick and Marie G. Sells. BA, Newcomb Coll., 1957; MS, Tulane U., 1960; PhD, Washington U., St. Louis, 1975. Diplomate clin. psychology Am. Bd. Profl. Psychology. Prof. dept. psychiatry Kans. U. Med. Ctr., Kansas City, 1980—, dir. divsn. psychology. Rsch. grantee Nat. Assn. Alcohol Abuse and Alcoholism, Washington, 1980-97. Mem. APA, Kans. Psychol. Assn. (dir.). Home: 12231 Charlotte Kansas City MO 64146 Office: Kans U Med Ctr Dept Psychiatry 3901 Rainbow Blvd Kansas City KS 66160 E-mail: epenick@kumc.edu.

PENICK, JOHN E., educator; b. Langley, Va., Jan. 2, 1944; s. Edgar and Bessie P.; m. Nell Inman, July 23, 1966; children: Lucas T., Megan J. Penick. BS, U. Miami, 1966, MA, 1969; PhD, Fla. State U., 1973. Sci. dept. head Miami (Fla.) Jackson High Sch., 1967-70; instr. Miami-Dade Community Coll., 1968, Fla. State U., Tallahassee, 1970-73; dir. tchr. edn. Loyola U., Chgo., 1973-75; prof. U. Iowa, Iowa City, 1975-97, head Sci. Edn. Ctr., 1982, 89-93; prof., head dept. math., sci. and tech. edn. N.C. State U., Raleigh, 1998—2009; v.p. r & d Sangari do Brasil, 2009—. Editor: (monograph series) Focus on Excellence, 1983—89; author: Biology: A Community Context, 2003; contbr. numerous articles to profl. jours. Named Disting. Alumnus Fla. State U., 1987; recipient Burlington No. award for outstanding career achievement U. Iowa, 1992; Fulbright fellow USIA, Portugal, 1985. Fellow Iowa Acad. Sci.; mem. NSTA (bd. dir. 1986-88, pres. 2003, Ohaus awards), Nat. Assn. for Rsch. in Sci. Tchg. (assoc. editor 1979-84), Coun. Sci. Soc. Prs. (sec. 1991-92, treas. 2003-04), Nat. Assn. Biology Tchrs. (pres. 1989, hon. mem. award, 2004), Assn. Sci. Tchr. Educators (pres. 2002, Outstanding Paper 1978, Outstanding Sci. Educator 1987, Outstanding Mentor 1997), Sigma Xi, Esilon Pi Tau (Dist. Svc. Citation, 2003). Office: 7750 SW 54 Ave Miami FL 33143

PENINGER, MICHAEL J., insurance company executive; Actuary Northwestern Nat. Life, 1977—85; corp. actuary Assurant Employee Benefits, 1985—91, sr. v.p., CFO, 1991—93, sr. v.p. fin., 1993—98, exec. v.p., 1998—99, pres., CEO, 1999—; exec. v.p. Assurant Inc., NYC, 1999—, interim CFO, 2007—09, CFO, 2009—. Fellow: Soc. Actuaries; mem.: Am. Acad. Actuaries. Office: Assurant Inc 1 Chase Manhattan Plz New York NY 10005*

PENISTEN, GARY DEAN, entrepreneur; b. Lincoln, Nebr., May 14, 1931; s. Martin C. and Jayne (O'Dell) P.; m. Nancy Margaret Golding, June 3, 1951; children: Kris D., Janet L., Carol E., Noel M. BS in Bus. Adminstrn., U. Nebr., Omaha, 1953; LLD (hon.), Concordia Coll., 1993. With Gen. Electric Co., 1953-74, mgr. group fin. ops. power generation group NYC, 1973-74; asst. sec. navy fin. mgmt., 1974-77; sr. v.p. fin., chief fin. officer, dir. Sterling Drug Inc., NYC, 1977-89; sr. v.p. fin., health group Eastman Kodak Co., NYC, 1989-90. Chmn. bd. dirs. Acme United Corp., 1996—2006, chmn. emeritus, 2007—08. Mem. corp. adv. bd. U. Nebr. Coll. Bus., Omaha. Recipient Disting. Public Service award Navy Dept., 1977; Alumni Achievement citation U. Nebr., Omaha, 1975. Mem. Navy League of U.S., Rotary, Ft. Lauderdale (Fla.) Country Club, White Eagle Golf Club (Naperville). Republican. Unitarian Universalist. Home and Office: 1409 Aberdeen Ct Naperville IL 60564-9787 Home Phone: 630-978-7093; Office Phone: 630-978-7093. Personal E-mail: asnfm@aol.com.

PENLAND, JOHN THOMAS, retired import/export and development company executive; b. Guntersville, Ala., Mar. 31, 1930; s. James B. and Kathleen (Bolding) P.; m. Carolyn Joyce White, May 30, 1961; children: Jeffrey K., Mark A., Michael J. BA, George Washington U., 1957. Vice pres., dir. Rouse, Brewer, Becker & Bryant, Inc., Washington, 1957-63; branch chief, staff mem. SEC, Washington, 1963—67; pres., dir. INA Trading Corp., Phila., 1968-69; v.p. INA Security Corp., Phila., 1967-69; from v.p. to pres. Shareholders Mgmt. Co., LA, 1969—75, v.p., dir. several mut. funds managed by, 1970-75; v.p. Shareholders Capital Corp., LA, 1972-73; pres., chmn., CEO, HMO Internat. and its subs., LA, 1975; founder, pres., chmn. Pendlar Corp., Atlanta, 1977-97; chmn., pres. Bella Vista Developers, Inc., Albuquerque, 1977-98; chmn., CEO, CompuComp Corp., Atlanta, 1977-81; chmn., pres. Fran Stef Corp., NYC, 1982-89; pres., chmn. Engineered Products Corp., Dandridge, Tenn., 1983-90; founder, chmn., CEO Am. Accessories Inc., Covington, Ga., 1983-98; founder, pres., chmn. United Am. Products Corp., Dandridge, 1983-89; founder, chmn., pres. Chamisa Properties, Inc., Albuqueque, 1988-94; founder, chmn. Glorieux Ltd., Atlanta, 1988-96; founder, pres. Ga. Ptnrs. Ltd., Covington, 1988—94; founder, chmn. Premier Trading Internat., Inc., Atlanta, 1989—98; founder, pres. Chamisa Enterprises, Inc., Covington, 1990—2001; founder, mng. ptnr. Ft. Hill Ptnrs., Knoxville, Tenn., 1990-93; chmn. Einson Freeman & Detroy Corp., Fair Lawn, NJ, 1978-83; founder, dir., pres. West Point Contract Packaging, Inc., Martinsville, Va., 1991-98; founder, mng. ptnr. Harbor View, Ltd., Fernandina Beach, Fla., 1992-94; founder, chmn. West Point Tech. Assembly, Inc., Winston-Salem, NC, 1993—2002; dir., pres. BKP Industries, Inc., Monroe, Ga., 1995-97; ret., 1998. With US Army, 1948—55. Republican. Episcopalian. Home: PO Box 549 Social Circle GA 30025-0549 Home Phone: 770-786-1007; Office Phone: 770-634-6817. Personal E-mail: cjpenland@bellsouth.net.

PENLEY, LARRY EDWARD, former academic administrator, finance educator; b. Bristol, Va., Feb. 9, 1949; s. William Edward and June (Caudill) P.; m. Yolanda Elva Sanchez, Nov. 25, 1977; children: Jonathan Andrew, Josephine Anna. BA, Wake Forest U., 1971, MA, 1972; PhD, U. Ga., 1976. Vis. prof. ITESM, Monterey, Mexico, 1977, Universidad de Carobobo, Valencia, Venezuela, 1978; assoc. dean U. Tex., San Antonio, 1980-85; prof., chmn. dept. Ariz. State U., Tempe, 1985—90, dean Coll. Bus., 1990—2003; pres. Colo. State U., 2003—08; chancellor Colo. State U. Sys., 2003—08. Contbr. articles to profl. jours. Mem. NCAA Task Force on Future of Athletics, Nat. Western Stock Show and Rodeo, Citizen of West Com.; mem. adv. counsel Group Ecole Superieure De Commerce de Toulouse, 1997; chmn. Assn. Advance Collegiate Sch. of Bus., 2000—01; bd. mem. dir. Greater Phoenix Econ. Coun., 1993—2003. Recipient Frank C. Carr Founders award, INROADS, 1997, Disting. Svc. award, Greater Phoenix Econ. Coun., 2002. Mem.: Assn. Advance Collegiate Schs. of Bus. (chmn. 2001—02), Rocky Mountain Bd., Inst. Internat. Edn., Mountain States Employers Coun. Bd., Greater Denver Metro Chamber Bd., Acad. Mgmt. (chmn. divsn. program 1986), Mountain West Conf. Bd., Colo. Inst. of Tech. Bd., Colo. Concern. Roman Catholic. Home: 4700 S Fulton Ranch Blvd Unit 75 Chandler AZ 85248-5037 Office Phone: 970-491-6211. E-mail: presofc@lamar.colostate.edu.

PENLEY, VIRGINIA LONG, social worker; b. Statesville, NC, July 3, 1955; d. Robert Long and Mary Joyce Broussard; m. Jeffrey Michael Penley. AA, Mitchell C.C., 1975; BA in Social Work, Greensboro Coll., 1977. LCSW; cert. Dir. Vol. Svcs. Social worker Moses H. Cone Hosp., Greensboro, 1987—94; dir. vol. svcs. and patient rels. Women's Hosp. Greensboro, NC, 1994—. Mem.: NASW (Piedmont rep. 1991—92), N.C. Soc. Dirs. Vol. Svcs. (chair publicity 2000—, corr. sec., edn. co-chair 1997—99), N.C. Zoologica. Presbyterian. Avocations: travel, antiques, reading. Office: Women's Hosp Greensboro 801 Green Valley Rd Greensboro NC 27408 Home Phone: 336-855-0353; Office Phone: 336-832-6586. Business E-Mail: ginger.penley@mosescone.com.

PENLIDIS, ALEXANDER, chemical engineering professor; b. Kozani, Greece, Feb. 12, 1957; Diploma in engring., U. Thessaloniki, 1980; PhD in Chem. Engring., McMaster U., 1986. Rsch. assoc. Polymer Prodn. Techs., McMaster Inst., Canada, 1985-86; from asst. prof. to assoc. prof. chem. engring. U. Waterloo, Ont., Canada, 1986-90, assoc. prof. Ont., 1990—95, prof. Ont., 1995—, assoc. dir. Inst. Polymer Rsch. Ont., 1990-95, dir., 1995—, assoc. dean rsch. & grad. studies, faculty engring. Ont., 1998—2004. Can. rsch. chair in poly. engring., 2002—; cons. in field. Founding co-editor Polymer Reaction Engring. Jour., 1990-2003. Fellow Chem. Inst. Can., Can. Acad. Engring.; mem. Can. Soc. Chem. Engring. Office: Univ Waterloo Inst Polymer Rsch Chem Engring Dept Waterloo ON Canada N2L 3G1 Office Phone: 519-888-4567 x36634. Business E-Mail: penlidis@uwaterloo.ca.

PENMAN, ROBBIE MAE, volunteer, political organization worker; b. Memphis, Feb. 25, 1903; d. Robert Rudolph and Emma Jimmie Franklin; m. Edward Thaddeus Penman Sr., June 28, 1922 (dec.); children: Vincent Robert, Edward Thaddeus Jr., Wallace Abraham, Horace Eugene. Student in English and Journalism, Alleghany Coll., Meadville, Pa.; student in Bus. Adminstrn., John Hay Bus. Coll., Cleve.; student in Social Svcs., Case Western Res. U., Cleve.; student in Housing and Cmty. Devel., Cleve. State U. Social svc. outreach worker; dir. day care ctr. Fellowship Bapt. Ch., Cleve. Author: Call Me Russell, 1995. Pres. George Washington Carver Elem. PTA, Cleve., John Borroughs Elem. PTA, Ctrl. Jr. H.S. PTA, East Tech. H.S. PTA; mem. Econ. Opportunity Anti-Poverty Bd., 1962—67; v.p. Model Cities Program, 1972—77, supr. dist. connectors; organizer Cmty. Responsive Dial A Bus; mem. bd. RTA; Am. rep. World Conf. Women, Copenhagen, 1980; asst. to Rev. Donald Jacobs Cleve. Black Ch. Ptnrs. in Ecumenism; mem. Cleve. Econ. Opportunity Anti-Poverty Bd., 1962—71; bd. mem. United St. Club, 1953, Cuyahoga County Welfare Bd., 1961, Vocational Guidance Rehabilitation Ctr., 1971, Regional Transit Authority, 1976, Sr. Project Cath. Commn., 1977, Hope House, St. Citizen Drop-In Ctr., United Labor Agency, 1980, Stop and Start Multi Purpose Homeless Ctr., 1981. Recipient Outstanding Svc. honors, Rep. Louis Stokes; named Outstanding Grandparent of Yr., Ch. LDS, 2005; named to Wall of Tolerance, Montgomery, Ala., 2005. Democrat. Ch. Lds. Achievements include first congressional sr. intern. Avocations: reading, exercise. Home: 6003 Thackeray Ave Cleveland OH 44103

PENN, AUDREY S., federal agency administrator; BA, Swarthmore Coll., Pa., 1956; MD, Columbia U., NYC, 1960. Intern, asst. resident Bronx Mcpl. Hosp. Ctr., Albert Einstein Coll. Medicine, 1960—62; asst. resident in neurology, Neurol. Inst. Columbia Presbyn. Med. Ctr., NYC, 1962—64, neurologist; asst. and instr. in neurology Coll. Physicians and Surgeons, Columbia U., NYC, 1964—67, assoc. prof. neurology, 1973—82, assoc. prof. to prof. neurology, 1973—95; dep. dir. Nat. Inst. Neurol. Disorders and Stroke, NIH, 1995—, acting dir., 1998, 2001—03. Bd. dirs. Am. Bd. Psychiatry and Neurology, 1975—82, exec. com, 1981—82; mem. immunological soc. study sect. NIH, 1982—86; mem. rev. panel for rsch. tng. fellowships Howard Hughes Med. Inst., 1989—91, chair rev. panel, 1992—94; mem. nat. adv. neurol. disorders and stroke coun. NIH, 1992—95. Mem.: AAAS, Assn. Rsch. in Nervous and Mental Disease, Harvey Soc., Am. Acad. Neurology, Am. Neurol. Assn. (pres. 1994). Office: Nat Inst Neurol Disorders & Stroke Bldg 31 8A52 31 Center Dr Bethesda MD 20892-2540 Office Phone: 301-496-3167.

PENN, BUDDIE J. (B.J. PENN), civilian military employee; b. Peru, Ind. BS, Purdue U.; MS, George Washington U. Cert. Aerospace Safety U. So. Calif., Nat. Security for Sr. Officials Harvard U. Former naval aviator; EA-6B pilot, 1972; held various leadership assignments including exec. officer/commdg. officer VAQ 33; battalion officer U.S. Naval Acad.; air officer USS Am.; spl. asst. to Cheif of Naval Ops.; commdg. officer NAS N. Island, Calif.; dep. dir. Navy Office Tech. Transfer and Security Assistance; dir. internat. bus. Loral Fed. Sys., 1995—98; with Naval Electronics and Surveillance Sys. Dept. Navy, US Dept. Def., 1998, dir. indsl. base assessments, 2001—05, asst. sec. for installations & environ., 2005—. Office: US Dept Def 1000 Navy Pentagon Rm 4E739 Washington DC 20350-1000 Office Phone: 703-693-4530. Office Fax: 703-693-1165.*

PENN, J. B., economist, former federal agency administrator; b. Lynn, Ark., Dec. 18, 1944; s. Jacob Bernard and Virginia Lucille (Martin) P.; m. Martha Ann Brannon (div.); children: Penny Alane, Kristin J. Rens. BS, Ark. State U., 1965; MS, La. State U., Baton Rouge, 1967; PhD, Purdue U., 1973. Rsch. economist Econ. Rsch Svc., USDA, Baton Rouge, W. Lafayette, Ind., 1967-75, leader policy group Washington, 1975-76, dep. adminstr. for econs., 1979-81; mem. sr. staff, Coun. Econ. Advisers Exec. Office of the Pres., Washington, 1977-78; pres. Econ. Perspectives, Inc., Washington, 1981-88; sr. v.p. Sparks Commodities, Inc., Washington, 1988—2001; under sec. for farm & foreign agr. services USDA, Washington, 2001—06; chief economist Deere & Co., Moline, Ill., 2006—. Co-author: (textbook) Agriculture and Food Policy, 3d edit., 1995. Mem. adv. bd. Ctr. for Nat. Policy, Washington, 1990; bd. dirs. Found. for Devel. of Polish Agr., Warsaw, 1990, Farm Found., 1995. Mem. Am. Agrl. Econs. Assn., Am. Econs. Assn. Office: Deere & Co 1 John Deere Rd Moline IL 61265-8098

PENN, KAL (KALPEN SURESH MODI), federal official, actor; b. Montclair, NJ, Apr. 23, 1977; Degree in Sociology, UCLA, 1999. Assoc. dir. Office Pub. Liaison & Intergovernmental Affairs The White House, Washington, 2009—. Adj. faculty mem. Asian Am. Studies Program U. Pa., 2008. Actor: (films) Express: Aisle to Glory, 1998, Freshmen, 1999, American Desi, 2001, Van Wilder, 2002, Badger, 2002, Where's the Party Yaar, 2003, Malibu's Most Wanted, 2003, Love Don't Cost a Thing, 2003, Ball & Chain, 2004, Harold & Kumar Go to White Castle, 2004, Dancing in Twilight, 2005, Son of the Mask, 2005, A Lot Like Love, 2005, Sueño, 2005, Man About Town, 2006, Bachelor Party Vegas, 2006, Superman Returns, 2006, The Namesake, 2006, Epic Movie, 2007, Harold & Kumar Escape from Guantanamo Bay, 2008, Harold & Kumar Go To Amsterdam, 2008, Under New Management, 2009; (TV films) Brookfield, 1999, Cosmopolitan, 2003, Regarding Ardy, 2003, Homeland Security, 2004, Awesometown, 2005; (TV series) All About the Andersons, 2003, 24, 2007, House M.D., 2007—09, (TV appearances) Buffy the Vampire Slayer, 1999, Sabrina, the Teenage Witch, 2000, Spin City, 2000, That's Life, 2001, Angel, 2001, ER, 2001, NYPD Blue, 2001, The Agency, 2001, Independent Lens, 2003, Tru Calling, 2003, Law & Order: Special Victims Unit, 2007; actor, assoc. prodr. (films) Hector, 2002, actor, exec. prodr. Van Wilder 2: The Rise of Taj, 2006. Office: The White House 1600 Pennsylvania Ave NW Washington DC 20500 also: c/o Artistry Mgmt 525 Westbourne Dr Los Angeles CA 90048

PENN, MARK J., public relations executive, pollster, political strategist; b. 1954; m. Nancy Jacobson. Grad., Harvard U., Cambridge, Mass., 1976. Co-founder, pres. Penn, Schoen & Berland Associates, NYC, 1975—; worldwide pres., CEO Burson-Marsteller, NYC, 2005—. Strategic cons. Ford Motor Co., Merck, Verizon, BP, McDonald's, Microsoft Corp., 1998—. Author: Microtrends: The Small Forces Changing the World; contbr. columns to The NY Times, The Washington Post, others; polit. analyst: CNN, Fox News, others. Polit. advisor Pres. Bill Clinton, Prime Minister Tony Blair, NYC Mayor Michael Bloomberg; chief campaign strategist US Senator Hillary Clinton, 2000—08. Recipient Pollster of Yr., Am. Assn. Political Cons., 1996, 2000; named one of The 50 Most Powerful People in DC, GQ mag., 2007; fellow, New Politics Inst. Democrat. Achievements include advising more than 25 elected leaders in the United States, Asia, Latin America and Europe. Office: Burson-Marsteller 230 Park Ave S New York NY 10003-1556 also: Penn Shoen & Berland Associates 245 E 92nd St New York NY 10128 Office Phone: 212-614-4446, 212-534-4000. Office Fax: 212-598-5679, 212-360-7423. Business E-Mail: markjpenn@bm.com.*

PENN, SEAN, actor; b. Burbank, Calif., Aug. 17, 1960; s. Leo and Eileen (Ryan) P.; m. Madonna Louise Ciccone, Aug. 16, 1985 (div. Jan. 10, 1989); m. Robin Wright Penn, April 27, 1996; 2 children: Dylan Frances, Hopper Jack. Actor: (plays) Heartland, 1981, Slab Boys, 1983, Hurlyburly, 1988; (films) Taps, 1981, Fast Times at Ridgemont High, 1982, Summerspell, 1983, Bad Boys, 1983, Crackers, 1984, Racing with the Moon, 1984, The Falcon and the Snowman, 1985, At Close Range, 1986, Shanghai Surprise, 1986, Color Blue, 1988, Colors, 1988, Judgment in Berlin, 1988, Casualties of War, 1989, We're No Angels, 1989, State of Grace, 1990, Carlito's Way, 1993, Dead Man Walking, 1995 (Golden Globe award nominee for best actor, 1995, Best Actor award Berlin Film Festival, 1996, Acad. award nominee for best actor, 1996), The Game, 1997, U Turn, 1997, Hugo Pool, 1997, The Thin Red Line, 1998, Hurly Burly, 1998, As I Lay Dying, 1998, Up at the Villa, 2000, Before Night Falls, 2000, The Weight of Water, 2000, I Am Sam, 2001, It's All About Love, 2003, Mystic River, 2003, (Golden Globe for best dramatic actor, 2004, Acad. Award for best actor, 2004, Golden Satellite award, 2004, London Critics Circle Film awards, 2004, Screen Actors Guild Award nomination for best actor, 2004), 21 Grams, 2003, The Assassination of Richard Nixon, 2004, The Interpreter, 2005, All the King's Men, 2006 (voice) Persepolis, 2007, Milk, 2008 (Best Actor NY Film Critics Cir., 2008, Boston Soc. Film Critics, 2008, Nat. Soc. Film Critics, 2009, 2008 Best Actor, Critics' Choice award, Broadcast Film Critics Assn., 2009, Best Actor, LA Film Critics Assn., 2009, Outstanding Performance by a Male Actor in a Leading Role, SAG, 2009, Acad. award for Best Actor in a Leading Role, 2009); actor, prodr.: Loved, 1997; actor, exec. prodr.: She's So Lovely, 1997; dir., writer: The Indian Runner, 1991; dir., prodr., writer: The Crossing Guard, 1995; dir., prodr., writer, actor: Into the Wild, 2007; dir., prodr.: The Pledge, 2001; actor (TV movies) Hellinger's Law, 1981, The Killing of Randy Webster, 1981. Recipient John Steinbeck award, San Francisco Chronicle, 2004, Desert Palm Achievement award, Palm Springs Internat. Film Soc., 2009. Office: Ste 2500 2049 Century Park E Los Angeles CA 90067-3127*

PENN, STANLEY WILLIAM, journalist; b. NYC, Jan. 12, 1928; s. Murray and Lillian (Richman) P.; m. Esther Aronson, July 12, 1952; children— Michael, Laurel. Student, Bklyn. Coll., 1945-47; B. Journalism, U. Mo., 1949. With Wall St. Jour., 1952-90; investigative reporter N.Y. bur., 1957-90. (Co-recipient Pulitzer prize for nat. reporting 1967). Home: 380 Riverside Dr New York NY 10025-1858 Personal E-mail: estan380@gmail.com.

PENN, WILLIAM M., finance educator, consultant; b. Balt., Sept. 16, 1942; s. William Melvin and June D. Penn; m. Marcia W. Woodward, Dec. 31, 1984; children: Emily G., Josh W. BA, McDaniel Coll., Westminster, Md., 1964; PhD, Duke U., Durham, NC, 1969. Fin. analyst Ford Motor Co., Dearborn, Mich., 1970—73; asst. prof. economics Loyola Coll., Balt., 1973—80; prof. economics & bus. Belhaven Coll., Jackson, Miss., 1981—. Pres. Citizens League Balt., 1975—78. Capt. US Army, 1968—70, Vietnam, Ft. Belvoir, Va. Decorated Bronze Star, Commendation medal US Army. Presbyterian. Home: 404 Eastpointe CV Madison MS 39110 Office: Belhaven Coll 1500 Peachtree St Jackson MS 39202 Office Fax: 601-968-9998. Business E-Mail: wpenn@belhaven.edu.

PENNELL, DANIEL MARK, researcher; b. Valparaiso, Ind., July 14, 1971; s. Lawrence Foster Pennell and Nancy Lea Rogan. BA, Ind. U., Bloomington, Ind., 1989—93, MA, 1997—99, MLS, 1999—2001. Bibliographer for Russian, east European, and Germanic studies U. of Pitts., Pitts., 2001—; asst. slavic bibliographer Ind. U., Bloomington, Ind., 1996—2001; program mgr. for edn. US Peace Corps., Saratov, Russia, 1995—96. Asst. dir. Inst. for the Study of Russian Edn., Bloomington, Ind., 1996—98; reviews editor Balkan Academic News, 2002—04, East European Politics and Societies, 2004—. Fgn. Lang. Area Studies fellowship, Ind. U., 1997-2000. Mem.: Southeastern European Studies Assn., Soc. for Romanian Studies, Am. Libr. Assoication, Am. Assn. for the Advancement of Slavic Studies, Phi Beta Kappa. Achievements include development of Slavic, East European, and Germanic Studies Research Collections; research in Modern Russian and Eastern European History. Office: University of Pittsburgh 3960 Forbes Avenue G-20X Hillman Library Pittsburgh PA 15260 Home: 1517 S Negley Ave Pittsburgh PA 15217 Personal E-mail: pennell@pitt.edu.

PENNELL, DANNY JOE, social worker; b. Aug. 31, 1945; s. Donald Louis and Lela Geneva (Murray) P.; m. Janis Evelyn Reynolds, Dec. 26, 1984; children: Joel, Jason, Jaime, Chad, Colter. BA, U. Ill., 1970, MSW, 1972. Social worker Dept. Child and Family Svcs., Danville, Ill., 1971-72, social worker supr. Rockford, Ill., 1972-74; instr. Rockford Coll., 1977-78; pres., CEO Goldie B. Floberg Ctr., Rockton, Ill., 1974—. Exec. dir. Found. Ft. Lewis Coll., Durango, Colo., 1986-87; bd. dirs. Winnebago County Child Protection Assn., Rockford, 1974-76; bd. dirs., mem. legis. affairs com., chmn. mental health devel. disabilities com., spl. edn. com. Child Care Assn. Ill., Springfield, Ill., 1980—; mem. child welfare adv. com. Ill. Dept. Children and Family Services; mem. devel. disabilities adv. com. Dept. Mental Health, mem. children's svcs. subcom.; cons. in field. Bd. dirs., v.p. H.O.P.E. Found., 2001—. Grantee Ill. Dept. Children and Family Svcs., 1970-72. Mem. Nat. Soc. Fund Raising Execs. (bd. dirs., sec. 1984-85, v.p. 1986-87), Nat. Soc. Fund Raising Dirs. (pres. bd. dirs. 1988, v.p. 1987, v.p. 1986, bd. mem. various coms. 1984, 85), Am. Assn. Mental Deficiency, Nat. Assn. Retarded Citizens, Coordinating Council for Handicapped Children, Nat. Assn. Devel. Disabilities Mgrs., Roscoe C. of C. (bd. dirs. 2000—). Home: 12080 N Ledges Dr Roscoe IL 61073-9600 Office: Goldie B Floberg Ctr PO Box 346 Rockton IL 61072-0346 Office Phone: 815-624-8431. Personal E-mail: dpenn58@aol.com.

PENNELL, WILLIAM BROOKE, lawyer; b. Mineral Ridge, Ohio, Oct. 28, 1935; s. George Albert and Katherine Nancy (McMeen) P. AB, Harvard U., 1957; LLB cum laude, U. Pa., 1961; m. Peggy Polsky, June 17, 1958; children: Katherine, Thomas Brooke. Bar: NY 1963, US Dist. Ct. (so. dist.) NY 1964, US Dist. Ct. (ea. dist.) NY 1964, US Ct. Appeals (2d cir.) 1966, US Ct. Claims 1966, US Tax Ct. 1967, US Supreme Ct. 1967. Clk. US Dist. Ct., (so. dist.) NY, NYC, 1961-62; assoc. Shearman & Sterling, NYC, 1962-71, ptnr., 1971-91. Recent case editor U. Pa. Law Rev., 1960-61. Bd. govs. Bklyn. Heights Assn., 1964-74, pres., 1969-71; chmn. bd. Willoughby House Settlement, 1972-95. Served with US Army, 1957. Fellow Salzburg Seminar Am. Studies, 1965. Mem. Rembrandt Club. Home and Office: PO Box 249 Canaan NY 12029-0249

PENNER, DUSTIN, professional hockey player; b. Winkler, Man., Can., Sept. 28, 1982; Attended, U. Maine, 2002—04. Left wing Cin. Mighty Ducks, 2004—05, Portland Pirates, 2005—06, Anaheim Ducks, 2005—07, Edmonton Oilers, 2007—. Named to All-Tournament Team, NCAA, 2004. Achievements include being a member of Stanley Cup Champion Anaheim Ducks, 2007. Office: Edmonton Oilers Hockey Club 11230 - 110 St Edmonton AB T5G 3H7 Canada*

PENNER, KEITH, former Canadian government official; b. Sask., Can., May 1, 1933; BA, U. Alberta, Can., 1955; MDiv, Toronto U., 1959; MEd, U. Ottawa, Can., 1971. Secondary sch. tchr., Dryden, Ont., Canada, 1961-68; mem. parliament Cochrane-Superior, Ont., 1968-88; mem. Can. Transp. Agy., Ottawa, 1988—2003; pres. dispute resolution Keith Penner & Assocs., Ottawa, 2003—. Past parliamentary sec. to Min. of State Sci. and Tech., past parliamentary sec. to Min. of Indian Affairs and No. Devel., past chmn. Standing Com. on Indian Affairs and No. Devel.; vis. fellow Sch. of Polit. Sci., Queen's U., 1987-88; chmn. Chartered Inst. Logistics and Transport, N.Am., 2004. Fellow: Chartered Inst. Logistics and Transport (chmn. 2004—08); mem.: Lic. Appeal Tribunal Ont. Office: Ottawa ON Canada Office Phone: 613-828-3067. Personal E-mail: keith.penner@rogers.com.

PENNER, REGINALD MARK, chemistry professor; b. Steinbach, Manitoba, Canada, Feb. 5, 1960; m. Theresa McIntire, July 14, 1995. BA in Chemistry, Gustavus Adolphus Coll., St. Peter, Minn., 1983; PhD, Tex. A & M U., Coll. Sta., 1987. Prof. U. Calif., Irvine, 1990—. Office: UCI Chemistry Univ Calif Irvine CA 92697-2025 Office Fax: 949-824-8571. Business E-Mail: rmpenner@uci.edu.

PENNER, STANFORD SOL, engineering educator; b. Unna, Germany, July 5, 1921; arrived in US, 1936, naturalized, 1943; s. Heinrich and Regina (Saal) P.; m. Beverly Preston, Dec. 28, 1942; children: Merilynn Jean, Robert Clark. BS, Union Coll., 1942; MS, U. Wis., 1943, PhD, 1946; Dr. rer. nat. (hon.), Technische Hochschule Aachen, Germany, 1981. Rsch. assoc. Allegany Ballistics Lab., Cumberland, Md., 1944-45; rsch. scientist Standard Oil Devel. Co., Esso Labs., Linden, NJ, 1946; sr. rsch. engr. Jet Propulsion Lab., Pasadena, Calif., 1947-50; mem. faculty Calif. Inst. Tech., 1950-63, prof. divsn. engring., jet propulsion, 1957-63; dir. rsch. and engring. divsn. Inst. Def. Analyses, Washington, 1962-64; prof. engring. physics, chmn. dept. aerospace and mech. engring. U. Calif., San Diego, 1964-68, vice chancellor for acad. affairs, 1968-69, dir. Inst. for Pure and Applied Phys. Scis., 1968-71, dir. Energy Ctr., 1973-91, disting. prof. engring. physics emeritus, 1991—. Bd. dirs. Optodyne Corp.; US mem. adv. group aero. rsch. and devel. NATO, 1952-68, chmn. combustion and propulsion panel, 1958-60; mem. adv. com. engring. scis. USAF-Office Sci. Rsch., 1961-65; mem. subcom. on combustion NACA, 1954-58; mem. rsch. adv. com. on air-breathing engines NASA, 1962-64; mem. coms. on gas dynamics and edn. Internat. Acad. Astronautics, 1969-80; nat. lectr. Sigma Xi, 1977-79; chmn. fossil energy rsch. working group Dept. Energy, 1978-82, chmn. advanced fuel cell commercialization working group, 1979-85; mem. assembly engring. NAE, 1978-82; chmn. NAS-NRC U.S. Nat. Com. IIASA, 1978-82; mem. commn. engring. tech. sys. NRC, 1982-84; spl. guest Internat. Coal Sci. Confs., 1983, 85, 87, 89, 91; mentor Def. Sci. Studies Group, 1985-93; chmn. studies mcpl. waste incineration NSF, 1988-89, Calif. Coun. Sci. Tech., 1992; pub. info. adv. com. Nat. Acad. Engring., 1994-98, Ind. Commn. on Environ. Edn., 1995-97, Environ. Literacy Coun., 1998-2005; sci. adv. bd., San Diego County, 1997—, chair, 2004-07. Author: Chemical Reactions in Flow Systems, 1955, Chemistry Problems in Jet Propulsion, 1957, Quantitative Molecular Spectroscopy and Gas Emissivities, 1959, Chemical Rocket Propulsion and Combustion Research, 1962, Thermodynamics, 1968, Radiation and Reentry, 1968; sr. author: Energy, Vol. I (Demands, Resources, Impact, Technology and Policy), 1974, 81, Energy, Vol. II (Non-nuclear Energy Technologies), 1975, 77, 84, Energy, Vol. III (Nuclear Energy and Energy Policies), 1976; editor: Chemistry of Propellants, 1960, Advanced Propulsion Techniques, 1961, Detonations and Two-Phase Flow, 1962, Combustion and Propulsion, 1963, Advances in Tactical Rocket Propulsion, 1968, In Situ Shale Oil Recovery, 1975, New Sources of Oil and Gas, 1982, Coal Combustion and Applications, 1984, Advanced Fuel Cells, 1986, Coal Gasification: Direct Applications and Syntheses of Chemicals and Fuels, 1987, CO2 Emissions and Climate Change, 1991, Commercialization of Fuel Cells, 1995, Advanced Nuclear Techs., 1998; assoc. editor Jour. Chem. Physics, 1953-56; founding editor Jour. Quantitative Spectroscopy and Radiative Transfer, 1960-92, Jour. Def. Rsch., 1963-67, Energy (The Internat. Jour.), 1975-98; sect. editor Energy and Power Systems, Ency. Phys. Sci. and Tech., 1998-2002. Recipient spl. award People-to-People Program, pub. svc. award U. Calif., San Diego, N. Manson medal Internat. Colloquia on Gasdynamics of Explosions and Reactive Systems, 1979, internat. Columbus award Internat. Inst. Comm., Genoa, Italy, 1981, disting. assoc. award US Dept. Energy, 1990, Edward Teller award for def. of freedom, 1997, Rockwell medal, 2003. Fellow Am. Phys. Soc., Optical Soc. Am., AAAS, NY Acad. Scis., AIAA (dir. 1964-66, past chmn. com., G. Edward Pendray award 1975, Thermophysics award 1983, Energy Systems award 1983), Am. Acad. Arts and Scis.; mem. NAE (Founders award, 2007), Internat. Acad. Astronautics, World Level Hall of Fame for Engring., Sci. and Tech., Am. Chem. Soc., Sigma Xi. Home: 5912 Avenida Chamnez La Jolla CA 92037-7402 Office: U Calif San Diego 9500 Gilman Dr La Jolla CA 92093-0411 Home Phone: 858-456-9421; Office Phone: 858-534-4284. Business E-Mail: spenner@ucsd.edu.

PENNER, SUSANNE MARY, communications executive; arrived in US, 1974; d. Franklyn Thomas and Paulette Penner; BS, Calif. Poly. State U., San Luis Obispo, 1998. With Weber Group, Palo Alto, Calif., 1998—99; rschr. Egon Zehnder Internat., Palo Alto, 1999—2000; mktg. mgr. Silicon Graphics, Mountain View, Calif., Trolltech, Palo Alto, Calif.; dir. Oracle, Redwood Shores, Calif. Author (contributor): (book) After the Morning Calm, 2002. Vol. Big Bros. Big Sisters, San Francisco, 1998—2003. Democrat-Npl. Avocations: travel, writing, reading. Office: Oracle 500 Oracle Pkwy Redwood City CA 94065 Personal E-mail: susanne.penner@oracle.com.

PENNEY, CHARLES RAND, lawyer, civic worker; b. Buffalo, July 26, 1923; s. Charles Patterson and Gretchen (Rand) P. BA, Yale U., 1945; JD, U. Va., 1951; DFA (hon.), SUNY, 1995, Niagara U., 2007. Bar: Md. 1952, NY 1958, U.S. Supreme Ct. 1958. Law sec. to US Dist. Ct. Judge W.C. Coleman, Balt., 1951-52; dir. devel. office Children's Hosp., Buffalo, 1952-54; sales mgr. Amherst Mfg. Corp., Williamsville, NY, 1954—56, Delevan Electronics Corp., East Aurora, NY; mem. firm Penney & Penney, Buffalo, 1958-61; pvt. practice Niagara County, NY, 1961—. Exhbns. include Mus. Modern Art, NYC, 1962, Whitney Mus. Am. Art, NYC, 1963, 79, 80, Burchfield-Penney Art Ctr., 1973, 92-2003, Meml. Art Gallery, Rochester, 1976, 78, 83, 88, U. Iowa, 1978, Columbus Gallery Fine Arts, Ohio, 1976, 78. Hon. life trustee Burchfield-Penney Art Ctr.; adv. bd. Found. Study of Arts and Crafts Movement at Roycroft; hon. bd. dirs. Buffalo-Lille/France Assn., Inc. 2d lt. U.S. Army, 1943-46. Recipient Pres.'s Disting. Svc. award Buffalo State Coll., 1991, Disting. Svc. to Culture award Coll. Arts and Scis., SUNY, Potsdam, 1983; named Disting. fellow Cultural Studies of the Burchfield-Penney Art Ctr., 1994, Outstanding Individual Philanthropist, Nat. Soc. Fund Raising Execs. Western NY, 1996, Individual Patron of the Arts award Buffalo and Erie County Arts Coun. and Buffalo C. of C., 1997, Citation for Outstanding Achievements and Svc. to Lockport Cmty., NY State Assembly, 1997; awarded Key to City of Lockport, 1997; named to Lockport Hist. Walk of Fame, 1999. Mem. AARP, YWCA Niagra (life), Albright-Knox Art Gallery Buffalo (life), Buffalo Mus. Sci. (Life), Buffalo and Erie County Hist. Soc. (life, Red Jacket award 2000), Niagara County Hist. Soc. (life), Old Ft. Niagara (life), Buffalo Soc. Artists (hon. trustee), Hist. Lockport (life), Landmark Soc. Western NY (life), Hist. Lewiston (life), Friends of U. Rochester Librs. (life) Meml. Art Gallery U. Rochester (hon. bd. mgrs., hon. life), Winslow Homer Soc. of Dirs. Cir. (hon. life), Smithsonian Instn. (benefactors cir.), Rochester Hist. Soc. (life), Am. Hist. Print Collectors Soc. (life), Burchfield Homestead Soc. (hon. life), Charles E. Burchfield Nature and Art Ctr., Archives Am. Art, Mark Twain Soc. (hon.), U. Rochester's Pres.'s Soc. (hon. life), U. Iowa's Pres.'s Club (hon. life), Va. Law Found., Nat. Geog. Soc. (life), World's Fair Collectors Soc., Hist. Soc. of Tonawandas (life), Pres.'s Cir. Buffalo State Coll. (hon. life), Buffalo State Alumni Assn. (life), Yale Sailing Assocs., Yale Glee Club Assocs., Peanut Pals, Grolier Club, Pan Am. Expo Collectors Soc., Buffalo Indsl. Heritage Com., Roycrofters-at-Large Assn. (life), Arctic Cir. Club, Order of the Alaska Walrus, Automobile Club (Lockport), Niagara County Antiques Club (hon.), Rochester Art Club (hon. life), Fine Arts Mus. San Francisco (patron), De Young & Legion of Honor Museums (patron), U. Cir., SUNY Buffalo, Chi Psi, Phi Alpha Delta. Office: 538 Bewley Building Lockport NY 14094-2944 *I have tried to strive for excellence in whatever I undertake, be it small or large. What success I may have achieved has required initiative, imagination, and dedication to the task at hand. Satisfaction comes from the hard work that leads to an objective. In all that I do I adhere to the Golden Rule and to fairness, honesty, and understanding in human relationships. I try to maintain a sense of humor at all times. And I enjoy living in a small community because it is from such areas that the strength of America comes.*

PENNEY, SHERRY HOOD, academic administrator, consultant; b. Marlette, Mich., Sept. 4, 1937; d. Terrance and B. Jean (Stoutenburg) Hood; m. Carl Murray Penney, July 8, 1961 (div. 1978); children: Michael Murray, Jeffrey Hood; m. James Duane Livingston, Mar. 30, 1985. BA, Albion Coll., 1959; MA, U. Mich., 1961; PhD, SUNY, Albany, 1972; LLD (hon.), Albion Coll., 1989; degree (hon.), Quincy Coll., 1999. Vis. asst. prof. Union Coll., Schenectady, NY, 1972-73; assoc. higher edn. NY State Edn. Dept., Albany, 1973-76; assoc. provost Yale U., New Haven, 1976-82; vice chancellor acad. programs, policy and planning SUNY System, Albany, 1982-88; acting pres. SUNY, Plattsburgh, 1986-87; chancellor U. Mass., Boston, 1988-95; pres. U. Mass. Sys., Boston, 1995; chancellor U. Mass. Boston, 1996-2000, endowed prof., 2001—. Chmn., bd. dirs. Nat. Higher Edn. Mgmt. Sys., Boulder, Colo., 1985-87; mem. commn. on higher edn. New Eng. Assn. Schs. and Colls., Boston, 1979-82, Mid. States Assn. Schs. and Colls., Phila., 1986-88; mem. commn. on women Am. Coun. Edn., Washington, 1979-81, commn. on govt. rels., 1990-94; bd. dirs. NSTAR, South Shore Hosp. Author: Patrician in Politics, 1974; co-author (with James D. Livingston) A Very Dangerous Woman: Martha Wright and Women's Rights, 2004; editor: Women and Management in Higher Education, 1975; contbr. articles to profl. jours. Nat. adv. com. Nat. Initiative for Women in Higher Edn., 2001—05; active Internat. Trade Task Force, 1994—96; exec. com. Challenge to Leadership, 1988, chair, 1995—98; trustee Berkeley Div. Sch., Yale U., 1978—82, John F. Kennedy Libr. Found., 1988—2001; chair Met. Affairs Coalition, 1999—2001; bd. trustees New Eng. Aquarium, 1990—2004; chair The Ednl. Resource Inst., 1996—; bd. visitors WEIU, 2002—06; bd. dirs. HERS, 1992—, Mary Baker Eddy Libr., Boston, 2001—06, Albany Symphony Orch., 1982—88, U. Mass. Found., 1988—2000, Mcpl. Rsch. Bur., Boston, 1990—2001, New Eng. Coun., 1990—2000, Greater Boston C. of C., 1989—2002, Met. Affairs Coalition, Greater Boston One to One Leadership Coun., 1990—2000, NASULGC Commn. Urban Affairs, 1990—2000, The Environ. Bus. Coun., 1991—97, South Shore Hosp., Mass., 2006—. Recipient Disting. Alumna award Albion Coll., 1978, Disting. Citizen award for racial harmony Black/White Boston, 1994, Am. Coun. on Edn./Nat. Identification Program award, Mass., Leadership award, 1995, New Eng. Women's Leadership award, 1996, Pinnacle award for Lifetime Achievement Greater Boston C. of C., 1998, Abigail Adams award, Mass. Women's Polit. Caucus, 2003. Mem. Comml. Club (Boston). Unitarian Universalist. Office: U Mass Boston 100 Morrissey Blvd Boston MA 02125-3300 Office Phone: 617-287-3890.

PENNIMAN, CLAYTON, biology professor; b. Boston, Mar. 24, 1952; m. Chris Emerich; 1 child, Eric. BS in Biology, U. Maine, Orono, 1973; PhD in Botany, U. NH, Durham, 1983. Rsch. prof. U. NH, Providence, 1984—90; asst. program mgr. Narragansett Bay Project, Providence, 1990—92; prof. dept. biology Ctrl. Conn. State U., New Britain, 1992—. Office: Ctrl Conn State Univ 1615 Stanley St New Britain CT 06053 Office Fax: 860-832-2658. Business E-Mail: penniman@ccsu.edu.

PENNIMAN, NICHOLAS GRIFFITH, IV, retired newspaper publisher; b. Balt., Mar. 7, 1938; s. Nicholas Griffith Penniman III and Esther Cox Lony (Wight) Keeney; m. Linda Jane Simmons, Feb. 4, 1967; children: Rebecca Helmle, Nicholas G. V. AB, Princeton U., 1960; MA, Washington U., 1999. Asst. bus. mgr. Ill. State Jour. Register, Springfield, 1964-69, bus. mgr., 1969-75; asst. gen. mgr. St. Louis Post-Dispatch, 1975-84, gen. mgr., 1984-86, pub., 1986-99; sr. v.p. newspapers ops. Pulitzer Pub. Co., 1986-99; pres., CEO Pulitzer Comm. Newspapers Inc., 1997-99; chmn. bd. Penniman & Browne, Inc., Balt., 2001—08. Chmn. Downtown St. Louis, Inc., 1988-90, Mo. Health and Ednl. Facilities Adminstrn., 1982-85, Ill. State Fair Bd., Springfield, 1973-75, Forest Pk. Forever, 1991-93, Pks. and Open Space Task Force St. Louis 2004, 1996-00, St. Louis Sports Com., 1992-93, Gateway Pks. and Trls. 2004, 1999-04; pres. Caring Found. Children, 1988-91; trustee St. Louis Country Day Sch., 1983-86, Nat. Recreation Found., 2003—, Merc. Libr. St. Louis, 1997-00; bd. dirs. Mo. Coalition for Environment, 1997-2000, Randall Rsch. Ctr., Pineland, Fla., 2001—, Friends of Rookery Bay, 2004—09; chmn. bd. Am. Rivers, 2004-06, Conservancy of SW Fla., 2007—; mem. Sons of Am. Revolution, 1982-, Collier County Environ. Adv. Coun., Fla., 2005-09. With US Army, 1962—67. Mem.: Rolling Rock Club, Elkridge Club, Noonday Club (pres. 1994), Grey Oaks Country Club. Home: 611 Portside Dr Naples FL 34103-4118 E-mail: ngpiv@aol.com.

PENNINGER, FRIEDA ELAINE, retired literature educator; b. Marion, NC, Apr. 11, 1927; d. Fred Hoyle and Lena Frances (Young) Penninger. AB, U. N.C., Greensboro, 1948; MA, Duke U., 1950, PhD, 1961. Copywriter Sta. WSJS, Winston-Salem, NC, 1948-49; asst. prof. English Flora Macdonald Coll., Red Springs, NC, 1950-51; tchr. English Barnwell, SC, 1951-52, Brunswick, Ga., 1952-53; instr. English U. Tenn., Knoxville, 1953-56; instr., asst. prof. Woman's Coll., U. N.C., Greensboro, 1956-58, 60-63; asst. prof., assoc. prof. U. Richmond (Va.), 1963-71; chair. dept. English Westhampton Coll., Richmond, 1971-78; prof. English U. Richmond, 1971-91, Bostwick prof. English, 1987-91, ret., 1991. Author: William Caxton, 1979, Chaucer's "Troilus and Criseyde" and "The Knight's Tale": Fictions Used, 1993, (novel) Look at Them, 1990; compiler, editor: English Drama to 1660, 1976; editor: Festschrift for Prof. Marguerite Roberts, 1976. Fellow Southeastern Inst. of Mediaeval and Renaissance Studies, 1965, 67, 69. Mem.: Friends of The Libr. U. NC Greensboro. Democrat. Presbyterian. Home: 2701 Camden Rd Greensboro NC 27403-1438

PENNINGTON, AUBREY EL, director; s. Elhanan and Rosie Mae Pennington; m. Kathy Lee Alstott, Dec. 28, 1985; children: Zachary El, Tyler Ray. BS, Campbellsville U., 1993; MA, Western Ky. U., 1999; Rank I, Union Coll., 2002. Cert. provisional secondary tchr. Ky. Dept. Edn., 1994, curriculum cons. Ky. Dept. Edn., 2005. History/social studies tchr. Casey Co. Pub. Schs., Liberty, Ky., 1993—99; region six social studies cons. Ky. Dept. Edn., Corbin, 2000—03; curriculum specialist Pulaski Co. Pub. Schs., Somerset, Ky., 2003—. Program cons. Am. Legacies Fed. History Grant, Frankfort, Ky., 2003—; mid. sch. social studies textbook editor McGraw-Hill Publishers, Inc., Englewood, NJ, 2005; vol. hist. interpreter Stones River Nat. Battlefield Pk., Murfreesboro, Tenn., 2006—; vol. oral historian U. Tex. Tech: Vietnam Oral History Project, Austin, 2005—. Mem.: Ky. Assn. Sch. Adminstrs. (assoc.), Assn. Supr. for Curriculum Devel. (assoc.), Ky. Assn. Tchrs. of History (assoc.), Ky. Coun. for Social Studies (assoc.), Nat. History in Edn. Assn. (assoc.), Am. Hist. Assn. (assoc.), Ky. Hist. Soc. (assoc.). Avocations: local historical research, photography, hiking. Personal E-mail: history2234@yahoo.com.

PENNINGTON, CHAD (JAMES CHADWICK PENNINGTON), professional football player; b. Knoxville, Tenn., June 26, 1976; s. Elwood and Denise Pennington; m. Robin Hampton; children: Cole, Luke. BA in Broadcast Jour., Marshall U., Huntington, W.Va., 2000. Quarterback NY Jets, 2000—08, Miami Dolphins, 2008—. Co-founder Share Your Soles Charity, 2003—. Named NFL Comeback Player of Yr., AP, 2006, 2008; finalist Rhodes Scholar. Achievements include setting Marshall University records at quarterback for touchdown passes & passing yards; setting the NY Jets team record for passer rating (104.2), 2002. Office: Miami Dolphins 7500 SW 30th St Davie FL 33314*

PENNINGTON, JODIE A., education outreach educator; b. Danville, Ky., Oct. 27, 1949; s. Emmett Clair and Edna Davis Pennington; m. Melinda Snider Pennington, June 10, 1972; children: Sara E., Ellen M. Pennington Steinmiller. BS, Western Ky. U., Bowling Green, 1971; MS, U. Ill., Urbana-Champaign, 1974, PhD, 1976. Asst. prof. animal sci. U. Wisconsin-River Falls, 1976—81, Purdue U., West Lafayette, Ind., 1981—85; asst. to assoc. prof. agr. Western Ky. U., Bowling Green, 1986—92; prof./dairy specialist Univ Ark. Coop Ext. Svc., Little Rock, 1993—. Contbr. more than 400 articles to profl. jours. Active United Meth. Ch., Conway, Ark., 1993—. Capt. USAR, 1971—83. Rsch. grantee, 1976—92, various grants, 1993—. Mem.: Nat. Mastitis Coun., Dairy Shrine (state coord. 2000—), Am. Dairy Sci. Assn. (3 com. chairmanships, bd. dirs. So. region), Am. Dairy Sci. Assn. Found. (charter mem.), Holstein Assn. Am., Ark. Assn. Registered Profl. Animal Scientists (pres. 1998—99), Ark. Assn. Coop. Ext. Specialists (pres., bd. mem. 1998—2002), Omicron Delta Kappa (life), Epsilon Sigma Phi (life), Gamma Sigma Delta (life), Sigma Xi (life), Phi Eta Sigma (life; advisor 1981—86), Alpha Gamma Rho (life; chpt. advisor 1976—81, Cert. of Merit 1981). Methodist. Avocations: gardening, landscaping, cattle and goat shows. Office: Univ Arkansas Coop Ext Svc 2301 S Univ Ave PO Box 391 Little Rock AR 72203 Home Phone: 501-336-8986; Office Phone: 501-671-2190. Office Fax: 501-671-2185. Business E-Mail: jpennington@uaex.edu.

PENNINGTON, JOHN ROBERT, biology educator, department chairman; b. East Cleveland, Ohio, May 7, 1950; s. William E. and Frances S. Pennington; m. Heather A. Pennington, May 29, 1993; children: Nathan, Michael, Gabrielle. AA, Lakeland Cmty. Coll., Kirtland, Ohio, 1976; BE magna cum laude, Lake Erie Coll., Painesville, Ohio, 1978. Cert. tchr. biology, sci., grades 7-12 Ohio. Sci. tchr. Willowick Jr. High, Ohio, 1978—82; biology tchr. Willoughby South High, Ohio, 1983—, chair sci. dept., 2001—. Staff sgt. USAF, 1971—75. Recipient Vietnam Svc. medal, USAF, 1973, Adell Knight Tchr. Excellence award, 2003, Tchr. Excellence award, Berlin Family Found., 2003. Avocations: travel, camping, nature photography. Home: 30214 Mildred St Willowick OH 44095 Office: Willoughby South HS 5900 Shankland Blvd Willoughby OH 44094 Office Phone: 440-975-3648. Personal E-mail: hjpenn@adelphia.net, hjpenn@roadrunner.com.

PENNINGTON, KAREN HARDER, lawyer; b. Amarillo, Tex., June 7, 1956; d. Alvin L. and Rosemary Herskowitz Harder; BS in Biology, W. Tex. State U., 1977; JD, U. Tex., 1986. Bar: Calif. 1986, Tex. 1998, US Patent and Trademark Office 1993, Hopi Tribal Ct. 1993. Assoc. atty. Thelen, Marrin, Johnson & Bridges, LA, 1986—89, Quinn, Emanuel & Urquhart, LA, 1989—91, Crosby, Heafey, Roach & May, LA, 1991—92; atty. Law Office of Karen H. Pennington, Long Beach, Calif., 1993—97, Cath. Charities Immigration Counseling Svcs., Dallas, 1998—2000; immigration atty. Law Office of Karen H. Pennington, Dallas, 2000—; of counsel Masih V. Mukasey. Recipient cover story, Sept. 9 issue, Tex. Lawyer mag., 2002. Mem.: Dallas Bar Assn., LA County Bar Assn., Tex. Bar Assn., Calif. Bar Assn., Am. Immigration Lawyers Assn., North Tex. Coalition Just Peace, United For Peace and Justice, Dallas Peace Ctr. Roman Catholic. Achievements include representation of post-Sept. 11 immigration/national security detainees both before the courts and in FBI interrogations. Office: Law Office of Karen H Pennington Ste 410 701 Commerce St Dallas TX 75202 Office Phone: 214-741-7711. Office Fax: 214-741-7733. Business E-Mail: penningtonlaw@yahoo.com.

PENNINGTON, ROBERT MICHAEL, marketing professional, consultant, communications educator, consultant; b. Chgo., Oct. 22, 1948; s. Charles Sheldon and Marcella Mary (Crossen) P.; m. Carol Sue-Chen Chang, Jan. 29, 1994. BA, U. Wis., Whitewater, 1981, MS, 1984; PhD, U. Wis., 1991. Advt. coord. Johnson Hill Press, Fort Atkinson, Wis., 1984-85; cons., 1985—; project asst. U. Wis., Madison, 1986-90; asst. prof. U. Okla., Norman, 1990-92, U. Tex., Arlington, 1992-98, N.Mex. State U., Las Cruces, 1998-2001; assoc. prof. Nat. Chung Hsing U., Taichung, Taiwan, 2003—05. Adv. com. Polit. Comm. Ctr., U. Okla., 1990-92. Bus. mgr. Jour. of Advt., 2001-02; contbr. articles to profl. jours. Vice chmn. Bd. Adjustment, Duncanville, Tex., 1995—98; co-chair Alliance for Responsible Growth, Las Cruces, N.Mex., 2005—07; assoc. prof. Fo Guang U. Jiaosi, Taiwan, 2008—. With US Army, 1973—74. Mem.: Soc. for Consumer Psychology, Am. Acad. Advt. (mem. rsch. com. 1992, internat. com. 1993—), Phi Beta Delta, Phi Kappa Phi. Avocations: competitive sailing, photography, music, Tae Kwon Do. Personal E-mail: pennington@zianet.com.

PENNINO, ANTHONY PAUL, playwright, educator; b. Plainfield, NJ, Feb. 12, 1967; s. Joseph Anthony and Dorothy Edith Pennino. BA, Columbia Coll., NYC, 1989; MA, Columbia U. Sch. Arts and Scis., NYC, 1990; MFA, Columbia U. Sch. Arts, NYC, 1993; PhD, U. London, 1999. Vis. prof. NJ. City U., Jersey City, 2003—07; parttime instr. Stevens Inst. Tech., Hoboken, NJ, 2007—08; sr. lectr. Kadir Has U., Istanbul, Turkey, 2008—. Dir. new works Met. Playhouse, NYC, 2002—; sec. and bd. mem. Actors' Shakespeare Co., Jersey City, 2006—07. Author: (musical) The Devil and Tom Walker, (play) Italian-American Cantos, Toby, Children's Crusader: A Parable of the Progressive Era; dir.: (play) A Soldier's Death (OOBR award, 2003). Fellow Fulbright Scholars Program, Coun. Internat. Exch. Scholars US Dept. State, 2008. Mem.: MLA, SSDC, Dramatists Guild America. Avocations: swimming, travel, cooking, theater, poker.

PENNISI, LIZ, women's health nurse; b. Bklyn., Nov. 20, 1953; d. Alexander and Marjorie (Soviero) Perillo; children: Stephen, Scott, Greg. Diploma, Beth Israel Sch. Nursing, NYC, 1974. RN, N.Y.; cert. ambulatory women's health nurse. Staff nurse Montefiore Hosp., Bronx, NY, 1974-75; mem. staff Beth Israel Med. Ctr., NYC, 1975-77; office nurse Martin Kurman, M.D., NYC, 1977-80, Adam Romoff, M.D. and Suzanne Yale, M.D., P.C, 1984—. Mem. AWHONN. Avocations: tennis, horseback riding, reading. Office: Drs Romoff and Yale 768 Park Ave New York NY 10021-4153 Personal E-mail: lizpennisi@hotmail.com.

PENNISTEN, JOHN WILLIAM, computer scientist, actuary, linguist; b. Buffalo, Jan. 25, 1939; s. George William and Lucy Josephine (Gates) P. AB in Math. and Chemistry with honors, Hamilton Coll., 1960; postgrad., Harvard U., 1960-61, U.S. Army Lang. Sch., 1962-63; MS in Computer Sci. with honors, NY Inst. Tech., 1987. Cert. Application Developer IBM, 2006, Assoc. Developer Oracle Corp., 2006, Linux adminstr. Novell Corp., 2008, in web devel. NYU, 2008; in Taxation NYU, 1982, in Asian Langs. NYU, 1992, in Profl. Banking Am. Inst. Banking, Am. Bankers Assn., 1988. Actuarial asst. New Eng. Mut. Life Ins. Co., Boston, 1965-66; asst. actuary Mass. Gen. Life Ins. Co., Boston, 1966-68; actuarial assoc. John Hancock Mut. Life Ins. Co., Boston, 1968-71; asst. actuary George B. Buck Cons. Actuaries, Inc., NYC, 1971-75, Martin E. Segal Co., NYC, 1975-80; actuary Laiken Siegel Co., NYC, 1980; cons. Bklyn., 1981—; timesharing and database analyst banklink corp. cash mgmt. div. Chem. Bank NYC, 1983-85; programmer analyst Empire Blue Cross and Blue Shield, NYC, 1986-88, Mt. Sinai Med. Ctr., NYC, 1988-89, French Am. Banking Corp. (subs. Banque National de Paris), NYC, 1989; sr. programmer analyst Dean Witter Reynolds, Inc., NYC, 1989-92; computer specialist for software NYC Dept. Fin., 1992—97, computer specialist, 2003—; sr. cons. Pinkerton Computer Cons., Inc., NYC, 1997-99; tech. officer J.P. Morgan Chase Co., NYC, 1999—2003. Enrolled actuary U.S. Fed. Pension Legis. Bklyn., 1976—. Contbr. articles to profl. jours. With US Army, 1961-64. Fellow: Soc. Actuaries; mem.: IEEE Computer Soc., MLA, AAAS, Bklyn. Heights Assn., Nat. Ry. Hist. Soc., Am. Chem. Soc., Math. Assn. Am., Am. Math. Soc., Nat. Model R.R. Assn. (life), Ry. and Locomotive Hist. Soc. (life), Assn. Computational Linguistics, Linguistic Soc. Am., Am. Assn. Artificial Intelligence, Assn. Computing Machinery, Met. Opera Guild, Harvard Club NY, Nat. Rep. Club Capitol Hill, Am. Legion, Phi Beta Kappa. Office: NYC Dept Fin Tech Solutions Group 59 Maiden Ln 25th Fl New York NY 10038 Business E-Mail: pennistenj@finance.nyc.gov.

PENNONI, CELESTINO R. (CHUCK PENNONI), civil engineer, academic administrator; b. Plains, Pa., Dec. 21, 1937; m. Annette Ribar, Oct. 24, 1959; children: David, Diane, Vincent, Andrew. BCE, Drexel U., 1963, MCE, 1966, PhD (hon.), 1992. Projects engr. City of Phila., 1961—64; with C&J Constrn. Co., 1964—66; founder Pennoni Assocs., Inc., Phila., 1966, pres., chmn., CEO; interim pres. Drexel U., Phila., 1994—95, 2009—, univ. trustee, 1993—2006, chmn. bd., 1997—2003. Trustee, pres. United Engring. Trustees, Inc.; pres. Accreditation Bd. Engring. and Tech.; mem. US Coun. for Internat. Engring. Practice; engring. adv. bd. Widener U., U. Pa., Drexel U.; vice chair bd. govs. Pa. Sys. of Higher Edn.; bd. mem. Parke Bank, GCA Svcs., Inc., Granite Group. Contbr. articles to profl. jours. Recipient A.J. Drexel Award, Drexel U., Bus. Leader of Yr. Award, Profl. Devel. Award, Nat. Soc. Profl. Engrs., George Washington Medal, Engineers Club of Phila., Robert Morris Citizenship award, Boy Scouts of Am., Excellence in Edn., March of Dimes Svc. to Humanity Award, Order of Merit of the Republic of Italy; named Drexel Honor Man of Yr., 1971; named to Legion of Honor, Chaplain of the Four Chaplains. Mem.: ASCE (former pres., dir., pres. ASCE Found., Edmund Friedman Profl. Recognition award, William H. Wisely Am. Civil Engineer award), NAE, Pa. Soc. Profl. Engrs., Golden Key Nat. Honor Soc. Achievements include development of innovative use of storm water management tech to control flooding in urban areas. Office: Pennoni Assocs Inc One Drexel Plz 3001 Market St Philadelphia PA 19104 also: Drexel U Office of Pres 3141 Chestnut St Philadelphia PA 19104 Fax: 215-222-0357.*

PENNOYER, PAUL GEDDES, JR., retired lawyer; b. NYC, Feb. 11, 1920; s. Paul G. and Frances (Morgan) P.; m. Cecily Henderson, Feb. 5, 1949; children: Jennifer, Deirdre, Paul T., Sheldon K., William M. BS, Harvard U., 1942, LLB, 1948. Bar: N.Y. 1949, U.S. Dist. Ct. (so. and ea. dists.) N.Y. 1952, U.S. Supreme Ct. 1972, U.S. Ct. Appeals (2d cir.) 1964, U.S. Ct. Appeals (4th cir.) 1986, U.S. Ct. Appeals (11th cir.) 1987. Assoc. Bingham Englar Jones & Houston, NYC, 1949-55, ptnr., 1955-63, Chadbourne & Parke, NYC, 1963-89; of counsel, 1989—. Trustee Frick Collection, 1975—2002, trustee emeritus, 2003—; trustee L.I. U., 1975-85, Morgan Meml. Park, 1970—, North Shore Wildlife Inc., 1980—. Lt. USN, 1942-45. Decorated Navy Cross, Air Medal, USN. Mem. ABA, N.Y. State Bar Assn., Assn. Bar City N.Y., N.Y. Bar found., Am. Coll. Trial Lawyers, N.Y. Yacht Club. Republican. Episcopalian. Office: Chadbourne & Parke 30 Rockefeller Plz New York NY 10112

PENNOYER, PETER MORGAN, architect; b. NYC, Feb. 19, 1957; s. Robert Morgan and Victoria (Parsons) P.; m. Katherine Lee Ridder, Sept. 24, 1988; children: Jane Delano, Anthony Ridder, Virginia Morgan. BA, Columbia U., NYC, 1979, MArch, 1983. Registered arch., NY. Designer Robert A.M. Stern Archs., NYC, 1979-83; pres. Peter Pennoyer Archs. P.C., NYC, 1990—. Contbg. author: Inside Architecture, 1997; prin. works include Mark Hotel, NYC, Waldorf Astoria, Mandarin Oriental, Hong Kong; co-author: The Architecture of Delano & Aldrich, The Architecture of Warren & Wetmore. Bd. dirs. Mcpl. Art Soc., NYC, 1994, Sir John Soane's Mus. Found., 1999, Morgan Libr., NYC, 2005-; pres. poetry project St. Marks Ch., NYC, 1994-97; dir. Whiting Found., NYC, 2002, Inst. NYC Classical Architecture, 2003. Recipient award Friends of Upper East Side Hist. Dists., 1992, NYC Landmarks award, 1994. Mem. AIA. Office: Peter Pennoyer Archs 432 Park Ave S 11th Fl New York NY 10016 Office Phone: 212-779-9765. E-mail: peter@ppapc.com.

PENNOYER, ROBERT M., lawyer; b. NYC, Apr. 9, 1925; BA, Harvard U., 1946; LL.B., Columbia U., 1950. Bar: N.Y. 1951, U.S. Supreme Ct. 1971. Asst. US atty. criminal divsn. (so. dist.) NY US Dept. Justice, 1953-55; asst. to gen. counsel US Dept. Def., Washington, 1955-57, spl. asst. to asst. sec. for internat. security affairs, 1957-58; ptnr. Patterson, Belknap, Webb & Tyler, NYC, 1962-95, of counsel, 1995—. Trustee Carnegie Instn., Washington, 1968-79, John Merck Fund, 1982—2007, Mrs. Giles Whiting Found., 1970—2000, Met. Mus. Art, 1966—, Pierpont Morgan Libr., 1969—, Columbia U., 1982-88, Boyce Thompson Inst. for Plant Rsch., Cornell U., 1974-97, Inst. Democracy Studies, 1999-2002, William C. Bullitt Found, 2007-. Lt. (j.g.) USNR, PTO, 1944-46. Recipient Lifetime Achievement award, The Am. Lawyer mag., 2006. Mem. ABA, N.Y. State Bar Assn., Assn. Bar City N.Y., Century Assn. Office: Patterson Belknap Webb & Tyler Rm 2200 1133 Ave of the Americas New York NY 10036-6731 Office Phone: 212-336-2700. Business E-Mail: rmpennoyer@pbwt.com.

PENNY, BRAD (BRADLEY WAYNE PENNY), professional baseball player; b. Blackwell, Okla., May 24, 1978; Pitcher Fla. Marlins, 2000—04, LA Dodgers, 2004—08, Boston Red Sox, 2009, San Francisco Giants, 2009—. Named to Nat. League All-Star Team, 2006—07. Achievements include member of the World Series Championship winning Florida Marlins, 2003; leading the National League in: wins (16), 2006. Avocations: fishing, hunting. Mailing: c/o San Francisco Giants AT&T Park 24 Willie Mays Plz San Francisco CA 94107*

PENNY, NICHOLAS BEAVER, museum director; b. London, Dec. 21, 1949; s. Joseph Noel and Agnes Celia (Roberts) P.; m. Anne Philomel Udy (div.), Mary Agnes crettier; children: Caroline Emil, Elizabeth Joan. MA, St. Catharines Coll., Cambridge, UK, 1971, Courtauld Inst., London, 1973, PhD, 1975. Leverhulme fellow Cambridge U., 1973-75; lectr. history of art dept. U. Manchester, 1975-82; sr. rsch. fellow King's Coll., Cambridge, 1982-84; keeper dept. Western art Ashmolean Mus., Oxford, Eng., 1984-89; dir. Nat. Gallery, London, 2008—, Clore curator Renaissance painting, 1990—2007; sr. curator sculpture Nat. Gallery of Art, Washington, 2002—08. Slade prof. U. Oxford, 1980-81. Author: Church Monuments in Romantic England, 1977, Reynolds, 1986, Piranesi, 1988, The Materials of Sculpture, 1996, Frames, 1997; co-author: Taste and The Antique, 1981, Raphael, 1983, Dürer to Veronese, 1999, Art of the Italian Renaissance Bronze, 2005, Collecting Sculpture in Early Modern Europe, 2008; editor exhbn. catalog Raphael: From Urbino to Rome, 2004. Fellow Am. Acad. Arts and Sciences. Office: Nat Gallery Trafalgar Sq London WC2N 5DN England

PENNY, ROGER PRATT, retired management consultant; b. Buffalo, July 13, 1936; s. George Albert and Louise (Mings) P.; m. Judith Stevens, Aug. 25, 1957; children: David, Sarah, Julia. BA in Adminstrv. Engring., Union Coll., 1958; grad., Wharton Bus. Sch., 1993. From supt. to pres. Bethlehem Steel Corp., Burus Harbor Plant, Lackawanna, NY, 1958—91; pres. Bethlehem Steel Corp., 1991—99, vice chmn., 1999—2000, ret., 2000. Mem. United Way, Buffalo, 1960-82; chmn. campaign United Way Porter County, Valparaiso, Ind., 1986; mem. Orchard Park Town Bd., 1970-82; mem. adv. bd. Purdue U., West Lafayette, Ind., 1985-86, Bus. Sch., Valparaiso U., 1986; bd. dirs. Minsi Trails coun. Boy Scouts Am., Lehigh Valley, Pa., 1988—, pres., 1996; trustee St. Luke's Hosp., 1998-2001. Mem. Am. Iron and Steel Inst., Assn. Iron and Steel Engrs., Valparaiso C. of C. (dir. 1985-86), Orchard Park C. of C., Buffalo C. of C., Sand Creek Club (pres. 1983-86), Buffalo Soccer Club (pres., sec. 1960-75), Saucon Valley Country Club, Wynstone Golf Club. Republican. Episcopalian. Office Phone: 847-756-4211.

PENNY, TIMOTHY JOSEPH, former congressman; b. Albert Lea, Minn., Nov. 19, 1951; s. Jay C. and Dona (Haukoos) P.; m. Barbara J. Christianson, Oct. 18, 1975; children: Jamison, Joseph, Molly, Marcus. BA, Winona State U., 1974; postgrad., U. Minn., 1975. Mem. Minn. Senate from Dist. 30, 1977-82, US Congress from 1st Minn. Dist., 1983—94; mem. agr. com., vets affairs com.; chmn. fgn. agr. and hunger subcom.; sr. fellow Ctr. for Study of Politics and Governance U. Minn., 1995—; sr. counselor Himle Horner Pub. Rels., 1995; pres. Southeastern Minn. Init Fund, 2007—. Author: Common Cents, 1995, Payment Due, 1996. Mem. Minn. State Univ. Bd., 1974-77; co-chmn. Dem. budget study group Whip-At-Large; bd. mem., policy chair Concord Coalition; adv. bd. mem. Minn. Compact Recipient Disting. Service award U. Minn., 1982, Spark Plug award Communicating for Agr., 1980, Nat. Comdr.'s award DAV, 1989. Mem. New Richland (Minn.) Jaycees, Waseca Pals, Inc., Waseca and Freeborn County Assn. for Retarded Citizens Democrat. Lutheran. Office: U Minn 138 Humphrey Center Minneapolis MN 55455 Office Phone: 612-624-8842.

PENROD, MARIAN PENUEL, wellness consultant, retired school librarian; b. Statesville, Tenn., May 11, 1930; d. Hayden L. Penuel and Zoie L. Cunningham; m. William T. Penrod, Jr., June 8, 1954 (div. Oct. 1979); children: Cheryl Anne Penrod Puryear, Paula Wynn, Laura Lynn Penrod Moseng. BS, Middle Tenn. State Coll., 1952; M of Religious Edn., So. Bapt. Theol. Sem., Louisville, 1955; EdM, U. Miami, 1958. Cert. specialist in pastoral care Pastoral Counseling Ctrs. Tenn., Inc., 2002. Tchr. Parma Elem., Mich., 1953—54, Golden Pond Elem., Ky., 1955—57, West Jackson Bapt., Tenn., 1965—66; tchr., libr. Madison County, Jackson, 1967—69; tchr. Dyer County, Dyersburg, Tenn., 1969—70; sch. libr. Murfreesboro City Schs., Tenn., 1972—98; wellness cons. Nikken, Inc., 1998—, Reliv Inc. Baptist. Avocations: reading, writing, travel, continued education. Home Phone: 615-893-7398.

PENSA, MARIANA, language educator; d. Tihomir and Enriqueta Elena Pensa; m. Stephen Michael Mulligan, July 1, 1994. Licenciada en Letras, Universidad de Buenos Aires, Argentina, Profesora en Letras, 1990; MA in Spanish, Carleton U., Ottawa Ont. Can., 1994, PhD Comparative Lit., 2002. Spanish instr. Inmaculada Concepción de María Inst., Buenos Aires, 1991, Educación y Cultura Inst., Buenos Aires, 1991—92; Spanish tchr. asst. Carleton U., 1992—94, 1997—2002; Spanish instr., tester Fgn. Lang. Inst. Ottawa, 1996—2004; asst. prof. Spanish Calif. U., Pa., 2004—. Contbr. articles to profl. jours. Recipient Carlos Somigliana Creative Writting award, Carlos Somigliana Found., Buenos Aires, 1992; grantee Comparative Lit. Studies grant, Latin Am. Theatre Rsch. Ctr., Carleton U., 1994—95; scholar Tchg. Assistantship, Carleton U., 1992—94, 1997—2002; FPDC Travel Fund grant, Calif. U., 2005, 2006, 2008, Dean Liberal Arts Office Travel grant, 2005, 2006, 2007, 2008. Mem.: MLA, Alpha Mu Gamma (hon.). Achievements include research in Latin American theatre with an specialty in Argentinean theater.

PENSE, ALAN WIGGINS, metallurgical engineer, academic administrator; b. Sharon, Conn., Feb. 3, 1934; s. Arthur Wilton and May Beatrice (Wiggins) P.; m. Muriel Drews Taylor, June 28, 1958; children: Daniel Alan, Steven Taylor, Christine Muriel. B.Metall. Engring., Cornell U., 1957; MS, Lehigh U., 1959, PhD, 1962. Research asst. Lehigh U., Bethlehem, Pa., 1957-59, instr., 1960-62, asst. prof., 1962-65, asso. prof., 1965-71, prof., 1971-96, chmn. dept. metallurgy and materials engring., 1977-83, assoc. dean Coll. Engring. and Applied Scis., 1984-88, dean, 1988-90, v.p., provost, 1990-96, prof. emeritus, 1996—. Assoc. dir. Ctr. Advanced Tech. for Large Structural Systems NSF, 1986-89; cons. adv. com. on reactor safeguards NRC, 1965-86; rsch. engr., 1997—; cons. Lehigh U., 1997—. Author: (with D. Henkel) Structure and Properties of Engineering Materials, 5th edit, 2001; also articles. Recipient Robinson award Lehigh U., 1965, Stabler award, 1972, Hillman award 1997, Materials Sci. and Engring. Disting. Alumni award, 2002; Danforth fellow, 1974-86. Fellow Am. Soc. Metals, Am. Welding Soc. (William Spraragan award 1963, Adams Membership award 1966, Jennings award 1970, Adams lectr. 1980, William Hobart medal 1982, Plummer lectr. 1995); mem. ASTM, Am. Soc. Engring. Edn. (Western Elec. award 1986), Internat. Inst. Welding, Nat. Acad. Engring. Republican. Evang. Congregationalist (bd. trustees Evang. Sch. Theology). Home: 2586 Lynhurst Dr Bethlehem PA 18017-3940 Office: The ATLSS Rsch Ctr 117 Atlss Dr Bethlehem PA 18015-4728 Office Phone: 610-758-6104. Business E-Mail: awp0@lehigh.edu. *Achievement of significant goals in our life must be balanced by the quality of that life itself, for what we are is as important as what we do.*

PENSHORN, JOHN S., insurance company executive; Stock analyst Piper Jaffray; dir. Capital Markets Comm. and Strategy UnitedHealth Grp., Minnetonka, Minn., 1998—, sr. v.p. Office: UnitedHealth Grp 9900 Bren Rd E Minnetonka MN 55343*

PENSLER, JAY MICHAEL, plastic surgeon, educator; b. Detroit, Apr. 29, 1954; BS Microbiology, U. Mich., 1976; MD, U. Chgo., 1980. Diplomate Am. Bd. Plastic Surgeons, Nat. Bd. Med. Examiners; lic. N.Y., Calif., Mass., Ill. Resident gen. surgery NYU Med. Ctr., 1980-83; resident plastic surgery U. Tex. Med. Br., Galveston, 1983-86; fellow craniofacial surgery Harvard U., Boston, 1986-87; plastic surgeon Northwestern Meml. Hosp., Chgo., 1987—; and assoc. prof. clin. plastic surgery Northwestern Univ. Med. Sch., Chgo. Assoc. prof. surgery Northwestern U., Chgo., 1987-93; plastic surgeon Children's Meml. Hosp., Chgo., 1987—; surf. staff Columbus-Cabrini Med. Ctr., Chgo., 1990—, Evanston (Ill.)-Glenbrook Hosps., 1992—. Featured on NBC, CBS, ABC, Fox-TV; contbr. more than 100 articles to profl. jours. Named one of Chgo.'s Top Doctors, Chgo. mag., 2003. Fellow Am. Coll. Surgeons (Met. Chgo. chpt.), Internat. Coll. Surgeons (Plastic Surgery); mem. AMA, Am. Acad. Pediatrics, Am. Assn. Pediatric Plastic Surgeons, Am. Burn Assn., Am. Cleft Palate-Craniofacial Assn., Am. Fedn. Clin. Rsch., Am. Soc. Bone and Mineral Rsch., Am. Soc. Maxillofacial Surgeons, Am. Soc. Plastic and Reconstructive Surgeons, Bioelec. Repair and Growth Soc., Blocker-Lewis Plastic Surgery Soc., Midwestern Assn. Plastic Surgeons, Chgo. Med. Soc., Chgo. Soc. Plastic Surgery. Office: 680 N Lake Shore Dr Ste 1125 Chicago IL 60611-8701

PENSON, JOHN B., JR., economics professor, consultant; b. Chgo., Sept. 1, 1941; s. John B. and Mary Elizabeth Penson; m. Donna Ruth Heagberg, Sept. 19, 1964; children: Matthew C., John B., Laura Elizabeth Patterson. BS in Agrl. Bus., Southern Ill. U., 1964, MS in Agrl. Bus., 1967; PhD in Agrl. Econ., U. Ill., Urbana Illinois, 1973. Economist US Dept. Agr., Washington, 1968—74; prof. regents and stiles Tex. A&M U., Coll. Sta., 1975—. CEO AgriLogic, Inc., Mansfield, Tex., 2005—07; vis. fgn. disting. prof. U. Korea, 2007; vis. prof. Kyushu U., Japan, 2008. Author: (textbook) Agricultural Finance, 1980, Personal Finance, 1983, Introduction to Agricultural Economics, 4th edit., 2006. Recipient Outstanding Doctoral award, Am. Agrl. Econs. Assn., 1974, Disting. Undergrad. Tchg. award, 1986, Disting. Policy Contbn. award, 1997, Presdl. award, 2007, Disting. Achievement Rsch. award, Tex. A&M Former Students Assn., 1984, Outstanding Undergrad. Tchg. award, Western Agrl. Econs. Assn., 1985, Outstanding Alumus award, Southern Ill. U., 1986, Disting. Achievement Award for Tchg., Tex. A&M U. Former Regents Students Assn., 1992, Honor Prof. award, Tex. A&M U., 1993, Regents Prof. award, Bd. Regents Tex. A&M U., 2000, Lifetime Achievement award, So. Agrl. Econs. Assn., 2007. Office: Texas A&M U 352 Blocker College Station TX 77843

PENTIUK, RANDALL ALAN, lawyer; b. Garden City, Mich., Mar. 15, 1955; s. Eugene Otto and Marjorie Bernice (Baynes) P.; children: Amanda Rene, Kristen Lynne, Stephanie Joyce; m. Cynthia Marie West, July 29, 1999; 1 child, Katheryn Alexandra. BSBA, Wayne State U., 1976; JD magna cum laude, Detroit Coll. Law, 1981. Bar: Mich. 1981, U.S. Dist. Ct. (ea. dist.) Mich. 1981, U.S. Ct. Appeals (6th cir.) 1984, U.S. Supreme Ct. 1984, D.C. 1985. Rsch. atty. Mich. Ct. Appeals, Detroit, 1981; ptnr. Logan, Huchla, Wycoff & Pentiuk and predecessor Logan, Huchla & Wycoff, P.C., Riverview, Mich., 1981-84, ptnr., 1984-89, Pentiuk, Miller & Waterman, P.C., 1989-93, Pentiuk, Couvreur & Kobiljak, 1993—; atty. City of Riverview, Mich.; corp. counsel City of Melvindale, Mich. Contbr. to profl. jours. Mem. Trenton Planning Commn., Mich., 1982-92, chmn. 1985-87. Down River Rep. Club, Trenton, 1983-85; exec. com. 16th Dist. Rep. Party Mich., 1989-91; pres. Rutherford Inst. Mich., 1987-89; bd. dirs. Detroit City Rescue Mission, chmn., 1992—; bd. dirs. Promise Village, chmn., 1996-97. Mich. Consol. Gas scholar Detroit Coll. Law, 1978, Burton scholar, 1979, Alumni scholar, 1980. Mem. ABA, State Bar Mich., Comml. Law League Am., Fed. Bar Assn., Nat. Inst. Mcpl. Legal Officers (com. federalism, sect. zoning and planning law), Nat. Assn. Housing Coops (bd. dirs.), Midwest Assn. Housing Coops. (bd. dirs.), Mich. Assn. Mcpl.

Attys., Christian Legal Soc. Baptist. Office: 2915 Biddle Ste 200 Wyandotte MI 48192 Home: 2915 Biddle Ave Ste 200 Wyandotte MI 48192-5267 Home Phone: 734-552-3600; Office Phone: 734-281-7100. Personal E-mail: kuitnep@aol.com. Business E-Mail: rpentiuk@pck-law.com.

PENTON-SMITH, TAMMY L., elementary school educator; b. Picayune, Miss., Apr. 26, 1963; d. Linda and Richard Culpepper; 1 child, Alaina. BS in Bus. Adminstrn., U. So. Miss., Hattiesburg, 2000; alternative rte. elem. tchr., William Carey Coll., Gulfport, Miss., 2001, M of Elem. Edn., 2004. Adminstrv. asst. Tulane U., New Orleans, 1983—96; supr. Kelly Svcs., Gulfport, 2000—01; tchr. 5th grade South Side Upper Elem., Picayune, 2001—05. Coord. sci. fair South Side Sch. Dist., 2002—06; chair grade level South Side Upper Elem., Picayune, 2005—06. Office: South Side Upper Elem 1500 Rosa St Picayune MS 39466

PENUEL, SUZANNE, literature and language professor; d. Arnold McCoy and Patricia Forbes Penuel; m. Christopher Bundrick, Aug. 1, 1998. Instr. U. Miss. English Dept., University, 2004—; lectr. U. SC Lancaster English Dept., 2008—. Contbr. articles to jours.

PENWARDEN, ANN P, assistant director; d. Henry M. and Hildegard H. Pinak; m. Brent H. Penwarden III, May 18, 1991; 1 child, Brent H. Penwarden IV. BA, U. Pa., Phila., 1984; MLS, U. Buffalo, 1987. Cert. pub. libr. Dept. Edn.,NY, 1987. Reference libr. Monroe CC, Rochester, NY, 1987—99, asst. dir. sys & ext. svcs., 1999—. Automation cons. COSTAATT, Port Spain, Trinidad and Tobago, 1999—2000. Trustee Landmark Soc. of Western NY, Rochester, 1998—. Recipient Outstanding Woman Recognition award, AAWCC, Monroe CC Chpt., 1998, Chancellor's award, SUNY, 2005; named Innovator of the Yr., League Innovation CC, 1991. Mem.: ALA (committees mem. 1994—95, Profl. Devel. award 1991), Assn. Coll. & Rsch. Libraries, WNY/O Chpt. (pres. 1997—98), NY Libr. Assn. (pres. SMART 2003—04). Roman Catholic. Avocations: skiing, sailing. Home: 23 Stony Brook Ln Fairport NY 14450 Office: Monroe CC 1000 E Henrietta Rd Rochester NY 14623 Office Fax: 585-292-3859. Business E-Mail: apenwarden@alumni.upenn.edu, apenwarden@monroecc.edu.

PENZER, MICHÈLE OLIVIER, lawyer; b. Nov. 22, 1968; AB, Harvard U., 1990; JD, Yale U., 1993. Bar: NY 1994. Ptnr. Latham & Watkins LLP, NYC, 2001—, mem. exec. com., 2005—09. Named one of 40 Under 40, Crain's NY Bus., 2007. Mem.: ABA, State Bar NY, NY State Bar Assn. Office: Latham & Watkins LLP 885 Third Ave, Ste 1000 New York NY 10022-4802 Office Phone: 212-906-1200. Office Fax: 212-751-4864.

PENZIAS, ARNO ALLAN, astrophysicist, information scientist, researcher; b. Munich, Apr. 26, 1933; arrived in U.S., 1940, naturalized, 1946; s. Karl and Justine (Eisenreich) Penzias; m. Sherry Chamove Levit, Aug. 2, 1996; children: David Simon, Mindy Gail, Laurie Shifra. BS in Physics, CCNY, 1954; MA in Physics, Columbia U., 1958, PhD in Physics, 1962; DHC (hon.), Observatoire de Paris, 1976; ScD (hon.), Rutgers U., 1979, Wilkes Coll., 1979, CCNY, 1979, Yeshiva U., 1979, Bar-Ilan U., 1983, Monmouth Coll., 1984, Technion-Israel Inst. Tech., 1986, U. Pitts., 1986, Ball State U., 1986, Kean Coll., 1986, U. Pa., 1992, Ohio State U., 1988, Iona Coll., 1988, Drew U., 1989, Lafayette Coll., 1990, Columbia U., 1990, George Wash. U., 1992, Rensselaer Univ., 1992, U. Pa., 1992, Bloomfield Coll., 1994, Rankin Tech. U., 1997, Hebrew Union Coll., 1997, Oxford U., 2002. Mem. tech. staff Bell Labs., Holmdel, NJ, 1961—72, head radiophysics rsch. dept., 1972—76, dir. radio rsch. lab., 1976—79, exec. dir. rsch., comm. scis. div., 1979—81, v.p. rsch., 1981—85; v.p., chief scientist Lucent Technologies, 1995—98, sr. tech. adv., 1998—2000; venture ptnr. New Enterprise Assocs., 1998—. Sr. advisor New Enterprise Assocs., 1997—98; adj. prof. earth and scis. SUNY, Stony Brook, 1974—84, Univ. Disting. lectr., 1990; lectr. dept. astrophys. Scis. Princeton U., 1967—72, vis. prof., 1972—85; rsch. assoc. Harvard Coll. Obs., 1968—80; Edison lectr. US Naval Rsch. Lab., 1979; Kompfner lectr. Stanford U., 1979; Gamow lectr. U. Colo., 1980; Jansky lectr. Nat. Radio Astronomy Obs.1983, 1983; Michelson Meml. lectr., 85; Grace Adams Tanner lectr., 87; Klopsteg lectr. Northwestern U., 1987; grad. faculties alumni Columbia U., 1987—89; Regents' lectr. U. Calif., Berkeley, 1990; Lee Kuan Yew Disting. vis. Nat. U. Singapore, 1991; mem. astronomy adv. panel NSF, 1978—79, mem. indsl. panel on sci. and tech., 1982—92, disting. lectr., 1987; affiliate Max-Planck Inst. for Radioastronomy, 1978—85; chmn. Fachbeirat, 1981—83; rschr. in astrophysics, info. tech., its applications and impacts; bd. dirs. Konarka Techs., Glacier Bay, Inc., Bloom Energy Corp. Patentee auction-based selection of telecom. carriers, participant tracking in conf. call, computer-based transp. sys., fraud prevention in calling cards, identifying telephone extensions in residence environment, double-encrypted identity verification sys.; author: Ideas and Information Managing in a High-Tech World, 1989, Harmony-Business, Technology and Life After Paperwork, 1995; editl. bd. Ann. Rev. Astronomy and Astrophysics, 1974—78, AT&T Bell Labs. Tech. Jour., 1978—84, chmn., 1981—84, assoc. editor Astrophys. Jour., 1978—82, contbr. over 100 articles to tech. jours. Bd. overseers U. Pa. Sch. Engring. and Applied Sci., 1983—86; mem. vis. com. Calif. Inst. Tech., 1977—77; mem. Com. Concerned Scientists, 1975—, vice chmn., 1976; mem. adv. bd. Union of Couns. for Soviet Jews, 1983—95; bd. dirs. Coun. on Competitiveness, 1989—92; bd. trustees Trenton (N.J.) State Coll., 1977—79. With US Army, 1954—56. Recipient Herschel medal, Royal Astron. Soc., 1977, Nobel prize in Physics, 1978, Townsend Harris medal, CCNY, 1979, Newman award, 1983, Joseph Handleman prize in the scis., 1983, Grad. Faculties Alumni award, Columbia U., 1984, Achievement in Sci. award, Big Bros. Inc., N.Y.C., 1985, Priestly award, Dickinson Coll., 1989, Pender award, U. Pa., 1992, N.J. Sci. and Tech. medal, 1996, Internat. Eng. Cons. Fell. award, 1997, Indsl. Rsch. Inst. medal, 1998; named to N.J. Lit. Hall of Fame, 1991. Mem.: AAAS, NAS (Henry Draper medal 1977), IEEE (hon.), NAE, World Acad. Arts and Sci., Internat. Astron. Union, Am. Phys. Soc. (Pake prize 1990), Am. Astron. Soc. Office: New Enterprises Assocs 2855 Sand Hill Rd Menlo Park CA 94025-7022*

PENZIEN, JOSEPH, structural engineering educator; b. Philip, SD, Nov. 27, 1924; s. John Chris and Ella (Stebbins) Penzien; m. Jeanne Ellen Hunson, Apr. 29, 1950 (dec. 1985); children: Robert Joseph, Karen Estelle, Donna Marie, Charlene May. Student, Coll. Idaho, 1942—43; BS, U. Wash., Seattle, 1945; ScD, MIT, Cambridge, Mass., 1950. Staff Sandia Corp., 1950—51; sr. structures engr. Consol. Vultee Aircraft Corp., Fort Worth, 1951—53; asst. prof. U. Calif. at Berkeley, 1953—57, assoc. prof., 1957—62, prof. structural engring., 1962—88, prof. emeritus, 1988—; dir. Earthquake Engring. Rsch. Ctr., 1968—73, 1977—80. Cons. engring. firms; chief tech. adv. Internat. Inst. of Seismology and Earthquake Engring., Tokyo, Japan, 1964-65; chmn. bd. Ea. Internat. Engrs., Inc., 1980-90, Internat. Civil Engring. Cons., Inc., 1990—2007, chmn. emeritus, ICEC Divsn. Paul C. Rizzo Assoc. Inc., 2007-. NATO Sr. Sci. fellow, 1969. Fellow Am. Acad. Mechanics; hon. mem. ASCE (Walter Huber Rsch. award, Alfred M. Freudenthal medal, Nathan M. Newmark medal, Ernest E. Howard award), Earthquake Engring. Rsch. Inst. (hon., dist. lectr. 2000, Hausner medal), IAEE (hon.), EERI (Alfred E. Alquist award, 1996, Dist. Lectr. 2000); Applied Tech. Coun. (Top Seismic Engr. 2006), Chinese Taiwan Soc. Earthquake Engring. (Hon. award 2006), mem. Am. Concrete Inst., Structural Engrs. Assn. Calif., Seismol. Soc. Am., Nat. Acad. Engring. Home: 800 Solana Dr Lafayette CA 94549-5004 Office: Paul C Rizzo Assoc Inc 2201 Broadway Oakland CA 94612-3017 Office Phone: 510-286-0214. Personal E-mail: josephpenzien@yahoo.com.

PEOPLES, JOHN ARTHUR, JR., former university president, consultant; b. Starkville, Miss., Aug. 26, 1926; s. John Arthur and Maggie Rose (Peoples) P.; m. Mary E. Galloway, July 13, 1951; children: Kathleen, Mark Adam. BS, Jackson State U., 1950; MA, U. Chgo., 1951, PhD, 1961. Tchr. math. Froebel Sch., Gary, Ind., 1951-58; asst. prin. Lincoln Sch., Gary, 1958-62; prin. Banneker Sch., Gary, 1962-64; asst. to pres. Jackson (Miss.) State U., 1964-66, v.p., 1966-67, pres., 1967-84; Trustees disting. prof. Univs. Ctr. of Jackson, 1984-85; asst. to pres. SUNY, Binghamton, 1965-66; cons. in higher edn., 1985—. Lectr. summers numerous univs. and colls. Contbr. articles to profl. jours. Active Boy Scouts Am.; bd. govs. So. Regional Edn. Bd.; bd. visitors Air U.; adv. com. U.S. Army Command and Gen. Staff Coll.; mem. Commn. Excellence Am. Assn. State Colls. and Univs.; bd. commrs. Jackson Airport Authority. Served with USMCR, 1944-47. Recipient Disting. Am. award Nat. Football Found., Presdl. citation, Lifetime Achievement award Nat. Black Coll. Alumni Found., 1993—, Miss. Medal of Svc. Gov. Haley Barbour, 2009; named to Southwestern Athletic Hall of Fame. Mem. Am. Council Edn. (chmn. dir. 1975), Am. Assn. Higher Edn. (dir. 1971-74), NEA, Miss. Tchrs. Assn., Jackson C. of C. (econ. council), Alpha Kappa Mu, Phi Kappa Phi, Phi Delta Kappa, Omega Psi Phi (Man of Year, Sigma Omega chpt. 1966), Sigma Pi Phi. Lodges: Masons (33 deg.).

PEOPLES, ROBERT WILLIAM, biomedical researcher; s. John Frederick and Janet S. Peoples; m. Kathleen Ann Peoples; children: Robert William, David Alexander, Daniel Frederick, Stephen John. BS in Biology, Purdue U., West Lafayette, Ind., 1983, MS in Pharmacology, 1986, PhD in Pharmacology, 1989. Contbr. articles to profl. jours. Rsch. grant, Alcoholic Beverage Mfrs. Rsch. Assn., 2004—05, Nat. Inst. on Alcohol Abuse and Alcoholism, 2005—. Mem.: Rsch. Soc. on Alcoholism, Soc. Neurosci. Office: Marquette Univ Schroeder Complex 446 Milwaukee WI 53201-1881 Business E-Mail: robert.peoples@marquette.edu.

PEOPLES-MARWAH, ANDREA MICHELLE, educational consultant, researcher; b. Akron, Oct. 19, 1972; d. Clinton Jr. and Josie Geneva Peoples; m. Sanjay Marwah, Mar. 24, 2003; 1 child, Aaniyah Lourdes. BA, Coll. Wooster, Ohio, 1995; MA, Trinity Coll., Washington, DC, 1997; EdD, George Washington U., Washington, DC, 2005. Tchr., rschr. Camino Nuevo Charter Acad., LA, 1999—2002, Alexandria City Pub. Schs., Va., 2002—05; rschr., cons. Self Incorporated, High Point, NC, 2006—. Rschr. MIND Inst., Irvine, 1999—2002, Akron Pub. Schs., 2003—06. Mem.: NEA, Am. Ednl. Rsch. Assn. (adv. bd. 2005). Avocations: rare book collector, gardening, running marathons, cooking. Home: 1413 Cantwell Ct High Point NC 27265 Office Phone: 301-728-4358. Personal E-mail: andsan3@yahoo.com, dr.andreaed@live.com.

PEPE, FRANK A., cell and developmental biology educator; b. Schenectady, May 22, 1931; s. Rocco and Margherita (Ruggiero) P. BS, Union Coll., 1953; PhD, Yale U., 1957. Instr. anatomy U. Pa., Phila., 1957-60, assoc. in anatomy, 1960-63, asst. prof., 1963-65, assoc. prof., 1965-70, prof., 1970-92, chmn. dept. anatomy, 1977-90, prof. cell. and devel. biology, 1992-96, emeritus prof., 1996—. Editor: Motility in Cell Function, 1979. Recipient Rsch. Career Devel. award USPHS, 1968-73, Raymond C. Truex Disting. Lecture award Hahneman U., 1988. Fellow AAAS; mem. Am. Assn. Anatomists, Am. Chem. Soc., Biophys. Soc., Microscopy Soc. Am., Sigma Xi. Home: 4614 Pine St Philadelphia PA 19143-1808 E-mail: fpepe@mail.med.upenn.edu.

PEPE, JOSEPH ANTHONY, bishop; b. Phila., Pa., June 18, 1942; s. Francis V. and Elvira (Fazio) Pepe. Attended, St. Charles Borromeo Sem.; JCD, Pontifical U., St. Thomas, 1976. Ordained priest Archdiocese of Phila., 1970; asst. pastor Our Lady of Loreta Parish; faculty mem. Cardinal O'Hara High Sch., Springfield, Pa.; defender of the bond, Met. Tribunal Archdiocese of Phila., 1976, prosynodal judge, 1977, vice chancellor, chancellor, 1990; vice promoter Cause of Blessed Katharine Drexel; tchr. canon law St. Charles Borromeo Sem., 1982—87; monsignor, 1991; pastor St. Justin Martyr Parish; jud. vicar Archdiocese of Santa Fe, N.Mex., 1993, chancellor, moderator of the curia, vicar for priests, 1998; ordained bishop, 2001; bishop Diocese of Las Vegas, Nev., 2001—. Roman Catholic. Office: Diocese of Las Vegas PO Box 18316 Las Vegas NV 89114-8316 Office Phone: 702-735-3500. Office Fax: 702-735-8941.

PEPE, LOUIS ROBERT, lawyer, educator; b. Derby, Conn., Mar. 7, 1943; s. Louis F. and Mildred R. (Vollaro) P.; m. Carole Anita Roman, June 8, 1969; children: Marissa Lee, Christopher Justin, Alexander Drew. B in Mgmt. Engring., Rensselaer Poly. Inst., 1964, MS, 1967; JD with distinction, Cornell U., 1970. Bar: Conn. 1970, U.S. Dist. Ct. Conn. 1970, U.S. Ct. Appeals (2d cir.) 1971, U.S. Supreme Ct. 1975, U.S. Ct. Claims 1978. Assoc. Alcorn, Bakewell & Smith, Hartford, Conn., 1970-75, ptnr., 1975-82; sr. ptnr. Pepe & Hazard, Hartford, 1983—. Adj. assoc. prof. Hartford Grad. Ctr., 1972-87; adj. prof. U. Conn. Law Sch., 2000-01. Mem. New Hartford Housing Authority, 1971-72, New Hartford Planning Zoning Commn., 1973-84, chmn., 1980-84, New Hartford Inland Wetlands Commn., 1975-78; dean's adv. coun. Cornell Law Sch., 1990—; dir. Greater Hartford Legal Aid Found., 1993-03, pres., 2004-05. 1st lt. U.S. Army, 1964-66. Decorated Army Commendation medal. Fellow Am. Bar Found., Conn. Bar Found. (bd. dirs. 2003—), Am. Coll. Const. Lawyers (bd. govs. 2006—09), Am. Coll. Trial Lawyers; mem. ABA, Am. Bd. Trial Advocates (pres., 2007-08), Conn. Bar Assn. (pres., 2005-06, chmn. constrn. law sect. 1989-92, chmn. pro bono com. 2003-04, chmn. standing com. on professionalism 2000-03, v.p. 2003-04, pres.-elect, 2004-05), Hartford County Bar Assn., Phi Kappa Phi. Home: 3 Metacom Dr Simsbury CT 06070-1851 Office: Pepe & Hazard Goodwin Sq Hartford CT 06103-4300 Office Phone: 860-241-2636. Office Fax: 860-522-5175. Business E-Mail: lpepe@pepehazard.com.

PEPE, NEIL, performing company executive; b. Bloomington, Ind., June 23, 1963; m. Mary B. McCann, 2000; 1 child. Artistic dir. Atlantic Theater Co., NYC, 1992—. Adj. asst. prof. Columbia U., NYC; instr. Atlantic Acting Sch., NYC. Dir.: (Broadway plays) The Beauty Queen of Leenane, 1998 (Drama Desk award for Outstanding New Play, 1998), The Lieutenant of Inishmore, 2006, Jay Johnston: The Two and Only, 2006, Spring Awakening, 2006 (Drama Desk award for Outstanding Musical, 2007, Tony award for Best Musical, 2007), Talk Radio, 2007, Speed-the-Plow, 2008; (plays) Shaker Heights, 1994, Clean, 1997, Mojo, 1997, American Buffalo, 2000, Further Than the Furthest Thing, 2002, Blue/Orange, 2002, The Night Heron, 2003, Sea of Tranquility, 2004, Romance, 2005, Celebration and the Room, 2005, Parlour Song, 2008, Almost an Evening, 2008; dir., actor: Five Very Live, 1992; actor: Three Sisters, 1991, The Virgin Molly, 1992, The Lights, 1993, Trafficking in Broken Hearts, 1994, Edmond, 1996, The Joy of Going Somewhere Definite, 1997; (films) Homicide, 1991, Assassination, 1994, Colin Fitz, 1997, The Spanish Prisoner, 1997, Last Days of May, 1998, Analyze This, 1999, Magnolia, 1999, Spartan, 2004, Melinda and Melinda, 2004, Choke, 2008. Recipient Spl. Drama Desk award, 2009. Office: Atlantic Theater Co 76 9th Ave Ste 537 New York NY 10011 Office Phone: 212-691-5919. E-mail: npepe@atlantictheater.org.*

PEPER, CHARLOTTE ANN, psychotherapist; b. Tucson, Oct. 30, 1949; d. Horace Eric and Marion Monier Bounds; children: Sonya, Jesse, Julie, John, Tina. AA, Pima C.C., Tucson, 1986; BA in Therapeutic Recreation, Prescott Coll., Ariz., 1994, MA in Counseling and Psychology, 2005. Therapeutic recreation provider City of Tucson, 1991—92; tchr. recreation therapy Ariz. Sch. for Deaf, 1992—95; cons. therapeutic recreation Westcenter Rehab. Ctr., 1999—2000; activity dir. Carondelet Holy Family Ctr., 1995—2000; dir. cmty. life Fountains at La Challa, 2000—02; tchr. music San Xavier Mission, 2002—04; exec. dir., cons. The Healing Bow, 1994—. Therapist homeless teens Teens is Transition, 2006—; psychiatric assessor Carondelet Hosp., 2007—, Tuscon Heart Hosp., 2007—. Recipient Carondelet Mission award, Canondelet Health Network, Tucson, 1998. Mem.: Assn. Creativity Counseling, Am. Counseling Assn. Democrat. Roman Catholic. Personal E-mail: healingbow2@yahoo.com.

PEPER, CHRISTIAN BAIRD, lawyer; b. St. Louis, Dec. 5, 1910; s. Clarence F. and Christine (Baird) Peper; m. Ethel C. Kingsland, June 5, 1935 (dec. Sept. 1995); children: Catherine K. Peper Larson(dec.), Anne Peper Perkins, Christian B.; m. Barbara C. Pleiter, Jan. 25, 1996. AB cum laude, Harvard U., 1932; LLB, Washington U., 1935; LLM, Yale U., 1937. Bar: Mo. 1934. Pvt. practice, St. Louis; of counsel Husch Blackwell Sanders LLP, St. Louis. Instr. Washington U. Law Sch., St. Louis, 1943—61; ptnr. A. G. Edwards & Sons, 1945—67; pres. St. Charles Gas Corp., 1953—72; bd. dirs. El Dorado Paper Bag Mfg. Co., Inc. Editor: (book) An Historian's Conscience: The Correspondence of Arnold J. Toynbee and Columba Cary-Elwes, 1986. Mem. vis. com. Harvard Div. Sch., 1964—70. Sterling fellow, Yale U., 1936. Mem.: ABA, East India Club (London), St. Louis Bar Assn., Mo. Bar Assn., Harvard Club, Order of Coif, Phi Delta Phi. Roman Catholic. Home: 1454 S Mason Rd Saint Louis MO 63131-1211 Office: Husch Blackwell Sanders LLP 190 Carondelet Plz Saint Louis MO 63105 Home Phone: 314-966-2863; Office Phone: 314-345-6000. Business E-Mail: cpeper@blackwellsanders.com, christianpeper@huschblackwell.com.

PEPICH, BRUCE WALTER, museum director, curator; b. Elmhurst, Ill., June 5, 1952; s. Walter Thomas and Joan (Dolly) P.; m. Lisa Englander, Apr. 21, 1983. BA in Art History, No. Ill. U., 1974. Art dir. Charles A. Wustum Mus., Racine, Wis., 1974—80, dir., 1981—; exec. dir., curator of collections Racine Art Mus., Racine, Wis., 2003—. Curator No. Ill. U. Student Assn., 1971-74, mem. art com. Univ. Ctr. Bd., 1972-74; juried many exhbns. in midwest, including Plaza Art Fair, Kansas City, scholastic art competitions, regional shows at Milw. Art Mus. Bd. dirs. Taylor Children's Home, Racine, 1991—; vice chmn. Racine United Arts Fund Drive, 1984; mem. Racine Arts Council, 1974—; bd. dirs. Racine Planning Council, 1982-84; v.p. Mayor's Discover Racine Com., 1979 Under his leadership the Wustum Mus. is now accredited by Am. Assn. Mus., Washington. Mem. Am. Assn. Museums, Am. Craft Coun. Office: Racine Art Mus PO Box 187 Racine WI 53401-0187 also: Charles A Wustum Mus 2519 Northwestern Ave Racine WI 53404-2242 Office Phone: 262-636-9177, 262-638-8300. Office Fax: 262-898-1045. E-mail: bpepich@ramart.org.

PÉPIN, JACQUES G., chef; b. Bourg-en-Bresse, France, Dec. 1935; arrived in U.S., 1959; m. Gloria Pépin. MA in 18th Century French Lit., Columbia U., 1972. Personal chef to three French heads of state, including Charles de Gaulle, 1956—58; employee Le Pavillon restaurant, NYC; dir. of rsch. and new devel. Howard Johnson Co.; dean French Culinary Inst., NYC. Adj. faculty mem. Boston U.; Founder Am. Inst. of Wine and Food; mem. Nat. Assn. of Cooking Profls.; bd. trustees James Beard Found. Former columnist New York Times, columnist Food & Wine mag., Host with daughter (PBS TV series) Jacques Pépin's Kitchen: Cooking with Claudine, 1998, Jacques Pépin's Kitchen: Encore with Claudine, 1998, Host with Julia Child, Julia and Jacques Cooking at Home (James Beard Found. award for Best Nat. Cooking Show, 2001; Daytime Emmy award, 2001); author: (cookbooks) La Technique, 1976, La Methode, 1979, Jacques Pépin Celebrates (James Beard award, 2002), 2001, Jacques Pépin's Complete Techniques, 2001, The Apprentice: My Life in the Kitchen, 2003, Jacques Pépin's Fast Food My Way, 2004, Jacques Pépin's: More Fast Food My Way, 2008, Chez Jacques: Traditions and Rituals of a Cook, 2007. Recipient Chevalier de L'Ordre du Mérite Agricole, France, 1992, Chevalier de L'Ordre des Arts et des Lettres, 1997, Disting. Alumni, Columbia Univ. Sch. of General Studies, Lifetime Achievement award, The James Beard Found., 2005. Avocation: painting.

PEPINE, CARL JOHN, physician, educator; b. Pitts., June 8, 1941; s. Charles John and Elizabeth (Hovan) P.; m. Lynn Dives, Aug. 3, 1963; children: Mary Lynn, Anne, Elizabeth. BS, U. Pitts., 1962; MD, N.J. Coll. Medicine (UMDNJ), 1966. Cert. Am. Bd. Internal Med., 1971, Am. Bd. Internal Med., Cardiovascular Disease, 1973. Intern Allegheny Gen. Hosp., U. Pitts., 1966-67; resident in internal medicine Jefferson Med. Coll. Hosp., Phila., 1967-68, naval med. ctr., 1968-69, fellow in physiology and cardiovasc. disease, 1969-71; asst. prof. medicine Jefferson Med. Coll., Phila., 1972-74, U. Fla., Gainesville, 1974-75, assoc. prof., 1975-79, prof., 1979—, co-dir. divsn. cardiovasc. medicine, 1982-88; chief cardiology VA Regional Med. Ctr., Gainesville, 1979-94, chief divsn. cardiovasc. medicine, 1998—2008. Dir. cardiology catheterization lab. Shands Hosp., U. Fla., Gainesville, 1974-86. Mem. editl. bds. Am. Heart Jour., 1997—, Am. Jour. Cardiology, 1981-94, 97—, Am. Jour. Geriat. Cardiology, 1992—96, Clin. Cardiology, 1995—, Circulation, 1980-83, 93—, Cardiac Chronicle, 1986—90, Heart Disease: A Jour. of Cardiovasc. Medicine, 1999—2003, Hypertension, 1999—2001, Jour. Am. Coll. Cardiology, 1981-85, 91-95, 98—2004, Jour. Preventive Cardiovasc. Medicine, 1997, Preventive Cardiology, 1998-2000; chief med. editor Cardiology Today, 1997—; contbr. articles to profl. jours.; developer catheters to measure blood flow and heart circulation. Comdr. USN, 1968-74. Recipient 7th Ann. Funk award for contrbn. to cardiovascular rsch., Soc. Federated Med. Agencies, 1974, clin. faculty Rsch. prize, U. Fla., 1989-90, Profl. Excellence Program (PEP) award, 1996-97, Disting. Internat. Educator, 2005, Pioneer Investigator award Internat. Soc. for Holter Monitoring, 1990, Rsch. Achievement awards U. Fla., 1990-93, Rsch. Found. Professorship award, 1999-2001, Paul Dudley White award Assn. Mil. Surgeons US, 1991, grantee Dept. of Def., 1971-74, VA, 1975-90, NHLBI, 1985-; named to America's Top Doctors, The Best Doctors in Am. and Am. Men and Women of Sci. Fellow Am. Coll. Cardiology (master, 1999, trustee 1986-88, 90-95, 2001—, v.p. 2001—, chmn. cardiac catheterization com. 1990-96, chmn. Fla. chpt. found. 1992—, chmn. bd. govs. 1986-87, chmn. ann. sci. sessions 1990, pres. 2003-04, Gifted Tchr. award (Fla. Chpt.), 2001), Am. Heart Assn. (coun. on clin. cardiology and on circulation, (Fla. affiliate bronze award for svc. recognition, 1983, Suncoast Chpt. for cardiovascular rsch. named Eminent Scholar of an endowed chair, 2001), Am. Fedn. Clin. Rsch., Soc. Cardiac Angiography, Am. Soc. Clin. Investigation; mem. Assn. Univ. Cardiologists, Am. Clin. and Climatol. Assn. (Theodore E. Woodward award 1998), Assn. of Profs. of Cardiology, European Soc. Cardiology, Pi Kappa Alpha, Alpha Omega Alpha. Office: U Fla 1600 SW Archer Rd PO Box 100277 Gainesville FL 32610-0277 Office Phone: 352-846-3292. Office Fax: 352-371-0370. Business E-Mail: pepincj@medicine.ufl.edu.

PEPONIS, HAROLD ARTHUR, insurance agent, portfolio manager; b. Chgo., Dec. 12, 1928; s. Arthur Harold and Ethel (Karambis) P.; m. Toula H. (Preketes), Mar. 1, 1952 (dec. Dec. 1984); one child, Arthur Harold II; m. Aphrodite E. (Stavros), May 26, 1990. BS, Loyola U., Chgo., 1950, postgrad., 1991. Treas. Plaza Cleaners and Dyers, Inc., Chgo., 1950—58; owner Exch. Cleaners, Chgo., 1958—63, Park West Plaza Cleaners, Chgo., 1963—69; ins. agt. Aetna Life and Casualty, Lisle, Ill., 1969—2006; ind. broker Registered Rep., Chgo., 1995—; ptnr. lecture series, pub. co. Images of Orthodoxy; instr. religion Plato Acad., Chgo., 1998—99. Pres. Tesera Assoc., Evanston, Ill., 1973-2004; dir. Faith Net, Inc., 2003-. Mem. editl. bd. Christianity and Arts mag., 1996-98; columnist Coyote Chronicle Newsletter, 2003-. Pres. parish coun. United Greek Orthodox Ch. of Chgo., 1963—64, Annunciation Cathedral, 1991—92, 1994; archon Order of St. Andrew, Greek Orthodox Ch., state comdr., 1994—2001, regional comdr., 2001—; mem. Greek Orthodox Metropolis Coun., 1998—; sec. Metroplis Coun. Greek Orthodox Metroplis of Chgo., 2004—07; mem. Ecumenical Millennium Com., 2006—; mem. local planning com. Nat. Workshop on Christian Unity, 2006—08. Recipient Medal of St. Paul, Greek Orthodox Archdiocese, 1999. Mem. Pan Arcadian Fedn. Am. (nat. pres. Chgo. 1963-64), Du Page Life Underwriters Assn., 2626 North Lakeview Condominium Assn. (bd. dirs. 2004-05, 2009-, sec. bd. dirs. 2005-06, v.p. 2006-2008, bd. dirs., 2009-, lectr. Chgo. neighborhood tours 2005—). Home: 2626 N Lakeview Apt 2503 Chicago IL 60614-1821 Office: 2626 No Lakeview Ste 806 Chicago IL 60614 Office Phone: 630-291-6865. Business E-Mail: hapeponis26@aol.com.

PEPONIS, JOHN, architect, educator; b. Athens, Greece, June 21, 1955; s. Anastassios Peponis and Mavra Kanaris; m. Evlabia Periklaki, Oct. 15, 1957; children: Elpida, Mavra Maria. BS in Architecture, U. Coll., London, 1976, MS in Architecture, 1977, PhD in Architecture, 1983. Assoc. prof. Ga. Inst. Tech., Atlanta, 1989—2003, prof., 2003—, dir. post profl. & PhD programs. Mem. editl. bd. Jour. Arch. Author: (book) Chorographies - Descriptions of Space (in Greek); editor: Contemporary Industrial Buildings in Greece, Proceedings, 3rd International Conference on Space Syntax; contbr. articles to profl. jours., chapters to books. With Greek Mil., 1984—85. Grantee, Minsitry Energy, Industry and Rsch., Greece, 1986—88, NSF, 2000—01, GSA, 2002—04, Steelcase Corp., 2004—05. Office: Georgia Inst Tech 247 Fourth St Atlanta GA 30332-0155 Business E-Mail: john.peponis@coa.gatech.edu.

PEPPAS, NICHOLAS ATHANASSIOU, chemical and biomedical engineering educator, consultant; b. Athens, Greece, Aug. 25, 1948; s. Athanassios Nikolaou Peppas and Alice Petrou Rousopoulou; m. Lisa Brannon, Aug. 10, 1988; children: Katherine, Alexander. Diploma in Engring., Nat. Tech. U., Athens, 1971; ScD, MIT, 1973; D honoris causa, U. Parma, Italy, 1999, U. Ghent, Belgium, 1999, U. Athens, 2000. Asst. prof. chem. engring. Purdue U., West Lafayette, Ind., 1976-78, assoc. prof., 1978-81, prof., 1981—2002, Showalter Disting. prof. of chem. and biomed. engring., 1993—2002; prof. chem. engring. U. Tex., Austin, 2003—, prof. biomed. engring., 2003, prof. pharmaceutics, 2003—, Fletcher S. Pratt disting. prof., 2003—. Vis. prof. U. Geneva, 1982-83, Calif. Inst. Tech., Pasadena, 1983, U. Paris, 1986, Hoshi U., Japan, 1994, Hebrew U., Jerusalem, 1994, U. Naples, 1995, Free U. Berlin, 2001, Complutense U. Madrid, 2001, Nanyang U., Singapore, 2007; adj. prof. U. Parma, Italy, 1987; cons. in field; mem. adv. bd. several cos. Author: Biomaterials, 1982, Hydrogels in Medicine and Pharmacy, 1987, One Hundred Years of Chemical Engineering, 1989, Pulsatile Drug Delivery, 1993, Biopolymers, 1993, Superabsorbent Polymers, 1994, Biomaterials for Drug and Cell Delivery, 1994, Polymer/Inorganic Interfaces, 1995, Physicochemical and Cellular Foundations of Biomaterials, 2004, Nanotechnology in Therapeutics, 2007; contbr. over 1100 articles and over 450 abstracts to jours.; editor: Biomaterials, 1982-2002; assoc. editor: AIChE Jour., 2008-, Biomedical Microdevices, 2007-, Pharmaceutical research, 2004. Active Austin Symphony Orch., Transfiguration Orthodox Ch. Austin. Recipient APV medal, Herbert McCoy award Purdue U., 2000, Sigma Xi award, 2002, Hamilton Book award, 2004; Career Rsch. Excellence award U. Tex., 2007 Fellow: AIChE (chmn. materials divsn. 1988—90, dir. bioengring. divsn. 1994—97, bd. dirs. 1999—2002, Inst. lectr. 2007, elected engr. modern era 2008, Materials Engring. Sci. award 1984, Bioengring. award 1994, Best Paper award 1994, William Walker award 2006, Jay Bailey award 2006, Founders award 2008, 2008, Top 100 Engrs. Modern Era 2008, Founders award 2008), Am. Phys. Soc., Italian Soc. Medicine and Scis., Soc. Biomaterials (pres.-elect 2002, pres. 2003—04, Clemson award 1992, Founders award 2005), Am. Phys. Soc., Am. Inst. Med. Biol. Engrs. (Pierre Galletti award 2008), Am. Assn. Pharm. Scientists (Rsch. Achievements Pharm. Tech. award 1999, Dale Wurster award 2002); mem.: Inst. Medicine, Inst. Medicine Nat. Acads., Tex. Acad. Scis., French Acad. Pharmacy, Biomed. Engring. Soc. (Best Rsch. award 2002), Polymer Pioneer, Am. Soc. Engring. Edn. (AT&T award 1982, Curtis McGraw award 1988, G. Westinghouse award 1992, GE Sr. Rsch. award 2002, Dow Chem. Engring. award 2006, fellowship 2008), Soc. Biomaterials, Controlled Release Soc. (pres. 1987—88, Founders award 1991, Eurand award 2002), Am. Chem. Soc. (Newsmaker of Yr. award 2002), Sigma Xi. Avocations: linguistics, opera, rare maps, classical record collecting. Office: U Tex Dept Chem Engring Austin TX 78712 Office Phone: 512-471-6644. Business E-Mail: peppas@che.utexas.edu.

PEPPER, DAVID M., scientist, educator; s. Harold and Edith Pepper; m. Denise D. Pepper, 1992. BS in Physics summa cum laude, UCLA, 1971; MS in Applied Physics, Calif. Inst. Tech., 1974, PhD in Applied Physics, 1980. Mem. tech. staff Hughes Rsch. Labs., Malibu, Calif., 1973—87, sr. staff physicist, 1987—91, head nonlinear and electro-optic devices sect., 1989—91, sr. scientist, 1991—94; sr. rsch. scientist HRL Labs. (formerly Hughes Rsch. Labs.), Malibu, 1994—2004; owner, scientist, tech. cons., intellectual property cons. Malibu Scientific, Malibu Photonics, 2004—. Adj. prof. math. and physics Pepperdine U., Malibu, 1981—; adv. panel NSF, Washington, 1997; panel advanced signal processing U. Va., 1999; mem. Def. Scis. Rsch. Coun., US Govt., Washington, 1999; panel invitee US Govt. Jason Panel, 2008; presenter in field. Author: Scientific American, 1986, 1990, Laser Handbook, Vol. 4, 1985; co-author: Optical Phase Conjugation, 1983, 1995, Spatial Light Modulator Technology, 1995, CRC Handbook of Laser Science and Technology, 1995; contbr. articles to profl. jours. Mem. Sons and Daughters of 1939 Club, 2d Generation of Martyrs Meml., Mus. Holocaust Recipient Rudolf Kingslake award Soc. Photo-Optical Instrumentation Engrs., 1982, Publ. of Yr. award Hughes Rsch. Lab., 1986, Inventor of Yr. award, 1997-2008, HRL Labs.; NSF trainee Calif. Inst. Tech., 1971; Howard Hughes Master and Doctoral fellow Hughes Aircraft Co., 1973-80 Fellow Optical Soc. Am. (conf. chair 1996-2001, adv. bd. topical conf. on nonlinear optics, Hawaii 1996, 98, 2000, invited tutorial meeting laser ultrasound 2001, Optics Letters: Top 10 most cited Paper award); mem. AAAS, IEEE (guest editor, assoc. editor, program com. US CLEO laser conf. 1997-2001, 2005, instr. laser tech. 1994-2000, invited tutorial laser tech. 2001, European CLEO laser conf. program com. 2003), SPIE (guest editor, conf. co-chmn. 1998-2000), NY Acad. Scis., Am. Phys. Soc., Laser Inst. Am., Internat. Coun. Sci. Unions (com. sci. and tech. in developing countries), Sigma Xi (v.p. 1986-87, chpt. pres. 1987-88, 90-92), Sigma Pi Sigma Jewish. Achievements include 59 patents in field; 12 patents pending in field. Avocations: classical music, travel, sports, astronomy, amateur radio. Office: Malibu Scientific P O Box 126 Malibu CA 90265-0126 Personal E-mail: dmpepper@atcharter.dot.net. *Personal philosophy: We all have a profound, meaningful purpose and mission in life—the challenge is to identify, appreciate, realize and embrace our dreams and goals.*

PEPPER, JEFFREY MACKENZIE, publishing executive; b. Dallas, June 11, 1957; s. Doris Jane (Mackenzie) P.; m. Christy Dale Pepper, Nov. 5, 2004; children: Katherine McRaven, Anne Mackenzie. BA, Coll. Wooster, 1979. Sales rep. Acad. Press, NYC, 1979-82; program editor Addison-Wesley Pub. Co., Reading, Mass., 1982-83, acquisitions editor, 1983-86; sr. editor Osborne McGraw-Hill, Berkeley, Calif., 1986-90, editor-in-chief, 1990-95; v.p., editl. dir. Acad. Press Profl., Chestnut Hill, Mass., 1995-97; v.p., editor-in-chief computer books Prentice Hall PTR, Upper Saddle River, NJ, 1997-98, v.p., pub., 1999—2005; exec. editor O'Reilly Media, Inc., 2005—07; asst. pub. Apress Inc., 2007. Contbr. articles to profl. jours. Avocations: storytelling, computers, gardening. Home: 5331 Burriss Ct Southport NC 28461

PEPPER, JOHN ENNIS, JR., entertainment company executive, former consumer products company; b. Pottsville, Pa., Aug. 2, 1938; s. John Ennis Sr. and Irma Elizabeth (O'Connor) P.; m. Frances Graham Garber, Sept. 9, 1967; children: John, David, Douglas, Susan BA, Yale U., 1960; PhD (hon.), Mt. St. Joseph Coll., St. Petersburg U., Russia, Xavier U. Staff asst. Procter & Gamble Co., Cin., 1963-64, asst. brand mgr., 1964-66, brand mgr., 1966-68, copy supr., 1968-69, brand promotion mgr., 1969-72, advt. mgr. bar soap and household cleaning products divsn., 1972-74, gen. mgr. Italy subs., 1974-77, divsn. mgr. internat., 1977-78, v.p. packaged soap and detergent divsn., 1978-80, group v.p. bar soap and household cleaning products divsn., 1980-81, group v.p. Europe, 1981-84, exec. v.p. U.S. bus., 1984-86, pres. U.S. Bus., 1986-90, pres. internat. bus., 1990-95, chmn., CEO, 1995-99, chmn., 1999—2002, mem. exec. com. of bd., 2000—03; v.p. fin. & adminstrn. Yale U., New Haven, 2004—05. Bd. dirs. Xerox Corp., 1990-2005, Motorola, Inc., 1994-2005, Boston Scientific Corp., 1999-2001, The Walt Disney Co., 2006-, non-exec chmn. 2007-. Chmn. U.S. Advisory Com. for Trade Policy and Negotiations; group chmn. Cin. United Appeal Campaign, 1980; bd. trustees Xavier U., 1985-89, mem. exec. com., 1989; trustee Cin. Coun. World Affairs, Cin. Art Mus., Ctr. Strategic & Internat. Studies, Christ Ch. Endowment Fund; fellow Yale Corp.; gen. chmn. United Way Campaign, 1994; mem. Gov.'s Edn. and Bus. Advisory Group, State of Ohio; mem. adv. coun. Yale Sch. Mgmt.; mem. schs. com. Cin. Bus. Com.; co-chmn., mem. exec. com. Cin. Youth Collaborative; mem. Total Quality Leadership steering com.; mem., bd. dirs. United Negro Coll. Fund; former v.p. Am. C. of C., Brussels, Belgium (1981-84); former mem. Cin. Symphony Bd. (1979-81), Cin. Art Mus; bd. mem. Population Services Internat.; honorary co-chair, Nat. Underground Railroad Freedom Ctr, CEO 2006-. Served to lt. USN, 1960—63. Mem. Am. Soc. Corp. Execs., Grocery Mfrs. Am., Nat. Alliance Businessmen (chmn. communication com.), Partnership for a Drug-Free Am., Soap and Detergent Assn. (bd. dirs.), The Bus. Coun., Bus. Roundtable, Yale Club, Queen City Club, Commonwealth Club, Comml. Club (former pres.). Office: Nat Underground Railroad Freedom Ctr 50 E Freedom Way Cincinnati OH 45202*

PEPPER, JOLINE ROMANO, psychologist, educator; b. Malden, Mass., Nov. 4, 1971; d. Leo Richard and Geraldine Kathleen Romano; m. Eric Edward Pepper; children: Erica Jade, Alexa Jo. BA, Merrimack Coll., 1993; MEd, U. Mass., 1995. Cert. advanced graduate study U. Mass., Boston, 1996. Sch. psychologist North Reading Pub. Schs., Mass., 1996—; lisason between dept. pub. health and dept. revenue Mass. Adj. faculty mem. Western New Eng. Coll., Mass., 1999—. Vol. food pantry outreach and citizenship com. Recipient Allen J. Ash award, Nat. Honor Soc. in Psychology. Mem.: Nat. Assn. Sch. Psychologists, Mass. Assn. Sch. Psychologists, Psi Chi. Democrat. Avocations: reading, skiing, rollerblading, travel. Personal E-mail: jolinepepper@msn.com.

PEPPER, JONATHON L., communications executive; b. Dearborn, Mich., Aug. 23, 1955; s. Joseph Daniel and Norma (McIntyre) P.; m. Diane Sharon Garelis, May 12, 1984; children: Jonathon Jay, Lauren Claire, Scott Joseph. BA, Mich. State U., 1977. Copywriter Detroit Free Press, 1977-84, reporter, 1984-87; nat. corr. Detroit News, 1987-91, bus. columnist, 1991-2000; host talk show Sta. WXYT, 1995-96; assoc. bus. editor Detroit News, 1997-2000; pres. Small Times Media LLC, Ann Arbor, Mich., 2000—02; dir. integrated comm. Ford Motor Co., Dearborn, Mich., 2002—04, dir. global corp. comm., 2005—07; v.p. corp. comm. Hess Corp., NYC, 2007—. Mem. Writers Guild Am., The Fairlane Club (vice chmn., past chmn.), Found. Am. Comm. (dir. bd. 2004-), Arthur W. Page Soc., PRS(NY)(seminar mem.) Business E-Mail: jpepper@hess.com.

PEPPER, PAMELA POE, psychologist; b. Erwin, NC, Feb. 21, 1953; d. Thomas Wesley Poe, Jr. and Norma Jean (Ferrell) Poe; m. Eugene Vance Pepper, Jr., May 15, 1976; children: Katherine McIver, Anna Faison. BA in Psychology & English, Salem Coll., 1975; MA in Counseling, U. NC, 1980; PhD in Sch. Psychology, U. NC-Chapell Hill, 1992. Lic. psychologist NC, health svcs. provider, psychologist NC, registered electroencephalography tech. Duke U., cert. provider psychol. svcs. traumatic brain injured students NC Dept. Public Instruction. Postdoctoral fellow in neuropsychology Wake Forest U., Bowman Gray Sch. Med., Winston-Salem, NC, 1993—95; rsch. technologist electroencephalography Epilepsy Rsch. Ctr., Va. Med. Ctr., Durham, NC, 1975—76; clin. assoc. biological psychiatry, program dir. electrophysiological tech. Duke U., Durham, 1978—81; mgr. staff edn. & devel. Durham Regional Med. Ctr., 1981—82; postdoctoral fellow in neurology, divsn. neuropsychology Wake Forest U. Bapt. Med. Ctr., Bowman Gray Sch. Medicine, 1993—95; adj. asst. prof. grad. studies edn. Salem Coll., Winston-Salem, 1994; clin. neuropsychologist Salem Psychiatric Assocs., P.A., Winston-Salem, 1995—97; clin. neuropsychologist, found. ptnr. TriCare, P.A., Winston-Salem, 1997—2003; clin. neuropsychologist Pepper Neuropsychol. Consulting., PLLC, Winston-Salem, 2004—. Spkr. in field. Bd. advisors quality assurance Qual Choice Behavioral Health, Winston-Salem, 1996—2001; mem. Jr. League Durham, 1975; pres. Durham/Chapel Hill Salem Coll. Alumnae Assn., 1975—76; bd. dirs. So. Soc. Electroencephalographic Technologists, Atlanta, 1980—81, Mental Health Assn. Forsyth County, Winston-Salem, 2000—02. Recipient Order of Scorpion, Salem Coll., 1973—75. Mem.: APA Clin. Neuropsychology Divsn., APA, Internat. Neuropsychol. Soc., Brain Injury Assn. NC (spkrs. bureau 1998—). Democrat. Presbyterian. Avocations: reading, writing, gardening, rock collecting, birdwatching. Office Phone: 336-409-4705. Business E-Mail: drpampepper@aol.com.

PEPPERDENE, MARGARET WILLIAMS, English educator; b. Vicksburg, Miss., Dec. 25, 1919; d. O.L. and Jane (Stocks) Williams. BS, La. State U., 1941; MA, Vanderbilt U., 1948, PhD, 1953; LHD (hon.), Agnes Scott Coll., 2006. Div. Instr. English U. Oreg., 1946-47; teaching fellow Vanderbilt U., 1948-50; instr., then asst. prof. Miami U., Oxford, Ohio, 1952-56; mem. faculty Agnes Scott Coll., 1956—, prof. English, chmn. dept., 1967—. Author articles.; Editor: That Subtile Wreath: Lectures Presented at the Quartercentenary Celebration of the Birth of John Donne, 1973. Served to lt. USNR, 1943-46. Fulbright fellow, 1950-51; Ford Found. grad. fellow, 1951-52; AAUW fellow, 1954-55; research fellow Dublin Inst. Advanced Studies, 1954-55; Guggenheim fellow, 1956-57; recipient Gov.'s Award in Humanities, Ga., 1987. Home: 418 Glendale Ave Decatur GA 30030-1922

PEPPER HENRY, JAMES, museum director; Grad., U. Oreg. Visual arts coord. Inst. Alaska Native Arts, Fairbanks, 1990—92; visual arts mgr. Interstate Firehouse Cultural Ctr., Portland, Oreg.; interim curator Am. Indian Art Portland Art Mus.; dir. Kanza Mus. of Kaw Nation, Okla., 1994—98; assoc. dir. cmty. and constituent svcs. Nat. Mus. of Am. Indian, Smithsonian Inst., Washington, 1998—2007; dir., CEO Anchorage Mus. at Rasmuson Ctr., Ala., 2007—. Founder/prodr. Nat. Pow Wow. Mem.: Kaw Nation of Okla. Office: Anchorage Mus at Rasmuson Ctr 121 W Seventh Ave Anchorage AK 99501 Office Phone: 907-343-4326. Office Fax: 907-343-6149. E-mail: museumdirector@anchoragemuseum.org.

PEPPERS, JERRY P., lawyer; b. Cleve., Mar. 8, 1946; s. Jerry P. and Katherine M. Peppers; m. Sue E. Schafer, June 14, 1969; children: Amy E., Erica K., Christina A., Michele S. BBA, Ohio U., 1968; JD, Duke U., 1971. Bar: N.Y. 1972, U.S. Dist. Ct. (so. dist.) N.Y. 1972, U.S. Ct. Appeals (2nd cir.) 1972. Assoc. Pillsbury Winthrop Shaw Pittman LLP, NYC, 1971-81, ptnr., 1982—; co-chair Mergers and Acquisitions Group, 2006—. Editor (booklet): Outline of Mergers and Acquisitions in the United States, 15th edit., 2003. Trustee Scarsdale Youth Soccer Club, Inc.; trustee emeritus, mem.alternative investment com. Ohio Univ. Found., Athens, 1991—; NY dir. Lincoln Hwy. Assn., 2008—; bd. dirs. Atheneum Venture Fund, Athens, 1996—; com. mem. Fields for Kids. Mem.: ABA, Soc. Automotive Engrs., Assn. Bar City NY, Internat. Bar Assn., India House, Fox Meadow Tennis Club (Scarsdale, NY). Avocation: coaching soccer. Office: Pillsbury Winthrop Shaw Pittman LLP 1540 Broadway New York NY 10036-4039 Office Phone: 212-858-1205. Business E-Mail: jerry.peppers@pillsburylaw.com.

PEPPERS, JULIUS (FRAZIER), professional football player; b. Wilson, NC, Jan. 18, 1980; BA in Afro-Am. Studies, U. NC, Chapel Hill, 2002. Defensive end Carolina Panthers, 2002—. Spokesperson Big Brothers Big Sisters of Greater Charlotte. Named NFL Defensive Rookie of Yr., AP, 2002, First Team All-Pro, 2004, 2006; named to Nat. Football Conf. Pro Bowl Team, NFL, 2004—06, 2008. Avocation: reading. Office: Carolina Panthers 800 So Mint St Charlotte NC 28202*

PEPPET, RUSSELL FREDERICK, accountant; b. Chgo., Oct. 3, 1939; s. George Russell and Elizabeth (Foster) P.; m. Rosemary Meyer, June 18, 1960 (dec. 2000); children: Cynthia, Jeffrey, Scott; m. Sandra S. Wharton, Feb. 2, 2002. BS in Math, Mich. State U., 1960; MBA, Northwestern U., 1963. C.P.A., Ill., Minn. Cons. Peat, Marwick, Mitchell & Co., Chgo., 1961-68, head mgmt. cons. dept. Mpls., 1968-72, partner, 1969-88; sr. cons. partner for Continental Europe, Paris, 1972-78, partner-in-charge mgmt. cons. dept., N.Y. office, 1978-81, vice chmn. mgmt. cons., 1981-86; mng. ptnr. San Jose Bus. Unit, 1986-88; v.p. internat. devel. Towers Perrin, NYC, 1989-90; vice-chmn. Quirk Carson Peppet Inc., NYC, 1990-98; prin. Churchill Capital Inc., NYC, 1999—2001; ptnr. Park Ave. Equity Ptnrs., 2005—; dir. Armstrong World Industries, 2006—. With U.S. Army, 1962-64. Mem. AICPA, Country Club of Darien (Conn.), Bonita Bay Club. Home: 5 Topping Ln Norwalk CT 06854-3418 Office: 12 E 49th St New York NY 10017 Office Phone: 212-758-4446.

PEPPLES, JASON JOHN, language educator; b. East Meadow, NY, May 27, 1973; s. Terry Wayne Pepples and Maureen Cummins; m. Kathleen Marie Wojtowicz, July 17, 1999; children: Abigail Julia, Olivia Maria, Ryan Jason. AA in Liberal Arts, Sullivan County CC, Loch Sheldrake, NY, 1994; BS in Elem. Edn. & Spanish, SUNY, Oneonta, 1997; MS in Edn. Spanish, SUNY, Binghamton, 2002. Cert. secondary Spanish and elem. edn. NY, 2002. Spanish tchr. Chenango Forks Mid. Sch., Binghamton, 1997—, Broome CC, Binghamton, 2006—08. Named Educator of Week, WBNG TV Sta. & NY State Lottery, 2002, 2006—07. Business E-Mail: pepples_j@sunybroome.edu.

PEPYNE, EDWARD WALTER, lawyer, psychologist, educator; b. Springfield, Mass., Dec. 27, 1925; s. Walter Henry and Frances A. (Carroll) P.; m. Carol Jean Dutcher, Aug. 2, 1958; children— Deborah, Edward, Jr., Susan, Byron, Shari, Randy, David, Allison, Jennifer, Jaymie Page. BA, Am. Internat. Coll., 1948; MS, U. Mass., 1951, Ed.D., 1968; postgrad., NYU, 1952-55; prof. diploma, U. Conn., 1964; JD, Western New Eng. Coll., 1978. Bar: Mass. 1978, U.S. Supreme Ct. 1981, Vt. 2004. Prin., tchr. Gilbertville Grammar Sch., Hardwick, Mass., 1948-49; sch. counselor West Springfield High Sch., Mass., 1949-53; instr. NYU, 1953-54; supt. schs. New Shoreham, RI, 1954-56; asst. prof. edn. Mich. State U., 1956-58; sch. psychologist, guidance dir. Pub. Sch. System, East Long, Mass., 1958-62; lectr. Westfield State Coll., 1961-65; dir. pupil services Chicopee Pub. Sch., 1965-68; assoc. prof. counselor edn. U. Hartford, West Hartford, Mass., 1968-71, prof., 1971-85, dir. Inst. Coll. Counselors Minority and Low Income Students, 1971-72, dir. Div. Human Services, 1972-77; cons. Aetna Life & Casualty Co., Hartford, 1962-75; hearing officer Conn. State Bd. Edn., 1980-99; exec. dir. Sinapi Assocs., 1959-78; pvt. practice, Ashfield, Mass., 1978—2005, Derby, Vt., 2004—. Co-author: Better Driving, 1958; assoc. editor: Highway Safety and Driver Education, 1954; chmn. editorial com.: Man and the Motor Car, 5th edit., 1954; contbr. numerous articles to profl. jours. Chief welfare svcs. Civil Def., Levittown, NY, 1953-54; chmn. Ashfield Planning Bd., Mass., 1979-83; moderator Town Ashfield, 1980-81, town counsel, Charlemont, Mass., 1983-84; mem. jud. nominating coun. Western Regional Com., 1993-99; mem. Mohawk Regional Sch. Com., 1999-2000; program chmn. Osher Lifelong Learning Inst., 2006-. Mem. ABA, APA, Mass. Bar Assn., Vt. Bar Assn., Mass. Acad. Trial Attys., Am. Pers. and Guidance Assn., New Eng. Pers. and Guidance Assn. (bd. dirs.), New Eng. Ednl. Rsch. Orgn. (pres. 1971), Am. Assn. Sch. Adminstrs., Am. Ednl. Rsch. Assn., Mt. Tom Amateur Radio Assn., Franklin County Amateur Radio Club, Elks, Kiwanis (pres. 1988-89, lt. gov. div. 12, 1991-92), Masons (master 1994-96, sec. 2007—), Shriners, Phi Delta Kappa. Home: 1585 Pine Hill Rd Newport VT 05855-9830 Personal E-mail: pepyne@earthlink.net.

PERADOTTO, JOHN JOSEPH, retired classics educator, editor; b. Ottawa, Ill., May 11, 1933; s. John Joseph and Mary Louise (Giacometti) P.; m. Noreen Doran, Aug. 29, 1959 (div. 1982); m. Marlene Rosen, Aug. 29, 1992; children: Erin, Monica, Noreen, Nicole. BA, St. Louis U., 1957, MA, 1958; PhD, Northwestern U., 1963. Instr. classics and English Western Wash. U., Bellingham, 1960-61; instr. Georgetown U., 1961-63, asst. prof. classics, 1963-66, SUNY, Buffalo, 1966-69, asso.

prof., 1969-73; prof., chmn. classics U. Tex., Austin, 1973-74; prof. classics SUNY-Buffalo, 1974-2000, Andrew V.V. Raymond prof. classics, 1984-99, Disting. tchg. prof., 1990-2000, Disting. tchg. prof. emeritus, 2000—, chmn. dept., 1974-77, dean div. undergrad. edn., 1978-82. Benedict Disting. vis. prof. Carleton Coll., 2003; Martin lectr. Oberlin Coll., 1987; dir. summer seminar for coll. tchrs. NEH, 1976, for secondary sch. tchrs., 1984; vis. scholar winter quarters U. Calif., San Diego, 2000—09. Author: Classical Mythology: An Annotated Bibliographical Survey, 1973, Man in the Middle Voice: Name and Narration in the Odyssey, 1990, also articles and revs.; founding assoc. editor: Arethusa, editor-in-chief:, 1974—95, mem. bd. editors: SUNY Press, 1978—81; editor: SUNY Press Classical Series, 1981—2000, Classical Literature and Contemporary Literary Analysis, 1977, Women in the Ancient World, 1978, 1983, Studies in Latin Literature, 1984, Under the Text; co-editor: Population Policy in Plato and Aristotle, 1975, The New Archilochus, 1976, Augustan Poetry Books, 1980, Indo-European Roots of Classical Culture, 1980, Vergil: 2000 Years, 1981, Texts and Contexts: American Classical Studies in Honor of J.P. Vernant, 1982, Semiotics and Classical Studies, 1983, Audience-oriented Criticism and the Classics, 1986, Herodotus and the Invention of History, 1987, Gonimos: Neoplatonic and Byzantine Studies Presented to L.G. Westerlink at 75, 1988, The Challenge of Black Athena, 1989, Pastoral Revisions, 1990, Reconsidering Ovid's Fasti, 1992, Bakhtin and Classical Studies, 1993, Rethinking the Classical Canon, 1994, Horace: 2000 Years, 1995, The New Simonides, 1996, The Iliad and its Contexts, 1997. Fellow Center for Hellenic Studies, 1972-73; recipient Chancellor's award for teaching excellence State U. N.Y., 1975, Disting. Retiring Editor award Coun. of Editors of Learned Jours., 1995. Mem. Am. Philol. Assn. (dir. 1974-77, pres. 1990), Classical Assn. Atlantic States (exec. com. 1976-78). Office: Dept Classics State U Ny Buffalo NY 14261-0026 Office Phone: 716-645-0462. Business E-Mail: peradott@buffalo.edu.

PERALES-PEREZ, OSCAR J., engineering educator; m. Martha B. Macedo-Llasa, Sept. 10, 1995; children: Diana Perales-Macedo, Andrea Perales-Macedo. PhD, Tohoku U., Sendai, Japan, 1998. Rsch. trainee, Japan Internat. Cooperation. Agy. Tohoku U., Sendai, Miyagi Prefecture, 1993—94, vis. assoc. prof., Ctr. Interdisciplinary Rsch., 1998—2001, rschr., 1998—2001; asst. prof. Nat. Engring. U., Lima, 1987—95, U. PR, Mayaguez, 2002—05, assoc. prof., 2005—, acad. senator, 2008; faculty fellow U. Wis., Dept. Materials Sci., Madison, 2004—09. Tech. panelist NSF, Washington, 2004. Recipient Disting. Prof. award, U. Puerto Rico, Coll. Engring., 2006—08; grantee, JICA-Japan, 1993—94, Govt. Japan-Monbusho, 1995—98, NSF, 2003—, DOD, 2006—09, DOE, 2008—. Achievements include development of new processes for high coercivity magnetic materials. Office: Univ Puerto Rico Mayaguez Engring Sci & Materials Mayaguez PR 00680-9044 Business E-Mail: oscarjuan.perales@upr.edu.

PERALTA, EVERETT FIGUEROA, college professor, department chairman; came to U.S., 1958; s. Everado Grijalva and Dora (Figueroa) P. BS in Soc. Sci., SUNY, Albany, 1985; MA in Edn. Administrn. and Supervision, U. Phoenix, 2000; EdD, Ariz. State U. Coll. Edn., Tempe, 2005. Cert. global edn. program U. London, Eng., 2003, in elem. edn. K-8, in secondary edn. 7-12, in endorsement social studies, supt., supr., prin., subsitute tchr., in std. adult edn., ESL tchr. Resident asst. Ariz. State U., Tempe, 1979—81; coord. leadership devel. program, summer conf. mgr., resident hall dir. U. Bridgeport, Conn., 1981—85; exec. dir. Grad. Student Assn. Ariz. State U., Tempe, 1985-87; vice-chmn. Ariz. State Bd. Econ. Planning and Devel., Phoenix, 1987-88; v.p., provost, registrar Ariz. Investment Insurance Sch., 1987—89; sr. mgmt. cons. Crystal Resources, Tempe, 1988—94; substitute tchr. Wilcox, Cochise, Pearce Sch. Dists., 1989—94; exec. dir. Coun. Family Concerns Resources, 1993—95; with Papago Elem. Sch., 1995—97; tchr., prin. Maricopa County Regional Schs., 1997—2001; prof. edn. Am. Indian Coll., Phoenix, 2001—, chmn. dept. edn., 2005—; prof. edn., soc. sci. Western Internat. U., Ottawa U., Phoenix, 2005—. Bd. dirs. FBI Citizens Acad.; bd. dirs. law related edn. We the People Program Ariz. Bar Assn.; exec. dir. Coun. Family Concerns and Resources, 1993—95; prof. Cochise C.C., 1990—94, We. Internat. U., 2005—; presenter in field; cons. in field. Author: College Study Skills, 1992, Organizational Development and Leadership Skills, 1985. Delegate Ariz. Boys State Am. Legion, 1971; bd. dirs. Rural Schs. Project, Willcox, 1972-73, ASU Bd. Equal Opportunity, ASU Task Force Student Recruitment Retention, ASU Student Affairs Bd., ASU Graduate Student Rsch. Grants Bd., ASU res. hall. govt., 1985, Cochise County Literacy Coun., Bisbee, Ariz., 1991-1994; election bd. clk. City of Willcox, 1992; mem. Tempe City Transp. Commn., 1989; precinct committeeman, dep. registrar Maricopa County, 1983-; Wilcox City Election Bd., 1994, state bd. Family Soc. Svcs., 1994, state bd. dir. Prevent Child Abuse, 1995; founder Bilingual Middle 5-8 Sch. Program 1997; Congressional adv. com. Soc. Security Nat. Health Plan, 1998, faculty senate academic affairs com., Am. Indian Coll. 2001. Mem. UN Assn. (state treas., bd. dirs. Conn. chpt. 1984-85), Ctr. for Study of Presidency, K.C. (3d degree knight), Am. Assn. Univ. Prof., Nat. Edn. Assn., Nat. Coun. Soc. Studies, Am. Ednl. Rsch. Assn., Assn. Study of Higher Edn., Omicron Delta Kappa, Phi Delta Kappa, Theta Kappa Epsilon. Conservative. Avocations: reading, writing, politics, public speaking, carpentry. Home: 10020 North 15th Ave Phoenix AZ 85021 Home Phone: 602-475-8712; Office Phone: 602-944-3335 ext. 269. Business E-Mail: eperalta@aicag.edu.

PERALTA-VIDEA, JOSE R., environmental scientist, researcher; b. Pueblo Nuevo, Nicaragua; MS, Tropical Agrl. Rsch. & Higher Edn. Ctr., Costa Rica, 1978; PhD, Postgraduate Coll., Mex., 1986, U. of Tex. at El Paso, 2002. Cert. Agronomist Nat. Sch. of Agrl., Managua, Nicaragua, 1975. Rschr. coffee program Ministry of Agr., Managua, Nicaragua, 1974—76; leader cocoa program Ctrl. Bank of Nicaragua, Managua, 1978—79; sub-leader agrl. rsch. Agrl. Devel. Ministry, Managua, Nicaragua, 1979—82; prof., rschr. grad. coll., plant breeding dept. "Hermanos Escobar" Agricultrural Sch., Ciudad Juarez, Mexico; HS prin. Monterey Inst. of Tech., Ciudad Juarez, Mexico, 1992—95; assoc. prof. Monterrey Inst. of Tech., Ciudad Juarez, Mexico, 1995—99; rsch. asst. U. of Tex. at El Paso, 1999—2001, rsch. specialist, 2001—. Recipient Best H.S. full prof., Monterrey Inst. of Tech., 1993, 1997, Outstanding Doctoral Student award, U. of Tex. at El Paso, 2002; grantee, U.S. Dept. of Energy, 2003—05, SW Ctr. For Environ. Rsch. and Policy, 2005—06, Stanford Synchrotron Radiation Lab. (Ssrl), 2005—. Mem.: Soc. for Advancement of Chicanos and Native Ams. in Sci. (assoc.), Am. Chem. Soc. (assoc.). Achievements include patents for Production of gold and silver nanoparticles by living plants; research in uptake and translocation of inorganic elements within the transport system of vascular plants exposed to excess heavy metals; use of growth factors and chelating agents to enhance the metal translocation from the roots to the leaves and the effects produced on the whole-plant element accumulation. Office: Univ of Texas at El Paso 500 West Univ Ave El Paso TX 79968 Business E-Mail: jperalta@utep.edu.

PERAMBAKAM, SUPRIYA, medical educator; d. Mohanakrishnan and Nalini Perambakam; m. Sujay Velegar, Oct. 16, 2007; children: Samay Velegar, Sidh Velegar. BS, U. Bombay, India, 1989; MS in Microbiology, M.S.U., Baroda, 1991; PhD, U. Bombay, Cancer Rsch. Inst., 1997. Cert. in health informatics U. Ill., Chgo., 2009. Vis. rsch. scientist Rush Cancer Inst., Rush Presbyn. St-Luke's Med. Ctr., 1997—99; vis. postdoc. rsch. assoc. U. Ill. Chgo., 1999—2002, rsch. asst. prof., 2002—. Invited sci. reviewer Peer Rev. Com. Dept. Def., Congressionally Directed Med. Rsch. Program, Frederick, Md., 2006—07, 2009; invited reviewer Pub. Elsevier, Amsterdam, 2006, Pub. Springer, NYC, 2006, Dove Med. Press, Macclesfield, 2006. Recipient Rsch. award, Milheim Found. Cancer Rsch., Denver, CO, 2007—08; Rsch. fellow, Coun. Sci. & Indsl. Rsch., 1991—96, Instl. Rsch. grant, Am. Cancer Soc., 2003—04. Mem.: Am. Assn. Immunologists (Faculty Travel award 2004, 2005, 2007). Achievements include patents pending for treating prostate cancer. Office: Univ Ill 909 S Wolcott Chicago IL 60612 Office Fax: 312-413-7963. Business E-Mail: speramba@uic.edu.

PERANTONI, ALAN O., medical researcher; PhD in Cell Biology, Catholic U., 1983. Asst. prof. Pathology Dept. U. Colo. Med. Sch.; acting lab. chief Cancer and Devel. Biology Lab., head Differentiation and Neoplasia Sect. Ctr. Cancer Rsch., Nat. Cancer Inst., NIH, Frederick, Md. Spkr. in field. Office: Nat Cancer Inst at Frederick Bldg 538, Rm 224 PO Box B Frederick MD 21702-1201 Office Phone: 301-846-6529, 301-846-5946. E-mail: peranton@ncifcrf.gov.*

PERCAS-PONSETI, HELENA, foreign language and literature educator; b. Valencia, Spain, Jan. 17, 1921; came to US, 1940, naturalized, 1950; m. Ignacio V. Ponseti, 1961. Baccalaureat, Paris, France, 1939; BA, Barnard Coll., 1942; MA, Columbia, 1943, PhD, 1951. Tchr. lang. and lit. Barnard Coll., 1942-43, Russell Sage Coll., 1943-45, Columbia U., 1945-47, Queens Coll., 1946-48; mem. faculty Grinnell Coll., 1948—, prof. lang. and lit., 1957—, James Morton Roberts Honor prof. modern fgn. langs., 1961-62, Seth Richards prof. modern fgn. langs., 1963-82, prof. emerita, 1982—. Author: Homage to Iowa: The Inside Story of Ignacio V. Ponseti, Dept. Orthop., U. Iowa, 2007; contbr. over 44 articles to profl. jours. Mem.: Assoc. Cervantistas Alcalá Henares Spain (charter 1987), Cervantes Soc. Am. (founding mem.), Hispanic Soc. Am. (hon.; hon. assoc. 2001). Home: 110 Oakridge Ave Iowa City IA 52246-2935

PERCUS, JEROME KENNETH, physicist, researcher; b. NYC, June 21, 1926; s. Philip M. and Gertrude B. (Schweiger) P.; m. Ora Engelberg, May 20, 1965; children: Orin, Allon. BSE.E., Columbia U., 1947, MA, 1948, PhD, 1954. Instr. elec. engring. Columbia U., NYC, 1952-54; asst. prof. Stevens Inst. Tech., Hoboken, NJ, 1955-58; assoc. prof. NYU, NYC, 1958-65, prof. physics, 1965—. Dir. Nat. Biomed. Research Found. Author: (book) Many-Body Problem, 1963, Kinetic Theory and Statistical Mechanics, 1969, Combinatorial Methods, 1971, Combinatorial Methods in Developmental Biology, 1977, Mathematical Methods in Developmental Biology, 1978, Mathematical Methods in Enzymology, 1984, Lectures on the Mathematics of Immunology, 1986, Mathematics of Genome Analysis, 2001; editor: (Jours.) Pattern Recognition, Jour. Statis. Physics, Jour. Statis. Mechanics, Open Math. Jour. With USN, 1944-46. Recipient Pregel Chemistry Physics award N.Y. Acad. Scis., 1975, Joel Henry Hildebrand award in the Theoretical and Exptl. Chemistry of Liquids, Am. Chem. Soc., 1993, Pattern Rec. Soc. award, 1992. Fellow AAAS, Am. Phys. Soc.; mem. Am. Math. Soc., Sigma Xi. Office: NYU 251 Mercer St New York NY 10012-1110 Business E-Mail: percus@cims.nyu.edu.

PERCY, HELEN SYLVIA, physician; b. Atlanta, May 7, 1923; d. George L. and Sophia (Toulchin) P.; 1 child, Valentina Stewart-Wajjon. BS, U. San Francisco, 1951; MD, Med. Coll. Pa., 1958. Intern Harbor Gen. Hosp., Torrance, Calif., 1958-59, resident, 1959; physician Maui Med. Group, Lahaina, Hawaii, 1968—; asst. prof. medicine U. Hawaii, Honolulu, 1978—2000. Adv. bd. Maui Community Health Ctr., 1986-89; v.p. Maui AIDS Found., 1986-89. Mem. AMA, Maui County Med. Soc. (pres. 1988-1989), Hawaii Med. Assn. (Maui councilor). Democrat. Buddhist. Avocation: dance. Office: Maui Med Group 130 Prison St Lahaina HI 96761-1247 Office Phone: 808-661-0051.

PERDEW, JOHN PAUL, physics professor; b. Cumberland, Md., Aug. 30, 1943; BS, Gettysburg Coll., 1965; PhD, Cornell U., 1971. Postdoctoral fellow U. Toronto, 1971-74, Rutgers U., New Brunswick, NJ, 1974-77; prof. physics Tulane U., New Orleans, 1977—, chair physics dept., 1991—94, 2001—03. Vis. scientist Nordita, Copenhagen, Argonne Nat. Lab., ETH Zurich, ITP Santa Barbara, Naval Rsch. Lab., Washington, Rice U.; invited lectr. numerous internat. confs. Contbr. more than 230 sci. articles to profl. jours. NSF Rsch. grantee, 1978—, Petroleum Rsch. Fund grantee 1998-2000; recipient Tulane LAS award for excellence in rsch., 1990. Fellow Am. Phys. Soc.; mem. Am. Chem. Soc., Am. Assn. Physics Tchrs., Internat. Acad. Quantum Molecular Sci., Phi Beta Kappa. Office: Tulane U Dept Physics New Orleans LA 70118 Business E-Mail: perdew@tulane.edu.

PERDIGÓ, LUISA MARINA, foreign language and literature educator; b. Havana, Cuba, Dec. 25, 1947; arrived in US, 1962, US citizen, 1970. d. Mario and Hortensia Dolores (Alvarez) P. AB, CUNY, 1971, MA, 1974, PhD, 1981; MA, Columbia U., 1987. LPN, 2005; cert. translator English/Spanish Am. Translators Assn., ins. and coding specialist. Asst. prof. Spanish, asst. dean St. Thomas Aquinas Coll., Sparkill, NY, 1982-87; asst. prof. Spanish and French CUNY, La Guardia, 1987-88, asst. prof. Spanish, City Coll., 1988-89; asst. prof. Spanish St. Peter's Coll., Jersey City, 1989-91; asst. prof. Spanish and French Clarion U., Pa., 1992-94, Rockland Coll. SUNY, 1995-96, Mercy Coll., 1998—2008, assoc. prof. Spanish and French, dir. fgn. languages program, 2007—08. Author: La Estética de Octavio Paz, 1975, The Origins of Vicente Huidobro's Creacionismo (1911-1916) and its Evolution (1917-47), 1994, The Lyrics of the Troubadour Perdigon, 2002, (poetry) Desde el Hudson/From the Hudson, 1993, Huellas/Footprints, 1997, 2d edit., 2006, America at the Millenium, 2000, The Best Poems and Poets of 2002, Theatre of the Mind, 2003, The M Poems, 2006, Songs of Honour, 2007, Centres of Expression, 2007; contbr. poetry to anthologies, articles to profl. jours. Participant seminar in poetry, NEH, U. Kans., 1991; Rsch. fellow Orgn. Am. States, Chile, 1981; grantee CUNY, 1975; scholar Columbia U., 1982-84. Mem.: MLA, Acad. Am. Poets, Clarion Hist. Soc., Circulo de Cultura Panamericano, Pi Delta Phi, Sigma Delta Pi.

PERDUE, BEVERLY EAVES, Governor of North Carolina; b. Grundy, Va., Jan. 14, 1948; d. Alfred P. and Irene E. (Morefield) Moore; m. Robert W. Eaves, Jr.; children from previous marriage: Garrett, Emmett. BA, U. Ky., 1969; MEd, U. Fla., 1974, PhD, 1976. Pvt. lectr., writer, cons., 1980-86; pres. The Perdue Co., New Bern, N.C., 1985—; mem. NC State Gen. Assembly from Dist. 3, Raleigh, 1987—90, NC State Senate from Dist. 3, Raleigh, 1991—2001; lt. gov. State of NC, Raleigh, 2001—09, gov., 2009—. Bd. dirs. Nations Bank, New Bern. Bd. dirs. N.C. United Way, Greensboro, 1990-92; exec. mem. N.C. Dem. Party, Raleigh, 1989—; mem. N.C. travel bd. Nat. Conf. State Legislators. Named Outstanding Legislator, N.C. Aging Network, 1989, 92, 100 to Watch, Dem. Leadership Coun. 2003; Toll fellow Nat. Conf. State Legislators, Lexington, Ky., 1992. Mem. Nat. Coun. on Aging, Bus. and Profl. Women, Rotary. Democrat. Episcopalian. Office: Office of Governor 20301 Mail Service Ctr Raleigh NC 27699 Office Phone: 919-733-4240. Office Fax: 919-733-2120. E-mail: bperdue@ncmail.net.*

PERDUE, DIANA S., mathematician, educator; d. James C. Perdue and Renate E. Perdue-Davenport; life ptnr. Toni R. Davis, Jan. 1, 1998. BA, Belmont U., 1988; MAT, Jacksonville U., 1991; PhD, U. Va., 1997. Dir. Edward Waters Coll., Jacksonville, Fla., 1989—90; tech. trainer Lockheed Martin, Rsch. Triangle Pk., NC, 1998—99; adj. faculty mem. Jacksonville U., 1990—91, U. Va., Charlottesville, 1991—97; asst. prof. math. edn. West Tex. A&M U., Canyon, 1999—2003; assoc. prof. math. edn. Va. State U., Petersburg, 2003—. Author of poems. Mem.: Rsch. Coun. Math. Learning, Math. Assn. Am., Nat. Coun. Tchrs. Math., Mensa. Democrat. Mem. United Ch. Of Christ. Avocations: kayaking, reading, white-water rafting. Office: Va State U Math Dept 1 Hayden Dr Petersburg VA 23806 Office Phone: 804-524-5437. E-mail: dperdue@vsu.edu.

PERDUE, GEORGE (SONNY PERDUE), Governor of Georgia; b. Perry, Ga., Dec. 20, 1946; s. Ervin and Ophie Perdue; m. Mary (Ruff); children: Leigh, Lara, Jim, Dan. PhD in Vet. Medicine, U. Ga. Mem. Ga. Senate (dist. 18), Atlanta, 1990—2002; pres. pro tem; mem. appropriations, ethics, rules, reapportionment coms.; also fin. and pub. utilities, health and human svcs. coms.; former chmn. higher edn., def. conversion com.; co-chair joint commn. legis. info. mgmt.; gov. State of Ga., Atlanta, 2003—. Capt. USAF, 1971-74, Vietnam. Democrat. Baptist. Office: Office of the Gov 203 State Capitol Atlanta GA 30334 Office Phone: 404-656-1776.

PERDUE, JOHN D., state treasurer; b. Manila, W.Va. s. Glenn and Mary Perdue; m. Robin Perdue; 2 children. BS in Agr., W.Va. U., 1972, State treas. State W.Va., 1997—. Chmn. W.Va. Coll. Agr., Forestry Visiting com. Mem. W.Va. Tech. Enterprise Investment Coun.; bd. mem. Coll. Savings Plan Network. Mem.: Nat. Assn. Unclaimed Property Adminstr. (former pres.), Nat. Assn. State Treas. (pres. 2004—05), W.Va. Forestry Assn., Leukemia Soc. Am. (W.Va. bd. trustees), Alpha Gamma Rho, Alpha Tau Alpha. Office: WVa State Treasurers Office 1900 Kanawha Blvd Capital Complex Bldg 1 Rm E-145 Charleston WV 25305 Office Phone: 304-558-5000. Business E-Mail: john.perdue@wvsto.com.*

PERDUE, PETER C., history professor; PhD, Harvard Univ., 1981. T.T. and Wei Fong Chao prof.Asian civilizations, prof. history MIT. Author: Exhausting the Earth, 1987, China Marches West, 2005. Fellow: Am. Acad. Arts & Scis. Office: MIT Bldg E51-291 77 Massachusetts Ave Cambridge MA 02139 Office Phone: 617-253-3064. Business E-Mail: pcperdue@mit.edu.

PEREIRA, KEVIN, pediatrician, director; MBBS, St John's Med. Coll., Bangalore, India, 1978—83. Cert. Otolaryngology Surgeon RCS Eng., 1992. Prof. otolaryngology & residency program dir. U. Tex., Houston, 2000—06; prof. & dir. pediatric otolaryngology U. Md., 2007—. Fellow: Am. Acad. Otolaryngology (Honor award 2006). Achievements include research in sleep apnea in children. Office: Univ MD Sch Medicin 16 S Eutaw St Ste 500 Baltimore MD 21201

PEREIRA, MARCIA ELISA, pathologist; b. Sao Bento do Sul, Santa Catarina, Brazil, June 27, 1976; d. Nelson Pereira and Maria Irene Zoellner. DVM, Santa Maria Fed. U., Brazil, 2001. Diplomate Am. Coll. Vet. Pathologist, 2008. Pathology resident Smithsonian Nat. Zool. Pk., Washington, 2004—07; pathologist Huntingdon Life Scis., East Millstone, NJ, 2007—. Mem.: ACVP.

PEREIRA, RENATO CLAUDIO COSTA, air transportation executive; b. Varginha, Brazil, Nov. 30, 1936; s. Ismael Costa Pereira and Mercedes de Carvalho Pereira; m. Maria Antonieta Arrojado Lisboa da Costa Pereira, June 27, 1964; children: Christiano A. L. Costa Pereira, Claudio A. L. Costa Pereira, André A. L. Costa Pereira, Ismael da Costa Pereira Neto. Degree, Air Force Acad., Brazil, 1959; postgrad., USAF, 1963, Brazilian Air Force, 1965, Brazilian Air Force Staff Sch., 1977, F.G.V., Brazil, 1983. Officer Brazilian Air Force, 1954-97; exec., project mgr. Centro Tecnico Aeroespacial, Sao Jose dos Campos, Brazil, 1975-85; officer Air Ministry Cabinet, head Procurement Office Ministry of Aeronautics, Brazil, 1985-89; pres. Latin Am. Civil Aviation Commn., 1993-97; chief negotiator CERNAI, Rio de Janeiro, 1990-97; former sec. gen., current cons. Internat. Civil Aviation Orgn., Montreal, Canada, 1997—2004; civil aviation cons., 2004—. Mem. Club Aeronautica, Planetary Soc. Avocations: reading, tennis, walking. Home: Rua Dona Cota 160/301 Varginha Minas Gerais CEP 37010-560 Brazil Home Phone: 55-35-32217617; Office Phone: 55-35-91977258. E-mail: rccp@rcpcorp.net, rccp@videotron.ca.

PEREIRA, ROBERTO M., entomologist; s. Evaristo M. and Jannette B. Pereira; m. Elisabete C. Cebim; children: Carolina C., Denise C. Degree, U. de São Paulo, Piracicaba, Brazil, 1981; MS, Cornell U., Ithaca, NY, 1987; PhD, U. Fla., Gainesville, 1991. Asst. prof. U. Tenn., Knoxville, 1997—2001; entomologist USDA-ARS-CMAVE, Gainesville, 2001—07; assoc. rsch. scientist - entomologist U. Fla. - Entomology & Nematology Dept., Gainesville, 2007—. Recipient Tech. Transfer award, USDA-ARS, 2006, Achievement award, Fla. Entomol. Soc., 2005. Mem.: Fla. Entomol. Soc., Soc. Invertebrate Pathology, Entomol. Soc. America. Achievements include patents for control of insects using microorganisms; research in microbial control of fire ants and other insects; control of urban pests; development of heat treatment method for control of bed bugs; patents for use of fire ant virus. Office: Univ Florida Entomology-Nematology Bldg 970 Natural Area Dr Gainesville FL 32611

PEREIRA, WELLESLEY, research scientist; PhD, Mich. Technol. U., Houghton, 2003. Adj. prof. Mich. Technol. U., 2004—; rsch. scientist ThermoAnalytics, Inc., Calumet, 2005—, bus. devel. mgr., rsch. devel., 2008—. Mem.: Am. Astron. Soc.

PEREIRAS, MARIBEL ALVARA, pharmacist, educator; d. Eulogio A. and Nora L. Rodriguez; m. Manuel Jose Pereiras, June 27, 2004; 1 child, Luke Manuel. PharmD, Rutgers State U. NJ, Piscataway, 2005. Cert. in pharmacotherapy Bd. Pharm. Specialties, 2007, in oncology pharmacy 2008. Staff pharmacist Johns Hopkins Hosp., Balt., 2006—07, Hackensack U. Med. Ctr., NJ, 2005—06, clin. pharmacy specialist, oncology, 2007—; clin. assoc. prof. Rutgers State U. NJ, 2007—. Youth min. St. Joseph and Michael Youth Group, Union City, NJ, 1999—2008. Mem.: Hematology Oncology Pharmacy Assn.

PEREL, JAMES MAURICE, pharmacology and healthcare educator, researcher; b. Buenos Aires, Mar. 30, 1933; came to U.S., 1947, naturalized, 1954; s. Aria and Bella (Silverberg) P.; m. July 18, 1959 (div. 1971); 1 child, Allan B.; m. Audrey Feldman, Apr. 9, 1972; children: Alissa A., Stephen M. BS, CUNY, 1956; MS, NYU, 1961, PhD, 1964. Nuclear chemist NY Naval Shipyard Lab., Bklyn.,

1956—58; assoc. rsch. scientist Goldwater Meml. Hosp. NYU, 1964—67; asst. prof. medicine and chemistry Emory U., Atlanta, 1967-70; asst. prof. psychiatry, pharmacology Columbia U. Coll. Physicians and Surgeons, NYC, 1970-76; assoc. rsch. scientist NY State Psychiat. Inst., NYC, 1970—76, assoc. prof. clin. pharmacology, chief psychiat. rsch., 1976-80; chief clin. pharmacology VA Med. Ctr. Highland Drive, Pitts., 1979-83; prof. psychiatry U. Pitts. Sch. Medicine, 1980—2001, acting chmn. dept. pharmacology, 1985-88, prof. pharmacology, 1980—2008, prof. pharmacology and chem. biology, 2008—, prof. emeritus psychiatry, 2001—; dir. clin. pharmacology Western Psychiat. Inst. & Clinic, Pitts., 1980—; prof. grad. neurosci., 1988—; postdoctoral fellow in clin. pharmacology NIH, 1964-67, NYU. Adj. faculty in chemistry CUNY, 1963-67; cons., mem. grant-awarding study sects. NIH, NIMH. Mem. editorial bd. Psychopharmacology, Neuropsychobiology, Therapeutic Drug Monitoring, Focus on Schizophrenia and Bipolar Disorders, Applied PHarmacokinetics and Pharmacodynamics, 4th edit.; contbr. over 400 articles to sci. jours., chpts. to books. Recipient Founders Day award, NYU, 1974, Julius Koch Meml. award, Rho Chi, 1983; named Psychopharmacologist of Yr., U. Toronto, 1993; named to Honor Roll, Century of Therapeutics and Sci. 1900-2000, Am. Soc. Clin. Pharmacology and Therapeutics; predoctoral fellow, NSF, 1958—60, numerous rsch. grants, including NIH, NIMH, Founds. Fund for Rsch. in Psychiatry, pharm. cos., pvt. founds. Fellow: Am. Inst. Chemists; mem. Am. Chem. Soc., World Fed. Neurology (co-founder, mem. neurotoxicology group), Internat. Assn. Therapeutic Drug Monitoring and Clin. Toxicology (com. chair), Am. Soc. Pharmacology and Exptl. Therapeutics, Am. Soc. Clin. Pharmacology and Therapeutics (sect. chair), Sigma Xi Jewish. Achievements include discovery of several widely-used pharmacotherapeutic agents. Office: U Pitts Sch Medicine 3811 Ohara St Pittsburgh PA 15213-2593 Office Phone: 412-246-6600. Business E-Mail: pereljm@upmc.edu, pereljm@pitt.edu.

PERELMAN, JEFFREY E., real estate company executive; BA with hon., Univ. Ill.; JD, Ill. Inst. Tech. Chgo. Kent Coll. Law. Former owner, mgr. Commodities Brokerage Firm; with Sterling Real Estate Ptnrs., Chgo., 1996—, now prin. Named one of Top 200 Art Collectors, ARTnews Mag., 2006—08. Avocation: collecting postwar and contemporary art. Office: Sterling Real Estate Ptnrs Ste 600 1033 Skokie Blvd Northbrook IL 60062

PERELMAN, LESLIE C., academic administrator; s. Noe Selig and Florence Cooper Perelman; m. Elizabeth Jane Garrels, Jan. 3, 1982; 1 child, David Noah. BA, U. Calif., Berkeley, 1970; MA, PhD, U. Mass., Amherst, 1980. Assoc. dean, undergraduate edn. MIT, Cambridge, 1995—2007, dir. writing across curriculum, 1999—. Liberal. Jewish. Office: Mass Inst Tech Rm 12-119 77 Massachusetts Ave Cambridge MA 02139 Office Phone: 617-253-3375. Business E-Mail: perelman@mit.edu.

PERELMAN, RONALD OWEN, consumer products company executive; b. Greensboro, NC, Jan. 1, 1943; s. Raymond and Ruth (Caplan) Perelman; m. Faith Golding, 1965 (div. 1983); 4 children; m. Claudia Cohen, Jan. 11, 1985 (div. 1994); 1 child, Sammantha; m. Patricia Duff, Dec. 20, 1995 (div. Sept. 10, 1998); 1 child, Caleigh Sophia; m. Ellen Barkin, June 28, 2000 (separated Jan. 19, 2006). BA, U. Pa., 1964; MBA, Wharton Sch. Fin., 1966. With Belmont Industries Inc., 1966-78; chmn., dir., CEO MacAndrews & Forbes Holdings Inc., Wilmington, Del., 1983—; chmn., CEO MacAndrews & Forbes Group Inc. (subs.), NYC, 1978—; chmn., dir., CEO Revlon Group Inc. (subs. MacAndrews & Forbes Group Inc.), NYC, 1985—, Revlon Inc. (subs.), NYC, 1985—; chmn. Nat. Health Labs. Inc., La Jolla, Calif., 1985—, Andrews Group Inc., La Jolla, 1985—; pres. bd. trustees Solomon R. Guggenheim Mus., La Jolla, 1995—. Named one of Top 200 Collectors, ARTnews mag., 2004, Forbes Richest Americans, 1999—, World's Richest People, Forbes Mag., 1999—. Jewish. Avocation: Collecting Contemporary Art. also: Solomark Guggenheim Mus 1071 5th Ave New York NY 10128-0173 Office: Revlon Consumer Products Corp 466 Lexington Ave Fl 13 New York NY 10017-3227

PERELSTEIN, EDUARDO M., pediatric nephrologist; b. Buenos Aires, Dec. 11, 1951; BA, U. Buenos Aires, 1968, MD, 1974. Cert. Am. Bd. Pediat., 1996, Am. Bd. Pediatric Nephrology, 1997. Resident in pediat. Children's Hosp., Buenos Aires, 1975—84; fellow in pediatric nephrology Saint Christopher's Hosp. for Children, Phila., 1984—87; assoc. attending pediatrician Weill Cornell Med. Coll., NYC, 1998—, assoc. prof. clinical pediat., 1998—. Recipient Chief Resident's award, NY Hosp. Pediatric Housestaff, 1995—96, Faculty award for Excellence in Tchg., NY Presbyn. Hosp.-Weill Cornell Med. Coll. Cornell U. Pediatric Housestaff, 2000, Excellence in Tchg. award, Joan and Sanford I. Weill Med. Coll. Cornell U., 2001—02, Outstanding Tchg. award, Weill Med. Coll. Pediatric Housestaff, 2002—03; named Tchr. of Yr., NY Hosp. Pediatric Housestaff, 1992—93, Physician of Yr., Weill Cornoil, Divsn. Nursing, 2005, Top Drs., NY, 2008; named to Best Doctors in America, 2007—08. Office: Dept Pediat Weill Cornell Med Coll 525 E 68th St New York NY 10065 Office Phone: 212-746-3260. Office Fax: 212-746-8861. Business E-Mail: emperels@med.cornell.edu.

PERENCHIO, ANDREW JERROLD, film and television executive; b. Fresno, Calif., Dec. 20, 1930; s. Andrew Joseph and Dorothea (Harvey) P.; m. Robin Green, July 16, 1954 (div.); children: Candace L., Catherine M., John Gardner; m. Jacquelyn Claire, Nov. 14, 1969 (div.); m. Margaret McHugh, 1987. BS, UCLA, 1954. V.p. Music Corp. Am., 1958-62, Gen. Artists Corp., 1962-64; pres., owner theatrical agy. Chartwell Artists, Ltd., LA, from 1964; chmn. bd. Tandem Prodns., Inc. and TAT Communications Co., LA, 1973-83; pres., CEO Embassy Pictures, LA, 1983—85; pres. Chartwell Partnerships Group, LA; chmn., CEO Univision Communications, 1992—2007. Promoter Muhammad Ali-Joe Frazier heavyweight fight, 1971, Bobby Riggs-Billie Jean King tennis match, 1973. Nat co-finance dir. McCain Presdl. Campaign, 2008. Served to 1st lt. USAF, 1954-57. Named one of Richest Americans, Forbes Mag., 1999—, World's Richest People, 2001—, 25 Most Influential Republicans, Newsmax Mag., 2008. Mem.: Bel-Air Country Club (LA); Westchester Country Club, NY; Friars Club, NYC.*

PERERA, LAWRENCE THACHER, lawyer; b. Boston, June 23, 1935; s. Guido R. and Faith (Phillips) P.; m. Elizabeth A. Wentworth, July 5, 1961; children: Alice V. Perera Lucey, Caroline F. Perera Barry, Lucy E.Perera Adams, Lawrence Thacher, Jr. BA, Harvard U., 1957, LL.B., 1961. Bar: Mass. 1961, U.S. Supreme Ct. 1973. Clk. Judge R. Ammi Cutter, Mass. Supreme Jud. Ct., Boston, 1961-62; assoc. Palmer & Dodge, Boston, 1962-69, ptnr., 1969-74; judge Middlesex County Probate Ct., East Cambridge, Mass., 1974-79; ptnr. Hemenway & Barnes, Boston, 1979—2007, of counsel, 2007—. Mem. nat. coun. Hon. Nat. Jud. Coll., Reno, prof., pres. Mass. CLE, Inc., 1988-90; trustee Mass. Investors Trust., 1981—2008; trustee, vice chmn. Boston Found., 1981-1996. Chmn. Boston Fin. Commn., 1969-71; overseer Boston Lyric Opera; chmn. bd. overseers Boston Opera Assn.; chmn. Back Bay Archtl. Commn., 1966-72; trustee emeritus Sta. WGBH Ednl. Found., Boston Athenaeum, Wang Ctr. Performing Arts. Fellow Am. Acad. Matrimonial Lawyers, Am. Coll. Trust and Estate Counsel; mem. ABA, Am. Bar Found., Am. Law Inst., Mass. Bar Assn., Mass. Bar Found., Boston Bar Assn., Boston Bar Found. Home: 18 Marlborough St Boston MA 02116-2101 Office: 60 State St Boston MA 02109-1800

PERERA, UNIL A.G., physics educator, researcher; b. Colombo, Sri Lanka, Nov. 12, 1956; came to U.S., 1982; s. Weymen and Daya (Daluwatta) P.; m. Shrima Y. Samaranayake, July 1, 1983; children: Nuwan, Nirosha. BS in Physics, U. Colombo, 1981; MS, U. Pitts., 1983, PhD, 1987. Asst. lectr. U. Colombo, 1981-82; tchg. asst. U. Pitts., 1982-83, rsch. asst., 1983-87, rsch. assoc., 1987-88, rsch. asst. prof., 1988-92; asst. prof. physics Ga. State U., Atlanta, 1992-95, assoc. prof., 1995-2001, prof., 2001—, grad. dir. physics, 1995—, dir. IRML, 1995—, assoc. chair, 2007—. Lectr. Nat. Rsch. Coun., Ottawa, Ont., Can., 1990, Indiana U. Pa., 1991, Calif. Inst. Tech., 1995, AAAS, Colombo, 1995, Emory U., Atlanta, 1995, U. Colombo, 1997, U. Peradeniya, Sri Lanka, 1997, Tech. U., Vienna, Austria, 1997, U. Linz, Austria, 1997, U. Ill., Chgo., 1998, U. Turkey, Istanbul, 1998, UCLA, 1998, CRL, Tokyo, 1998, Nat. U, Singapore, 1999, Inst. Fund Studies, Sri Lanka, 1999, Inst. for Physics of Microstructure, Nizhny Novogorod, Russia, 2000. Editor: Handbook of Thin Film Devices; contbr. more than 100 articles to profl. jours.; patentee in field. Mentor McNair Program, Atlanta, 1994-97. Grantee NASA, 1997—, NSF, 1990—, US Army, Ga. State U., 1992—, others. Fellow Am. Phys. Soc.; mem. IEEE (sr.), Soc. Photo Instrumentation Engrs. Buddhist. Office: Ga State U Dept Physics 29 Peachtree Center Ave NE Atlanta GA 30303-2515 Home Phone: 770-948-1505. Business E-Mail: uperera@gsu.edu.

PERES, JUDITH MAY, journalist; b. Chgo., June 30, 1946; d. Leonard H. and Eleanor (Seltzer) Zurakov; m. Michael Peres, June 27, 1972 (div. 2004); children: Dana, Avital. BA, U. Ill., 1967; M Studies in Law, Yale U., 1997. Acct. exec. Daniel J. Edelman Inc., Chgo., 1967-68; copy editor Jerusalem (Israel) Post, 1968-71, news editor, 1971-75, chief night editor, 1975-80, editor, style book, 1978-80; copy editor Chgo. Tribune, 1980-82, rewriter, 1982-84, assoc. fgn. editor, 1984-90, nat. editor, 1990-95, nat./fgn. editor, 1995-96, specialist writer, 1997—; Yale Law fellow, 1996-97. Recipient Media award, U. Mich., 2000, Soc. Women's Health Rsch., 2004. Office Phone: 312-222-4330. Business E-Mail: jperes@tribune.com.

PERES, SHIMON, President of Israel; b. Vishniev, Belarus, Aug. 1923; immigrated to Palestine, 1934; s. Isaac and Sarah Persky; m. Sonia Gelman; children: Zvia, Jonathan, Nechemia. Student, Harvard U. Mem. Mapai Secretariat, 1947; dir. gen. ministry def., 1953-59; mem. Knesset, 1959-2002; founder mem., sec.-gen. Rafi Party, 1965, mem. Labour Party, 1968-2005, chmn., 1977-1992, 95-97, 2003-05, mem. Kadima Party, 2005-; dep. min. def., 1959-65, min. econ. dept. in administered areas & for immigrant absorption, 1969-70, min. transport & communications, 1970-74, min. info., 1974, min. def., 1974-77, 1995-96, acting prime min., 1977; leader of opposition, 1977-84, min. interior & religious affairs, 1984-85, prime min., 1984-86, 95-96, vice prime min., 1986-90, min. fgn. affairs, 1986-88, 92-95, 2001-2002, min. reg. affairs, 1999-2001, dep. prime min., 2001-02, 2005-07, min. in charge of developing the Ngev & Galilee, 2006-07, pres. Israel, 2007-; chmn. Yad Ben-Gurion Author: In Between Hatred and Neighborhood, 1961, The Next Phase, 1965, David's Sling, 1970, Tomorrow is Now, 1978, From These Men, 1979, La Force De Vaincre, 1981, Entebbe Diary, 1991, The New Middle East, 1993, Reading Diary-Letter to Authors, 1994, Battling for Peace-Memoirs, 1995, For the Future of Israel, 1997, New Genesis, 1998, Le Voyage Imaginaire, 1998; contbr. articles to various jours. Creator Good Fence on Israel's border with Lebanon, 1976; founder Peres Ctr. Peace, 1996. Decorated officer Legion of Honor, 1959, Nobel Peace Prize, 1994. Office: Office of Pres 3 Hanassi St 92188 Jerusalem Israel

PERET, KAREN KRZYMINSKI, health facility administrator; b. Springfield, Mass., Mar. 8, 1950; d. Edward S. and Doris L. (Beaudry) Krzyminski; m. Robert J. Peret, June 19, 1971 (div. Sept. 2003); children: Heather, James, Kaitlin, Matthew. BSN, St. Anselm's, 1972; MS in Nursing Adminstrn., Boston U., 1980; EdD in Orgnl. Devel., U. Mass., 1993. RN, Mass. Staff nurse Boston VA's Hosp., 1972—73; staff nurse pediat. Harrington Meml. Hosp., Southbridge, Mass., 1973—74, instr. edn., 1974—75, relief day asst. dir. nursing, 1975; coord. continuing edn. Ctrl. Maine Med. Ctr., Lewiston, 1975—76; asst. dir. nursing Monson Devel. Ctr., Palmer, Mass., 1977—83, DON, 1983—94; exec. nursing cons. Liberty Healthcare, Waltham, Mass., 1994—98, v.p. ops. Phila., 1998—; ind. mgmt. cons., 1993—. Instr. Quinsigamond Cmty. Coll., Worcester, Mass., 1972-73. Contbr. articles to profl. jours. Mem. ANA, Mass. Nurses' Assn., Am. Assn. on Mental Retardation, Sigma Theta Tau. Home: 79 Sturbridge Rd Holland MA 01521-3123 Office: 401 E City Ave Ste 820 Bala Cynwyd PA 19004-1130 Home Phone: 413-245-9452; Office Phone: 800-331-7122. Personal E-mail: karenperet@aol.com.

PERETSMAN, NANCY BETH, investment banker; b. Worcester, Mass., Mar. 27, 1954; d. George Peretsman and Norma (Burofsky) O'Haire; m. Robert Williams Scully, Sept. 17, 1988. AB with hons., Princeton U., 1976; MPPM, Yale, 1979. V.p. Blyth, Eastman, Dillon & Co., NYC, 1979—83; dir., head of media group Salomon Bros., NYC, 1983—90, mng. dir., 1990—95; exec. v.p., mng. dir. Allen & Co., NYC, 1995—. Bd. dirs. Charter Comm., Inc., Priceline.com Inc. Charter trustee Princeton U., 1976; bd. dirs. Teach for America; mem. bd. trustees Princeton U., The New Sch.; trustee Inst. Advanced Study. Named one of 50 Women to Watch, The Wall St. Jour., 2005, 50 Most Powerful Women in Bus., Fortune mag., 2006, 2008, The 100 Most Influential Women in NYC Bus., Crain's NY Bus., 2007, The Top 50 Rainmakers, Dealmaker mag., 2007. Office: Allen & Co Inc 711 5th Ave 9th Fl New York NY 10022*

PERETT, WILLIAM GREGORY, historian; b. Lansing, Mich., Feb. 11, 1945; s. William Gregory and Virginia Swift Perett; m. Diane Beyer Beyer, Dec. 29, 1973; children: Daniel Gregory, Yvonne Louise. AB, Duke U., Durham, NC, 1967; MA, Stanford U., Calif., PhD, 1977. Fgn. svc. officer US Dept. State, Washington, 1977—2006. Lt. USN, 1968—72. Recipient Superior Honor award, US Dept. State, 1987, Meritorious Honor award, 1990, Disting. Pub. Svc. award, USN, 2005. Avocations: music, winemaking, travel. Home: 1705 N Patrick Henry Dr Arlington VA 22205 Office: History Dept George Wash Univ Phillips Hall 801 22nd St NW Washington DC 20052 Personal E-mail: wgperett@aol.com. Business E-Mail: wgperett@gwu.edu.

PERETTI, PETER ORAL, psychology professor, researcher; s. Peter Charles and Estelle Agnes (Janas) Peretti; children: Robert Peter, Kathryn June. BA, Lake Forest Coll., 1962; MA in Sociology, Roosevelt U., 1964, MA in Psychology, 1967; PhD in Psychology, Walden U., 1974. Prof. Purdue North Ctrl. U., Westville, Ind., 1964—66, Ill. Benedictine Coll., Lisle, 1966—69, North Park Coll., Chgo., 1969—72, City Coll. Chgo., 1972—. Author: 8 books, numerous poems, jour. articles. Recipient Regional and All City Science Fair Judge awards, 1974—, Golden Apple award for Tchg., 2002. Mem.: Assn. Advancement of Ethical Hypnosis, Assn. Supervision and Curriculum Devel., Assn. Rsch. Animal Behavior, Criterion Bar Assn., Quill and Scroll, Hugo's Companions, Mystery Writers Am., Chgo. Acad. Scis. (life), Field Mus. (life), The Hounds, Internat. Soc. Poets (Disting. Mem. award, Found. Laureate award 2005), Western Writers Am., Am. Players Theatre, Theater on the Lake, Caxton Club, Phi Theta Kappa (hon.). Avocations: book clubs, bicycling, jogging.

PERETZ, DON, political science professor; b. Balt., Oct. 31, 1922; m. Maya Frenkler, May 24, 1979. BA, U. Minn., 1944; MA, Columbia U., 1951, PhD, 1955. Fgn. corr. NBC, 1947-48; UN rep. for Am. Friends Svc. Com., fgn. corr. UN World, 1949-50; Middle East media evaluator Voice of America, U.S. Dept. State, 1952; rsch. dir. Regional Rsch. Analysis, 1954-56; lectr. in polit. sci. Dropsie Coll., 1956-59, Vassar Coll., 1959-62; assoc. dir. N.Y. State Edn. Dept.-Ctr. for Internat. Programs & Svcs., 1962-66; prof. polit. sci. SUNY, Binghamton, 1966-92; prof. emeritus, 1992—; dir. S.W. Asian-North African program, 1966-76, 84-88. Cons. on Middle East Am. Jewish Com., 1956-58; lectr. in polit. sci. Hofstra Coll., 1954; vis. prof. polit. sci. Williams Coll., 1966; cons. Syracuse U. Press, SUNY Press, Ind. U. Press, Breuner Found., Ford Found., U.S. Dept. Def., U.S. Dept. State, polit. sci. depts. SUC New Paltz, U. Vt., U. Ind., U. Calif.-Berkely, SUNY-Buffalo. Author, co-author 12 books including Israel and Palestine Arabs, 1955, The Middle East Today, 1963, 6th edit., 1994, The Middle East (with Hugo Jaeckel), 1963, Middle East Reader, 1968, A Palestine Entity?, 1970, Middle East Foreign Policy: Issues & Processes (with R. McLaurin & L.W. Snider), 1982, Islam-Legacy of the Past, Challenge of the Future (with R. Moench & S. Mohsen), 1984, The West Bank: History, Politics, Society and Economy, 1986, Intifada-The Palestinian Uprising, 1990, Palestinians, Refugees and the Middle East Peace Process, 1993, The Arab-Israel Dispute, 1996, (with Gideon Doron) The Government and Politics of Israel, 3d edit., 1997; also numerous articles. With U.S. Army, 1943-46, PTO. Grantee Ford Found., 1952-53, Rockefeller Found., 1962-63; Middle East Inst. fellow, 1965-75; Rockefeller Found. fellow, Bellaglo, Italy, 1989; nominated as Disting. Fellow Jennings Randolph Program for Internat. Peace, U.S. Inst. Peace, apptd. Vis. Peace Fellow, 1992. Mem. Coun. on Fgn. Rels. Home: 10450 Lottsford Rd 2111 Mitchellville MD 26721

PERETZ, MARTIN, publishing executive, educator; b. NYC, July 30, 1939; s. Julius and Ellen (Weberman) P.; m. Anne Labouisse, June 16, 1967; children— Jesse, Evgenia. BA, Brandeis U., 1959; MA, Harvard U., 1965, PhD, 1966; DHL (hon.), Bard Coll., 1982, Hebrew Union Coll., 2008; DLL (hon.), Coe Coll., 1983; PhD (hon.), Hebrew U., Jerusalem, 1987; DLL (hon.), Long Island Univ, 1988, Brandeis Univ, 1989, Hebrew Coll, 1990, Chgo. Theol. Sem., 1994. Instr. Harvard, 1965-68, asst. prof., 1968-72, lectr. social studies, 1972—; master Cabot House, 1972-75; chmn. editorial bd. New Republic mag., 1974-75; editor-in-chief New Republic, 1975—. Dir. Dreyfus Money Market Instruments, Dreyfus A Bonds, Dreyfus Instl. Money Market Fund, Dreyfus Balanced Fund, Dreyfus Global bond Fund, Dreyfus Growth and Income Fund, Dreyfus Internat. Funds, Dreyfus Variable Investment Fund and Premier Equity Funds, Dreytus Family Funds. Bd overseers YIVO Inst. Jewish Rsch., Chmn., Bd. govs. Hebrew U. Jerusalem; hon. chmn. Jerusalem Found.; dir. Leukosite; trustee Harvard Med. Sch., Immune Disease Inst.; chmn. The Street, Inc.; pres. Jerusalem Symphony Orch. Woodrow Wilson fellow, 1959-61; recipient medal excellence in journalism U. Mo. Sch. Journalism, 1982 Democrat. Jewish. Office: New Republic Ste 700 1331 H St NW Washington DC 20005 Office Phone: 202-508-4444.

PEREYRA-SUAREZ, CHARLES ALBERT, lawyer; b. Paysandu, Uruguay, Sept. 7, 1947; arrived in U.S., 1954, naturalized, 1962; s. Hector and Esther (Enriquez-Sarano) Pereyra-Suarez; m. Susan H. Cross, Dec. 30, 1983. BA in History magna cum laude, Pacific Union Coll., 1970; postgrad., UCLA, 1970-71; JD, U. Calif., Berkeley, 1975. Bar: Calif. 1975, DC 1980. Staff atty. Western Ctr. Law and Poverty, Inc., LA, 1976; trial atty. civil rights divsn. U.S. Dept. Justice, Washington, 1976—79, asst. U.S. atty., criminal divsn. LA, 1979—82; sr. litig. assoc. Gibson, Dunn & Crutcher, LA, 1982—84; pvt. practice LA, 1984—86, 1998—; ptnr. McKenna & Cuneo, LA, 1986—95, Davis Wright Tremaine, LA, 1995—98. Democrat. Avocations: tennis, jogging, travel. Office Phone: 213-623-5923. Business E-Mail: cpereyra@cpslawfirm.com.

PEREZ, ANNIE RIVERA, elementary school educator; d. Francisco Bontugan and Isabel Rivera Perez. BA in elem. edn., U. of Guam, 1975; MEd, U. Portland, 1994. Cert. Profl. II Elem.K-5, P.E. K-6 Guam Pub. Sch. Sys., 2005. Elem. tchr. Guam Pub. Sch. Sys., Hagatna, Guana Island, 1975—2000; elem. tchr. 5th grade San Vicente Cath. Sch., Barrigada, 2001—. Coord. elem. divsn. adminstrv. team San Vicente Cath. Sch., Barrigada, 2001—. Commr. Chamorro Land Trust, Hagatna, Guam, Guam, 2004—06. Mem.: Internat. Reading Assn. (assoc.). Roman Catholic. Office: San Vicente Cath School 196 Bejong Guam Barrigada 96913 Guana Island Personal E-mail: arp@guam.net.

PEREZ, ANTONIO M., imaging company executive; b. Spain; BSEE, Madrid U. Corp. v.p., mem. exec. coun., pres. consumer bus. Hewlett-Packard Co., pres., CEO inkjet imaging bus., 1995—99; pres., CEO Gemplus Internat., 2000—01; pres., COO Eastman Kodak Co., Rochester, NY, 2003—05, CEO, 2005—, chmn., 2006—. Dir. Schering-Plough Corp.; vice chair. Diversity Best Practices, CEO initiative, 2006—07, chmn., 2007—; house trustee George Eastman. Trustee George Eastman House. Mem.: Bus. Roundtable, Bus. Coun.*

PEREZ, EDITH ADALJISA, physician; b. Humacao, P.R., Apr. 30, 1956; d. Ruben and Edith (Maldonado) Perez; BS magna cum laude, U. P.R., 1975, MD, 1979. Diplomate Nat. Bd. Med. Examiners, Am. Bd. Internal Medicine. Resident in internal medicine Loma Linda U., 1979-82; physician Nat. Health Service Corps, 1982-84; fellow in hematology-oncology U. Calif.-Davis program Martinez VA Hosp., 1984-87, asst. prof. clin. medicine, 1987—; mem. staff hematology and oncology Martinez VA Hosp., 1987—. Mosby scholar, 1975. Mem. AMA, ACP, AAAS, Am. Soc. Clin. Oncology.

PEREZ, GLAD M., marketing executive; d. Luis and Delia Perez. BBA in Gen. Bus., Pace U., NYC, 1985; attended MBA mini-program, Am. Mgmt Assn., 1987; grad. Advanced Exec. Program, Northwestern U. J.L Kellogg Grad. Sch. Mgmt., 1998, grad. International Mktg. Program, 2000. Dir. brand mgmt. McGraw-Hill, NYC, 1977—85; dir. mktg. comm. AT&T, Basking Ridge, NJ, 1985—2004; v.p. mktg. and e-commerce Affinity Fed. Credit Union, Basking Ridge, 2005—. Bd. mem. Affinity Investment Svcs., Basking Ridge. Contbr. donations to Joyce Meyer Ministries. Recipient Silver awards, multicultural market, advt. and mktg. effectiveness, AME Internat., 1995, 2 Clio awards, 1996, NJ Gold medal, Art Dirs. Club NJ, 1996, Best Theme award, 1997, Multicultural Excellence award, Assn. Nat. Advertisers, 1999, 2001, Telly award, 2004. Mem.: NAFE, Am. Advt. Fedn. (ADDY award. 1999), Assn. Nat. Advertisers (Multicultural Excellence award 1999, 2001), Credit Union Execs. Soc., Advt. Women NY, The Advt. Club, Mktg. Execs. Networking Group, Nat. Assn. for Multi-ethnicity in Comm., Direct Mktg. Assn. (Gold Echo award 1999), Am. Mgmt. Assn.,

Am. Mktg. Assn. (Golf EFFIE award 1992), Ctr. for Creative Leadership (life). Avocations: travel, theater, art, holistic medicine. Home: 132 Constitution Way Basking Ridge NJ 07920 Office: Affinity Federal Credit Union 73 Mountain View Blvd Basking Ridge NJ 07920 Personal E-mail: gmperez@gmp-associates.com. Business E-Mail: gladp@affinityfcu.com.

PEREZ, JOHN D., lawyer; b. Cleve., Oct. 29, 1948; s. Isabel and Juan Perez; m. Lois Pasquariello, Dec. 1968 (div. 1995); children: John J., Bryan J., Jamie M. BS, William Paterson Coll., Wayne, NJ, 1974; JD, U. Bridgeport, Conn., 1980. Bar: NJ 1987, US Dist. Ct. NJ 1987, US Ct. Appeals (3rd cir.) 1997, US Ct. Appeals (5th cir.) 2000, US Ct. Appeals (2d cir.) 2003, US Ct. Appeals (11th cir.) 2005, US Supreme Ct. 1992. Pvt. practice, Paterson, NJ, 1987—92, West Paterson, NJ, 1995; of counsel H. Betti Industries, Carlstadt, NJ, 1992—93; asst. coutny counsel Passaic County, Paterson, NJ, 1994—96; prof. paralegal studies Berkley Coll., West Paterson, NJ, 1994—96; atty. Perez, Perez & Perez, PC, Newark, 1996—. Com. on character NJ Bd. Bar Examiners, 1992—2006. Mem.: Am. Immigration Lawyers Assn. (mentor 2003—, treas. NJ chpt. 2003—05), NJ State Bar Assn., Fed. Bar Assn. (pres. 2005—). Office: Perez Perez & Perez PC 41-51 Wilson Ave Ste 2A Newark NJ 07105-3214 Business E-Mail: info@perezlawyers.com.

PEREZ, JORGE M., real estate developer; b. Argentina; arrived in U.S., 1968; BS in Economics, C. W. Post, Long Island U.; MS in Urban Planning, U. Mich. Mng. gen. ptnr. Related Group of Fla., Miami, 1979—. Bd. dir. Regions Fin. Corp. Author: Powerhouse Principles: The Billionaire Blueprint for Real Estate Success, 2008. Past. mem. Dem. Nat. Com.; trustee Univ. Miami; vice chmn. Miami Dade Cultural Affairs Council; dir. Miami Film Festival, Miami Downtown Develop. Authority. Recipient Miami Bus. Leader of Yr. award, 2000, Ernst & Young Entrepreneur of Yr. award, 2002, Multifamily Exec. Builder of the Yr., 2003, Citizen of Yr. award, Miami C. Of C., 2004; named one of The 25 Most Influential Hispanics, TIME mag., 2005, Forbes' Richest Americans, 2006. Democrat. Avocations: art collecting, especially Latin Am. contemporary art, tennis. Office: Related Group of Florida 2828 Coral Way Miami FL 33145

PEREZ, JOSEPHINE, psychiatrist, educator; b. Tijuana, Mex., Feb. 10, 1941; came to the U.S., 1960, U.S. citizenship, 1968. BS in Biology, U. Santiago de Compostela, Spain, 1971, MD, 1975. Nuc. medicine technician, EEG technician, supr. Electrographic Labs., Encino, Calif., 1963—69; clerkships in internal medicine, gen. surgery, otorhinolaryngology, dermatology and venereology Gen. Hosp. of Galicia, Spain, 1972-75; resident in gen. psychiatry U. Miami, Jackson Meml. Hosp. and VA Hosp., Miami, Fla., 1976-78; practice medicine specializing in psychiatry, marital and family therapy, individual psychotherapy Miami, 1979—. Emergency room physician Miami Dade Hosp., 1975; attending psychiatrist Jackson Meml. Hosp., 1979—, asst. dir. adolescent psychiat. unit, 1979-83; mem. clin. faculty U. Miami Sch. Medicine, 1979—, clin. instr. psychiatry, 1979—. Mem. AMA (Physicians' Recognition award 1980, 83, 86, 89, 98, 2000, 01, 05), Am. Assn. for Marital and Family Therapy (cert. clin. mem., treas. 1982-84, pres.-elect 1985-87, pres. 1987-89), Am. Psychiat. Assn., Am. Med. Women's Assn., Assn. Women Psychiatrists, Fla. Psychiat. Soc., South Dade Women Physicians Assn. Office: 420 S Dixie Hwy Ste 4A Coral Gables FL 33146-2228 Office Phone: 305-666-7766, 305-857-9250.

PÉREZ, LOUIS A., JR., history professor; MA, U. Ariz., 1966; PhD, U. N.Mex., 1970. J. Carlyle Sitterson prof. history U. NC at Chapel Hill, dir. Inst. for the Study of the Americas. Author: Cuba: Between Reform and Revolution, 1995, The War of 1989: The United States and Cuba in History and Historiography, 1998, On Becoming Cuban: Identity, Nationality and Culture, 2000 (Bolton-Johnson prize, Conf. Latin Am. History, 2000), Winds of Change: Hurricanes and the Transformation of 19th-Century Cuba, 2001 (George Perkins Marsh prize, Am. Soc. Environ. History, 2001), Cuba and the United States: Ties of Singular Intimacy, 2003, To Die in Cuba: Suicide and Society, 2005 (Elsa Goveia prize, 2007), Cuba in the American Imagination, 2008. Fellow John Simon Guggenheim Meml. Found., 2000. Fellow: Am. Acad. Arts and Sciences. Office: U NC Chapel Hill Dept History CB 3195 Hamilton Hall Chapel Hill NC 27599-3195 Office Phone: 919-962-6880. E-mail: perez@email.unc.edu.

PEREZ, LOUIS ANTHONY, radiologist; b. NYC, June 11, 1939; s. Salvatore Lawrence and Valvadina Rose (Ruscillo) P.; divorced, 1988; children: Lisa, Gregg, Nicole; m. Patricia Ann McVey, May 19, 1990; 1 child, Kelsey. BEE, Manhattan Coll., 1962; MD, SUNY, Bklyn., 1966. Diplomate Am. Bd. Radiology (oral examiner), Am. Bd. Nuclear Medicine. Chief nuc. medicine Misericordia Hosp., Bronx, 1973-75, Norwalk Hosp., Conn., 1975-82; cons. Manhattan Coll., Radiology Inst., Riverdale, N.Y., 1974-81; dir. radiology Lawrence Hosp., Bronxville, NY, 1982—2004; asst. clin. prof. radiology Columbia U. Coll. Physicians and Surgeons, NYC, 1995—2006; with NE Radiology, Brewster, 2006—. Contbr. articles to profl. jours., chpts. to books. Lt. comdr. USN, 1963-77. Grantee, Am. Cancer Soc., 1968-70, USPHS, 1974-75. Fellow Am. Coll. Radiology; mem. Soc. Nuc. Medicine (trustee 1985-89, 92—, chmn. sci. subcom. 1988—, chpt. pres. 1982), NY State Med. Soc. Independent. Roman Catholic.

PEREZ, MARITZA E., special education educator; b. Bklyn., Nov. 18, 1977; d. Perez A. Jose and Carmen A. Perez (Stepmother), Irma Diaz; m. Steven Brown. Bachelor's, Clayton State U., Morrow, Ga., 2000; Master's, Ctrl. Mich. U., Atlanta, 2003; cert. ednl. specialist, postgrad., Argosy U., Atlanta, 2006—. Tchr. Kendrick Mid. Sch., Jonesboro, Ga., 2000—; tchr. devel. specialing, 2007—. Coach swimming Kendrick Mid. Sch., Jonesboro, Ga., 2000—, grade level chair, 2002—06, 1:1 wireless tchr., 2005—; profl. devel. facilitator Clayton County Pub. Schs., Jonesboro, 2002—, Ga. Performance Stds. trainer, 2004—. Named Tchr. of Month, Kendrick Mid. Sch., 2000, 2001, 2003, 2004, 2005, 2006; Hope grantee, State of Ga., 1995. Avocations: swimming, reading. Office: Kendrick Middle School 7971 Kendrick Rd Jonesboro GA 30238 Home: 402 Grandiflora Dr Mcdonough GA 30253-8014 Office Phone: 770-473-2795. Business E-Mail: mperez@clayton.k12.ga.us.

PEREZ, OLIVER, professional baseball player; b. Culiacan, Mex., Aug. 15, 1981; Pitcher San Diego Padres, 2002—03, Pitts. Pirates, 2004—06, NY Mets, 2006—. Pitcher Tometeros de Culiacan, 2002; mem. Mex. nat. team World Baseball Classic, 2006, 09. Achievements include member of Caribbean World Series Championship winning Tometeros de Culiacan, 2002; leading the National League in: strikeouts per nine innings (10.97), 2004; starts (34), 2008. Office: NY Mets Citi Field 126th St & Roosevelt Ave Flushing NY 11368*

PEREZ, PAMELA LINDSEY, language educator; d. Robert Avery Grey and Joanne Vaughn Baldey; m. William George Hare; 1 child, Joanna Isabel Grey-Perez. BA in Spanish Lit., Calif. State U., Northridge, 1997, M in Spanish, 2001; PhD in Polit. Sci. and Sociology, U. Complutense, Madrid, 1981. Lic. in polit. sci. and sociology U. Complutense, Madrid, 1976; cert. in basica edln. skills test Calif., 1986. Adj. prof. Mission Coll., Sylmar, Calif., 2004—05; prof. Calif. State U., LA Divsn. Extended Edn., LA, 2005; adj. faculty U. Complutense, 1976—80, Valley Coll., Calif., 2001—05, Citrus Coll., Azuza, Calif., 2001, Peppardine U., Malibu, Calif., 2003, Calif. State U. Northridge, 2001—, Pierce Coll., Woodland Hills, Calif., 2005—. Participant Conferencia La Frontera, La Paz, Baja California Sur, Mexico. Mem.: Royal Assn. Spanish Geographers, Assn. Spanish Geographers. Home: 18645 Hatteras St 270 Tarzana CA 91356 Office: Calif State Univ 18111 Nordhoff Northridge CA 91330-8247 Personal E-mail: pamelalperez@sbcglobal.net. Business E-Mail: pamela.l.perez@csun.edu.

PEREZ, PETER MICHAEL, food products executive; b. Aurora, Ill., Sept. 24, 1953; s. Peter Joseph and Marie Frances (Rogacs) P.; m. Cynthia Lou Perez, May 3, 1976; children: Peter Charles, Lisa Marie. BSBA, Ea. Ill. U., Charleston, 1976; MBA, Northwestern U., 1986. Mgr. plant Emerson Electric Co., Denver, 1985-86, Kraft, North Bergen, NJ, 1986-88, Allentown, Pa., 1988-91; regional mgr., dir. human resources Kraft/Phillip Morris, Deerfield, Ill., 1991-95; v.p., Human Resources Pepsi-Cola Gen. Bottlers, 1995—97, sr. v.p., Human Resources, 1997—2000; chief human resources officer Alliant Foodservice, 2001; sr. v.p. human resources W.W. Granger, 2001—03, ConAgra Foods, Inc., Omaha, 2003—07; exec. v.p., Human Resources ConAgra Foods Inc., 2007—. Bd. dirs. Constellation Brands Inc., 2008—. Mem. Biltmore Country Club. Republican. Roman Catholic. Avocations: sports, guitar. Office: ConAgra Foods Inc 1 ConAgra Dr Omaha NE 68102-5001 Office Phone: 402-595-4000. Office Fax: 402-595-4709.*

PEREZ, SUZANNE, art educator, consultant; b. Wichita, Kans., Aug. 23, 1968; d. Bryan and Patty Burris; m. Edwardo Perez, Dec. 22, 2007. MA, U. North Tex., Denton, 1997. Corp. art collection cons. Burlington Northern Santa Fe Rlwy., Ft. Worth, 1997—2004; coll. art instr. Tarrant County Coll., Hurst, Tex., 2000—. Artist in field. Exhbn., The Black Paintings. Guest lectr. Women's Caucus Art, Dallas, 2007. Named Best Lectr., Tarrant County Coll. NE Academic Event Com., 2005.

PEREZ, THOMAS EDWARD, state official, law educator; b. Buffalo, Oct. 7, 1961; m. Ann Marie Staudenmaier; children: Amalia, Susana, Rafael AB in Internat. Rels.-Polit. Sci., Brown U., 1983; JD cum laude, Harvard U., 1987; M in Public Policy, John F. Kennedy Sch. Govt., Harvard U., 1987. Bar: NY 1988, DC 1998. Law clk. to Hon. Zita L. Weinshienk US Dist. Ct. Colo., 1987-89; trial lawyer, criminal sect., civil rights divsn. US Dept. Justice, 1989-94, dep. chief criminal sect., civil rights divsn., 1994-97; spl. counsel to Senator Edward M. Kennedy US Senate, 1995-98; dep. asst. atty. for civil rights US Dept. Justice, 1998—99; dir. Office Civil Rights (OCR) US Dept. Health & Human Services, 1999—2002; asst. prof., dir. clin. law office U. Md. Sch. Law, Baltimore, 2001—07; sec. Dept. Labor, Licensing & Regulation (DLLR) State of Md., Annapolis, 2007—. Cons. Vera Inst. Justice, N.Y.C., 1997-99; tchr. Stanford U., Washington, 1994-96; part time faculty mem., George Washington Sch. Pub. Health Mem., Montgomery County Coun., 2002-06, coun. pres., 2005 Mem. Hispanic Bar Assn. (bd. dirs.). Office: Maryland Department Labor Licensing & Regulation 500 N Calvert St #401 Baltimore MD 21202 Office Phone: 410-230-6020. Office Fax: 410-333-0853.*

PEREZ, VICTOR MANUEL, physician, plastic surgeon; b. Cosamaloapan, Veracruz, Mex., Aug. 18, 1967; s. Tomas and Manuela Perez; m. Diana Marie Bobovnyik, July 14, 2000; children: Victor Manuel Jr., Ava Elizabeth. BS, U. Autonomous Nuevo Leon, Guadalupe, N.L. Mex., 1990. Cert. Am. Bd. Plastic Surgery, 2003. Gen. practitioner Ministry of Health, Benito Juarez, Nuevo Leon, Mexico, 1990—91, Mexican Inst. Social Security, Pal, Coahuila, 1991—92; resident Cook County Hosp., Chgo., 1994—95; resident in gen. surgery Western Res. Care Sys., Youngstown, Ohio, 1995—98; burn surgery fellow Shriners Burn Hosp., Galveston, Tex., 1998—99; resident in plastic surgery Loma Linda U. Med. Ctr., Calif., 1999—2002; chief, plastic surgery sect. VA Hosp., Kansas City, Mo., 2002—; asst. prof. plastic surgery U. Kans. Med. Ctr., Kansas City, 2002—. Presenter in field. Contbr. articles to profl jours. and book chpts. in field. Grant, Plastic Surgery Ednl. Found., 2001. Fellow: ACS; mem.: Kans. City Plastic Surgery Soc., Am. Burn Assn., Am. Soc. Plastic Surgeons. Roman Catholic. Achievements include invention of new techniques in abdominoplasty-umbilical insci. Avocation: dog shows. Office: Univ Kansas Medical Ctr 3901 Rainbow Blvd Kansas City KS 66160 Office Fax: 913-588-2061. Business E-Mail: vperez@kumc.edu.

PEREZ, WILLIAM D. (BILL PEREZ), candy company executive, former sports apparel company executive; b. Akron, Ohio, 1947; s. Dorothy Perez; m. Catherine A. Perez; 2 children. BA in Govt., Cornell U., 1969; B in Info. Mgmt., Am. Grad. Sch. Internat. Mgmt., 1970. Joined SC Johnson & Son, Inc., 1970, gen. mgr. SC Johnson Spain, gen. mgr. SC Johnson Iberia, v.p., regional dir. Latin America, v.p. home care bus., exec. v.p. N. Am. consumer products, pres., COO worldwide consumer products Racine, Wis., 1993-97, pres., CEO, 1997—2004, NIKE, Inc., Beaverton, Oreg., 2004—06, William Wrigley Jr. Co., Chgo., 2006—. Bd. dirs. May Dept. Stores Co., 1998—2004, Kellogg Co., 1999—. William Wrigley Jr. Co., 2006—, Hallmark Cards, Inc., Grocery Mfr. America, Inc. Mem. Cornell U. Council; advisory bd. Racine Youth Leadership Acad.; bd. dirs. Sustainable Racine. Recipient Out & Equal Champion for Workplace Equality award, Out & Equal Workplace Advocates, 2002. Mem.: Grocery Manufacturers of Am. (bd. dirs.). Achievements include 11 marathons. Avocations: running, golf. Office: William Wrigley Jr Co 410 N Michigan Ave Chicago IL 60611 E-mail: bill.perez@wrigley.com.

PEREZ-ABADIA, GUSTAVO A., medical educator; b. Salta, Argentina, Apr. 27, 1963; s. Fernando Perez and Vitalia Abadia; children: Gabriela M., Andres. MD, U. Nat. Tucuman, Argentina, 1989. Cert. pediat. surgeons Hosp. Ninios Santisima Trinidad, 1995. Rsch. fellow Inst. Bioelectronics, U. Nat. Tucuman, 1987—91; resident pediat. dept. Hosp. Ninios Santisima Trinidad, Cordoba, 1991—95; rsch. fellow Divsn. Plastic & Reconstructive Surgery & Urology, Dept. Surgery, U. Louisville, 1996—99, sr. rsch. fellow, 1999—; asst. prof. Dept. Physiology, U. Louisville, 2005—; vice pres. treasure Endoprotech, Inc., Louisville, 2009—; dir. instr. Microsurgical Tchg. Lab., Louisville, 2007—. Recipient Young Investigator award, 2002, Perkins prize, 2004, Excellence award, EndoProtech, Inc., 2008; grant, NIH, 2005—06, Devel. Direct Cellular Energy Delivery Sys. NIH, 2005—07, Ky. Sci. Transp., 2006—08, New Anti-Complement Therapy Reduce Reperfusion Injury NIH, 2008—. Mem.: Am. Physiol. Soc., Plastic Surgery Rsch. Coun. Office: Univ Louisville 500 S Preston St A Bldg Rm 1115 Louisville KY 40292 Office Fax: 502-852-6239. Business E-Mail: gustavo@louisville.edu.

PÉREZ-CARDONA, JOSÉ MANUEL, cardiologist; b. Mayaguez, PR, Feb. 26, 1977; s. Oscar Manuel Pérez-Ramos and Blanca Alicea Cardona-Cardona; m. Lorimar Jirau-Rodríguez; 1 child, Sebastián Manuel Pérez-Jirau. MD, U. PR, San Juan, 2003. Cert. med. dr. USMLE, Puerto Rico, 2003, in internal medicine ABIM, Puerto Rico, 2006. Chemistry rschr. Interamerican U. PR, Arecibo, 1996—99; internal medicine rschr. U. PR, 2003—06, internal medicine chief resident, 2006—07, cardiology fellow, 2007—. Office: Univ PR Dept Medicine PO Box 365067 San Juan PR 00936-5067 Office Phone: 787-759-8252. Office Fax: 787-754-1739. Personal E-mail: jopeca@hotmail.com.

PEREZ-CRUET, JORGE, geriatric psychiatrist, researcher; b. Santurce, PR, Oct. 15, 1931; s. Jose Maria Perez-Vicente and Emilia Cruet-Burgos; m. Anyes Heimendinger, Oct. 4, 1958; children: Antonio, Mick, Graciela, Isabelle. BS magna cum laude, U. PR, 1953, MD, 1957; diploma in psychiatry, McGill U., Montreal, Que., Can., 1976. Diplomate Am. Bd. Geriat. Psychiatry, Am. Bd. Psychiatry and Neurology, Nat. Bd. Med. Examiners, lic. Can. Coun. Med. Examiners, Med. Coun. Can., cert. in quality assurance, profl. in healthcare quality Health Quality Cert. Bd., eligible Am. Bd. Psychiatry and Neurology, psychiatrist Am. Bd. Psychiatry and Neurology, 1980, in Geriatric Psychiatry Am. Bd. Psychiatry and Neurology, 1991, re-cert. Am. Bd. Psychiatry and Neurology, 2001, in Addiction Psychiatry Am. Bd. Psychiatry and Neurology, 2006. Rotating intern Michael Reese Hosp., Chgo., 1957-58; fellow in psychiatry Johns Hopkins U. Med. Sch., 1958-60, instr., then asst. prof. psychiatry, 1962-73; psychiatrist neurophysiology and psychosomatic lab. Walter Reed Army Inst. Rsch., Washington, 1960—62, cons., 1963-65; rsch. assoc. lab. chem. pharmacology Nat. Heart Inst., NIH, Bethesda, Md., 1969-71; med. dir. USPHS adult psychiatry sect. lab. clin. sci. NIMH, Bethesda, 1971-73; psychiatry resident diploma course in psychiatry McGill U. Sch. Medicine, Montreal Gen. Hosp., 1973-76, Montreal Children's Hosp., 1975; prof. psychiatry, chief psychopharmacology lab. U. Mo.-Mo. Inst. Psychiatry, St. Louis, 1976—78; chief psychiatry svc. San Juan VA Hosp., PR, 1978—92, pharmacy and therapeutic com., 1978—2004; prof. psychiatry U. PR Med. Sch., 1978-92, U. Okla. Health Sci. Ctr., 1992—2004, Okla. City VA Med. Ctr., 1992—2004; pvt. practice. Spl. cons. NASA, Moffettfield, Calif., 1965-69; cons. divsn. narcotic addition and drug abuse NIDA, 1972-73; drug adv. com. FDA/NIDA, 1976-80, pharmacy and therapeutic com., 1992—; local organizer Internat. Coll. Neuropsychiatry, San Juan, PR, 1986, CINP, 1986; spl. advisor mental health PR Senate, PR sec. health, 1989; prin. investigator NASA biosatellite project JH Sch. Med., 1963-65.; staff sr. psychiatrist and supt. psychiatry ward, VA Med. Ctr., Oklahoma City, 1992-1995, sr. staff psychiatrist and physician substance abuse clinic, 1995-2004, med. dir. Opioid Treatment Ctr., 1995-2004. Editor: Catholic Physicians Guild Archiocese of Okla., 1997-98. Mem. Rep. Nat. Com., 1995; mem. Eisenhower Commn., 2001. Capt. M.C. USAR, 1960-62; sr. surgeon USPHS, 1969-71, med. dir., 1971-73. Recipient Coronas award, 1957, Ruiz-Arnau award, 1957, Diaz-Garcia award 1957, Geigy award, 1975, 76, AMA Recognition award 1971, 76, 81, Horner's award 1975, 76, Pavlovian award, 1978, Recognition cert. VA Svc. awards and commendations, 1980-98, Senate of PR, 1986, Cert. of Merit Gov. of PR, 1986, Cert. Recognition, Sec. Health, San Juan, Puerto Rico, Appreciation plaque Fifth World Congress of IRMA, Manila, Philippines, Eisenhower Commn., 1995; nominee Eisenhower Commn. award, 1995, 2001. Fellow Interam. Coll. Physicians and Surgeons, Royal Coll. Physicians and Surgeons Can. (sr., cert.), Am. Psychiat Assn. (Disting., life, 2001); mem. AAAS, Am. Coll. Med. Quality (bd. dirs. 2004), Am. Physiol. Soc., Am. Coll. Psychiatrists, Pavlovian Soc., Am. Fedn. Clin. Rsch., Am. Fedn. Med. Rsch., Am. Assn. Geriat. Psychiatry, Am. Geriat. Soc., Am. Coll. Preventive Medicine, Am. Soc. Clin. Pharmacology and Therapeutics, Am. Soc. Pharmacology and Exptl. Therapeutics, Am. Soc. Addiction Medicine (cert.), Am. Acad. Addiction Psychiatry (dir. Area VIII, 2002-), Soc. Neurosci., Nat. Assn. Healthcare Quality (mem. editl. bd. Jour. Health Quality, 2005), Internat. Soc. Rsch. Aggression, Okla. Psychiat. Assn., Am. Soc. Clin. Psychopharmacology, Menninger Found., Charles F. Menninger Soc., Okla. Assn. Health Care Quality, Alumni, UPR Sch. Med., Johns Hopkins Med. Surg. Inst., NY Acad. Scis., NIH Alumni (life), McGill, Okla. Hist. Soc.(life). Republican. Roman Catholic. Avocations: painting, writing. Home: 8311 SW Fitzroy Pl Lawton OK 73505 Home Phone: 405-751-0243, 580-531-4573; Office Phone: 405-834-3001, 405-818-4020. Personal E-mail: jperezcrue@aol.com.

PEREZ-CRUET, MICK JORGE (MIGUELANGELO JORGE PEREZ-CRUET), neurosurgeon, educator; b. Washington, May 3, 1961; s. Jorge Fortunato and Anyes Lilly Perez-Cruet; m. Donna Jeanne Roggenbuck, July 9, 1994; children: Kristin Magdalene, Joshua Michael, Rachel Elizabeth, David Gabriel. BA, Grinell Coll., 1983; MSc in Chemistry, U. South Fla., 1986; MD, Tufts U., 1991. Commd. 2d lt. USAF, 1987, advanced through grades to maj., 1997, ret., 2001; intern surg. svc. Baylor Coll. Medicine, Houston, 1991-92, resident in neurosurgery, 1992-97; attending neurosurgery, v. chmn. Wilford Hall Med. Ctr., San Antonio, 1997—2001; spinal fellow Rush U./CINN, Chgo., 2001—02; asst. prof., dir. minimally invasive spine surgery Rush U., Chgo., 2002—03; assoc. dir. Inst. Spine Care/CINN; dir., spinal surgery Mich. Head and Spine Inst., 2003—; assoc. prof. Oakland Univ.; dir. minimally invasive spine surgery, Providence Med. Ctr. William Beaumont Hosp., 2003—, vice chair dept. neurosurgery; dir. spine fellowship program Providence Med. Ctr., 2004—; pres., CEO, MI4Spine, LLC; founder, pres. Minimally Invasive Neurosurg. Soc., 2009—. Prin. investigator clin. trials; presenter in field; appointee Coun. State Neurosurg. Socs., 1997, chmn. young physicians com., chmn. workforce com., corr. sec., publs. com.; mem. sci. adv. bd. Neospine; founding surgeon US Spine CNS Publs. Com., 2002—; dir. socioecon. peer rev. articles AANS Bull. Editor: (textbooks) Outpatient Spinal Surgery, An Anatomical Approach to Minimally Invasive Spine Surgery, (DVD) AANS Minimally Invasive Spine Techniques, Minimally Invasive Spine Fusion: Techniques and Operative Nuances; asst. editor: AANS Bull. Com.; contbr. chapters to books, articles to profl. jours. Chmn. class reunion Tufts Sch. Medicine, 1995-96; dir. class fund Grinnell Coll., 1999—. Air Force Health Professions scholar, 1987—91. Mem. AMA, ACS, AAAS, Congress Neurol. Surgeons, Am. Assn. Neurol. Surgeons (dir. spine courses, editor-in-chief AANS Bull. Socioecon. Jour. 2005—), Mich. Med. Soc., Mich. Assn. Neurol. Surgeons (treas., pres. 2006-08), Sigma Xi (grantee 1985). Achievements include invention of spine instrumentation. Avocations: hunting, fishing, scuba diving, archery, poetry. Office: Mich Head and Spine Inst 22250 Providence Dr Ste 300 Southfield MI 48075 Office Phone: 248-440-2162. Personal E-mail: perezcruet@yahoo.com.

PÉREZ DAMERA, MYRA M., lawyer; b. Havana, Cuba, Sept. 15, 1952; arrived in US, 1959; d. Genovevo Pérez and Mirtha Acosta; AA, Miami Dade Jr. Coll., Fla., 1973; BS, Fla. Internat. U., Miami, 1987; JD, Cath. U. PR, Ponce, 1993. Legal asst. Lehman Brothers Inc., 1993—96; ptnr. Damera & Dreize, PA, Miami, 1996—. Spkr. Dade County Bar Assn., 2004; pres., CEO, founder Fla. Traffic Atty. Com., Miami, 2004—06; trainer, guest spkr. Traffic Magistrate Orientation, Miami, 2005—06. Mem.: Fla. Bar Assn. Avocations: tennis, boating, skiing. Office: Damera & Dreize PA 901 Ponce de Leon Blvd #506 Coral Gables FL 33134 Office Phone: 305-446-6760. Business E-Mail: briefdc@aol.com.

PEREZ DE ALONSO, MARCELA, human resources specialist, information technology executive; b. Chile; Grad., Cath. U., Chile. Various sr. level positions in human resources and ops. Citigroup, global consumer head human resources, 1996—99; divsn. head Citigroup North L.Am. Consumer Bank, 1999—2004; exec. v.p. human resources and workforce devel. Hewlett-Packard Co., Palo Alto, Calif., 2004—. Mem. adv. bd. Marshall Bus. Sch. U. So. Calif.; spkr. in field; bd. dirs. Catalyst, NYC, Hewlett-Packard Co. Fin. Svcs. Mem. adv. bd. U. So. Calif. Marshall Bus. Sch.; bd. mem. Next Door Solutions to Domestic Violence. Named Corp. Exec. of Yr., Hispanic-Net, 2005; named one of 50 Most Important Hispanics in Tech. and Bus., Hispanic Engr. & Info. Tech. mag. Office: Hewlett Packard Co 3000 Hanover St Palo Alto CA 94304*

PEREZ DE LA MESA, MANUEL JOSE, swimming pool company executive; b. Havana, Cuba, Mar. 20, 1957; came to the U.S., 1961; s. Manuel Adolfo Oscar and Olga Marta (Cuervo) Perez de la Mesa; m. Ana Lidia Vidal, June 19, 1982; children: Rosario, Manuel, Cristina. BBA in Fin., Fla. Internat. U., 1977; MBA in Controllership, St. John's U., 1980. Fin. analyst Latin Am. Sea-Land Svc., Inc., Ft. Lauderdale, Fla., 1977-79, sr. fin. analyst Edison, N.J., 1979-80, regional contr. Latin Am. Ft. Lauderdale, 1980-82; ops. auditor IBM, San Jose, Calif., 1982-85, advisory pricing staff Bethesda, Md., 1985-87; asst. corp. contr. Del Monte Fresh Produce Inc., Coral Gables, Fla., 1987-88, v.p. fin. and ops. Latin Am. San Jose, Costa Rica, 1988-90, v.p. ops. S.Am. Santiago, Chile, 1990-91, v.p. planning and devel. Coral Gables, 1991-94; v.p. fin. and ops. Gemaire Distbrs. Inc., Deerfield Beach, Fla., 1994-96; v.p. ops. Watsco, Inc., Miami, Fla., 1996—99; pres. and COO SCP Pool Corp., Covington, La., 1999—2001, pres., CEO, 2001—. Chmn. Agribusiness, Caribbean/Latin Am. Action, Washington, 1991-93; dir., investment banking consulting Latin Fin. Inc., N.Y.C., Miami, Mexico City, 1993—. Mem. Inst. Mgmt. Acctg. Avocations: sports, investment analysis. Office: SCP Pool Corp 109 Northpark Blvd Covington LA 70433-5005

PÉREZ-DÍAZ, VÍCTOR MIGUEL, sociology educator; b. Madrid, Dec. 8, 1938; s. Miguel Pérez-Poyo and Victoria Díaz-Alonso; m. Marina González Olivares, Apr. 2, 1938. PhD in Sociology, Harvard U., 1976, Complutense U., Madrid, 1978, PhD in Law, 1978. Fellow Inst. Advanced Study, Princeton U., 1976-77; rsch. dir. INI Found., Madrid, 1977-80, FIES Found., Madrid, 1980-86; founding dir. Ctr. Social Sci. Juan March Inst., Madrid, 1987-92; dir. rsch. ctr. Analistas Socio-Políticos, 1993; prof. sociology Complutense U., Madrid, 1978—. Vis. prof. MIT, Cambridge, 1988-89, U. Calif., LaJolla, 1987-93, Harvard U., Cambridge, 1992-93, Inst. for Advanced Study, Princeton, 1975-76, Inst. nat. des Scis. & Politiques, Paris, 1994-95; mem. adv. com. PRISA, Madrid, 1991, Spanish Min. Health, 1996, New Sch. for Social Rsch., N.Y., 1999, Hans Spier vis. prof., 1999; mem. adv. com., prof. King Juan Carlos Ctr., NYU, 2000; mem. adv. bd. REPSOL, Madrid, 1993. Author: State, Bureaucracy and Civil Society, 1978, Castilian Peasants, 1992, The Return of Civil Society, 1993, Spanish Democracy, 1996, Public Sphere and Civil Society, 1997, Spain at the Crossroads, 1999, La lezione spagnola, 2003. Mem. Commn. on Unemployment Spanish Govt., Madrid, 1987-88, Study Group on Social Policy: European Communities Brussels, 1991-93; com. mem. Social Sci. Rsch. Coun., N.Y., 1983-89; mem. Nat. Com. Rules Ethical Behavior, 1997-2000, Prize Libre Empresa, 2002, Fund Rafael del Pino. Mem. Acadmia Europaea, Am. Acad. Arts and Scis. (fgn. hon. mem.). Home: Comandante Fortea 3 28008 Madrid Spain Office: Analistas Socio-Políticos Gabinete de Estudios c/Quintana, 24-5 dcha 28008 Madrid Spain Home Phone: 34-91-5413959; Office Phone: 34 91 5414746. Personal E-mail: asp@ctv.es.

PEREZ ESQUIVEL, ADOLFO, human rights activist; b. Nov. 26, 1931; m. Amanda E., 1956; 3 children. Grad., Nat. Sch. Fine Arts, Buenos Aires and La Plata, Argentina, 1956. Sculptor, prof. art Manuel Belgrano Nat. Sch. Fine Arts, Buenos Aires, 1956—; prof. faculty arch. and urbanism U. Nat. de la Plata; now rector United Nations U. for Peace, Escalzu, Costa Rica. Founder Servico Paz y Justica, 1971, sec. gen., 1974-86; joined Oouddian (Militant Noviolence) group, 1973; founder mag. Paz y Justica; imprisoned for peace activities, 1977-79. Author: Christ in a Poncho: Testimonials of the Nonviolent Struggles in Latin America, 1983. Recipient Pope John XXIII award Pax Christi, 1977; Nobel prize for peace, 1980. Address: SERPAJ CR Paseo de los Estudiantes Apartido Postal 1190 1002 San José Costa Rica E-mail: aperezesquivel@gmail.com.

PEREZ-NIEVES, ROBERTO, plastic surgeon, educator; b. Arecibo, PR, Nov. 15, 1963; children: Benjamin Reinier, Roberto C., Mia M. BS, Internat. U., 1987; MD, Ponce Sch. Medicine, 1992. Gen. surgery specialty Ponce U. Hosp., 1997; gen. surgeon US Army South Korea, 1997—98; commd. humanitarian surg. missions US Army South, Honduras, 2002, humanitarian surgical missions Paraguay, 2004, Dominican Republic, 2005, advanced through grades to lt. col., 2005; subject matter expert US Army Med. Sch., San Antonio, 2003—05; asst. prof. U. Tex., San Antonio, 2004—05. Decorated Commendation medal US Army. Fellow: ACS; mem.: Am. Soc. Plastic Surgery. Avocations: scuba diving, parachuting, running, skiing, dance. Office: PO Box 388 Mercedita PR 00715-0388 Home Phone: 210-373-1964; Office Phone: 787-840-1114.

PÉREZ-RIVERA, FRANCISCO (FRANK RIVERA), writer; b. Vertientes, Cuba, Oct. 3, 1938; came to U.S., 1968, naturalized, 1974; s. Francisco Daniel Pérez and María Eloísa Rivera. BA, Camagüey Coll., Cuba, 1955; MA in Romance Langs., U. Munich, 1967. Newsman, script writer Bavarian Radio, Munich, 1964-68; newsman AP, NYC, 1968-92, arts and entertainment editor, 1992—2006, ret., 2006; dir. Spanish programs for lang. labs., 1987. Author: (poetry) Constructions, 1979; (novel) Bells Over the Prairies, 1986, 2d edit., 2004; (short stories) Cuban Short Stories, 1992; (short stories) Varadero and Other Cuban Short Stories, 1998; co-author: Introduction to Spanish Literature, 1976, 2d edit, 1982; short stories in the anthologies New Cuban Storytellers (in Spanish), 1961, Cuba: Nouvelles et contes d'aujourd'hui, 1985, Narrative and Liberty: Cuban Tales of the Dispersion, 1996, Prosa moderna del mundo hispánico, 1997; author, narrator audio books The Golden Age of Spanish Literature, 2002. Grantee German Academic Exchange Svc., Munich, 1961-67; fellow Cintas Found., N.Y., 1980; 1st prize short story Círculo de Escritores y Poetas Latinoamericanos, N.Y., 1997, Internat. Short Story award Círculo de Cultura Panamericano, N.J., 1997. Home: 212 E 77th St Apt 1G New York NY 10075-2111

PERFETTI, ROBERT NICKOLAS, educational consultant; b. Staples, Minn., Jan. 8, 1937; s. Nickolas Albert and Lila Bertha (Beurge) P. BS, St. Cloud State U., Minn., 1960; postgrad., Bemidji State U., Minn., 1961-62, Calif. State U., LA, 1964-68, Pepperdine U., Malibu, Calif., 1967-68; MA, La Verne U., Calif., 1970; postgrad., U. So. Calif., LA, 1972—73, Point Loma U., Pasadena, Calif., 1974-75; EdD, Pacific States U., LA, 1975; DD, Universal Life Ch., 2002. Cert. admistr., counselor, secondary, community coll., jr. high sch., adult, and elem. edn. Calif. Prin. Richmond Pub. Schs., Minn., 1960-62; elem. tchr. Sebeka Sch. Dist., Minn., 1962-63; team leader lang. arts, social sci. and summer sch. Rowland Unified Sch. Dist., Rowland Heights, Calif., 1965-76, coord. math. lab., 1976-79, secondary counselor, 1979-81, coord. work experience edn., career edn. and career ctr., 1981-95, home ind. study coord., ednl. cons., 1992-95; mental health counselor St. Gabriel's Hosp., Little Falls, Minn., 1999. Coord. Gender Equity, 1980-95, Job Tng. Partnership Act, 1980-95; advisor Nat. Vocat. Tech. Honor Soc., 1991-95; alumni dir. Sacred Heart Sch., Staples. Editor: (profl. newspaper) Reaction. Officer parish coun. Our Lady of the Assumption Ch., Claremont, Calif., chmn. edn. com.; chmn. PTA, Rowland Heights; rep. fed. project, Rowland Heights; scoutmaster, chmn. troop com. Boy Scouts Am. Recipient Svc. Commendation Rowland Unified Sch. Dist., 1978; named. L.A. County Tchr. of Yr. Calif. State Dept. Edn., 1975, Outstanding Secondary Educator of Am., 1974, Giano Tchr. of Yr. Giano Intermediate Sch., 1973, Tchr. of Yr. Rowland Unified Sch. Dist., 1974. Mem. NEA (life), Calif. Tchrs. Assn., Assn. Rowland Educators (v.p.), Calif. Assn. Work Experience Educators (Alpha chpt. v.p.), Alpha Phi Omega (pres.), Pi Delta Epsilon (pres.), KC (3d degree). Roman Catholic. Avocations: water sports, travel, research, writing. Home: 200 4th St SE Little Falls MN 56345-3116 E-mail: perfetti7@msn.com.

PERGER, DONNA SPAGNOLI, retired secondary school mathematics educator; b. Portsmouth, Va., Apr. 24, 1951; d. Delmo John and Lurline M. (Smith) Spagnoli; m. Steve John Perger Jr., June 9, 1980; 1 stepchild, Stephanie Lee. BS in Secondary Edn., Old Dominion U., 1973. Tchr. math. Manor H.S., Portsmouth, Va., 1973—74, Bettie Williams Sch., Virginia Beach, Va., 1974—78, Virginia Beach Jr. H.S., 1978—80, Queens Lake Sch., York County, Va., 1980—2003, chair dept. math. Lead tchr. VQUEST. Art work published in Stampers Sampler, Somerset Studio and Gallery mags. Elder Olive Br. Christian Ch. Named Mid. Sch. Tchr. of Yr. Daily Press Newspaper, Newport News, 1993. Avocations: paper embossing (repousse), needlecrafts, sewing, gardening. Personal E-mail: cardorft@cox.net.

PERHACH, JAMES LAWRENCE, pharmaceutical executive; s. James Lawrence and Elizabeth Louise (Hoffman) P.; m. Judith Irene Selter, Apr. 15, 1967; children: Laura Anne, Amy Elizabeth. BS, U. Dayton, 1966; MS, U. Pitts., 1969, PhD, 1971. Sr. scientist dept. pharmacology Mead Johnson Rsch. Ctr., divsn. Bristol Myers, 1971—74, sr. investigator dept. biol. rsch., 1974—76, sr. rsch. assoc. dept. biol. rsch., 1976—77, sr. rsch. assoc. dept. pathology and toxicology, 1977—78, prin. rsch. assoc. dept. pathology and toxicology, 1978—80; from dir. pharmacology to dir. biol. rsch. to dir. clin. investigation Wallace Labs. Divsn. Carter-Wallace, Inc., Cranbury, NJ, 1980—87, v.p. clin. pharmacology and pharmacokinetics, 1987—2001; sr. dir. clin. pharmacology Purdue Pharma, L.P., 2001—04; sr. dir. CNS Therapeutic Area Forest Rsch. Inst, 2004—05, exec. dir. clin. devel., 2005—. Adj. asst. prof. dept. pharmacy practice and adminstrn. Ernest Mario Coll. Pharmacy Rutgers U., 1993—; adv. bd. clin. rsch. ctr. U. Medicine and Dentistry NJ Robert Wood Johnson Med. Sch., 1995-2003; drug utilization rev. coun. State of NJ, 1983-2003, med. pharmacologist, 1983, sec., 1984, chmn., 1985-87. Fellow: Am. Coll. Clin. Pharmacology; mem.: Am. Soc. Pharmacology and Exptl. Therapeutics, Am. Soc. Clin. Pharmacology and Therapeutics. Achievements include research in drug discovery, elucidation of mechanism of action and safety evaluation of new therapeutic agents. Office: Forest Rsch Inst Harbor Side Fin Ctr Plaza V Jersey City NJ 07311 Home Phone: 609-716-9228; Office Phone: 201-427-8465. Business E-Mail: james.perhach@frx.com.

PERHAM, ROY GATES, III, industrial psychologist; b. Hackensack, NJ, Apr. 22, 1958; s. Roy Gates Jr. and Titania Joan (Robbitts) P. BA with honors, Bates Coll., 1980; MS, Stevens Inst. Tech., 1982, PhD, 1989. Intern Sen. Edmund S. Muskie, Washington, 1978; psychometrician Lab. Psychol. Studies Stevens Inst. Tech., Hoboken, NJ, 1981-83, instr., 1985, adj. asst. prof., 1990—95, Fairleigh Dickinson U., Rutherford, NJ, 1986; sr. assoc. AAI Orgnl. Performance Cons., Florham Park, NJ, 1990-94; assessment projects mgr. Tech. Employee Selection and Tng. Inc., Hasbrouck Heights, NJ, 1995—. WordStar coord. NY Computer Soc., NYC, 1985-88; adj. asst. prof. psychology John Jay Coll. Criminal Justice, NYC, 2006-. Chmn. Juvenile Conf. Com., Hasbrouck Heights and Wood-Ridge, NJ, 1985-95; mem. NJ State Juvenile Delinquency Commn., Trenton, NJ, 1988-91; county exec.'s rep. Bergen County Youth Svcs. Commn., 1990-2002, chair, 1994-96; chair Bergen County Task Force on Youth Violence, 1993-95; asst. Bergen County Exec. for Juvenile Justice, NJ, 1999—2002; mem. NJ Gov's. Juvenile Justice and Delinquency Prevention Com., 2001—. Named Citizen of Yr., Lions Club of Hasbrouck Heights, NJ, 1988. Mem. APA, Am. Psychol. Soc., Met. NY Assn. for Applied Psychology, NJ Property Owners Assn., Soc. for Indsl./Orgnl. Psychology, Inc., Phi Beta Kappa, Psi Chi. Home: 269 Raymond St Hasbrouck Heights NJ 07604-1723 Office: Technical Employee Selection & Tng Inc The Profl Bldg 248 Blvd Hasbrouck Heights NJ 07604 Office Phone: 201-288-0730.

PERIASWAMY, PADMINI, materials scientist, researcher; d. Nanjappa and Amirthavalli Periaswamy. BS in Applied Scis., PSG Coll. Tech., Coimbatore, 1988, MS in Materials Sci., 1990; PhD, Indian Inst. Sci., Bangalore, India, 1996. Postdoctoral rschr. Technische Universitaet, Dresden, Germany, 1997—98; asst. rsch. engr. U. Calif., Santa Barbara, 1998—2000; postdoctoral rschr. U. Ala., Tuscaloosa, 2000—01, asst. rsch. engr., 2001—02, assoc. rsch. engr., 2002—07; with US Patent and Trade Mark Office, 2008. Contbr. articles to profl. jours. Grantee, Dept. of Energy Exptl. Program to Stimulate Competitive Rsch., 2003—06, Office of Naval Rsch., 2003—06; Humboldt Rsch. fellow, Humboldt Found., Germany, 1997—98. Mem.: IEEE, Materials Rsch. Soc., Am. Phys. Soc. Achievements include patents in field. Avocations: travel, music, tennis, reading. Office Fax: 205-348-1685. Business E-Mail: padmini@bama.ua.edu.

PERIBERE, JEROME A., agricultural products executive; M in Bus. Econs. and Fin., Inst. D'Etudes Politiques, Paris. With Dow Chem. Co., 1977—, regional mktg. mgr. Ea. Europe, 1982—85, regional mgr. Mid. East and Africa, 1985—88, dir. European agr. bus., 1988—89, comml. dir. agr. bus. Europe, 1989—93, global comml. dir. Indpls., 1993—97, corp. strategy leader Dow AgroSciences, 1997—98, global leader Weed Mgmt. Global Bus. Unit European Trade area, 1998—2002, global leader agr. chems., 2002—04, pres., CEO Dow AgroSciences, 2004—, mem. Office of the Chief Exec., 2006—. Mem. bd. BioCrossroads. Named a Power Player in Life Sci. and Tech., Indpls. Bus. Jour., 2005. Office: Dow AgroSciences LLC 9330 Zionsville Rd Indianapolis IN 46268

PERICAK-VANCE, MARGARET A., medical geneticist, educator, health facility administrator; b. Buffalo, June 28, 1951; m. Jeff Pericak-Vance; 1 child. PhD in Med. Genetics, Ind. U., 1978. Dir. Ctr. Human Genetics Duke U. Med. Ctr., Durham, NC, 1996—2006, James B. Duke prof. medicine, chief, med. genetics sect.; prof. Dept. Medicine, dir. Inst. Human Genomics U. Miami, 2007—. Recipient Louis D. scientific prize, Inst. France Acad. Sci., 2001; co-recipient McKnight Memory & Brain Disorders award, 2001; named to Century Club: 100 People to Watch as We Move to the Next Millennium, Newsweek Mag., 1997. Mem.: Inst. Medicine, Am. Coll. Med. Genetics (founding fellow). Office: U Miami Dept Medicine PO Box 016760 Miami FL 33101-6760 E-mail: m.pericakvance@miami.edu.

PERICH, TERRY MILLER, retired secondary school educator; b. Greensburg, Pa., Sept. 22, 1948; s. Miller and Eleanor Ann (Schmuck) P.; m. Kathleen Ann Ferrari, July 26, 1975. BA in Elem. Edn., Edinboro U., 1970; elem. cert., Pa. State U., 1973; Masters equivalency degree, U. Pitts., 1994; postgrad., Carlow Coll., 1994. Trained student assistance profl., Pa.; cert. tchr. elem. edn. Tchr. sci. and math. Penn Trafford Schs., Harrison City, Pa., 1970—2003; v.p. Jeannette Area Hist. Soc., 2003—06. Mentor, tchr. Tchr. Enhancement Inst. St. Vincent Coll., Latrobe, Pa.; selected tchr. Watershed Restoration St. Vincent Coll., Latrobe. Author: Image of America, 2005; co-author: Postcard History, 2005, Postcard History Series. County committeeman Dem. Party, Penn Twp., Pa., 1994—; lion tamer Bushy Run Lions Club, Claridge, Pa., 1993—, 3rd v.p., 1995, 2d v.p., 1996, 1st v.p., 1997—. Recipient Commendation, Pres.-elect Clinton, Student Assistance Program award for working with students at risk St. Vincent Coll. Prevention Projects, 1991. Mem. NEA, ASCD, PACE, Nat. Sci. Tchrs. Assn., Pa. Tchrs. Edn. Assn., Pa. Sci. Tchrs. Assn., Westmoreland County Assn. Student Assistance Profls. (bd. dirs. 1992-94, mem. Westmoreland county student assistance team 1995-96, 96-97), Penn Trafford Edn. Assn. (exec. bd. dirs. 1990-91). Roman Catholic. Avocations: travel, education. Home: 13 Rizzi Dr Irwin PA 15642-8902 Office Phone: 724-205-1983. E-mail: middie22@aol.com.

PERICH, THOMAS J., lawyer; b. Galveston, Tex., 1945; BS, Georgetown U., 1967; MA with honors, in Economics, U. Tex., 1971, JD with honors, 1975. Bar: Tex. 1976, admitted to practice: US Ct. Appeals (5th Cir.), bar: US Ct. Appeals (11th Cir.). Ptnr. Dept. Bus. Transactions Andrews & Kurth LLP, Houston, mem. policy com. Mem. Tex. Law Rev., 1974—75. Mem.: Tex. Assn. Bank Counsel (dep. mng. ptnr. houston office), Houston Comml. Lawyer Forum, Houston Bar Assn., State Bar Tex., ABA, Order of Coif. Office: Andrews & Kurth LLP 600 Travis St Ste 4200 Houston TX 77002-3090 Home Phone: 713-818-3650; Office Phone: 713-220-4268. Office Fax: 713-238-7175. Personal E-mail: tperich@akllp.com. Business E-Mail: tperich@andrewskurth.com.

PERILLO, SALVATORE J., lawyer; b. Apr. 25, 1945; m. Elizabeth E. Perillo. BS, SUNY, Albany; JD, Woodrow Wilson Coll. Law. Gen. counsel Mohawk Industries Inc., Calhoun, Ga. Mem.: Am. Corp. Counsel Assn. Office: Mohawk Industries Inc 160 S Industrial Blvd PO Box 12069 Calhoun GA 30701 Office Phone: 706-624-2660. Office Fax: 706-624-3825.

PERIN, NOEL I., neurosurgeon; arrived in US, 1984; s. Rajes Perinpanayagam; m. Frances J. Baker, Nov. 30, 1985; children: Christopher D., Michelle N. MD, U. Colombo, Sri Lanka, 1973. Cert. neurosurgery Am. Assn. Neurol. Surgeons, 1994. Neurosurgeon, gen. surgeon Middlesex Hosp., London, 1986—90; spine fellowship NYU Med. Ctr., 1991; dir. trauma U. Cin., 1991—94; dir. spinal neurosurgery Mt. Sinai Med. Ctr., NYC, 1994—2001; dir. spine and minimally invasive spinal surgery St. Luke's- Roosevelt Hosp. Ctr., NYC, 2001—. Clin. assoc. prof. Roosevelt Hosp. Ctr., NYC. Co-author: Thorascopic Spinal Surgery, 1999. Fellow: ACS (assoc.), Royal Coll. Surgeons Edinburgh. Achievements include research in pharmacological treatment in spinal cord injury. Avocations: golf, tennis, travel. Office: Roosevelt Hosp Ctr Ste 5G 80 1000 10th Ave New York NY 10019 Office Fax: 212-523-6115. E-mail: nperin@slrhc.org, nperin@chpnet.org.

PERINGIAN, LYNDA ANN, dietician, writer; d. Mike and Clara A. Peringian. BS in Dietetics, U. Detroit, 1974; MS in Foods and Nutrition, Wayne State U., Detroit, 1976. Registered dietitian, cert. personnel cons. Clin. dietitian North Oakland Gen. Hosp.; chief dietitian Drs. Hosp., Detroit; dir. Healthcare divsn. Roth Young, Detroit, 1977—88; pres. Peringian & Assoc., Dryden, Mich., 1988—. Author: Healthcare Textbook, 1989, The MIRACLE ROSES - A True Story, 2007. Vol. Birmingham (Mich.) Cmty. House. Avocations: sports, piano, cooking, reading, gardening.

PERINO, DANA MARIE, public relations executive, former White House press secretary; b. Evanston, Wyo., May 9, 1972; d. Leo and Jan Perino; m. Peter McMahon, 1998. BA in Mass Comm., U. So. Colo., 1994; MA in Pub. Affairs Reporting, U. Ill., Springfield, 1995. Staff asst. for Rep. Scott McInnis US Congress, Washington, 1995, press sec. to Rep. Dan Schaefer, 1995—98; spokesperson US Dept. Justice, 2001; assoc. dir. comm. White House Coun. on Environ. Quality, 2002—05; spl. asst. to pres., dep. press sec. The White House, 2005—06, dep. asst. to Pres., dep. press sec., 2006—07, acting press sec., 2007, asst. to Pres., press sec., 2007—09; chief issues counselor Burson-Marsteller, Washington, 2009—. Recipient Disting. Alumni award, Colo. State U., 2003. Republican. Office: Burson-Marsteller 1110 Vermont Ave NW Ste 1200 Washington DC 20005 Office Phone: 202-530-0400. Office Fax: 202-530-4500.*

PERINPANAYAGAM, HIRAN, dental educator; b. Colombo, Sri Lanka, Aug. 15, 1967; s. Chris and Clarice Perinpanayagam; m. Meghan Kodweis Perinpanayagam; children: Thomah Kodweis, Marala Schaft. DDS, U. Otago, New Zealand, 1989; MS, U. Rochester, NYC, 1995; PhD, U. Iowa, Iowa City, 2003. Diplomate Am. Bd. Endodontics, 2003. Asst. prof. U. Buffalo, 2002—06; assoc. prof. U. Western Ont., London, Canada, 2007—. Mem.: Am. Assn. Endodontists (com. mem. 2006—). Office: Univ Western Ont Schulich Sch Medicine & Dentistry DSB 0079 London ON N6A 5C1 Canada Office Fax: 519-850-2459. Personal E-mail: doctor.hiran@gmail.com. Business E-Mail: hiran.perinpanayagam@schulich.uwo.ca.

PERIYASAMY, KASILINGAM, engineering educator; s. Periyasamy Narayanan and Seethalakshmi Periyasamy; m. Raji R. Rajendran, May 25, 1989; children: Sarvesh, Viswesh Raj. BS in Engring. with honors, U. Madras, India, 1981; MS in Engring., Anna U., Chennai, 1983; MS in Computer Sci., Concordia U., Montreal, Can., 1987, PhD, 1991. Asst. prof. U. Man., Winnipeg, Manitoba, Canada, 1991—96, assoc. prof., 1996—99, U. Wis., La Crosse, 1999—2004, prof., 2004—. Software cons. Self-business, La Crosse, Wis., 2003—08. Grant, Wis. Space Rsch. Consortium, 2000—01. Mem.: Assn. Computing Machinery. Office: Univ Wis-La Crosse 1725 State St La Crosse WI 54601 Office Fax: 608-785-6820. Business E-Mail: kasi@cs.uwlax.edu.

PERKEL, ROBERT SIMON, photojournalist, educator; b. Jersey City, Apr. 23, 1925; s. Louis Leo and Flora Sonia (Levin) Perkel. BS, NYU, 1948; MS, Barry U., 1964; postgrad., Columbia U. Owner, operator Gulfstream Color Labs., Miami Beach, Fla., 1955-61; graphics instr. Dade County Pub. Schs., 1962-66; freelance photojournalist, 1967—. Rep. News Events Photo Svc., Ft. Lauderdale, Fla.; instr. photography Broward CC, 1982—92; rep. Patch Comm., Titusville, Fla., 1985—88; pub. Biograph/Comm., North Miami Beach, Fla., 1987—90. Contbr. photos stories and photographs to numerous mags. and indsl. trade publs.; exhibitions include Met. Mus. and Art Ctr., Coral Gables, Fla., Mus. Fine Arts, Boston. Former publicity dir. Coun. Internat. Visitors Greater Miami. With US Army, 1943—46, ETO. Recipient Cmty. Spirit award, Zonta Club Greater Miami, 1980, Found. medal, Nat. Press Photographers Found., 2000. Mem.: VFW (life), DAV (life; trustee Jack Schwartz chpt., past comdr. Miami Beach-Surfside chpt., nat. citation for disting. svc. 1969, nat. svc. plaque 2000), Covenant Soc., Guardian Soc., Nielsen Media Rsch., Nat. Press Photographers Assn. (life), Barry U. Alumni Assn., Steamship Hist. Soc. Am. Found. (life; SE Fla. chpt.), NYU Alumni Fedn. (Leadership award for 1982-1983 fund campaign), World Ocean and Cruise Liner Soc., Silver Leader, Commander's Club, Am. Legion, Order of the Flame, Alpha Mu Gamma. Home: 280 Sierra DR Apt C206 Miami FL 33179-3852

PERKIEL, MITCHEL H., lawyer; b. NYC, Oct. 26, 1949; s. Frank and Ella Perkiel; m. Lois E. Perkiel, June 24, 1984; children: Joshua L., Alexa Kim, Griffin. BA, SUNY, Stony Brook, 1971; JD, New York Law Sch., 1974. Bar: N.Y. 1975, U.S. Dist. Ct. (so. and ea. dists.) N.Y. 1975, U.S. Ct. Appeals (2d cir.) 1975, Conn. 1988, Utah 1999. Law clk. to presiding justice N.Y. County Civil Ct., 1975; assoc. Levin & Weintraub & Crames, NYC, 1975-80, ptnr., 1980-90, Kaye, Scholer, Fierman, Hayes & Handler, NYC, 1990—2001, Jenkens & Gilchrist, Parker Chapin, NYC, 2001—05, Troutman Sanders LLP, NYC, 2005—. Notes and comments editor New York Law Rev., 1973-74. With USAR, 1969-73. Mem. ABA, Assn. of Bar of City of N.Y., Am. Bankruptcy Inst., Turnaround Mgmt. Assn. (dir.). Office Phone: 212-704-6016. Business E-Mail: mitchel.perkiel@troutmansanders.com.

PERKIN, RONALD MURRAY, pediatrician, educator; b. Denver, July 31, 1948; s. Robert Murray and Marion Kathryn (Thompson) P.; m. Susan Renee Sheer; children: Matthew Murray, Jeffrey Jay, Nickolas James, Thomas Mitchell, Benjamin Sheer, Savannah Paige. BS in Engring., U. Colo., 1970; postgrad., Johns Hopkins U., 1970-71; MD, U. South Fla., 1976; MA, Loma Linda Univ., 1997. Diplomate Am. Bd. Pediatrics. Resident in pediatrics Children's Med. Ctr., Dallas, 1976-79, fellow in pediatric intensive care, 1979-81, asst. dir. pediatric intensive care, 1981; clins. asst. prof. pediatrics U. Tex. Health Sci. Ctr. Southwestern Med. Sch., Dallas, 1981; asst. adj. prof. pediatrics U. Calif. Sch. Medicine, San Diego, 1982-84, co-dir. pediatric intensive care, 1982-84; dir. pediatric ICU attending physician Childrens Hosp. Orange (Calif.) County Hosp., 1984-88; attending physician newborn ICU St. Joseph's Hosp., Orange, 1984-88; assoc. prof. pediatrics Loma Linda Univ., 1988-90, prof. pediatrics, 1990-2000; prof., chmn. dept. pediats. Brody Sch. Medicine, East Carolina U., Greenville, NC, 2000—. Cons. Naval Hosp., San Diego, 1983-84; asst. adj. prof. pediatrics U. Calif., Irvine, 1984-88; dir. pediat. intensive care fellowship program U. Calif. Irvine and Children's Hosp. Orange County, 1984-88; critical care adv. com., critical care coun., Extra Corporeal Membrane Oxygenation found. So. Calif., emergency dept. com., ethics com., ethics cons. svc. critical care com., resident evaluation sub-com., respiratory care com.; dir. pediat. critical care Loma Linda U. Children's Hosp., 1988-2000, assoc. chair pediat. Sch. Medicine, 1993-2000; lectr. in field. Editor: (with others) Brain Insults in Infants and Children: Pathophysiology and Management; Emergency Management of the Critically Ill Child; Pediatric Hosp. Medicine: A Textbook of Inpatient Care, 2003, 2d edit., 2008, Primer on Pediatric Palliative Care, 2005, Pediatric Emergency Medicine Manual, 2007; reviewer Capistrano Press, Ltd., 1982-84, Jour. Pediatrics, 1982—; contbr. articles to profl. jours. With USN, 1971—73. Recipient student awards U. South Fla. Coll. Medicine, faculty awards U. Calif., Irvine, Lange Ann. award Lange Book Co., 1974; Mosby scholar Mosby Book Co., 1975-76. Fellow Am. Acad. Pediatrics, Am. Coll. Critical Care Medicine; mem. Soc. Critical Care Medicine, Calif. Children Svcs. (adv. com. rev. pediatric ICU's 1986-2000). Office: 3E-142 Brody Med Scis Bldg Greenville NC 27858-4354 Office Phone: 252-744-2540. Office Fax: 252-744-1376. Business E-Mail: perkinr@ecu.edu.

PERKINS, BRIAN D., consumer products company executive; b. 1954; m. Lois Perkins; children: D.J., Michael. Grad., U. Pa. Wharton Sch. Bus., 1980. Product dir. McNeil Consumer Products Co., 1980, mgmt. bd. consumer healthcare, 1989, v.p. mktg. consumer healthcare, 1991—93, pres., 1994—99; co. grp chmn. Consumer Pharms. Worldwide, 1999; pres. personal products N.Am. divsn. Johnson & Johnson, 1993—94, v.p. corp. affairs, mem. exec. com., 1999—. Bd. dirs. Advt. Coun., Inc., 2005—, chmn. bd. dirs., 2009—. Named a Power Player, Advt. Age, 2008. Mailing: Corp Hdqs One Johnson & Johnson Plaza New Brunswick NJ 08933*

PERKINS, CYNTHIA O., art educator; d. Donald R. and Z. Virgina Perkins. MA in Art History, U. Okla., Norman, 1996. Asst. prof. art Del Mar Coll., Corpus Christi, Tex., 2001—; vis. prof. art Okla. State U., Stillwater, 1998—2001. Contbr. articles to profl. jour. Mem.: Coll. Art Assn. Liberal. Roman Catholic. Office: Del Mar Coll 101 Baldwin Corpus Christi TX 78404 Office Phone: 361-698-1503.

PERKINS, DWIGHT HEALD, economics professor; b. Chgo., Oct. 20, 1934; s. Lawrence Bradford and Margery (Blair) P.; m. Julie Rate, June 15, 1957; children: Lucy Fitch, Dwight Edward, Caleb Blair. BA, Cornell U., 1956; AM, Harvard U., 1961, PhD, 1964. From instr. to assoc. prof. Harvard U., Cambridge, Mass., 1963-69, prof. econs., 1969-81, assoc. dir. East Asian Rsch. Ctr., 1973-77, chmn. dept. econs., 1977-80, H.H. Burbank prof. polit. economy, 1981—2006, dir. Asia Ctr., 2002—05; dir. Harvard Inst. Internat. Devel., Cambridge, 1980-95; H.H. Burbank Rsch. prof. of polit. economy Harvard U., 2006—. Trustee China Med. Bd., 1995—2004, chair, 2000—04; cons. permanent subcom. on investigations US Senate, 1974—80; H.M. Jackson vis. prof. Chinese studies U. Wash., 1985, Phi Beta Kappa lectr., 1992—93, Faculty Salzburg seminar, 1996; lectr. Fulbright tchg. policy program, Vietnam, 1997—2009; mem. Internat. Adv. Group to Prime Min. of Papua, New Guinea, 1991—92, 2000—02; cons. Korea Devel. Inst., 1972—80, 2006—, Govt. Malaysia, 1968—69, 2005—07; C. V. Star disting. fellow China Devel. Rsch. Found., 2008—09. Author (with M. Halperin): Communist China and Arms Control, 1965, Agricultural Development in China, 1368-1968, 1969, Market Control and Planning in Communist China, 1966, China: Asia's Next Economic Giant?, 1986; author: (with E.S. Mason and others) The Economic Modernization of Korea, 1980; author: (with S. Yusuf) Rural Development in China, 1984; author: (with S. Radelet and others) Economics of Development, 1983, 6th edit., 2006; editor: China's Modern Economy in Historical Perspective, 1975; editor: (with M. Roemer) Reforming Economic Systems in Developing Countries, 1991; editor: (with J. Stern and others) Industrialization and the State: The Korean Heavy and Chemical Industry Drive, 1995; editor: (with others) Assisting Development in a Changing World, 1997, Industrialization and the State: The Changing Role of the Taiwan Government in the Economy, 1945-1998, 2001, Innovative East Asia: The Future of Growth, 2003; editor: (with S. Yusuf and others) Under New Ownership: Privatizing China's State-Owned Enterprises, 2006. Vis. com. Far Ea. studies U. Chgo., 1973-77; bd. govs. East-West Ctr., Honolulu, 1979-82; co-moderator Aspen Inst. Seminar on Korea, Colo., 1980-83. Lt. (j.g.) USNR, 1956-58. Fgn. Area Tng. fellow, Ford Found., NY, 1958—62, NSF Sci. Faculty fellow, Tokyo, 1968—69. Mem. Am. Philos. Soc., Assn. Asian Studies, Assn. Comparative Econ. Systems (pres. 1999-2000), Am. Econ. Assn., Phi Beta Kappa. Home: 64 Pinehurst Rd Belmont MA 02478-1504 Office: Harvard Univ Dept Econs Cambridge MA 02138-5781 Business E-Mail: dwight_perkins@harvard.edu.

PERKINS, EDDIE, retired professional boxer; b. Clarksdale, Miss., Mar. 3, 1937; Profl. boxer, 1956—75; ret., 1975. Winner world title vs. Duilio Loi by unanimous decision, light welterweight divsn. World Boxing Assn., 1962, winner world title vs. Roberto Cruz by unanimous decision, light welterweight divsn., 63, winner world title def. vs. Yoshinori Takahashi by knockout, light welterweight divsn., 64, winner world title def. vs. Bunny Grant by unanimous decision, light welterweight divsn., 64; winner world title vs. Roberto Cruz by unanimous decision, light welterweight divsn. World Boxing Coun., 1963, winner world title def. vs. Yoshinori Takahashi by knockout, light welterweight divsn., 64, winner world title def. vs. Bunny Grant by unanimous decision, light welterweight divsn., 64; winner title vs. Armando Muniz by split decision, light welterweight divsn. N.Am. Boxing Fedn., 1973, winner title def. vs. Armando Muniz by unanimous decision, light welterweight divsn., 74. Named to Profl. Boxing Hall of Fame, 2006, Internat. Boxing Hall of Fame, 2008. Achievements include holding the light welterweight world title from 1963 to 1965; holding the North American light welterweight title from 1973 to 1974; acquiring 22 career knock-outs. Mailing: c/o Internat Boxing Hall of Fame 1 Hall of Fame Dr Canastota NY 13032

PERKINS, EDWARD JOSEPH, political science professor, retired ambassador; b. Sterlington, La., June 8, 1928; m. Lucy Liu; children: Katherine, Sarah. Student, U. Calif., Lewis and Clark Coll.; BA, U. Md., 1967; MPA, U. So. Calif., 1972, DPA, 1978; studied French, Fgn. Service Inst., 1983; LLD (hon.), U. Md., 1990, St. John's U., 1990, Lewis and Clark Coll., 1988; LHD (hon.), Winston-Salem State U., 1990, Bowie State Coll., 1993; HHD (hon.), St. Augustine Coll., 1991, Beloit Coll., 1990, U. So. Calif., 1995. Chief pers. Army and Air Force Exch. Svc., Taipei, Taiwan, 1958-62, dep. chief Okinawa, Japan, 1962-64; chief pers. & adminstrn. Army and Air Force Exchange Service, Okinawa, Japan, 1964-66; asst. gen. services officer Far East bur. US Agy. Internat. Devel. (USAID), 1967-69, mgmt. analyst, 1969-70; asst. dir. for mgmt. US Ops. Mission to Thailand, 1970-72; staff asst. Office of Dir. Gen. Fgn. Svc., 1972, personnel officer, 1972-74; adminstrv. officer Bur. Near Eastern & South Asian Affairs US Dept. State, 1974-75, mgmt. analysis officer Office Mgmt. Ops., 1975-78, counselor for polit. affairs Accra, Ghana, 1978-81, dep. chief of mission Monrovia, Liberia, 1981-83, dir. Office of West African Affairs, Bur. African Affair, 1983-85, US amb. to Liberia, 1985-86, US amb. to South Africa, 1986-89, dir. gen., dir. pers. Fgn. Svc. Washington, 1989-92, US amb. to UN NYC, 1992-93, US amb. to Australia Canberra, 1993-96. William J. Crowe prof. and exec. dir. Internat. Programs Ctr., U. Okla., Norman 1996-; mem. adv. bd. Inst. Internat. Pub. Policy, 1997-; mem. adv. coun. Univ. Office of Internat. Programs, Pa. State U., 1997; mem. White House Adv. Com. on Trade Policy and Negotiations, 2003-. Contbr. articles to profl. publs.; editor (with David Boren) Preparing American's Foreign Policy for the 21st Century, 1999, with (Joseph Ginat) Palestinian Refugees: Traditional Positions and New Solutions, 2001, (with David Boren) Democracy, Morality, and the Search for Peace in America's Foreign Policy, 2002, (with Joseph Ginat and Edwin G. Corr) Middle East Peace Process: Vision Versus Reality, 2002, (with Connie Cronley) Mr. Ambassador: Warrior For Peace, 2008 Trustee Lewis and Clark Coll., 1994—, Woodrow Wilson Nat. Fellowship Found., 1999—; bd. govs. Joint Ctr. for Polit. and Econ. Studies, 1996-2003; mem. steering com. Ctr. for Australian and New Zealand Studies, Georgetown U., 1996—; bd. Cranlana Programme; bd. visitors Nat. Def. U., 2002-. Recipient Superior Honor award US Dept State, 1983, Presdl. Meritorious Svc. award, 1987, Presdl. Disting. Svc. award, 1989, Meritorious Honor award US Agy. for Iinternat. Devel. (USAID), 1967, Award for Outstanding Svc. as Fgn. Svc. Officer Una Chapman Cox Found., 1989, Living Legend award The Links, Inc., 1989, Disting. Alumni award U. So. Calif., 1991, Achievement award So. U., 1991, Statesman of Yr. award George Washington U., 1992, Dir. General's Cup, US Dept. State, 2001; honoree U. Okla. chpt. Beta Gamma Sigma, 1998. Fellow Nat. Acad. Pub. Adminstrn.; mem. VFW, ASPA, Navy League, Am. Polit. Sci. Assn., Fgn. Policy Assn. (ambassadorial fellow), Internat. Studies Assn., Coun. on Fgn. Rels., Am. Acad. Diplomacy, Am. Consortium Internat. Pub. Adminstrn., Am. Fgn. Svc. Assn., Am. Legion, Ctr. Study of Presidency, Chester A. Arthur Soc., Pub. Svc. Comm., World Affairs Couns. Okla. and Washington, Am. Acad. Diplomacy, Pacific Coun. on Internat. Policy, Assn. for Diplomatic Studies and Tng. (bd. dirs. 1998—), Kappa Alpha Psi (Laurel Wreath award,1993, C. Rodger Wilson Leadership Conf. award, 1990, Disting. Svc. award 1989, Outstanding Achievement award for Fgn. Svc. 1986), Phi Kappa Phi. Office: U Okla Internat Programs Ctr 339 W Boyd St Rm 400 Norman OK 73019-5144 E-mail: eperkins@ou.edu.*

PERKINS, GEORGE WILLIAM, II, financial services executive, film producer; b. Salem, Mass., Sept. 10, 1926; s. George William and Daisy A. (Chase) P.; m. Mildred Boyle, Oct. 6, 1951; children: George William III, Clifton Alfred Dow, Mark Paige. Student, Northeastern U., 1944-49; BSc, Curry Coll., 1952; postgrad., Eastern Sch. Photography, Boston U.; cert., Coll. Financial Planning, Denver, 1974. Registered investment advisor; cert. meeting profl., sr. adv. Conv. Liaison Coun. Travel lectr., color cinematographer, 1946—; in charge road testing Renault auto, Alcan Hwy., Alaska, 1949; pres. Neily Film Prodns., Inc., 1953-55; Eastern regional v.p. Western Res. Life Assurance Co., Ohio, 1973-75; pres., chmn. bd. Fin. Mktg. Systems, Inc., Nashua, NH, 1974—; chmn. Holmes Travel Orgn., 1978—; chmn. bd., v.p. Fin. Cons. Group for Women, Inc., 1981—; registered prin. Fin. Cons., Stoneham, Mass., 1975-88, Linsco-Pvt. Ledger, Boston, 1988-96; div. mgr. Calif. Pacific Ins. Services Inc., 1977-80; pres. Fin. Benefits Planning Corp., 1983—; sr. v.p., treas. Penn Distbn. Co, Inc., 1983-87, Penn RE Life Ins. Co., 1984-88; v.p. Polymer Balloon Corp., 1984-88; dir., treas. Linsco Ins. Agy., Inc., 1987-96; registered prin. Linsco-Pvt. Ledger, 1988-96; sr. v.p. corp. rels. Capital Def. Corp., 1990—. Dir. Fin. Cons. Mgmt. Corp., Sonolite Corp., Contrex Co., FBP, Inc., FMSINC, Capital Defence Corp., Security Trust Ins. Co.; registered prin. IAC Sec., Inc., 1996—; spkr. on sales and svc. motivation; assoc. prof. bus. adminstrn. Curry Coll., until 1963, also sr. mem. bd. trustees, mem. coll. corp., also chmn. reorgn., 1963; pvt. trustee and executor, 1992—; cons. instr. Nat. Ctr. for Fin. Edn., 1992—; leadership coun. Nat. Fedn. of Ind. Bus., 1998—. Chief rsch. team, prodr. first feature length 16 mm Filmorama Wide Screen motion picture, 1954; narrator, film prodr.: Burton Holmes travelogues, 1950-70; appearances at Carnegie Hall, N.Y. Music Hall, Phila. Symphony Hall, Boston Nat. Geog. Soc., Washington, numerous other cities, U.S., Mexico and Can.; designer world's largest portable Filmorama Wide Screen motion picture screen; contbg. editor: monthly newsletter Fin. Strategies and Money Mgmt. for Women; contbr. articles to profl. jours. Served with USNR, World War II, PTO. Recipient Nat. Quality award Nat. Assn. Life Underwriters, Dirk Huston award for Outstanding Entrepreneurial Excellence and High Level Bus. Ethics ILONA, 1998. Mem. Merrimack Valley Life Underwriters Assn. (v.p., dir. 1968-69), Boston Life Underwriters Assn., Advt. Club Greater Boston, Internat. Assn. Fin. Planners (charter pres. No. Mass. chpt.), Nat. Assn. Security Dealers (prin.), Northeastern U., Curry Coll. Alumni Assn., Mass. Brokers Assn., Inst. Cert. Fin. Planners, Ins. Conf. Planners Assn., Am. Soc. Assn. Execs., Wealth Info. Planning Sys., Inc. (chmn. 2000—), Masons, Rotary (charter pres. Chelmsford, Mass. 1967-68). Home: 278 Lowell St Lynnfield MA 01940-1115 Office: 33 Main St Nashua NH 03064-2776 Home Phone: 781-334-3311; Office Phone: 603-889-0840. E-mail: george@consolpro.net. *Life tends to be what you encourage it to be as you live it day by day.*

PERKINS, HOMER GUY, manufacturing executive; b. New Haven, Oct. 23, 1916; s. Frank W. and Emily (Oesting) P.; m. Dorothy C. Stock, Jan. 24, 1942; children: Maribeth Perkins Grant, Homer Guy Jr., Hazel Mary Perkins Adolphson, Dorothy Catherine, Caroline Anne, Faith Elizabeth Perkins Crotteau, Ruth Emily Perkins Sico. BA in Internat. Rels., Yale U., 1938; LLD (hon.), Westfield U., Mass., 1977. With Enesco Group, Inc. (formerly Stanhome, Inc.), Westfield, 1939—, v.p., 1965-66, exec. v.p., 1966-70, pres., CEO, 1970-78, chmn., 1978-81. Bd. dir. Stanley Park of Westfield, 1949-2005, treas., 1955-69; pres. Citizens Scholarship Found., Easthampton, Mass., 1966-67, Easthampton Cmty. Chest, 1960-61; chmn. fin. com., bd. dirs. Western Mass. coun. Girl Scouts U.S., 1966-69; devel. com. Clarke Sch. Deaf, Northampton, 1965-68; fin. com. Town of Easthampton, 1962-70, chmn. fin. com., 1967-68; dir. Frank Stanley Beveridge Found., Westfield, 1956-95, pres., 1986-87; trustee Cooley Dickinson Hosp., Northampton, 1963-70, 84-92, chmn. bd. trustees, 1989-91; pres. bd. trustees Northampton Sch. for Girls, 1964-73; bd. dirs. Porter Phelps Huntington Found., Hadley, Mass., 1960-92, Guild of Holy Child, Westfield, 1969-76; bd. overseers Williston Acad., Easthampton, 1961-64, Old Sturbridge Village, Mass., 1970-76; v.p. bd. trustees Williston-Northampton Sch., 1970-75, pres., 1975-78; dir. Lathrop Communities, 2000-07, chair fin. com., 2001, pres. bd. dirs., 2005. With USAAF, 1942-46. Mem. Direct Selling Assn. (chmn. 1975, bd. dirs., mem. Hall of Fame), Paperweight Collectors Assn. (pres. 1991-95), Lions (past pres. Easthampton club). Home: 112 Bassett Brook Dr Easthampton MA 01027-1096

PERKINS, JACOB JAMES, structural engineer; b. Omaha, Aug. 23, 1980; s. Jim and Linda Perkins. BS in Civil Engring. Cum Laude, Kans. State U., Manhattan, 2006, BS in Constrn. Sci., 2008, MS in Civil Engring., 2008. Cert. in fundamental engring., State Kans., 2006. Grad. rsch. asst. Kans. State U., Manhattan, 2006—08; structural engr. TY Lin Internat., Olympia, Wash., 2008—. Contbr. articles to profl. jour. Cmty. project organizer Associated Gen. Contractors Student Chpt., 2003—03. Mem.: ASCE.

PERKINS, JAMES D., surgeon; b. Las Vegas, N.Mex., 1953; MD, U. Ark., 1979. Diplomate Am. Bd. Surgery. From intern to resident in gen. surgery St. Francis Regional Med. Ctr., Wichita, Kans., 1979-84; fellow in transplant surgery Mayo Grad. Sch., 1985. Office: Univ Washington Dept Surgery Box 356410 1959 NE Pacific St Seattle WA 98195-0001

PERKINS, JEREMY GOODRICH, hematologist, oncologist, researcher; MD, U. Health Scis., Bethesda, Md., 1997. Diplomate in internal medicine Am. Bd. Internal Medicine, 2000, in oncology Am. Bd. Internal Medicine, 2003, in hematology Am. Bd. Internal Medicine, 2004. Internal medicine resident Walter Reed Army Med. Ctr., Wash., 1997—2000, hematology and oncology fellow, 2000—03, chief, hematology and oncology clinic, 2004—08, dir., blood rsch. mil. casualty divsn. Silver Spring, Md., 2008—; staff hematologist and oncologist Eisenhower Army Med. Ctr., Augusta, Ga., 2003—04. Lt. col. US Army, 1993. Fellowship, ACP, 2007. Achievements include development of damage control resuscitation for trauma. Office: Walter Reed Army Med Ctr 6900 Georgia Ave NW Washington DC 20307 E-mail: jeremy.perkins1@us.army.mil.

PERKINS, JOE BOB, energy executive; Cons. McKinsey & Co.; dir. bus. develop. Tejas Gas, 1994—95; v.p. bus. develop. Coral Energy LLC, 1995—96; v.p. corp. planning Houston Industries, 1996—98; pres. & COO wholesale & power generation Reliant Resources, 1998—2002; ptnr. RTM Media, 2002—03; pres. Targa Resources Inc., Houston, 2004—. Office: Targa Resources Inc Ste 4300 1000 Louisiana Houston TX 77002*

PERKINS, JOHN ALLEN, lawyer; b. New Bedford, Mass., Sept. 13, 1919; s. Ralph Chamberlaine and Louise Bartlett (Allen) P.; m. Lydia Bullard Cobb, Sept. 9, 1944; children: John A., Susan W., Robert C., William B. AB, Harvard U., 1940, LL.B., 1943. Bar: Mass. Of counsel Edwards Angell Palmer & Dodge LLP, Boston; clk. Social Law Library, 1961-83; grad. researcher Univ. Coll., Oxford U., 1978. Bd. dirs. Greater Boston Legal Services, Inc., 1972-91. Author: The Prudent Peace— Law as Foreign Policy, 1981, The Heart of the Art: Reflections on the Human Side of Estate Planning, 2006; contbr. articles to profl. jours. Mem. Dedham (Mass.) Sch. Com., 1959-65, chmn., 1963-65, town counsel, Dedham, 1971-72. Mem. Am. Law Inst., Am. Coll. Trust and Estate Counsel, Mass. Bar Assn. (dir. 1973-75), Internat. Acad. Estate and Trust Law (exec. coun. 1990-94), Boston Bar Assn. (council 1972-75, v.p. 1981-82, pres. 1982-84). Home: 100 Newbury Court Ste 610 Concord MA 01742-5835

PERKINS, JOHN N., history professor; b. Carthage, Mo., May 28, 1949; s. Letitia L. Perkins; m. Betty S Perch, Oct. 21, 1949; children: Kristen S. Brasch, Jason N. MA in History, Mo. State U., Springfield, 1976. Adj. faculty mem. Crowder Coll., Neosho, Mo., 2003—; tchr. Aurora HS., 1974—2003, chmn. social studies, 1976—2003. Mem.: Mo. Ret. Teachers Assoc. Democrat. Avocations: golf, fishing. Business E-Mail: jperkins@crowder.edu.

PERKINS, KIMORA LEE See SIMMONS, KIMORA

PERKINS, LEEMAN LLOYD, musicologist, educator; b. Salina, Utah, Mar. 27, 1932; s. Milton Lloyd and Ida Margaret (Johnson) P.; m. Marianne Suzanne Contesse, Nov. 14, 1956; children: Eric Raymond, Bruce Philippe, Marc Christian (dec.), Patrick Thierry. BFA, U. Utah, 1954; PhD, Yale U., 1965. Instr. Boston U., 1964, Yale U., 1964-67, asst. prof., 1967-71, dir. undergraduate studies in music history, 1969-70; assoc. prof. music history, coord. for musicology U. Tex., Austin, 1971-75, grad. adv. for musicology, 1976; prof. music Columbia U., NYC, 1976—2003, prof. emeritus, 2003—, chmn. dept music, 1985-90. Instr. advanced seminar in Medieval History, Smith Coll., 1968; vis. assoc. prof. music Columbia U., 1975; vis. prof. Boston U., 1978; dir. NEH Summer Seminar, 1977. Editor: Johannes Lheritier Opera Omnia, 1969, (with Howard Garey) The Mellon Chansonnier, 1979, Music in the Age of the Renaissance, 1999; gen. editor: Masters and Monuments of Renaissance Music, 1978—. Chmn. grad. musicology com., Columbia U., 1980-84, 1993-96, 97-2001. Sgt., 7th Army Symphony, U.S. Army, 1957-59. Recipient James Morris Whiton Fund award Yale U., 1965, The Otto Kinkeldey award Am. Musicological Soc., 1980, la Médaille de la Ville de Tours, 1997; Trumbull Coll. fellow Yale U., 1966-71, Lewis-Farmington fellow Yale U., 1962-63, Morse fellow Yale U., 1967-68, Am. Coun. Learned Soc. fellow, 1973-74, NEH fellow,

1979, 1984-85, French Archival Scis. fellow Newberry Libr. Center for Renaissance Studies, 1991; Martha Baird Rockefeller grantee, 1963-64, Paul Mellon Found. grantee, 1972, Am. Coun. Learned Soc., 1972, 82, U. Tex. grantee, 1975, Mem. Am. Musicological Soc. (chmn. program com. 1979, bd. dirs. 1980-81, adv. bd., 1985-86, chmn. ad hoc sub com., 1985-86, exec. com. delegate, 1989-92, mem. fellowship com. 1995-98), Internat. Musicological Soc., The Renaissance Soc. of Am., Phi Beta Kappa, Phi Kappa Phi. Mem. Lds Ch. Business E-Mail: LLP1@columbia.edu.

PERKINS, MARCUS MATTHEW, special education educator; b. Cedar Rapids, Iowa, June 17, 1954; s. Frederick M. Perkins; 2 children. BA, McPherson Coll., Kans., 1977; MA, U. Iowa, Iowa City, 1992. Cert. k-12 art tchr. Iowa, 1979, secondary spl. edn. tchr. Iowa, 1982, wrestling coach Iowa, 2006, secondary prin. Minn., 1995. Juvenile corrections staff McPherson County, Kans., 1975—77; paraprofessional Cedar Rapids Cmty. Sch., Iowa, 1977, tchr., 1979—95, spl. edn. tchr., 2001—, coach, 2001—; tchr. Mpls. Pub. Sch., 1995—97, ednl. adminstrn., 1997—2001. Performer Iowa City Arts Coun., 1994—; security stage mgmt. Iowa City Jazz Festival, Iowa, 2005—; performer Cedar Rapids Freedom Fest, Iowa, 1990—95. Mem.: Cedar Rapids Edn. Assn. (life). Avocations: travel, music, painting, wrestling, sports. Office: Cedar Rapids Community Schools 931 Blairs Ferry Rd NE Ste C Cedar Rapids IA 52402-1271 Business E-Mail: mperkins@cr.k12.ia.us. E-mail: marcbfunky@gmail.com.

PERKINS, NANCY JANE, industrial designer; b. Phila., Nov. 5, 1949; d. Gordon Osborne and Martha Elizabeth (Keichline) P. Student, Ohio U., 1967—68; BFA, U. Ill., 1972. Indsl. designer Peterson Bednar Assocs., Evanston, Ill., 1972-74, Deschamps Mills Assos., Bartlett, Ill., 1974-75; dir. graphic design Cameo Container Corp., Chgo., 1975-76; indsl. design cons. Sears Roebuck & Co., Chgo., 1977-88; cons. indsl. design, 1988—; program mgr. indsl. design Jarden Consumer Solutions, Boca Raton, Fla., 2007—08; pres. Dallas Lighthouse for the Blind, 2009. Lectr. CUNY, 1995; founder Perkins Design Ltd., Anna Wagner Keichline Gallery, Bellefonte, Pa.; adj. prof. grad. design seminar U. Ill. Chgo., 1982, 88, 91, 93, adj. instr. undergrad. design, 1984, 88, 91, 93; adj. instr. Ill. Inst. Tech., 1987, 91; vis. assoc. prof. Carnegie-Mellon U., 1991; juror annual design rev. Indsl. Design mag., 1986; tech. rev. com. Ben Franklin Partnerships, 1991—; spkr. in field. Contbg. author: Design and Feminism, 1999; featured in Bard Grad. Ctrs.' Exhibit, NYC, 2000; contbr. articles to profl. jours. Co-leader Cadette troop DuPage County coun. Girl Scouts US, 1978-79. Recipient Outstanding Alumni award U. Ill. Alumni Jour., 1981, Goldsmith award, 1992; profiled in Indsl. Design mag., 1986, Feminine Ingenuity (by Anne L. Macdonald), 1992, Dun & Bradstreet Reports, 1993; profiled The Phila. Inquirer Mag., 1994; featured in Chgo. Athenaeum "33 plus 20", 1993, Pratt Manhattan Gallery, NYC, 1994. Fellow Indsl. Designers Soc. Am. (treas. Chgo. chpt. 1977-79, vice chmn. 1979-80, chmn. 1981, dist. membership com. 1982, ann. conf. com. 1983, publs. com. 1985-86, dir.-at-large 1987-88, v.p. Midwest dist. 1989-90, nat. sec.-treas. 1991-92, del. Internat. Coun. of the Socs. Indsl. Design 1989, co-founder women's sect. 1992, pres. design found. 2007, bd. dirs. design found.). Achievements include patents in field. Home: # 917 3225 Turtle Creek Blvd Dallas TX 75219-5488 Office Phone: 888-223-5211. Personal E-mail: njperkins@earthlink.net.

PERKINS, ROBERT EDWARD, retired secondary school educator; b. Hartford, Conn., Mar. 22, 1939; s. Alfred Warren and Montez Ordell (Rideout) P.; m. Jane Richmond Dickey; children: Ann, Margaret. BA, Harvard Coll., 1961; MA, U. Maine, 1964. M of French Deerfield (Mass.) Acad., 1968—90; tchr. French Flint Hill Sch., Oakton, Va., 1990—2004; ret., 2004. Organist, choir dir. South Congl. Ch., Amherst, Mass., 1966—80, 1st Ch. Deerfield, Mass., 1980—90; organist Little Falls Presbyn. Ch., Arlington, Va., 1991—2005; ret., 2005. Pres. PTO Old Deerfield (Mass.) Grammar Sch., 1972; treas., bd. dirs. Pioneer Valley Symphony, Greenfield, Mass., 1975—85; pres. Ballet Arts Regional Rep. Ensemble, Greenfield, 1978—82. Lt. comdr. USNR, 1961—63. Mem.: Am. Guild Organists (treas. Nova 1998—2001). Democrat. Home: 2304 Islander Ct Palm Harbor FL 34683 Personal E-mail: vaorganguy@aol.com.

PERKINS, ROBERT MITCHELL, JR., pediatrician; b. Balt., Apr. 26, 1946; s. Robert Mitchell Perkins Sr. and Lillie Ellen Perkins; m. Roseanna Francine Villa; children: Lauren Amy, Robert Mitchell III. BA, U. Miami, Coral Gables, Fla., 1969; MFA, NY U. Grad. Inst.Film & TV, NYC, 1971. Tech. writer Bendix Field Engring. Corp., Columbia, Afghanistan, 1978—82; prof. CC Balt., 1982—2008.

PERKINS, ROGER ALLAN, lawyer; b. Port Chester, NY, Mar. 4, 1943; s. Francis Newton and Winifred Marcella (Smith) P.; m. Katherine Louise Howard, Nov. 10, 1984; children: Marshall, Morgan, Matthew, Justin, Ashley. BA, Pa. State U., 1965; postgrad., U. Ill., 1965-66; JD with honors, George Washington U., 1969. Bar: Md. 1969, Mass. 1975. Trial atty. Nationwide Ins. Co., Annapolis, Md., 1969-72; assoc. Arnold, Beauchemin & Huber, PA, Balt., 1973; from assoc. to ptnr. Goodman & Bloom, PA, Annapolis, 1973-76; ptnr. Luff and Perkins, Annapolis, 1976-78; pvt. practice Anapolis, 1978—. Temp. adminstrv. hearing officer Anne Arundel County, 1984-2009; asst. city atty., Annapolis, 1980-82; atty. Bd. Appeals of City of Annapolis, 1986-2003, 2005—2008; mem. Appellate Jud. Nominating Commn., 1995—; mem. Md. Jud. Campaign Conduct Com., Inc., 2006-. Editl. adv. bd. Daily Record, 1996-97. Mem. Gov.'s Task Force on Family Law, 1991-94; adv. coun. on family legal need of low income persons MLSC, 1991; coach youth sports. Fellow Am. Acad. Matrimonial Lawyers, Am. Bar Found., Md. Bar Found. (bd. dirs. 1992-95); mem. ABA (ho. dels. 1991-93, 94-96, standing com. on solo and small firm practitioners 1993-97, chair 1996-97), Md. State Bar Assn. (pres. 1992-93, treas. 1988-91, bd. govs. 1985-87, chair membership com. 2002-04, chair spl. com. on lawyer profl. responsibility 1994-95, family and juvenile law sect. coun. 1983-89, chair 1987-88), Anne Arundel County Bar Assn. (pres. 1984-85). Home: 503 Bay Hills Dr Arnold MD 21012-2001 Office: The Courtyards 133 Defense Hwy Ste 202 Annapolis MD 21401-8907 Office Phone: 410-266-3558, 800-640-1469. Personal E-mail: roger@perkinslaw.com.

PERKINS, ROSWELL BURCHARD, lawyer; b. Boston, May 21, 1926; AB cum laude, Harvard U., 1945, LLB cum laude, 1949; LLD, Bates Coll., 1988. Bar: Mass. 1949, N.Y. 1949. Assoc. Debevoise, Plimpton & McLean, NYC, 1949-53; ptnr. Debevoise & Plimpton and predecessor firm, NYC, 1957-96; of counsel, head rep. office Debevoise & Plimpton LLC, Moscow, 1997-01. Asst. sec. U.S. Dept. HEW, 1954-56; counsel to Gov. Nelson A. Rockefeller State of N.Y., 1959; asst. counsel spl. subcom. Senate Commerce Com. to investigate organized crime in interstate commerce, 1950; chmn. N.Y.C. Mayor's Task Force on Transp. Reorgn., 1966; mem. Pres.'s Adv. Panel on Pers. Interchange, 1968, chmn. adv. com. Medicare Adminstrn. Contracting, Subcontracting HEW, 1973-74; dir. Fiduciary Trust Co., N.Y., 1963-2000; trustee Bowery Savs. Bank, 1975-82; mem. legal com. to bd. dirs. N.Y. Stock Exch., 1995-2000. Editor Harvard Law Rev., 1948-49. Mem. N.Y. Lawyers Com. Civil Rights, 1970-73; mem. nat. exec. com., 1973-1980, co-chmn. 1973-75; mem. adv. coun. Woodrow Wilson Sch. Pub. and Internat. Affairs, Princeton U., 1967-69; bd. dirs. The Commonwealth Fund, 1974-97, Sch. Am. Ballet, 1974-85, chmn. bd. 1976-80; dir., sec. N.Y. Urban Coalition, 1967-74; trustee Pomfret Sch., 1961-76; The Brearley Sch., 1969-75; dir. Salzburg Seminar Am. Studies, 1970-80; mem. overseers vis. com. Kennedy Sch. Govt., Harvard U., 1971-77, Harvard and Radcliffe Colls., 1958-64, 1971-77, Davis Ctr. for Russian and Eurasian Studies, 2000-05 Recipient Spl. Merit citation Am. Judicature Soc., 1989, Harvard Law Sch. Assn. award, 1994, 50 Yr. award Fellows of ABA, 2002. Mem. ABA (commn. on law and economy, 1975-79, mem. ho. of dels. 1980-93), N.Y. State Bar Assn., Assn. of the Bar of the City of N.Y. (chmn. spl. com. on fed. conflict of interest laws 1958-60). Harvard Alumni Assn. (pres. 1970-71), Am. Law Inst. (mem. coun. 1969, pres. 1980-93, chmn. coun. 1993-2008), Am. Arbitration Assn. (bd. dirs. 1966-71), Russian Inst. Dirs. (mem. expert coun. 2002-06), Ind. Dirs. Assn. (mem. adv. com. Russia 2002-06). Home: 1120 5th Ave New York NY 10128-0144 Office: Debevoise & Plimpton 919 3rd Ave 46th Fl New York NY 10022-3916 Home Phone: 212-722-3673; Office Phone: 212-909-6421. Business E-Mail: rbperkins@debevoise.com.

PERKINS, TOM (THOMAS JAMES PERKINS), venture capital company executive; b. Oak Park, Ill., Jan. 7, 1932; s. Harry H. and Elizabeth Perkins; m. Gerd Thune-Ellefsen, Dec. 9, 1961 (dec.); children: Tor Kristian, Elizabeth Siri; m. Danielle Steel, 1998 (div. 1999). BSEE, MIT, 1953; MBA, Harvard U., 1957. Founder Univ. Lab. (merged with Spectra Physics in 1960's); gen. mgr. computer div. Hewlett Packard Co., Cupertino, Calif., 1965-70, dir. corp. devel., 1970-72; co-founder, gen. partner Kleiner & Perkins, San Francisco, 1972-80; sr. ptnr. Kleiner Perkins Caufield & Byers, San Francisco, 1980—; chmn. bd. Tandem Computers, Inc., Cupertino, Calif., 1974—97. Founder, chmn. Genentech; bd. dirs. Spectra Physics., Symantec, Corning Glass Works, Collagen Corp., LSI Logic Corp., Hybritech Inc., Econics Corp., Vitalink Communications Corp., News Corp., Iolon, Philips Electronics NV, Compaq Computer, Hewlett Packard Co., 2002-04, 2005-06; chmn. Acuson, Tandem Computers. Author: Classic Supercharged Sports Cars, 1984, Sex and the Single Zillionaire, 2006, Valley Boy: The Education of Tom Perkins, 2007 Trustee San Francisco Ballet, 1980—. Mem. Nat. Venture Capital Assn. (chmn. 1981-82, pres. 1980-81) Clubs: N.Y. Yacht, Links, Am. Bugatti (pres. 1983—). Office: Kleiner Perkins Caufield & Byers 2750 Sand Hill Rd Menlo Park CA 94025

PERKINS, TROY, filmmaker; MFA, NYU, 1997. Dir.: (short film) Brothers (Gold Remi Award, UFVA Faculty Juried Finalist, 2008), Tractor For Sale (Gold Remi Award, 2008), (educational video) Encouraging a bright future for women in STEM (Aurora Gold Award, AEGIS Award, Gold Remi, 2008). Mem.: U. Film & Video Assn. (scriptwriting chair 2006—08). Office: UW Oshkosh-Radio TV Film Dept 800 Algoma Blvd Oshkosh WI 54901 Business E-Mail: perkins@uwosh.edu.

PERKINS, WILLIAM CLYDE, business educator; b. Lebanon, Ind., Aug. 2, 1938; s. Clyde Philip and Dorothy May (Finch) P.; m. Phyllis Louise Swinford, June 18, 1960; children: Bonnie Michele, Betsy Anne Hawkins, Jeffrey William. BS in Civil Engring., Rose Polytech. Inst., 1960; MBA, Ind. U., 1962, DBA, 1966. Instr. U.S. Mil. Acad., West Point, N.Y., 1964-65, asst. prof., 1965-66, Ind. U., Bloomington, 1966-69, assoc. prof., 1969-74, prof., 1974—2003, prof. emeritus, 2003—. Author: Managing Information Technology, 1991, 94, 99, 2002, 2005, 2008, FORTRAN for Business Students, 1981, Computers and Information Systems, 1973. Capt. U.S. Army, 1964-66. Fellow Decision Scis. Inst. (treas. 1984-86, v.p. 1982-84, pres. 1992-93, disting. svc. award 1988), Midwest Decision Scis. Inst. (pres. 1984-85, 25 yr. disting. svc. award 1994); mem. Assn. for Info. Sys. Mem. United Ch. of Christ. Avocations: hiking, travel, reading. Home: 4308 E Cambridge Dr Bloomington IN 47408-3109 Office: Ind U Kelley Sch Bus Bloomington IN 47405 Business E-Mail: perkinsw@indiana.edu.

PERKINS, WILLIAM H., JR., retired finance company executive; b. Rushville, Ill., Aug. 4, 1921; s. William H. and Sarah Elizabeth (Logsdon) P.; m. Eileen Nelson, Jan. 14, 1949; 1 child, Gary Douglas. Pres. Howlett-Perkins Assos., Chgo. Mem. Ill. AEC, 1963-84, sec., 1970-84; apptd. by Pres. to adv. bd. Nat. Armed Forces Mus., Smithsonian Instn., 1964-82; army aide to Anthony Eden and Lord Halifax of Great Britain, UN Conf., 1945. Sgt.-at-arms Democratic Nat. Conv., 1952, 56, del.-at-large, 1964, 68, 72; spl. asst. to chmn. Dem. Nat. Com., 1960; mem. Presdl. Inaugural Com., 1961, 65, 69, 73, ins. policy agent, 1961. With US Army, 1944-46 Mem. Ill. Ins. Fedn. (pres. 1965-84), Ill. C. of C. (chmn. legis. com. 1971), Chgo. Assn. Commerce and Industry (legis. com., Raoul Wallenberg Humanitarian award 1993), Sangamo Club, Masons, Shriners. Methodist. Home: 726 Community Dr La Grange Park IL 60526-1555

PERKINS-BANAS, MELISSA VERONICA, neuropsychologist; d. Roy Dennis and Marian Dana Perkins; m. Joseph Paul Banas, July 3, 1999. BA, U. RI, 1992; MA, U. Hartford, 1995, MS, 1996; PsyD, Yeshiva U., 2004. Cert. Psychologist 1999. Sch. psychologist Norwich Pub. Schools, Norwich, Conn., 1999—2003; neuropsychologist Wheeler Clinic, Conn., 2003—. Post- doctoral neuropsychology fellowship Fielding Inst., NYC, 2004—. Sponsored athlete Adidas Woodbridge Racing Team, Woodbridge, Conn., 2000—02. Recipient Conn. Distance Runner of the Yr., Hi Tek Racing Team, 2001; Cecilia Rothenberg scholarship, Yeshiva U., 2002—03. Mem.: Assn. Advancement of Applied Sport Psychology, Conn. Assn. Sch. Psychologists, NASP, Am. Psychology Assn. (Divsn. 60, clin. neuropsychology), Psi Chi Nat. Honor Soc. Psychology. Roman Catholic. Office: Wheeler Clinic 91 Northwest Dr Plainville CT 06062 Home: 22 Hill St Southington CT 06489

PERKINSON, ROBERT RONALD, psychologist, consultant; b. Richmond, Va., Aug. 8, 1945; s. Gordon Archibald and Sarah (Haskins) P.; m. Elizabeth Godfrey Fly, July 27, 1968 (div. 1984); children: Robert Reps, Nyshie Page, Shane William; m. Angela Kaufman, Sept. 20, 1991. BS, Colo. State U., 1968; MS, Ea. Wash. State U., 1970; PhD, Utah State U., 1974. Lic. psychologist, S.D.; cert. chem. dependency counselor level III, S.D.; nat. cert. gambling counselor; nat. cert. alcohol and drug counselor; lic. marriage and family counselor, S.D. Juvenile ct. psychologist, Cedar City, Utah, 1971-72; psychologist in pvt. practice Jackson, Wyo., 1974-83; dir. psychol. svcs. Western Wyo. Mental Health Assn., Jackson, 1977-78, psychologist, 1983—; psychologist, clin. dir. Keystone Treatment Ctr., 1988—. Cons. in field; chief psychologist Grand Teton Nat. Pk., Teton County Sheriff's Office and Police Dept. Copyrights: The Yellowstone Park Game, The Good Health Game, The Grizzly Control Team, Communication from God, Chemical Dependency Counseling, The Mystics, God Talks CD, Peace Will Come CD, The Treatment of Pathological Gambling: A Step By Step Approach. Author: Chemical Dependency Counseling: A Practical Guide, 1997, 2nd edit., 2002, 3rd edit, 2008, The Chemical Dependency Treatment Planner, 1998, God Talks to You, 2000, The Addiction Treatment Planner, 2001, 3rd edit., 2006, 4th edit., 2009, The Alcoholism and Drug Abuse Patient Workbook, 2003, The Gambling Addiction Patient Workbook, 2003, Treating Alcoholism: Helping Your Clients Find the Road to Recovery, 2004; contbr. articles to profl. jours. Mem. APA, S.D. Psychol. Assn., S.D. Chem. Dependency Assn., Biofeedback Soc. Am. (bd. dirs. Wyo. br.), Wyo. Bd. Psychologist Examiners (pres. 1997, bd. dirs. S.D. coun. problem gambling), Nat. Registere of Health Svc. Providers in Psychology. Address: PO Box 159 Canton SD 57013-0159 Personal E-mail: perk@iw.net.

PERKNER, STANISLAV, academic administrator, educator; b. Kladno, Czech Republic, Oct. 12, 1946; arrived in US, 1992; s. Alois Perkner and Karolina Poslednikova-Perknerova; m. Jitka Pulkrabkova, Oct. 1, 1966 (div.); m. Christine D. Willbanks, Feb. 6, 2006; children: Eva, Stanislav, Radim. MA in Social Scis. and Journalism, Charles U., Prague, 1970, PhD in History of Czechoslovakia, 1971; PhD in Gen. History, Comenius U., Bratislava, 1982. From asst. to assoc. prof. Sch. Journalism Charles U., Prague, 1971—90, head of radio and TV dept., dean Sch. Journalism, 1974—90; dir., assoc. prof. Internat. Inst. for the Tng. of Journalists, Prague, 1990—91; dir. libr. and learning ctr., prof. Humphreys Coll., Stockton, Calif., 2001—. Rsch. dir. Internat. Assn. for Mass Comm. Rsch. - Czechoslovak Nat. Com., Prague, 1983—90; vis. lectr. Indian Inst. for Mass Comm. Rsch., New Delhi, 1982; vis. rschr. Ind. U., Bloomington, 1986, vis. prof.; mass media rsch. cons. Fed. Ministry of Fgn. Affairs, Prague, 1983—86; vis. prof. Calif. State U., Univ. of the Pacific, Am. Univ., U. Pitts., Brigham Young U., U. Okla., Wichita State U., San Joaquin Delta Coll.; mem. editl. bd., chmn. The Journalist, Prague, Czech Republic, 1980—91, The Isues of Journalism, Prague, Czech Republic, 1980—91, The Journalist's Quar., Prague, Czech Republic, 1980—91. Co-author: (textbook) Theory and Practice of Radio Journalism (Czechoslovak Radio Ann. award, 1987), (nonfiction) The Language of Drama, Vols. I and II (Guild of Czech Dramatists Ann. award, 1989), A Passion for Radio, (specialized ency.) An Encyclopedia of Journalism. Mem., chair acad. coun. Humphreys Coll., Stockton, 1998—2006; mem. lit., arts, and media Nat. Com. for the State Awards, Prague, 1988—90. Business E-Mail: sperkner@humphreys.edu.

PERKOVIC, ROBERT BRANKO, retired international management consultant; b. Belgrade, Yugoslavia, Aug. 27, 1925; came to U.S., 1958, naturalized, 1961; s. Slavoljub and Ruza (Pantelic) P.; m. Jacquelyn Lee Lipscomb, Dec. 14, 1957; children: Bonnie Kathryn, Jennifer Lee. MS in Econs, U. Belgrade, 1954; B.F.T., Am. Grad. Sch. Internat. Mgmt., 1960; grad. Stanford exec. program, Stanford U., 1970. Auditor Gen. Foods Corp., White Plains, NY, 1960-62, controller Mexico City, 1962-64; dir. planning Monsanto Co., Barcelona, 1964-67, dir. fin. Europe, Brussels, 1967-70, dir. fin. planning-internat. St. Louis, 1970-71, asst. treas., 1971-72, Brussels, 1972-74; corp. treas. Fiat-Allis Inc. & BV, Deerfield, Ill., 1974-78; v.p., treas. TRW Inc., Cleve., 1978-88; pres. RBP Internat. Cons., Cleve., 1988—. Former dir. U.S. Bus. Coun. for Southeastern Europe, Inc. Active Cleve. Commn. on Fgn. Relations. Inc. Served with Yugoslavian Army, 1944-47. Mem. Fin. Execs. Inst., Cleve. Treas. Club (past bd. dirs., pres.), Latin Am. Bus. Assn. (co-founder), Mayfield Village (Ohio) Racquet Club. Office: RBP Internat Cons 26 Pepper Creek Dr Cleveland OH 44124-5248

PERKOWSKI, JAN LOUIS, language, literature and folklore educator; b. Perth Amboy, NJ, Dec. 29, 1936; m. Liliana Asenova Daskalova, May 24, 1989. AB magna cum laude, Harvard U., 1959, AM, 1960, PhD, 1965. Asst. prof. U. Calif., Santa Barbara, 1964-65; assoc. prof. U. Tex., Austin, 1965-74; prof. U. Va., Charlottesville, 1974—2009. Author: A Kashubian Idiolect in U.S., 1969, Vampires, Dwarves & Witches Among the Ontario Kashubs, 1972, Vampires of the Slavs, 1976, Gusle & Ganga Among the Hercegovinians of Toronto, 1978, The Darkling-A Treatise on Slavic Vampirism, 1989, Vampire Lore, 2006; contbr. over 65 articles to profl. jours. Grantee, fellow Ford Found., Harvard U., Kościuszko Found., U. Tex., Am. Philos. Soc., Nat. Mus. Man, U. Va., NEH, Kennan Inst., I.R.E.X., Fulbright, others. Mem. Am. Assn. for the Advancement of Slavic Studies, Am. Assn. Tchrs. of Slavic and East European Langs., Am. Assn. S.E. European Studies, Bulgarian Studies Assn.

PERKYNS, JANE ELIZABETH, music educator, composer; b. St. John, New Brunswick, Can., Jan. 17, 1960; arrived in U.S., 1990, naturalized, 2000; d. Joseph Archibald Gormley, Carmelita Anne Gormley; m. John Stephen Perkyns, Aug. 20, 1983; children: Stephen, Nicholas. MusB, Dalhousie U., Halifax, NS, Can., 1982; MusM, Juilliard Sch., 1983; D in Musical Arts, U. B.C., Vancouver, B.C., Can., 1990. Music adminstr., tchr. Jewish Cmty. Ctr., Houston, 1990—94; adj. music faculty Tex. So. U., Houston, 1990—96, asst. prof. music, 1996—2001, assoc. prof. music, 2001—. Founder, dir. Curtyn Calls Theatre and Pub. Co., Houston, 1995—; co-dir. spl. edn. programs Theatre Under the Stars, Houston, 2000—; dir. Charles P. Rhinehart Piano Festival, 2001—06. Composer: (Musical) The Gift, 1994, Pinnojokio, 1996, Love is a Disability, 1998, Medea's Children, 1999, musician Solo/collaborative recitals. Panelist Cultural Arts Coun. Houston/Harris County, 2000—02. Grantee Mayor's Initiative Grant, Cultural Arts Coun. Houston/Harris County, 2001, Gen. Assistance Grant, Cultural Arts Coun., 2003, Office Civil Rights, 2003. Mem.: Music Educators Nat. Conf., Music Educators Nat. Assn., Nat. Assn. for Music Edn., Royal Conservatory Music (coord. of exams Houston area 1994—2003), Houston Music Tchrs. Assn. (bd. mem., chair scholarship event 1995—2002), Tex. Music Tchrs. Assn., Music Tchrs. Nat. Assn. (cert.), Coll. Music Soc., Houston Tuesday Musical Club. Avocations: children's arts and crafts, cooking, yoga. Home: 5634 Benning Dr Houston TX 77096 Office: Tex So Univ 3100 Cleburne Houston TX 77004 Home Phone: 713-726-1050; Office Phone: 713-313-7529. Office Fax: 713-313-1869. Personal E-mail: perkyns_je@tsu.edu. Business E-Mail: perkyns-je@tsu.edu.

PERL, DON A., literature and language professor; b. Bringhamton, NY, Feb. 9, 1943; s. Jerome John and Julia Sall Perl; m. Annette Miriam Marshall, Mar. 28, 1998; children: Rashaun, Jonah, Justin, Cade. BA in English Lit., U. Rochester, NY, 1964; JD, Syracuse U., 1967; MA in Spanish, U. Northern Colo., 2001. Lic. tchr. Met. State Coll., Denver, 1981. Tchr. Englewood Pub. Schs., Colo., 1981—82, Greeley Pub. Schs., Colo., 1982—2001; Founder, Pres. Coalition Better Edn. Inc., Greeley, Colo., 2002—; Adj. Prof. Spanish U. Northern Colo., Greeley, 2002—. Faculty advisor Green Party Campus, Greeley, 2004—06. Sponsor-ballot initiative Coalition Better Edn. Inc., 2004. Recipient Outstanding Prof. award, 2008, Delta Zeta Soc., 2007. Mem.: Greely Tchrs. Assn. (life), Delta Zeta Sorority. Avocations: gardening, music, bicycling, writing. Home: 2424 22nd Ave Greeley CO 80631 Office: Univ Northern Colo Hispanic Studies Candelaria Hall Greeley CO 80639 Office Phone: 970-351-2746.

PERL, HAROLD, neonatologist, pediatrician; b. July 24, 1950; m. Esther Jayde Strauss, June 18, 1972; children: Ari, Sharona, Gil, Doniel. BA, Yeshiva Coll., 1972; MD, Albert Einstein Coll Medicine, 1975. Diplomate Am. Bd. Pediatrics, cert. in neonatal and perinatal medicine. Intern, resident Montefiore Hosp. and Med. Ctr., NYC, 1975-78; neonatology fellowship Albert Einstein Coll. Medicine, 1978—80; dir. neonatology Hackensack (NJ) U. Med. Ctr., 1991—2005; co-dir. SIDS Ctr. NJ; pres. Gateway-N.W. Consortium NJ, 2005—. Mem. biomed.

ethics com. Hackensack U. Med. Ctr., 1985—. Mem. health profls. adv. com. March of Dimes, No. N.J., 1982-97. Home Phone: 201-837-9182; Office Phone: 201-996-5362. E-mail: hperl@humed.com.

PERL, MARTIN LEWIS, physicist, educator, chemical engineer; b. NYC, June 24, 1927; children: Jed, Anne, Matthew, Joseph. B in Chem. Engring., Poly. Inst. Bklyn., 1948; PhD, Columbia U., 1955; ScD (hon.), U. Chgo., 1990. Chem. engr. Gen. Electric Co., 1948—50; asst. prof. physics U. Mich., 1955—58, assoc. prof., 1958—63; prof. Stanford U., 1963—. Author: High Energy Hadron Physics, 1975, Reflections on Experimental Science, 1996; contbr. articles on high energy physics and on relation of sci. to soc. to profl. jours. With U.S. Mcht. Marine, 1944—45, with US Army, 1946—47. Recipient Wolf prize in physics, Wolf Found., Israel, 1982, Nobel prize in physics, 1995. Fellow: Am. Phys. Soc.; mem.: NAS, Am. Acad. Arts and Scis. Home: 3737 El Centro St Palo Alto CA 94306-2642 Office Phone: 650-926-2652. Business E-Mail: martin@slac.stanford.edu.

PERLAK, KIMBERLEY SHELLEY, music educator; d. Edward and Patricia Perlak. MusB, Stetson U., DeLand, Fla., 1998; MusM, Yale U., New Haven, Conn., 2001; MusD, U. Tex., Austin, 2008. Faculty & intern coord. Nat. Guitar Workshop, New Milford, Conn., 1997—; faculty Stetson U. Cmty. Sch. Arts, DeLand, 1994—98, Neighborhood Sch. Music, New Haven, 2000—01, Victoria Coll., Tex., 2002—04, Austin CC, 2004—, Austin Guitar Sch., 2004—, Concordia U., Austin, 2008—. Musician: (presenter) Speaking Am.: The Lang.of the Am. Guitar Sound (Featured Presenter: Nat. Guitar Workshop, 2007). Advisor Friends McCallum Fine Arts Acad., Austin, 2001—08; dep. registrar voting DNC, Austin; musician St. David's Episcopal Celtic Musicians, Austin, 2006—08. Recipient The Eliot Fisk prize, Yale U. Sch. Music, 2001. Mem.: The Austin Classical Guitar Soc. (bd. dir. 2002—05), Guitar Found. Am., Pi Kappa Lambda. Liberal. Roman Cath. Home: 4505 Duval St #106 Austin TX 78751 Business E-Mail: kimperlak@yahoo.com.

PERLE, EUGENE GABRIEL, lawyer; b. NYC, Dec. 21, 1922; s. Philip and Simme (Meschenberg) P.; m. Ellen Carlotta Kraus, Nov. 26, 1953 (dec. 1964); 1 child, Elizabeth Anne Perle; m. Ruth Friedberg Lerner, May 23, 1972 (div. 1977); m. Patricia Fitzpatrick Sinnott, Jan. 24, 1981. BA, Queens Coll., 1943; JD, Yale U., 1949. Bar: NY 1950, Conn. 1995. Assoc. Cravath, Swaine & Moore, NYC, 1949-53; asst. counsel NY State Moreland Commn. Investigation Harness Racing, NYC, 1953-54; assoc. Gordon, Brady, Caffrey & Keller, NYC, 1954-56; assoc. gen. atty. Time Inc., NYC, 1956-66, pub. counsel, 1966-73, v.p. law, 1973-80, corp. v.p. law, 1980-85; counsel Proskauer & Rose, NYC, 1985-92, Chapman & Fennell, 1992-94; mem. Ohlandt, Greeley, Ruggiero & Perle, Stamford, Conn., 1995-97, sr. counsel, 1998—. Coauthor: Perle & Williams Publishing Law, 1988-2006; mem. editl. bd. Yale Law Jour., 1948-49; mem. adv. bd. Bur. Nat. Affairs Patent, Trademark and Copyright Jour., 1972-86; contbr. to Bull. Copyright Soc. USA. Trustee Baron deHirsch Fund, 1959-87, hon. trustee, 1988—; commr. Nat. Commn. New Technol. Uses Copyrighted Works, 1975-78; bd. dirs. NY Sch. Circus Arts, Inc., 1979-87, Am. Arbitration Assn., 1979-84; justice of peace City of Norwalk, Conn., 1960-63. Lt. USNR, 1943-46. Mem. ABA (chmn. copyright divsn. 1970-71, 86-87, chmn. com. copyright new tech. 1971-73, chmn. com. econs. profession 1976, coun. patent, trademark copyright sect. 1979-83, governing bd. forum com. comms. law 1979-85, chmn. related fields future devels. divsn. forum com. entertainment sports industries 1979), Copyright Soc. USA (trustee 1962-64, 69-70, 71-74, pres. 1976-78, hon. trustee 1978—), US Trademark Assn. (bd. dirs. 1969-72, 74-77, v.p. 1972-73), Assn. Bar City NY, Sunningdale Country Club, Century Assn., Banyan Golf Club of Palm Beach. Democrat. Office: Ohlandt Greeley Ruggiero & Perle One Landmark Sq Stamford CT 06901 Home (Summer): Putnam Hill #4C Greenwich CT 06830 Home Phone: 706-861-0948; Office Phone: 203-327-4500. Personal E-mail: egabrielperle@gmail.com. E-mail: egperle@ogrp.com.

PERLE, RICHARD NORMAN, political scientist, former federal agency administrator; b. NYC, Sept. 16, 1941; s. Jack Harold and Martha Gloria Perle; m. Leslie Joan Barr, July 31, 1977; 1 child, Jonathan. BA in Internat. Politics, U. So. Calif., 1964; postgrad. in econs., U. London, 1962-63; MA, Princeton U., 1967. Prof. staff mem. subcommittee nat. security US Senate Com. on Govt. Ops., Washington, 1970-72; profl. staff mem. to Senator Henry M. Jackson US Senate Armed Services Com., Washington, 1969-80; asst. sec. for internat. security policy US Dept. Def., Washington, 1981-87; resident fellow Am. Enterprise Inst. for Pub. Policy Rsch., Washington, 1987—. Fellow Princeton U., 1964—66, Social Sci. Research Coun. & America Coun. of Learned Soc., 1967—68; mem. Def. Policy Bd., 1987—2004, chmn., 2001—03; co-founder Project for the New Am. Century; former co-chmn., dir. Hollinger, Inc. Prodr.: (TV miniseries) The Gulf Crisis: The Road to War, 1992; author: Hard Line, 1992; co-author (with David Frum): An End to Evil: How to Win the War on Terror, 2004; editor: Reshaping Western Security, 1991. Office: Am Enterprise Inst Pub Policy Rsch 1150 17th St NW Washington DC 20036-4603 E-mail: rperle@aei.org.*

PERLER, BRUCE ALAN, vascular surgeon; b. New Bedford, Mass., Mar. 12, 1950; s. J. Leonard and Muriel Marcia (Katzman) P.; children: Mason, Rachel. AB in Zoology summa cum laude, Duke U., Durham, NC, 1972, MD, 1976; MBA, Johns Hopkins U., Balt., 2004. Diplomate Am. Bd. Gen. Surgery, cert. spl. qualificatons in gen. vascular surgery; lic. physician, Mass., Md. Surg. intern Mass. Gen. Hosp., Boston, 1976-77, surg. resident, 1977-81, clin. and rsch. fellow in vascular surgery, 1981-82; clin. fellow surgery Harvard Med. Sch., 1977-82; asst. prof. surgery Johns Hopkins U. Sch. Medicine, Balt., 1982-88, assoc. prof., 1988—97, prof., 1997—; asst. surgery Mass. Gen. Hosp., Boston, 1981-82; dir. noninvasive lab., mem. med. bd., vice-chmn. med. staff com. Johns Hopkins Hosp., Balt., 1982—, chief divsn. vascular surgery, 2002—, attending vascular surgeon, 1982—, med. dir. intermediate care unit, 1989-91, mem. med. bd., 1995—99; Julius H. Jacobson II prof. Johns Hopkins U. Sch. Medicine, Balt., 2002—. Cons. vascular surgery Johns Hopkins Bayview Med. Ctr., Balt., 1982—, circulatory system devices panel Ctr. Devices and Radiologic Health, FDA, Washington, 1989—, Rsch. Adv. Group, VA, Washington, 1993—; mem. diagnostic and therapeutic tech. assessment panel AMA, 1991; lectr. throughout U.S. and Can. Mem. editl. bd. Jour. Vascular Surgery, asst. editor, assoc. editor, 2006—, editor, 2009-; editl. bd. Jour. Vascular Endovascular Surgery, Annals of Vascular Surgery; contbr. articles to profl. jours., chpts. to books. Rsch. grantee NIH, 1986-87, 92-94. Mem. ACS, Am. Surg. Assn., Soc. Vascular Surgery (bd. dirs.), So. Assn. Vascular Surgery (program com. 1992-95, exec. coun. 2004—, pres 2009-), Ea. Vascular Soc. (membership com. 1991-94, sec. 2001-, pres. 2004-05), Soc. Univ. Surgeons, Assn. Acad. Surgery, Chesapeake Vascular Soc. (pres. 1992-93), Balt. Acad. Surgery, Duke Med. Alumni Assn., Phi Beta Kappa. Office: Johns Hopkins Hosp - Harvey 611 Dept Surgery 600 N Wolfe St Dept Surgery Baltimore MD 21287-8611 Office Phone: 410-955-2618.

PERLESS, ELLEN, advertising executive; b. NYC, Sept. 9, 1941; d. Joseph B. and Bertha (Messinger) Kaplan; m. Robert L. Perless, July 2, 1965. Student, Smith Coll., 1958-59; BA, Bard Coll., 1962. Copywriter Doyle, Dane Bernbach, NYC, 1964-70, Young & Rubicam, NYC, 1970-74, creative supr., 1974-76, v.p., creative supr., 1977, v.p., assoc. creative dir., 1978, sr. v.p., assoc. creative dir., 1979-84; v.p., assoc. creative dir. Leber Katz Ptnrs., 1984-85, sr. v.p., creative dir., 1986-87; sr. v.p., sr. creative dir. Foote Cone & Belding, NYC, 1987-93, sr. v.p., group creative dir., 1994—2002; sr. v.p., sr. creative dir. Euro RSCG Life Becker, NYC, 2003—04; creative cons. pvt. practice Greenwich, Conn., 2004—. Author: numerous poems. Recipient Clio awards, Andy awards, awards Art Dirs. Club N.Y., N.Y. Festivals, One Club. Home: 37 Langhorne Ln Greenwich CT 06831-2611 Personal E-mail: ellen@perless.com.

PERLESS, ROBERT L., sculptor; b. NYC, Apr. 23, 1938; s. Meyer and Ethel (Glassman) Perless; m. Ellen R. Kaplan, July 2, 1965. Student, U. Miami, Fla., 1955-59. One-man shows include Bodley Gallery, N.Y.C., 1968, 1970, Galerie Simonne Stern, New Orleans, 1969, Bernard Danenberg Gallery, N.Y.C., 1970—72, Bonino Gallery, 1976, exhibited in group shows at Bodley Gallery, 1970, Whitney Mus., 1970, Forum Gallery, N.Y.C., 1975, Bonino Gallery, 1975, Houston Gallery, Aldrich Mus., Ridgefield, Conn., 1978, 1987, 1994, 1997—98, Taft Mus., Cin., 1980, Stamford (Conn.) Mus., 1989, Bruce Mus., Greenwich, Conn., 1989, 2001, André Emmerich's Top Gallant Farm, 1991—96, Greenwich Art Soc., 2000, Sculpture Now, Stockbridge, Mass., 2003, Art Omi Internat. Arts Ctr., NY, 2004—06, Represented in permanent collections Whitney Mus., Aldrich Mus., Chrysler Mus., Norfolk, Va., Okla. Art Ctr., Oklahoma City, Phoenix Art Mus., Stamford Mus., Benton Mus., Storrs, Conn., Bard Coll., Annandale-on-Hudson, N.Y., Bucknell U., Lewisburgh, Pa., City of Corpus Christi, Tex., City of Palm Desert, Calif., Syracuse Hancock Internat. Airport, Miami U., Oxford, Ohio, Rusk Inst., NYC, Salt Lake C.C., Town of Port Chester, NY, U. Conn., Storrs, U. No. Iowa, Cedar Falls, Utah Valley State Coll., Heber City, others, one-man shows include Flinn Gallery Greenwich, Conn., 2006, exhibited in group shows at Sculpture in the Park White Plaens, NY, 2006, In Site Governors Island NY, 2008, Represented in permanent collections Howell Cheney Technical HS, Manchester, Conn. Mem.: Sculptors Guild. Address: 37 Langhorne Ln Greenwich CT 06831-2611 Office Phone: 203-869-0710. E-mail: robert@perless.com.

PERLIN, ARTHUR SAUL, chemistry professor; b. Sydney, NS, Can., July 7, 1923; s. Benjamin and Eva (Gaum) P.; m. Ruth Laurel Freedman, Nov. 18, 1950; children: Anna, Louise, Deborah, Myra, David BSc, McGill U., Can., 1944, MSc, 1946, PhD, 1949. Rsch. officer Nat. Rsch. Council Can., Ottawa, Ont., Can., 1948-67; E.B. Eddy prof. chemistry McGill U., Montreal, Que., Can., 1967-91, prof. chemistry emeritus, 1991—; rsch. scientist Pulp and Paper Rsch. Inst. Can., Montreal, Que., 1967—. Contbr. articles to profl. jours., chpts. to books; patentee in field Fellow Royal Soc. Can., Chem. Inst. Can.; mem. Am. Chem. Soc. (C.S. Hudson award 1979) Office: McGill U Dept Chemistry Montreal PQ Canada H3A 2K6 Office Phone: 514-398-6188.

PERLIN, GARY LAURENCE, diversified financial services company executive; b. Chgo., May 8, 1951; s. Maurice and Berna (Bardige) P.; m. Amy R., July 4, 1976; children: Jonah, Jacob. BS in Fgn. Svc., Georgetown U., 1972; MS, London Sch. Econs., 1974; MPA, Princeton U., NJ, 1975. Staff aide to US Senator Adlai Stevenson III, Washington, 1972-73; economist The World Bank, Washington, 1975-78, dir. fin. sector devel. dept., 1993—96, v.p., treas., 1996—99, sr. v.p., CFO, 1999—2003; trader J. Aron & Co., NYC, 1978-80; cons., v.p. Hadley Lockwood, NYC, 1980-82; v.p. risk mgmt. Fed. Nat. Mortgage Assn. (Fannie Mae), Washington, 1982-85, sr. v.p. fin., treas., 1985—93; sr. v.p., CFO, prin. acctg. officer Capital One Fin. Corp., McLean, Va., 2003—. Mem. Commodity Futures Trading Commn., Fin. Products Adv. Com., Washington, 1986-91; dir. Future Industry Assn., 1991—; treas. The European Inst., 1991—. Office: Capital One Fin Corp 1680 Capital One Dr Mc Lean VA 22102

PERLIN, JONATHAN BRIAN, health services company executive, former federal agency administrator; b. 1961; s. Seymour Perlin; m. Donna Perlin; 1 child, Benjamin. MS in Health Adminstrn., Va. Commonwealth U., Ph.D in Pharmacology & Toxicology. Med. dir. quality improvement Med. Coll. Va. Hosps. Va. Commonwealth U., assoc. dir. internal medicine residency tng. prog.; chief quality and performance officer US Dept. Veterans Affairs, Washington, 1999—2002, dep. under sec. health, 2002—04, acting chief rsch. & devel. officer, 2003—04, acting under sec. for health (Veterans Health Adminstrn.), 2004—05, under sec. for health, 2005—06; sr. v.p. quality, chief med. officer HCA Inc., Nashville, 2006—. Contbr. articles to profl. jours. Fellow: ACP. Office: HCA Inc One Park Plz Nashville TN 37203

PERLIN, SEYMOUR, psychiatrist, educator; b. Passaic, NJ, Sept. 27, 1925; s. Samuel and Fanny (Horowitz) P.; m. Ruth Joan Rudolph, Aug. 21, 1958; children: Jonathan Brian, Steven Michael, Jeremy Francis. Student, Johns Hopkins U., 1943-44; BA summa cum laude, Princeton U., 1946; MD, Columbia U., 1950; grad., Washington Psychoanalytic Inst. Diplomate Am. Bd. Psychiatry and Neurology. Intern Univ. Hosp., Ann Arbor, Mich., 1951-52; resident N.Y. State Psychiat. Inst., 1950-51, 53-54, Manhattan State Hosp., 1952; practice medicine specializing in psychiatry and psychoanalysis Bethesda, Md., 1954-59, Stanford, Calif., 1959-60, NYC, 1960-63, Balt., 1964-72, Bethesda, 1974—; chief div. psychiatry Montefiore Hosp., 1960-63; dir. clin. care and tng. Henry Phipps Psychiat. Clinic, Johns Hopkins Hosp., 1964-72; sr. research scholar Ctr. for Bioethics, Kennedy Inst., Georgetown U., Washington, 1974-78; clin. prof. psychiatry UCLA Sch. Medicine, 1973-74, George Washington U. Sch. Medicine, 1974-76, prof. to prof. emeritus, 1977-97, 97—, also dir. residency tng., 1977-93; lectr. psychiatry Columbia U., 1963-64; assoc. prof. psychiatry Johns Hopkins Sch. Medicine, 1964-65, prof., 1966-72, dep. chmn. dept. psychiatry and behavioral scis., 1969-72; program dir. Fellowship Program in Suicidology, 1967-72; adv. council Univ. health services Princeton, 1970-82. Vis. fellow Princeton U., 1973, Oxford U., 1974; Joseph P. Kennedy fellow medicine, law and ethics, 1974-75; chief sect. psychiatry Lab. Clin. Sci., NIMH, 1955-59, mem. clin. program-project com., 1967-70; fellow Ctr. Advanced Study in Behavioral Scis., 1959-60; chmn. mental health study sect. B, div. research grants NIH, 1964-66; cons. Community Mental Health Services, Md. Dept. Mental Hygiene, 1964-72; chmn. bd. dirs. Youth Suicide Nat. Ctr., 1985-87. Cons. editor: Jour. Suicide and Life Threatening Behavior, 1970-89; editorial bd.: Johns Hopkins Med. Jour, 1970-72; editor: Handbook for the Study of Suicide; co-editor: Ethical Issues in Death and Dying; contbr. numerous articles to med. jours. Served with USNR, 1944-46, with USPHS, 1954-58. Recipient Meirhoff award in pathology, 1950, Bicentennial Silver medal for achievement in psychiatry, 1967, both Coll. Phys. and Surg. Columbia. Fellow Am. Psychiat. Assn. (named Disting. Life fellow 2003); mem. Am. Coll. Psychiatry, Washington Psychoanalytic Soc., Med. Soc. D.C., Washington Psychiat. Soc., Am. Assn. Suicidology (pres. 1969-70, Dublin award 1978, ann. lectureship in suicidology in his name George Washington U. 1995), Phi Beta Kappa. Home and Office: 5125 Westbard Ave Bethesda MD 20816-1413 Office Phone: 301-229-5330.

PERLINGIERI, ILYA SANDRA, art historian, writer; b. NYC; d. Nathaniel Gordon and Naomi Miller Coval-Apel; children: Blake Andrew, Chemynne Alida. BA, U. Mo., 1966; MA, San Diego State U., 1984; PhD, Columbia Pacific U., 1999. Dir. Ilya Sandra Perlingieri Sewing and Design Sch., San Diego and Miami, Fla., 1973-92; asst. prof., chmn. dept. fashion design Marist Coll., Poughkeepsie, N.Y., 1984-85; mem. faculty Fashion Inst. Design, San Diego, 1986-87, LA, 1999—2000. Adj. prof. San Diego State U., 1989—92; dir. Textile Arts and Conservation Ctr., San Diego, 1979—83; guest lectr. Met. Mus. Art, NYC, Nat. Gallery, London, Art Inst. Chgo., Los Angeles County Mus. Art, Nat. Gallery, Washington, NYU, Yale U., others; environ. writer; guest Sta. PBS-TV, Sta. NPR, Sta. NBC-TV, BBC, London. Author: Sofonisba Anguissola: The First Great Woman Artist of the Renaissance, 1992, French. edit., 1992, The Uterine Crisis, 2003; contbg. editor: Threads mag.; contbr. articles to profl. jours.; environ. columnist:. Dir. edn. Nomad Mus. Tribal Art, Portland, 1999—2001. Recipient award, Prague Quadriennale, 1979, Gildred Found., 1980, Sameul H. Kress Found., 1989, 1999; grantee, Thanks be to Grandmother Winifred Found., 2001; French Fgn. Ministry Lecture grantee, 1995. Mem.: Am. Bot. Coun., Early Modern Women (charter), Met. Mus. Art Huntington Libr. and Art Collections, Renaissance Soc. Am. Avocations: playing classical piano, lyric soprano, organic gardening.

PERLIS, DONALD M., artist; b. NYC, July 29, 1941; s. Herman and Sylvia M. (Marks) P.; m. Theresa Brown, June 9, 1968. Student, Art Students League, 1961, Sch. Visual Arts, NYC, 1965, Skowhegan Sch., 1965. One-man show Sindin Gallery, N.Y.C., 1994, 95, Walter Wickiser Gallery, N.Y.C., 1996-97, Claudia Carr Gallery, N.Y.C., 1999; exhibited in group shows Whitney Mus., N.Y.C., Graham Gallery, 1971, 75, Sindin Galleries, 1993, 95, Charas-Elbohio, 1993; exhbns. include Nat. Mus. Poland, Gdansk, 2007, NAD, 2007; represented by Denise Bibro Gallery, N.Y.C.; documentary film on artist produced by Time Capsule Films, 1993; author: (monograph) Allegories of Love, 1995. Mem. NAD. Home: 110 Duane St #5R New York NY 10007

PERLIS, MICHAEL FREDRICK, lawyer; b. NYC, June 3, 1947; s. Leo and Betty F. (Gantz) Perlis; m. Colleen M. DeLee, Sept. 8, 2003; children: William Garrison, Grace Joanne;children from previous marriage: Amy Hannah, David Matthew. BS in Fgn. Svc., Georgetown U., 1968, JD, 1971. Bar: DC 1971, NY 1993, US Dist. Ct. 1971, US Ct. Appeals 1971, DC Ct. Appeals 1971, Calif. Ct. Appeals 1980, US Dist. Ct. (no. dist.) Calif. 1980, US Dist. Ct. (ctrl. dist.) Calif. 1985, US Ct. Appeals (9th cir.) 1980, US Supreme Ct. 1980, NY Supreme Ct. 1993. Law clk. DC Ct. Appeals, Washington, 1971—72, asst. corp. counsel, 1972—74; counsel divsn. enforcement US SEC, 1974—75, br. chief, 1975—77, asst. dir., 1977—80; ptnr. Pettit & Martin, San Francisco, 1980—89; ptnr. fedl. securities law litig. Stroock & Stroock & Lavan, LA, 1989—, mem. operating exec. com. Adj. prof. Cath. U. Am., 1979—80. Mem.: ABA (co-chmn. subcom. securities and commodities litig. 1982—83), Calif. State Bar Assn., DC Bar Assn. Office: Stroock & Stroock & Lavan 2029 Century Park E Ste 1800 Los Angeles CA 90067-3086 Office Phone: 310-556-5821. Business E-Mail: mperlis@stroock.com.

PERLMAN, BARRY ARNOLD, astronomy educator; b. New Bedford, Mass., July 21, 1947; s. Louis and Lorainne Rhoda (Benoit) P. BS, Boston U., 1970; MS, Nova Southeatern U., 1989. Cert. tchr. Fla. Adminstrv. law judge Fla. Dept. Labor, Miami, 1972-82; planetarium specialist, adj. prof. Broward Coll., Ft. Lauderdale, Fla., 1982-87, asst. prof., 1994—; planetarium dir. Mus. Sci. & History, Jacksonville, Fla., 1987-88, Dade Pub. Schs., Miami, 1989-94; dir. edn. South Fla. Sci. Mus., West Palm Beach, 1996-98; dir. Sci. Explorium, Boca Raton, Fla., 1998—2000; pres. & CEO E-Class Solutions Inc., Davie, Fla., 2005—. Ptnr. Rocket Tech. Fla., Ft. Lauderdale, 1982-87; pres. Ft. Lauderdale Acad. Sci., 1979; dir. Fox Observatory, Ft. Lauderdale, 1977-78; bd. of directors, Graves Museum of Natural History, 1995. Author: Applied Physical Science, 1989. Mem. Fla. Rocket Soc. (pres. 1989-90).

PERLMAN, BARRY STEVEN, sociologist, educator; b. Bklyn., Aug. 25, 1944; s. Aubrey and Grace Perlman; m. Joan Paul Perlman, Apr. 29, 1984; children: Adam, Ryan. AA, Queensborough C.C., 1964; BA, Queens Coll., CUNY, 1966; postgrad., Adelphi U., 1966—68, Temple U., 1968—71. Lectr. Chestnut Hill Coll., Phila., 1968—69, LaSalle U., Phila., 1968—70; instr. Temple U., Phila., 1968—71; assoc. prof. C.C. Phila., Phila., 1971—, chmn. Dept. Social Scis., 1983—89. Chmn. coms. C.C. Phila., 1973—; reviewer articles various publs.; presenter and session chair profl. meetings and confs. Contbr. articles to profl. jours. Founding mem. Am. Cancer Rsch. Ctr., 1978; key communicator Bensalem Twp. Schs., Pa., 1976—79. Recipient Outstanding Contbn. award, Human Svcs. Careers Student Assn., 1990; fellow, NIMH. Mem.: Human Svcs. Career Assn., Am. Sociol. Assn., Am. Fedn. Tchrs., Nat. Social Sci. Assn. Jewish. Office: Community College Phila 1700 Spring Garden St Philadelphia PA 19130 Office Phone: 215-751-8560.

PERLMAN, BARRY STUART, electrical engineer, researcher, director; b. Bklyn., Dec. 5, 1939; s. Harold Wallace and Jane (Cohen) P.; m. Carolyn Amelia Francis; 1 child, David Matthew. BEE, CCNY, 1961; MSEE, Poly. U. N.Y., 1964; PhD in Electrophysics, Poly. Inst. N.Y., 1973. Mem. tech. staff, comms. lab. RCA Corp., NYC, 1961-68; mem. tech. staff RCA Labs., Princeton, NJ, 1968-81, mgr. microwave rsch. lab., 1981-86, head design automation rsch., 1986-88; chief microwave photonic devices br. Electronics and Power Source Directorate, Army Rsch. Lab., Ft. Monmouth, NJ, 1988-95; dir. electronics divsn. Phys. Scis. Directorate, Army Rsch. Lab., Ft. Monmouth, 1995-96; chief RF and electronics divsn. Sensor and Electron Devices Directorate, Army Rsch. Lab., Ft. Monmouth and Adelphi, Md., 1996-97; R&D Engring. Ctr. staff Comm.-Electronics Command, Ft. Monmouth, 1997-98, chief applied comm., 1998-99; assoc. dir. for tech., prin. scientist Intel and Info Directorate, 1999—2002; assoc. dir. tech. & DARPA liaison office Comm. Electronics Rsch., Devel. and Engring. Ctr. Hdqrs. Rsch., Devel. and Engring. Command. Pres., mem. bd. dirs. INTEREX, Los Altos, Calif., 1981—83; rep. adv. group on electron devices, chmn. subpanel on RF Components Office of Undersec. of Def.; chmn. Computational Electronics and Nanoelectronics tech. area High Performance Computing Modernization Program, 1995—2005, program mgr. modeling and simulation Electronic Battlefield Environ. Portfolio, 2000—05; program mgr. Scalable Urban Simulation, 2005—07, Digital Array Radar, 2005—08, Adv. Digital Transceiver, 2008—, Electronic Network Sys. Tech. Area; agt. Intelligent RF Front End Program and Tech. Efficient Agile Microsys. Program High Performance Computing Modernization Program, 2005—07, sys. study team, modeling/simulation team for FCS comm. Def. Advanced Rsch. Projects Agy.; agt. analog Spectral Processors, 2006—; agent Disruptive Mfg. Tech., 2007—, MicroIsotope Power Sources, 2007—; Def. Advanced Rsch. Projects Agy. agt. Trusted Electronics, 2006—, Energy Starved Electronics and Subthreshold logic, 2006—; NASA/JPL adv. com. for SATCOM sys. on a chip U. Mich.; tech. adv. bds. UCLA; ind. adv. bd. Computer Applications to Electromagnetics Edn. NSF and U. Utah, 1990—94; mem. ind. adv. bd. Computer Applications to Electromagnetics Edn. MIMICAD Ctr., U. Colo., 1989—95; adv. bd. Elec. Engring./WAMI U. So. Fla.; ind. adv. bd. Wireless Comm. NJ Inst. Tech.; Ctr. prof. microwave/lightwave engring. Drexel U., Phila., 1992—2002; ind. adv. bd. U. Hawaii, Manoa, 2003—; advisor to NSF Connection One Inc. Ariz. State U., 2004—; advisor NJ Nanotech. Consortium; mem. R&D Coun. NJ; mem. TAB Conformal Antennas and Arrays Using Novel Electronic Materials Ohio State U., 2005—; mem. indsl. adv. bd. Multiscale Physics IMPACT Ctr U. Ill. Urbana-Champagne; advisor mobile radio program group Va. Tech., 2006—; advisor Ga. Electronic Design Ctr. Ga. Inst. Tech., 2006—; advisor high frequency electronics group Purdue U., 2006; transceiver Scalcblellrban Network Simulation, 2006—07; advisor, mem. Multifunction Phases Arrays Radar, MPAR Working Group, NOAA, FAA, DWS and DOD, 2008—. Editor: Advances in Microwaves, 1974; mem. editl. bd. Wiley Jour. MW.MMW CAD, 1992—; contbr. articles to profl. jours.; patentee in field. Bd. dirs. YMCA, Princeton, 1975-78; pres. Home Owners Assn., E. Windsor, N.J., 1976-78; instr. Am. Heart Assn., N.J., 1978-82; chief rescue squad, E. Windsor, 1978-82. Fellow: IEEE (life; admission and advancement com. 1987—92, tech. program chair Sarnoff Symposium 1999—2002); mem.: COMCAS (tech. program chair 2007—), Comm., Antennas & Propagation Soc., Automated RF Techniques Group (treas. 1984—88, v.p. 1990—91), Cirs. and Sys., Ultrasonics, Ferroelectrics and Frequency Control, Microwave Theory and Tech. Soc. of IEEE (IMS tech. program com. 1980—, editl. bd. chmn. CAD com. MTT-1 1985—92, MTT adcom. 1990—94, chmn. Intersoc. Liaison 1995—97, chmn. meetings and symposia com. 2002—04, MTT adcom. 2002—, chmn. membership svcs. com., repcom tech. adv. bd. 2005—07, pres. elect 2008, pres. MIT Adcom 2009). Avocations: woodworking, photography, pistol/rifle target competition, gardening, gourmet cooking. Office: Army Comm-Electronics Ctr RDEC Hdqrs AMSRD CER TSP Bldg 2700 Fort Monmouth NJ 07703-5000 Office Phone: 732-427-4883. Personal E-mail: bperlman@comcast.net. Business E-Mail: b.perlman@ieee.org.

PERLMAN, BURTON, judge; b. Dec. 17, 1924; s. Phillip and Minnie Perlman; m. Alice Weihl, May 20, 1956; children: Elizabeth, Sarah, Nancy, Daniel. BE, Yale U., 1945, ME, 1947; LLB, U. Mich., 1952. Bar: Ohio 1959, N.Y. 1953, Conn. 1952, U.S. Dist. Ct. (so. and ea. dists.) N.Y. 1954, U.S. Dist. Ct. (so. dist.) Ohio 1959, U.S. Ct. Appeals (2d cir.) 1953, U.S. Ct. Appeals (6th cir.) 1959. Assoc. Armand Lackenbach, NYC, 1952—58; pvt. practice Cin., 1958—61; assoc. Paxton and Seasongood, Cin., 1961—67; ptnr. Schmidt, Effton, Josselson and Weber, Cin., 1968—71; U.S. magistrate U.S. Dist. Ct. (so. dist.) Ohio, 1971—76, U.S. bankruptcy judge, 1976—. Chief bankruptcy judge so. dist. Ohio, 1986—93; adj. prof. U. Cin. Law Sch., 1976—. With US Army, 1944—46. Mem.: ABA, Cin. Bar Assn., Fed. Bar Assn. Office: US Bankruptcy Ct Atrium 2 8th Fl 221 E 4th St Cincinnati OH 45202-4124 Office Phone: 513-684-2572 ext. 131.

PERLMAN, DAVID, journalist; b. Balt., Dec. 30, 1918; s. Jess and Sara Perlman; m. Anne Salz, Oct. 15, 1941 (dec. 2002); children: Katherine, Eric, Thomas. AB, Columbia U., 1939; MS, Columbia U. Sch. Journalism, 1940. Reporter Bismarck Capital, ND, 1940, San Francisco Chronicle, 1940—41, reporter, sci. editor, 1951—77, city editor, 1977-79, assoc. editor, sci. editor, 1979—; reporter New York Herald Tribune, Paris, NYC, 1945-49; European corr. Colliers mag. and New York Post, 1949-51. Regents prof. human biology U. Calif., San Francisco, 1974; vis. lectr. China Assn. Sci. and Tech., Beijing, Chengdu, Shanghai, 1983; sci. writer-in-residence U. Wis., 1989. Contbr. articles to maj. mags. Founding dir. Squaw Valley (Calif.) Cmty. Writers; bd. dirs. Alan Guttmacher Inst., 1990—99; trustee Scientists Inst. Pub. Info., 1986—94; chmn. pub. svc. award com. Nat. Sci. Bd., 1998—2001. With inf. USAAF, 1941—45. Recipient Atomic Indsl. Forum award, 1975, Sci. Writing award, AAAS, 1976, Exploratorium award, 1977, Ralph Coates Roe medal, ASME, 1978, Margaret Sanger Cmty. Svc. award, 1981, Fellows' medal, Calif. Acad. Scis., 1984, Career Achievement award, Soc. Profl. Journalists, 1989, Glenn T. Seaborg award, Internat. Platform Assn., 1993, Sustained Achievement award for sci. journalism, Am. Geophys. Union, 1997, medal, U. Calif., San Francisco, 2000, Journalism award, Columbia U., 2000, award for disting. med. reporting, San Francisco Med. Soc., 2000, Grady-Stack award for sci. journalism, Am. Chem. Soc., 2001, John Wesley Powell award, U.S. Geol. Survey, 2004, Hearst Eagle award, 2004, Career Achievement award, Soc. Profl. Jours., 2008; Poynter Inst. fellow, Yale U., 1984, Carnegie Corp. fellow, Stanford U., 1987. Fellow: AAAS (mem. com. Pub. Understanding Sci. 1985—90, adv. bd. Science-81-86 mag., Career Excellence award 2009), Calif. Acad. Scis.; mem.: Astron. Soc. Pacific (bd. dirs. 1976—78), Nat. Assn. Sci. Writers (pres. 1970—71, Disting. Sci. Journalism award 1994), Coun. Advancement Sci. Writing (pres. 1976—80), Sigma Xi. Office: San Francisco Chronicle 901 Mission St San Francisco CA 94103-2905 Business E-Mail: dperlman@sfchronicle.com.

PERLMAN, HARVEY STUART, academic administrator; b. Lincoln, Nebr., Jan. 17, 1942; s. Floyd Ted and Rosalyn (Lashinsky) P.; m. Susan G. Unthank, Aug. 27, 1966; children: Anne, Amy. BA, U. Nebr., 1963, JD, 1966. Bar: Nebr. 1966, Va. 1980. Teaching fellow U. Chgo. Law Sch., 1966-67; mem. faculty U. Nebr. Sch. Law, 1967-74, prof., 1972-74; prof. law U. Va., Charlottesville, 1974-83; dean law sch. U. Nebr., Lincoln, 1983—98, interim sr. vice chancellor, 1995—96, interim chancellor, 2000—01, chancellor, 2001—; exec. dir. Nebr. Commn. on Law Enforcement. Author: (with Edmund Kitch) Legal Regulation of the Competitive Process, 1972, 79, 86; asso. editor: Jour. Law and Human Behavior, 1974-86. Named Ida Beam Distinguished Vis. Prof. Law, U. Iowa, 1981-86. Mem. Am. Bar Assn., Nebr. Bar Assn., Law-Psychology Assn., Am. Law Inst. Office: U Nebr Office of the Chancellor 201 ADM UNL Lincoln NE 68588 E-mail: hperlman1@unl.edu.*

PERLMAN, ITZHAK, violinist; b. Tel Aviv, Aug. 31, 1945; arrived in U.S., 1958; s. Chaim and Shoshana P.; m. Toby Lynn Friedlander, 1967; children: Noah, Navah, Miriam, Leora, Ariella. Student, Tel Aviv Acad. Music; studied with Ivan Galamian & Dorothy DeLay, Juilliard Sch.; student, Meadowmount Sch. Music.; degree in music (hon.), Tufts U., 1986; degree (hon.), Harvard U., Yale U., Brandeis U., Roosevelt U., Yeshiva U., Hebrew U. Appeared with numerous orchs. including NY Philharm., Cleve. Orch., Phila. Orch., Nat. Symphony Orch., Berlin Philharm., English Chamber Orch., London Symphony, London Philharm., Royal Philharm., BBC Orch., Vienna Philharm., Israel Philharm.; founder Perlman Music Program, NY, 1998—; prin. guest condr. Detroit Symphony, 2001-05; music advisor St. Louis Symphony, 2002-04; participant numerous music festivals including Ravinia Festival, Tanglewood Music Festival, Aspen Music Festival, Israel Festival, Wolf Trap Summer Festival; recital tours US, Can., S.Am., Europe, Israel, Australia, Far East; recorded for Angel, London, RCA Victor, DG, Telarc, Teldec, Sony. Albums include Vivaldi: The Four Seasons, 1977 (Grammy award best classical performance 1977), Beethoven: Sonatas For Violin And Piano, 1978 (Gramy award best chamber music performance 1978), Brahms: Concerto For Violin In D, 1978 (Grammy award best classical album 1978), The Spanish Album, 1980 (Grammy award best classical performance 1980), Brahms: Violin And Cello Concerto In A Minor, 1980 (Grammy award best classical performance 1980), Berg: Violin Concerto/Stravinsky: Violin Concerto In D, 1980 (Grammy award best classical performance 1980), Music For Two Violins, 1980 (Grammy award best chamber music performance 1980), Isaac Stern: 60th Anniversary Celebration, 1981 (Grammy award best engineered recording 1981, Grammy award best classical performance 1981), Tchaikovsky: Piano Trio In A Minor, 1981 (Grammy award best chamber music performance 1981), Elgar: Violin Concerto In B Minor, 1982 (Emmy award best classical performance 1982), Chausson: Violin Concerto, 1984, An Isaac Stern Vivaldi Gala, 1985, Beethoven: The Complete Piano Trios, 1987 (Grammy award best chamber music performance 1987), Bach: Double Concerto, 1987, Mozart Violin Concertos Nos.1 & 2, 1987 (Grammy award best classical performance 1987), Paganini & Giuliani: Duos for Violin and Guitar, 1987, The Italian Album, 1989, Brahms: The 3 Violin Sonatas, 1990 (Grammy award best small ensemble performance 1990), Dvorák In Prague: A Celebration, 1994, Bach: Violin Concertos, 1995, The American Album: Works Of Bernstein, Barber, Foss, 1995 (Grammy award best instrumental soloist performance with orch. 1995), Cinema Serenade, 1997, John Williams Greatest Hits 1969-1999 Cinema Serenade 2, 1999, Classic Yo-Yo, 2001, Classic Perlman: Rhapsody, 2002; appeared in PBS documentary Fiddling for the Future, 1998 (Emmy award outstanding cultural music-dance program 1999); TV specials Perlman in Russia, 1992 (Emmy award outstanding classical program 1992), Itzhak Perlman: In the Fiddler's House, 1996 (Emmy award outstanding cultural music-dance program 1996). Founder Perlman Music Program, 1995. Recipient Leventritt prize, 1964, Medal of Liberty, 1986, Nat. Medal of Arts, 2000, Kennedy Ctr. Honor, 2003, Golden Plate award, Acad. Achievement, 2005; named Musician of Yr., Musical Am., 1981; inductee Am. Classical Music Hall of Fame, 2001. Office: IMG Artists c/o Elizabeth Sobol Gomez Carnegie Hall Tower 152 W 57th St 5th Floor New York NY 10019*

PERLMAN, JON ARTHUR, plastic surgeon; b. NYC, Dec. 17, 1948; Bachelor, Lafayette Coll.; MD, Cornell U., 1973. Diplomate Am. Bd. Plastic Surgery, cert. Am. Bd. Surgery. Intern Mass. Gen. Hosp., Boston, 1973—74, resident in surgery, 1974—78; resident in plastic surgery UCLA Med. Ctr., 1978—80; pvt. practice plastic surgery Beverly Hills, Calif., 1980—. Attending plastic surgery Cedars-Sinai Med. Ctr., LA; chief divsn. plastic surgery Brotman Med. Ctr., 1985—; asst. clin. prof. plastic surgery UCLA Med. Ctr.; featured plastic surgeon ABC's Extreme Makeover. Fellow: Am. Coll. Surgeons; mem.: L.A. Soc. Plastic Surgeons, Calif. Soc. Plastic Surgeons, Am. Soc. Plastic Surgeons, Am. Soc. Aesthetic Plastic Surgeons. Office: 414 N Camden Dr 8th Fl Beverly Hills CA 90210 Office Phone: 310-854-0031. Office Fax: 310-275-5079. E-mail: jonap@ucla.edu.

PERLMAN, MIKE, mortgage company executive; b. Haifa, Israel, Apr. 2, 1951; BEME, CCNY, 1973; MBA, NYU, 1976. Cert. mgmt. cons., cert. systems profl. Mech., nuc. engr. Ebasco Svcs., NYC, 1973-76; treasury analyst Consol. Edison, NYC, 1976-78; cons., ptnr. Deloitte & Touche, NYC, Washington; founding ptnr. fin. services group AT&T Solutions; mng. dir. Morgan Stanley, 1997—2007; exec. v.p. ops., and tech. Freddie Mac, 2007—. Office: Freddie Mac 8200 Jones Br Dr Mc Lean VA 22102-3110 Office Phone: 703-903-2000.

PERLMAN, RICHARD WILFRED, economist, educator; b. Mt. Vernon, NY, Dec. 15, 1923; s. Uriel and Annie (Feitelberg) P.; m. Irma Lowenthal, Sept. 18, 1949; children: Abel, David, Laura, Jennifer. AB, Cornell U., 1947; PhD, Columbia U., 1953. Asst. prof. econs. Adelphi U., Garden City, N.Y., 1953-57, assoc. prof., 1957-64; prof. econs. U. Wis., Milw., 1964-97, prof. emeritus, 1997—, chmn. dept., 1965-68, 74-77; NRC prof. Brookings Instn., 1958-59. Fulbright lectr. Inst. Politecnico Nacional, Mexico City, 1964, Autonomous U. Madrid, 1972 Author: Economics of Education, 1973, Labor Theory, 1969, Economics of Poverty, 1976, (with others) An Anthology of Labor Economics, 1972, Economics of Unemployment, 1984, Issues in Labor Economics, 1989, Sex Discrimination in the Labor Market, 1994. Mem. President's Com. on EEO, 1963. Rsch. fellow U. Melbourne, Australia, 1985, hon. rsch. fellow U. Birmingham, 1990-93, sr. fellow, 1993-; Fulbright rsch. scholar, Australia, 1987, rsch. scholar Victoria U. Tech., Australia, 1997. Mem. Am. Econ. Assn., Indsl. Relations Research Assn., Phi Beta Kappa. Home: 3341 N Summit Ave Milwaukee WI 53211-2930 Business E-Mail: rperlman@uwm.edu.

PERLMAN, RON (RONALD FRANCIS PERLMAN), actor; b. NYC, Apr. 13, 1950; s. Dorothy Perlman; m. Opal Stone, Feb. 14, 1981; children: Blake Amanda, Brandon Avery. BFA in Theatre, Lehman Coll., NYC, 1971; MFA, U. Minn., 1973. Actor: (films) Quest for Fire, 1981, The Ice Pirates, 1984, The Name of the Rose, 1986, Sleepwalkers, 1992, Double Exposure, 1993, When the Bough Breaks, 1993, The Adventures of Huck Finn, 1993, Cronos, 1993, Romeo Is Bleeding, 1993, Police Academy: Mission to Moscow, 1994, Sensation, 1995, The City of Lost Children, 1995, Fluke, 1995, The Last Supper, 1995, The Island of Dr. Moreau, 1996, Betty, 1997, Prince Valiant, 1997, Tinseltown, 1997, Alien: Resurrection, 1997, Frogs for Snakes, 1998, The Protector, 1998, I Woke Up Early the Day I Died, 1998, Happy, Texas, 1999, Price of Glory, 2000, The King's Guard, 2000, Stroke, 2000; actor, actor: (films) Enemy at the Gates, 2001, Down, 2001, Night Class, 2001, Boys on the Run, 2001, Blade II, 2002, Crime and Punishment, 2002, Star Trek: Nemesis, 2002, Rats, 2003, Absolon, 2003, Two Soldiers, 2003, Hoodlum & Son, 2003, Looney Tunes: Back in Action, 2003, Hellboy, 2004, Quiet Kill, 2004, The Second Front, 2005, Missing in America, 2005, Local Color, 2006, How to Go Out on a Date in Queens, 2006, The Last Winter, 2006, 5ive Girls, 2006, No. 6, 2006, In the Name of the King: A Dungeon Siege Tale, 2007, (voice) Terra, 2007, Acts of Violence, 2008, Outlander, 2008, Hellboy II: The Golden Army, 2008; (TV films) Our Family Honor, 1985, A Stoning in Fulham County, 1988, Blind Man's Bluff, 1992, Arly Hanks, 1993, Original Sins, 1995, (voice) Tiny Toon Adventures: Night Ghoulery, 1995, The Adventures of Captain Zoom in Outer Space, 1995, The Second Civil War, 1997, A Town Has Turned to Dust, 1998, Supreme Sanction, 1999, Primal Force, 1999, Operation Sandman, 2000, The Trial of Old Drum, 2000, Desperation, 2006, (voice) Hellboy Animated: Blood and Iron, 2007,: (TV series) Beauty and the Beast, 1987—90 (Golden Globe award for Best Performance by an Actor in a TV-Series - Drama, 1989, Best Actor in a Quality Drama Series, Viewers for Quality Television Awards, 1988, 1989), Picture Windows, 1994, Mortal Kombat: Defenders of the Realm, The Magnificent Seven, 1998—2000, Justice League, 2003, Teen Titans, 2003—06, Danny Phantom, 2004—06, (voice) The Batman, 2004—08. Recipient Acting award of Excellence, Big Bear Lake Internat. Film Festival, 2004; named Male Discovery of Yr., Golden Apple Awards, 1989. Avocations: golf, jazz, pool. Office: c/o Kritzer Levine Wilkins Entertainment Llc 8840 Wilshire Blvd Ste 100 Beverly Hills CA 90211

PERLMUTH, WILLIAM ALAN, lawyer; b. NYC, Nov. 21, 1929; s. Charles and Roe (Schneider) P.; m. Loretta Kaufman, Mar. 14, 1951; children: Carolyn, Diane. AB, Wilkes Coll., 1951; LLB, Columbia U., 1953. Bar: N.Y. 1954. Assoc. Cravath, Swaine & Moore, NYC, 1955-61; ptnr. Stroock & Stroock & Lavan, NYC, 1962—97, of counsel, 1998—. Editor Columbia U. Law Rev., 1952-53. Trustee Aeroflex Found., NYC, 1965—, Harkness Found. for Dance, NYC, 1976—, Wilkes U., Wilkes-Barre, Pa., 1980—, Hosp. for Joint Diseases Orthopaedic Inst., NYC, 1980—, Weininger Found., 1985—, NYU Hosps. Ctr., 1994—, NYC Ctr., 1995—, Sch. Am. Ballet, 1997—, Bklyn. Acad. Music, 2004—; chmn. bd. trustees Hosp. Joint Diseases Orthop. Inst., 1994—2005. Mem. N.Y. State Bar Assn., Assn. of Bar of City of N.Y. Jewish. Home: 880 5th Ave New York NY 10021-4951 Office: Stroock & Stroock & Lavan 767 Third Ave New York NY 10017 Office Phone: 212-806-5001. Business E-Mail: bperlmuth@stroock.com.

PERLMUTTER, BARBARA S., retired public relations executive; b. Hartford, Conn., Oct. 7, 1941; d. Leon and Ethel (Zinman) Sondik; m. Louis Perlmutter, Dec. 11, 1966; children: Kermit, Eric. BA, Smith Coll., 1963; MA in History, Columbia U., 1965; MBA, NYU, 1979. Analyst Celanese Internat. Co., NYC, 1965-69; sr. econ. analyst Nat. Econ. Rsch. Assoc., White Plains, N.Y., 1979-85; dir. pub. affairs Marsh & McLennan Companies, Inc., NYC, 1985-88, v.p. pub. affairs, 1988-99, sr. v.p. pub. affairs chief comm. officer, 1999—2006; ret., 2007. Avocations: aerobics, reading, tennis.

PERLMUTTER, DAVID (DADI), computer company executive; BSc in Elec. Engring., Technion Israel Inst. Tech., 1980. Devel. team leader Intel Corp., Haifa, Israel, gen. mgr. microprocessor divsn., mgr. Israel devel. ctr. Haifa, gen. mgr. basic microprocessor divsn., v.p. microprocessor products group, gen. mgr. mobile platforms group, co-mgr. mobility group, v.p., gen. mgr. mobile platforms group, exec. v.p., gen. mgr. mobility group. Recipient Innovation award, Pres. of Israel, 1987. Achievements include patents for branch target buffers; multiprocessing cache coherency protocols. Office: Intel Corp 2200 Mission College Blvd Santa Clara CA 95054-1549 Office Phone: 408-765-8080.*

PERLMUTTER, DAVID H., physician, educator; b. Bklyn., May 11, 1952; s. Herman Arthur and Ruth (Jacobs) P.; m. Barbara Ann Cohlan, Feb. 7, 1981; children: Andrew, Lisa. BA, U. Rochester, 1974; MD, St. Louis U., 1978. Cert. Pediatrics, 1983, Pediatric Gastroenterology and Nutrition, 1990. Intern then resident in pediatrics U. Pa. Sch. Medicine, Phila., 1978-81; fellow in pediatric gastroenterology Harvard U. Sch. Medicine, Boston, 1981-84, instr. pediatrics, 1983-85, asst. prof. pediatrics, 1985-86; Donald Strominger prof. of pediatrics Washington U. Sch. Medicine, St. Louis, 1986-89, prof. cell biology, physiology, 1989—2001; dir. gastroenterology and nutrition divsn. St. Louis Children's Hosp., 1992—2001; Vira I. Heinz prof. and chair pediatrics U. Pitts. Sch. Medicine, 2001—, prof. cell biology and physiology, 2001—; physician in chief, sci. dir. Children's Hosp. Pitts., 2001—. Editl. bd.: Hepatology, Am. Jour. Physiology; cons. editor: Pediatric Rsch.; contbr. articles to profl. jours. Recipient Established Investigator award Am. Heart Assn., 1987, Rsch. Scholar award Am. Gastroent. Assn., 1985, RJR Nabisco Co., 1986, E. Mead Johnson award for Rsch. in Pediatrics, 1994. Mem. Inst. Medicine, Am. Pediatric Soc., Assn. Am. Physicians, Am. Assn. for the Study of Liver Disease, Soc. Pediatric Rsch. (coun. rep. 1990—, former pres.), Am. Soc. Cell Biology, Am. Soc. Clin. Investigation. Office: Dept Pediatrics Ste 3300 3705 5th Ave DeSoto Wing Pittsburgh PA 15213 Office Phone: 412-692-8071. E-mail: david.perlmutter@chp.edu.*

PERLMUTTER, ED (EDWIN GEORGE PERLMUTTER), United States Representative from Colorado, former state legislator, lawyer; b. Denver, May 1, 1953; m. Deana M. Perlmutter; children: Alexis, Abbey, Zoey. BA, U. Colo., Boulder, 1975; JD, U. Colo. Sch. Law, 1978. Atty. Berenbaum, Weinshienk & Eason, P.C., Denver, 1978—; mem. dist. 20 Colo. State Senate, Denver, 1994—2002, pres. pro tempore, 2001—03, mem. pub. policy & planning com., joint legal svcs. com.; mem. US Congress from 7th Colo. dist., 2006—, mem. fin. svcs. com., homeland security com. Bd. trustees First Jud. & Jud. Performance Commn., 1989—91, chair, 1991—93; fin. chair Jefferson County Dems. Active Jefferson Found., Girl Scouts of America, Am. Heart Assn.; PTA mem. Maple Grove Elem. Sch., Golden, Colo.; trustee Midwest Rsch. Inst.; mem. Applewood Cmty. Ch.; past bd. dirs. Nat. Jewish Med. & Rsch. Ctr. Mem.: ABA, Comml. Law League America, U. Colo. Alumni Assn., Colo. Trial Lawyers Assn., Colo. Oil & Gas Assn., Associated Gen. Contractors Colo., Applewood Bus. Assn., Am. Judicature Soc., Am. Bankruptcy Inst., Golden C. of C., West C. of C., Northwest Metro C. of C., Denver Bar Assn., Colo. Bar. Assn. (bd. govs.), Arvada Soccer Assn., Table Mountain Soccer Assn., Wheat Ridge Soccer Assn. Democrat. Office: 415 Cannon House Office Bldg Washington DC 20515 also: 12600 W Colfax Ave Ste 8400 Lakewood CO 80215*

PERLMUTTER, ISAAC, entertainment company executive; b. 1946; m. Laura Perlmutter. Ind. fin. investor; with Marvel Entertainment, Inc., NYC, 1990—, chmn., 1993—95, vice chmn., 2001—, CEO, 2005—. Bd. dirs. Marvel Entertainment, Inc., 1993—, Ranger Industries, Inc. Established (with Laura Perlmutter) the Laura and Isaac Perlmutter Professorship and Chair in Cell Biology (now Pathology) Skirball Inst. Biomolecular Medicine. Office: Marvel Entertainment Inc 417 5th Ave New York NY 10016

PERLMUTTER, LOUIS, investment banker, lawyer; b. Cambridge, Mass., Oct. 3, 1934; s. Kermit H and Rachel P (Ehrlich) Perlmutter; m. Barbara Patricia Sondik, Dec. 11, 1966; children: Kermit, Eric. BA, Brandeis U., Waltham, Mass., 1956, LHD (hon.), 1995; JD, U. Mich., 1959. Bar: Mass 1959, NY 1961. Law practice, NYC, 1960-65; asst. to pres. New Eng. Industries, NYC, 1965-67; pres. Octagon Assocs., NYC, 1967-75; sr. v.p. White Weld, NYC, 1975-78; mgn. dir. Merrill Lynch, White, Weld, NYC, 1978; exec. mng. dir. Lazard Freres & Co. LLC, NYC, 1978-99, ltd. mng. dir., 2000—05; sr. advisor Lazard Alternative Investments, 2005—09, Corp. Ptnrs., LLC, 2009—. Contbr. articles to profl jours. Bd. dirs. Charles H. Revson Found.; chmn. Transatlantic Inst.; bd. govs. Am. Jewish Com.; bd. dirs., treas. World Fedn. UNA; chmn. bd. trustees Brandeis U., Waltham, Mass., 1988—95, Am. Jewish Congress, NYC, 1988—94; bd. dirs., chmn. exec. com. UN Assn. USA, 1993—96; bd. fellows Harvard Med. Sch.; adv. bd. Fgn. Affairs; mem. Coun. Fgn. Relations., Admnistrv Coun., Blaustein Inst. Advancement Human Rights; bd. govs. State of USA; bd. dirs. Harvard Med. Internat., 2005—08. Recipient Human Rels. award, Am. Jewish Com., 1995, Pub. Svc. award, Phoenix H.S., 1999, tribute dinner, Israel Policy Forum, 2001, honoree, World Fedn. UN Assn., 2003. Home: 39 E 79th St New York NY 10075-0275 Office: Corp Ptnrs LLC 30 Rockefeller Plz New York NY 10112-5900 Business E-Mail: louis.perlmutter@corporatepartnersllc.com.

PERLMUTTER, ROGER, medical products executive; Chmn. dept. immunology U. Wash., 1989—97, prof. depts. immunology, biochemistry and medicine, 1991—97; investigator Howard Hughes Med. Inst., 1991—97; various positions including exec. v.p. Worldwide Basic Rsch. and Preclinical Devel. Merck Rsch. Labs., 1997—2000; exec. v.p. R & D Amgen, Inc., 2001—. Bd. dirs. Stem Cells, Inc. Office: Amgen Inc One Amgen Center Dr Thousand Oaks CA 91320-1799 Office Phone: 805-447-1000. Office Fax: 805-447-1010.

PERLMUTTER, SAUL, astrophysicist, educator; AB in Physics (magna cum laude), Harvard U., 1981; PhD in Physics, U. Calif. Berkeley, 1986. Postdoctoral rschr. Space Sci. Lab., Lawrence Berkeley Nat. Lab., 1987—88; sr. staff scientist, astrophysicist Lawrence Berkeley Nat. Lab.; prof., physics dept. U. Calif. Berkeley, 2004—. Leader Internat. Supernova Cosmology Project, 1998—. Contbr. articles to profl. jours., to Sky and Telescope mag.; guest appearances Pub. Broadcasting Sys., BBC documentaries on astronomy and cosmology. Recipient Henri Chretien award, Am. Astronomical Soc., 1996, Breakthrough of Yr. award, Science Mag., 1998, E.O. Lawrence award in Physics, Dept. Energy, 2002, John Scott award, 2005, Padua prize, 2005, Feltrinelli Internat. prize, Phys. and Math. Scis., Lincei Acad., Rome, 2006; co-recipient Shaw prize in Astronomy, Shaw Found., Hong Kong, 2006, Gruber Cosmology prize, 2007; named Scientist of Yr., Calif., 2003. Fellow: Am. Acad. Arts & Scis. Achievements include discovery of the universe's accelerating expansion using supernovae as "standard candles" to measure the cosmic expansion rate. Office: Lawrence Berkeley Lab 50-232 Univ Calif 392 LeConte Berkeley CA 94720 Office Phone: 510-486-5203, 510-642-3596. Office Fax: 510-486-5401. Business E-Mail: saul@lbl.gov.

PERLOFF, JOSEPH KAYLE, cardiologist, educator; b. New Orleans, Dec. 21, 1924; s. Richard and Rose (Cohen) P.; m. Marjorie G. Mintz; children: Nancy L., Carey E. BA, Tulane U., 1945; postgrad., U. Chgo., 1946-47; MD, La. State U., New Orleans, 1951; MA (hon.), U. Pa., 1973. Diplomate Am. Bd. Internal Medicine, Am. Bd. Cardiovascular Disease. Intern Mt. Sinai Hosp., NYC, 1951-52, resident in pathology, 1952-53, resident in medicine, 1953-54; Fulbright fellow Inst. Cardiology, London, 1954-55; resident in medicine Georgetown U. Hosp., Washington, 1955-56, fellow in cardiology, 1956-57; from clin. instr. to prof. Georgetown U. Sch. Medicine, Washington, 1957-72, dir. cardiac diagnostic lab., 1959-68, asst. dir. divsn. cardiology, 1968-72; prof. medicine and pediat. U. Pa. Sch. Medicine, Phila., 1972-77, chief cardiovascular sect., 1972-77; prof. medicine and pediatrics UCLA Sch. Medicine, 1977—, Streisand/AHA chair in cardiology, 1983. Cons. Nat. Heart, Blood and Lung Inst.; dir. UCLA Adult Congenital Heart Disease Ctr. Author: The Cardiomyopathies, 1988, Physical Exam Heart and Circulation, 1990, 4th edit., 2009, Clinical Recognition of Congenital Heart Disease, 5th edit., 2003, Congenital Heart Disease in Adults, 3rd edit., 2009. Ensign USN, 1943—46, PTO. Recipient The Best of UCLA award Chancellor's Selection, 1987; Residency Career Devel. award NIH, 1959-69, Sherman M. Mellinkoff award UCLA Med. Sch., 2000, Extraordinay Merit award, 2004, Fellow ACP, Am. Coll. Cardiology(Lifetime Achievement award 2008); mem. Am. Fedn. Clin. Rsch., Assn. Univ. Cardiologists, Alpha Omega Alpha. Office: UCLA Sch Medicine Cardiology 47 123 Chs Los Angeles CA 90024 Office Phone: 310-825-2019. Personal E-mail: josephperloff@earthlink.net.

PERLOFF, MARJORIE GABRIELLE, literature educator; b. Vienna, Sept. 28, 1931; arrived in U.S., 1998; d. Maximilian and Ilse (Schueller) Mintz; m. Joseph K. Perloff, July 31, 1953; children: Nancy Lynn, Carey Elizabeth. AB, Barnard Coll., 1953; MA, Cath. U., 1956, PhD, 1965; LittD (hon.), Bird Coll., 2008. Asst. prof. English and comparative lit. Cath. U., Washington, 1966-68, assoc. prof., 1969-71, U. Md., 1971-73, prof., 1973-76; Florence R. Scott prof. English U. So. Calif., LA, 1976—; prof. English and comparative lit. Stanford (Calif.) U., 1986—, Sadie Dernham prof. humanities, 1990—, prof. emerita, 2000. Vis. prof. U. Utah, 2002; scholar-in-residence U. So. Calif., 2004—; guest prof. Beijing Lang. and Culture U., 2004. Author: Rhyme and Meaning in the Poetry of Yeats, 1970, The Poetic Art of Robert Lowell, 1973, Frank O'Hara, Poet Among Painters, 1977, 2nd edit., 1998, The Poetics of Indeterminacy: Rimbaud to Cage, 1981, 2d edit., 1999, The Dance of the Intellect: Studies in the Poetry of the Pound Tradition, 1985, 2d edit., 1996, The Futurist Moment: Avant-Garde, Avant-Guerre and the Language of Rupture, 1986, 2d edit., 2003, Poetic License: Essays in Modern and Postmodern Lyric, 1990, Radical Artifice: Writing Poetry in the Age of Media, 1991, Wittgenstein's Ladder: Poetic Language and the Strangeness of the Ordinary, 1996, Frank O'Hara, 2d edit., 1998, Poetry On and Off the Page: Essays for Emergent Occasions, 1998, Twenty-first Century Modernism, 2001, The Vienna Paradox, 2004, Differentials, 2004; editor: Postmodern Genres, 1990; co-editor: John Cage: Composed in America, 1994; contbg. editor: Columbia Literary History of the U.S., 1987; contbr. preface to Contemporary Poets, 1980, A John Cage Reader, 1983. Guggenheim fellow, 1981-82, NEA fellow, 1985; Phi Beta Kappa scholar, 1994-95. Fellow Am. Acad. Arts and Scis.; mem. MLA (exec. coun. 1977-81, Am. lit. sect. 1993—, 1st v.p. 2005, pres. 2006), Comparative Lit. Assn. (pres. 1993-94, mem. adv. bd. Libr. of Am.), Lit. Studies Acad. Home: 1467 Amalfi Dr Pacific Palisades CA 90272-2752 Home Phone: 310-454-4835. Personal E-mail: mperloff@earthlink.net.

PERLOFF, ROBERT, psychologist, educator; b. Phila., Feb. 3, 1921; s. Myer and Elizabeth (Sherman) P.; m. Evelyn Potechin, Sept. 22, 1946; children: Richard Mark, Linda Sue, Judith Kay. AB, Temple U., 1949; MA, Ohio State U., 1949, PhD, 1951; DSc (hon.), Oreg. Grad. Sch. Profl. Psychology, 1984; DLitt (hon.), Calif. Sch. Profl. Psychology, 1985. Diplomate Am. Bd. Profl. Psychology. Instr. edn. Antioch Coll., 1950—51; with pers. rsch. br. Dept. Army, 1951—55, chief statis. rsch. and cons. unit., 1953—55; dir. R & D Sci. Rsch. Assocs., Inc., Chgo., 1955—59; vis. lectr. Chgo. Tchrs. Coll., 1955—56; mem. faculty Purdue U., 1958—59, prof. psychology, 1964—69; 1961field assessment officer univ. Peace Corps Chile III project, 1962; Disting. Svc. prof. bus. adminstrn. and psychology U. Pitts. Joseph M. Katz Grad. Sch. Bus., 1969—90, Disting. Svc. prof. emeritus, 1991—; dir. rsch. programs U. Pitts. Grad. Sch. Bus., 1969—77; dir. Consumer Panel, 1980—83. Bd. dirs. Book Ctr.; adv. com. assessment exptl. manpower R & D labs. NAS, 1972-74; mem. rsch. rev. com. NIMH, 1976-80, Stress and Families rsch. project, 1976-79; cons. in field. Contbr. articles to profl. jours.; editor Indsl. Psychologist, 1963-65, Evaluator Intervention: Pros and Cons; book rev. editor Personnel Psychology, 1952-55; co-editor: Values, Ethics and Standards Sourcebook, 1979, Improving Evaluations; bd. consulting editors Jour. Applied Psychology; bd. advs. Archives History Am. Psychology, Psychol. Svc. Pitts., Recorded Psychol. Jours.; guest editor Am. Psychologist, 1972, Edn. and Urban Soc., 1977, Profl. Psychology, 1977; adv. editor Contemporary Psychology, 1994—. Bd. dirs., v.p. Sr. Citizens Svc. Corp., Calif. Sch. Profl. Psychology; bd. dirs. Greater Pitts. chpt. ACLU, sec., 1997-98; chmn. nat. adv. com. Inst. Govt. and Pub. Affairs, U. Ill., 1986-89, sec. nat. adv. com., 1997—; mem. adv. com. Cornell Inst. for Rsch. on Children, 2002—. Decorated Bronze Star; recipient Legacy award, Greater Pitts. Psychol. Assn., 2001, Hist. Preservation award, City of Pitts., 2002; named in his honor, Robert Perloff Grad. Rsch. Assistantship in Inst. Govt. and Pub. Affairs, U. Ill., 1990, in his honor, Robert Perloff Career Achievement award, Knowledge Utilization Soc., 1991. Fellow: APA (mem.-at-large exec. com. divsn. consumer psychology 1964—67, coun. reps. 1965—68, pres. divsn. 1967—68, chmn. sci. affairs com., divsn. consumer psychology 1968—69, edn. and tng. bd. 1969—72, mem.-at-large exec. com. divsn. consumer psychology 1970—71, coun. reps. 1972—74, dir. 1974—82, chmn. fin. com., treas. 1975—84, chmn. investment com. 1977—82, pres. 1985, adv. bd., bd. sci. affairs 1994—96, task force intelligence and Intelligence Tests, author column Std. Deviations in jour., pres. address selected as one of 50 over 50 yrs.), AAAS, Ea. Psychol. Assn. (dir. 1977—80, pres. 1980—81); mem.: Coun. of Sci. Soc. (found. alumnus, pres. 1998—), Knowledge Utilization Soc. (pres. 1993—95), Soc. Psychologists in Mgmt. (pres. 1993—94, Disting. Contbn. to Psychology Mgmt. award 1989), Am. Evaluation Assn. (pres. 1977—78), Am. Psychol. Found. (v.p. 1988—89, pres. 1990—92, trustee 1995—98, Lifetime Achievement in Psychology Gold Medal award 2000), Assn. for Consumer Rsch. (chmn. 1970—71), Pa. Psychol. Assn. (Disting. Svc. award 1985), Internat. Assn. Applied Psychology, Am. Psychol. Soc., Phi Beta Kappa, Psi Chi, Beta Gamma Sigma, Sigma Xi (pres. U. Pitts. chpt. 1989—91). Home: 815 Saint James St Pittsburgh PA 15232-2112 Home Phone: 412-687-3807; Office Phone: 412-648-1554. Personal E-mail: rperloff@katz.pitt.edu. *Experiment. Innovate responsibly. Take risks judiciously. Do not shrink from new ventures for fear of failure. No one is immune from adversity. The hallmark of a successful achieving person is his or her ability to snap back after misfortune, and to benefit from and not be immobilized by failure.*

PERLOV, DADIE, management and executive search consultant; BA, NYU, 1950; postgrad., Adelphi U., 1963, Vanderbilt U., 1973. Cert. assn. exec., N.Y. Exec. dir. ops. Open City, NYC, 1962-64; field svcs. dir. Nat. Coun. Jewish Women, NYC, 1968-74; exec. dir. N.Y. State Libr. Assn., 1974-81, Nat. Coun. Jewish Women, NYC, 1981-90; founder, prin. Consensus Mgmt. Group, NYC and Indpls., 1989—. Cons. HEW 1975-76; pres.-elect Internat. Coun. Libr. Assn. Execs., 1979-80; exec. mem. Conf. of Pres., 1981-90; strategic planner, lectr., merger facilitator; bd. devel., structure/governance, ops., audits mgmt. cons. exec. search ABA, Am. Bankers Assn., ALA, Nat. Assn. Home Builders, Am. Coll. Healthcare Execs., Nat. Assn. Ind. Insurers, and more than 550 clients other maj. trade and profl. assns. Co-author: The Ultimate Association Diet: How to Stay Fit and Trim in the 21st Century; author monthly column Dear Dadie for Assoc. Trends; contbr. articles to profl. jours. Mem. N.Y. Zool. Soc., 1959—, adv. bd. Nat. Inst. Against Prejudice and Violence, 1985-89; bd. visitors Pratt Inst., Bklyn., 1980-84; bd. dirs. Pres. Coun. on Handicapped, 1981—; facilitator Nursing Summit, 1994, 2004. Recipient Recognition award N.Y. Libr. Assn., 1978, BUDDY award NOW Legal Def. and Edn. Found., 1989, cert. N.Y. State Legislature, 1978, Trends award, 2007; named N.Y. State Exec. of Yr., 1980, One of Am.'s 100 Most Important Women, Ladies' Home Jour., 1988. Fellow Am. Soc. Assn. Execs. (cert. 1978, evaluator 1980-91, bd. dirs. 1987-90, bd. found. 1990-92, Excellence award 1983); mem. LWV (chpt. pres. 1960-62), N.Y. Soc. Assn. Execs, (pres. 1985, Outstanding Assn. Exec. 1989, Outstanding Svc. award 1991), Global Perspectives in Edn. (bd. dirs.), Nat. Orgn. Continuing Edn. (coun.), Audubon Soc., N.Y. Citizens Coun. on Librs. (bd. dirs. 1981-84), Am. Arbitration Assn. (mem. panel). Avocations: writing, mycology, history, music, art. Office Phone: 212-712-2449. Fax: 212-874-8068.

PERLOVSKY, LEONID ISAACOVICH, magnetic resonance imaging research and development company researcher; b. Odessa, Ukrain, USSR, Nov. 11, 1948; came to U.S., 1978; s. Isaac E. and Riva B. (Bormashenko) P.; m. Diana Vinkovetsky; children— Ilya, Boris, Daniel. M.S. with honors, Novosibirsk U., 1971; Ph.D., Joint Inst. Nuclear Research, Dubna, 1975. Asst. prof. Siberia Civil Engring. Inst., Novosibirsk, U.S.S.R., 1975-77; assoc. prof., 1977-78; research prof. NYU, N.Y.C., 1979-80; sr. research physicist Exxon Prodn. Research, Houston, 1980-81, research specialist, 1981-83, sr. research specialist, 1983-85; prin. research scientist Advanced NMR Systems, Boston, 1985—; cons. Sibera Agrl. Inst., Novosibirsk, 1975-78, Software Foundry, Inc., N.Y.C., 1979-80, Earth Resources Lab., MIT, 1986; participant, speaker sci. confs. Contbr. articles to profl. jours. Mem. Soc. Exploration Geophysicists, Soc. Profl. Well Log Analysts, Soc. Indsl. and Applied Math., IEEE, Am. Statis. Assn. Research on magnetic resonance imaging. Home: 30 Griggs Rd Brookline MA 02446-4732 Office: 30 Sonar Dr Woburn MA 01801-5704

PERLSTADT, HARRY, medical sociology educator; b. Chgo., Aug. 23, 1942; s. Sidney M. and Mildred (Penn) Perlstadt; m. Tari Chrystal Taylor, Aug. 4, 1968; children: Emily, Roger. BA, U. Mich., 1963; MA, U. Chgo., 1966, PhD, 1973; MPH, U. Mich., 1979. Prof. med. sociology Mich. State U., East Lansing, 1968—, dir. program in bioethics, humanities and society, 2003—07. Evaluation cons. Kellogg Found., 1986-97, Mich. Dept. Pub. Health and Mich. State U., 1987-91, COSMOS Corp. and NIMH, Washington, 1988-90, Mott Children's Health Ctr., 1991-95, WHO, 2002-03, Mich. Dept. Cmty. Health and Health Resources and Svcs. Adminstrn., U.S. Dept HHS, 1999-2000. Chair Mich. Coalition Smoking or Health, Lansing, 1984-92; mem. Mich. Tobacco Reduction Task Force, Lansing, 1989, Tobacco Free Mich. Action Coalition, Lansing, 1990-94; chair Commn. on Applied and Clin. Sociology, 1995-2004; rsch. agenda com. Ctrs. for Disease Control, 2005-06. NIMH postdoctoral fellow, U. Mich., 1977-78; recipient Pub. Svc. Achievement award Am. Lung Assn. Mich., 1985. Mem. APHA (governing coun. 1990-95, 2004-06, exec. bd. 2002-04, sci. bd. 2000-08), Am. Sociol. Assn. (chair sociol. practice sect. 1998-99, Soc. Applied Sociology (editor The Useful Sociologist 1987-89), Mich. Pub. Health Assn. (pres. 1988-89), Am. Lung Assn. (nat. coun. 1999-2009, sci. adv. com. 2003—). Avocations: dance, reading, history. Office: Mich State U Sociology/Berkey Hall East Lansing East Lansing MI 48824-1111 Business E-Mail: perlstad@msu.edu.

PERLSTEIN, WILLIAM JAMES, lawyer; b. NYC, Feb. 7, 1950; s. Justin Sol and Jane (Goldberg) P.; m. Teresa Catherine Lotito, Dec. 20, 1970; children: David, Jonathan. Student, London Sch. Econs., 1969-70; BA summa cum laude, Union Coll., 1971; JD, Yale U., 1974. Bar: Conn. 1974, D.C. 1976, U.S. Dist. Ct. D.C. 1977, U.S. Ct. Appeals (D.C. cir.) 1978, U.S. Supreme Ct. 1993, N.Y. 2000. Law clk. to judge Marvin Frankel U.S. Dist. Ct., NYC, 1974-75; assoc. Wilmer, Cutler & Pickering, Washington, 1975-82, ptnr., 1982—2004, mem. mgmt. com., 1995—2004, chmn., 1998—2004; co-mng. ptnr. & co-chmn. mgmt. com. Wilmer Cutler Pickering Hale & Dorr, Washington, 2004—. Mng. editor Yale Law Jour., 1973-74; contbg. author The Workout Game, 1987. Dir. Neighborhood Legal Svcs. program. Mem.: Am. Bar Found., Am. Coll. Bankruptcy (gen. counsel), Am. Law Inst., Am. Bankruptcy Inst. (chmn. legis. com. 1986—89, bd. dirs. 1989—93, 1997—2002), ABA (bus. bankruptcy com 1983—, v.chmn. executory contracts subcom. of bus. bankruptcy com. 1988—90, bankruptcy cts. subcom. 1990—97, chmn. legislation subcom. 1997—), Yale Club NY, Econ. Club Wash., Met. Club Wash., Phi Beta Kappa. Jewish. Office: Wilmer Cutler Pickering Hale & Dorr 1875 Pennsylvania Ave NW Washington DC 20006-3642 Office Phone: 202-663-6274. Office Fax: 202-663-6363. Business E-Mail: william.perlstein@wilmerhale.com.

PERMINOV, ANATOLY, aerospace agency executive; b. Kirov, Russia, June 16, 1945; Grad., Perm Military Command & Engring. Coll., 1967, Dzerzhinsky Military Academy, 1976, Gen. Staff Academy, 1991. Comdr. Plesetsk Space Ctr., Russia, 1991—93; variety of staff positions Strategic Rocket Forces hq., 1993—2001; head Russian Space Forces, 2001—04, Russian Fed. Space Agy. (Roskosmos), Moscow, 2004—. From missile officer to comdr. Russian Military. Office: Russian Fed Space Agy 42 Shchepkin Str 107996 Moscow Russia Office Phone: 74956889905. Business E-Mail: perminov@roscosmos.ru.

PERMUTT, SOLBERT, physiologist, physician; b. Birmingham, Ala., Mar. 6, 1925; s. Harry and Rachel (Damsky) P.; m. Loretta Paul, Jan. 17, 1952; children— Nina Rachel, Thomas Joshua, Lisa Ellen. MD, U. So. Calif., 1949. Intern U. Chgo. Clinics, 1949-50, resident medicine, 1952, research assoc. dept. anatomy, 1950-52; resident medicine Montefiore Hosp., NYC, 1954-56; fellow medicine and environmental medicine Johns Hopkins Med. Sch., 1956-58; chief div. cardiopulmonary physiology Nat. Jewish Hosp., Denver, 1958-61; asst. prof. physiology Sch. Medicine, U. Colo., 1960-61; mem. faculty Sch. Hygiene and Pub. Health, Johns Hopkins, 1961, prof. environ. health sci., 1965—; prof. medicine Johns Hopkins U. Sch. Med., 1972—, dir. respiratory div. dept. medicine, 1972-81, prof. anesthesiology, 1978—; head physiology div., environ. health sci. John Hopkins Sch. Hygiene and Pub. Health, 1976-79; dir. pulmonary div. Francis Scott Key Med. Ctr. (John Hopkins Med. Instn.), 1981-87, dir. pulmonary rsch., div. pulmonary medicine, 1986-87, dir. rsch. div. pulmonary and critical care medicine, 1988-98; assoc. dir. Johns Hopkins Asthma and Allergy Ctr., 1990—. Cons. space sci. bd. Nat. Acad. Sci., 1966-67, mem. com. effects atmospheric contaminants human health, 1968-70; mem. project com. Heart and Lung Program, NIH, 1970-74; mem. sci. adv. council Children's Asthma Research Inst. and Hosp., Denver, 1973-75; mem. expert panel Nat. Inst. Allergy and Infectious Diseases, 1972-74; mem. nat. adv. com. for Cal. Primate Research Center, 1972-75; vice chmn. council on cardiopulmonary diseases Am. Heart Assn., 1974-75, chmn., 1976—, mem. research com., 1979-85; nat. adviser Aspen Lung Confs., 1974—; mem. pulmonary disease adv. com. HHS and NIH, 1979-83. Mem. editorial bd. publs. Am. Physiol. Soc. Circulation Research, 1965—, La Revue Française des Maladies Respiratories, 1975—; contbr. articles to profl. jours. Served with U.S. Army, 1943-46, 53-54. Recipient Gold medal Am. Coll. Chest Physicians, 1977, Louis and Artur Lucian award McGill U., 1980; fellow Nat. Found. Infantile Paralysis, 1956-58 Mem. Am. Lung Assn. (George Wills Comstock award 1988, Edward Livingston Trudeau medal 1992), Cardiovascular System Dynamics Soc., Am. Med. Assn. (reference panel for diagnostic and therapeutic tech. assessment-DATTA), Assn. Am. Physicians, Johns Hopkins Med. and Surg. Assn., Md. Soc. Med. Rsch., Am. Thoracic Soc., Am. Physiol. Soc., AAAS, Am. Heart Assn. (Citation for Disting. Svc. to Rsch. 1979-84, Disting. Achievement award Cardiopulmonary Coun. 1986). Home: 830 W 40th St Apt 114 Baltimore MD 21211-2121 Home Phone: 410-243-5599; Office Phone: 410-550-2512. Business E-Mail: spermut@jhmi.edu.

PERNICIARO, CHARLES VINCENT, dermatologist, educator, entrepreneur; b. New Orleans, June 15, 1957; s. Ernest Gabriel and Phereby Sheppard Perniciaro; children: Jamie Lynn, Kelly Gabrielle. BS, U. La., Lafayette, 1979; MD, La. State U., New Orleans, 1983. Diplomate Am. Bd. Dermatology, Am. Bd. Dermatology and Pathology. Staff physician Ochsner Clin. of Baton Rouge, La., 1987-90; sr. assoc. cons. and staff dermatologist Mayo Clinic, Jacksonville, Fla., 1990-93, cons., staff dermatologist and dermatopathologist, 1993-99; pvt. practice dermatology Brunswick, Ga., 1999—2008, Neptune Beach, Fla., 1999—2006, Ponte Vedra Beach, Fla., 2006—; dir. dermatopathology Bernhardt Labs., Jacksonville, Fla., 2001—. Pres., CEO Holiday Lighting Concepts, Inc., 1996-2000; lectr., presenter in field; adj. clin. assoc. prof. pathology U. Fla. Shands Jacksonville Med. Ctr., 1999-2001. Contbr. articles to profl. jours. Founder, bd. dirs. S.W. La. Skin Cancer Found., 1987. Recipient Outstanding Paper award Noah Worcester Dermatol. Soc., 1993, First Place Poster award 17th Internat. Colloquium Dermatopathology, 1996; named one of Best Doctors, 2000-08, How to Find the Best Fla. Doctors, 2000, Am. Top Physicians, 2003-05. Fellow: Am. Soc. Dermatopathology (chmn. membership com., bd. dirs. 2000—01), Am. Acad. Dermatology (com. on preventive dermatology 1988—90, task force on dermatologic oncology 1990—93, environ. coun. 1994—96, adv. coun. 1995—2001, adv. bd. 2006—07); mem.: So. Med. Assn. (vice chair sect. dermatology 1995—96, chair-elect 2001—06, chair 2006—07, Resident-in-Tng. award 1994), Fla. Soc. Dermatology (bd. dirs. 1998—2006, chmn. membership com. 1999—2002, v.p. 2002—03, pres. 2003—04, Practitioner of Yr. 2009), Jacksonville Dermatology Soc. (sec.-treas. 1995, pres. 1996, webmaster 2003—04), Lions (charter, bd. dirs. Ponte Vedra Beach 1997—98). Avocations: tennis, computers. Home: 514 Midway St Neptune Beach FL 32266

PERO, COLIN DANIEL, facial plastic surgeon researcher; b. Parma, Ohio, Jan. 21, 1976; s. Ernest Eugene and Pamela Jean Pero; m. Roxanne Elizabeth Girod, Oct. 17, 2008. MD, U. Tex-Houston Med. Sch., 1999—2003. Diplomate Board Eligible AAOHNS, 2008. Resident LSUHSC, Head & Neck Surgery, New Orleans, 2003—08; facial plastic surgery fellow Otolaryngology Dept, UI-Chgo. Med. Sch., 2008—. Contbr. articles and chpt. to books. Parishioner Holy Name Cathedral, Chgo. Mem.: Am. Rhino Logic Surgery, Am. Acad. Facial Plastic & Re Constructive Surgery, Am. Acad. Otolaryngology/Head & Neck Surgery (mem. 2004—08). Roman Catholic.

PERO, VICTORIA, performing arts educator; b. Englewood, NJ, June 9, 1964; d. Jack and Rose Pero; m. Peter Scanlan, Aug. 1, 1993; children: Declan Victor Scanlan, Sophia Kathleen Scanlan, Isabella Miranda Scanlan. BS, Northwestern U., Evanston, Ill., 1986; MFA, Ohio U., Athens, 1994. Cert. in acting London Acad. Music and Dramatic Art, 1988, tchr. NJ, 2006. Assoc. artistic dir. Am. Stage Co., Teaneck, NJ, 1989—91; asst. to artistic dir. Cleve. Play Ho., 1990—91; assoc. prodr. Drama League, NYC, 1994—95; assoc. artistic dir. Cir. Sq. Theater, NYC, 1995—97; owner, prodr. Shakespeare Summer Arts Inst., Closter, NJ, 2001—; performing arts tchr. Bergen County Acads., Hackensack, NJ, 2005—. Health club instr. CORE, Closter, NJ, 1998—. Asst. dir. (dramas) Broken Glass, Royal Nat. Theater, London, Death of a Salesman, Guthrie Theater; dir.: (dramas) The Lower Rooms, The Appointment, Scenes and Revelations, Big Cactus, Tales of the Lost Formicans, Woyzeck, The Grapes of Wrath, Romeo Meets Juliet, The Spirit of Life, (musical comedy) Consumer Behavior, (comedies) Bright Ideas, Trippin', The After Dinner Joke (Named to Top Ten Off Off Broadway Revs., 1999), (pre-broadway) The Alchemist; asst. dir. (musical) Purlie, Encores, NYC; dir.: (musicals) Sugar Dumpling, Stormy Weather, Pippin (Papermill Playhouse award, 2006), The Secret Garden (Papermill Playhouse award), The King and I, (outdoor farce) Alice In Wonderland. Prodr. Closter Arts Orgns., NJ, 1998—2008. Scholar Super Stipend, Ohio U., 1991—94. Mem.: Soc. Stage Dirs. and Choreographers. Liberal. Avocations: art, gardening, exercise. Home: 35 County Rd Demarest NJ 07627 Office: Bergen County Acads 200 Hackensack Hackensack NJ 07601 Business E-Mail: vicper@bergen.org.

PERONTO, JANICE LYNN, principal; d. Richard A. and Bonnie J. Sinkenbring; m. Karl Eric Peronto, June 10, 1995; children: Kolton Richard, Kolby Eric, Konnor Walter. BA in Edn., Purdue U., West Lafayette, Ind., 1991; MEd (hon.), Tarleton State U., Ctrl. Texas, Tex., 2001. Tchr. Cedar Valley Elem., Killeen, Tex., 1992—2002; campus instrnl. specialist Clifton Pk. Elem., 2002—05; asst. prin. Cedar Valley Elem., 2005—. Adv. panel Tex. SBEC, Austin, 1999—; goal III action rsch. coord. Killeen Ind. Sch. Dist., 2002—, mentor coord., 2002—; adv. panel Cedar Valley Elem., 1993—. Mem. Killeen Svc. League, 2003—04. Recipient Excellence Tchg., Killeen Daily Herald, 1997—98,

Tchr. of Yr., Walmart Found., 1997—98, Tchr. of Quarter, Exch. Club Killeen, 2001—02. Mem.: Tex. Edn. Assn., Tex. Elem. Prin. Assn. (assoc.), Delta Kappa Gamma (assoc.). Office: Cedar Valley Elementary 4801 Chantz Drive Killeen TX 76542 Office Fax: 254-680-6600. E-mail: janice.peronto@killeenisd.org.

PEROT, ROSS (H. ROSS PEROT, HENRY ROSS PEROT), real estate company, investment company, data processing executive; b. Texarkana, Tex., June 27, 1930; s. Gabriel Ross and Lulu May Perot; m. Margot Birmingham, 1956; children: Ross Jr., Nancy, Suzanne, Carolyn, Katherine. Ed., US Naval Acad., 1949—53. Data processing salesman IBM Corp., 1957-62; founder Electronic Data Systems Corp., Dallas, 1962-84, sold to GM, 1984, chmn., CEO, also dir., to 1986; founder The Perot Group, Dallas, 1986—, Perot Systems Corp., Washington, 1988—, bd. mem. Dallas, 1988—94, Plano, 1997—, chmn. Dallas, 1988—92, Plano, 2000—04, chmn. emeritus, 2004—. Ind. candidate US Presdl. Election, 1992, Reform Party candidate, 96. Author (books) United We Stand: How We Can Take Back Our Country, 1992, Not for Sale at Any Price: How We Can Save America for Our Children, 1993, Intensive Care: We Must Save Medicare and Medicaid Now, 1995, Preparing Our Country for the 21st Century, 1995, Ross Perot: My Life & the Principles for Success, 1996; co-author (with Pat Choate) Save Your Job, Save Our Country: Why NAFTA Must Be Stopped-Now!, 1993, (with Senator Paul Simon) The Dollar Crisis: A Blueprint to Help Rebuild the American Dream, 1996. Served with USN, 1953-57. Recipient Winston Churchill Award, 1986, Internat. Disting. Entrepreneur Award, U. Man., 1988, Raoul Wallenberg Award, Jefferson Award, Patrick Henry Award, Nat. Bus. Hall of Fame Award, Sarnoff Award, Eisenhower Award, Smithsonian Computerworld Award, Horatio Alger Award.; named one of Forbes' Richest Americans, 1999—, World's Richest People, Forbes mag., 1999—. Office: Perot Systems Corp 2300 W Plano Pkwy Plano TX 75075 also: Perot Family Trust PO Box 269014 Plano TX 75026-9014

PEROT, ROSS, JR., (HENRY ROSS PEROT JR.), real estate developer, professional sports team executive; b. Arlington, Tex. m. Sarah Fullinwider, 1984. BBA, Vanderbilt U., 1981. With Petrus Oil Co., Okla., 1981-83; mng. ptnr. The Perot Group, 1983—; owner Hillwood Devel., Dallas, 1988—; majority owner Dallas Mavericks basketball, 1996—2000; pres., CEO Perot Systems, Dallas, 2000—04, chmn., 2004—. Exec. com. Prince of Wales Bus. Leaders' Forum, Winston Churchill Found. Pilot, USAFR, 1983-1991. Achievements include completing first flight around the world in a helicopter. Office: Perot Systems 2300 W Plano Pkwy Plano TX 75075

PEROTTI, ROSE NORMA, lawyer; b. St. Louis, Aug. 10, 1930; d. Joseph and Dorothy Mary (Roleski) Perotti. BA, Fontbonne Coll., St. Louis, 1952; JD, St. Louis U., 1957. Bar: Mo. 1958. Trademark atty. Sutherland, Polster & Taylor, St. Louis, 1958-63, Sutherland Law Office, 1964-70, Monsanto Co., St. Louis, 1971-85, sr. trademark atty., 1985-91, assoc. trademark counsel, 1991-94, trademark counsel, 1994-96, Polster, Lieder, Woodruff & Lucchesi, 1996—. Honored with dedication of faculty office in her honor, St. Louis U. Sch. Law, 1980. Mem. ABA, Mo. Bar, Bar Assn. Met. St. Louis, Am. Judicature Soc., Friends St. Louis Art Mus., Mo. Bot. Garden. Business E-Mail: rperotti@patpro.com.

PERRAM FRANK, HEATHER, editor-in-chief; Grad., Tulane U., New Orleans. With CBS, E! Entertainment, Oprah Winfrey's Harpo Prodns., Warner Bros.; exec. dir. creative programming AOL; editor-in-chief Women's Lifestyle & Parenting Group Interactive Media, NYC; site dir. MORE.com Meredith Corp., 2005, editor-in-chief LHJ.com; v.p. programming Revolution Health, 2007—. Bd. dirs. Patricia M. Sitar Ctr. for the Arts. Office: LHJ Meredith Corp 375 Lexington Ave New York NY 10017

PERRAULT, PAUL A., bank executive; b. 1951; BS, Babson Coll., 1973; MBA, Boston Coll., 1975. Joined Shawmut Bank, 1975; pres. Bank of New England-Old Colony, Providence, 1989—90; CEO Chittenden Corp., 1990—98, chmn., CEO, 1998—2007; pres., CEO Sovereign Bancorp, Inc., 2009—. Mem. Am. Bankers Coun., Corp. Governance Task Force. Mem. SuperCommunity Bank Peer Group; bd. trustees, treas. Shelburne Mus. Office: Sovereign Bancorp Inc 75 State St Boston MA 02109 also: 1500 Market St Philadelphia PA 19102 E-mail: PPerrault@sovereignbank.com.*

PERRAULT, PENNI MARILYN, elementary school educator; b. Chgo., Mar. 25, 1952; d. Alex and Adeline Diana Matzkin; m. Arthur Norman Perrault, Apr. 17, 1982; children: Paris Danielle, Arthur Norman III. B, U. Pacific, Stockton, Calif., 1974; MEd, Nat. U., San Diego, 2000. Cert. instr. Calif., 1996. Gifted and talented instr. Saugus Union Sch. Dist., Calif., 1991—95; elem. sch. tchr. Newhall Sch. Dist., Santa Clarita, Calif., 1996—. Facilitator-conflict resolution program Newhall Sch., 1996—98; grade level team leader, founding mem. diversity com. Oak Hills Sch., Valencia, Calif., 2005—. Avocations: swimming, travel, cooking. Office: Newhall Sch Dist 25374 Orchard Village Rd Santa Clarita CA 91381 Personal E-mail: pper49@earthlink.net.

PERREAU GUIMARAES, MARCOS, medical researcher; b. Rio De Janeiro, Nov. 25, 1966; PhD, U. Rene Descartes, Paris, 1998. Faculty U. Rene Descartes, 1998—2000; rschr. INRIA, Grenoble, Savoie, France, 2000—. Rschr. Suppes Brain Lab, Stanford, Calif., 2001—. Office: Stanford Univ 220 PAnama St Stanford CA 94305 Personal E-mail: montereyunderwater@gmail.com. Business E-Mail: marcospg@csli.stanford.edu.

PERREAULT, WILLIAM DANIEL, JR., business administration educator; b. NYC, Apr. 7, 1948; s. William Daniel Sr. and Barbara Louise (Peckham) P.; m. Pamela Pittard, May 27, 1972; children: Suzanne Elizabeth, William Daniel III. BS, U. N.C., 1970, PhD, 1973. Asst. prof. U. Ga., Athens, 1973-76, U. N.C., Chapel Hill, 1976-79, assoc. prof., 1979-81, prof., 1981-83, Hanes prof., 1983-88. Vis. prof. Stanford (Calif.) U., 1986-87, assoc. dean, 1988-92. Kenan prof., 1988—; vis. prof. Cambridge (Eng.) U., 1997. Co-author: Essentials Marketing, 2008, The Marketing Game, 2001, Basic Marketing, 2007; editor: Jour. Mktg. Rsch., 1982-85; contbr. articles to profl. jours. Chmn. adv. com. Bur. Census, Washington, 1982—86. Mem. Am. Mktg. Assn. (v.p. 1986, 95, bd. dirs. 1986-89, 94-95, Odell award 1985, Disting. Educator award 1997, Churchill award 1997, Stern award, 2007, Lifetime Achievement award, Sales Rsch., 2008), Acad. Mktg. Sci. (Outstanding Edn. award 1995), Decision Scis. Inst. (coun. 1977), Assn. Dir. Consumer Rsch. Conf. (chmn. 1976—), Mktg. Sci. Inst. (trustee 1989-94), Phi Beta Kappa. Republican. Presbyterian. Office: U NC CB 3490 Mccoll Bldg Chapel Hill NC 27599-3490 Office Phone: 919-962-3171. Business E-Mail: bill_perreault@unc.edu.

PERRELLA, ANTHONY JOSEPH, electronics engineer; b. Boulder, Colo., Sept. 16, 1942; s. Anthony Vincent and Mary Domenica (Forte) Perrella; m. Pamela Smith, July 19, 1980; 1 child, Kathleen. BS, U. Wyo., 1964, postgrad., 1965, U. Calif., San Diego, 1966-67, U. Calif., Irvine, 1968-70. Flight engr. U.S. Naval Tng. Devices Ctr., San Diego, 1965-67; sch. engr. Collins divsn. Rockwell Internat. (formerly Collins Radio Co.), Newport Beach, Calif., 1967-69, electromagnetic interference and TEMPEST group head, 1969-74, supr., 1974-75, mgr., 1975-77, mgr. sys. integration, 1977, mgr. space comm. sys., 1977-78; sr. mem. tech. staff ARGOSys. Inc., Sunnyvale, Calif., 1978-81, program mgr., 1978-81, dep. dept. mgr. EW sys., 1980-83, divsn. EW staff engr., 1983-84, dept. mgr., 1984-87, Sun Microsys. Inc., Mountain View, Calif., 1987-89; prin. A. J. Perrella-Cons., Las Vegas, Nev., 1989—. V.p. R & D Things Unlimited, Inc., Laramie, Wyo., 1965—72, pres., 1972—75; bd. dirs., v.p. Columbian Credit Union, 1994—97. Bd. dirs. Bay Area Found. Mentally Retarded Children, 1994—2002, treas., 1996—2002; bd. dirs. Columbian Retirement Home, Inc., 1999—2002. Mem.: AAAS (life), IEEE (life), N.Y. Acad. Scis., Am. Mgmt. Assn., Assn. Old Crows KC (treas. San Jose chpt. 1992—93, sec. 1993—94, dep. dist. 22 1993—94, v.p. 1994—95, dist. 21 1994—97, pres. 1995—96, Calif. dist. sec. 1996—2000, trustee 1996—, Calif. youth dir. 1997—98, 2000—01, Calif. dist. master 2000—02, Calif. ch. dir. 2001—02, dir. Nev. shining armor 2003—04, Nev. state advocate 2004—05), Tau Kappa Epsilon. Roman Catholic. Office: 2550 Garcia Ave Mountain View CA 94043-1109 Home: 22 Cascade Lake St Las Vegas NV 89148-2791

PERRELLI, THOMAS JOHN, federal agency administrator, lawyer; b. Falls Church, Va., Mar. 12, 1966; AB magna cum laude, Brown U., 1988; JD magna cum laude, Harvard U., 1991. Bar: Va. 1991, DC 1993, Supreme Ct. Va. 1991, U.S. Dist. Ct. DC 1994, U.S. Ct. Appeals (Fed. cir.) 2002, U.S. Supreme Ct. 1996. Law clk. to Hon. Royce C. Lamberth US Dist. Ct. DC, 1991—92; assoc. Jenner & Block LLP, Washington, 1992—97; counsel to atty. gen. US Dept. Justice, Washington, 1997—99, dep. asst. atty. gen., 1999—2001, assoc. atty. gen., 2009—; ptnr. Jenner & Block LLP, Washington, 2001—09, mng. ptnr., co-chair entertainment & new media practice. Contbr. articles to profl. jours. Recipient Albert E. Jenner Pro Bono award, 2005; named one of The Top 40 Lawyers Under 40, The Nat. Law Jour., 2005. Mem.: Brown U. Club Washington (pres.). Office: US Dept Justice 950 Pennsylvania Ave NW Washington DC 20530*

PERRIELLO, TOM (THOMAS STUART PRICE PERRIELLO), United States Representative from Virginia; b. Ivy, Va., Oct. 9, 1974; s. Vito and Linda Perriello. BA, Yale U., New Haven, 1996, JD, 2001. Humanitarian aid worker, Sierra Leone; spl. advisor, spokesperson for the internat. prosecutor Liberia; nat. security analyst Century Found., Darfur, Sudan and Afghanistan; nat. security cons.; founder Catholics in Alliance for the Common Good, FaithfulAmerica.org; mem. US Congress from 5th Va. Dist., 2009—. Democrat. Roman Catholic. Office: US Congress 1520 Longworth House Office Bldg Washington DC 20515-4605 also: Dist Office 104 S 1st St Charlottesville VA 22902 Office Phone: 202-225-4711, 434-293-9631. Office Fax: 202-225-5681.*

PERRIER, NANCY, endocrinologist, educator; b. New Orleans, Dec. 29, 1966; m. Daniel Perrier; children: Daniel, Amelie. MD, LA State U. Med. Sch., New Orleans, 1993. Diplomate Am. Bd. Surgery 1999. Asst. prof. Wake Forest U. Bapt. Med. Ctr., Winston-Salem, NC, 1999—2004; assoc. prof. MD Anderson Cancer Ctr., Houston, 2004—, assoc. med. dir., endocrine ctr., 2006—, chief surg. endocrinology, 2007—, fellowship program dir., surg. endocrinology, 2007—. Recipient Dennis W. Jahnigen Career Devel. Scholars award, Am. Geriat. Soc., 2004, 2005. Mem.: ACS, Southern Surg. Assn., Am. Assn. Clin. Endocrinologists, Am. Assn. Endocrine Surgeons. Office: MD Anderson Cancer Ctr 1515 Holcombe Boulevard Unit 444 Houston TX 77030 Office Fax: 713-563-5727. Business E-Mail: nperrier@mdanderson.org.

PERRIER, PIÉRRE CLAUDE, aeronautical engineer, researcher; b. Paris, June 30, 1935; s. Georges Marie and Marguerite Marie (Pellissier) P.; m. Anne Congnard, July 15, 1967; children: Emmanuel, Agnes, Claire. Baccalaureat, Stanislas Coll., Paris, 1953; Engenieur Civil, Ecole Nationale Superieure Aeronautique, Paris, 1958; Ingenieur Docteur, Ecole Nationale Superiour Aeronautique, Paris, 1959. Researcher Centre Nat. Res. Scientifique, Meudon, France, 1958-59; engr. Dassault Aviation, Paris, 1959—; sec.-gen. French Acad. of Tech., Paris. Mem. com. applications l'Académé des Scis., Paris, 1987; pres., chmn. com.sci. and tech. CNRS, Paris, 1988, Brussels, 1989., vice chmn., founder European Rsch. Community Flow Turbulence and Combustion. Author: Karozoutha, Mshamshana; contbr. articles to profl. jours. Mem. coun. sci. def. Ministry of Armies, Paris, 1983-87. Recipient Médaile de l'Aéronautique award French Govt., Paris, 1980. Mem. AIAA, AAAF, NAE (fgn. assoc.), French Acad. Sci. (corr.), French Acad. Techs. (founding mem.), Acad. Air and Space, US Acad. Engring. (foreign amarte). Roman Catholic. Achievements include development of Computational Fluid Dynamics, Turbulence Modeling by Homogeneisation and basic principles of CAO; oral structures in thinking and sayings (application to gospel oral generation). Home: 16 Rue De Mouchy 78000 Versailles France Office: Daussalt Aviation 78 Quai Marcel Dassault 92240 Saint Cloud France also: French Acad Tech 28, rue Saint Dominique F-75007 Paris France

PERRILLES, ANGELA TERESE, physical therapist; b. Peoria, Ill., Apr. 27, 1969; d. William Ernest and Marilyn June Perrilles. BS in Fitness Leadership/Cardiac Rehab., No. Ill. U., DeKalb, 1992; MS in Athletic Tng./Exercise Physiology, Ill. State U., Normal, 1998; AAS, Ill. Ctrl. Coll., East Peoria, 2000. Aide phys. therapy St. Francis Med. Ctr., Peoria, 1988—89; front desk clerk/med. records Health Ctr. No. Ill. U., DeKalb, 1990—95; aide phys. therapy No. Rehab., DeKalb, 1993—95; fitness dir., personal trainer Landmark Health Club, Peoria, 1995—2002; athletic trainer Mustangs Jr. Hockey League, Peoria, 1999—2002; phys. therapist asst. Profl. Therapy Svcs., Peoria, 2000—02; phys. therapist asst./athletic trainer Orthop. Inst./Great Plains, Peoria, 2002—. Coord. cardiac rehab., therapist Jasper County Hosp., Rensselaer, Ind., 1996—97. Contbr.: newsletter Orthop. Inst. Ill., 2004—. Vol. spl. events Peoria Park Dist., 1997—; mem. Peoria Jaycees, 1998—; runner St. Jude Children's Hosp., Peoria, 1999—; chair, organizer Red Kettle campaign Salvation Army, Peoria, 2004—; vol. MS Soc., Arthritis Found., ARC, Peoria Humane Soc., Race for the Cure, Race for Life, Arthritis Walk, Diabetes Walk. Recipient Cmty. Svc. award, Peoria Park Dist., 2002. Mem.: Nat. Athletic Trainers Assn. Avocations: running, hot air ballooning, cross stitch, outdoor activities. Home: 617 Rohmann Ct Peoria IL 61604 Office: Orthopedic Inst Ill-Great Plains Rehab 303 N Kumpf Blvd Peoria IL 61605 E-mail: atpatc@insightbb.com.

PERRIMON, NORBERT JEAN PAUL, medical geneticist, educator; b. Bosguerard, France, Oct. 24, 1958; naturalized, US, 2005; s. Marcel Perrimon and Francine Ferret; m. Lizabeth A. Perkins; children: Pamela, Sarah. PhD, U. Paris VI, 1983; MS (hon.), Harvard U., 1996. Postdoctoral fellow Case Western Res. U., Cleve., 1983-86; asst. prof. genetics Harvard Med. Sch., Boston, 1986-93, assoc. prof. genetics, 1993-96, prof. genetics, 1996—; asst. investigator Howard Hughes Med. Inst., 1986—93, assoc. investigator, 1993—97, investigator, 1997—; assoc. mem. Broad Inst., Cambridge, Mass., 2006—. Mem. editl. bd. Mechanisms of Devel., 1999-, BioMed Ctrl. Devel. Biology, 2000-, Molecular and Cellular Biology, 2000-, Internat. Jour. Devel. Biology, 2002-, BioMed Ctrl. Genomics, 2005-, Genome Biology, 2008-, Sci. Signaling, 2008-; assoc. editor PLoS Genetics, 2008-. Recipient Chaire d'Etat, College de France, Paris, 2003, George W. Beadle medal, Genetics Soc. America, 2004; Lucille Markey scholar, 1985-86. Fellow: Am. Acad. Arts and Sciences. Office: Howard Hughes Med Inst Dept Genetics Harvard Med Sch 77 Ave Louis Pasteur Boston MA 02115 Office Phone: 617-432-7672. Office Fax: 617-432-7688. E-mail: perrimon@receptor.med.harvard.edu.

PERRIN, EDWARD BURTON, biomedical researcher, public health educator; b. Greensboro, Vt., Sept. 19, 1931; s. J. Newton and Dorothy E. (Willey) P.; m. Carol Anne Hendricks, Aug. 18, 1956; children: Jenifer, Scott. BA, Middlebury Coll., 1953; student in Stats., Edinburgh U., Scotland, 1953—54; MA in Math. Stats., Columbia U., 1956; PhD, Stanford U., 1961. Asst. prof. dept. biostats. U. Pitts., 1959-62; asst. prof. dept. preventive medicine U. Wash., Seattle, 1962-65, assoc. prof., 1965-69, prof., 1969-70, prof., chmn. dept. biostats., 1970-72, prof. dept. health svcs., adj. prof. dept. biostats., 1975-98, chmn. dept., 1983-94, prof. emeritus, 1999—; hon. prof. West China U. of Med. Scis., Szechwan, China, 1988-98; overseas fellow Churchill Coll., Cambridge U., 1991-92; sr. scientist Seattle Vets. Affairs Med. Ctr., 1994—2001. Biometrician VA Co-op Study on Treatment of Esophageal Varices, 1961—73; sr. cons. biostatistics Wash., Alaska regional med. programs, 1967—72; mem. epidemiology & disease control study sect. NIH, 1969—73; clin. prof. dept. cmty. medicine and internat. health Sch. Medicine, Georgetown U., Washington, 1972—75; dep. dir. Nat. Ctr. Health Stats. HEW, 1972—73, dir., 1973—75; rsch. scientist Health Care Study Ctr. Battelle Human Affairs Rsch. Ctr., Seattle, 1975—76, dir., 1976—78, Health & Population Study Ctr. Battelle Human Affairs Rsch. Ctr., 1978—83; chmn. health svcs. rsch. study sect. HEW, 1976—79; chmn. health svcs. R & D field program rev. panel VA, 1988—91; chmn. health svcs. info steering com. State of Wash., 1993—94; mem. nat. adv. coun. Agy. for Health Care Policy & Rsch. Dept. HHS U.S. Govt., 1994—97; mem. com. on nat. stats. NRC, NAS, 1994—2000; chmn. sci. adv. com. Med. Outcomes Trust, 1994—99; mem. report rev. com. NAS, 2005—; bd. dirs. Wash. State Acad. Scis., 2007—. Contbr. articles on biostats., health svcs. and population studies to profl. publs.; mem. editl. bd.: Jour. Family Practice, 1978-90, Pub. Health Nursing, 1992-98. Mem. tech. bd. Milbank Meml. Fund, 1974-76, Health Svcs. and Outcomes Rsch. Methodology, 1999-04. Recipient Outstanding Svc. citation HEW, 1975; Fulbright scholar 1953-54. Fellow AAAS, APHA (Spiegelman Health Stats. award 1970, program devel. bd. 1971, chmn. stats. sect. 1978-80, governing coun. 1983-85, stats. sect. recognition award 1989), Am. Statis. Assn. (mem. adv. com. to divsn. statis. policy 1975-77); mem. Assn. Health Svcs. Rsch. (pres. 1994-95, bd. dirs. 1991-2000), Inst. Medicine of NAS (chmn. membership com. 1984-86, mem. bd. on health care svcs. 1987-96, forum health stats. 1994-95, chmn. com. on clin. evaluation 1990-93), Biometrics Soc. (pres. Western N.Am. Region 1971), U. Wash. Retirement Assn. (bd. dirs. 2006—), Sigma Xi, Phi Beta Kappa. Home: 4900 NE 39th St Seattle WA 98105-5209

PERRIN, ROBERT, writer, consultant; b. Ann Arbor, Mich., Aug. 21, 1925; m. Barbara J. Groom, June 25, 1949; children: Stephen, Jennifer Perrin Hummel. BS, U. Minn., 1945. Reporter United Press Assn., Detroit, 1948-49, Detroit Free Press, 1949-55; adminstrv. asst. U.S. Senate, Washington, 1955-66; asst. dir. U.S. Office Econ. Opportunity, Washington, 1966-68, dep. dir., 1968-70; v.p. Mich. State U., East Lansing, 1970-79; vice-chancellor SUNY System, Albany, 1979-85; exec. v.p. Tchrs. Ins. and Annuity Assn.-Coll. Retirement Equities Fund, NYC, 1987-92; cons. Dept. State, 1993-94. Author: Piggy's Luck and More Tales of Evildoing, 1998, Keeping in Practice, 2001, To Talk of Many Things, 2008; contbr. articles to mags., newspapers. Mem. U.S.-Mex. Commn. on Border Devel., Washington, 1967-68. Lt. USNR, 1943-46, PTO. Fellow Reid Found., 1954; Pulitzer prize nominee Detroit Free Press, 1956. Home: 2435 Emerald Lake Dr East Lansing MI 48823-7256

PERRINE, RICHARD LEROY, environmental engineer, educator; b. Mountain View, Calif., May 15, 1924; s. George Alexander and Marie (Axelson) P.; m. Barbara Jean Gale, Apr. 12, 1945; children: Cynthia Gale, Jeffrey Richard. AB, San Jose State Coll., 1949; MS, Stanford U., 1950, PhD in Chemistry, 1953. Cert. environ. profl., 1987. Research chemist Calif. Research Corp., La Habra, 1953-59; assoc. prof. UCLA, 1959-63, prof. engring. and applied sci., 1963-92, prof. emeritus, 1992—, chmn. environ. sci. and engring., 1971-82; prin. Aspen Environ. Group, 1990-93. V.p. Sage Resources, 1988-91; cons. environ. sci. and engring., energy resources, flow in porous media; mem. Los Angeles County Energy Commn., 1973-81; mem. adv. council South Coast Air Quality Mgmt. Dist., 1977-82; mem. air conservation com. Los Angeles County Lung Assn., 1970-84; mem. adv. com. energy div. Oak Ridge Nat. Lab., 1987-90; mem. policy bd. William D. Ruckelshaus Inst. Environ. and Natural Resources U. Wyo., 1994-2004. Editor in chief The Environ. Profl., 1985-90. Served with AUS, 1943-46. Recipient Outstanding Engr. Merit award in environ. engring. Inst. Advancement Engring., 1975; ACT-SO award in field of chemistry West Coast region NAACP, 1984. Fellow AAAS; mem. Am. Chem. Soc., Soc. Petroleum Engrs., Am. Inst. Chem. Engrs., N.Am. Assn. Environ. Edn., Nat. Assn. Environ. Profls. (cert.), Air and Waste Mgmt. Assn., Am. soc. Civil Engrs., Sierra Club, Wilderness Soc., Audubon Soc., Sigma Xi, Tau Beta Pi, Phi Lambda Upsilon. Home: 22611 Kittridge St West Hills CA 91307-3609 Office: Univ Calif Engring Boelter Hall 6532 F Los Angeles CA 90095-0001 E-mail: rperrine@ucla.edu.

PERRINEAU, HAROLD, actor; b. Bklyn., Aug. 7, 1963; s. Harold Williams; m. Brittany Perrineau; children: Aurora, Wynter Aria. Studied, Shenandoah Conservatory. Actor: (films) Shakedown, 1988, King of NY, 1990, Smoke, 1995, Flirt, 1995, Blood and Wine, 1996, The Edge, 1997, Come To, 1998, Lulu On The Bridge, 1998, The Tempest, 1998, A Day in Black and White, 1998, The Best Man, 1999, Woman on Top, 2000, Overnight Sensation, 2000, Someone Like You, 2001, Prison Song, 2001, On Line, 2002, The Matrix Reloaded, 2003; (TV series) Fame, 1982, Oz, 1997, Lost, 2004—06 (Outstanding Performance by an Ensemble in a Drama Series, Screen Actors Guild award, 2006), 2008—. Office: c/o Agy for the Performing Arts LA 405 S Beverly Dr Beverly Hills CA 90212-4425

PERRON, EDWARD ADRIAN, lawyer; b. Washington, Jan. 19, 1954; s. Edward Joseph and Irene (Lum) P.; m. Julie Corman, June 29, 1980; children: Kelly Elizabeth, Christopher Edward. BA in Economics and East Asian Studies, Harvard U., 1975, JD, 1979. Bar: Calif. 1979, US Dist. Ct. (ctrl. dist.) Calif. 1979, US Ct. Appeals (9th cir.) 1980, DC 1995, NY 1996. Assoc. Lillick & McHose, Los Angeles, 1979-85, ptnr., 1985-90; ptnr., mem. exec. com., chair office mgmt. com. Pillsbury Madison & Sutro, Los Angeles, 1991—2001, vice chmn., ptnr. compensation com., 1996, chmn., ptnr. compensation com., 1997—98; (Pillsbury Madison & Sutro merged with Winthrop, Stimson, Putnam, 2001); ptnr., mem. mng. bd. & ptnr. compensation com. Pillsbury Winthrop LLP, Los Angeles, 2001—06; (Pillsbury Winthrop LLP merged with Shaw Pittman LLP, 2005); ptnr., corp. & securities dept., mem. mng. bd.

& ptnr. compensation com. Pillsbury Winthrop Shaw Pittman LLP, Los Angeles, 2005—06. Co-chmn. ptnr. compensation com. Pillsbury Winthrop LLP, 2004, chmn. ptnr. compensation com., 2007—09. Author: (book) Distributing Foreign Products in the United States, 2000. Mem. exec. adv. bd. Japan Am. Cmty. & Cultural Ctr., LA, 1990—, Asian Pacific-Am. Legal Ctr., LA, 1995—. Mem. Japan Am. Soc. So. Calif. (gen. counsel, dir. 1985-2006, chmn. 2007-09), Japan Bus. Assn. So. Calif., ABA, Calif. Bar Assn., Los Angeles County Bar Assn. Office: Pillsbury Winthrop Shaw Pittman LLP 725 S Figueroa St Los Angeles CA 90017-5524 Office Phone: 213-488-7352. Office Fax: 213-629-1033. Business E-Mail: edward.perron@pillsburylaw.com.

PERRON, WILLIAM FRANCIS, retired protective services official; s. Walter Pearle and Winifred Prescilla Perron; m. Nancy Arlene Chuplis, Aug. 21, 1981; children: Melinda Ann Hill, Stephen Reese, Jason Edmond. MS in Criminal Justice, Anna Maria Coll., Paxton, Ma., 1990. Police officer Town Auburn, Mass., 1971—94; police chief Town Boylston, Mass., 1994—98; ret. chief police Town West Boylston, 1998—2001. Bd. dir. mem. Shelter Homless Veterans, Worcester, Mass., 1994—96. Cpl. USMC, 1967—68, Vietman. Decorated Purple Heart award Presidential Unit Citation. Home: 3-2 Victoria Dr Auburn MA 01501 Office: Town West Boylston Prescott St West Boylston MA 01583 Personal E-mail: wperron@hotmail.com.

PERRONE, NICHOLAS, engineering company executive; b. NYC, Apr. 30, 1930; B. Aero. Engring., Poly. Inst. Bklyn., 1951, MS, 1953, PhD, 1958. Research asst., then assoc. applied mechanics Bklyn. Poly. Inst., 1951-58; asst. prof., then assoc. prof. Pratt Inst., 1958-62; sr. scientist Structural Mechanics br. Office Naval Research, Washington, 1962-67, acting head dept., 1967-68, dir. program, 1968-69, 71-82; pres. CASA Gifts Inc., 1983-85; dep. to pres. Advanced Tech. and Research Inc., 1986-87; pres. Perrone Forensic Cons. Inc., 1987—. Lectr. civil engring. Cath U. Am., 1962-64, adj. prof., 1965-91; spl. research fellow NIH, Georgetown U., 1969-70; participant numerous workshops, confs., symposia; lectr. in field. Contbg. author: Biodynamics, 1980; editor or co-editor numerous monographs; editorial adv. bd.: Advances in Engring. Software, Computers and Structures, Engineering Fracture, Pressure Vessels and Piping; contbr. numerous articles to profl. jours. Fellow AAAS, ASME, Am. Acad. Mechanics; mem. ASCE, AIAA, N.Y. Acad. Sci., Am. Soc. Engring. Edn., Soc. Automotive Engrs., Soc. Mfg. Engrs. Address: 8 Cherry Ln Newtown Square PA 19073-3949 Home Phone: 610-325-7324; Office Phone: 610-325-4447. E-mail: nicholasperrone@comcast.net.

PERRONI, CAROL, artist; b. Boston, July 28, 1952; d. Michael John and Mary Agnes (Collett) P.; m. John Richard Mugford, May 23, 1987; 1 child, Jonathan Perroni. Student, Boston Mus. Sch., 1970-71; BA in Art, Bennington Coll., 1976; student, Skowhegan Sch. Painting and Sculpture, 1978; MFA in Art, Hunter Coll., 1983; MEd, The Coll. Santa Fe, 2003. Studio asst. for artist Isaac Witkin, Bennington, Vt., 1973-74; libr. asst. Simmons Coll. Libr., Boston, 1977-78; studio asst. for artist Mel Bochner, NYC, 1979; bookkeeper Internat. House, NYC, 1979-80; studio asst. for Lee Krasner, East Hampton, NY, 1980; rsch. asst. Art News Mag., NYC, 1981; intern Greenespace Gallery, NYC, 1982-83; tech. asst. Avery Architectural and Fine Arts Libr. Columbia U., NYC, 1981-83; libr., rechr. Kennedy Galleries, Inc., NYC, 1984-86; program specialist, art tchr. Swinging Sixties Sr. Citizen Ctr., Bklyn., 1986-87; with Arts in Edn. Program, RI, 1993-96; tchr. St. Francis Cathedral Sch., Santa Fe, 2004—06; educator, program developer Santa Fe Pub. Libr., 2006—07. One-woman shows include Boston City Hall, 1978, Hunter Coll. Gallery, N.Y.C., 1983, Ten Worlds Gallery, N.Y.C., 1986, Gallery X, New Bedford, Mass., 1993-94, Hera Gallery, Wakefield, R.I., 1995, 98, AS220, Providence, 1996, C.C. of R.I., Lincoln, 1996, Boyden Libr., Foxboro, Mass., 1997; group shows include Salem State Coll., Mass., 1978, Fuller Mus. Art, Brockton, Mass., 1989-90, Danforth Mus. Art, Framingham, Mass., 1989, Attleboro Mus., Mass., 1989, Gallery One, Providence, 1992, Gallery X, New Bedford, Mass., 1992-98, Grove St. Gallery, Worcester, Mass., 1993, Bell St. Chapel, Providence, 1994-95, AS220, Providence, 1994, 98, Hera Gallery, Wakefield, R.I., 1993-99, 2000, 01, 04, St. Andrew's Sch., Barrington, R.I., 1994, McKillop Gallery, Salve Regina U., Newport, R.I., 1995, North River Arts Soc., Marshfield Hills Village, Mass., 1995, Providence Art Club, 1995, The Sarah Doyle Gallery, Brown U., Providence, 1995-96, R.I. Watercolor Soc. Slater Meml. Park, Pawtucket, 1995, Fed. Res. Bank, Boston, 1996, Art Adv./Boston, Quincy, Mass., 1996, Rotch-Jones-Duff Mus., New Bedford, Mass., 1997, Dryden Galleries, Providence, 1997, Renaissance Gallery, Fall River, Mass., 1997, 98, Island Arts Gallery, Newport, 1997, Harwood Art Ctr., Albuquerque, 1998, Branigan Cultural Ctr., Las Cruces, N.Mex., 1999, 2000, Atrium Gallery, Providence, 2000, New Haven Pub. Libr., 2000, Angelo State U., San Angelo, Tex., 2000, Rockport (Tex.) Ctr. Arts, 2001, Lorain C.C., Elyria, Ohio, 2001, Hiestand Galleries, Miami U., Oxford, Ohio, 2001, South Broadway Cultural Ctr., Albuquerque, 2001, N.Mex. State U. Art Gallery, Las Cruces, 2001, 06, Sedona (Ariz.) Arts Ctr., 2002, Cork Gallery, Avery Fisher Hall, Lincoln Ctr., N.Y., 2002, 03, 04, 05, Keystone Bldg., Santa Fe, 2003, Tishman Hall, Coll. of Santa Fe, 2004, Ctr. Contemporary Arts, Santa Fe, 2004, 05, 06, 07, 09, Roswell (N.Mex.) Mus. and Art Ctr., 2004, 05, 08, Stables Gallery, Taos, N.Mex., 2004, 07, Santa Fe Art Inst., 2004, Headwaters Arts and Conf. Ctr., Dubois, Wyo., 2004, U. N.Mex., Los Alamos, 2005, Peninsula Fine Arts Ctr., Newport News, Va., 2005, Cuyahoga Valley Art Ctr., Cuyahoga Falls, Ohio, 2006, Claremont Forum Gallery, Calif., 2006, Arts Alliance Gallery, Albuquerque, 2006, Art-at-the-Cathedral, Lexington, Ky., 2006, Ctr. for Arts, Evergreen, Colo., 2007, Art Dialogue Gallery, Buffalo, 2007, Internat. Women's Peace Conf., Dallas, 2007, Albuquerque Mus., 2007, Cultural Arts Ctr., Glen Allen, Va., 2008, N.Mex. Expo, Hispanic Arts Bldg., Albuquerque, 2009, Butler Inst. Am. Art, Yoonestown, Ohio, 2009, Western Colo. Ctr. The Arts, Grand Junction, Colo., 2009, Ouray Cmty. Ctr., Colo., 2009; represented in permanent collection at R.I. Hosp. Art Collection and pvt. collections. Bd. dirs. Hera Ednl. Found., 1994—2001. Grantee Artists Space, 1986, Flintridge Found., 1993, fellow Vt. Studio Ctr., Johnson, 1990, Dorland Mountain Arts Colony, 1993, Anderson Ranch Arts Ctr., Snowmass Village, Colo., 2004. Mem.: SOHO 20 Gallery (nat. affiliate mem.), Am. Acad. Women Artists (assoc.). Home and Office: 2089 Plaza Thomas Santa Fe NM 87505-5438 Personal E-mail: carolpi56@msn.com.

PERRONS, ROBERT K., engineer, researcher; b. Dryden, Canada, May 27, 1972; s. Robert T. G. Perrons and Barbara M. Kirby; m. Shannon M. Woodward, Aug. 13, 2005; children: Carson W., Aiden W. B in Mech. Engring. summa cum laude, McMaster U., Hamilton, Can., 1995; MS in Tech. and Policy, MIT, Cambridge, Mass., 1997; PhD in Engring., U. Cambridge, Eng., 2004. Cert. chartered European engr., 2001, chartered engr., UK Instn. Mech. Engrs., 2001. Prodn. engr. Shell Internat. Exploration and Prodn., 1997—2001, exec. coord. Rijswijk, Netherlands, 2004—06, smart fields cons. New Orleans, 2006—; indsl. rsch. fellow U. Cambridge, 2001—04. Affiliated rschr. Ctr. for Strategy and Performance, U. Cambridge, 2005—. Contbr. articles to numerous profl. and acad. jours. Recipient Fitzwilliam Coll. Grad. award, 2002—03, Grad. Rsch. award, Natural Sci. and Engring. Rsch. Coun. Can., 2002—04; Can. scholar, 1991—95, Dr. Harry Lyman Hooker scholarship, McMaster, 1991—95, Dalley scholarship, 1993, Yates scholarship, 1994, Gates Cambridge scholar, U. Cambridge, 2001—04. Mem.: Soc. Petroleum Engrs. Office: Shell Internat Exploration & Production PO Box 51510 New Orleans LA 70151-1510 Business E-Mail: robert.perrons@shell.com.

PERROT, PAUL NORMAN, museum director; b. Paris, July 28, 1926; came to US, 1946, naturalized, 1954; s. Paul and K. Norman (Derr) P.; m. Joanne Stovall, Oct. 23, 1954; children— Paul Latham, Chantal Marie Claire, Jeannine, Robert. Student, Ecole du Louvre, 1945-46, N.Y. U. Inst. Fine Arts, 1946-52. Asst. The Cloisters, Met. Mus. Art, 1948-52; asst. to dir. Corning (NY) Mus. Glass, 1952-54, asst. dir. mus., 1954-60, dir., 1960-72; editor Jour. Glass Studies, 1959-72; asst. sec. for mus. programs Smithsonian Instn., Washington, 1972-84; dir. Va. Mus. Fine Arts, 1984-91, Santa Barbara Mus. Art, 1991-94, mus. cons., 1995—. Lectr. glass history, aesthetics, museology; past v.p. Internat. Coun. Mus. Found.; past pres. N.E. Conf. Mus.; past pres. Internat. Centre for Study of Preservation and Restoration of Cultural Property, Rome, mem. coun., 1974-88. Author: Three Great Centuries of Venetian Glass, 1958, also numerous articles on various hist. and archael. subjects. Former trustee Winterthur Mus.; former trustee, treas. Mus. Computer Network; former mem. Internat. Cons. Com. for the Preservation of Moenjodaro; former chmn. adv. com. World Monuments Fund; former chmn. vis. com. Getty Conservation Inst. Mem. Am. Assn. Mus. (past v.p., coun. 1967-78, named to Centennial Honor Roll, 2006), NY State Assn. Mus. (past pres.), Internat. Assn. History Glass (past v.p.) Corning Friends of Library (past pres.), So. Tier Library System (past pres.). E-mail: paulnperrot@comcast.net.

PERROTTA, ANTONIO, trust company executive; arrived in U.S., 1993; BS in Engring., Mil. Inst. Engring., Rio de Janeiro, 1981; BS in Econs., Rio de Janeiro State U., 1982; MS in Computer Sci., Mil. Inst. Engring., Rio de Janeiro, 1985. Sr. tech. mgr. Bamerindus Bank, Rio de Janeiro, Rio de Janeiro, 1981—93; sr. mgr. Price Waterhouse, NYC, 1993—95; v.p. J.P.Morgan, NYC, 1995—2003; chief tech. officer Bessemer Trust, Woodbridge, NJ, 2003—.

PERRUCCI, ROBERT, sociologist, educator; b. NYC, Nov. 11, 1931; s. Dominic and Inez (Mucci) P.; m. Carolyn Land Cummings, Aug. 4, 1965; children: Mark Robert, Celeste Ann, Christopher Robert, Alissa Cummings, Martin Cummings. BS, SUNY, Cortland, 1958; MS, Purdue U., West Lafayette, Ind., 1959, PhD, 1962. Asst. prof. sociology Purdue U., West Lafayette, Ind., 1962-65, asso. prof., 1965-67, prof., 1967—, head dept., 1978-87. Vis. Simon prof. U. Manchester (Eng.), 1968-69; Bd. dirs. Ind. Center on Law and Poverty, 1973-76 Author: Sociology, 1983, Circle of Madness, 1974, Divided Loyalties, 1980, The Triple Revolution, 1971, Profession Without Community, 1968, The Engineers and the Social System, 1968, Mental Patients and Social Networks, 1982, Plant Closings: International Context and Local Consequences, 1988, Networks of Power, 1989, Japanese Auto Transplants in the Heartland: Corporatism and Community, 1994, The New Class Society, 1999, Science Under Siege?, 2000, The New Class Society: Goodbye American Dream, 2008, The Transformation of Work in the New Economy,2007, America at Risk: The Crisis of Hope, Trust and Caring, 2009; editor: The American Sociologist, 1982—84, Social Problems, 1993-96, Contemporary Sociology, 2000-2005; contbr. articles to profl. jours. Served with USMC, 1951-53. Recipient grants, NSF, 1966—68, 1976—78, NIMH, 1969—72, Sloan Found., 2002—05; fellow, Social Sci. Rsch. Coun., 1962. Mem. Am. Sociol. Assn., Soc. Study Social Problems (dir. 1980-83, v.p. 1996-97, pres. 1999-2000), N. Central Sociol. Assn. (pres. 1973-74) Home: 305 Leslie Ave West Lafayette IN 47906-2411 Office: Dept Sociology Purdue U West Lafayette IN 47907

PERRY, ALAN EUGENE, literature and language educator, department chairman; b. Athens, Tenn., June 8, 1956; s. Robert Eugene and Dorothy Coleman Perry. BS in English Edn. and Bus. Edn., Tenn. Wesleyan Coll., Athens, 1978; MA in English, East Tenn. State U., Johnson City, 1979; EdS in Ednl. Leadership, Berry Coll., Rome, Ga., 1999; EdD in Sch. Improvement, State U. W. Ga., Carrollton, 2005. English tchr. Chattooga HS, Summerville, Ga., 1979—. Named Star Tchr. Chattooga County, Rotary Club, 1982, 1990, 1996, 2006, 2007, Chattooga County Tchr. Yr., Optmist Club, 1990. Mem.: Nat. Coun. Tchrs. English (secondary steering com., standing com. on affiliates), Ga. Coun. Tchrs. English (conf. dir. 1998—, pres. 2000—06, Lifetime Achievement award 2007). Baptist. Avocations: photography, comic book collecting, painting, drawing. Home: 944 Hwy 114 Summerville GA 30747 Office: Chattooga HS 989 Hwy 114 Summerville GA 30747

PERRY, ANNE MARIE LITCHFIELD, educator; b. LaJunta, Colo., June 20, 1943; d. Robert Silas and Anne (Kennedy) Hovey, Robert Latta Litchfield (Stepfather); m. Franklin Haile Perry, Dec. 21, 1968; children: Kristina Marie, Tad Kennedy. BE, Drake U., 1966; MA, U. Tex., 1969; PhD, Tex. A&M U., 1977. Grade sch. tchr., San Antonio, 1966—67, Austin, 1967—68; rsch. assoc. R&D Ctr., U. Tex., Austin, 1968; grad. asst., instr. Tex. A&M U., 1969—70; kindergarten tchr., 1970—72; instr. U. St. Thomas, 1973—74; spl. edn. tchr., supr. Cypress, Cypress-Fairbanks Ind. Sch. Dist., Houston, 1974—77, supr. gifted/.talented, bilingual, English lang. devel. programs, 1977—80; mem. adj. grad. faculty U. Houston, 1979—80; lower sch. dir. curriculum and ednl. resources Kinkaid Sch., Houston, 1980—85, dir. young writers workshops, 1985—; tchr., chair lang. arts dept. Klein Intermediate Sch. Dist., Tex., 1986—2001. Vis. asst. prof. Tex. A&M U., 1988—89; cons. in field. Author (photographer): Riders Ready, 1985; author: Website Design and Maintenance, 2001—, Teacher Guide and Student Packet for Frindle, 2002, Just Like Always, 2005; editor: Travels in Mexico and California, 1988, Bluebonnet Books-Activities for 1996, Lonestar Books-Activities for 1993-1994 and 1994-1995. Named Tchr. of Yr., Hancock Elem. Sch., 1975. Mem.: NEA, Tex. Ret. Tchrs. Assn., Brazos Bluebonnet Quilt Guild, Tex. State Tchrs. Assn., Run for the Wall. Methodist.

PERRY, BLAIR LANE, lawyer; b. Oct. 2, 1929; s. Elwyn Lionel and Ruth Hubbard (Kelley) Perry; m. Margaret James, July 4, 1959; children: Jennifer E., Andrew B.; m. Theodora Pearson, Mar. 29, 1998. BA, Williams Coll., 1951; LLB, Harvard U., 1957. Bar: Mass. 1957, U.S. Dist. Ct. Mass. 1958, U.S. Dist. Ct. (no. dist.) Tex 1978, U.S. Ct. Appeals (1st cir.) 1958, U.S. Supreme Ct. 1971. Assoc. Hale and Dorr, Boston, 1957—63, jr. ptnr., 1963—68, sr. ptnr., 1968—90; of counsel Fish & Richardson, Boston, 1991—2002. Contbr. articles to profl. jours. With USMC, 1951—53. Mem.: ABA, Boston Patent Law Assn., Mass. Bar Assn. Home and Office: 193 Dromoland Ln Barnstable MA 02630-1804 Office Phone: 508-375-0653.

PERRY, CATHERINE, language educator; d. Whitall Nicholson and Barbara Perry; m. Gregory Vandenbroucke, May 2, 1999; m. Rachid Haddaoui, Dec. 30, 1971 (div. June 1983); children: Ahmed Haddaoui, Souleyma Haddaoui. PhD, Princeton U., NJ, 1995. Tchg. asst. Ind. U., Bloomington, 1987—89, Princeton U., 1990—91; instr. U. Notre Dame, Ind., 1993—95, asst. prof., 1995—2002, assoc. prof. French & francophone studies, 2002—. Fellow Nanovic Inst. European Studies, Notre Dame, 1994—; pres. Conseil Internat. d'Etudes Francophones, 2003—05; editor-in-chief Scholarly Jour. Nouvelles Etudes Francophones, 2004—; fellow Joan B. Kroc Inst. Internat. Peace Studies, Notre Dame, 2005—. Contbr. articles to profl. jours. Recipient Kaneb Tchg. award, U. Notre Dame, 2003, Disting. Woman award, 2004, Chevalier award, French Nat. Order Palmes Acad.; Summer Rsch. grant, Nat. Endowment Humanities, 1997. Mem.: Multiple Profl. Assn., Multiple Hon. Socs. Office: Univ Notre Dame 343 O'Shaughnessy Hall Notre Dame IN 46556 Business E-Mail: cperry@nd.edu.

PERRY, CHARLES OWEN, sculptor; b. Helena, Mont., Oct. 18, 1929; s. Owen Hindmarch and Margaret Carroll (Bache) P.; m. Sheila Alicia Henry, June 22, 1962; children— Paul, Carlo, Daniela, Patrick, Marco. Student, Columbia U., 1953; M.Arch., Yale U., 1958. Architect Skidmore Owings & Merrill, San Francisco, 1958-64, Prix de Rome Architecture, 1964-66. Sculptor-in-residence Dartmouth Coll., 1973. One-man shows include Hansen Gallery, San Francisco, 1964, Waddell Gallery, N.Y.C., 1967, 70, Dartmouth Coll., 1973, Arts Club, Chgo., 1973, Auguste st-Gaudens Mus., N.H.; exhibited in group shows at Whitney Mus., 1964, 66, Spoleto Festival, 1967, Venice Biennale, 1970, Quadrienalle di Arte de Roma, 1977, Katonah Gallery, N.Y.; represented in permanent collections at Mus. Modern Art, N.Y.C., Art Inst. Chgo., San Francisco Mus. Art, U. Ind. Mus. Art, Dartmouth Coll., U. Mich., Nat. Air and Space Mus., IBM, Charlotte, N.C., Hyatt Regency, San Francisco, Fed. Res. Bank, Mpls., Barnett Plaza, Tampa, Lincoln Ctr., Dallas, Shell Oil Bldg., Melbourne, Australia, GE Hdqrs., Fairfield, Conn., Bushnell Park, Hartford, Conn., Crystal City, Arlington, Va., Zeimu U., Tokyo, Kokubu Civic Ctr., Japan, Shell Plz. Singapore, Waterfront Pk., Louisville; patentee in furniture design field. Served with U.S. Army, 1951-53. Decorated Bronze star, Am. Iron & Steel Inst Citation for Excellende in Fine Art, 1969, 1971, Prix de Rome in Arch., 1964, Best of Show Nat. Acad. Design award sculpture, 1987, Product Design award, Inst. Bus. Designers, 1992, Internat Design Expo., Canada, 1990, 1998. Fellow Am. Acad. Rome, Nat. Acad. Design; mem. Century Assn. (N.Y.C.), Internat. Sculpture Ctr. Roman Catholic. Studio: 3 Raymond St Norwalk CT 06854-3107 Office Phone: 203-820-1011. Personal E-mail: coperry@aol.com. Business E-Mail: charles@charlesperry.com.

PERRY, CHARLES RICHARD, history professor; b. Atlanta, Sept. 29, 1946; s. James Hilliard and Mildred Perry; m. Dana Brumfield, July 6, 1985; children from previous marriage: Samuel M., Melissa P. Pluchos. BA, Davidson Coll., NC, 1968; MA, Harvard U., PhD, 1976. William R. Kenan, jr. prof. history U. of the South, Sewanee, Tenn., 2004—. Pres. Southern Conf. Brit. Studies, 2001—03. Author: (book) The Victorian Post Office. Fellow: Royal Hist. Soc.; mem.: Am. Hist. Assn. Office: Univ of the South University Ave Sewanee TN 37383 E-mail: cperry@sewanee.edu.

PERRY, DALE LYNN, chemist; b. Greenville, Tex., May 12, 1947; s. Francis Leon and Violet (Inabinette) P. BS, Midwestern U., 1969; MS, Lamar U., 1972; PhD, U. Houston, 1974. NSF fellow dept. chemistry Rice U., Houston, 1976-77; Miller Research fellow dept. chemistry U. Calif.-Berkeley, 1977-79; prin. investigator solid state chemistry and spectroscopy Lawrence Berkeley Lab. U. Calif., 1979—, sr. scientist, 1987—. Lectr. Ana G. Mendez Ednl. Found., 1988; rsch. mem. G.T. Seaborg Inst. for Transactinium Sci. Author, editor: Instrumental Surface Analysis of Geologic Materials, 1990, Applications of Analytical Techniques to the Characterization of Materials, 1992, Applications of Synchrotron Radiation Techniques to Materials Science, 1993, II, 1995, III, 1996, IV, 1998, V, 2001, VI, 2002, Handbook of Inorganic Compounds, 1995, Materials Synthesis and Characterization, 1997; contbr. articles to profl. jours. Named Outstanding Mentor for Undergrad. Rsch., US Dept. Energy, 2002. Fellow AAAS, Royal Soc. Chemistry (London); mem. Am. Chem. Soc. (chmn. materials chemistry and engring. subdivsn., indsl. and engring. chemistry divsn., 1992-96), Soc. Applied Spectroscopy, Coblentz Soc., Materials Rsch. Soc. (corp. participation com. 1991-96), Sigma Xi (nat. rsch. award 1974). Achievements include research in chem. and materials. Office: U Calif Lawrence Berkeley Nat Lab Mail Stop 70A 1150 Berkeley CA 94720-0001 Personal E-mail: dlperry@comcast.net.

PERRY, DEAN M., biologist; b. Springfield, Mass., Oct. 6, 1951; s. Roger H. and Irene M. Perry; m. Cheryl J. Perry, June 7, 1980; children: Matthew E., Sarah M. MS, Southern Conn. State U., New Haven, 1980. Rsch. fishery biologist Nat. Marine Fisheries Svc., Milford, Conn., 1976—. Contbr. articles to profl. jours. Mem.: NY Micros. Soc. Achievements include research in spawning marine fish in captivity & out of season. Avocations: fishing, hiking. Office: Nat Marine Fisheries Svc 212 Rogers Ave Milford CT 06460 Business E-Mail: dean.perry@noaa.gov.

PERRY, DOUGLAS, opera singer; B.M., Wittenberg U.; MA, Ball State U. Made debut as Don Basilio in Marriage of Figaro, with N.Y.C. Opera; appeared as King Kaspar in: Amahl and the Night Visitors; appeared as Timothy in: Help! Help! The Globolinks; appeared as Guillot in: Manon; Dancing Master and Brighella in: Ariadne auf Naxos; Met. Opera debut as scientist/first mate in: The Voyage (Philip Glass); European debut with Netherlands Opera as Mahatma Gandhi in Satyagraha (Philip Glass); appeared as analyst in A Quiet Place (Bernstein), La Scala and Vienna Stadtsoper, as Sailor 1, Scientist 3, Traveler 2 world premier Corvo Bronco, Teatro Camô, Lisbon, Portugal, Teatro Real, Madrid; featured soloist on tours and recs. with Gregg Smith Singers and Camerata Singers; performed with Sante Fe Opera, also performed with Ft. Worth Opera, Chatauqua Opera, N.Y.C. Opera, Opera Co. of Boston, Houston Grand Opera, Balt. Opera., Miami Opera, Chgo. Lyric Opera, Seattle Opera, San Francisco Opera, Opera Co. Phila.; recs. include Satyagraha, Songs from Liquid Days, A Quiet Place, Mother of Us All. Address: 170 W End Ave New York NY 10023-5401

PERRY, E. LYNN, lawyer; d. Eldon G. Perry and Doris E. Noonan BA, U. Ariz., 1970; JD, Loyola U., 1976. Bar: Ill. 1977, US Dist. Ct. (no. dist.) Ill. 1977, NY 1980, US Dist. Ct. (so. and ea. dists.) NY, Calif. 1980, US Dist. Ct. (no., ea. and cen. dists.) Calif., US Ct. Appeals (9th cir.), US Supreme Ct. Flight attendant Pan American World Airways, NYC and L.A., 1971-75; asst. state's atty. Cook County State's Atty., Chgo., 1977-79; assoc. Kass, Goodkind, Wechsler & Labaton, NYC, 1980-81; assoc. counsel MasterCard Internat., Inc., NYC, 1981-84; assoc. Townsend and Townsend and Crew, San Francisco, 1984-89, ptnr., 1989—2002, Thelen Reid & Priest, 2002—06, Perry IP Group, San Francisco, 2006—. Adj. prof. U. Calif. Hastings Coll. Law, 2005—07; spkr. in field. Scholar U. Ariz., Tucson, 1970, Loyola U., L.A., 1976. Mem. ABA (Governing Com. Forum Franchising 1991-93), Internat. Trademark Assn. (editl. bd. Trademark Reporter 1985—, profl. writing competition judge 1988-2005, panel of neutrals 2003—), Calif. State Bar (trademarks chair 1990-91, Exec. Com. Intellectual Property Sect. 1991-94), San Francisco Intellectual Property Law Assn. (program chair 1987-88). Avocations: tennis, yoga, skiing. Office: Perry IP Group Ste 3900 4 Embarcadero Ctr San Francisco CA 94111

PERRY, EDWIN CHARLES, lawyer; b. Lincoln, Nebr., Sept. 29, 1931; s. Arthur Edwin and Charlotte C. (Peterson) P.; m. Joan Mary Hanson, June 5, 1954; children: Mary Mills, Judy Phipps, James Perry, Greg Perry, Jack Perry, Priscilla Heffel Finger. BS, U. Nebr., 1953, JD, 1955. Bar: Nebr. 1955; U.S. Dist. Ct. Nebr., 1955; U.S. Ct. Appeals Nebr., 1968. Of counsel Perry, Guthery, Haase & Gessford, P.C., Lincoln, 1957—. Chmn. Lincoln Lancaster County Planning Com., Madonna Rehab. Hosp. Fellow Am. Bar Found., Nebr. Bar Found.; mem. Nebr. State Bar Assn. (chair ho. dels. 1987-88, pres. 1991-92), Nebr. Coun. Sch. Attys. (pres. 1978-79), Lincoln Bar Assn. (pres. 1982-83). Republican. Roman Catholic. Office: Perry Guthery Haase & Gessford PC 223 S 13th St Ste 1400 Lincoln NE 68508-2005 Office Phone: 402-476-9200.

PERRY, EVELYN REIS, communications company executive; b. NYC, Mar. 09; d. Lou L. and Bertl (Wolf) Reis; m. Charles G. Perry III, Jan. 7, 1968; children: Charles G. IV, David Reis. Student, Am. Acad. Dramatic Arts, 1958-59, U. N.Mex., 1963-64; BA, U. Wis., 1963. Lic. real estate broker, N.C. Vol. ETV project Peace Corps, Colombia, 1963-65; program officer-radio/tv Peace Corps, Washington, 1965-68; dir. Vols. in Svc. to Am. (VISTA), Raleigh, N.C., 1977-80; exec. dir. CETA Program for Displaced Homemakers, Raleigh, 1980-81; cons. exec. dir. to Recycle Raleigh for Food and Fuel, Theater in the Park, 1981-83; pres., CEO Carolina Sound Comms., MUZAK, Charleston, SC, 1984—, Ga. Sound Comms., 2003—; pub. rels. account exec. various cos. Washington, Syracuse, N.Y., 1969-71; cons. pub. rels. and orgn. Olympic Organizing Com., Mexico City, 1968; cons. pub. rels., fundraising, arts mgmt. pub. speaking Ill., Pa., N.C., 1971-77; orgnl. and pub. speaking cons. Perry & Assocs., Raleigh, 1980—. Spkr. Nat. Sys. Contrs. Assn., 1993, 95, 97; founder Nat. Assn. Women Bus. Owners, Charleston, S.C., 1998; bd. dirs. Charleston Area Br. Banking and Trust, 1999—; bd. dirs. Nat. Fedn. Ind. Bus., 1986-, mem. adv. bd., 1999-. Contbr. articles to Sound and Comm. mag. Mem. adv. bd. Gov.'s Office Citizen Affairs, Raleigh, 1981-85; mem. Involvement Coun. of Wake County, N.C., Raleigh, 1981-84; mem. Adv. Coun. to Vols. in Svc. to Am., Raleigh, 1980-84; mem. Pres.'s adv. bd. Peace Corps, Washington, 1980-82; v.p., bd. dirs. Voluntary Action Ctr., Raleigh, 1980-84, bd. dirs., Charleston, 1988-94; sec. bd. dirs. Temple Kahil Kadosh Beth Elohim, 1987-89, sec. fin., 1989-90, v.p. programming, 1990-93, v.p. adminstrn. 1993-95, v.p. sisterhood, 2001—; bd. dirs. Chopstik Theater, Charleston, 1989-90, SC Women's Bus. Ctr., 2003-; del., chmn. S.C. Delegation to White House Conf. Small Bus., 1995; S.C. del. Congl. Sml. Bus. Summit, 1998; mem small bus. regulatory rev. com. SC State Senate, 2004—; mem. Think Tank Entrepreneurship for Women, Columbia Coll., SC; v.p., SC Bus. Initiative, 2009-. Named Bus. Women Adv. of Yr., SBA, 2002. Mem. N.C. Coun. of Women's Orgns. (pres., v.p. 1982-84), Charleston Hotel and Motel Assn., N.C. Assn. Vol. Adminstrs. (bd. dirs. 1980-84), S.C. Restaurant Assn., Nat. Assn. Women Bus. Owners (founder lowcountry chpt. 1998, pres. 1998—2001), Internat. Planned Music Assn. (chmn. conf. 1993), bd. Branch Banking & Trust, 1999—, Nat. Fedn. Ind. Bus. (mem. adv. bd. 1987—, chmn. leadership coun. 1994-2000, del. Congl. Summit, Washington, pres. 2003, Small Bus. Champion award 2005), Internat. Platform Assn., Theaterworks (bd. dirs. 1994-96), Internat. Planned Music Assn. (bd. dirs. 2000—, v.p. 2001-2003, pres. 2003-05). Office: Carolina Sound Comm Inc 7630 Southrail Rd Bldg B North Charleston SC 29420 Business E-Mail: evelyn@carolina-sound.com.

PERRY, GEORGE, dean, neuroscientist, educator; s. George Richard and Mary Arlene (George) P.; m. Paloma Aguilar, May 21, 1983; children: Anne, Elizabeth. AA in Liberal Arts, Allan Hancock Coll., Santa Maria, Calif., 1973; BA in Zoology with high honors, U. Calif., Santa Barbara, 1974; PhD in Marine Biology, U. Calif., San Diego, 1979; PhD (hon.), Arturo Prat, Iquique, Chile, 2007. Postdoctoral fellow Baylor Coll. Medicine, Houston, 1979-82; from asst. prof. to prof. pathology Case Western Res. U., Cleve., 1982-94, prof., 1994—2005, interim chair dept., 2001—05; affiliated prof. chemistry and biochemistry U. Alaska, Fairbanks, 2001—; dean Coll. of Sciences U. Tex., San Antonio, 2006—. Tchg. asst. U. Calif., San Diego, 1977, Stanford U., 1978—79; memory task force on Alzheimer's disease Ohio Gov., 1987, 90; mem. sci. adv. bd. Familial Alzheimer's Disease Rsch. Found., 1988—; mem., chair neurology scis. study sect. NIH, Bethesda, Md., 1989—95; cons. Nymox, Inc., Panacea Pharms., Inc., Prion Devel. Labs., Voyager, Takada Pharms., Neurotez Labs., Alzheimer Rsch. Disease and Regeneration Forum; mem. Faculty of 1000 Biology, Neurobiology Sect., 2004—; spkr. in field; mem. numerous rev. bds. nationally/internationally. Author: The Neuronal Cytoskeleton, 1992, numerous publs. in field; co-author: Frontiers in Biosciences, 2002, Neurosignals, 2002, Brain Pathology, 2004, Microscopy Rsch. and Technique, 2005, Internat. Jour. Exptl. Pathology, 2005; assoc. editor: Am. Jour. Pathology, 1994-2000, Jour. Biomedicine and Biotechnology, 2004—; sr. assoc. editor: Microscopy Rsch. and Technique, 2002—; mem. editl. bd. Am. Jour. Pathology, 1992—, Alzheimer Disease and Associated Disorders, 1994—, Alzheimer's Disease Rev., 1995-98, Jour. Alzheimer's Disease, 1997—, Jour. Exptl. Neurol., 1997-99, Molecular Chem. Neuropathology, 1997-99, Jour. Neural Transmission, 1998-2003, Investigational Drugs Jour., 1998—, Brain Pathology, 1999—, Jour. Molecular Neurosci., 1999-2001, Antioxidant and Redox Signaling, 2000—, Research Signpost, 2000, Lab. Investigation, 2000—06, Brain Rsch., 2002—, Current Medicinal Chemistry, 2002—, Neurobiology of Lipids, 2003—, Jour. Biomed. Biotech., 2002—, Pathology, 2003—, Pharm. Devel. Regime, 2003—, Med. Chemistry Rev.-Online, 2003-05, Current Alzheimer Rsch., 2003—, NeuroSignals, 2003—, Disease Markers, 2003—, Neurobiology Disease, 2004—, Lett Drug Design Discovery, 2004—; reviewer: Expert Review of Neurotherapeutics, 2004—, Mini-Reviews in Medicinal Chemistry, 2005—, Future Neurology, 2005—, Jour. Biological Chemistry, 2006—, Developmental Microbiology and Molecular Biology, 2006—, CNS Agents in Medicinal Chemistry, 2006—, Jour. Clin. Pathology, 2007—, Molecular Neurodegeneration, 2007—, Open Medicinal Chemistry Jour., 2007—, Acta Neuropathol., Alan Liss Publ. Co., Am. Jour. Pathol., Ann Neurol, others; contbr. articles to Exptl. Cell Rsch., Jour Cell Biology, Devel. Biology, Brain Rsch., Am. Jour. Pathology, Jour. Neurosci., European Jour. Cell Biology, Nature, Annals Neurology, Lancet, Acta Neuropathology, Jour. Neurochemistry, Neurosci. Letters, Neuroreport, Med. Hypotheses, Nature Medicine, Neurodegeneration, Sci., others. Pres. Serra Club, 1995-97. Tng. corps. USAR, 1972—74, U. Calif. Santa Barbara. Recipient Bausch and Lomb medal, 1971, Rsch. Career Devel. award, NIH, 1988—93, Career Devel. award, 1988, Temple award, Alzheimer's Assn., 1999, Disting. Am. Portuguese Ancestry award, Portuguese-Am. Hist. Found., Inc., 2001, Mensch award, Alzheimer Rsch. Forum, 2003, Cmty. Svc. award, Cleve. Area Chpt. Alzheimer's Assn., 2004, Zenith award, Alzheimer Assn., 2007; grantee, NIH, 1985—, Am. Health Assistance Found., 1988—90, 1997—99, Alzheimer's Assn., 1989—90, 1998—2002, 2004—, United Mitochondrial Disease Fund, 2000—02; fellow, Kennecott Copper, 1974—75, Muscular Dystrophy Assn., 1980—82, Philip Morris, USA, 2003—06. Fellow AAAS, Iberoam. Molecular Biology Orgn. ISI Highly Cited Com. Neurosci.; mem. AAUP (case chapter exec. com. 1996—2006, membership chair 1996-98, v.p. 1998-99, pres. 1999—2006), Am. Soc. Cell Biology, Electron Microscopy Soc. N.E. Ohio (treas. 1986-88, trustee 1988-90, pres. 1990-91), Soc. Neurosci., Am. Assn. Neuropathologists (awards com. 1992-93, 95-2002, chmn. 2001-02, internat. congress neuropathology concilator 1995-2000, sec.-treas. 2003-08, pres. elect. 2007-08, pres. 2008-), Am. Soc. Investigative Pathology (program com. 1998-2001), Am. Soc. Neurochemistry, U.S. and Can. Acad. of Pathology, Hispanic Med. Assn. (com. on status of Portuguese in medicine and sci.), Soc. for Neurosci., Sigma Xi (pres. chpt. 2004-06), Iberoamerican Molecular Biology Orgn., Am. Aging Assn.(Harman Research award, 2008) Democrat. Roman Catholic. Avocation: genealogy. Office: U Tex San Antonio Coll Scis One UTSA Circle San Antonio TX 78249-0661 Office Phone: 210-458-4450. Business E-Mail: george.perry@utsa.edu.

PERRY, GEORGE WILLIAMSON, lawyer; b. Cleve., Dec. 4, 1926; s. George William and Melda Patricia (Arther-Holt) P. BA in Econs., Yale U., 1949; JD, U. Va., 1953. Bar: Ohio 1953, DC 1958, US Supreme Ct. 1958, US Ct. Appeals (DC cir.) 1959. Atty. US Dept. Justice, Washington, 1954—56; assoc. Roberts and McInnis, Washington, 1957-59; atty. assoc. counsel Com. on Interstate Fgn. Commerce, US Ho. Reps., Washington, 1960—65; atty., advisor ICC, Washington, 1965-68; assoc. dir. devel. Yale U., New Haven, 1968-70; trust officer The No. Trust Co., Chgo., 1970-71; dir. tax rsch. Pan Am. World Airways, NYC, 1973-75; hearing officer Indsl. Commn. Ohio, Cleve., 1978-81; sole practice Cleve., 1981—. With US Army, 1945-46. Mem. Soc. Cin. in State of Conn., Ancient and Hon. Artillery Co. (mem. Boston-hereditary), Phi Delta Phi, Chi Delta Theta. Home: 1801 E 12th St #1522 Cleveland OH 44114-3541 Personal E-mail: gperryxyz@yahoo.com.

PERRY, GEORGE WILSON, oil and gas company executive; b. Pampa, Tex., July 18, 1929; s. Frank M. and Ruth (Ingersoll) P.; m. Patricia Carberry Bowen, 1950 (dec. 2009); children: Sally Jett Perry Pemrick, Susan Jeanne Perry Bynder, Virginia Anne Perry Haynie, Tobe Jackson Perry. BS in Petroleum Engring., U. Tulsa, 1952. Registered profl. engr., Tex. Engr. Stanolind Oil & Gas Co., Oklahoma City, 1952—53, Parker Drilling Co., Tulsa, 1953—54, Holm Drilling Co., Tulsa, 1954—55; drilling engr. Mobil Oil, Victoria, Tex., 1955—61, engr. Lake Charles, La., 1955—61, Paris, 1961—68; ops. mgr. Anaco, Venezuela, 1968—72, NYC, 1972—73, Tehran, Iran, 1973—74, Stavanger, Norway, 1974—78, New Orleans, 1978—79; exec. v.p. Loffland Bros. Co., Tulsa, 1979—89; pres., CEO Gas Well Properties, Inc., Dallas, 1989—. Mem. Delta Tau Delta. Avocation: astronomy.

PERRY, GREGORY J., museum director; BA, U. Ill., Urbana-Champaign, 1982; JD, DePaul U., 1990; MA in modern art hist., theory and criticism, Sch. of Art Inst. Chgo., 2003. Assoc. Robert W. Smith & Assocs., Ill., Hillside, and Fein and Seeskin, Ill.; assoc. dir. devel. spl. projects Art Inst. Chgo.; assoc. dir. Jane Voorhees Zimmerli Art Mus., Rutgers U., NJ, 2000—02, acting dir., 2002, dir., 2003—07. Office: Allentown Mus Art 31 N 5th Ave Allentown PA 18101

PERRY, HELEN, medical/surgical nurse, secondary school educator; b. Birmingham, Ala., Mar. 4, 1927; d. Van Mary Ellenol (Thornton) Curry; m. Charlie Pitts, May 1960 (div.); 1 child, Charlenia Pitts; m. George Perry (dec. 1989); children: Hattie Mae(dec.), George Jr., Bishop, Jose Sr. Student, LaSalle Extension U., Chgo., 1968; MA in Nat. Security Criminal Justice, Georgetown U., 1979; Doctorate/Mayanuis Mosaic Soc., Duke Univ., San Antonio, 1979; student in Nursing, Syracuse U., 1983; BS in Nursing, Suracuse U., 1989. Cert. paramedic, of completion Ptnrs. in Health Sheperd Ctr. Am. South Side, 2006; LPN, lic. practical nurse, paramedic, Fla. Profl. Acad. Tchr. Wenona HS City Bd. Edn., Birmingham, 1977—2005, supply tchr., 2005—. Notary pub., Ala., 1975—; home health nurse U. Ala. Birmingham Hosp., 1988—; math. and reading tutor Princeton Elem. Sch., 2004; founding mem. Review Bd., 2009. Composer: (songs) Twas the Hour of Midnight, 1950. Trustee Nat. Crime Watch, 1989; mem. adv. bd. Am. Security Coun., Va., Washington, 1969—91; mem. Coalition for Desert Storm; others; vol. ARC, Birmingham, 1970—; mem. crime watch Am. Police, Washington, 1989; mem. Hall of Fame Pres. Task Force, Washington, 1983—91, Image Devel. Adv. Bd.; nominee Nat. Rep. Com., Washington, 1991, 1992; selected VIP guest del. Rep. Nat. Conv., Houston, 1992; life mem. Rep. Presdl. Task Force, Washington, 1992; mem. Jefferson Com., 2001; mem. adv. bd. Nat. Congl. Com., Washington; mem. fin. com. fundraiser Middleton for Congress Campaign, 1994, Dist. # 59 Bd. Reps.; mem. exec. com. Jefferson County Rep., chairperson legis. dist. 52; chair Harriet Tubman Rep. Com.; del. Commonwealth of Ky. So. Rep. Leadership Conf., 2000; min. Greater Emmanuel Temple Holiness Ch., Birmingham, 1957—, ordained elder, vice champion mother bd.; apptd. hon. mem. Internat. Women's Review Bd.; apptd. Profl. Women's Adv. Bd.; mem. Nat. Law Enforcement Officer's Assn., 1989. Recipient award, Ala. Sheriff Assn., 1989, Navy League, 1989—91, cert. of appreciation, Pres. Congl. Task Force, 1990, Rep. Nat. Com., 1994, Diamond award, U.S.A. Serve Am., 1992, Rep. Presdl. award, Legion of Merit, 1994, Royal Proclamation, Royal Highness Kevin, Prince Regent of Hutt River Province, 1994, Royal Ceremonial jewel, Svc. award, Ala. Bd. Nursing, Outstanding Sr. Citizen's cert. of recognition, Lifetime Achievement award, Fran Nicholas Law, World Congress Arts Ctr., Ret. Nurse Demonstator Leadership award, UAB Hosp., Svc. award, Ala. Bd. Nursing.; named Good Samaritan, Law Envforcement Officers, Amb., Am. Biog. Inst.; named to Police Hall of Fame, Nat. Crime Watch Pub. Svc.; nominee Presdl. Election Registry, Rep. Presdl. Task Force, 1992. Mem.: Nat. Rep. Com., ICC (clergyman), Am. Assn. Advancement Sci., Pres.'s Task Force, Hon. Sheriff's Assn., Am. Security Coun. (nat. adv. bd.), Nat. Fedn. Rep. Women (trustee bd.), Ala. Nurses Assn., Nat. Assn. Unknown Players, LaSalle Ext. U. Alumni (life), Nat. Rep. Women Assn., Notary Pub. and Notary Soc. Avocations: singing, writing, reading, gardening. Home: 2321 7th Ave N Apt 321 Pk Pl Birmingham AL 35203-2410 Home Phone: 205-715-2114.

PERRY, J. WARREN, health facility administrator, educator; b. Richmond, Ind., Oct. 25, 1921; s. Charles Thomas and Zona M. (Ohler) Perry. BA, DePauw U., 1944; postgrad., Harvard U., 1948—49; MA, Northwestern U., 1952, PhD, 1955; DSc (hon.), D'Youville Coll., 1990, Med. Coll. Ohio, 1996, DePauw U., 1998. Instr. St. John's Mil. Acad., Delafield, Wis., 1944—47; counselor, asst. prof. psychology U. Ill.-Chgo., 1953—56; dir. prosthetic-orthotic edn., asst. prof. orthopaedic surgery Northwestern U. Med. Sch., 1957—61; lectr. psychology U. Chgo., 1957—61; asst. chief div. tng. Vocat. Rehab. Adminstrn., HEW, 1961—64, dep. asst. commr. research and tng., 1964—66; prof. health scis. adminstrn. SUNY-Buffalo, 1966—95, founding dean Sch. Health Related Professions, 1966—77, dean and prof. emeritus, 1985—. Mary E. Switzer Meml. lectr., Dallas, 1977, Lexington, 91; mem. Task Force for Legislation for Allied Health Professions, 1966—67; com. edn. allied health professions and svcs., coun. med. edn. AMA, 1968—73; nat. adv. com. Am. Dietetic Assn., 1970—75, chmn., 1972—75; nat. rev. com., regional med. programs HEW, 1969—72; mem.steering com. on manpower policy for primary care bd. health promotion and disease prevention Inst. of Medicine-NAS, 1981—83, sr. advisor com. to study role allied health, com. to study med. manpower in VA, 1988—91; spl. med. adv. com. VA, 1974—77; mem. task force on manpower for prevention Fogarty Internat. Inst., NIH, 1975—76; mem. acad. planning com. Mass. Gen. Hosp. Founding editor Jour. Allied Health, 1972—78, editor emeritus, 1985—; contbr. articles to profl. jours. Mem. Legacy Soc.; charter mem. Cmty. Found. for Greater Buffalo, 1998—; patron of the arts Coun. of Buffalo and Erie County, 2000; bd. dirs., dir. com. opera edn. Lyric Opera Guild, Chgo., 1957—61; chmn. acad. divsn. dr., coun. trustees Buffalo Philharm. Orch., 1987—93; bd. dirs. Goodwill Industries, Buffalo, 1969—76; trustee Cmty. Music Sch. Buffalo, 1977—80; adv. bd., v.p. Sisters of Charity Hosp., Buffalo, 1969—87, pres., 1986—88; bd. visitors U. Pitts., 1977—80; coun. trustees D'youville Coll., Buffalo, 1978—88, trustee emeritus, 1989—95; bd. dirs. Am. Lung Assn. Western N.Y., 1975—92, pres., 1983; bd. dirs. ARC, Buffalo, Artpark State Performing Arts Ctr., Lewiston, NY, 1986—96, Am. Lung Assn. N.Y.State, 1981—85, exec. com., 1989—92; chmn. N.Y. State Coalition Smoking or Health, Albany, NY, 1987—91; trustee Theodore Roosevelt Inaugural Site Found., 1987, pres., 1991—94; bd. advisors Buffalo Coun. on World Affairs, 1987—88; trustee Buffalo Opera Co., 1989—94, chmn. opera adv. coun., 1995—97. Recipient Sustained Superior Svc. award, HEW, 1965, Disting. Svc. award, Am. Orthotics-Prosthetics Assn., 1966, Buffalo Opera Co., 1995, Chancellor's award for adminstrv. svc., SUNY, 1977, 1st Allied Health Leadership award, 1988, Disting. Author award, Jour. Allied Health, 1978, Cert. of Merit, AMA, 1979, Pres. Cir. Pin, Buffalo State Coll., 1993, 50th Anniversary Alumni citation, De Pauw U., 1994, Outstanding Svc. award, Theodore Roosevelt Inaugural Site Found., 1994, Theodore Roosevelt Exemplary Citizenship award, 1997, Brotherhood/Sisterhood award in health, NCCJ Western N.Y., 1995, Christmas Seal Hall of Fame award, ALA N.Y. State, 1995, Disting. Citizenship award, Mayor of Buffalo, 1995, Patron of the Arts award, Arts Coun. of Buffalo and Erie County, 2000, Alumni Achievement award, SUNY-Buffalo, 2000, Wisdom award of honor, 1999, Humanitarian award, Coordinated Care Assn. Buffalo, 2002, Clara Barton award, ARC (Greater Buffalo chpt.), 2004; named Outstanding Individual Philanthropist, Nat. Soc, Fundraising Execs. Western N.Y., 1992, Ky. Col., 1969, Nebr. Admn., 1964, Man of the Yr., Opera Found. Buffalo, Inc., 2000, J. Warren Perry Disting. Author award in his honor, Jour. Allied Health, Perry Scholarship in his honor, U. Buffalo Found., J. Warren Perry Outstanding Vol. Leadership award in his honor, Western N.Y. chpt. ALA, J. Warren Perry Meml. lectr. in his honor, SUNY, Buffalo, Buffalo Philharmonic Chorus, 2003; fellow Wisdom Hall of Fame fellow, Wisdom Soc., 1999; Perry Lecture Hall, D'Youville Coll. named in his honor, 2004. Fellow: Assn. Schs. of Allied Health Professions (pres. 1969—70, Cert. of Merit 1977, Pres.'s award 1978, Honors of Soc. award 1984); mem.: Nat. Rehab. Assn., Am. Pers. and Guidance Assn., Am. Dietetics Assn. (hon.), APA, Phi Beta Kappa, Delta Tau Delta, Phi Delta Kappa (pres. 1955). Home: 705 Renaissance Dr Apt 208 Williamsville NY 14221

PERRY, JACQUELIN, orthopedist, surgeon; b. Denver, May 31, 1918; d. John F. and Tirzah (Kuruptkat) P. BE, U. Calif., LA, 1940; MD, U. Calif., San Francisco, 1950; DSc (hon.), U. So. Calif., 1996. Intern Children's Hosp., San Francisco, 1950-57; resident in orthop. surgery U. Calif., San Francisco, 1951-55; orthop. surgeon Rancho Los Amigos Hosp., Downey, Calif., 1955—, chief stroke svc., 1972-75; chief pathokinesiology Rancho Los Amigos Med. Ctr., 1961—; mem. faculty U. Calif. Med. Sch., San Francisco, 1966—, clin. prof., 1973—; mem. faculty U. So. Calif. Med. Sch., 1969—, prof. orthop. surgery, 1972—, dir. polio and gait clinic, 1972—. Disting. lectr. for hosp. for spl. surgery and Cornell U. Med. Coll., NYC, 1977-78; Packard Meml. lectr. U. Colo. Med. Sch., 1970; Osgood lectr. Harvard Med. Sch., 1978; Summer lectr., Portland, 1977; Shands lectr.; cons. USAF; guest spkr. symposia; cons. Biomechanics Lab. Centinela Hosp., 1979—. Served as phys. therapist U.S. Army, 1941-46. Recipient Disting. Svc. award Assn. Rehab. Facilities, 1981, Pres.'s award, 1984, Isabelle and Lenard Goldensen award for tech. United Cerebral Palsy Assn., 1981, Jow Dowling award, 1985, Profl. Achievement award UCLA, 1988, Milton Cohen award Nat. Assn. Rehab., 1993, Tribute Pres. award Ruth Jackson Orthop. Soc., 2004; named Woman of Yr. for Medicine in So. Calif. LA Times, 1959, Alumnus of Yr. U. Calif. Med. Sch., 1980, Physician of Yr. Calif. Employment Devel. Dept., 1994; Jacquelin Perry Neuro Trauma Inst. Rancho Clin. Bldg. named in her honor, 1996. Mem. AMA, Am. Acad. Orthop. Surgeons (Kappa Delta award for rsch. 1977, orthop. rsch. svc., 1976), Am. Orthop. Assn. (Shands lectr. 1988), Western Orthop. Assn., Calif. Med. Soc., LA County Med. Soc., Am. Phys. Therapy Assn. (hon. Golden Pen award 1965), Am. Acad. Orthotists and Prosthetists (hon.), Scoliosis Rsch. Soc. (Lifetime Achievement award 2009), LeRoy Abbott Soc., Am. Acad. Cerebral Palsy, Gait & Clin. Movement Analysis Soc. (mem. emeritus, Lifetime Achievement award 2000), Orthop. Rsch. Soc. (Shands award 1998, 99). Home: 12319 Brock Ave Downey CA 90242-3503 Office: Rancho Los Amigos Med Ctr 7601 Imperial Hwy Downey CA 90242-3456 Office Phone: 562-401-7177. E-mail: pklab@larei.org.

PERRY, JAMES ALFRED, environmental scientist, academic administrator, educator, consultant; b. Dallas, Sept. 27, 1945; BA in Fisheries, Colo. State U., 1968; MA, Western State Coll., 1973; PhD, Idaho State U., 1981. Sr. water quality specialist Idaho Div. Environ., Pocatello, 1974-82; area mgr. Centrac Assocs., Salt Lake City, 1982; H.T. Morse disting. prof. water quality U. Minn., 1982—, head dept. fisheries, wildlife, conservation biol., 2000—06, dir. natural resources policy and mgmt., 1985—2002, spl. asst. to dean grad. sch., 1996-2000, interim assoc. v.p., dean internat. programs, 2006. Vis. scholar Oxford U., Green Coll., England, 1990—91; dep. dir. AID-funded Environ. Tng. Project for Ctrl. and Ea. Europe, 1992—96; assoc. Internat. Inst. Sustainable Devel., 2007—; cons. in field. Author: Water Quality Management of a Natural Resource, 1996, Ecosystem Management for Central and Eastern Europe, 2001; editor: Jour. Natural Resources and Life Scis. Edn., 1996—2004; mem. editl. bd. Mitigation and Adaptation Strategies for Global Change, 1998—2005. Charter mem. Leadership Devel. Acad., Lakewood, Minn., 1988; bd. dirs. Minn. Ctr. for Environ. Advocacy, 1995-2006, vice chmn., 2005. Fellow Pres.'s Academic Leadership Initiative, 2003-05; recipient Richard C. Newman Art of Tchg. award, 1998, Morse-Alumni award, 1999, Outstanding Svc. award U. Minn., 2001, Ctr. Integrative Study Writing award interdisciplinary tchg. of writing, 2003, Juror Brock Internat. Edn. prize, 2006; ACOP/ESCOP nat. leadership fellow, 1995-96, CIC acad. leadership fellow, 2000-01, Gordon L. Starr Leadership award, 2003-05. Fellow: Am. Inst. Fish Resource Biology; mem.: Acad. Disting. Tchrs., Nat. Assn. Univ. Fish and Wildlife Programs (sec./treas. 2001—), Soc. for Conservation Biology, Wildlife Soc., Am. Fisheries Soc., N.Am. Benthol. Soc. (exec. bd. Albuquerque 1990—91), Internat. Soc. Theoretical and Applied Limnology, Internat. Water Resources Assn., Am. Water Resources Assn., Minn. Acad. Scis. (bd. dirs. 1987—90), Gamma Sigma Delta (merit award 2001), Xi Sigma Pi, Sigma Xi. Office: Univ Minn Dept Fisheries Wildlife and Conservation Biology 320 Hodson Hall 1980 Folwell Ave Saint Paul MN 55108-1037 Office Phone: 612-625-4717. Business E-Mail: jperry@umn.edu.

PERRY, JAMES BENN, former hotel and gaming company executive; b. New Castle, Pa., Jan. 15, 1950; s. Samuel Wesley Jr. and Grace Elizabeth (Brumbaugh) P.; m. Cathy Ann Jackson, Dec. 27, 1982; children: James Benn Jr., Lauren Elizabeth, Julie Ann. BA in History, Ohio Wesleyan U., 1972; postgrad., Ariz. State U., 1975-76; student, Tulane U., 1968-70. CPA, N.J. Internal auditor Ramada Inns, Phoenix, 1976-78, regional controller, 1978-79, v.p., contr., 1985-87; asst. controller Tropicana Hotel & Casino, Las Vegas, Nev., 1979-80, controller Atlantic City, 1980-82, v.p. fin., 1982-85, sr. v.p., casino ops., 1987-89; exec. v.p./asst., gen. mgr. ops. TropWorld Casino and Entertainment Resort, Atlantic City, 1989-92, pres., gen. mgr., 1992—96; pres. Hospitality Group, Keating Bldg. Group, 1996—97, Argosy Gaming Co., Alton, Ill., 1997—2002, CEO, 1997—2003, Trump Entertainment Resorts, Inc., Atlantic City, 2005—07. Bd. dirs. Isle of Capri Casinos, Inc., 2007—. Mem. AICPA, N.J. Soc. CPAs (chmn. gaming conf. com. 1985-86). Avocation: golf.

PERRY, JAMES E.C., state supreme court justice; b. New Bern, NC; m. Adrienne M. Perry, 1971; children: Willis, Jaimon, Kamilah. BA, St. Augustine's Coll., 1966; JD, Columbia Univ., 1972. Sr. ptnr. Perry & Hicks PA; judge Fla. 18th Jud. Cir., 2000—09, chief judge, 2003—05; assoc. justice Fla. Supreme Ct., 2009—. Founder, pres. Jackie Robinson Sports Assn.; trustee Carter CME Tabernacle Church; treas. bd. trustees St. Augustine's Coll. Recipient Humanitarian award, Seminole County NAACP, Paul C. Perkins award, Orange County NAACP, Key to the City, New Bern, NC, 2004, Martin Luther King Drum Major award for social just., 2005, Williams-Johnson Outstanding Jurist award, Brevard & Seminole County Bar Associations, 2006. Office: Fla Supreme Ct 500 S Duval St Tallahassee FL 32399-1925 Office Phone: 850-921-1096.*

PERRY, JAMES FREDERIC, philosophy educator, writer; b. Washington, Jan. 21, 1936; s. Albert Walter and Helene Anna Maria (Neumeyer) P.; m. Sandra Jean Huizing, Feb. 18, 1957 (div. May 1972); children: Sandra Elaine, James Frederic Jr., Bartholomew; m. Roberta Schofield, June 6, 1984. Student, Princeton U., 1953-56, Marietta Coll., Ohio, 1958-60; BA with honors in Philosophy, Ind. U., 1962, PhD in Philosophy of Edn., 1972. NDEA fellow in philosophy U. N.C., 1962—65; instr. N.C. State U., Raleigh, 1965-66; Univ. fellow Ind. U., 1971, adj. lectr. Bloomington, 1972-75; prof. philosophy Hillsborough C.C., Tampa, Fla., 1975-97, 2005—, honors prof. philosophy, 1997—2005. Adj. prof. U. South Fla., 2000—, adj. honors prof., 2006—. Author: Random, Routine, Reflective, 1989; contbr. articles to profl. jours. Precinct committeeman Dem. Party, Tampa, Fla., 1988—2004. Mem. AAUP (pres. Fla. conf. 1986-89, chair com. "A" on acad. freedom 1989-2002), C.C. Humanities Assn. (so. divsn. exec. bd. 1981-89), Am. Philos. Assn., Fla. Philos. Assn. (pres. 2004-05), Internat. Soc. Philos. Enquiry, Internat. Congress for Critical Thinking and Moral Critiques (founding mem. S.E. coun. 1991), World Congress Philosophy (Boston 1998, Istanbul 2003, Seoul 2008), Princeton Alumni Assn. of Fla. Suncoast (sec. 1983-86, pres. 1986-95), Mensa, Authors Guild, Textbook and Acad. Authors Assn. Avocations: travel, genealogy. Office: Hillsborough C C PO Box 10561 Tampa FL 33679-0561 Office Phone: 813-253-7357. Business E-Mail: jperry@hccfl.edu.

PERRY, JAN, Councilwoman; BA cum laude, U. Southern Calif., 1977, MPA, 1981. Cert.: UCLA Ext. (in Litig.) 1979. Chief of staff, Dist. 9 LA City Coun., with legis. dept., 10th Dist., with sr. planning dept., 13th Dist., asst. pres. pro tempore, chair energy and environ. com., chair ad hoc homeless com., vice chair arts, parks, health, and aging com., vice chair ad hoc com. on recovering energy, natural resources, and econ. benefit from waste for LA, mem. housing, cmty., and econ. devel. com., mem. ad hoc LA river com., mem. ad hoc stadium com., councilwoman, Dist. 9, 2001—. With Hollywood Cmty. Housing Corp., 1990—93, African-Am./Jewish Leadership Connection, 1997, Coro Found., 1997, Japanese America Nat Mus, Black-Korean Alliance; exec. dir. Census 2000 Outreach Project, 1998; mem. bd. dirs. Cmty. Fin. Resources Ctr., LA Edn. Partnership, South Coast Air Quality Mgmt. Dist.; chair Light Rail Authority. Mem. bd. dirs. Metro region Nat. Women's Polit. Caucus, League of Women Voters, Santa Monica Mountains Conservancy, William O Douglas Outdoor Classroom, Jennessee Ctr. Vocational Edn. Com., Angels Flight Railway Found., Jewish Cmty. Rels. Com., Jewish Fedn. Coun. Mailing: City Hall 200 N Spring St Rm 420 Los Angeles CA 90012 Office: Dist Office 4703 S Broadway Ave Los Angeles CA 90037 Office Phone: 213-473-7009, 323-846-2651. Office Fax: 213-473-5946, 323-846-2656. Business E-Mail: Jan.Perry@lacity.org.*

PERRY, JEAN LOUISE, academic administrator; b. Richland, Wash., May 13, 1950; d. Russell S. and Sue W. Perry. BS, Miami U., Oxford, Ohio, 1972; MS, U. Ill., Urbana, 1973, PhD, 1976. Cons. ednl. placement office U. Ill., 1973-75; adminstrv. intern Coll. Applied Life Studies, 1975-76, asst. dean, 1976-77, assoc. dean, 1978-81, asst. prof. dept. phys. edn., 1976-81; assoc. prof. phys. edn. San Francisco State U., 1981-84, prof., 1984-90, chair, 1981-90; dean Coll. Human and Cmty. Scis. U. Nev., Reno, 1990—2006, spl. asst. to pres. for athletics, academics and compliance, 2006—. Named to Excellent Tchr. List, U. Ill., 1973—79. Mem.: AAHPERD (fellow rsch. consortium, pres. 1988—89), Nat. Assn. Girls and Women in Sports (guide coord., pres.), Nat. Assn. Phys. Edn. in Higher Edn., Am. Ednl. Rsch. Assn., Am. Assn. Higher Edn., Phi Delta Kappa, Delta Psi Kappa. Home: 3713 Ranchview Ct Reno NV 89509-7437 Office: U Nev Legacy Hal/ 232 Reno NV 89557-0001 Office Phone: 775-784-3505.

PERRY, JOHN, communications educator, researcher; b. Kingston, NY, Nov. 1937; s. Al John and E. Perry. BS, Syracuse U., NY, 1960, MA, 1964; PhD, Southern Ill. U., Carbondale, 1971. Spl. doctoral asst. Southern Ill. U., 1966—68; divsn. chmn. fine arts Blue Mountain Coll., Miss., 1972—74; instr. English U. Tex., 1987—88; prof. comm. arts U. Incarnate Word, San Antonio, 1988—. Author: (biography) James A. Herne: The American Ibsen, Jack London: An American Myth, (history) Texas: An Illustrated History. NDEA grant, Breadloaf Sch. English, Middlebury Coll., 1965. Avocation: antiques. Office: Univ Incarnate Word 4301 Broadway St San Antonio TX 78209-6318 Business E-Mail: perry@uiwtx.edu.

PERRY, JOSEPH NATHANIEL, bishop; b. Chgo., Apr. 18, 1948; Attended, Capuchin Sem. of St. Mary, Crown Point, Ind., 1967—71; BA in Philosophy, St. Joseph Coll., Rensselaer, Ind., 1971, BA in Theology, 1971; MDiv, St. Francis de Sales Major Sem., Milw., 1975; JCL, Cath. U. Am., Washington, DC, 1981. Ordained priest Archdiocese of Milw., 1975, priest, 1975—98, with Tribunal, 1976—95, chief judicial officer with Tribunal, 1983—95; assoc. pastor St. Nicholas Parish, Milw., 1975—76; instr. canon law studies Sacred Heart Sch. Theology, Hales Corners, Wis., 1983—98, Marquette U. Sch. Law, Milw., 1996—98, St. Mary of the Lake Sem., Mundelein, Ill., 1997—; pastor All Sts. Parish, Milw., 1995—98; episcopal vicar, Vicariate VI Archdiocese of Chgo., 1998—, aux. bishop, 1998—; ordained bishop, 1998. Mem. adv. bd. Archbishop Quigley Prep. Sem., 1998—, bd. mem., 1999—; liaison liturgy and liturgical tng. publs. Archdiocese of Chgo., 1999—, Episcopal liaison for Catechetics, 2003—; judge US Ct. Appeals, Province Chgo., 1999—. Mem.: Black Cath. Congress (v.p. bd. 2004—), Knights of St. Peter Claver and Ladies Auxiliary, US Conf. Cath. Bishops (mem. ad hoc com. for pienary coun. 2002—, secretariat for family, laity, women and youth 2002—, mem. ad hoc com. on Catholics' Use of Holy Scripture 2003—, mem. com. on edn. 2003—, chmn. com. on African Am. Catholics 2004—), Canon Law Soc. Roman Catholic. Office: PO Box 733 South Holland IL 60473-0733

PERRY, JUNE CARTER, United States Ambassador to Sierra Leone; b. Texarkana, Ark., Nov. 13, 1943; d. Bishop W. and Louise Pendleton Carter; m. Frederick M. Perry; children: Chad D., André F. BA cum laude, Loyola U./Mundelein Coll., Chgo., 1965; MA, U. Chgo., 1967. Nat. teaching fellow NC A&T State U., Greensboro, 1967-68; grad./undergrad. lectr. U. Md., College Park, 1969-70; dir. pub. affairs WGMS/RKO Radio, Washington, 1974-77; spl. asst. to dir. pub. affairs Cmty. Svcs. Adminstrn., Washington, 1977-79; dir. pub. affairs ACTION/Peace Corps, Washington, 1979-83; gen. svcs. officer US Dept. State, Lusaka, Zambia, 1984-86, polit./labor officer, US Embassy Harare, Zimbabwe, 1986-87, country office for Botswana Bur. African Affairs Washington, 1987-89, spl. asst. to dep. sec., 1989, chief internal polit. affairs and narcotics coord. US Embassy Paris, 1990—93, dep. amb. to Ctrl. African Rep., 1996—97, sr. adv. to asst. sec., 1997—98, dep. US amb. to Madagascar, 1998—2000, dir. Office Social and Humanitarian Affairs, Bur. Internat. Orgn., 2002—04, dep. dir. Office of Policy and Plans, Polit. Mil. Affairs Bur. Washington, US amb. to Kingdom of Lesotho Maseru, 2004—07, US amb. to Sierra Leone Freetown, 2007—. Diplomat-in-residence, Howard U., 2001-02; adv. coun. The Women's Inst., Bethesda, Md., 1983—. Producer, host: Soul of the Classics, WGMS Radio, 1974-77, Heritage Series, RKO Radio, 1974-77, DC Schs. Radio Project, 1973; commentator: WTOP Radio. Bd. dirs. Sign of the Times Art Gallery and Workshop, 1975-77, others in past. Recipient Spl. Achievement award, ACTION, 1981, Mundelein Disting. Alumnae, Mundelein Coll., 1981, Superior Achiever award, RKO Radio, 1977, Superior Honor, Sr. Performance awards State Dept., 1997, 98, 2003, 04, 05, 06, 07, 08, Coffey award, Loyola U., 2008; Diplomat-in-Residence of Yr. award, US Dept. State, 2002; Woodrow Wilson fellowship, 1965, UN Human Rights awardee, 1977, others. Mem. Am. Fgn. Svc. Assn., Cosmos Club, Delta Sigma Theta, Nat. Coun. Negro Women. Avocations: African art collecting, African-Am. and French history, classical music. Office: DOS Amb 2160 Freetown Pl Dulles VA 20189-2160

PERRY, KATY (KATHERYN ELIZABETH HUDSON), singer; b. Santa Barbara, Calif., Oct. 25, 1984; Singer: (albums) Katy Hudson, 2001, One of the Boys, 2008, (songs) I Kissed a Girl, 2008, Hot N Cold, 2008. Recipient Best New Act award, MTV Europe Awards, 2008, Favorite Pop Song, People's Choice Awards, 2009, Internat. Female Solo Artist, BRIT Awards, 2009. Office: c/o Mitch Rose Creative Artists Agy 20000 Ave of the STars Los Angeles CA 90067*

PERRY, KELLY ANN, research scientist; b. Meriden, Conn., Dec. 12, 1983; d. Marybeth Perry and Daniel Jr. Nitkowski. BS in Chemistry, U. Vt., Burlington, 2005; PhD candidate in Phys. Polymer Chemistry, Rensselaer Poly. Inst., Troy, NY, 2005—. Asst. child adv. bd. Chrysalis Domestic Violence Svcs., Meriden, Conn., 2000—05; pers. Diversity Ctr., ALANA Student Ctr., Burlington, 2003—05; overnight shelter adv. bd. Women Helping Battered Women, Burlington, 2004—05; tchg. asst. chemistry U. Vt., 2005; intern Oak Ridge Nat. Lab., Tenn., 2006—; fellow Integrated Rsch. and Edn. and Traineeship, Rensselaer Poly. Inst., 2006—08. Contbr. numerous presentations. Treas. Cadmium Iota Sigma Pi Treas., Troy, 2007—08, Women's Chemist Com., Troy, 2007—08. Recipient Dartmouth Book award, award, Am. Inst. Chemist, Merck Index award, award, UVM Cmty. Svc.; named Shiner ALANA Ally of Yr. Mem.: MSA, Am. Chem. Soc., Phi Beta Kappa (bd. mem. 2005). Office: Oak Ridge Nat Lab PO Box 2008 Ms6064 Oak Ridge TN 37831-6064 Office Fax: 865-576-5413. Business E-Mail: perryka@ornl.gov.

PERRY, KENNETH WILBUR, finance educator; b. Lawrenceburg, Ky., May 21, 1919; s. Ollie Townsend and Minnie (Monroe) P.; m. Shirley Jane Kimball, Sept. 5, 1942; 1 dau., Constance June (Mrs. Linden Warfel). BS, Eastern Ky. U., 1942; MS, Ohio U., 1949; PhD, U. Ill., 1953; LL.D., Eastern Ky. U., 1983. C.P.A., Ill. Instr. Berea Coll., 1949-50, U. Ky., summer 1950; teaching asst. U. Ill. at Champaign, 1950-53, asst. prof. accounting, 1953-55, asso. prof., 1955-58, prof., 1958—, Alexander Grant prof., 1975—. Vis. prof. Northeastern U., summer 1966, Parsons Coll., 1966-67, Fla. A. and M. U., fall 1971; Carman G. Blough prof. U. Va., fall 1975; dir. Illini Pub. Co. Author: Accounting: An Introduction, 1971, Passing the C.P.A. Examination, 1964, (with N. Bedford and A. Wyatt) Advanced Accounting, 1960; contbg. author: Complete Guide to a Profitable Accounting Practice, 1965, C.P.A. Review Manual, 1971; Editor: The Ill. C.P.A, 1968-70; contbg. editor: Accountants' Cost Handbook, 1960. Served to maj. AUS, 1942-46; col. Res. ret. Named outstanding alumnus Eastern Ky. U., 1969 Mem. Am. Accounting Assn. (v.p. 1963, Outstanding Educator award 1974), Am. Inst. C.P.A.'s, Am. Statis. Assn., Nat. Assn. Accountants (dir. 1969-71), Ill. Soc. C.P.A.s (chair in accountancy), Beta Alpha Psi, Beta Gamma Sigma (Distinguished scholar 1977-78), Omicron Delta Kappa. Methodist. Home: 2314 Fields South Dr Champaign IL 61822-9302 Office: Commerce W U Ill Champaign IL 61822

PERRY, KENNY (JAMES KENNETH PERRY), professional golfer; b. Elizabethtown, KY, Aug. 10, 1960; s. Ken Perry; m. Sandy Perry; children: Lesslye, Justin, Lindsey. Grad., Western Ky. U., Bowling Green, 1982. Profl. golfer, 1982—; mem. Pres. Cup team, 2003, 2005, Ryder Cup team, 2004, 2008. Deacon Ch. of Christ, Franklin, Ky. Achievements include winning PGA Tour events: New England Classic, 1994, Bob Hope Chrysler Classic, 1995, Buick Open, 2001, 2008, Bank of America Colonial, 2003, 2005, Meml. Tournament, 2003, 2008; Greater Milw. Open, 2003, Pres. Cup, 2003, Bay Hill Invitational, 2005, Ryder Cup, 2008, John Deere Classic, 2008, Travelers Championship, 2009. Avocation: auto racing. Office: PGA Tour 100 PGA Tour Blvd Ponte Vedra FL 32082*

PERRY, LEE ROWAN, retired lawyer; b. Chgo., Sept. 23, 1933; s. Watson Bishop and Helen (Rowan) P.; m. Barbara Ashcraft Mitchell, July 2, 1955; children: Christopher, Constance, Geoffrey. BA, U. Ariz., 1955, LLB, 1961. Bar: Ariz. 1961. Since practiced in, Phoenix; clk. Udall & Udall, Tucson, 1960-61; mem. firm Carson, Messinger, Elliott, Laughlin & Ragan, 1961-99. Mem. law rev. staff, U. Ariz., 1959-61. Mem. bd. edn. Paradise Valley Elem. and H.S. Dists., Phoenix, 1964-68, pres., 1968; mem. bd. edn. Osborn Elem. Sch. Dist., Phoenix, 2002; bd. dirs. Osborn Sch. Dist. Found., 2003—; treas. troop Boy Scouts Am., 1970-72; mem. Ariz. adv. bd. Girl Scouts U.S.A., 1972-74, mem. nominating bd., 1978-79; bd. dirs. Florence Crittenton Services Ariz., 1967-72, pres., 1970-72; bd. dirs. U. Ariz. Alumni, Phoenix, 1968-72, pres., 1969-70; bd. dirs. Family Service Phoenix, 1974-75; bd. dirs. Travelers Aid Assn. Am., 1985-89; bd. dirs. Vol. Bur. Maricopa County, 1975-81, 83-86, pres., 1984-85; bd. dirs. Ariz. div. Am. Cancer Soc., 1978-80, Florence Crittenton div. Child Welfare League Am., 1976-81; bd. dirs. Crisis Nursery for Prevention of Child Abuse, 1978-81, pres., 1978-80; Ariz. dir. Devereux Found., 1996-2000, vice chmn. 1996-98. 1st lt. USAF, 1955-58. Mem. State Bar Ariz. (conv. chmn. 1972), Rotary (dir. 1971-77, 95-96, pres. 1975-76, West Leadership award 1989), Ariz. Club (bd. dirs. 1994-2002, pres.-elect 1997-98, pres. 1998-99), Phoenix Country Club, Phi Delta Phi, Phi Delta Theta (pres. 1954). Republican. Episcopalian. Home: 106 N Country Club Dr Phoenix AZ 85014-5443

PERRY, LOUIS BARNES, retired insurance company executive; b. LA, Mar. 4, 1918; s. Louis Henry and Julia (Stoddard) P.; m. Genevieve Patterson, Feb. 8, 1942; children: Robert Barnes, Barbara Ann, Donna Lou. BA, UCLA, 1938, MA, 1940, PhD, 1950; fellow in econs., Yale U., 1941; LL.D., Pacific U., 1964; L.H.D., Whitman Coll., 1967, Linfield Coll., 1981; D.C.S., Willamette U., 1977. Teaching asst. UCLA, 1940-41, research teaching asst., 1946-47; faculty Pomona Coll., 1947-59, asst. to pres., 1955-57, prof. econs., 1957-59; pres. Whitman Coll., Walla Walla, Wash., 1959-67; v.p., treas. Standard Ins. Co., Portland, Oreg., 1967-68, exec. v.p., 1968-71, pres., 1972-83, chmn., 1983-85, also bd. dirs. Investment counselor, broker Wagenseller & Durst, L.A., 1951-59; rsch. coord. So. Calif. Rsch. Coun., 1952-54; cons. Carnegie Survey Bus. Edn., 1957-58. Author: (with others) Our Needy Aged, 1954, A History of the Los Angeles Labor Movement, 1963; Contbr. (with others) articles to profl. jours. Mem. Oreg. Bd. Higher Edn., 1975-87, pres., 1975-80. Served to maj. AUS, World War II; lt. col. Res. Mem. Am. Coll. Life Underwriters (trustee 1972-81), Rotary, Phi Beta Kappa, Beta Gamma Sigma, Phi Delta Kappa, Pi Gamma Mu, Alpha Gamma Omega, Artus. Methodist. Home: 1585 Gray Lynn Dr Walla Walla WA 99362-9282 *In looking back over the years, an unspoken and oftentime subliminal guiding principle has been to reach beyond one's realistic grasp. This concept coupled with an interest in treating others as one would like to be treated has made it possible to react to new challenges. Successfully meeting the latter has provided a varied career in a number of different fields of activity.*

PERRY, MALCOLM BLYTHE, biologist, researcher; b. Birkenhead, Cheshire, Eng., Apr. 26, 1930; s. Cyril A. and Hilda P. (Blythe) Perry; m. Eileen M. Perry, Aug. 10, 1956 (dec. Nov. 1981); children: Sara Jane, Judith Anne; m. Philomena C. Kingsley, July 25, 2001. B.Sc., U. Bristol, Eng., 1953; PhD, U. Bristol, 1956, D.Sc., 1969. Banting rsch. fellow Queen's U., Kingston, Ont., Canada, 1955, asst. prof., 1956-60, R.S. McLaughlin research prof., 1960-62; sr. resch. officer Nat. Rsch. Coun., Ottawa, 1962—81, prin. rsch. officer, 1981—. Scientist U. Cambridge, Eng., 1969, U. Paris, 1979; prof. U. Ottawa, 1982 Contbr. articles to profl. jours. Fellow Royal Soc. Can., Royal Inst. Chemistry; mem. Can. Soc. Microbiology (award 1991), Am. Soc. Microbiology, Internat. Endotoxin Soc. (award 2002). Office: NRC 100 Sussex Dr Ottawa ON Canada K1A 0R6 Home: 769 Hemlock Rd Ottawa ON Canada K1K 0K6 Office Phone: 613-990-0837. Business E-Mail: malcolm.perry@nrc.ca.

PERRY, MARGARET, librarian, writer; b. Cin., Nov. 15, 1933; d. Rufus Patterson and Elizabeth Munford (Anthony) P. AB, Western Mich. U., 1954; Cert. d'etudes Francaises, U. Paris, 1956; MSLS, Cath. U. Am., 1959. Young adult and reference libr. N.Y. Pub. Libr., NYC, 1954-55, 57-58; libr. U.S. Army, France and Germany, 1959-63, 64-67; chief circulation U.S. Mil. Libr., West Point, NY, 1967-70; head edn. libr. U. Rochester, NY, 1970-75, asst. prof. NY, 1973-75, assoc. prof. NY, 1975-82, asst. dir. librs. for reader svcs. NY, 1975-82, acting dir. librs. NY, 1976-77, 80; univ. libr. Valparaiso U., Ind., 1982-93; ret., 1993. Mem. Task Force on Coop. Edn., Rochester, 1972; freelance writer Mich. Land Use Inst., 1995-01. Author: A Bio-bibliography of Countee P. Cullen, 1903-1946, 1971, Silence to the Drums: A Survey of the Literature of the Harlem Renaissance, 1976, The Harlem Renaissance, 1982, The Short Fiction of Rudolph Fisher, 1987, short stories; contbr. articles to profl. jours. and children's mags. Bd. dirs. Urban League, 1978-80 Recipient 1st prize short story contest Armed Forces Writers League, 1966; 2d prize Frances Steloff Fiction prze, 1968, 1st prize short story Arts Alive, 1990, 2d prize short story Willow Rev., 1990; seminar scholar Schloss Leopoldskron, Salzburg, Austria, 1956, 3d prize short story West Shore C.C., Scottville, Mich., 1995. Mem. ALA. Democrat. Roman Catholic. Avocations: violin and viola, collecting book marks, gardening, reading, travel. Home: 8 Muriel St Ithaca NY 14850 Office Phone: 607-257-3997. Personal E-mail: mperry515@yahoo.com.

PERRY, MARION J.H., English educator; d. Armin Werner and Adah Hubbard (Porter) Helz; m. Franklyn Alfred Perry, Jr., July 17, 1971; children: Aurelia, Scott. BA, Ripon Coll., Wis., 1964; MA, U. Iowa, 1966; MFA, 1969; MA, U. Buffalo, 1979, PhD, 1986. Instr. West Liberty (W.Va.) State Coll., 1966-68, Albright Coll., Reading, Pa., 1968-70; lectr. SUNY-EOC, Buffalo, N.Y., 1970-74; mentor Empire State Coll., Buffalo, N.Y., 1978-81; prof. English Lit. Erie C.C., Orchard Park, N.Y., 1980—; founder & pub. Word Worth, Maryland 20878. Dir. Women's Ctr. Erie C.C., Orchard Park, N.Y., 1989-95. Author: (poetry) Establishing Intimacy, 1982, Dishes, 1989, The Mirror's Image, 1981, Icarus, 1980; pub., founder & pub. Word Worth Mag. Ideas & Arts, Md. 20878 Mag. Mem., v.p. League of Women Voters, E. Aurora, N.Y., 1987-92; sec. bd. dir. ECC Found., Buffalo, N.Y., 1989-99. Recipient Woman of Yr. award Bus. and Profl. Women, Orchard Park, N.Y., 1994, All Nations Poetry Contest Triton Coll., River Grove, Ill., 1980-81, Apex Grand award, 2008. Mem. Nat. Coun. Tchrs. English, Poetry Soc. Am., Phi Delta Kappa. Home: PO Box 221 East Aurora NY 14052

PERRY, MARK BRADLEY, lawyer, minister; b. Ft. Worth, Mar. 14, 1966; s. James Paul and Dorothy Nelle Perry; m. Cassie Lue Bond, Jan. 2, 2003; children: Michael Dean Marquez, Christian Lee Marquez, Madison Lue Marquez, Alexandria Rebecca Marquez, Ashley Danielle. BBA, Baylor U., Waco, Tex., 1988; JD, U. Wis., Madison, 1992; MDiv, Yale U., New Haven, 1995. Founding atty. Trustlaw Assocs., Farmington, N.Mex., 1996—; founding pastor United Ch. Farmington, 1998—2007; founding chaplain, bereavement counselor NW N.Mex. Hospice, Farmington, 1998—; pres., CEO BP Realty, LLC, Farmington, 2002—. Pres. Otero County Bar Assn., Alamogordo, N.Mex., 1997, San Juan County Bar Assn., Farmington, 2000. Maj. Res. USAF, 2006—. Mem.: Masons. Baptist. Avocations: German shepherds, firearms. Office: Trustlaw Associates 412 W Arrington Ave Farmington NM 87401 Business E-Mail: trustlawassociates@yahoo.com.

PERRY, MATTHEW, actor; b. Williamstown, Mass., Aug. 19, 1969; s. John Bennett Perry and Suzanne Morrison. Actor: (films) A Night in the Life of Jimmy Reardon, 1988, She's Out of Control, 1989, Getting In, 1994, Fools Rush In, 1997, Edwards and Hunt: The First American Road Trip, 1997, Almost Heroes, 1998, Three to Tango, 1999, The Whole Nine Yards, 2000, Disney's THe Kid, 2000, Serving Sarah, 2002, The Whole Ten Yards, 2004, 17 Again, 2009; actor, exec. prodr. (films) Numb, 2007; actor (TV series) Second Chance, 1987, Sydney, 1990, Home Free, 1993, Friends, 1994-2004, Studio 60 on the Sunset Strip, 2006-07; writer (films) Imagining Emily, 1999; actor (TV movies) Dance 'Til Dawn, 1988, Call Me Anna, 1990, Deadly Relations, 1993, L.A.X. 2194, 1994 Parallel Lives, 1994, The Ron Clark Story, 2006; (TV appearances) 240-Robert, 1979, Charles in Charge, 1985, Silver Spoons, 1986, The Tracey Ullman Show, 1987, Mr. Belvedere, 1988, Highway to Heaven, 1988, Empty Nest, 1988, Just the 10 of Us, 1988, Growing Pains, 1989, Who's the Boss?, 1990, Beverly Hills, 90210, 1990, Dream On, 1992, The John Larroquette Show, 1993, Caroline in the City, 1995, Ally McBeal, 2002, The West Wing, 2003, Scrubs, 2004; theater debut Sexual Perversity in London, 2003. Office: c/o Doug Chapin Mgmt 1416 Havenhurst Dr Apt Gf1 Los Angeles CA 90046-3884

PERRY, MICHAEL CLINTON, internist, academic administrator, educator; b. Wyandotte, Mich., Jan. 27, 1945; s. Clarence Clinton and Hilda Grace (Wigginton) P.; m. Nancy Ann Kaluzny, June 22, 1968; children: Rebecca Carolyn, Katherine Grace. BA, Wayne State U., 1966, MD, 1970; MS in Medicine, U. Minn., 1975. Diplomate Am. Bd. Internal Medicine, Am. Bd. Hematology, Am. Bd. Oncology. Intern in internal medicine Mayo Grad. Sch. Medicine, Rochester, Minn., 1970-71, resident, 1971-72, fellow, 1972-75; instr. Mayo Med. Sch., Rochester, 1974-75; asst. prof. U. Mo., Columbia, 1975-80, assoc. prof., 1980-85, prof., 1985—, chmn. dept. medicine, 1983-91, sr. assoc. dean, 1991-94, Nellie A Smith chair oncology, dir. div. hematology/oncology, 1994—. Prin. investigator Cancer and Leukemia Group B, Nat. Cancer Inst., Chgo., 1982—, exec. com., 1982-84, 1987-90. Author, co-author 30 book chpts.; editor: Toxicity of Chemotherapy, 1984, The Chemotherapy Source Book, 1992, 96, 2001, Comprehensive Textbook of Thoracic Oncology, 1996; contbr. articles to profl. jours. Recipient Faculty Alumni award U. Mo., Columbia, 1985, Disting. Alumnus award Wayne State U., 1995, Disting. Oncologist of Yr. award So. Assn. Oncology, 2000. Fellow ACP; mem. Am. Soc. Hematology, Am. Soc. Clin. Oncology, Cen. Soc. Clin. Research, Am. Soc. Internal Medicine (Young Internist of Yr. 1981), Sigma Xi, Alpha Omega Alpha. Office: U Mo-Columbia 516 Ellis Fischel Cancer Ctr 115 Business Loop 70 W Columbia MO 65203-3244 Home: 3111 S Bobcat CT Columbia MO 65201-3141 E-mail: perrym@health.missouri.edu.

PERRY, MURVIN HENRY, communications educator; b. Bruce, SD, Apr. 28, 1922; s. Earl Henry and Lorraine (Eichel) P.; m. Rita Clare Kaefring, Aug. 23, 1952; children— Gail, Mark, Scott, Todd, Chris. BS, S.D. State Coll., 1950; MA, U. Iowa, 1954, PhD in Mass Communications, 1959. High sch. tchr., Gregory, S.D., 1947-48; publicist, tchr. S.D. State Coll., 1949-51; with VA, 1952-56; asst. to dir. Sch. Journalism, State U. Iowa, 1956-59; asst. prof. journalism Kans. State U., 1959-63; prof., dir. journalism Kent State U., 1963-79; chmn. dept. communication E. Tenn. State U., Johnson City, 1979-88, ret., 1988. Served with USNR, 1943-46, South Pacific Theater. Mem. Soc. Profl. Journalists. Home: 307 Oak Ln Johnson City TN 37604-3109 Business E-Mail: mhpjctn@embarqmail.com.

PERRY, NANCY BLAND, accountant; b. Houston, Miss., Aug. 17, 1955; d. Charles Edward Bland, Minnie Lou Bland; 1 child, Cheryl Elizabeth Crisco; m. Paul D Perry. BS in Edn. with distinction, Miss. Coll., 1975, cert. acctg., 1988. CPA Miss. CPA, acct. various CPA firms, Jackson, Miss., 1983—89; pvt. practice CPA Clinton, Miss., 1989—91; sr. acct. Chem. First Inc., Jackson, 1991—2003; asst. v.p. acctg. Denmiss LLC, 2003—. Bd. dirs., various offices Girl Scouts U.S. Mid. Miss., Jackson, 1992—; team mem. Leadership Clinton, 1997—98; bd. dirs., various positions Clinton Pub. Sch. Dist. PTA, 1988—96; bd. dirs., sec. treas. ChemFirst Found., Inc., Jackson, 1996—2002; trustee Clinton Pub. Sch. Dist., 1998—2008; bd. dirs. Clinton Jr. Miss, 1997—2004; trustee Frances Rushton Meml. Scholarship Trust, 1998—, chair, 2001—. Recipient Metro Jackson's Finest award, Cystic Fibrosis Foundation, 1999, Thanks Badge, Girl Scouts U.S. Mid. Miss., 1995; named Parent of the Yr., Clinton Pub. Sch. Dist., 1995; nominee GIVE, Gov. of Miss., 1995. Mem.: AICPA, Miss. Soc. CPAs, Am. Soc. Women Accts. (bd. dirs., various positions 1996—2001), Jr. Aux. Clinton (bd. dirs., treas. 1996—2000, trustee Francecs Rushton Meml. Scholarship Trust 1999—, chair 2001—), Clinton C. of C. Ch. Of Christ. Business E-Mail: nperry@denkmann-ms.com.

PERRY, PHILIP J., lawyer, former federal agency administrator; b. San Diego, 1964; m. Elizabeth Cheney Perry, 1993; children: Katherine, Elizabeth, Grace, Philip, Richard. BA, Colo. Coll., 1986; JD, Cornell U., 1990. Ptnr. Latham & Watkins LLP, 1993—97; counsel US Senate Spl. Investigation of Campaign Fin. Abuses, 1997—98; policy adv. Bush-Cheney presidential transition team, 2000; acting assoc. atty. gen. US Dept. Justice, 2001—02, prin. dep. assoc. atty. gen., 2001—02; gen. counsel. Office Mgmt. & Budget Exec. Office of the Pres., 2002—03; ptnr. Latham & Watkins LLP, Washington, 2003—05, 2007—; gen. counsel US Dept. Homeland Security, Washington, 2005—07. Office: Latham & Watkins LLP 555 Eleventh St NW Ste 1000 Washington DC 20004 Office Fax: 202-637-2201. Business E-Mail: phil.perry@lw.com.*

PERRY, RALPH BARTON, III, lawyer; b. NYC, Mar. 17, 1936; s. Ralph Barton Jr. and Harriet Armington (Seelye) P.; m. Mary Elizabeth Colburn, Sept. 2, 1961; children: Katherine Suzanne, Daniel Berenson. AB, Harvard U., 1958; LLB, Stanford U., 1963. Bar: Calif. 1964. Assoc. and mem. Keatinge & Sterling, L.A., 1963—68; mem. firm Graven Perry Block Brody & Qualls, L.A., 1968—2006, Perry & Grossman, L.A., 2006—. Bd. dirs. Planning and Conservation League, 1968-2005, PLC Found., 2005—, Coalition for Clean Air, 1970-2007, pres. 1972-80, 85-88. Served with U.S. Army, 1956-58. Mem. ABA (ho. of dels. 1975-95), State Bar Calif., L.A. County Bar Assn., Lawyers Club L.A. County (gov. 1968-82), Nat. and Internat. Wildlife Fedns., Sierra Club, L.A. Athletic Club. Home: 296 Redwood Dr Pasadena CA 91105-1339 Office: 523 W 6th St Ste 723 Los Angeles CA 90014-1223 Office Phone: 213-680-9770. Personal E-mail: rbp3@live.com.

PERRY, RICHARD CAYNE, hedge fund manager; b. Feb. 9, 1955; s. Arnold and Merel Perry; m. Lisa Rachel Newberger; 2 children. BA, U. Pa. Wharton Sch. Bus., 1977; MBA, NYU, 1980. Equity trader Goldman, Sachs & Co., 1977—88; founder, chmn., CEO Perry Capital LLC, 1988—. Adj. assoc. prof. NYU Stern Sch. Bus.; chmn. bd. dirs. FTD.com Inc., 1999—; bd. dirs. Endurance Specialty Holdings Ltd./Endurance Specialty Insurance, Ltd., 2001—, Sears Holdings Corp., 2005—, Universal Am. Corp., 2009—, Republic Engineered Products, Inc. Bd. trustees Allen Stevenson Sch., NYC, Harlem Children's Zone; bd. dirs. Milton Acad., Mass.; mem. nat. adv. bd. Facing Hist. & Ourselves. Democrat. Avocation: art. Office: Perry Capital LLC 767 5th Ave 19th Fl New York NY 10153 Office Phone: 212-583-4000.*

PERRY, RICHARD S., legislative staff member; b. Aiken, SC, 1969; s. Robert "Skipper" Perry, Jr. BA, Washington and Lee U., Va., 1991. Office mgr. Lindsey O. Graham congressional campaign, Aiken, SC, 1994; legis. asst. to Lindsey O. Graham US House Representatives, Washington, 1995—96, chief of staff, 1996—2002, US Senate, Washington, 2003—. Office: Office of Senator Lindsey Graham 290 Senate Russelll Office Bldg Washington DC 20510-4003 Office Phone: 202-224-5972. E-mail: richard_perry@lgraham.senate.gov.*

PERRY, RICK (JAMES RICHARD PERRY), Governor of Texas; b. Paint Creek, Tex., Mar. 4, 1950; m. Anita Thigpen; children: Griffin, Sydney. BS in Animal Sci., A&M U., 1972. Farmer/rancher; mem. Tex. Ho. of Reps., 1985-90, mem. appropriations and calendars com.; commr. of agr. State of Tex., 1991-98, lt. gov. Austin, 1999-2000, gov., 2000—. Chmn. Republican Governors Assn., 2007—08, fin. chmn., 2008—. Active Boy Scouts Am. Capt. USAF, 1972-77 Recipient Disting. Eagle Scout Award, 1992, Gerald W Thomas Agriculturist Award, Pub. Servant of Yr., 1995, Outstanding Tex Leader, John Ben Shepperd Pub. Leadership Inst., 1996; named Man of Yr. in Tex. Agr., Tex. County Agr. Agents Assn., 1990; named an Most Effective Legislators, Dallas Morning News, 1989. Mem.: Tex. & Southwestern Cattle Raisers Assn., Tex. Firemen & Fire Marshals Assn. (life), Nat. Future Farmers of Am. Alumni Assn., Am. Legion. Republican. Methodist. Office: Office of Governor 1100 San Jacinto PO Box 12428 Austin TX 78711 Office Fax: 512-463-5571.

PERRY, ROBERT MICHAEL, lawyer, consultant, rancher; s. John Robert and Katherine Marie (McManus) Perry. BA in History, St. Mary's U., San Antonio, 1959, JD, 1959; LLM, Georgetown U., Washington, 1964; diploma, US Army Arty. and Missile Sch., Ft. Sill, Okla., 1959, JAG Sch. U. Va., Charlottesville, 1962, US Army Command and Gen. Staff Course, 1978. Bar: Tex. 1961, US Supreme Ct., US Ct. Appeals (2d cir.), US Ct. Appeals (3d cir.), US Ct. Appeals (4th cir.), US Ct. Appeals (5th cir.), US Ct. Appeals (7th cir.), US Ct. Appeals (9th cir.), US Ct. Appeals (10th cir.), US Ct. Appeals (DC cir.), US Ct. Mil. Appeals, US Ct. Claims, US Tax Ct. Served to col. US Army, 1959—94, legal officer 1st armored divsn. Ft. Hood, Tex., 1959—61; staff officer JAG Dept. of Army, Washington, 1961—64; trial atty. Land and Natural Resources Divsn. Dept. of Justice, 1964—69; trial counsel Exxon Co. USA, Houston, 1969—80; gen. counsel and adminstr. enforcement US EPA, Washington, 1981—83; legal cons. San Antonio, Washington and Garrison, NY, 1983—. Mobilization designee US Army, Washington, 1964—94; chmn. Oil and Gas Industry Litigation Com. Trans Alaskan Pipeline, Alaska Native Claims and Offshore Oil and Gas Leasing Litigation, Houston, Washington and Anchorage, 1971—80; co-chmn environ. orgn. study com. US Army, Washington, 1984—94. Co-author: Fed. Condemnation Handbook 3 vols., 1964—69; editor-in-chief: US Dept. Justice Land and Natural Resources Divsn. Jour., 1967—68, The Forum (Fed. Bar Assn. DC), 1967—68; contbr. articles to govt. jours. Pres. and CEO Perry-Gething Found., San Antonio, 1975—, pres., CEO Garrison, NY, 1975—; event pres. San Antonio Fiesta Commn., 1978—; pres. and CEO Frontier Times Mus., Bandera, 2001—07. Decorated Legion of Merit, Commendation medal with oak leaf cluster US Army, Meritorious Svc. medal; recipient Spl. Achievement award, Adminstr. US EPA, 1982. Mem.: Tex. and Southwestern Cattle Raisers Assn., Tex. Bar Assn. Avocation: raising rare Jacob sheep and hybrid cattle. Home: Perrymount Ranch PO Box 531 Bandera TX 78003 Office: Perry-Gething Found PO Box 830233 San Antonio TX 78283-0233 Office Phone: 210-227-9498.

PERRY, SCOTT, professional sports team executive; s. Lowell Perry; m. Kim Perry; 1 child, Chelsea. Attended, U. Oreg., Eugene; B in Mktg., Wayne State U., Detroit, 1986. Asst. coach U. Detroit Mercy Titans, U. Calif. Golden Bears, Berkeley, U. Mich. Wolverines; head coach Eastern Ky. U. Colonels, 1997—2000; scout Detroit Pistons, 2000—02, dir. player pers., 2002—07, v.p. basketball ops., 2008—; asst. gen. mgr. Seattle Supersonics, 2007—08. Organizer Ceciliaville Golf Outing; chmn. St. Cecilia's Athletic Bd. Office: Detroit Pistons 6 Championship Dr Auburn Hills MI 48326*

PERRY, STEPHEN A., museum administrator, former federal agency administrator; b. Ohio, 1945; m. Sondra Perry; 5 children. B in Acctg., U. Akron; M in Mgmt., Stanford U.; attended, U. Mich. Exec. Develop. program. Various acctg. positions including dir. acctg., dir. purchasing, sr. v.p. Timken Co., Canton, 1964, v.p. human resources, purchasing and communications, 1993—97, sr. v.p., 1997—2001; dir. Dept. Adminstrv. Services State of Ohio, 1991—93; adminstr. US Gen. Services Adminstrn., Washington, 2001—05; pres., exec. dir. Pro Football Hall of Fame, Canton, Ohio, 2006—. Chmn. Human Resources Coun. of the Mfrs. Alliance for Productivity and Innovation; served on Human Resources Policy Com. Steering Group, Nat. Assn. of Mfrs.; bd. dir. Labor Policy Assn. Chmn. Canton Scholar Fund, Stark County Dist. Libr. Bd., United Way Campaign Ctrl. Stark County, 1996, Jr. Achievement, 1999, Leadership Stark County Selection Com.; mem. Ohio Bd. Regents, 1993—2002; bd. trustees Canton Urban League, 1968—83, Profl. Football Hall of Fame, 1993—2001; gen. chmn. Profl. Football Hall of Fame Festival, 1999; bd. trustees Timken Mercy Med. Ctr., 1984—91; mem. Walsh U. Adv. Bd., 1987—91; served on the Mgmt. Improvement Commn. appointed by Ohio Gov. Bob Taft. Recipient Disting. Svc. award, Jaycees, 1977, Pres. Social Responsibility award, Kent State U., 1995, Disting. Alumni award, Kent State U., Stark Campus Alumni Coun., 1996, Dr. Frank L. Simonetti Disting. Bus. Alumnus award, U. Akron, Coll. Bus. Alumni Assn., 1999, Disting. Alumni award, Trimken High Sch. Alumni Assn., 1999, U. Akron, 2001; named Man of Yr., Canton Christian Hall of Fame, 2000. Office: Pro Football Hall of Fame 2121 George Halas Dr NW Canton OH 44708

PERRY, STEVEN L., lawyer; b. Okla. City, June 24, 1952; s. Ed and Marilyn Vick Perry; divorced; 1 child, Kyle Kubecka. BA in Polit. Sci., U. Okla., 1974; JD, Okla. City U., 1977. Claims, collection Trans-South, 2001—02; govt. claims CMR, 2003—05; atty. Wheat and Assocs., 2005—06; landman, atty. Triad Energy Inc., 2006—. Mem.: Okla. Bar Assn. Democrat. Methodist. Office: PO Box 18721 Oklahoma City OK 73154-8721 Office Phone: 405-605-0590. Business E-Mail: steveperry@steveperry08.com.

PERRY, STEVEN WAYNE, statistician; b. Edenton, NC, Feb. 9, 1971; s. Allen Ray and Josephine Spruill Perry; children: Dominique Lavon, Jullian Nolan. BA in Sociology, Norfolk State U., Va., 1996; MA in Sociology, Ohio State U., Columbus, 1998. Survey statistician US Dept. Commerce, Census Bur., Washington, 1998—2004; statistician US Dept. Justice, Bur. Justice Stats., Washington, 2004—. Author: (book) Census of Tribal Justice Agencies, 2002, (booklet) American Indians and Crime, A BJS Statistical Profile, 2002. Mem. New Creation AME Ch., Ft. Washington, Md., 2006. With US Army, 1990—92. Decorated Army Achievement medal US Army, Nat. Def. Svc. medal; recipient ROTC Cadet Outstanding Acad. Achievement award, Gen. Soc. War 1812, 1994, Spl. Achievement award, US Cenus Bur., 1999—2002, Spl. Activity award, Bur. Justice Stats., 2004—06; fellow, Va. Poly. and State U., 1994, Coll. William and Mary, 1995. Mem.: Am. Legion (assoc.). Achievements include development of tribal criminal history record improvement program. Avocations: coin collecting/numismatics, kite collecting. Office: US Dept Justice 810 Seventh St NW Washington DC 20531

PERRY, THOMAS EDMUND, novelist, television screenwriter, producer; b. Tonawanda, NY, Aug. 7, 1947; s. Richard Edmund and Elizabeth Marie P.; m. Jo Anne Lee Perry, Aug. 31, 1980; children: Alix Elizabeth, Isabel Rose. BA cum laude, Cornell U., Ithaca, NY, 1969; PhD in English Lit., U. Rochester, NYC, 1974. Adminstr. Coll. Creative Studies U. Calif., Santa Barbara, 1975-80, U. So. Calif., LA, 1980-84; tv writer, prodr., staff Universal Studios, Disney Studios, Viacom Entertainment, LA, 1984-90; freelance writer for tv Cannell Prodns., Paramount Studios, others, LA, 1990—. Author (novels): The Butcher's Boy, 1982 (Edgar award for best first novel Mystery Writers America 1983), Metzger's Dog, 1983, Big Fish, 1985, Island, 1987, Sleeping Dogs, 1992, Death Benefits, 2001, Pursuit, 2001, Dead Aim, 2002, Nightlife, 2006, Silence, 2007, Fidelity, 2008, (Jane Whitfield novels): Vanishing Act, 1995, Dance for the Dead, 1996, Shadow Woman, 1997, The Face-Changers, 1998, Blood Money, 2000, Runner, 2009. With Air Nat. Guard, 1970-76. Mem. Writers' Guild America, Internat. Assn. Crime Writers. Mailing: Lescher & Lescher Ltd c/o Robert Lescher 346 E 84th St New York NY 10028 Personal E-mail: perrycontact@aol.com.

PERRY, TROY D., retired minister, religious organization administrator; divorced; 2 children; m. Phillip Ray De Blieck, July 16, 2003. Student, Midwest Bible Sch., 1959; D in Ministry (hon.), Samaritan Coll., LA, 1982; D in Human Svcs., Sierra U., Santa Monica, Calif., 1985; DDiv (hon.), Episcopal Div. Sch., Cambridge, Mass., 2003. Former pastor Ch. of God of Prophecy, Santa Ana, Calif.; founder, moderator Universal Fellowship Met. Cmty. Chs., LA, 1968; ret., 2005. Rep. Met. Community Chs. and gay and lesbian rights movement numerous TV shows including 60 Minutes, Phil Donahue, The Mike Douglas Show; author: The Lord is My Shepherd and Knows I'm Gay, Don't Be Afraid Anymore, 1991, (video) God, Gays and The Gospel: This is Our Story; contbg. editor Is Gay Good? Mem. LA County Commn. Human Rels.; del. 1st White House Conf. on AIDS, 1993; del. 1st White House Conf. on Hate Crimes, 1997; trustee Chgo. Theol. Sem., 2002-06. Recipient Humanitarian award Gay Press Assn., Equality award Human Rights Campaign, 1996. Mem. Universal Fellowship Ch. Office: Universal Fellowship MCC PO Box 1374 Abilene TX 79604 Personal E-mail: revtroyperry@aol.com.

PERRY, TYLER A., playwright, actor, theater director and producer; b. New Orleans, Sept. 14, 1969; Writer (plays) I Know I've Been Changed, I Can Do Bad All By Myself, 2000, Meet the Browns, 2004, Diary of a Mad Black Woman, 2005 (BET Comedy award for Outstanding Lead Actor in a Theatrical Film, 2005, BET Comedy award for Outstanding Writing for a Theatrical Film, 2005), Why Did I Get Married?, 2007, writer, actor, dir. Madea's Family Reunion, 2002, Madea's Class Reunion-The Class That Had No Class, 2003, Madea Goes to Jail, 2005; writer, dir.: (plays) What's Done In The Dark, 2006; writer, dir., prodr. The Marriage Counselor, 2008; co-writer (with Bishop T. D. Jakes), dir., prodr. (plays) Woman, Thou Art Loosed, 1999, Behind Closed Doors, 2001, dir., writer, prodr. (films) Daddy's Little Girls, 2007, actor, prodr., writer, dir. Diary of a Mad Black Woman, 2005 (Black Movie award for Outstanding Achievement in Writing, 2006), Why Did I Get Married?, 2007 (Outstanding Supporting Actor in a Motion Picture, NAACP, 2008), Meet the Browns, 2008, The Family That Preys, 2008, Madea Goes to Jail, 2009, actor, exec. prodr., dir. Madea's Family Reunion, 2006, writer, dir. (TV series) House of Payne, 2007—; author: (books) Don't Make a Black Woman Take Off Her Earrings: Madea's Uninhibited Commentaries on Love and Life, 2006 (Quills award humor The Quills Literacy Found., 2006). Named one of Most Influential Black Americans, Ebony mag., 2006, Top 25 Entertainers of Yr., Entertainment Weekly, 2007, 50 Smartest People in Hollywood, 2007, The 100 Most Influential People in the World, TIME mag., 2008, The 100 Most Powerful Celebrities, Forbes.com, 2008; named to Power 150, Ebony mag., 2008.*

PERRY, VERNON G., research scientist, educator; b. Boaz, Ala., May 8, 1921; s. George and Bertie Orr Perry; m. Imogene Hyatt, Aug. 28, 1948; children: David K, Ronald L. BS, Auburn U., Ala., 1943, MS, 1949; PhD, U. Wis., Madison, 1955. Asst.nematologist ARS-USDA, Sanford, Fla., 1949—54, assoc. nematologist Madison, Wis., 1955—58; prof. U. Fla., Gainesville, 1959, asst. dean, 1976—87, prof., asst. dean, 1987, emeritus. Contbr. chapters to books; editor: (book) Tropical Nematology. 1st lt. US Army, 1943—46, PTO, Japan. Recipient Best Paper, Fla State Hort Soc, 1963, Am. soc. hort sci., 1969, Hon. award, Congress Italiano Nematologist, 1974. Fellow: Soc. Nematologists (pres. 1966—67). Presbyterian. Achievements include Elected Fellow Amer Assoc. Adv. Science. Avocations: golf, fishing, gardening. Home: 720 Sw 80th Blvd Gainesville FL 32607

PERRY, WILLIAM BRIAN, colorectal surgeon; b. Natchitoches, La., Dec. 18, 1963; s. William Nathaniel and Joyce Hargis Perry; m. Holly Christine Hundemer, June 27, 1987; children: Katherine Mitchell, Patrick William, Austin Joseph. BS, La. State U., 1986; MD, Duke U., 1990. Lic. colon and rectal surgery Am. Bd. of Colon and Rectal Surgery, gen. surgery Am Bd. of Surgery, Tex. State Bd. of Med. Examiners. Chief of colorectal surgery Wilford Hall Med. Ctr., Lackland AFB, Tex., 1997—2006, gen. surgery residency program dir., 2002—06. Cons. to USAF surgeon gen. for colorectal surgery USAF Med. Corps, Bolling AFB, DC, 1997—2004; chief med. ops., chief of staff 4407th Med. Group, Prince Sultan Air Base, Saudi Arabia, 1998; chief trauma surgeon 332d Expeditionary Med. Group, Balad Air Base/LSA Anaconda, Iraq, 2005, 07. Contbr. articles to med. jours. and texts. Lt. col. USAF, 1990—2008. Decorated Commendation Medal USAF Bronze Star. Fellow: ACS, Am. Soc. of Colon and Rectal Surgeons; mem.: VFW, Soc. of Air Force Clin. Surgeons (pres. 2004—06), Delta Tau Delta (treas. 1983—84). E-mail: william.perry.1@us.af.mil.

PERRY, WILLIAM FRANCIS, nurse, educator; s. William Warren Perry and Elsa de Jesus Meads, Philip Meads (Stepfather); m. Carmen Brandie Arsenault; children: William David, James Philip, Katherine Elizabeth, Matthew Alexander. AA, Cape Cod CC, West Barnstable, Mass., 1973; BS, Regents Coll., Albany, NY, 1990; MA, Wright State U., Dayton, Ohio, 1998. RN Ohio Bd. Nursing. Officer USAF Nurse Corps, 1976—96; clin. info. specialist Kettering Health Network, Ohio, 1996—. Staff nurse Mass. Gen. Hosp., 1973—76; adj. instr. Wright State U. Miami Valley Coll., Dayton. Roman Catholic. Office: Kettering Health Network 2110 Leiter Rd Miamisburg OH 45342

PERRY, WILLIAM JAMES, engineering educator, former United States Secretary of Defense; b. Vandergrift, Pa., Oct. 11, 1927; s. Edward Martin and Mabelle Estelle (Dunlap) Perry; m. Leonilla Green, Dec. 29, 1947; children: David, William, Rebecca, Robin, Mark. BS in Math., Stanford U., 1949, MS, 1950; PhD, Pa. State U., 1957. Instr. math. Pa. State U., 1951—54; sr. mathematician HRB-Singer Co., State College, Pa., 1952—54; dir. electronic def. labs. GTE Sylvania Co., Mountain View, Calif., 1954—64; founder, pres. ESL, Inc., Sunnyvale, Calif., 1964—77; tech. cons. US Dept. Def., Washington, 1967—77, under sec. for rsch. & engring., 1977—81; mng. dir. Hambrecht & Quist, San Francisco, 1981—85; chmn. Tech. Strategies & Alliances, Menlo Park, Calif., 1985—93; prof., co-dir. Ctr. for Internat. Security and Arms Control Stanford U., Calif., 1989—93, prof. mgmt. sci. & engring., 1997—, sr. fellow, Hoover Inst., 1997—, Michael and Barbara Berberian prof., co-dir. Preventive Def. Project, 1997—; dep. sec. US Dept. Def., Washington, 1993—94, sec., 1994—97. Chmn. Global Tech. Ptnrs. LLC; mem. Iraq Study Group, 2006, Def. Policy Bd. Advisory Com., 2007—. Served in US Army, 1946—47. Recipient Def. Disting. Svc. medal, US Dept. Def., 1980, 1981, Achievement medal, Am. Electronics Assn., 1980, Forrestal medal, 1994, Henry Stimson medal, 1994, Arthur Bueche medal, NAE, 1996, Eisenhower award, 1996, Presdl. Medal Freedom, The White House, 1997, Outstanding Civilian Svc. medals, U.S. Army, 1997, USN, 1997, USAF, 1997, USCG, 1997, NASA, 1981, Def. Intelligence Agy., 1997; sr. fellow, Freeman Spogli Inst. Internat. Studies, Stanford U., 1997—. Office: Stanford Univ CISAC Encina Hall Rm C229 Stanford CA 94305-6165 Office Phone: 650-725-6501. Office Fax: 650-725-0920.

PERSAD, CHADEE, information technology manager; b. Rio Claro, Trinidad and Tobago; s. Chandrika and Indardaye Persad; m. Tara Gopaul, Aug. 4, 1974; children: Govind, Geeta. BSME, U. West Indies, 1974; MSME, City U., London; PhD, U. Tex. at Austin, 1983. Rsch. assoc. Ctr. Materials Sci., U. Tex., 1984—90; rsch. scientist U. Tex., Austin, Tex., 1990—2000; sr. rsch. scientist U. Tex. Inst for Advanced Technology, Austin, Tex., 2001—; faculty, dept. mech. engring. U. West Indies. Vis. faculty U. Netherlands, Antilles, Currcao, 1983—84. Author: (technical publications) Performance of Advanced Materials (US State Dept. for contributions to the ISTC, 1996). Grantee Multidisciplinary - Friction and Wear Scis., Office of Naval Rsch., 2004-2007. Mem.: ASME. Achievements include research in high performance materials for sliding electrical contacts. Avocation: travel.

PERSAUD, TRIVEDI VIDHYA NANDAN, anatomy educator, researcher, consultant; b. Port Mourant, Berbice, Guyana, Feb. 19, 1940; arrived in Canada, 1972; s. Ram Nandan and Deen (Raggy) P.; m. Gisela Gerda Zehden, Jan. 29, 1966; children: Indrani Uta and Sunita Heidi (twins), Rainer Narendra. MD, Rostock U., Germany, 1965, DSc, 1974; PhD in Anatomy, U. West Indies, Kingston, Jamaica, 1970. Intern, Berlin, Germany, 1965-66; govtl. med. officer Guyana, 1966-67; lectr., sr. lectr. anatomy dept. U. West Indies, 1967-72; assoc. prof. anatomy dept. U. Man., Winnipeg, 1972-75, prof., 1975—, prof. ob-gyn., reproductive scis., 1979-99, prof. emeritus, 1999—, prof. pediatrics and child health, 1989—, prof., chmn./head dept. human anatomy & cell sci., 1977-93, dir. Teratology Rsch. Lab., 1972-97. Cons. in teratology, Children's Centre, Winnipeg, 1973—; mem. sci. staff Health Scis. Centre, Winnipeg, 1973—. Author, editor 22 med. textbooks, including: Early History of Human Anatomy: From Antiquity to the Beginning of the Modern Era, 1984, (with others) Basic Concepts in Teratology, 1985, Environmental Causes of Human Birth Defects, 1991, History of Human Anatomy: The Post-Vesalian Era, 1997, (with K.L. Moore) The Developing Human, 8th edit., 2008, Before We Are Born, 7th edit., 2008; rev. Medical Embryology, 6th edit., 2003, hon. mem. Am. Assn. Clin. Anatomists, 2008; contbr. numerous chpts. to books, over 200 articles to profl. jours. Recipient Carveth Jr. Scientist award Can. Assn. Pathologists, 1974, Albert Einstein Centennial medal German Acad. Scis., 1975, Dr. & Mrs. H.H. Saunderson award U. Manitoba, 1985, 12th Raymond Truex Disting. Lectureship award Hahnemann U., 1990, Queen Elizabeth II Golden Jubilee medal Govt. Can., 2003. Fellow Royal Coll. Pathologists of London; mem. Can. Assn. Anatomists (pres. 1981-83, J.C.B. Grant award 1991), Am. Assn. Anatomists, Teratology Soc., European Teratology Soc. Office: Univ Man Dept Anatomy & Cell Sci 745 Bannatyne Ave Winnipeg MB R3E OJ9 Canada Office Phone: 204-789-3333. Business E-Mail: persaud@cc.umanitoba.ca.

PERSCHBACHER, PETER WESLEY, environmental science educator, research scientist; b. Davenport, Iowa, Nov. 15, 1946; s. Wesley Adolph and Margaret Pohly Perschbacher; m. Viriginia Brady, Feb. 14, 1986. BS, U. Mich., Ann Arbor, 1968; MS, Auburn U., Ala., 1975; PhD, Tex. A&M U., College Station, 1985. Rsch. assoc. U. NC Inst. Marine Sci., Morehead City, 1975-79; grad. rsch. asst. Tex. A&M U., Baytown, 1980-85; Aquaculture Trainer-Peace Corps Rsch. Planning Inst., Ft. Pierce, Fla., 1983; aquaculture biologist Caribbean Marine Rsch. Ctr., Lee Stocking Island, Bahamas, 1985; aquaculture advisor Harza Engring. Internat., Mymensingh, Bangladesh, 1986-87; rsch. biologist Agrl. Rsch. Svc., USDA, Tishomingo, Okla., 1989-93; assoc. prof. U. Ark., Pine Bluff, 1993—. Cons. KTAADIN, Newton, Mass., Norwegian Govt., Trondheim, Norway; affiliate faculty NASA. Author: Recirculation-Aeration Bibliography for Aquaculture, 1993; editor, contbg. author: Small Scale Aquaculture, 2003; editor, contbg. author Asia Fisheries Sci. (top 10 papers, 2008), contbg. author: Third National Reservoir Symposium, 1997, Am. Chem. Soc. symposium in Agr., 2002, Third World Fisheries Congress, Beijing, 2000; contbr. article (named to top ten papers of 1998, 2007), others. Chair Clean and Beautiful Commn. Bd., Pine Bluff, 2000; active Racial Harmony Task Force, Pine Bluff, 1996—98; organizer Environ. Fair Grace Episcopal Ch., Pine Bluff, 1997—2005; organizer waste mgmt. and splty. animal prodn. workshop U. Ark., 1999, chair rural life conf., 2003—07. Grantee Mgmt. of Environmentally-Derived Off-Flavors in Warmwater, USDA, Stoneville, Miss., 1995-2000, USDA-CSRS, 2006- Mem. Am. Fisheries Soc., Am. Inst. Fisheries Rsch. Biologists, World Aquaculture Soc. (chair small-scale aquaculture spl. session 2002, 07), Asian Fisheries Soc., Sigma Xi ((pres. Ctrl. Ark. chpt. 2007), Nat. Diversity Com., Xi Sigma Pi, Gamma Sigma Delta (founding mem. U. Ark. chpt.) Democrat. Episcopalian. Achievements include development of sustainable aquaculture, cool weather algae in aquaculture; alligatar rearing. Avocations: native orchids, palms. Home Phone: 870-534-0650; Office Phone: 870-575-8145. Business E-Mail: pperschbacher@uaex.edu.

PERSCHBACHER, REX ROBERT, law educator; b. Chgo., Aug. 31, 1946; s. Robert Ray and Nancy Ellen (Beach) P.; children: Julie Ann, Nancy Beatrice. AB in Philosophy, Stanford U., 1968; JD, U. Calif., Berkeley, 1972. Bar: Calif. 1972, U.S. Dist. Ct. (no. dist.) Calif. 1973, U.S. Dist. Ct. (so. dist.) Calif. 1979, U.S. Ct. Appeals (9th cir.) 1980, U.S. Dist. ct. (ea. dist.) Calif. 1985. Law clk. to judge U.S. Dist. Ct. (no. dist.) Calif., San Francisco, 1973-74; asst. prof. law U. Tex., Austin, 1974-75; assoc. Heller, Ehrman, White & McAuliffe, San Francisco, 1975-78; asst. prof. law U. San Diego, 1978-79, assoc. prof. law, 1980-81; mem. faculty Inst. on Internat. and Comparative Law, London, 1984—88; acting prof. law U. Calif., Davis, 1981-85, prof., 1988—, assoc. dean, 1993-98, dean Law Sch., 1998—2008. Dir. clin. edn. Univ. Calif., Davis, 1981-93, acad. senate, law sch. rep., 1989-91; vis. prof. law Univ. Santa Clara (Calif.), summer 1986. Co-author: California Civil Procedure and Practice, 1996, The United States Legal system-An Introduction, 2002, 2d edit., 2007, California Legal Ethics, 7th edit., 2007, Problems in Legal Ethics, 9th edit., 2007, Cases and Materials on Civil Procedure, 5th edit., 2005; contbr. articles to legal jours. Bd. dirs. Legal Svcs. of No. Calif., 1990-96. Recipient Disting. Teaching Award, 1992. Mem. ABA (Section of Legal Edn. and Admissions to Bar, Accreditation Com., 2000-), Calif. Bar Assn., Am. Assn. Law Schs., Inn of Ct. Democrat. Avocation: travel. Office: UC Davis Sch Law 400 Mrak Hall Dr Davis CA 95616

PERSELL, CAROLINE HODGES, sociologist, educator, researcher; b. Ft. Wayne, Ind., Jan. 16, 1941; d. Albert Randolph and Katherine (Rogers) Hodges; m. Charles Bowen Persell III, June 17, 1967; children: Patricia Emily, Stephen David. BA, Swarthmore Coll., 1962; MA, Columbia U., 1967, PhD, 1971. Sr. assoc., then nat. coord. Nat. Scholarship Svc. and Fund for Negro Students, NYC, 1962-66; project dir. Bur. Applied Social Rsch., NYC, 1968-71; asst. prof. NYU, 1971-76, assoc. prof., 1976-86, prof., 1986—, dir. grad. studies dept. sociology, 1984-87, chair dept. sociology, 1987-93, Robin Williams Disting. lectr., 1993-94. Author: Education and Inequality, 1977, Understanding Society, 1984, 3d edit., 1990; author: (with Cookson) Preparing for Power, 1985, Making Sense of Society, 1992; author: (with Maisel) How Sampling Works, 1996; assoc. editor: Tchg. Sociology, 1983—85, Sociology of Edn., 1991—95, Gender & Society, 1992—95; contbr. articles to profl. jours. Carnegie scholar Advancement of Tchg., 2000-01; grantee Fund for Improvement of Postsecondary Edn., 1989-92, NSF Equipment Fund, 1993-96; recipient Faculty Devel. award NSF, 1978-79, Women Educators' Rsch. award, 1978. Mem.: Sociologists for Women in Soc., Ea. Sociol. Soc. (pres. 1995—96), Am. Sociol. Assn. (chair sect. 1983—84, chmn. publs. com. 1987—89, chair sect. 1988—89, v.p. 2004—05). Avocations: violin, gardening, opera, sports, photography. Office: NYU Dept Sociology 295 LafayetteSt New York NY 10012 Office Phone: 212-998-8350. Business E-Mail: chp1@nyu.edu.

PERSHAD, ASHISH, cardiologist; b. Hyderabad, India, Jan. 7, 1971; s. Kailash and Sheela Pershad; m. Nisha Waghray, Oct. 11, 1970; 1 child, Yash. MD, U. Bombay, 1994. Interventional cardiologist Heart and Vascular Ctr. Ariz., Phoenix, 2001—. Cons. WL Gore Inc, Flagstaff, Ariz., 2002—05, Care Hospitals, Hyderabad, Ap, India, 2003—. Med. adv. bd. Boston Sci. Inc, Natick, Mass., 2003—05. McLennon Acad. scholar, U. Bombay, 1994—95. Mem.: Soc. Coronary Angiography and Interventions, Am. Coll. Physicians, Am. Coll. Cardiology, Maricopa Med. Soc. (licentiate), Ariz. Med. Assn. (licentiate). Office: Heart and Vascular Ctr Ariz 1331 N7th St Ste #375 Phoenix AZ 85006 Office Fax: 602-307-0080. Business E-Mail: apershad1@cox.net.

PERSHAN, RICHARD HENRY, lawyer; b. NYC, Jan. 4, 1930; s. Benjamin and Sadie (Aronowsky) P.; m. Kathryn Schaefler, June 11, 1952; children: Lee S., Richard H. Jr., Pamela P. Hochman, Julia B. BA, Yale U., 1951, LLB, 1956. Bar: NY 1956, US Supreme Ct.1969. Assoc. Davis, Polk & Wardwell, NYC, 1956-60; ptnr. Finch & Schaefler, NYC, 1960-85, LeBoeuf, Lamb, Greene & MacRae (now Dewey & LeBoeuf LLP), NYC, 1986-94, of counsel, 1995—2009, Sullivan & Worcester LLP, NYC, 2009—. Counsel Mcpl. Art Soc., NYC, 1965-70, Fine Arts Fedn., NYC, 1975-80. Served to 1st lt. USAF, 1951-53. Fellow Am. Coll. Trust and Estate Counsel (author, editor, articles and studies 1960—); mem. Assn. of Bar of City of NY, Yale Club (NYC). Democrat. Avocation: fitness. Home: 1435 Lexington Ave New York NY 10128-1630 Office: Sullivan & Worcester LLP 1290 Avenue of America New York NY 10104 Home Phone: 212-348-7774; Office Phone: 212-660-3062. Personal E-mail: rpershan@yahoo.com. Business E-Mail: rpershan@sandw.com.

PERSHING, ROBERT GEORGE, retired telecommunications industry executive; b. Battle Creek, Mich., Aug. 10, 1941; s. James Arthur and Beulah Francis P.; m. Diana Kay Prill, Sept. 16, 1961 (div. Jan. 1989); children: Carolyn, Robert; m. Charlene Jean Reed Wallis, Mar. 18, 1989 (div. Dec. 1995); m. Luz F. Villalon Dreisbach, July 23, 2006. BSEE, Tri-State Coll., 1961. Comm. engr. Am. Elec. Power, Ind., NY, and Ohio, 1961-69; design supr. Wescom, Inc., Ill., 1969-74; dir. engring. Tellabs, Inc., Lisle, Ill., 1974-78; pres., CEO Teltrend, Inc., St. Charles, Ill., 1979-89, chmn. bd., 1979-88; CEO DKP Prodns., Inc., St. Charles, Ill., 1986-89; exec. cons. Teltrend, St. Charles, Ill., 1979-93; asst. treas. Magnekopy, inc., Villa Park, Ill. Bd. dirs. TI Investors, Inc.; advisor entrepreneurial studies U. Ill.; engring. cons. Recipient Chgo. Area Small Bus. award, 1986., INC 500 awards, 1987, 88. Mem. IEEE. Office: PO Box 3377 Show Low AZ 85902 Home Phone: 928-537-8952; Office Phone: 928-537-8952. E-mail: rpershing@frontiernet.net.

PERSICO, JOSEPH EDWARD, historian; b. Gloversville, NY, July 19, 1930; s. Thomas Louis and Blanche (Perrone) P.; m. Sylvia La Vista, May 23, 1959; children: Vanya, Andrea. BA, SUNY-Albany, 1952, PhD (hon.), 1996; postgrad., Columbia U., 1955. Writer on staff of Gov. State of NY, Albany, 1955-59; commd. fgn. service officer USIA, 1959, served in Buenos Aires, Rio de Janeiro, 1959-62; speechwriter to commr. Dept. Health State of NY, Albany, 1963-66, chief speechwriter for Gov., 1966-74; speechwriter for Vice Pres. Nelson Rockefeller The White House, Washington, 1975-77. Commr. Am. Battle Monuments Commn. Author: My Enemy My Brother: Men and Days of Gettysburg, 1977, Piercing the Reich: The Penetration of Nazi Germany by American Secret Agents During World War II, 1979, The Imperial Rockefeller: A Biography of Nelson A. Rockefeller, 1982, Edward R. Murrow: An American Original, 1988, Casey: William J. Casey, From the OSS to the CIA, 1990, Nuremberg: Infamy on Trial, 1994, Roosevelt's Secret War: FDR and World War II Espionage, 2001, Eleventh Month, Eleventh Day, Eleventh Hour: Armistice Day, 1918, 2004, Franklin and Lucy: President Roosevelt, Mrs. Rutherfurd, and the Other Remarkable Women in His Life, 2008; co-author: Colin Powell: My American Journey, 1995; author: (novels) The Spiderweb, 1979. Served to lt. (j.g.) USN, 1952-55. Recipient Disting. Alumnus award SUNY-Albany, 1982 Mem.: Coun. Fgn. Rels., Authors Guild, Inc. Office Phone: 518-452-5429.

PERSING, JOHN ARTHUR, surgeon; b. Burlington, Vt., Apr. 16, 1948; s. Raymond Maurice and Natalie (Vespucci) P.; m. Susan Powers Light, June 22, 1971; children: Sarah Merriman, John Scott. BA cum laude, U. Vt., 1970, MD, 1974; MA (hon.), Yale U., 1992. Diplomate Am. Bd. Plastic and Reconstructive Surgery, Am. Bd. Neurol. Surgeons. Resident gen. surgery Hosp. of U. Ariz., Tuscon, 1974-76; resident neurol. surgery Hosp. of U. Va., Charlottesville, 1976-82, resident plastic surgery, 1982-84, dir. cranial base surgery, 1988-92, vice chmn. dept. of plastic surgery, 1988-92, chief divsn. of craniofacial surgery, 1988-92; asst. prof. plastic and neurosurgery U. Va., Charlottesville, 1984-87, assoc. prof. of plastic and neurosurgery, 1987-89, prof. plastic and neurosurgery, 1989-92; prof. plastic surgery and neurosurgery Yale U. Sch. of Medicine, New Haven, Conn., 1992—, chief sect. of plastic surgery, 1992—; fellow Trumbull Coll. Yale U., New Haven, 1994—. Editor: Clinics in Plastic Surgery, July, 1995; co-editor Jour. of Craniofacial Surgery, 1992—, Scientific Foundations and Surgical Treatment for Craniosynostosis, 1989, Neurosurgery Clinics of North America, July, 1991; assoc. editor Plastic and Reconstructive Surgery, 1997-2005. Recipient Donald D. Matson award Am. Assn. of Neurol. Surgeons, 1981. Mem. Am. Assn. Pediatric Plastic Surgeons (pres. 1995-97), Am. Assn. Plastic Surgeons (membership com. 1994-95), Am. Soc. Plastic and Reconstructive Surgeons (trustee 2007-), Am. Cleft Palate-Craniofacial Assn. (coms.), Am. Soc. Maxillofacial Surgeons (coms., v.p. 2000-01,pres. 2002-03, Bernd Speissl award 1991, Maxillofacial Surgeons Found. Rsch. award 1992), Plastic Surgery Edn. Found. (sec. 2005-07, pres. elect 2009), Assn. Acad. Chmn. of Plastic Surgery (plastic surgery residency tng. evaluation com. 1993, chair issues com. 1994, v.p. 2002-03, pres. 2004-05), Northeastern Soc. Plastic Surgeons (program com. 1995), Plastic Surgery Rsch. Coun. (program com. 1991-94), Am. Bd. Plastic Surgery (chmn. 2005). Office: Yale Plastic Surgery 330 Cedar St # 2 New Haven CT 06510-8041 Office Phone: 203-785-2570. Business E-Mail: john.persing@yale.edu.

PERSINGER, DEL LOUIS, pharmaceutical company executive; b. Whiting, Iowa, Aug. 2, 1949; s. Ardell L. and Doris L. Persinger; m. Mary L. Tabor, Sept. 16, 1984; children: Christopher, Benjamin Hammerschlag, Sarah Hammerschlag. BSChemE with distinction, Iowa State U., 1971, MS in Journalism and Mass. Comm., 1975; MBA in Fin., Am. U., 1990. Refinery process engr. Exxon Co., Baton Rouge, 1971-73; environtl. and pub. affairs mgr. Am. Petroleum Inst., Washington, 1975-89, sr. assoc. refining, 1989-92, dep. dir. mfg., distbn. and mktg., 1992-94, dir. mgmt. and budget, 1994-96; v.p. fin. ops. Pharm. Rsch. and Mfrs. of Am., Washington, 1996—2006, sr. v.p., CFO, 2006—; pres., CEO PhRMA Found., Washington, 1999—. Trustee, past pres. Bethesda Jewish Congregation, 1992—2000. Mem. Fin. Execs. Inst., Am. Soc. of Assn. Execs., Am. Found. for Pharm. Edn. (bd. dirs. 1999—), Phi Kappa Phi, Tau Beta Pi, Omega Chi Epsilon. Office: Pharm Rsch and Mfrs of Am Ste 300 950 F St NW Washington DC 20004

PERSKY, DAVID WILLIAM, lawyer; b. Boston, Feb. 2, 1950; s. Lester and Mary Elizabeth (Connor) P.; m. Mary Easler, Nov. 28, 1980. B.A., So. Methodist U., 1972; M.S., Miami U., 1973; Ph.D., Fla. State U., 1979; postgrad. Stetson Coll. Law. Asst. dir. housing U. South Fla., Tampa, 1973-77; coordinator alcohol awareness Fla. State U., Tallahassee, 1977-79; asst. to v.p. acad. affairs U. South Fla., Tampa, 1979-80, asst. to v.p. student affairs, 1980-84, assoc. dean students, 1985—. Bd. dirs. Alcohol Community Treatment Services, Tampa, 1984-87, Tampa Bay Council on Alcoholism, 1984-86, DWI Counterattack, Inc., 1984-85. Mem. Nat. Assn. Student Personnel Administrs., Blue Key, Kappa Sigma, Omicron Delta Kappa. Jewish. Club: Civitan (pres. 1983-84). Avocations: tennis; running; rugby. Office: Saint Leo Univ 33701 SR 52 Saint Leo FL 33574-6665 Home: 9631 Norchester Circle Tampa FL 33647

PERSKY, MARLA SUSAN, lawyer; b. Pitts., Feb. 15, 1956; d. Bernard and Elaine (Matus) P.; m. Craig Heberton IV, May 20, 1984. BS, Northwestern U., 1977; JD, Washington U., St. Louis, 1982. Bar: Ill. 1982. Asst. dir. med. records Chgo. Lake Shore Hosp., 1978; sales/mktg. rep. Colgate-Palmolive Co., Chgo., 1978-79; mem. Lurie Sklar & Simon, Chgo., 1982-86; corp. counsel Baxter Healthcare Corp., Deerfield, Ill., 1986-91; lead litigation counsel Baxter Internat. Inc., 1991-94; assoc. gen. counsel Baxter Healthcare Corp., Deerfield, 1994—98, dep. gen. counsel, 1998—2004, gen. counsel, corp. sec., 2004—. Dir. Cytyc Corp. Sr. editor Urban Law Ann., 1981-82; contbr. articles to profl. jours. Mem. Chgo. Bar Assn., Ill. Bar Assn. (writing contest award 1983), ABA (vice chmn. medicine and law com. 1984-86), Am. Soc. Law and Medicine, Am. Acad. Hosp. Attys. Democrat.

PERSLIDEN, JAN R. G., physicist; b. Norrkoping, Sweden, July 13, 1950; s. Rune E.B. and Ruth E.M. (Roxne) P.; m. Lena K. Åman, Aug. 1, 1976; children: Sara, Hanna, Mikael, Persliden. PhD, Linkoping U., 1986. Rsch. asst. dept. radiation physics U. Linkoping, 1976-82; med. physicist Univ. Hosp., Linköping, Sweden, 1982-88, prin. med. physicist, 1988-99, assoc. prof., 1993, prof., 2002—. Cons. med. physicist Norrkoping Hosp., Motala Hosp., Sweden, 1994-99; head med. physics dept. U. Hosp., Orebro, Sweden, 1999-. Contbr. articles to profl. jours. Mem. Swedish Soc. of Radiation Physics (bd. dirs. 1994-2001, pres. 1999-2001), Swedish Electrotech. Commn. Baptist. Avocations: church activities, cross country skiing. Office: Dept Radiation Physics Univ Hosp 701 85 Örebro Sweden Office Phone: 4619 6021000. Personal E-mail: Jan.Persliden@orebroll.se.

PERSOFF, MYRON MAYER, plastic surgeon; b. West Palm Beach, Fla., Apr. 26, 1941; BS, U. Fla., Gainesville, 1963; MD, U. Miami, Fla., 1967. Cert. Am. Bd. Plastic Surgery, 1977. Rotating-2 intern Phila. Naval Hosp., 1967—68; resident gen. surgery U. South Fla. Sch. Medicine, Tampa, 1971—73, St. Joseph Hosp., Houston, 1973—74, resident plastic surgery, 1974—76; fellow Cronin-Brauer Clin. Assn., Houston, 1974—76; staff mem. North Broward Hosp., 1976—90, West Boca Med. Ctr., 1985—94, Northridge Med. Ctr., Ft. Lauderdale, Fla., 1993—95, Mercy Hosp., Coconut Grove, Fla., 1994—, Coral Gables Hosp., Fla., 1998—2001; active staff mem. Boca Raton Cmty. Hosp., Fla., 1976—93; clin. asst. U. Miami Sch. Medicine, 1977—2001. Contbr. articles to med. jours.; featured: magazines Plastic Surgery Products. Orthopedic surgeon USN, 1968—69, Navy Hosp., Pensacola, Fla., sea duty USN, 1968, USS Speigel Grove, attended Flight Surgeons Sch. USN, 1969, Pensacola, Fla., served in USN, 1969—71, US Naval Air Sta., Cubi Point, Philippines. Fellow: Am. Coll. Surgeons; mem.: AMA, Broward County Soc. Plastic Surgeons, Lipolysis Soc. N.Am., Miami Soc. Plastic Surgeons, Dade County Med. Assn., Palm Beach County Med. Soc., Fla. Med. Assn., Palm Beach County Soc. Plastic and Reconstructive Surgeons, Fla. Soc. Plastic and Reconsructive Surgeons, Southeastern Soc. Plastic and Reconstructive Surgeons, Am. Soc. Plastic and Reconstructive Surgeons, Am. Soc. Aesthetic Plastic Surgery. Office: Coconut Grove Plastic Surgery Mercy Output Ctr 3659 S Miami Ave Ste 4006 Miami FL 33133 Office Phone: 305-858-5255. Office Fax: 305-858-5235. Business E-Mail: info@drpersoff.com.

PERSOFF, NEHEMIAH, actor, artist; b. Jerusalem, Aug. 2, 1919; came to U.S., 1929; s. Samuel and Puah (Holman) P.; m. Thia Persov; children: Jeffrey Jonathan, Dan Deckel, Perry Erez, Dahlia. Student, Hebrew Tech. Inst., NYC, 1934-37. Ind. stage, screen and TV actor, 1945—. Actor: (Broadway prodns.) Sundown Beach, Galileo, Richard the 3d, King Lear, Peer Gynt, Peter Pan, Reclining Figure, Flahooly, Montserrat, Tiger at the Gate, Only in America, (local, regional prodns.) Fiddler on the Roof, Man of La Mancha, Oliver, I'm Not Rappaport, 1988, Death of a Salesman (Stratford, Ont.), Two, Drinking America, Rosebloom, Dybbuk (Best Actor L.A. Critics 1975), Glass Menagerie (Israeli prodn.), Volpone, Of Mice and Men, (films) In Search of the Real Jesus, The Harder They Fall, The Wrong Man, This Angry Age, Men in War, Some Like It Hot, Al Capone, Green Mansions, The Commancheros, The Greatest Story Ever Told, Voyage of the Damned, Yentl, The Hook, The Last Temptation of Christ, Twins, numerous TV shows including For Whom the Bell Tolls (Sylvania award for best supporting actor 1958), The Big Knife, Alfred Hitchcock Presents, Rawhide, Twilight Zone, The Untouchables, The Wild, Wild West, I Spy, Gunsmoke, Police Story, Columbo, Barney Miller, Six Million Dollar Man, Delta House, Littlest Hobo, Magnum P.I., Hotel, Adderly; (TV miniseries) The French Atlantic; (one-man show) Aleichem Sholem-Sholem-Alecheim, 1971 (L.A. Critics award, San Francisco Critics Circle award 1979); paintings exhibited at George Krevsky Fine Arts, San Francisco, Seago Gallery, Cambria, Calif. With US Army, 1942—45. Jewish.

PERSON, EVERT BERTIL, retired newspaper and radio executive; b. Berkele, Calif., Apr. 6, 1914; s. Emil P. and Elida (Swanson) P.; m. Ruth Finley, Jan. 26, 1944 (dec. May 1985); m. 2d, Norma Joan Betz, Mar. 12, 1986. Student, U. Calif., Berkeley, 1937; LHD, Calif. State Univ., 1983, LHD, 1993, Sonoma State U., 1993. Co-publisher, sec.-treas. Press Democrat Pub. Co., Santa Rosa, Calif., 1945-72, editor, 1972-73, pres., pub., editor-in-chief, 1973-85; sec.-treas. Finley Broadcasting Co., Santa Rosa, 1945-72, pres., 1972-89, Kawana Pubs., 1975-85; pub. Healdsburg Tribune, 1975-85; prin. Evert B. Person Investments, Santa Rosa, 1985—. Pres. Person Properties Co., Santa Rosa, 1945-70; v.p. Finley Ranch & Land Co., Santa Rosa, 1947-72, pres., 1972-79; pres. Baker Pub. Co., Oreg., 1957-67, Sebastopol (Calif.) Times, 1978-81, Russian River News, Guerneville, Calif., 1978-81; pres. publ. Kawana Pubs., 1978-85; mem. nominating com. AP, 1982-84, mem. auditing com., 1984-85 Bd. dirs Empire Coll., Santa Rosa, 1972-98, Sonoma County Taxpayers Assn., 1966-69, San Francisco Spring Opera Assn., 1974-79; bd. dirs. San Francisco Opera, 1986-95, v.p., 1988-95; pres. Calif. Newspaperboy Found., 1957-58; chmn. Santa Rosa Civic Arts Commn., 1961-62; pres. Santa Rosa Sonoma County Symphony Assn., 1966-68, Luther Burbank Meml. Found., 1979, Santa Rosa Symphony Found., 1967-77; adv. bd. Santa Rosa Salvation Army, 1959-67; commodore 12th Coast Guard Dist. Aux., 1969-70; trustee Desert Mus., Palm Springs, 1987-92, v.p. Nat. Bd. Canine Companions, Inc., 1989-92.

Decorated Knight of the Holy Sepulchre. Mem. Calif. Newspaper Pubs. Assn. (pres. 1981-82), Internat. Newspaper Fin. Execs. (pres. 1961-62), Bohemian Club, Sonoma County Press Club, Santa Rosa Golf and Country club, The Springs Club, Santa Rosa Rotary (past pres.), Masons (33 degree, Legion of Merit), Shriners. Roman Catholic. Home: 775 White Oak Dr Santa Rosa CA 95409-6155 Office: The Oaks 1400 N Dutton Ave Ste 12 Santa Rosa CA 95401-4644

PERSONICK, STEWART DAVID, electrical engineer; b. Bklyn., Feb. 22, 1947; s. Louis and Mamie (Katz) P.; m. Carol Ann Cooke, Apr. 12, 1986. B.E.E., CCNY, 1967; S.M., MIT, 1968, Sc.D., 1970. Engr. Bell Labs., Holmdel, N.J., 1967-75, engring. supr., 1975-78, dept. head, 1983-84; engring. mgr. Vidar div. TRW, Mountain View, Calif., 1978-81, research mgr. Tech. Research Ctr. El Segundo, Calif., 1981-83; cons. Pacific Palisades, Calif., 1983-84; com. mem. NRC, Washington, 1983—; div. mgr. Bell Communications Research, Red Bank, N.J., 1984-85, asst. v.p., 1985-95, v.p., gen. mgr., 1995—. Author: Optical Fiber Transmission Systems, 1981, Fiber Optics Technology and Applications, 1985; editor spl. issue on fiber optic systems, IEEE Trans., 1978, 83; IEEE misc. jours., 1975—; patentee fiber optics; contbr. chpts. in books. Fellow IEEE, Optical Soc. Am.; mem. NAE, IEEE Communications Soc. Office: Bell Communications Rsch 445 South St Rm 1c-201B Morristown NJ 07960-6454

PERSONS, JOHN WADE, lawyer; b. Fitchburg, Mass., Dec. 6, 1953; s. Roger W. and Vivian A. (Boudreau) P.; m. Marjorie L. Smith, July 18, 1980; children: Katherine A., Elizabeth W. BA in History magna cum laude, U. Conn., 1975, MA, 1977; JD, Albany Law Sch., 1980. Bar: N.Y. 1981, U.S. Dist. Ct. (no. dist.) N.Y. 1981, U.S. Dist. Ct. (ea. dist.) N.Y. 1985. From law clk. to assoc. Cade & Saunders, Albany, NY, 1978—84; legal rschr., writing instr. Albany Law Sch., 1979—80; assoc. Glynn and Mercep, Stony Brook, NY, 1984—86; ptnr. Glynn, Mercep and Persons, Stony Brook, NY, 1987—91; assoc. Faruolo, Caputi, Weintraub & Neary, Huntington, NY, 1991—96; from assoc. to ptnr. Grey & Grey, LLP, Farmingdale, NY, 1996—2003; assoc. Montfort, Healy, McGuire and Salley, Garden City, NY, 2004—. Law guardian Albany County Family Ct., 1984. Mem. N.Y. State Bar Assn. (ins. sect., negligence and compensation law sect.), Suffolk County Bar Assn. (ins., negligence and compensation), Killington Sch. for Instrs.(yoga shanti tchr. trainer) Democrat. Home: 53 Cedar St Stony Brook NY 11790-1732 Office: Montfort Healy McGuire & Salley PO Box 7677 1140 Franklin Ave Garden City NY 11530-7677 Office Phone: 516-747-4082. Business E-Mail: john_persons@mhms-law.com.

PERSONS, (W.) RAY (W. RAY PERSONS), lawyer, legal association administrator; b. Talbottan, Ga., July 22, 1953; s. William and Frances (Crowell) P.; m. Wendy-Joy Mottley, Sept. 24, 1977; children: Conrad Ashley, April Maureen. BS cum laude, Armstrong State Coll., 1975; JD, Ohio State U., 1978. Bar: Ga. 1979, US Dist. Ct. (so. dist.) Ga. 1980, US Dist. Ct. (no. dist.) Ga. 1986, US Ct. Appeals (11th cir.) 1986. Assoc. Troutman, Sanders, Lockerman & Ashmore, Atlanta, 1978-79; atty. NLRB, Atlanta, 1980-82; legis. counsel U.S Ho. Reps., Washington, 1983-86; atty. Mack & Bernstein, Atlanta, 1986-87; ptnr. Arrington & Hollowell LLP, Atlanta, 1987-95, Swift, Currie, McGhee & Hiers LLP, Atlanta, 1995-99, Hunton & Williams LLP, Atlanta, 1999—2001, King & Spalding LLP, Atlanta, 2001—. Adj. prof. litigation Ga. State U., Atlanta, 1989—; spl. asst. atty. gen. State of Ga., Atlanta, 1988—. Master Am. Inns of Ct. (Lamar chpt.); fellow Am. Coll. Trial Lawyers; mem. ABA, Internat. Soc. Barristers, Am. Bd. Trial Advocates, State Bar Ga., Atlanta Bar Assn. (bd. dirs., 1996-97, 2000-, sec., 2003-04, treas., 2004-05, 2nd v.p., 2005-06, pres.-elect, 2006-07, pres., 2007-) Lawyers Club of Atlanta. Roman Catholic. Office: King & Soalding LLP 1180 Peachtree St NE Atlanta GA 30309 Office Phone: 404-572-2494. Business E-Mail: rpersons@kslaw.com.

PERSSE, DAVID, emergency physician, director; s. John David and Mary Margaret Persse; married. MD, Georgetown U. Sch. Medicine, Washington, 1989. Med. lic. Tex., 1992. Physician Houston Fire Dept., 1996—, dir., emergency med. svcs., 1996—; with, pub. health authority Houston Dept. Health and Human Svcs., 2002—. Office: City Houston 500 Jefferson St Ste 1500 Houston TX 77002 Office Fax: 713-646-5310.

PERSSON, ERLAND KARL, retired electrical engineer, researcher, executive; b. Soderala, Sweden, Oct. 9, 1923; arrived in U.S., 1949, naturalized, 1953; m. Elaine Darm; children: Ann Monn, Eric. BSEE, U. Minn., 1955. Registered profl. engr., Minn. Prin. engr. Gen. Mills, Mpls., 1956-61; v.p. engring. Electro-Craft Corp., Hopkins, Minn., 1961-72, v.p. R & D, 1972-83, sr. v.p., chief tech. officer, 1983-86; pres. Erland Persson Co., Mpls., 1987—2008. Contbr. articles to profl., chapters to books. Mem. mech. engring. adv. com. U. Minn.; bd. dirs. Minn. High Tech. Coun., 1984—86, mem., 1987. Fellow: IEEE (life; mem. indsl. drives com.), Audio Engring. Soc. (life; founder midwest chpt. 1974); mem.: Eta Kappa Nu. Achievements include patents in field. Home Phone: 952-540-6520.

PERTUSA, INMACULADA, language educator; b. Albacete, Spain, Nov. 13, 1963; d. Antonio Pertusa and Trinidad Seva. PhD, U. Colo., Boulder, 1996. Assoc. prof. U. Ky., Lexington, 2003—04, Western Ky. U., Bowling Green, 2004—. Sec. AILCFH, 2007—. Recipient Outstanding Tchg. award, UK Provost, 2003. Office: Western Ky Univ 1906 College Heights Blvd #31029 Bowling Green KY 42101 Business E-Mail: inma.pertusa@wku.edu.

PERUMAL, OMATHANU PILLAI, research scientist, medical researcher, educator; b. Madurai, Tamil Nadu, India, June 29, 1974; arrived in USA, 2003; married; 1 child. BPharm, Tamil Nadu Dr. M.G. R. Med. U., Chennai, India, 1995; MPharm, Birla Inst. Tech., India, 1997; PhD, Nat. Inst. Pharm. Edn. and Rsch. (NIPER), Chandigarh, India, 2002. Jr. rsch. fellow Birla Inst. Tech., Ranchi, Jharkhand, India, 1995—97; lectr. Ultra Coll. Pharmacy, Madurai, Tamil Nadu, India, 1997—98; sr. rsch. fellow Nat. Inst. Pharm. Edn. and Rsch. (NIPER), Chandigarh, Punjab, India, 1998—2002; rsch. scientist Ranbaxy Rsch. Laboratories, Grugaon, Haryana, India, 2002—03; post doctoral scientist Coll. pharmacy, U. Ky., Lexington, Ky., 2003—04; rsch. assoc. Wayne State U., Detroit, 2004—05; asst. prof. Coll. Pharmacy, SD State U., Brookings, SC, 2005—. Reviewer Internat. Jour. TB and Lung Diseases, AAPS Pharm. Sci., Current Drug Delivery, Biorganic and Medicinal Chemistry, Biomacromolecules, Jour. Investigative Dermatology, Transactions of the Royal Soc. Tropical Medicine and Hygiene, others; presenter in field. Assoc. editor Jour. Biomed. Nanotech.; contbr. articles to profl. jours. Sec. Jr. Jaycess Wing of Madurai Jr. Chamber, Madurai, Tamil Nadu, India, 1993—94, chmn., 1994—95. Jr. rsch. fellow, U. Grants Commn., India, sr. rsch. fellow, Dept. Sci. and Tech., India, post-doctoral scholar, NIH. Mem.: Controlled Release Soc., Am. Assn. Colls. Pharmacy, Indian Pharm. Assn. (assoc.), Am. Assn. Pharm. Scientists (assoc. Travel award 2004), Rho Chi, Sigma Xi. Achievements include development of a new modified radioimmuno assay for analysis of insulin; a new gel system for the transdermal delivery of insulin; research in insulin delivery through skin using electrical current and chemical enhancers; new ways to improve the drug delivery across skin using various chemical and physical strategies. Avocations: table tennis, reading, cricket. Office: SD State U Coll Pharmacy Box 2202C Brookings SD 57007 Personal E-mail: omathanu@yahoo.com.

PERVAIZ, MOHAMMAD HASSAN, cardiologist; b. Lahore, Punjab, Pakistan, May 2, 1978; arrived in U.S., 2003; s. Pervaiz Akhtar Butt and Riffat Pervaiz; m. Maimoona Qamar. Degree, Govt. Coll., Lahore, Pakistan, 1997; MD, King Edward Med. Coll., Pakistan, 2002. Cert. Ednl. Commn. Fgn. Med. Grad., 2003. Clin. instr. Coll. Human Medicine Mich. State U., East Lansing, 2004—, resident internal medicine dept. medicine, 2004—, cardiology fellow, 2007—. Contbr. articles to med. jours. Grantee, Boston Sci., 2006. Mem.: AMA (assoc.), ACP (assoc.). Avocation: Aikido. Office: Mich State U Dept Medicine B301 Clinical Ctr East Lansing MI 48823 Home: 2932 Trappers Cove Trl Apt 2B Lansing MI 48910-8503 Business E-Mail: pervaiz@msu.edu.

PERVAN, NENAD NENO, theater educator; b. Sarajevo, Bosnia-Herzegovina, Feb. 16, 1966; s. Slavko and Divna Pervan; m. Milena Markovic, Apr. 17, 1993; 1 child, Andrej. BFA, Akademija Umetnosti, Yugoslavia, 1990; MFA, U. Tenn., Knoxville, 1997. Vis. asst. prof. Loyola Marymount U., LA, 2007—. Dir.: (theatre) The Balcony by Jean Genet, The Echoes by R.Nash, Powder Keg by Dejan Dukovski, The Emigrants by Slawomir Mrozek, Jedan Covjek i Jedna Zena; actor: Andora, The Trial, The Cherry Orchard, Tango, Much Ado About Nothing, La Cage Aux Folles (Best Supporting Actor-musical, 1995), Sarajevo. A Few More Stories, The Grease, The Country Wife, Lend Me A Tenor, Bluebeard's Castle, (television) Aleksa Santic, (film) Crni Bombarder, Granica, Najbolji, The Cavern, The Hunted, She Kept Silent. Mem.: Actor's Equity Assn., Screen Actor's Guild. Office: Loyola Marymount Univ 1 LMU Drive Los Angeles CA 90045 Office Fax: 310-338-1984. Business E-Mail: npervan@lmu.edu.

PERVOUCHINE, DMITRI, science educator; PhD, Moscow State U., 1999, MS, 1996, Boston U., 2002. Musician piano performances in various concerts. Mem.: Piano Class MGU. Personal E-mail: dpbostonus@yahoo.com.

PERZEK, PHILIP JOHN, lawyer; b. Chgo., Sept. 25, 1960; s. Thomas John and Dorothy (Malis) P.; m. Gayle Karon Scott, Aug. 17, 1985; 1 child, Rachel Karon. BS, No. Ill. U., 1982; JD, Northwestern U., 1986. Bar: Ill. 1986, U.S. Dist. Ct. (no. dist.) Ill. 1986. Law clk. to Hon. Nicholas J. Bua U.S. Dist. Ct. (no. dist.) Ill., Chgo., 1986-88; ptnr. Latham & Watkins LLP, Chgo., 1988—. Mem. Ill. State Bar Assn., Nat. Comml. Fin. Assn. Home: 207 W 8th St Hinsdale IL 60521-4448 Office: Latham & Watkins 5800 Sears Tower Chicago IL 60606 Office Phone: 312-876-7699. Business E-Mail: Philip.Perzek@lw.com.

PESCATORE, CHRISTOPHER, cosmetic dentist; DMD, U. Medicine and Dentistry, NJ. Instr. advanced aesthetic programs Baylor U., U. Ky., NYU; clin. co-dir. Las Vegas Inst. Advanced Dental Studies; clin. dir. MicroDental Labs.; pvt. practice Danville, Calif. Mem. editl. bd. REALITY; contbr. articles to profl. jours. Office: 903 San Ramon Blvd Ste 226 Danville CA 94526 Office Phone: 925-362-9330. Office Fax: 925-362-8789. Business E-Mail: chrisdmd@aol.com.

PESCATORE-SHIREY, HOPE JEAN, middle school reading educator; b. Hollywood, Fla., Sept. 12, 1966; d. Earle Milton Sr. and Faith Lucille Pescatore. BS, Nova U., 1987, MS, 1990. Cert. tchr., Fla. Tchr. 1st, 2d and 3d grades Sunland Park Elem. Sch., Ft. Lauderdale, Fla., 1987—92; tchr. reading Omni Mid. Sch., Boca Raton, Fla., 1992—99; tchr. reading I, II, III Lake Worth H.S., Fla., 1999—2001; reading coach Okeeheelee Mid. Sch., Greenacres, Fla., 2001—. Facilitator Regional League Mid. Sch. Conf., 2003, 04, Fla. Online Reading Devel., 2002—; prof. Fla. OnLine Reading Devel., 2002—; spkr. in field; trainer in field. Acad. scholar Nova U., Success grantee Citibank, 1995; named Greenacres Tchr. of Yr. Wal-Mart, 2005 Mem. CRISS Dist. trainee E-mail: shirey@palmbeach.k12.fl.us.

PESCH, ELLEN P., lawyer; BA, Barat Coll., 1986; JD, John Marshall Law Sch., 1989; LLM, DePaul U., 1991. Bar: Ill. 1989, U.S. Dist. Ct. (no. dist.) Ill. With Sidley Austin Brown & Wood, Chgo., 1989—, ptnr., 2001—. Mem.: ABA, Internat. Swaps and Derivatives Assn., Stable Value Investment Assn.

PESCH, LEROY ALLEN, physician, educator, health and hospital consultant, business executive; b. Mt. Pleasant, Iowa, June 22, 1931; s. Herbert Lindsey and Mary Clarissa (Tyner) P.; children from previous marriage: Christopher Allen, Brian Lindsey, Daniel Ethan; m. Donna J. Stone, Dec. 28, 1975 (dec. Feb. 1985); stepchildren: Christopher Scott Kneifel, Linda Suzanne Kneifel; m. Gerri Ann Cotton, Sept. 27, 1986; 1 child, Tyner Ford. Student, State U. Iowa, 1948—49, Iowa State U., 1950—52; MD cum laude, Washington U., St. Louis, 1956. Intern Barnes Hosp., St. Louis, 1956-57; rsch. assoc. NIH, Bethesda, Md., 1957-59; asst. resident medicine Grace-New Haven Hosp., New Haven, 1959-60; clin. fellow Yale Med. Sch., New Haven, 1960-61, instr. medicine, 1961-62, asst. prof. medicine, 1962-63, asst. dir. liver study unit, 1961-63; assoc. physician Grace-New Haven Hosp., 1961-63; assoc. prof. medicine Rutgers U., New Brunswick, NJ, 1963-64, prof., 1964-66, chmn. dept. medicine, 1965-66; assoc. dean, prof. medicine Stanford Sch. Medicine, 1966-68; mem. gen. medicine study sect. NIH, 1965-70, chmn., 1969-70; dean, dir. univ. hosps. SUNY, Buffalo, 1968-71; dep. asst. sec. manpower HEW, 1970-72, spl. cons. to sec. for health, 1970-75; prof. div. biol. scis. and medicine U. Chgo., 1972-77; prof. pathology Northwestern U., 1977-79; health and hosp. cons.; chmn., chief exec. officer Health Resources Corp. Am., 1981-84; chmn. bd. dirs. Republic Health Corp., 1985-88; chmn., chief exec. officer The Bora Health Group, Seattle, 1987-92; pres. Genus Tech. Corp., 1987—; chmn., chief exec. officer The Pesch Group Cos., Sun Valley, Idaho, 1989—. Contbr. articles on internal medicine to profl. jours. Bd. dirs. Buffalo Med. Found., 1969-72, Health Orgn., Western N.Y., 1968-71, Joffrey Ballet, N.Y.C., 1980—; trustee Michael Reese Hosp. and Med. Ctr., Chgo., 1971-76, pres., CEO, 1971-77; mem. exec. bd. Auditorium Theatre Coun., Chgo.; trustee W. Clement and Jessie V. Stone Found.; mem. adv. com. Congl. Awards; pres. Pesch Found. Sr. asst. surgeon USPHS, 1957-59. Mem.: AAAS, Am. Soc. Biol. Chemists, Am. Assn. for Clin. Rsch., Am. Assn. for Study of Liver Disease. Mailing: C/O Gerri Pesch PO Box 12 Sun Valley ID 83353 Personal E-mail: allen622@cox.net.

PESCI, JOE (JOSEPH FRANK PESCI), actor; b. Newark, Feb. 9, 1943; s. Angelo and Mary Pesci; m. Claudia Haro, 1988 (div. 1992); m. Garrett Warren; 1 child, Tiffany. Actor: (films) The Death Collector, 1976, Raging Bull, 1980 (Nat. Bd. Rev. award for Best Supporting Actor, Nat. Soc. Film Critics award for Best Supporting Actor, NY Film Critics Cir. award for Best Supporting Actor, BAFTA Award for Best Newcomer, Acad. award nominee, Golden Globe award nominee), Dear Mr. Wonderful, 1982, I'm Dancing as Fast as I Can, 1982, Easy Money, 1983, Once Upon A Time In America, 1984, Eureka, 1984, Tutti Dentro, 1984, Man on Fire, 1987, Moonwalker, 1988, The Legendary Life of Ernest Hemingway, 1988, Lethal Weapon 2, 1989, Betsy's Wedding, 1990, Goodfellas, 1990 (Acad. award for Best Supporting Actor, Golden Globe award nominee), Home Alone, 1990, The Super, 1991, JFK, 1991, My Cousin Vinny, 1992 (Am. Comedy award for Funniest Actor in a Motion Picture), Lethal Weapon 3, 1992, The Public Eye, 1992, Home Alone 2: Lost In New York, 1992, A Bronx Tale, 1993, Jimmy Hollywood, 1994, With Honors, 1994, Casino, 1995, Gone Fishin', 1997, 8 Heads in a Duffel Bag, 1997, Lethal Weapon 4, 1998, The Good Shepherd, 2006; (TV series) Half Nelson, 1985, Tales from the Crypt, 1992. Named Best Supporting Actor (for Goodfellas), Boston Soc. Film Critics, Chgo. Film Critics Assn., Kansas City Film Critics Cir., LA Film Critics Assn., Nat. Bd. Rev.*

PESCOVITZ, ORA HIRSCH, health facility administrator, medical educator; b. Carmel, Ind., Sept. 23, 1956; m. Mark David Pescovitz; children: Aliza Beth, Ari Samuel, Naomi Rachel. MS in Med. Edn., Northwestern U., Ill., 1978; MD, Northwestern U. Med. Sch., Ill., 1979. Cert. diplomate Am. Bd. Pediatrics, 1985, Am. Bd. Pediat. Endocrinology and Metabolism, 1986. Med. ward officer Children's Hosp. Nat. Med. Ctr., Washington, 1983—84, instr. pediat. endocrinology/metabolism, 1985—86; asst. prof. pediat. endocrinology, metabolism Dept. Pediat. U. Minn., 1986—97; assoc. prof. pediat., physiology and biophysics Ind. U. Sch. Medicine, 1988—92, prof. pediat., physiology and biophysics, 1992—2009, full mem. grad. sch. faculty, 1993, dir. sect. pediat. endocrinology, diabetology dept., 1990, Edwin Letzter prof. prof. pediat., 1998—2009, exec. assoc. dean rsch. affairs; pres., CEO Riley Hosp. for Children, 2004—09; exec. v.p. med. affairs U. Mich., 2009—; CEO U. Mich. Health Sys., 2009—. Editor (editl. bd.): Jour. Clin. Endocrinology and Metabolism, 1989—93, (jour.) Endocrine Reviews, 1995—98, Hormone Rsch., 1996—, Endocrine, 1997—, Pediat. Endocrinology: The Endocrinologist, 1998—; contbr. to devel. of movie on precocious puberty;, author 150 sci. publs., 101 abstracts. Mem. numerous nat. coms., 1987—; mem. Internat. Consensus Group on Growth Hormone Therapy: Workshop on Current Trends of Growth Related Rsch., 1989, Internat. Growth Forum II Organizing Com., 1996, 1997, Advances in Pediats. Course Planning Com., Mpls., 1985—88, Accident Prevention Com., AAP; mem. com. to draft a mission statement U. Minn., 1986—88, mem. residency selection com. dept. pediat., 1986—88, mem. gen. clin. rsch. ctr. sci. rev. com., 1986—88, mem. pediat. specialists bd. nominating com., 1986—88; mem. numerous coms. Ind. U., 1989—. Recipient Rsch. Career Devel. award, NIH, 1991—96, Forty Under 40, Indpls. Bus. Jour., 1993, Disting. Lectr., Mary E. Culbertson Symposium, Ind. U. Sch. Nursing, 2002; named one of Best Drs. in Am., Woodward and White, 1995, 1996, 1998, Am. Health, 1997, Indpls. Best Drs., 1995, The Influential Women in Indpls., Indpls. Bus. Jour. and Ind. Lawyer, 1999; nominee Women in the Lead, Indpls. Bus. Jour., 2002. Mem.: Women in Endocrinology, Soc. Pediat. Rsch., Midwest Soc. Pediat. Rsch., Lawson Wilkins Pediat. Endocrine Soc., Endocrine Soc., Am. Acad. Pediat. Achievements include patents for Use of GHRH-RP to stimulate stem cell factor production. Office: U Mich M7324 Med Scis Bldg Box 5626 1500 E Medical Center Dr Ann Arbor MI 48109 Office Phone: 734-647-9351. Business E-Mail: opescovi@umich.edu.

PESEC, DAVID JOHN, data systems executive; b. Cleve., Apr. 19, 1956; s. Rudolph Jan and Martha Garvel. (Kessler) P; m. Jan M. Garuer BS, Cleve. State U., 1988; MBA, U. Phoenix, 1999; PhD, Trinity Coll., 2000. Pvt. practice cons., Cleve., 1976—78; programmer Champion Svc. Corp., Cleve., 1978; sr. sys. programmer United Tel. of Ohio, Mansfield, 1978—89; dir. devel. Broderick Data Sys., Mansfield, 1989—97; prin. cons. Keane, Inc., Independence, Ohio, 1997—2000; pres. Pesec Creative Mgmt., Inc., Mansfield, 2000—. Adj. prof. Ashland U., 2001—, Am. Intercontinental U., 2001—; bd. dirs. Park Ave. Pets., Inc. Bd. dirs. ARC, Mansfield, 1989—, Mansfield Emergency Svc., 1986; assoc. pastor Cornerstone Grace Brethren Ch., 1995—; life mem. Rep. Nat. com., 1991—, Rep. Senatorial Inner Circle, 1991—. Recipient Senatoral medal of freedom, 1996. Mem. Am. Mgmt. Assn., Assn. Computing Machinery, Intercity Radio Club (pres. 1987-90), NRA, Gideons (v.p. 1992), Profl. Photographers. Republican. Mem. Grace Brethren Ch. Avocations: flying, auto racing. Office: 2152 Walker Lake Rd, Ste 127 Mansfield OH 44903 Office Phone: 419-589-7418. Business E-Mail: dpesec@pesecreativemanagement.com.

PESEK, TODD, physician, director; MD, Ohio State U. & Cleve. Clinic, 2004. Founding dir. ctr. healing across cultures Cleve. State U., 2004—. Office: Cleveland State Univ 2121 Euclid Ave HS 101 Cleveland OH 44115 Business E-Mail: t.pesek@csuohio.edu.

PESETSKY, BETTE, writer, educator; b. Milw., Nov. 16, 1932; d. Louis Block and Rose McKnight; m. Irwin Pesetsky, 1956; 1 child, David. BA, Washington U., St. Louis, 1954; MFA, U. Iowa, 1959. Vis. prof., Writers Workshop U. Iowa, Iowa City, 1990-91; vis. prof., dept. English and comparative studies U. Calif., Irvine, 1992-93; vis. prof. dept. English St. Lawrence U., Canton, N.Y., 1994; Disting. vis. fiction writer Wichita (Kans.) State U., 1994; Disting. vis. prof. dept. English U. Miami, 1997; Piaker vis. prof. dept. English, gen. lit. and rhetoric SUNY, Binghamton, 2002; writer-in-residence English dept. New Coll. of Fla., Fla. State U., Sarasota, 2004—. Author: (novels) Stories Up To a Point, 1982 (NY Times Notable Books, 1982), Author from a Savage People, 1983 (NY Times Notable Books, 1983), Digs, 1985, Midnight Sweets, 1988 (NY Times Notable Books, 1988), Confessions of a Bad Girl, 1989 (NY Times Notable Books, 1989), The Late Night Muse, 1991 (NY Times Notable Books, 1991), Cast a Spell, 1993 (NY Times Notable Books, 1993). Recipient Creative Artists Pub Serv Award, NY Coun Arts, 1980—81; fellow Creative Writing, NEA, 1979. Mem.: PEN. Home: Hilltop Park Dobbs Ferry NY 10522

PESETSKY, DAVID MICHAEL, linguist; b. Iowa City, Jan. 26, 1957; s. Irwin and Bette Pesetsky; m. Janis Melvold; children: Benjamin, Jonathan. BA summa cum laude, Yale U., 1977; PhD, MIT, 1982. Asst. prof. linguistics U. So. Calif., LA, 1982—83; assoc. prof. linguistics U. Mass., Amherst, 1983—88; Ferrari P. Ward prof. modern langs. and linguistics MIT, Cambridge, 1988—, Margaret Macvicar fellow, 2005—. Adv. bd. NSF, Divsn. Social, Behavioral and Econ. Scis., Washington, 1998—2000; com. visitors to linguistics program NSF, 1999—99, linguistics program rev. panel, 1990—93; vis. prof. Linguistic Soc. Am. Summer Inst., 1983, 96, 97, 99, 2003, LOT Grad. Sch. Linguistics, Netherlands, 1993—2000, Netherlands, 2000; vis. lectr. worldwide; editl. boards Linguistic Inquiry, Rivista di Grammatica Generativa, Natural Lang. Semantics, Oxford Surveys in Syntax, English Linguistics, Lang. Acquisition. Author: (scientific monograph) Zero Syntax, Phrasal Movement and its Kin; contbr. articles to profl. jours. Cons. for English lang. arts curriculum framework Dept. Edn., Mass., 1996; player New Philharm. Orch. of Mass. Recipient Ednl. Partnership award, Portsmouth Bd. Edn., N.H., 1998; grantee, NSF, 1991—96; fellow, Internat. Rsch. and Exchanges Bd., 1979—80. Mem.: AAAS (sect. member-at-large 1995—95, coun. del. 1996—99), Linguistic Soc. Am. (com. on lang. k-12 curriculum 2003—), Generative Linguists of Old Worlds (keynote spkr. 2003 2003), Phi Beta Kappa. Achievements include research in the nature of syntactic case marking and its relation to tense systems (with E.Torrego); established the existence and distinctness of three types of syntactic movement operations. Avocations: violin, chamber music, Russian language and culture. Office: Dept Linguistics & Philos 32-D862 MIT Cambridge MA 02139 E-mail: pesetsk@mit.edu.

PESHKIN, SAMUEL DAVID, retired lawyer; b. Des Moines, Oct. 6, 1925; s. Louis and Mary (Grund) P.; m. Shirley R. Isenberg, Aug. 17, 1947; children: Lawrence Allen, Linda Ann. BA, State U. Iowa, 1948, JD, 1951. Bar: Iowa 1951. Ptnr. Bridges & Peshkin, Des Moines, 1953-66, Peshkin & Robinson, Des Moines, 1966-82. Mem. Iowa Bd. Law Examiners, 1970—. Bd. dir. State U. Iowa Found., 1957—, Old Gold Devel. Fund, 1956—, Sch. Religion U. Iowa, 1966—. Fellow Am. Bar Found., Internat. Soc. Barristers; mem. ABA (chmn. standing com. membership 1959—, ho. of dels. 1968—, bd. govs. 1973—), Iowa Bar Assn. (bd. govs. 1958—, pres. jr. bar sect. 1958-59, award of merit 1974), Inter-Am. Bar Assn., Internat. Bar Assn., Am. Judicature Soc., State U. Iowa Alumni Assn. (dir., pres. 1957) Home and Office: 14500 N Frank Lloyd Wright Blvd Apt 310 Scottsdale AZ 85260-8822 Office Phone: 480-607-3136.

PESIC, RATNIK JOSIP, application developer, management consultant, mathematician, educator; b. Rijeka, Croatia, Oct. 1, 1945; arrived in South Africa, 1992, naturalized, 1992; s. Josip and Mary Pesic; m. Dunja Gasparov, May 17, 1970; 1 child, Ognjen. MSc in Computer Scis. and Info. Sys., Sch. Orgnl. Scis., South Africa, 1983; PhD in Computer Scis. and Mgmt., Ecole Supérieure Robert de Sorbon, France, 2007. Cert. in Internat. Bus. Mgmt. Program Manhattan Inst. Mgmt., NY, Math. Tchr. Faculty Scis. and Math., Belgrade, Yugoslavia, 1969, Cons. Mgr. Inst. Superieur de Guestion and IIM, Paris, 1991. Univac software engr. Inst. Expert Econs. Analysis, Belgrade, Zurich, 1969—71; mgr. software devel. group Govt. Fin. Auditing and Treasury Agy., Belgrade, 1971—73; head software dept. Inst. Planning and Mgmt., Belgrade, 1973—75; dir. Lab. Info. Sys. Medicine and Healthcare, Subotica, 1975—78; exec. mgr. Inst. Orgn. and Devel., Belgrade, 1978—82; CEO Consulting and Software Design Centre, Belgrade, 1982—93, OGI Sys. Internat. OSI, Johannesburg, 1993—. Founder, owner, CEO Consulting and Software Design Centre, Belgrade, 1982—93; advisor faculty natural scis. Technikon, Pretoria, South Africa, 1995—97; bus. sys. developing mgr. LIMON - Fin. Sys. and Cons., Johannesburg, 1997—98, MAK Sys., Paris, 1998—99, project leader database migration methodology; head devel., mem. co. sr. mgmt. bd. EHD, Johannesburg, 1999—2004; project co-leader testing and tng. icao internat. standards ELT-Internat., Oxford-Banbury, OGI Sys. Internat., Intersystems, Boston, 2004—05; project leader bus. sys. Kapa Reynolds, Paris, 2004—05; project leader database migration methodology OGI Sys. Internat., Intersystems, Boston, 2005—07, composite model of difference. Author: Introduction to Fortran, Consumers Credits for Furniture Industry, National Payment System - Model II, Health-Care and Medical Information Systems, Electronic Computer System-Tool-Yes or No, Programming Language-BASIC. Fellow: Royal Soc. Art, London; mem.: Healthcare Info. and Mgmt. Sys. Soc., Assn. Computing Machinery, Am. Assn. Artificial Intelligence, IEEE Computer Soc. Achievements include development of composite artificial intelligence bi-bm erp system. Avocations: classical music, swimming, cooking, tai chi. Office: OGI Sys Internat PO Box 717 Morningside Sandton Gauteng Johannesburg 2057 South Africa

PESKOWITZ, ED, professional sports team owner, communications executive; married; 2 children. Grad., SUNY; M in Internat. Rels., Grad. Sch. Pub. and Internat. Affairs, Pitts. Writer numerous publs. including NY Post and Stars and Stripes; co-founder United Comm. Grp., Rockville, Md., 1977—; prin. Atlanta Spirit, LLC (parent co. of NBA Atlanta Hawks and NHL Atlanta Thrashers). Served in 25th Inf. Divsn. US Army, Vietnam. Office: United Comm Grp Ste 1100 11300 Rockville Pike Rockville MD 20852-3030

PESMEN, SANDRA (MRS. HAROLD WILLIAM PESMEN), journalist, educator; b. Chgo., Mar. 26, 1931; d. Benjamin S. and Emma (Lipschultz) Zuckerman; m. Harold W. Pesmen, Aug. 16, 1952; children: Bethann, Curtis. BS, U. Ill., 1952. Reporter Radio and Community News Service, Chgo., 1952-53; wire editor Champaign-Urbana (Ill.) Courier, 1953; reporter, feature writer Lerner Chgo. N. Side Newspapers, 1953-55; stringer corr. Wayne (Mich.) Eagle, 1958-61; reporter, feature writer Chgo. Daily News, 1968-78; features editor Crain's Chgo. Business mag., 1978-89; corp. features editor Crain Communications, Inc., 1989-95; tchr. feature writing Northwestern U. Evening Sch., 1972-81; host www.widowslist.com, 2008—; owner Widlist Media. Author: Writing for the Media, 1983, Dr. Job's Complete Career Guide, 1995; editor: Career News Service; author syndicated column Dr. Job, 1985—, Host the Windows, 2009 Recipient Golden Key award, Ill. Mental Health Dept., 1966, 1971, award, Inst. Psychoanalysis, 1971, AP, 1975, Penny Mo. award, 1978, Stick o'Type award, Chgo. Newspaper Guild, 1978, Peter Lisagor award, Soc. Profl. Journalists, 1991; named to, Chgo. Journalism Hall of Fame, 1997, Illini Media Alumni Hall of Fame, 2008. Home: 2811 Fern Ave Northbrook IL 60062-5809 Office Phone: 847-272-7175. Personal E-mail: pesmensandra@sbcglobal.net. Business E-Mail: sandy@windowlist.com.

PESOLA, GENE RAYMOND, physician; b. Hancock, Mich., Oct. 21, 1952; s. Raymond Lloyd and Helen Eleanor Pesola; m. Helen Rostata, Jan. 5, 1991; children: Gene Richard, Glen Raymond, Gary Roger. BS in Biology magna cum laude, Mich. Technol. U., Houghton, 1974; MD, Wayne State U., 1979; MPH in Biostats. magna cum laude, Columbia U., 1998, MPhil in Epidemiology, 2006. Diplomate Am. Bd. Internal Medicine, also sub-bds. pulmonary medicine and critical care medicine; cert. in pub. health, 2008, BCLS, ACLS, ATLS, PALS. Intern Harlem Hosp., NYC, 1979-80; resident U. Tenn. Affiliated Hosps., Memphis, 1980-82; fellow in pulmonary medicine Mt. Sinai Hosp. and Affiliates, NYC, 1982-84; fellow in critical care medicine Meml. Sloan-Kettering Cancer Ctr., NYC, 1984-85, rsch. fellow, 1985-87; asst. prof. medicine and anesthesia Albert Einstein U., Bronx, NY, 1988-89; attending physician Mt. Vernon Emergency Room, NY, 1989-90; rschr. cell/molecular pharmacology and exptl. therapeutics Med. U. SC, Charleston, 1991-94; attending physician critical care and emergency medicine N.Y. Cmty. Hosp., Bklyn., 1989—; attending physician dept. emergency medicine St. Vincent's Hosp., NYC, 1994—2000; asst. prof. emergency medicine NY Med. Coll., 1995-2000, assoc. prof. emergency medicine, 2000; assoc. attending physician Divsn. Pulmonary and Critical Care Medicine, Harlem Hosp./Columbia U., NYC, 2001—; assoc. clin. prof. medicine Columbia U., NYC, 2001—; co-prin. investigator ACRN, NYC, 2001—04. Mem. editl. bd. Academic Emergency Medicine, 2002—, assoc. editor, 2006—, Internet Jour. Asthma, Allergy and Immunology, 2002—; contbr. chapters to books, articles to profl. jours.; reviewer numerous jours. including CHEST, Catheterization and Cardiovasc. Interventions, Annals of Emergency Medicine, The Lancet, Academic Emergency Medicine. Grantee Am. Fedn. Clin. Rsch., 1992; Pharm. Mfr. Found. fellow, 1992-94; named one of Am.'s Top Physicians Consumer's Rsch. Coun., 2004-06; named Tchr. of Yr. Dept. Medicine Harlem Hosp., 2006.

PESSL, MARISHA, writer, artist; b. Asheville, NC, Oct. 26, 1977; m. Nic Caiano. BA, Columbia Univ., NYC. Author: (novels) Special Topics in Calamity Physics, 2006 (recipient John Sargent Sr. First Book Award, 2006), Night Film, 2008. Achievements include being New York Times Best-Selling Author, several weeks. Office: The Penguin Group 80 Strand London WC2R ORL England*

PESTA, BEN W., II, lawyer, writer; b. Hagerstown, Md., Oct. 15, 1948; s. Ben W. and Ethel Irene (Kirkpatrick) P.; m. Monique Raphel High, Dec. 7, 1987; 1 stepchild, Nathalie Carroll. AB, UCLA, 1969; JD, U. Calif., Berkeley (Boalt Hall), 1972. Bar: US Supreme Ct., US Ct. Appeals, 9th Appellate Cir., US Dist. Cts. Central and Eastern Dist. Calif., Eastern Dist. Wis., Dist. Ariz., all Calif. Cts. Assoc. editor Esquire Mag., 1972—74; instr. grad. profl. writing program U. So. Calif., 1980—82; assoc. pub. Weider Health & Fitness, Woodland Hills, Calif., 1984—90; pvt. practice law LA, 1990—. Freelance writer. Contbr. articles and reviews to Esquire, Playboy, Rolling Stone, Crawdaddy, Sport, TV Guide, Cosmopolitan, Self, LA Style mags., etc., LA Times, LA Daily News, LA Weekly, Am. Bar assoc. Jour., Calif. Lawyer, jours. Calif. lawyer. Capt. USAF, 1973, 438th MAW. Mem.: ABA, ACLU, Authors Guild, Calif. Pub. Defenders Assn., Calif. Atty. for Criminal Justice, Nat. Assn. Criminal Def. Lawyers, Fed. Bar Assn., LA County Bar Assn., State Bar Calif. Office: 1901 Ave of the Stars Ste 390 Los Angeles CA 90067 Office Phone: 310-201-0666. Business E-Mail: pestalaw@aol.com.

PESTANA, CARLOS, surgeon, retired dean, educator; b. Tacoronte, Tenerife, Canary Islands, Spain, June 10, 1936; came to U.S., 1968, naturalized, 1973; s. Francisco and and Blanca (Suarez) P.; m. Myrna Lorena Serrato, Aug. 25, 1966; children— Becky Elizabeth, George Byron. BS, Nat. U. Mex., 1952, MD, 1959; PhD in Surgery, U. Minn., 1965. Intern St. Mary of Nazareth Hosp., Chgo., 1959-60; resident Mayo Clinic, Rochester, Minn., 1961-65; surgeon Hosp. 20 de Noviembre Mexico City; asst. prof. surgery Nat. U. Mex., 1966-67, U. Tex. Med. Sch. at San Antonio, 1968-70, asso. prof., 1970-74, prof., 1974—, asso. dean for acad. devel., 1971-73, asso. dean for student affairs, 1973-86, assoc. dean acad. affairs, 1986-97, clin. prof. surgery, 1998-2000, prof. emeritus, 2000—. Recipient Edward John Noble Found. award, 1965, Piper Prof. award Minnie Stevens Piper Founds., 1972, Nat. Golden Apple award Am. Med. Student Assn., 1999. Mem. Alpha Omega Alpha (Robert J. Glaser Disting. Tchr. award 1997). Home: 10123 N Manton Ln San Antonio TX 78213-1932 Office: 7703 Floyd Curl Dr San Antonio TX 78284-6200 Office Phone: 210-567-5700.

PESTORIUS, EILEEN MCGEE, art educator; d. Emmett Gregory McGee and Joanna Barbara Madis; m. Frederick Michael Pestorius, Aug. 18, 1962; children: Ellen M Kleinknecht, Michael J, Patrick P, Frederick P. BA in English, Nazareth Coll., Rochester, 1961; MA, U. Tex., Austin, 1992. Adj. prof., art Austin CC, Tex., 1992—; pres. elect Waterloo Watercolor Group, Austin, Tex.; docent emerita UT Blanton Mus. Art, Austin, Tex. Cmty. ed tchr. Eanes ISD, West Lake Hills, Tex., 1995—; painting trip coord., Italy & France Thewestmill.com, Tex. Painter in oil and watercolor, numerous art exhibitions; contbr. to The London Cronicles. Avocations: sports, music, art, travel, reading. Office: Austin Comm Coll Austin TX 78746 Home Fax: 328-3070. Personal E-mail: eileenthepainter@aol.com.

PESZKE, MICHAEL ALFRED, psychiatrist, writer; b. Deblin, Poland, Dec. 19, 1932; arrived in U.S., 1956; s. Alfred Bartlomiej and Eugenia Halina (Grebocka) Peszke; m. Alice Margaret Sherman, Sept. 20, 1958; children: Michele Halina Olender, Michael Alexander. BA, Trinity Coll., Dublin, Ireland, 1956; MB, BCh, BAO, Dublin U., 1956. Cert. Bd. cert. psychiatrist. Staff psychiatrist Yale Student Health Svc., New Haven, 1961-64; asst. prof. sch. medicine U. Chgo., 1964-68; cons. psychiatrist Wesleyan U., Middletown, Conn., 1968-70; asst. prof. Sch. Medicine U. Conn., Farmington, 1970-73, assoc. prof., 1973-80, prof. psychiatry, 1980-90; clin. prof. U. Md. Sch. Medicine, Balt., 1991-99; chief Psychiatry Svc. Perry Point (Md.) VA Med. Ctr., 1990-98, co-coord. R&D, 1998-99. Dir. psychiat. clin. svcs. John Dempsey Hosp. U. Conn. Health Ctr., Farmington, 1983—87; chief VA Med. Ctr., Newington, Conn., 1987—90; ind. rschr., 1999—; mem. com. to the endowed chair of Polish and Polish Am. studies Ctrl. Conn. State U., 2001—06; advisor Am. Polish Adv. Coun. Author: Involuntary Treatment of the Mentally Ill: The Problem of Autonomy, 1975, Battle for Warsaw, 1939-44, 1995, Poland's Navy: 1918-1945, 1999; co-author (edited by L.A. Pervin, L.R. Reik, W. Dalrymple): The College Drop-out and the Utilization of Talent, 1966; co-author: (edited by J. Zusman, E. Bertsch) The Future of Psychiatric State Hospitals, 1975; co-author: The Polish Underground Army, The Western Allies and the Failure of Strategic Unity in World War II, 2005; contbr.; book reviewer Am. Jour. Psychiatry, 1976—99. Advisor Am. Polish Adv. Coun., 2003—; prof. emeritus U. Ct. Sch. Medicine. Fellow: APA (life; disting.); mem.: Polish Inst. Arts and Scis. Am., Inc., Am. Coll. Psychiatrists, Royal United Svc. Inst. (London), Soc. for Mil. History.

PETACH, ANN MARIE, diversified financial services company executive; b. 1960; BA in Bus. & Spanish, Muhlenburg Coll., 1982; MBA, Carnegie-Mellon U., 1984. Fin. mgmt. positions Ford Motor Co., 1984—2007; asst. treas. Autolatina; treas. AutoEuropa; dir. global banking Ford Motor Co.; asst. treas. Ford Credit, Ford Motor Co., v.p., treas., 2004—07; mng. dir., head bus. fin. BlackRock Inc., NYC, 2007—08, CFO, 2008—. Office: BlackRock Inc 40 E 52d St New York NY 10022

PETAEV, MIKHAIL IVANOVICH, senior geologist, researcher; b. Kasimov, Russia, May 7, 1957; came to U.S., 1991; s. Ivan M. and Zinaida V. (Ivanova) P.; m. Vera N. Glodina, Mar. 6, 1982; 1 child, Ivan. MS, Moscow State U., 1979; PhD, USSR Acad. Scis., 1985. Staff scientist Lab. Thermodynamics of Natural Processes, Vernadsky Inst., Moscow, 1982-84, head meteorite rsch. group Lab. Comparative Planetology, 1984-91; sr. staff scientist Harvard-Smithsonian Ctr. for Astrophysics and dept. earth and planetary scis. Harvard U., Cambridge, Mass., 1992—. Dir. Precious Stones and Meteorites from the USSR Exhbn., Prague, Czechoslovakia, 1987-88; curator Nat. Meteorite Collection of USSR Acad. Scis., Moscow, 1988-92. Contbr. articles to profl. jours. Mem. Meteoritical Soc., Am. Geophys. Union, Geochem. Soc. Avocations: fishing, outdoor activity, reading, political analysis. Office: Harvard Univ Dept Earth Planetary Sci 20 Oxford St Cambridge MA 02138-1516 Business E-Mail: mpetaev@cfa.harvard.edu.

PETAK, WILLIAM JOHN, systems management educator; b. Johnstown, Pa., June 23, 1932; s. Val Andrew and Lola Agatha (Boroski) P.; m. Ramona Janet Cayuela, Dec. 28, 1957; children: Elizabeth Ann Petak-Aaron, William Matthew, Michael David. BS in Mech. Engring., U. Pitts., 1956; MBA, U. So. Calif., 1963, DPA, 1969. Engr. Northrop Corp., Hawthorne, Calif., 1956-59; test engr. Wyle Labs., El Segundo, Calif., 1959-63; we. regional mgr. Instrument div. Budd Co., Phoenixville, Pa., 1963-69; v.p., dir. J.H. Wiggins Co., Redondo Beach, Calif., 1969-81; prof. systems mgmt. U. So. Calif., LA, 1982-98, exec. dir. Inst. Safety and Sys. Mgmt., 1987-98, prof. policy, planning and devel., 1998—2005, prof. emeritus, 2006. Chmn. earthquake mitigation com. Nat. Com. on Property Ins., Boston, 1990-92; mem. com. on natural disasters NRC, Washington, 1985-91, mem. U.S. nat. com. for the decade for natural disaster reduction, 1989-92. Co-author: Natural Hazard Risk Assessment and Public Policy, 1982, Politics and Economics of Earthquake Hazard Reduction, 1986, Disabled Persons and Earthquake Hazards, 1988; editor spl. issue Pub. Adminstrn. Rev., 1985. Commr. County of Los Angeles, 1994—; mem. policy bd. So. Calif. Earthquake Prep. Project, L.A., 1986-92; trustee Marymount Coll., Palos Verdes, Calif., 1974-2009. Sgt. U.S. Army, 1950-52. Mem. Soc. for Risk Analysis, Earthquake Engring. Rsch. Inst., Am. Soc. for Pub. Adminstrn., Sigma Xi. Republican. Roman Catholic. Avocations: skiing, fishing, hiking. Office: 6044 Moss Bank Dr Rancho Palos Verdes CA 90275 Business E-Mail: petak@usc.edu.

PETCHESKY, ROSALIND POLLACK, social and political scientist, educator; b. Bay City, Tex., Aug. 16, 1942; BA, Smith Coll., 1964; MA, Columbia U., 1966, PhD, 1974, Prof., polit. sci. and women's studies, Hunter Coll. CUNY, 1987—, head, women's studies program, Hunter Coll., 1987—91. Bd. dirs. Women's Environ. and Develop. Orgn., 2000—. Author: The Individual's Rights and the International Organization, 1966, Abortion and Women's Choice: The State, Sexuality and Reproductive Freedom, 1984 (Joan Kelly Meml. prize Am. Hist. Assn., 1984), Abortion and Women's Choice: The State, Sexuality and Reproductive Freedom, 2d edit., 1990; co-editor: Negotiating Reproductive Rights: Women's Perspectives Across Countries and Cultures, 1998; serves governing bd. Jour. Reproductive Matters. Founder, first internat. coord. Internat. Reproductive Rights Rsch. Action Group. Fellow, MacArthur Found., 1995. Office: CUNY Hunter Coll Dept Polit Sci Hunter West 1726 695 Park Ave New York NY 10021-5024 Office Phone: 212-772-5500, 212-772-5682. E-mail: rpetches@igc.org.

PETE, ERIC E., writer, claims representative; b. Seattle, Oct. 1, 1968; s. Earl Joseph Pete and Edna Mae Bushnell; m. Marsha Bluin; 1 child, Chelsea. BS, McNeese State U., 1993. Assoc. in mgmt., assoc. in claims, sr. claims law assoc., assoc. in ins. svcs. Claim rep. State Farm Cos., 1994—; owner E-fect Pub., Houston, 2000—. Author: (novels) Real for Me, 2000, Someone's In the Kitchen, 2002, Gets No Love, 2004, Don't Get It Twisted, 2005, Lady Sings the Cruels, 2006, Blow Your Mind, 2007, Sticks And Stones, 2009, Reality Check, 2009. With US Army, 1987—89. Mem.: Toastmasters Internat., Delta Sigma Pi. Avocations: reading, travel, dance, weightlifting, art. Office: PO Box 670562 Houston TX 77267-0562 Home: 3139 Crossout Cr Spring TX 77373 Office Phone: 281-528-6150. Business E-Mail: heyeric@att.net.

PETER, BACH, epidemiologist, pulmonologist; MA in Pub. Policy, U. Chgo.; MD, U. Minn. Med. Sch. Cert. internal med., pulmonary med., critical care med. Resident Johns Hopkins Hosp.; former sr. adv. to adminstr. Centers for Medicare and Medicaid Svcs.; assoc. attending physician Meml. Sloan-Kettering Cancer Ctr.; mem. Health Outcomes Rsch. Group Meml. Sloan-Ketterin Cancer Ctr. Dept. Epidemiology & Biostatistics. Mem. Inst. Medicine's Nat. Cancer Policy Forum, Com. Performance Measurement of the Nat. Com. on Quality Assurance; camp physician Rwandan Civil War Refugee Camp, Goma, Democratic Republic of Congo. Author: (op-ed pieces) Wall St. Jour.; contbr. articles various medical publs. Office: 1275 York Ave New York NY 10065 Office Phone: 646-735-8137. Office Fax: 646-735-0011. E-mail: bachp@mskcc.org.*

PETER, JACK E., museum administrator; married; 1 child. Grad., Loyola U. With Airfax Productions, Optimus, Inc.; gen. mgr. & v.p. Post Group, Disney-MGM Studios; dir. prodn. PGA TOUR Productions, Ponte Vedra Beach, Fla., 1994—95, v.p., 1995—2000; gen. mgr. World Golf Hall of Fame, St. Augustine, Fla., 2000—01, v.p., 2000—04, COO, 2001—, sr. v.p., 2004—. Office: World Golf Hall Of Fame 12173 Ripken Cir N Jacksonville FL 32224-4638 Office Phone: 904-940-4000.

PETER, PHILLIPS SMITH, lawyer; b. Washington, Jan. 24, 1932; s. Edward Compston and Anita Phillips (Smith) P.; m. Jania Jayne Hutchins, Apr. 8, 1961; children: Phillips Smith Peter Jr., Jania Jayne Hutchins Stone. BA, U. Va., 1954, JD, 1959. Bar: Calif. 1959. Assoc. McCutchen, Doyle, Brown, Enerson, San Francisco, 1959-63; with GE (and subs.), various locations, 1963-94, v.p. corp. bus. devel., 1973-76, v.p. Washington, 1976-79, v.p. corp. govtl. rels., 1980-94; counsel, head govt. rels. dept. Reed Smith Shaw & McClay, Washington, 1994—. Chmn. bd. govs. Bryce Harlow Found., 1990-92, bd. dirs. Mem. editl. bd. Va. Law Rev., 1957-59. Trustee Howard U., 1981—89; bd. dirs., exec. com. Nat. Bank of Washington, 1981—86; v.p. Fed. City Coun., Washington, 1979—85; bd. dirs. Carlton, 1987—90, 1995—98, pres., 1995—96; bd. dirs. Tudor Place Found., 1999—, v.p., 2001—02, pres., 2002—03; mem. Kennedy Ctr. Internat. Com., 2007—. Mem. Calif. Bar Assn., Order of Coif, Wee Burn Club, Ea. Yacht Club, Farmington Country Club, Landmark Club, Congl. Country Club, Georgetown Club, Chevy Chase Club, Carlton Club (bd. dirs. 1990-98), Coral Beach and Tennis Club, Johns Island Club, The Windsor Club, Omicron Delta Kappa. Episcopalian. Home: 10805 Tara Rd Potomac MD 20854-1341 Address: Johns Island 1000 Beach Rd 690 Ocean Rd & 10656 Eton Way Windsor Vero Beach FL 32963-3429 Business E-Mail: ppeter@reedsmith.com.

PETER, SAMUEL (OKON), professional boxer; b. Akwaibom, Nigeria, Sept. 6, 1980; m. Enobong Peter, 2002; 2 children. Profl. boxer, 2001—. Winner vacant title vs. Jeremy Williams by knockout, heavyweight divsn. N.Am. Boxing Fedn., 2004, winner title def. vs. Taurus Sykes by knockout, heavyweight divsn., 05, winner vacant title vs. Julius Long by knockout, heavyweight divsn., 06, winner title def. vs. James Toney by split decision, heavyweight divsn., 06, winner title def. vs. James Toney by unanimous decision, heavyweight divsn., 07; winner vacant title vs. Yanqui Diaz by tech. knockout, heavyweight divsn. US Boxing Assn., 2005, winner title def. vs. Taurus Sykes by knockout, heavyweight divsn., 05; winner title vs. Taurus Sykes by knockout, heavyweight divsn. N.Am. Boxing Assn., 2005, winner title def. vs. Robert Hawkins by unanimous decision, heavyweight divsn., 05; winner title vs. James Toney by split decision, heavyweight divsn. Internat. Boxing Assn., 2006; winner vacant interim title vs. Jameel McCline by unanimous decision, heavyweight divsn. World Boxing Coun., 2007, winner world title def. vs. Oleg Maskaev by tech. knockout, heavyweight divsn., 08. Mailing: c/o Duva Boxing 409 Minnisink Rd # 3 Totowa NJ 07512

PETERA, ANNE PAPPAS, federal agency administrator; b. Richmond, Va., Feb. 13, 1950; d. Evangel Thomas and Margaret Theresa (McGuire) Pappas; m. Ronald Petera, Sept. 15, 1968; 1 child, Paul Evangel. BS, Va. Commonwealth U., 1980; grad., Realtors Inst. Br. officer Ctrl. Fidelity Bank, Richmond, 1972-79; asst. v.p. Signet Bank, Richmond, 1979-85; sales assoc. Hermitage Realty, Richmond, 1985-92; assoc. broker Napier Old Colony, Richmond, 1992-95, Bowers, Nelms & Fonville & Jefferson-Jones, Richmond, 1995-96; chair Va. Dept. Alcoholic Beverage Control, 1996-97; sec. Commonwealth of Va., 1998—2002; dir. adminstrn. Atty. Gen. of Va., 2002—06; asst. sec. intergovernmental programs US Dept. Homeland Security, 2006—. Mem. faculty Richmond Assn. Realtors Sch. Real Estate, 1991-96; bd. visitors Va.

Commonwealth U., 2001-04, vice rector, 2003-04, mem. exec. com., chair academic and health affairs com.; mem. bd. dirs. Health System Authority Va. Commonwealth U., chair audit com. Vice-chmn. Hanover (Va.) County Rep. Com., 1990-92, chmn., 1992-94; chmn. 1st Congl. Dist., Rep. Party Va., Richmond, 1994-98, budget dir., 1996-98, treas. 1998-2001; mem. Rep. Nat. Com., 2001—. Named Outstanding Young Woman of America, 1981, Disting. Achiever, Richmond Assn. Realtors, 1986, 87, 89, 90, 91, 92, 93, 94. Mem. Nat. Alcohol Beverage Control Assn. (dir. 1996-98), Nat. Assn. Realtors, Nat. Assn. Bank Women (pres. Richmond chpt.). Republican. Roman Catholic. Avocations: golf, reading, travel. Office: US Dept Homeland Security 12th & C St SW Washington DC 20024 E-mail: annepetera@aol.com.*

PETERLE, TONY JOHN, zoologist, educator; b. Cleve., July 7, 1925; s. Anton and Anna (Katic) P.; m. Thelma Josephine Coleman, July 30, 1949; children: Ann Faulkner, Tony Scott. BS, Utah State U., 1949; MS, U. Mich., 1950, PhD (univ. scholar), 1954; Fulbright scholar, U. Aberdeen, Scotland, 1954-55; postgrad., Oak Ridge Inst. Nuclear Studies, 1961. With Niederhauser Lumber Co., 1947—49, Macfarland Tree Svc., 1949—51; rsch. biologist Mich. Dept. Conservation, 1951—54; asst. dir. Rose Lake Expt. Sta., 1955—59; leader Ohio Coop. Wildlife Rsch. unit U.S. Fish and Wildlife Svc., Dept. Interior, 1959—63; asso. prof., then prof. zoology Ohio State U., Columbus, 1959—89, prof. emeritus, 1989, chmn. faculty population and environ. biology, 1968—69, chmn. dept. zoology, 1969—81, dir. program in environ. biology, 1970—71; liaison officer Internat. Union Game Biologists, 1965—93; chmn. internat. affairs com., mem. com., ecotoxicology co-organizer XIII Internat. Congress Game Biology, 1979—80; propr. The Iron Works, 1989—. Pvt. cons., 1989—; mem. com. rev. EPA pesticide decision making Nat. Acad. Scis.-NRC; mem. vis. scientists program Am. Inst. Biol. Scis.-ERDA, 1971-77; mem. com. pesticides Nat. Acad. Scis., com. on emerging trends in agr. and effects on fish and wildlife; mem. ecology com. of sci. adv. council EPA, 1979-87; mem. research units coordinating com. Ohio Coop. Wildlife and Fisheries, 1963-89; vis. scientist EPA, Corvallis, 1987. Author: Wildlife Toxicology, 1991; editor: Jour. of Wildlife Mgmt., 1969-70, 84-85, 2020 Vision Meeting the Fish and Wildlife Conservation Challenges of the 21st Century, 1992. Served with AUS, 1943-46. Named Internat. Scientists of Yr., 2002. Fellow AAAS, Am. Inst. Biol. Scis., Ohio Acad. Sci.; mem. Wildlife Disease Assn., Wildlife Soc. (regional rep. 1962-67, v.p. 1968, pres. 1972, Leopold award 1990, hon. mem. 1990, Profl. award of merit North Ctrl. sect. 1993), Nat. Audubon Soc. (bd. dirs. 1985-87), Ecol. Soc., INTECOL-NSF panel U.S.-Japan Program, Xi Sigma Pi, Phi Kappa Phi. Home: 4072 Klondike Rd Delaware OH 43015-9513 Office: Ohio State U Dept Evolution Ecology Organismal Bi 318 W 12th Ave Columbus OH 43210

PETERLIN, BORIS MATIJA, physician; b. Ljubljana, Slovenia, July 4, 1947; came to U.S., 1961; s. Anton and Leopoldina (Leskovic) P.; m. Anne Scheel-Larsen, July 21, 1984; children: Anton Alexander, Sebastian Bogomir. BS, Duke U., 1968; MD, Harvard U., 1973. Diplomate Am. Bd. Internal Medicine, Am. Bd. Rheumatology. Intern, resident Stanford (Calif.) Univ. Hosp., 1973-75, sr. resident, 1977-78; fellow in rheumatology, immunology Stanford (Calif.) U. Hosp., 1978-81; asst. prof. U. Calif., San Francisco, 1981-88, assoc. prof., 1988-94, prof., 1994—; asst. investigator HHMI, Bethesda, Md., 1984-89, assoc. investigator, 1989-95, investigator, 1995—2002. Vis. prof. U. Ljubljana, 1998—; fin. vis. disting. prof. 2009 Contbr. articles to Nature, Cell, Genes and Development, others. Lt. commdr. USPHS, 1975-77. Rosalind Russell Arthritis scholar U. Calif.; recipient Alexander von Humboldt prize, 1995, Ambassador of Sci. of Rep. of Slovema 2008. Fellow Am. Soc. for Clin. Investigation; mem. Am. Assn. Immunology, Am. Fedn. Clin. Rsch., Am. Soc. for Microbiology, Am. Coll. Rheumatology, Assn. Am. Physicians, Slovenian Acad. Arts & Scis., Phi Beta Kappa, Phi Lambda Upsilon. Democrat. Roman Catholic. Achievements include diagnosis of bare lymphocyte syndrome; discovery of mechanism of action of HIV Nef and Tat proteins; fundamental studies in replication of HIV. Home: 14 Hill Point Ave San Francisco CA 94117-3603 Office: U Calif San Francisco-HHMI 3D And Parnassus San Francisco CA 94143-0001 Home Phone: 415-665-2071; Office Phone: 415-502-1905. Business E-Mail: matija.peterlin@ucsf.edu.

PETERMAN, DONNA COLE, communications executive; b. St. Louis, Nov. 9, 1947; d. William H. Cole and Helen A. Morris; m. John A. Peterman, Feb. 7, 1970. BA in Journalism, U. Mo., 1969; MBA, U. Chgo., 1984. Mgr. employee comm. Sears Merchandise Group, Chgo., 1975-80; affairs and mktg. comm. Seraco Real Estate, Chgo., 1980-82; dir. corp. comm. Sears, Roebuck and Co., Chgo., 1982-85; sr. v.p., dir. corp. comm. Dean Witter Fin. Svcs. Group, NYC, 1985-88; sr. v.p., mng. dir. Hill and Knowlton, Inc., Chgo., 1988-94, exec. v.p. NYC, 1994-96; sr. v.p., dir. corp. comm. Paine Webber Group, Inc., NYC, 1996-2000; mng. dir., regional head comms. and mktg. The Americas, UBS Americas Inc., 2000—03; chief comm. officer PNC Fin. Svcs. Group Inc., 2003—. Media chair DeKalb County Comm., Ga., 1975; media dir., Mo. Atty. Gen., 1971, Rep. Govs. Conf., 1974; copywriter Govt. of Mo., 1971. Chmn. bd. trustees Found. for Investor Edn. Mem. Pub. Rels. Soc. Am., Arthur Page Soc., Pub. Rels. Seminar, Edgewood Country Club, Palmetto Pines Country Club, The Wise Men. Republican. Roman Catholic. Avocations: tennis, golf, sailing, skiing, bridge. Office: The PNC Fin Svcs Group Inc 1 PNC Plaza 249 5th Ave Pittsburgh PA 15222-2707

PETERMANN, HANS JÜRGEN, research scientist; b. Vienna, Feb. 2, 1942; MA in German, Calif. State U., 1971; PhD in Physics, 2d Phys. Inst., Vienna, Austria, 1976; PhD in Botany (hon.), Bot. Inst., Berlin, Germany, 1980. Prof. phys. scis. Coll. of Desert, Palm Desert, Calif.; rsch. scientist Palm Springs, Calif., 1991—. Chmn., sr. pr. Galaxy Energy Sys., Inc. Author: The Esoteric Sciences Vol. 1, 2d edit., 2001, Curiosities of Plant Kingdom Vol. 1, 2d edit., 2003, The Esoteric Sciences Vol. 2, 2003, Gravitation, Matter and Space Travel, 3d edit., 2008. With US Army, 1963—66. Achievements include development of magnetic generator; advanced gravity converter; patents in field. Avocations: hiking, tennis, scuba diving, mountain climbing, swimming. Office: PO Box 74 Palm Springs CA 92263-74

PETERS, ALAN, anatomy educator; b. Nottingham, Eng., Dec. 6, 1929; came to U.S., 1966; s. Robert and Mabel (Woplington) P.; m. Verona Muriel Shipman, Sept. 30, 1955; children: Ann Verona, Sally Elizabeth, Susan Clare. BSc, Bristol U., Eng., 1951, PhD, 1954. Lectr. anatomy Edinburgh (Scotland) U., 1958-66; vis. lectr. Harvard, 1963-64; prof., chmn. dept. anatomy and neurobiology Boston U., 1966-98, Waterhouse prof., 1998—. Anatomy com. Nat. Bd. Med. Examiners, 1971-75; mem. neurology B Study sect. NIH, 1975-79, chmn., 1978-79; affiliate scientist Yerkes Regional Primate Rsch. Ctr., 1984—. Author (with S.L. Palay and H. deF Webster): The Fine Structure of the Nervous System, 1970, The Fine Structure of the Nervous System, 3rd edit., 1991; author: Myelination, 1970; mem. editl. bd.: Anat. Record, 1972—81, Jour. Comparative Neurology, 1981—97, Neurocytology, 1972—89, 1993—2006, Cerebral Cortex, 1990—2005, Studies of Brain Function, Anat. and Embryology, 1989—92; editor (with E.G. Jones): (book series) Cerebral Cortex, 1984—2000; exec. prodr.(with B. Payne): Cat Visual Cortex, 2001; contbr. articles to profl. jours. Served to 2d lt. Royal Army Med. Corps, 1955-57. Recipient Henry Gray award, 1998, Sanford L. Palay award Jour. Comparative Neurology, 2004; grantee NIH, 1986. Mem. Anat. Soc. Gt. Britain and Ireland (Symington prize anatomy 1962, overseas mem. coun. 1969), Assn. Anatomy Chmn. (pres. 1976-77), Am. Anat. Assn. (exec. com. 1986-90, pres. 1992-93, Henry Gray award 1998), Am. Soc. Cell Biology, Soc. Neuroscis., Internat. Primatological Soc., Cajal Club (Harman lectr. 1990, Cortical Discoverer award 1991). Home: 1010 Waltham St # 589 Lexington MA 02421 Office: Boston U Sch Medicine Dept Anatomy and Neurobiology 80 E Concord St Roxbury MA 02118-2307 Home Phone: 781-862-1492; Office Phone: 617-638-4235. Business E-Mail: valan@bu.edu.

PETERS, BERNADETTE (BERNADETTE LAZZARA), actress; b. Queens, NY, Feb. 28, 1948; d. Peter and Marguerite (Maltese) Lazzara; m. Michael Wittenberg, July 20, 1996 (dec. Sept. 26, 2005). Student, Quintano Sch. for Young Profls., NYC. Ind. actress, entertainer, 1957—. Appeared on TV series All's Fair, 1976-77; frequent guest appearances on TV; (films) The Longest Yard, 1974, Silent Movie, 1976, Vigilant Force, 1976, W.C. Fields and Me, 1976, Silent Movie, 1976, The Jerk, 1979, Heartbeeps, 1981, Tulips, 1981, Pennies from Heaven, 1981 (Golden Globe award best actress), Annie, 1982, Slaves of New York, 1989, Pink Cadillac, 1989, Impromptu, 1991, Alice, 1990, Anastasia (voice), 1997, Cinderella, 1997, Snow Days, 1999, Prince Charming, 2001, Bobbie's Girl, 2002, A Few Good Years, 2002, It Runs in the Family, 2003; (TV movies) Cinderella, ABC-TV, 1997, Holiday in Your Heart, 1997; (stage appearances) This is Google, 1957, The Most Happy Fella, 1959, Gypsy, 1961, Curly McDimple, 1967, Johnny No-Trump, 1967, George M!, 1968 (Theatre World award, 1968), Dames at Sea, 1968 (Drama Desk award, 1968), La Strada, 1969, On the Town, 1971, Tartuffe, 1972, Mack and Mabel, 1974, Sally and Marsha, 1982, Sunday in the Park with George, 1983-85 (Tony nom., 1983), Song and Dance, 1985-86 (Drama League award best actress, 1985, Tony award best actress, 1986, Drama Desk award best actress, 1986), Into the Woods, 1987, The Goodbye Girl, 1992-93, Annie Get Your Gun 1998-1999 (Tony award best actress, 1999, Outer Critics Circle award best actress, 1999, Drama Desk award best actress, 1999), Gypsy, 2003; TV mini-series The Odyssey, 1997; rec. artist: (MCA Records) Bernadette Peters, 1980, Now Playing, 1981; CD's include I'll Be Your Baby Tonight, Angel Records, 1996 (Grammy nomination), Sondheim Etc: Bernadette Peters Live at Carnegie Hall, Angel Records, 1997 (Grammy nom.), solo concert Radio City Music Hall, 2002. Founder Ann. Broadway Barks fundraiser. Recipient Hasty Pudding Theatrical award, 1987 Woman of Yr. award, Sara Siddons Actress of Yr. award, 1993-94, Actors Fund medal for artistic achievement, 1999, NYC Parks Citizen award, 2006; named Woman of Yr., Police Athletic League, 1999; named to Theatre Hall of Fame. Office: William Morris Agency c/o Jeff Hunter 1325 Ave of the Americas 15th Fl New York NY 10019

PETERS, CALVIN RONALD, plastic and reconstructive surgeon; b. New Orleans, Jan. 27, 1940; s. Arthur Henry and Christine Cecile (Moldaner) P.; m. Pamela Alice Orth, Sept. 4, 1965; children: Brandon Scott, Kendall Kyle. BS, La. State U., 1961, MD, 1964. Diplomate Am. Bd. Surgery, Am. Bd. Plastic Surgery. Intern USN Hosp., Portsmouth, Va., 1964-65; gen. surg. resident Ochsner Clinic, 1968-72; plastic surgery resident Duke U. Med. Ctr., Durham, 1972-75, asst. prof. plastic surgery, 1975-78; program dir., plastic surgery Cleve. Clinic, 1978-79; pres., founder Ctr. for Plastic and Reconstructive Surgery, Orlando, Fla., 1979—. Chmn. dept. plastic surgery, Orlando Regional Med. Ctr., Orlando, 1981-86, Fla. Hosp. Med. Ctr., Orlando, 1981-86. Contbr. numerous articles, chpts. to profl. jours. and textbooks. With USN, 1965-68. Recipient Sr. Resident award Plastic Surgery Ednl. Found., Chgo., 1975. Fellow Am. Coll. Surgeons (bd. govs. 1980-86); mem. Am. Soc. Plastic and Reconstructive Surgeons, Am. Assn. Plastic Surgeons, Am. Soc. Maxillofacial Surgeons, Am. Soc. Aesthetic Plastic Surgeons, Orange County Med. Soc. (pres. 1989—), Fla. Soc. Plastic and Reconstructive Surgeons (pres. 1989—), Fla. Cleft Palate Soc. (pres. 1987-88), Interlachen Country Club, Winter Park Racquet Club. Republican. Episcopalian. Avocations: running, skiing, swimming, boating, golf. Home: 467 Lakewood Dr Winter Park FL 32789-3939 Office: Ctr Plastic/Recon Surgery 2501 N Orange Ave Ste 442 Orlando FL 32804-4642

PETERS, CAROL BEATTIE TAYLOR (MRS. FRANK ALBERT PETERS), mathematician; b. Washington, May 10, 1932; d. Edwin Lucius and Lois (Beattie) Taylor; B.S., U. Md., 1954, M.A., 1958; m. Frank Albert Peters, Feb. 26, 1955; children— Thomas, June, Erick, Victor. Group mgr. Tech. Operations, Inc., Arlington, Va., 1957-62, sr. staff scientist, 1964-66; supervisory analyst Datatrol Corp., Silver Spring, Md., 1962; project dir. Computer Concept, Inc., Silver Spring, 1963-64; mem. tech. staff, then mem. sr. staff Informatics Inc., Bethesda, Md., 1966-70, mgr. systems projects, 1970-71, tech. dir., 1971-76; sr. tech. dir. Ocean Data Systems, Inc., Rockville, Md., 1976-83; dir. Informatics Gen. Co., 1983-89; pres. Carol Peters Assocs., 1989—. Home and Office: 12311 Glen Mill Rd Potomac MD 20854-1928 E-mail: carol-peters@comcast.net.

PETERS, CHARLES A., electronics executive; married; 5 children. B in mech. engring., Cornell U.; MBA, Harvard U. Engring. coop. student Emerson Elec. Co., 1975—78, corp. planning, mgmt. positions through sr. v.p., 1978—98, exec. v.p., 1998—2000, sr. exec. v.p., 2000—. Office: Emerson Electric Company 8000 W Florissant Ave Saint Louis MO 63136

PETERS, CHARLES WILLIAM, nuclear energy industry executive; b. Pierceton, Ind., Dec. 9, 1927; s. Charles Frederick and Zelda May (Line) Peters; m. Katharine Louise Schuman, May 29, 1953; 1 child, Susan Kay; m. Patricia Ann Miles, Jan. 2, 1981; stepchildren: Bruce Miles Merkle, Leslie Ann Merkle Sanaie, Philip Frank Merkle, William Macneil Merkle. AB, Ind. U., 1950; postgrad., U. Md., 1952—58. Supervisory rsch. physicist Naval Rsch. Lab., Washington, 1950—71; physicist EPA, Washington, 1971—76; mgr. advanced sys. EATON-Consol. Controls Corp., Springfield, Va., 1976—89; v.p. Nuc. Diagnostic Sys., Inc., Springfield, Va., 1989—92; cons. Am. Tech. Inst., Memphis, 1993—. With US Army, 1945—47. Mem.: AAAS, IEEE, Am. Phys. Soc. Home and Office: 5235 N Whispering Hills Ln Tucson AZ 85704-2510

PETERS, DAVID ALLEN, mechanical engineering educator, consultant; b. East St. Louis, Ill., Jan. 31, 1947; s. Bernell Louis and Marian Louise (Blum) P.; children: Michael H., Laura A., Nathan C. BS in Applied Mechanics, Washington U., St. Louis, 1969, MS in Applied Mechanics, 1970; PhD in Aeros. and Astronautics, Stanford U., 1974. Assoc. engr. McDonnell Astronautics, 1969-70; rsch. scientist Army Aeronautics Lab., 1970-74; asst. prof. Washington U., 1975-77, assoc. prof., 1977-80, prof. mech. engring., 1980-85, chmn. dept., 1982-85; prof. aerospace engring. Ga. Inst Tech., Atlanta, 1985-91; dir. NASA Space Grant Consortium Ga. Inst. Tech., Atlanta, 1989-91; dir. Ctr. for Computational Mechanics Washington U., 1992—, prof. dept. mech. engring. St. Louis, 1991—, chmn. dept. mech. engring., 1997—2007, McDonnell Douglas prof. engring., 1999. Contbr. 150 articles to profl. jours. Recipient sci. contbn. award NASA, 1975, 76, Disting. Faculty award Washington U., 2006. Fellow AIAA, ASME, Am. Acad. Mechanics, Am. Helicopter Soc. (jour. editor 1987-90, Alexander Nikolsky award, 2008); mem. Am. Soc. for Engring. Edn., Internat. Assn. for Computational Mechanics (charter), Pi Tau Sigma (gold medal 1978). Baptist. Home: 7629 Balson Ave Saint Louis MO 63130-2150 Office: Wash U Dept Mech Engr Campus Box 1185 Saint Louis MO 63130 Office Phone: 314-935-4337. Business E-Mail: dap@me.wustl.edu.

PETERS, DENNIS GAIL, chemist; b. LA, Apr. 17, 1937; s. Samuel and Phyllis Dorothy (Pope) P. BS cum laude, Calif. Inst. Tech., 1958; PhD, Harvard U., 1962. Mem. faculty Ind. U., 1962—, prof. chemistry, 1974—, Herman T. Briscoe prof., 1975—. Co-author textbooks, contbr. articles profl. jours. Woodrow Wilson fellow, 1958-59; NIH predoctoral fellow, 1959-62; vis. fellow Japan Soc. for Promotion Sci., 1980; recipient Ulysses G. Weatherly award disting. teaching Ind. U., 1969, Disting. Teaching award Coll. Arts and Scis. Grad. Alumni Assn. Ind. U., 1984, Nat. Catalyst award for Disting. Teaching Chem. Mfrs. Assn., 1988, Henry B. Linford award The Electrochem. Soc., 2002; grantee NSF. Fellow Ind. Acad. Sci., Am. Inst. Chemists, Electrochem. Soc. 2007; mem. ACS (grantee, Div. of Analytical Chemistry award for excellence in teaching 1990, James Flack Norris award 2001). Home: 1401 S Nancy St Bloomington IN 47401-6051 Office: Dept Chemistry Ind U Bloomington IN 47405 Home Phone: 812-334-2487; Office Phone: 812-855-9671. Business E-Mail: peters@indiana.edu.

PETERS, DOUGLAS ALAN, appeals nurse supervisor; b. Portsmouth, Va., Oct. 4, 1968; s. Terrance Gene and Pamela P. BA in Philosophy, Va. Poly. Inst. and State U., 1992; BSN summa cum laude, James Madison U., 1995; JD, U. Md., Balt., 2003. RN Tenn.; cert. case mgr., legal nurse cons. Photojournalist CVNI/The Greene County Record, Stanardsville, Va., 1992; nursing asst. Rockingham Meml. Hosp., Harrisonburg, Va., 1993-95; clin. nurse Bapt. Hosp., Pensacola, Fla., 1995-96; nurse mgr. quality assurance Escambia County Jail Infirmary, Pensacola, 1996-97; case mgr./U.R. Total Health Care, Balt., 1997-98; case mgr. Blue Cross/Blue Shield of Md., Balt., 1998-2000, appeals analyst, 2000—01, sr. appeals analyst, 2001—04; jud. law clk. 23d Jud. Cir., W.Va., 2004—05; legal cons. CareFirst Blue Cross Blue Shield, 2005; nurse, case mgr. George Washington U. Hosp., 2006—07, Medicare Part D Appeals Grievances Healthspring Inc., Nashville, 2007—09, appeals nurse supervisor, 2009—. Vol. Middle Tenn. Med. Res. Corps. Mem.: ABA (health law sect.), Greater Nashville Darts Assn., Am. Assn. Legal Nurse Cons., Phi Alpha Delta, Sigma Theta Tau, Alpha Chi Sigma. Avocations: darts, eschatological studies. Personal E-mail: dapeters2006@yahoo.com.

PETERS, ELLEN ASH, retired judge; b. Berlin, Mar. 21, 1930; arrived in U.S., 1939, naturalized, 1947; d. Ernest Edward and Hildegard (Simon) Ash; m. Phillip I. Blumberg; children: David Bryan, James Douglas, Julie Haden Dreisch. BA with honors, Swarthmore Coll., 1951, LLD (hon.), 1983; LLB cum laude, Yale U., 1954, MA (hon.), 1964, LLD (hon.), 1985, U. Hartford, 1983, Georgetown U., 1984, Conn. Coll., 1985, N.Y. Law Sch., 1985; HLD (hon.), St. Joseph Coll., 1986; LLD (hon.), Colgate U., 1986, Trinity Coll., 1987, Bates Coll., 1987, Wesleyan U., 1987, DePaul U., 1988; HLD (hon.), Albertus Magnus Coll., 1990; LLD (hon.), U. Conn., 1992, U. Rochester, 1994, Detroit Mercy Coll. Law, 2001. Bar: Conn. 1957, US Dist. Ct. Conn. 1965. Law clk. to judge U.S. Circuit Ct., 1954-55; assoc. in law U. Calif., Berkeley, 1955-56; prof. law Yale U., New Haven, 1956-78, adj. prof., 1978-84; assoc. justice Conn. Supreme Ct., Hartford, 1978-84, chief justice, 1984-96; ret., 1996. Judge trial referee Appellate Ct., Hartford, Conn., 2000—. Author: Commercial Transactions: Cases, Texts, and Problems, 1971, Negotiable Instruments Primer, 1974; contbr. articles to profl. jours. Bd. dirs. Nat. Ctr. State Cts., 1992—96, chmn., 1994; bd. mgrs. Swarthmore Coll., 1970—81; trustee Yale-New Haven Hosp., 1981—86, Yale Corp., 1986—92; mem. conf. Chief Justices, 1984—, pres., 1994; hon. chmn. U.S. Constl. Bicentennial Com., 1986—91; mem. Conn. Permanent Commn. on Status of Women, 1973—74, Conn. Bd. Pardons, 1978—80, Conn. Law Revision Commn., 1978—84; bd. dirs. Hartford Found., 1997—2002. Recipient Ella Grasso award, 1982, Jud. award, Conn. Trial Lawyers Assn., 1982, citation of merit, Yale Law Sch., 1983, Pioneer Woman award, Hartford Coll. Women, 1988, Disting. Svc. award, U. Conn. Law Sch. Alumni Assn., 1993, Raymond E. Baldwin Pub. Svc. award, Quinnipiac Coll. Law Sch., 1995, Disting. Svc. award, Conn. Law Tribune, 1996, Nat. Ctr. State Cts., 1996; named Laura A. Johnson Woman of the Yr., Hartford Coll., 1996. Mem.: ABA, Am. Philos. Coun., Am. Acad. Arts and Scis., Am. Law Inst. (coun.), Conn. Bar Assn. (Jud. award 1992, Spl. award 1996). Office: Appellate Ct 75 Elm St Hartford CT 06106-4431 Home Phone: 860-232-2719. Office Fax: 860-713-2216.

PETERS, FREDERICK WHITTEN, lawyer; b. Omaha, Aug. 20, 1946; s. Jordan Holt and Elizabeth (O'Bryant) P.; children: Mary Irvin, Elizabeth Holt, Margaret Etheridge, Finian O'Bryant, Fiona Whitten. BA magna cum laude, Harvard U., 1968; MS with distinction, London Sch. Econs., 1973; JD magna cum laude, Harvard U., 1976. Bar: D.C. 1978, U.S. Dist. Ct. D.C. 1978, U.S. Dist. Ct. Md., 1994, U.S. Ct. Appeals (3d and D.C. cirs.) 1979, U.S. Ct. Claims 1981, U.S. Ct. Appeals (11th cir.) 1986, U.S. Ct. Mil. Appeals 1993. Law clk. to Hon. J. Skelly Wright U.S. Ct. Appeals (D.C. cir.), Washington, 1976-77; law clk. to justice William J. Brennan U.S. Supreme Ct., Washington, 1977-78; assoc. Williams & Connolly, Washington, 1978-84, ptnr., 1984-95, 2001—; prin. dep. gen. counsel Dept. of Defense, 1995-97, undersec., acting sec. USAF, 1997-99, sec. USAF, 1999-2001; ptnr. Williams & Connolly LLP, Washington, 2001—. Legal ethics com. DC Bar, 1988-94, chmn. rules rev. com., 1991-96; rules com. US Ct. Mil. Appeals, 1993-95. Pres. Harvard Law Rev., 1975-76. Bd. dirs. Cleveland Park Hist. Soc., Washington, 1986-91, 2001-02, Washington Area Lawyers for the Arts, 1987-93, Air Force Enlisted Found., 2001-06, Air Force Aid Soc., 2002—, AF Assn. 2009-; adv. com. on streamlining procurement laws DOD, 1991-93, vice chmn. adv. com. on future of US aerospace industry, 2001-2002. Lt. USNR, 1969-72. Fellow: Am. Bar Found.; mem.: ABA. Democrat. Episcopalian. Avocations: sailing, computer science, golf. Office: Williams & Connolly 725 12th St NW Washington DC 20005 Home: 2220 Windsor Rd Alexandria VA 22307-1020 Office Phone: 202-434-5440. Business E-Mail: wpeters@wc.com.

PETERS, GARY CHARLES, United States Representative from Michigan; b. Pontiac, Mich., Dec. 1, 1958; s. Herbert Garrett and Madeleine (Vignier) P.; m. Colleen Ochoa; children: Gary Jr., Madeleine, Alana. BA, Alma Coll., 1980; MBA, U. Detroit, 1984; JD, Wayne State U., 1989; MA in Philosophy, Mich. State U., East Lansing. Bar: Mich. 1990. Fin. cons., resident mgr., asst. v.p. Merrill Lynch, Pierce, Fenner & Smith, Inc., Rochester, Mich., 1980-89; v.p., br. mgr. Paine Webber, Inc., Rochester, Mich.; mem. Mich. State Senate from Dist. 14, Lansing, 1994—2002; commr. Mich. State Lottery; Griffin chair, Am. govt. Ctrl. Mich. U.; mem. US Congress from 9th Mich. Dist., 2009—. Securities arbitrator, mediator Nat. Assn. Securities Dealers, NY Stock Exchange, Am. Arbitration Assn.; adj. prof. Oakland U., Rochester, 1991-93, instr. Wayne State U., 1992-94; vice chair Mich. Senate Dem. Whip fin. com.; mem. edn. com., judiciary com., families, mental health and human svcs. com., econ. devel. & econ. trade com., law revision com. Mich. Sentencing Commn. Councilman City of Rochester Hills, 1992-94, mem. zoning bd. appeals and Paint Creek Trailways Commn., 1992-94; officer-at-large Mich. Dem. Party, 1996. Officer USNR, 1993—. Decorated Navy and Marine Corps Achievement medal, Mil. Outstanding Vol. Svc. medal. Mem. Mich. State Bar Assn., Sierra Club, Phi Beta Kappa. Democrat. Avocations: hiking, motorcycling, world travel, soaring, scuba diving. Office: US Congress 1130 Longworth House Office Bldg Washington DC 20515-2209 also: Dist Office PO Box 226 Bloomfield Hills MI 48303-0226 Office Phone: 202-225-5802, 248-737-2692. Office Fax: 202-226-2356.*

PETERS, GEOFFREY WRIGHT, lawyer, fundraising executive; b. Wilmington, Del., Oct. 30, 1945; s. William Ernest and Ann Miller Peters; m. Cecile Felicia Dziekonski, Aug. 26, 1967; children: Gregory Kent, Jessica Mohr. AB, Northwestern U., 1967; MA, JD, U. Denver, 1972. Bar: Colo. 1972, Nebr. 1972, Va. 1978, Minn. 1980, U.S. Supreme Ct. 1980. Sole practice, Denver, 1972; prof. law Creighton U., Omaha, 1972-78; dep. dir. Nat. Ctr. State Cts., Williamsburg, Va., 1978-80; pres., dean law William Mitchell Coll. Law, St. Paul, 1980-83; exec. v.p., gen. counsel Minn. Protective Life Ins. Co., Eden Prairie, 1983—86; v.p. ops. Garvey Industries, Wichita, 1986—90; pres. Corp. Investment Internat. (Garvey subs.), Phoenix, 1988-89, Firm One, Inc., Phoenix, 1988-89; chmn. Mid-Am. World Trade Ctr., Wichita, Kans., 1986—91; pres. Pres.'s Coll., 1989—91, Viguerie Co., Falls Ch., Va., 1990—91; exec. v.p. Amortibanc (Garvey subs.), 1989—91; pvt. practice Vienna, Va., 1991—; pres., mng. dir. Creative Dir. Mktg. Internat., Crofton, Md., 1992—2002; pres. Creative Direct Response, 2002—. Cons. Nat. Wiretap Commn., Washington, 1973—74; adj. prof. law William & Mary-Marshall Wythe Sch. Law, Williamsburg, 1978—80; gen. counsel Am. Charities Reasonable Fundraising Regulation, Vienna, 1995—; chmn., dir. Coun. Govt. Reform, Arlington, Va., 1992—2002; spkr. in field. With U.S. Army, 1969—71, West Point, NY. Decorated Army Commendation medal U.S. Army; recipient Pub. Svc. award, DMA Nonprofit Fedn.; named one of 50 Most Influential Persons in Nonprofit Sector, The Nonprofit Times, 2005, 2006; grantee prin. investigator more than 20 various grant funded projects, 1972-1980. Fellow: Am. Bar Found.; mem.: Minn. Bar Assn. (bd. govs. 1980—83). Achievements include first to create an international direct response fundraising agency operating in 25 countries. Avocations: flight instructing, commercial piloting, scuba diving, travel. Office: Am Charities for Reasonable Fundraising Regulation 9112 Tetterton Ave Vienna VA 22182 also: 16900 Science Dr Ste 210 Bowie MD 20715 Office Fax: 703-938-2207. E-mail: gpeters@cd-nfl.com.

PETERS, GERALD EUGENE, JR., dermatologist, surgeon; b. Cin., May 2, 1961; m. Antonia Marie Shalz. MD, U. Cin., 1988. Cert. intern U. Calif., San Francisco, 1989, dermatology residency Am. Coun. Grad. Med. Edn., 1998, in procedural dermatology, and mohs micrographic surgery Am. Coll. Mohs Surgery, 2005. Dermatologist, mohs surgery fellow Billings Clinic, Mont., 2002—05; mohs surgeon, dermatologist Bend Meml. Clinic, Oreg., 2005—. Dermatologist USAF, Ramstein, Germany, 1998—2001. Lt. col. USAF, 1990—2002, Beale AFB, Lackland, Ramstein, Travis. Named Flight Surgeon of Yr., SAC, 1991. Fellow: Am. Coll. Mohs Surgery, Am. Acad. Dermatology. Office: Bend Meml Clinic 1501 NE Med Center Dr Bend OR 97702 Home Fax: 541-322-3616.

PETERS, GORDON BENES, retired musician; b. Oak Park, Ill., Jan. 4, 1931; s. Arthur George and Julia Anne (Benes) P.; children: Rénee Kemper, Erica Kemper. Student, Northwestern U., 1949-50; studied with Pierre Monteux, 1952—63; MusB, Eastman Sch. Music, 1956, MusM, 1962. Founder, dir. Marimba Masters, 1954—59; percussionist Rochester (NY) Philharm. Orch., 1954—59; prin. percussionist, asst. timpanist Grant Park Symphony Orch., Chgo., 1954—58; mem. faculty Rochester Bd. Edn., 1956-57, Geneseo State Tchrs. Coll., 1957-58; acting prin. percussionist Rochester Philharm., NY, 1958-59; prin. percussionist and assoc. prin. timpanist Chgo. Symphony Orch., 1959—2001; condr., adminstr. Civic Orch. Chgo., 1966-87; condr. Elmhurst Symphony Orch., 1968-73. Instr. percussion instruments Northwestern U., 1963-68, lectr., 1991; guest condr. Bangor Symphony, Maine, 1993; lectr. Winthrop U., SC, 2006. Author, pub. Treatise on Percussion, 1962, rev., 1975 as The Drummer: Man, 1975, rev., 2003 (CD); arranger-pub. Marimba Ensemble arrangements; composer-pub.: Swords of Moda-Ling; editor: percussion column Instrumentalist mag, 1963-69; contbr. articles to profl. jours. Bd. dirs. Pierre Monteux Sch., Hancock, Maine, 1965-95. With U.S. Mil. Acad. Band, 1950-53. Recipient Pierre Monteux Disciple Conducting award, 1962; named Prin. Timpani chair GBP, Chgo. Youth Symphony Orch., 2000. Mem. Percussive Arts Soc. (pres. 1964-67, bd. dirs. Hall of Fame 2004), Am. Symphony Orch. League, Condrs. Guild (treas., exec. com. 1979-82, 86-90), Japan Xylophone Assn., Phi Mu Alpha Sinfonia (life). Home (Winter): 824 Hinman Ave Evanston IL 60202-5906 Home (Summer): PO Box 403 Hancock ME 04640-0403

PETERS, HOWARD NEVIN, foreign language educator; b. Hazleton, Pa., June 29, 1938; s. Howard Eugene and Verna P.; m. Judith Anne Griessel, Aug. 24, 1963; children: Elisabeth Anne, Nevin Edward. BA, Gettysburg Coll., 1960; PhD, U. Colo., 1965. Asst. prof. fgn. langs. Valparaiso (Ind.) U., 1965-69, assoc. prof., 1969-75, dir. grad. divsn., 1967-70, acting dean Coll. Arts and Scis., 1970-71, assoc. dean Coll. Arts and Scis., 1971-74, dean Coll. Arts and Scis., 1974-81, prof. fgn. langs., 1975—, prof. fgn. langs. and lits., chair dept. fgn. langs. and lits., 1994—95, prof. emeritus fgn. langs. and lits., 1995—. Author (poetry) Espejo De Son, 1997. NDEA fellow, 1960-63 Mem. Midwest MLA, Phi Beta Kappa, Sigma Delta Pi, Phi Sigma Iota. Lutheran. Home: 860 N Cr 500 E Valparaiso IN 46383 Office: Meier Hall Rm 113 Valparaiso U Valparaiso IN 46383 Business E-Mail: Howard.Peters@valpo.edu.

PETERS, JENNIFER R., music educator; b. Pontiac, Mich., Dec. 5, 1968; d. Larry Troy Moehlman and Marjorie Carol Sullivan. B in Music Edn., Mich. State U., 1991; M in Ednl. Adminstrn., Chapman U., Orange, Calif., 1995. Cert. tchr. Mich., Calif., N.D., Colo., Fla. Music tchr. Lompoc (Calif.) Unified Schs., 1992—95, Walhalla (N.D.) Sch. Dist., 1995—97; music store salesperson Colorado Springs (Colo.) Graner Music, 2001—02; music tchr. Brentwood Mid. Sch., Greeley, Colo., 2002—03; band dir. Brevard County Schs., Palm Bay, Fla., 1998—2001, 2003—. Mem. Humane Soc. of U.S., 1992—. Mem.: Colo. Music Educators Assn., Fla. Music Educators Assn., Music Educators Nat. Conf., Fla. Band Assn. Office Phone: 321-952-5800.

PETERS, JOHN G., academic administrator, political scientist; m. Barbara Cole Peters; 1 child, Russell. BA, John Carroll U.; MA in Govt., Ohio U.; PhD in Polit. Sci., U. Ill., Urbana-Champaign, 1974. Adminstr. U. Nebr.-Lincoln; provost, COO U. Tenn., Knoxville; pres. No. Ill. U., DeKalb, 2000—. Chair Mid Am. Conf. Coun. of Pres., 2003—04; bd. dirs. Ill. Coalition, East-West Corp. Corridor Assn., Castle Bank, N.A., Ill. Coun. on Econ. Edn.; co-chair Ctr. for Child Welfare and Edn.; polit. adviser Nat. Cattlemens Assn. Assoc. editor Great Plains Quarterly, 1986—93; contbr. articles to profl. jours. Recipient No. Leadership Inst. Award, 2001. Fellow: Ctr. for Great Plains Studies; mem.: Nat. Assn. Telecommunications Officers, Nat. Assn. State Land Grant Colls. and Univs., Nat. Fedn. Local Cable Programmers, Policy Studies Orgn., Coun. Colls. of Arts and Scis., Western Polit. Sci. Assn., Internat. Polit. Sci. Assn., Midwest Polit. Sci. Assn., Am. Polit. Sci. Assn., Pi Alpha Alpha (hon.), Phi Beta Kappa (hon.), Phi Kappa Phi (hon.). Office: Office of Pres No Ill U 1425 W Lincoln Hwy Dekalb IL 60115-2825 Office Phone: 815-753-9500. E-mail: b40jgp1@wpo.cso.niu.edu.

PETERS, JORG, professor; Prof. U Fla., Gainesville, 1998—. Office: Univ Fla CSE 328 Gainesville FL 32611

PETERS, JULIE ANNE, writer; b. Jamestown, NY, Jan. 16, 1952; BA, Colo. Women's Coll. Rsch. asst., computer programmer Tracom Corp., Denver, 1975—84; computer sys. designer Electronic Data Sys., 1985—88; ednl. asst. Jefferson County Sch. Dist., Lakewood, Colo., 1990—94; writer, 1994—. Author: The Stinky Sneakers Contest, 1992, Risky Friends, 1993, B.J.'s Billion-Dollar Bet, 1994, How Do You Spell G-E-E-K?, 1996, Revenge of the Snob Squad, 1998, Romance of the Snob Squad, 1999, Love Me, Love My Broccoli, 1999, Define Normal, 2000, A Snitch in the Snob Squad, 2001, Keeping You a Secret, 2002, Luna: A Novel, 2004 (Nat. Book Award finalist, 2004), Far from Xanadu, 2005, Between Mom and Jo, 2006, Grl 2 Grl, 2007. Recipient Top Hand Award, Colo. Authors' League, Lambda Lit. award. Address: 14 Twilight Dr Lakewood CO 80215 E-mail: juli@julieannepeters.com.

PETERS, KENNETH MICHAEL, urologist, researcher; b. Detroit, Apr. 1, 1964; s. William Thomas and Janet Ann Peters; m. Diane Lynn Hogeboom, July 15, 1988; children: Anna Rose, Amanda Leigh. MD, Case Western Res. U. Sch. Medicine, Cleve., 1991. Diplomate Am. Bd. Urology. Resident gen. surgery William Beaumont Hosp., Royal Oak, Mich., 1991—93, resident urology, 1993—97, fellow urology, 1997—98, dir. clin. rsch., dept. urology, 1999—2007, chmn. dept. urology, 2007—; pvt. practice clin. urologist Birmingham Urology Assoc., Mich., 1998—. Contbr. articles to profl. jours., chapters to books. Grantee NIH. Mem.: Internat. Soc. Pelvic Neuromodulation, Internat. Continence Soc., Soc. Urodynamics & Female Urology (Clin. Rsch. award), Mich. Urological Soc., Am. Urological Assn. (mem. rsch. coun.). Achievements include research in nerve rerouting surgery, interstitial cystitis and neuromodulation; the use of neuromodulation for the treatment of interstitial cystitis; pioneering the use of BCG for interstitial cystitis. Office: Comprehensive Urology 31157 Woodward Ave Royal Oak MI 48073-0926 Office Phone: 248-336-0123. Business E-Mail: kmpeters@beaumont.edu.

PETERS, LEO FRANCIS, environmental engineer; b. Melrose, Mass., Aug. 14, 1937; s. Joseph Leander and Mary Gertrude (Phalen) Peters; m. Joan Catherine Anderson, May 20, 1961; children: Elizabeth M., Susan J., Carolyn A., Jennifer L. BSCE, Northeastern U., Boston, 1960, MSCE, 1966; postgrad., Harvard U., 1989. Registered profl. engr., Mass., N.H., diplomate, Am. Acad. Environ. Engrs. Jr. engr. N.Y. Dept. Transp., Albany, 1960-61; chief engr. John M. Cashman, Weymouth, Mass., 1961-62; project engr. Metcalf & Eddy, Inc., Boston, 1962-65, Weston & Sampson, Boston, 1965-67, assoc., 1967-70, ptnr., 1970-76; exec. v.p. Weston & Sampson Engrs., Inc., Boston, 1976-82, pres., CEO Wakefield and Peabody, Mass., 1982-99, chmn., 1999—2002, chmn. emeritus, 2002—. Treas. Engring. Ctr., 1991—93; mem. corp. Northeastern U., Boston, 1992—, dir. nat. coun., 1993—; treas. Engring Ctr. Edn. Trust, 1992—94, chmn., 1994—95. Clk., mem. Melrose (Mass.) Planning Bd., 1969—91; mem. Conservation Commn., 2003—06, Designer Selection Bd. Commonwealth of Mass., 2004—, vice chair, 2006—07, chair, 2007—; bd. dir. Environ. Bus. Coun. New Eng., 1997—2002. Recipient Environ. Merit award, Environ. Bus. Coun. New Eng., Leadership award, Engring. Ctr., 2001; named Outstanding Civil Engr., Northeastern U. Civil Engring. Alumni, Young Engr. of the Yr., Mass. Soc. Profl. Engrs., Disting. Engring. Alumnus, Northeastern U., 2005. Fellow: Am. Coun. Engring. Cos. (v.p. 1995—96, sr. v.p. 1996—97, pres. 1999—2000); mem.: ASCE (life), Boston Soc. Civil Engrs. (hon. life), New Eng. Water Works Assn. (hon. life) (pres. 1989—90), Am. Coun. Engring. Couns. New Eng. (pres. 1990—91), Water Environ. Fedn., Am. Pub. Works Assn., Am. Water Works Assn. Roman Catholic. Home: 187 E Emerson St Melrose MA 02176-3534 Office: Weston & Sampson Engrs Inc 5 Centennial Dr Peabody MA 01960-7985 E-mail: leopeters@comcast.net.

PETERS, LEONARD K., environmental scientist; BS, MS, PhD, U. Pitts. Joined U. Ky., 1974, asst. prof. chem. engring. to v.p. rsch. and grad. studies; rschr. Alcoa Rsch. Labs., Cleve. State U.; with Va. Tech., 1993—2003, mgr. rsch. and grad edn. programs, sr. exec. rsch. divsn.; dir. Pacific NW Nat. Lab. operated by Battelle U.S. Dept. Energy, 2003—06; sr. v.p. Battelle, 2003—. Mem. adv. bd. Wash. State U. Coll. Engring. and Architecture; bd. dirs. Heritage Coll., VITEX Sys., Inc., Wash. Tech. Alliance, Wash. Roundtable, Wash. State U. Rsch. Found., Tri Cities Devel. Coun.; chmn. bd., pres. Va. Tech. Intellectual Properties, Inc.; chmn. rsch. com. Va. Rsch. and Tech. Adv. Commn. Adv. bd. Jr. Achievement Greater Tri-Cities; bd. dirs. United Way Benton and Franklin Counties; Tri-Cities Indsl. Devel. Coun. Recipient Recognition award for contributions to Sci. and Tech., Nat. Sci. Found., 1990. Mem.: AIChE, Oreg. Coun. Knowledge and Econ. Devel., Am. Soc. Engring. Edn., Am. Assn. Aerosol Rsch., Air and Waste Mgmt. Assn., Sigma Xi. Office: Battelle 505 King Ave Columbus OH 43201

PETERS, MARGARET ANNETTE, English language educator; BA in English, Tex. A&M U., College Station, 1988; MA in English, Claremont Grad. Sch., Calif., 1993. Assoc. prof. English, Santa Fe C.C., 1996—, chair dept. English and speech, 2004—. Adviser Phi Theta Kappa, Santa Fe, 2001—03. Achievements include Gov. of New Mexico declared December 12, 2001, Margaret A. Peters Day throughout the state of New Mexico to commend her work as a teacher. Avocations: book arts, crafts, painting and drawing, journaling. Office: Santa Fe CC 6401 Richards Ave Santa Fe NM 87508 Personal E-mail: margpeters@gmail.com. Business E-Mail: mpeters@sfccnm.edu.

PETERS, MARY ELIZABETH, former United States Secretary of Transportation; b. Phoenix, Dec. 4, 1948; d. Rose Peters; m. Terry Peters; children: Tammy, Terry, Tina. BA in Mgmt., U. Phoenix; attended, John F. Kennedy Sch. Govt. Program for State & Local Govt. Executives, Harvard U., 2000. Various positions Ariz. Dept. Transp., 1985—98, dir., 1998—2001; adminstr. Fed. Highway Adminstrn., US Dept. Transp., Washington, 2001—05; nat. dir. for transp. policy, cons. HDR, Inc., Phoenix, 2005—06; sec. US Dept. Transp., Washington, 2006—09. Vice chairwoman Nat. Surface Transp. Policy & Revenue Study Commn., 2006; bd. dirs. Aldis, Inc., 2009—. Past bd. dirs. Project Challenge, Nat. Guard; past chair adv. bd. Hwy. Expansion Loan Program; mem. Gt. Ariz. Develop. Authority; past mem. Growing Smarter Commn. Recipient George S. Bartlett award, 2005; named Women of Yr., Women's Transp. Seminar, 2004; named one of Most Influential Person in Ariz. Transp., Ariz. Bus. Jour. Mem.: We. Assn. State Hwy. Transp. Officials, Am. Assn. State Hwy. Officials (past chair standing com. on planning, assest mgmt. task force, reauthorization steering com. 2001). Republican.*

PETERS, MARYBETH, copyrights register; b. Pawtucket, RI, June 12, 1939; Student, U. R.I., 1957-58; BSc in Edn., R.I. Coll., 1961; JD (hons.), George Washington U., 1971. Bar: D.C. 1973. Tchr., Cranston, R.I., 1961-65; examiner Music Section, Cranston, R.I., 1966-69, sr. examiner, 1969-75; from sr. attorney to register Copyright Office, Washington, 1975-94, register of copyrights, 1994—. Cons. copyright law World Intellectual Property Orgn., Geneva, 1989—90; lectr. Communications Law Inst. Catholic U. Am. Columbus Sch. Law; adj. prof. U. Miami Sch. Law, Georgetown U. Law Ctr. Mem. ABA, Copyright Soc. U.S.A., Computer Law Assn. (bd. dirs.), D.C. Computer Law Forum. Office: Copyright Office Library of Congress 101 Independence Ave SE Rm 403 Washington DC 20540-0002

PETERS, MAX STONE, chemical engineer, educator; b. Delaware, Ohio, Aug. 23, 1920; s. Charles Clinton and Dixie Mae (Stone) Peters; m. Laurnell Louise Stephens, June 29, 1947; children: Margaret Dixie, M. Stephen. BSChemE, Pa. State U., 1942, MS, 1947, PhD (Shell Oil Co. grad. fellow 1949-51), 1951. Registered profl. engr., Pa., Colo. Prodn. supr. Hercules Powder Co., 1942-44; research asst. Pa. State U., 1946-47; tech. plant supr. George I. Treyz Chem. Co., 1947-49; mem. faculty U. Ill., 1951-62, prof. chem. engring., 1957-62, head dept., 1958-62; dean engring. U. Colo., 1962-78, prof. chem. engring., 1978-87, chmn. dept., 1981-85, emeritus prof. chem. engring., emeritus dean engring., 1987—. Mem. adv. com. engring. divsn. NSF, 1962—66; chmn. Pres.'s Nat. Medal Sci. Com., 1969—70, Colo. Environ. Commn., 1970—72. Author: Elementary Chemical Engineering, 1954, rev. edit., 1984, Plant Design and Economics for Chemical Engineers, 1958, rev. edit., 1968, 2003; cons. editor: McGraw-Hill series chem. engring., 1960—87. With US Army, 1944—46. Recipient Merit award, Am. Assn. Cost Engrs., 1969, Disting. Alumnus award, Pa. State U., 1974, U. Colo., 1971, Phillips Lecture award, Okla. State U., 1980. Mem.: AIChE (dir. 1961—64, pres. 1968, Founders award 1974, Lewis award 1979), Am. Assn. Cost Engring., Am. Chem. Soc. (adv. bd. jours. 1956—59), Am. Soc. Engring. Edn. (chmn. chem. engring. divsn. 1962, sec. engring. coll. adminstrn. coun. 1965—67, George Westinghouse award 1959, Lamme award 1973, Merry Field award 1985), Nat. Acad. Engring., Sigma Xi, Sigma Tau, Tau Beta Pi, Phi Lambda Upsilon, Phi Eta Sigma, Alpha Chi Sigma. Achievements include research in biomass, kinetics, mechanisms. Home: 4875 Sioux Dr No 004 Boulder CO 80303

PETERS, MERCEDES, psychotherapist; b. NYC; BS, L.I. U.; MS, U. Conn.; tng. in psychotherapy, Am. Inst. Psychotherapy; PhD in Psychoanalysis, Union Inst., 1989. Cert. in psychoanalysis Postgrad. Ctr. Mental Health. Sr. psychotherapist Cmty. Guidance Svc. Postgrad. Ctr. Mental Health; staff affiliate Postgrad. Ctr. for Mental Health, 1974-76; pvt. practice psychoanalysis and psychotherapy, Bklyn.; tchr., supr. psychoanalytic psychotherapy at various psychotherapeutic tng. ctrs., 1975—; cons. to advanced tng. program Jewish Bd. Family and Children's Svcs., 2000—06. Contbr. articles to profl. jours. Past bd. dirs. Brookwood Child Care Assn. Fellow: Am. Orthopsychiat. Assn.; mem.: NASW, NAACP, LWV, Assn. Psychoanalytic Self Psychology, Assn. Psychoanalytic, Postgrad. Psychoanalytic Soc., Nat. Assn. Advancement Psychoanalysis (past bd. dirs., chair UN com.), Wednesday Club. Office: 142 Joralemon St Brooklyn NY 11201-4709 Office Phone: 718-875-9874.

PETERS, MILTON EUGENE, retired educational psychologist; b. Anderson, Ind., July 22, 1938; s. Olen A. and Dorothy LaVerne (Lambert) P.; m. Carol Ann Dudycha, Aug. 27, 1960. BA, Wittenburg U., 1960; M in Div., Hamma Sch. Theology, 1963; MA, Bowling Green State U., 1965; PhD, U. Toledo, 1975. Lic. psychologist, Ohio. Pastor Luth. Ch. Am., 1966-69; instr. psychology Defiance Coll., Ohio, 1969-70, Bluffton Coll., Ohio, 1970-72; tchr., rsch. asst. U. Toledo, 1973-75, prof., 1975-76, U. Findlay, 1989—2007, dir. instl. rsch., asst. prof. psychology Ohio, 1976-85, assoc. prof. psychology, 1985-89. Cons., lectr. in field; ednl. rschr. Contbr. articles to profl. and religious jours. Mem. APA, Am. Assn. Univ. Prof. (pres. U. Findlay), Midwestern Psychol. Assn., Creative Edn. Found. (colleague), Findlay Beacon Club, Fostoria Power Squadron. Home: 1130 Country Club Dr Findlay OH 45840-6342 Home Phone: 419-424-0224.

PETERS, RALPH EDGAR, architectural firm and engineering executive; b. Harrisburg, Pa., Feb. 20, 1923; s. George Edward and Rebecca Flavia (Michener) P.; m. Roberta Jane Shaffer, June 12, 1948; children: Sheila Jane, Gail Marie, Ralph Jr., Bret Edward. Student, U. Pa., 1942; BA in Bus. Adminstrn., Pa. State U., 1948. From payroll supt. to asst. budget supr. Pa. State U., 1948-52; chief acct., pers. officer Haller, Raymond & Brown, State College, Pa., 1952-54; from contr. to CEO and chmn. bd. Benatec Assocs., Inc. (formerly Berger Assocs., Inc.), Camp Hill, Pa., 1954—. Chmn. bd. advisors Pa. State U., Harrisburg, 1979—; chmn. bd. dirs. Holy Spirit Hosp., Camp Hill, 1982—; past pres. Tri-County United Way, Harrisburg, 1978—; chmn. Pvt. Industry Coun., Harrisburg, 1982-87. With U.S. Army, 1943-46, ETO, 1952-53, Korea. Recipient Comty. Svc. award Salvation Army, 1980, Disting. Pennsylvanian award Greater Phila. C. of C., 1981, Catalyst award Capital Region Econ. Devel., 1992, James Skelly award for exceptional svcs. to the hwy. program Associated Constructors of Pa., 1993, Alexis de Tocqueville Humanitarian award United Way, 1999; named Transp. Adv. of Yr., Pa. Hwy. Info. Assn., 1994; finalist Ctrl. Pa. Entrepreneur of Yr., 1996; Paul Harris fellow Rotary Internat., 1997. Mem. Pa. C. of C. (bd. dirs., transp. com. chmn. 1972-90), Harrisburg Area C. of C. (pres., chmn. 1979-83), Ams. for Competitive Enterprise Sys. (pres. 1981-83), Cumberland County Transp. Authority, Susquehanna Valley Regional Airport Authority, Lions, Masons, Pa. Jaycees (pres. 1955-56, nat. v.p. 1956-57), Delta Sigma Pi. Lutheran. Office: Benatec Assocs Inc 200 Airport Rd New Cumberland PA 17070-2467 Home: 80 Sycamore Dr #111 Elizabethtown PA 17022-3011 Home Phone: 717-361-5430; Office Phone: 717-901-7055. Business E-Mail: rpeters@benatec.com.

PETERS, ROBERT K., dean, newscaster, journalist; b. Tyler, Tex., June 2, 1941; s. Robert K. and Ruth Bailey Peters; m. Judy D. Loden, Feb. 23, 1980; children: Jonathan W., Anne E. AA, Tyler Jr. Coll., 1961—; BA, Tex. Christian U., 1962; M in History, Stephen F. Austin State Coll., 1964; PhD, U. Tex., 1977. Staff writer, weather, and sci. Tyler Courier Times Telegraph, 1962—; newsreader weather KTBB Radio Sta., Tyler, 1962—; dean univ. studoes Tyler Jr. Coll., 1966—; observer, sta. keeper Nat. Weather Svc., Tyler, 1992—. Dir. bd. dirs. Horizon, Tyler, 1977—; trustee Tyler Mus. Art, 1999—. Author: Texas from Annexation to Succession: 1846-1861, 1977, Practicing Texas Politics, Instructor Resource Manual, 1994, 1995, 1997, 1998, 2000, 2001, 2003. Mem. Tex. Coun. Workforce and Econ. Competitiveness, Austin, 1999—2003, N.E. Tex. State Sub-Commrs. Revision, Austin, 1973—74, Tex. Commn. Blind Bd., Austin, 1985—91, 1999—2004, Tex. Coun. Disabilities, Austin, 1990—91, City of Tyler Rev. Bd., 1990—94, Tex. Planning Coun. Disabilities, Austin, 1991—93. Recipient Piper Prof. award, Piper Found., San Antonio, 1993, Nat. Weather Svc. Cooperating Observer award, Nat. Weather Svc., Shreveport, La., 2002. Mem.: Tex. State Hist. Soc., So. Hist. Soc., Orgn. Am. History,

Am. Hist. Soc. Republican. Episcopalian. Avocations: reading, cooking. Home: 3813 Brookwood Tyler TX 75701 Office: Tyler Jr Coll 1400 E 5th St Tyler TX 75711 Fax: 903-510-2708. E-mail: rpet@tjc.edu.

PETERS, ROBERT WAYNE, small business owner; b. LaPorte, Ind., Jan. 2, 1950; s. Harry Carl and Dorothy May (Fischer) P.; m. Frances Kay Cooley, Aug. 21, 1971; children: Carolyn Marie, Angela Lynn. BA, Purdue U., 1972. CLU. Mgr. pension adminstrn. Gen. Life Ins. Corp., Milw., 1973-75; dir. qualified plan devel. Cen. Life Assurance Co., Des Moines, 1976-84; v.p. individual ops. First Farwest Ins. Co., Portland, Oreg., 1984-90; pres. CAF Enterprises, Inc., Portland, 1990—. Lectr. in field. Contbr. articles to profl. jours. Mem. N.W. Vintage Thunderbird (v.p. 1988, pres. 1989-90, exec. bd. 1991, sec. 1992-93, 97-2002, treas. 1995-96, sec.-treas. 2000), N.W. Car Collectors Assn. (treas. 2002-09). Avocations: reading, vintage thunderbirds. Office: CAF Enterprises Inc PO Box 1529 Tualatin OR 97062-1529 Personal E-mail: bob@tbirdsanctuary.com.

PETERS, ROSEMARY ALISON, literature and language professor; b. Los Alamitos, Calif., Oct. 6, 1969; d. Fred Roy and Pamela E. Peters. AB, U. Calif., Davis, 1992; MA, PhD, Harvard U., Cambridge, Mass., 2003. Lectr. English Ecole Normale Supérieure-Lettres & Sciences Humaines, Lyon, Rhône-Alpes, France, 2000—02; asst. bd. undergraduate studies, dept romance lang. & lit. Harvard U., 2004—06; lectr. French Boston U., 2005—06; asst. prof. French Southern Ill. U., Carbondale, 2006—07; asst. prof. French studies La. State U., Baton Rouge, 2007—. Musician baton rouge symphony chorus. Coun. Rsch. Summer grant, La. State U., 2008. Mem.: MLA, Midwest MLA, Am. Comparative Lit. Assn. Avocations: running, travel, piano, guitar, violin.

PETERS, SARAH WHITAKER, art historian, writer; b. Kenosha, Wis., Aug. 17, 1924; d. Robert Burbank and Margaret Jebb (Allen) Whitaker; m. Arthur King Peters, Oct. 21, 1943; children: Robert Bruce, Margaret Allen, Michael Whitaker. BA, Sarah Lawrence Coll., Bronxville, NY, 1954; MA, Columbia U., NYC, 1966; student, L'Ecole du Louvre, Paris, 1967-68; diplome, Ecole des Trois Gourmandes, Paris, 1968; PhD, CUNY, 1987. Freelance critic Art in Am., NYC. Lectr.-in-residence Garrison Forest Sch., Owings Mills, Md.; adj. asst. prof. art history C.W. Post, U. L.I.; lectr. Bronxville (N.Y.) Adult Sch., Internat. Mus. Photography, 1979, Tufts U., 1979, Madison (Wis.) Art Ctr., 1984, Meml. Art Gallery, Rochester, N.Y., 1988, 91, Caramoor Mus., Katonah, N.Y., 1988, Yale U. Art Gallery, New Haven, 1989, The Cosmopolitan Club, N.Y.C., 1977, 91, Sarah Lawrence Coll., Bronxville, 1992, The Phillips Collection, Washington, 1993, 2006, Mpls. Inst. Arts, 1993, Whitney Mus. Am. Art, Champion, 1994, U. Wis., Parkside, 1994, Nat. Mus. Wildlife Art, Jackson Hole, Wyo., 1995, The Georgia O'Keeffe Mus., Santa Fe, 1997, 2006, Bronxville Pub. Libr., 1998, Weatherspoon Art Mus., Greensboro, NC, 2003, Amon Carter Mus, Ft. Worth, 2003, Vassar Coll., 2003, Pa. Acad. Fine Arts, Phila., 2004. Author: Becoming O'Keeffe: The Early Years, 1991, 2d edit., 2001, Pattern of the Past: A Kenosha Memoir, 2001; contbr. essays to Portraits of American Women, 1991, The Dictionary of Art, 1996, Frames of Reference; Works from the Whitney Museum of American Art, 1999, American Art Review, 2003, Georgia O'Keeffe: Color and Conservation, 2006, N.Mex. Hist. Rev., 2006, Seeing America: Painting and Sculpture, 2006; TV appearances include: BBC, London, The Late Show, 1993, A&E Network Biography series on Georgia O'Keeffe, 2004; radio interview: Art Today, Australia Broadcasting Corp., 1999; contbr. articles to profl. jours. Mem. Coll. Art Assn., Bronxville Field Club, The U. Club. Avocations: horseback riding, rock climbing, tennis, cooking. Home: 14 Village Ln Bronxville NY 10708-4806

PETERS, SUE ELLEN, retired elementary school educator; b. Rock Springs, Wyo., Oct. 1, 1951; d. Vernon A. Martin and Betty E. McCloy Honadel; m. Gary M. Peters, Sept. 5, 1980; children: David Blaine, Tessa Ellen. BS in Edn., Black Hills State Coll., 1973; MS in Natural Sci., U. Wyo., 1988. Substitute tchr. K-12 Edgemont (S.D.) Ind. Sch. Dist., 1973-77, tchr., 1977-79, Campbell County Sch. Dist 1, Gillette, Wyo., 1979—2008. Math curriculum com. Campbell County Sch. Dist., Gillette, 1982-2008, math. standards team, 1989-91, family math. team, 1993-2006, 6 traits of reading team, 2001-02, Wyo. Edgate team, 2002-03; mem. devel. team Wyo. State Test-PAWS. Liaison to Mayor's cmty. art coun. Powder River Symphony, 2005—, bd. dirs., 2001—06, pres., 2004—06. Recipient Vol. award St. Jude Children's Rsch. Hosp., Memphis, Tenn., 1988, '89, '90, '91. Mem. NEA, PEO (Wyo. state del. 2002, 07, chpt. rec. sec. 2003-05, chpt. chaplain 2005-07, chpt. pres. 2007-09), Wyo. Edn. Assn. (human rights com. mem. 1980-82), Campbell County Edn. Assn., Nat. Coun. Tchrs. of Math., Campbell County Reading Coun., Wyo. Coun. Tchrs. of Math., Epsilon Sigma Alpha (2d v.p. Wyo. chpt. 1991, sec. Omega Chi chpt. 1988-90). Avocations: travel, reading, vol. work. Personal E-mail: gspeters@vcn.com.

PETERS, SUSAN P., human resources specialist; married; 1 child. BA, St. Mary's Coll., Univ. Notre Dame, 1975; M Edn., Univ. Va., 1978. Mgmt. positions Gen. Electric, 1979—82; mgr. union rels., profl. rels. mgr. Trane Co., 1982—84; mgr. non-exempt rels. GE Plastics, Pittsfield, Mass., 1984—86, HR mgr. worldwide mktg., prod. mgmt., 1986—89, HR mgr. Europe Bergen op Zoom, Netherlands, 1989—90; mgr. HR staffing & develop. Gen Electric, Fairfield, Conn., 1990—91; mgr. human resources GE Plastics, Pittsfield, Mass., 1991—93; sr. human resources mgr. GE Appliances, Louisville, 1993—2000; exec. v.p. human resources NBC, 2000—01; v.p. exec. develop. Gen. Electric, Fairfield, Conn., 2001—. Office: General Electric 3135 Easton Turnpike Fairfield CT 06828*

PETERS, THEODORE, JR., emeritus research scientist, consultant; b. Chambersburg, Pa., May 12, 1922; s. Theodore and Miriam (Lenhardt) P.; m. Margaret Campbell, June 9, 1945; children: Theodore D., James C., Melissa Peters Barry, William L. BS in Chem. Engring. summa cum laude, Lehigh U., 1943; PhD in Biol. Chemistry, Harvard U., 1950. Diplomate Am. Bd. Clin. Chemistry. Grad. asst. MIT, Cambridge, 1943-44; rsch. fellow Harvard Med. Sch., Boston, 1948-50; instr. U. Pa. Sch. Medicine, Phila., 1950-51; biochemist U.S. VA Hosp., Boston, 1953-55; rsch. biochemist Mary Imogene Bassett Hosp., Cooperstown, N.Y., 1955-88, rsch. scientist emeritus, 1988—2009; vis. scientist Carlsberg Laboratorium, Copenhagen, 1958-59; guest worker NIH, Bethesda, Md., 1971-72; vis. rsch. prof. U. Western Australia, Perth, 1982. Chmn. classification panel FDA, Washington, 1976-79; bd. dirs. Nat. Com. for Clin. Lab. Standards, Villanova, Pa., 1986-87. Author: All About Albumin, Biochemistry, Genetics, and Medical Applications, 1996; chmn. bd. editors Clin. Chemistry, 1979-84; contbr. articles to profl. jours. Mem. Sewer Bd., Cooperstown, 1973—; mem. Water Bd., Cooperstown, 1973—, Watershed Supervisory Com., Cooperstown, 1999-; chmn. lake com. Otsego County Conservation Assn., Cooperstown, 1972-78. Comdr. USNR, 1944-47, 51-53. Recipient Gold medal Biol. div. Electron Microscope Soc. Am., 1966, Conservationalist of Yr. award, Otsego County Conservation Assn., 2006, Outstanding Achievement award, NY Rural Water Assn., 2008. Fellow Am. Assn. Clin. Chemistry (pres. 1988, awards 1976, 77, 91); mem. Am. Chem. Soc., Am. Soc. Biol. Chem. Molecular Biology (emeritus), Am. Soc. for Cell Biology (emeritus), Protein Soc. (emeritus), Nat. Acad. for Clin. Biochemistry (diplomate), Acad. Clin. Lab. Physicians and Scientists, Phi Beta Kappa. Avocations: tennis, hiking, music. Home: 85 Lake St Cooperstown NY 13326-1038 Personal E-mail: tedp@stny.rr.com.

PETERS, THOMAS JOSEPH, computer scientist, mathematician; b. Washington; s. Raymond Joseph and Mary Theresa (O'Neill) P. BA in Math., New Coll., 1973; MS in Math., U. R.I., 1978; PhD in Math., Wesleyan U., Conn., 1982. Environ. analyst Conn. Dept. Environ. Protection, Hartford, 1973-75; asst. prof. U. Hartford, 1982-83; mem. sr. tech. staff Prime/Computervision, Inc., Bedford, Mass., 1984-88; mem. rsch. staff C.S. Draper Lab., Cambridge, Mass., 1988-89; vis. assoc. prof. U. Conn., Storrs, 1989-90, asst. prof., 1990—96, assoc. prof., 1996—2006, prof., 2006—. Cons. No. Rsch. and Engring. Corp., Woburn, Mass., 1989, Prime/Computervision, Inc., Bedford, 1990. Author: (with others) Innovative Applications of Artificial Intelligence, 1991; contbr. articles to profl. jours. Mem. adv. bd. Conn. Lung Assn., East Hartford, 1982-84; advisor Community Child Guidance Clinic, Manchester, Conn., 1991. Conn. State scholar, 1968-73. Mem. Am. Math. Soc., Assn. for Computing Machinery, Soc. for Indsl. and Applied Math. Office: U Conn Dept Computer Sci & Engring U 155 Storrs CT 06269-3155 Office Phone: 860-486-5045.

PETERS, TODD, psychiatrist; MD, Pa. State U. Coll. Medicine, Hershey, 2006. Resident psychiatry Brown U., Providence, 2006—.

PETERSEN, ANNE C. (CHERYL PETERSEN), foundation administrator, educator; b. Little Falls, Minn., Sept. 11, 1944; d. Franklin Hanks and Rhoda Pauline (Sandwick) Studley; m. Douglas Lee Petersen, Dec. 27, 1967; children: Christine Anne, Benjamin Bradfield. BA, U. Chgo., 1966, MS, 1972, PhD, 1973. Asst. prof., rsch. assoc. Dept. Psychiatry U. Chgo., 1972-80, assoc. prof., rsch. assoc., 1980-82; prof. human devel., head Dept. Individual and Family Studies Pa. State U., University Park, 1982-87, dean Coll. Health and Human Devel., 1987-92, prof. health and human devel., 1987-92; dean grad. sch., v.p. for rsch. throughout state U. Minn., Mpls., 1992-94, prof. adolescent devel. and pediatrics, 1992-96; dep. dir., COO NSF, Arlington, Va., 1994-96; sr. v.p. programs W.K. Kellogg Found., 1996—2005; dep. dir. Ctr. Advanced Study Behavioral Scis. Stanford U., 2006—, prof. Dept. Psychology, 2006—. Vis. prof., fellow Coll. Edn., R&D Psychology, Roosevelt U., Chgo., 1973-74; cons. Ctr. for Health Adminstrn. Studies U. Chgo., 1976-78, Ctr. for New Schs., Chgo., 1974-78, Robert Wood Johnson Found. Mathtech, Inc., 1987-89; coord. clin. rsch. tng. program Michael Reese Hosp. and Med. Ctr., Chgo., 1976-80, dir. Lab. for Study of Adolescence, 1975-82; faculty Ill. Sch. for Profl. Psychology, 1978-79; statis. cons. Coll. Nursing U. Ill. Med. Ctr., 1975-83; assoc. dir. health program MacArthur Found., 1980-82, also cons. health program, 1982-88; chair sr. adv. bd. NIMH, 1987-88; nat. adv. mental health coun. NIH, 1997-2003; trustee Nat. Inst. Statis. Scis., 1998-2004. Author: Sex Related Differences in Cognition Functioning: Developmental Issues, 1979, Promoting Adolescent Health: A Diolog on Research and Practice, 1982, Firls at Puberty: Biological and psychosocial Perspectives, 1983, Brain Maturation and Cognitive Development: Comparative and Cross Cultural Perspectives, 1991, Narrowing the Margins: Adolescent Unemployment and the lack of a social role, 1991, Grofit: A Fortran Program for the Estimation of Parameters of a Human Growth Curve, 1972, Girls at Puberty: Biological and Psychosocial Perspectives, 1983, Adolescence and Youth: Psychological Development in a Changing World, 1984, Youth Unemployment and Society, 1994, Transitions Through Adolescence: Interpersonal Domains and Context, 1996; reviewer Jour. Youth and Adolescence, 1975-80, Devel. Psychology, 1979—, Sci., 1979—, Jour. Edn. Psychology, 1979—, Child Devel., 1980—, Jour. Edn. Measurement, 1980, Ednl. Rschr., 1980, Am. Ednl. Rsch. Jour., 1981—, Jour. Mental Imagery, 1982-92, Sex Roles, 1984—; cons. editor Psychology of Women Quar., 1978-82, assoc. editor, 1983-86; adv. editor Contemporary Psychology, 1985-86; mem. editl. bd. various profl. jours.; contbr. chpts. to books and articles to profl. jours. Bd. overseers Lewis Coll., Ill. Inst. Tech., 1980-82; mem. adv. bd. longitudinal data archive project Murray Ctr., Radcliffe Coll., 1985-91, mem. sci. adv. bd., 1983-91 Fellow: APA (chmn. task force on reproductive freedom 1979—81, program chmn. 1981—82, chmn. task force on long range planning 1986—89, pres. divsn. 7 1992—93), AAAS; mem.: NAS (nat. forum on future children and their families 1987—91, chmn. panel on child abuse and neglect 1991—93, mem. forum on adolescence Inst. of Medicine 1997—2000, chair bd. on behavioral, cognitive and sensory scis. 1997—, mem. nat. academics com. sci., engring., and policy 2003—), Global Phys. Therapy Alliance (pres. 2005—), Soc. for Rsch. on Adolescence (pres. 1990—92, past pres. 1992—94, chmn. nominations com. 1992—94, mem. fin. com. 2004—), Acad. Europaea, Psychometric Soc., Behavior Genetics Assn., Assn. Women in Sci. (bd. dirs. 1996—2000), Am. Ednl. Rsch. Assn. (various offices), Internat. Soc. for the Study of Behavioral Devel. (coun. mem. 1995—, pres.-elect 2002—06, pres. 2006—), Inst. for Medicine. Home: 3715 Blackberry Ln Kalamazoo MI 49008-3333 Office Phone: 650-321-2052. E-mail: globalphilliance@yahoo.com.

PETERSEN, BARRY REX, news correspondent; b. Norfolk, Va., Jan. 14, 1949; s. Kermit and Mavis Lucille (Sutton) P.; m. Sandra H. Petersen, June 7, 1971 (div. Dec. 1984); children: Emily Jensine, Juliette Rose; m. Jan Chorlton, Feb. 14, 1985. BS in Journalism, Northwestern U., 1970, MS in Journalism, 1972. Sports columnist Sidney (Mont.) Herald, 1964-66; city hall reporter Arlington Heights (Ill.) Day, 1968-69; columnist, copy editor Chgo. Today, 1970-71; pub. Daily Northwestern, Evanston, Ill., 1970-71; reporter Milw. (Wis.) Jour., 1971-72; investigative reporter Sta. WITI-TV, Milw., 1972-74; reporter, anchor Sta. WCCO-TV, Mpls., 1974-78; corr. CBS News, LA, 1978-81, San Francisco, 1981-85, Tokyo, 1986-88, Moscow, 1988-90, London, 1991-95, Tokyo, 1995—. Pres. AFRTA, Milw., 1973-74; Josephine B. and Newton N. Minow vis. prof. in communications Northwestern U., Evanston, Ill., 1991. Recipient Investigative Reporting award Wis. Press Assn., 1973, Nat. Emmy award, 1994, 97, World gold medal radio breaking news N.Y. Festivals, 1999, Edward R. Murrow award, 2004. Mem. Fgn. Corrs. Club Japan, Fgn. Club of China. Lutheran. Avocations: sailing, travel, international real estate. also: CBS News 5-3-6 Akasaka Minato-ku Tokyo 107 Japan Office Phone: 212-975-3019. Business E-Mail: bp3@cbsnews.com.

PETERSEN, BENTON LAURITZ, paralegal; b. Salt Lake City, Jan. 1, 1942; s. Lauritz George and Arleane (Curtis) P.; m. Sharon Donnette Higgins, Sept. 20, 1974 (div. Aug. 9, 1989); children: Grant Lauritz, Tashya Eileen, Nicholas Robert, Katrina Arleane. AA, Weber State Coll., 1966, BA, BA, Weber State Coll., 1968; M of Liberal Studies, U. Okla., 1980; diploma, Nat. Radio Inst. Paralegal Sch., 1991; JD, Monticello U., 1999. Registered paralegal. Announcer/news dir. KWHO Radio, Salt Lake City, 1968-70, KDXU Radio, St. George, Utah, 1970-73, KSOP Radio, Salt Lake City, 1973-76; case worker/counselor Salvation Army, Midland, Tex., 1976-84; announcer/news dir. KBRS Radio, Springdale, Ark., 1984-86; case worker/counselor Office of Human Concern, Rogers, Ark., 1986-88; announcer KAZM Radio, Sedona, Ariz., 1988-91; paralegal Benton L. Petersen, Manti, Utah, 1991—. Cons. Sanpete County Srs., Manti, 1992—. Award judge Manti City Beautification, 1992-96; treas. Manti Destiny Com., 1993-98; tourism com. Sanpete County Econ. Devel., Ephraim, Utah, 1993-96. Served with U.S. Army N.G., 1959-66. Mem.: Nat. Assn. Attys. in Fact (past pres.). Mem. Lds Ch. Avocation: reading. Home: 120 N 470 E Manti UT 84642 Office Phone: 435-835-8689. Personal E-mail: bpfreedom@hotmail.com.

PETERSEN, CAROLYN ASHCRAFT, retired psychologist; b. Waxhaw, NC; d. J. Carl and Carolyn (Ray) Wolfe; m. Thomas L. Ashcraft (div. 1973); children: Anne C., Thomas Wolfe; m. Marvin E. Petersen, Nov. 14, 1982. BS, U. N.C.; MA, Vanderbilt U., PhD, 1963. Lic. psychologist, Pa., Fla. Psychologist Peabody Child Study Ctr., Nashville, 1963-64; rschr. U.S. Dept. Edn.-Peabody, Nashville, 1964-65; assoc. prof. Tenn. State U., Nashville, 1965-66; asst. prof. U. Tenn., Nashville, 1966-69, LaSalle Coll., Phila., 1970-72; adj. instr. U. Pa., Phila., 1970-73; clin. psychologist Overbrook Sch. for Blind, Phila., 1974-76, Fla. Sch. for Deaf and Blind, St. Augustine, 1976-78; asst. prof. psychology U. Tampa, Fla., 1979-82; assoc., adj. prof. S.D. State U., Brookings, 1983-89; ret., 1995. Cons. Tenn. Dept. Edn., Cookeville, 1966-69, Charter Hosp., Tampa, 1979-82; organizer symposia for profl. meetings. Contbr. to profl. publs. Bd. dirs. Brookings Hosp. Aux., 1985-88; v.p. S.D. Art Mus. Guild, 1988-89. Fellow Am. Psychol. Soc., Pa. Psychol. Assn.; mem. APA, Southeastern Psychol. Assn., Nat. Register Psychologists. Republican. Avocations: bridge, travel, art. Home: 103 Silverbell Ct Sun City Center FL 33573-6215 Personal E-mail: drcarolynpetersen@yahoo.com.

PETERSEN, CHRIS, college football coach; b. 1964; m. Barbara Petersen; children: Jack, Sam. BA in Psychology, U. Calif. Davis, 1988, M in Edn. & Psychology. Freshman football coach U. Calif. Davis, 1987—88, receivers coach, 1989—91; quarterbacks coach U. Pitts., 1992, Portland St. U., 1993—94; offensive coord. U. Oreg., 1995—2000, Boise State U., 2000—05, head football coach, 2006—. Recipient Paul "Bear" Bryant award, Nat. Sportscasters & Sportswriters Assn., 2006; named WAC Coach of Yr., Sporting News, 2008. Achievements include coaching Boise St. to a perfect 12-0 record, 2006. Office: Boise State U Dept Athletics Boise ID 83725*

PETERSEN, DAVID L., lawyer; AA, Concordia Jr. Coll., Milw., 1963; BA, Concordia Sr. Coll., Ft. Wayne, Ind., 1965; JD, Valparaiso U., Ind., 1968. Bar: Wis. 1968, U.S. Dist. Ct. (ea. dist.) Wis. 1969, U.S. Ct. Appeals (7th cir.) 1972, U.S. Supreme Ct. 1988, Fla. 1989. Ptnr. Quarles & Brady, Milw. and Naples, Fla., 1968—2008. Author: Wisconsin Condominium Law, 1988, 98, 2003, 06; editor Valparaiso U. Law Rev., 1967-68; contbr. articles to profl. jours. Mem. Greater Milw. Com. Cmty. Devel., 1983; bd. dirs. Goals for Greater Milw. 2000, 1982, Broward Com. of 100; mem. nat. adv. bd. Nat. Ctr. for Missing and Exploited Children, Washington, Adam Walsh Children's Fund, Palm Beach, Fla.; dir. Boys and Girls Club Collier County. Lt. col., instr. pilot USAF/Wis. Air N.G., 1970-90. Mem. ABA, Wis. Bar Assn., Milw. Bar Assn., Fla Bar Assn., Broward County Bar Assn., Palm Beach County Bar Assn., Collier County Bar Assn., Am. Coll. Real Estate Lawyers, Milw. Yacht Club, Palm Beach Yacht Club. Office: Quarles & Brady LLP 1395 Panther Ln Naples FL 34109 also: Quarles & Brady LLP 411 E Wisconsin Ave Ste 2550 Milwaukee WI 53202-4409 Office Phone: 239-434-4959.

PETERSEN, DONALD SONDERGAARD, lawyer; b. Pontiac, Ill., May 14, 1929; s. Clarence Marius and Esther (Sondergaard) P.; m. Alice Thorup, June 5, 1954; children: Stephen, Susan Petersen Schuh, Sally Petersen Riordan. Student, Grand View Coll., 1946—48; BA, Augustana Coll., Rock Island, Ill., 1951; JD, Northwestern U., 1956. Bar: Ill. 1957. Assoc. Norman & Billick and predecessors, Chgo., 1956-64, ptnr., 1965-78; counsel Sidley & Austin, Chgo., 1978-80, ptnr., 1980-93, ret., 1993. Pres. Chgo. Exhibitors Corp., Chgo., 1972-85. Bd. dirs. Mount Olive Cemetery Co. Inc., Chgo., 1972-90; bd. dirs. Augustana Hosp., 1983-87, The Danish Home, 1976—; bd. dirs. Luth. Gen. Hosp., Park Ridge, Ill., 1968-2005, chmn., 1979-81, 89-91; bd. dirs. Luth. Gen. Health System and predecessors, Park Ridge, 1980-95, chmn., 1980-81, 83-85; bd. dirs., chmn. Parkside Health Mgmt. Corp., Parkside Home Health Svcs., 1985-88. With U.S. Army, 1951-53. Mem. Chgo. Bar Assn., Ill. State Bar Assn. Clubs: Union League (Chgo.). Home: 241 N Aldine Ave Park Ridge IL 60068-3009 Office: 9th Fl One S Dearborn St Chicago IL 60603 Office Phone: 312-853-7232.

PETERSEN, DOROTHY VIRGINIA, investment company executive; b. Milw., Sept. 22, 1929; d. Carl Arndt and Loretta Louise Laura (Bremer) Scherer; m. Glenn Charles Petersen, Aug. 27, 1949; children: Vicki Lynn Taylor, Larry Dean, Rick Randall. BS magna cum laude, U. Wis.-Parkside, 1975. Repair dept. clk. Eastman Kodak Co., Milw., 1946—47; sec. First Wis. Trust Co., Milw., 1947—49; head sec. art edn. dept. U. Wis., Madison, 1949—50, sec., asst, art edn. dept.; sec. and asst. Red Star Yeast Co., Milw., 1950—51; exec. sec. Boy Scouts Am., Milw., 1963—65, Applied Power, Pewaukee, Wis., 1965—67; sec., treas. Westshore Muffler Shops, Milw., 1983—2002; asst. sec., treas. Fastrack, Inc., Mequon, Wis., 2002—. Paintings (Honorable Mention, Wis. Art Show, Twin Lakes, 1976). Head fund drive Town of Greenfield ARC, 1956, helper fund drive, 1955, helper fund, 1957—59; leader Girl Scouts Am., Wauwatosa, Wis., 1960—61; cub pack sec. Boy Scouts Am., Wauwatosa, 1962—63; children's class tchr. Baha'i World Faith, Greenfield, Milw., Burlington, 1959—72, spkr. Milw., Burlington, 1970—99; mem., spkr. Baha'i Faith, 1959—72. Mem.: Order Ea. Star (Wauwatosa chpt. 219). Avocations: day trading, genealogy, reading, photography. Personal E-mail: dvpetersen29@hotmail.com.

PETERSEN, JAMES L., lawyer; b. Bloomington, Ill., Feb. 3, 1947; s. Eugene and Cathryn Theresa (Hemmele) P.; m. Helen Louise Moser, Nov. 20, 1971; children: Christine Louise, Margaret Theresa. BA, Ill. State U., 1970; MA, U. Ill., Springfield, 1973; JD magna cum laude, Ind. U., 1976. Bar; Ind. 1976, Fla. 1980, U.S. Dist. Cts. (no. and so. Ind.), U.S. Ct. Appeals (7th cir.), U.S. Supreme Ct. Admissions officer U. Ill., Springfield, 1970-71, asst. to v.p., 1971-72, registrar, 1972-73; assoc. Ice Miller, Indpls., 1976-83, ptnr., 1983—. Pres. United Cerebral Palsy of Ctrl. Ind., 1981-83, pres. Found., 1988-90, Stanley K. Lacy Leadership Series participant. Mem. ABA, Fla. Bar Assn., Ind. Bar Assn., Am. Coll. Trial Lawyers, Intl. Franchise Assn. (bd. mem. Symposium Organizing Cmte., 2003-04), Defense Trial Coun. Ind. (past co-chair, Prods. Liability Cmte; elected 1997 Diplomat), The Business Council, Inc., Ill. State U. Alumni Assn. (pres. 1990-92), Ind. U. Law Alumni Assn. (bd. dirs. 1992—, pres. 1998-99), Ind. U. Bd. Visitors 1998-99, Order of Coif. Home: 11827 Sea Star Dr Indianapolis IN 46256-9400 Office: Ice Miller LLP PO Box 82001 One American Sq Indianapolis IN 46282 Office Phone: 317-236-2308.

PETERSEN, JEAN SNYDER, retired educational association administrator; b. NYC, Oct. 16, 1931; d. Peter Eugene and Helyn Brownell (Parker) Snyder; m. Elton Reed Petersen, Sept. 16, 1954; children—Bruce Brownell, Craig Reed. Student, N.Y. U., 1949-51; degree fgn. banking, Am. Inst. Banking, 1952. Fgn. credit investigator Chase Nat. Bank Hdqrs., NYC, 1952-56; nat. exec. dir. Assn. Children and Adults with Learning Disabilities (name changed to Learning Disabilities Assn. of Am.), Pitts., 1972—; exec. dir., vol. Learning Disabilities Found. Am.; ret., 2001. Mem. exec. com., treas. Jr. League, Pitts.; bd. dirs.

Found. for Children with Learning Disabilities, N.Y.C., Children's Hosp., Pitts., Music for Mt. Lebanon, Vocat. Rehab. Ctr., Pitts.; bd. dirs., v.p., mem. exec. com. Assn. Retarded Citizens Pa.; ptnr. UN Internat. Yr. of Disabled; ruling elder Presbyn. Ch.Assn. Retarded Citizens Pa.; mem. exec. com. Pat Buckley Moss Nat. Children's Charity Found; chmn. bd. dirs. Masonic Learning Ctrs. for Children. Recipient Sustainers award Jr. League, 1977, Recognition award, 1975, Pres.'s award, 1978. Mem. AAUW, Meeting Planners Internat. (treas.), Am. Soc. Assn. Execs. Republican. Presbyterian.

PETERSEN, JESSICA M., biology professor; b. Bedford, Eng., Apr. 29, 1979; d. William and Deanna Paulk; m. Joshua Petersen; 1 child, Andrew. MS, Med. U. SC., Charleston, 2005. Biology tchr. Tate HS, Pensacola, Fla., 2005; biology instr. Pensacola Jr. Coll., Fla., 2005—. Mem.: HAPS, Phi Theta Kappa (Theta Chi advisor 2008—). Office: Pensacola Jr Coll 1000 College Blvd Pensacola FL 32504 Business E-Mail: jpetersen@pjc.edu.

PETERSEN, JOHN D., former academic administrator; m. Carol Petersen; 2 children. BS in Chemistry, UCLA, 1970; PhD in Inorganic Chemistry, U. Calif., Santa Barbara, 1975. Asst. prof. chemistry Kans. State U., 1975—80; head dept. chemistry, assoc. dean rsch. Coll. Scis. Clemson U., 1980—93; prof. chemistry, dean Coll. Sci. Wayne State U., 1994—2000; provost, exec. v.p. univ. affairs U. Conn., Storrs, 2000—04; pres., CEO U. Tenn. Sys., Knoxville, Tenn., 2004—09. Mem.: Nat. Assn. State Univ. and Land Grant Coll. (exec. com. for chief academic officers), Coun. Chem. Rsch., Am. Chem. Soc.

PETERSEN, KURT EDWARD, electrical engineer, researcher, entrepreneur; b. San Francisco, Feb. 13, 1948; s. William Ernest and Shirley Ann (Bailey) Petersen; m. Carol Tao, Sept. 24, 2000; children: Scott Edward, Brett William. BSEE cum laude, U. Calif., Berkeley, 1970; MS, MIT, 1972, PhD, 1975. Mem. rsch. staff IBM, San Jose, Calif., 1975-82; founder, v.p. tech. Transensory Devices, Inc., Fremont, Calif., 1982-85, NovaSensor, Fremont, Calif., 1985-95; founder, pres. Cepheid, Sunnyvale, Calif., 1996—2004; founder, CEO SiTime, Sunnyvale, Calif., 2004—. Cons. prof. Stanford (Calif.) U., 1994—. Fellow: IEEE (gen. chmn. solid state sensors workshop 1986, Simon Ramon medal 2001); mem.: Nat. Acad. Engring. Achievements include patents in micromachining technology. Avocations: skiing, travel. Office: SiTime 990 Almanor Dr Sunnyvale CA 94085 Office Phone: 408-328-4401. E-mail: kp@sitimecorp.com.

PETERSEN, LESLIE, political organization administrator; m. Hank Phibbs. Activist Teton County Dem. Party, Wyo., chairwoman; legis. liaison to Gov. Ed Herschler Office of the Gov., Wyo.; state committeewoman Teton County, commr.; fundraising organizer Senator John Kerry's Presdl. Campaign, Senator Barack Obama's Presdl. Campaign; chairwoman Wyo. Dem. Party, Casper, 2009—; ret. realtor. Dem. candidate Wyo. Sec. State, 1982, Wyo. House of Reps., 1990. Democrat. Office: Wyo Dem Party 254 N Center St Ste 205 PO Box 1963 Casper WY 82602-1963 Office Phone: 307-473-1457, 307-473-1459. Business E-Mail: leslie.petersen@wyoming.com.*

PETERSEN, MARTIN EUGENE, curator; b. Grafton, Iowa, Apr. 21, 1931; s. Martin S. and Martha Dorothea (Paulsen) P. AA, Mason City Jr. Coll., Iowa; BA, State U. Iowa, 1951, MA, 1957; postgrad., The Hague (Netherlands), 1964. Curator San Diego Mus. Art, 1957-96; advisor Olaf Wieghorst Mus., El Cajon, Calif., 1996—. Extension instr. U. Calif., 1958, lectr., 1960 Author art catalogues, books, articles in field. Served with AUS, 1952-54. Mem. So. Calif. Art Historians. Achievements include specialist in early southern California art.

PETERSEN, MATTHEW SPENCER, commissioner, lawyer; b. Utah, 1970; BA, Brigham Young U., Provo, 1993; JD, U. Va., 1999. Assoc., election law & govt. ethics practice Wiley Rein & Fielding LLP; counsel, com. on house adminstrn. US Ho. of Reps., Washington; Republican chief counsel, com. rules and adminstrn. US Senate, Washington; commr. Fed. Election Commn., Washington, 2008—. Republican. Office: Fed Election Commn 509 7th St NW Washington DC 20004 Office Phone: 202-694-1000. Business E-Mail: CommissionerPetersen@fec.gov.*

PETERSEN, NIELS HELVEG, Danish government official; b. Odense, Denmark, Jan. 17, 1939; s. K. Helveg and Lilly P. Petersen. LLB, U. Copenhagen, 1965, Stanford U., Calif., 1961. Mem. Danish Parliament Folketing Social-Liberal Party, 1966-74, 77—, cabinet chief Danish commn. European Commn., 1974-77, chmn. parliamentary group, 1978-88; minister econ. affairs Govt. of Denmark, Copenhagen, 1988-90, minister fgn. affairs, 1993-2000. Office: Folketinget Christiansborg 1240 Copenhagen Denmark Business E-Mail: rvnihe@ft.dk.

PETERSEN, ROGER GENE, biometrician, educator; b. Essington, Pa., July 22, 1924; s. Oliver Wendell and Lela (Schmidt) P.; m. Jean Napier Hurt, June 26, 1948; 1 child, David. BS, Iowa State Coll., 1949, MS, 1950; PhD, NC State Coll., Raleigh, 1954. Asst. statistician N.C. State Coll., 1952-55; asst. prof. Oreg. State Coll., Corvallis, 1955-57, assoc. prof., 1957-61, N.C. State U., Raleigh, 1961-64, prof., 1964-65; prof. dept. statistics Oreg. State U., Corvallis, 1965-90, prof. emeritus, 1990—. Cons. Ford Found., Cairo, 1973, Winrock Internat., Islamabad, Pakistan, 1988, 91; prin. biometrician ICARDA, Aleppo, Syria, 1978-80, 82-86. Author: Introduction to Statistical Inference, 1973, Design and Analysis of Experiments, 1985, Agricultural Field Experiments, 1994. With U.S. Army, 1943-46, ETO. Recipient award for excellence in teaching R.M. Wade Found., 1988. Mem. Am. Soc. Agronomy, Biometrical Soc. (sec.-treas. Western N.Am. region chpt. 1977-78, pres. 1983). Office: Oreg State U Dept Statistics Corvallis OR 97331 E-mail: ptrsen@peak.org.

PETERSEN, ROLAND, artist, printmaker; b. Endelave, Horsens, Denmark, 1926; came to US, 1928; m. Caryl Ritter, Mar. 4, 2003; children from previous marriage: Dana Mark, Maura Brooke, Julien Conrad, Karena Caia. BA, U. Calif., Berkeley, 1949, MA, 1950; postgrad., Han Hofmann's Sch. Fine Arts, 1950-51, S.W. Hayter's Atelier 17, Paris, 1950, 63, 70, Islington Studio, London, 1976, The Print Workshop, 1980. Tchr. State Coll. Wash., Pullman, 1952-56; faculty U. Calif., Davis, 1956-91, prof. art, 1991; ret., 1991. Exhibited one-man shows: Oakland At Mus., 1954, Calif. Palace Legion of Honor, San Francisco, 1961, Gump's Gallery, San Francisco, 1962, Staempfli Gallery, N.Y.C., 1963, 65, 67, Adele Bednarz Gallery, Los Angeles, 1966, 69, 70, 72, 73, 75, 76, Crocker Art Gallery, Sacramento, 1965, de Young Mus., San Francisco, 1968, La Jolla Mus., 1971, Phoenix Mus., 1972, Santa Barbara Mus., 1973, U. Reading, Eng., 1977, 80, U. Calif., Davis, 1978, 92, Brubaker Gallery, Sarasota, Fla., 1979, Rorick Gallery, San Francisco, 1981, 82, 83, 84, 85, Himovitz-Salomon Gallery, Sacramento, 1987-88, 91, Vanderwoude Tananbaum Gallery, N.Y.C., 1987-89, Harcourts Gallery, San Francisco, 1989, 91, 93, U. Calif., Davis, 1992, Maxwell Galleries, San Francisco, 1995, Endelave (Denmark) Mus., 1996, John Natsoulas Gallery, Davis, Calif., 1998, Hackett-Freedman Gallery, San Francisco, 2002, 2004, 2008; group shows include Calif. Palace Legion of Honor, San Francisco Art Inst., 1962, Mus. Art, Carnegie Inst., Pitts., 1964, Obelisk Gallery, Washington, John Herron Art Inst., Indpls., 1964, Pa. Acad. Fine Arts, Phila., Crocker Art Gallery, Sacramento, 1965, 81, Art Inst. Chgo., 1965, Va. Mus. Fine Arts, Richmond, 1966, U. Ariz. Art Gallery, Tucson, 1967, Am. Cultural Center, Paris, 1971, Nat. Gallery, Washington, 1972, Otis Art Inst. Gallery, Los Angeles, 1974, Auerbach Fine Art Gallery, London, 1977, U. Wis., Madison, 1977, Bklyn. Mus., 1978, U. Ill., 1978, U. Nev., Las Vegas, 1980, Brubaker Gallery, Sarasota, Fla., 1983, U.S.A. World Print Council, San Francisco, Nat. Mus., Singapore, Nat. Gallery, Bangkok, Thailand, Amerika Haus, Berlin, Malmo Konsthall, Sweden, Museo Carrillo Gil, Mexico City, all 1984-86, Crocker Art Mus., 1991, Fresno Met. Mus., 1992, Hall of Pictures, Uman, Russia, 1992, Calif. State U., L.A., 1992, San Bernardino, 1993 Pence Gallery, Davis, Calif., 1993, Artists Contemporary Gallery, Sacramento, 1994, Andre Milan Gallery, Sao Paulo, Brazil, 1995; represented in permanent collections: de Young Mus., San Francisco, San Francisco Mus. Modern Art, Va. Mus. Fine Arts, Richmond, Mus. Modern Art, N.Y.C., Phila. Mus. Art, Whitney Mus. Am. Art, Phoenix Mus., Santa Barbara Mus., Musée Municipal, Brest, France, Smithsonian Instn. Nat. Collection Fine Arts & Archives of Am. Art, Hirschorn Coll., Washington, San Jose Mus. Art, Calif., others. With USN, 1944-46, PTO. Guggenheim fellow, 1963, U. Calif. creative arts fellow, 1967, 70, 77; Fulbright grant, 1970. Home: 1148 Crespi Dr Pacifica CA 94044-3539

PETERSEN, RONALD C., neurologist, educator; BA, Hamline U., St. Paul; PhD, U. Minn.; MD, Mayo Clinic, Rochester, Minn. Cert. Am. Bd. Psychiatry and Neurology. Internship in internal medicine Stanford U. Med. Ctr., Palo Alto, Calif.; residency in neurology, Mayo Grad. Sch. Medicine Mayo Clinic, Rochester, Minn., prof. neurology, dir., Mayo Alzheimer's Disease Rsch. Ctr.; fellowship in behavioral neurology Harvard U. Med Sch./Beth Israel Hosp., Boston. Editor: Memory Disorders, Mayo Clinic on Alzheimer's Disease, Mild Cognitive Impairment: Aging to Alzheimer's Disease, Mayo Clinic Guide to Alzheimer's Disease; contbr. articles to profl. jours. Recipient MetLife award for med. rsch. in Alzheimer's disease, 2004, Potamkin prize, Am. Acad. Neurology, 2005, Leon Thal prize for excellence in dementia rsch., Lou Ruvo Brain Inst., 2007. Mem.: Nat. Alzheimer's Assn. (vice chmn., med. and sci. adv. com. 2005—08), Alzheimer's Assn. (chair, med. & sci. adv. com. 2008, Ronald and Nancy Reagan Rsch. Inst. award 2004). Office: Mayo Clinic 200 First St SW Rochester MN 55905 Office Phone: 507-284-2511, 507-538-0487. Office Fax: 507-284-0161.

PETERSEN, ULRICH, geology educator; b. Negritos, Peru, Dec. 1, 1927; s. Georg and Harriet (Bluhme) P.; m. Edith Martensen, Apr. 27, 1952 (dec. Aug. 1978); children: Erich, Armin (dec.), Heidi.; m. Eileen Bourque, June 19, 1982. Mining Engr., Escuela Nacional de Ingenieros, Lima, Peru, 1954; MA, Harvard U., 1955, PhD, 1963. Geologist Instituto Geológico del Peru and Instituto Nacional de Investigación y Fomento Mineros, 1946-51; geologist Cerro de Pasco Corp., Peru, 1951-54, asst. chief geologist, 1956-57, chief geologist, 1958-63; lectr. Harvard, 1963-66; assoc. prof. Harvard U., 1966-69, prof. mining geology, 1969-81, Harry C. Dudley prof. econ. geology, 1981-95; cons. geologist, 1963—; prof. emeritus, 1996—. Named Knight Comdr. Merit Order Disting. Svcs., Peru, 1968; recipient A. von Humboldt rsch. award, 1992-93, 2003-04; Merit award Colegio de Ingenieros del Peru, 2000, Torch Habich award U. Nacional de Ingenieria del Peru, 2005; named Engr. of Yr., Soc. de Ingenieros del Peru, 1996. Mem. Soc. Econ. Geologists (pres. 1988-89), Geol. Soc. Am., Soc. Geologica del Peru (hon.) Home: 414 Marsh St Belmont MA 02478-1109 Office: 20 Oxford St Cambridge MA 02138-2902 E-mail: ulrichp@aol.com.

PETERSEN, WILLIAM (WILLIAM LOUIS PETERSEN), actor; b. Evanston, Ill., Feb. 21, 1953; m. Joanne Brady, 1974 (div. 1981); 1 child, Maite; m. Gina Cirone, 2003. Attended, Idaho State U., Pocatello. Co-founder Remains Theater Ensemble, 1979; co-owner High Horse Prodns. Actor: (films) Thief, 1981, To Live and Die in L.A., 1985, Manhunter, 1986, Amazing Grace and Chuck, 1987, Cousins, 1989, Young Guns II, 1990, Hard Promises, 1991, Passed Away, 1992, In the Kingdom of the Blind, the Man with One Eye is King, 1995, Fear, 1996, Mulholland Falls, 1996, Gunshy, 1998, Kiss the Sky, 1999, The Skulls, 2000, The Contender, 2000 (Alan J. Pakula award, 2001); (TV series) The Twilight Zone, 1986, Fallen Angels, 1995, CSI: Crime Scene Investigation, 2000—09 (SAG award for best actor, 2005); (TV films) Long Gone, 1987, Keep the Change, 1992, Curacao, 1993, Present Tense, Past Perfect, 1995, The Beast, 1996, 12 Angry Men, 1997, The Staircase, 1998, The Rat Pack, 1998, Haven, 2001; (TV miniseries) The Kennedys of Massachusetts, 1990, Return to Lonesome Dove, 1993, (broadway play) The Night of the Iguana, 1996; prodr.: Hard Promises, 1991, Keep the Change, 1992, CSI: Crime Scene Investigation, 2000—02; co-exec. prodr. CSI: Crime Scene Investigation, 2002—03; exec. prodr.: CSI: Crime Scene Investigation, 2004—06.*

PETERSILIA, JOAN, law educator, criminologist; b. 1951; BA in Sociology, Loyola U., 1972; MA in Sociology, Ohio State U., 1974; PhD in Criminology, Law & Society, U. Calif., Irvine. Dir. Criminal Justice Program RAND Corp., Santa Monica, Calif., 1989—94; faculty co-dir. Stanford Criminal Justice Ctr.; prof. criminology, law & society U. Calif. Sch. Social Ecology, Irvine, Calif., 1992—2009, prof. emeritus, 2009—; founding dir. UCI Ctr. on Evidence Based Corrections, 2005—09; prof. law Stanford Law Sch., 2009—. Spl. adv. to Gov. Arnold Schwarzenegger State of Calif., 2003—; vis. prof. Stanford Law Sch., 2005—06. Mem.: Western Soc. Criminology, Am. Correctional Assn., Am. Probation & Parole Assn., Assn. for Criminal Justice Rsch. in Calif. (pres. 1984—85, v.p. 1982—83), Am. Soc. Criminology (v.p. 1985—86, pres. 1989—90). Office: Stanford Law School Crown Quadrangle 559 Nathan Abbott Way Stanford CA 94305-8610 Office Phone: 650-723-2465. Office Fax: 650-725-0253. E-mail: petersilia@law.stanford.edu.*

PETERSON, ADRIAN LEWIS, professional football player; b. Palestine, Tex., Mar. 21, 1985; s. Nelson Peterson and Bonita Jackson; 1 child, Adeja. Attended, U. Okla., Norman, 2004—06. Running back Minn. Vikings, 2007—. Recipient Hall Trophy, 2003, ESPY award, Best Breakthrough Athlete, ESPN, 2008; named 1st Team All-Freshman, AP, 2004, 1st Team All-Am., 2004, NFL Offensive Rookie of Yr., 2007, 1st Team All Pro, 2008, NFL Pro Bowl MVP, 2008, FedEx Ground NFL Player of Yr., 2008; named to Nat. Football Conf. Pro Bowl Team, NFL, 2007, 2008. Achievements include setting the NFL single-game rushing record (296 yards), 2007; leading the NFL in: rushing yards per game, 2007; touches, rushing yards, yards from scrimmage, 2008. Mailing: c/o Minn Vikings Metrodome 34 Kirby Puckett Pl Minneapolis MN 55415*

PETERSON, ALFRED EDWARD, retired family physician; b. Bridgeport, Conn., Mar. 23, 1922; s. Carl Emil Rudolf and Elin Maria (Lindholm) P.; m. June Meadows, May 27, 1944 (dec. Apr. 22, 2007); children: Christina, Elin (dec.), Martha, Amy. BA, Dartmouth Coll., 1946; MD, U. Vt., 1950. Diplomate Nat. Bd. Med. Examiners. Intern Binghamton City Hosp., NY, 1950-51; pvt. practice Binghamton, 1952—2005; ret., 2005. Sch. physician Chenango Forks (N.Y.) Ctrl. Schs., 1953-94; founding mem. Chenango Bridge Med. Group. Bd. dirs. Chenango Emergency Squad, Binghamton, 1980-85, Robert W. Smith Found., Rotary Club, 1980-2003; bd. dirs. med. records Broome CC, Binghamton, 1988-94. Capt. USAAF, 1943-45. Fellow Am. Acad. Family Physicians; mem. AMA, N.Y. State Med. Soc., Broome County Med. Soc., N.Y. State Acad. Family Physicians. Democrat. Avocations: cabinet making, environmental and animal welfare causes, travel, history.

PETERSON, ANDREA, elementary school educator; b. BC, Canada; d. Victor and Darlene Rahn; m. Joel Peterson. BA in Music Edn., U. Wash., 1996. Cert. in early and mid. childhood music Nat. Bd. Tchg. Standards, 2002. Music tchr. to elem. music specialist Monte Cristo Elem. Sch., Granite Falls, Wash., 1997—. Named Wash. Tchr. of Yr., Coun. Chief State Sch. Officers, 2007, Nat. Tchr. of Yr., 2007. Avocations: saxophone, singing (mezzo soprano). Office: Monte Cristo Elem Sch 1201 100th St NE Granite Falls WA 98252 Business E-Mail: apeterso@gfalls.wednet.edu.

PETERSON, ANN SULLIVAN, physician, consultant; b. Rhinebeck, NY, Oct. 11, 1928; AB, Cornell U., 1950, MD, 1954; MS, MIT, 1980. Diplomate Am. Bd. Internal Medicine. Intern Cornell Med. Divsn.-Bellevue Hosp., NYC, 1954—55, resident, 1955—57; fellow in medicine and physiology Meml.-Sloan Kettering Cancer Ctr., Cornell Med. Coll., NYC, 1957—60; instr. medicine Georgetown U. Sch. Medicine, Washington, 1962—65, asst. prof., 1965—69, asst. dir. clin. rsch. unit, 1962—69; assoc. prof. medicine U. Ill., Chgo., 1969—72, asst. dean, 1969—71, assoc. dean, 1971—72; assoc. prof. medicine, assoc. dean Coll. Physicians and Surgeons, Columbia U., NYC, 1972—80, Cornell U. Med. Coll., NYC, 1980—83; assoc. dir. divsn. med. edn. AMA, Chgo., 1983—86, dir. div. grad. med. edn., 1986—89, v.p. mgmt. cons. corp., 1989—93; ind. cons. Chgo., 1993—2005. Contbr. articles to med. jours. Mem. bd. regents Uniformed Svcs. U. of Health Scis., 1984—90. John and Mary R. Markle scholar, 1965—70, Alfred P. Sloan fellow, MIT, 1979—80. Fellow: ACP; mem.: Mortar Bd., Alpha Omega Alpha, Alpha Epsilon Delta.

PETERSON, ANNE ELIZABETH WALLACE, music educator, composer; b. Aurora, Ill., June 17, 1949; d. Vernon Ammon and Marjorie Lois (Loudon) Wallace; m. Thomas Leonard Peterson (dec. 1990); m. Tim Allen Gasser, Feb. 27, 1993. Attended, Macphail Sch. Music, 1964—67, San Francisco Conservatory Music, 1974—77, U. Edinburgh, 1979, Baroque Performance Inst., 1992; studied with Martha Ivory, 1970, studied with Charlene Brendler, 1978; BA in English and Music, U. Minn., 1971; MA in Music, Lone Mountain Coll., 1978; studied harpsichord, with Laurette Goldberg, 1974—78; studied harpsichord with Peter Williams. Cert. in Tech. Writing De Anza Coll., Cupertino, Calif., 1981. Music tchr. Pillsbury-Waite Cultural Arts Ctr., Mpls., 1971—72, Music Sch., Sunnyvale, Calif., 1991—; tech. writer, editor, rschr. SRI Internat., Menlo Park, Calif., 1973—90. Music tchr. Cmty. Sch. Music and Arts, Mountain View, Calif., 1973—78, Mountain View, 1979—2001; harpsichord performer No. Calif. Renaissance Faire, 1979—85, Minn. Renaissance Festival, 1982; mem. Soc. Tech. Communication, 1979—90, conv. spkr., 1983; keyboard gen. music instr. Boys' and Girls' Club, Redwood City, Calif., 1990—92; pvt. piano and harpsichord tchr., Redwood City, 1980—; musician, Palo Alto, San Francisco, Calif.; conf. workshop presenter in field. Author: (book) Harpsichord Tuning: An Easy Start, 1978, (book, CD) Follow the Rainbow, 2003; composer: (children's book and CD) 4 Cats, 2006, 3 Cats and a Dog, 2007, New Pet Friends, 2009, New Piano Suite for Pets, 2009; musician (harpsichordist): (albums) Then, 1997, Harpsichord at Hampstead, 1999, Starspirations, 2000; musician: Good Company (with Tudor Rose Ensemble), 1997; musician: (harpsichordist) Come and Adore! (Christmas-variety) Starspirations, 1999; musician: (harpsichordist, ensemblist, vocalist) Elizabeth Gambarini, 2000, Cougar Love, 2005; contbr. articles to profl. jours.; author: articles Teach Street.com. Mem.: Nat. Assn. Composers USA, Music Tchrs. Assn. (Appreciation award 2000), Music Tchrs. Assn. Calif. (program chair 2000—01), Toastmasters Internat. (Achievement award 1989), Phi Beta (pres. Pi Lambda chpt. 1993—95, program chair 1974—85, 2002—03, Grad. Grant-In Aid award, Marie Logan award 1979, Nat. Historian award 2004). Office Phone: 650-365-5375. Personal E-mail: awpgmusic@yahoo.com.

PETERSON, ARTHUR LAVERNE, foundation administrator; b. Glyndon, Minn., June 27, 1926; s. John M. and Hilda C. (Moline) P.; m. Connie Lucille Harr, June 14, 1952 (dec. July 26, 2002); children: Jon Martin, Rebecca Ruth, Donna Harr, Ingrid Bliss; m. Mary Kinum, Sept. 12, 2003. AB, Yale U., 1947; MSPA, U. So. Calif., 1949; postgrad., U. Chgo., 1949-50; PhD, U. Minn., 1962; LLD, Lebanon Valley Coll., 1988. Mem. Wis. State Legislature, 1951-55; from instr. to asst. prof. polit. sci. U. Wis., Eau Claire, 1954-60; assoc. prof. to prof. polit. sci. Ohio Wesleyan U., Delaware, 1961-65, 70-80; pres. Am. Grad. Sch. Internat. Mgmt., Phoenix, 1966-70; dean spl. programs Eckerd Coll., St. Petersburg, Fla., 1980-84, dir. Acad. Sr. Profls., 1987-94; pres. Lebanon Valley Coll., Annville, Pa., 1984-87; pres., CEO Ctr. for the Study of the Presidency, 1997-99; Scott prof. leadership Rocky Mountain Coll., Billings, Mont., 1999—2002; mem. Mont. Ho. Reps., 2001—03; pres. Thomas Wathen Found. Acad., Riverside, Calif., 2002—. Bd. dirs. Arnold Industries; asst. to chmn. Rep. Nat. Com., Washington, 1960-61; founding dir. Ctr. Internat. Bus., L.A., 1969-70; cons. Novin Inst. Polit. Affairs, Tehran, Iran, 1973; exec. dir. Fla. Assn. Colls. and Univs., 1988—96. Author: McCarthyism: Ideology and Foundations, 1962; co-author: Electing the President, 1968; contbr. articles to profl. jours. Chmn. Ohio Civil Rights Commn., 1963-65; dep. chmn. Republican Nat. Com., 1965-66; mem. Ohio Ethics Commn., 1976-80. Capt. USMC, 1951-52, Korea Citizenship Clearing House Nat. Faculty fellow, 1960; recipient citation for excellence Sigma Phi Epsilon, 1977, Marshall award Ohio Wesleyan Students, 1979. Mem. Am. Polit. Sci. Assn., Am. Judicature Soc. (dir. 1975—80), Soc. Polit. Enquiries (pres. 1985—88), Acad. Polit. Sci., Rotary, Masons, Pi Sigma Alpha (dir. 1972—76), Phi Mu Alpha Sinfonia, Omicron Delta Kappa Republican. Mem. United Ch. of Christ. Avocations: sailing, flying, music. Home: 26555 Chambers Ave Sun City CA 92586-2132 Office: Wathen Found 4130 Mennes Ave Riverside CA 92509 E-mail: apeter333@aol.com. *Give the most you can give, of what you are and what you believe, both talent and treasure - where you are - now!.*

PETERSON, BARBARA ANN BENNETT, history professor, television personality; b. Portland, Oreg., Sept. 6, 1942; d. George and Hope Bennett; m. Frank Lynn Peterson, July 1, 1967. BA, BS, Oreg. State U., 1964; MA, Stanford U., 1965; PhD, U. Hawaii, 1978; PhD (hon.), London Inst. Applied Rsch., 1991, Australian Inst. Coordinated R, 1995. From prof. history to prof. emeritus U. Hawaii, 1967—95, prof. emeritus, 1995—; prof. history Oreg. State U., 2000—03. Prof. Asian history and European colonial history and world problems Chapman Coll. World Campus Afloat Semester At Sea, 1974, European overseas exploration, expansion and colonialism U. Colo., Boulder, 1978, Modern China, Modern East Asia, The West in the World U. Pitts., 1999, Colonial America, & Am. Presidency, Calif. State U. Palm Desert Campus, San Bernardino, 2004-05; assoc. prof. U. Hawaii-Manoa Coll. Continuing Edn., 1981; Fulbright prof. history Wuhan (China) U., 1988-89; Fulbright rsch. prof. Sophia U., Japan, 1967; rsch. assoc.

Bishop Mus., 1995-98; lectr. Capital Spkrs., Washington, 1987—; prof. world civilization Hawaii State Ednl. Channel, U. Hawaii Sys., 1993-97; adj. fellow East-West Ctr., Honolulu, 1998-99; contbr. review editor, Biography jour., U. Hawaii at Manoa; prof. history U. Pitts. Semester at Sea, fall 1999; adj. prof. Hawaii Pacific U.; adj. fellow East-West Ctr., Hawaii, 1998-99, tchr. colonial Am. history and Am. Presidency Osher Inst., Calif. State U. 2004-05; vis. faculty Portland State U., 2006. Co-author: A Woman's Place is in the History Books, Her Story: A Curriculum Guide for American History Teachers, 1980; author: America in British Eyes, 1988, John Bull's Eye on America, 1995, Sarah Childress Polk, First Lady of Tennessee and Washington, 2002 (nominated for Pulitzer prize 2003, Avery O. Craven award 2003, Merle Curti award 2003, Albert J. Beveridge award 2003), Emalani, 2003, George Washington America's Moral Exemplar, 2005 (nominated for Pulitzer prize 2006), Franklin Delano Roosevelt, Preserver of Spirit and Hope, 2006, Ancestors, Icons and Memories, 2008; editor: Notable Women of Hawaii, 1984, (with W. Solheim) The Pacific Region, 1990, 91, American History: 17th, 18th and 19th Centuries, 1993, America: 19th and 20th Centuries, 1993, Notable Women of China, 2000 (nominated for Pulitzer prize 2001), Hawaii in the World, 2000,(with Donald O. Dewey) James Madison, Defender of the American Republic, 2009; assoc. editor Am. Nat. Biography, 1998 (Dartmouth medal); contbr. articles to profl. publs. Participant People-to-People Program, Eng., 1964, Expt. in Internat. Living Program, Nigeria, 1966; chmn. 1st Nat. Women's History Week, Hawaii, 1982; pres. Bishop Mus. Coun., 1993-94; active mem. Hawaii Commn. on Status of Women; fundraiser local mus. and children's activities. Fulbright scholar, Japan, 1967, sr. tchg. Fulbright scholar, China, 1988-89; NEH-Woodrow Wilson fellow Princeton U., 1980; recipient state proclamations Gov. of Hawaii, 1982, City of Honolulu and Hawaii State Legis., 1982, Outstanding Tchr. of Yr. award Wuhan U., China, 1988, Woman of Yr. award, 1991, U. Hawaii Bd. Regents Medal for Outstanding Tchr. of Yr., 1993, Disting. Alumni, U. Hawaii, 1997; inducted into the Women's Hall of Fame, Seneca Falls, NY, 1991; co-champion Hawaii State Husband and Wife Mixed Doubles Tennis Championship, 1985, Disting. Alumni award U. Hawaii, 1997. Fellow: World Lit. Acad. (Eng.); mem.: AAUW, Friends of History, Portland U. (pres.), Am. Studies Assn. (Hawaii chpt. pres. 1984—85), Women in Acad. Adminstrn., Hawaii Found. History and Humanities (mem. editl. bd. 1972—73), Fulbright Assn. (founding pres. Hawaii chpt. 1984—88, mem. nat. steering com. chairwoman ann. conf. 1990, pres. 1998—99), Am. Hist. Assn. (mem. numerous coms., nominated Albert J. Beveridge award 2003), Maison Internat. des Intellectuals, Phi Kappa Phi, Pi Beta Phi (mem. mortar bd.). Avocations: writing, cooking, fund raising for charity and children's organizations and museums, gardening, travel. E-mail: fandbpeterson@aol.com.

PETERSON, BART R. (BARTON R. PETERSON), pharmaceutical company executive, former mayor; b. Indpls., June 15, 1958; m. Amy Minick Peterson; 1 child, Meg. Grad., Purdue U., 1980; JD, U. Mich., 1983. Atty. Ice Miller Donadio & Ryan, Indpls.; exec. asst. environ. affairs to chief staff to gov. Evan Bayh Indpls., 1989—95; pres. Precedent Co., 1995; mayor Indpls., 2000—08; sr. v.p. corp. affairs & comm. Eli Lilly & Co., Indpls., 2009—. Fellow politics John F. Kennedy Sch. Govt., Harvard U., 2008; disting. vis. prof. pub. policy Ball State U., 2008—. Bd. mem. Ind. Nature Conservancy, Regenstrief Found. Democrat. Office: Eli Lilly & Co Lilly Corp Center 893 S Delaware Indianapolis IN 46285 also: Ball State U 2000 W University Ave Muncie IN 47306 Office Phone: 617-495-1360. Office Fax: 617-496-4344. E-mail: bart_peterson@ksg.harvard.edu.*

PETERSON, BETTY W., language educator, writer; b. Phil, Ky., Nov. 15, 1944; d. James Delno Withers and Mae Berniece Withers (Luttrell) Emerson, Glen Emerson (Stepfather); m. Danny F. Peterson, Aug. 11, 1962; children: Angela Yvette Jones, Alisa Yvonne, Brenton Franklin, Danny Keith. BA English high distinction, U. Ky., Lexington, 1982, MA English, 1986. Instrnl. specialist Somerset C.C., Ky., 1986—89, asst. prof. English, 1989—91, assoc. prof. English with tenure, 1991—2000; prof. English Somerset Cmty. and Tech. Coll., 2000—, tchg. cons., 2006—. Co-editor Ky. writing Somerset C.C., 1989—94, tchg. cons., 2006—. Contbr. articles short stories poems to profl. jours. anthologies,; author (produced pub.) plays. Tchr. Gov.'s Scholars Program No. Ky. U., 1996. Recipient Oswald Rsch. and Creativity Award, U. Ky., 1981, Dantzler-Dantzler Acad. Achievement award, 1982, Tchg. Assistantship, U. Ky., 1984—86, Commd. Ky. Col., Hon. Order Ky. Cols., 1996, NISOD Tchg. Excellence Award, Somerset C.C., 2001, NIZOD award, 2009; named to Who's Who Among Am. Tchrs., 2002, 2005, 2006; nominee New Horizons award, Somerser CC, 2008—09; scholar, U. Ky. Alumni Assn., 1976—77; Va. Ctr. for Creative Arts Fellow, Ky. Found. for Women, 1993, Al Smith fellow, Ky. Arts Coun., 2007. Mem.: Dramatists Guild Am., Inc. (assoc.), U. Ky. Alumni Assn., Jesse Stuart Found. Independent. Roman Catholic. Avocations: writing, reading, aerobics, theater, guitar.

PETERSON, BOB, III, animator, film director, scriptwriter; Animator (films) Toy Story, 1995, story artist A Bug's Life, 1998, Toy Story 2, 1999; actor(voice): (films) Monsters, Inc., 2001, The Incredibles, 2004, Cars, 2006, Finding Nemo Submarine Voyage, 2007, Toyko Mater, 2008, Tracy, 2009; writer, voice (films) Finding Nemo, 2003 (Annie award for Outstanding Writing in an Animated Feature Prodn., 2004), voice, writer, co-dir. Up, 2009. Office: Pixar Animation Studios 1200 Park Ave Emeryville CA 94608*

PETERSON, BRADY, literature and language professor; b. Ft. Sill, Tex., Oct. 4, 1946; s. Brady and Nellie Earline Peterson; m. Barbara Jo Sowell; children: Melinda, Emily, Meredith Louise Kuhn, Julie Elizabeth, Charley Rose. PhD, U. Tex., Austin, 1982. Assoc. prof. U. Mary Hardin Baylor, Belton, Tex., 1998—. Office: Univ Mary Hardin Baylor UMHB Box 8008 900 Coll St Belton TX 76513 Business E-Mail: bpeterson@umhb.edu.

PETERSON, BRUCE D., lawyer, energy executive; b. Chgo., Nov. 1956; BA, North Park Coll., 1978; JD, U. Notre Dame Law Sch., 1982. Fgn. svc. officer US State Dept., Washington, 1982; ptnr. Hunton & Williams, Washington, 1989—2002; sr. v.p., gen. counsel DTE Energy Co., Detroit, 2002—05. Mem. legal com. Am. Gas Assn., Edison Electric Inst. Bd. dirs. Detroit Symphony Orch.; trustee Cranbrook Ednl. Cmty.; bd. govs. Cranbrook Inst. Sci.

PETERSON, BRUCE ERNEST, social studies educator; s. Elmer G. and Gladys G. Peterson; m. Linda Helen Simpson, Oct. 18, 1997. BA, Lebanon Valley Coll., Annville, Pa., 1984; MA, Rutgers U., Newark, NJ., 1986. Cert. tchr. Social Studies NJ., Edn. Dept., 2004. Adj. prof. William Paterson U., Wayne, NJ, 2004—, Hudson County CC, Jersey City, 2007—. Mem.: Pi Sigma Alpha Polit. Sci. Nat.

PETERSON, CARL ERIC, metal products executive, banker; b. Wareham, Mass., Apr. 8, 1944; m. Frances Harkness, Sept. 7, 1966; children: Robin, Alec Harkness. BA, Brown U., 1966; MA, U. Pa., 1971. With R.I. Hosp. Trust Nat. Bank, Providence, 1971-82; with Engelhard Corp., Iselin, NJ, 1982-85, Dryvit System, Inc., West Warwick, RI, 1986, Gerald Metals, Inc., Stamford, Conn., 1987—2002. Mem. corp. Woods Hole Oceanographic Instn., 1981—92, 2004—, trustee, 2005—; pres. Woods Hole Oceanographic Inst. Assocs., 2005—. With USN, 1967—70. Mem.: NY Yacht Club.

PETERSON, CHARLES HAYES, lawyer; b. St. Louis, May 8, 1938; s. Edmund Herbert and Dorothy Marie (Brennan) P.; m. Auli Irene Ahonen, Nov. 28, 1981; children: Mika, Charles, Michael, Katja. BS, U.S. Naval Acad., 1960; MBA, Stanford U., 1971, JD, 1974. Commd. midshipman USN, 1956, advanced through grades to capt., resigned, 1969; with USNR, 1969-89, ret., 1998; counsel Gen. Electric, San Jose, Calif., 1973-79; divsn. counsel Syracuse, NY, 1980-83; v.p. COGEMA, Inc., Washington, 1983-87; pres. NUEXCO Trading Co., Washington, 1987-95; of counsel Morgan, Lewis & Bockius, LLP, 1995—2001; ptnr. Pillsbury Winthrop Shaw Pittman, Washington, 2001—. Recipient Meritorious Service medal State of Calif., 1986. Mem. Calif. Bar Assn., Washington DC Bar Assn. Lutheran. Office: Pillsbury Winthrop Shaw Pittman 2300 N'St NW Washington DC 20037 Office Phone: 202-663-8083. Office Fax: 202-663-8007.

PETERSON, CHARLES MARQUIS, medical educator; b. NYC, Mar. 8, 1943; s. Charles William and Elisabeth (Marquis) P.; m. Karen Pielop, Dec. 26, 1996; children: Caroline, Elisabeth, Christopher. BA in cum laude, Carleton Coll., 1965; MD, Columbia Coll., 1969; MBA, U. Calif., Irvine, 2000. Intern Harlem Hosp., NYC, 1969-70, resident, 1970-73, chief resident, 1972-73; guest investigator, asst. physician Rockefeller U., NYC, 1971-73, assoc. physician, 1973-78, asst. prof., 1973-78, assoc. prof., 1978-84; clin. prof. medicine U. So. Calif., LA, 1985-98; program dir. blood diseases program Nat. Heart, Lung and Blood Inst., NIH, Bethesda, Md., 1998—. Vis. clin. fellow Columbia Coll. Physicians and Surgeons, 1970-73; asst. vis. physician Harlem Hosp., 1973-84; cons. pediatrics Cornell U. Med. Ctr., 1975-84; assoc. attending medicine Beth Israel Med. Ctr., 1976-84; lectr. Mt. Sinai Sch. Medicine, 1977—; adj. assoc. prof. dept. medicine Cornell U. Med. Ctr., 980-84; assoc. attending physician dept. medicine N.Y. Hosp., 1980-84; attending physician in medicine Cottage Hosp., Santa Barbara, Calif., 1984-98; dir. rsch., med. dir. Sansum Med. Rsch. Found., 1984-96, sr. scientist, 1997-98; dir. diabetes Endocrine Clinic, Santa Barbara County, 1989-98; CEO, Sansum Med. Rsch. Found., 1995-96; program dir. Blood Diseases Program Nat. Heart Lung Blood Inst., NIH, 1998-2000, acting dir. and dir. divsn. blood diseases and resorces, 2000—. Author: Self Monitoring of Blood Glucose: A Physician's Guide, 1981, Take Charge of Your Diabetes, 1982, Diabetes Management in the 80's, 1982; co-author: The Diabetes Self-Care Method, 1990, A Touch of Diabetes, 1991, Vivere con il Diabete, 1992, and many others; mem. editorial bd. Diabetes Care, 1980-84, Diabetes in the News, 1985—, Diabetes News Bureau, 1985—, Diabetes Profl., editor-in-chief, 1988-91, Diabetic Nephropathy/Jour. of Diabetic Complications, 1982-91; contbr. numerous articles to Prensa Medica, Jour. Lab. and Clin. Medicine, New England Jour. Medicine, Annals of Internal Medicine, Archives of Neurology, Blood, Jour. Nat. Med. Assn., Am. Jour. Obstetrics and Gynecology, many others. Mem. med. adv. bd. Cooley's Anemia Vols., 1975-84; bd. mem. Diabetes Control Found., 1980-88; dir. Diabetes Self Care Program, 1978-84, med. dir., 1981-84; bd. mem. Leake and Watts, 1978-84, Gifts for Life, 1986-89; bd. dirs. Sports Tng. Inst., 1984-86, others. Fellow ACP; mem. Am. Chem. Soc., Am. Diabetes Assn., Am. Fedn. Clin. Rsch., Am. Med. Writers Assn., Am. Soc. Clin. Investigation, Am. Soc. Hematology, Am. Soc. Pharmacology and Experimental Therapeutics, Coun. Biology Editors, Diabetes and Pregnancy Study Group West (founder), N.Y. Acad. Scis., Rsch. Soc. Alcoholsim, Soc. Experimental Medicine and Biology, Am. Med. Writers Assn., Am. Diabetes Assn. (founding bd. mem. Santa Barbara chpt. 1988-98, pres. 1991-92), Sigma Xi. Office: 6701 Rockledge Dr # 7950 Bethesda MD 20817-1813

PETERSON, COLLIN CLARK, United States Representative from Minnesota; b. Fargo, ND, June 29, 1944; children: Sean, Jason, Elliott. BA in Bus. Adminstrn. and Acctg., Moorhead State U., 1966. CPA Minn. Mem. Dist. 10 Minn. State Senate, 1976-86; mem. US Congress from 7th Minn. dist., 1991—; chmn. US House Agrl. Com., 2007—. With U.S. Army N.G., 1963-69. Mem. Am. Legion, Ducks Unltd., Elks, Sportsmen's Club, Rural Caucus, Mainstream Forum, Cormorant Lakes Sportsmen Club, Congl. Sportsmen's Caucus, Mainstream Forum, Congl. Rural Caucus. Democrat. Lutheran. Office: US Congress 2159 Rayburn Ho Office Bldg Washington DC 20515-2307 also: Lake Ave Plaza Bldg Ste 107 714 Lake Ave Detroit Lakes MN 56501*

PETERSON, COURTLAND HARRY, law educator; b. Denver, June 28, 1930; s. Harry James and Courtney (Caple) P.; m. Susan Schwab, Gisvold, Jan. 28, 1966; children: Brooke, Linda, Patrick. BA, U. Colo., 1951, LLB, 1953; MCL, U. Chgo., 1959; JD, U. Freiburg, Germany, 1964. Bar: Colo. 1953. Mem. faculty U. Colo. Law Sch., 1959—, prof., 1963—, dean, 1974-79, Nicholas Rosenbaum prof., 1991-94, Nicholas Doman prof. emeritus, 1995—. Vis. prof. UCLA Law Sch., 1965, Max Planck Inst., Hamburg, Germany, 1969-70, U. Tex. Law Sch., Austin, 1973-74, Summer Program, Tulane U., Rodos, Greece, 1993, Summer Program, La. State U., Aix-en-Provence, France, 1996; bd. dirs. Continuing Legal Edn. in Colo., 1974-77. Author: Die Anerkennung Auslaendischer Urteile, 1964; Translator: (Bauer) An Introduction to German Law, 1965. Served to 1st lt. USAF, 1954-56. Fgn. Law fellow U. Chgo., 1957-59; Ford Found. Law Faculty fellow, 1964; Alexander von Humboldt Stiftung fellow, 1969-70. Mem. ABA, Colo. Bar Assn. (bd. govs. 1974-79), Boulder County Bar Assn., Am. Soc. Comparative Law (dir., bd. editors, treas. 1978-89, hon. pres. 1996-98), Internat. Acad. Comparative Law, Am. Law Inst., Boulder County Bar Found. (trustee 1995-2000), U. Colo. Ret. Faculty Assn. (pres. 1998-2000). Home: 4135 Caddo Pky Boulder CO 80303 Office: U Colo Law Sch Boulder CO 80309-0001 Personal E-mail: courtpeterson@comcast.net.

PETERSON, CYNTHIA L., communications educator; b. Kansas City, Mo., Nov. 2, 1952; d. C. Ray and Sara D. Bowman; m. Steven J. Peterson, Apr. 21, 1973; children: Daniel S., Andrea D. Stambaugh, R. David. PhD, U. Kans., Lawrence, 2005. Lic. pub. sch. tchg. Kans., 1980. TV prodr. Milhuff Ministries, Olathe, Kans., 1981—83; tchr. Bonner Springs HS, Kans., 1986—87; instr. MidAmerica Nazarene U., Olathe, 1987—88, theatre dir., 1987—, prof., 1991—; grad. tchg. asst. U. Kans., 1988—90. Children's theatre dir. Olathe Cmty. Theatre, 1990—93. Dir.: (more than 40 mainstage plays and musicals). Class leader Coll. Ch. Nazarene, Olathe, 2007—08. Recipient Excellence Grad. Tchg. award, 1990. Mem.: Nat. Comm. Assn. Avocation: travel. Office: MidAmerica Nazarene Univ 2030 E College Way Olathe KS 66062 Business E-Mail: cpeterso@mnu.edu.

PETERSON, CYNTHIA LYNN, library director, educator; d. Arthur Wayne and D'Alva Rae Peterson. BS in Edn., Baylor U., 1979; MLS, U. North Tex., Denton, 1983; BA, Mars Hill Coll., NC, 1989. Cert. tchr. State of Tex., Texas County libr. Tex. State Libr. Tchr. Richardson Ind. Sch. Dist., Richardson, Tex., 1979—83; libr. Wiley (Tex.) Pub. Libr., 1983—84; libr. instrnl. svcs., coord. music libr. Mars Hill Coll., 1984—89; head of cataloging Henderson State U., Arkadelphia, Ark., 1989—90; head of cataloging libr. U. of Tex. Southwestern Med. Ctr., Dallas, 1990—94, asst. mgr. database devel. and control libr., 1994—96, mgr. database devel. and control libr., 1996—97; dir. libr. svcs. Bluefield (Va.) Coll., 1997—2000, East Tex. Bapt. U., Marshall, 2001—. Faculty sponsor Delta Pi Theta, East Tex. Bapt. U., Marshall, 2003—; mem. work group Tex. Heritage Digitization Initiative, Austin, 2005—; mem. at large, rep. Tex. Coun. Acad. Librs., 2006—07, sec., treas., 2007—08. Author: (novels) Background of Eternity; indexer (book) Upper Laurel and Her People; contbr. articles to several profl. jours. Singer Plano Civic Chorus, 1982—83, Asheville Choral Soc., 1985—88; choir dir. Meml. Bapt. Ch., Bluefield, Va., 1999—2000; dir. children's choir Northway Bapt. Ch., Dallas, 1991—93, editor and author single adult newsletter, 1991—93; mem.choir 1st Bapt. Ch., Longview, Tex., 2006—, mem.ladies ensemble, 2006—; costumer Arkadelphia Little Theatre, 1989—90; reader North Tex. Taping and Radio for the Blind, Dallas, 1993—94; webmaster VikingNet - Alumni Web Page - Valhalla H.S., 1996—2004. Mem.: ALA, Texas Coun. Academic Libraries (Sec. 2007—, Treasurer 2007—), Holston Associated Librs. (bd. dirs. 1997—2000), Appalachian Coll. Assn. (mem. task force Appalachian Libr. and Info. Coop. 1998—2000), Tex. Libr. Assn., Assn. of Christian Librns., So. Bapt. Libr. Assn., Assn. Coll. and Rsch. Librs. (mem. leadership com. 2002—04), Beta Phi Mu. Republican. Southern Baptist. Avocations: reading, writing, singing, needlework/sewing, travel. Office: East Texas Bapt Univ 1209 N Grove St Marshall TX 75670 Office Fax: 903-935-3447. Business E-Mail: cpeterson@etbu.edu.

PETERSON, DAVID FREDERICK, retired government agency administrator; b. Washington, Apr. 4, 1937; s. Victor Henry and Alice Augusta (Vogle) P.; m. Laurie A. Cadigan, June 11, 1988. AB, Harvard U., 1959; LL.B., Cornell U., 1962. Bar: D.C. 1963. With Metromedia Inc., NYC and Los Angeles, 1963—70; exec. dir. consumer info. ctr. GSA, Washington, 1970—76, dir. consumer affairs, 1976—82, assoc. archivist for mgmt. Nat. Archives and Records Service, 1982—83; asst. archivist for Fed. Records Ctrs. Nat. Archives and Records Adminstrn., Washington, 1983—96; asst. archivist Presdl. Librs., 1996—2001; ret., 2001. Served with U.S. Army, 1963 Home: 2730 NE Sewalls Landing Way Jensen Beach FL 34957 Personal E-mail: lcdfpeterson@aol.com.

PETERSON, DAVID LYNN, research scientist; BSc in Mech. Engring., U. Utah, Salt Lake City, 1966; MS, Stanford U., Calif., 1969. Aerospace engr. Gasdynamics Branch, NASAAmes, 1966—71; ceramic engr. Thermal Protection Branch NASA Ames, 1971—76; rsch. scientist, earth & ecosystem NASA Ames Rsch. Ctr., Calif., 1976—2004, branch chief Calif., 1991—99; chief Earth Sci. NASA Ames Rsch. Ctr., Calif., 1999—2004. Mem. Global Change Earth Sci. Com. NASA, 1982—2004, Astrobiology Com NASA, 1994—2000; cons. Planetary Coral Reef Found., 1998—2004; reviewer Tropical Medicine Rsch. Ctr. Selection, 1997. Contbr. chapters to books, articles to profl. jours. Bldg. comm. chair St. Williams Ch., Calif., 1999; comm. mem. Coll. Notre Dame, Calif., 1988—93; spkr. Commonwealth Club, San Francisco, 2004. Mem.: Peninsula Rose Soc., Pi Tau Sigma. Avocations: guitar, music, writing, gardening.

PETERSON, DAWN MICHELLE, entrepreneur, writer; b. Rochester, Minn., Oct. 28, 1962; d. Kenneth Eugene and Lois Ann Silker; m. Bud Lamont Peterson, Feb. 14, 1981; children: Jacquline Ann Peterson, Holly Marie Schill, Cassie Jan Wilson. Student, Internet Svcs. Corp. Continuing Bus. Edn., 1985—2005, Legacy Bus. Group Bus. Edn., 2005—. Mgr. of fine dining restaurant and pvt. club Hilton Hotels, Ogden, Utah, 1983—85; pres. B & D Enterprise, Layton, Utah, 1985—; dir. of internat. divsn. Wilson Enterprises, Inc., Ogden, 1991—98; pres. Amma's Daycare, Layton, 2002—07, D. S. Peterson Lit. Co., Layton, 2004—, Wide Ink, 2007—. Directorship, Brazilian divsn. Wilson Enterprises, Inc., Ogden, Utah, 1993—95, directorship, Turkish divsn., 1994—96, directorship, Ctrl. Am. divsn., 1994—96, directorship, Polish divsn., 1993—96, directorship, UK divsn., 1993—98, directorship, German divsn., 1993—98, directorship, Mex. divsn., 1993—98, directorship, Australian divsn., 1994—98; US overseer Wilson Enterprises, Inc. and World Wide Dvsn., 1993—98, seminar spkr., 1993—; sr. bus. cons. Victory Devel., Guadalajara, Mexico, 1998—2007; com. mem. for internet services corp. India launch team Internet Services Corp./Wilson Enterprises, Inc., 1998; organizer and key note spkr. Germany's Women in Bus. Conf., 1996. Author: (novels) Code Breakers; author: (also actor and dir.) (plays) The Tale of the Pigs with the Folders on Their Heads, Barn Yard Animals (Sch. Creativity award, 1970), Laverne and Shirley go into Business; author/speaker (audio presentation) Empowering Women Business Owners, It's an Amazing Trip. Mem. Women In Bus., Ogden, Utah, 1983—85, Ogden C. of C., 1983—85, Rep. Nat. Com., 1987—2005; del. Utah Rep. Party, 1986. Recipient All Around Title, Buckaroo Rodeo, 1974, 1976, Appaloosa Horsemen's Assn., 1980, Endurance Champion, Utah Endurace Racing Assn., 1980, Lake Powell Fesitval of Lights Parade, Lake Powell Festival Com., 2002, 5th in Top 25 Producers, Quixtar Corp., 2002. Mem.: Ind. Bus. Owners Assn. (assoc.). R-Consevative. Christian. Avocations: travel, writing, reading. Office Phone: 801-510-9336. Personal E-mail: bpeterson5673@msn.com.

PETERSON, DONALD FRED, physiologist, educator; b. Great Bend, Kans., Aug. 4, 1941; s. Donald F. and Mary K. (Doerr) P.; m. Bonnie Jean Campbell, July 30, 1967; children: Corilynn, Bailey, Ronald. Student, U. Sorbonne, Paris, 1962-63; BS in Zoology, Kans. State U., 1965, PhD in Physiology, 1970. Postdoctoral fellow U. Utah Med. Ctr., Salt Lake City, 1969-71; instr. U. Tex. Health Sci. Ctr., San Antonio, 1971-73, asst. prof., 1973-77, assoc. prof., 1977-78, Oral Roberts U. Med. Ctr., Tulsa, 1978-88, prof., chmn. physiology, 1988-90; prof., chmn. physiology Kirksville (Mo.) Coll. Osteo. Medicine, 1990—. Mem. extra-curricular task force Kirksville (Mo.) Sch. Dist., 1995, pres. Kirksville Boosters, 1994-95, Kirksville Area Master Gardeners, 2008. Recipient Rsch. Career Devel. award NIH, 1976. Fellow Am. Physiol. Soc.; mem. Am. Heart Assn. (chmn. Mo. peer rev. com. 1995-96, chmn. Mo. rsch. com. 1996-97, bd. dirs. and exec. com. Mo. affil. 1996-98, bd. dirs. Heartland affiliate 1998-2000, Heartland rsch. com. 1997-2000, Mo. pub. advocacy com., 2001-), Sigma Xi. Mem. Ch. of Christ. Avocations: road-running races, triathlons, gardening, marathon. Home: 2201 Crestline Dr Kirksville MO 63501-5709 Office: Kirksville Coll Osteo Med Dept Physiology 800 W Jefferson St Kirksville MO 63501-1443 Office Phone: 660-626-2309. Business E-Mail: fpeterson@atsu.edu.

PETERSON, DONALD MATTHEW, insurance company executive; b. Mt. Vernon, NY, Dec. 22, 1936; s. Cornelius J. and Catherine M. (Carney) P.; m. Patricia A. Frusciante, Sept. 10, 1960; children: Daniel, Linda, David, Debra, James. BA in Econs., LaSalle U., 1958. CLU; ChFC; FSA, MAAA, EA, RHU. Actuarial analyst Met. Life, NYC, 1958-63; actuarial assoc. N.Am. Co. for Life and Health, Chgo., 1963-66; chmn. bd. dirs. Trustmark Ins. Co., Lake Forest, Ill., 1966—. Bd. dirs. Trustmark Ins. Co., Trustmark Life Ins. Co., Star Mktg. and Adminstrs., InfoTrust Coresource. Bd. dirs. Glenview (Ill.) Pub. Schs., 1973-76, Lake County (Ill.) United Way, 1989-96, Glenview Dist. 34 Found., 1990-93, Lake Forest Hosp., 1992-2001, Ill. Life Ins. Coun., 1990-94, Barat Coll., 1994-2001, Lake Forest Grad. Sch. Mgmt., 1995-2001. Mem. NALU, Nat. Assn. Health Underwriters, Am. Acad.

Actuaries, Health Ins. Assn. Am. (bd. dirs. 1992-99), Am. Coun. Life Ins. (bd. dirs. 1995-98), Econ. Club Chgo., North Shore Country Club, Conway Farms Golf Club, Pelican Nest Golf Club, Exec. Club. Republican. Roman Catholic. Avocations: golf, curling, swimming, running. Office: Trustmark Ins Co 400 N Field Dr Lake Forest IL 60045-4809

PETERSON, DOROTHY HAWKINS, artist, educator; b. Albuquerque, Mar. 14, 1932; d. Ernest Lee and Ethel Dawn (Allen) Hawkins; m. John W. Peterson, July 9, 1954; children: John Richard, Dorothy Anne. BS in Edn., U. N.Mex., Albuquerque, 1953; MA, U. Tex., 1979. Freelance artist, 1960—; educator, instr. Carlsbad (N.Mex.) Ind. Elem. Sch. Dist., 1953-54; instr. Charleston (S.C.) County Schs., 1955-56; instr. in painting Midland (Tex.) Coll., 1971-76, Roswell (N.Mex.) Mus. Sch., 1981-83, 91—; instr. in art history Ea. N.Mex. U., Roswell, 1989—2000; instr. painting N.Mex. Mil. Inst., Roswell, 1992—94. Bd. dirs. N.Mex. Arts Commn., Santa Fe; cons. Casa de Amigos Craft Guild, Midland, Tex., 1971-73. One woman shows include Art Inst., Permian Basin, Odessa, Tex., 1994. Tutor Roswell Literacy Coun., 1988-89; bd. dirs. N.Mex. Arts & Crafts Fair, Albuquerque, 1983-85. Named Best of Show, Mus. of the S.W., 1967, 69; recipient Top award, 1973, 75, Juror award N.Mex. Arts & Crafts Fair, 1986, 1st pl. award Profl. Watercolor N.Mex. State Fair, 1988, Talens-d' Arches award Tex. Watercolor Soc., 1998, Bd. Dirs. award San Diego Watercolor Soc., 1998, N.Mex. Watercolor Soc., 1998, others. Mem. Nat. Watercolor Soc. (San Diego Watercolor Soc. award 1988), N.Mex. Watercolor Soc. (2d pl. award 1981, 1st pl. award state fair 1988, Grumbacher award 1993, Wingspread award 1994, 1st pl. award 1995, 1st, 3rd and Graham award 1997, Best of Show 2001, Best of Show 2004, Masterworks award N.Mex. Tricentennial 2005, 3d pl. award 2006, 1st pl. Masterworks, 2006). Office: Dorothy Peterson Studio PO Box 915 Roswell NM 88202-0915 Personal E-mail: dhpeterson@dfn.com.

PETERSON, DOUGLAS BRIAN (PETE PETERSON), former ambassador, former United States Representative from Florida; b. Omaha, June 26, 1935; m. Carlotta Ann Neal (dec.); children: Michael, Paula, Douglas (dec.); m. Vi Peterson. Grad., Nat. War Coll., 1975; BA, U. Tampa, 1976; postgrad., U. Ctrl. Mich., 1977. Commd. USAF, 1954, advanced through grades to col., ret., 1980; exec. CRT Computers, 1984-90; mem. faculty Fla. State U., 1985-90; mem. US Congress from 2nd Fla. Dist., 1991-96; US amb. to Vietnam US Dept. State, Hanoi, 1997—2001; pres. Peterson Internat., Inc., 2001—. Founder, CEO The Alliance for Safe Children. Prisoner of war, Vietnam. Mem.: VFW, Am. Acad. Diplomacy, Coun. Am. Ambs., Am. Legion. Roman Catholic. Office: 27 Bowen St Camberwell VIC 3124 Australia Office Phone: 66-2-655-4811. E-mail: petevi@bigpond.net.au.

PETERSON, EDWARD ADRIAN, lawyer; b. St. Louis, May 19, 1941; s. Adrian J. and Virginia (Hamlin) P.; m. Catherine Frances Younghouse, Dec. 17, 1960; children: Kristin, Kendra. BSBA, Washington U., St. Louis, 1963; LLB, So. Methodist U., 1966. Bar: Tex. 1966, U.S. Dist. Ct. (no. and so. dists.) Tex. Instr. bus. law and acctg. Midwestern U., Wichita Falls, Tex., 1966-67; assoc. Schenk & Wesbrooks, Wichita Falls, 1966-67, Newman & Pickering, Dallas, 1967-72; ptnr. Moore & Peterson, Dallas, 1972-89, Winstead PC, Dallas, 1989—. Spkr. in field. Contbr. articles to legal jours. Bd. dirs. Leukemia Soc., 1970-71, North Tex. Commn., 1992-96, South Dallas/Fair Park Trust Fund, 1992, Tex. Ch. Extension Fund, Tex. Dist., Tex. Dist. Luth. Ch. Mo. Synod., 2002-07, Dallas Luth. Sch., 2007—. Fellow Am. Coll. Real Estate Lawyers (title ins. com., common interest com.), Am. Coll. Mortgage Attys., Tex. Bar Found. (life), Dallas Bar Found., Coll. State Bar Tex.; mem. ABA, State Bar Tex., Tex. Coll. Real Estate Attys., Dallas Bar Assn., Phi Alpha Delta, Sigma Alpha Epsilon. Lutheran. Home: Ste 205B 2808 McKinney Ave Dallas TX 75204-2562 also: 131 Hilton Head Island Dr Mabank TX 75156 Office: Winstead PC 5400 Renaissance Tower 1201 Elm St Dallas TX 75270-2199 Office Phone: 214-745-5642. Business E-Mail: epeterson@winstead.com.

PETERSON, EDWIN J., retired judge, mediator, educator; b. Gilmanton, Wis., Mar. 30, 1930; s. Edwin A. and Leora Grace (Kitelinger) P.; m. Anna Chadwick, Feb. 7, 1971; children: Patricia, Andrew, Sherry. BS, U. Oreg., 1951, LLB, 1957. Bar: Oreg. 1957. Assoc. firm Tooze, Kerr, Peterson, Marshall & Shenker, Portland, Oreg., 1957-61, mem. firm, 1961-79; assoc. justice Supreme Ct. Oreg., Salem, 1979-83, 91-93, chief justice, 1983—91; ret., 1993; disting. jurist-in-residence, adj. instr. Willamette Coll. of Law, Salem, 1994—. Chmn. Supreme Ct. Task Force on Racial Issues, 1992-94, Oreg. Law Enforcement Contacts Policy and Data Review Com., 2005-; standing com. on fed. rules of practice and procedure, 1987-93; bd. dirs. Conf. Chief Justices, 1985-87, 88-91; founder Understanding Racism Found., 1998; mem. Oreg. Joint Bench-Bar Commn. on Professionalism, 1996-, chair, 1996-97. Chmn. Portland Citizens Sch. Com., 1968-70; vice-chmn. Young Rep. Fedn. Oreg., 1951; bd. visitors U. Oreg. Law Sch., 1978-83, 87-93, chmn. bd. visitors, 1981-83; pres., bd. dirs. Understanding Racism Found., 1999-2002, bd. dirs., 2002—. 1st lt. USAF, 1952-54. Mem. Oreg. State Bar (bd. examiners 1963-66, gov. 1973-76, vice chmn. profl. liability fund 1977-78), Multnomah County Bar Assn. (pres. 1972-73), Phi Alpha Delta, Lambda Chi Alpha. Episcopalian. Office: Willamette Univ Coll Law 245 Winter St SE Salem OR 97301-3916 Home: 471 High St SE # 340 Salem OR 97301 Office Phone: 503-375-5399. Business E-Mail: epeterso@willamette.edu.

PETERSON, ELIZABETH HOLLY, art association administrator; b. Nyack, NY, Dec. 30, 1967; d. John Lawrence and Holly Winifred Peterson; life ptnr. Jean Dolan, Sept. 18, 2004. BA in Studio Art, Wells Coll., Aurora, NY, 1989; MS in Theory, Criticism and History of Art, Design and Architecture, Pratt Inst., Bklyn., 1997; postgrad., NYU, 2003. Exhbn. coord., asst. to the dep. dir. The Mus. of Modern Art, NYC, 1997—2004; dir. The Print Rsch. Found., Stamford, Conn., 2005—08; dir., coord., gallery and mus. scis. AKVS Gallery, Willimantic, Conn., 2008—. Exhbn. coord. Masterworks from the Mus. Modern Art, Strangely Familiar: Approaches to Scale in the Collection of The Museum of Modern Art, Masterworks from MoMA, 1900-1955, project coord. CAFE/ETC. Recipient award, Art Students League, 1986, Nat. Acad. Design, 1996, Distinction in the Spl. Field of Studio Art award, Wells Coll., 1989, Cert. of Excellence award for Outstanding Merit, Pratt Inst., 1997. Mem.: Coll. Art Assn., Am. Assn. of Mus. Avocations: singing, painting, travel, yoga. Office: AKVS Gallery Eastern Conn State Univ 83 Windham St Willimantic CT 06226 Office Phone: 860-465-0293. Business E-Mail: petersonel@easternct.edu.

PETERSON, ERIC H., lawyer; b. 1960; m. Tonya Peterson; 2 children. BA, So. Meth. U., JD, 1985. Bar: 1985. Ptnr. Worsham Forsythe & Wooldridge, Dallas; sr. v.p., gen. counsel DTE Energy, Mich., 2000—02; exec. v.p., gen. counsel TXU Corp., Dallas, 2002—06; exec. v.p., sec. gen. counsel Blockbuster Inc., Dallas, 2007—. Mem. legal com. Edison Electric Inst. Mem.: ABA (vice chmn. electricity com. pub. utility Comm. and Transp. Law Sect.). Presbyterian. Office: Blockbuster Inc 1201 Elm St Dallas TX 75270

PETERSON, ERIK CHARLES, prosecutor; BA, Drake U., 1992; JD, Marquette U. Law Sch., 1995. Asst. dist. atty. Richland County, 1995—98; dist. atty. Iowa County, 1999—2006; US atty. (we. dist.) Wis. US Dept. Justice, Madison, 2006—09.*

PETERSON, EVONNE STEWART, elementary school educator; d. Richard Allen and Theresa Johnson Stewart; m. Kelvin Osborne Peterson (div.); 1 child, Chelsey Denise. BA in Art Edn., N.C. Ctrl. U., 1979; MA in Art Edn., Winthrop U., 1998; MEd in Reading, Lang., and Literacy, U. N.C., 2001; postgrad., Western Carolina U., 2006—. Cert. K-12 Reading Education Charlotte-Mecklenburg Schools, Charlotte, NC, 2001, K-12 Art Education Charlotte-Mecklenburg Schools, Charlotte, NC, 1991. Adminstrv. svcs. clk. Bachelor Enlisted Quarters, Rota, Spain, 1985—88; tour cons. Am. Airlines, Cary, NC, 1989—90; tchr. afterschool enrichment program Bruns Ave. Elem., Charlotte, 1991—92; tchr. art Lincoln Heights Elem., 1992—2004, tchr. Title I literacy, 2004—, Title I summer sch. site coord., lead tchr., 2005—. Sch. leadership team chair Lincoln Heights Elem., Charlotte, 2002—, tchr. adv. coun. rep., 2001—, mentor, 2000—, literacy/writing com., 2002—, key communicator, 2002—04, diversity facilitator, 2002—04; selected participant Tchg. Fellows Inst., White Oaks, Charlotte, 2005; presenter in field. Recipient Tchr. of Month award, Coca-Cola, 2003; grantee, World Affairs Coun., 1998, IMPACTII, 2000, Charlotte-Mecklenburg Schs., 2001. Mem.: N.C. Educators Assn. (corr.), Internat. Reading Assn. (corr.), Kappa Delta Pi, Phi Kappa Phi. Baptist. Avocations: aerobics/strength training, travel, reading, arts and crafts. Office: Lincoln Heights Elem Sch 1900 Newcastle St Charlotte NC 28216

PETERSON, FRANKLIN DELANO, lawyer; b. Braham, Minn., Nov. 11, 1932; s. John Erick and Myrtle M. (Anderson) P.; m. Beverly Ann Crabb, Aug. 2, 1958; children: Heidi, Durward, Heather. Student, Augsburg Coll., Mpls., 1950—51; BA, St. Cloud State Coll., Minn., 1955; LLB, William Mitchell Coll. Law, St. Paul, 1961. Bar: Minn. 1961. Field claims adjuster Farmers Mut. Ins. Co., St. Paul, 1955-57; asst. dist. claims mgr. Minn. Farmers Ins. Group, Mpls., 1957-62; sole practice Kenyon, Minn., 1963—. Atty. City of Kenyon, 1964—82; v.p. Kenyon Devel. Corp., bd. dirs.; sec. Tri-Valley Constrn. Co., Kenyon, bd. dirs. Chmn. Goldwater for Pres. campaign, Village of Kenyon Reps., 1964, Goodhue County LeVander for Gov., 1966, Goodhue County Reps, 1969-70; sec. Goodhue Selective Service Bd., 1968—; pres. Mineral Springs Chem. Dependency Ctr., 1974-85; mem. Kenyon Pub. Sch. Bd. Edn., 1976-82, treas. 1980-82, Kenyon Booster Club (charter), v.p. 1983; mgr. mgr. Kenyon Legion Baseball, 1979—; bd. dirs. Kenyon Roseview Apts., 1967—, pres. 1985—; potentate Osman Shrine, St. Paul, Minn., 2007. Served with USAF, 1950-52. Mem. ABA, Minn. Bar Assn. (jud. dist. del., pres. 1st dist. 1979-80), Goodhue County Bar Assn., Minn. Assn. Plaintiffs Attys., Nat. Assn. Claimants Counsel, Sons of Norway (pres. Kenyon lodge 1969), Kenyon Comml. Club, Kenyon Country Club (pres. Osman Shrine Clowns 1993), Masons, Shriners, (potentate Osman Shrine, 2007), Lions (pres. Kenyon chpt.), Royal Order Jesters, Ct. of St. Paul and Shriner Clowns. Lutheran. Office: 634 2nd St Kenyon MN 55946-1334 Office Phone: 507-789-6141.

PETERSON, GALE EUGENE, historian; b. Sioux Rapids, Iowa, May 23, 1944; s. George Edmund and Vergene Elizabeth (Wilson) P. BS, Iowa State U., 1965; MA, U. Md., 1968, PhD, 1973. Instr. dept. history U. Md., College Park, 1971-72, Cath. U. Am., Washington, 1972-73; prin. investigator Gregory Directory project Orgn. Am. Historians, Bloomington, Ind., 1973-75; instr. dept. history Purdue U., West Lafayette, Ind., 1975-76; dir. U.S. Newspaper Project, Orgn. Am. Historians, Bloomington, Ind., 1976-78; exec. dir. Cin. Hist. Soc., 1978-96, exec. dir. emeritus, 1996—; exec. dir. Ohio Humanities Coun., 1998—. Author: (with John T. Schlebecker) Living Historical Farms Handbook, 1970, Harry S Truman and the Independent Regulatory Commissions 1945-52, 1985. Mem. Cin. Bicentennial Commn., 1983-88. Mem. Orgn. Am. Historians (treas. 1993-2003), Am. Assn. State and Local History, Am. Hist. Assn., Am. Assn. Mus., Assn. Midwest Museums (v.p.-at-large 1993-95, exec. v.p. 1995-96, pres. 1996-98), Nat. Coun. on Pub. History (bd. dirs. 1992-95). Office: Ohio Humanities Coun Ste 1620 471 E Broad St Columbus OH 43215-3857 Office Phone: 614-461-7802. Personal E-mail: galep@one.net.

PETERSON, GARY ANDREW, agronomics researcher; b. Holdrege, Nebr., Apr. 30, 1940; s. Walter Andrew and Evelyn Christine (Johnson) P.; m. Jacquelyn Charlene Flick, June 18, 1965; children: Kerstin, Ingrid. BS, U. Nebr., 1963, MS, 1965; PhD, Iowa State U., 1967. Research assoc. agronomy Iowa State U., Ames, 1964-67; prof. U. Nebr., Lincoln, 1967-84; prof. soil and crop scis. Colo. State U., Ft. Collins, 1984—, head dept. soil and crop scis., 2003—. Assoc. editor AGronomy Jour., 1979-81, tech. editor, 1981-83, editor, 1984-89, editor-in-chief, 1991-96; contbr. articles to profl. jours. Fellow Am. Soc. Agronomy (Ciba-Geigy Agr. Achievement award 1974, Agronomic Achievement award-Soils 1990), Soil Sci. Soc. Am. (prs. 2008, Applied Rsch. award 1987), Soil Conservation Soc. Am. Republican. Avocations: reading, hiking, skiing. Office: Colo State U Dept Soil Crop Scis Fort Collins CO 80523-0001 Home Phone: 970-224-5752; Office Phone: 970-491-6501. Business E-Mail: gary.peterson@colostate.edu.

PETERSON, GEORGE ANTHONY, psychologist, consultant; b. Jersey City, July 9, 1948; s. George Anthony and Margaret Agnes Peterson; m. Maria Gomez Souder, Apr. 2, 1983; children: Alysia Lynn Peterson Souder, Elliott William Peterson Souder, Christine Ann, George Anthony, John Joseph. BA, Seton Hall U., South Orange,NJ, 1971; MA, NJ. CIty U., Jersey CIty, 1978; Degree, 1981. Cert. tchr. NJ. CIty U., 1972, sch. psychologist NJ. CIty U., 1981, supr. Montclair State NJ, 2004. Capt. USArmy Caven Point, Edison, NJ, 1972—86; counselor Boys & GIrls Club, Jersey City, 1989—99, Gaint Steps, Hoboken, NJ, 1990—93; cons. Jersey Care, West Orange, 1992—2004. Decorated Meritorius award Us Army. Mem.: Rotary CLub. Home: 195 Christopher St Montclair NJ 07042 Office: Ps 20 160 Danforth Ave Jersey City NJ 07305 Personal E-mail: ittpbb@yahoo.com.

PETERSON, GEORGE FOLKE, retired insurance company executive, writer; b. Racine, Wis., June 4, 1926; s. George Edwin Peterson and Anna Zetterquist; m. Evelyn Marie Malcolm, Dec. 29, 1959. Student, Carthage Coll., 1945—48; BA, Ariz. State U., 1949. Mng. ptnr., co-pub. Opportunities Pub. Co., Racine, 1949—50; dir. mkt. rsch., dir. circulation Watson Publs., Chgo., 1955—58; circulation dir., rsch. mgr. Am. Aviation Pub. Co., Washington, 1958—62; editor, pub. Astrosci. News, Washington, 1962—64; mgmt. cons. Alexander Proudfoot Co., Chgo., 1964—66; field exec. Blue Cross of Fla., Inc., St. Petersburg, 1968—84; freelance writer Holiday, Fla., 1984—. Co-founder, CEO Inst. Cons. Engrs., Chgo., 1956—58; CFO Corp. Treas. Anchor Det. Co., Bristol, Va., 1962—64. Editor, pub.: Sci. Newsletter, 1964; author: Accounts Receivable Management, 1984; author: (as Lane Stevenson) (novel) To Las Vegas With Love, 2002, Searching for Krisztina, 2004. Bd. dirs. Health Sys. Agy., Fla., 1980—83; former mem. Fla. Health Sys. Agy. With Med. Corp US Army, 1950—52. Recipient Pub.'s Achievement award, Am. Aviation Pub. Co., 1960, Cert. of Recognition, Sec. of Def. William Cohen, 2000, Sec. of Def. Donald Rumsfeld, 2005. Mem.: NY Acad. Scis. Avocations: astronomy, cosmology, particle physics, string theory physics. Home and Office: 3538 Burntwood Ct Holiday FL 34691 Personal E-mail: george_peterson@rocketmail.com.

PETERSON, GEORGE P. (BUD PETERSON), academic administrator; b. Prairie Village, Kans. BS in Mech. Engring. and Math., Kans. State U., 1975, MS in Engring., 1980; PhD, Tex. A&M U., 1985. Engring. prof. Tex. A&M U., College Station, 1981—2000; provost Rensselaer Poly. Inst., Troy, NY, 2000—06; chancellor U. Colo., Boulder, 2006—09; pres. Ga. Inst. Tech., 2009—. Editor: Jour. Exptl. Thermal and Fluid Scis.; assoc. editor: ASME Jour. Heat Transfer, AIAA Jour. Thermophysics and Heat Transfer, Internat. Jour. Heat and Fluid Flow, Microscale Thermophysical Engring.; contbr. articles to profl. jours. Recipient Best Paper award, AIAA, 1990, award for outstanding mgmt., NSF, 1994, Ralph James and the O. L. (Andy) Lewis awards, ASME, Dow Outstanding Young Faculty award, ASEE, Pi Tau Sigma Gustus L. Larson Meml. award, ASME, Thermophysics award, AIAA, Meml. award, ASME, Sustained Svc. award, AIAA; fellow, Tex. Engring. Expt. Sta., 1986, 1988; sr. fellow, 1989. Fellow: Am. Inst. of Aeronautics and Astronautics, Am. Soc. of Mech. Engrs.; mem.: Phi Kappa Phi, Sigma Xi, Tau Beta Pi, Pi Tau Sigma. Office: Ga Inst Tech Office of Pres 225 N Ave NW Carnegie Bldg Atlanta GA 30332 E-mail: bud.peterson@gatech.edu.*

PETERSON, HERBERT BRYSON, obstetrician, gynecologist, educator; b. Maryville, Tenn., Sept. 24, 1951; BA in biology, Wittenberg U., 1973; MD, U. Pitts., 1977. Cert. Ob-Gyn., 1986, Pub. Health and Gen. Preventative Medicine, 1989. Intern U. NC, Chapel Hill, 1977—79, resident, 1979—81; chief, Epidemiologic Studies br. CDC, chief, Women's Health and Fertility br.; with Dept. Reproductive Health and Rsch. WHO; clin. prof. Emory U., Atlanta, 1994—2002; joint prof. U. NC Sch. Medicine, Chapel Hill, 1994—2004, prof. obstetrics and gynecology, 2004—; prof. and chair maternal and child health U. NC Gillings Sch. Global Pub. Health, Chapel Hill, 2004—, Kenan disting. prof., 2009—; fellow U. NC Cecil B. Sheps Ctr. Health Services Rsch., Chapel Hill. Recipient Disting. Svc. medal, USPHS, 1999. Fellow: Am. Coll. Epidemiology, Am. Coll. Preventive Medicine, Am. Coll. Obstetricians and Gynecologists; mem.: Inst. Medicine, Soc. Gynecol. Investigation, Am. Gynecol. and Obstet. Soc. Office: 430A Rosenau Hall Campus Box 7445 135 Dauer Dr Chapel Hill NC 27599 Office Phone: 919-966-5981. Office Fax: 919-966-0458. E-mail: herbert_peterson@unc.edu.*

PETERSON, HIKARU HANAWA, agricultural studies educator; PhD, Cornell U., Ithaca, NY. Asst. prof. Kans. State U., Manhattan, 2000—06, assoc. prof., 2006—.

PETERSON, JAMES ERLING, state legislator; b. Havre, Mont., July 19, 1946; s. Erling and Marrietta Peterson; m. Lorraine Mable Haynes; children: Jennifer James, Robert. BS, Mont. State U., Bozeman, 1968; MAgr, Tex. A & M U., Coll. Station, 1973; MBA in Fin., West Tex. State U., Canyon, 1979. Membership dir. Tex. Cattle Feeders Assn., Amarillo, 1973—84; v.p. First Nat. Bank, Amarillo, 1984—86; mem. Dist. 15 Mont. House of Reps., 2002—06, Mont. State Senate, 2007—, majority leader. Cheif fin. officer Tejon Ranch Co., Lebec, Calif., 1986—89; exec. v.p. Mont. Stock Growers Assn., Helena, 1989—2000; interim assoc. dean Mont. State U., 2003—08. Master: Mason; mem.: Meat Export Assn. Republican. Methodist. Office: PO Box 200500 Helena MT 59620-0500 Office Phone: 406-444-4800. Office Fax: 406-444-4875.

PETERSON, JAMES ROBERT, engineering psychologist; b. St. Paul, Apr. 16, 1932; s. Palmer Elliot and Helen Evelyn (Carlson) P.; m. Marianna J. Stockvig, June 26, 1954; 1 child, Anne Christine. BA in Psychology cum laude, U. Minn., 1954, MA in Exptl. Psychology, 1958; PhD in Engring. Psychology, U. Mich., 1965. Devel. engr. Honeywell Inc., 1961-65, sr. devel. engr., 1965-67, staff engr., 1967-90, sr. project staff engr., 1990-93, retired, 1993. Honeywell sponsor rep. Shuttle Student Involvement Program, 1982, 84; emeritus Human Factors and Ergonomics Soc. Contbr. articles to profl. jours. With USMC, 1954-57, USMCR, 1957-62. Mem. Air and Space Mus. (charter), Smithsonian Inst., Masons, Am. Legion, Delta Upsilon (life). Achievements include invention of Apollo translation hand controller; participation in development work in all U.S. Manned Space Programs (Mercury, Gemini, Apollo, Lunar Excursion Module, Manned Orbiting Laboratory, Space Shuttle and Space Sta.) as member/manager of associated human factors groups. Home: 3303 San Gabriel St Clearwater FL 33759-3341 Personal E-mail: bpeteputt@aol.com.

PETERSON, JEFFREY V., construction executive; b. 1946; m. Eva Peterson; 3 children. BS, U. So. Calif.; MBA, Stanford U., 1971. Mng. dir. investment banking Kidder, Peabody & Co., 1987—92; mng. dir. pvt. client services Trust Co. of the West, 1992—2005; bd. dir. Standard Pacific Corp., 2000—, lead ind. dir., 2004—08, chmn., pres., CEO, 2008. Am. Heart Assn.; bd. mem. Am. Hosp. in Paris, Pitzer Coll., Lowe Inst., Claremont McKenna Coll. Office: Standard Pacific Corp 26 Technology Dr Irvine CA 92618-2301*

PETERSON, JOEL C., investment company executive; b. May 20, 1947; m. Diana J. Hulme; 7 children. BS, Brigham Young U.; MBA, Harvard U., 1973. Treas. Trammell Crow Co., 1973—77, CFO, 1977—85, CEO, 1988—91; founding ptnr. Peterson Ptnrs., LP, Salt Lake City, 1995—; vice chmn. JetBlue Airways Corp., 2007—08, chmn., 2008—. Lectr. entrepreneurial mgmt. Stanford U. Grad. Sch. Bus., 1992—; bd. dirs. Asurion, Dallas Market Ctr., Texas Commerce Bank, Dallas, Franklin Covey Co., 1997—, JetBlue Airways Corp., 1999—. Bd. dirs. Covey Leadership Ctr., 1993—97, vice chmn., 1994—97. Office: Peterson Ptnrs, LP 2825 E Cottonwood Parkway, St 400 Salt Lake City UT 84121 Office Phone: 801-365-0180. Office Fax: 801-365-0181. E-mail: joel@petersonpartnerslp.com.

PETERSON, JOHN E., former United States Representative from Pennsylvania; b. Titusville, Pa., Dec. 25, 1938; s. Axel Benjamin and Mary Elizabeth (Baker) Peterson; m. Saundra June Watson, 1968; children: Richard D., Florence Waychoff. Grad. from rural leadership prog., Pa. State U. Owner retail food market, Pleasantville, Pa., 1958-84; mem. Pleasantville City Coun., Pa., 1969—77, Pa. State House Reps. from 65th dist., 1977-84, Pa. State Senate from 25th dist., 1984-96, US Congress from 5th Pa. dist., 1997—2009, mem. appropriations com., co-chair Congl. Rural Caucus. Mem. Pub. Health and Welfare Com., now chmn.;active PENNVEST Bd., Pa. Hardwoods Devel. Coun.; sec. Ctr. Rural Pa. Mem. regional adv. coum. Pitts. Cancer Inst.; bd. advs. Foxview Manor, Inc.; mem. adv. bd. U. Pitts., Titusville and Bradford campuses; mem. adv. coun. Ind. U. of Pa. Culinary Sch.; active Pa. Trauma Ctr. Found., Venango County Indsl. Bd. Served in US Army, 1957—63. Recipient John Heinz Meml. award; Presdl. Distinction medal U. Pitts. at Bradford, Recognition award Pa. Acad. Family Physicians, Appreciation award, Better Life award Pa. Health Care Assn., Guardian of Small Bus. award Nat. Fedn. Ind. Bus., Spl. Achievement award Pa. Bar Assn., Elected Officials award Pa. Home Health Assn., 1994, Congl. Partnership award Nat. Assn. Devel. Orgns.;

named Senator of Yr. Jewish Coalition, Legislator of Yr., Pa. Assn. County Human Svc. Adminstrs., 1993, Pa. Home Health Care Assn., 1993, Nat. Rural Health Assn., 2002, Policymaker of Yr. Assn. Career and Tech. Edn. Mem. Titusville Area C. of C., Pleasantville PTA, Lions. Republican. Methodist.*

PETERSON, JOHN KENNETH, elementary school educator; b. Devils Lake, ND, Nov. 9, 1950; s. John L. and Olive G. Peterson; m. Carol A. Wells, July 3, 1979; children: Kristin Wilton, Lori. BS, Dana Coll., Blair, Nebr., 1972; MA in Tchg., Colo. State U., Ft. Collins, 1976. Sales mgr., nat. accts. mgr. Lance Inc., Charlotte, NC, 1979—93; ind. sales agt. Cronatron Welding, Charlotte, 1993—99; tchr. 8th grade, coach Altar Valley Sch. Dist., Tucson, 1999—. Recipient New Sales Agt. award, Cronatron Welding, 1993, Rd. Runner Dist. Agt. of Yr., 1994; named Dist. Mgr. of Yr., Lance Inc., 1988, VFW Local & Dist. Outstanding Educator, 2007—08. Mem.: Nat. Coun. Social Studies. Republican. Lutheran. Avocations: reading, hunting, fishing, horseback riding. Home: PO Box 23040 Tucson AZ 85734 Office: Altar Valley Sch Dist #51 10150 S Sasa Be huny Tucson AZ 85736 Office Phone: 520-822-9343 ext. 146, 520-822-9343 146.

PETERSON, KEITH STANLEY, literature and language professor; b. Redding, Calif., Mar. 13, 1958; s. Richard Lyle and Marian Holbrook Peterson; m. Carol Anne Brown, Dec. 19, 1981; children: Jillian Rae, Joseph Scott, Amy Lynn, Kevin Neil. BA, Brigham Young U., Provo, Utah, 1985, MA, 1987; PhD, Tex. Christian U., Ft. Worth, 1990. Asst. prof. English and comm. studies Brigham Young U., Laie, Hawaii, 1990—96, assoc. prof. English, 1996—, coord. U. composition, 2000—08. Contbr. articles to profl. jours. Recipient Faculty Exemplary Svc. award, Brigham Young U., 2008; IDA Green fellowship, Tex. Christian U., 1988—89. Mem.: Nat. Coun. Tchrs. English. Mem. Lds Ch.

PETERSON, KENNETH ALLEN, JR., lawyer; b. Chgo., Sept. 14, 1966; s. Kenneth Allen Peterson, Sr. and Marilyn Peterson; m. Alice Irene Bruen, Jan. 10, 1997; children: Alexander Louis, Randall Tyler, Cameron Edward, Kaitlyn Samantha Bilotta. BA, Purdue U., West Lafayette, Ind., 1984—88; Jurisprudence D, Ind. U., Bloomington, Ind., 1988—91. Bar: Ill. 1991. Assoc. Chapman & Cutler, Chgo., 1991—96; mem. Bell, Boyd & Lloyd, LLC, Chgo., 1996—. Assoc. Ind. Law Jour., 1989—91. Chmn. Cub Scout Pack 173, Steger, Ill., 2005—06; mem. Kiwanis Internat., Steger, 2005—; dist. chmn. crossroads dist. Calumet Coun. Boy Scouts Am., Munster, Ind., 2006—; chmn. Bd. Fire & Police Commrs. of Village of Steger, Ill., 2001—03; village trustee Village of Steger, 2003—, chmn. Econ. Devel. Com., 2004—. Recipient Eagle Scout award, Boy Scouts Am., 1980. Fellow: Am. Coll. Investment Coun.; mem.: Order of Coif, Order of Arrow (life). Lutheran. Home: 3134 Sandy Ridge Dr Steger IL 60475 Office: Bell Boyd & Lloyd LLC 70 W Madison St Ste 3100 Chicago IL 60602 Business E-Mail: kpeterson@bellboyd.com.

PETERSON, KIM MOREAU, biology professor; b. Billings, Mont., Dec. 30, 1948; s. Clifford Barton Peterson and Lillian Nadine Speelmon; m. Claudia Victoria Vargas, July 15, 1992; children: Sasha Victoria, Lisa Clover Kay, Tessa Marie Green; m. Deborah Keys Peterson. PhD, Duke U., Durham, 1978. Rsch. assoc. Duke U., 1978—79; asst. prof. Biol. Scis. Clemson U., 1979—84, assoc. prof.; assoc. prof. biol. scis. U. Alaska Anchorage, 1992—96, prof., 1996—, chair dept., 1998—2002, vice provost, 2002—05, assoc. dean Rsch. Coll. Arts & Scis., 2007—. Avocation: sailing. Office: Univ Alaska Anchorage 3211 Providence Dr Anchorage AK 99508-4614

PETERSON, KURT C., lawyer; b. Salem, NJ, Mar. 31, 1953; BA in Econs. and Polit. Sci., Stanford U., 1975; JD, U. Calif. Hastings Coll. Law, 1978. Bar: Calif. 1978, US Dist. Ct. No. Dist. Calif., US Dist Ct. Ctrl. Dist. Calif. Law clk. to Hon. Robert Kane Calif. Ct. Appeal 1st Dist., 1978; with Crosby Heafey Roach & May (combined with Reed Smith in 2003), 1978—2003, opened L.A. office & served as first mng. ptnr., 1990, opened Century City office, 1997, mng. ptnr., 2000—03; ptnr., mem. exec. com. Reed Smith LLP, 2003—. Contbr. ABA Profl. Liability Litig. Newsletter. Bd. trustees Ctr. for Law in the Pub. Interest; bd. dirs. Music Ctr. of LA County and Techno. Named Alumnus of Yr., Hastings Alumni Assn. LA Chpt., 2001; named one of the top 25 lawyers under 45 in Calif., Calif. Law Bus., 1993. Mem.: ABA (vice chair litig. sect. legal malpractice subcom. 1989—92), Assn. Bus. Trial Lawyers, L.A. Bar Assn. Office: Reed Smith LLP 1901 Ave of the Stars, Ste 700 Los Angeles CA 90067-6078 Office Phone: 310-734-5201. Office Fax: 310-734-5299. Business E-Mail: kpeterson@reedsmith.com.

PETERSON, LANCE ROBERT, physician; b. Mpls., Sept. 2, 1947; s. Alvin Robert and Norma Lorraine (Soderlin) P.; m. LoAnn Charlotte Liukonen, Aug. 24, 1968; children: Anja Kristine, Kari Elizabeth. BS, U. Minn., 1970, MD, 1972. Diplomate Am. Bd. Internal Medicine, Am. Bd. Infectious Diseases, Am. Bd. Med. Microbiology. Intern U. Minn., 1972—73, resident, 1973—75; med. dir. home care VA Med. Ctr., Mpls., 1975—77, staff infectious diseases, 1977—92; dir. clin. microbiology Northwestern Meml. Hosp., Chgo., 1992—2002; dir. microbiology and infectious diseases rsch. NorthShore U., Evanston, 2002—, health care epidemiologist, 2005—. Prof. medicine U. Minn., Mpls., 1990—92, prof. lab. medicine, 1990—92; prof. pathology and medicine Northwestern U., Chgo., 1992—; chief microbiology VA Med. Ctr., Mpls., 1979—92, assoc. chief molecular biology, 1987—89; staff infectious diseases Northwestern Meml. Hosp., Chgo., 1992—2002, dir. prevention epicenter, 1999—2002. Co-editor: Diagnostic Microbiology, 9th edit.; editor: The Biologic and Clinical Basis of Infectious Diseases, 5th edit.; contbr. chpts. to books and articles to profl. jours. Pres. Greater Mpls. Day Care Assn., 1985-86; bd. dir. Cmty. Child Care Ctr., Mpls., 1986-89, VA Employees Child Care Ctr., Mpls., 1987-92, chair fund-raising com., 1987-92. Grantee, VA Dept., 1978—88, Bayer, Inc., 1985—2006, R.W. Johnson Rsch. Instn., 1990—2004, Ctrs. Disease Control, 1999—2004, Wyeth, Inc., 2003—, Wash. Sq. Health Found., 2003—04, 2006—08, Gene Ohm Scis., 2006—, Cepheid, Inc., 2006—, Nanosphere, Inc., 2006—, others. Fellow: Ctrl. Soc. Clin. Rsch. (chair. infectious diseases sect. 1995—97), Am. Soc. Clin. Pathologists, Infectious Diseases Soc. Am. (regional bd. 1991—92, sec.-treas. Chgo. area 2003—), Am. Acad. Microbiology; mem.: Brit. Soc. Antimicrobial Chemotherapy, Am. Soc. Microbiology (BD Rsch. Clin. Microbiology award 2005, NQF Eisenberg award 2007). Avocations: travel, jogging, dining, gardening. Office: NorthShore Univ 2650 Ridge Ave Evanston IL 60201 Home Phone: 847-835-2971; Office Phone: 847-570-1637. Business E-Mail: lpeterson@northshore.org.

PETERSON, LYNN MEISTER, engineering educator; d. Paul Albert and Anne Sophie Meister; 1 child, Eric Arnold. BA in Math., Wittenberg U., Springfield, Ohio, 1962; MA in Math., Duke U., Durham, NC, 1963; MA, U. Mich., Ann Arbor, 1967; PhD in Math. Scis., U. Tex. Southwestern Med. Sch., Dallas, 1978. Instr., math. Kent State U., Ohio, 1963—64; programmer analyst Johnson Rsch. Found. U. Pa., Phila., 1967—68, U. Tex. Southwestern Med. Sch., 1968—78, asst. prof., med. computer sci., 1978—82; asst. prof., computer sci. & engring. U. Tex. Arlington, 1982—86, assoc. prof., computer sci. & engring., 1986—96. Recipient Lockheed Martin award; named Outstanding Young Women of America, 1970. Mem.: Am. Assn. Engring. Edn. (chair, gulf SW sect. 2003—04), IEEE Computer Soc., Mortar Bd., Upsilon Pi Epsilon, Tau Beta Pi, Sigma Xi. Office: Univ Tex Arlington Box 19019 Arlington TX 76019

PETERSON, M. JEANNE, historian, educator; b. Minn., Nov. 26, 1937; d. Clifford Woodrow and Mildred Amelia (Kukas) P.; divorced. BA magna cum laude, U. Calif., 1966, PhD, 1972. Lectr., asst., assoc. prof. Ind. U., Bloomington, 1971-87, prof. history, 1987—, chairperson dept. history, 1987—93, exec. assoc. dean Coll. Arts and Scis., 1993—99, acting chair gender studies dept., 1999—2000, prof. emerita history, found. prof. emerita gender studies, 2001—. Cons. Jour. Women's History, Bull. Hist. Medicine, J. Brit. Studies, U. Mich. Press, Butler U., Indpls., Harvard U. Press, Princeton U. Press, Columbia U. Press, Ind. U. Press, SUNY Press, Food and Foodways, J. Brit. Studies, Med. History, ACLS, Am. Hist. Rev., Victorian Studies, NEH, NIH, Can. Coun., Adam Matthew Ltd., SUNY Brockport, Johns Hopkins U. Press, U. Va. Press, U. Toronto Press, Ligature, Inc., Am. Philos. Soc., Wellcome Trust (U.K.); external review com. Arts & Entertainment Network (TV) U. Nebr., Lincoln, 1992, U. Iowa, Iowa City, 1995; MA review com. U. N.C., Greensboro, 1993. Reviewer: Tenure Review, SUNY Brockport; Author: The Medical Profession in Mid-Victorian London, 1978, Family, Love, and Work in the Lives of Victorian Gentlewomen, 1989; assoc. editor: Oxford Dictionary of National Biography; co-editor: Lizzie Borden: A Case Book of Family and Crime in the 1890s, 1980; contbr. articles to profl. jours. NEH fellow, 1978-79, Guggenheim Found. fellow, 1984-85, Inst. for Advanced Study fellow Ind. U., 1984-85. Mem. Am. Hist. Assn., Soc. for the Social History Medicine, N.Am. Conf. Brit. Studies, Am. Assn. History Medicine, N.Am. Victorian Studies Assn., Phi Beta Kappa. Home: 1311 S Rechter Ct Bloomington IN 47401-6173 Office: Ind U Dept Gender Studies 742 Ballantine Rd Bloomington IN 47401-5022 Home Phone: 812-332-0458; Office Phone: 812-855-0101. Business E-Mail: petersom@indiana.edu.

PETERSON, MARTHA, artist; b. Flint, Mich., Sept. 26, 1927; d. Carl J. and Addie Amelia Primm; m. Edward Carlyle Peterson, Sept. 9, 1948; children: Mark, Laura, Michelle. Student, Corcoran Art Sch., Washington, 1966-68, Cath. U., 1966-67, Mich. State U., East Lansing, 1974-76. Art tchr. Forsyth CC, Winston-Salem, NC, 1995-96; pvt. art tchr. Winston-Salem, 1995—. Bd. dirs. Assoc. Arts Winston-Salem, 1995—97, 2007—; co-founder Quincy Valley Art Students League; mem. Davison County Arts Mus. Mem.: Middletown Art Guild, High Point Arts Coun., Surry County Arts Coun. Unitarian. Avocations: gardening, reading, travel.

PETERSON, MERRILL DANIEL, historian, educator; b. Manhattan, Kans., Mar. 31, 1921; s. William Oscar and Alice Dwinell (Merrill) P.; m. Jean Hymphrey, May 24, 1944 (dec. Nov. 1995); children: Jeffrey Ward, Kent Merrill. Student, Kans. State U., 1939-41; AB, U. Kans., 1943; PhD in History of Am. Civilization, Harvard U., 1950. Teaching fellow Harvard U., Cambridge, Mass., 1948-49; instr., then asst. prof. history Brandeis U., Waltham, Mass., 1949-55; asst. prof., bicentennial preceptor Princeton U., N.J., 1955-58; mem. faculty Brandeis U., Waltham, Mass., 1958-62, dean students, 1960-62; Thomas Jefferson Found. prof. U. Va., Charlottesville, 1962-87, prof. emeritus, 1987—, chmn. dept. history, 1966-72, dean faculty Arts and Scis., 1981-85; Mary Ball Washington prof. Am. History University Coll., Dublin, Ireland, 1988-89; vol. Peace Corps, Armenia, 1997. Scholar in residence Bellagio Study Ctr., 1974; faculty Salzburg Seminar in Am. Studies, 1975; Lamar lectr. Mercer U., 1975; Fleming lectr. La. State U., 1980; lectr. at 20 European univs., 40 Am. colls. and univs. Author: The Jefferson Image in the American Mind, 1960 (Bancroft prize, Gold medal Thomas Jefferson Meml. Found.), Major Crises in American History, 2 vols., 1962, Democracy, Liberty and Property: The State Constitutional Convention Debates of the 1820s, 1966, Thomas Jefferson and the New Nation: A Biography, 1970, James Madison: A Biography in His Own Words, 1974, Adams and Jefferson: A Revolutionary Dialogue, 1976, Olive Branch and Sword: The Compromise of 1833, 1982, The Great Triumvirate: Webster, Clay and Calhoun, 1987; editor: Thomas Jefferson: A Historical Profile, 1996, The Portable Thomas Jefferson, 1975, Thomas Jefferson Writings, 1984, Thomas Jefferson: A Reference Biography, 1986, The Virginia Statute for Religious Freedom: Its Evolution and Consequences in American History, 1988, Visitors to Monticello, 1989, Lincoln in American Memory, 1994 (History finalist, Pulitzer prize, PBK Book award U. Va.), Coming of Age with the New Republic, 1938-1950, 1999, The John Brown Legend Revisited, 1859-2000, 2002, Starving Armenians: America and the Armenian Genocide. 1915-1930 and After, 2004, The President and His Biographer: Woodrow Wilson and Ray Stannard Baker, 2007. Bd. dirs. Thomas Jefferson Found.; chmn. Thomas Jefferson Commemoration Commn., 1993-94. Guggenheim fellow, 1962-63, Ctr. for Advanced Study in Behavioral Scis. fellow, 1968-69, NEH and Nat. Humanities Ctr. fellow, 1980-81; recipient 20th Anniversary award Va. Found. for Humanities, 1994, Nat. First Freedom award First Freedom Coun., 1997, Career Achievement award, 2005, Libr. Va. Fellow Am. Acad. Arts and Scis.; mem. Am. Hist. Assn., Am. Antiquarian Soc., Mass. Hist. Soc., Phi Beta Kappa. Home and Office: 250 Pantops Mountain Rd Apt 212 Charlottesville VA 22911-8600 Home Phone: 434-972-2312.

PETERSON, PAM M., museum director; b. Phila, Pa. d. Warren Allen and Bernice Straub Matthias; m. John W Peterson, Sept. 14, 1968; children: Matthew Park, Joanna Joohee. BA, Chatham Coll., 1964—68; MEd, Boston U., 1974; cert. for advanced studies, Harvard U. Fogg Ctr. for Conservation, 1983. Conservator of art Isabella Stewart Gardner Mus., Boston, 1970—76, U. Heidelberg, Germany, 1976—79; conservator of art intern Fogg Mus., Harvard U., 1983; conservator of art Peabody Essex Mus., Salem, Mass., 1982—98; dir. exhibits and edn. Marblehead Mus. and Hist. Soc., Marblehead, Mass., 1998—2003, mus. dir., 2003—. Mem. bd. dirs. Marblehead Arts Assn., 2001—03; commr. Essex Nat. Commn., 2000—. Author: (book) J. O. J. Frost, 2003, Marblehead Myths Legands and Love, 2007. Pres. Marblehead Middle Sch. Parents Council, 1995—96. Grant, Marblehead Mass. Cultural Coun., 2000, 2003. Mem.: New England Mus. Assn., Marblehead C. of C., Marblehead Harbor Rotary Club. Democrat. Episcopalian. Avocations: painting, writing. Office: Marblehead Mus and Hist Soc 170 Washington St Marblehead MA 01945 Home: 21 Lincoln Park Marblehead MA 01945-2553 Office Phone: 781-631-1768. Business E-Mail: mmhspeterson@yahoo.com.

PETERSON, PETE See PETERSON, DOUGLAS

PETERSON, PETER GEORGE, retired investment company executive, former United States Secretary of Commerce; b. Kearney, Nebr., June 5, 1926; s. George and Venetia P.; m. Sally H., May 1953 (div. 1979); children: John, Jim, David, Holly, Michael; m. Joan Ganz Cooney, Apr. 26, 1980. BS, Northwestern U., 1947; MBA, U.Chgo., 1951; PhD (hon.), Colgate U., George Washington U., Northwestern U., Georgetown U., U. Rochester, New School U., Southampton Coll. at L.I. Exec. v.p. Market Facts, Chgo., 1948-52; v.p. McCann Erickson, Chgo., 1952-58; pres. Bell and Howell, Chgo., 1961—63, exec. v.p., 1961—63, chmn., CEO, 1963-71; asst. to Pres. for internat. econ. affairs The White House, Washington, 1961-63; sec. US Dept. Commerce, Washington, 1972-73; chmn., CEO Lehman Brothers Inc., NYC, 1973—77, Lehman Brothers Kuhn, Loeb, Inc., 1977—84; sr. chmn., co-founder The Blackstone Group, 1985—2008. Chmn., Fed. Res. Bank NY, 1999-2003, The Peter G. Peterson Found., 2008-; founding pres. The Concord Coalition co-chmn, The Conf. Bd. Comm. on Publ. Trust and Pvt. Enterprise Author: Facing Up: How to Rescue the Economy from Crushing Debt and Restore the American Dream, 1993, Will America Grow Up Before it Grows Old: How the Coming Social Security Crisis Threatens You, Your Family, and Your Country, 1996, Gray Dawn: How the Coming Age Wave Will Transform America--and the World, 1999, Running on Empty: How the Democratic and Republican Parties Are Bankrupting Our Future and What Americans Can Do About It, 2004, The Education of an American Dreamer: How a Son of Greek Immigrants Learned His Way from a Nebraska Diner to Washington, Wall Street and Beyond, 2009; editor: Readings in Market Organization and Price Policies; co-author: On Borrowed Time: How The Growth In Entitlement Spending Threatens America's Future, 1989. Founding mem. Bi-Partisan Budget Appeal; pres. The Concord Coalition; trustee Commn. for Econ. Devel., Mus. Modern Art, NYC; bd. dir. Pub. Agenda. Recipient Outstanding Service award Phoenix House, NYC, 1976, Stephen Wise award Am. Jewish Congress, 1981, U. Chgo. Alumni medal, 1983, Man of Vision award, 1994, Nebraskalander award, 1994, Harvard Bus. Sch. Leadership award, 2004, Coro N.Y. Leadership award, 2004, Woodrow Wilson award for Corporate Citizenship, Woodrow Wilson Internat. Ctr. for Scholars, 2006; named to Pres. Clinton's Bi-Partisan Comm. on Entitlement Reform, 1994. Mem. Coun. on Fgn. Rels. (chmn. bd. 1985-2007, chmn. emeritus, 2007-), Inst. Internat. Econ. (chmn. bd 1980), Nat. Bur. Econ. Rsch. (trustee), Japan Soc., Blind Brook Club (Purchase, NY), Deepdale Club (Manhasset, NY), Maidstone Club (Easthampton, NY), Chgo. Club, River Club, Links, Augusta Nat. Club, Friar's Head Golf Club (Riverhead, NY), Burning Tree (Washington), Quail Valley Golf Club, Atlantic Club, Windsor Club; fellow Am. Acad. Arts & Sciences Republican. Office: c/o The Blackstone Group 345 Park Ave Ste 3101 New York NY 10154-0004*

PETERSON, RALPH E., endocrinologist, researcher; b. Paola, Kans., Aug. 21, 1918; s. William Oscar and Alice Danial Peterson; children: Susan, Merrill, Larry, Patricia, Dean, Sandi. BS, Kans. State U., 1940, MS, 1941; postgrad., Brown U., 1941—42; MD, Columbia U., 1946. Resident U. Minn. Hosp., Mpls., 1946—48; asst. chief dept. chemistry Walter Reed Med. Ctr., Washington, 1950—52; sr. clin. investigator NIH, Bethesda, 1953—58; dir. divsn. endocrinology Cornell U. Med., NYC, 1958—83; prof. med. NY Hosp. Cornell U., NYC, 1958—83; dir. med. rsch. svc. VA, Washington, 1983—90; ret., 1990. Contbr. articles to profl. jours. Recipient Rsch. Career award, NIH, 1962—83, Foster Fuqua award, Am. Acad. Pediat., 1977, Nicholas Pichardo award, Santo Domingo, Dominican Rep., 1980; fellow Fulbright, How Florey Inst., 1964—65. Mem.: AAAS, Endocrine Soc., Am. Assn. Physician, Am. Soc. Clin. Investigation, Am. Fed. Clin. Res., Am. Chem. Soc. Avocation: scultpure. Home: 1309 Bellhook Pl NW Concord NC 28027-8059

PETERSON, RANDY, consumer products company executive, information technology professional; BS in Computer Sci., U. ND. Sr. sys. analyst positions Comtel Comm., AT&T Bell Labs.; joined Procter & Gamble Far East, Inc., Japan, 1993; various info. tech. positions Procter & Gamble Co., Korea, Singapore, Philippines, digital mktg. inovation mgr. Cin. Adv. bd. mem. Search Engine Strategies Conf. & Expn. Office: Hdqs 1 Procter & Gamble Plz Cincinnati OH 45202 Office Phone: 513-983-1100. Office Fax: 513-983-6369.*

PETERSON, RICHARD STEWART, theater director; b. Binghamton, NY, Feb. 10, 1947; s. Stewart Ervin and Frances Joesphine Peterson; m. Linda L. Zaragoza, Sept. 9, 1988; m. Linda S. Smutzinger, Aug. 22, 1970 (div. Sept. 12, 1987); children: Brenton Geoffrey, Amy Kristina, Gretchen Elizabeth. Candidate, Yankton Coll., SD, 1970; MA, Syracuse U., NY, 1977. Cert. facility exec. Internat. Assn. Auditorium Mgrs., Coppell, Tex, 2005. Ops. mgr. Clemens Performing Arts Ctr., Elmira, NY, 1977—81; mgr. stage ops. Cultural Resources Coun., Syracuse, 1981—91; asst. dir. Oncenter Converntion Ctr., Arena Performing Arts Ctr., Syracuse, 1991—95; exec. dir. performing arts ctr. Chesapeake Coll., Wye Mills, Md., 1996—. Mgr. Asian Ballet Tour, UBC, Italian/Austrian Tour, Ballet Co., Stars Bolshoi, Ballet Tour; treas. Caroline Arts Coun., Denton, Md., 1997—2002, bd. dirs., 1997—2002, Cmty. Alliance Performing Arts, Easton, Md., 1998—2004; panalist Md. State Arts Coun., Balt., 2003—08. Rev. hist. dist. housing renovation projects; bd. mem. Denton Hist. Rev. Bd., 2004—08. Mem.: US Inst. Theatre Tech., Internat. Assn. Auditorium Mgrs. Liberal. Roman Catholic. Avocations: photography, music, woodworking, antiques. Home: 209 S 5th Ave Denton MD 21629 Office: Chesapeake Coll Todd Performing Arts 1000 College Cir PO Box 8 Wye Mills MD 21629 Office Fax: 410-827-3221. Business E-Mail: dpeterson@chesapeake.edu.

PETERSON, ROBERT AUSTIN, retired manufacturing executive; b. Sioux City, Iowa, July 5, 1925; s. Austen W. and Theresa Peterson; m. Carol May Hudy, May 17, 1952; children: Roberta, Richard., Bruce. BS, U. Minn., 1946, BBA, 1947. Credit mgr. New Holland Machine div. Sperry Rand Corp., Mpls., 1952-61; from credit mgr. to treas. Toro Co., Mpls., 1961-70, v.p., treas. internat. fin., 1970-83; v.p. fin., pres. Toro Credit Co., 1983-93. Chmn. Prior Lake Spring Lake Watershed Dist., 1970-80; chmn., bd. dirs. Prior Lake Bd. Edn., 1965-71; chmn. Scott County Republican Party, 1969-70; bd. dirs. Scott Carver Mental Health Center, 1969-73, Minn. Watershed Assn., 1972-76. Served to ensign USNR, 1943-46. Mem.: Prior Lake Yacht Club (bd. dirs.).

PETERSON, ROBERT SCOTT, electrical engineer; b. McKeesport, Pa., Mar. 24, 1930; s. William James and Emma Elizabeth (Scott) P.; m. Betty Louise Oleska, Aug. 11, 1962 (dec. 1995). BSEE, Pa. State U., 1952; MSEE, U. Pitts., 1961. Lic. profl. engr., Pa. Sr. application, design engr. Westinghouse Elec., Pitts., 1952-63, devel. engr. Buffalo, 1963-85, Pitts., 1985-89, AEG Automation Corp., Pitts., 1989-94; cons. engr. CDI-Ctrl. Corp., Pitts., 1994—. Holder 30 U.S. patents. Coach Midget Football League, McKeesport, 1953-55. With U.S. Army, 1955-57. Mem. IEEE, NY Acad. Scis., Assn. Iron Steel Engrs. Achievements include patents in field. Avocations: gardening, woodworking, painting, dance, sports. Home: 972 Willow Dr, Rm 207 Pittsburgh PA 15237-2223 Office Phone: 412-767-4690.

PETERSON, ROBIN TUCKER, marketing educator; b. Casper, Wyo., July 31, 1937; s. Walfred Arthur and Mary Lurene Peterson; m. Marjorie K. Greenwald, June 25, 1963; children: Timothy, Kimberly. BS, U. Wyo., 1959, MS in Bus., 1961; PhD, U. Wash., 1967. Mem. faculty Idaho State U., Pocatello, 1963-73; prof. mktg., head mktg. dept. St. Cloud (Minn.) State U., 1973-76; prof. mktg. N.Mex. State U., Las Cruces, 1976—2007, head dept. mktg., 1976—, endowed disting. prof., 2007—. Fulbright lectr., Yugoslavia, 1973; vis. scholar Ea. Mont. State

Coll., 1985; Sunwest Fin. Svcs. Disting. Centennial prof. N.Mex. State U., 1991, 92; Norwest Disting. prof. N.Mex. State U., 1999, Wells Fargo Disting. prof., 2002;endowed prof., 2008, en vis. lectr. Nirma Inst. Ahmedabad, India, 1999, Chiang Moi U., Thailand, 2000; Fulbright lectr. Kathmandu U., Nepal, 2001. Author: Marketing-A Contemporary Introduction, 1976, Forecasting, 1976, edit., 1983, Personal Selling, 1977, Marketing in Action, 1977, Lernbook Marketing, 1984, Marketing: Concepts and Decision Making, 1987, Principles of Marketing, 1989, Argentina, 1990, Managing the Distributor Sales Network, 1990, Business Forecasting, 1992, Getting New Products to Market Rapidly, 1994; exec. editor Bus. Forecaster, 1993-94; editor Jour. Bus. and Entrepreneurship, 1994-98; contbr. articles to profl. publs. Served with USAR, 1962-63. Fellow Assn. Small Bus. Entrepreneurship; mem. Am. Mktg. Assn., Sales and Mktg. Execs. Internat., Acad. Mktg. Sci. (pres. 1977-78, 80-82), Am. Arbitration Assn. (Outstanding Educators Am. award), S.W. Small Bus. Assn. (pres. 1983-84, Outstanding Mktg. Educators award, Outstanding Educator, Assn. of Small Bus., 2002), S.W. Mktg. Assn., Western Mktg. Educators, Las Cruces C. of C., Las Cruces Sales and Mktg. Club, Beta Gamma Sigma, Phi Kappa Psi, Alpha Kappa Psi, Alpha Mu Alpha. Republican. Presbyterian. Home: 4350 Diamondback Dr Las Cruces NM 88011-7539 Office: NMex State U PO Box 5280 Las Cruces NM 88003-5280 Home Phone: 575-646-5748; Office Phone: 575-646-5200. Business E-Mail: ropeters@nmsu.edu.

PETERSON, ROBYN GAYLE, museum director; b. San Francisco, Jan. 17, 1958; BA, UCLA, 1979; MA, U. Wis., 1982, PhD, 1987. Goldsmith, 1974-80; collections acquisition asst. social studies bibliographer Meml. Libr./U. Wis., 1984-86; curator of collections The Rockwell Mus., Corning, N.Y., 1988-99; sr. dir. exhbns. and programs Turtle Bay Exploration Park, Redding, Calif., 1999—2006; exec. dir. Yellowstone Art Mus., Billings, Mont., 2006—. Author: American Frontier Photography, 1993, Edward Borein, 1997, Warp and Weft: Cross-cultural Exchange in Navajo Weavings, 1997, Transforming Trash: Bay Area Fiber Art, 2000, Second Nature: the Art of Michael Haykin, 2006; co-author: Sudden and Solitary: Mount Shasta and Its Artistic Legacy, 2008; contbg. author: Allgemeines Künstlerlexikon, 1998—; editor/contbr.: Collector's Choice Review: Masterpieces of Glassmaking; Frederick Carder and the Steuben Glass Works, 1993, Brilliance in Glass: The Lost Wax Glass Sculpture of Frederick Carder, 1993, Journey to Justice: The Wintu People and the Salmon, 2002, The Other Side of the Looking Glass: The Glass Body and Its Metaphors, 2003, Bug-Eyed: Art, Culture, Insects, 2004; mng. editor: Frederick Carder and Steuben Glass: American Classics (Thomas P. Dimitroff), 1998; contbr. articles to profl. jours.; peer reviewer IMLS. Mem. Coll. Art Assn., Am. Assn. Mus. (peer reviewer accreditation). Office: Yellowstone Art Mus 401 N 27th St Billings MT 59101 Office Phone: 406-256-6804. Business E-Mail: director@artmuseum.org.

PETERSON, ROGER, community bank executive, retired international investment banker, manufacturing executive, air force officer; b. Chgo., June 7, 1929; s. Milton Albert and LaVergne P.; m. Sally Ann Alder, Apr. 25, 1952; children: Bruce Roger, Dale Alder, Drew Alan. BS in Acctg., UCLA, 1955; MS in Mgmt., U. Colo., 1964; grad., Air Command and Staff Coll. Air U., Ala., 1965; grad. Exec. Program for Internat. and Nat. Security, J.F. Kennedy Sch. Govt., Harvard U., Cambridge, Mass., 1983. Joined USAF, 1950, advanced through grades to maj. gen., 1981, pilot, 1956-61, mgr. tactical missile site constrn., 1961; air officer comdg. 11th Cadet Squadron, Air Force Cadet Wing USAF Acad., 1961-64; asst. sec. Joint Chiefs of Staff and NSC matters for Hdqrs. Pentagon, 1965-68; transport pilot USAF, Vietnam, 1968, asst. chmn. US-Japan Joint Com., Adminstrn. of Status of Forces Agreement, 1968-73, chief program cost, dir. budget, 1973-76, chief plans, comptroller of Air Force, 1976-78, dir. mgmt. analysis, 1978-79, dir. programs, asst. chief of staff for research and devel., 1979-81; asst. dir. plans, policies and programs Def. Logistics Agy., Alexandria, Va., 1981-82, dep. dir., 1982-83; asst. dep. chief staff for logistics and engring. Hdqrs. USAF, Washington, 1983-84; pres., chief exec. officer advanced tech. rsch. & devel. firm, 1984—85; strategic planner United Techs. Corp., 1985-88; v.p., chief oper. officer Sikorsky Support Svcs. Inc., 1988-90; exec. asst. to mng. ptnr. O'Connor & Assocs., 1990-92; mng. dir. global ops. and svcs. Swiss Bank Corp., Zurich, 1992-96, chief of staff Chgo., 1996-99, br. mgr. Chgo. N.Am. and S.Am., 1996-99; mng. dir. UBS A.G. (formerly Swiss Bank Corp.), NY, 1996-99, UBS AG, NYC, 1999—2001; mng. dir. mktg. and strategic planning SunSouth Bank, Dothan, Ala., 2002—. Decorated D.S.M., Legion of Merit, Air medal with oak leaf cluster, Joint Service Commendation medal, Air Force Commendation medal with two oak leaf clusters. Mem. Air Force Assn., Beta Gamma Sigma, Phi Sigma Iota Epsilon. Presbyterian. Achievements include designing and negotiating consolidation of US Air Force bases in Tokyo, 1970-73; negotiating mil. and civil aviation agreement for return of Okinawa to Japan; created global bus. mgmt. system for Swiss Bank Corp. Home: 1602 Deerpath Rd Dothan AL 36303-2173 Office: SunSouth Bank 108 Jamestown Blvd Dothan AL 36302 Office Phone: 334-836-4201. Personal E-mail: sbcrogerp@aol.com. *Always with honor.*

PETERSON, RONALD ROGER, lawyer; b. Chgo., July 27, 1948; married; children: Elizabeth G., Ronald W. AB, Ripon, 1970; JD, U. Chgo., 1973. Bar: Ill. 1974, US Dist. Ct. (no. dist.) Ill. 1974, US Ct. Appeals (7th cir.) 1974, US Dist. Ct. (ea. dist.) Wis. 1975, US Dist. Ct. (no. dist.) Ind. 1978, US Dist. Ct. (ctrl. dist.) Ill. 1980, US Ct. Appeals (8th cir.) 1984, US Ct. Appeals (6th cir.) 1990, US Ct. Appeals (9th cir.) 1996, US Dist. Ct. (we. dist.) Mich. 1999, US Ct. Appeals (3d cir.) 2001, US Dist. Ct. (ea. dist.) Mich. 2004. Commd. 2d lt. US Army, 1968, advanced through grades to 1st lt., 1973, with mil. intelligence, 1968-78; ptnr. Jenner & Block, Chgo., 1974—. Editor: Consumer Bankruptcy in Illinois; contbr., articles to profl. jours. Trustee Ripon Coll.; mem. exec. bd. Northeast Ill. Coun. Boy Scouts of Am. Commd. 2d lt. US Army, 1968, advanced through grades to 1st lt. US Army, 1973, with mil. intelligence US Army, 1968—78. Named to, Best Lawyers in Am., Chambers USA: Ill. Super Lawyer. Mem.: ABA, Fed. Bar Assn., Am. Coll. Bankruptcy Lawyers, Am. Bankruptcy Inst., Comml. Law League, Internat. Soc. Insolvency Practitioners, Chgo. Bar Assn., US Supreme Ct. Hist. Soc. Avocation: skiing. Office: Jenner & Block 330 North Wabash Fl 4000 Chicago IL 60611-7603 Office Phone: 312-923-2981. Business E-Mail: rpeterson@jenner.com.

PETERSON, ROSETTA HICKS, retired music educator; b. Memphis, Dec. 23, 1932; d. Homer Jackson Hicks and Loretta Jones Hicks Kateo. BA, Spelman Coll., Atlanta, 1954; M in Music Edn., Memphis State U., 1975. Cert. tchr. Ga., Tenn. Music tchr. T.H. Slater Elem. Sch., Atlanta, 1954—60, Porter Jr. HS, Memphis, 1961—71, Vance Jr. HS, Memphis, 1971—94; elem. tchr. Douglas Elem. Sch., Memphis, 1960—61; ret., 1994. Organist Rush Meml. Ch., Atlanta, 1957—60; organist, dir. Mt. Pisgah Christian Meth. Episcopal Ch., Memphis, 1966—88, St. John Bapt. Ch., Memphis, 1988—. Singer: (opera chorus) Aida, Memphis Opera, 1969, Porgy and Bess, Lyric Theatre, 1972. Vol. VA Hosp., Memphis, 1964—88, Friends of the Orpheum, Memphis, 1978—82. Named Outstanding Secondary Tchr. Am., Washington, 1974. Mem.: Music Educators Nat. Conf., Zoo Soc., Zeta Phi Beta (life; state dir. 1969—71), Phi Delta Kappa (life; pres. Beta Eta chpt.).

PETERSON, RUSSELL WILBUR, environmental services administrator, Former Governor, Del; b. Portage, Wis., Oct. 3, 1916; s. John Anton and Emma (Anthony) P.; m. E. Lillian Turner, June 30, 1937 (dec. Apr. 28, 1994); children: Russell Glen, Peter Jon, Kristin, Elin; m. June B. Jenkins, Oct. 21, 1995. BS, U. Wis., 1938, PhD, 1942, LLD (hon.), 1984; DSc (hon.), Williams Coll., 1975, Butler U., Springfield Coll., Stevens Inst. Tech., 1979, Gettysburg Coll., 1980, Alma Coll., 1981, Ohio State U., SUNY-Syracuse, Northland Coll., Fairleigh Dickinson U., 1981; LLD (hon.), Monmouth Coll., 1982, Salisbury State U., 1988; LHD, Meadville-Lombard Theol. Sch., 1992; DHL, Colby-Sawyer Coll., 2000; DSc (hon.), U. Del., 2006. With E. I. DuPont de Nemours & Co., Inc., 1942-69, rsch. dir. textile fibers dept., 1954-55, 56-59, merchandising mgr. textile fibers, 1955-56, dir. new products divsn. textile fibers, 1959-62, dir. R & D divsn. devel. dept., 1963-69; chmn. exec. com. Textile Research Inst., Princeton, NJ, 1959-61, chmn. bd. dirs., 1961-63, fellow, 1969; gov. State of Del., 1969—73; chmn. exec. com. Nat. Commn. Critical Choices for Am., 1973; chmn. U.S. Council on Environ. Quality, 1973-76; pres. Nat. Audubon Soc., 1979-85; mem. Nat. Commn. Critical Choices for Am., 1973-74; dir. Office Tech. Assessment, U.S. Congress, 1978-79. Pres. New Directions, 1976-77; regional v.p. Nat. Mcpl. League, 1968-78; chmn. Edn. Commn. States, 1970; chmn. com. nuclear energy and space tech. So. Govs. Conf., 1970-71; chmn. Nat. Adv. Commn. on Criminal Justice Standards and Goals, 1971-73; chmn. com. law enforcement, justice and pub. safety Nat. Govs. Conf., 1970-73; v.p. Council State Govts., 1970-71; chmn. adv. bd. Solar Energy Research Inst., 1979-83; vis prof. Dartmouth Coll., 1985, Carleton Coll., 1986, U. Wis., Madison, 1987; chmn. Centennial Internat. Symposium, Nat. Geog. Soc., 1986-88. Author: Oral History, Russell W. Peterson, 1995, Rebel with a Conscience, 1999, Delaware Heritage Series, 1999, Patriots, Stand Up!, 2004, (CD) We Can Save the Earth, 2000; contbr. articles to profl. jours. Chmn. Del. River Basin Commn., 1971-72; founding chmn. Bio-Energy Coun., 1976-78; bd. dirs. World Wildlife Fund, 1976-82, Population Action Internat., 1973-97, Alliance to Save Energy, 1979-93, Global Tomorrow Coalition, 1981-91, chmn., 1981-87; regional councillor Internat. Union Conservation Nature and Natural Resources, 1981-88, v.p., 1984-88; mem. Pres.'s Commn. on Accident at Three Mile Island, 1979; pres. Nat. Audubon Soc., 1979-85, Internat. Coun. Bird Preservation, 1982-90; chmn. Ctr. on Consequences of Nuclear War, 1983-87; vice-chmn. Better World Soc., 1985-90, pres., 1985-87; vis. com. John F. Kennedy Sch. Govt., 1979-85; Goodwill amb. UN Environ. Program, 1984-2002, world environ. prize com., 1989-2002; mem. Gov. Cuomo's Environ. Adv. Bd., 1985-94; adv. bd. Pace U. Sch. Law, 1988-98, Earth Island Inst., 1988-2002; chmn. bd. Earth Lobby, 1992-96; co-chmn. gov.'s task force on rejuvenating Wilmington waterfront, 1992-95; exe. com. Del. Riverfront Devel. Corp., 1995-2006, mem. 2006—; founder Stand Up For What's Right & Just, 2001, hon. chmn. 2002—. Decorated Order of Golden Ark (The Netherlands); Disting. fellow U. Del., 2000; recipient Ann. award NCCJ, 1966, Gold medal World Wildlife Fund, 1971, Ann. award Comml. Devel. Assn., 1971, Gold Plate award Nat. Acad. Achievement, 1971, Audubon award Nat. Audubon Soc., 1977, Frances K. Hutchinson medal Garden Club Am., 1980, Spl. Recognition award Population Reference Bur., 1983, Robert Marshall award Wilderness Soc., 1984, Nat. Conservation medal DAR, 1989, Human and Civil Rights award Del. Human Rights Commn., 1989, Spl. Recognition award Del. State Human Rels. Commn., 1989, Environ. Law Inst. award, 1990, Dr. Martin Luther King, Jr. Citation, Mt. Joy Meth. Ch., 1991, Ann. award Am. Civil Liberties Found. Del., 1992, Lawrence Solid Waste award Assn. N.Am., 1993, Kiwanis Cmty. Svc. award, 1993, Lifetime Achievement award Global Tomorrow Coalition, 1994, Lifetime Achievement award League of Conservation Voters, 1995, Del. Nature Soc., 1997, Liberty Bell award Del. State Bar Assn., 1998, Green Century award Resource Renewal Inst., 1999, Spl. Recognition award Med. Soc. Del., 2000, Samual Baxter Meml. award Water Resources Assn., 2002, Presdl. medal Del. State U., 2003, Holmes Weatherly award Unitarian-Universalist Assn., 2004, Whitney Young award Met. Wilmington Urban League, 2009; Paul Harris fellow Rotary Internat., 2002; named Conservationist of Yr., Nat. Wildlife Fedn., 1972, Swedish-Am. of Yr., Vasa Order of Am. In Sweden, 1982, Lifetime Achievement award Creative Grandparenting, 1999, NAACP, 1999; named to Wis. Conservation Hall of Fame, 2007, Del. Hall of Fame, 2008, Delware Maritime Hall of Fame, 2009; Del. refuge named in his honor Russell W. Peterson Wildlife Refuge, 2000; bronze statue in his honor on Wilmington Waterfront, 2002, King Neptune award, Kalmar Hyopel Fedn., 2008, Kalmar Nyckel Found., 2008, Greater Wilmington Urban League award, 2008, 09; papers on file Libr. of Congress, 2006. Fellow Am. Inst. Chemists (hon.), AAAS (past bd. dirs.); mem. Am. Ornithologists Union, Linnaean Soc., Fedn. Am. Scientists, Am. Chem. Soc. (Parsons award 1974), Del. Acad. Sci., U.S. Assn. for Club of Rome, Cosmos Club (Cert. of Appreciation 2001), Phi Beta Kappa, Sigma Xi (Proctor prize 1978), Phi Lambda Upsilon, Phi Kappa Phi. Unitarian Universalist. Address: 11 E Mozart Dr Wilmington DE 19807-1942

PETERSON, STEVEN W., neonatal nurse; m. Melissa J. Peterson. AS, Allen County C.C., Iola, Kans., 1996; BSN, Baker U., Baldwin City, Kans., 2002. RN Kans., cert. legal nurse cons., Kans., critical care RN, AACN, TNCC. Staff nurse med./surg. unit Stormont-Vail Health Care, Topeka, 2002—03, staff nurse neonatal ICU, 2003—. Chair elect profl. devel. coun. Stormont Vali Health Care. Med. advisor Am. Legion Boys State Kans., Topeka, 1994—; vol. fireman Burlingame (Kans.) Fire Dept., 1995—97; mem. bd. edn. Unified Sch. Dist. 454, Burlingame, 1996. Mem.: Am. Assn. Legal Nurse Cons., AACN (cert. CCRN), AOPA, Kans. Bar Assn., Acad. Neonatal Nursing. Personal E-mail: stevep_rn@yahoo.com.

PETERSON, SUSAN CARL, secondary school educator, gifted and talented educator; b. Detroit, Mich., Aug. 27, 1942; d. Robert Oscar and Merna Beck Carl; m. David Wayne Peterson, Aug. 14, 1970; children: Gretchen Susan, Paul David. BA, Kalamazoo Coll., 1964; MA in Tchg., Northwestern U., 1965. Tchr. biology and gifted James B. Conant H.S., Hoffman Estates, Ill., 1965—. Blood dr. organizer Lifesource, Hoffman Estates, 1970—2002; teens against cancer trainer Am. Cancer Soc., Hoffman Estates, 1976—2002. Recipient Outstanding Sci. Tchr. award, Suburban Cook County Office Edn., 1997. Mem.: ASCD, Nat. Assn. Biology Tchrs. Office: James B Conant HS 700 E Cougar Trail Hoffman Estates IL 60194

PETERSON, THOMAS VIRGIL, religious studies educator; b. Wash., Apr. 14, 1943; s. Charles C. Peterson and Helen Ann Armstrong; 1 child, Eli Jordan. PhD, Stanford U., Calif., 1975. Prof., religious studies Alfred U., NY, 1975—. Author: Linked Arms: A Rural Community Resists Nuclear Waste, Ham and Japheth: The Mythic World of Whites in the Antebellum South; contbr. articles to publs. Mem.: Am. Acad. Religion (bd. dirs. 1997—2002). Home: 60 Southern Main St Alfred NY 14802 Office: Alfred Univ Divsn Human Studies Alfred NY 14802 Business E-Mail: fpett@alfred.edu.

PETERSON, VICTOR LOWELL, aerospace engineer, consultant; b. Saskatoon, Sask., Can., June 11, 1934; came to U.S., 1937; s. Edwin Galladet and Ruth Mildred (McKeeby) P.; m. Jacqueline Dianne Hubbard, Dec. 21, 1955; children: Linda Kay, Janet Gale, Victor Craig. BS in Aero. Engring., Oreg. State U., 1956; MS in Aerospace Engring., Stanford U., 1964; MS in Mgmt., MIT, 1973. Rsch. scientist NASA-Ames Rsch. Ctr., Moffett Field, Calif., 1956-68, asst. chief hypersonic aerodyns., 1968-71, chief aerodyns. br., 1971-74, chief thermo and gas dynamics div., 1974-84, dir. aerophysics, 1984-90, dep. dir., 1990-94; pvt. mgmt. cons., 1994—. Mem. nat. adv. bd. U. Tenn. Space Inst., Tullahoma, 1984-94. Contbr. numerous articles to profl. jours. Treas. Woodland Acres Homeowners Assn., Los Altos, Calif., 1978—. Capt. USAF, 1957-60. Recipient medal for outstanding leadership NASA, 1982; Alfred P. Sloan fellow MIT, 1972-73. Fellow AIAA. Republican. Methodist. Achievements include development of numerical aerodynamic simulation system for aerospace, of method for reconstructing planetary atmosphere structure from accelerations of body entering atmosphere, of theory for motions of tumbling bodies entering planetary atmospheres. Home: 484 Aspen Way Los Altos CA 94024-7100 Personal E-mail: vicpeterson@comcast.net. *Achievements in life are maximized by creating visions of success and focussing relentlessly on successful accomplishment of intermediate objectives.*

PETERSON GERSTNER, JANET, English professor; b. Normal, Ill., Nov. 5, 1963; d. Carroll Valleen and Lillian Maxine Peterson; m. Clilnton J. Gerstner, Aug. 1, 1992; children: Isabelle Olivia Gerstner, Alec James Gerstner. BA in English, Colo. State U., Denver, 1991; MA in English, Ariz. State U., Tempe, 1994, PhD in English, 2000. Prof. of English San Juan Coll., Farmington, N.Mex., 2001—, English program coord., 2007—. Recipient Tchg. Excellence award, Nat. Inst. for Staff and Orgnl. Devel., 2003; fellow, Preparing Future Faculty, Fall 1997-Spring 1999. Mem.: MLA, Nat. Coun. of Tchrs. of English, Two-Year Coll. Assn., League for Innovation in the C.C. Office: San Juan Coll 4601 College Blvd Farmington NM 87402

PETHICK, CHRISTOPHER JOHN, physicist; b. Horsham, Sussex, Eng., Feb. 22, 1942; s. Richard Hope and Norah Betty (Hill) P. BA, Magdalen Coll., Oxford U., Eng., 1962, DPhil, 1965. Fellow Magdalen Coll., Oxford U., 1965-70; research assoc. U. Ill., Urbana, 1966-68, research asst. prof., 1968-69, assoc. prof. physics, 1970-73, prof. physics, 1973-95, Nordita, Copenhagen, 1975—. A.P. Sloan research fellow, 1970-72. Fellow Am. Phys. Soc. (Lars Onsager prize 2008); mem. European Phys. Soc. Office: Nordita Blegdamsvej 17 DK-2100 Copenhagen Denmark Office Phone: 45 35 32 52 26. Business E-Mail: pethick@nbi.dk.

PETHLEY, LOWELL SHERMAN, retired management consultant; b. Tacoma, Wash., Nov. 14, 1928; s. Sherman and Faye Maude (Newton) P.; m. Agnes Lenore Hudgins, Feb. 21, 1953; children: Lynn Louise, Curtis Sherman, Christopher Lowell, Suzanne Elizabeth. BS, U. Wash., 1956, MBA, 1957. Cert. mgmt. cons., CPA. Sr. acct., cons. prin. Deloitte & Touche, Seattle, 1957-65, San Francisco, 1965-67, ptnr. in charge Midwest cons. Chgo., 1968-86, ptnr., 1968—86; ret., 1986. Author, editor: Bank Costing for Planning and Control, 1973; contbr. articles to profl. jours., A Study of The Decision Support and Managment Information System, 2007. Mem. AICPA (hon. life; cons.), Inst. Mgmt. Cons. (hon. life.), Ill. Soc. CPA, Inverness Golf Club (treas. 1971-73), PGA, Nat. Golf Club, PGA West Club, Phi Beta Kappa, Delta Upsilon, Beta Alpha Psi. Avocations: computers, art. Office: Deloitte & Touche 10 Westport Rd Wilton CT 06897-4522 Office Phone: 760-835-1211. Personal E-mail: elesspee@aol.com.

PETIET, CAROLE ANNE, psychologist; b. Newport News, Va., Mar. 1, 1952; d. Gaston Kaleski and Ann (Snyder) Pettit Johnson; m. Lawrence Phillip Bischoff III, Dec. 29, 1973 (div. 1979); m. Robert Jomax Brooks, May 4, 1984 (div. 1989); 1 child, Nicole; stepchildren: Gregory, Randall. BS in Nursing, Baylor U., 1975; MA, Calif. Sch. Profl. Psychology, Berkeley, 1980, PhD, 1982. RN Calif.; lic. psychologist Calif., Colo. Charge nurse Elizabeth Knutsson Hosp., Estes Park, Colo., 1975-76; nurse coordinator, staff nurse Alta Bates Hosp., Berkeley, Calif., 1976-83; pvt. practice psychotherapy, cons., sports psychology Berkeley, Calif., 1982—; tng./clin. cons., rsch. cons. Phoenix Recovery Ctrs., Alameda, Calif., 1980-88; staff psychologist Kaiser Permanente Med. Ctr., Vallejo, Calif., 1982-84. Sports psychology cons. Women's Ski Programs, Aspen, Colo., and B.C., Can., 1986-93; co-coord. women's studies splty., mem. faculty Rosebridge Grad. Sch., Walnut Creek, Calif., 1986-94; supr., mem. adj. faculty CSPP, Berkeley/Alameda, 1986-89; intern Eden Youth and Family Svcs., Hayward, Calif., 1978-79, No. Calif. State Correctional Med. Facility, Vacaville, 1979-80, Kaiser Vallejo, 1980-81, Kaiser San Francisco, 1981-82; rschr. in field. Contbr. articles, presentations to profl. pubs. Scholar Baylor Hosp. Women's Aux., 1974, Soroptimists, 1981; recipient Am. Coll. Scholarship, 1979. Mem. APA, Assn. Women in Psychology, World Fedn. Mental Health, NOW, Amnesty Internat. Democrat. Achievements include research on neuropsychological effects of altitude on women climbers; participant in the 1986 American Women's Expedition to Mount Kongur, China. Office: 2340 Ward St Ste 105 Berkeley CA 94705-1146 Office Phone: 510-843-6760.

PETILLO, JOHN J., former academic administrator, priest; b. Montclair, NJ, Mar. 19, 1947; s. Gennaro and Geraldine (Illaria) Petillo; m. Sabina M. Porcaro; 1 child. Earned undergraduate degree, Seton Hall U., 1969, MA in Counseling, 1971; profl. diploma in counselor edn., Fordham U., 1973, PhD in Counseling and Personnel Services, 1976; M.Div. in Pastoral Theology, Darlington Sch. Theology, 1975; M.P.A., Rutgers U., 1977. Ordained priest Roman Catholic Ch., 1973; left priesthood in 1990. Asst. dir. office research and planning Archdiocese Newark, Roman Cath. Ch., 1975-77, chancellor for adminstrn., 1978-83; dep. dir. Cath. Community Services, NJ, 1976-78; asst. to pres. Seton Hall U., South Orange, NJ, 1978, chancellor, chief exec. officer, 1983-90, also mem. bd. trustees and bd. regents, 1983—; chancellor, chief exec. officer Immaculate Conception Sem., 1983; CEO for several insurance companies Tribus Companies, Care Advantage, Inc., Blue Cross and Blue Shield, NJ (also pres.), 1990—2001; pres., CEO Newark Alliance, 2001—04; chmn. bd. trustee U. Medicine and Dentistry NJ, 2003—, interim pres., 2004, pres., 2004—06. Mem. Archdiocesan Bd. Adminstrn. Mem. long range-strategic planning com. United Way Am.; bd. dirs. Blue Cross NJ, Nat. Soc. Prevention Blindness, Nat. Commn. on Coop. Edn., Found. Ednl. Alternatives, Ind. Coll. Fund NJ, NJ State Police Meml. Library and Mus. Assn., labor-higher edn. council Am. Council on Edn. and AFL-CIO, Commn. for Pub. Responsibility for Ednl. Success, Washington Ctr. NJ Scholarship Program, Statue of Liberty Centennial Commn. State NJ, NJ Performing Arts Ctr., St. Joseph's Health System, Wachovia Regional Found., Lincoln Educational Svcs.; chmn. bd. Essex County Coll. Found. Mem. Assn. Ind. Colls. and Univs. NJ (bd. dirs.) Office: The Univ Med Dentistry 65 Bergen St Newark NJ 07103 Office Phone: 973-972-4400. Business E-Mail: petillo@umdnj.edu.

PETILLON, LEE RITCHEY, lawyer; b. Gary, Ind., May 6, 1929; s. Charles Ernest and Blanche Lurene (Mackay) Petillon; m. Mary Anne Keeton, Feb. 20, 1960; children: Andrew G., Joseph R. BBA, U. Minn., 1952; LLB, U. Calif., Berkeley, 1959. Bar: Calif. 1960, U.S. Dist. Ct. (so. dist.) Calif. 1960. V.p. Creative Investment Capital, Inc., LA, 1969—70; corp. counsel Harvest Industries, LA, Calif., 1970—71; v.p., gen. counsel, dir. Tech. Svcs. Corp., Santa Monica, Calif., 1971—78; ptnr. Petillon & Davidoff, LA, 1978—92, Gipson Hoffman & Pancione, 1992—93; pvt. practice Torrance, Calif., 1993—94; ptnr. Petillon & Hansen, Torrance, 1994—2003, Petillon & Hiraide LLP, Torrance, 2004—06, Petillon, Hiraide, Loomis & Katz LLP, Torrance, 2006—, Petillon Hiraide & Loomis LLP, 2008—. Co-author: R&D Partnerships, 2d edit., 1985, Representing Start-Up Companies, 1992, 16th edit., 2008; contbr. chapters to books. Chmn. Neighborhood Justice Ctr. Com., 1983-85, Middle Income Co., 1983085; active Calif. Senate Commn. on Corp. Governance, State Bar Calif. Task Force on Alternative Dispute Resolution, 1984-85; chmn. South Bay Sci. Found., Inc.; vice-chmn. Calif. Capital Access Forum, Inc.; dir., legal counsel ACE-Net.org, Inc. Recipient Cert. of Appreciation L.A. City Demonstration Agy., 1975, United Indian Devel. Assn., 1981, City of L.A. for Outstanding Vol. Svcs., 1984, Outstanding Vol. award Torrance C. of C., 2000, Small Bus. Adv. of Yr. award Torrance C. of C., 2001, Marvin Greene award Los Angeles County Bar Assn., 2005; named Small Bus. Adv. of Yr. Calif. C. of C., 2001. Mem.: ABA (venture capital and pvt. equity com.), Los Angeles County Bar Assn. (trustee 1984—85, alt. dispute resolution sect. 1992—94, bus. and corp. law sect. 2000—, chmn. law tech. sect., Griffin Bell Vol. Svc. award 1993), Los Angeles County Bar Found. (bd. dirs.), Calif. State Bar Assn. (pres., Pro Bono Svcs. award 1983). Avocations: backpacking, reading, music, painting. Office: Petillon Hiraide Loomis LLP 21515 Hawthorne Blvd Ste 1260 Torrance CA 90503-6503 Home Phone: 310-378-1852; Office Phone: 310-543-0500. Business E-Mail: lpetillon@corplawp-h.com.

PETINGA, CHARLES MICHAEL, transportation executive; b. Atlantic City, July 9, 1946; s. Thomas Joseph and Rose Marie (Merindino) P.; m. Velna Mae McVicker, June 7, 1969; children: Scott, Jeffery. BS in Geology, Geography, U. Wis., Superior, 1969. Ops. supr. Schneider Transport, Inc., Green Bay, Wis., 1973-74, prodn. mgr., 1974-76, safety dir., 1976-79; dir. safety Schneider Nat., Inc., Green Bay, Wis., 1979-82, dir. risk mgmt., 1982-87; gen. mgr. Petinga Candy Co., Atlantic City, 1987-89; sr. v.p., midwest practice leader Transp. Industry, Appleton, Wis., 1989-2000; exec. v.p. Smith Transport Inc., Roaring Spring, Pa., 2003—; prin. Transp. Assocs., Appleton, Wis., 2005—06; exec. dir. transp. HNI Risk Svcs., New Berlin, Wis., 2006—; prin. Cornerstone Asset Mgmt., 2007. Cons. local charitable groups, Green Bay, 1985-88; practice leader freight/logistics Global Transp. Industry; adviser, cons. Small Bus. Execs., Green Bay, 1989; mem. worker compensation task force Wis. Motor Carriers, Madison, 1991; nat.-internat. spkr. at univs., bus. schs., vocat. schs. and high schs.; speaker to motor carrier assns., bd. directors, and industry mgmt. groups, nat. and state assns. Co. liaison Green Bay United Way, 1985, 86. With US Army, 1971—73. Mem. Wis. Coun. Safety Suprs., Nat. Safety Mgmt. Soc., Wis. Motor Carriers Assn., Risk and Ins. Mgmt. Soc., Nat. Safety Coun., Am. Trucking Assn. Avocations: martial arts, physical fitness, weightlifting. Home: 842 Whisper Falls Ln Menasha WI 54952 Office: HNI Risk Svcs 4650 W Spencer St Ste 13 Appleton WI 54914-8230 Office Phone: 920-540-0647. Personal E-mail: cpetinga@new.rr.com. Business E-Mail: cpetinga@hni.com.

PETIT, PARKER HOLMES, health care corporation executive; b. Decatur, Ga., Aug. 4, 1939; s. James Percival and Ethel (Holmes) P.; m. Janet Lewis; children: William Wright, Patricia Monique, Meredith Katherine. BS in Mech. Engring., Ga. Inst. Tech., 1962, MS in Engring. Mechanics, 1964; MBA, Ga. State U., 1973. Engr. Gen. Dynamics Corp., Fort Worth, Tex., 1966-67; engring. project mgr. Lockheed-Ga. Co., Marietta, 1967-71; pres., founder, chief exec. officer Healthdyne, Inc., Marietta, 1971—. Bd. dirs. Atlantic S.E. Airlines, Atlanta, Healthdyne Technologies, Inc., Atlanta, Healthdyne Info. Enterprises, Inc., Marietta, Ga., Matria Healthcare, Inc., Marietta, Logility Corp., Atlanta, Intelligent Sys., Norcross, Ga. Author: Primer on Composite Materials, 1968; patentee in field Chmn. bd. dirs. Sudden Infant Death Syndrome Alliance, Washington, 1986; active nat. adv. coun. Emory U. Med. Sch., Coun. fellows for the Emory, Ga. Tech. Biomed. Tech. Rsch. Ctr.; bd. dirs. Ga. Rsch. Alliance, 1995. 1st lt. U.S. Army, 1964-67. Recipient Humanitarian award La SocieteFrancaise de Bienfaisance, 1981; mem. Tech. Hall of Fame of Ga.; mem. Ga. Tech. Acad. Disting. Alumni, 1994; Internat. Bus. fellow, 1986. Mem. Health Industry Mfrs. Assn., Cobb County C. of C. (bd. dirs. 1980-82), Atlanta C. of C. (bd. dirs. 1997—), Pi Kappa Phi. Republican. Methodist. Avocations: flying, painting, golf, tennis. Office: Healthdyne Inc 1850 Parkway Pl SE Marietta GA 30067-4439

PETITO, MARGARET L., foundation president; b. Dallas, Sept. 28, 1950; d. Jacob Charles and Eileen (Shank) Loehr; m. John Haven Petito, 1978 (div. 1984); children: John Christian Robert, David Nelson. BA, So. Meth. U., 1972; MA, Georgetown U., 2006. Mem. Action/Vista Program U.S. Govt., Middlesex, NY, 1972—74; dir., curator Oliver House Mus., Penn Yan, NY, 1975—77; staff asst. Williams & Jensen, P.C., Washington, 1986—89; dir. fed. rels. Chambers Devel. Co., Inc., 1989—92; dir. fed. affairs DSSI-U.S. Biotech., Washington, 1992—94; cons., dir. pub. affairs Embassy Ecuador, Govt. Ecuador, Washington, 1994—96; prin. Petito & Assocs., Washington, 1994—. Dir. external events Internat. Cancer Alliance, Bethesda, Md., 1996—97, Sch. of Bus., Georgetown U., Washington, 1998—99; pres., exec. dir. Friends of Rule of Law in Ecuador, Inc., 2001—. Spl. legis. advisor Drugwatch Internat., Chgo., 1993—; bd. dirs. Nyumbani Orphanage for Kenyan Children with AIDS, Washington, 1989—99; dir. Marshall Ho. Mus., Lambertville, NJ, 1980—82; founder, co-chair Forum for Environ., Washington, 1989—91; pres. Cultural Partnership of the Ams., Washington, 1999—. Mem.: Tex. State Soc. Roman Catholic. Avocations: squash, needlepoint, fishing. Home and Office: Friends of Rule of Law in Ecuador Inc 6008 34th Pl NW Washington DC 20015-1607 Office Phone: 202-537-1327. Business E-Mail: mlp3@starpower.net.

PETITTI, MICHAEL JOSEPH, JR., lawyer; b. Canton, Ohio, July 25, 1955; s. Michael Joseph and Shirley Darlene Petitti; m. Anita Jean Charley, Aug. 27, 1977; 1 child, Michael Joseph III. BA, Ariz. State U., Tempe, 1982, JD with cum laude, 1987. Bar: Ariz. Supreme Ct. 1987, US Dist. Ct., Dist Ariz., Ariz., US Ct. Appeals, 9th Cir. Atty. Evans, Kitchell & Jenckes, Phoenix, 1987—89, Beus, Gilbert & Morrill, Phoenix, 1989—90, Gomez & Petitti, P.C., 1990. Spkr. in field. Pedrick scholar, 1984, 85, 86. Mem. ABA, State Bar Ariz. (mem. exec. coun. state bar employment and labor law sect. 1997-, sec. 2002-03, budget officer 2003-04, chair elect 2004-05, chair 2005-06, past chair 2006-07), Maricopa County Bar Assn., Nat. Employment Lawyers Assn., Ariz. Employment Lawyers Assn. Democrat. Avocations: reading, running. Office: Gomez & Petitti PC 2525 E Camelback Rd Ste 860 Phoenix AZ 85016 Office Fax: 602-956-9854. Business E-Mail: mjp@gomezlaw.net.

PETKANICS, DONNA M., lawyer; BA, Northwestern U., 1980; JD, U. Calif., Boalt Hall Law Sch., 1985. Staff economist President Carter Administrn., Washington; with Wilson Sonsini Goodrich & Rosati, Palo Alto, Calif., 1985—, assoc. mng. ptnr., 1996—97, co-chmn., nominating com., 1997, 1998, mng. dir. ops., ptnr., mem. exec. mgmt. com. & policy com. Office: Wilson Sonsini Goodrich & Rosati 650 Page Mill Rd Palo Alto CA 94304-1050 Office Phone: 650-493-9300. Office Fax: 650-493-6811. Business E-Mail: dpetkanics@wsgr.com.

PETKOV, PETKO M., geneticist, researcher; s. M. Boev and R. Boeva; m. Stefka B. Petkova; 1 child, Michael P. PhD, Sofia U., Bulgaria. Assoc. rsch. scientist Jackson Lab., Bar Harbor, Maine, 2001—06, rsch. scientist, 2006—. Rsch. grant, NIGMS, 2006—. Mem.: AAAS. Achievements include research in three levels of regulation of mammalian recombination; development of first chromosome-wide recombination hotspot map; discovery of first mammalian gene regulating recombination hotspot placement; research in mouse family tree. Office: Jackson Lab 600 Main St Bar Harbor ME 04609 Business E-Mail: petko.petkov@jax.org.

PETKUN, RICHARD MICHAEL, lawyer; b. Cambridge, Mass., Oct. 20, 1947; s. Bertram Allen and Ruth (Grass) P.; m. Winifred Ann Walker, Dec. 30, 1979; 1 child, Julia Justine. BA cum laude, Harvard Coll., 1969; JD, Harvard Law Sch., 1972. Bar: NY 1974, Colo. 1982. Assoc. Dewey Ballantine, NYC, 1972—77; pvt. practice NYC, 1977—79; tax counsel Union Tex. Petroleum Corp./Allied Chem. Corp., Houston and Morristown (NJ), 1979—81; assoc. Davis, Graham & Stubbs, Denver, 1981-84; v.p. corp. affairs Denver Technol. Ctr., Denver, 1984—87; chief counsel EF Internat., Inc., Denver, 1987—99; exec. v.p. P&O Inc., Denver, 1999—2000; pres. P&O America, Inc., Denver, 2000—01; shareholder Isaacson Rosenbaum, Denver, 2001—03, Greenberg Traurig, LLP, Denver, 2004—. Recipient Best Lawyers in Am., 2007, 2008. Mem. ABA, Colo. Bar Assn., Denver Bar Assn. Office: Greenberg Traurig LLP 1200 17th St Ste 2400 Denver CO 80202 Office Phone: 303-572-6518. Office Fax: 720-904-7618.

PETNO, DOUGLAS B., investment company executive; b. Feb. 7, 1965; Mng. dir., group head energy JPMorgan Chase & Co., NYC, 2005—. Recipient Top Dealmaker, Dealmaker mag., 2006; named one of Top 50 Rainmakers for energy/power, 2007. Mem.: Mat. Petroleum Coun. Office: JPMorgan Chase & Co 1 Chase Manhattan Plaza Fifth Fl New York NY 10081 Office Phone: 212-622-6774. E-mail: douglas.b.petno@jpmorgan.com.

PETO, SIR RICHARD, medical researcher; b. May 14, 1943; s. Leonard Huntley and Carrie Clarinda Peto; m. Sallie Messum, 1970 (dissolved); 2 children; m. Gale Mead (dec. 2001); 2 children. MA in Natural Sci., Trinity Coll.; MSc in Statistics, Imperial Coll., London. Rsch. officer Med. Rsch. Coun., 1967—69, U. Oxford, 1969—72, lectr., 1972—75, reader in cancer studies, 1975—92, founder, co-dir. Clin. Trial Svc. Unit, 1975—, prof. med. statistics and epidemiology, 1992—. Recipient Charles S. Mott prize, GM Cancer Rsch. Found., 2002; co-recipient King Faisal International prize (medicine), King Faisal Found., 2005; knighted for services to epidemiology and cancer prevention, 1999. Fellow: Royal Soc. (Royal medal 2002), Acad. Med. Sciences; mem.: Inst. Medicine (fgn. assoc.). Achievements include research in the causes of cancer in general, the effects of smoking, the establishment of large-scale randomized trials of the treatment of heart disease, stroke, cancer, and a variety of other diseases; introduced combined "meta-analyses" of results from related trials that achieve uniquely reliable assessment of treatment effects. Office: Clin Trial Svc Unit Richard Doll Bldg Old Road Campus Oxford OX3 7LF England Office Phone: 44-1865-743801. Office Fax: 44-1865-743985. Business E-Mail: secretary@ctsu.ox.ac.uk.

PETRACCHI, ENRIQUE SANTIAGO, judge; b. Buenos Aires, Nov. 16, 1935; s. Enrique Carlos and Lilia Raño; children: Florencia, Enrique Juan, María, Francisco. Justice Supreme Ct., Argentina, 1983—89, chief justice, 1989—90, justice, 1990—2003, pres., 2004—07. Fluent in Spanish, English, French and Italian. Office: Corte Suprema de Justicia Talcahuano 550- 4 Piso oficina 4113 1013 Buenos Aires Argentina

PETRAEUS, DAVID HOWELL, career military officer; b. Cornwall, NY, Nov. 7, 1952; s. Sixtus and Miriam Sweet (Howell) Petraeus; m. Hollister Knowlton, July 6, 1974; children: Anne, Stephen. BS, US Mil. Acad., 1974; grad., US Army Command and Gen. Staff Coll., Ft. Leavenworth, Kans., 1983; M in Pub. and Internat. Affairs, Princeton U., 1985, PhD, 1987. Commd. 2nd lt. US Army, 1974, advanced through grades to gen., 2007; platoon leader, adjutant 1-509th Inf. (Airborne), Vicenza, Italy, 1975—79; co. comdr., ops. officer, aide-de-camp 24th Inf. Divsn., Ft. Stewart, Ga., 1979—87; asst. prof. internat. relations US Mil. Acad., West Point, NY, 1985-87; mil. asst. to supreme allied comdr. Europe NATO, Brussels, 1987-88; bn. and brigade ops. officer 3rd infantry divsn. US Army, 1988-89, asst. divsn. comdr. for ops., 82nd Airborne divsn., chief of staff, XVIII Airborne Corps. Ft. Bragg, NC, asst. chief of staff for military ops. Joint HQ Ctr., Allied Command Europe, 2001—02, comdr., 101st Airborne Divsn. Ft. Campbell, Ky., 2002—04, comdr. Multinational Security Transition Commd. Iraq Baghdad, Iraq, 2004—05, comdr. Combined Arms Ctr. Ft. Leavenworth, Kans., 2005—07; comdr. Multi-Nat. Force-Iraq, Baghdad, Iraq, 2007—08, US Ctrl. Command (USCENTCOM), 2008—. Mem. NATO Tng. Mission, Iraq. Author: The American Military and the Lessons of Vietnam, 1987; co-editor: NATO At Forty, 1989; contbr. Strategy, Democracy, and Vietnam, 1987, articles to profl. jours. Decorated DSM US Army, Def. Disting. Svc. medal, Bronze Star with v, Meritorious Svc. medal NATO; recipient Golden award of Iraqi Order of Date Palm, 2005; named one of The World's Most Influential People, TIME mag., 2007, The Global Elite, Newsweek mag., 2008. Mem.: Assn. US Army, Coun. Fgn. Relations, Army-Navy Arlington, Va., Phi Kappa Phi. Presbyterian. Avocations: distance running, writing. Office: US Central Command (USCENTCOM) 7115 S Boundary Blvd MacDill AFB Tampa FL 33621*

PETRAITIS, KAREL COLETTE, lawyer; b. Chgo., Apr. 4, 1945; d. Ferdinand John and Dolores (Karroll) P.; BA, U. Md., 1967, postgrad., 1967-68; JD, George Washington U., 1971. Bar: Md. 1972, U.S. Supreme Ct. 1977. Law clk. Prince George's County Office of Law, Md., 1971-72, atty., 1972-80; real estate agt. Harloff & Perkins, Riverdale, Md., 1978-82; pvt. practice law, College Park, Md., 1980—; past pres., v.p., treas, bd. dirs. Coll. Park Bd. Trade. Youth coord. Agnew for Gov., 1966, Mathias for Senate, 1968, Beall for Senate, 1970; nat. committeewoman Md. Young Reps., 1971-79, dir., 1979-81, legal counsel, 1972-79; mem. bd. trustees Elizabeth Seton H.S., 1991-95. Recipient cert. appreciation Prince George County Circuit Ct., 1979; cert. public service Prince George County, 1980; pres. Friends of Md. Summer Inst. for Creative and Performing Arts, 1983-86, 1997-98, trustee, 1986-2001. Mem. Md. Bar Assn., Prince George County Bar Assn., George Washington Law Alumni Assn. (bd. dirs. 1979-94, sec. 1982-84, pres. Md. chpt. 1985-87), U. Md. Alumni Assn. (pres. young alumni 1978-80, pres. Prince George's 1986-88, 2007—, bd.dirs. 1988-96, treas, 2004-07, mem. arts and humanities bd. 1999-2004, legis. com. advocacy 2003—), Hon. Agr. Alumni, Gridiron Club (membership com.), Terrapin Club (bd. dirs., 2005-), Fastbreakers, Rebounders, FOG Balt. County Rep. Women's Club, Gamma Phi Beta Alumnae (treas. DC 2006—), Sports legend Museum(bd. dir. 2008-) Roman Catholic. Home: 7307 Radcliffe Dr College Park MD 20740-3023 Office: 7100 Baltimore Ave Ste 205 College Park MD 20740 Office Phone: 301-277-1443. Personal E-mail: karelcp@aol.com.

PETRAKIS, HARRY MARK, author; b. St. Louis, June 5, 1923; s. Mark E. and Stella (Christoulakis) P.; m. Diane Perparos, Sept. 30, 1945; children: Mark, John, Dean. Student, U. Ill., Champaign, 1940—41, LHD (hon.), 1971, Gov.'s State U., Chgo., 1980, Hellenic Coll., Brookline, Mass., 1984, Roosevelt U., Chgo., 1987, Am. Coll. Greece, Athens, 2004, Ind. U., Bloomington, 2006. Freelance writer, tchr., lectr.; tchr. workshop classes in novel, short story; McGuffey vis. lectr. Ohio U., Athens, 1971; writer-in-residence Chgo. Pub. Library, 1976-77, Chgo. Bd. Edn., 1978-79; Kazantzakis Prof. San Francisco State U., 1992. Author: Lion at My Heart, 1959, The Odyssey of Kostas Volakis, 1963, Pericles on 31st Street, 1965 (nominated for Nat. Book award), The Founder's Touch: The Life of Paul Galvin of Motorola, 1965, A Dream of Kings, 1966 (Nat. Book award nomination), The Waves of Night, 1969, Stelmark: A Family Recollection, 1970, In the Land of Morning, 1973, The Hour of the Bell, 1976, A Petrakis Reader, 28 Stories, 1978, Nick the Greek, 1979, Days of Vengeance, 1983, Reflections on a Writer's Life and Work, 1983, Collected Stories, 1986, Ghost of the Sun, 1990, Tales of the Heart, 1999, Twilight of the Ice, 2003, The Orchards of Ithaca, 2004, Legends of Glory and Other Stories, 2007, (novel) The Shepherds of Shadows, 2008; writer (films) A Dream of Kings, 1969, Picture Windows, 1995; contbr. short stories to mags. including, Atlantic Monthly, Sat. Eve. Post, Harper's Bazaar, Country Beautiful. (Story included in Prize Stories, also O. Henry Award 1966). Recipient awards Friends of Am. Writers, Friends of Lit., Soc. Midland Authors, Carl Sandburg award, Ellis Island medal of honor, 1995, O'Henry award Mem. Authors Guild, PEN, Writers Guild Am.-West. Address: Dune Acres 80 East Rd Chesterton IN 46304-1035 Personal E-mail: hmp801@comcast.net. *"...The older I become, the more clearly I see that there is a stunning purity in the writing of a book that I cannot achieve in my own life with its frailty and desperation. The work takes over with a life of its own. In those moments, I wouldn't trade writing with all its loneliness and sometimes with its pain, for any other profession in the world.*

PETRAKIS, MYRON TITOS, retired mechanical engineer; b. Chgo., Apr. 6, 1922; s. Titos Myron and Elpis Lagovardos Petrakis; m. Catherine Theresa Rinaldi, Sept. 20, 1952; children: Stephen Paul, Barbara Jean, Mary Ann. BSME, Ill. Inst. Tech., Chgo., 1951. Tool and dye maker Republic Flow Meters Co., Chgo., 1941—44; project engr. Gen. Am. Plastics, East Chicago, Ind., 1951—53; mgr. plastic molding Fed. Tool Corp., Lincolnwood, Ill., 1953—67; sales engr. Application Engring. Corp., Elk Grove, Ill., 1967—69; pres. B/P Plastic Equipment Co., Rosemont, Ill., 1969—91. Civil def. dir. Village of Norridge, Ill., 1964—66; commn. sec. Bd. of Fire and Police Commn., Norridge, 1959—; publicist Norridge H.S. Problems Com., 1957—59; historian Village of Norridge, 1996—. With USN, 1944—46. Recipient Sheriff's Sr. Medal of Honor, Cook County Sheriff, Chgo., 2003. Mem.: Soc. Plastic Engrs. (dir., chair edn. 1970—73), K.C. (4th deg.). Achievements include design of accessories for plastic injection molding. Avocations: photography, woodworking, stained glass, fishing. Home: 4437 N Ottawa Ave Norridge IL 60706 Office: Norridge Board of Fire and Police Commrs 4000 N Olcott Ave Norridge IL 60706

PETRAKIS, NICHOLAS LOUIS, epidemiologist, medical researcher, educator; b. San Francisco, Feb. 6, 1922; s. Louis Nicholas and Stamatina (Boosalis) P.; m. Patricia Elizabeth Kelly, June 24, 1947; children: Steven John, Susan Lynn, Sandra Kay. BA, Augustana Coll., 1943; BS in Medicine, U. S.D., 1944; MD, Washington U., St. Louis, 1946. Intern Mpls. Gen. Hosp., 1946-47; physician, researcher U.S. Naval Radiol. Def. Lab., San Francisco, 1947-49; resident physician Mpls. Gen. Hosp., 1949-50; sr. asst. surgeon Nat. Cancer Inst., USPHS, San Francisco, 1950-54; asst. research physician Cancer Research Inst., U. Calif., San Francisco, 1954-56; asst. prof. preventive medicine U. Calif. Sch. Medicine, San Francisco, 1956-60, assoc. prof., 1960-66, prof., 1966-91, chmn. dept. epidemiology and internat. health, 1978-88, prof. emeritus, 1991—; prof. epidemiology U. Calif. Sch. Pub. Health, Berkeley, 1981-91. Assoc. dir. G.W. Hooper Edn., U. Calif., San Francisco, 1970-74, acting dir., 1974-77, chmn. dept. epidemiology and internat. health, 1979-89; co-dir. Breast Screening Ctr. of No. Calif., Oakland, 1976-81; cons. Breast Cancer Task Force, Nat. Cancer Inst., Bethesda, Md., 1972-76; chmn. Biometry & Epidemiology Contract Rev. Com., Bethesda, 1977-81; bd. sci. counselors, divsn. cancer etiology Nat. Cancer Inst., Bethesda, 1982-86; scientific adv. com. Calif. State Tobacco-Related Disease Rsch. Program, 1991-93; cons. U. Crete Sch. Medicine, Heraklion, Greece, 1984. Contbr. articles to profl. jours. Eleanor Roosevelt Internat. Cancer fellow Am. Cancer Soc., Comitato Reserche Nucleari, Cassacia, Italy, 1962; U.S. Pub. Health Service Spl. fellow Galton Lab., U. London, 1969-70; recipient Alumni Achievement award Augustana Coll., Sioux Falls, S.D., 1979, Axion award Hellenic-Am. Profl. Soc. of Calif., San Francisco, 1984, Lewis C. Robbins award Soc. for Prospective Medicine, Indpls., 1985, Otto W. Sartorius, MD, award from Susan Love MD Breast Cancer Found., 2001. Mem. Am. Soc. Preventive Oncology (founding, pres. 1984-85, Disting. Achievement award 1992), Soc. for Prospective Medicine (founding), Am. Assn. Cancer Rsch., Am. Epidemiol. Soc., Am. Soc. Clin. Investigation, Am. Bd. Preventive Medicine (cert.). Achievements include research in breast cancer, med. oncology and hematology. Office: U Calif Sch Medicine Dept Epidemiology & Biostats Box 0560 MU420W San Francisco CA 94143-0001 Home: 1450 Post St Apt 415 San Francisco CA 94109

PETRANOVICH, DANILO, political science professor; s. Mirjana and Dusan Petranovic. BA, Harvard Coll., Cambridge, 2000; PhD, Yale U., New Haven, 2007. Rsch. assoc. Nat. Rev., NYC, 2007—08; lectr. Yale U. Polit. Sci., New Haven, 2007—08; vis. prof. Duke U. Polit. Sci., Durham, NC, 2008—.

PETRANY, STEPHEN MICHAEL, medical educator, director; s. Ronald Martin and Grace Petrany; m. Nancy Ann Baumgardner, Dec. 9, 1978; children: Elizabeth Ann Quinn, Catherine Eileen, Mary Christine, Stephen John, Michael Joseph, Nicholas Andrew. MD, Georgetwon U., Washington, DC, 1980. Diplomate Am. Bd. Family Medicine, 1980. Prof. Marshall U. Joan C. Edwards Sch. Medicine, Huntington, W.Va., 1989—; family medicine residency dir. Marshall U. Family Medicine Residency Program, 1989—2004; med. dir. Ebenezer Med. Outreach Ctr., 2003—; pres., bd. dirs. Ebenezer Med. Outreach, Inc., Huntington, W.Va., 2008—. Pres. Ebenezer Med. Outreach, Huntington, 2008—. Avocations: guitar, films, painting. Office: 1600 Med Ctr Dr Huntington Huntington WV 25701 Office Fax: 304-691-1153. Business E-Mail: petrany@marshall.edu.

PETRASCHECK, MICHAEL, biologist, researcher; b. Zurich, Switzerland, Aug. 21, 1971; s. Armin Wilhelm and Eva Theresa Petrascheck; m. Ekaterina Nikolajevna Kanakina, Dec. 1, 2003; children: Pavel, Maria. Grad. student, Inst. Molecular Biology, Zurich, Switzerland, 1998—2001. Scientist Fred Hutchinson Cancer Rsch. Ctr., Seattle, 2002—09; asst. prof. Scripps Rsch. Inst., La Jolla, 2009—. Achievements include discovery of lifespan increasing antidepressants. Avocations: guitar, composing.

PETRASH, JEFFREY MICHAEL, lawyer; b. Cleve., Dec. 14, 1948; s. Robert Anthony and Naomi Marjorie (Close) P.; 1 child, Michael Stewart. AB, U. Mich., 1969, JD, 1973. Bar: Mich. 1974, D.C. 1975, Md. 1997. Assoc. Dickinson, Wright, McKean, Cudlip & Moon, Detroit, 1973-75, Hamel, Park, McCabe & Saunders, Washington, 1975-78; from assoc. to ptnr. Dickinson, Wright, Washington, 1978-99; sr. counsel Am. Gas Assn., Washington, 2000—. Served to capt. US Army, 1969—77. Mem. Soc. Barristers. Episcopalian. Avocation: sailing. Home: 6606 Hillandale Rd Bethesda MD 20815-6406 Office: 400 N Capitol St NW Washington DC 20001-1511 Office Phone: 202-824-7231. E-mail: jpetrash@aga.org.

PETRELLI, HEATHER MW, academic administrator, director; b. Pensacola, Fla., Aug. 3, 1972; d. Leroy Wende; m. Jonathan H. Petrelli, Sept. 28, 2003. MA, Towson U., Md., 1998. Pres. Coll. Edge, LLC, Bradenton, Fla., 2004—; dir. admissions, student svcs., assessment & faculty devel. LECOM, Bradenton, 2007—. Asst. dean student affairs U. Md., Sch. Pharmacy, Balt., 2005—07. Avocations: travel, dance, pottery, cooking, reading. Business E-Mail: info@collegeedge.net.

PETRELLI, THOMAS J., lawyer; s. Thomas J. and Kathleen M. Petrelli. MS in Environ. Law, Vt. Law Sch., S. Rolyalton, 1998—2001, JD, 1998—2001; LLM in Trial Advocacy, Temple U., Phila., 2005—06. Bar: Pa. 2002, NJ 2003, DC 2004, US Ct. Appeals (3d cir.), Pa. 2002, US Ct. Appeals (3d cir.), NJ 2004. Assoc. Obermayer, Rebmann, Maxwell & Hippel, LLP, Phila., 2001—02, Cooper Levenson, Atlantic City, 2003—04; solo practioner Law Offices Thomas J. Petrelli, Jr., Phila., 2004; prin. Petrelli Law, PC, 2004—. Mem.: Phila. Bar Assn., Bar Assn. DC, NJ Bar Assn., Pa. Bar Assn. Office: Thomas Petrelli 1616 Walnut St Ste 1910 Philadelphia PA 19103-5319 Office Fax: 215-966-8655. Business E-Mail: info@petrellilaw.com.

PETREN, CAROL ANN, lawyer, insurance company executive; m. Floyd Clarke. Grad. magna cum laude, Boston Coll.; JD, LLM, U. Mo. Sch. Law. Fed. prosecutor Jackson County, Kansas City, Mo.; asst. US atty. We. Dist. Mo.; counsel US Ho. Reps. Com. on Stds. of Ofcl. Conduct; mng. ptnr. Wilson, Elser, Moskowitz, Edelman & Dicker, Washington, 1994; dep. gen. counsel Sears, Roebuck and Co.; sr. v.p., dep. gen. counsel MCI, 2003—06; exec. v.p., gen. counsel CIGNA Corp., 2006—. Office: CIGNA Corp Two Liberty Pl 1601 Chestnut St Philadelphia PA 19192-1550 Office Phone: 215-761-1000.*

PETREQUIN, HARRY JOSEPH, JR., foreign service officer; b. Ste. Genevieve, Mo., July 1, 1929; s. Harry Joseph and Crescentia Ellen (Bechter) P.; m. Katharine McDonnell Drouin, Oct. 7, 1980; children: John Andrew, Marc Christopher, Paul Nicholas. AB, Westminster Coll., 1950; B of Fgn. Trade, Am. Grad. Sch. Internat. Mgmt., 1954; postgrad., Johns Hopkins U., 1960; MA, Tufts U., 1970. Joined U.S. Fgn. Svc., 1955; assigned AID and predecessor agys., 1955—; dep. dir. S.E. Asia Regional Econ. Devel. Office, Thailand, 1970-74; U.S. coord. Senegal River Basin Authority, Dakar, 1975-76; dir. ASEAN and South Pacific Affairs, 1977-80; dir. program devel. and evaluation staff Bur. Internat. Orgn. Affairs State Dept., 1980-81; dep. dir. AID Mission, Morocco, 1981-85; coord. AID Sr. Mgmt. Course, 1985-86, Indsl. Coll. of the Armed Forces, 1986-87; faculty dept. nat. security policy Nat. War Coll., Washington, 1987-89; internat. devel. cons. Black Mountain, NC, 1989—. Adj. prof. polit. sci. Warren Wilson Coll., Swannanoa, NC, 1993-94; faculty U. NC Coll. Srs., 1995—. Lt. (j.g.) USCGR, 1951-53, Comdr. Ready Res., 1973. Recipient Superior Honor award AID, 1979, State Dept. Superior Honor award, 1981, Comdrs. award for Civilian Svc., Dept. of the Army, 1989. Mem. Soc. Internt. Devel., World Federalist Assn. (nat. bd. dirs.), Am. Fgn. Svc. Assn., UN Assn. U.S., Acad. Polit. Sci., Cousteau Soc., Common Cause, Inst. Noetic Scis., World Future Soc., Amnesty Internat., Coast Guard Combat Vets Assn., Greenpeace, Vets. for Peace, The Land Inst., Phi Alpha Theta. Office Phone: 828-669-8404.

PETREY, SANDY, educator; b. Alexander City, Ala., Aug. 29, 1941; s. Donald Sanford and Gary Horne Petrey; m. Nancy K. Miller, June 24, 1983; children: Charlotte McRae, Donald Sanford. BA, Emory U., Decatur, Ga., 1962; PhD, Yale U., New Haven, 1966. Prof. SUNY, Stony Brook, 1980—. Vis. prof. Harvard U., Cambridge, Mass. Contbr. literary papers; translator: (novel) Emile Zola, THE SIN OF FATHER MOURET, Jules Valles, THE INSURRECTIONIST. Fellow, NEH, 1972—73. Mem.: MLA, AATF. Home: 6 Conscience Cir East Setauket NY 11733

PETRI, MICHELLE, medical educator; d. William Arthur and Ann Emmons Petri; m. Daniel Ware Goldman, Aug. 22, 1976; children: Megan Goldman-Petri, Jason Goldman-Petri. BA in Biochemistry, Harvard Coll., Boston, 1976, MD, 1980; MPH, Johns Hopkins U., Balt., 1990. Lic. in internal medicine Am. Bd. Internal Medicine, 1983, in allergy and immunology Am. Bd. Allergy and Immunology, 1985, rheumatologist Am. Bd. Internal Medicine, 1986. Intern & resident Mass. Gen. Hosp., 1980—83; prof. Johns Hopkins U. Sch. Medicine, Balt., 1987—. Fellow: Am. Coll. Rheumatology (Marion W. Ropes Meml. Lect. award 1997, Dubois Meml. award 1993); mem.: Lupus Found. Am. (bd. dirs. 2006—07). Avocations: travel, archaeology. Office: Johns Hopkins University 1830 E Monument St Ste 7500 Baltimore MD 21205 Office Fax: 410-614-0498. Business E-Mail: mpetri@jhmi.edu.

PETRI, PETER ALEXANDER, economist, educator, director; b. Budapest, Hungary, Oct. 17, 1946; came to U.S., 1959; s. George and Margaret (Fejer) P.; m. Jean H. Lawrence, June 19, 1976; children: Philip, Nicholas. BA, Harvard U., 1968, PhD, 1976. Prof. of Econ. Brandeis U., Waltham, Mass., 1974—; dean Grad. Sch. Internat. Econs. and Fin., Waltham, Mass., 1994—; dir. Lemberg Prog. in Internat. Econ. & Fin., Brandeis U., Waltham, 1986-94; Carl Shapiro prof. of internat. fin. Brandeis U., Waltham, 1989—. Fulbright rsch. scholar Keio U., Tokyo, 1991; cons. World Bank, Washington, OECD, Paris. Author: The Future of the World Economy, 1977, Modeling Japanese-American Trade, 1984, East Asia's Trade and Investment, 1994; editor: Wassily Leontief, 1982, The Economics of the Dollar Cycle, 1990, Regional Co-operation and Asian Recovery, 2000, ASEAN Econ. Bulletin, Jour. of Asian Econs., Singapore Econ. Rev. Grantee Study of Japanese Trade, U.S. State Dept., 1980, Study of U.S. Social Security, Social Security Adminstrn., 1982-83, Internat. Bus. Edn., U.S. Dept. Edn., 1989, 92, 94, Ctr. for Global Partnership, 1995—, NSF, 1995; Econ. Policy fellow Brookings Inst., 1979. Mem. Am. Econ. Assn., Acad. Internat. Bus.

PETRI, THOMAS EVERT, United States Representative from Wisconsin; b. Marinette, Wis., May 28, 1940; s. Robert and Marian (Humleker) Petri; m. Anne Neal, Mar. 26, 1983; 1 child, Alexandra. BA in Govt., Harvard U., 1962, JD, 1965. Bar: Wis. 1965. Law clk. to US Judge James Doyle US Dist. Ct. (we. dist.) Wis., Madison, 1965-66; vol. Peace Corps, Somalia, 1966-67; aide White House, Washington, 1969-70; dir. crime and drug studies Pres.'s Nat. Adv. Coun. on Exec. Orgn., 1969; lawyer pvt. practice, Fond du Lac, Wis., 1970-79; mem. Wis. State Senate, Madison, 1973-79, US Congress from 6th Wis. dist., 1979—, sr. mem. edn. and labor com., transp. and infrastructure com., ranking mem. on aviation subcom. Editor: Nat. Indsl. Policy: Solution or Illusion, 1984. Republican. Lutheran. Avocations: reading, swimming, hiking, bicycling, skiing. Office: US House Reps 2462 Rayburn House Office Bldg Washington DC 20515-0001 Office Phone: 202-225-2476.*

PETRIASHVILI, MARINA, physician; arrived in US, 1997; d. Linette Tsertsvadze. MD, Tbilisi State Med. U., Georgia, 1983—89; student, NYU Sch. Medicine. Diplomate Tbilisi State Med. U., 1989, Ednl. Commn. for Foreign Med. Graduates Ednl. Commn. For Fgn. Med. Graduates, 1998, cert. Anesthesiology Residency NY U. Sch. of Medicine/NY, 2004, Fellowship in Cardiac Anesthesiology NY U. Sch. of Medicine, 2005, Am. Bd. of Anesthesiology Written Test Am. Bd. of Anesthesiology, 2004. Attending physician Rehab. Ctr. Kartli, Tbilisi, Georgia, 1990—93, Dimitrov Hosp. and Clinics Found., Tbilisi, Georgia, 1994—97; residency in surgery Albert Einstein Coll. of Medicine, Bronx, 2000—01; residency in anesthesiology NY U. Med. Ctr., NY, 2001—04; fellowship in cardiac anesthesiology NY U. Sch. of Medicine, NY, 2004—05; with Woodhull Med. and Mental Health Ctr., Bklyn. Active mem. Am. Soc. of Anesthesiologists, 2001; mem. Soc. of Cardiovasc. Anesthesiologists, 2004, Am. Soc. of Echocardiography, NY State Soc. of Anestheiologists, NY, 2001. Recipient Honors Diploma, Tbilisi State Med. U. Mem.: AMA (corr.). Personal E-mail: petrim02@hotmail.com.

PETRICK, ALFRED, JR., economist, educator; b. Mt. Vernon, NY, Dec. 30, 1926; s. Alfred and Ruth (Updike) P.; m. Ruth Goodridge, Jan. 2, 1956; children: Elizabeth, Andrew Wayne. BS, BA, Columbia U., 1952, MS, 1962; MBA, Denver U., 1966; PhD, U. Colo., 1969. Registered profl. engr., Colo. Sales engr. Ingersoll Rand Co., NYC, 1953-54; project engr. U.S. AEC, Grand Junction, Colo., 1954-57; mining engr. Reynolds Metals Co., Bauxite, Ark., 1957-61, Guyana, 1957-61; mineral economist U.S. Bur. Mines, Denver, 1963-70; Coulter prof. Colo. Sch. Mines, Golden, 1970-84, emeritus prof., 1984—; dir. Petrick Assocs., Evergreen, Colo., 1974—2004; ret., 2004. Author: Economics International Development, 1977, Economics of Minerals, 1980, Preparacion y Evaluacion, 1982. Mem. com. tech. aspects strategic materials Nat. Acad. Sci., Washington, 1973-76, mem. com. surface mining and reclamation, 1979. Served with USAF, 1945-47, PTO. Fulbright research scholar U. Otago, Dunedin, New Zealand, 1986; recipient Edn. award Instituto Para Functionarios De Las Industrias Minera y Siderurgica, Mexico City, 1981; recipient Service award Office Tech. Assessment, U.S. Congress, 1981. Mem. AIME (chmn. council econs. 1977-78, Henry Krumb lectr. 1986, service award), Profl. Engrs. Colo. Presbyterian. Home: 5544 S Hatch Dr Evergreen CO 80439-7233 Office: Colo Sch Mines Golden CO 80401 Personal E-mail: peta33@comcast.net.

PETRICK, ERNEST NICHOLAS, mechanical engineer, researcher; b. Pa., Apr. 9, 1922; s. Aurelius and Anna (Kaschak) P.; m. Magdalene Simcoe, June 13, 1946; children: Deborah Petrick Healey, Katherine, Denise, Victoria Petrick Kropp. BS in Mech. Enging, Carnegie Inst. Tech., 1943; MS, Purdue U., 1948, PhD, 1955. Registered profl. engr., Mich. Faculty Purdue U., 1946-53; dir. heat transfer research Curtiss-Wright Corp., Woodridge, NJ, 1953-56; chief advanced propulson systems Curtiss-Wright Research divsn., Quehanna, Pa., 1957-60; chief research engr. Kelsey-Hayes Co., Detroit, 1960-65; sr. exec. US Civil Svc.; chief scientist, tech. dir. U.S. Army Tank-Automotive Command, Warren, Mich., 1965-82; chief scientist, dir. engring. labs. Gen. Dynamics, 1982-87; engring. cons., 1987—; panel mem. combat vehicles NATO, 1973-82; mem. adv. bd. on basic combustion research NSF, 1973; chmn. advanced transp. systems com. White House Energy Project, 1973; mem. adv. com. NSF-RANN research program Drexel U. Coll. Engring., 1976-78; mem. Army Sci. Bd., 1983-89; cons. Air Force Studies Bd. NRC, 1991-93, cons. Def. Sci. Bd., 1994-95; cons. NAS, 1997—99, US Army Tank Automotive Command, 2001—03, Bd. Army Sci. and Tech. Rev. NAS Naval Studies Bd., 2003; adj. prof. engring. Wayne State U., Detroit, 1972-82, U. Mich., Ann Arbor, 1982-83; con. Coun. Environ. Quality, White House, 1973. Contbr. articles on transp., ground vehicles, propulsion and project mgmt. to profl. jours. Lt., chief engr. destroyer USNR, 1942—46, WWII. Recipient certificate of achievement U.S. Army, 1967, Outstanding Performance awards, 1970, 71, 76, 82, Outstanding Mech. Engring. award Purdue U., 1991; named Disting. Engring. Alumnus Purdue U., 1966. Mem. Soc. Automotive Engrs. (nat. dir. 1978-80), Am. Def. Preparedness Assn. (chmn. land warfare survivability divsn. 1990-95, Silver medal 1992, Recognition award 1992), Assn. U.S. Army, Sigma Xi, Pi Tau Sigma. Home: 1540 Stonehaven Rd Ann Arbor MI 48104-4150 Office: ENP Cons 1540 Stonehaven Rd Ann Arbor MI 48104

PETRICK, MICHAEL JOSEPH, journalism educator; b. Antigo, Wis., Sept. 6, 1942; BS, U. Wis., Milw., 1965, MS, 1967; PhD, U. Wis., Madison, 1970. News editor Milw. South Times Star, 1966-67; disting. teaching fellow U. Wis., Madison, 1969-70; from asst. to assoc. prof. U. Md., College Park, 1970-78; copy editor Evening Star, Washington, 1974-75; chairperson dept. journalism Ctrl. Mich. U., Mt. Pleasant, 1978-84, prof., 1984-2000, prof. emeritus, 2000—. Writing and editing coach Ctrl. Mich. Newspapers, 1984-85; writing and reporting coach Greenville (Mich.) Daily News, 1997-99; chair bd. in control of student media Ctrl. Mich. U., 1997-99 Co-author: Using the Mass Media, 1975; contbr. articles to profl. jours Named to Ctrl. Mich. Jour. Hall of Fame, 2006. Mem. Md.-Del.-D.C. Press Assn. (chmn. freedom of info. com. 1972-73), Soc. Profl. Journalists (campus chpt. adviser 1970-99), Nat. Coun. Editl. Writers, Assn. for Edn. in Journalism and Mass Communication Office: PO Box 6 Mount Pleasant MI 48804-0006 Business E-Mail: michael.petrick@cmich.edu.

PETRICOFF, M. HOWARD, lawyer, educator; b. Cin., Dec. 22, 1949; s. Herman and Neoma P.; m. Hanna Sue, Aug. 11, 1974; children: Nicholas, Eve. BS, Am. U., 1967-71; JD, U. Cin., 1971-74; M in Pub. Adminstrn., Harvard U., 1980-81. Bar: Ohio, U.S. Ct. Appeals (D.C. cir.) 1977, U.S. Ct. Appeals (10th cir.) 1985, U.S. Ct. Appeals (6th cir.) 1989, U.S. Supreme Ct. 1989. Asst. city law dir. City of Toledo (Ohio), 1975-77; asst. atty. gen. Ohio Atty. Gen. Office, Columbus, 1977-82; ptnr. Vorys, Sater, Seymour & Pease, Columbus, 1982—. Adj. prof. law Capital U. Law Sch., Columbus, 1991—. Contbr. articles to profl. jours. Reginald Heber Smith Found. fellow Washnigton, 1974-75. Mem. Ohio Bar Assn., Columbus Bar Assn., Ohio Oil and Gas Assn. Office: Vorys Sater Seymour & Pease PO Box 1008 52 E Gay St Columbus OH 43215-3161 Office Phone: 614-464-6400. Business E-Mail: mhpetricoff@ussp.com.

PETRIDES, GEORGE ATHAN, ecologist, educator; b. NYC, Aug. 1, 1916; s. George Athan and Grace Emeline (Ladd) P.; m. Miriam Clarissa Pasma, Nov. 30, 1940; children: George H., Olivia L., Lisa B. BS, George Washington U., 1938; MS, Cornell U., 1940; PhD, Ohio State U., 1948; postdoctoral fellow, U. Ga., 1963-64. Naturalist Nat. Park Service, Washington and Yosemite, Calif., 1938-43, Glacier Nat. Park, Mont., 1947, Mt. McKinley Nat. Park, Alaska, 1959; game technician W.Va. Conservation Commn., Charleston, 1941; instr. Am. U., 1942-43, Ohio State U., 1946-48; leader Tex. Coop. Wildlife Unit; assoc. prof. wildlife mgmt. Tex. A. and M. Coll., 1948-50; assoc. prof. wildlife mgmt., zool. and African studies Mich. State U., 1950-58, prof., 1958—; research prof. U. Pretoria, S. Africa, 1965; vis. prof. U. Kiel, Germany, 1967; vis. prof. wildlife mgmt. Kanha Nat. Park, India, 1983; del. sci. confs. Warsaw, 1960, Nairobi and Salisbury, 1963, Sao Paulo, Aberdeen, 1965, Lucerne, 1966, Varanasi, India, Nairobi, 1967, Oxford, Eng., Paris, 1968, Durban, 1971, Mexico City, 1971, 73, Banff, 1972, Nairobi, Moscow, The Hague, 1974, Johannesburg, 1977, Sydney, 1978, Kuala Lumpur, 1979, Cairns, Australia, Mogadishu, Somalia, Peshawar, Pakistan, 1980. Participant NSF Expdn., Antarctic, 1972, FAO mission to, Afghanistan, 1972, World Bank mission to, Malaysia, 1975 Author: Field Guide to Trees and Shrubs, 1958, 2d edit., 1972, Field Guide to Eastern Trees, 1988, 98, Field Guide to Western Trees, 1992, 98, First Guide to Trees, 1993, Trees of the California Sierra Nevada, 1996, Trees of the Pacific Northwest, 1998, Trees of the Rocky Mountains and Intermountain West, 2000, Trees of the American Southwest, 2000; editor wildlife mgmt. terrestrial sect. Biol. Abstracts, 1947-72; contbr. articles to biol. publs. Served to lt. USNR, 1943-46. Fulbright research awards in E. Africa Nat. Parks Kenya, 1953-54; Fulbright research awards in E. Africa Nat. Parks Kenya, Uganda, 1956-57; N.Y. Zool. Soc. grantee Ethiopia, Sudan, 1957; N.Y. Zool. Soc. grantee Thailand, 1977; Mich. State U. grantee Nigeria, 1962; Mich. State U. grantee Zambia, 1966; Mich. State U. grantee Kenya, 1969; Mich. State U. grantee Africa, 1970, 71, 73, 81; Mich. State U. grantee Greece, 1974, 83; Mich. State U. grantee Iran, 1974; Mich. State U. grantee Botswana, 1977; Mich. State U. grantee Papua New Guinea, Thailand, 1979; Iran Dept. Environment grantee, 1977; Smithsonian Instn. grantee India and Nepal, 1967, 68, 75, 77, 83, 85; World Wildlife Fund grantee W. Africa, 1968 Mem. Am. Ornithologists Union, Am. Soc. Mammalogists, Wildlife Soc. (exec. sec. 1953), Wilderness Soc., Am. Comm. Internat. Wildlife Protection, Ecol. Soc., Fauna Preservation Soc., E. African Wildlife Soc., Internat. Union Conservation Nature, Zool. Soc. So. Africa, Sigma Xi. Presbyterian. Home: 4895 Barton Rd Williamston MI 48895-9305 Office: Mich State U Dept Botany East Lansing MI 48824 E-mail: petrides@msu.edu.

PETRIE, BRUCE INGLIS, lawyer; b. Washington, Nov. 8, 1926; s. Robert Inglis and Marion (Douglas) P.; m. Beverly Ann Stevens, Nov. 3, 1950 (dec. Oct. 1993); children: Laurie Ann Roche, Bruce Inglis, Karen Elizabeth Medsger. BBA, U. Cin., 1948, JD, 1950. Bar: Ohio 1950, U.S. Dist. Ct. (so. dist.) Ohio 1951, U.S. Ct. Appeals (6th cir.) 1960, U.S. Supreme Ct. Assoc. Kunkel & Kunkel, Cin., 1950-51, Graydon, Head & Ritchey, 1951-57, ptnr., 1957—. Exec. prodr. (sch. video) Classical Quest, 2000; author: How To Get the Most Out of Your Lawyer, 2002, Political patragr in ohio:governors judicial appointees, 2008; contbr. articles to legal jours. Pres. Charter Rsch. Inst., 2000—03; bd. edn. Indian Hill Exempted Village Sch. Dist., 1965—67, pres., 1967; adv. bd. William A. Mitchell Ctr., 1969—86; Green Areas adv. com. Village of Indian Hill, Ohio, 1969—80, chmn., 1976—80; charter mem. Ohio Ethics Com., 1974—75; founder Parents as Tchrs. Metro Housing Authority Commn., 1991—; a prin. advocate merit selection judges Ohio; trustee, mem. bd. Seven Hills Neighborhood Houses' Inst. for Learning in Retirement; organizer Late Gt. Lakes Book Distbn. project, global vol. tchr. China, 2003—07; elder, trustee, deacon Knox Presbyn. Ch.; bd. dirs. Charter Com. Greater Cin., 1952—, Hamilton County Good Govt. League, Murray Seasongood Good Govt. Fund, 1975—, chmn., 1989—; bd. dirs. Nat. Civic League, Cin. Vol. Lawyers for Poor Found., Linton Music Series, Amernet Chamber Music Soc.; co-founder Sta. WGUC-FM; mem. WGUC-FM Cmty. Bd., 1974—, chmn., 1974—76. Recipient Pres.'s award U. Cin., 1976, Disting. Alumnus award, 1995. Fellow: Am. Bar Found.; mem.: ABA, Ohio State Bar Assn. Found. (Outstanding Rsch. in Law and Govt. award 1986, Charles P. Taft Civic Gumption award 1988, Ohio Bar medal 1988), Am. Law Inst., Nat. Civic League (coun. 1984—, Disting. Citizen award 1985), Am. Judicature Soc. (dir., Herbert Lincoln Harley award 1973), Cin. Bar Assn. (pres. 1981, Trustee's award 2000), Ohio Bar Assn., Cin. Country Club, Univ. Club, Cincinnatus Assn., Lit. Club, Order of Coif. Avocations: tennis, squash, woodworking, writing, horticulture, music. Home: 2787 Walsh Rd Cincinnati OH 45208-3428 Office: Graydon Head & Ritchey 1900 Fifth 3d Ctr 511 Walnut St Ste 1900 Cincinnati OH 45202-3157

PETRIE, DONALD JOSEPH, banker; b. NYC, Sept. 2, 1921; s. John and Elizabeth (Thomson) P.; m. Jane Adams, Aug. 27, 1949; children: R. Scott, Anne, Elizabeth, Douglas, Susan. BBA, Manhattan Coll., 1950. Personnel mgr. Otis Elevator Co., NYC, 1951-59; personnel dir. Brown Bros. Harriman & Co., NYC, 1959-68; exec. v.p. U.S. Trust Co., NYC, 1968-79; sr. v.p. Marine Midland Bank, NYC, 1979-86, Drake Beam Morin Inc., NYC, 1986-90; chmn., chief exec. officer Webster Corp., NYC, 1990—. Lectr. Baruch Sch. Bus., Coll. City N.Y., 1955-58; pres., chmn. exec. and fin. coms., dir. Webster Apts., N.Y.C., 1973—2009, pres. emeritus 2009-; adj. prof. mgmt. Hofstra U., Hempstead, N.Y., 1986-93. Author: Explaining Pay Policy, 1969, Handling Employee Questions About Pay, 1976. Capt. USAAF, 1942-46. Mem. N.Y.C. Partnership and C. of C. (chmn. mgmt. edn. and adv. com. 1964-98). Home: 11 Fairview Ave Great Neck NY 11023-1462 Office: 419 W 34th St New York NY 10001-1596 Office Phone: 212-967-9000.

PETRIE, GEOFFREY MICHAEL, professional sports team executive, retired professional basketball player; b. Darby, Pa., Apr. 17, 1948; m. Anne-Marie Petrie; children: Mike, Anne-Marie, Susanne. Grad., Princeton U., NJ, 1970. Player Portland Trail Blazers, 1970—76, exec., 1976—89, sr. v.p. ops., 1989—93; v.p. basketball ops. Sacramento Kings, 1994—2006, pres. basketball ops., 2006—. Named NBA Rookie of Yr., 1971, NBA Exec. of Yr., The Sporting News, 1999, 2001; named to NBA All-Star Team, 1971, 74, NBA All-Rookie Team, 1971. Avocations: golf, tennis, guitar. Office: Sacramento Kings One Sports Pky Sacramento CA 95834*

PETRIE, GREGORY STEVEN, lawyer; b. Seattle, Feb. 25, 1951; s. George C. and Pauline P.; m. Margaret Fuhrman, Oct. 6, 1979; children: Kathryn Jean, Thomas George. AB in Polit. Sci and Econs., UCLA, 1973; JD, Boston U., 1976. Bar: Wash. 1976, U.S. Dist. Ct. (we. dist.) Wash. 1976. Adminstr. Action/Peace Corps, Washington, 1973, Fed. Power Commn., Washington, 1974; assoc. Oles Morrison et al, Seattle, 1976-80; ptnr. Schwabe Williamson Ferguson & Burdell, Seattle, 1981-94; mng. shareholder Krutch Lindell Bingham Jones & Petrie, Seattle, 1994—. Mem. Seattle-King County Bar Assn., Profl. Liability Architects and Engrs., Wash. Athletic Club. Avocations: woodworking, skiing. Office: Krutch Lindell Bingham Jones & Petrie 1420 Fifth Ave Ste 3150 Seattle WA 98101 Home Phone: 206-632-4555; Office Phone: 206-682-1505. Business E-Mail: gsp@krutchlindell.com.

PETRIE, THOMAS A., investment company executive; BS, US Mil. Acad., West Point, NY; MS in Bus. Adminstrn., Boston U.; PhD in Enging. (hon.), Colo. Sch. Mines, 2005. Chartered fin. analyst. Mng. dir., sr. oil analyst The First Boston Corp.; co-founder Petrie Parkman & Co., Denver, Houston; vice chmn., mem. exec. client coverage group Merrill Lynch & Co., Inc., 2006—. Adv. bd., oil and gas acctg. Securities and Exch. Commn.; contbr., analyst Barron's, Wall St. Week with Louis Rukeyser, The News Hour with Jim Lehrer, CNBC, Fox News; advisor

Kingdom of Saudi Arabia, State of Alaska, US Dept. Energy. Trustee Assn. of Grads., the US Mil. Acad. at West Point, Denver Art Mus., The Colorado Conservation Trust; nat. adv. bd. C.M. Russell Mus.; bd. dirs. The Gettysburg Found. Mem.: Nat. Assn. Securities Dealers (past chmn., dir., dist. 3 bus. conduct com.), Nat. Assn. Petroleum Investment Analysts (past pres., bd. dirs.). Office: Merrill Lynch & Co Inc Global Hdq 4 World Fin Ctr 250 Vesey St New York NY 10080 Office Phone: 212-449-1000.

PETRIE, WILLIAM MARSHALL, psychiatrist; b. Louisville, Oct. 19, 1946; s. Garner McReynolds and Claire (Samuels) P.; children: Christopher W., Ellen M., Shelley M.; m. Lori L. Molchin, Oct. 1, 1994; 1 child, Halle C. BA, Vanderbilt U., 1968, MD, 1972. Research psychiatrist NIMH, Rockville, Md., 1975-77; asst. prof. dept. psychiatry Vanderbilt Med. Ctr., Nashville, 1977-81, assoc. prof., 1981-82, assoc. clin. prof., 1982-87, clin. prof., 1992—; pvt. practice psychiatry Psychiat. Cons., P.C., Nashville, 1982—, pres., 1996—. Bd. dirs Psychiat. Solutions, Inc.; clin. instr. Georgetown U. Med. Ctr., 1975—77; cons. psychopharmacology rsch. br. NIMH, 1977—80; rschr. in geriatric psychopharmacology; med. dir. memory Study Ctr., 1987—; chmn. of psychiatry Parthenon Pavilion, 1994—96; bd. trustees Centennial Mutual Ctr., 1994—2000, vice-chmn. bd. trustees, 1998—2000; pres. Columbia Psychiat. Care Network, 1997—98, Psychiat. Cons., PC, 1999—2005; med. dir. Parthenon Pavilion, 2007—, Rolling Hills Hosp., 2009—. Mem. editl. bd. Gen. Hosp. Psychiatry, 1995—, Audio Digest Psychiatry, 1996-99; contbr. articles to profl. jours.; chpts. to books. Fellow Am. Psychiat. Assn. (disting. fellow, pres. mid. Tenn. dist. br. 1986-87); mem. AMA, Tenn. Med. Assn., Am. Assn. Geriatric Psychiatrists, Am. Coll. Psychiatrists, Tenn. Psychiat. Assn. (pres. 1999-2000). Democrat. Methodist. Office: Psychiat Cons PC 2014 Quail Hollow Cir Franklin TN 37067 Home Phone: 615-373-5033. Business E-Mail: wpetrie@psychiatricconsultants.com.

PETRIK, MICHAEL THOMAS, lawyer; b. Chgo., Jan. 13, 1957; s. Thomas J. and Bette J. (Sarich) P.; m. Susan Renée Prince, June 2, 1979; children: Michael Ray, Stephanie Renée. BS in Bus. Mgmt., Ea. Ill. U., 1979, BA in Econs., 1979; JD, Duke U., 1983. Bar: Ga. 1983, US Tax Ct. 1985. Assoc. Alston & Bird LLP, Atlanta, 1983—90, ptnr., 1991—, leader state and local tax group. Instr. constnl. law and tax, Atlanta Law Sch., 1984-92, state and local tax law, Ga. State U., 1992-98; tech. cons. Sales and Use Tax Alert, 1991-92. Edit. adv. bd.: State Income Tax Alert, 1991—, Ga. corr. State Tax Notes, Arlington, Va., 1990-97, interstate tax rep., 1996—, Corp. Bus. Taxation Monthly, 1999-; contbr. articles to profl. jours. Mem. emergency intervention svc. coun. United Way, Atlanta, 1984-90, bd. dirs. 1995-04; mem. Met. Atlanta Mentors' Coun., 1992-95, One-to-one Atlanta Leadership Coun., 1993-96; St. Joseph's Mercy Found. Leadership Coun., 2005-; bd. adv. United Way 211, 1992-03, chair; bd. advisors St. Pius Catholic HS, 2004-; Big Bros./Big Sisters, Atlanta, 2004-; United Way Pub. Policy Com.,2006-; United Way Cmty. Impact Coun., Atlanta, 2006-; active Vol. DeKalb, Atlanta, 1984-86; bd. dirs. Arrive Alive, Inc., Atlanta, 1987-91; bd. dirs. Duke Law Alumni Assn., 2005-; Delta Sigma Phi Found., 2006-; bd. trustees Brother Rice HS, Chgo., 2006-; trustee Lawyers Comm. Civil Rights, 2001-, United Way Pub. Policy Com., 2007-; bd. of trustees Vasser Woolley Found., 2002-, Leadership Atlanta, 2001-, chair, 2004-05; adv. bd. The Salvation Army of Metro Atlanta, 2007-, Ga. C. of C. Tax Com., 2008-. Mem. KC, Ga. Bar Assn. (state coun. 1983—), Atlanta Bar Assn., Federalist Soc., St. Thomas More Soc., Serra Internat., Commerce Club, Delta Mu Delta, Omicron Delta Epsilon, Ga. C. of C. Tax Cmty. Roman Catholic. Avocations: religion, literature, music. Office: Alston & Bird LLP 1201 W Peachtree St One Atlantic Ctr Atlanta GA 30309-3424 Office Phone: 404-881-7479. Office Fax: 404-253-8784. Business E-Mail: mike.petrik@alston.com.

PETRILLO, LEONARD PHILIP, lawyer, retired investment company executive; b. Toronto, Ont., Can., June 20, 1941; s. Philip and Bernice Petrillo; m. Linda née Hodgson; children: Larissa, Matthew, Stefanie, Ann-Marie, Karen. BSc, U. Toronto, 1964; LLB, Osgoode Hall Law Sch., Toronto, 1967. Bar: Ont. 1969. Ptnr. Robinson & Petrillo, 1969-79; corp. counsel Seel Enterprises Ltd., 1979-81; gen. counsel Toronto Stock Exch., 1981—84, v.p., gen. counsel, corp. sec., sec. to bd. dirs., 1984—2003; dir. Educators Group Fin. Inc., 2004—. E-mail: lppetnillo@rogers.com.

PETRINO, BOBBY, college football coach; b. Lewistown, Mont., Mar. 10, 1961; m. Becky Schaff; children: Kelsey, Nick, Bobby, Katie. BS in Math and Phys. Edn., Carroll U., 1983. Grad. asst. Carroll U., 1983, offensive coord., 1985—86; grad. asst. Weber State U., 1984, wide receiver, tight ends coach, 1987—88; quarterbacks coach Idaho U., 1989, offensive coord., 1990—91; quarterbacks coach Ariz. State U., 1992—93, Jacksonville Jaguars, 1999—2000, offensive coord., 2001, Auburn U., 2002, U. Nev., 1994, Utah State U., 1995—97, U. Louisville, 1998, head coach, 2003—06, Atlanta Falcons, Flowery Branch, Ga., 2007, U. Ark. Razorbacks, 2008—. Office: U Ark Razorbacks Broyles Athletic Ctr PO Box 7777 Fayetteville AR 72702

PETRINOVICH, LEWIS FRANKLIN, psychologist, educator; b. Wallace, Idaho, June 12, 1930; s. John F. and Ollie (Steward) Petrinovich. BS, U. Idaho, 1952; PhD, U. Calif., Berkeley, 1962. Asst. prof. San Francisco State Coll., 1957—63; from assoc. to prof. SUNY, Stony Brook, 1963-68; prof. U. Calif., Riverside, 1968-91, chmn. psychology, 1968-71, 86-89, prof. emeritus, 1991—2009. Bd. dirs. Eastman Med. Products, Cymed Corp. Author: Understanding Research in Social Sciences, 1975, Introduction to Statistics, 1976, Human Evolution, Reproduction and Morality, 1995, Living and Dying Well, 1996, Darwinian Dominion: Animal Welfare and Human Interests, 1999, The Cannibal Within, 2000; editor: Behavioral Development, 1981, Habituation, Sensitization and Behavior, 1984; cons. editor Behavioral and Neural Biology, 1972-90, Jour. Physiol. and Comparative Psychology, 1980-82, Jour. Comparative Psychology, 1983-90. Bd. dirs. Friends of Big Band Jazz, 2001—07. Fellow APA, Am. Psychol. Soc., Calif. Acad. Scis., Human Behavior and Evolution Soc., Western Psychol. Assn.; mem. Am. Ornithol. Union, Animal Behavior Soc., Sigma Xi Home: 415 Boynton Ave Berkeley CA 94707-1701 Office: U Calif Riverside Psychology Dept Riverside CA 92521-0001 Personal E-mail: lpetrin@aol.com.

PETRIS, ELLI, bankruptcy case manager; b. Oceanside, NY, July 29, 1982; d. George and Anastasia Petris. BA in History and Polit. Sci., Molloy Coll., Rockville Ctr., NY, 2004; MA in Govt. and Politics, St. John's U., Jamaica, NY, 2006. Cert.: St. John's U. (in internat. law, diplomacy and pub. adminstrn.) 2006, Hofstra U., Hempstead, NY (in paralegal studies) 2007. Bankruptcy case mgr. Epiq Bankruptcy Solutions, NYC, 2008—. Mem.: ASPA, Acad. Polit. Sci., Internat. Polit. Sci. Assn., Am. Polit. Sci. Assn., Am. Hist. Assn., Phi Alpha Theta. Home: 2438 Atlantic Blvd Wantagh NY 11793

PETRO, ALLISON N., language educator; d. Stedman B. Noble and Phyllis N. Smith, Paul G. Smith (Stepfather); m. Nicolai Petro, Oct. 13, 1985; children: Aleksandr N., Andrei N. BA, Harvard U., Cambridge, Mass., 1978—83; MA, U. RI, Kinston, 1993—95. Coord. ita program U. RI, 1995—2001, dir. English lang. studies, 2003—05; fulbright sr. lectr. Novgorod State U., Russia, 2001—02; instr. English Yale U., New Haven, 2002—03; asst. prof. English CC RI, Newport, 2005—. Cofounder New Eng. ITA Network, Storrs, Conn., 1998—2001. Contbr. chapters to books, articles to profl. jours. Recipient Hope & Heritage award, U. RI, 1999, 2000, 2004, 2006; fellow Fulbright Sr. lectureship, J. William. Fulbright Fgn. Scholarship Bd., 2001—02. Mem.: Internat. Tchg. Asst. (chair interest sect. 2004—07), TESOL (Profl. Devel. award 1998). Independent. Russian Orthodox. Avocation: travel. Office: CC RI One John H Chafee Blvd Newport RI 02840 Personal E-mail: anpetro@gmail.com.

PETRO, NICOLAI, political science professor, consultant; m. Allison Petro. PhD, U. Va., Charlottesville, 1984; PhD (hon.), Novgorod State U., Russia. Prof. U. RI, Kingston, 1991—. Greek Orthodox. Office: Univ RI Washburn Hall Kingston RI 02881 Office Fax: 208-693-5200. Personal E-mail: nnpetro@gmail.com.

PETROCELLI, DANIEL M., lawyer; b. East Orange, NJ; m. Alison Petrocelli; 4 children. BS cum laude, U. Calif., Los Angeles, 1976; JD magna cum laude, Southwestern U., 1980. Bar: Calif. 1981, US Ct. Appeals (9th cir.) 1981, US Dist. Ct. (ctrl. and no. districts.) Calif. 1981, US Supreme Ct. 1981, US Dist. Ct. Colo. 1998. Ptnr. (Century City office) O'Melveny & Myers LLP, LA, mem. policy com. Mem. The American Lawyer's Litigation Dept. of Yr.; nat. commentator on trials and other legal issues; spkr. to bus. groups, bar and judges associations, and citizen groups. Mem. Southwestern U. Law Review, 1978—79, editor-in-chief, 1979—80; author: Triumph of Justice: The Final Judgement on the Simpson Saga, 1998, Outside the Courtroom, Beyond a Reasonable Doubt, 2006; contbr. articles to profl. jours. Named Litigator of Yr., Century City Bar Assn., honoree, Columbus Citizens Found., Alumnus of Yr., Southwestern U., Trial Lawyer of Yr., Malibu Bar Assn., San Diego Trial Lawyers Assn., So. Calif. Super Lawyer, LA Mag.; named one of Los Angeles' Top 50 Litigators, LA Bus. Jour., Lawyers of Yr., Calif. Lawyer. Mem.: Assn. of Bus. Trial Lawyers, State Bar Calif. (antitrust and unfair competition sects.), ABA (litigation sect. and corp. counsel com.), LA County Bar (antitrust and unfair competition sects.). Office: O'Melveny & Myers LLP 1999 Avenue of Stars 7th Fl Los Angeles CA 90067-6035 Office Phone: 310-246-6850. Office Fax: 310-246-6779. Business E-Mail: dpetrocelli@omm.com.*

PETRONE, WILLIAM FRANCIS, pediatrician, microbiologist, corporate executive; b. Bklyn., Sept. 12, 1949; s. Arthur Carmen and Helen (Kenny) P.; m. Kathleen Anne Baron, Aug. 25, 1979; children; William Gaetano, Katherine Bridget, Jason Daniel. BA, U. Conn., 1972; MS, U. Mass., 1974; PhD, U. R.I., 1978; MD, U. South Ala., 1984. Diplomate Am. Bd. Pediatrics, Pediatric Emergency Medicine, Gen. Pediatrics. Rsch. assoc. Coll. Medicine U. South Ala., Mobile, 1978-80; resident in pediat. Orlando Regional Med. Ctr., Fla., 1984—85, W.Va. Univ. Med. Ctr., 1985—87; emergency rm. physician, pediat. emergency svcs. Mercy Hosp., Springfield, Mass., 1987—2006, Harrington Meml. Hosp., Southbridge, Mass., 2006—. Med. Simulation Software, Cmty. Pediat. Assoc. Contbr. articles on inflamation and white blood cell function to sci. jours. Fellow Am. Acad. Pediat., Am. Coll. Emergency Physicians; mem. AAAS, AMA, N.Y. Acad. Scis., Sigma Xi. Roman Catholic. Office: Mercy Hosp Emergency Unit PO Box 9012 Springfield MA 01102-9012

PETROPOULOS, DIMITRIOS, oncologist, hematologist, educator; s. Antonios Petropoulos and Maria Petropoulou; m. Sophia Tsakiri. MD, Nat. & Capodistrian U. Med. Sch., Athens, 1986; BS summa cum laude, U. Athens Med. Sch., 1986. Diplomate in pediat. Am. Bd. Pediat., 1994, in pediat. hematology, oncology Am. Bd. Pediat. Hematology, Oncology Subspecialty Bd., 1996. Attending physician Aghia Sophia Children's Hosp., Athens, 1997—2002; asst. prof. Md. Anderson Cancer Ctr., Houston, 2002—, staff physician, pediat., 2002—. Mem.: Am. Soc. Hematology, Am. Soc. Blood and Marrow Transplantation. Office: Md Anderson Cancer Ctr 1515 Holcombe Blvd Box 87 Houston TX 77030 Office Fax: 713-792-0608. Business E-Mail: dpetro@mdanderson.org.

PETROPOULOS, JONATHAN GEORGE, history professor; b. LA, Jan. 10, 1961; s. George Jonathan and Maureen Laura Petropoulos; m. Kimberly Ann Shiring, May 27, 1994; children: Astrid Sophia, Isabel Stella. PhD, Harvard U., Cambridge, Mass., 1990. John V. Croul prof. European history Claremont McKenna Coll., Calif., 1999—. Rsch. dir. art and cultural property Presdl. Commn. Holocaust Assets US, Washington, 1998—2000. Author: (books) Art as Politics in the Third Reich, 1996, Faustian Bargain: The Art World in Nazi Germany, 2000. Fellow, Alexander von Humboldt Found., 1993, Fulbright, 1999, German Academic Exch. Svc., 2000. Achievements include research in history of Nazi art looting and restitution. Office: Claremont McKenna Coll 850 Columbia Ave Claremont CA 91711 Business E-Mail: jpetropoulos@cmc.edu.

PETROPOULOS, KOSTAS, music educator; BA in Classical Studies, Villanova U., Pa., 2004, MA in Classical Studies, 2006. Pres. Kopos Prodns., Mt. Laurel, NJ, 2003—; adj. prof. classical studies Villanova U., 2006—. Composer: (album) Infusion, Fantasmagoria, The Return of Anteros. Recipient Howard A. Grelis, O.S.A. award, Villanova U., 2004. Mem.: Nat. Honor Soc., Phi Kappa Phi. Office: Villanova Univ 800 Lancaster Ave Villanova PA 19085 Business E-Mail: kostas.petropoulos@villanova.edu.

PETROPOULOS, MICHALIS, research scientist; s. Athanasios Petropoulos and Evaggelia Petropoulou; m. Mirjana Andjelkovic, May 25, 2008. Diploma, Tech. U. Crete, Chania, Greece, 1998; MS, U. Calif. San Diego, La Jolla, 2000, PhD, 2005. Sr. software engr. Enosys Software Inc., San Diego, 2000—01; intern. Bell Labs., Murray Hill, NJ, 2002, Microsoft Rsch., Redmond, Wash., 2003, IBM Almaden Rsch. Ctr., San Jose, Calif., 2004; asst. prof. U. Buffalo, 2006—08. Cons. App2you, Inc., La Jolla, 2007. Contbr. articles to publs. Mem.: Assn. Computing Machinery. Achievements include patents for flexible format query processing system for web browsers. Office: Univ Buffalo SUNY 201 Bell Hall Buffalo NY 14260 Business E-Mail: mpetropo@cse.buffalo.edu.

PETROSIAN, VAHÉ, astrophysicist, educator; b. Arak, Iran, Sept. 13, 1938; came to U.S., 1958; s. Armenak and Chnarik (Beglarian) P.; m. Maude Denney Voegeli, Aug. 21, 1965 (div. 1992); children: Gabrielle Elane, Meline Chnar; m. Patricia Evans Wipfler, 2005 B.E.E., Cornell U., 1962, MS, 1963, PhD, 1967. Research fellow Calif. Inst. Tech., Pasadena, Calif., 1967-69; vis. scientist Inst. Theoretical Astronomy, Cambridge, Eng., summer 1969; asst.prof. Stanford U., (Calif.), 1969-71, assoc. prof., 1972-79, prof., 1980—, chmn. astronomy program. Vis. cons. Kitt Peak Nat. Obs., Tucson Alfred P. Sloan fellow, 1972-74; NASA grantee, 1970—; NSF grantee, 1980—. Fellow Royal Astron. Soc.; mem. Internat. Astron. Union, Am. Astron. Soc., U.S. Volleyball Assn. Achievements include the co-discovery of giant luminous arcs and gravitational theory in clusters of galaxies. Home: 4114 Willmar Dr Palo Alto CA 94306-3835 Office: Stanford U Astronomy Program Varian 310 Stanford CA 94305-4060 Office Phone: 650-723-1435.

PETROSKEY, DALE ALAN, professional sports team executive, former museum director; b. Detroit, Aug. 17, 1955; s. Eugene Louis and Marie Therese (Boutain) P.; m. Ann Holiday Grover; children: Kathleen Mills, Frank, Claire. BA, Mich. State U., 1978. Asst. press sec. Mich. House Reps., Washington, 1978-81; press sec. to congressman Mark Siljander US House Reps., Washington, 1981, adminstrv. asst. to Bill Goodling, 1981-85; asst. press sec. White House, Washington, 1985-87; asst. sec. pub. affairs Dept. Transp., Washington, 1987-88; sr. v.p. Nat. Geographic Soc., 1988-99; pres., COO Nat. Baseball Hall of Fame & Mus., Cooperstown, NY, 1999—2008; exec. v.p. mktg. and cmty. devel. Tex. Rangers, 2008—. Founder Mayo Smith Soc., Mich. and Washington, 1983. Republican. Roman Catholic. Avocations: tennis, baseball, reading, travel. Office: Tex Rangers Rangers Ballpark in Arlington 1000 Ballpark Way Arlington TX 76011

PETROSKI, HENRY, engineering educator, writer; b. NYC, Feb. 6, 1942; s. Henry and Victoria Petroski; m. Catherine, July 15, 1966; children: Karen, Stephen. B Mech. Engring., Manhattan Coll., Riverdale, NY, 1963, DP (hon.), 2003; MS, U. Ill., 1964, PhD, 1968; DSc (hon.), Clarkson U., Potsdam, NY, 1990; DHL (hon.), Trinity Coll., Hartford, Conn., 1997; DSc (hon.), Valparaiso U., Ind., 1999. Registered profl. engr., Tex.; chartered engr., Inst. of Engrs. of Ireland. Instr. U. Ill., Urbana, 1965-68; asst. prof. U. Tex., Austin, 1968-74; engr. Argonne Nat. Lab., Ill., 1975-80; assoc. prof. civil engring. Duke U., Durham, NC, 1980-87, prof., 1987-93, Aleksandar S. Vesic prof., 1993—, prof. history, 1995—, chmn. dept. civil and environ. engring., 1991-2000, dir. grad. studies, 1981-86. Author: To Engineer is Human, 1985, Beyond Engineering, 1986, The Pencil, 1990, The Evolution of Useful Things, 1992, Design Paradigms, 1994 (Best Book award in engring., Am. Assn. U. Presses, 1994), Engineers of Dreams, 1995, Invention by Design, 1996, Remaking the World, 1997, The Book on the Bookshelf, 1999, Paperboy, 2002, Small Things Considered, 2003, Pushing the Limits, 2004, Success Through Failure, 2006, The Toothpick, 2007, (documentary) To Engineer is Human, 1987; columnist: Am. Scientist, 1991—, ASEE Prism, 2000—. Fellow NEH, 1987-88, Nat. Humanities Ctr., 1987-88, Guggenheim fellow, 1990-91; recipient Outstanding Engring. Grad. award Manhattan Coll., 1992, Alumni award for disting. svc. Coll. Engring. U. Ill. at Urbana-Champaign, 1994, Washington award Western Soc. Engrs., 2006, Disting. Svc. award Engring. Alumni Assn. Duke U., 2007. Fellow ASME (Ralph Coats Roe medal 1991), Am. Acad. Arts and Sci., Am. Philos. Soc., Inst. Engrs. Ireland, NAE, Soc. History Tech., The Moles (hon.), Sigma Xi, Tau Beta Pi; mem. ASCE (disting. mem., Civil Engring. History and Heritage award 1993). Office: Duke U Sch Engring PO Box 90287 Durham NC 27708-0287 Office Phone: 919-660-5203. Business E-Mail: petroski@duke.edu.

PETROSKY, MICHELE MARIE, school librarian; b. Honesdale, Pa., Mar. 15, 1968; d. Eugene and Carolyn Forbes; m. John Joseph Petrosky, June 21, 1997; 1 child, Victoria Elizabeth. BSc in Edn., Millersville U., Pa., 1990; MEd, Mansfield U., Pa., 2003. Exec. sec. LA Bank, Lake Ariel, Pa., 1990—91; sch. libr. & info. technologist Western Wayne Sch. Dist., South Canaan, Pa., 1991—. Catechist Parish St. Thomas More, St Mary, Lake Ariel, 1990—. Mem.: Pa. Sch. Librs. Assn., Pi Lamda Theta. Home: 308 J&J Rd Moscow PA 18444 Office: Western Wayne Sch Dist 1970B Easton Turnpike Lake Ariel PA 18436 Personal E-mail: chelesfaeriedust@aol.com. Business E-Mail: mpetrosky@westernwayne.org.

PETROSKY, TOMIO YAMAKOSHI, research scientist; b. Tokyo, Mar. 30, 1947; s. Joseph Petrosky and Shima Yamakoshi; m. Misako Yamakoshi Ochi, May 4, 1975; children: Keiko Yamakoshi, Emiko Yamakoshi. PhD, Tokyo U. Sci., 1979. Rsch. scientist Ilya Prigogine Ctr. Studies Statis. Mechanics and Complex Sys., U. Tex., Austin, 1980—92, sr. rsch. scientist, 1992—2006, Ctr. Quantum Complex Sys., U. Tex., 2006—. Cons. Internat. Solvay Inst. Physics and Chemistry, Brussels, 1992—2003; vis. prof. Nat. Inst. Fusion Sci., Toki, Gifu, Japan, 2005—06; invited fgn. scholar Inst. Indsl. Sci., U. Tokyo, 2006, Yukawa Inst. Theoretical Physics, Kyoto U., 2008; guest prof. Osaka Prefecture U., Sakai, Japan, 2007—08. Recipient Métropole award, 10th Internat. Sovlay Conf. Chemistry, Brussels, 1995, Peter the Gt. medal, Russian Acad. Natural Scis., 2000; Rsch. grant, Dept. Energy, 1991—2006. Mem.: Am. Physics Soc., European Acad. Arts, Scis. and Humanities (Paris). Avocations: hiking, kayaking. Home: 8503 Bisbee Ct Austin TX 78745 Office: Univ Tex Dept Physics 1 Universy Sta C1609 Austin TX 78712 Business E-Mail: petrosky@physics.utexas.edu.

PETROVIC, BOJAN, nuclear engineer, educator; b. Zagreb, Croatia, 1955; arrived in U.S., 1991; s. Gajo and Asja Petrovic; m. Senka Petrovic, 1976; children: Nada, Sonja. BSc in Theoretical Math., U. Zagreb, Croatia, 1979; MSc in Nuc. Engring., Pa. State U., U. Park, 1987, PhD in Nuc. Engring., 1995. Rsch. staff Rudjer Boskovic Inst., Zagreb, Croatia, 1979—91; rsch. asst. Pa. State U., U. Pk., 1992—95, rsch. faculty, 1995—99; sr. scientist Westinghouse Electric Co., Pitts., 1999—2004, prin. scientist, 2004—05, fellow scientist, 2005—07; prof. Ga. Inst. Tech., Atlanta, 2007—. Participant expert/specialist confs. Internat. Atomic Energy Agy., Vienna, 1988—; assoc. dir. Penn State Transport Theory Group, U. Pk., Pa., 1995—99; cons. in field, 1997—99, 2007—; chair tech. program com. Internat. Conf. Advances in Nuc. Fuel Mgmt. III, Hilton Head, SC, 2003, ANS Ann. Meeting, Atlanta, 2009; author-presenter internat. confs. and symposia; guest editor Nuclear Technology, 2005; reviewer profl. jours. and confs., 1996—. Mem. editl. adv. bd.: Nuc. Tech., 2006—. Fellow, Internat. Atomic Energy Agy., 1986—87. Mem.: ASME (session organizer and chair 2000—06), ASTM (mem. sci./tech. program com. 1996—), Am. Nuc. Soc. (mem. 19.10 stds. com. 1993—, reviewer 1996—, mem.exec. com. reactor physics divsn.), Am. Soc. Engring. Edn. (co-recipient Best Paper Reactor Physics Divsn. 1993, 2008, co-recipient Best Paper Math. and Computation Divsn. 1995, co-recipient George Washington Signature award 2006). Office: Ga Inst Tech George Woodruff Sch 771 Ferst Dr Atlanta GA 30332-0405

PETROVIC, BOJAN D, diagnostic radiologist; s. Dragan P and Vera M Petrovic; m. Polina V Vinnik, June 11, 2004. MD, U. Ill., Chicago, 2004. Resident physician Northwestern U. Dept. Radiology, Chicago, Ill., 2005—. Mem.: Alpha Omega Alpha. Avocations: swimming, travel, films.

PETROVIC, KIMBERLY ANN, nursing researcher, educator; d. Joseph Felix and Janet Marie Petrovic. B in Biology, Wheaton Coll., Ill., 1994; M in Sociology, N.Mex. State U., Las Cruces, 1998; MSN, Vanderbilt U., Nashville, 2000; postgrad., U. Conn., Storrs, 2003—. RN Oreg., cert. gerontological nurse practitioner, Oreg. Grad. student rschr. Oreg. Health and Scis. U., Portland, 2000—02; unit mgr., supr. geriatrics Crestview, Portland, 2002—03; supr., weekend mgr. Harborside Healthcare, West Hartford, Conn., 2003—. Program dir. Ctr. on Aging and Human Devel. U. Conn., Storrs, 2003—05, instr. gerontology dept. human devel. and family studies, 2004—, instr., faculty mem. Sch.

Nursing, 2005—; rsch. asst. Ctr. for Devel. Disabilities U. Conn. Health Ctr., Farmington, 2003—05; geriatrics rschr. Hartford Hosp., Conn., 2004—, rsch. mentor geriatric nursing, 2005—; presenter in field. Author: Nursing Care Management of Older Adults with HIV/AIDS and Chronic Depression, 2006; co-author (with others): Physician Attitudes and Practices on Providing Care To Individuals with Intellectual Disabilities: An Exploratory Study, 2004, Complementary and Alternative Medicine for Older Adults with Intellectual Disabilities, 2004, Cautious Optimism and the Care of Older Adults with Disabilities, 2004; co-author: Respite Care Manual, 2005, Adverse Events Associated with the Presence of Delirium in Hospitalized Older Adults, 2007, Medical Conditions and Medication Use in Adults with Down Syndrome: A descriptive Analysis, 2007; guest editor: Jour. Conn. State Med. Soc., 2004, reviewer: N.C.L.E.X. (Nursing) Questions, 2005—. Recipient Nat. Rsch. Svc. award in geriatric nursing, NIH, 2000—02, Shelia Packard Nursing Rsch. award, 2006; named to, Conn. Geriatric Edn. Consortium; rsch. fellow, U. Conn. Dept. Human Devel. and Family Studies, 2006, Pauline Toner grantee, U. Conn. Sch. Nursing, 2006. Mem.: Conn. Geriatrics Soc., Nat. Coun. on Family Rels., Gerontol. Soc. Am. (campus rep. U. Conn. 2003—04), Am. Geriatrics Soc., Sigma Theta Tau. Avocations: running, pilates, travel, windsurfing, writing. Office: U Conn Sch Nursing Dept Human Devel and Family Studies Storrs Mansfield CT 06269

PETROVICH, ALISA VLADIMIRA, historian, educator; b. Midland, Mich., Mar. 18, 1961; d. Vladimir and Mildred (Desnica) P. BA in English, U. Houston-Ctrl., 1985; DDS, U. Tex., Houston, 1989; MA in History, U. Tex., 1992, PhD in History, 1997. Prof. history Brazosport Coll., Lack Jackson, Tex., 1993—, U. Houston-Ctrl., 1997, U. Houston-Clear Lake, 1997—. Presenter in field. Contbr. articles to profl. jours. Mary Miller scholar, 1995, 96, C.W. Moores fellow, 1996-96. Mem. French Colonial Hist. Assn., Am. Hist. Soc., Am. Soc. for Ethnohistory (travel grantee 1993), S.E. Social Sci. Soc., East Tex. Hist. Soc., Phi Alpha Theta. Avocations: foreign travel and archival research, opera, animal rights, charities. Home: 128 Flag Dr W Lake Jackson TX 77566-6008 Office: U Houston-Clear Lake 2700 Bay Area Blvd Houston TX 77058-1002

PETROW, GEORGE J., lawyer; b. 1953; BA cum laude, U. Neb., Lincoln, 1976; JD, U. Utah, 1979. Bar: Calif. 1979, Utah 1980, Conn. 1983, NY 1988. Law clk. Hon. Bruce S. Jenkins, US Dist. Ct., Dist. of Utah, 1980—81; ptnr., securitization and structured fin. Sidley Austin LLP, NYC, 1997—, co-mng. ptnr. NYC office, mem. mgmt. and exec. coms. Exec. editor Utah Law Rev., 1978—79. Mem.: ABA. Office: Sidley Austin LLP 787 Seventh Ave New York NY 10019 Office Phone: 212-839-5300. Office Fax: 212-839-5599. Business E-Mail: gpetrow@sidley.com.

PETROWSKI, JOSEPH H., oil industry executive; BA in Econ. and Govt., Harvard Univ., 1976. Former pres., CEO Louis Dreyfus Energy Co. No. Am.; former exec. pres. Duke Louis Dreyfus; former pres., CEO Consolidated Natural Gas Energy Svcs.; mng. dir. JHP Assoc., LLP; pres., CEO Gulf Oil Partnership, Newton, Mass., 2005—. Contbr. articles to numerous profl. jours. Office: Gulf Oil Partnership Ste 300 275 Washington St Newton MA 02458-1646

PETRU, SUZANNE MITTON, retired health care finance executive; b. Shawano, Wis., Sept. 26, 1947; d. William Wallace and Gertrude Priscilla Mitton; m. W. James Petru, Jan. 2, 1987. BSBA, Northwestern U., 1970, MBA, 1971. CPA, Ill., Wis. Life Fellow Am. Coll. Healthcare Execs. Sr. acct. Arthur Andersen & Co., Chgo., 1971-77; v.p. fin. Thorek Hosp. and Med. Ctr., Chgo., 1977-82; sec./treas. La Grange (Ill.) Meml. Health Sys., 1982-85; v.p. fin. La Grange Meml. Hosp., 1982-85; audit prin. Deloitte & Touche (formerly Touche Ross & Co.), Chgo., 1985-88; sr. v.p. fin., treas. SSM Health Care Sys., St. Louis, 1988-95; pres. healthcare divsn. Am. Home Assurance Co. (subs. Am. Internat. Group, Inc.), 1995-96; v.p., CFO, treas. Group Health Plan (subs. Coventry Corp.), 1996-98; v.p. Petru Enterprises, Petru Internat., 1998—; sr. v.p. fin., CFO Rockford (Ill.) Health Sys., 2000—05; ret., 2005. Mem. investment com. Sisters of Charity Healthcare Sys., Cin., 1993-96, mem. fin. com., 1994-96; mem. assoc. bd. La Grange Meml. Hosp., 1988-95; advisor Jr. Achievement, 1971-76. Fellow Healthcare Fin. Mgmt. Assn. (bd. dirs. 1989-91, principles and practices bd. 1992-95, nat. matrix 1985-86, 88-89, pres., pres.-elect, sec., bd. First Ill. chpt. 1979-86, compliance officers forum adv. coun. 1998—, Follmer Bronze award 1982, Reeves Silver award 1985, Muncie Gold award 1988, Alice V. Runyan chpt. 1988); mem. Fin. Execs. Inst., Country Club at Legends (adv. bd. 1991-93), St. Louis Club (house com. 1991-95). Republican. Presbyterian. Avocations: golf, travel. Personal E-mail: spetru@quixnet.net.

PETRUNGER, DENNIS KEITH, school system administrator, educator; s. James and Alice Petrunger; m. Veronica Campos. Bachelor, Edinboro U., Pa., 1975. Tchr. Gen. Mclane Sch. Dist., Edinboro, 1975—86; adminstr. Palm Beach County Sch. Bd., West Palm Beach, 1986—. Personal E-mail: samuraiden@aol.com.

PETRUS, SALLY A., elementary school educator; b. Parma, Ohio, Sept. 20, 1965; d. Salvatore Charles Scherma and Carmie Lizzini-Scherma; m. Ronald M. Petrus, Oct. 13, 1990; children: triplets, Arianne Lee, Brianne Lynn, Carlianne Marie. BFA, Ohio U., Athens, 1987; MEd, Baldwin Wallace Coll., Berea, Ohio, 1991. Tchr. Parma City Sch. Dist., 1989—. Advisor student coun., Parma, 2004—, h.s. cheerleading, 1991—98. Recipient Cleve. Crystal Apple award, Cleve. Plain Dealer, 2001. Mem.: PTA (assoc.), Parma Edn. Assn. (assoc.), Nat. Tchrs. Assn. (assoc.). Home: 14572 Walking Stick Way Strongsville OH 44136 Office: Parma City Sch Dist 5210 Loya Pky Parma OH 44134 Personal E-mail: sallypabc@aol.com.

PETRUSA, JOSHUA H., librarian; b. Joliet, Ill., 1978; s. John Petrusa and Terre Houte; m. Leila Breton; children: Julieta, Marco. MLIS, U. Ill., Champaign; BA, DePaul U., Chgo. Collection devel. asst. DePaul U., Chgo., 2005—07; electronic resources libr. Norwich U., Northfield, Vt. Mem.: ALA. Avocation: music. Office: Norwich Univ 23 Harmon Dr Northfield VT 05663 Business E-Mail: jpetrusa@norwich.edu.

PETRUSKA, PAUL ERIC, lawyer; b. Topeka, Kans., Dec. 12, 1969; s. Paul Joseph and Margaret Rose Petruska; m. Laura Allison Petruska; children: Kathryn, Grant. BA, St. Louis U., Mo., 1992, JD, 1995. Atty Brown & James, St. Louis, 1995, Brasher Law Firm, St. Louis, 1996—2001, Williams Venker & Sanders, 2001—. Tax asst. Preparers Assn., St. Louis, 1997—2002; young leaders Bd. Wyman, St. Louis, 2007—. Mem.: Mo. Bar, Bar Assn. Met., NARTC. Office: Williams Venker & Sanders LLC 100 N Broadway 21st floor Saint Louis MO 63102 Home Phone: 314-984-0682; Office Phone: 314-345-5007. Office Fax: 314-345-5055. Business E-Mail: ppetruska@wvslaw.com.

PETRUSKA, STEVEN C., construction executive; Grad. in Acctg., Ctrl. Mich. U., Mt. Pleasant, 1981. V.p. fin. South Tex. divsn. Pulte Homes Inc., 1984, pres. Las Vegas divsn., pres. SW region, area pres. Ariz. and Nev. ops., exec. v.p., COO Bloomfield Hills, Mich., 2004—. Dow Corning Exec.-in-Residence Ctrl. Mich. U., 2004—05. Office: Pulte Homes Inc 100 Bloomfield Hills Pky Ste 300 Bloomfield Hills MI 48304-2946

PETRUZZELLI, JULIE A., lawyer; b. Glen Ridge, NJ, Apr. 18, 1957; BS in Chemistry/Biochemistry, Brown Univ., 1979; JD, Univ. Va., 1982. Bar: NY 1983, DC 1989, US Patent & Trademark Office. Ptnr. Venable LLP, Washington. Mem.: ABA, NY Bar Assn., Women's Bar Assn. DC, NY Patent, Trademark, and Copyright Law Assn., Am. Intellectual Property Law Assn. Office: Venable LLP 575 Seventh St NW Washington DC 20004 Office Phone: 202-344-4010. Office Fax: 202-344-8300. Business E-Mail: japetruzzelli@venable.com.

PETRUZZI, CHRISTOPHER ROBERT, business educator, consultant; b. Peoria, Ill., July 28, 1951; s. Benjamin Robert and Mary Katherine (Urban) P.; m. Georgina Sailer, June 20, 1992; children: Lillian Caroline, Vivian Audrey. BA, Wabash Coll., 1972; MBA, U. Chgo., 1974; PhD, U. So. Calif., 1983. Lectr. bus. U. Wis., Milw., 1975-77; cons. H.C. Wainwright, Boston, 1978-79; lectr. U. So. Calif., 1978-81; prof. bus. U. Pa., Phila., 1981-84; prof. acctg. NYU, 1984-89, Calif. State U., Fullerton, 1989—. Pres. ECON Investment Software, San Clemente, Calif., 1987-2000; pres. Smart Execution LLC, 2001-. Earhart fellow, 1972-73, U. Chgo. fellow, 1974-76. Libertarian. Christian. Office: Ste 302B 629 Camino de los Mares San Clemente CA 92673 Home: 1527 Via Tulipan San Clemente CA 92673

PETSCHEK, ROLFE GEORGE, physics professor; b. Los Alamos, N.Mex., Aug. 25, 1954; s. Albert George and Marilyn Adiene Petschek; m. Jane Paquette, May 31, 1980; 1 child, Iris Hua. PhD, Harvard U., Cambridge, Mass., 1981. Prof. physics Case Western Res. U., Cleve., 1983—. Mem.: Am. Phys. Soc. Independent. Achievements include patents for electrode patterns for liquid crystal displays. Avocations: hiking, skiing. Home: 2866 Woodbury Rd Shaker Heights OH 44120-2624 Office: Case Western Res Univ Dept Physics Cleveland OH 44106-7079 Office Fax: 216-368-4671. Business E-Mail: rolfe.petschek@case.edu.

PETTENER, EMANUELE, literature and language professor; b. Venice, Italy, Apr. 30, 1971; s. Giorgio Pettener and Marie-Therese Dakskobler; m. Ilaria Serra, Jan. 2, 2002; children: Ida Maria, Gabriele Julian. PhD, Fla. Atlantic U., Boca Raton, 2004. Cert. tchr. Fla. Atlantic U., 2003. Instr. Fla. Atlantic U., 2003—, dir. study abroad program, 2003—06; novelist Corbo Editore, Ferrara, Italy, 2007—. Author: (novel) E' Sabato mi hai Lasciato e sono Bellissimo; contbr. articles to profl. jours.

PETTERSEN, KEVIN WILL, investment company executive; b. Yonkers, NY, July 4, 1956; s. Kjell Will and Marilyn Ann (Stevens) Pettersen; m. Mary Elizabeth Murphy, Aug. 30, 1981; children: Kelly, Elizabeth, Erin. Diploma academia, Chaminade, Mineola, NY, 1974; BA in Econs., SUNY, Stony Brook, 1978. Buyer JC Penney Co., Inc., NYC, 1979-82; nat. sales mgr. Randa Corp., Inc., NYC, 1982-83; dir. sales Wemco, Inc., NYC, 1983-86; mng. dir., sr. v.p. D.H. Blair & Co., Inc., NYC, 1986—89; exec. v.p. Brean Murray, Foster Securities, Inc., NYC, 1989—90; v.p., br. mgr., corp. office Chmn.'s Coun., A.G. Edwards and Sons, Inc., Huntington, NY, 1990—2006; pres. Harborview Fin. Advisors, Inc., 2006—; br. mgr., registered prin. Raymond James Fin. Svcs., 2006—, mem. exec. coun., 2009; mem. Fin. Svc. Inst., 2008—. Mem. pres. coun. A. G. Edwards, mem. Million Dollar Club, mem. chmn.'s coun., 1998; mem. exec. coun. Oppenheimer Funds Group. Active Oyster Bay Supr.'s Adv. Com. Crime, 1993—95; basketball coach girls team Cath. Youth Orgn., 1998—2007; del. Rep. Planning Com.; bd. dirs. Harbour Green L.I. Assn., 1990—94, pres., 1991. Recipient Outstanding Character award, Chaminade, 1974, Coach of Yr., Cath. Youth Orgn., 2007. Mem.: Tri Stage Golf Assn., Kellenberg Meml. HS Devel. Fund Com., Chaminade Wall St. Assn., Monarch Soc., St. Rose of Lima Father's Guild, Soc. Friendly Sons St. Patrick, Unqua Corinthian Yacht Club, Chaminade Torch Club, Green Harbour Beach Club (bd. dirs. 1994—98, treas. 1999). Republican. Roman Catholic. Avocations: golf, skiing, boating. Home: 85 Biltmore Blvd Massapequa NY 11758-8142 Office: Raymond James Fin Svcs Inc 5510 Merrick Rd Massapequa NY 11758 Office Phone: 516-795-5500.

PETTERSEN, KJELL WILL, securities trader, consultant; b. Oslo, June 19, 1927; came to US, 1946, naturalized, 1957; s. Jens Will and Ragna O. (Wickstrom) P.; m. Marilyn Ann Stevens, Aug. 16, 1952; children: Thomas W., Maureen, Kevin W., Maryann, Kathleen. Student, Zion Theol. Sch., 1945—49, NY Inst. Finance, 1955—56. Mgr. A.M. Kidder & Co., NYC, 1954-64; sr. v.p., sec., dir. Halle & Stieglitz, Fillor Bullard Co., Inc., 1964-73; sr. v.p., dir. mktg. Parrish Securities, Inc., NYC, 1973-74; cons. Loeb, Rhoades & Co., NYC, 1974-79; mng. dir. Prudential Securities, NYC, 1979-89; pres. Arbitration Recovery Cons., Marco, Fla., 1992-93; vice chmn. Noddings Investment Group, Inc., Oakbrook Terrace, Ill., 1993-95; mem. City Coun., Marco Island, Fla., 1997—2002, chmn., 2001—02. Dir. Ski for Light Inc., Mpls., Creative Arts Rehab. Ctr. Inc., NYC. Dem. candidate NY State Assembly, Nassau County, 1962; past dir. Guadalupe Ctr., Marco YMCA; pres. Quest for Peace Internat.; co-chmn. Marco Island Celebration 2000. Mem. Nat. Assn. Security Dealers (bd. arbitrators), NY C. of C., Norwegian-Am. C. of C. (dir. Guadalope Ctr.), Scandinavian Found., Bankers Club of Am., Norwegian Club (NYC), Rotary. Home: c/o Kevin Pettersen 5510 Merrick Rd Massapequa NY 11758 Personal E-mail: marcokjell@aol.com.

PETTERSEN, SUZANN, professional golfer; b. Oslo, Apr. 7, 1981; Profl. golfer, 2000—; mem. Evian Ladies European Tour, 2001—02, LPGA, 2003—. Mem. European team Solheim Cup, 2002, 03, 05, 07. Named Rookie of Yr., Ladies European Tour, 2001. Achievements include winning LPGA tour events including the Michelob Ultra Open, 2007, McDonald's LPGA Championship, 2007, Longs Drugs Challenge, 2007, Honda LPGA Thailand, 2007, Hana Bank-Kolon Championship, 2007; winner, French Open, 2001, and the SAS Masters, 2007, on the Ladies European Tour; winner, World Amateur Championship, 2000; winner, British Girls Championship, 1999; winner, Norwegian Amateur Championship, 1996-2000. Avocation: skiing. Mailing: HNP AS Huysman Nystuen & Ptnrs Gladengveien 3b 0661 Oslo Norway

PETTERSON, GOSTA, surgeon; b. Sweden; MD, Gothenburg U., Sweden, 1971, PhD. Bd. cert. in gen. and thoracic surgery Sweden, Denmark, Norway and England, cert. European Bd. Thoracic and Cardiovascular Surgery. Residency in gen. surgery Sahlgrenska U. Hosp., Gothenburg, 1971—76, residency in cardiothoracic surgery, 1977—81, staff cardiothoracic surgeon, 1981—90; clin., rsch. fellowship, dept. surgery U. Ill. Coll. Medicine, Chgo., 1979—80; prof. cardiothoracic surgery U. Copenhagen, 1990; chief surgeon, dept. cardiothoracic surgery State U. Hosp. Rigshospitalet, Copenhagen; chief cardiothoracic surgery Hamlet Pvt. Hosp., 1998—99; staff cardiothoracic surgeon Cleve. Clinic Found., 1999—, vice chmn. dept. thoracic & cardiovascular surgery, surg. dir. lung transplantation. Chmn. endocarditis working group Internat. Soc. Chemotherapy; mem. OPTN/UNOS Thoracic Organ Transplantation Com., Region 10; expert on cardiothoracic surgery Sweden, Denmark; guest prof. China, Romania, US. Author: My Heart Needs Repair, You Have Touched My Heart; contbr. articles to profl. jours. Mem.: Soc. Thoracic Surgeons, Am. Assn. Thoracic Surgery, Internat. Soc. Heart and Lung Transplantation, European Assn. Cardiothoracic Surgery, Finnish Surg. Soc. (hon.), Lithuanian Soc. Cardiothoracic Surgery (hon.), Romanian Acad. Sci. (hon.), Romanian Acad. Med. Sciences (hon.), European Congenital Heart Surgeons Club (hon.). Avocations: running, skiing, horseback riding, hunting. Office: Cleveland Clinic Found 9500 Euclid Ave # F25 Cleveland OH 44195-0002 Office Phone: 216-444-2035. Office Fax: 216-445-3294.

PETTEWAY, SAMUEL BRUCE, college president; b. Fayetteville, NC, July 18, 1924; s. Walter Bernard and Margaret Maysie (Cole) P.; m. Eleanor Glenn Sugg, Nov. 27, 1948; children— Margaret Petteway Small, Samuel Bruce. BS, N.C. State U., 1949, MEd, 1966, EdD, 1968. Gen. mgr. Homeowners Ins. and Realty Co., 1960-63; engring. tech. dept. chmn., dean occupational and transfer programs, dir. evening programs Lenoir County Community Coll., 1963-68; pres. Coll. of the Albemarle, Elizabeth City, NC, 1968-75, N.C. Wesleyan Coll., Rocky Mount, 1975-86; br. mgr. Sherwin Williams, 1953—60; first class radio engr. Radio WFTC-AM, 1949—53. Prof. Va. Poly. Inst. and State U., 1973-75, East Carolina U., 1994-99; pres. Philanthropic Cons., Inc., Kinston, N.C., 1986-96; sec. Coll. Mgmt. Svcs., Inc., Raleigh, N.C., 1989; lic. amateur radio operator, 1992—. Pres. chpt. Am. Cancer Soc., 1960-61, Boys' Club Lenoir County, 1987-91, Westminster Homeowners Assn., 1997; bd. dirs. Rocky Mount Acad., 1979-80, Triangle East, Inc., 1985-86, Cypress Glen Retirement Home, chmn. 1996; chmn. deferred giving com. N.C. Meth. Found., 1979-86; chmn. coun. on ministries 1st United Meth. Ch., Rocky Mount, 1980-81, Westminster United Meth. Ch., 1989-90, chmn. bd. trustees, 1994-99, chmn. adminstrv. bd., 2001-03; chmn. bd. trustees Art Edn. Found., 1980; mem. Nash County Bd. Health, 1985-86; bd. trustees United Meth. Retirement Homes, Inc., 1996-99; treas. Meth. Home for Children, 1997-2002. With USN, 1943—46, with USNR, 1946—51. Named Tar Heel of Week News and Observer, 1975, Today's Outstanding N.C. Citizen WNCT-TV, 1975; NSF fellow U. Ill., 1963 Mem. Nat. Assn. for Hosp. Devel., N.C. Assn. Colls. and Univs., N.C. Conf. United Meth. Ch. (chmn. bd. trustees 1973-79), Nat. Soc. Fund Raising Execs. (cert.), Rocky Mount C. of C. (bd. dirs. 1980-84), Rotary (scholarship com. dist. 7730 1995-2004), Phi Kappa Phi, Theta Alpha Phi. Clubs: Benvenue Country, Galaxy Social; Kinston Country. Lodges: Rotary (pres. 1980-81, bd. dirs. Kinston chpt. 1988-92). Republican. Office: 708 Westminster Ln Kinston NC 28501-2770 Home Phone: 252-527-7982. Personal E-mail: bpetteway@suddenlink.net.

PETTIBONE, PETER JOHN, lawyer; b. Schenectady, NY, Dec. 11, 1939; s. George Howard and Caryl Grey (Ketchum) P.; m. Jean Kellogg, Apr. 23, 1966; children: Stephen, Victoria. AB summa cum laude, Princeton U., 1961; JD, Harvard U., 1964; LLM, NYU, 1971. Bar: Pa. 1965, D.C. 1965, N.Y. 1968, U.S. Supreme Ct. 1974, Russia (fgn. legal cons.) 1995. Lectr. Heidelberg (Fed. Republic Germany) U., 1965-67; assoc. Cravath, Swaine & Moore, NYC, 1967-74, Lord Day & Lord, Barrett Smith, NYC, 1974-76, ptnr. NYC and Washington, 1976-94, Patterson, Belknap, Webb & Tyler LLP, NYC and Moscow, 1994-99, Hogan & Hartson LLP, NYC and Moscow, 2000—. Pres. 1158 Fifth Ave. Corp., N.Y.C., 1991-94; pres. North Ferry Co., Shelter Island, N.Y., 1987-90; bd. dirs., vice-chmn. N.Y. State Facilities Devel. Corp., N.Y.C., 1983-89. Editor USSR Legal Materials, Columbia U., 1990-92. Trustee, treas. Hosp. Chaplaincy Inc., N.Y.C., 1980-86, Civitas, N.Y.C., 1984-92; mem. Coun. Fgn. Rels., 1993—; trustee Union Chapel, Shelter Island, N.Y., 1990—, CEC Internat. Ptnrs., 1996-2002; bd. dirs., vice chmn. Geonomics Inst., Middlebury, Vt., 1991-98; mem. vestry Ch. of Heavenly Rest, N.Y.C., 1987-93; mem. Nat. Adv. Coun. Harriman Inst. Columbia U., 1996—; mem. Russia com. Episcopal Diocese of N.Y.; bd. dirs. Transatlantic Ptnrs. Against AIDS. Capt. U.S. Army, 1965-67, Heidelberg, Germany. Mem. ABA, Assn. Bar City NY (chmn. com. on CIS affairs 1991-94), US-USSR Trade and Econ. Coun. Inc. (US co-chmn. legal com. 1980-92), US-Russia Bus. Coun. (bd. dirs.), Soc. of Cin., Anglers Club NYC, NY Yacht Club, Shelter Island Yacht Club, Moscow Country Club, Amateur Ski Club NY (pres. 1980-82), Canterbury Choral Soc. (pres. 1983-84), Internat. Tax and Investment Ctr. (bd. dirs.), Phi Beta Kappa. Episcopalian. Home: 1158 5th Ave New York NY 10029-6917 also: 10 Wesley Ave Shelter Island Heights NY 11965 Office: Hogan & Hartson LLP 875 3rd Ave New York NY 10022 Office Phone: 212-918-3510. Business E-Mail: pjpettibone@hhlaw.com.

PETTIGREW, L. EUDORA, retired academic administrator; b. Hopkinsville, Ky., Mar. 1, 1928; d. Warren Cicero and Corrye Lee (Newell) Williams; children: Peter W. Woodard, Jonathan R. (dec.). MusB, W.Va. State Coll., 1950; MA, So. Ill. U., 1964, PhD, 1966; PhD honoris causa, U. Pretoria, South Africa, 2002, Holy Family Coll., 2002, Western Conn. State U., 2004. Music/English instr. Swift Meml. Jr. Coll., Rogersville, Tenn., 1950-51; music instr., librarian Western Ky. Vocat. Sch., Paducah, 1951-52; music/English instr. Voorhees Coll., Denmark, SC, 1954-55; dir. music and recreation therapy W.Ky. State Psychiatric Hosp., Hopkinsville, 1956-61; research fellow Rehab. Inst., So. Ill. U., Carbondale, 1961-63, instr., resident counselor, 1963-66, coordinator undergrad. ednl. psychology, 1963-66, acting chmn. ednl. psychology, tchr. corps instr., 1966; asst. prof. to assoc. prof. dept. psychology U. Bridgeport, Conn., 1966-70; prof., chmn. dept. urban and met. studies Coll. Urban Devel. Mich. State U., East Lansing, 1974-80; assoc. provost, prof. U. Del., Newark, 1981-86; pres. SUNY Coll. at Old Westbury, 1986-98. Cons. for rsch. and evaluation Hill Neighborhood House Day Care Tng. Project, Bridgeport, 1966-68, U.S. Ea. Regional Lab., Edn. Devel. Ctr., Newton, Mass., 1967-69; coordinator for edn. devel., 1968-69; cons. Bridgeport Public Schs. lang. devel. project, 1967-68, 70; Lansing Model Cities Agy., Day Care Program, 1971; U. Pitts., 1973, 74, Leadership Program, U. Mich. and Wayne State U., 1975, Wayne County Pub. Health Nurses Assn., 1976, Ill. State Bd. Edn., 1976-77; assoc. prof. U. Bridgeport, 1970, Ctr. for Urban Affairs and Coll. of Edn., Mich. State U., East Lansing, 1970-73; program devel. specialist Lansing Public Schs. Tchr. Corps program, 1971-73; coord. workshop Conflict Resolution The Woman's Role in Our World, 4th Internat. UN Conf. on Women, Beijing, China, 1995; lectr. in field; condr. workshops in field; guest spkr. Internat. Conf. on The New Role of Higher Edn. in the Context of an Ind. Palestinian State, An-Najah Nat. U., Nablus, Palestine, 1996; mem. exec. com. UN Non-Govtl. Orgn., Dept. Pub. Info., 2004—. Tv/radio appearances on: Black Women in Edn, Channel 23, WKAR, East Lansing, 1973, Black Women and Equality, Channel 2, Detroit, 1974, Women and Careers, Channel 7, Detroit, 1974, Black Women and Work: Integration in Schools, WITL Radio, Lansing, 1974, others; editor: Universities and Their Role in World Peace, 2003; contbr. articles to profl. jours. Mem. exec. com. UN Non Govtl. Orgns. Dept. Public Info., 2004. Recipient Diana award Lansing YWCA, 1977, Outstanding Profl. Achievement award, 1987, award L.I. Ctr. for Bus. and Profl. Women, 1988, Educator of Yr. 100 Black Men of L.I., 1988, Black Women's Agenda award, 1988, Woman of Yr. Nassau/Suffolk Coun. of Adminstrv. Women in Edn., 1989,

Disting. Ednl. Leadership award L.I. Women's Coun. for Equal Edn. Tng. and Employment, 1989, L.I. Disting. Leadership award L.I. Bus. News, 1990, Disting. Black Women in Edn. award Nat. Coun. Negro Women, 1991; named Outstanding Black Educator, NAACP, 1968, Oustanding Woman Educator, Mich. Women's Lawyers Assn. and Mich. Trial Lawyers Assn., 1975, Disting. Alumna, Nat. Assn. for Equal Opportunity in Higher Edn., 1990, Woman of Yr., Nassau County League of Women Voters, 1991, Disting. Alumna So. Ill. U., 1997, N.Y. State Senate resolution of commendation, 1998; Elected to Achievers Hall of Fame: Long Island Bus. and Profl. Women's Orgn., 2001 Mem. AAAS, Nat. Assn. Acad. Affairs Adminstrs., Internat. Assn. Univ. Pres. (exec. com.), Phi Delta Kappa, Rotary Club (Wilmington, Del.).

PETTIGREW, RODERIC I., federal agency administrator, radiologist, researcher; BS in Physics, cum laude, Morehouse Coll., Atlanta, 1972; MS in Nuc. Medicine and Engring., Rensselaer Poly. Inst., Troy, NY, 1973; PhD in Applied Radiation Physics, MIT, 1977; MD, U. Miami, 1979. Intern/resident internal medicine Emory U., Atlanta; resident nuc. medicine U. Calif., San Diego; clin. rsch. scientist Picker Internat.; Robert Wood Johnson Found. fellow Emory U., 1985; prof. radiology, medicine (cardiology) & bioengring. Emory U. Sch. Medicine, dir. Ctr. Magnetic Resonance Rsch.; dir. Nat. Inst. Biomed. Imaging & Bioengring. NIH, Bethesda, Md., 2002—. Contbr. articles to profl. jours. Recipient Benjamin E. Mays award, 1989; named a Most Disting. Alumnus, U. Miami, 1990. Fellow: Am. Inst. Med. & Biomed. Engring., Internat. Soc. Magnetic Resonance in Medicine, Am. Coll. Cardiology, Am. Heart Assn.; mem.: Inst. Medicine, Phi Beta Kappa. Achievements include research in dynamic three-dimensional imaging of the heart using magnetic resonance; development of first computer software package specifically designed for cardiac imaging using MRI. Office: NINIB 6707 Democracy Blvd Bethesda MD 20892 Office Phone: 301-496-8859. Office Fax: 301-480-4973. E-mail: pettigrr@mail.nih.gov.*

PETTIGREW, THOMAS FRASER, social psychologist, educator; b. Richmond, Va., Mar. 14, 1931; s. Joseph Crane and Janet (Gibb) Pettigrew; m. Ann Hallman, Feb. 25, 1956; 1 child, Mark Fraser. AB in Psychology, U. Va., 1952; MA in Social Psychology, Harvard U., 1955, PhD, 1956; DHL (hon.), Governor's State U., 1979; DSN (hon.), Philipps U., Germany, 2008. Rsch. assoc. Inst. Social Rsch., U. Natal, Republic South Africa, 1956; asst. prof. psychology U. N.C., 1956-57; asst. prof. social psychology Harvard U., Cambridge, Mass., 1957-62, lectr., 1962-64, assoc. prof., 1964-68, prof., 1968-74, prof. social psychology and sociology, 1974-80; prof. social psychology U. Calif., Santa Cruz, 1980-94, rsch. prof. social psychology, 1994—; prof. social psychology U. Amsterdam, 1986-91. Adj. fellow Joint Ctr. Polit. and Econ. Studies, Washington, 1982—; adv. bd. women's studies program Princeton (N.J.) U., 1985-2001; vis. prof. Westfaelishe Wilhelms-U., Germany, 1993, Philipps U., Germany, 2000, 01, 04, 06, Schiller U., Germany, 2002; Glynn Resident scholar, Washington & Lee U., 2008; disting. vis. prof. Flinders U., Australia, 1997; sr. fellow Rsch. Inst. for the Comparative Study of Race and Ethnicity, Stanford U., 2001-02, mem. German govt. adv. com. Intercultural Conflicts and Social Integration, 2003-2006 Author: (with E.Q. Campbell) Christians in Racial Crisis: A Study of the Little Rock Ministry, 1959, A Profile of the Negro American, 1964, Racially Separate or Together?, 1971; (with Frederickson, Knobol, Glazer and Veda) Prejudice, 1982; (with Alston) Tom Bradley's Campaigns for Governor: The Dilemma of Race and Political Strategies, 1988, How to Think Like a Social Scientist, 1996; editor: Racial Discrimination in the United States, 1975, The Sociology of Race Relations: Reflection and Reform, 1980; (with C. Stephan & W. Stephan) The Future of Social Psychology: Defining the Relationship Between Sociology and Psychology, 1991; mem. editorial bd. Jour. Social Issues, 1959-64, Social Psychology Quarterly, 1977-80; assoc. editor Am. Sociol. Rev, 1963-65; adv. bd. Integrated Edn, 1963-84, Phylon, 1965-93, Edn. and Urban Society, 1968-90, Race, 1972-74, Ethnic and Racial Studies, 1978-95, Rev. of Personality and Social Psychology, 1980-85, Cmty. and Applied Social Psychology, 1989-2004, Individual and Politics, 1989-93, Jour. Ethnic and Migration Studies, 1994—, 21st Century Afro Rev., 1994—; contbr. articles to profl. jours. Chmn. Episcopal presiding Bishop's Adv. Com. on Race Relations, 1961-63; v.p. Episcopal Soc. Cultural and Racial Unity, 1962-63; mem. Mass. Gov.'s Adv. Com. on Civil Rights, 1962-64; social sci. cons. U.S. Commn. Civil Rights, 1966-71; mem. White House Task Force on Edn., 1967; mem. nat. task force on desegregation policies Edn. Commn. of States, 1977-79; trustee Ella Lyman Cabot Trust, Boston, 1977-79; Emerson Book Award com. United Chpts. Phi Beta Kappa, 1971-73; com. status black Ams. NRC, 1985-88. Guggenheim fellow, 1967-68, Sr. Scientist fellow NATO, 1974, Ctr. Advanced Study in Behavioral Scis. fellow, 1975-76, Sydney Spivack fellow Am. Sociol. Assn., 1978, Netherlands Inst. Advanced Study fellow, 1984-85, Bellagio (Italy) Study Ctr. resident fellow, Rockefeller Found., 1991; Fulbright New Century scholar, 2003-04; recipient Kurt Lewin Meml. award Soc. for Psychol. Study Social Issues, 1987, (with Martin) Gordon Allport Intergroup Rels. Rsch. prize, 1988, Faculty Rsch. award U. Calif., Santa Cruz, 1988, (with Tropp) Gordon Allport Intergroup Rels. Rsch. prize, 2003, Disting. Social Scis. Emeriri Faculty award, 2008. Fellow APA (Weiss meml. lectr., 2003), Am. Sociol. Assn. (coun. 1979-82), Iternat. Acad. Intercultural Rsch. (Lifetime Achievement award, 2008, U. Calif. Panunzio Disting. award, 2009); mem. Soc. Psychol. Study Social Issues (coun. 1962-66, pres. 1967-68, Disting. Svc. award 1998), Soc. Exptl. Social Psychology (Disting. Scientist award 2002), European Assn. Social Psychology. Home: 524 Van Ness Ave Santa Cruz CA 95060-3556 Business E-Mail: pettigr@ucsc.edu.

PETTINELLA, NICHOLAS ANTHONY, corporate financial executive; b. Little Falls, NY, Sept, 9, 1942; s. Nicholas and Rose (Zuccaro) P.; m. Nancy C. Whitehouse, Oct. 28, 1978; children: Albert J., Michael A. BS, Bentley Coll., 1968; MBA, Babson Coll., 1975; postgrad., Harvard U., 1979, Stanford U., 1983. CPA. Mass. auditor Coopers & Lybrand, Boston, 1970-76; treas. Courier Corp., Lowell, Mass., 1976-80; controller corp. ops. Digital Equipment Corp., Maynard, Mass., 1980-81; dir. fin. Intermetrics, Inc., Burlington, Mass., 1981-83, sr. v.p. fin., chief fin. officer, treas., 1983-98; sr. v.p. fin., treas. Averstar, Inc., Burlington, 1999-2000; v.p., CFO IronBridge Networks, Inc., Lexington, Mass., 2000—01; CFO ideaLogix, Inc., Framingham, Mass., 2001—02, Accordare, Arlington, Mass., 2002—04; exec. v.p., CFO Harmony Line, Inc., Cambridge, Mass., 2004—. Bd. dirs. The Computer Mus., Boston, treas. 1988-98, bd. overseers 1997-99, Mus. Scis., Boston, 1999-2003. Chmn. fin. com. Town of Ashland, Mass., 1980-82. Served with U.S. Army, 1964-66. Mem. Fin. Execs. Inst., AICPA, Inst. Mgmt. Accts., Mass. Soc. CPAs, Treas. Club Boston, Pacioli Soc. Roman Catholic. Home: 141 South St Ashland MA 01721-2263

PETTIS, PATRICIA AMANDA, secondary school educator, farmer; b. Red Wing, Minn., Jan. 28, 1967; d. Albert A. and Marilyn June (MacAdams) Berg; m. Pettis Steven Mark, Sept. 5, 1992; children: Steven Joseph, Nathan Carl, Allie Amanda, Christopher Mark, Matthew Albert. BS in Edn., St. Cloud State U., Minn., 1990. English instr. LeSueur-Henderson H.S., Minn., 1997—98, Waterville Elysian Morristown Sch. Dist., Waterville, Minn., 1998—. Declamation head coach LeSueur-Henderson H.S., 1997—98; yearbook advisor WEM H.S., Waterville, 1998—2002, lit. mag. advisor, 1998—2003, class advisor, 1998—2006, nat. honor soc. advisor, 2000—. Sunday sch. educator St. Peters Cath. Ch., St. Peter, Minn. Mem.: Minn. Edn. Assn. (assoc.). Avocations: running, gardening, coaching and playing sports. Home: 46364 327th Ave Kasota MN 56050 Office: Waterville-Elysian-Morristown HS 500 East Paquin St Waterville MN 56096

PETTIS-ROBERSON, SHIRLEY MCCUMBER, former US Representative, California; b. Mountain View, Calif. d. Harold Oliver and Dorothy Susan (O'Neil) McCumber; m. John J. McNulty (dec.); m. Jerry L. Pettis (dec. Feb. 1975); children: Peter Dwight Pettis, Deborah Pettis Moyer; m. Ben Roberson, Feb. 6, 1988. Student, Andrews U., Berrien Springs, Mich., 1942—43, student, 1945, U. Calif., Berkeley, 1944—45; PhD (hon.), Loma Linda U., Calif., 2002. Mgr. Audio-Digest Found., LA, Glendale, 1958—61; sec. treas. Pettis, Inc., Hollywood, Calif., 1958-68; mem. U.S. Congress, Calif., 1975—79. Pres. Women's Rsch. Edn. Inst., 1979—80; bd. dirs. Lumbermens Mut. Ins. Co., Kemper Corp., Am. Motors, Am. Mfg. Co., 1980—97. Mem. Former Mems. Congress, 1980—, Pres.'s Commn. Arms Control Disarmament, 1982—85, Commn. Presdl. Scholars, 1990—93; chair bd. Loma Linda U. Children's Hosp. Found.; trustee U. Redlands, Calif., 1980—83, Loma Linda U. Med. Ctr., Calif., 1990—95, bd. mem.

PETTIT, DONALD R., astronaut, flight engineer, researcher; b. Silverton, Oreg., Apr. 20, 1955; m. Micki Pettit; 2 children. BSChemE, Oreg. State U., 1978; PhD in Chemical Engring., U. Ariz., 1983. Staff scientist Los Alamos Nat. Lab., Los Alamos, N.Mex., 1984—96, mem. synthesis group, slated with assembling the technology to return to the moon and explore Mars, 1990, mem. Space Station Freedom Redesign Team, 1993; mission specialist, Lyndon B. Johnson Space Ctr. with technical duties in the Astronaut Office Computer Support Branch NASA, Houston, 1996—. Projects included: Reduced gravity fluid flow and materials processing experiments aboard the NASA KC-135 airplane, atmospheric spectroscopy measurements on noctolucent clouds seeded from sounding rocket payloads, volcano fumarole gas sampling on active volcanos, investigated problems in the detonation physics applied to weapons systems; completed first space flight as NASA ISS science officer and flight engineer aboard the International Space Station, Expedition-6 (launched in the STS-113 Space Shuttle Endeavour and returned to Earth on Soyuz TMA-1), Nov. 23, 2002 to May 3, 2003, logged over 161 days in space and 2 EVAs (spacewalks) totalling 13 hours and 17 minutes. During the 5 1/2 months aboard the ISS, the crew worked with numerous US and Russian science experiments; crew mem. for STS-126 Endeavour Mission, 2008. Avocations: photography, swimming. Office: NASA Johnson Space Center 2101 NASA Pwky Houston TX 77058*

PETTIT, FREDERICK SIDNEY, metallurgical engineering educator, department chairman; b. Wilkes Barre, Pa., Mar. 10, 1930; s. Edwin Humes and Edith Mae (Barnecut) P.; m. Lou-Jean Mary Corso, Aug. 30, 1958; children: Frederick N., Theodore E., John C., Charles A. B in Engring., Yale U., 1952, M in Engring., 1960, D in Engring., 1962. Jr. engr. Westinghouse Electric Corp., Pitts., 1952-54; engr. Avco-Lycoming, Stratford, Conn., 1957-58; postdoctoral student Max Planck Inst. Phys. Chemistry, Gottingen, Fed. Republic Germany, 1962-63; sr. staff scientist Pratt & Whitney Aircraft Co., East Hartford, Conn., 1963-79; prof. metall.-material engring. dept., chmn. U. Pitts., Pa., 1979-88, prof., 1988—2006, prof. emeritus, 2006—, Harry S. Tack prof. materials engring., 1992—2006; mem. adv. bd. Jour. Oxidation of Metals, Plenum Press, N.Y., 1975—. 1st lt USMC, 1954-57. Fellow, NSF, 1962—63. Mem. Metall. Soc. (program dir. 1982-83), Electrochem. Soc. (sec.-treas. high temperature materials div. 1979-83), Am. Soc. Metals, Materials Rsch. Soc. Roman Catholic. Office: U Pitts 848 Benedum Hall Pittsburgh PA 15261-2208 Home: 21 Lost Brook Ln Wallingford CT 06492-5706 Home Phone: 203-626-5351; Office Phone: 412-624-9730. Business E-Mail: pettit@pitt.edu.

PETTIT, GEORGE HUNTER, lab administrator, researcher; b. Austin, Tex., Apr. 19, 1960; s. Rowland and Flora Hunter Pettit; m. Michelle Zumwalt, Aug. 9, 1986; children: Valerie Zumwalt, Rowland West. BA in Biochemistry, Rice U., Houston, 1982, PhD in Elec. Engring., 1990; MD, U. Tex. Southwestern Med. Sch., Dallas, 1986. Med. rsch. officer FDA Ctr. Devices & Radiol. Health, Rockville, Md., 1990—96; chief scientist Alcon Orlando Tech. Ctr., Orlando, Fla., 1996—2008; v.p., vision sci. rsch. Alcon Labs., Ft. Worth, 2008—. Methodist. Avocations: raising children, travel. Home: PO Box 34085 Fort Worth TX 76162 Office: Alcon Labs 6201 S Freeway Fort Worth TX 76134 Business E-Mail: george.pettit@alconlabs.com.

PETTIT, GEORGE ROBERT, chemist, educator, cancer researcher; b. Long Branch, NJ, June 8, 1929; s. George Robert and Florence Elizabeth (Seymour) P.; m. Margaret Jean Benger, June 20, 1953; children: William Edward, Margaret Sharon, Robin Kathleen, Lynn Benger, George Robert III. BS, Wash. State U., 1952; MS, Wayne State U., 1954, PhD, 1956. Tchg. asst. Wash. State U., 1950-52, lecture demonstrator, 1952; rsch. chemist E.I. duPont de Nemours and Co., 1953; grad. tchg. asst. Wayne State U., 1952-53, rsch. fellow, 1954-56; sr. rsch. chemist Norwich Eaton Pharms., Inc., 1956-57; asst. prof. chemistry U. Maine, 1957-61, assoc. prof. chemistry, 1961-65, prof. chemistry, 1965; vis. prof. chemistry Stanford U., 1965; prof. chemistry Ariz. State U., 1965—, chmn. organic chemistry divsn., 1966-68, disting. rsch. prof., 1978-79, Dalton prof. medicinal chemistry and rsch., 1986—2005, Regent's prof. chemistry, 1990—. Vis. prof. So. African, Univs., 1978; dir. Cancer Rsch. Lab., 1974-75, 2005, Cancer Rsch. Inst., 1975-2005; co-dir. Ariz. Prostate Cancer Task Force, 2000-05; lectr. various colls. and univs.; cons. in field. Contbr. articles to profl. jours. Mem. adv. bd. Wash. State U. Found., 1981—85. With Res. USAF, 1949—53. Recipient Alumni Achievement award, Wash. State U., 1984; named to Academic Hall of Fame, Pub. Schs., City of Long Br., NJ, 2009. Fellow: Am. Inst. Chemists (Guenther award in chemistry of natural products 1998, Pioneer award 1989, Ariz. Gov.'s Excellence award 1993); mem.: Am. Soc. Oncology, Am. Assn. Cancer Rsch., Am. Soc. Pharmacognosy (Rsch. Achievement award 1995), Chem. Soc. London, Am. Chem. Soc. (mem. awards com. 1968—71), Phi Lambda Upsilon, Sigma Xi. Office: Ariz State U Dept Chemistry and Biochemistry Tempe AZ 85287-2404 Office Phone: 480-965-2461.

PETTIT, GHERY ST. JOHN, electronics engineer; b. Woodland, Calif., Apr. 6, 1952; s. Ghery DeWitt and Frances Marie (Seitz) P.; m. Marilyn Jo Van Hoose, July 28, 1973; children: Ghery Christopher, Heather Kathleen. BS in Electrical Engring., Wash. State U., 1975. Cert. EMC engr., NARTE, EIT Wash., Colo. Nuclear engr. Mare Island Naval Shipyard, Vallejo, Calif., 1975-76; electronics engr. Naval Electronic Systems Engring. Ctr., Vallejo, 1976-79; sr. engr. Martin Marietta Denver Aerospace, 1979-83; staff engr. Tandem Computers Inc., Santa Clara, Calif., 1983-90, mgr. electromagnetic capability Cupertino, Calif., 1990-91, electromagnetic compatibility lead engr., 1991-95; electromagnetic compatibility engr. Intel Corp., Hillsboro, Oreg., 1995-96, Dupont, Wash., 1996—. Mem. U.S. tech. adv. group subcom. I, Spl. Com. on Radio Frequency Interferences subcom. Internat. Electrotechnical Commn.; mem. CISPR SC I, WG2, WG3 and WG4. Asst. cubmaster Boy Scouts Am., San Jose, Calif., 1985-86, cubmaster, 1986-88, ast. scoutmaster, 1988-90, scoutmaster, 1990-93. Mem. IEEE (sr.), Nat. Rsch. Coun. (bd. assessment of NIST programs 1999—2005), EMC Soc. (bd. dirs. 1999-2004, 2006—, v.p. commn. svcs. 2003—08, v.p. conferences, 2009-), Electromagnetic Capability Soc. (sec.-treas. Littleton, Colo. chpt. 1983, sec. Santa Clara Valley chpt. 1985-87, vice chmn. 1987-89, chmn. 1989-91, sec. Santa Clara Valley sect. 1991-92, treas. 1992-93, vice chmn. 1993-94, chmn. 1994-95), IEEE Electromagetic Capability Soc. (chmn. Seattle chpt. 1997-2000). Republican. Presbyterian. Avocations: flying, amateur radio, sailing. Office: Intel Corp 2800 Center Dr Dupont WA 98327-9773 Business E-Mail: ghery.pettit@intel.com.

PETTIT, JOHN DOUGLAS, JR., management educator; b. Alice, Tex, Aug. 19, 1940; s. John Douglas and Vivian Iola (Beaman) P.; m. Suzanne McLeod, Aug. 23, 1964; children: Melanie Ann Wilson, David Bryant. BBA, U. North Tex., 1962, MBA, 1964; PhD, La. State U., 1969. Instr. mgmt. Miss. State U., Starkville, Miss., 1964-65; grad. asst. La. State U., Baton Rouge, 1965-67, instr. mgmt., 1967-68; asst. prof. bus. Tex. Tech. U., Lubbock, Tex., 1968-69; assoc. prof. mgmt. U. North Tex., Denton, Tex., 1969-78, prof. mgmt., 1978-95; chair excellence in free enterprise Austin Peay State U., Clarksville, Tenn., 1995-96; interim chair and prof. dept. info. and decision scis. U. Tex., El Paso, Tex., 2000-2001, vis. prof. Dept. Mktg. and Mgmt., 2005—, interim chmn., 2005—06. Bd. dirs. Capital Instnl. Svcs., Dallas and NYC, mem. audit com., 2003—; cons. various orgns., 1969—98; mgr., co-owner Pettit's Cleaners/Hatters, Alice, 1992—96; vis. prof. mgmt. Wichita (Kans.) State U., 1994—95; vis. prof. Ecole Superieure de Commerce et de Mgmt., Poitier and Tours, France, 2002—03, U. Kuopio, Finland, 2003—04. Kuopio, Finland, 2002, Co-author: Business Communication: Theory and Application, 7th edit. 1993, Report Writing for Business, 10th edit. 1998, Lesikar's Basic Business Communication, 8th edit. 1999; mem. editl. bd. Organl. Comm. Abstracts, 1980-85; mem. editl. bd. Jour. Bus. Comm., 1987-90, mng. editor, 1990-94. Mem. choir Trinity Presbyn. Ch., Denton, 1985-2006; docent, Bass Performance Hall, Ft. Worth, 2006, usher, 2006; trainer, Metroport Meals on Wheels, Argyle, Tex., 2002-, driver, 2002-; actor, singer Denton Cmty. Theater Summer Prodn., 1988-95. Recipient Master's Degree award Chgo. Bd. Trade, 1963. Fellow Assn. Bus. Comm. (pres., 1st v.p., exec. dir., 1990-94); mem. Southwestern Fedn. Adminstrv. Disciplines (pres., v.p.), Acad. Mgmt., Denton Country Club (bd. dirs.), Blue Key Nat. Hon. Fraternity, Beta Gamma Sigma (hon.), Phi Kappa Phi (hon.), Delta Sigma Pi. Presbyterian. Avocations: music, tennis. Home: 9122 David Fort Rd Argyle TX 76226-2953 Business E-Mail: jpettit@utep.edu.

PETTIT, JOHN W., health facility administrator; b. Detroit, Mar. 6, 1942; s. John W. and Clara (Schartz) P.; m. Kathleen Endres, Aug. 8, 1970; children: Julie, Andrew, Michael. BBA, U. Notre Dame, 1964; MBA, Mich. State U., 1974. CPA, Mich.; CFP, 2001. Acct. Ernst & Ernst, Detroit, 1964-67; chief acct. Detroit Inst. Tech., Detroit, 1967-69; controller, dir. adminstrn. & fin. Mich. Cancer Found., Detroit, 1969-80; chief adminstrv. officer Dana-Farber Cancer Inst., Boston, 1980-94; exec. v.p., chief oper. officer John Wayne Cancer Inst., Santa Monica, Calif., 1995-97; fin. cons. LA, 1998—. Grant reviewer Nat. Cancer Inst., Bethesda, Md., 1979-94. Pres. advanced mgmt. program Mich. State U., 1978-79; mem. adv. bd. Arthritis Found. So. Calif. chpt., 1999—2004; mem. Town Meeting, Wellesley, Mass., 1991-94. Avocations: sailing, woodworking, photography, music. Home and Office: 4518 Winnetka Ave Woodland Hills CA 91364 Office Phone: 818-226-3832. E-mail: john@jwpfinancial.com.

PETTIT, LAWRENCE KAY, university president; b. Lewistown, Mont., May 2, 1937; s. George Edwin and Dorothy Bertha (Brown) P.; m. Sharon Lee Anderson, June 21, 1961 (div. Oct. 1976); children: Jennifer Anna, Matthew Anderson, Allison Carol, Edward McLean; m. Elizabeth DuBois Medley, July 11, 1980 (div. Dec. 1998). BA cum laude, U. Mont., 1959; AM, Washington U., St. Louis, 1962; PhD, U. Wis., 1965. Legis. asst. US Senate, 1959-60, 62; asst. & assoc. prof. dept. polit. sci. Pa. State U., 1964-67; assoc. dir. fed. rels. Am. Council Edn., Washington, 1967-69; chmn. dept. polit. sci. Mont. State U., 1969-72; adminstrv. asst. to gov. State of Mont., 1973; chancellor Mont. Univ. System, Helena, 1973-79; pvt. practice ednl. cons. Mont., 1979-81; dep. commr. for acad. affairs Tex. Coordinating Bd. for Higher Edn., 1981-83; chancellor Univ. System of South Tex., 1983-86; chancellor (now pres.) So. Ill. U., Carbondale, Edwardsville, 1986-91, Disting. svc. prof., 1991-92; pres. Indiana U. Pa., 1992—2003, ret., 2003. Mem. adv. bd. S & T Bancorp., 1997-2003; mem. regional adv. bd. Nat. City Bank, 1997-99; bd. dirs. Ind. Healthcare Corp., 1992-2007. Author: (with H. Albinski) European Political Processes, 2d edit., 1974, (with E. Keynes) Legislative Process in the U.S. Senate, 1969, (with S. Kirkpatrick) Social Psychology of Political Life, 1972, (with J. Goetz and S. Thomas) Legislative Process in Montana, 1975; mem. editl. bd. Ednl. Record, 1985-98. Mem. adv. bd. Leadership Ctr. Ams., 1988-90, Ill. Coalition, 1989-92; dem. primary candidate for 2d dist. US Ho. of Reps., Mont., 1980; mem. Ill. Gov.'s Com. on Sci. and Tech., 1986-90; bd. dirs. Tex. Guaranteed Student Loan Corp., 1985-86, Reschini Found., 2003-07, Humanities Mont., 2008-; chmn. Ill.-Niigata Commn. on Edn. and Econ. Devel., 1990-92; chair bd. dirs. Nat. Environ. Edn. and Tng. Ctr., 1994-04; mem. adv. bd. Princeton Rev., 2003-04. U. Wis. fellow 1962-63, Vilas fellow U. Wis., 1963-64. Mem. AAUP (pres. Mont. conf. 1971-72), Nat. Assn. Sys. Heads (pres. 1989), Am. Coun. on Edn. (chmn. leadership commn. 1989-90, sr. fellow 1991-92), Am. Assn. Higher Edn., Am. Assn. State Colls. and Univs. (Disting. Svc. award 1991), Newcomen Soc., Duquesne Club Pitts., 1993-2007, World Affairs Coun. Pitts., 1993-2008, Pa. Soc. (life), Rotary (Paul Harris fellow), Ind. C. of C. (bd. dirs. 1992-03), Sigma Chi (Significant Sig award 1988), Phi Kappa Phi, Mont. Club. Episcopalian. Home: 2567 Overlook Blvd Helena MT 59601 Office Phone: 724-388-2543. Personal E-mail: lpettit@bresnan.net.

PETTIT, MARILYN HILLEY, historian, educator, archivist, consultant; b. Dallas, Oct. 30, 1942; d. Wofford Neal and Lavalle Shipper Hilley; 1 child, Rachel A. Pettit Reich. BA, U. Tex., Austin, 1964; MA, NYU, 1980, PhD, 1991. Cert. in Archival Mgmt. NYU, NY State, 1980. Asst. dir. archival program NYU, 1982—88, dir. archival program, 1988—93; asst. prof. U. Md., Coll. Pk., 1993—97; univ. archivist St. John's U., NYC, 1997—99; dir. archives and Columbiana Libr. Columbia U., NYC, 1999—2004; v.p. collections Bklyn. Hist. Soc., Bklyn., 2004—. Adj. prof. Columbia U., 2000—04, Pratt Inst. Sch. Info. and Libr. Sci., Bklyn., 2003. Co-author: New York University & the City, 1997; contbr. articles to profl. jours. Trustee The Old Stone House, Bklyn., 1998—; mem. The Heights Casino, Bklyn. Mem.: DAR, Orgn. Am. Historians, Soc. Am. Archivists, Soc. for Hist. of Early Am. Republic. Democrat. Presbyterian. Avocations: theater, music.

PETTITT, JAY S., architect, consultant; b. Redford, Mich., Jan. 6, 1926; s. Jay S. and Florence Marian (Newman) P.; m. Ruth Elizabeth Voigt, June 21, 1947; children— J. Stuart, Laura Ellen, Patricia Lynn, Carol Ann B.Arch., U. Mich., 1951. Registered architect, Mich. Draftsman Frank J. Stepnoski and Son, Fond du Lac, Wis., 1951; project architect Albert Kahn Assocs., Inc., Detroit, 1951-62, chief archtl. devel., 1962-67, v.p., 1967-88, dir. architecture, 1975-88; archtl. cons. Beulah, Mich., 1988—. Active Jr. Athletic Assn., Redford, Mich., 1959-63; com. chmn. Boy Scouts Am., 1960-65; supr. Benzonia Twp. Served with U.S. Army. 1943-46, ETO. Fellow AIA; mem. Mich. Soc. Architects (pres. 1967), Am. Arbitration Assn., Am. Assn. Hosp. Planning, Engring. Soc. Detroit, U. Mich. Pres.' Club Avocations: sailing, skiing. Office Phone: 231-882-4040. Personal E-mail: jaypettitt@bignetnorth.net.

PETTITTE, ANDY (ANDREW EUGENE PETTITTE), professional baseball player; b. Baton Rouge, June 15, 1972; m. Laura Pettitte, Jan. 9, 1993; children: Joshua Blake, Jared, Lexy Grace, Luke Jackson. Student, San Jacinto Coll., Tex. Pitcher NY Yankees, 1995—2003, 2007—. Houston Astros, 2004—06. Co-author (with Bob Reccord, Mark Tabb): (autobiography) Strike Zone: Targeting a Life of Integrity & Purity, 2005. Recipient Warren Spahn Award, 2003; named Am. League Championship MVP, 2001; named to MLB All-Star Game, 1996, 2001. Achievements include being a member of World Series Champion New York Yankees, 1996, 1998, 1999, 2000. Office: NY Yankees Yankee Stadium One E 161st St Bronx NY 10451 Office Phone: 718-293-4300.

PETTMAN, BARRIE OWEN, entrepreneur; b. Hessle, Eng., Feb. 22, 1944; m. Norma Edwards, Apr. 10, 1987 (dec. 1991); m. Maureen Crowther, 1992. BSc, Hull Tech. Coll., 1966; MSc, PhD, City U., London, 1970; DLitt, Internat. Mgmt. Centres, 1991. Asst. lectr., lectr. U. Hull, Eng., 1970-82; dir. manpower unit U. Rhodesia, 1978-79; registrar Internat. Mgmt. Ctr. from Buckingham, 1983—; mng. dir. Emmasglen Ltd., 1970—96; dir. MCB Unv. Press Ltd., 1974—2004; ptnr. Barmarick Publs., 1980—2004; pres. Burke's Landed Gentry of Great Britain Ltd., 1999—. Vis. prof. Can. Sch. mgmt., 1983—2003; hon. v.p. Br. Soc. Commerce, 1975—; chmn. Inst. of Sci. Bus., 1972-79, Insts. of Tng. and Devel., Humberside Br., 1990—. Editor: Internat. Jour. Social Econs. 1973-79, Internat. Jour. of Manpower, 1980-84, Mgmt. Rsch. News, 1981—2005, Equal Opportunities Internat. 1981—2005, Internat. Jour. Sociology and Social Policy, 1984—2005, Internat. Jour. of New Ideas, 1992—2005, others; author: Training and Retraining, 1973, Labour Turnover and Retention, 1975, Equal Pay, 1975, Manpower Planning Workbook, 1976, 84, Industrial Democracy, 1984, Discrimination in the Labour Market, 1980, Management: A Selected Bibliography, 1983, The New World Order, 1996, Social Economies in Transition, 1996, Self Development, 1997, The Internationalisation of Franchising, 1998, The Ultimate Entrepreneur's Book, 1999, What Self-Made Millionaires Really Think, Know & Do, 2002, other publs. Acceded to title of The Baron of Bombie, 1999. Fellow Brit. Soc. Commerce (hon. v.p.), Inst. of Mgmt., Internat. Inst. Social Econs., Royal Geog. Assn., Royal Soc. Arts, Inst. Pers. and Devel., Inst. Mfg., Inst. Mgmt. Specialists; mem. Internat. Inst. Social Econs. (pres. 1972—), Brit. Univs. Indsl. Rels. Assn. Office: Enholmes Hall Patrington Hull HU12 0PR England Fax: 01964 631716. E-mail: bopmpettman@btinternet.com.

PETTUS, MILDRED LOUISE, retired history professor, writer; b. Lancaster County, SC, Feb. 1, 1926; d. Calvin Hall and Bessie Kathryn (Rodgers) Pettus. BA in History, Winthrop Coll., 1946; MA in History, U. S.C., 1954. Tchr. Kershaw (S.C.) H.S., 1947-48; cotton gin mgr. Pettus Gin Co., Ft. Mill, S.C., 1949-54; tchr. Spartanburg (S.C.) Jr. Coll., 1955-56, Douglas (Ariz.) H.S., 1956-63, Ajo (Ariz.) H.S., 1964-65, Orlando (Fla.) Jr. Coll., 1965-67; asst. prof. Winthrop Coll., Rock Hill, S.C., 1967-89; ret., 1989. Author: Pictorial History of Lancaster County, South Carolina, 1984, The Springs Story, 1986, The Palmetto State, 1989, The Waxhaws, 1993, A Roddey Family, 1998, Leasing Away a Nation - The Flawed System of Catawba Indian Land Leases, 2005; columnist: Nearby History, Charlotte Observer, 1985—2006, Carolina Gateway, 2006. Recipient Achievement of Merit award, Am. Assn. Colls. Tchr. Edn., 1973, Outstanding Publ. Editor award, SC Confederation of State and Local History Socs., 1994, Preservation award, Hist. Rock Hill, 2003, York County SC Culture and Heritage Commn. Keeper of the Culture award, 2000, History award, Nat. Soc. DAR, 2001, Alumni Profl. Achievement award, Winthrop U., 2006; named archives in her honor, 2006. Mem.: York County Geneal. and Hist. Soc. (bd. dirs., editor The Quar. 1989—2006). Democrat. Home: 9227 Whistling Straits Dr Indian Land SC 29707-5867 Home Phone: 803-396-0208. Personal E-mail: mlpettus@comporium.net.

PETTY, ELIZABETH MARIE, geneticist; b. Chgo., July 13, 1959; d. Ralph David and Joyce Elizabeth (Carlson) P.; life ptnr. Karen Kay Milner, Dec. 15, 1985. BA, Clarke Coll., 1981; MD, U. Wis., 1986. Diplomate Nat. Bd. Med. Examiners, Am. Bd. Pediats., Am. Bd. Med. Genetics, Molecular Genetics and Clin. Genetics. Pediat. intern and resident U. Wis., Madison, 1986-89; genetics fellow Yale U., New Haven, 1989-93; prof. U. Mich., Ann Arbor, 1994—, med. dir. genetic counseling program, 1996—, dir. med. genetics outpatient clinic, 1996—2006, assoc. dean student programs Med. Sch., 2006—. Expert witness DNA testing in State of Ohio and Mich., 1995—; presenter regional, nat. and internat. confs. on genetics, 1991—. Contbr. chpt. to books, articles, editls. to profl. jours.; peer reviewer various jours., 1994—. Participant Gay and Lesbian Health Group, Ann Arbor, 1994—; apptd. to State of Mich.'s Gov.'s Commn. on Genetic Privacy and Progress, 1997-98. Recipient Clin. Investigator award NIH-NCI, 1995-2000, RO1 award, 1997—, Am. Cancer Rsch. Fund award, 1997-98, U. Mich. award for Disting. Pub. Svc., 2000, Breast Cancer award Dept. Def., 2001, 06. Fellow Am. Soc. Human Genetics, Am. Coll. Med. Genetics; mem. AMA, Am. Acad. Scis., European Soc. Human Genetics, Human Genome Orgn., Alpha Omega Alpha. Democrat. Roman Catholic. Avocations: flute, photography. Office: U Mich 5220 MSRB III Ann Arbor MI 48109-0640

PETTY, GEORGE OLIVER, retired lawyer; b. LA, Mar. 31, 1939; s. Hugh Morton and May (Johnson) P.; m. Sandra Diane Kilpatrick, July 14, 1962; children: Ross Morton, Alison Lee, Christopher Henry. AB, U. Calif., Berkeley, 1961; LLB, U. Calif., 1964. Bar: Calif. 1965, Eng. and Wales 1986, U.S. Supreme Ct. 1976. Atty. Huovinen & White, Oakland, Calif., 1967-69; counsel Bechtel Power Corp., San Francisco, 1969-83; prin. counsel Bechtel Ltd., London, 1983-86; gen. counsel Sun-Diamond Growers of Calif., Pleasanton, Calif., 1987-95; pvt. practice, 1995—96; gen. counsel Tone Bros. Inc., 1997—2008; ret., 2009. Leader Arlington Ave. Utilities Undergrounding Com., 1987—2001. Capt. US Army, 1965—67. Mem. Calif. State Bar Assn., Alameda County Bar Assn., Eng. and Wales Bar Assn., Middle Temple Inn. Office Phone: 510-528-1721. Personal E-mail: gopetty@aol.com.

PETTY, M. S. MARTY, publisher; b. St. Louis, Mo., Dec. 17, 1952; married; 2 children. BA in Journalism, Univ. Mo., 1975; MS in Mgmt., Hartford Grad. Ctr. (Rensselaer), 1989. Asst. mng. editor Kansas City Star and Times; mng. editor Hartford (Conn.) Courant, 1983—89, de. exec. editor, assoc. pub., 1989, sr. v.p., gen. mgr.; pub., CEO Hartford (Conn.) Courant, 1997—2000; exec. v.p. St. Petersburg (Fla.) Times, 2000—, pub., 2004—. Trustee Poynter Inst. for Media Studies, Tampa Bay Newspapers Inc.; juror Pulitzer Prize awards; pres. Soc. of Newspaper Design, 1985; bd. dir. Wm. Randolph Hearst Found. journalism bd., 1987—89. Trustee Congressional Quarterly, Governing Mag., Fla. Trend Mag. Named Bus. Woman of Yr., Women's Coun., St. Petersburg Area C. of C., 2005; named a Woman of Distinction, Girl Scouts of Suncoast Coun., 2004. Mem.: Nat. Assn. Minority Media Executives, Newspaper Assn. Am. (diversity bd.), Am. Press Inst. (adv. bd.), Florida Press Assn. (bd. dir.). Office: St Petersburg Times 490 1st Ave S Saint Petersburg FL 33701

PETTY, MARGARET, elementary school educator; BA in Elem. Edn., Incarnate Word Coll., San Antonio; MS in Spl. Edn./Learning Disabilities, Ala. A&M Univ., Huntsville. Cert. Nat. Bd. Tchg. Standards, 2004. Lead tchr., spl. edn. Rainbow Elem. Sch., Madison, Ala., Liberty Mid. Sch., Madison, Ala. Named Ala. Elem. Tchr. of Yr., 2006, Ala. Tchr. of Yr., 2006; nominee Disney Am. Tchr. award, 2002. Office: Rainbow Elem Sch 50 Nance Rd Madison AL 35758 Office Phone: 256-830-4673. Business E-Mail: mpetty@madisoncity.k12.al.us, Mpetty@ALSDE.edu.

PETTY, MARSHA, chemistry educator; BA cum laude, Ouachita Baptist Univ., Arkadelphia, MA, 1977; postgrad. study, Henderson State Univ., Hendrix Coll., Univ. Ctrl. Ark. Tchr., 1976—; chemistry tchr. Ark. H.S., Texarkana, 1993—. Named Ark. H.S. Tchr. of Yr., Rotary Club, 2005, Ark. Tchr. of Yr., 2006. Mem.: Nat. Sci. Tchr. Assn. Office: Ark High Sch 3512 Grand Ave Texarkana AR 71854

PETTY, MARTY, publishing executive; b. 1953; m. Mark Petty; children: Lindsay, Skip. BJ, U. Mo., 1975; MS in Mgmt., Harvard Grad. Ctr., 1989. Asst. mng. editor Kansas City Star and Times; mng. editor The Hartford Courant, 1983-86, v.p., dep. exec. editor, 1986-89, assoc. pub. for projects and planning, 1989, sr. v.p., gen. mgr., pub., CEO, 1997—2000; exec. v.p. St. Petersburg Times, Fla., 2000—09, pub., 2004—09. Bd. dirs. St. Petersburg Times, Tampa, Fla.; chmn. Barnes Scholarship com. St. Petersburg Times Fund; trustee Poynter Inst. Media Studies, Congl. Quarterly, Governing mag., Fla. Trend mag., Tampa Bay Newspapers, Inc. Editor The Electronic Times, 1991-92. Mem. journalism bd. Wm. Randolph Hearst Found., 1987-89; mem. CEO adv. bd. Greater Hartford Arts Coun.; pres. bd. Camp Courant; bd. dirs. Hartford Courant Found., Hartford Hosp. Holding Co.; mem. The MetroHartford Growth Couns. millennium mgmt. com.; bd. dirs. Tampa Bay Partnership, Leadership Fla.; trustee Jr. Achievement, Acad. Prep, Kids Voting USA; mem. pres.'s coun. Eckerd Coll. Named Disting. Bus. Woman of Yr., St. Petersburg Area C. of C., 2005, Bus. Woman of Yr., Tampa Bay Bus. Jour., 2005; named a Woman of Distinction, Girl Scouts of Suncoast Coun., 2004. Mem. Newspaper Assn. of Am. (Ptnrs. 2000 com., Copyright Clearance Ctr. adv. bd.), Soc. Newspaper Design (pres. 1985, active cons.), Am. Soc. Newspaper Editors, Am. Press Inst. (adv. bd.), AP Mng. Editors, Poynter Inst., Fla. Press Assn. (bd. dirs.), Nat. Assn. Minority Media Execs. Office: St Petersburg Times 490 1st Ave S Saint Petersburg FL 33701-1121 Office Phone: 727-893-8792. Office Fax: 727-892-2328. E-mail: mpetty@sptimes.com.*

PETTY, RICHARD, retired race car driver; b. Level Cross, NC, July 2, 1937; s. Lee and Elizabeth T. P.; m. Lynda Owens, 1958; children: Kyle, Sharon, Lisa, Rebecca. Profl. race car driver, 35 years; ret., 1992; co-owner, Car #43 Petty Enterprises Inc., Richard Petty Motorsports, 2009—. Actor(voice): (films) Cars, 2006, Swing Vote, 2008. Mem. Pres.'s Coun. Fitness and Sport. Recipient Myers Bros. award Nat. Motorsports Press Assn., 1961, 67, 71, Excellence award NASCAR, 1987; named Grand Nat. Rookie of Yr., 1959; Most Popular Driver in Grand Nat., 1962, 64, 68, 70, 74, 75, 76, 77, 78; Martini & Rossi Am. Driver of Yr., 1971; Driver of Yr. Nat. Motorsport Press Assn., 1974-75; Driver of Quarter Century, 1991; named one of Most Influential People in the World of Sports, Bus. Week, 2008; inducted into NC Athletic Hall of Fame, 1973. Mem. Nat. Assn. Stock Car Auto Racing (7 time champion; Winston Cup grand nat. champion 1964, 67, 71, 72, 74, 75, 79) Achievements include entered 1015 Grand Nat. Races, winner 200, 1958-86, with 55 Superspeedway wins; winner Daytona 500, 1964, 66, 71, 73, 74, 79, 81; 1000th career Winston Cup start June 15, 1986 at Mich. Internat. Speedway; 500th consecutive start on Aug. 21, 1988 in Champion Spark Plug 500. Office: Richard Petty Motorsports 112 Byers Creek Rd Mooresville NC 28117*

PETTY, THOMAS LEE, internist, educator; b. Boulder, Colo., Dec. 24, 1932; s. Roy Stone and Eleanor Marie (Kudrna) P.; m. Carol Lee Piepho, Aug. 7, 1954; children: Caryn, Thomas, John. BA, U. Colo., 1955, MD, 1958. Intern Phila. Gen. Hosp., 1958-59; resident U. Mich., 1959-60, U. Colo., Denver, 1960-62, pulmonary fellow, 1962-63, chief resident medicine, 1963-64, instr. medicine, 1962-64, asst. prof., 1964-68, assoc. prof., 1968-74, prof. medicine, 1974—; pres. Presbyn./St. Luke's Ctr. for Health Scis. Edn., 1989-95; practice medicine, specializing in internal medicine, pulmonary medicine Denver, 1962—; prof. medicine Rush Univ., 1992—. Cons. Kindred Hosp., 1991-. Author: For Those Who Live and Breathe, 1967, 2d edit., 1972, Intensive and Rehabilitative Respiratory Care, 1971, 3d edit., 1982, Chronic Obstructive Pulmonary Disease, 1978, 2d edit., 1985, Principles and Practice of Pulmonary Rehabilitation, 1993, Enjoying Life With COPD, 1995, 3d edit., Pulmonary Disorders of the Elderly, 2007, others; contbr. articles to profl. jours. NIH and Found. grantee, 1966-88. Master ACP, Am. Coll. Chest Physicians (master, pres. 1982); mem. Assn. Am. Physicians, Assn. of Pulmonary Program Dirs. (founding pres. 1983-84, chmn. nat. lung health edn. program 1995—, co-chmn. 2000-04), Am. Bd. Internal Medicine (bd. govs. 1986-92), Am. Thoracic Soc. (Disting. Achievement award 1995), Phi Beta Kappa, Phi Delta Theta, Alpha Omega Alpha, Phi Rho Sigma (pres. 1976-78). Home: 1325 Clermont Street Denver CO 80220 Office: 899 Logan St Ste 103 Denver CO 80203 Home Phone: 303-717-0325. Personal E-mail: tlpdoc@aol.com.

PETTY, TOM (THOMAS EARL PETTY), musician, composer; b. Gainesville, Fla., Oct. 20, 1950; s. Earl and Katherine Petty; m. Jane Benyo, 1974 (div. Sept. 9, 1996); children: Adria, Kim; m. Dana York, June 3, 2001. With band the Sundowners (1964) which later was called the Epics (1965-69) and Mudcrutch (1970-74), Gainesville, Fla.; songwriter, musician for Leon Russell, 1974—75; lead singer, guitarist Tom Petty and the Heartbreakers, 1975—. Singer:(albums with the Heartbreakers) Tom Petty and the Heartbreakers, 1976, You're Gonna Get It, 1978, Damn the Torpedoes, 1979, Hard Promises, 1981, Long After Dark, 1982, Southern Accents, 1985, Pack Up the Plantation-Live!, 1986, Let Me Up (I've Had Enough), 1987, Into the Great Wide Open, 1991 (Grammy nomination for Best Rock Performance by a Duo or Group with Vocal, 1992), Tom Petty and the Heartbreakers' Greatest Hits, 1993, Playback, 1995, Echo, 1999 (Grammy nomination for Best Rock Album, 2000), Anthology: through the Years, 2000, The Last DJ, 2002, Live at the Olympic: The Last DJ and More, 2003; (soundtrracks) She's The One, 1996; (with The Traveling Wilburys) Traveling Wilburys Vol. 1, 1989 (Grammy Award for Best Rock Performance by a Duo or Group with Vocal, 1990, Grammy nomination for Album of Yr., 1990), Traveling Wilburys Vol. 3, 1990; (albums with Mudcrutch) Mudcrutch, 2008; (solo albums) Full Moon Fever, 1989 (Grammy nomination for Album of Yr., 1990), Wildflowers, 1994 (Grammy nomination for Best Rock Album, 1996), Highway Companion, 2006; hit singles include Breakdown, 1978, Here Comes My Girl, 1979, Refugee, 1979, (duet with Stevie Nicks) Stop Dragging My Heart Around, 1981, The Waiting, 1981, You Got Lucky, 1982, Don't Come Around Here No More, 1985, Jammin' Me, 1987, Free Fallin', 1989, Running Down A Dream, 1989, I Won't Back Down, 1989, Into the Great Wide Open, Learning to Fly, 1991, Mary Jane's Last Dance, 1993, You Don't Know How It Feels, 1994, You Wreck Me, 1994, Walls, 1996, Free Girl Now, 1999, Swingin', 1999; Actor: (films) Made in Heaven, 1987, The Postman, 1997; (TV appearances) (voice only) The Simpsons, 2002, (voice only), King of the Hill, 2005; host (radio show) Buried Treasure, 2005—; subject of documentary: Tom Petty and the Heartbreakers: Runnin' Down a Dream, 2007 (Grammy award for Best Long Form Music Video, 2009). Grammy nomination for Best Rock Performance by a Duo or Group with Vocal (with Stevie Nicks for Stop Draggin' My Heart Around), 1982, Grammy nomination for Best Rock Song (Learning to Fly), 1992, Grammy nomination for Best Rock Performance by a Duo or Group with Vocal (with Bob Dylan, Roger McGuinn, Neil Young, Eric Clapton, and George Harrison for My Back Pages), 1994, Grammy nomination for Best Rock Song (with the Heartbreakers for Room At The Top), 2000, Grammy Award for Best Male Rock Vocal Performance (for You Don't Know Hot It Feels), 1996, MTV Video Music Award for Best Male Video (with the Heartbreakers for Mary Jane's Last Dance), 1994, Video Vanguard Award, MTV Video Music Awards, 1994, MTV Video Music Award for Best Male Video (for You Don't Know How It Feels), 1995, Songwriter Award, ASCAP, 1990, Golden Note Award, ASCAP, 1996, Nat. Veteran's Foundation Special Award of Recognition, 1995, UCLA George & Ira Gershwin Award, 1996, Bill Graham Lifetime Achievement Award, CA Music Awards, 1998, Hollywood Walk of Fame Star (with the Heartbreakers), 1999, inducted, Rock & Roll Hall of Fame (with the Heartbreakers), 2002, Legend Award, Radio Music Awards, 2003, Century award, Billboard Music Awards, 2005. Office: Warner Bros Records 3300 Warner Blvd Burbank CA 91505-4694

PETZ, EDWIN V., real estate company executive, lawyer; b. Beatrice, Nebr., May 14, 1935; s. Virgil Leonard and Ruth Elenor (Thomsen) P.; m. Daphne Cross, May 17, 1958 (div. June 1964); 1 dau., Katherine J.; m. Anne Higgins, Dec. 3, 1964 (div. Sept. 1993); 1 son, W. Christopher; m. Louise Loosli, Jan. 9, 1997. BA, Principia Coll., Elsah, Ill., 1955; JD, Harvard U., 1958. Bar: N.Y. 1959, Mass. 1976. Assoc. Chadbourne, Parke, Whiteside & Wolff, NYC, 1958-62; asst. gen. counsel Martin Marietta Corp., Bethesda, Md., 1963-64, 1965-75; gen. atty. sec. Bunker-Ramo Corp., Oakbrook, Ill., 1964-65; asst. gen. counsel United Brands Co., NYC, 1975-82, v.p., gen. counsel, sec., 1982-84; sr. v.p., gen. counsel Milstein Properties Corp., 1985—2003; sr. v.p., gen counsel The Milstein Group Inc., 1992—; sr. v.p., gen. counsel Ogden CAP Properties, LLC, 2003—. Mem. ABA, Assn. of Bar of City N.Y. Clubs: University (N.Y.C.). Republican. Episcopalian. Office: Ogden CAP Properities LLC 390 Park Ave New York NY 10022

PETZAL, DAVID ELIAS, retired editor, writer; b. NYC, Oct. 21, 1941; s. Henry and Aline Born (Bixer) P.; m. Arlene Anne Taylor, May 29, 1974. BA, Colgate U., 1963. Editor Maco Publs., NYC, 1964—69; mng. editor Davis Publs., NYC, 1969—70; features editor Hearst Publs., NYC, 1970—72; mng. editor CBS Publs., NYC, 1972—79, editor, 1979—83, exec. editor, 1983—2001, Field & Stream Mag., NYC, 1983—2001, mng. editor, 2001—03, dep. editor, 2002—08; ret., 2008. Author: The .22 Rifle, 1972; editor: The Experts Book of the Shooting Sports, 1972, The Experts Book of Upland Game and Waterfowl Hunting, 1975, The Experts Book of Big-Game Hunting in North America, 1976, The Ency. of Sporting Firearms, 1991.

PETZEL, FLORENCE ELOISE, textiles educator; b. Crosbyton, Tex., Apr. 1, 1911; d. William D. and Eloise Petzel. PhB, U. Chgo., 1931, AM, 1934; PhD, U. Minn., 1954. Instr. Judson Coll., 1936—38; asst. prof. textiles Ohio State U., 1938—48; assoc. prof. U. Ala., 1950—54; prof. Oreg. State U., Corvallis, 1954—61, 1967—75, prof. emeritus, 1975—, dept. head, 1954—61, 1967—75; prof., divsn. head U. Tex., 1961—63; prof. Tex. Tech. U., 1963—67. Vis. instr. Tex. State Coll. for Women, 1937; vis. prof. Wash. State U., 1967 Author: Textiles of Ancient Mesopotamia, Persia and Egypt, 1987; contbr. articles to profl. jours. Effie I. Raitt fellow, 1949—50. Mem. Met. Opera Guild, Sigma Xi, Phi Kappa Phi, Omicron Nu, Iota Sigma Pi, Sigma Delta Epsilon, New Eng. Hist. & Geneal. Soc. Home: 150 Downs Blvd Apt D114 Clemson SC 29631

PETZOLD, CAROL STOKER, state legislator; b. St. Louis, July 28; d. Harold William and Mabel Lucille (Wilson) Stoker; m. Walter John Petzold, June 27, 1959; children: Ann, Ruth, David. BS, Valparaiso U., Ind., 1959. Tchr. Parkwood Elem. Sch., Kensington, Md., 1960-62; legis. aide Md. Gen. Assembly, Annapolis, 1975-79; legis. asst. Montgomery County Bd. Edn., Rockville, Md., 1980; cmty. sch. coord. Parkland Jr. H.S., Rockville, 1981-87; mem. Md. Ho. of Dels., Annapolis, 1987—2007, mem. constl. and adminstrv. law com., 1987-93, mem. judiciary com., 1994—2006, chair subcom. on criminal justice, 2003—06, vice chair Montgomery County del., 1995—2006, dep. majority whip, 1999—2002. Mem. spl. com. drug and alcohol abuse Md. Ho. Dels., 1999—07, chair, 2007; mem. transp. planning bd. Nat. Capitol Region, 1989—07; vice chmn. assembly on fed. issues Nat. Conf. State Legislatures, 1996-97, chair adv. coun. on energy, 1997-99, chair energy and transp. com., 1998-99, pres. women's legis. network, 2004-05, chair transp. com., 2004-05; mem. State Adv. Coun. Adminstrv. Hearings, 1990-2007, chair, 1996-2001, Md. State Rd. Commn., 2008-, Md. Transp. Commn., 2008-. Editor Child Care Sampler, 1974, Stoker Family Cookbook, 1976; author, editor Stoker-Rauch Family History, 2007. Pres. Montgomery Child Care Assn., 1976-78; mem. Md. State Scholarship Bd., 1978-87, chmn. 1985-87; chmn. Legis. Com. Montgomery County Commn. for Children and Youth, 1979-84; mem., v.p. Luth. Social Services Nat. Capitol Area, Washington, 1980-86; mem. exec. com. coun. Montgomery United Way, 1981-2000; bd. dirs. Wheaton-Kensington C. of C., 2007-08, Nat. Capital Trolley Mus., 2008—. Recipient Statewide award, Gov.'s Adv. Bd. on Homelessness, 1994, recognized for outstanding commitment to children, US Dept. HEW, 1980, Recognized Exceptional Svc. award, Valparaiso U. Alumni Assn., 1988, Excellence Edn. Alumni award, Valparaiso U., Award of Excellence, MADD, 2002, Disting. Legislator award, 2003, Impaired Driving Coalition, 2003, Legis. award, Md. Network Against Domestic Violence, 2003; named Mother of Yr., March of Dimes, 2000; named one of Top 100 Md. Women, Daily Record, 2002, 2004. Mem.: AAUW (honoree Kensington br. 1971, 2002, honoree Md. divsn. 1981), Women Legislators of Md., Women's Polit. Caucus (chmn. Montgomery County 1981—83). Democrat. Lutheran.

PETZOLD, JOHN PAUL, judge; b. 1938; BA, U. Maine, 1961; LLB, Washington & Lee U., 1962. Bar: Ohio 1962, Va. 1962. Pvt. practice law, Ohio, 1962-91; asst. atty. gen. State of Ohio, 1964-71; law dir. City of Miamisburg, Ohio, 1979-91; judge Montgomery County Common Pleas Ct., Dayton, Ohio, 1991—. Bd. tax appeals City of Kettering, Ohio, 1971-91. Mem. ABA, Ohio State Bar Assn. (bd. govs., former chairperson young lawyers sect., chairperson pub. rels. com., vice chairperson lawyers assistance com., eminent domain com., banking, comml., and bankruptcy law com., pres. 1998-99), Dayton Bar Assn.

(pres. 1989-90), Common Pleas Judge Assn. (mem. bd. commrs. on grievances and discipline 1995-97). Avocations: golf, swimming, writing, teaching, reading, genealogy. Office: Montgomery County Common Pleas Ct 41 N Perry St Dayton OH 45402-1431

PETZOLD, MARK CARL, electrical engineer, educator; s. Lester and Rachel Petzold; m. Deanna Loomis, Mar. 19, 1994; children: David, Steven. PhD in Elec. Engring., U. Colo., Colo. Springs, 2001. Engr. Varian Assocs. Med. Equipment, Palo Alto, Calif., 1988—94; sr. staff engr. Pericle Comm. Co., Colo. Springs, 2000—01; assoc. prof. St. Cloud State U., Dept. Elec. and Computer Engring., St. Cloud, Minn., 2001—. Den leader Boy Scouts America, St. Cloud, 2008—. Mem.: IEEE, Am. Soc. Engring. Edn. Achievements include research in serial concatenated convolutional codes. Office: Saint Cloud State Univ 720 Fourth Ave S ECC 211 Saint Cloud MN 56301 Business E-Mail: mcpetzold@stcloudstate.edu.

PEUGEOT, PATRICK, insurance executive; b. Paris, Aug. 3, 1937; s. Jacques Louis and Edith (Genoyer) P.; m. Catherine Dupont, 1963; children: Hubert, Thomas, Camille. Degree, Ecole Poly., Paris, 1959, Ecole Nat. D'Adminstrn., 1965. Ins. auditor Ministry of Fin., Paris, 1962-65; auditor Cour des Comptes, Paris, 1965-83; spl. asst. Bur. Planning, Paris, 1966-70; sr. v.p. EMC, Toulouse, France, 1970-72, Hachette Inc., Paris, 1972-74; exec. v.p. ops. AGF Life, Paris, 1974-78; exec. v.p. AGF Reims, Paris, 1979-82; pres. Caisse Cen. de Reassurance, Paris, 1983-85; chmn., CEO Scor S.A., Paris, 1983-94, hon. chmn., 1994, 1994—, La Mondiale Groupe, 2005—; dir. SCOR U.S., 1994—; vice-chmn., CEO La Mondiale, Paris, chmn., CEO, 1996—2005, hon. chmn., 2005—; chmn. La Mondiale Partenaire, 2005—08, Cimade Decumenial Svc. Mutual Aid. Home: 99 Rue du Faubourg du Temple 75010 Paris France Office Phone: 0033153057714, 0176608953. Business E-Mail: francoise.masquelier@lamondiale.com.

PEVEAR, ROBERTA CHARLOTTE, state legislator; b. Bethel, Maine, July 4, 1930; d. Frank Albert Sr. and Thirza Estella (Hickford) Gibson; m. Edward Gordon Pevear, Aug. 21, 1971. Diploma in Comml. Art, Gould Acad., 1947. Sec. Wilner Wood Products, South Paris, Maine, 1947-50; sec. export dept. Whitaker Cable, North Kansas City, Mo., 1951-56; sec. br. and dist. Anheuser-Busch, Inc., Kansas City, Mo., 1957-59; legal sec. Johnson & Johnson, New Brunswick, NJ, 1960-65, St. John, Ronder & Bell, Kingston, NY, 1966; sec., adminstrv. asst. Sears-Roebuck & Co., Overland Park, Kans., 1967-70, Exeter, NH, 1971-77; salesman Avon Products, Hampton Falls, NH, 1978-86; mem. ho. reps. State of N.H., 1979-88, ret., 1988. Commr. Rockingham Planning Commn., N.H., 1979-88, N.H. Planning Com., 1985-88; clk. Environment and Agrl. Com. N.H. Ho. Reps., 1983-88; del. mem. Rockingham County, 1979-88, exec. bd., 1984-88; chmn. Rockingham County Home, 1987-88. Civil Def. dir., Hampton Falls, NH, 1980—88. Recipient Community Citizen award Hampton Falls Grange, 1982, Seacoast Retired Sr. Service award, 1985. Mem. Nat. Order Women Legislators, N.H. Order of Women Legislators, DAR. Avocations: writing, genealogy.

PEVEC, ANTHONY EDWARD, bishop emeritus; b. Cleve., Apr. 16, 1925; s. Anton and Frances Darovec P. MA, John Carroll U., Cleve., 1956; PhD, Western Res. U., Cleve., 1964. Ordained priest Diocese of Cleve., Ohio, 1950; assoc. pastor St. Mary Church, Elyria, Ohio, 1950—52, St. Lawrence Ch., Cleve., 1952—53; rector-prin. Borromeo Sem. HS, Wickliffe, Ohio, 1953—75; adminstrv. bd. Nat. Cath. Edn. Assn., 1972—75; pastor St. Vitus Ch., Cleve., 1975—79; rector-pres. Borromeo Coll., Wickliffe, 1979—82; ordained bishop, 1982; aux. bishop Diocese of Cleve., 1982—2001, aux. bishop emeritus, 2001—. Mem. v.p. Slovenian-Am. Heritage Found., Cleve., 1975—. Recipient honoree, Heritage Found., Cleve., 1982, Alumni medal, John Carroll U., 2004; named Man of Yr., Fedn. Slovenian Nat. Homes, Cleve., 1985, Cath. Man of Yr., KC, 1998, Man of Yr., Pioneer Assn., 2001, Cathedral Latin Alumni Assn., 2003; named to Hall of Fame, St. Vitus Alumni Assn., 1989, Wickliffe Hall of Fame, 2000. Mem.: KC (state chaplain 2003—05), Cath. Order Foresters (state chaplain 2000—04), U.S. Cath. Conf. (nat. adv. coun. 1996—97), Nat. Conf. Cath. Bishops (com. on vocations 1984—86, com. on pro-life activities 1990—92, com. on priestly formation 1993—95, com. on sci. and human values 1993—96). Democrat. Roman Catholic. Avocations: reading, music. Home and Office: Diocese of Cleveland 28700 Euclid Ave Wickliffe OH 44092-2527 Home Phone: 440-944-1400. Business E-Mail: bpaepevec@dioceseofcleveland.org. *Ultimately I must always remember that the Lord is totally in control of my life, no matter how complicated it may seem to be. I am here to do the Lord's will, and wherever I go I come to do His will.*

PEW, JOHN GLENN, JR., lawyer; b. Dallas, Apr. 18, 1932; s. John Glenn Sr. and Roberta (Haughton) P. BA, U. Tex., 1954, LLB, 1955. Bar: Tex. 1955, U.S. Dist. Ct. (no. dist.) Tex. 1959, U.S. Supreme Ct. 1959, U.S. Ct. Appeals (5th cir.) 1961, U.S. Ct. Appeals (10th cir.) 1982. Ptnr. Jackson Walker LLP, Dallas, 1964—. With USNR, 1955-58. Mem.: Order of Coif, Phi Beta Kappa. Republican. Presbyterian. Office: Jackson Walker LLP 901 Main St Ste 6000 Dallas TX 75202-3797 Office Phone: 214-953-6000. E-mail: jpew@jw.com.

PEW, ROBERT ANDERSON, retired real estate and equipment leasing corporation officer; b. Phila., Aug. 22, 1936; s. Arthur Edmund and Mary Elizabeth (Elliott) P.; children from previous marriage: Robert Anderson (dec.), James Cunningham, Glenn Edgar, Joan Elliott; m. Daria S. Decerio, June 19, 1993; 1 child, Richard Westerman. Student, Princeton U., 1954-56; BS, Temple U., 1959; MS in Mgmt. (Alfred P. Sloan fellow), MIT, 1970; LLD (hon.), Widener U., 1982; DPS (hon.), Temple U., 1983; LHD (hon.), Gettysburg Coll., 1984. Ops. asst. prodn. div. Sun Oil Co., Premont, Tex., 1959-60, ops. asst. prodn. div. Morgan City, La., auditor internal audit dept. Phila., 1960-65, staff asst. treasury dept., 1965-69, asst. to exec. v.p. corp. projects group, 1970-71, sec.-treas., mgr. financial control of products group, 1971-74, corp. sec., 1974-77; pres. Helios Capital Corp., 1977-96; CEO Radnor Corp., 1995-96; bd. dirs. Glenmede Corp., Phila., chmn., 1997—2004. Bd. dirs. Pew Charitable Trusts, Phila., Glenmede Trust Co. N.A., Phila., Sunoco Inc, Phila., 1978—2009. Trustee Children's Hosp., Phila., vice chmn., 1991—. Served Pa. Air N.G., 1956—59. Recipient R. Kelso Carter award Widener U., 1971 Mem. Aircraft Owners and Pilots Assn. (trustee, chmn. 1974-77, 85-2002, vice-chmn. 1979-85), Am. Hosp. Assn. (hon.), Coll. Physicians Phila., Union League Club, Harbor Club (pres. 1992-96), Phila. Aviation Country Club, Merion Cricket Club, N.E. Harbor Fleet, Seal Harbor Yacht Club. Republican. Presbyterian. Home: 916 Muirfield Rd Bryn Mawr PA 19010-1921 Personal E-mail: dungarnem@aol.com.

PEWEN, WILLIAM F., legislative staff member; b. Pasadena, Calif. BS in Health Edn., Southern Oreg. State U.; MPH in Epidemiology, U. Pitts., 2001, PhD in Infectious Diseases and Microbiology, 2003. Sr. health policy advisor, Senator Olympia Snowe US Senate, Washington, 2004—. Congl. fellow, Am. Soc. Microbiology, 2003—04. Republican. Office: 154 Rayburn Senate Office Bldg Washington DC 20515 Office Phone: 202-224-5344. Office Fax: 202-224-1946.*

PEWITT, JAMES DUDLEY, retired academic administrator; b. Franklin, Tenn., July 28, 1930; s. James Isaac and Eleanor (Dudley) P.; m. Betty Louise Hightower, Oct. 31, 1952; children: Ransom D., James P., Thomas E. Student, Vanderbilt U., 1948-51; MBA, MS, U.S.C., 1964, D in Bus. Adminstrn., 1967. Commd. lt. USAF, 1952, advanced through grades to col., 1969; AMC test pilot, 1958—62; spl. asst. for econ. analysis Office of Sec. of Air Force, 1967; exec. to asst. sec. Air Force for Fin. Mgmt. Nat. War Coll., 1971; asst. Da Nang Air Base, Vietnam, 1972; dep. comdr. for ops. Vietnam, 1972; vice comdr. Gunfighters, 1972; chief linebacker ops. Staff of Dir. of Ops., Vietnam, 1972; dir. mgmt. analysis USAF, 1973, ret., 1973; dir. grad. sch. bus. U. Ala., Birmingham, 1973-74, asst. v.p. ops. and planning, 1974-77, v.p. adminstrn., 1977-84, sr. v.p. adminstrn., 1984-90, Disting. prof., 1990—94, emeritus, 1994—. Bd. dir. Birmingham Cable Communications, Allied Products Co. Mem. Birmingham Airport Authority, 1986-93; chmn. bd. So. Mus. of Flight, 1993-2005; faculty rep. Sun Belt Conf., 1983-90, pres., 1989-90; mem. NCAA Coun., 1990-94. Decorated D.F.C. with 3 oak leaf clusters, Bronze Star, Legion of Merit with 2 oak leaf clusters, Air medal with 11 oak leaf clusters, 10 other awards and fgn. decorations; named to Ala, Aviation Hall of Fame, 2003. Mem. Birmingham C. of C. (bd. dirs. 1977-84, pres. 1983, chmn. 1984), Birmingham Country Club, Skull & Dagger, Phi Kappa Phi, Beta Gamma Sigma, Sigma Xi, Omicron Delta Kappa, Kappa Alpha, Order of Daedalians, Order of Quiet Birdmen. Avocations: flying, golf. Home Phone: 205-870-5470.

PEYREFITTE, ASHTON GEORGE, JR., meteorologist, educator; b. New Orleans, Oct. 5, 1942; s. Ashton Gonzalo Peyrefitte and Melba Catherine Parpal. BS, Fla. State U., Tallahassee, 1967, MS, 1969; PhD, U. Utah, Salt Lake City, 1986. Mem. faculty St. Aloysius H.S., New Orleans, 1964—65; rsch. asst. Fla. State U., Tallahassee, 1967—70; instr. U. Lowell, Mass., 1971—72, SUNY, Oneonta, 1972—80; assoc. instr. U. Utah, Salt Lake City, 1980—81; assoc. prof. meteorology Plymouth State U., NH, 1985—2000, faculty emeritus; asst. prof. meteorology Ctrl. Mich. U., Mt. Pleasant, 2000—. Contbr. articles to profl. jours. Named Outstanding Tchg. Asst., U. Utah, 1981; fellow, NSF, 1969. Mem.: Nat. Weather Assn., Am. Meteorol. Soc. (banquet held in honor 2006). Office: Ctrl Mich Univ Dept Geology 314 Brooks Hall Mount Pleasant MI 48859

PEYTON, JOHN, Mayor, Jacksonville, Florida; b. July 28, 1964; m. Kathryn Pearson; children: John Conner, Kent Thomas. Grad. Exec. Edn. Program, Harvard Bus. Sch.; BA, Mercer U., 1986. V.p. Gate Petroleum Co., Fla.; mayor City of Jacksonville, Fla., 2003—. Mem. Harry S. Truman Scholarship Found., 2007—. Past pres. Greenscape of Jacksonville, 1998—99; chmn. Jacksonville Symphony Assn.; mem. St. John's Episcopal Ch.; bd. mem. Jacksonville Transp. Authority, 1996—99, chmn., 1999—2003. Recipient James Patterson Pageturner award, 2005, Children's Champion award, Episcopal Children's Services, 2005. Republican.*

PEZESHK, VIOLET, psychologist, educator; d. Mohammad and Gowhar Pezeshk; children: Jhanna Shaghaghi, Natasha Shaghaghi. PhD, Alliant Internat. U., 2000. Cert. hypnotherapist Calif.; DV specialist Minn., 1998. Mem. adj. faculty Dept. Clin. Psychology and MFT Alliant Internat. U., San Diego, 2001—; clin. psychologist Palomar Family Counseling, Escondido, Calif., 2003—04. Program dir. St. Clare's Home, Escondido, 2002—03. Author: (self-help book) Psychological Development of Children from Birth to Adolescence, (children's novel) Ziba, editor weekly clin. article for mag.; exhibitions include Peace on Earth. Mem.: APA (assoc.). Personal E-mail: drpezeshk@yahoo.com.

PEZZELLA, JERRY JAMES, JR., investment and real estate company executive; b. Chesapeake, Va., Sept. 30, 1937; s. Jerry James, Sr. and Mabel (Aydlett) Pezzella; m. Carolyn Blades; children: James M., Stanley J., Julie Pezzella Scanlon. BS, U. Richmond, 1963; MBA, U. Pa., 1964. Asst. v.p. Va. Nat. Bank (now Bank of Am.), Norfolk, 1964-68; chmn. bd., pres. First Am. Investment Corp., First Ga. Investment Corp., Atlanta, 1968-74; v.p. Great Am. Investment Corp., Atlanta, 1974-78; sr. exec. v.p., 1984-85; exec. v.p. Equity Fin. & Mgmt. Co., Chgo., 1978-99; pres., chmn. bd. First Capital Fin. Corp., Chgo., 1983-85; pres. GAFGI Holdings Inc., Chgo., 1983-98; chmn. bd. 1st Property Mgmt. Corp., 1990-92; dir., fin. officer, treas., vice chairman Bear Paw Svc. Dist., 2002—08. Instr. fin. Old Dominion U., 1965—67, Ga. State U., 1970—73; adj. prof. U. Richmond, 1975—77; real estate cons., 1997—2001; bd. dirs. Great Am. Mgmt. and Investment, Inc. Mem. exec. com. Nat. Multi Housing Coun., 1991—93, bd. dirs., 1992—94. Mem.: Brasstown Valley Golf & Country Club, Met. Club (Chgo.). Home: 1240 Village Rd Murphy NC 28906-1763

PEZZOLESI, LINDA S.W., science educator; d. Donald and Grace Wilhelm; m. Timothy Pezzolesi, July 24, 1991. BS, SUNY Coll. Environ. Sci. and Forestry, Syracuse, 1991; MS, Tex. Tech U., Lubbock, 1994; PhD, SUNY Binghamton, 2000. Faculty Skidmore Coll., Saratoga Springs, NY, 2002—03; asst. prof. Hudson Valley CC, Troy, NY, 2003—. Pvt. practice, burrowing owl relocation cons., Denver, 2000—01. Mem.: Animal Behavior. Office: Hudson Valley CC 80 Vandenburgh Ave Troy NY 12180 Business E-Mail: l.pezzolesi@hvcc.edu.

PEZZULLO, RALPH MICHAEL, writer, playwright; b. NYC, Dec. 27, 1954; s. Lawrence Anthony Pezzullo and Josephine DeMattia; m. Alice Palmisano, Aug. 8, 1980 (div. Jan. 1994); children: John Lawrence, Michael Richard; m. Jessica Rae Pezzullo, May 19, 1994; children: Francesca Sophia, Alessandra Sabina. M in Pub. and Internat. Affairs, George Washington U., 1975. Grants specialist Nat. Endowment Arts, Washington, 1975—79. Author: At the Fall of Somoza, 1994, Eve Missing, 2003, Jawbreaker, 2005, Plunging Into Haiti, 2006, The Walk-In, 2008, Most Evil, 2009, (plays) From Behind the Moon, 1984, The Tail of the Tiger, 1985, Eating the Shadow, 1990, Wilderness of Mirrors, 1994, Hide Mother in My Heart, 1996, Gauquin's Parrot, 1997, Spain, 1998, Stakes, 1999, Okeechobee Split, 2000, Murder Sketched Gently, 2000, Most Evil, 2009, (radio drama/series) The Life and Times of Swamp Fox, 1985. Recipient Spl. citation Kesselring award, 1986, Screenwriting award, Writer's Guild Am. E. Found., 1987, award, Ctr. Theater, 1994, Douglas Dillon prize, 2006; Playwriting fellow, Jerome Found., 1997, 1998, 1999, 2001. Mem.: PEN USA, Writer's Guild Am., Pvt. Eye Writers Am., Mystery Writers Am., Author's League Am., Art Student's League, Dramatists Guild. Avocations: painting, sports. Home: 10055 Reevesbury Dr Beverly Hills CA 90210 E-mail: pezzullo@mindspring.com, ralph@ralphpezzullo.com.

PEZZUTO, JOHN MICHAEL, dean, pharmacology educator; b. Hammonton, NJ, Aug. 29, 1950; s. Michael L. and Elizabeth (Brown) Pezzuto; m. Mimi Rotstein, Aug. 29, 1986; children: John-Henry Albert, Elisabeth Lee, Michael Joseph Ivan; 1 child from previous marriage, Jennifer Anne. AB, Rutgers U., NJ, 1973; PhD, U. Medicine & Dentistry NJ, 1977. Postdoc. assoc. MIT, Cambridge, 1977-79; instr. chemistry U. Va., Charlottesville, 1979-80; asst. prof. U. Ill., Chgo., 1980-84, assoc. prof., 1984-91, prof., Coll. Pharmacy, 1991—2002, prof., Coll. Medicine, 1994—2002, Disting. Univ. prof., 2002; prof. medicinal chemistry/molecular pharmacology Purdue U. Coll. Pharmacy, Nursing & Health Scis., West Lafayette, Ind., 2002—06, dean, 2002—06; founding dean, prof. chemistry U. Hawaii Coll. Pharmacy, Hilo, 2006—. Assoc. dir. U. Ill. Cancer Ctr., 1991—95, dep. dir., 2000—02; head dept. med. chemistry/pharmacognosy U. Ill. Coll. Pharmacy, 1992—95, interim head, 2000—01, dir. prog. collaborative rsch. in pharm. scis., 1995—98, assoc. dean rsch. & grad. edn., 1998—2002; pres., co-founder Internat. Therapeutics Inc., River Forest, Ill. Editor-in-chief Jour. Pharmacognosy, 1991—95, Combinatory Chemistry and High Throughput Screening, 1996—97, Pharmaceutical Biology, 1997—; contbr. articles to profl. jours. Recipient Career Devel. award, NIH, 1984—89; grantee Nat. Inst. Dental Rsch., 1984—85; fellow NIH, 1977—80, Alexander von Humboldt Found., 1990—91. Mem.: AAAS, Am. Soc. Biol. Chemists, NY Acad. Scis., Am. Assn. Cancer Rsch., Am. Soc. Pharmacognosy, Am. Chem. Soc. Office: U Hawaii Coll Pharmacy 34 Rainbow Dr Hilo HI 96720-4091 Office Phone: 808-933-2909. Business E-Mail: pezzuto@hawaii.edu.*

PEZZUTO, MIMI, pharmacist, educator; b. Chgo., Jan. 5, 1962; d. Sherwin Rotstein and Lynda Silverman, Mark Heister (Stepfather), Howard Silverman (Stepfather); m. John Pezzuto, Aug. 29, 1986; children: John-Henry, Elisabeth, Michael. Degree, U. Ill. Coll. Pharmacy, Chgo., 1986. Registered pharmacist Ill., Hawaii, 1986. Pharmacist, pharmacy mgr. Walgreen Co., Deerfield, Ill., 1986—95; sr. cons. Blue Cross and Blue Shield Assn., Chgo., 1995—97, mgr. pharmacy programs, 1997—2002, Blue Cross Blue Shield Ill.(HCSC), 1997—2002; instr. pharm. scis. pharmacy practice U. Hawaii, Hilo, 2008—. Cons. Rxaminer (now DestinationRX), Chgo., 2000—02, Pharm. Industry, Law Firms. Office: Univ Hawaii 34 Rainbow Dr Hilo HI 96720 Personal E-mail: mimipezzuto@yahoo.com.

PFAELZER, MARIANA R., federal judge; b. LA, Feb. 4, 1926; AB, U. Calif., 1947; LLB, UCLA, 1957. Bar: Calif. 1958. Assoc. Wyman, Bautzer, Rothman & Kuchel, 1957-69, ptnr., 1969-78; judge U.S. Dist. Ct. (ctrl. dist.) Calif., 1978—. Mem. Jud. Conf. Adv. Com. on Fed. Rules of Civil Procedure. Pres., v.p., dir. Bd. Police Commrs. City of L.A., 1974-78. UCLA Alumnus award for Profl. Achievement, 1979, named Alumna of Yr., UCLA Law Sch., 1980, U. Calif. Santa Barbara Disting. Alumnus award, 1983. Mem. ABA, Calif. Bar Assn. (local adminstrv. com., spl. com. study rules procedure 1972, joint subcom. profl. ethics and computers and the law coms. 1972, profl. ethics com. 1972-74, spl. com. juvenile justice, women's rights subcom. human rights sect.), L.A. County Bar Assn. (spl. com. study rules procedure state bar 1974), Ninth Cir. Dist. Judges Assn. (pres.). Office: US Dist Ct 312 N Spring St Ste 152 Los Angeles CA 90012-4703

PFAFF, BRUCE, legislative staff member; b. Cin. Grad. in mktg. and pub. rels., U. Cin. Dep. campaign mgr. Rob Portman's Congl. Campaign; dep. dir. fundraising Thomas Kindness's Congl. Campaign; dir. Supreme Ct. campaigns Ohio Republican Party, 1994; campaign mgr. John Gillespie's Senatorial Campaigns, Cate Zeuske's Senatorial Campaigns; polit. dir. Scott McCallum's Gubernatorial Campaign; chief of staff to Senator Ted Kanavas Wis. State Senate; ptnr., sr. v.p. and dir. client devel. Pub. Affairs Strategies, Inc.; campaign mgr. Milw. County Exec. Scott Walker's Gubernatorial Campaign, 2005—06; comm. dir. to Rep. Jean Schmidt US House of Reps., Washington. Served with Ohio Army Nat. Guard. Republican. Office: 418 Cannon House Office Bldg Washington DC 20515 Office Phone: 202-225-3164. Office Fax: 202-225-1992.*

PFAFF, JUDY, artist; b. London, Eng., 1946; Student, Wayne State U., 1965—66, Southern Ill. U., 1968—69; BFA, Washington U., St. Louis, 1971; postgrad., Yale U., 1970, MFA, 1973. Prof. arts Columbia U., 1992—94; Milton Avery Disting. prof. art Bard Coll., 1989, 1991, 1994—. Exhibited in group shows at Whitney Mus. Am. Art, NY, 1975, 1988, Whitney Mus. Am. Art, Champion, Stamford, Conn., 1993, Hallwalls Gallery, Buffalo, 1976, Art Mus. U. Calif., Santa Barbara, 1979, Neuberger Mus. SUNY, Purchase, 1979, Contemporary Arts Mus., Houston, 1980, Contemporary Arts Ctr., Cin., 1980, Mus. Modern Art, NYC, 1984, Venice Biennale, 1984, Rotunda Gallery, Bklyn., 1984, Bklyn. Mus., 1985, Mis. Modern Art, 1989, Internat. Art Projects, Asia, 1990, Inst. Contemporary Art, Phila., 1991, Cultural Space, NY, 1992, Henie-Onstad Art Ctr., Norway, 1992, Drawing Ctr., NY, 1993, one-woman shows include Webb and Parsons Gallery, New Canaan, Conn., 1974, Artists Space NY, 1975, Theatre Gallery U. Southern Fla., Tampa, 1977, LA Contemporary Exhbn., 1978, Holly Soloman Gallery, NY, 1980, 1986, Daniel Weinberg Gallery, LA, 1984, Wacoal, Japan, 1985, Nat. Mus. Women in the Arts, Washington, 1989, Cleve. Ctr. for Contemporary Art., 1990, Fabric Workshop, NY, 1991, Rotunda Gallery, 1993, commd. works, Spokane City Hall, 1984. Recipient Merit medal for Sculpture, Am. Acad. Arts and Letters, 2002; grantee, Nat. Endowment for the Arts, 1979; Guggenheim fellow, 1983, MacArthur fellow, 2004. Office: Bard Coll PO Box 5000 Annandale On Hudson NY 12504-5000 E-mail: pfaff@bard.edu.

PFAFF, WILLIAM WALLACE, medical educator; b. Rochester, NY, Aug. 14, 1930; s. Norman Joseph and Eleanor Blakesley (Wells) P.; m. Patricia Ann Clark; children: Nancy, Karen, Margaret, Mary Catherine. AB, Harvard U., 1952; MD, SUNY, 1956. Intern U. Chgo., 1956-58; sr. asst. surgeon NIH, Bethesda, Md., 1958-60; resident Stanford U. Med. Ctr., Palo Alto, Calif., 1960-65; asst. prof. U. Fla., Gainesville, 1965-68, assoc. prof., 1968-71, prof. surgery, 1971-95, prof. emeritus, adj. prof., 1995—, dir. organ transplant programs, 1971-95. Bd. dirs. United Network for Organ Sharing, Richmond, Va., pres. elect, 1997-98, pres., 1998-99; pres., com. chmn. Southeastern Organ Procurement Found., Richmond, 1973-95. Fellow Am. Coll. Surgeons; mem. Am. Surg. Assn., Am. Soc. Transplant Surgeons, So. Surg. Assn., Transplantation Soc., Alachua County Med. Soc. (pres. 1977-78). Home: 2445 NW 15th Pl Gainesville FL 32605-5148 Office: U Fla Dept Surgery PO Box 100286 Gainesville FL 32610-0286 Home Phone: 352-378-2240; Office Phone: 352-265-0606. Personal E-mail: puffer12@aol.com. Business E-Mail: pfaff@surgery.ufl.edu.

PFALTZ, HUGO MENZEL, JR., lawyer; b. Newark, Sept. 23, 1931; s. Hugo M. and Mary E. (Horr) Pfaltz; m. Marilyn M. Muir, Sept. 29, 1956; children: Elizabeth W., William M., Robert L. BA, Hamilton Coll., 1953; JD, Harvard U., 1960; LLM, NYU, 1965. Bar: NJ 1960, US Dist. Ct. NJ 1960, US Supreme Ct. 1977. Assoc. McCarter & English, Newark, 1960—61, Bourne & Noll, Summit, NJ, 1961—74; sole practice Summit, 1974—82; ptnr. Pfaltz & Woller, 1983—. Mem. Battleship NJ Commn., 1985—2001, NJ Law Revision Commn., 1986—2003. Assoc. editor NJ Law Jour., 1966—2002, editor, 1984—86. Chmn. Summit Rep. City Com., 1966; mem. NJ Constl. Conv., 1966, NJ Assembly, 1968—72. Served to lt. USNR, 1953—62. Mem.: ABA, Summit Bar Assn., Union County Bar Assn., NJ Bar Assn., Beacon Hill Club (Summit), Baltusrol Club (Springfield, NJ), Univ. Club (Washington), Univ Club (NYC). Home: 118 Prospect St Summit NJ 07901-2472 Office: 382 Springfield Ave Summit NJ 07901-2707 Home Phone: 908-273-5000; Office Phone: 908-273-1974. Personal E-mail: hugopf@aol.com.

PFALTZGRAFF, ROBERT LOUIS, JR., political scientist, educator; b. Phila., June 1, 1934; s. Robert L. and Mary (Warriner) P.; m. Diane A. Kressler, May 20, 1967; children: Suzanne Diane, Robert Louis III. BA with honors, Swarthmore Coll., 1956; MBA in Internat. Bus., U. Pa., 1958, PhD in Polit. Sci. (Penfield fellow), 1964; MA in Internat. Relations, 1959. Research assoc. Fgn. Policy Research Inst., 1964-71; asst. prof. polit. sci. U. Pa., Phila., 1964-70; dep. dir. Fgn. Policy Research Inst., 1971-73; assoc. prof. internat. politics Fletcher Sch. Law and Diplomacy, Tufts U., Medford, Mass., 1971-78; pres. Inst. for Fgn. Policy Analysis, Cambridge, Mass., 1976—; prof. internat. politics Fletcher Sch. Law and Diplomacy, Tufts U., Medford, Mass., 1978-83, Shelby Cullom Davis prof. internat. security studies, 1983—. Vis. lectr. Fgn. Svc. Inst. Dept. State, 1970—71; George C. Marshall prof. Coll. of Europe, Bruges, Belgium, 1970—71; short term acad. guest prof. Nat. Def. Coll., Tokyo, 1981; hon. prof. U. St. Andrews; pres. U.S. Strategic Inst., Washington, 1977—79, Inst. Fgn. Policy Analysis, Cambridge, Mass., 1976—; mem. internat. security adv. bd. U.S. Dept. State, 2006—. Author: Britain Faces Europe, 1957-1967, 1969, Politics and the International System, 1969, The Atlantic Community: A Complex Balance, 1969, The Study of International Relations, 1977, Power Projection and the Long Range Combat Aircraft: Missions, Capabilities and Alternative Designs, 1981, Contending Theories of International Relations: A Comprehensive Survey, 1981; co-editor: Contrasting Approaches to Strategic Arms Control, 1974, SALT: Implications for Arms Control in the 1970s, 1973, The Other Arms Race: New Technologies and Non Nuclear Conflict, 1975, Arms Transfers to the Third World: The Military Build-up in Less Industrial Countries, 1978, Intelligence Policy and National Security, 1981, Projection of Power: Perspectives, Perceptions and Problems, 1982, The U.S. Defense Mobilization Infrastructure: Problems and Priorities, 1983, International Dimensions of Space, 1984, National Security Policy: The Decision-Making Process, 1984, The Peace Movements in Europe and the United States, 1985, American Foreign Policy: FDR to Reagan, 1986, co-editor: Selling the Rope to Hang Capitalism? The Debate on West-East Trade and Technology Transfer, 1987, Emerging Doctrines and Technologies: Implications for Global and Regional Political-Military Balance, 1987, Protracted Warfare--The Third World Arena: A Dimension of U.S.-Soviet Conflict, 1988, Guerrilla Warfare and Counter-Insurgency: U.S.-Soviet Policy in the third World, 1988, U.S. Defense Policy in an Era of Constrained Resources, 1989, Contending Theories of International Relations: A Comprehensive Study, 1990, 4th edit., 1998, National Security Decisions: The Participants Speak, 1990, The United States Army: Challenges and Missions for the 1990s, 1991, The Future of Air Power in the Aftermath of the Gulf War, 1992, Naval Forward Presence and the National Military Strategy, 1993, Ethnic Conflict and Regional Instability: Implications for U.S. Policy and Army Roles and Missions, 1994, Naval Expeditionary Forces and Power Projection: Into the 21st Century, 1994, Roles and Missions of Special Operations Forces in the Aftermath of the Cold War, 1995, War in the Information Age: New Challenges for U.S. Security, 1997, NATO and Southeastern Europe: Security Issues for the Early 21st Century, 2000, The Role of Naval Forces in 21st Century Operations, 2000, Strategy and International Politics, 2000, Contending Theories of International Relations, 5th edit., 2001, others; contbr. articles to profl. jours., chpts. to books. Guggenheim fellow, 1968-69; Relm Found. grantee, 1969 Mem.: Internat. Inst. Strategic Studies, Coun. Fgn. Rels., Internat. Studies Assn., Army and Navy Club (Washington). Office: The Fletcher Sch Tufts Univ 160 Packard Ave Medford MA 02155 Business E-Mail: rlp@ifpa.org.

PFAU, JAMES MICHAEL, lawyer; b. Milw., Aug. 22, 1958; s. Raymond and Patricia Ann P.; children: Gretchen Canright, Anna Katharine. BS in Journalism with distinction, Northwestern U., 1979; JD magna cum laude, U. Mich., 1983. Bar: Minn. 1983, U.S. Dist. Ct. Minn. 1983. Ptnr. Faegre & Benson, Mpls., 1983—. Contbr. articles to profl. jours. Bd. dirs. St. Anthony Pk. Cmty. Coun., St. Paul, 1989-92. Mem. Minn. State Bar Assn. Episcopalian. Home: 2140 Fairmount Ave Saint Paul MN 55105 Office: Faegre and Benson LLP 90 S 7th St Ste 2200 Minneapolis MN 55402-3901 Office Phone: 612-766-8616. E-mail: jpfau@faegre.com.

PFAU, RICHARD ANTHONY, retired university president; b. NYC, Feb. 19, 1942; s. Hugo and Irene Beatrice P.; m. Nancy Ann DiPace, Sept. 12, 1964; children: Bradley Madison, Aleksandra Nicole. AB, Hamilton Coll., 1964; MA, U. Va., 1973, PhD, 1975. Systems analyst Equitable Life Ins. Co., NYC, 1964-66; asst. prof. history Dickinson Coll., Carlisle, Pa., 1975-80; assoc. prof., assoc. dean U. Miami, Coral Gables, Fla., 1980-85; dean of faculty, provost Emory (Va.) and Henry Coll., 1985-93; pres. Ill. Coll., Jacksonville, Ill., 1993—2002, Averett U., Danville, Va., 2002—. Author: No Sacrifice Too Great: The Life of Lewis L. Strauss, 1985. Contbr. articles, book revs. to profl. publs. Vestryman St. Thomas Episc. Ch., Abingdon, Va., Epis. Ch. Epiphany, Denville, Va.; chmn., sec.-treas., exec. com., bd. dirs. Va. Found. for Humanities and Pub. Policy; mem. bd. trustees Carlisle Sch., Martinsville, Va.; mem. adv. bd. Salvation Army, Jacksonville, Ill. Capt. USAF, 1966-71. DuPont fellow, 1974-75; Hoover fellow, 1982. Mem. Danville Golf Club, Danville Rotary Club, Omicron Delta Kappa, Alpha Psi Omega, Pi Delta Epsilon. Home: PO Box 134 597 Rt 20 Sharon Springs NY 13459

PFEFFER, CYNTHIA ROBERTA, psychiatrist, educator; b. Newark, May 22, 1943; d. Edward I. and Ann Pfeffer. BA, Douglas Coll., 1964; MD, NYU, 1968. Assoc. dir. child psychiatry inpatient unit Albert Einstein Coll. Medicine, Bronx, NY, 1973-79; chief child psychiatry inpatient unit N.Y. Hosp. Cornell Med. Ctr., White Plains, NY, 1979-95; assoc. prof. clin. psychiatry Weill Med. Coll. Cornell U., NYC, 1984—. Prof. psychiatry Cornell U. Med. Coll., 1989—; pres. N.Y. Coun. on Child and Adolescent Psychiatry, N.Y.C., 1989—; dir. childhood bereavement program Weill Med. Coll. Cornell U., 1999—. Author: The Suicidal Child, 1986, Difficult Moments in Child Psychotherapy, 1988; editor: Youth Suicide: Perspectives on Risk and Prevention, 1989, Intense Stress and Mental Disturbance in Children, 1996; co-editor: Neurologic Disorders: Developmental and Behavioral Sequelae for Child and Adolescent Psychiatric Clinics of North America, 1999. Recipient Erwin Stengel award Internat. Assn. Suicide Prevention, 1987, Wilford Hulse award N.Y. Coun. on Child & Adolescent Psychiatry, 1989, Sigmund Freud award Am. Soc. Psychoanalytic Physicians, 1994., William Shonfeld award Am. Soc. Devel. Psychology, 2009 Fellow Am. Psychiat. Assn., Am. Acad. Child and Adolescent Psychiatry (councillor-at-large 1989—, Norbert Rieger award 1988), Am. Psychopathological Assn.; mem. Am. Assn. Suicidology (pres. 1987, Young Contbrs. award 1981, 82). Office: NY Hosp Westchester Div 21 Bloomingdale Rd White Plains NY 10605-1504 also: 1100 Madison Ave New York NY 10028-0327 Office Phone: 914-997-5849, 212-717-2334. Business E-Mail: cpfeffer@med.cornell.edu.

PFEFFER, DAVID H., lawyer; b. NYC, Mar. 15, 1935; B. Chem. Engring., CCNY, 1956; JD, NYU, 1961, LL.M. in Trade Regulation, 1967. Bar: N.Y. 1961. With patent dept. U.S. Rubber Co., Wayne, NJ, 1957-61; assoc. Watson, Leavenworth, Kelton & Taggart, NYC, 1961-63, Morgan & Finnegan, LLP, NYC, 1963-70, ptnr., 1971—2007, of counsel, Lock Lord Bissell & Liddell, 2009—. Village prosecutor Roslyn Harbor, N.Y., 1976-78, village justice, 1979-2003; panel of arbitrators Am. Arbitration Assn, Ctr. Dispute Resolution, NY Civil Ct., Nat. Arbitration Forum, CPI Inst. Dispute Resolution, Tech. & Health Panel Mem. ABA (litigation sect.), N.Y. State Bar Assn., Assn. Bar City N.Y., Am. Intellectual Property Law Assn. (com. alt. dispute resolution), N.Y. Intellectual Property Law Assn. (com. on alt. dispute resolution), Order of Coif. Office: Locke Lord Bissell & Liddell LLP 3 World Financial Ctr New York NY 10281-2101 Office Phone: 616-217-7700. E-mail: dpfeffer@lockelord.com.

PFEFFER, JEFFREY, business educator; b. St. Louis, July 23, 1946; s. Newton Stuart and Shirlee (Krisman) P.; m. Kathleen Frances Fowler, July 23, 1986. BS, MS, Carnegie Mellon U., 1968; PhD, Stanford U., 1972. Tech. staff Rsch. Analysis Corp., McLean, Va., 1968-69; asst. prof. U. Ill., Champaign, 1971-73; from asst. prof. to assoc. prof. U. Calif., Berkeley, 1973-79; prof. Grad. Sch. Bus., Stanford (Calif.) U., 1979—. Dir. Audible Magic, Inc.; vis. prof. Harvard U. Sch. Bus., Boston, 1981—82, London Bus. Sch., 2005, IESE, Barcelona, 2006—09, Singapore Mgmt. U., 2006. Author: The External Control of Organizations, 1978, Organizational Design, 1978, Power in Organizations, 1981, Organizations and Organization Theory, 1982 (Terry Book award 1984), Managing with Power, 1992, Competitive Advantage Through People, 1994, New Directions for Organization Theory, 1997, The Human Equation, 1998, The Knowing-Doing Gap, 1999, Hidden Value, 2000, Hard Facts, Dangerous Half-Truths, and Total Nonsense, 2006, What Were They Thinking?, 2007. Bd. dir. San Francisco Playhouse, Quantum Leap Healthcare. Fellow Acad. Mgmt. (bd. govs. 1984-86, New Concept award 1979, Richard D. Irwin award for scholarly contbns. to mgmt. 1989); mem. Labor and Employment Rels. Assn. Jewish. Avocations: cooking, music. Home: 425 Moseley Rd Hillsborough CA 94010-6715 Office: Stanford U Grad Sch Bus Stanford CA 94305 Home Phone: 650-340-7331; Office Phone: 650-723-2915. E-mail: pfeffer_jeffrey@gsb.stanford.edu.

PFEFFER, LAWRENCE MARC, cell biologist; b. NYC, Nov. 28, 1951; s. Paul and Bess (Wilkins) P.; m. Susan Ritterstein, Sept. 19, 1976; children: Jessica Rachel, Elyssa Danielle. BS (magna cum laude), SUNY, Albany, 1972; PhD, Cornell U., 1977. Undergrad. fellow SUNY, Albany, 1971-72; grad. fellow Cornell U. Grad. Sch. Med. Sci., NYC, 1972-77; postdoctoral fellow Rockefeller U., NYC, 1977-80, rsch. assoc., 1980—81, asst. prof., 1981-87, assoc. prof., 1987-91; assoc. prof. dept. pathology U. Tenn. Coll. Medicine, Memphis, 1991-92, prof., 1992—, Muirhead prof., 2002—; dir. Ctr. Cancer Rsch., 2007—. Ad hoc reviewer for Sci. Procs. NAS, Cancer Rsch., Interferon Rsch., Jour. Immunology, Molecular Cellular Biology. Editor: Mechanisms of Interferon Actions, 1989; mem. editl. bd. Jour. Interferon Cytokine Rsch., 1992—, Jour. Biol. Chemistry, 2002-08. Recipient Jr. Faculty Rsch. award Am. Cancer Soc., 1982-85, Leukemia Scholar award Leukemia Soc. Am., 1986-91. Mem. Harvey Soc., Interferon Soc., Sigma Xi, Am. Soc. for Microbiology. Democrat. Jewish. Achievements include research on signal transduction of cytokines, cytokine receptors, mechanism of interferon action, and regulation of gene expression by interferon. Office: Univ Tenn Dept Pathology Coll Medicine 19 South Manassas Ave Rm 154 Memphis TN 38113-3400 Home Phone: 901-758-0624; Office Phone: 901-448-7855. Business E-Mail: lpfeffer@utmem.edu.

PFEFFER, PATRICK, architect; PhD, U. Paris, 1984—90. Dir. Alcatel, Petaluma, Calif., 1996—2000, Gluon Networks, Petaluma, 2000—03; chief network arch. Detecon, San Mateo, Calif., 2003—. Contbr. scientific papers. Achievements include patents for pattern matching. Office: Detecon Inc 128 Spear St Fl 4 San Francisco CA 94105-5147

PFEFFER, PHILIP ELLIOT, biophysicist; b. NYC, Apr. 8, 1941; s. Charles and Della (Smith) P.; m. Judith Stadlen, Dec. 22, 1962; children: Charles, Ari, Shira. AB, Hunter Coll., 1962; MS, Rutgers U., 1964, PhD, 1966. Rsch. asst. dept. chemistry Rutgers U., New Brunswick, NJ, 1964-66; rsch. fellow dept. chemistry U. Chgo., 1966-68; rsch. scientist Ea. Regional Rsch. Ctr. USDA, Phila., 1968-88, rsch. leader Ea. Regional Rsch. Ctr., 1976-88, lead scientist Ea. Regional Rsch. Ctr., 1988—; emeritus, 2006. Editor-at-large Marcel Dekker, N.Y.C., 1990—; adj. prof. dept. biosci. and biotech. Drexel U., Phila., 1996—; vis. prof. U. Bordeaux, France, 1998. Editor: Nuclear Magnetic Resonance in Agriculture, 1989, Nuclear Magnetic Resonance in Plant Biology, 1996; mem. editl. bd. Jour. Carbohydrate Chemistry, 1985—, Jour. Magnetic Resonance Analysis; contbr. articles to profl. jours. including Plant Physiology, Carbohydrate Rsch., Biochemica Acta, Biophysica, Jour. Magnetic Resonance. Recipient Bond award Am. Oil Chemists Soc., 1976, Fed. Svcs. award Phila. Fed. Assn., 1979, Science and Edn. award USDA, 1982; fellow Orgn. for Econ. Cooperation and Devel., 1989; Agrl. Rsch. Svc. rsch. fellow, 1989; vis. scientist grantee Centre d'Etudes Nucleaires de Grenoble, 1986, Oxford U., 1989; Nat. Rsch. Initiative grantee, 1997, 2002. Mem. AAAS, Internat. Soc. for Magnetic Resonance, Am. Chem. Soc. (Phila. sect. Scientist of Yr. 1982), Soc. for Applied Spectroscopy. Achievements include patents and publs. concerning use of alpha-anions; discovery of deuterium isotope shift NMR method for determining carbohydrate structures; development of P-31 NMR in vivo methodology for studying metal ion transport and C-13 NMR for studying plant/microbe interactions in nitrogen fixing plant nodules and symbiotic mycorrhizae. Office: USDA 600 E Mermaid Ln Wyndmoor PA 19038-8598 Business E-Mail: philip.pfeffer@ars.usda.gov.

PFEIFER, MICHAEL DAVID, bishop; b. Alamo, Tex., May 18, 1937; s. Frank and Alice (Savage) P. Student, Oblate Sch. Theology. Ordained priest Missionary Oblates of Mary Immaculate, 1964; priest Roman Cath. Ch., Mexico City, 1964-1981, provincial-superior of Oblate Southern US Province San Antonio, 1981-85; ordained bishop, 1985; bishop Diocese of San Angelo, Tex., 1985—. Roman Catholic. Address: PO Box 1829 804 Ford St San Angelo TX 76902 Office Phone: 325-651-7500. Office Fax: 325-651-6688. Business E-Mail: mdpomi@aol.com.

PFEIFER, PAUL E., state supreme court justice; b. Bucyrus, Ohio, Oct. 15, 1942; m. Julia Pfeifer; 3 children. BA, Ohio State U., 1963, JD, 1966. Asst. atty. gen. State of Ohio, 1967-70; mem. Ohio House of Reps., 1971-72; asst. prosecuting atty. Crawford County, 1973-76; mem. Ohio State Senate, 1976-92, minority floor leader, 1983-84, asst. pres. pro-tempore, 1985-86; ptnr. Cory, Brown & Pfeifer, 1973-92; justice Ohio Supreme Ct., 1992—. Mem. Grace United Meth. Ch., Bucyrus. Republican. Office: Supreme Court of Ohio 65 S Front St Columbus OH 43215-3431 Office Phone: 614-387-9020.*

PFEIFER, POLLY LEE, elementary school educator; d. Gerald Edward and Nancy Lee Pfeifer. BA in Edn., Coll. Saint Benedict, St. Joseph, Minn., 1987; MA in Edn., St. Mary's U., Winona, Minn., 1994; student in Libr. Media Scis., Mankato State U., Minn., 2006—. Cert. tchr. Minn., 1987. Tchr. sci. Minnetonka (Minn.) Pub. Schs., 1987—. Mem.: NEA, Minn. Ednl. Media Orgn., Nat. Assn. Sci. Tchrs., Minnetonka (Minn.) Tchrs. Assn. (v.p. 1996). Roman Cath. Avocations: reading, basketball, golf. Office: Minnetonka Mid Sch West 6421 Hazeltina Blvd Excelsior MN 55331

PFEIFER, TRACY M., plastic surgeon; b. Yonkers, NY, Dec. 20, 1960; d. Adrienne K and William A Pfeifer. BA, Rutgers U., 1982—84; MS, Calif. State U., Los Angeles, 1984—85; MD, U. of Medicine and Dentistry of NJ, 1987—91. Bd. cert. Am. Bd. of Plastic Surgery, 2001, Am. Bd. of Surgery, 1999. Plastic surgeon, pvt. practice Pfeifer Plastic Surgery, PLLC, NYC, 1999—. Fellow: Am. Coll. Surgeons; mem.: Am. Soc. Aesthetic Plastic Surgery, Am. Soc. Plastic Surgeons, NY Regional Soc. of Plastic Surgeons (exec. bd. mem. 2000—). Office: Pfeifer Plastic Surgery PLLC 565 Park Ave New York NY 10021 Office Fax: 212-593-8823. E-mail: tpfeifer@drpfeifer.com.

PFEIFFER, DANIEL H., federal official; b. Wilmington, Del., Dec. 24, 1975; s. Gary Malick and Lear Pfeiffer; m. Sarah Elizabeth Feinberg, July 15, 2006. BA in Govt. magna cum laude, Georgetown U., Washington, DC, 1998. N.E. comm. dir. Dem. presdl. campaign, Nashville, 2000; adv. to Senator Tim Johnson US Senate, Sioux Falls, SD, 2002, press sec. to Senator Tom Daschle SD, 2003—05, comm. dir. to Senator Evan Bayh Washington, 2005—06; comm. dir. Barack Obama's Presdl. Campaign, 2008; dep. comm. dir. The White House, Washington, 2009—. Democrat. Office: The White House 1600 Pennsylvania Ave NW Washington DC 20500*

PFEIFFER, ERIC ARMIN, psychiatrist, gerontologist, writer; b. Rauental, Germany, Sept. 15, 1935; came to U.S., 1952; naturalized, 1957; s. Fritz and Emma (Saborowski) P.; m. Natasha Maria Emerson, Mar. 21, 1964; children: Eric Alexander, Michael David, Mark Armin. AB, Washington U., 1956, MD, 1960. Intern Albert Einstein Coll. Medicine, Bronx, NY, 1960-61; resident in psychiatry U. Rochester, NY, 1961-64; practice medicine specializing in psychiatry Durham, NC, 1966-76, Denver, 1976-78; asst. prof. Duke U., Durham, 1966-69, assoc. prof., 1969-72, prof., 1973-76, project dir., 1971-76, assoc. dir., 1974-76; dir. Davis Inst. Care and Study Aging, Denver, 1976-77; prof. psychiatry U. Colo., Denver, 1976-78; prof. psychiatry, chief div. geriatric psychiatry U. South Fla. Coll. Medicine, Tampa, 1978—, dir. Suncoast Gerontology Ctr., 1980—. Chief psychiatry svc. Tampa VA Med. Ctr., 1979-80; cons. in field; chmn. bd. Social Systems, Inc., 1975-76; chmn. com. on mental health and mental illness of elderly HEW, 1976-77. Author: Disordered Behavior, 1968, (with E.W. Busse) Behavior and Adaptation in Late Life, 1970, 3d edit., 1977, Successful Aging, 1974, Multidimensional Functional Assessment, 1977, Alzheimer's Disease, 1989. With USPHS, 1964-66. Markle Found. scholar acad. medicine, 1968-73; Eric Pfeiffer Chair in Alzheimer's Disease Rsch. named in his honor, U. S. Fla., 1985. Fellow Gerontol. Soc. (chmn. clin. medicine sect. 1975-76), Am. Psychiat. Assn.; mem. Am. Geriatrics Soc. (Allen Gold medal 1977), So. Psychiat. Soc., Phi Beta Kappa. Office: 12901 Bruce B Downs Blvd Tampa FL 33612-4742 Office Phone: 813-839-5769. Business E-Mail: epfeiffe@health.usf.edu.

PFEIFFER, ISOBEL LORRAINE, education educator; b. Warsaw, Ind., Aug. 30, 1921; d. Franklin Otis and Ethel Faun (Shilling) Rarick; m. Robert Thomas Pfeiffer, June 9, 1945. MA, Ind. U., 1948; PhD, Kent State U., Ohio, 1966. Tchr. Warsaw Jr. High Sch., 1942-45, 46-48, South San Francisco (Calif.) High Sch., 1945-46, West Aurora (Ill.) Schs., 1948-49; instr. Aurora Coll., 1949-51; tchr. Martinsville (Ind.) Schs., 1951-53, East Lansing (Mich.) Schs., 1953-56, Tallmadge (Ohio) Schs., 1956-57; tchr., dean of girls Kent Schs., 1957-66; prof. U. Akron, Ohio, 1966-82, West Ga. Coll., Carrollton, 1982-88, U. Ga., 1989—91. Cons. instrnl. supervision, Cuyahoga County, Ohio, 1970-72, U. Akron Ednl. Research and Devel. Ctr., 1978-82; adviser Northeastern Ohio Sch. Supervisors Assn., Akron, 1972-80. Author: Supervision of Teachers, 1982; contbr. articles to profl. jours. Mem. AAUW (pres. local br. 1961-63), Coun. of Profs. of Instrnl. Supervision (pres. 1990-91), Ga. Assn. Supervision and Curriculum Devel. (editor newsletter 1983-84), Am. Ednl. Rsch. Assn., Kappa Delta Pi, Delta Kappa Gamma (pres. local chpt. 1970-72), Phi Delta Kappa (chpt. editor 1984-85). Avocations: travel, reading, bridge. Home: 1310 E Island View Dr Warsaw IN 46580-5078 Home Phone: 574-269-3952.

PFEIFFER, JANE CAHILL, former broadcasting company executive, consultant; b. Sept. 29, 1932; d. John Joseph and Helen (Reilly) Cahill; m. Ralph A. Pfeiffer, Jr., June 3, 1975. BA, U. Md., 1954; postgrad., Cath. U. Am., 1956—57; LHD (hon.), Pace Coll., 1978, U. Md., 1979; LHD (hon.), Manhattanville Coll., 1979, Amherst U., 1980, Babson Coll., 1981, U. Notre Dame, 1991; LHD (hon.), Bryant Coll., 1995, St. Thomas Aquinas Coll., 2006. With IBM Corp., Armonk, NY, 1955-76, sec. mgmt. rev. com., 1970, dir. comm., 1971, v.p. comm. and govt. rels., 1972-76, bus. cons., 1976-78; chmn. NBC, Inc., NYC, 1978-80; bus. cons., 1980—. Sr. advisor The Conf. Bd., 1991. Pres.'s adv. com. White House Fellows, 1966, Pres.'s Gen. Adv. Commn. on Arms Control and Disarmament, 1977-80, Pres.'s Commn. Mil. Compensation; trustee Rockefeller Found., U. Md., Carnegie Hall, 1981-1986, U. Notre Dame; bd. dirs. Catholic Univ. of Am., 1973-1978, Rockefeller Found., 1973-1985, White House Fellows, 1976-1981, Kettering Found., 1975-1979; bd. mem. Internat. Paper, 1984-2004, J.C. Penney Co., 1977-2004, Ashland Inc., 1984-2004, Mutual of NY, 1986-2004. Recipient Achievement award Kappa Kappa Gamma, 1974-80, Eleanor Roosevelt Humanitarian award NY League for Hard of Hearing, 1980, Disting. Alumna award U. Md., 1975, Humanitarian award NOW, 1980, Centennial Alumna medallion U. Md., 1988; White House fellow, Washington, 1966, Making Waves award, Greatest 50 Women in Radio and Television-AWRT, 2002. Mem. Coun. Fgn. Rels., Overseas Devel. Coun., Econ. of N.Y. Club. Office: C/O Jonathan L Smith Chesapeake Asset Mgmt LLC 1 Rockefeller Plz Rm 1210 New York NY 10020-2002 Home: Johns Island 1050 Beach Rd Apt 1G Vero Beach FL 32963-3413 Office Phone: 212-218-4044.

PFEIFFER, MARGARET KOLODNY, lawyer; b. Elkin, NC, Oct. 7, 1944; d. Isadore Harold and Mary Elizabeth Kolodny; m. Carl Frederick Pfeiffer II, Sept. 2, 1968. BA, Duke U., 1967; JD, Rutgers U., 1974. Bar: NJ 1974, NY 1976, DC 1981, US Supreme Ct. 1979. Law clk. to Hon. F.L. Van Dusen U.S. Ct. Appeals 3d cir., Phila., 1974-75; assoc. Sullivan & Cromwell, NYC and Washington, 1975-82, ptnr. litigation, antitrust, intellectual property, internat. trade and investment practice area, criminal def. and investigations, 1982—. Contbr. articles to profl. jours. Trustee Nat. Law Ctr. on Homelessness and Poverty. Mem. ABA, Internat. Bar Assn., DC Bar Assn., NY State Bar Assn., Assn. of Bar of City of NY, Am. Soc. of Internat. Law. Avocations: gardening, reading, music. Office: Sullivan & Cromwell 1701 Pennsylvania Ave NW Washington DC 20006-5866 Office Phone: 202-956-7540. Business E-Mail: pfeifferm@sullcrom.com.

PFEIFFER, MARY LOUISE, artist, educator; b. Troy, Ohio, Feb. 14, 1944; d. John Edward Dunnick and Helen Elizabeth Johnson-Dunnick; children: William G. II, Scott Edward. AS magna cum laude, Tidewater Coll., Virginia Beach, Va., 1976; BA, Fla. Internat. U., Miami, 1986, MA in Religious Studies, 2004; LLM, St. Thomas U. Sch. Law, Miami, 2002. Owner, operator Pfeiffer Originals, Art Glass Designs, Miami,

1976—; adj. prof. dept. religious studies Fla. Internat. U., 2002—, faculty fellow the honors coll., 2005—. Pres. friends environ studies Fla. Internat. U., pres. women's studies adv. bd., bd. advisors coll. arts and scis. Author: (technical textbook) Basic Radiography, NCHC Monograph. Acting chmn. Navy Relief Soc., Meridian, Miss., 1968—69; pres., sec.-treas. Officers' Wives Club, 1968—69; POW-MIA com. NAS Oceana, Virginia Beach, 1970—75; hospitality coord. Performing Arts Cmty. and Edn., Miami, 1982—84; mem. steering com. 5th-7th tribal symposia St. Thomas U. Sch. of Law, 2002—06. Recipient Alumni Assn. Torch award, Fla. Internat. U. Alumni Assn., 2000, Outstanding Svc. award dept. religious studies, Fla. Internat. U., 2000, 2002. Fellow: The Honors Coll. (faculty); mem.: Phi Theta Kappa, Theta Alpha Kappa. Avocations: swimming, sailing, golf, travel. Home: 19160 NE 19 Pl North Miami Beach FL 33179-4316 Office: Florida Internat U UP Campus 11200 SW 8th St DM 233 Miami FL 33199 Office Fax: 305-348-2118. Business E-Mail: pfeiffer@fiu.edu.

PFEIFFER, MICHELLE, actress; b. Santa Ana, Calif., Apr. 29, 1957; d. Dick and Donna P.; m. Peter Horton, 1981 (div. 1988); 1 adopted child, Claudia Rose; m. David Kelley, Nov. 13, 1993, 1 child. Student, Golden West Coll., Whitley Coll. Actress: (feature films) Falling in Love Again, 1980, Hollywood Knights, 1980, Charlie Chan and the Curse of the Dragon Queen, 1981, Grease II, 1982, Scarface, 1983, Ladyhawke, 1985, Into the Night, 1985, Sweet Liberty, 1986, Amazon Women on the Moon, 1987, Witches of Eastwick, 1987, Married to the Mob, 1988, Tequila Sunrise, 1988, Dangerous Liaisons, 1988 (Acad. award nominee for best supporting actress, 1989, BAFTA award, 1990), The Fabulous Baker Boys, 1989 (L.A. Film Critics Assn. award for best actress, 1989, D.W. Griffith award Nat. Bd. Rev., 1989, N.Y. Film Critics award, 1989, Nat. Soc. Film Critics award for best actress, 1990, Golden Globe award for best actress drama, 1990, Acad. award nominee for best actress, 1990), The Russia House, 1990, Frankie & Johnny, 1991, Love Field, 1992 (Acad. award nominee for best actress, 1993), Batman Returns, 1992, The Age of Innocence, 1993, Wolf, 1994, Dangerous Minds, 1995, Up Close and Personal, 1996, To Gillian on her 37th Birthday, 1996, One Fine Day, 1996, A Thousand Acres, 1997, The Prince of Egypt (voice), 1998, The Story of Us, 1998, A Midsummer Night's Dream, 1999, Deep End of the Ocean, 1999, What Lies Beneath, 2000, I Am Sam, 2001, White Oleander, 2002, Sinbad: Legend of the Seven Seas (voice), 2003, I Could Never Be Your Women, 2007, Hairspray, 2007, Stardust, 2007, Chéri, 2009; (TV movies) The Solitary Man, 1979, Callie and Son, 1981, The Children Nobody Wanted, 1981, Splendor in the Grass, 1981, One Too Many, 1983, Tales from the Hollywood Hills: Natica Jackson, 1987, Power, Passion and Murder, 1987; (TV series) Delta House, 1979, B.A.D. Cats, 1980; prodr: (films) A Thousand Acres, 1997; exec. prodr.: (films) One Fine Day, 1996. Named Woman of the Yr., Harvard's Hasty Pudding Theater Club, 1995; recipient Crystal award, Women in Film, 1993. Office: c/o Wolf-Kasteler Pub Rels 355 N Maple Dr Ste 351 Beverly Hills CA 90210*

PFEIFFER, PHYLLIS KRAMER, publishing executive; b. NYC, Feb. 11, 1949; d. Jacob N. and Estelle G. Rosenbaum-Pfeiffer; m. Stephen M. Pfeiffer, Dec. 21, 1969; children: Andrew Kramer, Elise Kramer. BS, Cornell U., 1970; postgrad., U. San Diego, 1976-78. Instr. Miss Porter's Sch., Farmington, Conn., 1970; tchr. Dewey Jr. HS NYC Bd. Edn., 1970—73; rschr. Hunter Coll., NYC, 1971—72; account exec. La Jolla (Calif.) Light, 1973—75, advt. dir., 1975—77, gen. mgr., 1977-78, pub., 1978-87; exec. v.p. Harte Hanks So. Calif. Newspapers, 1985—87; gen. mgr. San Diego edit. L.A. Times, 1987—93; pres., pub. Marin Ind. Jour., Novato, Calif., 1993—2000; v.p. advt. and mktg. Contra Costa Times, 2000—04; sr. v.p. advt. San Francisco Chronicle, 2005—07; pub. Sun Diego Suburban Newspapers, 2008—. Dir. comm. ctr. San Diego State U., 1980-93. Bd. dirs. La Jolla Cancer Rsch. Found., 1979-82, YMCA, San Diego Ballet, 1980, Dominican Coll., San Rafael, Calif, 1994—, Marin Theater Co., Alvarado Hosp., 1981-88, chmn. fin. com., 1986, sec. bd., 1986; co-chmn. Operation USS La Jolla, USN, 1980—; mem. mktg. com. United Way, 1979-81, chmn., 1983; trustee La Jollan's Inc., 1975-78, Nat. Pk. Trust, 2000-02, Dogs for the Blind, 2001-.; mem. Conv. and Visitors Bur. Blue Ribbon Com. on Future, 1983; mem. resource panel Child Abuse Prevention Found., 1983—; bd. overseers U. Calif., San Diego; mem. violent crimes task force San Diego Police Dept.; dir. Guide Dogs for the Blind, Oakland Mus. Grantee N.Y. Bd. Edn., 1971-72; named Pub. of Yr., Gannet Co., Inc., 1995. Mem. Newspaper Assn. Am., Calif. Newspaper Pubs. Assn. (bd. dirs., exec. com.), Chancellor's Assn. U. Calif.-San Diego, Clairemont Club. Home: 6333 La Jolla Blvd Unit 370 La Jolla CA 92037-6622 Office Phone: 858-875-5940. Business E-Mail: ppfeiffer@lajoualight.com. E-mail: ppfeiffer@sfchronicle.com.

PFEIFFER, STEVEN BERNARD, lawyer; b. Orange, NJ, Jan. 19, 1947; s. Bernard Victor and Elizabeth Sophia (Bissell) P.; m. Kristin Reagan, June 27, 1970; children: Victoria Pfeiffer Metz, Rachel Catherine, Emily Dorothea, Stephanie Kristin Bissell, Andrew Steven Bernard. BA in Govt., Wesleyan U., 1969; BA in Jurisprudence, Oxford U., 1971, MA, 1983; MA in African Studies, U. London, 1973; JD, Yale U., New Haven, Conn., 1976. Bar: NJ 1976, DC 1978. Assoc. Fulbright & Jaworski, Houston, London, 1976—83, ptnr. London, Washington, 1983—, ptnr.-in-charge London, 1983—86, 1989—2002, head internat. dept., 1989—2003, ptnr.-in-charge Washington office, 1998—2002, chmn. exec. com., 2003—. Bd. dirs. The Africa Am. Inst., NYC, Project HOPE, Washington, Barloworld Ltd., Johannesburg, Iridium Holdings LLC, Washington, NAACP Legal Defense and Ednl. Fund, NYC. Contbr. articles to profl. jours. Alumni-elected trustee Wesleyan U., Middletown, Conn., 1976-79, charter trustee, 1980-92, vice chmn. bd. trustees, 1986-87, chmn. bd. trustees, 1987-92, chmn. emeritus, 1992—; trustee St. Andrews Sch., Middletown, Del., 1995—. With USN, 1969, 72-74; asst. cinceur plans officer, Office of CNO, Washington, 1972-73; spl. asst. to Sec. of Navy, Washington, 1973-74. Rhodes scholar, 1969-72; Thomas Watson Travel fellow, The Watson Found., 1969. Mem. ABA, NJ State Bar Assn., Am. Soc. Internat. Law, Internat. Bar Assn. (past chmn. sect. energy and natural resources law 1992-94), Naval Res. Assn., Internat. Inst. Strategic Studies (London), Coun. Fgn. Rels. NY. Avocations: tennis, history, fishing, books. Office: Fulbright & Jaworski LLP Market Sq 801 Pennsylvania Ave NW Washington DC 20004-2623 Office Phone: 202-662-4585. Office Fax: 202-662-4643. Business E-Mail: spfeiffer@fulbright.com.

PFEIFLE, MARK D., federal official; b. Wishek, ND, Mar. 30, 1972; BA in Polit. Sci. and Comm., U. ND. Gen. mgr. KDRQ Radio, Wishek, ND, 1994—95; mktg. & advt. sales dir. Grand Forks Air Base Leader, 1995—97; corr. AP, Bismarck, Grand Forks, 1996—97; dir. radio comm. Rep. Nat. Com., Washington, 1997—99, dep. press sec., 1998—99, dep. comm. dir., 2000—07; sr. comm. adv. US Dept. Def.; comm. advisor White House; dir. Social Security Info. Ctr. US Dept. Treasury; dep. asst. to Pres., dep. nat. security adv. for strategic comm. & global outreach NSC, 2007—; with S4 Inc., 2009; dep. commns. dir. Reb. Nat. Com., 1997—2001; dir. Social Security Information Ctr., US Dept. Treasury. Panelist, spkr. Rock the Vote MTV. Radio guest host Gary Nolan Show; freelance writer: USA Today, Grand Forks Herald; contbr. articles to Rising Tide. Republican. Office: Nat Security Coun 1600 Pennsylvania Ave NW Washington DC 20500 Office Phone: 202-863-8665, 703-850-6058. Personal E-mail: markpfeifle@aol.com.

PFENDER, EMIL, mechanical engineering educator; b. Stuttgart, Germany, May 25, 1925; came to U.S., 1964, naturalized, 1969; s. Vinzenz and Anna Maria (Dreher) P.; m. Maria Katharina Staiger, Oct. 22, 1954; children: Roland, Norbert, Corinne. Student, U. Tuebingen, Germany, 1947-49; diploma in physics, U. Stuttgart, Germany, 1953, D Ing. in Elec. Engring., 1959. Assoc. prof. mech. engring. U. Minn., Mpls., 1964-67, prof., 1967—2000, prof. emeritus, 2000—. Contbr. articles to profl. jours.; patentee in field. Fellow: ASME; mem.: NAE. Home: 1947 Bidwell St Saint Paul MN 55118-4417 Office: U Minn Dept Mech Engring 111 Church St SE Minneapolis MN 55455-0150 Office Phone: 612-625-6012. Business E-Mail: pfender@tc.umn.edu.

PFENING, FREDERIC DENVER, III, manufacturing executive; b. Columbus, Ohio, July 28, 1949; s. Frederic Denver Jr. and Lelia (Bucher) P.; m. Cynthia Gordon, July 1, 1978 (div. 1999); children: Lesley, Frederic Denver IV; m. Janet Evans, 1999. BA, Ohio Wesleyan U., 1971; MA, Ohio State U., Columbus, 1976. Various positions Fred. D. Pfening Co., Columbus, 1976-88, pres., 1988—. Bd. dirs. Friends of Ohio State U. Librs., 1988-94, 1998-2009, pres. 2004-06, Columbus State C.C. Devel. Found., 1991-99, Hist. Sites Found., Baraboo, Wis., 1984-2004, 2008-, pres., 1987-91. Mem. Am. Soc. Bakery Engrs., Orgn. Am. Historians, Bakery Equipment Mfrs. Assn. (bd. dirs. 1985-91), Young Pres.'s Orgn., World's Pres.'s Orgn., Circus Hist. Soc. (pres. 1986-89, mng. editor Bandwagon Jour.), Rotary. Office: 1075 W 5th Ave Columbus OH 43212-2629 Home Phone: 614-451-2939; Office Phone: 614-294-5361 ext 102. Business E-Mail: fpfening@pfening.com.

PFENNIG, DAVID WILLIAM, biology professor; b. San Antonio, Tex., Nov. 6, 1955; s. Clarence William and Betty Augusta Pfennig; m. Karin Susan Congdon, May 20, 1995; children: Katrina Sonora, Elsa Kai. BS, U. Tex., Austin, 1979, PhD, 1989; MS, U. Tex., San Antonio, 1982. Postdoc. fellow Ariz. State U., Tempe, 1989—91, Cornell U., Ithaca, NY, 1991—93; asst. prof. U. Ill., Urbana Champaign, 1993—96, U. NC, Chapel Hill, 1996—, assoc. prof., 1996—, prof., 1996—. Recipient Zachary Taylor Smith Disting. Term Prof. award, U. NC, 2007—. Mem.: Soc. Study Evolution. Office: Univ NC Coker Hall CB#3280 Chapel Hill NC 27599-3280 Business E-Mail: dpfennig@unc.edu.

PFENNIGSTORF, WERNER, lawyer; b. Hamburg, Germany, Sept. 28, 1934; s. Walter and Ilse (Schroeter) Pfennigstorf; m. Heika Helene Droenner, Apr. 6, 1963. Habilitation, U. Hamburg, 1974, JD, 1960; MCL, U. Mich., 1961. Bar: Germany 1962. Wissenschaftl asst. U. Hamburg, 1963—66, rsch. fellow, 1970—72; staff atty. Ins. Laws Rev. Commn., State Wis., Madison, 1967—70; project dir. Am. Bar Found., Chgo., 1973—86; pvt. practice, 1986—. Author: Legal Expense Insurance, 1975, A Comparative Study of Liability Law and Compensation Schemes in Ten Countries and the US, 1991, German Insurance Laws, 3rd edit., 1995, Public Law of Insurance, 1996; editor: Personal Injury Compensation, 1993, Pollution Insurance, 1993; co-editor: Legal Service Plans, 1977. Mem.: ABA (assoc.), Internat. Assn. Ins. Law, Deutscher Verein fur Versicherungswissenschaft. Lutheran. Office: Roethkampstr 3 21709 Duedenbuettel Germany

PFEUFFER, ROBERT JOHN, musician; b. Cleve., Dec. 25, 1925; s. Henry Vincent and Elmo Alice (Burger) P.; m. Betty June Weller, Sept. 21, 1946; children— Barbara (Mrs. Steven Mosley), Jeanne, Susan, Catherine. B.Mus. in Edn, U. Mich., 1950, M.Mus. in Edn, 1951. Contrabassoonist, bassoonist Detroit Symphony Orch., 1951-61, Phila. Orch., 1962-91; instr. bassoon Wayne State U., 1957-61, New Sch. Music, Phila., 1969—; prin. bassoon Lynchburg Symphony, 1994—, Roanoke Opera, 1996—, Milford Cmty. Band, Del. Served with AUS, 1942-44. Mem. U.S. Power Squadron, Kappa Kappa Psi, Pi Mu Alpha. Roman Catholic. Home: 6 Sharp Ln Camden Wyoming DE 19934-4526 Office: Cadbury at Cherry Hill 2150 Rt 38 Apt 445 Cherry Hill NJ 08002 E-mail: rjp567@verizon.net.

PFIFFNER, JAMES PRICE, political science professor; b. Stevens Point, Wis., June 24, 1946; s. James Sturtevant and Alice Price Pfiffner; m. Debra Ann Jones, Aug. 11, 1979; children: Megan Cyr, Katherine Courtney, Morgan Meehan. BA in Polit. Sci., U. Wis., 1968, MA in Polit. Sci., 1972, PhD in Polit. Sci., 1975. Tchg. asst. U. Wis., Madison, 1971-74; rsch. fellow Brookings Inst., Washington, 1974-75; asst. prof. U. Calif., Riverside, 1975-78, Calif. State U., Fullerton, 1978-80, assoc. prof. polit. sci., 1980-84, John Brown Mason prof., 1983-84; spl. asst. to dir. Office Pers. Mgmt., Washington, 1980-81; assoc. prof. govt. and pub. policy George Mason U., Fairfax, Va., 1984-87, prof., 1987—, univ. prof., 2003—; S.T. Lee Profl. fellow Sch. Advanced Study, U. London, 2007. Author: The President, the Budget, and Congress: Impoundment and the 1974 Budget Act, 1979, The Strategic Presidency: Hitting the Ground Running, 1988, 2d edit., 1996, The Modern Presidency, 1998, 5th edit., 2007, The Character Factor: How We Judge America's Presidents, 2004, (book) Power Play: The Bush Presidency Constitution, 2008; editor: The President and Economic Policy, 1986, The Managerial Presidency, 1991, 2d edit., 1999, Governance and American Politics: Classic and Current Perspectives, 1995; co-editor: The Presidency in Transition, 1989, The Presidency and the Gulf War, 1993, Understanding the Presidency, 1997, 5th edit., 2008, The Future of Merit, 2000, Intelligence Nat. Security Policy Making on Iraq, British Am. Perspectives, 2008. With U.S. Army, 1969-70, Vietnam. Decorated Army Commendation medal for Valor, Vietnam/Cambodia, 1970; Brookings Instn. fellow, 1974-75, vis. scholar, 1983, 97; Nat. Assn. Sch. Pub. Affairs and Adminstrn. faculty fellow, 1980-81; S. T. Lee Professorial fellow Sch. for Advanced Study, U. London, 2007. Mem. Nat. Acad. Pub. Adminstrn., Cosmos Club. Office: George Mason U Sch Pub Policy 3C6 Fairfax VA 22030-4444

PFIFFNER, PATRICK MEEHAN, musician, educator; b. Stevens Point, Wis., Mar. 19, 1948; s. James Sturtevant and Alice Mary (Price) Pfiffner; m. Linda Sue Ridenour, Aug. 6, 1972; children: James Stanley, Jeffrey Allen. MusB, San Diego State U., 1976, MusM, 1977. Extra percussionist/timpanist San Diego Symphony, 1972—; percussionist Nederlander Orgn., San Diego, 1976—; resident drummer/percussionist/contractor Starlight Light Opera, San Diego, 1981—; extra percussionist/timpanist San Diego Opera, 1982—; prin. percussionist/timpanist San Diego Chamber Orch., 1985—; prof. music Point Loma Nazarene U., San Diego. Percussionist Sammy Davis, Bob Hope, George Burns, Mickey Rooney, Robert Goulet, Andre Bocelli, Johnny Mathis, Milton Berle, 1981—; dir. Grand Pacific Band, 1986—, Grossmont Coll. concert and jazz bands, 1979—86, Heartland Youth Orch., 1983—84. Author: The Ancestors of Patrick Meehan Pfiffner, 2002; contbr. articles to profl. jours.; performer: (CD) Those Hollywood Marches, with Lalo Shifrin, 1990, Russian CD, San Diego Chamber Orch., 1989, French CD, 1991, Berlioz: Symphonie Fantastique, San Diego Symphony Orch., Malcolm Arnold CD, 1992, Magnification CD, Rock Group Yes, 2001, nat. tours Broadway shows, including Beauty and the Beast, Hello Dolly, King and I, Ragtime, The Producers, Hairspray, others. Musician 2d class USN, 1967—71, USS Little Rock, Mediterranean Sea. Mem.: ASCAP, Percussive Arts Soc., Am. Fedn. Musicians Local 325. Avocations: long distance running, genealogy. Home: 13138 Beechtree St Lakeside CA 92040-3307 Office: Pt Loma Nazarene U 3900 Lomaland Dr San Diego CA 92106 Personal E-mail: patpfiffner@cox.net.

PFISTER, MARC, consumer products company executive, physician, researcher; s. Erwin and Gertrud Pfister; m. Susanna Pfister, Sept. 9, 1999; children: Ayo Marc Lewis, Elia Marc. BS, U. Berne, 1983, MD, 1988; diploma in Pub. Health, U. Basel, Switzerland, 1991. Cert. in strategic mktg. U. Berkeley, San Francisco, 2001. Clin. fellow Hosp. Interlaken, Berne, 1992—94; rsch. fellow U. Hosp. Berne, 1994, med. officer, clin. fellow, 1995—99; clin. rsch. post doctoral fellow U. Calif., San Francisco, 1999—2002; assoc. dir. Sanofi Aventis Pharm., Bridgewater, NJ, 2002—04; global head, exec. dir. Bristol-Myers-Squibb, Princeton, NJ, 2004—. Founder Modeling And Simulation Applications in Clin. Pharmatherapy Orgn., co-chair, ACOP, 2008, ACCP, 2009. Contbr. articles to profl. jours.; section editor JCP. Fellow: Am. Coll. Clin. Pharm.; mem.: Am. Soc. Nephrology, Am. Soc. Hypertension. Achievements include design of new methods for quantitative decision making; novel computer models for clinical research. Avocations: piano, jazz, classical music. Office: Bristol-Myers-Squibb Rsch Inst PO Box 4000 Rt 206 Princeton NJ 08540 Office Phone: 609-252-5322. Office Fax: 609-252-7822. Personal E-mail: mpfisterusa@aol.com.

PFISTER, RAYMOND LAWRENCE, otolaryngologist; b. Newport, Ky., Apr. 13, 1925; s. Frederick Charles Pfister and Goldie Furnish; m. Barbara Schlenck, May 31, 1946; children: Debbie, Robyn, Holly, Michael. MD, U. Cin., 1948; postgrad., Harvard U., 1950. Asst. for otolaryngology Cin. Gen. Hosp., 1952—73; chief of staff Naples Cmty. Hosp., Fla., 1988—90, chmn. bd. dirs., 1990. Capt. USAF, 1952—54. Fellow: Am. Coll. Surgeons, Am. Bd. Head and Neck Surgery; mem.: Naples Yacht Club (commodore). Republican. Episcopalian. Avocations: sailing, horse racing. Home: 1325 7th St S Naples FL 34102 Personal E-mail: pfis13@aol.com.

PFISTERER, MARILYN, councilwoman; b. Pa. married; 5 children. Grad., Lugar Excellence in Pub. Svc. Series. Sales mgr. and trainer; contr. for the sec. of state State of Ind.; small bus. owner; councillor, dist. 14 Indpls.-Marion County City-County Coun. Mem. internal audit com. City of Indpls., coun. liaison, Charter Sch. Initiative, mem. med. history mus. bd., mem. econ. adv. com., active, Early Intervention Planning Coun., active, Re-entry Program Com.; mem. exec. bd. Ind. Assn. Counties and Towns; chmn. adminstrn. and fin. com. Indpls.-Marion County City-County Coun. State del. Rep. State Convention, Ind.; campaign vol. Rep. Party, Ind., ward chmn., precinct com. woman; mem. trustees bd. Wayne Township, Ind., 1999—, GOP mem. Mem.: Greater Indpls. Rep. Women's Club (past pres.), Speedway Lion's Club. Republican. Office: 1001 Mt Auburn Dr Indianapolis IN 46224 also: Indpls Marion County City County Coun 241 City County Bldg 200 E Washington St Indianapolis IN 46204 Office Phone: 317-244-7156, 317-327-4242. Business E-Mail: cpfist1061@aol.com.*

PFLAUM, JEFFREY D., lawyer; JD, William Mitchell Coll. Law; MBA, U. Minn. Atty. Popham Haik Schnobrich Kaufman; assoc. gen. counsel ADC Telecom. Inc., 1996—99, v.p., gen. counsel & sec., 1999—. Office: ADC Telecommunication Inc 13625 Technology Dr Minneapolis MN 55440 Office Phone: 952-938-8080. Office Fax: 952-917-1717.*

PFLAUM, STEVEN F., lawyer; b. Chgo., Aug. 25, 1955; s. Donald A. and Sharon R. (Satin) P. BA, U. Ill., 1976; JD magna cum laude, U. Mich., 1979. Bar: Calif. 1979, Ill. 1984, U.S. Dist. Ct. (ctrl. and no. dists.) Calif. 1980, U.S. Dist. Ct. (no. dist.) Ill. 1985, U.S. Dist. Ct. (ea. dist.) Wis. 1986, U.S. Dist. Ct. (ctrl. dist.) Ill. 1994, U.S. Ct. Appeals (9th cir.) 1985, U.S. Ct. Appeals (7th cir.) 1986, U.S. Ct. Appeals (6th cir.) 1988, U.S. Ct. Appeals (8th cir.) 1994, U.S. Ct. Claims 1984, U.S. Supreme Ct. 1986, registered Chgo. Bar Assn., City of Waterville. Assoc. Beardsley, Hufstedler & Kemble, LA, 1979-81, Hufstedler, Miller, Carlson & Beardsley, LA, 1981-82, O'Donnell & Gordon, LA, 1982-83, ptnr., 1984-85, Chgo., 1985-87, McDermott, Will & Emery, Chgo., 1988—. Author: Forced Dissemination of Information About Consumer Organizations: Lessons from Illinois Experience, 1988, Solicitation of Business from Corporate Clients, 1991, Client Solicitation: What You Can Do and What You Can Do About It, 1993, Beyond the 65 dB DNL Standard: The Future Efforts to Determine the Significance of Airport Noise Impacts, 1994, High Court Takings Rulings Has Implications ofr airport Noise, 1994, Successful Practice Under the New Illinois Civil Discovery Rules, 1995, Should Justice Heiple Be Impeached?, 1997, Justice James D. Heiple: Impeachment and the Assault on Judicial Independence, 1998. Mem. Deerfield Bd. Zoning Appeals, 1989-93. Mem. ABA, Chgo. Bar Assn. (bd. mgrs. 1993-95, profl. responsibility com. 1986—, chair 1990-91, chair spl. com. Ill. discovery rules 1995, fin. com. 1995—, spl. com. Supreme Ct. redistricting 1997, mem. gen. coun. 1996—2009), Ill. Jud. Ethics Com., Chgo. Coun. Lawyers, Appellate Lawyers Assn. (bd. dirs. 2008-), Order of Coif, Ill. Supreme Ct. Com. on Prof. Reps. (chair 2009-), Phi Beta Kappa. Avocations: tennis, skiing, music. Office: McDermott Will & Emery 227 W Monroe St Ste 3100 Chicago IL 60606-5096 Office Phone: 312-984-3641. *Notable cases include: representing City of Newport Beach, Calif. in connection with dispute regarding proposed expansion of John Wayne Airport; represented Ill. Citizens Utility Bd. in connection with litigation and legislation regarding constitutionality of distbn. of Cub promotional materials.*

PFLUM, BARBARA ANN, retired allergist; b. Cin., Jan. 10, 1943; d. James Frederick and Betty Mae (Doherty) P.; m. Makram I. Gobrail, Oct. 20, 1973 (dec.); children: Christina, James. BS, Coll. Mt. St. Vincent, 1967; MD, Georgetown U., 1971; MS, Coll. Mt. St. Joseph, 1993. Cons. Children's Med. Ctr., Dayton, Ohio, 1975—2006, dir. allergy clinic, 1983-89; dir. allergy divsn. Hopeland Splty. Clinic, Dayton, 1998-2000; ret., 2006. Fellow Am. Acad. Pediatrics, Am. Acad. Allergy and Immunology, Am. Coll. Allergy and Immunology; mem. Ohio Soc. Allergy and Immunology, Western Ohio Pediatric Soc. (pres. 1985-86) Roman Catholic. Home Phone: 937-293-2079. Personal E-mail: bapflum@hotmail.com.

PFLUM, WILLIAM JOHN, retired physician; b. NYC, July 30, 1924; s. Peter Arthur and Caroline (Schmidt) P.; m. Roseann Sarah Stubing, Oct. 13, 1956; children: Carol Jean, Jeanine, Suzanne, Denise, Peter. BS, Georgetown U., 1947; MD, Loyola U., Chgo., 1951. Diplomate Am. Bd. Allergy & Immunology. Intern St. Vincent's Hosp, NYC, 1951-52; resident in internal medicine NYU div. Goldwater Meml. Hosp., NYC, 1952-53; resident in allergy Inst. Allergy Roosevelt Hosp., NYC, 1956; attending internist allergy & immunology Overlook Hosp., Summit, NJ, 1958—. Assoc. attending Inst. Allergy, Immunology and Infectious Diseases, Roosevelt Hosp., N.Y.C., 1957-92; pvt. practice medicine, specializing in allergy and immunology, Summit, 1957-92; ret.; cons. in field. With USAAF, 1943—45, ETO. Decorated Purple Heart, air medal with two clusters, POW medal. Fellow Am. Acad. Allergy, Am. Coll.

Allergists, Am. Assn. Clin. Immunology and Allergy; mem. Summit Med. Soc., Am. Assn. Clin. Immunology and Allergy (pres. Mid-Atlantic region 1975-76), Disabled Am. Vets., Mil. Order Purple Heart, Am. Ex-Prisoners of War, 8th Air Force Hist. Soc., World Marathon Runners Assn., Robert A. Cooke Allergy Alumni Assn. Achievements include completion of 26 consecutive Boston Marathons, 1971-1996 with Am. Med. Athletic Assn. Home: 1104 Presa Pl Lady Lake FL 32159 Home Phone: 352-205-8186.

PFOTENHAUER, JOHN M., engineering educator, researcher; s. C. Donald and Martha L. Pfotenhauer; m. Nadine M. Gramsey, June 1, 1979; children: Donald P., Beth M., Lydia R., David J. PhD, U. Oreg., Eugene, 1984. Scientist U. Wis., Madison, 1984—93, asst. prof., 1993—99, assoc. prof., 1999—2005, prof., 2005—; guest rschr. Nat. Inst. Sci. & Tech., Boulder, Colo., 2001—02; vis. faculty, rschr. Oak Ridge Nat. Lab., Tenn., 2002. Pres. Cryogenic Engring. Conf. Bd., Madison, 2005—. Contbr. articles to profl. jours. (Best Paper of Yr., 2005). Ch. elder Springs Hope Fellowship, Madison, 1998—2008. Grant, USAF, 1994—96, 2003—05, US Dept. Energy, 1998—, NASA, 2003—05, Office Naval Rsch., 2003—05. Mem.: ASME, Am. Soc. Engring. Educators, Cryogenics Soc. Am., Am. Phys. Soc., Sigma Pi Sigma. Achievements include patents for cryogenic cooling apparatus with voltage isolation. Office: Univ Wis-Madison 1500 Engineering Dr Madison WI 53706 Office Fax: 608-262-8464. Business E-Mail: pfot@engr.wisc.edu.

PFOTENHAUER, KURT PAUL, trade association administrator; b. Richmond, Va., June 23, 1960; s. Fredrick William and Carolyn Ann (Viets) P.; m. Nancy M. Pfotenhauer; children: Jonathan, Benjamin, Kelsey, Johnny, Adam. BA, U. Notre Dame, 1982; MA, Yale U., 1985. Legis. asst. to Rep. Denny Smith US Congress, Washington, 1985-87, chief of staff to Rep. Denny Smith, 1989-90; legis. asst. Union Pacific Corp., Washington, 1987-88; ops. mgr. United Parcel Svc., Chantilly, Va., 1990-91, v.p. pub. affairs Washington, 1991—96; chief of staff to Senator Gordon Smith US Senate, 1996—2002; sr. v.p. govt. affairs & pub. policy Mortgage Bankers Assn., 2002—07; CEO Am. Land Title Assn., Washington, 2008—. Lutheran. Office: Am Land Title Assn 1828 L St NW Ste 705 Washington DC 20036 Office Phone: 800-787-2582.

PFOUTS, RALPH WILLIAM, economist, consultant; b. Atchison, Kans., Sept. 9, 1920; s. Ralph Ulysses and Alice (Oldham) P.; m. Jane Hoyer, Jan. 31, 1945 (dec. Nov. 1982); children: James William, Susan Jane Pfouts Portman, Thomas Robert (dec.), Elizabeth Ann Pfouts Klenowski; m. Lois Bateson, Dec. 21, 1984 (div.); m. Felicia Sprincenatu, 1993 (div.); m. June St. James, July 14, 2001 BA, U. Kans., 1942, MA, 1947; PhD, U. NC, 1952. Rsch. asst., instr. econs. U. Kans., Lawrence, 1946—47; instr. U. NC, Chapel Hill, 1947—50, lectr. econs., 1950—52, assoc. prof. econs., 1952—58, prof. econs., 1958—87; pvt. practice Chapel Hill, 1987—2005, Boise, Idaho, 2005—. Vis. prof. U. Leeds, 1983; vis. rsch. scholar Internat. Inst. for Applied Sys. Analysis, Laxenberg, Austria, 1983; prof. Ctrl. European U., Prague, 1991; chmn. grad. studies dept. econs. Sch. Bus. Adminstrn. U. NC, Chapel Hill, 1957-62, chmn. dept. econs. Sch. Bus. Adminstrn., 1962-68 Author: Elementary Economics-A Mathematical Approach, 1972; editor: So. Econ. Jour, 1955-75; editor, contbr.: Techniques of Urban Economic Analysis, 1960, Essays in Economics and Econometrics, 1960; mem. editl. bd. Metroeconomica, 1961-80, Atlantic Econ. Jour, 1973—; contbr. articles to profl. jours Served as deck officer USNR, 1943—46. Social Sci. Rsch. Coun. fellow U. Cambridge, 1953-54; Ford Found. Faculty Rsch. fellow, 1962-63 Mem. AAAS, Am. Statis. Assn., NC Statis. Assn. (past pres.), Am. Econ. Assn., So. Econ. Assn. (past pres.), Internat. Atlantic Econ. Soc. (v.p. 1973-76, pres. 1977-78, Lifetime Achievement award, 2008), Population Assn. Am., Econometric Soc., Math. Assn. Am., Phi Beta Kappa, Pi Sigma Alpha, Alpha Kappa Psi, Omicron Delta Epsilon Home and Office: 2308 W Norcrest Dr Boise ID 83705 Office Phone: 208-331-1234. Personal E-mail: rwpfouts@msn.com.

PFUND, RANDY (RANDALL C. PFUND), former professional sports team executive; b. Oak Park, Ill., Dec. 29, 1951; Student, Wheaton Coll. Tchr., coach Glenbard South HS, Ill.; asst. coach, dir. booster orgn. Westmont Coll., Santa Barbara, Calif.; asst. coach LA Lakers, 1985—92, head coach, 1992—94; gen. mgr. Miami Heat, Fla., 1994—2008.

PFUNTNER, WALTER ALAN, JR., marketing executive, educator; PhD in Systems Engring., Clarkson U., Potsdam, NY, 1986. Cert. profl. engr., NY. Power application developer NYPP, Schenectady, 1989—92, IT mgr., 1992—2007, NYISO, Rensselaer, 1992—2007, sr. planning engr., 2007—08, prin. market trainer, 2008—. Boy scout adult leader BSA, Albany, NY, 2000—08. Mem.: IEEE (sect. chmn., pes chpt. chmn. 1989—92). Avocations: art, Tae Kwon Do.

PHADKE, ARUN G., engineering educator; b. Gwalior, M.P., India, Aug. 27, 1938; came to U.S., 1959; s. Gajanan G. and Indira G. Phadke; m. Kusum K. Joglekar, Sept. 14, 1964; 1 child, Ajit A. BS, Agra U., India, 1955; B in Tech. with honors, Indian Inst. Tech., 1959; MSEE, Ill. Inst. Tech., 1961; PhD, U. Wis., Madison, 1964. Systems engr. Allis Chalmers, Milw., 1963-67; asst. prof. elec. engr. dept. U. Wis., Madison, 1967-69; cons. engr. Am. Elec. Power Svc. Corp., NYC, 1969-82; univ. disting. prof. Va. Poly Inst. & State U., Blacksburg, 1982—, 2000—. Cons. various electric utilities, equipment mfrs., 1980—. Co-author: Computer Relaying for Power Systems, 1988; contbr. several articles to profl. jours. Disting. Svc. citation, 1987, Centennial medal U. Wis., 1991; co-recipient Benjamin Franklin medal in Elec. Engring., Franklin Inst., 2008. Fellow IEEE (chmn. power sys. relaying com., outstanding educator Power Engring. Soc. 1991, Millennium medal, Herman Halperin Electric Transmission and Distribution award, Power Engring. Soc. Technical Com. Disting. award); mem. Edison Elec. Inst. (outstanding educator 1986), Conf. Internat. Grand Reseaux Electrique (chmn. working groups), NAE. Achievements include patents in field. Avocations: painting, tailoring. Office: Va Poly Inst & State U Elec Engring Dept 426 Whittemore Hall Blacksburg VA 24061-0111 E-mail: aphadke@vt.edu.

PHALEN, ROBERT FRANKLYNN, environmental scientist; b. Fairview, Okla., Oct. 18, 1940; married, 1966; 2 children. B in Physics, San Diego State U., 1964, M in Physics, 1966; PhD in Biophysics, U. Rochester, 1971. Engring. aide advanced space systems dept. Gen. Dynamics/Astronautics, San Diego, 1962-63; asst. to radiation safety officer, lab. teaching asst. San Diego State U., 1964-66, instr. physics dept., 1966; mem. summer faculty biology dept. Rochester (N.Y.) Inst. Tech., 1970-72; rsch. assoc. aerosol physics dept. Lovelace Found. for Med. Edn. and Rsch., Albuquerque, 1972-74; from adj. asst. prof. to assoc. prof. in residence dept. community and environ. medicine U. Calif., Irvine, 1974-84, prof., dir. Air Pollution Health Effects Lab., 1985—2008, faculty Ctr. for Occupl. Environ. Health, 1985—, prof. dept. medicine, 2008—. Editor Aerosol Sci. and Tech., mem. editl. bd., 2002-05; reviewer Am. Rev. Respiratory Disease, Applied Indsl. Hygiene, Bull. Math. Biology, Exptl. Lung Rsch., Jour. Toxicology and Environ. Health, Jour. Toxicology and Applied Pharmacology, Jour. Aerosol Sci., Sci., Toxicol. Scis.; reviewer, mem. editl. bd. Fundamental and Applied Toxicology, 1986-92, Inhalation Toxicology, 1988-04, Jour. Aerosol Medicine, 1988-98; mem. safety and occupl. health study sect. NIH, 1988-01, mem. spl. study sects., 1980, 81, chmn. spl. study sects., 1982-84, 87, 88, 92, mem. site visit teams, 1980-01; mem. expert panel on sulfur oxides EPA, mem. inhalation toxicology divsn. peer rev. panel, 1982, session chmn., 1983, participant workshop on non-oncogenic lung disease, 1984, mem. grants rsch. sci. rev. panel on health rsch., EPA advisor, 1985-88, 93-98, 03; mem. com. animal models testing interventions against aerosol agts. Nat. Acad. Sci., 2005-06; mem. task group on respiratory tract kinetic model Nat. Coun. Radiation Protection, 1978-97; mem. adv. panel on asbestos APHA, 1978; chmn. atmospheric sampling com. Am. Coun. Govtl. Indsl. Hygienists, 1982-92; chmn. NIOSH spl. study sect., 1983; panelist workshop NHLBI, 1982; sci. advisor Prentice Day Sch., 1986-04; mem. Clean Air Sci. Adv. Ctr., EPA, 2007-; mem. bd. dirs. Calif. BioMed. Rsch. Assoc.; dir. four internat. confs. on health effects of particulate air pollution; dir. internat. conf. on inhaled aerosol doses. Author: Inhalation Studies: Foundations and Techniques, 1984, The Particulate Air Pollution Controversy, 2002, 2nd edit., 2009, (with others) Advances in Air Sampling, 1988, Concepts in Inhalation Toxicology, 1989, Deposition, Retention and Dosimetry of Inhaled Radioactive Substances, 1997; editor: Methods in Inhalation Toxicology, 1997; contbr. numerous articles to profl. jours. Am. Legion scholar. Fellow Acad. Toxicol. Scis., Southern Calif. Acad. Scis.; mem. Am. Assn. Aerosol Rsch. (charter, chmn. ann. meeting 1985), Am. Conf. Govtl. Indsl. Hygienists, Am. Indsl. Hygiene Assn. (jour. reviewer, chmn. ann. conf. 1981, 85, 86), Brit. Occupl. Hygiene Soc., Internat. Soc. Aerosols in Medicine, Soc. for Aerosol Rsch., Health Physics Soc., Internat. Hormesis Soc. (charter), Soc. Toxicology, Career Achievement award 2000). Achievements include research in nasal, tracheobronchial and pulmonary transport of inhaled deposited particles and effects of pollutant exposure on transport kinetcs, laboratory simulation and characterization of airborne environmental pollutants, respiratory tract deposition and clearance models for inhaled particles, including species comparisons and body size effects, behavior of highly-concentrated aerosols with respect to deposition in the respiratory tract. Office: U Calif Air Pollution Health Effects Lab Cmty & Environ Medicine Irvine CA 92697-1825 Business E-Mail: rfphalen@uci.edu.

PHAM, CHRISTOPHER HOANG, application developer, educator; naturalized; s. Le Pham and Nhung Thi Hoang; m. Vivian Trang Nguyen; children: Christopher Jr. HuyVu, Ariel ThuyTien, Elise Cat-Tien. MSEE, San Jose State U., 1995, BSEE, 1994; postgrad., U. Calif., Davis, 1998—2000. Tech. support Hewlett Packard, Mountain View, Calif., 1987—88, NovTek Inc., San Jose, 1989—90; assoc. design engr. Ancot Corp., Menlo Park, Calif., 1990—92; devel. engr. and nuclear scientist Quantrads Sensors Corp., Santa Clara, Calif., 1993—94; sofware devel. & performance engr. Adaptec Inc., Milpitas, Calif., 1994—95; software devel. engr. Credence Systems Inc., Fremont, Calif., 1995—96; mem. of tech. staff SUN Microsystems Inc., Menlo Park, Calif., 1997—98; sr. software engr. Cisco Systems Inc., San Jose, Calif., 1998—2000, software mgr. I and II, 2000—01, engring. mgr. III, 2002—; engring. mgr. III, sr. tech. lead, adj. prof. San Jose State U. Adj. prof. Evergreen Valley Coll., San Jose, 1998—2000, San Jose State U., 1995—. Contbr. articles to profl. jours. Pres.-elect VACETS, San Jose, 2006—, bd. dirs., 2006—. Recipient Asian Am. Engr. of the Yr. award, CIE-USA, 2005, Medal of Edn., MOE VN, 2007. Master: IEEE (sr.). Republican. Achievements include patents for technologies. Avocations: travel, language art. Home: SJSU EE Dept One Washington Sq San Jose CA 95192-0084 Personal E-mail: phamc@email.sjsu.edu. Business E-Mail: chpham@cisco.com.

PHAM, DAVID LAN, secondary school educator, writer; b. Binh Chuan, Thudaumot, Vietnam, Feb. 1, 1940; s. Khoai Van Pham and Chuc Thi Le; m. Tam Thi Nguyen, Nov. 22, 1965; children: Albert, Elizabeth, Wellington, An, Victoria. BEd, Faculty of Pedagogy, Saigon Vietnam, 1963; BA in History, Faculty of Letters, Saigon Vietnam, 1965; M in Libr. Sci, Faculty of Pedagogy, Saigon Vietnam, 1973. Tchr., chief libr. Ly Thuong Kiet Comprehensive H.S., Hoc Mon, Gia Dinh, Vietnam, 1963—75; social svcs. coord. Cath. Social Svcs. Refugee Resettlement Program, Bayou La Batre, Ala., 1987—96. Advisor Binh Duong Bo De Sch., 1968—75; advisor Binh Duong Confedn, Vietnamienne du Travail, 1968—75; vis. Thailand for Libr. Sci. Observation, 1973; advisor, founder Mutual Assistance Assn., Bayou La Batre, Ala., 1988—89. Columnist Thoi Bao Daily, Saigon, Vietnam, 1963—64, columnist Point South, Mobile, Ala., 1991—94; columnist: Binh Duong News, 2000— (award of apperciation, 2003); editor: (Bulletin) Bulletin Tin Viet, Dac San Que Huong, 1987—96; author: Two Hamlets in Nam Bo, 1999, Earthy Life, 2001, Vietnam History Dictionary, 2002, International Politico - Cultural Influences on Vietnam in the 20th Century, 2004. Gen. sec. Assn. Vietnamese Tchrs. of History and Geography, 1967—69, Viet. Libr. Assn, 1973—74; founder Tutorial Program, Bayou La Batre, Ala., 1992—96. Buddhist. Avocations: reading, travel, walking, writing, zen. Home: 1341 Leith Dr Toledo OH 43614 E-mail: davidlanpham@hotmail.com.

PHAM, KHANH DAI, aerospace engineer, researcher; s. Viet Son Pham and Linh Kim Bang; m. Huong Dieu Nguyen, Dec. 18, 2003; 1 child, An Duy. D Elec. Engring., U. Notre Dame, 2004. Registered profl. engr., Nebr. Postdoctoral rschr. U. Notre Dame, Ind., 2003—04; aerospace and rsch. engr. Air Force Rsch. Lab., Kirtland AFB, N.Mex., 2004—. Recipient Best Paper Presentation award, IEEE, 2000, 2004; Arthur J. Schmidt Presdl. fellow, U. Notre Dame, 1998—2002, Ctr. Applied Math. Grad. Rsch. fellow, 2000, 2003. Mem.: ASME, AIAA, SPIE (program com. 2005—06), AAS (nat. chmn. 2005—06), Golden Key Nat. Honor Soc., Phi Theta Kappa, Eta Kappa Nu, Tau Beta Pi. Achievements include research in statisical control theory. Office: AF Rsch Lab 3550 Aberdeen Ave SE Kirtland AFB NM 87117 Office Fax: 505-846-7877. Business E-Mail: khanh.pham@kirtland.af.mil.

PHAM, LEE, literature and language professor, consultant; s. Doanh Manh Pham and Hong Thi Phan; m. Vanlan Pham, Apr. 10, 1962; children: Mylinh, Julie, Linh Xuan, Joanne, Linh Trong, Vanlinh Pyle. BA, Nat. U. Saigon, Vietnam, 1961; diploma, U. Sydney, 1972; MEd, U. Houston, 1984, EdD, 1989. Tchr. English Chu Van An H.S., Saigon, Vietnam, 1961—75, Houston Ind. Sch. Dist., 1985—93; instr. US citizenship Inst. R & D, Houston, 2003—05; reader sat essay NCS Pearson Ednl. Measurement, Bloomington, Minn., 2005—. Cons. Radio Free Asia, Washington, DC, DC, 2003—; adj. faculty English as 2d lang. San Jacinto Coll. South Campus, Houston, 2004—05, Lone Star Coll. Sys., Houston, 2006—. Author of poems; translator: (radio broadcasting program) News Reports & Interviews; art photography, Landscapes. Scholar, Australian Govt., 1971; Fulbright Grad. Study grantee, US Govt. Inst. Internat. Edn., 1975. Mem.: Tex. CC Tchrs. Assn., Assn. Tex. Profl. Educators. Buddhism. Avocations: travel, photography, poetry. Personal E-mail: lee_pham01@yahoo.com.

PHAM, SI MAI, cardiothoracic surgeon; b. Ninh Hoa, Khanh Hoa, Vietnam, Oct. 6, 1955; arrived in US, 1975; s. Tro Pham and Nhung Thi Mai; m. Marie Christine Pham, Sept. 9, 1987; children: Benjamin Bartley, Anthony Ninh, Vivienne Elisabeth, Victoria B.H. Student, U. Saigon Sch. Pharmacy, Vietnam, 1973-75; BS in Chem. magna cum laude, Lebanon Valley Coll., Annville, Pa., 1979; MD, U. Pitts., 1983; D (hon.), U. Morón, 2002. Diplomate, surg. critical care Am. Bd. Surgery, Am. Bd. Thoracic Surgery. Intern, resident gen. surgery U. Pitts., 1983-86, rsch. fellow, cardiothoracic surgery, 1986-87, sr. and chief resident gen. surgery, 1987-89, resident cardiothoracic surgery, 1989-92, asst. prof. surgery, Sch. Medicine, 1992—98, dir. adult cardiac transplant program, Sch. Medicine, 1993-97, assoc. dir. heart transplant and artificial heart program, 1997-98, dir. cardiothoracic transplant rsch., 1997-98; dir. extracorporeal membrane oxygenation svc. Presbyn. U. Hosp., Pitts., 1993-98; dir. cardiopulmonary transplantation and artifical heart program, divsn. cardiothoracic surgery U. Miami Sch. Medicine, 1998—; assoc. prof. surgery U. Miami Sch. Medicine, 1998—2002, prof., 2002—. Prof. surgery U. Miami Sch. Medicine, 2002—; reviewer various med. jours. Contbr. articles to profl. jours., chapters to books, scientific papers. Recipient Am. Chem. award, 1979, Radiology award U. Pitts., 1983, Dalsemer rsch. scholar award Am. Lung Assn., 1997-99; ACS Faculty fellowship award, 1994-96, Health Care Heroes award Greater Miami C. of C., 2007; grantee Children's Hosp. Pitts., 1987, Am. Heart Assn., 1987-89, 94-96, 96-99, Thoracic Surgery Found., 1996-97, 97-98, Am. Lung Assn., 1997—, Presbyn. U. Hosp., 1987-89, NIH, 1999—, Vietnamese Am. Med. Rsch. Found. sci. award, 2005. Fellow Am. Coll. Surgeons, Am. Heart Assoc. (cmty. bd. mem.); mem. Am. Soc. Artificial Internal Organs, Internat. Soc. Heart and Lung Transplantation, Soc. Critical Care Medicine, Am. Assn. Advancement of Sci., Am. Soc. Transplant Surgeons, Soc. Thoracic Surgeons, Am. Assn. Thoracic Surgery, Extracorporeal Life Support Organization, Assn. for Acad. Surgery, Phi Alpha Epsilon, Transplant Found. South Fla. (adv. bd. mem.). Avocations: reading, gardening. Office: U Miami Sch Medicine Highland Profl Bldg 1801 NW 9th Ave Ste 5th Fl Miami FL 33136 Office Phone: 305-355-5070. Business E-Mail: spham@med.miami.edu.

PHAM, WELLINGTON, radiologist, educator; b. Saigon, Saigon, Vietnam, Sept. 4, 1969; s. David and Tammy Nguyen Pham; m. Michiyo Koyama, Oct. 14, 2004. PhD in Medicinal and Biol. Chemistry, U. Toledo, 2000. Rsch. fellow UCLA Sch. Medicine, 2000—01, Harvard Med. Sch., Boston, 2001—05, radiology instr., 2005—06; asst. prof. radiology Vanderbilt U. Sch. Medicine, Nashville, 2006—. Dir. chemistry Vanderbilt U. Inst. Imaging Sci., Nashville, 2006—. Recipient Jr. Faculty award, Neuro-Imaging, 2006—. Mem.: Am. Assn. Avancement Sci., NY Acad. Scis., Soc. Exptl. Biology and Medicine, Soc. Molecular Imaging, Am. Assn. Cancer Rsch., Am. Chem. Soc., Sigma Xi. Office: Vanderbilt Univ Sch Medicine 1161 21st Ave S Nashville TN 37232 Personal E-mail: wellington.pham@vanderbilt.edu.

PHAN, ANH-VU, adult education educator, researcher; b. Saigon (Ho Chi Minh City), Vietnam, Aug. 16, 1959; s. Tinh Van Phan and Hao Thi Ly; m. Tran-Nam Phan, Jan. 4, 1995; children: Jerrick Dac-Huy children: Johann Anh-Huy. B in Mech. Engring., Ho Chi Minh City U. of Tech., Vietnam, 1977—82; DEA (MS equivalent), Institut Nat. Polytechnique de Grenoble, France, 1992—93; PhD, Ecole Polytechnique, U. of Montreal, Can., 1994—97. Asst. lectr., dept. mech. engring. Ho Chi Minh City U. of Tech., Vietnam, 1982—84, lectr., dept. mech. engring., 1984—92; consulting engr. RENAULT, Ho Chi Minh City, 1993—93; lectr., assoc. chair, dept. mech. engring. Ho Chi Minh City U. of Tech., Vietnam, 1993—94; post-doctoral rschr., dept. mech. engring. Ecole Polytechnique de Montreal, 1998—99; post-doctoral rsch. assoc. Computer Sci. and Math. Divsn., Oak Ridge Nat. Lab., Tenn., 1999—2001; rsch. staff mem. Computational Scis. and Engring. Divsn., Oak Ridge Nat. Lab., 2002; asst. prof., dept. mech. engring. U. South Ala., 2002—06, assoc. prof., dept. mech. engring., 2006—. Contbr. numerous articles in profl. jours. Recipient Ralph E. Powe Jr. Faculty award, Oak Ridge Associated Univs., 2004, Best Faculty Mem. award, U. South Ala. Coun. Internat. Students Orgn., 2004—05; grantee Bourse d'Excellence, Govt. of Que., 1994-1997, post-doctoral fellowship, Ecole Polytechnique de Montreal, 1998—99, Bourse de Stage, French Govt., 1992—93, post-doctoral rsch. assocs. fellowship, Oak Ridge Associated Universities, 1999—2001. Mem.: Am. Soc. Mech. Engrs., Internat. Assn. for Computational Mechanics, US Assn. for Computational Mechanics, Internat. Soc. of Structural and Multidisciplinary Optimization (assoc.). Achievements include research in Further development of the Boundary Contour Method for applications in Stress Analysis, Shape Optimization and Linear Fracture Mechanics; mutli-scale modelling of composite materials; modeling the growth of nanostructures and the simulation of machining processes; invention of Development of a new crack tip element for Fracture Mechanics using the Boundary Element Methods. Office: U of South Alabama EGCB 212 307 University Blvd Mobile AL 36688-0002 E-mail: vphan@usouthal.edu.

PHAN, MANH-HUONG, materials scientist; b. Thai Binh, Vietnam, May 15, 1978; s. Anh Lien and Ty Thi Phan; m. Ngoc Bich Nguyen; 1 child, Chau Minh. PhD, U. Bristol, Eng., 2006. Cert. in physics, U. Bristol, 2006. Sr. rschr. Hanoi Nat. U., Vietnam, 2000—01; rsch. project adviser Chungbuk Nat. U., Cheongju, Republic of Korea, 2001—, advisor, 2002—07, rsch. scientist, 2003; rsch. fellow U. Bristol, 2006—07, rsch. project adviser, 2003—, advisor, 2007—; rsch. specialist U. South Fla., Tampa, 2007—, rsch. project adviser & tchr., 2007—. Reviewer phys. jours. Am. Inst. Physics Pubs., Coll. Pk., Md., 2003—; rsch. project adviser Hanoi U. Tech., 2007—; editl. bd. mem. Open Indsl. & Mfg. Engring. Jour., 2007. Contbr. chapters to books to peer-reviewed papers. Recipient, Korea, 2007, Internat. Symposium Magnetism, Russia, 2008, Session chair, Austin, 2008; grantee, Republic of Korea, 2007. Mem.: Am. Phys. Soc. (Session Chair 2008). Achievements include discovery of new giant magnetoimpedance materials for sensor applications & magnetic refrigeration technology; invention of new technique to improve GMI materials properties; research in leading expert in GMC materials research. Office: Univ South Fla 4202 E Fowler Ave Tampa FL 33620 Office Fax: 813-974-5813. Personal E-mail: huongcmsvn@yahoo.com.au. Business E-Mail: mphan@cas.usf.edu.

PHAN, PHILLIP HIN CHOI, business educator, consultant; b. Singapore, Feb. 23, 1963; arrived in US, 1982; s. Bryan K. and Rosaline (Teo) Phan; m. Soo-Hoon Lee, Feb. 13, 1988. BBA with distinction, U. Hawaii, 1984; PhD, U. Wash., 1992. Cost contr. Westin Hotels & Resorts, Dallas and Singapore, 1984—88; assoc. prof. York U., Toronto, 1992—2000; cons. World Bank, 1998—2001, OECD, 1998—2000; Bruggeman prof. Rensselaer Poly. Inst., Troy, NY, 1998—2007; Bosch public policy fellow Am. Acad. Berlin, 2006—07; prof. John Hopkins U., Balt., 2008—. Asst. prof. CUNY, 1997; vis. prof. Nat. U. Singapore, 1998—2003, Singapore Mgmt. U., 2003—, Thammasat U., Thailand, 1997; Haniel Found. vis. prof. Humboldt U., Germany, 2004—05; ptnr. Core Competence Cons., Inc., Toronto, 1993—98; dir. Blood Trac Sys. Internat., Edmonton, 1996—98; mem. multi-nat. enterprises and investment com. Can. Coun. Internat. Bus., 1993—2000. Mem. editl. bd. Jour. Bus. Venturing, 1998—, Acad. Mgmt. Jour., 2002—, Jour. Fin. Stability, 2003—, Jour. Tech. Transfer, 2003—; co-editor: Asia Pacific Jour. Mgmt., 1999—2001. Recipient Endowment Excellence award, Boeing Corp., 1992, Schulich Sch. Faculty Rsch. award, 1996; named MBA Educator of the Yr., RPI, 2004; Rsch. grantee, Social Scis. and

Humanities Rsch. Coun. Can., 1997, John Broadbent Rsch. Fund, 2000—, Kauffman Entrepeneur Found., 2002, Edna G. Benson fellow, 1992, Michael G. Foster fellow, 1992, Bosch Pub. Policy fellow, Am. Acad. in Berlin, 2006—07, George W. Tyler scholar, 1992. Mem.: Acad. Internat. Bus. (mem. senatorial com.), Inst. Mgmt. Scis., Acad. Mgmt. Republican. Avocations: reading, bicycling, tennis, scuba diving. Home: 250 S President St # 900 Baltimore MD 21202 Office: John Hopkins Univ Carey Bus Sch Baltimore MD 21202 Office Phone: 518-276-2319. E-mail: pphan@rpi.edu.

PHANEUF, DION, professional hockey player; b. Edmonton, Alta., Can., Apr. 10, 1985; s. Paul and Amber Phaneuf. Defenseman Calgary Flames, 2005—. Recipient Bill Hunter Trophy, 2004, 2005, All-Rookie Team, NHL, 2006; named to NHL All-Star Game, 2008, First All-Star Team, NHL, 2008. Achievements include being a member of Gold Medal Team Canada, World Junior Championships, 2005. Office: Calgary Flames PO Box 1540 Stn M Calgary AB T2P 3B9 Canada

PHANEUF, RONALD ARTHUR, physics professor; b. Windsor, Ontario, Canada, Jan. 26, 1947; s. Arthur Lawrence and Eleanor Blanche Phaneuf; m. Jimmie Lee McNatt, May 31, 1980; children: Shane Royle Benedict, Peter Timothy Benedict. PhD, U. Windsor, Ontario, 1973. Postdoc. fellow JILA U. Colo., Boulder, 1973—75; rsch. staff program mgr. Oak Ridge Nat. Lab., Tenn., 1975—92; dept. chair U. Nev., Reno, 1992—2001, prof., 1992—. Adv. group atomic and molecular data fusion IAEA, Vienna, 1983—93, atomic and molecular data ctr. network, 1983—92; com. atomic, molecular and optical sci. NRC, Washington, 1990—93, commn. phys. sci., math. and applications, 1992—93; lawrence award screening panel Dept. Energy, Washington, 1994—94. Mentor Big Bros. Big Sisters, Reno, 2006—08. Recipient Alexander von Humboldt Rsch. award, David A. Shirley award; Physics Rsch. grants, Dept. Energy, 1998—2008, NASA, 1998—2008, Nat. Inst. Standards and Tech., 2003—05. Fellow: Am. Phys. Soc. (sec. treas. 1993—96); mem.: Am. Assn. Physics Tchrs. Office: Univ Nevada Dept Physics 220 Reno NV 89557 Office Fax: 775-784-1398. Business E-Mail: phaneuf@unr.edu.

PHANG, MAY, music educator; MusB with honors, McGill U., Montreal, Can., 1992, MusM, 1994; D of Musical Arts, Temple U., 2004. Grad. asst. McGill U., 1992—94; instr. secondary piano Temple U., 1994—97; instr. piano Manayunk Cmty. Ctr. for the Arts, 1997, Settlement Music Sch., 1997; pianist, cello auditions Curtis Inst. Music, 1998; pianist Drexel U., 1999—2000; asst. prof. piano Carroll Coll., Wis., 2000—03; faculty piano Wis. Conservatory Music, Wis., 2001—03; asst. prof. piano DePauw U., Ind., 2003—. Guest artist Montreal Internat. Music Camp, Canada, 2002; faculty New Eng. Music Camp, 2000—01, Adult Chamber Music Workshop, Milw., 2002—03. Singer: DePauw Symphony Orch., MIMC Orch., Wis. Wind Orch., Ambler Symphony Orch., Phila. Orch., Singapore Symphony Orch., Temple U. Chamber Orch., Orch. Symphonique de Trois-Rivières, Banff Festival Chamber Players, Montreal Symphony Orch., McGill Symphony Orch., Temple U. Symphony Orch. Juror Piano Arts Wis. Competition, Wis., 2003; juror, clinician Carroll HS Piano Competition and Masterclass, 2003; juror Waukesha Symphony Concerto Competition, 2001, 2003, Polish Fest Chopin PIano Competition, Milw., 2001—02. Recipient 1st pl., Chopin Young Pianists Competition, Buffalo, 1990, Montreal Classical Music Festival, 1990—91, Concours d'orchestre Symphonique de Montréal, 1991, Can. Music Competition, 1991, Prix du Cercle du cent Associés, 1993, Concours d'orchestre Symphonique de Trois-Rivières, 1994, 2d pl., Pontoise Internat. Young Artists Competition, 1995; Clara Lichtenstein fellow, McGill U., 1992, Maureen Forrester-Montreal Musicians Guild scholar, 1991, Russel Conwell fellow, Temple U., 1994—96, Herbert A. Morse scholar, 1993. Mem.: Coll. Music Soc., Ind. Music Tchrs. Assn. (chair collaborative arts), Music Tchrs. Nat. Assn., Phi Kappa Lambda Soc. Office: Depauw Univ 313 S Locust St Greencastle IN 46135 Office Phone: 765-658-4403. Business E-Mail: mphang@depauw.edu.

PHANSALKAR, SHOBHA, health facility administrator, researcher; b. Kirkee, Maharashtra, India, Oct. 26, 1978; d. Sahib Das and Prem Pyari Satsangi; m. Amit Phansalkar, Dec. 20, 2003. PharmB, U. Pune, 2000; MS, U. Utah, Salt Lake City, 2003, PhD, 2007. Rsch. asst. U. Utah, 2002—06, NLM fellow, informatics, 2006—07; informaticist Ptnrs. Healthcare, Wellesley, Mass., 2007. Oil and acrylic on canvas; contbr. scientific papers. Recipient Tehmi Irani award, John D. Morgan award; numerous Travel grants.

PHARES, ALAIN JOSEPH, physicist, researcher; b. Beirut, Apr. 20, 1942; came to U.S., 1975, naturalized, 1982; s. Joseph Michel and Renee Cecile (Doummar) P.; m. Claude Tawa, July 27, 1968; children—Caroline, Denis, Pascal. BS in Engring., St. Joseph U., 1964; Docteur-es-Sciences, U. Paris, 1971; PhD, Harvard U., 1973. Research fellow Nat. Council Sci. Research, Lebanon, 1973-75; assoc. prof. Lebanese U., 1973-75; research fellow Internat. Centre Theoretical Physics, Trieste, Italy, 1974, Harvard U., 1975-76; vis. asst. prof. U. Mont., 1976-77; asst. prof. physics Villanova U., Pa., 1977-79, assoc. prof. Pa., 1979-82, prof. Pa., 1982—, chmn. dept. Pa., 1981-91, dir. secondary sch. sci. Pa., 1981-94. Contbr. articles to profl. jours. Grantee, NSF, 1991—, PSC, 1991—, SDSC, 2002—03; fellow, IAEA, 1974; French Govt. fellow, 1964—66. Mem. Am. Phys. Soc., Internat. Assn. Math. and Computers in Simulation, Sigma Xi Office: Villanova U Dept Physics Villanova PA 19085 Office Phone: 610-519-4889. Business E-Mail: alain.phares@villanova.edu.

PHARES, DEE ANNA, literature and language professor; b. Northridge, Calif., Mar. 15, 1972; d. Johanna Mae Sizemore and Dale Sumner Phares; m. Timothy Andrew Ryan, Jan. 13, 2007. BA in English & Anthropology, U. Nev., Reno, 1997, MA in English Lit., 2000, PhD student, 2001—; MA in Shakespeare Studies, King's Coll., London, 2001. Actress Pk. City Shakespeare Festival, Pk. City, Utah, 1990; assoc. editor, royal Shakespeare co.'s complete works Palgrave/Macmillan, London, 2004—07, textual editor, Othello and Macbeth, 2004—09, Random House, 2004—09, assoc. editor, royal Shakespeare co.'s complete works, 2004—09; dramaturg Oreg. Shakespeare Festival, Ashland, Oreg., 2005—06; vis. asst. prof. Northern Ill. U., DeKalb, 2007—; adj. faculty Aurora U., 2008—. Recipient Disting. Tchg. Asst. award, Core Humanities Program U. Nev., 2003—04; Humanities and Social Scis. Dissertation Yr. fellowship, UNR Grad. Sch., 2005—06. Mem.: MLA, Ill. Philol Assn., Brit. Shakespeare Assn., Shakespeare Assn. Am., Golden Key Nat. Honor Soc. Office: Northern Ill Univ Reavis Hall 215 Dekalb IL 60115 Business E-Mail: dphares@niu.edu.

PHARES, JAMES KENNETH, retired electronics engineer; b. Elkins, W.Va., Feb. 19, 1925; s. Dewey Paul and Cora Belle (Yokum) Phares; m. Lorna Jean Gibson, June 12, 1950; 1 child, Michael. BS in Electronics Engring., Davis and Elkins Coll., 1957. Comm. technician W.Va. State Police, Elkins, 1947—57; electronics engr. Goodyear Aerospace, Akron, Ohio, 1957—87; part-time instr. Goodyear Tech. Coll., Akron, 1967—97; ret., 1997. Author: Hunter-Killer Group WWII Anti-Submarine Warfare, 2006. With USN, 1943—46. Achievements include patents for money changing device; power control system. Avocations: amateur radio, astronomy, writing. Home: 610 Deborah Dr Akron OH 44319

PHARIES, STEPHEN ANDREW, lawyer; b. Oakland, Calif., Apr. 2, 1967; s. Stephen Earl and Fumiko Pharies; m. Kathy Lynne Jones, Jan. 9, 1993; children: Jonathan Ryan, Abigail Lynne. BS, U. Calif., Riverside, 1989; JD, U. Oreg., Eugene, 1992. Cert.: State Bar Calif. Bd. Legal Specialization (in estate planning, probate and trust Law) 2003. Assoc. Thomas, Snell, Jamison, Russell & Asperger, Fresno, Calif., 1992—93, Musick, Peeler & Garrett, LLP, LA, 1993—96; ptnr. Procopio, Cory, Hargreaves & Savitch LLP, San Diego, 1996—2001, Ferrette, Alcorn, Pharies & Dorgan, ALC, San Diego, 2001—08, Procopio Cory Hargreaves & Savitch LLP, San Diego, 2009—. Editor-in-chief Oreg. Law Rev., Eugene, 1991—92; dir. Boys and Girls Club LA, 1994—96; chmn. Cmty. Property Com., Real Property Probate and Trust Sect., ABA, Washington, 1996—98; dir. Palomar Pomerado Health Found., San Diego, 2008, mem., 08; exec. com. mem. State Bar Calif., Trusts and Estates Sect., San Francisco, 2008. Contbr. articles to profl. jours. (Excellence Writing award, 1999). Recipient AV Rating award, Martindale Hubbell, 2001; named one of Super Lawyer, Law and Politics Mag.,San Diego, 2008. Mem.: State Bar Calif., San Diego County Bar Assn., ABA. Avocation: golf. Office: Procopio Cory Hargreaves & Savitch LLP 530 B St Ste 2100 San Diego CA 92101 Office Phone: 619-515-3216. Office Fax: 619-398-0197. Business E-Mail: sap@fapdlaw.com, sap@procopio.com.

PHARIS, RUTH MCCALISTER, retired bank executive; b. San Diego, Feb. 13, 1934; d. William L. and Mary E. (Beuk) McC.; m. E. Edwin Pharis, Mar. 14, 1953; children: Beth, Tracey, Todd. Grad., Del Mar Coll., Corpus Christi, Tex., 1979. Asst. cashier Parkdale State Bank, Corpus Christi, 1970-72, asst. v.p., 1972-76, v.p., 1976-79, Cullen Center Bank & Trust, Houston, 1979-81, sr. v.p., 1982-93; dir. human resources Scooter Store, Inc., New Braunfels, Tex., 2001—03. Instr. Am. Inst. Banking, 1977—79. Mem. adv. coun. Houston C.C. Mem. Human Resource Mgmt. Assn., Bank Adminstrn. Inst. (v.p. Coastal Bend chpt. 1979), Nat. Assn. Bank Women (ednl. chmn. Coastal Bend group), Am. Inst. Banking (rep.), Tex. Bankers Assn. (coun. 1983-84, instr.), Coastal Bend Personnel Soc. (v.p.), Houston Personnel Assn., New Braunfels (Tex.) Rep. Women (pres. 1999-2002), Corpus Christi C. of C. (mem. women's com. 1976-79), Order Eastern Star. Republican. Baptist. Home: 2779 Morning Star New Braunfels TX 78132-4722

PHELAN, MARILYN ELIZABETH, law educator; b. Lubbock, Tex., July 12, 1938; m. Harold L. Phelan, Sept. 1, 1960; children: Pat, Scott, Kimberly. BA, Tex. Tech U., 1959, MBA, 1967, PhD, 1971; JD, U. Tex., 1972. Bar: Tex. 1961; CPA. Assoc. prof. Tex. Tech U., Lubbock, 1971-77, prof. law, 1977—, Paul Whitfield Horn prof. law, 1993—. Author: Law of Cultural Property, 1998, Nonprofit Enterprises--Corporations, Trusts, and Associations, 2008, Representing Tax Exempt Organizations, 2008, Museum Law., 2007, 3d edit., Nonprofit Organizations, 2003;: 2d edit., 2007. Mem. ABA, AICPA, Nat. Conf. Commrs. Uniform State Laws, Am. Law Inst., State Bar Tex., Internat. Coun. Mus. (legal affairs com. mem.). Office: Tex Tech Univ Sch Law 18th & Hartford Sts Lubbock TX 79409 Home Phone: 817-579-5179; Office Phone: 806-742-3787 ext 251, 806-742-3990 362. Business E-Mail: marilyn.phelan@ttu.edu.

PHELAN, ROBIN ERIC, lawyer; b. Steubenville, Ohio, Dec. 28, 1945; s. Edward John and Dorothy (Borkowski) P.; m. JoAnn Keach, June 27, 1970 (dec. May 18, 1994); children: Travis McCoy, Tiffany Marie, Trevor Monroe; m. Melinda Jo Ricketts, May 27, 1995; 1 child, Taezja Monet. BSBA, Ohio State U., 1967, JD, 1970. Bar: Tex. 1971, U.S. Ct. Appeals (5th cir.) 1981, U.S. Ct. Appeals (11th cir.) 1981, U.S. Ct. Appeals (6th cir.) 1986, U.S. Ct. Appeals (10th cir.) 1988, U.S. Supreme Ct. Ptnr. Haynes and Boone, Dallas, 1970—. Co-author: Bankruptcy Practice and Strategy, 1987, Cowans Bankruptcy Law and Practice, 1987, Annual Survey of Bankruptcy Law, 1988, Bankruptcy Litigation Manual; contbr. articles to profl. jours. Mem. ABA (chmn. insolvency and secured transactions com. internat. law sect.), Internat. Bar Assn., Internat. Insolvency Inst. (bd. dirs.), Am. Bankruptcy Inst. (dir., past pres.), Am. Coll. Bankruptcy, State Bar Tex. (chmn. bankruptcy law com. sect. bus. law 1989-91), Dallas Bar Assn. Roman Catholic. Avocation: athletics. Home: 4214 Woodfin Dr Dallas TX 75220-6416 Office Phone: 214-651-5612. Business E-Mail: robin.phelan@haynesboone.com.

PHELAN, STEPHANIE ELLEN, artist, graphics designer; b. Montclair/Glen Ridge, NJ, Apr. 25, 1946; d. James Richard and Ellen Irma (McGeehan) P.; m. Richard Kubicz, Jan. 26, 1979 (div. 1983). Student, George Washington U., 1964-65. Asst. buyer, adminstrv. asst. Doyle Dane Bernbach, NYC, 1965-66; asst. art dir. Eye Mag., NYC, 1967-69; assoc. art dir. Nat. Lampoon, NYC, 1969-72; art dir. Grapevine Newspaper, Martha's Vineyard, Mass., 1972-75, Martha's Vineyard C. of C., 1976-78; assoc. art dir. Connoisseur Mag., NYC, 1983-88; dir. print prodn. Calvin Klein Cosmetics, NYC, 1989-90; sr. designer Money Mag., NYC, 1990—2002; creative dir. Mamm Mag., NYC, 2002—05; art dir. Consumer Reports Money Advisor, NYC, 2003—04; freelance designer and dog portraitist NYC, 1991—. Drawing, "Black Dog" logo for the Black Dog Tavern Co., 1976, featured in, NY Mag., County Living Mag., Am. Airlines Mag., Best for Pets Digest. Aux. police officer N.Y.C. Police Dept., 1981—. Recipient commendations N.Y.C. Police Dept., 1983, 86, award of merit, 1989, Dog Art award Westminster Kennel Club, 1993. Roman Catholic. Office Phone: 212-620-0652. E-mail: tucker@phelandogart.com.

PHELIZON, JEAN FRANCOIS, finance company executive; b. Paris, Apr. 28, 1946; s. Christian and Anne (Camuset) P.; m. Isabelle Delatour, July 3, 1971; children: Camille, Constance, Charlotte. MBA and MS, Paris U., 1970, PhD in Econ. Sci., 1975. Contr. Flat Glass div. St. Gobain, Paris, 1979; CFO St. Gobain Spain, Madrid, 1983-85; CFO paper wood div. St. Gobain, Paris, 1985-89; CEO, Lembacel, Lyon, France, 1988-89; CFO, Compagnie St. Gobain, Paris, 1989-2000, sr. v.p., 1998—; pres., CEO, Saint-Gobain Corp., 2000—07; CEO, Certain Teed, 2000—04. Editor: Economica, 1970, 4th edit. 1998, Masson, 1981, 2d edit. 1984, Citic (China), 2003, 04, Praeger, 2006. Dir. French-Am. C. of C., Nat. Assn. Mfrs. Decorated chevalier Order of Merit, Legion of Honor. Office: SG Corp PO Box 860 750 E Swedesford Rd Valley Forge PA 19482 Home: 347 Spring Mill Rd Villanova PA 19085 Home Phone: 610-527-8801; Office Phone: 610-341-7699. Personal E-mail: jfphelizon@yahoo.com. E-mail: jfp@sgcna.com.

PHELPS, ARTHUR VAN RENSSELAER, physicist, consultant; b. Dover, NH, July 20, 1923; s. George Osborne and Helen (Ketchum) P.; m. Gertrude Kanzius, July 21, 1956 (dec. Jan. 3, 2003); children: Wayne Edward, Joan Susan. ScD in Physics, MIT, 1951. Cons. physicist rsch. labs. Westinghouse Elec. Corp., Pitts., 1951-70; sr. rsch. scientist Nat. Bur. Standards, Boulder, Colo., 1970-88; fellow Joint Inst. Lab. Astrophysics U. Colo., Boulder, 1970-88, adjoint fellow, 1988—, chmn., 1979-81. Chmn. Gordon Rsch. Conf., Plasma Chemistry, 1990. Recipient Silver Medal award Dept. Commerce, 1978. Fellow Am. Phys. Soc. (Will Allis prize 1990). Achievements include patent for Schulz-Phelps ionization gauge; research on electron and atomic collision processes involving low energy electrons, molecules, ions, metastable atoms and resonance radiation; on laser processes and modeling; on gaseous electronics. Office: U Colo JILA Campus Box 440 Boulder CO 80309-0440 Home: 1331 E Hecla Dr Unit 247 Louisville CO 80027-2341

PHELPS, ASHTON, JR., newspaper publisher; b. New Orleans, Nov. 4, 1945; s. Ashton Sr. and Jane Cary (George) Phelps; m. Suzanne Dupuy Phelps; children: Cary Clifton, Mary Louise, Sanders. BA, Yale U., 1967; JD, Tulane U., 1970. Trainee Times-Picayune Pub. Corp., New Orleans, 1970—71, asst. to pub., 1971—79, pres., pub., 1979—97, pub., 1997—. Chmn. Audit Com. of Associated Press, 1986—90, mem. nominating com., 1996—2002; bd. dirs. Bur. Govtl. Rsch., New Orleans, 1973—89, Xavier U. La., New Orleans, 1974—82, Internat. House, New Orleans, 1981—83, Coun. for Better La., 1982—85, Ochsner Found. Hosp., New Orleans, 1982—, Pub. Affairs Rsch. Coun., New Orleans, 1982—85, 2000—, La. Children's Mus., New Orleans, 1983—90, Yale Alumni Assn. La., 1985, Newspaper Advt. Bur. Future of Advt. Com., 1986—89, Met. Area Com., New Orleans, UNCF, 2004—. Mem.: La. Press Assn. (bd. dirs. 1984—93, v.p. 1989—90, pres. 1991—92), So. Newspaper Pubs. Assn. (bd. dirs. 1982—85, found. bd. dirs. 1982—83, pres. 1990—91). Avocation: tennis. Office: The Times-Picayune 3800 Howard Ave New Orleans LA 70125-1429

PHELPS, BONNIE NOREEN, retired secondary school educator; d. Norton Robert and Joyce Madelaine Phelps. B, U. Colo., 1966; M, Rivier Coll., 1974. Cert. tchr. NH, 1974. Sr. English tchr. Nashua HS North, NH, 1966—2007; ret., 2007. Running start faculty mem. NH Cmty. Tech. Coll., Claremont, 2000—; mem. faculty leadership com. High North Site Coun., 2005. Author: (poetry) The 14th (Illiand Lit. Presdl. Lit. award and hon. award, 1994), Hurricane Bonnie in POETRY'S ELITE Poetry.com, (poem) Sibilance (semifinalist N.Am. Open Poetry contest, 1993); poetry project: The Ripple Effect (performed by Nashua Symphony), 2006—07. Judge Yankee Pen Poetry Contest, Boston Writing Project in Nantucket, 2004; vol. Penguin Plunge Spl. Olympics, NH, 2005. Recipient Creative Comms. Poetic Achievement award, Nashua H.S. Nortn, 2005. Mem.: Am. Fedn. Tchrs., Nat. Coun. Tchrs. English (assoc.), Poetry Soc. N.H. (corr.; sec. of round robins 1987—88). Independent. Avocations: reading, writing, research on alternative health. Personal E-mail: bnphelps@msn.com.

PHELPS, CARMEN LANETTE, literature educator; b. St. Louis, Mar. 3, 1971; d. Johnnie Lamont Phelps and Dorothy Jean Neal. BS, U. Kans., Lawrence, 1994; MA, Chgo. State U., 1997; PhD, George Wash. U., 2004. Asst. prof. ethnic Am. lit. Longwood U., Farmville, Va., 2004—08, U. Toledo, 2008—. Home: 1206 Hidden Ridge Rd Toledo OH 43615 Office: Univ Toledo 2801 Bancroft St Toledo OH 43606 Business E-Mail: carmen.phelps@utoledo.edu.

PHELPS, CHARLES ELLIOTT, economics professor, director; b. NYC, Apr. 20, 1943; s. McKinnie L. and Carolyn (McCleery) P.; m. Dale L. King, Sept. 2, 1967; children: Darin H., Teresa A. BA in Math., Pomona Coll., 1965; MBA in Hosp. Adminstrn., U. Chgo., 1968, PhD in Bus Economics, 1973. Rsch assoc., Ctr. for Health Adminstrn. Studies U. Chgo., 1969—71; rsch. economist, economics dept. RAND Corp., Santa Monica, Calif., 1971—79, dir., regulatory policies and institutions program, sr. staff economist, faculty mem., RAND Grad. Inst., 1979—84; prof. polit. sci. & econs. U. Rochester, NY, 1984—, dir., pub. policy analysis program NY, 1984—89, faculty mem., Rochester Ctr. for Economics Rsch. NY, 1984—, prof., cmty. and preventative medicine, Sch. Medicine and Dentistry NY, 1989—, chair, cmty. and preventative medicine, Sch. Medicine and Dentistry NY, 1989—94, provost NY, 1994—. Cons. JUREcon, Inc., LA, 1977-86; pvt. cons., Rochester, NY, 1986-; dir., pub. policy analysis program, U. Rochester, 1984-89, chair, health and soc. com., 1984-94, mem. academic computing exec. com., 1988-94, mem. exec. com. and informal exec. com., Sch. Medicine and Dentistry, 1989-94, chair, dept. cmty. and preventive medicine, 1989-94, chair, faculty adv. com. for presdl. search, 1993; mem. Nat. Adv. bd. Leonard Davis Inst. Health Economics, U. Pa., 1988-93; commr. Rochester Health Commn., 1995-2000; bd. trustee, Ctr. for Governmental Rsch., 1998-99; mem. Nat. Adv. Commn. for Digital Strategies, Libr. Congress, 2001-02; mem. report review com., NRC, 2002-. Co-editor Transforming Ideas: Selected Profiles in University of Rochester Research and Scholarship, 2000; Author Health Economics, 1st edit 1992, 2nd edit. 1997, 3rd edit., 2002; mem. editl. bd. Journal Health Economics, Journal Risk and Uncertainty, 1990-2000; founding assoc. editor, Economic Bulletin, 2000; contbr. articles to profl. jours. Mem. Greater Rochester Fights Back Against Drugs, 1990—91. Assoc. Nat. Bur. for Econ. Rsch.; mem. Inst. Medicine(mem. com. on med. technologies, 1985-86, com. for priority setting in med. tech., 1989-90, com. on Gulf War illnesses, 1999-2000), Am. Econ. Assn., Nat. Acad. Social Ins., Soc. for Med. Decision Making (trustee 1990-92), Assn. for Pub. Policy Analysis and Mgmt.(sec. 1980-91), Agy. for Health Care Policy and Rsch. (health care tech. study sect 1990-94). Avocations: photography, archery, astronomy, canoeing, woodworking. Home Phone: 585-381-2429; Office Phone: 585-275-5931. Office Fax: 585-461-1046. Business E-Mail: charles.phelps@rochester.edu.

PHELPS, CHARLOTTE DEMONTE, retired economics professor; b. East Orange, NJ, Jan. 26, 1933; d. Robert William and Marian Ethel (Page) DeMonte; m. Edmund Strother Phelps, 1957 (div. 1969). BA magna cum laude, Radcliffe Coll., 1955; MA, Yale U., 1956, PhD, 1961. Instr. Conn. Coll., New London, 1961; rsch. staff economist Cowles Found. and Econ. Growth Ctr. Yale U., 1963—65; postdoctoral rsch. fellow com. on econ. stblzn. Social Sci. Rsch. Coun., 1965—68; asst. prof. dept. econs. Temple U., Phila., 1967—68, assoc. prof., 1969—97, prof., 1998—2000; ret., 2000. Cons. Hay/McBer, 1999—2000. Author: Unconscious Motivation and Economic Choice, 1981; mem. editl. bd.: Jour. Econ. Behavior and Orgn., 1998—2008, Jour. Socio-Econs., 2001—; contbr. articles to profl. publs. Active Phila. Cmty. Coordinated Child Care Coun., 1970-72; schs. and scholarships com. Harvard-Radcliffe Clubs Phila., 1977-82. Named to Fulbright Sr. Specialist Roster, 2002—; grantee Murray Rsch. Ctr., Radcliffe Coll., 1998—2000, Smith Richardson Found., 1998—2000, Fulbright Sr. Specialists grant in Econs., Max Planck Inst. Rsch. in Econ. Sys., 2003; vis. fellow, Yale U., 1998—99, pre-doctoral grantee, Comm. on Money and Credit, 1959—60. Mem. Am. Econ. Assn., Soc. Advancement Behavioral Econs. (bd. dirs.), Internat. Soc. New Instl. Econs., Internat. Assn. for Rsch. in Econ. Psychology, Assn. Yale Alumni (del. 1994-97), Yale Club Phila., Cosmopolitan Club Phila., Harvard Club Phila., Phi Beta Kappa. Home: 604 S Washington Sq Apt 2505 Philadelphia PA 19106-4129 Office: Temple U Dept Econs 879 Ritter Annex Philadelphia PA 19122 Home Phone: 215-922-2160; Office Phone: 215-204-1677. Business E-Mail: cdphelps@temple.edu.

PHELPS, CONNIE LEA, special education gifted educator; b. Sioux City, Iowa, Aug. 4, 1953; d. Robert William and Carol Lea (Yaryan) Rice; m. Ronald Wayne Phelps, May 31, 1975. Diploma fgn. missions with honors Moody Bible Inst., 1977; BS in Bibl. Studies, Dallas Bible Coll., 1981; MEd in Elem. Edn., East Tex. State U., 1982; EdD in Elem. Edn. U. Ark., 1987; MS in Spl. and Gifted Edn., Emporia State U., 2002. Tchr. Pleasant Wood Christian Sch., Dallas, 1979-82, Beverly Hills Christian Sch., Dallas, 1982-83; tchr., elem. coordinator Three Lakes Christian Sch., Troy, Mont., 1983-85; grad. asst. U. Ark., 1985-87; sub. tchr. Wichita Pub. Schs., 1999; gifted facilitator Truesdell Mid. Sch., 1999-2004, West HS, 2001-04, Kelly Elem. and Cleve. Traditional Magnet, 2001-03; asst. prof. gifted spl. edn. Emporia State U., 2004-; Missionary appointee Alaska Bible Coll., Glennallen; with SEND Internat., 1987-90; advisor Educators Mus. Adv. Coun., Dallas, 1981-83; adj. faculty Baker U., Wichita, 1999-2004, Wichita State U., 2002-04; dir. gifted program Emporia State U., 2004-. Presenter in field. Contbr. articles to profl. jours. Active Dallas Mus. Fine Arts, 1980-82. Mem. AAUW, World Coun. Gifted and Talented Children, Nat. Assn. for Gifted Children (counseling and guidance network sec., curriculum studies network, computers and tech. profl. devel. network, rsch. stds. com.), Assn. Edn. Gifted Underachieving Students, Supporting Emotional Needs of the Gifted, Kans. Assn. for the Gifted, Talented and Creative (historian, bd. mem.), Coun. Exceptional Children, Assn. Gifted Divsn., Am. Ednl. Rsch. Assn. and Postsecondary Divsn., Rsch. on Fiftedness Talent Spl. Internet Group, Phi Delta Kappa (chpt. mem. liaison), Region Club. Home: 1737 Rural St Emporia KS 66801-5549 Home Phone: 620-340-0142; Office Phone: 620-341-5817.

PHELPS, EDMUND STROTHER, economics professor; b. Evanston, Ill., July 26, 1933; s. Edmund Strother and Florence Esther (Stone) P.; m. Viviana Regina Montdor, Oct. 1, 1974. BA, Amherst Coll., 1955, DLitt (hon.), 1985; MA, Yale U., 1956, PhD, 1959. Economist Rand Corp., Santa Monica, Calif., 1959-60; asst. prof. Yale U., Cowles Found., 1960-62, assoc. prof., 1963-66; vis. assoc. prof. M.I.T., 1962-63; prof. econs. U. Pa., Phila., 1966-71, Columbia U., 1971-78, 79-82, McVickar prof. polit. economy, 1982—; scholar Russell Sage Found., 1993-94; prof. NYU, 1978-79. Fellow Ctr. for Advanced Study in Behavioral Scis., 1969-70; sr. advisor Brookings Inst., 1976—; econ. advisor European Bank for Reconstrn. and Devel., 1991-94; mem. econ. policy panel Observatoire Francais des Conjonctures Economiques, 1991—. Author: numerous books including Golden Rules of Economic Growth, 1966, Microeconomic Foundations of Employment and Inflation Theory, 1970, Economic Justice, 1973, Studies in Macroeconomic Theory, Vol. I, 1979, Vol. II, 1980, Political Economy, 1985, The Slump in Europe, 1988, Structural Slumps, 1994, Rewarding Work, 1997, Designing Social Inclusion:Tools to Raise Low-End Pay and Employment in Private Enterprise, 2003. Recipient Kenan Enterprise award, William R. Kenan Charitable Trust, 1996, Nobel prize in Economics, Nobel Found., 2006; fellow Social Sci. Rsch. Coun., 1966; Guggenheim fellow, 1978. Fellow: AAAS, Econometric Soc., Am. Econ. Assn. (disting. exec. com. 1976—78, v.p. 1983); mem.: Nat. Acad. Scis., Phi Beta Kappa. Home: 45 E 89th St New York NY 10128-1251 Office: Columbia Univ Dept Economics Rm 1004 New York NY 10027*

PHELPS, MARK, men's college basketball coach; Grad., Old Dominion U., Norfolk, Va., 1996. Head coach Rock Ch. Acad., Va. Beach, Va., 1991—94, Atlantic Shores Christian HS, Chesapeake, Va., 1994—96; dir. basketball ops. NC State U. Wolfpack, 1996—2000, asst. coach, 2000—05, recruiting coord., dir. scouting, asst. coach, 2005—06; asst. coach Ariz. State U. Sun Devils, 2006—08; head coach Drake U. Bulldogs, 2008—. Office: Drake U c/o Dept Athletics 2507 University Ave Des Moines IA 50311 Office Phone: 515-271-3894.

PHELPS, MARK D., music educator; b. Audubon, Iowa, Apr. 17, 1955; s. Arnold and Ruth Phelps. MusB, Northwestern U., Evanston, Ill., 1978; MusM, Ind. U., Bloomington, 1982. Pvt. vocal practice, Bloomington, Ind., 1980—; asst. prof. opera studies Ind. U., Bloomington, 1980—, song lit. tchr., 2000—. Pianist: vocal recitals and master classes; musician: (world premieres piano) Art Inst. Chgo., 1976, Orchestra Hall; singer: Chgo. Symphony Chorus, 1975—78. Pres. Windermere Woods Homeowners Assn., Bloomington, 2008—. Recipient 1st prize, Piano Competition, Iowa Fedn. Pianists, 1975. Liberal. Unitarian Universalist. Avocations: gardening, travel, clocks. Business E-Mail: phelpsm@indiana.edu.

PHELPS, MARSHALL C., JR., computer software company executive; m. Eileen Phelps; 2 children. BA, Muskingum Coll.; MS, Stanford Grad. Sch. Bus.; Doctorate, Cornell Law Sch. With IBM Corp., 1972—2000, v.p. intellectual property & licensing, dir. govt. rels.; chmn., CEO Spencer Trask Intellectual Capital Co. LLC; dep. gen. counsel, Legal & Corp. Affairs group Microsoft Corp., 2003—06, corp. v.p. IP policy & strategy, 2006—. Exec.-in-residence Fuqua Sch. Bus., Duke U., bd. visitors; bd. dirs. Internat. Intellectual Property Inst. Recipient Career Achievement award, IBM Corp., 1999; named to Intellectual Property Hall of Fame, 2006. Office: Microsoft Corp 1 Microsoft Way Redmond WA 98052-6399 also: Fuqua Sch Bus Duke U 1 Towerview Dr Durham NC 27708*

PHELPS, MICHAEL, Olympic swimmer; b. Balt., June 30, 1985; s. Fred and Debbie Phelps. Student, U. Mich. Mem. US Men's Olympic Swim Team, Sydney, 2000, Athens, 2004, Beijing, 2008, Team Speedo, 2001—. Co-author (with Brian Cazeneuve): Michael Phelps: Beneath the Surface, 2008. Hon. bd. mem. Pathfinders for Autism; spokesperson Boys & Girls Clubs of America; hon. bd. mem. Boys & Girls Club, Harford County, Md. Recipient James Sullivan award, AAU, 2003, Gold medal, 200m butterfly, World Championships, 2001, Gold medal, 200m butterfly, 200m, 400m individual medley, 400m medley relay; Silver medal, 100m butterfly, 800m freestyle relay, 2003, Gold medal, 200m freestyle, 200m individual medley, 400m medley relay, 400m, 800m freestyle relay; Silver medal, 100m butterfly, 2005, Gold medal, 100m, 200m freestyle, 100m, 200m butterfly, 200m, 400m individual medley, 400m, 800m freestyle relay, 2007, Gold medal, 100m, 200m butterfly, 400m, 800m freestyle relay, 400m medley relay; Silver medal, 200m freestyle, 2009, Gold medal, 200m, 400m individual medley, 400m medley relay; Silver medal, 200m butterfly, 800m freestyle relay, Pan Pacific Championships, 2002, Gold medal, 400m, 800m freestyle relay, 2006, Gold medal, 100m, 200m butterfly, 200m, 400m individual medley, 400m medley relay, 800m freestyle relay, Athens Olympic Games, 2004, Bronze medal, 200m freestyle, 400m freestyle relay, 2004, Gold medal, 200m freestyle, 200m butterfly, 200m, 400m individual medley, 400m, 800m freestyle relay, 400m medley relay, Beijing Olympic Games, 2008; named Swimmer of Yr., USA Swimming, 2001, 2003—04, Athlete of Yr., 2007, Am. Internat. Athlete of Yr., 2004, Sportsman of Yr., US Olympic Com., 2004, Sports Illus., 2008; named one of The Most Influential People in the World of Sports, Bus. Week, 2008, The Ten Most Fascinating People of 2008, Barbara Walters, 10 People Who Mattered, Newsweek, 2008. Achievements include holding individual world records in: 200m individual medley, 400m individual medley, 200m butterfly, 2008, 100m butterfly, 2009; being a member of world record setting: 400m freestyle relay, 2008, 800m freestyle relay, 2008, 400 medley relay, 2009; breaking the world record for Gold medals in a single Olympic games (8), Beijing, 2008; breaking the all-time record for most career Olympic Gold medals (14), 2008. Office: USA Swimming 1 Olympic Plaza Colorado Springs CO 80909 Mailing: PO Box 1734 Olney MD 20830-1734*

PHELPS, MICHAEL EDWARD, biophysics professor; b. Cleve., Aug. 24, 1939; s. Earl E. and Regina Bridget (Hines) P.; m. Patricia Emory, May 15, 1969; children: Patrick, Kaitlin. BA in Chemistry and Math., Western Wash. State U., 1965; PhD in Chemistry, Washington U., St. Louis, 1970. Asst. prof. Washington U. Sch. Medicine and Engring., 1970-73, assoc. prof., 1973-75; assoc. prof. dept. radiology U. Pa., Phila., 1975-76; prof. radiological sciences UCLA, 1976—92, prof. biomathematics, 1980—84, chief divsn. biophysics, 1981—84, Jennifer Jones Simon prof., 1983—86, Norton Simon prof., 1996—, chief div. nuclear medicine, 1984—92, dir. Crump Inst. for Biol. Imaging, 1989—, chmn., dept. molecular and med. pharmacology, 1992—, chief, divsn. nuclear medicine, dept. molecular and med. pharmacology, 1992—2000; assoc. dir. UCLA/DOE Lab. Structural Biology and Molecular Medicine, 1984—2002; dir. UCLA/DOE Inst. Molecular Medicine, 2002—. Mem. study sect. NIH, Bethesda, Md., 1974-78. Author: Reconstruction Tomography in Diagnostic Radiology and Nuclear Medicine, 1977, Physics in Nuclear Medicine, 1980, 1987, 2002, Principles of Tracer Kinetics, 1983, PET: Molecular Imaging and its Biological Applications, 2004; contbr. articles to profl. jours. Recipient Von Hevesy Found. award, 1975,George Von Hevesy prize Von Hevesy Found., Zurich, 1978, 82, Oldendorf award, Soc. for Computerized Tomography and Neurologicval Imaging, 1981, S. Weir Mitchell award, Am. Acad. of Neuology, 1981, Ernest O. Lawrence award US Dept. Energy, 1984, Spec. award for Individual Distinction, Am. Nuclear Soc., 1984, Landauer Mem. award, Am. Assn. for Physicists in Medicine, 1988, Robert J. and Claire Pasarow Found. award, 1992, Disting. Scientists award, Inst. for Clin. PET, 1995, Enrico Fermi Presdl. award, 1999, Charles F. Kettering prize, GM Cancer Rsch. Found., 2001; holder Norton Simon endowed chair, 1983-; named Disting. Alumnus Western Wash. State U., 1980 Fellow Am. Heart Assn.; mem. ACP (Richard and Hinda Rosenthal award 1987), Inst. Medicine NAS (elected), Nat. Acad. Scis. (elected 1999), Soc. Nuclear Medicine (Paul Aebersold award 1983, Ted Block Mem. award, 1989), Internat. Soc. Cerebral Blood Flow and Metabolism (Cert. Excellence award 1979), NY Acad. Scis. (Sarah L. Poiley award 1984), Soc. Neuroscis. Roman Catholic. Business E-Mail: mphelps@mednet.ucla.edu.

PHELPS, NORRIS D., biology professor; s. Lewis A. and Muriel Phelps; m. Beth Cluff, Oct. 20, 1972; children: Christina Hale, Lori Roberts, Rachel Kempton, Benjamin, Scott, Stephen. BS in Zoology, Ariz. State U., Tempe, 1975, MS in Natural Scis., 1977; PhD, Tex. Tech U., Lubbock, 1989. Soybean breeder Ring Around Rsch. OXY, Hale Center, Tex., 1981—92; sci. tchr. Mesa Pub. Schs. Taylor J.H., Ariz., 1992—2007; prof. Mesa CC Life Sci., Ariz., 2004—. Scout master, cub master, ADC Boy Scouts America, Mesa, Ariz., 1993—2004; bpric coun., exec sec, high councilor Ch. Jesus Christ LDS, Mesa, 1995—2009. Spec 5 Phoenix Hosp. USAR, 1971—76. Mem.: CSSA. Mem. Lds Ch. Home: 57 N Fraser Dr W Mesa AZ 85023 Office: Mesa CC Life Sci RM 1833 W Southern Ave Mesa AZ 85202 Personal E-mail: ndpsoya@juno.com.

PHELPS, STEVEN, editor; BA, U. Tex. Dallas, Richardson, 1999. Cert. AAGD Art Inst. Dallas, 2003. Photography editor Tex. Lawyer, Dallas, 2000—06. Clk. & contbr. Dallas Morning News. Office: Cowboys & Indians Mag 6688 N Ctrl Expy Ste 650 Dallas TX 75206 Business E-Mail: sphelps@cowboysindians.com.

PHEMISTER, ROBERT DAVID, veterinary medical educator; b. Framingham, Mass., July 15, 1936; s. Robert Irving and Georgia Nora Phemister; m. Ann Christine Lyon, June 14, 1960; children: Katherine, David, Susan. D.V.M., Cornell U., 1960; PhD, Colo. State U., Ft. Collins, 1967. Diplomate: Am. Coll. Vet. Pathologists. Research assoc. U. Calif., Davis, 1960-61, vis. rsch. pathologist, 1974-75; staff scientist Armed Forces Inst. Pathology, Washington, 1962-64; sect. leader to dir. collaborative radiol. health lab. Colo. State U., 1964-77; mem. faculty Coll. Vet. Medicine and Biomed. Scis., 1968-85, prof. vet. pathology, 1973-85, assoc. dean, 1976-77, assoc. dir. expt. sta., 1977-85, dean, 1977-85, interim acad. v.p. Univ., 1982, interim pres. Univ., 1983-84, spl. counselor to pres., 1984-85; vis. prof. Colo. State U., 1995-96; prof. vet. pathology Cornell U., 1985-99, dean and prof. emeritus, 1999—, dean Coll. Vet. Medicine, 1985-95. Cons. Miss. State U., 1977-81; commr. Colo. Advanced Tech. Inst., 1983-84; mem. governing bd. N.Y. Sea Grant Inst., 1985-95, vice chmn., 1990-92; mem. vet. medicine adv. com. FDA, 1984-88; mem. joint coun. on food and agrl. scis. USDA, 1988-92, mem. exec. com., 1989-92; chmn. Zweig Meml. Fund for Equine Rsch., 1985-95; mem. adv. panel for vet. medicine Pew Health Professions Commn., 1991-93. Author papers in field. Served to comdr. USPHS, 1960-68. Named Disting. Practitioner Nat. Acad. Practice, 1985, Honor Alumnus, Colo. State U., 1989; recipient Charles A. Lory award and Disting. Univ. Leadership award Colo. State U., 1984, Regional Health Adminstr.'s award, 1985. Mem. AVMA (coun. on edn. 1985-91, adv. bd. vet. specialities 1985-89), Assn. Am. Vet. Med. Colls. (pres. 1982-83), Colo. Vet. Med. Assn. (Disting. Svc. award 1985), N.Y. State Vet. Med. Soc. (Centennial award 1990), Sigma Xi, Phi Zeta, Phi Kappa Phi, Gamma Sigma Delta (Merit award for Adminstrn. 1995). Home: 3136 Rock Park Dr Fort Collins CO 80528

PHEMISTER, THOMAS ALEXANDER, lawyer; b. Framingham, Mass., June 2, 1940; s. Robert Irving and Georgia Nora (Savignac) P.; m. Lois Ann Devol, Dec. 28, 1963; children: Michael Anderson, Elizabeth Lynn, Mary Nicole, Virginia Noel. BA, Carleton Coll., 1962; JD, U. Chgo., 1965. Bar: Ill., Colo. 1965. Pvt. practice law, Chgo., 1965—69; gen. atty. Western R.R. Assn., Chgo., 1969—71; in law practice with Richard J. Hardy, Washington, 1972—73; gen. atty. Assn. Am. R.R.s, Washington, 1973—79; dir. Bur. Explosives Assn. Am. Railroads, 1979—85; sole practice Washington, 1985—87; with Office Chief Counsel Fed. R.R. Adminstrn., Washington, 1987—2002; sr. hazardous materials specialist Office of Safety, 2002—, liaison to Assn. Am. Rds. com. on tank cars, 2003—, mgr. tank car safety program fed. R.R. adminstrn., 2006—. Mem. dept. of transp. intermodal hazardous materials attys. group, 1989-2002; mem. com. on transp. of hazardous materials Transp. Rsch. Bd., 1980-86; mem. nat. motor carrier adv. com. Fed. Hwy. Adminstrn., 1982-86; mem. Can. Nat. Rail Task Force for Movements of Dangerous Commodities, 1985; mem. hazardous materials control course oversight com. Tex. A&M U., 1981-87; mem. bd. correction mil. records USCG, 1992-2002. Pub.: Emergency Handling of Hazardous Materials in Surface Transportation, 1981, Hazardous Materials Regulations Excerpted for Railroad Employees, 1981, Emergency Action Guides, 1983; author: A Report on Tank Cars: Federal Oversight of Design Construction and Repair, 1990, Forward through the 90s: A Report on Selected Issues in the Transportation by Rail of Hazardous Materials, 1994, Safe Placement of Train Cars: A Report, 2005, Delegations of Authority: Concepts of Stewardship, 2006. Mem. Fairfax County Drug Task Force chpt. Parents Alliance to Neutralize Drug and Alcohol Abuse (PANDAA), 1987—89, Kairos Prison Ministries, 1997—; mem. teams 1, 2, 3, 4, 5, 8, 10 lead percussionist, teams 2, 3, 4, 5, 8, 10 Va. Augusta Correctional Ctr., 1997—; adult advisor Fairfax County 4-H Horse Forum, 1988—; adult overall advisor Fairfax County 4H Fair Horse Show, 1988—2002, show steward, 2002—; treas. Ill. Lawyers for McCarthy, 1968; trustee First Congregational Ch., Western Springs, Ill., 1970—71; mem. program ministries coun. United Christian Parish of Reston, Va., 1980—82, mem. South Lakes vestry Va., 1984—87, mem. parish bd. Va., deacon, ministries com. Va., 1987—93; bd. dirs. Upper Room Emmaus of nat. capital area, 1989—90, lay leader, 1990. Recipient Holden Profrock award, Assn. Am. Railroads, Bureau Explosives, 2009. Mem. Assn. Am. R.R. (liaison to tank car com. 2003—), Hunter Valley Riding Club (bd. dirs., v.p. 1993-94). Home: 10802 Dayflower Ct Reston VA 20191-5110 Office: 1200 New Jersey Ave SE Washington DC 20590-0001 Home Phone: 703-362-0254; Office Phone: 202-493-6050. Business E-Mail: thomas.phemister@dot.gov. *Integrity is an absolute essential - both preserving my own and dealing with other people so that they, too, do not have to compromise on matters of principle.*

PHETTEPLACE, GARY, mechanical engineer; BS in Mech. Engring., Northeastern U., Boston, 1975; PhD, Stanford U., Calif., 1994; MS in Engring. Scis., Dartmouth Coll., Hanover, NH, 1981. Cert. profl. engr., State NH., 1980, State Calif., 2004, State Md., 2004, State Alaska, 2005, State Vt., 2008, State Mass., 2008. Rsch. mech. engr. US Army Cold Regions Rsch. and Engring. Lab., Hanover, 1975—2007; pres. GWA Rsch. LLC, Lyme, NH, 2007—, cons. and expert witness. Contbr. articles to profl. jours. Mem. Lyme Energy Com., Lyme, NH, 2008—08, Grafton County Alt. Energy Com., Haverhill, NH, 2008—08; volunteeer Habitat for Humanity, Lebanon, NH, 2002—04. Mem.: Am. Soc. Heating Refrigerating and Air-Conditioning Engrs. (mem. 1978—2008), Internat. Dist. Energy Assc., ASHRAE Geothermal Energy Tech. Com. (mem., past chair 2006—), ASHRAE Dist. Heating and Cooling Tech. Com. (chmn. 2008—). Achievements include research in steam and hot water heat distributions systems and ground source heat pump systems. Home: 7 Masa Morey Ln Lyme NH 03768 Office: GWA Rsch LLC 7 Masa Morey Ln Lyme NH 03768 E-mail: phet@valley.net.

PHIBBS, CLIFFORD MATTHEW, surgeon, educator; b. Bemidji, Minn., Feb. 20, 1930; s. Clifford Matthew and Dorothy Jean (Wright) P.; m. Patricia Jean Palmer, June 27, 1953; children— Wayne Robert, Marc Stuart, Nancy Louise BS, Wash. State U., Pullman, 1952; MD, U. Wash., Seattle, 1955; MS, U. Minn., 1960. Diplomate Am. Bd. Surgery. Intern Ancker Hosp., St. Paul, 1955—56; resident in surgery U. Minn. Hosps., 1956—60; practice medicine specializing in surgery Oxboro Clinic, Mpls., 1962—, pres., 1985—; cons. to health risk mgmt. corps., 1994—. Mem. Children's Hosp. Ctr., Northwestern-Abbott Hosp., Fairview-Southdale Hosp., Fairview Ridges Hosp.; clin. asst. prof. U. Minn., Mpls., 1975-78, clin. assoc. prof. surgery, 1978—; med. dir. Minn. Protective Life Ins. Co. Contbr. articles to med. jours. Bd. dirs. Bloomington Bd. Edn., Minn., 1974—, treas., 1976, sec., 1977-78, chmn., 1981-83; mem. adv. com. jr. coll. study City of Bloomington, 1964-66, mem. cmty. facilities com., 1966-67, advisor youth study commn., 1966-68; vice chmn. bd. Hillcrest Meth. Ch., 1970-71; mem. Bloomington Adv. and Rsch. Coun., 1969-71; bd. dirs. Bloomington Symphony Orch., 1976—, Wash. State U. Found., trustee, 1990—; dir. bd. mgmt. Minnesota Valley YMCA, 1970-75; bd. govs. Mpls. Met. YMCA, 1970—; bd. dirs. Bloomington Heart-Health Found., 1989—, Martin Luther Manor, 1989; pres. Oxboro Clinics, 1985—; bd. dirs. Bloomington History Clock Tower Assn., 1990—; bd. dirs. Fairview Hosp. Clinic, 1994—, Bloomington Sister city Orgn., 1999-, Bloomington Cmty. Found., 1997-, v.p., Bloomington Health Adv. Bd., 2000-, MMA Minority and Cross-Cult. Affairs Com., 2000-, Com. on Cult. Competence Minnesota Med. Assn., 1986. Capt. MC, US Army, 1960-62; mem. Minn. Med. Assn. Minority and Cultural Affairs Com., 2007. Recipient Minority Affairs Meritorious Svc. award, Minn. Med. Soc., 2007. Mem. ACS, AMA (Physician Recognition awards 1969, 73, 76, 79, 82, 85, 88, 91, 94), Assn. Surg. Edn., Royal Soc. Medicine, Am. Coll. Sports Medicine, Minn. Med. Assn. (del. 1991-94, Minority Affairs Meritorius Svc. award, 2007), Minn. Surg. Soc., Mpls. Surg. Soc., Hennepin County Med. Soc., Pan-Pacific Surg. Assn., Jaycees, Bloomington C. of C. (chmn. bd. 1984, chmn. 1985-86), Bloomington Adv. Bd. health, Bloomington Sister City Bd., Bloomington Cmty. Found. (bd. dirs. 1996-). Achievements include development of program for Bloomington Public Schools to encourage minority students interest in careers in healthcare fields. Home: 9613 Upton Rd Minneapolis MN 55431-2454 Office: 600 W 98th St Minneapolis MN 55420-4773 Personal E-mail: kphiibs@aol.com.

PHIFER-STARKS, KIM D., paralegal, educator; d. Kenneth and Virginia Davis; m. John Starks, Jr., Jan. 27, 2001; 1 child, Brett Phifer. BA, U. Southern Miss., Hattiesburg, 1989, MS, 1992; JD, Miss. Coll. Sch. Law, Jackson, 1996. Pvt. practice atty. Law Office Kim D. Phifer-Starks, Ocean Springs, Miss., 1998—2001; prosecutor City of Gulfport, Miss., 2002—04; paralegal tech. instr. Miss. Gulfport CC, 2004—. President-elect/mem. Gulf Coast Women's Ctr. for Nonviolence, 2005—. Mem.: Miss. Bar. Office: Mississippi Gulf Coast CC 2226 Switzer Rd Gulfport MS 39507 Business E-Mail: kimberly.starks@mgccc.edu.

PHILBECK, JOHN HEYDT, lawyer; s. Bob H. and Sue N. Philbeck. BA, Elon U., 1989; JD, Valparaiso U. Sch. Law, 1992. Bar: NC 1992, US Dist. Ct., NC 1993, US Dist. Court (ea. and mid. dist.) NC 2000, US Dist. Ct. (we. dist.) NC 2000, US Ct. Appeals (4th cir.) 2000, US Tax Ct. 2000, US Ct. Internat. Trade 2000, US Supreme Ct. 2000, All NC State Trial and Appellate Cts. Atty. J. Heydt Philbeck, Atty. at Law, Raleigh, NC, 1992—96, Murphy & Philbeck, PLLC, Raleigh, 1996—2000, Allen & Pinnix, P.A., Raleigh, 2000—06, Bailey & Dixon LLP, Raleigh, 2006. Barrister Braxton Craven Am. Inn Ct., Raleigh-Durham, 2000—. Recipient 40 Under 40 Leadership award, Triangle Bus. Jour., 2005; named NC Super Lawyers, Law and Politics Mag., 2006—09, Top 100 Lawyers, NC Super Lawyers, 2009; named one of Legal Elite, Bus. NC, 2007—09. Fellow: Trial Counsel Am., NC Inst. Polit. Leadership; mem.: Leadership NC, Nat. Employment Lawyer's Assn., NC Acad. Trial Lawyers, Wake County Bar Assn. (bd. dirs.), NC Bar Assn. Office: Bailey & Dixon LLP 434 Fayetteville St 25th Fl Raleigh NC 27602 Office Fax: 919-828-6592.

PHILBIN, CHRISTOPHER R., legislative staff member; b. Worcester, Mass., Nov. 11, 1971; BA, Syracuse U., NY, 1993; JD, New Eng. Sch. Law, Boston, 1999. Bar: Mass. 2000. Dir. econ. devel., Clinton, Mass., 1993—98; legis. dir. for Senator Robert A. Bernstein Mass. State Senate, 1999—2000; assoc. Bernstein, Burwick and Tucker, LLC, Worcester, 2001—02; legis. counsel for Rep. James P. McGovern US House of Reps., Washington, 2002—04, chief of staff, 2004—. Bd. dirs. Dr. Franklin Perkins Sch., Lancaster, Mass., 2000—. Mem.: Mass. Bar Assn., Town of Clinton (mem. Mass. dem. town com. 1998—), Emerald Club Worcester County. Roman Catholic. Avocations: sports, reading, travel. Office: Office of Congressman James P McGovern 131 Cannon House Office Bldg Washington DC 20515 Office Phone: 202-225-6101. Business E-Mail: christopher.philbin@mail.house.gov.*

PHILBIN, PATRICK FRANCIS, lawyer, former federal agency administrator; b. 1967; BA summa cum laude, Yale U., 1989; JD magna cum laude, Harvard U., 1992; Diploma in Legal Studies, Cambridge U., 1995. Bar: Mass. 1995, DC 1997. Law clk. for Hon. Laurence H. Silberman US Ct. Appeals (DC Cir.), 1992—93; law clk. for Justice Clarence Thomas US Supreme Ct., 1993—94; assoc. Kirlmand & Ellis LLP, Washington, 1995—98, ptnr., 1998—2001, 2006—; dep. asst. atty. gen. Office Legal Counsel US Dept. Justice, Washington, 2001—03, assoc. dep. atty. gen., 2003—05. Spkr. in field. Recipient Exceptional Civilian Svc. Award, Office Sec. Def., 2002, Atty. Gen.'s Award for Excellence in Furthering the Interests of US Nat. Security, US Dept. Justice, 2004. Office: Kirkland & Ellis LLP 655 Fifteenth St, NW Washington DC 20005-5793 Office Phone: 202-879-5030. Office Fax: 202-879-5200. E-mail: pphilbin@kirkland.com.*

PHILBIN, REGIS (FRANCIS XAVIER), television personality; b. NYC, Aug. 25, 1931; s. Frank and Florence P.; m. Kay Faylan, 1957 (div. 1968); children: Amy, Danny; m. Joy Senese, Mar. 1, 1970; children: Joanna, Jennifer. Student, U. Notre Dame. Hollywood stagehand, NBC page The Tonight Show; truck driver, newswriter, sportscaster. Co-host The Joey Bishop Show, 1967-69, host Sta. KABC A.M. LA., 1975-83, Sta. WABC TV Morning Show, 1983-88 (with Kathy Lee Gifford in 1985); co-host (syndicated show) Live! With Regis and Kathie Lee, 1988-2000, Live! With Regis and Kelly, 2001—, exec. prodr., 2001—, Miss Am. Pageant, 1991, 92, 95; host, Who Wants to be a Millionaire, 1999-2002; co-author: Cooking with Regis and Kathie Lee, 1993, Entertaining with Regis and Kathie Lee, 1994; host (TV show) America's Got Talent, 2006-; author: I'm Only One Man, 1995, Who Wants to Be Me?, 2003; TV appearances include The Danny Thomas Hour, 1968, Get Smart, 1968, The Big Valley, 1968, Rowan & Martin's Laugh-In, 1968, Love, American Style, 1969, 71, That Girl, 1970, The Silent Force, 1970, The Jimmy Stewart Show, 1972, The Neighbors, 1975, The San Pedro Beach Bums, 1977, CHiPs, 1978, Lucan, 1978, Fantasy Island, 1979, 83, Ryan's Hope, 1987, 1988, Mad About You, 1993, Seinfeld, 1994, The Larry Sanders Show, 1994, The Cosby Mysteries, 1995, Hope & Gloria, 1995, The Fresh Prince of Bel-Air, 1996, Life's Work, 1996, Spin City, 1997, 99, 2000, Diagnosis Murder, 1998, Caroline in the City, 1998, The Simpsons, 1998, Becker, 2001, One Life to Live, 2002, Hope and Faith, 2003, 2005, 2006 The Apprentice, 2004, Extreme Makeover: Home Edition, 2004, Less Than Perfect, 2005; TV Film appearances SST:Death Flight, 1977, Mad Bull, 1977, Mirror, Mirror, 1979, Perry Mason: The Case of the Telltale Talk Show Host, 1993; Film appearances include The Bad News Bears Go To Japan, 1978, The Emperor's New Clothes, 1993, The Man Who Loved Women, 1983, Night and the City, 1992, Dudley Do-Right, 1999, Little Nicky, 2000, People I Know, 2002, Cheaper by the Dozen, 2003, The Breakup Artist, 2004, Miss Congeniality 2: Armed and Fabulous, 2005; (voice roles) Happily Ever After: Fairy Tales for Every Child, 1995, Mother Goose: A Rappin' and Rhymin' Special, 1997, Hercules, 1998, Family Guy, 2002, Pinocchio, 2002, Lilo & Stitch: The Series, 2004; albums It's Time For Regis!, 1968, When You're Smiling, 2004; host Walt Disney World Very Merry Christmas Parade, 1991, 1992, Walt Disney World Christmas Day Parade, 2002-05, Walt Disney World Happy Easter Parade, 1992, New Year's Rockin' Eve 2005, Fox New Year's Eve Live 2006. Recipient Four Daytime Emmy awards, Broadcasting & Cable Lifetime Achievement award, Crystal Apple award for contributions to the NY TV industry, Mayor Rudolph Giuliani, Star on Hollywood Walk of Fame, 2003; named Personality of Yr., TV Guide, 2001; named one of The 100 Most Powerful Celebrities, Forbes.com, 2007, 2008; named to Guinness Book of World Records for the most hours on camera, 2004, Acad. TV Arts & Sciences Hall of Fame, 2006, Broadcasting Hall of Fame, Nat. Assn. Broadcasters, 2006. Achievements include setting Guinness World Record in 2004 for Most Hours on Camera (15,188 hours). Office: Regis & Kelly 7 Lincoln Sq New York NY 10023-5900

PHILIP, A. G. DAVIS, astronomer, educator, editor; b. NYC, Jan. 9, 1929; s. Van Ness and Lillian (Davis) P.; m. Kristina Drobavicius, Apr. 25, 1964; 1 dau., Kristina Elizabeth Elanor. BS, Union Coll., 1951; MS, N.Mex. State U., 1959; PhD, Case Inst. Tech., 1964. Tchr. physics, math. and chemistry Brooks Sch., 1954-59; instr. Case Inst. Tech., 1962-64; asst. prof. astronomy U. N.Mex., 1964-66, SUNY-Albany, 1966-67, assoc. prof., 1967-76, mem. exec. com. Arts and Scis. Coun., 1975-76; rsch. prof. astronomy Union Coll., Schenectady, NY, 1976—, astronomer Dudley Obs., 1967-81, Frank L. Fullam chair astronomy, 1980-81, editor Dudley Obs. Reports, 1977-81; astronomer Van Vleck Obs. Wesleyan U., 1982-94; editor contbns. VVObs., 1982-94; pres. Inst. for Space Observation, 1986—. Guest Acad. Scis. Lithuania, 1973, 76, 79, 86, 03, Stellar Data Ctr., Strasbourg, France, 1978, 79, 80, 82, 85, 86; vis. astronomer Moletai Obs., 1988, 94, 99, 00, Vatican Advanced Tech. Telescope, 1996—, CASLEO, Argentina, 2000—; bd. dirs., sec.-treas. N.Y. Astron. Corp., 1969-01; pres., treas. L. Davis Press, Inc., 1982—; trustee, chmn. Grants award com. Fund Astrophys. Rsch., 1985—; dir. Shapley Vis. Lectureships Program, 1994-05; rsch. bd. advisors Am. Biog. Inst., 1996-; Elected Lithuanuan Acd. Sci., 1997. Exhibited: 2d Ann. Photography Regional, Albany, 1980; author: (with M. Cullen and R.E. White) UBV Color - Magnitude Diagrams of Galactic Globular Clusters, 1976; (with A. Robucci, M. Frame, K.W. Philip) Mm, Fractal Series, Vol. 1, Midgets on the Spike, 1991; editor: The Evolution of Population II Stars, 1972, (with D.S. Hayes) Multicolor Photometry and the Theoretical HR Diagram, 1975, (with T. M. Miller, L. J. Relyea) An Analysis of the Hauck Mermilliod Catalogue of Four Color Data, 1976, (with M.F. Mc Carthy) Galactic Structure in the Direction of the Galactic Polar Caps, 1977, (with D. H. DeVorkin In Memory of Henry Norris Russell, 1977, (with Hayes) The HR Diagram, 1978, Problems in Calibration of Multicolor Systems, 1979, (with M.F. McCarthy and G.V. Coyne) Spectral Classification of the Future, 1979, X-Ray Symposium, 1981, (with Hayes) Astrophysical Parameters for Globular Clusters, 1981, (with A.R. Upgren) The Nearby Stars and the Stellar Luminosity Function, 1983, (with N. Sanduleak) A Deep Objective Prism Survey of the Large Magellanic Cloud for OB and Supergiant Stars, 1983, (with Hayes and L. Pasinetti) Calibration of Fundamental Stellar Quantities, 1985, (with D.W. Latham) Stellar Radial Velocities, 1985, Horizontal-Branch and UV-Bright Stars, 1985, Spectroscopic and Photometric Classification of Population II Stars, 1986, (with J. Grindley) IAU Symposium No. 126, Globular Cluster Systems in Galaxies, 1987, (with Hayes and Liebert) IAU Colloquium No. 95, The Second Conference on Faint Blue Stars, 1987, (with Hayes and Adelman) New Directions in Spectrophotometry, 1988, Calibration of Stellar Ages, 1988, (with A.R. Upgren) Star Catalogues; A Centennial Tribute to A.N. Vyssotsky, 1989, (with P. Lu) The Gravitational Force Perpendicular to the Galactic Plane, 1989, (with D.S. Hayes and S.J. Adelman) CCDs in Astronomy. II. Precision Photometry: Astrophysics of the Galaxy, 1991, (with Robucci, Frame and Philip K.) Midgets on the Spike, vol. I, 1991, (with A.R. Upgren) Objective-Prism and Other Surveys, 1991, N.Y. State Astronomy, 1992, (with B. Hauck and A.R. Upgren) Workshop on Databases for Galactic Structure, 1993, (with K.A. Janes and A.R. Upgren) IAU Symposium No. 167, New Developments in Array Technology and Applications, 1995, (with V. Straizys) Photometric Systems and Standard Stars, 1996, 30 Years of Astronomy at Van Vleck Observatory, 1997, (with Peter Boyce) Electronic Publishing: Now and the Future, 1997, (with J. Liebert and R. Saffer) The Third Conference on Faint Blue Stars, 1997, (with W. van Altena and A. Upgren) Anni Mirabiles: A Symposium Celebrating the 90th Birthday of Dorrit Hottleit, 1999, The Kth Reunion, 2000, (with R.A. Koopmann) The Starry Universe: The Cecilia Payne-Gaposchkin Centenary, 2001, (with R.O. Gray and C. Corbally) The Garrison Festschrift, 2003, (with J. Sudzius and V. Straizys) Stellar Photometry: Past, Present and Future, 2003, (with William van Altena and Rebecca Koopmann) The Hottleit Centennial: A Year of Celebration, 2006; mem. editl. bd., 1994—, co-editor, 1998—, Baltic Astronomy, Astrometric and Photometric Group, Wesleyan U., 1997-03; lectr. tours (with K.W. Philip) An Introduction to the Mandelbrot Set, 1988-91; contbr. chpts. to books, articles to profl. jours.; worked with Dr. Irving Langmuir on "The Pathology of Science", 1950. Served with AUS, 1951-53. Yale U. vis. fellow, 1976; rsch. grantee Rsch. Corp., NSF, NASA, Nat. Rsch. Lab., NAS, Am. Astron. Soc. Fellow AAAS, Royal Astron. Soc., Am. Phys. Soc.; mem. Am. Astron. Soc. (Harlow Shapley lectr. 1974—, auditor 1977, 79-85), Am. Math. Soc., Can. Astron. Soc., Internat. Astron. Union (chmn., sec. various coms. and commns., pres. commn. 30 1982-85, chmn. working group on spectroscopic and photometric data 1985-94, chmn. sci. organizing com. symposium # 167, mem. working group on pub. 2000-), N.Y. Acad. Scis., Astron. Soc. Pacific, Astron. Soc. N.Y. (sec.-treas. 1969-2001, editor newsletter 1974-2001), Capital Computer Club (bd. dirs. 1990—, v.p. 1993—), H. Rider Haggard Soc., Sigma Xi. Achievements include being 1st U.S. observer Soviet 6M telescope, 1980. Home: 1125 Oxford Pl Schenectady NY 12308-2913 Office: Union Coll Physics Dept Schenectady NY 12308

PHILIP, GEORGE MICHAEL, academic administrator, former pension fund administrator; b. Kingston, NY, June 7, 1947; s. Michael and Margarita Philip; m. Sandra Philip, Aug. 22, 1970; children: Matthew, Michael, Robert. BA, SUNY, Albany, 1969, MA, 1972; JD, Western New Eng. Coll., Springfield, Mass., 1977. Bar: NY 1978, US Dist. Ct. (no. dist.) NY 1978. Tchr. HS Schnectady City Sch. Dist., NY, 1969-71; pub. info. rep. NY State Tchrs. Retirement Sys., Albany, 1971-73, mgr. facilities and administry. svcs., 1973-77, mgr. mem. and employer svcs., 1977-82, chmn. task force, 1982, divsn. mgr. mgmt. and fin., 1982-86, dir. investor rels., pub. info., and budget, 1986-88, chief real estate investment officer, 1988-92, asst. exec. dir., 1992-95, chief investment officer, 1992—2007, exec. dir., 1995—2007; interim pres. U. at Albany - SUNY, 2007—09, pres., 2009—. Bd. dirs., sec. Pension Real Estate Assn., Glastonbury, Conn., 1989-95; mem. real estate adv. com. Babson Coll., Wellesley, Mass.; past pres. Nat. Coun. on Tchr. Retirement, Sacramento; mem. State Acad. for Pub. Administrn., Albany; past chair exec. com. Coun. Instl. Investors, Washington; mem. pension mgrs. adv. com. NY Stock Exch. Chair bd. dirs., chmn. investment com. St. Peter's Hosp., Albany; chmn. investment com. Cath. Health East, Phila.; chmn. univ. coun. SUNY, Albany; bd. dirs. Univ. at Albany Found., Univ. at Albany Alumni Assn., SUNY Rsch. Found.; bd. dirs., chair investment com. Saratoga Performing Arts Ctr. Office: U at Albany University Hall, Rm 302A 1400 Washington Ave Albany NY 12222 Office Phone: 518-956-8010. E-mail: presmail@uamail.albany.edu.*

PHILIP, PETER VAN NESS, former trust company executive; b. NYC, Feb. 23, 1925; s. Van Ness and Lilian (Davis) P.; m. Sabina FitzGibbon, May 3, 1952; children: William Van Ness, Thomas Winslow, Peter Sandys. AB, Yale U., 1945; MBA, NYU, 1950. With Price, Waterhouse & Co., NYC, 1947-52; W.H. Morton & Co., Inc., NYC, 1952-73; pres., CEO Equitable Securities, Morton & Co., Inc., 1970-73; sr. v.p., dir. White Weld & Co., Inc., NYC, 1974-76; v.p. Morgan Guaranty Trust Co., NYC, 1977-88, ret. With 86th inf. div. AUS, 1943-45. Decorated Purple Heart, Bronze Star. Mem.: Racquet and Tennis (N.Y.C.); Links; Yale (N.Y.C.), Downtown Assn. (N.Y.C.), Bond (N.Y.C.); Bedford ((N.Y.); Golf and Tennis; Ekwanok (Manchester, Vt.). Home: Box 395 740 Guard Hill Rd Bedford NY 10506-1042

PHILIPP, KARLA ANN, musician, educator, conductor; b. Milw., Sept. 12, 1955; d. John William and Catherine Ann Philipp. MusB, U. Ariz., 1977; MusM, Memphis State U., 1979. Tchr. itinerant strings Memphis City Schs., 1979—2009; condr. youth string ensemble and youth sinfonia Memphis Youth Symphony, 1997—; adj. instr. U. Memphis, 2009—. Sect. bass player Tucson Symphony Orch., 1977—78, Memphis Symphony Orch., 1979—89; prin. bass Jackson Symphony Orch., 1989—2007; note reading tchr., condr. Am. Suzuki Inst., Stevens Point, Wis., 1993—2005; dir. orch. Intermountain Suzuki String Inst., Salt Lake City, 2001—04; notereading tchr., dir. orch. Suzuki Inst. U. Memphis, 2005—, dir. orch. Summer String Camp, 2006—; presenter in field. Mem. Integrity, Memphis, 2003—. Recipient award for tchr. excellence, Rotary Club, Memphis, 1998, Outstanding Tchr. award, Tenn. Gov.'s Sch. for Arts, 1991, 1994, 1995; grantee, Rotary Club, Memphi, 1991, 1997; Haldeman scholar, U. Ariz. Sch. Music, 1974—78. Mem.: Suzuki Assn. of Ams., West Tenn. Sch. Band and Orch. Assn., Tenn. Music Educators Assn., Music Educators Nat. Conf., Am. String Tchrs. Assn. (west Tenn v.p. 1993—95), Am. Fedn. Musicians Local 71. Episcopalian. Avocations: reading, travel. Office: Ridgeway High Sch 2009 Ridgeway Rd Memphis TN 38119 Personal E-mail: philippbass@aol.com.

PHILIPPE, BOIS ROGER JEAN, science educator, researcher; b. Guérande, Loire-Atlantique, France, Aug. 29, 1970; s. Jean-Claude and Lyliane Janne Bois; m. Tina Izard, Apr. 23, 2001. PhD, U. Paris, 1996. Asst. prof. Scripps Rsch. Inst., Scripps Fla., Jupiter, 2007—, prin. investigator, 2007—. Office: Scripps Rsch Inst Scripps 130 Scripps Way #2C1 Jupiter FL 33458 Business E-Mail: pbois@scripps.edu.

PHILIPPON, MARC JOSEPH, orthopaedic surgeon; b. Quebec City, Can., May 9, 1965; arrived in U.S., 1990; s. Pontien Aderville and Micheline (Lortie) P.; m. Senenne Catalina Reid, Mar. 25, 1995; children: Michèle, Marc-Christophe, Mia-Véronique. BA with honors, Fla. Atlantic U., 1987; MD, McMaster U., Hamilton, Ont., Can., 1990. Lic. physician, Fla., Pa.; diplomate Am. Bd. Orthopaedic Surgery. Orthop. surgery resident U. Miami, Jackson Meml. Hosp., 1995; orthopaedic surgeon Holy Cross Hosp., Ft. Lauderdale, Fla., 1995, chief orthopaedic surgery, 2000-01; chief orthopaedic surgeon humanitarian mission to Ukraine Kiev Orthopaedic Inst., 1997; orthopaedic surgeon Broward Gen. Hosp., Ft. Lauderdale, 1998—2002; dir. sports medicine/hip disorders dept. orthopaedic surgery U. Pitts. Med. Ctr.; dir. fellowship program U. Pitts. Med. Ctr. for Sports Medicine, dir. hip arthroscopy fellowship, dir. golf medicine program, dir. Fla. site; orthop. surgeon, ptnr. Steadman-Hawkins Clinic, Vail, Colo., 2005—. Cons. Howmedica Inc., Rutherford, N.J., 1996-97, Smith & Nephew Inc., Memphis, 1998-99, Zimmer (Bristol-Myers Squibb), NHL, NFL, NBA and MLB profl. teams and has treated PGA golfers; clin. adv. bd. Oratec Interventions, Inc., Menlo Park, Calif., 1998-2002; clin. asst. prof., U. Pitts. Med. Ctr.; med. cons. Ctr. for Sports Medicine; orthop. surgeon Nat. Hockey League Players Assn.; lectr. in field. Contbr. chapters to books, articles to profl. jours. Bd. dirs. Svc. Agy. for Sr. Citizens, Ft. Lauderdale, 1996-2000. Farquharson scholar Can. Med. Rsch. Coun., 1989. Fellow Internat. Coll. Surgeons, Am. Acad. Orthop. Surgeons; mem. AMA, Fla. Med. Assn., Am. Orthop. Soc. for Sports Medicine, Arthroscopy Assn. N.Am. (master instr.), Herodicus Soc., Phi Kappa Phi. Roman Catholic. Achievements include invention of orthopaedic surgery instrument and devices. Avocations: skiing, tennis, sailing, hockey, soccer, golf. Office: Steadman Hawkins Clinic 181 W Meadow Dr Ste 400 Vail CO 81657 Office Phone: 970-476-1100.*

PHILIPPONE, DAVID J., lawyer; b. Rochester, NY, Oct. 28, 1968; s. John Edward and Eileen Marie Philippone; m. Mary C. Philippone, Aug. 7, 1993; children: Michael V., Maura E. BA magna cum laude, St. John Fisher Coll., Rochester, 1989; JD cum laude, Syracuse U., NY, 1992. Bar: N.Y. 1993, N.J. 1992, U.S. Dist. Ct. (no. dist.) N.Y. 1993. Assoc. atty. Mackenzie Law Firm, Syracuse, NY, 1992—95, Thaddeus B. Oot & Assocs., Syracuse, 1995—2001; mem. Oot & Assocs. PLLC, Syracuse, 2001—. Editor-in-chief Legis. Rsch. Bur., Syracuse U. Coll. Law, 1992. Coach baseball West Genesee Athletic Club, Camillus, 2004—; coach soccer We. Onandaga Youth Soccer Assn., Camillus, 2005—; mem. Camillus Optimists; bd. dirs. Camillus Youth Hockey Assn., NY, 2006—, We. Area Vol. Emergency Svcs. Inc., 1999—2004. Mem.: Injured Workers Bar Assn., NY State Bar Assn., Onondaga County Bar Assn. (co-chair young lawyers sect. 1994), Workers Compensation Bar Assn. Ctrl. NY (pres. 2002—05, v.p. 1999—2002). Home: 5411 Anvil Dr Camillus NY 13031 Office: Oot and Associates PLLC 503 E Washington St Syracuse NY 13202

PHILIPPS, EDWARD WILLIAM, former banker, real estate appraiser; b. NYC, Dec. 19, 1938; s. Edward Charles and Eleanor Elizabeth (Eisenger) P.; m. Diane Rose DiCuffa, June 12, 1960; children: James Michael, Robert Christopher. Appraiser Dry Dock Savs., NYC, 1956-70, Nat. Bank of West, White Plains, NY, 1970-72, Aires Real Estate, Yonkers, NY, 1972-74; sr. v.p. Am. Savs. Bank (merger Empire Savs. Bank), NYC, 1974-92; self employed real estate appraiser Yonkers, 1992-93; sr. v.p., chief lending officer LaJolla (Conn.) Bank, 1993-99; cons., 1999—. Mem. mortgage com. Cmty. Preservation Corp., N.Y.C., 1990-92. Mem. Am. Inst. Real Estate Appraisers, Homebuilders Assn. Fairfield County (bd. dirs.). Avocations: wood working, fishing. Home and Office: 261 Kimball Ave Yonkers NY 10704-3030 E-mail: ephilipp@optonline.net.

PHILIPS, BRIAN D., delivery service executive; b. Toledo, 1967; Grad., Miami U., Oxford, Ohio, 1988; MBA, Ind. U., 1992. With mktg. dept. Kimberly Clark Corp.; with svc. devel. mktg. dept. FedEx Express, mng. dir. mktg. Latin Am. and Caribbean divsn., mng. dir. segment and sponsorship mktg.; v.p. US mktg. FedEx Services; exec. v.p., COO FedEx Office, pres., CEO, 2008—. Mem. exec. com. The United Way Met. Dallas. Office: FedEx Office 13155 Noel Rd Ste 1600 Dallas TX 75240

PHILIPS, GEORGE K., parochial school educator; b. Johnson City, NY; s. George C. and Mary Lou Phillips; m. Diana Philips, 2005; 1 child, George Joseph. BA in History, Villanova U., Pa., 1998; MA in Edn., U. Notre Dame, Ind. With microelectronics divsn. IBM, Endicott, NY; tchr. Loyola Coll. Prep, Shreveport, La.; with govt. rels. divsn. Sallie Mae Inc., Washington; long term substitute tchr. Ea. Sr. HS, Washington; congl. aide Congressman Chris Smith, Washington; tchr. Seton Cath. Ctrl. HS, 2005—; lectr. in govt. Broome CC, 2005—; small bus. owner D&G Phillips' Graphic Design, 2005—. Mem. Our Lady of Angels Ch. Mem.: Alpha Phi Omega. Republican. Office: Seton Cath Ctrl HS 70 Seminary Ave Binghamton NY 13905

PHILIPS, LAURA ALMA, former pharmaceutical executive; b. San Francisco, Sept. 4, 1957; d. Irving and Mary Elizabeth (Gray) P.; m. Mark Maroncelli, Jule 29, 1979 (div. 1989); m. John Arnold Elliott, May 5, 1994. BA, Williams Coll., 1979; PhD, U. Calif., Berkeley, 1985; MBA, Cornell U., 1997. Postdoctoral fellow U. Chgo., 1985-87; asst. prof. Cornell U., Ithaca, NY, 1987-94; fellow, Office Senator Joseph Lieberman US Senate, Washington, 1994; fellow Office Sci. & Tech. Policy The White House, Washington, 1995; sr. policy adv. to sec. US Dept. Commerce, Washington, 1994—96; mgr. strategic analysis Corning Inc., NY, 1997—2002; v.p., program mgmt. AMDeC Found., 2002—03; COO, acting CFO NexGenix Pharmaceuticals, 2003—06. Cons. in field, Ithaca, 1996-97; bd. dirs., Delcath Systems, Inc. 2007-. Contbr. articles to profl. jours. Bd. dirs. Boyce Thompson Inst., Planned Parenthood NY, 2003- Democrat.

PHILIPSEN, DIRK PETER, history professor, consultant; b. Heidenheim, Ala., Mar. 20, 1959; s. Hans and Ina Philipsen; m. Wesley Hogan, Dec. 30, 2005; children: Niklas, Sven. PhD, Duke U., Durham, NC, 1992. History prof. Va. State U., Petersburg, 1996—. Project dir. Nat. Endowment Humanities, Petersburg, Va., 2007—. Founder, co-dir. Inst. Study Race Rels., Petersburg, Va., 1997. Recipient Outstanding Faculty award, State Coun. Higher Edn., 2005; Race Rels. fellow, Va. Found. Humanities, 1999, Oral History Program fellow, Gwathmey Found., 2004. Mem.: Am. Hist. Assn. Independent. Avocations: tennis, hiking. Home: 2519 Cherrytree Ln Richmond VA 23235 Office: Va State Univ 1 Hayden Dr Petersburg VA 23806 Office Fax: 804-524-5802. Business E-Mail: dphilips@vsu.edu.

PHILLIPPE, RYAN, actor; b. New Castle, Del., Sept. 10, 1974; s. Richard and Susan Phillippe; m. Reese Witherspoon, June 5, 1999 (div. Oct. 5, 2007); children: Ava Elizabeth, Deacon. Student, New Castle Bapt. Acad., 1992. Co-founder, ptnr. Lucid Films, 2002—. Actor: (films) Crimson Tide, 1995, Invader, 1996, White Squall, 1996, Nowhere, 1996, Little Boy Blue, 1997, I Saw What You Did Last Summer, 1997, Homegrown, 1998, 54, 1998, Playing by Heart, 1998, Cruel Intentions, 1999, The Way of the Gun, 2000, Antitrust, 2001, Gosford Park, 2001, Igby Goes Down, 2002, The I Inside, 2003, Crash, 2004, Five Fingers, 2005, Chaos, 2005, Flags of Our Fathers, 2006, Breach, 2007, Stop Loss, 2008; (TV series) One Life to Live, 1992—93; (TV miniseries) The Secrets of Lake Success, 1993, (TV appearances) A Perry Mason Mystery: The Case of the Grimacing Governor, 1994, Matlock, 1994, Due South, 1994, Chicago Hope, 1996, The Outer Limits, 1996, (voice only) King of the Hill, 2000. Office: c/o William Morris Agy Attn: John Fogelman 151 El Camino Dr Beverly Hills CA 90212

PHILLIPS, AMY J., lawyer; b. Scranton, Pa., Aug. 15, 1975; d. Protus Eugene and Barbara Carol Phillips; m. Walter Scott Baker, June 8, 2002 (div. July 2007). BA, Allentown Coll. St. Francis de Sales, Center Valley, Pa., 1997; JD, Pa. State U., Carlisle, 2000. Bar: Pa. 2000. Law clk. Hon. Jerome P. Cheslock, Stroudsburg, Pa., 2000—01; sr. assoc. Hoffmeyer & Semmelman, LLP, York, 2001—. Fundraiser Union Pk. Assn., Gouldsboro, Pa., 2000—; sec. YWCA, York, 2006—; sec., treas. Shadowfax Found., 2003—. Recipient Pa. Rising Star, Phila. Mag., 2006, 2007, 2008. Mem.: York County Bar Assn. (domestic rels. liaison 2003—05, legis. liaison 2007—), Pa. Bar Assn. (Pa. Rising Star 2004, 2007, 2008). Home: 4115 Locust Point Ct Dover PA 17315 Office: Hoffmeyer & Semmelman LLP 30 North George St York PA 17401 Office Fax: 717-852-8780. E-mail: aphillips@hoffsemm.com.

PHILLIPS, ANTHONY GEORGE, neurobiology researcher; b. Barrow, Cumbria, Eng., Jan. 30, 1943; came to Can., 1953; s. George William and Mabel Lilian (Wood) P. BA, U. Western Ont., London, Can., 1966, MA, 1967, PhD, 1970. Asst. prof. psychobiology U. B.C.,

Vancouver, Canada, 1970-75, assoc. prof., 1975-80, prof., 1980—, head dept. psychology, 1994-99, prof. dept. psychiatry, 1999—, founding dir. U. B.C. Inst. Mental Health. Founder Quadra Logic Tech., Inc., Vancouver. Contbr. numerous papers to sci. jours. Chair inst. adv. bd. CIHR Inst. for Neurosci. Mental Health & Addiction, 2001—; bd. dirs. Tibetian Refuge Aid Soc., 1980—; chmn. Can.-India Village Aid, Vancouver, 1981—86, 2003—05. Recipient Killam Rsch. prize Can. Coun., 1977, D.O. Hebb award Can. Psychol. Assn.; Steacie fellow Nat. Scis. and Engring. Rsch. Coun. Can., 1980. Fellow Royal Soc. Can.; mem. Soc. Neurosci., Can. Soc. for Neurosci., Can. Coll. Neuropsychopharmacology. Office: U BC Dept Psych 2255 Wesbrook Mall Vancouver BC Canada V6T 1Z4 Office Phone: 604-822-4624. Business E-Mail: aphillips@psych.ubc.ca.

PHILLIPS, BARRY, lawyer; b. Valdosta, Ga., Feb. 16, 1929; s. W. Otis and Gypsy (Mercer) P.; m. Grace Greer, Aug. 3, 1957; children: Mary Grace, Barry Jr., Greer, Quinton. AB, U. Ga., 1949, LLB, 1954. Bar: Ga. 1951, D.C. 1977. Assoc. Kilpatrick Stockton, Atlanta, 1954-60, ptnr., 1960-97, of counsel, 1997—. Bd. dirs., mem. exec. com., credit com. Bank South Corp., 1978-96. Mem. bd. regents Univ. Sys. Ga., 1988-94, vice chmn., 1991-93, chmn., 1993-94; trustee U. Ga. Found., Atlanta, 1983-87, treas., 1985-87; mem. bd. visitors U. Ga. Law Sch., 1983-87, chmn., 1985; dir. Ctrl. Atlanta Progress, 1985-86; dir. USA-ROC Econ. Coun., 1985-91; bd. dirs. Ga. Coun. Internat. Visitors, Atlanta, 1986-93, sec., 1986-87, pres., 1987-88; bd. dirs. Atlanta Conv. and Visitors Bur., 1986-91, sec., 1986-87, v.p., 1987-88; bd. dirs. Ga. Region NCCJ, 1980-98, co-chair, 1982-83; chmn. Met. Atlanta Olympic Games Authority, 1990-91; bd. dirs. Ga. Sports Hall of Fame, 1990—, vice chmn., 1993-95, chmn., 1995-96; attache Can. Olympic Team for 1996 Olympics, 1995-96. 1st lt. U.S. Army, 1951-53, Korea. Decorated Air medal; recipient Brotherhood-Sisterhood award Ga. Regional NCCJ, 1993. Fellow Am. Coll. Investment Counsel (bd. dirs. 1986-88), Ga. Bar Found., Soc. Internat. Bus. Fellows; mem. Ga. Bar Assn. (chmn. corp. and banking law sect. 1977-78), Atlanta Bar Assn., D.C. Bar Assn., Lawyers Club Atlanta, U. Ga. Law Sch. Alumni Assn. (trustee 1979-84, pres. 1982-83), Can. Am. Soc. (bd. dirs. 1981-90, pres. 1981-83), Brit. Am. Bus. Group (bd. dirs. 1985-95), Sphinx, Gridiron, Phi Beta Kappa, Phi Kappa Phi, Omicron Delta Kappa. Democrat. Methodist. Avocations: reading, travel. Home: 4850 Tanglewood Ct NW Atlanta GA 30327-4558 Office: Kilpatrick Stockton 1100 Peachtree St NE Ste 2800 Atlanta GA 30309-4530 Home Phone: 404-255-6521; Office Phone: 404-815-6380. Business E-Mail: bphillips@kilstock.com. E-mail: bphilatl@aol.com.

PHILLIPS, BETTY LOU (ELIZABETH LOUISE PHILLIPS), writer, interior designer; b. Cleve. d. Michael N. and Elizabeth D. (Materna) Suvak; m. John S. Phillips, Jan. 27, 1963 (div. Jan. 1981); children: Bruce, Bryce, Brian; m. John D.C. Roach, Aug. 28, 1982. BS, Syracuse U., 1960; postgrad. in English, Case We. Res. U., 1963—64. Cert. elem. and spl. edn. tchr., NY; cert. interior designer, Calif. Tchr. pub. schs., Shaker Heights, Ohio, 1960—66. Sportswriter Cleve. Press, 1976-77; spl. features editor Pro Quarterback Mag., NYC, 1976-79; bd. dirs. Cast Specialties Inc., Cleve., 1960-2007. Author: Chris Evert: First Lady of Tennis, 1977, Picture Story of Dorothy Hamill, 1978 (ALA Booklist selection), American Quarter Horse, 1979, Earl Campbell: Houston Oiler Superstar, 1979, Picture Story of Nancy Lopez, 1980 (ALA Notable book), Go! Fight! Win! The NCA Guide for Cheerleaders, 1981 (ALA Booklist), Something for Nothing, 1981, Brush Up on Your Hair, 1981 (ALA Booklist), Texas.The Lone Star State, 1989, Provençal Interiors-French Country Style in America, 1998, French by Design, 2000, French Influences, 2001, Villa Décor: Decidedly French and Italian Style, 2002 (Foreword Mag. Best Non-Fiction Book, 2003), Unmistakably French, 2003, Emily Goes Wild, 2003 (Tex. Inst. Letters Best Children's Book, 2004), Secrets of French Design, 2004, The French Connection, 2005, Emily Works Out, 2005, Emily's Manners, 2005, Inspirations From France & Italy, 2007 (Forward Mag. Silver medal), The French Room, 2008; contbr. articles popular mags.;, author. Mem.: Am. Soc. Interior Designers (profl. mem., cert.), Soc. Children's Book Writers, Delta Delta Delta. Republican. Roman Catholic. Home: 4200 Saint Johns Dr Dallas TX 75205-3718

PHILLIPS, BRANDON EMIL, professional baseball player; b. Raleigh, NC, June 28, 1981; Infielder Cleve. Indians, 2002—05, Cin. Reds, 2006—. Recipient Fielding Bible award, 2008, Gold Glove award, 2008, Roberto Clemente award, Cin. Reds, 2008. Office: Cin Reds Great Am Ball Pk 100 Main St Cincinnati OH 45202-4109*

PHILLIPS, CARL, poet, educator; b. 1959; BA in Greek and Latin magna cum laude, Harvard U., 1981; MA in Latin and Classical Humanities, U. Mass., Amherst, 1983; MA in Creative Writing, Boston U., 1993. Latin tchr., 1983—91; asst. prof. English Washington U., St. Louis, 1993—95, assoc. prof., 1995—, dir. creative writing prog., 1996—98, 2000—02. Author: In the Blood, 1992 (Samuel French Morse Poetry prize, 1992), Cortege, 1995, From the Devotions, 1998, Pastoral, 2000 (Lambda Lit. award), The Tether, 2001 (Kingsley Tufts Poetry award), Rock Harbor, 2002, The Rest of Love: Poems, 2004, Riding Westward, 2006, Quiver of Arrows: Selected Poems, 2007. Recipient Lit. Award, AAAL, Pushcart prize, Acad. Am. Poets prize; named a Witter Bynner fellow, 1998, 2006; Witter Bynner Found. fellowship, Libr. Congress, 1997, Guggenheim fellowship. Fellow: Am. Acad. Arts & Sci. Office: Washington U Campus Box 1122 One Brookings Dr Saint Louis MO 63130 Office Phone: 314-935-7133. Business E-Mail: cphillips@wustl.edu.

PHILLIPS, CAROLINE L., lab administrator; b. Washington, Oct. 7, 1955; d. Elinor and Frank duBose Phillips; m. Raymond L. Baumler, Oct. 1, 1983; 1 child, Irene Caroline Baumler. MS, Va. Commonwealth U., Richmond, 1981. Computer programmer/analyst Nat. Inst. Aging, Bethesda, Md., 1986—2000, info. tech. specialist data mgmt., 2001—. Vol. Sunday sch. tchr. Seven Locks Bapt. Ch., Potomac, Md., 2001—06; mem. Heritage Cir. Children Christian Children's Fund, Richmond, Va., 2005—06. Recipient NIA Group award for publ. of a resource data book, Nat. Inst. Aging, 1990, Pub. Health Svc. On-the-Spot award, NIH/Nat. Inst. Aging, 1992, 1998, 1999, NIH award of Merit, 1994; named Sec.'s Employee of the Month, Nat. Inst. Aging, 1989, 1996. Mem.: Psi Chi. Achievements include development of specifications for database of neuropsychological tests for a large epidemiologic study in Iceland; data management for a large epidemiologic sstudy of elderly people in Italy. Avocations: drawing, painting, jogging, swimming, music.

PHILLIPS, CARTER GLASGOW, lawyer; b. Canton, Ohio, Sept. 11, 1952; s. Max Dean and Virginia Scott (Carter) P.; m. Sue Jane Henry, June 5, 1976; children: Jessica, Ryan. BA summa cum laude, Ohio State U., 1973; MA, Northwestern U., 1975, JD magna cum laude, 1977. Bar: Ill. 1977, DC 1979, US Dist. Ct. (no. dist.) Ill., US Dist. Ct. (DC dist.), US Ct. Appeals (1st, 2d, 3d, 4th, 5th, 6th, 7th, 8th, 9th, 10th, 11th, DC and Fed. cirs.), US Supreme Ct. Law clk. to hon. Judge Robert Sprecher US Ct. Appeals (7th cir.), Chgo., 1977—78; law clk. to chief Justice Warren E. Burger US Supreme Ct., Washington, 1978—79; asst. prof. law U. Ill., Champaign, 1979—81; asst. solicitor gen. US Dept. Justice, Washington, 1981—84; ptnr. Sidley & Austin, Washington, 1984—. Mng. ptnr. DC office, mem. mgmt. com. Sidley Austin Brown & Wood LLP, Washington, 1995—; chmn. dean's adv. bd. Northwestern U. Law Sch., 2002—04, mem. dean's adv. bd., 2002—, adj. prof. law, 2006—; chmn. Fed. Cir. Adv. Coun., U.S. Ct. Appeals, 2003—05, mem., 2003—; pres., master Edward Coke Appellate Inn of Ct.; mem. adv. bd. Coll. Arts and Scis., Ohio State U. Contbr. articles to profl. jours. Bd. advs. Georgetown Univ. Law Ctr.'s Supreme Ct. Inst.; bd. trustees Supreme Ct. Hist. Soc., Fed. City Coun.; bd. dir. Inst. Judicial Adminstrn., NYU Sch. Law; mem. adv. com. US Ct. Appeals, Fed. Cir.; mem. adv. coun. U. Calif. Irvine. Recipient Alumni Merit Award, Northwestern U., 1998, Alumni Svc. Award, 2006, Rex Lee Advocacy award, 2001; named one of Top 45 Lawyers Under 45, Am. Lawyer Mag., 1995, 100 Best Lawyers in Am., Nat. Law Jour., 1995, 100 Most Influential Lawyers, 2006, Top 10 Newsmakers of 2006, IP Law and Bus., Best Appellate Lawyers in Am., 2007, Lewis F. Powell award, Nat. Chamber Litig. Ctr., 2007, OSU Alumni Profl. Achievement award, 2007, 90 Greatest Washington Lawyers of the Last 30 Yrs., Legal Times. Fellow: Am. Coll. Trial Lawyers; mem.: Am. Acad. Appellate Lawyers, Am. Law Inst., Order of the Coif, Phi Beta Kappa. Republican. Episcopalian. Office: Sidley Austin LLP 1501 K St NW Fl 10 Washington DC 20005-3705 Home Phone: 703-734-0985; Office Phone: 202-736-8270. E-mail: cphillips@sidley.com.

PHILLIPS, CARYL, writer; b. St. Kitts, West Indies, Mar. 13, 1958; BA with honors, The Queen's Coll., Oxford, Eng., 1979; AM (hon.), Amherst Coll., Mass., 1995; DUniv (hon.), Leeds Metro. U., 1997; D (hon.), U. York, 2003; DLitt (hon.), U. Leeds, 2003; AM (hon.), Yale U., 2006. Writer in residence Factory Arts Ctr. Arts Coun. Great Britain, London, 1980-82; writer in residence U. Mysore, India, 1987, U. Stockholm, 1989; vis. writer Amherst Coll., 1990-92, writer in residence, 1992—98, co-dir. creative writing ctr., 1994-97, prof. English, writer-in-residence, 1994-98; prof. English, Henry R. Luce prof. migration and social order Barnard Coll., Columbia U., NYC, 1998—2005, dir. Initiatives in the Humanities, 2003—05; prof. English Yale U., 2005—. Vis. lectr. U. Ghana, 1990, U. Poznan, 1991; vis. writer Humber Coll., 1992, 93; writer-in-residence Nat. Inst. Edn., Singapore, 1994; vis. prof. English NYU, 1993; vis. prof. humanities U. W.I., 1999—2000; mem. arts coun. Gt. Britain Drama Panel, 1982—85; mem. prodn. bd. Brit. Film Inst., 1985—88, Bush Theatre, 1985—89; mem. Caribbean Writer bd. U.S. V.I., 1989—; hon. sr. mem. U. Kent, 1988—; cons. editor Faber & Faber, Inc., 1992—94, Caribbean series editor, 1996—2000; participant, keynote spkr 12 ann. confs. German-speaking countries New Lits. in English, Giessen, Germany, 1989; resident writer Hull (Engl.) Internat. Lit. Festival, 1992; instr. writing Arvon Found., summers, 1983—; reader, lectr. in field. Author: The Final Passage, 1985 (Malcolm X prize for lit., 1985), A State of Independence, 1986, The European Tribe, 1987 (Martin Luther King Meml. prize, 1987), Higher Ground, 1989, Cambridge, 1991, Crossing the River, 1993 (James Tait Black meml. prize), The Nature of Blood, 1997, The Atlantic Sound, 2000, A New World Order: Selected Essays, 2001, A Distant Shore, 2003 (PEN/Faulkner Award for Fiction nominee, 2004, Commonwealth Writers prize, 2004, Hurston/Wright Legacy award finalist, Nat. Book Cir. Critics finalist in fiction), Dancing in the Dark, 2005 (PEN Beyond the Margins prize, 06), Foreigners, 2007; editor: Extravagant Strangers: A Literature of Belonging, 1997, The Right Set: A Tennis Anthology, 1999; author: (plays) Strange Fruit, 1980, Where There Is Darkness, 1982, The Shelter, 1983, Rough Crossings, 2007, (TV documentary screenplays) Welcome to Birmingham, 1983, The Hope and Glory, 1984, Lost in Music, 1984, The Record, 1985, Darker Than Blue: Curtis Mayfield, 1995, BBC Profile Spl. Caryl Phillips Interviews Chinua Achebe, 2003, South Bank Show: Caryl Phillips, ITV, 2003, (films) Playing Away, 1986, The Final Passage, 1996, The Mystic Masseur, 2001 (Mar Del Plata Film Festival Silver Ombu for Best Screenplay), (radio plays) The Wasted Years, 1984 (Best Radio Play of Yr. award BBC, 1984), Crossing the River, 1985, The Prince of Africa, 1987, Writing Fiction, 1991, A Kind of Home: James Baldwin in Paris, BBC Radio 4, 2004, Hotel Cristobel, 2005, (radio documentaries) St. Kitts (Pride of Place), 1983, Sport and the Black Community, 1984, No Complaints: James Baldwin at Sixty, 1985, Archive Hour: I Too am America BBC Radio, 2003; contbr. (documentary programs) Bookmark, 1984, Black on Black, London Weekend TV, 1983, others; contbr. articles to periodicals. Recipient Young Writer of Yr. award, London Sunday Times, 1992, award, Lannan Lit., 1994, Caribbean Am. Heritage award for outstanding contbn. to lit., 2004; fellow, Guggenheim, 1992, 50th Anniversary, Brit. Coun., 1984, Royal Soc. Lit., 2000; Mel and Lois Tukman fellow, N.Y. Pub. Libr. Ctr. for Scholars and Writers, 2003, hon. fellow, The Queen's Coll. Oxford, 2006. Address: care G Garrett AP Watt Ltd 20 John St London WC1N 2DR England Office: Yale U English Dept 315 Linsly Chittenden Hall 63 High St New Haven CT 06520 Business E-Mail: Ggarrett@apwatt.co.uk.

PHILLIPS, CHANDLER ALLEN, biomedical engineer, human factors engineer; b. LA, Dec. 21, 1942; s. Chandler A. and Ann P.; m. Jane Draper, Feb. 14, 1980. AB in Biol. Scis., Stanford U., 1965; MD, U. So. Calif., 1969; AB in Classical Langs., Wright State U., 1982; PhD (hon.), U. Human Studies, Las Vegas, 1985. Registered profl. engr., Ohio, Calif. Rsch. physician U. Dayton, Ohio, 1972-74; asst. prof. physiology Wright State U., Dayton, 1975-79, assoc. prof. biomed. engring., 1979-84, prof. biomed. engring., 1984-91, prof. biomed. and human factors engring., 1991—99, prof. biomed. indsl. and human factors engring., 1999—, Brage Golding disting. prof. rsch., 2007—. Author: Functional Electrical Rehabilitation, 1991, Human Factors Engineering, 2000; sr. editor: Mechanics of Skeletal and Cardiac Muscle, 1983, Effective Extremity Prostheses, 1989; regional editor Auto Medica, 1997-03; mem. editl. bd. Jour. Biomechanics, 1984-87, Jour. Clin. Engring., 1984-98, Auto Medica, 1988-97, Prosthetics-Orthotics Engring., 1995-98. Amateur radio operator W6SWV. Capt. USAF, 1970—72. Fellow: IEEE (life Harry Rowe Mimno award 1984), Aerospace Med. Assn. (John Paul Stapp award 2002), Am. Inst. Med. and Biol. Engring., Am. Acad. Neurologic Orthopedic Surgeons (hon.). Avocations: commercial-instrument pilot, fishing, classical philology. Office: Dept Biomed Indsl Human Factors Engring Wright State U Dayton OH 45435 Office Phone: 937-775-5044.

PHILLIPS, CHARLES DAVID, gerontologist, health services researcher, public health professional; b. Abilene, Tex., Nov. 3, 1948; s. Willie Everette and Mary Charlene Phillips; m. Catherine Hawes, June 2, 1978; 1 child, Anna Michelle Tankersley. BA, Tarleton State U., Stephenville, Tex., 1971; MPH, U. NC, Chapel Hill, 1987; PhD, U. Tex., Austin, Tex., 1979. Asst. prof., dept. polit. sci. U. N.C., Chapel Hill, 1980—87; rsch. scientist RTI Internat., Rsch. Triangle Park, NC, 1988—96; dir. Myers Rsch. Inst., Beachwood, Ohio, 1996—2000; regents prof. dept. health policy and mgmt. Sch. Rural Pub. Health, Coll. Sta., Tex., dir. health svcs. rsch. program, 2000—, head doctoral studies, 2001—07. Mem. grad. faculty Tex. A&M U., 2000—. Mem. editl. bd.: The Gerontologist, 2000—09. Recipient Pub. Svc. award, Nat. Citizens Coalition Nursing Home Reform, 2005, Alumni Academic Forum honoree, Tarleton State U., 2006, Regents Prof. award, TAMU Sys. Bd. Regents, 2008; named Gerontologist of Yr., U. Tex., Houston Ctr. Aging, 2001; named to Rschr. Honor Roll, Nat. Citizens Coalition Nursing Home Reform, 2000, ISI Highly Cited Authors Social Scis. Fellow: Gerontol. Soc. Am., interRAI; mem.: APHA, Nat. Pub. Health Honor Soc., AcademyHealth, Delta Omega. Democrat. Office: Sch Rural Pub Health TAMUSHSC 1266 Tamu College Station TX 77843 Business E-Mail: phillipscd@srph.tamhsc.edu.

PHILLIPS, CHARLES E., JR., computer software company executive; b. Little Rock, Ark., 1960; BS in Computer Sci., USAF Acad., 1981; MBA in Fin., Hampton U., Va.; JD, NY Law Sch. CFA; bar: Ga., DC. Prin. Morgan Stanley & Co., Inc., 1994—95, mng. dir., 1995—2003; exec. v.p. strategy, partnerships & bus. devel. Oracle Corp., Redwood City, Calif., 2003—04, pres., 2004—, co-pres. PeopleSoft Calif., 2004. Bd. dirs. Oracle Corp., 2004—, Viacom Corp., 2004—, Morgan Stanley, 2006—; mem. President's Econ. Recovery Advisory Bd., 2009—. Trustee Joint Ctr. for Polit. and Econ. Studies, Washington, NY Law Sch., bd. dirs., Jazz at Lincoln Ctr., NYC. Capt. USMC. Named one of 50 Black Profls. on Wall Street, Black Enterprise Mag., 50 Who Matter Now, Business 2.0, 2007. Office: Oracle Corp 500 Oracle Pky Redwood City CA 94065 Office Phone: 650-506-7000. Office Fax: 650-506-7200.*

PHILLIPS, CHARLES FRANKLIN, JR., retired economist; b. Geneva, NY, Nov. 5, 1934; s. Charles Franklin and Evelyn (Minard) P.; m. Marjorie Hancock, June 22, 1957; children: Charles Franklin, Susan Hancock, Anne Davis. BA, U. N.H., 1956; PhD, Harvard U., 1960. Asst. prof. econs. Washington and Lee U., Lexington, Va., 1959-63, assoc. prof., 1963-66, prof., 1966—2003, Robert G. Brown prof., 1979—2003; ret., 2003. Mem. adv. bd. Shenandoah Valley area, First Union, 1971—; econ. cons. pub. utilities. Author: Competition in the Synthetic Rubber Industry, 1963, The Economics of Regulation, 1965, rev. edit., 1969, The Regulation of Public Utilities, 1984, 3d edit., 1993; editor: Competition and Monopoly in the Domestic Telecommunications Industry, 1974, Competition and Regulation-Some Economic Concepts, 1976, Expanding Economic Concepts of Regulation in Health, Postal and Telecommunications Services, 1977, Regulation, Competition and Deregulation-An Economic Grab Bag, 1978, Regulation and the Future Economic Environment-Air to Ground, 1980. Mem. city coun. Lexington, 1969-71, mayor, 1971-88; mem. Va. Rep. Ctrl. Com., 1974-76, 77-96; trustee Hebron Acad., Maine, 1971-82; mem. Presbyn. Ch., 1959—, elder, 1993-98, trustee, 1994—; mem. Commn. on Rev. of Nat. Policy Toward Gambling, 1972-76; chmn. Valley Program for Aging Svcs., 1993-95, treas., 1996-99; bd. dirs. Rockbridge Area Presbyn. Home, 1973—, Nat. Regulatory Rsch. Inst., 1992-95, Stonewall Jackson Found., 1997-2000, 2001-06, treas., 2003-04, pres, 2004-06; pres. United Way of Lexington-Rockbridge County, 1996-98, crusade chmn., 1999; pres. Hist. Lexington Found., 1997-2000, bd. dir. Maury River Sr. Ctr., 2004-, treas.; bd. dir. Rockbridge Area Free Clinic, 2007-, treas. Recipient award McKinsey Found., 1962, J. Rhoads Foster award, 1995, Hist. Hexington Found., 2004. Mem. Am. Econ. Assn. (Disting. Mem. award transp. and pub. utility group 1997), So. Econ. Assn., Am. Mktg. Assn., Kiwanis, Phi Beta Kappa, Omicron Delta Epsilon (pres. 1976-77, 78-79, 96-97, Outstanding Regional Dir. award 1971). Home: 414 Morningside Dr Lexington VA 24450-2739 Home Phone: 540-463-5409. E-mail: phillipscf@wlu.edu.

PHILLIPS, CHRISTOPHER, history professor, researcher; s. Kenneth Wayne and Ruth Anne Phillips; m. Jill M. Mitchell, Mar. 19, 1994; children: Grayson Clay, Maddox Turner. PhD, U. Ga., Athens, 1992. Assoc. prof. history Emporia State U., Kans., 1992—99; prof. history U. Cin., Cin., 1999—. Recipient Eagleton-Waters Book award, 2001, Md. Hist. Soc. Book award, 1998; named Outstanding Academic Title, 1991. Mem.: So. Hist. Assn. Liberal. Avocations: woodworking, art, travel. Office: Univ Cin PO Box 210373 Cincinnati OH 45221-0373

PHILLIPS, CLAY THOMAS, legislative staff member; Chief of staff for Rep. Kathy Castor, US House of Reps., Washington, 2007—; assoc. staff US House Rules Com., 2007—. Office: Office of Congresswomen Kathy Castor 317 Cannon House Office Bldg Washington DC 20515 Office Phone: 202-225-3376. Office Fax: 202-225-5652. E-mail: clay.phillips@mail.house.gov.*

PHILLIPS, DAVID P., grocery company executive; CFO Publix Super Markets, Lakeland, Fla., 1999—, treas. Office: Publix Super Markets PO Box 407 Lakeland FL 33802-0407 Office Phone: 863-688-1188.

PHILLIPS, DOROTHY K., lawyer; BS, U. Pa.; MA, NYU; JD, Villanova Law Sch., 1978. Bar: Pa. 1978, NJ 1978, US Dist. Ct. (east dist.) Pa., US Dist. Ct. NJ, US Ct. Appeals (3d cir.), US Supreme Ct. Lectr. Marriage Coun. Phila., U. Pa., Hahnemann Med. Sch., Phila., 1970-75; atty. Adler, Barish, Daniels, Levin & Creskoff, Phila., 1978-79, Astor, Weiss & Newman, Phila., 1979-80; ptnr. Romisher & Phillips. P.C., Phila., 1981-86; prin. Dorothy K. Phillips & Assocs., LLC, 1986—. Judge Reimel Moot Ct. Competition, Villanova Law Sch., 1986; faculty Pa. Bar Inst., CLE Temple U. Sch. Law, 1987-89, Nat. Bus. Inst., lectr. 1998-2006, Sterling Edn. Sem., 2008, with Louis D. Brandeis Soc., Nat. Found. Celiac Awareness. Author: The Legal Intelligencer, The Phila. Lawyer, 1998; family law columnist: Pa. Law Weekly Domestic Dispute, 2005-08; contbr. articles to profl. jours. Named a Super Lawyer Phila. Mag., 2005-08; named one of Top 50 Lawyers Phila. Mag., 2006, 2007, Top 50 Female Attys. Phila.; featured in Wall St. Jour., Phila. Inquirer, Phila. Bus. Jour., Harper's Bazaar, WPVI-ABC6, KYW-CBS3, WCAU-NBC10, FOX Phila., CN8. Mem.: ATLA, ABA, Nicholas A. Cipriani Family Law Am. Inn Ct., Phila. Trial Lawyers Assn., Custody Rules Drafting Com. (Sup. Ct. Pa. faculty), Lawyers Club, Montgomery County Bar Assn., Phila. Bar Assn. (Supreme Ct. Pa., faculty), NJ State Bar Assn., Pa. Bar Assn., Pa. Trial Lawyers Assn.

PHILLIPS, EDWARD JOHN, consulting firm executive; s. Harold E. and Mary C. P.; m. Kathleen A. Everett, July 23, 1960; children: Elizabeth J., Edward J. B of Mech. Engring., Villanova U., 1973; MBA, Widener U., 1975. Registered profl. engr., Ill., Pa., Ohio; chartered engr., U.K. Tech. ops. mgr. Motorola, Inc., Franklin Park, Ill., 1976-81; v.p. engring. Rival Mfg. Co., Kansas City, Mo., 1981-82; prin., sr. cons. Richard Muther & Assocs., Kansas City, 1982-85; chmn. KANDE, Inc., Overland Park, Kans., 1983-86; pres., CEO Sims Cons. Group Inc., Lancaster, Ohio, 1986—; chmn. bd. dirs., pres. Sims Consulting Group, Lancaster, Ohio. Bd. dirs. KANDE, Inc., Wilmington, Del. Author: Manufacturing Plant Layout, 1997; contbr. articles to profl. jours. Recipient Profl. Achievement award, Villanova U., 2006. Mem. NSPE, ASME (chmn. material handling divsn. 1989-91, internat. mgmt. com. 1977), MIMechE, Soc. Mfg. Engrs., Tau Beta Pi, Pi Tau Sigma. Office: Sims Cons Group Inc PO Box 968 Lancaster OH 43130-0968

PHILLIPS, ELAINE ANDERSON, religious studies educator; d. Donald Wesley and Marie Pauline Anderson; m. Perry Gust Phillips, Dec. 23, 1972. PhD, Dropsie Coll. Hebrew and Cognate Learning, Phila., 1991. Assoc prof and academic dean Pinebrook Jr. Coll., Coopersburg, Pa., 1979—92; prof. bibl. studies Gordon Coll., Wenham, Mass., 1993—. Field instrn. Jerusalem U. Coll., 1997—. Tchr. Pk. St. Ch., Boston, 1998—2008. Recipient Jr. Disting. Faculty award, Gordon

Coll., 1996, Sr. Disting. Faculty award, 2006. Fellow: Interdisciplinary Bibl. Rsch. Inst. (exec. bd. 1990—2008); mem.: Inst. Bibl. Rsch. (exec. com. 2001—03), Soc. Bibl. Lit. Avocations: travel, reading, writing.

PHILLIPS, ERNIE HOWARD, music educator; b. Gainesville, Ga., Apr. 5, 1957; s. Ernest Cecil and Charlotte (Inez) Phillips; m. Connie Harrison, June 5, 1982; children: Matthew, Ryan, Hamilton. MusB, U. Ga., 1979, MusM in Music Edn., 1981. Grad. asst. U. Ga. Bands, 1979—81; asst. band dir. East Hall HS, Gainesville, 1981—88; band dir., fine arts dept. head West Hall HS, Gainesville, 1988—. Guest honor band condr. U. Ga. Music Festival, 1998, Ga. Music Educators In-Svc. Conf., 1998; guest condr. U. Ga. Redcoat Band, 2001. Musician (prin. tubist): Gainesville Symphony Orch., 1982—, North Winds Symphonic Band, 1985—; musician: (chmn., bd. dirs.). Dir. Soc. Preservation and Encouragement Barber Shop Quartet Singing in Am., Gainesville, 1983—95; donor U. Ga. Scholarship Fund, Athens, 1993—; bass sect. mem. Lakewood Baptist Worship Choir, Gainesville, 1984—. Recipient Legion of Honor award, John Philip Sousa Found., 2001. Mem.: Ga. Music Educators Assn. (9th dist. instrumental chmn. 2005—), Nat. Band Assn., Music Educators Nat. Conf., U. Ga. Alumni Soc., Phi Beta Mu. Baptist. Home: 5024 Jay Creek Rd Oakwood GA 30566 Office: West Hall HS 5500 McEver Rd Oakwood GA 30566 Office Phone: 770-967-9826 ext 250. Business E-Mail: ernie.phillips@hallco.org.

PHILLIPS, EUAN HYWEL, publishing executive; b. Chipstead, Surrey, Eng., Mar. 31, 1928; s. Edgar Aneurin and Elsie Llewella (Davies) P.; m. Margaret June Savage, June 12, 1954; children: David John, Janet Margaret. BA, Emmanuel Coll., Cambridge, Eng., 1949, MA, 1965. Cost acct. J. Lyons & Co. Ltd., London, 1950-53; dispatch mgr. Pickerings Produce Canners Ltd., Manchester, Eng., 1953-56; mgmt. cons. P.A. Mgmt. Cons. Ltd., London, 1956-65; mng. dir. Unwin Bros. Ltd., Old Woking, England, 1965-73; univ. printer designate Cambridge U. Press, England, 1973-74, univ. printer, 1974-76, dir. Am. br. NYC, 1977-82; exec. dir. Assn. Am. U. Presses, 1987-90. Gov. Guildford Sch. Art, 1966-69, Cambridge Coll. Arts and Tech., 1974-76; dir. East Asian History of Sci., Inc., 1978-81 Contbr. to scholarly pub. With Royal Navy, 1946-48. Mem. Brit. Printing Industries Fedn. (coun. 1966-73, pres. Home Counties Alliance 1970-71), Troupers Light Opera Co., Connestee Falls Golf Assn. (pres. 1996-97), Connestee Falls Property Owners Assn. (bd. dirs. 2001—04). Home: 2637 Connestee Trl Brevard NC 28712

PHILLIPS, FRANK M., orthopedic surgeon; b. Johannesburg, Aug. 10, 1960; arrived in USA, 1987; s. David Montagu and Helen Shirley Phillips; m. Denise Walt, Apr. 25, 1985; children: Gina Laurie, Jason Daniel. MBBCh, U. Witwatersrand, Johannesburg, 1983. Diplomate Am. Bd. Orthopaedic Surgery, lic. Ill., Ohio. Intern in gen. surgery and internal medicine U. Witwatersrand, Johannesburg, 1984, sr. house officer, orthop. surgery, 1985—87; orthop. rsch. fellow U. Chgo. Hosp., 1988—89, orthop. resident, 1989-94, spine surgeon, med. dir. spine ctr., 1995—2003, assoc. prof. surgery; spine fellowship Case Western Res. U. Sch. Medicine, Cleve., 1994—95; orthop. surgeon, Midwest Orthopaedics Rush Univ. Med. Ctr., Chgo., 2003—, dir. sect. minimally invasive spine surgery, co-dir. spine fellowship, prof. orthop. surgery. Contbr. articles to profl. jours., chapters to books. Recipient Charles Herndon Residency Rsch. award, Orthopaedic Rsch. & Edn. Found., 1992, Zimmer Residents Travel award, Am. Orthopaedic Assn., 1994; named one of Chgo. Top Doctors, Chgo. Mag., 2006. Mem.: Am. Orthopaedic Assn., Mid-Am. Orthopaedic Assn., Ill. Orthopaedic Soc., Cervical Spine Rsch. Soc., Internat. Soc. Study of Lumbar Spine, Orthopaedic Rsch. Soc., No. Am. Spine Soc., Am. Acad. Orthopaedic Surgeons. Office: Rush Univ Med Ctr Midwest Orthopaedics 1725 W Harrison St Ste 1063 Chicago IL 60612-3841 Office Phone: 312-243-2422.*

PHILLIPS, FREDERICK FALLEY, architect; b. Evanston, Ill., June 18, 1946; s. David Cook and Katharine Edith (Falley) P.; m. Gay Fraker, 1983 (div. 1993); m. Linda Gardner, 2002; children: Daniel Gardner, Alice Katharine. BA, Lake Forest Coll., 1969; MArch, U. Pa., 1973. Registered architect, Ill., Wis. Intern Harry Weese & Assocs., 1974, 75; architect pvt. practice, Chgo., 1976-81; pres. Frederick Phillips and Assocs., Chgo., 1981—; adj. prof. Ill. Inst. Tech., 2008. Bd. dirs. Landmarks Preservation Coun., 1981-85, Chgo. Acad. Sci., 1988-97, Friends of Ceuros de Escazu, Costa Rica, 1992-95, Project Rush Chgo., 2001--; mem. aux. bd. Chgo. Architecture Found., 1975-89. Recipient award Townhouse for Logan Sq. Competition, AIA and Econ. Redevel. Corp. Logan Sq., 1980, Gold medal award Willow St. Houses, Ill. Ind. Masonry Coun., 1981, Silver award for pvt. residence, 1989, Gold medal award pvt. residence, 1994, Three Record Houses awards Archtl. Record, 1990, 95, award 2d Compact House Design Competition, 1990, award of exellence for pvt. residence AIA/Nat. Concrete Masonry Assn., 1992, 98, award pvt. residence Am. Wood Coun., 1993, Honorable mention-Best in Am. Living award Profl. Builders Mag., 1995, Builder's Choice award pvt. residence, Builder Mag., 1996, Jury's Choice award pvt. residence Chgo. Athenaeum, 1996, 2001, Am. Architecture award Chgo. Athenaeum, 2001, Grand award Residential Architecture Mag., 2003, award Custom Builder Mag., 2003, award Am. Inst. Steel Construction, 2004, Excellence Housing Design award Homebuilder Assn. Greater Chgo., 2007. Fellow AIA (chmn. task group mfg. housing Nat. Com. Design 1994-96, mem. awards task group 1998-01, chmn. 2000-01, Disting. Bldg. award for Willow St. Houses, Chgo. chpt. 1982, for Pinewood Farm 1983, for Pvt. Residences 1990, 92, 98, for Tower House, 2001, for Sawyer Studio, 2008, Housing Com. award 2006, 08); mem. Chgo. Archtl. Club, Racquet Club (bd. govs. 1983-89), Arts Club, Cliff Dwellers Club (bd. govs. 1985-88). Office: Frederick Phillips & Assocs 1456 N Dayton St Ste 200 Chicago IL 60642

PHILLIPS, GARY STEPHEN, lawyer; b. Far Rockaway, NY, June 26, 1957; s. Lawrence and Ilene (Kaufman) P.; m. Debbie J. Kanner, Mar. 27, 1983; children: Joshua Charles, Allison Ilyse. BA with high honors, U. Fla., 1978, JD with honors, 1981. Bar: Fla. 1982, U.S. Dist. Ct. (so. dist.) Fla. 1982, U.S. Ct. Appeals (11th cir.) 1982, U.S. Supreme Ct. 1986. With Sparber, Shevin, Shapo & Heilbronner, Miami, Fla., 1981-87; pvt. practice law Miami, 1987-90; with Buchanan Ingersoll P.C., Miami, 1990-95, Phillips, Eisinger & Brown, P.A., Hollywood, Fla., 1996—2005, Phillips, Cantor & Berlowitz, 2006. Contbr. editor U. Fla. Law Rev., 1980-81. Named one of Leading Fla. Attys.-Comml. Litig., Best of the Bar, South Fla. Bus. Jour., 2003, Top Lawyers, South Fla. Legal Guide, 2003—09, States Legal Leaders, Fla. Legal Elite, 2005—09, Fla. Super Lawyers, 2006—09, 2007, 2009; finalist Daily Bus. Reviews Most Effective Lawyers, 2008. Mem.: ABA, Broward County Bar Assn., North Dade Bar Assn. (treas. 1992), Dade County Bar Assn., Fla. Bar Assn. (litig., real property, probate and trust law sects.), Am. Judicature Soc., Omicron Delta Epsilon, B'nai B'rith, Omicron Delta Kappa, Phi Beta Kappa. Democrat. Jewish. Office: 4000 Hollywood Blvd Ste 375 Hollywood FL 33021-6782

PHILLIPS, GARY WILSON, physicist; b. Golden City, Mo., June 11, 1940; s. Phillip Pemberton and Teresa Colleen (Wilson) P.; m. Virginia Louise, July 20, 1963; children: Carol Tracy, Julie Michelle, Brian Scott. BS, MIT, 1962; PhD, U. Md., 1967. Rsch. assoc. U. Wash., Seattle, 1966-69; rsch. scientist assoc. U. Tex., Austin, 1969-71; scientist Teledyne Isotopes, Westwood, N.J., 1971-73; rsch. physicist U.S. Naval Rsch. Lab., Washington, 1973-84, supr. rsch. physicist, 1985—. Contbr. articles to profl. jours. Vol. Springfield (Va.) Youth Club, 1976-88, coach, 1982; vol. West Springfield Little League, 1981-84; leader Webelos Scouts, 1981. Mem. Am. Phys. Soc., Sigma Xi, Sigma Phi Sigma. Avocations: skiing, swimming, bridge. Office: Naval Rsch Lab 4555 Overlook Ave SW Washington DC 20375-0001

PHILLIPS, GENE DANIEL, language educator; b. Springfield, Ohio, Mar. 3, 1935; s. Ira Granville and Johanna Catherine (Davoran) P. BA, Loyola U., 1957, MA, 1959; Licentiate in Theology, Bellarmine Sch. Theology, 1965; PhD in English, Fordham U., 1970. From asst. prof. to assoc. prof. English dept. Loyola U., 1970-81, prof. English dept., 1981—. Author: (books) Fiction, Film, and Faulkner, 1988, Conrad and Cinema, 1995, Exiles in Hollywood: Major European Directors in America, 1998, Creatures of Darkness: Raymond Chandler and Film Noir, 2000, Godfather: Francis Ford Coppola, 2004, Beyond the Epic: The Life and Films of David Lean, 2006. Fiction and Film grantee Am. Philos. Soc., 1974. Mem. MLA, Lit./Film Soc. Office: Loyola U English Dept 6525 N Sheridan Rd Chicago IL 60626

PHILLIPS, GERALD BAER, internal medicine scientist, educator; b. Bethlehem, Pa., Mar. 20, 1925; s. Abel H. and Cecilia (Blum) P.; m. Maria Bonzi Lewis, July 15, 1970; children: Abigail, Elizabeth. AB, Princeton U., 1946; MD, Harvard U., 1948. Diplomate Am. Bd. Internal Medicine. Intern Presbyn. Hosp., NYC, 1948-50; rsch. fellow Thorndike Meml. Lab., Med. Sch. Harvard U., Boston, 1950-53; vis. fellow biochemistry Columbia U. Coll. Physicians and Surgeons, NYC, 1954-56, from assoc. in medicine to assoc. prof., 1956-73, prof., 1973—. Sr. attending physician St. Lukes-Roosevelt Hosp.; attending physician NY-Presbyn. Hosp. Sr. asst. surgeon USPHS, 1952-54. Mem.: Am. Soc. for Biochemistry and Molecular Biology, Am. Soc. for Clin. Investigation, Alpha Omega Alpha. Home: 196 E 75th St New York NY 10021-3257 Office: 1000 10th Ave New York NY 10019-1147 E-mail: gbp1@columbia.edu. *I attribute any success I may have had to heredity and luck.*

PHILLIPS, GORDON LEIGH, II, oncologist; s. Alan and Bess Long; m. Donna Reece; children: Drew, Madeline. MD, Okla. U. Sch. Medicine, 1971. Internal med. physician U. NC Sch. Medicine, Chapel Hill, 1972—74; clin. fellow Wash. U. Sch. Medicine, St. Louis, 1974—75, rsch. fellow, 1975—77, instr. medicine, 1977—78, asst. prof. of medicine & radiation ontology, 1978—84; assoc. prof. medicine U. Brit. Columbia, Vancouve, Canada, 1984—89, prof. medicine, 1989—94, U. Ky. Coll. Medicine, Ky., 1994—2002, James P. Wilmot Cancer Ctr, Rochester, NY, 2002, prof. ontology, 2004, dir. leukemia blood & marrow transplant program. Recipient Physiology award, U. Okla. Sch. Medicine, 1972, Oustanding Resident awards, U. NC Sch. Medicine, 1974, Jr. Faculty award, Am. Cancer Soc., 1978—80, Bringing Clin. award, Vancouver Gen. Hosp. Academic Awards, 1989; grant, U. Brit. Columbia Health Care Rsch. Found., 1987—88, U. Brit. Columbia Faculty Med. Rsch. Com., 1988—89, Brit. Columbia Health Care Rsch. Found., 1984—86, 1990—91, Nat. Cancer Inst. Can., 1988—90, 1989—99, 1998, grants, 1992—95, grant, Health & Welfare Can., 1988—89, Nat. Inst. Health, 1998, ACP fellowship, Am. Soc. Internal Medicine, 1999. Office: James P Wilmot Cancer Ctr SMH 601 Elmwood Ave Box 704 Rochester NY 14642 Office Fax: 585-276-0350.

PHILLIPS, HAROLD JOHN, III, protective services official, consultant; b. Rochester, NY, Jan. 13, 1949; s. Harold John Jr. Phillips; m. Georgann Faulkner, Jan. 8, 1983; children: Tamara Lee, Sherri Ann Streb, Harold John IV, Nicole Marie, Ashley Dawn. Cert. fire protection tech., Monroe CC, Rochester, NY, 1989. Fire officer Ridge Rd. Fire Dist., Rochester, NY, 1968—2000, fire chief, exec. fire officer, 2000—. Pres. Pub. Safety Mgmt. Cons. Group, Rochester, 1990—. Mem.: Nat. Fire Protection Assn., Nat. Soc. Exec. Fire Officers, Internat. Assn. Fire Chiefs, NY State Assn. Fire Chiefs (com. chmn. 1985—), Greece C. of C. Home: 104 Pearson Ln Rochester NY 14612 Office: Ridge Road Fire Dist 1299 Long Pond Rd Rochester NY 14626 Office Fax: 585-227-4040; Home Fax: 585-225-0815. Personal E-mail: bphillips@publicsafetymngt.com. Business E-Mail: hphillips@rrfd.org.

PHILLIPS, HARVEY G., musician, performing arts educator; b. Aurora, Mo., Dec. 2, 1929; s. Jesse E. and Lottie A. (Chapman) P.; m. Carol A. Dorvel, Feb. 22, 1954; children: Jesse E., Harvey G., Thomas A. Student, U. Mo., 1947-48, Juilliard Sch. Music, 1950-54, Manhattan Sch. Music, 1956-58; MusD (hon.), New England Conservatory of Mu, 1971; HHD (hon.), U. Mo., Columbia, 1987. Founder, v.p. Mentor Music, Inc., NYC, 1958—79; v.p. Wilder Music, Inc., NYC, 1964-77, Magellan Music, Inc., NYC, 1971—, Peaslee Music Inc., 1971—; established faculty position Aspen Sch. Music, summer 1962, U. Wis., summer 1963, Hartt Sch. Music, Hartford, Conn., 1962-64, Mannes Sch. Music, NYC, 1964-65; exec. v.p. Orch. USA, NYC, 1962-65; exec. v.p., pers. mgr., tubist Symphony of the Air N.Y.C., 1957-66; v.p. Brass Artists, Inc., NYC, 1964—; adminstrv. asst. to Julius Bloom, Rutgers U., New Brunswick, NJ, 1966-67; v.p. fin. affairs New Eng. Conservatory of Music, Boston, 1967-71; mem. faculty Sch. Music, Ind. U., Bloomington, 1971-94, disting. prof. music, trustee, 1979, disting. prof. emeritus, 1994. Adv. bd. Am. Brass Chamber Music, Inc., 1971—; chmn. bd. Summit Brass/Keystone Brass Inst., 1985—92, Rafael Mendez Brass Inst., 1993—; cons. Margun Music, Inc., 1977—; bd. dirs. Summit Brass. Brass coach Festival at Sandpoint, Idaho, 1986-94; mem. faculty Joven Orch., Spain, 1987-94, Festival Casal Orch., San Juan, P.R., 1964-76; dir. 1st Internat. Tuba Symposium Workshop, Ind. U., 1973, Brass-Wind Music Studios, Carnegie Hall, N.Y.C., 1961-67; tubist, King Bros. Circus Band, 1947, Ringling Bros. & Barnum & Bailey Circus Band, 1948-50, N.Y.C. Ballet Orch., 1951-71, N.Y.C. Opera Orch., 1951-62, Voice of Firestone Orch., 1951-53, Sauter-Finegan Orch., 1952-53, Band of Am., 1952-54, NBC Opera Orch., 1956-65, Bell Tel. Hour Orch., 1956-66, Goldman Band, 1957-62; founding mem., tubist N.Y. Brass Quintet, 1954-67; condr., co-prodr. Burke-Phillips All Star Concert Band, 1960-62; co-founder, tubist Matteson-Phillips Tubajazz Consort, 1976—; founding mem. TubaShop Quartet, 1996—; rec. artist Crest Records, 1958-78—; originator Octubafest, TubaChristmas, Tubasantas, Tubajazz, TubaEaster, Tubacompany, Summertubafest; exec. editor Instrumentalist mag., 1986-96, bd. advisors, 1996—. Founder, pres. Harvey Phillips Found., Inc., N.Y.C., 1977—; bd. dirs. Mid-Am. Festival of the Arts, 1982-90, Bloomington Area Arts Coun., 1983-90; judge 1st Internt. tuba competition of CIEM Internat. Competition for Musical Performers, Geneva, 1991. Served with U.S. Army Field Band, 1955-56. Recipient Disting. Svc. to Music award Kappa Kappa Psi, 1978, Cmty. Svc. award City of Bloomington, 1978, Nat. Assn. Jazz Educators award, 1977, 78, Nat. Music Conf. award, 1977, T.U.B.A. award, 1978, MI Hummel The Tuba Player award, 1990, Disting. Achievement award Ednl. Press Assn. Am., 1991, Mentor Ideal award Assn. Concert Bands, 1994, Lifetime Achievement award United Music Instruments, 1995, Sudler award medal of the Order of Merit Sousa Found., 1995, Summit Brass Outstanding Svc. and Support Internat. Brassfest, 1995, Orpheus award Phi Mu Alpha Sinfonia, 1997, Ind. U. President's medal, 2008; elected to Acad. Wind and Percussion Arts Nat. Band Assn., 1995; recipient Edwin Franko Goldman citation Am. Bandmasters Assn., 1996, Devel. of Mus. Artistry and Opportunities for Future Generations award Colonial Euphonium Tuba Inst., 1998, Lifetime Achievement award Rafael Mendez Brass Inst., 1998, Platinum Piston Lifetime Achievement award, U. Ga., 1999; Legion of Hon., Goldman Meml. Band, 2002; Harvey Phillips Day proclaimed New England Conservatory Music, 1971, Harvey Phillips Day proclaimed Marionville, Mo. Bicentennial, 1976, Harvey Phillips Weekend Gov. of Mo., 1982; named hon. mem. U.S. Army Band Pershings Own, 1984, Highest Pres.'s award, Ind. U., 2008; named to Am. Classical Music Hall of Fame, 2007-08. Mem. Am. Fedn. Musicians, Tubists Universal Brotherhood Assn. (bd. advs. 1973—, pres. 1984-87, hon.), Hoagy Carmichael Jazz Soc. (founder, acting pres. 1983—), Tau Beta Sigma, Phi Mu Alpha Sinfonia (Orpheus award 1997), Kappa Gamma Psi. Home and Office: Tubaranch 4769 S Harrell Rd Bloomington IN 47401-9028 Office: Sch of Music Ind U Bloomington IN 47405 Office Phone: 812-824-8833. Business E-Mail: philliph@indiana.edu. *The role of a performer and teacher is to give, to share skills and knowledge. My primary goal in life is to create new opportunities in the music profession, to develop, expand, and preserve the music arts.*

PHILLIPS, HOLLY L., internist, medical reporter; b. Jan. 19, 1971; BA cum laude in English Lit., Williams Coll.; MD, Columbia U., 2000. Resident Lenox Hill Hosp., NYC, pvt. practice, tchr. Dept. Internal Medicine; medical reporter WCBS-TV, 2007—. Contbr., medical expert NBC News, ABC News, CNN, MSNBC, CNBC, Fox News. Contbr. (health columns) Vogue, Town and Country, Cosmo, Gotham; contbr. articles to med. jours. Vol. Park Ave. Women's Shelter. Office: Lenox Hill Hosp 120 E 87th St #P20A New York NY 10128*

PHILLIPS, HOWARD WILLIAM, investment banker; b. NYC, May 16, 1930; s. Louis and Helen (Klein) P.; children: Jan Davis, Richard Louis; m. Carol Napack, June 9, 1985. BA, Dartmouth Coll., Hanover, NH, 1951, MBA, 1952; JD, Harvard U., Cambridge, Mass., 1957. Bar: NY 1957. Assoc. Cahill, Gordon, Reindel & Ohl, NYC, 1957-64; v.p., gen. counsel McCall Corp., NYC, 1964-68, sr. v.p., 1968-69; ptnr. Oppenheimer & Co., NYC, 1969-81; chmn. Holmes, Phillips & Co., NYC, 1981-83; dir. corp. fin. D.H. Blair Investment Banking Corp., 1983-95. Bd. dirs. Pioneer Behavioral Health, Boston; pres. Asolo Theatre Co., Sarasota, Fla., 2004-06. Served to lt. (j.g.) USNR, 1952-54. Mem. Easthampton Tennis Club (NY), Longboat Key Club (Sarasota), Sara Bay Country Club (Sarasota). Home: Box 2047 3 Cove Hollow Farm Rd East Hampton NY 11937 Office: 500 S Palm Ave PHT Sarasota FL 34236 Office Phone: 941-365-1995.

PHILLIPS, JAMES CHARLES, physicist, researcher; b. New Orleans, Mar. 9, 1933; s. William D. and Juanita (Hahn) P.; m. Joanna Vandenberg, Mar. 1, 1996. BA, U. Chgo., 1952, BS, 1953, MS, 1955, PhD, 1956. Mem. tech. staff Bell Labs., 1956-58; NSF fellow U. Calif. at Berkeley, 1958-59, Cambridge (Eng.) U., 1959-60; faculty U. Chgo., 1960-68, prof. physics, 1965-68; mem. tech. staff Bell Labs., 1968-96; cons. Bell Labs., Lucent Tech., 1996—. Sloan fellow, 1962-66; Guggenheim fellow, 1967. Fellow Am. Phys. Soc. (Buckley prize 1972), Minerals, Metals and Materials Soc. (William Hume-Rothery award 1992); mem. NAS. Home: 204 Springfield Ave Summit NJ 07901-3909

PHILLIPS, JAMES DICKSON, JR., retired federal judge; b. Scotland County, NC, Sept. 23, 1922; s. James Dickson and Helen (Shepherd) Phillips; m. Jean Duff Nunalee, July 16, 1960; children: Evelyn, James Dickson III, Elizabeth Duff, Ida Wills. BS cum laude, Davidson Coll., 1943; JD, U. N.C., 1948. Bar: N.C. 1948. Asst. dir. Inst. Govt., Chapel Hill, NC, 1948—49; ptnr. Phillips & McCoy, Laurinburg, NC, 1949—55, Sanford, Phillips, McCoy & Weaver, Fayetteville, NC, 1955—60; from asst. prof. to prof. law U. N.C., 1960—78, dean Sch. Law, 1964—74; judge US Ct. Appeals (4th Cir.), 1978—94, sr. judge, 1994—. Vice-chmn. N.C. Cts. Commn.; chmn. N.C. Bd. Ethics, 1977—78. With US Army, 1943—46. Decorated Bronze Arrowhead, Bronze Star, Purple Heart; recipient John J. Parker Meml. award, Thomas Jefferson award, Disting. Alumnus award, U. N.C., 1993. Mem.: Am. Law Inst. Democrat. Presbyterian.

PHILLIPS, JAMES EDGAR, lawyer; b. NYC, Aug. 30, 1949; s. Jack Louis Phillips and Jacqueline (Kasper) Ehrman; children: Zachary J., Mark H. BA, Boston U., 1971; JD, Case Western Reserve U., 1975. Bar: Ohio 1975, US Supreme Ct. 1977, US Dist. Ct. (so. dist.) 1978, US Ct. Appeals (6th cir.) 1981, US Dist. Ct. (no. dist.) 1982, US Ct. Appeals (7th cir.) 2001. Asst. prosecutor Franklin County Prosecutor Office, Columbus, Ohio, 1975-77, sr. asst. prosecutor, 1977-79; assoc. Vorys, Sater, Seymour & Pease, Columbus, 1979-84, ptnr., 1984—; spl. prosecutor State of Ohio, 1993—. Gen. counsel Nat. Fraternal Order of Police, Washington, 1987-2002, Conrail Police #1, US Postal Police #2; mem. Bd. Profl. Law Enforcement Certification; mem. Wong Sun Soc., 1997—; adj. prof. Ohio State U. Moritz Sch. Law, 2005—. Author: Civil Recovery in Ohio, 1986, Collective Bargaining in the Pub. Sector, 1988; editor Bar Briefs; contbr. articles Jours., 1987-89. Pres. bd. dir. Ohio Ctr. for Law-Related Edn., 1985—95; bd. dirs. Schottenstein Stores Corp., 2002—, Alvis House, 2005—06. Fellow Ohio Bar Found., Columbus Bar Found., Ohio Bar Assn. (chmn. com. law-related edn. 1982-86), Columbus Bar Assn. (bd. govs. 2008-), Sixth Cir. Jud. Conf. (life); Ohio Assn. Criminal Defense Lawyers (bd. dirs., treas.). Avocations: travel, photography. Office: Vorys Sater Seymour & Pease PO Box 1008 52 E Gay St Columbus OH 43216-1008 Office Phone: 614-464-5610. Business E-Mail: phillips@vorys.com.

PHILLIPS, JAMES HAROLD, retired lawyer; b. Dec. 18, 1934; s. Frank Carroll and Mabel Lorraine (James) Phillips; m. Jean Keir Woodruff, Oct. 2, 1959 (dec.); children: Susan, John(dec.), Sara, Jamie; m. Patricia Kay Elder Densford, Dec. 28, 2007. BSEE, Rose-Hulman Inst. Tech., 1960; JD, George Washington U., 1967. Bar: Ariz. 68, U.S. Dist. Ct. Ariz. 68, U.S. Patent Office 68, U.S. Supreme Ct. 72, U.S. Ct. Customs & Patent Appeals 74, Tex. 80, U.S. Ct. Appeals (fed. cir.) 82. Patent atty. GE, 1967—68; ptnr. Drummond, Cahill & Phillips, Phoenix, 1968—73; asst. patent counsel NCR Corp., Dayton, Ohio, 1973—76; sr. profl. atty. Sun Co. Inc., Dallas, 1976—84; ptnr. Cates & Phillips, Phoenix, 1984—88; asst. patent counsel Bull HN Info. Sys., Phoenix, 1988—95; patent cons. Bull NH Info. Sys., Phoenix, 2000—05; counsel Squire, Sanders and Dempsey, Phoenix, 1995—2000, ret., 2000. Author: Paderewski Discovers America, 2006; contbr. articles to profl. jours. Charter mem. Phoenix Symphony Coun.; pres. AMICA-Tex. chpt. With USN, 1952—55. Mem.: Tex. Bar Assn., Ariz. Bar Assn. (chmn. patent, trademark and copyright sect. 1985—86). Personal E-mail: speedyjim@cox.net.

PHILLIPS, JANET COLLEEN, retired educational association administrator, editor; b. Pittsfield, Ill., Apr. 29, 1933; d. Roy Lynn and Catherine Amelia (Wills) Barker; m. David Lee Phillips, Feb 7, 1954; children— Clay Cullen, Sean Vincent. BS, U. Ill, 1954. Reporter Quincy (Ill.) Herald Whig, 1951, 52, soc. editor, 1953; editorial asst. Pub. Info. Office U. Ill.-Urbana, 1953-54, asst. editor libr., 1954-61; asst. editor Assn. for Libr. and Info. Sci. Edn., State College, Pa., 1960-61, mng. editor, 1961-89, exec. sec., 1970-89; adminstrv. dir. Interlibr. Delivery

Svc. of Pa., 1990-99; ret. Mem. Palmer Mus. Arts, State Coll. Cmty. Theatre, Mt. Nittany Med. Ctr. Aux. Mem. Assn. Libr. and Info. Sci. Edn., Embroiderer's Guild Am., Pa. State Blue Golf Course Club, Univ. Women's Club (Pa. State), Ctr. Hills Country Club, Am. Wine Soc., Osher Lifelong Learning Inst., Delta Zeta. Presbyterian. Avocations: travel, golf, sewing, needlecraft. Address: 471 Park Ln State College PA 16803-3208 E-mail: janph2@aol.com.

PHILLIPS, JOHN EDWARD, zoologist, educator; b. Montréal, Que., Can., Dec. 20, 1934; s. William Charles and Violet Mildred (Lewis) P.; m. Eleanor Mae Richardson, Sept. 8, 1956; children: Heather Anne, Jayne Elizabeth, Jonathan David, Catherine Melinda, Wendy Susannah. BSc with honors, Dalhousie U., Halifax, NS, 1956, MSc, 1957; PhD, Cambridge U., Eng., 1961. Asst. prof. Dalhousie U., Halifax, N.S., 1960-64; assoc. prof. U. B.C., Vancouver, Canada, 1964-71, prof., 1971—, head dept. zoology, 1991-96. Vis. rschr. Cambridge (Eng.) U., 1972, 76, 81; chair grant selection com. Nat. Rsch. Coun. Can., Ottawa, Ont., 1969-71; mem. coun. Nat. Sci. and Engring. Rsch. Coun., Ottawa, 1983-87. Mem. editorial bd.: Can. Jour. Zoology, 1971-75, Am. Jour. Physiology, 1978-93, Jour. Experimental Biology, 1981-85, Am. Zool., 1996-01; contbr. articles to profl. jours. Mem. grant selection com. Can. Cystic Fibrosis Found., Toronto, 1989-91; active Vancouver Bach Choir. Named to James chair St. Francis Xavier U., Antigonish, N.S., 1993; recipient Killam Rsch. prize U. B.C. Fellow Royal Soc. Can.; mem. Can. Soc. Zoologists (sec. 1972-76, v.p. 1976-78, pres. 1979, Fry medal 2000), Am. Soc. Zoologists (exec. 1983-85, chair divsn. comp. physiol. biochemistry 1983-85). Avocations: music, singing. Home: 12908 22 B Ave White Rock BC Canada V4A 6Z3 Home Phone: 604-538-0527. Personal E-mail: jephillips@telus.net.

PHILLIPS, JOHN L., astronaut; b. Fort Belvoir, Va., Apr. 15, 1951; m. Laura Jean Doell; 2 children. BS in Math. and Russian, U.S. Naval Acad., Annapolis, Md., 1972; MS in Aero. Systems, U. W. Fla., 1974; MS in Geophysics and Space Physics, UCLA, 1984, PhD in Geophysics and Space Physics, 1987. Commd. ensign USN, Annapolis, 1972; advanced through grades to Capt. USNR; Navy Corsair pilot USN, Lemoor, Calif., 1975—76, resigned, 1982; postgrad studies UCLA, 1982—89; Oppenheimer fellow Los Alamos Nat. Lab., N.Mex., 1987—89, rschr., 1989—93; prin. investigator Solar Wind Plasma Experiment aboard Ulysses Spacecraft, 1993—96; navy reservist, as A-7 pilot, 1982—2002; ret. as Capt. USNR, 2002; astronaut NASA, Houston, 1996—; ascent/entry flight engr. STS-100 Endeavour, 2001; flight engr., NASA sci. officer Expedition 11, 2005; mission specialist STS-119 Discovery Mission, 2009. Contbr. scientific papers on plasma environs. of sun, earth, other planets, comets etc, 1992. Recipient NASA Space medal, 2000, Disting. Performance award, Los Alamos Nat. Lab., 1996. Avocations: exercise, hiking, kayaking, skiing. Office: Astronauts Office NASA Johnson Space Ctr 2102 NASA Parkway Houston TX 77058*

PHILLIPS, JOHN P., neurologist, educator; s. John C. and Jean G. Phillips; m. Jan K. Amelang; children: Michael G., Marisa S. MD, Madison, Wis., 1986. Assoc. prof. neurology U. N.Mex, Albuquerque, 1998—; med. dir. Mind Rsch. Network, Albuquerque, 2006—. Mem. Firefly Children's Network, Washington, 2002—07. Med. Rsch. grant, NIH, 2002—05. Mem.: Am. Soc. Neurorehabilitation, Child Neurology Soc., Am. Acad. Cerebral Palsy and Devel. Medicine (Subcom. Rsch. awards 2000—08). Achievements include research in cerebral palsy, brain development, neuroimaging. Office: Univ N Mex Neurology MSC 10 5620 1 University New Mexico Albuquerque NM 87131 Business E-Mail: jpphillips@salud.unm.edu.

PHILLIPS, JOHN P(AUL), retired neurosurgeon; b. Danville, Ark., Oct. 14, 1932; s. Brewer William Ashley and Wave Audrey (Page) P.; m. June Helen Dunbar, Dec. 14, 1963; children: Todd Eustace, Timothy John Colin, Tyler William Ashley. AB cum laude, Hendrix Coll., 1953; MD, U. Tenn., 1956. Diplomate Am. Bd. Neurol. Surgeons. Intern Charity Hosp. La., New Orleans, 1957; resident surgery U. Tenn. Hosps., 1958; resident neurol. surgery U. Tenn. Med. Units, 1958-62; practice medicine, specializing in neurol. surgery Salinas, Calif., 1962-93; ret., 1993. Chief of staff, chief of surgery Salinas Valley Meml. Hosp.; mem. staffs Community Hosp. Monterey Peninsula, U. Calif. Hosp., San Francisco; asst. clin. prof. U. Calif., 1962—. Commd. Ky. col. Mem. AMA, ACS, Internat. Coll. Surgery, Harvey Cushing Soc., Congress Neurol. Surgery, Western Neurosurg. Assn., San Francisco Neurol. Soc., Pan Pacific Surg. Assn., Stanford U. Faculty Club (emeritus), Alpha Omega Alpha, Phi Chi, Alpha Chi.

PHILLIPS, JOHN RICHARD, engineering educator; b. Albany, Calif., Jan. 30, 1934; s. Eric Lester and Adele Catherine (Rengel) P.; m. Joan Elizabeth Soyster, Mar. 23, 1957; children: Elizabeth Huntley, Sarah Rengel, Catherine Hale. BS, U. Calif., Berkeley, 1956; M in Engring., Yale U., 1958, PhD in Engring., 1960. Registered profl. engr., Calif. Chem. engr. Stanford Rsch. Inst., Menlo Park, Calif., 1960; rsch. engr. Chevron Rsch. Co., Richmond, Calif., 1962-66; mem. faculty Harvey Mudd Coll., Claremont, Calif., 1966—2002, James Howard Kindleberger prof. engring., 1991—2002, prof. engring., 1974—2002, prof. emeritus, 2002—, dir. engring. clinic, 1977-93, chmn. engring. dept., 1993-99. Vis. prof. U. Edinburgh, Scotland, 1975, Cambridge (Eng.) U., 1981, ESIEE, France, 1981, Naval Postgrad. Sch., 1984-85, Calif. Poly. U., San Luis Obispo, 1992, 99, U. Canterbury, New Zealand, 2000, Smith Coll., 2001; vis. scientist So. Calif. Edison Co., 1980; founder Claremont Engring., 1973; cons. in field. Contbr. articles to profl. jours. 1st lt. AUS, 1960-62. Mem. Am. Inst. Chem. Engrs., Am. Soc. Engring. Edn., Sigma Xi, Alpha Delta Phi, Tau Beta Pi. Home: 911 W Maryhurst Dr Claremont CA 91711-3320

PHILLIPS, JOHN TAYLOR, judge; b. Greenville, SC, Aug. 20, 1921; s. Walter Dixon and Mattie Sue (Taylor) P.; m. Mary Elizabeth Parrish, Dec. 18, 1954; children: John Allen, Susan, Linda-Lea, Julia. AA, Glenville State Coll., 1952; JD, Mercer U., 1955; LLD, Asbury Coll., 1992. Bar: Ga. 1954, U.S. Supreme Ct. 1969. Mem. Ho. of Reps. State of Ga., Atlanta, 1959-62, Senate, 1962-64. With USMC, 1942-51. Methodist. Home: 1735 Winston Dr Macon GA 31206-3241 Office: State Ct Bibb County PO Box 6242 Macon GA 31208 Home Phone: 478-781-1888; Office Phone: 478-621-6676.

PHILLIPS, JOSEPH BRANTLEY, JR., lawyer; b. Greenville, SC, Dec. 5, 1931; BS in Bus. Adminstrn., U. S.C., 1954, JD, 1955. Bar: SC 1955. Assoc. Leatherwood, Walker, Todd & Mann, Greenville, 1958-63, ptnr., 1963—2006; ret. Chmn. bd. deacons Presbyn. Ch., 1970-71, pres. Men of Ch., 1968-69, chmn. Christian Svc. Ctr., 1972-73; bd. dirs. Greenville Urban Ministry, 1978. Mem. ABA, S.C. Bar Assn., Greenville Bar Assn., Greenville Young Lawyers Club (pres. 1961-62), Lawyers Pilots Bar Assn., Kiwanis (pres. 1973). Clubs: Greenville Country (pres. 1977). Home: 207 Butler Springs Rd Greenville SC 29615-2261 Office: PO Box 87 Greenville SC 29602-0087

PHILLIPS, JOSEPH ROBERT, museum director; b. Utica, NY, Mar. 14, 1950; m. Dixie Anne Stedman, 1988. BS in Marine Transp., SUNY Maritime Coll., 1972; MA in History Mus. Studies, SUNY, Cooperstown, 1981; MBA, NH Coll. (now Southern NH U.), 1990. Capt., exec. dir. Hudson River Sloop Clearwater, Poughkeepsie, NY, 1972-75; capt., assoc. project dir. NY Bicentennial Barge, Albany, 1975-76; various project positions Maine Maritime Mus., Bath, 1978-81; various program mgmt. and mktg. positions Bath Iron Works Corp., Shipbuilders, 1982-92; mus. dir. Maine State Mus., Augusta, 1992—. Bd. dirs. Friends of Maine State Mus., 1992—, Maine Archives and Museums, 1996—2002; mem. Maine State Cultural Affairs Coun., 1992—, State House and Capitol Pk. Commn., 1992—, Blaine House Commn., 1994—, Maine-Aomori Sister State Coun., 2001—; exec. com. Maine Ctr. for Arts, 2006—07. Mem.: Brunswick Naval Mus. & Meml. Gardens (bd. dirs. 2009—), Friends of Blaine Ho. (bd. dirs. 2005—). Office: Maine State Mus 83 State House Sta Augusta ME 04333-0083 Office Phone: 207-287-6607. Business E-Mail: joseph.phillips@maine.gov.

PHILLIPS, JOSEPH THEODORE, JR., neurologist, educator; b. Austin, Tex., Sept. 14, 1952; s. Joseph Theodore and Maxine Phillips; m. Janey Benfield, Aug. 24, 1974; children: Lauren Therese, Tara Eileen. BS in Chemistry, U. Tex., Austiin, 1974; MD, U. Tex., Dallas, PhD, 1981. Cert. Am. Bd. Neurology and Psychiatry. Academic faculty mem. U. Tex. Southwestern Med. Ctr., Dallas, 1984—93, clin. prof. neurology, 2008—; med. dir. MS Ctr. Tex. Neurology, Dallas, 1993—. Mem.: Nat. MS Soc., Med. Adv. Bd., Phi Beta Kappa. Achievements include research in clinical trials for new treatments. Avocations: astronomy, archaeology, paleontology. Office: MS Ctr Tex Neurology 6301 Gaston Ste 400 West Dallas TX 75214

PHILLIPS, JOY LAMBERT, lawyer, banker; b. Ft. Bragg, NC, Sept. 25, 1955; d. Jurloew Lambert and Mary Carolyn (Gregory) Trivette; m. Frank Warren Phillips, May 10, 1975. AA, N.E. Miss. Jr. Coll., Booneville, 1974; BA, U. Miss., 1976, JD, 1980. Bar: Miss. 1980. Assoc. Daniel, Coker, Horton & Bell, P.A., Jackson, Miss., 1980-85; sr. v.p., asst. gen. counsel Deposit Guaranty Nat. Bank, Jackson, 1985—98; gen. counsel Hancock Bank, Gulfport, Miss., 1999—. Seminar speaker, 1990-91. Treas., Miss. Opera Guild, Jackson, 1990-92; mentor Miss. Coll. Sch. Law, Jackson, 1989-92. Mem. ABA, Miss. Bar Assn. (pres. 2005-06), Hinds County Bar Assn., Harrison County Bar Assn., Miss. Women Lawyers (pres. 1989-90), Jackson Young Lawyers, Kiwanis (dir. 1991-93, pres. 1966). Avocations: reading, walking, dogs, biking. Home: PO Box 819 Gulfport MS 39502-0819 Office: Hancock Bank One Hancock Plz Gulfport MS 39501 Home Phone: 228-044-6044; Office Phone: 228-563-5755. E-mail: joy_phillips@hancockbank.com.

PHILLIPS, JOYCE A., insurance company executive; MBA, NYU, 1982. Analyst Nissho-Iwai Corp., Tokyo, 1986—90; internat. product mgr. Western Union Fin. Services; various position within Global Consumer Fin. divsn. GE Capital Corp., 1995—99; pres., rep. dir. Citicorp Card Svcs., 1999—2001; pres., CEO Citicorp Diner Club Japan, 2000—01; country bus. mgr. consumer ops., dir. retail bank Citigroup Japan, 2001—05; head Internat. Retail Banking Citigroup Global Consumer Group, 2005—07; pres., COO, Am. Life Ins. Co. (ALICO) Am. Internat. Group (AIG), Del., 2007—. Named one of 25 Most Powerful Women in Banking, US Banker, 2006, Top 20 Nonbank Women in Fin., 2007, 2008. Office: ALICO One ALICO Plz 600 King St Wilmington DE 19899*

PHILLIPS, JULIA MAE, physicist; b. Freeport, Ill., Aug. 17, 1954; d. Spencer Kleckner and Marjorie Ann (Figi) Phillips. BS, Coll. William and Mary, Williamsburg, Va., 1976; PhD, Yale U., New Haven, Conn., 1981. Mem. tech. staff AT&T Bell Labs., Murray Hill, 1981-88, supr. thin film rsch. group, 1988-95; dept. mgr. materials process computation and modeling dept. Sandia Nat. Labs., Albuquerque, 1995-2000, dep. dir. materials and process scis. ctr., 2000-01, dir. phys. and chem. sci. ctr. & nano sci. ctr., 2001—. Program mgr. Consortium Superconducting Elecs., 1989-92; mem. com. on condensed matter and materials physics NRC, 1996-99, mem. solid state scis. com., 1998-2001, mem. nat. materials adv. bd., 1999-2004, chair, 2002-2004, mem. com. on materials rsch. for def.-after-next, 1999-2002; vice chair Solid State Scis. com., 1999-2001, mem. bd. on physics and astronomy, 2000-06; mem. adv. com. math. and phys. scis. NSF, 2000-03. Editor: Heteroepitaxy on Silicon Technology, 1987, Epitaxial Oxide Thin Films and Heterostructures, 1994; prin. editor Jour. Materials Rsch., 1990-2005; mem. editl. bd. Applied Physics Letters and Jour. Applied Physics, 1992-94, Applied Physics Revs., 1998-2001; contbr. articles to profl. jours. Recipient Horizon award, U.S. Dept. Labor Women's Bur., 2002, Wilbur Cross medal, Yale U., 2004. Fellow Am. Acad. Arts and Scis., Am. Phys. Soc. (exec. com. divsn. materials physics 1997-2000, exec. com. condensed matter physics, 2005—09), Am. Assn. Advance Sci. (coun. 2003-06, bd. dirs., 2009-); mem. NAE (councillor 2008-), Materials Rsch. Soc. (sec. 1987-89, councillor 1991-93, 2d v.p. 1993, 1st v.p. 1994, pres. 1995), Fedn. Materials Soc. (exec. com. 1997), Sigma Xi, Phi Beta Kappa.

PHILLIPS, JULIEANNE APPLESON, history professor; b. Cleve., Jan. 15, 1952; d. Nick Appleson and Patricia Kepic (Appleson) Zajac; m. William Harold Phillips, July 2, 1977; children: Kristen Ann, Amy Lynn. AA, Cuyahoga C.C., Parma, Ohio, 1987; BA in History, Baldwin-Wallace Coll., Berea, Ohio, 1989; MA in History, Cleve. State U., 1990; PhD in Am. History, Case Western Res. U., 1996. Cert. history secondary edn. Ohio. Grant coord. Dayton-Tchg. Am. History, 2003—05; asst. prof. Urbana U., Ohio, 2005—. Author: (ency.) U.S. Aging Policy Interest Groups Institutional Profiles, (Web project) The History Place, (Web resource) Workshop for Teachers: Celebrating the 150th Anniversary of the Women's Rights Movement 1848-1998, (tchg. resource) Dayton Public Schools Social Studies Instructional Guide, (ency.) Encyclopedia of New England Culture, The Eleanor Roosevelt Encyclopedia, Organizing Black America, African American Women in the United States, The Historical Encyclopedia of World Slavery, Slavery in the US; contbr. articles to numerous profl. jours. Judge Nat. Spelling Bee, Dayton, 2005, Nat. History Day, Cleve, 1986—2005; dir. Women Historians of Western Ohio, Dayton, 2000—05; independent evaluator Fairfield City and Northwest Sch. Dist. Tchg. Am. History Grant Miami U.-Hamilton, Hamilton, Ohio, 2006; moderator, steering com. mem. Buckeye Coun. for History Edn., 2006; panelist numerous profl. confs.; mem. Coord. Coun. Women in History; advisor, Urbana U. chpt. Phi Alpha Theta, 2005—. Recipient Elizabeth S. Magee Doctoral fellowship, Case Western Res. U., 1990—95, All Am. scholarship, US Achievement Acad., 1989, award, Nat. Collegiate Edn., 1989; fellow, Ohio Bd. of Regents, 1989—91. Mem.: Ohio Acad. of History (assoc.), Nat. Coun. for History Edn. (assoc.), Orgn. of Am. Historians (assoc.), Am. Hist. Assn. (assoc.), Order Lance History Club, Urbana U. (advisor 2005—). Office: Urbana Univ 579 College Way Urbana OH 43078 Business E-Mail: jphillips@urbana.edu.

PHILLIPS, JULIEN L., theater educator; d. Iver C. and Florence Brill Lind; m. Jeffrey Hill Phillips, Aug. 10, 1968; children: Katherine Norelle, Alison Elizabeth. BA, U. Minn., 1967; PhD, 1977; MA, U. Ill., Urbana, 1968. Instr. theatre arts U. Minn., 1971—76; cons. oral presentation U. Minn. Law Sch., 1984—91; prof. speech & theatre arts North Hennepin CC, Bklyn. Park, 1990—. Contbr. articles to profl. publs. Recipient Disting. Svc. award, Pillsbury United Cmtys. Mem.: Pillsbury, United Cmtys., Minn. (life).

PHILLIPS, KAREN DIANE, surgeon; b. Dayton, Ohio, Jan. 11, 1968; d. Charles Joseph and Theresa Olwen Muscato; m. Ian Daniel Same, Sept. 24, 1999; children: Luke Daniel, Mason Charles. BS in Chemistry, Mary Washington U., Fredericksburg, Va., 1990; MD, Med. U. Ohio, Toledo, 1995. Diplomate Am. Bd. Surgery, 2001. Chief resident U. SC, Columbia, 1995—2000; intern, resident U. SC, Richland Meml. Hosp. and the Dorn Vets. Adminstrn. Hosp., 1996—2000; gen. surgeon Alamogordo Surg. Assocs., Alamogordo, N.Mex., 2001—04, So. Surg. Group, Lexington, SC, 2004—. Fellow: ACS; mem.: AMA, Soc. S.C. Surgeons, So. Med. Assn., Am. Soc. Breast Surgeons. Office: So Surg Group 2728 Sunset Blvd West Columbia SC 29169 Home: 600 N Overlook Dr Alexandria VA 22305-1220 Home Fax: 803-251-3382. Personal E-mail: kphillipsmd@hotmail.com.

PHILLIPS, KATHARINE ANNE, psychiatrist; b. Bronxville, NY, Apr. 17, 1955; d. Harry Scott and Mary (Bryan) P. AB summa cum laude, Dartmouth Coll., 1977, MD, 1987. Lic. med. doctor. Dep. editor Harvard Rev. of Psychiatry, Belmont, Mass., 1990-94; prof. psychiatry Brown U. Sch. Medicine, Providence, 2003—. Recipient Outstanding Resident award NIMH, 1989;, Outstanding Psychiatrist award for clin. psychiatry Mass. Psychiat. Soc., 1994, one of Best Drs. in America, Nat Edit., 2001-03, 2005-. Mem. AMA, Am. Psychiat. Assn. (disting. fellow, spl. presdl. commendation award 2004), Phi Beta Kappa, Alpha Omega Alpha.

PHILLIPS, KATHLEEN GAY, small business owner; b. Clarkston, Wash., Nov. 7, 1952; d. Cecil Martin Phillips and Nellie Florance Robertson; 1 child, John Cecil Dickeson-Phillips. Student, Lewis and Clark State Coll., Lewiston, Idaho, 1973, student, 1992, Walla Walla C.C., 1990—91; grad., H&R Tax Course, 2003. Cert. notary State of Idaho. Accounts clk. Lewis and Clark State Coll., Lewiston, 1975; co-founder Christina's Creations, Altus, Okla., 1982—, Funmates, Lewiston, 1982; dir. TK Springer, Inc., 1981; asst. mgr. Circle Drive Mobile Home Park, 1982—87. Surveyor Consumer Mail Panel, Palatine, Ill., 2000; restorer Gray Hut Apt. - Hist. Baughman House, Lewiston, 1993—99; rep. Western Modern Jewelry and Jewelry by Kathleen G. Phillips; history cons. Corps. Engrs. at Clarkston. With Medic Alert, 1979—; established Memory Walk & Safe Return, Alzheimer's Assn., 2005; worked with Gov. Kerathoun, Senator Craig, Senator Crapio, House of Rep. Helen Cheenawith, CL Otter. Pvt. US Army, 1991, Gulf War, with USNR. Recipient Oldest Tree award, Pks. and Recreation Bd., 1999. Mem.: Idaho Hist. Soc., Lewiston C. of C., The Planetary Soc., Clan Donald U.S. A., Am. Legion, Order of Ea. Star (life), Pi Beta Lambda. Methodist. Avocations: needlecrafts, painting, archaeology. Home: 718 N 6th Ave # 207 Yakima WA 98902 Home Phone: 509-823-5921. E-mail: johndickeson@msn.com.

PHILLIPS, KEITH WENDALL, minister; b. Portland, Oreg., Oct. 21, 1946; s. Frank Clark and Velma Georgina (Black) P.; m. Mary Katherine Garland, July 16, 1973; children: Joshua, Paul, David. BA, UCLA, 1968; MDiv, Fuller Theology Sem., 1971, D. of Ministries, 1972; LHD (hon.), John Brown U., 1990; LHD (hon.), Sterling Coll., 2002. Dir. Youth For Christ Clubs, LA, 1965-71; pres. World Impact, LA, 1971—. Commencement speaker Tabor Coll., 1969, 91, John Brown U., 1990, Sterling Coll., 2002. Author: Everybody's Afraid in the Ghetto, 1973, They Dare to Love the Ghetto, 1975, The Making of a Disciple, 1981, No Quick Fix, 1985, Out of Ashes, 1996. Chmn. L.A. Mayor's Prayer Breakfast Com., 1985—; bd. dirs. Christian Cmty. Devel. Assn., 1992—; founder/coord. Crowns of Beauty Confs.; spkr. Promise Keeper. Named Disting. Staley lectr., 1969. Mem. Evangelistic Com. of Newark (pres. 1976—), World Impact of Can. (pres. 1978—), The Oaks (pres. 1985—), Faith Works (pres. 1987—) Baptist. Office: World Impact 2001 S Vermont Ave Los Angeles CA 90007-1279 *Our knowledge of God's Word outruns our obedience. The challenge for Christians is to live what we know.*

PHILLIPS, KENNETH EDWARD, history educator, writer; b. Elamville, Ala., Dec. 29, 1947; s. Counce A. and Alma Ruth Phillips; m. Veva Elaine Roberts, May 4, 1973; 1 child, Haley Leigh. AA, George C. Wallace State Cmty. Coll., 1978; BSc, Troy State U., 1979; MA, Auburn U., 1982, PhD, 1999. History instr. Gordon Jr. Coll., Barnesville, Ga., 1986—87, Martin Meth. Coll., Pulaski, Tenn., 1988—89; archivist hist. U.S. Army Missile Command, Redstone Arsenal, Ala., 1989—90; history instr. Auburn U., Ala., 1990—91, George C. Wallace State Cmty. Coll., Dothan, Ala., 1991—. Contbg. author: Encyclopedia of Alabama. Councilman Ariton City Coun., 1976—78. E5 USN, 1968—71. Recipient Malcolm C. McMillan History award, Auburn U., 1981, Colonel Dames award, 1984, Robert L. Partin award, 1986. Mem.: Ala. Hist. Assn., Southern Hist. Assn., Agrl. Hist. Assn. Democrat. Meth. Avocations: reading, writing, films. Office: Wallace Cmty Coll Wallace Hall 102 1141 Wallace Dr Dothan AL 36303

PHILLIPS, KEVIN PRICE, political historian, writer; b. NYC, Nov. 30, 1940; s. William Edward and Dorothy Virginia (Price) Phillips; m. Martha Eleanor Henderson, Sept. 28, 1968; children: Andrew, Alexander. AB, Colgate U., 1961; postgrad., U. Edinburgh, Scotland, 1959-60; JD, Harvard U., 1964. Bar: NY 1965, DC 1965. Adminstrv. asst. to Congressman Paul Fino, 1964—68; spl. asst. atty. gen. US US Dept. Justice, 1969—70; newspaper columnist syndicated King Features, 1970—83; contbg. columnist LA Times, Wall St. Jour.; nat. elections commentator CBS TV News, 1984—96. Spl. asst. to campaign mgr. Nixon for Pres. Com., 1968; pres. Am. Polit. Rsch. Corp., 1971—98; commentator Nat. Pub. Radio, 1984—2004; spkr. in field. Author: The Emerging Republican Majority, 1969, Electoral Reform and Voter Participation, 1975, Mediacracy, 1975, Post-Conservative America, 1982, The Business Case for a National Industrial Strategy, 1984, The Politics of Rich and Poor, 1990, Boiling Point: Democrats, Republicans and the Decline of Middle-Class Prosperity, 1993, Arrogant Capital: Washington, Wall Street and The Frustration of American Politics, 1994, The Cousins' Wars: Religion, Politics and the Triumph of Anglo-America, 1999, Wealth and Democracy: A Political History of the American Rich, 2002, American Dynasty: Aristocracy, Fortune, and the Politics of Deceit in the House of Bush, 2004, American Theocracy: The Peril and Politics of Radical Religion, Oil, and Borrowed Money in the 21st Century, 2006, Bad Money: Reckless Finance, Failed Politics, and the Global Crisis of American Capitalism, 2008; editor, pub. The American Political Report, 1971—98. Home: PO Box 1542 Litchfield CT 06759-1542

PHILLIPS, LARRY EDWARD, lawyer; b. Pitts., July 5, 1942; s. Jack F. and Jean H. (Houghtelin) P.; m. Karla Ann Hennings, June 5, 1976; 1 child, Andrew H.; 1 stepchild, John W. Dean IV. BA, Hamilton Coll., Clinton, NY, 1964; JD, U. Mich., 1967. Bar: Pa. 1967, Fla. 2004, US Dist. Ct. (we. dist.) Pa. 1967, US Tax Ct. 1969. Assoc. Buchanan Ingersoll & Rooney PC, Pitts., 1967—73, shareholder, 1973. Mem. ABA (sect. taxation, com. on corp. tax and sect. real property, probate and trust law), Am. Coll. Tax Counsel, Pa. Bar Assn., Fla. Bar, Tax Mgmt. Inc. (adv. bd.), Pitts. Tax Club, Allegheny County Bar Assn., Collier County Bar Assn., Duquesne Club. Republican. Presbyterian. Office: Buchanan Ingersoll & Rooney PC One Oxford Ctr 301 Grant St Fl 20 Pittsburgh PA 15219-1410 Office Phone: 412-562-8846. Business E-Mail: larry.phillips@bipc.com.

PHILLIPS, LAUGHLIN, retired museum director, editor; b. Washington, Oct. 20, 1924; s. Duncan and Marjorie Grant (Acker) P.; m. Elizabeth Hood, 1956 (div. 1975); children: Duncan Vance, Elizabeth Laughlin; m. Jennifer Stats Cafritz, 1975. Student, Yale U., 1942-43; MA, U. Chgo., 1949. Fgn. svc. officer, 1949—64, Hanoi, Vietnam, 1950—53, Tehran, Iran, 1957—59; co-founder Washingtonian mag., 1965, editor, 1965-74, editor-in-chief, 1974-79; pres. Washington Mag., Inc., 1965-79; dir. Phillips Collection, 1972-92, chmn. bd., 1967—2002, chmn. emeritus, 2002—. Trustee Nat. Com. for an Effective Congress, 1966—, MacDowell Colony, 1977-79; bd. dirs. UN Assn. Am., 1997-2001. With AUS, 1943-46, PTO. Decorated Bronze Star; comendador Orden de Mayo al Mérito (Argentina); chevalier de l'Ordre de la Couronne (Belgium), knight's cross 1st class Order of Danebrog (Denmark); officier Arts et Lettres (France). Mem.: Rolling Rock Club (Ligonier, Pa.), Met. Club (Washington), Cosmos Club (Washington). Personal E-mail: locphil@aol.com.

PHILLIPS, LEO HAROLD, JR., lawyer; b. Jan. 10, 1945; s. Leo Harold and Martha C. (Oberg) P.; m. Patricia Margaret Halcomb, Sept. 3, 1983. BA summa cum laude, Hillsdale Coll., 1967; MA, U. Mich., 1968, JD cum laude, 1973; LLM magna cum laude, Free U. of Brussels, 1974. Bar: Mich. 1974, NY 1975, US Supreme Ct. 1977, DC 1979. Fgn. lectr. Pusan Nat. U., Korea, 1969-70; assoc. Alexander & Green, NYC, 1974-77; counsel Overseas Pvt. Investment Corp., Washington, 1977-80, sr. counsel, 1980-82, asst. gen. counsel, 1982-85, Manor Care, Inc., Gaithersburg, Md., 1985-91, asst. sec., 1988-99, assoc. gen. counsel, 1991-99, v.p., 1996-99. Vol. Peace Corps, Pusan, Korea, 1968-71; mem. program for sr. mgrs. in govt. Harvard U., Cambridge, Mass., 1982. Contbr. articles to legal jours. Chmn. legal affairs com. Essex Condominium Assn., Washington, 1979-81; mem. fin. com., bd. trustees Miami City Ballet, 2001-06; deacon Chevy Chase Presbyn. Ch., Washington, 1984-87, moderator, 1985-87, supt. ch. sch., elder, trustee, 1987-90, pres., 1988-90, mem. nominating com., 1995-96; trustee, sec.-treas., Independence Grove, 2006-08; trustee Scholastic Achievement Found. Palm Beach County, 2007-, pres. 2008-; pres. men's club, Delray Beach Presbyn. Ch., Fla., 2007-08, Nominating com. 2007-. Recipient Alumni Achievement award Hillsdale Coll., 1980; Meritorious Honor award Overseas Pvt. Investment Corp., 1981, Superior Achievement award, 1984. Mem. ABA (internat. fin. transactions com., vice-chmn. com. internat. ins. Law), Am. Soc. Internat. Law (Jessup Internat. Law moot ct. judge semi-final rounds 1978-83, chair corp. counsel com. 1993-97), Internat. Law Assn. (Am. br.; com. sec. 1982), DC Bar, NY State Bar Assn., Royal Asiatic Soc. (Korea br.), State Bar Mich., Washington Fgn. Law Soc. (sec.-treas. 1980-81, bd. dirs., program coord. 1981-82, v.p. 1982-83, pres.-elect 1983-84, pres. 1984-85, chmn. nominating com. 1986, 88), Washington Internat. Trade Assn. (bd. dirs. 1984-87), Assn. Bar City NY, Hillsdale Coll. Alumni Assn. (co-chmn. Washington area 1977-90), Univ. Club (NYC), Rotary (Delray Beach treas. 2003-2004, pres.-elect 2004-05, pres. 2005-06, asst. dist. gov. 2006-08, dist. gov. elect 2008-09, dist. gov. 2009-), Beach Property Owners Assn.(trustee 2006—, v.p. 2008-), Drug Abuse Found. Palm Beach County (trustee 2007-), Mae Volen Sr. Ctr. (dir. 2009-).

PHILLIPS, LINDA, museum director; BA in Art Hist., Middlebury Coll., 1971—75; Doctoral Prog. in Art Hist., CUNY Grad. Ctr., 1975—80. Helena Rubinstein fellow Whitney Mus. Am. Art, NYC, 1976, sr. fellow, 1977, mgr. downtown br. NYC, 1977—80, assoc. cur. br. museums, 1980—83, assoc. cur., 1985—88, cur., 1988—98; asst. dir. exhibitions Phila. Coll. Art, 1977; Henry Luce III dir. New Mus. Contemporary Art, NYC, 1999—. Panelist, juror Visual Arts panel, Nat. Endowment for Arts, 1985, Overview panel, Nat. Endowment for Arts, 1986, Art in Pub. Places panel, 1987, Mass. Coun. Arts Review Com., 1987, NYC Pub. Art Commn., 1987, Brandeis U. Creative Arts Awards, 1989, Frederick R. Weisman Awards in Arts, 1989, Fulbright Fellowship Review Com., 1989—93, Nat. Assn. for Advancement in Arts, 1999, Sao Paolo Bieñal, 1996; bd. mem. White Columns, 1980—84, Lower Manhattan Cultural Coun., 1982—88, Fabric Workshop Adv. Bd., 1985—, Gallery Assn. NY State, 1985—90, L.A.C.E. Adv. Bd., 1998—, Frederick Kiesler Found., 1999—; cons. Peat Marwick, Chase Manhattan Bank, FIAR Found., Milan. Office: New Mus Contemporary Art 235 Bowery New York NY 10002 Office Phone: 212-219-1222.*

PHILLIPS, LISA, museum director; b. NY, 1955; d. Warren H. and Barbara Phillips; m. Leon Falk, Mar. 1995. Grad. cum laude, Middlebury Coll., Vt. Curatorial asst. to curator Whitney Mus. Am. Art, NYC, 1977—99; dir. New Mus. Contemporary Art, NYC, 1999—. Author: The American Century: Art and Culture 1950-2000, 1999. Named an The 100 Most Influential Women in NYC Bus., Crain's NY Bus., 2007. Mailing: New Mus Contemporary Art 235 Bowery New York NY 10002 Office Phone: 212-219-1222.

PHILLIPS, M. IAN, physiologist, educator; b. London, July 30, 1938; arrived in US, 1967; s. Robert Leonard and Winifred Maud (Wheatley) Phillips; m. Blanca Aguiar, Nov. 29, 2004; m. Kate Phillips (div.). BSc with honors, U. Exeter, Eng., 1962; PhD, U. Birmingham, Eng., 1967, DSc, 1985. Vis. asst. prof. U. Mich., Ann Arbor, 1967—69; fellow Calif. Inst. Tech., Pasadena, 1969—70; prof. U. Iowa, Iowa City, 1970—80; chmn., prof. U. Fla., Gainesville, 1980—2003; v.p. rsch. U. South Fla., Tampa, 2003—06; Norris prof. Keck Grad. Inst., Claremont, Calif., 2006—. Program dir. neuro. NSF, Washington, 1990; chmn. cardiovascular study sect. NIH, Washington, 1992—94. Editor: Regulatory Peptides, 1990—2006, Gene Therapy, 2002, Antisense Therapeutics 2d edit., 2005; co-author: Principles of Hormone & Behavior, 2005; author: (plays) Rembrandt, 11 books, 300 papers. Bd. dirs. Moffit Cancer Ctr., Tampa, Fla., 2003—06. Recipient Lucian award, McGill U., Can., 1989, Frank Annunzio award, Christopher Columbus Fedn., 2002, Merit award, NIH, 1995—2006; named Norris Prof. Life Scis., 2007. Fellow: Am. Heart Assn. Achievements include discovery of brain peptides in hypertension; research in gene therapy for hypertension, stem cell rsch. on heart failure. Office: Keck Grad Inst 535 Watson Dr Claremont CA 91711 Home: 616 McKenna St Claremont CA 91711 Home Phone: 727-507-1190; Office Phone: 909-607-7487.

PHILLIPS, MARION GRUMMAN, civic volunteer, writer; b. NYC, Feb. 11, 1922; d. Leroy Randle and Rose Marion (Werther) Grumman; m. Ellis Laurimore Phillips, Jr., June 13, 1942; children: Valerie Rose (Mrs. Adrian Parsegian), Elise Marion (Mrs. Edward E. Watts III), Ellis Laurimore III, Kathryn Noel Phillips, Cynthia Louise (Mrs. Charles Prosser). Student, Mt. Holyoke Coll., 1940-42; BA, Adelphi U., 1981. Civic vol. Mary C. Wheeler Sch., 1964-68, Historic Ithaca, Inc., 1972-76, Ellis L. Phillips Found., 1960-91. Bd. dirs. North Shore Jr. League, 1960-61, 64-65, 68-69, Family Svc. Assn. Nassau County, 1963-69, Homemaker Svc. Assn. Nassau County, 1959, 61. Author: (light verse) A Foot in the Door, 1965, The Whale-Going, Going, Gone, 1977, Doctors Make Me Sick (So I Cured Myself of Arthritis), 1979; editor: (with Valerie Phillips Parsegian) Richard and Rhoda, Letters from the Civil War, 1982, Wooden Shoes the story of my Grandfather's Grandfather (F.M. Sisson), 1990, Irish Eyes, family hist. of McTarsneys and Sissons, 1990, The Log Chapel, A History of the Congregational Community Church, Rockwood, Maine, 1999; editor Jr. League Shore Lines, 1960-61, The Werthers in America-Four Generations and their Descendants, 1987; A B-Tour of Britain, 1986; contbr. articles on fund raising to mags. Mem. New Eng. Hist. Geneal. Soc., N.Y. Geneal. Biographical Soc., Hannah Adams Womens Club, PEO Sisterhood, Medfield Garden Club. Congregationalist. Mailing: Apt 374 20 Longwood Dr Westwood MA 02090-1149

PHILLIPS, MARY GUTIERREZ, biology professor; d. Tomas Victor and Josephine Gutierrez; m. Lance Phillips. BA, Occidental Coll., LA, 1974; MA, U. Calif. Santa Barbara, 1981. Cert. in life secondary tchg. State of Calif. Assoc. prof. biology Tulsa CC, Okla., 1981—. Mem. fundraising Lymphoma and Leukemia Found., NYC, 2006—. Recipient Student Assn. Outstanding Tchr. award, Student Body - Tulsa CC, 1987, Tchg. Excellence award, Tulsa CC, 2001, Poetry award, 2007; grant, NSF, 2006—. Mem.: Okla. Acad. Sci., AAAS, NSTA, Nat. Assn. Biology Tchrs. Office: Tulsa CC 10300 E 81st St Tulsa OK 74133 Business E-Mail: mphillip@tulsacc.edu.

PHILLIPS, MELANNIE, medical educator; d. Scott and Norma Bohms; m. Nathan Phillips, Oct. 14, 2000. BS, Mich. State U., East Lansing, 2000; M in Public Health, Davenport U. Lic. vet. technician State Lic. Mich., 2000. Adj. prof. Davenport U., Caro, Mich., 2006—, tutor, 2005—; patient adminstrv. svcs. Marlette Regional Hosp., 2005—.

PHILLIPS, OLIVER, tropical forest ecologist, researcher; BA in Natural Scis., U. Cambridge, Eng., 1987, MA in Natural Scis., 1991; PhD in Population Biology, Washington U., St. Louis, 1993. NERC Rsch. fellow U. Leeds, England, 1996-99, lectr., 1999—2003, reader in tropical ecology, 2003—06, prof. tropical ecology, 2006—. Rsch. assoc. Mo. Bot. Garden, 1997—. Recipient Edmund H. Fulling award Soc. Econ. Botany, 1992. Mem. Soc. for Econ. Botany (mem. coun. 1996-99), Assn. Trop. Biology, Brit. Ecol. Soc. (Founder's Prize, 2004). Office: U Leeds Geography Sch Earth & Biosphere Inst Leeds LS2 9JT England Office Phone: 44 113 343 6832. Business E-Mail: o.phillips@leeds.ac.uk.

PHILLIPS, PAMELA KIM, lawyer; b. San Diego, Feb. 23, 1958; d. John Gerald and Nancy Kimiko (Tabuchi) Phillips; m. R. Richard Zanghetti, Sept. 16, 1989. BA cum laude, The Am. U., 1978; JD, Georgetown U., 1982. Bar: N.Y. 1983, U.S. Dist. Ct. (so. dist.) N.Y. 1983, Fla. 1994, U.S. Dist. Ct. (mid. dist.) Fla. 1994, US Supreme Ct., 2007. Assoc. Curtis, Mallet-Prevost, Colt & Mosle, NYC, 1982-84, Dewey & Leboeuf (formerly LeBoeuf, Lamb, Greene & MacRae), NYC, 1984—90, ptnr., 1991—. Mng. editor The Tax Lawyer, Georgetown U. Law Sch., Washington, 1980-81. Mem. coun. The Fresh Air Fund, 1991-94, Youth Leadership Jacksonville, 1999—; bd. dirs. Jacksonville Zool. Soc., Inc., 1996—, sec., 1997—; pres. First Coast Venture Capital Group, Inc., 1996-98; bd. trustees Beaches Episcopal Sch., 2004-, chair 2007-09. Am. Univ. scholar, Washington, 1976-78. Mem. ABA, Bar Assn. City N.Y. (sec. young lawyers com. 1987-89, chmn. 1989-91, second century com. 1990-93, banking law com. 1991-94), Jacksonville Bar Assn., River Club. Democrat. Roman Catholic. Home: 109 Carriage Lamp Way Ponte Vedra Beach FL 32082-1903 Office: Dewey & LeBoeuf 1301 Ave Americas New York NY 10019-5369 Office Phone: 212-259-8087. Business E-Mail: phillips@dl.com.

PHILLIPS, PAUL EVERARD, medical educator, rheumatologist; b. London, Feb. 2, 1937; came to U.S., 1940; s. Ralph Francis and Barbara Alison (Reeves) P.; m. Charlotte Wood, 1962 (div. 1981); children: Christopher, Diane, Hugh; m. Sharon Patricia Sullivan, Mar. 10, 1984; 1 child, Margaret Helen. AB, Princeton U., 1958; MD, Albany Med. Coll., 1962. Diplomate Am. Bd. Internal Medicine, Am. Bd. Rheumatology. Resident in Medicine Roosevelt Hosp., NYC, 1962-63; assoc. in Virology NIH, Bethesda, Md., 1963-65; resident in Medicine Bellevue Hosp., NYC, 1965-67; fellow in rheumatology Columbia-Presbyn. Hosp., NYC, 1967-69, assoc. in medicine, 1969-70; from asst. to assoc. prof. medicine Cornell U. Med. Coll., NYC, 1970-81; prof. medicine SUNY Upstate Med. U., Syracuse, 1981—; also prof. pediatrics assoc. prof. rehab. medicine SUNY, Syracuse, 1981—, chief divsn. rheumatology, 1981-2001. Attending physician Univ. Hosp., Crouse-Irving Meml. Hosp., Syracuse, 1981—; cons. VA Med. Ctr., Syracuse, 1981—. Editor Clin. and. Exptl. Rheumatology, 1982-2000; contbr. 70 articles to profl. jours. Trustee Everson Mus., 1998—. Recipient 40 rsch. grants various sources, N.Y.C., Syracuse, 1967—. Fellow Am. Coll. Physicians, Am. Coll. Rheumatology, Dewitt Fish and Game Club (pres. 1993-95). Avocation: shooting sports. Office: SUNY Upstate Med U 750 E Adams St Syracuse NY 13210-2306 Home Phone: 315-682-6607; Office Phone: 315-464-4194. Business E-Mail: phillipp@upstate.edu.

PHILLIPS, PEGGIE L., medical educator; d. Travis Virgil and Elaine Root Phillips. MA, San Francisco State U., 1986. Lectr. San Francisco State U., 1976—82; instr. Indian Valley Coll., Novato, Calif., 1980—83, City Coll. San Francisco, 1981—, Calif. Coll. Podiatric Medicine, San Francisco, 1979—80; prof. Life Chiropractic Coll. West, Hayward, Calif., 1983—. Rsch. asst. Calif. Acad. Sci., San Francisco, 1976—81.

PHILLIPS, PETER CHARLES BONEST, economist, educator, researcher; b. Weymouth, Dorset, Eng., Mar. 23, 1948; came to U.S., 1980; s. Charles Bonest and Gladys Eileen (Lade) P.; m. Emily Dowdell Birdling, Feb. 10, 1971 (div. 1980); 1 child, Daniel Lade; m. Deborah Jane Blood, June 13, 1981; children: Justin Bonest, Lara Kimberley. BA, Auckland U., New Zealand, 1969, MA, 1971; PhD, London U., 1974; MA (hon.), Yale U., 1979. Teaching fellow U. Auckland, 1969-70, jr. lectr., 1970-71; lectr. in econs. U. Essex, Colchester, Eng., 1972-76; prof. econs. U. Birmingham, Eng., 1976-79, Yale U., New Haven, Conn., 1979-85, Stanley Resor prof. econs., 1985-89, Sterling prof. econs., 1989—; Alumni disting. prof. econs. U. Auckland, 1991—; pres. Predicta Software Inc., Madison, Conn., 1994—. Vis. scholar Ecole Polytechnique, Paris, 1977; univ. vis. prof. Monash U., Melbourne, Australia, 1986; vis. prof. Inst. Advanced Studes, Vienna, Austria, 1989; disting. visitor London Sch. Econs., 1989. Editor Econometric Theory jour., 1985; joint editor Asia Pacific Economic Review, 1995-2000; contbr. over 230 articles, book revs., notes to profl. jours. Recipient award for promotion of sci. Japan Soc., 1983, New Zealand medal Sci. and Tech., 1998, Plura Scripsit, 1997, Plurima Scripsit Econometric Theory award, 2000, Nzier Qantas Economist of Yr., 2000; Commonwealth Grants Com. scholar, Eng., 1971, Guggenheim fellow, N.Y., 1984-85. Fellow Am. Acad. Arts & Scis., Royal Soc. New Zealand (hon.), Econometric Soc., Jour. Econometrics, Am. Statis. Soc., Inst. Math. Stats., British Acad., 2008, Modsim Soc. (Biennial Medal, 2003). Avocations: running, building, poetry, reading, native plant restoration. Office: Cowles Found PO Box 208281 New Haven CT 06520-8281 Home: PO Box 208281 New Haven CT 06520-8281 E-mail: peter.phillips@yale.edu.

PHILLIPS, PHIL E., professor, academic administrator; m. Joan Phillips; children: Kelly, Mark, Paul. BS in Art Edn., Appalachian State U., Boone, NC, 1971; MA in Art Edn., U. Ill., Champaign-Urbana, 1973, EdD in Art Edn., 1979. Pres. East Carolina U., Greenville, NC, 2006—. Co-investigator Eisenhower Math. and Sci. Network, 1996, 1998—99. Contbr. articles to profl. jours. Mem.: Nat. Art Edn. Assn., NC Art Edn. Assn. (bd. dirs. 2000—05, Higher Edn. Educator of Yr. 2002). Office: Sch Art and Design East Carolina U Greenville NC 27858

PHILLIPS, RICHARD, cargo ship captain; m. Andrea Coggio; children: Mariah, Danny. Grad., Mass. Maritime Acad., Buzzards Bay, 1979. Captain MV Maersk Alabama, 2009—. Named one of The World's Most Influential People, TIME mag., 2009. Achievements include being internationally recognized for his bravery after his crew and cargo ship were hijacked by armed Somali pirates on April 8, 2009; to save his crew of 20 sailors, Captain Phillips agreed to be held hostage by the pirates and was rescued by US Navy Seals on April 12, 2009; the MV Maersk Alabama cargo ship was the first US flagged vessel hijacked by pirates since about 1815 during the Second Barbary War. Office: c/o Maersk Line Ltd One Commercial Pl 20th Fl Norfolk VA 23510*

PHILLIPS, RICHARD A., retired literature and language educator; b. Chester, Pa., June 6, 1949; s. Albert Phillips and Florence (Dunn) P. BS, Cheyney U., Pa., 1971. Cert. tchr., Del. Tchr. Colonial Sch. Dist., New Castle, Del., 1971-87, 1991—2005, HighCroft Sch., Williamstown, Mass., 1986; exec. dir. Sylvan Learning Ctrs., Wilmington, Del., 1987-90; ret., 2005. Cmty. rels. vol. PAWS for People, Elkton, Md., bd. mem. NEA, Del. State Edn. Assn. Retired (bd. dirs. 2006—, chmn. publicity 2000—06), New Castle County Edn. Assn. (bd. dir. 1991—2005, v.p. 1998—2005), Colonial Edn. Assn. (exec. com. 1971—84), Nat. Coun. Tchrs. English.

PHILLIPS, ROBERT, engineering educator, researcher; BS, U. Minn., 1986; PhD, Wash. U., 1989. Clark Millikan vis. asst. prof. Caltech, 1997—2000, prof. mech. engring. and applied physics, 2000—. Contbr. articles to profl. jour. Recipient Pioneer award, NIH, 2004. Achievements include research in exploring nanoscale mechanics in biol. systems; the way DNA binding proteins that control gene expression expert mechanical forces on DNA resulting in the formation of loops. Office: Calif Inst Tech 159 Broad MC 128-95 Office 221 Steele 1200 E Calif Blvd Pasadena CA 91125 Office Phone: 626-395-3374. Office Fax: 626-583-4963. Business E-Mail: phillips@aero.caltech.edu.

PHILLIPS, ROBERT F., economics professor, department chairman; BA, U. Calif., Berkeley, 1978; PhD, Columbia U., NYC, 1985. Asst. prof. economics George Washington U., Washington, 1985—91, assoc. prof. economics, 1991—2000, prof. economics, 2000—, chair dept. economics, 2006—. Cons. US Bur. Census, 1985—86, World Bank, 1987, DRI, McGraw-Hill, 1997—98. Contbr. articles to numerous bus. & econ. jours. Mem.: Econometric Soc., Am. Econ. Assn., Omicron Delta Epsilon. Office: George Washington Univ 2115 G St NW Ste 340 Washington DC 20052

PHILLIPS, ROBERT KENNEY, retired english literature and language professor; b. Jacksonville, Fla., Jan. 13, 1945; s. Robert Isadore and Swannanoa Kenney Phillips; m. Sharon Muckenfuss Phillips; children: Anna Lena, Marsha Kathleen Price, Robert Merwan MacKenney. BA, U. SC., Columbia, 1967, MA, 1970; PhD, U. Va., Charlottesville, 1977. Chair, English, fgn. langs. dept. Lander U., Greenwood, SC, 2004—06, emeritus prof., English, 2008—. Jr. co-editor Weevils in the Wheat: Narratives of Virginia Ex-Slaves; contbr. articles to numerous profl. jours. Master Boy Scouts America, Due West, SC, 1998—2001. With USN, 1969—71, Mayport, Fla. Recipient Navy Achievement medal, 1970, Meritorious Unit Citation - Jordanian Crisis, 1971, Disting. Prof. award, Lander Coll., 1980. Mem.: AAUP, Sungian Soc. Scholarly Studies, Internat. Arthurian Soc., Jungian Soc. Scholarly Studies (treas. 2007—), Haw River Assembly, Sierra Club, Meher Baba, Phi Beta Kappa. Democrat. Avocations: gardening, hiking, canoeing, fishing, hunting. Office: Lander Univ English & Fgn Lang Dept 320 Stanley Ave Greenwood SC 29649-2099 Office Phone: 864-388-8265.

PHILLIPS, RONALD FRANK, academic administrator; b. Houston, Nov. 25, 1934; s. Franklin Jackson and Maudie Ethel (Merrill) P.; m. Jamie Jo Bottoms, Apr. 5, 1957 (dec. Sept. 1996); children: Barbara Celeste Phillips Oliveira, Joel Jackson, Phil Edward. BS, Abilene Christian U., 1955; JD, U. Tex., 1965. Bar: Tex. 1965, Calif. 1972. Bldg. contractor Phillips Homes, Abilene, Tex., 1955-56; br. mgr. Phillips Weatherstripping Co., Midland and Austin, Tex., 1957-65; corp. staff atty. McWood Corp., Abilene, 1965-67; sole practice law Abilene, 1967-70; mem. adj. faculty Abilene Christian U., 1967-70; prof. law Pepperdine U., Malibu, Calif., 1970—, dean Sch. Law, 1970-97, dean emeritus, 1997—, vice chancellor, 1995—. Mem. Nat. Conf. Commrs. on Uniform State Laws, 1988—2003. Deacon North A and Tenn. Ch. of Christ, Midland, 1959-62; deacon Highland Ch. of Christ, Abilene, 1965-70; elder Malibu Ch. of Christ, 1978-95; mgr., coach Little League Baseball, Abilene, Huntington Beach and Malibu, 1968-78, 90-95; coach Youth Soccer, Huntington Beach, Westlake Village and Malibu, 1972-80, 85-86, 91. Recipient Alumni citation Abilene Christian U., 1974 Fellow Am. Bar Found. (life); mem. ABA, State Bar Tex., State Bar Calif., Christian Legal Soc., L.A. Bar Assn., Assn. Am. Law Schs. (chmn. sect. on adminstrn. law schs. 1982, com. on cts. 1985-87), Am. Law Inst. Republican. Office: Pepperdine U 24255 Pacific Coast Hwy Malibu CA 90263-4951 Business E-Mail: ronald.phillips@pepperdine.edu.

PHILLIPS, RONALD LEWIS, plant geneticist, educator; b. Huntington County, Ind., Jan. 1, 1940; s. Philemon Lewis and Louise Alpha (Walker) P.; m. Judith Lee Lind, Aug. 19, 1962; children: Brett, Angela. BS in Crop Sci., Purdue U., 1961, MS in Plant Breeding and Genetics, 1963, Doctorate (hon.), 2000; PhD in Genetics, U. Minn., 1966; postgrad., Cornell U., 1966-67. Rsch. and tchg. asst. Purdue U., 1961—62; rsch. asst. U. Minn., St. Paul, 1962—66, rsch. assoc., 1967—68, asst. prof., 1968—72, assoc. prof., 1972—76, prof. genetics and plant breeding, 1976—93, Regents prof., 1993—, McKnight presdl. chair in genomics, 2000—. Vis. prof., Italy, 1981, Canada, 83, China, 86, Japan, 90, Morocco, 96; program dir. Competetive Rsch. Grants Office USDA, Washington, 1979, chief scientist, 1996—98, mem. adv. grant panels, NSF, DOE; chmn. Gordon Conf. on Plant Cell and Tissue Culture, 1985; mem. sci. adv. coun. U. Calif. Plant Gene Expression Ctr., Berkeley, 1986—93, chair, 1992—93; program adv. com. Palm Oil Rsch. Inst. Malaysia, 1992—2001; non-resident fellow Noble Found., 2001—06; sci. adv. bd. Donald Danforth Plant Sci. Ctr., St. Louis, 2000—; sci. liaison officer Internat. Rice Rsch. Inst. USAID, 2000—03, bd. trustees, 2004—, mem. adv. grant panels; dir. Plant Molecular Genetics Inst., 1991—94; trustee Biol. Stain Commn.; mem. Nat. Plant Genetic Resources Bd.; dir. Ctr. Microbial and Plant Genomics U. Minn., 2000—05. Co-editor: Cytogenetics, 1977, Molecular Genetic Modification of Eucaryotes, 1977, Molecular Biology of Plants, 1979, The Plant Seed: Development, Preservation and Germination, 1979, Genetic Improvement of Crops: Emergent Techniques, 1980, DNA-Based Markers in Plants, 1994, 2d edit., 2001; assoc. editor Genetics,

1978—81, Can. Jour. Genetics and Cytology and Genome, 1985—90, mem. editl. bd. Maydica, 1978—, In Vitro Cellular and Devel. Biology, 1988—92, Cell Culture and Somatic Cell Genetics of Plants, 1983—91, Jour. of the Oil Palm, 1994—, Proc. NAS, 1996—98; contbr. chpts. to Maize Beeding and Genetics, 1978, Staining Procedures, 1981, Chromosome Structure and Function, 1987, Corn and Corn Improvement, 1988, Plant Transposable Elements, 1988, Chromosome Engring. in Plants, 1991, Maize Handbook, 1994, sci. articles to profl. jours. Mem. chmn. coun. on ministries, lay leader United Meth. Ch., 1968, dir. Project AgGrad, 1983—; Cub Scout Pack co-chmn. Boy Scouts Am., 1976-77; judge Minn. Regional and State Sci. Fair, 1970-80. Recipient Purdue Agrl. Alumni Achievement award, 1961, Purdue Disting. Agrl. Alumni award, 1993; NSF fellow, 1961; NIH fellow, 1966-67; recipient Northrup King Oustanding Faculty Performance award, 1985, DeKalb Genetics Crop Sci. Disting. Career award, 1997. Fellow: AAAS (program com. 2003—06, chair sect. O), Crop Sci. Soc. Am. (awards com., divsn. chmn., bd. rep. 1988—91, pres.-elect 1998—99, pres. 1999—2000, past pres. 2000—01, Rsch. award 1988), Am. Soc. Agronomy (Caleb-Dorr award); mem.: NAS (chair sect. 62 1999—2002, nominating com. 2002, Wolf Agr. prize 2007), Coun. Sci. Soc. (pres chair 2006), Am. Soc. Agronomy (award student sect.), Genetics Soc. Am., Sigma Xi, Alpha Zeta, Gamma Sigma Delta (award of merit 1994), Gamma Alpha (nat. treas.). Office: U Minn Dpt Agronomy-Plant Genetics Saint Paul MN 55108 Business E-Mail: phill005@umn.edu.

PHILLIPS, RUTH ANN, retired secondary school educator; b. Greensboro, NC, Nov. 26, 1948; d. Paul Frank and Agnes Elizabeth (Butler) P. AB, Elon U., 1971. Cert. health and phys. edn. tchr., N.C. Tchr. health and phys. edn., chmn. dept. Sellars-Gunn Jr. H.S., Burlington, NC, 1972-81, coach tennis, basketball, softball, 1973-81; tchr., coach varsity softball, chmn. health and phys. edn. Walter M. Williams Sr. H.S., Burlington, 1981—2001, ret., 2001. Participant Summer Nat. Sr. Olympic Games, 2007—. Named Tchr. of Yr., Sellars-Gunn Jr. High Sch., 1975, Secondary Phys. Edn. Tchr. of Yr., N.C., 1998, Eight Who Make A Difference, Homer Thompson Meml., 2001. Mem.: Why Nots Sr. Softball Team (NC Sr. Games Gold medalist 2005—08), State Employees Assn. NC, N.C. Assn. Educators, Sr. Games. Democrat. Methodist. Avocations: racquetball, softball. Home: 2027 S Mebane St Burlington NC 27215-7617

PHILLIPS, RUTHANNE, special education administrator; d. George and Margaret Ann Mitro. BA in Psychology, cum laude, Wittenberg U., Springfield, Ohio, 1979; MS in Spl. Edn., Calif. Luth. U., Thousand Oaks, 1983; MA in Ednl. Leadership, Calif. State U., LA, 2004. Multiple subjects tchg. credential Calif., learning handicapped specialist tchg. credential Calif., severely handicapped specialist tchg. credential Calif., resource specialist cert. of competence Calif., adminstrv. svcs. credential Calif., computers in edn. cert. Calif. Luth. Coll., child mental health specialist Calif. Luth. Coll. and Camarillo State Hosp., specially designed acad. instrn. in English Calif. Grad. student asst. Camarillo State Hosp. and Devel. Ctr., Calif., 1979—80, tchg. asst., 1980—81, spl. edn. tchr., 1981—96, Calif. Dept. Youth Authority at Fred C. Nelles Sch., Whittier, 1996—97, LA County Office Edn. Divsn. Spl. Edn. at High Desert Prin.'s Adminstrv. Unit, Palmdale, 1999—2000; spl. edn. resource specialist tchr. LA County Office Edn. Divsn. Juvenile Cts. and Cmty. Schs. at Pacific Lodge Boys Home, Woodland Hills, 1997—99; spl. edn. program specialist Antelope Valley Spl. Edn. Local Plan Area, Palmdale, 2000—07; spl. edn. program specialist moderate/severe disabilities Palmdale Sch. Dist., 2007—08, spl. edn. program specialist II moderate/severe disabilities, 2008—. Mem. Calif. Svcs. Tech. Assistance and Tng. Region 11 Coordinating Coun., LA, 2000—07, sec., 2001—02, chairperson, 2002—04; mem. adv. bd. Antelope Valley Family Focus Resource and Empowerment Ctr., Palmdale, 2003—05; mem. Calif. Sys. Pers. Devel. Adv. Coun., Sacramento, 2003—05, Pacific Lodge Sch. Site Coun., Woodland Hills, 1997—99; campus adv. bd. Chapman U., Antelope Valley, Palmdale, 2001—03; bd. dirs. Very Spl. Arts of Calif., Sacramento, 2006—07. Mem. Friends of the Acton-Agua Dulce Libr., Acton, Calif., 2005—, Friends of Acton Park, Calif., 2005—; liturgy coord. St. Mary's Acton-Agua Dulce Mission, Acton, 2002—, historian, 2000—, lector, 2000—; religious edn. tchr. St. Mary's Acton-Aqua Duice Mission, 2001—03; asst. religious edn. coord. St. Mary's Acton-Agua Dulce Mission, Acton, 2004—05; literacy tutor Camarillo, 1992—97, Acton, Palmdale, 2002—08. Recipient Wittenberg Alumni scholarship, Wittenberg U., 1975—79. Mem.: ASCD, CEC, L.A. County Adminstrs. of Spl. Edn., Assn. Calif. Sch. Adminstrs., Antelope Valley Astronomy Club, Psi Chi, Alpha Xi Delta (Zeta chpt. historian 1978—79). Democrat. Roman Catholic. Avocations: scrapbooking, cardmaking, reading, travel, collecting 1st editions by Stephen King and Dean Koontz. Office: Palmdale Sch Dist Spl Edn and Student Svcs 39139 10th St E Palmdale CA 93550

PHILLIPS, SAUL, men's college basketball coach; b. Reedsburg, Wis., Oct. 11, 1972; m. Nicole Phillips; children: Jordan, Charlie. B in Bus. & Psychology, U. Wis., Platteville, 1996. Grad. asst. Wayne State Coll. Wildcats, Nebr., 1996—97; asst. coach Lake Superior State U. Lakers, 1997—99, U. Wis. Milw. Panthers, 1999—2001; dir. ops. U. Wis. Badgers, 2001—04; asst. coach ND State U. Bison, 2004—07, head basketball coach, 2007—. Achievements include coaching the University of North Dakota Bison to a NCAA tournament bid in its first year of Division I eligibility, 2009. Office: ND State U Basketball Bison Sports Arena 1600 N University Dr Fargo ND 58108 Office Phone: 701-231-7805. Business E-Mail: Saul.Phillips@ndsu.edu.*

PHILLIPS, SIDNEY FREDERICK, gastroenterologist, educator; b. Melbourne, Australia, Sept. 4, 1933; s. Clifford and Eileen Frances (Fitch) P.; m. Decima Honora Jones, Mar. 29, 1957; children: Penelope Jane, Nichola Margaret, David Sidney. M.B.BS, U. Melbourne, 1956, MD, 1961. Resident med. officer Royal Melbourne Hosp., 1957-61, asst. sub-dean clin. sch., 1961-62; research asso. Central Middlesex Hosp., London, 1962-63; rsch. assoc. Mayo Clinic, Rochester, Minn., 1963-66, cons. in gastroenterology, 1966-2000; prof. medicine Mayo Med. Sch., 1976-2000, prof. medicine emeritus, 2000—, dir. gastroenterology rsch. unit, 1977-94; program dir. Mayo Gen. Clin. Rsch. Ctr., 1974-87; dir. Mayo Digestive Diseases Core Ctr., 1984-90; Karl F. and Marjory Hasselman prof. rsch., 1994-2000. Editor: Digestive Diseases and Sciences, 1977-82, Gastroenterology International, 1990-95; sr. assoc. editor: Gastroenterology, 1991-96; contbr. chpts. to books, articles to profl. jours. Fellow ACP, Royal Coll. Physicians, Royal Australian Coll. Physicians; mem. Am. Motility Soc. (pres. 1994-96), Am. Soc. Clin. Investigation (emeritus), Gastroenterology Soc. Australia (hon.), Am. Gastroenterology Assn. Assn. Am. Physicians, Brit. Soc. Gastroenterology (hon.). Office: St Mary's Hosp Gastroenterology Unit 200 1st St SW Rochester MN 55905-0001 Home: Dakota on the Park 209 8th St E #411 Saint Paul MN 55101-3389 Personal E-mail: decimasidney@aol.com.

PHILLIPS, STACY D., lawyer; b. NYC, Sept. 5, 1958; d. Gerald F. and Francine Anne (Kantor) Phillips. AB cum laude with high distinction, Dartmouth Coll., 1980; JD, Columbia U., 1983. Cert.: Family Law Specialist, bar: Calif. 1984, US Dist. Ct. Ctrl. and So. Districts Calif., US Ct. Appeals 9th Cir. Law clk. to Hon. Edward Rafeedie US Dist. Ct., LA, 1983-84; assoc. Wyman, Bautzer, Rothman, Kuchel & Silbert, LA, 1984-85, Jaffe & Clemens, Beverly Hills, Calif., 1986—90; founding ptnr. Mannis & Phillips, LA, 1995—2000, Phillips Lerner, Lauzon & Tamra LLP, LA, 2000—. Guest commentator various TV programs including Good Morning America, Hard Copy, Inside Edition; contbr. Divorce Mag., adv. bd.; bd. dirs. Legal Momentum (previously NOW Legal Def. and Edn. Fund); co-chair Calif. Leadership Coun. Author: Divorce: It's All About Control - How To Win the Emotional, Psychological and Legal Wars; co-author: Mother Knows Best-Family Law Practitioners Must Nurture, Not Wield Poison Pens; contbr. articles to profl. jours. Bd. dirs. Vista del Mar Child and Family Services, Levitt & Quinn Family Law Ctr., Bnai Zion Found. Inc.; bd. trustees Alternative Living for the Aging; bd. govs., bd. dirs. Legal Momentum; past chair, bd. dirs. ALA. Recipient Women of Action Award, Israel Cancer Rsch. Fund, 2000, Women of Achievement Award, Bnai Zion Found. Inc., 2001, Women Who Make a Difference Award, LA Bus. Jour., 2001, Patricia McClure Award, Asthma & Allergy Found. Am., 2001, Women of Achievement Award in Family Law and Mediation, Century City C. of C., 2001, 2002, Women to Watch award, Jewish Women Internat., 2005; named one of 50 Most Powerful Women in LA Law, LA Bus. Jour., 1998, Top 20 Attorneys Under 40 Years Old, LA Daily Jour., 1998, Top 50 Women Litigators in Calif., 2003; grantee Policy Study Internship, Dartmouth Coll., 1978. Mem.: ABA (mem. family law sect.), Beverly Hills Bar Assn. (mem. family law sect., mem. alternative dispute resolutions com.), LA Bar Assn. (mem. family law sect.), State Bar Calif. (mem. child custody and visitation com.), National Partnership of Women & Families, Chancery Club of LA. Avocations: cooking, tennis. Office: 2029 Century Park E Ste 1200 Los Angeles CA 90067 Office Phone: 310-277-7117. Business E-Mail: sdpdissoqueen@plljlaw.com.

PHILLIPS, STANLEY DAVIS (DAVE), United States Ambassador to Estonia; b. High Point, NC; Attended, U. N.C., Chapel Hill. CEO Phillips Industries, Inc.; ptnr. Market Square Partnership; sec. commerce State of NC, 1993—97; chmn. NC Econ. Develop. Bd., 1997—2000; bd. mem. NC Dept. Transp.; US amb. to Estonia Tallinn, 2007—. Chmn. Piedmont Triad Partnership, Econ. Develop. Corp. of High Point. Chair World Games of Special Olympics, 1999; bd. mem. Smithsonian Inst., Duke U., Wake Forest U. Med. Ctr. Office: Market Sq Tower High Point NC 27260

PHILLIPS, STEFANIE PANNELL, school system administrator; b. Oakland, Calif., Nov. 5, 1968; d. Steven Alexander and Elaine Ruth Pannell; m. Bryan Kelvin Phillips, July 31, 1993; children: Brandyn, Blayke. BS, U. Calif., Davis, 1992, MBA, 1994; EdD, U. Southern Calif., LA, 2005. Sales assoc. Best Foods, Pleasanton, Calif., 1994—95; mktg. mgr. Wornel Simpson and Assoc., Sacramento, 1995—97; acct. Money Store, Sacramento, 1997—98; analyst Calif. Dept. Fin., Sacramento, 1998—2000; dir. fin. Grant Joint Union HS Dist., Sacramento, 2000—02; asst. supr. Ontario-Montclair Sch. Dist., Ontario, Calif., 2002—06; assoc. supr. Chino Valley Unified Sch. Dist., Calif., 2006—07. Adj. prof. U. Southern Calif., 2004—07, Nat. U., Ontario, 2007, Calif. State Poly., Pomona, 2007; dept. supr. Chino Valley Unified Sch. Dist., 2007—08, Business E-Mail: stefanie_phillips@chino.k12.ca.us.

PHILLIPS, STEPHEN S., lawyer; b. Phila., 1946; BA, Wesleyan U., 1968; JD, Dickinson U., 1971. Bar: Pa. 1971, U.S. Ct. Appeals (3d cir.) 1971, U.S. Supreme Ct. 1980, Tenn. 1998. Sr. ptnr. Pepper Hamilton LLP, Phila., 1979-97; exec. v.p., gen. counsel, sec. Sofamor Danek Group, Inc., Memphis, 1998-99; spl. counsel Medtronic, Inc., 1999. Bd. dirs. Schindler Enterprises, Inc., Franke Holding USA, Inc., eResearch Tech., Inc., Plexus Biomed., Inc. Mem. ABA, Internat. Bar Assn., Pa. Bar Assn., Order of Barristers (pres. 1971-72), Phila. Country Club. Address: 976 Derring Ln Bryn Mawr PA 19010-1749

PHILLIPS, STEVE, electronics executive; arrived in US, 2001; BSc with honors in Electronic Engring., U. Essex, Eng.; postgraduate diploma in Mgmt. Studies, Thames Valley U., Eng. Various leadership positions Thorn EMI, 1984—96; info. tech. dir. European foods divsn. Diageo, 1996—99; v.p. info. tech. to sr. v.p., chief info. officer Gateway, Dublin, 1999—2003, sr. v.p., chief info. officer, 2003—04, Memec, 2004—05, Avnet, Inc., Phoenix, 2005—. Bd. dirs. Ariz. Tech. Coun., 2007—. Named one of Top 100 Chief Info. Officers, eWeek, 2007. Fellow: Instn. Elec. Engrs. Office: Avnet Inc 2211 S 47th St Phoenix AZ 85034-6403 Office Phone: 480-643-2000.

PHILLIPS, STONE (STONE STOCKTON PHILLIPS), newscaster; b. Texas City, Tex., Dec. 2, 1954; m. Debra Phillips; 1 child, Streeter. BA in Philosophy with honors, Yale U., 1977. Past prodr., reporter WXIA-TV, Atlanta; formerly with documentary unit Close-Up ABC News, assignment editor Washington, 1979—81, gen. assignment corr., 1982—86, corr. 20/20, 1986—92; prin. anchor Dateline NBC-TV, NYC, 1992—2007; contbg. corr. MSNBC. Past remedial-reading tchr. Fulton County Juvenile Ct., Atlanta; substitute host Good Morning America, 1986; guest sports anchor World News Sunday, 1986; past substitute anchor NBC Nightly News, Today, Meet the Press. Recipient F. Gordon Brown award for Outstanding Acad. & Athletic Leadership, Yale U., 1976, 3 Nat. Headliner awards for Outstanding Journalism, Overseas Press Club award, Nat. Assn. Black Journalists award, AMA award, Am. Psychol. Assn. award, B'nai B'rith award; named to Scholar Athlete Hall of Fame, Nat. Football Found.; NCAA Post-Grad. scholar.

PHILLIPS, SUSAN DIANE, secondary school educator; b. Shelbyville, Ky., Aug. 28, 1955; d. James William and Catherine Elizabeth (Jones) P. B Music Edn., Ea. Ky. U., 1977; postgrad., U. Ky., 1987; AA Christian Ministry, United Christian Minstry Inst., 2001. Tchr. music Breckinridge County Schs., Hardinsburg, Ky., 1978, Perry County Schs., Hazard, Ky., 1980—83, Music on the Move, Louisville, 1985—86, Cooter R-4 Sch., Mo., 1987—90, Lewis County Schs., Vanceburg, Ky., 1990—. Staff cavalcade of bands Ky. Derby Festival, Louisville, 1984-86 Dir. handbell choirs Simpsonville (Ky.) United Meth. Ch., 1985-86 Named Ky. Col. Gov. Commonwealth Ky., 1979 Mem. NEA, Ky. Educators Assn., Ky. Music Educators Assn., Music Educators Nat. Conf., Internat. Soc. Tech. in Edn. Office: Lewis County Mid Sch Lions Ln Vanceburg KY 41179 E-mail: susan.phillips@lewis.kyschools.us.

PHILLIPS, SUSAN MEREDITH, dean, economist, educator; b. Richmond, Va., Dec. 23, 1944; d. William G. and Nancy (Meredith) Phillips. BA in Math., Agnes Scott Coll., 1967; MS in Fin. and Ins., La. State U., 1971, PhD in Fin. and Economics, 1973. Asst. prof. La. State U., 1973—74, U. Iowa, 1974—78; econ. fellow Directorate of Econ. and Policy Rsch., SEC, 1976—78; assoc. prof. fin. dept. U. Iowa, 1978—83, assoc. v.p. fin. & univ. services, 1979—81; commr. Commodity Futures Trading Commn.; 1981—83, chmn., 1983—87; prof. fin. dept., v.p. fin. and univ. svcs. U. Iowa, Iowa City, 1987—91; bd. govs. Fed. Res. Sys., Washington, 1991—98; dean Sch. of Bus., prof. fin. dept. George Washington U., Washington, 1998—. Trustee Fin. Acctg. Found., Norwalk, 2006—; bd. dirs. Chgo. Bd. Options Exch., Nat. Futures Assn., Kroger Co., State Farm Mutual Auto. Co. Co-author (with J. Richard Zecher): The SEC and the Public Interest; contbr. articles to profl. jours. Fellow Brookings Econ. Policy fellow, 1976—77. Office: George Washington U Sch Bus Ste 660 2201 G St NW Washington DC 20052 Office Phone: 202-994-6380. Business E-Mail: gwsbdean@gwu.edu.*

PHILLIPS, TED RAY, advertising executive; b. Am. Falls, Idaho, Oct. 27, 1948; s. Virn E. and Jessie N. (Aldous) P.; m. Dianne Jacqulynne Walker, May 28, 1971; children: Scott, Russell, Stephen, Michael. BA, Brigham Young U., 1972, MA, 1975. Account exec. David W. Evans, Inc., Salt Lake City, 1972-75; dir. advt. divsn. continuing edn. U. Utah, Salt Lake City, 1975-78; sr. v.p. Evans/Lowe & Stevens, Inc., Atlanta, 1978, exec. v.p., 1979; pres., CEO David W. Evans/Atlanta, Inc., 1979-80; dir. advt. O.C. Tanner Co., Salt Lake City, 1980-82; pres. Thomas/Phillips/Clawson Advt., Inc., Salt Lake City, 1982-86, Hurst & Phillips, Salt Lake City, 1986-94; CEO, chmn. The Phillips Agy., Salt Lake City, 1994-2000; CEO Virtual Ad Agy., 2000—. Advt. instr. divsn. continuing edn. Brigham Young U., 1983-85. Dir. comms. Salt Lake County Mayor's Office, 2002-04. Recipient Silver Beaver award Boy Scouts Am., 1994, Spurgeon award, 1995. Mem. Am. Advt. Fedn. (8 Best-in-West awards, 2 nat. Addy awards, Clio finalist 1984, Telly award 1991, 92, 2002), Utah Advt. Fedn. (bd. dirs. 1976-78, 80-87, pres. 1984-85). Mem. Lds Ch. Home: 1792 Cornwall Ct Sandy UT 84092-5436 Office: 1792 E Cornwall Ct Ste A Sandy UT 84092 Office Phone: 801-550-1808. Personal E-mail: phillips66er@earthlink.net, ted@phillipsad.com.

PHILLIPS, TERENCE MARTYN, immunologist; b. Amersham, Eng., Aug. 2, 1946; came to U.S., 1977; s. Bertram Henry and Irene Edith (Martin) P.; m. Elizabeth Ann Thom, May 31, 1975 (div. Aug. 1988); 1 child, Thomas; m. Jennifer Holly Madans, Oct. 23, 1988. M.I. in Biology, U. London, Eng., 1969, MPhil, 1975, PhD, 1977, DSc, 1986. Cert. clin. lab. dir. Jr. lectr. London Sch. Hygiene and Tropical Medicine, 1972-75; rsch fellow McGill U., Montreal, Quebec, Can., 1975-77; asst. prof. Georgetown U., Washington, 1977-81; assoc. prof. George Washington U., Washington, 1981-89, dir. immunochemistry lab., 1981—, prof. medicine, 1989—, prof. microbiology and immunology, 1998—. Dir. Tissue Typing Lab., George Washington U., Washington, 1985—; cons. FDA, Washington, 1986—, Congl. Office of Tech. Assessment, Washington, 1988—; reviewer Nat. Cancer Inst., Bethesda, Md., 1986—, Metallobiochemistry, Gen. Medicine, NIH, 1990—; rsch. fellow Smithsonian Inst., Washington, 1997—. Author: Winning the War Within, 1986, Analytical Techniques in Immunochemistry, 1992, The Immune System, 1998, Affinity and Immunoaffinity Purification Techniques, 1999; editor: Analytical Immunology, 1988; mem. editl. bd. Nephron, Clin. Nephrology, Biomed Chromavogr, BioTechniques; contbr. articles to profl. jours. Mem. Nat. Kidney Found., Washington, 1985—, Nat. Heart Found., Washington, 1986—. Recipient McDonald prize, U. London, 1975. Fellow Nat. Acad. Clin. Biochemists; mem. Am. Chem. Soc., Soc. Clin. Scis., Assn. Med. Lab. Immunologists, N.Y. Acad. Scis. Avocation: fishing. Office: NIH 13 South Dr, 13/3N15 Bethesda MD 20892 Home: 4330 River Rd NW Washington DC 20016 Office Fax: 301-496-6608. Personal E-mail: tmphil46@yahoo.com. Business E-Mail: phillipt@mail.nih.gov.

PHILLIPS, TERRY LEMOINE, investment advisor; b. Washington, July 27, 1938; s. Clifford LeMoin and Dorothy Louise (Schuman) P.; m. Lynne Ann Bruce, Aug. 12, 1962; children: Susan Rae, Stephen Kirk. BS, Purdue U., 1964, MS, 1966. CPA Ind., pers. fin. specialist, Ind. Assoc. program leader, data processing Purdue U. Lab. Applications of Remote Sensing, West Lafayette, Ind., 1966-71, program leader, 1971-74, dep. dir., 1974-85; mgr. personal computer svcs. Purdue U. Computing Ctr., West Lafayette, 1986-92; adminstr. Continuing Edn. Ctr., West Lafayette, 1992-2000; investment advisor rep. Diesslin & Assocs., West Lafayette, 2000—. Cons. AID, Computer Scis. Corp. Scoutmaster, explorer advisor Boy Scouts Am., bd. dirs. Sagamore Coun.; sports coord. youth sports Battleground, Ind.; elder, deacon, trustee, treas. Presbyn. Ch.; bd. dirs. Tippecanoe chpt. Am. Diabetes Assn. With USN, 1956-59. Recipient Most Innovative Idea award Am. Diabetes Assn., 1987. Mem. IEEE (sr.), AICPA, Assn. Inst. for Certification of Computer Profls. (cert. in date processing), Assn. Computing Machinery, Data Processing Mgmt. Assn. (internat. dir., co-founder, v.p., pres., treas. Sagamore chpt., Individual Performance award 1983, 85, 88), Rotary (bd. dirs., treas.), Tau Beta Pi, Eta Kappa Nu. Home: 3711 Brixford Dr West Lafayette IN 47906-8705 also: 3711 Brixford Ln West Lafayette IN 47906-8705 Home Phone: 765-463-2789; Office Phone: 765-497-7744. E-mail: terry@diesslin.com, tl.phillips@insightbb.com.

PHILLIPS, THEODORE LOCKE, radiologist, educator; b. Phila., June 4, 1933; s. Harry Webster and Margaret Amy (Locke) Phillips; m. Joan Cappello, June 23, 1956; children: Margaret, John, Sally. BSc, Dickinson Coll., 1955; MD, U. Pa., 1959. Intern Western Res. U., Cleve., 1960; resident in therapeutic radiology U. Calif., San Francisco, 1963, clin. instr., 1963—65, asst. prof. radiation oncology, 1965—68, assoc. prof., 1968—70, prof., 1970—, chmn. dept. radiation oncology, 1973—98. Rsch. radiobiologist U.S. Naval Radiologic Def. Lab., San Francisco, 1963—65; rsch. physician Lawrence Berkeley Lab. Contbr. numerous articles to profl. pubis. With USNR, 1963—65. Grantee, Nat. Cancer Inst., 1970—99. Mem.: Inst. Medicine, No. Calif. Radiation Oncology Assn., Radium Soc., Radiation Rsch. Soc. (pres. 1977), Am. Coll. Radiology, Calif. Med. Assn., Am. Assn. Cancer Rsch., N.Am. Hyperthermia Soc. (pres. 1994), Radiol. Soc. N.Am., Am. Soc. Clin. Oncology, Am. Soc. Therapeutic Radiology and Oncology (pres. 1984), Alpha Omega Alpha, Phi Beta Kappa. Republican. Office: U Calif San Francisco Dept Radiation Oncology 1600 Divisidero St ste H1031 San Francisco CA 94143-1708

PHILLIPS, THOMAS EDWORTH, JR., financial advisor, investment management consultant; b. Danville, Va., July 7, 1944; s. Thomas Edworth Sr. and Jean (Worley) P.; m. Claudia Mitchell, July 23, 1966; children: Kelly Marie, Melissa Joyce. BS in Econs., Va. Tech., 1966; cert. in investments, N.Y. Inst. Fin., 1969; MS in Bus., Va. Commonwealth U., 1973; postgrad., U. Pa., 1989. Cert. investment mgmt. analyst; registered investment adviser. Edn. coord. Prince William County Schs., Manassas, Va., 1966-67; investment broker Conrad and Co., Richmond, Va., 1967-68; investment exec. UBS Paine Webber, Inc., Richmond, 1968—, divisional v.p., 1980-99, sr. v.p. and prime cons., 2000—; registered prin. NY Stock Exch., Nat. Assn. Securities Dealers, 1987—. Access program nat. com. UBS Paine Webber, N.Y.C., Inc., 1989-90, mem. dir.'s coun., 1987-88, managed accounts nat. adv. bd., 1991-93; mem. mut. fund Nat. Adv. Coun., 1996—, pres.' council, 1997—; bd. dirs. Madison Group, Inc., Richmond, Meadowbrook Assocs., Inc., Richmond; speaker in field. Bd. dirs. Va. Non-Profit Housing Coalition, pres., 1992—; chmn. bd. deacons. Mt. Olivet Ch., Hanover, Va., 1984-85; trustee Hanover Acad., Ashland, Va., 1980-84; pres. alumni bd. Va. Commonwealth U., Richmond, 2003-05. Rotary Found. fellow, 1989. Mem. Investment Mgmt. Cons. Assn., Capital Soc., Va. Tech. Alumni Assn., Va. Commonwealth U. Alumni Assn., Rotary, Bull and Bear Club, Omicron Delta Epsilon. Avocations: horses, tennis, golf. Office: UBS PRIME Consulting Group 1021 E Cary St Ste 1800 Richmond VA 23219-4000 Home: 13464 Lakeview Farms Pl Ashland VA 23005 Office Phone: 804-775-1501. Business E-Mail: tom.phillips@ubs.com.

PHILLIPS, THOMAS JOHN, lawyer; b. Mpls., Nov. 24, 1948; BA, U. Minn., 1970; JD, U. Utah, 1973; LLM in Taxation, NYU, 1974. Bar: Wis. 1974. Ptnr. Quarles & Brady, Milw., 1991—. Co-author: Wisconsin Limited Liability Company Forms and Practice Manual, 1999. Mem. ABA (tax sect. corp. tax corp. coms. bus. law sect,), Wis. Bar Assn., Profl. Inst. Taxation, Mil. Tax Club, North Shore Country Club, Order of Coif. Avocations: gardening, golf. Office: 411 E Wisconsin Ave Ste 2040 Milwaukee WI 53202-4497 Home Phone: 262-241-5314; Office Phone: 414-277-5831. Business E-Mail: tjp@quarles.com, thomas.phillips@quarks.com.

PHILLIPS, TODD, film director, film producer; b. Bklyn., 1970; Attended, NYU. Director, prodr.: (films) Hated, 1994; Frat House, 1998; Bittersweet Motel, 2000; dir., writer, actor Road Trip, 2000; dir., prodr., writer, actor Old School, 2003; dir., writer Starsky & Hutch, 2004; dir., prodr., writer School for Scoundrels, 2006; exec. prodr.: All the King's Men, 2006; prodr., dir., actor (films) The Hangover, 2009; actor: (TV series) Film School, 2004. Office: c/o Creative Artists Agy 2000 Ave of the Stars Los Angeles CA 90067 Office Phone: 323-822-4300. E-mail: toodstf@aol.com.*

PHILLIPS, TYLER BRADSTREET, retired business executive; b. Flushing, NY, Nov. 29, 1937; s. Joseph H. and Genevieve (Tyler) P.; m. Katherine Lawrence Bitter, Nov. 23, 1968; children— Tyler Bradstreet Jr., Katherine Lawrence, Christopher Bradstreet. BA, Wittenberg U., 1960, postgrad. Northwestern U., Chgo. Product mgr. Packaging Corp Am., Evanston, Ill., 1963-65, mktg. mgr. H.P. Hood & Co., Boston, 1965-73; account supr. Compton Advt., NYC, 1973-78; mgmt. supr. Ogilvy & Mather, NYC, 1978-82; v.p. account services LCF Co., NYC, 1982; corp. dir. mktg. Jac Pac Foods, Manchester, NH, mng. dir., Red-L Foods, Inc., Pomfret, Conn.; exec. v.p. Joseph Kirschner Co., Augusta, Maine; pres., CEO, trustee Angostura Internat. Ltd., Cranford, NJ; Angostura Ltd., Toronto, Can., cons. CL Fin., Trinidad, BWI; inventor Pharmaceutical Dispensing Package, 1963. Trustee Lakes Region Conservation Trust, Ctr. Harbor, NH, 1984—; dir., Waldheim Trust, Mirror Lake, NH. Served with med. corps. U.S. Army. Avocations: yachting, swimming, mountain climbing, car collecting. Home: Mirror Lake Farm Mirror Lake NH 03853

PHILLIPS, VICKI L., foundation administrator, former school system administrator; b. Marion, Ind., Jan. 15, 1958; d. Denver Phillips and Vivian (Burnette) Fuqua. BS in Edn., Western Ky. U., 1980, MA in Psychology, 1987; doctoral student, U. Ky., 1988—; EdD in instrnl. leadership, U. of Lincoln, Eng., 2002. Dir. devel. tng. dept. Panorama, Bowling Green, Ky., 1978—80; tchr. learning and behavior disorders Simpson County Bd. Edn., 1981—85; exceptional child cons. Ky. Dept. Edn. Office Edn. for Exceptional Children, 1986—90; chief exec. asst. to edn. commr. Ky. Dept. of Edn., 1986—93; dep. dir./chief of staff Nat. Alliance for Restructuring Edn., Wash., DC, 1993—95; dir. Greater Phila. First Partnership for Reform; exec. dir. Children Achieving Challenge, 1995—98; supt. Sch. Dist. of Lancaster, 1998—2003; sec. of edn. Pa. Dept. Edn., Harrisburg, 2003—04; supt. Portland Pub. Schools, Oreg., 2004—07; dir. edn. College Ready in US Program Bill & Melinda Gates Found., 2007—. Mem. ASCD, Nat. Coun. for Exceptional Children, Coun. for Behavior Disorders, Nat. Assn. for Sch. Psychologists, Ky. Assn. Sch. Adminstrs., Ky. Assn. for Psychology in the Schs., Ky. Assn. for Family-Based Svcs., Ky. Families for Family-Based Svcs., Ky. Families as Allies. Office: Bill & Melinda Gates Found US Program PO Box 23350 Seattle WA 98102*

PHILLIPS, VIRGINIA, retired federal employee; b. Glenmora, La., July 22, 1933; d. Leon Bunyan Phillips and Linnie Scott Rountree. BS, La. State U., Baton Rouge, 1953. Cert. tchr. La. Tchr. Hermansville HS, Hermansville, Mich., 1953—54, Washougal HS, Wash., 1955—56, El Dorado County HS, Placerville, Calif., 1956—57; sec. USAID, Tripoli, Libya, 1957—59, Seoul, Republic of Korea, 1959—61; sec. various law firms, temp. employment agys. Washington, 1963—69; fed. employee, 1969—94. Tutor Dept. Interior, Washington Pub. Schs., 1988—90. Contbr. to review bd. 9-11 mag. Bd. mem. Glenmora Cemetery Assn., 2003—05, pres., 2005; mem., Civilian Rev. Bd. Selective Svc. Sys., Washington, 1981—94; driving instr. AARP, Alexandria, La., 2002—; bd. dirs. Marlyn Condominium, Washington, 1986—88, Westchester Corp., Washington, 1992—93. Mem.: DAR, Nat. Assn. Ret. Fed. Employees (contbr. to Retirement Life mag.), First Families Tenn., Sovereign Colonial Soc. Americans of Royal Descent, Colonial Order of the Crown, Plantagenet Soc., Soc. Descendants Knights of Most Noble Order of the Garter, Magna Charta Dames, First Families Miss., United Daus. Confederacy, Sons and Daus. of Pilgrims. Democrat. Avocations: genealogy, writing, photography. Home: 1016 A Nye Dr Alexandria LA 71303-5758

PHILLIPS, WADE, professional football coach; b. Orange, Tex., June 21, 1947; s. Oail Andrew (Bum) and Helen Phillips; m. Laurie Phillips; children: Tracey, Wesley. Student, U. Houston, 1965—68. Asst. football coach U. Houston, 1969; football coach Orange (Tex.) High Sch., 1970-72, Okla. State U., 1973-74, U. Kans., 1975; linebacker coach Houston Oilers, 1976, defensive line coach, 1977-80; defensive coord. New Orleans Saints, 1981-85, Phila. Eagles, 1986-88, Denver Broncos, 1989-93, head coach, 1993-94, Buffalo Bills, 1998—2000; def. coord. Atlanta Falcons, 2001—04, interim head coach, 2003—04; def. coord. San Diego Chargers, 2004—07; head coach Dallas Cowboys, 2007—. Office: Dallas Cowboys One Cowboys Pkwy Irving TX 75063*

PHILLIPS, WALTER MILLS, III, psychologist, educator; b. NYC, Sept. 29, 1947; s. Walter Mills and Grace Mary (Mullen) P.; m. Anne Marie Boyle, July 3, 1971; children: Jonathan, Elizabeth. BS, Fordham U., 1970; MA, U. S.D., 1973, PhD, 1975. Lic. clin. psychologist, Conn.; diplomate Am. Coll. Forensic Examiners, Am. Bd. Disability Evaluators, Am. Bd. Disability Analysts; cert. sr. disability analyst. Adolescent resident counselor Hawthorne (N.Y.) Cedar Knolls Sch., 1970—71; NIMH tng. fellow, 1971—75; clin. psychology intern Inst. of Living, Hartford, Conn., 1974—75, clin. staff psychologist, 1975—79, sr. staff psychologist, 1979—82, asst. dir. dept. clin. psychology, 1980—82, dir. clin. psychology tng., 1980—82; co-dir. outpatient psychiatry U. Conn., Farmington, 1982—88; asst. prof. psychiatry, dir. psychiatry evaluation svc. U. Conn. Health Ctr., 1982—88, dir. Anxiety Rsch. and Treatment Ctr., 1985—88; pvt. practice psychotherapy Hartford, 1976—; dir. adolescent/young adult svc. Grandview Psychiat. Resource Ctr., Waterbury, Conn., 1988—90; dir. psychology Waterbury Hosp., 1990—98; pvt. practice clin. psychology Waterbury and Middlebury, Conn., 1990—. Asst. clin. prof. psychiatry Sch. Medicine Yale U., New Haven, Conn., 1988-2006; ret. psychiatry faculty, 2007-; mem. psychology exec. com. Sch. Medicine Yale U., New Haven, 1990-98. Contbr. articles to profl. jours. Mem. APA, Am. Psychotherapy Assn. (diplomate), Conn. Psychol. Assn., Soc. Psychotherapy Rsch., Soc. Personality Assessment, Conn. Hosp. Assn. (chmn., dir. psychology conf. 1992-96), N.Y. Acad. Scis., Sigma Xi. Office: 415 Middlebury Rd Middlebury CT 06762 Office Phone: 203-758-8333. Business E-Mail: phillips.walter@comcast.net.

PHILLIPS, WALTER RAY, law educator; b. Democrat, NC, Mar. 19, 1932; s. Walter Yancey and Bonnie (Wilson) P.; m. Patricia Ann Jones, Aug. 28, 1954; children: Bonnie Ann, Rebecca Lee. AB, U. N.C., 1954; LL.B., Emory U., 1957, LL.M., 1962, JD, 1970; postgrad., Yale U., 1965-66. Bar: Ga. 1957, Fla. 1958, Tex. 1969, Mo. 2001, U.S. Supreme Ct. 1962. With firm Jones, Adams, Paine & Foster, West Palm Beach, Fla., 1957-58; law clk. to chief judge U.S. Dist. Ct., Atlanta, 1958-59; with firm Powell, Goldstein, Frazer & Murphy, Atlanta, 1959-60; bankruptcy judge U.S. Cts., Atlanta, 1960-64; prof. law U. N.D., 1964-65; teaching fellow Yale U., 1965-66; prof. law Fla. State U., 1966-68, Tex. Tech. U., Lubbock, 1968-71; Disting. vis. prof. law Baylor U., 1971; atty. Commn. on Bankruptcy Laws of U.S., Washington, 1971-72; dep. dir., adminstrv. officer, 1972-73; prof. Sch. Law, U. Ga., 1973-2000, assoc. dean, 1975-83, acting dean, 1976, Joseph Henry Lumpkin prof., 1977-94, also dir. univ's self. study, 1978, Herman E. Talmadge prof., 1994-2000. Chapman disting. vis. prof. law U. Okla., 1985-86; vis. prof. law U. Okla., 1990, U. Mo., Columbia, 1993, 94, 2001—; reporter Gov.'s Legislation for Ga., 1973; v.p., dir. Killearn Estates, Inc.; mem. Conf. on Consumer Fin. Law; prof. London Law Consortium, 1999. Author: Florida Law and Practice, 1960, Encyclopedia of Georgia Law, 1962, Seminar for Newly Appointed Referees in Bankruptcy, 1964, Damages: Cases and Materials, 1967, (with James William Moore) Debtors' and Creditors' Rights, Cases and Material, 1966, 5th edit., 1979, The Law of Debtor Relief, 1969, 2d edit., 1972, supplement, 1975, (with James William Moore) Rule 6, Moore's Federal Practice, 1969, Adjustment of Debts for Individuals, 1979, 2d edit., 1981, supplement, 1982, 84, 85, Liquidation Under the Bankruptcy Code, 3d edit., 1988, supplement, 1989, 90, 91, 92, 93, 94, Cases and Materials on Corporate Reorganization, 1983, 3d edit., 1986, 4th edit., 1988, 5th edit., 1990, 7th edit., 1996, 8th edit., 1998, Family Farmer and Adjustment of Individual Debts, 1987, supplement, 1988, 89, 90, 91, 92, 93, 94, A Primer of Chapters 12 and 13 of the Bankruptcy Code, 1995. Bd. dirs. Lubbock Day Nurseries, 1969, pres., 1970-71. Served with USAF, 1950. Mem. ATLA, ABA (consumer bankruptcy com. 1973—, chmn. 1986-90), Fed. Bar Assn., Fla. Bar Assn., Tex. Bar Assn., Western Circuit Bar Assn., Ga. Bar Assn. (vice chmn. publs. com. 1977-89, com. on profl. responsibility 1983—2002), Mo. Bar Assn., Am. Judicature Soc., Phi Alpha Delta (chief tribune) Baptist. Home: 3800 Wakefield Dr Columbia MO 65203-5630

PHILLIPS, WANDA CHARITY, secondary school educator, writer; b. Gettysburg, Pa., Apr. 1, 1947; d. Roy Homer and Frances Marie (White) Kuykendall; m. James E. Phillips; children: Jenny, Peter, Micah. BS in Secondary Edn., Shippensburg U., Pa., 1968; cert. elem. edn., Grand Canyon Coll., 1973; MA in Adminstrn., No. Ariz. U., Flagstaff, 1993; EdD, George Fox U., Newberg, Oreg., 2007. Tchr. Littlestown H.S., Pa., 1969, Phoenix Indian Sch., 1971-72, Peoria Sch. Dist., Ariz., 1973—99; author ISHA Enterprises, Inc., Scottsdale, Ariz., 1985—. Ednl. seminar presenter ISHA Enterprises, Scottsdale, Ariz., 1986—, Assn. Christian Sch. Internat., Calif., 1988—. Author: Easy Grammar, 1986, Daily Grams: Guided Review Aiding Mastery Skills, 1986, Daily Grams: Guided Review Aiding Mastery Skills for Grade 3, 2003, Grade 4, 2003, Grade 5, 2003, Easy Writing, 1991, Easy Grammar Daily: Guided Teaching and Review for Grade 2, 2006, Easy Grammar, Grades 5 and 6, 1994 (children's book) My Mother Doesn't Like to Cook, 1993, Easy Grammar Plus, 1995, Easy Grammar: Grades 4 and 5, 1996, Easy Grammar: Grades 3 and 4, 1998, Grades 3, 4, 5, 6, 2006, Daily Grams: Grades 3, 4, 5, 6, and 7, 2002, Easy Grammer Ultimate Teaching Series Grade 8, 9, 11, 12 and Above, 2008. Raspberry Cottage Tearoom Ministries. Mem.: Peoria Ednl. Enrichment Found. (bd. mem. 2008, mem., Peoria Schs., Ariz. 2008—09), Nat. Trust for Hist. Preservation, Paradise Valley Women's Club. Office: ISHA Enterprises Inc Easy Grammar Systems PO Box 25970 Scottsdale AZ 85255 Office Phone: 480-502-9454. E-mail: info@easygrammar.com.

PHILLIPS, WILLIAM DANIEL, physicist; b. Wilkes-Barre, Pa., Nov. 5, 1948; s. William Cornelius and Mary Catherine (Savine) Phillips. BS, Juniata Coll., Huntingdon, Pa., 1970; PhD, MIT, 1976. Rsch. asst. MIT, Cambridge, 1970—76, Chaim Weizmann fellow, 1976—78; physicist Nat. Inst. Standards and Tech., Gaithersburg, Md., 1978—90, group leader, 1990—95, fellow, 1995—. Vis. prof. Ecole Normale Superieure, Paris, 1989—90; disting. prof. physics U. Md., College Park, 1991—. Editor (author): Laser Manipulation of Atoms and Ions, 1992; contbr. articles to profl. jours. Recipient Sci. Achievement award, Wash. Acad. Scis., 1982, Silver medal, Dept. Commerce, 1983, Gold medal, US Dept. Commerce, 1993, Pa. Soc., 1999, Albert A. Michelson medal, Franklin Inst., 1996; co-recipient Nobel Prize for physics, 1997, Schawlow prize in laser sci., APS, 1998; named Outstanding Young Scientist, Md. Acad. Sci., 1982. Fellow: Am. Acad. Arts and Scis., Am. Phys. Soc.; mem.: NAS, Potifical Acad. Sci. (apptd. academician 2004), Optical Soc. Am. (hon.), Soc. Physics Students, Sigma Xi. Achievements include demonstrated laser cooling of atomic beams; electromagnetic trapping of neutral atoms; discovery of sub-doppler laser cooling; produced submicrokelvin 3D kinetic temperatures. Office: Nat Inst Stds & Tech 216 B123 100 Bureau Dr Stop 8424 Gaithersburg MD 20899-8424 Business E-Mail: william.phillips@nist.gov.

PHILLIPS, WILLIAM E., advertising agency executive; b. Chgo., Jan. 7, 1930; s. William E. and Alice N. Phillips; children: Michael, Tom, Sarah; m. Barbara Smith, Nov. 27, 1997. BS, Cornell U., 1951; MBA, Northwestern U., 1955. Brand mgr. Procter & Gamble, Cin., 1955-59; with Ogilvy & Mather, NYC, 1959-90; CEO Ogilvy Group, 1981-88; exec. in residence, prof. Johnson Grad. Sch. Mgmt. Cornell U., 1989-90. Bd. dirs. Gen. Housewares, Sun Glass Hut, Inc., Alliance Nat. Office Ctrs. Chmn. emeritus Outward Bound Internat.; chair Outdoor Edn., Cornell U., 1990—; co-chair Cayuga Soc. for Planned Giving at Cornell U.; trustee emeritus Cornell U.; trustee Internat. Tennis Hall of Fame, Newport, R.I., Florence Griswold Mus., Old Lyme, Conn., 1991—; active in Dem. politics. Lt. (j.g.) USN, 1951-54, Korea/Pacific/Mediterranean. Recipient Disting. Svc. award, Singapore Outward Bound, 1997, Kurt Hahn award, Outward Bound, 1998, Rhodes Exemplary Alumni Svc. award, Cornell U., 2001. Mem. Old Lyme Country Club, Am. Alpine Club, Explorers Club, Cornell Club, Univ. Club, Naval Mil. Club (London), Achilles Club N.Y.C. (bd. dirs.). Avocations: skiing, tennis, bicycling. Home: 200 N Cove Rd Old Saybrook CT 06475-2537 Office Phone: 212-237-4241. Business E-Mail: bill.phillips@ogilvy.com.

PHILLIPS, WINFRED MARSHALL, academic administrator, professor, mechanical engineer; b. Richmond, Va., Oct. 7, 1940; s. Claude Marshall and Gladys Marian (Barden) P.; children: Stephen, Sean. BSME, Va. Poly. Inst., 1963; MA in Engring., U. Va., 1966, DSc, 1968. Mech. engr. U.S. Naval Weapons Lab., Dahlgren, Va., 1963; NSF trainee, tchg. and rsch. asst. dept. aerospace engring. U. Va., Charlottesville, 1963—67, rsch. scientist, 1966—67; asst. prof. dept. aerospace engring. Pa. State U., University Park, 1968-74, from assoc. prof. to prof., 1974—80, assoc. dean rsch. Coll. Engring., 1979—80; head Sch. Mech. Engring. Purdue U., West Lafayette, Ind., 1980-88; dean Coll. Engring. U. Fla., Gainesville, 1988-99, assoc. v.p. engring., 1989—99, v.p. rsch. and Don and Ruth Eckis prof. biomed. engring., 1999—. Bd. dir. Wachovia Bank, Gainesville; vis. prof. U. Paris, 1976—77; adv. com. Nimbus Corp., 1985—90, Hong Kong U. Sci. and Tech., 1990—93, AvMed Inc.; co-founder, v.p. CEO Inc., 1990—; acad. adv. coun. Indsl. Rsch. Inst., 1990—93; exec. com. Accreditation Bd. on Engring. and Tech., 1991—96; sci. adv. com. Electric Power Rsch. Inst., 1994—99; vice-chmn. Southeastern Coalition for Minorities in Engring., 1995—2000, chmn., 2001—04, chair Washington Accord, 2007—; internat. revs. for univs. in Saudi Arabia, Russia, Netherlands, Kuwait, Mexico, China, France Accreditation Bd. on Engring. and Tech., 1995—; bd. dirs Oak Ridge Associated Univs., 2002—, chair coun., mem. exec. com., 2002—; mem. US Pres.'s Commn. on Nat. Medal of Sci., 2003—. Sect. editor Am. Soc. Artificial Internal Organs Jour., 1985-99; contbr. over 175 articles to profl. jours., chpts. to books. Mem. Ind. Boiler and Pressure Vessel Code Bd., 1981—88; bd. dirs. Ctrl. Pa. Heart Assn., 1974—80, U. Fla. Found., 1989—91, 1995—2001. Recipient Career Rsch. award, NIH, 1974—78, NIH Surgery and Bioengring. Study sect., 1988—91, Fla. High Tech. and Industry Coun., 1990—94, Nat. Engring. award, Am. Assn. Engr. Socs., 2000, Linton Grinter award, 2000, Global Messenger award, Southeastern Consortium for Minorities in Engring., 2003; named Disting. Hoosier Ind., 1987, Sagamore of the Wabash, 1988. Fellow AAAS, AIAA, ASEE (vice chair 2001-02, chmn. bd. 2002—, Lamme award 2003), ASME (sr. v.p. edn. 1986-88, bd. dirs. 1995-2000, pres. 1998-99, ABET (pres. 1996-97), Dedicated Svc. award 2001, Ralph Coates Roe medal 2005), Biomed. Engring. Soc., NY Acad. Scis., Am. Astron. Soc., Am. Inst. Med. and Biol. Engring. (founding fellow, chair coll. fellows 1994-95, pres. 1996-97), Am. Soc. Engring. Edn. (past chmn. long range planning soc. awards 1990-92, vice chmn. engring. deans coun. 1991-93, chair 1993—, bd. dirs. 1994-98, 1st v.p. 1994-95, pres. 1996-97), Royal Soc. Arts, Am. Soc. Artificial Internal Organs (trustee 1982-90, sec.-treas. 1986-87, pres. 1988-89, adv. bd. 1998—), ABET (hon.; pres. 1996-97); mem. Nat. Assn. State Univs. and Land-Grant Colls. (com. quality of engring. edn.), Univ. Programs in Computer-Aided Engring., Design and Mfg. (bd. dirs. 1985-91), Wash. Accord Wash. IEA (chair 2008-09), Am. Phys. Soc., Internat. Soc. Biotheology, Fla. Engring. Soc., Cosmos Club, Fla. Blue Key, Rotary (pres. Lafayette 1987-88), Sigma Xi, Phi Kappa Phi, Phi Tau Sigma, Sigma Gamma Tau, Tau Beta Pi (eminent engr.), Washington Accord of IEA(chair, 2008-09). Achievements include research in artificial heart pumps; reentry aerodynamics; blood rheology; modeling blood flow; fluid dynamics of artificial hearts; use of smooth blood contacting surface; prosthetic valve fluid dynamics; laser Doppler studies of unsteady biofluid dynamics. Home: 4140 NW 44th Ave Gainesville FL 32606-4518 Office: U Fla Rsch and Grad Programs 223 Grinter Hall Gainesville FL 32611 Office Phone: 352-392-9271.

PHILLIPS, WINIFRED PATRICIA, composer; b. Mobile, Ala., Apr. 13, 1972; d. Winifred Waldron Phillips. BA summa cum laude in Comms., Kean U., 1994. Composer, prodr., actress, writer Nat. Pub. Radio, Washington, 1992—2002; composer, prodr., actress, writer Radio Tales XM Satellite Radio Dramas, Washington, 2002—; owner music and audio prodn. co. Gens. Prodns.; composer Take Two Interactive, NYC, 2005—06, Activision, Santa Monica, Calif., 2006—07. Composer Sony Computer Entertainment Am., Santa Monica, Calif., 2004. Composer, prodr., actress, writer (National Public Radio dramas) Generations Radio Theater Presents: Radio Tales, 1996—2002, (radio dramas) Radio Tales, XM Satellite Radio, 2002—, composer, prodr., actress (radio drama) The Odyssey Trilogy, 2003, Arabian Nights Trilogy, 2003, The Gift of the Magi, 1996, The Yellow Wallpaper, 1996, The Fall of the House of Usher, 1998, Sleepy Hollow, 1998, The Time Machine, 1999, Gulliver's Travels, 1999, The Mummy, 1999, The Island of Doctor Moreau, 2000, Dr. Jekyll and Mr. Hyde, 2000, Journey to the Center of the Earth, 2000, The Pit and the Pendulum, 2000, The Hunchback of Notre-Dame, 2001, Jason and The Argonauts, 2001, War of the Worlds, 2001, Phantom of the Opera, 2001, Beowulf, 2001, Twenty Thousand Leagues Under the Sea, 2001, The Invisible Man, 2001, The Lost World, 2002, composer, actress, author (radio musicals) Celtic Hero, 2000; composer, actress, author: radio musicals Lord of the Celts, 1998; author: (short stories) Breaking Point, 1991, Celtic Beauty for Sword and Sorceress 20 book anthology, 2003, (radio drama script) Light of Truth, 1985; composer: (video games) God of War, 2004, Charlie and the Chocolate Factory, 2005, The Da Vinci Code, 2006, Shrek the Third, 2007; singer, musician: Best of the Best: A Tribute to Game Music, 2007, Go Mario! (Super Mario Brothers), 2007, composer, singer, musician: God of War Video Game Soundtrack, 2004. Recipient GRACIE award for best nat./network drama series, Am. Women in Radio and TV, 2001, 2003, 2004, N.Y. Festivals award, Internat. Radio Festivals, 1997, AUDIE Honors award, Audio Pubs. Assn., 1999, GOLDEN REEL Merit award, Nat. Fedn. Cmty. Broadcasters, 2001, GRACIE award for outstanding achievement by an actress, Am. Women in Radio and TV, 1998, N.Y. Festivals award, Internat. Radio Festivals, 2001, N.Y. Festivals World medal, 2004, Outstanding Achievement in Original Music Composition for Videogame, Acad. Interactive Arts Sci., 2005, Best Original Score of Yr. awrd, Game Zone, 2005, Best Original Music award, Game Spot, 2005, Best Original Score award, IGN PS2, 2005, Music of Yr., Game Audio Network Guild, 2005, Best Interactive Score, 2005, Best Cinematic/Cut Scene Audio, 2005, Audio of Yr., 2005; grantee Endowment grantee, Wallace - Reader's Digest Funds, 1996—2002, NEA, 1996—2002, Durkin Hayes Publ., 1998. Mem.: SAG, BMI, NARAS, Game Audio Network Guild, Ind. Game Developers Assn., Am. Fedn. Musicians. Avocations: reading, Web design, computer art, travel. Business E-Mail: phillips@radiotales.com.

PHILLIPS-BROWN, EXA, educator; BS, Calumet Coll., Whiting Ind., 1975; grad., U. Calif., Riverside, 2000; MEd, Calif. State U., San Bernardino, 2009. Cert. educator Adkins Life Skills, NY, 1981. Civilian Dept. Def., Chgo., 1966—71; with DHHS, Social Security Adminstrn., Hammond, Ind., 1971—78, technician LA, 1981—90; customer svc. rep. Fed. Express, Fullerton, Calif., 1990—95; educator tchg. Moreno Valley Unified Sch. Dist., Calif., 1996—2009. Spl. svcs. coord. NW Ind. Pub. Sch. Study Coun., Crown Point, Ind., 1980—81. Recipient Civilian Svc. medal, Republic of Vietnam, 1968—69. Mem.: Moreno Valley Educators Assn., Assn. Calif. Sch. Administr., Am. Assn. Ret. Persons, Golden Key Internat. Honor Soc. (Membership 2008). Democrat. Avocation: teaching. Office: Moreno Valley Unified Sch Dist 25634 Alessandro Blvd Moreno Valley CA 92553-4395 Personal E-mail: exa.phillips@verizon.net.

PHILLIPSON, DONALD E., lawyer; b. Denver, July 22, 1942; BS, Stanford U., 1964, JD, 1968; MS, U. Calif., Berkeley, 1965. Former mem. Davis, Graham & Stubbs, Denver; now cons., writer. Mem. Nat. Soccer Hall of Fame (builder). Office: 14325 Braun Rd Golden CO 80401-1431 Office Phone: 303-279-1577.

PHILLIS, JOHN WHITFIELD, physiologist, educator; b. Port of Spain, Trinidad, Apr. 1, 1936; came to U.S., 1981; s. Ernest and Sarah Anne (Glover) P.; m. Pamela Julie Popple, 1958 (div. 1968); children: David, Simon, Susan; m. Shane Beverly Wright, Jan. 24, 1969. B in Vet. Sci., Sydney U., Australia, 1958, D in Vet. Sci., 1976; PhD, Australian Nat. U., 1961; DSc, Monash U., Australia, 1970. Sr. lectr. Monash U., 1963-69; vis. prof. Ind. U., Indpls., 1969; prof. physiology, assoc. dean rsch. U. Man., Winnipeg, Canada, 1970-73; prof., chmn. dept. physiology U. Sask., Saskatoon, Canada, 1973-81, asst. dean rsch., 1973-75;

prof. physiology Wayne State U., Detroit, 1981—2004, prof. emeritus, 2004—, chmn. dept. physiology, 1981-97; courtesy prof. U. Fla., Gainsville, 2004—. Mem. scholarship and grants com. Can. Med. Rsch. Coun., Ottawa, Ont., 1973-79, rsch. prof., 1980; mem. sci. adv. bd. Dystonia Med. Rsch. Found., Beverly Hills, Calif., 1980-85, Curtis Rsch. Inst., Risingsun, Ohio, 1998-2000; mem. sci. adv. panel World Soc. for Protection of Animals, 1982-98; Wellcome vis. prof. Tulane U., 1986; mem. acad. scholars Wayne State U., 1995. Author: Pharmacology of Synapses, 1970; editor: Veterinary Physiology, 1976, Physiology and Pharmacology of Adenosine Derivatives, 1983, Adenosine and Adenine Nucleotides as Regulators of Cellular Function, 1991, The Regulation of Cerebral Blood Flow, 1993, Novel Therapies for CNS Injuries: Rationales and Results, 1996; editor Can. Jour. Physiology and Pharmacology, 1978-81, Progress in Neurobiology, 1973-97. Mem. grants com. Am. Heart Assn. of Mich., 1985-90, mem. rsch. coun., 1991-92, mem. rsch. forum com., 1991-96, chair, 1992-93; mem. Brain/Stroke Consortium Study Group, Am. Heart Assn., 1998. Wellcome fellow London, 1961-62; Can. Med. Rsch. Coun. grantee, 1970-81; NIH grantee, 1983-2000. Mem. Brit. Pharmacol. Soc., Am. Physiol. Soc., Soc. Neurosci., Internat. Brain Rsch. Orgn. Office: Wayne State U Sch Medicine Dept Physiology 540 E Canfield Ave Detroit MI 48201-1928 Personal E-mail: jphillis@med.wayne.edu.

PHILLIS, MARILYN HUGHEY, artist; b. Kent, Ohio; d. Paul Jones and Helen Margaret Hughey; m. Richard Waring Phillis, Mar. 19, 1949; children: Diane E., Hugh R., Randall W Student, Kent State U., 1945; BS, Ohio State U., 1949. Chemist Battelle Meml. Inst., Columbus, Ohio, 1949—53; illustrator periodical We. Res. Hist. Mag., Garrettsville, Ohio, 1974—79; illustrator book AAUW, Piqua, Ohio, 1976; instr. art Edison State C.C., Piqua, 1976; instr. watermedia Springfield Mus. Art, Ohio, 1976—84. Juror art exhbns. state and nat. art groups, 1980—; instr. painting state and nat. orgns., 1980—; lectr. art healing Wheeling Jesuit Coll., W.Va., 1994—96; founder, coord. Nat. Creativity Seminar, Stretching Boundaries for Creative People, 1993, 1995, 1997, 1999, 2002, 07. Author: Watermedia Techniques for Releasing the Creative Spirit, 1992; contbr. chapters to books, articles and illustrations to profl. jours.; one-woman shows include Stifel Fine Art Ctr., Wheeling, Springfield Art Mus., Zanesville Art Ctr., Ohio, Ohio U., Lancaster, Ohio U. East St. Clairsville, Cleve. Inst. Music, Columbus Mus. Art, Cheekwood Mus. Art, Bot. Hall, Nashville, Idaho Falls Art Ctr., Monroe C.C., Mich., exhibitions include Butler Mus. Am. Art, Youngstown, Ohio, Taiwan Art Edn. Inst., Taipei, 1994, Represented in permanent collections Ohio U., Lancaster and St. Clairsville, W.Va. No. CC, Wheeling, Springfield Mus. Art, Ohio, Heritage Hall mus., Talladega, Ala., Ohio Watercolor Soc., W.Va. Women Artists, U. Charleston, Monroe C.C., Mich., also corp. collections. Co-chmn. Cmty. Health and Humor Program, Wheeling, 1992 Recipient First awards Watercolor West, Riverside, Calif., 1990, Hudson Soc. award Nat. Collage Soc., 1995, Art Masters award Am. Artist Mag., 1996; named to Hall of Fame, Kent, Ohio, 2000, Hall of Fame, Wheeling, 2000 Mem. Internat. Soc. Study of Subtle Energies and Energy Medicine (art cons. sci. jour. 1992-2006, art and healing workshop 1995), Am. Watercolor Soc. (dir. 1991-93, newsletter editor 1992—, chmn. Jury of Awards, 2003, Jury of Selection, 2008, Osborne award 1975), Soc. Layerists in Multi-Media (nat. v.p. 1988-93), Ohio Watercolor Soc. (sec. 1979-82, v.p. 1982-89, pres. 1990-96, Gold medal, Best of Show 1993), Nat. Watercolor Soc. (chmn. selection jury 2001), Internat. Noetic Sci., Western Ohio Watercolor Soc. (pres. 1979-80, 2d award 1982), Allied Artists NY, W.Va. Watercolor Soc. (1st award 1993), Ky. Watercolor Soc., Ga. Watercolor Soc., So. Watercolor Soc. (pres. 1997-98, Silver award 1999) Avocations: hiking, reading, genealogy, music, travel. Home and Office: Phillis Studio 72 Stamm Cir Wheeling WV 26003-5549 Personal E-mail: mhphillis@yahoo.com.

PHILOGENE, BERNARD J. R., academic administrator, science educator; b. Beau-Bassin, Mauritius, May 4, 1940; came to Can., 1961; s. Raymond Pierre and Simone Marie (Ruffier) P.; m. Hélène Marie Lebreux, July 7, 1964; children: Simone, Catherine. BS, U. Montreal, 1964; MS, McGill U., 1966; PhD, U. Wis., 1970; DSc (hon.), Compiègne, 1995; DSc (hon.), U. de Pau, France, 2005. Rsch. officer Can. Forestry Svc., Que., 1966—70, rsch. scientist Que., 1970—71; asst. prof. U. B.C., Vancouver, 1971-74; asst. prof., assoc. prof., then prof. entomology U. Ottawa, Canada, 1974—2005, vice dean sci. and engring., 1982—85, dean faculty of sci., 1986—90, acad. vice rector, 1990—97, acting dean, 1985—86, prof. emeritus, 2005—; pres. Can. Consortium of Sci. Socs., 1992—94. Cons. OAS, Washington, 1979-80, Agence de Coop. Culture & Tech., Paris, 1982-83, Can. Internat. Devel. Agy., Ottawa, 1983-85, UN Environ. Program, Geneva, Switzerland, 1985-86, Internat. Devel. Research Ctr., Ottawa, 1985—. Mem. Ont. Pesticide Adv. Com., 1987-91. Decorated commandeur de l'Ordre des Palmes Académiques (France); knight of merit Order of St. John of Jerusalem. Fellow Entomol. Soc. Can. (bd. dirs. 1977-80); mem. Am. Inst. Biol. Scis., Entomol. Soc. Am., Can. Pest Mgmt. Soc., Assn. Can.-Française Advancement Sci. (bd. dirs. 1984-86), Internat. Soc. Chem. Ecology, Entomol. Soc. of Can. (Gold Medal 2000). Office: U Ottawa PO Box 450 30 Marie Curie St Ottawa ON Canada K1N 6N5 Home Phone: 613-742-1827; Office Phone: 613-562-5800. E-mail: bphilog@uottawa.ca.

PHILOSOPHE, BENJAMIN, surgeon; MD, Boston U., PhD, 1990. Diplomate Md., 1997. Head, divsn. transplantation U. Md., Balt., 2005—. Office: Univ Md Med Ctr 29 S Greene St Ste 200 Baltimore MD 21201 Business E-Mail: bphilosophe@smail.umaryland.edu.

PHILP, RICHARD NILSON, writer, editor, journalist, historian; b. Plainfield, NJ, July 7, 1943; s. Lester Perry and Gladys Emma Linea (Nilson) P. BA in English and Theater cum laude, U. N.C., 1965; MFA in Theater Lit. and Playwriting, Yale U., 1968. Lectr. Yale U., Princeton U., Fordham U., Juilliard, U. Utah, U. Wyo., others; faculty Summer Dance Festival U. Wyo., 1995-97. Author 8 plays, produced 1963-72; author: To Move, To Learn, 1973, Danseur: The Male in Ballet, 1977, Romeo and Juliet, Romeos Dancing, Shakespeare Without Words, 2003, Vladimir Malakov, 2003, Dracula the Ballet, 2004, Peter Pan: A Ballet Scenario, 2005, Alice in Wonderland: A Ballet Scenario, 2005, Village, A Biocentennial Celebration of the Village of Catskill, 2006, Catskill Village, 2009; editor and contbg. author: Memoirs of a Dancer: Shadows, Dreams, Memories, 1979, The Gospel According to Dance, 1980, Alvin Ailey American Dance Theater, 1993, Passion & Line, 1997; exec. editor: Dance Books, 1981-86; founding bd. dirs. World Dance Alliance, 1993; chmn. Dance Mag. Prize for Reportage, Video Danse, 1992, 93, 96, 99; mng. editor Dance Mag., 1970-88, editor-in-chief, 1989—99, exec. editor, 2000-02, editor-in-chief emeritus, 2002-; assoc. editor Critics Choice, 1969-70, assoc. editor After Dark, Magazine of Entertainment, 1970-75; contbr. monthly column Kickoff, 1989—2002; contbr. articles to profl. jours. Treas. Dance Mag. Found., 1984-93; co-chmn. internat. adv. bd. Jackson Ballet Competition, Miss., 1989-2004; selection com. ann. Broadway Astaire awards, 1989-2005; bd. dirs. Israel Dance Collection Libr., 1989—95, Joffrey Ballet Sch., 1994—, Video Danse, Paris, Lively Art Christ Ch. Episcopal, Hudson, NY; treas., bd. dirs. Beattie-Powers Pl., 2006-, Beatles Powers Pl. historian, 2006-; adv. bd. Juilliard Sch., 1994-2002; bd. advisors Thomas Cole's Cedar Grove, 1999—; docent Thomas Cole's Cedar Grove, 2001—; active Catskill Bicentennial Com., 2006; historian Catskill Village, 2006—, Town of Catskill Historian, 2008-, curator Catskill River Views, 2009 Recipient Spl. citation Soc. Illustrators, Bronze medal 28th Internat. Film and TV Fest, NYC, 1985, Silver medal Chgo. Internat. Film Festival, 1985, TV Documentary Writing award Am. Film Festival, 1986, Nijinsky award, 1994, Ellen Rettus Planning Achievement award for cmty. svc., 2006. Mem. Catskill Writers Group (founder 1978), Devon Beekeepers Assn. (Eng.), Mountain Beekeepers Assn., 2006-. Home and Office: 166 Bridge St Catskill NY 12414-1404 Home: The Towers Apt 22 33-15 80th St Jackson Heights NY 11372 also: Vista Harbor Apt 10C 2800 Indian River Blvd Vero Beach FL 32960 Office Phone: 518-943-5308. Personal E-mail: richardphilp@mhcable.com.

PHILPOTT, LARRY LA FAYETTE, retired horn player; b. Alma, Ark., Apr. 5, 1937; s. Lester and Rena (Owens) P.; m. Elise Robichaud, Nov. 24, 1962 (div. June 1975); children: Daniel, Stacy; m. Anne Sokol, Feb. 14, 1984. BS, Ga. So. Coll., 1962; MusM, Butler U., 1972. Instr. in horn Butler U., De Pauw U.; dir. music Cedarcrest Sch., Marysville, Wash., 1991—2007; instr. horn Western Wash. U., Dept Music, Bellingham, 1995-98. Mem., N.C. Symphony, 1960, Savannah (Ga.) Symphony, L'Orchestre Symphonique de Quebec, Que., Can., 1962-64, prin. horn player, Indpls. Symphony Orch., 1964-89, Flagstaff Summer Festival, 1968-; artist in-residence Ind.-Purdue Indpls.; appeared with, Am. Shakespeare Theatre, summer 1965, Charlottetown Festival, summers 1967-68, Flagstaff Summer Festival, 1968-85, Marrowstone Music Festival, 1985—. Served with USN, 1956-60. Mem. Music Educators Nat. Conf., Am. Fedn. Musicians, Internat. Conf. Symphony and Opera Musicians, Internat. Horn Soc., Coll. Music Soc., Phi Mu Alpha Sinfonia. Home: 8 Calahorra Way Hot Springs Village AR 71909-5401 Personal E-mail: larryphilpott@hotmail.com.

PHILPOTT, LINDSEY, civil engineer, researcher, educator; b. Bridestowe, Devonshire, Eng., Aug. 2, 1948; came to U.S., 1983; s. George Anthony and Joyce Thirza (Teeling) P.; m. Christine May Pembury, Aug. 20, 1974 (div.); children: David, Elizabeth; m. Kathleen Linda Matson, Feb. 17, 1982 (div.); children: Nicholas, Benjamin; m. Kim Elaine Moore, Nov. 24, 1991. Higher Nat. Cert. in Civil Engring., Bristol Poly., Eng., 1973; BSCE, U. Ariz., 1986, MSCE, 1987, U. Norwich, 2008. Registered profl. engr., Calif.; lic. water treatment plant operator, Calif.; USCG lic. operator 100 ton master. Area structural engr. Dept. Environment (Property Svcs. Agy.), Bristol, 1971-73; civil engr. Webco Civil Engring., Exeter, Eng., 1973-75; tech. mgr. Devon & Cornwall Housing Assn., Plymouth, Eng., 1975-79; prin., architect S.W. Design, Plymouth, 1979-81; archtl. engr. United Bldg. Factories, Bahrain, 1981-83; jr. engr. Cheyne Owen, Tucson, 1983-87; civil engr. Engring. Sci. Inc., Pasadena, Calif., 1987-89; project engr. Black & Veatch, Santa Ana, Calif., 1989-90; sr. engr. Brown & Caldwell, Irvine, Calif., 1990-91; environ. engr. Met. Water Dist. So. Calif., LA, 1991—2002; instr. USCG and marlinespike seamanship Orange Coast Coll. Sailing Ctr., Newport Beach, Calif., 1999—; mgr. vol. support svcs. Ocean Inst., Dana Point, Calif., 2002—03; instr. Calif. Sailing Acad., Marina del Rey, 2003—. Adj. prof. hydraulics and instrumentation, San Antonio Coll., Walnut, Calif., 1995-2000, ACC instr., Calif. Sailing Acad., Marina del Rey, 2002—; cons. forensic specialist, Garrett Engrs., Inc., Long Beach, Calif., 2003—. Author: Knots-A Complete Guide, 2004, Pocket Guide to Knots, 2006, The Complete Book of Fishing Knots, Leaders and Lines, 2008. Foster parent Foster Parents Plan, Tucson, 1985-87; vol. reader tech. books Recording for the Blind, Hollywood, Calif., 1988-89, South Bay, Calif., 1990-91, Pomona, Calif., 1991—; vol. sailor/tchr. L.A. Maritime Inst. Topsail Youth Program, 1994—, Ocean Inst., 1998—; instr. Calif. Sailing Acad., Marina delRay, Calif., 2002—. Mem.: ASCE, Calif. Sailing Acad., ACCI, Am. Sailing Assn., Engrs. Soc. (pres. 1985—96), Water Environment Fedn., Am. Water Resources Assn. (water quality com. 1990—), Am. Water Works Assn., Santa Monica Bay Power Fleet (sec. Marina del Rey chpt. 2000—), Mensa, Internat. Guild of Knot Tyers (pres. Pacific Am. br. 2000—04, 2006—08, editor, J. Knotting Matters 2008—), Marina Venice Yacht Club (commodore 1999), South Bay Yacht Racing Club (Marina del Rey, Calif., commodore 1996), Internat. Order of Blue Gavel (treas. dist. 11 2002, sec. 2009). Avocations: hiking, bicycling, sailing, crosswords, knot-tying. Office: Garrett Engrs Inc Atlantic Ave Long Beach CA 90807 Home Phone: 562-595-8854; Office Phone: 800-229-3647. Personal E-mail: marline.man@verizon.net.

PHINNEY, WILLIAM CHARLES, retired geologist; b. South Portland, Maine, Nov. 16, 1930; s. Clement Woodbridge and Margaret Florence (Foster) P.; m. Colleen Dorothy Murphy, May 31, 1953; children— Glenn, Duane, John, Marla. BS, MIT, 1953, MS, 1956, PhD, 1959. Faculty geology U. Minn., 1959-70; chief geology br. NASA Lyndon B. Johnson Space Center, Houston, 1970-82, chief planetology br., 1982-89, ret., 1994. NASA prin. investigator lunar samples. Contbr. articles to profl. jours. Served with C.E. AUS, 1953-55. Recipient NASA Exceptional Sci. Achievement medal, 1972, NASA Cert. of Commendation, 1987; NASA rsch. grantee, 1972-94, NSF rsch. grantee, 1960-70. Mem. Am. Geophys. Union, AAAS, Mineral. Soc. Am., Geol. Soc. Am., Minn. Acad. Sci. (dir.), Sigma Xi. Home: 18063 Judicial Way S Lakeville MN 55044-8895

PHIPPS, BENJAMIN KIMBALL, II, lawyer; b. Boston, Jan. 16, 1933; s. Benjamin Kimball and Bertha Elizabeth (Forsyth) P.; m. Phyllis Jarrett Anderson, Jan. 10, 1962; children: Lisa Jarrett, Christina Caroline. BS in Commerce, U. Va., 1955, LLB, 1958. Bar: Fla. 1964, U.S. Dist. Ct. (no. dist.) Fla., U.S. Claims Ct., U.S. Ct. Appeals (5th and 11th cirs.), U.S. Tax Ct.; cert. Inst. Profls. in Taxation, 2004. Pvt. practice, Tallahassee, 1965—; chmn. & sr. ptnrs. Phipps & Havell. Counsel tax com. Fla. Ho. of Reps., 1966-72, counsel to spkr., 1973-74, mem. adv. com. fin. & tax com., 1983-84; mem. Legis. Task Force Taxpayers' Bill Rights, 1989-91; elected dir. Fla. Coun. Property Tax Lawyers, 2003 Contbr. articles to profl. jours.; columnist Tallahassee Democrat. Chmn. Hist. Tallahassee Preservation Bd., 1970-91; mem. Tallahassee Trust for Hist. Preservation, 1997—, treas., 1998—. Served to capt., U.S. Army, 1958-64. Mem. ABA (tax sect. state and local tax com.), Tallahassee Bar Assn., Fla. Bar Assn. (treas., vice chmn., chmn. tax sect. 1985-86, editl. bd. Fla. Bar Jour. News, chmn. 1975-76), Inst. Profls. Taxation, CMI, Gov.'s Club, Univ. Ctr. Club, Cosmos Club, Exch. Club, Tiger Bay Club (dir.), Fla. Econ. Club, St. Andrews Soc. (pres. 1978-79), Sigma Alpha Epsilon, Phi Alpha Delta, Pi Delta Epsilon. Republican. Episcopalian. Office: PO Box 1351 Tallahassee FL 32302-1351 Office Phone: 850-222-7000. Business E-Mail: bkp@thephippsfirm.com.

PHIPPS, JOHN RANDOLPH, retired army officer; b. Kansas, Ill, May 16, 1919; s. Charles Winslow and Kelsey Ethel (Torrence) P.; m. Pauline M. Prunty, Feb. 8, 1946; children: Charles W., Kelsey J. Phipps-Selander. BS in Econs. with honors, U. Ill., 1941; M.P.A., Sangamon State U., 1976; A course, Command and Gen. Staff Coll., 1959, nuclear weapons employment course, 1962; course, U.S. Army War Coll., 1973, U.S. Nat. Def. U., 1978. Owner, operator chain shoe stores in, Ill., 1946-70; commd. 2d lt. F.A. U.S. Army, 1941, advanced through grades to capt., 1943; service in Philippines and Japan; discharged as maj., 1946; organizer, comdr. Co. E, 130th Inf., Ill.; N.G., Mattoon, 1947, comdg. officer 2d Bn., 130th Inf., 1951, lt. col. 2d Bn., 130th Inf., 1951; called to fed. service, 1952; adv. (29th Regt., 9th Republic of Korea Div.), 1952-53; comdr. officer 1st Bn., 130th Inf., Ill. N.G., 1954, col., 1959; comdg. officer 2d Brigade, 33d Div., 1963-67; asst. div. comdr. 33d Inf. Div., 1967, brig. gen., 1967; comdr. 33d Inf. Brigade, Chgo., 1967-70, Ill. Emergency Ops. Hdqrs., 1970, asst. adj. gen. Ill., 1970-77, acting adj. gen., 1977-78, adj. gen., 1978, promoted to maj. gen., 1978, now maj. gen. ret. Decorated Silver Star, Bronze Star, Disting. Service medal, Combat Infantry Badge, Army Disting. Service medal Ill., various Philippine and Korean decorations; State of Ill. Long and Honorable Service medal. Mem. VFW, Adj. Gens. Assn. U.S., N.G. Assn. U.S., N.G. Assn. Ill., Am. Legion, Amvets. Home: 100 Wabash Ave Mattoon IL 61938-4524

PHIPPS, ROBERT LEE, information technology manager; b. Oxnard, Calif., Mar. 16, 1963; m. Beatriz Phipps, Sept. 9, 1995; children: Cynthia, Stephanie. AS in Engring., Ventura Coll., Calif., 1993; BS in Computer Sci., Calif. State Poly. U., Pomona, 1989, MBA, 2003. Cert. computing profl. Inst. Cert. Computing Profls., 1995, CISM Info. Sys. Audit Control Assn., 2005; wilderness 1st responder Wilderness Med. Assocs., 2006. Computer programmer Wilsey Foods, Industry, Calif., 1987—90; programmer-analyst Sirena Swimwear, El Monte, Calif., 1990—92; sr. programmer analyst Disney Consumer Products, Burbank, Calif., 1992—95, info. tech. mgr. Glendale, Calif., 1995—. Bd. mem., dir. mem. svcs. Inst. Cert. Computing Profls., Chgo., 1998—99; mem. Mt. SAC RISSC Adv. Bd., 2004—. Team mem. Cmty. Emergency Response Team, Pomona, Calif., 2005—; mem. Cal Poly. Pomona Computer Sci. Industry Adv. Bd., 2007—. Mem.: ISACA, Am. Inst. Aeronautics & Astonautics (life), Air Force Assn. (life), Planetary Soc., MENSA, Toastmasters Internat. (Advanced Toastmasters Gold award 2003). Avocations: aerospace, hiking, scouting.

PHIPPS, SHAWN CHRISTOPHER, occupational therapist; s. John Phipps and Judith Scheifley. BS, U. Southern Calif., LA, 1997; MS, San Jose State U., Calif., 2002; PhD, Touro U., Cypress, Calif., 2005. Registered Occupl. therapist Nat. Bd., 1998, lic. Calif. Bd. Occupl. Therapy, 2001. Occupl. therapy supr. & clin. specialist Rancho Los Amigos Nat. Rehab. Ctr., Downey, Calif., 1998—2008; asst. prof. occupl. therapy Calif. State U., Dominguez Hills, LA, 2003—; occupl. therapist Childrens's Hosp., LA, 2005—; therapy mgr. Calif. Children's Svc., LA, 2008—. Chair LA Occupl. Therapy Leadership Forum, 2007—08. Contbr. articles to jours. (Cordelia Myers Writer's award, 2008), chapters to books. Mem.: World Fedn. Occupl. Therapist, Am. Occupl. Therapy Assn. (alt. rep. 2006—08, chair calif. conf. com. 2007—08), Occupl. Therapy Assn. Calif. (dir. 2002—07, pres. 2008, Occupl. Therapy Practice award 2005). Avocations: piano, tennis, travel. Office: Occupational Therapy Assn Calif PO Box 276567 Sacramento CA 95827-6567

PHITAYAKORN, ROY, surgeon; BS, Allegheny Coll., Meadville, Pa., 1998; MD, U. Pitts., Pa., 2002; MHPE, U. Ill., Chgo., 2006. Chief resident gen. surgery Case Western Res. U., Cleve., 2002—. Contbr. scientific papers to profl. jours. Recipient "Rookie of Yr. award", Allegheny Coll., 1995, "Inspiration award", 1996, "Dedication award", 1997, "Dean's award for Leadership", 1998, award, U. Pitts. Sch. Medicine, 2002, Sheehan Cheke Meml. prize, 2002, Best MHPE Thesis award, U. Ill., 2007; Surg. Edn. Rsch. fellowship, Assn. Surg. Edn., 2005—06. Mem.: ACS, Soc. America Gastrointestinal Endoscopic Surgeons, Assn. Academic Surgeons, Assn. Surg. Edn.

PHOENIX, BETHANY JOYCE, healthcare educator; d. Charles Victor and Marilyn Joyce Quinn; children: Stephanie Kay Kasten, Aurora Arianne Kasten. BSc, U. Calif., San Francisco, 1988, MSc, 1990, PhD, 1997. Cert. clin. nurse specialist, Calif. Bd. Registered Nursing, 1997. Assoc. health scis. clin. prof. U. Calif. Sch. Nursing, 1997—; behavioral health educator Kaiser Health Plan, San Francisco, 2003—. Chpt. women's leader Soka Gakkai Internat., San Mateo, Calif., 2004—08, culture dept. academic divsn. leader, 2006—08. Named Myrtle Crawford Lectr., Coll. Nursing U. Sask., 2005; Traineeship, Natl. Inst. Mental Health, 1988—92, Advanced Edn. Nursing Tng. grant, Health Resources and Svcs. Adminstrn., 2000—. Mem.: Am. Psychiat. Nurses Assn. (chair, advanced practice com. 2006—07). Buddhist. Office: Univ Calif San Francisco 2 Koret Way UCSF Box 0608 San Francisco CA 94143-0608 Business E-Mail: beth.phoenix@nursing.ucsf.edu.

PHOENIX, DAVID D., special education educator; b. Greensboro, NC, Mar. 21, 1945; s. David D. Phoenix and Gladys Corrine Apple; m. Pearl Z. Phoenix, Aug. 13, 1976; children: Karen Deborah Tarlton, David Irvin Fox, Heather Shanti-Dhana. BA in Speech and Drama, U. Nev., Reno, 1968, EdS, 1975, MA in English, 1974. Cert. in learning disabilities Calif. Chancellors Office, 1984. Helitack foreman Bur. Land Mgmt., Carson City, Nev., 1964—72; supr. vocat. evaluation ctr. Bur. Rehab., Reno, 1972—82; human resources specialist U. Nev., 1984—85, instr.; prof. spl. edn. Pierce Coll., Woodland Hills, Calif., 1985—. Office: Pierce Coll 6201 Winnetka Ave Woodland Hills CA 91371 Home Fax: 818-710-4219. Business E-Mail: phoenid@piercecollege.edu.

PHOENIX, G. KEITH, lawyer; b. Centralia, Ill., Aug. 13, 1946; BA in Liberal Arts, So. Ill. U., 1968; JD, St. Louis U., 1973. Bar: Mo. 74, U.S. Dist. Ct. (so. dist.) Ill. 75, U.S. Ct. Appeals (7th and 8th cirs.) 82. Assoc. Coburn, Croft & Shepherd & Putzell, St. Louis, 1974—79; sr. counsel, pres. Sandberg, Phoenix & von Gontard, St. Louis, 1979—. Legal cons. Am. Acad. Pedist. Contbr. articles on med./legal topics to profl. jours. Mem. bd. trustees St. Louis U., 2005—. 1st lt. US Army, 1968—71, Vietnam. Decorated Bronze Star with cluster, Air medal with cluster, Vietnam medal; named one of Mo. and Kans. Civil Litig. Super Lawyers, 2005—08; named to Best Lawyers in Am., 2003—08. Mem.: Product Liability Adv. Coun. (lead trial coun., Mo. Lawyers Top Verdicts 2007), Am. Bd. Trial Advocacy (past pres.), Lawyer's Assn. (past pres.), St. Louis Bar Assn., Mo. Bar Assn., Ill. Bar Assn. (Named One of the Top Trial Lawyers in Am. 2002, 2003). Office: Sandberg Phoenix & von Gontard One City Centre 1500 Saint Louis MO 63101-1880 Office Phone: 314-231-3332. Business E-Mail: kphoenix@sandbergphoenix.com.

PHOENIX, JOAQUIN RAPHAEL, actor; b. San Juan, Oct. 28, 1974; s. John Bottom and Arlyn Dunetz. Actor: (TV films) Backwards: The Riddle of Dyslexia, 1984, Kids Don't Tell, 1985, Secret Witness, 1988; (TV series) Morningstar/Eveningstar, 1986; (films) SpaceCamp, 1986, Russkies, 1987, Parenthood, 1989, Walking the Dog, 1991, To Die For, 1995, Inventing the Abbotts, 1997, U Turn, 1997, Return to Paradise, 1998, Clay Pigeons, 1998, 8MM, 1999, The Yards, 2000, Gladiator, 2000, Quills, 2000, Buffalo Soldiers, 2001, Signs, 2002, It's All About Love, 2003, (voice) Brother Bear, 2003, The Village, 2004, Ladder 49, 2004, Hotel Rwanda, 2004, Walk the Line, 2005 (Best Performance by an Actor in a Motion Picture-Musical or Comedy, Hollywood Fgn. Press Assn. (Golden Globe award), 2006), We Owen the Night, 2007, Reservation Road, 2007, Two Lovers, 2008. Named Favorite Leading Man, People's Choice Awards, 2008. Office: c/o Anonymous Content 3532 Hayden Ave Culver City CA 90232

PHOLSENA, KHEMPHENG, finance and administration bank executive; Grad. Engr., Moscow Energy Inst., 1971; grad., Foreign Trade Acad., Moscow, 1983. Vice-min. Trade and External Econ. Relations, 1989—93; sec.-gen. Official Devel. Assistance Mgmt. Com., 1993—96; vice-min. Prime Min. Office, 1996—2001; v.p. Com. for Planning and Cooperation, 1993—96, 1998—2003; vice-min. Foreign Affairs, Lao PDR, 2003—04; v.p. (Fin. and Adminstrn.) Asian Devel. Bank, 2004—. Mem.: Commission for Econ., Sci., and Technical Cooperation with Socialist Countries (v.p.), Joint-Commission for Cooperation with the Federation of Russia (v.p.), Lao-Japan Friendship Assn. (v.p.), Lao-Luxembourg Partnership Commission (v.p.). Office: Asian Development Bank PO Box 789 Manila 0980 Philippines Office Phone: (63-2) 632-5025. Office Fax: (63-2) 636-2444. E-mail: information@adb.org.

PHOMMAHAXAY, PHANTHONG, ambassador; b. Vientiane, Laos, Mar. 2, 1941; m. Amphanh Luangrath; 4 children. Grad. in fgn. affairs, Centre Nat. d'Etudes Politiques Administratives et Juriques, Vientiane, Laos; diploma of fgn. affairs, London. With Lao Min. of Fgn. Affairs, Vientiane, 1962—, embassy attache Beijing, 1965—68, head passport sect., head polit. sect. Vientiane, 1968—73, 2d sec., 1st sec. and chargé d'affaires Lao embassy Paris, 1974—78, dir. NGO sect., dept. internat. orgns. Vientiane, 1978—80, 1st sec., dept. head mission Bangkok, 1980—84, dep. dir. gen., dir. gen. press dept. Vientiane, 1984—90, amb. to Indonesia, 1990—94, dir. gen. Asia Pacific and Africa dept. Vientiane, 1994—95, amb. to Australia and N.Z., 1995—98, amb. to Germany, the Netherlands, Switzerland and Austria, 1998—2001, amb. to US Washington, 2001—. Avocations: reading, golf. Office: Embassy of the Laos 2222 S St NW Washington DC 20008 E-mail: laoemb@verizon.net.

PHONGKUSOLCHIT, KIATTISAK, finance educator, researcher; s. Jitt Phongkusolchit and Vilai Phongkusoljit. BS in Material Sci., Srinakharinwirot U., Bangkok, 1999; MS in Mfg. Sys., So. Ill. U., Carbondale, 2003; PhD in Bus. Adminstrn., So. Ill. U., 2003. Asst. prof. U. Tenn., Martin, 2007—; tchg. & rsch. asst. So. Ill. U., 2001—07. Consultant Bangplakhod Concrete Pipe Co. Ltd., Prasamutjadee, 2007—, Thai Lotus Indsl. Co. Ltd., Bang Bua Thong, Nonthaburi, 2007—. Contbr. articles to profl. publs. Vol. judge Ill. Jr. Acad. Sci., Carbondale, 2006; vol. gear program Internat. Student and Scholar So. Ill. U., 2003. Grant, Pontikes Ctr. Mgmt. Info., 2006—07. Mem.: Prodn. & Ops. Mgmt. Soc., Decision Scis. Insts., Thai Student Assn. at So. Ill. U. Carbondale (v.p. 2003—07), Golden Key Internat. Honor Soc., Internat. Honor Soc. Beta Gamma Sigma, Honor Soc. Phi Kappa Phi. Office: Univ Tennessee Martin 231 Lovelace St Martin TN 38238 Office Fax: 731-881-7231.

PHUNG, NGUYEN DINH, medical educator; b. Ninh Binh, Vietnam, Sept. 25, 1950; came to U.S., 1975; s. Thu Dinh Nguyen and Minh Tuyet Le; m. Thuy Thanh Tran, Sept. 25, 1974; children: The-Ngoc, Khoi-Nguyen, Thien Huong. MD, Saigon Med. Sch., 1973. Diplomate Am. Bd. Internal Medicine, Am. Bd. Allergy and Immunology. Clin. instr. medicine, staff physician U. Okla. Health Scis. Ctr. & Vets. Hosp., Oklahoma City, 1982-84; clin. asst. prof. medicine U. Tex. Med. Sch., Houston, 1989—. Co-author: Practical Allergy & Immunology, 1983; contbr. articles to profl. jours. Mem. ACP, Am. Acad. Allergy and Immunology. Avocations: writing, music. Office: Allergy and Asthma Clinic 2905 Milam St Houston TX 77006-3609

PI, EDMOND HSIN-TUNG, psychiatry educator; MD, Cath. U. Coll. Medicine, 1972. Cert. in subspecialty psychosomatic medicine, Am. Bd. Psychiatry and Neurology. Chief resident U. Ky. Med. Ctr., Lexington, 1977-78; instr. psychiatry U. So. Calif. Sch. Medicine, LA, 1978-80, asst. prof., 1980-83; assoc. prof. Med. Coll. Pa., Phila., 1983-85, U. So. Calif. Sch. Medicine, 1985-88, prof. clin. psychiatry, 1988—98; prof. Charles R. Drew U. Medicine and Sci., 1998—2003; clin. prof. psychiatry Sch. Medicine, UCLA, 1999—2005; prof. clin. psychiatry Sch. Medicine, U. So. Calif., 2005—, assoc. chair for clin. affairs, dept. psychiatry, 2006—. Asst. dir. psychopharmacology U. So. Calif. Sch. Medicine, 1978-80; asst. dir. adult psychiat. clinic L.A. County and U. So. Calif. Med. Ctr., 1980-83; dir. adult psychiat. clinic Med. Coll. Pa., Phila., 1983-85; dir. Adult Psychiat. Inpatient Svcs., L.A. County and U. So. Calif. Med. Ctr., 1985-91, dir. Adult Psychiat. Outpatient Svcs., 1995-97; dir. transcultural psychiatry U. So. Calif. Sch. Medicine, 1991-98; med. dir. State of Calif. Dept. Mental Health, 1997-98; dir. Consultation and Liaison Svcs., L.A. County and U. So. Calif. Med. Ctr., 1998; exec. vice-chmn., assoc. ctr. dir. Augustus F. Hawkins Mental Health Ctr., Martin Luther King. Jr./Charles R. Drew U. Med. Ctr., 1998-2003; dir. psychiat. inpatient svc. Harbor/UCLA Med. Ctr., 2003-05; dir. psychiat. consultation and liaison svcs. L.A. (Calif.) County and U. So. Calif. Med. Ctr., 2005—, assoc. chair clin. affairs, 2006—. Author: Reactions to Psychotropic Medications, 1987, (book chpts.) Transcultural Psychiatry, Clinical Psychopharmacology, 1985—; contbr. articles to profl. jours. Mem. Calif. Gov.'s Com. Employment Disabled Persons, Sacramento, 1993—2007; bd. dirs. Chinese Bus. Assn., LA, 1990—92, Com. of 100, NYC, 1993—98, San Gabriel chpt. ARC, Calif., 1994—97, Mental Health Assn., LA County, Calif., 1995—97, 1998—2001. Vis. scholar Com. on Scholarly Comm. with People's Republic of China U.S. Nat. Acad. Scis., Washington, 1987-88; Treval fellow Am. Coll. Neuropsychopharmacology, 1982. Fellow Am. Psychiat. Assn. (chair com. Asian-Am. psychiatrists 1998-2000), Am. Soc. Social Psychiatry, Pacific Rim Coll. Psychiatry (treas. 1991-97), Am. Coll. Psychiatrists; mem. Soc. Study Psychiatry and Culture, Pacific Rim Assn. Clin. Pharmogenetics, Assn. Chinese Am. Psychiatrists (pres. 1995—). Avocations: photography, writing, travel, tennis, media communications. Office: LAC & USC Med Ctr Dept Psychiatry 2010 Zonal Ave # 1P1 Los Angeles CA 90033 Office Phone: 323-226-7975. Business E-Mail: ehpi@usc.edu.

PIAGENTINI, SUSAN, music educator; PhD, Northwestern U., Evanston, Ill. Asst. prof. Valley City State U., ND, Elmhurst Coll., Ill.; coord., theory & aural skills Northwestern U. Sch. Music, Evanston, Ill., 2000—. Recipient Faculty Honor Roll, Northwestern U. Student Govt., 2006—07. Mem.: Soc. Music Theory, Coll. Music Soc. (treas.,regional chpt. 2006—), Omicron Delta Kappa, Pi Kappa Lambda.

PIANALTO, SANDRA, bank executive; b. Valli del Pasubio, Italy, Aug. 4, 1954; B in Econs., U. Akron, Ohio, 1976; M in Econs., George Washington U., 1985; grad. advanced mgmt. prog., Duke U. Fuqua Sch. Bus., Durham, NC; LHD (hon.), U. Akron, Baldwin-Wallace Coll., Kent State U., Ursuline Coll., Notre Dame Coll.; LLD (hon.), John Carroll U.; D of Bus. Adminstrn. (hon.), Cleve. State U. Economist bd. govs. Fed. Reserve Sys.; staff mem. budget com. U.S. Ho. of Reps.; economist rsch. dept. Fed. Res. Bank Cleve., 1983—84, asst. v.p. pub. affairs, 1984—88, v.p., sec. bd. dirs., 1988—93, first v.p., COO, 1993—2003, pres., 2003—. Bd. dirs. Cleve. Found., Gr. Cleve. Partnership, U. Hosp. Health Sys., Rock & Roll Hall of Fame and Mus., N.E. Ohio Coun. Higher Edn., Cath. Diocese Cleve. Found., Ohio Bus. Alliance for Higher Edn. & Economy; chmn. bd. dirs. United Way Greater Cleve. Office: Fed Res Bank Cleve PO Box 6387 Cleveland OH 44101-1387 Office Phone: 216-579-2000.*

PIANKA, ERIC RODGER, population biologist, educator; b. Hilt, Calif., Jan. 1939; s. Walter and Virginia P.; m. Helen Dunlap, Dec. 20, 1965 (div. Dec. 1980); children: Karen, Gretchen. BA, Carleton Coll., 1960; PhD (NIH fellow), U. Wash., 1965; DSc, U. We. Australia, 1990. NIH postdoctoral fellow Princeton U., 1965-68, U. Western Australia, Nedlands, 1966-67; asst. prof. zoology U. Tex., Austin, 1968-72, assoc. prof., 1972-77, prof., 1977—, Denton A. Cooley Centennial prof. zoology, 1986—. Vis. prof. U. Kans., 1978, U. P.R., 1981 Author: Evolutionary Ecology, 6th edit., 2000, also Greek, Japanese, Spanish, Polish and Russian transl., Ecology and Natural History of Desert Lizards, 1986, The Lizard Man Speaks, 1994; co-editor: Lizard Ecology: Studies of a Model Organism, 1983, Lizard Ecology: Historical and Experimental Perspectives, 1994, Lizards: Windows to the Evolution of Diversity, 2003, Varanoid Lizards of the world, 2004; mng. editor The Am. Naturalist, 1971-74; mem. edit. bd. BioSci, 1975-80; bd. editors Nat. Geog. Rsch., 1985—; contbr. articles to profl. publs. Named Disting. Herpetologist, 2004, Disting. Tex. Scientist, 2006; Fulbright Sr. Rsch. scholar, 1990-91; Guggenheim fellow, 1978-79; NSF grantee, 1966-94; Nat. Geog. Soc. grantee, 1975-79, 89-90, 95-96. Fellow AAAS; mem. Am. Soc. Naturalists, Ecol. Soc. Am., Am. Soc. Ichthyologists and Herpetologists, Soc. for Study Evolution, Herpetologists League, Western Australian Naturalists Club, French Varanid Assn. (hon.). Research on ecology and diversity of desert lizards. *Differential reproductive success is all pervasive, but awfully short sighted. The disparity between what humans could be versus what we, in fact, have achieved is simply pitiful. For the first time in the history of life on Earth, a product of natural selection has looked back at itself and said "Ah ha, I see you!" Yet we are totally unable to put this wisdom to use to save ourselves, let alone the other creatures sharing this poor beleaguered planet. A wild rattlesnake has as much "right to life" as you or I. Watch as Homo the sap outreproduces himself right to extinction, a victim of natural selection running blindly to its beat just like all other forms of life.*

PIANKA, GEORGE, orthopedic surgeon; arrived in US, 1964; s. Antoni and Aleksandra Pianka; m. Audrone Julia Raskys, Aug. 16, 1986; children: George, John Paul, Mark, Matthew. BS, Cornell U., Ithaca, NY, 1980; MD, U. Conn., Farmington, 1984. Intern Lenox Hill Hosp., NYC, 1984, resident orthopedics, 1985—89, attending physician orthopedics, 1990, chief hand surgery; fellow hand surgery Hosp. for Joint Diseases, NYC, 1989—90; attending physician orthopedics Phelps Meml. Hosp., Sleepy Hollow, NY, 1995. Contbr. chapters to books. Recipient Resident Tchg. award, Lenox Hill Orthopedic Dept., 1995, 2000. Fellow: Am. Soc. for Surgery of Hand, Am. Acad. Orthopedic Surgeons; mem.: NY Soc. for Surgery of Hand. Avocations: tennis, fishing, skiing. Office: Hudson Valley Bone and Joint Surgeons 24 Saw Mill River Rd Hawthorne NY 10532 also: 73 E 71st St New York NY 10021 Office Phone: 914-631-7777, 212-472-5899. Personal E-mail: aidadrpianka@hotmail.com.

PIANKO, THEODORE A., lawyer; b. Dennville, NJ, Sept. 5, 1955; s. Theodore and Pasqualina (Liguori) Pianko; m. Beatriz Maria Olivera (div. Dec. 1985); m. Kathryn Anne Lindley, Feb. 18, 1990; children: Matthew James, Samuel Wahoo, Zoe Wahoo. BA, SUNY, 1975; JD, U. Mich., 1978. Bar: Mich. 1978, Ill. 1979, Calif. 1980. Atty. Ford Motor Co., Dearborn, Mich., 1978-80; assoc. Lillick McHose & Charles, LA, 1980-83; ptnr. Sidley & Austin, LA, 1983-94, Christie, Parker & Hale, Newport Beach, Calif., 1994—2006; gen. counsel TGR Group Asia, 2007—. Home: 60/11 Moo 4 Cherngtalay Thalang Phuket 83110 Thailand Office: TGR Group Asia 164-19 Moo 6 Paklock Thalang Phucket 83110 Thailand Home Phone: 66-84-8501304; Office Phone: 66-76-60426. Business E-Mail: ted@pianko.com.

PIANO, RENZO, architect; b. Genoa, Italy, Sept. 14, 1937; m. Magda Arduino, 1962; m. Emilia Rossato, 1992; children: Carlo, Matteo, Lia, Giorgio Anthony. Dip.Arch., Poly. of Milan, 1964; PhD in Fine Arts (hon.); Pratt Inst., NY, 2002. Worked with Franco Albini, Milan, 1962-64, E. Piano, Genoa, 1964-65, Z.S. Makowsky, London, 1965-70; ptnr. Piano and Rogers Architects, London, Paris and Genoa, 1970—, Piano and Rice, Genoa, Paris and London, 1977—93, Renzo Piano Building Workshop, Genoa, Paris and London, 1994—. Lectr. Poly. of Milan, 1965-68; vis. lectr. Columbia U., NYC, 1967, U. Pa., Phila., 1967, U. Bucharest, Romania, 1968, Poly. of Delft, Netherlands, 1969, Unesco, Paris, 1973, Oslo Sch. Architecture, 1976; prof. architecture Archtl. Assn. Sch., London, 1971, Poly. Cen. London, 1971, created with Harvard U., Architecture Workshop Found., 2001-. Prin. works include Italian Industry Pavilion, Expo '70, Japan, 1970, Fitzroy St. Comml. Ctr., Cambridge, UK, 1970, B&B Italia Offices, Como, 1971, Universal Oil Products U.K. Head Office and UOP Fragrances Ltd. Lab., Tadworth, Surrey, 1972, Aston Martin Lagonda Ltd. Offices, Showroom, Restaurant, etc., London, 1973, PATScentre, Cambridge, 1975, Inst. de Recherche et de Coordination Acoustique, Paris, 1977, Centre Beaubourg, Paris, 1977, Kronenbourg factory, Strasbourg, 1978, Quartiere Il Rigo housing estate, Corciano, Perugia, Italy, 1978-82, Civic Ctr. and Libr., Loano, Savona, Italy, 1980, Nationalgalerie extensions & housing, West Berlin, 1981, De Menil Collection bldg., Houston, 1981-83, Bance Agricola Comml. bldg., Reggio Emilia, Italy, 1981-83, IBM travelling exhbn. pavilions, 1982, Palazzo a Vela conversion, 1982, Centocelle/Torrespaccata Bus. Ctr., Rome, 1982, Banca Agricola Comml. br. bldg., Modena, Italy, 1982, 5 Met. Rwy. Stas., Genoa, 1983, Il Prometeo music rsch. lab., Venice, 1984, Centre Georges Pompidou cinema extensions, Paris, 1984, Comml. Ctr. office bldgs., Naples, Italy, 1984, Kenya Energy Tech. Inst., Nairobi, 1984, Leisure Ctr., Cremona, Italy, 1984, Columbus Expedition 500th Anniversary designs, Genoa, 1984, Office Bldg. for Lowara factory, Vicenza, Italy, 1985, Mus. for Menil Collection, Houston, 1986, Hdqs. for Light Metals Exptl. Inst., Novara, Italy, 1987, Nicola Football stadium, Bari, Italy, 1990, Bercy Comml. Ctr., Paris, 1990, IRCAM Extension, Paris, 1990, Cruise Ships for P&O, USA, 1990, Housing City of Paris, 1991, Thomson factories, Guyancourt, France, 1991, Underground stas. for Ansaldo, Genoa, Italy, 1991, Hdqrs. Credito Indsl. Sardo, Cagliari, Italy, 1992, Kansai Internat. Airport, Osaka, 1994, Lingotto Congress-Concert Hall, Turin, Italy, 1994, Renzo Piano Bldg. Workshop Office, Genoa, 1994, Cy Twombly Pavilion, Houston, 1995, Meridien Hotel at Lingotto and Bus. Ctr., Torino, Italy, 1995, Hdqs. Harbour Authorities, Genoa, 1995, Cinema, Offices, Contemporary Art Mus., Congress Ctr., Landscape, Cité Internat., Lyon, France, 1996, I Portici (Shopping St. at Lingotto), Turin, 1996, Ushibuka Bridge, Kumamoto, Japan, 1997, Mus. Sci. and Tech., Amsterdam, The Netherlands, 1997, Mus. Beyeler Found., Riehen, Basel, Switzerland, 1997, Mercedes Benz Design Ctr., Stuttgart, Germany, 1998, Lodi (Italy) Bank Hdqs., 1998, The NY Times Bldg., NYC, 2000; Renovation and expansion of the Calif. Acad. Sciences, 2000, Morgan Pierpont Library, NYC, 2000, U. of Mich. Law Sch., 2002, High Mus. Expansion, Atlanta, 2005, Morgan Libr. and Mus., 2006, NY Times bldg., 2007, Harvard Art Mus., 2008, Broad Contemporary Art Museum numerous others; exhbns. include Triennale, Milan, 1967, Archtl. Assn., London, 1970, Musée des Arts Decoratifs, Paris, 1973, IBM Travelling Exhbn. in Europe, 1986, Columbus Internat. Exposition, Aquarium and Congress Hall, Genoa, 1992, Out of the blue, Kunst-und Ausstellungshalle, Bonn, Germany, 1997, Out of the blue, Villa Pignatelli, Naples, Italy, 1997, Out of the blue, Gallery MA, Tokyo, 1998, Renzo Piano: The architect's studio, La. Mus. of Modern Art, Humlebaek Copenhagen, Denmark, 2003. Recipient 1st prize Place Beaubourg Competition, Paris, 1971, Auguste Perret prize Internat. Union Architects, 1978, Compasso d'Oro award, Milan, 1981, Arnold W. Brunner Memorial Prize in Architecture Am. Acad. of Arts and Letters, 1994, Erasmus prize, Netherlands, 1995, Art pirze Akademie Künste, Berlin, 1995, Premio Capo Circeo, 1996, Diploma European award for steel structures for elevated heliport structure at Lingotto (Italy), 1997, Pritzker Arch. prize, The White House, 1998, Wexner Prize, Wexner Ctr. for the Arts, 2001, Médaille D'Or, International Union of Architects, Berlin, 2002, Michelangelo Antonioni for the Arts, Rome Auditorium, Italy, 2002, Gold medal Italian Architecture, Milan, 2003, Bus. Cultural award, Italy-Am. C. of C., NY, 2003, McKim prize, Am. Acad. in Rome, 2005, Gold medal, AIA, 2008, Sonning prize, U. Copenhagen, 2008; decorated officer Nat. Order Legion of Honor (France), 2000; named one of 100 Most Influential People, Time Mag., 2006. Fellow: AIA (hon.). Office: Atelier Piano 34 rue des Archives 75004 Paris France also: Studio Renzo Piano Via Rubens 29 16158 Genoa Italy E-mail: italy@rpbw.com, france@rpbw.com.

PIAZZA, MIKE (MICHAEL JOSEPH PIAZZA), retired professional baseball player; b. Norristown, Pa., Sept. 4, 1968; s. Vince and Veronica Piazza; m. Alicia Rickter, Jan. 29, 2005; 1 child, Nicoletta Veronica. Attended, Miami-Dade CC. Catcher LA Dodgers, 1992—97, Fla. Marlins, 1998, NY Mets, 1998—2005, San Diego Padres, 2006, Oakland Athletics, 2007; ret., 2008. Hitting coach, Italian nat. team World Baseball Classic, 2009. Recipient Silver Slugger award, 1993—2002, Ted Williams award, 1997; named Nat. League Rookie Player of Yr., Sporting News, 1993, Nat. League Rookie of Yr., Baseball Writers' Assn., 1993, All-Star Game MVP, 1996; named to Nat. League All-Star Team, 1993—2002, 2004, 2005, Nat. League Slugger Team, 1993. Achievements include holding the Major League record for career home runs hit by a catcher (427). Avocation: heavy metal music.*

PIAZZA, TONY, theater educator; m. Terri Piazza; children: Emma, Alexander. MA in Theatre, San Diego State U., 1992. Dir. theatre Allen CC, Iola, Kans., 1999—. Office: Allen CC 1801 N Cottonwood St Iola KS 66749 Business E-Mail: piazza@allencc.edu.

PICARD, IRVING H., lawyer; b. 1941; BS, U. Pa. Wharton Sch. Finance, 1963; JD, Boston U. Sch. Law, 1966; LLM, NYU Sch. Law, 1967. Bar: Mass. 1966, Mass (US Dist. Ct.) 1974, (4th cir.) (US Ct. Appeals) 1975, (2nd, 7th & 10th cirs.) 1976, (1st & 9th cirs.) 1977, NY 1982, NY (US Dist. Ct. (so. & ea. dist.)) 1982, NY (US Dist. Ct. (no. dist.)) 1986. Ptnr. Baker & Hostetler LLP. Mem.: Assn. Insolvency & Restructuring Advisors, Nat. Assn. Bankruptcy Trustees, Turnaround Mgmt. Assn., Registry Mediators for the US Bankruptcy Ct., Fed. Bar Coun., Commercial Law League America, Am. Bankruptcy Inst., Am. Bar Assn, NY Bar Assn. Office: Baker & Hostetler LLP 45 Rockefeller Plaza 11th Fl New York NY 10111 Office Phone: 212-589-4688. Office Fax: 212-589-4201. E-mail: ipicard@bakerlaw.com.*

PICARD, M(EREDITH) DANE, geologist; b. Washburn, Mo., Aug. 7, 1927; s. Vincent Hayes and Velma Vestal Picard; m. Virginia Reitz Picard, July 5, 1958 (div.); children: Marion, Jacqueline, Dane, Bennet. Student, Swarthmore Coll., 1945; BS, U. Wyo., 1950; AM, Princeton U., 1962, PhD, 1963. Surveyor U.S. Soil Conservation Svc., Worland, Wyo., 1947; geologist Texaco Inc., Casper, Wyo., 1950; geologist, dist. stratigrapher Shell Oil Co., Salt Lake City, 1950-56; geologist St. Helens Petroleum Corp., Casper, 1956-57; dist. mgr. Am. Stratigraphic Co., Durango, Colo., 1957-60; from assoc. prof. to prof. geology U. Nebr., Lincoln, 1963-68; prof. geology and geophysics U. Utah, Salt Lake City, 1968—2002, prof. emeritus, 2002—. Vis. prof. U. Tex., Austin, 1967-68; cons. Utah Geol. Survey, Salt Lake City, 1969-74, Mountain Fuel Supply Co., Salt Lake City, 1972-75. Author: Grit and Clay, 1975, Mountains and Minerals, Rivers and Rocks, 1993, A Late Roundup, 2007; co-author: (with L.R. High Jr.) Sedimentary Structures of Ephemeral Streams, 1973, (with W.L. Stokes and Sheldon Judson) Introduction to Geology, 1978; editor: Henry Mountains Symposium, 1980, Geology and Energy Resources, Uinta Basin of Utah, 1985; co-editor:(with M.F. Miller and A.A. Ekdale) Trace Fossils and Paleoenvironments, 1984. With USN, 1945-46. Named Outstanding Alumnus, Coll. Arts and Scis., U. Wyo., 1994; recipient award for outstanding contbns. to pub. understanding of geology Am. Geol. Inst., 1998. Fellow AAAS, Geol. Soc. Am. (gen. chmn. nat. meeting 1975); mem. Am. Assn. Petroleum Geologists (hon.), Soc. Econ. Paleontologists and Mineralogists (pres. 1984-85), Nat. Assn. Geosci. Tchrs. (pres. 1988-89, Shea award 1997), Utah Geol. Assn. (hon.), Wyo. Geol. Assn. (hon.), Soc. for Sedimentary Geology (hon.; Francis J. Pettijohn medal 2002). Avocations: tennis, climbing. Home: 3520 S Westwood Dr Salt Lake City UT 84109 Office: Dept Geology & Geophysical U Utah Salt Lake City UT 84112 Home Phone: 801-277-3015; Office Phone: 801-440-3696. Business E-Mail: dane.picard@utah.edu.

PICARD, ROBERT GEORGES, writer, educator; b. Pasadena, Calif., July 15, 1951; s. Robert William and Roberta Marlene (Robertson) P.; m. Terry Jean Haverstock, Dec. 28, 1971 (div. May 1979); m. Elizabeth Louise Carpelan, Sept. 15, 1979; children: Anna Elisabeth, Helena Caroline, Alexander William. BA, Loma Linda U., 1974; MA, Calif. State U., Fullerton, 1980; PhD, U. Mo., 1983. Editor Riverside (Calif.) Community News, 1977-79; copy editor, wire editor Ontario (Calif.) Daily Report, 1979-80; publs. editor Freedom of Info. Ctr., Columbia, Mo., 1980-83; from asst. to assoc. prof. La. State U., Baton Rouge, 1983-87; assoc. prof., dir. communication industries mgmt. Emerson Coll., Boston, 1987-90; prof. Calif. State U., Fullerton, 1990—98, Turku Sch. Economics, 1998—2003; Hamrin prof. media econs. Jonkoping Internat. Bus. Sch., Sweden, 2003—. Chair Com. for Media Diversity, Boston, 1987-2003; vis. prof. Turku (Finland) Sch. Econs., 1993-94. Author: The Press and the Decline of Democracy, 1985, The Ravens of Odin: The Press in the Nordic Nations, 1988, Media Economics: Concepts and Issues, 1989, In the Camera's Eye: News Coverage of Terrorist Events, 1991, Media Portrayals of Terrorism, 1993; editor: Press Concentration and Monopoly, 1988, The Cable Network's Handbook, 1993, Media Firms: Structures, Operations and Performance, 2002, The Economics and Financing of Media Companies, 2004, Strategic Responses to Media Market Changes, 2004, Ditigal Terrestrial Television in Europe, 2005; Media Product Portfolios: Issues Mgmt. Multiple Products and Svcs., 2005; Internet and Mass Media, 2008; editor Jour. Media Econs., 1988-96, Jour. Media Bus. Studies, 2004—; assoc. editor Polit. Communication and Persuasion, 1988-91. Chpt. pres. ACLU, Baton Rouge, 1985-87; bd. dirs. New England Inst. for Peace, Boston, 1988-90; coord. publicity Habitat for Humanity, Riverside, 1991-92. Recipient Internat. Rsch. award Assn. for the Advancement of Policy, Rsch. and Devel., 1984, Outstanding Rsch. award Phi Kappa Phi, 1986, Joan Shorenstein Ctr. on Press, Politics, Public Policy fellowship Harvard Univ., 2006. Mem. Assn. for Edn. in Journalism and Mass Communication (chair profl. freedom and responsibility com. 1992-93). Avocations: stamp collecting/philately, sailing. Office: Jönköping Internat Bus Sch Media Mgmt and Transformation Ctr PO Box 1026 SE-551 11 Jönköping Sweden Office Phone: +46 36 15 75 80. Business E-Mail: robert.picard@robertpicard.net.

PICARELLO, ANTHONY R., JR., lawyer; b. 1969; m. Martha Picarello. BA in Social Anthropology, Harvard U., 1991; MA in Religious Studies, U. Chgo. Divinity Sch., 1992; JD, U. Va., 1995. Bar: Va., DC. Law clk. to Hon. Gene Carter US Dist. Ct. Maine, Portland, Maine, 1995—96; assoc. Covington & Burling LLP, Washington, 1996—2000; v.p., gen. counsel The Becket Fund for Religious Freedom, Washington, 2000—07; gen. counsel The US Conf. Catholic Bishops, 2007—. Named one of Litigation's Rising Stars, The Am. Lawyer, 2007. Avocation: gardening. Office: The US Conf Catholic Bishops 3211 4th St NE Washington DC 20017

PICASSO, PALOMA, fashion designer; b. Paris, Apr. 19, 1949; d. Pablo Picasso and Françoise Gilot; m. Rafael Lopez-Cambil, 1978. Student, U. Sorbonne, Paris; studied jewellry design and fabrication. Designer jewellery Yves St. Laurent, 1969, Zolotas, 1971; founder Paloma Picasso Botique, Paris, Japan, Hong Kong. Founder Paloma Picasso Found. Designed costumes and sets for L'Interprétation, 1975, Success, 1978; creations designed by her for Paloma Picasso brand include: jewellery for Tiffany & Co., 1980; fragrances Paloma Picasso, 1984, Minotaure, 1992; cosmetics for L'Oréal; women's accessories for Lopez-Camil Ltd., 1987; hosiery and eyewear for Carrera; bone china, crystal, silverware and tiles for Villeroy & Boch; home linens for Martex; fabrics and wallcoverings for Motif; appeared in film Immoral Tales, 1974. Office: Lopez-Cambil Ltd 37 W 57th St Fl 12 New York NY 10019-3411 also: Nourithe Serraf Martine Herbin 13 cité de Pusy 75017 Paris France

PICAVET, ROBERT CLEMENT, retired lawyer; b. Boston, July 15, 1922; s. Edgar and Jeanne (Gelan) Picavet; m. Marjorie Catherine McKenney Picavet, July 25, 1943; 1 child, Kenneth Robert. AB, Tufts U., 1944; JD, Suffolk U., 1959. Bar: Mass. 1959, US Dist. Ct. Mass. 1962, Maine 1980, US Dist. Ct. Maine 1980, US Supreme Ct. 1981. Claim mgr. Travelers Ins. Co., Danvers, Mass., 1947—82; sole practice Kennebunkport, Maine, 1982—89. Bd. dirs. Plan E Civic Assn., Medford, Mass., 1959—64; chmn. Planning Bd., Medford, 1964—66; rep. Met. Area Planning Coun., Boston, 1969—72; mem. Bd. Appeals, Medford, 1976—80; corporator Lawrence Meml. Hosp., Medford, 1976—80. Served with USAAF, 1943—45, MTO, PTO. Mem.: Masons, Disabled Am. Veterans, Maine Trial Lawyers Assn., Maine Bar Assn. Democrat. Home: Ward Road Ext Kennebunkport ME 04046 also: PO Box 7021 Cape Porpoise ME 04014-7021

PICAZIO, KIM LOWRY, lawyer; b. Greenville, NC, Jan. 8, 1969; d. Harry Etheridge and Marion Thomas Lowry; m. Michael James Picazio, Mar. 25, 1995. BS, U. Miami, 1991; JD, Fla. State U., 1995. Bar: Fla. 1995. Lawyer Heinrich, Gordon, Hargrove, Weihe & James, P.A., Ft. Lauderdale, Fla., 1995-96; atty. Law Offices of Robert D. Hertzberg, P.A., Miami, Fla., 1996—2007, pvt. practice, 2007—. Recipient: Corpus Juris Secundum award (Contract Law), Am. Jurisprudence award (Contract Law); named on of Top Lawyers, South Fla. Legal Guide., 2005-07. Mem. ATLA, Am. Acad. Matrimonial Lawyer, Dade County Bar Assn., First Family Law Inns Ct., Fla. Bar (Family Law Sect.), Fla. Acad. Matrimonial Lawyers. Office: Law Office Kim L Picazio PA One Fin Plaza 100 SE 3rd Ave Ste # 2500 Fort Lauderdale FL 33394 Office Phone: 954-467-5558. Office Fax: 954-462-1335. Personal E-mail: picazio@bellsouth.net. Business E-Mail: kim@picaziolaw.com.

PICCININI, GUALTIERO, philosopher, educator; b. Milan, Nov. 11, 1970; s. Norberto Piccinini and Lucia Vetrano; m. Lori Lea Shelley, July 28, 2004; children: Violet Star Shelley-Pettinelli, Brie Minerva Shelley-Piccinini. PhD, U. Pitts., 2003. Postdoc. fellow Wash. U., St. Louis, 2003—05; asst. prof. U. Mo., St. Louis, 2005—. Office: Univ Mo St Louis 1 University Blvd Saint Louis MO 63121-4400 Business E-Mail: piccininig@umsl.edu.

PICCININO, ROCCO MICHAEL, librarian; b. Phila., Aug. 21, 1949; s. Rocco Anthony and Ida Marie (Minicozzi) P. BA in History magna cum laude, LaSalle Coll., 1971; postgrad., U. NC, 1971—73; MSLS, Drexel U., 1981. Ednl. resources specialist CC of Phila., 1973-74; asst./assoc. libr. United Engrs. & Constructors Inc. (A Raytheon Co.) Libr., Phila., 1974-81, head libr. Boston, 1981-84; asst./assoc. dir. Wentworth Inst. of Tech. Libr., Boston, 1984-89; sci. libr. Smith Coll. Librs., Northampton, Mass., 1989-91, coord. br. libr. svcs., sci. libr., 1991—2006, assoc. dir. br. libr., head young sci. libr., 2007—. Mem. ALA (Assn. Coll. Rsch. Librs. divsn. instruction sect. policy com. 2002-04, nom. com. 2005-07, sci. and tech. sect. coun., co-chair coll. libr. discussion group 1998-02, forum for sci. and tech. libr. rsch. 2000-02, comparison of sci. and tech. com. 2002-04, conf. program planning com. 2003-05, nominating com. 2004-06, info. literacy com. 2006-), Libr. Adminstrn. and Mgmt. Assn. (bldg. and equipment sect., bldgs. for coll. and univ. librs. com., 2000-02, sys. and svcs. sect. program com. 2004-06), Libr. and Info. Tech. Assn., Spl. Librs. Assn. (sci.-tech. divsn., Boston chpt. adv. coun. 1996-04, chair We. Outreach 1996-2004, nominating com. 2004-05), IEEE (libr. adv. coun. 2002-03), Phi Alpha Theta, Beta Phi Mu. Democrat. Roman Catholic. Avocations: travel, bicycling, reading, films. Home: 104 Woods Rd Northampton MA 01062-3507 Office: Smith Coll Young Sci Libr Northampton MA 01063-0001 Office Phone: 413-585-2951. Business E-Mail: rpiccini@smith.edu.

PICCIRILLI, THOMAS EDWARD, writer; b. 1965; Author: (novels) Dark Father, 1990, Shards, 1996, Inside the Works, 1997, Hexes, 1999, The Deceased, 2000, The Night Class, 2000 (Bram Stoker award for Best First Novel, 2003), A Lower Deep, 2001, Grave Men, 2002, Lie Down Already, 2003, A Choir of Ill Children, 2003, Coffin Blues, 2004, Thrust, 2005, November Mourns, 2005, Headstone City, 2006, The Dead Letters, 2006, Frayed, 2007, The Midnight Road, 2007, The Fever Kill, 2007, The Cold Spot, 2008, (non-fiction) Welcome to Hell: A Working Guide for the Beginning Writer, 2000, Deconstructing Tolkien: A Fundamental Analysis of the Lord of the Rings, 2004, (Felicity Grove series) The Dead Past, 1997, Sorrow's Crown, 1998, (story collections) Pentacle, 1995, The Hanging Man and Other Strange Suspensions, 1996, The Dog Syndrome and Other Sick Puppies, 1997, Deep into that Darkness Peering, 1999, Four Dark Nights, 2002, Mean Sheep, 2003, (collection of poems) A Student of Hell, 2000, This Cape Is Red Because I've Been Bleeding, 2002, Waiting My Turn to Go Under the Knife, 2005; contbr. numerous short stories to anthologies; editor: (anthologies) The Devil's Wine, 2004, Midnight Premiere, 2007. Recipient Bram Stoker award for Outstanding Achievement in Poetry. Mailing: c/o Bantam Dell Pub Group Random House Inc 1745 Broadway 3rd Fl New York NY 10019 E-mail: Picself1@aol.com.*

PICCOLI, DAVID ANTHONY, pediatrics educator; b. Pitts., Apr. 9, 1953; s. William A. and Therese (Schirmer) P.; m. Catherine Welch, Aug. 22, 1981; children: Matthew, Cara, Laura. BA, Johns Hopkins U., 1975; MD, Harvard U., 1979. Diplomate Am. Pd. Pediatrics, also in pediatric gastroenterology and nutrition. Intern Children's Hosp., Boston, 1979-80, resident in pediatrics, 1980-82, chief resident in pediatrics, 1982-83; fellow in pediatric gastroenterology and nutrition Children's Hosp. of Phila., 1983-86; asst. prof. pediatrics U. Pa. Sch. Medicine, Phila., 1986—; mem. staff div. gastroenterology Children's Hosp. Phila., 1986—. Mem. Am. Gastroent. Assn., Am. Assn. for Study of Liver Disease, N.Am. Soc. for Pediatric Gastroenterology and Nutrition. Office: Children's Hosp Phila Div Gastroenterology Philadelphia PA 19104

PICCOLI, GIULIANO, paleontologist, educator; b. Buie d'Istria, Italy, June 13, 1927; s. Emilio Piccoli and Ines Fazio; m. Margherita Gentile, June 30, 1960; children: Gregorio, Antonio, Maria, Benedetto, Giovanni. Degree in Mech. Engring., Padova U., Italy, 1953, degree in Geol. Scis., 1957. Univ. asst. Padova U., 1954—67, prof. geology, 1967—74, prof. paleontology, 1974—2002; ret., 2002. Dir. U. Inst. Geology, Padova, 1970—74; dean, tchr. Geology Somali Nat. U., Mogadishu, Somalia, 1974—82; vis. prof. Tohoku U., Sendai, Japan, 1990. Founder (internat. symposium) Shallow Tethys, 1982—; author: (math model) Paleo Biogeography Palaeo-3, 1991—; editor: (Eocene Fossils of Java) Memorie di Scienze Geologiche Padova, 2001—. Recipient Forti prize, Inst. Veneto Sci. Letters and Arts, Venice, 1968. Fellow: Italian Paleontological Soc. (advisor 1970—76), Italian Geol. Soc. (advisor 1963—67); mem.: Internat. Commn. Hist. Geology (Italian rep. 1980—2008). Roman Catholic. Home: Riviera San Benedetto 27 35139 Padua Italy Office Phone: 01139 49 8722055. Personal E-mail: giulianopiccoli@hotmail.com.

PICHARD, AUGUSTO D., cardiologist, medical educator; b. Santiago, Chile, Sept. 26, 1945; came to U.S., 1971; s. Roberto M. Pichard and Eliana Merino Descalzi; m. Nancy L. Prendergast, June 29, 1973; children: Nicole, Dominique, Alicia, Robert. Grad., Cath. U. Chile, MD, 1969. Cert. Am. Bd. Internal Med., 1975, Am. Bd. Internal Med., Cardiovascular Disease, 1977, Am. Bd. Internal Med., Interventional Cardiology, 1999. Intern Catholic Univ. Chile, 1968—69, resident, 1969—70, resident in cardiology, 1970—71; fellow Cleveland Clinic, 1971—73, assoc. mem. staff, 1973-75; lab. dir. Mt. Sinai Hosp., NYC, 1975-81; assoc. prof. medicine Mt. Sinai Med. Sch., NYC, 1978-81, Cath. Univ. Chile, 1981-82; cardiologist, dir. cardiac catheterization lab. Washington Hosp. Ctr., Washington, 1983—; prof. medicine George Washington U., Washington, 1983-89, clin. prof. medicine, 1990—; cardiologist Washington Cardiology Ctr. Mem. med. bd. Washington Hosp. Ctr., 1997, 99; chmn. bd. Medlantic Rsch. Inst., Washington, 1998—. Mem editl. bd. Am. Jour. Cardiology, 1992-98. Named Hon. Mem. Faculty Cath. U. Chile, 1994. Fellow ACP, Am. Coll. Cardiology, Am. Heart Assn., Soc. Cardiac Angio and Intervention. Roman Catholic. Avocations: tennis, ski, yoga. Office: Washington Cardiology Ctr 110 Irving St NW Washington DC 20010-2976 Office Phone: 202-877-5975. Office Fax: 202-877-3339.

PICHASKE, DAVID RICHARD, language educator; b. Kenmore, NY, Sept. 2, 1943; s. Donald Richard Pichaske and Martha Theresa Schisa; m. Elaine Ezekian (div.); children: Stephen Geoffrey, Kristin Diane; m. Michelle Lynn Payne, Sept. 3, 1991. BA, Wittenberg U., 1965; PhD, Ohio U., 1969. Asst. to assoc. prof. Bradley Polytech. Inst., Peoria, Ill., 1969—; assoc. to prof. S.W. Minn. State U., Marshall, 1980—. Sr. Fulbright lectr. U. Lodz, Poland, 1989—91, U. Latvia, Riga, 1996—97, Mongolian Nat. U., 2003. Author: Beowulf to Beatles: Approaches to Poetry, 1972, Writing Sense: A Handbook of Composition, 1975, A Generation in Motion: Popular Music and Culture in the Sixties, 1979, Chaucer's Literary Pilgrimage: Movement in the Canterbury Tales, 1977, Beowulf to Beatles and Beyond: The Varieites of Poetry, 1981, The Poetry of Rock, 1981, The Jubilee Diary: April 10, 1980-April 19, 1981, 1982, Visiting the Father and Other Poems, 1987, Late Harvest: Rural American Writing, 1992, Poland in Transition: 1989-91, 1994, Southwest Minnesota: The Land and the People, 2000, UBO3: A Season in Outer Mongolia, 2003, Hallelujah Anyway!, 2004, The Father Poems, 2005, Rooted: Seven Midwest Writers of Place, 2006; co-author (with Joseph Amato and Richard Davies): A Place Called Home, 2003. Recipient Minn. Book award, Minn. Humanities Commn., 2003. Mem.: Jour. Popular Music and Soc. (adv. editor 1995—), Minn. Machinery Mus. (bd. dirs. 2003—). Office: Southwest Minn State Univ Marshall MN 56258 Home: 10489 810th Ave Granite Falls MN 56241-4024 Home Phone: 320-564-2424; Office Phone: 507-537-6463. Personal E-mail: pichasked@hotmail.com.

PICHÉ, GREGORY RUSSELL, lawyer; b. Grosse Pt. Farms, Mich., May 12, 1945; s. Russell Forrest Piché and Marie Anne Heoenroether; m. Tamara Katherine Vincelette, Mar. 5, 1954. Degree, Mich. U., Ann Arbor, 1963—67; JD, Mich. State U., 1970—72. Atty. Spurgeon, Aman & Hanes, Colo. Springs, 1972—76, Spurgeon, Haney & Howbert, Colo. Springs, 1976—86, Holland & Hart, Denver, 1986—. Adv. bd. U. Colo., Denver, 1995—. Pres., trustee Mus. Contemporary Art, Denver, 2001—06; trustee Mus. De Las Amer., Denver, 2006; pres., dir. Coloradans Against Death Penalty, Denver, 2004—06. 1st lt. US Army, 1969. Office: Holland & Hart LLP PO Box 8749 Denver CO 80201 Office Phone: 303-295-8014.

PICHÉ, LEE ANTHONY, bishop; b. Mpls., Minn., May 8, 1958; s. LeRoy and Cecilia Piché. STB, MA, Saint Paul Sem.; MPh, Columbia Univ. Ordained priest Archdiocese of Saint Paul & Mpls., 1984; assoc. pastor Saint Mark parish, Saint Paul, Minn., 1984—87; instr. in philos. Univ. St. Thomas, 1994—97; pastor St. Joseph parish, W. St. Paul, Minn., 1999—2005; chmn. commn. for ecumenism & interreligious affairs Archdiocese of Saint Paul & Mpls., 2000—08; pastor All Saints parish, Lakeville, Minn., 2005—08, St. Andrew parish, Como Lake, Minn., 2008—09; vicar gen., moderator of curia Archdiocese of Saint Paul & Mpls., 2008—09; ordained bishop, 2009; aux. bishop Archdiocese of Saint Paul & Mpls., 2009—. Roman Catholic. Office: Archdiocese of Saint Paul & Mpls 226 Summit Ave Saint Paul MN 55102-2197 Office Phone: 651-291-4400. Office Fax: 651-290-1629.*

PICHETTE, PATRICK, information technology company executive; b. Can., 1962; BA in Bus. Adminstrn., U. du Québec à Montréal, Can., 1987; MA in Philosophy Politics and Econs., Oxford U., Eng., 1989. Assoc. McKinsey & Co., Toronto, Canada, 1989—94, ptnr., lead mem. N.Am. telecom practice Montréal, Canada, 1996—2000; v.p., CFO Call-Net Enterprises, 1994—96; exec. v.p., planning and performance mgmt. Bell Can. Enterprises, 2001—02, CFO, 2002—03, exec. v.p., Bell Can., 2003—04, pres. ops., Bell Can., 2004—08; sr. v.p., CFO Google, Inc., Mountain View, Calif., 2008—. Bd. mem. Engineers Without Borders, The Trudeau Found. Rhodes Scholar, 1987—89. Office: Google Inc 1600 Amphitheatre Pky Mountain View CA 94043 Office Phone: 650-253-0000. Office Fax: 650-253-0001.*

PICHLER, SHAUN, statistician, educator; b. Royal Oak, Mich., Apr. 6, 1980; s. Gary and Michele Pichler. PhD student, Mich. State U., East Lansing. Rsch. asst. U. Mich., Ann Arbor, 2001—02, Loyola U., Chgo., 2002—03, Mich. State U., 2004—, instr., 2007—. Rsch. statistician Prep. Profile Sys. Inc., Bend, Oreg., 2008—. Contbr. articles to profl. jours. Vol. and mentor Lansing Sch. Hosts Program, 2000. Recipient Distinguished Alumni award, Loyola U. Mem.: Soc. Indsl. and Orgnl. Psychology, Acad. Mgmt., Golden Key, Phi Kappa Phi. Democrat. Avocation: reading short fiction. Office: Mich State Univ 241 S Kedzie Hall MSU East Lansing MI 48824

PICHOT, MICHEL, language educator, department chairman; b. Tonypandy, Wales, Eng., June 22, 1957; s. Marcel Elisee and Hilary Pichot; m. Vivan Isabel Steemers, Nov. 9, 2001; children: Jonathan, Emilie Sabrina. PhD, Pa. State U., State Coll., 1991. Cert. in stage theorique et pedagogique Chambre Commerce et d'Industrie Paris, 1997. Asst. prof. French Andrews U., Berrien Springs, Mich., 1993—2001; assoc. prof. French Aquinas Coll., Grand Rapids, Mich., 2002—, chairperson dept. modern langs., 2006—. Office: Aquinas Coll 1607 Robinson Road SE Grand Rapids MI 49506 Business E-Mail: pichomic@aquinas.edu.

PICK, DONALD LOWELL, urologist; s. James Donald Pick and Pearl Jane Lea; m. Yumi Yoshinaga, Oct. 29, 2005. BA, UC Berkeley, Calif., 1998; MD, UC Irvine Coll. Medicine, Orange, Calif., 2003. Lic. Calif., 2005; cert. basic sci. Cert.excellence U. Irvine Coll. Medicine, 2001. Residental urologist U, Coll. Irvine Med. Ctr., Dept. Urology, 2004—08, minimally invasive urol. surgery fellow, 2008—. Contbr. scientific papers. Recipient Golden Key Honor Soc. award, 1998, Best Poster award, Am. Urol. Assn., 2008; NIH Summer Rsch. Grant, Nat. Inst. Health, 2000. Mem.: Soc. Endourology, Am. Urol. Assn. Democrat-Npl. Avocations: bass, guitar, hiking. Personal E-mail: dpick@uci.edu.

PICK, JAMES BLOCK, business professor, writer; b. Chgo., July 29, 1943; s. Grant Julius and Helen (Block) Pick. BA, Northwestern U., 1966; MS in Edn., No. Ill. U., 1969; PhD, U. Calif., Irvine, 1974. Cert. computer profl. Asst. rsch. statistician, lectr. Grad. Sch. Mgmt., U. Calif., Riverside, 1975-91, dir. computing, 1984-91; co-dir. U.S.-Mex. Database Project, 1988-91; assoc. prof. mgmt. and bus., dir. info. mgmt. program U. Redlands, Calif., 1991-95, 99-01, prof. bus., 1995—, chair dept. mgmt. and bus., 1995-97, 98-99, chair faculty assembly Sch. Bus., 2001—04. Vis. prof. U. Iberoam., Mexico City, 1997, Mexico City, 2001; cons. internat. divsn. U.S. Census Bur., 1978; mem. Univ. Commons. Bd., 1982—86; mem. nat. curriculum task force IS, 1997; mem. U. Commn. Future Bus. Programs, 1998—2000; pres. Orange County chpt. Assn. Sys. Mgmt., 1978—79; mem. bd. govs. PCCLAS, Assn. Borderlands Studies, 1989—92, v.p., 2000—01, pres., 2002—; bd. profls. advisors demographic analysis U. Calif, Irvine, 2002—; mem. exec. coun. Info. Resources Mgmt. Assn., 2003—07; vis. rschr. Ctr. for Rsch. on Immigration, Population, and Pub. Policy U. Calif., Irvine, 2005; external faculty rsch. assoc. CRITO, U. Calif., Irvine, 2006—; vis. rschr. dept. sociology U. Calif., Irvine, 2009. Author: Geothermal Energy Development, 1982, MicroManual, 1986, Computer Systems in Business, 1986, Atlas of Mexico, 1989, The Mexico Handbook, 1994, Mexico Megacity, 1997, Mexico and Mexico City in the World Economy, 2001, Geographic Systems in Business, 2004, Exploring the Urban Community: A GIS Approach, 2005, Geo-Business: GIS in the Digital Organization, 2008; mem. editl. bd. Jour. Borderlands Studies, 1999—, Jour. Info. Tech. Cases and Applications, 2002—, Frontera Norte, 2006; mem. editl. bd.: Jour. Info. Tech. for Devel., 2007, Revista Latinoamericana y del Caribe de la Asociación de Sistemas de Información, 2008; condr. rsch. info. sys., population, environ. studies; contbr. articles to profl. jours. Trustee Newport Harbor Art Mus., 1981—87, 1988—96, mem. acquisitions com., 1987—91, v.p., 1991—96; trustee, chmn. collection com. Orange County Mus. Art, 1996—; mem. com. Block Mus., 1999—2001, mem. bd. advisors, 2006—; trustee Berkeley Art Mus. and Pacific Film Archives, 2003—. Recipient Thunderbird award, Bus. Assn. L.Am. Studies, 1993, Outstanding Alumnus award, No. Ill. U., 2004; grantee co-principal investigator grant, US Small Bus. Adminstrn., 2006—08; vis. scholar, Lingnan U., Hongkong, 2009; Ford Found. grantee, 1998—99, Sr. Fulbright scholar, 2001. Mem.: AAAS, Assn. for Info. Sys., Assn. Am. Geographers, Sociedad de Demografia Mexicana, Internat. Union Sci. Study Population, Population Assn. Am., Am. Statis. Assn., Am. Sociol. Assn., Assn. for Info. Systems, Assn. Computing Machinery, Standard Club (Chgo.). Office: U Redlands Sch Bus 1200 E Colton Ave Redlands CA 92374-3755 Business E-Mail: james_pick@redlands.edu.

PICKARD, ANN, oil industry executive; b. Cheyenne, Wyo., Oct. 15, 1955; d. Clinton Arnold Pickard and Betty Darlene Garton; m. Daniel Martin Smith, Nov. 8, 1979; children: Nathan, Rebecca. BA, U. Calif., San Diego, 1979; MA, U. Pa., 1983. Middle East analyst Beri, S.A., LA, 1983-85, v.p. Washington, 1985-89; internat. affairs analyst Mobil Corp., Fairfax, Va., 1989-92, strategic ventures mgr., 1992-94, new bus. devel. mgr. Russia, 1994-95, issues mgr., 1995-97, v.p. S.Am., 1997—2000; joined Royal Dutch Shell, 2000, pres. So. Cone Gas & Power Rio de Janeiro, dir. global businesses and strategy, mem. Shell Gas & Power Exec. Com., 2002, mem. exploration and prodn. leadership team, regional v.p. exploration and prodn. Africa Nigeria, 2005—. Trustee Eurasia Found., Washington, 1995—; bd. dirs. Mobil Found., Fairfax. Mem. Leadership Am. Avocations: tennis, golf, travel. Office: Royal Dutch Shell Ca 207a Kesslerpark 1 Rijswijk Netherlands*

PICKARD, ROBERT EVINS, history professor; s. Robert Harville Pickard and Kathryn George Parrote; m. Milagros Salao, Sept. 15, 1979; 1 child, Maria. BS, Mid. Tenn. State U., Murfreesboro, 1976; MA, East Mich. U., Ypsilanti, 1978; MPA, George Wash. U., Washington, 1989. Adj. prof. Mid. Tenn. State U., 2003—; adj. prof., US history Tenn. State U., Nashville, 2007—. UN vol. Peace Corp, Somalia, 1978—84, Philippines, 1978—84. Contbr. articles to profl. jours. Vol. Gore Campaigns, Nashville; staff mem., comm. coord. Al Gore Presdl. Campaign, Washington, 1988. Mem.: Tenn. Hist. Soc., St. Edwards Cath. Ch., Friends Warner Pks., Friends Radnor Lake. Democrat. Home: 6301 Vaughn's Gap Ct Nashville TN 37205 Office: Tenn State Univ 3500 John A Merritt Nashville TN 37209 Personal E-mail: uncleb920@hotmail.com.

PICKARD, WILLIAM FRANK, plastics company executive; b. LaGrange, Ga., Jan. 28, 1941; s. William H. and Victoria (Woodward) P. AS, Mott Community Coll., 1962; BS, Western Mich. U., 1964; MSW, U. Mich., 1965; PhD, Ohio State U., 1971; PhD in Bus. Adminstrn. (hon.), Cleary Coll., 1980. Dir. employment and edn. Urban League Cleve., 1965-67; exec. dir. NAACP, Cleve., 1967-69; assoc. dir. dept. urban studies Cleve. State U., 1971-72; assoc. prof. Wayne State U., Detroit, 1972-74; owner, operator McDonald's Restaurants, Detroit, 1971—; chmn., chief exec. officer Regal Plastics, Roseville, Mich., 1985—. Vis. lectr. Cleve. State U., U. Chgo., Hiram Coll., U. Toledo, U. Mich., Case Western Res. U., Ohio State U., Wayne County Community Coll., McDonald's Hamburger U.; participant mgmt. seminar Case Western Res. U., Greater Cleve. Associated Found. and Rockefeller Found., 1968; chmn. Gov.'s adv. com. on minority bus., pres. 1976; bd. dirs. First Ind. Nat. Bank, Mich. Nat. Bank Corp., Farmington Hills. Mem. Pres.-elect Ronald Regan's transition team to SBA; chmn. econ. devel. com. Nat. Black Rep. Council, 1978, bd. dirs. com. to elect Gov. Ronald Reagan Pres., 1980, chmn. congl. liaison com., 1982; chmn. Mich. Reps. Urban Campaign to elect Gov. Reagan Pres., 1980; vice chmn. Mich. Rep. State Com., 1981; bd. control Grand Valley State Coll., Allendale, Mich.; bd. dirs. Oakwood Hosp., Kirkwood Gen. Hosp., Detroit, Detroit Black Causes, Detroit Econ. Devel. Corp., 1977, Nat. Minority Purchasing Council, Washington, Detroit Urban League, vice chmn.; appointed by Pres. Ronald Regan, and confirmed by U.S. Senate Chmn. of African Devel. Found., 1983. Named one of Ten

Outstanding Young Men Cleve., Jaycees, 1969; Alice W. Gault schlor, 1962-63; Nat. Urban League fellow, 1964. Mem. Booker T. Washington Bus. Assn., NAACP, Jaycees, Alpha Phi Alpha. Home: 335 Pine Ridge Dr Bloomfield Hills MI 48304-2140

PICKEL, ALAN SCOTT, lawyer; b. Cleve., Sept. 28, 1965; BS, Syracuse U., 1987, JD cum laude, 1990. Bar: Conn. 1990, N.Y. 1991, U.S. Dist. (ea. and so. dists.) N.Y. 1991, U.S. Dist. Ct. Conn. 1991. Assoc. Law Office of Jeffrey S. Stephens, Greenwich, Conn., 1990—91, Cooper Liebowitz Royster & Wright, Elmsford, NY and Stamford, Conn, 1991—93, Piazza Melmed & Berkowitz, Stamford, 1993—96; ptnr. Piazza & Melmed, Stamford, 1996—98, Piazza & Pickel, Stamford, 1998—2003, Law Offices of Alan Scott Pickel, Stamford, 2003—. Andrews scholar, Spl. Master, Attorney, Trial Referee, Fact Finder, Arbitrator., 1988—90. Mem. ATLA, Conn. Trial Lawyers Assn., Conn. Bar Assn., N.Y. Bar Assn., Westchester County Bar Assn., Stamford/Norwalk Bar Assn. Office: Law Offices Alan Scott Pickel 1700 Bedford St Stamford CT 06905 Office Phone: 203-348-4100. Business E-Mail: apickel@alanpickel.com.

PICKEL, DIANE DUNN, education educator; d. Donald and Janice Dunn; m. David E. Pickel, May 30, 1987; 1 child, Emily N. BS in mktg., Pa. State U., 1976—80, MBA, 1985—86. Pub. rels. coord. Huth/PSC Engrs., Lancaster, Pa., 1987—91; mktg. rep. Brinjac, Kambic & Assocs., Harrisburg, Pa., 1991—94; adj. faculty Harrisburg Area C.C., Pa., 1993—2000; prof., bus. adminstrn. Ctrl. Pa. Coll., Summerdale, Pa., 1997—; cons. Entrepreneurial Devel. Ctr., 1998—99, 2004. Vol. Elizabethtown Boys Club Cheerleading Competition, Elizabethtown, Pa., 1997—2003; parent vol. Elizabethtown area sch., 1994—2007; vol. Jr. Achievement. Sam M. Walton Free Enterprise fellow, 1999—2002. Mem.: Am. Mktg. Assn., Penn State Alumni Assn. Office: Ctrl Pa Coll College Hill and Valley Rd Summerdale PA 17093 E-mail: dianepickel@centralpenn.edu.

PICKEL, JOYCE KILEY, psychologist; b. Dec. 20, 1939; m. Edward McDonald, Aug. 24, 1960 (div. Mar. 1977); children: Catherine, Maureen, Edward; m. Mark Pickel, Apr. 6, 1982. BS in Edn., Boston State Coll., 1961; MEd, R.I. Coll., 1968; MA, Mich. State U., 1969; EdD, No. Ill. U., 1990. Tchr., Mass., R.I., 1962-66; guidance counselor Grand Ledge (Mich.) schs., 1966-67; diagnostician Eaton County Intermediate Sch. Dist., Charlotte, Mich., 1968-69; psychometrist Hammond, Ind., 1969-70; coord. programs, sch. psychometrist N.W. Ind. Spl. Edn. Coop., Highland, 1970-72; instr. Ind. U., Gary, 1970-72; program dir. Trade Winds Rehab. Ctr., Gary, 1972-73; supv. sch. psychologist Thornton Fractional Twp. H.S. 215, Calumet City, Ill., 1973—. 1st v.p. Greater Hammond Cmty. Coun., 1974-76; treas. Colonial Club Condominium ASsn., 2003-06, pres., 2006—; regional spkr. teen suicide various confs. Recipient award Hammond Cmty. Coun., 1974, 75, 76, Cmty. Svc. award Greater Hammond Cmty. Coun., 1975; NDEA fellow R.I. Coll., 1967, NDEA fellow Mich. State U., 1967-68. Mem. Nat. Assn. Sch. Psychologists, Coun. Exceptional Children, Am. Fedn. Tchrs., S. Met. Assn. Sch. Psychologists (pres. 1982-83, bd. dirs. 1985-86, v.p. 1994-95), Ill. Sch. Psychol. Assn. (dir. region VIII, mem. governing bd., pres. 1990-91, historian 1995—, Ted Smith Meml. award 1986), Phi Delta Kappa. Office: 1601 Wentworth Ave Calumet City IL 60409-6309 Personal E-mail: pickelj@bellsouth.net.

PICKENS, ALEXANDER LEGRAND, retired education educator; b. Waco, Tex., Aug. 30, 1921; s. Alex LeGrand and Elma L. (Johnson) P.; m. Frances M. Jenkins, Aug. 20, 1955. BA, So. Meth. U., 1950; MA, North Tex. U., Denton, 1952; EdD, Columbia U., 1959. Tchr. art public schs., Dallas, 1950-53, Elizabeth, N.J., 1953-54; instr. Coll. Architecture and Design U. Mich., 1954-59; assoc. prof. dept. art U. Ga., Athens, 1959-62; assoc. prof. Coll. Edn. U. Hawaii, Honolulu, 1962-68, prof. edn., 1969—2001, chmn. doctoral studies curriculum instrn. Coll. Edn., 1984-89, asst. to dean for alumni affairs coll. devel., 1989-01, ret., 2001, emeritus prof., 2002—. Dir. children's classes Ft. Worth Children's Mus., 1951-53; head art Nat. Music Camp, Interlochen, Mich., summers, 1957-58, U. Oreg., Portland, summers 1959-60, 62; cons. youth art activities Foremost Dairies, Honolulu, 1964-74; cons. art films United World Films, 1970-75; art edn. cons. Honolulu Paper Co., 1970-76, Kamehameha Sch., Bishop Estate, 1978-95. Exhibited ceramics, Wichita Internat. Exhbn., Syracuse (N.Y.) Nat. Exhbn., St. Louis Mus., Dallas Mus., San Antonio Mus., Detroit Art Inst., Hawaii Craftsmen, also others; editorial bd.: Arts and Activities mag, 1955-82; editor: U. Hawaii Ednl. Perspectives, 1964-99; contbr. articles to profl. jours. Mem. adult com. Dallas County chpt. Jr. ARC, 1951-53; mem. exec. com. Dallas Crafts Guild, 1950-53; v.p., publicity chmn. U. Ga. Cmty. Concert Assn., 1960-62, program chmn. Gov.'s Commn. Observing 150 Yrs. Pub. Edn. in Hawaii, 1990-91; bd. dirs. Honolulu Theatre for Youth, 1998-2003; bd. dirs. Honolulu Symphony, 1998—; bd. dirs. Chamber Music Hawaii, 2003—. Served with USAAF. Recipient award merit Tex. State Fair, 1957, All-Am. award Ednl. Press Assn. Am., 1968, 70, 72, 75, 79, Regents' medal for tchg. U. Hawaii, 1989, Gov.'s Commn. Observance of 150 Yrs. Pub. Edn., 1990-91, COE Individual Benefactor award, 2008. Mem. AAUP, NEA, Internat. Soc. Edn., Nat. Art Edn. Assn., Coun. for Advancement and Support of Edn., Assn. Fundraising Profls., Nat. Planned Giving Coun., Hawaii Planned Giving Coun., Phi Delta Kappa, Kappa Delta Pi. Address: 1471 Kalaepohaku St Honolulu HI 96816-1804 Personal E-mail: apickens@hawaii.rr.com.

PICKENS, JAMES B., science educator; b. Billings, Mont., Apr. 29, 1951; s. Bernie A. and Olga V. Pickens; m. Miriam Dobrofsky, Aug. 10, 1983. BS, Ea. Mont. Coll., Billings, 1975; MS, U. Ga., Athens, 1980, PhD, 1985. Prof. Mich. Technol. U., Houghton, 1985—. Recipient Hardwood Rsch. award, Nat. Hardwood Lumber Assn., 1996. Mem.: Soc. Am. Foresters. Achievements include patents for HW Buck optimal hardwood log bucking software system. Office: Mich Tech Univ 1400 Townsend Dr Houghton MI 49931

PICKENS, ROBERT BRUCE, retired accountant; b. Uniontown, Pa., May 20, 1926; s. Joseph Abraham and Margaret Gertrude (Brown) P.; m. Mary Ellen Evans, Sept. 9, 1950; children: Laura Gail Martin, Rachel Diane Rosen, David Bruce. BS in Bus. Adminstrn, Waynesburg Coll., 1950. C.P.A., Pa., Ill., Ind. Vice pres. Home Bottle Gas Corp., Uniontown, 1950-51; jr. accountant to sr. accountant Tenney & Co., Uniontown, 1951-56; mgr. Hosp. Service Assn. Western Pa., Pitts., 1956-57; auditor U. Pitts., 1957-58; sr. accountant Eugene A. Conniff Co., Pitts., 1958-59; mgr. Sheppard & Co., Pitts., 1959-63; supr. Alexander Grant & Co., Chgo., 1963-65; asst. to treas. CTS Corp., Elkhart, Ind., 1965, gen. auditor, controller, chief acctg. officer, 1966-81; ret., 1981; self-employed as acct., 1981-86; sec., controller, chief acctg. officer SEA Group, Inc. and SEA-ILAN, Inc., 1987-88; pvt. cons., 1989—; ret., 1999. Mem. Bower Hill Civic League, 1956-62; active Boy Scouts Am., 1938-62. Served to cpl. USAAC, 1944-45; USAF Res., 1947-50. Mem. AICPA, Pa. Inst. CPAs, Ill. CPA Soc., Ind. CPA Soc. Republican. Presbyn. (elder, trustee 1959-61, treas. 1960-61). Home: 73 Rogers Rd Carmel IN 46032-1467

PICKENS, RUPERT TARPLEY, III, French language educator; b. High Point, NC, Feb. 20, 1940; s. Rupert T. Jr. and Ida (Munyan) P.; m. Nancy Shore Clinard, May 13, 1942; children: John Armfield, Edward Munyan. AB, U. N.C., 1961; postgrad., U. de Rennes (France), 1961-62; MA, U. N.C., 1964, PhD, 1966. Asst. prof. French U. N.C., Chapel Hill, 1966-69, U. Ky., Lexington, 1969-70, assoc. prof. French, 1970-78, prof. French, 1978—, chair dept. French, 1984-92, 1998—2001. Author: The Welsh Knight, 1977; editor: The Sower and His Seed, 1983, In Honor of Hans-Erich Keller, 1993, The French Canon, 1994; editor, co-author: The Songs for Jaufre Rudel, 1978, Perceval by Chrétien de Troyes, 1990; translator: The Story of Merlin, 1993. Vestry mem. Ch. of St. Michael the Archangel, Lexington, 1978-82, 87-90, 2005, 08, sr. warden, 1980-82, 88-90, 2008-. Fulbright fellow U.S. Govt., 1961-62; rsch. grantee Nat. Endowment for the Humanities, 1989-90. Mem. Soc. Guillaume IX (pres. 1992-94), Internat. Marie de Franco Soc. (pres. 2007-09), Fulbright Assn., Internat. Arthurian Soc., Internat. Country Literature Soc., Soc. Rencesvals. Episcopalian. Office: U Ky 1021 Patterson Towers Lexington KY 40506-0006 Home: 968 Hammock Oak Ln Lexington KY 40515-6455 Office Phone: 859-257-3133. E-mail: rtpickens@insightbb.com.

PICKENS, T. BOONE (THOMAS BOONE PICKENS JR.), hedge fund manager, former oil industry executive; b. Holdenville, Okla., May 22, 1928; s. Thomas Boone Pickens and Grace Molonson; m. Lynn O'Brien, 1949 (div. 1971); 4 children; m. Beatrice Louise Carr, Apr. 21, 1972 (div.); 1 adopted child; m. Nelda Cain, 2000 (div. 2004); m. Madeleine Paulson, July 16, 2005. Student, Tex. A&M U.; BS in Geology, Okla. State U., Stillwater, 1951. Geologist Phillips Petroleum Co., 1951-54; co-founder Mesa Petroleum Co. (formerly Petroleum Exploration, Inc.), 1956, chmn. bd. dirs., pres., 1964—96; gen. ptnr., CEO Mesa Ltd. Partnership, 1985—96; founder, chmn. BP Capital Mgmt., 1996—. Mem. Nat. Petroleum Coun.; founder, chmn. United Shareholders Assn.; bd. dirs. Clean Energy Fuels Corp., 2001—, Exco Resources Inc., 2005—. Author: Boone, 1987, The Luckiest Guy in the World, 2001, The First Billion is the Hardest: Reflections on a Life of Comebacks and America's Energy Future, 2008. Adv. Nat Campaign for Drug Free America; founder, chmn. T. Boone Pickens Found. Recipient Disting. Am. award, Nat. Football Found., 2008, Bower award for bus. leadership, Franklin Inst., Phila., 2009; named Texan of Yr., Tex. Legis. Conf., 2008; named one of Forbes' Richest Americans, 2006—, 25 Most Influential Republicans, Newsmax Mag., 2008, The World's Most Influential People, TIME mag., 2009. Republican. Office: BP Capital 8117 Preston Rd Ste 260 Dallas TX 75225*

PICKER, SEBASTIÁN, artist; Exhibitions include Gallery 355, Boston, 1976—77, 1980, Ctr. Culturel de Villeparisis, Paris, 1978, Kunstamt Kreutzberg, Berlin, 1979, Galería Skandia, Bogotá, Colombia, 1979, Galería D'Art Mestral, L'Escala, Spain, 1983, Cleveland Mus. Contemporary Art, 1986, Mass. Coll. Art, Boston, 1987, The Space, 1987, 1991, Bunker Hill Cmty. Coll., 1988, Optica Gallery, Montreal, 1990, Artists Found., Boston, 1990, Red Mesa, Gallup, N.Mex., 1993, Mills Gallery, Boston Ctr. for Arts, 1994, Crashing Thunder Gallery, Gallup, N.Mex., 1996, Meredith Kelly, Santa Fe, 1996—97, Arden Gallery, Boston, 1995, 1997, 2000, 2002, 2004—05, Brewster Arts, NY, 1998, Art Miami, 1999—2000, Turner Carroll Gallery, Santa Fe, 1999—2000, Museo Carlos Cruz Diez, Caracas, Venezuela, 2000, Arte Am., Miami, 2004—06, Brea Gallery, LA, 2005, Museo Raúl Anguiano, Guadalajara, 2006, Mason Murer Fine Art, Atlanta, 2006, Galería Pablo Guerrero, Guadalajara, 2006, Museo de Arrte Contemporáneo, Jorge Chávez Carrillo, Colima, Mex., 2007, Represented in permanent collections Fundació Vila Casas, Barcelona, Mus. Latin Am. Art, Longbeach, Calif., El Museo Cultural de Santa Fe, Albuquerque Mus. Recipient First prize, Macworld Art Contest, 1985; grantee Barcelona Sister City Travel Grant, Boston, 1984, Mass. Coun. on Arts and Humanities Grant, 1988, Mass. Artist Fellowship Prog., 1991. Office: Arden Gallery 129 Newbury St Boston MA 02116

PICKERELL, JAMES HOWARD, photojournalist; b. Dayton, Ohio, June 9, 1936; s. Howard and Frances (Harrison) P.; m. Mary Louise Fisher, June 26, 1965; children: Cheryl Elizabeth, Stacy Rae. Student, Ohio U., 1954-56; BA, UCLA, 1963. Comml. photographer, 1963—; ind. photographer Vietnam, 1963-67. Author: Vietnam in the Mud, 1966, Marketing Photography in the Digital Environment, 1994, Negotiating Stock Photo Prices, 5th edit., 2001; writer, pub.: newsletter Selling Stock. With USN, 1956-60. Mem. Nat. Press Photographers Assn. (1st Pl. Spot News award 1965), Am. Soc. Mag. Photographers (nat. bd. 1987-89), Profl. Photographers Assn., Beta Theta Pi. Address: 8104 Cindy Ln Bethesda MD 20817-6915 Office Phone: 301-251-0720. Personal E-mail: jim@scphotos.com.

PICKERING, CHIP (CHARLES WILLIS PICKERING JR.), former United States Representative from Mississippi; b. Laurel, Miss., Aug. 10, 1963; m. Leisha Jane Prather (separated); children: Will, Ross, Jackson, Asher, Harper. BA in Bus. Adminstrn., U. Miss., 1986; MBA, Baylor U., Waco, Tex., 1989. Liaison USDA, 1989—90; legis. asst. to Senator Trent Lott US Senate, Miss., 1992—96; mem. US Congress from 3rd Miss. Dist., 1997—2009. Co-chmn. Miss. for Bush, 2000, 04; mem. energy and commerce com. US Congress, asst. minority whip. Appeared in: (films) Borat: Cultural Learnings of America for Make Benefit Glorious Nation of Kazakhstan, 2006. Republican.*

PICKERING, HOWARD WILLIAM, metallurgy engineer, educator; b. Cleve., Dec. 15, 1935; s. Howard William and Marian (Vittes) P.; m. Judith Anne Burch, Apr. 20, 1963; children: John, Kim, Scott, Carolyn. BS in Metall. Engrng., U. Cin., 1958; MS, Ohio State U., 1959, PhD, 1961. Scientist U.S. Steel Corp., Monroeville, Pa., 1962-69, sr. scientist, 1969-72; postdoctoral U.S. Steel fellow Max-Planck Inst., Gottingen, Fed. Republic Germany, 1964-65; assoc. prof. metall. engrng. Pa. State U., University Park, 1972-76, chmn., 1975-80, prof., 1976-90, disting. prof., 1990—. Cons. Ga. Pacific Corp., Newark, 1983-88, Argonne Nat. Lab., 1986-88, Allegheny Ludlum Corp., 1992—; mem. external adv. panel Corrosion Research Ctr., U. Minn., 1980-86. Co-author: Atom Probe Field Ion Microscopy and Its Applications, 1988; editor Corrosion Sci. Jour., 1975-95; contbr. numerous articles to profl. jours. Recipient Disting. Alumnus award Coll. Engrng. U. Cin., 1988, Coll. Rsch. award Pa. State U., 1989, Disting. Alumnus award Coll. Engrng. Ohio State U., 1990; numerous rsch. grants. Fellow Nat. Assn. Corrosion Engrs. (rsch. com. 1980-89, A.B. Campbell award 1964, Willis Rodney Whitney award 1985), Electrochem. Soc. (chmn. edn. com. 1979, Young Author award 1967, H.H. Uhlig award 1987); mem. AAAS, Metall. Soc. (edn. and profl. affairs com. 1979-83, corrosion resistant metals com. 1974—), Tau Beta Pi, Phi Lambda Upsilon.

PICKERING, JAMES HENRY, III, academic administrator, educator; b. NYC, July 11, 1937; s. James H. and Anita (Felber) P.; m. Patricia Paterson, Aug. 18, 1962; children: David Scott, Susan Elizabeth. BA, Williams Coll., 1959; MA, Northwestern U., 1960, PhD, 1964. Instr. English Northwestern U., 1963-65; mem. faculty Mich. State U., East Lansing, 1965-81, prof. English, 1972-81, grad. and assoc. chmn. dept., 1968-75, dir. Honors Coll., 1975-81; dean Coll. Humanities and Fine Arts U. Houston, 1981-90, sr. v.p., provost, 1990-92, pres., 1992-95, Martha Gano Houstoun prof. lit. criticism, 2008—; historian laureate Estes Park, Colo., 2006. Author: The Spy, 1971, The Harper Reader, 1971, Fiction 100, 1974, 1978, 1982, 1985, 1988, 1992, 1995, 1998, 2001, 2004, 2007, The World Turned Upside Down: Prose and Poetry of the American Revolution, 1975, The Spy Unmasked, 1975, The City in American Literature, 1977, Concise Companion to Literature, 1981, Literature, 1982, 86, 90, 94, 97, Mountaineering in Colorado, 1987, Wild Life on the Rockies, 1988, A Mountain Boyhood, 1988, The Spell of the Rockies, 1989, Purpose and Process, 1989, Poetry, 1990, In Beaver World, 1990, Rocky Mountain Wonderland, 1991, A Summer Vacation in the Parks and Mountains of Colorado, 1992, Fiction 50, 1993, Knocking Round the Rockies, 1994, Drama, 1994, Frederick Chapin's Colorado, 1995; This Blue Hollow: Estes Park, The Early Years, 1859-1915, 1999, Mr. Stanley of Estes Park, 2000, In the Vale of Elkanah, 2003, 07, The Ways of the Mountains, 2003, Early Estes Park Historical Narratives, 4 vols., 2004, America's Switzerland: Estes Park and Rocky Mountain National Park, The Growth Years, 2005, Enos Mill's Colorado, 2005, Estes Park and Rocky Mountain National Park, Then and Now, 2006, Rocky Mountain Celts, 2006, The MacGregors of Black Canyon: An American Story, 2008. Historian laureate Town of Estes Park. Mem. Coll. English Assn. (pres. 1980-81), Phi Beta Kappa, Phi Kappa Phi, Omicron Delta Kappa. Office: U Houston Dept English Houston TX 77204-0001 Personal E-mail: jhpick@earthlink.net.

PICKERING, KRISTINA, state supreme court justice; m. Steve Morris; 2 children. BA, Yale U., 1974; JD, U. Calif. Davis, 1977. Law clk. to Judge Bruce R. Thompson US Dist. Ct., Reno; assoc. Lionel Sawyer & Collins, 1980—84, ptnr., 1985—92; co-founder, ptnr. Morris Pickering & Peterson, 1992—; adj. faculty William S. Boyd Sch. Law, U. Nev., 2000, 2002; settlement judge Nev. Supreme Ct., judge, 2008—. Mem. Nev. Bd. Bar Examiners, 1992—2007. Named to Best Lawyers in America, Super Lawyers. Mem.: Am. Law Inst. Office: Nev Supreme Ct 201 South Carson St Carson City NV 89701-4702 Office Phone: 775-684-1600.*

PICKERING, LARRY KENNETH, pediatrician, researcher; m. Margaret Jane Thompson, July 8, 1967; children: Margaret Anne, Andrew Michael. MD, W.Va. U. Sch. Medicine, 1970. Diplomate Am. Bd. Pediat. in Pediats. and Infectious Diseases, Nat. Bd. Med. Examiners. Intern pediat. svc. St. Louis Children's Hosp., 1970-71, resident pediat. svc., 1971-72; fellow pediat. infectious diseases St. Louis Children's Hosp. and Washington U. Sch. Medicine, 1972-74; asst. prof. pediat. U. Tex. Med. Sch., Houston, 1974-77, assoc. prof. pediat., 1977-82, prof. pediat. dept. pediat. divsn. infectious diseases, 1982-92, prof. program in immunology, 1982-92. Cons. M.D. Anderson Hosp. and Tumor Inst., Houston, 1974-78, St. Joseph Hosp., Houston, 1975-89, Meml. Hosp. Sys., Houston, 1977-92, AMA; assoc. prof. pediat. M.D. Anderson Hosp. and Tumor Inst., U. Tex. Cancer Ctr., 1978-83, prof. pediat., 1983-92; infection control med. advisor Speech and Hearing Inst., U. Tex. Health Sci. Ctr., Houston, 1978-87, prof. Grad. Sch. Biomed. Scis., 1982-89; adj. prof. pharmaceutics dept. pharmaceutics Coll. Pharmacy, U. Houston, 1983-92; dir. Ctr. for Pediat. Rsch., Ea. Va. Med. Sch., Children's Hosp. of The King's Daus., Norfolk, 1992-2001; David R. Park prof. pediat., 1989-92, dir. divsn. infectious diseases dept. pediat., 1975-1992; prof., CHKD chair in pediatric rsch. Ea. Va. Med. Sch., Norfolk, 1992-2001; prof. pediats. dept. pediats. Emory U. Sch. Medicine, Atlanta, 2001-; external examiner and reviewer dept. pediat. U. Jordan, Amman, 1984; mem. subboard pediat. infectious diseases Am. Bd. Pediat., 1991-96; mem. planning com. First Internat. Pediat. Infectious Diseases Conf., Monterey, Calif., 1995; mem. sci. com. First World Congress of Pediat. Infectious Diseases, 1995; mem. steering com. E. Mead Johnson Award for Rsch. in Pediat., 1996-99; presenter in field; assoc. dir. spl. projects, nat immunization project, immunization program Ctrs. for Disease Control and Prevention, Atlanta, 2000-01, sr. advisor to dir. Nat. Ctr. for Immunization and Respiratory Diseases, 2001-, exec. sec. Adv. Comm. Immmir Practices Ctr. Dieses Ctrl. & Prevention, Atlanta, 2005-. Author: (with H.L. DuPont) Infections of the Gastrointestinal Tract, 1980, Infectious Diseases of Children and Adults; editor: (with R.R. Howell and F.H. Morriss) Human Milk in Infant Nutrition and Health, 1986, (with M.T. Osterholm, J.O. Klein and S.S. Aronson) Infectious Diseases in Child Day Care: Management and Prevention, 1987, Infections in Day Care Centers Seminars in Pediatric Infectious Diseases, 1990, Diarrheal Disease, 1994, (with S. Long and C. Prober) Principles and Practice of Pediatric Infectious Diseases, 1997, 3rd edit., 2008; contbg. editor: Infectious Disease Clinics in North America, 1992; editor-in-chief Pediat. Infectious Diseases: Clin. Updates, Nat. Found. for Infectious Diseases, 1994-2000; mem. editl. bd. Infectious Diseases Newsletter, 1985-89, Infection, 1988, Pediat., 1990-93, Report on Pediat. Infectious Diseases, 1990-95, co-editor, 1993-95, Pediatric. Infectious Disease Jour., 1987-96, 2001--, Seminars in Pediat. Infectious Diseases, 1997—, Vaccine Bull., 1997-2001, Infectious Diseases in Children, 1997-09; editor; contbr. articles to profl. jours. Med. adv. com. Met. Houston chpt. March of Dimes, 1974-76, bd. dirs., 1975-80, chmn. profl. adv. com., 1977-79; mem. rsch. com. Nat. March of Dimes, 1999-2004. Named Disting. Alumnus, W.Va. U. Sch. Medicine, Morgantown, 1995, Edward J. van Liere Rsch. award. Fellow Infectious Diseases Soc. Am. (exec. com. Emerging Infections Network 1997-2000, mem. com. 2003--06); mem. AAAS, Am. Acad. Pediats., Intersci. Conf. on Antimicrobiol Agts. and Chemotherapy, Internat. Soc. for Rsch. in Human Milk and Lactation, Am. Soc. for Clin. Pharmacology and Therapeutics, Am. Soc. for Tropical Medicine and Hygiene, Am. Pediat. Soc., Am. Soc. Microbiology, Am. Acad. Pediat. (com. on infectious diseases 1990-96, assoc. editor RedBook 1990-97, editor 1997-, exec. com. sect. breastfeeding 2001—03), Am. Fedn. for Clin. Rsch., Nat. Found. of Infectious Diseases (bd. dirs. and treas. 1997—, chair continuing med. edn. com. 1999—2003), Va. Pediat. Soc., Tex. Pediat. Soc., Tex. Med. Assn., Tex. Infectious Diseases Soc. (coun. mem. 1982-84), Harris County Pediat. Soc. (edn. com. 1975-79), Harris County Med. Soc., Houston Acad. Medicine, Houston Pediat. Soc. (constn. and by-laws com. 1978-82), So. Soc. for Pediat. Rsch. (coun. mem. 1981-83, Founder's award 1994), Soc. for Pediat. Rsch. (chair infectious diseases subspecialty sect. 1995, co-chair seminar Epidemiology 1995), Pediat. Infectious Diseases Soc. (pres.-elect 1993-95, pres. 1995-97, Disting. Physician award, 2007), The Milk Club (exec. com. 1995-99), ICAAC (program com. 1997-2002), AAP (chair rsch. com. and exec. com. sect. on breastfeeding), Infectious Diseases Soc. Am. (coun. mem. 2003-06), Sci. Program Com., 2007-, chair panel). Avocations: tennis, biking, canoeing. Office: CDC and Prevention Nat Ctr Immunization Respiratory Disease 1600 Clifton Rd NE # MsE05 Atlanta GA 30333 Office Phone: 404-639-8562. Office Fax: 404-639-8626. Business E-Mail: LPickering@cdc.gov.

PICKERING, THOMAS REEVE, retired aerospace transportation executive; b. Orange, NJ, Nov. 5, 1931; s. Hamilton R. and Sarah C. (Chasteney) P.; m. Alice J. Stover, Nov. 24, 1955; children: Timothy R., Margaret S. AB, Bowdoin Coll., 1953; MA, Fletcher Sch. Law and Diplomacy, 1954, U. Melbourne, Australia, 1956. Joined US Fgn. Svc., 1959; fgn. affairs officer ACDA, 1961; polit. adviser U.S. del. 18 Nation Disarmament Conf., Geneva, 1962-64; consul Zanzibar, 1965-67; counselor of embassy, dep. chief mission Am. Embassy, Dar es Salaam, Tanzania, 1967-69; dep. dir. Bur. Politico-Mil. Affairs US Dept. State,

1969-73, spl. asst. to sec., 1973-74, exec. sec., 1973-74, US amb. to Jordan Amman, 1974-78, asst. sec. for oceans, internat. environ. & sci. affairs Washington, 1978-81, US amb. to Nigeria Lagos, 1981-83, US amb. to El Salvador San Salvador, 1983-85, US amb. to Israel Tel Aviv, 1985-88, US permanent rep. to UN NYC, 1989-92, US amb. to India New Delhi, 1992-93, US amb. to Russia Fedn. Moscow, 1993-96, under sec. for polit. affairs Washington, 1997—2000; pres. Eurasia Found., 1996-97; sr. v.p. internat. relations Boeing Co., 2001—06; vice chmn. Hills and Co. Served to lt. comdr. USNR, 1956-59. Recipient Woodrow Wilson Award for Pub. Svc., Woodrow Wilson Internat. Ctr. for Scholars, 2005. Mem. Council Fgn. Relations, Internat. Inst. Strategic Studies, Phi Beta Kappa.

PICKERING, WILLA EARLINE, electrical engineer, educator; d. Earl and Martha Pickering; children: Robert William Lucas, Christopher Lucas. BA in Math., Okla. State U., Stillwater, 1963; MS in Elec. Engring., U. N.Mex, Los Alamos, 1977; PhD, Sch. Info. Tech. & Engring. George Mason U., Fairfax, Va., 2003. Cert. info. system arch. Lockheed Martin, Bethesda, Md., 2001. Fellow rschr. Lockheed Martin, 1977—; adj. assoc. prof. U. Md. U. Coll., Adelphi, 2001—. Contbr. scientific papers. Recipient Phi Kappa Phi award, 1977, Gold Medal, Martin Marietta, 1979, Info. and Communication Sys. Tech. award, 1987, Individual Spl. Recognition award, Lockheed Martin, 2004. Mem.: IEEE, Soc. Women Engrs. Personal E-mail: willapickering@gmail.com. Business E-Mail: willa.e.pickering@lmco.com.

PICKETT, A. DEAN, lawyer; b. Casper, Wyo., June 25, 1949; s. A. Foy and Esther L. (Nieman) Pickett; m. Lucinda M. Wayne, July 3, 1971; children: Amanda M. Pickett-Williams, Gregory D. Allen-Pickett. BA, No. Ariz. U., Flagstaff, 1971; JD, U. Ariz., Tucson, 1974. Bar: Ariz. 1974, Wash. 1975, Colo. 1999. Of counsel Mangum, Wall, Stoops & Warden, PLLC, Flagstaff, 1980—. Lectr. edn. law Ariz. Sch. Bds. Assn., 1983—; judge Pro Tem Ariz. Ct. Appeals, 1992. Chmn. Coconino County Rep. Com., 1986-88; trustee Mus. No. Ariz., 1983-91, 92-99, chmn., 1998-99; bd. dirs. Flagstaff Federated Cmty. Ch., 1987. Lt. USN, 1974—78. Decorated Navy Achievement medal USN. Mem. State Bar Ariz., Wash. State Bar Assn., Nat. Assn. Coll. and Univ. Attys., Nat. Sch. Bds. Assn. Coun. Sch. Attys. (dir. 2002-, chair 2009), Coconino County Bar Assn., Malpais Kiwanis (pres. 1982-83). Presbyterian. Avocation: travel. Office: Mangum Wall Stoops & Warden PLLC 100 North Elden St Flagstaff AZ 86001

PICKETT, DONN PHILIP, lawyer; b. Chgo., May 3, 1952; s. Philip Gordon and Gloria Joan (Hansen) P.; m. Janet Benson, Aug. 25, 1973; children: Jessica Kelly, William Benson. BA magna cum laude, Carleton Coll., Minn., 1973; JD, Yale U., 1976. Bar: Calif. 1976, US Dist. Ct. (no. dist.) Calif. 1976, US Dist. Ct. (ctrl. dist.) Calif. 1980, US Dist. Ct. (ea. dist.) Calif. 1983, US Ct. Appeals (9th cir.) Calif. 1979, US Ct. Appeals (5th cir.) Tex. 1994, US Supreme Ct. 1991, US Dist. Ct. Ariz. 1997, US Dist. Ct. Colo. 1997, US Ct. Appeals (fed. cir.) 1997, US Ct. Appeals (11th cir.) 1998, US Ct. Appeals (1st cir.) 2006. Assoc. McCutchen, Doyle, Brown & Enersen, San Francisco, 1976-83, ptnr., 1983—2002, chair, 2001—02; ptnr. Bingham McCutchen LLP, San Francisco, 2002—, vice chmn., 2002—08; co chair Bingham Litigation Area, 2008—. Mem. U.S. Dist. Ct. Civil Justice Reform Act adv. group, 1995-99; bd. dirs. Equal Justice Works, 2005—, Legal Aid Soc., San Francisco, 2006—. Bd. dirs. Bay Area Coun., 2003—. Mem. ABA (chmn. civil practice com. antitrust sect. 2001-04, vice chmn. trial practice com. 2004-), State Bar Calif. (com. on adminstrn. of justice 1988-91, vice chmn. 1992-93, chmn. 1993-94, legis. chmn. 1994-96), San Francisco Bar Assn. (judiciary com. 1988-92, exec. com. conf. of dels. 1993-96, 2000, bd. dirs. 1997-99), Phi Beta Kappa. Office: Bingham McCutchen LLP 3 Embarcadero Ctr San Francisco CA 94111 Home Phone: 415-435-2313; Office Phone: 415-393-2082. Business E-Mail: donn.pickett@bingham.com.

PICKETT, EUGENIA VALDIVIA, retired social worker; b. Balt., Mar. 26, 1938; d. Robert Thomas and Eugenia King Valdivia; children: Jennifer Pickett Connoley, Juliana Ewing Harris; 1 stepchild, Jennifer Greenwald. BS, Towson U., 1959; MA, Antioch U., 1975. Diplomate psychotherapy Nat. Bd. Med. Psychotherapy; LCSW MD, cert. group psychotherapy Am. Group Psychotherapy Assn. Educator Balt. City Pub. Schs., 1960—69; staff coord. Greenmount Ave. Medical, Mental Health Clinic, Balt., 1970—76; psychiat. social worker pvt. practice, Balt., 1976—2008. Educator women's studies, childhood edn. Balt. CC, Essex, 1978—79; primary trainer Assn. Music, Imagery, Salina, Kans., 1979—2003; cons. Ctr. Living Head Trauma, Balt., 1986—91; primary trainer Creative Therapies Inst., Massapeagua, NY, 1991—2003. Editor: Women: A Journal of Liberation, Journal of the Association for Music and Imagery. Mem. Balt. Def. Com., 1960; mem., pub. spkr. Women's Consciousness Raising Group, Balt., 1965—72; staff counselor, therapist Women's Growth Ctr., Balt., 1970—84; educator, meditation instr. Lotus Garden Buddhist Ctr., Stanley, Va., Balt. Shambhala Ctr., Balt., 1976—. Mem.: Md. Soc. Clin. Social Workers (sec. 1999—2002). Buddhist. Personal E-mail: epicdharma@aol.com.

PICKETT, OWEN BRADFORD, lawyer, former congressman; b. Richmond, Va., Aug. 31, 1930; BS, Va. Poly. Inst., 1952; JD, U. Richmond, Va., 1955. CPA Va.; bar: Va. 1955, D.C. 1962. Pvt. practice, Virginia Beach, Va., 1964—86; mem. Va. Ho. of Dels., Richmond, 1972—86, US Congress from 2d Va. dist., Washington, 1987—2001; of counsel Troutman, Sanders, LLP, Virginia Beach, 2001—. Chmn. Va. Dem. State Ctrl. Com., 1980—82. Mem.: AICPA, ABA, DC Bar Assn., Va. Bar Assn. Democrat. Baptist. Office: Troutman Sanders LLP Ste 2000 222 Ctrl Pk Dr Virginia Beach VA 23462 Home Phone: 757-481-0979; Office Phone: 757-687-7525. Personal E-mail: obpickett@msn.com. Business E-Mail: owen.pickett@troutmansanders.com.

PICKETT, STEPHEN WESLEY, academic administrator, consultant; b. Billings, Mont., May 27, 1956; s. Wesley William and Carol Ann (Bollum) P. BA, Houston Bapt. U., 1980; MS, U. North Tex., 1988. Cert. elem. tchr., rehab. counselor, Tex. Hosp. tchr. Houston Ind. Sch. Dist., 1981-85; asst. to assoc. dean of students U. North Tex., Denton, 1988-90, asst. coord. disabled student svcs., Office Student Devel., 1990-91, dir. Office Disability Accommodation, 1991—2001, univ. mentor/advisor, 1992—2001; dir. disability svcs. U. Oreg., Eugene, 2002—08. Assoc. dir. office of acad. advising U. Oreg., 2002—08; academic access cons., 2008—. Co-author: curriculum guide The Newspaper as a Student Communicator, 1982 (Exxon Found.'s Impact Two award). Chair Mayor's Com. on Employment of Persons with Disabilities, Denton, 1990; mem. coun.-at-large Sam Houston Area Coun. Boy Scouts Am., Houston, 1975—; grad. Denton C. of C. Leadership Program, 1992; pub. rels. chair leadership Denton Steering Com., 1993-94; mem. ad. bd. city of Denton Transit, 1990-2001; exec. bd. Svc. provision for Aging Needs, a United Way Agy., 1997-2001; mem. U. of North Tex. Adv. Bd. for ADA Access, 1992-2001, co-chair UNT ADA adv. com., 2000-01; mem. budget com. Denton County United Way, 1998-2001. Recipient Cmty. Svc. award U. North Tex., 1992, award for svcs. to persons with disabilities North Tex. Rehab. Assn., 1993, Disting. Alumnus award Houston Bapt. U., 1994, Outstanding Alumnus award Ctr. for Rehab. Studies, U. North Tex., 1995. Mem. Assn. Higher Edn. and Disability, Nat. Assn. Student Pers. Adminstrs., Tex. Assn. Coll. and Univ. Student Pers. Adminstrs. (chair multicultural com. 1994-95, v.p. 1995-96, co-chair endowment found. com. 1996-97), Tex. Assn. Higher Edn. and Disabilities (sec. 1998-99, conf. co-chair 1999). Presbyterian. Avocations: reading, travel, stamp collecting/philately. Office: U Oreg Disability Svc 164 Oregon Hall 5278 U Oreg Eugene OR 97403-5278 Office Phone: 541-747-5794. Office Fax: 541-988-1824. Personal E-mail: stevewp@att.net.

PICKETT, TERRY HILL, language professional educator; b. Washington, Ga., Apr. 19, 1941; s. William Lewis and Katherine (Hill) P.; m. Gisela Vollprecht; children: Jessica Victoria, Cortland Alexander. AB, U. Ga., 1966; postgrad, U. Kiel, 1966-67; MAD, U. Ala., 1968; PhD, Vanderbilt U., 1970. Prof. German and Russian U. Ala., Tuscaloosa, 1970—. Author: The Unseasonable Democrat: K.A. Varnhagen v. Ense 1785-1858, 1985; co-author: (with Francoise de Rocher) The Letters of the American Socialist Albert Brisbane to K.A. Varnhagen fon Ense, 1986; contbr. articles to profl. jours. Grantee 1977, 83, 93, rsch. grantee 1972, 76, 87; recipient Fulbright award 1989-90, 1980-81, 1972-73; German Exch. award 1974, 66-67. Mem. SAMLA, AATG, Modern Lang. Assn., German Studies Assn., Christianity and Lit.

PICKHOLTZ, RAYMOND LEE, electrical engineering educator, consultant; b. NYC, Apr. 12, 1932; s. Isidore and Rose (Turkish) P.; m. Eda Rebecca Mittler, June 30, 1957; children: Robin, Andrew, Julie. BEE, CUNY, 1954, MEE, 1958; PhD, Poly. U. N.Y., 1966. Research engr. RCA Labs., Princeton, NJ, 1954-57, ITT Labs., Nutley, NJ, 1957-61; assoc. prof. Poly. Inst. Bklyn., 1962-71; prof. elec. engring., chmn. dept. George Washington U., Washington, 1977-80, prof., 1971—2004, prof. emeritus, 2004—; pres. Telecommunication Assocs., Fairfax, Va., 1963—; cons. Inst. Def. Analyses, 1971-90, IBM Research, Yorktown Heights, NY, 1968-72; del. Union Radio Scientifique, Geneva, 1979—, vice chmn., 1987; del. NRC, Washington, 1980-83; cons. Motorola, CBC, NAB, USADR, Lucent, Verizon, 1996—. Vis. prof. U. Que., 1977; vis. scholar U. Calif., 1983; chmn. U.S. Nat. Commn. C, Union Radio Sci. Internat., 1990-92; mem. sci. and indsl. adv. bd. Telecom. Inst. Ont., Can. and Inst. Nacionale de la Recherches Scientique; vice chair, wireless panel World Tech. Evaluation Ctr. Editor: book series Computer Science Press, 1979—; IEEE Trans., 1975-80; editor-in-chief Jour. of Comms. and Networks, 2005—; author: Local Area and Multiple Access Networks, 1986; contbr. articles to profl. jours.; patentee in field. Recipient rsch. award RCA Labs., 1955; rsch. grantee Office of Naval Research, Washington, 1982, E-Systems, Falls Church, Va., 1983-96, MCI, Falls Church, Va., Instelsat, Washington, Nortel Networks, 1996—, DARPA, NSF, 1999—. Fellow IEEE (bd. govs. 1979-82, digital comm. com., Centennial medal 1984), AAAS, Washington Acad. Scis.; mem. IEEE Comm. Soc. (v.p. 1986-88, pres. 1990-92, Donald W. McLellan award, 1994, Erskine fellow New Zealand 1997, Third Millennium medal 2000, ACM MSWIN prize paper award, 1999, Best paper of 1999 in Jour. of Comms. and Networks, 2000, gen. chair, Infocom, Kobe, Japan 1997, gen. chair, ACM Mobicom Y2K, Boston, 2000), Math. Assn. Am., Cosmos Club, Sigma Xi, Eta Kappa Nu. Home: 3613 Glenbrook Rd Fairfax VA 22031-3210 Office: George Washington U Dept Elec Computer Engring Washington DC 20052-0001

PICKHOLZ, JASON R., lawyer; b. NYC, Jan. 10, 1970; s. Marvin Gerald and Joyce (Merrick) Pickholz. BA magna cum laude, Colgate U., Hamilton, NY, 1991; JD, NYU Sch. Law, 1994. Bar: NY 1995, US Dist. Ct. (ea. and so. dists.) NY 1995, US Ct. Appeals (2nd cir.), US Ct. Appeals (DC), US Supreme Ct. Jud. clk. to hon. Kevin Thomas Duffy, US Dist. Ct. (so. dist.) NY, 1994-95; litigator Morvillo, Abramowitz, Grand, Iason & Silberberg, P.C., NYC, 1995-97, Paul, Weiss, Rifkind, Wharton & Garrison, NYC, 1997—2002; founding ptnr. Pickholz Law Firm LLP, NY, 2002—05; shareholder Akerman Senterfitt LLP, NY, 2005—07; ptnr. Duane Morris LLP, NYC, 2007—. Mem. adv. bd., bd. dirs. Akerman Senterfitt LLP, 2007—. Contbr. articles to profl. jours. Founder Pickholz Family Scholarship NYU Sch. Law/Colgate U. Mem.: ABA (sr. editor Trial Practice Jour. 2002—09, Outstanding Editor award 2002—03, Outstanding Newsletter award 2005—06), Fed. Bar Coun., Assn. Bar City of NY, Nat. Assn. Criminal Def. Lawyers, NYU Sch. Law Alumni Assn. (hon.; bd. dirs. 2001—04), Phi Beta Kappa. Office: Duane Morris LLP 1540 Broadway New York NY 10036 Office Phone: 212-692-1017. Office Fax: 212-214-0829. Business E-Mail: jrpickholz@duanemorris.com.*

PICKHOLZ, MARVIN G., lawyer; b. NYC, Apr. 18, 1942; children: Jason, Michael. AB, NYU, 1963; LLB, NYU Sch. Law, 1967, LLM, 1968. Bar: NY 1967, DC 1975. Trial atty. SEC, NYC, 1967—69, chief br. enforcement, 1969—72, nat. asst. dir. divsn. enforcement Washington, 1975—76, asst. chief trial atty., 1976—78, asst. dir., 1978—79; ptnr. Camhy Karlinsky & Stein, NYC, 1995; now ptnr. Duane Morris LLP, NYC. Contbr. articles to profl. jours., chapters to books; guest appearances include CNBC, NBC, Fox News, BBC. Named a SuperLawyer, Law & Politics mag., 2007, 2008; named one of Washington's 50 Best Lawyers, Washington Mag., 1992. Mem.: ABA (vice chmn./chmn. com. white-collar crime 1983—87, coun. mem. 1985—89, coun. liaison 1989—), Assn. SEC Alumni (founder, first pres., bd. dirs.). Office: Duane Morris LLP 1540 Broadway New York NY 10036-4315 Office Phone: 212-692-1050. Office Fax: 212-208-2641. Business E-Mail: mgpickholz@duanemorris.com.*

PICKLE, JERRY RICHARD, lawyer; b. Paris, Tex., Feb. 2, 1947; s. Joseph Rambert and Martha Marie (Biggers) P.; m. Helen Leigh Russell, May 3, 1975; children: Jonathan Russell, Stephen Richard (dec.), Sarah Elizabeth. BA in History, U. Houston, 1969, JD, 1971. Bar: Tex. 1972, U.S. Dist. Ct. (no. dist.) Tex. 1974. Mem. Luna, Ballard & Pickle, Garland, Tex., 1972-74; assoc. Hightower & Alexander, Dallas, 1974-76, Cuba & Johnson, Temple, Tex., 1976-77; sr. corp. counsel Scott & White Clinic, Temple, 1977—. Asst. prof. Tex. A&M U. Coll. of Medicine, Temple, 1986—. Contbr. articles to profl. jours. V.p. The Caring House, Temple, 1989; v.p. Tex. divsn. Am. Cancer Soc., Temple, 1976—77; adv. bd. R.R. & Pioneer Mus., Temple, 1982—84; hist. preservation bd. City of Temple, 1979—90; chmn. Bell County Hist. Commn., 1980—82; bd. dirs. Bell County Mus., 1992—96, Temple Coord. Child Care Coun., 1991—93, Sr. Citizens Activities Ctr., Temple, 1993—94, pres., 1992—96; bd. dirs. Temple Cultural Activities Ctr., 1992—98, 2001—06, pres., 1994—95; chair Heart o'Tex. Coun., Chisholm Trl. Dist., Boy Scouts Am., 1987—88; mem. U. N.C.-Chapel Hill Parents Coun., 2001—05; trustee Temple Ind. Sch. Dist., 2005—, sec., 2006—07, v.p., 2007—; dir. Temple Edn. Found., 2007—, Tax Appraised Bd. Bell County, Tex., 2006—. Mem.: ABA, Temple C. of C. (bd. dirs. 1983—85, 1988—90), Coun. Med. Group Practice Attys. (chair 2001—02), Am. Health Lawyers Assn. (chair tchg. hosp. and acad. med. ctrs. 1997—99), Bell-Lampasas-Mills Counties Young Lawyers Assn. (pres. 1980—81), Bell-Lampasas-Mills Counties Bar Assn. (bd. dirs. 1985—90, pres. 1988—89), State Bar Coll., Tex. Bar Found., Tex. Young Lawyers Assn., State Bar Tex. (health law sect. councilman 1980—84, chmn. 1983—84), Jaycees (chpt. dir. 1977—78), Rotary (chpt. dir. 1981—85, 1986—87). Democrat. Episcopalian. Avocations: reading, golf, music. Office: Scott & White Clinic 2401 S 31st St Temple TX 76508-0001 Office Phone: 254-724-3001. Office Fax: 254-724-4501. Business E-Mail: jpickle@swmail.sw.org.

PICKLE, JOSEPH WESLEY, JR., religious studies educator; b. Denver, Apr. 8, 1935; s. Joseph Wesley and Wilhelmina (Blacketor) P.; m. Judith Ann Siebert, June 28, 1958; children: David E., Kathryn E., Steven J. BA, Carleton Coll., 1957; B.D., Chgo. Theol. Sem., 1961; MA, U. Chgo., 1962, PhD, 1969. Ordained to ministry Am. Bapt. Conv., 1962. Asst. pastor Judson Meml. Ch., NYC, 1959-60; acting dean summer session Colo. Coll., Colorado Springs, 1969-70, from asst. prof. to prof. religion, 1964—2002, faculty dir. internat. studies, 1994-98; prof. emeritus, 2002. Vis. prof. theology Iliff Sch. Theology, Denver, 1984, 2003; vis. prof. religious studies U. Zimbabwe, Harare, 1989; cons. Colo. Humanities Program, Denver, 1975-89; coord. Sheffer Meml. Fund, Colo. Coll., Colorado Springs, 1983-2001. Co-editor Papers of the 19th Century Theology Group, 1978, 88, 93. Pres. bd. dirs. Pikes Peak Mental Health Ctr., Colorado Springs, 1975; chmn. Colo. Health Facilities Rev. Coun., Denver, 1979-84; mem. Colo. Health Facilities Rev. Coun., Denver, 1976-84, Colo. Bd. Health, Denver, 1986-91; bd. dirs. Marson Found., Colorado Springs, 1994—, Colo. Springs Choral Soc., 2005-, pres. 2008-. Am. Bapt. Conv. scholar, 1953-59; Fulbright Hays Grad. fellow U. Tübingen, Fed. Republic Germany, 1963-64, Danforth fellow, 1957-63, Joseph Malone fellow, 1987. Fellow Soc. for Values in Higher Edn.; mem. Am. Theol. Soc. (pres. 1996-97), Am. Acad. Religion (regional pres. 1983-84, 92-93), Cath. Theol. Soc. Am., Fulbright Assn., Phi Beta Kappa. Democrat. Home: 20 W Caramillo St Colorado Springs CO 80907-7314

PICKLE, LINDA WILLIAMS, biostatistician; b. Hampton, Va., July 19, 1948; d. Howard Taft and Kathryn Lee (Riggin) Williams; m. James B. Pearson, Jr., Oct. 14, 1984; 1 child from previous marriage, Diane Marie. BA, Johns Hopkins U., 1974, PhD in Biostats., 1977; postgrad., George Washington U., 1986—87. Computer programmer Comml. Credit Computer Corp., Balt., 1966-69; systems analyst, computer programmer Greater Balt. Med. Ctr., 1969-72; grad. tchg. asst. biostats. Johns Hopkins U., Balt., 1974-77; adj. asst. prof. divsn. biostats. and epidemiology Georgetown U. Med. Sch., Washington, 1983—88, assoc. prof., 1988-91, dir. biostats. unit V.T. Lombardi Cancer Rsch. Ctr., 1988-91; biostatistician Nat. Cancer Inst. NIH, Bethesda, Md., 1977-88, sr. math statistician divsn. cancer control/population scis., 1999—2007; math. statistician office rsch. methodology Nat. Ctr. Health Stats., Hyattsville, Md., 1991-99; chief statistician StatNet Consulting LLC, Gaithersburg, Md., 2007—; adj. prof. dept. geography and pub. health scis. Pa. State U., 2008—. Author: Atlas of U.S. Cancer Mortality Among Whites: 1950-80, 1987, Atlas of U.S. Cancer Mortality Among Nonwhites: 1950-1980, 1990, Atlas of United States Mortality, 1996, U.S. Predicted Cancer Incidence, 2003; contbr. articles to profl. jours. Recipient Hammer award, US Govt., 2000. Fellow: Am. Statis. Assn.; mem.: Biometric Soc., Sigma Xi, Phi Beta Kappa. Achievements include research in statistical methods in epidemiology, mapping health statistics.

PICKLER, KELLIE DAWN, country singer; b. Albemarle, NC, June 28, 1986; d. Cynthia Morton and Clyde Pickler. Contestant American Idol, 2005; signed to 19 Recordings/BNA Records, 2006—. Singer: (albums) Small Town Girl, 2006, Kellie Pickler, 2008, (songs) Red High Heels, 2006, I Wonder, 2006 (Breakthrough Video of Yr., Tearjerker Video of Yr., & Performance of Yr., Country Music TV, 2008). Office: c/o Fitzgerald Hartley Co 1908 Wedgewood Ave Nashville TN 37212

PICKREL, PAUL, language educator; b. Gilson, Ill., Feb. 2, 1917; s. Clayton and Inez (Murphy) P. AB, Knox Coll., 1938; MA, Yale U., 1942, PhD, 1944. Instr. English Lafayette Coll., 1941-42; instr. Yale U., 1943-45, asst. prof., 1945-50, lectr. English, 1954-66, chmn. Scholar of House Program, 1959-60, 61-66; fellow Morse Coll., 1962-66; adviser John Hay fellows, 1959-66; vis. prof. English Smith Coll., Northampton, Mass., 1966-67, prof., 1967-87, prof. emeritus, 1987—, chmn. dept., 1972-75, 81-82. Author: (novel) The Moving Stairs, 1948; also essays on fiction, numerous book revs.; mng. editor: Yale Rev., 1949-66; chief book critic: Harper's mag., 1954-65. Mem. Aurelian Honor Soc., Elizabethan Club (New Haven), Faculty Club (Northampton), Phi Beta Kappa.

PICKRELL, GARY R., engineering educator, director; married. PhD, Va. Tech, Blacksburg, 1994. Assoc. dir., Ctr. Photonics Tech. Va. Tech, 1999—, assoc. prof., 2004—, dir. Nano Bio Materials Lab, 2004—. Contbr. articles to profl. jours. Mem. Prime Photonics, Blacksburg, 2004—09. Recipient Asst. Prof. award, Va. Tech, 2004. Mem.: IEEE. Achievements include patents for optical fibers, sensors & materials; invention of random hole optical fiber at home applications. Home: 3631 Isabel Ct Blacksburg VA 24060

PICKREN, WADE EDWARD, historian; b. Alma, Ga., Nov. 29, 1952; s. Bill and Merle Pickren; m. Alexandra Rutherford, June 26, 2004; children: Emily Jane, Graham Wesley; m. Mary Jane Tarzwell, May 27, 1977 (div.). PhD, U. Fla., Gainesville, 1995. Historian APA, Washington, 1998—; assoc. chair, psychology Ryerson U., Toronto, Ontario, Canada, 2006—. Author: (book) A Historical Analysis of Training, Research, Practice & Advocacy, A Historical Analysis of Science, Practice, and Policy, Evolving perspectives on the history of psychology; contbr. articles to profl. jours. Donor NY Soc. Study Psychol. Issues, 2004—09. Fellow: Soc. Psychol. Study Social Issues; mem.: APA, Eastern Psychol. Assn. (historian 2005—09), History Sci. Soc. Achievements include research in history of race and ethnic issues in psychology. Avocations: music, reading, hiking. Office: Ryerson Univ 350 Victoria St Toronto ON Canada M5B 2K3 Business E-Mail: wpickren@psych.ryerson.ca.

PICOTT, JERRY LEE, JR., music educator; b. Philadelphia, Pa., June 24, 1968; s. Jerry and Deloris Picott; m. Tikija Picott; children: Jerry, Jasmine, Jordan. BA Music Ed., Bethune Cookman U., 1990; MS Ed. in Leadership, Nova Southeastern U., 1997. Band dir. Campbell Mid. Sch., Daytona Beach, Fla., 1990—98, Mainland H.S., Daytona Beach, 1998. Recipient Outstanding Young Educator, Daytona Beach Jaycees, 1999. Mem.: MENC, VTO, Fla. Bandmasters Assn., Internat. Masons Daytona Beach, King Soloman (life), Phi Delta Honor Soc., Omega Psi Phi Frat. Baptist. Office: Mainland High School 125 South Clyde Morris Blvd Daytona Beach FL 32114-3954

PICOTTE, SUSAN CARROLL, lawyer; b. Brighton, Mass., Sept. 2, 1954; d. John Dennis, Jr., and Patricia (Curran) Carroll; m. William Burgess Picotte, Aug. 12, 1978; children: David Hunter, Philip Burgess. BA in Econs. magna cum laude, Russell Sage Coll., 1976; JD, Union U., Albany, N.Y., 1979. Bar: N.Y. 1980, U.S. Dist. Ct. (no. dist.) N.Y. 1980, U.S. Dist. Ct. (we. dist.) N.Y. 1985, U.S. Supreme Ct. 1988. With O'Connell & Aronowitz, P.C., Albany, 1978-79; assoc. firm Cooper, Erving & Savage, Albany, 1979-82, ptnr., 1983-86; ptnr. Cooper, Erving, Savage, Nolan & Heller, LLP, 1987-2001, Cooper, Erving & Savage

LLP, 2002—. Mem. Albany Law Rev., 1977-78. Bd. dirs., 1st v.p. Coun. Cmty. Svcs. N.E. N.Y., Albany, 1980-86; trustee Shaker Heritage Soc., 1983-86; mem. Jr. League Troy, Inc., 1981-86; bd. dirs. Univ. Found. Albany, Inc., 1987-91; trustee Emma Willard Sch., 1990-95. Fellow N.Y. State Bar Found.; mem. ABA, N.Y. State Bar Assn. (ho. dels. 1992-96, nominating com. 1996—98), Albany County Bar Assn. (dir. 1983-94, sec. 1989-90, treas. 1990-91, v.p. 1991-92, pres. elect 1992-93, pres. 1993-94), N.Y. State Women's Bar Assn., Albany County Bar Found. (bd. dirs. 1995-2004), Emma Willard Sch. Alumnae Assn. (dir. 1982-88, v.p. 1988-90, pres. 1990-92), Albany Roundtable (dir. chpt. 1990—2006), Estate Planning Coun. Ea. N.Y. Inc. (bd. dirs. 2006—), Schuyler Meadows Club (bd. govs. 1993-96), Phi Kappa Phi. Roman Catholic. Office: 39 N Pearl St Albany NY 12207-2785 Business E-Mail: spicotte@coopererving.com.

PICOULT, JODI LYNN, writer; b. LI, NY, May 19, 1966; m. Tim Van Leer; children: Sammy, Kyle, Jake. BA, Princeton U., NJ, 1988; MEd, Harvard U. Former textbook editor, 8th grade English tchr. Author: (novels) Songs of the Humpback Whale, 1992, Harvesting the Heart, 1993, Picture Perfect, 1995, Mercy, 1996, The Pact, 1998, Keeping Faith, 1999, Plain Truth, 2000, Salem Falls, 2001, Perfect Match, 2002, Second Glance, 2003, My Sister's Keeper, 2004 (Publishers Weekly bestseller), Vanishing Acts, 2005 (Publishers Weekly bestseller), The Tenth Circle, 2006, Nineteen Minutes, 2007 (Debut #1 NY Times bestseller, Publishers Weekly bestseller), Change of Heart, 2008 (Debut #1 NY Times bestseller), Handle With Care, 2009 (#1 Publishers Weekly bestseller), (comic books) Wonder Woman Series, 2007. Recipient New Eng. Bookseller award for fiction, 2003. Avocation: ice hockey. Office: PO Box 508 Etna NH 03750 Business E-Mail: jodi@jodipicoult.com.*

PICOWER, WARREN MICHAEL, editor; b. NYC, Aug. 21, 1934; s. Abraham and Nell (Bloom) P.; divorced; children: Jenny Emelia, Eve Julie. BA, Queens Coll., 1956; MA, New Sch. for Social Rsch., 1978; PsyD in Psychology, Heed U., LA, 1982. Editorial asst. Newsweek mag., NYC, 1956-59; assoc. editor Zimmerman Pub. Co., NYC, 1961-63; assoc., mng. editor Fawcett Pubs., NYC, 1963, 64-65; mng. editor Tuesday Publs., NYC, 1965-67, exec. editor, v.p., 1967-73; sr. editor King Features Syndicate, NYC, 1974-78; mng. editor Food & Wine Mag., NYC, 1978-93; consulting editor Travel Holiday Mag., NYC, 1993-94; mng. editor Zagat Survey restaurant and hotel guides, NYC, 1994-97; sr. project editor Money Mag., NYC, 1997-98. Cons. in field. Contbr. articles to profl. jours.

PICRAUX, SAMUEL THOMAS, physicist, researcher; b. St. Charles, Mo., Mar. 3, 1943; s. Samuel F. and Jeannette D. Picraux; m. Danice R. Kent, July 12, 1970; children: Jeanine, Laura, Samantha. BS in Elec. Engring., U. Mo., 1965; postgrad., Cambridge U., Eng., 1965-66; MS in Engring. Sci., Calif. Inst. Tech., 1967, PhD in Engring. Sci. and Physics, 1969. Mem. tech. staff Sandia Nat. Labs., Albuquerque, 1969-72, div. supr., 1972-86, dept. mgr., 1986-96, dir., 1996-2001; prof. materials engring., exec. dir. materials rsch. Ariz. State U., 2001—05; chief scientist Ctr. Integrated Nanotech., Los Alamos Nat. Lab., 2005—. Mem. solid state scis. com. NRC, 1996-98; vis. scientist dept. physics Aarhus U., Denmark, 1975; NATO lectr., 1979, 81, 83, 86.; NSF lectr. 1976, 81. Author: Materials Analysis by Ion Channeling, 1982; editor: Applications of Ion Beams to Metals, 1974, Metastable Materials Formation by Ion Implantation, 1982, Surface Alloying by Ion Electron and Laser Beams, 1986, Beam-Solid Interactions and Transient Processes, 1987; editor Nuclear Instruments and Methods International Jour. B, 1983-91; contbr. numerous articles to profl. jours. Recipient Ernest Orlando Lawrence Meml. award U.S. Dept. Energy, 1990, 3 Basic Energy Scis. Outstanding Rsch. awards U.S. Dept. Energy, 1985, 92, 94, Mo. Honor award disting. svc. in engring., 2006; Fulbright fellow, 1965-66. Fellow AAAS, Am. Phys. Soc. (chmn. materials physics divsn. 1990), Materials Rsch. Soc. (pres. 1993); mem. IEEE (sr.), Am. Vacuum Soc. Office: Los Alamos Nat Lab Ctr Integrated Nanotech MST-CINT MSK771 Los Alamos NM 87545 Home Phone: 505-232-2977; Office Phone: 505-665-8554. Business E-Mail: picraux@lanl.gov.

PICTON, EARLA WISE, retired music educator, director; b. San Antonio, Jan. 8, 1954; d. Beverly Ann and Gordon Guy Wise; m. Jerry Francis Picton, June 14, 1985; children: Jeremiah Francis, Jordanne Kathleen. AS, San Antonio Coll., 1974, Del Mar Coll., Corpus Christi, Tex., 1976; BS, Tex. A&M U., Corpus Christi, 1978. Cert. in music Tex. Edn. Agy., 1978, prek-4th grade tchg. Tex. Edn. Agy., 2005, in 6th-8th grade English lang. arts, reading 2008. Band dir. Chula Vista Acad. Fine Arts, Corpus Christi, 1978—81, Cunningham Jr. High, Corpus Christi, 1981—84, Rockport-Fulton HS, 1984—94, 2005—08, Aransas Pass HS, Tex., 1994—2004; tchr. ABC Learning Ctr., Rockport, 2004—05. Mem.: Aransas County Ret. Tchrs. Assn., Assn. Tex. Small Sch. Bands, Tex. Band Masters Assn., Tex. Music Educators Assn.

PIDAPARTI, RAMANA M., engineering educator; s. Murthy P. S. N. and Satyavathi P.; m. Chitra Pidaparti; children: Rohan, Reena. PhD, Purdue U., West Lafayette, Ind., 1989. Prof. mech. engring. Va. Commonwealth U., Richmond, 1989—; prof. dir. academic programs Ind. U. Purdue U. Indpls. Recipient Frank Burley Disting. Prof. award, Purdue Sch. Engring. and Tech., Ind. U. Purdue U. Indpls., 2002. Fellow: ASME. Office: Va Commonwealth Univ 401 W Main St Richmond VA 23284-3015 Business E-Mail: rmpidaparti@vcu.edu.

PIDERIT, JOHN J., educational consultant and author, former university president; b. NYC, Feb. 26, 1944; BA in Math. and Philosophy magna cum laude, Fordham Univ., 1967; Lic. in Sacred Theology cum laude, Philosophische und Theologische Hochschule Sankt Georgen, Frankfurt, West Germany, 1971; MPhil, Oxford Univ., 1974; MA, PhD in Econ., Princeton Univ., 1979. Tchr. math. Regis High Sch., NYC, 1967-68; ordained Catholic priest, Soc. of Jesus Frankfurt, Germany, 1971; asst. campus minister Fordham Univ., Bronx, NY, 1971-72, Princeton Univ., 1975-78, preceptor, 1976-77; asst. prof. econ. Fordham Univ., Bronx, NY, 1978-89, assoc. prof. econ., 1989-90, asst. chmn. econ. dept., 1979-82, 88-89, dir. program internat. polit. econ. and devel., 1981-83, 87-88, asst. chmn. grad. studies, 1984-88; corp. v.p. Marquette Univ., Milw., 1990-93; pres. Loyola Univ., Chgo., 1993—2000, Catholic Edn. Inst., Bronx, NY. Vis. fellow Woodstock Theol. Ctr., Washington, summer 1982; sabbatical Santa Clara U., 1989-90; master Queen's Ct. Residential Coll., 1987-90; chmn. responsible investment com. N.Y. province SJ, 1986-88, mem. fin. com., 1986-88; mem. joint commn. govtl. rels. of Am. Coun. Edn., 1994; mem. exec. com. Nat. Planning Com. Jesuit Assembly '89, 1988-90. Author: The Ethical Foundations of Economics, 1993; co-author (with Melanie Morey): Catholic Higher Education: A Culture in Crisis, 2006, Renewing Parish Culture: Building For a Catholic Future, 2008; contbr. articles to profl. jours. Founder, moderator Friends of Loyola, 1987-90; pres. Univ. Neighborhood Housing Corp., 1986-90, Maroon Enterprises, Inc., 1986-90; trustee Canisius Coll., Buffalo, 1983-88, 89-94, Loyola Marymount U., L.A., 1996—, John Carroll U., Univ. Heights, Ohio; bd. dirs. Corp. Cmty. Schs. of America; promoter PIVOT H.S. and Middle Sch. with Milw. Pub. Schs., 1990-93; mem. Greater Milw. Edn. Trust, 1990-93; mem. steering com., chair edn. task force Milw. Cmty. Traffic Safety Com., 1991-93; mem. steering com. Libr. Literacy Soc. Milw., 1991-93; mem. scholarship com. Knitworkers Union Local 155, N.Y.C., 1982-90; mem. Princeton Schs. Com. N.Y. Region, 1985-88, chmn. Federation of Indp. Colls. and Univs., 1999. Mellon grantee Fordham U., summer 1983, summer grantee Fordham U., 1979, Princeton U. fellow, 1974-78. Office: Catholic Edn Inst St Helena Hall Ste 202 925 Hutchinson River Pkwy Bronx NY 10465 Office Phone: 718-823-8565.*

PIDOT, WHITNEY DEAN, retired lawyer; b. NYC, Mar. 2, 1944; s. George B. and Virginia (Ulrich) P.; m. Jeanne Stoddard, April 23, 1973; children: Whitney Dean Jr., Philip Martin, Seth Thayer. AB magna cum laude, Harvard U., 1966; JD, MBA, Columbia U., 1970. Bar: N.Y. 1971. Ptnr. Shearman & Sterling, NYC, 1970, global mng. ptnr., 1998—2002, mem. exec. goup, 1998—2003, Asia mng. ptnr., 2001—03, of counsel, 2004—05; chair, CEO Goelet Co. LLC, 2004—. Mem. adv. bd. Barclays Bank N.Y., 1989-92, Molecular Tool, Inc. (biotech.) Balt., 1991-96, Equine Genetic Rsch. Ptnrs., Balt., 1991-95; trustee, vice chair Winthrop Univ. Hosp., Mineola, NY. Mayor, Village of Matinecock, Locust Valley, N.Y., 1977-92; vice chmn. North Shore Mayors Com., Long Island, N.Y., 1980-92; bd. dirs. Nassau County (N.Y.) Village Officials Assn., 1978-80; commr. Locust Valley Fire Dist., 1979-93. Mem. N.Y. Bar Assn., Piping Rock Club (pres. 1988-94), Jupiter Island Club (pres. 2006-), Union Club N.Y.C., Phi Delta Phi. Republican. Home: Matinecock Farms PO Box 653 Locust Valley NY 11560 Office: Goelet Co LLC 425 Park Ave New York NY 10022 Business E-Mail: wpidot@shearman.com, wpidot@goeletcorp.com.

PIECUCH, DIANE MARIE, music educator; b. Ironwood, Mich., Mar. 25, 1950; d. John H. Meyer and Betty E. Meyer-Lundberg. MusB, Mich. State U., East Lansing, 1972; MusM, George Mason U., Fairfax, Va., 1998. Cert. Orff Schulwerk George Mason U., 1988. Music tchr. Loudoun County Pub. Schs., Sterling, Va., 1972—75, Fairfax County Pub. Schs., Alexandria, Va., 1975—77, 1986—. V.p. PQ Prodns., Alexandria, 1977—96. Composer: (multiple songs) For Corporations And School. Min. of cmty. care St. John's Luth. Ch., Alexandria, 2005—06. Recipient Supts. award, Sch. Bd., 1991—92. Mem.: Fairfax Gen. Music Educators Assn. (assoc.; pres. 1995—97), Am. Orff Schulwerk Assn (assoc.; social chmn. 1989—91). R-Consevative. Lutheran. Avocation: jogging. Home: 6543 Kelsey Point Cir Alexandria VA 22315 Office: Rose Hill Elementary Sch 6301 Rose Hill Dr Alexandria VA 22310 Personal E-mail: dpq@cox.net. E-mail: diane.piecuch@fcps.edu.

PIECUCH, JIM, history professor, writer; b. Manchester, NH, Oct. 6, 1959; s. Boleslaw and Yvette Piecuch; m. Lori Warfield, Mar. 28, 1987; 1 child, Joseph. PhD, Coll. William & Mary, Williamsburg, Va., 2005. Firefighter City of Manchester, NH, 1980—93; asst. prof. history Kennesaw State U., Ga., 2006. Writer, cons. interpretive signage Palmetto Conservation Found., Camden, SC, 2007—. Author: (nonfiction history) Three Peoples, One King: Loyalists, Indians, and Slaves in the Revolutionary South, The Battle of Camden: A Documentary History. Roman Catholic.

PIEDIMONTE, GIOVANNI, pediatrician; m. Miriam Perez. MD, U. Rome, 1986. Cert. MD Bd. of Medicine, 2006. Dir., pediatric pulmonary medicine Jackson Meml. Med. Ctr., Miami, Fla., 1995—2006; chmn. dept. pediat. W.Va. U., Morgantown, 2006—; pediatrician in chief W.Va. U. Children's Hosp., 2006—. Achievements include research in pediatric pulmonary. Business E-Mail: gpiedimonte@hsc.wvu.edu.

PIEFER, THOMAS R., history educator; b. Auburn, Wash., Dec. 15, 1952; s. Raymond Andrew and Marion Piefer; m. Teresa Kay Willard, Dec. 26, 1971; children: Rebecca, Christina, Craig. BA in Edn., Ctrl. Wash. U., Ellensburg, 1987; MS in Edn., Walla Walla Coll., College Place, Wash., 1993, Antioch Coll., Seattle, Wash., 2003. Cert. lifeguard, advanced lifesaving. Tchr. Ctrl. Mid. Sch., Milton-Freewater, Oreg., 1987—2006, chair, social studies, 2004—06; tchr. Christian Edn. Trinity Bapt. Ch., Walla Walla, Wash., 1987—2006; trainer in social studies, state of Oreg. Teach Tchrs. Author: (book) Helping Hispanic Parents Through the Education Maze. Mentor Oreg. Youth Guard, Milton-Freewater, Oreg.; youth worker Trinity Baptist Ch., Oreg., 1988—2006, vol., Awana, 1987—2006. With USAF, 1971—2002. Recipient Non-commissioned Officer of Quarter award, USAFR, 1973, 1975, 1985, 2006, Tchr. of Quarter award, Ctrl. Mid. Sch., Milton-Freewater, Oreg., 2003, 2004. Mem.: Milton-Freewater Edn. Assn., Walla Walla Hot Wheels Car Club. Avocations: jogging, camping, woodworking, teaching. Home: 84608 Eastside Rd Milton Freewater OR 97862 Personal E-mail: piefert@neofast.net.

PIEGARI, JAMES A., psychologist; b. Bklyn., Aug. 4, 1951; s. Vincent and Olympia Piegari. BS in Psychology, Georgetown U., 1972; MA in Clin. Psychology, St. John's U., 1975; MA in Psychology, Rutgers U., 1995, New Sch. Social Rsch., 1995; PhD in Psychology, Saybrook Grad. Sch. and Rsch. Ctr., 1999. Lic. psychologist NY, cert. sch. psychologist NY. Ops. rsch. analyst USPHS Hosp., SI, NY, 1976—78; applied behavioral scis. specialist United Cerebral Palsy Assns. NY State, SI, 1978—80, Terence Cardinal Cooke Health Care Ctr., NYC, 1980—2001, psychologist, 2002—; pvt. practice psychologist SI, 2002—. Mem. publs. com. Flower Hosp., NYC, 1980—81; cons. Vietnamese refugee program Mission of Immaculate Virgin, Mt. Loretto, SI, 1986—96; assoc. prof. Mercy Coll., Arthur Kill Correctional Facility, SI, 1989—90; supt. provider psychol. svcs. NYC Dept. Edn., 2002—; cert. mediator S.I. Cmty. Dispute Resolution Ctr.; mem. alumni admissions program Georgetown U. Contbr. articles to profl. jour., chapters to books. Mem. health and hosps. com. NYC Cmty. Bd., SI, NY, 1979—80; charter mem. Friends of South Beach Psychiat. Ctr., SI, NY, 1980—81, bd. dirs., 1980—81, chmn. mental health symposium com., 1980—81; mem. appellate divsn. panel mental health profl. psychologist Supreme Ct., NY. Recipient Employee Recogition award, Terence Cardinal Cooke Health Care Ctr., 2001. Mem.: APA, NY State Psychol. Assn. Avocations: Civil War antiques, photography, travel, motorcycle touring. Home and Office: 7 Azalea Ct Staten Island NY 10309

PIEL, ELEANOR JACKSON, lawyer; b. Santa Monica, Calif., Sept. 22, 1920; d. Louis Harris and Blanche Melicent (Virden) Jackson; m. Gerard Piel, June 24, 1955; 1 child, Eleanor Womack. Student, UCLA, 1936-39; BA, U. Calif., Berkeley, 1940, JD, 1943; postgrad., U. So. Calif., 1940-41. Bar: Calif. 1943, N.Y. 1956. Law clk. U.S. Dist. Ct., San Francisco, 1943-44; dep. atty. gen. State of Calif., 1944; clk. U.S. Senate Civil Svc. Com., 1945; atty. Internat. Prosecution Sect., Tokyo, 1945-46; legal adviser Supreme Command Allied Powers, Japan, 1945-48; practice law LA, 1948-55; atty. Legal Aid Soc., NYC, 1957-58; practice in N.Y.C., 1957—. Trustee NYU Med. Ctr., 1969—; bd. dirs. Overseer Ctr. Rsch. on Women, Wellesley Coll., 1994-2000; mem. alumnae bd. Boalt Hall Sch. Law, U. Calif., Berkeley. Fellow ABA (life); mem. Assn. Bar City N.Y. (mem. spl. com. to revise criminal code 1970-83, com. on penology 1971-76, grievance com. 1973-76, com. on state cts. of superior jurisdiction 1989-92, civil rights com., chair spl. com. capital representation 1993-98, mem. spl. com. drugs and the law, v.p. 2000, vice pres.), N.Y. State Bar Assn., N.Y. County Lawyers Assn., Fortune Soc. Women's Forum, Cosmopolitan Club, Women's City Club (counsel), Century Club. Home: 1115 5th Ave New York NY 10128-0100 Office: 2 E 93rd New York NY 10128-0100 Office Phone: 212-423-0797. E-mail: e.jacksonpiel@verizon.net.

PIEL, JOHN A., education educator; b. Indpls., Mar. 2, 1948; s. Alfred H. Piel and Margot (Thom) Walker; m. Charlotte Calvert, Aug. 12, 1979; children: Abbie, Christopher, Amanda. BA, U. No. Colo., 1970, MA, 1976; PhD, Fla. State U., 1980. Dir. early childhood edn. Idaho State U., Pocatello, 1981—. Contbr. numerous articles to profl. jours. Mem. Nat. Assn. Edn. Young Children, Assn. Childhood Edn. Internat. Democrat. Avocation: golf. Home: 1855 Jean St Pocatello ID 83201-2558 Office: Idaho State U Dept Consumer Sci Pocatello ID 83209-0001

PIEN, GRACE, medical educator; d. Shui-hsien and Arlene C. Pien. MD, Columbia U., NYC, 1994; MS, U. Pa., Phila., 2004. Residency prog. medicine Boston U. Sch. Medicine, 1994—97; hospitalist Jordan Hosp., Plymouth, Mass.; clin. fellow Pulmonary Critical Care U. Pa., Phila., 1998—99, rsch. fellow sleep med., 2000—01; asst. prof. medicine U. Pa. Sch. Medicine, Phila., 2002—. Office: Hosp Univ Pa Sleep Medicine Divsn 3624 Market St Ste 205 Philadelphia PA 19104 Office Fax: 215-615-4874.

PIEN, HOWARD, pharmaceutical executive; b. 1958; BS, MIT; MBA, Carnegie Mellon U. With Abbott Laboratories, Merck; v.p. & dir. product mktg.-US SmithKline Beecham, 1992—93, v.p. & dir. new product devel.-US, 1991—92, v.p. & dir. mktg.-US, 1993—95, mng. dir. & sr. v.p.-UK, 1995—97, sr. v.p. & dir.-North Asia, 1997; pres. pharm. internat. GlaxoSmithKline, 2001—03; CEO & dir. Chiron Corp., Emeryville, Calif., 2003—07, chmn., 2004—07; pres., CEO Medarex, Inc., Princeton, NJ, 2007—. Bd. dirs. ImmunoGen, Inc., 2007. Office: Medarex, Inc 707 State Rd Princeton NJ 08540-1437 Office Phone: 609-430-2880. Office Fax: 609-430-2850.

PIENAAR, RUDOLPH, biomedical researcher; b. Epson, Surry, July 2, 1970; s. Rudolph Johannes Francois and Martha Hendrika Pienaar; m. Lara Seven Odendaal, Mar. 15, 1997; children: Reza Kay, Chloe, Quinten Rudolph. B in Elec. & Electronic Engring., U. Pretoria, South Africa, 1992, M in Elec. & Electronic Engring., 1996; Deng in Applied Biomed. Engring., Cleve. State U., 2002. Postdoc. rsch. fellow Mass. Gen. Hosp., Boston, 2003—05, asst. med. imaging, 2005—; instr. radiology-newborn medicine Harvard Med. Sch., Cambridge, Mass., 2005—; tech. dir. fetal-neonatal neuroimaging & devel. sci. ctr. Childrens Hosp., Boston, 2009—. Mem.: IEEE, ISMRM, HBM, ACM. Home: 505 Washington St Winchester MA 01890 Office: Children's Hosp Boston 300 Longwood Ave Boston MA 02115 Personal E-mail: rudolph.pienaar@gmail.com. Business E-Mail: rudolph.pienaar@childrens.harvard.edu.

PIENE, CHLOE, artist, filmmaker; BA in Art History, Columbia U., NYC, 1993. Exhibitions include Me & More, Kunstmuseum, Luzern, 2003, Whitney Biennial, Whitney Mus. Am. Art, NY, 2004, Spirit, Galerie Nathalie Obadia, Paris, 2004, Videodrome II, Bates Coll. Mus. Art, 2004, Boys Will Be Boys?, Mus. Contemporary Art, Denver, 2005, Getting Emotional, 2005, Mus. Contemporary Art, Denver, 2005, Chloe Piene Galleries Nathalie Obadia, Sandroni Rey Gallery, LA, Klemens Gasser and Tanja Grunert, NYC. Syrian Orthodox. Avocation: golf. Studio: 66 Washington Ave 3rd Fl Brooklyn NY 11205 Business E-Mail: cpstudio@verizon.net.

PIEPER, DANIEL ROY, neurosurgeon; b. Beech Grove, Ind., Oct. 2, 1964; s. Roy L. and Shirley A. P.; m. Donna E. Pieper, May 25, 1991; children: Stephanie, Lindsey, Brett. BS in Chemistry, Coll. William and Mary, Williamsburg, Va., 1987; MD, Med. Coll. Va., 1991. Diplomate Am. Bd. Neurol. Surgery, Nat. Bd. Med. Examiners. Intern in gen. surgery Baylor Coll. Medicine, Houston, 1991-92, resident in neurosurgery, 1992-97; staff neurosurgeon McClellan VA Med. Ctr., Little Rock, 1997-99, Ark. Childen's Hosp., Little Rock, 1997-99, U. Ark. Med. Scis., Univ. Hosp., Little Rock, 1997-99; fellow in neurosurgery, clin. instr. neurosurgery & skull base surgery U. Ark. Med. Scis., Little Rock, 1997-98, asst. prof. neurosurgery, 1998-99; staff neurosurgeon William Beaumont Hosp., Royal Oak, Mich., 1999—, Providence Hosp., Southfield, Mich., 1999—, Botsford Hosp., Novi, Mich., 1999—. Mem. quality rev. com. U. Hosp. Ark., 1998-99, physicians adv. com., 1998-99; dir. neurol. grand rounds dept. neurosurgery U. Ark. Med. Scis., 1998-99, coord. neurol. interest group sch. medicine, 1998-99; mem. adv. bd. Rhone-Poulenc Rorer, Collegeville, Pa., 1998—, mem. spkrs. bur., 1999—; lectr. in field. Contbr. articles to profl. jours. Recipient 2nd Place award Assn. Operating Room Nurses award, 1997. Fellow ACS (assoc.); mem. AMA, Am. Assn. Neurol. Surgeons (sgt. at arms ann. meeting 1997, cerebrovascular surgery sect. 1998—), Congress Neurol. Surgeons (registration com. ann. meeting 1998, cerebrovascular surgery sect. 1998—), North Am. Skull Base Soc., Michael E. DeBakey Internat. Surg. Soc., Phi Eta Sigma, Alpha Lambda Delta. Avocations: hiking, camping, golf. Home: 22250 Providence Dr Ste 300 Southfield MI 48075-6211 Fax: 248 569 2436. E-mail: pieperd@usa.net.

PIEPER, DAROLD D., lawyer; b. Vallejo, Calif., Dec. 30, 1944; s. Walter A. H. and Vera Mae (Ellis) P.; m. Barbara Gillis, Dec. 20, 1969; 1 child, Christopher Radcliffe. AB, UCLA, 1967; JD, USC, 1970. Bar: Calif. 1971. Ops. rsch. analyst Naval Weapons Ctr., China Lake, Calif., 1966-69; assoc. Richards, Watson & Gershon, LA, 1970-76, ptnr., 1976—2005; gen. counsel Foothill Transit, 2000—, Greater L.A. County Vector Control Dist., 2001—05, Tri-City Mental Health Ctr., 2003—; spl. counsel L.A. Unified Sch. Dist., 2000—04; city atty. City of Vista, Calif., 2005—. Spl. counsel L.A. County Transp. Commn., 1984-93, L.A. County Met. Transp. Authority, 1993-94; commr. L.A. County Delinquency and Crime Commn., 1983-94, pres., 1987-94; chmn. L.A. County Delinquency Prevention Planning Coun., 1987-90. Contbr. articles to profl. jours. Peace officer Pasadena (Calif.) Police Res. Unit, 1972-87, dep. comdr., 1979-81, comdr., 1982-84; chmn. pub. safety commn. City of La Canada Flintridge, Calif., 1977-82, commr. 1977-88; bd. dirs. La Canada Flintridge Coordinating Council, 1975-82, pres. 1977-78; exec. dir. Cityhood Action Com., 1975-76; chmn. Youth Opportunities United, Inc., 1990-96, vice-chmn. 1988-89, bd. dirs. 1988-96; mem. L.A. County Justice Systems Adv. Group, 1987-92; trustee Lanterman Hist. Mus. Found., 1989-94, Calif. City Mgmt. Found., 1992—. Recipient commendation for Community Service, L.A. County Bd. Suprs., 1978, Commendation for Svc. to Youth, 1996. Mem. ABA, Calif. Bar Assn., L.A. County Bar Assn., San Diego County Bar Assn., City Attys. Assn. San Diego County (v.p. 2006, pres. 2007), La Canada Flintridge C. of C. and Cmty. Assn. (pres. 1981, bd. dirs. 1976-83), Peace Officers Assn., L.A. County, UCLA Alumni Assn. (life), U. So. Calif. Law Alumni Assn. Office Phone: 760-795-6042.

PIEPER, JOHN ALBERT, dean, educator; b. Colo. Springs, Colo., June 13, 1952; s. John Louis and Dorothy Anne Pieper; m. Patrice Colleen Shoaf, July 15, 1978; children: Katharine Leona, John Lough. BS in Biology, U. Colo., Boulder, 1974; BS in Pharmacy, U. Wyo., Laramie, 1977; PharmD, SUNY, Buffalo, 1979. Cert. pharmacotherapy specialist Bd. Pharm. Specialists, 1991; registered pharmacist State Bd.

Pharmacy, Wyo., 1979. Chmn. and prof. Divsn. Pharmacotherapy, Sch. Pharmacy, U. NC, Chapel Hill, 1994—2002; postdoc. fellow Sch. Pharmacy, SUNY, Amherst, 1979—80; asst. prof. Coll. Pharmacy, U. Fla., Gainesville, 1980—84; vice chmn. and assoc. prof. Coll. Pharmacy, U. Tenn., Memphis, 1984—88; assoc. dean and assoc. prof. Sch. Pharmacy, U. Colo., Denver, 1988—94; dean and prof. Coll. Pharmacy, U. N.Mex., Albuquerque, 2002—; v.p. interdisciplinary rsch. U. N.Mex. Health Scis. Ctr., Albuqeurque, 2005—. Chair, external adv. bd. Sch. Pharmacy, U. Pitts., 1996—; exec. dir. N.Mex. Ctr. Isotopes in Medicine, Albuqeurque, 2004—; dir. Sci. Tech. Corp., U. N.Mex., 2004—. Contbr. scientific papers. Chmn. N.Mex. Bd. Acupuncture and Oriental Medicine, Santa Fe, 2008; dir. Farmers State Bank, Calhan, Colo., 1992—2008. Fellow: Am. Coll. Clin. Pharmacy (pres. 1993—94, chmn. bd. trustees, Rsch. Inst. 1994—95); mem.: Commn. on Credentialing, Am. Soc. Health Sys. Pharmacists (apptd. mem. 2004—08), Nat. Assn. Chain Drug Stores (pharmacy edn. adv. com. 2003—08), Am. Found. Pharm. Edn. (mem. grant selection com. 1996—2008). Office: Univ NMex Coll Pharmacy 2502 Marble NE Albuquerque NM 87131-0001 Business E-Mail: jpieper@salud.unm.edu.

PIEPER, MICHAEL JOSEPH, television producer, actor, talk show host; b. Detroit, July 12, 1958; s. Frank John Pieper and Marie Yolanda Dansereau; m. Barbara Marie Michalik (div. Feb. 1990); children: Melanie Lynn, Heather Irene. Student, Marygrove Coll., 1976—78, Specs Howard Sch. Broadcast Arts, 1988. Ordained min. Universal Life Ch., 2000. Owner, prodr. Quixote Video, Huntington Beach, Calif., 1981—. Actor (TV series) T-bone Playhouse, 1981—82, actor, co-prodr. comedy soap opera, Daze of Our Wives, 1982—85; performer: (TV series) game show, Out-patient Bonanza, 1984—85; actor: (radio series) Proceed With Caution, 1985—86; (TV films) Streetlevel, 1983, The Banana Republic, 1983; actor, co-prodr. (TV films) Bartolo's Cafe, 1984, The Paper, 1992, host, co-prodr. (talk show) Forum, 1983—85, host Detroit Metro Magazine, 1985, songwriter Feathersong, 1996; songwriter: Legacy, 2006. Mem.: Internat. Platform Assn. (life). Avocations: singing, painting, photography, metaphysics. Home and Office: Quixote Video 500 Scribner Dr Apt 309 New Albany IN 47150 Office Phone: 812-944-3533. Personal E-mail: magikrhino@gmail.com.

PIEPGRAS, DAVID G., neurosurgeon, educator; b. Luverne, Minn., 1940; MD, U. Minn., 1965. Diplomate Am. Bd. Neurol. Surgery. Intern Mary Hitchcock Hosp., Hanover, Minn., 1965—66; resident in surgery Hennepin County Gen. Hosp., Mpls., 1969—70; resident in neurol. surgery Mayo Grad. Sch. Medicine, Rochester, 1970—74; staff St. Mary's Hosp., Rochester, 1974—, Rochester Meth. Hosp., 1974—; staff cons. dept. neurosurgery Mayo Clinic, Rochester, 1974—, prof. neurol. surgery. Bd. dirs. Am. Bd. Neurol. Surgery, 2002—. Fellow: ACS; mem.: AMA, Congress of Neurol. Surgeons, Am. Acad. Neurol. Surgeons. Office: Mayo Clinic Dept Neurol Surgery Rochester MN 55905-0001

PIEPHO, LEE (EDWARD LEE PIEPHO), humanities educator; b. Detroit, Jan. 10, 1942; s. Edward Ernest and Dolores Faye (Dowis) P.; m. Susan Brand, June 13, 1964. AB, Kenyon Coll., 1964; MA, Columbia U., 1966; PhD, U. Va., 1972. Instr. Sweet Briar Coll., Va., 1969—72, asst. prof., 1972—78, assoc. prof., 1978—83, prof., 1983—94, Shallenberger Brown prof., 1994—2006, rsch. prof., 2006—, dept. chmn., 2000—01, coord. European civilization program, 1986—89. Author: Holofernes' Mantuan, 2001; translator, editor: Adulescentia: The Eclogues of Mantuan, 1989; contbr. articles to profl. jours. Grantee, NEH, 2007; fellow, SIMRS, 1979, NEH, 1985, 1997; Dulin fellow, Folger Shakespeare Libr., 1989—90, Mednick fellow, 1996. Mem. Internat. Assn. for Neo-Latin Studies, Modern Lang. Assn. Am., Renaissance Soc. Am. Avocations: golf, scuba diving. Home: 137 Woodland Rd Sweet Briar VA 24595 Office: Sweet Briar Coll Dept English Sweet Briar VA 24595 Business E-Mail: lpiepho@sbc.edu.

PIEPHO, ROBERT WALTER, pharmacy educator, researcher; b. Chgo., July 31, 1942; s. Walter August and Irene Elizabeth (Huybrecht) Apfel; m. Mary Lee Wilson, Dec. 10, 1981. BS in Pharmacy, U. Ill.-Chgo., 1965; PhD in Pharmacology, Loyola U., Maywood, Ill., 1972. Registered pharmacist, Ill., Mo. Assoc. prof. U. Nebr. Med. Ctr., Omaha, 1970-78; prof. pharmacy, assoc. dean Sch. Pharmacy U. Colo., Denver, 1978-86; prof. pharmacol., dean U. Mo. Sch. Pharmacy, Kansas City, 1986—. Contbr. articles to profl. jours., chpts. to books. Pres. Club Monaco Homeowners Assn., Denver, 1980-82. Named Outstanding Tchr. U. Nebr. Coll. Pharmacy, 1975; recipient Arthur Hassan Colo. Pharmacal Assn., 1983, Excellence in Teaching U. Colo. Med. Sch., 1983 Fellow Am. Coll. Clin. Pharmacology (regent 1983-88, 91-96, pres. 1998-2000); mem. Am. Soc. Hosp. Pharmacists, Am. Soc. Pharmacology and Exptl. Therapeutics, Rho Chi Roman Catholic. Office: U Mo Sch Pharmacy 2464 Charlotte St Kansas City MO 64108-2718 Office Phone: 816-235-1609. Business E-Mail: piephor@umkc.edu.

PIERANGELI, SILVIA SUSANA, medical educator, consultant; b. Buenos Aires, Oct. 10, 1955; d. Hector Raul Pierangeli and Nelida Susana Vega de Pierangeli; m. Alvaro Schleh, Jan. 16, 2003; children: Maria Cecilia Miranda, Maria Eugenia Miranda. PhD, U. of Louisville, 1990. Lab. dir. Coll. of Am. Pathologists. Rsch. assoc. U. of Louisville, 1990—96; prof. Morehouse Sch. of Medicine, Atlanta, 1996—2006, U. Tex. Med. Br., Galveston, 2006—. Tech. dir. Louisville APL Diagnostics, Inc, Doraville, Ga., 1993—. Contbr. scientific papers to profl. publs. Recipient Fulbright scholarship, USIA, 1985—88. Mem.: Am. Coll. of Rheumatology. Achievements include research in Mechanisms of thrombosis induced by antiphospholipid antibodies in the antiphospholipid syndrome; discovery of better antigen for detection of antiphospholipid antibodies; development of better laboratory assay for diagnosis of antiphospholipid syndrome. Business E-Mail: sspieran@utmb.edu.

PIERARD, RICHARD VICTOR, history educator; b. Chgo., May 29, 1934; s. John Perkins and Diana Florence (Russell) P.; m. Charlene Burdett, June 15, 1957; children: David, Cynthia. BA, Calif. State U., LA, 1958, MA, 1959; PhD, U. Iowa, 1964. Prof. history Ind. State U., Terre Haute, 1964-2000, emeritus, 2000—. Vis. prof. Greenville (Ill.) Coll., 1972-73, Free Theol. Acad., Seeheim, Fed. Republic Germany, 1971, 78, Regent Coll., Vancouver, B.C., Can., 1975, Trinity Evang. Div. Sch., Deerfield, Ill., 1982, No. Bapt. Theol. Sem., Lombard, Ill., 1987, Fuller Theol. Sem., Pasadena, Calif., 1988, 91, Moscow Theol. Sem., 1997, 99, 2001, 2003, 2004 Gordon Coll., Wenham, Mass., 2000-2001; scholar-in-residence Gordon Coll., 2000—2007; vis. prof. U. Otego, New zealand, 2002; South Asia Inst. Advanced Christian Studies, India, 2007-; Fulbright prof. U. Frankfurt, Fed. Republic Germany, 1984-85; Fulbright prof. U. Halle, German Dem. Republic, 1989-90; pres. Greater Terre Haute Ch. Fedn., 1987-88; del. Lausanne II Congress on World Evang., Manila, Philippines, 1989; mem. Bapt. Heritage & Identity Study Commn., Bapt. World Alliance, 1990. Author: The Unequal Yoke: Evangelical Christianity and Political Conservatism, 1970, 2006 new edit., Bibliography on the Religious Right in America, 1986; co-author: Twilight of the Saints: Biblical Christianity and Civil Religion, 1978, Civil Religion and the Presidency, 1988, Two Kingdoms: The Church and Culture through the Ages, 1993, The Revolution of the Candles: Christians in the Revolution of the German Democratic Republic, 1996, The New Millennium Manual, 1999, Baptists Together in Christ, 2005, The American Church Experience, 2008, Blues Music and Gospel Proclamation, 2008; contbr. articles to religious and hist. publs. Del. White House Conf. on Librs., Washington, 1979, Ind. Dem. Party Convention, Indpls., 1980, 88; precinct committeeman Dem. Party, Terre Haute, 1978-80, 90—2000; mem. Ind. Gov.'s Adv. Com. on Librs., 1980-81. With U.S. Army, 1954-56. Recipient Terre award for cmty. svc., Terre Haute, Ind., 1991; Fulbright scholar U. Hamburg (Fed. Republic Germany), 1962-63; rsch. fellow U. Aberdeen (Scotland), 1978; Chavanne scholar Baylor U., 1988. Mem. Conf. on Faith and History (sec.-treas. 1967—2004), Evang. Theol. Soc. (pres. 1985), Am. Hist. Assn., Am. Soc. Ch. History, Am. Soc. Missiology, Internat. Assn. Mission Studies, Soc. for Encouragement and Preservation of Barbershop Quartet Singing in Am., Am. Bapt. Hist. Soc. (bd. mgrs. 1993—2003). Democrat. Home: 1031 Indian Hill Rd Hendersonville NC 28791 Office Phone: 828-694-3779. Personal E-mail: charrichp@aol.com.

PIERCE, ALLAN DALE, engineering educator, researcher, editor; b. Clarinda, Iowa, Dec. 18, 1936; s. Franklin Dale and Ruth Pauline (Wright) P.; m. Penelope Claffey, Oct. 27, 1961; children: Jennifer Irene, Bradford Loren. BS, N.Mex. Coll. Agrl. and Mechanic Arts, 1957; PhD, MIT, 1962. Registered profl. engr., Mass. Staff rschr. Rand Corp., Santa Monica, Calif., 1961-63; sr. staff scientist Avco Corp., Wilmington, Mass., 1963-66; asst. prof. MIT, Cambridge, 1966-68, assoc. prof., 1968-73; prof. mech. engring. Ga. Inst. Tech., Atlanta, 1973-76, Regent's prof., 1976-88; Leonhard chair in engring. Pa. State U., University Park, 1988-93; chmn. dept aerospace and mech. engring. Boston U., 1993-99, prof., 1993—. Vis. prof. Max Planck Inst., Goettingen, Fed. Republic Germany, 1976-77; vis. scientist Woods Hole Oceanographic Inst., 2002-03, adj. scientist, 2003-; cons. in field. Author: Acoustics: An Introduction to Its Physical Principles and Applications, 1981; editor phys. acoustics monograph series, 1988-97; editor Jour. Computation Acoustics, 1992-99; contbr. articles to profl. jours. Recipient Sr. U.S. Scientist award Alexander von Humboldt Found., 1976, Cert. of Recognition Nat. Aeronautics and Space Adminstrn., 1984, Per Bruel Gold medal for noise control and acoustics ASME, 1995; NSF fellow, 1957-60, Shell Oil fellow, 1960-61, Faculty fellow U.S. Dept. Transp., 1979-80. Fellow Acoustical Soc. Am. (editor-in-chief 1999—, Silver medal 1991, Rossing prize in acoustics edn. 2004, Gold medal 2005), ASME (Rayleigh lectr. 1992, Per Bruel Gold medal 1995, chair Noise Control and Acoustics Divsn. 1999-2000), Acoustical Found. India (Gold Medal 2007); mem. IEEE, AIAA, DEGA. Home: PO Box 339 East Sandwich MA 02537-0339 Office: Boston U Dept Mech Engring 110 Cummington St Boston MA 02215-2407 Business E-Mail: adp@bu.edu.

PIERCE, ANTONIO, professional football player; b. Ontario, Calif., Oct. 26, 1978; s. Cleo Burrows; m. Jocelyn Maldonado, May 24, 2008; 3 children. Attended, Mt. San Antonio Coll., Walnut, Calif., U. Ariz., Tucson. Linebacker Washington Redskins, 2001—05, NY Giants, 2005—. Comm. intern Howard Stern Show, 2008. Named Man of Yr., United Way, 2007, Minority Athletes Networking Inc., 2008; named to Nat. Football Conf. Pro Bowl team, NFL, 2006. Achievements include member of Super Bowl XLII championship winning NY Giants, 2008. Office: NY Giants Giants Stadium East Rutherford NJ 07073*

PIERCE, BARBARA A., elementary school educator; b. Memphis, Mar. 17, 1943; d. Charlie Lewis Pierce and Rita Mae Brown. BS in Edn., Cheyney State Coll., 1968; MS in Edn. & Reading, Coll. New Rochelle, 1974. Tchr. Mt. Vernon Sch. Sys., NY, 1968—2003, ret., substitute, 2003—. Author: Whichever Way The Wind Blows, 2006, From an Anthill Springs a Mountain, 2007, Just South of the Rainbow, 2007, (new children's book) The Emperor's Regret, 2008. Recipient Jenkins award, PTA, Mt. Vernon. Mem. Lds Ch. Avocations: poetry, beading.

PIERCE, BENJAMIN ALLEN, biologist, educator; b. Birmingham, Ala., Nov. 15, 1953; s. John Rush and Amanda (Allen) P.; m. Marlene Francis Tyrrell, July 19, 1980; children: Sarah Elizabeth, Michael Stephen. BS in Biology, So. Meth. U., 1976; PhD, U. Colo., 1980. Rsch. asst. U. Colo., Boulder, 1979-80; asst. prof. biology Conn. Coll., New London, 1980-84, Baylor U., Waco, Tex., 1984-88, assoc. prof. biology, 1988—2005; prof. biology Southwestern U., Georgetown, Tex., 2005—, prof. Lillinn Nelson Pratt chair. Author: The Family Genetic Source Book, 1990, Genetics, A Conceptual Approach,1st, 2nd, 3rd Edit.; contbr. articles to profl. publs. Achievements include research in population genetics and evolution. Office: Biology Dept Southwestern U Georgetown TX 78626 Business E-Mail: pierceb@southwestern.edu.

PIERCE, CHARLES ELIOT, JR., retired library director, educator; b. Springfield, Mass., Dec. 25, 1941; s. C. Eliot and Dora Mason (Redway) P.; m. Barbara G. Hanson, Oct. 18, 1969; children: Sheila H., Charles Eliot III BA, Harvard U., 1964, MAT, 1966, PhD, 1970. Prof. English Vassar Coll., Poughkeepsie, NY, 1970-87; dir. Pierpont Morgan Libr. & Mus., NYC, 1987—2007; ret., 2008. Mem. vis. com. Vassar Coll. Art Gallery, Sherman Fairchild Found. Author: (literary criticism) The Religious Life of Samuel Johnson, 1983 Trustee Canadian Ctr. Architecture; vis. com. Harvard Art. Mus. Mem. Canadian Ctr. Arch., Johnsonians, Century Assn., Grolier Club, Walpole Soc., Knickerbocker Club. Episcopalian. Personal E-mail: charlespiercejr@yahoo.com.

PIERCE, CHESTER MIDDLEBROOK, retired psychiatrist, educator; b. Glen Cove, NY, Mar. 4, 1927; s. Samuel Riley and Hettie Elenor (Armstrong) P.; m. Jocelyn Patricia Blanchet, June 15, 1949; children: Diane Blanchet, Deirdre Anona. AB, Harvard U., 1948, MD, 1952; ScD (hon.), Westfield Coll., 1977, Tufts U., 1984; D in Engring. Tech. (hon.), Wentworth Inst. Tech., 1997. Instr. psychiatry U. Cin., 1957-60; asst. prof. psychiatry U. Okla., 1960-62, prof., 1965-69; prof. edn. and psychiatry Harvard U., 1969—; pres. Am. Bd. Psychiatry and Neurology, 1977-78; ret., 1997. Mem. Polar Rsch. Bd.; cons. USAF. Author publs. on sleep disturbances, media, polar medicine, sports medicine, racism; mem. editl. bds. Advisor Children's TV Workshop; chmn. Child Devel. Assn. Consortium; bd. dirs. Action Children's TV. With M.C. USNR, 1953-55. Fellow: Brit. Royal Coll. Psychiatrists (hon.), Royal Australian and New Zealand Coll. Psychiatrists (hon.); mem.: Am. Acad. Arts and Scis., Am. Orthopsychiat. Assn. (pres. 1983—84), Black Psychiatrists Am. (chmn.), Inst. Medicine of NAS. Democrat. Home: 17 Prince St Jamaica Plain MA 02130-2725 Office Phone: 617-495-4929.

PIERCE, DANIEL ROBERT, lawyer; b. Lowell, Mass., June 14, 1972; BA cum laude, U. Mass., 1995; JD magna cum laude, Boston U., 1998. Bar: Mass. 1998, US Dist. Ct. (Dist. Mass.). Assoc. Schnader Harrison Goldstein & Manello, Boston, 1998—2002, Duane Morris LLP, Boston, 2003—06, ptnr., 2007—. Mem.: Boston Bar Assn. Office: Duane Morris LLP Ste 500 470 Atlantic Ave Boston MA 02210 Office Phone: 857-488-4247. Office Fax: 857-401-3076. E-mail: DRPierce@duanemorris.com.*

PIERCE, DANIEL THORNTON, physicist; b. LA, July 16, 1940; s. Daniel Gordon Pierce and Celia Francis Thornton Thayer; m. Barbara Harrison, Nov. 19, 1988; children: Jed, Maia, Stephen. BS, Stanford U., 1962, PhD in Applied Physics, 1970; MA, Wesleyan U., Middletown, Conn., 1966. NSF rsch. asst. materials sci. dept. Stanford U., 1961; lectr in physics U.S. Peace Corps, Kathmandu, Nepal, 1962-64; rsch. asst. Wesleyan U., 1964-66, Stanford Electronics Lab., 1966-70, rsch. assoc., 1970-71; rsch. staff Solid State Physics Lab., Swiss Fed. Inst. Tech., 1971-75; physicist Nat. Inst. Standards and Tech. (formerly Nat. Bur Standards), Gaithersburg, Md., 1975—, fellow, 1994—. Contbr. chpts. to books, numerous articles to profl. jours. Trustee Unitarian Ch. of Rockville, Md., 1994-96 Recipient IR-100 award R&D Mag., 1980, 85, Gold medal Dept. Commerce, 1987, William P. Schlichter award Nat. Inst. Standards and Tech., 1992. Fellow Am. Phys. Soc. (exec. com. Materials Physics Divsn. 1998-2001), Am. Vacuum Soc. (surface sci. exec. com. 1984-88, Gaede-Langmuir prize 1994). Achievements include patents for source of spin polarized electrons, absorbed current and low energy spin polarization detectors; development of scanning electron microscopy with polarization analysis. Office: Nat Inst Standards and Tech Mail Stop 6202 Bldg 216 Rm A223 Gaithersburg MD 20899-6202 Office Phone: 301-975-3711. Business E-Mail: daniel.pierce@nist.gov.

PIERCE, DAVID, information technology executive; With Universal Pictures, MGM; with New World Home Entertainment New World Pictures, 1984; sr. v.p. Columbia Tristar Home Video Sony Pictures Entertainment, 1989—94; exec. v.p., gen. mgr. Sony Wonder SONY BMG Music Entertainment; pres., CEO Atari, Inc., NYC, 2006—. Office: Atari Inc 417 Fifth Ave New York NY 10016-2204 Office Phone: 212-726-6500.

PIERCE, DAVID HYDE, actor; b. Albany, NY, Apr. 3, 1959; m. Brian Hargrove, Oct. 24, 2009. BA in Theatre & English, Yale U., 1981. Appeared in plays Beyond Therapy, 1982, Holiday, 1982, Summer, 1983, That's It, Folks! 1983, Candida, 1984, The Seagull, 1984, The Grand Hysteric, 1984, The Three Zeks, 1984, Tartuffe, 1984, Donuts, 1985, Hamlet, 1986, The Author's Voice, 1987, The Maderati, 1987, Camille, 1987, The Cherry Orchard, 1988, Zero Positive, 1988, Much Ado About Nothing, 1988, The Heidi Chronicles, 1989, Elliot Loves, 1990, It's Only a Play, 1991, Monty Python's Spamalot, 2005, Curtains, 2006 (Tony award best performance by a leading actor in a musical, 2007), Accent on Youth, 2009; films include Bright Lights, Big City, 1988, Crossing Delancey, 1988, Rocket Gibraltar, 1988, The Fisher King, 1991, Little Man Tate, 1991, Sleepless in Seattle, 1993, Addams Family Values, 1993, Wolf, 1994, Nixon, 1995, Hercules, 1998, A Bug's Life, 1998, Jackie's Back!, 1999, Mating Habits of the Earthbound Human, 1999, Isn't She Great, 2000, Chain of Fools, 2000, Wet, Hot, American Summer, 2001, Osmosis Jones, 2001; TV series include The Powers That Be, 1993, Frasier, 1993-2004 (seven Am. Comedy awards), Laud Weiner, 2001, Full Frontal, 2002, Treasure Planet (voice), 2002, Down with Love, 2003. Recipient Emmy award, 1995, 1998, 1999, 2004, SAG Award, 1996, 2000, Q Award 1994, 95, 96, 98, TV Guide award, 2000, TV Critics Assn. award 1997, 1998. Am. Comedy award 1995-2000.

PIERCE, DONALD FAY, lawyer; b. Bexley, Miss., Aug. 28, 1930; s. Percy O. and Lavada S. (Stringfellow) Pierce; m. Norma Faye Scribner, June 5, 1954; children: Kathryn Pierce Tuttle, D. F. Jr., John S., Jeff G. BS, U. Ala., 1956, JD, 1958. Bar: Ala. 1958, U.S. Ct. Appeals (5th cir.) 1958, U.S. Dist. Ct. (no., mid. and so. dists.) Ala. 1958, U.S. Ct. Appeals (11th cir.) 1982. Law clk. to presiding judge U.S. Dist. Ct. (so. dist.) Ala., 1958—59; ptnr. Hand, Arendall, Bedsole, Greaves & Johnston, Mobile, Ala., 1964—91, Pierce, Carr, Alford, Ledyard & Latta, P.C., 1991—; pvt. practice; of counsel Butler Pappas LLP. Mem. Products Liability Adv. Coun., 1990—; bd. overseers Vanderbilt Cancer Ctr., 1994—. Contbr. articles to profl. jours. Trustee UMS Prep Sch., 1980—87. 1st lt. US Army, 1951—53. Mem.: Def. Research Inst. (pres. 1987, chmn. 1988), Def. Counsel Trial Acad. (bd. dir. 1983—84), Internat. Assn. Def. Counsel, Am. Acad. Hosp. Attys., Fedn. Ins. and Corp. Counsel, Ala. Def. Lawyers Assn. (past pres.). Baptist. Home: 4452 Winnie Way Mobile AL 36608-2221 Office: Butler Pappas LLP 1110 Montlimar Dr Ste 1050 Mobile AL 36608 Home Phone: 251-344-0170; Office Phone: 251-338-1313. Business E-Mail: d.pierce@butlerpappas.com.

PIERCE, DONALD SHELTON, retired orthopedic surgeon, educator; b. Castine, Maine, May 21, 1930; s. Frederick Ernest and Jeannie (Emmet) P.; m. Janet Ten Broeck, Dec. 29, 1956; children: Donald Shelton, Stanton ten Broeck, Frederick Ernest, Jennifer Emmet. AB cum laude, Harvard U., 1953, MD, 1957. Diplomate Am. Bd. Spine Surgery, Am. Bd. Orthop. Surgery; lic. lay eucharistic minister Episcopal Ch., 2004. Intern U. Hosp., Cleve., 1957-58, resident, 1958-62; rsch. assoc. biomechanics lab. U. Calif., San Francisco, 1962-64; practice medicine specializing in orthopedic surgery San Francisco, 1962-64; instr. orthopedic surgery U. Calif. Med. Sch., San Francisco, 1962-64, Harvard Med. Sch., 1964-66; clin. and rsch. assoc. J.P. Kennedy Jr. Meml. Hosp., Brighton, Mass., 1964-66; clin. assoc. in orthopedics Harvard Med. Sch., 1966-67, clin. asst. prof. orthopaedic surgery, 1979-87, clin. assoc. prof., 1987-2000; ret., 2000; sr. orthopedic surgeon Mass. Gen. Hosp., Boston. Chief dept. rehab. medicine Mass. Gen. Hosp., Boston, 1965-72, assoc. orthopedic surgeon, 1969—, vis. orthopedic surgeon, 1969—; lectr. dept. mech. engring. MIT, 1970-72. Co-author: Amputees and Their Porstheses, 1971; author: The Total Care of Spinal Cord Injuries, 1977; contbr. articles in field to profl. jours. Pres. Wellesley (Mass.) Friendly Aid Assn., 1965-67, dir., 1967-70; dir. Family Svc. Counseling Region West, Wellesley, 1965-67; mem. exec. com., task force chmn. Mass. Rehab. Planning Commn., 1966-68; pres. Maine Ret. Skippers Race, 2003-05; co-chmn. capital campaign com. Trinity Espic. Ch., Maine. With USAF, 1951-52. Fellow ACS, Am. Acad. Orthopedic Surgeons, Royal Soc. Health, Pan Am. Med. Assn., Soc. Internat. Chirurgerie, Ortopaedie et Traumatologie; mem. NAS (mem. skeletal com. 1965-68, mem. subcom. basic projects, mem. com. prosthetics R & D 1966-68), NRC (musculoskeletal com., mem. subcom. basic projects, mem. com. prosthetics R & D), Othopedic Rsch. Soc., Am. Orthopaedic Assn., Cervical Spine Rsch. Soc. (pres. 1986), Fedn. Spine Assns. (pres. 1987), N.E. Med. Assn. (pres.), Ezekiel Hersey Coun., Harvard Med. Sch. (mem. Dean's Coun.). Personal E-mail: treetops-1@comcast.net.

PIERCE, FRANK POWELL, lawyer, judge; b. San Antonio, Dec. 28, 1953; s. Arnold Leigh and Marie Pierce; m. Ernestine Pierce; 4 children. BA in Polit. Sci., U. Houston, 1977; JD, Tex. So. U., 1980. Bar: Tex. 1980, U.S. Dist. Ct. (so. and we. dists.) Tex. 1982, U.S. Ct. Appeals (5th cir.) 1982, U.S. Supreme Ct. 1984. Atty. Bexar County Legal Aid, San Antonio, 1980-83; asst. city atty. City of San Antonio, 1983-87; judge County Ct. at Law No. 2, San Antonio, 1987—; asst. atty. gen., 1993—2001; judge Child Support Ct. 2, Harris County, 2001—. Mem. Bexar County Bail Bond Bd., 1987-88; mem. faculty St. Philip's Coll., part-time; adj. prof. South Tex. Coll. Law. Mem. speaker's bur. San Antonio Literacy Coun., 1988, mediation bd. Bexar County, 1989—; deacon Mt. Zion 1st Bapt. Ch., San Antonio; alumnus Leadership San Antonio; mem. minority recruitment task force Dental Sch., U. Tex.

Health Sci. Ctr.; mem. Palmer Drug Abuse Bd., 1987—; bd. mgrs. Alamo br. YMCA, San Antonio; bd. dirs. Halfway House San Antonio, 1989; city councilman, San Antonio, 1991-93. Named Black Achiever in Govt., Iota Phi Lamda, 1984; recipient Citizen of Yr. award Omega Psi Phi, 1987, Man of Yr. award Mission Lodge, San Antonio, 1988. Mem. Tex. Bar Assn. Office: Family Law Ctr Ct Two 1115 Congress Ste 411 Houston TX 77002 Office Phone: 713-755-2910.

PIERCE, HILDA (HILDA HERTA HARMEL), painter; b. Vienna; arrived in U.S., 1940; m. Herman J. Slutzky; 1 child, Diana Rubin Daly (dec.). Student, Art Inst. Chgo.; studied with Oskar Kokoschka, Salzburg, Austria. Art tchr. Highland Park (Ill.) Art Ctr., Sandburg Village Art Workshop, Chgo., Old Town Art Ctr., Chgo.; owner, operator Hilda Pierce Art Gallery, Laguna Beach, Calif., 1981-85. Guest lectr. maj. art mus. and art tours, Carribean cruises South America, Argentina, Brazil, Israel, Egypt, France, Switzerland, Austria, Italy, Mex., San Diego, China, India, 1998—2002, Russian river cruise and major art mus., St. Petersburg, Moscow, 1994; lectr., Mexico, 1994—2008, U. Calif. Geisel Libr., San Diego, 2003—08; founder, chmn. Art Encounters, San Diego. One-woman shows include Fairweather Hardin Gallery, Chgo., Gotthelf Gallery, La Jolla, Calif., Sherman Art Gallery, Chgo., Marshall Field Gallery, exhibited in group shows at Old Orchard Art Festival, Skokie, Ill., Union League Club, Chgo., North Shore Art League, Winnetka, Ill., Art Inst. Chgo., Represented in permanent collections U. Calif. San Diego Art Libr., La Jolla, Carnival Cruise Lines megaliner M.S. Fantasy, megaliner M.S. Imagination, Rebecca and John Moores Cancer Ctr., U. Calif. San Diego, U. Calif. San Diego Geisel Libr.; featured (video) Survivors of the Shoah, Stephen Spielberg Found., 1996; author: Hilda: A True Story of Terror, Tears and Triumph, 2007; contbr. articles to profl. jours. and periodicals; Represented in permanent collections Painting Saint Hilda, St. Paul's Cathedral, San Diego; actor: (TV miniseries, several interviews) San Diego Insider Chambord and NBC, 2009. Recipient Outstanding Achievement in Art award, Chgo. Immigrants Svc. League, 1964. Office Phone: 858-558-7556. Personal E-mail: hildapierce@aol.com. *An artist's most precious quality is curiosity. It has kept me young for many years, kept me searching, experimenting and never being complacent, in my life and my work.*

PIERCE, JAMES CLARENCE, surgeon, educator; b. Huron, SD, Aug. 5, 1929; s. Henry Montraville and Carrie Bernice (Matson) P.; m. Carol Sue Wilson, 1967; children: Henry MacDonald, Richard Matson, Elizabeth Gail. BA, Carleton Coll., 1951; MD, Harvard U., 1955; MS, U. Minn., 1963, PhD in Surgery, 1966. Diplomate Am. Bd. Surgery. Surg. intern Peter Bent Brigham Hosp., Boston, 1955-56; surg. fellow U. Minn., 1959-66; instr. surgery Med. Coll. Va., Richmond, 1966, prof. surgery and microbiology, 1972-75; dir. Tissue Typing Lab., 1969-75; attending surgeon, dir. surg. research, dir. transplantation service St. Luke's Hosp. Center, NYC, 1975-78; prof. surgery Columbia U., 1976, Ailsa Mellon Bruce prof. surgery, 1977-78; clin. prof. surgery Pa. State U. and, 1979-88; chmn. dept. surgery Geisinger Med. Center, Danville, Pa., 1979-90, chmn. emeritus, 1990—. Clin. prof. surgery Jefferson U., 1990—. Contbr. articles to profl. jours. Elder Presbyn. Ch. With M.C., USAF, 1957-59. NIH fellow, 1963-65; Royal Soc. Medicine Found. travelling fellow, 1971; James IV Assn. Surg. traveller, 1978 Mem. ACS (pres. Ctrl. Pa. chpt. 1981-82), Transplant Soc., Am. Soc. Transplant Surgeons, Ea. Surg. Soc., JCP Soc., Soc. Univ. Surgeons, Sigma Xi. Republican. Home: 1906 Red Ln Danville PA 17821-8415

PIERCE, JANIS VAUGHN, insurance executive, consultant; b. Memphis, Dec. 23, 1934; d. Jesse Wynne and Dorothy Arnette (Lloyd) Vaughn; m. Gerald Swetman Pierce, May 27, 1956; children: Ann Elizabeth Swetman, John Willard. BA, U. Miss., 1956, MA, 1964. High sch. tchr., 1957-58; mem. faculty Memphis Univ. Sch., 1965-66, Memphis State U., 1968-75; agent Aetna Life Ins. Co., Memphis, 1977-80, career supr., 1980—, mgr., 1983, supr. prime, career, 1984, chmn. Aetna Women's Task Force, 1980-85; coord. agency tng. specialist Union Ctr. Life Ins. Co., Memphis, 1985-88; agent, v.p., dir., bus. cons. Cons. Sys., Inc., 1975-84, pres., 1984—. Pres. Women's Resource Ctr., Memphis, 1974-77; sec. Tenn. chpt. Women's Polit. Caucus, 1975-76; bd. dirs., treas., mem. exec. com. Memphis YMCA, 1979—; mem. bd. commr. Memphis Area Trans Auth., 1982—; chmn. fin., adminstrn. com., 1983—, chmn. bd. commn., 1990—; pres., bd. dirs. The Support Ctr., Memphis, 1986-87, Supprt Ctrs. Am., 1987—; mem. Tenn. adv. com. U.S. Civil Rights Commn., 1980-85, steering com. Big Break, 1978; mem. adv. bd. Porter Leath Children's Ctr., 1984—, bd. dirs., 1986—; mem. planned giving com. Girl Scouts U.S., 1990—; mem. citizens adv. bd. St. Joseph Hosp., 1991—; mem. Leadership Memphis, 1981. Univ. scholar U. Miss., 1952-56. Mem. AAUW, LWV, United Daus. Confederacy (pres. Albert Sidney Johnson chpt. 1961), Women Leaders Roundtable, Nat. Assn. Life Underwriters, Tenn. Life Underwriters Assn., Am. Pub. Transp. Assn. (bd. dirs. 1991—, gov. bds. com. 1985—, sec. 1987-88, v.p. 1988-90, mem. task force transp. handicapped 1987, pres. 1989, legis. com. 1985—, region III rep. 1991—), Women's Life Underwriters Conf. (bd. dirs., pres. 1985), Memphis Life Underwriters Assn. (bd. dirs. 1982, edn. chmn. 1982, pub. svc. com. 1983, law and legis. chmn. 1984, pres. 1986), Memphis PTA (coun. 1971-72), Memphis Soc. CLUs, Mortar Bd. (regional coord. 1972-78), Memphis CLU Assn., C. of C. (ambassador 1980), Alpha Lambda Delta, Sigma Delta Pi, Le Bonheur Club (bd. dirs.), Memphis State U. Women's Club (pres. 1978). Episcopalian. Republican. Home: 1613 Lyttleton St Camden SC 29020-2906

PIERCE, JERRY EARL, publishing executive; b. Hindsdale, Ill., Aug. 3, 1941; s. Earl and Adeline A. (Zaranski) P.; m. Carol Louise Martin, Aug. 15, 1964; children: Patricia, Barbara, Linda. Bradley. BS, U. Ill., 1964. With R.R. Donnelley & Sons, Chgo., 1964-70, Western Pub. Co., Racine, Wis., 1970—, nat. pubs. acct. exec., 1975—. Chair bd. Pierce Sale Co., Inc., Restaurant Equipment World, Inc., Heat Transfer Engring. Inc.; chmn. bd. Tech Industries & Millwork, Inc., 1989-93; pres. B.J. Installation Co., Inc., 1989-91, ROI World Equipment, 1993—; v.p., sec. Savers Clubs Am., Inc.; v.p. Pierce Aviation, 2000—; chmn. adv. bd. Greater Winter Park, Bankfirst Bank, Winter Park, Fla. Chmn. Leadership Trust of Nat. Fedn. Ind. Bus. 1st lt. US Army, 1968—70. Mem.: Stetson U. Family Enterprise Ctr. (chmn. adv. bd.), Nat. Fed. Ind. Bus. Fla. (chmn. safe trust, Small Bus. Person of Year 2006), Goldenrod C. of C. (bd. dirs. 2007—08), Nat. Bus. Aviation Assn., Food Equipment Distbrs. Assn. (bd. dirs. 1997—98), Food Svc. Cons. Soc., Cleve. Advt. Club, Interlachen Country Club (treas. Winter Pk., Fla.), Ctrl. Fla. Veterans Mem. Found. (chmn. 2008—), Ctrl. Fla. Vets. Inc. (past pres.). Republican. Episcopalian. Achievements include patents for refrigeration-to-water utility cost control system; invention of E-Commerce business model. Home: 2639 Ultra Vista Dr Maitland FL 32751 Office: 2413 N Forsyth Rd Orlando FL 32807-6455 Office Phone: 407-679-9004.

PIERCE, JOHN ALBERT, retired medical educator; b. Little Rock, Ark., Mar. 10, 1925; s. Albert Proffitt Pierce and Mary Helen Baldwin; m. Susan Kay Ellis, May 23, 1984. MD, U. Ark., Little Rock, 1948. Diplomate Am. Bd. Internal Medicine, 1954. Instr. to prof. Dept Medicine, U. Ark Sch. Medicine, Little Rock, 1954—67; assoc. prof. to prof. Wash. U. Sch Medicine, St Louis, 1967—93, dir., pulmonary disease divsn., 1967—85. Contbr. scientific papers to profl. jours. Recipient Disting. Svc. award, Wash. U., 2008. Home: 836 Wheelright Dr Ballwin MO 63021 Office Fax: 314-454-5571; Home Fax: 636-394-7827. Business E-Mail: john.a.pierce@sbcglobal.net.

PIERCE, JOHN GERALD (JERRY), lawyer; b. Winter Haven, Fla., Jan. 12, 1937; s. Francis E. and Margaret (Butler) P.; m. Kathleen E., Dec. 1, 1989; children: Kathleen M. Cooke, Nancy A., John Gerald Jr., Michael J. BChemE, U. Fla., Gainesville, 1959, JD with honors, 1965. Bar: Fla. 1966, US Dist. Ct. (mid. dist.) Fla. 1966, US Ct. Appeals (11th cir.) 1983. Assoc. Anderson & Rush, Dean & Lowndes, Orlando, Fla., 1966—68, Arnold, Matheny & Eagen, Orlando, 1968—70; ptnr. Pierce, Lewis & Dolan, Orlando, 1970—74; pvt. practice Orlando, 1974—2002; prin., owner Pierce & Assocs. PL, Orlando, 2003—. Served to 1st lt. US Army, 1959—65. Named Businessman of Yr., Nat. Rep. Congl. Com., 2004. Mem. ABA, Fla. Bar Assn., Orange County Bar Assn. Republican. Roman Catholic. Avocations: golf, boating, skiing. Home: 605 Fox Valley Dr Longwood FL 32779-2417 Office: 800 N Ferncreek Ave Orlando FL 32803-4127 Office Phone: 407-898-4848. Business E-Mail: jerry@johnpierce.com.

PIERCE, JOHN RANDALL, medical inspector, pediatrician; b. Nashville, May 9, 1947; MD, U. Tenn., 1971. Cert. Pediatrics, 1977, Neonatal-Perinatal Medicine, 1981. Chief Dept. Pediatrics, residency program dir. U.S. Army Med. Corps.; dep. comdr. clin. svcs., dir. med. edn. Walter Reed Army Med. Ctr.; cons. pediatrics US Surgeon Gen.; dep. med. inspector Veterans Health Adminstrn., US Dept. Veterans Affairs, Washington, 2002—04, med. inspector, 2004—. Asst. prof. pediatrics Uniformed Svcs. U. of Health Scis.; historian Walter Reed Soc. Co-author: Yellow Jack: How Yellow Fever Ravaged America and Walter Reed Discovered Its Deadly Secrets, 2005; contbr. articles to profl. jours. Col. med. corps US Army. Decorated Legion of Merit, Meritorious Svc. Medal, Joint Svc. Commendation Medal, Army Commendation Medal, Army Achievement Medal, Order of Mil. Med. Merit Surgeon Gen. Fellow: Am. Acad. Pediatrics. Office: US Dept Veterans Affairs Vets Health Adminstrn 810 Vermont Ave NW Washington DC 20420 Office Phone: 202-461-4094. E-mail: john.pierce@va.gov.*

PIERCE, LAWRENCE WARREN, retired federal judge; b. Phila., Dec. 31, 1924; s. Harold Ernest and Leora (Bellinger) Pierce; m. Wilma Taylor, 1948 (dec. May 1978); m. Cynthia Straker, July 8, 1979; children: Warren Wood, Michael Lawrence, Mark Taylor. BS, St. Joseph's U., Phila., 1948, DHL, 1967; JD, Fordham U., 1951, LLD, 1982, Fairfield U., 1972, Hamilton Coll., 1987, St. John's U., 1990. Bar: N.Y. 1951, U.S. Supreme Ct. 1968. Civil law practice, NYC, 1951—61; asst. dist. atty. Kings County, NYC, 1954—61; dep. police commr. NYC, 1961—63; dir. N.Y. State Divsn. for Youth, Albany, 1963—66; chmn. N.Y. State Narcotic Addiction Control Commn., 1966—70; vis. prof. criminal justice SUNY, Albany, 1970—71; dist. judge U.S. Dist. Ct., So. Dist. N.Y., 1971—81; judge U.S. Fgn. Intelligence Surveillance Ct., Washington, 1979—81; cir. judge U.S. Ct. Appeals 2d Cir., 1981—95; ret., 1995. Dir. Cambodian ct. tng. project Internat. Human Rights Law Group, 1995. Past bd. dirs. CARE, Havens Fund Soc., Lincoln Hall for Boys, S-R and S.A.R., N.Y. chpts., Cath. Interracial Coun., Practising Law Inst. Mem.: ABA (com. on corr. svc. and facilities 1970—71, alt. observer U.S. Mission to UN 1988—90, site evaluation com., sec. legal edn. 1996—98), Spl. Com. Army Confinement Facilties (Office of Sec. of Army 1970), Urban League, Nat. Bar Assn., Am. Law Inst., Coun. Fgn. Rels.

PIERCE, MARY E., retired elementary school educator, public relations consultant; b. Chgo. d. Henry Harris and Eva Irene (Hanes) P. BE, Chgo. Tchrs. Coll., 1944. One room sch. tchr. Will County, Monee, Ill.; tchr. 5th grade Peotone (Ill.) Sch. Dist.; tchr. elem. and jr. h.s. Steger (Ill.) Sch. Dist., chair lang. arts dept.; ret., 1979; chair sch. improvement plan; pub. rels. cons. Former pres. Steger Edn. Assn.; chmn. bd. dirs. #194 Employee Credit Union, Steger, 1972-95. Village clk. Village of Richton Park, 1992—; pres. Friends of Libr., Richton Park, 1980-2007, v.p.; bd. dirs. So. Suburban Cancer Soc., Tinley Pk., Ill., 1994—, S.E. Chpt. Ill. Credit Union, Calumet City, Ill., 1994-95. Recipient Cmty. Svc. award Cook County Sheriff's Office, Chgo., Merit award S.E. chpt. Ill. Credit Union League. Mem. Delta Kappa Gamma Soc. (Lambda State Beta Beta chpt. treas. 1979-2003). Avocation: golf. Home: 22147 Karlov Ave Richton Park IL 60471-1227

PIERCE, MICHAEL NORMAN, internist; b. NYC, May 1, 1955; s. Samuel and Ingeborg Pierce. BA in Biology, SUNY, Binghamton, 1977; MD, U. Vt., 1982. Diplomate Am. Bd. Internal Medicine. Intern, gen. surg. resident L.A. County/U. So. Calif. Med. Ctr., LA, 1982—84; intern, resident in internal medicine Calif.-Pacific Med. Ctr., San Francisco, 1985—88; attending physician St. Francis Meml. Hosp., San Francisco, 1989—96, Montefiore Med. Ctr., East Elmhurst, NY, 1997—98, St. Barnabas Hosp./CHS/HHC, East Elmhurst, 1998—2001; asst. attending physician St. Luke's Roosevelt Hosp. Ctr., NYC, 2002—05, assoc. attending physician, 2005; dir. HIV medicine All Med Med. and Rehab. NY, 2006—, dir. internal medicine attending, 2006—. Chair Spring conf. St. Luke's Roosevelt Hosp. Ctr., 2003; judge, mem. abstract rev. bd. for resident's poster competition NY Downstate ACP-ASIM sci. meetings, 1997—; mem. CME med. bd. com. St. Luke's Roosevelt Hosp. Ctr., NYC, 2002—05, key faculty, internal medicine residency program; asst. clin. prof. medicine Columbia U. Coll. Physicians and Surgeons, NYC, 2002—05; active HIV mgmt. preceptorship program Johns Hopkins U. Sch. Medicine, Balt., 2001; mem. Infectious Disease Soc. Am., Infectious Disease Soc. Am. HIV Med. Assn.; HIV med. specialist State of NY; prin. investigator Pfizer clin. trial of Maravaroc. Mem. editl. bd. Johns Hopkins U. Sch. Medicine Advanced Studies in Medicine, 2002—. Recipient Physician's Recognition award, AMA, 1991—; Pharm. Mfrs. Assn. grantee, 1979. Fellow: ACP (com. on med. students 2001—), Soc. Gen. Internal Medicine; mem.: AMA, N.Y. County Med. Soc., Med. Soc. State N.Y. (surveyor-reviewer hosp. CME programs 1998—, mem. com. on edn.). Office Phone: 718-292-0100.

PIERCE, MORTON ALLEN, lawyer; b. Liberec, Czechoslovakia, June 25, 1948; m. Nancy Washor, Dec. 14, 1975 (dec.); children: Matthew J., Nicholas L. BA, Yale Coll., 1970; JD, U. Pa., 1974; postgrad., Oxford U., 1974-75. Bar: N.Y. 1975. Assoc. Reid & Priest, NYC, 1975-83, ptnr., 1983-86, Dewey Ballantine, NYC, 1986—2008, vice-chmn., 2002—03, co-chmn., 2003—05, chmn., 2005—08; ptnr. Dewey & LeBoeuf, 2008—. Mem. mgmt. com. 1988—, chmn. corp. dept., 1999-2003, global chmn., mergers and acquisitions group, 1990—, mem. exec. com., 2001—. Contbr. articles to profl. jours. Mem. ABA (chmn. subcom. on internat. securities matters 1985-91, adv. com. to fed. regulation of securities com. 1991-2000, task force on rev. of the fed. securities law 1991-2000), Assn. of the Bar of the City of N.Y. (securities law com. 1988-91, chmn. subcom. on securities and exch. commn. enforcement matters 1990-91), Internat. Bar Assn. (com. on securities transactions), Legal Aid Soc. (bd. dirs.), Gordon A. Rich Found. (bd. dirs.). Home: 188 E 76th St New York NY 10021-2826 Office: Dewey LeBoeuf LLP 1301 Ave Of The Americas New York NY 10019-6022 Office Phone: 212-259-6640. Office Fax: 212-259-6333. Business E-Mail: mpierce@dl.com.

PIERCE, PATRICIA ANN, retired university administrator; b. Harriman, Tenn., Feb. 13, 1949; d. Fred Ernest and Lela Nora (Jones) P.; m. Jacky Albert Goss, Sept. 21, 1991; children: Wesley Matthew Goss, James Michael Goss. BS, U. Tenn., 1973; cert., Bryn Mawr Coll., 1991. Cert. secondary edn. tchr., Tenn.; cert. diversity trainer. Field rep. Tenn. Human Rights Commn., Nashville, 1973-76, compliance dir., 1976-78; assoc. dir.Opportunity Devel. Ctr. Vanderbilt U., Nashville, 1978-81, dir., 1981—2007; ret. Cons. Pierce Consulting, Nashville, 1985—; presenter in field. Contbr. articles to profl. jours. Chair Mayor's Adv. Com. for People with Disabilities, Nashville, 1988-89; pres. bd. dirs. League for Hearing Impaired, Nashville, 1994-95, Nashville YWCA, 1996-98; spkr. Nat. Intramural Recreation Sports Assn., Nashville, 1994; del. People to People Internat. Learning Disability Del., Beijing, 1995; nongovtl. rep. NGO Forum, 4th World Conf. on Women, Beijing, 1995; People to People Internat. del. to Cuba, 2003; active Gov. Adv. Com. on Equal Employment Opportunity, 1992-96; mem. Leadership Nashville, 2003; commr. Tenn. Human Rights Commn., 2005—; bd. dirs. Internat. ATHENA, 2004—. Recipient Jean Harris award Rotary 1998, Mary Jane Werthern award Vanderbilt 1997, Nashville ATHENA award, 2003, Excellence and Equity award Tenn. Econ. Coun., 2006; named to Leadership America 2000; inducted in Acad. of Women of Achievement, 2002. Tenn. State U. Woman of Legend and Merit award, 2008. Mem.: Women in Higher Edn. in Tenn. (historian 1999—, pres.), CABLE Profl. Womens Networking Orgn. (pres. 1991—92, historian 2000—, Promote Women award 1993), Am. Coun. Edn. (state facilitator 1994—95, bd. mem. 1994—, mem. Tenn. planning com., Outstanding Contbns. cert. 1995), Internat. Assn. Higher Edn. and Disability (pres. 1988—89, Ronald Blosser Dedicated Svc. award 1989), Internat. Women's Forum, Women's Polit. Caucus (v.p. 2001—02), Women in Numbers (bd. mem. 2000—, pres. 2003). Avocations: hiking, tennis, photography. E-mail: ppierce954@comcast.net.

PIERCE, PAUL ANTHONY, professional basketball player; b. Oakland, Calif., Oct. 13, 1977; s. Lorraine Hosey. Student in Crime and Delinquency Studies, U. Kans., Lawrence, 1995—98. Forward-guard Boston Celtics, 1998—. Mem. USA Basketball Men's Sr. Nat. Team, 2002, 06. Founder The Truth Fund, 2002—. Recipient Home Team Cmty. Svc. award, NBA, 2002; named NBA Finals MVP, 2008, Bostonian of Yr., The Boston Globe mag., 2008; named to All-Rookie First Team, NBA, 1999, Eastern Conf. All-Star Team, 2002—06, 2008, 2009. Achievements include leading the NBA in: scoring (2144 points), 2002; free throws (604), free throw attempts (753), 2003; member of the NBA Championship winning Boston Celtics, 2008. Avocation: music. Office: Boston Celtics 226 Causeway St 4th Fl Boston MA 02114-4720*

PIERCE, PHILIP SARGENT, clinical psychologist; b. Medford, Mass., Aug. 25, 1941; s. Elmer Grandville and Pauline Dudley Pierce; m. Rae Foster, Oct. 10, 1967; children: Jennifer, Jessica, John, Jill. BA, U. Maine, 1963; MA, U. N.H., 1965; PhD, U. S.C., 1971. Lic. psychologist, Maine. Clin. psychologist Pineland Ctr., Pownal, Maine, 1965-77, Togus (Maine) Vets. Med. and Regional Office Ctr., 1977-83, sr. psychologist, 1983—, acting chief mental health svc., 2003. Vis. prof. psychology U. So. Maine, Portland, 1971-72; asst. prof. psychology St. Joseph's Coll., North Windham, Maine, 1972-78, U. Maine, Augusta, 1977-78; clin. assoc. psychology U. Maine, Orono, 1981—; lectr. on psychology grad. program in sch. and health psychology U. New Eng., Biddeford Pool, Maine; adj. clin. faculty mem. Antioch New Eng. Grad. Sch., 1996-2000; cons., spkr., presenter in field; northeastern regional exam. coord. Am. Bd. Clin. Psychology, 1993-95, nat. credential rev. officer, 1995-97; mem. Am. Bd. Profl. Psychology, Inc. Contbr. numerous articles to profl. jours. Trustee Falmouth Congl. Ch., 1981-84, chmn. bd. trustees, 1983-84, sec. mem. giving and investments subcom., 1982-84, mem. Christian enlistment com., 1985-88, chmn., 1987-88, mem. nominations com., 1989-92, chmn. ch. coun., 1990-93, mem. bylaws com., 1994-97; bd. dirs. Falmouth Little League, 1984-90, coach, 1983-85, treas., 1984-90, umpire, 1983-93; bd. dirs. Maine Running Hall of Fame, 1994—, vice chmn., 1995-96, chmn., 1996-2004; bd. dirs. Maine Sports Hall of Fame, 1994—2004, 1st v.p., 1995-2001, chmn. honors and selection com., 1996-2002, pres. 2001-02. With U.S. Army, 1966 Fellow APA (divsn. newsletter editor 1981-84, exec. bd. 1981-82, pres. 1985-86, chmn. fellow com. 1990-96, coun. of reps. 1977-79, coun. liaison to Maine Psychol. Assn. 1995-97, coun. reps. for Maine and Vt., 1998-2001, chmn. rural caucus), Maine Psychol. Assn. (newsletter editor 1971-74, mem. exec. bd. 1971-88, pres. 1975-77, chmn. ethics com. 1992-98, policy coun. 1992-2002), Am. Psychol. Soc., Acad. Clin. Psychology (bd. dirs. 1993-2002, v.p. 1998-2002); mem. AAAS, N.Y. Acad. Sci., Assn. VA Lead Psychologists (chmn. gero-psychology task force 1983-84, chmn. APA-VA interaction task force 1984-85), Soc. Maine Psychologists (chmn. continuing edn. com. 1990-92, 98-2000, pres. 1992-94, treas. 1994-98), Maine Soc. Forensic Psychologists, Maine Track Club (sec. 1985-86, v.p. 1986-87, pres. 1987-88, race dir. 1984-2006), New Eng. 65 Plus Running Club (v.p. 2008-, chair, Hall of Fame 2008-) Democrat. Avocation: long distance running. Home: 79 Waites Landing Rd Falmouth ME 04105

PIERCE, RANDY G., state supreme court justice; m. Gayla Smith; 3 children. BS in acctg., Univ. So. Miss., 1987, MBA; JD, Univ. Miss. CPA; bar: Miss. 1997. Atty. private practice, 1997—2005; mem., Dist. 105 Miss. House Reps., 2000—05; chancery ct. judge Miss. 16th Dist.; assoc. justice Miss. Supreme Ct., 2009—. Bd. mem. Jones County Jr. Coll. Found. Mem.: Am. Inst. CPAs, Miss. Soc. CPAs, Miss. Bar Assn. Baptist. Office: Miss Supreme Ct 450 High St Jackson MS 39201 Office Phone: 601-359-2093.*

PIERCE, RICHARD HARRY, oceanographer; PhD in Chem. Oceanography, U. R.I., 1973. Sr. scientist, dir. Ctr. for Eco-Toxicology, Mote Marine Lab., Sarasota, Fla. Office: Mote Marine Lab 1600 Ken Thompson Pkwy Sarasota FL 34236-1096 E-mail: rich@mote.org.

PIERCE, RUDOLPH F., lawyer; b. Boston, Aug. 12, 1942; s. Fred D. and Edna M. (Owens) P.; m. Mildred C. Pierce, Apr. 29, 2000; children from previous marriage: Kristen, Khari. BA, Hampton Inst., 1967; JD, Harvard U., 1970. Bar: Mass. 1970, DC 2002. Ptnr. Crane, Inker & Oteri, Boston, 1972-75, Keating, Perretta & Pierce, Boston, 1975-76; magistrate U.S. Dist. Ct. Mass., Boston, 1976-79; justice Mass. Superior Ct., Boston, 1979-85; ptnr. LeBoeuf, Lamb, Leiby & MacRae, Boston; dir., bus. & securities litig. Goulston & Storrs, Boston & Washington. Chmn. bd. dir. Nat. Inst. Trial Advocacy. Contbr. articles to profl. jours. Trustee Children's Hosp., Boston, 1986—, Inst. Healthcare Improvement; past chmn. New Eng. Aquarium. Fellow Am. Coll. Trial Lawyers; mem. Internat. Acad. Trial Lawyers, ABA, Mass. Bar Assn. (bd. dels.), Boston Bar Assn. (pres. 1989-90). Office: Goulston & Storrs Ste 1100 2001 K St NW Washington DC 20006 Office Phone: 202-721-1153. Business E-Mail: rpierce@goulstonstorrs.com.

PIERCE, SUSAN RESNECK, academic administrator, literature educator, consultant; b. Janesville, Wis., Feb. 6, 1943; d. Elliott Jack and Dory (Block) Resneck; 1 child, Alexandra Siegel. BA, Wellesley Coll., 1965; MA, U. Chgo., 1966; PhD, U. Wis., 1972. Lectr. U. Wis., Rock County, 1970-71; from asst. prof. to prof. English Ithaca (N.Y.) Coll., 1973-82, chmn. dept., 1976-79; program officer Nat. Endowment for Humanities, 1982-83, asst. dir., 1983-84; dean Henry Kendall Coll. Arts and Scis. U. Tulsa, 1984-90; v.p. acad. affairs, prof. English Lewis and Clark Coll., Portland, Oreg., 1990-92; pres. U. Puget Sound, Tacoma, 1992—2003, Boca Raton Comty. Hosp. Found., 2004—05; pvt. practice, 2005—; sr. cons. Academic Search, 2006—. Vis. assoc. prof. Princeton (N.J.) U., 1979; bd. dirs. Janet Elson Scholarship Fund, 1984-1990, Tulsa Edn. Fund, Phillips Petroleum Scholarship Fund, 1985-90, Okla. Math. & Sci. High Sch., 1984-90, Hillcrest Med. Ctr., 1988-90, Portland Opera, 1990-92, St. Joseph's Hosp., 1992—, Seattle Symphony, 1993—; cons. U. Oreg., 1985, Drury Coll., Springfield, Mo., 1986; mem. Middle States and N. Cen. Accreditation Bds.; mem. adv. com. Fed. Women's Program, NEH, 1982-83; participant Summit Meeting on Higher Edn., Dept. Edn., Washington, 1985; speaker, participant numerous ednl. meetings, sems., commencements; chair Frederick Ness Book Award Com. Assn. Am. Colls., 1986; mem. award selection com. Dana Found., 1986, 87; mem. Acad. Affairs Council, Univ. Senate, dir. tchr. edn., chmn. adv. group for tchr. preparation, ex-officio mem. all Coll. Arts and Scis. coms. and Faculty Council on Internat. Studies, all U. Tulsa; bd. dirs. Am. Conf. Acad. Deans; bd. trustees Hillcrest Med. Ctr.; participant Aspen Inst. Md. 1999, Annapolis Group Media Roundtable, 1996, Harvard Seminar, 1992; former bd. dirs. Assn. Am. Colls. and Univs., 1989-92, Am. Conf. of Academic Deans, 1988-91, Am. Assn. Colls., 1989-92. Author: The Moral of the Story, 1982, also numerous essays, jour. articles, book sects., book revs.; co-editor: Approaches to Teaching "Invisible Man"; reader profl. jours. Bd. dirs. Arts and Humanities Coun., Tulsa, 1984-90, Mizener Pk., 2004-; trustee Hillcrest Hosp., Tulsa, 1986-90; mem. cultural series com., community rels. com. Jewish Fedn., Tulsa, 1986-90; bd. dirs. Tulsa chpt. NCCJ, 1986-90, Kemper Mus. 1996—, Seattle Symphony, 1993-96, St. Joseph Hosp., 1992-93, Portland Opera, 1990-92, Ctr. for Arts, Boca Raton, 2004—. Recipient Best Essay award Arix. Quar., 1979, Excellence in Teaching award N.Y. State Edn. Council, 1982, Superior Group Service award NEH, 1984, other teaching awards; Dana scholar, Ithaca Coll., 1980-81; Dana Research fellow, Ithaca Coll., 82-83; grantee Inst. for Ednl. Affairs, 1980, Ford Found., 1987, NEH, 1989. Mem. MLA (adv. com. on job market 1973-74), South Ctrl. MLA, NIH (subcom. on college drinking), Assn. Governing Bds. (coun. of pres.), Nat. Inst. on Alcohol Abuse (presl. advisory group), Soc. for Values in Higher Edn., Assn. Am. Colls. (bd. dirs.), Am. Conf. Acad. Deans (bd. dirs. 1988-91), Coun. of Presidents, Assn. Governing Bds., The Annapolis Group (mem. exec. com.), Phi Beta Kappa, Phi Kappa Phi, Phi Gamma Kappa. Office Phone: 561-212-5103. Business E-Mail: srpconsulting@comcast.net.

PIERCE, TAMORA, writer; b. South Connellsville, Pa., Dec. 13, 1954; d. Wayne Franklin Pierce and Jacqueline Sparks; m. Timothy Erving Liebe, Dec. 14, 1985. BA, U. Pa., 1977. Data collector Office Assessment, Kingston, NY, 1976—77; sec. Office Town Assessor, Hardenburgh and Denning, 1977—78; housemother McAuley Home for Girls, Buhl, Idaho, 1978—79; lit. agt. asst. Harold Ober Assocs., NYC, 1979—83; sec. Chase Manhattan Bank, NYC, 1983—89, Joseph Conklin, NYC, 1990—92; freelance writer NYC, 1992—. Author: Alanna: The First Adventure, 1983, In the Hand of the Goddess, 1984, The Woman Who Rides Like A Man, 1986, Lioness Rampant, 1988, Wild Magic, 1992, Wolf-Speaker, 1994, The Emperor Mage, 1995, The Realms of the Gods, 1996, Sandry's Book, 1997, Tris's Book, 1998, Daja's Book, 1998, Briar's Book, 1999, First Test, 1999, Plain Magic in Flights of Fantasy, 1999, Magic Steps, 2000, Page, 2000, Testing in Lost and Found, 2000, Street Magic, 2001, Squire, 2001, Folquin's Folly in Disney Adventures, 2001, Elder Brother in Half Human, 2001, Cold Fire, 2002, Lady Knight, 2002, Shatterglass, 2003, Trickster's Choice, 2003, Trickster's Queen, 2004, The Will Of The Empress, 2005, The Hidden Girl in Dreams and Visions, 2006, Huntress in Firebirds Rising, 2006, Terrier in 2006, 2006; co-author: White Tiger, 2007, Melting Stones, 2007, Blood Hound, 2009, The Dragons Tale In the Dragon Book, 2009; contbr. articles to profl. jours. and the Ultimate Book Guide; narrator, dir. (CD) Full Cast Audio Books; co-editor: Young Warriors, 2005, Student of Ostriches in Young Warriors, 2005. Mem. Greenpeace, 2001, World Wildlife Fedn., 1998—, Internat. Wolf Ctr., Ely, Minn., 1998—, N.Y. Ctr. Wildlife Conservation, NYC, 1997—. Recipient Edward E. Smith Meml. Skylark award, Boskone 42, 2005, Lit. Lights award, Boston Pub. Libr., 2006, Muriel becker Literacy award, AJ Coun. Tchrs. English, 2008. Mem.: ACLU, Soc. Childrens Book Writers and Illustrators, The Authors Guild, Amnesty Internat. Avocations: audio theatre and books, military and civil history, wildlife, gemology. Personal E-mail: tampierce@aol.com.

PIERCE, TERRY JO, medical/surgical nurse; b. Winchester, Ind., Dec. 31, 1953; d. Kenneth Eugene and Ilene Marie (Ward) Heltzel; children: Amy Jo, J. Aaron; m. Johnny R. Pierce, Apr. 29, 1995. Cert., Ivy Tech., Richmond, Ind., 1983. LPN, Ind. Nursing asst. Henry County Meml. Hosp., New Castle, Ind., 1982-84; charge nurse Heritage House Convalescent Ctr., New Castle, 1984-89; office nurse, lab. technician McAllister Family Practice, New Castle, 1989—2003, Samantha Meeks Family Practice, Inc., New Castle, 2003—07; staff New Castle Family Physicians, Ind., 2007—. Mem.: Am. Assn. Office Nursing. Home: 2852 E US Highway 40 Lewisville IN 47352-9730 Office: New Castle Family Physicians 2200 Forest Ridge Pky Ste 310 New Castle IN 47362 Office Phone: 765-599-3400.

PIERCE, THRESIA KORTE (TISH PIERCE), primary school educator; b. Maize, Kans. d. Herman and Marie Adeline (Lubbers) Korte; children: Judith, John, Mark. BS, Friends U., 1955; MS, U. Nev., Las Vegas, 1978. Cert. tchr., Nev., Nev. Life Ins. lic. Office worker Internat. Trust Co., Denver, Colo., 1951, Motor Equipment Co., Wichita, Kans., 1952-53; tchr. Wichita Pub. Schs., 1960-69, Clark County Sch. Dist., Las Vegas, Nev., 1970-2000. Author short stories; contbr. articles to profl. jours. Senator Clark County Edn. Assn., Clark County Classroom Tchrs. Nominee Wichita Women of Yr., 1967. Mem. NEA, Epsilon Sigma Delta (v.p. 1962). bd. dirs. Kansas Newman U., Wichita, 1966-68. Home: Bldg 6 Unit 1106 1600 S Valley View Blvd Las Vegas NV 89102-0547

PIERCE, WILLIAM SCHULER, cardiac surgeon; b. Wilkes-Barre, Pa., Jan. 12, 1937; s. William Harold and Doris Louis (Schuler) P.; m. Peggy Jayne Stone, June 12, 1965; children: William Stone, Jonathan Drew. BS, Lehigh U., 1958; MD, U. Pa., 1962. Intern U. Pa., 1962—63; resident in surgery Hosp. U. Pa., 1963—70; asst. prof. M.S. Hershey Med. Ctr., Pa. State U. Coll. Medicine, Hershey, 1970—73, assoc. prof., 1973—77, prof. surgery, 1977—, chief divsn. cardiothoracic surgery, 1991—95; assoc. chmn. dept. surgery, dir. rsch., dept. surgery, 1995—97. Contbr. over 300 articles to profl. jours. With USPHS, 1965—67. Fellow: ACS; mem.: AAAS, AMA, Soc. Clin. Surgery., Am. Surg. Assn., Soc. Univ. Surgeons, So. Pa. Assn. Thoracic Surgery, Inst. Medicine, Assn. Acad. Surgery, Am. Heart Assn., Soc. Vascular Surgery, Am. Soc. Artificial Internal Organs, Internat. Cardiovascular Soc. Achievements include invention of inventor cardiac valve, blood pump. Office: Milton S Hershey Med Ctr PO Box 850 Hershey PA 17033-0850 Office Phone: 717-531-8328. Business E-Mail: wpierce@hmc.psu.edu.

PIERCY, EARL, social sciences educator; s. Lloyd Piercy and Lois Stewart; m. Nancy Piercy; 1 child, James. PhD, Cornell U., Ithaca, NY, 1982. Cert. in peace studies European U. Ctr., 2008. Dean Calif. U. Advanced Studies, Petaluma, 1990—92; prof. sociology Truckee Meadows CC, Reno, 1992—. Cons. Environ. Sci. Assocs., San Francisco, 1982—84. Mem. United Way, Reno, 2002—04. Office: Truckee Meadows CC 7000 Dandini Blvd Reno NV 89512 Business E-Mail: epiercy@tmcc.edu.

PIERCY, GORDON CLAYTON, bank executive, educator; b. Takoma Park, Md., Nov. 23, 1944; s. Gordon Clayton and Dorothy Florence (Brummer) Piercy; m. Roberta Margaret Walton, 1985; children: Elizabeth Anne, Kenneth Charles, Virginia Walton, Zachary Taylor Walton. BS, Syracuse U., 1966; MBA, Pace U., 1973. Mgmt. trainee Suburban Bank, Bethesda, Md., 1962-66; mktg. planning assoc. Chemical Bank, NYC, 1966-70; sr. market devel. officer Seattle-First Nat. Bank, 1970-74; product expansion adminstr., mktg. planning mgr. VISA, Inc., San Francisco, 1974-76; v.p., dir. mktg. Wash. Mutual Bank, Seattle, 1976-82; v.p., mktg. dir. First Interstate Bank Wash. N.A., Seattle, 1983-86; sr. v.p. mktg., dir. Puget Sound Nat. Bank, Tacoma, 1986-92; sr. v.p., dir. mktg. and sales Key Bank, Tacoma, 1993-94; dir. corp. sales KIRO-TV, Seattle, 1994; sr. v.p., dir. mktg. and sales Pacific N.W. Bancorp, 1994—2004; pres. Whidbey Western R.R., 1995—; prin. Whidbey Mktg., 2004—; mktg. and fin. instr. Embry-Riddle U., Oak Harbor, Wash., 2005—. Bd. dirs., treas. Whidbey Gen. Hosp. Found.; chair, bd. trustee Skagit Valley Coll. Mem.: S.W. Railcar Ltd. (mem. exec. com.), Island County Econ. Devel. Assn. (bd. dirs.), Pacific Railcar Operators, Mktg. Comm. Exec. Internat. (v.p.), Ctrl Whidbey Lions, Delta Mu Delta, Alpha Kappa Psi, Sigma Nu (treas.). Episcopalian. Home and Office: 750 N Snowberry Ln Coupeville WA 98239-3110 Office Phone: 360-678-4488.

PIERCY, MARGE, poet, writer; b. Detroit, Mar. 31, 1936; d. Robert Douglas and Bert Bernice (Bunnin) Piercy; m. Ira Wood, 1982. AB, U. Mich., 1957; MA, Northwestern U., 1958; DHL (hon.), Hebrew Union Coll., 2004, Union Coll., 2004, Eastern Conn. State U., 2005. Instr. Gary ext. Ind. U., 1960—62; poet-in-residence U. Kans., 1971; disting. vis. lectr. Thomas Jefferson Coll., Grand Valley State Colls., 1975, 1976, 1978, 1980; vis. faculty Women's Writers Conf., Cazenovia Coll., NY; Elliston poetry fellow U. Cin., 1986. DeRoy Disting. vis. prof. U. Mich., 1992; editor Leapfrog Press, 1997—2008; poetry editor Lillith, 1999—; fiction editor Seattle Rev., 2003. Author: Breaking Camp, 1968, Hard Loving, 1969, Going Down Fast, 1969, Dance the Eagle to Sleep, 1970, Small Changes, 1973, To Be of Use, 1973, Living in the Open, 1976, Woman on the Edge of Time, 1976, The High Cost of Living, 1978, Vida, 1980, The Moon is Always Female, 1980, Braided Lives, 1982, Circles on the Water, 1982, Tri-Colored Blocks for a Quilt, Essays, 1982, Stone, Paper, Knife, 1983, My Mother's Body, 1985, Gone to Soldiers, 1988, Available Light, 1988 (May Sarton award 1991), Summer People, 1989, He, She and It, 1991, Body of Glass, 1991 (Arthur C. Clarke award 1993), Mars and Her Children, 1992, The Longings of Women, 1994, Eight Chambers of the Heart, 1995, City of Darkness, City of Light, 1996, What Are Big Girls Made Of?, 1997 (Notable Book award ALA 1997), Storm Tide, 1998, The Art of Blessing the Day, 1999, Early Grrrl, 1999, Three Women, 1999, Sleeping With Cats, A Memoir, 2002, expanded edit., 2005, Colors Passing Through Us, 2003, Third Child, 2003, Sex Wars: A Novel of the Turbulent Post-Civil War Period, 2005, The Crooked Inheritance, 2006, Pesach for the Rest of Us, 2007; co-author: (with Ira Wood) So You Want to Write: How to Master the Craft of Writing Fiction and the Personal Narrative, 2001, 2d edit., 2005; (CD) Louder: We Can't Heed You Yet, 2004; author of poetry (17 vols.). Cons. N.Y. State Coun. on Arts, 1971, Mass. Found. for Humanities and Coun. on Arts, 1974; mem. Writer Bd., 1985-86; bd. dirs. Mass. Found. Humanities and Pub. Policy, 1978-85, Am. ha-Yam, 1988-98, v.p., 1995-96; gov.'s appointee to Mass. Cultural Coun., 1990-91, Mass. Coun. on Arts and Humanities, 1986-89; artistic adv. bd. ALEPH Alliance for Jewish Renewal, Am. Poetry Ctr., 1988—; lit. adv. panel poetry NEA, 1989, mem. fiction and creative nonfiction panel, 2007; mem. adv. bd. Carrie A. Seaman Animal Shelter. Recipient Borenstone Mountain Poetry award, 1968, 74, Lit. award Gov. Mass. Commn. on Status of Women, 1974, Nat. Endowment of Arts award, 1978, Carolyn Kizer Poetry prize, 1986, 90, Shaeffer-Eaton-PEN New Eng. award, 1989, Golden Rose Poetry prize, 1990, Brit ha-Dorot award The Shalom Ctr., 1992, Notable Book award, 1997, Paterson poetry prize, 2000. Mem.: ARS, NOW, PEN, Wellfleet Coun. Aging Bd. (friends coun.), Am. Poetry Soc., Nat. Writers Union, Authors League, Authors Guild, Lower Cape Rose Soc., Citizens for the Preservation of Wellfleet, Mass. Audubon Soc., New Eng. Rose Soc., New Eng. Poetry Club. Address: PO Box 1473 Wellfleet MA 02667-1473 Personal E-mail: hagolem@c4.net.

PIERETTI, RAFAEL VICENTE, urologist, pediatrician; s. Rafael Vicente and Frine Pieretti; m. Cristina Vanmarcke, Dec. 4, 1970; children: Maria Cristina, Rafael Vicente, Patricia Cristina, Diana Estefania Cristina, Alberto Christian. MD, Luis Razetti, Ctrl. U. Venezuela, 1965. Diplomate in gen. surgery Royal Coll. Physicians & Surgeons, 1974, in pediatric surgery Royal Coll. Physicians & Surgeons, 2004. Chief pediatric urology Mass. Gen. Hosp., Boston, 2004—; cons. pediatric urologist Newton Wellesley Hosp., Mass., 2004—. Cons. pediatric urologist Shriner's Hosp., Boston, 2004. Contbr. scientific papers to profl. jours. Lt. col. Army, 1971—87, Venezuela. Mem.: Am. Urol. Assn. (assoc.). Achievements include pediatric urology, pediatric surgery, reconstructive surgery of the genito-urinary system. Office: Mass Gen Hosp 55 Fruit St Boston MA 02114 Office Fax: 617-726-2167. Personal E-mail: rpieretti@gmail.com. Business E-Mail: rpieretti@partners.org.

PIERI, DAVID C., research scientist; s. Nazareth and Margaret Pieri; m. Colleen Rea Utting, Aug. 2, 2008; 1 child, Erika N. BS in Physics, Villanova U., Pa., 1972; PhD in Geol. Sci., Cornell U., Ithaca, NY, 1979. Geologist US Geol. Survey, Flagstaff, Ariz., 1972—74; rsch. scientist Jet Propulsion Lab., Pasadena, Calif., 1980—. Project scientist NASA Viking Mars Lander Continuation Mission, Pasadena, 1980—82. Author: (screenplay) Rio Grande New Jersey (Screenwriting award, 1999). Sgt. USAF, 1970—76, Willow Grove, Pa. & Syracuse, NY. Mem.: Soc. Sci. Exploration (editl. bd. 2002—08), Am. Geophys. Union. Office: Jet Propulsion Lab MS183-501 4800 Oak Grove Dr Pasadena CA 91109 E-mail: dave.pieri@jpl.nasa.gov.

PIERIBONE, VINCENT ALLEN, medical researcher, educator; s. David Marcia and Frances Pieribone; m. Julia Tsai, Oct. 15, 2006. PhD, NYU, 1992. Assoc. fellow John B. Pierce Lab., Yale U., New Haven, 1997—; assoc. prof. Yale U. Sch. Medicine, 1998—. Assoc. mem. Mystic Aquarium, Conn., 2008—. Author: (book) Aglow in the Dark: the revolutionary science of biofluorescence. Office: John B Pierce Lab Yale Univ 290 Congress Ave New Haven CT 06519 Business E-Mail: vap5@email.med.yale.edu.

PIERLUISI, PEDRO R., Resident Commissioner from Puerto Rico, United States House of Representatives; b. San Juan, PR, Apr. 26, 1959; s. Jorge A. and Doris (Urrutia) Pierluisi; m. María Elena Carrión; children: Anthony, Michael, Jacqueline, Rafael. BA, Tulane U., 1981; JD, George Washington U., 1984. Bar: D.C. 1984, U.S. Dist. Ct. D.C. 1985, U.S. Ct. Appeals (D.C. cir.) 1985, P.R. 1990, U.S. Dist. Ct. P.R. 1990, U.S. Supreme Ct. 1990, U.S. Ct. Appeals (1st cir.) 1993. Assoc. Verner, Liipfert, Bernhard, McPherson & Hand, Washington, 1984—85, Cole, Corette & Abrutyn, Washington, 1985—90; ptnr. Pierluisi Pierluisi & Mayol-Bianchi, San Juan, 1990—93; atty. gen. Govt. of P.R., 1993—96; ptnr. O'Neill & Borges, San Juan, 1997—2007; resident commr. US Congress from Puerto Rico, 2009—. Mem.: ABA (house dels. 1995—96, standing com. on substance abuse 1995—98, coordinating com. on gun violence 1998—2001, state membership chmn. 2000—03), Am. Arbitration Assn. (arbitrator), Internat. Ctr. Dispute Resolution (arbitrator), George Washington U. Internat. Law Soc. (pres. 1982—83), Nat. Assn. Attys. Gen. (chair ea. region 1996), Jose Jaime Pierluisi Found. (pres. 2003—06), Puerto Rico Homebuilders Assn. (bd. dirs. 1999—2003), Phi Alpha Delta (hon.; Munoz chpt.). Democrat. Avocation: jogging. Office: US Congress 1218 Longworth HOB Washington DC 20515 also: 250 Calle Fortaleza Viejo San Juan PR 00901 Office Phone: 202-225-2615, 787-723-6333. Office Fax: 202-225-2154.*

PIERNO, ANTHONY ROBERT, lawyer; s. Anthony M. and Mary Jane (Saporita) P.; m. Beverly Jean Kohn, 1954 (dec. 2008); children: Kathryn Ann, Robert Lawrence, Linda Jean Derengowski, Diane Marie Leonard. BA with highest honors, Whittier Coll., 1954; JD, Stanford U., 1959; LLD (hon.), Whittier Coll., 2000. Bar: Calif. 1960, DC 1979, Tex. 1994. Assoc. Adams, Duque & Hazeltine, LA; ptnr. Poindexter & Barger, LA; chief dep. commr. State of Calif., 1967-69, commr. of corps., 1969-71; ptnr. Wyman, Bautzer, Rothman & Kuchel, Beverly Hills, Calif.; sr. ptnr. Memel, Jacobs, Pierno & Gersh, LA, 1976-86, Pillsbury, Madison & Sutro, LA, 1986-89; sr. v.p., gen. counsel MAXXAM, Inc., L.A. and Houston, 1989-97. Author: Corporate Disaggregation, 1982; editor Stanford U. Law Rev. Trustee Whittier Coll., 1977-2000, chmn. bd. trustees, 1994-2000, chmn. presdl. selection com., 1989-90, trustee emeritus, 2005-; chmn. Marymount Coll., Palos Verdes, Calif., 1989-92, trustee, 1976-2000, trustee emeritus, 2006-; past mem. Los Angeles County Children's Svcs. Commn. With US Army, 1954-56. Recipient Emcalian award Marymount Palos Verdes Coll., 1983, Whittier Coll. Lancer Soc. Lifetime Achievement award, 1984—, Lifetime Svc. award, 2004. Mem. ABA, LA County Bar Assn., State Bar Calif. (chmn. com. on corps. 1971-75, advisor to com. on corps. 1975-76, mem. exec. com. bus. law sect. 1976-80, chmn. spl. com. on franchise law), Calif. Club (LA), Am. Inns of Ct. Republican. Roman Catholic. Office: 92 Avenida Lirio Blanco Rancho Mirage CA 92270 Office Phone: 760-341-7595. E-mail: arplaw@msn.com.

PIERONI, ROBERT EDWARD, internist, educator, military officer; b. Portland, Maine, June 20, 1937; s. Ansel Kirby and Agnes Mary (Dumais) P.; m. Dorothy Louise McDonnell, Oct. 3, 1970; children: Michelle Kirby, Robert Francis. BS, Boston Coll., 1959; MD, Pa. State U., 1971. Diplomate Am. Bd. Internal Medicine, Am. Bd. Family Practice, Am. Bd. Allergy and Immunology, Am. Bd. Quality Assurance, Am. Bd. Geriatric Medicine. Chemist Mass. Dept. Pub. Health, Boston, 1962-71, sr. bacteriologist, 1971-74; asst. prof. internal medicine U. Ala., Tuscaloosa, 1974-76, assoc. prof. dept. internal medicine and family practice, 1976-81, prof. internal medicine and family practice, 1981—; enlisted U.S. Army, 1961, advanced through grades to col., 1981. Prior cons. VA Hosp., Tuscaloosa, T. Hardin Med. Facility and Partlow State Hosp., Tuscaloosa, 1974—; cons. FDA, Dept. Def. Contbr. articles to profl. jours., chapters to books. Decorated Bronze Star, 1991, Commendation for Valor; recipient Golden Stethoscope award, 1982, Faculty Recognition award, 1986, Ala. Golden Eagle Humanitarian award Ala. Sr. Citizens Hall of Fame, 1988 and Physicians award, 1998, Wright A. Garner scientist award Ala. Acad. Sci., 1997, Designator A Proficiency award Army Surgeon Gen., 2001. Mem. AMA, ACP, Am. Coll. Allergy, Asthma and Immunology, Am. Geriatric Soc., Gerontol. Soc. Am., Am. Acad. Family Physicians, Physicians for Human Rights, VFW, Am. Legion. Democrat. Roman Catholic. Avocations: mountain trekking, scuba diving, studying medical and military history, reading. Home: 398 Riverdale Dr Tuscaloosa AL 35406-1814 Office: U Ala Dept Internal Medicine PO Box 870326 Tuscaloosa AL 35487-0001 Office Phone: 205-348-1287. Personal E-mail: dp398@comcast.net.

PIERRE, JUAN, professional baseball player; b. Mobile, Ala., Aug. 14, 1977; Attended, Galveston Coll., Tex., U. South Ala., Mobile. Outfielder Colo. Rockies, 2000—02, Fla. Marlins, 2003—05, Chgo. Cubs, 2006, LA Dodgers, 2007—. Recipient Cool Papa Bell award, Negro Leagues Baseball Mus., 2003; named Player of Yr., Sun Belt Conf., 1998. Achievements include leading the National League in: stolen bases, 2001, 03; singles, 2001, 03, 04, 06, 07; games played, 2003-07; at-bats, 2003, 04, 06; hits, 2004, 06; triples, 2004; member of the World Series championship winning Florida Marlins, 2003. Office: LA Dodgers 1000 Elysian Pk Ave Los Angeles CA 90012-1199*

PIERRE, SAMUEL J., engineering educator; b. Haiti, Oct. 5, 1955; BEng. in Civil Engring., Ecole Polytechnique of Montreal, 1981; BSc in Math. and Computer sci., U. Que., Montreal, 1984, MSc in Math. and Computer Sci., 1985; MSc in Econs., U. Montreal, 1987; PhD in Elec. Engring., Ecole Polytechnique of Montreal, 1991. Registered profl. engr., Order of Engrs. of Que. Full prof. Ecole Polytechnique of Montreal, 1998—. Dir. Mobile Computing and Networking Rsch. Lab., Montreal, 1999—, Mobile Computing and Networking Rsch. Group, Montreal, 2003—; NSERC/Ericsson indsl. rsch. chair in next-generation mobile networking sys. Ecole Polytechnique of Montreal, 2002—. Recipient Sligos-Avignon award for the best rsch. paper, Ninth Internat. Conf. on Expert Sys. and their Applications, 1989, Disting. Paper award, OPNETWORK, 2003, 2005, Knight Nat. Order Que. Fellow: Can. Acad. Engring. (Knight of Nat. Order of Que.), Engring. Inst. Can.; mem.: IEEE, Assn. for Computing Machinery, IEEE Computer Soc., IEEE Comm. Soc. Achievements include patents for Mobile Computing Systems. Office: Ecole Polytechnique of Montreal PO Box 6079 Station Centre-ville Montreal PQ Canada H3C 3A7 Office Fax: 514 340 5159. Business E-Mail: samuel.pierre@polymtl.ca.

PIERRET, ROBERT F., electrical engineering educator; b. E. Cleveland, Ohio, Aug. 20, 1940; s. Frank Sylvester and Elsie Ann (Svoboda) P.; m. Linda Jane Pierz, Aug. 22, 1965; children: Ross, Suzanne, John. BS, Case Inst. of Technology, 1962; MS, U. Ill., 1963, PhD, 1966. Rsch. assoc. U. Ill., Urbana, 1966-67, asst. prof., 1967-70; assoc. prof. Purdue U., West Lafayette, Ind., 1970-77, prof., 1977—, asst. head of ECE, 1996—2004. Cons. editor Prentice Hall, Inc., Upper Saddle River, N.Y., 1999—; editl. adv. bd. Solid-State Electronics jour., 1985—. Author: (book) Semiconductor Device Fundamentals, 1996, (four vols.) Modular

Series on Solid State Devices, 1983, 87, 91. Grad. fellow NSF, 1962-66. Mem. IEEE (sr.). Avocations: personal computer, playing accordion. Office: Purdue U/Sch ECE 465 Northwestern Ave West Lafayette IN 47907-2035 Office Phone: 765-494-3507. Business E-Mail: pierret@purdue.edu.

PIERRO, RICHARD SALVATORE, electrical engineer; s. Carmine and Elvira (Coccetti) Pierro; m. Diana Zannella, June 6, 1970; children: Richard C, Christopher T. BEE, NYU, 1965, MSEE, 1967. Radar rsch. engr. United Technologies Corp.-Norden Sys., Norwalk, Conn., 1967-72; sr. radar sys. engr. Sperry Rand Corp.-Def. Products Group, Great Neck, N.Y., 1972-86; owner, engrng. cons. Rivere Radar Cons. Co., Bayville, N.Y., 1986-97; sr. prin. sys. engr. Raytheon-Electronic Systems, Bedford, Mass., 1997-99; mem. corp. sr. staff Tech. Svc. Corp., Trumbull, Conn., 1999—. Contbr. numerous articles to profl. jours. Mem.: IEEE (sr.; subject matter expert), Eta Kappa Nu. Independent. Roman Catholic. Achievements include invention of Probability Density Function Gen; Low Angle, Air-Ground Ranging Radar. Avocations: health, exercise, sports, music, collectibles. Office Phone: 516-628-3156, 203-601-8309. Personal E-mail: rspierro@optonline.net. Business E-Mail: rich.pierro@tsc.com.

PIERSKALLA, WILLIAM PETER, dean, finance and engineering educator; b. St. Cloud, Minn., Oct. 22, 1934; s. Aloys R. and Hilda A. Pierskalla; m. Carol Spargo, Children: Nicholas, William, Michael. AB in Econs., Harvard U., 1956, MBA, 1958; MS in Math., U. Pitts., 1962; PhD in Ops. Rsch., Stanford U., 1965; MA, U. Pa., 1978. Assoc. prof. Case Western Res. U., Cleve., 1965-68, So. Meth. U., Dallas, 1968-70; prof. dept. indsl. engrng. and mgmt. scis. Northwestern U., Evanston, Ill., 1970-78; exec. dir. Leonard Davis Inst. U. Pa., Phila., 1978-83, prof., chmn. health care sys. dept., 1982-90, prof. decision sci. and systems engrng., dep. dean acad. affairs Wharton Sch., 1983-89, Ronald A. Rosenfield prof., 1986-93; dir. Huntsman Ctr. Global Competition and Leadership U. Pa. Wharton Sch., 1989-91; John E. Anderson prof. UCLA, 1993—99, dean John E. Anderson Grad Sch. Mgmt., 1993-97, disting. prof. to disting. prof. emeritus, 1999—. Cons. HHS, Bethesda, Md., 1974-87, MDAX, Chgo., 1985-91, MEDICUS, Evanston, 1970-75, Sisters of Charity, Dayton, Ohio, 1982-83, Project Hope, 1990; bd. dirs., chmn. The Bush Found.; bd. dirs. No. Wilderness Adventures, Informs. Contbr. articles to various publs. Mem. adv. bd. Lehigh U., 1986-93, U. So. Calif. Bus. Sch., 1987-93; regent St. Mary's Coll., 1998-2001, Hong Kong U. Sci. and Tech., 1992-2005. Recipient Harold Larnder Meml. prize Can. Oper. Rsch. Soc., 1993; grantee NSF, 1970-83, HHS, Washington, 1973-82, Office Naval Rsch., Arlington, Va., 1974-77. Fellow Inst. Ops. Rsch. and Mgmt. Scis. (v.p. publs. 2000-03); Mem. Ops. Rsch. Soc. Am. (pres. 1982-83, editor 1979-82, Kimball Disting. Svc. medal 1989), Inst. Mgmt. Scis. (assoc. editor 1970-77), Internat. Fedn. Operational Rsch. Socs. (pres. 1989-91), NAE, Omega Rho.

PIERSOL, LAWRENCE L., federal judge; b. Spirit Mound Township, SD, Oct. 21, 1940; s. Ralph Nelson and Mildred Alice (Millette) P.; m. Catherine Anne Vogt, June 30, 1962; children: Leah C., William M., Elizabeth J. BA, U. S.D., 1962, JD summa cum laude, 1965. Bar: S.D. 1965, U.S. Ct. Mil. Appeals, 1965, U.S. Dist. Ct. S.D. 1968, U.S. Supreme Ct. 1972, U.S. Dist. Ct. Wyo. 1980, U.S. Dist. Ct. Nebr. 1986, U.S. Dist. Ct. Mont. 1988. Ptnr. Davenport, Evans, Hurwitz & Smith, Sioux Falls, SD, 1968-93; judge U.S. Dist. Ct. SD, Sioux Falls, 1993—, chief judge, 1999—2005. Mem. budget com. Jud. Conf. U.S., 1996-2003, chair economy subcom., 2001-03; chmn. tribal ct. com., security com. 8th Cir. Jud. Coun.; editor-in-chief Law Rev.; mem. Judl. Conf. US, 2005-, exec. com., 2006-. Majority leader S.D. Ho. of Reps., Pierre, 1973-74, minority whip, 1971-72; del. Dem. Nat. Conv., 1972, 76, 80; S.D. mem. del. select commn. Dem. Nat. Com., 1971-75. Mem. ABA, State Bar S.D., Fed. Judges Assn. (bd. dirs., pres.). Avocations: reading, running, painting, sailing. Office: US Dist Ct 400 S Phillips Ave Sioux Falls SD 57104-6824 Home Phone: 605-338-7245; Office Phone: 605-330-6640.

PIERSON, AL See **PIZZAMIGLIO, ALBERT**

PIERSON, ANNE BINGHAM, physician; b. NYC, June 9, 1929; d. Woodbridge and Ursula Wolcott (Griswold) Bingham; m. Richard N. Pierson Jr., July 10, 1954 (div. Aug. 1974); children: Richard N. III, Olivia Tiffany Jacobs, Alexandra deForest Griffin, Cordelia Stewart Comfort Smela; m. Richard Taliaferro Wright, Nov. 25, 1978 (div. Sept. 1997); m. Paul H. Altrocchi, May 9, 1998 (div.). Student, Katharine Branson Sch., Ross, Calif., 1943-47; BA, Vassar Coll., 1951; MD, Columbia U., 1955, MPH, 1972. Intern Lenox Hill Hosp., NYC, 1955-56; substitute internship AUH, Beruit, Lebanon, 1955; mem. staff 7th Day Adventist Hosp., Taipei, Taiwan, 1957; clinic physician, med. dir. Planned Parenthood of Bergen County, Hackensack, N.J., 1960-74, also bd. dirs., 1966-69; asst. clin. prof. dept. ob-gyn. Columbia U. Coll. Physicians and Surgeons, Internat. Inst. Study of Human Reproduction, 1972-74; med. dir. Memphis Assn. for Planned Parenthood, Inc., 1974-75; staff physician N.Y. Telephone Co., 1976-87; med. dir. Planned Parenthood Assn. Hudson County, 1976-79; physician Sonalysts, Waterford, Conn., 1988—. Mem. nat. med. adv. com. Planned Parenthood-World Population, 1966-69. Pres. Vassar Class 1951, 1986-91; artist mem. Clinton Art Soc., 1989—, East Lyme Art League, 1991—; active Jr. League, 1964-69, sustainer, 1969—. Mem. AMA (Physicians Recognition award 1973—), Nat. Soc. Colonial Dames (life, asst. sec. 1991-94, 2d v.p. 1994-97), Cosmopolitan Club, Lyme Art Assn. (treas. 1998-99, pres. 1999—), Mystic Art Assn., Essex Art Assn. Office: Sonalysts 215 Parkway N Waterford CT 06385-1209

PIERSON, DIANA LEE, librarian, educator; b. Ann Arbor, Mich., Feb. 27, 1952; d. Robert Harris Pierson and Irena Cooper; m. Kurt Michael Compeau; 1 child, Hannah Marie Pierson-Compeau. BA, Hope Coll., Holland, Mich., 1974; MLS, Western Mich. U., Kalamazoo, 1975. Cert. in profl. edn. Mich., 2005. Asst. dir. Loutit Libr., Grand Haven, Mich., 1975—87; dir. Coopersville Dist. Libr., 1987—90; libr.,tchr. Hillsdale HS, 1997—. Pres. Hillsdale AAUW, Mich., 1992—94. Fellow: Delta Kappa Gamma (newsletter editor). Office: Hillsdale High Sch 30 S Norwood Hillsdale MI 49242 Business E-Mail: dpierson@hillsdaleschools.org.

PIERSON, EDWARD SAMUEL, engineering educator, consultant; b. Syracuse, NY, June 27, 1937; s. Theodore and Marjorie O. (Bronner) P.; m. Elaine M. Grauer, June 6, 1971; 1 child, Alan. BS in Elec. Engrng., Syracuse U., 1958; SM, MIT, 1960, ScD, 1964. Asst. prof., fellow MIT, 1965-66; assoc. prof., assoc. dept. head U. Ill., Chgo., 1966-75; program mgr. Argonne Nat. Labs., Ill., 1975-82; head dept. engrng. Purdue U. Calumet, Hammond, Ind., 1982-95, spl. asst. to chancellor for environ. programs, 1995—2005. Cons. Argonne Nat. Lab., 1972-75, 82-93, Solmecs Corp., 1982-88, HMJ Corp., Washington, 1983-88, LM Mfg., 1994—. Contbr. articles to profl. jours. NSF fellow, 1958-60 Mem. IEEE, ASME, Am. Soc. Engrng. Edn. Office: Purdue Univ Calumet Hammond IN 46323 Home Phone: 773-327-9188; Office Phone: 219-989-2467. E-mail: pierson@calumet.purdue.edu.

PIERSON, RICHARD NORRIS, JR., medical educator; b. NYC, Sept. 22, 1929; s. Richard Norris and Dorothy (Stewart) Pierson; m. Alice Roberts, Aug. 26, 1974; children from previous marriage: Richard N., Olivia Tiffany, Alexandra de Forest, Cordelia S.C. stepchildren: Alice W. Dunn, Eric C.W. Dunn. BA, Princeton U., 1951; MD, Columbia U., 1955. Diplomate Am. Bd. Internal Medicine, Am. Bd. Nuclear Medicine. Resident St. Luke's Roosevelt Hosp., NYC, 1955—61, assoc. dir., 1961—65, dir. div. nuclear medicine, 1965—89, dir. body composition unit, 1965—2003, attending physician, 1975—; prof. clin. medicine Columbia U., 1980—; dir. medicine Hackensack Hosp., 1973—74; staff assoc. Brookhaven Nat. Lab., 1970—2002; rsch. scholar Lawrence Radiation Lab., Berkeley, Calif., 1970—71. Bioengrig. inst. Columbia U., 1976—, chmn., 1989—94. Editor: Quantitative Radiocardiography, 1975; contbr. articles to profl. jours. Warden St. Paul's Ch., 1980—82; bd. dirs. Englewood Health Dept., NJ, 1966—74, Empire Blue Cross/Blue Shield, NY, 1978—91, v.p. NY, 1990—91. NIH grantee, 1973—76, 1986—2003, John A. Hartford grantee, 1967—70. Fellow: ACP, NY Acad. Medicine; mem.: AAAS, Nat. Physicians Alliance, NY County Med. Soc. (pres. 1978—79), Soc. Nuclear Medicine (greater NY area pres. 1982—83, del. to AMA 1991—2001, trustee 1991—, Berson-Yalow award 1995), Alliance for Continuing Med. Edn. (pres. 1987—89), Am. Med. Rev. Rsch. Ctr. (AMA del. NY State 1978—90, chmn. 1984—89), Am. Bur. Med. Advancement in China (pres. 1979—87), NY County Health Svc. Rev. Orgn. (chmn. 1980—82), Am. Inst. Nutrition, Am. Physiol. Soc., Physicians for a Nat. Health Program, NY Metro Chpt. (bd. mem., spkr. 2003—), Century Assn., P&S Alumni Assn. (pres. 1989—91), Englewood Field Club. Home: 60 Lincoln St Englewood NJ 07631-3117 Office: St Lukes Roosevelt Hosp Ctr 1111 Amsterdam Ave New York NY 10025-1716 Home Phone: 201-569-3562; Office Phone: 212-523-3385. Business E-Mail: RNP1@columbia.edu.

PIERSON, ROBERT DAVID, investor; b. Orange, NJ, Mar. 5, 1935; s. Carleton Wellington and Muriel Browning (Potter) Pierson; m. Virginia Duncan Knight, Apr. 30, 1960; children: Lisa Boles, Alexandra Mead, Robert Wellington. BA, Lehigh U., 1957. Exec. asst. 1st Nat. City Bank N.Y., NYC, 1958-61; asst. to pres. Cooper Labs. Inc., NYC, 1961-65; dir. mktg. svcs. Arbrook divsn. Johnson & Johnson, Somerville, NJ, 1965-69; v.p. Klemtner Advt. Inc., NYC, 1969-71; sr. v.p. Bowery Savs. Bank, NYC, 1972-80; vice chmn., dir. Carteret Bancorp, Inc., Wilmington, Del., 1980-90; pres. No. Divsn. Collective Bank, 1990-96, Collective Fin. Svcs., Inc., Harbor Mortgage Co. divsn. Collective Bank, Montclair, NJ, 1997-98; pvt. investor, 1998—. Mem. town coun. Twp. of Mendham, NJ, 1992—2006, mayor, 1995—96, 2003—04. With USCG, 1958—63. Mem.: Morristown Club, Morris County Golf Club. Republican. Presbyterian. Home: Green Hills Rd Mendham NJ 07945-3305

PIERSON, WAYNE GEORGE, trust company executive; b. LA, Nov. 5, 1950; s. Norman Einar and Annabelle Florence (McLay) P.; m. Margaret Aileen Boyle, Mar. 18, 1972; children: Heather, Dawn, Mark, Michael. BS in Bus. Adminstrn. with honors, Calif. State U., Northridge, 1973. CPA, Oreg., Calif. Audit supr. Ernst & Whinney (now Ernst & Young), L.A. and Portland, Oreg., 1973-80; treas. Gregory Affiliates, Beaverton, Oreg., 1980-82; chief fin. & investment officer Meyer Meml. Trust, Portland, 1982—. Pres. Acron Investors, LLC, 2005-; bd. dirs. Oaktree Capital Group LLC, 2007-; mem. adv. com. Power Voyager Capital, Onset Ptnrs. Chair investment com. Columbia Cascade Scout Coun. Mem. AICPA, Chartered Fin. Analysts Inst., Oreg. Soc. CPAs, Portland Soc. Fin. Analysts, Found. Fin. Officers Group (bd. dirs.). Avocations: tennis, scouting, travel. Office: Meyer Memorial Trust STE 400 425 NW 10th Ave Portland OR 97209-3128

PIERSTORFF, ERIK, biomedical engineer; s. Bruce and Carol Pierstorff; m. Trish Kaiser; 1 child, Simone Kaiser-Pierstorff. BS, Emory U., Atlanta, 1996; PhD, U. Calif., Berkeley, 2003. Postdoc. rschr. NIH, Bethesda, Md., 2005—06, Northwestern U., Evanston, Ill., 2006—08; chief tech. officer Biotic Labs., Culver City, Calif., 2008—. Vol. US AID, Moscow, 2004, Sustainable Sci. Insts., Asuncion, Paraguay, 2004. Contbr. articles to profl. jours. Recipient Nat. Biology Honors Soc. award, Phi Sigma, Emory U., 1996, Venture Challenge semifinalist award, Northwestern U., 2007, Venture Challenge winner, 2008; Pre-Intramural Rsch. Tng. fellowship, NIH, 1996—97, Intramural Rsch. Tng. fellowship, 2005—06. Office: Biotic Labs 6140 Bristol Pky Culver City CA 90230-6604

PIETAMBARAM, SRINIVAS V., engineer; s. Venkatacharyulu and Rajya Lakshmi Venkata Peetambaram; m. Suvarna Pappu, May 8, 2004. BE, Nat. Inst. Tech., Rourkela, India, 1996; PhD, U. Fla., Gainesville, 2001. Sr. staff engr. Freescale Semiconductor, Chandler, Ariz., 2001—08; mem. tech. staff Everspin Technologies, Inc., 2008—. Contbr. articles to profl. jours. Recipient Metall. Engrng. Assn. Gold Medal, Nat. Inst. Tech. Rourkela, India, 1992—96. Achievements include patents for High K dielectric film; amorphous alloys for magnetic devices; synthetic antiferromagnet structures for use in MTJs in MRAM technology; method of making amorphous alloys for semiconductor device; low power magnetoelectronic devices utilizing enhanced permeability materials; patents pending for methods and apparatus for a synthetic anti-ferromagnet structure with reduced temperature dependence; MRAM synthetic anitferomagnet structure; enhanced permeability device structures and method. Office: Everspin Technologies Inc 1300 N Alma Sch Rd Chandler AZ 85224 Office Fax: 480-814-2170. Business E-Mail: srinivas.pietambaram@everspin.com.

PIETRAFACE, WILLIAM JOHN, biology professor; s. William and Antoinette Pietraface; m. Marjorie Miller, May 20, 1978. BS, Pa. State U., Univ. Pk., 1971; MS, East Stroudsburg State Coll., Pa., 1973; PhD, W.Va. U., Morgantown, 1979. Prof. & chair biology SUNY Coll., Oneonta, 1998—. Pres. Coll. Oneonta Found., NY, 2009. Recipient Chancellor's award, SUNY, 1986. Office: SUNY Coll Biology Dept Oneonta NY 13820

PIETRO, KATHLEEN C., environmental scientist; b. Ohio; Cert. profl. wetland scientist Soc. Wetland Scientists, 1998. Sr. environ. scientist South Fla. Water Mgmt. Dist., West Palm Beach, Fla., 1987—. Wildlife, Fla. Treasures. Mem.: Sigma XI (treas. 1999—2008). Office: S Fla Water Mgmt Dist 3301 Gun Club Rd West Palm Beach FL 33406 Business E-Mail: kpietro@sfwmd.gov.

PIETROCARLO, NICK, artist, consultant, information technology director; b. Buffalo, May 11, 1971; s. Shirley and Nick Pietrocarlo. BS in Mgmt., Calif. Coast U., 2003, MBA in Bus., 2007. Program Mmgt. Profl. Project Mgmt. Inst., 2008; cert. Citizen's Police Acad. Miami Police Dept., 2003, notary public Dept. State of Fla., 2004, neighborhood leadership acad. City of Miami Beach, 2004. Graphic artist Arvin Calspan Corp., Buffalo, 1988—89; film intern Hallwalls Contemporary Arts Ctr., Buffalo, 1989—90, tech. asst., 1990—92; photo lab mgr. U. Buffalo, 1991—91; treas. Topsy Turvy, Inc, Buffalo, 1992—94; video programmer Royal Caribbean Cruises, Ltd., Miami, 1994—97, interactive tv specialist, 1997—99, project mgr., 1999—2002, program mgr., 2002—; global info. tech. ops. mgr. Island Cruises, Brighton, England, 2005—, dir. info. tech., 2006—; chairperson Miami Beach Citizen's Police Acad., 2008. Freelance artist, Miami, 1990—; cons. Cruise Industry and Info. Tech., Miami, 2000—; mem. cmty. emergency response team, Miami Beach, Fla. Prodr.: (multimedia show) Etc, 1990, (music video) Game of Fools, 2005; assoc. prodr. (video prodn.) Casino Royale, 1996; editor: (video documentary) Riding on the hair of a buffalo, 1992, (video wallpaper exhibits) Topsy Turvy, 1992—94, (pub. svc. announcement) AIDS Trilogy, 1993, (local TV talk show) The Pink Flamingo Show, 1993—94; dir.: (segment for Jerry Lewis Telethon) Charo, 1995; exec. prodr.: (video documentary) Laffoley's Odyssey, 2005. Grantee Video Prodn. grant, Owego Experimental T.V. Ctr., 1991, Rochester Visual Arts Ctr., 1992;, NY State Coun. of Arts, 2005. Mem.: Cmty. Emergency Response Team (Miami Beach, chair person, strategy bd. 2007), CIO (exec. bd., corporate exec. bd. 2007), Project Mgmt. Inst. Roman Catholic. Achievements include production of conceptual device. Avocations: walking, photography. Personal E-mail: nick@pietrocarlo.com. Business E-Mail: npietrocarlo@rccl.com.

PIETROFESA, JOHN JOSEPH, psychologist, educator; b. NYC, Sept. 12, 1940; s. Louis John and Margaret P.; m. Cathy Marks, June 22, 1985; children: John, Paul, Maria, Dolores. EdB cum laude, U. Miami, 1961; MEd, 1963, Ed.D., 1967. Diplomate Am. Bd. Sexology; cert. cognitive behavior therapist, forensic counselor, sex therapist; lic. psychologist, social worker. Counselor Dade County (Fla.) pub. schs., 1965-67; prof. edn. Wayne State U., Detroit, 1967—; div. head theoret. and behavioral founds., 1977-83; dept. chair counselor edn., 1999—. Cons. Nat. Football League, 2003—; cons. to various schs., hosps. and univs. Author: The Authentic Counselor, 1971, 2nd edit., 1980, School Counselor as Professional, 1971, Counseling and Guidance in the Twentieth Century, 1971, Elementary School Guidance and Counseling, 1973, Career Development, 1975, Career Education, 1976, College Student Development, 1977, Counseling: Theory Research and Practice, 1978, Guidance: An Introduction, 1980, Counseling: An Introduction, 1984; mem. editl. bd. Counseling and Values, 1972-75. 1st lt. Mil. Police Corps, AUS, 1963-65. Mem. APA, ACA, Mich. Counseling ASsn., Assn. Counselor Edn. and Supervision, Phi Delta Kappa. Home: PO Box 99 Bloomfield Hills MI 48303-0099 Office: Wayne State U 321 Education Detroit MI 48202 Home Phone: 248-646-0821; Office Phone: 248-642-6066.

PIETROPAOLI, ANGELO EUGENE, social studies educator, musician; b. Little Falls, NY, Aug. 16, 1953; s. Angelo Gino and Mary Louise Pietropaoli; m. Suzanne Rosemary Rizos Pietropaoli, Jan. 7, 1977; children: Elizabeth, John, Thomas, Matthew, Mary Catherine. BA magna cum laude, LeMoyne Coll., Syracuse, NY, 1975. Cert. in secondary social studies NY State Cert., 1982. Social studies tchr. Notre Dame Sch., Malone, NY, 1978—84, Brushton-Moira Ctrl. Sch., NY, 1984—, chmn. dept. social studies, 1996—; adj. history instr. North Country CC, Malone, 1994—; regional summer sch. tchr. B.O.C.E.S., Malone, 2004—. Family life educator Diocese of Ogdensburg, NY, 1981—; choir mem. Ecumenical Choir Christmas Concert for Am. Cancer Soc., Malone, 1994; vol. Knights of Columbus, Malone, 2002—; musician Notre Dame Ch., Malone, 1980—, vol. tchr., 1977—95; soccer coach and asst. coach Malone Youth Soccer League, 1996—2001. Named Tchr. of Yr., Adirondack Chpt. DAR, Melone, 2002; nominee Outstanding Tchr., Adirondack Chpt. DAR, Malone, 1992. Mem.: Brushton-Moira Tchrs. Assn., NY State United Tchrs., Brushton-Moira Chpt. Nat. Jr. Honor Soc. (advisor 2005—). Independent. Roman Catholic. Avocations: gardening, music, hiking, kayaking. Office: Brushton-Moira Ctrl Sch 787 County Rt 7 Brushton NY 12916

PIETRUSKI, JOHN MICHAEL, JR., pharmaceutical executive; b. Sayreville, NJ, Mar. 12, 1933; m. Roberta Jeanne Talbot, July 3, 1954; children: Glenn David, Clifford John, Susan Jane. BS with honors, Rutgers U., 1954; LLD (hon.), Concordia Coll., 1993. With Proctor and Gamble Co., 1954-63; pres. med. products div. C.R. Bard, Inc., 1963-77; with Sterling Drug, Inc., NYC, 1977-88; pres. Pharm. Group, 1977-81, corp. exec. v.p., 1981-83, pres., COO, 1983-85, chmn., CEO, 1985-88; pres. Dansara Cons., 1988—; chmn. Encysive Pharms., Inc., 1990—2008. Bd. dirs. PDI, Inc., Xylos Corp., Trial Card, Inc. 1st lt. US Army, 1955—57. Mem.: Union League Club (N.Y.C.), Phi Beta Kappa. Home: 27 Paddock Ln Colts Neck NJ 07722-1266 Office: One Penn Plaza Ste 3408 New York NY 10119 Office Phone: 212-268-5510. Personal E-mail: jmpco4@aol.com.

PIETRZAK, ALFRED ROBERT, lawyer; b. Glen Cove, NY, June 26, 1949; s. Alfred S. and Wanda M. (Wapniarski) P.; m. Sharon Esther Chizek, July 9, 1978; children: Eric A., Daniel J. BA cum laude in cursu honorem, Fordham U., 1971; JD, Columbia U., 1974. Bar: NY 1975, US Dist. Ct. (so., ea., we. and no. dists.) NY 1975, (no. dist.) Calif. 1983, US Ct. Appeals (2d. cir.) 1975, (9th cir.) 1983, (11th cir.) 1985, US Supreme Ct. 1985. Assoc. Brown & Wood (formerly Brown, Wood, Ivey, Mitchell & Petty), NYC, 1974-82, ptnr., 1983—2001; also head litigation practice group; ptnr. and mem. exec. com. Sidley Austin Brown & Wood LLP (following merger), NYC, 2001—, and co-chair profl. responsibility com. Mem. fin. products adv. com. Commodity Futures Trading Commn.; mem. CLE faculty Fordham U. Sch. Law.; mem. litig. adv. com. Bond Market Assn.; bd. advisors Rev. of Securities and Commodities Regulation; bd. editors Futures Internat. Law Letter; adv. bd. Fordham Internat. Law Jour. Editl. adv. bd. Fordham Internat. Law Jour., Review of Securities and Commodities Regulation.Contbr. articles to legal journals. Named one of World's Leading Litig. Lawyers, Euromoney mag. Mem. ABA, Assn. Bar City NY (securities regulation com., chmn. futures regulation com., retail fin. svcs. com.), Am. Law Inst. (lectr.), Securities Industry Assn., Futures Industry Assn., Bond Mkt. Assn. Democrat. Roman Catholic. Office: Sidley Austin Brown & Wood LLP 787 Seenth Ave New York NY 10019-6018 Office Phone: 212-839-5537. Office Fax: 212-839-5599. Business E-Mail: rpietrzak@sidley.com.

PIETRZAK, RONA, dean, director; d. William Pietrzak and Sophie Ronnie Ostoich; life ptnr. Amiel Braverman; 1 child, Alexis Choice Pietrzak Braverman. JD, U. Pitts. Sch. Law, 1983. Caseworker Allegheny County DYS, Pitts., 1969—74; staff rep. AFSCME DC 84, Pitts., 1974; law clk. US Ct. Appeals 7th Cir., Chgo., 1983—84; asst. prof., law Rutgers Law Sch., Camden, NJ, 1884—1991; instr., grad. sch. soc. wk & rsch. Bryn Mawr Coll., Pa., 1991—2001, asst. dean & dir., McBride scholars program, 1995—2002, assoc. dean & dir., McBride scholars program, 2002—; trustee Salfrod Quarry Custodial Trust, Phila., 1993—. Vol. Obama for Change, Phila., 2008; exec. bd. mem. Germantown Jewish Ctr., Phila., 2008—. Mem.: AAUW. Liberal. Jewish. Avocations: gardening, kayaking, quilting, travel. Office: Bryn Mawr Coll 101 N Merion Ave Bryn Mawr PA 19010 Office Fax: 610-526-7560. Business E-Mail: rpietrza@brynmawr.edu.

PIETRZAK, TED S., art gallery director; b. Kitchener, Ont., Can., Sept. 18, 1952; m. Marlene C. Longdon, Aug. 25, 1990; 1 child, Christina. BA in Arts Mgmt., U. Guelph, Banff, Alta., Can.; attended, Mus. Mgmt. Inst., Berkeley, Calif. Asst. to dir. Art Gallery Hamilton, Ont., 1976-80; dir. Burlington Cultural Ctr., 1980-91, Art Gallery Hamilton, 1992—97, Burchfield-Penney Art Ctr., 1998—. Active Roswell Pk. Cancer Inst.; chair, cultural tourism com. Buffalo Niagara

Convention and Visitor Bureau, bd. dirs., Burchfield Nature and Art Ctr. Mem. Ont. Assn. Art Galleries (pres. 1983-84), Can. Art Mus. Dirs. Orgn. (chair govt. and arts com., treas. 1991-95). Avocations: cooking, reading, music. Office: Burchfield-Penney Art Ctr Buffalo State Coll 1300 Elmwood Ave Buffalo NY 14222 Office Phone: 716-878-3909. Business E-Mail: pietrzts@buffalostate.edu.

PIETRZEN, JULIE LYNN, lawyer; b. Southfield, Mich., Mar. 13, 1974; d. Eugene Victor Pietrzen and Joan Diane Bragg. BA, Albion Coll., Albion, Mich., 1996; JD, Case Western Res. U., Cleve., 2004. LCSW Mich. Patient advocate L&S Assocs., Inc., Haslett, Mich., 1996—97; program coord. YWCA of Western Wayne County, Mich., 1997—2000; atty. Frantz Ward LLP, Cleve., 2004—. Mem.: Cuyahoga County Bar Assn., Cleve. Bar Assn., Ohio State Bar Assn., Phi Delta Phi (province pres. 2004—, Balfour scholar 2003, Grad. of the Yr. 2004). Democrat. Avocations: volleyball, reading, writing, skiing. Office: Frantz Ward LLP 127 Public Sq 2500 Key Center Cleveland OH 44114

PIETZSCH, MICHAEL EDWARD, lawyer; b. Burlington, Iowa, Aug. 1, 1949; s. Walter E. and Leanna (Moore) P.; m. Ellen G. Hart; children: Christine E., Catherine M. AB, Stanford U., 1971; JD, U. Chgo., 1974. Bar: Ill. 1974, Ariz. 1976. Ptnr. McCabe & Pietzsch, Phoenix, 1975-90, Pietzsch & Williams, Phoenix, 1990-95, Polese, Pietzsch, Williams & Nolan, Phoenix, 1995—2007, Pietzsch, Bonnett and Womack, Phoenix, 2008. Contbr. articles to profl. jours.; speaker at profl. confs. Del. White House Conf. Small Bus., Washington, 1986, White House Savs. Summit, 1998; chmn. bd. trustees Ariz. Sci. Ctr., 1994-98; pres. The Group, Inc., 1995-98. Fellow Am. Coll. Tax Counsel, Am. Coun. on Tax Policy, Am. Coll. Employee Benefits Counsel; mem. ABA (chmn. personal svc. orgns. com. tax sect. 1986-90), Stanford Phoenix Club (pres. 1982-84). Office: 2702 N Third St Ste 3000 Phoenix AZ 85004 Office Phone: 602-604-6250. E-mail: pietzsch@usbenefitslaw.com.

PIGA, STEPHEN MULRY, retired lawyer; b. Bklyn., Apr. 9, 1929; s. Stephen Paul and Ella (Mulry) P.; married, Feb. 23, 1952 (div.); children: Maureen, Stephen, Susan, Elizabeth; m. Emilie Halliday, Aug. 1, 1975 (dec. Aug. 2003); 1 dau., Margaret. AB, Princeton U., 1950; LLB, Columbia U., 1955. Bar: N.J. 1955, N.Y. 1956. Assoc. White & Case, NYC, 1955-63, ptnr., 1964-92; ret., 1992. Lectr. Practicing Law Inst. N.Y. and various insts., bar assns. Served to capt. USMCR, 1951-53. Mem. ABA, N.Y. State Bar Assn. (exec. com. tax sect. 1981-89, chmn. employee benefits com.), Assn. of Bar of City N.Y., N.J. Bar Assn., Am. Contract Bridge League (life master), Profl. Bowlers' Assn. Am., High Mt. Golf Club. Republican. Avocations: fishing, golf, bowling, bridge.

PIGFORD, THOMAS HARRINGTON, nuclear engineering educator; b. Meridian, Miss., Apr. 21, 1922; s. Lamar and Zula Vivian (Harrington) P.; m. Catherine Kennedy Cathey, Dec. 31, 1948 (dec. 1992); children: Cynthia Pigford Naylor, Julie Earnest; m. Elizabeth Hood Weekes, Nov. 12, 1994. BS in Chem. Engring., Ga. Inst. Tech., 1943; S.M. in Chem. Engring., M.I.T., 1948, Sc.D. in Chem. Engring., 1952. Asst. prof. chem. engring., dir. Sch. Engring. Practice, M.I.T., 1950-52, asst. prof. nuclear and chem. engring., 1952-55, assoc. prof., 1955-57; head engring., dir. nuclear reactor projects and asst. dir. research lab. Gen. Atomic Co., La Jolla, Calif., 1957-59; prof. nuclear engring., chmn. dept. nuclear engring. U. Calif., Berkeley, 1959—; sr. rsch. scientist Lawrence Berkeley Lab., 1959—. Mem. panel Nat. Atomic Safety Licensing Bd. AEC-Nuclear Regulatory Commn., 1963-77; mem. Pres.'s Commn. on accident at 3-Mile Island, 1979; mem. bd. radioactive waste mgmt. and energy engring. bd., NAS-NAE, chmn. waste isolation systems panel, waste isolation pilot plant panel, fusion hybrid panel, separations and transmutations panel, transmutation of military plutonium panel, panel on health standard for radioactive waste disposal, chmn. adv. coun. Inst. Nuclear Power Op.; mem. Sec. of Energy's expert cons. group on Chernobyl accident; chmn. nuclear oversight com. Sacramento Mcpl. Utility Dist.; chmn. nuclear safety com. Gulf States Utilities Co.; mem. expert cons. group Swedish Nuclear Power Inspectorate; mem. peer rev. group for waste isolation pilot plant; mem. corp. rev. com. Oak Ridge Nat. Lab; lectr. Taiwan Nat. Sci. Found., 1990; vis. prof. Kyoto U., 1975, Kuwait U., 1976; cons. in field. Author: (with Manson Benedict) Nuclear Chemical Engineering, 1958, 2d edit., 1981; contbr. numerous articles to profl. jours.; patentee in field. Served with USNR, 1944-46. Recipient John Wesley Powell award U.S. Geol. Survey, 1981; named Outstanding Young Man of Greater Boston, Boston Jaycees, 1955; E. I. DuPont DeNemours rsch. fellow, 1948-50; Berkeley citation U. Calif., 1987; Japan Soc. for Promotion Sci. fellow, 1974-75; grantee NSF, 1960-75, EPA, 1973-78, Dept. Energy, 1979-92, Ford Found., 1974-75, Electric Power Rsch. Inst., 1974-75, Mitsubishi Metals Corp., 1989-90; named to Ga. Tech. Hall of Fame, 1995. Fellow Am. Nuclear Soc. (bd. dirs., Arthur H. Compton award 1971); mem. AIME, NAE, Am. Chem. Soc., Am. Inst. Chem. Engrs. (Robert E. Wilson award 1980, Service to Society award 1985), Atomic Indsl. Forum (dir.), Sigma Xi, Phi Kappa Phi, Tau Beta Pi. Home: 166 Alpine Ter Oakland CA 94618-1823 Office: U Calif Dept Nuclear Engring Berkeley CA 94720-0001 Office Phone: 510-652-0393. Business E-Mail: pigford@nuc.berkeley.edu.

PIGGE, JOYCE A., political science professor; AA, Rend Lake Coll., Mt. Vernon, Ill., 1965; BA, Maryville Coll., Tenn., 1967; DA, Lehigh U., Bethehem, Pa., 1979. Prof., polit. sci. Bethany Coll., Lindsborg, Kans., 1970—. Office: Bethany Coll 335 East Swensson St Lindsborg KS 67456 Business E-Mail: piggej@bethanylb.edu.

PIGGOTT, MICHAEL RANTELL, chemical engineer, educator; b. Cheadle Hulme, Eng., Feb. 13, 1930; s. Henry Alfred and Ethel (Rantell) P.; m. Norma Clark, July 9, 1955; children: Diana, Andrew, Stephen. BS, Imperial Coll., London, 1951, PhD, diploma, Imperial Coll., London, 1955. With R&D GE, England, 1955-58; sr. rsch. staff Bexford Ltd., England, 1958-60; rsch. officer Gillette, England, 1960-64, Chalk River Nuclear Labs., Canada, 1964-68; prof. chem. engring. U. Toronto, Ont., 1968-95, chmn. Ctr. Study of Materials, 1979-83, prof. emeritus, 1995—. Pres. MERP Enhanced Composites Inc. Author: Load Bearing Fibre Composites, 1980, 2d edit., 2001, What Engineers Should Know About Fibre Composites, 2006; contbr. articles to profl. publs.; patentee in field. Mem. Am. Soc. Composites (founding mem.), Alpine Club Can. Home: 23 Lorraine Dr #1508 Willowdale ON Canada M2N 6Z6 Office: U Toronto 200 College St Toronto ON Canada M5S 3E5

PIGNATELLI, DEBORA BECKER, state official; b. Hoboken, NJ, Oct. 25, 1947; d. Edward and Frances (Fishman) Becker; m. Michael Albert Pignatelli, Aug. 22, 1971; children: Adam Becker, Benjamin Becker. AA, Vt. Coll., 1967; BA, U. Denver, 1969. Exec. dir. Girl's Club Greater Nashua, NH, 1975-77; dir. tenant svcs. Nashua Housing Authority, 1979-80; vocat. counselor Comprehensive Rehab. Assocs., Bedford, NH, 1982-85; specialist job placement Crawford & Co., Bedford, 1985-87; mem. N.H. Ho. of Reps., Concord, 1986—91; mem. appropriations com., 1986-91, asst. minority leader, 1989—91; mem. N.H. Senate, Concord, 1992—2003, v.p. policy, Dem. whip, chair judiciary com., mem. capital budget com., chair enrolled bills com., long range capital budget overview com.; elected mem. N.H. Govs. Exec. Coun., 2005—; co-chair NH Women Hitlary. Del. Am. Coun. Young Polit. Leaders, Germany, 1987. Asst. coach Little League Baseball, Nashua, 1987—90; del. Dem. Nat. Conv., 1988, Gore del., 2000; mem. steering com. Gephardt for Pres. campaign, NH, 1987—88; bd. dirs. Sky Meadow Condominium Assn. Recipient Meritorious Svc. award, NH Women's Lobby, 1997, John F. Kennedy award, Hillsborough County Dems., 2001, Anita and Norman Freedman award, N.H. Dems., 2004, William Paine Domestic Violence award, 2005; named one of 10 Most Powerful Women in NH, NH Editions mag., 1995. Mem.: Women's Lobby, N.H. Children's Lobby. Jewish. Avocations: skiing, swimming, boating. Home: 22 Appletree Grn Nashua NH 03062-2252 Office Phone: 603-271-3632.

PIGNATELLI, DONNA M., legislative staff member; BA, Mt. Holyoke Coll., South Hadley, Mass., 1977. Legis. corr. for Rep. George Danielson US House of Reps., Washington, 1977—78, adminstrv. asst. for Rep. Jim Shannon, 1979—82, chief of staff for Rep. Sherrod Brown, 1995—2004, chief of staff for Rep. Martin T. Meehan, 2005, chief of staff for Rep. Bart Gordon, 2007—; staff govt. rels. The New Eng., Boston, 1982—90; with Am. Coun. Life Ins., Washington, 1990—95. Avocations: golf, reading, travel. Office: Office of Congressman Bart Gordon 2306 Rayburn House Office Bldg Washington DC 20515 Office Phone: 202-225-4231. Business E-Mail: donna.pignatelli@mail.house.gov.*

PIGOTT, EUGENE F., JR., state appeals court judge; b. Rochester, NY, Sept. 27, 1946; m. Peggy Pigott; 2 children. BA, LeMoyne Coll., 1968; JD, SUNY Buffalo Sch. Law, 1973. Bar: NY 1974. Atty. Offermann, Fallon, Mahoney & Adner, Buffalo, 1974—82; Erie County atty., 1982—86; chief trial counsel Offermann, Cassano, Pigott & Greco, 1986; judge NY State Supreme Ct., 1997—98; justice Appellate Divsn., 4th Dept., 1998—2000, presiding justice, 2000—06; assoc. judge NY State Ct. Appeals, 2006—. Office: State of NY Court of Appeals 20 Eagle St Albany NY 12207-1095*

PIGOTT, MARK C., automotive executive; BS in Indsl. Engring., Stanford U., Calif., MBA. V.p. Paccar Inc., Bellevue, Wash., 1988—89, sr. v.p., 1990—93, exec. v.p., 1993—95, bd. dirs., 1994—, vice chmn., 1995—96, chmn., CEO, 1997—. Mem. exec. com. Washington Roundtable. Named Mgr. of Yr., Truck & Off-Hwy. Ledger, 2004; named a Top CEO, Instl. Investor mag., 2005. Office: PACCAR PO Box 1518 Bellevue WA 98009 Office Phone: 425-468-7400. Office Fax: 425-468-8216.

PIIRMA, IRJA, chemist, educator; b. Tallinn, Estonia, Feb. 4, 1920; came to U.S., 1949; d. Voldemar Juri and Meta Wilhelmine (Lister) Tiits; m. Aleksander Piirma, Mar. 10, 1943; children: Margit Ene, Silvia Ann. Diploma in Chemistry, Tech. U., Darmstadt, Fed. Republic of Germany, 1949; MS, U. Akron, 1957, PhD, 1960. Rsch. chemist U. Akron, Ohio, 1952-67, asst. prof., 1967-76, assoc. prof., 1976-81, prof., 1981-90, prof. emerita, 1990—, dept. head, 1982-85. Author: Polymeric Surfactants, 1992; editor: Emulsion Polymerization, 1982; contbr. articles to profl. jours. Recipient Extra Mural Rsch. award BP Am., Inc., 1989. Mem. Am. Chem. Soc. Avocations: swimming, skiing. Home: 3528 Adaline Dr Cuyahoga Falls OH 44224-3929 Office: U Akron Inst Polymer Sci Akron OH 44325-3909 Home Phone: 330-688-4834. Personal E-mail: irjapiirma@sbcglobal.net.

PIJEAUX, LAWRENCE J., JR., museum director; b. New Orleans; m. Maxine J. Pijeaux; 5 children. BS, Southern U., Baton Rouge; MA in Tchg., Tulane U., New Orleans; EdD, U. Southern Miss., Hattiesburg. Mgr., Lila Wallace Grant Indpls. Mus. Art; exec. dir. Birmingham Civil Rights Inst., Ala., 1995—. Spkr. in field. Mem. adv. bd. Ala. Bur. Tourism and Travel; bd. dirs. United Way of Ctrl. Ala., Inc., Ala. Symphony Orchestra, Birmingham Internat. Festival, Ala. Sch. Math. and Sci., 2007—. Recipient Mus. Leadership award, Smithsonian Inst., Am. Hero in Edn. award, Reader's Digest; named Ala. Tourism Exec. of Yr., 2006. Mem.: Ala. Mus. Assn., Am. Assn. Mus., Am. Assn. for State and Local History, Assn. African-Am. Mus. (pres., Svc. and Achievement award), 100 Black Men of Birmingham, Rotary Internat., Omega Psi Phi (Edn. Leader of Yr. award). Office: Birmingham Civil Rights Inst 520 Sixteenth St N Birmingham AL 35203 Office Phone: 205-328-9696. Office Fax: 205-251-6104. Business E-Mail: lpijeaux@bcri.org.

PIKE, DIANE KENNEDY, writer, educator; b. Norfolk, Nebr., Jan. 24, 1938; d. G. Edward and Arlene Alice (Wyant) Kennedy; m. James Albert Pike, Dec. 20, 1968 (dec. Sept. 1969). BA with distinction, Stanford U., 1959; MA, Columbia U., 1964. Tchr. Crandon Inst., Montevideo, Uruguay, 1960-62, Willow Glen H.S., San Jose, Calif., 1964-65; dir. youth and children's work First United Meth. Ch., Palo Alto, Calif., 1965-67; exec. dir. New Focus Found., Santa Barbara, Calif., 1967-69, Bishop Pike Found., Santa Barbara, 1969-72, The Love Project, San Diego, 1972-89, Teleos Inst., San Diego, 1989-93, Scottsdale, Ariz., 1993—. Author: Search, 1971, Cosmic Unfoldment: The Individualizing Process as Mirrored in the Life of Jesus, 1976, Life is Victorious! How to Grow Through Grief, 1976, The Process of Awakening, 1985, Life As A Waking Dream, 1997, rev. edit., 2008, Four Paths to Union, 2001, Awakening to Wisdom, 2003, The House of Self: A Description of the Structure and Function of the Individual's Energy Field, 2006; co-author: The Other Side, 1968, The Wilderness Revolt, 1972, Channeling Love Energy, 1974, The Love Project Way, 1980. Avocations: tennis, swimming, travel. Personal E-mail: dkpike@aol.com.

PIKE, GEORGE HAROLD, JR., religious organization administrator, clergyman; b. Summit, NJ, Jan. 14, 1933; s. George Harold and Ann Aurelia (Brewer) P.; m. Pauline Elizabeth Blair, Aug. 27, 1955; children: Elizabeth, George 3d, James. BA, Trinity Coll., Hartford, Conn., 1954; MDiv, Dubuque Theol. Sem., Iowa, 1957; DDiv (hon.), U. Dubuque, 1998. Ordained to ministry Presbyn. Ch. USA., 1957. Pastor 1st PResbyn. Ch., Kasson, Minn., 1956-59, 3d Presbyn. Ch., Dubuque, 1959-64; sr. pastor Presbyn. Ch., Bettendorf, Iowa, 1964-68, 1st Presbyn. Ch., Vancouver, Wash., 1968-78, Cranford, NJ, 1978-88; exec. chair Presbyn. Ch. USA, Louisville, 1988-93; co-dir. Bicentennial Presbyn. Ch. USA; interim pastor 2d Presbyn. Ch., Kansas City, Mo., 1993-95; dir. sem. devel. U. Dubuque, Iowa, 1995-98; retired, 1998; interim pastor Valley Presbyn. Ch., Green Valley, Ariz., 2000, interim sr. pastor, 2008. Mem. exec. com. Consultation on Ch. Union, Princeton, 1980-89, pres., 1984-88. Dir. Bettendorf Bd. Edn., 1964-68, pres. 1967-68; bd. dirs. Southwest Wash. Hosps., Vancouver, 1969-78. Named Citizen of Yr., Jaycees, Bettendorf, 1967, Citizen of Yr., B'nai B'rith, Cranford, 1988; named to Honorable Order of Ky. Cols., 1989 Presbyterian. Avocations: golf, photography. Home: 928 W Union Bell Dr Green Valley AZ 85614-5928 Personal E-mail: Ghpike@aol.com.

PIKE, KERMIT JEROME, cultural organization administrator; b. East Cleveland, June 19, 1941; s. Frank James and Pauline Frances (Prijatel) P.; m. Joyce Rita Massillo, June 27, 1964; children: Christopher James, Laura Elizabeth. BA, Case Western Res. U., 1963, MA, 1965. Rsch. asst. Western Res. Hist. Soc., Cleve., 1965-66, curator manuscripts, 1966-72, chief libr., 1969-75, dir. libr., 1976—2002, COO, 1997—2007, capital campaign mgr., 2006—07, sr. v.p., 2007—. Adj. prof. history, libr. sci. Case Western Res. U., 1975-84. Author: Guide to the Manuscripts and Archives, 1972, Guide to Shaker Manuscripts, 1974; editor: Guide to Jewish History Sources, 1983; Compiler: Guide to Major Manuscript Collections, 1987. Mem. Super Sesquicentennial Com., Cleve., 1971, Cleve. Bicentennial History Com., 1992—96, Ohio Preservation Coun., 1997—, Ohio Hist. Records Adv. Bd., 2002—07; chmn. Family Heritage Adv. Bd., Numa Corp., 1995—99; chmn. vis. com. on humanities and arts Cleve. State U., 1980—82; trustee Nationalities Svc. Ctr., Cleve., 1978—86. Recipient Achievement award No. Ohio Live, Cleve., 1987; Spl. Recognition award Gov. Richard F. Celeste of Ohio, 1990. Mem. Soc. Ohio Archivists (co-founder 1968, pres. 1971-72), Black History Archives (founder 1970), Orgn. Am. Historians, Soc. Am. Archivists, Manuscripts Soc., Midwest Archives Conf., Ohio Geneal. Soc., Early Settlers Assn. of the Western Res., Rowfant Club, Lake County Farmers' Conservation Club, Lambda Chi Alpha. Roman Catholic. Office: Western Res Hist Soc 10825 East Blvd Cleveland OH 44106-1777 Office Phone: 216-721-5722. Business E-Mail: kjpinmentor@sbcglobal.net.

PIKE, LARRY SAMUEL, lawyer; b. Savannah, Ga., Feb. 23, 1939; s. Abram and Ida (Feinberg) P.; m. Bonnie Jo Haykin, June 21, 1959; children: Douglas, Stacey, Scott. BA, Emory U., 1960, LLB, 1963; postgrad., Leeds U., Eng., 1960-61. Assoc. L. Jack Swertfeger Jr. Atty., Decatur, Ga., 1963-65; ptnr. Swertfeger, Scott, Pike & Simmons, Decatur, 1966-75, Simmons, Pike & Warren, Decatur, 1975-76, Lefkoff, Pike & Sims, Atlanta, 1976-85, Branch, Pike & Ganz, Atlanta, 1985-95, Holland & Knight LLP, Atlanta, 1995—. Pres. Ansley Park Civic Assn., Atlanta, 1977-79, Northshore Homeowners Assn., Tybee Island, Ga., 1992-95, The Temple, Atlanta, 1979-81, trustee, 1977—, Am. Cancer Soc., DeKalb County, Ga. unit, 1970-71, crusade chmn., 1969-70; trustee Ansley Park Beautification Found., Inc., Atlanta, 1984—, treas., 2000-06, v.p. 2006—; trustee The Temple Endowment Fund, Atlanta, 1979-87, Atlanta Jewish Cmty. Ctr., 1973-76; bd. overseers Hebrew Union Coll., Cin., 1987-93; alumni coun. Emory U., Atlanta, 1966-72; bd. trustees Union of Am. Hebrew Congregations, 1991-99; mem. Rabbinical Placement Commn., 1994-2000; mem. St. Joseph's Hosp. Leadership Coun., 2003—; mem. planned giving adv. bd. Cmty. Found. Greater Atlanta, 2005-08; mem. gift planning adv. coun. Emory U., 2006—. Editor-in-chief law jour. and newspaper; contbr. articles to profl. jours. Named Outstanding Young Man of Yr., North DeKalb Jaycees, 1968, Super Lawyer, Atlanta Mag.; named one of Legal Elite, Ga. Trend mag.; Fulbright fellow, 1960—61. Mem. ABA, State Bar Ga. (exec. coun. Young Lawyers sect. 1968-72), Atlanta Bar Assn., Decatur-DeKalb Bar Assn. (sec. 1965-66), Atlanta Legal Aid Soc. (pres. 1974-75, past bd. dirs.), Atlanta Tax Forum, Lawyers Club Atlanta, B'nai B'rith (pres. Atlanta lodge 1970-71, Ga. pres. 1974-75, dist. 5 bd. govs. 1973-76, chair Youth Orgn. Bd. 1971-73), Bryan Soc., Phi Beta Kappa, Omicron Delta Kappa. Office: Holland & Knight LLP 2000 One Atlantic Ctr Atlanta GA 30309 Business E-Mail: larry.pike@hklaw.com.

PIKE, LYNN A., bank executive; Grad., Duke U. Fuqua Sch. Bus. Exec. Sch. Mktg., Durham, NC. With Bank of Boston; mgr., Fla., NY and NJ cmty. banking units First Nationwide Bank; dir. nat. sales GMAC Mortgage Corp.; exec. v.p., regional pres., LA met. divsn. Wells Fargo Bank; mng. dir. consumer banking & distbn. FleetBoston, 2002—04; pres. banking bus. Bank of America, 2004—07; pres. Bank of America Calif.; COO banking bus. Capital One Fin. Corp., McLean, Va., 2007, pres., 2007—. Mgmt. operating com. Bank of America; dir. Capital One Nat. Assn.; mem. br. bd. Fed. Res. Bank San Francisco. Mem. Calif. Businesses Edn. Excellence, Calif. Bus. Roundtable; bd. trustees Bank of America Found.; mem. exec. com. Operation Hope, mem. nat. bd. dirs., 2001, northeastern bd. mem., 2007—; bd. dirs. Phoenix Houses Calif.; bd. trustees Autry Mus. Named one of 25 Women to Watch, US Banker, 2007, 2008. Office: Capital One Financial Corp 1680 Capital One Dr Mc Lean VA 22102 Office Phone: 703-720-1000.*

PIKE, RALPH WEBSTER, chemical engineer, educator, academic administrator; b. Tampa, Fla., Nov. 10, 1935; s. Ralph Webster and Macey (Adams) P.; m. Patricia Jennings, Aug. 23, 1958. B in Chem. Engring., Ga. Inst. Tech., 1957, PhD, 1962. Rsch. chem. engr. Exxon R & D Co., Baytown, Tex., 1962—64; Paul M. Horton prof. chem. engring. and sys. sci. La. State U., Baton Rouge, 1964—, assoc. vice chancellor rsch., 1967—96, dir. La. Mineral Inst., 1979—, dean engring., 1999—2001. Cons. to chem. and petroleum refining industry, fed. govt. and State of La., 1964—. Author: Formulation and Optimization of Mathematical Models, 1970, Optimization for Engineering Systems, 1986, Optimizacion en Ingenieria, 1989, Computational Transport Phenomena for Engineering Analyses, 2009. Active various civic, ch. and cmty. orgns., Baton Rouge, 1964—. 2d lt. U.S. Army, 1958-60. Recipient more than 100 rsch. grants, including NASA, NSF, Dept. Interior, Dept. Def., EPA, NOAA, state agys. and pvt. industry, 1964—. Fellow AIChE (chmn. nat. program com. 1984, local sect. 1985); mem. Am. Chem. Soc. (Charles E. Coates Mem. Award, 1994), Sigma Xi. Democrat. Methodist. Avocation: skiing. Home: 6063 Hibiscus Dr Baton Rouge LA 70808-8844 Office: La State U 1139 Energy Coast and Environment Bldg Baton Rouge LA 70803-0001 Office Phone: 225-578-3428. Business E-Mail: pike@lsu.edu.

PIKE, THOMAS HARRISON, plant chemist; b. West Palm Beach, Florida, Oct. 9, 1950; s. Rufus Draper and Dora Marie (Thomason) P.; m. Julie Lynn (Simpson), Aug. 19, 1972; one child, Thomas Simpson. BS, Baylor Univ., 1972; MS, Calif. State U., 2001. Sci. instr. Valliant Pub. Sch., Okla., 1975—76; sch. adminstr. Swink Pub. Sch., Okla., 1976—81; plant chemist Western Farmers Electric Coop., Ft. Towson, Okla., 1981—2004; tech. editor Penn Well Pub., 2004—. Instr. dept. sci. and engring., Eastern Okla. State Coll., 1997—; mem. adv. bd. Kiamichi Vo-Tech. Sch., Idabel, Okla., 1985-87; tech. editor Penn Well Pub. Mem. adv. bd. Kiamichi Vo-Tech. Sch., Idabel, Okla., 1997—. Mem. ASME (co-chmn. task force, 1988-90); ASTM; Nat. Assn. Corrosion Engr. Achievements include rsch. in corrosion control of condensers, case history of turbine problems, improving boiler efficiency, preservation of turbines during extended outages, metal oxide transport, and water clarification; two patents in chemical process control technology. Home: R R 1 Box 299 Garvin OK 74736-9755 Office: Western Farmers Electric Coop PO Box 219 Fort Towson OK 74735-0219 Business E-Mail: t_pike@wfec.com.

PIKE, WILLIAM EDWARD, retired banking executive; b. Ft. Collins, Colo., Jan. 25, 1929; s. Harry H. and Alice Francis (Swinscoe) P.; m. Catherine Broward Crawford, June 26, 1965; children: Elizabeth Catherine, Robert Crawford, Daniel William. Student, U. Colo., 1947-48; BS, U.S. Naval Acad., 1952; MBA, Harvard, 1960. Commd. ensign USN, 1952, advanced through grades to lt., 1958; ret., 1958; asst. treas. Morgan Guaranty Trust Co., NYC, 1962-64, asst. v.p., 1964-66, v.p., 1966-71, sr. v.p., 1971-74, chmn. credit policy com., 1974-86; exec. v.p. J.P. Morgan & Co. Inc., 1986-89; corp. dir., trustee, pvt. investor. Mem. Harvard Club N.Y.C. Clubs: Country (New Canaan, Conn.). Episcopalian. Home: Indian Waters Dr New Canaan CT 06840 Office: William E Pike 79 Indian Waters Dr New Canaan CT 06840-6107

PIKITCH, ELLEN KAREN, science educator; d. Benjamin and Ruth Pikitch; m. Allen Saul Zwickler, May 24, 1997; children: Adam Craig Zwickler, Randi Beth Zwickler; 1 child from previous marriage, Scott Merritt Emlen. BS, MA, CUNY, NYC, 1977; MS, Ind. U., Bloomington, 1982, PhD, 1983. Asst. prof. Oreg. State U., Newport, 1983—87, Sch. Fisheries, U. Wash., Seattle, 1987—90, assoc. prof., 1990—96, assoc. dir. rsch., dir. fisheries rsch. inst., 1992—96; dir. fisheries programs Wildlife Conservation Soc., NYC, 1996—98, dir. marine conservation programs, 1998—2002, dir. ocean strategy, 2002—03; exec. dir. Pew Inst. for Ocean Sci., NYC, 2003—; prof. U. Miami Rosenstiel Sch., Fla., 2003—. Mem. Pres. Clinton's Panel on Ocean Exploration, 2000—01; mem. sturgeon specialist group Internat. Union for the Conservation of Nature, 2002—; task force mem. Millennium Project Task Force on Environ. Sustainability, 2003—05; conservation com. mem. Sea Change Investment Fund, San Francisco, 2005—; co-founder Caviar Emptor Campaign, lead scientist. Contbr. articles to profl. jours. Recipient Nehemiah Gittleson award, City Coll., CUNY, 1977, Kenyon prize for Excellence in Pure and Applied Math., 1977, Emerging Scholar award, Phi Kappa Phi, Oreg. State U. Chpt., 1987, Disting. Svc. award, Coll. Ocean and Fisheries Sci., U. Wash., 1992, Silver Anvil award, Pub. Rels. Soc. Am., 2004; named one of, Outstanding Young Women Am., 1986; Breckenridge fellow, Ind. U., 1982, Eigenmann fellow, 1982—83, Pew fellow in marine conservation, 2000—04. Mem.: AAAS, Soc. for Conservation Biology, Am. Fisheries Soc. Achievements include research in fisheries management and ocean conservation. Office: Pew Institute for Ocean Science 126 East 56th St Mezzanine New York NY 10022 Business E-Mail: epikitch@miami.edu.

PIKOV, VICTOR, physiologist; m. Olga Bespalova, Dec. 12, 1997. PhD, Georgetown U., Washington, 2000. Postdoc. Calif. Inst. Tech., Pasadena, 2000—02; staff scientist Huntington Med. Rsch. Inst., Calif., 2002—. Dir. summer rsch. program Huntington Med. Rsch. Institutes, 2004—. Grants, NIH, 2002—. Office: Hmri 734 Fairmount Ave Pasadena CA 91105

PIKUZ, SERGEY, physicist, researcher; b. Dnepropetrovsk, USSR, Apr. 8, 1950; s. Aleksandr and Lidia Pikuz; m. Irina Abramova, Mar. 15, 1993; 1 child, Svetlana. BS in Physics, Moscow State U., 1973; PhD in Physics, P.N. Lebedev Phys. Inst., Moscow, 1977. Scientist P.N. Lebedev Phys. Inst., 1973—95, leding staff scientist, 1995—. Vis. scientist Cornell U., Ithaca, NY, 1993—2001, vis. prof., 2002—. Contbr. articles to profl. jours. Achievements include research in laser-produced plasma; fast Z pinches; design of new types of x-ray spectrographs; new sources of x-ray; new laser interferometrs; invention of X pinch; patents for X pinch point-projection radiography; discovery of foam-like structure of exploded wire dense core; mesurements of hot spot parameters in X pinch. Office: Cornell Univ 439 Rhodes Hall Ithaca NY 14853 Office Fax: 607-255-3004. Business E-Mail: jlo4@cornell.edu, sap17@cornell.edu.

PILACHOWSKI, DAVID M., library director; s. Michael Pilachowski and Janice Esther Ripley; m. Marsha Lee Reiter, Aug. 8, 1970; children: Justin A., James M., Evan D. Degree in Polit. Sci. and Asian Area Studies, U. Vt., Burlington, 1971; MLS, U. Ill., Urbana, 1973. Reference libr. U. Vt., Burlington, 1973—81, online search coord., 1977—81; head reference svc. Colgate U., Hamilton, NY, 1981—85, asst. u. libr. for pub. services, 1983—85, acting libr., 1985—86, assoc. libr., 1986—91; dir. libraries Denison U., Granville, Ohio, 1991—98; coll. libr. Williams Coll., Williamstown, Mass. Librs. cons., 1995. Contbr. articles to numerous profl. jours. Mem.: ALA, Boston Library Consortium (bd. dirs.), Phi Beta Kappa. Office: Williams Coll Librs 55 Sawyer Library Dr Williamstown MA 01267 Office Phone: 413-597-2502. Business E-Mail: dpilacho@williams.edu.

PILAFIAN, AUDREY KALENIAN, music educator; b. Chgo., Sept. 19, 1929; d. Hagop and Adrine Kalenian; m. Harry Pilafian, Sept. 10, 1949; children: Martin, Jack David, Robert John, Mary Katherine. Student, Northwestern U., 1947—49; MusB, U. Miami, 1951, MEd in Supervision and Adminstrn., 1972. Cert. supr./adminstr., gifted edn., music edn., elem. edn. tchr. Fla. Elem. sch. tchr. Miami/Dade Pub. Schs., 1962—76, gifted students tchr., 1976—92; adj. supr. Fla. Internat. U., Miami, 1994—. Musician U. Miami Symphony Orch., Coral Gables, Fla., 1953—56; pvt. cello tchr., Miami, 1970—; cellist Chamber Music Prof. Agy., Miami, 1995—. Vol. co-dir. strings ensemble Leewood Elem. Sch., Miami, 1992—2005; state bd. mem. Odyssey of the Mind, Inc., Fla., 1983—98; supt. Sunday Sch. St. Mary Armenian Ch., Hollywood, Fla., 1953—. Recipient Pontifical Blessing Encyclical, His Holiness Karenkin I, Catholicos of all Armenians, 1998; named Dade County Tchr. of Yr., Fla. Fedn. Woman's Clubs, 1968. Mem.: Phi Delta Kappa (tchr.), Sigma Alpha Iota (musician/performer, editor, historian), Alpha Delta Kappa (internat. chmn. Fine Arts Grants Bd. 1991—97, internat. music chmn. 2005). Avocations: cello, chamber music, amateur radio, travel, camping. Home and Studio: 9940 SW 60 St Miami FL 33173

PILAFIAN, CHRISTOPHER, choreographer; s. Suren Pilafian and Grace Elizabeth Jones; Diploma, Juilliard Sch., NYC, 1974. Guest choreographer Dance Colloquium, NYC, 1985—86, Bat Dor Dance Co., Tel Aviv, 1985; guest instr. Cornish Inst., Seattle, 1985, Jean Isaacs' San Diego Dance Theater, 1997—2008; panelist Calif. Arts Coun., Sacramento, 1992; mem. Juilliard Dance Ensemble, NYC, 1972—74, Kathryn Posin Dance Co., NYC, 1972—74, Elizabeth Keene Dance Co., NYC, 1972—74, Rush Dance, NYC, 1973—74, Sara Sugihara & Friends, NYC, 1973—74; guest instr. Princeton U., 1974; founding mem., assoc. artistic dir. Jennifer Muller,The Works, NYC, 1974—89; faculty Dancerschool, NYC, 1979—81; guest artist Diamond Dance Co., NYC, 1980—82; faculty Peridance Ctr., NYC, 1981—88; featured dancer Bounce Nat. Comml., NYC, 1986—88, PBS, Alive,Off Ctr, NYC, 1988; guest choreographer Jennifer Muller, NYC, 1991—2000; continuing lectr. U. Calif., Santa Barbara, 1996—2008; choreographer Boy Culture Llc, LA, 2005—06, Reprise Broadway's Best, LA, 2008; sr. lectr. U. Calif., 2008—. Panelist Calif. Arts Coun., Sacramento, 1992. Choreographer Santa Barbara Dance Theatre, 1990—2009, The Joyce Theater, NYC; costume, sound & scenic designer Sight Unseen; choreographer Points of Departure, Santa Barbara Dance Alliance, numerous orgn. Bd. mem. Santa Barbara Dance Alliance, 1995—2009, adjudicator, 2000—08; adv. SUMMERDANCE, Santa Barbara, 1997—2002. Recipient Choreography award, Interlochen Arts Acad., 1970—71, Media, Visual & Performing Arts award, U. Calif., 2008; Doris Humphrey scholarship, Juilliard Sch., 1972—73, Louis Horst fellowship, 1973—74. Mem.: AFTRA, SAG, UCSB. Office: Dept Theater & Dance Univ Calif Santa Barbara CA 93106 Business E-Mail: pilafian@theaterdance.ucsb.edu.

PILAND, NEILL FINNES, health services economist, researcher, educator; b. Pomona, Calif., Nov. 6, 1943; s. Finnes Elmer and Sylvia Beatrice (Renick) PiL.; m. Diane Lynn Fiedor, Aug. 12, 1977; children: Evan Neill, Spencer Lowell, Arden Geneva. BA, UCLA, 1965, MPH, 1970, PhD, 1979; MA, U. Calif., Davis, 1966. Rsch. assoc. Sch. Pub. Health UCLA, 1971-73, sr. rsch. assoc., 1973; health economist Stanford Rsch. Inst., Menlo Park, Calif., 1973-77, asst. mgr. health svcs. rsch., 1974-77; dir. health ctr. study Jicarilla Apache Tribe, Dulce, N.Mex., 1978-82; dir. health systems evaluation program Lovelace Med. Found., Albuquerque, 1982-83, dir. health svcs. rsch. and edn., 1983-91; dir. Ctr. Health & Population Rsch., Albuquerque, 1991-94, Lovelace Inst. for Health and Population Rsch., Albuquerque, 1994-96; rsch. dir. Ctr. Rsch. Med. Group Mgmt. Assn., Englewood, Colo., 1996—2002; prof. and dir. Inst. Rural Health, Idaho State U., Pocatello, 2002—, rsch. prof., 2005—08, rsch. prof. and dir., 2008—; clin. assoc. prof. U. Colo. Sch. Medicine; rsch. prof. U. Denver; dir. policy and rsch. Colo. Health Inst., Denver, 2004—05; rsch. prof. Inst. Rural Health Idaho State U., 2005—08; sr. rsch. assoc. MGMA Ctr. Rsch, 2002—; dir. Rsch. Proffession Inst. Rural Health, Idaho State U., 2008—. Clin. asst. prof. medicine U. N.Mex., Albuquerque, 1981, clin. assoc. prof., 1994—; vis. prof. U. N.H., Durham, 1989-90; mem. commn. tobacco control, Idaho, 2003-04 Co-author: Strategic Nursing Management: Power and Responsibility in a New Era; mem. editorial bd. Jour. Managerial Issues, 1991—; co-editor: Physician Profiling: A Sourcebook for Adminstrators, Chart Accounts for Healthcare Organizations, Reinventing Medical Practice; contbr. over 100 articles to profl. jours. Mem. rsch. com. N.Mex. HealthNet, 1986-88; chair econ. issues N.Mex. Com. on Pub. Health Impact of Smoking, 1988; bd. dirs. Am. Geriat. and Gerontology, 1984-87, Healthcare for Homeless, 1988-92; mem. exec. coun. N.Mex. ASSIST Com., 1992—, sci. adv. com. N.Mex. ASSIST Project, 1992—; mem. steering com. Group Practice Improvement Network, 1996—; mem. workgroup smoking control Colo. Dept. Health and Environment, 1999-2002; scholarship interviewer NHSC, 2003-04; mem. Idaho State Commn. Tobacco Control, 2004—; bd. dirs. Vets. Med. Rsch. Found., 2002—. Recipient traineeship, USPHS, 1968-70. Mem. APHA, Am. Econ. Assn., Soc. Rsch. Adminstrs., Assn. Health Svcs. Rsch. Avocations: tennis, hockey, hiking, biking. Home: 2 Rice Ave Pocatello ID 83201 Office: Inst Rural Health Idaho State U Graveley Hall 205 Campus Box 8174 Pocatello ID 83209-8174 Office Phone: 208-282-5021. Business E-Mail: pilaneil@isu.edu.

PILANT, CHARLES ALAN, history professor; b. Colorado Springs, Maine, Nov. 16, 1950; s. Norman Arthur and Mona Ilene Pilant; m. Melva Jean Kinney; children: Jedediah Alan, Nathaniel Adam(dec.). PhD, Marquette U., Milw., 1989. Prof. U. Cumberlands, Williamsburg, Ky., 1987—. Petty officer 2nd class USN, 1968—73. Independent. Mem.Christian Church. Avocations: fishing, hunting. Home: 1060 Old Hickory Blvd Williamsburg KY 40769 Office: Univ Cumberlands 7502 College Sta Dr Williamsburg KY 40769 Office Fax: 606-539-4490. Business E-Mail: apilant@ucumberlands.edu.

PILARCZYK, DANIEL EDWARD, archbishop; b. Dayton, Ohio, Aug. 12, 1934; s. Daniel Joseph and Frieda S. (Hilgefort) Pilarczyk. Student, St. Gregory Sem., Cin., 1948—53; PhB, Pontifical Urban U., Rome, 1955, PhL, 1956, STB, 1958, STL, 1960, STD, 1961; MA, Xavier U., 1965; PhD, U. Cin., 1969; LLD (hon.), Xavier U., 1975, Calumet Coll., 1982, U. Dayton, 1990, Marquette U., 1990, Thomas More Coll., 1991, Coll. Mt. St. Joseph, 1994, Hebrew Union Coll., 1997. Ordained priest Archdiocese of Cin., Ohio, 1959, asst. chancellor, 1961—63; synodal judge Archdiocesan Tribunal, 1971—82; faculty Athenaeum of Ohio, St. Gregory Sem., 1963—74; v.p. Athenaeum of Ohio, 1968—74, trustee, 1974—; rector St. Gregory Sem., 1968—74; ordained bishop, 1974; aux. bishop Archdiocese of Cin., 1974—82, vicar gen. Ohio, 1974—82, dir. ednl. services Ohio, 1974—82, archbishop, 1982—. V.p. Nat. Conf. Cath. Bishops, 1986—89, pres., 1989—92, chmn. com. on doctrine, 1996—2000; U.S. rep. Episc. bd. Internat. Commn. on English in Liturgy, 1987—97, chmn., 1991—97; jt. com. Orthodox and Cath. Bishops, 2002. Author: Praepositini Cancellarii de Sacramentis et de Novissimis, 1964—65, Twelve Tough Issues, 1988, We Believe, 1989, Living in the Lord, 1990, The Parish: Where God's People Live, 1991, Forgiveness, 1992, What Must I Do?, 1993, Our Priests: Who They Are and What They Do, 1994, Sacraments, 1994, Bringing Forth Justice, 1996, 1999, Thinking Catholic, 1998, Practicing Catholic, 1999, Believing Catholic, 2000, Live Letters, 2001, Twelve Tough Issues and More, 2002, Being Catholic, 2006, When God Speaks, 2006. Trustee Cath. Health Assn., 1982—85, Cath. U. Am., 1983—91, 1997—2000, Pontifical Coll. Josephinum, 1983—92. Recipient Bishop John England award, 2009; Ohio Classical Conf. scholar, Athens, 1966. Mem.: Am. Philol. Assn. Roman Catholic. Home and Office: 100 E Eighth St Cincinnati OH 45202-2129 Office Phone: 513-421-3131.

PILAT, JANET LOUISE B. OBERHOLTZER, adult education educator; b. Cleve., Apr. 7, 1942; d. Merton Bradley and Shirley Adeline (Jasper) Bartter; m. John Clayton Oberholtzer, June 20, 1965 (div. 1989); children: Julie Lynne Oberholtzer Chatfield, John Jacob, Joy Ellen Oberholtzer Martin; m. Paul Michael Pilat, Jr., May 20, 1995. BS in Edn., Baldwin Wallace Coll., 1964, MEd, 1987. Cert. reading tchr., Ohio. Tchr. Buckeye Schs., Medina, Ohio, 1964-65, East Cleveland (Ohio) Schs., 1965-67; substitute tchr. Medina City Schs., 1983-87; adj. prof. U. Akron, Ohio, 1987-95, Lorain County C.C., 1993-98. Adj. prof. Ashland U. at Grafton (Ohio) Prison, 1994; pvt. tutor and cons., Medina, 1992—. Officer bd. dirs. Girl Scouts U.S.A., Akron, 1968-83; water safety instr. ARC, Medina, 1962-97, trainer, 1976-97, bd. dirs., 1975-83, 91-93; dep. dir. Bd. Elections, 1995—; dir. Medina County Bd. Elections, 2008-. Recipient Western Res. award Girl Scouts U.S.A., 1983, Thanks Badge, 1978, Disting. Svc. award ARC, 1989, Jaycees, 1978. Mem. Internat. Reading Assn., Nat. Assn. Devel. Edn., Delta Kappa Gamma. Democrat. Methodist. Avocations: swimming, reading, sewing, baking. Office: Box 506 Medina OH 44258 Home: 410 Lafayette Rd # 1 Medina OH 44256 E-mail: jbp5644p@aol.com.

PILAT, MICHAEL JOSEPH, engineering educator; b. Longview, Wash., Feb. 19, 1938; s. Joseph Michael and Mary Veronica (Lazor) Pilat. BS in Chem. Engring., U. Wash., 1960, MS in Chem. Engring., 1963, PhD in Civil Engring., 1967. Registered profl. engr., Wash. Engr. Boeing Co., Seattle, 1961—64; mem. faculty U. Wash., Seattle, 1967—71, assoc. prof. civil engring., 1971—78, prof., 1978—. Mem.: AIChE, Tau Beta Pi, Am. Assn. Aerosol Rsch., Air Pollution Control Assn., Am. Inst. Chem. Engrs., Seattle Mountaineers, Sigma Xi. Achievements include patents in field of air pollution control. Home: 7306 57th Ave NE Seattle WA 98115-6231 Office: U Wash Dept Civil Engring Box 35700 Seattle WA 98195-2700

PILATI, STEFANO, apparel designer; b. Milan; Intern Nino Cerruti; menswear asst. Giorgio Armani, 1993—95; fabric and rsch. devel. Prada, 1995—98, asst. designer womenswear/menswear Miu Miu, 1998—2000; design dir. Yves St. Laurent, 2000—04; creative dir. Yves St. Laurent Rive Gauche, 2004—. Named a Maverick, Details mag., 2008. Office: Yves Saint Laurent 3 E 57th St New York NY 10022-2557

PILBEAM, DAVID ROGER, paleoanthropology educator, curator; b. Brighton, Sussex, Eng., Nov. 21, 1940; came to U.S., 1968; s. Ernest Winton and Edith (Clack) P.; m. Maryellen Ruvolo, Dec. 18, 1982; 1 child, Katharine Alexandra. BA, Cambridge U., 1962, MA, 1966; PhD, Yale U., 1967; MA (hon.), Harvard U., 1982. Demonstrator in anthropology Cambridge U., Eng., 1965-68; asst. prof. anthropology Yale U., 1968-70, assoc. prof., 1970-74, prof., 1974-81, prof. anthropology, geology and geophysics, 1974-81, prof. anthropology, 1981-90; dean undergrad. edn. Harvard U., Cambridge, Mass., 1987—92, 1996—97, Henry Ford II prof. social sci., 1990—, sr. advisor to dean Harvard Coll., interim dean Harvard Coll., 2007—08; dir. Peabody Mus., 1990, curator paleoanthropology. Author: Evolution of Man, 1970, Ascent of Man, 1972; co-author: Human Biology, 3d edit., 1988; co-editor: Cambridge Encyclopedia of Human Evolution, 1992. Fellow Am. Anthropol. Assn.; mem. Am. Acad. Arts and Scis., Nat. Acad. Scis. (fgn. assoc.). Office: Harvard U Peabody Mus 11 Divinity Ave Cambridge MA 02138-2019 Office Phone: 617-495-4736. Office Fax: 617-496-8041. E-mail: pilbeam@fas.harvard.edu.

PILCHER, CHRISTIE W., retired special education educator; b. Jackson, Tenn, Dec. 17, 1944; d. Charles Arthur Sr. and Ruby Mazie (Pope) Walker; m. David Wayne Pilcher, Mar. 20, 1966 (div. 1974); children: David Andrew, Clayton Everett. Student, Mercer U., 1962-63; BA, North Ga. Coll., 1966; MEd, Ga. State U., 1976. Tchr. reading US Army Edn. Ctr., Munich, 1967; tchr. K.G. US Dependent Sch., Munich, 1967-68; tchr. Ga. Acad. for the Blind, Macon, 1974-79; tchr. for visually impaired Bibb County Bd. Edn., Macon, 1979-91, spl. edn. K.G., 1991-94; tchr. visually impaired Troup County Bd. Edn., LaGrange, Ga., 1994—2000, Bartow County Sch. Sys., Cartersville, Ga., 2000—01; tchr. spl. needs kindergarten Bibb County Bd. Edn., Macon, 2001—02, 2004—05, tchr. mildly intellectually disabled, 2004—05; ret., 2005. Parent advisor Ga. Parent Infant Network for Ednl. Svc., Clarkston, 1985—2004; tchr. summer program Ga. Bapt. Children's Home, Baxley, 1991. Vol. Ga. Radio Reading Svc., 2003—; mem. choir Mt. Zion Bapt. Ch., 2004—, Sunday sch. tchr., 2004—. Avocations: painting, reading, baking, travel, gardening. Home: 939 Clairmont Pl Macon GA 31204-1099 Personal E-mail: christiep@bellsouth.net.

PILCHER, JAMES BROWNIE, lawyer; b. Shreveport, La., May 19, 1929; s. James Reece and Martha Mae (Brown) P.; m. Lorene Pilcher; children: Lydia, Martha, Bradley. BA, La. State U., 1952; JD summa cum laude, John Marshall Law Sch., 1955; postgrad., Emory U., 1957. Bar: Ga. 1955. Legal aide to Spkr. of Ho. of Reps., Ga., 1961-64; assoc. city atty. City of Atlanta, 1964-69; pvt. practice law Atlanta, 1969—. Exec. com. Dem. Exec. Com. of Fulton County, Ga., 1974-86; bd. dirs. Whitehead Boys Club, 1961-89; trustee Ga. Inst. Continuing Legal Edn., 1988-89; pres. Atlanta Jaycees, 1961-62. Fellow, Lawyers Found. Ga., 1996—. Mem. ABA, Ga. Assn. Criminal Def. Lawyers (pres. 1980-82), State Bar Ga. (chmn. 1988-89, gen. practice and trial sect., chmn. criminal law sect. 1986-87), Atlanta Bar Assn., Ga. Trial Lawyers Assn. (life), Ga. Claimants Attys. Assn. (pres. 1983-84), Nat. Assn. Criminal Def. Lawyers (bd. dirs. 1980-85), Ga. Inst. Trial Advocacy (bd. dirs. 1986-89), South Fulton Bar Assn. (pres. 1987-88), Trial Lawyers for Pub. Justice (life), Atlanta Consumer Bankruptcy Attys. Group (life, pres. 2001-03), Kiwanis (Peachtree, Atlanta pres. 1983-84, gov. Ga. dist. 1992-93), Sierra Club Am. (life), Barristers Club of Emory U. Law Sch. Presbyterian. Home and Office: 1195 W Wesley Rd NW Atlanta GA 30327-1407 Office Phone: 404-352-3440. Personal E-mail: pilcherlaw@netzero.net, pilchers@comcast.com, pilcherlaw@comcast.com.

PILCHER, JAMES ERIC, physicist; b. Toronto, Ont., Can., Apr. 23, 1942; came to US 1965; s. Francis Eric and Isabel (Brand) P.; m. Carla Grosso, Aug. 31, 1970; children: Marc R., Daniel E., Erica M. BASc, U. Toronto, 1964, MSc, 1966; PhD, Princeton U., 1968. Rsch. assc. Princeton U., Princeton, NJ, 1968-69; vis. scientist CERN, Geneva, 1969-70, sci. assoc., 1979—80; asst. prof. Harvard U., Cambridge, Mass., 1970-72; asst./assoc. prof. U. Chgo., 1972-79, prof., 1979—, dir. Enrico Fermi Inst., 2001—. Member Physics Adv. Com., SSC, Dallas, 1990-. Author numerous articles to profl. jours. Fellow Alfred P. Sloan Found., 1972—76. Fellow Am. Phys. Soc. Achievements include discovery that there are exactly 3 families of light neutrinos. Office: University of Chicago EFI Box 47 5640 S Ellis Ave Chicago IL 60637 Office Phone: 773-702-7443. Office Fax: 773-702-1914. E-mail: j-pilcher@uchicago.edu.

PILDES, RICHARD H., law educator; AB, Princeton U., 1980; JD, Harvard Law Sch., 1983. Bar: Mass. 1987. Law clk. to Judge Abner Mikva US Ct. Appeals DC Cir., 1983—84; law clk. to Justice Thurgood Marshall US Supreme Ct., 1984—85; assoc. Foley, Hoag & Eliot, Boston, 1986—87; asst. prof. U. Mich. Law Sch., 1988—93, prof., 1993—2000, NYU Sch. Law, 2000—03, An-Bryce prof. law, 2003—04, Sudler Family prof. constl. law, 2004—; co-dir. NYU Ctr. Law and Security, 2003—. Vis. prof. U. Chgo. Law Sch., 1997, NYU Sch. Law, 1999—2000, Harvard Law Sch., 2004; sr. fellow Program in Ethics & the Professors Harvard U., 1998—99. Author (with others): The Law of Democracy: Legal Structure of the Political Process, 2001; co-editor: The Future of the Voting Rights Act, 2006. Carnegie scholar, 2004. Fellow: Am. Acad. Arts and Sciences. Office: NYU Sch Law Vanderbilt Hall Rm 507 40 Washington Sq S New York NY 10012-1099 Office Phone: 212-998-6377. E-mail: rick.pildes@nyu.edu.

PILEGGI, ANNAMARIA, theater director, educator; b. Kans. City, Mo., Mar. 23, 1961; d. Felix Anthony and Theresia Claire Pileggi; life ptnr. Opal Andrews. MFA, Brandeis U., Waltham, Mass., 1988. Vis. asst. prof. St. Lawrence U., Canton, NY, 1990—91; sr. lectr. Wash. U., St. Louis, 1991—. Dir.(co-producer): (hotcity theatre). Recipient Excellence in Tchg. award, Wash. U., Coll. Arts and Scis., 1994, 1999, 2001. Office: Wash Univ St Louis One Brookings Dr Saint Louis MO 63130 Office Fax: 314-935-4955. Business E-Mail: apileggi@wustl.edu.

PILEGGI, DOMINIC F., state legislator; b. Chester, Pa., Dec. 15, 1957; s. Francis and Mary Pileggi; m. Diana Pileggi; children: Elisa, Gabrielle, Michael. BA in Economics, St. Joseph's U., 1979; JD, Villanova Sch. Law, 1982. Atty. Pileggi & Pileggi, 1982—; councilman City of Chester, 1994—98, mayor, 1998—2002; mem. Dist. 9 Pa. State Senate, 2002—, majority leader, 2007—, fl. leader. Dir. Chester-Upland Sch. Dist.; city councilman, dir. pub. safety, 1994—98; ptnr. Law Firm of Pileggi & Pileggi. Bd. dirs. J. Lewis Crozer Libr., 1989—; mem. Chester Salvation Army Bd. of Advisors; mem., chmn. of exec. com. Rep. Party; bd. dirs. Del. County Indsl. Devel. Corp. Recipient T.M. Thomas Achievement award, 2001, Rev. Jesse F. Anderson award, 2002. Mem.: Rotary Club of Chester (past pres., Rotarian of Yr. 1995). Republican. Roman Catholic. Office: 350 Capitol Bldg Senate Box 203009 Harrisburg PA 17120-3009 Mailing: 100 Evergreen Dr Ste 113 Glen Mills PA 19342 Office: 100 Granite Dr Ste 105 Media PA 19063 Office Phone: 717-787-4712, 610-358-5183, 610-565-9100. Office Fax: 717-783-7490, 610-358-5184, 610-566-2010. Business E-Mail: dpileggi@pasen.gov.*

PILEGGI, DOMINIC J., electronics executive; BA, Rutgers U. Sales & mgmt. positions Thomas & Betts, Memphis, 1979—88, pres. electronics, 1988—94, pres. elec. products group, 1994—95; sr. exec. positions with Casco Plastic, Inc., Jordan Telecommunications, 1995—98; pres. EMS div. Viasystems Inc., 1998—2000; sr. v.p. Thomas & Betts, Memphis, 2000—02, group pres. electrical, 2000—03, pres., COO, 2003—04, pres., CEO, 2004—05, chmn., CEO, 2006—. Office: Thomas & Betts 8155 T&B Blvd Memphis TN 38125 Office Phone: 901-252-8000.

PILEGGI, JENNIFER WENDY, lawyer, transportation services executive; b. NYC, July 27, 1964; d. Jerome E. Rosenfeld. BA in Art History, cum laude, Yale U., 1986; JD, NYU, 1990. Bar: Calif. 1990. Assoc. Heller, Ehrman, White & McAuliffe, San Francisco, Marron, Reid & Sheehy, San Francisco; joined CNF Inc., Palo Alto, Calif., 1996; corp. counsel Menlo Worldwide Logistics subs., Redwood City, Calif., 1996—99, v.p., corp. counsel, 1999—2003, Menlo Worldwide subs., Redwood City, Calif., 2003—04; sr. v.p., gen. counsel, corp. sec. Con-Way Inc., 2004—09, exec. v.p., gen. counsel, sec., 2009—. Mem.: ABA, Calif. State Bar Assn. Office: CNF Inc 2855 Campus Dr Ste 300 San Mateo CA 94403 Office Phone: 650-378-5200. Office Fax: 650-357-9160.*

PILEWSKI, JOSEPH MARK, medical and cell biology educator; b. Erie, Pa., June 10, 1961; s. Robert M. and Angeline R. (Rizzo) P.; m. Anne M. Maxwell; children: Katherine E., Christine M., Matthew J., Claire A. BA, Holy Cross Coll., Worcester, Mass., 1983; MD, U. Rochester, 1987. Diplomate Am. Bd. Internal Medicine, Am. Bd. Pulmonary Disease, Am. Bd. Critical Care Medicine. Intern in internal medicine U. of Pa., 1987-88; resident in internal medicine U. Pa., Phila., 1988—90, pulmonary and critical care fellow, 1990-94; asst. prof. medicine U. Pitts., 1994—2004, asst. prof. cell biology, 1994—2004, assoc. prof. medicine, pediatrics, cell biology and physiology, 2004—. Harry Schwachman Clin. Investigator award Cystic Fibrosis Found., 1995. Mem. ACP, AAAS, Am. Thoracic Soc., Alpha Omega Alpha. Office: U Pitts NW 628 MUH 3459 Fifth Ave Pittsburgh PA 15213-2500 Office Phone: 412-692-2210.

PILGERAM, LAURENCE OSCAR, biochemist; b. Great Falls, Mont., June 23, 1924; s. John Rudolph and Bertha Roslyn (Phillips) P.; m. Cynthia Ann Moore, Apr. 16, 1971; children: Karl Erich, Kurt John. AA, U. Calif., Berkeley, 1948, BA, 1949, PhD, 1953. Instr. dept. physiology U. Ill. Profl. Coll., Chgo., 1954-55; asst. prof. dept. biochemistry Stanford (Calif.) U. Sch. Medicine, 1955-57; dir. arteriosclerosis rsch. lab. U. Minn. Sch. Medicine, Mpls., 1957-65, Santa Barbara, Calif., 1965-71; dir. coagulation lab., assoc. dir. Cerebrovascular Rsch. Ctr., Baylor Coll. Medicine, Tex. Med. Ctr., Houston, 1971-75; dir. Thrombosis Control Labs., Palo Alto, Calif., 1975-79, Santa Barbara, 1979—; prof. dept. molecular biology U. Calif., Santa Barbara, 2004—. Cons. NIH, Bio-Sci. Labs., FDA; del. Coun. on Thrombosis and Coun. on Strokes, Am. Heart Assn. Assembly. Co-editor: Nutrition and Thrombosis for the Nat. Dairy Coun., 1973; contbr. sci. articles to profl. jours. Recipient CIBA award, London, 1958, Karl Thomae award, Germany, 1973; NIH grantee, 1954-75; Life Ins. Med. Rsch. Fund fellow, 1952-54. Mem. Am. Soc. for Biochemistry and Molecular Biology. Office: PO Box 1583 Goleta PO Santa Barbara CA 93116 Office Phone: 805-967-5994.

PILGRAM, SUZANNE, artist, educator; b. Montclair, NJ, Feb. 25, 1945; d. Hans J. and Florence Ketchum Pilgram; m. Hassan Ghavam, Sept. 3, 1973. BA in Art, Am. U., 1967, MFA in Painting, 1970. Artist, clk. US Com. for UNICEF Children's Culture Ctr., 1970—73; prof. Coll. Translation, Tehran, Iran, 1973—80, Farah Pahlavi U., Tehran, 1977—78, Trenton State Coll., NJ, 1983; assoc. prof. Georgian Court U., Lakewood, NJ, 1981—. Printmaking coun. NJ Exhibit Intolerance, 2006—; lectr., presenter in field. One-woman shows include Phoenix Gallery, NYC, 2007, exhibitions include Columbia U., 2001, Trenton Artists Workshop Assn., 2006—09, Phoenix Gallery, NYC, 2004—08. Grantee Fullbright-Hays Group Projects Abroad, U.S. State Dept., Jamaica, 1983, Faculty Rsch. grant, Georgian Ct. U., 2004; Art fellowship, Womens Studio Workshop, 2007. Mem.: Nat. Assn. Art Educators Higher Edn., Trenton Artists Workshop, N.J. Exhbn. (Grant 1987—). Avocation: gardening. Home: 9 Robin Rd Howell NJ 07731 Office: Georgian Ct Univ 900 Lakewood Ave Lakewood NJ 08701 Office Phone: 732-987-2330. Business E-Mail: pilgrams@georgian.edu.

PILGRIM, LONNIE (BO PILGRIM), food products executive; b. May 8, 1928; married. Ptnr. Pilgrim's Pride Corp., Pittsburg, Tex., 1953-68, CEO, 1968—98, chmn., CEO, 1998—2004, chmn., 2004—. Chmn. First State Bank Pitts. Served with U.S. Armed Forces, 1951-53. Office: Pilgrim's Pride Corp 4845 US Hwy 271 N Pittsburg TX 75686 Mailing: Pilgrim's Pride Corp PO Box 93 Pittsburg TX 75686-0093

PILISUK, MARC, psychology educator; b. NYC, Jan. 19, 1934; s. Louis and Charlotte (Feferholtz) P.; m. Phyllis E. Kamen, June 16, 1956; children: Tammy, Jeff. BA, Queens Coll., 1955; MA, U. Mich., 1956, PhD, 1961. Asst. prof., assoc. rsch. psychologist U. Mich., Ann Arbor, 1961-65, founder teach-in, 1965; assoc. prof. Purdue U., West Lafayette, Ind., 1965-67; prof.-in-residence U. Calif., Berkeley, 1967-77, prof. cmty. psychology Davis, 1977—. Vis. prof. U. Calif., Wright Inst., 1991—93; cons. Ctr. for Self Help Rsch., Berkeley, Calif., 1991—93; prof. psychology Saybrook Grad. Sch. & Rsch. Ctr., San Francisco, 1993—. Author: (textbooks) International Conflict and Social Policy, 1972, The Healing Web: Social Networks and Human Survival, 1986, Who Benefits from Global Violence and War: Uncovering a Destructive System, 2008; editor: The Triple Revolution, 1969, Poor Americans, 1970, Triple Revolution Emerging, 1972, How We Lost the War on Poverty, 1973. Grantee, NSF, 1962—66;, NIMH fellow, 1959—60, tng. grantee, Nat. Inst. Alcoholism and Drug Abuse, 1973—77. Fellow: APA (pres. divsn. peace psychology 1996—97, cadre experts on violence, Presdl. award 2005, Lifetime Contbn. award 2005), Am. Orthopsychiat. Assn., Soc. for Psychol. Study Social Issues (coun., Sage award 2004—05); mem.: ACLU, APHA, Faculty for Human Rights in C.Am., Psychologists for Social Responsibility (adv. bd. mem., Disting. Svc. award 2001, Anthony Marsalla Peace and Justice award 2006), Am. Soc. on Aging, Soc. for Cmty. Rsch. and Action. Home Phone: 510-526-1788; Office Phone: 510-526-0876. Business E-Mail: mpilisuk@saybrook.edu.

PILLA, ANTHONY MICHAEL, bishop emeritus; b. Cleve., Nov. 12, 1932; s. George and Libera (Nista) P. Student, St. Gregory Coll. Sem., 1952—53, Borromeo Coll. Sem., 1955, St. Mary Sem., 1943, student, 1956—59; BA in Philosophy, John Carroll U., Cleve., 1961, MA in History, 1967. Ordained priest Diocese of Cleve., 1959; assoc. St. Bartholomew Parish, Middleburg Heights, Ohio, 1959—60; prof. Borromeo Sem., Wickliffe, Ohio, 1960—72, rector-pres., 1972—75; mem. Diocese Cleve. Liturgical Commn., 1964—69, asst. dir., 1969—72; sec. for svcs. to clergy and religious pers. Diocese of Cleve., 1975—79, aux. bishop, vicar Eastern region, 1979—80, apostolic adminstr., 1980—2006, bishop, 1981—2006, bishop emeritus, 2006—; ordained bishop, 1979. Trustee Borromeo Sem., 1975—79, Cath. U., 1981—84; trustee, mem. bd. overseers St. Mary Sem., 1975—79; mem. adv. bd. permanent diaconate program Diocese of Cleve., 1975—79, hospitalization and ins. bd., 1979. Bd. dirs. NCCJ, 1986—. Mem.: Greater Cleve. Roundtable (trustee 1981—), Cath. Conf. Ohio, Nat. Conf. Cath. Bishops (pres. 1995—98), U.S. Cath. Conf., Nat. Cath. Edn. Assn. (dir. 1972—75). Roman Catholic. Home and Office: Chancery Office Diocese of Cleveland 1027 Superior Ave E Ste 300 Cleveland OH 44114-2503

PILLA, VENKATA, systems analyst; married. PhD, U. Tex., Arlington, 2006. Ops. rsch. sr. analyst Am. Airlines, Ft. Worth, 2006—; supplemental instrn. leader U. Tex. Contbr. scientific papers. Vol. Tarrant Area Food Bank, Ft. Worth, 2006—08. Mem.: INFORMS.

PILLAERT, E(DNA) ELIZABETH, museum director; b. Baytown, Tex., Nov. 19, 1931; d. Albert Jacob and Nettie Roseline (Kelley) P. BA, U. St. Thomas, 1953; MA, U. Okla., 1963; postgrad., U. Wis., 1962-67, 70-73. Asst. curator archaeology Stovall Mus., Norman, Okla., 1959-60, ednl. liaison officer, 1960-62; research asst. U. Okla., Norman, Okla., 1962, U. Wis., Madison, 1962-65, cons. archaeol. faunal analysis, 1965—; curator osteology Zool. Mus., Madison, 1965—, chief curator, 1967-92, assoc. dir., 1992—2007, disting. rschr., 2000—, dir., 2007—. Bd. dirs. Lysistrata Feminist Coop., Madison, 1977-81, Univ. YMCA, Madison, 1974-77 Mem. Wis. Archaeol. Soc., Okla. Anthrop. Soc., Am. Assn. Mus., NOW, Stoughton Hist. Soc., Am. Ornithological Union, Friends of Stoughton Libr., Friends of Stoughton Auditorium. Home: 216 N Prairie St Stoughton WI 53589-1647 Office: U Wis Zool Mus 434 Noland Bldg 250 N Mills St Madison WI 53706-1708 Office Phone: 608-262-3766. Business E-Mail: pillaert@facstaff.wisc.edu.

PILLAI, HARI, electronics executive; BS in Mgmt., U. Dublin; MS in Bus., Nat. Univ. Ireland. Various op., product devel. and gen. mgmt. roles Solectron Corp.; staff networks & comm. divsn. Digital Equipment Corp.; v.p. assembly ops. Sanmina-SCI Corp., 1994, various mfg. mgmt. positions, then pres., gen. mgr. EMS divsn., 2002—04, pres. global EMS ops., 2004—08, pres., COO, 2008—. Office: Sanmina SCI Corp 2700 N First St San Jose CA 95134 Office Phone: 408-964-3555. Office Fax: 408-964-3636.*

PILLALAMARRI, SESHASAYI, computer scientist and engineer, researcher; b. Masulipatam, India, Mar. 4, 1946; s. Ramadas and Umabala Pillalamarri; m. Indira Dantu, Feb. 5, 1977; children: Sandhya, Sirisha, Vamsee. BS, Osmania U., 1964; B in engring., Indian Inst. Sci., 1967; M in tech., Indian Inst. Tech., 1969; MS, SUNY Stonybrook, 1972; PhD, U. Linz, 2000. Sci. officer Indian Inst. Tech., Madras, 1974—76, asst. mgr., 1976—87, mgr., computer ctr., 1987—96; rsch. scientist Siemens AG, Munich, Bavaria, 1992—93, ICSI, U. Calif., Berkeley, 1993—94, Ariz. State U., Phoenix, 1996—2002; software engr. Computer Info. Tech. Corp., 1996—2002, City of Phoenix, 2002—. Cons. Indian Inst. of Tech., Madras, Tamil nadu, India, 1976—96. Contbr. chapters to books, 2000. Mem.: Assn. for Computing Machinery (assoc.), IEEE (assoc.). Independent. Achievements include invention of the impact of source traffic distribution on quality of service (QOS) in ATM networks; stability of RYNSORD, a decentralized algorithm for railway networks; fundamental attributes of high speed networks. Avocations: music, poetry. Home: 3524 W Buckhorn Tr Phoenix AZ 85083 Office: City of Phoenix 300 W Washington St Phoenix AZ 85003 Business E-Mail: sesh.pilla@phoenix.gov.

PILLARISETTI, ANAND, mechanical engineer; b. Berhampur, Orissa, India, Mar. 12, 1980; s. Ranga Rao and Rajeshwary Pillarisetti. BTech, Nat. Inst. Tech., Warangal, India, 2002; MS, Drexel U., Phila., 2006; PhD, U. Md., Coll. Pk., 2008. Grad. tchg. asst. Drexel U., 2003—04, grad. rsch. fellow, 2003—06, mech. engr. grad. students assn., 2004—05, pub. rels. officer Indian grad. students assn., 2004—05, treas. engr. grad. students assn., 2005—06; grad. rsch. asst. U. Md., 2007—08; postdoc. rschr. U. Pa., Phila., 2009—. Contbr. articles to profl. jours. Home: 108 Levering St C3 Philadelphia PA 19127 Office: Dept Mech Engring Room 216 Towne Bldg 220S 33rd St Philadelphia PA 19104 Personal E-mail: anand.setti@gmail.com.

PILLAY, GAUTAM, chemical engineer, chemist, academic administrator; b. Buffalo, Jan. 28, 1967; s. Sivasankara K. K. and Revathi (Krishnamurthy) Pillay; m. Amy Matthews, 2004. BS, N.Mex. State U., Las Cruces, 1988; PhD, Tex. A&M U., 1993. Grad. rschr., staff mem. Los Alamos Nat. Lab., 1984-87, mem. tech. staff, 1997—2001; grad. rschr. Tex. A&M U., College Station, 1988-92; rsch. engr. Pacific N.W. Lab., Richland, Wash., 1992-95, sr. rsch. engr., 1995-97; adj. faculty Wash. State U., Richland, 1993-97; exec. dir. Inland N.W. Rsch. Alliance, Idaho Falls, Idaho, 2001—04; v.p. rsch. S.D. Sch. Mines and Tech., Rapid City, 2004—08; assoc. provost rsch. Rowan U., 2008—. Contbr. articles to profl. jours. Recipient Fed. Lab. Consortium award for excellence in tech. transfer, 1997; NSF Grad. Rsch. fellow, 1988—91. Mem.: AIChE (symposium chair), N.Y. Acad. Scis., Am. Nuc. Soc., Am. Chem. Soc., Electrochemical Soc. (symposium chair 1993—, mem. exec. com. 1994—, pres. Pacific N.W. sect. 1996—97, v.p. IE & EE divsn. 2002—04, pres. 2004—06), Phi Kappa Phi, Alpha Chi, Omega Chi Epsilon, Tau Beta Pi. Avocations: general aviation, musician. Office: Rowan Univ 201 Mullica Hill Rd Glassboro NJ 08028 Office Phone: 856-256-5150. Business E-Mail: pillay@rowan.edu.

PILLAY, SRINIVASAN, psychology professor, consultant; s. Savabathy and Raz Pillay; m. Umadevi Naidoo, Dec. 14, 1993. Degree in Psychiatry, Harvard Med. Sch., Boston, 1999; MD, U. Natal, 1990. Cert. psychiatrist ABPN, 2000; master coach Behavioral Coaching Inst., 2007. Cons., brain imaging U. Utah; brain imaging rschr. McLean Hosp., Belmont, Mass., 1995—2008; instr. psychiatry Harvard Med. Sch., 2001—06, asst. prof. psychiatry, 2006—08, asst. clin. prof. psychiatry, 2007—; faculty Behavioral Coaching Inst., NY, 2009. Dir. anxiety disorders outpatient program McLean Hosp.,Harvard Med. Sch.; cons. Neuro Business Group, Cambridge, Mass., 2008—. Contbr. scientific papers to profl. jours. Recipient New Investigator award, NIMH, 1994, Outstanding Resident award, 1997, award, Am. Assn. Geriatric Psychiatrists, 1997, Kaplen award, Harvard Med. Sch., 1999, Young Investigator award, NARSAD, 2002, Travel award, ADAA, ACNP, 2005; named Psychiatry Resident of Yr., Janssen, APA, 1999; Laughlin fellowship, Am. Coll Psychiatry, 1998, fellowship, Soc. Biol. Psychiatry, Lily, 1998, Am. Psychoanalytic Assn., 1998. Mem.: Am. Psychiat. Assn., Mass. Med. Soc. Achievements include research in structural brain imaging in depression and also on brain changes in anxiety disorder. Office: Neuro Business Group 119 Mount Auburn St Cambridge MA 02138 Business E-Mail: boundariless@mac.com.

PILLER, CHARLES LEON, journalist; b. Chgo., Jan. 9, 1955; s. Jack H. and Alice (Shakow) P.; m. Surry Piller Bunnell, Aug. 21, 1984; 1 child, Nathan Bunnell Piller. BA, Lone Mountain Coll., 1977. Editor, writer U. Calif., San Francisco, 1982-89; sr. editor Macworld mag., San Francisco, 1990-96; exec. editor PC World Mag., San Francisco, 1996—97; tech. writer L.A. Times, 1996—2002, science writer, computer tech. and biology, 2002—06, bus. & tech. reporter, 2006—. Chair Ctr. Pub. Integrity, Washington, 1988—, also bd. dirs.; cons. US Senate, Washington, 1989-92. Author: Gene Wars, 1988, The Fail-Safe Society, 1991; contbr. numerous articles to newspapers and mags. Recipient of the John Swett Journalism award, 1993, Benjamin Fine Journalism award, 1995, Runner-Up Lincoln Steffens Journalism award, 1994, Am. Soc. of Business Press Editors (various awards). Office: LA Times 202 W First St Los Angeles CA 90012 Office Fax: 213-237-4712. Business E-Mail: charles.piller@latimes.com.

PILLIOD, JAMES P., state legislator; b. NYC, Aug. 9, 1930; s. James J. and Mary Alice (Phillips) Pillod; m. Judith Bean; children: Charly, David, Jay, Linda, Mary, Sharon, Susan. BA, Yale U., 1952; MD, Duke U., 1960. Diplomate American Bd. Pediatrics. Staff physician Midland Mich. Gen. Hosp. and U. Hosp., 1960—64, Lake Regional Gen. Hosp., 1964; physician pvt. practice, 1964—96; mem. Belknap, Dist. 05 NH House of Reps., Concord, 1996—. Lt. (j.g.) USN. Diplomate Acad. of Pediatrics; mem. AMA (past del.), NH Med. Soc. (past pres.), NH Hosp. Assn. (Physician Staff Mem. of Yr. 1988), NH Pediat. Soc. (Pub. Servant of Yr. 1997). Republican. Home: 504 Province Rd Belmont NH 03220-3723 Office: State House 107 N Main St Concord NH 03301 Office Phone: 603-271-2548. Home Fax: 603-528-1935. E-mail: jimp3047@metrocast.net.

PILLSBURY, GEORGE STURGIS, retired investment advisor; b. Crystal Bay, Minn., July 17, 1921; s. John S. and Eleanor (Lawler) P.; m. Sally Whitney, Jan. 4, 1947; children: Charles Alfred, George Sturgis, Sarah Kimball, Katharine Whitney. BA, Yale U., 1943. Mem. Lafayette Club, Woodhill Club, Minnetonka Yacht Club, Mpls. Club, River Club (NYC). Home: 1300 Bracketts Point Rd Wayzata MN 55391-9393 Office: 601 Carlson Pkwy Ste 800 Minnetonka MN 55305 Home Phone: 952-473-9634; Office Phone: 952-405-7945. Personal E-mail: gspbury@aol.com.

PILLSBURY, HAROLD CROCKETT, III, otolaryngologist; b. Balt., Dec. 5, 1947; m. Carol Higgins Pillsbury; children: Matthew, Benjamin, Thomas. BA, George Washington U., Washington, 1970, MD, 1972. Diplomate Nat. Bd. Med. Examiners, Am. Bd. Otolaryngology; lic. Conn., N.C. Resident gen. surgery U. N.C., Chapel Hill, 1972-73, resident otolaryngology, 1973-76; fellow Kantonsspital, Zurich, Switzerland, 1977; asst. prof. otolaryngology Yale U., New Haven, Conn., 1977-81, assoc. prof. otolayngology, 1981-82; assoc. prof. surgery, otolayngology, head and neck surgery U. N.C. Sch. Medicine, Chapel Hill, 1982-86, prof. surgery, otolaryngology, head and neck surgery, 1986—, Thomas J. Dark Disting. Prof., 1991—. Civilian cons. USAF Surgeon Gen. for Otolaryngology-Head and Neck Surgery, 1993; hon. guest lectr. Alpha Omega Alpha Induction Ceremonies, U. N.C., Chapel Hill, 1990, 91, Sch. of Medicine Commencement Ceremony, U. N.C., 1990., Whitehead lectr. Whitehead Med. Soc., U. N.C., 1994. Countbr. numerous articles to profl. jours. Recipient John A Kirchner Tchg. award, 1980, Disting. Alumni Achievement award George Washington U., 2006. Mem. Am. Acad. Otolarygology-Head and Neck Surgery (past pres. 1998-99, Honor award 1985, Disting. Svc. award 1994, Harris Mosher award 1986), Am. Bd. Otolaryngology (pres. 2004-06), Am. Laryngol., Rhinol. and Otol. Soc. (pres. 2007), Am. Laryngol. Assn. (past pres. 2000-01), Soc. Univ. Otolaryngologists (past pres. 1997-98), Alpha Omega Alpha, Triological Soc. (pres. 2008). Office: Univ NC Dept Otolaryngology Head & Neck Surgery G125 Physicians Office Bldg 170 Manning Dr Chapel Hill NC 27599-7070 Office Phone: 919-966-3342.*

PILNICK, GARY H., food products executive, lawyer; b. Forest Hills, NY, Sept. 17, 1964; m. Helen Pilnick. Grad., Lafayette Coll., 1986; law degree with honors, Duke U., 1989. Atty. Jenner and Block, Chgo., 1989—95; v.p., chief corp. counsel Specialty Foods Corp., 1995—97; chief counsel corp. devel. and fin. Sara Lee Corp., 1997—99; v.p., chief counsel Sara Lee Branded Apparel, 1999—2000; v.p., dep. gen. counsel, asst. sec. Kellogg Co., 2000—03, sr. v.p., gen. counsel corp. devel., sec., 2003—. Office: Kellogg Co Box 3599 1 Kellogg Sq Battle Creek MI 49016-3599 E-mail: gary.pilnick@kellogg.com.

PILSON, MICHAEL EDWARD QUINTON, oceanography educator; b. Ottawa, Ont., Can., Oct. 25, 1933; came to U.S., 1958; s. Edward Charles and Frances Amelia (Ferguson) P.; m. Joan Elaine Johnstone, July 6, 1957; children: Diana Jane, John Edward Quinton. BSc, Bishops U., Lennoxville, Que., Can.; MSc, McGill U., Montreal, Que., Can., 1958; PhD, U. Calif., San Diego, 1964. Chemist Windsor Mills (Can.) Paper Co., 1954-55; asst. chemist Macdonald Coll. of McGill U., 1955-58; biologist Zool. Soc. San Diego, 1963-66; asst. prof. U. R.I., Narragansett, 1966-71, assoc. prof., 1971-78, prof., 1978-2000, prof. emeritus, 2000—. Dir. Marine Ecosystems Rsch. Lab., Narragansett, 1976-97. Contbr. articles to profl. and popular jours.; author chpts. for 11 books, 1 textbook. Grantee NSF, NOAA, EPA, NIH. Mem. AAAS, AGU, ASLO, Oceanography Soc., Am. Soc. Mammalogists, Saunderstown Yacht Club (bd. govs. 1974-87, commodore 1985-87), Brome Cougar Spotters (pres. emeritus). Home: PO Box 27 Saunderstown RI 02874-0027 Office: U RI Grad Sch Oceanography Narragansett RI 02882

PILTNER, REINHARD, engineering educator; b. Bochum, Germany; s. Richard and Irmgard Piltner. Dr.Ing., Ruhr U., Bochum, 1982. Asst. prof. dept. engring. mechanics U. Nebr., Lincoln, 1996—. Office: Georgia Southern University Dept Math Sci Statesboro GA 30460-8093

PILTZ-SEYMOUR, JODY ROBIN, ophthalmologist; b. NYC, Nov. 12, 1959; d. Theodore and Harriet Piltz; m. Barry Seymour, Sept. 11, 1983; children: Sofie, Emma. BS, Tufts U., 1980; MD, Albert Einstein Coll. Medicine, NYC, 1984. Diplomate; lic. physician, Pa. Asst. prof. U. Pa. Health Sys./Scheie Eye Inst., Phila., 1990—; dir. glaucoma svc. Scheie Eye Inst., Phila., 1990—. Grantee Nat. Eye Inst., NIH, 1993—, 95—, 97—, William Penn Found., Phila., 1996-97. Fellow Am. Acad. Ophthalmology (com. mem. 1990—), Phila. Acad. Medicine; mem. Am. Glaucoma Soc., Internat. Perimetric Soc., Assn. Rsch. in Vision and Ophthalmology, Pa. Med. Soc. Avocations: family time, skiing, cooking, travel. Office: Scheie Eye Inst U Pa 51 N 39th St Philadelphia PA 19104-2689

PILZ, ALFRED NORMAN, manufacturing executive; b. Evergreen Park, Ill., Oct. 12, 1931; s. Alfred and Erma Louise (Deane) P.; m. Constance Ney, Nov. 1957; children: Kerry, Kurt, Stephen, Matthew. BS, Ill. Inst. Tech., 1953; MBA, Harvard U., 1960. Registered profl. engr., Mass. Indsl. engr. Harnischfeger Corp., Milw., 1956-58; cons. Arthur D. Little Co., Cambridge, Mass., 1959-60; asst. to exec. v.p., mgr. prodn. engring. Nat. Forge Co., Irvine, Pa., 1960-62; mgmt. cons. McKinsey & Co., NYC and Cleve., 1962-67; pres., gen. mgr. Ajax Iron Works Divsn., Corry, Pa., 1967-72; pres., chief exec. officer WDP, Inc., 1972-79, Swank Refractories Co., Johnstown, Pa., 1972-77, Hyde Park (Pa.) Foundry & Machine Co., 1974-79, Shepard-Niles Corp., Montour Falls, NY, 1979-82, Acco Babcock Materials Handling, Frederick, Md., 1982-85; ptnr. Fagan and Co., Ligonier, Pa. Bd. dirs. Acco Babcock, Inc., Babcock Internat., Chemung Foundry, Parnell Precision Products Co., Carre-Orban and Partners, Liberty Mut. Ins. Co., Ind. Steel and Engring. Corp., Bedford Crane Co., Shepard Niles Corp., Marine Bank, WDP, Inc., Ligonier Valley (Pa.) R.R. Soc.; chmn. Parnell Precision Products, 1980-82, Ind. Steeland Engring., Bedford Crane Co., 1981-82, pres., chmn., CEO, Greenway Products. With USN, 1948—56, Korea. Mem.: Ligonier Railroad Assn. (bd. dirs.), Ligonier Railroad Hist. Soc., Petroleum Equipment Supplies Assn., Modern Railroad Industry Assn., Conveyor Equipment Mfg. Assn., Hoist Mfrs. Assn., Crane Mfrs. Assn., Ligonier Railroad Hist. Soc., Ft. Ligonier Assn., Navy League, Tin Can

Sailors Assn., Nat. Trust Soc., Auburn-Cord-Duesenberg Club, HYP (Pitts.). Home: 139 Ramsey Rd Ligonier PA 15658-2204 Office: 223 E Main St Ligonier PA 15658-1347 Office Phone: 724-238-6268.

PIMENTA, SIMON IGNATIUS CARDINAL, cardinal, archbishop emeritus; b. Bombay, Mar. 1, 1920; Studied, St. Pius Coll., Bombay; B in math. & pedagogy, State UNiv., Bombay; D in canon law, Pontifical Urban Univ., Rome, 1954. Ordained priest Archdiocese of Bombay, India, 1949, parish priest, sec. to archbishop, vice-chancellor, 1954—59, parish priest of cathedral, 1959—70; prof. liturgy, rector Seminary St. Pius X, Bombay, 1959—70; ordained bishop, 1971; aux. bishop Archdiocese of Bombay, 1971—77, coadjutor archbishop, 1977—78, archbishop, 1978—97; elevated to cardinal, 1988; cardinal-priest S. Marian Regina Mundi a Torre Spaccata, 1988—; archbishop emeritus Archdiocese of Bombay, 1997—. Roman Catholic. Address: Archbishops House 21 Nathalal Parekh Marg Maharashtra Bombay 400001 India

PIMENTEL, ARMANDO, energy executive; BS in Acctg., Fla. State U., Tallahassee. Profl. acctg. fellow Office the Chief Accountant, US Securities and Exch. Commn., 1996—98; ptnr. acctg. rsch. dept. Deloitte & Touche LLP, audit ptnr., head power & utilities segment, sr. ptnr., regulatory and pub. policy group; sr. engagement ptnr. FLP Group, Inc., Miami, Fla., exec. v.p. fin., CFO, 2008—. Spkr. in field. Office: FPL Group Inc PO Box 025576 Miami FL 33102*

PIMIENTO, JOSE MARIO, physician; s. Heriberto Pimiento and Sonia Echeverri; m. Natalia Carolina Reyna, Dec. 3, 2006. MD, Universidad Nacional de Colombia, Bogota, 2000. Resident St. Mary's Health Sys., Waterbury, Conn., 2003—.

PIMLEY, KIM JENSEN, financial training consultant; b. Abington, Pa., Apr. 29, 1960; d. Alvin Christian Jensen and Helen Marie (Kairis) Meinken; m. Michael St. John Pimley, Nov. 10, 1988; 1 child, Oliver Jensen Pimley. BA, Emory U., 1982, MA magna cum laude, 1982; postgrad., U. Chgo., 1985—. Mgr. tng. ops. Continental Bank, Chgo., 1986-88, mgr. coll. rels., 1988-90; mgr. client svcs. The Globecon Group, NYC, 1990-92; prin. Pimley & Pimley, Inc., Princeton, NJ, 1992-93; pres. P&P Tng. Resources, Inc., Princeton, 1993—. Owner Jr. League Designer Showhouse, 1997; mem. bd. trustees Pennington Sch., 2009-. Contbr. poetry to various jours. Trustee Dem. Com., 1997—; chmn. silent auction Princeton Friends Sch., 2002-04; trustee Opera Festival NJ, 2000-03; bd. dirs., v.p. fin. Jewish Ctr. Princeton, 1999—, pres. 2004-05; NJ bd. dir. Am. Jewish Com., 2007-, pres., 2009; bd. dirs. Princeton Healthcare Sys. Found., 2005—, United Jewish Fedn., Princeton, Mercer, Bucks, 2006; co-chmn. Nov. Night, 2006, bd. dir. Penning Sch., 2009 Scholarship U. Chgo., 1984. Mem. ACLU (NJ bd. dirs.), Princeton Cmty. Dem. Orgn. (treas.), Oxford & Cambridge Club, Nassau Club. Office: P&P Tng Resources Inc 117 Library Pl Princeton NJ 08540-3019

PIMM, STUART L., ecology educator; b. Derbyshire, Eng., Feb. 27, 1949; naturalized, U.S. m. Julia Killeffer, June 2, 1990; 2 children. BA second class honors, Oxford, Eng., 1971; PhD, New Mex. State Univ., 1974. Asst. prof. Clemson Univ., SC, 1974—75, Tex. Tech Univ., Lubbock, 1975—79, assoc. prof., 1979—82; assoc. prof. ecology and evolutionary biology Univ. Tenn., Knoxville, 1982—86, prof., 1986—99, Columbia Univ., NYC, 1999—2002; Doris Duke chair of conservation ecology Duke Univ., NC, 2002—. Vis. prof. Griffith Univ., Queensland, Australia, 1983—84, Inst. for Nonlinear Sci., Univ. Calif., San Diego, 1987, Sch. of Ecosystem Mgmt., Univ. New Eng., Australia, 1987, Ctr. for Population Biology, Imperial Coll., Silwood Park, England, 1990, Mammal Rsch. Inst., Pretoria, South Africa, 1996, Pretoria, 2000; sr. vis. scholar Nat. Rsch. Coun., 1995; disting. assoc. in rsch. Bernice P. Bishop Mus., Honolulu, 1997—. Contbr. articles to profl. journals. Recipient Pew Fellowship, 1993—96, Kemp prize for disting. ecologists, 1994, Aldo Leopold Leadership Fellow, 1999; named one of world's most highly cited scientists, Inst. Sci. Info., 2002. Fellow: Am. Acad. Arts & Sci. Office: Nicholas Sch Environ and Earth Sci Duke Univ Box 90328 Durham NC 27708 Office Phone: 919-613-8000. Office Fax: 919-684-8741.

PINALS, ROBERT STANTON, physician; b. Elizabeth, NJ, Aug. 23, 1931; s. Herman and Goldie (Kotler) P.; m. Emanuella DiAssisi, June 20, 1953; children: Deborah, David, Stephen. BA, Cornell U., 1952; MD, U. Rochester, 1956. Diplomate in internal medicine and rheumatology Am. Bd. Internal Medicine. Chief rheumatology Lemuel Shattuck Hosp., Boston, 1961—63; from instr. to asst. prof. medicine Tufts U. Sch. Medicine, Boston, 1963—69; from assoc. prof. to prof. medicine SUNY, Syracuse, 1969—79; prof. medicine U. Tenn., Memphis, 1978—84, U. Med. Dentistry N.J.-Robert Wood Johnson Med. Sch., Piscataway, 1984—. Mem., cons. arthritis adv. com. FDA, Wasington, 1985-93, chmn., 1986-89; mem. rheumatology subsplty. com. Am. Bd. Internal Medicine, 1988-95; vice chmn. dept. medicine U. Med. Dentistry N.J., 1997—; chmn. dept. medicine Princeton Med. Ctr., 1984-97 Contbr. numerous chpts. to books, more than 100 articles to profl. jours. Bd. dirs. Ctrl. N.Y. chpt. Arthritis Found., 1969-78, pres., 1976-77. Capt. USAF, 1957-59. Rheumatology fellow, Mass. Gen. Hosp., Boston, 1961—63. Master: Am. Coll. Rheumatology; fellow: ACP. Office: UMDNJ-Robert Wood Johnson Med Sch Dept Medicine PO Box 19 New Brunswick NJ 08903-0019 Personal E-mail: bob@pinals.com.

PINCHING, DEBORAH ANNE ODELL, special education educator; b. Travis AFB, Calif., June 28, 1954; d. John R. and Ruth A. (Patchell) Dawson; married, Jan. 6, 1996. BS in edn., N.Mex. State U., Las Cruces, N. Mex., 1976; post grad., U. N.Mex., 1991. Cert. in elem. and spl. edn. teaching, N.Mex. Tchg. asst. Las Cruces Pub. Sch., Las Cruces, N.Mex., 1976-77; tchr. spl. edn. Ft. Stanton Sch. and Hosp., N.Mex., 1977-79, Carlsbad Mcpl. Sch., N.Mex., 1979—2004. Ednl. assistive technologist Carlsbad Mcpl. Sch., 1991-2004; owner Deb's Techs., 1994—; instr. assistive tech. tchg. courses U. N.Mex., Albuquerque, 1992; presenter at profl. conf.; ret., 2004. Foster parent trainer, N.Mex. Human Svc. Dept., Carlsbad, N Mex., 1988-91, foster parent, 1984-91, bd. dirs. 2001-. Mem.: NEA, Choices (bd. mem.), Pilot Club Internat. Mem. Nazarene. Avocations: crocheting, computer programming, cooking. Home: PO Box 3190 Carlsbad NM 88221-3190 Personal E-mail: dpinching@hotmail.com.

PINCHUK, NICHOLAS THOMAS, manufacturing executive; b. Troy, NY, Oct. 11, 1946; s. Nicholas Thomas and Mildred Frances Pinchuk; m. Lee Joyce Pinchuk, Aug. 8, 1970; children: Madeline Pinchuk Boehning, Tanya, Thomas. BSEE, Rensselaer Poly. Inst., Troy, 1968, MEE, 1969; MBA, Harvard U., Cambridge, Mass., 1976. Various fin. and engring. mgmt. positions Ford Motor Co., 1972—83; v.p., CFO Carrier Internat. Corp., Syracuse, NY, 1985-86; v.p. strategic planning Carrier Corp. (subs. of United Techs. Corp.), Syracuse, 1986-87, pres. Asia-Pacific Ops. Singapore, 1987-97, pres. global refrigeration ops.; sr. v.p., pres. Worldwide Comml. and Indsl. Group Snap-On, Inc., 2002—07, pres., COO, 2007, pres., CEO, 2007—09, chmn., pres., CEO, 2009—. Mem. mgmt. adv. bd. Syracuse U., 1997; bd. dirs. Columbus McKinnon Corp., 2007-, Snap-On, Inc., 2007- 1st lt. US Army, 1970—71, Vietnam. Mem. Am. Soc. Refrigeration and Air Conditioning Engrs. Office: Snap-On Inc PO Box 1410 Kenosha WI 53141-1410 Office Phone: 262-656-5200. E-mail: nicholas.t.pinchuk@snapon.com.*

PINCKNEY, CHARLES COTESWORTH, lawyer; b. Richmond, Va., Oct. 23, 1939; s. Thomas and Charlotte (Kent) P.; m. Helen Raney, Aug. 13, 1966; children: Sarah Whitley, Thomas. BA, Yale U., 1961; LLB, U. Va., 1967. Bar: Va. 1967. Assoc. Mays, Valentine, Davenport & Moore, Richmond, 1967-72; ptnr. Mays & Valentine, LLP, Richmond, 1972-2000, Troutman Sanders LLP, Richmond, 2001—07, counsel, 2008—. Bd. dirs. Sweet Briar Coll., 1996-2000; pres. Sheltering Arms Hosp., Richmond, 1986-87, bd. dirs., 1970-99, 2004-; trustee William H.-John G.-Emma Scott Found., 1974-, sec., 1994-99, 2008-, v.p., 1999-2004, pres. 2005-08; campaign chmn. United Way Svcs., 1998, bd. dirs., 1997-2009. Lt. (j.g.) USNR, 1961-63. Mem. Country Club of Va., Commonwealth Club (bd. govs. 1986-92, pres. 1991-92), Richmond German (pres. 1996-98, sec.-treas. 2006-), Soc. of Cin., fellow Va. Law Found. Republican. Episcopalian. Home: 2 Roslyn Rd Richmond VA 23226-1610 Office: Troutman Sanders LLP 1001 Haxall Pt PO Box 1122 Richmond VA 23218-1122 Home Phone: 804-288-3367; Office Phone: 804-697-1383. E-mail: cotes.pinckney@troutmansanders.com.

PINCKNEY, NEAL T., psychologist, retired educator; b. NYC, July 26, 1935; s. Leo Allen and Jean P.; children: Andrew Allen, Jennifer Elizabeth, Matthew Ian. Cert. polit. social and hist. issues, King's Coll., U. Durham, 1957; AB, U. So. Calif., 1958, postgrad., 1958—61; PhD, Oxford U., 1966; postgrad., U. Vienna, U. Hiroshima, Stanford U. Mem. Pub. Welfare Commn., LA County, 1958—60; tchr. pub. schs., LA, 1960—61; tchr., counselor Las Vegas, 1961—62; admninstr. therapist psychiat. clinic, 1962—63; educator, dir. guidance svc. Dept. Def. Overseas Dep. Schs., Eng. and Japan, 1963—67; pvt. practice clin. psychology, 1967—87; lectr. Calif. State U., Sacramento, 1967—68, asst. prof., 1968—71, assoc. prof., 1971—77, prof. psychology and edn., 1977—87, prof. emeritus, 1987—, chmn. dept. behavioral scis., 1980—82, prof. counseling psychology, coord. grad. studies, dept. adminstrn., counseling and policy studies, 1992—; founder, clin. dir. Healing Heart Found., 1993—. Vis. prof. U. Calif.-Davis, 1979—; psychologist, instr. enforcement psychology and human rels. Calif. Hwy. Patrol, 1967-80; dir. Univ. Software Evaluation Project, 1987; tech. cons., adv. Ministry Edn. and Culture, Govt. Brazil, Brasilia, 1974-76; cons. psychologist Calif. Med. Facility, Vacaville, various law enforcement agys.; prof. U. Hawaii, lectr. U. Hawaii, Leeward CC, 1992-93; mem. profl. treatment team Preventive Medicine Rsch. Inst.-Ornish Residential Retreat for Reversing Heart Disease, 1996; sponsor, builder Makaha Chartres Labyrinth; webmaster Healing Heart Website, moderator, sponsor internet discussion group; dir. Judge Rotenberg Ednl. Ctr., 2004-06. Author: Healthy Heart Handbook, 1994, Law and Ethics in Counseling and Psychotherapy, A Casebook, 1961, 86; pub. USER, a Software Report Card, 1987; editor: Incite Newsletter of Hawaii Portable Computer Users Assn., 1987-88; editor: Ency. of Psychology, 2d edit. Served with 3d Armored Divsn. U.S. Army, 1954-55. Queen's scholar Eng., 1956-57; scholar Dept. State Fgn. Svc. Inst., 1974; fellow Ford Found., 1960-61. Mem. APA, Brit. Psychol. Assn., Japanese Psychol. Assn., Brazilian Psychol. Assn., Am. Ednl. Rsch. Assn., Am. Assn. Counseling and Devel., Am. Radio Relay League (life), Hawaii Personal Computer Users Group (pres. 1989-91, sys. operator Electronic Bulletin Bd. Svc.), Quarter Century Wireless Assn. (life), Vegetarian Soc. of Hawaii (bd. dirs.), No. Calif. DX Club, Hawaii DX Assn., Phi Delta Kappa, Delta Phi Epsilon, Commonwealth Club San Francisco, Oxonian Club Tokyo, Toastmasters (area gov. 1962-63), Mason Home: Ste 1601 1650 Ala Moana Blvd Honolulu HI 96815-1411 *Those who rush through life are merely hurrying toward their death. When one pauses to savor its many subtle varieties one begins to gain some insight and to be in awe of the wonder of it all. Then we begin to place ourselves in perspective and everything has meaning.*

PINCUS, HOWARD J., geologist, engineer, educator; b. NYC, June 24, 1922; s. Otto Max and Gertrude (Jankowsky) Pincus; m. Maud Lydia Roback, Sept. 6, 1953; children: Glenn David, Philip Ethan. BS, CCNY, 1942; PhD, Columbia U., 1949. Cert. profl. geol. scientist Ind., 1964, profl. engr. Wis., 1981, profl. geologist Am. Inst. Profl. Geologists, 1981. Rsch. assoc. Lamont Geol. Obs., Columbia U., 1949-51; geologist Ohio Dept. Natural Resources, summers 1950-61; faculty Ohio State U., 1949-67, from instr. to assoc. prof., 1949-59, prof., 1959-67, chmn. dept. geology, 1960-65; rsch. geologist U.S. Bur. Mines, 1963—67, geologist, rsch. supr., 1967-68; prof. geol. sci. and civil engring. U. Wis., Milw., 1968-87, prof. emeritus, 1987—, dean Coll. Letters and Sci., 1969-72; cons. geology and rock mechanics, 1954-67, 68—. Sr. postdoctoral fellow NSF, 1962; mem. U.S. nat. com. tunneling tech. NAE, 1972—74; mem. U.S. nat. com. rock mechanics NAS/NAE, 1975—78, 1980—89, chmn., 1985—87; mem. U.S. com. Internat. Assn. Engring. Geology/NAS, chmn., 1987—90. Tech. editor: Geotechnical Testing Jour., 1992—95; mem. editl. bd. Geotechnical Testing Jour., 1996—2007. Served to 1st lt. C.E. US Army, 1942—46. Recipient award for tchg. excellence, U. Wis.-Milw. Alumni Assn., 1978. Fellow: AAAS, ASTM (Frank W. Reinhart award 1987, Merit award 1989), Geol. Soc. Am. (chmn. engring. geology divsn. 1973—74); mem.: Am. Inst. Profl. Geologists (pres. Ohio sect. 1965—66), Assn. Engring. Geologists, Am. Rock Mechanics Assn., Internat. Soc. Rock Mechanics, Internat. Assn. Engring. Geology, Soc. Mining Engrs., Geol. Soc. Am., Am. Geophysical Union, Sigma Xi, Phi Beta Kappa (pres. Ohio State U. chpt. 1959—60, pres. U. Wis.-Milw. chpt. 1975—77). Home and Office: 3480 Stream Side Ln Apt 120 Thousand Oaks CA 91360-8477 Home Fax: 805-241-2877. Personal E-mail: hpincus@san.rr.com. Business E-Mail: hjpincus@uvtomail.com.

PINCUS, LIONEL I., financial executive, entrepreneur; b. Phila., Mar. 2, 1931; s. Henry and Theresa Celia (Levit) P.; m. Suzanne Storrs Poulton (dec.). BA, U. Pa., 1953; MBA, Columbia U., 1956. Assoc. gen. ptnr. Ladenburg, Thalmann & Co., NYC, 1955-63; pres. Lionel I. Pincus & Co., Inc., NYC, 1964-66; pres., CEO E.M. Warburg & Co., Inc., NYC, 1966-70; chmn., CEO E.M. Warburg, Pincus & Co., LLC, 1970—2002, chmn. emeritus, 2003—. Trustee NY Presbyn. Hosp.; trustee, chmn. emeritus Columbia U.; trustee German Marshall Fund USA, 1982-88; mem. bd. overseers Columbia Grad. Sch. Bus.; bd. dirs. Am. Mus. Natural History, Nat. Park Found., 1995-01; mem. Partnership for NYC; emeritus dir. Sch. Am. Ballet. Mem. Coun. Fgn. Rels., Nat. Venture Capital Assn. (Lifetime award), World Wildlife Fund (nat. coun.), Nat. Golf Links Am. Club, Meadow Club. Office: Warburg Pincus LLC 450 Lexington Ave Fl 10 New York NY 10017-3147

PINCUS, THEODORE, microbiologist, rheumatologist, educator; AB, Columbia U., 1961; MD, Harvard U., 1966. Assoc. Sloan-Kettering Inst., NYC, 1973-75; asst. prof. medicine/immunology, dir. clin. immunology lab. Stanford (Calif.) U., 1975-76; prof. Wistar Inst., Phila., 1976-80; adj. assoc. prof. medicine-rheumatology U. Pa., Phila., 1976-80; prof. medicine and microbiology Vanderbilt U., Nashville, 1980—. Fellow ACP, Am. Rheumatism Assn., Am. Soc. Microbiology. Achievements include description of morbidity and mortility of rheumatoid arthritis; analyses of host genetic and psychosocial variables in chronic diseases; description of host genetic control of experimental retrovirus infection; description of psychological and economic consequences of chronic disease; analysis of "mind body" explanations of associations between socioeconomic status and chronic disease. Office: Vanderbilt U Divsn Rheumatology & Immunology 203 Oxford House Nashville TN 37232-0001

PINCUS, THEODORE HENRY, public relations executive; b. Chgo., Sept. 15, 1933; s. Jacob T. and J. (Engel) Pincus; m. Sharon Barr, Jan. 16, 1988; children: Laura, Mark, Susan, Anne, Jennifer. BS in Journalism, Ind. U., 1955. Free-lance bus. writer, 1955—58; sr. exec. Harshe Rotman & Druck, Chgo., 1958—62; owner Theodore Pincus & Assocs., Chgo., 1962—, prin., owner, 2003—; chmn., CEO Fin. Rels. Bd., Inc., Chgo., 1965—98; vice chmn. BSMG Worldwide divsn. Interpub. Group, NYC, 1998—2001; fin. columnist Chgo. Sun Times, 2002—; mng. ptnr. Stevens Gould & Pincus, 2007—. Pub. affairs advisor to Nelson Rockefeller, NYC, 1960, NYC, 68; advisor U.S. Info. Agy., 1993—; adj. prof. fin. MBA Sch., DePaul U., 2002—; former mem. adv. bd. NASDAQ, USIA; former mem. Obama Econ. Policy Com., 2008; ind. comm. cons., 2003—. Author: Giveaway Day, 1977, On the Offensive, 2001; contbr. artcles to profl. jours. including Wall St. Jour., Fortune and N.Y. Times; author: Read at Your Own Risque, 2007. Active presdl. nomination campaigns; vice-chmn. Midwest Region Am. Jewish Com.; mem. adv. bd. Ind. U. Bus. Sch., The Ill. Coalition; mem. Obama Economics Policy Com., 2008. With USAF, 1955—57. Recipient numerous nat. awards for profl. excellence in investor rels. and corp. pub. rels., including Silver Anvil award, Pub. Rels. Soc. Am., 1966, Civic Achievement award, Am. Jewish Com., 1993, Pub. Rels. Profl. of Yr., Pub. Rels. Soc. Am., 2002; named Entrepreneur of Yr., Ernst and Young Merrill Lynch, 1998. Mem.: Nat. Investor Rels. Inst. (founding), Young Pres.'s Orgn., Union League, Standard Club. Office: 400 E Ohio St Chicago IL 60611-3322 Office Phone: 312-321-1202.

PINCUS, WALTER HASKELL, news editor; b. Bklyn., Dec. 24, 1932; s. Jonas and Clare (Glassman) Pincus; m. Betty Meskin, Sept. 12, 1954; 1 child, Andrew John; m. Ann Witsell Terry, May 1, 1965; children: Ward Haskell, Adam Witsell, Cornelia Battle Terry. BA, Yale U., 1954; JD, Georgetown U., 2001. With Wall St. Jour., 1957—58; cons. Senate Fgn. Rels. Com., 1962-63; spl. writer Washington Evening Star, 1963-66; editor, reporter Washington Post, 1966-69; chief cons. Symington subcom. Senate Fgn. Relations Com., 1969-70; assoc. editor New Republic, 1972-74, exec. editor, 1974-75; spl. writer Washington Post, 1975—; cons. NBC News, 1971-79, CBS News, 1979-86, NBC News, 1987-88, Washington Post Co., 1989—. Vis. lectr. Yale U., 1988, 2002, Stanford U., 2003—. Trustee Shakespeare Theater, 1988—, co-chmn. edn. com., 1989—91, chmn. nominating com., 1992—96, mem. exec. com., 1992—2007. With US Army, 1955—57. Recipient Page One award, 1960, George Orwell award, 1977, George Polk award, 1978, Emmy award, 1981, Stewart Alsop award, 1999, Edwin Weintal award, 2008; co-recipient Pulitzer prize, 2001. Mem.: Coun. Fgn. Rels., Yale Club Washington. Home: 3202 Klingle Rd NW Washington DC 20008-3403 Office: Washington Post 1150 15th St NW Washington DC 20071-0001 Office Phone: 202-334-7429. E-mail: pincusw@washpost.com.

PINCZOWER, KENNETH EPHRAIM, lawyer; s. Joachim and Dinah Pinczower; m. Julie Pinczower; children: Devorah, David C., Chana, Fayga Tziporah, Samuel Joseph, Sarah. BA, Queens Coll., 1985; postgrad., Rabbinical Sem. Am., NYC, 1983-86; JD, Benjamin N. Cardozo Sch. Law, 1989. Bar: N.Y. 1990, N.J. 1990, DC 1991, Fla. 1993, U.S. Dist. Ct. (so. and ea. dists.) N.Y. 1990, U.S. Dist. Ct. N.J. 1990, U.S. Ct. Appeals (2d cir.) 2004, U.S. Supreme Ct. 2004. Auditor Seidman & Seidman/B.D.O., NYC, 1986-87; summer assoc. U.S. Attys. Office, So. Dist. N.Y., NYC, 1988; Alexander jud. fellow U.S. Dist. Judge, So. Dist. N.Y., NYC, 1987-88; asst. corp. counsel N.Y.C. Law Dept., 1989-95; atty. Barron, McDonald, Carroll & Cohen, NYC, 1995—. Editor: Cardozo Arts & Entertainment Law Jour., 1988—89. Com. mem. Nat. Conf. Synagogue Youth, 1991—; vol. instr. Jewish Edn. Program, NYC, 1983—86; instr. Aish Ha Torah, 1994—98; Shulchan Aruch Sar Eleph Machon Yerushalayim, 2000—; Talmud assoc. Mesorah Heritage Found., 1993—; chmn. Torah Chesed Fund Yeshiva U., 1993—. Avocations: talmudic law, tennis, basketball. Home: 725 W 231st St Bronx NY 10463 Office: Barron McDonald et al 1 Whitehall St New York NY 10004-2109 Office Phone: 212-510-9221. Personal E-mail: kejewels@aol.com. Business E-Mail: pinczok@nationwide.com.

PINCZUK, ARON, physicist; b. San Martin, Argentina, Feb. 15, 1939; s. Faiwel and Ester (Wejeman) P.; m. Gladys Norma Teitelman, June 14, 1962; children: Ana Gabriela, Guillermo Fabian. Licenciado, U. Buenos Aires, Argentina, 1962; PhD, U. Pa., 1969; D (hon.), U Autonoma, Madrid, 1997. Staff mem. Nat. Rsch. Coun., Argentina, 1971-76; head physics dept. Faculty of Scis., U. Buenos Aires, Argentina, 1974; vis. scientist Max Planck Inst., Stuttgart, Germany, 1976, IBM Rsch., Yorktown Heights, NY, 1976-77; staff mem. Bell Labs., Murray Hill, NJ, 1978—; prof. Columbia U., NYC, 1998—. Sec. Argentina Phys. Soc., Buenos Aires, 1972-75; editor Solid State Communications, 1989-92, assoc. editor in chief, 1992-2004, editor in chief, 2005—. Contbr. over 200 articles to profl. jours. and numerous chpts. to books. Recipient Oliver E. Buckley Condensed-Matter Physics prize Am. Physical Soc., 1994. Fellow: AAAS, Am. Phys. Soc.; mem.: Am. Acad. Arts & Scis., Optical Soc. Am., Materials Rsch. Soc. Achievements include use and devel. novel optical methods in studies of structural phase transitions, semiconductor interfaces and interactions of free electrons in semiconductors; discovered novel phenomena in studies of quantum electron fluids. Office: Columbia U Dept Physics and Applied Physics New York NY 10027 Office Phone: 212-854-9632. Business E-Mail: aron@phys.columbia.edu.

PINDER, GEORGE FRANCIS, engineering educator, research scientist; b. Windsor, Ont., Can., Feb. 6, 1942; s. Percy Samuel and Stella Marie P.; m. Phyllis Marie Charlton, Sept. 14, 1963; children— Wendy Marie, Justin George. B.Sc., U. Western Ont., 1965; PhD, U. Ill., 1968. Research hydrologist U.S. Geol. Survey, 1968-72; mem. faculty dept. civil engring. Princeton U., 1972-89, prof., 1972-89, chmn. dept., from 1980, dir. water resources program, 1972-80; dean Coll. Engring. and Math. U. Vt., Burlington, 1989-96, dir. Rsch. Ctr. for Groundwater Remediation Design, 1993—, disting. prof. Coll. Engring. and Math., 2005—. Recipient O.E. Meinzer award Geol. Soc. Am., 1975, WUC medal, 1992; U. Vt. Univ. scholar, 1993. Fellow: Wessex Inst., Am. Geophys. Union (Robert E. Horton award 1969); mem.: ASCE (Julian Hinds medal 2002), Vt. Acad. Sci. and Engring. Home: 188 Bishop Rd Shelburne VT 05482-6933 Office: U Vt Coll Engring And Math Burlington VT 05405-0001

PINDLE, ARTHUR JACKSON, JR., philosopher, researcher; b. Macon, Ga., May 26, 1942; s. Arthur Jackson Sr. and Beatrice Rosetta (Williams) P.; 1 child, Zhinga D. BS in Physics, Morehouse Coll., 1964; MA in Philosophy, Yale U., 1973, MPhil, 1974, PhD in Philosophy, 1978. Physicist IBM, Inc., Poughkeepsie, NY, 1964, Naval Ordinance Station, Indian Head, Md., 1966-69, Satellite Experiment Lab, Suitland, Md., 1970-71; philosophy prof. Fayetteville (N.C.) State U., 1976-83;

pres. HRG, Inc., New Orleans, 1983—; dir. rsch. NITRT, Inc., New Orleans, 1993—; pres. Grael Electronics, Inc., 1998; prof. philosophy Spelman Coll., 2006. Mem. bd. advs. Inst. Philosoph. Rsch., Boulder, Colo., 1980-83. Contbr. articles to profl. jours.; patentee personal computer console. Mem. Dem. Nat. Com., 1993-98. Avocations: yoga, chess. Home: 260 18th St NW Apt 10216 Atlanta GA 30363 Personal E-mail: apindle@aim.com.

PINDYCK, BRUCE EBEN, lawyer, corporate financial executive; b. NYC, Sept. 21, 1945; s. Sylvester and Lillian (Breslow) P.; m. Mary Ellen Schwartz, Aug. 18, 1968; children: Ashley Beth, Eben Spencer, Blake Michael Lawrence. AB, Columbia U., 1967, JD, 1970, MBA, 1971. Bar: N.Y. 1971, Wis. 1987. Assoc. Olwine, Connelly, Chase, O'Donnell & Weyher, NYC, 1971-80; asst. gen. counsel Peat, Marwick, Mitchell & Co., NYC, 1980-82; ptnr. Hollyer, Jones, Pindyck, Brady & Chira, NYC, 1983-87; pres., CEO Meridian Industries, Inc., Milw., 1985—, also chmn. bd. dirs.; CEO Majilite Corp., Dracut, Mass., 1987—, also chmn. bd. dirs. Mem. capital campaign com. Columbia U., 1984-87. Mem. bd. visitors Columbia Coll., 2001—, U. Wisconsin-Milwaukee, Sch. Bus., 2007—; bd. dirs. Harambee Cmty. Sch., 1991—96, Milw. Ballet Co., 1993—97, Milw. Pub. Mus., 1994—98, The Private Bank, Milw., 2005—, Jr. Achievement, 2005—. Mem. Columbia Coll. Alumni Assn. (regional dir. 1988-94, v.p. 1994-98, exec. com., 1994-98), World Pres.'s Orgn. Office: 100 E Wisconsin Ave Milwaukee WI 53202-4107 Home Phone: 414-352-9196; Office Phone: 414-224-0610. E-mail: bpindyck@meridiancompanies.com.

PINE, CHARLES JOSEPH, clinical psychologist; b. July 13, 1951; s. Charles E. LaVern (Upton) P.; m. Mary Day, Dec. 30, 1979 (div. 1996); children: Charles Andrew, Joseph Scott, Carolyn Marie; m. Inga Marie Talbert, Feb. 11, 1998. BA in Psychology, U. Redlands, 1973; MA in Psychology, Calif. State U., LA, 1975; PhD in Clin. Psychology, U. Wash., 1979; postdoc. in Psychology Am. and Indian studies, UCLA, 1981. Diplomate in clin. psych. Am. Bd. Profl. Psychology; lic. psychologyist, Calif., Fla. Psychology technician Seattle Indian Health Bd., USPHS Hosp., 1977-78; psychology intern VA Outpatient Clinic, LA, 1978-79; instr. psychology Okla. State U., 1979-80, asst. prof., 1980; asst. prof. psychology and Native Am. studies program Wash. State U., 1981-82; dir. behavioral health svcs. Riverside-San Bernardino County Indian Health Inc., Banning, Calif., 1982-84; clin. psychologist VA Med. Ctr., Long Beach, Calif., 1984-85, clin. psychologist, psychology coord. psychiatry divsn. Sepulveda, Calif., 1985-93; clin. dir. Traumatic Stress Treatment Ctr., Thousand Oaks, Calif., 1985-93; assoc. clin. prof. UCLA Sch. Medicine, 1985-93, Fuller Grad. Sch. Psychology, Pasadena, Calif., 1985-93; pvt. practice Orlando, Fla., 1993-94; rsch. assoc. Nat. Ctr. Am. Indian and Alaska Native Mental Health Rsch., Denver, 1989—; psychologist Vets. Counseling Ctr., San Bernardino, Calif., 1997—2003, clin. coord., 1997—2003; psychologist Calif. Dept. Youth Authority, Norwalk, Calif., 2003—04, psychologist Heman G. Stark Youth Correctional Facility Chino, Calif., 2004—. Adj. assoc. prof. Calif. Sch. Profl. Psychology, L.A., 1989-95; adj. faculty mem. U. Ctrl. Fla., 1993-94; psychologist, adminstrv. coord. alcohol and drug abuse treatment program Orlando VA Outpatient divsn. Tampa VA Med. Ctr., 1993-94; cons. NIH, 1993-96; psychologist stress treatment programs Bay Pines (Fla.) VA Med. Ctr., 1994-96; mem. L.A. County Am. Indian Mental Health Task Force, 1987-92; editl. cons. White Cloud Jour., 1982-85; cons. Dept. HHS, USPHS, NIMH, 1980. Contbr. articles to profl. publs. Vol. worker Variety Boys Clubs Am., 1973-75; coach Rialto Jr. All-Am. Football League, 1974, Conejo Valley Little League, Dr. Phillips Little League, 1993—; coach Conejo Youth Flag Football Assn., pres., 1990; coach, bd. dirs. Westlake Youth Football, 1991-92; co-commn. Dr. Phillips Pop Warner football, 1993—; ret. U.S. Dept. Vet. Affairs, 2003-. Grantee U. Wash. Inst. Indian Studies, 1975-76, UCLA Inst. Am. Cultures, 1981-82: Fellow APA (chair task force on svc. delivery to ethnic minority populations bd. ethnic minority affairs 1988, bd. ethnic minority affairs 1985-87); mem. Soc. Indian Psychologists (pres. 1981-83), Nat. Register Health Svc. Providers in Psychology, Calif. Psychol. Assn. Found. (bd. dirs. 1990-92), Soc. for Psychol. Study Ethnic Minority Issues (exec. com. 1987-88, pres. 1995-96), Sigma Alpha Epsilon, Chi Sigma Chi. Roman Catholic.

PINE, CHRIS WHITELAW, actor; b. LA, Aug. 29, 1980; s. Robert Pine and Gwynne Gilford. Actor: (films) Why Germany?, 2004, The Princess Diaries 2: Royal Engagement, 2004, Confession, 2005, The Bulls, 2005, Just My Luck, 2006, Blind Dating, 2006, Smokin' Aces, 2006, Bottle Shock, 2008, Star Trek, 2009, Carriers, 2009; (TV films) Surrender Dorothy, 2006. Office: c/o PMK/HBH 700 San Vicente Blvd West Hollywood CA 90069*

PINEDA, ALBERT ANTHONY, obstetrician, gynecologist, educator; b. NYC, Feb. 15, 1937; MD, N.Y. Med. Coll., 1963. Diplomate Am. Bd. Ob-gyn. Intern St. Vincents Hosp., NYC, 1963-64; resident in ob-gyn. Flower-Fifth Ave Hosp.-N.Y. Med. Coll., NYC, 1964-68; fellow in gynecol. oncology Met. Hosp., NYC, 1968-69; med. staff St. Joseph's Hosp. Med. Ctr., Paterson, N.J.; clin. assoc. prof. N.Y. Med. Coll., 1976, Seton Hall U. Grad. Sch. Med. Edn., 1991—; clin. prof. St. George's U. Sch. Medicine, 1995—; pvt. practice Clifton, N.J. Mem. ACOG, Soc. Gynecol. Oncology, N.J. Med. Soc., Passaic County Med. Soc.

PINELLI, THOMAS EDWARD, information scientist; b. Johnston, RI, Nov. 8, 1947; s. Anthony and Florence (Vowell) P. BS, Old Dominion U., 1970, MS in Edn., 1976; MS, Clemson U., 1972; MPA, Golden Gate U., 1978; MSLS, Cath. U., 1983; PhD, Ind. U., 1990. Tchr., dept. chmn. Virginia Beach (Va.) City Pub. Schs., 1970-72; ednl. programs officer NASA Langley Rsch. Ctr., Hampton, Va., 1972-74, adminstrv. ops. specialist, 1974-78; internat. programs officer NASA Hdqrs., Washington, 1978-79; chief tech. info. div. NASA Ames Rsch. Ctr., Moffett Field, Calif., 1980-82; asst. chief rsch. info. and application div. NASA Langley Rsch. Ctr., Hampton, 1983-93, head visual imaging br., 1994—. Chair Am. Nat. Standards Inst., 1987, 91. Assoc. editor Jour. of Soc. for Tech. Communications, 1980—; contbr. chpts. to books, articles to profl. jours. Recipient Scholarly Publ. award Nat. Coun. Tchrs. English, 1985, others. Mem. AIAA, Am. Soc. Engrng. Edn., Spl. Librs. Assn. (George Mandel award 1989), Soc. for Tech. Communications, Am. Soc. for Info. Sci. Home: 302 Lynns Way Yorktown VA 23692-4967

PINERO, MARIA ANABEL, language educator; BA in Romance Langs., U. Oregon, 1971; MA in Tchg. English, Brigham Young U., 1975, PhD in Tchg. Methodology, 1977. Adj. asst. prof. U. Utah, 1979—95; dir., bilingual edn. Davis Dist. Sch., Farmington, 1977—96, supr. multicultural edn., 1996—97, supr. foreign langs., 1992—2006; instr., multicultural edn. Brigham Young U., 1992—98, instr., Spanish, 1992—; assoc. instr. Westminster Coll., 1998—. Sec. Editl. Fabril Argentina, Buenos Aires, 1960, translator, 60, Colo. State U., Ft. Collins, 1968—69; clerk. Bank of America, LA, 1961—63; teller Walker Bank and Trust Co., Salt Lake City, 1963—66, Nat. Bank of Oregon, Eugene, 1969—71; pres. Utah Assn. Bilingual Edn., 1985—86, exec. bc. mem., 1986—87. Contbr. articles to profl. jours. Mem.: NABE, ITESOL (pres. 1989—99, v.p. 1997—98), TESOL, UFLA, ACTFL, AATSP, State Foreign Lang. Suprs. (com. mem. 1983—91), Phi Delta Kappa.

PINES, ALEXANDER, chemistry educator, researcher, consultant; b. Tel Aviv, June 22, 1945; came to US, 1968. US citizen in 1981. s. Michael and Neima (Ratner) P.; m. Ayala Malach, Aug. 31, 1967 (div. 1983); children: Itai, Shani; m. Ditsa Kafry, May 5, 1983; children: Noami, Jonathan, Talia. BSc, Hebrew U., Jerusalem, 1967; PhD in Chemical Physics, MIT, 1972; D (hon.), U. Paris "Pierre et Marie Curie", 1999, U. Rome "La Sapienza", 2001. Asst. prof. chemistry U. Calif., Berkeley, 1972-75, assoc. prof., 1975-80, prof., 1980—, Pres.'s chair, 1993-97, Chandellor's rsch. prof., 1997-99, Miller rsch. prof., 1998-99, Glenn T. Seaborg prof. chemistry, 1999—. Faculty sr. scientist materials scis. div. Lawrence Berkeley Nat. Lab., 1975—; cons. Mobil Oil Co., Princeton, N.J., 1980-84, Shell Oil Co., Houston, 1981—; chmn. Bytel Corp., Berkeley, Calif., 1981-85; vis. prof. Weizmann Inst. Sci., 1982; adv. prof. East China Normal U., Shanghai, People's Rep. of China, 1985; sci. dir. Nalorac, Martinez, Calif., 1986-92; Joliot-Curie prof. Ecole Superieure de Physique et Chemie, Paris, 1987; Walter J. Chute Disting. lectr. Dalhousie U., 1989, Charles A. McDowell lectr. U. B.C., 1989, E. Leon Watkins lectr. Wichita State U., 1990; Hinshelwood lectr., U. Oxford, 1990, A.R. Gordon Disting. lectr. U. Toronto, 1990, Venable lectr. U. N.C., 1990, Max Born lectr. Hebrew U. of Jerusalem, 1990; William Draper Harkins lectr. U. Chgo., 1991, Kolthoff lectr. U. Minn., 1991; Md.-Grace lectr. U. Md., 1992; mem. adv bd. Nat. High Magnetic Field Lab., Inst. Theoretical Physics, U. Calif. Santa Barbara, Ctr. Pure and Applied Math. U. Calif., Berkeley; mem. adv. panel chem. Nat. Sci. Found.; Randolph T. Major Disting. Lectr. U. Conn., 1992; mem. bd. sci. govs. Weizemann Inst. Sci., 1997—; Peter Smith lectr. Duke U., 1993, Arthur William Davidson lect. U. Kansas, 1992, Arthur Birch lect. Australian Nat. U., 1993, Richard C. Lord Meml. lectr. MIT, 1993, Steacie lectr. Nat. Rsch. Coun. Can., 1993, Morris Loeb lectr. Harvard U., 1994, Jesse Boot Found. lectr., U. Nottingham, 1994, Frontiers in Chemistry lectr. Tex. A&M U., 1995, Bergman lectr. Weizmann Inst. Sci., 1995, faculty rsch. lectr. U. Calif., Berkeley, 1996, Raymond & Beverly Sackler lectr. Tel Aviv U., 1996; Priestley lectr. Pa. State U., 1997; Amy Mellon lectr. Purdue U., 1997; Rsch. frontiers chemistry lectr. U. Iowa, 1998, Moses Gomberg lectr. U. Mich., 1998, J and N Max T. Rogers, Mich. State U., 1998, Frontiers in Chemistry lectr., Wayne State U., 1998, Lord Todd Prof., Cambridge U., 1999, Abbot lectr., U. N.D., 2000, John D. Roberts lectr., Calif. Tech. U., 2000, Willard lectr., U. Wis., 2000, Cliford lectr., U. Pitts., 2000, William Lloyd Evan lectr. Ohio State U., 2000, Jacob Bigeleisen lectr. Stony Brook U., 2001, Laird lectr. U. B.C., 2001; Alan S. Tetelman fellow Yale U., 2001, Regitze Vold Meml. lectr. U. Calif., San Diego, 2001, Sammet guest prof. Goëethe U., Frankfurt, 2001. Editor Molecular Physics, 1987-91; mem. bd. editors Chem. Physics, Chem. Physics Letters, Nmr: Basic Principles and Progress, Advances in Magnetic Resonance, Accounts Chemistry Research, Concepts in Magnetic Reson; adv. editor Oxford U. Press; contbr. articles to profl. jours.; patentee in field. Recipient Strait award North Calif. Spectroscopy Soc., Outstanding Achievement award U.S. Dept. of Energy, 1983, 87, 89, 97, 98, R & D 100 awards, 1987, 89, Disting. Teaching award U. Calif., Ernest O. Lawrence award, 1988, Pitts. Spectroscopy award, 1989, Wolf prize in chemistry, Wolf Found., Israel, 1991, Donald Noyce Undergrad. Teaching award U. Calif., 1992, Robert Foster Cherry award for Great Tchrs. Baylor U., 1995, F.A. Cotton Medal for Excellence in Chemical Rsch., 1998, Dickson prize Carnegie Mellon U., 2001; Guggenheim fellow, 1988, Christensen fellow St. Catherine's Coll., Oxford, 1990; named in honor of his 50th birthday, Ampere Advanced Inst., Varenna, Italy; named to Scientific American 50 List, 2002. Fellow Am. Phys. Soc. (chmn. divsn. chem. physics), Inst. Physics; foreign fellow Royal Soc.; mem. NAS, Am. Chem. Soc. (mem. exec. com. divsn. phys. chemistry, Nobel Signature award in Graduate Edu. 1982, Baekeland Medal for Pure Chemistry, 1985, Harrison Howe award 1991, Centennial Spkr., Jour. Physical Chemistry, 1997, Langmuir award in Chemical Physics, 1998, Remsen award (Md. sect.) 2000, Dickson prize 2001), Royal Soc. Chemistry (Bourke lectr., Bourke Medal, 1988, Centenary lectr. and medal 1994), Internat. Soc. Magnetic Resonance (v.p., pres. 1993-96), Lawrence Hall Sci. Outreach Com. Achievements include pioneering contributions to the development of nuclear magnetic resonance (NMR) spectroscopy; his techniques are widely used in chemistry and materials science. Office: U Calif Chemistry Dept D64A Hildebrand Hill Berkeley CA 94720-0001 Office Phone: 510-642-1220. Office Fax: 510-486-5744. Business E-Mail: pines@berkeley.edu.

PINES, BURTON YALE, media executive; b. Chgo., Apr. 6, 1940; s. Hyman and Mary Pines. BA, U. Wis., 1961, MA, 1963, PhD, 1967. Instr. U. Wis., Madison, 1962-65; corr., bur. chief Time mag., Bonn, Saigon and Vienna, 1966-73, editor NYC, 1973-81; sr. v.p. Heritage Found., Washington, 1981-92; chmn. Nat. Ctr. for Pub. Policy Rsch., Washington, 1982-94; co-founder, exec. v.p. COO NET Polit. Newstalk Network (later known as America's Voice Cable TV Network), Washington, 1992-95; pres., CEO Booknet Cable TV Network, NYC, 1995—; exec. editor Internet ops. GOP Nat. Conv., 2000; sr. v.p. Nat. Exec. Svc. Corps, 2005—. Author: Back to Basics, 1982, Out of Focus, 1994; editor: Mandate for Leadership II, 1984, Mandate for Leadership III, 1988. Recipient Page One award N.Y. Newspaper Guild, 1976, 77, 78, Freedom's Found. award, 1983. Jewish. Office: BookNet 150 W 51st St Ste 1804 New York NY 10019-6848

PINES, WAYNE LLOYD, public relations executive, author; b. Washington, Dec. 31, 1943; s. Jerome Martin and Ethel (Schnall) Pines; m. Nancy Freitag, Apr. 16, 1966 (div. 2003); children: Noah Morris, Jesse Mireth; m. Carol Cole Kleinman, Jan. 7, 2007. BA, Rutgers U., 1965; postgrad., George Washington U., 1969—71. Reporter, city editor Middletown Times Herald-Record, NY, 1965—68; copy editor Reuters News, 1968—69; assoc. editor FDC Reports, Washington, 1969—72; chief consumer edn. and info. FDA; also editor FDA Consumer Mag., 1972—74, dep. asst. commr. for pub. affairs, chief press rels. Rockville, Md., 1975—79, assoc. commr. pub. affairs, 1978—82; exec. editor Product Safety Letter and Devices and Diagnostics Letter, Washington, 1974—75; spl. asst. to dir. NIMH, 1982—83; sr. v.p., sr. counselor Burson-Marsteller, 1983—97, exec. v.p., dir. med. issues, 1987—93; pres. regulatory svc. APCO Worldwide, Washington, 1993—; sr. counselor Grey Healthcare Group, 1993—2004; mng. dir. Comms. Ptnr. and Assoc., 1999—2005; exec. v.p. Garden City Group, 1996—2006; pres. Bio-pharm. Forum George Washington U., 2002—04. Adj. prof. Washington Pub. Affairs Ctr., U. So. Calif., 1980—81; instr. NYU Sch. Continuing Edn., 1982—84, Profl. Devel. Inst., 1983—85; columnist Med. Advt. News, 1985—90, WebMD, 1999—2001; chmn. Theramentrix, Inc., 1999—2001; ethics bd. Patient Channel, 2002—; bd. dirs. Scolr Pharma Inc., Medstar Rsch. Inst., chmn., 2006—; bd. dirs. FDA Alumni Assn., FDA Alliance, pres., 2006—07; bd. mem. Excel Life Scis., 2007—; pres. Alliance for a Stronger FDA, 2008—. Author: The Sermons of Jerome Martin Pines, 1978, FDA Advertising and Promotion Manual, 1992, When Lightning Strikes: A How-to Crisis Manual, 1994, A Practical Guide to Food and Drug Law and Regulation, 1998, How to Work with the FDA, 2001, Crisis Communication in Healthcare: A Delicate Balance, 2002, A Framework for Pharmaceutical Risk Management, 2003, Making Your Case to the FDA, 2005, FDA Advisory Committees Perils and Profits, 2005, DTC Advertising and Promotion: The Changing Environment, 2005, FDA: A Century of Consumer Protection, 2006, Communicating in a Healthcare Crisis, 2006, Pharmaceutical Risk Management: Practical Applications, 2008, Marketing Compliance Guide for Drug and Device Manufacturers, 2008; contbr. articles to profl. jours. Home: 5610 Wisconsin Ave Apt 908 Chevy Chase MD 20815 Office: APCO Worldwide 700 12th St NW Washington DC 20005 Home Phone: 301-654-2675.

PINEYRO, MICHELE, psychologist; b. Manhattan, NY, Apr. 14, 1968; d. Carlos and Ines Pineyro; m. Gregory Colao, July 16, 2004; 1 child, Frances Colao-Pineyro. M in Sch. Psychology, Interamerican U., San Juan, PR, 1998; PhD student in Psychology, St. John's U., Queens, NY. Cert. bilingual sch. psychologist NY State, 1999. Bilingual sch. psychologist NYC Dept. Edn., Queens, 1999—2005, Carmel Ctrl. Sch. Distrtic, NY, 2005—, Bilinguals, Inc., Hartsdale, NY, 2007—. Grant, NYC Dept. of Edn., 1995.

PING, CHIEN-LU, soil scientist, educator; s. Chia-Yeh Ping and ShuChun Chao; m. Sandy Wu, July 20, 1969; children: Andrew, Dennis. PhD, Wash. State U., Pullman, 1976. Cert. profl. soil scientist Am. Registry Profl. Agronomy, Crop and Soil Scientists, 2008. Prof. U. Alaska Fairbanks, Palmer, 1982—. Rsch. grants, Nat. Sci. Found., 1993—2008. Mem.: Soil Sci. Soc. Am. Office: Univ Alaska Fairbanks 533 E Fireweed Ave Palmer AK 99645

PING, LARRY LEE, history professor; s. Robert Theodore and Myrtle Ping; m. Nancy Carol Smith, Dec. 22, 1995; 1 child, Jenna Melissa Newberry. PhD in History, U. Oreg., Eugene, 1994. Asst. prof. history U. Nev., Las Vegas, 1988—; prof. history Southern Utah U., Cedar City, 1989—. Contbr. articles to profl. jours.; author: (book) Gustav Freytag and the Prussian Gospel: Novels, Liberalism, and History, 2006. Academic German Studies Assn., Utah. Named Outstanding Educator, Southern Utah U., 2005—06; Fulbright scholar, US Fulbright Com., 1983—84, Quadrille Ball fellowship, Germanistic Soc. Am., 1983—84. Mem.: German Studies Assn. Liberal. Avocations: hiking, travel. Office: Southern Utah Univ 351 West Center St Cedar City UT 84721

PINGITORE, REGINA, psychologist, researcher; m. Daniel von der Embse, Oct. 3, 1998. MA, Edinboro U., Pa., 1984; PhD, Loyola U. Chgo., 1990. Lic. in clin. psychology Ill., in psychology Utah. Health sci. officer Vets. Affairs Med. Ctr., North Chgo., 1990—94; rsch. asst. prof. U. Ill., Chgo., 1992—2000; dir. rsch. planning and rsch. Publicis, Salt Lake City, 2000—02; chief rsch. officer JD Power and Assocs., Westlake Village, Calif., 2002—. Contbr. articles to profl. publs. Rsch. grants, NIH, Va., NIMH, ACA, 1991—2000. Mem.: APA, INFORMS, MRA. Office: JD Power and Assoc 2625 Townsgate Westlake Village CA 91361

PINGPANK, ROBERT CHARLES, retired mathematics educator; b. Waterbury, Conn., May 27, 1937; s. Henry Frederick and Mabel Jenny Pingpank; m. Richard Thomas Nolan, June 4, 2009. BS, Trinity Coll., Hartford, Conn., 1959; MEd, U. of Hartford, 1964; CAS, Hartford Sem., 1970. Cert. secondary sch. adminstr. Conn., 1964. Math. tchr. Thomaston H.S., Thomaston, Conn., 1959—65, 1990—94, math. dept. head, 1967—90; tchr. Hamden Pub. Schs., Hamden, Conn., 1965—66, Cheshire Acad., Cheshire, Conn., 1966—67; adj. lectr. in math. Mattatuck C.C., Waterbury, Conn., 1970—80. V.p. The Litchfield Inst., Inc., Litchfield, Conn., 1984—96; guest spkr. Sr. Lifestyles radio program, 2005; guest lectr. Fla. Atlantic U., 2006. Author (with Richard T. Nolan): Soul Mates: More Than Partners, 2004. Active Compass of Lake Worth, Fla., 2004—; soc. of regents Cathedral of St. John the Divine, NYC, 2002—; mem. Integrity-Palm Beach, Lake Worth, Fla., 2001—; treas. St. Paul's Episcopal Ch., Bantam, Conn., 1975—87, asst. treas., 1987—94; mem. Lambda Legal, NYC, 2002—; notary pub. State of Fla., 1988—. Co-recipient award for Exceptional Leadership and Cmty. Svc., Palm Beach County Chapt. ACLU, 2008; named Outstanding Secondary Educators of Am., 1973. Fellow: ELMS Soc. Trinity Coll.; mem.: NEA, PFLAG, Flagler Mus., Norton Mus. Art, St. Andrew's Episcopal Ch. (eucharistic minister 2007—), Harwood Soc. Cheshire Acad., Yale Legacy Ptnrs., Assn. Tchrs. Math. in Conn., Conn. Edn. Assn., Thomaston Edn. Assn. (treas.), Christ Ch. Cathedral (friends legacy cir.), Soc. Torch NYU, Cathedral Founders Soc. Wash. Nat. Cathedral Compassion & Choices. Independent. Episcopalian. Avocations: automobiles (history, design, mechanical, costs), Cavalier King Charles Spaniels. Home: 2527 Egret Lake Dr West Palm Beach FL 33413-2161 Personal E-mail: litchinst@aol.com.

PINGREE, BRUCE DOUGLAS, lawyer; b. Salt Lake City, June 6, 1947; s. Howard W. and Lois (Ivie) P.; m. Lorraine Bertelli, Oct. 11, 1981; children: Christian James, Matthew David, Alexandra Elizabeth, Meredith Gillian, Lauren Ashley, Geoffrey Nicholas. BA in Philosophy, U. Utah, 1970, JD, 1973. Bar: Ariz. 1973, Tex. 1990. Ptnr. Snell & Wilmer, Phoenix, 1973—89; shareholder Johnson & Gibbs, Dallas, 1989—93; ptnr. Gardere & Wynne, Dallas, 1993—95, Baker Botts, LLP, Dallas, 1995—. Lectr. in field. Contbr. articles to profl. jours. Served to capt. USAR Fellow Am. Coll. Employee Benefit Counsel, Inc. (charter); mem. ABA (tax sect., past chair employee benefits com., past vice chair, past chmn. various sub-coms., 1993-94, chair joint com. on employee benefits 1994-95), Tex. State Bar Assn. (chair, tax sect. benefits and compensation com. 2000), Dallas Bar Assn. (chair employee benefits sect. 2001-2002), S.W. Benefits Conf., Nat. Assn. Stock Plan Profls., Order of Coif. Episcopalian. Office: Baker & Botts LLP 2001 Ross Ave Ste 600 Dallas TX 75201-2900 Home: 4218 Rosa Ct Dallas TX 75220 Office Phone: 214-953-6878. Business E-Mail: bruce.pingree@bakerbotts.com.

PINGREE, CHELLIE M. (ROCHELLE M. PINGREE), United States Representative from Maine; b. Mpls., Apr. 2, 1955; divorced; children: Hannah, Cecily, Asa. Attended, U. Southern Maine, Outward Bound, 1970; BA, Coll. of Atlantic, 1976; attended Summer Fellows Program, Kennedy Sch. Govt., 1996. Farmer North Island Farm, 1977—80; owner, founder North Island Designs, 1981—93; mem. Maine State Senate from Dist. 12, 1992—2000, majority leader, 1996—2000; pres., CEO Common Cause, 2003—07; founder, mng. ptnr. Nebo Lodge, 2006—09; mem. US Congress from 1st Maine Dist., 2009—. Mem. North Haven Grange, 1981—; founder, pres. North Haven Arts and Enrichment Fund, 1999—2000; mem. adv. bd. Main Businesses for Social Responsibility, 2000—; bd. dirs. Wal-Mart Watch, 2005—. Author; photography, design, and prodn. coord. Maine Island Classics: Sweaters and Stories From Offshore, 1988, Sweaters from the Maine Islands, 1990, North Island Designs, 1992, Maine Island Classics, 1992, North Island Designs 5: A Scrapbook of Sweaters from a Maine Island, 1993. Mem. Spl. Com. to Study Nursing Home Rates, 1995—96, Commn. to Study Poverty Among the Working Poor, 1995—96, Adv. Com. on Mental Retardation, 1995—96; co-chair Maine Econ. Growth Coun., 1995—98; former chair SAD 7 Sch. Bd.; Chair North Haven Tax Assesors, 1980—94; mem. North Haven Planning Bd., 1989—94; senator Maine State Senate, 1992—2000. Democrat. Lutheran. Office: US Congress 1037 Longworth House Office Bldg Washington DC 20515-1901 also: Dist Office 57 Exchange Ave Ste 302 Portland ME 04101 Office Phone: 202-225-6116, 207-774-5019. Office Fax: 202-225-5590, 207-871-0720.*

PING-ROBBINS, NANCY REGAN, musician, writer, artist; b. Nashville, Dec. 19, 1939; d. Charles Augustus and Ruby Phyllis (Perdue) Regan; m. Robert Leroy Ping, June 19, 1959 (div. 1980); children: Robert Alan, Michael Regan, Bryan Edward; m. William Edward Robbins, Jr., Mar. 14, 1981. BMusic, Ind. U., 1964; MA, U. No. Colo., 1972; PhD, U. Colo., 1979. Pvt. instr. piano and flute, 1960—; organist Armed Forces Chapels, Frankfurt, Kaiserslautern, Germany, 1962-66; staff pianist US Armed Forces Spl. Svcs. Theater, Frankfurt, 1963-65; music tchr. Fayetteville Pub. Schs., Ind., 1966-67, Stratton Pub. Schs., Colo., 1967-70; instr. piano, staff piano accompanist U. No. Colo., Greeley, 1970-72; instr. music history U. Colo., Boulder, 1974; instr., asst. prof. music U. NC, Wilmington, 1974-79; assoc. prof. music, coord. music Shaw U., Raleigh, NC, 1979-87; dir. Atlantic CC Com. Arts Sch., 1987-88. Profl. harpsichord accompanist Internat. Inst. in Early Music, 1983; adj. prof. Atlantic Christian Coll. (now Barton Coll.), 1987—88, assoc. prof., 1987—95; mem., pianist Chekker Duo, 1996—2003, 2006—07; founder mem. Susato Sounds Early Music Group, 2009. Recs. include: Early Popular Music on Piano/Harpsichord, 1984, Christmas at the Piano, 1997, En Blanc et Noir, 2001; author: The Piano Trio in the Twentieth Century, 1984, Scott Joplin: A Guide to Research, 1998, (memoir) Why the Circle Broke, 2006, (novel) Rachel's Choices, 2006; editor, compiler: The Music of Gustave Blessner, 1985; music reviewer: News and Observer, Raleigh, 1981-96, head music critic, 1989-95; artist: (painting) The White Show, Visual Arts Exch., Raleigh, NC, 2007, North Carolina Woods in Fall, Luna Bean, Wilson, 2007, 500 under 50, Harnett County Arts Coun., 2007, Art for the Masses, Creative Wilmington.com, 2007, Holiday Invitational Wilson Arts Ctr., 2008, Tales Retold, Punchline, Unfettered, 2009, Visual Arts Exch., 2009, Small Treasures, Cary Gallery Artists, 2009; contbr. articles to profl. jours. Sec. Bach Festival Com., Raleigh, 1984; dir. music Bailey United Meth. Ch., N.C., 2000-07. John H. Edwards fellow Ind. U., 1961; U. Colo. grad fellow, 1972-74; Mellon Found. grantee, 1982; N.C. Arts Coun. grantee, 1985; NEH summer seminar fellow, 1984. Mem. Am. Musicol. Soc. (sec.-treas. chpt. 1981-83), Soc. for Ethnomusicology (chmn. regional chpt. 1983-84), Wilson Piano Tchrs. Assn. (pres. 1988-90, 95-98, 2009-), Soc. Am. Music (formerly Sonneck Soc., program com. 1999), Wilson Active Artist Assoc.(newsletter editor, 2008-09), Alpha Lambda Delta, Pi Kappa Lambda, Sigma Alpha Iota. Personal E-mail: npr@japakco.com, nanart@japakco.com.

PINGS, ANTHONY CLAUDE, architect; b. Fresno, Calif., Dec. 16, 1951; s. Clarence Hubert and Mary (Murray) P.; m. Carole Clements, June 25, 1983; children, Adam Reed, Rebecca Mary. AA, Fresno City Coll., 1972; BArch, Calif. Poly. State U., San Luis Obispo, 1976. Lic. architect, Calif.; cert. Nat. Council Archtl. Registration Bds. Architect Aubrey Moore Jr., Fresno, 1976-81; architect, prin. Pings & Assocs., Fresno, 1981-83, 86—, Pings-Taylor Assocs., Fresno, 1983-85. Prin. works include Gollaher Profl. Office (Masonry Merit award 1985, Best Office Bldg. award 1986), Fresno Imaging Ctr. (Best Instnl. Project award 1986, Nat. Healthcare award Modern Health Care mag. 1986), Orthopedic Facility (award of honor Masonry Inst. 1987, award of merit San Joaquin chpt. AIA 1987), Modesto Imaging Ctr. (award of merit San Joaquin chpt. AIA 1991), Peachwood Med. Ctr. (award of merit San Joaquin chpt. AIA). Mem. Calif. Indsl. Tech. Edn. Consortium Calif. State Dept. Edn., 1983, 84. Recipient Excellence in Bus. award Fresno, 1999. Mem. AIA (bd. dirs. Calif. chpt. 1983-84, v.p. San Joaquin chpt. 1982, pres. 1983, Calif. Coun. evaluation team 1983, team leader Coalinga Emergency Design Assistance team), Fresno Arts (bd. dirs., counsel 1989—, pres. 1990-93), Fig Gardens Home Owners Assn. (bd. dir. 1991—, pres. 1994—). Republican. Home: 4350 N Safford Ave Fresno CA 93704-3509

PINHEIRO, JOAQUIM MANUEL BERNARDINO, pediatrician, educator; b. Lisbon, Portugal, Mar. 22, 1958; s. Manuel Henriques and Maria Helena (Bernardino) P.; m. Alexandra Lori Auld, Mar. 17, 1991; children: Gabriela, Isabel, Sofia. BA summa cum laude, Rutgers U., 1978; MD, NYU, 1982. Resident in pediatrics Johns Hopkins Hosp., Balt., 1982-85; fellow in neonatology Yale-New Haven Hosp., 1985-88; asst. prof. pediatrics Albany (N.Y.) Med. Coll., 1988-92, assoc. prof. pediatrics, 1992—. Mem. admissions com. Albany Med. Coll., 1992—, dir. neonatology fellowship program, 1994—; cons., peer reviewer N.Y. State Dept. of Health, Albany, 1995—. Active health profls. adv. bd. March of Dimes, Albany, 1988—. Am. Heart Assn. grantee, 1992-95; Neonatal Hearing Screening grantee N.Y. State Dept. of Health, 1994—; recipient Cardiovascular Disease Rsch. award Margaret Finnerty Found., 1995—. Fellow Am. Acad. Pediatrics; mem. Am. Thoracic Soc., Soc. Pediat. Rsch., Phi Beta Kappa, Alpha Omega Alpha. Avocation: soccer. Home: 42 Folmsbee Dr Albany NY 12204-1222 Office: Albany Med Ctr A-101 47 New Scotland Ave Albany NY 12208-3412

PINHEIRO, JOHN C., historian, educator; b. Calif. s. Albert and Patricia Pinheiro; m. Cassandra Pinheiro. BA, Calif. State U., Bakersfield, 1992, MA, 1994; PhD, U. Tenn., Knoxville, 2001. Asst. editor Papers George Wash. U. Va., Charlottesville, 2002—04, consulting editor Miller Ctr. Pub. Affairs, 2008—; assoc. prof. history Aquinas Coll., Grand Rapids, Mich., 2004—. Author: (book) Manifest Ambition: James K. Polk and Civil-Military Relations during the Mexican War; contbr. articles to profl. jours. (Russell B. Nye award, 2003). Jerry and Edgar Wilson fellowship, 2000—01, fellowship, Filson Hist. Soc., 2000. Mem.: So. Hist. Assn., Soc. Historians Early Republic, Phi Alpha Theta. Office: Aquinas Coll 1607 Robinson Rd SE Grand Rapids MI 49506-1799 Business E-Mail: pinhejoh@aquinas.edu.

PINIELLA, LOU (LOUIS VICTOR PINIELLA), professional baseball team manager; b. Tampa, Fla., Aug. 28, 1943; m. Anita Garcia, Apr. 12, 1967; children: Lou, Kristi, Derrick. Student, U. Tampa. Outfielder various minor-league teams, 1962-68, Cleve. Indians, 1968, Kans. City Royals, 1969-73, NY Yankees, 1974-84, coach, 1984-85, mgr., 1985-87, 1988, gen. mgr., 1987-88, spl. adviser, TV announcer, 1989; mgr. Cin. Reds, 1990-92, Seattle Mariners, 1992—2002, Tampa Bay Devil Rays, 2003—05; baseball analyst ESPN, 2005—06; mgr. Chgo. Cubs, 2006—. Recipient Ellis Island Medal of Honor, 1990; named Am. League Rookie of Yr., Baseball Writers' Assn. America, 1969, Am. League Mgr. of Yr., 1995, 2001, Nat. League Mgr. of Yr., 2008; named to Am. League All-Star Team, Maj. League Baseball, 1972. Achievements include leading the American League in: doubles (33), 1972; member of the World Series Championship winning New York Yankees, 1977, 78; manager of the World Series Championship winning Cincinnati Reds, 1990. Office: Chgo Cubs Wrigley Field 1060 W Addison St Chicago IL 60613*

PINJARI, ABDUL R., assistant professor; b. Kurnool, Andhra Pradesh, India, July 4, 1979; s. Abdul Jaleel and Murthuja Bi Pinjari; m. Sultana Shaikh, Dec. 16, 2007. B.Tech, Indian Inst. Tech. Madras, Chennai, 2002; M.S.C.E, U. South Fla., Tampa, 2004; PhD, U. South Fla., Austin, Tex., 2008, U. Tex., Austin. Grad. rsch. asst. U. South Fla., 2002—04, Ctr. Transp. Rsch. UT Austin, 2004—08, rsch. project mgr., 2007—08. Contbr. numerous articles to profl. jours. Vol. Vibha, Austin, 2005. Recipient Profl. Devel. award, Grad. Sch. UT Austin, 2006, Charley Wootan award, 2008; fellow, Internat. Rd. Fedn., 2007; Mary Collins Meml. Endowed Presdl. fellowship, Dept. Civil Engring. UT Austin, 2006—07. Mem.: UT Chpt. Inst. Transp. Engrs. (treas. 2005—06), Tau Beta Pi. Office: Univ S Fla Civil Engring 4202 E Fowler Ave Tampa FL 33612 Business E-Mail: apinjari@eng.usf.edu.

PINK, MICHAEL, performing company executive; b. York, Eng. Trained as classical dancer, Royal Ballet Sch. Dancer English Nat. Ballet, 1975—85; founding dir. Ballet Ctrl., London, 1987—91; assoc. dir. Northern Ballet, 1988; artistic dir. Milw. Ballet, 2002—. Internat. tchr. Norwegian Nat. Ballet, Aterballetto, Balletto di Toscanna Italy, The Hartford Ballet, Rozas Dance Co., London Contemporary Dance Co., White Oaks Dance Project, Ballet Rambert, English Nat. Ballet, Phoenix Dance Co., London Ballet. Recipient First Pl. in inaugural, Ursula Moreton Choreographic Competition, First Pl., Royal Soc. of Arts Competition, Choreography Performance award, Wis. Dance Coun., 2008. Office: Milwaukee Ballet 504 W National Ave Milwaukee WI 53204 E-mail: michael@milwaukeeballet.org.*

PINK, (ALECIA BETH MOORE), singer; b. Doylestown, Pa., Sept. 8, 1979; d. James and Judy (Kugel) Moore; m. Carey Hart, Jan. 7, 2006 (separated Feb. 2008). With Arista Records, 2001—. Singer: (albums) Can't Take Me Home, 2000, M!ssundaztood, 2001, Try This, 2003, I'm Not Dead, 2006, (songs) Funhouse, 2008, There U Go, 2000, Most Girls, 2000, (with Mya, Lil' Kim, Christina Aguilera) Lady Marmalade, 2001 (Grammy award Song Yr., 2002, 2 MTV Video Music awards, 2001), You Make Me Sick, 2001, Get the Party Started, 2001 (2 MTV Video Music Awards, 2002), Don't Let Me Get Me, 2002, Just Like a Pill, 2002, Family Portrait, 2002, Feel Good Time, 2003, Trouble, 2003 (Grammy award, Best Female Rock Performance, 2004), God is a DJ, 2003, Stupid Girls, 2006 (MTV Video Music award for Best Pop Video, 2006); actor: (films) Ski to the Max, 2000, Rollerball, 2002, Charlie's Angels: Full Throttle, 2003, Catacombs, 2007. Recipient World Music award for Best Am. Pop Female Artist, 2003; named one of 100 Sexiest Artists, VH1, 2002. Office: Box #390 5701 E Circle Dr Cicero NY 13039

PINKAEW, PRACHYA, film producer and director; b. Thailand, Sept. 2, 1962; Grad. in Architecture, Nakornratsima Tech. Coll., 1985. Art dir. Pack Shot Entertainment, 1990, creative dir.; head Baa-Ram-Ewe. Dir. Thai Film Assn. Writer, prodr., and dir. (films) Ong-Bak, 2003 (Action Asia award Deauville Asian Film Festival, 2004, Orient Express award Catalonian Internat. Film Festival, 2003), Tom Yum Goong, 2005; dir.: (films) The Magic Shoes, 1992, Darkside Romance, 1994; prodr.: Body Jumper, 2001, Heaven 7, 2002, 999-9999, 2002, Hoedown Showdown, 2002, Sayew, 2003, The Unborn, 2003, Fake, 2003, Pisaj, 2004, Kerd ma lui, 2004, Cherm, 2005. Mailing: c/o Sahamongkol Film International Co 288 SP Bldg (IBM) Phahonyothin Rd Samsennai Phayathai Bangkok 10400 Thailand Office Phone: 662-9335665.

PINKEL, DONALD PAUL, pediatrician; b. Buffalo, Sept. 7, 1926; s. Lawrence William and Ann (Richardson) P.; m. Marita Donovan, Dec. 26, 1949 (div. 1981); children: Rebecca, Nancy, Christopher, Mary, Thomas, Anne, Sara, John, Ruth; m. Cathryn Barbara Howarth, May 16, 1981; 1 child, Michael. BS, Canisius Coll., 1947; MD, U. Buffalo, 1951. Diplomate Am. Bd. Pediatrics, Pediatric Hematology and Oncology, Nat. Bd. Med. Examiners. From intern to resident to chief resident Children's Hosp., Buffalo, 1951-54; research fellow Children's Hosp. Med. Ctr., Boston, 1955-56; chief. of pediatrics Roswell Park Meml. Inst., Buffalo, 1956-61; founding dir. St. Jude Children's Rsch. Hosp., Memphis, 1961-73; chmn. pediatrics Med. Coll. Wis., Milw., 1974-78; pediatrician-in-chief Milw. Children's Hosp., 1974-78; founding dir. Midwest Children's Cancer Ctr., Milw., 1974; chief. of pediatrics City of Hope Med. Ctr., Duarte, Calif., 1978-82; chmn. pediatrics Temple U. Sch. Medicine, Phila., 1982-85; prof., Kana Rsch. chair, dir. pediatric leukemia program M.D. Anderson Cancer Ctr. U. Tex., Houston, 1985-93; prof. pediat. U. Tex. Med. Sch., Houston, 1985-99; prof. emeritus U. Tex.-M.D. Anderson Cancer Ctr., Houston, 1994—. Clin. prof. pediats. U. So. Calif., LA, 2002—; adj. prof. biol. scis. Calif. Polytechnic State U., San Luis Obispo, Calif., 2001—. Contbr. articles to profl. jours. Bd. dirs. Lee County Coop. Clinic, Mariana, Ark., 1972-74. Served with USN, 1944-45, served to 1st lt. U.S. Army, 1954-55. Recipient Albert Lasker award for Med. Rsch., Lasker Found., 1972, Windermere Lectureship Brit. Pediatric Assn., 1974, David Karnofsky award Am. Soc. Clin. Oncology, 1978, Zimmerman prize for Cancer Rsch. Zimmerman Found., 1979, Charles Kettering prize Gen. Motors Cancer Rsch., 1986, Clin. Rsch. award Am. Cancer Soc., 1988, Return of the Child award Leukemia Soc. Am., 1992, Pollin prize in pediat. rsch. N.Y. Presbyn. Hosp., 2003. Mem. Am. Soc. Clin. Oncology, Am. Pediat. Soc., Am. Assn. Cancer Rsch., Soc. Exptl. Biology and Medicine, Am. Soc. Hematology. Democrat. Roman Catholic. Avocations: swimming, sailing. Home: 275 Marlene Dr San Luis Obispo CA 93405 E-mail: donpinkel@yahoo.com.

PINKEL, GARY, college football coach; b. Akron, Ohio, Apr. 27, 1952; m. Vicki Pinkel; children: Erin, Geoff, Blake. BS in Edn., Kent St. Univ., 1973, grad. studies, Bowling Green. Grad. asst. Kent State U. Golden Flashes, 1974—75; tight ends coach Washington U. Huskies, 1976, wide receivers coach, 1979—83, offensive coord., 1984—90; wide receivers coach Bowling Green St. U. Falcons, 1977—78; head coach U. Toledo Rockets, 1991—2000, U. Mo. Tigers, 2001—. Named to Kent State Hall of Fame, 1997. Office: Univ Mo c/o Tigers Athletics Columbia MO 65211*

PINKER, STEVEN ARTHUR, psychology professor; b. Montreal, Que., Can., Sept. 18, 1954; arrived in US, 1976; s. Harry and Roslyn (Wiesenfeld) P.; m. Rebecca Goldstein BA in Exptl. Psychology, McGill U., Montreal, 1976; PhD, Harvard U., 1979; DSc (hon.), McGill U., 1999; DPhil (hon.), Tel Aviv. U., 2003, U. Newcastle, 2005; DUniv (hon.), U. Surrey, 2003. Postdoctoral fellow Center for Cognitive Sci., MIT; asst. prof. psychology Harvard U., Cambridge, Mass., 1980-81, Stanford U., Palo Alto, Calif., 1981-82, MIT, Cambridge, 1982—85, assoc. prof. brain & cognitive sci., 1985—89, prof., 1989—, co-dir. Center for Cognitive Sci., 1985—94, dir. McDonnell-Pew Center for Cognitive Neuroscience, 1994—99, Peter de Florez prof., 2000—03; Johnstone Family prof. psychology Harvard U., 2003—. Cons. Cognitive and Instructional Scis. Group, Xerox Corp. Palo Alto Rsch. Centers, 1981—82; vis. scholar, dept. of psychology Harvard Univ., 1987—88; vis. scholar, cognitive devel. unit Med. Rsch Coun., London, 1988; vis. scholar, dept. of psychology and linguistics Univ. Calif., Santa Barbara, 1995—96; hon. vis. prof., dept. of psychology Univ. of Auckland, New Zealand, 2001—04; inst. advisor Allen Inst. for Brain Sci., Seattle; spkr. in field. Author: Language Learnability and Language Development, 1984, Learnability and Cognition, 1989, The Language Instinct, 1994, How the Mind Works, 1997 (LA Times Science Book Prize, 1998, finalist for Pullitzer prize, 1998), Words and Rules: The Ingredients of Language, 1999, The Blank Slate: The Modern Denial of Human Nature, 2002 (finalist for Pulitzer prize, 2003), The Stuff of Thought: Language As a Window Into Human Nature, 2007; assoc. editor Cognition, 1984—; advisor, Am. Heritage Dictionary; serves on several advisory and editorial bds., contbr. articles to sci. jours. and chapters in books. Recipient Troland Rsch. award NAS, 1993, Golden Plate award, Am. Acad. of Achievement, 1999, Henry Dale prize Royal Instn. Gt. Britain, 2004, Henry Dale prize Royal Instn. of Gt. Britain, 2004; named Humanist Laureate Internat. Acad. Humanism, 2001, Humanist of Yr., Am. Humanist Assn., 2006. Fellow AAAS, APA (Disting. Early Career award 1984, Boyd McCandless award 1986, William James Book prize 1995, 99, 2003, Eleanor Maccoby Book prize 2003), Am. Acad. Arts and Scis., Linguistics Soc. Am. (Linguistics, Lang. and Pub. Svcs. award 1997), Am. Psychol. Soc. Office: Dept Psychology Harvard Univ William James Hall 970 33 Kirkland St Cambridge MA 02138 Office Phone: 617-495-0831. Office Fax: 617-495-3278. Business E-Mail: pinker@wjh.harvard.edu.*

PINKERT, DEAN A., federal official; BA with high honors, Oberlin Coll., Ohio, 1978; JD with honors, U. Tex.; ML, London Sch. Economics and Polit. Sci. Sr. assoc. King & Spalding, Washington, 1998—2000; trade and judiciary counsel to Senator Robert C. Byrd, 2001; atty. advisor Office of Chief Counsel for Import Adminstrn., US Dept. Commerce, sr. atty.; commr. US Internat. Trade Commn., Washington, 2007—. Office: US Internat Trade Commn 500 E St SW Washington DC 20436*

PINKERTON, MARJORIE JEAN, librarian, library science educator; b. Chgo., June 15, 1934; d. Michael Seretto and Evelyn Isabel (Scott) Glass; m. James Ronald Pinkerton, June 29, 1957; children— Steven James, Kathryn Lynn. B.A. in Spanish and History, Carroll Coll., 1956; MA in Spanish, U. Wis., Madison, 1964; MA in Library Sci., U. Mo., 1973. Tchr. high sch., Pardeeville, Wis., 1956-57, Preble, Wis., 1958-59; libr. asst. Meml. Libr., U. Wis., Madison, 1959-64; substitute tchr., librarian Columbia Pub. Schs., Mo., 1965-73; ednl. materials librarian, asst. prof. William Woods Coll., Fulton, Mo., 1973-81, assoc. prof., 1985-93, ret., 1993, dir. Dulany Libr. 1981-1993. Co-author: Outdoor Recreation and Leisure, 1969. Contbr. articles to profl. jours. Mem. Bd. Adjustment, City of Columbia, 1971-75, chmn., 1973-74; dir. Nat. Ghost Ranch Found., United Presbyterian Ch., Santa Fe, N.Mex., 1981-84; active Columbia Safety Coun., 1967, pres., 1969-70. Recipient award for cmty. svc. New Democratic Coalition, Columbia, 1976, Outstanding Young Woman award, 1969. Mem. ALA, Mo. Assn. Coll. and Rsch. Libraries (chmn. 1984-85), Mo. Libr. Assn. (com. chmn. 1978-79), Mid-Mo. Associated Colls. and Univs. (chmn. libr. com. 1984-85), Nat. Coun. Tchrs. English, LWV (v.p. 1967-68, 2002-06, dir. 2008-), Nat. Geneal. Soc., Beta Phi Mu (pres. 1974-76, 85-86), Peace Studies Inst., Phi Alpha Theta, Kappa Delta Pi. Presbyterian. Clubs: UN (pres. 1970), Friends of the Libr. (Columbia, sec.-treas. 1977-78), Gertrude Matthews Soc., Jefferson Club, U. Mo. Libr. Soc. Avocations: genealogy, reading, travel. Home: 20 Springer Dr Columbia MO 65201-5425 Home Phone: 573-445-2052. Personal E-mail: mpmidge@aol.com.

PINKERTON, RICHARD LADOYT, retired management educator, writer; b. Huron, SD, Mar. 5, 1933; s. Abner Pyle and Orral Claudine (Arneson) P.; m. Sandra Louise Lee, Aug. 28, 1965 (div. 1992); children: Elizabeth, Patricia. BA, U. Mich., 1955; MBA, Case Western Res. U., 1962; PhD, U. Wis., 1969. Sr. market rsch. analyst Harris-Intertype Corp., Cleve., 1957-61; mgr. sales devel. Triax Corp., Cleve., 1962-64; coord. mktg. program Mgmt. Inst., U. Wis., 1964-67; dir. exec. programs Mgmt. Inst., U. Wis. (Grad. Sch. Bus.), also asst. prof. mktg., 1969-74; prof. mgmt., dean Grad. Sch. Adminstrn., Capital U., Columbus, Ohio, 1974-86; prof. mgmt., dir. Univ. Bus. Ctr., Craig Sch. Bus. Calif. State U., Fresno, 1986-89, prof. mktg., 1989-2000, chmn. mktg. and logistics dept., 1996-2000, dir. London semester, prof. emeritus, mem. bd., 2000—. Adj. prof. Case Western Res. U., 2004-; trustee Ohio Coun. Econ. Edn., 1976-87; cons. to govt. and industry, 1960—. Co-author: The Purchasing Manager's Guide to Strategic Proactive Procurement, 1996; contbr. articles to profl. jours. Bd. govs. Hannah Neil Home for Children, Columbus, 1975—78; mem. indsl. and cmty. devel. commn. City of Strongsville, Ohio; bd. dirs. The Fresno Townhouse Assn., 1992—2001. Officer USAF, 1955—57, lt. col. USAF, 1957—78. La Verne Noyes scholar, 1952—55, Nat. Assn. Purchasing Mgmt. fellow, 1967—68. Mem.: Am. Mktg. Assn. (chpt. pres. 1972—73), Nat. Assn. Purchasing Mgmt. (chmn. acad. planning 1979—84, rsch. symposium 1992), Nat. Assn. Contract Mgmt. (chmn. validation cert. com. 1990), Air Force Assn., Res. Officers Assn., Marines Meml. Club, Columbia Hills Country Club, Phi Gamma Delta, Alpha Kappa Psi, Beta Gamma Sigma. Home: 18487 Woodside Crossing South Strongsville OH 44149-6891 Office Phone: 440-846-1430.

PINKERTON, ROBERT BRUCE, mechanical engineer; b. Detroit, Feb. 10, 1941; s. George Fulwell and Janet Lois (Hedke) P.; m. Barbara Ann Bandfield, Aug. 13, 1966; 1 child, Robert Brent. BSME, Detroit Inst. Tech., 1965; MA in Engring., Chrysler Inst. Engring., 1967; JD, Wayne State U., 1976. From mech. engr. to emissions and fuel economy planning specialist Chrysler Engring. Office Chrysler Corp., Highland Park, Mich., 1967-80; dir. engring. Replacement div. TRW, Inc., Cleve., 1980-83; v.p. engring. TRW Automotive Aftermarket Group, 1983-86; v.p. engring. and rsch. Blackstone Corp., Jamestown, NY, 1986-89, pres., CEO, 1989-90, Athena Corp., Beaufort, SC, 1990—, Cedar Crest Corp., Beaufort, SC, 1990—; chmn., CEO Beaufort Land Co., 1998—. Bd. dirs. VRI, LLC, Coastal Banking Co., Inc., Low Country Nat. Bank, Village Renaissance, Inc., Carpenters Hall, Coastal Banking Co., Inc.; chmn. redevelopment commn. City Beaufort, 2004—. Mem. exec. com. Beaufort Schs. Oversight Com., 1995-99, Pvt. Industry Coun., 1996-99. Mem.: Greater Beaufort C. of C. (bd. dirs. 1997—98), Beaufort Roundtable (pres. 2000—02), Rotary (asst. dist. gov. 1997—98). Episcopalian. Home: 5-D Rising Tide Dr Beaufort SC 29902 Office: PO Box 2115 1203 Boundary St Beaufort SC 29902 Business E-Mail: rbp@athenacorp.com.

PINKETT-SMITH, JADA, actress; b. Balt., Sept. 18, 1971; m. Will Smith, Dec. 31, 1997; 2 children. Actor (films) Menace II Society, 1993, The Inkwell, 1994, Jason's Lyric, 1994, A Low Down Dirty Shame, 1994, Demon Knight, 1995, The Nutty Professor, 1996, Set It Off, 1996, Blossoms and Veils, 1997 (also exec. prodr.), Scream 2, 1997, Woo, 1998, Return to Paradise, 1998, Bamboozled, 2000, Kingdom Come, 2001, Ali, 2001, The Matrix Reloaded, 2003, The Matrix Revolutions, 2003, Collateral, 2004, (voice) Madagascar, 2005, Reign Over Me, 2007, The Women, 2008, (voice) Madagascar: Escape 2 Africa, 2008, (TV films) If These Walls Could Talk, 1996, Maniac Magee, 2003, (TV series) A Different World, 1992-93, exec. prodr. All of Us, 2003-; exec. prodr. (films) The Seat Filler, 2004; author (children's book): Girls Hold Up This World, 2004 (NY Times Bestseller list, NAACP Image award for outstanding lit. work-children's 2006). Office: c/o Overbrook Entertainment Inc 450 North Roxbury Dr 8th Fl Beverly Hills CA 90210

PINKWATER, JULIE, publishing executive; BA, Boston U. With Sotheby's Internat. Realty, Network TV Assn; with advertising agency McCaffrey & McCall, Penchina Selkowitz, McCann Erickson; mgr. position Ladies Home Jour.; beauty dir. Allure; advertising dir. More, 1998—2000, pub., 2000—01, Fitness Mag., G&J USA, NY, 2001—04; v.p., pub. Ladies Home Jour., NY, 2004—. Office: Ladies Home Jour 125 Park Ave 20th Floor New York NY 10017-5529 Office Phone: 212-551-7153. Office Fax: 212-455-1313. E-mail: julie.pinkwater@meredith.com.*

PINN, VIVIAN W., federal agency administrator, pathologist; b. Halifax, Va., 1941; BA, Wellesley Coll., Mass., 1963; MD, U. Va. Sch. Medicine, 1967. Intern pathology Mass. Gen. Hosp., Boston, 1967-68, rsch. fellow, 1968-70; asst. pathologist Tufts U. New Eng. Med. Ctr. Hosp., Boston, 1970-77, pathologist, 1977-82; asst. to assoc. prof. pathology Tufts U. Sch. Medicine, 1971-82, asst. dean student affairs, 1974-82; prof., dept. chair pathology Howard U. Coll. Medicine, Washington, 1982-91; dir. Office Rsch. on Women's Health (ORWH), NIH, Bethesda, Md., 1991—, assoc. dir. rsch. women's health, ORWH, 1994—. Pres. Nat. Med. Assn., 1989—90; co-chair NIH Working Group Women in Biomed. Careers. Recipient Disting. Alumna award, U. Va. Sch. Medicine, 1992, Walter Reed Alumni Achievement award, 2007, Walter Ridley Trailblazer award, 2007, Alumni Achievement award, Wellesley Coll., 1993, Excellence in Leadership award, Dominion Resources Svcs., Inc., 2008, James D. Bruce Meml. award, ACP, Catherine McFarland award for disting. svc. in women's health, Med. Coll. Pa., Women in Medicine Leadership Devel. award, Assn. Am. Med. Colleges, Margaret E. Mahoney award for outstanding svc. in advancing the quality of health care for women, Commonwealth Fund, Pres.'s Achievement award, Am. Med. Women's Assn., Lifetime Achievement award, Jacobs Inst.; named an Alumni Luminary, U. Va. Sch. Medicine, 1998. Fellow: Am. Acad. Arts & Scis. Office: NIH OWHR 6707 Democracy Blvd Ste 400 Bethesda MD 20892 Office Phone: 301-402-1770. Office Fax: 301-402-1798.*

PINNELL, SABRINA L., political science professor; d. Robert P. and Sharron G. Pinnell; m. Edward F. Collins, Aug. 1, 2004. BA, U. Calif., Santa Cruz, 1992; MPA, Monterey Inst. Internat. Studies, Calif., 1995; PhD, U. Calif., Santa Barbara, 2007. Part-time lectr. Dept. Polit. Sci., Santa Clara U., Calif., 2006; lectr. Dept. Polit. Sci., San Jose State U., 2007—; part-time instr. Dept. Polit. Sci., Mission Coll., Santa Clara, 2008—. Mem.: Internat. Polit. Sci. Assn., Am. Polit. Sci. Assn. Avocations: music, martial arts. Office: San Jose State Univ One Washington Square San Jose CA 95192

PINO, JEFFREY P., manufacturing executive; b. Aberdeen, Md. B in Psychology, U. Ariz., Tucson, 1976; M in Bus. Adminstrn. and Mgmt., Webster U., St. Louis, 1985; disting. honor grad., US Army Armor Sch., US Army Aviation Sch. Cert. airline and helicopter instr. pilot. With Bell Helicopter Textron, 1985—2002, program mgr. for prodn. Kiowa Warrior (OH-58D) and Cobra (AH-1S) modernization programs, program mgr. team bidding on LHX competition, v.p. sales and mktg., exec. dir. Europe, dir. L.Am., regional mgr. S.Am., sr. v.p.; sr. v.p. mktg. and comml. programs Sikorsky Aircraft Corp., Stratford, Conn., 2002, sr. v.p. corp. strategy, mktg., and comml. programs, pres., 2006—. Chmn. bd. dirs. Fairfield, Westchester County affiliate INROADS; mem. bd. dirs. Bridgeport Hosp., Conn. Ret. master Army aviator US Army, devel. test pilot/project officer US Army, Yuma Proving Ground, Ariz., mem. Nat. Guard US Army, mem. USAR. Office: Sikorsky Aircraft 6900 Main St Stratford CT 06615

PINO, VERONICA WOODARD, humanities educator; d. Elizabeth Louise Woodard; m. Hector Rafael Pino; children: Rafael, Nikita Carlene Toppin. PhD, Fla. Atlantic U., Boca Raton, 2008. Assoc. prof. Indian River State Coll., Fort Pierce, Fla., 1982—. Bus.-info. tech. adv. com. Ft. Pierce Ctrl. HS, Fort Pierce, 2008—09; state common course number chair office sys. tech. Fla. Dept. Edn., Tallahassee, 2006—08. Mem., corr. sec. Links, Inc., Fort Pierce, 1994—2009. Recipient Pioneer award, Indian River State Coll., 2002, IMPAC award, Fla. Atlantic U., 1998—99. Mem.: AAUP (sec. & contract negotiator 2001—09), Fla. Assn. Cmty. Colls. (pres. 2000—01), Gold Key Internat., Alpha Kappa Alpha. Democrat. Baptist. Avocations: cooking, travel. Home: 1425 SW Robys Way Palm City FL 34990 Office: Indian River State Coll 3209 Virginia Ave Fort Pierce FL 34981 Personal E-mail: vtoppin@hotmail.com. Business E-Mail: vpino@irsc.edu.

PINSKY, DREW (DAVID DREW PINSKY), television personality, psychotherapist; b. Pasadena, Calif., Sept. 4, 1958; s. Morton and Helene; m. Susan Pinsky, July 20, 1991; children: Jordan Davidson, Douglas Drew, Paulina Marie. BS in Biology, Amherst Coll., Mass., 1980; MD, U. Southern Calif., 1984. Chief resident Huntington Meml. Hosp.; med. dir. dept. chem. dependency svcs. Aurora Las Encinas Hosp., Pasadena, Calif.; pvt. practice; asst. clin. prof. psychiatry Keck U. Southern Calif. Sch. Medicine. Spokesperson Musicians Assistance Prog.; works with Advocates for Youth, Ind. Women's Forum, Media Project, Entertainment Industry Coun., Hillside Home for Children. Host (radio) Loveline, 1982—, (TV series), MTV, 1996—2000, Men Are from Mars, Women Are from Venus, 2000, Strictly Sex with Dr. Drew, 2005, Strictly Dr. Drew, 2006, Sex...With Mom and Dad, host, prodr. Celebrity Rehab with Dr. Drew, 2008—, Sober House, 2009, appearances on Dawson's Creek, 2003, Family Guy, 2005, The Adam Carolla Project, 2005, Minoriteam, 2006, Robot Chicken, 2006, Code Monkeys, 2007; actor: (films) New York Minute, 2004, Wild Hogs, 2007, Big Stan, 2007; author: Cracked: Putting Broken Lives Together Again, 2003, When Painkillers Become Dangerous, 2004. Recipient Kaiser Sexual Health in Entertainment award, Planned Parenthood of Am. award, PRISM award, Claire Found. award. Mem.: Am. Soc. Internal Medicine, Calif. Med. Assn., Am. Soc. Addiction Medicine, AMA, Am. Coll. Physicians. Avocations: opera, running, skiing, surfing. Office: Aurora Las Encinas Hospital 2900 E Del Mar Blvd Pasadena CA 91107*

PINSKY, ROY DAVID, lawyer; b. Syracuse, NY, Feb. 1, 1948; s. Norman M. and Rose C. Pinsky; m. Stephanie V. Pinsky, June 9, 1968; children: Alissa Jill, Todd Justin. BS, Syracuse U., 1969, JD, 1971. Bar: NY 1972, Fla. 1981. Ptnr. Pinsky, Canter and Pinsky, Syracuse, 1972, Pinsky and Pliskin, Syracuse, 1972-88, Pinsky & Skandalis, 1988—. Spl. cons. Syracuse Bd. Edn., 1972-74; mem. atty. grievance com. Fifth Jud. Dist. Contbr. articles to profl. jours. Bd. dirs. Young Israel-Shaarei Torah of Syracuse; trustee Jewish Home of Ctrl. NY Served with US Army, 1969-75. Mem. NY State Bar Assn., Fla. Bar Assn., Onondaga County Bar Assn., Transp. Lawyers Assn. (past trustee), Def. Rsch. Inst., Can. Transport Lawyers Assn., Conf. Freight Counsel, Syracuse U. Sch. Mgmt. Alumni Assn. (past. nat. pres.). Home: 4623 Glencliffe Rd Manlius NY 13104-2378 Office: Ste 250 5790 Widewaters Pkwy Syracuse NY 13214-0250 Office Phone: 315-446-2384. Business E-Mail: rpinsky@pinskyskandalis.com.

PINSON, CHARLES WRIGHT, surgeon, educator, academic administrator; b. Albuquerque, May 29, 1952; s. Ernest Alexander and Jean Elizabeth Pinson. Student, Miami U., Oxford, Ohio, 1970-72; BA, U. Colo., Boulder, 1974, MBA, 1976; MD, Vanderbilt U., 1980. Diplomate Am. Bd. Surgery, Am. Bd. Surg. Critical Care, Nat. Bd. Med. Examiners. Resident in gen. surgery Oreg. Health Sci. U., Portland, 1980-86; fellow gastrointestinal surgery Lahey Clinic, Burlington, Mass., 1986-87; fellow transplant surgery Harvard U., Boston, 1987-88; dir. liver transplant program VA Western region, Portland, 1989-90, Oreg. Health Sci. U., Portland, 1988-90; interim chmn. dept. surgery Vanderbilt U., Nashville, 1993-95, chief divsn. hepatobiliary surgery and liver transplantation, 1990—2004, vice-chmn. dept. surgery, 1995-2001; dir. Vanderbilt Transplant Ctr., Nashville, 1993—; chmn. med. bd. Vanderbilt U. Med. Ctr., Nashville, 1997-99; chief of staff Vanderbilt U. Hosp., Nashville, 1997—2004; H. William Scott prof., chmn. dept. surgery Vanderbilt U., Nashville, 2001—04; chief med. officer, assoc. vice chancellor for clin. affairs Vanderbilt U. Med. Ctr., Nashville, 2004—09; dep. vice chancellor health affairs CEO Vanderbilt Hosp. & Clinics; pres. Vanderbilt Health Svc.; sr. assoc., dean Vanderbilt Med. Ctr. Adv. bd. Pacific N.W. Transplant Bank, Portland, 1989—90, Tenn. Donor Svcs., Nashville, 1991—, sec., 2003—05. Mem. editl. bd. Annals Surgery, Jour. Gastrointestinal Surgery, Liver Transplantation, HPB; contbr. articles to profl. jours., chapters to books. Chair liver and intestine allocation com. United Network Organ Sharing, 2003—05; bd. dirs. ARC, Nashville, 1992—94, Am. Liver Found., 1992—96, Ronald McDonald House, 2002—, United Network Organ Sharing, 2000—02, Hosp. Hospitality House, Nashville, 2005—. Fellow, Am. Heart Assn., 1983—84. Mem.: Internat. Hepatopancreatobiliary Assn. (mem. sci. com. 2000—03, mem. exec. com. 2003—, treas. 2004—08, pres. elect. 2008—), Internat. Liver Transplantation Soc., Soc. Surgery Alimentary Tract, Assn. Acad. Surgery, N. Pacific Surg. Assn. (mem. sci. program 1990—92), Western Surg. Assn., So. Surg. Assn., Am. Surg. Assn., So. Med. Assn. (chmn. sect. surgery 1997—2001), Am. Physiologic Soc., Am. Hepatopancreatobiliary Assn. (mem. exec. com. 1997—, treas. 1999—2003, pres. elect 2001—03, pres. 2003—05), Am. Gastroent. Assn., Am. Soc. Study Liver Diseases, Am. Soc. Transplant Surgeons, Soc. Surg. Oncology, Halsted Soc., Soc. Univ. Surgeons, Phi Beta Kappa, Sigma Xi, Alpha Omega Alpha. Office: Vanderbilt U Med Ctr D3300 MCN Nashville TN 37232-5545

PINSON, LARRY LEE, pharmacist, state agency administrator; b. Van Nuys, Calif., Dec. 5, 1947; s. Leland J. and Audrey M. (Frett) Pinson; m. Margaret K. Pinson, Mar. 18, 1972; children: Scott C., Kelly E. Student, U. Calif., Davis, 1969; AA, Am. River Coll., Sacramento, 1968; PharmD, U. Calif., San Francisco, 1973. Lic. pharmacist Calif., Nev. Staff pharmacist/asst. dir. pharm. svcs. St. Mary's Hosp., Reno, 1973-77; chief pharmacist May Ang Base USAF, 1973-77; owner & mng. pharmacist Silverda Pharmacy, 1979—2001; mng. pharmacist Scolari's Food & Drug, Reno, 2001—05; exec. sec. Nev. State Bd. Pharmacy, 2005—, pres., 1996—2004, exec. sec., 2005—; pharm., therapeutics com. State Nev., 2004—06. Cons. pharmacist Physicians Hosp., 1974—93, Reno Med. Plz., 1973—2001, Rural Calif. Hosp. Assn., 1973—74, Ford Ctr. Foot Surgery, 1980—2007; pharmacy coord. Intensive Pharm. Svcs., 1986—87; cons. Calif. Dept. Health & Corrections, Susanville, 1975—76, Nev. Med. Care Adv. Bd., Carson City, 1984—87; provider, reviewer Nev. State Bd. Pharmacy, Reno, 1975—84; instr. Nev. CC, 1974—76; adj. prof. Idaho State U., Pocatello, 1989—, ND State U., 2006—. Co-author: Care of Hickman Catheter, 1984. Softball coach Reno/Sparks Recreation Dept., 1973—92; bd. dirs. Am. Cancer Soc., 1986—90; mem. State of Nev. Pharmaceutics and Therapy Com., 2004—05, Nev. Arthritis Found.; cubmaster Pack 153 Boy Scouts Am., Verdi, Nev., scoutmaster com. chmn. Reno troop 1, 1988—92. Recipient Bowl of Hygeia award, Nev. Pharmacists Assn. and A. H. Robbins Co., 1984; named Pharmacist of the Yr., Nev. Pharm. Alliance, 1999. Mem.: U. Calif. San Francisco Alumni Assn. (pres. 2009—), Greater Nev. Heatlh Sys. Agy., Nev. Profl. Stds. Rev. Orgn., Nev. Pharmacists Assn. (pres. 1981—82), Am. Pharm. Assn., Nat. Assn. Bds. Pharmacy, Kappa Psi. Avocations: skiing, fishing, backpacking, softball, golf. Home: PO Box 478 Verdi NV 89439-0478 Office: 431 W Plumb Ln Reno NV 89509 Office Phone: 775-850-1440. Personal E-mail: Rx2005@aol.com.

PINSON, VICKI FAYE, music educator, director; d. Ned B. and Ellen Faye Pinson. MusB, Jacksonville State U., Ala., 1979; MusM, Ga. State U., Atlanta, 1988. Band dir. Haroldson County High, Tallapoosa, Ga., 1979—80, Dacula High & Mid., Ga., 1980—89, Meadowcreek High, Norcross, Ga., 1989—2000, Habersham County High, Mt. Airy, Ga., 2000—07; applied instr., music apprec. Gainesville State Coll., Ga., 2007—. Mem.: Northwinds Symphonic Band, Nat. Band Assn., Women Band Dirs. Internat. Assn., Am. Sch. Band Dirs. Assn., GMEA, Phi Beta Mu, Pilot Club Internat. Assn. Office: Gainesville State Coll PO Box 1358 Gainesville GA 30503 Office Fax: 678-717-3832. Business E-Mail: vpinson@gsc.edu.

PINSON, WILLIAM MEREDITH, JR., pastor, writer, administrator, professor; b. Ft. Worth, Aug. 3, 1934; s. William Meredith and Ila Lee (Jones) P.; m. Bobbie Ruth Judd, June 4, 1955; children: Meredith Pinson Creasey, Allison Pinson Hopgood. BA, U. N. Tex., 1955; BD, Southwestern Bapt. Theol. Sem., Ft. Worth, 1959, ThD, 1963, MDiv, 1973; LittD (hon.), Calif. Bapt. Coll., Riverside, 1978; DD (hon.), U. Mary Hardin-Baylor, Belton, Tex., 1984; LHD (hon.), Howard Payne U., Brownwood, Tex., 1986; LittD (hon.), Dallas Bapt. U., 1990; LLD (hon.), Hardin Simmons U., 1999. Ordained to ministry Bapt. Ch., 1955. Assoc. sec. Christian Life Commn., Dallas, 1957-63; prof. Christian ethics Southwestern Bapt. Theol. Sem., Ft. Worth, 1963-75; pastor First Bapt. Ch., Wichita Falls, Tex., 1975-77; pres. Golden Gate Bapt. Theol. Sem., Mill Valley, Calif., 1977-82; vol. dir. Tex. Bapt. Heritage Ctr., 2000—; disting. prof. Dallas Bapt. U., 2001—; disting. vis. prof. Baylor U., 2001—. Exec. dir. Bapt. Gen. Conv. Tex., 1982—2000, exec. dir. emeritus, 2000—; chmn. program com. Christian Life Commn. So. Bapt. Conv., spl. rschr. for home mission bd., nat. task force planned growth in giving, 1984—94, stewardship commn., 1986—96; bd. dirs. T.B. Maston Found.; adj. prof. Southwestern Bapt. Theol. Sem., 1976—77; chmn. study commn. freedom, justice and peace Bapt. World Alliance, 1975—80, study commn. on ethics, 1990—95, commn. on racism, 1992—, com. on polity and heritage, 2000—; v.p. Bapt. Gen. Conv. Tex., 1972—73, state missions commn., 1976—77, vice chmn. urban strategy com., chmn. order of bus. com., 1976, chmn. steering com. Good News Tex., 1976—77, chmn. resolutions com.; spkr. in field; bd. dirs., chair centennial com. Baylor U. Health Care Sys., 2002—. Contbr. articles to profl. jours., chapters to books. Adv. bd. Bapt. History and Heritage Soc., 2002—; mem. adv. com. Sch. Leadership Dallas Bapt. U., 2003—. Named Lilly Found. scholar Southwestern Bapt. Theol. Sem., 1960-62; recipient Disting. Alumni award Southwestern Bapt. Theol. Sem., 1979, U. North Tex., 1980, Mosaic Missions award Home Mission Bd., 1984, Parabolani award Tex. Bapt. Men, 1999, Spirit of Excellence award Houston Bapt. U., 2000, Tex. Bapt. Missions award State Missions Commn., 2000, Pioneer award Tex. Bapt. Missions Found., 2001, W. Winfred Moore award for lifetime achievement in ministry Baylor U., 2001, Officers' award Bapt. History and Heritage Soc., 2003, Elder Statesman award Independence. Assn., 2005, George W. Truett award, Baylor U., 2008. Mem. So. Bapt. Assn. Colls. and Schs., So. Bapt. Assn. of State Exec. Dirs. (pres. 1996-97). Baptist. Avocations: travel, reading. Office: Bapt Gen Conv Tex 333 N Washington Ave Dallas TX 75246-1782 Home Phone: 972-298-7371; Office Phone: 214-370-9471. Office Fax: 214-370-0228. Business E-Mail: william.pinson@bgct.org.

PINTAR, ELIZABETH, anthropologist, educator; Degree in Anthropology, U. Buenos Aires, Argentina, 1987; MA in Anthropology, U. Tulsa, Okla., 1990; PhD in Anthropology, Southern Meth. U., Dallas, Tex., 1996. Assoc. prof. anthropology Austin CC, 1998—. Mem.: Soc. Argentina Antropologia, Soc. Am. Archaeology. Office: Austin CC 11928 Stonehollow Dr Austin TX 78758 Business E-Mail: lpintar@austincc.edu.

PINTAR, JENNIFER A., healthcare educator; d. John and Janet Ayers Peoples; m. Kevin Pintar, Oct. 2, 1998; children: Jordan, Reagan. PhD, U. Pitts., 2001, MPH, 2004. Cert. Nat. Strength and Conditioning Assn., 2001, health fitness instructor Am. Coll. Sports Medicine, Ind., 2001. Instr. Youngstown State U., Ohio, 1999—2002, asst. prof., 2002—05, assoc. prof., 2005—. Bd. mem. Glen Montessori Sch., Emsworth, Pa., 2003—08; fitness dir. vol. Rich Ctr. Study and Treatment Autism, Youngstown, 2000—07. Recipient Disting. Prof. award, Youngstown State U., 2003; grant, Rich Ctr. Study and Treatment Autism, 2000—06, U. Rsch. Coun., 2000—07. Mem.: Nat. Strength and Conditioning Assn., Am. Coll. Sports Medicine. Avocations: exercise, reading, travel. Office: Youngstown State Univ 235 Beeghly Ctr Youngstown OH 44555 Office Fax: 330-941-2280. Business E-Mail: japintar@ysu.edu.

PINTAUER, TOMISLAV, chemistry professor; b. Zagreb, Croatia, May 9, 1974; s. Juraj and Barica Milcic Pintauer. BSChemE, U. Pa., Phila., 1997, MS in Chemistry, 1998; PhD in Chemistry, Carnegie Mellon U., Pitts., 2002. Asst. prof. Duquesne U., Pitts., 2005—. Mem.: Am. Chem. Soc., Sigma Xi. Achievements include research in metal mediated atom transfer radical addition, cyclization and polymerization reactions. Office: Duquesne Univ 600 Forbes Ave 308 Mellon Hall Pittsburgh PA 15282 Home Phone: 412-427-7709.

PINTER, GABRIEL GEORGE, retired physiology educator; b. Bekes, Hungary, June 23, 1925; came to U.S., 1958; s. Lajos and Regina (Szilagyi-Farkas) Pinter; m. Berit Helgesen, Dec. 19, 1958 (dec. May 1980); children: Renee Astrid, Eva Ingelill; m. Vera Lederer Dallos, May 24, 1984. MD, U. Sch. Medicine, Budapest, Hungary, 1951. Asst. prof. U. Sch. Medicine, Budapest, Hungary, 1951-56; rsch. assoc. U. Inst. Med. Rsch., Oslo, Norway, 1957-58; asst. prof. U. Tenn., Memphis, 1958-61; from asst. prof. to prof. U. Md., Balt., 1961-92; retired. Vis. prof. King's Coll., London, 1990-94. Contbr. articles to profl. jours.; translator (with wife) philos. and lit. works into Hungarian. Recipient A.V. Humboldt prize, Germany, 1980; Swedish Royal Med. Soc. fellow, Uppsala, 1972. Mem. Am. Physiol. Soc., Physiol. Soc. Gt. Brit., Scandinavian Physiol. Soc., European Soc. Microcirculation.

PINTO, FREIDA, actress; b. Bombay, Oct. 18, 1984; Studied, St. Xaviers Coll., Mumbai, India. Model. Anchor (TV series) Full Circle, 2006—07, actress (films) Slumdog Millionaire, 2008 (Outstanding Performance by a Cast in a Motion Picture, SAG, 2009). Recipient Breakthrough Performance award, Palm Springs Internat. Film Festival, 2008, Best Actress award, Elle Mag., 2009. Office: c/o Creative Artists Agy 2000 Ave of the Stars Los Angeles CA 90067*

PINTO, JERALD E., financial analyst, director; b. NYC, Apr. 4, 1953; s. Jesse E. and Rosalind Pinto; m. Rosemarie Angella Spence, Jan. 29, 2005. BA, Laurentian U., Sudbury Ont.; MBA, Bernard Baruch Coll., CUNY; MPhil, PhD, NYU Stern Sch. Bus. Cert. CFA Inst. Prin. TRM Svcs., NYC, 1995—2002; dir. CFA Inst., Charlottesville, Va., 2002—. Author: (book) Quantitative Investment Analysis, Equity Asset Valuation; editor: Managing Investment Portfolios: A Dynamic Process. Sec. treas. Friends Laurentian U. Inc., Washington, 1985—2001. Willensky fellowship, NYU Stern Sch. Bus., C. W. Nichols Found. fellow. Mem.: Fin. Mgmt. Assn. Office: CFA Inst 560 Ray C Hunt Dr Charlottesville VA 22903

PINTO, MARK R., manufacturing executive; B, Rensselear Poly. Inst., Troy, NY; M, PhD, Stanford U., Calif. V.p., gen. mgr. network product IC divsn., chief tech. officer Bell Labs. and Lucent Microelectronics Group (later Agere Systems); sr. v.p., chief tech. officer, gen. mgr. New Bus. and New Products Group Applied Materials, Inc., 2004—, chmn. Venture Investment Com. Adj. prof. Yale U., New Haven. Contbr. articles to sci. jours. Named a Bell Labs fellow. Fellow: IEEE. Achievements include patents in field. Office: Applied Materials Inc PO Box 58039 Santa Clara CA 95052-8039 Office Phone: 408-727-5555.

PINTO, NICHOLAS JOAQUIM, physics professor; s. Thomas Celstino Pinto and Agatha Louie Fernandes; m. Carmen Ines Sanchez, Aug. 30, 1997; 1 child, Victoria Ines. BSc in Physics, Bombay U., 1985; MS in Physics, Bowling Green State U., Ohio, 1987; PhD in Physics, Mont. State U., Bozeman, 1992. Postdoctoral rschr. Wichita State U., Kans., 1992—94; prof. U. PR, Humacao, 1995—. Mem.: AAAS, Am. Chem. Soc., Am. Phys. Soc. Achievements include patents for conducting polymers. Home: Urb Santa Cecilia # 55 C/Stma Trinidad Caguas PR 00725 Office: PR 100 Rd # 908 Humacao PR 00791 Business E-Mail: nicholas.pinto@upr.edu.

PINTO, ROSALIND, retired secondary school educator, volunteer; b. NYC; d. Barney and Jenny Abrams; m. Jesse E. Pinto (dec.); children: Francine, Jerry, Evelyn. BA in Polit. Sci. cum laude, Hunter Coll.; MA in Polit. Sci., History, Columbia U.; postgrad., Queens Coll., LaGuardia C.C.; diploma (hon.), Internat. Order Clairvoyancy, Astrology and Numerology, 2007. Lic. social studies tchr. jr. HS, NY, per diem substitute; cert. secondary sch. social studies grades 7-12, NY. Substitute tchr., 1966-69, 90, 91—; tchr. social studies I.S. 126Q, LI, NY, 1969-88, Jr. HS 217 Briarwood, NYC, 1988-89; ret., 1989; part-time cluster tchr. social studies and communication arts Pub. Sch. 140, Bronx, NY, 1990-92; substitute tchr. I.S. 227Q, 1992-93. Participant seminars and workshops. Author curriculum materials; contbr. study guide for regent's competency test, 1990; author numerous poems; contbr. articles to profl. jours. Enrollment asst. Insight Heart Team, 1989; vol. receptionist Whitney Mus., NYC; mem. com. on pub. transp. Cmty. Bd. 6, Queens, 1990—96, mem. com. on history, 1990—, chmn. beautification com., 1992—, mem. com. on planning and zoning, 1996—, mem. com. on environ. sanitation, 1999—; mem. Forest Hills Action League, 1999; advocate Census 2000 participation; active Gt. Smokies Song Chase Warren-Wilson Coll., NC, 1992; mem. Queens Hist. Soc., Forest Hills Van Ct. Homeowners Assn.; bd. dirs. Ctrl. Queens Hist. Soc.; past mem. Rego Park Coalition Against Crime; mem. Forest Hills Civic Assn., 1996—97; vol. local polit. campaigns. Recipient Project award, Beautification Com., 1995, Women's History Month Rosemary Gunning award, Queens Borough Pres., 2000, Editor's Choice award, Best Poems and Poets, 2001, 2002, 2004, 2005, 2007, Poet Merit award, Poetry Conv., 2002—03, 2005, 2006, 2007, Poetry Divsn. award, Noble House, 2006, Appreciation Cert., Night Out Against Crime, 2002, 2003, 2004, 2007, NY State Senate, 2004—05. Fellow: Mcpl. Art Soc. (hon. mention design 2000 award); mem.: NAFE, Internat. Soc. Poets (life; adv. panel, Internat. Poet of Merit award 1993, 2000, Editor's Choice award 2001), Ctr. for Sci. in the Pub. Interest, Robert F. Kennedy Dem. Assn. (bd. dirs., RFK Assn. cert. of appreciation for dedication 2005, Hon. Diploma Internat. Order Clairvoyancy, Astrology and Numerology 2007), Hunter Coll. HS Alumni Assn., Hunter Coll. Alumni Assn., Columbia U. Grad. Sch. Arts and Scis. Alumni Assn., NY Insight Alumni Assn. Avocations: poetry, reading, walking, art shows, plays. Home Phone: 718-268-2739, 703-841-1517. *Loving people and having faith in them and the possibility of happy outcomes is the greatest motivation toward achievement of goals.*

PINTO-MARTIN, JENNIFER ANNE, epidemiologist, educator; b. Colma, Calif., Mar. 17, 1957; d. Douglas Wellman Pinto and Elizabeth Kathleen (O'Hara) Hazard; m. Muscoe Burnett Martin, Aug. 17, 1986; children: Emily Grace Martin, Nora Mills Martin, Charlotte Elizabeth Martin, Muscoe (Jack) Burnett Martin. BS, Stanford U., 1974—78; MPH, U. Calif., Berkeley, 1980—82, PhD, 1982—84. Asst. prof. Columbia U., NYC, 1984—90, U. Pa., Phila., 1990—97, assoc. prof., 1998—2005, prof., 2005—, dir., Masters in Pub. Health Program, 2007—. Dir., Ctr. for Autism and Develop. Disabilities Rsch. and Epidemiology U. Pa.; cons., Interagency Autism Coordinating Com. NIH; mem. scientific review com. Nat. Inst. Neurological Diseases and Stroke, Am. Pub. Health Assn., Soc. for Epidemiological Rsch.; mentor and advisor to numerous grad. and undergraduate students. Mem. editl. bd. Pediatric and Perinatal Research. Grantee Ctr. for Autism Rsch., CDC, 2001. Mem.: Soc. for Pediat. Epidemiologic Rsch. (former pres.), Internat. Soc. for Autism Rsch. (sec.). Office: Univ Pennsylvania Sch Nursing 418 Curie Blvd Philadelphia PA 19104-4217 Business E-Mail: pinto@nursing.upenn.edu.*

PIOLI, SCOTT, professional sports team executive; b. Washingtonville, NY, Mar. 31, 1965; m. Dallas Pioli; 1 child, Mia Costa Pioli. B in Comm., Ctrl. Conn. State U., New Britain, 1988; M, Syracuse U. S.I. Newhouse Sch. Pub. Comm., NY. Grad. asst. Syracuse U. Orange, 1988—90; offensive line coach Murray State U. Racers, 1990, defensive line coach, 1991; pro pers. asst. Cleve. Browns, 1992—95; dir. pro pers. Balt. Ravens, 1996, NY Jets, 1997—99; pers. dir. New Eng. Patriots, 2000—01, v.p. player pers., 2002—08; gen. mgr. Kansas City Chiefs, 2009—. Founder Rose Pioli Scholarship; bd. dirs. Coll. for Every Student Found. Recipient George Young NFL Exec. of Yr. award, The Sporting News, 2003, 2004, Award for Exec. Achievement, NFL Players Assn., 2004; named NFL Exec. of Yr., Dallas Morning News, 2001, 2007, Pro Football Weekly, 2003, 2007, Sports Illus., 2003, USA Today, 2004, San Francisco Chronicle, 2004, 2007, SI.com, 2004; named to Ctrl. Conn. State U. Hall of Fame, 2005. Achievements include member of Super Bowl XXXVI, XXXVIII, XXXIX Championship winning New England Patriots. Office: Kansas City Chiefs One Arrowhead Dr Kansas City MO 64129*

PIORKOWSKI, JOSEPH D., JR., lawyer, physician, educator, military officer; b. Chester, Pa., Nov. 21, 1956; s. Joseph D. Piorkowski and Elizabeth C. Bell; m. Marjorie Eldridge, Aug. 4, 1984; childre, Joseph and Alexandra. BA cum laude, Hofstra U., 1976; DO, Phila. Coll. Osteo. Medicine, 1980; JD magna cum laude, Georgetown U., 1988; MPH, Johns Hopkins U., 1992. Diplomate Am. Bd. Preventive Medicine, Am. Bd. Legal Medicine, Am. Osteo. Bd. Family Practice, Nat. Bd. Examiners for Osteo. Physicians and Surgeons; lic. physician, Md., D.C.; bar: Md., D.C., Tex., U.S. Dist. Ct. D.C., U.S. Dist. Ct. Md., U.S. Ct. Appeals (4th and D.C. cirs.), US Supreme Ct.; cert. instr. advanced trauma life support; cert. advanced cardiac life support. Commd. ensign USN, 1977, advanced through grades to capt., 1996, flight surgeon fighter squadron 31/carrier air wing THREE, staff physician U.S.S. Kennedy, substance abuse coord., 1982-84, flight surgeon Naval Air Facility, peer review coord. Navy Med. Clinics Washington, 1984-88, head Naval Air Facility Med. Clin., 1986-88; intern in psychiatry Nat. Naval Med. Ctr., Bethesda, Md., 1980-81; law clk. to Hon. Oliver Gasch US Dist. Ct. DC, 1988-89; ptnr. Williams & Connolly, Washington, 1997—2000, Shook, Hardy & Bacon, Washington, 2001—04; prin. Piorkowski Law Firm, PC, Washington, 2004—. Instr. Mil. Tng. Network, Dept. Def., 1986—; adj. prof. law Georgetown U. Law Ctr., Washington, 1992—, clin. asst. prof. dept. surgery Georgetown U. Med. Ctr., 1995-2004 Contbr. articles to profl. jours. Coach Great Falls Youth Basketball, 2005—07; leader Daily Bread Food Pantry McLean Bible Ch. Decorated Meritorious Svc. medal; named one of 75 Best Lawyers in Washington, Washingtonian mag., 2002; acad. honors scholar, Hofstra U., 1976. Fellow Am. Coll. Preventive Medicine, Am. Coll. Legal Medicine, Aerospace Med. Assn. (assoc.); mem. ABA (litigation sect.), Soc. of U.S. Naval Flight Surgeons, Internat. Soc. Pharmacoepidemiology, Regulatory Affairs Profl. Soc., Assn. of Mil. Surgeons of U.S., Am. Osteo. Assn., Am. Coll. Family Practitioners, Internat. Assn. Defense Counsel, Order of Coif, Delta Omega, Psi Chi. Office: Piorkowski Law Firm 910 17th St NW Ste 800 Washington DC 20006 Home Phone: 703-757-7560; Office Phone: 202-223-5535. Business E-Mail: JPiorkowski@lawdoc1.com.

PIOT, PETER (BARAN), global health professor; b. Leuven, Belgium, Feb. 17, 1949; MD, U. Ghent, 1974; PhD in Microbiology, U. Antwerp, 1981, PhD (hon.), 1997, Free U., 1995; DSc (hon.), U. West Indies, 2005, Clark U., 2007, U. Liege, 2008. Sr. fellow microbiology and infectious diseases U. Washington, 1978—79; prof. microbiology Inst. Tropical Medicine, 1980—92; prof. pub. health Free U., Brussels, 1989—94; assoc. dir. Global Program AIDS/WHO, Geneva, 1995; exec. dir. Joint UN Program on HIV/AIDS, Geneva, 1995—2008; under sec.-gen. UN, 2002—08; prof. global health, dir. Imperial Coll., London; sr. fellow Gates Found., Seatle, 2009; scholar in residence Ford Found., 2009; prof. Coll. France, Paris, 2009—. Dir. WHO Collaborating Ctr. AIDS, Antwerp, Project SIDA, Kinshasa; assoc. prof. U. Nairobi, STD/AIDS Project, Kenya; co-discoverer Ebola virus; Socrates chair, European Acad., Yuste, Spain, 2004; pres., mem. bd. King Boudouin Found., Terrence Higgins Trust, London, Vlerick Sch. Mgmt., Ghent, Belgium. Editor: (with others) Chlamydial Infection, 1982, (with J.M. Mann) AIDS and HIV Infection in the Tropics, 1988, (with P. Lamptey) Handbook on AIDS Prevention in Africa, 1990, 2d edit. 1991, (with others) Basic Laboratory Procedures in Clinical Bacteriology, 1991; co-author: AIDS in Africa: A Handbook for Physicians, 1992, Reproductive Tract Infections in Women, 1992, (with K.K. Holmes)Sexually Transmitted Diseases, 1999, 2008 (with M. Carael) L'Epidemie de Sida et la Mondialisation des Risques, 2005. Knighted baron King Albert II, 1995; decorated officier l'Ordre Nat. du Léopard (Zaïre), comdr. l'Ordre du Lion (Sénégal), Nat. Order Burkina Faso Mali and Madagascar; NATO fellow, 1978-79; recipient Kerkheer prize Medicine, 1989, Health award Flemish Cmty., 1990, AMICOM award Medicine, 1991, H. Breurs prize, 1992, A. Jauniaux prize, 1992, van Thiel award, 1993, Glaxo award infectious diseases, 1995, Nelson Mandela award, 2001, Gold medal Royal Acad. Arts and Scis., Belgium, 2002, E. Calderone medal Columbia U., 2003, Vlerick award, Belgium, 2004, Congl. Achievement award, Philippines, 2005, Grand Ofcl. Order Infante Don Enrique, Portugal, 2005, Acad. Alliance Found. Global Health Leadership award, NY, 2005; named Outstanding Physician, AMA, Chgo., 2004. Fellow Royal Coll. Physicians (London); mem. Royal Acad. Medicine, Royal Acad. Overseas Scis., Internat. AIDS Soc. (pres. 1992), Inst. Medicine, US Nat. Acad. Scis., other European, US, and African socs. Achievements include co-discovering the Ebola virus. Office: Inst Global Health Imperial Coll 15 Prince's Gardens London SW7 1NA England Office Fax: 22 7914179. Business E-Mail: globalhealthpa@imperial.ac.uk.

PIOU-BREWER, MAGALIE, psychotherapist, educator, small business owner; b. Arthabaska, Que., Can., Apr. 26, 1971; d. Edouard Louis and Jacqueline Dorcal Piou; m. Michael Alexander Brewer, July 21, 2003; children: Anya Lilly Brewer, Jasmine Rosa Brewer. Student, Cath. U., Leuven, Belgium, 1991—92; BA in Comm., Loyola Coll., Balt., 1993, MS in Pastoral Counseling, 2000; PhD in Clinical Psychology, George Washington U., 2004. Lic. counselor. Assoc. dir. admissions Loyola Coll., Balt., 1994—2001; child psychotherapist Stevenson Psychol. Svcs., Columbia, Md., 2001—03; clin. dir. Bridgeway Counseling Svcs., Columbia, 2004—; exec. dir. MPB Group, Inc., Columbia, 2004—. Adj. asst. prof. Loyola Coll. Grad. Ctr., Columbia, 2005—; spkr. in field. Acad. fellow, George Washington U., 2000—03, Maternal/Child Health grant, Kennedy Kreiger Inst., Balt., 2003. Mem.: APA, Am. Counselors Assn., Am. Mental Health Counselors Assn. Avocations: reading, travel. Office: MPB Group Inc 9650 Santiago Rd Ste 11 Columbia MD 21045 Office Phone: 410-730-2385.

PIPER, ADRIAN MARGARET SMITH, philosopher, artist, educator; b. NYC, Sept. 20, 1948; d. Daniel Robert and Olive Xavier (Smith) P.; m. Jeffrey Ernest Evans, June 27, 1982 (div. 1987). AA, Sch. Visual Arts, 1969; BA in Philosophy, CCNY, 1974; MA, Harvard U., 1977, PhD, 1981; student, U. Heidelberg, Germany, 1977-78; LHD (hon.), Calif. Inst. Arts, 1992, Mass. Coll. Art, 1994. Asst. prof. U. Mich., Ann Arbor, 1979-86; Mellon rsch. fellow Stanford (Calif.) U., 1982-84; assoc. prof. Georgetown U., Washington, 1986-88, U. Calif., San Diego, 1988; prof. philosophy Wellesley (Mass.) Coll., 1990—. Disting. scholar Getty Rsch. Inst., 1998—; speaker, lectr. on both philosophy and art. Artist: one-woman exhbns. include NY Cultural Ctr., NYC, 1971, Montclair State Coll., NJ, 1976, Wadsworth Atheneum, Hartford, Conn., 1980, Nexus COntemporary Art Ctr., Atlanta, 1987, The Alternative Mus., NYC, 1987, Goldie Paley Gallery, Phila., 1989, Power Plant Gallery, Toronto, 1990, Lowe Art Mus., Coral Gables, Fla., 1990-91, Santa Monica (Calif.) Mus. Contemporary Art, 1991, John Weber Gallery, NYC, 1989, 90, 91, 92, Whitney Mus. Am. Art, NYC, 1990, Hirschorn Mus., Washington, 1991, Ikon Gallery, Birmingham, Eng., 1991, Cornerhouse, Manchester, Eng., 1992, Cartwright Hall, Bradford, Eng., 1992, Kunstverein, Munich, Germany, 1992, Indpls. Ctr. Contemporary Art, 1992, Manasterio de Santa Clara, Moguer, Spain, 1992, Grey Art Gallery, NYC, 1992, Paula Cooper Art Galler, 1992, 94; group exhbns. include Paula Cooper Gallery, 1969, Dwan Gallery, NYC, 1969, 70, Seattle Art Mus., 1969, Stadtisches Mus., Leverkusen, Germany, 1969, Kunsthalle Berne, Berne, Switzerland, 1969, NY Cultural Ctr., 1970, Allen Mus., Oberlin, Ohio, 1970, Mus. Modern Art, NYC, 1970, 88, 91, Musee d'Art Moderne, Paris, 1971, 77, 89, Inhibodress Gallery, New South Wales, Australia, 1972, Calif. Inst. Arts, Valencia, 1973, Samuel S. Fleischer Art Meml., Phila., 1974, Mus. Contemporary Art, Chgo., 1975, Newberger Mus., Purchase, NY, 1978, Mass. Coll. Art, Boston, 1979, Artemesia Gallery, Chgo., 1979, A.I.R. Gallery, NYC, 1980, Inst. Contemporary Arts, London, 1980, The New Mus., NYC, 1981, 83, 85, Kenkeleba Gallery, NYC, 1983, The Studio Mus. Harlem, NYC, 1985, 89, Mus. Moderner Kunst, Vienna, Austria, 1985, Intar Gallery, NYC, 1988, Whitney Mus. Downtown, NYC, 1988, Art Gallery Ont., Toronto, 1988, Long Beach (Calif.) Art Mus., 1989, Simon Watson Gallery, NYC, 1990, Feigen Gallery, Chgo., 1990, Barbara Krakow Gallery, Boston, 1990, Milw. Art Mus., 1990, Contemporary Arts Ctr., Houston, 1991, John Weber Gallery, 1991, Anne Plumb Gallery, NYC, 1991, Hirschorn Mus., 1991, The Albuquerque Mus. Art, 1991, The Toledo Mus. Art, 1991, Denver Art Mus., Fukui Fine Arts Mus., Fukyui-ken, Japan, 1992-93, NJ State Mus., Trenton, 1992-93, Philippe Staib Gallery, NYC, 1992, New Loom House, London, 1992, Espace-Lyonnais D'Art Contemporain, Lyon, France, 1993, Am. Acad. Inst. Arts and Letters, NYC, 1993; permanent collections include Met. Mus. Art, Whitney Mus., LA Mus. Contemporary Art, San Francisco Mus. Modern Art, The Bklyn. Mus., Denver Art Mus., Kunstmuseum Berne, Musee d'Art Moderne, The Mus. Contemporary Art, Chgo., The Wadsworth Atheneum, Met. Mus. Art; art performances include RISD, 1973, The Whitney Mus. Am. Art, 1975, Kurfurstendamm, Berlin, 1977, Hauptstrasse, Heidelburg, Germany, 1978, Allen Meml. Mus., Oberlin, Ohio, 1980, Contemporary Art Inst. Detroit, 1980, San Francisco Art Inst., 1985, Calif. Inst. Art, 1984, The Studio Mus. Harlem, 1988; performances on video, 1987—; contbr. articles to profl. jours. Recipient NY State Coun. on Arts award, 1989, Visual Arts award, 1990, Skowhegan medal for sculptural installation, 1995, Dance Theatre Workshop award for New Genres, 2000; NEH Travel fellow, 1979, NEA Visual Artists' fellow, 1979, 82, Andrew Mellon Postdoctoral fellow, 1982-84, Woodrow Wilson Internat. Scholars fellow, 1988-89, Guggenheim Meml. fellow, 1989, non-resident fellow NY Inst. for Humanities, NYU, 1996—, Wissanschftskolleg zu Berlin Inst. Adv. Study fellow, 2005-; NEA Artists Forums grantee, 1987; rsch. fellowship NEH, 1998, Getty Rsch. Inst. Disting. scholarship, 1998-99, Internat. Forschungszentrum Kulturwissenschaften fellow Vienna, fellow Wissenschetskolleg zu Berlin Inst. Advanced Study, 2005-. Mem. AAUP, Am. Philos. Assn. (mem. ea. divsn.), Am. Soc. Polit. and Legal Philosophy, N.Am. Kant. Soc. Avocations: Medieval and Renaissance music, fiction, poetry, yoga, German. Office: Adrian Piper Rsch Archives Postfach 54 02 04 D-10042 Berlin Germany Office Phone: 49-30-308-253-18. E-mail: contact@adrianpiper.com, contack@adrianpiper.com.

PIPER, CRYSTAL NICOLE, medical researcher; b. Columbia, SC, Oct. 15, 1979; d. Jacqueline Elizabeth Stover. BS, SC State U., Orangeburg, 2001; MPH, Des Moines U. Osteo. Med. Ctr., Iowa, 2002, MHA, 2003; PhD, U. SC, Columbia, 2007. Rsch. asst. Iowa Dept. Pub. Health, Des Moines, 2001—02; policy intern Iowa State Governor's Office, Des Moines, 2002; tech. mgmt. SC Dept. Health, Columbia, 2003—04; grants mgr. Benedict Coll., Columbia, 2004—05, adj. faculty, 2005—09; rsch. asst. U. SC, 2004—07, rsch. assoc., 2007—; registration rep. Palmetto Health Hosp., Columbia, 2005—06. Governing coun. APHA, Washington, 2009—. Avocations: travel, reading. Office: Univ SC Inst Health Disparities 220 Stoneridge Dr Ste 208 Columbia SC 29210 Business E-Mail: piper@mailbox.sc.edu.

PIPER, DON COURTNEY, political scientist, educator; b. Washington, July 29, 1932; s. Don Carlos and Alice (Courtney) Piper; m. Rowena Inez Wise, July 6, 1956; children: Sharon, Valarie. BA, U. Md., 1954, MA, 1958; PhD (James B. Duke fellow), Duke U., 1961. Research assoc. Duke U., 1961-62; exec. sec. Commonwealth-Studies Center, 1962-64; asst. prof. dept. govt. and politics U. Md., College Park, 1964-67, assoc. prof., 1967-69, prof., 1969-97, prof. emeritus, 1997—, head dept. govt. and politics, 1968-74, dir. grad. studies dept., 1982-95, mem. coun. of system faculty, 1989-90; chmn. faculty council College Park Faculty Assembly, 1974-75, chmn. campus senate, 1975-77, 89-90, univ. marshal, 1981-97, mem. Athletic Council, 1986-93, mem. senate ad hoc com. on undergrad. edn., 1986-88, chmn. chancellor's ad hoc com. on campus ceremonies, 1986-87, chmn. acad. com. of Athletic Council, 1986-89; chmn. campaign for College Park, 1988-89; chmn. retention review com. U. Md., 1990-91, chmn. budget and facilities com. athletic coun., 1991-93, chmn. senate com. on programs courses and curriculi, 1991-93, co-chair Mid. States self-study exec. com., 1995-97; tchg. fellow Lilly Ctr. for Tchg. Excellence, 1994—95. Rsch. asst. Am. Coun. Edn., 1966—68; mem. faculty adv. com., mem. adv. com. Md. State Bd. Higher Edn., 1977—82. Author: International Law of Great Lakes, 1967; co-author: International Law Standard and Commonwealth Developments, 1966, De Lege Pactorum, 1970, Foreign Policy Analysis, 1975; editor (with R. Taylor Cole): Post-Primary Education and Political and Economic Development, 1964; editor, author (with Ronald Terchek): Interaction: Foreign Policy and Public Policy, 1983; bd. editors World Affairs, 1971—94, mem. editl. adv. com. Internat. Legal Materials, 1977—78. Served to 1st lt. USAF, 1955—58. Mem.: Phi Beta Kappa (pres. Gamma chpt. 1978—79), Pi Sigma Alpha, Omicron Delta Kappa (faculty advisor 1990—97), Phi Kappa Phi (chpt. pres. 1982—83). Methodist. Home: 6312 Oakview Ct Hillsborough NC 27278

PIPER, GEORGE CHILTON, lawyer; b. Lexington, Ky., Feb. 23, 1939; s. Lewis Allie and Anna (Zink) Piper; children: Jennifer A., Geoffrey C. AB, Harvard U., 1960; JD, U. Ky., 1967; MPH, Harvard Sch. Pub. Health, 1984. Ptnr. Martin, Ockerman & Brabart, Lexington, 1966—91; founding ptnr. Piper, Wellman & Bowers, Lexington, 1991—. Gen. counsel Planned Parenthood of Bluegrass, Inc., Lexington, 1971—2004. Sgt. E-4 US Army, 1961—64. Recipient Samdperil Essay award, Harvard Sch. Pub. Health, 1984. Home: 147 E 3Rd Ave Lexington KY 40508-1825 Office Phone: 859-231-1012. Office Fax: 859-231-1015. Business E-Mail: pwb@pwblaw.net.

PIPER, JAMI KATHLEEN, music educator, composer, musician; b. Oakland, Calif., Dec. 31, 1955; d. Barry Eugene Piper and Margaret Letitia (Weis) Smythe; children: Stephanie June Hauck, Matthew Lewis Hook. MusB, U. Pacific, Stockton, Calif., 1976; MFA, Mills Coll., Oakland, Calif., 1987; postgrad. in Piano Pedagogy and Performance, U. Colo., Boulder, 1998. Cert. pre-sch. through 12 tchg. credential in music U. Colo., Boulder, 1997, lifetime credential music Calif. CC, 1987, Nat. Music Tchrs. Assn., in piano Lifetime Profl. Cert., 2009. Piano accompanist, soloist contracted, Calif., 1962—; piano tchr. self employed, Calif., 1976—94, 2005—, Colo., 1996—2002; adj. educator Music Tchr. Assn. Calif., Calif., 1989—, Music Tchr. Nat. Assn., Colo., 1994—2002; vocal, instrumental music tchr. Boulder Valley Sch., Colo., 1999—2002; gen. music, theory, history & piano tchr. Boulder Arts Acad., Colo., 1995—98; piano accompanist, soloist contracted, Colo., 1995—2002; organist & music dir. St. Clement's Episcopal Ch., Rancho Cordova, Calif., 2008—. V.p., treas. Music Tchr. Assn. Calif., Alameda County, 1990—92, pres., 1992—94; v.p. Boulder Area Music Tchr. Assn., Colo., 1994—95; chair of auditions Colo. Music Tchr. Assn., Colo., 1996—98; Am. advisor Kitumusote, Tanzania, 2005. Composer: (hymn) Benediction, 1986, Give Him the Praise, 1986, God Almighty, God of Love, 1987; musician: (solo concert debut U.S.) Oakland, Calif., 1973, (solo concert debut Europe) Mendemblik, Noord-Holland, 1988; arranger: Doulos, 1986, performer, co-arranger, project cons.: albums Look into the Word, 1986. Pres. Daughters of the King, Prince of Peace Chpt., Fair Oaks, Calif., 2006—09. Recipient Mary M. Henry prize, Mills Coll., Oakland, Calif., 1985—87; named Artist of the Session, Festival Noord Holland, 1988; scholar, State of Calif., 1973—76; Music grant, U. Pacific, Stockton, Calif., 1973—76. Mem.: Am. Guild Organists, Nat. Piano Guild, Calif. Assn. Profl. Music Tchrs. (pres. Sacramento chpt. 2007—09, state exec. bd. mem. northern Calif. rep. 2008—09), Nat. Music Tchr. Assn., Music Tchr. Assn. Calif., Pi Lambda Theta, Kappa Delta Pi. Democrat. Episcopalian. Achievements include world premier performance of "Awaken", by Ken McCaw 1986 & Wondrous Love premier performance 2009 by Jami K. Piper. Avocations: sewing, gardening, ballet, figure skating. Home and Office: 5643 Chris Ann Ct Sacramento CA 95841-2800

PIPER, LLOYD LLEWELLYN, II, engineer, government and service industry executive; b. Wareham, Mass., Apr. 28, 1944; s. Lloyd Llewellyn and Mary Elizabeth (Brown) P.; m. Jane Melonie Scruggs, Apr. 30, 1965; 1 child, Michael Wayne. BSEE, Tex. A&M U., 1966; MS in Indsl. Engring, U. Houston, 1973. Registered profl. engr., Tex.; bd. cert. hazardous waste mgmt. Am. Acad. Environ. Engrs. With Houston Lighting & Power Co., 1965—74; project mgr. Dow Chem. Engring. & Constrn Svcs., Houston, 1974—78, Ortloff Corp., Houston, 1978, mgr. engring., 1979—80, v.p., 1980—83; pres., CEO Plantech Engrs. & Constructors, Inc. subs. Dillingham Constrn. Corp., Houston, 1983—86; pres. Delta Plantech Co., Houston, 1985—86; dir. on-site tech. devel. Chem. Waste Mgmt., Inc., Oak Brook, Ill., 1986—88, mgr. projects Houston, 1988—94, dir. facility devel., 1994—95; asst. mgr. Richland Ops. U.S. Dept. Energy, Wash., 1995—96, dep. mgr., 1996—99, adminstr., 1999—2002, asst. mgr., 2002—03; dep. mgr. Carlsbad Field Office US Dept. Energy, 2003—07; mgr. Piper & Associates, LLC, 2007—. Bd. dirs., pres. Harris County Water Control and Improvement Dist., 1973—83; bd. dirs. Environ. Sci. and Tech. Found., 1997—99, United Way, 1998—2003, exec. com., 1998—2001, treas., 2000—01, bd. dirs., 2004—07, Ponderosa Joint Powers Agy. Harris County, 1977—83, pres., 1977—83; pres. bus. and industry adv. coun. North Harris Montgomery C. C. Dist., 1991—92. Contbr. articles to profl. jours. Recipient Disting. Svc. award Engrs. Coun. Houston, 1970; named Tex. Young Engr. of Yr., 1976, Nat. Young Engr. of Yr., 1976. Mem. IEEE (Outstanding Svc. award Houston sect. 1974), NSPE (chpt. pres. 1978, nat. chmn. engrs. in industry divsn. 1977, nat. v.p. 1977, chmn. nat. polit. action com. 1979-82, vice chmn. nat. engrs. week 1988-92, nat. trustee edn. found. 1988-90), Phi Kappa Phi, Tau Beta Pi. Office: PO Box 6353 Bryan TX 77805

PIPER, MARK HARRY, retired banker; b. Flint, Mich., Apr. 17, 1931; s. James U. and Dorothy (Weed) P.; m. Wanda L. Hubbard, June 20, 1953; children: Mark T., Kathryn L. BS, St. John's Mil. Acad., 1949; AB with distinction and honors in Econs, U. Mich., 1953, JD cum laude, 1956. Bar: Mich. 1956. With Clark, Klein, Winter, Parsons & Prewitt, Detroit, 1956-57, Genesee Mchts. Bank & Trust Co., Flint, 1957-88, v.p., sr. trust officer, 1966-72, sr. v.p., 1972-88, NBD Genesee Bank (formerly United Mich. Corp.), 1985-88, cashier, sec. bd. dirs., 1985-88. Adj. instr. bus. adminstrn. U. Mich., Flint, 1976-80; interim co-pension officer Detroit Conf. United Meth. Ch, 1993-99; pres. Flint Estate Planning Coun., 1969-70; mem. Flint citizens adv. coun. U. Mich., 1974-82; vice chmn., 1975-82. Bd. dir. Retirement Homes of Detroit Ann. Conf. Meth. Ch., 1964-76, vice chmn. profl. ministry and support, 1975, mem. bd. support systems, 1975, coun. fin. and adminstrn., 1976-84, chmn. coun. fin. and adminstrn., 1980-84; bd. dirs. United Meth. Devel. Fund, 1986-90; gen. bd. pensions United Meth. Ch., 1988-96, mem. investment com., gen. bd. pensions, 1988-00; mem. investment com. United Meth. Found. of Detroit. Conf. of United Meth. Ch., 1993-2004, interim exec. dir., 2004; trustee Flint YMCA Boysfarm Found., 1964-78, chmn., 1976-78; bd. mgmt. Flint YMCA Boysfarm, 1968-74; mem. Detroit Conf. Bd. P. United Meth. Ch., 1968-76, chmn., 1972-75, 88-02, mem., 1986-02; bd. dirs. U. Mich. Devel. Coun., 1980-82; bd. dirs., asst. treas., sec.-treas. Flint Area Young Life Found., 1979-2006, Mich. Area Young Life Com., 1980-88; bd. dirs., vice chmn. The Crim Road Race Inc., 1985-87; bd. mem. Stewardship Found. Mich., 2002-06. Mem. Mich. Bar Assn., Genesee County Bar Assn., Inst. Continuing Legal Edn., U. Mich.-Flint Club (bd. dirs., pres. 1973-74), Rotary Club. Home: 13380 Purple Finch Cir Lakewood Ranch FL 34202 also: 13307 Supreme Ct Linden MI 48451 Home Phone: 941-751-4642, 810-735-5035. Personal E-mail: mhpiper3@aol.com.

PIPER, ROBERT JOHNSTON, retired architect, urban planner; b. Byron, Ill., Feb. 2, 1926; s. Leo Edward and Helen Anna (Johnston) P.; m. Carol Jane White, June 23, 1951; children— Christopher White, Brian Douglas, Eric Johnston. BS in Archtl. Engring, U. Ill., 1951; M. City and Regional Planning, Cornell U., 1953. Architect, planner Orput & Assos., Rockford, Ill., 1953-61; dir. profl. services AIA, Washington,

1961-67; partner, v.p. Perkins & Will, Chgo., 1967-74; dep. dir. Northeastern Ill. Planning Commn., Chgo., 1974-76; asso. Metz, Train, Olson & Youngren, Inc., Chgo., 1976-79; dir. community devel. City of Highland Park, Ill., 1980-91; ret., 1991; coord. Chgo. '93 and Chgo. Design Consortium Chgo. Cultural Ctr., 1992—. Pres. Landmarks Preservation Council Ill., Chgo., 1976-80 Author: Careers in Architecture, vocat. guidance manuals, 1967, 71, 75, 80, 85, 93; author, editor: Architect's Handbook of Professional Practice, 7th edit., 1963; prin. works include Regional Open Space Plan, Northeastern Ill., Spring Valley Operations Breakthrough Housing Complex, Kalamazoo, CBD Streetscape and Skokie Corridor Master Plan, Highland Park. Trustee Village of Winnetka, Ill., 1978-83; mem. Potomac Planning Task Force Dept. Interior, 1967-68, Commn. on Fed. Procurement, Washington, 1970-71; mem. nat. advisory bd. cmty. characteristics HEW, 1970-78; mem. Burnham Plan 1909 Centennial Com., 1999-2008. Served with USNR, 1944-46, PTO. Fellow AIA (mem. Task Force Future of Inst. 1974-75, various coms., pres. AIA Ill. coun. 1986, Disting. Achievement awards AIA Ill., AIA Chgo. 1993), Am. Inst. Cert. Planners; mem. Lambda Alpha (Chgo. Chpt. Mem. of Yr. award 1999, Daniel H. Burnham Disting. Svc. award, 2004). Episcopalian. Home: 2323 McDaniel Ave 4109 Evanston IL 60201-2583 Home Phone: 847-328-5041. Personal E-mail: piper1132@comcast.net.

PIPER, THOMAS LAURENCE, III, banker; b. Washington, June 20, 1941; s. Thomas Laurence and Edna (Milewski) P.; m. Ann Runnette, Apr. 8, 1967; children: Thomas Laurence IV, Andrew Kerr. Student, U. Va., 1959—61. Assoc. Hodgdon & Co., Inc., Washington, 1962-65; sr. v.p., dir. Hayden Stone Inc., NYC, 1966-73; mng. dir. New Court Securities Corp., NYC, 1974-81, Dillon, Read & Co., Inc., NYC, 1981—97, UBS Warburg LLC, 1997—2000, Citigroup Pvt. Bank, 2000—03; sr. advisor The Nassau Group, 2003—04; sr. v.p. W.P. Stewart Asset Mgmt. (NA), Inc., 2005—. Chmn. fund dir. New Canaan chpt. ARC, 1978; bd. dirs. Manhattan coun. Boy Scouts Am., Waveny Care Ctr., New Canaan, Our Lady Queen of Angels, Manhattan; vice-chmn. adv. bd. U. Va. Art Mus., Charlottesville. Mem.: Bond Club NY, Investment Assn. NY (pres. 1974), Quail Valley Club, Red Stick Golf Club, Blind Brook Club, Country Club of New Canaan, Brook Club (N.Y.C.), Racquet and Tennis Club (N.Y.C.). Home: 14 Westmere Ave Norwalk CT 06853 Office Phone: 212-702-3248. Business E-Mail: tom@wpstewart.com. E-mail: tpiper3@optonline.net.

PIPER, WILLIAM H. (BILLY PIPER), legislative staff member; b. Louisville, Jan. 3, 1969; Grad. in polit. sci., U. Richmond, Va., 1991. Personal asst., Senator Mitch McConnell US Senate, Washington, legis. aide, Senator Mitch McConnell, polit., fin. dir., Senator Mitch McConnell's re-election campaign, 1996, sr. legis. asst. and appropriations coord., Senator Mitch McConnell, chief of staff to Senator Mitch McConnell. Republican. Office: 361A Russell Senate Office Bldg Washington DC 20510-1702 Office Phone: 202-224-2541.*

PIPES, DORIS PERRY, secondary school educator, consultant; b. Tyrone, NY, Dec. 21, 1923; d. Raymond James and Mildred (Wood) Perry; m. Vernon Thomas Pipes, 1951 (div. 1965); 1 child, Vernon Thomas, Jr. AA, Cerritos Coll., 1962; BA, U. Calif., Fullerton, 1964; MA, U. Calif., LA, 1972. Cert. secondary sch. tchr. Coord. spl. programs, dept. chair program Pioneer High Sch., Whittier, Calif., 1964-65, dir. reading program, coord. tchr. tng., dept. head, 1966-67; instr. grad. sch. Whittier Coll., 1967-71; tchg. cons., classroom materials cons. Scholastic Mag., NYC, 1969-73; resource splst. Calif. High Sch., Whittier, 1973-90, cons. math dept., 1988-90; ret., 1990. Vis. guest lectr., dir. elem. reading clinic Loyola U., L.A., 1967-70; cons. Inglewood High Sch., 1971-72; adminstr. field testing parallel tests in Spanish and English, 1971, 77; reading tchr. Whittier Adult Sch., 1962-66. Contbr. article to jour. Mem. PTA Calif. High Sch., 1964-90 Recipient PTA award, 1989; named Outstanding Secondary Sch. Reading Program Nat. Assn. Secondary Sch. Prins., 1972, Outstanding Secondary Educator of Yr. Outstanding Secondary Educators, 1973. Mem. Internat. Reading Assn. (pres. Rio Hondo coun. 1967), Calif. Tchrs. Assn. (chair), Calif. High Sch. Tchrs. Assn., Alpah Gamma Sigma. Avocations: travel, reading, gardening. Home: 1581 Northwood Rd Apt 274H Seal Beach CA 90740

PIPES, RICHARD EDGAR, historian, educator; b. Cieszyn, Poland, July 11, 1923; arrived in US, 1940, naturalized, 1943; s. Mark and Sophia Haskelberg Pipes; m. Irene Eugenia Roth, Sept. 1, 1946; children: Daniel, Steven. Student, Muskingum Coll., 1940-43; AB, Cornell U., 1945; PhD, Harvard U., 1950; LLD (hon.), Muskingum Coll., 1988; LHD (hon.), Adelphi U., 1991; Dr.h.c., U. Silesia, Poland, 1994. Mem. faculty Harvard U., 1950—96, prof. history, 1958-75, Frank B. Baird Jr. prof. history, 1975-96, Baird prof. emeritus, 1996-98, Baird Rsch. Prof., 1998-2001, Baird prof. emeritus, 2001—. Fellow Am. Coun. Learned Socs., 1965, Ctr. for Advanced Study in Behavioral Scis., Stanford, Calif., 1969—70; assoc. dir. Russian Rsch. Ctr., 1962—64, dir., 1968—73; sr. cons. Stanford Rsch Inst., 1973—78; dir. East European and Soviet affairs NSC, 1981—82; lectr. Norwegian Nobel Peace Inst., Oslo, 1993. Author: (books) The Formation of the Soviet Union, Communism and Nationalism, 1917-1923, 1954, The Russian Intelligentsia, 1961, Social Democracy and the St. Petersburg Labor Movement, 1885-1887, 1963, Struve: Liberal on the Left, 1970, Russia Under the Old Regime, 1974, Soviet Strategy in Europe, 1976, Struve: Liberal on the Right, 1905-1944, 1980, U.S.-Soviet Relations in the Era of Détente: a Tragedy of Errors, 1981, Survival is Not Enough: Soviet Realities and America's Future, 1984, Russia Observed: Collected Essays on Russian and Soviet History, 1989, The Russian Revolution, 1990, Russia Under the Bolshevik Regime: 1919-1924, 1993, Communism, the Vanished Specter, 1994, A Concise History of the Russian Revolution, 1995, The Three "Whys" of the Russian Revolution, 1995, The Unknown Lenin: From the Secret Archive, 1996, Property and Freedom, 1999, Communism: A History, 2001, Vixi: Memoirs of a Non-Belonger, 2003, The Degaev Affair: Terror and Treason in Tsarist Russia, 2003, Russian Conservatism and Its Critics, 2006. Chmn. Govt. Team B to Rev. Intelligence Estimates, 1976; mem. Reagan transition team Dept. State, 1980; exec. mem. Com. on Present Danger, 1977—92. Served with USAAF. Recipient George Louis Beer prize, Am. Historical Assn., 1955, Comdr.'s Cross of Merit, Republic of Poland, 1996, Nat. Humanities medal, NEH, 2007; Guggenheim fellow, 1956, 1965, Walter Cabot Channing fellow, Harvard U., 1990—91. Fellow: Acad. Arts and Scis.; mem.: Polish Acad., Coun. Fgn. Rels. Home: 17 Berkeley St Cambridge MA 02138-3409

PIPES, ROBERT BYRON, mechanical engineer, educator; b. Shreveport, La., Aug. 14, 1941; s. Walter H. and Mattye Mae (Wilson) P.; m. Ruth Ellen Franz, June 27, 1964; children: Christopher Franz, Mark Robert. BS, La. Poly. Inst., 1964, MS, 1965; MSE, MA, Princeton U., 1969; PhD, U. Tex., 1972. Registered profl. engr., Del. Sr. structures engr. Gen. Dynamics Corp., 1969-72; asst. prof. mech. engring. Drexel U., 1972-74; assoc. prof. mech. and aerospace engring. U. Del., 1974-80, prof., 1980-91, also dir. Center Composite Materials, 1978-85, dean Coll. Engring., 1985-91, provost, v.p. acad. affairs, 1991-93; pres. Rensselaer Polytech. Inst., NY, 1993-98; disting. vis. scientist Coll. William and Mary, 1998—2001; Goodyear prof. polymer engring. U. Akron, Ohio, 2001—04; John C. Bray disting. prof. engring. Purdue U., 2004—. Cons. in field; com. mem. NRC. Author: Experimental Mechanics of Fiber Reinforced Composite Materials, 1982, Characterization of Advanced Composite Materials, 1987, 3d edit., 2002; series editor 12 vols. Composite Materials; contbr. articles to profl. jours. Bd. dirs. Omnova Solutions, Inc., Fairlawn, Ohio, 1993—2005. Recipient Gustus Larson award, ASME, 1987. Mem. ASME (Gustus Larson award 1983), Soc. Mfg. Engrs., Soc. Advancement of Material and Processing Engring., Nat. Acad. Engring. (elected 1987), Swedish Acad. Engring., Am. Soc. Composites, ASTM, Sigma Xi, Tau Beta Pi, Pi Tau Sigma, Omicron Delta Kappa. Methodist. Achievements include pioneering work in the field of composite materials. Home and Office: 4509 Sugar Maple Dr Lafayette IN 47905 Office Phone: 765-494-5767. E-mail: bpipes@purdue.edu.

PIPINOS, IRAKLIS ILIAS, surgeon; s. Elias and Margarita Pipinos; m. Kostoula Panousopoulou; children: Elias, Margarita, Anna. MD, U. Crete, Greece, 1992. Diplomate Am. Bd. Surgery, Am. Bd. Vascular Surgery. Intern Henry Ford Hosp., Detroit, resident in gen. surgery, vascular surgery fellow; endovascular surgery fellow Stanford Med. Ctr.; assoc. prof. surgery U. Nebr. Med. Ctr., Omaha, 2001—. Fellow: ACS; mem.: Soc. Vascular Surgery. Achievements include NIH funded rsch. in mitochondria physiology. Office: Univ Nebr Dept Surgery 983280 Univ Nebr Med Ctr Omaha NE 68198

PIPKIN, JAMES HAROLD, JR., lawyer; b. Houston, Jan. 3, 1939; s. James Harold and Zenda Marie (Lewis) P. BA, Princeton U., 1960; JD, Harvard U., 1963; Diploma in Law, Oxford U., Eng., 1965. Bar: D.C. 1964, U.S. Supreme Ct. 1969, D.C. Ct. Appeals, 1972. Law ck. to assoc. justice U.S. Supreme Ct., Washington, 1963-64; assoc. Steptoe and Johnson, Washington, 1965-70, ptnr., 1971-93, spl. coun., 2007—09; counselor to The Sec. of the Interior U.S. Dept. of the Interior, 1993-98; U.S. spl. negotiator for Pacific Salmon, Dept. of State, 1994-2001; rank of amb. Dept. of State, 1995-96; dir. office policy analysis U.S. Dept. Interior, 1998-2001; fgn. affairs officer U.S. State Dept., 2001—02. Counsel Friends of Music, Smithsonian Inst., Washington, 1984-88; mem. Nat. Arbitration Panel, 1983-94. Author or co-author: The English Country House: A Grand Tour, 1985, The Country House Garden: A Grand Tour, 1987, Places of Tranquility, 1990; contbr. photographs and articles to mags. including House & Garden, Smithsonian mag., The Mag. Antiques, Archtl. Digest. Grand officier Confrérie des Chevaliers du Tastevin, 1989—. Mem. ABA, D.C. Bar Assn., Met. Club. Home: 6109 Davenport Ter Bethesda MD 20817-5827

PIPPENGER, MICHAEL KIRK, economics professor, researcher; b. Indpls., Aug. 10, 1957; s. Joseph Irwin and Shirley Pippenger; m. Joanne Pippenger, Dec. 31, 2000. BS, Ball State U., Muncie, Ind., 1980; MA, U. Chgo., 1985; MS, PhD, Purdue U., West Lafayette Ind., 1990. Vis. asst. prof. economics Ball State U., 1989—90, Miami U., Oxford, Ohio, 1990—91, U. Alaska, Fairbanks, 1991—92, asst. prof. economics, 1992—97, chair, dept. economics, 1997—2007, assoc. prof. economics, 1997—. Rec. sec. United Academics AAUP, AFT, Fairbanks, 1996—98, orgnl. v.p., 1998—2002; chair, bd. dirs. Spirit Alaska FCU, 2001—07. Contbr. articles to numerous profl. jours. Com. mem. revenue task force Fairbanks North Star Borough, 1999—2000. Home: 102 Pepperdine Fairbanks AK 99709 Office: University of Alaska Box 6080 Fairbanks AK 99775-6080 Personal E-mail: mpippenger@gci.net. Business E-Mail: ffmkp@uaf.edu.

PIPPENGER, NICHOLAS JOHN, mathematician, Computer Scientist Researcher Educator; b. Abington, Pa., Mar. 14, 1947; s. Robert and Mary Emma Pippenger; m. Maria Margaret Klawe, May 12, 1980; children: Janek Evan Klawe, Sasha Kathleen. BS, Shimer Coll., 1965, MIT, 1967, MS, 1969, PhD, 1974. Mem. tech. staff Charles Stark Draper Lab., Cambridge, Mass., 1969—73; mem. rsch. staff IBM Corp., Yorktown Heights, NY, 1973—80, San Jose, Calif., 1980—87, fellow, 1987—89; prof. U. BC, Vancouver, Canada, 1988—2000, rsch. chair, 2000—03; prof. Princeton U., NJ, 2003—06, Harvey Mudd Coll, Claremont, Calif., 2006—. Fellow: IEEE, Assn. Computing Machinery, Acad. Sci., Royal Soc. Can.; mem.: Math. Assn. of Am., Am. Math. Soc., Soc. Indsl. and Applied Math. Office: Harvey Mudd Coll Dept Math 1250 N Dartmouth Ave Claremont CA 91711 Business E-Mail: njp@math.hmc.edu.

PIPPIN, ROBERT B., philosopher, educator; b. 1948; BA with honors, Trinity Coll., Hartford, Conn., 1970; MA, Penn. State Univ., 1972, PhD in Philosophy, 1974. Asst. prof. New Coll., Sarasota, Fla., 1974—75, Univ. Calif., San Diego, 1975—81, assoc. prof., 1981—89, prof., 1989, 1989—92, dept. chair, 1990—92; prof. Univ. Chgo., 1992—, Raymond W. and Martha Hilpert Gruner disting. svc. prof. Author: Hegel's Idealism, 1989, Modernism as a Philosophical Problem, 1991. Recipient Disting. Achievement award, Andrew Mellon Found., 2001. Fellow: Am. Acad. Arts & Scis. Office: Dept Philosophy Univ Chgo 1115 E 58th St Chicago IL 60637 Office Phone: 773-702-5453. Business E-Mail: r-pippin@uchicago.edu.

PIPREK, JOACHIM, solid state physicist; b. Potsdam, Germany, Dec. 6, 1956; came to U.S., 1993; MS, Humboldt U., Berlin, 1980, PhD, 1986. Prin. scientist Werk Fernsehelektronik, Berlin, 1986-90; rsch. assoc. Humboldt U., Berlin, 1990-93; asst. prof. U. Del., Newark, 1993-97; adj. prof. U. Calif., Santa Barbara, 1997—2005; pres. NUSOD Inst., 2005—. Author Semiconductor Optoelectronic Devices, 2003, co-author: (chpts.) Laser Diodes, 1998—; editor Optelectronic Devices, 2005, Nitride Semiconductor Devices, 2007; contbr. articles to profl. jours. Mem. IEEE (sr.), Am. Phys. Soc., German Phys. Soc. Achievements include inventions and observations in optics and semiconductor devices. E-mail: piprek@ieee.org.

PIRAINO, THOMAS ANTHONY, JR., lawyer; b. Cleve., July 12, 1949; s. Thomas Anthony and Margaret (Stephens) P.; m. Barbara McWilliams, Sept. 4, 1976; children: Margaret, Ann, Mary. BA in History, magna cum laude, Allegheny Coll., 1971; JD, Cornell U., 1974. Bar: Ohio 1974. Assoc. counsel Parker-Hannifin Corp., Cleve., 1981-84, asst. gen. counsel, 1984-98, v.p., gen. counsel, sec., 1998—. Contbr. articles to legal jours. Mem. ABA, Ohio Bar Assn., Am. Corp. Counsel (sec. 1985—), Am. Soc. Corp. Secs. (past pres., Ohio chapter.) Avocations: tennis, jogging. Office: Parker Hannifin Corp 6035 Parkland Blvd Cleveland OH 44124-4141

PIRCHER, LEO JOSEPH, lawyer, director; b. Berkeley, Calif., Jan. 4, 1933; s. Leo Charles and Christine (Moore) P.; m. Phyllis McConnell, Aug. 4, 1956 (div. Apr. 1981); children: Christopher, David, Eric; m. Nina Silverman, June 14, 1987. BS, U. Calif., Berkeley, 1954, JD, 1957. Bar: Calif. 1958, (N.Y.) 1985, cert.: Calif. Bd. Legal Specialization (cert. specialist taxation law). Assoc. Lawler, Felix & Hall, L.A., 1957-62, ptnr., 1962-65, sr. ptnr., 1965-83, Pircher, Nichols & Meeks, L.A., 1983—. Adj. prof. Loyola U. Law Sch., LA, 1959—61; corp. sec. Am. Metal Bearing Co., Gardena, Calif., 1975—; dir. Varco Internat., Inc., Orange, Calif.; spkr. various law schs. and bar assns. edn. programs. Author (with others): (novels) Definition and Utility of Leases, 1968. Chmn. pub. fin. and taxation sect. Calif. Town Hall, LA, 1970—71. Mem.: ABA, Nat. Assn. Real Estate Investment Trusts Inc. (cert. specialist taxation law), L.A. County Bar Assn. (exec. com. comml. law sect.), N.Y. State Bar, Calif. State Bar, Regency (L.A.). Republican. Office: Pircher Nichols & Meeks Ste 1700 1925 Century Park E Los Angeles CA 90067-6022 Home Phone: 310-274-2455; Office Phone: 310-201-8901. Personal E-mail: lpircher@pircher.com.

PIRCHNER, HERMAN, JR., foreign policy specialist; b. Cleve., June 26, 1946; s. Herman Sr. and Constance Pirchner; m. Elizabeth Scull Wood. BBA, U. Toledo, 1970. Dir. fin. Chuck Grassley for U.S. Senate, Des Moines, 1979-80; dir. legislation U.S. Senator Roger Jepsen, Washington, 1981-82; pres. Am. Fgn. Policy Coun., Washington, 1982—. Cons. to polit. campaigns Roger Jepsen for U.S. Senate, Iowa, 1982-84, Bob Kasten for U.S. Senate, Wis., 1982-86, George Voinovich for U.S. Senate, Ohio, 1988. Bd. dirs. Herbert Hoover Presdl. Libr. Assn., 1998—. Mem. Univ. Club. Republican. Avocations: pocket billiards, chess, squash. Business E-Mail: pirchner@afpc.org.

PIRIE, ROBERT BURNS, JR., defense analyst; b. San Diego, Sept. 10, 1933; s. Robert Burns and Gertrude May (Freeman) P.; m. Joan Adams, Dec. 23, 1960; children: John Winthrop, Carl Joseph Emil, Susan Gilman. Student, Princeton U., 1950-51; BS, U.S. Naval Acad., 1955; BA, Magdalen Coll., Oxford U., 1959, MA, 1963. Commd. ensign U.S. Navy, 1955, advanced through grades to comdr., 1969; comdg. officer (U.S.S. Skipjack), 1969-72; dep. asst. dir. Congl. Budget Office, 1975-77; prin. dep. asst. sec. for manpower, res. affairs and logistics Dept. Def., Washington, 1977-79, asst. sec., 1979-81; mgmt. cons., 1981—; def. analyst Ctr. for Naval Analyses, Alexandria, Va., 1981-83; asst. v.p. Inst. for Def. Analyses, Alexandria, 1983-86, v.p., 1986-87; exec. v.p. Essex Corp., Alexandria, 1987, pres., 1987-88; sr. economist Rand Corp., Washington, 1989; dir. strategic studies group U.S. Naval War Coll., 1989-92; v.p. Ctr. Naval Analyses, Alexandria, 1992-94; asst. sec. of Navy for Installations and Environ. USN, Washington, 1994-2000, undersec. of Navy, 2000—01; sr. fellow Ctr. for Naval Analysis, 2001—. Chmn. bd. advisors Nat. Infrastructure Inst., 2004—06. Vestryman St. John's Episcopal Ch., Chevy Chase, Md., 1973-76, 81, jr. warden, 1982-84, sr. warden, 1984-87; trustee U.S. Naval Acad. Found., 1980-94. Rhodes scholar, 1956 Mem. U.S. Naval Inst., U.S. Naval Acad. Alumni Assn. (trustee 1967-70), Vincent's Club, Cosmos Club. Home: 4405 Stanford St Chevy Chase MD 20815-5207 Personal E-mail: rpirie@aol.com.

PIRKL, JAMES JOSEPH, industrial designer, educator, writer; b. Nyack, NY, Dec. 27, 1930; s. James and Ida Bertha (Gigrich) Pirkl; m. Sarah B. W. Woolsey, June 8, 1974; children: Theo, James, Philip. Cert. in advt. design, Pratt Inst., 1951, B in Indsl. Design cum laude, 1958. Design staff GM, Warren, Mich., 1958-65, sr. designer, 1961-64, asst. chief designer, 1964-65; instr. indsl. design Center Creative Studies, Detroit, 1963-65; faculty dept. design Syracuse (N.Y.) U., 1965-92, assoc. prof., 1969-73, prof. indsl. design, 1974-92, prof. emeritus, 1992—, coord. indsl. design program, 1979-84, chmn. dept. design, 1985-91; exec. council chmn. Sch. Art, 1976-78, 80-81; sr. rsch. fellow All-U. Gerontology Ctr., 1990-92. Prin. James J. Pirkl/Design, 1965—; cons. GE, 1967—70, N.Y. State Coun. Arts, 1968—69, Loretto Geriatric Ctr., Pulos Design Assocs., 1972—80, Fed. Prison Industries, 1974, Xerox Corp., 1975, Am. Soc. Aging, 1995, Ford Motor Design Ctr., 1992, Arthritis Found., 1993—96, Age Wave, Inc., 1993—96, GE Appliances, 1994, ProMatura Group, 1994—98, universal kitchen product R.I. Sch. Design, 1996—98, Boeing Co., 2004; chmn. accreditation coun. Design Found., 1982—84; designer, project dir. Transgenerational House, 2000—03; exec. dir. Transgenerational Design Matters, 2004—; lectr. in field. Author: Trangenerational Design: Products for an Aging Population, 1994; co-author: Guidelines and Strategies for Designing Transgenerational Products, 1988; co-designer GM Futurama Exhbn., N.Y. World's Fair, 1964—65; contbr. articles to profl. jours. Design mem. Everson Mus. Art, 1977—85; chmn. planning commn. Town of Cazenovia, 1988—93; mem. exhbns. com. Syracuse Cultural Resources Coun., 1992—93; coord. Tylenol/Arthritis Found. Student Design Awards Program, 1993—95; mem. senate Syracuse U., 1973—80, mem. adv. bd. SEARS Project, 1989—91, chmn. chancellor's citation, 1988—92. With SeaBees USN, 1951—55. Recipient Gold Indsl. Design Excellence award, Indsl. Designers Soc. Am. and Bus. Week Mag., 1994. Fellow: Indsl. Designers Soc. Am. (nat. bd. dirs. 1977—81, chmn. Ctrl. N.Y. chpt. 1977—81, v.p. Mid-East region 1978—81, chmn. NASAD liaison com. 1984—88, archives com. 1988—92, U.S. rep., del. Internat. Congress Socs. Indsl. Design 1989, chmn. universal design com. 1991—94, Edn. award 2001); mem.: Author's Guild, Am. Soc. Aging (contbr. articles to jour.), Nat. Ctr. Barrier Free Environment (adv. task force 1981), Human Factors Soc. (life), Nat. Assn. Schs. Art and Design (accreditation evaluator 1985—95), The Design Found. (chmn. accreditation coun. 1982). Achievements include originating the concept of Transgenerational Design and design of the world's first Transgenerational House. Home: 2007 Quail Run Dr NE Albuquerque NM 87122 Business E-Mail: jjp@transgenerational.org.

PIRKLE, EARL CHARNELL, retired geologist; b. nr. Buckhead, Ga., Jan. 8, 1922; s. Early Charnell and Eva Lee (Collins) P.; m. Valda Nell Armistead, July 9, 1942; children: Betty Jean, William A., Fredric L. AB, Emory U., 1943; MS, 1947; postgrad., U. Tenn., 1947-50; PhD, U. Cin., 1956. Certified profl. geologist. Prodn. coordinator, research crystallographer Pan-Electronics Labs., Inc., Atlanta, 1942-45; instr. geology U. Tenn., 1947-50; mem. faculty dept. phys. scis. and geology U. Fla., Gainesville, 1950-93, prof. emeritus, 1993—, prof., 1963—, chmn. dept. phys. scis., 1972-79; dir. Phys. Scis., 1979-82. Cons. in field; vis. prof. geology Emory U., summers 1959-65; rsch. cons. Fla. Dept. Nat. Resources Bur. Geology, 1950-70. Author: Natural Regions of the United States, 1977, 4th edit., 1985; Editor: Physical Science- Our Environment, 1968, Our Physical Environment, 1980; Contbr. articles to profl. jours. Served with AUS, 1945-46. Fellow Geol. Soc. Am., Soc. Econ. Geologists; mem. Am. Assn. Petroleum Geologists, Am. Soc. Mining, Metall. and Petroleum Engrs., Fla. Acad. Scis., Southeastern Geol. Soc., Phi Beta Kappa, Sigma Gamma Epsilon, Gamma Theta Epsilon, Sigma Chi. Democrat. Methodist.

PIRKUL, HASAN, dean, management educator; BS in Industrial Engring., Bogazici U., 1977; MS in Mgmt. Sci., U. Rochester, 1980, PhD in Computer Info. Sys., 1983. Asst. prof. Max M. Fisher Coll. Bus., Ohio State U., 1981—87, assoc. prof., 1987—91, prof. accounting and info. sys., 1991, dir. info. sys. programs, founding dir. Ctr. for Info. Technologies in Mgmt.; now dean, Caruth chair of mgmt. Sch. Mgmt., U. Tex., Dallas. Mem. Dallas Com. on Fgn. Rels.; chair Coll. on Info. Sys., Inst. for Ops. Rsch. and Mgmt. Sci. Founding editor-in-chief Jour. of Info. Tech. and Mgmt. Office: U Tex at Dallas Sch Mgmt SM 40 800 W Campbell Rd Richardson TX 75080-3021 Office Phone: 972-883-2705.*

PIRODSKY, DONALD MAX, psychiatrist, educator; b. Freeport, NY, Feb. 2, 1945; s. Max and Doris Geilhard (Biedermann) P.; m. Gail Giufre Pallotta, Jan. 4, 1997; children: Laura Anne, Jason Donald. BA, Hofstra U., Hempstead, NY, 1966; MD, SUNY, Syracuse, 1970. Diplomate Am.

Bd. Psychiatry and Neurology, Nat. Bd. Med. Examiners. Intern Northwestern U. Med. Ctr., Chgo., 1970-71; resident in psychiatry Strong Meml. Hosp., Rochester, NY, 1973-74, U. Ariz. Med. Ctr., Tucson, 1974-76; instr. psychiatry SUNY Health Sci. Ctr., Syracuse, 1976-78, attending psychiatrist, 1976-91, asst. prof. psychiatry, 1978-85, mem. exec. com. of med. coll. assembly, 1979-82, clin. assoc. prof., 1985—2006, adj. attending psychiatrist, 1991—2006; pvt. practice Syracuse and Fayetteville, NY, 1976—2006, Canastota, NY, 2006—; staff psychiatrist, dir. consultation/liaison svc. Syracuse VA Med. Ctr., 1976-87, chmn. pharmacy rev. and therapeutic agts. com., 1980-86. Psychiat. cons. Ariz. Sch. Deaf and Blind, Tucson, 1975-76, Syracuse Devel. Ctr., 1977-2006, Rochester Sch. Deaf, 1978-81; ex-officio mem. Family Counseling Agy., Tucson, 1975-76; adj. attending psychiatrist SUNY Health Sci. Ctr., Syracuse, 1991-2006. Author: Primer of Clinical Psychopharmacology: A Practical Guide, 1981, (with Jerry S. Cohn) Clinical Primer of Psychopharmacology: A Practical Guide, 2d edit., 1992; contbr. articles to profl. jours., chpts. to med. books. Lt. comdr. USPHS, 1971-73. Fellow Am. Psychiat. Assn. (Disting., mem. cen. NY dist. br.); mem. Am. Psychosomatic Soc., Am. Assn. Mental Retardation, Med. Soc. State of NY, NY State Psychiat. Assn., Onondaga County Med. Soc. Episcopalian. Avocations: sports, collecting baseball cards and other sports memorabilia. Office Phone: 315-247-9681.

PIRRIS, STEPHEN MONTGOMERY, neurosurgeon; b. Washington, Pa., Jan. 5, 1976; s. John Pirris and Pirris Montgomery Sally; m. Kristin Marie Grudowski, Mar. 25, 1981. BS in Biology, U. NC, Chapel Hill, 1998; MD, U. Pitts., 2002. Cert. physician Pa., 2004. Resident U. Pitts. Med. Ctr., 2002—. Clin. Travelling Spine fellowship, N.Am. Spine Soc., 2007—08. Mem.: Congress Neurosurgeons. Conservative. Roman Catholic. Home: 506 Bingham St Pittsburgh PA 15203 Office: Univ Pitts Med Ctr Dept Neurosurgery 200 Lothrop St Ste B-400 Pittsburgh PA 15213 Business E-Mail: pirrissm@upmc.edu.

PIRRO, ALFRED ANTHONY, JR., emergency physician; b. Stamford, Conn., May 17, 1961; s. Alfred Anthony, Sr. and Frances (Battaglia) Pirro. BA in Natural Scis., Johns Hopkins U., Balt., 1983; MD, U. Conn., Storrs, 1987. Diplomate Am. Bd. Anesthesiology, Am. Bd. Critical Care Medicine. Resident in surgery Hosp. of St. Raphael, New Haven, 1987-90; fellow in neurosurgery Hartford Hosp., Conn., 1991-92, resident in anesthesiology, 1992-95, critical care fellow, 1995-97, staff anesthesiologist, 1997-99; emergency medicine physician Windham Hosp., Willamantic, Conn., 1991—; instr. anesthesiology John Dempsey Hosp.-U. Conn. Sch. Medicine, Hartford, 1997-99; owner Hosp. Physician Specialists, Elkton, Md., 2006—08; med. dir. hospitalist program Union Hosp. Cecil County, Elkton, 2004—, chmn. dept. hospitalist medicine, 2007—, med. dir. ICU. Chmn. critical care, chmn. med. records com. Union Hosp. Cecil County, 2002—, mem. med. exec. com., 2007—; med. dir. Calvert Manor Nursing and Rehab Ctr., Rising Sun, Mo., 2007—; sec., treas. & med. staff U. Hosp., 2008—. Advisor Lally for Congress campaign, Mineola, NY, 1994. Scholar, Pitney Bowes, 1979; Beneficial-Hodson scholar, Johns Hopkins U., 1979. Mem.: AMA, Soc. Critical Care Medicine, Md. State Med. Soc. Republican. Office Phone: 443-350-4544. Personal E-mail: aapjrmd@aol.com.

PIRRO, JEANINE FERRIS, television personality, former prosecutor; b. Elmira, NY, June 2, 1951; d. Leo and Esther Ferris; m. Albert J. Pirro, Aug. 23, 1975 (separated 2007); children: Christi, Alexander. BA, U. Buffalo, 1972; JD, Albany Law Sch., 1975. Bar: NY 1975. Legis. aide NY State Senate, Albany, 1973-75; asst. dist. atty. Westchester County Dist. Atty. Office, White Plains, NY, 1975-78, chief Victim Witness Unit, 1978-79, chief domestic violence/child abuse bur., 1978-90, dist. atty., 1994—2006; county court judge Westchester County, White Plains, NY, 1990-93. Numerous appearances as legal analyst Fox News, CNN, ABC, NBC, CBS. Author: To Punish and Protect, 2003; judge (TV series) Judge Jeanine Pirro, 2008—. Chair Gov. Pataki's NY State Commn. on Domestic Violence Fatalities Rev. Bd., 1996; Rep. party candidate for NY State atty. gen., 2006; bd. dirs. My Sister's Place, 1990—; bd. vis. Pace U. Sch. Law, 1994— Named one of 50 Most Beautiful People, People mag., 1997. Mem. NY State Dist. Attys. Assn. (pres. 1999-2000), Nat. Mus. Women's History (bd. adv.). Republican. Roman Catholic.*

PISANI, ANTHONY MICHAEL, architect; b. Cambridge, Mass., May 18, 1943; s. Anthony Joseph and Josephine Ann (Tortorella) P.; m. Emilia D'Agostino, Aug. 27, 1967; children: Emiliabianca, Giancarlo Diploma, Mus. Sch., 1966; BFA, Tufts U., 1966; MArch., Harvard U., 1971. Registered architect, Mass., Calif., Maine, Mich., N.Y., N.H., Tex., Vt. Project architect Kallmann & McKinell, Architects, Boston, 1971-73, Charles G. Hilgenhurst & Assocs., Boston, 1973-74, Desmond & Lord, Architects, Boston, 1974-77; pres. Anthony M. Pisani & Assocs., Architects, Boston, 1978—. Instr. design Boston Archtl. Center, 1971-74; vice- chmn. Boston Landmarks Commn., 1987-95. Major works in Eastern U.S., Ireland, Can., Mex., P.R., Japan; contbr. articles to profl. jours. Mem. Boston Zoning Bd. Appeal, 1998—. Mem. AIA, Boston Soc. Architects, Constrn. Specifications Inst., Urban Land Inst., Nat. Council Archtl. Registration Bds., Soc. Archtl. Historians Home: 95 Robinwood Ave Boston MA 02130-2110 Office: 374 Congress St Boston MA 02210-1807 Home Phone: 617-522-6692; Office Phone: 617-423-1022. E-mail: apisani@pisani.com.

PISANI, MICHAEL VINCENT, music educator; b. Gary, Ind., Mar. 16, 1954; s. Mario Donato Pisani and Dolores Joan Stefanelli. BFA; MusM, Oberlin Coll., Ohio, 1977; PhD, Eastman Sch. Music, U. Rochester, NY, 1996. Asst. condr. Houston Grand Opera, 1979—86; artistic coord. Eckardt Gramatte Found., Winnipeg, Manitoba, Canada, 1990; prof. music Vassar Coll., Poughkeepsie. Author: (book) Imagining Native America Music; contbr. articles. Mem.: Soc. Am. Music, Am. Musicological Soc. Home: Vassar Coll Box 595 Poughkeepsie NY 12604

PISANO, ETTA D., radiologist, educator; AB cum laude, Dartmouth Coll., 1979; MD, Duke U. Cert. Diagnostic Radiology Am. Bd. Radiology, 1988. Radiology resident Beth Israel Hosp., Boston, 1984—88, chief resident, 1986—87, dir. mammography, 1988—89; med. dir. Carolina Screening Mammography, 1989—93; residency program dir. Dept. Radiology U. NC Sch. Medicine, 1992—96, section chief Breast Imaging Sect., 1989—2005, program dir. Post-grad. Continuing Med. Edn. Course in Breast Imaging, 1989—2005, Kenan prof. radiology and biomedical engring., dir. Biomed. Rsch. Imaging Ctr., 2003—, vice dean academic affairs, 2006—. Contbr. articles to profl. jours. Recipient Francis W. Gramlich Philosophy Prize, 1979, Health Breakthrough award, Ladies' Home Jour., 2006; named one of 20 Most Influential People in Radiology, Diagnostic Imaging, 2002, America's Best Breast Cancer Doctors, Redbook, 2001. Fellow: Soc. Breast Imaging; mem.: Inst. Medicine, Assn. Profl. Women in Medicine and Sci. (mem. Nominating and Salary Equity Com. 1994—), Assn. Univ. Radiologists, Am. Coll. Radiology, Am. Assn. Women's Radiologists, Am. Med. Women's Assn. (Women in Sci. Award 2005), Radiological Soc. North Am., Internat. Digital Mammography Devel. Group (chair 1996—, pres. pro tem 2001—), Am. Roentgen Ray Soc. Office: U NC Chapel Hill Sch Medicine 503 Old Infimary Chapel Hill NC 27599-7510 Home: 105 Majestic Ct Chapel Hill NC 27517-8345 Home Phone: 919-942-1166; Office Phone: 919-966-4397. E-mail: etpisano@med.unc.edu.*

PISANO, JANE G., museum administrator; BA in Polit. Sci., Stanford U.; MA in Internat. Rels., PhD in Internat. Rels., John Hopkins U. White House fellow Nat. Security Coun.; faculty Sch. Fgn. Svc., Georgetown U.; head LA 2000, The 2000 Partnership; dean, Sch. Pub. Adminstrn. U. Southern Calif., v.p. external rels., sr. v.p. external rels., 1998—2001; pres., dir. Natural Hist. Mus. LA County, 2001—. Chair bd. govs. Calif. Cmty. Found.; pres. bd. trustees John Randolph Haynes and Dora Haynes Found.; bd. chair Nat. Acad. Pub. Adminstrn.; mem. Coun. Fgn. Rels.; bd. dirs. WellPoint, Inc. Office: Natural Hist Mus LA County 900 Exposition Blvd Los Angeles CA 90007

PISANO, LINDA MAUREEN, costume designer, educator; d. Theodore Jack and Patricia Kindred; m. Paul Warren Pisano, Sept. 1, 1990; children: Massimiliano Alessandro, Liam Lucian. BFA in Performance, Utah State U., 1990, MA in Theatre, 1993; MFA in Costume Design & Tech., Ohio State U., Columbus, 1996. Asst. prof. theatre Iowa State U., Ames, 1999—2002; prof. costume design Ind. U. Theatre & Drama, Bloomington, 2002—. Designer for balletmet columbus, Dracula, Beauty & the Beast, Aladdin, Alice in Wonderland (World Design Exhbn., Prague Quadrenniel, 1999), Ind. repertory theatre, Romeo & Juliet, To Kill A Mockingbird & Others, Utah Shakespearean festival, Doctor Faustus, Room Service (USITT Nat. Jury Winner, 2006). Recipient Meritorious award, Kennedy Ctr.-Am. Coll. Theatre Festival, 2000, 2001; grantee Rsch. & Travel Commedia Del Arte Masks, Coll. Arts & Humanities Inst. Ind. U., 2007. Mem.: US Inst. Theatre Tech. (Peggy Ezekiel award 1997, 2000, 2004, 2006, Nat. Jury Winner 1997, 1999, 2006), Costume Soc. Gt. Britain, Costume Soc. Am., United Scenic Artists.

PISARCZYK, RICHARD V., oil industry executive; m. Mary Pisarczyk; 1 child, Michael. B in Chem. Engring., Mich. State U., 1968. Engr. Mobil Oil Corp., 1968, mgr. Ferndale Refinery Wash., 1984—86, v.p., gen. mgr. olefins and aromatics, petrochemicals divsn., Mobil Chem. Co., 1986—88, mgr. planning and fin. analysis, mfg. Fairfax, Va., 1988, mgr. Chalmette Refinery La., 1989, mgr. planning coordination, corp. planning and economics Fairfax, 1992, mng. dir. Mobil Oil Australia Pty Ltd., 1994—97, v.p. East/Gulf Coast bus., North America mktg. & refining, 1997—99; regional dir. Americas, ExxonMobil Chem. Exxon Mobil Corp., 1999—2001, sr. v.p. basic chemicals, 2001—03, sr. v.p. basic chemicals and intermediates, 2003—05, pres. ExxonMobil Rsch. & Engring. Co., 2005—. Rep. Indsl. Rsch. Inst.; mem. Rsch., Innovation and Enterprise Coun. Recipient Red Cedar Cir. award in Chem. Engring. and Materials Sci., Mich. State U., 2007. Avocations: golf, woodworking. Office: Exxon Mobil Corp Hdqs 5959 Las Colinas Blvd Irving TX 75039-2298*

PISCHINGER, FRANZ FELIX, engineer, researcher, educator; b. Waidhofen, Austria, July 18, 1930; s. Franz and Karoline (Bentz) P.; m. Elfriede Pischinger-Goessler, 1957 (2001); children: Gerhard, Martin, Stefan, Thomas, Alice; m. Elisabeth Pischinger-Froehlich, 2003. Diploma in Engring., Tech. U., Graz, Austria, 1952, DR in Internal Combustion Engines, 1954, Habilitation degree, 1958, Dr (hon.), 1994. Asst. Tech. U., Graz, 1953-58; head rsch. dept. Inst. Internal Combustion Engines (AVL), Graz, 1958-62; leading positions in rsch., devel. Kloeckner-Humboldt-Deutz AG, Cologne, Germany, 1962-70; dir. Inst. Applied Thermodynamics RWTH, Aachen, Germany, 1970-97; CEO FEV Motorentechnik, Aachen, Germany, 1978—2003, chmn. bd., 2003—; v.p. Deutsche Forschungsgemeinschaft, Bonn-Bad Godesberg, Germany, 1984—90; hon. prof. Dalian U., China, 2005. Exec. bd. mem. Coun. Tech. Scis. Union German Acad. Scis. Humanities. Contbr. articles to profl. jours. Decorated Ehrenring Sub asupiciis praesidentis republicae (Austria), 1954, Bundesverdienstkreuz 1st class (Germany), 1978; recipient Herbert Akroyd Stuard award Inst. Mech. Engrs., 1962, Carl-Engler-Medaille DGMK, Deutsche Wissenschaftliche Gesellschaft Erdöl, Erdgas Kohle, Hamburg, 1990, Austrian cross of Honor for Sci. and Art First Class, 1998, Hon. Prof., Dalian U. Tech., China, 2005. Fellow Soc. Automotive Engrs. U.S.A.; mem. ASME Internat. (Soichiro Honda medal 2000), NAE (USA) (fgn. assoc.), Verein Deutscher Ingenieure (medal of honor 1993, decoration of honor 1997), Deutsche Gesellschaft Mineralölwissenschaft U. Kohlechemie, Rheinisch-Westfälische Akademie Wissenschaften, Aachen-Frankenburg Club, Rotary. Office: FEV Motorentechnik Neuenhofstrasse 181 52078 Aachen Germany

PISCHL, ADOLPH JOHN, school administrator; b. East Orange, NJ, Mar. 28, 1920; s. Adolph and Anna (Ellerman) P.; m. Tennessee Wild, Sept. 9, 1947; 1 child, Sallyann. Certificate, Drake Coll., 1940. With Juilliard Sch. Music, NYC, 1962-86, asst. concert mgr., 1962-66; dir. pub. relations Juilliard Sch. Music, NYC, 1966-68; concert mgr. Juilliard Sch. Music, NYC, 1966-86; adminstr. Sch. Strings, NYC, 1987-88. With The Dance Mart, NYC, 1950-2005, pub. dir. Am. Dance Festival, Conn. Coll., 1964-68; mgr. Betty Jones Dances I Dance, 1966-68, Ruth Currier Dance Co., 1966-68, Anna Sokolow Dance Co., 1966-68, Julliard Sch. Bookstore, 1971-86. Founder, editor: Dance Perspectives, 1958-64, Dance Data, 1977; editor: Juilliard News Bull. and Rev. Ann, 1964-85; pub.: Dance Horizons, 1965-86 (Dance mag. award 1999); Contbr. articles to dance mags. Bd. dirs. Dance Notation Bur.; sec. bd. dirs. Walter W. Naumburg Found., Inc. With AUS, 1940-46. Home: 603 Valley View Pompton Plains NJ 07444 Personal E-mail: ajpischl@aeitv.net.

PISCIOTTA, HENRY ANDREW, librarian, researcher; s. Jack and Mary Pisciotta; m. Erika Carol Linke; 1 child, Rachel Nora Linke. BFA, Drake U., Des Moines, 1973; MA Libr. Sci., U. Minn., Mpls., 1981, MA in Art History, 1982; grad. in Coursework, U. Pitts., 1999. Rsch. fellow, acting bibliographer U. Minn. Librs., Mpls., 1979—81; fine arts libr. Carnegie Mellon U. Librs., Pitts., 1982—87; adj. asst. prof. Canegie Mellon U. Dept. Art, Pitts., 1998; head fine arts and spl. collections Carnegie Mellon U. Librs., Pitts., 1987—2000, interim mgmt. team, 1996—98; arts & architecture libr. Penn. State U. Librs., University Park, Pa., 2000. Exec. bd. Art Librs. Soc. N.Am., 1991—93; coord. Visual Image User Study, Penn State U., 2001—03; cons. Assn. Coll. and Rsch. Librs. Contbr. articles to profl. jours. Adv. bd. Palmer Mus. Art, University Park, 2007. Mem.: Assn. Coll. and Rsch. Librs., Visual Resources Assn. (comm.), Art Libraries N.Am. (midwest rep. 1991—93, and other committees and appointments since 1979). Home: 915 Metz Ave State College PA 16801 Office: Penn State Univ Librs State College PA 16801 Business E-Mail: henryp@psu.edu.

PISCITELLI, FELICIA ANN, librarian, musician, musicologist; b. Tinker Air Force Base, Oklahoma City, Okla., Sept. 21, 1956; d. Domenic Ralph and Frankie Lee Piscitelli. BA in Fine Arts, U. N.Mex, 1979, MusM, 1983; MLS, U. Ariz., 1990. Piano tchr., Albuquerque, 1982—84; libr. tech. asst. U. N.Mex, Albuquerque, 1984—89; original cataloger, assoc. prof. Tex. A&M U., College Station, 1991—, asst. dir. cataloging, 2004—. Contbr. articles to profl. jours., chapters to books (Walter Gerboth award music bibliography, 1994);, author program notes musical concerts. Part-time organist St. Thomas Aquinas Cath. Ch., College Station, 1993—2005. Grantee Hymnody Am. Protestantism Project, Inst. Study Am. Evangelicalism, 1998. Mem.: Am. Guild Organists, Music Libr. Assn., Brazos Valley Chorale, Sigma Alpha Iota (life). Roman Catholic. Avocations: music, travel, languages. Office: Tex A&M U Sterling C Evans Libr Cataloging College Station TX 77843-5000 Office Fax: 979-862-1166. Business E-Mail: f-piscitelli@tamu.edu.

PISKOTI, CAROL LEE, art educator; b. Stockton, Calif., Jan. 13, 1949; d. Kyman and Clara Lee; m. James Piskoti, June 16, 1984. BA in Fine Art, Calif. State U. Stanislaus, Turlock, 1971. Tchg. credential Calif. Tchr. Sacramento City Sch. Dist., 1973—. Facilitator, staff Calif. Consortium for Arts Edn., Sacramento, 2002—05. Recipient Hon. Svc. award, PTA-John F. Kennedy H.S., 1989. Mem.: Crocker Art Mus. (tchg. adv. bd. 2002—), Nat. Art Edn. Assn., Calif. Art Edn. Assn. (chair vols. 2001, chair no. area youth art month 2004—06, Award of Merit 2001, Ruth Jansen Outstanding Visual Arts Educator of Yr. award 2004). Avocations: painting, drawing. Office: John F Kennedy HS 6715 Gloria Dr Sacramento CA 95831 Office Phone: 916-433-5200 ext 1602.

PISNEY, RAYMOND FRANK, international consulting services executive; b. Lime Springs, Iowa, June 2, 1940; s. Frank A. and Cora H. P. BA, Loras Coll., 1963; postgrad., Cath. U. Am., 1963; MA, U. Del., 1965. Asst. adminstrn. and rsch., Mt. Vernon, Va., 1965-69; hist. sites adminstr. N.C. Archives and Hist. Dept., Raleigh, 1969; asst. adminstr. divsn. hist. sites and museums N.C. Dept. Art, Culture and History, Raleigh, 1969-72; cons. Cannon Mills Co., Kannapolis, NC, 1972-73; exec. dir. Woodrow Wilson Birthplace Found., Staunton, Va., 1973-78, Mo. Hist. Soc., St. Louis, 1978-87; sr. v.p., cons. svcs. ETI Internat., Washington, 1987—2000; commentator WMAL-ABC Radio, Washington, 1999—2000; v.p. Brakeley, Inc., Stamford, Conn., 2000—03; pres., CEO, Aurora Internat. Inc., Alexandria, Va., 2001—. Pres. Va. History and Museums Fedn., 1977-78; pres. Mo. Museums Assoc., 1982-84; cons. assoc. Battelle, Washington, 1994. Author: Historical Markers: A Bibliography, 1977, Historic Markers: Planning Local Programs, 1978, A Preview to Historical Marking, 1976, Old Buildings: New Resources for Work and Play, 1976; editor: Virginians Remember Woodrow Wilson, 1978, Woodrow Wilson in Retrospect, 1978, Woodrow Wilson: Idealism and Realty, 1977, Historic Preservation and Public Policy in Virginia, 1978, Nonprofit Strategic Planning, 2004, Funding for Nonprofits, 2004, Case Studies in Nonprofit Funding, 2005, Nonprofit Board Development, 2005. Trustee James Clerk Maxwell Mus. and Found., Edinburgh, Scotland, 1993—, Internat. Human Rights Monument and Mus., Moscow, 1991—; sec., trustee Scotland WorldWide Heritage, Glasgow, 1993—; mem. internat. com. Charles A. Lindbergh Anniversary, Paris, 1987; sec. Internat. Assn. Consulting Firms, 1994-96; bd. dirs. Nat. History Day, 2002-05, Internat. Coun. of Caring Cmtys./U.N., 2002-. Recipient Bertha Black Rhoda award NAACP, 1985; Hagley fellow U. Del., 1963-65; Seminar for Hist. Adminstrs. fellow, 1965. Mem. Internat. Assn. Consulting Firms (sec. 1994-96), Washington Ind. Writers, Am. Assn. Museums, Nat. Trust Hist. Preservation U.S., Am. Assn. State and Local History, Can. Museums Assn., Brit. Museums Assn., Internat. Coun. Monuments and Sites, Internat. Coun. Museums, Lindbergh Anniversary Assn. (internat. com. 1987), Phi Alpha Theta. Roman Catholic. Home: PO Box 7201 Falls Church VA 22040-7201 Office: Catholic Religious Formation Conference 8820 Cameron St Silver Spring MD 20910-4152 *Words that have guided my career were written more than two millennia ago by Marcus Tullius Cicero (106-43 B.C.); the highest level of our work is to 'criticize by creating, rather than by finding fault.".*

PISONI, LORENZO, actor; Grad. with honors, Vassar Coll. Circus performer, 1978—99. Actor: (Broadway plays) Henry IV, 2003, Equus, 2008; (plays) Troilus and Cressida, 2001, As You Like It, 2003, Last Dance, 2003, Much Ado About Nothing, 2004, Election Day, 2007, The Devil's Disciple, 2007; creator, actor: Humor Abuse, 2009 (Lucille Lortel award for Outstanding Solo Show, 2009, Drama Desk award for Outstanding Solo Performance, 2009, Obie award for Performance, Village Voice, 2009); choreographer (plays) The Harlequin Studies, 2003; actor: (films) Cirque du Soleil: Journey of Man, 2000, Read You Like a Book, 2006, South of Pico, 2007, Company Retreat, 2008; stuntman: Daredevil, 2003. Office: c/o Sarah Fargo Paradigm Agy 360 Park Ave S 16th Fl New York NY 10010 also: c/o Lisa Loosemore Viking Entertainment 445 W 23rd St Ste 1A New York NY 10011*

PISTELL, TIMOTHY K., manufacturing executive; b. Long Branch, NJ, 1947; B in Acctg., Miami U. of Ohio, 1969; MBA, Baldwin-Wallace Coll., Berea, Ohio, 1984. Corp. acctg. trainee Parker-Hannifin Corp., Cleve., 1969, various positions including dir. bus. planning, v.p. fin./controller internat. England, then treas., 1993—2003, v.p., 2001—03, v.p. fin. & adminstrn., 2003—05, exec. v.p. fin. & adminstrn., CFO, 2003—. Mem. exec. bd. Northeast Ohio Multiple Sclerosis Soc., Great Lakes Theater Festival. Mem.: MAPI CFO Coun., Assn. Fin. Professionals, Nat. Assn. Accountants, Fin. Execs. Inst. Office: Parker Hannifin Corp 6035 Parkland Blvd Cleveland OH 44124 Office Phone: 216-896-2130. Office Fax: 216-896-4057. Business E-Mail: tpistell@parker.com.*

PISTER, KARL STARK, engineering educator; b. Stockton, Calif., June 27, 1925; s. Edwin LeRoy and Mary Kimball (Smith) P.; m. Rita Olsen, Nov. 18, 1950; children: Francis, Therese, Anita, Jacinta, Claire, Kristofer. BS with honors, U. Calif., Berkeley, 1945, MS, 1948; PhD, U. Ill., 1952; D of Pub. Policy (hon.), U. Fla., 2004; LHD (hon.), U. Colo., 2005. Instr. theoretical and applied mechanics U. Ill., 1949-52; faculty U. Calif., Berkeley, 1952-62, prof. engring. scis., 1962-96, Roy W. Carlson prof. engring., 1985-90, dean Coll. Engring., 1980-90, Roy W. Carlson prof. emeritus, chancellor Santa Cruz, 1991-96, pres., chancellor emeritus, 1996—, sr. assoc. to pres. Oakland, 1996-99, v.p. edn1. outreach, 1999-2000. Richard Merton guest prof. U. Stuttgart, Germany, 1978; cons. to govt. and industry; bd. dirs. Monterey Bay Aquarium Rsch. Inst.; trustee Am. U. Armenia, Grad. Theol. Union, Berkeley; chmn. bd. Calif. Coun. Sci. and Tech.; bd. dirs. Ctr. Future Tchg. and Learning. Contbr. articles to profl. jours.; mem. editl. bd. Jour. Optimization Theory and Applications, 1982, Ency. Phys. Sci. and Tech. With USNR, WWII. Fulbright scholar, Ireland, 1965, West Germany, 1973; recipient Wason Rsch. medal Am. Concrete Inst., 1960, Vincent Bendix Minorities in Engring. award Am. Soc. for Engring. Edn., 1988, Lamme medal, 1993, Alumni Honor award U. Ill. Coll. Engring., 1982, Disting. Engring. Alumnus award U. Calif. Berkeley Coll. Engring., 1992, Berkeley medal, 1996, U. Calif. Presdl. medal, 2000, World Tech. Network award for policy, World Tech. Coun., London, 2002 Alumnus of Yr. award Calif. Alumni Assn., Berkeley, 2006, Clark Kerr award U. Calif. Berkeley, 2007. Fellow: AAAS, ASME (Applied Mechanics award 1999, Internat. Pres.'s award 2000), Am. Acad. Arts and Scis., Am. Acad. Mechanics, Calif. Acad. Sci. (hon.); mem.: ASCE, NAE. Office: U Calif Dept Civil & Environ Engr Berkeley CA 94720 Office Phone: 510-642-3066. Business E-Mail: pister@ce.berkeley.edu.

PISTOLE, JOHN S., federal agency administrator; b. 1956; married; 2 children. BA, Anderson U., 1978; JD, Ind. U. Law Sch., 1981. Pvt. practice, Anderson, Ind., 1981—83; spl. agent Mpls. divsn. FBI, 1983—85, spl. agent NY divsn., 1985—90, supr. organized crime sect. Washington, 1990—94, field supr. white collar crime and civil rights squad, undercover coord. Indpls., 1994—99, asst. spl. agent in charge Boston, 1999—2001, inspector Washington, 2001—02, dep. asst. dir. counterterrorism divsn., 2002—03, asst. dir. counterterrorism divsn., 2003, exec. asst. dir., counterterrorism and counterintelligence, 2003—04, dep. dir., 2004—. Instr. Internat. Law Enforcement Acad., Budapest, Hungary, 1995—96; FBI rep. state dept. delegation, Sofia, Bulgaria; dir. Blue Team info. soc. working group, 2001. Recipient Presdl. Rank award for Disting. Exec., 2005, Edward H. Levy award for Outstanding Professionalism & Exemplary Integrity, 2007. Office: FBI J Edgar Hoover Bldg 935 Pennsylvania Ave NW Washington DC 20535-0001*

PISTOLE, THOMAS GORDON, microbiology professor, researcher, department chairman; b. Detroit, Sept. 17, 1942; s. Leotis Merton Pistole and Lillian Nell (Bosley) Besser; m. Donna Dulcie Straw, Sept. 11, 1965; children: James Alexander, Jennifer Katharine. PhB, Wayne State U., 1964, MS, 1966; PhD, U. Utah, 1969. Postdoctoral fellow U.S. Army, Frederick, Md., 1969-70; research assoc. U. Minn., Mpls., 1970-71; asst. prof. U. NH, Durham, 1971-77, assoc. prof., 1977-83, prof., 1983—, chmn., 1983-92, dist. prof., 2006, co-dir. discovery program undergrad. edn., 2007—08, dir., 2008—09. Vis. scientist Weizmann Inst., Rehovot, Israel, 1979; vis. prof. U. Edinburgh, Scotland, 1986; faculty fellow Office of V.P. for Acad. Affairs U. N.H., 1996-99; mem. ad hoc study sect. U.S. Dept. Agr., 2002. Co-editor: Biomedical Application of the Horseshoe Crab, 1979; mem. editl bd.: Jour. Invertebrate Pathology, 1988—90. NRC fellow, 1969-70; NIH sr. internat. fellow, 1986; grantee NIH, 1975-77, 89-93, 96-2006, NSF, 1981-84. Mem.: Soc. for Leukocyte Biology, Am. Assn. Immunologists, Am. Soc. for Microbiology. Avocations: singing, collecting old sheet music, walking, cooking. Office: U NH Rudman Hall Dept Microbiology Durham NH 03824-2617 Home Phone: 603-868-5766; Office Phone: 603-862-0111. Business E-Mail: thomas.pistole@unh.edu.

PISTORIUS, GEORGE, language educator; b. Prague, Czechoslovakia, Mar. 19, 1922; came to U.S., 1958, naturalized, 1964; s. Theodor and Blazena (Jiranek) P.; m. Marie Skokan, June 30, 1945; 1 dau., Erika. Student, Charles U., Prague, 1945-48; postgrad., Université de Paris, 1948-50; certificats d'etudes superieures, Université de Strasbourg, France, 1950, 51; PhD, U. Pa., 1963. Asst. dept. comparative lit. Charles U., 1946-48; instr. Lafayette Coll., Easton, Pa., 1958-61, asst. prof. French, 1961-63; asso. prof. Williams Coll., 1963-68, prof. Romanic langs., 1968-92, chmn. dept., 1971-82, prof. emeritus, 1992—. Instr. French, Colby Coll. Summer Sch. Lang., 1959-65 Author: Bibliography of the works of F.X. Salda, 1948, Destin de la culture francaise dans une democratie populaire, 1957, L'Image de l'Allemagne dans le roman francais entre les deux guerres (1919-1939), 1964, Marcel Proust und Deutschland, Eine Bibliographie, 1981, 2d edit. 2002, André Gide und Deutschland: Eine internationale Bibliographie, 1990. Home: 54 Cluett Dr Williamstown MA 01267-2805

PISZEL, ANTHONY S. (BUDDY PISZEL), mortgage company executive; b. 1954; BA in Economics, Rutgers U., NJ; MBA in Acctg., Golden Gate U., San Francisco. Practice fellow Fin. Acctg. Stds. Bd., 1988—90; audit ptnr. Deloitte & Touche, 1990—93; CFO individual life ins. Prudential Fin. Inc., 1993—95, CFO inst. life ins., 1995—97, corp. v.p., 1997—98, sr. v.p., contr., 1998—2004; exec. v.p., CFO Health Net, Inc., Woodland Hills, Calif., 2004—06, Freddie Mac (Fed. Home Loan Mortgage Corp.), McLean, Va., 2006—08; CFO, treas. The First Am. Corp., Santa Ana, Calif., 2009—. Bd. dirs. RehabCare Group, Inc., 2005—. Mem.: AICPA, NJ State Soc. CPAs. Office: The First American Corporation 1 First American Way Santa Ana CA 92707*

PITASKY, SCOTT, computer software company executive; m. Rena Pitasky; 3 children. BSc in Engring. Fin. and Mgmt., U. Pa. Wharton Sch., Phila. Investment banker Citicorp; strategy cons. Corp. Decisions, Inc., Boston; dir. human resources AlliedSignal, Inc.; prin. iQuantic, Inc., San Francisco; v.p., sr. dir. human resources Amazon.com, Seattle; joined Microsoft Corp., Redmond, Wash., 2001, dir. MSN, sr. dir. server & tools, gen. mgr. global staffing, corp. v.p. human resources talent & orgn. capability group, 2008—. Mem. adv. bd. Mich. State U.; mem. talent mgmt. coun. Corp. Leadership Coun.; mem. U. So. Calif. Ctr. Effective Organs. Office: Microsoft Corp One Microsoft Way Redmond WA 98052-6399*

PITCHER, GRIFFITH FONTAINE, lawyer; b. Balt., Nov. 1, 1937; s. William Henry and Virginia Griffith (Stein) P.; children: Virginia T. Pitcher Ballinger, L. Brooke Pitcher Fick, William T.B., Margaret W. Pitcher Saylors. BA, Johns Hopkins U., 1960; JD, U. Va., 1963. Bar: Ala. 1963, Fla. 1971, Ga. 1996. Assoc. Bradley, Arant, Rose & White, Birmingham, Ala., 1963-71; mem. Van den Berg, Gay & Burke, Orlando, Fla., 1971-76, Mahoney, Hadlow & Adams, Jacksonville, Fla., 1976-82; ptnr. Squire, Sanders & Dempsey, Miami, Fla., 1982-93; of counsel Mershon, Sawyer, Johnston, Dunwoody & Cole, Miami, Fla., 1994-95, Chamberlain, Hrdlicka, White, Williams & Martin, Atlanta, 1996—2002, Seyfarth Shaw LLP, Atlanta, 2002—. Contbr. articles to profl. jours. Vice chmn. Winter Park (Fla.) Planning & Zoning Bd., 1974-75. With Army N.G., 1961-64. Fellow: Am. Coll. Bond Counsel (founding fellow, past treas., past dir.); mem.: Ga. State Bar, Nat. Assn. Bond Lawyers, Order of Coif, Delta Phi. Republican. Personal E-mail: grifpitcher@charter.net.

PITCHER, MEGAN LOUISE, dancer, director; d. Steven Pitcher and Jane Bagnall. BFA in Modern Dance Choreography, Ohio U., Athens, 2002. Artistic dir. MegLouise Dance, Cleve., 2002—; asst. vol. coord. Ottawa Co. United Way, Holland, Mich., 2002—04; dance faculty, outreach coord. Richland Acad., Mansfield, Ohio, 2004—05; adj. dance faculty Ohio State U., Mansfield, 2004—05; dance faculty Beck Ctr. Arts, Lakewood, Ohio, 2005—08; adj. dance faculty Cuyahoga CC, Parma, Ohio, 2006—. Guest artist and choreographer Muskegon Civic Theater, Mich., 2002—04, Ft. Hayes Sch., Columbus, Ohio, 2002, Muskegon Cath. Ctrl. Sch., 2003—03, Hathaway Brown Sch., Shaker Heights, Ohio, 2006—, Shaker Heights Ensemble Program, 2006—08, Orange Schs., Pepper Pike, Ohio, 2007—08; guest artist Holland Area Arts Coun., 2003—04, West Fest Dance Festival, Grand Haven, Mich., 2004, Ohio Dance Festival, Columbus, 2007—08, NASA Glen Rsch. Ctr., Cleve., 2007—08. Dancer (modern dance) Nothing Too Bad Ever Happened & Dance Choice, Nearly Nude: Deconstructing Beauty, Companions, Forever Solo, (improvisational performance & dance) Directed By You, Dance Choice, iNput. AmeriCorps Promise fellow, Points Light Found., 2003—05. Mem.: Ohio Arts Presenters Network, Columbus Movement, Ohio Dance Festival. Office: Cuyahoga CC 11000 Pleasant Valley Rd Parma OH 44130 Personal E-mail: meglouisedance@yahoo.com.

PITCHER, STEPHEN M., finance company executive, museum director; b. 1943; m. Cynthia N. Pitcher. Dir., fin. and sys. Norton Advanced Ceramics, Worcester, Mass.; v.p. fin., controller Vetrotex, Phila.; founder Compass Ptnrs., LLC, 1995—. Trustee Higgins Armory Mus., Worcester; bd. chair Music Worcester; interim exec. dir. Preservation Worcester, EcoTarium, Worcester, 2005—. Address: EcoTarium 222 Harrington Way Worcester MA 01604 Office Phone: 508-929-2700.

PITCHUMONI, CAPECOMORIN SANKAR, gastroenterologist, educator; b. Madura, India, Jan. 20, 1938; came to U.S., 1967; s. Sankara and Jaya (Lekshmi) Iyer; m. Prema Iyer, Nov. 11, 1964; children: Sheila, Shoba, Suresh. Student, St. Xavier Coll., India, 1953-55; MB BS, Trivandrum Med. Coll., India, 1959, MD, 1965. Intern Med. Coll., Trivandurm, India, 1961-63; resident in gastroenterology Yale U., 1967-69; N.Y. Med. Coll., 1969-72; practice medicine specializing in gastroenterology NYC, 1972—; asst. prof. medicine Kottayam Med. Coll., India, 1967, N.Y. Med. Coll., 1972-75, assoc. prof., 1975-80, prof. clin. medicine, 1980-85, prof. medicine, 1985—, assoc. prof. preventive and social medicine, 1975-86, prof. community and preventive medicine, 1986—; chief sect. gastroenterology Our Lady of Mercy Med. Ctr., NYC, 1980—, assoc. dir. medicine, 1985—, program dir. internal medicine, 1987—, dir. medicine, 1992, chmn. emeritus dept. medicine, 2002—; chief divsn. gastroenterology St. Peters U. Hosp., New Brunswick, NJ, 2002—. Contbg. author med. textbooks; contbr. articles to profl. jours. Recipient Om Prakash award Indian Soc. Gastroenterology, 1976, Outstanding Scientist of Yr. award MV Spltys., Madras, 1994, Oration award Thangavelu Endowment, 1994. Master ACP, Am. Coll. Gastroenterology (gov. 1996-2000), ACP; fellow Royal Coll. Physicians and Surgeons Can., Am. Coll. Nutrition, Am. Gastroent. Assn.; mem. Assn. Physicians India, India Soc. Gastroenterology (life), Am. Inst. Nutrition, Gastrointestinal Endoscopy, Am. Soc. for Clin. Nutrition. Hindu. Home: 1 Nevius Pl Somerset NJ 08873 Office: St Peters U Hosp New Brunswick NJ Personal E-mail: drpitchumoni@gmail.com.

PITCOCK, JAMES ALLISON, retired pathologist; b. Little Rock, Sept. 13, 1929; s. Radford Bolling and Anne (Whitelaw) P.; m. Cynthia Jean Dehaven, June 18, 1954; children: Allison P. Mays, James Dehaven. BS, MIT, 1951; MD, Washington U., 1955. Diplomate Am. Bd. Pathology. Intern Vanderbilt U., Nashville, 1955-56; resident Barnes Hosp., St. Louis, 1956-59, 61-62; asst. pathologist St. Vincents Hosp., Little Rock, 1963, Bapt. Meml. Hosp., Memphis, 1964-75, asst. dir. labs., 1975-87, dir. labs., 1987-95; ret. Vol. faculty U. Tenn. Med. Sch., Memphis, 1965-96, acting chair pathology, 1986-89; com. chair, mem. Am. Heart Assn., Memphis, 1976-84, exec. com., 1983-87, pres., 1985-86. Contbr. chpts. to books and articles to profl. jours. Capt. USAF, 1959-61. Mem. Alpha Omega Alpha, Sigma Xi. Episcopalian. Achievements include experimental and scholarly work in experimental hypertension and surgical pathology. Home Phone: 901-767-4224.

PITEGOFF, PETER ROBERT, dean, law educator; b. NYC, Mar. 6, 1953; s. Joseph and Libbie (Shapiro) P.; m. Ann Casady, Mar. 22, 1986; children: Maxwell Jacob, Elias Samuel. AB, Brown U., 1975; JD, NYU, 1981. Bar: Mass 1981, NY 1988; cert. tchr., RI. Tchr. Hope High Sch., Providence, 1974-75; community organizer Nat. Assn. for So. Poor, Petersburg, Va., 1975-76, Citizens Action League, Oakland, Calif., 1976-78; gen. counsel ICA Group, Boston, 1981-88; ptnr. Arrington & Pitegoff, Somerville, Mass., 1986-88; assoc. prof. U. Buffalo Law Sch., SUNY, 1988—94, prof., 1994—2005, vice dean academic affairs, 1998—2005; dean, prof. U. Maine Sch. Law, Portland, 2005—. Adj. asst. prof. law NYU, 1986-88; instr. Harvard Law Sch., 1985; cons. in field, 1978—; legal counsel cmty. devel. worker purchases of bus. corp. fin. dem. corp. structures child care policy and welfare policy. Contbr. to profl. publs. Root-Tilden scholarship NYU, 1978; grantee Pub. Interest Law Found., NYC, 1981; grantee Berkeney Law Found., 1982. Democrat. Jewish. Avocations: athletics, travel, music. Office: Univ Maine Sch Law 246 Deering Ave Portland ME 04102 Office Phone: 207-780-4344. E-mail: pitegoff@usm.maine.edu.*

PITERNICK, ANNE BREARLEY, librarian, educator; b. Blackburn, Eng., Oct. 13, 1926; arrived in Can., 1956, naturalized, 1965; d. Walter and Ellen (Harris) Clayton; m. Neil Brearley, 1956 (div. 1971); m. George Piternick, May 6, 1971. BA, U. Manchester, Eng., 1948, F.L.A., 1983. Mem. library staff U. B.C., Vancouver, Can., 1956-66, head sci. div., 1960-61, head social scis. div., 1965-66, prof. Sch. Library, Archival and Info. Studies, 1966-91, prof. emerita, 1991—, assoc. dean Faculty of Arts, 1985-90. Pres. Can. Assn. Spl. Librs. Info. Svcs., 1969-70, Can. Libr. Assn., 1976-77; organizer Confs. on Can. Bibliography, 1974, 81; mem. Nat. Com. Bibliog. Svcs. Can., 1975-80, chmn. com. on bibliography and info. services social scis. and humanities, 1981-84; adv. bd. Nat. Libr. Can., 1978-84; adv. acad. panel Social Scis. and Humanities Rsch. Coun., 1981-84; mem. Nat. Adv. Com. Culture Stats., 1985-90; pres. adv. com. on campus enhancement U. BC, 2001-. Contbr. articles to profl. jours. Bd. dirs. Vancouver Friends of Chamber Music, 2001—. Recipient Queen's Silver Jubilee medal, 1977, award for Spl. Librarianship Can. Assn. Spl. Librs. and Info. Svcs., 1987, 75th Anniversary medal U.B.C., 1990, Can. 125 medal, 1993; fellow Coun. on Libr. Resources, 1980. Fellow Libr. Assn.; mem. Assn. Profs. Emeriti U. B.C. (pres. 2003-04), Coll. and Univs. Retiree Assns. Can. (bd. dirs. 2005-07) Achievements include research in electronic info. svcs. and scholarly comm. Home: 1849 W 63rd Ave Vancouver BC Canada V6P 2H9 Personal E-mail: annebp@interchange.ubc.ca.

PITHAWALLA, YEZDI BAHADUR, chemist; b. Mumbai, Maharashtra, India, Oct. 4, 1970; s. Bahadur Nusserwanji and Aban Bahadur Pithawalla; m. Sharmine Yezdi Pithawalla, Mar. 22, 2002; 1 child, Anosh Yezdi. BS in Chemistry, U. Mumbai, India, 1991; MS in Phys. Chemistry, U. Mumbai, 1993; PhD in Chemistry, Va. Commonwealth U., Richmond, 1999. Postdoctoral fellow Va. Commonwealth U., 1999—2000, Philip Morris USA, Richmond, 2000—02, assoc. rsch. scientist, 2002—04, rsch. scientist, 2004—06, sr. rsch. scientist, 2006—. Sec. Va. Sect. of the Am. Chem. Soc. (ACS), Richmond, Va., 2007—. Contbr. chapters to books, articles to profl. jours. Team capt. Am. Poolplayers Assn. Nat. Team Championships, Las Vegas, Nev., 2004—05; ballroom dancer Commonwealth Games Va., Roanoke, 1998. Mem.: Am. Chem. Soc. (chair pub. rels. com., Va. sect. 2002—03, chair academic & indsl. awards com., Va. sect. 2004—06, session 230th nat. meeting 2005), Materials Rsch. Soc., Sigma Xi. Achievements include patents for discovering novel methods to synthesize nanomaterials; patents pending for in the area of nanomaterials and modification of cigarette filters and papers. Office: Philip Morris USA 4201 Commerce Rd Richmond VA 23261 Personal E-mail: sharmine_yezdi@yahoo.com. Business E-Mail: yezdi.b.pithawalla@pmusa.com.

PITICI, FELICIA, biophysicist; b. Timisoara, Romania, Nov. 20, 1964; d. Grigore and Ecaterina Milian; m. Mircea Ioan Pitici, June 16, 1987; 1 child, Ioana Emina. Degree in physics (hon.), U. Bucharest, 1988, MS in Physics, 1997; PhD, Mt. Sinai Sch. of Medicine of N.Y. U., NYC, 1999. Physicist Institute for Nuc. Power Reactors, Pitesti, Arges, Romania, 1988—90; asst. prof. U. Bucharest, Physics Dept., Bucharest, Romania, 1990—92; rsch. assoc., vis. asst. prof. Wesleyan U., Chemistry / Physics Dept., Middletown, Conn., 1999—2002; vis. asst. prof. Wesleyan U., Physics Dept., Middletown, Conn., 2003—04; rsch. assoc. NIH, Ithaca, NY, 2004—. Contbr. articles pub. to profl. jour., scientific papers. Achievements include research in computational studies of biomolecular systems. Avocation: classical music. Personal E-mail: fpitici@cs.cornell.com.

PITINO, RICK, men's college basketball coach; b. NYC, Sept. 18, 1952; m. Joanne Pitino; children: Michael, Christopher, Richard, Ryan, Jacqueline. Grad., U. Mass., 1974. Grad. asst. U. Hawaii, 1974, asst. coach, 1975-76, Syracuse U., 1976-78; head coach Boston U., 1978-83; asst. coach NY Knicks, 1983-85, head coach, 1987-89, Providence U., 1985—87, U. Ky., Lexington, 1989-97; head coach, pres. Boston Celtics, 1997—2001; head coach U. Louisville, 2001—. Co-author: (with Bill Reynolds) Born to Coach: A Season with the New York Knicks, 1988, Success Is a Choice: Ten Steps to Overachieving in Business and Life, 1997, Lead to Succeed, 2000, (with Dick Weiss) Full Court Pressure: A Year in Kentucky Basketball, 1992; (with Pat Forde) Rebound Rules: The Art of Success 2.0, 2008 Named New Eng. Coach of Yr., 1979, 1983, Coll. Coach of Yr., The Sporting News, 1987; named to NYC Hall of Fame, 2006. Achievements include leading the Kentucky Wildcats to the 1996 NCAA Championship as head coach; achieved his 500th career victory as college basketball coach on Dec. 17, 2007. Office: Mens Basketball Athletics Dept U Louisville Louisville KY 40292 Office Phone: 502-852-6651. E-mail: rick.pitino@louisville.edu.*

PITKIN, EDWARD THADDEUS, aerospace engineer, consultant; b. Putnam, Conn., Dec. 14, 1930; s. Thaddeus Eugene and Florence Mabel (Brown) P.; m. Clara Lucy Modliszewski, June 13, 1953; children—Gayle Linda, Dale Edward. BS, U. Conn., 1952; MS (Guggenheim fellow), Princeton, 1953; PhD (NASA fellow), UCLA, 1964. Project engr. Astro Div. Marquardt Co., Los Angeles, 1956-59, mgr. space propulsion, 1959-61; engring. cons. Los Angeles, 1961-64; asso. prof. aerospace engring. U. Conn., Storrs, 1964-70, prof. mech. and aerospace engring., 1970-90, prof. emeritus, 1990—; cons. engr., 1990—; asst. dean U. Conn., Storrs, 1977-87. Contbr. articles to profl. jours. Served as lt. USAF, 1953-55. Asso. fellow AIAA Home: 115 Brookside Ln Mansfield Center CT 06250-1001 Office: U Conn Dept Mech Engring U-139 191 Auditorium Rd Storrs Mansfield CT 06269-3139

PITKIN, HOWARD F., state banking agency administrator; With Office of State Comptr., Conn., Conn. Dept. Banking, Hartford, 1977—, dir. bank exam. divsn., 1989—2000, adminstr. depository instns., 2000, chief. adminstrn., 2004—06, acting bank commr., 2006—07, bank commr., 2007—. Bd. mgrs. Downtown Hartford YMCA. Recipient Disting. Mgr. of Yr. award, State of Conn., 2000. Office: Conn Dept Banking 260 Constitution Plz Hartford CT 06103-1800 Office Phone: 860-240-8299. Office Fax: 860-240-8178. E-mail: howard.pitkin@ct.gov.*

PITKIN, ROY MACBETH, retired obstetrician, educator; b. Anthon, Iowa, May 24, 1934; s. Roy and Pauline Allie (McBeath) Pitkin; m. Marcia Alice Jenkins, Aug. 17, 1957; children: Barbara, Robert Macbeth, Kathryn, William Charles. BA with highest distinction, U. Iowa, 1956, MD, 1959. Diplomate Am. Bd. Ob-Gyn. Intern King County Hosp., Seattle, 1959—60; resident in ob-gyn U. Iowa Hosps. and Clinics, Iowa City, 1960—63; asst. prof. ob-gyn U. Ill., 1965—68; assoc. prof. ob-gyn U. Iowa, Iowa City, 1968—72, prof., 1972—87, head dept. ob-gyn, 1977—87; prof. UCLA, 1987—97, head dept. ob-gyn., 1987—95, prof. emeritus, 1997—. Mem. residency rev. com. ob-gyn., 1981—87; chmn., 1985—87. Author: The Green Journal 50 Years On, 2003, Whom the Gods Love Die Young: A Modern Medical Perspective on Illness that Caused the Early Death of Famous People, 2008; co-editor: The Best of After Office Hours, 2003; editor-in-chief Year Book of Obstetrics and Gynecology, 1975—86, Clinical Obstetrics and Gynecology, 1979—2000; editor: Obstetrics and Gynecology, 1985—2001; editor emeritus Obstetrics and Gynecology, 2001; contbr. articles to med. jours. Served to lt. comdr. M.C. USNR, 1963—65. Recipient NIH career awardee, 1972—77, Disting. Alumni Achievement award, U. Iowa, 2002. Fellow: Royal Ob-Gyn. (ad eundem); mem.: Coun. Sci. Editors (Dist. Svc. award 2002), Inst. Medicine, NAS, Soc. Perinatal Obstetricians (pres. 1978—79), Soc. Gynecol. Investigation (pres. 1985—86), German Soc. Gyn-Ob. (hon.), Ctrl. Asn. Ob-Gyn., Am. Gyn-Ob. Soc. (pres. 1994—95), Am. Coll. Ob-Gyns., AMA (Goldberger award in clin. nutrition 1982). Presbyterian. Home: 78900 Rancho La Quinta Dr La Quinta CA 92253-6252 Personal E-mail: r.pitkin@earthlink.net.

PITLUK, ELLEN EIDELBACH, lawyer, mediator; d. Mark Adrian and Baylor Merle Eidelbach; m. Lee Dean Pitluk, Feb. 1, 1985; children: Jessie, Mason. BA in Journalism, Tex. A&M U., College Station, 1981; JD, St. Mary's U., San Antonio, 2002, postgrad. Bar: Tex. 2003, U.S. Dist. Ct. (we. dist.) Tex. 2003. Grad. recruiter Trinity U., Dept. Health Care Adminstrn., San Antonio, 1990—94, 1997—99; rsch. asst. St. Mary's U., Sch. Law, 2000; law clk. Walsh, Anderson, Brown,. Schulze & Aldridge, 2001; law clk. hon. Frank Montalvo 288th Jud. Dist. Ct., Bexar County, 2002; atty., mediator pvt. practice, San Antonio, 2003—. Contbr. articles to profl. jours.;, author of poems. Mem.: ABA, San Antonio Bar Assn., San Antonio Bar Found., Coll. State Bar Tex., State Bar Tex. Office: PO Box 780895 San Antonio TX 78278

PITMAN, GARY ROBERT, oil industry executive; b. Sandys, Bermuda, Oct. 18, 1948; s. Robert Knoll and Patricia Anne (Howes) P.; m. Martha Jean MacKenzie, May 27, 1972; children: Rebecca, Megan. BBA, U. N.B., Can., 1971. Cert. Gen. Acct., Can. Supr. internat. investments Bank of Bermuda Ltd., Hamilton, 1972—75; mgr. acctg., asst. sec. Kupan Internat., Hamilton, 1975—77; comptr. Kupan Internat. Ltd., Hamilton, 1977—79; asst. treas. Kupan Internat. & Insco Ltd., Hamilton, 1979—80, v.p., treas., 1980—85; sr. v.p., treas. Chevron Internat. Ltd., Hamilton, 1985—90, pres., 1990—; mem. parliament, 1998—2002. Dir. 150 Chevron subs. worldwide; shadow min. Environment, Planning and Natural Resources, 1998-2001, Transport, 2001-2002. Former dep. chmn. bd. govs. Warwick Acad., Bermuda, 1987-96; chmn. United Bermuda Party, 1993-98; senator Bermuda Govt., 1994-97, parliamentary sec., 1994-97, justice of the peace, 1995, cabinet minister, govt. senate leader, 1997; chmn. Bermuda Bd. Immigration, 1989-98; pres. U. New Brunswick Bermuda Alumni Chpt., 1997-99; former Senate spokesman for Tourism and Marine Svcs. Ministry, Works, Engring. Parks and Housing Ministry, Info. and Tech. Ministry; trustee Packwood Srs. Home, 1999—. Mem.: Cert. Gen. Accts. Assn. (pres. 1992—93), Sandys Rotary Club (pres. 1994—95). Roman Catholic. Avocations: deep sea fishing, gardening, travel. Office: Chevron Internat Ltd 11 Church St POB HM 2082 Hamilton HM HX Bermuda Home: 17 Belmont Heights Harbour Rd Warwick WK 06 Bermuda

PITMAN, GERALD H., plastic surgeon; AB, Williams Coll.; MD, U. Pa. Diplomate Am. Bd. Plastic Surgery. Resident in surgery Columbia divsn. NY Presbyn. Hosp., NYC; resident in plastic surgery NYU Med. Ctr., fellow in microsurgery, attending plastic surgeon, Tisch Hosp./Manhattan Eye, Ear and Throat Hosp. Clin. prof. surgery NYU Sch. Medicine; lectr. in field. Author: Liposuction and Aesthetic Surgery,

1993; contbr. numerous articles to profl. jours. Fellow: ACS, NY Acad. Medicine; mem.: Am. Soc. Plastic and Reconstructive Surgeons, NY State and County Med. Socs., NY Regional Soc. Plastic and Reconstructive Surgeons, NE Soc. Plastic Surgeons, Am. Soc. Aesthetic Plastic Surgery, Am. Soc. Plastic Surgeons. Achievements include pioneering the use of power-assisted liposuction and considered one the best in the world for this procedure. Avocations: boating, fishing, skiing, triathlons. Office: 170 E 73rd St New York NY 10021 Office Phone: 212-517-2600. Office Fax: 212-628-0774. Business E-Mail: info@drpitman.com, drpitman@drpitman.com.

PITMAN, GROVER ALLEN, music educator; b. Corpus Christi, Tex., Nov. 1943; s. John William and Mae Belle Pitman; m. Jacqueline Kay Pitman, 1966; children: William Dunn, Karen Joanne. MusB, U. Tex., 1965, MusM, 1967; PhD, Cath. U. Am., 1973. Tchr. Fredericksburg (Tex.) Pub. Schs., 1966-67; instr. Muskingum Coll., New Concord, Ohio, 1967-68; solo hornist US Naval Acad. Band, Annapolis, Md., 1968-72; asst. prof. Winthrop Coll., Rock Hill, SC, 1972-78; prof. Westminster Coll., New Wilmington, Pa., 1978—, chmn. Dept. Music, 1978—2005. Prin. hornist Austin (Tex.) Symphony Orch., 1961-67, Annapolis (Md.) Symphony Orch., 1968-72; hornist Annapolis Brass Quintet, 1968-72, Youngstown (OH) Symphony Orch., 1988—. Grantee Winthrop Found., Rock Hill, 1977, Watto award, Westminster Coll., 2005. Mem. Pa. Collegiate Bandmasters Assn. (pres. 1983-84), Pa. Music Educators Assn. (pres. dist. 5 1984-85), Rotary (pres. New Wilmington chpt. 1986). Episcopalian. Office: Westminster Coll New Wilmington PA 16172-0001 Office Phone: 724-946-7274.

PITMAN, JIM, professional sports team executive; m. Linda Pitman; children: Amy, Kyle. Grad. in Acctg., U. Ill., 1987. With audit divsn. Arthur Andersen, Phoenix, 1987—92; asst. contr. to corp. contr., v.p. fin. Phoenix Suns, 1992—99, exec. v.p. fin. and adminstrn., 1999—. Treas. Phoenix Suns Charities; bd. mem. US Airways Ctr. Edn. Found., Valley of the Sun YMCA. Avocations: basketball, softball, golf. Office: Phoenix Suns 201 E Jefferson St Phoenix AZ 85004*

PITMAN, LAVERN FRANK, librarian; b. Poynette, Wis., June 8, 1943; s. George and Carolyn (Hutchinson) P.; m. Rosa Papist, Sept. 8, 1973 (dec. Oct. 1996); 1 child, Christina. BA, Wis. State U., 1965; MSLS, Catholic U. Am., 1973; MA, Frostburg State U., 1985. Cataloger copyright office Libr. Congress, Washington, 1966-71, Spanish/Italian cataloger shared divsn., 1971-79; libr. Frostburg (Md.) State U., 1980-98. Author: The Family of John and Deborah Flick Meyers, 1989, The Robertsons: A Norwegian Family in America, 1993; co-author: A Century of Commitment: Frostburg State University, 1997; editor: Civil War Diary of Jesse Meyers, Co. I, 23d Regiment, Wisconsin Volunteer Infantry, 2002. Historic Interpreter, Mt. Vernon, 1999-2004; curator Wayside Found., 1999-2000; libr. Md. Bur. Mines, 2000-02; trustee Shenandoah County Pub. Libr., Va., 2004—. Mem. Geneal. Soc. Allegany County, Geneal. Soc. Wis., State Hist. Soc. Wis., Frostburg Mus. Assn., Strasburg Mus., Norwegian-Am. Geneal. Ctr. and Naeseth Libr., Sons of Norway, Vesterheim Norwegian-Am. Mus., Clan Rose Soc. Am.

PITMAN, URSULA WALL, curator, educator; d. Thomas Joseph and Emily Hruby Wall; m. Lawrence Clymer Pitman, Aug. 19, 1961 (dec. Jan. 1996). BS in History, Northeastern U., 1968, BS in Art History, 1983; MA in History, Boston Coll., 1971, PhD in History, 1978. Cert. history tchr., IBM sys. svc. rep. Computer demonstrator, lectr. IBM, NYC, 1956—59, data processing instr. Boston, 1959—61; art educator Fitchburg Art Mus., Mass., 1978—83, curator, 1979—89, dir., instr. docent program, 1982—2000, developer in-mus. and outreach programs, 1982—2000. Advisor on fundraising activities Fitchburg Art Mus., 1978—2000, dir. funded lectr. series, 1980—90, mem. edn. com., 1983—2000; art lectr. Jr. League Boston Sch. Program, Lincoln, Mass., 1976—77; co-dir. Tchrs. Workshop DeCordova Mus., Lincoln, 1980; co-grant writer, implementer Nat. Endowment for the Arts, Washington, 1982—2000. Vol. Harvard U. docent Sachler Mus., Fogg Art Mus., Busch Reisinger Mus., Cambridge, Mass., 1983—93; vol. docent DeCordova Mus., Lincoln, 1976—83; vol. libr. asst. Lahey Clinic, Burlington, Mass., 1996; vol. Nat. Heritage Mus., Lexington, Mass., 1997—. Avocations: reading, museums, theater. Home: 61 Willard Grant Rd Sudbury MA 01776

PITMAN-GELLES, BONNIE LOUISE, museum administrator, educator; b. Stamford, Ct., Apr. 24, 1946; d. Benjamin Pitman and Margaret (Hackett) Perry; m. George Gelles, Jan. 1, 1976 (div. 1985); 1 child, David Alexander. AB, Pine Manor Coll., 1966; BA cum laude, Sweet Briar Coll., 1968; MA, Tulane U., 1971. Curator of edn. Winnipeg Art Gallery, Canada, 1968-71, New Orleans Mus. Art, 1971-75; faculty New Orleans Ctr. for Creative Arts, 1975-76; cons. Nat. Endowment for Arts, Washington, 1976-80, panelist Arts in Edn., 1978-84; cons. NEH, Washington, 1977-79, panelist, 1978-79; market rep. Parker Bros., Inc., Salem, N.Y., 1980; cons. Bklyn Ednl. Cultural Alliance, 1980-81, Lincoln Ctr., NYC, 1980-81; assoc. dir. Seattle Art Mus., 1981—, acting dir., 1986-87; mem. faculty mus. mgmt. program U. Colo., Boulder, 1986; dep. dir. U. Art Mus. U. Calif., Berkeley, 1990—95; exec. dir. Bay Area Discovery Mus., Sausalito, Calif., 1995—2000; dep. dir. Dallas Mus. of Art, 2000—08, Eugene McDermott dir., 2008—. Mem. nat. adv. com. Getty Ctr. for Edn. in the Arts, 1988—; cons. numerous mus. Author: Watermelon, 1973, Pumpkins into Coaches: Handbook on Youth Education in Museums, 1977, Museums as Educational Instruments, 1980, Museums, Magic and Children, 1981, Taking a Closer Look: Evaluation in Art Museums, 1992. Excellence and Equity: Education & The Public Dimension of Museums, Presence of Mind: Museums and the Spirit of Learning, 1999; editor: Southeast Regional Resource Book for Museums, 1973; numerous articles in field. Panelist Office of Edn., Washington, 1976-77, Nat. Mus. Act, Washington, 1975-7; assoc. mem. bd. dirs. Children's Hosp., Seattle; Sausalito C. of C. Recipient Leadership Tomorrow award United Way, C. of C., 1985, Disting. Svc. award Music & Art Found., Seattle, 1988; named to Centennial Honor Roll, Am. Assn. Museums, 2006. Am. Assn. Mus. (councilor at large 1976-79, 85-88, chmn. edn. com. 1976-80, v.p. 1979-80, 88-92), Internat. Com. Mus. (accreditation commr. 1985—, exec. com. 1977-83), Nat. Hist. Trust, Western Mus. Assn. (Director's Chair award 1992), Phi Beta Kappa, Delta Kappa Phi. Democrat. Avocation: sailing. Office: Dallas Mus of Art 1717 N Harwood Dallas TX 75201 E-mail: bpitman@DallasMuseumofArt.org.

PITOFSKY, ROBERT, federal agency administrator, law educator; b. Paterson, NJ, Dec. 27, 1929; s. Morris and Sadye (Katz) P.; m. Sally Levy; children: Alexander, David, Elizabeth. BA, NYU, 1951; LLB, Columbia U., 1954; LLD (hon.), Georgetown U., 1989, Nyenrode U., Netherlands, 2002. Bar: N.Y. 1956, D.C. 1973, U.S. Supreme Ct. 1972. Atty. Dept. Justice, Washington, 1956-57; assoc. Dewey, Ballantine, Bushby, Palmer & Wood, NYC, 1957-64; prof. law NYU, 1964-70; dir. Bur. Consumer Protection, FTC, 1970-73; prof. law Georgetown U. Law Ctr., Washington, 1973—83, 1989—, dean, exec. v.p. law ctr. affairs, 1983-89; commr. FTC, Washington, 1978-81, chmn., 1995-2001; of counsel Arnold & Porter, Washington, 1973-78, 81-95, 01—. Guest scholar Brookings Instn., Washington, 1989-90; vis. prof. law Harvard Law Sch., 1975-76, Columbia Law Sch., 2005; faculty mem. Salzburg (Austria) Seminar in Am. Studies, 1975; chmn. Def. Sci. Bd. task force on antitrust aspects of def. industry downsizing, 1994. Editor: How the Chicago School Overshot the Mark: The Effect of Conservative Economic Analysis on U.S. Antitrust, 2008; co-author: Cases on Antitrust Law, 1967, Cases on Trade Regulation, 5th edit. 2003; co-editor: Revitalizing Antitrust in Its Second Century, 1991; contbr. articles on consumer protection and antitrust to profl. publs. Served with U.S. Army, 1954-56. Recipient Disting. Service award FTC, 1972, Hart Pub. Svc. award Cons. Fedn. Am., 2001, Kirkpatrick Lifetime Achievement award FTC, 2002; named One of Ten Outstanding Mid-Career Law Profs. Time Mag., 1977, Disting. Columbia Law Grad. in Tchg., 2005. Mem. ABA (coun. antitrust sect. 1986-89), Am. Acad. Arts and Scis., Am. Law Inst., Assn. Am. Law Schs., Columbia U. Ctr. for Law Econ. Studies (adv. bd. 1975-95). Democrat. Jewish. Office Phone: 202-942-5662. Business E-Mail: robertpitofsky@aporter.com.

PITOT, HENRY CLEMENT, III, pathologist, educator; b. NYC, May 12, 1930; s. Henry Clement and Bertha (Lowe) Pitot; m. Julie S. Schutten, July 29, 1954; children: Bertha, Anita, Jeanne, Catherine, Henry, Michelle, Lisa, Patrice. BS in Chemistry, Va. Mil. Inst., 1951; MD, Tulane U., 1955, PhD in Biochemistry, 1959, DSc (hon.), 1995. Instr. pathology Med. Sch. Tulane U., New Orleans, 1955-59; postdoctoral fellow McArdle Lab. U. Wis., Madison, 1959-60, mem. faculty Med. Sch., 1960—, prof. pathology and oncology, 1966-99, prof. emeritus, 1999—, chmn. dept. pathology, 1968-71, acting dean Med. Sch., 1971-73, dir. McArdle Lab., 1973-91. Recipient Borden Undergrad. Rsch. award, 1955, Leaderle Faculty award, 1962, Career Devel. award, Nat. Cancer Inst., NIH, 1965, Parke-Davis award, 1968, Noble Found. Rsch. award, 1984, Esther Langer award, U. Chgo., 1984, Hilldale award, U. Wis., 1991, Founders award, Chem. Industry Inst. Toxicology, 1993, Midwest Regional chpt. Soc. Toxicology award, 1996, Emeritus Faculty award, U. Wis. Med. Sch., 2001, Disting. Lifetime Toxicology award, Soc. Toxicology, 2003, Gold-headed Cane award, Am. Soc. Investigative Pathology, 2005, Lifetime Disting. Alumnus award, Tulane Med. Sch., 2005, Disting. Svc. award, Assn. Pathology Chairs, 2005. Fellow: AAAS, N.Y. Acad. Scis.; mem.: Soc. Toxicologic Pathologists, Soc. Toxicology, Soc. Surg. Oncology (Lucy J. Wortham award 1981), Soc. Exptl. Biology and Medicine (pres. 1991—93), Am. Soc. Investigative Pathology (pres. 1976—77), Am. Cancer Soc. (life), Japanese Cancer Soc. (hon.), Am. Chem. Soc., Am. Soc. Biochemistry and Molecular Biology, Am. Assn. Cancer Rsch., Am. Soc. Cell Biology. Roman Catholic. Home: 314 Robin Pkwy Madison WI 53705-4931 Office: U Wis McArdle Lab Cancer Rsch 1400 University Ave Madison WI 53706-1599 Office Phone: 608-262-3247. Business E-Mail: pitot@oncology.wisc.edu. *Where and who we are today is the result of those whom we have met and known and loved until now.*

PITPITAN, CONSUELO LOPEZ, pharmacist, educator; 1 child, Amelia Bryson Reyes-Crozier. MEd in bilingual, bicultural, U. Ariz., Tucson, 1987. Cert. pharmacy technician Pharmacy Certification Bd. & Ariz. State, 1995. Adj. faculty Pima County CC, Tucson, 1986—. Coord. bilingual interpreter Spanish, English Kino Cmty. Hosp., Tucson, 1974—2004; cons., facilitator Ariz. Area Health Edn. Ctrs., Tucson, 1987—90. Translator (English, Spanish): (Bilingual Interpreter) Med. Field Comm. Trainer Nat. Pharm. Stockpile Met. Med. Response Sys., Tucson, 2002. Mem.: Ariz. Pharmacy Alliance. Avocations: travel, gardening, reading, music, yoga. Office: Pima CC 2202 W Anklam Rd Tucson AZ 85709-0170

PITT, BERTRAM, cardiologist, educator, consultant; b. Kew Gardens, NY, Apr. 27, 1932; s. David and Shirley (Blum) P., m. Elaine Liberstein, Aug. 10, 1962; children: Geoffrey, Jessica, Jillian BA, Cornell U., 1953; MD, U. Basel, Switzerland, 1959. Diplomate Am. Bd. Internal Medicine, Am. Bd. Cardiology. Intern Beth Israel Hosp., NYC, 1959-60, resident Boston, 1960-63; fellow in cardiology Johns Hopkins U., Balt., 1966-67, from instr. to assoc. prof., 1967-77; prof. medicine, dir. div. cardiology U. Mich., Ann Arbor, 1977-91, prof. medicine Sch. Medicine, 1991—2005, prof. medicine emeritus Sch. Medicine, 2005—; chmn., steering com. NHLBI JOPCAT Trial, 2008—. Author: Atlas of Cardiovascular Nuclear Medicine, 1977; editor: Cardiovascular Nuclear Medicine, 1974; co-editor: Clinical Trials in Cardiology, 1997, Current Controlled Trials in Cardiovascular Medicine, 1999—. Served to capt. U.S. Army, 1963-65. Mem. ACP, Am. Coll. Cardiology, Am. Soc. Clin. Investigation, Assn. Am. Physicians, Am. Physiol. Soc., Am. Heart Assn. (James. B. Herrick award 2005), Assn. Univ. Cardiologists, Am. Coll. Chest Physicians, Johns Hopkins U. Soc. Scholars. Home: 24 Ridgeway St Ann Arbor MI 48104-1739 Office: U Mich Divsn Cardiology 1500 E Medical Center Dr Ann Arbor MI 48109-0005 Office Phone: 734-936-5260. Business E-Mail: bpitt@umich.edu.

PITT, BRAD, actor; b. Shawnee, Okla., Dec. 18, 1963; s. Bill and Jane Pitt; m. Jennifer Aniston, July 29, 2000 (div. Oct. 2, 2005); adopted children: Maddox Chivan Jolie-Pitt, Zahara Marley Jolie-Pitt, Pax Thien Jolie-Pitt children: Shiloh Nouvel Jolie-Pitt, Knox Leon Jolie-Pitt, Vivienne Marcheline Jolie-Pitt. Co-founder Maddox Jolie-Pitt Found. (MJP), 2006—; founder Make It Right Foundation New Orleans, 2007—. Actor: (films) No Man's Land, 1987, Less Than Zero, 1987, Cutting Glass, 1989, Happy Together, 1990, Across the Tracks, 1991, Thelma and Louise, 1991, Johnny Suede, 1991, Contact, 1992, Cool World, 1992, A River Runs Through It, 1992, Kalifornia, 1993, True Romance, 1993, The Favor, 1994, Interview with the Vampire, 1994 (MTV Movie awards for Best Male Performance, Most Desirable Male, 1995), Legends of the Fall, 1994, Se7en, 1995 (MTV Movie award, Most Desirable Male, 1996), 12 Monkeys, 1995 (Best Supporting Actor, Acad. Sci. Fiction, Fantasy & Horror Films, 1996, Golden Globe award, Best Supporting Actor, 1996, Best Supporting Actor, Sci-Fi Universe Mag., 1996, Favorite Supporting Actor in sci. fiction, Blockbuster Entertainment awards, 1997), Sleepers, 1996, Seven Years in Tibet, 1997 (Best Actor, Rembrandt awards, 1998), The Devil's Own, 1997, Dark Side of the Sun, 1997, Meet Joe Black, 1998, Fight Club, 1999, Snatch, 2000, The Mexican, 2001, Spy Game, 2001, Ocean's Eleven, 2001, Full Frontal, 2002, Confessions of a Dangerous Mind, 2002, Sinbad: Legend of the Seven Seas (voice only), 2003, Troy, 2004 (Choice Movie Actor in Drama/Action Adventure, Teen Choice awards, 2004), Ocean's Twelve, 2004, Mr. & Mrs. Smith, 2005 (MTV Movie award, Best Fight Scene, 2006), Babel, 2006, Ocean's Thirteen, 2007, Burn After Reading, 2008, The Curious Case of Benjamin Button, 2008, Inglourious Basterds, 2009; (TV films) A Stoning in Fulham County, 1988, Too Young to Die, 1990; (TV series) Another World, 1987, Glory Days, 1990, (TV appearances) Growing Pains, 1987, 1989, Dallas, 1987, 1988, 21 Jump Street, 1988, Head of the Class, 1989, Freddy's Nightmares, 1989, thirtysomething, 1989, Tales from the Crypt, 1992, Friends, 2001, King of the Hill (voice only), 2003, Getaway, 2005; prodr.: (films) The Departed, 2006, Running with Scissors, 2006; actor, prodr.: (films) The Assassination of Jesse James by the Coward Robert Ford, 2007; exec. prodr.: (films) God Grew Tired of Us: The Story of Lost Boys of Sudan, 2004, Year of the Dog, 2007; co-prodr.: (films) A Mighty Heart, 2007. Named Male Star of Tomorrow, ShoWest Convention, 1993, Favorite Leading Man, People's Choice Awards, 2006, Favorite On Screen Match-Up (with George Clooney), 2008, Favorite Leading Man, 2009; named one of 50 Most Powerful People in Hollywood, Premiere mag., 2004—06, Barbara Walters 10 Most Fascinating People of 2006, The World's Most Influential People, TIME mag., 2007, 2008, 2009, The 100 Most Powerful Celebrities, Forbes.com, 2007, 2008. Office: c/o Plan B Entertainment Inc 9150 Wilshire Blvd Ste 350 Beverly Hills CA 90212-3427*

PITT, GEORGE, lawyer, investment banker; b. Chgo., July 21, 1938; s. Cornelius George and Anastasia (Geocaris) P.; m. Barbara Lynn Goodrich, Dec. 21, 1963 (div. Apr. 1990); children: Elizabeth Nanette, Margaret Leigh; m. Pamela Ann Pittsford, May 19, 1990. BA, Northwestern U., 1960, JD, 1963; hon. grad., US Army Intelligence Sch., Ft. Holabird, Md., 1964; Leading Strategic Change course, U. Va., 1999. Bar: Ill. 1963. Assoc. Chapman and Cutler, Chgo., 1963-67; ptnr. Borge and Pitt, and predecessor, 1968-87, Katten Muchin & Zavis, Chgo., 1987-97; sr. mng. dir. Banc One Capital Markets, Inc. (formerly First Chgo. Capital Markets, Inc.), Chgo., 1998-2000; mng. dir. UBS Fin. Svcs. Inc. (formerly UBS PaineWebber Inc.), Chgo., 2000—04, Morgan Keegan & Co., Inc., Chgo., 2004—07; of counsel Greenberg Traurig LLP, Chgo., 2007—. Conf. chmn. Bond Buyer's 3d Ann. Midwest Pub. Fin. Conf., 1994; conf. co-chmn. Bond Buyer's 8th Ann. Midwest Pub. Fin. Conf., 1999, conf. co-chmn. Bond Buyer's 11th, 2005. Notes and comments editor Northwestern U. Law Rev., 1962-63. 1st lt. AUS, 1964. Fellow: Am. Coll. Bond Counsel; mem.: Ill. State Bar Assn., Phi Gamma Delta, Phi Delta Phi, Eta Sigma Phi. Office Phone: 312-456-1022. Business E-Mail: pittg@gtlaw.com.

PITT, HARVEY LLOYD, risk management consultant, former federal agency administrator; b. Bklyn., Feb. 28, 1945; s. Morris Jacob and Sara (Sapir) P.; m. Saree Ruffin, Jan. 7, 1984; children: Robert Garrett, Sara Dillard; children from previous marriage: Emily Laura, Jonathan Bradley. BA, CUNY, 1965; JD with honors (Univ. scholar), St. John's U., NYC, 1968; LLD (hon.), St. John's U., 2002. Bar: N.Y. 1969, U.S. Supreme Ct. 1972, D.C. 1979. Legal asst. to commr. US Securities & Exchange Commn. (SEC), Washington, 1969, spl. counsel, 1971-72, chief counsel divsn. market regulation, 1972-73, exec. asst. to chmn., 1973-75, gen. counsel, 1975-78; editor Instl. Investor Study, 1970-71; ptnr. Fried, Frank, Harris, Shriver & Jacobson, Washington, 1978—2001; chmn. US Securities & Exchange Commn. (SEC), Washington, 2001—03; CEO Kalorama Ptnrs., LLC, 2003—. Adj. prof. law George Washington U. Nat. Law Ctr., 1974-82, U. Pa. Law Sch., 1983-84, vis. practitioner, 1984, Georgetown U. Law Ctr., 1976-84; comml. arbitrator Am. Arbitration Assn. Contbr. articles to profl. jours. V.p. Glen Haven Civic Assn., Silver Spring, Md., 1972-73, pres., 1974. Recipient Learned Hand award Inst. for Human Rels., 1988, Presdl. medal, Bklyn. Coll., 2003. Mem. ABA (past chmn. subcom. SEC practice and enforcement, past co-chmn. subcom. state takeover laws), Fed. Bar Assn. (Outstanding Young Lawyer award 1975), Adminstrv. Conf. U.S., Am. Law Inst. (project advisor on restatement law on corp. governance), Delta Sigma Rho, Tau Kappa Alpha, Phi Delta Phi. Office: Kalorama Ptnrs LLC Ste 800 1130 Connecticut Ave NW Washington DC 20036-3915 Office Phone: 202-721-0000. Business E-Mail: harvey@kaloramapartners.com.

PITT, WILLIAM ALEXANDER, cardiologist; b. July 17, 1942; came to U.S., 1970; s. Reginald William and Una Sylvia (Alexander) P.; children: William Matthew, Joanne Katharine. MD, U. B.C., Vancouver, 1967. Diplomate Royal Coll. Physicians Can. Intern Mercy Hosp., San Diego, 1967-68, resident, 1970-71, assoc. dir. cardiology, 1972-92; resident Vancouver Gen. Hosp., 1968-70, U. Calif., San Diego, 1971-72; with So. Calif. Cardiology Med. Group, San Diego, 1984—; pvt. practice Clin. Cons. Cardiology. Bd. trustees San Diego Found. for Med. Care, 1983-89, 91—, pres., chmn. bd. trustees, 1986-88, med. dir., 1991-96; trustee Pacific Found. for Med. Care, 1996—, med. dir., 1996—; bd. dirs. Mut. Assn. for Profl. Services, Phila., 1984-92; pres. Alternet Med. Svcs., Inc., 1992-95; pres. and med. dir. San Diego IPA, 1995-2005. Fellow Royal Coll. Physicians Can., Am. Coll. Cardiology (assoc.); mem. AMA, Am. Heart Assn., Calif. Med. Assn., San Diego County Med. Soc., San Diego County Heart Assn. (bd. dirs. 1982-88). Episcopalian. Office: So Calif Cardiology Med Group 6386 Alvarado Ct Ste 101 San Diego CA 92120-4906 Home Phone: 619-596-0894. Personal E-mail: wmapitt@aol.com, wmapitt@sbcglobal.net.

PITTELKO, ROGER DEAN, clergyman, theology studies educator; b. Elk Reno, Okla., Aug. 18, 1932; s. Elmer Henry and Lydia Caroline (Nieman) Pittelko. AA, Concordia Coll., 1952; BA, Concordia Sem., St. Louis, 1954, MDiv, 1957, STM, 1958; postgrad., Chgo. Luth. Theol. Sem., 1959-61; ThD, Am. Div. Sch., Pineland, Fla., 1968; DMin, Faith Evang. Luth. Sem., Tacoma, 1983. Ordained to ministry Luth. Ch., 1958. Vicar St. John Luth. Ch., SI, NY, 1955—56, asst. pastor New Orleans, 1958-59; pastor Concordia Luth. Ch., Berwyn, Ill., 1959-63, Luth. Ch. Holy Spirit, Elk Grove Village, Ill., 1962—87; chmn. Commn. on Worship, Luth. Ch.-Mo. Synod, 1982—92, chmn. commn. worship, 1994—98, asst. bishop Midwest region English dist., 1983, pres., bishop English dist., 1987-97, 3d v.p., 1997—2001; prof. pastoral theology Concordia Theol. Sem., Ft. Wayne, Ind., 1997—2003; pastor Trinity Luth. Ch., Villa Park, Ill., 2003—05, Grace English Luth. Ch., Chgo., 2005—06. Author: Guide to Introducing Lutheran Worship; contbr. articles to jours. Mem.: Luth. Acad. for Scholarship, Concordia Hist. Inst., Itasca Country Club (Ill.), Maywood Sportsmans Club (Ill.). Republican. Lutheran. Office: Trinity Luth Ch 300 S Ardmore Ave Villa Park IL 60181-2699 Office Phone: 630-834-3440. Personal E-mail: emep@juno.com.

PITTELKOW, MARK ROBERT, physician, dermatologist, educator, researcher; b. Milw., Dec. 16, 1952; s. Robert Bernard and Barbara Jean (Thomas) P.; m. Gail L. Gamble, Nov. 26, 1977; children: Thomas, Cameron, Robert. BA, Northwestern U., 1975; MD, Mayo Med. Sch., 1979. Intern then resident Mayo Grad. Sch., 1979-84, post-doctoral exptl. pathology, 1981-83; from asst. to assoc. prof. dermatology Mayo Med. Sch., Rochester, Minn., 1984-95, prof. dermatology, 1995—, assoc. prof. biochemistry and molecular biology, 1992—. Cons. Mayo Clinic/Found., Rochester, 1984— Fellow Am. Acad. Dermatology; mem. AAAS, Am. Dermatol. Assn., Soc. Investigative Dermatology, Am. Burn Assn., Am. Soc. Cell Biology, N.Y. Acad. Scis., Chi Psi. Achievements include discovery of skin and epidermal growth control; autocrine growth factor production; growth and differentiation of keratinocytes. Office: Mayo Clinic 200 1st St SW Rochester MN 55905-0002 Home: 2759 Braeburn Ln Sw Rochester MN 55902-3489 Office Phone: 507-284-2555. Business E-Mail: pittelkow.mark@mayo.edu.

PITTENGER, ARTHUR O., JR., mathematics educator; b. Indpls., Oct. 24, 1936; s. Arthur O. Sr. and Barbara (Sherman) P.; m. Judith MacGillivray, Apr. 24, 1965; children: Laurence, Christopher, Elise. BS, Stanford U., 1958, PhD, 1967. Vis. scholar Moscow State U., 1967-68; rsch. assoc. Rockefeller U., NYC, 1968-70; asst. prof. U. Mich., Ann Arbor, 1970-72; assoc. prof., then prof. U. Md. Baltimore County, Balt., 1972—, dean Arts and Scis., 1988-93, interim provost, 1993-94. Cons. IDA, Princeton, N.J., 1973-75; vis. prof. Oxford U., Eng., 1999-2000.

Contbr. articles to profl. jours. Lt. U.S. Army, 1960. Fellow Inst. Math. Stats.; mem. Am. Math. Soc., Phi Beta Kappa, Phi Kappa Phi. Office: U Md Baltimore County Dept Math Baltimore MD 21250-0001

PITTENGER, DAVID M., aquarium administrator; BS, Cornell, 1971; MS, Pa., 1976. Tchr. Antioch Coll., 1972—76; tchr., naturalist Acad. Natural Sciences, 1972—77; park ranger Everglades Nat. Park, 1978; exec. dir. Gulf of Maine Aquarium, 1985—86, Nat. Aquarium in Balt. Office: Nat Aquarium 501 E Pratt St Pier 3 Baltimore MD 21202-3194 Office Phone: 410-576-3822. Office Fax: 410-576-8238. Business E-Mail: dpittenger@aqua.org.

PITTMAN, AMANDA NELSON, music educator; d. General Lee and Amanda Hopkins Nelson; m. Marvin Benjamin Pittman, 1964; 1 child, Marvin Benjamin Jr. BMus, U. So. Calif., LA, 1948, MMus, 1961, DMA, 2003. Gen. tchg. credential in elem. edn. Calif. Tchr. elem. edn. Ft. Worth Schs., 1949—51; tchr. elem. music LA City Schs., 1957—64, Montgomery County Schs., Rockville, Md., 1964—66, LA City Schs., 1966—75, Beverly Hills Unified Schs., Calif., 1975—90, LA City Schs., 1990—91, Clark County Sch. Dist., Las Vegas, Nev., 1992—98, LA City Schs., 1999—. Instr. music edn. Pepperdine U., LA, 1967—70, U. So. Calif., 1975—77, Calif. State U., LA, 2002—03. Adminstrv. officer USAFR, March AFB, Calif., 1959—64. Capt. USAF, 1951—56. Mem.: Calif. Music Educators Assn., LA City Elem. Schs. Music Assn. (v.p. 2004—06), Internat. Assn. for Jazz Edn., Music Educators Nat. Conf. (presenter 1960—2006), Women in Mil. Svc. for Am. Found. (charter mem.). Home: 8957 Haas Ave Los Angeles CA 90047

PITTMAN, CONSTANCE SHEN, endocrinologist, educator; b. Nanking, China, Jan. 2, 1929; arrived in US, 1946; d. Leo F.-Z. and Pao Kong (Yang) Shen; m. James Allen Pittman, Jr., Feb. 19, 1955; children: James Clinton, John Merrill. AB in Chemistry, Wellesley Coll., 1951; MD, Harvard U., 1955. Diplomate Am. Bd. Internal Medicine, sub-bd. Endocrinology. Intern Baltimore City Hosp., 1955-56; resident U. Ala., Birmingham, 1956-57; instr. in medicine U. Ala. Med. Ctr., Birmingham, 1957—59, fellow dept. pharmacology, 1957-59, from asst. prof. to assoc. prof., 1959-70, prof., 1970—. Prof. medicine Georgetown U., Washington, 1972—73; mem. diabetes and metabolism tng. com. NIH, Bethesda, Md., 1972—76, mem. nat. arthritis, metabolism and digestive disease coun., 1975—78, mem. gen. clin. rsch. ctrs. com., 1979—83, 1987—90; bd. dirs., mem., exec. dir. Internat. Coun. for Control of Iodine Deficiency Diseases, 1994—; mem. Iodine Deficiency Disorders Elimination Steering Com. Kiwanis Internat., 2002—. Interim editor: ICCIDD Newsletter, 2004—06. Master ACP; mem. Assn. Am. Physicians, Am. Soc. for Clin. Investigation, Endocrine Soc. (coun., 1978-79, pres. women's caucus 1978-79), Am. Thyroid Assn. (pres. 1990-91), Kiwanis (mem. iodine deficiency disorders steering com.). Achievements include research in activation and metabolism of thyroid hormone; kinetics of thyroxine conversion to triiodothyrine in health and disease states; control of iodine deficiency disorders. Emails. Office: UAB Div Endocrinology/Metab Lab Med Ctr Birmingham AL 35294-0001 Office Phone: 205-934-0800. Business E-Mail: cpittman@uab.edu.

PITTMAN, JACQUELYN, retired mental health nurse, nursing educator; b. Pensacola, Fla., Dec. 22, 1932; d. Edward Corry Sr. and Hettie Oean (Wilson) P. BS in Nursing Edn., Fla. State U., 1958; MA, Columbia U., 1959, EdD, 1974. Physician asst. Med. Ctr. Clinic, Pensacola, 1953-55; clin. instr., asst. dir. nursing svc. Sacred Heart Hosp., Pensacola, 1955-56; instr. psychiat. nurse Fla. State Hosp., Chattahoochee, 1958; instr. psychiat. nursing Pensacola Jr. Coll., 1959-60, 62-63; chmn. div. nursing Gulf Coast C.C., Panama City, Fla., 1963-66; asst. prof. U. Tex., Austin, 1970-72, assoc. prof., 1972-80; prof. nursing, coord. curriculum and tchg. grad. program La. State U. Med. Ctr., New Orleans, 1980-99, rep. faculty senate, 1997-99; pres.-elect faculty assembly Sch. Nursing La. State U. Med. Ctr. Sch. Nursing, New Orleans, 1997-98, pres., 1998-99; ret., 1999. Curriculum cons. Nicholls State U., Thibodaux, La., 1982, Our Lady of Lake Sch. Nursing, Baton Rouge, 1983; rsch. liaison So. Bapt. Hosp., New Orleans, 1987-89, Med. Ctr. La., 1992-99; mem. adv. bd. Sister Henrietta Guyot Professorship; mem. planning com. Nichols State U./La. State U. Med. Ctr. Partnership, 1996-99. Mem. ethics com., trustee Hotel Dieu Hosp., New Orleans, 1987—91; judge Internat. Sci. and Engring. Fair Assn., 1990, 1992; del. La. State Nurses' Assn. State Conv., 1992, 1994; assoc. Libr. of Congress, Smithonian Instn.; mem. Dem. Nat. Comm., Presdl. Task Force, 1992, Ctr. for Study of Presidency; tchr. Christian edn. program for mentally retarded St. Ignatius Martyr Ch., 1979—80; tchr. initiation team Rite of Christian Initiation of Adults, Our Lady of the Lake Cath. Ch., Mandeville, La., 1983—86; v.p., bd. dirs. St. Tammany Guidance Ctr., Inc., Mandeville, 1987—91; mem. parish outreach meals-on-wheels program St. Tammany, Covington, La., 2001—02. Mem. ANA, LWV, Am. Assn. Adv. Sci. Directory, N.Y. Acad. Scis., Acad. Polit. Sci., Libr. of Congress Assocs., Nat. Trust for Hist. Preservation, La. Endowment for Humanities, La. Nurses Assn. (archivist 1987-99, state task force com. to preserve hist. documents 1987-99), So. Nursing Rsch. Soc., Nat. League Nursing, Boston U. Nursing Archives, Women's Inner Cir. Achievement N.Am. Cmtys., Internat. Order of Merit, World Found. Successful Women, Wilson Ctr. Assocs., Kappa Delta Pi, Sigma Theta Tau. Democrat. Roman Catholic. Avocations: swimming, golf, travel, reading, louisiana history. Address: 204 Woodridge Blvd Mandeville LA 70471-2604 Personal E-mail: jpit204@att.net.

PITTMAN, JAMES ALLEN, JR., endocrinologist, educator; b. Orlando, Fla., Apr. 12, 1927; s. James Allen and Jean C. (Garretson) Pittman; m. Constance Ming-Chung Shen, Feb. 19, 1955; children: James Clinton, John Merrill. BS, Davidson Coll., 1948, DSc (hon.), 1981; MD, Harvard, 1952; DSc (hon.), U. Ala., Birmingham, 1984, Chung Shan Med U., Taichung, Taiwan, 2005. Intern, asst. resident medicine Mass. Gen. Hosp., Boston, 1952—54; tchg. fellow medicine Harvard U., 1953—54; clin. assoc. NIH, Bethesda, Md., 1954—56; instr. medicine George Washington U., 1955—56; chief resident U. Ala. Med. Ctr., Birmingham, 1956—58, instr. medicine, 1956—59, asst. prof., 1959—62, assoc. prof., 1962—64, prof. medicine, 1964—92, dir. endocrinology and metabolism divsn., 1962—71, co-chmn. dept. medicine, 1969—71, also prof., physiology and biophysics, 1967—92, dean, 1973—92, Disting. prof., 1992—. Mem. endocrinology study sect. NIH, 1963—67; mem. nat. adv. rsch. resources coun. NIH, 1991—95; asst. chief med. dir. rsch. and edn. in medicine U.S. VA, 1971—73; prof. medicine Georgetown U. Med. Sch., Washington, 1971—73; mem. grad. med. edn. nat. adv. com. HEW, 1976—78; mem. HHS Coun. on Grad. Med. Edn., 1986—90; hon. prof. Chung Shan Med. and Dental Coll., Taiwan, 1994; sr. advisor Internat. Coun. on Ctrl. of Iodine Deficiency Diseases, 1994—96. Author: Diagnosis and Treatment of Thyroid Diseases, 1963; contbr. articles in field to profl. jours. Master: Am. Coll. Endocrinology; fellow: AAAS; mem.: ACP, Stearman Restorers Assn., Hist. Sci. Soc., Am. Soc. for the History of Medicine, So. Soc. Clin. Investigation (Founder's medal 1993), Am. Fedn. Clin. Rsch. (pres. So. sect., nat. coun. 1962—66), Am. Chem. Soc., Am. Diabetes Assn., Am. Ornithologists Union (life), NY Acad. Scis. (life), Endocrine Soc. Ecuador (hon.), Soc. Nuc. Medicine, Am. Thyroid Assn., Am. Assn. Clin. Endocrinologists, Endocrine Soc., Assn. Am. Physicians, Inst. Medicine of NAS, Harvard U. Med. Alumni Assn. (pres. 1986—88), Wilson Ornithol. Club (life), Alpha Omega Alpha, Phi Beta Kappa, Omicron Delta Kappa. Office: U Ala Sch Med Pittman CAMS 1924 7th Ave S Birmingham AL 35294-0007 Office Phone: 205-934-3414. Personal E-mail: japdoc@msn.com. Business E-Mail: japdoc@uab.edu. *I hope that each time I meet a person, both of us leave the encounter the better for it.*

PITTMAN, JAMES MORRIS (JACK PITTMAN), cartoonist, illustrator, character designer, consultant; b. Sanford, NC, Oct. 22, 1952; s. James Berdine and Merry Louise (Thomas) P.; m. Patricia Lynne Smith, Nov. 27, 1977; children: Jay Scott, Jonathan Patrick, Joy Elizabeth. B of Environ. Design in Arch. with honors, N.C. State U., 1974. Sports and editl. cartoonist, illustrator, courtroom artist The News and Observer, Raleigh, NC, 1974-83; freelance cartoonist, illustrator Raleigh, 1983—. Adj. prof. Meredith Coll., Raleigh, 1993-94; advtsg. illustrator for Am. Express, Coca-Cola, Procter & Gamble, GMC, Palace Entertainment, Kellogg's, Wendy's, Carolina Hurricanes, NHL, Ericsson, Inc., Gatorade, GlaxoSmithKline, Nortel Networks, Touchstone Energy coops. Illustrator: (book) A Dust of Snow, 1980, Are You Smart, Or What?, 2001, If You're So Smart, Prove It!, 2007, Discover Your Inner Sloth, Darren Dwayne DeBakey and His Amazing Inventions, mags. include Nat. Geographic World, Wildlife in NC, Carolina Country, Focus on the Family Publication, Reader's Digest, (CD-ROM) Heavenword Children's Bible, 1997, The Birth of Kidd Millennium, 2001, (comic strip) Kidd Millennium, 2001-05; permanent collections include The Internat. Mus. of Cartoon Art, N.C. Mus. History, 2002-03, NC Wildlife Resources Commn. Offices, NC State U. Centennial Campus, 2006—, Animation Exhibit, John E. Pechmann Fishing Edn. Ctr., 2008—, drummer, Adjustyd Bluz Band, 2006—. Deacon So. Bapt. Ch. Recipient various ADDY awards Triangle Advtsg. Fedn., 1983-97, 69th Exhbn. Merit; Best in Mag. Illustration award. Mem. Nat. Cartoonists Soc. (chmn. SE chpt. 2009-, Best in Advt. and Illustration award Reuben divsn. 1995, 98, 2004), Raleigh Civitan Club. Mem. So. Bapt. Ch. Avocations: percussion, computers. Home: PO Box 10711 Raleigh NC 27605-0711 Office: J Pittman Illustrator 1740 Brooks Ave Raleigh NC 27607-6618 Office Phone: 919-785-1966. E-mail: jptoonist@aol.com, jack@jackpittman.net.

PITTMAN, ROBERT TURNER, retired newspaper editor; b. Gates, NC, Sept. 24, 1929; s. Thomas Everett and Lillian (Turner) P.; m. Ruth Fike, Aug. 25, 1956; children— Laura Emily, Mary Ann, Lillian Elizabeth. BA, Washington and Lee U., 1951; MA, U. N.C., 1957. Reporter Times Dispatch, Richmond, Va., 1951; editor, pub. Daily Ranger, Glendive, Mont., 1957-58; writer editorials Times Union, Jacksonville, Fla., 1958-63; editorial editor Times, St. Petersburg, Fla., 1963-92; dir. Times Pub. Co., 1968-92. Trustee Poynter Inst. Media Studies, St. Petersburg, 1978-92. Editor: (jour.) Masthead, 1980—81. Active St. Petersburg Charter Revision Com., 1992-93; dir. Fla. Bar Found., 1994-96. Lt. (j.g.) USNR, 1951-55. Recipient Pinellas Civil Liberties award, 1993; U. N.C.-Chapel Hill scholarship established in honor, 1994, Liberty Bell award St. Petersburg Bar Assn., 1995. Mem. Nat. Conf. Editl. Writers (pres. 1978, life), Nat. Conf. Editl. Writers Found. Inc. (pres. 1984) Methodist. Home: 736 18th Ave NE Saint Petersburg FL 33704-4608

PITTMAN, ROBERT WARREN, investor; b. Jackson, Miss., Dec. 28, 1953; s. Warren E. and Lanita (Hurdle) P.; m. Sandra Hill, July 27, 1979; 1 child, Robert Thomas; m. Veronique Choa, Nov. 28, 1997; children: Andrew Forest, Lucy Li. Student, Millsaps Coll., 1971-72, Oakland U., 1972-73, U. Pitts., 1973-74; AMP, Harvard U., 1984-85. Disc. jockey Sta. WJDX-FM, Jackson, Miss., 1970-72, Sta. WRIT, Milw., 1972; rsch. dir. Sta. WDRQ, Detroit, 1972-73; prog. dir. Sta. WPEZ, Pitts., 1973-74, Stas. WMAQ-WKQX NBC, Chgo., 1974-77, Sta. WNBC, NYC, 1977-79; exec. prod. Album Tracks, NBC TV, NYC, 1977-78; dir., v.p., then sr. v.p. MTV Networks, NYC, 1979-82, exec. v.p., COO, 1983-85, pres., CEO, 1985-86, Quantum Media, Inc., NYC, 1987-89; exec. adv. Warner Comm., Inc., NYC, 1989-90; pres., chief exec. officer Time Warner Enterprises, NYC, 1990-95; CEO, Six Flags Entertainment, 1991-95; mng. ptnr., CEO, Century 21 Real Estate, 1995-96; pres., CEO Am. Online Networks, 1996-97; pres., COO Am. Online, Inc., 1997-2001; CO-COO AOL Time Warner, 2001, COO, 2002—; ptnr. Pilot Grp., 2003—. Bd. dirs. Spot Runner, 2006—, Cendant Corp. Bd. dirs. Elec. Arts, N.Y.C. Ballet, N.Y. Shakespeare Festival, chmn., 1987—94; bd. dir., vice-chmn. Robin Hood Found.; bd. dir. Alliance Lupus Rsch. Recipient Prog. Mgr. of Yr. Billboard, 1977, Prog. Dir. of Yr. Hall Radio Report, 1978, Entrepreneur award White House SB Conf., 1986, Golden Plate award Am. Acad. Achievement, 1990, medal of Excellence Miss. U. Women, 1992, Vision award Retinitis Pigmentosa International, 1992, Lifetime Achievement Internat. Monitor award Internat. Teleproduction Soc., 1993, Gold Medal award Internat. Radio and TV Soc., 2002, Cablevision Mags. 20/20 Vision award, Pres. award Bank St. Coll. Edn.; named Innovator of Yr. Performance Mag., 1981, Humanitarian of Yr., AMC, 1984, Time Mag. Man of Yr. runner-up, 1984, Esquire Mag. Under 40 Leadership, 1985; named one of Pioneers of New Am. Start-Up, Success mag., One of Five Original Thinkers of 80s, Life Mag., 1990, 8 of 50 Most Influential Baby Boomers, Life Mag., 1996, Bus. Week's Top 25 Exec. of 1998, one of 50 Pioneers and Visionaries of TV, 2002; inducted Broadcast & Cable Hall of Fame, 1999. Methodist. Office: Pilot Group LLC 75 Rockefeller Plaza 23 Fl New York NY 10019

PITTMAN, ROY CLINTON, JR., neurosurgeon, theologian, lawyer, philosopher; b. Florence, SC, Oct. 12, 1931; s. Roy Clinton and Edna Hester (Altman) P.; m. Therese Huguette Lamarche Pittman, Apr. 1958 (div. May 1976); 1 stepdaughter, Michele Lois Young; children: Charlotte Elisabeth, Clinton Christopher, Russell Roy; m. Jeanne Elmore Waters Pittman, Oct. 10, 1976. BS magna cum laude, Wofford Coll., Spartanburg, SC, 1952; MD, Med. U. S.C., Charleston, 1956; JD, Washburn U. Coll. Law, Topeka, Kans., 1991; MDiv with honors, Emory U. Candler Sch. Theology, Atlanta, 1995; DSc (hon.), The London Inst., 1973. Diplomate Am. Bd. Neurol. and Orthopedic Surgery; ordained to ministry Ea. Orthodox Ch., 2000; bar: Fla. 1992, U.S. Dist. Ct. (mid. dist.) Fla. 1992. Intern U.S. Naval Hosp., Newport, RI, 1956-57; resident in neurology U.S. Naval Hosp.-Nat. Naval Med. Ctr., Bethesda, Md., 1957-58; neurologist East Coast Neuropsychiat. Ctr.-U.S. Naval Hosp., Phila., 1958-59, head neurology br., 1959; resident in neurosurgery Jefferson Med. Coll. Hosp., Phila., 1959-61, chief resident, 1961-62; resident in gen. surgery Hahnemann Med. Coll. Hosp., Phila., 1962-63; pvt. practice neurol. surgery Morton Plant and Mease Hosps., Clearwater-Dunedin, Fla., 1963-82, Cmty. Hosp. of New Port Richey, New Port Richey, Fla., 1978-88; pvt. practice legal medicine, med. jurisprudence & bioethics Pittman Profl. Assn., Clearwater, Fla., 1995-98, Tarpon Springs, Fla., 1995-98; pres., gen. counsel The Quintessential Corp., Tarpon Springs, 1998-2000; founder, prior Trinity House Retreat, Greek Orthodox Monastery of the Holy Trinity, 2001—. Protestant chaplain Morton Plant/Mease Countryside Hosp., Clearwater, Fla., 1997-98. Contbr. articles to profl. jours. Pres. St. Petersburg (Fla.) Coll. Alumni Assn., 1973-75. Lt. MC, USN, 1956-59, lt. comdr., 1962. Recipient Top Paper Bioethics and The Law award Washburn U. Coll. Law, Topeka, Kans., 1990, Top paper Comparative Civil Law award Cumberland Sch. Law and U. Heidelberg Germany Faculty of Law, 1990; endowed Jeanne Pittman ann. Bioethics and the Law Top Paper award Washburn U. Coll. Law, Topeka, 1995. Fellow Internat. Coll. Angiology, Royal Soc. Health, Internat. Coll. Surgeons, Am. Coll. Legal Medicine; mem. AMA, Congress Neurol. Surgeons, Fla. Med. Assn., Fla. Bar, Phi Beta Kappa, Phi Delta Phi. Jeffersonian Democrat. Avocations: stamp collecting/philately, anthropology, travel. Office Phone: 727-992-4502. Home Fax: 727-934-6799.

PITTMAN, WILLIAM CLAUDE, electrical engineer; b. Pontotoc, Miss., Apr. 22, 1921; s. William Claude and Maude Ella (Bennett) P.; m. Eloise Savage, Apr. 20, 1952; children: Patricia A. Pittman Ready, William Claude III, Thomas Allen. BSEE, Miss. State Coll., 1951, MSEE, 1957. Cert. svc. holder US Govt. From electronic engr. to supr. elec. engring. dept. U.S. Army Labs., Redstone Arsenal, Ala., 1951-59; supr. electronic engr. to aero. engring. supr. NASA/Marshall Space Flight Ctr., 1960; electronic engr. Army Missile Labs., 1962-82; program mgr. Army Labs. and R&D Ctr., Redstone Arsenal, 1982-99; vol. cons. Army Aviation and Missile Rsch., Devel. and Engring. Ctr., 1999—. Organizer numerous sci. and tech. confs.; mem. Launch Team First Redstone Missile Cape Canaveral, 1953. Author patents, reports, papers, Flag of United States Flown Over Capitol, 1997. Sgt. USMC, 1940-46, PTO. Recipient Medal of Honor, DAR, Meritorious Civilian Svc. award Dept. Army, 1993, Numerous award & Commendation Letters. Fellow AIAA (assoc.; chmn. Miss.-Ala. chpt. 1981-82, Martin Schilling award 1980); mem. IEEE (sr. life; Cert. Svc. Holder), First Marine Div. Assn., DAV, IRE (chmn. Huntsville sect. 1957-58), Madison Hist. Soc., SAR (pres. Tenn. Valley chpt. 1984-85, Ala. Soc. 1990-91, Cert. 1991, Patriot medal), Tau Beta Pi, Phi Kappa Phi, Kappa Mu Epsilon. Avocations: history, genealogy. Home: 704 Desoto Rd SE Huntsville AL 35801-2032 Office: US Army Aviation Missile Command Huntsville AL 35898-5000 Office Phone: 256-876-1778. Personal E-mail: bill.pittman@amrdec.army.mi, wcpittman@comcast.net.

PITTNER, JOHN R, electrical engineer, researcher; BS in Elec. Engring., Carnegie Mellon U., Pitts., 1963; MS in Elec. Engring., U.Pitts., 1999; PhD in Elec. Engring., 2006. Cert. registered profl. engr., Pa., 1992. Engr. Westinghouse Systems Control Divsn., Buffalo, 1963—72, sr. engr., Westinghouse Advanced Energy Systems Divsn., Madison, Pa., 1972—88; sr. controls engr. Westinghouse/AEG Process Systems, Pitts., 1988—99; sr. process,controls engr. Alstom Process Industries, Pitts., 1999—2001; tchg. fellow U. Pitts., 2005—06, rsch. assoc., 2006—. Peer reviewer tech. articles Internat. Fedn. Automatic Control, Control Engring. Practice, Laxenburg, Austria, 2006—, Internat. Fedn. Automatic Control Automatica, 2008—. Contbr. articles to profl.jours. Tchg. fellowship, U. Pitts., 2005, Rsch. grant, Pa. Infrastructure Tech. Alliance, 2006—07, 2007—. Mem.: Inst. Elec. & Electronic Engrs., Industry Applications Soc. (Meritorious Paper award 2008—), Inst. Elec. & Electronic Engrs., Control Sys. Soc. (life). Achievements include patents for torque control of DC motor with field weakening; process line control with reduced size reel motors and tension control at a winding reel; patents pending for System for Controlling a Rolling Mill; research in improved system for control of tandem cold rolling; development of method for control of rotary crop shear for hot metal rolling mill, system for control of heat transport system in advanced nuclear reactor plant; design of control systems for metal strip process lines. Home: 217 Lincoln Ave Pittsburgh PA 15237 Office: Univ Pitts 3700 O'Hara St Pittsburgh PA 15261 Office Fax: 412-624-8003. Personal E-mail: jrpst16@hotmail.com. Business E-Mail: jpittner@engr.pitt.edu.

PITTONI, LUKE M., lawyer; b. Rockville, NY, May 14, 1945; s. Mario and Grace (Henjes) P.; m. Mary Jo Rocque, July 8, 1972; children: Elizabeth, Katherine, Ellen. BA in Econs., Holy Cross Coll., 1967; JD, Fordham U., 1971. Bar: N.Y. 1972, U.S. Ct. Appeals (2d. cir.) 1975, U.S. Dist. Ct. (so. and ea. dists.) N.Y. 1975, U.S. Supreme Ct. 1976, U.S. Dist. Ct. Conn. 1977, Conn. 1986. Assoc. Martin, Clearwater & Bell, NYC, 1972-75; trial atty. Anthony L. Schiavetti, NYC, 1975-78; assoc. Alexander & Green, NYC, 1978-79; ptnr. Heidell, Pittoni, Murphy & Bach, P.C., NYC, 1979—. Mem. ABA, Conn. Bar Assn., N.Y. State Bar Assn., Am. Bd. Profl. Liability Attys., Am. Bd. Trial Advocates (past pres. NYC chpt.), N.Y. State Med. Def. Bar Assn. (founder, past pres. 1995-97), Def. Rsch. Inst., Internat. Assn. Def. Counsel. Office: Heidell Pittoni Murphy & Bach 99 Park Ave Fl 7 New York NY 10016-1506 Office Phone: 212-286-8585. Personal E-mail: lpittoni@hpmb.com.

PITTS, JAMES ATWATER, finance company executive; b. Greenwich, Conn., Apr. 8, 1940; s. Jeremiah Patrick and Mary Louise (McGregor) P.; m. Noreen Mary Kiggins, July 20, 1963; children: Paul, Andrew, Sarah. BBA with honors, Niagara U., 1962; MBA, U. Conn., 1971; student in Advanced Mgmt. Program, Harvard Bus. Sch., Cambridge, Mass., 1985. CPA, N.Y. Staff acct. Price Waterhouse, Stamford, Conn., 1962; tax specialist Deloitte Haskins & Sells, Rochester, NY, 1965-68; div. contr. Xerox Corp., Stamford, 1968-76; asst. corp. contr. Digital Equipment Corp., Maynard, Mass., 1976-81; v.p., corp. contr. Data Gen. Corp., Westboro, Mass., 1981-86; exec. v.p. fin. adminstrn. and strategic planning Cullinet Software, Inc., Westwood, 1986-88; v.p., chief fin. officer Bain & Co. Inc., Boston, 1988-91; sr. v.p. fin. and adminstrn., treas., CFO Clean Harbors Inc., 1992-96; v.p. for fin. and adminstrn. The Boston Found., 1996—2004, chief investment officer, 2004, treas., 2004; ret., 2004. Bd. dirs. Wainright Bank & Trust Co., 2005—, mem. audit com., 2005—, chmn. audit com., 2008—, mem. exec. com., 2005—; bd. dirs. Macquarie Asset Mavacement Inc., 2009—, Boston Coach Inc., 2009—. Chmn. Sudbury Town Fin. Com., Mass., 1984; v.p., mem. exec. com. Children's Mus. Boston, 1984-96; bd. dirs. Mus. Wharf Inc., 1988-96, Lake Winniepesaukee Assn., Wolfeboro, NH; chmn. Sudbury Long Range Capital Expenditures Com., 1981; trustee Lake Regional Conservation Trust, Meridith, NH; pres. Springfield Point Assn., 2000-. With US Army, 1963-64, USAR, 1965-90, Desert Storm, 1991. Decorated Meritorious Svc. medal, 1991; recipient Internat. Exec. Mgmt. award Internat. Mgmt. Inst. U. Geneva, 1980. Mem. AICPAs, Conn. CPA Soc., N.Y. Soc. CPAs, Fin. Execs. Inst., Harvard Bus. Sch. Assn. Boston (bd. govs. 1992-96, alumni treas. 2005—08, audit com.), Nat. Assn. Corp. Dirs. (bd. dirs. New Eng. chpt. 2005-, chair audit com. New Eng. chpt., 2005-08), Res. Officers Assn. (life), Soc. Mil. Compts., Bald Peak Colony Club, Officers Club Mailing: 139A Charles St 222 Boston MA 02114 Home Phone: 617-227-5544. Personal E-mail: jamesapitts@aol.com.

PITTS, JIM (JAMES L. PITTS), lobbyist; Grad., U. S.C. Spl. asst. to the adminstr. US Dept. Labor, 1981—83; spl. asst. to the sec. Congl. rels. HUD, 1983—88; sr.-level exec. br. position US Dept. Energy; dir. polit. affairs, Office of the V.P. The White House, 1990—93; chief of staff US Senator Spence Abraham, 1996—2001; exec. dir. Fin. Svcs. Coordinating Coun., 2001—03; founding prin., mem. exec. com. Navigators Global, Washington, 2003—. Dep. pub.: The Weekly Standard, 1995—97. Polit. dir. Bush-Quayle Re-election Campaign. Named to Top Washington Lobbyists, The Hill, 2002—07. Republican. Office: Navigators Global 901 7th St NW Ste 200 Washington DC 20001 Office Phone: 202-315-5100. Office Fax: 202-315-5010.*

PITTS, JOSEPH R. (JOE PITTS), United States Representative from Pennsylvania; b. Lexington, Ky., Oct. 10, 1939; s. Joseph S. and Pearl Jackson Pitts; m. Virginia Pratt, 1961; children: Karen R., Carol J., Daniel J. AB in Philos. and Religion, Asbury Coll., Wilmore, Ky., 1961; MEd in Comprehensive Sci., West Chester U., Pa., 1972. Tchr. math., sci., english and phys. ed. Mortonsville Elem. Sch., Versailles, Ky., 1962—63; tchr. math. and sci. Great Valley HS, Malvern, Pa., 1969—72; mem. Pa. State Ho. Reps. from Dist. 158, 1973—97; owner, operator landscape nursery, Unionville, Pa., 1974—90; mem. US Congress from 16th Pa. dist., 1997—, mem. energy and commerce com., 2001—. Transp. com. State of Pa., 1977-80, appropriations com., 1979-82, rep. policy com., chmn. labor rels. com., transp. and joint legis. budget and fin. coms., chmn. rep. appropriations com., 1989. 2nd lt. to capt. USAF, 1963—69. Decorated Air medal with five oak leaf clusters; recipient Pub. Servant award Chester-Del. Pomona Grange, 1980, Cmty. Leadership award Pa. for Biblical Morality, 1984, Disting. Govt. Svc. award Am. Mushroom Inst., 1985, Defender of Life award Pro Life Coalition S.E. Pa., 1985, William Penn award Pa. FACTS, 1985, Small Bus. Champion award Small Bus. Survival Com., 1999-2003, Best and Brightest award Am. Conservative Union, 2000, Friend of the Shareholder award Am. Shareholders Assn., 2000-2003, Taxpayer's Friend award Nat. Taxpayer's Union, 2000-2003, Silver Eagle award Pakistani Assn. N.Am., 2001. Mem.: NRA, Brandywine Valley Assn., VFW Post 5467, Rotary. Republican. Office: PO Box 837 Unionville PA 19375 Office Phone: 202-225-2411, 610-444-4581. Office Fax: 610-444-5750.*

PITTS, ROGER L., psychologist; b. Kansas City, Kans., May 25, 1953; s. Claude and Beverly Pitts; 1 child, Erica. Cert. ednl. specialist Kans. U., 1978. Sch. psychologist Olathe Dist. Schs., Kans., 1978—. Mem.: NASP.

PITTS, SHARON ANN GAMMAGE, nursing director; b. Plainview, Tex., Oct. 23, 1956; d. David and Letha Juanita (Howard) Gammage; m. Billy Lee Pitts, May 20, 1978; 1 child, Billy Luke. Diploma, NW Tex. Hosp. Sch. Nursing, Amarillo, 1977. Med. supr. Cen. Plains Regional Hosp., Plainview, Tex., asst. dir. nurses, supr., dir. quality assurance, oper. rm. circulator, dir. Mem. Assn. Oper. Rm. Nurses. Home: 2900 W 17th St Plainview TX 79072-4759

PITTS, TERENCE RANDOLPH, museum director, consultant; b. St. Louis, Feb. 5, 1950; s. Benjamin Randolph and Barbara Avalon (Gilliam) P.; children: Jacob Richard, Rebecca Suzanne. BA, U. Ill., 1972, MLS, 1974; MA in Art History, U. Ariz., 1986. Registrar Ctr. for Creative Photography, Tucson, 1976-77, curator, 1978-88, dir., 1989-2000; exec. dir. Cedar Rapids (Iowa) Mus. Art, 2000—. Cons. Art and Architecture Thesaurus, Getty Mus., 1984—. Author: (with others) George Fiske: Yosemite Photographer, 1981, Edward Weston: Color Photography; author exhbn. catalogs Four Spanish Photographers, 100 Years of Photography in the American West, Photography in the American Grain, Reframing America. Fellow Nat. Endowment Arts, 1983; travel grantee Nat. Mus. Act, 1979, rsch. grantee U. Ariz., 1983. Office: Cedar Rapids Mus Art 410 3d Ave SE Cedar Rapids IA 52401 E-mail: pitts@crma.org.

PITTS-CUTLER, MELISSA ANNE, counselor, social worker; b. LA, Aug. 20, 1964; d. William E. and Sadie Lee Pitts; m. Kevin Bernard Cutler, June 7, 1998; children: Allanah Mirelle Cutler, Aniah Drew Cutler. BS, Calif. State U., 1987, MSW, 1993. Cert.: Deliquency Control Inst., U. So. Calif. 2000. Youth counselor Calif. Youth Authority, Norwalk, 1987—91, Whittier, 1991—93, parole agt. LA, 1993—94, asst. supervising parole agt. Westminster, 1994—. Cons. Artshare LA, 2000—05. Author: (fiction) All Men Are.But What About You My Sister, 2005. Donor So. Poverty Law Ctr., 2004. Mem.: Alpha Kappa Alpha. Democrat. Avocations: sports, travel. Office: Calif Youth Authority 8311 Westminster Blvd #260 Westminster CA 92683 Office Phone: 714-890-3381. Office Fax: 562-633-5837. Business E-Mail: kcnmiss@sbcglobal.net.

PITYNSKI, ANDRZEJ PIOTR, sculptor; b. Ulanow, Poland, Mar. 15, 1947; naturalized citizen, 1987; s. Aleksander and Stefania (Krupa) P.; m. Christina Teresa Gacek, Aug. 6, 1976; 1 child, Alexander Mark. MFA in Sculpture, Acad. Fine Arts, Cracow, Poland, 1974; postgrad., Art Students League, NYC, 1975. Cert. tchr., NJ; supr. modeling, mold, enlarging, resin crafts. Supr. and instr. sculpture Tech. Inst. of Sculpture - Johnson Atelier, Mercerville, NJ, 1979—; instr. sculpture Rider U., Lawrenceville, NJ, 1992—97, Rutgers U., NJ, 1998—2002. Asst. to sculptor Alexander Ettl, Sculpture House, NY, 1975-79 Bronze/granite monumental sculptures include Monument for The Book, 2008, Book Monument, 2008, Bronze/Granite Lesko, Poland, Shield of Honor, Ulanow, Poland, 2004, Count J. Tarnowski, Tarnobrzeg, Poland, 2003, General Kosciuszko, St. Petersburg, Fla., 2002, Sarmatian - Spirit of Freedom, Hamilton, NJ, 2001, Flame of Freedom, Balt., 2000, Blue Army-1998, Warsaw, Poland, Katyn-1940, Jersey City, NJ, 1991-92, Pope John Paul II, Manhattan, NY, 1991, Ulanow, Poland, 1989, General Anders, Doylestown, Pa., 1995, Father J. Popieluszko, Trenton, NJ, 1987, Avenger, Doylestown, Pa., 1987, Portrait Bust M Curie, 1986, Bayonne, NJ; aluminum sculpture Partisans II, Hamilton, NJ, 1999, Partisans, Boston, 1983, Ignacy Paderewski, Cracow, Poland, 1973; one-man show at Hamilton, NJ, 2000, NY, 2001; exhbn. Mus. of Polish Army, Warsaw, 1995, Contemporary Artists Guild, Lever House, NY, 1991—, Zacheta Nat. Art Gallery, Warsaw, 1991, Fedn. Internat. De La Medaille/Brit. Mus., London, 1992, Cast Iron Gallery, Soho, NY, 1992, Alt. Ext. Gallery, Phila., 1992, Audubon Exhibits-54th Ann. Exhbn., Fed. Hall, NYC, others. Recipient Polonia Restituta Cross, R.P. London, 1989, Gold Order of Merit, Rep. of Poland, 1990, Cultural award Am. Inst. Polish Culture, Washington, 1992; named Comdr. Order Merit of Republic of Poland, 1996, The Monuments Conservancy's Perennial Wisdom award-medal, NYC, 1999, Honorary Citizen of Balt., 2001. Fellow Nat. Sculpture Soc.; mem. Allied Artists of Am. (Silver medal of honor 1985, Elliot Liskin Meml. award 1989, Mems. and Assocs. award 1994), Audubon Artists (Gold Medal of Honor 1996, Silver Medal of Honor 1997, 98), Contemporary Artists Guild, Am. Medallic Sculpture Assn. Republican. Roman Catholic. Avocations: horse jumping, hunting, Judo. Office: PO Box 220380 Brooklyn NY 11222 Office Phone: 609-510-8926. Personal E-mail: andrewpitynski@comcast.net. E-mail: ap@atelier.org.

PITZER, RUSSELL MOSHER, chemistry educator; b. Berkeley, Calif., May 10, 1938; s. Kenneth Sanborn and Jean Elizabeth (Mosher) P.; m. Martha Ann Seares, Sept. 3, 1959; children: Susan M., Kenneth R., David S. BS, Calif. Inst. Tech., 1959; AM, Harvard U., 1961, PhD, 1963. Instr. Calif. Inst. Tech., Pasadena, 1963-66, asst. prof., 1966-68; assoc. prof. Ohio State U., Columbus, 1968-79, prof., 1979—2008, prof. emeritus, 2008—, chmn. dept. chemistry, 1989-94. Acting assoc. dir. Ohio Supercomputer Ctr., Columbus, 1986-87; interim dir. 2001-03, cons. Lawrence Livermore (Calif.) Nat. Lab., 1981-86; cons. Pitzer Coll., Claremont, Calif., 1988—. Contbr. articles to profl. jours. Mem. AAUP, Am. Chem. Soc., Am. Phys. Soc. Office: Ohio State U Dept Chemistry 100 W 18th Ave Columbus OH 43210-1106

PIVEN, FRANCES FOX, political scientist, educator; b. Calgary, Alta., Can., Oct. 10, 1932; arrived in U.S., 1933, naturalized, 1953; d. Albert and Rachel (Paperny) F.; 1 dau., Sarah. BA, U. Chgo., 1953, MA, 1956, PhD, 1962; L.H.D. (hon.), Adelphi U., 1985. Mem. faculty Columbia, 1966-72; prof. polit. sci. Boston U., 1972-82, Grad. Ctr., CUNY, 1982—. Co-author: Regulating the Poor: The Functions of Public Welfare, 1971, 2d edit., 1993, The Politics of Turmoil: Essays on Poverty, Race and the Urban Crisis, 1974, Poor People's Movements, 1977, New Class War, 1982, The Mean Season, 1987, Why Americans Don't Vote, 1988; editor: Labor Parties in Post Industrial Societies, 1992, The Breaking of the American Social Compact, 1997, Why Americans Still Don't Vote, 2000, Work, Welfare and Politics, 2002, The War at Home, 2004, Challenging Authority, 2006, Keeping Down The Black Vote, 2009. Recipient C. Wright Mills award Soc. Study Social Problems, 1971, Fulbright Disting. Lectureship award U. Bologna, 1990, President's award APHA, 1993, Annual award Nat. Assn. Sec. of State, 1994, Lifetime Achievement award Pol. Sociology Am. Sociological Assn., 1995, Disting. Career award, 2000, Pub. Understanding of Sociology award, 2003; Guggenheim fellow, 1973-74; Am. Coun. Learned Socs. awardee, 1982. Mem. ACLU, Am. Polit. Sci. Assn. (v.p. 1981-82), Soc. Study Social Problems (pres. 1980-81, Lee founders award 1992), Am. Sociol. Assn. (pres. 2006-07). Home: PO Box N Millerton NY 12546-0651 Office: CUNY Grad Sch 365 5th Ave New York NY 10016-4309

PIVEN, JEREMY, actor; b. New York, New York, July 26, 1965; s. Byrne and Joyce Piven. Student, Drake U. Actor: (films) Lucas, 1986, One Crazy Summer, 1986, Say Anything, 1989, Elvis Stories, 1989, The Grifters, 1990, White Palace, 1990, The Player, 1992, Body Chemistry II: The Voice of a Stranger, 1992, Bob Roberts, 1992, Singles, 1992, There Goes the Neighborhood, 1992, Judgement Night, 1993, Twenty Bucks, 1993, Car 54, Where Are You?, 1994, Floundering, 1994, PCU, 1994, Twogether, 1994, The Ticket, 1994, Miami Rhapsody, 1995, Dr. Jekyll and Ms. Hyde, 1995, Heat, 1995, Larger Than Life, 1996, Layin' Low, 1996, E=mc—2, 1996, Just Write, 1997, Grosse Pointe Blank, 1997, Livers Ain't Cheap, 1997, Kiss the Girls, 1997, Phoenix, 1998, Very Bad Things, 1998, Music From Another Room, 1998, Red Letters, 2000, The Crew, 2000, The Family Man, 2000, Rush Hour 2, 2001, Serendipity, 2001, Black Hawk Down, 2001, Highway, 2002, Me and Daphne, 2002, Old School, 2003, Runaway Jury, 2003, Scary Movie 3, 2003, Chasing Liberty, 2004, Two for the Money, 2005, Keeping Up with the Steins, 2006, Smokin' Aces, 2006, (voice) Cars, 2006, The Kingdom, 2007, RocknRolla, 2008, The Goods: Live Hard, Sell Hard, 2009; (TV films) 12:01, 1993, Don King: Only in America, 1997, Partners, 1999; (TV series) Carol & Company, 1990, Rugrats (voice), 1991, The Larry Sanders Show, 1992—93, Pride and Joy, 1995, Ellen, 1995—98, Cupid, 1998, Entourage, 2004— (Emmy award for Outstanding Supporting Actor in a comedy series, 2006, Primetime Emmy for Outstanding Supporting Actor in a Comedy Series, Acad. TV Art and Scis., 2007, 2008, Best Performance by an Actor in a Supporting Role in a Series, Mini-Series or Motion Picture Made for TV, Golden Globe award, 2008); (Broadway plays) Fat Pig, 2004, Speed-the-Plow, 2008; exec. prodr. Jeremy Piven's Journey of a Lifetime, 2006. Office: c/o Tracy Brennan Creative Artists Agy LCC 2000 Avenue of the Stars Los Angeles CA 90067

PIVEN, JOSEPH, psychiatrist, educator; BS in Psychology, U. Md., MD. Intern Good Samaritan Hosp., Phoenix; resident in psychiatry Johns Hopkins Hosp., fellow in child & adolescent psychiatry; fellow in psychiatric genetics Johns Hopkins U. Sch. Medicine; prof. psychiatry UNC Sch. Medicine. Office: 101 Manning Dr Chapel Hill NC 27514 Office Phone: 919-843-8641. E-mail: jpiven@med.unc.edu.*

PIVEN, PETER ANTHONY, architect, management consultant; b. Bklyn., Jan. 3, 1939; s. William Meyer and Sylvia Lee (Greenberg) P.; m. Caroline Cooper, July 9, 1961; children: Leslie Ann, Joshua Lawrence. AB, Colgate U., Hamilton, NY, 1960; MArch, U. Pa., Phila., 1963; MS, Columbia U., NYC, 1964. Diplomate: cert. Nat. Coun. Archtl. Registration Bds.; registered arch., NY, Pa., NJ. Arch. Westermann-Miller Assocs., NYC, 1964-66, Bernard Rothzeid, A.I.A., NYC, 1967-68; v.p. Caudill Rowlett Scott, NYC, 1968-72; prin. Geddes Brecher Qualls Cunningham, Phila., 1972-87; pres. The Coxe Group, Inc., Phila., 1980-90, dir., prin. cons., 1980—. Adj. prof. U. Pa. Grad. Sch. Fine Arts, 1989—, Rensselaer Poly. Inst. Sch. Architecture, 1994—; vis. instr. Harvard U. Grad. Sch. Design.; lectr. U. Pa. Sch. Design, 2005; mem. 14th edit. com. Architects Handbook Profl. Practice; dir. PennPraxis, 2008. Author: Compensation Management: A Guideline for Small Firms, 1982, Architect's Essentials of Ownership Transition, 2002; co-author: Success Strategies for Design Professionals, 1987, Architect's Essentials of Starting a Design Firm, 2003, Architect's Essentials of Starting, Assessing and Transitioning a Design Firm, 2008; contbg. editor: Archtl. Record and Design Intelligence; author (contbg.): Architects Handbook of Professional Practice, 1994, 2001, 2008, Architects Handbook of Professional Practice Update, 2004, 2005, 2006. Mem. NYC Cmty. Planning Bd., 1969-72. Recipient Thomas U. Walter award, Phila., 2008. Fellow AIA (chmn. fin. mgmt. com. 1976-80, chmn. Fellows Jury 1998, mem. conv. task force 1998, mem. Nat. Ethics Coun. 1998-2004, chmn. 2004, pres. Phila. chpt. 1980); mem. Phila. C. of C. (dir. 1980-81), The Carpenters Co. of City and County of Phila. (mng. com. 1989-91). Home: Apt 10 201 Queen St Philadelphia PA 19147 Office: The Coxe Group Inc 1904 3rd Ave Seattle WA 98101-3097 Home Phone: 215-952-2780. Business E-Mail: ppiven@coxegroup.com.

PIVER, M. STEVEN, gynecologic oncologist; b. Washington, Sept. 29, 1934; s. Harry Samuel and Sonia (Bard) P.; m. Susan Myers, June 25, 1958; children: Debra Ellen, Carolyn Jan, Kenneth Stuart. BS, Gettysburg Coll., 1957; MD, Temple U., 1961. Diplomate Am. Bd. Ob-Gyn, Am. Coll. Surgeons. Intern Nazareth Hosp., Phila., 1961—62; resident Johns Hopkins U. Hosp., Balt., 1962; resident ob-gyn. Pa. Hosp. U. Pa., Phila., 1965—68; fellow gynecologic oncology Hosp. Tumor Inst. U. Tex., Houston, 1968—70; asst. prof. gynecologic oncology UNC Sch. Medicine, 1970—71; assoc. chief gynecologic oncology Roswell Park Cancer Inst., Buffalo, 1972—83, founder, dir. Gilda Radner Familial Ovarian Cancer Registry, 1981—, chief gynecologic oncology, 1984—97; clin. prof., dir. divsn. gynecologic oncology SUNY, Buffalo, 1986—87, prof. gynecology, 1998—, chair emeritus gynecologic oncology, 1998—. Cons., editor Yearbook of Cancer, 1972-88; assoc. editor Nat. Cancer Inst., PDQ, 1984—; mem. editl. bd. The Female Patient, 1989—, Oncology Reports, 1993—; author: Ovarian Malignancies: Clinical Care of Adults and Adolescents, 1983, Gilda's Disease: Sharing Personal Experiences and a Medical Perspective on Ovarian Cancer, 1996, Myths and Facts About Ovarian Cancer, 1997; editor: Ovarian Malignancies: Diagnostic and Therapeutic Advances, 1987, Manual of Gynecologic Oncology/Gynecology, 1989, Conversations About Cancer, 1990, Handbook of Gynecologic Oncology, 1995; contbr. more than 300 articles to profl. jours. Bd. dirs. United Way Buffalo Erie County, 1986-91; chmn. bd. trustees D'Youville Coll., Buffalo, 1989—; pres. Friends Night People, Buffalo, 1988-97. Capt. USAF, 1962-64. Hon. fellow Phi Beta Kappa, Gettysburg Coll., 1956, Tex. Assn. Obstetricians Gynecologists, 1983, Alpha Omega Alpha, Temple U. Sch. Medicine, 1995; named Citizen Yr., Buffalo News, 1989; recipient YMCA Leadership award Buffalo YMCA, 1990, Brotherhood/Sisterhood Award Medicine (Western NY Region), NCCJ, 1991, St. Marguerite D'Youville Coll. Cmty. Svc. award, 1992. Fellow ACS, Am. Coll. Obstetricians and Gynecologists; mem. Am. Soc. Clin. Oncology, Soc. Gynecologic Oncologists, Soc. Surg. Oncology, Am. Radium Soc., Phi Beta Kappa, Alpha Omega Alpha. Achievements include documentation of hydroxyurea as a radiation sensitizer in cervix cancer that significantly improves cure rate and that ovarian cancer can be inherited; patent for method of enhancing the efficacy of anti-tumor agents. Home: 315 Lincoln Pky Buffalo NY 14216-3127 Office: Sisters Hosp 2157 Main St Buffalo NY 14214-2692 Business E-Mail: mpiver@chsbuffalo.org.

PIWNICA-WORMS, HELEN M., cell biologist, educator; BA, St. Olaf Coll.; PhD in Microbiology, Immunology, Duke Univ.; postdoctoral study, Dana-Farber Cancer Inst. Faculty Tufts Univ. Med. Sch., Harvard Med. Sch.; staff Beth Israel Hosp., Boston; prof. cell biology, physiology, internal medicine Washington Univ., St. Louis; and investigator Howard Hughes Med. Inst., 1994—. Former investigator Am. Heart Assn. Fellow: Am. Acad. Arts & Scis. Office: 554 McDonnell Med Sci Bldg Box 8228 Washington Univ Saint Louis MO 63110 Office Phone: 314-362-6834. Business E-Mail: hpiwnica@cellbiology.wustl.edu.

PIXLEY, JOHN SEYMOUR, immunology educator; b. New Haven, Conn., Sept. 6, 1950; s. John Seymour and Catherine (Orr) P.; m. Janice A. Coburn, Nov. 2, 1975; children: Aaron Ross and Jedediah Harris. BS, Tufts U., 1972; MD, N.Y. Med. Coll., 1975. Diplomate Am. Bd. Internal Medicine and Rheumatology. Intern Westchester County Med. Ctr., Valhalla, N.Y., 1975-76, resident, 1978-81; fellow rheumatology/immunology SUNY, Stony Brook, 1982-84; gen. med. officer USPHS Indian Health Svc., Parker, Ariz., 1976-78; attending physician Montefiore Med. Ctr., Bronx, N.Y., 1981-82, Cen. N.J. Med. Group, New Brunswick, 1984-85, Fallston (Md.) Gen. Hosp., 1985-87; asst. prof. U. Nev. Sch. Medicine, Reno, 1987-96, assoc. prof., 1996—. Med. liaison North Nev. Arthritis Found., 1989—, North Nev. Lupus Found., 1988—. Contbr. articles to profl. jours. Recipient rsch. grant Reno Cancer Ctr., 1988—. Fellow ACP, AAAS, Am. Coll. Rheumatology, Am. Fedn. Clin. Rsch. Unitarian/Universalist. Office: 1500 E 2nd St Ste 302 Reno NV 89502-1198 Office Phone: 775-784-7500.

PIZA, ARTHUR LUIZ, painter; b. Brazil, Jan. 13, 1928; came to France, 1951; One-man exhbns.: Brazil, Germany, Yugoslavia, U.S., France, Switzerland, Sweden, Spain, Belgium, Italy; represented in permanent mus. and pvt. collections. Decorated Chevalier Des Arts Et Lettres; recipient Purchase prize, 1953; Nat. prize for Prints São Paulo Biennale, 1959, Nat. prize Brazilian critics, 1994; prizes at biennales at Ljubljana, 1961, Santiago, 1966, Venice, 1966, Grenchen triennale, 1961, biennales of Norway and Mex., 1980, biennale San Juan, Puerto Rico, 1990. Address: 16 rue Dauphine 75006 Paris France Personal E-mail: 28azip3@wanadoo.fr. Business E-Mail: avec.piza@netcourrier.com.

PIZANA, ORLANDO AKHIEM, communications educator; b. Boston, Aug. 26, 1973; s. Armando Mark and Annette Pizana. BA in English, Howard U., Washington, 1999; MS in English Edn., Fla. State U., Tallahassee, 2004. Tchg. asst. Sch. Edn. Computer Learning Ctr. Fla. State U., 2002—04; instr. Sylvan Learning Ctr., Tampa, Fla., 2004—06; instr., comm. St. Petersburg Coll., Fla., 2004—. English tutor, St. Petersburg, 2004—. Mem.: Omega Psi Phi Frat. Inc. (Eta Rho Chpt.) (co-chmn., scholarship com. 2007—08, Superior Svc. award 2003). Baptist. Office: St Petersburg Coll PO Box 13489 Saint Petersburg FL 33733 Personal E-mail: opizana@hotmail.com. Business E-Mail: pizana.orlando@spcollege.edu.

PIZARRO, CHRISTIAN, surgeon, department chairman; married. MD, U. Chile, Santiago, 1985. Chief, pediat. cardiothoracic surgery Alfred I duPont Hosp. Children, Wilmington, Del., 2004—. Fellow: ACS; mem.: Euroean Assn. Cardiothoracic Surgeons, Internat. Soc. Heart & Lung Transplantation, Congenital Heart Surgeons Soc., Soc. Thoracic Surgeons. Office: Alfred I duPont Hosp Children 1600 Rockland Rd Wilmington DE 19803

PIZER, DONALD, author, educator; b. NYC, Apr. 5, 1929; s. Morris and Helen (Rosenfeld) P.; m. Carol Hart, Apr. 7, 1966; children— Karin, Ann, Margaret. BA, UCLA, 1951, MA, 1952, PhD, 1955. Mem. faculty Tulane U., 1957—2001, prof. English, 1964-72, Pierce Butler prof. English, 1972—2001, Mellon prof. humanities, 1978-79. Author: Hamlin Garland's Early Work and Career, 1960, Realism and Naturalism in Nineteenth-Century American Literature, 1966, The Novels of Frank Norris, 1966, The Novels of Theodore Dreiser, 1976, Twentieth-Century American Literary Naturalism: An Interpretation, 1982, Dos Passos "USA": A Critical Study, 1988, The Theory and Practice of American Literary Naturalism, 1993, American Expatriate Writing and the Paris Moment, 1996, Am. Naturalism and the Jews, 2008. Served with AUS, 1955-57. Guggenheim fellow, 1962; Am. Council Learned Socs. fellow, 1971-72; Nat. Endowment Humanities fellow, 1978-79 Mem. MLA. Home: 6320 Story St New Orleans LA 70118-6340

PIZER, HOWARD CHARLES, sports and entertainment executive; b. Chgo., Oct. 23, 1941; s. Edwin and Estyr (Seeder) P.; m. Sheila Graff, June 14, 1964; children: Jacqueline, Rachel. BBA, U. Wis., 1963; JD magna cum laude, Northwestern U., 1966. Assoc. McDermott, Will & Emery, Chgo., 1966-72; ptnr. Katten, Muchin, Zavis, Chgo., 1972-74; exec. v.p., gen. counsel Balcor Co., Skokie, Ill., 1975-80; exec. v.p. Chgo. White Sox, Chgo., 1981—. Exec. v.p. United Ctr. Joint Venture. Past pres. Chgo. Spl. Olympics; bd. dirs. Chgo. Conv. and Tourism Bur., Inc., 1983—, Spl. Children's Charities, 1984—, Chgo. Baseball Cancer Charities, 1983—, Near West Side Cmty. Devel. Corp. Mem. Chgo. Bar Assn., Standard Club Chgo., Briarwood County. Home: 300 Euclid Ave Winnetka IL 60093-3606 Office: Chgo White Sox 333 W 35th St Chicago IL 60616-3651

PIZITZ, RICHARD ALAN, retail executive, real estate company officer; b. Birmingham, Ala., Feb. 24, 1930; s. Isadore and Hortense (Hirsch) P.; m. Joan Black; children: Richard Alan Jr., Jill Carole, Susan Lyn. BA, Washington & Lee U., 1951; MBA, Harvard U., 1953. Mdse. mgr. Pizitz Dept. Stores, Birmingham, 1953-59, v.p., 1959-66, pres., 1966-86, chmn. bd., 1986-87; chmn. Pizitz Mgmt. Group, Birmingham, 1987—. Pres. United Way, Birmingham, 1988, Ala. Commn. on Higher Edn., 1987-95; pres. Better Bus. Bur., Birmingham, 1962; mem. Ala adv. commn. U.S. Commn. on Civil Rights, 1985. Recipient Erskine Ramsay award, 1974; named Mktg. Man of Yr., Am. Mktg. Assn., 1966, Man of Yr., Young Men's Bus. Club, 1970. Mem. Ala. Commn. on Higher Edn., Birmingham C. of C. (pres. 1970), Ala. Retail Assn. (pres. 1965). Avocations: flying, skiing, tennis, scuba diving. Office: Pizitz Mgmt Group 2112 11th Ave S Ste 528 Birmingham AL 35205-2850 Address: 2936 Redmont Park Ln Birmingham AL 35205-2136

PIZOT-HAYMORE, FABIENNE, language educator, translator; m. Maury Haymore, Nov. 21, 1998. MA in French, Case Western Res U., Montpellier, France, 2006. Cert. didactics in tchg. ESL Montpellier,

1998. Lectr. French Case Western Res. U., Cleve., 2000—; instr. French Lakeland CC, Kirtland, Ohio, 2002—05. Transl., proofreading, alignments, non linear audio and video editing pvt. practice in numerous countries, 1994—; cons. Time Keeping Sys., Inc., Garfield Heights, Ohio, 2001; rsch., scripting, story boarding, cons. Digital Multi Media, LLC, Cleve., 2004—, voice over artist, 2006—; linguist TippingSprung, LLC, NYC, 2008. Translator: (novels) Un Spasme de Vacuité. Merit and Resources scholarship, French Govt., 1992—98. Mem.: Transl. Zone, ProZ, Aquarius, French Am. C. of C. Office: Case Western Res Univ 10900 Euclid Ave Cleveland OH 44106-7118 Personal E-mail: fabienne.pizothaymore@gmail.com. Business E-Mail: fgh2@case.edu.

PIZZAGALLI, JAMES, construction and real estate company executive; b. Burlington, Vt., Nov. 23, 1944; s. Angelo and Theresa (Moalli) P.; m. Judy Rock, June 21, 1969; 1 child, Michael. BS, U. Vt., 1966; JD, Boston U., 1969. Treas. Pizzagalli Constrn. Co., Burlington, Vt., 1969—76, v.p., 1976—91, chmn., CEO, 1991—98, co-chmn., 1998—; pres. Pizzagalli Properties, LLC, 1971—. Dir. Chittenden Corp., Burlington, 1982-2007, AGC Edn. Found., Washington, 1992-2004, Shelburne (Vt.) Mus., 1983-92, 2000—; life dir. Assn. Gen. Contractors, Washington, 1976—, atty.-at law. Trustee U. Vt., 2000—05. Mem.: The Moles. Republican. Roman Catholic. Office: Pizzagalli Properties LLC PO Box 2009 South Burlington VT 05407 E-mail: jpizzagalli@pizzagalliproperties.com.

PIZZAMIGLIO, ALBERT THEODORE (AL PIERSON), conductor; b. Ill. m. Nancy Alice Gilman, Mar. 27, 1978; five children. Studied music theory and composition; BA, MA, Ill. State U.; advanced music studies, U. Ill. Condr. Al Pierson Big Band U.S.A., 1975-89, Guy Lombardo's Royal Canadians, Aubrey, Tex., 1989—. Nat. youth music dir. Am. Inst. of Cooperation; co-host, owner TV show, Bloomington, Ill.; tchr. high sch. and coll., amb. music Ill. State U. Musician, composer, arranger, vocalist, band leader; founder Al Pierson & Big Band U.S.A. (Best New Dance Band in the Country 1975, America's Number One Dance Band 1977), performed for fourteen yrs. at numerous famous ballrooms in the midwest and many prestigious pvt. parties, on twenty internat. dance tours including Europe, the Orient, the Middle East, the Caribbean, Mexico, Hawaii, Alaska and Tahiti; released 15 albums; recorded Guy Lombardo music album, 2000, now with Guy Lombardo's Royal Canadians performing throughout the continental U.S. and Can. and 44 other fgn. countries; condr. PBS TV series (past three yrs. and continuing), 1977, PBS TV spls., 1994, 95, 96, 97, 2000, Presdl. Inauguration Festivities, 1994. Mem. Pres. George Bush Inauguration, 2004, Pres. Bill Clinton's Inauguration, 1992. Recipient Superman award for helping save 32 lives in snowstorm, 1997, 98, 99, Ill. State U. Disting. Alumni award, 2004; inducted into Ballroom Dancers' Hall of Fame, 1976; named amb. Music for World pres. Ill. State U., 1998, Alumnus of Yr. Ill. State U., 2004-, Mens Club award, Ill. Club Office: Gilman Inc Artists Mgmt RR 1 Aubrey TX 76227-9801 Personal E-mail: apglo@aol.com.

PIZZINGRILLI, KIM, state official; BBA in Econs., U. Pitts., Johnstown, 1981; M Govtl. Adminstrn., U. Pa., 1988. Auditor, acct., and asst. dir. bur. of audits Pa. Treasury Dept., 1981-87; sr. regulatory analyst Pa. Ind. Regulatory Rev. Commn., 1987-95; spl. asst. to sec. Dept. of State, Harrisburg, Pa., 1995-96, dep. sec. regulatory programs, 1996-98, acting sec., 1998-99, sec. of the commonwealth, 1999—2002; commr. Pa. Pub. Utility Comm., 2002—. Mem. Bd. of Property, Bd. of Fin. and Revenue, State of Pa.; mem. Pa. State Athletic Commn., Pa. State Nav. Commn. for the Delaware River and its Navigable Tributaries, mem. Pa. Mcpl. Retirement Bd.; keeper Great Seal of the Commonwealth. Mem. Nat. Assn. Sec. of State, Women Exec. in State Govt. Republican. Office: Pennsylvania Pub Utility Commn PO Box 3265 Harrisburg PA 17105-3265*

PIZZO, PHILIP A., dean, pediatrician, educator; b. NYC, Dec. 6, 1944; BA, Fordham U., 1966; MD, U. Rochester, 1970. Diplomate Am. Bd. Pediat., Am. Bd. Hematology/Oncology. Intern Children's Hosp. Med. Ctr., Boston, 1970-71, jr. asst. resident, 1971-72, sr. resident, 1972-73; clin. assoc. Pediatric Oncology Br. of Nat. Cancer Inst., 1973-75, investigator, 1975-76, sr. investigator, 1976-80; head infectious disease sect. Pediatric Br. of Nat. Cancer Inst., 1980-96, chief pediat., 1982-96; sci. dir. divsn. clin. scis. Nat. Cancer Inst., 1994-96; prof. pediat. Sch. Medicine, Uniformed Svcs. U. Health Sci., 1987-96; Thomas Morgan Rotch prof., chmn. dept. pediat. Harvard U. Sch. Medicine, Boston, 1996—2001; dean Stanford U. Sch. Medicine, 2001—. Mem. Elizabeth Glaser Pediatric AIDS Found. (bd. dirs. 1996-2006), Internat. Immunocompromised Host Soc., IDSA (bd. dirs. 1996-99), Calif. Healthcare Inst. (bd. dirs. 2003-), NIH Blue Ribbon Panel, Admin Boal, HAMC, Ind. Citizen Oversight Com., AAHC (bd. dirs. 2006-), Inst. Medicine (coun. mem. 2006-). Office: Stanford U Sch Med 300 Pasteur Dr, Ste M121 Palo Alto CA 94305 also: 730 Welch Rd Palo Alto CA 94304 Office Phone: 650-724-5688. Office Fax: 650-725-8040. E-mail: philip.pizzo@stanford.edu.*

PIZZO, SALVATORE VINCENT, pathologist; b. Phila., June 22, 1944; s. George J. Pizzo and Aida (Alcaro) Lepore; m. Carol Ann Kurkowski, Dec. 28, 1968 (div. 1987); children: Steven, David, Susan. PhD, Duke U., 1972; BS, St. Joseph's Coll., 1966; MD, Duke U., 1973. Asst. prof. Duke U. Med. Ctr., Durham, NC, 1976-80, assoc. prof., 1980-85, prof., 1985—, disting. prof. pathology, 2006—, dir. med. scientist tng. program, 1987—2007, chmn., 1991—. Mem., chmn. program rev. com. NIH, Bethesda, Md., 1986-90; vice chmn. Gordon Conf. Proteases, Holderness, N.H., 1990, chmn., 1992-96; cons. in field, 1980—; mem. Cellular and Molecular Basis of Disease Rev. Com., 1990-96. Contbr. articles to profl. jours. Grantee NIH, 1976—, Am. Cancer Soc., 1976—; Disting. Faculty award, Duke U., 2004, Dean's award for excellence in mentoring, 2004; named one of the top 150 cited authors for jours. in the life sciences. Fellow AAAS; mem. Am. Heart Assn. (exec. com. Thrombosis coun. 1990, 92), Am. Chem. Soc., Am. Assn. Pathologists (program com. 1985-88, long range planning com. 1990-92), Am. Soc. Biological Chemists, Alpha Sigma Nu, Phi Beta Kappa, Alpha Omega Alpha, Sigma Xi. Achievements include patents in field; research in lipoproteins in coagulation and fibronolysis, a link to atherosclerosis, anticoagulation drug development; identification of ATP synthase as the target for Angiostatin action. Office: Duke U Med Ctr PO Box 3712 Durham NC 27710-0001 Office Phone: 919-684-3528, 919-421-3058. Business E-Mail: pizzo001@mc.duke.edu.

PIZZORNO-SIMPSON, MARIE C., biology professor, department chairman; b. Covina, Calif., Aug. 27, 1963; d. Albert Lawrence and Antoinette Fogliani Pizzorno; m. Thomas E. Simpson, Aug. 11, 2001. BA, Whittier Coll., Calif., 1985; PhD, Johns Hopkins Sch. Medicine, Balt., 1991. Predoctoral fellow Johns Hopkins Sch. Medicine, 1985—91; postdoctoral fellow Princeton U., NJ, 1991—95; vis. asst. prof. Vassar Coll., Poughkeepsie, NY, 1995—96; asst. prof. biology Bucknell U., Lewisburg, Pa., 1996—2002, assoc. prof. of biology, 2002—, chair, dept. biology, 2007—. Contbr. articles to sci. jourls. Recipient William Pierce Bogar Jr. MD award, Bucknell U., 2007. Mem.: Am. Soc. Virology, Am. Soc. Microbiology. Episcopalian. Avocations: painting, reading, needlecrafts. Office: Bucknell Univ Dept Biology Lewisburg PA 17837

PIZZUTI, RONALD A., real estate developer; m. Ann Pizzuti; 3 children. BS, Kent State U., 1962. Chmn., CEO Pizzuti Cos., Columbus, Ohio, 1976—. Mem. Ohio Arts & Sports Facilities Commn.; bd. trustees Kenyon Coll.; chair bd. trustees Kent State U.; bd. dir. Kent State Found. Recipient Shining Stars of Seminole County. Lifetime Achievement award, 2002; named one of Top 200 Collectors, ARTnews Mag., 2003—08. Mem.: Columbus C. of C. (exec. com.). Avocation: Collecting modern and contemporary art. Office: Pizzuti Cos Ste 800 Two Miranova Pl Columbus OH 43215 Business E-Mail: rpizzuti@pizzuti.com.

PLA, ARTHUR JAMES, school system administrator; s. Amelio Pla Jr. and Alice Pla Walls; m. Aline Cloud Pla, July 7, 2000; children: Cyndra Miles, Renea Smith, Arthur James Jr. BS in Edn., Fla. A&M U., Tallahassee, 1970, MEd, 1972; postgrad., Fla. State U., Tallahassee, 1972—74. Cert. life ins. agt. Fla.; tchr. Fla., lic. real estate agt. Fla. Tchr., coach Leon HS, Tallahassee, 1970—72, asst. prin., 1973—78; dir. student svcs. Leon County Schs., Tallahassee, 1977—85, dir. alternative edn. ctr., 1985—87, dir. transp., 1999—; asst. prin. Lincoln HS, Tallahassee, 1987—97, Raa Mid. Sch., Tallahassee, 1997—99. Cons. in field. Mem. exec. com. North Fla. Edn. Credit Union, Tallahassee, 1976—80, ARC, Tallahassee, 1978—81, chmn. Tallahassee chpt., 1981—84; coach Little League Football and Baseball, Tallahassee, 1987—90. Recipient Centurion award, Franklin Ins. Co., 1985, Work Horse award, Turner Heritage Homes, 1995, Diversified Coop. Edn. Svc. award, Lincoln HS, 1989—90, Pride award, Lincoln HS PTO, 1990, Outstanding Adminstr. award, Leon County Schs., 1993, Disting. Minority Educator award, 1993; named Rookie of Yr., Turner Heritage Homes, 1993, Salesman of Mo., 1994, 1995, 1996, Prodr. of Mo., 1995, Outstanding Asst. Prin., Leon HS, 1973—78. Mem.: NAACP (Black Achievers award 2004), Fla. Assn. Pupil Transp., Fla. Assn. Sch. Adminstrs., So. Assn. Secondary Schs. (mem. accreditation com.). Democrat. African Methodist Episcopal. Avocations: camping, fishing, football. Office: Leon County Schs 3395 W Tharpe St Tallahassee FL 32303 Business E-Mail: plaa@mail.leon.k12.fl.us.

PLACEK-ZIMMERMAN, ELLYN CLARE, school system administrator, educator, consultant; b. Chgo., Sept. 3, 1951; d. Clarence Joseph and Jerrine LaMarr (Ruhlow) Placek; m. Allan John Zimmerman, Aug. 10, 1974; 1 child, Alissa Jan. BS, No. Ill. U., 1973, MS, 1977, cert. in advanced study, 1978, EdD, 1982. Tchr. Arlington Heights (Ill.) Pub. Schs., 1973-75, 75-76, dir. libr. and learning ctr., 1976-81, tchr. lang. arts and reading jr. high sch., 1981-84, tchr. kindergarten, 1984-86; prin. Orchard Street Sch., Fox River Grove, Ill., 1988-89, Pritchett Sch., Buffalo Grove, Ill., 1989-90, Round Lake (Ill.) Pub. Schs., 1992-93, asst. supt. curiculum and instrn., 1993-2001; asst. to supt. curriculum and instrn. Wood Dale (Ill.) Pub. Schs., 2001—03, prin., 2003—07, ednl. cons., 2008—; cons. Lake County Regional Office Edn., Ill., 2008—. Dir. Ill. State grant "At Risk Program" for pre-sch. children, Cary Pub. Schs., 1986-87; mem. part-time faculty Coll. Edn., Roosevelt U., Chgo., 1983-84, 88-89; tchr. jr. high social, reading and lang. arts studies, 1988; cons. in field; mem. steering com. Curriculum 2000 Conf., De Kalb, Ill., 1985; lectr. in field; supr. student tchrs. Ill. State U., Normal, 1986, Roosevelt U., Chgo., 1988-89, Elmhurst Coll., 1992; freelance writer Daily Herald newspaper. Contbg. author Feeling Good About Food. Sec. Scarsdale Estates Assn., 2009, pres., Arlington Heights, 1983; bd. dirs. ABC/25 Found., 1991-92. Mem. Ill. ASCD (registration com. for fall conf. 1987, triple I arrangements com. 1988), Ill. Assn. Tchrs. English (cons., spkr. conf. 1984), Ill. Women Adminstrs. (publicty com. conf. 1985), PTA (hon. life). Avocations: playing guitar, calligraphy. Home: 402 E Orchard St Arlington Heights IL 60005-2660

PLACENTI, FRANK MICHAEL, lawyer; b. Columbus, Ohio, Sept. 2, 1953; s. Anthony Joseph and Evelyn (Piteo) P.; m. Tobi M. Placenti, Apr. 29, 1971. BA cum laude, Ohio State U., 1975, JD summa cum laude, 1979. Bar: Ariz. 1979, U.S. Dist. Ct. Ariz. 1979, U.S. Ct. Appeals (9th cir.) 1979. Ptnr., transactions and corp. governance Squire, Sanders and Dempsey LLP, Phoenix. Chmn., Phoenix Childrens Hosp. Found. Chmn. Super Bowl Kick-Off Luncheon, 1996, NBA All Star Kick-Off Luncheonj, 1995, Phoenix C. of C., 1991—92, Boys & Girls Clubs Met. Phoenix, 1992—93; chmn. bd. dirs. Phoenix Children's Hosp. Found., 2005—. James K. Barton Meml. scholar Ohio State U., 1977-79; named one of Outstanding Young Men in Am., 1981. Mem. ABA (litigation, communication law and young lawyers sects.), Maricopa County Bar (chmn. com., lectr. on litigation 1985-86), Greater Phoenix Leadership, Phoenix C. of C., Order of Coif, Phi Kappa Theta, Phi Kappa Tau, Phi Eta Sigma. Avocations: golf, travel, wine. Office: Squire Sanders and Dempsey LLP 40 North Central Ave Phoenix AZ 85004-4498 Office Phone: 602-528-4000.

PLACERES, MARTHA, music educator; d. Alfonso Placeres and Martha Gonzalez. MA, U. Tex., 2005. Lectr. Conservatorio Musica, Puebla, 1999—2001; asst. master tech. instr. U. Tex., Brownsville, 2001—. Contbr. articles to profl. jours.

PLACIK, OTTO JOSEPH, plastic surgeon; b. June 26, 1962; BS in Medicine, Northwestern U., 1985, MD with distinction, 1987. Cert. Nat. Bd. Med. Examiners, 1988, diplomate Am. Bd. Plastic Surgery. Resident in gen. surgery Northwestern U., 1987—90, resident in plastic surgery, 1990—93; adj. staff Evanston Hosp. Corp., Glenview, Ill., 1991—92, 1994, locum tenens staff, 1995, attending staff, 1996—; fellow Shriners Hosp. for Crippled Children, 1992, consulting staff, 1995—; fellow in aesthetic reconstruction, surgical house officer St. Joseph Hosp., Chgo., 1993; fellow microvascular and hand surgery Davies Med. Ctr., U. Calif., San Francisco, 1994; non-voting attending staff Northwest Cmty. Hosp., Arlington Heights, Ill., 1995—; courtesy staff Meth. Hosp., Chgo., 1995—; plastic surgeon MD Aesthetics Skin Care Ctr., Arlington Heights, Ill., 1995—; courtesy staff Holy Family Hosp., Des Plaines, Ill., 1996—2003; asst. prof. clin. surgery Northwestern U., 1997—; vice chief Sect. Plastic Surgery, Northwest Cmty. Hosp., 1998, 1999, chief, 2000, 2001; consulting staff St. Elisabeth Hosp., Chgo., 1999—. ASPRS resident del. Coun. Med. Splty. Socs., 1993, mem. resident task force, 93; mem. interdisciplinary cancer com. Northwest Cmty. Hosp., 1995, mem. emergency care com., 98; mem. ISMIE Plastic Surgery Subcommittee, 2000; treas. plastic surgery edn. rsch. Northwestern U., 2002; mem. Enhance Ednl. Found. Scholarship Com., 2006—. Assoc. editor Chicago Health Mag., Chicago Image, 2003—. Named to Consumers' Guide to Top Doctors, 2002, 2005—07, America's Cosmetic Doctors and Dentists, 2003, The Best of the US, 2007. Mem.: Soc. Laparoendoscopic Surgeons, Am. Soc. Aesthetic Plastic Surgery, Am. Acad. Facial Plastic and Reconstructive Surgery, Lipoplasty Soc., Ill. State Med. Soc., AMA (Physician's Recognition award 1996—99), Chgo. Soc. Plastic Surgery, Midwest Assn. Plastic Surgeons, Alpha Omega Alpha (co-pres. 1986, Honor Med. Soc. 2005). Office: Assoc Plastic Surgeons SC MD Aesthetics Skin Care Ctr 880 W Central Rd Ste 3100 Arlington Heights IL 60005-2467 also: 680 N Lake Shore Dr Ste 830 Chicago IL 60611-2201 also: MD Aesthetics LLC 845 N Michigan Ave Ste 923E Chicago IL 60611 also: Northwestern U Montgomery Ward Meml Bldg 303 E Chicago Ave Evanston IL 60208 Office Phone: 847-398-1660, 312-787-5313, 312-335-2070. Office Fax: 847-398-1784. Business E-Mail: bodysculptor@asprsdial.org, o-placik@northwestern.edu.

PLACILLA, CHRISTINA DAWN, music educator; b. Troy, NY, July 2, 1974; d. Melford and Kathleen Placilla; m. Ryan William Peller, Feb. 10, 2006. MusB, Calif. State U., Long Beach, 1996; MusM, Hartt Sch., U. Hartford, Conn., 2000; MusD, U. Colo., Boulder, 2004. Asst. prof. strings Winston-Salem State U., NC, 2005—; artist viola and chamber music U. NC Sch. Arts Summer Session, Winston-Salem, 2006; violist Ensemble Argos, Winston-Salem, 2006—, Ko-Lab Projekt, Winston-Salem, 2007—. Contbr. articles to musical jour. (David Dalton Rsch. award, 2000); musician: (recording) Remembrances From Home (Winston-Salem Arts Coun. Regional Artist grant, 2007). Organizer and clinician Winston-Salem Forsyth County Schs., 2005—07. Achievements include research in pdagogy of chamber Music. Office: Winston-Salem State Univ Fine Arts Bldg Rm 208 Winston Salem NC 27110 Business E-Mail: placillac@wssu.edu.

PLACKE, JAMES ANTHONY, retired diplomat; b. Grand Island, Nebr., June 14, 1935; s. Gerhard F. and Florence E. (McCormick) P.; m. Mary Sabina Shea, July 25, 1959; children— Elizabeth, Stephen, Carolyn B.Sc., U. Nebr., 1957, MA, 1959. Commd. fgn. service officer Dept. State, 1958; econ. counselor Am. Embassy, Tripoli, Libya, 1970-71, Ottawa, 1977-79; fgn. service insp. Dept. State, Washington, 1971-73, dir. office food policy, 1974-76; minister Am. Embassy, Jiddah, Saudi Arabia, 1979-82; dep. asst. sec. Nr. Eastern and South Asian Affairs Bur., Dept. State, Washington, 1982-85; pvt. practice, 1986—90; dir. Cambridge Energy Rsch. Assoc., 1991-2000, sr. assoc., 2001—09. Del. UN World Food Conf., 1974; mem. econ. expert working group Iraq Study Group, 2006. Recipient Meritorious Honor award Dept. State, 1969, 71; Presdl. Meritorious Service award, 1985

PLAEGER, FREDERICK JOSEPH, II, lawyer; b. New Orleans, Sept. 10, 1953; s. Edgar Leonard and Bernice Virginia (Schiwetz) P.; m. Kathleen Helen Dickson, Nov. 19, 1977; children: Douglas A., Catherine E. BS, La. State U., 1976, JD, 1977. Bar: La. 1978, Tex. 1999, U.S. Dist. Ct. (ea. dist.) La. 1978, U.S. Ct. Appeals (5th cir.) 1981, U.S. Supreme Ct. 1989. Law clk. U.S. Dist. Ct. (ea. dist.) La., New Orleans, 1977-79; assoc. Milling, Benson, Woodward, Hillyer, Pierson & Miller, New Orleans, 1979-85, ptnr., 1985-89; v.p., gen. counsel, corp. sec. La. Land and Exploration Co., New Orleans, 1989-97; v.p., gen. counsel Burlington Resources Inc., Houston, 1997—2006; sr. v.p., gen. counsel EOG Resources, 2007—. Selected mem. Met. Area Com. Leadership Forum, 1986; bd. dirs. Soc. Environ. Edn., La. Nature and Sci. Ctr., 1992—94; trustee Houston Ballet, 2001—; bd. dirs. New Orleans Speech and Hearing Ctr., 1985—91, pres., 1988—90; bd. dirs. Children's Oncology Svcs. La. (Ronald McDonald Ho. of New Orleans), 1987—90. Recipient Service to Mankind award Sertoma, 1989; named Tex. Super Lawyer, Tex. Monthly Mag., 2004, 05, 06, 07, Magna Stella Lifetime Achievement award, 2007. Mem.: ABA, Tex. Gen. Counsel Forum (pres. Houston chpt. 2005—06, statewide chmn. 2006—07), Am. Corp. Counsel Assn. (bd. dir. New Orleans chpt. 1995—98), La. Bar Assn., Inst. Energy Law (adv. bd. 2001—, exec. com. 2002—, chmn. 2005—08), Houston City Club. Republican. Roman Catholic. Avocations: computers, fishing. Home: 5105 Longmont Dr Houston TX 77056-2417

PLAFKER, SCOTT, medical educator; b. South Amboy, NJ; m. Kendra Plafker. PhD, Johns Hopkins U., Baltimore. Asst. prof. U. Okla. Health Scis. Ctr., 2003—. Office: Univ Okla Health Scis Ctr 940 Stanton L Young Blvd BMSB 538 Oklahoma City OK 73104 Office Phone: 405-271-8001. Business E-Mail: scott-plafker@ouhsc.edu.

PLAGER, S. JAY, federal judge; s. A. L. and Clara L. Plager; children: Anna Katherine, David Alan, Daniel Tyler. AB, U. N.C., 1952; JD, U. Fla., 1958; LLM, Columbia U., 1961. Bar: Fla. 1958, Ill. 1964. Asst. prof. law U. Fla., 1958—62, assoc. prof., 1962—64; assoc. prof. law U. Ill., Champaign-Urbana, 1964—65, prof., 1965—77; dir. Office Environ. and Planning Studies, 1972—74, 1975—77; dean, prof. law Ind. U. Sch. Law, Bloomington, 1977—84, prof. law, 1984—90; counselor to undersec. US Dept. Health and Human Svcs., 1986—87; assoc. dir. Office of Mgmt. and Budget Exec. Office of the Pres., 1987—88, adminstr. info. and regulatory affairs, 1988—89; cir. judge US Ct. Appeals (fed. cir.), 1989—2000, sr. judge, 2000—. Vis. rsch. prof. law U. Wis., 1967—68; vis. scholar Stanford U., 1984—85. Author (with others): Water Law and Administration, 1968; author: Social Justice Through Law-New Approaches in the Law of Property, 1970; author: (with others) Florida Water Law, 1980. Chmn. Gainesville (Fla.) Planning Commn., 1962—63; active Urbana Plan Commn., 1966—70, nat. air pollution manpower devel. adv. com., 1971—75; cons. Ill. Inst. for Environ. Quality, US EPA; chmn. Ill. Task Force on Noise, 1972—76; vice chmn. Nat. Commn. on Jud. Discipline and Removal, 1991—93; budget com. Jud. Conf. US Cts., 1996—2003. With USN, 1948—70. Office: US Ct Appeals for Fed Cir The National Courts Bldg 717 Madison Pl NW Washington DC 20439-0002*

PLAINE, LLOYD LEVA, lawyer; b. Washington, Nov. 3, 1947; d. Marx and Shirley P. Leva; m. James W. Hill. BA, U. Pa., 1969; postgrad., Harvard U.; JD, Georgetown U., 1975. Bar: DC 1975. Legis. asst. to US Rep. Sidney Yates, 1971-72; with Sutherland, Asbill & Brennan, Washington, 1975-82, ptnr., 1982—. Fellow Am. Bar Found., Am. Coll. Trust and Estate Counsel (past regent), Am. Coll. Tax Counsel; mem. ABA (past chmn. real property, probate and trust law sect., past coun. sect. of taxation). Office: Sutherland Asbill & Brennan Ste 6 1275 Pennsylvania Ave NW Washington DC 20004-2415 Office Phone: 202-383-0155.

PLAISANCE, MELISSA C., consumer products company executive; b. Feb. 12, 1960; BSBA cum laude, Bucknell U., 1982; MBA, UCLA, 1990. With Bankers Trust Co. Corp. Fin., LA, 1982—90; dir., investor rels. Safeway Inc., 1990—93, v.p., investor rels., 1993—94, v.p., investor rels. & pub. affairs, 1994—95, sr. v.p. fin., investor rels. & pub. affairs Pleasanton, Calif., 1995—2000, sr. v.p., fin. & investor rels., 2000—03, 2004—; sr. v.p., fin. & corp. comm. Del Monte Foods Co., San Francisco, 2004. Office: Safeway Inc PO Box 99 5918 Stoneridge Mall Rd Pleasanton CA 94566-0009*

PLAKS, ALBERT I., electrical engineer, educator; b. Minsk, Russia, Apr. 17, 1941; came to U.S., 1990; s. Israel and Genia P.; children: Elena, Victoria, Giller; m. Anna Toporovsky. MSEE, Polytech. U., Minsk, 1963, PhD in Electrical Engring., 1973. Profl. engr., Israel. Designer, rschr. Inst. Automotive Industry, Minsk, 1963—67; asst. prof. Polytech. U., Minsk, 1970—76; pres., owner Electromat, Inc., Tel-Aviv, Israel, 1977—81; sr. lectr. Singalovsky Tech. Coll., Tel-Aviv, 1980—90; sr. project engr. Dept. Pub. Works, Rishon-le-Zion, Israel, 1981—90; control specialist Murray Corp., Hunt Valley, Md., 1990—2007; prof.

Balt. Hebrew U., 1992—2003. Adviser Inst. Standards, Tel-Aviv, 1985-87, Ministry of Edn., Tel-Aviv, 1983-90; inspector edn. divsn. Min. of Labor, Jerusalem, Israel, 1985-90. Author: Electric Machines for Servo Systems, 1989, Power Electronics Basics, 2000, Israel and Espionage, 2001, Weapon of Retribution, 2006; patentee in field. Program dir., host (radio show) Star of David, Washington-Balt., 1996. Mem. Internat. Acad. Ecology Man and Nature Protection Scis. Avocations: swimming, theater, cinema, paper writer. Office Phone: 410-526-0290. Personal E-mail: aastardavid@gmail.com.

PLAMANN, ALFRED A., wholesale distribution executive; Pres., CEO Cert. Grocers Calif., Unified Grocers Inc. (formerly Unified Western Grocers), Commerce, Calif., 2000—. Office: Unified Grocers Inc 5200 Sheila St City Of Commerce CA 90040

PLANAS-SILVA, MARICARMEN DELIA, cancer researcher; b. Lima, Peru, Nov. 12, 1962; d. Pedro Guido Planas and Olga Maria Silva de Planas. PhD, Baylor Coll. Medicine, Houston, 1991. Postdoc. fellow Whitehead Inst. Biomed. Rsch., Cambridge, Mass., 1993—2000; asst. prof. Penn State Coll. Medicine, Hershey, Pa., 2000—07. Named Local Hero, Idearc Media, 2008; finalist Coll. Venture Challenge Grad., Harrisburg Market Keystone Innovation Zone, 2008; Hershey Foods Corp. Grad. fellowship, Penn State Harrisburg Sch. Bus., 2008—. Mem.: AAAS, Am. Assn. Cancer Rsch., Beta Gamma Sigma. Roman Catholic. Home: 13 Chevy Chase Hershey PA 17033 Business E-Mail: mcplanas@psu.edu.

PLANK, JULIE, professional basketball coach; Grad., Ohio State U., Columbus, 1983. Asst. coach Capital U. Crusaders, Columbus, Ohio, 1984—86, Stanford U. Cardinal, Calif., 1986—95, Vanderbilt U. Commodores, Nashville, 1997—99, US Women's Nat. Team, 1999—2000; asst. coach, dir. scouting Ind. Fever, 2000—07; asst. coach Minn. Lynx, 2008; head coach Washington Mystics, 2008—. Named Asst. Coach of Yr., WNBA, 2008. Office: Washington Mystics Verizon Ctr 601 F St NW Washington DC 20004*

PLANK, KEVIN A., apparel executive; b. Kensington, Md., Aug. 13, 1972; s. William and Jayne Plank; m. Desiree Jacqueline Guerzon, Mar. 2003; 1 child, Kevin James. BBA, U. Md., 1996. Founder, chmn., pres., CEO Under Armour Inc., Balt., 1996—2008, chmn., CEO, 2008—. Bd. trustees U. Md. Coll. Park Found. Named Entrepreneur of Yr. for Md. Mfg., Ernst & Young, 2003; named one of Most Influential People in the World of Sports, Bus. Week, 2008. Office: Under Armour Inc Investor Relations 1020 Hull St Baltimore MD 21230-2080 Office Phone: 617-587-8911.

PLANK, ROGER B., energy executive; BA, Colgate Univ.; MBA, Univ. St. Thomas. With Apache Corp., Houston, 1981—, v.p., CFO, 1997-2000, exec. v.p., CFO, 2000—09, pres., 2009—. Bd. dir. Parker Drilling Co.; past pres. Tex. Independent Producers & Royalty Owners Assn.; dir. Okla. Independent Petroleum Assn., Domestic Petroleum Council. Bd. mem. Alley Theatre, Houston, Ucross Found. Office: Apache Corp 2000 Post Oak Blvd Ste 100 Houston TX 77056-4400*

PLANT, ALBIN MACDONOUGH, lawyer; b. Balt., July 30, 1937; s. Albin Joseph and Ruth E. (Frech) P.; m. Anne Warwick Brown, June 17, 1961; children: Katherine, Albin MacDonough Jr., Elizabeth Ashby. BA, Princeton U., NJ, 1959; LLB, U. Va., Charlottesville, 1963; MLA, Johns Hopkins U., Balt., 1978. Bar: Md. 1963, U.S. Dist. Ct. Md. 1963, U.S. Ct. Appeals 1970. Assoc. Semmes, Bowen & Semmes, Balt., 1963-71, ptnr., 1971-91, Stewart, Plant & Blumenthal, Balt., 1991—. Bd. dir. T. Rowe Price Savs. Bank; adj. prof. law U. Balt., 1979, U. Md., 1979—83, 1984—85. Bd. dir. Balt. Choral Arts Soc. Mem.: Am. Coll. Trust and Estate Counsel, Am. Bar Found. (life), Wednesday Law Club, Md. Club, Lawyers Roundtable. Democrat. Office: 7 St Paul St Baltimore MD 21202-1626 Office Phone: 410-347-0511. Business E-Mail: amplant@spblaw.com.

PLANT, EWAN P., research scientist; b. Oamaru, North Otago, New Zealand, Jan. 3, 1971; s. Bruce E. and Yvonne Plant; m. E Sarah Fraser, Nov. 27, 2004; 1 child, Zeke Simon Edward Fraser-Plant. PhD, U. Otago, Dunedin, 1989. Postdoc fellow U. Medicine and Dentistry, Piscataway, NJ, 2000—01; rsch. assoc. U. Md., Coll Pk, 2002—05; orise fellow FDA, Bethesda, Md., 2006—. Active mem. South Ctrl. Cmty. Assn., Washington, 2006—08. Mem.: Am. Soc. Virology. Achievements include research in discoveries and descriptions concerning ribosome fidelity. Office: Fda 8800 Rockville Pike HFM 310 Bethesda MD 20892 Office Fax: 301-480-4757. Business E-Mail: ewan.plant@fda.hhs.gov.

PLANT, JACKSON VAUGHN, minister; s. Harry Jackson and Caroline Plant. Ordained pastor Ch. of God, 2006. Founder, pastor For This Time Ministries, Glen Burnie, Md., 1999—. With USN, 1988. Mem.: Alpha Tau Omega (life; v.p. 1984—85). Republican. Business E-Mail: jplant@jacksonplant.com.

PLANT, JEFF, architecture educator; m. Stacey Plant. BS in Human Ecology, Tenn. Tech U., Cookeville, 1986; MS in Housing and Design, Va. Tech., Blacksburg, 1998; PhD, U. Ill., Carbondale, 1997. Cert. commissioned tchr. Trinity Assembly, 2008. Human ecol. full prof. Tenn. Tech. U., Cookeville, 2000—. Vp external rels. AAFCS, Cookeville. Personal E-mail: jeffplant@gmail.com.

PLANT, JOHN CHARLES, automotive executive; b. West Bromwich, West Midlands, Eng., Aug. 1, 1953; s. John and Florence (Harrison) P.; m. Christine Ann; children: Alexa Jayne, John Alexander. B in Commerce, Econs., Acctg. and Law, Birmingham U., Eng., 1974. Auditor Touche Ross, Birmingham, 1974-77; financier Lucas Auto Ltd., Birmingham, 1977—, Burnley, England, 1983—; mng. dir. Lucas Varity Elec. and Electronics, 1991—97; pres. Lucas Varity Automotive, 1999; pres., CEO TRW Chassis; gen. mgr. TRW Automotive, exec. v.p., 1999—2001, co-CEO, pres., CEO Livonia, Mich., 2001—. Bd. dirs. Martin Currie Portfolio Investment Trust PLC. Fellow Inst. Chartered Accts. in Eng. and Wales (mng. dir., FCA award 1981). Avocation: tennis. Office: TRW Automotive 12025 Tech Center Dr Livonia MI 48150

PLANT, JOHN MAXIME, educator; m. Teresa Plant. MA, U. South Fla., Tampa. Lic. pilot F.A.A, 1962, cert. tchr. State Fla., 1964. Col., spl. forces (ret.) US Army, Bad Tolz, Fort Bragg, NC, 1956—94; coll. prof. Pasco-Hernando CC, New Port Richey, Fla., 2005—. GS-13 civilian analyst US Mil., Cuidad Panama, Panama, 1998—2005. Com. mem. Boy Scouts Am., Tampa, 1947—. Avocations: flying, computers, writing. Home: 5282 Tanner Rd Spring Hill FL 34609 Office: Pasco-Hernando CC 10230 Ridge Rd New Port Richey FL 34654 Personal E-mail: sofretjmp@aol.com. Business E-Mail: plantj@phcc.edu.

PLANT, RANDALL LESLIE, otolaryngologist; MD, U. Ill., Chgo., 1987. Otolaryngologist Alaska Native Med. Ctr., Anchorage, 2002—. Office: Alaska Native Med Ctr 4315 Diplomacy Dr Anchorage AK 99508 Personal E-mail: rlplant@gci.net. E-mail: rlplant@anthc.org.

PLANT, ROBERT ANTHONY, singer; b. Bromwich, Staffordshire, Eng., Aug. 20, 1948; m. Maureen Wilson, Nov. 9, 1969 (div. Aug. 1983); children: Carmen Jane, Karac (dec. July 26, 1977), Logan Romero, Jesse Lee Lead singer Crawling King Snakes, Band of Joy, 1966—68, Led Zeppelin, 1968—80. Singer: (albums with Led Zeppelin) Led Zeppelin, 1968, 1969, Led Zeppelin III, 1970, Led Zeppelin IV, 1971, Houses of the Holy, 1973, Physical Graffiti, 1975, The Song Remains the Same, Presence, 1976, In Through the Out Door, 1979, Coda, 1982, Remasters, 1990, BBC Sessions, 1997, Early Days: The Best Of Led Zeppelin Volume One, 2000, Latter Days: The Best Of Led Zeppelin Volume Two, 2002, How the West Was Won, 2003, Mothership, 2007, (solo albums) Pictures at Eleven, 1982, The Principle of Moments, 1983, Shaken 'n' Stirred, 1985, Now and Zen, 1988, Manic Nirvana, 1990, Fate of Nations, 1993, Sixty Six to Timbuktu, 2003, Mighty Rearranger, 2005, Nine Lives, 2006, (albums with The Honeydrippers) The Honeydrippers: Volume One, 1985, (albums with Jimmy Page) No Quarter: Jimmy Page and Robert Plant Unledded, 1994, (albums with Strange Sensation) Dreamland, 2002, Enchanter, 2005, (albums with Alison Krauss) Raising Sand, 2007 (Wide Open Country Video of Yr., Country Music TV, Musical Event of Yr., Country Music Assn., 2008, Record of Yr., Album of Yr., Best Pop Collaboration with Vocals, Best Country Collaboration with Vocals, Best Contemporary Folk Album, Grammy Awards, 2009); performer: (films) The Song Remains the Same, 1976, (TV films) Unledded, 1994. Recipient Grammy award for Best Hard Rock Performance, 1999, Polar Music prize, Royal Swedish Acad. Music, 2006, Grammy award for Best Pop Collaboration with Vocals, 2008, Grammy Lifetime Achievement award; named a Comdr. of the Most Excellent Order of the British Empire (CBE), Prince Charles of Wales, 2009; named to Rock and Roll Hall of Fame (as mem. of Led Zeppelin), 1995. Office: c/o Bill Curbishley Trifold Mgmt 12 Oval Rd London NW1 7DH England Office Phone: 44-20-7419-4300. Fax: 44-20-7419-4325. E-mail: trinuk@globalnet.co.uk.*

PLAPINGER, WILLIAM A., lawyer; b. Washington, July 23, 1952; s. Jerome S. and Alice E. Plapinger; m. Kathleen J. Murray, Oct. 11, 1982; children: Alexander S., Elizabeth L., Thomas A. Student, Westfield Coll., U. London, 1972—73; AB, Vassar Coll., 1974; JD, NYU, 1978. Bar: NY 1979, US Dist. Ct. (ea. dist.) NY 1979, US Dist. Ct. (so. dist.) NY 1979, US Supreme Ct. 1983. Assoc. Sullivan & Cromwell, NY, 1978—86, ptnr., 1986—87, London, 1987—, mng. ptnr. London office, 1995—2008, coord. European offices, 2000—. Trustee Vassar Coll., Poughkeepsie, 1996—, chair bd. trustees, 2006—; trustee Am. Sch., London, 1996—. Mem.: India Ho., Queenwood Golf Club, Vineyard Golf Club, Links Club. Office: Sullivan & Cromwell LLP 1 New Fetter Ln London EC4A 1AN England Mailing: 125 Broad St 32nd Fl New York NY 10004-2498 Office Phone: 44 0 20 7959 8900. Business E-Mail: plapingerw@sullcrom.com.

PLAPP, BRYCE VERNON, biochemistry educator; b. DeKalb, Ill., Sept. 11, 1939; s. Vernon Edgar and Eleanor Barbara (Kautz) P.; m. Rosemary Kuhn, June 13, 1962; children— Brendan Bryce, Laurel Andrea BS, Mich. State U., East Lansing, 1961; PhD, U. Calif.-Berkeley, 1966. Research assoc. J.W. Goethe U., Frankfurt/Main, Germany, 1966-68; research assoc. Rockefeller U., NYC, 1968-70; faculty U. Iowa, Iowa City, 1970—, prof. biochemistry, 1979—. Contbr. articles to profl. jours.; mem. editorial bd. Archives Biochemistry and Biophysics. Am. Cancer Soc. fellow, 1966-68 Mem. Am. Soc. for Biochemistry and Molecular Biology, Am. Chem. Soc., Sigma Xi Avocations: travel, sports. Office: Univ Iowa Dept Biochemistry 4-712 Iowa City IA 52242 Office Phone: 319-335-7909. E-mail: bv-plapp@uiowa.edu.

PLASCENCIA, JOSE J., social worker, consultant; s. Jesus G. Plascencia and Maria De La Luz Garcia; m. Maria Esther Aguayo; children: Krystal Marie, Ariel Monique, Dulce Lizbeth. BA in Psychology, San Diego State U., 1997, MSW (hon.), 2000. EOPS counselor Imperial Valley Coll., Calif., 1998—. Recipient Appreication & Recognition award, No. Ariz. U., 2007, GLEAM award, Imperial Valley Coll., 2008. Office: Imperial Valley Coll 380 E Aten Rd PO Box 158 Imperial CA 92251 Office Fax: 760-355-6107. Business E-Mail: jose.plascencia@imperial.edu.

PLASEK, SUSAN G., academic administrator; d. Charles R. Skarke and Mercedes W. Carpenter, James E. Pourchot (Stepfather) and Lorraine Wimhurst (Stepmother); m. Lawrence Leroy Pourchot; children: Lawrence Leroy Jr., Jeffrey Allan, Darin Anthony. MS, U. Houston, Clear Lake City. Cert. susan gale plasek Tex. Edn. Agy., 1980. Prin. Queen Peace Sch., La Marque, Tex., 1983—89. Pres. Gulf Coast Assn. Edn. Young Children, Tex., 2002—03. Office: Coll Mainland 1200 Amburn Texas City TX 77591 Business E-Mail: splasek@com.edu.

PLASIL, FRANZ, physicist; b. Prague, Czechoslovakia, May 17, 1939; came to U.S., 1960; s. Frank and Eva (Wenger) P.; m. Catherine Logan, Feb. 15, 1964 (div. Sept. 1979); two children: Maia (dec. Feb. 26, 2008), David; m. Carol Baratz, Apr. 12, 1980. BS, Queen Mary Coll., U. London, 1960; PhD, U. Calif., Berkeley, 1964. Chemist Lawrence Berkeley (Calif.) Lab., 1964-65; rsch. assoc. Brookhaven Nat. Lab., Upton, NY, 1965-67; rsch. staff physics div. Oak Ridge (Tenn.) Nat. Lab., 1967-78, group leader physics div., 1978-86, sect. head physics div., 1986-99; fellow U. Tenn.-Battelle, 1999—2002; hon. rsch. prof. dept. physics and astronomy U. Tenn., Knoxville, 2002—. Contbr. articles to Annals of Physics, Phys. Rev., Phys. Rev. Letters, Nuc. Phys., Phys. Letters. Ct. appointed spl. advocate for abused and neglected children. Recipient Alexander von Humboldt award 1985, E. Mach medal of honor Acad. of Sci. of the Czech Republic, 1998. Fellow Am. Phys. Soc. Achievements include rsch. in fission-imposed limits on the stability of rotating nuclei and in nucleus-nucleus collisions at ultrarelativistic energies. Home: 964 W Outer Dr Oak Ridge TN 37830-8607 Personal E-mail: plasil@comcast.net.

PLASKETT, THOMAS GEORGE, transportation executive, director; b. Raytown, Mo., Dec. 24, 1943; s. Warren E. and Frances S. P.; m. Linda Lee Maxey, June 8, 1968; children: Kimberly, Keith. B in Indsl. Engring., Kettering U.; MBA, Harvard U. Supr. indsl. engring. GM, Flint, Mich., 1968, supt. indsl. engring., 1969-73, sr. staff asst., treas. NYC, 1973; asst. contr. Am. Airlines, NYC, 1974, v.p. mktg. adminstrn., 1975-76, sr. v.p. fin., 1976-80, sr. v.p. mktg. Dallas, 1980—86; pres., CEO Continental Airlines Inc., Houston, until 1988; chmn., CEO, pres. Pan Am Corp., NYC, 1988—91; chmn. Fox Run Capital Assocs., 1991—; dir., interim pres., CEO, acting CFO Greyhound Lines, Inc., Dallas, 1994-95, chmn., 1995—99; vice-chmn. Legend Airlines, Dallas, 1997—2001, exec. v.p., 1999—2001; pres., CEO Probex Corp., Dallas, 1999—2000, chmn., 1999—2000. Bd. dirs. Radioshack Corp., Ft. Worth, Novell, Inc. 2002-; Waltham, Mass., Provo, Utah, Alcon Inc., Ft. Worth, Platinum Rsch. Orgn., Dallas, non-exec. chair, 2002-08. Avocations: golf, skiing, squash. Office: PO Box 141111 Irving TX 75014-1111 Office Phone: 972-333-4751. Business E-Mail: tom@foxruncapital.com.

PLATFOOT, CHRISTOPHER W., systems administrator, information technology executive; b. Greenville, Ohio, June 18, 1966; s. Willard Ralph Platfoot and Shiela Ann Coffield. A of Applied Bus., Edison State Coll., 2001. Shift supr. Clopay Corp., Russia, Ohio, 1990—99; pc coord. Upper Valley Med. Ctr., Troy, 1999—2006, sys. adminstr., 2005—. Condr. Fraternal Order Eagles, Minster, Ohio, 2004—06. With USN, 1998—2006. Decorated Mil. Outstanding Vol. Svc. medal USN, Coast Guard Spl. Ops. Ribbon USCG, Coast Guard Meritorious Unit Commendation, Sea Svc. Deployment Ribbon USN, Navy & Marine Corps Commendation medal Dept. of Navy, Navy & Marine Corps Achievement medal, Navy Achievement medal, Navy Conduct medal, Navy Res. Meritorious Svc., Nat. Def. medal, War on Terrorism Svc. medal USN, Armed Forces Res. medal; scholar, Local Sponsor, 2001. Mem.: Phi Theta Kappa (life Internat. Scholastic Order 2001). Roman Catholic. Avocations: travel, softball, skiing. Office: Upper Valley Med Ctr 3130 N Dixie Hwy Troy OH 45373 Business E-Mail: cplatfoot@uvmc.com.

PLATIS, CHRIS STEVEN, adult education educator; b. East Chicago, Ind., May 21, 1926; s. Sam and Myra (Theodore) P.; m. Jeanette Brown. BS in Phys. Edn., Ind. U., 1955, MS in Edn., 1964, postgrad., 1965—68. Gen. foreman Cast Armor, Inc., East Chicago, 1951—53; tchr. East Chgo. and Ind. Pub. Schs., 1955—. Asst. sports editor East Chgo. Calumet News, 1973-78; asst. dir. No. Ind. State Sports Mus., 1984-95, 96, 97, 98, 00. Appearances include (films) A Bridge Too Far, The Longest Day, Bridge at Remagan, D-Day, The Battle of the Bulge; author: Teaching Kids of Tomorrow, 1978, Are Teachers Adequate for Today's Students?, 1997. Master Boy Scouts Am., East Chicago, 1965-87; asst. recreational dir. North Twp., Northern Ind., 1993; All-Pacific Army, Football, Basketball, Track, 1946. With U.S. Army, 1944-46. Named to East Chgo. Hall of Fame All Am. Amateur Baseball Congress, 1955, 56, 57, Ind. Amateur Baseball Hall of Fame, 1962, US Masters Track and Field All Am., 1995-98 (ranked 8 times # 1 and 2 in the country in masters track and field, 8 times ranked # 1 and 2 in the world in masters track and field, 1996-98, 10 nat. sr. Olympic medals), 35 (20 gold) individual Ind. Hoosier State Games Regional Medals, 35 (20 gold) individual Ind. Hoosier State Games Final Medals, 1996, 97, 98, 2000, 01, 2 Alltime State Records; Nat. Sr. Olympic track and field qualifier, 1997-99; 90 Yr. Greatest Athletes in East Chgo.'s History, Individual and Team Records Baseball Hall of Fame Archives, Cooperstown, NY, 2003; mem. team won 53 league championships, 54 playoff championships, 41 Ind. State baseball championships, 7 world regional titles, 2 runner-up world championships, Nat. C.I.O. baseball championship, 1950, 1949 Big Ten Baseball Champions, Ind. U.; conf. baseball champions, 1942-44; all-conf. team, 1942-44, capt., 1942-44; named Most Valuable Player, Best Infielder award, Batting Champ, All-Star Team, 1950; Ind. State Jr. Legion champions, all-state, Midwest All-Star team, 1942, Ind.-Ill. Bi-State champions, 1950, Most Valuable, Batting Champion, Best Infielder award, 1950; career and team records in Baseball Hall of Fame Archives, 2003; named Northwest Ind. Intriguing Family of Yr., 2002; recipient 15 league batting titles, 11 MVP awards, 22 times Ind. All State in Baseball, 21 times League Mgr. of Yr., 8 Decades Baseball, 1936-2000, Nat./European Tchr. of Yr., 1984, Life Time Achievement award Ind. U., 2007. Fellow VFW (charter mem. World War II Meml. 1998), Am. Legion, Normandy Invasion Club, Nat. Assn. of Basketball Coaches, Nat. Wildlife Assn. Republican. Avocations: reading, writing, baseball, tennis, golf.

PLATIS, JAMES GEORGE, secondary school educator; b. Detroit, Mar. 23, 1927; s. Sam and Myra (Theodore) P.; m. Mary Lou Campbell, Aug. 16, 1974. BS in Physical Edn., Ind. U., 1955, MS in Edn., 1965; postgrad., Ind. State U., Terre Haute, 1967. Cert. physical edn. tchr., Ind. Foreman Cast Armor, Inc., East Chicago, Ind., 1951-53, Youngstown Sheet & Tube, East Chicago, 1953-54; dir., tchr. East Chicago Pub. Schs., 1955—. Sports editor East Chicago Globe/Calumet News, 1973-78, Herald Newspapers, Merrillville, Ind., 1973-78; asst. dir. No. Ind. State Sports Mus., 1984-99. Contbr. articles to newspapers, jours. Founder East Chicago Hall of Fame, 1975, Little Olympics, East Chicago, 1956; pres. Ind. Am. Amateur Baseball Congress, 1954-57, commr., 1984-98; dir. No. Ind. State Sports Mus., 1988-00. With AUS, 1945-47, ETO. Named to Ind. Amateur Baseball Hall of Fame, 1962, East Chicago Hall of Fame, 1976, All-Am. Amateur Baseball Congress, 1955, 56, The Athletic Congress Masters All-Am., 1986-98, 99, 2000, 2001-02; selected to 90 Yr. Greatest Athletes in East Chicago History, Nat. Athletic Congress, 1990; named Amateur Coach of Yr., US Baseball Fedn. Ind., 1990, Amateur Runner-up Coach of Yr., 1988; recipient 53 World and 61 Nat. No. 1 track rankings, Athletic Congress Masters, 17 World Records, 1987-2002, 16 League Batting Titles, 12 MV League Players awards; Ind. Jr. Legion State Champions, All-State Batting Champions, MVP in tournament, Conf. Baseball Champions, 1943, 44, 45, All-Conf. Team, 1944-45, Conf. Batting Champion, 1944, Team Cptn., 1945, All-Midwest team, Best Outfielder, 1944; 23 times Ind. all-state team; Ind. Nat. Baseball State Champions; mem. team won 53 League Championships, 54 Playoff championships, 41 Ind. State Baseball Championships, 5 Ind. State Champions Runner Up, 7 World Regional Titles, 5 World Finalists, 2 runner-up World Champions, Big Ten baseball champions Ind. U., 1949, Best Outfielder Congress All-State team, Ill., Ind. Bi-State Champions, 1950; Nat. C.I.O. Baseball Championship, 1951, 12 Times League Mgr. Of The Year, 1982-96; Big Ten Baseball Champions, Ind. U., 1949; named Athlete of Yr. Ind. Masters Track and Field, 1992, World Sr. Olympic Masters Track & Field Champion, Spain, 6 gold medals, named Best Performer, 3 Masters Track & Field World Records, 1992, Fla. Masters Track and Field Athlete of Yr., 1994-98; recipient 76 State Ind. Track and Field Individual Gold medals, 1983-99, 2000-02, 86 Ind. state regional individual gold medals, 1983-98, 2000-02, 322 All Am. Masters Track and Field Certs., 1986-99, 2000-02, 39 Ill. Grand Prix individual titles, 1989-92, 45 Mid-West Track and Field individual titles, 1989-92, 5 gold medals, silver medal World Sr. Olympic Masters Track & Field, 1996, Ga., 5 Masters Track & Field World Records, 1997, 2 Masters Track & Field World Records, 1998, Nat. Senior Olympics Qualifer, 1991, 93, 95, 97, 99, 2001, 03, 4 Gold medals, 2 World Records Nat. Sr. Olympics, 1999-2001, 7 gold medals World Sr. Olympic Masters Track and Field, Sydney, Australia, 2000, 5 World Records, selected Best Performer; named Internat. Man of the Yr. in Edn., 1991-92, 93, Profl. of the Yr. in Edn., 1991, Master Track and Field All-Am., 1986-2003, Northwest Ind. Intriguing Family of the Yr., 2002, 8 Decades of Baseball, Individual & Team Records in Baseball Hall of Fame, Cooperstown, NY, 2003, Youth award Chgo. Profl. Pitch & Hit Club, 2005. Fellow Nat. Assn. Basketball Coaches, Am. Assn. Health, Phys. Edn. and Recreation; mem. Athletic Dirs. Assn. Sportswriters Guild, VFW, Am. Legion, WWII Meml. (82nd Airborne Divsn., 1st Inf. Divsn. 1998), Mens Club Ind. U., Lifetime Achievment award, Ind. U., 2007. Republican. Avocations: reading, running, baseball, writing.

PLATIS, MARY LOU, media specialist; b. East Chicago, Ind., Jan. 21, 1946; d. Walter James and Mary Helen (Taus) Campbell; m. James George Platis, Aug. 16, 1974. BS, Ind. State U., 1972, MS, 1974. Tchr. 4th grade Holy Trinity Sch., East Chicago, Ind., 1968-72; tchr. phys. edn. Washington Elem. Sch., East Chicago, Ind., 1972-86; media specialist Ctrl. High Sch. Libr., East Chicago, Ind., 1986—. Recipient 72 Ind. track and field individual state medals, 1983-2001, 72 Ind. state regional individual medals, 1983-2002, 25 All Am. certs., 12 times Masters track and field All Am., 1989-98, 37 Ill. Grand Prix individual titles, 1989-93, 43 Midwest track and field individual titles, 1989-95, 3 times Nat. Masters track and field champion, 7 times Nat. runner-up, Bronze medal Nat. Sr. Games, Pitts., 2005; nat. sr. Olympics qualifier, 1997, 99, 2001, 03, 05; 6th pl. ribbons (2) Nat. Sr. Olympics, 1999; nat. and world ranked masters track and field, 1989-98; individual championship titles in racquetball; named to East Chicago Sports Hall of Fame, 1992; named NW Ind. Most Intriguing Family, Times Newspaper, 2002. Mem. Nat. Assn. Basketball Coaches. Avocations: racquetball, tennis, working out. Home: 938 Troon Ct Schererville IN 46375 Office: Ctrl High Sch Libr 1100 W Columbus Dr East Chicago IN 46312-2582 Home Phone: 219-322-8012; Office Phone: 219-391-4046. E-mail: mlplatis@aol.com.

PLATNICK, NORMAN I., curator, entomologist; b. Bluefield, W.Va., Dec. 30, 1951; s. Philip and Fannie (Kascenewsky) P.; m. Nancy Stewart Price, June 14, 1970; 1 child, William Durin. BS in Biology, Concord Coll., 1968; MS in Zoology, Mich. State U., 1970; PhD in Biology, Harvard U., 1973. Asst. curator Am. Mus. Natural History, NYC, 1973-77, assoc. curator, 1977-82, curator, 1982-98, chmn. dept. entomology, 1987-94, Peter J. Solomon Family curator, 1998—; program dir. biotic surveys and inventories NSF, 2002—03. Sci. attaché Consulate of Gondwana, N.Y.C., 1976—. Author: The World Spider Catalog; co-author: Systematics and Biogeography, 1981; co-editor: Advances in Cladistics, 1983. V.p. Ctr. Internat. de Documentation Arachnologie, 1986-89 (pres. 1995-98). Fellow Willi Hennig Soc. (founder, pres. 1990-92); mem. Am. Arachnological Soc. (charter, membership sec. 1976—2002). Office: Am Mus Natural History Central Pk W At 79th St W New York NY 10024 Office Phone: 212-769-5612. Business E-Mail: platnick@amnh.org.

PLATOW, RAPHAELA, museum director, curator; b. Munich; BA in Art History, Albert-Ludwig U., Freiburg, Germany; MA in Art History, Bus. Adminstrn., and German Lit., Humboldt U., Berlin. Internat. curator in residence Contemporary Art Mus., Raleigh, NC; curator Rose Art Mus., Brandeis U., Mass., 2002—06, chief curator, 2006—07; Alice & Harris Weston dir., chief curator Contemporary Arts Ctr., Cin., 2007—. Staff Internat. Biennale di Venezia, 1999; interim dir. Rose Art Mus., Brandeis U., 2005; adj. curator Kunstforum München Found., Munich; mgr. Projektraum Berlin. Editor: (book) Clare Rojas: Hope Springs Eternal, 2007. Office: Contemporary Arts Ctr 44 E Sixth St Cincinnati OH 45202 Office Phone: 513-345-8410. Office Fax: 513-721-7418. Business E-Mail: rplatow@cacmail.org.

PLATSOUCAS, CHRIS DIMITRIOS, immunologist; b. Athens, Greece, Apr. 17, 1951; came to U.S., 1973; s. Dimitrios Evagelos and Maria (Tsonidis) P.; m. Emilia L. Oleszak, Oct. 18, 1985. BS, Patras U., Greece, 1973; postgrad., Purdue U., 1974; PhD, MIT, 1978. Rsch. fellow/assoc. Meml. Sloan-Kettering Cancer Ctr., NYC, 1978—81, asst. mem., 1982—85, asst. prof., 1981-85, head lab. biol. response modifiers, 1981-85; assoc. prof. dept. immunology M.D. Anderson Cancer Ctr., Houston, 1985-89, prof., dep. chmn., 1989-93, Ashbel Smith professorship, 1991-92, H.L. and O. Stringer professorship in cancer rsch., 1992-93; L.H. Carnell prof. dept. microbiology, immunology Temple U. Sch. Medicine, Phila., 1993—2007, chmn. dept. microbiology and immunology, 1993—2006; acting dean Coll. Sci. and Tech. Temple U., Phila., 1998-2000, dean Coll. Sci. and Tech., 2000—04, Old Dominion U., Norfolk, Va., 2007—; dean Coll. Sci.; dir. Ctr. Mol. Medicine; prof. Biol Sci. Biotech. cons., sci. reviewer study sects. NIH, Bethesda, Md., 1982—. Contbr. numerous articles to profl. jours. Nat. Rsch. Svc. award NIH, 1978-79; grantee NIH, Am. Cancer Soc., State of Tex., many others. Mem. Am. Assn. Immunologists, Am. Soc. Hematology, Am. Assn. Biochem & Molecular Biology, Soc. Investigative Pathology, Am. Assn. Cancer Rsch. Greek Orthodox. Achievements include patents in field; research on human T cell immunology, on T-cell antigen receptors, on tumor-infiltrating lymphocytes in malignant melanoma and ovarian carcinoma, on organ transplantation, on chronic rejection, on AIDS, on multiple sclerosis, schlerodema, osteoarthritis, and other autoimmune diseases. Office: Old Dominion Univ Office of Dean, Coll Sci 4600 Elkhorn Ave OCNPS Rm 143 Norfolk VA 23529 Office Phone: 757-683-3277. Business E-Mail: cplatsoucas@odu.edu, cplatsoucas@cox.edu.

PLATT, DONALD OLIVER, literature and language professor; b. Coral Gables, Fla., July 22, 1957; s. Donald Oliver and Martha Caroline Luecht Platt; m. Dana Brookes Roeser, Aug. 8, 1987; children: Eleanor Grace, Lucy Clara. BA, Hampshire Coll., Amherst, Mass., 1985; MFA, U. Va., Charlottesville, 1987; PhD, U. Utah, Salt Lake City, 1995. Asst. prof. English State U. West Ga., Carrollton, Ga., 1995—2000; prof. English and poetry Purdue U., West Lafayette, Ind., 2000—. Author: (book of poetry) Dirt Angels, My Father Says Grace (Runner-up Midland Authors Poetry award, 2008), Cloud Atlas, Fresh Peaches, Fireworks, & Guns. Recipient Pushcart prizes, Pushcart Anthology, 2003, 2005, Best Am. Poetry, 2006; named, 2000; fellow, Nat. Endowment Arts, 1996. Home: 325 Lawn Ave West Lafayette IN 47906 Office: Dept English Purdue Univ 500 Oval Dr West Lafayette IN 47907 Office Fax: (765) 49403780. Business E-Mail: plattd@purdue.edu.

PLATT, JAN KAMINIS, former county official; b. St. Petersburg, Fla., Sept. 27, 1936; d. Peter Clifton and Adele (Diamond) Kaminis; m. William R. Platt, Feb. 8, 1963; 1 child, Kevin Peter. BA, Fla. State U., 1958; postgrad., U. Fla. Law Sch., 1958-59, U. Va., 1962, Vanderbilt U., 1964. Pub. sch. tchr. Hillsborough County, Tampa, Fla., 1959-60; field dir. Girl Scouts Suncoast Coun., Tampa, 1960-62; city councilman Tampa City Coun., 1974-78; county commr. Hillsborough County, 1978—94, country commr., 1996—2004; chmn. Hillsborough County Bd. County Commrs., 1980-81, 83-84, 98-99, ret., 1994, re-elected, 1996, chmn., 1998-99, County Charter Rev. Bd., 2005—06; cp-chair Countrywide Cultural Plan, 2006—. Chmn. Tampa Bay Regional Planning Coun., 1982, West Coast Regional Water Supply Authority, Tampa, 1985, Hillsborough County Coun. Govts., 1976, 79, Agy. Bay Mgmt., Hills Environ. Protection Commn., Sunshine Amendment Drive 7th Congrl. Dist., Tampa, 1976, Cmty. Action Agy., Tampa, 1981, 83-84,chmn. pro tem Tampa Charter Revision Commn., 1975, chmn. Prison Sitting Task Force, Tampa, 1983, Tampa Housing Study Com., 1983, Met. Planning Orgn., Tampa, 1984, Bd. Tax Adjustment, Tampa, 1984, chmn. Hartline, 2002-03, Friendship Trailbridge Oversight Com., 2002-03, Tampa Bay Water, 2003-04; appointee Constn. Revision Commn., Fla., 1977, HRS Dist. IV Adv. Coun., Fla.; mem. Hillsborough County Expy. Authority, Taxicab Commn., Ch. Hills Cmty. Youth Coun.; vice chmn. steering com. Nat. Counties Environ. Task Force; pres. Suncoast Girl Scout Coun., 1973-74, Ch. Head Start Cmty. Coun., 2005-09; chmn. County Charter Rev. Bd., 2005-. Bd. dirs. March of Dimes, Tampa, The Fla. Orch., Tampa, Tampa Bay Sierra, Tampa Audubon; trustee Hillsborough County Hosp. Authority, Tampa, 1984-94; pres. Citizens Alert, Tampa, Bay View Garden Club, Rose Garden Cir., 2007-09; v.p. Hillsborough County Bar Aux.; adv. bd. Northside Cmty. Mental Health Ctr.: Access House, Tampa, KeepHillsbrough County, 2007-; active Arts Coun. Tampa-Hillsborough County, 1983-85, 96-2001, Drug Abuse Coordinating Coun. Orgn., Tampa, Bd. Criminal Justice, Tampa, Fla. Coun. on Aging, Inebriate Task Force, Tampa, Tampa Downtown Devel. Authority Task Force, Tampa Sports Authority, Tampa Area Mental Health Bd., Children's Study Commn., Manahill Area Agy. on Aging, Tampa, Athena Soc., Tampa Area Com. Fgn. Affairs, LWV; v.p. Life Enrichment Ctr.; bd. dirs. Arts Coun.; exec. com. Tampa Performing Arts Ctr., chmn. charter rev. bd.; co-founder, v.p. Ybor Fresh Market; pres. Keep Hillsburough Beautiful, 2007-09, Waverly Home-owners Assn., 2007-09; mem. Com. of 100, pres. Friends of Liberty Coun. Recipient Athena award, Women in Comm., 1976, Spessard Holland Meml. award, Tampa Bay Com. for Good Govt., 1979, First Lady of Yr. award, Beta Sigma Phi, 1980, First Ann. Humanitarian award, Nat. Orgn. of Prevention of Animal Suffering, 1981, Women Helping Women award, Soroptimist Internat. Tampa, 1983, Good Govt. award, Tampa Jaycees, 1983, LWV, 1983, John Books Meml. award, Fla. Audubon Soc., 1989, Girl Scout Woman of Distinction award, 1996, Girl Scout Thanks award, 1996, Libery Bell award, Hillsborough County Bar Assn., 2000, Black Bear award, Suncoast and Tampa Bay Groups of the Sierra Club, 2001, Eliza Wolff award, Tampa United Meth. Ctrs., Outstanding Leadership in Local Environ. Protection, Fla. Local Environ. Resource Agys., 2002, Lifetime Achievement award for outstanding leadership in local environ. protection, 2004, Communicator of Yr., Tampa Ednl. Cable Consortium, 2005, Disting. Alumna award, Fla. State U., 2005, Tampa Bay Ethics award, Tampa U. Ctr. Ethics, 2005, Dan Hanson Conservationist Yr., Frank Sergeant Fishing Expo, 2006, Zonta Status of Women award, 2006. Mem. Am. Judicature Soc., State Assn. County Commrs. Fla. (at-large dir.), AAUW (bd. dirs.), Mortar Board (Disting. Liftetime Mem. award 2006), Garnet Key, Phi Beta Kappa (past pres. local alumni), Phi Kappa Phi. Democrat. Episcopalian. Home: 3531 Village Way Tampa FL 33629-8914

PLATT, JEFFREY LOUIS, experimental surgeon, immunologist, pediatric nephrologist, educator; b. New Rochelle, NY, Mar. 21, 1949; s. Charles Alfred and Paula Platt. BA in Politics with honors, NYU, 1971; postgrad., Columbia U., 1971-73; MD, U. Southern Calif., 1977. Diplomate Am. Bd. Pediatrics, Nat. Bd. Med. Examiners. Pediatrics intern Children's Hosp. LA, 1977-78, resident, 1978-79, Della M. Mudd resident, 1979-80; med. fellow in pediatric nephrology U. Minn., Mpls., 1980-85, instr. dept. pediatrics, 1985-86, asst. prof., 1986-88, assoc. prof. pediatrics and cell biology and neuroanatomy, 1988-92; prof. surgery, pediatrics and immunology depts. Duke U., Durham, NC, 1992—98, Dorothy W. and Joseph W. Beard prof. exptl. surgery, 1994—98; prof. surgery immunology and pediatrics Mayo Clinic, Rochester, Minn., 1998—2008, dir. transplantation biology, 2006—08; prof. surgery U. Mich., 2008—, prof. microbiology and immunology, 2008—. Mem. editl. bd.: Transplantation, Transplant Immunology, Xenotransplantation, Jour. Immunology, Cellular Immunology; mem. editl. bd. Human Immunology, editor Innate Immunity; contbr. over 500 articles to med. jours.; author: 4 books. Recipient Clinician-Scientist award Am. Heart Assn., 1983-88, Established Investigator award Am. Heart Assn., 1988-93, Inst. Medicine of NAS. Mem. AAAS, NIH (Merit award), Assn. Am. Physicians, Fellow Am. Heart Assn (coun. kidney in cardiovasc. disease, coun. basic sci.), Internat. Soc. Nephrology, Am. Assn. Immunologists, Am. Fedn. Clin. Rsch., Am. Soc. Nephrology, Am. Assn. Pathologists, Soc. for Devel. Biology, Clin. Immunology Soc., Soc. Pediatric Rsch., Soc. Glycobiology, Soc. Exptl. Biology and Medicine, Alpha Omega Alpha. Office: Dept Surgery Univ Mich Biomedical Sciences Res Bldg 109 Zina Pitcher Pl Ann Arbor MI 48109 Office Phone: 734-615-6819. Business E-Mail: plattjl@umich.edu.

PLATT, JONATHAN JAMES, lawyer; b. Southampton, NY, Aug. 3, 1950; s. William Bangs Jr. and Edith Elizabeth (Guldi) P.; m. Linda Lee Tiska, Sept. 23, 1978. BS in Fgn. Svc., Georgetown U., 1972; JD, Fordham U., 1976. Bar: N.Y. 1977, U.S. Dist. Ct. (ea. dist.) N.Y. 1988, U.S. Ct. Appeals (2d cir.) 1988. Assoc. William B. Platt, Jr., Southampton, 1977-78; ptnr. Platt & Platt, Southampton, 1978-80, Platt, Platt & Platt, Southampton, 1980-2000; pvt. practice Southampton, 2001—. Counsel Elks, Southampton, 1983—. Mem. ABA (gen. practice sect., probate and trust sect., real property sect., 1985—, sect. of law practice mgmt. 1993—), N.Y. State Bar Assn. (real property sect., trusts and estates law, gen. practice sect. 1977—, invited participant statewide conf. solo and small firm practitioners 1991), Suffolk County Bar Assn. (real property com., solo and small firm task force 1992-97, Pres.' award of merit 1994), Elks (hon., exalted ruler 1982-83, hon. life, dist. govt. rels. chmn. 1991-94, esquire to dist. dep. 1993-94). Republican. Roman Catholic. Avocations: photography, videography, golf, scuba diving. Office: 99 Sanford Pl Southampton NY 11968-3338 Home Phone: 631-283-9031; Office Phone: 631-283-0099. Personal E-mail: jplattesq@aol.com.

PLATT, JOSEPH BEAVEN, former college president; b. Portland, Oreg., Aug. 12, 1915; s. William Bradbury and Mary (Beaven) P.; m. Jean Ferguson Rusk, Feb. 9, 1946; children: Ann Ferguson Walker, Elizabeth Beaven Garrow. BA, U. Rochester, 1937; PhD, Cornell U., 1942; LLD, U. So. Calif., 1969, Claremont McKenna Coll., 1982; DSc, Harvey Mudd Coll., 1981. Instr. physics U. Rochester, NY, 1941-43, from asst. prof. to prof., 1946-56, assoc. chmn. dept. physics, 1954-56; staff mem. Radiation Lab. MIT, Cambridge, 1943-46; founding pres. Harvey Mudd Coll., Claremont, Calif., 1956-76; pres. Claremont Grad. U., 1976-81. Trustee Aerospace Corp., 1972-85, Consortium for Advancement of Pvt. Higher Edn., 1985-92; chief physics br. AEC, 1949-51; cons. US Office Ordnance Rsch., NSF, 1953-56; mem. com. on sci. in UNESCO, NAS-NRC, 1960-62, mem. com. on internat. orgns. and programs, 1962-64, sci. advisor US Del., UNESCO Gen. Conf., Paris, 1960, alt. del., 1962, chmn. Subcom. on Sino-Am. Sci. Cooperation, 1965-79; mem. panel on internat. sci. Pres.'s Sci. Adv. Com., 1961; trustee Analytic Svcs., Inc., 1958-89, chmn., 1961-89; mem. adv. com. on sci. edn. NSF, 1965-70, 72-76, chmn., 1969-70, 73-74, 74-75; bd. dirs. Lincoln Found., 1979-85, Bell & Howell Corp., 1978-88, Am. Mut. Fund, 1981-88, DeVry, Inc., 1984-87, Sigma Rsch., 1983-87, Jacobs Engring. Co., 1978-86. Author: Harvey Mudd College: The First Twenty Years, 1994. Trustee China Found. for Promotion of Edn. and Culture, 1966—, Carnegie Found. for Advancement Tchg., 1970-78, Ancient Bibl. Manuscript Ctr., 1980-2005; chmn. select com. Master Plan for Higher Edn. Calif., 1971-73; mem. Carnegie Coun. for Policy Studies in Higher Edn., 1975-80. Fellow Am. Phys. Soc.; mem. IEEE, Automobile Club So. Calif. (bd. dirs. 1973-90, chmn. bd. dirs. 1986-87), Calif. Club, Sunset Club, Twilight Club, Cosmos Club, Bohemian Club, Phi Beta Kappa, Sigma Xi, Phi Kappa Phi. Home: 452 W 11th St Claremont CA 91711-3833 Business E-Mail: joseph_platt@hmc.edu.

PLATT, LESLIE A., lawyer; b. Bronx, NY, Aug. 7, 1944; s. Harold and Ann (Bienstock) P.; m. Marcia Ellin Berman, Aug., 1969; 1 son, Bill Lawrence. BA, George Washington U., 1966; JD, NYU, 1969. Bar: N.Y. 1970, U.S. Dist. Ct. D.C. 1972. Atty. advisor Office Gen. Counsel HUD, Washington, 1971-72, legis. atty., 1972-75, asst. gen. counsel for legis. svcs., 1975-78, assoc. gen. counsel for legis., 1978-80; dep. gen. counsel-legal counsel HEW (HHS 1980) Office Gen. Counsel, Washington, 1980-81, legal counsel and staff dir. White House Agent Orange group, 1980-81; pvt. practice Washington, 1982-91; exec. asst. to dir. NIH, 1991-92; exec. v.p., COO, gen. counsel The Inst. for Genomic Rsch., Gaithersburg, Md., 1992-95; sr. v.p. strategic devel., gen. counsel Am. Type Culture Collection, Manassas, Va., 1996-98; prin. assurance and adv. bus. practice Ernst & Young LLP, McLean, Va., 1999—2004; counsel Pillbury Winthrop Shaw Pittman, LLP, Washington, 2007—09; mng. dir., healthcare practice leader Daylight Forensic & Adv. LLC, Washington, 2009—. Pres, dir. Found. for Genetic Medicine, Inc., 1997—2004; adj. prof. George Mason U., 2005—. Patentee in field. Chmn. cmty. adv. bd. Fairfax Hosp. Assn. Cameron Glen Facility; chair steering com. Reston/Herndon Bus.-H.S. Partnership; mem. Loudoun County Sci. and Tech. Cabinet, 2002—04, chair, 2006—; bd. dirs. No. Va. Tech. Coun., 2002—05. Recipient Disting. Svc. award HUD, 1978. Mem. ABA, Fed. Bar Assn., Am. Jud. Soc., Fed. Sr. Exec. Svc. (charter), Internat. Bar Assn. Home: 11901 Triple Crown Rd Reston VA 20191-3015 Office: Daylight Forensic & Adv LLC 1155 Connecticut Ave NW 4th Fl Washington DC 20036 Office Phone: 202-552-8392. Business E-Mail: lplatt@daylightforensic.com.

PLATT, NICHOLAS, retired ambassador; b. NYC, Mar. 10, 1936; s. Geoffrey and Helen (Choate) P.; m. Sheila Maynard, June 28, 1957; children: Adam, Oliver, Nicholas. BA cum laude, Harvard U., 1957; MA, Johns Hopkins U., 1959. Commd. fgn. svc. officer Dept. State, 1959; vice consul Windsor, Ont., Canada, 1959-61; Chinese lang. trainee, 1962-63; polit. officer consulate gen. Hong Kong, 1964-68; chief Asian Communist areas divsn. Bur. Intelligence and Rsch., Dept. State, Washington, 1969, chief North Asia div., 1970, dept. dir. Exec. Secretariat staff, 1971, dir. staff, 1972-73; chief polit. sect. U.S. Liaison Office, Peking, China, 1973-74; 1st sec. Am. embassy, Tokyo, 1974-77; dir. Office of Japanese Affairs, Dept. State, 1977-78; mem. staff Nat. Security Council, White House, 1978-79; dep. asst. sec. for internat. security affairs Dept. Def., 1980-81; dep. asst. sec, for internat. orgn. affairs Dept. State, 1981-82; amb. Lusaka, Zambia, 1982-84; exec. sec., spl. asst. to sec. state Dept. State, 1985-87; amb. to The Philippines Am. Embassy, Manila, 1987-91, amb. to Pakistan, 1991-92; pres. Asia Soc., NYC, 1992—2004, pres. emeritus, 2004—. Bd. dirs. Fiduciary Trust Internat., Scenic Hudson. Recipient Meritorious award exemplary achievement pub. adminstrn. William A. Jump Found., 1973, Disting. Civilian Svc. medal Dept. Def., 1981, Presdl. Merit award, 1985, 87, Disting. Honor award U.S. Dept. State, 1987, 91, Wilbur Carr award, 1992. Mem. N.Y. Com. Fgn. Rels., Met. Club (Washington), Century Club, Union Club. Home: 131 E 69th St New York NY 10021-5158

PLATT, OLIVER, actor; b. Windsor, Ont., Can., Jan. 12, 1960; s. Nicholas Platt and Sheila Maynard; m. Camilla Campbell, 1993; children: Lily, George, Claire. Attended, Tufts U. Actor: (films) Crusoe, 1988, Married to the Mob, 1988, Working Girl, 1988, Flatliners, 1990, Postcards from the Edge, 1990, Beethoven, 1992, Diggstown, 1992, Benny & Joon, 1993, Indecent Proposal, 1993, The Temp, 1993, The Three Musketeers, 1993, Tall Tale, 1995, Funny Bones, 1995, Executive Decision, 1996, A Time to Kill, 1996, Venice, 1997, Bulworth, 1997, Dangerous Beauty, 1998, Doctor Dolittle, 1998, A Small Miracle, 1998, The Impostors, 1998, Simon Birch, 1998, Three to Tango, 1999, Gun Shy, 1999, Lake Placid, 1999, Bicentennial Man, 1999, Gun Shy, 2000, Ready to Rumble, 2000, Don't Say a Word, 2001, Liberty Stands Still, 2002, ZigZag, 2002, Ash Wednesday, 2002, Pieces of April, 2003, Hope Springs, 2003, Kinsey, 2004, Loverboy, 2005, The Ice Harvest, 2005, Casonova, 2005, The Ten, 2007, Martian Child, 2007, Frost/Nixon, 2008, Wonder Woman (voice), 2009, Year One, 2009, (TV films) The Infiltrator, 1995, Cinderelmo, 1999, (TV series) Deadline, 2000-01, Queens Supreme, 2003, Huff, 2004-, (Broadway plays) Shining City, 2006, Guys and Dolls, 2009; assoc. prodr. (film) Big Night, 1996. Office: c/o William Morris Agy 151 S El Camino Dr Beverly Hills CA 90212-2704*

PLATT, ROBERT L., retired industrial hygienist, consultant; b. Storm Lk., Iowa, Nov. 29, 1943; s. James Herbert Platt and Rita Catherine Hienrick; m. Nancy Benning Kelly, June 11, 1994. MS, U. Idaho, Moscow, 1973. Registered industrial hygienist Tenn., 1993. Supervisory hygienist US Army, Rock Island, Ill., 1979—2004. E-5 US Army, Edgewood Arsenal Md., 1969-71, served in 3 major mil. campaigns to include SE Asia, Iraq/Afghanistan. Decorated Order Mil. Merit Medicine US Army Med. Dept., Civilian Meritorious Achievement award US Army; recipient 3 Comdr. awards for Excellence, 2 Army Achievement awards. Mem.: VFW, Am. Legion. Conservative. Achievements include defined process, procedure and destination for containers of nerve agent and mustard gas stockpiles in the Department of Defense. Avocations: golf, travel, fishing, hunting, gardening. Personal E-mail: rbplatt@iowatelecom.net.

PLATT, THOMAS COLLIER, JR., federal judge; b. NYC, May 29, 1925; s. Thomas Collier and Louise Platt; m. Ann Byrd Symington, June 25, 1948; children: Ann Byrd, Charles Collier, Thomas Collier, III, Elizabeth Louise. BA, Yale U., 1947, LL.B., 1950. Bar: N.Y. 1950. Assoc. Root, Ballantine, Harlan, Bushby & Palmer, NYC, 1950-53; asst. U.S. atty. Bklyn., 1953-56; assoc. Bleakley, Platt, Schmidt, Hart & Fritz, NYC, 1956-60, ptnr., 1960-74; judge U.S. Dist. Ct. (ea. dist.) N.Y., 1974—, chief judge Bklyn., 1988-95. Former dir. Phoenix Mut. Life Ins. Co., RAC Corp., McIntyre Aviation, Inc.; atty. Village of Laurel Hollow, N.Y., 1958-74; acting police justice Village of Lloyd Harbor, N.Y., 1958-63 Alt. del. Republican Nat. Conv., 1964, 68, 72; del. N.Y. State Rep. Conv., 1966; trustee Brooks Sch., North Andover, Mass., 1968-82, pres., 1970-74. Served with USN, 1943-46 Mem. Fed. Judges Assn. (sec., bd. dirs. 1982-91). Clubs: Phelps Assn. (New Haven) (bd. govs. 1960-98); Cold Spring Harbor Beach (N.Y.) (bd. mgrs. 1964-70); Yale of N.Y.C. Episcopalian. Office: US Dist Ct PO Box 9014 Central Islip NY 11722-9014

PLATT, WARREN E., lawyer; b. McNary, Ariz., Aug. 5, 1943; BA, Mich. State U., 1965; JD, U. Ariz., 1969. Bar: Ariz. 1969, Calif. 1991, Texas 1993. Atty. Snell & Wilmer, Phoenix. Mng. editor Ariz. Law Rev., 1968—69. Fellow Am. Coll. Trial Lawyers; mem. Blue Key, Order of Coif, Phi Alpha Delta Office: Snell & Wilmer One Arizona Ctr Phoenix AZ 85004-0001 also: 600 Anton Blvd Ste 1400 Costa Mesa CA 92626 Office Phone: 602-382-6292, 714-427-7475. Business E-Mail: wplatt@swlaw.com.

PLATT, WILLIAM HENRY, judge; b. Allentown, Pa., Jan. 25, 1940; s. Henry and Genevieve (McElroy) P.; m. Maureen Hart, Nov. 29, 1969; children: Meredith H., William H., James H. AB, Dickinson Coll., 1961; JD, U. Pa., 1964. Bar: Pa. 1967, U.S. Supreme Ct. 1971. Ptnr. Yarus and Platt, Allentown, 1967-77; asst. pub. defender Lehigh County (Pa.), 1972-75, chief pub. defender, 1975-76, dist. atty., 1976-91; ptnr. Eckert, Seamans, Cherin & Mellott, 1991-95; city solicitor City of Allentown, 1994-95; judge Ct. Common Pleas of Lehigh County, Allentown, 1996—, pres. judge, 2002—07, 2008—. Mem. criminal procedural rules com. Supreme Ct. Pa., 1982-92, chmn., 1986-92; mem. Gov.'s Trial Ct. Nominating Commn. Lehigh County, 1984-87; mem. Pa. Commn. on Crime and Delinquency Victim Services Adv. Com., 1983-91. Served with M.P., U.S. Army, 1964-66. Mem.: ABA, Pa. Conf. of State Trial Judges (edn. com. 1997—2002, chmn. criminal law sect. 2001—), Pa. Bar Inst. (bd. dirs. 1989—2000, exec. com. 1994—2000, pres. 1997—98, hon. life dir.), Pa. Assn. Dist. Attys. (exec. com. 1980—86, pres. 1983—84, chmn. 1986—87, tng. inst. mem. 1986—91), Nat. Assn.

Dist. Attys. (state dir. 1982—84), Lehigh County Bar Assn. (bd. dirs. 2007—), Pa. Bar Assn. Office: Lehigh County Courthouse 455 W Hamilton St Allentown PA 18101-1614 Office Phone: 610-782-3393.

PLATTNER, MARC FLOREA, foundation administrator, editor; b. NYC, May 8, 1945; s. Irving Herman and Claire Yvette (Bakst) P.; m. Jacqueline Suzanne Stark, Sept. 19, 1976; children: David Marshall, Laura Wolcott. AB summa cum laude, Yale U., 1966; PhD in Govt., Cornell U., 1974. Mng. editor The Pub. Interest, NYC, 1971-75; program officer The Twentieth Century Fund, NYC, 1975-81; adviser econ. and social affairs US Mission to UN, NYC, 1981-83; fellow Nat. Humanities Ctr., Rsch. Triangle Pk., NC, 1983-84; dir. program Nat. Endowment Democracy, Washington, 1984-89, counselor, 1989—2002, v.p. rsch. studies, 2002—; editor Jour. Democracy, 1989—; dir. Internat. Forum Dem. Studies, 1994—. Adj. prof., Touro Coll., N.Y.C., 1973-75; cons. Exec. Coun. on Fgn. Diplomats, Armonk, N.Y., 1984-90; vis prof. Robert Schuman Ctr. Adv. Studies European U. Inst., Florence, Italy, 2002-03. Author: Rousseau's State of Nature, 1979, Democracy Without Borders?, 2008; editor: Human Rights in Our Time, 1984; co-editor: The Global Resurgence of Democracy, 1993, Capitalism, Socialism and Democracy Revisited, 1993, Nationalism, Ethnic Conflict, and Democracy, 1994, Democratization in Africa, 1999, The Democratic Invention, 2000, The Global Divergence of Democracies, 2001, Islam and Democracy in the Middle East, 2003, World Religions and Democracy, 2005, Electoral Systems and Democracy, 2006, The State of India's Democracy, 2007, Latin America's Struggle for Democracy, 2008, How People View Democracy, 2008; contbr. numerous articles to various publs. Dir. issues rsch., Moynihan for Senate campaign, N.Y.C., 1976. Herbert H. Lehman fellow, 1966-70; Earhart Found. fellow, 1970-71. Mem. Am. Polit. Sci. Assn., Coun. on Foreign Relations, Phi Beta Kappa. Office: Nat Endowment Democracy 1025 F St NW 8th Fl Washington DC 20004 Office Phone: 202-378-9900. Business E-Mail: marc@ned.org.

PLATTS, HOWARD GREGORY, cultural organization administrator, non for profit trustee; b. Aug. 14, 1947; s. Thayer Horton and Anne Elizabeth (Gregory) P.; m. Elizabeth Hertzler Murray, June 7, 1969; children: James Thayer, Christopher Wilke. AB, Harvard U., 1969; M. Pub. and Pvt. Mgmt., Yale U., 1980. Tchr. Potomac Sch., McLean, Va., 1969-72; investment officer First Am. Bank, Washington, 1972-78; fin. analyst Yale U., New Haven, 1979; fin. asst. to pres. Nat. Geog. Soc., Washington, 1980-82, asst. treas., 1982-91, sr. v.p., treas., 1992—. Trustee Nat. Presbyn. Sch., Washington, 1988-91, Decatur House, Washington, 1994-2004, Ctr. for the Study of the Presidency, Washington, 2004—; chmn., trustee regional blood svcs. ARC, Balt., 1992-2000; treas., bd. dirs. Friends of Fort Dupont, Washington, 1995-2002; governing bd. St. Albans Sch., Washington, 1997-2003 Trustee Westmoreland Congl. Ch., 1988-91. Mem. Washington Soc. Investment Analysts (pres., bd. dirs. 1985-91). Home: 5302 Portsmouth Rd Bethesda MD 20816-2929 Office: Nat Geog Soc 1145 17th St NW Washington DC 20036-4701 Office Phone: 202-857-7417. Business E-Mail: platts@aya.yale.edu.

PLATTS, TODD RUSSELL, United States Representative from Pennsylvania, state legislator; b. York, Pa., Mar. 5, 1962; m. Leslie Platts; 2 children. BS summa cum laude in Pub. Adminstrn., Shippensburg U. Pa., 1984; JD cum laude, Pepperdine U. Sch. Law, Malibu, Calif., 1991. Atty. Barley, Snyder, Senft & Cohen; mem. Pa. State Ho. Reps. from Dist. 196, 1993-2001, US Congress from 19th Pa. dist., 2001—, mem. transp. and infrastructure com., mem. edn. and labor com., ranking mem. healthy families and cmtys. subcommittee, mem. oversight and govt. reform com. Mem. aging and youth edn. com. State of Pa., 1993. Republican. Episcopalian. Office: US House Reps 1032 Longworth House Office Bldg Washington DC 20515 Office Phone: 202-225-5836. Office Fax: 202-226-1000.*

PLATTS-MILLS, THOMAS ALEXANDER EVELYN, immunologist, educator, researcher; b. Colchester, Essex, Eng., Nov. 22, 1941; arrived in US, 1982; s. John Faithful and Janet Katherine (Cree) Platts-Mills; m. Roberta Rosenstock, Apr. 9, 1970; children: Eliza, Timothy, James, Oliver. BA in Animal Physiology, Balliol Coll., Eng., 1963; PhD, London U., 1982. Fellow in medicine Johns Hopkins U., Balt., 1971-74; staff mem. Med. Rsch. Coun., England, 1975—79; hon. cons. physician Northwick Park Hosp., London, 1978-82; Oscar Swineford, Jr. prof. medicine & microbiology, head divsn. allergy & immunology U. Va., Charlottesville, 1982—, dir. Asthma & Allergic Diseases Ctr., 1993—. Mem. immunological scis. study sect. NIH, 1988—92. Mem. editl. bd. Am. Jour. Respiratory Critical Care Medicine, Clin. & Exptl. Immunology, Clin. Allergy, Jour. Immunological Methods; contbr. articles to profl. jours. Fellow: Royal Coll. Physicians; mem.: Southeastern Allergy Assn. (pres. 1987—88, Hal Davidson award 1986), Brit. Soc. Allergy & Clin. Immunology, Am. Acad. Allergy, Asthma & Immunology (v.p. 2004—05, pres.-elect 2005—06, pres. 2006—07), Assn. Am. Physicians. Office: U Va Med Sch PO Box 801335 Charlottesville VA 22908-0225 Office Phone: 434-924-2209. Office Fax: 434-924-5779. E-mail: tap2z@virginia.edu.*

PLATUS, LIBBY, journalist, art educator, sculptor, artist; b. LA, Aug. 18, 1939; d. Benjamin Lyon and Gertrude Goldman; children: Julie Linda, Diana Lisa. BA, UCLA, 1961. Interviewer, writer Restaurant Hospitality Mag., 2005—09, Sante Mag., 2007—09; writer Moving Pictures Mag., 2006—07, Cheers Mag., 2007—08, Valley Mag., 2007, Grit Mag., 2009, Fit Pregnancy Mag., 2009. Lectr., condr. workshops numerous internat., nat., regional meetings and meetings in all 50 states, World Craft Conf., Kyoto, 1978, Vienna, 80, Glasgow Sch. Art, Scotland, 1980, 84, Loughborough Coll. Art., England, 1980, 84, RI Sch. Design, 1982, Parsons Sch. Design, NYC, 1982, Arrowmont, Gatlinburg, Tenn., 1978, Gatlinburg, 83, Gatlinburg, 87, Konstfackakolan, Sweden, 1984, Goldsmith's Coll., England, 1984, Taldeteo Linen Koneakoulo, Finland, 1984, Fairbanks Art Assn., Alaska, 1985, 95, 97, 2000, 04, Savannah Coll. Art and Design, Ga., 1987, 89, 90, 92, 94, 99, E. NC U., Greenville, 1989, Greenville, 92, Greenville, 97, Greenville, 2000, Greenville, 02, Navajo CC, Shiprock Reservation, N.Mex., 1992, World Wildfowl Carving Exhbn., Ward Found., Md., 1990, Kansas City Art Inst., 1990, 92, So. Ute Tribal Hdqrs., Ignacio, Colo., 1993, U. Western Sydney Design Dept., 1993, Sydney Coll. Art, 1993, Victorian Coll. Art, Melbourne, Australia, 1993, U. S. Australia, Underdale, Australia, 1993, Australian Nat. U., Canberra, 1993, Walariki Poly. Coll., Rotorua, New Zealand, 1993, Actearoa Inst., South Auckland, New Zealand, 1993, numerous others; cons. Millstream Arts Festival Coll. St. Benedict, St. Joseph, Minn., 1992, Mountain State Art and Crafts Festival, Cedar Lakes, W.Va., 1992, Grand Junction area C. of C., Home Based Bus. Trade Fair, Colo., 1992, Yavapal Coll. Creative Comm. Convergence, Sedona, Ariz., 1995; judge regional exhbn. Fairbanks Art Assn., 1984, Art Harvest Jr. League Clearwater-Dunedin, Fla., 2000, Greater Gulf Coast Art Festival, Pensacola, Fla., 1999; judge culinary competition Mont. Dept. Commerce, 1999, Western Food Svc. and Hospitality Expo., LA, 2001, Roma Pizza Competition, LA, 2007, Long Beach, Calif., 08; panel moderator Calif. Restaurant Assn., Western Food Svc. and Hospitality Expo., LA, 2004; juror Millstream Arts Festival, Coll. St. Benedict, St. Joseph, 1992; participant Charmin Care TV comml., 1989; judge Roma Pizza Competition, 2006, LA Conventional, Calif., 2007, San Diego Bay Wine & Food Festival, 2007, Jack Daniel World Barbeque Championship, Lynchburg, Tenn., 2008. Exhibited in group shows at Richmond Designer Craftsmen, Calif., 1971, Crocker Gallery, Sacramento, 1973, Comsky Gallery, Beverly Hills, Calif., 1973, Galeria del Sol, Santa Barbara, Calif., 1973, Laguna Beach Mus. Art, Calif., 1973, Riverside Art Ctr., 1974, Calif. State U., Northridge, 1974, Fullerton, 1974, Calif. Design, LA, 1976, Cleve. Mus. Art, 1977, Represented in permanent collections Tex. Christian U., Faberge Hdqrs., NYC, pub. and pvt. collections, prin. works include Big Canyon Country Club, Newport Beach, Calif., Carolando Hyatt Hotel, Victorville, Calif., Blue Cross So. Calif., LA. Mem., mem. citizens adv. commn. LA Olympics Cultural and Fine Arts Commn., 1980—84; adv. bd. Crafts Report Edn. Fund, 1985—86; participant Rotary Internat. Group Study Exch., Bangalore, India, 1998. Recipient Graphic Achievement award, Fox River Paper Corp., 1974; named winner, Tex. Christian U. Nat. Invitational Fiberwork Competition, 1977. Mem.: Artists Equity (adv. bd. L.A. chpt. 1981—87). Home and Office: PO Box 55026 Sherman Oaks CA 91413-0026 Office Phone: 818-906-3989. Personal E-mail: libbyplatus@gmail.com.

PLAUCHE, NANCY CAROLINE, retired counselor; b. Lima, Ohio, Oct. 31, 1938; d. Willis Sylvanis and Mabel Louise (Neiswander) Siferd; m. Jack Plauche (div. 1979); children: Michel, Jacqueline, Jon. BFA, Ohio U., 1960; MS, Nova U., Ft. Lauderdale, Fla., 1984; PhD, The Union Inst., Cin., 1989. Counselor Pinellas county Schs., St. Petersburg, Fla., 1980—2002; smoke stopper's instr. Nat. Ctr. for Health Promotion/Morton Plant Hosp., Clearwater, Fla., 1986-92; ret., 2002. Co-dir. Counseling & Profl. Cons. Svcs., St. Petersburg, 1984-88. Co-author: All About Me, 1985, Safer Parenting, 1985; contbr. articles to profl. jours. Mem. Dem. Exec. Com., Wood City W.Va., 1977-79; sustainor Jr. League St. Petersburg. Mem. APA, So. Assn. Coll. Counselors, Am. Psychol. Soc., Am. Arbitration Assn., People to People Internat., Fla. Counseling Assn., Fla. Sch. Counselors Assn., Clearwater Area Panhellenic Assn. Democrat. Avocations: painting, drawing, travel, cultural exchange.

PLAUD, JOSEPH JULIAN, psychology educator; b. Worcester, Mass., Mar. 25, 1965; s. Henry Emile and Barbara Ann (Perry) P.; m. Christine Marie Therlault, Mar. 14, 1987 (div. Mar. 1990); 1 child, Brianna Marie; m. Deborah Muench, Jan. 30, 1999. BA summa cum laude, Clark U., 1987; PhD in Psychology, U. Maine, 1993. Lic. clin. psychologist, Mass.; bd. cert. behavior analyst Behavior Analyst Cert. Bd. Psychology resident U. Miss. Med. Ctr., Jackson, 1992-93; asst. prof. psychology U. ND, Grand Forks, 1993-97; dir. rsch., webmaster Cambridge Ctr. for Behavioral Studies, Mass., 1999—2003; pres. Franklin D. Roosevelt Am. Heritage Ctr., Inc. Cons. ND Devel. Ctr., Grafton, 1994—, State of NH, 1999—; forensic cons., 1993—; vis. scholar Brown U., 1998—; COO New Sch. for Learning Scis.; forensic psychology cons. Applied Behavioral Cons., Inc. Author: From Behavior Theory to Behavior Therapy, 1997; editor-in-chief Jour. Behavioral Analysis and Therapy, Jour. Sexual Offender Civil Commitment: Science and the Law; contbr. articles to profl. jours. Pres. Franklin D. Roosevelt Am. Heritage Ctr., Inc. Lt. comdr. Med. Svc. Corps, USNR, 2002. Fellow APA, Behavior Therapy and Rsch. Soc. (clin.); mem. AAAS, Assn. for Advancement of Behavior Therapy, Am. Psychol. Soc., Phi Beta Kappa, Psi Chi. Democrat. Roman Catholic. Home: 44 Hickory Ln Whitinsville MA 01588-1356 E-mail: plaud@fdrheritage.org.

PLAUT, JONATHAN VICTOR, rabbi; b. Chgo., Oct. 7, 1942; s. W. Gunther and Elizabeth (Strauss) P.; m. Carol Ann Fainstein, July 5, 1965; children: Daniel Abraham, Deborah Maxine. BA, Macalester Coll., St. Paul, Minn., 1964; postgrad., Hebrew Union Coll., Jerusalem, 1967-68; BHL, Hebrew Union Coll., Cin., 1968, MA, 1970, DHL, 1977, DD (hon.), 1995. Ordained rabbi, 1970. Rabbi Congregation Beth-El, Windsor, Ont., Canada, 1970-84; sr. rabbi Temple Emanu-El, San Jose, Calif., 1985-93; dir. comty. outreach and involvement Jewish Fed. of Met. Detroit, 1993-95; pres. JVP Fund Raising Cons., Inc., Farmington Hills, Mich., 1994—. Lectr. Assumption Coll. Sch., 1972-84, St. Clair Coll., 1982-84, U. Windsor, Ont., Can., 1984; adj. asst. prof. Santa Clara U., 1985-93; adj. prof. U. Detroit Mercy, 2002—; vis. Rabbinic scholar Temple Beth El, 1993—95; pres. JVP Fund Raising Cons., 1994—; rabbi emeritus Congregation Beth El, Traverse City, Mich., 1999—2004; rabbi Temple Beth Israel, Jackson, Mich., 2000—. Contbg. author: Reform Judaism in America: A Biographical Dictionary and Sourcebook, 1993; author: The Jews of Windsor 1790-1990: A Historical Chronicle, 2007; editor: Through the Sound of Many Voices, 1982, Jour. Can. Jewish Hist. Soc., 1976-83, One Voice: The Selected Sermons of W. Gunther Plaut, 2007, Eight Decades: The Selected Writings of W., 2008; The Plaut Family Tracing the Legacy, 2007, also articles; host weekly program Religious Scope, Sta. CBET-TV, Religion in News, Sta. CKWW, 1971-84. Pres. Jewish Nat. Fund Windsor, 1978-81, chmn. bd. dirs., 1981-84; chmn. United Jewish Appeal Windsor, 1981-83, State of Israel Bonds, Windsor, 1980; nat. bd. dirs. Jewish Nat. Fund Can., 1972-84; pres. Reform Rabbis of Can., 1982-84; bd. dirs. Can. Jewish Congress, 1978-84, Jewish Family Svc. Santa Clara County, 1987-90, Jewish Fedn. Greater San Jose, 1986-93; chaplain San Jose Fire Dept., 1987-93; mem. exec. cabinet United Jewish Appeal, Windsor, 1971-84, mem. nat. rabbinic cabinet, 1993-95; mem. exec. com. Windsor Jewish Community Coun., 1970-84, chmn. 1975-84; mem. adv. coun. Riverview unit Windsor Hosp. Ctr., 1972-81; pres. Credit Counselling Svc. Met. Windsor, 1977-79. Honoree Jewish Nat. Fund, 1985. Mem. NCCJ, Can. Jewish Congress (nat. exec. bd. 1978-84), Can. Jewish Hist. Soc. (nat. v.p. 1974-84), Calif. Bd. Rabbis, Rabbinic Assn. Greater San Jose (chmn. 1986-87), Ctrl. Conf. Am. Rabbis, Nat. Assn. Temple Educators. Home and Office: 30208 Kingsway Dr Farmington Hills MI 48331-1648 Office Phone: 248-505-8888. Fax: 248-788-4144. Personal E-mail: jvplaut@earthlink.net.

PLAVE, LEE JONATHAN, lawyer; s. Seymour and Matty P.; m. Ilene P. BA, Clark U., 1980; JD cum laude, NY Law Sch., 1983. Bar: NY 1983, DC 1987, Va. 2004. Atty., Used Car Rule program coord. FTC, Washington, 1983—87; assoc. to ptnr. Brownstein & Zeidman, P.C., Washington, 1987—96; ptnr. DLA Piper (formerly Piper Rudnick), Washington, 1996—2007; ptnr., chmn. Domain Name practice group DLA Piper, Washington, 2005—07; co-founding ptnr. Plave Koch PLC, Va., 2007—. Assoc. editor NY Law Sch. Jour. Internat. and Comparative Law, 1982-83; contbr. articles to profl. jours. Mem. ABA, Internat. Bar Assn., Va State Bar Assn., DC Bar Assn., NY State Bar Assn., Internat. Franchise Assn. Jewish. Avocations: ice hockey, stamp collecting/philately, politics. Office: Plave Koch PLC 12355 Sunrise Valley Dr Ste 230 Reston VA 20191 Office Phone: 703-774-1203. Office Fax: 703-774-1201. Business E-Mail: lplave@plavekoch.com.

PLAYER, THELMA B., librarian; b. Owosso, Mich. d. Walter B. and Grace (Willoughby) Player. BA, Western Mich. U., 1954. Reference asst. USAF Aero Chart and Info. Ctr., Washington, 1954-57; reference libr. USN Hydrographic Office, Suitland, Md., 1957-58, asst. libr., 1958-59; tech. libr.br. head USN Spl. Project Office, Washington, 1959-68, Strategic Sys. Project Office, Washington, 1969-76. Mem. AAUW, English Speaking Union, Nat. Geneal. Socl, Ohio Geneal. Soc. Royal Oak Found., Daus of Union Vets. of Civil War, David Ackerman Descs. Episcopalian. Home: 730 24th St NW Washington DC 20037-2519

PLAYFAIR, JIM, professional hockey coach; b. Vanderhoof, BC, Can., May 22, 1964; m. Roxanne Playfair; children: Dylan, Jackson, Austyn. Defenseman Portland Winter Hawks, 1981—83, Calgary Wranglers, 1983—84, Edmonton Oilers, 1984, Nova-Scotia Oilers, 1984—87, Saginaw Hawks, 1987—89, Chgo. Blackhawks, 1987—89, Indpls. Ice, 1989—92; head coach Dayton Bombers (ECHL), 1993—96, Michigan K-Wings (IHL), 1996—98, Saint John Flames (AHL), 2000—02; asst. coach Calgary Flames, 2003—06, head coach, 2006—07, assoc. coach, 2007—09; head coach Abbotsford Heat (AHL), 2009—. Recipient Minor Profl. Coach of Yr., The Hockey News, 2001. Achievements include being the head coach of Calder Cup Champion Saint John Flames, 2001. Office: c/o Calgary Flames PO Box 1540 Stn M Calgary AB Canada T2P 3B9

PLAYS, DANA, film director, educator; d. Paul Irwin and Edith Fiore; children: Corbin Theo, Nathan Eliot Heintz. BFA with distinction, Calif. Coll. Arts, Oakland, 1978, MFA with high distinction, 1987. Cert. avid profl. Video Symphony, Burbank, Calif., 2005. Humanities symposia coord. San Francisco Art Inst., 1984—90; asst. prof. Syracuse U., 1990—96; assoc. prof. Occidental Coll., LA, 1996—2004, U. Tampa, Fla., 2005—. Dir.: (film) Rhizome (1st prize, Santa Fe Winter Film Expo, 1983, 1st prize, Black Maria Film Festival, Juror's Choice, 2002, Dir.'s Citation, Black Maria Film and Video Festival, 2007), Shards (Exptl. Film award, San Francisco Art Inst. Film Festival, 1990), Via Rio (1st prize, Ann Arbor Film Festival, 1986), Don't Means Do, Across the Border (Bronze award, Houston Internat. Film Festival, 1983), Santa Fe Winter Film Expo, Silverfish, Nuclear Family (Dir.'s Choice, Black Maria Film and Video Festival, 1995, 1st prize, Empire State Film Festival, 2002), Grain Graphics (1st prize, UICA San Francisco Art Inst. Festival, 1978), Arrow Creek, Love Stories My Grandmother Tells (3rd prize, Big Muddy Film Festival, 1995), Zero Hour (Dir.'s Choice, Sinking Creek Film Celebration, 1982, Tom Berman award, 1992). Mem. Film Forum LA, 1997—2006; bd. trustees Putney Sch., Vt., 2002—05. Recipient Alumni Faculty Rsch. award, U. Tampa, 2007—08, Mellon award, Occidental Coll., 1999, Nuclear Family Irror's Choice award, Black Maria Film & Video Festival, 2002, Rhizome Dir's Citation award, 2007, First Prize, Santa Winter Film Expo, 1983, Bronze award, Houston Internat. Film Festival, 1983; David Delo Faculty Rsch. grant, U. Tampa, 2007—08, 2008—. Mem.: Canyon Cinema, Filmmaker's Coop., Assn. Am. U. Profs., Coll. Art Assn., Soc. Cinema and Media Studies (mem. 2007—08). Democrat. Office: Univ Tampa Film and Media 401 W Kennedy Blvd Tampa FL 33606 Home: 777 N Ashley Dr Tampa FL 33602 Personal E-mail: dplays@yahoo.com. Business E-Mail: dplays@ut.edu.

PLAZEK, DONALD JOHN, materials scientist, educator; b. Milw., Jan. 12, 1931; s. Stanley and Marian (Parker) Plazek; m. Patricia Lenore Filkins, Oct. 29, 1955; children: Mary, Joseph, Caroline, Daniel, John, David, Anne. BS in Chemistry, U. Wis., 1953, PhD in Phys. Chemistry, 1957. Postdoctoral rsch. fellow U. Wis., Madison, 1957-58; fellow Mellon Inst., Pitts., 1958-67; assoc. prof. materials engring. U. Pitts., 1967-74, prof., 1974-93, prof. emeritus, 1993—. Adj. prof. chemistry Carnegie-Mellon U., Pitts., 1987—. Mem. adv. bd. Jour. Polymer Sci., 1991—98; assoc. editor: Rubber Chemistry and Tech., 1993—97; contbr. scientific papers to profl. jours. Fellow, Brit. Rsch. Coun., 1976—77, Japan Soc. Promotion Sci., 1987—88, Polymer and Materials Sci. Engring., 2006. Fellow: Am. Phys. Soc.; mem.: Soc. Rheology (Bingham medal 1995), Am. Chem. Soc. (George Stafford Whitby award for disting. tchg. and rsch. Rubber divsn. 1993, Fernley H. Banbury award Rubber Divsn. 2009). Avocations: tennis, tropical fish, mushrooms. Office: U Pitts Dept Mech Engring and Materials Sci Dept Pittsburgh PA 15261-0001 Home Phone: 412-766-0247. Business E-Mail: plazek@engr.pitt.edu.

PLEASANT, JAMES CARROLL, mathematician, computer sciences educator; b. Greenville, NC, Jan. 9, 1936; s. George Lemuel and Elizabeth Pleasant; m. Louise D. Pleasant, Feb. 22, 1957; children: Carroll, Gary, Scott. BS, East Carolina U., Greenville, NC, 1958, MA, 1960; PhD, U. S.C., 1965. Prof. math. East Carolina U., Greenville, 1960-61, 63-65, East Tenn. State U., Johnson City, 1966-85, prof. computer scis., 1985—2003; prof. math. Milligan Coll., 2003—04; tchg. prof. East Carolina U., 2004—. Rsch. assoc. Oak Ridge (Tenn.) Nat. Lab., 1975-80. Orch. player Johnson City Symphony, 1970-85. Mem. Assn. Computing Machinery. Avocations: fishing, rv-ing, horseback riding. Home: 5025 County Home Rd Greenville NC 27858-9667 Home Phone: 252-321-2649; Office Phone: 252-328-4253. Business E-Mail: pleasantj@ecu.edu. E-mail: ljplez@usit.net.

PLEASANT, JAMES SCOTT, lawyer; b. Anniston, Ala., July 14, 1943; s. James C. and Barbara (Scott) P.; m. Susan M. Pleasant, May 17, 1966; children: Deborah Kaye, Carol Ann, Julie Ruth. BS, Oreg. State U., 1965; JD summa cum laude, Williamette U., 1972. Bar: Tex. 1972, U.S. Dist. Ct. (no. dist.) Tex. 1973, U.S. Ct. Appeals (5th cir.) 1975, U.S. Supreme Ct. 1977. Ptnr. Gardere Wynne Sewell, LLP, Dallas, 1972—. Mem. Smithsonian Assn., Washington, 1985—, Dallas Mus. of Art, 1987—. Capt. U.S. Army, 1966-69, Vietnam. Mem. ABA (partnership law sect. 1969—), Tex. Bar Assn. (partnership law sect. 1989—), Vietnam Pilots Assn., Dustoff Assn. Office: Gardere Wynne Sewell LLP 1601 Elm St Ste 3000 Dallas TX 75201-4761 Office Phone: 214-999-4690. Business E-Mail: pleasant@gardere.com.

PLEASANT, JOHN RUFFIN, JR., retired literature and language professor; b. Shreveport, La., Oct. 26, 1938; s. John Ruffin and Margaret Noble Pleasant; m. Deborah Tramel Pleasant, June 30, 2000; children: Elizabeth Alice Hudson, Margaret Evelyn, Leslie Carrington Cantrell, Catherine Brooke Alexander, John Kirk. PhD, La. State U., Baton Rouge, 1976. Assoc. prof. English Southeastern La. U., Hammond, 1965—97, assoc. prof. emeritus. Adj. instr. LSU, Shreveport. Actor: (plays) The Oldest Living Graduate. Pres. United Meth. Men, Hammond, 1987—90. Capt. US Army, 1963—67, Baton Rouge. Decorated Parachute Badge US Army. Mem.: Thomas Wolfe Soc. Democrat. Methodist. Avocations: travel, reading, golf. Home: 5921 Fern Ave Shreveport LA 71105

PLEASANTS, JOHN F., electronics executive; b. 1965; m. Jennifer Pleasants; children: Jack, James. BA in Polit. Sci., Yale U., 1987; MBA, Harvard U., 1993. With Frito-Lay divsn. PepsiCo; with Hygiene Industries; gen. mgr., new mkts. divsn. City Search IAC / InterActive Corp, 1996; exec. v.p. new markets Ticketmaster Online-CitySearch (divsn. IAC/InterActiveCorp), Pasadena, Calif., pres. ticketing & transactions; pres. info. sys., CEO Ticketmaster, Pasadena, Calif., 2000—03; pres., CEO Ticketmaster, Reserve Am., Ticketweb, Pasadena, 2003—05, Revolution Health Group, 2005—08; pres. global publishing, COO Electronic Arts, Inc., Redwood City, Calif., 2008—. Bd. dir. Ticketmaster7, Australia, The Active Network, La Jolla, Calif. Office: Electronic Arts Inc 209 Redwood Shores Pky Redwood City CA 94065

PLEASANTS, JULIAN MCIVER, history educator, summer school director; b. Pinehurst, NC, Nov. 12, 1938; s. James McIver and Jean (McIver) P.; m. Donna Marie Bishop, Feb. 28, 1987. BA, Davidson Coll., Chapel Hill, NC, 1960; MA, U. NC, 1962, PhD, 1971. Asst. prof. Western Carolina U., Cullowhee, NC, 1966-67; from asst. prof. to prof. U. Fla., Gainesville, 1969—. Instr. Converse Coll., Spartanburg, SC, 1962; dir. summer sch. U. New Orleans, U. Fla., 1976-97, dir., proctor oral history program, 1996-; cons. Documentary on Frank P. Graham, 1991. Author: Frank P. Graham and The Senate Election of 1950 in North Carolina, 1990 (Best Book in NC History 1991), Buncombe Bob: The Life and Times of Robert Rice Reynolds, 2001, Orange Journalism: Voices From Florida Newspapers, 2003, Hanging Chads: The Inside Story of the 2000 Presidential Recount in Florida, 2004, Gator Tales: An Oral History of the University of Florida. Dir. Upward Bound program, Gainesville, 1971. 1st lt. US Army, 1962-64. Rotary Internat. fellow, 1965-66, fellow Archie K. Davis Found., 1990-91; recipient award of merit City of Innsbruck, Austria, 1985, 91; named one of 10 Outstanding Profs., Interfraternity Coun.-Omicron Delta Kappa, 1972; named Most Inspiring Prof. U. Fla., 1989. Mem. Fla. Hist. Assn., So. Hist. Assn., Golden Key (hon.), Phi Alpha Theta. Avocations: reading, walking, travel. Office: U Fla History Dept 4103 Turlington Hall Gainesville FL 32611 Home: 4051 Fearrington Post Pittsboro NC 27312 Business E-Mail: jpleasan@history.ufl.edu.

PLEAU, LARRY (LAWRENCE WINSLOW PLEAU), professional sports team executive; b. Boston, June 29, 1947; s. Ernest and Norma (Knowles) Pl.; m. Wendy Sargent MacDougall, May 3, 1969; children, Steven Lawrence, Shannon Lynn. Grad. high sch. Center Montreal Canadiens, 1969-72, New England Whalers, Hartford, Conn., 1972-79; asst. coach Hartford Whalers, 1979-80, coach, gen. mgr., 1980-83, asst. gen. mgr., 1983-84, coach, 1988-89; coach, gen. mgr. Binghamton Whalers, NY, 1984-88; asst. gen. mgr. player devel. NY Rangers, 1989, asst. gen. mgr., v.p. player personnel; sr. v.p., gen. mgr. St. Louis Blues, 1997—. Player US Olympic Hockey Team, Grenoble, France, 1968, US Nat. Hockey Team, Stockholm, 1969, USA Hockey Team, Providence, 1976; radio, TV commentator, ESPN, Hartford, 1979-80; owner Bridge Marina Inc. With US Army, 1967-69. Named Coach of Yr., Am. Hockey League, 1986—87, NHL Exec. of Yr., Sporting News, 2000; named to NHL All-Star Team, 1973—75, US Hockey Hall of Fame, 2000. Democrat. Achievements include being a member of Stanley Cup Champion Montreal Canadiens, 1971. Avocations: deep sea fishing, golf, tennis. Office: St Louis Blues Hockey Club Savvis Ctr 1401 Clark Ave Saint Louis MO 63103

PLEHN, JONATHAN FREEMAN, internal medicine and cardiology educator; b. NYC, Feb. 12, 1952; MD, NYU, 1977. Bd. cert. in internal medicine, 1981; bd. cert. in cardiovasc. disease, 1983. Intern Montefiore Hosp.-U. Pitts., 1977-78, resident in internal medicine, 1978-80, resident in cardiology, 1980-81; fellow in cardiology Rush-Presbyn.-St. Luke's Hosp., Chgo., 1981-83; staff physician Boston City Hosp., 1983-88, Mary Hitchcock Meml. Hosp., Lebanon, N.H., 1988—; asst. prof. internal medicine Boston U. Sch. Medicine, 1983-88, Dartmouth Med. Sch., Hanover, N.H., 1988-91, assoc. prof. internal medicine, 1991—. Mem. Am. Coll. Cardiology, Am. Heart Assn., Am. Fedn. Clin. Rsch., Am. Soc. Echocardiography. Office: Dartmouth Hitchcock Med Ctr Lahey-Hitchcock Clinic Sect Cardiology Lebanon NH 03756

PLEICONES, COSTA M., state supreme court justice; b. Greenville, SC, Feb. 29, 1944; s. Mike and Lecha Pleicones; m. Donna Singletary; 2 children. BA in English, Wofford Coll., Spartanburg, SC, 1965; JD, U. SC, 1968. Bar: SC 1968. Pub. defender Richland County, SC; atty. Lewis, Babcock, Pleicones and Hawkins; municipal judge City of Columbia, SC; county atty. Richland County, SC; resident cir. ct. judge 5th Judicial Cir., 1991—2000; assoc. justice SC Supreme Ct., 2000—. With JAG US Army, 1968—73, with USAR, 1973—99. Office: 1231 Gervais St Columbia SC 29201-3206 also: PO Box 11330 Columbia SC 29211*

PLEITEZ, CONCEPCION MARIA, elementary school educator; d. Isaac and Luar Salcedo Ramos; children: Nuria Sofia, Sarah Marina, Cristina. BA, Calif. State U., LA, 1996; postgrad., Calif. Poly. U., Pomona, 1997—2005. Receptionist Mattier, Annigian & Minto, West Covina, Calif., 1979—80; legal asst. Gloria Lorez-Hickson, Esquire, LA, 1980—81, Moseley & Carroll, El Monte, Calif., 1981—85; legal asst., office mgr. Richard F. Hernandez, Esquire, West Covina, Calif., 1985—96; elem. sch. tchr. Hacienda-La Puente Sch. Dist., La Puente, Calif., 1996—. Sch. site rep. HLPTA, Industry, Calif., 2003—, bargaining team mem., 2005—, bd. dirs. Author: (childrens book) If I Could Go to the Moon, 2007, Jaine and the Birds, 2007. Simultaneous interpreter Faith Cmty. Ch., West Covina, 2001—. Recipient Who award, CTA Orange Svc. Ctr. Coun., 2006. Mem.: Calif. State U. LA Alumni, Golden Key. Republican. Office: Wing Lane Elem Sch 16605 Wing Ln La Puente CA 91744

PLENDL, HANS S., retired physicist, editor; arrived in U.S., 1948; s. Hans N. and Anna Katherina Plendl; m. Marion Setsuko Ito, Aug. 3, 1957 (div. Dec. 8, 1990); children: Konrad Alexander, David Christopher, Kathrin Francesca, Leilani Ann. BA, Harvard U., 1952; PhD, Yale U., 1958. Tchg. asst. physics dept. Yale U., New Haven, 1952—53, rsch. asst. Cyclotron Lab., 1954—56; from asst. to assoc. to prof. physics dept. Fla. State U., Tallahassee, 1956—95, prof. emeritus physics dept., 1995—. Vis. staff mem. Nuc. Rsch. Ctr. Karlsruhe and Max Planck Inst. for Nuc. Physics, Heidelberg, Germany, 1960—62; vis. prof. physics dept. Tech. U., Munich, 1985—86; guest scientist Rsch. Ctr., Juelich, Germany, 1989—98; sr. rsch. fellow Inst. for Internat. Coop. Environ. Rsch., Tallahassee, 1995—2004; vis. scientist Oak Ridge Nat. Lab., 1957—87, Brookhaven Nat. Lab., 1985—87, Los Alamos Nat. Lab., 1985—87; program adv. com. NASA Space Radiation Effects Lab., Newport News, Va., 1969—78; edn. adv. com. US Senate, Washington, 1983—85; bd. trustees Nautilus Found., Tallahassee, 1991—99; adv. com. Internat. Conf. on Mesons and Nuclei, Dubna, Russia, 1994; co-chair Internat. Workshop on Nuc. Methods for Transmutation of Nuc. Waste, Dubna, 1996; adv. com. Internat. Symposia on Environ. Contamination in Ea. and Ctrl. Europe, Warsaw and Prague, 1998, 2000, 03; co-chair Internat. Workshop on Techs. in Nuc. Separations, Prague, 2000; mem. Recon Inc., Tallahassee, 1965—69; writer, editor Ricordiarte and LEM Art Pubs., Milan, 2000—06; dir. German Sch. Tallahassee, 2004; bd. dirs. Univ. Enterprises Internat. Inc.; presenter, cons. in field. Co-author: (textbook) Hands-on Astronomy; editor: Nuclear Transmutation Methods for Disposition of Long-Lived Radioactive Materials, Accelerator Driven Systems, Science and Technology without Borders, Philosophical Problems of Modern Physics; contbr. articles to sci. jours. Recipient Travel award, Fulbright Found., 1963, Award for Excellence in Tchg., Amoco Found., 1975, Rsch. stipend, Deutsche Forschungsgemeinschaft, 1985. Achievements include discovery of several isomeric states in scandium and titanium isotopes and elucidation of pion-nucleus interactions. Avocation: languages. Home: #29 2949 Shamrock N Tallahassee FL 32309 Office: Fla State U Physics Dept Tallahassee FL 32306 Business E-Mail: plendl@phy.fsu.edu.

PLEPLER, RICHARD L., broadcast executive; b. Manchester, Conn., Dec. 17, 1958; s. Sanford Jay and Constance (Federman) Plepler. BA in Govt., Franklin and Marshall Coll., 1981. Spl. asst. spl. projects Office US Senator Christopher J. Dodd, Washington, 1981-84; pres. RLP Inc., NYC, 1985-92; sr. v.p. corp. comm. HBO Inc., NYC, 1992—97, exec. v.p. corp. comm., 1997—2002, exec. v.p., 2002—07, co-pres., 2007—. Office: HBO 1100 Avenue of the Americas New York NY 10036*

PLESCH, ANDREAS, geologist, consultant; b. Würzburg, Unterfranken, Germany, Jan. 4, 1968; s. Wilhelm and Hanna (Vogel) Plesch; m. Silke Urban, Aug. 9, 2003. MS, SUNY, Albany, 1994; PhD, Freie Universität Berlin, Berlin, 1999. Rsch. assoc. Harvard U. (EPS), Cambridge, Mass., 2006—, post-doc. rschr., 1999—2006. Cons., Watertown, Mass., 2006—08. Mem.: Am. Geophys. Union, Am. Assn. Petroleum Geologists. Lutheran. Achievements include first to construct a regional 3d fault model for earthquake research: the Southern California Earthquake Center Community Fault Model; co-developed new 3d mechanical structural restoration method, applied to giant oil fields. Home: 115 Putnam St FL2 Watertown MA 02472 Office: Harvard Univ 20 Oxford St Cambridge MA 02138 Personal E-mail: andreasplesch@gmail.com. E-mail: andreas_plesch@harvard.edu.

PLĒSUMS, GUNTIS, architect, retired educator; b. Riga, Latvia, Dec. 17, 1933; came to U.S., 1950, naturalized 1954; s. Valdemārs and Velta Plēsums; m. Māra Mazutis, Aug. 28, 1965; children: Jāna, Kārla. BArch, U. Minn., 1961; MArch, MIT, 1964. Registered architect, N.Y., Oreg. Arch. Affleck, Desbarats, Dimakopoulos, Lebensold & Sise, Montreal, Que., Can., 1964-66; instr. RISD, Providence, 1967-69; prof. arch. U. Oreg., Eugene, 1969—95, prof. emeritus, 1995—; pvt. practice arch. Eugene, 1980—; arch. emeritus, 2003. Vis. assoc. prof. Kans. State U., Manhattan, 1976; adj. assoc. prof. Oreg. Sch. Design, Portland, 1983; vis. prof., dir. MArch program Chinese U. Hong Kong, 1993-99; lectr. U.S., Eng., Japan, China, Latvia, Denmark, Tunisia. Author: Townframe: Environments for Adaptive Housing, 1978, (with Heino Engel, others) Structure Systems; contbr. articles to profl. publs., including Ency. of Vernacular Arch. of the World; prin. works include: theme pavilion Man the Producer for Expo 67, Montreal, 1964-66. With Affleck, Desbarats, Dimakopoulos, Lebensold Sise, Architects. Served as sgt. U.S. Army, 1953-56. Fulbright fellow, 1966-67, NEA fellow, 1982, 90; Graham Found. for Advanced Studies in Fine Arts grantee, 1974. Home: PO Box 1009 Lorane OR 97451-1009 Office Phone: 541-767-3772. Business E-Mail: gplesums@uoregon.edu.

PLETCHER, ELDON, retired cartoonist; b. Goshen, Ind., Sept. 10, 1922; s. Arthur and Dora (Cripe) P.; m. Barbara Jeanne Jones, Jan. 29, 1948; children— Thomas Lee, Ellen Irene. Student, Chgo. Acad. Fine Arts, 1941-42, U. Aberdeen, Scotland, 1945, John Herron Art Sch., Indpls., 1946-47. Editl. cartoonist Sioux City Jour., Iowa, 1949-66, The Times-Picayune, 1966-85; free-lance gag cartoonist Sat. Eve. Post, Rotarian, Nat. Enquirer, other publs. Rep. permanent exhbns., Syracuse U., U. South Miss., U. Cin., Boston Mus. Art, Harry S. Truman Library, Lyndon B. Johnson Library, Wichita State U., John F. Kennedy Libr., Richard M. Nixon Libr., U. Mo.; cartoons appeared in The Continental Edit. of Yank (Army Weekly). Served with AUS, 1943-46. Recipient Christopher award, 1955, Freedoms Found. award, 12 years Mem. VFW, Assn. Am. Editorial Cartoonists. Democrat. Presbyterian. Personal E-mail: epletch@aol.com.

PLETSCH, MARIE ELEANOR, plastic surgeon; b. Walkerton, Ont., Can., May 3, 1938; came to U.S. 1962; d. Ernest John and Olive Wilhemina (Hossfeld) P.; m. Ludwig Philip Breiling, Aug. 25, 1967; children: John, Michael, Anne. MD, U. Toronto, 1962. Diplomate Am. Bd. Plastic Surgery. Intern Cook County Hosp., Chgo., 1962-63, resident, gen. surgery, 1963-64, St. Mary's Hosp., San Francisco, 1964-66; resident in plastic surgery St. Francis Hosp., San Francisco, 1966-69; practice med. specializing in plastic surgery Santa Cruz, Calif., 1969—; Monterey, Calif., 1990—; adminstr. Plasticenter, Inc., Santa Cruz, 1976-88, med. dir., 1987-88. Mem. AMA, Am. Soc. Plastic and Reconstructive Surgeons, Calif. Soc. Plastic Surgeons (mem. coun. 1986-89, sec. 1989-93, v.p. 1994-95, pres. elect 1995-96, pres. 1996-97), Am. Soc. Aesthetic Plastic Surgeons, Calif. Med. Assn., Assn. Calif. Surgery Ctrs. (pres. 1988-92), Santa Cruz County Med. Soc. (bd. govs. 1983-88, 1992-94), Santa Cruz Surgery Ctr. (bd. dirs. 1988-93, 2004—). Roman Catholic.: 24571 Silver Cloud Ct Monterey CA 93940 Office: Santa Cruz Can Am Medical 223A Mount Hermon Rd Scotts Valley CA 95066- Office Phone: 831-462-1000. Personal E-mail: pletsch@pacbell.net.

PLETZ, THOMAS GREGORY, lawyer; b. Toledo, Oct. 3, 1943; s. Francis G. and Virginia (Connell) P.; m. Carol Elizabeth Connolly, June 27, 1969; children: Anne M., John F. BA, U. Notre Dame, 1965; JD, U. Toledo, 1971. Bar: Ohio 1971, U.S. Ct. Appeals (6th cir.) 1978, U.S. Supreme Ct. 1985. Ct. bailiff Lucas County Common Pleas Ct., Toledo, 1967-71; jud. clk. U.S. Dist. Ct. (no. dist.) Ohio, Toledo, 1971-72; assoc. Shumaker, Loop & Kendrick, Toledo, 1972-76, litigation ptnr., 1976—. Acting judge Sylvania (Ohio) Mcpl. Ct., 1990—; mem. Ohio Bar Bd. Examiners, 1993-2003, chmn., 1996-99. Active Toledo Parish Coun., 1987-2003; mem. Nat. Conf. Bar Examiners Com., 1996-2001. With USNR, 1965-92; ret. CDR. Recipient Toledo Jr. Bar award, 1995. Mem. ABA, Ohio State Bar Assn., Toledo Bar Assn. (trustee 1981-93), Diocesan Attys. Bar Assn., 6th Cir. Jud. Conf. (life). Roman Catholic. Office: Shumaker Loop & Kendrick 1000 Jackson St Toledo OH 43604-1573 Office Phone: 419-321-1231. Business E-Mail: tpletz@slk-law.com.

PLEVAN, BETTINA B., lawyer; b. Oceanside, NY, Nov. 21, 1945; BA, Wellesley Coll., 1967; JD magna cum laude, Boston U., 1970. Bar: NY 1971, US Dist. Ct., (ea. dist.) NY, US Ct. Appeals, (2nd cir.), 1975, US Supreme Ct. 1977, US Ct. Appeals, (DC cir.), 1977, US Ct. Appeals, (3rd. cir.), 1978, US Dist. Ct. (So. dist.) NY, 1979, US Tax Ct., 1979, US Ct. Appeals, (5th. cir.), 1982, US Ct. Appeals (9th cir.), US Dist. Ct. (No. dist.) NY, 1983, US Ct. Appeals, (4th cir.), 1986, US Dist. Ct. (We. dist.) NY, 1993, US Ct. Appeals, (6th cir.). Editor Boston U. law Review, 1968—70; mem. Proskauer Rose LLP (formerly Proskauer Rose Goetz & Mendelsohn), NYC, 1974—. Pres. Fed. Bar Coun., 1996—98, pres. emeritus, 1998—. Named one of The Best Lawyers in NY, NY mag., The 50 Most Influential Women Lawyers in Am., Nat. Law Jour., 2007. Fellow: Am. Acad. Appellate Lawyers, Am. Coll. Trial Lawyers; mem.: ABA (mem. Ho. Delegates 1986—91, bd. govs. 2006—09), NY County Lawyers Assn., NY State Bar Assn., Assn. Bar of the City NY (mem., com. on state courts of superior jurisdiction 1975—78, chair 1978—81, mem. exec. com. 1981—85, chair coun. on jud. adminstrn. 1985—88, mem., long range planning com. 1988—90, chair 1992—95). Office: Proskauer Rose LLP 1585 Broadway Fl 27 New York NY 10036-8299 Office Phone: 212-969-3065. Office Fax: 212-969-2900. E-mail: bplevan@proskauer.com.*

PLEVYAK, LINDA HUETHER, education educator, researcher; d. Carl and Carol Huether; m. Howard Plevyak, Sept. 19, 1987. PhD, Ohio State U., Columbus, 1997. Lic. in tchg. Calif. & Ohio, 1990. Tchr. Mojave Sch. Dist., Calif., 1989—92; asst. prof. Ga. So. U., Statesboro, 1997—2000; assoc. prof. U. Cin., 2000—. Dog rescue Golden Retriever, Cin., 2003—. Grantee fellow, Excellence in Tchg. & Learning Ctr., 2007. Office: Univ Cincinnati One Edwards Center Room 2150Q Cincinnati OH 45221-0105 Business E-Mail: linda.plevyak@uc.edu.

PLEW, MARK G., archaeologist, educator; b. Bloomington, Ind., June 19, 1949; m. Sarah Saras. PhD, Ind. U., Bloomington, 1985. Archaeologist Idaho State Hist. Soc., Boise, 1977—84; prof. anthropology Boise State U., 1984—. Dir., Denis Williams archeol. field sch. U. Guyana, Georgetown, 2006—. Mem. Idaho Archeol. Soc., Boise, 1985—. Recipient Found. Outstanding Rsch. award, Boise State U., 2001. Achievements include 30 years archaeological research on the Snake River Plain. Home: 3389 Crosspoint Boise ID 83706 Office: Boise State Univ 1910 University Dr Boise ID 83725 Business E-Mail: mplew@boisestate.edu.

PLEWS-OGAN, MARGARET L., pediatrician, department chairman; b. Chgo., Apr. 10, 1956; d. George Montague and Jean Mccorkell Plews; m. James Linn Plews-Ogan, June 12, 1978; children: Erin Jean, William Mcmillan. BA, Coll. Wooster, Ohio, 1977; MD, Harvard Med. Sch., Boston, 1991. Diplomate Am. Bd. Internal Medicine, 1996. Assoc. prof. U. Va., Charlottesville, 2004, chief, geriat., palliative medicine, 2004—. Dir. UVA Inst. Quality & Patient Safety, Charlottesville, 2007—. Contbr. articles to profl. jours.

PLIANBANGCHANG, SAMLEE, world organization administrator; b. Samutprakarn, Thailand, June 6, 1940; s. Boonta and Boonreon (Em-siri) P.; m. Duangratana Intakanok, Aug. 7, 1970; children: Pinyupa, Kraitos. MD, U. Med. Scis., Bangkok, 1965; MPH, TM, Tulane U., 1970, DrPH, 1972; cert. in health planning, Johns Hopkins U., 1972. Med. officer Ministry Pub. Health, Bangkok, 1965-74, dir. tech. div., 1974-81; sec. Nat. Adv. Bd. for Disease Prevention and Control, Bangkok, 1981-84; cons. WHO, New Delhi, 1984-85, regional planning officer, 1985-94; dir. prevention and control diseases WHO Searo, 1994—96; deputy regional dir. and dir. of programme mgmt., 1996—2000; sr. analyst, special advisor budget mgmt. reforms WHO, Geneva, 2001—04, regional dir. South East Asia Region, 2004—, pres., 2004—; dean Coll. Pub. Health Chulalongkorn U., 2001—04. Pub. health cons. Ministry Pub. Health, Bangkok, 1984—. Fellow APHA, Am. Coll. Preventive Medicine,; mem. Thai Med. Coun., Thai Health Assn., Delta Omega Soc. Buddhist. Avocations: reading, gardening, boating, driving, fishing. Office: World Health Orgn Mahatma Gandhi Rd New Delhi 110002 India Home Phone: 662-2391-1547; Office Phone: 91-11-2334-0804. Business E-Mail: samleep@neayo.who.int.

PLIMACK, ELIZABETH R., oncologist; MD, NYU Sch. Medicine, 2002; MS in Patient Based Biologic Rsch., U. Tex. Grad. Sch. Biomedical Sci., 2008. Cert. Am. Bd. Internal Medicine. Intern & resident NYU Med. Ctr.; fellow in med. oncology U. Tex. MD Anderson Cancer Ctr.; attending physician dept. medical oncology Fox Chase Cancer Ctr. Mem.: Am. Soc. Clinical Oncology, Am. Assn. for Cancer Rsch. Office: Fox Chase Cancer Center 333 Cottman Ave Philadelphia PA 19111-2497 Office Phone: 215-728-2570.*

PLIMPTON, THOMAS E., automotive executive; BS in Acctg., U. Kans.; MBA, Rockhurst Coll. Asst. gen. mgr. Peterbilt, Newark, Calif., gen. mgr., 1992—96; with Foden Truck Co. PACCAR Inc., England, exec. v.p. Bellevue, Wash., 1998—2002, pres., 2002—08, vice-chmn., prin. fin. officer, 2008—. Dir. PACCAR Fin. Corp. Avocations: golf, college football, basketball, reading. Office: Paccar Inc 777 106th Ave Bellevue WA 98004 Mailing: Paccar Inc PO Box 1518 Bellevue WA 98009*

PLINE, JENNIFER ALICE, trust company executive; BA, Boston Coll., 1982, MBA, 1987. Chartered fin. analyst CFA Inst., 1990, chartered investment counselor Investment Counsel Assn. Am., 1990. Dir. client svc. Standish Mellon Asset Mgmt., Boston, 1987—2005; v.p. trusts Harvard Mgmt. Co., Boston, 2005—. Mem. adv. bd. Fin. Dept. Boston (Mass.) Coll., 2002—06. Mem. com. fgn. rels. City Boston; trustee Beth Israel Hosp., Needham, Mass., 2005—06; chmn.'s account exec. United Way Mass. Bay, Boston, 2004—06; mem. adv. bd. Horizons for Homeless Children, Boston, 2003—06. Office: Harvard Management Company 600 Atlantic Avenue Boston MA 02210

PLINSKE, KATHLEEN A., educational association administrator associate vice president; b. McHenry, Ill., July 4, 1980; d. Peter and Eileen Plinske. BA, Ind. U., Bloomington, 2001; MA, Roosevelt U., Chgo., 2004; EdD, Pepperdine U., Malibu, Calif., 2008. Instrnl. media specialist McHenry County Coll., Crystal Lake, Ill., 2001—04, coord. media devel. and tech. tng., 2004—06, dir. distance edn. and profl. devel., 2006—07, exec. dir. instl. effectiveness, 2007—08; assoc. v.p. Instl. Effectiveness, 2009—. Peer reviewer Higher Learning Commn., Chgo., 2006—. Recipient 10 Under 40 award, McHenry County Bus. Jour., 2006; Herman B. Wells scholarship, Ind. U., 1997—2001, C.C. Leadership Devel. Doctoral fellowship, Pepperdine U., 2006—07, Glen and Gloria Holden scholarship, 2007—08. Office: McHenry County Coll 8900 US Highway 14 Crystal Lake IL 60012 Office Phone: 815-455-8694. Office Fax: 815-455-3684. Business E-Mail: kplinske@mchenry.edu.

PLISCHKE, LE MOYNE WILFRED, chemist, researcher; b. Greensburg, Pa., Dec. 11, 1922; s. Fred and Ruth Naomi (Rumbaugh) P.; m. Joan Harper, Mar. 11, 1966. BS, Waynesburg U., 1948; MS, W.Va. U., 1952. Rsch. chemist U.S. Naval Ordinance Test Sta., China Lake, Calif., 1952-53; asst. prof. chemistry Commonwealth U., Richmond, Va., 1953-54; rsch. chemist E.I. du Pont, Gibbstown, N.J., 1955-57, Monsanto Chem. Co., Pensacola, Fla., 1957—. Mem.: Am. Chem. Soc. Achievements include 18 U.S. patents and 51 foreign patents in field. Home: 2100 Club House Dr Lillian AL 36549-5402 Office: Monsanto Co The Chem Group PO Box 97 Gonzalez FL 32560-0097 E-mail: plis123@gulftel.com.

PLISKIN, BERENICE RITA CHAPLAN, artist; b. NYC, May 21, 1932; d. Bernard Chaplan and Frances Ettinger Chaplan; m. Robert Pliskin, May 11, 1953. BS, CCNY, 1954; MFA, Lehman Coll., 1978. Elem. and art tchr. Bd. Edn., NYC, 1954—90. Author (illustrator): A TrainLoad of Fun, 1981; author: Spanish Word Game Masters, 1987, French Word Game Masters, 1988; co-author: Top 20 ESL Word Game Hits, 1990. Recipient First prize nat. watercolor, Scholastic Arts, 1949, award in oil painting, 1950, Edn./Cmty. award, Westchester Arts Coun., 2002, Digital Delights award, Surface Design Assn., 2003. Mem.: Nat. Mus. Women in the Arts (Archival File). Avocation: travel.

PLOMBON, JOHN JOSEPH, electronics engineer; s. Julian James and Willette Odessa Plombon; m. Sara Katheryn Gardiner, Dec. 28, 1997; children: Alexandra Anne, Audrey Odessa. PhD, U. Calif., Santa Barbara, 1992. Sr. process engr. Intel Corp., Hillsboro, Oreg., 2002—. Personal E-mail: john.plombon@gmail.com.

PLOMONDON, JOHN EDMUND, literature and language professor; b. Topeka, Kans., Sept. 29, 1954; s. Ernest Edmund and Flora Kathleen Plomondon; m. Suzanne Nielsen, Sept. 6, 1997; children: Taylor Murphy, Evan Murphy. MS, U. Minn., Mpls., 1982. Tchg. asst. U. Minn., 1978—91; cmty. faculty Met. State U., St. Paul, 1981—2008; faculty Mpls. Cmty. & Tech. Coll., 1987—. Mem. Miss. Market Coop., St. Paul, 1984—85. Liberal. Avocations: music, computers. Office: Mpls Cmty & Tech Coll 1501 Hennepin Ave Minneapolis MN 55403 Business E-Mail: john.plomondon@minneapolis.edu.

PLOSSER, CHARLES IRVING, bank executive, economics professor; b. Birmingham, Ala., Sept. 19, 1948; s. George Gray and Dorothy (Irving) Plosser; m. Janet Schwert, June 26, 1976; children: Matthew, Kevin, Allison. B in Engring., cum laude, Vanderbilt U., Nashville, 1970; MBA, U. Chgo., 1972, PhD, 1976. Cons. Citicorp Realty Cons., NYC, 1972-73; lectr. Grad. Sch. Bus., U. Chgo., 1975-76; asst. prof. Grad. Sch. Bus. Stanford U., Calif., 1976-78; asst. prof. econs. W.E. Simon Grad. Sch. Bus., U. Rochester, NY, 1978-82, assoc. prof., 1982-86, prof., 1986-89, Fred H. Gowen prof. econs., 1989-92, John M. Olin Disting. prof. econs. and pub. policy, 1992—2006, acting dean, 1990-91, 92-93, dean, 1993—2003; pres. Fed. Res. Bank, Phila., 2006—. Chmn. bd. dirs. Consortium Grad. Study in Mgmt., St. Louis, 1995—97; bd. dirs. ViaHealth, Inc., 1995—2000, RGS Energy Grp., 1996—2002, Rochester Gas & Electric Corp.; rsch. assoc. Nat. Bur. Econ. Rsch.; adv. bd. mem. Rochester New Enterprise Forum, Univ. Tech. Seed Fund, LLC; Met. adv. bd. Chase Manhattan Bank. Editor: Jour. Monetary Econs., 1983—2006; contbr. articles to profl. jours. 1st lt. US Army, 1972—73. Research grantee, NSF, 1982, 1984. Mem.: Am. Fin. Assn., Econometrics Soc., Am. Econs. Assn., Beta Gamma Sigma, Tau Beta Pi. Office: Fed Res Bank Phila Ten Independence Mall Philadelphia PA 19106-1574

PLOTCH, WALTER, management consultant, fund raising counselor; b. NYC, July 19, 1932; s. Harry and Belle (Lebowsky) P.; m. Yvette Gabrielle Lambert, Mar. 20, 1957; children: Allison, Jennifer, Adrienne. AB, Queens Coll., 1957; MA, Harvard U., 1959; postgrad., 1959-62. Analyst L.F. Rothschild & Co., NYC and Boston, 1962-64; cmty. cons., 1964-65; edn. dir. New Eng. Anti-Defamation League, 1965-68; nat. edn. dir., 1968-76; v.p. Brakeley, John Price Jones Inc., NYC, 1976-79; sr. v.p., dir., 1979-89; sr. v.p. The Oram Group, Inc., NYC, 1989-92; exec. v.p.; pres., CEO Walter Plotch Assocs., Inc., Croton-On-Hudson, NY, 1992—2005. Mem. faculty Grad. Sch. Mgmt. and Urban Affairs, New Sch. U.; lectr. Harvard U. Grad. Sch. Edn.; cons. Harcourt, Brace, Plenum Pubs. Co-editor: Pluralism in a Democratic Society, 1977; gen. editor: The Job Corps Intergroup RElations Series, 1974; contbr. articles to profl. jours.; contbg. editor mag., Jour. Sponsored Rsch. Bd. dirs. Schizophrenia Found., 1975-90; nat. bd. dirs. NCCJ, 1980-84, Nat. Charitable Info Bur.,mem. exec. com. 1986-94. Served with USCGR, 1953-55, Korea. Grantee U.S. Office Edn., Dept. Labor, N.Y. Coun. Humanities; tchg. fellow Harvard U., 1959-61. Mem. Princeton Club, Phi Alpha Theta. Democrat. Jewish. Office: 39 Furnace Dock Rd Croton On Hudson NY 10520-1406

PLOTKIN, ALLEN, aerospace engineer, educator; b. NYC, May 4, 1942; s. Oscar and Claire (Chasick) P.; m. Selena Berman, Dec. 18, 1966; children: Samantha Rose, Jennifer Anne. BS, Columbia U., 1963, MS, 1964; PhD, Stanford U., 1968. Asst. prof. aerospace engring. U. Md., College Park, 1968-72, assoc. prof., 1972-77, prof., 1977-85; prof. dept. aerospace engring. San Diego State U., 1985—, chmn. dept., 1985-90, 93-96, 2008—. Vis. assoc. Calif. Inst. Tech., Pasadena, 1975-76; cons. Naval Surface Weapons Ctr., White Oak, Md., 1981-84. Co-author: Low-Speed Aerodynamics, 1991, 2d edit., 2001. Recipient Engring. Sci. award Washington Acad. Scis., 1981; rsch. grantee NASA, NSF; NASA-Am. Soc. Engring. Edn. summer faculty fellow, 1969, 70. Fellow AIAA (assoc., assoc. editor jour. 1986—, Young Engr.-Scientist award Nat. Capital sect. 1976, Sustained Svc. award 2003, J. Leland Atwood award, 2005), ASME; mem. Soc. Naval Architects and Marine Engrs., Am. Soc. Engring. Edn., Aerospace Dept. Chairmen's Assn. (chmn. 1989-90), Sigma Xi, Tau Beta Pi. Democrat. Jewish. Avocations: jogging, reading, country music. Home: 17364 St Andrews Dr Poway CA 92064-1231 Office: San Diego State U Dept Aerospace Engring San Diego CA 92182 Office Phone: 619-594-7019.

PLOTKIN, HORACIO, pediatric endocrinologist, orthopedic surgeon, educator; b. Buenos Aires, Dec. 23, 1964; arrived in US, 2002; m. Carola Rabuffetti, Mar. 23, 1999; children: Sophie Adele, Lucas Jay, Olivia Robin. BS, J.J. Urquiza, Buenos Aires, 1981; MD, U. Buenos Aires, 1987. Resident in pediats. T. Alvarez Hosp., Buenos Aires, 1988—92; fellow in pediat. endocrinology J.P. Garrahan Hosp., Buenos Aires, 1991—92; fellow in metabolic bone diseases IDIM, Buenos Aires, 1992—96; fellow in endocrinology Yale U., New Haven, 1996—97; fellow in pediat. metabolic bone diseases McGill U., Montreal, Que., Canada, 1997—2002; asst. prof. pediats. U. Nebr. Med. Ctr., Omaha, 2002—07, asst. prof. orthop. surgery, 2002—07, assoc. prof. pediats., 2007—, assoc. prof. orthop. surgery, 2007—; dir. Metabolic Bone Diseases Clinic Children's Hosp., Omaha, 2002—, dir. Osteogenesiss Imperfecta Clinic, 2002—. Contbr. articles and cartoons to humorous publs. Named Home Town Hero, City of Omaha, 2005. Fellow: Am. Acad. of Pediats.; mem.: Endocrine Soc., Internat. Bone and Mineral Soc., Am. Soc. for Bone and Mineral Rsch. Office Fax: 402-559-4001.

PLOTKIN, IRVING H. (IRVING HERMAN PLOTKIN), economist, consultant; b. Bklyn., July 19, 1941; s. Samuel H. and Dorothy (Falick) P.; m. Janet V. Bufe, July 26, 1969; children: Aaron Jacob, Joshua Benjamin. BS in Econs., U. Pa., 1963; PhD in Math. Econs., MIT, 1968. Corp. planning analyst Mobil Oil Co., NYC, 1962-63, Mobil Oil Italiana, Genoa, Italy, 1965; ind. cons. econs. and ops. rsch. to banks, mut. funds, ins. cos., govt. agys. Cambridge, Mass., 1965-68; sr. economist Arthur D. Little, Inc., Cambridge, 1968—2002. Dir. regulation and econs., 1974-2002, v.p., 1979-2002; bd. dirs. Arthur D. Little Valuation, Inc.; trustee Arthur D. Little, Inc., ESOP, 1988-2002; mgr. dir. tax svc. PricewaterhouseCoopers LLP, Boston, 2002—; instr. fin. and computer scis. MIT, 1965-68; lectr. maj. univs. U.S. and abroad; expert witness U.S. Ho. of Reps. and Senate coms., U.S. Ct. Claims, U.S. Tax Ct. I.C.C., FTC, Fed. Martime Commn., Fed. Dist. Cts., Fed. Res. Bd., other fed. and state govt. agys., 1967—. NASA fellow, 1963-66, NSF fellow, 1967, Am. Bankers Assn. fellow, 1968. Mem. Am. Econ. Assn., Econometric Soc., Am. Fin. Assn., Beta Gamma Sigma, Pi Gamma Mu, Tau Delta Phi (chpt. pres. 1962-63). Home: Apt 910 975 Memorial Dr Cambridge MA 02138-5754 Office: 125 High St Boston MA 02110 Office Phone: 617-530-5332. Business E-Mail: irving.h.plotkin@us.pwc.com.

PLOTKIN, LOREN H., lawyer; b. Bklyn., Feb. 8, 1943; s. Arthur and Betty Ann (Strugatz); m. Carol Baxter, Aug. 25, 1990; children: Lily, Kate. BA, Harpur Coll., SUNY, Binghamton, 1963; JD, St. John's U., NYC, 1966. Bar: NY 1966, U.S. Dist. Ct. (so. and ea. dists.) N.Y. 1972, U.S. Tax Ct. 1976. Law asst. appellate divsn., first dept. N.Y. State Supreme Ct.; ptnr. Lans Feinberg & Cohen, NYC, 1969-81; mem. Levine & Thall, P.C., NYC, 1981-84, Levine Thall and Plotkin, N.Y.C., 1984-96, Levine Thall, Plotkin & Menin, L.L.P., NYC, 1996-99, Levine, Plotkin & Menin, L.L.P., NYC, 2000—. Lectr. on entertainment law. Notes and comments editor St. John's U. Law Rev., 1965-66. Home: 34 Lawrence Ln Palisades NY 10964-1604 Office: Levine Plotkin & Menin LLP 1740 Broadway Fl 22 New York NY 10019-4315

PLOTKIN, MANUEL D., management consultant, educator, former corporate executive, government official; s. Jacob and Bella (Katz) P.; m. Diane Fern Weiss, Dec. 17, 1967; 1 child, Lori Ann. BS with honors, Northwestern U., 1948; MBA, U. Chgo., 1949. Price economist, survey coordinator U.S. Bur. Labor Statistics, Washington, 1949-51, Chgo., 1951-53; sr. economist Sears Roebuck & Co., Chgo., 1953-61, mgr. market research, 1961-66, chief economist, mgr. mktg. rsch., 1966-73, dir. corp. planning and research, 1973-77, exec. corp. planner, 1979-80; dir. U.S. Bur. Census, Washington, 1977-79; v.p., dir. group practice Divsn. Mgmt. Cons. Austin Co., Evanston, Ill., 1981-85; pres. M.D. Plotkin Research & Planning Co., Chgo., 1985—. Tchr. statistics Ind. U., 1953-54; tchr. econs. Wilson Jr. Coll., Chgo., 1954-55; tchr. quantitative methods and managerial econs. Northwestern U., 1955-63; tchr. mktg. rsch. and mktg. mgmt. DePaul U., Chgo., 1992-95; mem. Conf. Bd. Mktg. Rsch. Adv. Coun., 1968-77, chmn.-elect, 1977; chmn. adv. com. U.S. Census Bur., 1974-75; trustee Mktg. Sci. Inst., 1968-77; mem. Nat. Commn. Employment and Unemployment Stats., 1978-79, Adv. Coun. Edn. Stats., 1977-79, Interagy. Com. Population Rsch., 1977-79; mem. adv. coun. Kellstadt Ctr., DePaul U., 1987-92; trustee U.S. Travel Data Ctr., 1977-79. Contbr. articles to profl. jours. Served with AUS, 1943-46, ETO. Decorated Bronze Star medal with oak leaf cluster. Mem. Am. Mktg. Assn. (pres. Chgo. 1968-69, nat. dir. 1969-70, nat. v.p. mktg. rsch. 1970-72, nat. v.p. mktg. mgmt. 1981-83, pres., CEO 1985-86), Am. Statis. Assn. (pres. Chgo. 1966-67, Forecasting award 1963), Am. Econ. Assn., Nat. Assn. Bus. Economists, Planning Execs. Inst., World Future Soc., Midwest Planning Assn., U. Ill. Businessmen Rsch. Adv. Group, Chgo. Assn. Commerce and Industry, Beta Gamma Sigma, Alpha Sigma Lambda, Delta Mu Delta. Home and Office: 2650 N Lakeview Ste 3910 Chicago IL 60614-1831

PLOTKIN, SHARON LEE, protective services official, educator; b. Miami Beach, Fla., Feb. 9, 1963; d. Herbert Levin and Esther Evelyn Levin-Passero; m. David Jacob Plotkin (div.); children: Alexandra Faye, Andi Raye. AA, Broward CC, Pembroke Pines, Fla., 1983; BS, Fla. Internat. U., Miami, 1985, MS, 1990. Counselor Jewish Cmty. Ctr., Miami, 1982—88; co-owner Ralph Rottens Not Pound, Miami Lakes, Fla., 1989—95; crime scene investigator North Miami Police Dept., Fla., 1995—. Advisor William Turner Tech. HS, Miami, 2003—06; pub. spkr., trainer various colls. and HS, Fla., 2004—; adj. faculty mem. Am. Intercontinental, Weston, Fla., 2005—. Co-author: Crime Scene Children, 2006. Vol. Camilos House, Miami, 2005—. Acad. grantee, Fla. Internat., 1986. Mem.: S. Fla. Forensic Assn., Assn. Bloodstain Pattern Analysts, Internat. Assn. Identification. Republican. Jewish. Avocations: reading, music, travel. Office: North Miami Police 700 NE 124 St North Miami FL 33161 Office Phone: 305-218-6949. Personal E-mail: slplotkin@bellsouth.net.

PLOTKIN, STANLEY ALAN, virologist; b. NYC, May 12, 1932; s. Joseph and Lee (Fishbein) P.; m. Susan Lannon, Nov. 24, 1979; children: Michael, Alec. BA, NYU, 1952; MD, SUNY, NYC, 1956; MA (hon.), U. Pa., 1974; D (hon.), U. Rouen, 2006, Complutense U. Madridf, 2009. Diplomate Am. Bd. Pediat., Am. Acad. Pediat. Intern Cleve. Met. Gen. Hosp., 1956-57; resident pediat. Phila. Children's Hosp., 1961—62, dir. divsn. infectious diseases, sr. physician, 1969—90; registrar Hosp. for Sick Children, London, 1962-63; assoc. mem. Wistar Inst., Phila., 1963-74, prof. virology, 1974—; asst. prof. pediat. U. Pa., Phila., 1966-71, assoc. prof., 1971-74, prof., 1974-91; prof. emeritus, 1991—; assoc. chmn. dept. pediat. U. Pa., Phila., 1986-88; med. and sci. dir. Pasteur-Mérieux-Connaught Labs. (now Sanofi-Pasteur), Marnes-la-Coquette, France, 1991-97; advisor to pres. Sanofi Pasteur, Swiftwater, Pa., 1997—. Adj. prof. internat. health Johns Hopkins U., Balt., 2000—. Assoc. editor: Am. Jour. Epidemiology, 1967-87, Proc. Soc. Exptl. Biology and Medicine, 1968-85, Pediatric Infectious Disease jour., 1982-87, Vaccine jour., 1983—, Biologicals, 2000—, Human Vaccines, 2005—, Clin. Vaccine Immunology, 2006—, Clin. Infectious Diseases, 2007—. Served as med. officer USPHS, 1957-60. Decorated Legion of Honor (France); recipient Bruce medal, ACP, 1987, Clin. Virology award, Pan Am. Group Rapid Viral Diagnosis, 1995, Gold medal, Sabin Found., 2002, Children's Hosp., Phila., 2006, Fleming award, Infectious Diseases Soc. Am., 2004, Marshall award, European Soc. Pediat. Infectious Diseases, 2006, medal, Fondation Mérieux, Finland award, Nat. Found. Infectious Diseases, 2009, Halleman prize, Am. Soc. Microbiology, 2009; named Disting. Physician, Pediat. Infectious Diseases Soc., 1993, Disting. Alumnus, Children's Hosp., Phila., 2001; grantee, Joseph P. Kennedy Found., 1964—66, Hartford Found., 1971—73, NIH, 1973—. Fellow: AAAS; mem.: NAS (Inst. of Medicine), French Acad. Medicine (foreign mem.), World Soc. Pediat. Infectious Diseases (pres. 2003—06), Am. Acad. Pediat. (chmn. infectious diseases com. 1987—90), Am. Soc. Microbiology (Hilleman prize 2009), Am. Epidemiology Soc., Am. Pediat. Soc., Soc. Pediat. Rsch., Hungarian Soc. Microbiology (hon.). Achievements include pioneering work on vaccine strains for protection against polio, rabies, rubella, rotavirus and cytomegalovirus. Office Phone: 215-297-9321. Personal E-mail: stanley.plotkin@vaxconsult.com.

PLOTNICK, HARVEY BARRY, publishing executive; b. Detroit, Aug. 5, 1941; s. Isadore and Esther (Sher) Plotnick; m. Susan Regnery, Aug. 16, 1964 (div. Apr. 1977); children: Andrew, Alice; m. Elizabeth Allen, May 2, 1982; children: Teresa, Samuel. BA, U. Chgo., 1963. Editor Contemporary Books, Inc., Chgo., 1964-66, pres., pub., 1966—94; pres., CEO Paradigm Holdings, Inc., Chgo., 1994—. CEO Molecular Electronics Corpn., 2000. Trustee U. Chgo., 1994—, bd. gov., Argonne Nat. Lab., 2001—. Named one of Top 200 Collectors, ARTnews mag., 2005—08. Avocations: collecting old master prints, collecting Islamic ceramics. E-mail: harvey1844@aol.com.

PLOTNICK, ROBERT DAVID, economic consultant, educator; b. Washington, Aug. 3, 1949; s. Theodore and Jean (Hirshfeld) P.; m. Gay Lee (Jensen), Dec. 22, 1972. BA, Princeton U., 1971; MA, U. Calif., Berkeley, 1973, PhD, 1976. Rsch. assoc. Inst. Rsch. on Poverty, Madison, Wis., 1973—75; asst. prof. Bates Coll., Lewiston, Maine, 1975—77, Dartmouth Coll., Hanover, NH, 1977—84; assoc. prof. U. Wash., Seattle, 1984—90, prof., 1990, assoc. dean, 1990—95, acting dean, 1994—95. Vis. scholar Russell Sage Found., 1990, U. NSW, 1997, London Sch. Econs., 2004; rsch. affiliate Inst. Rsch. Poverty, 1989—, Nat. Poverty Ctr., 2004—; chmn. Population Leadership Program, 1999—2005; dir. Ctr. for Studies in Demography and Ecology, 1997—2002; adj. fellow Pub. Policy Inst Calif., 1998—2000; cons. Wash. Dept. Social and Health Svcs., Olympia, 1984—86, 1990—96, 2000; cons. in field; rsch. affiliate West Coast Poverty Ctr., 2005—, assoc. dir., 2008—09; v.p. Assn. Policy Analysis & Mgmt., 2009—. Author: Progress Against Poverty, 1975; contbr. articles to profl. journals. Recipient Teaching Excellence Award U. Wash., 1985, 89. Mem. Am. Econ. Assn., Assn. Policy Analysis and Mgmt., Population Assn. Am. Avocations: hiking, birdwatching. Office: U Wash Evans Sch Pub Affairs PO Box 353055 Seattle WA 98195-3055 Office Phone: 206-685-2055. Business E-Mail: plotnick@u.washington.edu.

PLOTNIK, ARTHUR, writer, columnist; b. White Plains, NY, Oct. 1, 1937; s. Michael and Annabelle P.; m. Meta Von Borstel, Sept. 6, 1960 (div. 1979); children: Julia Nicole, Katya Michelle.; m. Mary Phelan, Dec. 2, 1983. BA, State U. N.Y., Binghamton, 1960; MA, U. Iowa, 1961; MS in L.S, Columbia U., 1966. Gen. reporter, reviewer Albany (N.Y.) Times Union, 1963-64; freelance writer, 1964-66; editor Librarians Office, Library of Congress, 1966-69; assoc. editor Wilson Library Bull., Bronx, NY, 1969-74; editor-in-chief Am. Libraries, Chgo., 1975-89; assoc. pub. ALA, 1989-97; editl. dir. ALA Editions, 1993-97; writer, 1997—. Adj. instr. journalism Columbia Coll., Chgo., 1988-89; speaker in field. Author: The Elements of Editing: A Modern Guide for Editors and Journalists, 1982, Jacob Shallus, Calligrapher of the Constitution, 1987, Honk If You're a Writer, 1992, The Elements of Expression, 1996, 2d edit., 2006, The Urban Tree Book, 2000, The Elements of Authorship (reprint of Honk if You're a Writer), 2000, Spunk & Bite: A Writer's Guild to Punchier, More Engaging Language and Style, 2005, Paperback, 2007, Subtitled A Writers Guide to Bold Contemporary Style, gen. articles, fiction and poetry; contbg. editor: The Writer, 2000—07; mem. editl. bd.:, 2007—; exec. prodr.: Libr. Video mag., 1986—91; columnist: Editorial Eye, 1995—2001; contbr. articles to profl. jours. Bd. dirs. Am. Book Awards, 1979-82; bd. advs. Univ. Press of Am., 1982—1997. Served with USAR, 1962-67. Fellow Iowa Writers Workshop Creative Writing, 1961; recipient award Ednl. Press Assn. Am., 1973 (3), 77, 82, 83; cert. of excellence Internat. Reading Assn., 1970, First Pl. award Verbatim essay competition, 1986, award Am. Soc. Bus. Press Editors, 1987, First Pl. award poetry competition Irish-Am. Heritage Ctr., Chgo., 2005, William Stafford award, 2008. Mem. ALA, ACLU, Treekeepers (Openlands Project). Home and Office: 2120 W Pensacola Ave Chicago IL 60618-1718 also: N E Pub Assocs Literary Agents PO Box 5 Chester CT 06412-0005

PLOTTEL, JEANINE PARISIER, foreign language educator; b. Paris, Sept. 21, 1934; came to U.S., 1943; m. Roland Plottel, 1956; children: Claudia S., Michael E., Philip B. Baccalauréat lettres, Lycée Français de N.Y., 1952; BA with honors, Barnard Coll., 1954; MA, Columbia U., 1955, PhD with distinction, 1959. Lectr. dept. French and Romance philology Columbia U., NYC, 1955-59; rsch. assoc. fgn. lang. program MLA of Am., NYC, 1959-60; lectr. dept. romance langs. CUNY, NYC, 1960; asst. prof. div. humanities Julliard Sch. Music, NYC, 1960-65; dir. lang. labs. Hunter Coll. CUNY, 1965-69, asst. prof. dept. romance langs., 1965-69, assoc. prof. dept. romance langs., 1969-81, prof. dept. romance langs., 1981—2000, assoc. prof. French doctoral program grad. sch., univ. ctr., 1980-81, prof. French doctoral program grad. sch., univ. ctr., 1981—2000, prof. emeritus, 2000—. Exec. dir. AAVP NY state conf., 2002-07; mem. president's adv. coun. Barnard Coll., 2006-, bd. trustees; with dept. Romance langs. CUNY. Author: Les Dialogues de Paul Valéry, 1960; pub., editor N.Y. Literary Forum, 1978-88; contbr. articles to profl. jours., chpts. to books. Pres. Maurice I. Parisier Found., Inc.; bd. trustees Barnard Coll., 2007-.pres. Assn. du Mécénat de Inst. de France, 2007- Named Officer des Palmes Acad., 1999; recipient NEH fellowship, 1979; grantee N.Y. Coun. for the Humanities, 1986, Helena Rubenstein Found., 1986, Florence J. Gould Found., 1986, 88, N.Y. Times Found., 1986. Mem. AAUP (exec. dir. N.Y. State Conf. 2002-06), Maison Française (bd. dirs. Columbia U.), Peyre Inst., CUNY, Soc. French Am. Cultural Svcs. & Ednl. Aid, Hunter Coll. Art Galleries, Inst. French Studies. Home: 50 E 77th St Apt 14A New York NY 10075 Office: Hunter Coll-CUNY 695 Park Ave New York NY 10021-5024 Personal E-mail: plottel1@att.net, plottel1@mac.com.

PLOTZ, CHARLES MINDELL, physician, educator; b. NYC, Dec. 6, 1921; s. Isaac and Rose (Bluestone) P.; m. Lucille Weckstein, Aug. 5, 1945; children: Richard, Thomas, Robert. BA, Columbia U., 1941, D.Sc., 1951; MD, L.I. Coll. Medicine, 1944. Diplomate: Am. Bd. Internal Medicine. Intern New Haven Hosp., 1944-45; resident internal medicine Kings County Hosp., 1945-46, Maimonides Hosp., 1948-49; postdoctoral research fellow USPHS, Columbia Coll. Phys. and Surgs., 1949-50; practice medicine, specializing in internal medicine Bklyn., 1950—; chief Arthritis Clinic, attending physician Kings County Hosp. Center, 1950-85; chief L.I. Coll. Hosp. (Arthritis Clinic), 1950-65; asst. attending physician Mt. Sinai Hosp., 1955—; chief Mt. Sinai Hosp. (Arthritis Clinic), 1955-65, Arthritis Clinic, State U., Hosp., 1967-85; asst. physician Columbia-Presbyn. Med. Center, 1949-71; attending physician Bklyn. State Hosp.; dir. ambulatory care Bklyn. Hosp.Ctr., 1991-93; emeritus prof. medicine SUNY, 1991—; professorial lectr. Mt. Sinai Sch. Medicine, 1992—; emeritus prof. in medicine SUNY, 1991—. Cons. physician Peninsula Gen. Hosp., Jamaica Hosp.; cons. on rheumatology VA Hosp., Bklyn., L.I. Coll. Hosp.; cons. family practice Luth. Med. Ctr.; vis. cons. internal medicine Jewish Gen. Hosp., Mont., Que., Can., 1965; cons. internal medicine Avicenna Hosp. and Wazir Akbar Hosp., Kabul, Afganistan, 1965; prof. medicine, dir. continuing edn., chmn. dept. family practice SUNY Downstate Med. Ctr., 1967-91, prof. emeritus medicine and family practice, 1991—; Fulbright lectr. U. Paris, 1984, 91; professorial lectr. Mt. Sinai Sch. Medicine, 1992—. Editorial adv. bd.: Pakistan Med. Forum; editor-in-chief: Clin. Rheumatology in Practice, 1981—; editor-in-chief: Advances in Rheumatology, 1986—, Rheuma21st.com, 1998—. Mem. nat. bd. govs. Arthritis Found., 1964-82, bd. govs. N.Y. chpt., 1965—, v.p., 1971-83, trustee, 1977-82, N.Y. chpt. sr. v.p., 1977-82, vice chmn. bd. trustees, 1983-85, 87—, pres., 1985-87; trustee Leo N. Levi Meml. Nat. Arthritis Hosp., Alumni Fund-Alumni Assn. SUNY Downstate Med. Center, Bklyn. Inst. Arts and Scis., Bklyn. Bot. Garden; mem. adv. bd. MEDICO, corp. mem., 1977—; treas. Internat. League Against Rheumatism, 1981-89; trustee Internat. League Against Rheumatism Trust, 1981-89. Served to capt. AUS, 1946-48. WHO fellow U. Negev, 1974; master Am. Coll. Rheumatology, 1991—; recipient Gold medal Am. Coll. Rheumatology, 1992. Master Am. Coll. Rheumatology (Gold medal 1992), fellow ACP, Am. Acad. Family Physicians (charter), N.Y. Acad. Medicine (chmn. edn. com. 1976-78); mem. AMA, (N.Y. chpt.), AAUP, Internat. Soc. for Rheumatic Therapy (chmn. 1987-89), Am. Fedn. Clin. Rsch., Am. Rheumatism Assn. (past sec.-treas.), N.Y. Rheumatism Assn. (past pres., exec. com.), Harvey Soc., (N.Y. chpt.), Kings County med. socs., Bklyn. socs. internal medicine, Soc. Tchrs. Family Medicine, N.Y. State Acads. Family Physicians, Soc. Urban Physicians, Mystery Writers Am., Sigma Xi, Alpha Omega Alpha; hon. mem. Rheumatology Soc. France, Rheumatology Soc. Japan, Rheumatology Soc. Mex., Rheumatology Soc. Brazil, Rheumatology Soc. Yugoslavia, Rheumatology Soc. Norway, Rheumatology Soc. Egypt, Med. Soc. Czechoslovakia, Cosmos Club, Heights Casino Club. Home: 184 Columbia Hts Brooklyn NY 11201-2105 also: 450 Clarkson Ave Brooklyn NY 11203-2056 E-mail: rheuma21st@aol.com.

PLOUFFE, DAVID, political strategist; b. 1967; m. Olivia Morgan; 2 children. Attended, U. Del., 1985—88. Dep. field dir. Senator Tom Harkin's Re-Election Campaign, Iowa, 1990; state field dir. Senator Tom Harkin's Presdl. Campaign, Iowa, 1992; campaign mgr. Congressman John Olver's Re-Election Campaign, Mass., 1992, Atty. Gen. Charlie

Oberly's Senatorial Campaign, Del., 1994; campaign dir. Democratic Senatorial Campaign Dir., 1995; campaign mgr. Bob Torricelli's Senatorial Campaign, NJ, 1996; dep. chief of staff Congressman Richard Gephardt, 1997—98, presdl. campaign sr. strategist, 2004; exec. dir. Democratic Congl. Campaign Com., 1999—2000; assoc. AKP&D Message and Media, Chgo., 2000—04, ptnr., 2004—; campaign mgr. Senator Barack Obama's Presdl. Campaign, 2006—08. Spkr. in field. Democrat. Office: AKP&D Message and Media 730 N Franklin St Ste 404 Chicago IL 60610 Office Phone: 312-664-7500. Office Fax: 312-664-0174.*

PLOURD, CHRISTOPHER JOHN, lawyer, consultant; b. 1955; BA, Butler U., Indpls., 1977; JD, Thomas Jefferson Coll. Law, San Diego, 1980. Bar: Calif. 1981, US Dist. Ct. (so. dist. Calif.) 1981, cert.: State Bar Calif. (criminal law) 1991, bar: US Dist. Ct. (dist. Ariz.) 1995. Atty. Plourd, Blume, Scoville, Strickland & Breeze, P.C., El Centro, Calif., 1980—82; asst. pub. defender Imperial County Pub. Defenders Office, El Centro, 1983—86; staff atty. Defenders Inc., 1986—88; prin. Law Office of Christopher J. Plourd, San Diego, 1988—. Forensic sci. evidence cons. Mem.: San Diego Lawyers Club, Calif. Pub. Defenders Assn., NY Acad. Scis., Calif. Attys. for Criminal Justice, San Diego County Bar Assn., Am. Soc. Forensic Odontology, AAAS, Am. Acad. Forensic Scis. Office: Law Office of Christopher J Plourd 1168 Union St Ste 303 San Diego CA 92101 Office Phone: 619-615-6200. Office Fax: 619-615-6204. E-mail: dnacjp@flash.net.

PLOURDE, WILLIAM E., secondary school educator; s. Robert Joseph and Angela Anne Plourde. BA in Theology, Loyola Marymount U., 1982; MA in Asian Religions, U. Hawaii, 1994; MA in Theology, U. Notre Dame, 2000. Travel agt. Decker Internat., LA, 1978—84; driver Arrow Charter Lines, 1980—84; tchr. theology Sacred Hearts Acad., Honolulu, 1984—; dir. music campus ministires U. Hawaii, 1993—; sound/light tech. IATSE Local 665, 1998—. Sailing coach Sacred Hearts Acad., 1999—, student coun. advisor, 2003—06. Vol. Hospice Hawaii, Honolulu, 1994—; mem. chorus Hawaii Opera Theatre, 1988, 1989, 1995. Mem.: Am. Acad. Religion, Am. Choral Dirs. Assn. (life), Hawaii Yacht Club. Roman Catholic. Avocations: sailing, horseback riding, archery, travel. Office: Sacred Hearts Acad 3253 WaialaeAve Honolulu HI 96816

PLOVNICK, MARK STEPHEN, business educator; b. NYC, June 8, 1946; s. Jacob and Dorothy Edith Plovnick; m. Daisy Shulan Chan, Mar. 13, 1982. BSME, Union Coll., 1968; BA in Econs., Union Coll., 1968; MS in Mgmt., MIT, 1970, PhD in Mgmt., 1975. Instr., rschr. MIT, Cambridge, 1970—76; asst. prof. Clark Univ., Worcester, Mass., 1976—79, assoc. prof., 1979—89, chmn. dept. mgmt., 1979—82, assoc. dean Grad. Sch. Mgmt., 1982—89; prof. and dean Eberhardt Sch. Bus. U. Pacific, Stockton, Calif., 1989—2006, dir. economic devel., 2006—. Cons. to various orgns., 1970—; dir. Devel. Rsch. Assocs., Reston, Va., 1979—82; adj. assoc. prof. U. Mass. Med. Sch., Worcester, Mass., 1982—89; adj. asst. prof. Boston Univ. Sch. Medicine, 1974—75; clin. instr. Harvard Med. Sch., Boston, 1977—78. Author: 5 books; contbr. numerous articles to profl. jours. Mem. Civil Svc. Commn., San Joaquin County, 1989—94; mem. gen. plan action team City of Stockton, 2004—; editl. bd. Comstock's Mag., 2006—; bd. dirs. United Way, 1991—94, Goodwill Industries, 1992—, Stockton Symphony, 1995—2001, Stockton Rotary Endowment, 2005—, No. Calif. World Trade Ctr., 2006—, Bank of Agrl. and Commerce, 2006—. Mem.: San Joaquin Angels (bd. dirs., chmn. 2008—, pres.), San Joaquin County Pub. Facilities Financing Corp. (bd. dirs. 2006—), Greater Stockton C. of C. (bd. dirs. 1990—94, 2006—), Yosemite Club (bd. dirs. 2004—09). Office: Univ Pacific Stockton CA 95211-0001 E-mail: mplovnic@pacific.edu.

PLOWDEN, DAVID, photographer; b. Boston, Oct. 9, 1932; s. Roger and Mary Russell (Butler) P.; m. Pleasance Coggeshall, June 20, 1962 (div. 1976); children: John, Daniel; m. Sandra Oakes Schoellkopf, July 8th, 1977; children: Philip, Karen. BA Econs., Yale U., 1955; pvt. studies with Minor White and Nathon Lyons, Rochester, NY, 1959-60. Asst. O. Winston Link Studio, NYC, 1958-59, George Meluso Studio, NYC, 1960-62; photographer, writer, 1962—. Assoc. prof. Inst. Design, Ill. Inst. Tech., Chgo., 1978-86; lectr. U. Iowa Sch. Journalism, 1985-88; vis. prof. Grand Valley State Univ., 1988-90, 91-2007; artist-in-residence U. Balt., 1990-91. Author and photographer: Farewell to Steam, 1968, Lincoln and His America, 1970 (Benjamin Barondess award 1971), The Hand of Man on America, 1971, 2d edit, 1974, The Floor of the Sky: the Great Plains, 1972, Bridges: the Spans of North America, 1974, 2d edit. 1984, 3d edit., 2002, Commonplace, 1974, Tugboat, 1976 (notable Children's books ALA 1976, Children's Book Showcase 1976), Steel, 1981, An American Chronology, 1982 (Notable Books ALA 1982, Booklist's Best of the 80s 1989), Industrial Landscape, 1985, A Time of Trains, 1987, A Sense of Place, 1988, End of an Era: The Last of the Great Lakes Steamboats, 1992, Small Town America, 1994, Imprints: The Photographs of David Plowden, 1997, David Plowden: The American Barn, 2003, A Handful of Dust, 2006, David Plowden: Vanishing Point Fifty Years of Photography, 2007; co-author, photographer, Nantucket, 1970, Cape May to Montauk, 1973, Desert and Plains, the Mountains and the River, 1975, The Iron Road, 1978 (notable children's books 1978, Honor list Horn Books 1979), Wayne County: the Aesthetic Heritage of a Rural Area, 1979; introduction The Gallery of World Photography/the Country, 1983; commd. illustrator Gems, 1967, The Freeway in the City, 1968, America the Vanishing, 1969, New Jersey, 1977, North Dakota, 1977, Vermont, 1979, New York, 1981, A Place of Sense, 1988; contbr. articles to numerous jours. including Time, Newsweek, Life, Audubon, Fortune, Smithsonian, Camera Arts, Lenswork; one-man shows include Columbia U., 1965, Smithsonian Instn., 1970-71, 75-76, 81, 89, Internat. Ctr. Photography, NY, 1976, Witkin Gallery, NYC, 1979, Cin. Art Acad., 1979, Gilbert Gallery, Chgo., 1980-81, Chgo. Ctr. Contemporary Photography, 1982, Fed. Hall Mus., NYC, 1982, Calif. Mus. Photography, Riverside, 1982-83, Chgo. Hist. Soc., 1985, Martin Gallery, Washington, 1987, Kunstmuseum, Luzern, Switzerland, 1987, Burchfield Ctr., Buffalo, 1987-88, Iowa State Mus., Des Moines, 1988-89, Catherine Edelman Gallery, Chgo., 1990, Grand Valley State U., 1993, Ewing Gallery, Washington, 1994, Beinecke Rare Book and Manuscript Lib. Yale U., 1997, Albright-Knox Art Gallery, 1997, Mus. Contemporary Photography, Chgo., 1998, Albin O. Kuhn Libr. & Gallery, U. Md., Balt., 1998, Tatar/Alexander Photogallery, Toronto, 1999, Lawrence Miller Gallery, NYC, 2000, 08, The Chgo. Cultural Ctr., 2002, Peter Fetterman Gallery Photog. Works of Art, Santa Monica, Calif., 2004-05, Copia, Napa, Calif., 2004, Catherine Edelman Gallery, Chgo., 2007; exhibited in group shows at Met. Mus. Art, NYC, 1967, Kodak Gallery, NYC, 1976, Currier Gallery Art, Manchester, NH, 1978, Whitney Mus., 1979, Art Inst. Chgo., 1983-87, Witkin Gallery, NYC, 1988, Davenport (Iowa) Mus. Art, 1992, Mus. Contemporary Photography, Chgo., 1996, 98-99, City, 2000, Fay Gold Gallery, Atlanta, 2003-04, Catherine Edelman Gallery, Chgo., 2007; represented in permanent collections Albright-Knox Gallery, Art Inst. Chgo., Calif. Mus. Photography, Ctr. Creative Photography, Chgo. Hist. Soc., Libr. Congress, Smithsonian Instn., U. Md., J.B. Speed Mus., Iowa Humanities Bd., Iowa State Hist. Dept., Burchfield Art Ctr., Buffalo and Erie County Hist. Soc., Internat. Mus. Photography George Eastman House, Internat. Ctr. Photography, Ekstrom Libr. U. Louisville, Beinecke Rare Book and Mauscript Libr., Yale U., 1995—, Mus. Contemporary Photography, Chicy, Bayly Mus. U. Va., Charlottesville. John Simon Guggenheim fellow, 1968; grantee N.Y. State Coun. Arts, 1966, 87, Smithsonian Inst., 1970-71, Dept. Transp. and Smithsonian Inst., 1975-76, H. E. Butt Found., 1977, United Bd. Homeland Ministries, 1976, Chgo. Hist. Soc., 1980-84, Seymour H. Knox Found., 1987, Baird Found., 1987, State Hist. Soc. Iowa, 1987-88, Iowa Humanities Bd., 1987-88; recipient R.R. History award, 1989, Honored Imagemaker, Soc. for Photographic Edn., 2002; subjectof PBS documentary: David Plowden: Light, Shadow & Form, 2000. Mem. Am. Soc. Media Photographers. Home and Office: 609 Cherry St Winnetka IL 60093-2614 Office Phone: 847-446-2793. Home Fax: 847-446-2795. Personal E-mail: david@davidplowden.com.

PLOWMAN, JACK WESLEY, lawyer; b. Blairsville, Pa., Sept. 12, 1929; s. Ralph Waldo, Sr., and Ethel Beatrice (Nicely) P.; m. Barbara Ellen Brown, Apr. 5, 1952; children: Linda Ellen, Judith Lynn AB, U. Pitts., 1951, LL.B. with honors, 1956. Bar: Pa. 1956, U.S. Dist. Ct. (we. dist.) Pa. 1956, U.S. Ct. Appeals 1960, U.S. Supreme Ct. 1978. Assoc. Campbell, Houck & Thomas, Pitts., 1956-57; ptnr. Rose, Houston, Cooper & Schmidt, Pitts., 1957-63, Plowman & Spiegel, Pitts., 1963-2000; of counsel Bentz Law Firm, P.C., Pitts., 2000—. Adj. prof. emeritus Duquesne U. Sch. Law, 1963—80, 1983—2002. Editor-in-chief Pitts. Legal Jour., 1971—81, U. Pitts. Law Rev., 1955—56. Bd. dir. United Meth. Pub. House, 1984-96, Ward Home for Children, United Meth. Ch. Union, 1977-83, Wesley Inst., 1977-81, Neighborhood Legal Svcs. Assn., 1969-74; chancellor emeritus Western Pa. Ann. Conf., United Meth. Ch. Capt. JAG, USAFR, 1979-2000. Fellow Am. Bar Found. (life mem.), Am. Coll. Trial Lawyers, Allegheny County Bar Found. (trustee, sec.); mem. ABA, Pa. Bar Assn. (house del., 1982-88), Allegheny County Bar Assn. (pres. 1982), Pa. Bar Inst. (bd. dir. 1988-92), Am. Law Inst., Supreme Ct. Pa. Hist. Soc. (trustee, pres.). Republican. Office: Washington Ctr Bldg 680 Washington Rd Pittsburgh PA 15228 Home: 706 Bower Hill Rd Pittsburgh PA 15243-2040 Office Phone: 412-563-4500. E-mail: jplowman@bentzlaw.com.

PLOWMAN, LINCOLN, councilman, protective services official; married. Police officer Marion County Sheriff's Dept., Ind.; councillor, dist. 25 Indpls.-Marion County City-County Coun., 2004—; head, second and third shift robbery Indpls. Met. Police Dept., comdr., vice investigations sect., asst. comdr., investigations divsn.; majority leader Indpls.-Marion County City-County Coun. Chmn. met. devel. com. Indpls.-Marion County City-County Coun. Mem. Marion County-Indpls. Bd. Zoning Appeals. Served with US Army. Republican. Office: 7915 S Emerson Ave #296 Indianapolis IN 46237 also: Indpls Marion County City County Coun 241 City County Bldg 200 E Washington St Indianapolis IN 46204 Office Phone: 317-557-7594, 317-327-4242. Business E-Mail: lincolnplowman@comcast.net.*

PLOWMAN, TRAVIS S., education educator, consultant; s. Travis L. and Clare Hall Plowman; m. Sandra J. Cimorelli. BA, Charleston So. U., SC, 1979; MS in Edn., Old Dominion U., Norfolk, Va., 1994; EdS in Higher Edn. Adminstrn., George Wash. U., Washington, 2003; PhD in Edn., Warnborough U., Canterbury, England, 2005. Dir. Chief Naval Edn. and Tng., Starbase Atlantis, Norfolk Pub. Schs., Norfolk, Va., 1995—99; program coord. Navy Coll., Norfolk, 1999—2000; assoc. prof. ednl. tech. Coll. St. Rose, Albany, NY, 2000—. Bias rev. com. NY State Tchr. Certification Examinations, Malta, 2002—; adj. prof. Hampton U., Va., 1997—2000. Contbr., articles to profl. jours. Tutor Rensselear Literacy Vols. Am., Troy, NY, 2006—06. Lt. USN, 1975—94. Recipient Partnership Edn. award, Va. Gov., 1996, Excellence Edn. Award, Va. Tech U., 1997, Navy Pers. Excellence Partnership Flagship award, Dept. Navy, 1998; scholar, Warnborough U., 2003. Mem.: Am. Assn. Computers Edn., Assn. Ednl. Computing and Telecom., Internat. Soc. Tech. Edn., Internat. Soc. Self-Directed Learning, Internat. Tech. Edn. Assn., Epsilon Phi Tau (hon.). Avocations: rollerskating, reading, writing. Office: The College of Saint Rose 432 Western Ave Albany NY 12203 Home: PO Box 173 Guilderland NY 12084-0173

PLOWRIGHT, JOAN ANN, actress; b. Brigg, Lincolnshire, Eng., Oct. 28, 1929; d. William and Daisy (Burton) P.; m. Roger Gage, 1953 (div. 1961); m. Sir Laurence Olivier, Mar. 17, 1961 (dec. July 11, 1989); 3 children. Student, Old Vic Theatre Sch. Mem. Old Vic Co., toured S. Africa, 1952-53; 1st leading role in the Country Wife London, 1956; mem. English Stage Co., 1956, Nat. Theatre, 1963-74. Appearances include (plays) The Chairs, 1957, The Entertainer, 1958, Major Barbara and Roots, 1959, A Taste of Honey, 1960 (Tony Best Actress award 1961), Uncle Vanya, 1962-64, St. Joan, 1963 (London Evening Standard Best Actress award 1964), Hobson's Choice, 1964, The Master Builder, 1965, Much Ado About Nothing, 1967, Tartuffe, 1967, Three Sisters, 1967, 68, 69, The Advertisement, 1968, 69, Love's Labour's Lost, 1968, 69, The Merchant of Venice, 1970, 71-72, Rules of the Game, 1971-72, Woman Killed with Kindness, 1971-72, Taming of the Shrew, 1972, Doctor's Dilemma, 1972, Rosmersholm, 1973, Saturday Sunday Monday, 1973, Eden's End, 1974, The Sea Gull, 1975, The Bed Before Yesterday, 1975 (Variety award 1976), Filumena, 1977 (Soc. West End Theatres Best Actress award 1978), Enjoy, 1980, Who's Afraid of Virginia Woolf?, 1981, Cavell, 1982, The Cherry Orchard, 1983, The Way of the World, 1985, The House of Bernada Alba, 1986-87, Time and The Conways, 1991, If We Are Women, 1995, Absolutely! (Perhaps)!, 2003, (films) Much Ado About Nothing, 1969, Equus, 1976, Richard Wagner, 1982, Brimstone and Treacle, 1982, Brittania Hosp., 1983, Revolution, 1985, The Dressmaker, 1987, Drowning By Numbers, 1987, I Love You To Death, 1990, Avalon, 1990, Enchanted April, 1992 (Acad. award nominee Best Supporting Actress, Golden Globe award 1992), Dennis the Menace, 1993, A Pin for the Butterfly, 1993, Last Action Hero, 1993, The Summer House, 1993, Widows' Peak, 1994, The Scarlet Letter, 1994, Pyromaniacs: A Love Story, 1995, The Grass Harp, 1995, Hotel Sorrento, 1995, Jane Eyre, 1995, Surviving Picasso, 1996, 101 Dalmations, 1996, Mr. Wrong, 1996, The Assistant, 1997, Tea with Mussolini, 1998, The Last Spy, 1998, Bailey's Mistake, 2000, Global Heresy, 2000, Back to the Secret Garden, 2001, Callas Forever, 2001, George and the Dragon, 2002, Bringing Down the House, 2002, I Am David, 2003, Mrs. Palfrey at the Claremont (AARP award), George and the Dragon, 2004, Goose!, 2004, Mrs. Palfrey at the Claremont, 2005, Spidermerk Cronicles, 2007, (voice) Curious George, 2006; (TV films) Merchant of Venice, 1973, Daphne, Laureola, 1977, Saturday Sunday Monday, 1977, The Importance of Being Earnest, 1988, The Birthday Party, 1987, House of Bernarda Alba, A Nightingale Sang, 1989, Stalin, 1992 (Golden Globe Awd. 1992, Emmy nomination, supporting actress - miniseries, 1993), A Place for Annie, 1994, On Promised Land, 1994, Return of the Natives, This Could Be the Last Time, 1998, Encore, Encore, 1998, Frankie and Hazel, 2000, Bailey's Mistake, 2001. Office: Ind Talent Agy Ltd Paul Lyon Maris 76 Oxford St London WIN 0AX England

PLUCIENNIK, THOMAS CASIMIR, lawyer, former assistant county prosecutor; b. Irvington, NJ, Apr. 8, 1947; s. Casimir Stanley and Helen Victoria (Sienicki) P.; m. Maria Anna Soriano, June 16, 1974. BS in Acctg., Seton Hall U., 1969, JD, 1983; MA in Criminal Justice, CUNY, 1976. Bar: N.J. 1983, U.S. Ct. Mil. Appeals 1986, U.S. Dist. Ct. N.J. 1983, D.C. 1994, U.S. Supreme Ct. 1995, N.Y. 1996, U.S. Ct. Appeals (3rd cir.), U.S. Dist. Ct. (So., Ea., fed. dists.) N.Y. 1998, (10th cir.) 1995, 2000-; cert. criminal trial atty. N.J. Supreme Ct., mil. trial atty.; lic. pvt. investigator. Mng. ptnr. Joe Bell's Tavern & Restaurant, Newark, 1979; police officer City of Newark, 1972-79; criminal investigator Essex County Prosecutor, Newark, 1980-84, asst. prosecutor, 1984-88; sr. asst. prosecutor Warren County, NJ, 1988-89; atty. Voorhees & Acciavatti Esq., Morristown, NJ, 1989-94; defense atty. Picillo Caruso, 1994-96; assoc. Netchert, Dineen & Hillman, 1996-97; litigator Francis J. Dooley, 1998-99; pvt. practice Morristown, 1999—. Cert. instr. N.J. State Police Tng. Commn., Trenton, 1984; asst. dir. instruction Officers Candidate Sch. N.J. Mil. Acad., Sea Girt. Committeeman South Orange Republican Club, N.J., 1978-83; treas., founder Tuxedo Park Neighborhood Assn., South Orange, 1977; fin. sec. J. T. Kosciusko Assn., Irvington, N.J., 1979. Served to 1st lt. U.S. Army, 1969-71, maj. (ret.) JAGC, USAR, 1985-90. Ret. maj., judge adv. gen. USAR. Recipient Class C. Commendations, Newark Police Dept., 1973, 74, 75, Command Citations, 1973, 74, 75, 77, 78. Master: Worrall F. Mountain Inn of Ct. (dist. X ethics com. mem. 1991—95); mem.: ABA, ATLA, DC Bar Assn., NY State Bar Assn. (dist. X fee arbitration com. mem. 2001—05), Morris County Bar Assn., NJ State Bar Assn., Trial Attys. NJ (trustee), Mil. Officers' Assn. Am., Polish U. Club, South Orange Lions Club (charter mem.), Picatinny Officers Club, Mil. Officers Club (pres. Sea Girt, N.J. 1979—81), Congdon-Overlook Lodge (163 F&AM) (master), Am. Legion (merit badge counsellor, BSA). Republican. Roman Catholic. Home: 11 Laurel Ln Morris Plains NJ 07950-3216 Office Phone: 973-267-0067. Personal E-mail: tcpluciennik@yahoo.com.

PLUMB, MARJORIE JANE, social worker, consultant; b. Hinsdale, Ill., Feb. 27, 1959; d. Richard Louis and Emily Joyce Plumb; m. Tracy Ann Weitz. DPH, U. Calif., Berkeley, 2006. Policy dir. Gay and Lesbian Med. Assn., San Francisco, 1997—99; owner, cons. Plumbline Coaching and Consulting, Berkeley, 1999—. Dir. Women's Policy Inst., San Francisco, 2001—08. Mem.: APHA. Progressive. Avocations: travel, golf.

PLUMEZ, JEAN PAUL, advertising executive, consultant; b. NYC, Oct. 31, 1939; s. Jean Paul and Marie Antoinette (Compagne) P.; m. Jacqueline Hornor, Feb. 20, 1965; children: Jean Paul, Nicole. BS in Chem. Engring., Bucknell U., 1962, BA in Chemistry, 1962; MBA, U. Pa., 1968. Product engr. Mobil Oil Co., Paulsboro, NJ, 1965-66; account mgr. Dancer Fitzgerald, Sample, Inc., NYC, 1968-86, exec. v.p., 1979-86; pres. Leadership on Paper, Larchmont, NY, 1986—; founding ptnr. The Right Direction, 1987—. Capt. Signal Corps U.S. Army, 1962-64. Mem. Alpha Chi Sigma, Beta Gamma Sigma, Kappa Delta Rho Clubs: Larchmont Yacht, Wharton of N.Y., Princeton of N.Y. Home and Office: 90 Beechtree Dr Larchmont NY 10538-1202 Home Phone: 914-833-0332; Office Phone: 914-833-0332. Personal E-mail: jplumez@aol.com.

PLUMMER, ANITA ELLESCAS, artist; b. San Pedro, Calif., June 5, 1944; d. Henry Declison and Helen Robles Ellescas; m. Walter Allen Plummer III, July 25, 1964; children: Sean Allen, Kira Elise, Eric Drew. BA, Calif. State U., Fullerton, 1984, MA, 1994. Illustrator DC Cook Pub. Co., Elgin, Ill., 1969—80; illustrator textiles Funny Bunny Cache Cache, Santa Ana, Calif., 1982—94; illustrator designer Playskool, N. Vale, NJ, 1988—92; conceptual illustrator Mattel Toys, El Segundo, Calif., 1988—92; illustration instr. Learning Tree U., Irvine, Calif., 1994—95; design instr. Calif. State U., Fullerton, 1994—96; book illustrator Scholastic, NYC, 1995—96. Designer illustrator Nat. Christmas Seal Assn. Author in field. Mem.: Calif. Art Club, Laguna Plein Air Painters Assn., Nat. Assn. Women Artists. Avocations: antiques, aerobics, walking.

PLUMMER, CHRISTOPHER (ARTHUR PLUMMER), actor; b. Toronto, Ont., Can., Dec. 13, 1929; s. John and Isabella Mary (Abbott) P.; m. Tammy Grimes, Aug. 19, 1956 (div. 1960); 1 child, Amanda; m. Particia Audrew Lewis, May 4, 1962 (div. 1967); m. Elaine Taylor, 1970. Student pub. and pvt. schs., Can.; pupil, Iris Warren, C. Herbertcasari; LLD (hon.), U. We. Ont., 2004; DFA (hon.), NY Julliard Sch.; PhD (hon.), U. Toronto, Ryerson and Western Ont. Stage debut in The Rivals with Can. Repertory Theatre, 1950; Broadway debut in Starcross Story, 1954, J.B.; London debut in Becket, 1961; leading actor Cymbeline, Am. Shakespeare Theatre, Stratford, Conn., 1955, Royal Shakespeare Co., London and Stratford, Avon, Eng., 1961-62, Stratford (Ont.) Shakespeare Festival, 1956, 57, 58, 60, 62, 67, Nat. Theatre Co., London; radio roles include Shakespeare, Canada; plays include Home is the Hero, 1954, Twelfth Night, 1954, 70-71, Dark is Light Enough, The Lark, Julius Caesar, The Tempest, 1955, (rearranger with Sir Neville Mariner) Henry VI, 1956, Hamlet, 1957, Winter's Tale, 1958, Much Ado About Nothing, 1958, J.B., 1958, King John, 1960, Romeo and Juliet, 1960, Richard III, 1961, Arturo Ui, 1963, The Royal Hunt of the Sun, 1965, Antony and Cleopatra, 1967, Danton's Death, 1971, Amphitryon 38, 1971, The Constant Wife, The Dark is Light Enough (Theatre World award), Medea, The Lark; (musicals) Cyrano, 1973 (Tony award for Best Actor in a Musical, 1974), The Good Doctor, 1973, Love and Master Will, 1975; performer (with Sir Neville Mariner and rearranged by Michael Lankester) A Midsummer's Night's Dream; Othello, 1982, Macbeth, 1988, No Man's Land, 1993, Barrymore, 1996 (Tony award for best actor in a play, 1997, Drama Desk, Outer Critics Cr. award, Edwin Booth award, Boston Critics' award, Chgo.'s Jefferson award, LA Ovation award best actor 1997-98), King Lear, 2004 (Tony nom. best actor in a play, 2004), Inherit the Wind, 2007; made TV debut 1953; TV prodns. include Little Moon of Alban, Johnny Belinda, 1958, Cyrano de Bergerac, 1962, Oedipus Rex, After the Fall, 1974, The Doll's House, The Prince and the Pauper, Prisoner of Zenda, Hamlet at Elsinore, BBC, 1964, Time Remembered, Capt. Brassbound's Conversion, The Shadow Box, 1981, The Thornbirds, 1983, Little Gloria-Happy at Last, A Hazard of Hearts, 1987, Crossings, 1986, Danielle Steele's Secrets, 1992, Liar's Edge, 1992, On Golden Pond, 2001, Night Flight, 2002; star TV series The Moneychangers, 1977, Harrison Bergeron, 1995, We the Jury, 1996, The Conspiracy of Fear, 1996; actor: (films) Stage Struck, 1957, Wind Across the Everglades, 1958, The Fall of the Roman Empire, 1963, Inside Daisy Clover, 1965, Sound of Music (Acad. award), 1965, Triple Cross, 1967, Nobody Runs Forever, 1969, The Battle of Britain, 1969, The Royal Hunt of the Sun, 1969, Lock up your Daughters, 1969, The Phyx, 1970, Waterloo, 1971, The Man Who Would Be King, 1975, The Return of the Pink Panther, 1975, Conduct Unbecoming, 1975, International Velvet, 1978, Murder By Decree, 1979, Starcrash, 1979, The Silent Partner, 1979, Hanover Street, 1979, Somewhere in Time, 1980, Eyewitness, 1981, The Disappearance, 1981, The Amateur, 1982, Dreamscape, 1984, Ordeal by Innocence, 1984, Lily in Love, 1985, The Boss' Wife, 1986, The Boy In Blue, 1986, An American Tail, 1986 (voice), Souvenir, 1987, Dragnet, 1987, Light Years (voice), 1988, Where the Heart Is, 1989, Fire Head, 1991, Star Trek: VI: The Undiscovered Country, 1991, Rock a Doodle, 1992 (voice), Malcolm X, 1992, Wolf, 1994, Dolores Claiborne, 1994, Twelve Monkeys, 1995, Skeletons, 1996, The Arrow, 1997, Hidden Agenda, 1998, The Clown at Midnight, 1998, Blackheart, The Insider (Boston, L.A., Chgo., Las Vegas and Nat. Critics's awards), 1999, All the Fine Lines, 1999, The

Dinosaur Hunter, 2000, Dracula 2000, A Beautiful Mind, 2001, Nicholas Nickleby, 2002, Ararat, 2002, Blizzard, 2003, Cold Creek Manor, 2003, National Treasure, 2004, Alexander, 2004, Tma, 2005, Must Love Dogs, 2005, Syriana, 2005, The New World, 2005, Inside Man, 2006, The Lake House, 2006, (voice) Up, 2009; (TV movies) Winchell, 1998, Four Minute Mile, 2005, Our Fathers, 2005; (TV mini-series) Celebrate the Century, 1999, Nuremberg, 2000, American Tragedy, 2000; Author: In Spite of Myself: A Memoir, 2008 Decorated companion Order of Can., 1968; recipient Theatre World award, 1955, Evening Std. Theatre award, 1961, Delia Austrian medal, 1973, 2 Drama Desk awards, 1973, 82, Antoinette Perry award, 1974, Emmy award Nat. Acad. TV Arts and Scis., 1977, Genie award, Can., 1980, Golden Badge of Honor, Austria, 1982, Maple Leaf award Nat. Acad. Arts and Letters, many honors Eng., Austria, Can., Two Tony awards (seven nominations), Two Emmy awards (six nominations), Gt. Britain's Evening Std. award, Can.'s Genie award, Gov. Gen's Lifetime Achievement award, 2001, William Shakespeare award (Will award) classical theatre, Nat. Bd. Rev. Career Achievement award, NY., Jason Robard's award excellence in memory great friend, 2002; inducted in Am.'s Theatre's Hall of Fame, 1986, Can.'s Walk of Fame, 1997. Office: c/o Lou Pitt The Pitt Group 9465 Wilshire Blvd Ste 480 Beverly Hills CA 90212-2612*

PLUMMER, DIRK ARNOLD, chemical, electrical, and electronics engineer; b. Stamford, Conn., Apr. 18, 1930; s. Charles Arnold Plummer and Edwina Woodling Johnson; m. Janis Susan Lowery Stuart, Feb. 18, 1967 (div. 1973); 1 child, Julie. SBChemE, MIT, 1952; BSEE, U. Calif., Berkeley, 1961; MSEE, Monmouth U., 1995. Registered profl. engr., Conn., N.J.; cert. nondestructive test examiner of inspectors for radiography, magnetic particle, liquid penetrant and ultrasonic testing methods; cert. comml. pilot. Chem. engr. Foster Wheeler Corp., NYC, 1952; engr. The M.W. Kellogg Co., NYC, 1954; project engr. Am. Machine & Fdry. Co., Greenwich, Conn., 1955-56; devel. engr. Aerojet-Gen. Corp., Azusa, Sacramento, San Ramon, Calif., 1956-61; sr. mem. tech. staff Aerospace Comm. & Controls Divsn. RCA, Burlington, Mass., 1961-62; engr. Elec. Boat Divsn., Gen. Dynamics Corp., Groton, Conn., 1963; electronics engr. US Civil Svc., various locations, 1963-88; constrn. inspector Bd. Chosen Freeholders, Freehold, NJ, 1994; pvt. practice Sea Bright, NJ, 1988—. Contbr. articles to profl. jours. Archtl. control officer Sea Bright Village Assn., 1991. 1st lt. US Army, 1952-54; col. USAR ret. Recipient Meritorious Svc. medal Pres. of U.S., 1982, Cert. Commendable Svc. Def. Supply Agy., 1972. Mem. AAAS, NSPE, ASCE, ASME, AIChE (profl. devel. officer 1990), IEEE (chmn. nuc. and plasma sci. chpt. 1990), Am. Phys. Soc., Am. Math. Soc., Math Assn. Am., Internat. Soc. Logistics, Am. Chem. Soc. Home and Office: 45 Village Rd Sea Bright NJ 07760-2233 Office Phone: 732-842-1863. Business E-Mail: dap@alum.mit.edu.

PLUMMER, ELLEN, museum director; BA, Mount Holyoke; MA, PhD, Mich. Exec. dir. Artrain, Inc., 1989—90; asst. dir. programs U. Mich. Mus. Art, 1990—96; programs adminstr. Toledo Mus. Art, 1996—99, head edn., 1999—2002; exec. dir. Ark. Arts Ctr., Little Rock. Office: Ark Arts Ctr PO Box 2137 Little Rock AR 72203-2137 Office Phone: 501-372-4000. Office Fax: 501-375-8053. Business E-Mail: nplummer@arkarts.com.

PLUMMER, JAMES D., electrical engineering educator, dean; BS in elec. engring., UCLA, 1966; MS in elec. engring., Stanford U., 1967, PhD in elec. engring., 1971. Rsch. assoc. Stanford U., 1971—74, sr. rsch. assoc., 1974—78, assoc. dir. integrated circuits lab., 1974—84, dir. integrated circuits lab., 1984—93, assoc. prof. elec. engring., 1978—83, prof. elec. engring., 1983—, John M. Fluke Prof. Elec. Engring., 1988—, prof. (by courtesy) materials sci. and engring., 1996—, sr. assoc. dean. Sch. Engring., 1993—96, Frederick Emmons Terman dean. Sch. Engring., 1999—, chmn. elec. engring. dept., 1997—99, dir. Stanford Nanofabrication Facility, 1994—2000; nat. dir. NSF Nat. Nanofabrication Users Network, 1995—2000. Cons. to numerous semiconductor and other companies, 1970—; mem. bd. dirs. Internat. Rectifier, 1995—; mem. Cypress Semiconductor Tech. Adv. Bd., 1995-; Herbert H. Johnson lectr. in materials sci. and engring. Cornell U., 1998. Author, co-author of over 300 publs.; patentee in field. Recipient Outstanding Paper Award, Internat. Solid-State Circuits Conf., 1970, 1976, 1978, Outstanding Svc. Award, Elec. Engring. Dept., Stanford U., 1988, 2 Inventor Recognition Awards, Semiconductor Rsch. Corp., Tau Beta Pi Undergrad. Tchg. Award, Sch. Engring., Stanford U., 1992, Best Tchr. Award, Soc. Women Engineers, 1995, J.J. Ebbers award, IEEE, 2003, Aldert Van der Ziel award, 2003, Jacob Millman award, McGraw/Hill, 2004. Fellow: Am. Acad. Arts and Sciences, IEEE (Third Millenium Medal 2000); mem.: NAE, Materials Rsch. Soc., Am. Phys. Soc., Electrochem. Soc. (Solid State Sci. and Tech. Award 1991), Sigma Xi, Tau Beta Pi. Office: Stanford U Sch Engring 380 Panama Mall, 214 Terman Stanford CA 94305-4027

PLUMMER, MICHAEL DAVID, mathematics professor; b. Akron, Ohio, Aug. 31, 1937; s. Lewis Benjamin and Marguerite Lizabeth Plummer; m. Sara Fletcher Lee, Aug. 17, 1968; children: Carrie Elizabeth, Ian Benjamin. BA, Wabash Coll., Crawfordsville, Ind., 1959; MS, U. Mich., Ann Arbor, 1961, PhD, 1966. Instr. math. Yale U., New Haven; asst. prof. computer sci. CUNY, 1968—70; prof. math. Vanderbilt U., Nashville, 1970—2008. Editl. bd. Utilitas Math., Thai Jour. Math. Co-author: (math. book) Matching Theory; contbr. over 100 rsch. articles pub. Recipient Niveau prize, Hungarian Acad. Scis., 1991; grantee, NSF, NAS, Internat. Rsch. Exch. Fellow: Inst. for Combinatorial Analysis (mem. coun. 2002—07); mem.: Am. Math. Soc., Pi Delta Epsilon, Tau Kappa Alpha, Sigma Xi, Sigma Pi Sigma, Phi Beta Kappa. Home: 4612 Villa Green Dr Nashville TN 37215 Office: Dept Math Vanderbilt Univ Nashville TN 37240

PLUMMER, ORA BEATRICE, nursing educator, consultant; b. Mexia, Tex., May 25, 1940; d. Macie Idella (Echols); children: Kimberly, Kevin, Cheryl. BSN, U. N.Mex., 1961; MS in Nursing Edn., UCLA, 1966. Nurse's aide Bataan Meml. Meth. Hosp., Albuquerque, 1958—60, staff nurse, 1961—62, 1967—68; staff nurse, charge nurse, relief supr. Hollywood Cmty. Hosp., Calif., 1962—64; instr. U. N.Mex. Coll. Nursing, Albuquerque, 1968—69; sr. instr. U. Colo. Sch. Nursing, Denver, 1971—74, asst. prof., 1974—76; staff assoc. III We. Interstate Commn. for Higher Edn., Boulder, Colo., 1976—78; DON Garden Manor Nursing Home, Lakewood, Colo., 1978—79, nurse surveyor, cons., 1979—87; ednl. coord. Colo. Dept. Health, Denver, 1987—96. Active in faculty devel. Colo. Cluster of Schs.; bd. dirs. Domestic Violence Initiative, Aurora Mental Health Ctr., 2008. Contbr. articles to profl. jours. Mem. adv. bd. Affiliated Children's and Family Svcs., 1977; mem. Colo. Instnl. Child Abuse and Neglect Adv. Com., 1984-92; trustee Colo. Acad., 1990-96; mem. planning com. State Wide Conf. on Black Health Concerns, 1977; mem. staff devel. com. Western Interstate Commn. for Higher Edn., 1978, mem. minority affairs com., 1978, mem. coordinating com. for baccalaureate program, 1971-76; active in minority affairs, U. Colo. Med. Ctr., 1971-72; mem. ednl. resources com., pub. rels. com., rev. com. for reappointment, promotion and tenure U. Colo. Sch. Nursing, 1971-76, mem. regulatory tng. com., 1989-93; mem. gerontol. adv. com. Met. State Coll., 1989-94; mem. expert panel long term care tng. manual Health Care Financing Adminstrn., Balt., 1989; mem. employee diversity com. Colo. Dept. Health, 1989-96; mem. Nurse Del. to Cuba, 2000, People to People Peace Initiative to Egypt, 2008; bd. dir., Aurora Mental Health Ctr., Colo., 2008-. Nominee Nightingale award, Colo., 2003. Avocations: public speaking, teaching, coaching mentoring, consultation. Office: 4300 Cherry Creek South Dr Denver CO 80246-1523 Office Phone: 303-692-2890.

PLUMMER, WILLIAM B., rental company executive, former publishing executive; b. Oct. 12, 1958; BS, MIT, 1980, MS in Aeronautics & Astronautics, 1982; MBA, Stanford U., 1986. With Kidder, Peabody & Co., Goldman, Sachs & Co.; v.p. equity capital group GE Capital Corp., 1995—97; treas. Mead Corp., 1997—98, vice pres. corp. strategy and planning, 1998—2000, pres. Gilbert Paper Div., 2000; v.p., treas. Alcoa Inc., 2000—06; exec. v.p., CFO Dow Jones & Co., NYC, 2006—07, United Rentals Inc., Greenwich, Conn., 2008—. Bd. dirs. John Wiley & Sons, Inc., 2003—. Office: United Rentals Inc Five Greenwich Office Park Greenwich CT 06830*

PLUMMER, WILLIAM HAMILTON, III, museum director, editor; b. Syracuse, NY, Sept. 3, 1944; s. William Hamilton and Anne Dorothy (Stolar) Plummer; Student, U. Maine, 1964-65; BS, Ind. U., 1973; postgrad., U. Okla., 1983-84. Scholastic sports writer Syracuse Herald-Jour., 1968-69, sports writer, summers 1968-73, Riverside (Calif.) Press-Enterprise, 1973-74, Syracuse Herald-Jour., 1975-79; dir. pub. rels., media Amateur Softball Assn., Oklahoma City, 1979—96, mgr. Nat. Softball Hall of Fame, 1996—, historian, trade show mgr. Press officer US Olympic Com., Colorado Springs, Colo. and Houston, 1979-86, Syracuse and Chapel Hill, NC, 1981-87, Baton Rouge, 1985-91, Colorado Springs, 1983-90, Mpls./St. Paul, 1990 and La., 1991, San Antonio, Tex., 1993, St. Louis, 1994, Denver, 1995, (Pan Am Games) Indpls., 1982, 87, Parana, Argentina, 1995; softball info. mgr. for 1996 Olympic Games; press officer for 1987 and 1995 Pam Am. Games, and for US Olympic Festivals 1979, 81, 82, 83, 85, 86, 87, 89, 90, 91, 93, 94, and 95; press officer for Tex. State U. Games, 1989; stringer for AP, NCAA Coll. World Series, 1991-96, 97-98, 2000-07; umpire 2 Am. Softball Assn. Regionals, selected for 1995 Am. Softball Assn. 16-under Girls' Slow Pitch Nat. Championship; voting mem. James E. Sullivan award, Dial award; sec. ISF Press Commn., 1987; mem. Olympic Results Info. Svcs. Working Grp. for softball, 2000 Olympic Games. Contbr.: The Worth Book of Softball, 1994, Encyclopedia of World Sport, 1996, The Irresistible American Softball Book, 1978, Greatest Athletes of the 20th Century, 1991, The Complete Book of Softball, The Loonies Guide to Playing and Enjoying the Game, 1984,J our. of West, 1991, The Volvo Halls of Fame Guide, 1995, The Zollner Piston Story, 1995, Inside CNY Softball, 1995-97, The Joy of Keeping Score, 1996, The Masterful Art of Fast Pitch Pitching, 1996, 2000 Sydney Olympic Games official prog.; editor, The Inside Pitch, Okla. City; scriptwriter, voiceovers, rschr. (TV series) Softball 360, Fox, 2004, scriptwriter Greatest Softball Moments, 2005; preteens and tenns book cons., 2006, author: The Game America Plays, 2008. Mem. Steering com. Sooner State Games, Oklahoma City, 1984. Sgt. USAF, 1964-68. Recipient Cert. of Merit Civil Air Patrol, 1966, Outstanding Softball Coverage, Softball Writers and Broadcasters Assn., 1970, 71, 75, So. Calif. Wrestling Assn., 1974, Cert. Appreciation, Pan Am. Games, 1987, 95, NCAA Women's Coll. Softball World Series, 1988, 89, 90, Atlanta Organizing Com., 1996, SODA President's award, 1995, Outstanding Publ. award Okla. Mus. Assn., 2006; named Outstanding Sports Reporter, USAF, 1968, Softball Writer for Atlantic Coast, Amateur Softball Assn., 1971, Softball Writer of Yr., Softball Insight Mag., 1983, Outstanding Umpire, Oklahoma City Metro Amateur Softball Assn., 1996; Ernie Pyle scholar Ind. U., 1971; named to Ind. Amateur Softball Assn. Hall of Fame (hon.), 1998, Nat. Softball Hall of Fame, 1999, NY State Amateur Softball Assn. Hall of Fame, 2003. Mem. Ind. U. Alumni Assn., Cosida, Olympic Pub. Rels. Assn., Okla. City Softball Assn. (sec., 1998), Sigma Delta Chi. Avocations: photography, jogging, umpiring, reading, freelance writing. Office: Amateur Softball Assn 2801 NE 50th St Oklahoma City OK 73111-7203 Office Phone: 405-425-3433. E-mail: dplummer@softball.org.

PLUMMER, WILLIAM TORSCH, optical physicist; s. William Edwin and Margaret Fairchild (Torsch) P.; m. Susan Bowman White, Sept. 9, 1961; children: Kathryn, Hilleary. BA, Johns Hopkins U., 1960, PhD, 1965. Lens designer Muffoletto Optical Co., Towson, Md., 1963-69; sr. dir. optical engring. Polaroid Corp., Cambridge, Mass., 1969—2001; pres. WTP Optics, Inc., Concord, Mass., 2002—. Asst. prof. astronomy U. Mass., Amherst, 1967-69; vis. prof. Tufts U., Medford, Mass., 1984-88; sr. lectr. MIT, 1991—. Capt. signal corps USAR, 1965—67. Recipient David Richardson medal, 1980, Joseph Fraunhofer award, 1997, Robert M. Burley prize, 1997, Steve Benton Meml. award, 2006. Fellow SPIE, Nat. Speleological Soc., Optical Soc. Am.; mem. Nat. Acad. Engring., Phi Beta Kappa. Achievements include central optical and opto-mechanical developments in Polaroid SX-70 folding SLR camera, model 600 LMS camera, spectra camera, captiva camera, and in laser-based printing devices; implemented new concepts for precision in high-volume manufacture; 98 US patents in field for optical, mechanical, electronic, and chemical inventions. Home: 129 Arena Ter Concord MA 01742-4413 Personal E-mail: plummew@yahoo.com.

PLUMMER-D'AMATO, PRUDENCE, medical educator; d. John Daly and Sue Plummer; m. Daniel Lawrence D'Amato, Nov. 19, 2005. BSc in Physiotherapy with honors, La Trobe U., Melbourne, Victoria, Australia, 2000, PhD, 2004. Postdoc. rsch. asst. Nat. Stroke Rsch. Inst., Melbourne, 2003—04; coord., SIRROWS clin. trial U. Calif. LA, 2006—, postdoc. rschr., 2006—08, U. Fla. Brooks Ctr. Rehab. Studies, Jacksonville, Fla., 2006—08; asst. prof. Northeastern U., Boston, 2008—. Editl. bd. mem. Internat. Jour. Therapy and Rehab., London, 2007—. Contbr. scientific papers to profl. jours. (Physiotherapy Found. Rsch. prize, 2000). Recipient Rsch. prize, Australian Physiotherapy Assn., 2003. Mem.: World Fedn. Neuro Rehab., Am. Soc. Neuro Rehab., Internat. Soc. Posture and Gait Rsch., Golden Key Internat. Soc. Office: 6 Robinson Hall Northeastern Univ 360 Huntington Ave Boston MA 02115 Office Fax: 617-373-3161. Business E-Mail: pplummer@neu.edu.

PLUSQUELLIC, DONALD L., Mayor, Akron, Ohio; b. Akron, Ohio, July 3, 1949; m. Mary Plusquellic; children: David, Michelle. BS, Bowling Green State U., 1972; JD, U. Akron, 1981. Councilman Akron City Council, 1973-81, councilman-at-large, 1982-86, council pres., 1984—87; mayor City of Akron, Ohio, 1987—. Trustee U.S. Conf. of Mayors; mem task force for funding homeland security in US cities US Dept Homeland Security, 2006—. Pres. 62nd United States Conf. Mayors, 2004; mem. Mayors Against Illegal Guns Coalition; v.p. Internat. Mayors for Peace; hon. mem. Internat. Raoul Wallenberg Found.; pres. Ohio's Big City Mayors. Recipient Leadership award, Internat. Econ. Devel. Council, 2008, Grand award, Nat. Assoc. Home-builders, 1986, Civil Livability award, U.S. Conf. Mayors, 1999, Meritorious Svc. award, United Negro Coll. Fund, Bravo award, Ohio Ballet, Honor award, U. Akron's Alumni, Tree of Life award, Jewish Nat. Fund; named Municipal Leader of the Year, American City & County Magazine, 2003, Exec. of the Year, Sales & Mktg. Assoc., 1997, Sports Person of Yr., Dapper Dan Club, 1997, Citizen of Yr., Akron Bd. Realtors. Mem.: Omicron Delta Kappa (hon.). Achievements include development of the funding mechanism used to ensure appropriate monies are allocated to communities following the attack on September 11, 2001; the Joint Econonmic Development District program. Office: Office of the Mayor 200 Municipal Bldg 166 S High St Akron OH 44308-1626 Office Phone: 330-375-2345. Office Fax: 330-375-2468. Business E-Mail: mayor@ci.akron.oh.us.*

PLUTA, JOSEPH EDWARD, economics professor; b. Chgo., Aug. 11, 1946; s. Joseph Walter and Anna Wrobel Pluta; m. Margo Michelle Provost, July 28, 1973; children: Kathryn Therese Simmons, Andrew Joseph. BA, U. Notre Dame, Ind., 1967, MA, 1968; PhD, U. Tex., Austin, 1972. Asst. prof. economics U. North Fla., Jacksonville, 1973—74; assoc. prof. economics Naval Postgrad. Sch., Monterey, Calif., 1974—77; editor, tex. bus. rev. U. Tex., 1979—84; prof. economics St. Edward's U., Austin, 1984—. Econ. cons. Govt. South Vietnam, Saigon, 1974, Govt. Taiwan, Taipei, 1975; rsch. economist Comptr. Pub. Accts., Austin, 1977—79; host radio program KUT-FM, Austin, 1979—80; cons. numerous small bus., Austin, 1998—. Author: (book) The Market: Mainstream and Evolutionary Views, over 50 articles in acad. jours. Spkr. City Govt., Westlake Hills, Tex., 2003—05; sponsor, hurricane Katrina Evacuee, Austin, Tex., 2006—. Recipient Sears Found. Disting. Tchg. award, 1999, Disting. Tchg. Career award, 2006, Presdl. Scholarly Excellence award, 2008. Mem.: Assn. Instl. Thought, History Economics Soc., Assn. Evolutionary Economics. Democrat. Office: St Edwards Univ 3001 S Congress Ave Austin TX 78704 Office Fax: 512-233-1622. Business E-Mail: joep@stedwards.edu.

PNEUMAN, LINDA JACKSON, retired physician; b. Memphis, July 9, 1938; d. John Thomas Jackson, Jr. and Winnie Griffin Jackson; m. Gerald Warnick Pneuman, June 16, 1978 (dec.); m. Terry Robert Cobb, Nov. 8, 1957 (div. 1974); children: Kimberly Winn Kirby, Elizabeth Lankford Fredricksmeyer. BS magna cum laude, U. Memphis, 1961; MD, Meharry Med. Coll., Nashville, 1976. Tchr. chemistry and biology St Mary's Episcopal Sch., Memphis, 1960—62; rsch. asst. Vanderbilt U. Psychopharmacology Rsch. Ctr., Nashville, 1966—67; intern, resident St. Joseph's Hosp., Denver, 1976—77; physician Denver U. Student Health Svc., Denver, 1977—81, US Dept. Def., Bad Aibling, Bavaria, Germany, 1978—79, U. Colo. Student Health Svc., Boulder, 1981—88, Calif. State U., Chico, Calif., 1988—2002; ret. Chair quality assurance U. Colo. Student Health Svc., Boulder, 1985—88; chair human subjects com. U. Colo., Boulder, 1986—88; chair quality assurace Calif. State U., Chico Student Health Svc., 1988—97, acting dir., 2000—01; chief clin. medicine Calif. State U. Chico, 1997—2001. Vol. naturalist City of Boulder Open Space and Mountain Parks, 2005—06; bd. mem. Boulder Valley Women's Clinic, 1986—88; fund raiser Friendship Bridge, Evergreen, Colo., 2005—06. Outstanding Student scholar, Hill Family Found., 1974, 1975. Mem.: Alpha Omega Alpha (life). Democrat. Episcopalian. Home: 937 W Plum Cir Louisville CO 80027 Personal E-mail: lpneuman@csuchico.edu.

PNIAKOWSKI, ANDREW FRANK, structural engineer; b. Grodno, Poland, Aug. 18, 1930; s. Josef Leon and Janina (Kodzynski) Pniakowski; m. Margaret M. Czajkowski, Aug. 15, 1957; 1 child, Mary. Diploma Engr., Politechnika Warszawska, 1952. Registered profl. engr., Ont., Mass., Maine, N.H. Bridge design and field engr. Govt. of Poland, Ministry of R.R., Warsaw, 1952—57; bridge design engr. Dept. Hwys. of Ont., Toronto, Canada, 1958—66; sr. structural engr. Sverdrup & Parcel Assocs., Inc., Boston, 1967—71; chief structural engr. Louis Berger & Assocs., Inc., Needham, Mass., 1972—96; cons. engr. in transp., bridges, hwys., railroads, pub. bldgs., others. Mem.: Assn. Profl. Engrs. of Province of Ont., Prestressed Concrete Inst., Am. Concrete Inst., Am. Inst. Steel Constrn. Roman Catholic.

POAG, CLAUDE WYLIE, geologist, researcher; b. Deland, Fla., Aug. 12, 1937; s. Mary Elisabeth and Francis Black (Stepfather); m. Martha Murray; children: Tracy Elizabeth, Marla Denise, Graham Murray. BS, Fla. State U., Tallahassee, 1959; MS, La. State U., Baton Rouge, 1962; PhD, Tulane U., New Orleans, 1970. Micropaleontologist Chevron Oil Co., Lafayette, La., 1962—63, New Orleans, 1963—70; field officer NSF, Washington, 1963—64; asst. prof. oceanography Tex. A&M U., Coll. Sta., 1963—70; rsch. geologist US Geol. Survey, Woods Hole, Mass., 1974—2004, scientist emeritus, 2004—. Author: (nonfiction book) Chesapeake Invader (Shoemaker Comm. Award, 2000); contbr. articles to profl. jours. Fellow: AAAS, Geol. Soc. America; mem.: Am. Assn. Petroleum Geologists, Cushman Found. (editor 1986—88), Meteoritical Soc. Achievements include discovery of America's largest meteorite crater buried beneath Chesapeake Bay. Home: 14 Sandpiper Cir East Falmouth MA 02536 Office: US Geol Survey 384 Woods Hole Rd Woods Hole MA 02543-1598 Office Fax: 508-457-2310. Personal E-mail: bolide14@verizon.net. Business E-Mail: wpoag@usgs.gov.

POCALYKO, MICHAEL NICHOLAS, investment banker, venture capitalist; b. Fountain Hill, Pa., Dec. 24, 1954; s. Walter and Anna Margaret (Pagats) P.; m. Barbara Wilson Snelbaker, Dec. 26, 1976; children: James Kenneth, Kathryn Laura. AB, Muhlenberg Coll., 1976; MPA, Harvard U., 1985; MBA, U. Pa., 1995. Commd. ensign USN, 1976, advanced through grades to comdr., 1992; aviation detachment officer in charge USS Pharris, 1983-84; mem. strategic concepts group Office of Chief of Naval Ops., Washington, 1985-86, spl. asst. to Dep. Chief of Naval Ops., 1986-87; aviation detachment officer in charge USS Boone, 1988-90; with Office of Sec. of Navy, Washington, 1990-92; sr. fellow Atlantic Coun. U.S., Washington, 1992-93; with Office of Sec. Def., Washington, 1993—95; founder, prin. M.N. Pocalyko Investment Bankers, 1995—97; mng. dir., CEO Monticello Capital, 1997—, corp. dir., chmn., 1997—. Corp. dir., audit com. chmn. Challenger Corp., 2002—08; chmn. Advanced Environ. Resources Inc., 2003—08, Erdevel Europa S.à r.l., 2003—08, Erdevel Europa in the Kingdom of Saudi Arabia, 2004—08, Erdevel Water Sys. S.r.l. (later International Sys. S.r.l.), 2004—08, TherimuneX Pharms., Inc., 2008—; trustee Fairleigh Dickinson U., 2000—06; founder, corp. dir. Envambien, S.A., 2007—08; bd. adv. Financial Investments Inc., 2009—. Co-editor, contbr.: A John Hawkes Symposium: Design and Debris, 1977; contbr.: Reconstituting America's Defense, 1992, In Support of Arab Democracy, 2005; rapporteur: The Future of Russian-American Relations in a Pluralistic World, 1992, The Future of Ukrainian-American Relations in a Pluralistic World, 1992; co-author: The NATO Infrastructure Program, 1993; author: The New Trade Order, 1994, Trends in the International Business Competition Environment, 2001; contbr. articles, essays, op-eds to profl. publs., books, newspapers. Apptd. Fairfax County Industrial Devel. Authority, 1999—2000; apptd. mem. exec. coun. Boy Scouts Am. Nat. Capital Area Coun., 2002—; apptd. mem. Va. Commonwealth Competition Coun., 2000—03; mem. Fairfax County Rep. Com., 1996—2004, Va. Ho. Delegates 36th dist. Rep. Com., 1996—2001, chmn., 2001—06. Recipient Eagle Scout award, 1968, Vincent Astor Found. award U.S. Naval Inst., 1983, Lamb award, Evangelical Lutheran Ch. Am., 1998, Silver Beaver award, Boy Scouts Am., 2002; decorated Navy Commendation Medal, Navy Achievement Medal, Meritorious Svc. Medal (3 awards), 16 other decorations. Mem. U.S. Naval Inst., Internat. Inst. Strategic Studies, Coun. on Fgn. Rels., Assn. Naval Aviation, Muhlenberg Coll. Alumni Assn. (exec. coun. 1986-90, chmn. com. 1986-90), Metropolitan Club (New York), Tower Club (Tysons Corner Va.), Am. Legion, V.F.W., Beirut Veterans of Am., Masons, Sovereign Military Order Temple Jerusalem (gran officier), Military Order Foreign Wars, Military Order Carabao, Sigma Phi Epsilon, Sigma Tau Delta. Republican. Lutheran. Avocations: fly fishing, horseback riding. Office: Monticello Capital Lindbergh Ctr - Dulles Business Park 3901 Centerview Dr Ste R Chantilly VA 20151-3299 Office Phone: 703-674-0500, 703-674-0501. Business E-Mail: pocalyko@monticellocapital.com.

POCHI, PETER ERNEST, physician; b. Boston, Mar. 8, 1929; s. Anesti and Alice (Peterson) P.; m. Barbara Orlob, June 11, 1955; children: Alan, Rena. AB cum laude, Harvard Coll., 1950; MD, Boston U., 1955. Diplomate Am. Bd. Dermatology. Intern Boston City Hosp., 1955-56, vis. dermatologist, 1978-91, assoc. dir., 1967-74, 78-84, acting chief dermatology, 1984-85; resident in dermatology Boston U. Hosp., 1958-61, vis. dermatologist, 1977-91, acting chief dermatology, 1984-85; assoc. in medicine Peter Bent Brigham Hosp., Boston, 1972-78; sr. cons. in dermatology Lemuel Shattuck Hosp., Boston, 1975-91; Herbert Mescon prof. dermatology Sch. Medicine, Boston U., 1988-91, prof. emeritus, 1991—, interim chmn. dept. dermatology, 1984-85. Cons. med. service in dermatology Boston VA Hosp., 1978-82; lectr. dermatology Sch. Medicine, Tufts U., 1980-91; assoc. staff New Eng. Med. Ctr. Hosp., 1981-91. Assoc. editor Jour. Investigative Dermatology, 1968-73; contbg. editor Year Book of Dermatology, 1983-90; mem. editl. bd. Archives of Dermatology, 1979-84, Jour. Am. Acad. Dermatology, 1981-90; hon. editor Acta Dermatovenerologica Albanica, 2004—; contbr. articles to med. jours Bd. dirs. Cmty. Music Ctr., 1973-77, 97-2003, corp. mem., 1994-97, 2005—; governing bd. Boston Musical Theater, 2000-03. With USN, 1956-58. USPHS fellow, 1960-62, 62-63; USPHS grantee, 1965-84 Fellow Am. Acad. Dermatology (bd. dirs. 1981-85); mem. Am. Fedn. Clin. Rsch., AMA, Boston Dermatol. Club (sec.-treas. 1967-69), Boston U. Sch. Medicine Alumni Assn. (pres. 1979-80), Boston U. Nat. Alumni Coun., Dermatology Found., Evans Med. Found. (dir., sec.), Internat. Soc. Dermatology, Mass. Acad. Dermatology, Mass. Med. Soc. (chmn. sect. dermatology 1977-78), New Eng. Dermatol. Soc., Soc. Investigative Dermatology (bd. dirs. 1976-81, v.p. 1986-87), Am. Acne and Rosacea Soc. Home: 333 Commonwealth Ave Boston MA 02115-1933 Personal E-mail: pepderm@bu.edu.

POCHICK, FRANCIS EDWARD, financial consultant; b. Metuchen, NJ, May 28, 1931; s. Frank Stephen and Bertha Barbara Pochick; m. Shirley Ann Elliott, Feb. 16, 1957; children: Bonnie Lynn, Keith Francis. Student, Rutgers U., 1949-50, 54-55. Agt. New Eng. Mut. Life. Ins. Co., Newark and New Brunswick, NJ, 1958-61, Lambert M. Huppeler Co., Inc., NYC, 1962-64, cons., 1964, sr. cons. employee benefits, 1967-87; fin. cons. Francis E. Pochick Assocs., NYC, 1987—. Mem. adv. bd. Mercer Fund, Cmty. Found. N.J., 1986—, Rec. for the Blind, Princeton, 1989, charitable devel. officer Nat. Found., Inc., 1992, Nat. Coun. on The Aging, Planned Giving Coun. 1994; mem. com. bd. dirs. health Princeton Coun. Planned Giving, 1993; v.p. The Benefits Planning Co., Ltd., Charlottesville, Va., 1995. With USMC, 1951-54. Mem. Am. Soc. Pension Actuaries, Nat. Assn. Life Underwriters, Fin. Planning Assn., Estate Planning Coun., Nat. Assn. Philanthropic Planners, Lions, Glenmore Country Club. Home: 1451 Bremerton Ln Keswick VA 22947-9147 Office: PO Box 518 Keswick VA 22947-0518 also: No Jersey Br 30 Two Bridges Rd Fairfield NJ 07004-1550 Office Phone: 434-295-7173. Personal E-mail: blmccann118@aol.com, fepassoc@embarqmaic.com. Business E-Mail: fepassoc@earthlink.net.

POCIUS, ALPHONSUS VYTAUTAS, physical chemist; b. Emsdetten, Fed. Republic of Germany, May 20, 1948; came to U.S., 1950; s. Aleksandras and Sofija (Venckute) P.; m. Janice Lynn Amato, Aug. 9, 1970; children: Nicholas Stephen, Amanda Kathleen. BA, Knox Coll., 1970; PhD, U. Ill., 1974. With 3M Co., St. Paul, 1974—, div. scientist Adhesive Tech. Ctr., 1989—. Mem. tech. adv. com. Ctr. for Interfacial Engring., U. Minn., Mpls., 1988-92, resident indsl. fellow, 1990. Author course on adhesion and adhesives, 1985; mem. editorial adv. bd. Jour. Adhesion Sci. and Tech., 1990—; contbr. articles to profl. jours.; inventor in field. 1st lt. U.S. Army, 1974, capt. Res. ASTM (mem. com.), Adhesion Soc. Avocations: reading, carpentry, home improvement. Office: 3M Adhesive Tech Ctr 3M Center Bldg 236 Saint Paul MN 55144-1001

POCOCK, J. MICHAEL, communications executive; B in Telecomm., U. Ky., Lexington. Various sr. mgmt. pos., consumer products divsn. GE Co., Fairfield, Conn.; mem. mgmt. team Epson Am., Torrance, Calif.; variuos sr. mgmt. pos. Murata Bus. Systems, Dallas; variuos sr. mgmt. positions including pres., CEO Quadmark Ltd. Xerox Corp., Rochester, NY, 1992—94; v.p., gen. mgr. Digital Equipment Corp., Acton, Mass., 1994—96; v.p., gen. mgr. N.Am. sales Compaq Computer Corp., Houston, 1996—99, gen. mgr. comml. products computer group, 1999, v.p. corp. strategy; pres., CEO Polaroid Corp., Waltham, Mass., 2003—06; sr. v.p., gen. mgr. Linksys Cisco Systems, Inc., Irvine, Calif., 2006—.

POCOSKI, DAVID JOHN, cardiologist; b. Waterbury, Conn., July 15, 1945; s. Edward J. and Stella E. (Kolpa) Pocoski; m. Madelyn M. Pocoski, Sept. 25, 1971; 1 child, Sarah C. BS, U. Conn., Storrs, 1967; MD magna cum laude, Upstate Med. Ctr., Syracuse, NY, 1971. From intern to fellow in cardiology U. Rochester, NY; founder, pres. Osler Clinic of Medicine, Melbourne, Fla.; chief of staff, dir. cardiac rehab. Sea Pines Rehab. Hosp.; chmn. dept. cardiology Holmes Regional Med. Ctr., Melbourne. Commr. Holy Name Jesus Cath. Ch. Maj. USAF, 1974-76. Recipient Outstanding Scientist of the 20th Century award. Fellow Am. Coll. Cardiology; mem. AMA, Alpha Omega Alpha, Phi Beta Kappa. Republican. Roman Catholic. Avocations: music, art, running, community service. Home: 930 S Harbor City Blvd Melbourne FL 32901-1963 Office: Chmn Dept Cardiology Holmes Regional Med Ctr Melbourne FL 32901 Home Phone: 321-984-7707; Office Phone: 321-725-5050. Personal E-mail: fdhp93a@aol.com.

PODARIU, IULIA ANCA, physics professor, researcher; b. Pitesti, Romania, July 28, 1970; d. Georgel and Mariana Anita; m. Silviu Podariu, Sept. 12, 1993; children: Maria Irina, Ana Elena, Rebecca Magdalena. PhD in Physics, Kans. State U., Manhattan, 2002. Asst. prof. North Pk. U., Chgo., 2002—03, UNO, Omaha, 2003—. Judge sci. fairs. Contbr. scientific papers. Grantee, UNO, 2004, NSF-EPS Corp., 2005. Mem.: ACS, KSU ALumni Club. Achievements include research in nanoparticles, block copolymers and small particles mixtures, dynamics and equilibrium in bulk and nanofilms. Office: Univ Nebr Omaha 6001 Dodge St Omaha NE 68182

PODBERESKY, SAMUEL, lawyer; b. Cremona, Italy, Mar. 16, 1946; came to U.S., 1947; s. Noah and Mina (Milikowsky) P.; m. Rosita Rubinstein, March 8, 1970; children: Daniel J., Michael J. BS in Aeronautical Engring., U. Md., 1967; JD, U. Md., Balt., 1971. Bar: Md. 1972. Flight test engr. Vertol div. Boeing Co., Phila., 1967-68; regulatory atty. FAA, Washington, 1971-78; dep. asst. gen. counsel U.S. Dept. Transp., Washington, 1978-86, asst. gen. counsel aviation enforcement and proceedings, 1986—. Author: Never the Last Road, 2003. Office: US Dept Transp 1200 New Jersey Ave SE Washington DC 20590-0001

PODBOY, ALVIN MICHAEL, JR., law librarian, director; b. Cleve., Feb. 10, 1947; s. Alvin Michael and Josephine Esther (Nagode) P.; m. Mary Ann Gloria Esposito, Aug. 21, 1971; children: Allison Marie, Melissa Ann. AB cum laude, Ohio U., 1969; JD, Case Western Res. U., 1972, MLS, 1977. Bar: Ohio 1972, US Dist. Ct. (no. dist.) Ohio 1973, US Supreme Ct. 1992. Assoc. Joseph T. Svete Co. LPA, Chardon, Ohio, 1972-76; dir. pub. svcs. Case Western Res. Sch. Law Libr., Cleve., 1974-77, assoc. law libr., 1977-78; libr. Baker & Hostetler, LLP, Cleve., 1978-88, dir. librs., 1988—. Instr. Notre Dame Coll. of Ohio, Cleve., 1991-2002, Ursuline Coll., Cleve., 2003-, Am. Inst. Paralegal Studies, Cleve., 1991-96, libr. rels. adv. bd., Lexis Nexis, 2007-. Mem. (editl. adv. bd.) Law Tech. News, 1999—; Practice Innovations, 2001—. Bd. overseers Case Western Res. U., 1981-87, vis. com. sch. libr. sci., 1980-86, Westlaw adv. bd., 1987-92, bd. govs. law sch. alumni assn., 1992-95, West's Legal Directory Ohio Adv. Panel, 1990-91; adv. com. West's Info. Innovators Inst., 1995-97; chmn. Case Western Res. Libr. Sch. Alumni Fund, 1979-80; Rep. precinct committeeman Cuyahoga County, Cleve., 1981-95, exec. com., 1984-87; Rep. precinct committeeman Portage County, Aurora, 2004—; treas. Aurora Meml. Libr. Trust, 2004-08; 2nd vice comdr. Aurora Am. Legion Post 803, 2006-, Am. Legion Portage County Coun., 2007-, Am. Legion 14th Disting, 2008-, 1st lt. USAF, 1972. Mem.: ABA, Arnold Air Soc., Case Western Res. U. Libr. Sch. Alumni Assn. (pres. 1981), Ohio Regional Assn. Law Librs. (pres. 1985), Am. Assn. Law Librs. (chmn. pvt. law librs. spl. interest sect. 1994—95, exec. bd. 2001—04, cert.), Cleve. Bar Assn., Ohio State Bar Assn. (chmn. librs. com. 1989—91), Phi Alpha Theta, Pi Gamma Mu. Roman Catholic. Avocation: alpine skiing. Home: 417 East Parkway Blvd Aurora OH 44202 Office: Baker & Hostetler LLP 3200 National City Ctr Cleveland OH 44114-3485 Business E-Mail: apodboy@bakerlaw.com.

PODESTA, HEATHER MILLER, lobbyist, lawyer; m. Anthony Podesta, 2003. BA, U. Calif., Berkeley; JD, U. Va., 1997. Gen. counsel Airlines Clearing House, Air Transport Assn.; legis. aide trade and transp. to Senator Bill Bradley; legis. aide tax, trade, and pension policy to Rep. Earl Pomeroy; tax and trade counsel to Robert Matsui; prin. Blank Rome Govt. Rels. LLC, 2004; ptnr. Blank Rome LLP; founder, ptnr. Heather Podesta + Ptnrs., 2007—. Adv. bd. mem. Peggy Guggenheim Collection, 2005—. Bd. trustees Nat. Museum of Women in the Arts. Named one of 50 Top Lobbyists, Washingtonian mag., 2007. Democrat. Avocation: art collector. Office: Heather Podesta & Partners LLC 626 E ST NW # 200 Washington DC 20004-2203 Office Phone: 202-628-8953. Office Fax: 202-468-2930.*

PODESTA, JOHN DAVID, think-tank executive, law educator, former White House chief of staff; b. Chgo., Jan. 8, 1949; s. John David, Sr. and Mary (Kokoris) Podesta; m. Mary Spieczny, Nov. 4, 1978; children: Megan Rouse, Mae, Gabriel. BS, Knox Coll., 1971; JD, Georgetown U., 1976. Bar: DC 1976. Trial atty. US Dept. Justice, Washington, 1976-77; spl. asst. to dir. ACTION, Washington, 1978-79; counsel Senate Judiciary Com., Washington, 1979-81; chief minority counsel Senate Judiciary Subcom., Washington, 1981-86; chief counsel Senate Agrl. Com., Washington, 1987-88; pres., gen. counsel Podesta Associates, Inc., Washington, 1988-93; asst. to pres., staff sec. The White House, Washington, 1993-95, asst. to pres., dep. chief of staff, 1997-98, chief of staff to Pres., 1998—2001; pres., CEO Ctr. Am. Progress, Washington, 2001—; co-chmn. Barack Obama Presdl. Transition Team, 2008—09. Vis. prof. law Georgetown U. Law Ctr., Washington, 1983, Washington, 1995—97, Washington, 1998—2000, Washington, 2001—; chair US Senate subcom., Task Force Privacy and Tech., Washington, 1991; mem. coun. Adminstrv. Conf. US, Washington, 1993—95; mem. Com. Protecting and Reducing Govt. Secrecy, Washington, 1995. Author: Protecting Electronic Messaging, 1990. Named one of The 50 Most Powerful People in DC, GQ mag., 2007. Fellow: Natural Resources Def. Coun. (sr.); mem.: ABA (coun., sec. individual rights and responsibilities 1994—, chair 2002—03), DC Bar (chair adminstrv. law sect. 1982—83), League Conservation Voters (bd. dirs. 2001—). Democrat. Office: Ctr Am Progress 1333 H St NW 10th Fl Washington DC 20005 also: Georgetown U Law Ctr 574 McDonough Hall Washington DC 20001-2075*

PODESTA, TONY (ANTHONY T. PODESTA), lobbyist; b. Chgo., Ill., Oct. 24, 1943; s. John David and Mary (Kokoris) Podesta; m. Heather Miller. BA, U. Ill. Co-founder, pres. The Podesta Group, Washington, 1988—. Vis. prof. Georgetown U. Law Ctr. Named Power Collector, The Washington Post; named one of 50 Top Lobbyists, Washingtonian mag., 2007. Democrat. Avocation: art collecting. Office: Podesta Group Ste 900 E 1001 G St, NW Washington DC 20001 Office Phone: 202-393-1010. Office Fax: 202-393-5510. E-mail: tpodesta@podesta.com.*

PODEWILS, LAURA JEAN, epidemiologist, researcher; d. Robert A. and Nancy J. Podewils. BS, U. Nev., Reno, 1995; MS, San Diego State U., Calif., 1998; PhD, Johns Hopkins Bloomberg Sch. Pub. Health, Balt., 2003. Rsch. assoc. Johns Hopkins Sch. Nursing, Balt., 1999—2001; co-investigator, clin. trial Johns Hopkins Sch. Medicine, Balt., 2001—03; rsch. asst., dept. hosp. epidemiology Johns Hopkins Hosp., Balt., 2002; epidemic intelligence svc. officer Ctr. Disease Control and Prevention, Atlanta, 2003—05, epidemiologist, 2005—; short-term cons., stop polio team 18 WHO, Manila, 2005, Cons., mdr-tb rsch. subgroup Geneva, 2007—. Assoc. editor Jour. Pediatric Infectious Diseases, 2008—. Contbr. articles to med. jours. Big sibling Johns Hopkins Hosp. Intensive Primary Care Clinic, Balt., 2000—09; global village vol. Habitat for Humanity, Guatemala, 2006—07. Recipient US Pub. Health Svc. Achievement medal, HHS, 2005; Aging Tng. grant, Johns Hopkins Bloomberg Sch. Pub. Health, 1998—2003, grant, 2003. Mem.: Internat. Union Against Tb and Lung Diseases. Democrat. Avocations: hiking, pilates, travel. Office: Ctrs Disease Control 1600 Clifton Rd NE MS E-10 Atlanta GA 30333 Personal E-mail: lpodewil@yahoo.com. Business E-Mail: lpp8@cdc.gov.

PODEWILS, ULRICH, academic administrator; b. Hildesheim, Germany, Sept. 13, 1947; s. Erich and Gisela (Kohne) P.; m. Vaneeta Kumari Khosla, Mar. 27, 1954; 1 child, Indra Sarah. 1st state exam in law, U. Heidelberg, 1972; 2nd state exam in law, State of Baden-Wuerttemberg, 1975. Jr. lawyer State of Baden-Wuerttemberg, Germany, 1972-75; dept. head U. Mannheim, 1975-78; internat. affairs Ministry Sci., Stuttgart, Germany, 1978-83; head pub. rels. Fed. Ministry Edn., Bonn, Germany, 1983-86; sec. gen. Villa Vigoni, Como, Italy, 1986-87; head univ. affairs Fed. Ministry Edn., Bonn, 1987-88; chancellor Tech. U., Berlin, 1988-98; dir. Berlin office, Berlin Artist Program German Acad. Exch. Svc., 1998—2003, dir. New Delhi office, 2003—. Decorated Order of Merit Cavalier. Mem. Rotary Club New Delhi Midtown. Office: DAAD 72 Lodi Estate New Delhi 110 003 India Business E-Mail: podewils@daaddelhi.org.

PODGORNY, GEORGE, emergency physician; b. Tehran, Iran, Mar. 17, 1934; s. Emanuel and Helen (Parsian) P.; came to U.S., 1954, naturalized, 1973. B.S., Maryville Coll., 1958; postgrad. Bowman Gray Sch. Medicine, 1958; M.D., Wake Forest U., 1962; m. Ernestine Koury, Oct. 20, 1962; children: Adele, Emanuel II, George, Gregory. Intern in surgery N.C. Bapt. Hosp., Winston-Salem, 1962-63, chief resident in gen. surgery, 1966-67, in cardiothoracic surgery, 1967-69; sr. med. examiner Forsyth County, N.C., 1972—; dir. dept. emergency medicine Forsyth Meml. Hosp., Winston-Salem, 1974-80; sec.-treas. Forsyth Emergency Services, Winston-Salem, 1970-80; clin. prof. emergency medicine East Carolina U. Sch. Medicine, Greenville, 1984—, chmn. residency rev. com. on emergency medicine, 1980-88; mem. Accreditation Coun. for Grad. Med. Edn. Dir. Emergency Med. Svcs. Project Region II of N.C., 1975—; chmn. bd. trustees Emergency Medicine Found.; chmn. residency rev. com. emergency medicine Accreditation Coun. Grad. Med. Edn.; founder Western Piedmont Emergency Med. Svcs. Coun., 1973; mem. N.C. Emergency Med. Svcs. Adv. Coun., 1976-81; assoc. prof. clin. surgery Bowman Gray Sch. Medicine, Wake Forest U., Winston-Salem, 1979—. Bd. dirs. Piedmont Health Systems Agy., 1975-84; trustee Forsyth County Hosp., Authority, 1974-75; bd. dirs. N.C. Health Coordinating Coun., 1975-82, Medic Alert Found. Internat. Fellow Internat. Coll. Surgeons, Internat. Coll. Angiology, Royal Soc. Health (Great Britain), Royal Soc. Medicine, Southeastern Surg. Congress; mem. Am. Coll. Emergency Physicians (charter, pres. 1978-79), AMA, (chmn. coun. of sect. emergency medicine 1978-90, alt. del. for Am. Coll. Emergency Physicians, 1990—), Am. Bd. Emergency Medicine (pres. 1976-81). Contbr. articles to profl. publs. on trauma, snake bite and history of medicine; editorial bd. Annals of Emergency Medicine, Med. Meetings. Home and Office: 2115 Georgia Ave Winston Salem NC 27104-1917 Office Phone: 336-727-1161.

PODGORSAK, ERVIN B., medical physicist, educator, administrator; b. Vienna, Sept. 28, 1943; arrived in Slovenia, 1946, came to U.S., 1968, Can., 1973; s. Franc and Gabriella Podgorsak; m. Mariana Ambrozic, Oct. 23, 1965; children: Matthew, Gregor. Dipl.Ing. in Physics, U. Ljubljana, Slovenia, 1968; MSc in Physics, U. Wis., 1970, PhD in Physics, 1973. Diplomate Am. Bd. Med. Physics. Rsch. asst. U. Ljubljana, 1965-68, U. Wis., Madison, 1968-73; postdoctoral fellow U. Toronto, Ont., Canada, 1973-74; asst. prof. McGill U., Montreal, Que., Canada, 1975-79, assoc. prof., 1980-84, prof. med. physics, 1985—, dir. med. physics unit, 1991—2009; dir. dept. med. physics Montreal Gen. Hosp., 1979—2009. Hon. vis. prof. U. Ljubljana, 1995—; presenter in field. Author Radiation Physics for Medical Physicists, 2005; editor Review of Radiation Oncology Physics: A Handbook for Teachers and Students, 2005; contbr. numerous articles to sci. jours., chpts. to books. Recipient (with C. Zankowski) Sylvia Fedoruk prize in Med. Physics, 1997, (with C. Zankowski) Farrington Daniels award in Med. Physics, 1997, Agora Award, Le Palais des Congres, Montreal, 1998. Fellow Can. Coll. Physicists in Medicine (bd. dirs. 1981-89, v.p. 1984-87, pres. 1987-89), Am. Assn. Physicists in Medicine (bd. dirs. 1990-93, assoc. editor Med. Physics Jour. 1989-2005, radiother. com. 1994-96, Lifetime Achievement in Med. Physics award Upstate NY chpt. 2005, William D. Coolidge award 2006), Am. Coll. Med. Physics (bd. chancellors 1997-99, sec. 2007-09); mem. Can. Orgn. Med. Physicists (Gold medal, 2008), Can. Assn. Radiation Oncologists, Can. Radiation Protection Assn., Internat. Stereotactic Radiosurgery Soc. (bd. dirs. 1991-95) Home: 1540 croissant Seville Brossard PQ Canada J4X 1J4 Office: Montreal Gen Hosp Dept Med Physics 1650 Cedar Ave Montreal PQ Canada H3G 1A4 Office Phone: 514-934-8052. E-mail: epodgorsak@medphys.mcgill.ca.

PODHAJSKY, RONALD J., biomedical engineer, researcher; s. Albert and Agnes Podhajsky; m. Lisa Rachel Podhajsky, Aug. 15, 1987. BS, Rensselaer Poly. Inst., Troy, NY, 1987; MS, U. Calif., San Diego, 1989, PhD, 1992. R & D engr. ADAC Labs., San Jose, Calif., 1982—84; rsch. assoc. scientist, bioengr. Anesthesiology and Neuropathology, U. Calif., 1987—92; rsch. scientist, biomed. engr. Neurosurgery, Sch. Medicine, U. NC, Chapel Hill, 1993—97; R & D bio-instrument engr., project mgr. MedTec, Hillsborough, NC, 1998—99; prin. rsch. scientist Energy-Base Devices, Covidien, Boulder, Colo., 2000—. Engring. cons. NerveX, Hillsborough, 1998—99. Contbr. articles to sci. publs. Recipient TriVerse Team, V-mode Definition award, Energy-Based Devices, Covidien, 2008. Achievements include patents for electrosurgical pencils with improved Controls; method and system for controlling output of RF medical generator; surgical testing instrument and system; patents pending for medical devices. Office: Energy-Based Devices Covidien 5920 Longbow Dr Boulder CO 80301 Business E-Mail: ron.podhajsky@covidien.com.

PODICHETTY, VINOD KUMAR, medical researcher; arrived in U.S., 2000; s. Haricharan and Vasantha Podichetty. MBBS, Maharastra Inst. Med. Sci. & Rsch., India, 1998; MS, Cleve. State U., 2002; cert. in Protection of Human Research Subjects, U. Miami, 2002. Diplomate Indian Med. Coun., 1999. Staff physician Aware Hosps., Hyderabad, Andhra Pradesh, India, 1998; chief med. officer Aware Cancer Rsch. Inst., Hyderabad, Andhra Pradesh, India, 1999—2000; rsch. asst. Cleve. (Ohio) Clinic Found., 2000—02; coord., rsch. assoc. Cleve. Clinic Fla., Weston, Fla., 2003—04, project dir., 2004—; project lead U. Hosp. West Eng., Bristol, England, 1999. Co-director, spine symposium Cleve. Clinic Fla., Weston, Fla., 2003; dir. Primary Health Care Ctr. - Pulse Polio Program, Latur, Maharastra, India, 1997. Contbr. articles to profl. jours. Grantee, Pharm. Industry, 2002—05; scholar, Dept. Health Scis. Cleve. State U., 2000—02. Mem.: Am. Med. Writers Assn., Assn. Clin. Rsch. Profls., Am. Coll. Health Assn., Indian Soc. Human Genetics, Indian Med. Coun., Nat. Assn. Spine Specialists, N.Am. Spine Soc., Indian Student Orgn. (pres. 2002), Continuing Med. Edn. Com. Achievements include research in effectiveness of calcitonin nasal spray in the treatment of lumbar canal stenosis; thoracic microendoscopic discectomy; chronic non-malignant musculoskeletal pain in older adult: clinical issues and opioid intervention; age-based comparative outcomes of elderly patients receiving lumbar decompression surgery; ASA class, not age, predicts complications after minimally invasive spine surgery.

PODKUL, THEODORE B., JR., healthcare executive; s. Theodore B. and Ida C. Podkul; m. Joan Kline, June 10, 1973; children: Jennifer, Timothy. AB, Franklin and Marshall Coll., 1967; MA, George Washington U., 1974. Cert. compliance profl. Health Ethics Trust, med. adminstr. Am. Acad. Med. Administrators, Healthcare Compliance Assn. Adminstrv. resident US Dept. Vets. Affairs, Martinez, Calif., 1973—74, mgmt. analyst, 1974—75, med. dist. coord. Buffalo, 1976—78, health sys. specialist, 1979—2008. Mem. citizens bd. Nat. Alliance for Mentally Ill in Buffalo and Erie County, Buffalo, 1990—2005. First lt. US Army, 1967—70. Decorated Combat Inf. Badge US Army, Bronze Star, Army Commendation medal, Vietnam Campaign medal, Vietnam Svc. medal, Nat. Defence Svc. medal, Jungle Expert badge, Conspicuous Svc. Cross NY State, DSM State of NJ. Fellow: Am. Inst. Inst. Healthcare Quality, Assn. Behavioral Healthcare Mgmt. (cert., bd. dirs. 1988—89, Harold C. Piepenbrink award for Exemplary Leadership and Significant Accomplishments in Behavioral Healthcare Mgmt. 2004), Am. Acad. Med. Adminstrs. (life), Am. Coll. Health Care Adminstrs. (life); mem.: VFW (life), DAV (life), AMVETS (life), Am. Bd. Quality Assurance and

Utilization Rev. Physicians (cert. healthcare and mgmt., bd. dirs. 1989—2006), Health Care Compliane Assn., Assn. of Mil. Surgeons of Am. (life), Leadership VA (life), Am. Coll. Healthcare Execs. (cert. healthcare exec., cert. nursing home adminstr.), Leadership Buffalo (bd. dirs. 1989—90), Vietnam Veterans Am. (life), Combat Infantryman's Assn. (life), Am. Legion (life), 101st Airbourne Divsn. Assn. (life), Buffalo Ambassadors (hon.).

PODOLNY, JOEL M., academic administrator, management educator, former dean; AB magna cum laude, Harvard U., 1986, AM, 1989, PhD in Sociology, 1991. Asst. prof. orgnl. behavior Stanford U., 1991—95, assoc. prof., 1995—96, assoc. prof. strategic mgmt. and orgnl. behavior, 1996—99, prof., 1999—2000, William R. Timken prof. orgnl. behavior and strategic mgmt., 2000—02, sr. assoc. dean for academic affairs, 2000—02; prof. sociology and bus. adminstrn. Harvard U., Cambridge, 2002—05, Novartis prof. leadership and mgmt.; dir. rsch. Harvard Bus. Sch., Cambridge, 2003—05; dean, William S. Beinecke prof. mgmt. Yale Sch. Mgmt., New Haven, 2005—08; v.p., dean Apple U., Apple Inc., 2009—. Author: Status Signals: A Sociological Study of Market Competition, 2005; co-author: Strategic Management, 2001; cons. editor American Journal of Sociology, 1992—94, mem. editl. bd. Administrative Science Quarterly, 1999—2000; mem. editl. bd. American Sociological Review, 2005; assoc. editor Industrial and Corporate Change, 1999—; contbr. articles to profl. jours. Bd. mem. Greenwich Assocs. Mem.: Am. Sociol. Assn. Office: Apple Inc 1 Infinite Loop Cupertino CA 95014*

PODONSKY, GLENN S., federal agency administrator; Grad., U. Md., 1974. Dir. US Nuc. Regulatory Commn., 1978—79; pvt. cons., 1979; analytical evaluator UN Internat. Atomic Energy Agency; dep. asst. sec. security evaluations US Dept. Energy, Washington, dep. asst. sec., Office of Oversight, 1994—99, dir., Office Ind. Oversight and Performance Assurance, 1999—2004, dir., Office Security and Safety Performance Assurance, 2004—06, dir., Office Health, Safety and Security, 2006—. Officer USAF, 1974—78. Recipient Presdl. Disting. Rank award, Pres. William J. Clinton, 1996, Pres. George Bush, 2001; named Disting. Mil. Grad., U. Md., 1974, Command Officer of Yr., USAF Hdqs., 1976. Office: US Dept Energy Office Health Safety and Security 1000 Independence Ave SW EH-1 Washington DC 20585 Business E-Mail: Glenn.podonsky@oa.doe.gov.*

PODUSLO, SHIRLEY ELLEN, neuroscientist; b. Richeyville, Pa., Dec. 24, 1941; d. Joseph Poduslo and Helen Kondor. BS, Ohio State U., 1963; M, Johns Hopkins U., 1976, PhD, 1980. Biology tchr. Woodbridge (N.J.) Sr. High Sch., 1963; asst. Albert Einstein Coll. Medicine, NYC, 1964-73, Johns Hopkins U. Sch. Medicine, Balt., 1973-76, asst. prof., 1976-84, assoc. prof., 1984-90; prof. Tex. Tech. U. Health Scis. Ctr., Lubbock, 1990—. Contbr. articles to profl. jours. Grantee Kroc Found., 1979-82, NIH, 1980—, Multiple Sclerosis Soc., 1980-86. Mem. Am. Soc. Neurochemistry, Soc. for Neuroscience, Am. Soc. for Cell Biology, Am. Soc. Biological Chemists. Avocation: gardening. Office: Tex Tech U Health Scis Ctr Dept Neurology Lubbock TX 79430-0001

PODWALL, KATHRYN STANLEY, biology professor; b. Chgo., Oct. 14; d. Frank and Marie C. Stanley. BS, U. Ill.; MA, NYU. Prof. biology Nassau C.C., Garden City, NY. Developmental reviewer West Ednl. Pub., Amesbury, Mass. and Highland Park, Ill., 1989, 91-92; reviewer AAAS, Washington, 1970—; exec. bd., advisor Women's Faculty Assn., Nassau C.C., 1990—, pres, 2000-2002; lectr. in field. Author: Tested Studies for Laboratory Teaching, vol. 5, 1993; editor: (books and cassettes) Rhyming Simon Books and Cassettes, 1990, Sight Reading Syncopation, 1998, Today's Way To Play the Standards, 2000, Today's Way To Play the Classics, 2000, (book and CD) Cartoons & Car Tunes, 2001, Cartoons & Kid Tunes, 2002, Cartoons and Christmas Tunes, 2003, Rhythms and Blues, 2006, 50 Jazz Duets, 2006. Recipient L.I. Alzheimer's Found. Svc. award, 2002, Excellence award, Nat. Inst. for Staff and Orgnl. Devel., 2003, Chancellor's award excellence in tchg., SUNY, 2004. Mem. AAUW, Am. Soc. Mammalogists (life), Am. Assn. for Women in Cmty. Colls., Am. Inst. Biological Sci. (life), Ill. Forestry Assn. (life), Nat. Assn. Biology Tchrs. (life), Nat. Sci. Tchrs. Assn. (life), Soc. for Coll. Sci. Tchrs., Met. Assn. Coll. and Univ. Biologists, Nat. Cathedral Assn., N.Y. Acad. of Scis., Friends of Archives (charter), Xerces Soc., Southampton Colonial Soc., LaSalle County Hist. Soc. (life), Garden City Hist. Soc. (life), Soroptimists (bd. dirs. dist. 1 1994-96, club pres. 1992-94, Nassau County Pres. award 2001), U. Ill. Alumni Assn. (life). Avocations: travel, gardening, zoological pursuits. Office: Nassau Community College One Education Dr Garden City NY 11530 Office Phone: 516-572-7575. Business E-Mail: podwalk@ncc.edu.

POE, AMY FIELD, legislative staff member; Spl. asst. for scheduling for Rep. Roy Blunt, US House of Reps., Washington, 2000—02, adminstrv. asst., 2002—05, chief of staff, 2005—, House Office of Majority Whip, 2004. Office: Office of Congressman Roy Blunt 2229 Rayburn House Office Bldg Washington DC 20515 Office Phone: 202-225-6536. Office Fax: 202-225-5604. E-mail: amy.poe@mail.house.gov.*

POE, DAVID RUSSELL, lawyer; b. Columbia, Mo., Sept. 4, 1948; s. Russell Warren and Chloe Ardith (Prichard) P.; m. Constance Elizabeth Vaught, Aug. 3, 1974; children: Meghan Elizabeth, Michael Lewis. BS in Mechanical and Aerospace Engring., U. Mo., 1970; JD, Duke U., 1974. Bar: NY 1975, NC 1977, US Supreme Ct. 1985, DC 1991, US Ct. Appeals (1st, 2d, 4th, 6th and DC cirs.), US Dist. Ct. (so., ea. dists.) NY, US Dist. Ct. (ea. dist.) NC. Network engr. Southwestern Bell Telephone Co., St. Louis, 1970-71; assoc. LeBoeuf, Lamb, Leiby & MacRae, NYC, 1974-82, ptnr., 1983-89, Washington, 1989-93, LeBoeuf, Lamb, Greene & MacRae, LLP, Washington, 1994—, chmn. hydroelectric practice. Adj. faculty Columbus Sch. Law, Cath. U. Am., 1992-98. Vestry St. Paul's Ch., Englewood, NJ, 1986-89; legal advisor First Presbyn. Pre-Sch. and Kindergarten, Englewood, 1984-88; vestry St. John's Ch., McLean, Va., 1996-97, 1999-2001, jr. warden, 2000-01. Mem. ABA (pub. utility sect., chmn. adminstrv. law com. 1988-89, chmn. cable TV com. 1989-92, mem. coun. 1990-93, chmn. publs. com. 1993-95, chmn. ann. mtg. 1997, vice-chair 2001-02, chair-elect 2002-03, sect. chair 2003-04, sect. delegate to House of Delegates 2005-), Fed. Comm. Bar Assn., Fed. Energy Bar Assn. (vice chmn. jud. rev. com. 1994-95, chmn. 1995-96). Office: LeBoeuf Lamb Greene MacRae LLP Ste 1200 1875 Connecticut Ave NW Washington DC 20009-5728 Office Phone: 202-986-8039. Office Fax: 202-956-3237. Business E-Mail: dpoe@llgm.com.

POE, GEORGE WILKINSON, literature, culture and language professor; b. Greenville, SC, Mar. 28, 1952; s. Frank Swift and Rosalie (Haynes) P.; m. Sylviane Rosello, Jan. 8, 1977. AB with high honors in French, Davidson Coll., NC, 1974; postgrad., U. Paris IV, Inst. d'études politiques de Paris, 1974—75; MA, Middlebury Coll., Vt., 1975; PhD, Duke U., 1981. Part-time instr. French Duke U., Durham, NC, 1976—78; instr. to asst. prof. Davidson Coll., 1978—82; asst. prof. Hanover Coll., 1982—87, Sewanee: The U. of the South, Tenn., 1987—, assoc. prof., 1990—97, dept. chair, 1994—2000, prof. French and French Studies, 1997—. Faculty dir. Jr. Yr. in France Davidson Coll., 1979-81; study abroad dir. Dept. French Hanover Coll., 1982-87; founder Sewanee in France summer prog., 1988, dir., 1989-96; elected del. Assembly of Modern Lang. Assn., 1988-1991; elected to Conseil d'Adminstrn. Soc. Marivaux, 1989-1995; Camargo Found. scholar-in-residence, vis. prog. dir., 1995. Author: The Rococo & 18th Century French Literature, 1987; co-editor: The French Novel, 1995; editl. bd. Synthesis: An Interdisciplinarhy Jour. and the Synthesis Book Series, 1994-2006; contbr. articles and revs. to profl. jours. Alumni coord. meml. fund Ghigo-Embry-Meeks Fund Davidson Coll., 1987-. Recipient Tchr. of Yr. award, Sewanee: The U. of the South, 2004, US Prof. of Yr. award for Tenn., Carnegie Found. for Advancement of Tchg., Coun. for Advancement and Support of Edn., 2006; fellow Camargo Found., 1992. Mem. MLA, Am. Assn. Tchrs. French, Am. Soc. 18th Century Studies, Tenn. Fgn. Lang. Tchg. Assn., South Atlantic MLA. Avocations: theater, cinema, travel, golf. Office: Dept French and French Studies Sewanee The U of the South 735 University Ave Sewanee TN 37383 Office Phone: 931-598-1522. Business E-Mail: gpoe@sewanee.edu.

POE, LUKE HARVEY, JR., lawyer; b. Richmond, Va., Jan. 29, 1916; s. Luke Harvey and Alice Morris (Reddy) Poe; m. Josephine Jaster, Mar. 20, 1998. BS in Math, U. Va., 1938, JD, 1941; postgrad. (Rhodes scholar), Oxford U., Eng., 1939; D.Phil., Christ Ch., 1957. Bar: Va. bar 1940, D.C. bar and D.C. Ct. Appeals bar 1967, U.S. Supreme Ct. bar 1969, Md. bar 1974. Assoc. Cravath, Swaine & Moore, NYC, 1941—42; tutor St. John's Coll., Annapolis, Md., 1946—50, asst. dean, 1947—49, tenure tutor, 1953—60, dir. physics and chemistry lab., 1959—60; asst. chmn. Nat. Citizens Com. for Kennedy and Johnson and chmn. Citizens Com., Pres.'s Inaugural Com., 1960—61; asst. to chmn. bd. Aerojet-Gen. Corp., El Monte, Calif., 1961—63; divsn. pres. Internat. Tech. Assistance and Devel. Co., Washington, 1963—66; ptnr. Howard, Poe & Bastian, Washington, 1966—83; pvt. practice law, 1983—. Bd. dirs. First Am. Bank of Md.; cons. Dept. Transp., Dept. State, NEH; lectr. War Coll. of USAF, Gen. Studies program U. Va.; seminar leader Aspen Inst. Humanistic Studies; guest panelist Panel on Sci. and Tech. of Com. on Sci. and Astronautics, U.S. Ho. of Reps., 1970; pres. bd. dirs. Watergate East, Inc., 1976-79, 90-92; organizer U. Va. Unified Liberal Arts Program, 1988—. Author: The Combat History of the Battleship U.S.S. Mississippi, 1947, The Transition From Natural Law to Natural Rights, 1957; (with others) lab. manuals Einstein's Theory of Relativity, 1957, Electro-Magnetic Theory, 1959; editor: (with others) Va. Mag., 1936-38, U. Va. Law Rev., 1940-41. Dean's adv. coun. Lehigh U., 1962-65, mem. Seminar on Sci., Tech. and Pub. Policy, Brookings Instn., 1964-66; coun. on trends and perspectives U.S. C. of C., 1966-69; chmn. bd. Bristol Property Mgmt. and Svcs., Inc., 1967-88; chmn. Annapolis Bd. Zoning Appeals, 1966-75; mem. Annapolis Mayor's Task Force, 1967-74, Md. Gov.'s Commn. on Capital City, 1970-76. Lt. comdr. USNR, 1942-46. Decorated Jhalavada Order of Durbargadh, Dhrangadhara. Mem. Am. Law Inst., AAUP, Raven Soc. (pres.), Soc. of Cincinnati, Sr. Common Room and High Table (Christ Church), Met. Club (Washington), Travellers Club (London), Brook Club (N.Y.C.), New Providence Club (Annapolis), Vincent's Club (Oxford), Phi Beta Kappa, Phi Delta Phi. Episcopalian. Home: 139 Market St Annapolis MD 21401-2628 also: 2500 Virginia Ave NW Washington DC 20037-1901 Home Phone: 410-263-6245. Personal E-mail: lharveypoe@aol.com.

POE, RANDALL ELLSWORTH, public relations executive, author; b. Colorado Springs, Colo., Nov. 2, 1935; s. Everett E. and Emilie (Hamburger) P.; m. M. Catherine Ferguson, June 12, 1959 (div. July 1988); 1 child, Andrea Catherine. BA in Journalism, U. Calif., San Jose, 1958. Exec. dir. The Conf. Bd., NYC, 1961-68, news dir., 1968-74, news dir./media mgr., 1974-88, dir. comm., exec. dir., 1988—. Contbr. articles to maj. mags., chapters to books; columnist bus. pubs. Office: The Conf Bd 845 3rd Ave 2nd Fl New York NY 10022-6601

POE, ROBERT ALAN, lawyer; b. Bracken County, Ky., Apr. 25, 1951; Student, U. Ky.; BA, Centre Coll., 1973; JD, U. Va., 1976. Bar: Colo. 1976. Mem. Holland & Hart, Denver, 1976—. Adj. prof. taxation U. Denver, 1986-88. Articles editor Va. Law Rev., 1974-76. Mem. ABA, Order of Coif, Phi Beta Kappa. Office: Holland & Hart 8390 E Crescent Pkwy Ste 400 Greenwood Village CO 80111-2822 Home Phone: 303-766-7694; Office Phone: 303-290-1616. E-mail: apoe@hollandhart.com.

POE, TED, United States Representative from Texas, former judge; b. Temple, Tex., Oct. 13, 1948; m. Carol Poe. BA in Polit. Sci., Abilene Christian U., 1970; JD, U. Houston Law Ctr., 1973. Asst. dist. atty. Harris County, Tex., 1973—81, criminal ct. judge Tex., 1981—2003; mem. US Congress from 2nd Tex. dist., 2005—, mem. transp. and infrastructure com., mem. internat. rels. com., mem. small bus. com., founder Victims' Rights Caucus. Instr. U. Houston, FBI Nat. Acad., Quantico, Va., US Mil. Acad., West Point. Bd. mem. Nat. Children's Alliance; past bd. mem. Children's Assessment Ctr. Houston, CASA Child Advocates, Child Abuse Prevention Coun., Parents of Murdered Children, MADD, Drug Abuse Resistance Edn., Roseate Women's Ctr. for Abused Women, Abilene Christian U. Served Res. C-130 Unit USAF, 1970—76. Recipient Spirit of Enterprise award, US C. of C., Congl. Partnership award, S.E. Tex. Regional Planning Commn., 2006, Social Change award, Tex. Assn. Against Sexual Assault, Morton Bard award, Nat. Orgn. Victims Assistance; named Outstanding Nat. Victim Adv., Nat. Victim Ctr., Outstanding Judge, Found. for Improvement of Justice, Outstanding Instr., Tex. Dist. Atty. Assn., Best Judge, Kans. Peace Officers Assn., Outstanding Dist. Judge, Houston Police Officers Assn., Harris County Dep. Sheriffs Assn., Outstanding Young Lawyer, Houston Bar Assn. Republican. Christian. Office: US Ho Reps 1605 Longworth Ho Office Bldg Washington DC 20515-4302 Office Phone: 202-225-6565.*

POE, TERRY LYNN, music educator; b. Asheboro, NC, Mar. 30, 1952; s. George McLamb and Christine Teague Poe. B in music edn., Wake Forest U., 1970—74. Assoc. dir. Raleigh Boychoir, Raleigh, NC, 1974—94; chapel organist St. Mary's Coll., Raleigh, 1979—84; church organist Trinity U. Meth. Ch., Raleigh, NC, 1976—; choral music tchr. Wake County Pub. Schools, 1974—2008. Mentor coord. Carroll Mid. Sch., Raleigh, NC, 1995—2008, fine arts chmn., 1979—2008, beta club coun. chmn., 1994—2008. Mem. Wake County Exec. PTA Coun., 1988—89, Boy Scouts Am., 1965—70. Recipient Secondary Tchr. of Yr., Wake Cty. Pub. Sch., 1988. Mem.: Am. Guild Organists, Nat. Edn. Assn. Democrat. Bapt. Avocation: flying. Home: 704 Hampstead Pl Raleigh NC 27610 Office: Trinity United Meth Ch 824 N Bloodworth St Raleigh NC 27604 Personal E-mail: terrylpoe@aol.com.

POEHLEIN, CHRISTIAN HEINRICH, medical researcher; s. Heinrich and Hildegrad Ziegler Poehlein; m. Deborah Gail Jacobson; 1 child, Christian Jacob. MD magna cum laude, Ludwig-Maximilians U. Med. Sch., Munich, 1998. Cert. Bayrische Aerztekammer, Bayern, Germany, 1999. Surg. resident, dept. surgery Tech. U. Rechts der Isar, Munich, 1998—99; post-doc. rschr., lab. molecular & tumor immunology Earle A. Chiles Rsch. Inst., Providence Portland Med. Ctr., Oreg., 1999—2005, sr. rsch. scientist, lab. molecular & tumor immunology, 2005—08; sect. chief Lab. Translational Tumor Immunotherapy, Lab. Molecular Tumor Immunology, 2008—. Contbr. articles to profl. jours. Recipient Presdl. award, Internat. Soc. Biol. Therapy Cancer, 2003; co-recipient, 2006; grantee, NIH, NCI, 2004—; fellow, Chiles Found., 1999—2002. Mem.: Am. Assn. Cancer Rsch., Internat. Soc. Biol. Therapy of Cancer (Presdl. award 2003). Roman Catholic. Achievements include research in exploiting lymphopenia to augment the adoptive immunotherapy of melanoma patients; characterizing and regulating tumor-induced regulatory T Cells; patents pending for selective manipulation of tumor-induced regulatory T cells during reconstitution of lymphopenic hosts; characterization of the critical mechanisms necessary for therapeutic effector T cells to curatively eliminate tumor in vivo. Avocations: fly fishing, travel, golf, astronomy, history. Office: Earle A Chiles Rsch Inst Providence Cancer Ctr 4805 NE Glisan St Rm 2N57 Portland OR 97213 Office Fax: 503-215-6841. Personal E-mail: chpoehlein@aol.com. Business E-Mail: christian.poehlein@providence.org.

POEHLEIN, GARY WAYNE, retired chemical engineering professor; b. Tell City, Ind., Oct. 17, 1936; s. Oscar Raymond and Eva Lee (Dickman) P.; m. Sharon Eileen Wood., Jan. 1, 1958; children: Steven Ray, Timothy Wayne, Valorie Ann, Sandra Lee. BSChemE, Purdue U., 1958, MSChemE, 1961, PhD, 1966. Design engr. Proctor & Gamble, Cin., 1958-61; from asst. prof. to assoc. prof. Lehigh U., Bethlehem, Pa., 1965-75, prof. chem. engring., 1975-78, co-dir. emulsion polymers inst., 1973-78; dir. sch. chem. engring. Ga. Inst. Tech., Atlanta, 1978-86, assoc. v.p. rsch., dean grad. studies, 1986-91, v.p. interdisciplinary programs, prof. chem. engring., 1991-95; prof. chem. engring., 1978-96; dir. Chem. and Transport Systems Divsn. NSF, 1996-2000; ret., 2000. Bd. dirs. Flexible Products Co., Marietta, Ga.; interim chair chem. engring. dept., vis. prof. Lehigh U., 2001—02. Contbr. over 100 articles to tech. publs. Mem. sch. bd. Bethlehem Area Sch. Dist., 1969-75. Recipient Honor Scroll award Phila. br. Am. Inst. Chemists, 1977, Mac Pruitt award Coun. for Chem. Rsch., 1989, Outstanding ChE Alumni award Pudue U., 2008. Fellow AIChE. Avocations: woodworking, sailing. Home: 407 S Henry St Alexandria VA 22314-5901 Personal E-mail: gspoehlein@aol.com.

POEHLER, AMY, comedienne, actress; b. Burlington, Mass., Sept. 16, 1971; m. Will Arnett, Aug. 29, 2003; 1 child, Archie Arnett. Grad., Boston Coll. Performer Second City comedy troupe, Chgo., 1993—96, Improv Olympic, LA. Actor: (films) Saving Manhattan, 1998, Tomorrow Night, 1998, Deuce Bigalow: Male Gigolo, 1999, The Devil and Daniel Webster, 2001, Wet Hot American Summer, 2001, Martin & Orloff, 2002, Mean Girls, 2004, Envy, 2004, Southland Tales, 2006, Man of the Year, 2006, Blades of Glory, 2007, (voice) Horton Hears a Who!, 2008, Baby Mama, 2008 (Best WTF Moment, MTV Movie Awards, 2009), Hamlet 2, 2008, (voice) Monsters vs. Aliens, 2009; actor, writer, prodr. (films) Wild Girls Gone, 2005, actor, writer (TV series) Upright Citizens Brigade, 1998—2000; actor: (TV series) Saturday Night Live, 2001—08; appearances include (TV series) Late Night with Conan O'Brien, 1998—2000, Apt. 2F, 1997, Spin City, 1998, Undeclared, 2002, Arrested Development, 2004. Named a Maverick, Details mag., 2008; named one of The 50 Most Powerful Women in NYC, NY Post, 2008. Office: c/o 3 Arts Entertainment 9460 Wilshire Blvd 7th Fl Beverly Hills CA 90212*

POEHLING, KATHERINE, pediatrician; d. Gary Poehling; m. Timothy Peters, May 4, 1996; children: Jennifer Peters children: Robert Peters. MD, Wake Forest Sch. of Medicine, Winston-Salem, NC, 1995; MPH, Vanderbilt U. Sch. of Medicine, Nashville, Tenn., 2001. Lic. NC Med. Bd., 2007, cert. Bd. Am. Acad. Pediat., 1998. Fellow Vanderbilt U., Nashville, 1999—2002, asst. prof. of pediat., 2002—07; assoc. prof. pediats. Wake Forest U. Med. Ctr., Winston-Salem, NC, 2007—. Mem. NC Med. Bd., 2007. Fellow: Am. Acad. Pediat.; mem.: Soc. Pediatric Rsch., Acad. Pediat. Assn., Infectious Disease Soc. Am., Alpha Omega Alpha. Achievements include research in Clin. rsch. on pediat. respiratory infections.

POEHNER, RAYMOND GLENN, retired bank executive; b. Cleve., Oct. 2, 1923; s. Raymond Frank and Winifred (Kirchbaum) P.; m. Frances E. Dunaway Gillespie, Jan. 4, 1958 (dec. 1993); children: R. David, Jacqueline Diane, Leslie Marie, Jon Anthony, Rebecca Glen; stepchildren: Bruce Gillespie, Tony Gillespie. Student, pub. schs., Chgo. and Cleve. Enlisted USN, 1941, advanced through grades to chief petty officer, 1957, ret., 1965; with Security Pacific Nat. Bank, San Diego, 1966-80, loan officer, 1971-74, credit card officer, 1975-80, asst. br. mgr., 1974-80, asst. mgr.; ret., 1980. Mem. VFW, U.S. Naval Inst. (assoc.), Fla. Sheriff's Assn., Am. Biog. Soc. (nat. bd. advisors), R.I. Rsch. (cert. assoc.), Fleet Res. Assn., Rep. Legion of Merit, Nat. Geographic Soc., Nat. Assn. Civilian Conservation Corps Alumni, Optimist Club (dir. 1978), Fraternal Order Police (booster Fla. chpt.). Republican.

POESCH, JESSIE JEAN, art historian; b. Postville, Iowa, May 19, 1922; parents: Edward H. and Vina (Meier) P. BA, Antioch Coll., Yellow Springs, Ohio, 1944; MA, U. Del., Newark, 1956; PhD, U. Pa., Phila., 1966. Relief worker Am. Friends Svc. Com., France, Germany, Phila., 1946—54; curatorial asst. H.F. DuPont Winterthur Mus., Del., 1956-58; from asst. prof. to prof. art history Tulane U., New Orleans, 1963-92, Maxine and Ford Graham chair in fine arts, 1988-92. Guest curator Painting in the South, Va. Mus. Fine Arts, Richmond, 1980-84, Jefferson's America and Napoleon's France, New Orleans Mus. Art, 2003; curator Newcomb Pottery: An Enterprise for So. Women, 1895-1940, Newcomb Coll. Tulane U. and Smithsonian Instn. traveling exhbn. svc., 1984-87. Author: Titian Ramsay Peale, 1799-1885, and His Journals of the Wilkes Expedition, 1961, The Art of the Old South: Painting, Sculpture, Architecture and the Products of Craftsmen, 1560-1860, 1983, (with John Cuthbert) David Hunter Strother: One of the Best Draughtsmen the Country Possesses, 1997; (book/exhbn. catalogue) The Early Furniture of Louisiana, 1972, Newcomb Pottery: An Enterprise for Southern Women 1895-1940, 1984, Will Henry Stevens, 1987; editor: (with Barbara Bacot) Louisiana Buildings 1720-1948, 1997, (with Nancy E. Green) Arthur Wesley Dow and American Arts and Crafts, 1999, Newcomb Pottery and Crafts, 2003, Printmaking in New Orleans, 2006; also numerous articles and book revs. Fellow U. Del., 1954-56; Fulbright scholar U. London, 1960-62; NEH grantee, London, 1969-70. Mem. Soc. Archtl. Historians (bd. dirs. 1986-89), Coll. Art Assn., Am. Antiquarian Soc., La. Endowment for the Humanities (bd. dirs. 1984-90, La. Humanist of Yr. 1992), Victorian Soc. Am. (bd. dirs. 1988-92). Office: Tulane U Dept Newcomb Art New Orleans LA 70118 Home Phone: 504-862-5597; Office Phone: 504-314-2225. Business E-Mail: jpoesch@tulane.edu.

POETA, SALVATORE J., literature and language professor; b. Piazza Armerina, Enna, Italy, July 18, 1952; s. Fillipo and Salvatrice Poeta; m. Valerie D. Nelsen, June 17, 1978; children: Lauren Nelsen, Kristen Nelsen. PhD, U. Pa., Phila., 1982. Assoc. prof. Spanish lang. and lit. Villanova U., Pa., 1987—. Contbr. articles to profl. jours. Recipient Cross Alfonso X Sabio award, Spain's Ministry Edn. and Culture, 1999.

Mem.: Am. Assn. Tchrs. Spanish and Portuguese (past vice pres. 1993, past pres. 1994—97). Office: Villanova Univ 800 Lancaster Ave Villanova PA 19085 Office Fax: 610-519-6695. Business E-Mail: salvatore.poeta@villanova.edu.

POETHIG, EUNICE BLANCHARD, clergywoman; b. Hempstead, NY, Jan. 16, 1930; d. Werner J. and Juliet (Stroh) Blanchard; m. Richard Paul Poethig, June 7, 1952; children: Richard Scott, Kathryn Aileen, Johanna Klare, Margaret Juliet, Erika Christy. BA, De Pauw U., 1951; MA, Union Theol. Sem., 1952; MDiv, McCormick Theol. Sem., NYC, 1975, STM, 1977; PhD, Union Theol. Sem., 1985. Ordained to ministry Presbyn. Ch., 1979. Missionary United Presbyn. Ch. USA to United Ch. of Christ, The Philippines, 1956-72; mem. faculty Ellinwood Coll. Christian Edn., Manila, 1957-61; mem. faculty, campus ministry Philippine Women's U., Manila, 1962-68. Bd. dirs. Jane Addams Conf., Journey's End Refugee Resettlement Agy., Coun. of Bishops and Execs. of Buffalo Area Met. Ministries; trustee Presbyn. Found., 1991-94, Gen. Bd. Nat. Coun. Chs. Christ, 1995-97; editor New Day Pubs., Manila, 1969-72; curriculum editor Nat. Coun. Chs., Manila, 1962-72; assoc. exec. Presbytery Chgo., 1979-85; exec. Presbytery of Western N.Y., 1986-93; dir. congl. ministries divsn. gen. assembly Gen. Assembly Coun., Presbyn. Ch. (U.S.A.), 1994-98; mem. Coun. Execs., Ill. Coun. Chs., 1980-85. Author: Bible Studies in Concern Response, A.D., 1975, Good News Women, 1987, Sing, Shout and Clap for Joy: Psalms in Worship, 1989, Friendship Press Study on Philippines, 1989, Liturgy 9:1, 1990, Hunger Program Workbook, 1991; editor: (hym book series) Everybody, I Love You, 1971—72, 150 Plus Tomorrow: Churches Plan for the Future, 1982, 2s edit., 1985, Our Living Tradition, 1994, Women of Faith: 1986-1996, 1997, From Slavery to Promised Land, 1999, The Struggle for Equality: Women in Mission, 1999; prodr., dir.: DVD Women's Ordination: Past, Present and Future, 2006. Active Environ. Def. Fund, Erie County Environ. Mgmt. Coun., NY, 1990—93, NGO Forum UN Fourth World Conf. Women, Beijing, 1995; planning com. Celebrate Adult Curriculum, 1987—93, Transatlantic Dialogue, 2003—04; chmn. governing bd. Stony Point Ctr., 2002—04, PC USA; chmn. PC USA Celebrating the Ordination of Women, 2005—; bd. dirs. Ch. Women United, Chgo., 1974—79, More Light Presbyns., 2000—03; trustee McCormick Theol. Sem., Chgo., 1974—75; bd. dirs., exec. com. Presbyn. Cmty. Ctr., Louisville, 1999—2001; active Women's Ordination Conf. Nat. Presbyn. Ch. Com., Presbyn. Gen. Assembly Challenge to the Ch. Fund., 1989; design team Covenant People Curriculum, 1997; futures com. Highland Presbyn. Ch., chair, 1997—99; organizing bd. Asian Ctr. Theology and Strategy, Chgo., 1974. Recipient Walker Cup, DePauw U., 1951; Nettie F. McCormick fellow in Old Testament Hebrew, McCormick Sem., Chgo., 1975; recipient Disting. Alumni award DePauw U., 2003. Mem. Internat. Platform Assn., Soc. Bibl. Lit., Soc. Ethnomusicology, Assn. Exec. Presbyters (bd. dirs., chairperson 1991-93), Am. Schs. Oriental Rsch., Witherspoon Soc., Nat. Assn. Religious Women, Internat. Assn. Women Mins., Nat. Assn. Presbyn. Clergywomen. Home: 1000 E 53rd St #613 Chicago IL 60615 E-mail: poethig@sbcglobal.net.

POETTKER, MARY THERESE, music educator; b. Belleville, Ill., Aug. 29, 1950; d. Delmar Julius and Catherine Rita Thouvenot; m. Robert H. Poettker, Aug. 12, 1972; children: Christina, Scott, Jason, Jennifer. B in Music Edn., So. Ill. U., Edwardsville, 1972, M in Music Edn., 1974. Cert. tchr. vocal and instrument music tchr. K-12 Mo. Vocal music tchr. Ferguson-Florissant Sch. Dist., Mo., 1972—79, St. Elizabeth-St. Robert Regional Sch., St. Charles, Mo., 1981—. Dir. music St. Elizabeth Ann Seton Ch., St. Charles, 1983—. Nominee Disney Am. Tchr., Disney Co., 2001. Mem.: Mo. Music Educators Assn. (v.p. jr. high vocal and gen. music St. Louis Metro Dist. 8 1988—2000, 2006—08, sec. 2008—, Merit award St. Louis Metro Dist. 8 2001), Music Educators Nat. Conf., Nat. Pastoral Musicians (chpt. dir. 1998—2004, asst. chpt. dir. 2004—09, Outstanding Sch. Music Edn. 1996). Roman Catholic. Avocations: gardening, camping, crafts. Home: 112 Travelers Trail Saint Peters MO 63376-7149 E-mail: mpoettker@setonscene.org.

POGAL, MEREDITH A., dentist; BA, DMD, Wash. U. Gen. practice resident U. Rochester; pvt. practice Rochester, NY. Mem.: ADA, Dental Orgn. Conscious Sedation, NY State Dental Soc., Seventh Dist. Dental Soc., Monroe County Dental Soc., Am. Acad. Cosmetic Dentistry (former treas.), Acad. Gen. Dentistry. Office: 324 Greece Ridge Center Dr Rochester NY 14626 Office Phone: 585-227-4390. Office Fax: 585-227-5215.

POGGENPOHL, TERESA LOYOLA, marketing executive; b. Omaha, Apr. 17, 1961; d. Robert Paul and Clara Margaret (Hill) P. BS in Bus. Adminstrn., U. Nebr., 1983; MBA, U. Ill., 1986. Teaching asst. U. Ill., Champaign, 1985-86; staff cons. Arthur Andersen, Chgo., 1986-88; sr. cons. Andersen Cons. (now Accenture), London, 1988-90, mktg. mgr. Chgo., 1990-91, dir. mktg. rsch., 1991-94, worldwide dir. advt. and rsch., 1995; leader, renaming and branding initiative Accenture, Chgo., 2001, ptnr., global advt. and brand mgmt., exec. dir. global image, 2007—. Vol. Girl Scouts USA, Chgo., 1986-88. Mem. Am. Mktg. Assn., Evening Assocs. of Art Inst. Chgo. Republican. Roman Catholic. Avocation: travel. Office: Accenture 161 N Clark St Chicago IL 60601*

POGGI, LUIGI CARDINAL, cardinal, archbishop emeritus, archivist; b. Piacenza, Italy, Nov. 25, 1917; Attended, Alberoni Coll., Piacenza, Italy; grad., Pontifical Ecclesiastical Acad., Rome. Ordained priest Diocese of Piacenza, Italy, 1940; parish priest, 1940—45; diplomatic positions Secretariat of State, Vatican City, 1945—65; chaplain Regina Coeli prison, Rome, 1947—50; ordained bishop, 1965; archbishop, apostolic del. to Ctrl. Africa, 1965—69; apostolic nuncio to Peru, 1969—73; apostolic nuncio with spl. responsibilities for contacts with Ea. European states Rome, 1973—75; apostolic del. to Poland, 1975—86; apostolic nuncio to Italy, 1986—92; pro-archivist Vatican Secret Archives, Rome, 1992-94, archivist, 1994—98, archivist emeritus, 1998—; pro-librarian Vatican Libr., Rome, 1992—94, librarian, 1994—98, librarian emeritus, 1998—; elevated to cardinal, 1994; cardinal-deacon S. Maria in Dominica, 1994—2005; cardinal-priest S. Lorenzo in Lucina, 2005—. Roman Catholic. Office: Archbishop 00120 Vatican City

POGO, GUSTAVE JAVIER, cardiothoracic surgeon, educator; b. Buenos Aires, Feb. 7, 1957; came to US, 1964; s. Angel Oscar and Beatriz (Garcia-Tuñon) P.; m. Janis Teitler, Feb. 17, 1983; children: Michael Tyler, Katherine Elizabeth. BA cum laude, NYU, 1979, MD, 1983. Cert. Am. Bd. Surgery, Am. Bd. Thoracic Surgery. Intern gen. surgery North Shore Univ. Hosp., Manhasset, NY, 1983—84, resident gen. surgery, 1984—88, mem. provisional surg. staff, 1991—94, asst. attending surgeon to sr. attending surgeon, 1994—; resident cardiothoracic surgery Mt. Sinai Med. Ctr., NYC, 1988—91; adj. assoc. prof. surgery NYU Sch. Medicine. Contbr. articles to profl. jours. Fellow ACS, Am. Coll. Chest Physicians, Am. Coll. Cardiology; mem. Soc. Thoracic Surgery. Office: North Shore Univ Hosp 300 Community Dr Manhasset NY 11030-3801 Office Phone: 516-562-4970. Office Fax: 516-562-3787.

POGORELOV, NIKOLAI, physicist, researcher; b. Poltava, Ukraine, Dec. 31, 1951; s. Vladimir Pogorelov and Lyudmila Pogorelova; m. Lidia Gulyaeva, Apr. 12, 1977; 1 child, Natalia Pogorelova. MS, Moscow Inst. Physics and Tech., Dolgoprudny, Russia, 1975; PhD in Physics and Math., Inst. for Problems in Mechanics, Russian Acad. Scis., 1984; DSc in Physics and Math., Highest Certification Com. Russian Fedn., 2001. Rsch. scientist Inst. for Problems in Mechanics, Russian Acad. Scis., Moscow, 1977—90; assoc. prof. Moscow Aviation Inst. (State Tech. U.), 1985—91; sr. rsch. scientist Inst. for Problems in Mechanics, Russian Acad. Scis., Moscow, 1990—96, 1997—98, 1999—2002, prin. rsch. scientist, 2002—03; assoc. prof. Kobe (Japan) U., 1996—97, 1998—99; rsch. physicist U. Calif., Riverside, 2003—. Vis. prof. Max-Planck-Inst. Astrophysics, Garching, Germany, 1999—2002; vis. rschr. Solar-Terrestrial Environment Lab., Nagoya U., Toyokawa, Japan, 2002—03; chmn. organizing com. 1st Inst. Physics and Planetary Physics-CalSpace Internat. Conf., Palm Springs, Calif., 2006. Author: (book) Mathematical Aspects of Numerical Solution of Hyperbolic Systems; editor: Mathematical Problems of Numerical Solution of Hyperbolic Systems; contbr. articles to profl. jours.; dir.:. Grantee, NASA, 2005—, NSF, 2004—. Mem.: AAAS, Russian Nat. Com. Theoretical and Applied Mechanics, Am. Geophys. Union. Achievements include development of one of the most sophisticated numerical models of the heliospheric interface based on high-resolution shock-capturing methods, adaptive mesh refinement techniques and Monte Carlo simulations; performed a detailed analysis of nonevolutionary MHD shocks behavior in numerical plasma flow simulations; research in high-speed, non-equilibrium airflows near complex-shaped bodies at high angle of attack; global MHD-Boltzmann model of the outer heliosphere; multi-scale combined hybrid-magnetohydrodynamic-neutral atom code. Office: IGPP University of California 900 University Ave Riverside CA 92521 Business E-Mail: nikolaip@ucr.edu.

POGORELOV, VADIM ALEKSEEVICH, engineer; b. Rostov-on-Don, Russia, Dec. 12, 1970; s. Aleksey Ivanovich Pogorelov and Elena Sergeevna Lapshina. PhD, Secondary # 50, Rostov-on-Don, 1988; degree in info. mgmt., Rostov State Bldg. Engrs. U., 2003. Engr. Rostov Mil. Inst. Missile Corps, 1993—94, tchr., 1997—99, sr. tchr., 1999—2007, asst. prof., 2007—. Contbr. articles to profl. jours. Lt. col. missile corps Russian mil., 1994—, Rostov-on-Don. Presdl. scholar, 1996. Mem.: Acad. Navigation and Motion Control (assoc.). Russian Orthodox. Achievements include patents for automatic control, optical computers. Avocations: swimming, travel, photography. Mailing: Kozlova 61B Apt 39 344018 Rostov-on-Don Russia Office: Rostov Mil Inst Missile Corps Pr Mikhaila Nagibina 24/50 344027 Rostov-on-Don Russia Personal E-mail: locman@ctsnet.ru.

POGREBNYAK, VICTOR ALEXANDROVICH, physicist, researcher; s. Alexander D. Pogrebnyak and Klavdia Mischenko; m. Lyudmyla A. Krasilnikova, 1975; children: Vsevolod, Igor. PhD, Inst. Radio Physics and Electronics, Kharkiv, Ukraine, 1974; DSc, U. Latvia, Riga, 1991. Sr. rsch. scientist Inst. Radio Physics and Electronics, Kharkiv, 1970—98; prof. Çukurova U., Adana, Turkey, 1998—2006; assoc. prof. SUNY, Buffalo, 2007—. Office: SUNY Elec Engring Dept 332D Bonner Hall Buffalo NY 14260-1237 Office Phone: 716-645-1042. Office Fax: 716-645-3656. Personal E-mail: pogrebnyak@verizon.net.

POGUE, DONALD CARL, federal judge; BA, Dartmouth Coll., 1969; MA, JD, Yale U., 1974. Bar: Conn. 1974. Pvt. practice, 1974-75; ptnr. Kestell, Pogue & Gould, 1976-89; commr. Conn. Commn. Hosps. and Health Care, 1989-94; judge Conn. Superior Ct., 1994-95, US Ct. Internat. Trade, NYC, 1995—. Office: US Ct Internat Trade One Federal Plz New York NY 10278-0001*

POGUE, JOHN MARSHALL, physician; b. Washington, Sept. 21, 1945; s. L(loyd) Welch and Mary Ellen (Edgerton) P. AB with honors, Princeton U.; MD, Georgetown U. Diplomate Nat. Bd. Med. Examiners. Intern, resident Georgetown U. Hosp., Washington; editor, author Bradford Jour., 1983—; historian Gov. William Bradford Compact, 1996—, surgeon, 1999—, v.p., 2005—08, pres., 2008—. Spkr. and lectr. in field of cardiology. Author: Herbert Martin Giffin, M.D., A Role Model Physician and a Doctor's Doctor: From Princeton to Johns Hopkins, Mayo Clinic, USN, and Yater Clinic, 2000, Sir William Osler, M.D., The Preeminent Physician: From McGill to the University of Pennsylvania, Johns Hopkins, and Oxford, 2004, Caldwell Blakeman Esselstyn, Jr., M.D. of the Cleveland Clinic, Defeater of Coronary Artery Heart Disease Through Low-Fat, Plant-Based Nutrition, 2008; designer Ofcl. Gov. William Bradford Flag, 1987 (New Constellation award Nat. Flag Found., 1996), Ofcl. Order of Descs. of Colonial Physicians and Chirurgiens Flag, 2005; editor, contbr.: Pogue/Pollock/Polk Genealogy as Mirrored in History, From Scotland to Northern Ireland/Ulster, Ohio, and Westward, 1990 (recipient 5 First Pl. Genealogy awards, recipient 2 Meritorious History awards), assoc. editor: Hereditary Soc. Blue Book, 1997—, 1998, 1999, 2000; dir.(of film): Hugo Victor Rizzoli, Preeminent Neurosurgeon, A.B. and M.D., Johns Hopkins, Neurosurg. Tng. at Johns Hopkins Hosp., 2005; contbr. articles on cardiology to med. jours. Fellow Royal Soc. Medicine, Royal Microscopical Soc. Oxford, Royal Statis. Soc., Royal Geog. Soc., Royal Soc. Arts, Internat. Soc. Holter and Noninvasive Electrocardiology; mem. British Cardiovascular Soc., Am. Heart Assn. (coun. clin. cardiology, coun. arteriosclerosis, thrombosis & vascular biology, coun. basic cardiovasc. scis.), AMA, Royal Soc. Medicine (cardiology sect., cardiothoracic sect.), European Soc. Cardiology, Laennec Cardiovasc. Sound Soc., Brit. Soc. Echocardiography, Am. Soc. Echocardiography (coun. cardiac sonography, coun. intraoperative echocardiography, coun. pediat. & congenital heart disease, coun. Vascular Ultrasound), Internat. Soc. Cardiovasc. Ultrasound, Internat. Cardiac Doppler Soc., Internat. Soc. Electrocardiology (Glasgow U.), Internat. Soc. Holter and Noninvasive Electrocardiology, Internat. Acad. Cardiovasc. Scis., Can., British Soc. Cardiovascular Magnetic Resonance, Soc. Cardiovasc. Magnetic Resonance, Internat. Atherosclerosis Soc., Capital Area Heart Failure Soc. (founding mem. 2002), British Soc. for Heart Failure, Heart Failure Soc. Am., Heart Valve Soc. Am. (cardiac imaging coun.), Internat. Soc. Cardiovasc. Pharmacotherapy, Switzerland, British Soc. for Cardiovascular Rsch., Internat. Soc. Heart Rsch., Can., Cardiac Muscle Soc., World Heart Fedn., Switzerland, European Assn. Cardiovasc. Prevention and Rehab., European Microscopy Soc. (Netherlands), Friends Nat. Libr. Medicine (founding mem. 1988), Friends McGill U. Osler Med. Libr., Friends Oxford U. Mus. History Sci., Ashmolean Natural History Soc. Oxford, Oxford Hist. Soc., Internat. Shakespeare Assn. (Stratford-upon-Avon), Princeton U. Alumni Assn., Princeton Tigertones Alumni, DC Soc. Mayflower Descs. (surgeon 1998-), Order Descs. Colonial Physicians and Chirurgiens (surgeon gen. 1994-2000, 2006-, chmn. hon. membership com. 1994-, v.p. gen. 2000-03, pres. gen. 2003-06, hon. pres. gen. life, 2006—), Nat. Gavel Soc., Hereditary Order of Descs. of Colonial Govs. (rec. sec. gen. 2005-), Provincial Families Md., Kenwood Citizens Assn., Royal Soc. Medicine Club, London, Royal Soc. Medicine Med. Art Soc., RSM Music Soc., Royal Soc. Medicine Music Club, Royal Soc. Medicine Book Club, Princeton U. Club, Washington, Oxford Bibliographical Soc. of Oxford U. Bodleian Libr. Avocations: classical music, reading. Home and Office: 5204 Kenwood Ave Chevy Chase MD 20815-6604

POGUE, LINDA SUE, science educator; d. Carl E. and Charlene W. Amidon; m. Charles Pogue, Nov. 28, 1975; children: Susan D. Elliott, Scott A. BS in Computer Info. Sys., U. Ark., Monticello, 2001, AA, 2001; MS in Computer Info. Sys., U. Phoenix, Ariz., 2003. Advanced mainframe programmer Wal-Mart ISD, Bentonville, Ark., 2001—04; coll. instr. U. Ark., 2004—06, NorthWest Ark. CC, Bentonville, 2006—; CEO web designer Pogue Web Svc., Liberty Hill, Tex., 2008—. Personal E-mail: lpogue@poguewebservices.com. Business E-Mail: lpogue@nwacc.edu.

POGUE, RICHARD WELCH, lawyer; b. Cambridge, Mass., Apr. 26, 1928; s. Lloyd Welch and Mary Ellen (Edgarton) P.; m. Patricia Ruth Raney, July 10, 1954; children: Mark, Tracy, David. BA, Cornell U., 1950; JD, Mich. Law Sch., 1953. Bar: Mich. 1953, Ohio 1957, U.S. Dist. Ct. (no. dist.) Ohio 1960, U.S. Ct. Appeals (6th cir.) 1972, U.S. Ct. Appeals (D.C. and 9th cirs.) 1979. Assoc. Jones, Day, Reavis & Pogue, Cleve., 1957-60, ptnr., 1961—94, mng. ptnr., 1984-92, sr. ptnr., 1993-94, cons., 2004—; sr. advisor Dix & Eaton, Cleve., 1994—2003. Vis. prof. Mich. Law Sch., 1993-95; bd. dirs. Rotek Inc., Aurora, Ohio With Continental Ab, 1993-2003, Key Corp, 1975-2003, TRW, 1994-2001;Chmn. Cleve. Found., 1985-89, Greater Cleve. Roundtable, 1986-89, Greater Cleve. Growth Assn., 1991-93, Univ. Hosps., 1994-99, United Way Cleve., 1989, Kulas Found., 1998—, Bus. Vol. United, 1998-2001, Nat. Inventors Hall of Fame, 1996—, Newcomen Soc. U.S., Phila., 2000-05; mem. commn. higher edn. and econ. Gov., 2003-04; mem. Adminstrv. Conf. U.S., 1974-80; vice chmn. Cleve. Tomorrow, 1988-93; trustee Case Western Res. U., 1989-2003, U. Akron, 2004—; active Coun. Fgn. Rels., 1989—, Am./EC Assn. Bus. Adv. Coun., 1988-93; trustee Rock and Roll Hall of Fame and Mus., 1986-99; co-chmn. 1996 Cleve. Bicentennial Commn., interim chmn. Cleve. Inst. Music, 1994; chmn. dean's adv. coun. U. Mich. Law Sch., 2006—. Capt. U.S. Army, 1954-57. Recipient Outstanding Alumnus award U. Mich. Club, Cleve., 1983, Torch of Liberty award Anti-Defamation League, 1989, Leadership Cleve. Vol. of Yr. award, 1990, 1st Econ. Devel. Workshop award Nat. Coun. on Urban Econ. Devel., 1992, Humanitarian award Nat. Conf. Christians and Jews, 1992; named Cleve. Bus. Exec. of Yr., 2000, Cleve. United Way Vol. of Yr., 2002. Mem. ABA (chmn. antitrust sect. 1983-84), Ohio State Bar Assn. (chmn. antitrust sect. 1969-73). Clubs: Bohemian (San Francisco), Soc., Union (Cleve.). Republican. Mem. United Ch. of Christ. Office: Jones Day North Point 901 Lakeside Ave Cleveland OH 44114-1190 Office Phone: 216-586-7300. Office Fax: 216-586-7960. Business E-Mail: rwpogue@jonesday.com.

POGUE, WILLIAM REID, retired astronaut, foundation administrator, aerospace scientist, consultant; b. Okemah, Okla., Jan. 23, 1930; s. Alex W. and Margaret (McDow) P.; m. Jean Ann Pogue; children: William Richard, Layna Sue, Thomas Reid. BS in Secondary Edn., Okla. Bapt. U., 1951, D.Sc. (hon.), 1974; MS in Math., Okla. State U., 1960. Commd. 2d lt. USAF, 1952, advanced through grades to col., 1973; combat fighter pilot Korea, 1953; gunnery instr. Luke AFB, Ariz., 1954; mem. acrobatic team USAF Thunderbirds, Luke AFB and Nellis AFB, Nev., 1955-57; asst. prof. math. USAF Acad., 1960-63; exchange test pilot Brit. Royal Aircraft Establishment, Ministry Aviation, Farnborough, Eng., 1964-65; instr. USAF Aerospace Research Pilots Sch., Edwards AFB, Calif., 1965-66; astronaut NASA Manned Spacecraft Center, Houston, 1966-75; pilot 3d manned visit to Skylab space sta.; ret. Decorated Air medal with oak leaf cluster, D.S.M.; named to Five Civilized Tribes Hall of Fame, Choctaw descent; recipient Distinguished Service medal NASA, Collier trophy Nat. Aero. Assn.; Robert H. Goddard medal Nat. Space Club; Gen. Thomas D. White USAF Space Trophy Nat. Geog. Soc.; Halley Astronautics award, 1975; de la Vaalx medal Fedn. Aeronautique Internat., 1974; V.M. Komarov diploma, 1974; inducted into Okla. Aviation and Space Hall of Fame, 1980, U.S. Astronaut Hall of Fame, 1997. Fellow Acad. Arts and Scis. of Okla. State U., Am. Astron. Soc.; mem. Soc. Exptl. Test Pilots, Explorers Club, Sigma Xi, Pi Mu Epsilon. Baptist (deacon). Home: 709 Greenwood Way Bentonville AR 72712-7906 Personal E-mail: wrpogue@cox.net.

POHAN, ARMAND, transportation executive, professional hockey club executive, lawyer; b. Langley Field, Va., Apr. 28, 1944; s. Armen and Helen (Turner) P.; m. Margaret A. Neigel, Dec. 18, 1976; children: Andrew Stephen, Alicia Margaret, Amanda Turner AB, Harvard U., 1964, JD, 1967. Bar: N.J. 1967. Assoc. McCarter & English, Newark, 1968-70; asst. prosecutor Hudson County, N.J., 1970-72; assoc. McCarter & English, 1973-76, ptnr., 1976-77; v.p. A-P-A Transport Corp., North Bergen, N.J., 1977-83, pres., 1983—, Colo. Rockies Hockey Club, Denver, 1978-81; chmn. bd. dirs. NY Waterway, 2001—. Mem. Fort Lee Bd. Adjustment, N.J., 1977-78; mem. Fort Lee Planning Bd., 1979, 2002—, borough atty., Fort Lee, 1973-76, councilman, 2003—; bd. govs. Nat. Hockey League, 1978-81; trustee Bede Sch., Englewood, N.J., 1984-90; trustee Dwight-Englewood Sch., 1984-92, pres., 1985-92; trustee Fontainebleau Assn., 2002—, treas., 2003—. Mem. N.J. Bar Assn. Office: NY Waterway 115 River Rd Ste 120 Edgewater NJ 07020 Personal E-mail: apohan@aol.com.

POHAN, CATHY ANN, education educator, consultant; d. Aram and Seroy (Sue) (Hachadourian) Pohan. BA, Calif. State U., Fresno, 1975—80, MA, 1989—90; PhD, U. Nebr., Lincoln, 1991—94. Cert. Tchr. Calif. Tchg. Commn., 1980. Elem. sch. tchr. Fresno Unified, Calif., 1981—82, LA Christian Sch., 1982—89; prof. U. No. Colo., Greeley, Calif., 1994—96, San Diego State U., 1996—. Dir., coord. SDSU/CVESD Partnership Tchr. Preparation program, Chula Vista, Calif., 1998—. Contbr. articles pub. to profl. jour. Bd. mem. Asters Collection Home Owners Assn., Chula Vista, Calif., 2001—03. Recipient Outstanding Tchr. Yr., Delta Kappa Gamma, Colo., 1995. Mem.: ASCD, Am. Ednl. Rsch. Assn. (mem. and proposal reviewer 1995—2003). Office: Texas A & M - Corpus Christi College of Education 6300 Ocean Dr Corpus Christi TX 78412 Business E-Mail: pohan@mail.sdsu.edu.

POHL, CHRISTINE D., Christian ethics educator; d. Gunther E. and Dorothy E. Pohl. BS, Syracuse U., NY, 1972; MA in Theol. Studies, Gordon-Conwell Theol. Sem., S. Hamilton, Mass., 1986; PhD in Ethics and Soc., Emory U., Atlanta, 1993. Prof. social ethics Asbury Theol. Sem., Wilmore, Ky., 1989—. Bd. dirs. Louisville Inst., 2001—07, Soc. Christian Ethics, 2006—. Author: (book) Making Room: Recovering Hospitality as a Christian Tradition; co-author (Nicola Hoggard-Creegan): Living on the Boundaries: Evangelical Women, Feminism, and the Theological Academy; contbr. articles to profl. jours. Grant, Lilly Endowment, 2003—06. Mem.: Soc. Christian Ethics (bd. dirs. 2006—). Office: Asbury Theol Seminary 204 N Lexington Ave Wilmore KY 40390

POHL, FREDERIK, freelance/self-employed writer; b. NYC, Nov. 26, 1919; s. Fred George and Anna Jane (Mason) P.; m. Carol Ulf, Sept. 15, 1953 (div. 1981); children— Ann, Karen, Frederik, Kathy; m. Elizabeth Anne Hull, July 27, 1984 Editor Popular Pubs., NYC, 1939-43; editor Popular Sci., NYC, 1946-49; freelance writer NYC, 1950-60, 80—; editor Galaxy Pubs., NYC, 1961-69, Bantam Books, NYC, 1973-80. Author: Man Plus, 1977 (Nebula award), Gateway, 1978 (Nebula, Hugo, Campbell awards, Prix Apollo award), Jem, 1979 (Am. Book award), The Years of the City (Campbell award 1985), Chasing Science, 2000, The Boy Who Would Live Forever, 2004, Platnum Pohl, 2005; Co-author: (with Sir Arthur C. Clarke) The Last Theorem, 2008. Served to sgt. USAAF, 1943-45; Italy Recipient Popular Culture Assn. award, 1982 Fellow AAAS; mem. Sci. Fiction Writers of Am. (pres. 1974-76, Grand Master award 1993), World Sci. Fiction (pres. 1980-82), Authors Guild, Astron. Soc. Pacific. Democrat. Unitarian Universalist. Home: 855 Harvard Dr Palatine IL 60067-7026

POHL, JENS GERHARD, architecture educator, director; b. Wetzlar, Hessen, Germany, Sept. 18, 1940; s. Ernst Richard and Hildegard Wilhelmine Pohl; m. Barbara Moyra Penrose; children: Sonya Karen, Kym Jason. BArch, U. Melbourne, Australia, 1965; MS in Blgs. Sci., U. Sydney, 1967, PhD, 1970; Dr. Honoris Causa (hon.), Internat. Inst. Advanced Studies Sys. Rsch. and Cybern, Germany, 1998. Lic. VIC and NSW, Australia, 1968. Prof., architecture Calif. Poly. State U., San Luis Obispo, 1972—; exec. dir. Collaborative Agt. Design Rsch. Ctr., San Luis Obispo, 1986—; chief tech. officer CDM Technologies Inc., San Luis Obispo, 2002—. Recipient Recognition award, NASA, 1977, Archtl. Competition Honor award, State Calif., 1977, Architecture Dept. Faculty Merit award, Calif. Poly. State U., 1985, Meritorious Performance and Profl. Promise award, Calif. State U. Sys., 1987, Millennium award, Internat. Inst. Advanced Studies Sys. Rsch. and Cybernetics, 2000. Achievements include patents for three dimensional tracking solar energy concentrator; portable linear focused solar thermal energy collecting system. Office: Calif Poly State Univ 1 Grand Ave San Luis Obispo CA 93407

POHL, MICHAELA, historian, educator; BA, Evergreen State Coll., Olympia, 1989; PhD, Ind. U., Bloomington, 1999. Assoc. prof. Vassar Coll., Poughkeepsie, NY, 1999—. Office: Vassar Coll 124 Raymond Ave Poughkeepsie NY 12604

POHL, ROBERT OTTO, physics professor; b. Gottingen, Germany, Dec. 17, 1929; came to U.S., 1958; s. Robert Wichard and Auguste Eleonore (Madelung) P.; m. Karin Ursula Koehler, May 6, 1961; children: Helen M., Robert S., Otto C. Vordiplom, U. Freiburg, Fed. Rep. Germany, 1951; diploma, U. Erlangen, Fed. Rep. Germany, 1955, Dr. rer. nat., 1957. Asst. U. Erlangen, 1957-58; rsch. assoc. Cornell U., Ithaca, NY, 1958-60, asst. prof., 1960-63, assoc. prof., 1963-68, prof., 1968-2000, Goldwin Smith prof. physics emeritus, 2000—. Vis. prof. Tech. Hochschule Stuttgart, 1966-67, Tech. U. Munchen, 1973-74, Konstanz U., Regensburg U., 1987-88, all Fed. Republic Germany; vis. scientist Nuc. Research Ctr., Juelich, Fed. Rep. Germany, 1980-81, Hahn-Meitner Inst., Berlin, 1995. Contbr. articles on solid state physics to profl. jours. Recipient Sr. Scientist award Alexander von Humboldt Found., 1980; Guggenheim Found. fellow, 1973, Erskine fellow U. Canterbury, New Zealand, 1988. Fellow AAAS, Am. Inst. Physics (O.E. Buckley award 1985); mem. NAS, Internat. Thermal Conductivity Confs. Office: Cornell U Physics Dept Ithaca NY 14853-2501 Office Phone: 607-255-3303. Business E-Mail: pohl@ccmr.cornell.edu.

POHL, TIMOTHY R., investment company executive, lawyer; b. Cleve., July 4, 1966; s. Marc A. and Carol S. Pohl; m. Mary Kaye Sinclair; children: Kathryn Ruth, Jacob Irwin. BA, Amherst Coll., Mass., 1988; JD, U. Chgo., 1991. Bar: Ill. 1991, U.S. Dist. Ct. (no. dist.) Ill. 1991. Atty. Jones, Day, Reavis & Pogue, Chgo., 1991—99; ptnr., head bankruptcy practice Skadden, Arps, Slate, Meagher & Flom LLP, 1999—2008; mng. dir. restructuring group Lazard Ltd., Chgo., 2009—. Office: Lazard Ltd 190 LaSalle St 31st Fl Chicago IL 60603 Office Phone: 312-407-6629. Business E-Mail: tim.pohl@lazard.com.

POHL, ZACK, legislative staff member; BA in English, Mich. State U., East Lansing, 2006. Comm. & design coord. Mich. Interfaith Trust Fund, Lansing, 2006—07; comm. advisor Mich. Senate Dem. Caucus, 2007—08; comm. dir. Mark Schauer's Congl. Campaign, 2008; comm. dir. to Rep. Mark Schauer US House of Reps., Washington, 2008—. Mem.: Phi Beta Kappa. Democrat. Office: 1408 Longworth House Office Bldg Washington DC 20515 Office Phone: 202-225-6276. Office Fax: 202-225-6281.*

POHLAD, ROBERT C., consumer products company executive; Dir. Mesaba Holdings Inc.; v.p. N.W. area Pepsi-Cola Bottling Group; pres. Pohlad Cos., 1987—2000; CEO PepsiAmericas, 2000—, vice chmn., 2001—02, chmn., 2002—. Office: PepsiAmericas 4000 Dain Rauscher Plaza 60 S Sixth St Minneapolis MN 55402

POIAN, EDWARD LICIO, historian; b. Trieste, Friuli-Venezia Giulia, Italy, June 10, 1946; arrived in U.S., 1954, naturalized, 1960; s. Angelo Del Picollo and Zaira (de Bourbon-Comelli) Poian; m. Maria del Carmen Lopez Clinton, Nov. 22, 1969 (div. Mar. 1980); children: Jeanne Marie, Nicole Anna; m. Nancy Flynn, Sept. 18, 1982. AS, U.S. Govt. Inst., 1965; BS, Mercy Coll., Dobbs Ferry, NY, 1988; MS, LI U., Bklyn., 1989; PhD, U. Ariz., Tucson, 1992. Chief exec. Budget Fin. Inc., Pittsfield, Mass., 1968-70; acting postmaster U.S. Postal Svc., Chappaqua, 1971-80; v.p. Lehman Bros Khun Loeb, NYC, 1980-83; CEO Cosmopolitan Armaments, NYC, 1983-90; intern The UN Univ., 1989-90; prof. history Mercy Coll., Dobbs Ferry, N.Y., 1991—, prof. history and polit. sci., 1991—. Cons. in field; intern UN U., 1990. Author: On the Outside Looking In, 1972, Peace and Regional Security Through Education in Africa, 1992, Problems in Coordination Among Western Donor Governments in Relations to Multilateral and Social Programmes of the United Nations System, 1990; contbr. articles to profl. jours. Rector, CEO Internat. Ednl. Rsch. Found., Inc., Yonkers, NY, 1991—; trustee archeology dept. U. Trieste, 1986—; dir. history and govt. assn. Mercy Coll., 1988. With USCG, 1963—67, served to capt. USCG Res., 1968—98. Decorated Knight of Malta Cross of Gregory the Great Vatican City; recipient UN award, 1988. Fellow: World Assn. Former UN Interns and Fellows; mem.: VFW, Naval War Coll. Alumni Assn., Am. Soc. Polit. Sci., Yonker Hist. Soc., Mil. Officers Assn. Am., U.S. Naval Inst. (life), Navy League (N.Y. chpt.) (life), Fleet Res. Assn. (life), Am. Legion (life), Phi Gamma Mu, Phi Alpha Theta. Republican. Roman Catholic. Avocations: archaeology, historical research, art collector, philanthropy. Office: Mercy Coll Dept History and Polit Sci 555 Broadway Dobbs Ferry NY 10522-1134 Home: PO Box 50 Hastings On Hudson NY 10706 Personal E-mail: doctorpoian@email.com. Business E-Mail: captainedpoian@moaamail.org.

POILE, DAVID ROBERT, professional sports team executive; b. Toronto, Ont., Can., Feb. 14, 1949; s. Norman Robert and Margaret Poile; m. Elizabeth Ramey, July 4, 1971; children: Brian Robert, Lauren Elizabeth. BS, Northeastern U., 1971. Asst. mgr. Atlanta Flames, 1971-80, Calgary Flames, Alta., Can., 1980-82; gen. mgr., v.p. Washington Capitals, Landover, Md., 1982-95; exec. v.p., gen. mgr., pres. hockey ops. Nashville Predators, Nashville, 1997—. Recipient NHL Exec. of Yr., Sporting News, 1983, 1984, Lester Patrick Award, 2001; named NHL Exec. of Yr., Sporting News, 2007. Office: Nashville Predators Nashville Arena 501 Broadway Nashville TN 37203-3932

POINDEXTER, ALAN, astronaut; b. Pasadena, Calif., Nov. 5, 1961; s. John M. and Linda A. Poindexter; m. Lisa A. Pfeiffer; 2 children. B of Aerospace Engring., Ga. Inst. Tech., 1986; MS in Aeronautical Engring., Naval Postgrad. Sch., 1995. Commd. 2d lt. USN, 1986, advanced through grades to comdr.; with Hypervelocity Wind Tunnel Facility, Naval Surface Weapons Ctr., White Oak, Md.; naval aviator, Fighter Squadron 124 Naval Air Sta., Miramar, Calif., 1988; wing qualified landing signal officer Fighter Squadron 211, Miramar, Calif., Arabian Gulf, Operation Desert Storm, Operation So. Watch; test pilot, project officer Naval Strike Aircraft Test Squadron, Naval Air Sta., Patuxent River, Md., 1995, lead test pilot, F-14 Digital Flight Control Sys.; dept. head Fighter Squadron 32, Naval Air Sta., Oceana, Va.; astronaut NASA, Houston, 1998—, tech. advisor Astronaut Office Shuttle Ops. Br. Pilot Atlantis STS-122 Mission to deliver the European Space Agency's Columbus Lab. to Internat. Space Station, 2008. Mem.: Soc. Exptl. Test Pilots, Tau Beta Pi. Achievements include logged over 2,000 hours in 30 different aircraft; logged over 450 carrier landings. Avocations: motorcycling, running, weightlifting, water-skiing, boating, hunting, fishing. Office: Astronaut Office/CB NASA Johnson Space Ctr Houston TX 77058

POINDEXTER, MARK CAREY, university administrator communications educator, critic; b. St. Charles, Mo., Dec. 31, 1951; s. Russell L. and Jeanne Marie (Klinghammer) P.; 1 child from previous marriage: Claire Estelle; m. Bernadette Rahariarimpanahy, June 27, 1995; children: Matthew Tahiry, Anastasia Marie. BA, Lindenwood Coll., 1973; MA, Ctrl. Mich. U., 1980; PhD, U. Minn., 1987. Mng. editor Lexington Advertiser-News, Mo., 1974-75; news dir. KCUR-FM, Kansas City, Mo., 1975-79; dir. broadcasting N.D. State U. KDSU-FM, Fargo, 1980-87; prof. mass. comm. Ctrl. Mich. U., Mt. Pleasant, 1987—, exec. dir. internat. affairs, 2008—. Acad. specialist U.S. Info. Agy Haiti, 1989; lectr. USIA, Madagascar, 1989, Rwanda, 1990, Ethiopia, 1993, Chad, 1993; radio cons., Madagascar, 1994, Burkina Faso, 1997, Mali, 1997; Fulbright lectr. Institut Superieur de Journalisme in Rabat, Morocco, 1990; seminar leader Centre Africain des Journalistes et Communicateurs, Tunis, Tunisia, 1991; prodr. radio documentaries, including Migrant Workers (RFK Jour. award 1980); published Subscription Television in the Third World: The Moroccan Experience, 1991, Radio in Paris: Can Community Stations Survive?, 1997, Beyond Libido: Stalking the Beast in Cat People, 1997, ABC's the Path to 9/11 Terror Management Theory and the Am. Monomyth, 2008; dir. Ctrl. Mich. Internat. Film Festival, 2003-05. Contbr. articles to profl. jours. Recipient award for Best Radio Documentary, N.D. AP Broadcasters Assn., 1982, 1st pl. awards Mo. Broadcasters Assn., 1977-80. Mem. Popular Culture Assn., Broadcast Edn. Assn. E-mail: poind1m@cmich.edu.

POINSETTE, DONALD EUGENE, engineering executive, management consultant; b. Ft. Wayne, Ind., Aug. 17, 1914; s. Eugene Joseph and Julia Anna (Wyss) P.; m. Anne Katherine Farrell, Apr. 15, 1939 (dec.); children: Donald J., Eugene J., Leo J., Sharon Poinsette Smith, Irene Poinsette Snyder, Cynthia Poinsette West, Maryanne Poinsette Stohler, Philip J. Student, Purdue U., 1934, Ind. U., 1935-37, 64. With GE Corp., RCA, Stewart Warner Corp., 1937-39; metall. rsch. and field sales cons. P.R. Mallory Corp., 1939-49; dist. sales mgr. Derringer Metall. Corp., Chgo., 1949-50; plant engr. Cornell-Dubilier Electric Corp., Indpls., 1950-53; with Jenn-Air Corp., Indpls., 1953-74, purchasing dir., 1953-71, mgr. value engring. and quality control, 1969-74; bus. mgmt. cons. Mays and Assocs., Indpls., 1974-76. Pres. Marian Coll. Parents Club, Indpls., 1969-70; com. mem. Boy Scouts Am.; nat. trustee Xavier U., 1972-73, Dad's Club, Cin.; mem. Triad choral groups. Recipient Testimonial Golden Anniversary award Purdue U., 1987; named to U.S. Finder's List, Nat. Engrs. Register, 1956, Army Navy E award for excellence in engring. and prodn., 1944. Mem. Nat. Assn. Purchasing Mgmt., Indpls. Purchasing Mgmt. Assn., Soc. Am. Value Engrs. (cert. value specialist, sec.-treas. Ctrl. Ind. chpt. 1972-73), Soc. Ret. Execs. Indpls., Ind. U. Alumni Assn., Purdue U. Alumni Assn., Columbian (pres. 1972-73), Internat. Platform Assn., Tau Kappa Epsilon, K.C. (4 deg.). Home: 4802 E 65th St Indianapolis IN 46220

POINTURIER, YVAN, computer scientist; Diplôma in engring., Ecole Ctrl. Lille, 2000; MS, U. Va., Charlottesville, 2002, PhD, 2006. Postdoctoral fellow McGill U., Montreal, Canada, 2006—08; sr. rschr. Athens Info. Tech., Greece, 2008—. Recipient Best Paper award, IEEE Internat. Conf. Comm., 2006. Mem.: IEEE. Achievements include research in crosslayer design of transparent optical networks.

POIRIER, LOUIS JOSEPH, neurology educator; b. Montreal, Que., Can., Dec. 30, 1918; s. Gustave Joseph and Calixta (Brault) P.; m. Liliane Archambault, June 11, 1947; children: Guy, Michel, Louise, Esther. BSc, U. Montreal, 1942, MD, 1947; PhD, U. Mich., 1950; D (hon.), U. Rennes, France, 1973. Asst. prof. U. Montreal, 1950-55, assoc. prof., 1955-58, prof. faculty of medicine, 1958-65; chmn. dept. anatomy Faculty of Medicine, Laval U., Cité Universitaire, Que., 1970-78, prof. exptl. neurology, 1970-83; dir. Centre de Rsch. in Neurobiology, Laval U. and Hosp. de l'Enfant-Jesus, 1977-85, prof. emeritus, 1985—. Editor: Advances in Neurology, vol. 24, 1979; contbr. articles to profl. jours. Pres. Que. Health Scis. Research Council, 1978-81. Decorated officer Order of Can.; recipient Que. sci. award, 1975; Killam commemorative scholar, 1977, 78 Mem. AAAS, Royal Soc. Belgium (hon.), Neurol. Soc. France (hon.), Am. Assn. Anatomists, Am. Physiol. Soc., Soc. for Neuroscis., Internat. Brain Research Orgn., Can. Med. Assn. (emeritus). Address: 603 Chemin Caron Lac Simon Montpellier PQ Canada J0V 1M0

POIRIER, THERESE IRENE, pharmacist, pharmacy educator; b. St. Johns, Que., Can., Dec. 3, 1954; came to U.S., 1957; d. Antonio and Annette (Duquette) P. BS in Pharmacy, Albany Coll. Pharmacy, NY, 1977; PharmD, U. Mich., 1979; MPH, U. Pitts., 1985. Registered pharmacist, Pa., N.Y. Resident in pharmacy U. Mich. Hosp., Ann Anbor, 1977-79; pharmacist Mercy Hosp., Pitts., 1980-84; asst. prof. Sch. Pharmacy Duquesne U., Pitts., 1979-83, assoc. prof., 1983—93, prof., 1993—; dir. clin. pharmacy svcs. St. Francis Med. Ctr., Pitts., 1984—96; assoc. dean & prof. Southern Ill. U. Edwardsville, 2004—. Soul dir. life long learning Duquesne U., 1998. Contbr. chpt. to book, articles to profl. jours. Trainer Evangelism Explosion Ministry, Pitts., 1984. Named Alumnus Albany Coll. Pharmacy, 1982; recipient Univ. Creative Teaching award, Congressional fellowship, 1996-97.

POITIER, CONSTANCE RENA, music specialist, educator; b. Quincy, Fla., June 1, 1955; d. Leroy Cornelius and Dorothy Louise Parker Harris; m. James Poitier, July 22, 1995; children: Carla Felicia DuPont, Carl Franklin DuPont, Jr. BA, Bethune-Cookman Coll., 1977; ME, Fla. Atlantic U., 1984; ednl. specialist magna cum laude, Nova U., 2004. Nat. bd. cert. tchr. 2004, cert. nat. bd. cert. minority recruiter. Choral dir., gen. music Roosevelt Jr. H.S., West Palm Beach, Fla., 1977-81; drama coach Jupiter (Fla.) H.S., 1985; music specialist Roosevelt Elem., 1981-86, Riverview (Fla.) Elem., 1986-96; min. of music Spring Hill Bapt. Ch., Tampa, Fla., 1994-96; choral dir. Atlantic H.S., Port Orange, Fla., 1996-97; choral dir. Daytona Beach Gospel Choir Daytona Beach Bapt. Ch., Fla., 1996—; music specialist Palm Terrace Elem., Daytona Beach, Fla., 1997—, Bonner Elem., 2004—; asst. to the choral dir. Bethune Cookman Coll., 2003; proprietor Poitier Fin. Svcs. Choral dir. Progress M&E Bapt. State Conv., 1973-76; choral dir., pianist 1st Bapt. Ch. College Hill, Tampa, 1986-96; choir cons., guest dir., clinician for choral workshops; concert and rec. artist; pvt. instr., voice and piano; choral festival judge; gospel music workshop clinician. Author: My Book of Poems, 1996. Fellow NEA, NAACP, Am. Choral Dirs., Westside Bus. and Profls., Fla. Vocal Assn., Fla. Music Educators Assn., Fla. Music Educators Nat. Conf., Zeta Phi Beta. Home: 3801 Birch Mtn Rd Port Orange FL 32129 Office: Bonner Elem Sch George Ingram Blvd Daytona Beach FL 32114-1253 E-mail: connie8082@bellsouth.net.

POITIER, SIDNEY, actor, film director; b. Miami, Fla., Feb. 20, 1927; Grew up on Cat Island, The Bahamas. At age 15 moved to Miami, and at age 16 to NYC. s. Reginald and Evelyn (Outten) Poitier; m. Juanita Hardy, Apr. 29, 1960 (div. 1965); children: Beverly, Pamela, Sherri, Gina; m. Joanna Shimkus, Jan. 23, 1976; children: Anika, Sydney. Student, The Bahamas. Accepted to Am. Negro Theatre, NYC, on second audition and made debut in Days of Our Youth, 1945. Amb. to Japan from the Bahamas, 1997; bd. dirs. Walt Disney Co., 1994—2003. Performer: (Broadway plays) Lysistrata, 1946; Anna Lucasta, 1974; A Raisin in the Sun, 1959—60 (Tony Award nomination for best actor in a play, 1960); dir.: Carry Me Back to Morningside Heights, 1968; actor: (films) No Way Out, 1950, Cry, the Beloved Country, 1951, Red Ball Express, 1952, Go, Man, Go!, 1954, Blackboard Jungle, 1955, Goodbye, My Lady, 1956, Edge of the City, 1957, Something of Value, 1957, Band of Angels, 1957, The Mark of the Hawk, 1958, The Defiant Ones, 1958 (Acad. award nomination for best actor in a leading role, 1959), Virgin Island, 1958, Porgy and Bess, 1959, All the Young Men, 1960, A Raisin in the Sun, 1961, Paris Blues, 1961, Pressure Point, 1962, Lilies of the Field, 1963 (Acad. Award for best actor in a leading role, 1963, Golden Globe Award for best motion picture actor - drama, 1964), The Long Ships, 1963, The Bedford Incident, 1965, The Greatest Story Ever Told, 1965, A Patch of Blue, 1965, The Slender Thread, 1965, Duel at Diablo, 1966, To Sir, with Love, 1967, In the Heat of the Night, 1967, Guess Who's Coming to Dinner, 1967, The Lost Man, 1969, The Call Me Mister Tibbs!, 1970, Brother John, 1971, The Organization, 1971, The Wilby Conspiracy, 1975, Shoot to Kill, 1988, Little Nikita, 1988, Sneakers, 1992, The Jackal, 1997; (TV films) Separate but Equal, 1991 (Emmy Award nomination for outstanding lead actor in a miniseries or special, 1991), Children of the Dust, 1995, To Sir, with Love II, 1996, Mandela and de Klerk, 1997 (Emmy Award nomination for outstanding lead actor in a miniseries or special, 1997), David and Lisa, 1998, The Simple Life of Noah Dearborn, 1999, The Last Brickmaker in America, 2001; actor, prodr. (TV films) East of Eden, 1999, actor, dir. (films) Buck and the Preacher, 1972, A Warm December, 1973, Uptown Saturday Night, 1974, Let's Do It Again, 1975, A Piece of the Action, 1977, actor, writer (story) For Love of Ivy, 1968; dir.: (films) Stir Crazy, 1980, Hanky Panky, 1982, Fast Forward, 1985, Ghost Dad, 1990; author: (autobiography) This Life, 1980, The Measure of a Man: A Spiritual Autobiography, 2000, Life Beyond Measure, Letters to My Great-Granddaughter, 2008. Served 1267th Med. Deatchment US Army, 1944—45, veteran's hosp., LI. Decorated Hon. Knight Comdr. of the Most Excellent Order of the British Empire Her Majesty Queen Elizabeth II; recipient Golden Globe Award for World Film Favorite - Male, 1969, Cecil B. DeMille Award, Golden Globe Awards, 1982, Lifetime Achievement Award, Am. Film Inst., 1992, Kennedy Ctr. Honors, 1995, Lifetime Achievement Award, Screen Actors Guild, 2000, Hall of Fame Award, NAACP, 2001, Hon. Acad award, Acad. Motion Pictures Arts & Sciences, 2002, Presdl. Medal of Freedom, The White House, 2009, Star on Hollywood Walk of Fame. Achievements include First black person to win an Acad. Award for a leading role, 1964. Office: Creative Artists Agency 2000 Avenue Of The Stars Los Angeles CA 90067-4700*

POITRAS, GILLES LEE, librarian; b. Dupuy, Quebec, Canada, May 7, 1951; s. Roger Poitras and Edith Davis. ThM, Pacific Sch. Religion, Berkeley, Calif, 1982; MLS, U. Calif., Berkeley, 1982. Reference libr. Grad. Theol. Union, Berkeley, 1982—98, Golden Gate U., U. Libr., San Francisco, 1998—2000, access svcs. libr., 2002—; dir. Exploratorium Mus., San Francisco, 2000—02. Internet advisor BayNet Exec. Bd., San Francisco, 1994—, pres., 2000—01. Contbr. articles to profl.jours. Office: GGU Univ Library 536 Mission St San Francisco CA 94105-2968 Business E-Mail: gpoitras@ggu.edu.

POJETA, JOHN, JR., geologist, researcher; b. NYC, Sept. 9, 1935; s. John and Emilie (Pilat) P.; m. Mary Louise Eberz, June 23, 1957; children: Kim Louise, John Martin. BS, Capital U., Columbus, Ohio, 1957; MS, U. Cin., 1961, PhD, 1963. Teaching fellow U. Cin., 1957-63; geologist U.S. Geol. Survey, 1963—, chief lower paleozoic studies unit, 1969-74, chief br. paleontology and stratigraphy, 1989-94. Assoc. prof., lectr. George Washington U., 1965-74; research assoc. Smithsonian Instn., 1969—; U.S. Geol. Survey-Australian Bur. Mineral Resources exchange scientist, 1974-75 Author papers in field. Pres. Potomac Woods Citizens Assn.; mem. area 4 coun. Montgomery County (Md.) Bd. Edn.; mem. bd. Citizens for Good Govt.; trustee Paleontol. Rsch. Instn., 1976—85, 1999—, v.p., 1978—79, pres., 1980—82. Fellow: AAAS (coun.), Geol. Soc. Am. (sr.); mem.: Australasian Paleontologists, Paleontol. Soc. (sec. 1982—88, pres. 1989—90, bus. mgr. spl. studies 1989—). Home: 1492 Dunster Ln Rockville MD 20854-6119 Office: US Geol Survey Smithsonian Instn Rm E-308 MRC121 Mus Natural History Washington DC 20560-0137 Office Phone: 202-633-1347. Business E-Mail: pojetaj@si.edu.

POKALA, NAVEEN, urologist; b. Kurnool, Andhra Pradesh, India, Feb. 28, 1971; s. Satyanarayano Rao and Ramadevi Pokala; m. Suhasini Pokala, Sept. 12, 1999; 1 child, Sriya C. MBBS, Osmania Med. Coll., India, 1995; MS in Gen. Surgery, U. Health Scis., India, 1999. House staff, gen. surgery Bronx-Lebanon Hosp. Ctr., NYC, 2004—07; house officer, urology Henry Ford Hosp., Detroit, 2007—. Rsch. fellow Cleve. Clinic Found. Recipient Gold medal. Fellow: Royal Coll. Glasgow.

POKOL, ALBERT RONALD, librarian; b. Donora, Pa., Oct. 15, 1928; s. Alexander and Mary Pokol; m. Gayle M. Sanders, Aug. 12, 1954; children: Bruce Albert, Clifford Albert. BS in Edn., Calif. U., Pa., 1949; MEd, Duquesne U., Pitts., 1966; MLS, U. Pitts., 1969. Cert. in teaching Pa. Dept. Pub. Instrn., 1950. Libr. West Allegheny Sch. Dist., Imperial, Pa., 1952—54, Donora Sch. Dist., 1954—62, Robert Morris U., Pitts., 1962—65; reference libr. Calif. U., 1965—2007, archives/spl. collections libr., 2008—. Pastoral coun. mem. St. Sebastian Ch., Belle Vernon, Pa., 2008. Mem.: Pa. State Coll. & U. Faculties Assn., Calif. U. Pa. Alumni Assn., U. Pitts. Alumni Assn. Democrat. Roman Catholic. Home: 223 Bonnie St Belle Vernon PA 15012 Office: Calif Univ Pa 250 Univ Ave California PA 15419 Office Fax: 724-938-5901. Business E-Mail: pokol@cup.edu.

POKORNY, JOSEPH WENCESLAUS, III, engineer; b. Park Ridge, Ill., July 11, 1979; s. Joseph Wenceslaus Pokorny, Jr. and Marlene Pokorny. BS, U. Ill., Champaign, 2001, MS, 2003. Tchg. asst. U. Ill., Champaign, 2001—03; application support engr. The MathWorks, Inc., Natick, Mass., 2003—04, tng. engr., 2004—. Presenter in field. Recipient Lincoln Arc Welding award, James F. Lincoln Arc Welding Found., 2001. Mem.: IEEE. Democrat. Roman Catholic. Avocations: sports, fishing, travel. Office: The MathWorks Inc 3 Apple Hill Dr Natick MA 01760

POKOTILOW, MANNY DAVID, lawyer, educator; b. Patterson, NJ, June 26, 1938; s. Samuel Morris and Ruth (Fuchs) P.; children: Mali, Charyse, Mona, Andrew. BEE, Newark Coll. Engring., 1960; LLB, Am. U., Washington, DC, 1964. Bar: Pa. 1964, US Supreme Ct. 1969. Examiner Patent Office, Washington, 1960-64; ptnr. Caesar, Rivise, Bernstein, Cohen & Pokotilow Ltd., Phila., 1965—. Lectr. Pa. Bar Inst., various trade assns., expert witness on protection of computer software, patents, trademarks, trade secrets and copyrights; faculty Temple U. Sch. Law, 1985-94; mem. Pa. Bar Inst. Intellectual Property com. Vol. Support Ctr. for Child Advs., Phila., 1979—; bd. dirs., organizer Phila. Bar Assn. 10k Race, Phila., 1980-, Packard Press Road Run Grand Prix, 1986; bd. dirs. Hist. Soc. U.S. Dist. Ct. (ea. dist.) Pa., 1989-, v.p. 1998-2002, pres. 2002-03. Recipient Chair award for vol. excellence Am. Diabetes Assn., 1991; honored by Support Ctr. for Child Advs., 1992 and Am. Diabetes Assn., 1997; named to Million Dollar Club, Am. Diabetes Assn., 2002; named one of Best Lawyers in Greater Phila. area Phila. Mag., 1999, Best Lawyers in Am., 2006, 07-09; named to Top Tier of Am. Leading Lawyers for Bus., 2003-09. Fellow Litigation Counsel America (Named 100 Pa. Lawyer, 2004-09); mem. ABA (chmn. proprietary rights in software com., coun. sci. and tech. sect. 1989—97), IEEE, Assn. Trial Lawyers Am., Phila. Bar Assn. (bd. govs. 1982-84, chmn. sports and recreation com. 1977—, Mid-Size law firm mgt. com., 2009; hon. trustee campaign for qualified judges 1993), Phila. Patent Law Assn. (bd. govs. 1982-84, chmn. fed. practice and procedure com. 1983-88), Phila. Trial Lawyers (chmn. fed. cts. com. 1986-90), Lawyers Club Phila. (bd. govs. 1984-94, chmn. publicity 1994-98), Pa. Trial Lawyers, Tau Epsilon Rho (vice chancellor Phila. grad. chpt. 1986-88, chancellor 1988-90). Office: Caesar Rivise Bernstein Cohen & Pokotilow Ltd 1635 Market St Fl 12 Philadelphia PA 19103-2212 Home Phone: 610-664-8411; Office Phone: 215-567-2010. Business E-Mail: mpokotilow@crbcp.com.

POKRAS, SHEILA FRANCES, retired judge; b. Newark, Aug. 5, 1935; m. Norman M. Pokras, 1954; children: Allison, Andrea, Larry. Student, Beaver Coll., 1953-54; BS in Edn., Temple U., 1957; JD cum laude, Pepperdine U., 1969. Bar: Calif. 1970, U.S. Dist. Ct. D.C. 1970, U.S. Dist. Ct. Calif. 1970, U.S. Supreme Ct. 1975. Tchr. elem. and secondary schs., Phila. and Newark, 1957-59; pvt. practice law Long Beach, Calif., 1970-78; city councilwoman Lakewood, Calif., 1972-76; judge Long Beach Mcpl. Ct., 1978-80, L.A. Superior Ct., 1980-98; ret., 1998. Supervising judge, 1986; del. Calif. State Dem. Cen. Com., 1975, Calif. State Conv., 1975; mem. Com. on Gender Bias in Calif. Courts, 1986-89 Advisor Jr. League, 1980-85; mem. early childhood adv. bd. Long Beach City Coll.; bd. dirs. Long Beach Alcoholism Coun., 1979-80, Boys and Girls Club Am., 1981-89, Long Beach Symphony, 1985, Jewish Community Fedn., 1982-86, past mem. community rels. com.; active Nat. Women's Polit. Caucus, LWV. Recipient Torch of Liberty award, B'nai B'rith Anti-Defamation League, 1974; named Woman of Yr., NOW, Long Beach, 1984; honoree, Nat. Conf. Christians and Jews, 1986. Mem. ABA, AAUW, Nat. Assn. Women Judges (dist. supr. 1986), Calif. Bar Assn. (judges div.), Calif. Judges Assn. (mem. ann. seminar com. 1981-89), Mcpl. Cts. Judges Assn. (mem. Marshall com. 1979-80), L.A. County Bar Assn. (judges div., mem. arbitration com.), Women Lawyers Assn., L.A. (judges sect.), Women Lawyers Assn. Long Beach, Long Beach Legal Aid Found. (v.p. 1976-78), Long Beach Bar Assn. (active various coms., bd. govs. 1977-78, Judge of Yr. 1987), Long Beach C. of C. (bd. dirs.). Avocations: swimming, golf, jogging, classical music, movies. Personal E-mail: spokras@socal.rr.com.

POKROVSKY, VALERY LEONIDOVICH, physicist, researcher; b. Kirovograd, Ukraine, Jan. 1, 1931; s. Leonid Grigoryevich Pokrovsky and Raisa Yakovlevna Razumovsky; m. Svetlana Petrovna Krylova, Apr. 7, 1953; children: Sergei Pokrovsky, Olga Volpert. Degree in physics, Kharkov State U., 1953; PhD of Physics and Math., Tomsk State U., 1957; PhD of Physics and Math. (hon.), Russian Acad. Sci., 1962. Rsch. scientist, then chief of lab. Inst. Radiophysics Russian Acad. Sci. Siberian Br., Novosibirsk, 1957—66; prof. theoretical physics Novosibirsk State U., 1957—66; from chief divsn. to prin. scientist Landau Inst. for Theoretical Physics, Chernogolovka, 1966—; prof. theoretical physics Moscow Inst. Physics and Tech., Dolgoprudny, 1966—92; from vis. prof. to prof. dept. physics Tex. A&M U., College Station, 1992—99, Disting. prof., 1999—. Vis. prof. ETH, Zürich, 1995; vis. scientist Brookhaven Nat. Lab., Upton, N.Y., 1991-92, Kernforschunganlage, Jülich, Germany, 1990-91. Co-author Fluctuation Theory of Phase Transitions, 1979, Theory of Incommensurate Crystals, 1984, Theory of Two-Dimensional Crystals, 1992; editor Internat. Jour. Modern Physics and Letters, 1989—. Grantee NSF, 1997—; recipient Landau prize Russian Acad. Scis., 1984, Humboldt Rsch. award, 2000. Fellow Am. Phys. Soc. (Onsager prize 2005) Achievements include hypothesis of self-similarity in the theory of phase transitions, prediction of a new type of critical behavior associated with proliferation of linear defects in 2 dimensions, method to calculate transition probability in quantum mechanics beyond all orders of perturbation theory. Office: Tex A&M U Dept Physics College Station TX 77843-0001 E-mail: pokrovsky@physics.tamu.edu.

POLACHEK, DORA EISENBERG, humanities educator; d. Nathan and Toni Cumpana Eisenberg; m. Solomon William Polachek; 1 child, Nathaniel Joseph. BA, Barnard Coll., NYC; MA, NY U., NYC; PhD, U. NC, Chapel Hill. Asst. prof. of French Ithaca Coll., Ithaca, NY, 1985—86; lectr., asst. prof. of Frenc, sr. lectr. Cornell U., Ithaca, NY, 1986—97; vis. asst. prof., 1997—2001; vis. assoc prof., French Binghamton U., 2001—. Cons. reader, advanced placement french exam. Ednl. Testing Svc., Princeton, NJ, 2002—06; content adv. com. cons., NYS french certification exam Nat. Evaluation Svcs., Malta, NY, 2003—05; external project proposal evaluator Social Scis. & Humanities Rsch. Coun. Can., 2005; interim dir. Ctr. Medieval & Renaissance Studies, Binghamton U., NY, 2007—08. Contbr. articles to profl. jours. Editl. bd. reporter Jewish Fedn. Broome County, Binghamton. Recipient Chancellor's award, SUNY Ctrl., State U. NY, 2004, Excellence Internat. Edn. award, Binghamton U., 2005, Athanor prize, Italy's Assn. Culturale Progetto Athanor, 2007; Internat. Travel Grant, Cornell U., 1992, grant, Borchardt Found., 2002. Master: Phi Sigma Iota (faculty advisor 1998—); mem.: MLA (exec. com. mem. 1998—2003), Sixteenth Century Soc. (Bainton lit. book prize com. mem., chair 2001—), Am. Assn. Tchrs. French (v.p. 1989—93). Office: Binghamton Univ Romance Langs & Lits Libr Tower 510 Binghamton NY 13902-6000 Office Fax: 607-777-2644. Business E-Mail: dpolachk@binghamton.edu.

POLAK, ELIJAH, engineering educator, computer scientist; b. Bialystok, Poland, Aug. 11, 1931; came to US, 1958, naturalized, 1977; s. Isaac and Frama (Friedman) P.; m. Virginia Ann Gray, June 11, 1961; children: Oren, Sharon. BSEE, U. Melbourne, Australia, 1957; MSEE, U. Calif., Berkeley, 1959, PhD in Elec. Engring., 1961. Instrument engr. ICIANZ, Melbourne, Australia, 1956-57; summer student IBM Rsch. Labs., San Jose, Calif., 1959-60; vis. asst. prof. MIT, fall 1964; assoc. dept. elec. engring. and computer scis. U. Calif., Berkeley, 1958-61, asst. prof. elec. engring. and computer scis., 1961-66, assoc. prof., 1966-69, prof., 1969-94, prof. grad. Sch., 1994—. Author: (with L.A. Zadeh) System Theory, 1969, (with E. Wong) Notes for a First Course on Linear Systems, 1970, (with others) Theory of Optimal Control and Mathematical Programming, 1970, Computational Methods in Optimization, 1971, Optimization: Algorithms and Consistent Approximations, 1997. Guggenheim fellow, 1968; UK Sci. Rsch. Coun. Sr. fellow, 1972, 76, 79, 82 Fellow IEEE; mem. Soc. Indsl. and Applied Math. (assoc. editor Jour. Theory and Applications Optimization 1972—), Soc. Math. Programming. Jewish. Avocation: cross country skiing. Home: 38 Fairlawn Dr Berkeley CA 94708-2106 Office: U Calif Dept Elec Engring Cp S Berkeley CA 94720-0001 Office Phone: 510-642-2644. Business E-Mail: polak@eecs.berkeley.edu.

POLAK, EMIL JOSEPH, history professor, researcher; b. Bay Shore, NY, Aug. 16, 1936; s. Emil Frank and Mary Rose (Comitsky) Polak; m. Patricia Faith Leuzzi, Aug. 3, 1968. AB cum laude, U. Albany, 1957; AM, Columbia U., 1958, PhD, 1970. Lectr. Bklyn. Coll., 1961—65; instr. St. John's U., Jamaica, NY, 1965—66; lectr. S.I. C.C., 1966—67; instr. CCNY, 1967—70; asst. prof. Queensborough CC, Bayside, NY, 1970—76, assoc. prof., 1977—81, prof. dept. history, 1982—. Author: A Textual Study of Jacques de Dinant's Summa dictaminis, 1975, Medieval and Renaissance Letter Treatises and Form Letters: A Census of Manuscripts Found in Eastern Europe and the Former U.S.S.R., 1993, Medieval and Renaissance Letter Treatises and Form Letters: A Census of Manuscripts Found in Part of Western Europe, Japan and the United States of America, 1994; editor: A Medievalist's Odyssey: Helene Wieruszowski Scholar, 2004. Recipient Performance Excellence award, Queensborough CC, 2000, Excellence in Faculty scholarship award, 2002; grantee, Am. Coun. Learned Socs./USSR Acad. Scis., 1981, Gladys Krieble Delmas Found., 1995, NEH, 1997, Renaissance Soc. Am., 2000; fellow, Am. Acad. Rome, 1963, CUNY Rsch. Found., 1977—2009, Internat. Rsch. Exchanges Bd., 1978, 1981, 1996; fellowship, Vatican Film Libr. Mellon, 2009. Mem.: L.I. Maritime Mus., Internat. Soc. Classical Tradition, Medieval Latin Studies Group, Medieval Club N.Y., Am. Assn. Neo-Latin Studies, Early Book Soc., Internat. Assn. Neo-Latin Studies, Soc. Fellows Am. Acad. Rome, Am. Soc. History of Rhetoric, Internat. Soc. History of Rhetoric, Am. Hist. Assn., Medieval Acad. Am., Renaissance Soc. Am., Am. Phil. Assn., Bohemia Hist. Soc., Bayport Heritage Assn., Sayville Hist. Soc., Columbia U. Grad. Sch. Arts and Scis. Alumni Assn., U. Albany Alumni Assn., Pi Gamma Mu, Kappa Phi Kappa. Avocations: travel, theater, films. Office: Queensborough CC Dept History 222-05 56 Ave Oakland Gardens NY 11364-1497 Office Fax: 718-631-6372.

POLAK, SARAH, museum association administrator, educator; BA, Rockhurst U.; MA, U. Nebr., Lincoln. Instr. applied history Chadron State Coll, dir., Mari Sandoz High Plains Heritage Ctr., 2002—; pres. Nebr. Mus. Assn. Mem. Nebr. State Hist. Records Adv. Bd. Mem.: Mountain-Plains Mus. Assn., Mari Sandoz Heritage Soc., Assn. Coll. and Univ. Mus. and Galleries, Am. Assn. State and Local History, Am. Assn. Mus., Nebr. Travel Assn. Office: Mari Sandoz High Plains Heritage Ctr Chadron State Coll 1000 Main St Chadron NE 69337 Office Phone: 308-432-6066. Office Fax: 308-432-6464. Business E-Mail: spolak@csc.edu.

POLAK, VIVIAN LOUISE, lawyer; b. NYC, Nov. 1, 1952; d. Henri and Greta Etty (Querido) P. BA cum laude, Barnard Coll., 1974; JD, Harvard U., 1977. Bar: NY 1978, DC 1978, US Dist. Ct. (ea. and so. dists.) NY 1978. Assoc. Donovan, Leisure, Newton and Irvine, NYC, 1977-86; ptnr. LeBoeuf, Lamb, Greene & MacRae, NYC, 1986—2007, Dewey & LeBoeuf LLP, NYC, 2007—. Editor-in-chief Alley Way Newsletter (inside look new media law. NY law jour.), 2000—01; co-editor-in-chief Start-Up and Emerging Co. Strategist Am. Lawyer Media, 2001—03. Contbr. articles to profl. jours. Participant Sedona Conf. Working Group on Electronic Document Retention and Production, 2003—; co-chair Sedona Legacy Data Spl. Project Team, 2005—, Dewey & LeBoeuf IT and IP Practice Group; chair Dewey & LeBoeuf Diversity Com., 2007—. Mem. NY State Bar Assn. (sec. antitrust sect. 1991-92, mem. exec. com. 1992-95, chmn. internat. trade com. 1985-90), Assn. Bar City NY (com. copyright & lit. property) 1987-1988. Office: Dewey & LeBoeuf LLP 1301 Avenue of the Americas New York NY 10019 Office Phone: 212-259-8289. Office Fax: 212-649-9474. Business E-Mail: vpolak@dl.com.

POLAKIEWICZ, LEONARD ANTHONY, foreign language and literature educator; b. Kiev, Ukraine, Mar. 30, 1938; came to the U.S., 1950; s. Wladyslaw and Aniela (Ossowska) P.; m. Marianne Helen Swanson, Sept. 7, 1963; children: Barbara, Kathryn, Janet. BS in Russian with distinction, U. Minn., 1964, BA in Internat. Rels., 1964; MA in Russian, U. Wis., 1968; cert. Russian area studies, 1969; PhD in Slavic Langs./Lit., U. Wis., 1978; diploma in Polish Curriculum and Instrn., Curie-Sklodowska U., Lublin, Poland, 1981. Instr. U. Minn., Mpls., 1970-78, asst. prof., 1978—90, assoc. prof., 1990—, Morse Alumni disting. teaching assoc. prof. Slavic langs. and literatures, dir. Inst. Langs., 1991-93, chair Slavic dept., 1993—97, 1999—2000, 2006—08. Vis. asst. prof. U. London, 1984; dir. U. Minn. Polish Lang. Program, Curie-Sklodowska U., Lublin, Poland, summers 1984-89, dir. Russian Faculty Exch., Herzen Pedagogical U., St. Petersburg, Russia, 1993—; mem. selection com. Fulbright Tchr. Exch. Program, USIA, 1989, Title VI Dept. Edn., 1990, NEH Tchr.- Scholar Program, 1994; reviewer divn. ednl. programs NEH, 1990, translation program, 1993, 94; mem. rev. bd. Ctr. Applied Linguistics Polish Proficiency Test, 1990; mem. exec. com. Coun. on Internat. Edn., N.Y.C., 1991-94; mem. Russian Lang. Program Acad. Policy Com. CIEE, N.Y.C., 1994-2002; mem. nat. task force Polish Studies in Am., Ind. U., 1995-96; project dir. Nat. Coun. Orgns. of Less Commonly Taught Langs. Polish Lang. Learning Framework, 1995-2001; Polish examiner Yale U. Ctr. Lang. Study, 2006-2008; dir. U. Minn. Curie Sklodowska U. Faculty Exch., 1988—, U. Minn. Cath. U. of Lublin Faculty Exch., 1995-2001; coord. Def. Lang. Inst. Polish Proficiency Testing, 1998; apptd. adv. bd. Am. U. Poland, 2004-2008; mem. nat. screening com. Fulbright-Hays Program, US Dept. State, 2006; mem. rev. panel Boren fellowship, Nat. Security Edn. Program, 2007-09. Author: Supplemental Materials for First Year Polish, 1991, Supplemental Materials for Fifteen Modern Polish Short Stories, 1994, Directory of US Institutions of Higher Education and Faculty Offering Instruction in Polish Language, Literature and Culture, 1996-97, Intermediate Polish: A Cultural Reader with Exercises, 1999, (with Joanna Radwanska Williams and Waldemar Walczynski) Polish Language Learning Framework, 2002; assoc. editor Slavic and East European Jour., 1988-94; complier, editor, contbr. Can.-Am. Slavic Studies, Vol. 42, 2008, Devoted Chekhov Scholarship; mem. editl. bd. The Learning and Tchg. of Slavic Langs. and Cultures: Toward the 21st Century, 1996-2000; reviewer Choice Mag., Modern Lang. Jour., Canadian Slavonic Papers, Russian Review, Slavic and East European Jour., Soviet and Post-Soviet Rev. Bd. dirs. Immigration Hist. Rsch. Ctr., Mpls., 1984-89, Am. Univ. in Poland, 2004-08; co-founder Polish-Am. Cultural Inst., Mpls., 1986; vice-chair Polish Am. Congress' Commn. Edn., 1987; mem. gov.'s Commn. on Ea. Europe, St. Paul, 1991. With U.S. Army, 1961-63. Ford Found. fellow, 1964-65, NDEA fellow, Title IV, 1966-68; grantee Kościuszko Found., 1981, Coun. for European Studies grantee Columbia U., 1981, 84, 86, Rsch. Assoc. grantee Russian and East European Ctr., U. Ill., 1982, 83, 84, Wasie Found. grantee, 1983, IREX Collaborative Activities and New Exchs. grantee, 1984, Ireland Travel grantee Trinity Coll., Dublin, 1984, Bush Found. Rsch. grantee, 1986-87, grantee U.S. Dept. Edn., 1988-91; Fulbright-Hays Group Projects Abroad grantee for Poland, 1989, USIA U. Linkage grantee for Poland, 1989-93, IREX Short Term Travel grantee, 1995, USIA Coll. and Univ. Affiliations grantee for Poland, 1995-2000; recipient Polanie Club of the Twin Cities Merit award, 1982, Curie-Sklodowska U. medal for acad. linkage devel., 1992, Cavalier's Cross of Order of Merit of Republic of Poland, 1999, Disting Svc. award Herzen Pedagogical U., St. Petersburg, Russia, 2002, Pres.'s Outstanding Svc. award, 2003, A. Ronald Walton award Nat. Coun. Less Commonly Taught Langs., 2006. Mem. AAUP, Am. Assn. for the Advancement Slavic Studies, Am. Assn. Tchrs. Slavic and East European Langs. and Lits. (com. on testing and profl. devel. 1997—, Excellence in Tchg. in U.S. award 1994), Internat. Czeslaw Milosz Soc. (pres. 1984-85), N.Am. Chekhov Soc., Am. Coun. Tchrs. of Russian, Polish Inst. Arts & Scis. Am. (N.Y.C., Waclaw Lednicki Humanities award com. 1996), Assn. Literary Scholars & Critics, Soc. of Lovers of the Russian Book, Irish Assn. of Russian and East European Studies, Polish Tchrs. Assn. of Am., Polish Studies Assn. (mem. biannual prize jury 1998), Bristol Group Internat. Assn. Tchrs. Polish, U. Minn. Acad. Disting. Tchrs., The Australia and New Zealand Slavists' Assn. Roman Catholic. Avocations: reading, philatelics, genealogy, touring, gardening. Home: 466 Oak Creek Dr S Vadnais Heights MN 55127-7008 Office Phone: 612-625-1384. Business E-Mail: polak001@tc.umn.edu.

POLAKOFF, ABE, baritone; b. Bucharest, Rumania; s. Sam and Mary P. Ousherenkova; children: David Fred, Mark Evan, Robert Ira; m. Judyth Kanner, Dec. 5, 1992. Civil engring. student, CCNY; profl. tng. program, Am. Theater Wing, 1952-54; student, N.Y. Coll. Music, 1955-57. Dir. Island Opera Players; opera lectr. Arts Couns. (municipalities and schs.); cantor Progressive Shaari Zedek synagogue, Bklyn., 1972-77, Temple Emanuel, Denver, 1984-94. Debuts include Marcello in La Boheme, Milan, Florence, 1960; leading baritone Zurich Opera, 1961-63, numerous appearances with N.Y. Met. Opera, City Opera N.Y., Phila. Lyric Opera, Pitts. Opera, Seattle Opera, Berlin Deutsche Opera, Frankfurt Opera, Cinn. Opera, Hamburg, Munich Staatsoper, Stuttgart Staatsoper, The Netherlands Opera, Cin. Opera, Kansas City Lyric Opera, Canadian Opera Co., others; soloist with Mex. State Symphony Orch., Kalamazoo Symphony Orch., Winston-Salem (N.C.) Symphony, numerous concert and recital appearances Sgt. U.S. Army, 1943-46. 1st prize winner Am. Theatre Wing Vocal Profl. Scholarship award, 1954, 1st prize winner Am. Opera Auditions, 1960, Silver medal Vercelli (Italy) Internat. singing contest, 1960; Rockefeller Found. grantee, 1961-62; Bayreuth Festival Masterclass scholar. Mem. Cen. Opera Service, Am. Guild Musical Artists, Actors Equity Assn. Address: 11132 76th Ave Apt 7H Forest Hills NY 11375-6409 Personal E-mail: polakoffabe1@gmail.com. E-mail: judyth@nvbb.net.

POLAMALU, TROY (TROU AUMUA POLAMALU), professional football player; b. Garden Grove, Calif., Apr. 19, 1981; Grad., U. So. Calif., 2003. Safety Pitts. Steelers, 2003—. Named 1st Team All-Pro, AP, 2005, 2008; named to Am. Football Conf. Pro-Bowl Team, NFL, 2004—08. Achievements include member of Super Bowl Championship winning Pittsburgh Steelers, 2006, 2009. Office: c/o Pittsburgh Steelers 3400 S Water St Pittsburgh PA 15203*

POLANCO, PLACIDO ENRIQUE, professional baseball player; b. Santo Domingo, Dominican Republic, Oct. 10, 1975; m. Lily Polanco; children: Aide Rose, Ishmael. Student, Miami-Dade Wolfson CC, Fla. Draft pick St. Louis Cardinals, 1994, player, 1998—2002, Phila. Phillies, 2002—05, Detroit Tigers, 2005—. Mem. Dominican Republic Team World Baseball Classic, 2006. Recipient Stockton/Broeg award, Baseball Writers' Assn. of Am., St. Louis chpt., 2000—01, Gold Glove award, 2007, Silver Slugger award, 2007, MLB.com's Defensive Player of Yr. award, 2007; named Am. League Championship Series MVP, 2006; named to Am. League All-Star Team, 2007. Achievements include setting a Major League Baseball record for second basemen by playing 144 straight games without an error, August 13, 2007. Avocation: golf. Mailing: Detroit Tigers Comerica Park 2100 Woodward Ave Detroit MI 48201

POLAND, GREGORY A., medical professor, researcher; b. Quantico, Va., Aug. 16, 1955; s. James Poland; m. Jean Marie Poland; children: Caroline Marie, Eric Gregory, Matthew Gregory. BA in Biology, magna cum laude, Ill. Wesleyan U., Bloomington, 1977; MD, So. Ill. U., Springfield, 1980. Diplomate Am. Bd. Internal Medicine. Chief resident, instr. internal medicine Abbott-Northwestern Hosp., Mpls., 1984-85; asst. prof. internal medicine East Tenn. State U., Johnson City, 1985-87, VA Med. Ctr., Mpls., 1987-88; asst. prof. medicine Mayo Clinic Coll. Medicine, Rochester, Minn., 1988-93, assoc. prof. medicine, 1993-97, prof. medicine, infectious diseases, molecular pharmacology and experimental therapeutics, 1997—, Mary Lowell Leary prof. medicine, 2004; assoc. chair rsch., dept. medicine Mayo Clinic & Found., 1999—, dir. Vaccine Rsch. Group, Immunization Clinic and Prog. in Translational Immunovirology & Biodefense. Vis. prof. Capital Med. Coll., Beijing, 1994, Mich. State U., East Lansing, 1995, Santa Clara Valley Hosp, Stanford U., San Jose, Calif., 1995, U. Wis., Milw., 1997, So. Ill. U., 1997; mem. exec. com., chmn. Nat. Coalition Adult Immunization; bd. dirs. Nat. Found. Infectious Diseases, 1997—; mem. steering com. Nat. Network Immunization Info. Am. editor (med. jour.) Vaccine, 2000—; contbr. articles to profl. jours., chapters to books. Recipient US Surgeon Gen. award, Ctrs. Disease Control & Prevention and Health Care Fin. Adminstrn., 1998, Outstanding Pub. Svc. Medal, US Sec. Defense, 2003; named Outstanding Clin. Investigator of Yr., Mayo Clinic & Found., 1997; grantee Nat. Fund Med. Edn., 1988. Fellow: ACP; mem.: AMA, Internat. Soc. Vaccines (pres.), Infectious Diseases Soc. of America, Am. Soc. Clin. Pharmacology & Therapeutics, Internat. Soc. Travel Medicine, Am. Soc. Microbiology, Am. Fedn. Med. Rsch., Assn. Prog. Dirs. Internal Medicine, Minn. Med. Assn. Office: Mayo Clinic Dept Internal Medicine 200 First St SW 611 B Guggenheim Bldg St SW Rochester MN 55905-0001 Office Phone: 507-284-9039. Business E-Mail: poland.gregory@mayo.edu.*

POLAND, RICHARD CLAYTON, law educator; b. Hartland, Maine, June 23, 1947; s. Richard and Viola (Gardiner) P.; m. Judy Raithel, Feb. 2, 1978; 1 child, Brooke. BA, Taylor U., Upland, Ind., 1969; MS in Bus., Thomas Coll., 1993; JD, Northeastern U. Sch. Law, 1974. Bar: Maine, US Dist. Ct. Maine, US Supreme Ct. Sole practice law, Skowhegan, Maine, 1974-94; prof. law, dir. pre-law program Flagler Coll, St. Augustine, Fla., 1994—. Probate judge Somerset County, Skowhegan,

1977-94; Maine Family Ct. Commn., Augusta, 1981; mem. Maine Jud. Coun., Portland, 1989-93. Author: Pre-Law Handbook for Undergrads., 2000, 4th edit., 2007. Chmn. faculty welfare com. Flagler Coll. Cpl. Maine Nat. Guard, 1970-76. Mem. So. Assn. Pre-Law Advisors (pres. 2000-02, bd. dirs. 2002-06), Pre-Law Adv. Nat. Conf. (exec. bd. 2000-02). Avocations: travel, reading. Office: Flagler Coll 74 King St Saint Augustine FL 32084-4342 Office Phone: 904-819-6338. Business E-Mail: polandrc@flagler.edu.

POLANSKI, ROMAN, film director, writer, actor; b. Paris, Aug. 18, 1933; s. Ryszard and Bule (Katz-Przedborska) P.; m. Barbara Lass, Sept. 19, 1959 (div. 1962); m. Sharon Tate, Jan. 20, 1968 (dec. Aug. 9, 1969); m. Emmanuelle Seigner, Aug. 30, 1989 Student, Art Sch., Cracow, State Film Coll., Lodz. Appeared in (children's radio show) The Merry Gang, (stage prodn.) Son of the Regiment, When Angels Fall, 1958, Le Gros et le Maigre, 1960, Knife in the Water, 1962 (Venice Film Festival award), The Mammals, 1963 (Tours Film Festival award), Repulsion, 1965 (Berlin Film Festival award), Cul-de-Sac, 1966 (Berlin Film Festival award), Rosemary's Baby, 1968, Macbeth, 1971, Tess, 1980 (Cesar award), Pirates, 1986, Frantic, 1988, Bitter Moon, 1994, Death and the Maiden, 1994, The Ninth Gate, 1999, The Pianist, 2002 (Best Dir. Acad. award, 2003, Best Film, British Acad. Film Award (BAFTA), 2003, The David Lean Award for Achievement in Direction, 2003, 2003), Oliver Twist, 2005; actor, dir. (films) The Fearless Vampire Killers, 1967, Chinatown, 1974 (Best Dir. award Soc. Film and TV Arts, Priz Raoul-Levy, 1975), What?, 1972, The Tenant, 1976, appeared in (documentaries) Roman Polanski: Wanted and Desired, 2008; actor: (films) A Generation, 1955, End of the Night, 1957; dir., actor: (films) Two Men and a Wardrobe, 1958, See You Tomorrow, 1960, The Innocent Sorcerers, 1960, The Magic Christian and Andy Warhol's Death, 1969, Back in the U.S.S.R., 1992, A Pure Formality, 1994; actor, dir.: (plays) Amadeus; Warsaw, 1981; Paris, 1982; Amadeus/Italy, 1999; dir.: (Operas) Lulu, 1974, Rigoletto, 1976; (Operas, (musical comedy) Tales of Hoffman, Master Class, 1996—97; (Operas) Tanz der Vampire, 1997, 2000; author: (autobiography) Roman, 1984. Recipient Lifetime Achievement award, European Film Awards, 2006. Office: ICM 8942 Wilshire Blvd Beverly Hills CA 90211-1934

POLANSKY, LARRY PAUL, legal association administrator; b. Blkyn., July 24, 1932; s. Harry and Ida (Gershgorn) P.; m. Eunice Kathryn Neun; children: Steven, Harriet, Bruce. BS in Acctg., Temple U., 1958, JD, 1973. Bar: Pa. 1973, U.S. Dist. Ct. (ea. dist.) Pa. 1973, U.S. Ct. Appeals (3d cir.) 1973, D.C. 1978, U.S. Supreme Ct. 1980. Acct., systems analyst City of Phila., 1956-63; data processing mgr. Jefferson Med. Coll. and Hosp., Phila., 1963-65; systems engr. IBM Corp., Phila., 1965-67; dep. ct. adminstr. Common Pleas Cts. of Phila., 1967-76; dep. state ct. adminstr. Pa. Supreme Ct., Phila., 1976-78; exec. officer D.C. Cts., Washington, 1979-90. Presdl. appt. to bd. dirs. State Justice Inst., 1985-89; bd. dirs. Search Group, Inc. Author: A Primer for the Technologically Challenged Judge, 1995; contbr. articles to profl. jours. Elected supervisor, Kidder Twp., 2003-, chmn. 2005-08; served as cpl. U.S. Army, 1951-53, Korea. Fellow Inst. for Ct. Mgmt., Denver, 1984; recipient Reardon award Nat. Ctr. for State Cts., 1982, Disting. Svc. award Nat. Ctr. for State Cts., 1986, Justice Tom C. Clark award Nat. Conf. of Metro. Cts., 1991, award of merit Nat. Assn. Ct. Mgmt., 1996. Mem. ABA (jud. adminstrn. divsn., chmn. tech. com. 1991-93, 95, exec. com. lawyers conf. 1985-98, chmn. 1991-92, JAD coun. 1994-97), Conf. State Ct. Adminstrn. (bd. dirs. 1980-86, pres. 1984-85). Republican. Jewish. Avocations: tennis, skiing, computers, golf. Home and Office: PO Box 752 Lake Harmony PA 18624-0752 Home Phone: 570-722-9288; Office Phone: 570-722-9288.

POLANYI, JOHN CHARLES, chemist, educator; b. Berlin, Jan. 23, 1929; s. Michael and Magda Elizabeth (Kemeny) Polanyi; m. Anne Ferrar Davidson, 1958; children: Margaret, Michael; m. Brenda Bury, 2004. BSc, Manchester U., Eng., 1949, MSc, 1950, PhD, 1952, DSc, 1964; DSc (hon.), U. Waterloo, 1970, Meml. U., 1976, McMaster U., 1977, Carleton U., 1981, Harvard U., 1982, Rensselaer U., Brock U., 1984, Lethbridge U., Sherbrooke U., Laval U., Victoria U., Ottawa U., 1987, Manchester U. and York U., Eng., 1988, U. Montreal, Acadia U., 1989, Weizmann Inst., Israel, 1989, U. Bari, Italy, 1990, U. B.C., 1990, McGill U., 1990, Queen's U., 1992, Free U. Berlin, 1993, Laurentian U., 1995, U. Toronto, 1995, U. Liverpool, 1995; LLD (hon.), Trent U., 1977, Dalhousie U., 1983, St. Francis-Xavier U., 1984, Concordia U., 1990, Calgary U., 1994. Mem. faculty dept. chemistry U. Toronto, Ont., Canada, 1956—, prof., 1962—. William D. Harkins lectr. U. Chgo., 1970; Reilly lectr. U. Notre Dame, 1970; Purve lectr. McGill U., 1971; F.J. Toole lectr. U. N.B., 1974; Philips lectr. Haverford Coll., 1974; Kistiakowsky lectr. Harvard U., 1975; Camille and Henry Dreyfus lectr. U. Kans., 1975; J.W.T. Spinks lectr. U. Sask., Canada, 1976; Laird lectr. U. We. Ont., 1976; CIL Disting. lectr. Simon Fraser U., 1977; Gucker lectr. Ind. U., 1977; Jacob Bronowski Meml. lectr. U. Toronto, 1978; Hutchinson lectr. Rochester (N.Y.) U., 1979; Priestley lectr. Pa. State U., 1980; Barré lectr. U. Montreal, 1982; Sherman Fairchild disting. scholar Calif. Inst. Tech., 1982; Chute lectr. Dalhousie U., 1983; Redman lectr. McMaster U., 1983; Wiegand lectr. U. Toronto, 1984; Edward U. Condon lectr. U. Colo., 1984; John A. Allan lectr. U. Alta., 1984; John E. Willard lectr. U. Wis., 1984; Owen Holmes lectr. U. Lethbridge, 1985; Walker-Ames prof. U. Wash., 1986; John W. Cowper disting. vis. lectr. SUNY, Buffalo, 1986; vis. prof. chemistry Tex. A&M U., 1986; Disting. vis. spkr. U. Calgary, 1987; Morino lectr. U. Japan, 1987; J.T. Wilson lectr. Ont. Scil. Ctr., 1987; Welsh lectr. U. toronto, 1987; Spiers Meml. lectr. Faraday divsn. Royal Soc. Chemistry, 1987; Polanyi lectr. Internat. Union Pure and Applied Chemistry, 1988; W.B. Lewis lectr. Atomic Energy of Can. Ltd., 1988; Consol. Bathurst vis. lectr. Concordia U., 1988; Priestman lectr. U. N.B., 1988; Killam lectr. U. Windsor, 1988; Herzberg lectr. Carleton U., 1988; Falconbridge lectr. Laurentian U., 1988; DuPont lectr. Ind. U., 1989; Luther lectr. U. Regina, 1989; Franklin lectr. Rice U., 1990; Laurier lectr. Wilfred Laurier U., 1990; Pratt lectr. U. Va., 1990; Goodrich lectr. Case Western Reserve U., 1990; Phillips lectr. U. Pitts., 1991; Albert Noyes lectr. U. Tex., 1992; John and Lois Dove Meml. lectr. U. Toronto, 1992; Fritz London lectr. Duke U., 1993; Castle lectr. U. South Fla., 1993; Linus Pauling lectr. Calif. Inst. Tech., 1994; Hagey lectr. U. Waterloo, 1995; Larkin Stuart lectr. U. Toronto, 1995; Hungerford lectr. York Club, 1995; disting. lectr. ser. Meml. U., 1995; John C. Polanyi Nobel Laureate lectr. U. Toronto, 1995; Floyd E. Bartell Meml. lectr. U. Mich., 1996; Christian Culture award lectr. Assumption U., 1996; Liversidge lectr. U. Sydney, 1996; disting. scientist lectr. Apotex, Inc., 1996; mem. sci. adv. bd. Max Planck Inst. Quantum Optics, Germany, 1982—92; mem. nat. adv. bd. on Sci. and Tech., 1987—89; hon. cons. Inst. Molecular Sci., Okazaki, Japan, 1989—94; bd. dirs. Steacie Inst. Molecular Scis., Ottawa, Ont.; founding mem., pres. Can. Com. of Sci. and Scholars; Beam Disting. vis. prof. U. Iowa, 1992; Charles M. and Martha Hitchcock prof. U. Calif., Berkeley, 1994; Young Meml. visitor Royal Mil. Coll., 1994; mem. Bd. of Premier's Coun., 1994; co-chair Internat. Consultative Group on Improving UN Rapid Reaction Capability. Editor (with F.G. Griffiths): The Dangers of Nuclear War, 1979; contbr. articles to jours., mags., newspapers; prodr. (film) Concepts in Reaction Dynamics, 1970. Mem. Queen's Privy Coun. for Can., 1992; founding mem. Can. Pugwash Com., 1960; Can. Ctr. for Arms Control and Disarmament. Decorated Officer Order of Can., Companion, knight Grand Cross Order St. John of Jerusalem; recipient Marlow medal, Faraday Soc., 1962, Centenary medal, Chem. Soc. Gt. Brit., 1965, Norandaaward, Chem. Inst. Can., 1967, award, Brit. Chem. Soc., 1971, Mack award and lectureship, Ohio State U., 1969, medal, Chem. Inst. Can., 1976, Remsen award and lectureship, Am. Chem. Soc., 1978, Nobel prize in Chemistry, 1986, Izaak Walton Killam Meml. prize, 1988, C. Polanyi award, Can. Soc. Chemistry, 1992, Floyd E. Bartell Meml. lectureship, U. Mich., 1996, Liversidge lectureship, U. Sydney, 1996, Christian Culture award and lectureship, Assumption U., 1996; co-recipient (with N. Bartlett) Steacie prize, 1965, Wolf prize in chemistry, Wolf Found., 1982; fellow Sloan Found., 1959—63, Guggenheim, 1979—80, Geoffrey Frew, 1996, Disting. Anniversary, Australian Nat. U., 1996. Fellow: Royal Soc. Chemisry (Michael Polanyi medal 1989), Royal Soc. Edinburgh, Royal Soc. Can. (founding mem., pres., com. on scholarly freedom, Marshall Tory medal 1977), Trinity Coll., U. Toronto (hon.), Royal Soc. London (Royal medal 1989, Bakerian lectureship and award 1994), Chem. Inst. Can. (hon.); mem.: NAS (fgn. mem.), Croation Acad. Scis. and Arts, Russian Acad. Scis. (foreign mem.), Pontifical Acad. Scis. (Rome), Am. Acad. Arts and Scis. (mem. com. on internat. security studies, hon. fgn.). Office: U Toronto Dept Chemistry Rm 262 80 St George St Toronto ON Canada M5S 3H6

POLAY, BRUCE, musician, conductor, educator; b. Bklyn., Mar. 22, 1949; s. Benjamin and Joan Polay; m. Louise Phillips, Dec. 17, 1983; children: Elizabeth, Adam, Rachel, Jacob, Julia. MusB, U. So. Calif., 1971; MA, Calif. State U., 1977; DMA, Ariz. State U., 1989. Music dir. So. Calif. Philharm., Long Beach, 1971-81; grad. asst. in theory and orch., asst. condr. univ. symphony Ariz. State U., Tempe, 1981-83; condr. Phoenix Symphony Guild Youth Orch., 1981-83; music dir. Knox-Galesburg (Ill.) Symphony, 1983—; prof. music Knox Coll., Galesburg, 1983—, chair music dept., 2001—05. Guest condr. in Belarus, Italy, Eng., Mexico, Romania, Russia, Ukraine, Spain; bd. dirs. Ill. Coun. of Orchs., 1992—; mem. adv. bd. Found. for New Music, 1996—; bd. advisors Barlow Endowment for Music Composition, 1999-2004; mem. music panel Ill. Arts Coun., 2004—. Orchestral compositions include Enconium, 1986, Perspectives, 1989, Concerto for Tenor Trombone, 1990, Tranquil Cycle for Tenor and Orch., 1992, Cathedral Images, 1993, Bondi's Journey: An Orchestral Rhapsody on Jewish Themes, 1994, Pictures For an Exhibition Piano, 1995, Anniversary Mourning for a cappella choir, 1996, Sandburg Cycle for Soprano, Tenor and Piano, 2000, Semi-Suite for Vin, Cello and Piano, 2001, Golden Oldie for Orchestra, 2001, Elegy for Violin and Small Orchestra, 2002, Suite of Preludes for Organ, 2002, Illumination for Orchestra, 2003, Suite on Catalonian Folksongs for String Orchestra, 2004, 3 Violin Duets on Catalonian Folksongs, 2005, 5 novelettes for harp and string orchestra, 2006, Sparkle for Orchestra, 2007, (solo piano) Ebb & Flow, 2007, String Quartet, 2008, Etude #1 Hommage, 2009. Recipient Ill. Condr. of Yr. award Ill. Coun. Orchs., 1997, 2004, Exceptional Achievement award Knox Coll., 1999, 2004, Programming of the Yr. award, 2006; named Ill. Orchestra of Yr. Knox-Galesburg Symphony, 1986, 2003, 2008, Cultural Leadership award Ill Coun. Orchestra, 2008. Mem. ASCAP, Am. Music Ctr., Phi Kappa Phi. Mem. Lds Ch. Avocations: reading, American history. Home: 1577 N Cherry St Galesburg IL 61401-1820 Office: Knox Coll Campus Box 5 Galesburg IL 61401-4999 Office Phone: 309-341-7208. Business E-Mail: bpolay@knox.edu.

POLDEN, DONALD, dean, law educator; BBA, George Washington U.; JD cum laude, Ind. U. Sch. Law. Law clerk for Hon. William C. Hanson, Chief Justice U.S. Dist. Ct. for So. Dist. Iowa, 1975—76; of counsel Hawkins and Norris, 1978—90; prof. law Drake U. Sch. Law, 1976—93; assoc. dean U. Memphis Sch. Law, 1991—93, dean, prof law, 1993—2003, Santa Clara U. Sch. Law, 2003—. Vis. prof. U. Louisville Sch. Law, 1984. Co-author: Employment relationships: law and practice, 1998; contbr. articles to law jours. Fellow: Coll. Labor and Employment Lawyers; mem.: Am. Law Inst. (elected mem. 1993), ABA (life). Office: Santa Clara U Sch Law El Camino Real Santa Clara CA 95053 Office Phone: 408-554-4362. E-mail: dpolden@scu.edu.*

POLEMITOU, OLGA ANDREA, accountant; b. Nicosia, Cyprus, June 28, 1950; d. Takis and Georgia (Nicolaou) Chrysanthou. BA with honors, U. London, 1971, PhD, Ind. U., Bloomington, 1981. CPA Ind. Asst. productivity officer Internat. Labor Office/Cyprus Productivity Ctr., Nicosia, 1971-74; cons. Arthur Young & Co., NYC, 1981; mgr. Coopers & Lybrand, Newark, 1981-83; dir. Bell Atlantic, Reston, Va., 1983-97; v.p. corp. auditing Columbia Energy Group, Herndon, 1997—2000; pres., CEO Aristion, Inc., Reston, Va., 2000—. Chairperson adv. coun. Extended Day Care Cmty. Edn., West Windsor Plainsboro, NJ, 1987—88. Contbr. articles to profl. jours. Bus. cons. project bus. Jr. Achievement, Indpls., 1984—85. Mem.: AICPAs, NAFE, Princeton Network Profl. Women, Va. Soc. CPAs, N.J. Soc. CPAs (sec. mem. in industry com.), Ind. CPA Soc., Nat. Trust Hist. Preservation. Avocations: water-skiing, tennis. Home: PO Box 2744 Reston VA 20195-0744 Office: 11921 Freedom Dr Ste 550 Reston VA 20190 Business E-Mail: opolemitou@aristion.com.

POLENSEK, SHARON HARTMAN, speech pathology/audiology services professional; b. Memphis, Nov. 24, 1962; d. Montague and Betty Shannon; m. Robert Polensek, Sept. 30, 2006; children: David, Danielle; m. David Hartman; children: Jonathan Hartman, Benjamin Hartman. BS in Audiology & Speech Pathology, Fla. State U., Tallahassee, 1984; MS in Hearing Sci., Purdue U., West Lafayette, IN, 1988; PhD in Anatomy, Ind. U., Indianapolis, 1993; MD, Med. Coll. Ohio, 1995. Cert. in Adult Neurology Am. Bd. Psychiatry & Neurology, 2004. Resident house officer otolaryngology U. Mich., Ann Arbor, 1995—2000; resident house officer neurology Baylor Coll. Medicine, Houston, 2000—03. Fellow otoneurology Emory U., Atlanta, 2003—04, asst. prof. neurology; acting chief audiology & speech pathology Atlanta VA Med. Ctr., Decatur, Ga., 2008—09, chief audiology & speech pathology, 2009—. Contbr. articles to profl. jours., chapters to books. Recipient VA Rehab. R&D nat. career devel. award, VA Rehab. R&D, 2005—08; Otologic Rsch. fellowship, Deafness Rsch. Found., 1989—90, fellowship, Ind. U., 1990—91. Mem.: Barany Soc., Am. Acad. Neurology, Alpha Omega Alpha. Office: Atlanta VA Med Ctr 1670 Clairmont Rd Decatur GA 30033 Office Phone: 404-321-6111 3140. Business E-Mail: sharon.polensek@va.gov.

POLENSKE, KAREN ROSEL, economics educator; b. Lewiston, Idaho, Mar. 20, 1937; d. Albert T. and Helen M. Polenske. BA in Home Econs., Oreg. State U., 1959; MA in Pub. Adminstrn. and Econs., Syracuse U., 1961; PhD in Econs., Harvard U., 1966. Instr., lectr. Harvard U., Cambridge, Mass., 1966-70, rsch. assoc. econ. rsch. project, 1966-72; sr. visitor faculty of econs. King's Coll., Cambridge U., Cambridge, Eng., 1970-71; assoc. prof. dept. urban studies and planning MIT, Cambridge, Mass., 1972-81, prof. dept. urban studies and planning, 1981—. Sr. econs. cons. World Bank (in China), Washington, 1988-90, CMT (in Kuwait), Cambridge, 1987-88, Devel. Alternatives Inc. (in Pakistan), Washington, 1987-88, Asian Devel. Bank (in China), Manila, 1988, 92, Boston Inst. for Developing Econs., Washington, 1990-91, UN Devel. Programme (in India), 1993; del. System of Nat. Accounts Revisions, UN, Vienna, Austria, 1988; vis. scholar exch. program NAS, Beijing, 1986; vis. prof. U. Queensland, Brisbane, Australia, 1983, U. Montpellier, France, 1985, Chinese Acad. Scis., 1988, 90-92, 94, U. Brasilia, 1994, Keio U., 1996; dir. Spl. Program in Urban and Regional Studies (SPURS), 1973-74, 91-94. Co-author: (with mem. of rsch. staff) State Estimates of the Gross National Product, 1947, 58, 63, State Estimates of Technology, 1963; author: The U.S. Multiregional Input-Output Accounts and Model, 1980; editor: Multiregional Input-Output Analysis, 1972, 73; co-editor: (with Jiri V. Skolka) Advances in Input-Output Analysis, 1976, (with Ronald E. Miller, Adam Z. Rose), Frontiers of Input-Output Analysis, 1989, (with Chen Xi Kang) Chinese Economic Planning and Input-Output Analysis, 1991; rev. editor Internat. Panel on Climate Control. Mem. Cambridge (Mass.) Com. on the Status of Women, 1978-80. Recipient Walter Isard Disting. Scholar award, 1996; Netherlands Inst. for Advanced Study fellow, 1980. Mem. Am. Econ. Assn., Regional Sci. Assn. (councillor at large 1990-93), Internat. Assn. for Rsch. in Income and Wealth, Internat. Input-Output Assn. (v.p. 1992-96, pres. 1997—). Avocations: birding, photography. Office: MIT 77 Massachusetts Ave Rm 9-535 Cambridge MA 02139-4307

POLER-BUZALI, GABRIELA, performing arts association administrator; b. Venezuela; arrived in US, 1995; BA in dance, Boston Conservatory; MA in arts adminstrn., Columbia U. Tchrs. Coll. Dancer, choreographer Infinity Dance Theater, NYC; exec. asst., mgr. NY Internat. Ballet Competition, 2000—05; devel. officer Tribeca Performing Arts Ctr., NYC, 2005—06; exec. dir. Philharm. Orch. of the Americas, NYC, 2006—09, José Limón Dance Found., NYC, 2009—. Office: José Limón Dance Found Ste 1105 307 W 38th St New York NY 10018 Office Phone: 212-777-3353. Office Fax: 212-777-4764. E-mail: info@limon.org.*

POLESE, KIM, software company executive; BS, U. Calif., Berkeley, 1984; student, U. Wash. Product mgr. Sun Microsys., 1988—95; co-founder, pres., CEO Marimba, Inc. (acquired by BMC Software), 1996—2000; chmn. Marimba, Inc. (acquired by BMC Software), 1996—2004; CEO SpikeSource, Inc., Redwood City, Calif., 2004—. Exec. coun. TechNet; bd. dirs. Technorati, Inc., 2004—06. Bd. dirs. Do Something, Global Security Inst., Long Now Found., U. Calif. President's Bd. Sci. and Innovation, Carnegie Mellon Computer Sci. Advisory Coun. Named one of Time Mags. Most Influential Ams., Most Influential Women in Technology, Fast Company, 2009; Fellow at Carnegie Mellon University's Ctr. for Engineered Innovation. Mem.: Silicon Valley Mfg. Group. Achievements include a pivotal role in launching Java. Office: SpikeSource Inc 2000 Seaport Blvd 2nd Fl Redwood City CA 94063*

POLESKIE, STEPHEN FRANCIS, retired art educator, artist, writer, publisher; b. Pringle, Pa., June 3, 1938; s. Stephen Francis and Antoinette Elizabeth (Chludzinski) P.; m. Jeanne Mackin, 1979. BS, Wilkes Coll., 1959; postgrad., New Sch. for Social Research, 1961. Owner Chiron Press, NYC, 1961-68; instr. Sch. Visual Arts, NYC, 1968; prof. art Cornell U., Ithaca, NY, 1969-2001, prof. emeritus, 2001—. Vis. critic Pratt Graphic Arts Center, N.Y.C., 1965-68; vis. artist Colgate U., Hamilton, N.Y., 1973, USSR, 1979, Escuela de Bellas Artes, Honduras, 1980, Loughborough Coll. Art and Design, Eng., 1989; vis. prof. U. Calif., Berkeley, 1976; reviewer in field. Contbr. short stories to mags. and book; one-man shows include Louis K. Meisel Gallery, N.Y.C., 1978-80, Galerie Kupinski, Stuttgart, Germany, 1979, Palace of Culture and Sci., Warsaw, Poland, 1979, Sky Art Presentation, MIT, 1981, Am. Ctr., Belgrade, 1981, William and Mary Coll., 1983, McPherson Art Gallery, Victoria, B.C., Can., 1984, Studio D'Ars, Milan, 1985, Gallery Flaviana, Locarno, Switzerland, 1985, Il Salatto Gallery, Como, Italy, 1985, Galleria Schneider, Rome, 1987, Mus. Sztuki Lodz, Poland, 1987, Alternative Mus., Lido di Spina, Italy, 1987, Galerie Klaus Lea, Munich, 1987, Patricia Carega Gallery, Washington, 1988, Nine Columns Gallery, Palermo, Italy, 1988, John Hansard Gallery, Southampton, Eng., 1989, Quai Art Gallery, Isle of Wight, Eng., 1989, Lee Art Gallery, Clemson (S.C.) U., 1990, Apogeeairway, N.Y.C., 1991, Nine Columns Gallery, Brescia, Italy, 1991, Glenn Curtiss Mus., Hammondsport, N.Y., 1993, Caproni Mus., Trento, Italy, 1995, Temple U., Rome, 1995, Gallery Modern Art, Maribor, Slovenia, 1995, Palazzo Communale, Todi, Italy, 1995, Upstairs Gallery, Ithaca, NY, 2006, Palazzo Della Pretura, Piacenza, Italy, Internat. Art Ctr., Kyoto, Japan, 2006, Terrain Gallery, NYC, 2007; represented in collections at Met. Mus., N.Y.C., Mus. Modern Art, N.Y.C., Victoria and Albert Mus., London, Whitney Mus., N.Y.C., Walker Art Ctr., Mpls., Tate Gallery, London, Fort Worth Art Center, Nat. Collection, Washington, State Mus., Lodz, Poland, others; pub. Onager Edits., 2004, publ. The Balloonist The Story of T.S. C. Lowe, 2005; pub., The Third Candidate, 2008, Grater Life, 2009. Am. Fedn. of Arts grantee, 1965; Carnegie Found. grantee, 1967; Nat. Endowment for Arts grantee, 1973; N.Y. State Council on Arts grantee, 1973; Creative Artists Public Service Program grantee, 1978; Best Found. grantee, 1985 Home: PO Box 849 Ithaca NY 14851-0849 Office Phone: 877-275-6388. Personal E-mail: onagereditions@aol.com.

POLETAEVA, ELENA, mathematician, researcher; b. Moscow, Oct. 15, 1960; MS in Math., Moscow State U., Russia, 1983; PhD in Math., Pa. State U., University Park, 1992; Docent in Math., Lund U., Sweden, 2002. Vis. rsch. instr. Mich. State U., East Lansing, 1992—93; postdoctoral fellow U. Paris 7, 1993—94; vis. rsch. instr. Mich. State U., East Lansing, 1994—95; guest prof. Max-Planck-Institut fur Mathematik, Bonn, Germany, 1996—97; rsch. assoc. in math. Lund U., Sweden, 1998—2002, temp. assoc. prof., 2002—. Contbr. articles to profl. jours. Recipient Rsch. Fellowship in Math., Sonderforschungsbereich 170, Gottingen, Germany, 1990, Institut des Hautes Etudes Scientifiques, Bures-sur-Yvette, France, 1998, 2003, Inst. for Advanced Study, 1999, Max-Planck-Institut fur Mathematik, Bonn, Germany, 1999, Math. Scis. Rsch. Inst., 2002, Rsch. grant, Anna-Greta and Holger Crafoords Found., Royal Swedish Acad. of Scis., 2001. Mem.: Lund U. Math. Soc. Office: Univ of Texas Pan American Dept of Math 1201 W University Dr Edinburg TX 78539 Office Fax: 46-46-222-4213. E-mail: elena@maths.lth.se.

POLEVOY, NANCY TALLY, lawyer, social worker, genealogist; b. NYC, May 27, 1944; d. Charles H. and Bernice M. (Gang) Tally; m. Martin D. Polevoy, Mar. 19, 1967; children: Jason Tally, John Gerald. Student, Mt. Holyoke Coll., 1962—64; BA, Barnard Coll., 1966; MSW, Columbia U., 1968, JD, 1986. Bar: N.Y. 1987. Caseworker unmarried mothers' svc. Louise Wise Svcs., NYC, 1967, caseworker adoption dept., 1969-71; caseworker Youth Consultation Svc., NYC, 1968-69; asst. rsch. scientist, psychiat. social worker NYU Med. ctr., NYC, 1973-81; adv. ct. apptd. spl. advs. Manhattan Family Ct., NYC, 1981-82; cons. social work, 1981-86; matrimonial assoc. Ballon, Stoll & Itzler, 1987, Herzfeld & Rubin, P.C., 1987-88; practice NYC. Contbr. articles to profl. jours. Mem. parents' adv. bd. Riverdale Country Sch., 1988—93; mem. outreach bd. Manhattan divsn. United Jewish Appeal Fedn., 1990—94, exec. bd. Manhattan divsn., 1992—94, mem. met. campaign cabinet, 1994—95, mem. task force aging, 2004—; trustee Jewish Assn. Svcs. to Aged, 1996—, v.p., 1999—2003; bd. dirs. Ctr. Jewish History, 1996—; archives com. Ctrl. Synagogue, 1991—2005, chair, 1994—2005; trustee Am. Jewish Hist. Soc., 1992—, asst. treas.,

1995—98, v.p., 1998—2003, 2005—. Recipient French Govt. prize, 1963, honor for lifetime cmty. svc., United Jewish Appeal Fedn. N.Y., 2003. Mem.: NASW, Acad. Cert. Social Workers, N.Y. State Bar Assn., Assn. Bar City of N.Y., Barnard Coll. Alumni Assn. (v.p. 1966, class pres. 1966 1996—). Home and Office: 1155 Park Ave New York NY 10128-1209

POLEWAY, CHRISTOPHER J., former publishing executive; b. Bklyn., 1958; m. Poleway; 2 children. BA, St. Bonaventure Univ., Olean, NY; MBA, Fordham Univ. Mgr. fin. sys. HBO, 1982—88; gen. mgr. Corp. Fin. Reporting, 1988—91; Circulation Planning Mgr. Fortune, 1991—92, asst, bus. mgr., 1992—94, advertising bus. mgr., 1994—97, dir. of fin. and op., 1997—99, v.p. and gen. mgr., 1999—2000, chief op. officer, 2000—01; pres. Fortune/Money Group, 2001—07.

POLFLIET, SARAH JEAN, physician; b. Austin, Minn., July 4, 1975; d. Richard John and Charlotte Bertha Polfliet. BS in Physiology, U. Calif., Santa Barbara, 1998; MD, U. Va., Charlottesville, 2002; MD in Psychiat., Law, U. Calif., San Francisco, 2006. DEA Certification Med. Bd. of Calif., 2003, lic. MD Med. Bd. of Calif., 2003. Sec. in cmty. rels. U. Calif., 1997—98, asst. instr. of biology lab., 1998, resident physician San Francisco, 2002—06; physician Schuman-Liles Cmty. Psychiatry Clinic, Oakland, Calif., 2003—06; pvt. practice in psychiat. and psychopharmacology, San Francisco, 2006—; chief resident intensive svcs. Langley Ptnr. Psychiat. Inst., 2006. Rsch. asst. U. Va., Dept. of Psychiatry, Charlottesville, Va., 1999; co-leader for long-term women's depression group U. Calif., San Francisco, 2004—, psychiatry physician, women's mood and hormone clinic, 2004—05, jr. attending, 2005—, rsch. co-investigator, dept. psychiatry, 2005—; psychiatry physician, women's high-risk obstetric clinic San Francisco Gen. Hosp., 2004—05. Contbr. numerous articles and presentation to profl. jours. and confs.; author: Where Do Seagulls Go at Night, 2003. Vol. for cmty. outreach program St. Thomas Aquinas Ch., Charlottesville, Va., 1998—2002; vol. Magic Cir. Protective Shelters, Charlottesville, Va., 1999—2002; med. student selection com. U. of Va., Sch. of Medicine, 2001—02; vol. spkr. Med. Youth Soc., San Francisco, 2003—06; vol. St. Elizabeth's Ho. for Battered Women, 2006—. Recipient Julius R. Krevans award for Clin. Excellence, U. Calif., San Francisco, 2003, Pathology Honors, U. Va., Sch. of Medicine, 1999—2000, Edwin Alston award, U. Calif. San Francisco Psychiatric Residency Program, 2006; Bowman's scholarship, U. Va., Sch. of Medicine, 1999—2000, Forensic Fellow, U. Calif. San Francisco, Psychiatry and Law Program, 2006—07. Fellow: Am. Psychiat. Assn. (hon.); mem.: Am. Assn. Psychiat. and Law, U. Calif., Santa Barbara, Alumni Assn. (hon.), Alpha Omega Alpha (hon.), Assn. Women Psychiatrists (hon.), No. Calif. Psychiat. Assn. (hon.), U. Va., Sch. of Medicine, Alumni Assn. (hon.). Achievements include research in evaluating training of psychiatry residents about neuroleptic medications; rural suicide outreach programs in Virginia, including composition of suicide outreach survey and meta-analysis of data to further assist tele-psychiatry program.

POLHAMUS, BARBARA, behavioral scientist; d. Helen and Leslie Polhamus. PhD, MPH, U. N.C., Chapel Hill, 1991—97. Registered dietitian Am. Dietetic Assn., 1982. Nutrition dir. Dorchester Ho. Multi-Svc. Ctr., Mass., 1982—84; nutrition dir., maternal and child health Mass. Dept. Pub. Health, Boston, 1984—91; rsch. assoc. U. N.C., Chapel Hill, 1998—2000; behavioral scientist CDC, Nat. Ctr. for Chronic Disease Prevention and Health Promotion, Divsn. Nutrition Phys. Activity & Obsesity, Atlanta, 2000—. Tech. cons., Ukraine micronutrient survey CDC, Atlanta, 2002. Contbr. chapters to books, articles to profl. jours., sci. material for web sites. Recipient award of Excellence Pub. Health Tng. and Nutrition Team award, 2005; grantee, Inst. Nutrition, 1994; fellow, Dannon Inst., 1998. Mem.: APHA (elected sect. mem. 2002—04). Liberal. Avocations: yoga, hiking, travel. Office: CDC 4770 Buford Hwy NE MS K-25 Atlanta GA 30341 Personal E-mail: bfp9@cdc.gov.

POLI, KENNETH JOSEPH, editor, writer, photographer; b. Bklyn., June 8, 1921; s. Joseph H. and Irene (Seeman) P.; m. Virginia Osk, Dec. 14, 1946; 1 child, Bruce. Student, Goddard Coll., 1938-40. Writer, photographer North Atlantic Area Office ARC, NYC, 1946-49. Editorial cons., 1965— Author Critical Focus Column, 1972-83; editor: External House Mags., Internat. Nickel Co., N.Y.C., 1949-53, Leica Photography mag., E. Leitz, Inc., N.Y.C., 1953-65; assoc. editor Popular Photography mag., Ziff-Davis Pub. Co., N.Y.C., 1965-68, sr. editor, 1968-1970, editor, 1970-83, cons. 1983-87; cons. editor Photography Ann., 35-mm Photography, Photography Directory and Buying Guide, 1970-83; contbr. articles to photog. jours. and encys. With inf. U.S. Army, 1942-45, PTO. Decorated Purple Heart medals, Bronze Star. Mem. Am. Photog. Hist. Soc., Photographic Adminstrs., Circle of Confusion, Mensa. Home and Office: Apt 6167 1 Jefferson Ferry Dr South Setauket NY 11720-4727

POLI, ROBERTO, oil industry executive; b. 1938; Degree in econs., Florence U., 1963. Prof. bus. fin. U. Cattolica, Milan, 1966—98; founder, pres. Poli-Morelli & Ptnrs. S.p.A.; pres. Prof. Roberto Poli e Associati S.p.A.; chmn. Rizzoli Corriere delle Sera Group, 1983—84, Publitalia, 1995—96; mem. bd. dirs. IRI, 1994—97; chmn. Eni S.p.A., Rome, 2002—. Bd. dirs. Fininvest S.p.A., Mondadori S.p.A., Merloni Termosanitari S.p.A., G.D. S.p.A., Brafin S.A.P.A.; cons. in field; pres. Publitalia S.p.A. Office: Eni SpA Piazzale Enrico Mattei 1 00144 Rome Italy

POLIAKOFF, GARY A., lawyer, educator; b. Greenville, SC, Nov. 25, 1944; s. Herman and Dorothy (Ravitz) P.; m. Sherri D. Dublin, June 24, 1967; children: Ryan, Keith. BS, U. S.C., 1966; JD, U. Miami, 1969. Bar: Fla. 1969, DC 1971, Colo. 1999. Founding prin. Becker & Poliakoff, P.A., Hollywood, Coral Gables, Naples, Sarasota, West Palm Beach, Orlando, Ft. Walton Beach, Fla., Prague and Beijing, 1973—, Boca Raton, Ft. Lauderdale, Fla., Ft. Myers, Melbourne, Port St. Lucie, Tallahasse, Tampa Bay, NYC, mng. shareholder, 1973—2008. Adj. prof. condominium law and practice Nova Southeastern U.; panelist Nat. Confs. Cmty. Assn.; testified before coms. of the US Senate on Condominiums; lectr. condominium seminars Fla. Bar; participant Fla. Law Revision Council; cons. to State Legis. and the White House in drafting Condominium and Coop. Abuse Relief Act, 1980; mem. condominium study commn. State of Fla., 1990; chmn. State of Fla. Advisory Coun. on Condominiums, 1992, 93.; atty. Town of Southwest Ranches. Author: The Law of Condominium Operations, 1988; co-author: Florida Condominium Law and Practice, 1982, The Florida Bar Continuing Legal Education, 1982, 2007; co-author: New Neighborhoods: The Consumer's Guide to Condominium, Co-op and HOA Living, 2009; contbr. articles to legal jour. Mem. pres. adv. group U. SC, U.S.C. Ednl. Found., 1999-2001. Recipient Judge Learned Hand award Am. Jewish Com. for devel. of co-ownership housing law, 1999; Legal Elite award Fla. Trend Mag., 2004, 05, 06, 08, Diamond award Honoree for Excellence in Bus. Leadership So. Fla. Bus. Jour., 2002, 04-06, 08; named Outstanding Adj. Prof. of Yr., Best Lawyers of America, Best Mcpl. Law Practitioners in America.; named one of Top Fla. Lawyers. Mem. ABA (adv. nat. conf., nat. conf. commr., Uniform State Laws), Fla. Bar, Coll. Cmty. Assn. Lawyers (bd. gov.), Scribes. Home Phone: 954-434-7375; Office Phone: 954-985-4150. Personal E-mail: gpoliakoff@becker-poliakoff.com.

POLIAN, BILL, professional football team executive; b. NYC, Dec. 8, 1942; m. Eileen Polian; children: Lynn, Chris, Brian, Dennis. Grad., NYU. Asst. coach Manhattan Coll., 1965-67; asst. football coach U.S. Mcht. Marine Acad., 1968-70, head baseball coach, 1971-75; scout Kansas City Chiefs, 1978-82; dir. player pers. Winnipeg Blue Bombers, Canada, 1983; dir. pers. Buffalo Bills, 1984-85, gen. mgr., v.p. adminstrn., 1985—93; gen. mgr. Carolina Panthers, 1994—96; pres., gen. mgr. Indpls. Colts, 1997—. Mem. competition com. NFL, 1989—. Named NFL Exec. of Yr., 1988, 91, 95, 96, 99. Office: Indianapolis Colts 7001 W 56th St Indianapolis IN 46254*

POLICANO, ANDREW J., dean, finance educator; b. July 4, 1949; m. Pamela Z. Policano; children: Emily, Keith. BS in math., SUNY, Stony Brook, 1971; MA in economics, Brown U., 1973, PhD in economics, 1976. Asst. prof. U. Iowa, Iowa City, 1975-79, assoc. prof. dept. economics, 1979-81, prof., chair dept. economics, 1984-87, sr. assoc. dean academic affairs, 1987-88; prof. dept. economics Fordham U., NYC, 1981-84, asst. chair, dir. grad. studies, 1982-83; rsch. assoc. Ctr. for Study of Futures Markets Columbia U., NYC, 1982-86; dean divsn. social & behavioral sci. SUNY, Stony Brook, 1988-91; dean Sch. Bus., U. Wis., Madison, 1991—2001, Kuechenmeister Prof. Bus., 2001—04; dean Pual Merage Sch. Bus., U. Calif., Irvine, 2004—, prof. economics/pub. policy, 2004—. Guest prof. Inst. Advanced Studies, Vienna, Austria, 1985; dir. Nat. Guardian Life, Madison, 1991-2004, PIC Wis., 1995-2002, Badger Meter, 1997—; mem. Wis. Glass Ceiling Commn., 1995-2000. Recipient Disting. Alumnus award SUNY, Stony Brook, 1994. Mem. Assn. to Advance Collegiate Schools of Bus. (bd. dirs., 1997-98). Office: U Calif Paul Merage Sch Bus 350 SB Irvine CA 92697-3125 Office Phone: 949-824-8470. Business E-Mail: dean@merage.uci.edu.*

POLICASTRO, FELICE, research scientist; b. Ciudad Bolivar, Bolivar, Venezuela, July 31, 1967; s. Pietro and Antonietta Policastro; m. Miriam Mariela Marfisi; children: Pietro, Felice. MBA (hon.), Edgewood Coll., Madison, Wis., 1997; BS cum laude, U. de Oriente, 1993. CPA Venezuela. Incoming auditor, restaurant mgr., fin. advisor Hoteles Gaetas C.a., Puerto La Cruz, Anzoategui, Venezuela, 1987—89; co-owner, adminstrv. mgr. Maquinas Games C.a., Puerto La Cruz, 1990—92; auditor Amundaray, Villalta & Assocs., Puerto La Cruz, Venezuela, 1993; tchg. asst. U. de Oriente, Puerto La Cruz, 1989—92, lectr., 1993; tchg. and rsch. asst. U. Tex. Pan Am., Edinburg, 1998—. Supr. Oscar Rennebohm Libr., Edgewood Coll., Madison, 1996; internat. cons. Le Tre Sorelle Restaurant, West Palm Beach, Fla., 2000. Mem.: Anzoátegui Coll. of Bachelors in Pub. Acctg., Venezuelan Fedn. of Bachelors in Pub. Acctg., Fin. Mgmt. Assn.

POLICELLI, MAURA, legislative staff member; BA, Coll. of the Holy Cross, Worcester, Mass. Staff mem., Rep. Rosa DeLauro US House of Reps., Washington, dist. advisor new members office, Office of the Minority Leader, chief of staff to Rep. Jane Harman, 2001—03, chief of staff to Rep. Gabrielle Giffords, 2007—. Democrat. Office: 502 Cannon House Office Bldg Washington DC 20515 Office Phone: 202-225-2542. Office Fax: 202-225-0378. Business E-Mail: maura.policelli@mail.house.gov.*

POLICINSKI, CHRIS, food products executive; BA, Univ. Notre Dame, 1980; MBA, NYU. Mgmt. positions with Pillsbury Co., Kraft Gen. Foods; v.p. strategy, bus. & internat. develop. Land O'Lakes Inc., Arden Hills, Minn., 1997—99, exec. v.p. COO dairy foods value added group, 1999—2002, exec. v.p., COO dairy foods, 2002—05, pres., CEO, 2005—. Bd. dirs. Grocery Manufacturers Am.; bd. dir. Nat. Milk Prod. Fedn., Nat. Coun. Farmer Cooperatives. Bd. dirs. Greater Twin Cities United Way, Minn. Bus. Partnership; trustee Grad. Inst. Cooperative Leadership. Office: Land O'Lakes Inc 4001 Lexington Ave N Saint Paul MN 55126-2998 Mailing: Land O'Lakes Inc PO Box 64101 Saint Paul MN 55164-0101

POLICINSKI, EUGENE FRANCIS, non-profit organization executive, syndicated columnist, editor, radio and television personality, producer; b. South Bend, Ind., Aug. 31, 1950; s. E.T. and Margaret C. (O'Neill) P.; m. Kathleen Beta O'Donnell Powell, Aug. 19, 1972; children: Ryan, David. Degree in Journalism and Polit. Sci., Ball State U., 1972; student, Nashville Sch. Law, 2005—07. Corr. Gannett News Svc., Washington, 1979-82; Wash. editor USA Today, Arlington, Va., 1982-83, page one editor, 1983-85, mng. editor sports, 1989—96; spl. asst. to chmn./CEO Freedom Forum, Arlington, Va., 1996-98; Wash. editor Freedom Forum website, 1998-99; dep. dir. First Amendment Ctr., Nashville, 1999—2004, exec. dir., 2004—; v.p., 2006—. Host, commentator USA Today Sky Radio, Arlington, 1992—95; host Newseum Radio, 1998—2001; adj. faculty Winthrop U., 1999—; exec. prodr. Speaking Freely (PBS), 2001—05; host Freedom SIngs, 2003—. Founding editor USA Today Baseball Weekly, 1991. Bd. advisors Ctr. Study Sport in Soc., 1995—; trustee US Sports Acad., 1997—2006, Watkins Coll. Art and Design, 2001—04; dir. J-IDEAS program Ball State U., 2003—04. Named one of 100 Most Important People in Sports Sporting News, 1992-93, 95, Sports Person of Yr., U.S. Sports Acad., 1996; named to Journalism Hall of Fame, Ball State U., 1989, Alumni of Yr., 1996. Mem. NATAS (gov. 2004), Am. Soc. Newspaper Editors, Soc. Profl. Journalists, Assn. Educators in Journalism and Mass Comms, Internat. Press Inst., Newspaper Assn. Am. Found. Avocations: sailing, bicycling, golf. Office: First Amendment Center Office of Exec Dir 1207 18th Ave S Nashville TN 37212-2807 Home Phone: 615-460-9314; Office Phone: 615-727-1600. Business E-Mail: gpolicinski@fac.org.

POLICY, CARMEN A., professional sports team executive; b. Youngstown, Ohio, Jan. 26, 1943; s. Albert and Ruby (Tisone) P.; m. Aug. 8, 1964 (div. Mar. 1989); children: James, Daniel, Edward, Kerry, Kathy; m. Gail Marie Moretti, June 27, 1991. Grad., Youngstown State U., 1963; JD, Georgetown U., 1966. Bar: Ohio 1966, Va. 1966, D.C. 1966. Assoc. Nadler & Nadler, Youngstown, 1966-68; asst. prosecutor City of Youngstown, 1968-69; ptnr. Flask & Policy, Weimer & White, Youngstown, 1969-90; spl. counsel to atty. gen. State of Ohio, 1970-91; v.p., gen. counsel San Francisco 49ers, NFL, 1983-90, pres., 1990-99; pres. CEO SF4, 1990—98; pres., CEO & co-owner Cleve. Browns, 1998—2004, consultant, 2004—; prodr. Casa Piena Cabernet Sauvignon, Napa Valley. Mem. various coms. NFL, 1990—; bd. dirs. World League Am. Football, N.Y.C., 1991—. Com. mem. various charities, Youngstown, 1969-90, San Francisco, 1990—. Mem. Va. Bar Assn., Ohio Bar Assn., D.C. Bar Assn. Roman Catholic. Avocations: scuba diving, hiking. Home and Office: 1330 Jones St Apt 503 San Francisco CA 94109

POLIMENI, JOHN MATTHEW, economics professor; b. Schenectady, NY, Nov. 21, 1972; s. John Joseph and Catherine Marie Polimeni. BS in Math., Rensselaer Poly. Inst., 1994; MA in Econs., SUNY, Albany, 1996; PhD in Ecol. Econs., Rensselaer Poly. Inst., 2002. Cert. graduate studies in Econs. NY State Public Svc. Commn. Asst. prof. econs. Albany (N.Y.) Coll. Pharmacy, 2004—. Hon. mem. Scientific Coun. Romanian Nat. Acad. Sci., 2006—. Contbr. Young Faculty Rsch. award, Rensselaer Polytech. Inst., 2004, Fulbright scholar. Fellow Internat. Congress Chemistry and Environ.; mem. Acad. Political Sci., Am. Assn. Advancement of Sci., Am. Econ. Assn., Am. Health Econs. Assn. (charter mem.), Am. Statistical Assn., European Soc. Ecol. Econs., Game Theory Soc., Global Health Edn. Consortium, Internat. Assn. Energy Econs., Internat. Health Econ. Assn., Internat. Soc. Ecol. Econ., Internat. Studies Assn., Soc. European Anthropology, Soc. Industrial and Applied Maths., US Assn. Energy Econs., US SOc. Ecol. Econs. (charter mem.). Presbyterian. Office: Albany Coll Pharmacy 106 New Scotland Ave Albany NY 12208 Office Phone: 518-694-7384.

POLIN, JANE L., foundation official; b. NYC, Sept. 30, 1958; BA, Wesleyan U., Middletown, Conn., 1980; MBA, Columbia U., 1988. Asst. dir. ann. giving Wesleyan U., 1980—82; centennial fund assoc. Met. Opera Assn., NYC, 1982—84; devel. officer Columbia U., NYC, 1984—88; program mgr., comptr. GE Fund, Fairfield, Conn., 1988—99; v.p. cmty. devel. and corp. affairs Sperry & Hutchinson, Inc., 1999—2000, philanthropic advisor, 2001—. Author: Acts of Achievement: The Role of Performing Arts Centers in Education, 2003, Transforming Arts Teaching: The Role of Higher Education, 2007. Panelist arts-in-edn. Nat. Endowment for Arts, Washington, 1989—90, 1994—95, NEH, 1997; adv. bd. mem. ARC, 1991—99, United Way Am., 1991—99, Inst. for Internat. Econs., 1995—99, Young Audiences, NYC, 1991—2000, mem. Advt. Coun., 1998—2003; judge Frances Hesselbein Cmty. Innovation Fellows Program, 2001—02, Peter F. Drucker Award for Nonprofit Innovation, 1996—2000; bd. dirs. Fred Friendly Seminars, 2005—08. Mem.: Alpha Delta Phi. Home and Office: 67 Riverside Dr Apt 7D New York NY 10024-6136 Office Fax: 212-873-1568. Personal E-mail: janepolin@aol.com.

POLINER, GARY A., insurance company executive; Joined as atty. Northwestern Mutual Life Ins. Co., Milw., 1977, sr. v.p., CFO, sr. v.p., CFO, chief investment officer, 2007—08, exec. v.p., pres. IPS & affiliates, 2008—. Office: Northwestern Mutual 720 E Wisconsin Ave Milwaukee WI 53202-4797

POLING, KERMIT WILLIAM, minister; b. Elkins, W.Va., Oct. 1, 1941; s. Durward Willis and Della Mae (Boyles) P.; m. Patricia Ann Groves, June 12, 1965; children: David Edward Elson, Mikael Erik. Diploma in Bible, Am. Bible Sch., 1966; BA in Bible, Reed Coll. Religion, 1968; AA, W.Va. U., 1970; ThD, Zion Theol. Sem., 1971; postgrad., Wesley Theol. Sem., 1974; LLD, Geneva Theol. Coll., 1980; DSL (hon.), Berean Christian Coll., 1981; postgrad., Mansfield Coll., U. Oxford, Eng., 1986, Mansfield Coll., U. Oxford, 1990, postgrad., 1991; D Ecumenical Rsch., St. Ephrem's Inst. for Oriental Studies, 1989; BRE, Am. Bible Coll., 1991; M of Herbology, Emerson Coll., 1994. Ordained to ministry United Meth. Ch., 1967. Pastor Parkersburg-Crossroads (W.Va.) Cir., 1967-70; asst. sec. W.Va. Ann. Conf., 1967-69; pastor Hope-Halleck Morgantown Cir., 1970-76, Trinity-Warren Grafton (W.Va.) Charge, 1976-83, 1st Trinity Pennsboro (W.Va.) Charge, 1983-97, South Parkersburg United Meth. Ch., 1997—2004. Editor local ch. news; instr. Bible Bodkin Bible Inst., 1975-75, United Meth. Lay Acad., 1992—2004; mem. staff Taylor County Coop. Parish, 1976-83; coord. Hughes River Coop. Parish, 1983-86; mem. chaplains com. Grafton City Hosp., 1976-82; mem. coun. Ctr. d'Etudes et d'Action Oecumeniques, 1972-74; bishop in Partibus of Tayma. Author: A Crown of Thorns, 1963, A Silver Message, 1964, History of the Halleck Church, 1970, Eastern Rite Catholicism, 1971, From Brahmin to Bishop, 1976, Cult and Occult: Data and Doctrine, 1978, The Value of Religious Education in Ancient Traditional Churches, 1993, Anniversary History of Trinity Church, Pennsboro, 1997; editor: Jane's Heirs; contbr. articles and poems to religious jours. Decorated Royal Afghanistan Order of Crown of Amanullah, Royal Order of the Golden Eagle of Napoca, Byzantine Order of Leo the Armenian, Order of Polonia Resitutia, Mystical Order of St. Peter, knight Grand Cross of the Order of St. Dennis of Zante, companion Naval Order of U.S.; recipient Good Citizenship award Doddridge County, 1954, Silver medal Ordre Universel du Merit Humain, Geneva, 1973, Commendation for Outstanding Achievement in Ministry, Ohio Ho. of Reps., 1988; recipient U.S. Heritage award, 2002, St. Eugene Medal of Merit, 2009; named Chief of Dynastic Ho. of Polanie-Patrikios, 1988, Prince of the Holy Roman Empire, 2005. Mem. SAR, Assn. Bible Tchrs. (founder), Internat. Platform Assn., Naval Order U.S., Sovereign Order St. John Jerusalem, Ritchie County Ministerial Assn. (pres. 1984-97), Order Sacred Cup, Knights of Malta, Order of the Crown of Lauriers. Home: 101 E Myles Ave Pennsboro WV 26415

POLING, PARKER HAMILTON, legislative staff member; Comm. coord. House Edn. & Workforce Com., Washington, 2003; dep. chief of staff to congressman Patrick McHenry US House of Reps., 2007, chief of staff, 2007—. Republican. Mailing: US House Reps 224 Cannon House Office Bldg Washington DC 20215 Office Phone: 202-225-2576. Office Fax: 202-225-0316.*

POLIS, JARED SCHUTZ, United States Representative from Colorado, entrepreneur, philanthropist; b. Boulder, Colo., May 12, 1975; s. Stephen and Susan (Polis) Schutz. BA in Polit. Sci, Princeton U., NJ. Sales mgr. Blue Mountain Arts; exec. dir. internet startups Bluemountain.com, FrogMagic, Dan's Chocolates; founder Proflowers.com/Proflowers Inc., San Diego, 1998, Sonora Entertainment Grp., 2001, TechStars, 2006; mem. US Congress from 2nd Colo. dist., 2009—. Mem. exec. com. Colo. Dem. Party, 2000—07, Boulder County Dems., 2000—07; former chmn. Colo. State Bd. Edn.; co-chair Colo. Commn. HS Improvement; chair fin. literacy study grp. Nat. Assn. Sate Bds. Edn.; bd. mem. Latin Am. Rsch. & Svc. Agy., Colo. Anti-Defamation League, Colo. Consumer Health Initiative, Colo. Conservation Voters. Founder Jared Polis Found., 2000, Cmty. Computer Connection, Aurora, Colo.; founder, superintendent New America Sch., Thornton, Colo., 2004; co-founder Acad. Urban Learning, Denver, 2005; bd. dirs. Watershed Sch., Boulder. Recipient Pacesetter award in edn., Boulder Daily Camera, 2007, Ohtli award, Denver consul gen. of Mex., Cmty. Builder award, Anti-Defamation League, Cmty. award, Kauffman Found., Martin Luther King, Jr. Humanitarian award; named an Ernst & Young Entrepreneur of Yr., 2000, Outstanding Philanthropist, State of Colo., 2006, Outstanding Young Coloradoan, Colo. Jaycees; named one of Forty Under 40, Denver Bus. Journal, 2000. Democrat. Office: US Congress 501 Cannon House Office Bldg Washington DC 20515-0602 also: Dist Office 4770 Baseline Dr Ste 220 Westminster CO 80303 Office Phone: 202-225-2161, 303-484-9596. Office Fax: 202-226-7840.*

POLIS, NANCY E., automotive executive; b. Dayton, Ohio, Dec. 22, 1953; BS, Wright State Univ., 1976; MBA, Univ. Dayton, 1979. Fin. mgmt. positions in Delco Moraine div., GM tech. staff, GM of Canada group, GM comptroller's staff, fin. dir. corp. & legal staff GM Corp., Detroit, 1976—96, sec. public policy com., corp. sec., 1996—. Bd. mem. Visiting Nurse Assn. Mem.: Soc. Corp. Secretaries & Governance Professionals. Office: GM Corp 300 Renaissance Ctr Detroit MI 48265*

POLISH, SHELDON S., lawyer; b. Cleve., Feb. 14, 1943; BS in Acctg., Ohio State U., 1965; JD, Cleve. State U., 1969. CPA Fla., 1974; bar: Ohio 1969, Fla. 1974. Dir. tax., office mng. ptnr. Ernst & Young, Ft. Lauderdale, Fla.; shareholder, chmn. Ft. Lauderdale tax dept. Greenberg Traurig, P.A.; shareholder Berger Singerman, Ft. Lauderdale, Fla., 2003—. Grievance com. Fla. Bar, 2008—. Recipient Pres.'s award for Outstanding Svc. to the Jewish Fedn., Cmty. Svc. award, Jewish Cmty. Ctr., Esther Lowenthal Cmty. Svc. award, Jewish Fedn. Young Leadership award; named one of Top 100 Attys., Worth mag., 2005, Top Lawyers in Tax, Estates and Trusts, South Fla. Legal Guide, 2005—07. Mem.: Fla. Inst. CPA, AICPA, Fla. Bar Assn., ABA, Greater Ft. Lauderdale Tax Coun. Office: Berger Singerman 350 E Las Olas Blvd Ste 1000 Fort Lauderdale FL 33301 Office Phone: 954-712-5132. Business E-Mail: spolish@bergersingerman.com.

POLISI, JOSEPH WILLIAM, academic administrator; b. NYC, Dec. 30, 1947; m. Elizabeth Polisi; 3 children. BA in Polit. Sci., U. Conn., 1969; MA in Internat. Relations, Tufts U., 1970, MusM, 1973, M of Mus. Arts, 1975; DMA, Yale U., 1980; DHL (hon.), Ursinus Coll., Collegetown, Pa., 1986; MusD (hon.), Curtis Inst. Music, 1990; DMA, New England Conservatory Music, 2001; DHL (hon.), Juilliard Sch., 2005; DFA (hon.), Fordham U., Bronx, NY, 2006. Exec. officer Yale Sch. of Music, New Haven, 1976-80; dean of faculty Manhattan Sch. of Music, NYC, 1980-83; dean Coll. Conservatory of Music U. Cin., 1983-84; pres. The Juilliard Sch., NYC, 1984—. Spkr. in field. Performances as bassoonist throughout the U.S.; contbr. articles to various publs. in U.S. and France; author: The Artist as Citizen, 2005, American Muse: The Life & Times of William Schuman, 2008 Dir. Edward John Noble Foundation, Irene Diamond Fund, Samuels Found. Named Educator of Yr., Musical Am. Internat. Dir. Performing Arts, 2005. Fellow: Am. Acad. Arts and Sciences; mem.: Royal Acad. Music London (hon.). Office: Juilliard Sch Office of Pres 60 Lincoln Center Plz New York NY 10023-6588

POLITE, EVELYN C., retired elementary school educator, evangelist; b. Pineland, SC, Dec. 25, 1937; d. Martin and Mary Brantley Coger; m. Horace Polite, Jan. 1, 1958 (dec. Jan. 1987); children: Horace Lenton, Tracy Polite Floyd. BS, Allen U., 1960; M in Elem. Edn., Armstrong-Savannah (Ga.) State U., 1976; cert. specialist of arts in theology, Zoe U., Jacksonville, Fla., 2000; PhD in Christian Counseling, Zoe U., 2001. Tchr. math. Beaufort County Bd. Edn., Bluffton, SC, 1960—61, Florence County Bd. Edn., Florence, SC, 1961—63, Jasper County Bd. Edn., Ridgeland, SC, 1963—64, 1991—92, Savannah Pub. Schs., 1964—90; math. tutor Dept. Family and Children, Savannah, 1992—94; ret., 1994. Test-item writer Ednl. Testing Svc., Princeton, NJ, 1990; dir. Widows Harvest Ministries, Savannah, Ga.; care and counseling min. Coastal Cathedral Ch. of God. Pres. 42d St Civic Club, Savannah, 2000—03; exec. v.p. Cuyler-Brownsville Neighborhood Orgn., Savannah, 2001—02; chmn. bd. dirs. House of Hope Cmty. Outreach Ctr. Recipient Outstanding Tchr. award, Math.-Sci. Roundtable, Atlanta, 1990. Mem. Ch. Of God. Avocations: world missions, travel, physical fitness, reading Christian literature. Home: 33 Wild Heron Villas Rd Savannah GA 31419-8981 Office: PO Box 23485 Savannah GA 31403 Office Phone: 912-341-4220. Personal E-mail: evelyn33@bellsouth.net.

POLITE, LETTIE WILSON, retired middle school educator, librarian; b. Asheville, NC, Jan. 5, 1930; d. Lester Vernon and Argatha Foster Wilson; m. Harold Malverse Polite (dec.); children: Harold M. II, Joyce P. Carson. BS in Math. and Social Studies, NC Coll. (now NC Ctrl. U.), Durham, 1951; cert. in libr. sci., Allen U., Columbia, SC, 1955; MEd, NC U., Cullowhee, 1981. Tchr. libr. Asheville (NC) City Schs., 1953—64, tchr. 7th grade. math., 1965—72, tchr. 7th grade math., 8th grade sci., 1972—73, tchr. 6th grade math., 1973—91, tchr. 7th grade math., 1991—92; libr. St. Martin De Porres Sch., New Haven, 1964—65. Tutor, mentor Delta Ho. of Asheville, 1982—; co-chair Uniting for Racial Justice, Women's Internat. League of Peace and Freedom, Asheville, 1994—2005; del. Non-Governmental Orgn./World Conf. on Racism, Durban, South Africa, 2001; vol. Reuter Ctr. for Creative Retirement, 1998—; 1st v.p., asst. treas. Asheville Alumnae of Delta Ho., Inc., 1982—; adv. bd. African Am. Affairs Ministry Diocese of Charlotte, NC, 1972—; eucharistic min., mem. choir, pastoral coun., Cath. Daus. of Am. Ct. 412 Basilica of St. Lawrence, Asheville. Recipient cert. of excellence, Leadership Asheville Forum, 2004, NC Black Cath. Recognition award, Diocese of Charlotte, 2004. Mem.: NAACP, Nat. Coun. Negro Women, Links, Delta Sigma Theta. Democrat. Avocations: reading, crafts, travel, singing. Home: 33 Erskine Ave Asheville NC 28801

POLITI, BETH KUKKONEN, publishing services company executive; b. Englewood, NJ, Sept. 18, 1949; d. Andrew and Beatrice G. (Druskin) Kukkonen; m. Joseph Politi, Oct. 21, 1982; children: Andrew, Joseph. BS in Mktg., Miami U., Oxford, Ohio, 1971. Media buyer Schwab, Beatty & Porter, Inc., 1971-72; media planner Adler, Schwartz & Connes, 1972-73; media buyer/planner Schwab Beatty divsn. Marstellar, 1973-74; dir. insert advt. Benjamin Co., Inc., Elmsford, NY, 1975-78, prodn. mgr., 1978-80, editor supr., 1979-83, v.p. client svcs., 1980-83, assoc. pub., 1981—83; v.p. Bergen County Profl. Svcs., Ft. Lee, NJ, 1983—2007; pres. MarketValue Appraisal Svcs, Inc., 2007—08. Freelance proofreader Montage Media, Mahwah, NJ, 1999—2003. Trustee bd. edn. Pascack Valley Regional HS Dist., 1999—; v.p. Pascack Valley Regional H.S. Dist., 2002—06, pres., 2006—08; dist. fee artibration com. Office of Atty. Ethics of Supreme Ct. NJ, 2001—05, ethics com., 2006—; tax assessor Borough Bogota, NJ, 2004—07; del. exec. com. Bergen County Sch. Bd. Assn., 2003—, v.p. exec. com., 2005—06, pres., 2006—08. Home: 4 Smoke Rise Ct Montvale NJ 07645-1139 Personal E-mail: bkpoliti@hotmail.com.

POLITO, ANTHONY PETER, law educator; b. Bklyn., Feb. 8, 1964; s. Silvestro and Antonietta Barbara (Vairo) P.; m. Kristin Cecile, June 19, 1999. SB, MIT, 1986; JD, Harvard U., 1989; LLM, NYU, 1995. Bar: NY 1990, US Tax Ct. 1990. Clk. hon. Jack B. Jacobs Del. Ct. of Chancery, Wilmington, 1989—90; assoc. Debevoise & Plimpton, NYC, 1990—93, Richards & O'Neil, NYC, 1993—94, Willkie Farr & Gallagher, NYC, 1994-95; asst. prof. law Suffolk U., Boston, 1995-98, assoc. prof. law, 1998—2002, prof., 2002—. Vis. prof. law Boston Coll. Law Sch., 1999-2000, Bklyn. Law Sch., 2007-08. Exec. editor: Harvard Jour. Law & Pub. Policy. Mem. Phi Beta Kappa, Sigma Xi. Office: Suffolk U Law Sch 120 Tremont St Ste 260 G Boston MA 02108-4977 Office Phone: 617-573-8518. Office Fax: 617-573-8143. Business E-Mail: apolito@suffolk.edu.

POLITZER, HUGH DAVID, physicist, educator; b. NYC, Aug. 31, 1949; s. Alan A. and Valerie T. (Diamant) P. BS, U. Mich., 1969; PhD, Harvard U., 1974. Jr. fellow Harvard U. Soc. Fellows, 1974-77; mem. faculty Calif. Inst. Tech., 1975—, prof. theoretical physics, 1979—, exec. officer for physics, 1986-88. Author: Asymptotic Freedom: An Approach to String Interactions, 1974; appeared in Fat Man and Little Boy, 1989. Recipient J.J. Sakurai prize, 1986; fellow NSF, 1969-74, Sloan Found., 1977-81, Woodrow Wilson grad. fellow, 1969-74, Guggenheim fellow, 1997-98; co-recipient High Energy and Particle Physics prize European Phys. Soc., 2003, Nobel Prize in Physics, 2004. Mem. Am. Physical Soc., Harvard Soc. Fellows, Phi Beta Kappa. Achievements include discovery of asymptotic freedom in the theory of the strong interaction. Office: Calif Inst Tech High Energy Physics 1201 E California Blvd Mail Code 452-48 Pasadena CA 91106-3368 Business E-Mail: politzer@theory.caltech.edu.*

POLIZZOTTI, BRIAN DAVID, medical researcher; b. Meadowbrook, Pa., May 2, 1978; s. David Matthew and Agatha Judith Polizzotti. Degree in Chem. Engring., Pa. State U., 1998; BSc, Temple U., Phila., 2000; MS in Materials Sci. & Engring., U. Del., Newark, 2002, PhD, 2006. Cert. in GE green belt six sigma, 2008, in TRIZ basic course, GE, 2008; intellectual property scientists 2008. Rsch. assoc. Howard Hughes Med. Inst., Boulder, Colo., 2006—07; lead scientist Gen. Electric Co.'s Global Rsch. Ctr., Niskayuna, NY, 2007—; rsch. fellow Harvard Med. Sch. & Children's Hosp., Boston, 2009—. Dean fellowship, U. Del., 2000—01. Mem.: Materials Rsch. Soc., Am. Chem. Soc. Office: Children's Hosp Boston 320 Longwood Ave Boston MA 02115 Personal E-mail: brian.polizzotti@gmail.com.

POLK, DAVID BRENT, pediatrician, educator; BS in Chemistry and Biology summa cum laude, Ouachita U., 1980; MD, U. Ark., Little Rock, 1984. Diplomate Am. Bd. of Pediat., 1999. Dean's prof. of pediat. and cell and devel. biology Vanderbilt U., Nashville, 1990—, dir., Vanderbilt digestive disease rsch. ctr. Office: Vanderbilt University 2215 Garland Ave MRBIV 1025 Nashville TN 37232 Office Fax: 615-343-5323. E-mail: d-brent.polk@vanderbilt.edu.

POLK, DENNIS, electronics executive; BS acctg., Santa Clara Univ. CPA. Audit mgr. Grant Thornton LLP; fin. mgmt. positions from corp. contr. to sr. v.p., CFO Savoir Technology Group Inc., 1995—2000; v.p. fin. DoveBid Inc., 2000—01; sr. v.p. corp. fin., CFO SYNNEX Corp., Fremont, Calif., 2002—06, CFO, COO, 2006—07, COO, 2007—. Office: SYNNEX Corp 44201 Nobel Dr Fremont CA 94538-3178

POLK, JAMES RAY, journalist; b. Oaktown, Ind., Sept. 12, 1937; s. Raymond S. and Oeta (Fleener) P.; m. Bonnie Becker, Nov. 4, 1962; children: Geoffrey, Amy; m. Cara Bryn Saylor, June 21, 1980; 1 child, Abigail. BA, Ind. U., 1962. With A.P., Indpls., 1962-65, Milw., 1965, Madison, Wis., 1966-67, Washington, 1967-71; investigative reporter Washington Star, 1971-75; correspondent NBC News, Washington, 1975-92; sr. producer CNN Spl. Assignment, 1992—. Pres. Investigative Reporters and Editors, Inc., 1978-80, chmn. bd., 1980-82, nat. coll. chmn., 1983-90. With U.S. Navy, 1955-58. Recipient Pub. Affairs Reporting award, Am. Polit. Sci. Assn., 1961, Raymond Clapper Meml. award, 1972, 1974, Pulitzer prize for nat. reporting on Watergate, 1974, Sigma Delta Chi award, 1974, Nat. Headliner awards, 2d pl. award TV documentary, 1996, 2003, investigative reporting, 1993, Emmy award for coverage of Oklahoma City bombing, 1996, Ind. U. Disting. Alumni award, Journalism award, Nat. Air Disaster Found., 2007, Peabody award, 2007, Dupont-Columbia award, 2008; named to Ind. Journalism Hall of Fame, 1994. Mem. Phi Kappa Psi. Office: CNN Center Atlanta GA 30303

POLK, MICHAEL B., consumer products company executive; b. 1960; married. BS in Ops. Rsch. & Indsl. Engring., Cornell U., 1982; MBA in Mktg. & Gen. Mgmt., Harvard Bus. Sch., 1987. Mfg., rsch. & devel. The Procter & Gamble Co., 1982—85; joined Kraft Foods, Inc., 1987, various position brand mgmt. & sakles, 1987—97, v.p. category sales mgmt. & strategy, 1997—98, pres. Asia Pacific Region, 1999—2001, pres. biscuits, snacks, & confections segment, 2001—03; exec. v.p., gen. mgr. Post cereal divsn. Kraft Foods N.Am., 1998—99, group v.p., 2001—03, Kraft Foods Internat., 2000—01; sr. v.p. mktg., pres. Unilever Best Foods N.Am. Unilever, 2003—05; pres. Unilever USA, 2005—07, Unilever Americas, 2007—. Bd. dirs. The Yankee Candle Co., Inc., 2003—, Retail Industry Leadership Assn., Grocery Mfrs. America & Food Products Assn., GS1, Yellowstone Nat. Park. Office: Unilever Americas 800 Sylvan Ave Englewood Cliffs NJ 07632 Office Phone: 201-894-7760.*

POLL, ROBERT EUGENE, JR., bank executive; b. Urbana, Ill., Apr. 16, 1948; s. Robert E. Sr. and Dorothy (Baker) P.; children: Alexandra, Bianca. BA, Kenyon Coll., 1970; MBA, Ind. U., 1972. V.p. Chase Manhattan Bank, NYC, 1972-78; assoc. Lazard Freres & Co., NYC, 1978-82, mng. dir., mgr. mcpl. divsn., 1985-98; gen. ptnr. William Blair & Co., Chgo., 1982-84; sr. mng. dir. Poll Financial, LLC, 1998—; CEO Deane Group, 2009—; co-chmn. Chief Consol. Mining Co., 2002; pres., CEO Bernard Techs., Inc., 2002; mng. dir., chief investment officer Castleton Ptnrs., 2005—06; mng. dir. Kingspoke Fin., 2008—; pres. Starrett City Assn., 2009—. Adv. bd. Pub. Fin. Inst., N.Y.C., 1976, Worldvest. Trustee Citizens Budget Commn.; chmn. Ind. U. Bus. Conf. Mem. N.Y. Acad. Sci., Tavern Club (Chgo.), N.Y. Athletic Club, Ind. U. Kelley Sch. Bus. Alumni Assn. (pres.). Home: Starrett City Assn 150 E 58th St New York NY 10155 Personal E-mail: rppollfin@att.net. Business E-Mail: rpoll@deanegroup.com.

POLLACK, DANIEL H., real estate company executive; s. Michael Alan Pollack. BA in Real Estate, Ariz. State U., Tempe, 2002, BA in Mgmt., 2002. Cert. real estate sales Calif. Dept. Real Estate, qualified lic. gen. contractor Ariz. Registrar Contractors. V.p. Pollack Investments, Mesa, Ariz., 2002—. Com. mem. Jewish Fedn. Real Estate Affinity, Scottsdale, 2005; bd. dirs. Gainey Ranch Cmty. Assn., Scottsdale, Ariz., 2006. Named Bus. Person of the Yr., Ariz. Future Bus. Leaders Am., 2006. Mem.: Internat. Coun. Shopping Ctrs. (assoc.; state next generation divsn. chairperson 2005). Office: Pollack Investments 1136 W Baseline Rd Mesa AZ 85210

POLLACK, ELISA ERALI, language educator; d. David Rudolph Erali and Barbara Joan English; m. Travis Pollack, May 4, 1992; children: Rebecca Erali, Sarah Erali. MA, PhD, U. NC, Chapel Hill, 2004. Zertifikat Deutsch als Fremdsprache U. Bonn, Germany, 1991. Rsch. fellow deutscher akademischer austausch dienst Ctr. Gen. Linguistics, Berlin, 1997—98; asst. prof. German and Spanish Wofford Coll., Spartanburg, SC, 2007—. Mem.: Philol. Assn. Carolinas, Am. Assn. Tchrs. German, Soc. Germanic Linguistics, Phi Beta Kappa. Office: Wofford Coll 429 North Church St Spartanburg SC 29303 Office Fax: 864-597-4549. Business E-Mail: pollackee@wofford.edu.

POLLACK, EUNICE G., history professor; b. NYC; d. Hyman and Jennie Pollack; m. Stephen Harlan Norwood, June 1975. PhD, Columbia U., NYC. Editor: Encyclopedia of American Jewish History (Editor's Choice award, 2007), Antisemitism in America; contbr. articles. Mem.: Assn. Jewish Studies, Orgn. Am. Historians, Am. Hist. Assn. Office: Univ N Tex History Dept 1121 Union Cir Denton TX 76201 Personal E-mail: egpollack@aol.com. Business E-Mail: epollack@unt.edu.

POLLACK, GERALD ALEXANDER, economist, educator, federal agency administrator; b. Vienna, Jan. 14, 1929; came to US 1938, naturalized 1944; s. Stephen J. and Tini (Herschel) P.; m. Patricia E. Sisterson; children: Nora P. Silverman, Carol A. BA, Swarthmore Coll., Pa., 1951; MA, MPA, Princeton U., 1953, PhD, 1958. Corp. economist Leeds & Northrup Co., Phila., 1958-62; officer in charge internat. payments U.S. Dept. State, Washington, 1962-63; internat. economist Joint Econ. Com. of Congress, Washington, 1963-65; chief economist Office Spl. Rep. for Trade Negotiations, 1964; dep. asst. sec. U.S. Dept. Commerce, Washington, 1965-68; v.p. Loeb, Rhoades & Co., NYC, 1968-69, Bendix Corp., Southfield, Mich., 1969-70, Citibank, NYC, 1970-71; internat. economist Exxon Corp., NYC, 1971-86; v.p., chief economist Overseas Shipholding Group, NYC, 1986-89; assoc. prof. fin. Pace U., NYC, 1990-94; assoc. dir. for internat. econs. Bur. Econ. Analysis, U.S. Dept. Commerce, 1994-99. Contbr. articles to profl. jours. Bd. dirs. Jamaica Estates Assn., 1976-80, Oakwood Friends Sch., Poughkeepsie, N.Y., 1979-89; trustee Lindley Murray Fund, 1990-94; mem. Greenwich Dem. Town Com., 1992-94, 2001—; clk. Flushing Monthly Meeting Soc. of Friends, 1990-94; mem. Greenwich Rep. Town Meeting, 1999-2003; bd. mem. Greenwich Forum on War and Peace, 2006-. With US Army, 1953—55. Mem.: Violoncello Soc., Coun. on Fgn. Rels., Fairfield County Symphony Soc., Phi Beta Kappa. Democrat. Mem. Soc. Of Friends. Avocations: cello, classical music, photography, hiking, bicycling. Personal E-mail: gapollack@hotmail.com.

POLLACK, GERALD LESLIE, physicist, researcher, educator; b. Bklyn., July 8, 1933; s. Herman and Jennie (Tenenbaum) P.; m. Antoinette Amparo Velasquez, Dec. 22, 1958; children: Harvey Anton, Samuela Juliet, Margolita Mia, Violet Amata. BS, Bklyn. Coll., 1954; Fulbright scholar, U. Gottingen, 1954-55; MS, Calif. Inst. Tech., 1957, PhD, 1962. Physics student trainee Nat. Bur. Standards, Washington, 1954-58, solid state physicist, 1961-65, cons. Boulder, Colo., 1965-70; assoc. prof. dept. physics Mich. State U., East Lansing, 1965-69, prof., 1969—2005, prof. emeritus, 2005—; cons. NRC, Ill. Dept. Nuclear Safety; physicist Naval Med. Rsch. Inst., Bethesda, Md., summer 1979. Physicist USAF Sch. Aerospace Medicine, San Antonio, Tex., summer 1987; adj. prof. Dept. Physics, Colo. Sch. Mines, Golden, 2005-06. Co-author (with D.R. Stump): Electromagnetism, 2002; contbr. articles to profl. jours. Fellow Am. Phys. Soc.; mem. Am. Assn. Physics Tchrs. Business E-Mail: pollack@msu.edu.

POLLACK, IAN FREDRIC, physician, researcher; b. Holliswood, NY, Aug. 26, 1960; s. Jonah and Roberta Minnie (Wainick) P.; m. Constance Shenk, Aug. 15, 1982; children: Benjamin Nathan, Andrew Maxwell. BS magna cum laude, Emory U., 1980; MD, Johns Hopkins U., 1984. Intern in surgery U. Pitts., 1984-85, resident in neurosurgery, 1985-91, postgrad. fellow dept. neurobiology, 1988-90, asst. prof. dept. neurosurgery, 1990-96, assoc. prof., 1996—99, prof., 1999—. Walter Dandy prof., 2001—, co-dir. Brain Tumor Ctr., 1996—. Chmn. brain tumor strategy group. Contbr. articles to New Eng. Jour. Medicine, Cancer Rsch., Exptl. Neurology, Jour. Neurosurgery, Cancer, Jour. Neurosurgery Rsch., Neurosurgery, Brain Rsch., others. Van Wagenen fellow Am. Assn. Neurol. Surgeons, 1991; recipient Resident Rsch. award ACS, 1990, Pitts. Neurosci. Soc., 1989, Preuss award Am. Assn. Neurol. Surgeons and Congress Neurological Surgeons Joint Sect. on Tumors, 1989, Young Clinician Investigator award Am. Assn. Neurol. Surgeons, 1992. Mem. AAAS, Congress of Neurol. Surgeons, Phi Beta Kappa, Alpha Omega Alpha. Achievements include research in the growth factor response properties of human brain tumor cells in culture, the role of selective inhibitors on tumor growth in culture, molecular markers of brain tumor prognosis and immunotherapeutic strategies for brain tumors. Office: U Pitts Dept Neurosurgery 9402 Presbyn Univ Hosp 230 Lothrop St Pittsburgh PA 15213-2536 also: Childrens Hosp Pitts Dept Neurosurgery 3705 5th Ave Pittsburgh PA 15213-2583 E-mail: ian.pollack@chp.edu.

POLLACK, JOE, retired columnist, critic, writer; b. Bklyn., Feb. 3, 1931; s. Samuel H. and Anna (Weisman) P.; m. Joan Henriksen, Mar. 6, 1952 (div. 1964); children: Wendy, Dara, Sharon; m. Carol Atchison, Dec. 1, 1964 (dec. 1993); m. Ann Lemons, Nov. 20, 1994. BJ, U. Mo., 1952. Sports writer St. Louis Globe-Democrat, 1955-61; dir. pub. rels. St. Louis Football Cardinals, 1961-72; critic, columnist St. Louis Post-Dispatch, 1972-95. Critic Sta. KSDK-TV, St. Louis, 1973-88, Sta. KMOV-TV, St. Louis, 1988-92; commentator Sta. KMOX, St. Louis, 1960-85, Sta. KWMU, St. Louis, 1994—. Author: Joe Pollack's Guide to St. Louis Restaurants, 1988, updated, 1992, (with Ann Lemons Pollack) Beyond Toasted Ravioli, 1998, Beyond Gooey Butter Cake, 2001, The Great St. Louis Eats Book, 2005; contbr. numerous articles to mags. Recipient St. Louis Media Hall of Fame. Mem. Am. Theatre Critics Assn., Profl. Football Writers Assn., Am. Soc. Profl. Journalists. Home: 7417 Oxford Dr Saint Louis MO 63105-2915 Office Phone: 314-862-3321. Personal E-mail: jpalfood@aol.com.

POLLACK, JONATHAN DUKER, political science professor; b. New London, Conn., June 23, 1947; s. Dale Pollack and Esther Duker-Pollack; m. Barbara Marom, Jan. 8, 1989; children: Joshua Hoffman, Deena Marom Messinger, Noah Duker. BA in Polit. Sci., Rutgers Coll., New Brunswick, NJ, 1969; MA, U. Mich., Ann Arbor, 1975; PhD, U. Mich., 1976. Rsch. fellow Harvard U., Cambridge, Mass., 1975—78; staff mem. RAND Corp., Santa Monica, Calif., 1978—84, sr. staff mem., 1984—88, chmn. polit. sci. dept., 1988—90, corp. rsch. mgr. internat. policy, 1990—94, sr. advisor internat. policy, 1994—2000; chmn. strategic rsch. dept. Naval War Coll., Newport, RI, 2000—04, prof. of asian and pacific studies, 2000—. Bd. mem. U. RI Hillel, Kingston, 2006—08. Mem.: Nat. Com. U.S.-China Relations, Com. Internat. Security and Arms Control, Nat. Acad. Sci., Internat. Inst. Strategic Studies, Coun. Fgn. Rels., Phi Beta Kappa.

POLLACK, MARSHA, secondary school educator; d. Harry and Rose Grunberg; m. Bertram Pollack, July 14, 1944; 1 child, Meredith Pollack-Richman. BA, Bklyn Coll., 1968, MS, 1973; Specialist Diploma in Adminstrn. and Supervision, Queens Coll., 2003. Cert. tchr. Nat. Bd. Profl. Tchg. Standards, 2001. Tchr. N.Y.C. Dept. of Edn., Bklyn. and Queens, 1968—2002, asst. prin. Queens, 2002—03, tchr./coach/staff devel., 2003—. L.E.A.D. tchr. N.Y.C. Dept. of Edn., 1998—2002, nat. staff devel., 2000; profl. devel. Jericho Mid. Sch., 2003; lesson plan-abstract evaluator Internat. Reading Assn., 2003—05. CAL grantee, Chase Manhattan, 2001. Mem.: Am. Fedn. Tchrs., Nat. Coun. Tchrs. English, Phi Delta Kappa, Internat. Reading Assn., ASCD. Avocations: law, educational research, writing. Office Fax: 718-831-4008. Personal E-mail: bjmphp@aol.com. Business E-Mail: mpollac2@nycboe.net.

POLLACK, ROBERT ELLIOT, biologist, educator, writer; b. Bklyn., Sept. 2, 1940; s. Ephraim Hyman and Molly (Pollack) P.; m. Amy Louise Steinberg, Dec. 23, 1961; 1 child, Marya BA in Physics, Columbia U., 1961; PhD in Biology, Brandeis U., 1966. Asst. prof. pathology Med. Sch. NYU, NYC, 1969-70; sr. scientist Cold Spring Harbor Lab., NY, 1971-75; prof. microbiology Med. Sch., SUNY-Stony Brook, 1975-78; prof. biol. sci. Columbia U., NYC, 1978—; dean Columbia Coll., NYC, 1982-89. Bd. dirs., chmn. sci. adv. bd. Tapestry Pharms., 1994-; instr. Pratt Archtl. Sch., Bklyn., 1970; lectr. psychiatry Ctr. for Psychoanalytic Tng., Columbia U., 1999—, dir. Ctr. for the Study of Sci. and Religion, 1999—; vis. prof. pharmacology Albert Einstein Coll. Medicine, Bronx, N.Y., 1977-92; dean's disting. lectr. in Humanities, Columbia Med. Sch., 2000; lectr. Rosenthal Colloquium, March of Dimes, 1989; McGregory lectr. Colgate U., 1979; du Vigneaud lectr. Med. Sch., Cornell U., 1983.

Co-editor: Readings in Mammalian Cell Culture, 1973, 3d rev. edit., 1981, Signs of Life, 1984 (translations in 7 langs., Lionel Trilling award 1995), The Missing Moment, 1999, The Faith of Biology and the Biology of Faith, 2000; mng. editor BBA Revs. on Cancer, 1980-86; contbr. numerous rsch. articles on molecular cell biology to profl. jours. Trustee N.Y. Found., 1988-96, Brandeis U., 1989-94, Solomon Schechter Sch. of N.Y.C., 1996-98; fellow World Econ. Forum, 1995—; bd. overseers List Coll. of the Jewish theol. Sem. of Am., 1996-99; pres. Jewish Campus Life Fund, Columbia U., 1997-2001. Recipient Rsch. Career Devel. award NIH, 1974, Alexander Hamilton medal, 1989, Lionel Trilling award Columbia U., 1995; NIH spl. fellow Weizmann Inst., Rehovot, Israel, 1970-71; grantee Nat. Cancer Inst., NIH, 1968-92, Am. Cancer Soc., 1985-94; John Simon Guggenheim fellow, 1993. Fellow AAAS; mem. N.Y. Acad. Scis., Am. Soc. Microbiology. Office: Columbia U Fairchild Hall 1212 Amsterdam Ave # Mc2419 New York NY 10027-7003 Office Phone: 212-854-2409. Business E-Mail: pollack@columbia.edu.

POLLACK, ROBERT HARVEY, psychology professor; b. NYC, June 26, 1927; s. Solomon and Bertha (Levy) P.; m. Martha Dee Katz, Aug. 20, 1948; children: Jonathan Keith, Lance Michael, Scott Evan. BS, CCNY, 1948; MS, Clark U., Worcester, Mass., 1950, PhD, 1953. Lectr. U. Sydney, Australia, 1953-61; spl. rsch. fellow Columbia U., NYC, 1960-61; chief div. cognitive devel. Inst. Juvenile Rsch., Chgo., 1961-63, dep. dir. rsch., 1963-69; from clin. asst. prof. to clin. assoc. prof. rsch. U. Ill. Coll. Medicine, Chgo., 1962-67; prof. psychology U. Ga., Athens, 1969-96, chair grad. program. exptl. psychology, 1970-78, chair grad. study com., 1978-86; prof. emeritus, 1996—; chair grad. program in life-span psychology U. Ga., Athens, 1988-96. Editor: The Experimental Psychology of Alfred Binet, 1969; contbr. over 100 articles and chpts. to profl. publs. Cpl. U.S. Army, 1945-46. Grantee Nat. Inst. Child Health and Human Devel., 1965, 67, 72, 78. Fellow AAAS, Am. Psychol. Assn.; mem. Am. Assn. Sex Edn., Counsellors and Therapists, Gerontol. Soc. Am., Australian Psychol. Soc., Soc. for Researching Child Devel., Soc. for Sci. Study Sex, Sigma Xi. Democrat. Avocations: travel, stamp collecting/philately, opera, military history. Office: U Ga Dept Psychology Athens GA 30602 Office Phone: 706-542-3084. Business E-Mail: bpollack@uga.edu.

POLLACK, RONALD FRANK, healthcare organization executive, lawyer; b. NYC, Feb. 21, 1944; s. Max Louis and Hanna Esther (Borchardt) Pollack Baruch; m. Rebecca Lucy Bolling, Jan. 8, 1972; children: Sarah Shoshana, Abraham Max, Martin Landrum. BA, Queens Coll., 1965; JD, NYU, 1968. Bar: N.Y. 1968, D.C. 1978, U.S. Ct. Appeals (D.C. cir) 1970, U.S. Ct. Appeals (5th cir.) 1971, U.S. Ct. Appeals (6th cir.) 1974, U.S. Supreme Ct. 1973. Atty. Ctr. on Social Welfare Policy and Law, NYC, 1968-73; founder, exec. dir. Food Research and Action Ctr., NYC, 1970-80; dean Antioch Sch. Law, Washington, 1980-83; exec. dir. Families U.S.A., Washington, 1983—. Sec. treas., bd. dirs. Food Research and Action Ctr., Washington, 1980—; mem. civil legal services D.C. Jud. Conf. Com., 1980-83; appointee Pres.'s Adv. Commn. on Consumer Protection and Quality in the Health Care Industry, 1997-98. Author: If We Had Ham, We Could Have Ham and Eggs...If We Had Eggs: A Study of the National School Breakfast Program, 1972, Out to Lunch: A Study of USDA's Child Care Feeding and Summer Feeding Programs, 1974; co-author: On the Other Side of Easy Street: Myths and Facts About the Economics of Old Age, 1987. Treas. Jewish Fund for Justice, 1985-88, bd. dirs., 1985-93; bd. dirs. Am. Jewish World Service, Self-Help Community Services, 1974-77; mem. domestic adv. bd., project rev. bd. U.S.A. for Africa/Hands Across Am., 1986-88; v.p. of bd. dirs. Burgundy Farm Country Day Sch., 1988-90, pres. 1990-91; bd. dirs. Americans for Health, 1986-91. Arthur Garfield Hays Civil Liberties fellow, 1967-68; research fellow Legal Services Corp., Washington, 1978-80 Office: Families USA 1201 New York Ave Washington DC 20005

POLLACK, SEYMOUR VICTOR, computer science educator; b. Bklyn., Aug. 3, 1933; s. Max and Sylvia (Harrison) P.; m. Sydell Altman, Jan. 23, 1955; children: Mark, Sherie. BChemE, Pratt Inst., 1954; MChemE, Bklyn. Poly. Inst., 1960. Lic. chem. engr., Ohio. Engr. Schwarz Labs., Mt. Vernon, NY, 1954-55; design engr. Curtiss-Wright, Wood-Ridge, NJ, 1955-57, Fairchild Engines, Deer Park, NY, 1957-59, GE, Evendale, Ohio, 1959-62; rsch. assoc. U. Cin., 1962-66; prof. computer sci. Washington U., St. Louis, 1966-95, prof. emeritus, 1995—. Cons. Mo. Auto Club, St. Louis, 1969-82, United Van Lines, Fenton, Mo., 1984-86, Computer Sci. Accreditation Bd., N.Y.C., 1985-93. Author: Structured Fortran, 1982, UCSD Pascal, 1984, Studies in Computer Science, 1983, The DOS Book, 1985, Turbo Pascal Programming, 1991; cons. editor Holt Rinehart & Winston, N.Y.C., 1979-86. Bd. dirs. Hillel orgn., Washington U., 1983-84. Recipient Alumni Achievement award Pratt Inst., 1966, Outstanding Teaching award Burlington Northern Found., 1987. Mem. Assn. for Computing Machinery, Am. Assn. for Engring. Edn. Jewish. Avocations: trombone, walking, classical and jazz piano, jogging. Office: Washington U PO Box 1045 Saint Louis MO 63188-1045 Personal E-mail: shepsl@hotmail.com. Business E-Mail: svp@cse.wustl.edu.

POLLACK, STANLEY P., lawyer; b. NYC, Apr. 23, 1928; s. Isidor and Anna (Shulman) P.; m. Susan Aronowitz, June 16, 1974; 1 child, Jane. BA, NYU, 1948; JD, Harvard U., 1951; LLM in Taxation, NYU, 1959. Bar: N.Y. 1951, U.S. Dist. Ct. (so. dist.) N.Y. 1955. Sole practice, NYC, 1955-61; v.p., gen. counsel James Talcott, Inc., NYC, 1961-73; sr. exec. v.p. Rosenthal & Rosenthal Inc., NYC, 1973—. Served to j.g. lt. USNR, 1951-54. Mem. Bklyn. Bar Assn. (banking com., bankruptcy com.), Fed. Bar Council, Assn. Comml. Fin. Atty.'s (pres. 1968), Factors Chain Internat. Clubs: Harvard (N.Y.C.). Home: 6 Peter Cooper Rd New York NY 10010-6701 Office: Rosenthal & Rosenthal Inc 1370 Broadway # 2 New York NY 10018-7302

POLLACK, STEPHEN J., investment company executive, stockbroker; b. NYC, Aug. 25, 1937; s. Harold S. and Gladys H. P., m. Joan Honig Scott, May 18, 2008 BS in Econs., U. Pa., 1960; grad., Wharton Sch. Bus. V.p. retail sales Drexel Burnham Lambert, NYC, 1960-77; 1st v.p. investments Dean Witter Reynolds Inc., NYC, 1978-98; 1st v.p., fin. advisor Morgan Stanley, NYC, 1998—, v.p., fin. advisor, 2001—03; with Pollack Asset Mmgt., 2004—06; sr. v.p. investments Lempert Bros. Internat. USA, NYC, 2006—, mng. dir., 2007—08, Pollack Asset Mgmt., 2008—, Pollack Asst. Mgmt., 2009. Pres. B'nai B'rith Gotham, NYC; exec. v.p. Cosmopolitan League City of Hope; v.p. cir. mem. Whitney Mus., NYC; treas. Sutton Pl. Synagogue, pres. Havurah Group. With USAR, 1966. Recipient Double Chai Citation, State of Israel Bonds, 1984, Appreciation award City of Hope, 1984, Kiter Key Club award Franklin Funds, Million Dollar Club Svc. award, B'nai B'rith Internat. award. Mem. NASD, Securities Investor Protection Corp., Internat. Assn. Fin. Planners, Assn. Investment Brokers (bd. dirs.), Youngmen's Philanthropic League (bd. dirs.), Internat. Study Rsch. Inst., Exec. Forum, Fin. Investment Analysts Group, Fin. Analysts-Money Mgrs. Soc., Town Club, Atrium Club, Schuylkill Country Club, Wharton Sch. Club, U. Pa. Club, Yale Club, East River Tennis Club, Fresh Meadow Country Club, Matterhorn Sports Club, East Side Rep. Club, Knickerbokker Rep. Club, Berks County Tennis Club, Penn. Club (charter), Friars Club. Home: 245 E 40th St Apt 14E New York NY 10016-1714 Office: Pollack Asset Mgmt 245 E 40th St New York NY 10016 Personal E-mail: stevejpollack@gmail.com.

POLLAK, DAVE J., investment company executive, former political organization administrator; BA in Polit. Sci. & Economics, Colorado Coll., 1986; MA in Pub. Policy, Harvard U., 1990. V.p. Donaldson, Lufkin & Jenrette, 1990—95; 1st v.p. PaineWebber, 1995—2000; investment banker UBS, 2000—07; founder Dem. Leadership for the 21st Century; co-chair NY State Dem. Com., 2007—08; NY state dir. Obama for America, 2008; dir. Wetherly Capital Group, LLC, NYC, 2009—. Mem. Democratic Nat. Com., 2006—; bd. mem. NYC Dept. Youth & Cmty. Devel. Bd. mem. Advocates for Children, Ctr. for Arts Edn. Named one of The Top Fresh Faces in New York, The NY Daily News, NY's Power Babies, The NY Observer. Mem.: Saxophone Club (NY chmn. 1996). Democrat. Office: Wetherly Capital Group LLC 300 Park Ave #17 New York NY 10022 Office Phone: 212-572-4884.*

POLLAK, LISA, radio producer; Grad., U. Mich., 1990. Reporter News & Observer, Raleigh, NC, Charlotte (NC) Observer; columnist Balt. Sun, 1997—2004. Prodr.: This American Life, 2004—. Recipient Pulitzer prize for feature writing, 1997. Office: This American Life WBEZ Radio 848 E Grand Ave Chicago IL 60611

POLLAK, MARK, lawyer; b. Paris, July 16, 1947; came to U.S., 1955; s. Joseph and Zofia (Berkowitz) P.; m. Joanne Elizabeth Harris, Dec. 26, 1976; children: Joshua David, Jonathan Stephen, Benjamin Eric, Rebecca Lynn. BA, Bklyn. Coll., 1968; MA in City Planning, U. Pa., 1972, JD, 1972. Bar: Md. 1972. Assoc. Piper & Marbury, Balt., 1972-81, ptnr., 1981-99, Wilmer, Cutler & Pickering, Washington, 1999—2004, Wilmer Cutler Pickering Hale and Dorr LLP, Washington, 2004—07, Ballard Spahr Andrews & Ingersoll, LLP, Balt., 2007—. Bd. dirs. Jack Kent Cook Found. Author: Sports Leagues and Teams--An Encyclopedia 1871 to 1996, 1997. Bd. dirs. Balt. Children's Mus., Downtown Partnership of Balt., Inc. Mem. ABA, Md. Bar Assn., Am. Coll. Real Estate Lawyers. Office: Ballard Spahr Andrews & Ingersoll LLP 300 E Lombard Baltimore MD 21202-3268 Home Phone: 410-366-0925; Office Phone: 410-528-5563. Business E-Mail: pollakm@ballardspahr.com.

POLLAK, MARTIN MARSHALL, lawyer, training company executive; b. NYC, July 31, 1927; s. Edward and Jennie (Horowitz) P.; m. Ellen R. Spiegel, Sept. 16, 1929; children: David W., Richard M., Barbara S. AB, Syracuse U., 1950; LLB, St. John's U., Bklyn., 1953. Bar: N.Y. 1953, U.S. Dist. Ct. (ea. and so. dists.) N.Y. 1957, U.S. Supreme Ct. 1959. Ptnr. Feldman & Pollak, Attys., NYC, 1953-59; atty. N.Y. State, 1953—; founder, exec. v.p., treas. G.P. Strategies Corp. (formerly Nat. Patent Devel. Corp.), NYC, 1959-99. Trustee Worcester Found. for Exptl. Rsch., Shrewsbury, Mass., 1977—; cons. Allergan Optical Corp., Irvine, Calif., 1988-89; chmn. bd. Czechoslovak-U.S. Econ. Coun., Washington, 1987-96, vice-chmn., 1996—; pres. Internat. Hydron Corp., Woodbury, N.Y., 1981-88, NPO Trading USA, Inc., N.Y.C., Washington, Prague, Czechoslovakia, 1990-98, Am. Drug Co., Washington, N.Y.C., Moscow, 1993-98, Millennium Cell Corp., 1998-2000; bd. dirs. GSE Sys., Inc. Vice chmn. bd. Worcester Found., 2000—. With USN, 1945-47. Recipient gold medal Czechoslovakian Rep. C. of C., 1984. also: Gen Physics Corp 6700 Alexander Bell Dr Ste 300 Columbia MD 21046-2185 Office: GP Strategies Corp 120 White Plaines Rd Ste 425 Tarrytown NY 10591-5522

POLLAN, MICHAEL, author, journalist, professor; b. LI, NY, Feb. 6, 1955; s. Stephen and Corky Pollan; m. Judith Belzer, Sept. 6, 1987; 1 child, Isaac. Student, Mansfield Coll., U. Oxford, Eng.; BA, Bennington Coll., Vt., 1977; MA in English, Columbia U., NYC, 1981. Former exec. editor Harper's Mag.; now Knight prof. journalism U. Calif., Berkeley, also dir. Knight Prog. Sci. & Environ. Journalism. Author: Second Nature: A Gardener's Education, 1991, Place of My Own: The Education of an Amateur Builder, 1997, The Botany of Desire: A Plant's-Eye View of the World, 2001, The Omnivore's Dilemma: A Natural History of Four Meals, 2006 (Named one of Five Best Nonfiction Books of Yr., NY Times, 2006, One of 10 Best Books of Yr., Washington Post, 2006, James Beard award for best food writing, 2007, Calif. Book award), In Defense of Food: An Eater's Manifesto, 2008 (Publishers Weekly bestseller); contbg. writer NY Times Mag., articles anthologized Norton Book of Nature Writing, 1990, Best American Essays, 1990, 2003, American Science Writing, 2004, The Animals: Practicing Complexity, 2006; contbr. numerous articles/essays to periodicals. Recipient Reuters World Conservation Union Global award for environ. journalism, 2000, James Beard award for best mag. series, 2003, Am. Humane Assn. Genesis award. Office: U Calif Grad Sch Journalism 121 N Gate Hall #5860 Berkeley CA 94720 Office Phone: 510-642-8240.*

POLLAN, STEPHEN MICHAEL, lawyer, life coach, finance expert, journalist; b. NYC, May 19, 1929; m. Corinne Staller; children: Michael, Lori, Tracy, Dana. LLB, Bklyn. Law Sch., 1951; BBS, LI U., 1985. Bar: NY 1951. Asst. prof. Marymount Coll., 1960-70; pres. Royal Bus. Funds AMEX, 1970-76; sr. real estate cons. Nat. Westminster Bank, 1976-78; asst. prof. fin. C.W. Post Coll., LI U. Sch. Bus., 1994-96; prin. Stephen M. Pollan, P.C., NYC, 1980—; pvt. practice NYC, 2006—. Mem. President's Commn. on Small Bus. Co-author: Die Broke, Live Rich, Lifescripts, 1996, Second Acts, 2003, It's All in Your Head, 2006, Lifelines, 2007, other personal fin. books; contbr. numerous articles to nat. bus. publs. Pres. Gay Head Cmty. Coun., 1975; vice chmn. UN Com. for UN Day, 1971-72. Mem. Nat. Assn. Small Bus. Investment Cos. (regional pres. 1975, bd. govs.). Home: 1095 Park Ave New York NY 10128-1154 Office: 400 Park Ave Ste 1420 New York NY 10022 Office Phone: 212-688-8333. Personal E-mail: stephenpollan@stephenpollan.com. Business E-Mail: stephen@stephenpollan.com.

POLLAND, ANTHONY TRAVIS, engineering company executive, director; b. Prescott, Ariz., Nov. 27, 1974; s. Jasper Leon Mace and Dawnette Lynn Polland; m. Deanna Marie LeClaire, Mar. 3, 1998 (div. Nov. 14, 2005); 1 child, Travor Anthony. Dir., global pre sales engring. Tele Tech Holdings, Englewood, Colo., 2006—. Office: TeleTech Holdings 9197 S Peoria St Englewood CO 80112 Personal E-mail: tpolland@gmail.com. Business E-Mail: travispolland@teletech.com.

POLLARD, DANIEL L., financial analyst; s. Alan Payson Pollard and Hinda Leah Greyser. BA, U. Mass., Boston, 1990; JD, Harvard U., Cambridge, Mass., 1994. Bar: Mass. 1995. Mgmt., program analyst, office student fin. assistance and direct loans US Dept. Edn., Washington, 1996—99, policy, legislative analyst, 1999—2004, sr. portfolio analyst, 2004—. Contbr. articles to profl. jours. Recipient Disting. Toastmaster, 2009. Mem.: Toastmasters (FSA pres. 2006—07, area gov. 2007—08, divsn. gov. 2008—09). Achievements include knowledge of the facets of student loan programs - legislation, policy, budget, operations, systems, data mining, and portfolio assessment - has provided a resource for study groups and committees. Office: US Dept Edn 830 First St NE Washington DC 20202 Business E-Mail: daniel.pollard@ed.gov.

POLLARD, FRED DON, finance company executive, director; b. Proctorsville, Vt., Sept. 15, 1931; s. Bryant Frank and Millie Viola (Brobst) P.; m. Sandra Jean Norton, Oct. 19, 1957; children: Fred Don, Bruce Gardiner, Mark Bryant. BA, Dartmouth Coll., 1953, MBA, 1954. CPA, N.Y. Staff auditor Touche, Niven, Bailey & Smart, Chgo., 1954-55, 57-58; with Hertz Corp., Chgo., 1958-60, London, 1960-62, Paris, 1962-64, NYC, 1964-65; European controller Avis Rent A Car, London, 1965-69, internat. treas., 1969-71, asst. v.p., dir. fin. Garden City, NY, 1971-72, asst. treas., 1972-75; treas. Garcia Corp., Teaneck, NJ, 1975-78; v.p. fin., treas. Augsbury Orgn., Inc., Ogdensburg, NY, 1978-79, sr. v.p. fin., treas., 1979-83; pres. Corp. Fin. Assocs. No. N.Y., Canton, 1983—, Agrl. Processing Corp., Canton, 1983—; pres. and treas. AG Pro Ltd., Massena, NY, 1998—. Vis. lectr. sch. of mgmt. Clarkson U., Potsdam, 1986-87, dept. econs. St. Lawrence U., Canton, N.Y., 1987-88; cons. Whalen, Davey & Looney LLP, 1990-2000. Served with U.S. Army, 1955-57. Mem. N.Y. State Soc. CPAs, Am. Inst. CPAs., St. Lawrence county C. of C. (bd. dirs. 1997—). Lodges: Masons; Shriners. Presbyterian. Home: Old Stone House 1129 County Route 25 Canton NY 13617-6539 Office: 24 Commerce Dr Massena NY 13662 Home Phone: 315-386-3916; Office Phone: 315-764-5611. Business E-Mail: president@agprosoy.com.

POLLARD, HARVEY B., medical educator, neuroscientist; b. San Antonio, May 26, 1943; BA in Biology, Rice U., 1964; MS in Biochemistry, U. Chgo., 1969, MD, 1969, PhD, 1973. Rsch. assoc. NIH-Nat. Inst. Arthritis and Metabolic Diseases, Bethesda, Md., 1969-71, sr. investigator, 1972-74, 1977-79, sect. chief, 1979-81; lab. chief Nat. Inst. Diabetes, Digestive and Kidney Diseases, Bethesda, 1981-96; prof., chair dept. anatomy, physiology and genetics Uniformed Svcs. U. Sch. Medicine, Bethesda, 1997—. Contbr. over 275 articles to profl. jours. With USPHS, 1969-96. Recipient Commendation medal USPHS, 1982, Alumni award for Disting. Svc., U. Chigo. Alumni Assn., 1989, NIH Inventor's award, 1991. Mem. Biophys. Soc., Soc. for Neurosci., Am. Soc. for Pharmacology and Exptl. Therapeutics, Soc. for Cell Biology, Endocrine Soc., Am. Coll. Psychoneuropharmacology, Am. Soc. for Biochemistry and Molecular Biology, Am. Assn. Anatomists., Am. Physiol. Soc., Institute of Medicine of Washington, D.C. Office: USU Sch Med Dept Anatomy Physiology and Genetics Bethesda MD 20814-4712 E-mail: hpollard@usuhs.mil.

POLLARD, HERSCHEL NEWTON, artist, psychologist; s. Herschel Newton and Lora Frances Pollard; m. Luz Mariela Gomez Bolanos, Oct. 10, 1997; m. Margaret Lila Kathleen Innes, 1962 (div. 1972); children: Joanna Sophia, Steven Morton, Christopher Charles, Charles William, Heather Dianne, Herschel Newton. BA, Vanderbilt U., 1960; postgrad., Ga. State U., 1963—63, U. of Tenn., 1963—64, Vanderbilt Divinity Sch., 1963—64; PhD, Vanderbilt U., 1972; postgrad., Chattanooga State Tech. Coll., 1992—94. Lic. clin. psychology Tenn., forensic psychology Tenn., clin./cons. psychology Miss., Ark., Alaska, Fla. Counselor Inter-University Psychol. and Counseling Ctr., Nashville, 1964—72; prof. Grad. Sch. Murray State U., Ky., 1967—69; adj. prof. St. Thomas Aquinas Coll., Nashville, 1970—71; intern Nashville Cmty. Mental Health Ctr., 1971—72; pvt. practice psychologist Memphis, 1972—74; clin. dir. NW Miss. Regional Mental Health Sys., Clarksedale, Miss., 1975—76; dir. Kuskokwim Mental Health Svcs., Aniak, Alaska, 1976—77; clin. dir. Anchorage Cmty. Mental Health Svcs., 1977—78; pvt. practice clin. and consulting psychologist Naples, Fla., 1979—86; pvt. practice psychologist Chattanooga, 1986—; owner, dir. Montlake Studios, Chattanooga, 1990—; instr. Von Liebig Ctr. for the Arts, Naples, 1990—2003, Art League of Bonita Springs, Fla., 1995—98, Cape Coral Arts Studio, Fla., 2002—04, Visual Arts Ctr., Punta Gorda, Fla., 2003—07; pres. Art Inst. of Fla., Inc., Punta Gorda, 2006—; lectr. Fla. Gulf Coast U. Renaissance Acad., 2007—, Ringling Coll. Art and Design Continuing Edn., 2007—; clin. dir. Family Counseling and Recovery Ctrs., Inc., Conway, Little Rock, 2008—09; psychologist Tenn. Valley Health Care Sys., Chattanooga, 2009—. Contbg rschr. Pres.'s Commn. to Investigate Civil Disturbances, Nashville, 1970; mem. Pres.'s Commn. on Mental Health, Washington, 1976—78; instr. Visual Arts Ctr., Punta Gorda, Fla., 2002—; founder Nat. Aviation Art Exhbn., Nat. Air Show, Punta Gorda, 2006. Author, dir., prodr.: (films) Dealing with Conflict (1st award Religion and Ethics Divsn., EFLA Am. Film Festival, 1964); author: (biographical commentary and docudrama) Vincent van Gogh: Love, God and Art, (rsch. monograph) The Re-emergence of a Noteworthy Baroque Painting, (drama) The Madman of Arles, (book) Pollard's Brief Handbook for Painters, (novels) Wait for the Thunder, (biography) The Art of Frances Morton Pollard; co-author (with Ruth Banles Morton): A Life Remembered; author: (ednl. audio-visual) The Nineteen Friends of Robbie McNee (Excellence award Ednl. Film Libr. Assn., 1964), (film) Turning Point, 1971; designer, pub. Pollard's Infinite Palette; exhibitions include Von Liebig Ctr. for the Arts, Naples, Cape Coral Arts Studio, Naples Nat. Art Festival, Mus. of the Everglades, Robb and Stucky Atrium, Ft. Myers, Fla., No. Trust, Naples, Impac U., Punta Gorda, Goff Gallery, Visual Arts Ctr., Ave Maria U., Naples, 1st Cmty. Nat. Bank, Port Charlotte, Preseller Gallery, Punta Gorda, Alla Prima Pastel Invitational, Naples, The 2005 H. Pollard Retrospective Exhibit, Art and Humanities Gallery, Port Charlotte, Parthenon Mus., Nashville, Hunter Mus., Chattanooga, Larson Gallery, Northern Trust, Naples, Parthenon Mus., Nashville, others, Represented in permanent collections Portrait of Sir Denis Mahon, Nat. Gallery, Gt. Britain, The Entombment of Christ, Ave Maria U. Mus., Naples. Rep. SW Fla. Arts Coun., Ft. Myers, Fla., 2003—04; originator children's art exhbn. Early Edn. Project, 2003; bd. dirs. Early Edn. Project Policy Coun., Punta Gorda, 2002—03; pres. Von Liebig Ctr. for the Arts, Naples, 2003—04, Ctr. for the Visual Arts, Punta Gorda, 2005; bd. dirs. Charlotte Artists Guild, 2004—05, pres., 2005—. Lt. (j.g.) USN, 1960—62. Recipient Mitchell scholarship, Vanderbilt U., 1956—60, Tchg. fellowship, NIMH, 1964—72, 1st Prize, 2003 Plein Aire Festival, 2003, 1st Award, Visual Art Ctr., 2004, 1st Judge's award, Charlotte Nat. Art Competition, 2004, 1st Prize, Tenn. State Fair Art Competition, 1965, 1st Award, Collier County Fair Art Competition, 1970, Bowles award for portraiture, 2005, 1st award comml. aviation divsn., Nat. Aviation Art Exhbn., others; named Artist of Month, Charlotte County Bd. Commrs., 2005. Mem.: APA (licentiate), Nat. Rehab. Assn., Ark. Psychol. Assn., Charlotte Artists Guild (pres. 2005—), Naples Art Assn. (pres. 2003—04), Am. Numis. Assn. Achievements include development of The Pollard Pain Scale; design of Pollard's Infinite Palette. Avocations: Pre-Columbian archaeology, coin collecting/numismatics, ceramics, psychology of art, art. Office: CESA Pub 179 Maria Ct Punta Gorda FL 33950 Personal E-mail: hnpollard@aol.com. E-mail: artinstituteoffl@aol.com.

POLLARD, KATE, photographer, art educator; d. Douglas and Donna Pollard. BA, Pa. State U., Univ. Pk., 2002; MA in Design, U. Edinburgh, 2006. Adj. instr. Rowan U., Glassboro, NJ, 2008, Bucks County CC, Newtown, Pa., 2008—, Rutgers U., NB, NJ, 2009—. Exhibitions include Passing: Atticsalt Gallery, Edinburgh, The Female Gaze: Gallery

10G, NYC, This Woman's Movement: Rosier Gallery, San Francisco, This Woman's Movement: Kirsten Roschlaub Gallery, Hamburg, Germany, Memento Mori: ClayPool-Young Gallery, Morehead, Ky., IRevelar: Naomi Silva Gallery, Atlanta, Juried Photography Exhibition: Academy of Fine Arts, Lynchburg, Va., Emerging Photographer, New Orleans Darkroom Gallery, New Orleans, 2008, Raging Against The.: Micro Museum, Bklyn., Traditions, Visions and Herstory: Rhonda Schaller Studio, NYC, Small Rays of Hope: Rhonda Schaller Studio; contbr. articles to profl. publs. and mags. (Images of Yr., 2008). Recipient Internat. Photography awards, 2008, IPA Lucie awards, 2008. Personal E-mail: info@katepollard.com.

POLLARD, MICHAEL ROSS, lawyer, health science association administrator; b. Flint, Mich., Apr. 14, 1947; s. Gail Winton Pollard and Evelyn Georgeanna (LeMire) Goplen; m. Penelope Brigham, Aug. 22, 1970. AB in Polit. Sci., U. Mich., 1969; JD, Harvard U., 1972, MPH, 1974. Bar: Mass. 1972, D.C. 1975. Profl. assoc. for program devel. Nat. Acad. Scis. Inst. Medicine, Washington, 1974-77, dir. law and ethics div., 1977-78; atty. advisor Office of Policy Planning, FTC, Washington, 1978-81, asst. dir. Bur. Consumer Protection, 1981-83; dir. Office of Policy Analysis, Pharm. Mfrs. Assn., Washington, 1983-88; exec. dir. Am. Pharm. Inst., Washington, 1988-89; counsel Michaels, Wishner & Bonner, P.C., Washington, 1988-89, ptnr., 1989—2000; cons. fed. policy & regulation Medco Health Solutions, Inc., 2000—09. Cons. Nat. Ctr. for Health Svcs. Rsch., Rockville, Md., 1975-80, Office Tech. Assessment U.S. Congress, 1984-95; dir. Inst. for Health Policy Solutions, 1992-2009; sr. fellow, 2009-. Contbr. articles to profl. jours. Treas. Nat. Leadership Coalition on AIDS, 1988-93; treas. and dir.-at-large Nat. Commn. on Cert. of Physician Assts., 1991-97, James B. Angell scholar U. Mich., 1967, 68, 69; docent Hendricks Hill Mus., 2001—; vis. com. Harvard U. Sch. Pub. Health, 2002—08; mem. nat. adv. com. Calif. Health Benefits Rev. Program, 2004—; pres. Southport Island Assn., 2006—07. Mem. Rotary Internat., Phi Beta Kappa, Pi Sigma Alpha, Boothbay Harbor Yacht club, Harvard club, Southport Yacht club. Democrat. Avocations: running, bicycling, gardening, drawing, architecture. Home: 7300 Maple Ave Chevy Chase MD 20815-5108 also: 29 Paradise Lane Southport ME 04576-0340

POLLARD, MORRIS, microbiologist, educator; b. Hartford, Conn., May 24, 1916; s. Harry and Sarah (Hoffman) P.; m. Mildred Klein, Dec. 29, 1938 (dec. 2001); children: Harvey, Carol, Jonathan. D.V.M., Ohio State U., 1938; MS, Va. Poly. Inst., 1939; PhD (Nat. Found. Infantile Paralysis fellow), U. Calif.-Berkeley, 1950; DSc (hon.), Miami U., Ohio, 1981. Mem. staff Animal Disease Sta., Nat. Agrl. Research Center, Beltsville, Md., 1939-42; asst. prof. preventive medicine Med. br. U. Tex., Galveston, 1946-48, assoc. prof., 1948-50, prof., 1950-61; prof. biology U. Notre Dame, Ind., 1961-66, prof., chmn. microbiology, 1966-81, prof. emeritus, 1981—, 2001—, dir. Lobund Lab., 1961-85, Coleman dir. Lobund Lab., 1985—, Coleman Found. prof., 1985—2001. Vis. prof. Fed. U. Rio de Janeiro, Brazil, 1977; vis. prof. Katholieke U., Leuven, Belgium, 1981; mem. tng. grant com. NIH, 1965-70; mem. adv. bd. Inst. Lab. Animal Resources NRC, 1965-68; mem. adv. com. microbiology Office Naval Research, 1966-68, chmn., 1968-70; cons. U. Tex., M.D. Anderson Hosp. and Tumor Inst., 1958-66; mem. colon cancer com. Nat. Cancer Inst., 1972-76, chmn. tumor immunology com., 1976-79; mem. com. cancer cause and prevention NIH, 1979-81; program rev. com. Argonne Nat. Lab, 1979-85, chmn., 1983-85; lectr. Found. Microbiology, 1978 Editor: Perspectives in Virology Vol. I to XI, 1959-80; contbr. articles to profl. jours. Served from 1st lt. to lt. col. Vet. Corps, AUS, 1942-46. Recipient Disting. Alumnus award Ohio State U., 1979, Army Commendation medal, Presdl. citation, Hope award Am. Cancer Soc., 2000; named Hon. Alumnus U. Notre Dame, 1989; McLaughlin Faculty fellow Cambridge U., 1956; Raine Found. prof. U. Western Australia, 1975; vis. scientist Chinese Acad. Med. Scis., 1979, 81; hon. prof. Chinese Acad. Med. Scis., 1982. Mem. Am. Acad. Microbiology (charter), Brazilian Acad. Scis., Soc. Exptl. Biology and Medicine, Am. Soc. Microbiology (Acad. Sci. Achievement award 1990), Am. Soc. Investigative Pathology, Am. Assn. Cancer Rsch., Am. Soc. Lab. Animal Sci., Am. Soc. Virology, Assn. Gnotobiotics (pres.), Internat. Commn. Lab. Animal Sci., AAAS, Internat. Assn. Gnotobiology (pres.), Internat. Assn. Gnotobiotics (hon. pres. 1987), Sigma Xi, Phi Delta Epsilon (hon.), Phi Zeta (hon.). Office: Lobund Lab U Notre Dame Notre Dame IN 46556 Home: 1025 Park Pl Apt 137 Mishawaka IN 46545-3537 Office Phone: 574-631-7564.

POLLARD, OVERTON PRICE, retired lawyer; b. Ashland, Va., Mar. 26, 1933; s. James Madison and Annie Elizabeth (Hutchinson) Pollard; m. Anne Aloysia Meyer, Oct. 1, 1960; children: Mary O., Price, John, Anne, Charles, Andrew, David. AB in Econs., Washington and Lee U., 1954, JD, 1957. Bar: Va. Claims supr. Travelers Ins. Co., Richmond, Va., 1964-67; asst. atty. gen. State of Va., Richmond, 1967, 70-72; spl. asst. Va. Supreme Ct., Richmond, 1968-70; exec. dir. Pub. Defender Commn., Richmond, 1972—2003; ptnr. Pollard & Boice and predecessor firms, Richmond, 1972-87. Bd. govs. Va. Criminal Law Sect., Richmond, 1970—72; pres. Met. Legal Aid, Richmond, 1978; chair sr. lawyers sect. Va. State Bar, 1999—2000. Del. State Dem. Conv., Richmond, 1985; mem. Va. Commn. Family Violence Prevention, 1995; bd. dirs. Henrico County Housing Corp., 1999. With USN, 1957—59. Recipient Svc. award, Criminal Law Bd. of Govs. Pub. Defender Study, 1971, Outstanding Svc. award, Pub. Defender Commn., 1998, Carrico Professionalism award, Va. State Bar Criminal Law Sect., 2005. Fellow: ABA Found., Va. Law Found.; mem.: ABA, Va. Bar Assn. (Pro Bono Publico award 1995, Walker award 2005), Nat. Legal Aid and Defender Assn. (Reginald Heber Smith award 1991), Richmond Bar Assn., Va. Bar Assn. (chmn. criminal law sect. 1991—93). Democrat. Baptist. Avocation: fishing. Home: 7726 Sweetbriar Rd Richmond VA 23229-6622

POLLARD, ROYCE, Mayor, Vancouver, Washington; Ret. comdr. US Army Vancouver Barracks, 1961—88; councilman City of Vancouver, Wash., 1988—96, mayor Wash., 1996—. Rep. Bi-State Transp. Com., SW Wash. Regional Transp. Coun., Columbia River Edn. Workforce Coun., Joint Policy Adv. Com. Transp., Growth Mgmt. Act Steering Com. of Countrywide Elected Officials; bd. mem. Vancouver Fire Pension Bd., Vancouver Police Pension Bd., CRESA Bd. Dirs. Mem.: Vietnam Veterans of America, Ret. Officers Assn. (Columbia River Chpt.), Am. Legion Post 14, La Societe des Quarante Hommes at Huit Chevaux (Forty & Eight). Mailing: PO Box 1995 Vancouver WA 98668-1995 Office: City Hall 210 E 13th St Vancouver WA 98668 Office Phone: 350-487-8629. Business E-Mail: mayor@ci.vancouver.wa.us.*

POLLARD, THOMAS DEAN, cell biologist, educator; b. Pasadena, Calif., July 7, 1942; s. Dean Randall and Florence Alma (Dierker) Pollard; m. Patricia Elizabeth Snowden, Feb. 7, 1964; children: Katherine, Daniel. BA cum laude, Pomona Coll., Claremont, Calif., 1964; MD cum laude, Harvard Med. Sch., 1968. Intern Mass. Gen. Hosp., Boston, 1968—69; staff assoc. lab. biochemistry Nat. Heart and Lung Inst., Bethesda, Md., 1969—72; asst. prof. anatomy Harvard Med. Sch., Boston, 1972—75, assoc. prof., 1975—78; Bayard Halsted prof., dir. dept. cell biology and anatomy Johns Hopkins U. Sch. Medicine, Balt., 1977—96; pres. Salk Inst. Biol. Studies, La Jolla, Calif., 1996—2000, prof., 1996—2001, U. Calif., San Diego, 1996—2001; Eugene Higgins prof. molecular, cellular and devel. biology and cell biology Yale U., New Haven, 2001—06, prof. cell biology, 2002—, prof. molecular biophysics and biochemistry, 2003—, Sterling prof. molecular, cellular and devel. biology and cell biology, 2006—. Vis. scientist Med. Rsch. Coun. Lab. Molecular Biology, Cambridge, England, 1984; mem. NRC Commn. Life Sci., 1990—97, chair, 1993—97; mem. coun. NIH Nat. Inst. Gen. Med. Sci.; adj. prof. biology, bioengineering and chemistry and biochemistry U. Calif., San Diego, 1997—2001; chair dept. molecular, cellular and devel. biology Yale U., 2004—. Contbr. articles to profl. jours.; mem. editl. bd.: Cell Biology - Internat. Reports, 1976—81, Jour. Cell Biology, 1977—82, Jour. Submicroscopic Cytology, 1978—82, Cell Motility and the Cytoskeleton, 1980—94, Jour. Muscle Rsch. and Cell Motility, 1980—88, Microscopy Rsch. and Technique, 1981—93, Current Opinion in Cell Biology, 1988—, Current Biology, 1991—, Protein Profile, 1994—97, Trends in Biochemical Scis., 1995—, Procs. NAS, 1996—98, assoc. editor: Molecular Biology of the Cell, 1991—. Recipient Rsch. Career Devel. award, US Pub. Health Svc., 1974—78, MERIT award, Nat. Inst. Gen. Med. Sci., 1988—98; co-recipient Lewis S. Rosentiel Disting. Work in Basic Med. Rsch. award, Brandeis U., 1996, Gairdner Found. Internat. award, 2006; Winston Churchill Overseas fellowship, Churchill Coll., UK, 1984, Guggenheim fellowship, 1994. Fellow: Am. Acad. Microbiol., AAAS (bd. dirs. 2006—), Inst. Medicine, Biophys. Soc. (mem. coun. 1977—80, pres. 1992—93, Pub. Svc. award 1997), NAS, Am. Acad. Arts & Scis.; mem.: Am. Soc. Biochemistry and Molecular Biology, Marine Biol. Lab. (trustee 1991—97), Am. Soc. Cell Biology (mem. exec. com. 1976—77, mem. coun. 1976—79, pres. 1987—88, K.R. Porter lectr. 1989, E.B. Wilson medal 2004). Achievements include patents in field. Office: Dept Molecular Cellular and Devel Biology Yale U PO Box 208103 New Haven CT 06520-8103 E-mail: thomas.pollard@yale.edu.

POLLATSEK, ALEXANDER, retired psychology professor; b. NYC, Jan. 26, 1941; s. Frank and Toini Pollatsek; m. Harriet Suzanne Katcher, May 2, 1964; children: Elena Shura, David Eric. MS, Harvard U., Cambridge, Mass., 1963; MA, U. Mich., Ann Arbor, 1965, PhD, 1969. Prof. psychology U. Mass., Amherst, 1969—. Grant, NIH, 1980—. Office: Dept Psychology Univ Mass Amherst MA 01003 Personal E-mail: pollatsek@psych.umass.edu.

POLLEI, DANE F., museum director; b. Fond du Lac, Wis., Oct. 28, 1964; s. Gerald E. and Barbara May (Bassett) P.; M. Lynn Pollei; children: Marley, Chase, Odie BA in Anthrop., Mus. Studies, Beloit Coll., Wis., 1986; cert. in Non-Profit Mgmt., U. Wis., Parkside, 1990; cert. in Archival Adminstr., U. Wis., 1995. Mus. asst. Logan Mus. of Anthrop., Beloit, Wis., 1983-85; asst. to dir. Beloit Coll. Mus., 1985-86; dir., curator Freeport Art Mus., Ill., 1987-89; exec. dir. Kenosha County Hist. Soc., Wis., 1989-97; dir. adminstrn. John Michael Kohler Arts Ctr., Sheboygan, Wis., 1997—2004; dir. Brevard Mus. Art and Sci., Melbourne, Fla., 2004—06; dir., chief curator Mabee-Gerrer Mus. Art, Shawnee, Okla., 2006—. Instr. Highland C.C., Freeport, IL, 1988-89; adv. com. Wis. Fedn. Museums, 1990-92; cons. Font Bank On-Line, Evanston, IL, 1994. Author, editor: W.E.S.T. Word Traveller, 1992-96, co-author: Focus on Louis Thiers: A Photographers View of Kenosha, 1998 Pres. bd. dirs. Kenosha (Wis.) Unified Sch. Dist., 1993-96; mem. Hist. Preservation Commn., Kenosha; founder, pres. H.M.G.G. Festival of Arts and Culture, 1986—. Mem. Am. Assn. Museums. Populist Progressive. Office: Mabee-Gerrer Mus Art 1900 W MacArthur Dr Shawnee OK 74804 Personal E-mail: danepollei@yahoo.com.

POLLEY, HARVEY LEE, retired missionary, math and science educator; b. Wapato, Wash., Aug. 14, 1924; s. Edward Prestley and Alda June Polley; m. Corinne Weber; children: Catherine, David, Corinne, Robert. BA, Whitworth Coll., 1951; postgrad., East Wash. Coll., 1953, Berkeley Bapt. Div. Sch., 1958—59; MEd, Ctrl. Wash. Coll., 1958; postgrad., Ecole d'Adminstrn. des Affaires Africaines, Brussels, 1959—60. Tchr. Quincy Pub. Schs., Wash., 1953—57, N.W. Christian Schs., Spokane, 1958; missionary Am. Bapt. Fgn. Missionary Soc., Democratic Republic of Congo, 1958—89; tchr. Evang. Pedagogical Inst., Kimpese, Democratic Republic of Congo, 1961—69, asst. legal rep., dir., prin., supt., 1969—72; dir. BIM Hostel, Kinshasa, Democratic Republic of Congo, 1972—73; mem. staff Ctr. Agrl. Devel. Lusekele, Democratic Republic of Congo, 1975—85, dir., 1976—79, 1983—85, Plateau Bateke Devel. Program, Kinshasa, 1985—89; ret., 1989. Author: Mpila Kele, a rural development guide written in the Kituba lang., 1989. Mem. Coun. Elders, Kimpese, 1969-72; pres. bd. adminstrn. Vanga (Zaire) Hosp., 1981-83; mem. exec. com. Nat. Human Nutrition Planning Coun. Govt. Zaire-USAID, Kikwit, 1983-85. With U.S. Army, 1946-47, USAF, 51-53. Home: 2405 W Johannsen Rd Spokane WA 99208-9616

POLLEY, RICHARD DONALD, microbiologist, chemist; b. Bklyn., Feb. 23, 1937; s. George Weston and Evelyn (Tuttle) P.; m. Linda R. Radford, Sept. 21, 1991; children from previous marriage: Gordon MacHeath, Jennifer Elizabeth, Tabitha Isabelle, Sean Sullivan. Student, Trinity Coll., 1954-57; BS, Hofstra U., 1960. Lic. nuclear radiation tech. U.S. Govt., 2003. Asst. advt. mgr. tech. Sun Chem. Corp., 1961-63; tech. advt. mgr. Celanese Plastics Co., Newark, 1963-67; account dir. McCann Indsl. Tech. Sci. Mktg., NYC, 1967-68, v.p., gen. mgr. Miami, 1968-70; pres. Intercapital Belgium S.A., Brussels, Nassau, Bahamas, Panama City, Panama, 1970-72; cons. Nuclear Regulatory Commn., Atomic City, Idaho, 1975—76; founder, pres., tech. dir. Iodinamics Corp., Lancaster, Pa., El Paso, Tex., El Paso, Tex., 1973-76; founder, CEO, COO, tech. dir., bd. dirs., chmn. Hydrodine Corp., Miami, 1976—2002, chmn., CEO, tech. dir., 1986—2002, also bd. dirs. Founder, chmn. CEO, COO, tech. dir. Polymorphic Polymers Corp., Miami, 1978—90; founder, COO, tech. dir., CEO, bd. dirs. Omnidine Corp., Miami, 1980—98, bd. dirs.; pres., tech. dir. Skin Care Labs., Inc., Miami, Fla., 1979—90; tech. dir. Hydrodine Biotech (Far East) Ltd., Bangkok, Thailand, Hong Kong, Singapore and Kuala Lumpur, 1989—98; CEO, tech. dir. Polllabs., Sao Paulo, Brazil, 1990—2000; tech. dir. Ecology Tech. do Brasil, Sao Paulo, 1993—2000; tech. dir., environ. and agrl. mgr. Environ. Tech. do Brasil, Sao Paulo, 1995—; chief internat. tech. dir. environ. microbiology Gen. Environ. Sci. Corp., Solon, Ohio, 1993—2000; chmn., co-founder Peer Group Influencers Ltd., London, Miami, 1988—98; v.p., bd. dirs. Internat. Airlines, Long Beach, Calif., 1984—2000; COO, tech. dir. Swiver Corp., Miami, 1994—2002; tech. dir. chief scientist Infinity Techs., Ltd., Panama City, 1996—98; founder, bd. dirs., CEO, pres., tech. dir. PolleyTech Corp., Pembroke Pines, Fla., 1998—; overseas dir. field Iodine Deficiency Disease med. demonstration projects Beth Israel Hosp., Harvard U. Med. Sch., 1977—88; lectr. Harvard Bus. Sch., 1980; cons. water disinfection control, water environments Pan Am. Health Orgn., others; med. and tech. dir. Enzymes Brasil, Ltd., Sao Paulo, 2001—, med. mgr., tech. dir., Guayaquil, Ecuador, 2001—; chmn. med./sci. adv. bd., found. tech. dir. RAH Med. Rsch. Found., Napa Valley, Calif., 2001—; cons. IGFA Wetlands Project, 2001—; founder, CEO, COO, chmn. bd. dirs. Xurex Nano-Coatings Corp., Davie, Fla., 2005—. Mem. editl. adv. bd. Chem. Week, 1988; contbr. articles to profl. jours.; patentee. Mem. cmty. bd. Am. Heart Assn., Am. Stroke Assn., Broward County, PR. Recipient R. Buckminster Fuller Home of the Future award for paints and water system, 1976. Mem. AAAS, NRA, Am. Concrete Inst., N.Y. Acad. Scis., Internat. Iodine Inst. (chmn. bd. and tech. dir. 1976—), Associaçao de Ciencia e Tecnologia Ambiental (bd. dirs. Sao Paulo 1993—), The Nature Conservancy, World Wildlife Fund, Sierra Club, Audubon Soc., Wilderness Soc., Defenders of Wildlife, Environ. Defense Org., Fla. Wildlife Fedn., Internat. Game Fish Assn., others. Achievements include patents for farm, industrial, commercial, medical, environmental and household protective coatings and water treatment devices, nuclear industries; fields of medicine, environmental protection, agriculture and enzymes soil road building, asphalt and soil enzymes roads, lagoons, aquaculture, ponds; drinking water reservoirs, hazardous waste containment area soil reservoirs; soil aircraft landing strips; coinventor, foundational nano-molecular protective coatings. Office: Xurex Nano-Coatings Corp 531 Gallatin Place NW Albuquerque NM 87121 E-mail: rpolley@xurex.com.

POLLEY, SARAH, actress; b. Toronto, Canada, Jan. 8, 1979; d. Michael and Diane Polley; Attended, Canadian Film Centre. Actor: (films) One Magic Christmas, 1985, The Adventures of Baron Munchausen, 1988, Babar: The Movie, 1989, Exotica, 1994, Joe's So Mean to Josephine, 1996, The Sweet Hereafter, 1997, The Hanging Garden, 1997, The Planet of Junior Brown, 1997, Guinevere, 1999, eXistenZ, 1999, Go, 1999, The Life Before This, 1999, The Weight of Water, 2000, Love Come Down, 2000, No Such Thing, 2001, The I Inside, 2003, My Life Without Me, 2003, Luck, 2003, Dawn of the Dead, 2004, Don't Come Knocking, 2005, The Secret Life of Words, 2005, Beowulf & Grendel, 2005; (TV series) Road to Avonlea, 1990—96; (TV miniseries) John Adams, 2008, (TV appearances) Night Heat, 1985, Friday the 13th, 1987, Ramona, 1988, Slings and Arrows, 2006; dir.: (films) The Best Day of My Life, 1999; dir., writer (films) I Shout Love, 2001, Away from Her, 2006 (Best Dir. award, Directors Guild of Canada awards, 2007, Best First Film, NY Film Critics Circle, 2007), dir., prodr.,writer Don't Think Twice, 1999. Recipient Screen Actors Guild awards, 2007, NY Film Critics Online awards, 2007, LA Film Critics award, 2007, Nat. Bd. Review award, 2007, Sarasota Film Festival award, 2007, Genie award, 2008, numerous awards, 2007—08; named one of 50 Smartest People in Hollywood, Entertainment Weekly, 2007; nominee Acad. award, 2008, Oscar. Office: Celia Chassels Gary Goddard Agy Ltd 10 Saint Mary St Ste 305 Toronto ON M4Y 1P9 Canada

POLLICK, G. DAVID, academic administrator, philosopher; b. Kansas City, Mo., Oct. 13, 1947; children: Dayna, Landon; m. Karen Bentley Pollick, 2002. BA in Philosophy, U. San Diego, 1971; PhL in Philosophy, St. Paul U., Ont., Can., 1973; MA in Philosophy, U. Ottawa, Can., 1973, PhD in Philosophy, 1981. Lecturer, philosophy U. San Diego, San Diego, 1972-73; tchr.-counselor, neurologically and physically handicapped Aseltine Sch. Neurol. Handicapped, 1972-73; dir. heroin rehab. ctr. Imperial County Diversion Program, El Centro, Calif., 1973-74; tchr.-counselor, emotionally handicapped Finley Elem Sch, Holtville, Calif., 1974-75; lecturer, philosophy U. Ottawa, Ottawa, Ont, Canada, 1975-77; asst. prof. philosophy, dept. chrm., acad. coordinator St. John's U., Collegeville, Minn., 1977-84; assoc. prof., dean coll. arts and scis. Seattle U., 1984—89; acting pres., provost, v.p. for acad. affairs SUNY, Cortland, 1989—93; co-CEO, pres. Art Inst. Chgo., Sch. Art Inst. Chgo., 1993—95; pres. Lebanon Valley Coll., Annville, Pa., 1996—2004, Birmingham So. Coll., 2004—. Pres. Big South Conf., 2004—. Author: The Work of Roman Ingarden, 1977, (with others) The Aesthetics of Roman Ingarden, 1982; co-editor Supplementary Volume on Aesthetics, 1977. With USN, 1966—68. Fellow philosophy and fine arts, Inst. Ecumenical and Culture Rsch., 1976-77; Koscjusko Found. award, 1978. Avocations: sculpture, art history, archaeology. Office: Birmingham-Southern Coll 900 Arkadelphia Rd Birmingham AL 35254 Office Phone: 717-867-6100.

POLLIN, ABE, professional sports team owner, construction executive; b. Phila., Dec. 3, 1923; s. Morris and Jennie (Sack) P.; m. Irene S. Kerchek, May 27, 1945; children: Robert Norman, James Edward. BA, George Washington U., 1945; student, U. Md., 1941-44. Engaged in home bldg. bus., 1945—; pres. Abe Pollin Inc., Balt., 1962—; chmn. Balt. Bullets Basketball Club, Inc. (now Washington Wizards), 1964-97, NBA Washington Wizards, 1997—; chmn. bd., CEO Washington Sports & Entertainment, Washington. Dir. County Fed. Savs. & Loan Assn., Rockville, Md. Bd. dirs. United Jewish Appeal, Nat. Jewish Hosp., Jewish Cmty. Ctr.; bd. dirs., adv. com. John F. Kennedy Cultural Ctr. Recipient Duke Ziebert Capital Achievement award, Disting. Civilian Svc. award, US Army, Robert F. Kennedy-Martin Luther King, Jr. award, Coalition to Stop Gun Violence, 1996, United Cerebral Palsy Achievement award, 1996, Jewish Leadership award, 1997. Mem. Nat. Assn. Home Builders, Assn. Builders and Contractors Md., Washington Bd. Trade. Jewish. Office: Washington Wizards Verizon Ctr 601 F St NW Washington DC 20004*

POLLIN, BURTON RALPH, language educator; b. Worcester, Mass. s. Louis and Rae (Cohen) P.; m. Alice Pollin, Jan. 30, 1944; children: Diana Claire, Myles Clement. BA, CCNY, 1936; PhD, Columbia U., 1962. Tchr. English NYC Bd. Edn., 1936-62, chmn. dept. English, 1956-62; lectr. English CUNY, 1957-62, assoc. prof. to full prof., 1962-73, prof. emeritus, 1973—. Lectr. on Poe NY State Coun. Humanities, 1996—99, 2003—05. Author: Education and Enlightenment in the Works of William Godwin, 1962; edited Four Early Pamphlets, 1966, Godwin Criticism: A Synoptic Bibliography, 1967, Dictionary of Names and Titles in Poe's Collected Works, 1968, Discoveries in Poe, 1970, Benjamin Constant's Translation of Godwin's Political Justice, 1972, The Music for Shelley's Poems: An Annotated Bibliography of 1309 Compositions, 1974, Poe, Creator of Words, 1974, The Imaginary Voyages, vol. 1 of Collected Writings of...Poe, 1994, Word Index to Poe's Fiction, 1982, The Brevities of Poe, vol. 2 of Collected Writings of Poe, 1985, Poe's Writings in the Broadway Jour., vols. 3-4 of Collected Writings, 1986, Insights and Outlooks: Essays on Great Writers, 1986, Images of Poe's Works: A Comprehensive Descriptive Catalogue of Illustrations, 1989, The German Face of Poe (with Thomas Hansen), 1995, Poe's Writings in the Southern Literary Messenger, vol. 5 of Collected Writings of Poe (with J.V. Ridgely), 1986, Poe's Seductive Influence on Great Writers, 2004, The Letters of Edgar Allan Poe, 2009; adv. bd. editors Poe Studies, 1980—, Poe Rev., 2000-04; contbr. over 200 articles to profl. jours. Founder, continuing bd. dirs. Bronxville Beautification Coun., 1980—; active Friends of NY Pub. Libr., Carnegie Hall, Libr. of Bronxville, Eastchester Arts Coun., Columbia U. Libr. Friends, Supporters of Guggenheim Found.; bd. trustees Poe Mus., Richmond, Va. Recipient Poe award, Bronx County Hist. Soc., 2001, Rotary Club award, 2002, Alice and Burton Pollin for effective beautification of Bronxville, 2002; grantee Am. Philos. Soc., US, 1964—65, London, 1965, 1968, NY State U. Rsch. Found., 1966, Carl and Lily Pforzheimer, 1966, 1969, SUNY, 1967—73, Am. Coun. Learned Socs., 1968, 1975, 1984, Guggenheim Found., 1973—74, CUNY Rsch. Found., 1973, 1980, 1986, NEH, 1983—84, Lectureship on Poe, NY State Humanities Coun., 1996—99, 2003—05; fellow John Hay Whitney, 1947. Mem. MLA (life), Poe Studies Assn. (hon., life), Am. Lit. Assn. Avocations: literary research, piano playing, environmentalism. Home: 3 Stoneleigh Plz Apt 4D Bronxville NY 10708-2638

POLLIN, TONI I., endocrinologist, educator; MS in Molecular, Cellular & Devel. Biology, U. Minn., 1997; PhD in Human Genetics, U. Md., 2004. Diplomate Am. Bd. Genetic Counseling, 1999. Asst. prof. divsn. endocrinology, diabetes & nutrition U. Md. Sch. Medicine. Office: 660 W Redwood St Rm 445C Baltimore MD 21201 Office Phone: 410-706-1630. Office Fax: 410-706-1622. E-mail: tpollin@medicine.umaryland.edu.*

POLLINGER, TERESITA A., multi-cultural resource educator; arrived in US, 1974; d. Pedro Norberto Gomez and Teresa Sanchez-Gomez; m. Stephen Paul Pollinger, Apr. 11, 1947. BS in Spanish Lit., Bklyn. Col., NYC, 1982; MS in Edn., Columbia U., NYC, 1985. Cert. master chef New Orleans Culinary Inst., 1990, English spkr. of other langs. Fla. Dept. Edn., 1992. 2nd grade bilingual edn. tchr. PS 161, NYC, 1982—91; bilingual resource tchr. Sch. Bd. Broward County, Ft. Lauderdale, Fla., 1992—. Editor, proofread cons. Hampton Brown Pub. Co. Recipient Merit award, Cmty. Sch. Dist. 5, NYC, 1989; named Bilingual Tchr. of Yr., NYC Sch. Dist. Five PS 161, 1987. Mem.: Broward-Dade Fla. Bilingual Tchrs. Assn., Broward-Dade County Multicultural Educators, Bilingual Educators Am., Internat. Reading Assn. Home: 752 Lake Blvd Weston FL 33326 Office: Sch Bd Broward County Fla KC Wright Bldg 201 SE 3rd Ave Fort Lauderdale FL 33326 Office Phone: 754-323-0000. Personal E-mail: stephenppnyc@myacc.net.

POLLITT, BYRON H., JR., finance company executive, former retail executive; b. 1951; BS in Bus. Econs., U. Calif.; MBA, Harvard U. Mgmt. cons. McKinsey & Co.; v.p. corp. ops. planning Walt Disney Co., 1990—92, v.p. bus. planning, 1992—94, CFO, 1994—95, sr. v.p., CFO Disneyland Resorts, 1995—99, exec. v.p., CFO Walt Disney Pks. and Resorts, 1999—2003; exec. v.p., CFO Gap, Inc., San Francisco, 2003—07; CFO Visa Inc., Foster City, Calif., 2007—. Bd. mem. ARC Bay Area Chpt. Office: Visa Inc 900 Metro Ctr Blvd Foster City CA 94404 Office Phone: 650-952-4400.

POLLNER, LESLIE, legislative staff member; d. Melvin and Judy Pollner; m. Noam Levey. BA, Pomona Coll., Claremont, Calif., 1997; attended, Harvard U. Kennedy Sch. Govt., Mass., 2000—02. Assoc. Calif. Cmty. Found., 1998—2000; legis. dir., Councilwoman Wendy Greuel LA City Coun., dep. chief of staff, Councilwoman Wendy Greuel, 2002—06; comm. dir., Rep. Tim Mahoney US House of Reps., Washington, 2008, chief of staff to Rep. Suzanne Kosmas, 2008—. Coro fellow, Coro Southern Calif., 1997—98. Democrat. Office: 238 Cannon House Office Bldg Washington DC 20515 Office Phone: 202-225-2706. Office Fax: 202-226-6299.*

POLLOCK, ALEXANDER JOHN, banker; b. Indpls., Jan. 28, 1943; s. Alex S. and Doris L. (VanHorn) P.; m. Anne M. Fryfogle, Jan. 27, 1968; children: Elizabeth, Alexander, Evelyn, James. BA, Williams Coll., 1965; MA, U. Chgo., 1966; M.P.A., Princeton U., 1969. Instr. philosophy Lake Forest Coll., Ill., 1967; with internat. banking dept. Continental Ill. Nat. Bank, Chgo., 1969-77, v.p., 1977-82, sr. v.p., 1982-85; prin. Nolan Norton & Co., Chgo., 1985-86; chief fin. officer Marine Corp., Milw., 1986; pres. Marine Bank N.A., Milw., 1987; pres., CEO Cmty. Fed. Savs., St. Louis, 1988-90; vis. scholar Fed. Res. Bank of St. Louis, 1991; pres., CEO Fed. Home Loan Bank Chgo., 1991—2004; fellow Am. Enterprise Inst. Pub. Policy Rsch., Washington, 2004—. Bd. dirs. Gt. Lakes Higher Edn. Corp., Allied Capital Corp., CME Group; past pres. Internat. Union for Housing Fin. Chmn. bd. dirs. Great Books Found. Mem.: Union League Club(Chgo.), Univ. Club-(Washington), Phi Beta Kappa. Office: Am Enterprise Inst 1150 Seventeenth St NW Washington DC 20036 Office Phone: 202-862-7190. Business E-Mail: apollock@aei.org. *Omnia superans vi rationis et arte loquendi.*

POLLOCK, BRUCE GODFREY, psychiatrist, educator; s. Ira Justus and Sheila Joy (Godfrey) P.; m. Judith Arluk, May 18, 1982; children: Debra, Ariel. BS, U. Toronto, 1975, MD, 1979; PhD, U. Pitts., 1987. Chief resident Clarke Inst. Psychiatry, Toronto, 1982-83; fellow U. Pitts., 1983-84, asst. prof. dept. psychiatry, 1984-90, assoc. dir. clin. pharmacology dept. psychiatry, 1987-95, assoc. prof. dept. psychiatry and pharmacology, 1990-96, dir. geriat. psychopharm. dept. psychiatry and pharmacology, 1995—, prof. depts. psychiatry, pharmacology and pharm. scis., 1997—, chief acad. divsn. geriatrics and neuropsychiatry, 2001, Sandra A. Rotman chair neuropsychiatry, 2005—; head divsn. geriatric psychiatry U. Toronto, 2005—; v.p. rsch. CAMH, 2008—. Contbr. chapters to books, articles to profl. jours. Centennial fellow Med. Rsch. Coun. of Can., Ottawa, 1983, Merck fellow geriatric clin. pharmacology, Am. Fedn. for Aging Rsch., N.Y.C., 1988; recipient Geriat. Mental Health award NIMH, Bethesda, Md., 1992, Ind. Scientist award, 1997, Sr. Investigation Award, Am. Assoc. for Geriatric Psychiatry, Bethesda, Md., 2003. Fellow Royal Coll. Physicians Can., Am. Psychiat. Assn. (disting., Jack Weinberg Meml. award, 2009). Office: Ctr Addiction & Mental Health 33 Russell St Rm T109 Toronto ON M5S 2S1 Canada

POLLOCK, DAVID DANIEL, biologist, educator, research scientist; b. Calif. s. Alan Pollock and Urashan; m. Anabel E. Adler; children: Heather E. Adler-Pollock, Liam D. Adler-Pollock, Gabriel Adler-Pollock. BA in BioChemistry, U. Calif., Berkeley, 1986; PhD, Stanford U., 1995. Burroughs-Wellcome Fund fellow Nat. Inst. for Med. Rsch./Cambridge (England) U., 1997—99, U. Calif., Berkeley, 1999—2000; dir.'s fellow Los Alamos (N.Mex.) Nat. Lab.; asst. prof., adj. La. State U., Baton Rouge, 2000—01, asst. prof., 2001—. Grantee Rsch. Competitiveness Subprogram, State of La. Bd. of Regents, 2001—04; Hitchings-Elion fellow, Burroughs-Wellcome Fund, 1997—2000, R24 Glue grantee, NIH, 2002—, R22/R33 Innovation/Devel. grantee, 2002—. Mem.: AAAS, Internat. Soc. Computational Biologists, Protein Soc., Soc. Systematic Biology. Avocations: guitar, hiking. Office: La State U 202 Life Scis Bldg Baton Rouge LA 70803 E-mail: dpollock@lsu.edu.

POLLOCK, DONALD, communications educator, filmmaker; b. NYC, Dec. 18, 1953; s. Bernice Sylvia Pollock; m. Frances Gonzales Gonzales, Feb. 18, 1988; children: Ariella Flora Gonzales, McKinley Morganfield Gonzales. BA, SUNY, Binghamton, 1974; MA in Social Work, U. Hawaii, Honolulu, 1978; MFA, U. Southern Calif., LA, 1987. Cert. in ultimedia Cal Poly Pomona, 1995. Sta. mgr. LVTV-3 La Verne Cmty. TV, Calif.; prof. U. La Verne, Calif., 1991—. Prodr.(director,writer,camera): (documentaries) Temple Beth Israel: Celebrating 75 Years (Telly and Pegasus, 2008), (director,writer) University of La Verne College of Law Founders Gala (Pegasus, 2008), Sarah and Michael Abraham Profile (Telly and Pegasus and Broadcast Edn. Assn., 2008), James Swift Profile (Pegasus, 2008), Terry Deal Profile (Pegasus and Telly and Broadcast Edcuation Assn., 2007), (promotional video) Leroy Haynes Center (Pegasus and Alliance for Cmty. Media, 2008). Mem. religious sch. com. and brotherhood Temple Beth Israel, Pomona, Calif., 1999—2006. Recipient Robert Bennett Award, Am. Film Inst., 1994, Cable Ace, CCA, 1988; Faculty Fellowship, Nat. Assn. TV Program Executives, 2008, Artist in Residence, Calif. Arts Coun., 1990—91. Home: PO Box 1947 Claremont CA 91711 Office: Univ of La Verne 1950 Third St La Verne CA 91750

POLLOCK, ELLEN JOAN, editor; b. Mar. 4, 1955; Reporter Am. Lawyer mag., NYC; editor Manhattan Lawyer; with Wall St. Jour., 1989—2007, legal issues editor, 1989, sr. writer, dep. page one editor; exec. editor BusinessWeek, 2007—. Author: Turks and Brahmins: Upheaval at Milbank, Tweed Wall Street's Gentlemen Take Off Their Gloves, 1990, The Pretender: How Martin Frankel Fooled the Financial World and Led the Feds on One of the Most Publicized Manhunts in History, 2002. Office: BusinessWeek 43rd Fl McGraw-Hill Bldg 1221 Ave of Americas New York NY 10020

POLLOCK, GALE SUSAN, career military officer; b. Kearny, NJ, 1954; BS in Nursing, U. Md., Balt., 1976; MBA, Boston U., 1984; M in Healthcare Adminstrn., Baylor U., 1987; MA in Nat. Security & Strategy, Nat. Def. U., 1997; D in Pub. Svc. (hon.), U. Md., Balt., 2005; grad., US Dept. Def. CAPSTONE Program, Sr. Svc. Coll. at Idsl. Coll. Armed Forces, Air War Coll., Interagency Inst. Fed. Health Care Execs., Milt. Health Sys. CAPSTONE Program, Principles Advanced Nurse Adminstrs., NATO Staff Office Course. Cert. Registered Nurse Anesthetist. Enlisted US Army, advanced through grades to maj. gen., 2004, spl. asst. to surgeon gen. for info. mgmt. and health policy; comdr. Martin Army Cmty. Hosp., Ft. Benning, Ga., US Army Med. Activity, Ft. Drum, NY; staff officer Strategic Initiatives Command Group for Army Surgeon Gen.; healthcare advisor to Congl. Commn. to Svc. Mems. and Vets. Transition Assistance US Dept. Def.; health fitness advisor Nat. Def. U.; sr. policy analyst in health affairs US Dept. Def.; chief Anesthesia Nursing Svc., Walter Reed Army Med. Ctr., Washington, DC; lead agent TRICARE Pacific, Honolulu; commdg. gen. Tripler Army Med. Ctr. of Pacific Regional Med. Command, Honolulu; chief Army Nurse Corps, 2004—06; dep. surgeon gen. US Army, 2006—07, acting surgeon gen., 2007, dep. surgeon gen. for force mgmt., 2007—. Decorated Disting. Svc. medal US Army, Legion of Merit with 2 oak leaf clusters, Def. Meritorious Svc. medal, Meritorious Svc. medal with 4 oak leaf clusters, Joint Svc. Commendation medal, Army Commendation medal, Army Achievement medal, Expert Field Med. Badge, Parachutist Badge, Army Staff Identification Badge, German Armed Forces Milt. Efficiency Badge in Gold. Fellow: Am. Coll. Healthcare Execs. Office: Tripler Army Med Ctr 160 Krukowski Rd Honolulu HI 96859 Office Phone: 808-433-5716.

POLLOCK, JOHN PHLEGER, retired lawyer; b. Sacramento, Apr. 28, 1920; s. George Gordon and Irma (Phleger) P.; m. Juanita Irene Gossman, Oct. 26, 1945; children: Linda Pollock Harrison, Madeline Pollock Chiotti, John, Gordon. AB, Stanford U., 1942; JD, Harvard U., 1948. Bar: Calif. 1949, U.S. Supreme Ct. 1954. Ptnr. Musick, Peeler & Garrett, LA, 1953-60, Pollock, Williams & Berwanger, LA, 1960-80, Rodi, Pollock, Pettker, Christian & Pramov, LA, 1980—89, of counsel, 1989—. Contbr. articles to profl. publs. Trustee Pitzer Coll., Claremont, Calif., 1968-76, Fletcher Jones Found., 1969—, Good Hope Med. Found., 1980-2006, Pacific Legal Found., 1981-91; pres. LA area coun., Boy Scouts Am., 1970. Fellow Am. Coll. Trial Lawyers; mem. ABA, LA County Bar Assn. (trustee 1964-66). Home: 30602 Paseo Del Valle Laguna Niguel CA 92677-2317 Home Phone: 949-495-2948. Personal E-mail: phleger1@msn.com.

POLLOCK, KAREN ANNE, computer analyst; b. Elmhurst, Ill., Sept. 6, 1961; d. Michael Paul and Dorothy Rosella (Foskett) Pollock. BS, Elmhurst Coll., 1984; MS, North Ctrl. Coll., 1993. Formatter Nat. Data Corp., Lombard, Ill., 1985; computer specialist Dept. VA, Hines, Ill., 1985—. Lutheran. Avocations: cross-stitch, mystery books, bowling, bicycling, softball.

POLLOCK, LAWRENCE IRA (LARRY POLLOCK), investment company executive; b. 1947; BS in Mktg. & Retailing, Ohio State U., 1969. Pres., CEO Karten's Jewelers, 1990—94; pres., COO Zale Corp., 1994—96; exec. v.p., COO Home Place Inc., 1997—98, pres., CEO, 1998—99; pres. Cole Nat. Corp., 2000—03, pres., CEO, 2003—04; pres., mng. ptnr. Lucky Stars Partners, LLC, Cleve., 2004—; non-exec. chmn. Borders Group Inc., Ann Arbor, 2006—09. Bd. dirs. New West Eyeworks, Inc., 1990—98, Zale Corp., 1994—96, Borders Group Inc., 1995—, Cole Nat. Corp., 2000—04, Gemesis Corp., 2007—, Cardinal Commerce Corp. Chmn. Bellefaire JCB; trustee Musical Arts Assn. (Cleveland Orch.), Nat. Conf. for Cmty. & Justice No. Ohio region, WVIZ/PBS & 90.3 WCPN ideastream. Office: Lucky Stars Partners LLC 18100 S Pk Blvd Cleveland OH 44120*

POLLOCK, MARTIN L., state agency administrator; b. Paterson, NJ, July 3, 1954; s. Irving N. and Selma Pollock; m. Angeli S. Sancho, July 3, 1993; children: Sarah A., Abby M. BS, Rutgers U., New Brunswick, NJ, 1979; MS in Nuc. Pharmacy, U. So. Calif., LA, 1979; MS in Biochemistry & Biophysics, Oreg. State U., Corvalli, 1987; PharmD, U. Ark., Little Rock, 1999. Drug safety evalulator Food & Drug Adminstrn., Silver Spring, Md., 2000—08. Home: 6413 Lochridge Rd Columbia MD 21044 Office: Food & Drug Administrn 10903 New Hampshire Ave Silver Spring MD 20993-0002 Personal E-mail: mlpollock1@earthlink.net. Business E-Mail: martin.pollock@fda.hhs.gov.

POLLOCK, MICHAEL E., mathematics educator, football coach, director; b. Americus, Ga., Apr. 10, 1971; s. Donald Eugene and Brenda Floyd Pollock; m. Jane Watson, Dec. 31, 2003; children: Ragan Wingate, Jade Whitney Murray, Jalen Watson Murray, Brennan Victoria. BSED, U. Ga., Athens, 1993; MEd, U. Scranton, Pa., 2006. Cert. ednl. leadership Ga., 2008. Asst. athletic dir. asst. head football coach Valdosta HS, Ga., 2006—. Mem.: Ga. Athletic Coaches Assn. (Region Coach of Yr. 1997, 2000—01), Profl. Ga. Educators. Conservative. Baptist. Avocations: hunting, fishing, music, sports. Home: 4884 Twin Shadows Rd Valdosta GA 31602 Office: Valdosta HS 3101 N Forrest St Valdosta GA 31602 Business E-Mail: mpollock@gocats.org.

POLLOCK, R. JEFFREY, lawyer; b. San Francisco, Jan. 5, 1946; BA, DePauw U., 1968; MT, Harvard U., 1971; JD, Northeastern U., 1976. Bar: Ohio 1976, Mich. 2002. Asst. sec. dept. community devel. Commonwealth of Mass., 1972—73; assoc. Burke, Haber & Berick, Cleve., 1976—84, ptnr., 1984—90; atty. McDonald, Hopkins LLC, prin., 1990—; gen. counsel Metaldyne Corp., 2001—05. Mem. ABA, Ohio State Bar Assn., Cleve. Bar Assn. Office: McDonald Hopkins LLC 600 Superior Ave E Ste 2100 Cleveland OH 44114-2653 Home Phone: 216-321-2565; Office Phone: 216-348-5400. E-mail: jpollock@mcdonaldhopkins.com.

POLLOCK, ROBERT B., insurance company executive; BBA, Univ. Wis., Madison, 1976. Actuary CUNA Mutual Ins. Co., 1974—81; staff actuary through sr. v.p. Assurant Employee Benefits, 1981—93; pres., CEO Assurant Employee benefits, 1993—99; exec. v.p., CFO Assurant Inc., 1999—2005, pres., COO, 2005—06, pres., CEO, 2006—07, on adminstrv. leave, 2007—08, pres., CEO, 2008—. Past chmn., disability ins. com. Health Ins. Assn. Am. Fellow: Soc. of Actuaries; mem.: Am. Acad. of Actuaries. Office: Assurant Inc 1 Chase Manhattan Plz New York NY 10005

POLLOCK, ROBERT ELWOOD, nuclear scientist; b. Regina, Sask., Can., Mar. 2, 1936; s. Elwood Thomas and Harriet Lillian (Rooney) Pollock; m. Jean Elizabeth Virtue, Sept. 12, 1959; children: Bryan Thomas, Heather Lynn, Jeffrey Parker, Jennifer Lee. BSc (hon.), U. Man., Can., 1957; MA, Princeton U., 1959, PhD, 1963. Instr. Princeton (N.J.) U., 1961—63, asst. prof., 1964—69, rsch. physicist, 1969—70; Nat. Rsch. Coun. Can. postdoctoral fellow Harwell, England, 1963—64; assoc. prof. Ind. U., Bloomington, 1970—73, prof., 1973—84, disting. prof., 1984—2001, prof. emeritus, 2001—, dir. Cyclotron Facility, 1973—79, mem. nuc. sci. adv. com., 1977—80. Recipient Alexander von Humboldt Sr. U.S. Scientist award, 1985—88. Fellow: Am. Phys. Soc. (Bonner prize 1992). Home: 2811 Dale Ct Bloomington IN 47401-2414 Office: Ind U Swain Hall Dept Physics Bloomington IN 47405

POLLOCK, STEWART GLASSON, lawyer, state supreme court justice; b. East Orange, NJ, Dec. 21, 1932; BA, Hamilton Coll., 1954, LLD (hon.), 1995; LLB, NYU, 1957; LLM, U. Va., 1988. Bar: NJ 1958. Asst. U.S. atty., Newark, 1958-60; ptnr. Schenck, Price, Smith & King, Morristown, NJ, 1960-74, 76-78; commr. N.J. Dept. Pub. Utilities; counsel to gov. State of N.J., Trenton, 1978-79; assoc. justice N.J. Supreme Ct., Morristown, 1979-99; of counsel Riker Danzig Hyland & Perretti, Morristown, 1999—. Mem. NJ Commn. on Investigation, 1976-78; chmn. commn. on the rules of profl. conduct NJ Supreme Ct., 2000-09; co-chmn. Govs. Judicial Adv. Panel, Govs. Ethics Advisors Commn., Govt. Adv. Panel on Ethics, 2009- Contbr. articles to profl. jours. Fellow Am. Coll. Comml. Arbitrators; mem. ABA (chmn. appellate judges conf. 1991-92), N.J. Bar Assn. (trustee 1973-78), Morris County Bar Assn. (pres. 1973). Office: Riker Danzig Scherer Hyland & Perretti LLP Hdqs Plz 1 Speedwell Ave Morristown NJ 07962-1981 Business E-Mail: spollock@riker.com.

POLLY, DAVID W., JR., surgeon; b. Stuttgart, Germany, Mar. 14, 1957; m. Shirley Polly, June 23, 1984. BS, US Mil. Acad., West Point, NY, 1979. Cert. med. dr. USUHS, 1985. Col. USAR, Walter Reed, 1983—2003; chief orthop. surgery Walter Reed Army Med. Ctr., Washington, 2001—03, chief spine surgery, 1992—2001, U. Minn., Mpls., 2003—. Sec. Scoliosis Rsch. Soc., Milw., 2005—. Decorated Legion of Merit USAR. Office: Dept Orthop Surgery Univ Minn 2450 Riverside Ave S R200 Minneapolis MN 55454

POLOMSKY, MICHAEL DOUGLAS, psychology professor; b. Cleve., Utah, Sept. 24, 1954; s. John Paul and Nancy June Polomsky; m. Juanita L. Berr; children: Michael Ray, Jennifer Cathrine Esterle, Douglas Anthony. PhD, U. Akron, Ohio, 1991. V.p., gen. mgr. Barrett & Assoc., Inc., Akron, 1987—2001; prof. Cleve. State U., 1991—. Named Outstanding Prof., Nance Coll. Bus. Mem.: APA.

POLONSKY, ARTHUR, artist, educator; b. Lynn, Mass., June 6, 1925; s. Benjamin and Celia (Hurwitz) P.; children: Eli, D.L., Gabriel. Diploma with highest honors, Sch. Mus. Fine Arts, Boston, 1948. Instr. painting dept. Sch. Mus. Fine Arts, Boston, 1950-60; asst. prof. dept. fine arts Brandeis U., 1954-65; assoc. prof. Boston U., 1965-90, prof. emeritus, 1990—. One-man shows include Boris Mirski Gallery, Boston, 1950, 1954, 1956, 1964, Durlacher Gallery, NYC, 1965, Mickelson Gallery, Washington, 1966, 1974, Boston Pub. Libr., 1969, 1990, 1993, 1996, 1999, Boston Ctr. for Arts, 1983, Starr Gallery, Boston, 1987, Fitchburg Art Mus., 1990, Kantar Fine Arts, Newton, Mass., 2002, St. Botolph Club Gallery, Boston, 2004—05, exhibitions include Danforth Musuem, Framingham, Mass., 2008, Met. Mus., NYC, 1950, exhibited in group shows at The Salon Des Jeunes Peintres, Paris, 1950, Stedelijk Mus., Amsterdam, The Netherlands, 1950, Carnegie Internat. Expn., 1951, Boston Arts Festival, 1954—55, 1985, Inst. Contemporary Art, Boston, 1960, Boston Mus. Fine Arts, 1976, Expressionism in Boston, Decordova Mus., Lincoln, Mass., 1986, Palais Univ. de Strasbourg, France, 1992, Boston's Honored Artists, Danforth Mus., Framingham, Mass., 1995, 2007, DeCordova Mus., Lincoln, Mass., 2002, Sagendorph Gallery, Keene State Coll., Keene, NH, 2003, Francesca Anderson Gallery, Lexington, Mass., 2004, Represented in permanent collections Mus. Fine Arts, Boston, Fogg Mus., Harvard U., Addison Gallery of Am. Art, Andover, Mass., Stedelijk Mus., Amsterdam, Walker Art Ctr., Mpls., Zimmerli Art Mus., Rutgers U., New Brunswick, NJ, Honolulu Acad. Arts, DeCordova Mus., Lincoln, Mass., High Mus. Art, Atlanta, The Danforth Mus., Framingham, Mass. Recipient Louis Comfort Tiffany award for painting, 1951, 1st prize Boston Arts Festival, 1954; European travelling fellow Sch. Mus. Fine Art, Boston, 1948-50; named Copley Master, Copley Soc. Boston, 1986. Address: 364 Cabot St Newtonville MA 02460-2252 Office Phone: 617-969-6789.

POLOUJADOFF, MICHEL EUGENE, electrical engineering educator; b. Asnières, France, Apr. 2, 1932; s. Léon and Marguerite Blanche (Guillot) Poloujadoff; m. Jacqueline Suatton, Mar. 21, 1964; children: Muriel, Marie-Pierre. Degree, Ecole Superieure d'Electricité, Paris, 1955; MS, Harvard U.; DSc in Physics, U. Paris, 1960; Doct.h.c., Liége U., 1983, Budapest U., 1989, Bucharest U., 1996. Prof. U. Grenoble, France, 1961-83, 84-85, U. Pierre et Marie Curie, Paris, 1985—97, emeritus prof., 1997—; prof., chair Ecole Centrale, Paris, 1985-96; disting. Hooker vis. prof. McMaster U., Hamiton, Ont., Can., 1983-84. Author: The Theory of Linear Induction Machinery, 1980; author: (Chinese transl.), 1985; author: (3 tutorial books); author: (Spanish transl.); editl. bd. mem. 3 internat. revs. in field; contbr. more than 200 papers. Lt. Armée de l'Air, 1960—61, France. Decorated Officer of the Crown King of Belgium, Chevalier de la le'gion d'honneur French Pres.; recipient Charles Saulces de Freycinet award, Acad. Sci. Paris, 1987, Cert. of Appreciation, Assn. Elec. Engring. Specialists of Tunisia and Tunis Higher Sch. for Sci. and Tech., 2004; named Hon. Mem., Romanian Acad. Tech. Scis., 2004. Fellow: IEEE (Nikola Tesla award 1991, Lamme medal 1994), N.Y. Acad. Scis.; mem.: Soc. Electriciens et Electr. (émérite). Roman Catholic. Avocations: skiing, photography, gardening. Home: 2 Rue Duméril 75013 Paris France Office: U Paris 4 Place Jussieu 75252 Paris France Office Phone: +33-1-4427-9629. Business E-Mail: michel.poloujadoff@upmc.fr. E-mail: mpo@ccr.jussieu.fr.

POLOVINA, GINA BRI-ANNE, casino gaming company executive; d. Brian James and Marilyn Polovina, Jack David Bulavsky (Stepfather); m. Ira David Sternberg, Jan. 4, 2003; stepchildren: Sarah Sternberg, Michael Sternberg, Aaron Sternberg. BA in Polit. Sci., U. Nev., Las Vegas, 1991, MA in Polit. Sci., 1994. Account exec. & polit. cons. Joyce Advt., Las Vegas, 1992—94; v.p., govt. affairs Boyd Gaming Corp., Las Vegas, 1994—. Chair Leadership Las Vegas, 2002—04, Nev. Vol. Commn., 2006—; bd. trustee Las Vegas C. of C., 2002—; past pres. UNLV Coll. Liberal Arts Cmty. Adv. Bd., Las Vegas, 2002—; founder & past chair Nevadagives, Las Vegas, 2004—09; vol. dir. United Way Southern Nev., Las Vegas, 2006—, Three Square, Las Vegas, 2007—; co-chair United Way Commitment Edn. Coun., Las Vegas, 2007—;

mem., cmty. stakeholders adv. bd. Regional Transp. Commn., Las Vegas, 2008—. Recipient Recognition award, Global Gaming Bus., 2003, Outstanding Alumnus award, U. Nev. Las Vegas Coll. Liberal Arts, 2004, Athena award, Women's C. of C. Nevada, 2007; named Most Influential Women in Southern Nev., InBus. Las Vegas, 2004, Alumni of Yr., Coll. Liberal Arts U. Nev. Las Vegas Alumni Assn., 2008; named to Leadership Las Vegas Hall of Fame, Las Vegas C. of C., 2007. Mem.: Women's C. of C. Avocations: travel, current events. Office: Boyd Gaming Corp 3883 Howard Hughes Pky 9th Fl Las Vegas NV 89169 Office Fax: 702-792-7263. Business E-Mail: ginapolovina@bodygaming.com.

POLSBY, ALLEN ISAAC, retired lawyer; b. New Haven, Nov. 4, 1937; s. Daniel II and Edythe (Woolf) Polsby; m. Gail Kissling, Aug. 30, 1963; children: Daniel Laurence, Abigail Starr. AB, Brown U., Providence, 1959; JD, George Wash. U., Washington, 1962. Bar: DC 1962, US Ct. Appeals (DC cir.) 1963, US Supreme Ct. 1979. Assoc. Denning & Wohlstetter, Washington, 1962—63; trial atty. CAB, 1963—66; asst. counsel rsch. Com. Govt. Ops.; tech. programs subcom. US Ho. Reps., 1966; atty. Office Gen. Counsel, HUD, Washington, 1966—2003, acting gen. counsel, 1996, assoc. gen. counsel legis. and regulations, 2000—03.

POLSBY, DANIEL D., dean, law educator; b. Norwich, Conn., Mar. 14, 1945; BA, Oakland U., 1964; JD magna cum laude, U. Minn., 1971. Bar: Minn. 1971, D.C. 1972, Ill. 1977, N.Y. 1982. Law clk. to Judge Harold Leventhal U.S. Ct. Appeals (D.C. cir.), 1971-72; assoc. Wilmer, Cutler & Pickering, Washington, 1972-74; legal adviser to commr. FCC, Washington, 1974-76; asst. prof. law Northwestern U., Chgo., 1976-78, assoc. prof., 1978-79, prof., 1979—99, Kirkland & Ellis prof., 1990—99; prof. law George Mason U., Sch. Law, 1999—, assoc. dean, 1999—2004, acting dean, 2004—05, dean, 2005—. Vis. prof. Cornell U., 1981-82, U. Mich., 1982, U. So. Calif., 1990, Chgo. corr., The Economist, 1990-1994, legal. Author: The False Promise of Gun Control, 1994. Mem. ABA, ALI, Order of Coif. Office: George Mason U Sch Law 3301 Fairfax Dr Arlington VA 22201-4426 Office Phone: 703-993-8087. E-mail: polsby@gmu.edu.*

POLSGROVE, CAROL CLAXON, writer, retired communications educator; b. Louisville, Feb. 19, 1945; d. William Neville and Emma Osborne Claxon; 1 child, Cora. BA, Wake Forest U., Winston-Salem, NC, 1966; MA, U. Louisville, 1969, PhD, 1973. Instr. Maysville CC, Maysville, Ky., 1973—74; asst. prof. Eastern Ky. U., Ky., 1974—77; lectr. San Jose State U., Calif., 1978—80, 1982—83, Calif. State U., Hayward, 1987—89; prof. Ind. U., Bloomington, 1989—2008; ret., 2008. Author: It Wasn't Pretty Folks, But Didn't We Have Fun? Esquire in the Sixties, 1995, Divided Minds: Intellectuals and the Civil Rights Movement, 2001, Ending British Rule in Africa: Writers in a Common Cause, 2009; assoc. editor: The Progressive, 1980—81; editor: Mother Jones, 1983—85; mem. adv. bd.: Reporting Civil Rights, 2003; contbr. articles to Sierra, The Atlantic, The Progessive, Oceans, The American Prospect, The Nation.

POLSTER, JAMES, writer, film producer; b. Cleve., Sept. 14, 1947; s. Harold and Ethel Polster; m. Carol Pulitzer, Oct. 29, 1982; 1 child, Nick. BS, Tulane U., 1969; MA, Columbia U., 1973; EdM, Harvard U., 1982. Free lance journalist L.A. Times, San Francisco Examiner, Boston Globe, others, 1977-89; screenwriter Columbia/Tri-Star, Hollywood, Calif., 1988; prodr. Columbia Pictures, Burbank, Calif., 1991-95, NBC, Burbank, 1991-95. Advisor Indira Ghandi, New Delhi, 1979; spokesman Save the Rain Forest, 1987; lectr. in field. Author: A Guest in the Jungle, 1987 (MacDowell award 1988), Brown, 1995 (Critics Choice award 1995, Publishers Weekly Best Book of the Yr., Cable Radio Network Best Book of the Yr., Grad. Student, 2009); prodr. moves: Hart to Hart, others. Named to Shaker Heights (Ohio) Hall of Fame, 1996; recipient New Orleans Press Club awards, 1980, 81, Spl. Jury prize Internat. Film Festival, 1987; Wurlitzer Found. fellow, 1988; Calif. Arts Coun. grantee, 1995. Fellow Explorers Club; mem. Internat. Soc. Philos. Inquiry, Writers Guild Am., Vintage Auto Racing Assn., Fgn. Corr. Club (hon.), London Press Club (hon.). Avocations: auto racing, bobsled racing, hydroplane racing, drums.

POLSTON, RICKY L., state supreme court justice; m. Deborah Ehler Polston; four children, six adopted children. BS summa cum laude, Fla. State Univ., 1977, JD with high honors, 1986. CPA 1978; bar: Fla. 1987, US Dist. Ct., No., Middle & So. Fla. Districts, US Tax Ct., US Ct. Appeals 11th Cir., US Ct. Appeals Fed. Cir., US Ct. Fed. Claims, US Supreme Ct. Pub. acctg. practice, 1977—84; private law practice, 1987—2000; judge Fla. Ct. Appeal, 1st Dist., 2001—08; assoc. justice Fla. Supreme Ct., 2008—. Mem.: Tallahassee Bar Assn., Tallahassee Inn of Ct., Am. Inst. CPAs, Fla. Inst. CPAs, Beta Alpha Psi, Order of the Coif. Office: Fla Supreme Ct 500 S Duval St Tallahassee FL 32399-1925 Office Phone: 850-488-2361.*

POLUDASU, SHYAM SUNDER, cardiologist; s. Basaviah and Koteswari Poludasu; m. Srilekha Tiruvuri, Sept. 5, 2007. MBBS, Osmania Med. Coll., Hyderabad, BChir, 2000; MD, AMA, 2006. Chief resident VA Med. Ctr., Bklyn., 2006—07; fellow cardiology SUNY Downstate Med. Ctr., Bklyn., 2007—. Contbr. articles to profl. sci. jours. (Bristol-Myers Squibb Travel award, 2009). Recipient Henry I. Russek Travel award, Am. Coll. Cardiology, 2008. Mem.: ACP, AMA, Am. Heart Assn., Am. Coll. Cardiology. Office: SUNY Downstate Med Ctr 450 Clarkson Ave 1199 Brooklyn NY 11229 E-mail: shyam.poludasu@downstate.edu.

POLVERINI, PETER J., dean, dental educator; m. Carol Polverini. B in Biology, Marquette U., 1969, DDS in Dental-Oral Pathology, 1973; DMS, Harvard U. Cert. in oral and maxillofacial pathology Harvard U. Asst. prof. dept. diagnostic and surgical sciences U. Pittsburgh Sch. Dental Medicine, 1977—81; various positions Northwestern U. Med. and Dental Sch., 1981—92; prof. dentistry and chief oral and maxillofacial pathology U. Mich. Sch. Dentistry, 1992—95, chair dept. oral medicine, pathology, and surgery, 1995—96, chair dept. oral medicine, pathology, and oncology, 1996—2000, Donald A. Kerr Endowed Collegiate Prof., 1996—2000; dean U. Minn. Sch. Dentistry, 2000—03, U. Mich. Sch. Dentistry, 2003—. Mem. editl. bd. Lab. Investigation, Jour. Oral Pathology and Medicine; assoc. editor Angiogenesis. Address: U Mich Sch Dentistry 1011 N Univ Ave Ann Arbor MI 48109-1078

POLYAK, KORNELIA, oncologist, researcher; MD, Albert Szent-Gyorgyi Med. U., Hungary, 1991; PhD, Cornell U., 1995. Fellow Johns Hopkins Oncology Ctr.; assoc. prof. dept. med. oncology Harvard Med. Sch.; researcher Dana Farber Cancer Inst. Recipient Scholar award, V Found., 2001. Mem.: Am. Assn. Cancer Rsch. Office: Dana-Farber Cancer Institute 44 Binney St Dana 740C Boston MA 02115 Office Phone: 617-632-2106. Office Fax: 617-580-8490. E-mail: kornelia_polyak@dfci.harvard.edu.*

POLYAKOV, SERGEY VLADIMIROVICH, physicist, researcher; b. Moscow, Dec. 24, 1974; arrived in U.S., 1998; s. Vladimir Sergeevich Polyakov and Irina Nikolaevna Samoylova. MS in Physics, Moscow State U., 1998; PhD in Optics, U. Ctrl. Fla., 2003. Rsch. asst. Sch. of Optics U. Ctrl. Fla., Orlando, Fla., 1998—2003; post doctoral fellow Quantum Optics Group Calif. Inst. of Tech., Pasadena, Calif., 2003—05; mem. faculty dept. physics U. Md., College Park, 2005—. Contbr. articles to profl. jours. Grantee, Internat. Soros Found., 1995, 1997, 1998. Mem.: Optical Soc. of Am. (New Focus award). Achievements include measurement of world record-breaking non-classical (quantum) violation of over 300 for Cauchy-Schwarz inequality, demonstrating strong quantum character of light from a cold atomic ensemble; discovery of 4 photon absorption in polymers (polydiacetylens); design of world's most accurate calibration of single photon detectors; first to establish experimental proof of single photon generation from a cold atomic ensemble; demonstrate the creation storage, transferring and verification of entangled states in macroscopic physically separated systems held 2.8 meters apart. Office: 100 Bureau Dr Stop 8441 Gaithersburg MD 20899 Business E-Mail: sergey.polyakov@nist.gov.

POLYAKOV, YURIY SERGEYEVICH, engineer, researcher; b. Moscow, Sept. 3, 1980; s. Sergey Vladimirovich Polyakov and Lyubov Ivanovna Polyakova. BS in Computer Info. Systems summa cum laude, Excelsior Coll., Albany, NY, 2002; MS in Computer Sci., NJ Inst. Tech., Newark, 2003; PhD in Chem. Engring., Moscow State U. Environ. Engring., 2004; DSc in Physics and Mathematics, Karpov Inst. of Phys. Chemistry, Moscow, Russia, 2007. MCSE, cert. computing prof. Rsch. asst. Moscow State U. Environ. Engring., 1997—98; field engr. Cross Country Land Svcs., Leavenworth, Wash., 1998—99, network adminstr., software engr., 1999—2001; network engr., software engr. Envision Technologies Inc., Wenatchee, 2001—02; rschr., engring. cons. US Poly Rsch., Ashland, Pa., 2002—. Contbr. articles to profl. jours., chapters to books. Recipient Young Scientist award, Moscow Mayor's Office, 2005. Mem.: AIChE, North Am. Membrane Soc., Am. Filtration Soc. Achievements include patents pending for Hollow Fiber Membrane Adsorber and Process for the Use Thereof; research in the theory of novel filtration processes; study of nonuniform particle deposition on the inner and outer surfaces of ultrafiltration and microfiltration membranes; mathematical modeling of coupled turbulent heat and mass transfer with chemical conversions; development of approximate method for nonlinear differential and integrodifferential equations; phenomenological analysis of natural time and space series with stochastically varying components; development of feedback algorithm for switch location with application to network design. Office: USPolyResearch 906 Spruce St Ashland PA 17921 Business E-Mail: ypolyakov@uspolyresearch.com.

POLYCHRONAKOS, ALEXIOS PANTELIS, theoretical physics educator; b. Athens, Greece, June 28, 1959; m. Rodanthy Tzani, Oct. 5, 1990; 1 child, Iason Panteleimon. Elec. engring. diploma, Nat. Tech. U., Athens, 1982; MSc in Physics, Calif. Inst. Tech., Pasadena, 1983, PhD in Physics, 1987. Rsch. fellow U. Fla., Gainesville, 1987-90; rsch. scientist Columbia U., NYC, 1990-92; rsch. assoc. European Ctr. for Nuc. Rsch., Geneva, 1992-95; acad. visitor Norwegian Acad. Sci., Oslo, 1995-96; univ. lectr. Uppsala (Sweden) U., 1995—; assoc. prof. U. Ioannina, Greece, 1996—. Contbr. articles to profl. jours. Office: City College of NY Physics Dept Marshak 419 160 Convent Ave New York NY 10031

POMA, JOHN M., mining company executive, lawyer; BA, MBA, Coll. William and Mary; JD, Emory U. Atty. Jenkins Fenstermaker Krieger Kayes & Farrell, Huntington, W.Va., Midkiff & Hiner, Richmond, Va.; corp. counsel Massey Energy Co., 1996—2000, sr. corp. counsel, 2000—03, v.p., human resources, 2003—09, v.p., chief adminstrv. officer, 2009—. Office: Massey Energy Co 4 N 4th St Richmond VA 23219 Office Phone: 804-788-1800. Office Fax: 804-788-1801.*

POMAHAC, BOHDAN, plastic surgeon, educator; b. Mar. 8, 1971; MD, Palacky U. Sch. Medicine, Czech Republic, 1996. Diplomate Am. Bd. Plastic Surgery. Intern gen. surgery Brigham & Women's Hosp., Boston, 1996—99, resident gen. surgery, 1999—2001, resident plastic surgery, 2001—03, chief resident plastic surgery, 2004, assoc. dir. BWH Burn Ctr., 2004—; asst. prof. Harvard Med. Sch. Contbr. articles to profl. jours. Grantee Greenwall Found. Mem.: Am. Soc. Reconstructive Transplantation (founding mem.), Plastic Surgery Rsch. Coun., Am. Burn Assn., Am. Soc. Reconstructive Microsurgery, Am. Soc. Plastic Surgery. Achievements include leading 35-member medical team that performed the second facial transplant surgery operation in the US on April 9, 2009, a 17 hour procedure in which doctors donated their time while the hospital donated the other costs related to the operation. Office: Brigham & Womens Hosp Divsn Plastic Surgery 75 Francis St Boston MA 02115 Office Phone: 617-732-7796. Office Fax: 617-732-6387. Business E-Mail: bpomahac@partners.org.*

POMBO, RICHARD WILLIAM, former congressman, rancher, farmer; b. Tracy, Calif., Jan. 8, 1961; s. Ralph and Onita Pombo; m. Annette Rina Cole, 1983; children: Richie, Rina, Rachel. Student, Calif. State U., Pomona, 1979—82. Councilman City of Tracy, 1991-92; mayor pro-tem Tracy City Coun., 1992; mem. US Congress from 11th Calif. dist., 1993—2007; mem. agrl. com., resources com., transp. and infrastructure com., chmn. subcom. on livestock and horticulture. Chmn. Pvt. Property Rights Task Force, 1993-94, Endangered Species Act Task Force, 1995-96; co-chmn. Spkr.'s Environ. Task Force, 1996. Author (with Joseph Farah) This Land Is Our Land: How to End the War on Private Property, 1996 Co-founder San Joaquin County Citizen's Land Alliance, Calif., 1986—; active San Joaquin County Econ. Devel. Assn., Tracy Bus. Improvement Dist., City Coun. (vice chmn. Cmty. Devel. Agy., Cmty. Parks Com., and Waste Mgmt. Com.), San Joaquin County Rep. Ctrl. Com. Mem. Rotary Club. Republican. Roman Catholic.

POMERANTZ, MARK F., lawyer, former prosecutor; b. Bklyn., May 3, 1951; BA, Harvard U., 1972; JD magna cum laude, U. Mich., 1975. Bar: N.Y. 1977, U.S. Dist. Ct. (so. dist.) N.Y. 1982, U.S. Ct. Appeals (2nd cir.) 1982, U.S. Ct. Appeals (3rd and 4th cirs.) 1983, U.S. Ct. Appeals (11th cir.) 1988, U.S. Supreme Ct. 1988. Law clk. to Hon. Edward Weinfeld US Dist. Ct. (so. dist.) N.Y., 1975-76; law clk. to Justice Potter Stewart US Supreme Ct., 1976-77; assoc. Davis, Polk & Wardwell, 1977-78; asst. US atty. (so. dist.) N.Y. US Dept. Justice, 1978-82, chief appellate atty., 1981-82, mem. ctrl. screening com., appellate divsn., first dept., 1984-90, chief criminal divsn., 1997—99; ptnr. Clifford Chance Rogers & Wells, NYC, 1990—97, 1999—2000, Paul, Weiss, Rifkind, Wharton & Garrison, 2000—. Assoc. prof. law Columbia U., 1983-84, lectr., 1984-86, Harvard U., 1992. Editor-in-Chief Mich. Law Rev., 1974-75. Mem. ABA, N.Y. Coun. Def. Lawyers, Assn. of Bar of City of N.Y. (criminal cts. com. 1982-83, fed. cts. com. 1983-86, criminal advocacy com. 1986-89), Order of the Coif; fellow, Am. Coll. Trial Lawyers Office: Paul Weiss Rifkind Wharton & Garrison 1285 Ave of the Americas New York NY 10019 E-mail: mpomerantz@paulweiss.com.*

POMERANTZ, MARTIN, chemistry educator, researcher; b. NYC, May 3, 1939; s. Harry and Pauline (Sietz) P.; m. Maxine Miller, June 4, 1961; children: Lee Allan, Wendy Jane, Heidi Lauren. BS, CCNY, 1959; MS, Yale U., 1961, PhD, 1964. NSF postdoctoral fellow U. Wis.-Madison, 1963-64; asst. prof. Case Western Res. U., Cleve., 1964-69; assoc. prof. chemistry Yeshiva U., NYC, 1969-74, prof., 1974-76, chmn. dept., 1971-72, 73-76; prof. chemistry U. Tex.-Arlington, 1976—; co-dir. Ctr. for Advanced Polymer Rsch., 1988-91; dir. Ctr. for Advanced Polymer Rsch., 1991—; vis. assoc. prof. U. Wis.-Madison, 1972; vis. prof. Columbia U., NYC, 1970-75, Ben Gurion U. of the Negev, Beer Sheva, Israel, summers 1981, 85; program officer NSF, 2005—07. Contbr. articles to sci. jours. Fellow Alfred P. Sloan Found., 1971-76, NSF and Sterling, 1962-63, Leeds and Northrup Found., 1960-62, Woodrow Wilson fellow, 1959-60; grantee NSF, Robert A. Welch Found., Def. Adv. Rsch. Projects Agy., Air Force Office Sci. Rsch., Dept. Energy, Petroleum Rsch. Fund, Tex. Advanced Tech. program, Tex. Advanced Rsch. program, Disting. Record of Rsch. award U. Tex., Arlington, 1997, also others. Mem. Am. Chem. Soc. (Wilfred T. Doherty award Dallas-Fort Worth sect. 1997), Phi Beta Kappa, Sigma Xi. Achievements include research in synthesis, reactions and properties of organo lambda-5-phosphazenes, reactions of carbenes with other molecules, with themselves and with diazo precursors; design, synthesis and study of electronically conducting polymers with enhanced properties, synthesis and study of electroluminescent (light emitting) polymers, synthesis and study of potentially planar bithiophenes and trithiophenes, preparation and study of polymeric ionic self-assembled monolayers (ISAMs), non-linear optical materials. Home: 5521 Williamstown Rd Dallas TX 75230-2127 Office: U Tex Dept Chemistry-Biochemistry PO Box 19065 Arlington TX 76019-0065 Office Phone: 817-272-3811. Business E-Mail: pomerantz@uta.edu.

POMERANTZ, MARTIN ARTHUR, astronomer, educator, physicist; b. Bklyn., Dec. 17, 1916; AB, Syracuse U., 1937; MS, U. Pa., 1939; PhD, Temple U., 1951; Fil. Dr. (hon.), U. Uppsala, Sweden, 1967; ScD (hon.), Swarthmore Coll., 1973; DSc (hon.), U. Del., 2001, Syracuse U., 2007. Rsch. asst. Bartol Rsch. Found., 1938—41, rsch. fellow, 1941—43, physicist, 1943—59, dir., 1959—85, pres., 1985—87; v.p. The Franklin Inst., 1967—85, exec. v.p., 1985—87, Bartol prof., 1968—89; prof. emeritus U. Del., 1990—, pres. emeritus, 1987—. Fulbright scholar, vis. prof. Muslim U., Aligarh, India, 1952—53; leader Nat. Geog. Soc. expeditions, 1948—59; chmn. U.S. Com. for Internat. Yrs. of the Quiet Sun Nat. Acad. Scis., 1962—66, mem. Com. on Polar Rsch., 1959—71, mem. Space Sci. Bd., 1963—70, mem. Geophysics Rsch. Bd., 1959—73; v.p. Com for Internat. Yrs. of the Quiet Sun Internat. Coun. Sci. Unions, v.p. Com. Internat. Geophysique, 1962—66; mem. Com. on Solar-Terrestrial Rsch. Nat. Acad. Scis., 1981—86; vis. prof. astronomy Swarthmore Coll., 1961, 64, 67; vis. prof. U. Tokyo, 1983, Potchefstroom U., South Africa, 1987; Sigma Xi nat. lectr., 68; OAS vis. prof., 73. Editor: Jour. of the Franklin Inst.; mem. editl. bd.: Space Sci. Revs.,: Antarctic Rsch. Series. Recipient Centennial Gold medal, Syracuse U., 1970, Prix de la Belgica, Acad. Royal des Scis., des Lettres et des Beaux Arts de Belgique, 1985, Disting. Pub. Svc. award, NSF, 1987, medal for disting. sci. achievement, NASA, 1990. Fellow: AAAS, Am. Geophys. Union, Am. Phys. Soc.; mem.: Am. Polar Soc. (hon.), Rotary Internat., Cosmos Club, Explorers Club, Sigma Pi Sigma (hon.). Home: 100 Deer Valley Rd Apt GE San Rafael CA 94903 Personal E-mail: mapomeratz@sbcglobal.net.

POMERANTZ, MARVIN, thoracic surgeon; b. Suffern, NY, June 16, 1934; s. Julius and Sophie (Luksin) Pomerantz; m. Margaret Twigg, Feb. 26, 1966; children: Ben, Julie. AB, Colgate U., 1955; MD, U. Rochester, 1959. Diplomate Nat. Bd. Med. Examiners, Am. Bd. Surgery, Am. Bd. Thoracic Surgery (bd. dirs. 1989-95). Intern Duke U. Med. Ctr., Durham, NC, 1959—60, resident, 1960—61, instr. surgery, 1966—67; asst. prof. surgery U. Colo. Med. Sch., Denver, 1967—71, assoc. prof. surgery, 1971—74, assoc. clin. prof. surgery, 1974—93, prof. surgery, chief gen. thoracic surgery, 1992—; chief thoracic and cardiovascular surgery Denver Gen. Hosp., 1967—73, asst. dir. surgery, 1967—70, assoc.dir. surgery, 1970—73; pvt. practice Arapahoe CV Assocs., Denver, 1974—92; prof., chief gen. thoracic surgery sect. U. Colo. Health Sci. Ctr., 1992—; resident Duke U. Med. Ctr., Durham, NC, 1963—67. Clin. assoc. surgery br. NCI, 1961—63; mem. staff Univ. Hosp., Denver, Denver Gen. Hosp., Rose Med. Ctr., Denver, Denver VA Med. Ctr., Children's Hosp., Denver, U. Coll. Health Sci. Ctr., 1992—, bd. dirs., 1990—96; vice chmn. Am. Bd. Thoracic Surgery, 1995—97, chmn., 1997—99, Guest editor Chest Surgery Clinics N.Am., 1993; contbr. numerous articles to profl. publs., chapters to books. Master: AMA; fellow: ACS, Am. Coll. Chest Surgeons; mem.: Soc. Vascular Surgeons, Soc. Thoracic Surgeons (nomenclature/coding com. 1991—95, standards and ethics com., govt. rels. com., chmn. program com. 1994—95), Rocky Mtgn. Traumatologic Soc., rgery Soc., Internat. Cardiovascular Soc., Denver Acad. Surgery (pres. 1980), Colo. Med. Soc., Am. Heart Assn. (bd. dirs. Colo. chpt. 1993), Am. Assn. Thoracic Surgeons (program com. 1991), Western Thoracic Surg. Assn. (v.p. 1992, pres. 1993—94, counselor-at-large 1988—90). Office: UCHSC Divsn CTS 4200 E 9th Ave # C310 Denver CO 80262-0001 Business E-Mail: marvin.pomerantz@uchsc.edu.

POMERANTZ, NORA E., lawyer; b. NYC, Nov. 3, 1954; d. Frank Pomerantz and Jane Monell (Cooper) Newman; m. Alan Singer, June 22, 1985; children: Alexandra, Anna. BA cum laude, Kenyon Coll., Gambier, Ohio, 1976; JD summa cum laude, Temple U. Sch. Law, Phila., 1989. Bar: Pa. 1990, NJ 1990, US Tax Ct. 1991. Assoc. Drinker Biddle & Reath LLP, Phila., 1989-98, ptnr., 1998—2005, Duane Morris LLP, Phila., 2005—. Contbg. editor: Estates, Gifts & Trusts Jour. Recipient Israel Packel Meml. award, Temple U. Sch Law, 1989. Mem.: ABA, Phila. Bar Assn. Office: Duane Morris LLP 30 S 17th St Philadelphia PA 19103 Office Phone: 215-979-1929. Office Fax: 215-689-3793. Business E-Mail: NEPomerantz@duanemorris.com.*

POMERANTZ, FELIX, accounting educator; b. Vienna, Mar. 28, 1926; s. Joseph and Irene (Meninger) P.; m. Rita Lewin, June 14, 1953; children: Jeffrey Arthur, Andrew Joseph. BBA, CCNY, 1948; MS, Columbia U., NYC, 1949; PhD, U. Birmingham, Eng., 1992. Diplomate Am. Bd. Forensic Acctg.; CPA, NY, Va., La., NC; cert. computer profl., fraud examiner, govt. fin. mgr. Audit staff Coopers & Lybrand, CPAs, NYC, 1949-56; mgr. Marks, Grey & Shron (now Ernst & Young, CPA's), NYC, 1956-58; asst. chief auditor Am.-Standard, NYC, 1958-62; mgr. systems Westvaco Corp., NYC, 1962-66; dir. operational auditing Coopers & Lybrand, CPAs, NYC, 1966-68, ptnr., 1968-85; disting. lectr./dir. Ctr. for Acctg., Auditing, Tax Studies Fla. Internat. U., Miami, 1985-93, prof. acctg., 1993—2002, assoc. dir. sch. acctg., 1993—99, affil. faculty dept. religious studies, 1996—2002, prof. emeritus, 2003—. Author: Managing Capital Budget Projects, 1984; The Successful Audit: New Ways to Reduce Risk Exposure and Increase Efficiency, 1992; co-author: Pensions-An Accounting and Management Guide, 1976; Auditing in the Public Sector: Efficiency, Economy, and Program Results, 1976; Comparative International Auditing Standards, 1985; contbr. articles to profl. jours. Emeritus trustee Nat. Ctr. for Automated Info. Rsch.; founding mem. Ctr. for Study of Islam and Democracy; founder Afghan Inst. Accts.; mem. rev. panel Inst. Chartered Fin. Analysts of India Jour. Audit Practice. 1st lt. AUS, 1944-46, 51-52. Recipient Spear Safer Harmon faculty fellow Coll. Bus. Administrn., 1987, Outstanding Svc. award, 1998, Matriculation Merit award, 2000. Mem. AICPA, NY State Soc. CPA, Assn. Sys. Mgmt., Acad. Acctg. Historians, Assn. Govt. Accts., NY Acad. Scis., Am. Acctg. Assn.,

Inter-Am. Acctg. Assn., Assn. Cert. Fraud Examiners, Beta Gamma Sigma, Beta Alpha Psi (Most Disting. and Most Outstanding Prof. awards 1993, Most Supportive Prof. award 2002), Alpha Kappa Psi (Dr. Felix Pomeranz Faculty of Yr. award, Endless Work award, Loyal Mem. award 2006). Home: 250 Jacaranda Dr Apt 406 Fort Lauderdale FL 33324-2532 Office: Fla Internat U Sch Acctg University Park Miami FL 33199-0001 Office Phone: 954-370-3276.

POMEROY, CLAIRE, dean, academic administrator, medical educator; m. William Preston Robertson. MD, U. Mich. Coll. Medicine; MBA, U. Ky. Resident in internal medicine and infectious disease U. Minn., fellow internal medicine and infectious diseases, faculty mem., established HIV clinic at Mpls. Veterans' Adminstrn. Med. Ctr.; chief divsn. infectious diseases U. Ky. Coll. Medicine, asst. dean clin. affairs, assoc. dean rsch. informatics, prof.; exec. assoc. dean U. Calif. Davis Sch. Medicine, 2003, prof. infectious diseases and microbiology and immunology, vice chancellor human health sciences, 2005—, dean, 2005—. Faculty senate coun. U. Ky.; reviewer Nat. Institutes of Health, Dept. Veterans' Affairs. Bd. trustee U. Ky. Office: Office of Dean UC Davis Health Sys 2315 Stockton Blvd Sacramento CA 95817 Office Phone: 916-734-3578. E-mail: cpomeroy@ucdavis.edu.*

POMEROY, EARL RALPH, United States Representative from North Dakota, retired commissioner; b. Valley City, ND, Sept. 2, 1952; s. Ralph and Myrtle Pomeroy; 2 children. Student, Valley City State U.; BA in Polit. Sci., U. ND, 1974, JD, 1979. Bar: ND 1979. Atty. Sproul, Lenaburg, Fitzner and Walker, Valley City, 1979-84; mem. ND State Ho. Reps., 1980—84; ins. commr. State of ND, Valley City, 1984-92; mem. US Congress from ND (at large), 1993—, mem. ways and means com., mem. agr. com., co-chair Ho. Dem. Social Security Task Force, co-chair Rural Health Care Coalition. Recipient Found. award Rotary, 1975, Rural Health Champions Legis. award Nat. Rural Health Assn. 2004; named Outstanding Young North Dakotan ND Jaycees, 1982. Mem. Nat. Assn. of Ins. Commrs. (chmn. midwest zone 1987-88, exec. com. 1987-88), Phi Beta Kappa. Democrat. Presbyterian. Office: US House Reps 1501 Longworth House Office Bldg Washington DC 20515 Office Phone: 202-225-2611. Office Fax: 202-226-0893.*

POMEROY, HEATHER ALINE, sales and marketing executive; b. Laconia, NH, Mar. 4, 1977; d. Robert Dan and Mary Eleanor Pomeroy. BA, Dickinson Coll., Carlisle, Pa., 1999. Asst. to French dieticians Dickinson Coll. en France, Toulouse, 1998; tour cons. EF Edn., Cambridge, Mass., 1999—2001, regional sales mgr. Portland, Oreg., 2001—02; account exec. Internat. Data Collection, Chula Vista, Calif., 2002—03, dir. bus. devel., 2003—04, v.p. sales and mktg., 2004—; dir. bus. devel. Datascension, Brea, Calif., 2005—. Newsletter chair person Market Rsch. Assn., San Diego, 2004—. Editor, writer (newsletter) SoCal MRA Newsletter (Cert. of Appreciation, 2004). Grantee, Dickinson Coll., 1995—99. Mem.: Am. Mktg. Assn. (assoc.), Coun. Am. Survey Rsch. Orgns. (assoc.), Mktg. Rsch. Assn. (assoc.), So. Calif. 2002—05, bd. dirs. 2006—), Tri-Delta Sorority (assoc.). Democrat. Avocations: travel, speaking French, running, yoga, drawing. Office Fax: 619-628-2371. Personal E-mail: hpomeroy1@cox.net.

POMEROY, NAOMI, chef; b. Corvallis, Oreg., 1974; m. Michael Hebb (div.). Grad., Lewis & Clark Coll., Portland, Oreg. Co-owner, caterer Ripe; owner, exec. chef Beast, Portland, Oreg., 2007—. Named one of America's Best New Chefs, Food & Wine Mag., 2009. Office: Beast 5425 NE 30th Ave Portland OR 97211*

POMEROY, ROBERT CORTTIS, lawyer; b. Syracuse, NY, Sept. 17, 1943; s. Stuart E. and Elizabeth (Corttis) Pomeroy; m. Sandra Campbell; children: Lisa, Robert Jr., Heather. AB, Hamilton Coll., 1965; LLB, Harvard U., 1968. Bar: Mass. 1968, Fla. 1981. Assoc. Goodwin Procter LLP (formerly Goodwin, Procter & Hoar LLP), Boston, 1968-76, ptnr., 1977—2005, of counsel, 2005—. Mem.: Am. Coll. Trust and Estate Counsel. Avocations: skiing, golf, sailing. Office: Goodwin Procter LLP Exchange Pl Boston MA 02109-2881 Home: PO Box 596 Quechee VT 05059 Home Phone: 802-296-7973; Office Phone: 617-570-1150. Business E-Mail: rpomeroy@goodwinprocter.com.

POMFRET, BONNIE, music educator; d. Richard and Carolyn D. Pomfret; m. Arthur Lewis (div.); 1 child, Cara R. Lewis. State music exam., Musikhoschule Freiburg, Germany, 1977; MusM, Boston Conservatory, 1980; MusD, Ind. U., Bloomington, 1992. Assoc. prof. music Ill. State U., Normal, 1986—97; dir. vocal studies Emory U., Atlanta, 1997—2004; mem. music faculty Shorter Coll., Rome, Ga., 2004—06; dir. opera U. Ala., Birmingham, 2006—07; music faculty Salve Regina U., Newport, RI, 2007—. Cons. in field; pres. McClosky Inst. Voice, Maynard, Mass., 2007—. Singer: (CD) De Toda La Eternidad, 2005. Fellow, NEH, NY and Bayreuth, 1994; Ambassadorial fellow, Rotary Internat., Rome and Berlin, 1980—81. Mem.: Coll. Music Soc., Nat. Assn. Tchrs. Singing, Pi Kappa Lambda. Avocations: walking, gardening, knitting.

POMFRET, DAVID B., medical educator, internist; b. Somerset, Mass., Nov. 22, 1937; s. David B. Pomfret and Rhea Chouinard; m. Anna Rafferty, Mar. 31, 1964; children: Mark, Bruce, Scott, Heidi. BS, Stonehill Coll., 1959; MD, Univ. Coll., Dublin, Ireland, 1964. Diplomate Am. Bd. Internal Medicine. Chief medicine Leonard Morse Hosp., Natick, Mass., 1968—71, chief staff, 1976—80; clin. prof. Tufts U., Boston, 1976—; prof. medicine Tumaini U., Moshi, Tanzania, 1996—2000. Author: Computer Science, 1998, Dispatches From Kilimanjaro, 2006. Recipient Gold medal in surgery, UCD Sch. Medicine, 1964, Silver medal in medicine, 1964; named Outstanding Alumnus, Stonehill Coll., 2003. Fellow: ACP. Republican. Roman Catholic. Avocations: skiing, sailing, offshore racing. Home: 20 Grey Gull Rd Jamestown RI 02835-2808 Office: 15 Rolling Ridge Box 48 Bartlett NH 03812-0048 Home Phone: 401-423-0291; Office Phone: 603-374-2705. Personal E-mail: pomfret1@cox.net.

POMMER, JOHN (JACK POMMER), state legislator; m. Jane Pommer; children: Addie, Brock. BA in Philosophy, U. Colo., Boulder, 1986. TV/video prodr.; adj. prof. U. Colo. Sch. Journalism; mem. Dist. 11 Colo. House of Reps., Denver, 2002—. Active Big Brothers of Colo. Democrat. Office: Colo State Capitol 200 E Colfax Rm 271 Denver CO 80203 Office Phone: 303-866-2780. Business E-Mail: jack.pommer.house@state.co.us.

POMMIER, YVES GEORGES, medical researcher; b. Caen, Calvados, France, Apr. 1, 1951; came to U.S., 1988; s. Roger Pommier and Marie-Therese Blais; m. Françoise Champey, Jan. 4, 1988; children: Gabriel, Elie. MS in Pharmacology, U. Paris, 1978, MD cum laude, 1981, PhD, 1986. Cert. radiation safety authorized user NIH. Resident Paris Hosps., 1978-81; pharmacology asst. U. Paris., 1979-81; vis. fellow Nat. Cancer Inst., NIH, Bethesda, Md., 1981-84, vis. scientist, 1984-95, prin. investigator, 1995—; chief Lab. Molecular Pharmacology, Ctr. Cancer Rsch. NIH, Nat. Cancer Inst., Bethesda, Md., 1997—. Organizer internat. conf. HIV-1 Integrase Inhibitors, 1996; lectr. in field. Mem. editl. bd. Cancer Rsch., Molecular Pharmacology, Anticancer Drug Design, others; contbr. articles to med. jours.; patentee in field. Recipient Impact Medicine Med. Dr. for Yr. 2000, 1992, Fed. Tech. Transfer award, 1994; competitive tng. grantee French Found. for Biol. Rsch., 1981, NIH intramural grantee AIDS Targeted Antiviral Program of Office of Dir., 1993-94, 95-96, 97-98. Mem. French Soc. Pharmacology, Am. Fedn. for Clin. Rsch., Am. Assn. for Cancer Rsch. (program com. 1996-99, chmn. CaiN award 1998), N.Y. Acad. Scis., NIH Apoptosis Interest Group. Democrat. Avocations: painting, tennis, coaching soccer team. Office: Ctr Cancer Rsch Lab Molecular Pharmacology Bldg 37 Rm 5068 37 Convent Dr Bethesda MD 20892-4255 Office Phone: 301-496-5944. Office Fax: 301-402-0752. E-mail: pommier@nih.gov.*

POMORSKI, STANISLAW, lawyer, educator; b. Lwow, Poland, Nov. 23, 1934; arrived in U.S., 1972, naturalized, 1983; s. Juliusz and Maria (Ziemba) Pomorski; m. Patricia Smith; children: Lukasz, Christopher, Maria. M.Law, U. Warsaw, 1956, D.Law, 1968. Law clk., 1958-61; pvt. practice law Warsaw, 1961-64; vis. scholar Harvard U. Law Sch., Cambridge, Mass., 1964-66; rsch. assoc. Polish Acad. Scis., 1966-72; mem. faculty Rutgers U. Law Sch., Camden, NJ, 1973—, prof. law, 1977-81, disting. prof. law, 1981—2006, disting. prof. law emeritus, 2006—. Fellow Soviet law U. Leyden, Netherlands, 1980—81; trustee Nat. Coun. Soviet and East European Rsch., Washington, 1988—94. Author: (book) American Common Law and the Principle Nullum Crimen Sine Lege, 2d edit., 1975, Restructuring the System of Ownership in the USSR, 1991, On Multiculturalism, Concepts of Crime and the De Minimis Defense, 1997, Justice in Siberia, 2001, Modern Russian Criminal Procedure: The Adversarial Principle and Guilty Plea, 2006. Fellow, Ford Found., 1972—73. Office: Rutgers U Law Sch 5th And Penn St Camden NJ 08102 Office Phone: 856-225-6395. Business E-Mail: pomorski@camden.rutgers.edu.

POMP, ALFONS, medical educator; b. Can., Nov. 2, 1954; m. Rachel Chartrand; children: Audrey Chartrand, Genevieve Chartrand. BSc, McGill U., Montreal, 1971—76; MD, Sherbrooke U., 1980. Cert. Am. Bd. Surgery, 1987. Fellow surg. nutrition and metabolism R.I. Hosp./Brown U., 1986—88; assoc. prof. surgery U. Montreal/Hotel Dieu Hosp. Montreal, 1988—99, Mount Sinai Med. Sch., NYC, 1999—2003, Cornell Med. Coll., 2003—07, prof. surgery, 2007—. Contbr. articles to profl. jours. Fellow: ACS. Office: Weill Med Coll Cornell 525 E 68th St Box 294 New York NY 10021 E-mail: alp2104@med.cornell.edu.

POMPA, MARK A., construction executive; married; 3 children. B, Pace U., NY. CPA. Accountant, auditor, bus. advisor Arthur Andersen LLP; v.p., contr. EMCOR Group, Inc., 1994—2003, treas., 2003—07, sr. v.p., chief acctg. officer, 2003—06, exec. v.p., CFO, 2006—. Mem.: AICPA, Conn. State Soc. Cert. Pub. Accountants, Fin. Executives Internat. Office: EMCOR Group Inc Corp Hdqs 301 Merritt Seven Norwalk CT 06851 Office Phone: 203-849-7800. Office Fax: 203-849-7900.*

POMPADUR, I. MARTIN, communications executive; b. Bklyn, June 25, 1935; s. Jack and Florence (Raitbord) P.; m. Joan Lynn Krassner, Dec. 18, 1960 (div. 1986); children: F. Douglas (dec.), Jana Sue; m. Marian Hackett, Dec. 23, 1987 (div. 2003); 1 child, Chelsea Rae. BA, Williams Coll., 1955; LLB, U. Mich., 1958. Bar: Conn. 1958, NY 1961. Atty. ABC-TV Network, NYC, 1960-61, 61-66, chief adminstrv. officer, 1966-68, gen. mgr., 1968-70, v.p. broadcast div., 1970-72, corp. v.p., 1972; pres. ABC Leisure Group I, 1973-75, asst. to pres. parent co., 1975-76; also dir. parent co.; sr. v.p. Ziff Corp., 1977-78, pres., 1978-82; chmn., chief exec. officer GP Sta. Ptnr., 1982-96; mng. gen. ptnr. TV Sta. Ptnr., 1982-96; chmn., CEO PBTV, Inc., 1984-96; mng. gen. ptnr. Northeastern TV Investors Ltd. Partnership, 1984-96; prin. owner, sec. Caribbean Internat. News Corp., 1985—, also bd. dir.; CEO, COO RP Media Mgmt., Inc., 1986—97; CEO ML Media Ptnr., L.P., 1986—97; CEO, COO RP Opportunity Mgmt., 1988—2002; CEO ML Media Opportunity Ptnr., L.P., 1988—2002; exec. v.p. News Corp., 1998—2008; pres. News Corp. Ea. Ctrl. Europe, 1998—2000; chmn. News Corp. Europe, 2000—08; advisor to several cos., 2008—. Bd. dir. Nexstar, RP Coffee Ventures; prin. shareholder Hispanic Media Inc., 1986-90; prin. shareholder, vice-chmn. Hunter Pub. L.P., 1986-94; co-trustee Lidan Trust, 1983-85; atty. Young & Rubicam, Inc., advt. agy., NYC, summer 1961. Mem. Stamford bd. reps., chmn. legis. and rules com., 1959-60. Office: News Corp 28 Fl 1211 Ave of the Americas New York NY 10036 Home Phone: 203-661-0172. Personal E-mail: mpompadur@gmail.com.

POMPEO, ELLEN, actress; b. Everett, Mass., Nov. 10, 1969; d. Joseph and Kathleen Pompeo; m. Chris Ivery, Nov. 9, 2007. Actor: (films) 8 1/2 x 11, 1999, Coming Soon, 1999, Eventual Wife, 2000, In the Weeds, 2000, Moonlight Mile, 2002, Catch Me If You Can, 2002, Daredevil, 2003, Old School, 2003, Undermind, 2003, Nobody's Perfect, 2004, Art Heist, 2004; (TV series) Grey's Anatomy, 2005— (Outstanding Performance by an Ensemble in a Drama Series, SAG, 2007), (TV appearances) Strangers with Candy, 1999, Law and Order, 1996, 2000, Get Real, 2000, Strong Medicine, 2001, The Job, 2001. Office: c/o Creative Artists Agency 2000 Avenue of the Stars Los Angeles CA 90067

POMPER, BRIAN, lawyer, lobbyist; m. Anne Kim Pomper; children: Alexander, Elliot. BS in Mech. Enging., MIT; JD magna cum laude, Cornell U. Law clerk for the Hon. Sidney R. Thomas US Ct. Appeals (9th cir.) Mont.; atty. Skadden, Arps, Slate, Meagher & Flom; chief international trade counsel for chmn. Max Baucus, Fin. Com. US Senate; founding ptnr. Parven Pomper Strategies Inc., Washington. Adj. prof. internat. trade and policy George Washington U. Grad. Sch. Polit. Mgmt.; spkr. in field. Office: Parven Pomper Strategies Inc 1155 21st Street NW, Ste 202 Washington DC 20036 Office Phone: 202-351-6820. Office Fax: 202-223-9805.*

POMPER, PHILIP, historian, educator; b. Chgo., Apr. 18, 1936; s. Solomon and Rebecca (Fenigstein) P.; m. Alice N. Epstein, Aug. 27, 1961 (div.); children: Erica, Stephen, Karen; m. Emily Meyer, June 26, 1994 (dec. July 2003); m. Linda R. Shulsky, March 11, 2007. BA, U. Chgo., 1959, MA, 1961, PhD, 1965. Instr. history Wesleyan U., Middletown, Conn., 1964-65, asst. prof., 1965-71, assoc. prof., 1971-76, prof., 1976—, chmn. dept. history, 1981-84; William F. Armstrong prof. history, 1992—. Author: The Russian Revolutionary Intelligentsia, 1970, 2nd edit., 1993, Peter Lavrov and the Russian Revolutionary Movement, 1972, Sergei Nechaev, 1979 (Choice award 1979), The Structure of Mind in History: Five Major Figures in Psychohistory, 1985, Trotsky's Notebooks, 1933-35: Writings on Lenin, Dialectics and Evolutionism, 1986, Lenin, Trotsky, and Stalin: The Intelligentsia and Power, 1990; assoc. editor History and Theory, 1991—; editor: World History: Ideologies, Structures, and Identities, 1998; co-editor: History and Theory, Contemporary Readings, 1998; co-editor: The Return of Science: Evolution, History and Theory, 2002; contbr. articles on Russian history and theory of history to profl. jours. Fellow, Ford Found., 1963—64, Social Scis. Rsch. Coun., 1968, Hoover Instn., 1987, Wilson Ctr., 1988; Russian Rsch. Ctr. scholar, 1987—. Mem.: Am. Assn. for Advancement of Slavic Studies, Conn. Acad. Arts and Scis. Home: 13 Red Orange Rd Middletown CT 06457-4916 Office: History Dept Wesleyan U Middletown CT 06459-0001 Home Phone: 860-344-1847; Office Phone: 860-685-2398. Business E-Mail: ppomper@wesleyan.edu.

POMPONIO, XUN Z., economics professor; d. Bi Zhang and Quiya Jiang; m. Carmen John Pomponio. PhD, Pa. State U., 1991. Rsch. asst. Youngstown State U., Ohio, 1984—85; tchg. asst. Pa. State U., Univ. Pk., 1986—90. Vis. prof. China Ctr. Econ. Rsch., Beijing, 1998—99; editor Chinese Economist Soc. N.Am. Faculty Devel. grant, St. Olaf Coll., 2007, Freeman grant, 1997, 2002, 2004. Mem.: Western China Devel. Consortium (chinese economist soc. 1994—95). Dfl. Home: 1115 Maple St Northfield MN 55057 Office: St Olaf College 1520 St Olaf Ave Northfield MN 55057 Office Fax: 507-786-3523. Business E-Mail: pomponio@stolaf.edu.

POMYKALA, JOSEPH STEVEN, economics professor; b. Washington, June 28, 1962; s. Ronald Adam and Anne Maureen Pomykala. BA in Economics with Honors, U. Md., College Park, 1985; PhD, U. Pa., Phila., 1997. Econ. analyst Battelle Meml. Inst., Pacific NW Labs., Washington, 1986—87; lectr. Towson U., Md., 1998—. Cons. Ministry Privatization, Warsaw, 1991. Author: The Division and Destruction of Value: An Economic Analysis of Bankruptcy Law. Congress candidate Libertarian Party, Md., 2000. Mem.: Am. Economics Assn. Libertarian. Home: 744 Anneslie Rd Baltimore MD 21212 Office: Towson Univ 8000 York Rd Towson MD 21252

PONCE, FERNANDO AGUSTIN, physics professor; b. Huaraz, Ancash, Peru, May 4, 1949; s. Julio Alberto Ponce and Carmen Rosa Antúnez de Mayolo; m. Sharon Lee Miles; children: Francisco A., Daniel A., Tomás E. PhD, Stanford U., Calif., 1981. Rsch. scientist Hewlett-Packard Labs., Palo Alto, Calif., 1980—84, Palo Alto Rsch. Ctr., 1984—98; prof., dept. physics Ariz. State U., Tempe, 1999—. Fall meeting chair Materials Rsch. Soc., Boston, 1999; hon. prof. U. Nat. Ingenieria, Lima, Peru, 2002, Nat. U., Cuzc; chair Internat. Conf. Physics Semiconducors, Flagstaff, Ariz., 2004, Internat. Symposium Semiconductor Light Emitting Devices, Phoenix, 2008. Recipient medal, Eduardo Habich, Lima, 1999. Fellow: Am. Phys. Soc. Achievements include patents in field. Office: AZ State Univ Dept Physics Tempe AZ 85287-1504 Business E-Mail: ponce@asu.edu.

PONCE - ORTIZ, ESTEBAN, literature and language professor; b. Quito, Pichincha, Ecuador, Nov. 13, 1967; s. Francisco José Raúl Ponce and Ortiz María Mercedes; m. Rut Roman; 1 child, Alejandro Esteban Armas. AS, U. Tecnológica Equinoccial, Quito, 1990; MA, PhD, U. Md., Coll. Pk., 2007. Lic. Pontificia U. Católica del Ecuador, 2000. Spanish tchg. asst. U. Md., 2001—07; asst. prof. Spanish U. Va. Coll., Wise, 2007—08. Author: La idea del mal en el siglo 19 latinoamericano. Mem.: Latin Am. Studies Assn. Office: Univ Va Coll Wise One Colelge Ave Wise VA 24293 Office Fax: 276-328-0173. Business E-Mail: ep5j@uvawise.edu.

POND, PATRICIA BROWN, library and information science educator; b. Mankato, Minn., Jan. 17, 1930; d. Patrick H. and Florence M. (Ruehle) Brown; m. Judson S. Pond, Aug. 24, 1959. BA, Coll. St. Catherine, St. Paul, 1952; MA, U. Minn., 1955; PhD, U. Chgo., 1982. Sch. libr., Minn., NYC, 1952-62; asst. prof. libr. sci. U. Minn., 1962-63; reference libr. U. Mont., 1963-65; asst. prof. U. Oreg., 1967-72, assoc. prof., 1972-77; prof., dept. chair, assoc. dean Sch. Libr. and Info. Sci. U. Pitts., 1977-85. Mem. ALA (life), Phi Beta Kappa, Beta Phi Mu, Delta Phi Lambda, Kappa Gamma Pi. Home: 12520 SW Hart Rd Apt 223 Beaverton OR 97008-5785 Personal E-mail: ppond1@mindspring.com.

POND, RANDY, computer company executive; B in acctg. & fin., Ball State Univ. Fin. & mgmt. positions Versatec, David Systems, Xerox, Schlumberger, Arthur Andersen; v.p. fin., CFO, v.p. ops. Crescendo Comm.; joined Cisco Systems Inc., San Jose, Calif., 1993, dir. mfg. ops., 1994—95, v.p. mfg., 1995—2000, sr. v.p. We. Coast & Asia ops., 2000—01, sr. v.p. worldwide mfg. ops. & logistics, 2001—03, sr. v.p. ops. processes & systems, 2003—07, exec. v.p. ops. processes & systems, 2007—. Bd. mem. Islamic Networks Group, Am. Leadership Forum Silicon Valley; pres. Children's Discovery Mus., San Jose. Office: Cisco Systems Inc 170 W Tasman Dr San Jose CA 95134-1706*

POND, THOMAS ALEXANDER, physics professor, academic administrator; b. LA, Dec. 4, 1924; s. Arthur Francis and Florence (Alexander) P.; m. Barbara Eileen Newman, Sept. 6, 1958; children: Arthur Phillip Ward, Florence Alexandra. AB, Princeton U., 1947, AM, 1949, PhD, 1953; DSc, SUNY, Stony Brook, 1998. Instr. physics Princeton U., 1951-53; asst. prof., then assoc. prof. physics Washington U., St. Louis, 1953-62; prof. physics SUNY, Stony Brook, 1962-81, prof. emeritus, 1982—, chmn. dept., 1962-68, exec. v.p., 1967-79, acting pres., 1970, 75, 78; prof. physics Rutgers U., New Brunswick, NJ, exec. v.p., chief acad. officer, 1982-91, exec. v.p., chief acad. officer emeritus, 1991—, acting pres., 1990, prof., 1991-97, prof. emeritus, 1997—; acting sr. v.p. for acad. affairs U. Medicine and Dentistry N.J., New Brunswick, 1998. Bd. dirs. Action Com. for L.I., 1978-80, Tri-State Regional Planning Commn., 1979-82; trustee Univs. Research Assn., 1985-87; bd. dirs. Fermilab, 1987-89. Served to ensign USNR, 1943-46. Fellow AAAS; mem. Am. Phys. Soc., Phi Beta Kappa, Sigma Xi. Home: 144 Fox Run Arlington VT 05250

PONDER, ANNE, academic administrator; b. Asheville, NC, Apr. 26, 1950; d. Herschel Doyle and Mary Eleanor (Israel) Ponder; m. John Christopher Brookhouse, Mar. 3, 1973; children: Stephen Christopher, Nathaniel. AB, U. NC, 1971, MA, 1973, PhD, 1979. Dir. honors Elon Coll., NC, 1977-85; assoc. acad. dean Guilford Coll., Greensboro, NC, 1985-89; acad. dean, prof. Kenyon Coll., Gambier, Ohio, 1989—96, v.p. info. tech.; pres. Colby-Sawyer Coll., New London, NH, 1996—2005; chancellor U. NC, Asheville, 2005—. Mem.: NC Honors Assn. (pres. 1983), Nat. Collegiate Honors Coun. (pres. 1988—89), Order of Valkyries. Episcopalian. Office: U NC - Chancellor's Office Phillips Hall, CPO # 1400 One University Heights Asheville NC 28804-8503 Office Phone: 828-251-6500. Office Fax: 828-251-6495.

PONDER, CATHERINE, clergywoman; b. Hartsville, SC, Feb. 14, 1927; d. Roy Charles and Kathleen (Parrish) Cook; 1 child, Richard. Student, Worth Bus. Coll., 1948; BS in Edn., Unity Ministerial Sch., 1956; doctorate (hon.), Unity Sch., 1976. Ordained to ministry Unity Sch. Christianity, 1958. Min. Unity Ch., Birmingham, Ala., 1958-61, founder, min. Austin, Tex., 1961-69, San Antonio, 1969-73, Palm Desert, Calif., 1973—. Author: (books) The Dynamic Laws of Prosperity, 1962, The Prosperity Secret of the Ages, 1964, The Dynamic Laws of Healing, 1966, The Healing Secret of the Ages, 1967, Pray and Grow Rich, 1968, The Millionaires of Genesis, 1976, The Millionaire Moses, 1977, The Millionaire Joshua, 1978, The Millionaire from Nazareth, 1979, The Secret of Unlimited Prosperity, 1981, Open Your Mind To Receive, 1983, Dare To Prosper!: The Prospering Power of Prayer, 1983,

The Prospering Power of Love, 1984, Open Your Mind to Prosperity, 1984, The Dynamic Laws of Prayer, 1987, (memoir) Prosperity Love Story, From Rags to Enrichment, 2003. Office: 73-669 US Hwy 111 Palm Desert CA 92260-4033

PONDER, HERMAN, geologist; b. Light, Ark., Jan. 31, 1928; s. Herman Cook and Sylvia Adell (Cameron) P.; m. Barbara Elaine Sando, May 10, 1947; children: Teresa Elaine, David Mark. BA, U. Mo., 1955, PhD, 1959. Rsch. engr. A.P. Green Refractories Co., Mexico, Mo., 1959-61, lab mgr., 1961-63; project engr. Colo. Sch. Mines Rsch. Inst., Golden, 1963—67, mngr. mining divsn., 1967—70, pres., 1970—85; v.p. Copper Range Co., White Pine, Mich., 1985—89; chmn. bd. dirs. Analytica, Inc., 1985—98. Served with USN, 1946-47. Recipient Disting. Alumnus award U. Mo., 1993. Home: 2725 E Papago Trl Sierra Vista AZ 85650-8112

PONDER, JACQUELINE A., legislative staff member; Strategist, campaign mgr. Colo. Republican Party; chief of staff to Rep. Tom Tancredo US House of Reps., Washington, counsel, Rep. Tom Tancredo, 2006, chief of staff to Rep. Mike Coffman, 2008—; dep. dir. licensing Colo. Dept. of State, 2007, chief adminstrv. officer, 2007—08. Republican. Office: 1508 Longworth House Office Bldg Washington DC 20515 Office Phone: 202-225-7882. Office Fax: 202-226-4623.*

PONDER, MARIAN RUTH, mathematics educator; b. Waterloo, Iowa, July 12, 1932; d. Lee Roland and Leone Hyacinth (Holdiman) Rigdon; m. Joseph Glen Ponder, June 28, 1953; children: Dwight Lee, David Glen, Dean Joseph. BA (Purple and Gold math. scholar), U. No. Iowa, 1952; MSE, Drake U., 1960; postgrad., U. Wis., 1961—62, San Diego State U., 1980—81, Carleton Coll., 1980—81, U. No. Iowa, 1961—66, Drake U., 1971—75, Chico State U., 1985—86, U. Iowa, 1988, U. Tex., 1990, Des Moines Area C.C., 2003. Tchr. math., sci., Anamosa, Iowa, 1952—53, Monroe, Iowa, 1953—56, Newton, Iowa, 1956—64, 1966—92; head dept. math. Newton Schs., 1978—92; ret., 1992. Libr. Monroe HS, 1953—54; summer tchr. civics NHS, 1957. Ch. treas. Cmty. Heights Alliance Ch., 1980-87, Sunday sch. secretariat, 1966-82, fin. sec., 1993-94, 97-98, women's ministries treas., 1997-2001. Maytag scholar, 1960; Maytag Corp. grantee; Delta Kappa Gamma scholar, 1960, 81, 95, 2002, 07; Iowa State Delta Kappa Gamma Achievement award, 2005. Mem. NEA, Nat. Coun. Tchrs. Math., Iowa Ret. Sch. Pers. Assn., Iowa Edn. Assn., Newton Cmty. Edn. Assn. (chief negotiator 1985-87, pres. 1985-87), Iowa Coun. Tchrs. Math., Jasper County Hist. Soc., Jasper County Geneaol. Soc., Delta Kappa Gamma (state treas. 1978—2004, internat. fin. chmn. 1990-92, trustee edni. found. 1992-98, Annual Achievement award State chpt., 2005), Jasper County Ret. Sch. Pers. Assn. (treas. 1992-96, v.p. 1996-98, pres. 1998-2000), Kappa Mu Epsilon, Kappa Delta Pi, Lambda Delta Lambda, Delta Kappa Gamma. Republican. Mem. Christian and Missionary Alliance Ch. Home: 3791 Highway F36 W Newton IA 50208-8061 Home Phone: 641-792-6482.

PONDEXTER, CAPPIE, professional basketball player; b. Jan. 7, 1983; d. Leo and Vanessa Pondexter. Grad. in Africa Studies, Rutgers U., NJ. Guard Phoenix Mercury, 2006—, Fenerbahce, Turkey, 2006. Mem. USA Basketball Sr. Nat. Team, 2006, Beijing, 08. Recipient Gold medal, women's basketball, Beijing Olympic Games, 2008; named Nat. Player of Yr., Women's Basketball News Svc., 2006, Player of Yr., Big East Conf., 2006, Finals MVP, WNBA, 2007; named to All-Am. First Team, Kodak/Women's Basketball Coaches Assn., 2006, ESPN.com, 2006, Women's Basketball News Svc., 2006, All-Am. Team, US Basketball Writers Assn., 2006, Women's Wooden Award, 2006, Western Conf. All-Star Team, WNBA, 2006, All-Rookie Team, 2006. Achievements include being a member of the WNBA Championship winning Phoenix Mercury, 2007. Office: Phoenix Mercury 201 E Jefferson St Phoenix AZ 85004

PONEMAN, DANIEL BRUCE, federal agency administrator, lawyer; b. Toledo, Mar. 12, 1956; s. Meyer and Delores Suzanne (Shapiro) P.; m. Susan Anne Danoff, Aug. 12, 1984; children: Claire Gillian, Michael Bruder, William Meyer. AB in Govt. and Econs. magna cum laude, Harvard Coll., 1978; MLitt in Politics, Lincoln Coll., Oxford, Eng., 1981; JD cum laude, Harvard U., 1984. Bar: D.C. 1985, N.Y., 1985. Vis. fellow Internat. Inst. Strategic Studies, London, 1980-81; rsch. fellow ctr. sci. and internat. affairs Kennedy sch. govt. Harvard U., 1981-84; assoc. Covington & Burling LLP, 1985-89; White House fellow US Dept. Energy, 1989-90; dir. def. policy & arms control NSC, Washington, 1990-93, spl. asst. to the Pres., sr. dir. nonproliferation & export controls, 1993-96; counsel Hogan & Hartson LLP, 1996-97, ptnr., 1999—2002; prin. The Scowcroft Group, 2001—09; dep. sec. US Dept. Energy, Washington, 2009—. Author: Nuclear Power in the Developing World, 1982, Argentina: Democracy on Trial, 1987, (with Joel S. Wit) Going Critical: The First North Korean Nuclear Crisis (Douglas Dillon Award for Disting. Writing on Am. Diplomacy, 2005), 2003; contbr. articles to profl. jours. and newspapers including N.Y. Times, Washington Post, Wall Street Jour., L.A. Times, Boston Globe, Fin. Times. Mem. Commn. to Asses the Orgn. of Govt. to Combat the Proliferation of Weapons of Mass Distruction, 1997-99; mem. Pres.' Export Coun. Subcom. on Export Adminstrn. Grantee Corp. Pub. Broadcasting; Lord Crewe scholar. Mem. D.C. Bar, N.Y. Bar, Coun. Fgn. Rels., Phi Beta Kappa. Office: US Dept Energy Forrestal Bldg 1000 Independence Ave SW Rm 7B-252 Washington DC 20585*

PONGSREE, SAHARAT OAK, economics professor; s. Dheera and Subharat Pongsree; m. Chayawan Sonchaeng, May 24, 2007. BEE, Chulalongkorn U., Bangkok, 1993; MBA, Western Mich. U., Kalamazoo, 1995; PhD in Economics, Mich. State U., East Lansing, 2006. Instr. economics Mich. State U., 1998—2002, Western Mich. U., 2004—06; asst. prof. economics Wesley Coll., Dover, Del., 2006—. Mem.: Ludwig von Mises Inst., Eastern Econ. Assn., Southern Econ. Assn., Midwest Economics Assn., Am. Econ. Assn., Beta Gamma Sigma. Office: Wesley Coll 120 N State St Dover DE 19901 Office Fax: 302-736-2543. Business E-Mail: pongsrsa@wesley.edu.

PONITZ, DAVID H., former academic administrator; b. Royal Oak, Mich., Jan. 21, 1931; s. Henry John and Jeanette (Bouwman) P.; m. Doris Jean Humes, Aug. 5, 1956; children: Catherine Anne, David Robinson. BA, U. Mich., 1952, MA, 1954; EdD, Harvard U., 1964; PhD (hon.), U. Dayton, 1996, Wright State U., Dayton, Ohio, 2009. Prin. Waldron (Mich.) Area Schs., 1956-58, supt., 1958-60; cons. Harvard U., Boston Sch. Survey, 1961-63; supt. Freeport (Ill.) Pub. Schs., 1962-65; pres. Freeport C.C., 1962-65, Washtenaw C.C., 1965-75, Sinclair C.C., 1975-97, pres. emeritus, 1997—. Cons. to CC, Daha, Qatar; chmn., pres. Ohi Advanced Tech. Ctr.; ednl. cons., 1997—. Mem. editl. adv. bd. Nations Schs., 1963-70; chmn. adv. bd. C.C. Rev., 1978-89. Past chmn. Dayton Mayor's Coun. on Econ. Devel., 1977-85; mem. Nat. Adv. Coun. on Nursing; former co-chair Performing Arts Edn. Task Force; bd. dirs. Alliance for Edn.; former campaign chmn. Ann Arbor and Dayton United Way; past vice chmn. Dayton Citizens Adv. Coun. for Desegregation Implementation; v.p. Miami Valley Rsch. Park; mem., past chmn. Area Progress Coun., Dayton; bd. dirs. Dayton Devel. Coun.; mem. F.S.B. bd. Citizens Fed. Banks, Universal Energy Systems Bd.; past chmn. Miami Valley Joint Labor/Mgmt. Profls., Area Progress Coun.; chmn. bd. dirs Ctr. Occupational R&D; bd. chair Wright Tech. Network; bd. dirs. Dean Family Funds; trustee Thomas B. Fordham Found., pres., 2006—; mem. Midwestern Higher Edn. Commn.; vice chair Miami Valley Rsch. Found.; past chmn. bd. dirs. League Innovation C.C.; bd. dirs. Miami Valley Regional Planning Commn. Served with US Army, 1954-56; chair found. bd. USAF, chair Nat. Mus., 2006-08. Recipient Presdl. medallion, Patron emeritus Horry-Georgetown Tech. Coll., Bogie Buster Red Jacket award, 1987, Thomas J. Peters award for Excellence, Assn. Cmty. and Jr. Colls., 1988, Marie N. Martin Chief Exec. Officer award, ACCT, 1989, The Living Legend award, Martin Luther King Jr. Holiday Celebration Com., 1991, Hon. Alumnus award, Sinclair, 1991, honor, India Found., 1992, Disting. Eagle Scout award, Nat. Eagle Scout Assn., 1993, Smitty award, Anti-Defamation award, Anti-Defamation League, 1996, Citizen Legion of Honor award, 1997, hon. award, Citizen Legion, 1997, Edn. award, Gov., 1999; named Outstanding Alumnus, U. Mich., One of Top 100 Pres. in U.S. Coun. for Advancement and Support of Edn., Exec. of Yr., Bd. Realtors; named to Hall of Fame, Nat. Mgmt. Assn., 2001. Mem. Am. Assn. Cmty. and Jr. Colls. (nat. future commn., bd. dirs., chmn. 1988-89, Nat. Leadership award 2002), Ohio Tech. and C.C. Assn. (pres. 1979-80), Nat. Mgmt. Assn. (Hall of Fame award 2001), Rotary. Methodist. Home Phone: 937-434-6713; Office Phone: 937-434-6640. Business E-Mail: dponitzsinclair@woh.rr.com.

PONNAMBALAM, ANANTHASEKAR, pediatrician, gastroenterologist; arrived in U.S., 1997; s. Arumugam Ponnambalam and Lalitha Krishnaswamy; m. Kalpana Ananthasekar, July 1, 1993; children: Shivani Ananthasekar, Skandan Ananthasekar. MB, BChir, Stanley Med. Coll., Madras, 1985; Diploma in Child Health, Madras Med. Coll., 1987, MD, 1990, DM, 1993. Diplomate Am. Bd. Pediat., 2000, cert. pediat. gastroenterology Am. Bd. Pediat., 2005. Attending physician Primary Health Care, Tamilnadu, India, 1990—91; attending physician in pediat. and gastroenterology India, 1993—94; attending physician in pediat. Ministry of Health, Oman, 1994—97; resident in pediat. SUNY Downstate Med. Ctr., Bklyn., 1997—2000, fellow pediat. gastroenterology, 2000—03, rschr.; prof. pediat. U. South Albama, 2009—. Question writer Am. Bd. Pediats. Contbr. chapters to books. Fellow: Am. Acad. Pediat.; mem.: Am. Coll. Gastroenterology, Am. Gastroenterology Assn., N.Am. Soc. for Pediat. Gastroenterology Hepatology and Nutrition. Achievements include research in mast cells. Home: 110D Du Rhu Dr Mobile AL 36608-1209 Office: Univ South Ala 1504 Springhill Ave Mobile AL 36608 Personal E-mail: ananthasekarp@hotmail.com.

PONOMAREV, ARTEM LVOVICH, physicist, senior research scientist; s. Faina Vasilyevna Ponomaryova and Lev Timofeyvich Ponomarev; m. Amelia Lee Rugland, May 15, 1998. Diploma in Theoretical Physics, Moscow Inst. Physics Tech., 1993; MS in Physics, Columbia U., NYC, 1995, PhD in Physics, 1998. PhD fellowship internship Los Alamos Nat. Lab., 1997; Postdoc Fellowship U. of Calif. Berkeley, 1998—99; rsch. scientist NASA Johnson Space Ctr., Houston, 2003—06, sr. rsch. scientist, 2006—, radiation jour. club leader, 2008—. Recipient Space Act award, NASA Johnson Space Ctr., 2004, Advanced standing for PhD studies, Columbia U., 1998; scholar East Ctrl. European Leadership Fellowship, McLaine Found., 1993-1996; fellowship with stipend, Columbia U., 1993-1998. Mem.: Radiation Rsch. Soc., Sigma Xi (Elected mem.). Achievements include research in 3-D model of radiation of human tissue; stochastic model of DNA of damage patterns due to radiation on astronauts; automated image segmentation algorithm of microscopy images to reconstruct tissue; selected to work with Nobel prize winning physicist Vitaly Ginzburg for 3 years; winner of math and science olympics in Russia. Avocations: space, chess, water-skiing, scuba diving, dancing. Office: NASA Lyndon Johnson Space Ctr 2101 NASA Parkway Mail Code SK Houston TX 77058 Office Phone: 281-483-0089. Business E-Mail: artem.l.ponomarev@nasa.gov.

PONOROFF, LAWRENCE, dean, law educator, consultant; b. Chgo., Sept. 10, 1953; s. Charles Melvin and Jean Eileen (Kramer) P.; m. Monica J. Moses, July 25, 1981; children: Christopher J.; Devon E., Laura J., Scott C. BA summa cum laude, Loyola U., Chgo., 1975; JD, Stanford U., 1978. Bar: Colo. 1978, Ohio 1988, US Dist. Ct. Colo., US Dist. Ct. (no. dist.) Ohio, US Ct. Appeals (10th cir.). Assoc. Holme Roberts & Owen, Denver, 1978-84, ptnr., 1984-86; asst. prof. law U. Toledo, 1986-88, assoc. prof. coll. of law, 1988-90, prof. law, assoc. dean academic affairs, 1990-92, prof., 1990-95, Tulane U. Sch. Law, New Orleans, 1995-00, J. Mitchell Franklin prof. pvt. and comml. law, 2000—09, vice dean, 1998-2001, dean, 2001—09; dean, Samuel M. Fegtly prof. comml. law U. Ariz. James E. Rogers Coll. Law, 2009—. Vis. prof. Wayne State U. Law Sch., 1993, U. Mich. Law Sch., 1997; lectr. fed. juc. ctr.; cons. long range planning subcom. of com. on adminstrn. of bankruptcy sys. Jud. Conf. US, mem. adv. com. on bankruptcy rules, 2004—; mem. fed. jud. Ctr. Adv. Com. Bankruptey Judge Edn., 2008—; dir. Am. Bd. Cert., 2000—06; bd. advisors editors Am. Bankruptcy Inst. Law Rev., 2000—03; bd. dirs. La. Supreme Ct. Hist. Soc.; exec. dir. For the Children Literacy Program. Co-author: (with S.E. Snyder) Commerical Bankruptcy Litigation, 1989; (with J. Dolan) Basic Concepts in Commercial Law, 1998; (with Epstein and Markell) Making and Doing Deals: Contracts in Context, 2002, 2d edit., 2006; (with J. Dolan and B. Markell) Core Concepts of Commercial Law: Past, Present and Future, 2004. Bd. dir. La. Supreme Ct. Hist. Soc. Recipient L. Hart Wright Tchg. award, U. Mich. Law Sch., Felix Frankfurter Tchg. award, Tulane U. Law Sch. Fellow Am. Coll. Bankruptcy, Am. Bar Found.; mem. ABA, Am. Bar Inst., Am. Law Inst., La. State Bar Assn. (bd. govs. 2001-03). Home: 6025 Pitt St New Orleans LA 70118-6010 Office: Univ Ariz James E Rogers Coll Law 1201 E Speedway Blvd Tucson AZ 85721 Business E-Mail: lponoroff@law.arizona.edu.*

PONTE-CASTAÑEDA, PEDRO, mechanical engineering educator; b. Santa Cruz, Tenerife, Spain, Jan. 5, 1961; came to U.S., 1977; s. Pedro Ponte-Pedreira and Glenda (Castañeda) De Ponte. BS, BA, Lehigh U., 1982; SM, Harvard U., 1983, PhD in Applied Math., 1986. Rsch. officer U. Bath, England, 1986-87; asst. prof. Johns Hopkins U., Balt., 1987-90, U. Pa., Phila., 1990-94, assoc. prof., 1994—98, prof., 1998—, Ecole Polytech., Paris, 2003—08. Vis. prof. Ecole Polytechnique, Paris, 1994, 2001; vis. fellow Corpus Christi Coll., Cambridge U., 1994. Contbr. articles to profl. jours. Recipient Rsch. Initiation award NSF, 1988; grantee NSF, Air Force Office of Sci. Rsch. Mem. ASME (Spl. Achievement award for Young Investigators in Mechanics 2000), Soc. for Indsl. Applied Math., Phi Beta Kappa. Office: U Pa 220 S 33rd St Philadelphia PA 19104-6315 Office Phone: 215-898-5046. Business E-Mail: ponte@seas.upenn.edu.

PONTICELLI, CHARLOTTE MARIE (CHARLIE PONTICELLI), federal agency administrator; b. 1951; m. Anthony M. Ponticelli. BA cum laude, Hood Coll., Frederick, Md., 1973; MA in Spanish Lit., NYU, Madrid, Spain. Dir. congl. corr. Office Legis. Affairs The White House; congl. liaison officer L.Am./Caribbean US AID; commr. asst. US Commn. Civil Rights; dir. lectures & seminars Heritage Found., Washington, 2001—02; dir. human rights/women's affairs, Bur. Internat. Orgn. Affairs US Dept. State, dep. sr. coord. internat. women's issues, 2002—03, sr. coord. internat. women's issues, 2003—06, sr. adv. to asst. sec. population, refugees & migration, 2006—07; dep. under sec. internat. affairs US Dept. Labor, Washington, 2007—. Recipient Outstanding Young Alumna award, Hood Coll., 1984, Veritas Award, Albertus Magnus Coll., 1996, Afghan-Am. Sisterhood award, Ariana Outreach, 2006. Office: US Dept Labor Frances Perkins Bldg 200 Constitution Ave NW Rm C-4325 Washington DC 20210 Personal E-mail: cmponticelli@gmail.com.

PONTIOUS, ROBERT RONALD, literature and language professor; b. Crooksville, Ohio, Sept. 20, 1954; s. Pearl Junior and Geraldine Catherine Pontious; m. Renae Louise Drake, June 15, 1974; children: Sean Robert, Michelle Renee. AB in English, Kenyon Coll., Gambier, Ohio, 1976; degree, Duke U., Durham, NC, 1977; MS in Sci. Edn., Southern Ill. U., Edwardsville, 1989. Cert. in Devel. Edn. Appalachian State U., Boone, Nat. Ctr. Devel. Edn., 2002. English tchr. William T. Sutherlin Acad., Danville, Va., 1976—77, Fieldale Collinsville HS, Va., 1977—78; store mgr. Tandy Radio Shack, Toledo, 1978—82, dist. mgr. O'Fallon, Ill., 1982—86; English tchr. Highland HS, Ill., 1988—90, Bethalto City Schs., Ill., 1988—89; tchg. parent Boys and Gilrls Home NC, Lake Waccamaw, 1996—98; facutly senate pres. Brunswick CC, Supply, NC, 2001—05, prof. English, 1998—; English tchr. Newark HS, Newark, 1990—93. Cub scout den leader Boy Scouts Am., Wilmington, NC, 2006—09; sunday sch. supt. Southside Bapt. Ch., Wilmington, 2006—09; chmn. Carolina Canines Svc., Wilmington, 2003—05. Recipient R.J. Reynolds Excellence Tchg. award, Inst. Yr. NC Cmty. Coll. Sys., 2006. Mem.: NC English Instr., NC CC Facutly Assn. Avocations: travel, photography. Office: Brunswick CC 50 College Rd Supply NC 28462 Home: 4813 Lelituer Dr Wilmington NC 28409 Home Phone: 910-805-0709; Office Phone: 910-755-7362. Personal E-mail: purplelords@yahoo.com. Business E-Mail: pontiousr@brunswickcc.eud.

PONTUAL, ROMULO, broadcast executive; V.p. space tech. News Corp., 1996—98, sr. v.p., 1998—99, exec. v.p. news tech., 1999—2002, exec. v.p. TV platforms, 2002; with Hughes Electronics Corp.; exec. v.p., chief tech. officer DIRECTV Group, El Segundo, Calif., 2004—. Vice chmn. Innova S de RL, 2000; mem. mgmt. bd. Sky Brasil Servicos Ltd., 2001. Office: DIRECTV Group 2230 E Imperial Hwy El Segundo CA 90245 Office Phone: 310-964-5000.

PONTURO, ANTHONY T. (TONY PONTURO), former brewery company executive; b. May 29, 1952; m. Ruth Ponturo. BA in Economics, Villanova U., 1974. Dir., media svcs. Anheuser-Busch, Inc., 1982—91, v.p./dir., corp. media and sports mktg., 1991—98, chmn., chief exec., Busch Media Group, 1994—2008, v.p., global media & sports mktg., 1998—2008. Mem. strategy com. Anheuser-Busch, Inc., mem. mgmt. com.; bd. dirs. Anheuser-Busch Internat., Inc. Bd. dirs. Variety the Children's Charity of St. Louis. Named The Most Influential Person in Sports Mktg., Sports Bus. Jour., 2004; named one of The Most Powerful People in Sports, The Sporting News, 2004, The Most Influential People in the World of Sports, Bus. Week, 2007, 2008.*

PONTY, JEAN-LUC, violinist, composer, producer; b. Avranches, Normandy, France, Sept. 29, 1942; arrived in U.S., 1973; Grad., Conservatoire National Superieur de Musique, Paris, 1960. Classical violinist to 1964, played with Concerts Lamoureux Symphony Orch, jazz violinist Europe, 1964—69, night club and music festivals with George Duke Trio, U.S., 1969, toured with own group, Europe, 1970—72, recorded with Elton John, Honky Chateau, 1972, with Frank Zappa and the Mothers of Invention, 1973, Mahavishnu Orch., 1974—75, pioneer of electric violin Jazz innovator, headlining internat. concerts with own group since, 1975, appearances (music festivals) in the U.S. including Meadowbrook, Artpark, Wolf Trap, and in Europe Montreux, North Sea Festival, Paris Jazz Festival, spl. appearance as guest soloist with Montreal Symphony Orch., 1984, Toronto Symphony Orch., 1986, New Japan Philharm., 1987, Radio City Orch. N.Y., 1990, Oklahoma City, 1995, world tour with Stanley Clarke and Al DiMeola The Rite of Strings, 1994, 1995, own-produced (albums) Upon the Wings of Music, Aurora, Imaginary Voyage, Enigmatic Ocean, Cosmic Messenger, Jean-Luc Ponty: Live, Civilized Evil, A Taste for Passion, Mystical Adventures, Individual Choice, Open Mind, Fables, The Gift of Time, Storytelling, Tchokola (with African musicians), No Absolute Time, Live at Chene Park, The Very Best of Jean-Luc Ponty, 2000, appearances (with Doug Kershaw and Itzhak Perlman TV series) Fiddlers Three, Soundstage, Rock Concert, The Tonight Show, The Merv Griffin Show, Solid Gold, Pat Sajak Show CNN Entertainment, (TV series) throughout Europe, Brazil, Chile and Venezuela. Recipient internat. awards. Office: Gary S Kleinman 217 E Alameda Ave Ste 306 Burbank CA 91502-2621

PONVELLE, BRITTANY GOMEZ, elementary school educator; b. Metairie, La., Feb. 10, 1983; d. Wendi St.Amant and Terence Neil Gomez; m. Jason Paul Ponvelle, Aug. 7, 2004. BA, Nicholls State U., Thibodaux, La., 2005. Cert. tchr. La., 2005. Tchr. Elem. Sch., Houma, La., 2006—. Office: Bayou Blue Elem 1916 Bayou Blue Rd Houma LA 70364

POOL, MARY JANE, writer, editor; d. Earl Lee and Dorothy (Matthews) P. Grad., St. de Chantal Acad., 1942; BA in Art with honors, Drury Coll., 1946; LHD (hon.), Drury U., 2002. Mem. staff Vogue mag., NYC, 1946-68, assoc. merchandising editor, 1948-57, promotion dir., 1958-66, exec. editor, 1966-68; editor House and Garden mag., 1969, editor-in-chief, 1970-80. Cons. Baker Furniture Co., 1981-94, Aves Advt., Inc., 1981-94, bd. dirs.; mem. bd. govs. Decorative Arts Trust; past mem. bd. govs. Fashion Group, Inc., N.Y.C Author: The Gardens of Venice, 1989, The Gardens of Florence, 1992, Gardens in the City-New York in Bloom, 1999; co-author: The Angel Tree, 1984, The Angel Tree—A Christmas Celebration, 1993, The Christmas Story, 2001, editor: 20th Century Decorating, Architecture, Gardens, Billy Baldwin Decorates, 26 Easy Little Gardens. Mem. bus. com. N.Y. Zool. Soc., 1979-86; trustee Drury Univ., 1971—2009; bd. dirs. Isabel O'Neil Found., 1978—2008. Recipient award Nat. Soc. Interior Designers, Disting. Alumni award Drury Coll., 1961, Edith Wharton Women of Achievement award, 1999; Pool Art Ctr. at Drury U opened 2004. Address: 1 E 66th St New York NY 10021-5854

POOLE, CONNIE, medical librarian; d. William Davis and Dolores Ann Poole; m. Thomas James Dorst, Aug. 4, 1974; 1 child, Matthew Clark Poole Dorst. BA, Grinnell Coll., Iowa, 1973; AMLS, U. Mich., Ann Arbor, 1974. Sci. libr. Mich. State U., East Lansing, 1974—77; staff specialist Am. Hosp. Assn., Chgo., 1977—78, asst. to dir., 1978—82, asst. dir., resource ctr., 1982—90; head, tech. svc. Southern Ill. U., Springfield, 1990—95, dir., med. libr., 1996—, assoc. dean, info. resources and chair, info. and comm. scis., 2000—. Program participant Leadership Springfield, Ill., 1998—99, bd. dirs., 2008—. Mem.: Med. Libr. Assn. (nat. program com., chair 1999—2002, nominating com.

mem. 2003—04), Assn. Academic Health Scis. Libr. (bd. dirs. 2001—04, pres. 2009—). Home: 112 Pinehurst Dr Springfield IL 62704-3123 Office: Southern Ill Univ 801 N Rutledge P O Box 19625 Springfield IL 62794-9625

POOLE, DAVID P., lawyer, utilities executive; b. Houston, Mar. 13, 1962; s. Preston L. and Shari J. Poole; children: Aubrey, Reese. BSc in Petroleum Engring., Tex. Tech. U., Lubbock, 1984, JD, 1988. Bar: Tex. 1988, DC 1989, US Dist. Ct. (ND Tex.) 1988. Assoc. Worsham, Forsythe Woodridge, Dallas, 1988—97, ptnr., 1997—2002, mng. ptnr., 2001—02; ptnr., mng. ptnr. Hunton & Williams LLP, Dallas, 2002—04; assoc. gen. counsel, sr. v.p. TXU Corp., Dallas, 2004—06; gen. counsel, exec. v.p. Energy Future Holdings, Dallas, 2006—08; sr. v.p., gen. counsel, sec. Range Resources Corp., Fort Worth, 2008—. Mem. exec. bd. Cir. 10 Coun. Boy Scouts of Am., Dallas, 2003—. Mem.: Dallas Bar Assn. (co-chair CLE Com. 2003—04). Office: Range Resources Corp Ste 1200 100 Throckmorton St Fort Worth TX 76102*

POOLE, EVA DURAINE, librarian; b. Farrell, Pa., Dec. 20, 1952; d. Leonard Milton and Polly Mae (Flint) Harris; m. Tommy Lynn Cole, May 15, 1970 (div. Sept. 1984); 1 child, Tommy Lynn Cole, Jr.; m. Earnest Theodore Poole, Sept. 22, 1990; 1 child, Aleece Remelle Poole. BA in LS, Tex. Woman's U., Denton, 1974, MLS, 1976; postgrad., U. Houston, 1989. Libr. asst. Emily Fowler Pub. Libr., Denton, Tex., 1970-74; children's libr. Houston Pub. Libr., 1974-75, 1st asst. libr., 1976-77; children's libr. Ector County Libr., Odessa, Tex., 1977-80; head pub. svcs. Lee Davis Libr. San Jacinto Coll., Pasadena, Tex., 1980-84; libr. dir. San Jacinto Coll. South, Houston, 1984-90; libr. svcs. mgr. Emily Fowler Pub. Libr., Denton, 1990-93, interim dir., 1993; dir. librs. Denton Pub. Librs., 1993—. Mem. Libr. Svcs. Constrn. Act Adv. Coun., 1994-97, Libr. Svcs. Tech. Act Adv. Coun., 1997-2000; mem. TEXSHARE adv. bd. Tex. State Libr. and Archives Commn., 1999-2005, chmn., 2003-2004; bd. dirs. Denton Area Tchrs. Credit Union, 2003-06, Denton Area Tchrs. Credit Union, 2007—; treas., 2008-; mem. adv. bd. U. North Tex. Sch. Libr. and Info. Sci., 2000—, chair, 2006-07; mem. members coun. Online Computer Libr. Ctr., 2004-07; mem. presdl. search adv. com. U. North Tex., 2005-06; mem. external constituent bd. Tex. Woman's U. Sch. Libr. and Info. Studies, 2005—. Bd. dirs. Amigos Libr. Svcs., 2000-03, Girl Scouts Cross Timbers Coun., 2002-04, United Way of Denton County, 2002—, exec. com., bd. pres., 2006-07, Friends of Librs. U.S.A., 2003-2007,. Named to Outstanding Young Women of Am., 1991. Mem. ALA (chair Loleta Fyan jury com. 1999-2000) Allied Profl. Assn.(chmn. cert. pub. libr. adminstr. program 2005-06, mem. com. orgn., 2005-06), Pub. Libr. Assn. (mem. budget and fin. com. 1999-2002, chair budget and fin. com. 2001-2003, 2004-05, nat. conf. com. 2002-04, chair bylaws and orgn. 2002-03, mem. instnl. scholarships task force 2006-2007, bd. dirs. 2006-09), mem. Grow your own Instl. Scholarship Award Jury (chair) Libr. Adminstrn. and Mgmt. Assn. (program com. 1994-97, mem.-at-large bd. dirs. 2000-02, chair cultural diversity com. 2000-01, com. on orgn. 2002-05, rep. to Freedom to Read Found. 2002-03, strategic planning com. 2005-06), Tex. Libr. Assn. (pub. libr. divsn. sec. 1995-96, chair 1997-98, leadership devel. com. 1995-97, leadership devel. com. chair 1996-97, alumnae 1st class Tex. Accelerated Libr. Leaders 1994, legis. com. 1997-99, Dist. 7 coun. 1996-99, exec. bd. 1998-2000, 2002-05, ad hoc comn. on pub. lib. stds. com. chair 1998-2000, 2002 conf. local arrangements com. 2001-02, chair 2000 conf. program com. 1998-2000, chair awards com. 2001-02, pres.-elect 2002-03, pres. 2003-04, chair Tocker Found. com. 2006-08), Pub. Libr. Adminstrs. North Tex. (vice chair 1994-95, chair 1995-96), Tex. Mcpl. Libr. Dirs. Assn. (pres. 1995-96, grantee 1993, Libr. of Yr. 1998), Denton Rotary Club (mem. bd. dirs., 2006—, pres.-elect, 2007-08, pres., 2008-09), Tex. Mcpl. League (bd. dirs. 1997-2000), Greater Denton Arts Coun. (bd. dir., 2008-), Denton Regional Med. Ctr. (bd. dirs. 2009-). Office: Denton Pub Libr 502 Oakland St Denton TX 76201 Home Phone: 940-484-8963; Office Phone: 940-349-8750. Business E-Mail: eva.poole@cityofdenton.com.

POOLE, NANCY GEDDES, art gallery curator, writer; b. London, Ont., Can., May 10, 1930; d. John Hardy and Kathleen Edwards (Robinson) G.; m. William Robert Poole, Aug. 15, 1952; 1 child, Andrea Mary. BA, U. Western Ont., 1956, LLD, 1990. Owner, dir. Nancy Poole's Studio, Toronto, Ont., Canada, 1969-78; acting dir. London Regional Art Gallery, Ont., Canada, 1981—, exec. dir. Ont., 1985-89; dir. London Regional Art and Hist. Museums, Ont., Canada, 1989-95. Chair governing coun. Ont. Coll. Art, 1972-73; bd. dirs. Robarts Rsch. Inst., 1995. Author: The Art of London 1939-1980, 1984; editor Jack Chambers, 1978, The Collection, 1990. Bd. govs. U. Western Ont., 1974-85; bd. dirs. Western Area Youth Svcs., 1996; chair Western Area Youth Svcs. Found., 2004-06, Hazel Cryderman-Wees Found., 2004. Fellow Ont. Coll. Art. Mem.: Order of Can. Office: 420 Fanshawe Park Rd London ON Canada N5X 2S9

POOLE, RICHARD WILLIAM, economist; b. Oklahoma City, Dec. 4, 1927; s. William Robert and Lois (Spicer) Poole; m. Bertha Lynn Mehr, July 28, 1950; children: Richard William, Laura Lynne, Mark Stephen. BS, U. Okla., 1951, MBA, 1952; postgrad., George Washington U., 1957—58; PhD, Okla. State U., 1960. Rsch. analyst Okla. Gas & Electric Co., Oklahoma City, 1952- 54; mgr. sci. and mfg. devel. dept. Oklahoma City C. of C., 1954—57; mgr. Office of J.E. Webb, Washington, 1957-58; from instr. to prof. econs. Okla. State U., Stillwater, 1960-65, prof. econs., dean Coll. Bus. Adminstrn., 1965-72, v.p., prof. econs., 1972-88, Regents Disting. Svc. prof., prof. econs., 1988-93, emeritus v.p., dean, Regents Disting. Svc. prof./prof. econ., 1993—. Cons. to adminstr. NASA, Washington, 1961—69; adviser subcom. govt. rsch. U.S. Senate, 1966—69; lectr. Intermediate Sch. Banking, Ops. Mgmt. Sch., Okla. Bankers Assn., 1969—88; lectr. internat. off-campus programs Oklahoma City U., 1994—96. Author (with others): The Oklahoma Economy, 1963, County Building Block Data for Regional Analysis, 1965. Mem. Gov.'s Com. Devel. Ark.-Verdigris Waterway, 1970—71, Gov.'s Five-Yr. Econ. Devel. Plan, 1993; past v.p., bd. dirs., past chmn. Mid-Continent R & D Coun., 1966—78. 2d lt. arty. US Army, 1946—48. Recipient Delta Sigma Pi Gold Key award, Coll. Bus. Adminstrn. U. Okla., 1951, Tchg. award on Am. free enterprise sys., Merrick Found., 1992, Disting. Alumni award, Okla. State U., 1995, Henry G. Bennett Disting. Svc. award, 1999; named to Coll. Bus. Adminstrn. Hall of Fame, Okla. State U., 1993, Stillwater Hall of Fame, Payne county Hist. Soc. and Stillwater C. of C., 1996, Okla. Higher Edn. Hall of Fame, 1998. Mem.: Southwestern Bus. Adminstrn. Assn. (past pres.), Nat. Assn. State Univs. and Land Grant Colls. (past chmn. commn. edn. for bus. professions), Am. Assembly Collegiate Schs. Bus. (past bd. dirs.), Southwestern Econ. Assn. (past pres.), Stillwater C. of C. (past bd. dirs., pres.), Santa Fe Trail Assn. (bd. dirs. 2001—02), Okla. C. of C. (past bd. dirs.), Okla. Heritage Assn. (bd. dirs. 2000—05), Omicron Delta Kappa, Phi Eta Sigma, Phi Kappa Phi, Beta Gamma Sigma (past bd. dirs.). Home: 14901 N Pennsylvania Apt 336 Oklahoma City OK 73134

POOLE, SCOTT, architect, educator; b. Jan. 1, 1951; MArch, U. Tex., 1983. Registered arch., Va. Faculty mem. Va. Tech., Blacksburg, 1986—, prof. arch., dir. Sch. Arch. & Design, 2004—. Lectr. Yale U., U. Va., Sch. arch., Aarhus, Denmark; Gilmore vis. lectr. U. Calgary, 2000; vis. prof. Royal Danish Acad. Art, Copenhagen, Royal Inst. Tech., Stockholm; bd. dirs. Va. Soc. Am. Inst. Archs. Recipient Tchg. Excellence award, Va. Tech. Coll. Arch. and Urban Studies, 2002; Fulbright scholar, Finland. Mem.: AIA (v.p. Va. Soc.). Office: Va Tech Sch Arch Design 201 Cowgill Hall Blacksburg VA 24061 Business E-Mail: spoole@vt.edu.

POOLE, TODD W., legislative staff member; Degree, U. NC, Chapel Hill, 1993; BS in Polit. Sci., Appalachian State U., Boone, NC, 1997, MBA, 2002. With sales dept. Systel Office Automation, 1997; constituent adv. for Rep. Richard M. Burr US House of Reps., Washington, 1997—2003, dist. asst. for Rep. Virginia Foxx, 2000—03, dist. dir., 2005—06, dep. chief of staff, 2006—07, chief of staff, 2007—; campaign mgr. Office of Jay Helvey for Congress, 2003—04; field rep. Bush/Cheney Campaign, 2004. V.p. SGA, 1997. Office: Office of Congresswoman Virginia Foxx 1230 Longworth House Office Bldg Washington DC 20515 Office Phone: 202-225-2071. Business E-Mail: todd.poole@mail.house.gov.*

POOLE, WILL, computer company executive; BS in Computer Sci., Brown U. Sr. mktg. & engring. mgmt. Sun Microsystems Inc., 1985—90; co-founder, pres., CEO eShop Inc., 1991—96; joined Microsoft Corp., 1996, corp. v.p. new media platforms divsn., sr. v.p. Windows Client bus., 2003—07, corp. v.p. unlimited potential group, 2007—08. Co-chmn., mem. bd. dirs. NComputing, Inc., Redwood City, Calif., 2008—. Avocations: bicycling, sailing, building furniture. Office: c/o NComputing Inc 1 Lagoon Dr Ste 110 Redwood City CA 94065*

POOLE, WILLIAM, retired bank executive; b. Wilmington, Del., June 19, 1937; s. William and Louise (Hiller) P.; m. Mary Lynne Ahroon, June 26, 1960 (div. May 1997); children: William, Lester Allen, Jonathan Carl; m. Geraldine S. Stroud, July 12, 1997. AB, Swarthmore Coll., 1959, LLD (hon.), 1989; MBA, U. Chgo., 1963, PhD, 1966. Asst. prof. polit. economy Johns Hopkins U., Balt., 1963-69; professorial lectr. Am. U., Washington, 1970-71; assoc. professorial lectr. George Washington U., Washington, 1971-73; professorial lectr. Georgetown U., Washington, 1972; vis. lectr. Harvard U., Cambridge, Mass., 1973, MIT, Cambridge, 1974, 77; Bank Mees and Hope vis. prof. econs. Erasmus U. Rotterdam, 1991; prof. econs. Brown U., Providence, 1974-98, dir. ctr. for study fin. markets and insts., 1987-92, chmn. econs. dept., 1981-82, 85-86; economist Fed. Res. Sys., Washington, 1964, 69-70, sr. economist, 1970-74; pres., CEO Fed. Res. Bank St. Louis, 1998—2008; sr. fellow The Cato Inst., 2008—; Disting. fellow in residence U. Del., 2008—. Adviser Fed. Res. Bank, Boston, 1973-74, cons., 1974-81; vis. economist Res. Bank of Australia, 1980-81; mem. Coun. Econ. Advisers, 1982-85; adj. scholar Cato Inst., 1985-98. Author: (book) Principles of Economics, 1991; contbr. articles to profl. jours. Dir. United Way Gr. St. Louis; bd. trustees Webster U. Recipient Adam Smith award, Nat. Assn. Bus. Econs., 2006. Mem. Am. Econ. Assn., Western Econ. Assn. (mem. internat. exec. com. 1986-89, mem. nominating com. 1995). Office: The Cato Inst 1000 Massachusetts Ave NW Washington DC 20001

POOLER, ROSEMARY S., federal judge; b. 1938; BA, Bklyn. Coll., 1959; MA, U. Conn., 1961; JD, U. Mich. Law Sch., 1965; cert. in Sr. Mgmt. in Govt., Harvard U., 1978; degree (hon.), SUNY, Albany, 1986. With Crystal, Manes & Rifken, Syracuse, 1966—69, Michaels and Michaels, Syracuse, 1969—72; asst. corp. counsel Dir. of Consumer Affairs Unit, Syracuse, 1972—73; common counsel City of Syracuse Pub. Interest Rsch. Group, 1974—75; chmn., exec. dir. Consumer Protection Bd., 1975—80; commr. NY State Pub. Services Commn., 1981—86; staff dir. NY State Assembly, Com. on Corps., Authorities and Commns., 1987—94; judge Supreme Ct., 5th Jud. Dist., 1991—94, US Dist. Ct. (no. dist.) NY, Syracuse, 1994—98, US Ct. Appeals, (2nd cir.), 1998—. Vis. prof. Syracuse Univ. Coll. of Law, 1987—88; v.p. legal affairs Atlantic States Legal Found., 1989—90. Mem.: Assn. of Supreme Ct. Justices of the State of NY (sec. 1993—94), Women's Bar Assn. of the State of NY, NY State Bar Assn., Onondaga County Bar Assn. Office: Federal Bldg 100 S Clinton St Syracuse NY 13261-7395 also: 40 Foley Square New York NY 10007*

POON, ALAN MING WANG, sports association executive, director; s. Chung and Chai Poon; m. Grace Wong, 1980; 1 child, Arthur. MBA, Pacific We. U., 1984. Dir., sales mgr. Ed's News and Confectionery Ltd., Canada, 1984—87; dir., bus. mgr. Alanica Foodservices Ltd., Canada, 1988—94; product and export mgr. Hop Hing Group, Hong Kong, 1995—97; regional dir. Seawide Internat. Group, Hong Kong, 1997—2002; export mgr. Sunnyside Ltd., Hong Kong, 2002—05; regional dir. BTL Sports Inc., Toronto, Canada, 2005—. Part-time trainer BTL Sports Inc., 2005—. Author: Mechanic Tennis Training Program (cert. Hong Kong Tennis Assn., 2002). Recipient Quality Assurance Sys. award, Sunnyside Ltd., 2002. Fellow: Inst. Administrative Mgmt. (Internat. Essay Contest award 2000, Total Quality Management award 1992), Brit. Inst. Adminstrv. Mgmt. (hon. cert. 1982). Achievements include research in direct-mailing-orders as a marketing strategy. Office: BTL Sports Inc 4211 Sheppard Avenue East Unit A111 Toronto ON Canada M1S 5H5 Business E-Mail: btlsl2005@yahoo.ca.

POON, CHRISTINE A., dean, business educator, retired pharmaceutical company executive; b. Cin., June 23, 1952; d. James and Virginaia Poon; m. Mike Tweedle. BS in Biology, Northwestern U., 1973; MS in Biology & Biochemistry, St. Louis U., 1973; MBA in Fin., Boston U., 1982. Various mgmt. positions Bristol-Myers Squibb Co., 1985—2000, v.p., sr. v.p. for Can. and L.Am. pharm. ops., pres., gen. mgr. Squibb Diagnostics' Can. operation, 1994, pres. Med. Devices, 1997—98, pres. internat. medicines, 1998—2000; co. group chmn. pharm. group Johnson & Johnson, New Brunswick, NJ, 2000—01, worldwide chmn. pharms. group, 2001—03, worldwide chmn. medicines and nutritionals, 2003—09, vice chmn., mem. exec. com., 2005—09; dean, John W. Berry, Sr. chair in bus. Max M. Fisher Coll. Bus., Ohio State U., Columbus, 2009—. Bd. dirs. Johnson & Johnson, 2005—09, Prudential Fin., Inc., 2006—; bd. adv. Healthcare Businesswomen's Assn. Bd. dirs. Fox Chase Cancer Ctr., Phila. Named Woman of Yr., Healthcare Businesswomen's Assn., 2004; named one of 50 Women to Watch, Wall St. Jour., 2005, 2006, 100 Most Powerful Women, Forbes mag., 2005, 2007, 2008, 10 Most Powerful Women in NJ Bus., Star-Ledger, 2006, 50 Most Powerful Women in Bus., Fortune mag., 2006, 2007. Office: Ohio State U Fisher Coll Bus 201 Fisher Hall 2100 Neil Avenue Columbus OH 43210 Office Phone: 614-292-2666. E-mail: poon.36@osu.edu.*

POON, PETER TIN-YAU, engineer, physicist; b. Hengyang, Hunan, China, May 31, 1944; came to U.S., 1967; s. Sam. Chak-Kwong and Lai (Yiu) P.; m. Mable Tsang, Apr. 13, 1974; children: Amy Wei-Ling, Brian Wing-Yan. BS, U. Hong Kong, 1965; MA, Calif. State U., Long Beach, 1969; PhD, U. So. Calif., 1974. Advanced project mgmt. program cert. Stanford U., 2009. Tech. mgr. and sr. engr. advanced tech. and missions Jet Propulsion Lab./Calif. Inst. Tech., Pasadena, 1974—83; advisor Space Sta. Ada Task NASA, 1984—85, task leader software mgmt. and assurance program, software mgmt. stds., 1986—88, element mgr. software info. sys.; from multimission sys. mgr. to telecom. and mission sys. mgr. Cassini and Mars missions Jet Propulsion Lab., 1988—2001, telecom. and mission sys. mgr. global surveyor Mars Odyssey mission, 2001—09, telecomm. and mission sys. mgr. Voyager Interstellar mission, 2001—09, telecomm. and mission sys. mgr. Ulysses mission, telecom. and mission sys. mgr. European Very Long Baseline Interferometry Network Project, Space Geodesy Program, 2001—09. Del. various confs.; US chmn., program mgmt. com., panel chair Internat. Software Engring. Stds. Symposium, UK, Canada, Brazil and US, 1992—99, Canada, 1992—2009, Brazil, 1992—99, England, 1992—99, United States, 2000—09; mem. Internat. Orgn. for Standardization in Info. Tech. Subcom. and US Tech. Adv. Group, 1995—2007. Mem. editl. bd.: Software Quality Profl., Am. Soc. for Quality, 1998—; contbr. articles to profl. jours. Active JPL steering com. United Way, Pasadena, Calif., 1998—2005. Recipient Group awards NASA, 1977-2006, Recognition cert. Inventions and Contbns. Bd., award from Mars Global Surveyor and Mars Odyssey, 2002, European Space Agy, 2008, German Space Operations Ctr., 2009 Mem. IEEE (exec. com. software engring. stds. 1993-2000), Arcadia Music Club (pres. 1994-95), Sigma Xi, Eta Kappa Nu, Phi Kappa Phi, Athenaeum. Avocations: music, hiking, theater. Personal E-mail: petertpoon@yahoo.com.

POONS, LARRY, artist; b. Tokyo, Oct. 1, 1937; arrived in USA, 1938; Student, New Eng. Conservatory Music, 1955-57, Boston Mus. Fine Arts Sch., 1958. Mem. vis. faculty N.Y. Studio Sch., 1967. Lectr. in field. Author: The Structure of Color, 1971; exhibitions include Green Gallery, NYC, 1963—65, Art Inst. Chgo., 1966, Corcoran Gallery Art, Carnegie Inst., 1967, Leo Castelli Gallery, 1967—68, Documenta IV, Kassel, W. Germany, 1968, Whitney Mus. Am. Art, 1968, 1972, Lawrence Rubin Gallery, 1970—73, Whitney Biennial, 1973, Knoedler & Co., 1973—78, Knoedler Contemporary Art, N.Y.C., 1974—78, Andre Emmerlich Gallery, 1979—87, Albright-Knox Art Gallery, Buffalo, 1968, 1970, Pasadena Art Mus., 1969, Gallery 99, Bar Harbor Islands, Fla., 1981, Mus. Fine Arts, Boston, 1981—82, Galerie Montaigne, Paris, 1990, Helander Gallery, Palm Beach, Fla., 1990, Gallery Afinsa, Madrid, 1991, Salander-O'Reilly Galleries, N.Y.C., 1991—96, 1998, Frederick Spratt Gallery, San Jose, 1996—97, Ruth Bachofner Gallery, Santa Monica, 1996, Art Pub., Geneva, Switzerland, 1997, Claudia Carr Gallery, 1997, Larry Evan/James Willis and Frederick Spratt Gallery, San Francisco, 1997, exhibited in group shows at Matthew Mark, Pat Hearn, 1998, Sideshow 195, Bklyn., 1998, Sideshow, 2008, Denver Museum, 2007, Smithsonian Museum, 2008, Art and the Am. Experience, Kalamazoo Inst. of the Arts, 1998, Staatliche Kunsthalle, Baden-Baden, Germany, 1999, Ameringe Howard Fine Art, N.Y.C., 2000, Bernard Jacobson, 2002, Jacobson Howard, NYC, 2003—04, Side Show Gallery, Bklyn., 2003, 2006, Studio 18 Gallery, NYC, 2004, Albright Knox, Buffalo, 2005, David Nolam Gallery, NYC, 2009, Danese Gallery, 2009, Represented in permanent collections Mus. Modern Art, N.Y.C., Allen Meml. Art Mus., Oberlin Coll., Cleve. Mus. Art, Hirschhorn Mus. and Sculpture Garden, Washington, Milw. Art Ctr., Solomon R. Guggenheim Mus., N.Y.C., Harn Museum, Gainesville, FL, Tate Gallery, London, Whitney Mus. Am. Art, Met. Mus. Art, Chgo. Art Inst., Denver Mus., Boston Mus. Fine Arts, Albright-Knox Art Gallery, Stedelijk Mus., Amsterdam, Woodward Found., Washington, David Mirvish Gallery, Toronto, Bernard Jacobson Gallery, London, one-man shows include Salander-O'Reilly Gallery, N.Y.C., 2001, Theo Waddington, Boca Raton, Fla., 2000, Galleria Metta, Madrid, 2000, Perrella Gallery, Johnstown, N.Y., 2000, Bernard Jacobson, 2002, Bernard Jacobson Gallery, London, 2004, 2007, Jacobson Howard Gallery, 2004—05, Side Show Gallery, Bklyn., 2005—06, Bernard Jacobson Gallery, London, 2007, Danese Gallery, NYC, 2007, 2009, Jacobson Howard Gallery, 2008, exhibited in group shows at First Ctr. Arts, Nashville, 2008. Address: 831 Broadway New York NY 10003-4706

POOR, HAROLD VINCENT, engineering educator; b. Columbus, Ga., Oct. 2, 1951; s. Harold Edgar and Virginia (Hardin) P.; m. Connie Irene Hazelwood, Sept. 1, 1973; children: Kristin Elizabeth, Lauren Alissa. BEE with highest honors, Auburn U., 1972; PhD, Princeton U., 1977. From asst. prof. to prof. U. Ill., Urbana, 1977—90; prof. dept. elec. engring. Princeton U., NJ, 1990—, George Van Ness Lothrop prof. engring., 2003—05, Michael Henry Strater univ. prof. elec. engring., 2005—, dir. Ctr. for Innovation in Engring. Edn., 2005—06, dean engring. and applied scis., 2006—. Acad. visitor Imperial Coll. London U., 1985, 2003; vis. prof. Newcastle (Australia) U., 1987, Stanford U., 2004; vis. scholar Harvard U., 2004; sr. vis. fellow Imperial Coll., London U., 1993; cons. in field. Author: An Introduction to Signal Detection and Estimation, 1988, 2d edit., 1994, Wireless Communication Systems: Advanced Techniques for Signal Reception, 2004, Wireless Networks: Multiuser Detection in Cross-Layer Design, 2005, MIMO Wireless Communications, 2007, Quickest Detection, 2009; co-editor: Wireless Communications: Signal Processing Perspectives, 1998; contbr. articles to profl. jours. Grantee NSF, Office Naval Rsch., Army Rsch. Office, Darpa, 1978—; recipient Dir.'s Disting. Tchg. scholars award NSF, Aaron D. Wyner award, IEEE Info. Theory Soc., 2008, Disting. Alumnus award Tau Beta Pi 2005, Tech. Achievement award, Signal Processing Soc., 2007; John Simon Guggenheim Meml. Found. fellow, 2002-04. Fellow IEEE (bd. dirs. 1991-92, pres. Info. Theory Soc. IEEE 1990, editor-in-chief IEEE Transaction Info. Theory, 2004-07, Disting. Mem. award Control Sys. Soc. 1994, Third Millennium medal 2000, Joint Paper award with IEEE com. soc., 2001, Grad. Tchg. award 2001, EAB Major Ednl. Innovation award, 2004, James H. Mulligan Jr. Edn. medal 2005, Marconi Prize Paper award, 2007, Tech. Achievement award Signal Processing Soc., 2007), AAAS, Acoustical Soc. Am., Am. Soc. Engring. Edn. (Terman award 1992, Centennial cert. 1993), Inst. Math. Stats., Optical Soc. Am.; mem. NAE, Am. Acad. Arts and Scis., Cosmos Club (Washington), Eta Kappa Nu (eminent mem., 2008). Office: Princeton Univ Sch Engring and Applied Sci Princeton NJ 08544-0001 Office Phone: 609-258-2260.

POOR, JANET MEAKIN, III, landscape designer; b. Cin., Nov. 27, 1929; d. Cyrus Lee and Helen Keats (Meakin) Lee-Hofer; m. Edward King Poor III, June 23, 1951; children: Edward King IV, Thomas Meakin. Student, Stephens Coll., 1947-48, U. Cinn., 1949-51, Triton Coll., 1973-76. Pres. Janet Meakin Poor Landscape Design, Winnetka, Ill., 1975—. Chmn. bd. dirs. Chgo. Botanic Garden. Author, editor: Plants That Merit Attention Vol. I: Trees, 1984, Vol. II: Shrubs; contbr. articles to profl. jours. Participant in long range planning City of Winnetka, 1978-82, archtl. and environ. bd., 1980-84, beautification commn., 1978-84, garden coun., 1978-82; adv. coun., Sec. of Agr. Nat. Arboretum, Washington; nat. adv. bd. Filoli, San Francisco; trustee Ctr. Plant Conservation at Mo. Bot. Garden, St. Louis, also mem. exec. com.; mem. adv. coun. The Garden Conservancy, 1989—, chmn. Open Days Program Garden Conservancy; trustee Winnetka Congl. Ch., 1978-80; bd. dirs. Lady Bird Johnson Wildflower Ctr., Austin, Tex., McKee Bot. Garden, Vero Beach, Fla. Recipient merit award Hadley Sch. Blind, 1972; named Vol. of Yr. Hadley Sch. Blind. Mem. Chgo. Hort. Soc. (chmn. bd. dirs. 1987-93, medal 1984, gold medal garden design, exec. com., chmn. rsch. com., women's bd., designer herb garden Farwell Gardens at Chgo. Botanic Garden, Hutchinson medal 1994), Am. Hort. Soc. (bd. dirs., Catherine H. Sweeney award 1985), Garden Club Am. (chmn. nat. plant exchange 1980-81, chmn. hort. com. 1981-83, bd. dirs., 1983-85, corresponding sec. 1985-87, Horticulture award Zone XI 1981, Creative Leadership award 1986), Fortnightly Club, Garden Guild (bd. dirs.), Garden Club Am. (v.p. 1987-89, medal awards chmn. 1991-93, Medal of Honor 1994). Republican. Avocations: gardening, writing, music, lecturing, horticulture research. Home Phone: 847-446-2898.

POOR, PETER VARNUM, television producer and director; b. NYC, May 17, 1926; s. Henry Varnum and Bessie Breuer (Freedman) P.; m. Eloise Marcovicci Miller, Sept. 27, 1950; children: Candida Eustacia, Anna Maria, Graham Varnum. BA, Harvard U., 1947; postgrad., Centro Sperimentale di Cinematografia, Rome, 1951-52. Prodn. asst. New World Films, NYC, 1948; editor, dir. Willard Pictures, NYC, 1948-51; film editor, dir. and producer CBS News-Airpower, 1954-57, 7 Lively Arts, 1957-58, Twentieth Century, 1958-66, 21st Century, 1966-69, 60 Minutes, 1970-71, CBS Reports, 1971-75; sr. producer NBC News, Monitor, First Camera, White Paper, 1977-87; freelance producer and dir. Crow House Prodns., NYC, 1988—. Instr. in TV journalism Fordham U., 1976-78; screening com. Fulbright Grants in Film, TV and Radio, 1965-67, chmn., 1967, 70; adj. assoc. history of documentary Columbia U. Grad. Sch. Journalism, 1987; adj. asst. prof. visual arts NYU, 1991-92. Producer-dir.: (TV documentary films) What's New at School, 1972, The IQ Myth, 1975, The Biggest Lump of Money in the World, 1985, The Japan They Don't Talk About, 1986, Nuclear Power in France, 1987, The Cronkite Report, 1993. Served with USAF, 1944-45. Recipient Emmy award Acad. TV Arts and Sci., 1961-62, 67, Lasker TV award Lasker Found., 1968-69, U.S. CEA Forum award, 1967, 87; hon. mention Robert Kennedy Journalism Award in TV, 1976; Fulbright scholar, 1951-52. Mem. Dirs. Guild Am. (coun. 1980-90), Film Editors Union, Writers Guild Am. East. Clubs: Phoenix S-K (Cambridge, Mass.). Avocations: bicycling, reading, photography, gardening. Home and Office: 1150 5th Ave New York NY 10128-0724 Office Phone: 212-722-3836. E-mail: p.poor@worldnet.att.net.

POORMAN, ROBERT LEWIS, retired academic administrator; b. Germantown, Ohio, Dec. 9, 1926; s. Dale Lowell and Bernice Velma (Krick) P.; m. Lois May Romer, Dec. 26, 1949; children: Paula Beth, Janice Marie, Mark Leon, John Alex, Lisa Ann, Daniel Romer. Student, Ohio Wesleyan U., 1944-45, U. Va., 1945-46; BSEd., Ohio State U., 1948, MA, 1950; postgrad., U. So. Calif., 1951-53; Ed.D. (Kellogg fellow 1960-62, Disting. Scholar Tuition grantee 1960-62), UCLA, 1964. Tchr., counselor, adminstr., secondary schs., Colo., Mo., Ariz., 1948-57; registrar Phoenix Coll., 1957-60; intern Bakersfield Coll., 1960-63, asst. to pres., 1963-64, asso. dean instrn., 1964-65, dean students, 1965-67; founding pres. Lincoln Land C.C., 1967-88, pres. emeritus; edn. cons. MARA of Malaysia, 1983; higher edn. cons. Springfield, Ill., 1988—; interim pres. Parkland Coll., Champaign, Ill., 1989-90. Vis. assoc. prof. Fla. Internat. U., 1994-95, Fulbright Sr. Specialist peer reviewer, 2007-; lectr. in field; cons. in field. Contbr. articles to profl. jours. Bd. dirs. (past) United Way of Springfield, bd. dirs. Urban League of Springfield, Good Will Industries of Springfield, Springfield (Ill.) Symphony, Catholic Youth Orgn., Springfield, Gov.'s Prayer Breakfast, Springfield Mental Health, Griffin H.S. Bd., Diocesan Sem.; mem. adv. bd. Sacred Heart Acad., Springfield Commn. on Internat. Visitors, Sister Cities Assn. With USNR, 1944—46. Recipient Midwest region CEO of Yr. Assn. C.C. Trustees, 1988, recognition Ill. C.C. Trustees Assn., 1988; named an Outstanding CEO for Ill. Cmty. Colls. U. Tex. Leadership Program, 1987; named a leader in shaping the century State Jour. Register, 1999; Phi Theta Kappa fellow, 1981; Fulbright Sr. scholar, Lithuania, 1993, Ukraine, 1996, China, 2000; Fulbright sr. specialist, Tanzania, 2003-08. Mem. Am. Assn. Cmty. and Jr. Colls., Ill. Coun. Pub. C.C. Pres. (sec. 1973-74, vice chmn. 1974-75, chmn. 1975-76), Coun. North Ctrl. Cmty. and Jr. Colls. (exec. bd. 1979-81), North Ctrl. Assn. (cons., evaluator 1984-88) Republican. Roman Catholic. Home and Office: 2206 Augusta Dr Springfield IL 62704-3105 Office Phone: 217-546-1936. Business E-Mail: rpoorman@att.net.

POOS, JACQUES FRANCOIS, former foreign minister, member of European Parliament; b. Luxembourg, June 3, 1935; s. Adolphe and Catherine (Weimerskirch) P.; m. Monique Lorang, July 3, 1969; children: Daniel, Yasmine, Xavier. Dipl. fin. d et sec., Athenee, Luxembourg, 1954; Lic. ès Sc. Ec. et Commn. H.E.C., Switzerland, 1958; Dipl. Sup. Ec. Comparée, U. Internat., Luxembourg, 1960; Docteur ès Sciences Comm. et Ec., U. Lausanne, Switzerland, 1961. Seconded to Ministry of Nat. Economy, 1959-62. Mem. Rsch. at Nat. Statis. Office (STATEC), 1962-64; mng. dir. Imprimerie Coopérative and newspaper Tageblatt, 1964-76; mng. dir. Banque Continentale de Luxembourg S.A., 1980-82, Banque PARIBAS, Luxembourg S.A., 1982-84; City counsellor of Esch/Alzette, 1969-76; mem. Parliament, 1974-76, head of Socialist Workers Party Group; v.p. Socialist Workers Party, 1976-95; min. of fin. Luxembourg, 1976-79, v.p. of govt., min. for external trade, coop. min. of economy, min. of treasury, 1984-89, vice prime min., 1984-99, min. of def., 1989-94, min. for fgn. affairs, 1984-99, vice prime min., min. fgn. affairs, 1994-99; acting chmn. Coun. European Union, 1985, 91, 97; mem. European Parliament, 1999-04. Author: Le Luxembourg dans le Marché Commun, 1961; Le Modèle Luxembourgeois, 1977. E-mail: jpoos@europarl.eu.int.

POPAT, SAURIN RAJNIKANT, oncologist, surgeon; b. Kampala, Uganda, Aug. 19, 1969; s. Rajnirant Nagi and Bharti Rajnirant Popat; m. Katharine Elizabeth Herbert, Sept. 11, 1999; children: Alexander Shivam, Evan Kavi, Carys Meera Rose. BA, Queen's U., Kingston, Ont. Can., 1990; MD, U. Western Ont., 1992. Asst. prof. surgery U. Rochester, NY, 2000—04, asst. prof. otolarynology, 2004—06, asst. prof. oncology, 2003—06; asst. prof. surg. oncology Roswell Park Cancer Inst., Buffalo, 2006—07, assoc. prof. surg. oncology, 2007—. Dir. head and neck surg. oncology U. Rochester Med. Ctr., 2000—06; bd. dir. Univera Health, Buffalo, 2007—; self-employed med. legal cons., Rochester, 2002—06, Buffalo, 2006—. Contbr. scientific papers to profl. jours., chapters to books. Vo. physician med. aid mission U. Toronto, Thailand, 1996. Recipient Roundtree prize, U. Western Ont., 1990. Fellow: Am. Bd. Otolaryngology - Head & Neck Surgery, Am. Head and Neck Soc., Royal Coll Physicians and Surgeons Can., Am. Coll. Surgeons, Royal Coll. Surgeons Can., Royal Coll. Physicians. Avocations: hockey, golf, sailing. Office: Roswell Park Cancer Inst Elm and Carton Sts Buffalo NY 14263 Home Phone: 716-875-3158.

POPE, ANDREW JACKSON, JR., (JACK POPE), retired judge; b. Abilene, Tex., Apr. 18, 1913; s. Andrew Jackson and Ruth Adella (Taylor) Pope; m. Allene Esther Nichols, June 11, 1938; children: Andrew Jackson III, Walter Allen. BA, Abilene Christian U., Tex., 1934, LLD (hon.), 1980; LLB, U. Tex., 1937; LLD (hon.), Pepperdine U., Malibu, Calif., 1981, St. Mary's U., San Antonio, 1982, Okla. Christian U., Oklahoma City, 1983. Bar: Tex. 1937. Practice law, Corpus Christi, 1937-46; judge 94th Dist. Ct., Corpus Christi, 1946-50; justice Ct. Civil Appeals, San Antonio, 1950-65, Supreme Ct. Tex., Austin, 1965-82, chief justice, 1982-85; ret., 1985. Author: John Berry & His Children, 1988; chmn. bd. editors Appellate Procedures in Texas, 1974; contbr. articles to profl. jours. Pres. Met. YMCA, San Antonio, 1956—57; chmn. Tex. State Law Libr. Bd., 1973—80; trustee Abilene Christian U., 1954—. With USNR, 1944—46. Recipient Silver Beaver award, Alamo Coun. Boy Scouts Am., 1961, Disting. Eagle award, 1983, Rosewood Gavel award, 1962, Outstanding Alumnus award, Abilene Christian U., 1965, St. Thomas More award, St. Mary's U., San Antonio, 1982, Greenhill Jud. award, Mcpl. Judges Assn., 1980, citation, Houston Bar Found., 1985, award, San Antonio Bar Found., 1985, Disting. Jurist award, Jefferson County Bar, 1985, Oustanding Alumnus award, U. Tex. Law Alumni Assn., 1988, George Washington Honor medal, Freedom Found., 1988, Disting. Lawyer award, Travis County, 1992. Fellow: Tex. Bar Found. (Law Rev. award 1979—81); mem.: ABA, Tex. Ctr. for Legal Ethics and Professionalism (Outstanding Svc. award 2007), State Bar Tex., Tex. Supreme Ct. Hist. Soc. (v.p.), Tex. State Hist. Assn., Am. Judicature Soc., Tex. Philos. Soc., Bexar County Bar Assn., Travis County Bar Assn., Nueces County Bar Assn. (pres. 1946), State Bar Tex. (pres. jud. sect. 1962, Oustanding Fifty Yrs. Lawyer award 1994), Christian Chronicle Coun. (chmn.), KP (grand chancellor 1946), Masons, Sons Rep. of Tex., Austin Knife and Fork (pres. 1980), Order of Coif, Pi Sigma Alpha, Phi Delta Phi, Alpha Chi. Mem. Ch. Of Christ. Home: 2803 Stratford Dr Austin TX 78746-4626

POPE, C. ARDEN, III, economics professor; b. Logan, Utah, Sept. 30, 1955; s. Clive Arden Pope Jr. and Vivian Harper Pope; m. Ronda Lou Gneiting, Aug. 5, 1977; children: Jaren Clive, Devin Garret, Weston Arden, Nolan Gneiting, Bryson Ron, Dallin Kimball, Collin Harper. BS, Brigham Young U., Provo, Utah, 1978; MS, PhD, Iowa State U., Ames, 1981. Rsch. assoc., staff economist Iowa State U., 1980—82; asst. prof. Tex. A&M U., College Station, 1982—84; asst. to assoc. prof. Brigham Young U., 1984—94, prof. econs., 1994—. Vis. scientist Harvard Sch. Pub. Health, Boston, 1992—93. Author: (book chapter) Acute respiratory effects of particulate air pollution, Epidemiology of acute health effects, Epidemiology of chronic health effects, Outdoor Air: Particles, Epidemiology of Particle Effects, Effects of particulate air pollution exposures, Epidemiological evidence of relationship between particle exposure and cardiovascular outcomes, Air Pollution: Coronary Heart Disease Epidemiology; contbr. articles to numerous profl. jours. Recipient Creative Achievement award, Brigham Young U., 1986, Karl G. Maeser, Excellence in Rsch. and Creative Arts award, 1995, Karl G. Maeser Disting. Faculty Lectr., 2006, Mary Lou Fulton Professorship, 2005-, Clarence Olds Sappington Meml. Lectr., Am. Coll. Occupl. and Environ. Medicine, 1997, Lectr. award, Sigma Xi, 2000, Thomas T. Mercer Joint prize, Am. Assn. Aerosol Rsch. and the Internat. Soc. Aerosols in Medicine, 2001, Governor's medal Sci. & Tech., Utah Governor's Office, 2004; fellow Interdisciplinary Programs in Health, Harvard U., 1992-1993. Honorary, Am. Coll. Chest Physicians, 2008. Avocations: running, backpacking, community and church youth leader. Office: Brigham Young Univ 130 Fob Provo UT 84602 E-mail: cap3@byu.edu.

POPE, C. LARRY, food products executive; BBA, Coll. William & Mary, 1975, EMBA, 1994. Controller Smithfield Foods Inc., Smithfield, Va., 1980—99, v.p. fin., 1999—2000, CFO, 2000—01, pres., COO, 2001—06, pres., CEO, 2006—. Bd. mem. Coll. William & Mary Bus. Sch. Found. Office: Smithfield Foods Inc 200 Commerce St Smithfield VA 23430-1204

POPE, FRED WALLACE, JR., lawyer; b. Sanford, Fla., Feb. 9, 1941; s. Fred Wallace and Dorothy (Marshall) P.; m. Jane Laird Miller, Dec. 27, 1962 (div. Oct. 1986); children: Catherine W., Gregory W.; m. Christine R. Fredrick, Jan. 4, 1991. BA in Polit. Sci., U. Fla., 1962, JD with honors, 1969; AM in Internat. Rels., Boston U., 1965. Bar: Fla. 1970, U.S. Dist. Ct. (so., mid. and no. dists.) Fla., U.S. Supreme Ct. 1975, U.S. Ct. Appeals (11th cir.) 1983. Rsch. aide 2d Dist. Ct. Appeal, Lakeland, Fla., 1970; assoc. Trenam, Simmons, Kemker, Scharf & Barkin, Tampa, Fla., 1970-74; ptnr. Johnson, Pope, Bokor, Ruppel & Burns, P.A., Clearwater, Fla., 1974—. Dir. Citizens Bank Clearwater, 1986-98, First Nat. Bank of Fla., 1998-01. Trustee The Fla. Orch., Tampa, 1984—, chmn. bd. trustees, 1991-93; bd. dirs. Pinellas County Arts Coun., Clearwater, 1988-93. Capt. U.S. Army, 1962-67. Mem. ABA (coun. mem. sect. litigation 1983-86, editor, chief Litigation 1979-80), The Fla. Bar (gov. 1982-86), Clearwater Bar Assn. (pres. 1980-81). Office: Johnson Pope Bokor Ruppel & Burns LLP 911 Chestnut St Clearwater FL 33756-5643 E-mail: wallyp@jpfirm.com.

POPE, HARRISON GRAHAM, JR., psychiatrist, educator; b. Lynn, Mass., Dec. 26, 1947; s. H. Graham and Alice (Rider) P.; m. Mary M. Quinn, June 7, 1974; children: Kimberly, Hilary, Courtney. AB summa cum laude, Harvard U., 1969, MPH, 1972, MD, 1974. Diplomate Am. Bd. Psychiatry and Neurology. Resident in psychiatry McLean Hosp., Belmont, Mass., 1974-77, clin. rsch. fellow Mailman Rsch. Ctr., 1977-79, asst. psychiatrist, 1979-84, assoc. psychiatrist, 1984-92, psychiatrist, 1992—, chief biol. psychiatry lab., 1984—; Dupont-Warren rsch. fellow Harvard Med. Sch., Boston, 1976-77. Instr. psychiatry Harvard Med. Sch., Boston, 1977-82, asst. prof., 1982-85, assoc. prof., 1985-99, prof. 1999—; staff psychiatrist Hampstead (N.H.) Hosp., 1976-80; vis. fellow The Maudsley Hosp., London, 1977, Hôpital. Ste. Anne, Paris, 1977; mem. Am. Psychiat. Assn., 1976-80, adv. com. on schizophrenic, paranoid and affective disorders, 1979, adv. com. on preparation of DSM-III-R, 1984, task force on nomenclature and stats., 1979, 84. Author: Voices from the Drug Culture, 1971, The Road East, 1974, (with J.I. Hudson) New Hope for Binge Eaters: Advances in the Understanding and Treatment of Bulimia, 1984; co-editor: The Psychobiology of Bulimia, 1987, Use of Anticonvulsants in Psychiatry: Recent Advances, 1988, Psychology Astray: Fallacies in Studies of "Repressed Memory" and Childhood Trauma, 1997; The Adonis Complex: The Secret Crisis of Male Body Obsession, 2000; mem. editl. bd. European Psychiatry, Paris, 1984—. Internat. Jour. of Eating Disorders, 1984—. Jour. Clin. Psychiatry, 1993-; contbr. numerous articles to profl. jours. Named one of Outstanding Americans under 40 Esquire mag., 1984; fellow Scottish Rite Schizophrenia Program, No. Masonic Jurisdiction, 1977-81, Charles A. King Trust, Boston, 1977-79. Avocation: weightlifting. Office: McLean Hosp 115 Mill St Belmont MA 02478-1048

POPE, INGRID BLOOMQUIST, sculptor, poet, painter; b. Arvika, Sweden; became U.S. citizen. d. Oscar Emanuel and Gerda (Henningson) Brostrom; m. Howard Richard Bloomquist, Feb. 14, 1941 (dec. Nov. 1982); children: Dennis Howard, Diane Cecile Connelly, Laurel Ann Shields; m. Marvin Hoyle Pope, Mar. 9, 1985 (dec. June 1997). BA cum laude, Manhattanville Coll., 1979, MA in Humanities, 1981; MA in Religion, Yale U., 1984. Exhbns. include Manhattanville Coll., Purchase, N.Y., Yale Div. Sch., Ch. of Sweden in N.Y.C., First Ch. of Round Hill; author: (books) Musings, 1994, Hosannah, Help Please, 1999, Blessings, 2003. Past bd. dirs. N.Y.C. Mission Soc., Greenwich YWCA, Greenwich Chaplaincy, Greenwich Acad. Parents' Assn., past pres; past trustee First Ch. Round Hill, Greenwich; pres. Ch. Women United, Greenwich, 1989-91. Mem. AAUW, Nat. Assn. Pen Women, English Speaking Union, Nat. Wildflower Assn., Yale Club N.Y.C., Lakeview Club (Austin, Tex.), Acad. Am. Poets, Nat. Mus. of Women in Arts, Yale Alumnae Club (Austin and Greenwich, Conn.). *I need to share my feelings deep inside be it in verse or prose or form or line. I need to say it, do it, show, or write and so creatively I try to do my best. I lift up brush and paint a scene, I struggle with a stone or mold in clay or write my verse just as I do today.*

POPE, JACQUELINE PRIVETTE, music educator; b. Darlington, SC, Aug. 13, 1936; d. Leo Thomas Privette and Ophelia Mae Norris; m. George Wallace Kilpatriok (div.); children: George Ashley, Laurie Dawn, Andrew Wallace; m. James L. Pope, June 21, 1997. BA, Furman U., 1958; student, Bapt. Internat. Sem., 1960—61; studied with Powell Everhart, Atlanta, Ga., 1964—67, studied with Irene Harrower, 1972—74, studied with Claude Shirley, 1980—81; MusM in Voice Performance, Ga. State U., 1987; studied with Joseph Meeks, Kennesaw State U., 1995. Minister music and edn. Westminster (S.C.) Bapt. Ch., 1958—59; tchr. music Louisville (Ky.) City Schs., 1959—60, Jefferson County Schs., Louisville, 1961—62; substitute tchr. Houston (Tex.) City Schs., 1962—63; pvt. voice and piano tchr. Austell, Ga., 1964—; dir. music Southminster Presbyn. Ch., Marietta, Ga., 1983—91; music specialist Cobb County Pub. Schs., Marietta, 1987—98; chancel choir dir. Luth. Ch. Nativity, 1992—2009. Chmn. caring ministry Luth. Ch. Nativity, 1992—2004; dir. of music Cobb Children's Theater, 1972—82. Performer: (CD) Jacqueline P. Pope Sings for You. Mem.: Nat. Assn. Tchrs. Singing, Nat. Music Tchrs. Assn., Ga. Music Tchrs. Assn. (chmn. voice auditions 1980—81), South Cobb Arts Alliance, Alpha Delta Kappa (pres. 1999—2001, state pianist 2002—09). Democrat. Lutheran. Avocations: gardening, painting. Home: 2565 Sloan St Austell GA 30106 Office Phone: 770-732-8666.

POPE, JOHN, retired law educator; s. Robert A. and Winifred E. Pope; 1 child, Michele Elizabeth Woolbert. BA, Richard Stockton Coll., Pomona, NJ, 1976; MS, Fairleigh Dickinson U., Teaneck, NJ, 2002. Cert. police officer NJ. Police Tng. Commn., 1979. Ocean lifeguard Atlantic City Beach Patrol, Atlantic City, 1968—78; law enforcement officer Egg Harbor Twp. Police Dept., NJ, 1979—2007; adj. instr. Fairleigh Dickinson U., Teaneck, NJ, 2002—08. Vol. rowing coach Egg Harbor Twp. HS, NJ, 2006—08. Mem.: FBI Nat. Acad. Assoc. Avocations: rowing, sailing, music. Personal E-mail: jpope1532@comcast.net.

POPE, JOHN A., alderman; b. Chgo. m. Debbie Pope; children: Madelyn Rose, James William. Analyst, Office Budget and Mgmt. City of Chgo., dir. demolition, Bldg. Dept., asst. to Mayor Richard M. Daley; alderman, 10th ward Chgo. City Coun., 1999—. Co-chair spl. events com. Chgo. City Coun. Active CAPS: Chgo. Alternative Policing Program; mem. Hegewisch, East Side, South Chgo. Chambers of Commerce, Hegewisch Cmty. Com., South Chgo. Parents and Friends Fundraising Com., Calumet Area Indsl. Commn.; 10th ward committeeman Dem. Party, Chgo., 2000—; bd. mem. YMCA, Chgo. Mem.: Calumet Ecol. Pk. Assn. Democrat. Office: 3522 E 106th St Chicago IL 60617 also: City Hall 121 N La Salle St Chicago IL 60602 Office Phone: 773-721-1999, 312-744-3078. Office Fax: 773-721-5945. Business E-Mail: ward10@cityofchicago.org.*

POPE, JOHN CHARLES, former airline company executive; b. Newark, Mar. 30, 1949; s. John Aris Coutant and Eleanor Laura (Hillman) P. BA, Yale U., New Haven, 1971; MBA, Harvard U., Cambridge, Mass., 1973. Dir. profit analysis and capital analysis GM, NYC, 1973-77; sr. v.p. fin., treas., CFO Am. Airlines, Inc., AMR Corp., Dallas-Fort Worth, 1977-88; exec. v.p., CFO UAL Corp., United Airlines (subs.), Chgo., 1988-91, pres., COO, 1991-94. Bd. dirs. Fed. Mogul Corp., Detroit, R.R. Donnelley & Sons, Chgo., Dollar Thrifty Automotive Group, Inc., Tulsa, CNF Inc., San Mateo, Calif., Dollar Thrifty Automotive Group, Inc., Tulsa, Fed. Mogul Corp., Detroit, Kraft Foods, Northfield, Ill., R.R. Donnelley, Chgo.; chmn. bd. Waste Mgmt., Houston; bd. trustees, treas. Shedd Aquarium, Chgo. Office Phone: 847-735-0112.

POPE, JOHN EDWIN, editor, columnist; b. Athens, Ga., Apr. 11, 1928; s. Henry Louis and Rose (McAfee) P.; m. Eileen Pope; children: Shirley, Susan, Eddie, David. BA in Journalism, U. Ga., 1948. Sports editor Banner-Herald, Athens, Ga., 1943-48; So. sports editor UPI, Atlanta, 1948-50; sports writer Atlanta Constn., 1950-54; exec. sports editor Atlanta Jour., 1954-56; asst. sports editor Miami (Fla.) Herald, 1956-67, sports editor, 1967—2001, sports columnist, 2001—. Author: Football's Greatest Coaches, 1956, Baseball's Greatest Managers, 1960, Encyclopedia of American Greyhound Racing, 1963, Ted Williams: The Golden Year, 1970, (with Norm Evans) On the Line, 1976, The Edwin Pope Collection, 1988; contbr. articles to popular mags. and Ency. Brittanica, World Book. Recipient Bill Corum Meml. award Thoroughbred Racing Assn., 1962, top sports column award Nat. Headliners Club, 1962, 79, 82, 86, Eclipse award Thoroughbred Racing Assn., 1976, 82, 86, Red Smith award AP Sports Editors, 1989; named to Internat. Churchmen's Sports Hall of Fame, 1976; recipient Knight-Ridder editl. excellence award, 1996, Nat. Sportswriters and Sportscasters Assn. Hall of Fame, 1995, Fla. Sports Hall of Fame, 1996, Bert McGrane award Coll. Football Hall of Fame, 2000, Dick McCann award NFL Pro Football Hall of Fame, 2002, A.J. Liebling award Boxing Writers Assn. Am., 2005; named Orange Bowl Hall of Hon., 2003. Mem. Profl. Football Writers Am. (pres. 1968-69), Football Writers Assn. Am., Golf Writers Am., Nat. Turf Writers, U.S. Tennis Writers. Presbyterian. Office: Miami Herald 235 Harbor Dr Key Biscayne FL 33149 Home Phone: 305-361-9786. Personal E-mail: edwinpope@aol.com. E-mail: epope@herald.com.

POPE, JOHN MARVIN, journalist; b. Hattiesburg, Miss., Nov. 5, 1948; s. Paul M. Jr. and Mary Lee (Scott) P.; m. Diana Pinckley, May 19, 1984. BA cum laude, U. Tex., 1970, MA, 1972. Copy editor The States-Item, New Orleans, 1972-73, reporter, 1973-80, The Times-Picayune, New Orleans, 1980-86, med.-health reporter, 1986—2005, higher edn. reporter, 2005—. Hearst Found. vis. fellow U. Tex., 2005. Co-author: American First Ladies: Their Lives and Their Legacy, 1996. Recipient Med. Writing award, La. State Med. Soc., 1990, 1998, 2005, Frank Allen award, La.-Miss. AP, 1989, Louise McFarland award for excellence in pub. health comm., La. Pub. Health Assn., 2003; fellow Knight Found., Ctrs. for Disease Control and Prevention, 2001; Knight Ctr. for Specialized Journalism fellow, 1999. Fellow Phi Beta Kappa; mem. Soc. Profl. Journalists, Nat. Assn. Sci. Writers, Investigative Reporters and Editors, Press Club New Orleans (4 1st pl. awards 1978-87, Alex Waller award 1987). Avocations: running, travel, aerobics. Office: The Times-Picayune 3800 Howard Ave New Orleans LA 70125-1429 Business E-Mail: jpope@timespicayune.com.

POPE, KATHERINE COLLINS, former broadcast executive; b. Glencoe, Ill., Oct. 15, 1972; d. Michael A. and Christine Pope; m. Richard A. Robbins, June 2, 2001. Grad., Sarah Lawrence Coll. Assoc. prodr. A&E; writer & prodr. documentaries CBS; writer & prodr. VH1, 1999—2000; mgr. primetime series NBC Studios, 2000—01, dir. primetime series, 2001—02, v.p. primetime series, 2002—04, v.p. drama devel. NBC Entertainment, 2003—04, exec. v.p., 2006—07; sr. v.p. drama series NBC Universal TV Studio (name changed to Universal Media Studios, 2007), 2004—06, pres., 2007—08. Assoc. prodr. (TV series) Biography, writer & prodr. Behind the Music, 1999—2000. Named one of The 100 Most Powerful Women in Entertainment, The Hollywood Reporter, 2006, 2007, 2008. E-mail: katherine.pope@nbcuni.com.*

POPE, KENNETH SAYLE, psychologist; b. Tex. s. William Kenneth Pope and Kate Sayle; m. Karen Olio. MA, Harvard U., Cambridge, 1972; PhD, Yale U., New Haven, 1977. Diplomate clin. psychology Am. Bd. Profl. Psychology, Washington, 1988. Psychologist in ind. practice, LA, 1979—95, Norwalk, Conn., 1996—. Chair, ethics com. APA, Washington, 1988, Am. Bd. Profl. Psychology, 1989. Author: (book) Ethics in Psychotherapy & Counseling, 3rd Edit., What Therapists Don't Talk About; contbr. articles to profl. publs. Recipient Disting. Profl. Contributions award, APA Divsn. Clin. Psychology, 1994; fellow, Woodrow Wilson Found., 1971—72. Fellow: Assn. Psychol. Sci.

POPE, KITTY, library director; b. Canada; MLS, U. Western Ont. Asst. dir. & mgr. customer svcs. Calgary Pub. Libr., Alta., Canada, 2001—04; exec. dir. Alliance Libr. Sys., East Peoria, Ill., 2004—. Co-recipient Network Libr. of Yr. award, Libr. of Congress Nat. Libr. Svc. for the Blind & Physically Handicapped, 2005, 2006, Leadership Achievement award, Assn. Specialized & Coop. Librs. Agys., 2007, Libr. of the Future award for Alliance Second Life Libr. 2.0, ALA, 2007. Office: Alliance Libr Sys 600 High Point Lane East Peoria IL 61611 Office Phone: 309-694-9200 ext. 2101, 800-700-4857. Office Fax: 309-694-9230. E-mail: kpope@alliancelibrarysystem.com.

POPE, LISTON, JR., writer, journalist; b. New Haven, Dec. 26, 1943; s. Liston and Bennie (Purvis) P. BA in English, Duke U., 1965; postgrad., Sorbonne, Paris, 1965-70, U. Vienna, 1966-67. Probation officer Bronx (N.Y.) Supreme Ct., 1972-73; freelance journalist NYC, 1972—; war correspondent World Coun. of Chs., Beirut, 1978-79, Nat. Cath. News Svc., Managua, Nicaragua, 1983-84; radio prodr. Pacifica Radio, NYC, 1983-90; critic art/lit. Pacifica News, NYC, 1984-89; sr. editor N.A. Gilbert & Sons Publs., NYC, 1993—; pub. Mantis Press, NYC, 1995—. Press agent Liston Pope & Assocs., NYC, 1983—90; media dir. Casa Nicaragua, NYC, 1983—90. Author: Redemption: A Novel of War in Lebanon, 1994, Living Like the Saints: A Novel of Nicaragua, 1996, Floriane: Stages of Love, 1998, (plays) Somoza's Niece, 1987, Oratorio, 1987, Canto Epico, 1989, The Van Gogh Testament, 2005, Pushkin Russian Tragedy, 2008, Wherefore Tragedy, 2008, (trilogy) Newell Gilbert's Boyhood: American Wine, Journey on the Needing, Infernal Innocence, 2006, (novels) Manifest Oedipus: America At War, 2009, (plays) Manifest Oedipus: American Tragedy, 2009, Anthology of Socialist Poetry, 2009, On The Unities, 2009. Vis., supporting vol. Meml. Sloan-Kettering, 1972-78; recreation dir., tutor Cath. Guardian Group Home, 1975-90; life skills tchr. Harlem I Men's Shelter, N.Y.C., 1991-93; AIDS support worker St. Vincent's Supportive Care, Bellevue Visitation Program, Bellevue Pediatrics. Recipient Narrative Poetry award, NY Poetry Soc., 1972, Grand prize, Am. Poetry Assn., 1986. Home and Office: 126 W 73rd St Apt 11A New York NY 10023-3031 Office Phone: 212-874-6017. E-mail: liston4949@yahoo.com.

POPE, MARK ANDREW, lawyer, academic administrator; b. Munster, Ind., May 22, 1952; s. Thomas A. and Eleanor E. (Miklos) P.; m. Julia Risk Pope, June 15, 1974; children: Brent Andrew, Bradley James. BA, Purdue U., 1974; JD cum laude, Ind. U., 1977. Bar: Ind. 1977, U.S. Dist. Ct. (so. dist.) Ind. 1977, U.S. Ct. Appeals (7th cir.) 1984. Assoc. Johnson & Weaver, Indpls., 1977-79, Rocap, Rocap, Reese & Young, Indpls., 1980-82, Dutton & Overman, Indpls., 1982-88, ptnr., 1988-89; asst. gen. counsel Lincoln Nat. Corp., Fort Wayne, Ind., 1989-91, sr. counsel, 1991-95, v.p. govt. rels., 1995-2001; dir. athletics Ind. U.-Purdue U., Ft. Wayne, 2001—07, U. St. Francis, 2007—. Bd. dirs. Ft. Wayne Bicentennial Coun.; pres., bd. dirs. ARCH, Inc., 1994-97. Bd. editors, devel. editor Ind. U. Law Rev., 1976-77 Mem. pres.'s coun. Purdue U., 1977—; applied econs. cons. Jr. Achievement, 1989—95; bd. dirs. Jr. Achievement of No. Ind., 1992—94; grad. Leadership Ft. Wayne, 1992; adv. coun. Ind. U. Bus. Sch., Purdue U., Ft. Wayne, 2000—02; trustee Allen County War Meml. Coliseum, 2002—; bd. mem. Ft. Wayne Urban League, 2006—; mem. parish coun. St. Elizabeth Ann Seton Ch., 1993—96, pres., 1993—95; bd. edn. mem. Bishop Luers HS, 2000—03, pres., 2002—03; mem. bd. trustees Allen County War Meml. Coliseum, 2002—; mem. bd. dirs. Ft. Wayne Urban League, 2006—. Named Disting. Hoosier, Gov. of Ind., 1974. Fellow Ind. Bar Found., Indpls. Bar Found. (disting.); mem. ABA (dist. rep. young lawyers divsn. 1981-83, dir. 1983-84, liaison coord. 1985-86, 87-88, exec. coun. 1981-88, cabinet 1982-88, gen. practice sect. coun. mem. 1986—, membership chmn. 1987-89, chmn. career and family com. 1990-92, dir. 1991-93), Indpls. Bar Assn. (v.p. 1983, chmn. young lawyers divsn. 1981), 500 Festival Assocs. (vice-chmn. of 500 festival parade 1985-89), Orchard Ridge Country Club (bd. dirs. 1995-2001, sec. 1996-97, pres. 1999-2001), Nat. Assn. Intetcollegiate Athletics (mem. nat. adminstrv. coun., 2008-, vice-chair championship competition com., 2009-, mem. football play off com., 2008-09; Mid-Ctrl. Coll. Cof. Atheletic Dir. of Yr., 2009). Avocations: golf, running. Office: Univ of St Francis 2701 Spring St Fort Wayne IN 46808 Office Phone: 260-399-7700 ext. 6202. Business E-Mail: mpope@sf.edu.

POPE, MARTIN, chemist, educator; b. NYC, Aug. 22, 1918; s. Philip and Anna (Frimet) P.; m. Lillie Bellin, June 27, 1946; children: Miriam, Deborah Judith. BS in Chemistry, CCNY, 1939; PhD in Phys. Chemistry, Poly. Inst. Bklyn., 1950. Scientist Radiation Lab. Bklyn. Navy Yard, 1941—42; rsch. scientist Balco Rsch. Lab., Newark, 1946—47, tech. dir., 1951-56; sr. rsch. scientist NYU Radiation and Solid State Physics Lab., NYC, 1956-60, rsch. assoc. prof., 1960-65; assoc. prof. chemistry NYU, 1965—68, prof., 1968—88, prof. emeritus phys. chemistry, 1988—. Co-dir. NYU Radiation and Solid State Physics Lab., 1968—83, dir., 1983—88; vis. prof. U. Alexandria, Egypt, 1981. Contbr. articles to sci. jours., chapters to books; mem. editl. bd.: Molecular Crystals, 1965—97; co-author: Electronic Processes In Organic Crystals, 1982, Electronic Processes in Organic Crystals and Polymers, 1999. Pres. Ezra Jack Keats Found., NYC, 1983—. Pvt. to 1st lt. USAAF, 1942—46, WWII. Recipient Townsend Harris medalist, CUNY, 1996, Davy medal, Royal Soc., UK, 2006; grantee, Dept. Energy, 1958—88, NSF, 1960—75; honored at internat. conf., NYU, 1988, 2007, U. Rochester, 1998. Fellow: AAAS, NY Acad. Scis., Am. Phys. Soc.; mem.: Am. Chem. Soc., Sigma Xi. Achievements include patents in field. Avocation: mineralogy. Office: Dept Chemistry NYU New York NY 10003

POPE, RANDOLPH D., literature and language professor; b. Viña del Mar, Chile, Oct. 31, 1946; s. David Pope and Adriana Costa; m. María-Inés Lagos, Dec. 14, 1967; 1 child, Leslie Victoria. MA, Columbia U., NY, 1969, PhD, 1973. Lectr. Spanish U. Bonn, Germany, 1973—76; assoc. prof. Spanish Dartmouth Coll., Hanover, NH, 1976—83; prof. Spanish Vassar Coll., Poughkeepsie, NY, 1982—85; prof. Spanish and comparative lit. Wash. U., St. Louis, 1985—2001, chair comparative lit., 1990—97; dir. comparative lit. U. Va., Charlottesville, commonwealth prof. Spanish and comparative lit., 2002—, chair dept. Spanish, Italian and Portuguese, 2004—07. Dir. Spanish summer sch. Middlebury Coll., Vt., 1982—86; editor Revista Estudios Hispánicos, 1991—99; pres. Assn. Depts. Fgn. Langs., NYC, 2008—. Grant, Nat. Endowment Humanities, 1991, 1993, Yr. Rsch. fellowship, 1993—94. Mem.: MLA. Office: Univ Va Dept Spanish 115 Wilson Hall Charlottesville VA 22904-4777 Business E-Mail: rpope@virginia.edu.

POPE, ROBERT DEAN, lawyer; b. Memphis, Mar. 10, 1945; s. Ben Duncan and Phyllis (Drenner) P.; m. Elizabeth Dante Cohen, June 26, 1971; 1 child, Justin Nicholas Nathanson. AB, Princeton U., 1967; Diploma in Hist. Studies, Cambridge U., 1971; JD, Yale U., 1972, PhD, 1976. Bar: Va. 1974, D.C. 1980. Assoc. Hunton & Williams, Richmond, Va., 1974-80, ptnr., 1980—. Mem. steering com. Bond Attys. Workshop, 1994—98; lectr. in law U. Va. Law Sch., 2000—02; advisor, com. on govtl. debt and fiscal policy Govt. Fin. Officers Assn., 1993—99; adj. prof. law William & Mary Law Sch., 2004—. Author: Making Good Disclosure: The Role and Responsibilities of State and Local Officials Under the Federal Securities Laws, 2001; co-author: Disclosure Rules of Counsel in State and Local Government Securities Offerings, 2d edit., 1994. Mem. adv. com. Va. Sec. of Health and Human Svcs. on Continuing Care Legislation, 1992-94; mem. Anthony Commn. on Pub. Fin.; adv. coun. dept. history Princeton U., 1987-91; mem. Mcpl. Securities Rulemaking Bd., 1996-99, vice chmn. 1998-99. Mem.: Nat. Council Cmty. Justice, Nat. Conf. Cmty. Justice (bd. dirs. Richmond), Yale Law Sch. Assn. (exec. com. 1985—88), Va. Bar Assn. (chmn. legal problems of elderly 1982—88), Am. Coll. Bond Counsel (bd. dir. 2003—, sec. 2004—06, treas. 2006—08, v.p. 2008—), Am. Acad. Hosp. Attys., Nat. Assn. Bond Lawyers (bd. dirs. 1982—89, treas. 1984—85, sec. 1985—86, pres. 1987—88, coordinating coun. 2005—, Bernard P. Friel medal for contbns. to pub.fin. 1994), Bond Club Va. (bd. dirs. 1990—98, v.p. 1993—94, pres. 1994—95), Phi Beta Kappa. Republican. Episcopalian. Avocations: history, golf, music, book reviews. Office: Hunton & Williams 951 E Byrd Richmond VA 23219-4074 Home: 9704 Old Country Trace Richmond VA 23238 Office Phone: 804-788-8438. Business E-Mail: dpope@hunton.com.

POPE, ROBERT E(UGENE), fraternal organization administrator; b. Wellington, Kans., Sept. 10, 1931; s. Samuel E. and Opal Irene (Davis) P. BSChemE with honors, U. Kans., 1952, MS, 1958. Registered profl. engr., Kans. Asst. instr. U. Kans., Lawrence, 1952-56; lab. technician Monsanto Co., St. Louis, 1952; project engr. Mallinckrodt, Inc., St. Louis, 1953-59; traveling sec. Theta Tau, St. Louis, 1959-62, exec. sec., 1963-84, exec. dir., 1984-96, exec. dir. emeritus, 1996—. Carillonneur, Grace United Meth. Ch., St. Louis, 1985—, chmn. adminstrv. coun., 1991-95, trustee, 1997-99; lay mem. Mo. Conf., United Meth. Ch., 2000-06; trustee Theta Tau Ednl. Found., 1997-2002; bd. dirs. St. Louis Cmty. Tower Bells, 2000—. Mem. Am. Soc. Assn. Execs. (life), Profl. Fraternity Execs. Assn. (charter), Profl. Fraternity Assn. (exec. sec. 1977-86, Disting. Svc. award 1995), Theta Tau (Alumni Hall of Fame 1988, mem. bd. editors The Gear of Theta Tau 1993—2001, editor-in-chief 1996—2001), Tau Beta Pi, Phi Lambda Upsilon, Omicron Delta Kappa. Democrat. United Methodist. Avocations: physical fitness, sports, photography, stamp collecting, writing. Home: 13 Sona Ln Saint Louis MO 63141-7742

POPE, STEPHEN BAILEY, mechanical engineer, educator; b. Nottingham, Eng., Nov. 26, 1949; came to U.S., 1977; s. Joseph Albert and Evelyn Alice (Gallagher) P.; m. Linda Ann Syatt, Aug. 16, 1979; children: Sarah Evelyn, Samuel Joseph. BS in Engring., Imperial Coll., London, 1971; MS, Imperial Coll., 1972, PhD, 1976; DSc in Engring., U. London, 1986. Rsch. asst. Imperial Coll., London, 1972-77; rsch. fellow Calif. Inst. Tech., Pasadena, 1977-78; asst. prof. MIT, Cambridge, Mass., 1978-81, assoc. prof., 1981, Cornell U., Ithaca, N.Y., 1982-87, prof. engring., 1987-98, Sibley Coll. prof. mech. engring., 1998—. Cons. GE, Schenectady, N.Y., 1984—, GM, Warren, Mich., 1985—, Allison Engine Co., Indpls., 1986—. Editor: Combustion Theory and Modelling; assoc. editor Physics of Fluid; contbr. articles to profl. jours. Overseas fellow Churchill Coll, Cambridge, Eng., 1989; awards NSF, Army Rsch. Office, Air Force Office Sci. Rsch., U.S. Dept. Energy. Fellow Royal Soc., Am. Phys. Soc., Combustion Inst., Am. Acad. Arts & Scis. Office: 254 Upson Hall Cornell U Ithaca NY 14853 Business E-Mail: s.b.pope@cornell.edu.

POPE, THADDEUS MASON, law educator; b. Pitts., Aug. 2, 1969; s. Lawrence Sheldon and Reina Gloria Pope; m. Linda Louise Bosse, May 2, 1998; 1 child, Phineas Lawrence. JD, MA, Georgetown U., 1997, PhD, 2003. Bar: Calif. 1999. Jud. law clk. U.S Ct. Appeals, (7th cir.), Milw., 1999—2000; atty. Arnold & Porter LLP, LA, 2000—05; prof. law U. Memphis, 2005—. Contbr. articles to profl. jours. Pro bono adv. medicaid benefits City of L.A., 2003—05. Recipient Wiley W. Manuel award, State Bar Calif., 2004, Hon. Benjamin Aranda III Outstanding Pub. Svc. award, L.A. County Bar Assn., 2005. Mem.: Kennedy Inst. Ethics, APHA, Am. Soc. Law, Medicine & Ethics. Office: U Memphis School Law 3715 Central Ave Memphis TN 38152 Office Fax: 901-202-7549. Business E-Mail: tmpope@memphis.edu.

POPE, WILLIAM L., lawyer, judge; b. Brownsville, Tex., 1960; s. William E. and Maria Antonieta P.; m. Sandra Solis, May 16, 1992; children: Ana Lauren, William E.H. AA, Tex. Southmost Coll., 1980; postgrad., U. Tex., 1980-81, Tex. Christian U., 1982, Tex. Coll. Osteo. Medicine, 1982-83; JD, Baylor U., 1986; MD (hon.), Cosmopolitan U. & Rsch. Inst., Vina del Mar, Chile, 1998. Bar: Tex. 1986, US Dist. Ct. (so. dist.) Tex. 1988, US Supreme Ct. 1990, US Tax Ct. 2007. Assoc. Adams & Graham, Harlingen, Tex., 1986-91, ptnr., 1991—; mcpl. ct. judge & state magistrate City of La Feria, Tex., 1987—. Bd. trustees Episcopal Day Sch., Brownsville, Tex., 1999—2000. Mem.: Tex. Bar Jour. (bd. editors 2009—), Cameron County Bar Assn., Am. Coll. Legal Medicine, Tex. State Bar Assn. (mem. judiciary rels. com. 1999—2005). Mem. Ch. Of Christ. Office: Adams & Graham LLP 134 E Van Buren Ave Ste 301 Harlingen TX 78550 Office Phone: 956-428-7495. Business E-Mail: pope@adamsgraham.com.

POPEO, R. ROBERT, lawyer; b. Boston, Apr. 9, 1938; AB, Northeastern U., 1958; JD, Boston Coll., 1961. Bar: Mass. 1961, DC 1972. Law clerk US Dist. Ct. Mass., 1961-63; instr. Sch. Law Boston U., 1964-67; U.S Commr., 1967-71; asst. atty. gen. Commonwealth of Mass., 1970-74; chmn., pres. Mintz, Levin, Cohn, Ferris, Glovsky and Popeo, PC, Boston, 1989—, mem. policy com. Editor: Boston Coll. Indsl. and Comml. Law Rev., 1960—61; student editor Ann. Survey Mass. Law, 1960—61. Trustee Boston Coll.; mem. bd. overseers Boston Coll. Law Sch., Northeastern U.; mem. bd. advisors Boston Coll. Carroll Sch. Mgmt., Birmingham Bus. Sch.; mem. exec. comm. Mass. Bus. Round Table. Named one of top 100 Lawyers in Am., Nat. Law Jour. Fellow: Am. Coll. Trial Lawyers; mem.: ABA, Mass. Bar Assn., DC Bar Assn., Boston Bar Assn., Practising Law Inst. Office: Mintz Levin Cohn Ferris Glovsky & Popeo PC One Financial Center Boston MA 02111 Home Phone: 781-444-8013; Office Phone: 617-348-1716. Office Fax: 617-542-2241. Business E-Mail: rrpopeo@mintz.com.

POPE ROBBINS, LAURA E., librarian; d. Henry and Martha A. Pope; m. Steven M. Robbins, July 11, 1992; children: Alessandro P. Robbins, Corwin T. Robbins. BA, SUNY, Stony Brook, 1991; MLS, U. Wash., Seattle, 1995; MBA, Dowling Coll., Oakdale, NY, 2004. Cert. in web techs. Internat. Webmasters Assn., HTML Writers Guild, 2006; in pub. libr. profl. NY, 1998. Reference libr. Embry-Riddle Aero. U., Daytona Beach, Fla., 1995—98, Dowling Coll., 1999—, part time reference libr., 1998—99. Mem.: ALA, Internat. Web-Masters Assn., NY Libr. Assn., Assn. Coll. & Rsch. Librs., Ctr. Book Arts. Achievements include development of google gadget, Dowling College library catalog search; firefox search box plug-in; links database; FT options at dowling resolver. Avocations: hiking, travel. Office: Dowling Coll 150 Idle Hour Blvd Oakdale NY 11769 Business E-Mail: pope-rol@dowling.edu.

POPESCU, MIHAELA, elementary school educator, researcher; d. Constantin and Aurica Popescu; 1 child, Ileana Alexandra Klein. BS in Math., U. Bucharest, Romania, 1991, BS in Biology, 1997; MS, U. Fla., 2004, PhD, 2005. Mathematician Nuclear Energy Reactor Inst., Bucharest, 1991—93; hs math. tchr. Bucharest, 1994; mid. sch. math. tchr. Buzau, 1997—99; rsch. asst. U. Fla., Gainesville, 1999—2005; post doc. Sintef, Tondheim, Norway, 2005—06, rsch. scientist, 2006—. Cons. U. Bucharest, 1994—97. Contbr. articles to profl. jours. Sci. fair judge Sch. Bd. Alachua County, Gainesville, Fla., 1999, 2001. Alumni Fellowship, U. Fla. Mem.: ASME, AIAA, Norwegian Soc. Chartered Tech. Sci. Profls. Avocations: music, mountain climbing, skiing. Office: SINTEF A Getz vei 2 B 7465 Trondheim Norway

POPESCU, OTILIA, engineering educator; PhD, Rutgers U., New Brunswick, NJ; Diploma in Engring., Poly. Inst. Bucharest, Romania. Asst. lectr. Poly. U. Bucharest, Romania; grad. asst. Rutgers U., Piscatway, NJ; postdoc. fellow U. Tex., Dallas, Richardson; lectr. Old Dominion U., Norfolk, Va. Mem.: IEEE. Office: Old Dominion Univ 231 Kaufman Hall Norfolk VA 23529 Business E-Mail: otilia.popescu@ieee.org.

POPKIN, ALICE BRANDEIS, lawyer; b. NYC; d. Jacob H. and Susan Brandeis Gilbert; m. Jordan J. Popkin; children: Susan Cahn, Anne, Louisa. AB magna cum laude, Radcliffe Coll., 1949; JD, Yale U., 1953. Bar: NY 1953, US Dist. Ct. (so. dist.) NY 1956, US Ct. Appeals (2nd cir.) 1959, US Supreme Ct. 1962, DC 1972, Mass. 1987. Assoc. Cahill Gordon & Reindel, 1953—61; dir. internat. programs Peace Corps, 1961—63; project co-dir. Georgetown Inst. Criminal Law and Procedure, 1967—72; spl. counsel Senate Sub-Com. to Investigate Juvenile Delinquincy, 1972—74; atty., prof. Antioch Sch. Law, 1974—77; assoc. adminstr. EPA, 1977—79; pvt. practice cons. on internat. environ. issues, 1979—81; practicing atty., 1981—87; of counsel Toabe and Riley, Chatham, Mass., 1987—. Fellow Brandeis U.; trustee Radcliffe Coll.; active Chatham Harbor Mgmt. Com.; trustee Eldredge Pub. Libr., 1994—, pres. bd. trustees, 2005—. Mem. ABA, Mass. Bar Assn., Barnstable County Bar Assn., Estate Planning Coun. Cape Cod, Planned Giving Coun. Cape Cod. Office: Toabe & Riley Box 707 154 Crowell Rd Chatham MA 02633-2800 Home Phone: 508-945-0523. Personal E-mail: adee.abp@comcast.net.

POPLAU, RONALD W., social studies educator; AA, St. Lawrence Coll., 1957; BA, St. Paul Sem., 1959; MA, Emporia State Univ., 1968. Dir., continuing edn. Ottawa Univ., 1976—; social sci. tchr. St. Paul, 1962—64, Brazil, 1964—65, Ward H.S., Kans. City, Kans., 1965—69, Shawnee Mission Sch. Dist., 1969—; now social sci. tchr. NW H.S., Shawnee Mission, Kans. Recipient Penney's Golden Rule award, 1993, Kiwanis John Trembly award, 1993, Kans. City Star Honor, 1994, Wooster Coll. Excellence in Tchg. award, 1997, Disney Teacher award, 2005; named Shawnee Citizen of Yr., 1994, Kans. Tchr. of Yr., 2006; named a US Army Outstanding Citizen, 1997; named to Nat. Tchr. Hall of Fame, 1999; finalist Nat. Tchr. of Yr., 2006. Office: Shawnee Mission Northwest HS 12701 W 67th St Shawnee KS 66216 Business E-Mail: nwpoplau@smsd.org.

POPLER, KENNETH, behavioral health services administrator, psychologist; BA in Psychology, CUNY, 1967; MA in Psychology, New Sch. Social Rsch., NYC, 1969, PhD in Psychology, 1974; MBA, Wagner Coll., 1994. Diplomate Am. Bd. Profl. Psychology. Case worker N.Y.C. Dept. Social Svcs., 1967-70; intern Bklyn. Psychiat. Ctrs., 1970-72; sch. psychologist N.Y.C. Bd. Edn., 1972-73; psychologist Mid Nassau Cmty. Guidance Ctr., Hicksville, NY, 1973-77; dir. St. Mary Cmty. Mental Health Ctr., Hoboken, NJ, 1978-81; pres., CEO S.I. Mental Health Soc., Inc., 1981—. Asst. rsch. scientist N.Y. State Psychiat. Inst., NYC, 1971; psychometrician LI Jewish Hillside Med. Ctr., Queens, NY, 1972—73; vol. rsch. Manhattan Sch. Seriously Disturbed Children, NYC, 1972—73; instr. CUNY, Bklyn., 1972—73; sr. psychologist dir. psychol. svcs. HHC Gouverneur Hosp., NYC, 1973—78; pvt. practice, NYC, 1976—85; asst. clin. prof. psychiatry Mt. Sinai Med. Sch., NYC, 1978—95; apptg. by mayor N.Y.C. Bd. Health, 2003—. Apptd. by mayor N.Y.C. Cmty. Svcs. Bd., 1984—, chmn., 2003—; pres. Coalition Voluntary Mental Health Agys., Inc., 1991—94; founding bd. pres. Citywide Behavioral Network, Inc., Mental Health Provider Orgn., 1996—, Staten Island Behavioral Network, Inc., Case Mgmt. Provider, 2000—, Staten Island Not-For-Profit Assn., Inc., 2004—; sec. Head Start Sponsoring Bd. Coun., NYC, 1985—92; chmn. S.I. United Way Execs. Com., 1985, Mental Health Coun., SI, 1987—89. Mem.: Rotary. Office: SI Mental Health Soc Inc 669 Castleton Ave Staten Island NY 10301-2099 Business E-Mail: kpopler@simhs.org.

POPOFSKY, MELVIN LAURENCE, lawyer; b. Oskaloosa, Iowa, Feb. 16, 1936; s. Samuel and Fannye Charlotte (Rosenthal) P.; m. Linda Jane Seltzer, Nov. 25, 1962; children: Mark Samuel, Kaye Sylvia. BA in History summa cum laude, U. Iowa, 1958; BA in Jurisprudence (first class honors), Oxford U., Eng., 1960; LLB cum laude, Harvard U., 1962. Bar: Calif. 1962. Assoc. Heller, Ehrman, White & McAuliffe, San Francisco, 1962-69, ptnr., 1969—2008, mem. exec. com., 1980-93, co-chair, 1988-93; sr. ptnr. Orrick, Herrington & Sutcliffe, LLP, 2008—. Contbr. articles to law jours. Bd. dirs. Mt. Zion Hosp., San Francisco, 1982-88, U.S. Dist. Ct. (no. dist.) Calif. Hist. Soc., 1988-2004, Jewish Home for Aged, San Francisco, 1989-96, Golden Gate U., 1997-2000, Jewish Cmty. Fedn., 1997-2001. Recipient Anti-Defamation League's Disting. Jurisprudence award, 2000; named State Bar of Calif. Antitrust Lawyer of the Yr., 2000, Best Lawyers in Am. Calif., 1988-2008, Sr. Statesman Antitrust, Chambers, 2007-2008; Rhodes scholar, 1958. Fellow Am. Bar Found., Am. Coll. Trial Lawyers; mem. ABA, Calif. Bar Assn., San Francisco Bar Assn., Bur. Nat. Affairs (adv. bd. antitrust sect.), Calif. Acad. Appellate Lawyers. Democrat. Jewish. Home: 1940 Broadway Apt 10 San Francisco CA 94109-2216 Office: Orrick Herrington & Sutcliffe LLP 405 Howard St San Francisco CA 94105 Home Phone: 415-928-7780; Office Phone: 415-773-4590. Business E-Mail: lpopofsky@orrick.com.

POPOV, BRANKO NESTOR, engineering educator, educator; s. Nestor Kosta Popovski; m. Snezana Nikola Tagasova, Dec. 29, 1981; children: Irena Branko Popova, Nestor Branko, Biljana Branko Popova. PhD, U. Zagreb, Croatia, 1972; MS, U. Ill., Urbana, 2008. Resaerch prof. U. SC, Columbia, 1993—2000, dir., ctr. electrochem. engring., 2000—03, prof., 2003—05, carolina disting. prof., 2003—. Contbr. scientific papers. Recipient Fuel Cell South Crystal Flame Inovation award, Fuel Cell South, 2005; grant, ONR, 1993—2005, DOE, 2003, Fuji Film, 2003, NASA, 2007, PSCOR, 2007. Achievements include patents for carbon based composite catalyst. Office: Dept Chemical Engring 301 Main St Columbia SC 29208 Office Fax: 803-777-8265. Business E-Mail: popov@engr.sc.edu.

POPOVA, MARINA, engineering educator; d. Vladimir Navakovskiy and Svetlana Navakovskaya. BS, St. Petersburg State U., Russia, 1995, MS, 1997, PhD, 2002. Postdoc. fellow Dept. Mech. Engring., U. N.Mex., Albuquerque, 2002—05, rsch. prof., 2005—; asst. prof. computer and engring. dept. Northern N.Mex. Coll., Espanola, 2008—. Contbr. scientific papers (NSF - NATO Postdoc. Rsch. fellowship, 2002). Mem.: Am. Phys. Soc., Materials Rsch. Soc. Achievements include research in interfacial sliding in the presence of fluid flow: fundamental mechanics and applications; atomistic simulations of material deformation and fracture, computational nano-mechanics of materials; nano-scale physics and near-contact hydrodynamics. Office Fax: 505-277-1571. Business E-Mail: mpopova@unm.edu.

POPOVA, NINA, retired dancer, choreographer, director; b. Novorossisk, USSR, 1922; Student in Paris, studied ballet with Olga Preobrajenska, Lubov Egorova, Anatole Vilzak, Anatole Oboukhov, Igor Schwezoff. Ballet debut with Ballet de la Jeunesse, Paris, London, 1937-39; soloist Original Ballet Russe, 1939-41, Ballet Theatre (now Am. Ballet), 1941-42, Ballet Russe de Monte Carlo, 1943, 47, Ballet Alicia Alonso, Cuba; faculty Sch. Performing Arts, NYC, 1954—; later artistic dir. Houston Ballet, 1975; tchr. Nat. Acad. Arts, Champaign, Ill., also NYC, 1975—, now Eglevsky Ballet Sch., L.I.; tchr. ballet Mexico City, Mex.; asst. choreographer mus. comedy Birmingham So. Coll., Ala., 1960; numerous appearances on Broadway stage, TV; former mem. regular cast Your Show of Shows; currently tchg. NYC. Address: 33 Adams St Sea Cliff NY 11579-1614

POPOVIC, ZORAN, environmental engineer, educator; s. Branko and Ljiljana Popovic; m. Monica Ulseth, Feb. 14, 2003; children: Iska Ulseth, Amai Ulseth. PhD, Carnegie Mellon U., 1999. Prof. U. Wash., Seattle, 1999—. Contbr. scientific papers (ACM SIGGRAPH, 2004). Alfred P. Sloan, 2003, CAREER award, NSF, 2001, Schlumberger Found., 1997. Office: Dept CSE Univ Wash 101 Allen Ctr Seattle WA 98195 E-mail: zoranp@gmail.com.

POPOVICH, GREGG, professional basketball coach; b. Chgo., Jan. 28, 1949; m. Erin Popovich; children: Micky, Jill. BA in Soviet Studies, USAF Acad., 1970; MA in Phys. Edn. & Sports Scis., U. Denver. Asst. coach USAF Acad., 1973—79; head coach Pomona-Pitzer Coll., Claremont, Calif., 1979—87; asst. coach San Antonio Spurs, 1988-92, gen. mgr., 1994—2002, exec. v.p. basketball ops., 1994—2008, head coach, 1996—, pres. Spurs basketball, 2008—; asst. coach Golden State Warriors, 1992—94. Asst. USA Men's Sr. Nat. Team, 2002—04. 2nd lt. USAF, 1970—75. Recipient Daily Point of Light award, Pres. George H.W. Bush, 1992, Disting. Grad. award, Air Force Acad., 2008; named NBA Coach of Yr., 2003. Achievements include winning NBA Championships as head coach of the San Antonio Spurs, 1999, 2003, 2005, 2007; one of five NBA coaches with four or more championship titles. Office: San Antonio Spurs One AT&T Ctr San Antonio TX 78219*

POPOVICI, ADRIAN, law educator, emeritus professor; b. Bucharest, Rumania, Sept. 6, 1942; came to Can., 1951; s. Adrian and Alice (Moruzi) P.; children— Adrian, Alexandra. BA, Stanislas Coll., Montreal, 1959; B.C.L., McGill U., 1962; D.E.S., U. Paris, 1965. Bar: Que. 1963. Prof. law U. Montreal, Que., Canada, 1968—2008, emeritus prof.; Arnold Wainwright sr. fellow U. Mcgill. Author: L'Outrage au Tribunal, 1977, La Couleur du Mandat, 1995; editor: Problèmes de Droit Contemporain, 1974 Waimwright Sr. fellow, McGill Sch. Law, Montreal. Home: 5589 Canterbury Montreal PQ Canada H3T 1S8 Home Phone: 514-342-6839. E-mail: adrian.popovici@umontreal.ca.

POPOVICS, SANDOR, civil engineer, educator, researcher; b. Budapest, Hungary, Dec. 24, 1921; came to U.S., 1957; s. Milan and Erzsebet (Droppa) P.; m. Lea M. Virtanen, Aug. 29, 1960; children: John, Lisa. 1st Degree in Civil Engring., Poly. U., Budapest, Hungary, 1944; Advanced Degree in Civil Engring., Poly. U., 1956; PhD, Purdue U., 1961. Registered profl. engr. Ariz., Pa. Rsch. engr. Met. Lab., Budapest, 1944-48; adj. prof. Tech. Coll., Budapest, 1949-52; rsch. engr., mgr. Inst. for Bldg. Scis., Budapest, 1949-56; grad. asst. Purdue U., Lafayette, Ind., 1957-59; prof. engring. Auburn (Ala.) U., 1959-69; prof. civil engring. No. Ariz. U., Flagstaff, 1968-76; prof. engring. King Abdulazziz U., Jeddah, Saudi Arabia, 1977-78; Samuel S. Baxter prof. civil engring. Drexel U., Phila., 1979-92, rsch. prof., 1992—. Pres. Optimum Engring. Rsch. Author: Fundamentals of Portland Cement Concrete, 1982, Concrete Materials, 2d edit., 1992, Strength and Related Properties of Concrete, 1998, over 300 tech. papers. Recipient numerous grants and awards. Fellow ASCE (life), Am. Concrete Inst.; mem. ASTM, Ala. Acad. Scis., Ariz. Acad. Scis., Sigma Xi, Chi Epsilon. Avocations: jogging, music, fine art. Home and Office: 283 Congress Ave Lansdowne PA 19050-1206 Office: Drexel U Dept Civil Archtl & Environ Engring 32nd and Chestnut Philadelphia PA 19104 Home Phone: 610-649-1606; Office Phone: 610-623-0116. Personal E-mail: spopovics@gmail.com. Business E-Mail: popovics@coe.drexel.edu.

POPP, BERNARD FERDINAND, bishop emeritus; b. Nada, Tex., Dec. 6, 1917; s. Ferdinand and Anna Staff Popp. Attended, St. John's Sem., San Antonio. Ordained priest Archdiocese of San Antonio, 1943, sec. to archbishop Robert E. Lucey, 1945—68, aux. bishop, 1983—93, aux. bishop emeritus, 1993—; rector San Fernando Cathedral; ordained bishop, 1983. Roman Catholic.

POPP, JOSEPH BRUCE, manufacturing executive; b. Chgo., July 9, 1919; s. Peter Leon and Anna (Chomyz) P.; m. Mabel Lydia Szymanski, Oct. 23, 1941 (dec. Mar. 1993); m. Elinor A. Maves, Jan. 27, 1996 (dec. May 24, 2009); children: Dianne, Lydia, Bruce, Anita, Gregory. Founder, owner Poultry Farm, Westville, Ind., 1941-48, Gary (Ind.) Undercoating Co., 1948-51; survey analyst George S. May Co., Chgo., 1952-54; gen. sales mgr. Maurey Instrument Corp., Chgo., 1958-64; founder, owner Joe Popp Sales Co., North Riverside, Ill., 1964-89, Chart Pool USA Inc., Portage, Ind., 1966—. Bd. dirs. YMCA Camp Tecumseh, Brookston, Ind., 1973—2008. Sgt. US Army, 1942—46. Mem. Nat. Fedn. of Ind. Bus., Greater Portage C. of C., The Gideons Internat., Nat. Inst. Animal Agr. Republican. Achievements include patents for Bloodhound Property Security System. Home: 1133 Lincoln St Hobart IN 46342-6039 Office: Chart Pool USA Inc 5695 Old Porter Rd Portage IN 46368-1194

POPP, LILIAN MUSTAKI, writer, educator; b. NYC; d. Peter and Mae Claire (Cary) Mustaki; m. Robert J. Popp. BA, Notre Dame Coll.; postgrad., Columbia U.; MS in Edn., Hunter Coll. Tchr. English McKee Vocat. and Tech. H.S., SI, NY, 1946-63, chmn. acad. studies, 1963-71; prin. William Howard Taft H.S., Bronx, NY, 1971-79; adj. prof. Wagner Coll., SI, 1960-85; instr. Richmond Coll., CUNY, 1968-70; prof. St. John's U., 1991-93. Mem. Cmty. Sch. Bd., 1980—93, chmn., 1989—90; examiner N.Y.C. Bd. Edn., 1960—85. Author, editor: Journeys in Science Fiction, 1961, Four Complete World Novels, 1961, Gertrude Lawrence as Mrs. A., 1961, Four Complete Modern Novels, 1962, Four Complete Heritage Novels, 1963, Four Complete Novels of Character and Courage, 1964; contbr. articles to profl. jours. Chmn. vols. N.Y.C. Child Abuse Prevention Program, 1984—86; regional dir., mem. exec. bd. March of Dimes; book discussion leader Snug Harbor Cultural Ctr., 1981—; pres. Com. for a Nuclear-Free Island, 1986—91; v.p. Staten Islanders Against Nuclear Weapons, 1991—95; pres. SI chpt. Brandeis U. Nat. Women's Com., 1996—, leader News and Shmews; founder, pres. Coalition of S.I. Women's Orgns., 1996—; mem. edn. com. Staten Island Cmty. TV; mem. Libr. com. Staten Island Hist. Richmond Town; pres. Staten Island Youth Coun.; mem. libr. com. Coll. Staten Island; cmty. outreach chair Women for Women of Sierra Leone, 2001; bd. dirs. Staten Island Mental Health Soc., McKee HS Alumni and Friends Assn. Recipient Women Helping Women award Soroptimists, 1985, Thomas Wilson award for Substance Abuse Prevention, 1990, SI Advance Woman of Achievement award, 1994, Cmty. Hero award S.I. Register, 1996, Woman of Distinction award World of Women, 1998, Paul O'Dwyer Humanitarian award Staten Is. Dem. Assn., 1999, Honour award Am. Assn. U. Women Bd., 2009; named Outstanding Woman, NY State Sen. Vincent J. Gentile, 1998, Women's History Month award NY City Coun. Spkr. Peter Vallone and Councilmen Jeremiah O'Donovan, Oddo and Fiala, 2001, Bus. and Profl. Women's Club S.I. award of distinction, 2004, Woman of Distinction award, Second Chance Gospel Choir, 2005, NAACP, Staten Island Br, William A. Morris Humanitarian award, 2005, Named to Hall of Fame, McKee HS, 2008. Mem. AAUW (pres., Honor Cert. award, 2009), Belles Lettres Lit. Soc. (pres.), S.I. Hist. soc., NYC Assn. Tchrs. English (pres. 1967-71), Nat. Coun. Tchrs. English (bd. dirs. 1968-69), Acad. Pub. Edn., McKee Tchrs. Assn. (pres. 1969), HS Prins. Assn. (exec. bd.), Arista Hon. Soc. (hon.), Delta Kappa Gamma (pres. Alpha Beta chpt.), Phi Delta Kappa (v.p. 1990-92). Avocations: travel, reading, photography, jewelry making.

POPP, NATHANIEL, archbishop; b. Aurora, Ill., June 12, 1940; s. Joseph and Vera (Boytor) P. BA, St. Propcopius Coll., 1962; MDiv, Pontifical Gregorian U., Rome, 1966; PhD, U. Oradea, Romania, 2003. Ordained priest Romanian Greek Cath. Ch., 1966; consecrated bishop Romanian Orthodox Episcopate of Am., 1980; elevated to archbishop, 1999. Asst. pastor St. Michael Byz Ch., Aurora, 1967; parish priest Holy Cross Romanian Orthodox Ch., Hermitage, Pa., 1975-80; aux. bishop Romanian Orthodox Episcopate of Am., Orthodox Ch. in Am., Jackson, Mich., 1980-84, ruling bishop Detroit, 1984—; mem. Holy Snyod Orthodox Ch. in Am., Syosset, NY, 1980—; Episcopal moderator Pastoral Life Ministries, O.C.A., 1991—2000. Bd. dirs. Moldovita Romanian Orthodox Ch., Hayward, Calif, 1982; tchr. summer youth programs Romanian Diocese; confessor to sisterhood Holy Transfiguration Monastery; rep. Conf. on Monasticism, Cairo, 1978; participant Monastic Consultation, Cairo, 1979, Seventh Assembly, Vancouver, Can., 1983; active mem. diocesan liturgical commn.; spkr., lectr. in field. Author: Holy Icons, 1969; editor newspaper Solia; contbr. numerous articles to profl. jours. Chmn. Romanian-Am. Heritage Ctr., Grass Lake, Mich.; organizer, chmn. Help for Romania Nat. Relief Fund and Help the Children of Romania Relief Fund; chmn. Congress of Romanian Ams., 1991—; mem. adv. bd. Orthodox Christian Laity, 1999—; pres. Ctr. for Orthodox Christian Studies, St. Andrew, Detroit, 2000; Dr. Honoris Causa, U. Oradea, Romania, 2003; chmn. bd Orthodox Witness, 2003-. Romanian Orthodox. Home and Office: Romanian Orthodox Episcopate Am 2535 Grey Tower Rd Jackson MI 49201-9120 also: PO Box 305 Grass Lake MI 49240-0309 Office Phone: 517-522-4800.

POPPE, LAURIE CATHERINE, matrimonial lawyer, social worker, real estate executive; b. Fairfax, Va., Jan. 31, 1964; d. Loren Edward Brunner, Jr. and Elizabeth May Carper, Edward Monroe Peffly, Jr. (Stepfather); m. Christopher Carsten Poppe; 1 child, Sarah Elizabeth. A.Arch., No. Va. C.C., Annandale, 1985; AAS in Restaurant Mgmt., The Restaurant Sch., Phila., 1988; BA in Psychology, Rutgers U., New Brunswick, NJ, 1999; MSW, Rutgers U., 2005; JD, Rutgers U., Newark, 2005. Bar: N.J. 2005; LCSW N.J., 2005. Owner, mem. Dominion Properties, LLC, McLean, Va., 1994—; law clk. to Hon. Ann R. Bartlett, Superior Ct. NJ State Judiciary, Somerville, 2005—; with Norris, McLaughlin & Marcus, P.A., Bridgewater, NJ, 2006—. Scholarship founder for ind. rsch. Douglass Coll., Mabel Smith Honors Program, New Brunswick, 1999—2002. Grantee, Mabel Smith Honor Program, 1998. Mem.: AAUW, NASW, ABA, Somerset County Bar Assn., N.J. State Bar Assn., Psi Chi. Achievements include research in utilization of early intervention programs. Avocations: martial arts, singing, culinary arts, travel. Office Phone: 908-252-4312. Business E-Mail: lcpoppe@nmmlaw.com.

POPPE, PAMELA J., accountant; b. Breckenridge, Minn., Oct. 25, 1948; d. John T. and Anita Ruth (Knudsen) Sanker; m. James Wayne Kelly, May 10, 1969 (div. May 1993); children: Jamison Marc, Brian Lee m. James E. Poppe, Jan. 19, 2000. BA in Music Edn., Concordia Coll., Moorhead, Minn., 1969; BS in Indsl. Adminstrn., Iowa State U., 1980. CPA, Iowa. Band and choir tchr. Danube (Minn.) Ind. Schs., 1969-70; orch. tchr. Raleigh (N.C.) City Schs., 1972-73; French and English tchr. Bethel Acad., Kinston, N.C., 1974; jr. high sch. music tchr. Lenoir County Schs., Kinston, 1974-76; in-charge staff auditor McGladrey Pullen, Des Moines, 1980-82; with internal auditing dept. Am. Fed. Savs. & Loan, Des Moines, 1982-84; v.p. fin. Gentry, Ltd., Des Moines, 1984-89; dir. property mgmt. adminstrn. R&R Investors, Ltd., West Des Moines, Iowa, 1989—96; controller Venter Spooner Inc., Johnston, Iowa, 1997—2006; cons. RH Mgmt. Resources, Des Moines, 2006—07; acct. RSM McGladrey, Des Moines, 2007—. Mem. acct. adv. bd. Am. Inst. Bus., Des Moines, 1988-94. Chairperson Holy Trinity Luth. Ch., Ankeny, Iowa, 1991. Recipient Elijah Watts Sells award AICPA, 1980. Mem. Cert. Financial Mgrs. Assn., Iowa Timberline Users Group, Iowa Soc. CPAs, Mensa, Phi Beta Kappa. Avocations: reading, needlecrafts, quilting, dance, bicycling. Home: 909 SE Kensington Rd Ankeny IA 50021-3960 Office: 400 Locust St Ste 640 Des Moines IA 50309 Home Phone: 515-965-1265; Office Phone: 515-558-5547. Business E-Mail: pam.poppe@rsmi.com.

POPPEL, HARVEY LEE, management consultant, investment banker; b. Bklyn., Dec. 18, 1937; s. Frank M. and Fannie (Axenzow) P.; m. Emily A. Daigneault, Jan. 2, 1959; children: Marc F., Clinton S. BS, Rensselaer Poly. Inst., 1958, MS, 1959. Sr. info. systems analyst Westinghouse Electric Corp., Pitts., 1959-65; mgr. industry systems Western Union, Paramus, NJ, 1965-67; from assoc. to mem. operating coun. Booz, Allen & Hamilton, NYC, 1967-84; gen. ptnr. Poptech, LLC, Sarasota, Fla., 2003—. Bd. dirs. Larscom, Santa Clara, Calif., 1996-02; mng. dir. Broadview Assocs., Ft. Lee, 1984-96; mem. panel, lectr. on computers, comms. and info. industry; judge Entrepreneur of Yr., 1991, 93, 94, 95, 96; investor in start-ups. Co-author: Information Technology: The Trillion-Dollar Opportunity, 1987. Mem. Aspen Inst. Fellows, Inst. Mgmt. Cons., Israel Cancer Assn. (exec. com.), Rep. Jewish Coalition, Palm Beach Civic Assn. (bd. dirs. 2006—), Banyan Golf Club, Marin Country Club, Breakers Ocean Club, Zeta Psi Personal E-mail: hpoppel@msn.com.

POPPENSIEK, GEORGE CHARLES, retired veterinary scientist, educator; b. NYC, June 18, 1918; s. George Frederick and Emily Amelia (Miller) P.; m. Edith M. Wallace, July 3, 1943; children: Neil Allen, Leslie Marion. Student, Cornell U., 1936-37, MS, 1951; student, U. Pa., 1937-42, V.MD, 1942. Diplomate Am. Bd. Microbiology, Am. Coll. Vet. Microbiology (charter), Am. Coll. Vet. Preventive Medicine (hon.). Asst. instr. medicine U. Pa. Sch. Vet. Medicine, 1943; asst. prof. vet. sci. U. Md., 1943-44; head dept. vet. virus vaccine prodn. Lederle Labs. div. Am. Cyanamid Co., 1944-49; dir. diagnostic lab. N.Y. State Coll. Vet. Medicine Cornell U., 1949-51, research assoc. Vet. Virus Research Inst., 1951-55; veterinarian Plum Island Animal Disease Ctr., animal disease and parasite research div. Agrl. Research Service, U.S. Dept. Agr., 1955-56, acting-in-charge diagnostic investigations, 1956-58, charge immunological investigations, 1958-59; dean and prof. microbiology N.Y. State Coll. Vet. Medicine, Cornell U., 1959-74, James Law prof. comparative medicine, 1974-88, dean emeritus, James Law prof. comparative medicine emeritus, 1988—; guest prof. U. Bern, Switzerland, 1975; ret., 1988. Exam. com. Nat. Bd. Vet. Med. Examiners, 1976-79; bd. dirs. Cornell Rsch. Found., 1963-74; chmn. bd. dirs. Cornell Veterinarian, Inc., 1976-86 Recipient Certificate of Merit award U.S. Dept. Agr., 1958; citation Sch. Vet. Med., U. Pa., 1978, Centennial medals U. Pa., 1984, Ohio State U., 1985; others. Fellow AAAS, Am. Acad. Microbiology (charter); mem. AVMA, Am. Soc. Virology (charter), NY State Vet. Med. Soc. (disting. life), Am. Bd. Microbiology, US Animal Health Assn., Assn. Am. Vet. Med. Colls. (pres. 1970-71), So. Tier Vet. Med. Assn., Am. Vet. Radiology Soc., Am. Soc. for Microbiology, NY Agrl. Soc. (life), Argentine Nat. Acad. Agronomy and Vet. Medicine (hon.), Soc. Polona Medicinae Veterinariae (hon.), Sigma Xi, Phi Kappa Phi, Alpha Psi, Omega Tau Sigma, Phi Zeta. Congregationalist. Home: 32 Horizon Dr Ithaca NY 14850-9769 Home Phone: 607-257-7621. Personal E-mail: poppensiek@gmail.com.

POPPERS, PAUL JULES, anesthesiologist, educator; b. Enschede, Netherlands, June 30, 1929; arrived in USA, 1958, naturalized, 1963; s. Meyer and Minca (Ginsburg) P.; m. Ann Feinberg, June 3, 1969; children: David Matthew, Jeremy Samuel. MD, U. Amsterdam, 1955. Diplomate Am. Bd. Anesthesiology. Instr. anesthesiology Columbia U., NYC, 1962-63, assoc., 1963-65, asst. prof. anesthesiology, 1965-71, assoc. prof. anesthesiology, 1971-74; prof., vice chmn. dept. anesthesiology NYU, 1974-79; prof., chmn. dept. anesthesiology Stony Brook U., NY, 1979—97, disting. prof., chmn. dept anesthesiology, 1997—2000, disting. prof. emeritus, 2000—. Cons. Brookdale Med. Ctr., Bklyn., 1975-2000, VA Med. Ctr., Northport, N.Y., 1979-2000, The N.Y. Hosp. Med. Ctr. of Queens (formerly Booth Meml. Hosp.), Flushing, N.Y., 1979-98, L.I. Jewish Med. Ctr., New Hyde Park, N.Y., 1980-98, Ea. L.I. Hosp., Greenport, N.Y., 1995-99, Am. Hosp. Paris, 1989-93; cons., lectr. USN, 1968-85 Author: Regional Anesthesia, 1977; editor: Beta Blockade and Anaesthesia, 1979; sect. editor Jour. Clin. Anesthesia, 1990-2000; mem. editl. bd. Internat. Jour. Clin. Monitoring and Computing, 1990-2000, Anaesthesiology Digest, 1991-94, Gynecologic and Obstetric Investigation, 1996-2001; contbr. over 200 articles to profl. jours. Rsch. fellow NIH, 1961; recipient medal Polish Acad. Scis., Poland, 1987, Univ. medal Jagiellonian U., Krakow, Poland, 1987, 1st Sci. award Post-grad. Assembly in Anesthesiology; named Hon. Prof. Anesthesiology, U. Leiden, The Netherlands, 1977. Fellow Am. Coll. Anesthesiology, Am. Coll. Ob-gyns., Royal Soc. Medicine, Post-grad. Assembly in Anesthesiology (hon. chmn. 1989-2005); mem. Am. Soc. Anesthesiologists, Assn. Univ. Anesthesiologists, Internat. Anesthesia Rsch. Soc., Soc. Obstetric Anesthesia and Perinatology, Am. Soc. Regional Anesthesia, Jerusalem Acad. Medicine, Am. Soc. Pharmacology and Exptl. Therapeutics, Fedn. Am. Soc. Exptl. Biology, Sigma Xi. Home Phone: 212-396-9026. Personal E-mail: paulpoppers@hotmail.com.

POPPLETON, JANET WATERS, legislative staff member; b. Camden, Ark., Dec. 5, 1950; d. William J. and Sybil (Butcher) Waters; m. Glenn A. Perry, May 20, 1972 (div. Jan. 1993); 1 child, Marcus Perry; m. Miller John Poppleton Jr., Mar. 20, 1999; stepchildren: Ashley, Aubrey. BA with highest honors, So. State Coll., Magnolia, Ark., 1972; MA, Stephen F. Austin State U., 1976. Press sec. Office of Rep. Ralph Hall, US House of Reps., Washington, 1993-96, chief staff, 1996—, chief staff minority Sci. Com., 2007—. Bd. dirs., fundraiser Habitat for Humanity, Am. Cancer Soc., Longview, 1985-91; bd. dirs. Jr. League, Longview, 1988-91; pres., bd. dirs. Gregg County Early Childhood Devel. Ctr., Longview, 1990-92; precinct chmn. Gregg County Dems., Longview, 1990-92; trustee Trinity Sch. Tex., Longview, 1991-92. Mem. U.S. Ho. Rep. Adminstrv. Asst. Assn. Lutheran. Avocations: travel, performing arts, skiing, writing. Office: Rep Ralph Hall 2221 Rayburn Washington DC 20515-0001 Office Phone: 202-225-6673. E-mail: janet.poppleton@mail.house.gov.*

POPRAWA, ANDREW, diversified financial services company executive, accountant; b. Toronto, Ont., Can., Nov. 13, 1952; s. Mieczyslaw and Wanda P.; m. Rita Poprawa, Oct. 10, 1981; children: Alexandra, Jason. B in Commerce, U. Toronto, 1975. Chartered dir., Can., cert. govt. fin. mgr. CEO St. Stanislaus Credit Union, Toronto, 1980-82; dir. Toronto Ops. Office of Supt. of Fin. Instns., Canada, 1982—92; dir. Credit Unions and Cooperatives Ministry of Fin., Province of Ont., Toronto, 1992—93; pres., CEO Deposit Ins. Corp. of Ont., Toronto, 1993—. Mem. Toronto Bd. Trade; mem. governance com. Canadian Cooperative Assn.; mem. conf. bd. Can. Governance Adv. Com., Can. Nat. Award for Governance Pub. Sector. Mem.: Inst. Charter Accountants Ont., Lakeshore Yacht Club. Roman Catholic. Avocations: scuba diving, sailing, skiing, hockey. Office: Deposit Insurance Corp of Ontario 4711 Yonge St #700 Toronto ON Canada M2N 6K8 Home Phone: 905-624-2818; Office Phone: 416-325-9580. Business E-Mail: apoprawa@dico.com.

POPSON, LUCY (MARIA D. POPSON), elementary school educator; BS, Pacific Union Coll., MA in Edn. with Reading emphasis. Tchr. Walter Douglas Elem. Sch., Tucson, 1994—. Named Ariz. Tchr. of Yr., 2006. Office: Walter Douglas Elem Sch 3302 N Flowing Wells Tucson AZ 85705 Business E-Mail: popsonm@flowingwells.k12.az.us.

PORAT, M. MOSHE, dean, management educator; m. Rachel Porat; 1 child. BA with distinction in Econs. and Statistics, Tel Aviv U., MBA magna cum laude; PhD, Temple U. Instr. Sch. Mgmt., Tel Aviv U., 1971—73; dep. gen. mgr. Ihud Insurance Group, 1972—76; faculty mem. Temple U., 1981—, former Joseph E. Boettner prof. risk mgmt. & insurance and chmn. Risk Mgmt., Insurance and Actuarial Sci. Dept., dean Fox Sch. Bus. Mgmt., 1996—, dean Sch. Tourism and Hospitality, Laura H. Carnell prof. Vis. prof. Grad. Sch. Commerce, Meiji U., Toyko, 1993; bd. advisors Samsung Fire and Marine Insurance Co., Republic of Korea; com. chair Com. Fin., Resources, and Fiscal Impact, Phila. Edn. Adv. Taskforce. Contbr. articles to profl. jours. Bd. dirs. United America Indemnity, Ltd. Recipient Adam Smith Leadership Award, Academic Excellence and Ednl. Leadership by Econ. Pa., 2002; named Internat. Dean of Yr., Acad. Internat. Bus., 2001. Mem.: Pa. Economy League, America-Israel C. of C. Office: Fox Sch Bus and Mgmt, Temple U Alter Hall 367 1810 N 13th St Philadelphia PA 19122 Office Phone: 215-204-1836. E-mail: porat@temple.edu.*

PORAT, RUTH M., investment bank executive; d. Dan I. and Frieda Porat; m. Anthony Paduano, Dec. 17, 1983. AB, Stanford U., Calif.; MS in Econs., London Sch. Econs. and Polit. Sci.; MBA, U. Pa. Wharton Sch., Phila., 1987. Mgmt. cons. Yankelovich, Skelly & White, NYC; with mergers & acquisitions dept. Morgan Stanley, NYC, 1987, chair equity capital markets tech. bus., co-head global tech. group, vice chmn.

investment banking divsn., global head fin. instns. group, 2006—. Mem. bus. com. Met. Mus. Art. Mem. Humanities and Sci. Coun. Stanford U. Named one of 50 Women to Watch, The Wall St. Jour., 2008. Office: Morgan Stanley 1585 Broadway New York NY 10036*

PORCA, SANELA, economics professor; PhD in Economics, U. Tenn., Knoxville, 2002. Prof. economics U. SC, Aiken. Recipient Disting. Tchr. award, SC Govt., 2006, Excellence Tchg. award, U. SC, 2006, Svc. award, Internat. Acad. Bus. & Pub. Adminstrn. Disciplines, 2009, Best Paper award, Internat. Applied Bus. Rsch., 2003. Office: 471 Univ SC Aiken SC 29801 Office Phone: 803-641-3232. Business E-Mail: sanelap@usca.edu.

PORCARI, JOHN D., federal agency administrator; b. Rochester, NY, Dec. 14, 1958; m. Heidi Porcari. BA in Polit. Sci., U. Dayton, Ohio, 1981; MPA, SUNY, Albany, 1985. Environ. planner Dept. Environ. Resources, Prince George's County, Md., 1986—87; devel. review coord. Office County Exec., Prince George's County, 1987—89, devel. mgr., 1989—95; Gov.'s ombudsman, asst. sec. for econ. devel. policy Dept. Bus. & Econ. Devel., 1995—96; dep. sec. Md. Dept. Transp., 1997—98, sec., 1999—2003, 2007—09, acting sec., 2007; v.p. adminstrv. affairs U. Md., College Park, 2003—07; dep. sec. US Dept. Transp., Washington, 2009—. Democrat. Office: US Dept Transp 1200 New Jersey Ave SE Washington DC 20590 Office Phone: 202-366-4000.*

PORCARO, MICHAEL FRANCIS, advertising executive; b. NYC, Apr. 3, 1948; s. Girolamo M. and Marianna (DePasquale) P.; m. Bonnie Kerr, Apr. 7, 1972; children: Sabrina, Jon. BA in English, Rockford Coll., Ill., 1969. Broadcaster Sta. KFQD-AM; KENI-AM/TV, Anchorage, 1970-71, Sta. KENI-AM/TV, Anchorage, 1972-73; v.p. ops. Cook Inlet Broadcasters, Anchorage, 1973-74; owner Audio Enterprises, Anchorage, 1974-75; asst. Alaska Pub. Broadcasting Commn., Anchorage, 1975-76, exec. dir., 1976-81; CEO, ptnr. Porcaro Blankenship Advt. Corp., Anchorage, 1981-97; CEO Porcaro Comms., Anchorage, 1997—; chmn. bd. Bernholz & Graham, Pub. Rels., 2001—07, NY, 2007; ptnr. Porcaro Vancouver Ad and Pub. Rels., 2003, Porcaro LA (Calif.) Ad and Pub. Rels., 2004—06. Cons. Arco Alaska TV sta., Anchorage, 1981; expert witness U.S. Senate Subcom. on Telecom., Washington, 1978; chmn. citizens adv. com. dept. journalism U. Alaska, 1995-96; pub. rels. Bernholz & Graham, N.Y., 2007. Afternoon talk show host KENI, 2000—. Chmn. Municipality of Anchorage Urban Design Commn., 1990-93; mem. mayor's transition team Municipality of Anchorage, 1987-88; bd. dirs. Anchorage Glacier Pilots Baseball Club, 1987-88, Anchorage Mus. History and Art, Alaska Ctr. Internat. Bus., 1996, Commonwealth North, 1996-2000, Friends of Alaska Children's Trust, 1996-97, Anchorage Symphony Orch.; chmn. bd. dirs. Brother Francis Shelter for the Homeless, Anchorage, 1993-96; mem. mktg. com. gov.'s transition team, 1995; mem. United Way Anchorage Cabinet, 1996; bd. dirs. Alaska Spl. Olmpics, 2001, Anchorage Econ. Devel. Corp., 2001, Alaska Moving Image Preservation Assn., 2001, United Way Cabinet, 2008-09, Police Chief Selection Commn. Anchorage, 2009. Recipient Silver Mike award Billboard mag., 1974, Bronze award N.Y. Film Critics, 1981, Best of North award Ad. Fedn. Alaska, 1982—, Addy award, 1985, 91, Grand Addy award 1990, Cable TV Mktg. award 1986; Paul Harris fellow. Mem. Advt. Fedn. Alaska, Anchorage C. of C. (bd. dirs.), Alaska Moving Image Preservation Assn. (bd. dirs. 2001). Republican. Roman Catholic. Avocations: softball, hockey, travel, exercise. Office: Porcaro Comm 433 W 9th Ave Anchorage AK 99501-3519 Office Phone: 907-276-4262. Personal E-mail: mike.porcaro@porcaro.ca.

PORCELLO, LEONARD JOSEPH, engineering research and development executive; b. NYC, Mar. 1, 1934; s. Savior James and Mary Josephine (Bacchi) P.; m. Patricia Lucille Berger, July 7, 1962 (dec. Sept. 1991); children: John Joseph, Thomas Gregory; m. Victoria Roberta Smith, June 21, 1996. BA in Physics, Cornell U., 1955; MS in Physics, U. Mich., 1957, MSEE, 1959, PhD in Elec. Engring, 1963. Research asst. U. Mich., Ann Arbor, 1955-58, instr. elec. engring., 1958-61; research engr. Radar & Optics Lab., 1968-72; asso. dir. Willow Run Labs., 1970-72, asso. prof., 1969-72, prof., 1972-73, adj. prof., 1973-75. Dir. radar and optics divsn. Environ. Rsch. Inst. of Mich., Ann Arbor, 1973-76, v.p., 1973-76, trustee, 1975; asst. v.p., mgr. sensor sys. operation Sci. Applications Internat. Corp., Tucson, 1976-79, v.p., 1979-85, corp. v.p., 1985-87, mgr. def. sys. group, 1986-95, sr. v.p., 1987—, dep. mgr. tech. and advanced sys. sector, 1993-97, mgr. applied sys. group, 1995-2000, dep. mgr. space and tech. solutions sector, 1997-99; CFO TIAS ARMS, 2004-08, bd. dirs., 2004-09. Bd. dirs. Tucson Jr. Strings, 1977-79, chmn., 1978-79 Fellow IEEE; mem. Optical Soc. Am., AAAS, Sigma Xi, Eta Kappa Nu. Roman Catholic. Achievements include research on imaging radar, synthetic aperture radar systems and radar remote sensing. Home: 5072 Grandview Ave Yorba Linda CA 92886-4216 Office: Sci Applications Internat Corp Attn LJ Porcello PO Box 820 Yorba Linda CA 92885-0820 Office Phone: 714-695-1465. Business E-Mail: leonard.j.porcello@saic.com.

PORCH, WILLIAM MORGAN, physicist; b. Athens, Ohio, Nov. 8, 1944; s. Virgil and Nellie (Evans) Porch; m. Laura Virginia Lee Porch, Nov. 20, 1978. BA, U. Utah, 1966; MA, U. Wash., 1968, PhD, 1971. Optical engr. Boeing Co., Seattle, 1966—68; rsch. assoc. U. Wash., Seattle, 1968—72; physicist Lawrence Livermore Nat. Lab., Livermore, Calif., 1972—87; cons. reviewer Rsch. Edn. Assocs., Washington, 1983. Contbr. articles to profl. jours. Vol. Astron. & Minority Edn. Program, Chabot Obs., Oakland Sch. Dist., Calif., 1974—. Mem.: East Bay Astron. Soc., Am. Meteorol. Soc. (chmn. spl. com. meteorology & air pollution), Optical Soc. America, Am. Geophys. Union. Achievements include patents in field; discovery of nighttime valley wave oscillations in complex terrain, meteorological profile associated with a ship-trail cloud. Home: 1138 Big Rock Loop Los Alamos NM 87544-2805 Office: Los Alamos Nat Lab PO Box 1662 Los Alamos NM 87544 Office Phone: 505-667-0941. Business E-Mail: wporch@lawl.gov.

PORCHER, ROBERT, III, entrepreneur, retired professional football player; b. 1969; BA in Criminal Justice, South Carolina State U., 1992; grad., Nat. Automotive Dealers Acad., 2007. Cert. in bus. course Stanford Sch. Bus., 1999. Former profl. football player Detroit Lions, 1992—2004; pres. Southern Hospitality Restaurant Grp., Detroit Football Classic L.L.C., 2002—; founder Porcher Cancer Relief Fund; apprentice Honda Bloomfield, Mich., 2007—. Bd. mem. Super Bowl XL Host Com., NFL Players Assn. Exec. Bd., 2000—06, Detroit Econ. Growth Corp.; NFL bd. players rep., 1997—2000; mem. NFL Players Assn. Diversity Com., 2003—06, NFL Agent Disciplinary Com., 2005—; chmn. Cmty. Rels. Action Team, 2006; steering com. NAACP, 2006. Hon. chairperson Detroit Tribute to Local Initiatives Support Corp. Silver Anniversary event; involved with The Heat and Warmth Fun, Police Athletic League, Skillman Found., Focus: HOPE. Recipient NFL Extra Effort award, NFL Walter Payton Man of Yr.; named Detroit News Michigander of Yr., 2006, Nat. Father of Yr., Nat. Fatherhood Initiative, 2000; named one of 40 Under 40, Crain's Detroit Bus., 2006. Office: Rp3 Inc PO Box 492 Northville MI 48167-0492 Office Phone: 313-963-1940, 313-962-4277. Office Fax: 313-963-1947, 313-962-4380.

PORDON, WILLIAM PHILIP, music educator; b. Buffalo, Aug. 4, 1925; s. William Peter Pordon and Victoria Regina (Valenches) Dobson; m. Eleanor Grace Haggett, Sept. 28, 1951; children: Judith, Dorothy, Gregory. MusB, Chgo. Conservatory of Music, 1950, MusM, 1951. Violinist Atlanta Symphony, 1951-55; music tchr. Augusta (Ga.) Pub. Schs., 1955-59; dir. music Wayland (Mass.) Pub. Schs., 1960-69; asst. prof. music edn. U. Lowell, Mass., 1969-85. Author: String Starter, 1983; author/composer: Midnight Tango, 1990. With U.S. Army, 1942-44, ETO. Recipient Lowell Mason award Mass. Music Educators Assn., 1981. Mem. Am. String Tchrs. Assn. (pres. San Diego sect. 1985-2004). Achievements include designed and implemented the Point Loma String Project at Point Loma Nazarene University for training string teachers. Avocation: oil and watercolor painting. Home: 1672 Main St Ramona CA 92065-5257 Personal E-mail: casapoema@hotmail.com.

PORDUM, FRANCIS J., supervisor, former state legislator, educator, marketing professional; b. Lackawanna, NY; m. Rebecca Pordum; 1 child, Carolyn. BA, Colgate U., 1968; MEd, State U. Coll., Buffalo. Formerly tchr. and coach; mem. N.Y. State Assembly, 1983-96, mem. majority steering com., chmn. local govts. com., chmn. com. on state and local rels., chmn. ethics com.; v.p. mktg. and profl. svcs. Capitol Hill Mgmt. Svcs., Inc., Albany, NY, 1997—. Former mem. banking com., corrections com., ins. com., racing and wagering com., transp. com., commn. on critical transp. choices and hazardous wastes and toxic substances N.Y. County. Legislator, Erie County. Recipient Pub. Servant of Yr. award Erie County Fedn. Sportsmen, 1983, Citizen of Yr. award Am.-Polish Eagle, 1984, Legislator Citation of Merit award Nat. Columbus Day Com., 1985, Friend of Edn. award Hamburg Tchrs. Assn., 1986, others. Mem. Profl. and Businessmen's Assn. Western N.Y., Chopin Singing Soc., Polish Am. Congress, Lackawanna Tchrs. Fedn. Address: 7476 Derby Rd Derby NY 14047-9687 Office Phone: 716-549-5787.

POREMBKA, DAVID THOMAS, anesthesia and surgery educator; b. Latrobe, Pa., Nov. 28, 1953; m. Diane Irene Siefert; children: Daniela, Nathanael, Anna, Sarah. BS in Biology/Chemistry cum laude, U. Pitts., 1975; DO, Mich. State U., 1981. Diplomate Nat. Bd. Examiners, Am. Bd. Anesthesiology, Am. Bd. Critical Care Medicine subspecialty; cert. advanced trauma life support; lic. Mich., Ohio. Intern Botsford Gen. Hosp., Detroit, 1981-82, anesthesiology resident, 1982-83, Cleve. Clinic Found., 1984-86, anesthesiology chief fellow, surgical intensive care medicine, 1986-87, clin. fellow A, SICU rsch. assoc., 1987-88; assoc. prof. clin. anesthesiology, critical care medicine Univ. Cin. Coll. of Medicine, 1988—; assoc. dir. trauma/surg. intensive care unit Dept. Anesthesiology, Univ. Cin. Coll. of Medicine, 1988—; dir. transesophageal echocardiography Univ. Cin. Coll. of Medicine, 1988—, acting dir. cardiac anesthesia, 1989-90, 90—, asst. prof. clin. surgery, 1990-93, assoc. prof. of anesthesia, 1993—, assoc. prof. of surgery, 1994—. Anesthesiology rsch. assoc., dept. anesthesiology Univ. Pitts. (Pa.) Sch. of Medicine, 1977-78; cons. Baxter-Edwards, Advanced Tech. Labs.; vis. prof., presenter and lectr. in field. Contbr. articles to profl. jours.; patentee method for automatic contar extraction with echocardiography. Fellow Soc. Critical Care Medicine (chair anesthesia sect. 1995—, program com. 1993—, workforce com. 1994—, continuing edn. com. 1994—, multidisciplinary rev. bd. 1994—), Coll. Chest Physicians; mem. Am. Coll. Chest Physicians, Am. Heart Assn., Am. Soc. Anesthesiology, Am. Soc. Critical Care Anesthesiologists, Am. Soc. Echocardiography, Internat. Anesthesia Rsch. Soc., Mich. Soc. Critical Care Medicine, Ohio Soc. Anesthesiologists, Soc. Cardiovascular Anesthesiologists (edn. com. 1990—), Cin. Soc. Anesthesiology. Office: Univ of Cincinnati Coll of Med 231 Albert Sabin Way ML-0531 Cincinnati OH 45267 Business E-Mail: david.porembka@uc.edu.

POREMBKA, MICHAEL RICHARD, assistant principal, supervisor; b. Latrobe, Pa., Dec. 30, 1974; s. Richard D. and Carmella J. Porembka. BA in History Edn., St. Vincent Coll., Pa., 1997; MEd, Gannon U., Erie, Pa., 2002, Prin. Certification, 2004. Cert. Tchr. Pa., 1997, Adminstrv. Pa., 2002, Adminstrv. Prin. Pa., 2004, prin. cert. Gannon U., Pa., 2004. Tchr. Greater Latrobe (Pa.) Jr. HS, 1998—2006; social studies dept. coord. Greater Latrobe (Pa.) Sch. Dist., 2002—; asst. prin. Greater Latrobe (Pa.) Jr. HS, 2006—; sports/radio broadcaster WCNS Radio, Latrobe, Pa., 2001—. Track coach Greater Latrobe (Pa.) Jr. HS, 1997—2003, football coach, 1998—99, student assistance team mem., 2000—; strategic planning com. Greater Latrobe (Pa.) Sch. Dist., 2001—; asst. softball coach Greater Latrobe (Pa.) Sr. HS, 2005—06. Prodr.(co-host): (radio show) The Sunday Evening Polka Cafe; sports commentator (radio broadcast) Greater Latrobe High School Football on 1480 WCNS Radio. Platelet donor ARC, Greensburg, Pa., 1998—2006; com. mem. Westmoreland County Courthouse Com., Greensburg, Pa., 2005—06; lector St. Rose Roman Cath. Ch., Latrobe, Pa., 2002—06. Mem.: Nat. Assn. Secondary Sch. Principals (assoc.), Internat. Polka Assn. (assoc.), NEA (assoc.), Am. Greek Beneficial Soc. (assoc.), B.P.O. Elks (assoc.). Roman Catholic. Avocations: golf, cars, music. Office: Greater Latrobe Sch Dist 410 Main St Latrobe PA 15650

PORETTO, JODI, art dealer; BA, Loyola U., 1976. Comml. casualty underwriter, mktg. Continental Ins. Cos., New Orleans, 1976—85; fine art cons. Kurt Schon Galleries, New Orleans, 1987—89; dir. European art Manheim Galleries, New Orleans, 1989—94; fin. advisor Morgan Stanley, NYC, 1998—2001; art dealer Jodi Poretto Fine Art LLC, New Orleans, 2002—. Home and Office: Jodi Poretto Fine Art LLC 818 Bourbon St New Orleans LA 70116 Personal E-mail: jporetto@hotmail.com.

PORFILIO, JOHN CARBONE, federal judge; b. Denver, Oct. 14, 1934; s. Edward Alphonso Porfilio and Caroline (Carbone) Moore; m. Joan West, Aug. 1, 1959 (div. 1983); children: Edward Miles, Joseph Arthur, Jeanne Kathrine; m. Theresa Louise Berger, Dec. 28, 1983; 1 stepchild, Katrina Ann Smith. Student, Stanford U., 1952—54; BA, U. Denver, 1956, LLB, 1959, LLD (hon.), 2000. Bar: Colo. 1959, US Supreme Ct. 1965. Asst. atty. gen. State of Colo., Denver, 1962—68, dep. atty. gen., 1968—72, atty. gen., 1972—74; US bankruptcy judge Dist. of Colo., Denver, 1975—82; judge US Dist. Ct. Colo., Denver, 1982—85, US Ct. Appeals (10th cir.), Denver, 1985—99, sr. judge, 1999—. Instr. Colo. Law Enforcement Acad., Denver, 1965—70, State Patrol Acad., Denver, 1968—70; guest lectr. U. Denver Coll. Law, 1978. Committeeman Arapahoe County Rep. Com., Aurora, Colo., 1968; mgr. Dunbar for Atty. Gen., Denver, 1970. Mem.: ABA. Roman Catholic. Office: US Ct Appeals Byron White US Courthouse 1825 Stout St Denver CO 80238*

PORGES, AMELIA, lawyer; BA, Cornell U., 1973; MPP, Harvard U., 1980, JD cum laude, 1980. Bar: DC 1980, US Ct. Appeals, Fed. Cir., US Ct. Internat. Trade. Sr. counsel for dispute settlement, head enforcement, assoc. gen. counsel US Trade Rep., 1980—90, 1994—2000; sr. legal officer, counsellor for legal affairs Gen. Agreement on Tariffs and Trade; secretariat, 1990—94; of counsel Powell Goldstein Frazer & Murphy, Washington, 2000—02; counsel Sidney Austin LLP, Washington, 2002—. Vis. fellow Kyoto U. Faculty of Law, 1977—78; vis. lectr. Sophia U., Tokyo, 1985; adj. prof. Johns Hopkins U. Sch. Advanced Internat. Studies, 1999—; program co-chair Internat. Trade Update, Georgetown U. Law Ctr., 2002—. Author: Analytical Index/Guide to GATT Law and Practice, 1995; contbr. articles to profl. jours. Commr. Japan-US Friendship Commn.; mem. US-Japan Conf. on Cultural and Ednl. Interchange, 2007—; mem. adv. bd. Stanford U. GATT Digital Archive, 2003—; mem. chpt. 19 panelists NAFTA, 2001—07; bd. mem. Trade Policy Forum, 2005—08, gen. consel, 2008—. Fellow, Coun. on Fgn. Relations, Internat. Affairs, 1988—89; Fulbright fellow, 1985. Mem.: ABA (mem. internat. trade steering group 1994—), Am. Soc. Internat. Law (exec. coun. 1990—95, co-chair Internat. Econ. Law Interest Group 2007—09, editor insights 2008—). Office: Sidley Austin LLP 1501 K St NW Washington DC 20005 Office Phone: 202-736-8361. Office Fax: 202-736-8711. Business E-Mail: aporges@sidley.com. E-mail: amelia.pages@gmail.com.

PORIES, WALTER JULIUS, surgeon, educator; b. Munich, Jan. 18, 1930; s. Theodore Francis and Frances (Lowin) P.; m. Muriel Helen Aronson, Aug. 18, 1951; children: Susan E., Mary Jane, Carolyn A., Kathy G.; m. Mary Ann Rose McCarthy, June 4, 1977; children: Mary Lisa, Michael McCarthy. BA, Wesleyan U., Middletown, Conn., 1952; MD with honors, U. Rochester, 1955. Diplomate Am. Bd. Surgery, Am. Bd. Thoracic Surgery. Intern Strong Meml. Hosp., Rochester, NY, 1955—56, resident, 1958—62; chmn. dept. surgery Wright-Patterson AFB, Ohio, 1952—67; asst. prof. surgery and oncology U. Rochester, 1967—69; prof. surgery and assoc. chmn. dept. surgery Case Western Res. U., 1969—77; prof. surgery, biochemistry, exercise and sport medicine East Carolina U., Greenville, NC, 1977—, chmn. dept. surgery, 1977—96, dir. Metabolic Inst., 2005—08; chief surgery Pitt County Meml. Hosp., 1977—96, prof. surgery U. Health Scis. of Uniformed Svcs., 1982—; founder, assoc. dir. Rochester Cancer Ctr., 1967—69; founder, dir. Cleve. Cancer Ctr., 1972—77, Hospice of Cleve., 1975; founder, chmn. bd. Hospice of Greenville, 1981; med. dir. Home Health Care of Greenville, 1978—83; pres. Surg. Rev. Corp., Raleigh, 2003—. Founder, chmn. bd. Ctr. for Creative Living, 1985-91; pres., chmn. Echo Mgmt. Orgn., 1994—; vis. scholar NIH, 1996; sec. treas., pres. N.C. Med. Bd., 1997-2003. Author: Clinical Applications of Zinc Metabolism, 1974; editor: Operative Surgery series, vols. 1-4, 1979-83, Office Surgery for Family Physicians, 1985; editor in chief Current Surgery, 1990-2005; editor Nat. Curriculum for Residency in Surgery, 4th edit., 1988—. Bd. dirs. Boy Scouts Am., Cleve., 1974-77, Greenville Arts Mus., 1980-82; pres. Sequoiah, Inc., 1999—; bd. dirs. East Carolina U. Found., United Meth. Homes, 2003-. Maj. USAF, 1955-67; col. USAR, 1979-91, comdr. USAF Hosp., Durham, N.C.; activated Desert Shield, 1990. Decorated Legion of Merit; Thorndyke scholar, 1948-51; recipient McLester award USAF, 1966, Miss. Magnolia Cross, 1989, Presdl. citation for Desert Shield, 1994; named to Hon. Order of Ky. Cols., 1965. Fellow ACS, Am. Coll. Cardiology, Am. Coll. Chest Physicians; mem. Soc. for Vascular Surgery, Soc. Surg. Oncology, Soc. Univ. Surgeons, Am. Surg. Assn., Soc. Environ. Geochemistry (past pres.), Residency Rev. Com. for Surgery (vice-chair 1992-98), So. Surg. Assn., Soc. for Thoracic Surgery, Ea. Carolina Health Orgn. (pres., chmn. bd. 1994-99), Assn. Programs Dirs. in Surgery (pres. 1995-96), N.C. Surg. Assn. (pres. 1995-96), Am. Soc. Bariatic Surgery (pres. 2002), Sigma Xi (O. Max Gardner prize), Phi Kappa Phi. Home: Deep Sun Farm 7464 NC 43 N Macclesfield NC 27852 Office: East Carolina U Dept Surgery Greenville NC 27858 Office Phone: 252-744-3290. Business E-Mail: poriesw@ecu.edu.

POROMANSKA, MARGARITA KIRILOVA, environmental scientist, educator; b. Gabrovo, Bulgaria, Nov. 3, 1960; arrived in U.S., 2000; d. Kiril Georgiev Poromanski and Liliana Dimitrova Ralcheva; 1 child, Viktor Dimitrov Arabadjiev. MSc in Biology/Zoology, U. Sofia, Bulgaria, 1983; MSc in Environ. Sci., Ctrl. European U., Budapest, Hungary, 2000. Cert. substitute tchr. Ill. Environ. sci. expert Union Nature Conservation, Sofia, Bulgaria, 1998—99, Pearson Custom Pub., Indpls., 2004—; instr. biology Coll. DuPage, Glen Ellyn, Ill., 2001—, Waubonsee CC, Sugar Grove, 2001—07, Columbia Coll., Chgo., 2002—, Nat. Louis U., 2004—. Sci. and fgn. langs. tutor Ednl. Svcs. Glen Ellyn, Ill., 2001—, W. Suburban Ednl. Assocs., Naperville, Ill., 2002—; rsch. fellow Inst. Ecology Bulgarian Acad. Scis., Sofia, 1988—96; sr. reviewer AP Environ. Sci. Coll. Bd. Edn., 2006—. Author, editor: New Portals to Appreciating Our Global Environment, 2005. Judge science competition Malcolm X Coll., Chgo., 2004; sr. reviewer, AP Course Audit Environ. Sci. Coll. Bd. Edn., 2006—08. Grantee, Open Soc. Found., 1992; scholar, 1999, Carl-Duisberg Found., 1994. Mem.: NEA, Ill. Edn. Assn., Ctrl. European U. Alumni Assn. Avocations: hiking, bicycling, birdwatching. Home: 1662 Monticello Ct # C Wheaton IL 60189 Office: Coll DuPage Natural Applied Sci Dept 425 Fawell Blvd Glen Ellyn IL 60137-6599 Personal E-mail: m_poromanska@yahoo.com.

POROSOFF, HAROLD, chemist, science administrator, research and development company executive; b. Bklyn., Apr. 3, 1946; s. Solomon and Ruth (Goldberg) P.; m. Leslie Pamela Freiman, May 19, 1948; children: Lauren, Stephen, Marc. BS, MIT, 1966; PhD, Brown U., 1970. Various rsch. and mgmt. positions fibers div. Am. Cyanamid Co., Stamford, Conn. and Milton, Fla., 1970-78, various mgmt. positions Shulton Rsch. div. Clifton, NJ, 1978-83, dir., 1983-88, v.p. R & D chem. rsch. divsn. Stamford, 1989-93; v.p. R & D Cytec Industries Inc., Stamford, 1993-95; v.p., chief tech. officer Cytec Industries, Inc., Stamford, 1995-98, cons., 1998—. Patentee in field. Chmn. Scarsdale Cable TV Commn. Mem. AAAS. Office: 22 Olmsted Rd Scarsdale NY 10583-2324 E-mail: hpphd@optonline.net.

POROWSKI, ANNE M., management consultant; b. Urbana, Ill., Aug. 9, 1950; d. Thaddeus and Elsie Dibble Porowski. BA, Am. U. Sch. Pub. Affairs, Washington, DC, 1974. Organization Development Georgetown U., DC, 2004. Legis. analyst Office Congressman Tom Railsback, Washington, 1978—83; assoc. Flanagan and Assocs., 1983—86; budget analyst US Dept. Treasury, 1986—2003; program mgmt. analyst US Dept. of the Treasury, 2003—06; cons. Anne Porowski LLC, Chicago, 2005—. Facilitator America Speaks, 2007—; co-chair Think Peace, Take Action Seminar, Chgo., 2007. Mem.: UN Assn. Greater Chgo. Chpt. (v.p. 2007—), Orgn. Devel. Network of Chgo. (treas. 2008—), Orgn. Devel. Network, Soka Gakkai Internat., USA. Independent. Buddhist. Office: Anne Porowski LLC 400 E Randolph St Ste1403 Chicago IL 60601 Office Fax: 312-819-9658. Personal E-mail: aporowski@aol.com. Business E-Mail: anne@anneporowskiconsulting.com.

PORRAS, JESS, special education educator; s. Felipe and Dolores Porras; m. Margaret Morrell; children: Rina Michelle, Joaquin. MEd, La Verne U., Calif., 1995. Cert. in edn. therapy U. Calif. San Diego, 1996. Speech& lang. specialist South Bay Union Sch. Dist., Imperial Beach, Calif., 1975—78, resource specialist, 1978—98; learning disabilities specialist San Diego State U., 1998—. Adj. faculty San Diego State U., 2004—. Home: 6321 Caminito Del Cervato San Diego CA 92111 Office: San Diego State Univ 5500 Campanile Dr San Diego CA 92111

PORRAS, VICKI, language educator; d. Luisa and Alberto Porras. MA in Edn., U. Md., Coll. Pk., 1969. Prof. Spanish Prince George's CC, Largo, Md., 1967—97, chair foreing lang. dept., coord. ESL, dir.

Spanish, 1987—97; lectr. Spanish Am. U., Washington, 1997—2000; prof. Spanish Monterey Inst. Internat. Studies, Monterey, Calif., 2000—. Business E-Mail: vicki.porras@miis.edu.

PORRATI, MASSIMO, physicist, educator; b. Genoa, Italy, June 9, 1961; s. Bruno Porrati and Argelia Aspromonte. Laurea in Fisica, U. Pisa, Italy, 1984; diploma in Sci., Scuola Normale Superiore, Pisa, 1985. Ricercatore INFN, Pisa, 1990—96; prof. physics NYU, 1992—. Editor Letters Math. Physics, 2000—, Jour. High Energy Physics, 2004—. Contbr. articles to profl. jours. Recipient Sigrav award, 1998; Rsch. grant, Bi-Nat. Sci. Found., Israel & USA, 1997—2000, NSF, 1997—, Excellence Chair grant, European Union Marie Curie Actions, 2004—07. Achievements include research in advance theoretical high-energy physics. Office: Dept Physics NYU 4 Washington Pl New York NY 10003 Office Phone: 212-998-7733. Business E-Mail: massimo.porrati@nyu.edu.

PORRECO, RICHARD PATRICK, physician; b. Borinquen Field, PR, Aug. 27, 1946; s. Andrew Roger and Nancy Tendera Porreco; m. Terese Irene Kaske, Oct. 24, 1992; m. Jacqueline Anne Davis, June 8, 1968 (div. Apr. 29, 1989); children: Richard Christopher, Allison Christine. MD, U. Colo. Med. Ctr., Denver, Colo., 1971. Lic. Am. Bd.of Ob-gyn, 1977, Am. Bd. of Ob-gyn, Maternal-Fetal Med, 1981, Am. Bd. of Med. Genetics, 1984. Staff physician Naval Regional Med. Ctr., San Diego, 1975—77; fellow, maternal-fetal medicine U. Calif., San Diego, 1977—79; staff perinatalogist Kaiser-Permanente Med. Group, San Diego, 1979—81. Dir., maternal-fetal medicine Presbyn./St. Luke's Med. Ctr., Denver, 1981—. Joint venture com. HealthOne/HCA Joint Venture, Denver, Colo., 1999—2002. Lt. comdr. USNR, 1975—77, San Diego, Calif. Recipient Most Outstanding Faculty Tchg. Award, U. Colo. OBGYN Dept., 1990; grantee Rsch. In Genetics, Bank of Am., Giannini, 1977-79; scholar Med. Scholarship, Clara C. Wolleson Trust, Colo. Springs, 1967-71. Fellow: ACOG (pres., colo. gyn-ob soc. 1996—97, Outstanding Program Chmn. 1989); mem.: Denver Clin. and Path. Soc., Soc. Maternal Fetal Medicine, Alpha Omega Alpha (life), Alpha Tau Omega (life; v.p. 1966—67). Achievements include research in Over 80 various contbn. to clin. obstetrics lit; 25 years high risk obstet. care in Rocky Mtn region. Office: Obstetrix Med Group of Colo 1601 East 19th Ave Ste 5050 Denver CO 80218

PORSTEINSSON, ANTON P., medical educator, director; s. Porsteinn Sigurdsson and Inga Lilly Bjarnadottir; m. Sigridur Hauksdottir, Apr. 15, 1994; children: Inga Margret Antonsdottir, Orri Thor Antonsson. MD, U. Iceland Sch. Medicine, Reykjavik, 1987. Lic. state med. NY, 1994, diplomate in psychiatry Am. Bd. Neurology and Psychiatry, 1994, in geriatric psychiatry 1995. Sr. instr. psychiatry U. Rochester, NY, 1993—97, asst. prof. psychiatry, 1997—2003, assoc. prof. psychiatry, 2003—; dir. Alzheimers Disease Care, Rsch. and Edn. Program AD-CARE, Rochester, NY, 2006—. Dir. U. Rochester Memory Disorders Clinic, NY, 2006—, Dept. Psychiatry, Monroe Cmty. Hosp., Rochester, 2006—. Mem.: Am. Assn. Geriatric Psychiatry. Office: Ad-Care 435 E Henrietta Rd Rochester NY 14620 Office Fax: 585-760-6572.

PORT, LILLY BRUCK LIEB, retired advocate, columnist, commentator; b. Vienna, May 13, 1918; came to U.S., 1941, naturalized, 1944; d. Max and Sophie M. Hahn; m. Sandor Bruck, Mar. 7, 1943; 1 child, Sandra Lee (Mrs. John David Evans III); m. David L. Lieb, Dec. 7, 1985; m. Charles S. Port, Nov. 22, 1998. PhD in Econs., U. Vienna; postgrad., Sorbonne, Paris, Sch. of Econs., London, Sch. of Bus., Columbia U., 1941-42, Sch. of Social Work, NYU, 1964-66. Dir. consumer edn. Dept. Consumer Affairs, City of N.Y., 1969-78; project dir. Am. Coalition of Citizens with Disabilities, 1977-78; consumer advisor, broadcaster In Touch Networks, NYC, 1978-90; consumer affairs commentator Nat. Pub. Radio, 1980-82; ret. Author: Access, The Guide to a Better Life for Disabled Americans, 1978; contbr. articles to disability and rehab. to books, ency. and mag. Presid. Scarsdale Hadassah, 1960-68. Chmn. Westchester county, Bonds for Israel, 1960-68; trustee Kol AMI-JCC, White Plains, N.Y.; assoc. Jewish Mus.; sponsor Lilly Bruck Lieb Creative Writing Program, Purchase Coll., SUNY; mem. pres.'s coun. White Plains (N.Y.) Hosp. Recipient Woman of Yr. award Anti Defamation League, 1972. Democrat. Home: 25 Murray Hill Rd Scarsdale NY 10583-2829 Personal E-mail: lblone@aol.com.

PORT, ROBERT FREDERICK, linguist; b. Chgo., June 24, 1943; s. Frederick James and Edith Whitney Port; m. Diane Keeley, June 11, 1967; children: Nicholas, Cynthia, Juliet. MA, Columbia U., NYC, 1971; PhD in Linguistics, U. Conn., Storrs, 1976. Prof. Ind. U., Ind., 1976—. Author: (book) Mind as Motion. Home: 5975 Handy Rd Bloomington IN 47401 Office: Ind Univ Bloomington IN 47405 Office Fax: 812-855-5363. Business E-Mail: port@indiana.edu.

PORT, TAMARA LYNNE, biology professor, writer; b. Grand Rapids, Mich., Sept. 10, 1967; d. Glades Fredrick and Sue Carol Guy; m. David Foster Port, Aug. 4, 2004; children: Leo Foster, Kayla Nicole Belmont, Sophie Evelyn. BS, Grand Valley State U., Allendale, Mich., 1991; MS, Bucknell U., Lewisburg, Pa., 1994. Feature writer microbiology Suite101.com, Vancouver, British Columbia, Canada, 2007—; adj. biology prof. Kalamazoo Valley CC, 2007—; sci. & nature channel guide Lestout.com, 2008—. Learning Tech. Innovation grant, Kalamazoo Valley CC, 2009. Office: Kalamazoo Valley CC 6767 W O Ave Kalamazoo MI 49009 Personal E-mail: tamiport@yahoo.com. Business E-Mail: tport@kvcc.edu.

PORT, WHITNEY EVE, television personality, apparel designer; b. LA, Mar. 4, 1985; d. Jeffery and Vicki Lyn (Woskoff) Port. BA in Gender Studies, U. So. Calif., 2007. Intern Women's Wear Daily; intern, fashion contbr. Teen Vogue, LA, 2005—07; stylist The Peoples Revolution, 2007—08; intern in-house pub. rels. Diane von Furstenberg (DVF), NYC, 2008—; designer Whitney Eve collection, 2008—. Co-star (TV reality series) The Hills, 2006—08, star The City, 2009—. Office: Diane von Furstenberg 874 Washington St New York NY 10014-1723*

PORTAL, GILBERT MARCEL ADRIEN, oil industry executive; b. Paris, Aug. 2, 1930; came to U.S., 1982; s. Emmanuel Jules and Henriette Josephine (Bonnard) P.; m. Monique Janine Adam, July 12, 1951; children: Dominique, Veronique, Marc-Emmanuel. Baccalaureate, Lycee Charlemagne U., Paris, 1949; Ingenieur Civil des Mines, Sch. of Mines, St. Etienne, 1955; diplome du C.P.A., Ctr. Advanced Bus., Paris, 1969; auditeur 30 eme session IHEDN, Higher Studies Nat. Defense, Paris, 1978. Geophysicist Societe Nationale Elf Aquitaine, Sahara, Algeria, 1957-63; exploration mgr. north sea, 1963-65, dep. exec. v.p. Europe, 1965-68, dep. exec. v.p. North and South Am., 1968-70, chief exec. officer Iraq, 1970-72, dir., chief exec. officer Gabon, Africa, 1972-76, dep. exec. v.p. hydrocarbons, 1976-78, exec. v.p. North Africa, Mid. East, Far East, 1978-82; pres. Elf Aquitaine Petroleum, Houston, 1982-89; chmn., chief exec. officer Elf Exploration, Inc., Houston, 1989-90; sec.-gen. European Petroleum Industry Assn., 1990-95; ptnr. G.M.H. Internat. Oil and Gas Consulting, Paris, 1995—; pres. internat. devel. Howard Energy Internat. LLC, 1999—2002. Served to lt. French Army, 1955-57. Decorated Legion of Honor (France), Nat. Merit Order (France); Equatorial Star (Gabon). Mem. Cercle Royal Gaulois Artistique et Littéraire. Roman Catholic. Office Phone: (33) 1 45 58 01 02. Business E-Mail: gmh@portal-consult.com.

PORTALE, ALFRED, chef, restaurant owner; b. 1958; married. Grad., Culinary Inst. Am., 1981. Exec. chef Gotham Bar and Grill, NYC, 1985—87, exec. chef, ptnr., 1987—; ptnr. One Fifth Avenue, NYC, 1992—. Mem. Singapore Airlines Internat. Chef Panel; guest judge Top Chef, 2007. Author: (cookbooks) Gotham Bar and Grill Cookbook, 1997 (Julia Child Cookbook award, 1998), 12 Seasons Cookbook, 2001, Simple Pleasures, 2004. Recipient Ivy award, Restaurants & Institutions mag., 1990; named Best Chef in NY, 1993, Most Outstanding Chef in Nation, James Beard Found., 2006; named to Who's Who in Food & Beverage in Am., 1989. Office: Gotham Bar & Grill 12 E 12th St New York NY 10003-4498 Office Fax: 212-627-7810.

PORTELA, ANTONIO GOUVEA, retired mechanical engineer, researcher; b. Lisbon, Portugal, Jan. 26, 1918; s. Raul Lello Portella and Esther Gouvea Portela; married, Sept. 29, 1965; 2 children. Engr. degree, Inst. Superior Tecnico, Lisbon, 1960; prof. degree, Inst. Sup. Tecn., Lisbon, 1958. Cert. mech. engring. Contbr. articles to profl. jours. Mem. AAAS, ASME, Am. Nuclear Soc., N.Y. Acad. Scis., Academia de Engenharia of Portugal. Office: Inst Superior Tecnico Av Rovisco Paes Lisbon Portugal

PORTE-LEWIS, AMI LYNN, special education educator, school psychologist; b. Hammond, Ind., Aug. 27, 1975; d. James Edward and Debra Lynn Porte; m. Andrew Michael Lewis, June 15, 2002. BA in Psychology, Ind. U., Bloomington, 1998; MEd, ednl. specialist in sch. psychology with highest distinction, Valparaiso U., Ind., 2003. Mental health advisor St. Margaret Mercy Hosp., Dyer, Ind., 1998—2002; sch. psychologist Lincoln-Way Co-op 843, New Lenox, Ill., 2003—06; asst. pupil pers. dir. New Lenox Sch. Dist. 122, Ill., 2006—08, dir. pupil pers. senate. Adv. mem. Valparaiso U., 2001—03; new psychologist mentor New Lenox Sch. Dist., 2005—06. Named one of Those Who Make a Difference, New Lenox Sch. Dist., 2005. Mem.: Ill. Alliance Adminstrn. Spl. Edn., Nat. Assn. Sch. Psychologists. Avocations: travel, bicycling, wine tasting.

PORTELL, KEITH S, application developer, consultant; s. Sherman Melvin and Caroline Margaret Portell; m. Claudia Kane Epting, July 14, 1996; children: Andrew Justin, Aaron Michael. BS in info sys. mgmt., U. Of Md. U. Coll., 1995—97; Database Systems Technologies Grad. Cert., U. of Md. U. Coll., 2001—03, MS in computer sys. mgmt., 2001—04. MCSE Microsoft, 1997, cert. Novell Master Network Engineer Novell, 1994. Supr. Six Flags Corp., Houston, 1982—88; sys. analyst Giant Food, Inc., Landover, Md., 1988—94; lan/wan engr. Bus. Network Assoc., Annapolis, Md., 1994—95; network adminstr. Micros Systems, Inc., Beltsville, Md., 1995; lead network engr. Zurich Personal Ins., Balt., 1996—97; meta data architect Mayo Clinic, Jacksonville, Fla., 1997—. Contbr. articles. Mgmt. dir. Jaycees, Annapolis, Md., 1996—98. Mem.: Health Data Warehousing Assn. (assoc.), Am. Med. Informatics Assn (assoc.). Independent. Christian. Achievements include invention of Medical Data Trust - Mayo Clinic. Avocations: travel, reading, computers. Home: 6935 La Loma Dr Jacksonville FL 32217 Office: Mayo Clinic 4500 San Pablo Rd #VAS153A Jacksonville FL 32224 Personal E-mail: keith@keithportell.net. Business E-Mail: portell.keith@mayo.edu.

PORTENIER, WALTER JAMES, aerospace engineer; b. Davenport, Iowa, Oct. 9, 1927; s. Walter Cleveland and Doris Lucile (Williams) P.; m. Martha L. Dallam, Aug. 26, 1950 (dec. Apr. 1986); children: Andrea Ellen, Renee Suzanne; m. Patty Grosskopf Caldwell, Oct. 3, 1992. B in Aero Engring., U. Minn., 1950; MS in Aero Engring., U. So. Calif., 1958, Engr. in Aerospace Engring., 1969. Sr. engr. aerodynamics N.Am. Aviation, LA, 1951-61; MTS project engr., mgr. The Aerospace Corp., El Segundo, Calif., 1961-85; instr. U. So. Calif., LA, 1979; cons. L-Systems, Inc., El Segundo, 1985-89. Pres., bd. dirs. First United Meth. Ch., Santa Monica, Calif., 1988-90; judge, range officer Internat. Shooting Union, 1989—. Recipient Bronze medal Internat. Shooting Union, 1990, Silver medal Internat. Shooting Union, 1996. Fellow Am. Inst. Aeronautics and Astronautics (assoc.). Republican. Achievements include discovery of F-100 wing transonic buffet solution, blowing definition and test, design definition and test of area variation, F-108 mach 3 cruise canard and shock lift effectiveness, XB-70 transport wing definition for subsonic lift and supersonic cruise; re-entry systems analysis of vehicle design, payload, observables for systems procurement and technical direction; development of re-entry technology support for nosetip shape change, boundary layer transition, flow field codes, maneuvering technology; DoD-space transportation system support for space transportation system management (program definitions, manpower); launch on demand requirements; support of new booster systems performance options; reliability review of current systems; re-entry systems test in arms control environment; definition of space transportation system DoD reference missions and mission modeling for cost effectiveness, effective V/STOL aircraft implementation options. Home and Office: 7334 Donatello Ct Naples FL 34114

PORTER, AMY M., legislative staff member; BA in Internat. Politics, Pa. State U., 1993. Adminstrv. asst., legis. dir., Rep. Ed Royce US House of Reps., Washington, chief of staff to Rep. Ed Royce, 2002—, profl. staff, fgn. affairs com., 2008. Republican. Office: 2185 Rayburn House Office Bldg Washington DC 20515 Office Phone: 202-225-4111. Office Fax: 202-226-0335.*

PORTER, ANDREW CALVIN, dean, psychologist, educator; b. Huntington, Pa., July 10, 1942; s. Rutherford and Grace (Johnson) P.; children: Matthew, Anna, John, Joe, Kate. BS, Ind. State U., 1963; MS, U. Wis., 1965, PhD, 1967. Vis. asst. prof. Ind. State U., 1967; asst. prof. ednl. psychology Mich. State U., East Lansing, 1967—70, dir. office rsch. consultation, 1967—73, assoc. prof. ednl. psychology, 1970—74; vis. scholar Nat. Inst. Edn., Washington, 1973—74, chief measurement and methodology divsn., 1974—75; prof. ednl. psychology Mich. State U., East Lansing, 1974—88; assoc. dir. basic skills group Nat. Inst. Edn., Washington, 1975—76; dir. Sch. Advanced Studies Coll. Edn. Mich. State U., East Lansing, 1979—81, assoc. dean rsch. and grad. study Coll. Edn., 1981—85; Anderson-Bascom prof. edn., prof. ednl. psychology U. Wis., Madison, 1988—2003, dir. Wis. Ctr. Edn. Rsch., 1988—2003; Patricia and Rodes Hart prof. ednl. leadership and policy Vanderbilt U., Nashville, 2003—07, dir. Learning Scis. Inst., 2003—07; dean Grad. Sch. Edn., U. Pa., 2007—. Mem adv. com. What Works Clearinghouse Inst. Edn. Scis., 2002-, steering com. math./sci. partnerships, Nat. Acad. Sci., 2003-2005, nat. assessment governing bd., 2004-; chmn. adv. coun. on edn. stats., U.S. Dept. Edn., 1994-2001; chair bd. Internat. Studies, Nat. Acad. Sci., Nat. Rsch. Coun., 1998-2001 Editor: (with A. Gamoran) Methodological Advances in Cross-National Surveys of Educational Achievement, 2002; mem. editl. bd. Tchrs. Coll. Record, 1995—, Am. Ednl. Rsch. Jour., 2004—. Bd. dirs. Madison Urban League, 1992-96. Recipient Disting. Alumni award, Ind. State U., 1994, Sch. Edn. Dean's Club Faculty Disting. Achievement Award, U. Wis.-Madison, 1996, Crystal Apple Award, Mich. State U., 2000, Alumni Achievement award, U. Wis., Madison, 2005. Mem. Am. Ednl. Rsch. Assn. (pres. 2001, Outstanding Reviewer award 2003), Nat. Coun. Edn. Measurement, Nat. Coun. Tchrs. Math., Nat. Acads. (lifetime nat. mem.), Nat. Acad. Edn. (v.p. 2005), Phi Delta Kappa (life). Office: U Pa Grad Sch Edn 3700 Walnut St Philadelphia PA 19104 Office Phone: 215-898-7014. E-mail: andyp@gse.upenn.edu.

PORTER, BIGGS C., corporate financial executive; B in Acctg., Duke U.; M in Profl. Acctg., U. Tex., Austin. CPA. Audit prin. Arthur Young & Co.; corp. controller, asst. treas. Vought Aircraft; CFO integrated systems sector Northrop Grumman, CFO comml. aircraft divsn.; sr. v.p., corp. controller TXU Corp., Dallas; v.p., corp. controller Raytheon Co., Waltham, Mass., 2003—, acting CFO, 2005—06; CFO Tenet Healthcare Corp., Dallas, 2006—. Mem.: AICPA. Office: Tenet Healthcare Corp 13737 Noel Rd Dallas TX 75240 Office Phone: 781-522-3000.

PORTER, BLAINE ROBERT MILTON, sociology professor, psychology professor; b. Morgan, Utah, Feb. 24, 1922; s. Brigham Ernest and Edna (Brough) P.; m. Elizabeth Taylor, Sept 27, 1943 (dec.); children: Claudia Jackson, Roger B., David T., Patricia A. Hintze, Corinna; m. Myrna Katherine Kennedy, Feb. 26, 1988. Student, Utah State U., 1940-41; BS, Brigham Young U., 1947, MA, 1949; PhD (Grant Found. fellow family life edn. 1951-52), Cornell U., 1952. Instr. sociology Iowa State Coll., 1949-51; asst. prof. sociology and child devel. Iowa State U., 1952-55; prof., chmn. dept. human devel. and family relationships Brigham Young U., 1955-65, dean Coll. Family Living, 1966-80, univ. prof., 1980-87. Vis. prof. Fulbright rsch. scholar U. London, 1965-66; vis. prof. U. Wurzberg, 1980-81, 83; facilitator human rels. workshops for the Human Devel. Inst., Denver, 1988-98, pres., CEO Families for Children Internat., Inc., 2001—. Editor: The Latter-day Saint Family, 1963, rev. edit., 1966; editor quar. jour.: Family Perspective, 1966-82; contbr. articles to profl. jours. Pres. elect Iowa Coun. Family Rels., 1954-55; pres. Utah Coun. Family Rels. Coun., 1957-58; chmn. sect. marriage counseling Nat. Coun. Family Rels., 1958-59, bd. dirs., 1957-60, exec. com., 1958-72, pres., 1963-64; bd. dirs. Am. Family Soc., 1975-85. Pilot USAAF, 1942-45. Recipient Prof. of Yr. award Brigham Young U., 1964. Mem. Am. Home Econs. Assn. (vice chmn. sect. family relations and child devel. 1955-56), Am. Sociol. Assn. (sec. sect. on family 1964-67), Am. Assn. Marriage and Family Therapy, Am. Psychol. Assn., Soc. Research in Child Devel., Sigma Xi, Phi Kappa Phi (chpt. pres. 1969-71) Home: 1675 Pine Ln Provo UT 84604-2163 Office: 4505 HBLL Brigham Young U Provo UT 84602 Personal E-mail: porter22@comcast.net.

PORTER, BRUCE JACKMAN, computer engineer, application developer, portfolio manager, civil engineer; b. El Paso, Tex., Aug. 7, 1954; s. Covington Baskin and Carolyn Fee (Bruce) P.; m. Janette Anne Brown, Oct. 19, 1985; children: Laura, Holly, Travis. BS, US Mil. Acad., 1976; MS in Computer Sci., Stanford U., 1985, MS in Civil Engring., 1985; grad., U.S. Army War Coll., 1997. Engr. in tng., Pa. Commd. 1st lt. U.S. Army, 1979-80, advanced through grades to lt. col., 1993, co-commdr. 17th armored engr. bn. Ft. Hood, Tex., 1977-80, constrn. engr. Misawa, Japan, 1981-83, orgnl. evaluator Ft. Leavenworth, Kans., 1989-90, ops. officer 5th engr. combat bn. Saudi Arabia and Iraq, 1990-91; assoc. prof. mathematics U.S. Mil. Acad., West Point, NY, 1985-88; chief concepts officer USA Engr. Sch., Ft. Leonard Wood, Mo., 1991-93; logistics assistance officer 1st Cavalry Divsn., Ft. Hood, Tex., 1993-94; comdg. officer 20th Engr. Bn., 1st Cavalry Divsn., Ft. Hood, Tex., 1994-96; sr. engr. trainer Nat. Tng. Ctr., Ft. Irwin, Calif., 1997-98; cmdr., engr. brigade 4th Infantry Divn., Ft. Hood, Tex., 1998—99; exec. officer Army chief of staff for ops. Pentagon, Washington, 1999—2001; investment rep. Edward Jones & Co., Buellton, Calif., 2001—. Pioneer new courses in computer theory and discrete math. U.S. Mil. Acad., 1987-88; proponent Army Engr. Restructive Initiative, 1991-92; panel mem. Army Study Team for Battle Dynamics, 1992; mem. Summer Study for Chief of Staff of Army, 1992. Co-author: Army Keystone Operations Field Manual, 1993; pub. papers on combat engr. reorgn., 1991-92, 98. Decorated DSM, Bronze Star, Legion of Merit. Home: 345 Meadowlark Rd Santa Ynez CA 93460 Office: 175 H McMurray Rd Buellton CA 93427 Office Phone: 805-688-9079.

PORTER, CHARLES KING, advertising executive; b. Mpls., Oct. 10, 1945; s. King E. and Bernetta Porter Andrews; m. Margit Gammeltoft, Feb. 26, 1972; children: Kristin, Catherine, James. BS in Journalism, U. Minn., 1967. Ptnr. Breen & Porter Co., Miami, Fla., 1974-85; pres. Porter Creative Svcs., Miami, 1985-88, Crispin, Porter & Bogusky Advt., Miami, 1988-97, chmn., ptnr., 1997—. Dir. Miami Ad Sch. Trustee Beacon Coun., Miami, 1988—. Recipient Nat. Addy award Am. Advt. Fedn., 1991, 92, Andy award Advt. Club N.Y., 1993, 94. Mem. Am. Assn. Advt Agys. (forum, Nat. A Plus award 1991, 94, 95, 96). Presbyterian. Avocations: skiing, travel, history. Office: Crispin Porter & Bogusky Advt 2699 S Bayshore Dr Miami FL 33133-5408

PORTER, DAN A., biology professor, director; MS in Biology, West Tex. A&M U., Canyon, 1990. Rsch. assoc. West Tex. A&M U., 1990—92; prof. biology Amarillo Coll., Tex., 1992—, dir. natural history mus., 1995—. Cons. Region 16 Edn. Svc. Ctr., Tex., 1995—2008. Mem.: Tex. CC Tchrs. Assn., Southwestern Assn. Naturalist, Tex. Assn. Biology Tchrs., Nat. Assn. Biology Tchrs. Business E-Mail: daporter@actx.edu.

PORTER, DANIEL J., oil industry executive; B in Chem. Engring., U. Akron, Ohio. Mgmt. positions Std. Oil Ohio, BP/Amoco; regional pres. No. Gt. Plains Region, mgr. Mandan, ND refinery Tesoro Corp., 2001—02, pres. NW region Tesoro Refining and Mktg. Co., 2002—05, mgr. Anacortes refinery, 2002—05, sr. v.p. mktg., 2005—07, sr. v.p. supply & optimization, 2007—08, sr. v.p. refining, 2008—. Office: Tesoro Corp 300 Concord Plz San Antonio TX 78216-6999 Office Phone: 210-283-2000.

PORTER, DARWIN FRED, writer; b. Greensboro, NC, Sept. 13, 1937; s. Numie Rowan and Hazel Lee (Phillips) P. BA, U. Miami, 1959. Bur. chief Miami Herald, 1959-60; v.p. Haggart Assoc., NYC, 1961-64; editor, author Arthur Frommer Inc., NYC, 1964-67, Frommer/Pasmantier Pub. Corp., NYC, 1967-86, Prentice Hall Press, NYC, 1987-90, Simon & Schuster, NYC, 1991—. Author: Frommer Travel Guides to: England, 1964, Spain, 1966, Scandinavia, 1967, Los Angeles, 1969, London, 1970, Lisbon/Madrid, 1972, Paris, 1972, Morocco, 1974, Rome, 1974, Portugal, 1968, England, 1969, Italy, 1969, Germany, 1970, France, 1970, Caribbean, Bermuda, the Bahamas, 1980, Switzerland, 1984, Austria and Hungary, 1984, Bermuda and the Bahamas, 1985, Scotland and Wales, 1985, the Virgin Islands, 1991, Scotland, 1992, Jamaica/Barbados, 1992, Puerto Rico, 1992, the Caribbean, 1993, Bermuda, 1993, the Bahamas, 1993, Austria, 1993, Madrid & the Costa del Sol, 1993, San Francisco, 1996, California, 1996, Caribbean Cruises, 1996, Caribbean Ports of Call, 1996, Georgia and the Carolinas, 1996, Charleston and Savannah, 1996, Munich and The Bavarian Alps, 1996, Vienna & the Danube, 1996, Guide to Caribbean Cruises, 1997, Frommer's Europe, 1997, Frommer's Venice, 1997, Barcelona, Madrid & Seville, 1997, Frommer's Portable London, 1998,

Frommer's Portable Bahamas, 1998, Frommer's Portable Paris, 1998, Frommer's Portable Berlin, 1999; author: Butterflies in Heat, 1976, Marika, 1977, Venus, 1982, Razzle-Dazzle, 1998, Blood Moon, 1998, Frommer's Sweden, 1999, Frommer's Denmark, 1999, Midnight in Savannah, 2000, Hollywood's Silent Closet, 2000, Frommer's Frankfurt, 2001, Frommer's Great Britain, 2001, Bahamas for Dummies, 2002, Caribbean for Dummies, 2002, Rhinestone Country, 2002, Frommer's Charleston, 2003, Frommer's Savannah, 2003, Frommer's Sicily, 2003, Frommer's Norway, 2003, France for Dummies, 2003, Frommer's Cayman Islands, 2003, Frommer's Dominican Republic, 2003, The Secret Life of Humphrey Bogart, 2003, Katharine the Great, 2004, Fommer's Europe By Rail, 2004, Howard Hughes: Hell's Angel, 2004, Frommer's Seville and Southern Spain, 2005, Frommer's Andalusia, 2005, Irreverent Paris, 2005, Brando Unzipped, 2006, Frommer's Tuscany Day by Day, 2006, Jacko: His Rise & Fall, 2007, Frommer's Dream Vacations, 2007, Hollywood Babylon- It's Back, 2008, Merv Griffin: A Life In The Closet, 2009, Paul Newman: the Man Behind the Baby Blues. Recipient Silver award Internat. Film and TV Festival NY, 1977. Mem. Soc. Am. Travel Writers, Smithsonian Assoc., Nat. Trust for Hist. Preservation, Sigma Delta Chi. Home: 75 Saint Marks Pl Staten Island NY 10301-1606 Home Phone: 718-556-9410. Personal E-mail: porterandprince@hotmail.com.

PORTER, DAVID, computer software company executive; BS in Fin., East Ctrl. Okla. State U. Joined as clk./cashier Wal-Mart Stores, Inc., Broken Bow, Okla., 1981, various roles of increasing responsibility in store ops., merchandising & info. tech., then v.p., gen. mdse. mgr. entertainment; head worldwide product distbn. DreamWorks Animation SKG, Glendale, Calif., 2007—09; corp. v.p. retail stores Microsoft Corp., Redmond, Wash., 2009—. Office: Corp Hdqs One Microsoft Way Redmond WA 98052 Office Phone: 425-882-8080. Office Fax: 425-936-7329.*

PORTER, DAVID HUGH, musician, classicist, academic administrator, music educator; b. NYC, Oct. 29, 1935; s. Hugh B. and Ethel K. (Flentye) P.; m. Laudie Ernestine Dimmette, June 21, 1958 (dec. Nov., 1986); children: Hugh, Everett, Helen, David; m. Helen Louise Nelson, Aug. 24, 1987. BA with highest honors, Swarthmore Coll., 1958; PhD (Danforth Grad. fellow, Woodrow Wilson Grad. fellow), Princeton U., 1962; student, Phila. Conservatory Music, 1955-61. Instr. in classics and music Carleton Coll., Northfield, Minn., 1962-63, asst. prof., 1963-68, assoc. prof., 1968-73, prof., 1973-87, William H. Laird prof. liberal arts, 1974-87, pres. faculty, 1980-82, coll. pres., 1986-87; pres. Skidmore Coll., Saratoga Springs, NY, 1987—99, prof. classics, 1987—99; vis. prof. classics Williams Coll., Williamstown, Mass., 1999—2008, Harry C. Payne vis. prof. liberal arts, 2000—08; Case disting. vis. prof. classics Ind. U., 2008; Tisch Family disting. prof. Skidmore Coll., 2008—. Phi Beta Kappa vis. lectr., 1979-92, vis. scholar, 1994-95; vis. prof. classics Princeton U., 1986; recitalist, lectr., especially on contemporary music, at colls., univs. throughout U.S., U.K., on radio and TV; chmn. Hudson-Mohawk Assn., 1990-92, Inst. for Internat. Edn. of Students, 2004—. Author: Only Connect: Three Studies in Greek Tragedy, 1987, Horace's Poetic Journey: A Reading of Odes I-III, 1987, Virginia Woolf and Logan Pearsall Smith, 2002, Virginia Woolf and the Hogarth Press, 2004, The Omega Workshops and the Hogarth Press, 2008, On the Divide: The Many Lives of Willa Cather, 2008, Seeking Life Whole: Willa Cather and the Brewsters, 2009; editor: Carleton Remembered, 1909-86, 1987, The Not Quite Innocent Bystander: Writings of Edward Steuermann, 1989; contbr. articles to profl. jours. Rsch. fellow NEH, 1969-70, 83-84, Am. Coun. Learned Socs., 1976-77 Mem. Am. Philological Assn., Classical Assn. Atlantic States. Democrat. Avocations: hiking, reading, collecting rugs and books. Home: 5 Birch Run Dr Saratoga Springs NY 12866-1023 Personal E-mail: ddodger@skidmore.edu.

PORTER, DAVID LINDSEY, history and political science professor, writer; b. Holyoke, Mass., Feb. 18, 1941; s. Willis Hubert and Lora Frances (Bowen) P.; m. Marilyn Esther Platt, Nov. 28, 1970; children: Kevin, Andrea. BA magna cum laude, Franklin Coll., 1963; MA, Ohio U., 1965; PhD, Pa. State U., 1970. Asst. prof. history Rensselaer Poly. Inst., Troy, NY, 1970-75, co-dir. Am. studies program, 1972-74; ednl. adminstrv. asst. Civil Svc. Office State of N.Y., Troy, 1975-76; asst. prof. history William Penn U., Oskaloosa, Iowa, 1976-77, assoc. prof. history, 1977-82, prof. history and polit. sci., 1982-86, Louis Tuttle Shangle prof. history and polit. sci., 1986—, chmn. Sperry & Hutchinson Found. lectureship series, 1980-82, acting chair social and behavioral scis. divsn., 2000—01. Supr. legis. internship program Iowa Gen. Assembly, 1978—, records inventory project Mahaska County, 1978-79, internship program Washington Ctr., 1985—; active Franklin D. Roosevelt Meml. Commn.; chpt. adviser Phi Alpha Theta, 1977—. Author: The Seventy-sixth Congress and World War II, 1939-40, 1979, Congress and the Waning of the New Deal, 1980, Michael Jordan: A Biography, 2007; co-author: The San Diego Padres Encyclopedia, 2002; contbr. Dictionary of American Biography, 1981, 1988, 1994, 1995, Directory of Teaching Innovations in History, 1981, The Book of Lists #3, 1983, Biographical Dictionary of Internationalists, 1983, The Hero in Transition, 1983, Herbert Hoover and the Republican Era: A Reconsideration, 1984, The History of Mahaska County, Iowa, 1984, Franklin D. Roosevelt, His Life and Times: An Encyclopedic View, 1985, The Rating Game in American Politics: An Interdisciplinary Approach, 1987, Sport History, 1987, Book of Days, 1988, Sports Encyclopedia North America, 1988, The Harry S. Truman Encyclopedia, 1989, Encyclopedia of Major League Baseball Team Histories: The National League, 1991, Twentieth Century Sports Champions, 1992, Statesmen Who Changed the World, 1993, Ency. Modern Social Issues, 1996, Advanced Placement U.S. History 2, 1996, Encyclopedia of United States Popular Culture, 1997, Encyclopedia of Civil Rights, 1997, Encyclopedia of Propaganda, 1997, Total Padres, 1997, The Scribner Encyclopedia of American Lives, 1998, 1999, 2001, 2004, 2007, American National Biography, 1999, The Sixties in America, 1999, Racial and Ethnic Relations in America, 1999, History of Mahaska County, Iowa, 2000, Great Athletes, rev. edit., 2001, The Scribner Encyclopedia of American Lives, Sports Figures, 2002, Great Events: 1900-2001, rev. edit., 2002, The Scribner Encyclopedia of American Lives, The 1960's, 2003, Encyclopedia of American History, The Development of the Industrial United States, 1870—99; contbr.:; contbr. Dictionary of American History, 3rd. edit., 2003, Encyclopedia of the Great Depression, 2003, Native Americans in Sports, 2004, The Fifties in America, 2005; contbr.: The Seventies in America, 2006, Great Events from History: The 20th Century, 1941—70; editor, contbr. Biographical Dictionary of American Sports: vols. Baseball, 1987, Football, 1987, Outdoor Sports, 1988, Basketball and Other Indoor Sports, 1989, 1989-92 Supplement for Baseball, Football, Basketball and Other Sports, 1992, 1992-95 Supplement for Baseball, Football, Basketball and Other Sports, 1995, African-American Sports Greats, 1995, Baseball, revised and expanded edit., 3 vols., 2000, Latino and African American Athletes Today, 2004, Basketball: A Biographical Dictionary, 2005, compiler A Cumulative Index to the Biographical Dictionary of American Sports, 1993, assoc. editor (with others) American National Biography, 24 vols., 1999; contbr. articles to profl. jours., local newspapers. Mem. Franklin D. Roosevelt Meml. Commn.; participant Green Bay Packers Project, 1992; historian United Meth. Ch.; official scorer Babe Ruth State Tournament, 2000, 03. Grantee NSF, 1967, NEH, 1974, Rensselaer Poly. Inst., 1974, Eleanor Roosevelt Inst., 1981, William Penn Univ., 1986, 89, 92; recipient Choice Outstanding Acad. Book awards, 1989. Mem. AAUP, Am. Hist. Assn., Orgn. Am. Historians, N.Am. Soc. for Sport History, Soc. History Am. Fgn. Rels., Ctr. for Study of the Presidency, Soc. Am. Baseball Rsch., Friends of the Nat. Baseball Hall of Fame, Popular Culture Assn., Profl. Football Rschrs. Assn., Coll. Football Rschrs. Assn., Coll. Football Hist. Soc., State Hist. Soc. Iowa, Mahaska County Hist. Soc. (v.p.), Iowa State UN Assn. (chmn. ann. assembly 1982, nat. soc. Disting. Svc. award 1981), Mahaska County UN Assn. (v.p.), Oskaloosa Babe Ruth League (bd. dirs.), Oskaloosa Cmty. Choir, Friends of Oskaloosa Pub. Libr. (mem. nominating com.), Friends of the Nat. Baseball Hall of Fame, Phi Alpha Theta, Kappa Delta Pi. Home: 2314 Ridgeway Ave Oskaloosa IA 52577-9109 Office: William Penn Univ Dept Social and Behavioral Scis Divsn Oskaloosa IA 52577-1757

PORTER, DIXIE LEE, retired insurance company executive, consultant; b. Bountiful, Utah, June 7, 1931; d. John Lloyd and Ida May (Robinson) Mathis. BS, U. Calif., Berkeley, 1956, MBA, 1957. CLU. Personnel aide City of Berkeley, 1957-59; employment supr. Kaiser Health Found., LA, 1959-60; personnel analyst UCLA, 1961-63; personnel mgr. Reuben H. Donnelley, Santa Monica, Calif., 1963-64; personnel officer Good Samaritan Hosp., San Jose, Calif., 1965-67; fgn. svc. officer AID, Saigon, Vietnam, 1967-71; gen. agt. Charter Life Ins. Co., LA, 1972-77, Kennesaw Life Ins. Co., Atlanta, 1978—2007, Phila. Life Ins. Co., San Francisco, 1978—2007; pres. Womens Ins. Enterprises, Ltd., 1976—2007; ret., 2007. Cons. in field. Co-chair Comprehensive Health Planning Commn. Santa Clara County, Calif., 1973-76; bd. dirs. Family Care, 1978-80, Aegis Health Corp., 1977-92, U. Calif. Sch. Bus. Adminstrn., Berkeley, 1974-76; task force on equal access to econ. power U.S. Nat. Womens Agenda, 1977—, Lake County Transp. Coun., 2000—. With USMC, 1950-52. Mem. AAUW, CLU Soc., U. Calif. Alumni Assn., U. Calif. Sch. Bus. Adminstrn. Alumni Assn., Bus. and Profl. Women, Prytanean Alumni, The Animal Soc. Los Gatos/Saratoga (pres. 1987-90), The Am. Legion, Beta Gamma Sigma, Phi Chi Theta. Republican. Episcopalian. Office Phone: 707-263-9271.

PORTER, DOUGLAS W., health products executive; V.p. transformation CIGNA HealthCare, 1999—2001, v.p. employer svcs., 2001—02; sr. v.p. client svcs. Express Scripts, Inc., 2002—04, sr. v.p. client and patient svcs., 2004—. Office: Express Scripts Inc 13900 Riverport Dr Maryland Heights MO 63043 Office Phone: 314-770-1666.

PORTER, GEORGE HOMER, III, physician, medical foundation executive; b. Charlotte, NC, Sept. 7, 1933; s. George Homer Jr. and Sallie Mapp (Jacob) P.; m. Virginia Pillow, Apr. 5, 1958; 1 child, Virginia Mapp (dec.). AB magna cum laude, Duke U., 1954, MD with honors, 1958. Diplomate Am. Bd. Internal Medicine, Am. Bd. Hematology, Am. Bd. Med. Oncology. Intern internal medicine Duke U. Med. Ctr., Durham, NC, 1958-59; asst. resident medicine, instr. medicine Barnes Hosp., Washington U. Sch. Medicine, St. Louis, 1959-60; sr. resident physician The Peter Bent Brigham Hosp., Boston, 1960-61; clin. assoc. medicine, fellow hematology NIH, Bethesda, Md., 1961-64; staff hematologist-oncologist Ochsner Clinic, New Orleans, 1964—; chmn. emeritus, dept. hematology/oncology Ochsner Health Sys., New Orleans; trustee, mem. exec. com. Alton Ochsner Med. Found., New Orleans, 1973—, pres., chief exec. officer, 1980—2001; pres. Ochsner Clinic Found., New Orleans, 2001—. Prin. investigator Southeastern Cancer Study Group, 1973-78; bd. dirs. Eye, Ear, Nose and Throat Hosp., New Orleans, 1986—, Hibernia Corp., Hiberna Nat. Bank, New Orleans, 1980-92. Bd. dirs. Am. Cancer Soc., New Orleans, 1978-89, La. Cancer and Lung Trust Fund, 1980—, Leukemia Soc. Am., 1968-72, The Chamber, New Orleans, 1984-88, Bus. Task Force on Edn., New Orleans, 1985—, Bur. Govtl. Rsch., New Orleans, 1988—, Metrovision Partnership, New Orleans, 1990—. Named Tchr. of Yr., Alton Ochsner Med. Found., l967. Fellow ACP (life), Internat. Soc. Hematology; mem. AMA, ABA (mem. sect. on med. schs.), AAAS, Internat. Assn. for Study Lung Cancer (founding), Am. Fedn. Clin. Rsch., Am. Hosp. Assn., Am. Assn. Clin. Oncology, Am. Assn. Hematology, Am. Soc. Internal Medicine, Internat. AIDS Soc., La. Med. Soc., Am. Cancer Soc., Orleans Med. Soc. Soc. Surg. Oncology, Am. Coll. Legal Medicine (assoc.-in-medicine, bd. trustees NO/AIDS Task Force, bd. dirs. Acad. Med. Ctr. Consortium), Internat. Soc. for AIDS Edn., Assn. for Health Care Rsch., Mensa, SAR, Royal Soc. St. George, Milton Soc., Confrerie chevaliers du Tastevin, New Orleans Country Club, Boston Club, Century Assn. (N.Y.C.), Pickwick Club, Phi Beta Kappa. Office: Ochsner Clinic Found 1516 Jefferson Hwy New Orleans LA 70121-2429

PORTER, GERALD JOSEPH, mathematician, educator; b. Elizabeth, NJ, Feb. 27, 1937; s. Fred and Tillie Florence (Friedman) P.; m. Judith Deborah Revitch, June 26, 1960; children: Daniel, Rebecca, Michael. AB, Princeton U., 1958; PhD, Cornell U., 1963; MA (hon.), U. Pa., 1971. Instr. MIT, Cambridge, 1963-65; asst. prof. math. U. Pa., Phila., 1965-69, assoc. prof., 1969-75, prof., 1975—2005, prof. emeritus, 2006—, chmn. undergrad. affairs dept. math., 1971-73, assoc. dean computing Sch. Arts and Scis., 1981-91, dir. Interactive Math. Text Project, 1991-96. Chair-elect faculty senate U. Pa., 1992-93, chair, 1993-94, past chair, 1994-95, 2001-02; prin. investigator NSF MAC-MATC Grant, 1997-2001; chair U. Pa. Social Responsibility Adv. Com., 2005-08; chair-elect Pa. Assn. Sr. Emeritus Faculty, 2007-08, chair, 2008-09, past chair, 2009-. Author: (with D.R. Hill) Interactive Linear Algebra, 1996. Mem. Dem. Com., Haverford Twp., Pa., 1976-82, ward leader, 1980-84, treas., 1984-87. Postdoctoral fellow Office Naval Rsch., 1965-66. Mem. Am. Math. Soc., Math. Assn. Am. (chmn. com. computers in math. edn. 1983-86, chmn. investment com. 1986-2003, bd. govs. 1980-83, 86-2002, mem. fin. com. 1986-2000, exec. com. 1992-2002, chmn. audit and budget com. 1988-90, 92, treas. 1992-2002, chair com. on profl. devel. 1995-2001, chair membership com. 2004-07), Nat. Assn. Mathematicians. Democrat. Jewish. Home: 161 Whitemarsh Rd Ardmore PA 19003-1698 Office: U Pa 4N69 DRL 209 S 33rd St Philadelphia PA 19104-6395 Office Phone: 215-898-8467. Business E-Mail: gjporter@math.upenn.edu.

PORTER, GRANT A., investment banker; married. Natural resources group Lehman Brothers, Inc., NYC and London, 1985—2000, now vice chmn. NYC. Corp. trustee The Taft Sch., Watertown, Conn. Named a Top Dealmaker, Dealmaker mag., 2006. Office: Lehman Brothers Inc 745 Seventh Ave New York NY 10019 Office Phone: 212-526-2027. Office Fax: 212-520-0801. Business E-Mail: gporter@lehman.com.

PORTER, JAMES MORRIS, retired judge; b. Cleve., Sept. 14, 1931; s. Emmett Thomas and Mary (Connell) P.; m. Helen Marie Adams, May 31, 1952; children: James E., Thomas W., William M., Daniel J. AB, John Carroll U., 1953; JD, U. Mich., 1957. Bar: Ohio 1957. Assoc. firm M.B. & H.H. Johnson, Cleve., 1957-62, McAfee, Hanning, Newcomer, Hazlett & Wheeler, Cleve., 1962-67; ptnr. firm Squire, Sanders & Dempsey, Cleve., 1967-92; judge Ohio Ct. Appeals, 8th Dist., Cleve., 1993-2000, Cuyahoga County Common Pleas Ct., Cleve., 2001. 1st lt. U.S. Army, 1953-55. Fellow Am. Coll. Trial Lawyers; mem. The Country Club (Cleve.). Republican. Roman Catholic.

PORTER, JEAN MCRAE, counselor; b. Augusta, Ga., Aug. 1, 1949; d. Hugh Burrell and Ruby Collins McRae; m. Ralph S. Porter, Jr., Aug. 17, 1975; children: Bradford Sloan, Jonathan James. BS, Augusta Coll., Ga., 1970; MEd, Clemson U., SC, 1973. Cert. secondary adminstrn., guidance, biology, elem., sci. tchg. Tchr. Davenport Jr. HS, Greer, SC, 1970—71, Greer Middle Sch., 1971—73; counselor Hillcrest Middle Sch., Simpsonville, SC, 1973—75; counselor, tchr. Hughes Middle Sch., Greenville, SC, 1975—84; counselor Wade Hampton HS, Greenville, 1984—90, Bryson Middle Sch., Simpsonville, 1990—94, Woodmont HS, Piedmont, SC, 1994—95, Northwood Middle Sch., Taylors, SC, 1995—, 504 accommodations coord., 2002—. Facilitator Christmas Knights, 1995—. Mem.: NEA, Nat. Assn. Mental Illness, Greenville County Edn. Assn., SC Counselors Assn., SC Edn. Assn. Democrat. Avocations: reading, hiking, raising dogs. Home: 111 Brigham Creek Dr Greer SC 29650 Office: Northwood Middle School 710 Ikes Rd Taylors SC 29687 Office Phone: 864-355-7005. Business E-Mail: jporter@greenville.k12.sc.us.com.

PORTER, JEFFREY R., lawyer; b. 1963; m. Jill Porter; 2 children. BA with high honors in Polit. Sci., cum laude, Bates Coll., 1985; JD, Cornell U., 1988. Bar: Mass. 1988, US Dist. Ct. (Dist. Mass.). Ptnr., chair environ. law sect. Mintz, Levin, Cohn, Ferris, Glovsky & Popeo PC, Boston. Vice chair, bd. dirs. Boston Harbor Island Alliance; vice chair, bd. trustees Nature Conservancy Mass. Chpt.; bur. waste site clean up adv. com. Mass. Dept. Environ. Protection. Mem.: AIM, NAIOP, ABA (environ., energy and resources sect., litig. sect.), Boston Bar Assn., Phi Beta Kappa. Avocations: scuba diving, skiing, politics. Office: Mintz Levin Cohn Ferris Glovsky & Popeo PC One Financial Center Boston MA 02111 Office Phone: 617-348-1711. Office Fax: 617-542-2241. Business E-Mail: jporter@mintz.com.

PORTER, JILL, journalist; b. Phila., Aug. 5, 1946; d. Sidney and Mae (Merion) Chalfin; m. Eric Porter, Mar. 7, 1970 (div. 1975); m. Fred Hamilton, Oct. 28, 1983; 1 child, Zachary. BA, Temple U., 1968. Pub. rels. Manning Smith P.R., Phila., 1968-69; reporter Norristown Times Herald, Norristown, Pa., 1969-72, The Trentonian, Trenton, NJ, 1972-75, The Phila. Daily News, Phila., 1975-79, columnist, 1979—. Instr. Temple U., 1976—80. Contbr. articles to numerous mags. Vol. Phila. Futures, 1994, 95, 96, Phila. Cares, 1997, Career Wardrobe, 2006. Recipient numerous journalism awards. Avocations: dance, biking, reading, flying. Home: 134 Rolling Rd Bala Cynwyd PA 19004-2615 Office: Phila Media Holding LLC Phila Daily News 400 N Broad St Philadelphia PA 19130-4015 Office Phone: 215-854-5850. E-mail: porterj@phillynews.com.

PORTER, JOHN EDWARD, lobbyist, lawyer, former congressman; b. Evanston, Ill., June 1, 1935; s. Harry H. and Beatrice V. P.; 5 children. Attended, MIT; BSBA, Northwestern U., 1957; JD with distinction, U. Mich., 1961; degree (hon.), Northwestern U., Tufts U., Mt. Sinai Sch. Medicine, Oreg. Health Scis. U., Howard U., Rush U. Bar: Ill. 1961, D.C. 2005, U.S. Supreme Ct. 1968. Former honor law grad. atty., appellate div. US Dept. Justice, Washington; mem. Ill. Ho. of Reps., 1973—79, US Congress from 10th Ill. Dist., 1980—2001; ptnr. Hogan & Hartson, Washington, 2001—. Founder, co-chmn. Congl. Human Rights Caucus; legis. sponsor Radio Free Asia; founder Congl. Coalition on Population and Devel.; chmn. Global Legislators Organized for a Balanced Environment; mem. Commn. on Security and Cooperation in Europe; chmn. com. future roles acad. health ctrs.; chmn. com. on presdl. and fed. adv. com. sci. and tech., 2004, 08; co-chmn. Ctr. for Global Devel. Commn. on Weak States and Nat. Security Past editor: Mich. Law Rev. Bd. dirs., chair PBS, trustee, RAND Corp.;vice chair Rsch.! Am., Found. NIH; bd. dirs. Chgo. Botanic Gardens, J.S.Kemper Fed.; hon. trustee Brookings Inst.; trustee emeritus John F. Kennedy Ctr. for Performing Arts; former dir. Rand Corp., Am. Heart Assn., Population Resource Ctr., Princeton, NJ. Recipient Best Legislator award League of Conservation Voters, 1973, Ind. Voters Ill., 1974, Chgo. Crime Commn., 1976, Lorax award Global Tomorrow Coalition, 1989, Spirit of Enterprise award U.S. C. of C., 1988, 89, 90, Golden Bulldog award Watchdogs of the Treasury, 12 times, Taxpayer's Friend award Nat. Taxpayers Union, Taxpayer Superhero award Grace Commn.'s Citizens Against Government Waste, Mary Wood Lasker award for pub. svc., Edwin C. Whitehead award Rsch! Am., Carter award Nat. Found. Infectious Diseases, Pub. Svc. award Fedn. Am. Socs. for Exptl. Biology, Svc award Am. Soc. Cell Biology, Disting. Pub. Svc. award Am. Soc. Microbiology, Pub. Svc. Excellence award Assn. Am. Med. Colls., Lifetime Achievement award Juvenile Diabetes Found., Decade of Brain award Nat. Found. Brain Rsch., Lifetime Achievement award Am. Psychiat. Assn. and Acad. Consortium, Dr. Nathan Davis award AMA, Morris K. Udall Pub. Svc. award Michael J. Fox Found., Pub. Health Continuum award Coalition, Named one of 50 Top Lobbyists, Washingtonian mag., 2007. Mem.: Inst. Medicine, Inter-Am. Dialogue, Coun. Fgn. Rels. Republican. Office: Hogan & Hartson 555 13th St NW Washington DC 20004 Home Phone: 708-684-0890; Office Phone: 202-637-5695. Office Fax: 202-637-5910. E-mail: jeporter@hhlaw.com.

PORTER, JOHN FRANCIS, III, banker; b. Wilmington, Del., Sept. 17, 1934; s. John Francis, Jr. and Eloise Wilhelmina (Berlinger) P.; m. Ann Mayfield, Sept. 8, 1956; children: Leslie Gibson, Nina Porter Winfield, Sophie Porter Rohrer. BA, U. Va., 1956; MBA, U. Del., 1965. With Del. Trust Co., Wilmington, 1958-97, asst. treas., 1960-66, sec., 1966-68, v.p., sec., 1968-72, sr. v.p., sec., 1972-75, exec. v.p., 1975-79, pres., 1979-88; chmn., chief exec. officer Del. Trust Co. (now Wachovia), 1988-97; vice chmn. BANKPAC, 1982-86, chmn., 1986-88, Del. Trust Capital Mgmt., 1988-97. Mem. Ct. on Judiciary Preliminary Investigatory Com., 1991-97. Mem. bank adv. bd. State of Del., 1969-71; mem. coun. banking State of Del., 1970-2005, chmn., 1976-2005; trustee Alfred I. duPont Testamentary Trust, 1995—; pres. Wilmington and Brandywine Cemetery, 1974—; bd. dirs., trustee, mem. fin. com. mem. exec. com., chmn. audit com. Christiana Care, 1985-99; bd. dirs. Penjerdel, 1989-97, state v.p., 1990-97; bd. gov. Winterthur Corp. Coun., 1989-95, chmn., 1993-95; bd. dirs. Winterthur Mus., 1993-95; bd. dirs. Nemours Found., 1995—, chmn., 2005-07, The Glenmede Trust Co. N.A., 2000—. Capt. arty., U.S. Army, 1957. Mem. Am. Bankers Assn. (govt. rels. coun. 1984-88), Del. Bankers Assn. (pres. 1984-85, bd. dirs. 1981-87), Del. Bus. Roundtable (vice chmn. exec. coun. 1989-92, chmn. 1993-94), Wilmington Country Club (bd. dirs. 1970—, pres. 1973-74), Wilmington Club (bd. govs. 1980-89), Nassau Club, Wilmington Country Club (bd. dir.), Wilmington Club (bd. govs. 1980-89), Hole In The Wall Golf Club (Naples, Fla.), Naples Yacht Club. Office: The Nemours Found 1600 Rockland Rd Wilmington DE 19803-3607 Home Phone: 302-658-9482; Office Phone: 302-651-6048.

PORTER, JOHN RIDGELY, III, lawyer; b. Va., Apr. 28, 1948; s. John Ridgely and Mary Manning (Barclay) P.; m. DeLane Williams, June 24, 1978; 1 child, Eleanor Madison Macon. BA, U. Va., 1970; JD, Washington & Lee U., 1973. Law clerk to US judge US Dist. Ct., 1973—74; assoc. Carr & Porter, 1974—77, ptnr., 1978—2005, of counsel, 2005—06; pvt. practice Law Offices J. Ridgely Porter, III, Orange, Va., 2006—. Dir. Va. Internat. Terminals, 1985—92, pres., 1987—88; dir. Chesapeake Gen. Hosp., 1986—90, 1992—96, chmn. bd., 1994—95; owner Cattle Farms; dir. English Speaking Union,

Charlottesville, Va., Alliance Francaise, Charlottesville, Va. Dir. Boy's and Girl's Club, Orange, Va. Mem.: Va. State Bar (mem. sec. int. law). Episcopalian. Office Phone: 540-661-4127. Personal E-mail: ridgeporter@aol.com.

PORTER, JOHN WESTON, counselor, consultant, administrator; b. Fostoria, Ohio, Dec. 26, 1939; s. William Thomas and Ida Elizabeth (Carter) Porter. Student, U. Cin., 1958; BA, Heidelberg Coll., 1961; MA in Cmty. Psychology, U. DC, 1973, MA in Counseling, 1975; postgrad., Antioch Coll., Yellow Springs, Ohio, 1974, Frostburg U., Md., 1970, George Washington U., Washington, DC, 1968. Cert. Nat. Bd. Cert. Counselors, DC. Claims rep. Social Security Adminstrn., Cleve. and Akron, Ohio, 1961-62; office mgr. Phoenix Cos., Washington and LA, 1966-70; rschr. Frostburg U., U. DC, 1970-73; edn. and career devel. specialist DC Pub. Schs., 1973-79, career edn. unit, 1979-83, Career Assessment Ctr., 1983-85, asst. dir. guidance and counseling, 1985-95; mem. cmty. adv. coun. Washington Hosp. Ctr., 1987—. Counseling mentor DC Pub. Schs., 1998—2003; dir. Westport Consulting, 2001—; cons. DC Pub. Sch. HiScip program, New Couns. Mentor, 2001—02. Contbr. articles to profl. jours. Vice chmn. adv. coun. Group Health Assn., Washington, 1977—79, 1981—83; sec. Md.-DC Am. Coll. Testing Coun., 1987—88, vice chair, 1988—90, chair, 1990—91, mem. exec. com., 1991—; mem. adv. com. Children's Edn. Found., 1989—93, mem. fund raising com., 1989—, exec. bd., 1992—, asst. treas., 1992—93, treas., 1993—95; pres. N.E. Hill Found., 1990—92; mem. com. DC Career and Tech. Edn. Task Force, 2000; team chmn. Wilson HS, 2002, mem. student mgmt. task force, 2002—03, grant rev. panelist, 1998, 2002—03; mem. planning com. Friends of Turkey Thicket Rec. Ctr., 2005, cons., 2005—; treas. Tues. Evening Square Dance Group, 2006—08, exec. com. mem., 2008—. Lt. (j.g.) USN, 1962—66, lt. USNR. Recipient award, Ohio Acad. Sci., 1954—57, Cleve. Plain Dealer Operation Demonstrate, 1956, Svc. award, Heidelberg Coll. Publs., 1961, Recognition cert., DC Assn. Career Devel., 1975, 1976, DC City Coun., 1982, Children's Edn. Found., 1990, Recognition award Outstanding Contbn. to Guidance and Counseling, 1987, Commn. Svc. award, Advisory Neighborhood Commn., 2004, 2005. Mem.: ACA (counselor adv.-legis.), Coun. Accreditation Counseling and Related Ednl. Programs (site visit team 2000—), Assn. Counselor Edn. and Supervision, DC Career Devel. Assn. (exec. bd. 1983—90, treas. 1983—86), DC Sch. Counselors Assn. (Outstanding Leadership award 1994), Nat. Career Devel. Assn. (assembly del. 1984, master career coun. 2003), Am. Sch. Counselors Assn. (chair rsch. com. 1990—91, career guidance com., leadership recognition cert. 1987), Am. Counseling Assn. (chmn. govt. rels. N. Atlantic region 1980—81, cert. Outstanding Contbn. in Govt. Rels. 1982, Recognition award 1987), DC Counseling Assn. (treas. 1975—77, exec. bd. 1975—80, sec. 1977—78, pres. 1979—80, trustee 1989—92, treas. 1991—92, trustee 2003—04, exec. bd. mem. 2008—, trustee 2008—, counselor adv.-legis., Mem. of the Yr. 1980, Outstanding Leadership award 1980), Phi Delta Kappa (edn. found. rep. 1993—95, v.p. membership 1995—96, pres. 1996—97, MACI project adv. coun. Hosp. Sick Children 1997—98, rev. panel DC vocat. edn. grants 1998, lic. profl. counselor, DC). Home: 821 Taylor St NE Washington DC 20017-2009 Personal E-mail: jw.wb.porter@erols.com.

PORTER, JOHN WILSON, educational association administrator, director; b. Ft. Wayne, Ind., Aug. 13, 1931; BA, Albion Coll., Mich., 1953, D (hon.) in Pub. Adminstrn., 1973; MA, Mich. State U., East Lansing, 1957, PhD, 1962, LLD (hon.), 1977, Cleary Coll., Howell, Mich., 1987, LLD, 1989; LHD, Adrian Coll., Mich., 1970, U. Detroit, 1979; LLD, Western Mich. U., Kalamazoo, 1971, Ea. Mich. U., Ypsilanti, 1975; HHD, Kalamazoo Coll., 1973, Detroit Coll. Bus., 1975, Madonna Coll., Livonia, Mich., 1977; DEd, Detroit Inst. Tech., 1978; AA, Schoolcraft Coll., Livonia, Mich., 1979; DBA, Lawrence Inst. Tech., 1988. Counselor Lansing Pub. Schs., Mich., 1953-58; cons. Mich. Dept. Pub. Instrn., 1958-61; dir. Mich. Higher Edn. Assistance Authority, 1961-65; assoc. supt. for higher edn. Mich. Dept. Edn., 1966-69, state supt. schs., 1969-79; pres. Ea. Mich. U., Ypsilanti, 1979-89; v.p. Nat. Bd. for Profl. Teaching Standards, 1989; gen. supt. Detroit Pub. Schs., 1989-91; CEO Urban Edn. Alliance, Inc., Ypsilanti, Mich., 1991—2003. Mem. numerous profl. commns. and bds., 1959—, including Commn. on Financing Postsecondary Edn., 1972-74, Commn. for Reform Secondary Edn., Kettering Found., 1972-75, Edn. Commn. of States, 1973-79, Nat. Commn. on Performance-Based Edn., 1974-76, Nat. Commn. on Manpower Policy, 1974-79, Mich. Employment and Tng. Svcs. Coun., 1976-79, Nat. Adv. Coun. on Social Security, 1977-79, Commn. on Ednl. Credit, Am. Coun. on Edn., 1977-80; task panel on mental health of family Commn. on Mental Health, 1977-80; mem. Nat. Coun. for Career Edn. (HEW), 1974-76; pres. bd. dirs. Chief State Sch. Officers, 1974-79; pres. Coun. Chief State Sch. Officers, 1977-78; bd. dirs. Comerica Bank, 1986-2002; former chmn. bd. Coll. Entrance Exam. Bd., 1984-86; apptd. by Gov. John Engler, Mich. Sch. Dist. Accountability Bd., 1999, Gov. Jennifer M. Granholm, Lt. Gov.'s Commn. on Higher Edn. and Econ. Growth, 2004, Gov. Granholm to State Emergency Fin. Adv. Panel, 2007. Author: Mich. Internat. Student Problem Inventory, 1962, Educational Leadership for the 21st Century, 2006. Mem. East Lansing Human Relations Commn., 1965-69, Mich. Martin Luther King, Jr. Holiday Commn., 1986-90, Gov. James Blanchard's Blue Ribbon Commn. on Welfare Reform, Nat. Measurement Coun., 1972-78, Mich. Sch. Dist. Accountability Bd., 1999, Catherine McAuley Health Systems Bd., 1990-2000, Lt. Gov.'s Commn. Higher Edn. and Econ. Growth, 2004; trustee East Lansing Edgewood United Ch., 1963-79, Nat. Urban League, 1973-79, Charles Stewart Mott Found., 1981—, Albion Coll., 1989-; bd. dirs. Mich. Congress Parents and Tchrs., 1958-68, Mich. Internat. Council, 1977—; chmn. Am. Assn. State Colls. and US Task Force on Excellence in Edn., 1983; mem. bd. overseers com. for Grad. Sch., Harvard U., 1980-88; mem. edn. com. NAACP; convener goal 6 Nat. Edn. Goals Panel, 1990-2000. Recipient numerous awards including Disting. Svc. award Mich. Congress Parents and Tchrs., 1963, Disting. Svc. award NAACP, Lansing, 1968; cert. of outstanding achievement Delta Kappa chpt. Phi Beta Sigma, 1970; award for disting. svc. Assn. Ind. Colls. and Univs. Mich., 1974; Disting. Alumni award Coll. Edn., Mich. State U., 1974; award for disting. svc. to edn Mich. State U., 1974; Disting. Alumni award, 1979; award for disting. svc. to edn. in Mich. Mich. Assn. Secondary Sch. Prins., 1974; Pres.'s award as disting. educator Nat. Alliance Black Sch. Educators, 1977; Marcus Foster Disting. Educator award, 1979; recognition award Mich. Ednl. Rsch. Assn., 1978; recognition award Mich. Assn. Secondary Sch. Prins., 1978; recognition award Mich. Assn. Intermediate Sch. Adminstrs., 1979; recognition award Mich. Assn. Sch. Adminstrs., 1979; Mich. Sch. Bus. Ofcls., 1979; resolution Mich. State Legislature, 1978; Anthony Wayne award Coll. Edn., Wayne State U., 1979; Educator of Decade award Mich. Assn. State and Fed. Program Specialists, 1979; Spirit of Detroit award Detroit City Coun., 1981; Disting. Svc. award Ypsilanti Area C. of C., 1988; Philip A. Hart award Mich. Women's Hall of Fame, 1988; Summit award Greater Detroit C. of C., 1991; Mich. State C. of C. award 1991; Olivet Coll. award for Leadership and Social Responsibility, 2001; Lifetime Achievement award Albion Coll., 2003; inducted Mich. Edn. Hall of Fame, 1992; John W. Porter Disting. Chair endowed at Eastern Mich. U., 1999; Coll. of Edn. bldg. at Ea. Mich. U. named for him, 1999; bestowed 1st ever John W. Porter Leadership award Detroit Pub. TV, 2006. Mem.: NAACP (life), East Mich. U. (Martin Luther King Jr. Honor award 2007), Am. Assn. Sch. Adminstrs., Am. Assn. State Colls. and Univs. (pres.'s coun., chmn. task force on excellence in edn. 1983), Greater Detroit C. of C. (Summit award 1991), Tuskegee Airmen (Disting. Svc. award 1991), Ea. Mich. U. Alumni Assn. (disting. svc. award 1997), Mich. PTA (hon. life), Mich. State C. of C. (Disting. Svc. and Leadership award 1991), Econ. Club (dir. 1979), Sigma Pi Phi, Phi Delta Kappa.

PORTER, JON CHRISTOPHER, SR., lobbyist, former United States Representative from Nevada; b. Ft. Dodge, Iowa, May 16, 1955; m. Laurie Porter; children: J. Christopher, Nicole. Student, Briar Cliff Coll. Electronic appliance repair-distbn. store mgr., 1978—81; agt. Farmers' Ins. Grp. Corp., 1982—88, dist. mgr., 1988—2003; mem. City Coun., Boulder City, Nev., 1983—93, mayor, 1987—91; mem. Nev. State Senate from Dist. 1, 1995—2002, US Congress from 3rd Nev. Dist., 2003—09; dir. pub. policy Akerman Senterfitt, Washington, 2009—. Mem. U. Nev. Inst. for Ins. & Risk Mgmt., Las Vegas. Chair bd. dirs. Las Vegas Events, pres., 1993-95; charter bd. dirs. So. Nev. Water Authority; bd. dirs. Las Vegas Conv. and Visitors Authority; bd. dirs. Nev. League of Cities; mem. civilian mil. coun. Nellis AFB. Recipient Crystal Apple award, Clark County, Nev. Sch. Dist., 1998, Friend of the Shareholder award, Am. Shareholders Assn., 2004, Hero of the Taxpayer award, Americans for Tax Reform, 2004, Small Bus. Adv. award, Small Bus. Survival Com., 2004; named Elected Official of Yr., Nev. League of Cities, 1988. Mem.: Boulder City Rotary Club. Republican. Roman Cath. Office: Akerman Senterfitt 801 Pennsylvania Ave NW Ste 600 Washington DC 20004 Office Phone: 202-393-6222. Office Fax: 202-393-5959. E-mail: jon.porter@akerman.com.*

PORTER, JOSEPH EUGENE (JOEY PORTER), professional football player; b. Bakersfield, Calif., Mar. 22, 1977; m. Christy Porter; children: Jayle, Jasmine, Joey Jr., Jacob. Attended, Colo. State U., Fort Collins. Linebacker Pitts. Steelers, 1999—2006, Miami Dolphins, 2006—. Founder Joey Porter Boot Camp. Named First Team All-Pro, AP, 2002; named to Am. Football Conf. Pro Bowl Team, NFL, 2002, 2004, 2005, 2008. Office: Miami Dolphins 7500 SW 30th St Davie FL 33314*

PORTER, JUDITH DEBORAH REVITCH, sociologist; b. Phila., Mar. 26, 1940; d. Eugene and Esther (Tulchinsky) Revitch; m. Gerald Joseph Porter, June 26, 1960; children: Daniel, Rebecca, Michael. Student, Vassar Coll., 1958-60; BA, Cornell U., 1962, MA, 1963; PhD, Harvard U., 1967. Lectr. Bryn Mawr (Pa.) Coll., 1966-67, asst. prof., 1967-73, assoc. prof., 1973-79, prof. sociology, 1979—2006, chair dept. sociology, 1987-93, prof. emeritus, 2006—. Author: Black Child, White Child: The Development of Racial Attitudes, 1971; contbr. articles to profl. jours. Committeeperson Haverford Twp. Dem. Party, 1976-96; bd. dirs. Phila. AIDS Fund, 1992-98, Phila. Com. End Homelessness, 1984-, Women Against Abuse, 1995-; vice-chmn. exec. com. drugs and alcohol, Mayor, Phila.; vol. Congreso de Latinos Unidos, Inc., Greater Phila. Coalition Against Hunger. Recipient Shannon award NIMH, 1992-94; Ford Found. fellow, 1973-74; NSF fellow, 1967; NIDA grant Co-PI, 1998-2001. Mem. APHA, Am. Sociol. Assn., Phi Beta Kappa, Phi Kappa Phi. Jewish. Address: 161 Whitemarsh Rd Ardmore PA 19003-1634 Office: Bryn Mawr Coll Dept Sociology Bryn Mawr PA 19010 Office Phone: 610-526-5657. Business E-Mail: jporter@brynmawr.edu.

PORTER, KATHY LEE, marriage and family therapist, minister; b. St. Louis, Nov. 30, 1953; d. John Elmer and Mabel Elizabeth Porter. BA, Ctrol. Methodist, Fayette, Mo., 1976; MDiv, St. Paul Sch., Kansas City, Mo., 1983; MSW, St. Louis U., 2000. LCSW Mo. State com. Social Workers, 2006; ordained min. United Ch. Christ, 1991. Min. United Ch. Christ, Hancock, Minn., 1989—91, Payson Congl. Ch. and Bluff Hall, Ill., 1991—94, Hope United Ch. of Christ, Desoto, Mo., 1994—97; case mgr. BJC Behavioral Health, Farmington, Mo., 2000—02; in-home specialist, therapist Comtrea Mental Health, Festus, Mo., 1998—; children, youth therapist Comtrea Mental Health Ctr., Arnold, Mo., 2007—, child youth and family therapist, marriage therapist. Bd. mem. Neighborhood Houses, St. Louis, 1995—2001; mem. nat. Assn. of Soc. Workers, Washington, 2000—. Mem. DeSota Lions Club, DeSota, Mo., 1996—98, Mo. Coalition Against Domestic Violence, Jefferson City, Mo., 2003—; coord. Cmty. Singles, 1997—; mem. St. Luke's United Ch. Christ, Imperial, Mo. Mem.: Nat. Assn. Soc. Workers (Wash. and Mo. chpts.). United Church Of Christ. Avocations: swimming, horseback riding, reading. Home: 705 Stewart St De Soto MO 63020 Office: Comtrea 21 Municipal Dr Arnold MO 63010 Office Phone: 636-296-6206 ext. 337. E-mail: kleeporter@juno.com.

PORTER, KEVIN, professional hockey player; b. Detroit, Mich., Mar. 12, 1986; s. John and Sue Porter. BA, U. Mich., 2008. Center U. Mich. Wolverines, 2004—08, capt., 2007—08; center Phoenix Coyotes, 2008—. Mem. Team USA, IIHF Under-18 Championship, 2003, 04, Team USA, IIHF World Jr. Championship, 2005, capt., 06. Recipient Hobey Baker Meml. Award, 2008, RBK West All-Am. First Team, 2008; named Ctrl. Collegiate Hockey Assn. (CCHA) Player of Yr., 2008, Hockey Commrs. January Nat. Player of Month, 2008; named to All-CCHA First Team, 2008. Office: c/o Phoenix Coyotes Hockey Club 6751 N Sunset Blvd, #200 Glendale AZ 85305*

PORTER, LILIANA ALICIA, artist, photographer, painter, printmaker, filmmaker; b. Buenos Aires, Oct. 6, 1941; came to U.S., 1964, naturalized, 1982; d. Julio and Margarita (Galetar) P.; m. Luis Camnitzer, 1965 (div. 1978); m. Alan B. Wiener, May 28, 1980 (div. 1991). Grad., Nat. Sch. Fine Arts, Argentina, 1963. Co-dir., instr. Studio Camnitzer-Porter summer workshops, Lucca, Italy, 1974, 75, 76, 77; prof. art Queens Coll., CUNY, NYC, 1991—2007, ret., 2007. Adj. lectr. SUNY Coll., Old Westbury, N.Y., 1974-76, Purchase br., 1987; co-dir. Studio Porter-Wiener, N.Y.C., 1979-87. One-woman shows of prints/paintings/photographs include Galeria Artemultiple, Buenos Aires, Argentina, 1977, 78, Galleria Arte Comunale, Adro, Brescia, Italy, 1977, Hundred Acres Gallery, NYC, 1977, Mus. Modern Art, Cali, Colombia, 1978, Center for Interamerican Relations, NYC, 1980, Galeria Arte Nuevo, Buenos Aires, 1980, Barbara Toll Fine Arts, NYC, 1979, 81, 82, 84, Galerie Jolliet, Montreal, 1983, Museo de Arte Contemporaneo, Panama City, Panama, 1984, Dolan/Maxwell Gallery, Phila., 1985, U. Alta., Edmonton, 1985, Dolan/Maxwell Gallery, Phila., 1985, Galería Luigi Marrozzini, San Juan, PR, 1986, Galería-Taller, Museo de Arte Moderno, Cali, Colombia, 1987, The Space, Boston, 1988, Syracuse U., NY, 1990, Steinbaum-Krauss Gallery, NYC, 1993, Galeria Ruth Benzacar, Buenos Aires, 1994, 2009, U. Art Gallery, N.Mex. State U., Las Cruces, 1995, Monique Knowlton Gallery, 1996, Ruth Benzacar Gallery, NY, 1997, Mus. de Bellas Artes Juan Manuel Blanes, Montevideo, Uruguay, 1997, Espacio Minimo, Murcia, Espana, 1998, 2000, Annina Nosei Gallery, NY, 1999, 2000, 02, 04, Artcore Gallery, Toronto, Can., 1999, Ruth Benzacar Gallery, Buenos Aires, 2000, Sicardi Gallery, Houston, 2000, 02, 06, 09, Ctr. Photography, Woodstock, NY, 2000, Phoenix Mus., 2000, Galeria Espacio/Mimimo, Madrid, 2000, 03, 04, Brito-Cimino, Sao Paulo, Brazil, 2001, Casas Riegner Gallery, Miami, Fla., 2003, Hosfelt Gallery, San Francisco, 2003, 06, 08, Centro Cultural Recoleta, Buenos Aires, 2003, Palacio Aguirre, Cartagena, Spain, 2004, Eli Marsh Gallery, Amherst Coll., Mass., 2004, Annina Nosei Gallery, NYC, 2004, Galeria Ruth Benzacar, Buenos Aires, 2005, Carrie Secrist Gallery, Chgo., 2005, 08, Sala de Veronicas, Murcia, Spain, 2005, Galeria Petrus, San Juan, PR, 2005, Galeria Casas Riegner, Bogota, Colombia, 2005, Goya-Girl Contemporary, Balt., 2006, Hosfelt Gallery, NYC, 2007, Galleria Valentina Bonomo, Rome, 2007, Galeria Espacio Mimimo, Madrid, Spain, 2007, Barbara Krakow Gallery, Boston, 2008; retrospective exhibits 1968-90 Fundacion San Telmo, Buenos Aires, 1990, Museo Nacional de Artes Plasticas, Montevideo, Uruguay, 1991, Centro de Recepciones del Gobierno, San Juan, PR, 1991, Bronx Mus. Art, NYC, 1992, retrospective exhibit Archer Huntington Art Gallery U. Tex. Austin, 1993, Staller Ctr. for the Art SUNY at Stony Brook, NY, 1998, Centro Cultural Recoleta, Sala Cronopios, Buenos Aires, Argentina, 2003, Muses Tamayo, Mex., 2009; exhibited in numerous group shows including most recently El Mus. del Barrio, NYC, 2000, Casa de America, Madrid, 2000, Contemporary Mus., Balt., 2000, NY, others, Mass. Coll. Art, Huntington Gallery, Boston, 2001, ARCO, Madrid, 2001. Centro Cultural Borges, Buenos Aires, 2001, Peter Lewis Theater, Guggenheim Mus., NY, 2001, Hosfelt Gallery, San Francisco, 2001, Fundacion Telefonica, Madrid, 2001, Fundacion Joan Miro, Barcelona, 2001, Carrie Secrist Gallery, Chgo., 2001, Contemporary Art Ctr., NY, 2001, The Mahady Contemporary Gallery at Marywood U., Scranton, Pa., 2002, Kunst Werke, Berlin, 2003; represented in permanent collections Mus. Phila., Mus. Modern Art, NYC, RCA Corp., NYC, NY Public Libr., NYC, La Biblioteque Nationale, Paris, France, Museo del Grabado, Buenos Aires, Museo Universitario, Mexico City, Mexico, Museo de Art Moderno, Cali, Colombia, Museo de Bellas Artes, Caracas, Venezuela, Met. Mus. Art, NYC, Daros Collection Zurich, Tate Modern, London; (solo exhibit) Galeria Brito-Cimino, Sao Paulo, Brazil, 2008, Simmons Visual Art Ctr. Brenau U., Gainsville, Ga., 2009. Recipient 1st prize Argentinian Art 78 Mus. Fine Arts, Buenos Aires, 1978, Grand Prix XI, Internat. Print Biennial, Cracow, Poland, 1986, 1st prize VII Latin Am. Print Biennial, San Juan, Puerto Rico, 1986; fellow Guggenheim Found., 1980-81, N.Y. Found. for the Arts, 1985, grantee, 1999. Studio: 720 Greenwich St 10G New York NY 10014 Personal E-mail: lilianaporter@gmail.com. E-mail: lilianaporter@earthlink.net.

PORTER, LISA, sociologist, educator; b. Chadron, Nebr., June 22, 1971; d. Gene Strom and Nancy Kirkmeyer; m. Shannon Porter, July 19, 1994. PhD, Claremont Grad. U., Calif., 2007. Asst. prof. U. La Verne, 2000—05; performing arts instr. Country Day Sch., Brasilito, Santa Cruz, Costa Rica, 2005—07; asst. prof. sociology Bridgewater Coll., Va., 2007—. Trustee mem. La Paz Cmty. Sch., Flamingo, 2007—09. Mem.: Am. Anthrop. Assn. Liberal. Avocations: hiking, travel. Office: Bridgewater Coll 402 E College St Bridgewater VA 22812 Business E-Mail: lporter@bridgewater.edu.

PORTER, MARTY, museum director; m. Bill Porter; children: Patrick, Joel. BS in Speech and Hearing, Ctrl. State U., Edmond, Okla., 1974; M in Hearing Impaired Edn., U. Kans., Kansas City, 1977; grad. in Mus. Mgmt. Program, U. Colo., Boulder, 1995. Hearing impaired tchr. Kansas and Olathe Pub. Sch. Dists., 1974—82; exec. dir. Children's Mus. of Kansas City, 1989—. Mem. Jr. League Wyandotte and Johnson Counties, Kans.; mem. spl. adv. coun. Wyandotte County Spl. Edn. Cooperative, 1987—90, past pres.; past mem. bd. trustees, edn. and fin. coms. Trinity United Meth. Ch.; bd. dirs. Children's Campus of Kansas City. Recipient Outstanding Young Educator award, Kansas City Jaycee's, 1978; named Outstanding Woman of Yr., 1991. Mem.: Inst. Mus. Svcs., Assn. Children's Mus. (past mem. program com.), Mountain/Plains Mus. Assn., Downtown Shareholders Assn., Women's Chamber of Kansas City, Kiwanis Club. Office: Childrens Mus Kansas City 4601 State Ave Kansas City KS 66102 Office Phone: 913-287-8888. Business E-Mail: mporter@kidmuzm.org.

PORTER, MICHAEL PELL, lawyer; b. Indpls., Mar. 31, 1940; s. Harold Troxel and Mildred Maxine (Pell) P.; m. Alliene Laura Jenkins, Sept. 23, 1967 (div.); 1 child, Genevieve Natalie Porter Eason; m. Janet Kay Smith Hayes, Feb. 13, 1983 (div.). Student, DePauw U., Greencastle, Ind., 1957-58; BA, Tulane U., New Orleans, 1961, LLB, 1963. Bar: La. 1963, U.S. Ct. Mil. Appeals 1964, N.Y. 1969, Hawaii 1971. Clk. U.S. Ct. Appeals (5th cir.), New Orleans, 1963; assoc. Sullivan & Cromwell, NYC, 1968-71, Cades Schutte Fleming & Wright, Honolulu, 1971-74, ptnr., 1975-94; mem. faculty Addis Ababa (Ethiopia) U. Sch. Law, 1995-99; sr. regulatory advisor Egyptian Capital Market Authority, Cairo, 1999—2002; advisor capital market Palestinian Nat. Authority, 2002—03; lectr. Arab Acad. Banking and Fin. Scis., 2003; legal adv. Securities and Exch. Commn. Bangladesh, 2004—05. Legal advisor St. Matthews Anglican Ch., Addis Ababa, Ethiopia, 1995—99; cons, Rep. of Yemen, 1997; mem. deans coun. Law Sch. Tulane U., 1981—88; dep. vice chancellor Episcopal Diocese Hawaii, 1980—88, chancellor, 1988—94, Episcopal Ch., Micronesia, 1988—95. Author: Hawaii Corporation Law & Practice, 1989; Hawaii reporter State Limited Partnership Laws, 1992-94. Bd. dirs. Jr. Achievement Hawaii, Inc., 1974-84, Inst. Human Svcs., Inc., 1980-88; donor Michael P. Porter Dean's Scholastic Award, U. Hawaii Law Sch., 1977—. With JAGC, U.S. Army, 1963-66, Vietnam. Fulbright scholar, 1997-99; Tulane U. fellow, 1981. Mem.: Hawaii Bar Assn. E-mail: porterconsultant@yahoo.com.

PORTER, PHILIP THOMAS, retired electrical engineer; b. Clinton, Ky., Mar. 18, 1930; s. Philip Henry and Ruth Frances (Pennebaker) P.; m. Louise Monroe Jett, July 3, 1957; children: Philip C., Sara Shelby Porter Taylor. BA in Physics, Vanderbilt U., 1952, MA in Physics, 1953. Mem. tech. staff Bell Telephone Labs., Murray Hill, NJ, 1953-62, Holmdel, NJ, 1962-70, supr., 1971-78, West Long Branch, NJ, 1979-83; dir. wireless and wireline network compatiblity studies Telcordia Tech., Red Bank, NJ, 1984-94; ret., 1994. U.S. del. Consultative Com. for Internat. Radio, Geneva, 1984-93. Contbg. author: Electronics Engineers' Handbook, 1982, History of Science and Technology in the Bell System, 1985, Digital Communications, 1986; patentee in field. Fellow IEEE. Unitarian Universalist. Avocations: group singing, bridge. Personal E-mail: ptporter8@att.net.

PORTER, PHILIP WAYLAND, geography educator; b. Hanover, NH, July 9, 1928; s. Wayland Robinson and Bertha Maria (LaPlante) P.; m. Patricia Elizabeth Garrigus, Sept. 5, 1950; children: Janet Elizabeth, Sara Louise, Alice Catherine. AB, Middlebury Coll., 1950; MA, Syracuse U., 1955; PhD, U. London, 1957. Instr. geography U. Minn., Mpls., 1957-58, asst. prof., 1958-64, assoc. prof., 1964-66, prof., 1966-2000, prof. emeritus, 2000—; assoc. to v.p. acad. affairs, also dir. Office Internat. Programs, 1979-83. Geography panel Com. on Space Programs for Earth Observations Nat. Acad. Scis., 1967-71; liaison officer Midwest Univs. Consortium for Internat. Activities, 1979-83 Author: (with Eric S. Sheppard) A World of Difference: Society, Nature, Development, 1998, Challenging Nature: Local Knowledge, Agroscience and Food Security in Tanga Region, Tanzania, 2006, (with Eric Sheppard, David B. Frust and Richa Nagar) A World of Difference: Encountering and Contesting Development, 2nd edit., 2009; contbr. articles to profl. jours. With AUS, 1952-54. Grantee Ctrl. Rsch. Fund, 1955-56, NSF, 1961-62, 78-80, 92-93, Social Sci. Rsch. Coun., 1966-67, Rockfeller Found., 1969, 71-73, Gen. Svc. Found., 1981-83, Exxon Edn. Found., 1983-84, Fulbright, 1992-93; Bush Sabbatical fellow, 1985-86.

Mem. Assn. Am. Geographers (Lifetime Achievement award 2004), Phi Beta Kappa (alumni mem.). Home: 10 Burkehaven Terr Sunapee NH 03782-2402 Office: U Minn Dept Geography Minneapolis MN 55455 Office Phone: 603-653-0161. Personal E-mail: pwporter@myfairpoint.net.

PORTER, RICHARD JAMES, real estate broker, art historian, actor, voice over artist; b. Bellefonte, Pa., Jan. 2, 1950; s. David Louis and Anna Louise (McGarry) P.; m. Jeanne Chenault, Apr. 16, 1977; children: Andrew C., Julia M. BA, Pa. State U., 1971, MA, 1973, PhD, 1983. Instr. Middle Tenn. State U., Murfreesboro, 1973-76; registrar, curator Pa. State U. Mus. Art, University Park, 1977-85; chair grad. program in mus. studies Syracuse (N.Y.) U., 1985-86; sales assoc. Villager Realty, State College, Pa., 1986-88, Associated Realty, State College, 1988-91, assoc. broker, 1991-92; founder, broker, co-owner Re/Max Centre Realty, State College, 1992—2005; dir. Wally Findlay Galleries, NYC, 2005—07. Instr. Polley Real Estate Schs., Greensburg, Pa., 1991—99; assoc. broker Prudential Douclas Elliman, NYC, 2007-, freelance actor, 2008-, cons. local not-for-profit orgns., State College, 1986—; dir. Ctr. County, Pa. Bd. Realtors, State College, 1989-1995, v.p., 1992-94, pres. 199495—. Author exhbn. catalogs and articles in field, 1973—. Dir. Nittany Valley Symphony, State College, 1990-1994; chmn. Columbus Quincentenary Preservation Com., Ctr. County, 1990-91, Kish Bank Advisory Bd.,2002-2007. Recipient CRS designation Nat. Mktg. Inst., 1991,CRB designation 1993 Mem. Nat. Assn. Realtors, Pa. Assn. Realtors (recipient Grad. Realtors Inst. designation 1989, Pa. Assn. Realtors Excellence Life award, 1991, Owner of Yr., 1993, 96, 2003), Ctr. County Hist. Soc. (mem. exhbn. com. 1988-91), State College Choral Soc., State College Community Theatre, Torch Internat. (pres. 1990-91), Am. Assn. Museums (nat. coun. 1982-85), English Speaking Union, NY, Nat. Arts Club, NY. Episcopalian. Office: Re/Max Centre Realty 1375 Martin St State College PA 16803-3091 Home: 455 Windmere Dr Apt Llb State College PA 16801-7671 Personal E-mail: rporter567@aol.com.

PORTER, ROBERT CARL, JR., lawyer; b. Cin., Sept. 21, 1927; s. Robert Carl and Lavinia (Otte) P.; m. Joanne Patterson, July 5, 1952; children: Robert Carl III, David M., John E. BA with distinction, U. Mich., 1949; JD, Harvard U., 1952. Bar: Ohio 1952, U.S. Dist. Ct. (so. dist.) Ohio 1954, U.S. Ct. Appeals (6th cir.) 1954, U.S. Ct. Mil. Appeals 1956, U.S. Tax Ct. 1980, U.S. Supreme Ct. 1956. Ptnr. Porter & Porter, Cin., 1953-54; sole practice Cin., 1954-63; sr. ptnr. Porter & McKinney, Cin., 1963-88, Porter & Porter, Cin., 1989—. Dir. and officer numerous cos. Served with JAGC, USAF, 1952-53. Mem. ABA, Ohio State Bar Assn., Cin. Bar Assn., Cin. Country Club, Univ. Club, U. Mich. Club, Harvard Law Sch. Assn., Masons, Scottish Rite, Shriners, Phi Beta Kappa. Presbyterian. Home: 2365 Bedford Ave Cincinnati OH 45208-2656 Office: Porter & Porter 2100 4th and Vine Tower Cincinnati OH 45202 Home Phone: 513-871-5447; Office Phone: 513-621-3993. E-mail: rcpjr@porterlawoffices.com.

PORTER, ROGER BLAINE, federal official, educator; b. Provo, Utah, June 19, 1946; s. Blaine Robert and Elizabeth M. (Taylor) P.; m. Ann Robinson, Jan. 6, 1972; children: Robert Roger, Stacy Ann, David R., Rachel Elizabeth. BA in History and Polit. Sci., Brigham Young U., 1969; PhB, Oxford U., 1971; MA, PhD, Harvard U., 1978; PhD (hon.), Weber State U., 2003. Asst. dean, tutor in politics Queen's Coll., Oxford U., 1971-72; spl. asst. to pres. The White House, 1974-77; rsch. assoc. Kennedy Sch. Govt. and Grad. Sch. Bus., Harvard U., Cambridge, Mass., 1977-79, asst. prof. pub. policy, 1979-81, assoc. prof., 1981, prof. govt. and bus., 1985—; spl. asst. to Pres. of U.S., 1981-82; dep. asst. to Pres. of U.S., 1982-85; dir. White Ho. Office of Policy Devel., Washington, 1982-85; counselor to sec. U.S. Treasury, 1981-85; exec. sec. Nat. Productivity Adv. Com., 1981-85, Cabinet Coun. on Econ. Affairs, 1981-85, Econ. Policy Coun., 1985; asst. to U.S. Pres. for econ. and domestic policy, 1989-93. Exec. sec. Pres.'s Econ. Policy Bd., 1974—77; sr. scholar Woodrow Wilson Internat. Ctr. for Scholars, 1993—; dir. Ctr. for Bus. and Govt. Harvard U., 1995—2000, 2008—, master Dunster House, 2001—; mem. Pres.'s Commn. on White House Fellowships, 1976—2001, 2008—; bd. dirs. Zions Bancorp., Pactiv Corp., Nat. Life Ins. Co., Tenneco, Inc., Mutual of Am., Extra Space Storage, Packaging Corp. Am. Author: Presidential Decision Making, 1980, U.S.-USSR Grain Agreement, 1984, Efficiency, Equity, Legitimacy: The Multilateral Trading System at the Millenium, 2001; asst. editor: Public Policy, 1979—81. Mem. Utahns for Effective Govt., Salt Lake City, 1971-72; mem. Rep. Nat. Com. Econ. Adv. Com., 1977-81; trustee Gerald R. Ford Found.; mem. adv. bd. George Bush Sch. Govt. and Pub. Svc., Tex. A&M U. Rhodes scholar, 1969; Woodrow Wilson fellow, 1969; White House fellow, 1974; recipient spl. citation U.S. Sec. Treasury, 1977, Rolex Intercollegiate Tennis Achievement award, 1996; named One of 10 Outstanding Young Men in Am., 1981 Fellow Nat. Acad. Pub. Adminstrn.; mem. White House Hist. Assn. (bd. dirs. 1993—), Phi Kappa Phi, Pi Sigma Alpha, Phi Eta Sigma, Phi Alpha Theta. Republican. Mem. Lds Ch. Avocations: classical music, basketball, tennis, travel. Home: 12 Clifton St Belmont MA 02478-3363 Office: Harvard U Kennedy Sch Govt 79 JFK St Cambridge MA 02138-5801

PORTER, ROGER JOHN, research and development company executive, neurologist, pharmacologist; b. Pitts., Apr. 4, 1942; s. John Keaggy and Margaret (Parker) P.; m. Candace Marie Leland, Feb. 17, 1968; children: David, Stacey. BS, Eckerd Coll., 1964; MD, Duke U., 1968; DSc (hon.), Eckerd Coll., 2008. Diplomate Nat. Bd. Med. Examiners, Am. Bd. Neurology, Am. Bd. Electroencephalography. Intern U. Calif., San Diego, 1968-69; resident in neurology U. Calif., San Francisco, 1971-74; fellow rsch. tng. program Duke U., Durham, NC, 1966-67; staff assoc. sect. epilepsy Nat. Inst. Neurol. Diseases and Stroke, NIH, Bethesda, Md., 1969-71; investigator U. Calif., San Francisco, 1972-73; sr. rsch. assoc. epilepsy br. neurol. disorders program Nat. Inst. Neurol. and Communicative Disorders and Stroke, NIH, Bethesda, 1974-78, asst. chief epilepsy br., 1977-79, acting chief, 1979-80, acting chief clin. epilepsy sect., IRP, 1979-84, chief epilepsy br. neurol. disorders program, 1980-84, chief med. neurology br. and clin. epilepsy sect. IRP, 1984-87; dep. dir. Nat. Inst. Neurol. Disorders and Stroke, NIH, Bethesda, 1987-92; v.p., clin. pharmacology Wyeth-Ayerst Rsch., Radnor, Pa., 1992-97, v.p. clin. rsch., 1997—99, v.p., dep. head clin. rsch., 1999—2002; cons., 2002—. Adj. prof. neurology U. Pa., 1993—; prof. neurology Uniformed Svcs. U. Health Scis., Bethesda, 1980-93, adj. prof. pharmacology, 1982—; cons.-lectr. neurology Nat. Naval Med. Ctr., Bethesda, 1978-93; chmn. White House Subcom. on Brain and Behavioral Scis., 1990-92; scholar-in-residence Assn. Am. Med. Colls., Washington, 1989-90; mem. NIMH/Nat. Inst. Neurol. Disorders and Stroke Coun. of Assembly of Scientists, 1983-86, pres., 1985-86; mem. pharmacy and therapeutics com. NIH, 1977-86, chmn., 1978; mem. instnl. rev. bd. human subjects Nat. Inst. Neurol. Disorders and Stroke, 1984-87, chmn., 1986-87. Mem. editl. bd. Acta Neurologica Scandanavica, 1991-97, Annals of Neurology, 1987-92, Epilepsia, 1982-86; contbr. articles to profl. jours., chpts. to books; author 13 books, writer, contbr. 5 motion pictures, 1 exhibit. Bd. trustees Eckerd Coll., 1994—97; commd. officer USPHS, 1969—92. Recipient MacArthur Outstanding Alumnus award Eckerd Coll., 1977, Fulbright Disting. Prof. award, 1985, Disting. Alumnus award Duke Duke U. Med. Ctr., 1989, USPHS Dist. Svc. Medal, 1991, USUHS Commendable Svc. Award, 2001. Fellow Coll. Physicians Phila. (trustee 2006—, sec. 2008-), Am. Acad. Neurology, Am. Neurol. Assn.; mem. Am. Electroencephalographic Soc., Am. Epilepsy Soc. (pres. 1989-90), Soc. Neurosci., Am. Soc. Clin. Pharmacology and Therapeutics, Am. Soc. Exptl. Neurol. Therapeutics (pres. 2008-), Internat. League Against Epilepsy (sec. gen. 1989-93), Am. Soc. Pharmacology and Exptl. Therapeutics. Home and Office: 461 Timber Ln Devon PA 19333-1232 Office Phone: 610-989-3767. Business E-Mail: rjportermd@aol.com.

PORTER, SCOTT E., orthopedist; BS, Morehouse Coll., Atlanta, 1993; MD, Yale U. Sch. Medicine, New Haven, 1998. Cert. ABOS, 2004. Orthop. surg. fellow Carolinas Med. Ctr., 1999—2000; physician, fellowship, divsn. orthop. surgery U. Chgo., 2004—05; inductee AOA Kellogg Emerging Leadership Program, Rosemont, Ill., 2004—; apptd. bd. appeals for orthop. surgery ACGME, Chgo., 2008—. Contbr. scientific papers. Howard Hughes Rsch. fellow, Yale U. Sch. Medicine, 1996—98, Orthop. Surg. Rsch. fellow, Carolinas Med. Ctr., 1996—2000. Mem.: AMA. Office: Univ Miss Med Ctr 2500 N State St Jackson MS 39216-4505 Business E-Mail: sporter@orthopedics.umsmed.edu.

PORTER, STEPHEN CUMMINGS, geologist, educator; b. Santa Barbara, Calif., Apr. 18, 1934; s. Lawrence Johnson Porter Jr. and Frances (Cummings) Seger; m. Anne Mary Higgins, Apr. 2, 1959; children: John, Maria, Susannah. BS, Yale U., 1955, MS, 1958, PhD, 1962. Asst. prof. geology U. Wash., Seattle, 1962-66, assoc. prof., 1966-71, prof., 1971—2002, dir. Quaternary Research Ctr., 1982-98, prof. emeritus, 2002—. Bd. earth scis. Nat. Acad. Sci., Washington, 1983-85; adv. com. divsn. polar programs NSF, Washington, 1983-84; vis. fellow Clare Hall Cambridge (Eng.) U., 1980-81; guest prof. Chinese Acad. Scis., People's Republic of China, 1987—; v.p. Internat. Union Quaternary Rsch., 1992-95, pres., 1995-99. Co-author: Physical Geology, 1987, The Dynamic Earth, 1989, 5th edit., 2004, The Blue Planet, 1995, 2d edit., 1999, Environmental Geology, 1996, Dangerous Earth, 1997; editor: Late Quaternary Environments of the United States, 1983, Quaternary Rsch., 1976—2000; co-editor: The Quaternary Period in the U.S., 2004; assoc. editor Radiocarbon, 1982—89, Am. Jour. Sci., 1997—, mem. editl. bd. Quaternary Sci. Revs., 1988—, Quaternary Internat., 1989—2005. Served to lt. USNR, 1955-57. Recipient Benjamin Silliman prize Yale U., 1962; Willis M. Tale lectr. So. Meth. U., 1984, S.F. Emmons lectr. Colo. Sci. Soc., 1996; Fulbright Hays sr. rsch. fellow, New Zealand, 1973-74; Einstein Professorship Chinese Acad. Scis., 2007. Fellow Geol. Soc. Am. (Kirk Bryan award 2004, Disting. Career award 2005), Arctic Inst. N.Am. (bd. govs.), AAAS; mem. Am. Quaternary Assn. (coun., pres. 1992-94, Disting. Career award 2004). Avocations: photography, genealogy. Home: 18034 15th Ave NW Shoreline WA 98177-3305 Office: U Wash Dept Earth and Space Scis Seattle WA 98195-1310

PORTER, TERRY, former professional basketball coach, retired professional basketball player; b. Milw., Apr. 8, 1963; m. Susie Porter; children: Brianna, Franklin, Malcolm. Student, U. Wis., Stevens Point, 1981-85. Guard Portland Trail Blazers, 1985-97, Minn. Timberwolves, Mpls., 1997-98, Miami Heat, 1998-99, San Antonio Spurs, 1999—2002; asst. coach Sacramento Kings, 2002—03; head coach Milw. Bucks, 2003—05; asst. coach Detroit Pistons, 2006—08; head coach Phoenix Suns, 2008—09. Founder Milw.Scholars Fund, 1994—. Recipient Citizenship award, 1993; named to NBA All-Star team, 1991, 93. Avocation: golf.*

PORTER, THEODORE MARK, history educator; b. Kelso, Wash., Dec. 3, 1953; s. Charles Clinton and Shirley Isobel (Tolle) P.; m. Diane Rita Campbell, Aug. 19, 1979; 1 child, David Campbell. AB, Stanford U., 1976; PhD, Princeton U., 1981. Postdoctoral instr. Calif. Inst. Tech., Pasadena, 1981-84; rsch. mem. Zentrum fur interdisziplinaere Forschung der U. Bielefeld, Germany, 1982-83; asst. prof. history U. Va., Charlottesville, 1984-91; assoc. prof. history UCLA, 1991—95, prof. history, 1995—, chair Ctr. Cultural History of Sci., Tech. and Medicine, 1992—94, 1995—98, academic vice chair, 1997—98, vice chair undergraduate affairs. Vis. chair history of sci. U. Utrecht, Netherlands, 1999. Author: The Rise of Statistical Thinking, 1986, Trust in Numbers: The Pursuit of Objectivity in Science and Public Life, 1995, Karl Pearson: The Scientific Life in a Statistical Age, 2004; co-author: The Empire of Chance: How Probability Changed Science and Everyday Life, 1989; contbr. numerous articles to profl. jours. Grantee Guggenheim Found., 1989-90, NSF, 1991-92, 94-96. Fellow Am. Acad. Arts and Sciences; mem. History of Sci. Soc. (mem. coun. 1991-93), Am. Hist. Assn. Avocations: mountain climbing, tennis, bicycling. Office: UCLA Dept of History UCLA Box 951473 6265 Bunche Hall Los Angeles CA 90095-1473 Office Phone: 310-206-2352. Office Fax: 310-206-9630. Business E-Mail: tporter@history.ucla.edu.

PORTER, THOMAS R., cardiologist; b. Fremont, Nebr., Aug. 25, 1958; s. Donald William and Lois (Naber) P.; m. Lee A. Porter; children: Austin, Evan, Kaitlin, Dawson, Megan. BS, U. Nebr., 1980, MD, 1984. Diplomate Am. Bd. Internal Medicine. Intern, then resident Med. Coll. Va., Richmond, 1984-88, fellow in cardiology, 1988-91; co-dir. non-invasive cardiology lab., asst. prof. medicine McGuire VA Med Ctr., Richmond, 1991-92; dir. non-invasive cardiology lab., asst. prof. medicine U. Nebr. Med. Ctr., Omaha, 1992—. Fellow Am. Coll. Cardiology (Bristol Travel award 1991 Young Investigator award 1992); mem. Am. Heart Assn., Am. Soc. Echocardiography (sessions chmn. 1995, Young Investigator award 1994). Office: U Nebr Med Ctr 600 S 42nd St Omaha NE 68198-1002

PORTER, THOMAS W.B., lawyer; b. Ann Arbor, Mich., July 15, 1957; s. James Morris and Helen Marie (Adams) P.; m. Anne R.P. Ballew, Aug. 2, 1980; children: Devin B., Clare B., Keith B. BA, John Carroll U., 1977; JD, U. Mich., 1980. Bar: D.C. 1980, Mich. 1985, U.S. Ct. Claims 1980, U.S. Dist. Ct. (ea. dist.) Mich. 1985, U.S. Ct. Appeals (4th cir.) 1981, U.S. Ct. Appeals (fed. cir.) 1982, U.S. Ct. Appeals (6th cir.) 1986, U.S. Ct. Appeals (9th cir.) 1991, U.S. Ct. Appeals (7th cir.) 1992, U.S. Ct. Appeals (1st cir.) 1994. Trial atty. U.S. Dept. Justice Civil Div., Washington, 1980-85; assoc. Dykema Gossett PLLC, Detroit, 1985-87, ptnr., 1988-93, mem., 1994-98; gen. counsel Barton Malow Co., Southfield, Mich., 1997—98, v.p., gen. counsel, 1998—2001, sr. v.p., gen. counsel, 2001—04, exec. v.p., sec., chief legal officer, 2004—; chmn. United Integrity Assurance, Ltd., 2004—, sec., 2008—. Bd. dirs. Met. Affairs Coalition, 2004—, Design Build Inst. Am., 2005—, treas., 2007, vice chair, 2008, chair, 2009. Recipient Spl. Achievement award U.S. Dept. Justice Civil Div., Washington, 1984. Mem. Fed. Bar Assn. (mem. chpt. exec. bd. 1992-95, program chair 1995-96, treas. 1996-97, sec. 1997-98, v.p. 1998-99, pres.-elect 1999-2000, pres. 2000-01). Office: Barton Malow Co 26500 American Dr Southfield MI 48034 Office Phone: 248-436-5040.

PORTER, THOMAS WILLIAM, III, lawyer; b. Dallas, Aug. 23, 1941; s. Thomas William and Ruth Mae (Campbell) P.; m. Sally Ann Shell, May 10, 1963 (div. July 1983); children: Elizabeth Elisse, Laura Christina; m. Patty Ann Sanders, Nov. 2, 1985. BBA in Fin., So. Meth. U., Dallas, 1963; LLB, Duke U., Durham, NC, 1966. Bar: Tex. 1966, U.S. Dist. Ct. (no. dist.) Tex. 1967, U.S. Dist. Ct. (so. dist.) Tex. 1975, U.S. Dist. Ct. (we. dist.) Tex. 1977, U.S. Ct. Appeals (5th cir.) 1977. Assoc. Jackson & Walker, Dallas, 1966-72; ptnr. Bracewell & Patterson, Houston, 1972-74, Foreman & Dyess, Houston, 1974-81; sr. ptnr. Porter & Hedges LLP, Houston, 1981—, chmn., 2000—. Bd. dirs. US Concrete, Helix Energy Solutions, Copano Energy. Life mem. bd. visitors Duke U. Law Sch.; trustee Tex. Heart Inst.; dir. Alley Theatre, Hobby Ctr. Performing Arts. Fellow: Tex. Bar Found.; mem.: ABA (fed. regulation of securities com. 1979—, com. on law firms 1981—), State Bar Tex. Assn. (securities and investment banking com. 1976—2005, coun. mem. sect. bus. law 1984—86), Coronado Club, River Oaks Country Club. Republican. Methodist. Office: Porter & Hedges LLP Reliant Energy Plz 36th Fl 1000 Main St Houston TX 77002-6336 Business E-Mail: bporter@porterhedges.com.

PORTER, VERNA LOUISE, lawyer; b. May 31, 1941; BA, Calif. State U., 1963; JD, Southwestern U., 1977. Bar: Calif. 1977, U.S. Dist. Ct. (ctrl. dist.) Calif. 1978, U.S. Ct. Appeals (9th cir.) 1978; cert. Dispute Resolutions Programs Act Mediator, L.A. County Bar Assn., 2005. Ptnr. Eisler & Porter, LA, 1978-79, mng. ptnr., 1979-86; pvt. practice, 1986—. Judge pro-tempore LA Mcpl. Ct., 1983—, LA Superior Ct., 1989—, Beverly HIlls Mcpl. Ct., 1992—; mem. subcom. landlord tenant law, State Calif., panelist conv.; mem. real property law sect. Calif. State Bar, 1983; mem. client rels. panel, vol. LA County Bar Dispute Resolution; ct. appointed arbitrator civil cases, fee arbitrator LA Superior Ct.; mem. BBB Abitrator Automobile Lemon Laws, 2000—. Editl. asst., contbr. Apt. Bus. Outlook, Real Property News, Apt. Age. Mem. adv. coun. Freddie Mac Vendor, 1995—; mem. World Affairs Coun. Mem. ABA, LA County Bar Assn. (client-rels. vol. dispute resolution fee arbitration 1981—; arbitrator lemon law claims), LA Trial Lawyers Assn., Wilshire Bar Assn. Women Lawyers' Assn., Landlord Trial Lawyers Assn. (founding, pres.), Da Camera Soc. Office: 2500 Wilshire Blvd Ste 1226 Los Angeles CA 90057-4365 Office Phone: 213-385-1568.

PORTER, VERNA R., neurologist, educator; m. Dr. William G. Buxton; children: William Buxton, John Buxton, Andrew Buxton. MD, UCLA, 1994. Diplomate Am. Bd. of Psychiatry and Neurology, 2000. Chief neurology divsn. Santa Monica/UCLA Med. Ctr., 2002—; asst. clin. prof. dept. neurology UCLA, 2002—. Contbr. articles to profl. jours. Named one of America's Top Physicians, Consumer Rsch. Coun. of Am., 2004—05, 2006—07, 2008—. Mem.: Am. Acad. Neurology (life). Achievements include research in Dementia and Alzheimer's disease. Office: UCLA/Santa Monica Neurological Associate 1245 16th St Ste 309 Santa Monica CA 90404 Office Fax: 310-319-4552.

PORTER, W. THOMAS, retired bank executive; b. Jan. 8, 1934; s. Walter Thomas and Mary Rebecca (Brookes) P.; m. Dixie Jo Thompson, Apr. 3, 1959; children: Kimberlee Paige, Douglas Thompson, Jane-Amy Elizabeth. BS, Rutgers U., 1954; MBA, U. Wash., 1959; PhD, Columbia U., 1964. CPA, Wash., N.Y. Staff cons. Touche Ross & Co., NYC, 1959-61, dir. edn., 1964-66; NDEA fellow Columbia U., 1961-64; assoc. prof. U. Wash., 1966-70, prof., 1970-74; vis. prof. N. European Mgmt. Inst., Oslo, 1974-75; nat. dir. planning Touche Ross & Co., Seattle, 1975-78, dir. exec. fin. counseling, 1978-84; exec. v.p., mgr. pvt. banking Rainier Nat. Bank, 1984-87, exec. v.p., mgr. capital mgmt. and pvt. banking, 1987-88, vice-chmn., 1988—92, Security Pacific Bank Washington, 1989-92; exec. v.p., mgr. capital mgmt. group Bank of Am., Seattle, 1992-99; chmn. Porter Investments LLC, 1999—. Vis. lectr. taxation U. Wash., 1978—85; vis. lectr. strategic planning Nat. U. Ireland, 2003; bd. dirs. Coldstream Capital Mgmt., Charter Bank Wash.; lectr. financial planning U. Wash., 2007—. Author: The Bank of America Guide to Personal Financial Solutions, 2d edit., 1998, The Glory of Washington: The People and Events That Shaped the Husky Athletic Tradition, 2001, Husky Stadium: Great Games and Golden Moments, 2004, A Football Band of Brothers: Forging the University of Washington's First National Championship, 2007. Mem. Seattle adv. bd. Salvation Army, 1975-83, 89-97, pres., 1993-95; trustee Ryther Child Ctr., 1975-85, pres., 1979-81; trustee Lakeside Sch., 1977-87, pres., 1984-86; trustee Va. Mason Med. Ctr., 1986-97, chair bd. govs., 1994-96; chair Nat. Campaign for Student Athlete U. of Wash., 1995-2000, Mus. History and Industry, 1982-83, Olympic Park Inst., 1996-2001. With U.S. Army, 1955-57. Mem. Sand Point Country Club. Congregationalist.

PORTER, WALTER ARTHUR, retired judge; b. Dayton, Ohio, June 6, 1924; s. Claude and Estella (Raymond) P.; m. Patricia Reeves Higdon, Dec. 3, 1947; children— Scott Paul, David Bryant. BS in Engring, U. Cin., 1948, LL.B., 1949. Bar: Ohio 1949. Legal dep. Montgomery County Probate Ct., 1949-51; asst. pros. atty. Montgomery County, 1951-56; with Albert H. Scharrer (atty.), Dayton, 1956-61; mem. firm Smith & Schnacke, Dayton, 1962-85, pres., 1980-85; judge Montgomery County Common Pleas Ct., 1985-95; of counsel Thompson Hine & Flory, Dayton, 1996-2001. Served with inf. U.S. Army, 1943-45, ETO. Mem. ABA, Ohio Bar Assn. (pres. 1973-74), Dayton Bar Assn., Am. Coll. Trial Lawyers, Am. Coll. Probate Counsel, Phi Alpha Delta, Omicron Delta Kappa. Clubs: Mason. Democrat. Presbyterian. Home: 872 Timberlake Ct Kettering OH 45429-3494 Personal E-mail: wapphp@aol.com.

PORTER, WAYNE RANDOLPH, dermatologist; b. Washington, Jan. 10, 1948; s. James Randolph and Betty Rose (Burgess) P. BS, MIT, 1970; MD, Duke U., 1973. Diplomate Am. Bd. Internal Medicine, Am. Bd. Dermatology. Intern U. Miami (Fla.) Affiliated Hosps., 1973-74; resident in internal medicine U. Miami Sch. Medicine, 1973-76, resident in dermatology, 1976-78, clin. instr., then asst. prof. dermatology (vol.), 1978-85, assoc. prof. (vol.), 1985—2005, prof., 2005—. Adj. prof. Barry U. Sch. Grad. Medicine, 2000—; practice medicine specializing in dermatology, North Miami Beach, 1978—; mem. staff U. Miami-Jackson Meml. Hosp. Mem. med. adv. bd. Dade-Broward chpt. Lupus Found. Am. Fellow Internat. Soc. for Dermatologic Surgery, Am. Acad. Dermatology, Am. Assn. Dermatologic Surgeons; mem. AMA, ACP, Internat. Soc. Pediat. Dermatology, Fla. Med. Assn., Fla. Dermatology Soc., Miami Dermatol. Soc. (pres.), Dade County Med. Assn., So. Med. Assn., Bath Club (Miami Beach), Coral Reef Yacht Club. Office: 909 N Miami Beach Blvd Miami FL 33162-3712 Home Phone: 305-285-8983; Office Phone: 305-949-4223. E-mail: wrpmd@bellsouth.net.

PORTER, WILLIAM LYMAN, architect, educator; b. Poughkeepsie, NY, Feb. 19, 1934; s. William Quincy and Lois (Brown) Porter; m. Lynn Rogers Porter; children: Quayny Lyman, Zoe Lynn, Eve Lyman. BA, Yale U., 1955, M.Arch., 1957; PhD, MIT, 1969. Designer, job capt. Louis I. Kahn (architect), Phila., 1960-62; urban designer, asst. chief of design Ciudad Guayana project Joint Center for Urban Studies of Harvard and MIT, Caracas, Venezuela, 1962-64; Mellon fellow dept. urban studies and planning MIT, 1964-65; Samuel Stouffer fellow Joint Center for Urban Studies, Harvard and MIT, 1966-67; asst. prof. urban design, depts. architecture and urban studies and planning MIT, 1968-70, assoc. prof. urban design, 1970-71, prof. architecture and planning, 1971—2004, Norman B. and Muriel Leventhal prof. architecture and planning, 1988—2004, prof. emeritus, 2004—, head. dept. architecture, 1987-91, dean Sch. Architecture and Planning, 1971-81; co-dir. Aga Khan Program for Islamic Architecture Harvard U.-MIT, 1979-85. Cons. in field; mem. Nat. Archtl. Accrediting Bd., 1978—80, pres., 1979; mem. Mass. Designer Selection Bd., 1978—79, chmn., 1979; mem. steering com. Aga Khan Award for Architecture, 1977—86, mem. master jury, 1989; prin. Four Architecture Inc., Boston, 1994—2007, Anderson Porter Design, Cambridge, 2008—. Co-author: Excellence by Design: Transforming Workplace and Work Practice, 1999; co-founder, co-editor: Places: A Quar. Jour. Environ. Design, 1982—88, Facilities Engineering and Management Handbook: Commercial, Industrial and Institutional Buildings, 2000, Design Representation, 2003. Trustee Milton Acad., Mass., 1989—2001; mem. bd. overseers Coll. Fine Arts, U. Pa., 1984—90, Mus. Fine Arts, Boston, 1992—94. Fellow: AIA; mem.: Boston Soc. Archs. (dir. 1969—73, 1977—81), Harvard Musical Assn. (Boston), Phi Beta Kappa (hon.). Home: 17 Concord Ave Cambridge MA 02138-2321 Office: MIT Sch Architecture & Planning 77 Massachusetts Ave Cambridge MA 02139-4307 Business E-Mail: wlporter@mit.edu.

PORTER, WILMA JEAN, retired educational consultant; b. Sylacauga, Ala., May 30, 1931; d. Harrison Samuel and Blanche Leonard Butcher; m. Douglas Taylor Porter, Apr. 18, 1953; children: Daria Cecile, Blanche Evette, Douglas Vincent. BS, Tuskegee U., 1951; MS, Mich. State U., 1966; PhD, Iowa State U., 1980. Asst. dietitian Miss. State Tb Sanatorium, 1951-52; therapeutic dietitian dept. of hosp. City of N.Y., SI, 1952-53; libr. asst. Mississippi Valley State Coll., Itta Bena, Miss., 1963-65; asst. prof. Grambling (La.) State U., 1966-75, Howard U., Washington, 1976-80; country dir. U.S. Peace Corps, Tonga, 1980-82; asst. dir. internat. programs Ft. Valley (Ga.) Coll., 1983-84, dir. Inst. Advancement, 1984-88; dir. Sch. Home Econs., Tenn. Technol. U., Cookeville, 1989-96; ret., 1996. Project dir. Capitol Hill Health and Homemaker, Washington, 1982-83; interim dir. Inst. Advancement Alcorn State U., Lorman, Miss., 1988-89. Author lab. manual for quantity foods, 1977; editor: (cookbook) Some Christmas Foods and Their Origins from Around the World, 1983. Convenor Nat. Issues Forums, Ga. and Tenn., 1985-90; citizen participant Nat. Issues Forums Soviet Dialogue, Newport Beach, Calif., 1988; bd. dirs. Leadership Putnam, Cookeville, 1990-94; chmn. Tenn. Technol. U. campaign United Way, 1989; mem. devel. and planning com. Peach County Ft. Valley, 1985-87; mem. Peach County Heart Fund Dr., 1986-88; participant People to People Internat. to China; ct. apptd. spl. adv. for children vol. CASA N.E. La. Title III grantee U.S. Dept. Edn., 1986, 87; Tenn. Dept. Human Svcs. grantee, 1993, 94. Mem. AAUW (program chair 1991-92, pres. Cookeville br. 1993-94), Am. Family and Consumer Scis. Assn., Am. Dietetic Assn., La. Assn. Family and Consumer Scis., La. Dietetic Assn. Democrat. Roman Catholic. Avocations: writing, vegetable and flower gardening. Home: 1415 ML King Jr Ave Grambling LA 71245

PORTERFIELD, CHRISTOPHER, magazine editor, writer; b. Weston, W.Va., Apr. 3, 1937; s. James Herman and Irene (Smith) P.; m. Stephanie Brown, Jan. 20, 1962; children: Christopher Brown, Tessa Louise, Kevin Stephenson. BA, Yale U., 1958; MA, Columbia U., 1965. Music critic Time mag., NYC, 1967-69, cultural correspondent London, 1969-72; exec. producer Daphne Prodns., NYC, 1974-79; sr. editor Time mag., NYC, 1980-93, asst. mng. editor, 1993-96; exec. editor, 1996—2003; contbr., 2003—. Co-Author: (with Dick Cavett) (books) Cavett, 1973, Eye on Cavett, 1983; contbr. articles to popular mags. and periodicals, 1975—. Mem. Writers Guild of Am. Avocations: reading, music, tennis. Home and Office: 315 Central Park W New York NY 10025-7664

PORTERFIELD, SUSAN AZAR, literature and language professor; d. Alfred George and Betty Jo Azar; m. Christopher Cole Porterfield, July 24, 1976. PhD, Northern Ill. U., Dekalb, 1986. Assoc. prof. English dept. Rockford Coll., Ill., 1994—2000, prof., 2000—. Contbr. to anthology. Fellowship, Ill. Arts Coun., 2006. Mem.: Writing Programs. Avocations: reading, travel, cooking. Office: Rockford Coll 5050 E State St Rockford IL 61108 Business E-Mail: sporterfield@rockford.edu.

PORTERFIELD, WILLIAM WENDELL, chemist, educator; b. Winchester, Va., Aug. 24, 1936; s. Donald Kennedy and Adelyn (Miller) P.; m. Dorothy Elizabeth Dail, Aug. 24, 1957; children: Allan Kennedy, Douglas Hunter. BS, U. N.C., 1957, PhD, 1962; MS, Calif. Inst. Tech., 1960. Sr. research chemist Hercules, Inc., Cumberland, Md., 1962-64; asst. prof. chemistry Hampden-Sydney Coll., Va., 1964-65, assoc. prof., 1965-68, prof. chemistry, 1968—, Charles Scott Venable prof. chemistry, 1989—, chmn. natural sci. div., 1973—77, chmn. dept. chemistry, 1982-85, 93-96, 2002—06. Vis. fellow U. Durham (U.K.), 1984 Author: Concepts of Chemistry, 1972, Inorganic Chemistry, 1984, 2d edit., 1993; contbr. articles to profl. jours. Mem. Am. Chem. Soc., Royal Chem. Soc. (London, Eng.), Phi Beta Kappa Home: PO Box 697 Hampden Sydney VA 23943 Office Phone: 434-223-6179. Business E-Mail: wporterfield@hsc.edu.

PORTERFIELD-PYATT, CHAUMONDE R., music educator, advocate; b. Visalia, Calif., Oct. 18, 1943; d. Roy E. and Zoisla Saladin; m. Melvin E. Pyatt, June 16, 1984; children: Michelle R. Pyatt children: Brian K. Porterfield, Erik D. Porterfield, Kevin G. Porterfield. AA, Coll. Sequoias, Visalia, Calif., 1963; post grad. with Stanley Glasser, U. London, 1981; BS, U. San Francisco, 1988; degree (hon.), Wessex Theology Coll. Cert. C.C. supr. Calif., 1988, C.C. instr. Calif., 1987, Wellstone Actions Adv. Campaign Mgmt. Sch., 2006. Prof. music Coll. Sequoias, Visalia, Calif., 1981—. Exec. dir. 49th Mozart Festival, 1982; guest soloist Grieg Piano Concerto, No. 1, Opus 16 Kings County Symphony, 1988; state legislative advocate Faculty Assn. Calif. Cmty. Colleges, 1994; conf. presenter Copyright Laws II, Lobbying 101: How to Stalk the Wild Legislator, 2002. Accompanist and singer: Desert Song, 1963, Music Man, 1963; performer (with Maestro Igor Stravinsky): Von Himmel Hoch and Symphony of Psalms, 1965; performer: (with Maestro Aaron Copland) Musica Viva with the San Francisco Symphony, 1966; performer: New J. S. Bach Chorales Premiere, 1988, recitals featuring Composers of Chopin, Rachminoff, Liszt, Debussy, J. S. Bach, and Beethoven, Piano Dedication Concert-Visalia United Methodist Church, 1984; singer: San Francisco Chorale, 1967; contbr. articles to profl. jours. Recipient cert. Appreciation, Fine Arts Divsn. Coll. Sequoias, 2000; Music fellow, Wessex Theol. Coll., Eng., 1989. Mem.: NEA, C.C. Assn. (advocacy chair 1994—, polit. action com. 1994—, lobbying com 1994—, legislation com. 1994—, exec. bd 1998—, advocate 1998—, bd. dir. dist D, W. H. O. award 2004), Coll. Sequoias Tchrs. Assn. (sec. 1989, state rep. 1998—, W. H. O. award 2004), Music Assn. Calif. Cmty. Colleges (legis. advocacy rep. 1984, exec. bd. 1984—), Am. Theatre Organ Soc., Am. Guild Organists (conf. presenter 1984), Calif. State Tchrs. State Coun. (higher edn. rep. 2001), Calif. Teachers Assn. (life; exec. bd. 1989, advocate 1998—, higher edn. dir. at large 2004, com. higher edn. 2004, state dir. 2004—), Calif. Scholastic Fedn. (life), Mu Phi Epsilon (pres. 1967). Achievements include Invited guest to sail on the QE2 from New York to Southampton, England; featuring piano artists Eugene Istomin, Peter Orth, Michael LaGrand, Leonard Pennario and Charles Strauss; Invited guest performer on Steinway pianos once belonging to Vladimir Horowitz, Van Cliburn and Ignace Paderewski. Office: Coll Sequoias 915 S Mooney Blvd Visalia CA 93277 Business E-Mail: chaumondep@cos.edu.

PORTES, ALEJANDRO, sociologist, educator; b. Havana, Cuba, Oct. 13, 1944; came to U.S., 1960; s. Helio B. Portes and Eulalia Cordtada; m. Nancy Brazie, Jan. 28, 1966 (div. Dec. 1974); children: Elizabeth, Charles A., Andrea; m. Patricia Fernandez Kelly, Mar. 31, 1985. Attended, U. Havana, 1959—60, Catholic U. Argentina, Buenos Aires, 1963; BA summa cum laude, Creighton U., 1965; MA in Sociology, U. Wis., Madison, 1967, PhD in Sociology, 1970, DSc honoris causa, 1998; LHD honoris causa, New Sch. for Social Rsch., 1998; PhD honoris causa in Ednl. Scis., U. Genova, Italy, 2004. Lectr., sociology U. Wis., Madison, 1969-70; asst. prof., sociology U. Ill., Urbana-Champaign, 1970-71; assoc. prof., sociology U. Tex., Austin, 1971-75; prof., sociology Duke U., Durham, NC, 1975-80, Johns Hopkins U., Balt., 1980-87, John Dewey chair, prof. sociology, Sch. Arts and Scis., 1988—96; prof., sociology Princeton U., NJ, 1997—2002, chair, dept. sociology NJ, 2003—06. Prog. advisor, social scis., Ford-Found.-Brazil, 1976-77; Patricia and Phillip Frost disting. vis. prof. Fla. Internat. U., Miami, 1988-91, Emilo Bacardi Moreau disting. vis. prof., U. Miami, 1997; Walker-Ames disting. vis. prof., U. Wash., Seattle, 1999; vis. prof., Rural Sociology and Sociology, U. Wis.-Madison, 1986, Latin-Am. Sch. Social Scis., FLASCO-Ecuador, 1990-92; Inst. Polit. Scis., Paris, 2005, Nat. U. Gen. Sarmiento, Aregentina, 2006; mem. Internat. Com. on Migration and Develop., Social Sci. Rsch. Coun., 2006-07; mem. adv. bd., Centre on Migration, Policy, and Soc., Oxford U., 2003-; dir., Ctr. for Migration and Develop., Princeton U., 1999-2007, mem. exec. com., Prog. in Latin Am. Studies, 2005-07; mem. external review com., sociology dept., Vanderbilt U, 2001, Com. on Internat. Migration, Social Sci. Rsch. Coun., 1997-2004; cons. Ford Found., 1977, 79, 89, U.S. Congress Com. for Study of Immigration, 1988-90, Ministries of Labor and Social Welfare of Spain, Immigration Policy, 1990—; vis. fellow, Oxford U., 2000; invited lectr. in field. Author: Urban Latin America, 1976, Labor, Class and the International System, 1981, Latin Journey, 1985, Immigrant America, a Portrait, 1990, City on the Edge, the Transformation of Miami, 1993 (Robert Park award, Anthony Leeds award); bd. dirs. Ethnic and Racial Studies; referee for several peer-reviewed publications 2004-2006; contbr. several articles to peer-reviewed publications; mem. editl. bd. Ethnic and Racial Studies, 1995-, Jour. Ethic and Migration Studies, 1998-, Revista Mexicana De Sociologia, 1999-, Studies in Comparative Internat. Develop., 2000-, Global Networks, 2000-, City and Cmty., 2000-, Anuario Social y Politico de Am. Latina, 2001-, Internat. Migration Review, 2001-, Actes de la Recherche en Scis. Sociales, 2004-, Revista Migraciones, 2005-, Proceedings of the NAS, 2005-, Am. Sociol. Review 2006-. Guest Witness U.S. Congress Sub-com. on Immigration, 1983, 86; del. Internat. Sociol. Assn., Madrid, Spain, 1990-; bd. dirs. Spencer Found. 1997-2002. Recipient Manford Kuhn award, Midwest Sociol. Soc., Des Moines, 1967, Anthony Leeds award for best book in urban anthropolgy (City on the Edge), Soc. for Urban Anthropology, Am. Anthropological Assn., 1995, Disting. Alumnus award, Creighton U., 1999; fellow Ctr. for Advanced Studies in the Behavioral Scis., 1980—81, Ctr. for US-Mexican Studies, U. Calif., San Diego, 1984—85, Russell Sage Found., 1992—93; Internat. Fellow, Coun. on Fgn. Relations, 1972—73, Spencer Found. Sr. Scholar award, 1997. Fellow Am. Acad. Arts and Scis.; mem. Am. Sociol. Assn. (pres., sect. on polit. economy of the World Sys., 1985-86, coun. mem., 1993-96, pres. 1998-99, Robert E. Park award for the best book in urban sociology (City on the Edge), Cmty. and Urban Sociology Sect., 1995, Disting. Career award, Internat. Migration Sect., 1998, Disting. Scholarly Publication award for Legacies: The Story of the Immigrant Second Generation, 2002, William I. Thomas and Florian Znaniecki Disting. Scholarship award (Legacies), Internat. Migration Sect., 2002), Latin Am. Studies Assn. (mem. jt. com. Social Sci. Rsch. Coun. 1985-88), Sociol. Rsch. Assn., NAS (award for scientific reviewing, 2008). Avocations: sailing, motor boating. Office: Dept Sociology Princeton University Princeton NJ 08544-1010 Office Phone: 609-258-4436. Office Fax: 609-258-1520.

PORTES, RICHARD DAVID, economics professor; b. Chgo., Dec. 10, 1941; s. Herbert and Abra (Halperin) P.; m. Barbara Diana Frank, 1963 (div. 2005); children: Jonathan, Alison; m. Helene Mireille Rey, 2006; child: Ana. BA summa cum laude, Yale U., 1962; MA, Balliol and Nuffield Colls., Oxford, 1965, DPhil, 1969; DSc honoris causa, U. Libre de Bruxelles, 2000, London Guildhall U., 2000. Official fellow Balliol Coll., 1965—69; asst. prof. econs. and internat. affairs Princeton U., 1969-72; prof. econs. U. London, 1972-94; head dept. econs. Birkbeck Coll., 1975-77, 80-83; pres. Ctr. for Econ. Policy Rsch., 1983—; dir. Ecole des Hautes Etudes, Paris, 1978—; prof. econs. London Bus. Sch., 1995—. Vis. prof. Harvard U., Cambridge, 1977—78; assoc. Nat. Bur. Econ. Rsch., Cambridge, Mass., 1980—; mem. Bellagio Group on Internat. Economy, 1992—, Group Econ. Policy Advisors to Pres. of European Commn., 2001—; disting. global vis. prof. U. Calif., Berkeley, 1999—2000; dir. European Corp. Governance Inst., 1999—2005; Joel Stern disting. vis. prof. internat. fin. Columbia Bus. Sch., 2003—04. Editor, author: Planning and Market Relations, 1971, The Polish Crisis, 1981, Deficits and Detente, 1983, Threats to International Financial Stability, 1987, Global Macroeconomics, 1987, Blueprints for Exchange Rate Stability, 1989, Macroeconomic Policies in an Interdependent World, 1989, External Constraints on Macroeconomic Policy, 1991, The Path of Reform in Central and Eastern Europe, 1991, Economic Transformation in Central Europe, 1993, European Union Trade with Eastern Europe, 1995, Crisis? What Crisis? Orderly Workouts for Sovereign Debtors, 1995, Crises de la dette, 2003, European Government Bond Markets, 2006, European Corporate Bond Markets, 2006; Internation Financial Stability, 2007, Macroeconomic Stability and Financial Regulation, 2009,contbr. articles to profl. jours. Pres. Richard and Margaret Merrell Found. Decorated Comdr. Brit. Empire; Rhodes scholar; Guggenheim fellow, 1977-78. Fellow Brit. Acad., European Econ. Assn., Econometric Soc.; mem. Royal Econ. Soc. (exec. com. 1987-92, sec. gen. 1992—2008, v.p.), Econ. Policy (bd. govs., sr. editor 1985—), Coun. on Fgn. Rels. Office: London Bus Sch Regents Pk London NW1 4SA England Office Phone: 44 0 20 70008424. Business E-Mail: rportes@london.edu.

PORTIER, GUIDO MARCEL, lawyer; b. Amsterdam, June 2, 1970; m. Mascha Koopmans, Feb. 5, 1999. M, Vrije U., Amsterdam, 1994. Lic.: Royal Dutch Civil Law Profl. Orgn. (lawyer) 1995. Corp. lawyer Loyens & Loeff, Rotterdam, Netherlands, 1995—2005, head Dept. Corp. Law NYC, 2005—. Contbr. articles to profl. jours. Mem.: ABA, Royal Dutch Civil Law Profl. Orgn., Dutch Trade Law Assn., Internat. Bar Assn. Office: Loyens Loeff 555 Madison Ave Fl 27 New York NY 10022-3313

PORTIER, KENNETH MICHAEL, statistics educator; b. Houma, La., Nov. 7, 1951; s. Clovis Joseph and Lois Marie (Chauvin) P.; m. Mary Lee Stevens, Nov. 24, 1976; children: Sarah Elizabeth, Russell Joseph. BS in Math., Nicholls State U., Thibodaux, La., 1973; MS in Stats., U. N.C., 1976, PhD in Biostats., 1979. Statistician Nat. Inst. Environ. Health Scis., NIH, Research Triangle Park, 1976; stats. cons. Inst. Environ. Studies, U. N.C., Chapel Hill, 1977-78; asst. rsch. scientist stats. U. Fla., Gainesville, 1979-81, asst. prof., 1981-86, assoc. prof., 1986—, acting asst., v.p. acad. affairs, 1989-91. Cons. USAID/ECUADOR, Quito, 1983-84, Everglades Nat. Park, Homestead, Fla., 1985-89, St. Johns Water Mgmt. Dist., Palatka, Fla., 1987-88, Rookery Bay Nat. Esruarine Rsch., Naples, Fla., 1991. Contbr. numerous articles to profl. jours. Cubmaster Cub Scouts Am., Gainesville, 1990-94. Grantee Gas Rsch. Inst., Chgo., 1981-88, St. Johns Water Mgmt. Dist., 1987-88, 94, Everglades Nat. Park, 1985-89, U.S. Fish and Wildlife Svc., Gainesville, 1988-91, USDA, 1994—; recipient contract USAID/Ecuador, 1983-84. Mem. Biometric Soc., Am. Statis. Assn. Democrat. Roman Catholic. Home: 610 SW 127th St Newberry FL 32669-5405 Office: U Fla Dept Stats 401 Rolfs Hall Gainesville FL 32611-0327

PORTIS, CHARLES MCCOLL, reporter, writer; b. El Dorado, Ark., Dec. 28, 1933; s. Samuel Palmer and Alice (Waddell) P. BA, U. Ark., 1958. Reporter The Comml. Appeal, Memphis, 1958, Ark. Gazette, Little Rock, 1959-60, N.Y. Herald Tribune, NYC, 1960-64. Author: Norwood, 1966, True Grit, 1968, The Dog of the South, 1979, Masters of Atlantis, 1985, Gringos, 1991. Sgt. USMC, 1952-55, Korea. Presbyterian. Home: 7417 Kingwood Rd Little Rock AR 72207-1734

PORTIS, CLINTON, professional football player; b. Laurel, MS, Sept. 1, 1981; Degree, U. Miami. Running back Denver (Colo.) Broncos, 2002—03, Washington Redskins, 2004—. Named NFL Offensive Rookie of Yr., AP, 2002; named to Am. Football Conf. Pro-Bowl Team, NFL, 2003, Nat. Football Conf. Pro-Bowl Team, 2008. Achievements include being a member of NCAA Division I Championship winning University of Miami Hurricanes, 2001; leading the NFL in: yards per rush attempt, 2003, rushing attempts, 2007. Office: 21300 Redskins Park Dr Ashburn VA 20147*

PORTLAND, RENE (MAUREEN PORTLAND), retired women's college basketball coach; b. 1953; d. Margaret Muth; m. John Portland; 1 adopted child, Delisa children: Christine, John Jr, Stephen. BA in Social Sci., Immaculata Coll., 1975. Asst. coach, women's basketball team Immaculata Coll., 1975—76; head coach St. Joseph's U., Phila., 1976—78, U. Colo., Boulder, 1978—80, Pa. State U., University Park, 1980—2007. Named Atlantic 10 Conf. Coach of Yr., 1983, Women's Basketball Coaches Assn. (WBCA) Coach of Yr., 1991, 2004, Converse/US Basketball Writers Assn. Nat. Coach of Yr., 1992, Newspaper Enterprise Assn. Nat. Coach of Yr., 1993, Big 10 Conf. Coach of Yr., 1994, 2000, USA Basketball's Developmental Coach of Yr., 1997, Women's Basketball Jour. Nat. Coach of Yr., 2000, IKON/WBCA Dist. 6 Coach of Yr., 2000, Big Ten Coach of Yr. (Coaches & Media), 2003, 2004, Renaissance Person of Yr., Pa. State U., 2005; named to Pa. Sports Hall of Fame, 2001, Mount Nittany Soc., 2002. Mem.: Women's Basketball Coaches Assn. (WBCA) (pres. 1989—90). Achievements include being a member of three consecutive national championship teams at Immaculata University, 1972-75; as a women's basketball coach, has won seven conference championships & eight conference tournament titles.

PORTMAN, GLENN ARTHUR, lawyer; b. Cleve., Dec. 26, 1949; s. Alvin B. and Lenore (Marsh) P.; m. Katherine Seaborn, Aug. 3, 1974 (div. 1984); m. Susan Newell, Jan. 3, 1987. BA in History, Case Western Res. U., 1968; JD, So. Meth. U., 1975. Bar: Tex. 1975, U.S. Dist. Ct. (no. dist.) Tex. 1975, U.S. Dist. Ct. (so. dist.) Tex. 1983, U.S. Dist. Ct. (we. and ea. dists.) Tex. 1988, Ct. of Appeals, Ffith Cir., 1998. Assoc. Johnson, Bromberg & Leeds, Dallas, 1975-80, ptnr., 1980-92, Arter, Hadden, Johnson & Bromberg, Dallas, 1992-95, Arter & Hadden LLP, Dallas, 1996—2003, Bennett, Weston & LaJone, PC, Dallas, 2003—. Chmn. bd. dirs. Physicians Regional Hosp., 1994-96; mem. exec. bd. So. Meth. U. Sch. Law, 1994—; lectr. bankruptcy topics South Tex. Coll. Law, State Bar Tex.; mem. vis. com. Coll. Arts and Scis., Case Western Res. U., 1999-2004. Asst. editor-in-chief Southwestern Law Jour., 1974-75; contbr. articles to profl. jours. Firm rep. United Way Met. Dallas, 1982-92; treas. Lake Highlands Square Homeowners Assn., 1990-93. Mem. ABA, Am. Bankruptcy Inst., State Bar Tex., Dallas Bar Assn., Turnaround Mgmt. Assn., So. Meth. U. Law Alumni Assn. (coun. bd. dirs., v.p. 1980-86, chmn. admissions com., chmn. class agt. program 1986-89, chmn. fund raising 1989-91), 500 Club Inc., Assemblage Club. Republican. Methodist. Office: 1750 Valley View Ln Ste 120 Dallas TX 75234 Home: 1306 Bradford Dr Coppell TX 75019 Office Phone: 214-691-1776 ext. 207, 214-691-1336. Office Fax: 214-393-4007. Personal E-mail: glennportman@tx.rr.com. Business E-Mail: gportman@bwlpc.com.

PORTMAN, NATALIE, actress; b. Jerusalem, June 9, 1981; d. Avner and Shelley Hershlag. BS in Psychology, Harvard U., 2003. Founder HandsomeCharlie Films, 2008—. Designer Té Casan Vegan Shoe collection, 2008. Actress: (films) The Professional, 1994, Developing, 1995, Heat, 1995, Beautiful Girls, 1996, Everyone Says I Love You, 1996, Mars Attacks!, 1996, Star Wars: Episode I-The Phantom Menace, 1999, Anywhere But Here, 1999, Where the Heart Is, 2000, Zoolander, 2001, Star Wars Episode II-Attack of the Clones, 2002, Cold Mountain, 2003, Garden State, 2004, True, 2004, Closer, 2004 (Golden Globe award for best supporting actress, 2005), Domino One, 2005, Star Wars: Episode III-Revenge of the Sith, 2005, Free Zone, 2005, V for Vendetta, 2006, Paris, je t'aime, 2006, Goya's Ghosts, 2006, My Blueberry Nights, 2007, The Darjeeling Limited, 2007, Mr. Magorium's Wonder Emporium, 2007, The Other Boleyn Girl, 2008, (short films) Hotel Chevalier, 2007; dir. (short films) Eve, 2008; appeared in stage prodns. including Diary of Anne Frank, 1997 (Nominee Tony award), The Seagull, 2001. Recipient Movie for Humanity award, Venice Film Festival, 2008; named one of The 50 Most Powerful Women in NYC, NY Post, 2008. Office: Creative Artists Agency 2000 Avenue Of The Stars Los Angeles CA 90067-4700

PORTMAN, ROBERT JONES, lawyer, former United States Representative from Ohio; b. Cin., Dec. 19, 1955; m. Jane D. Portman; children: Jed, Will, Sally BA, Dartmouth Coll., 1979; JD, U. Mich., 1984. Assoc. Patton Boggs LLP, Washington, 1984—86; ptnr. Graydon Head & Ritchey LLP, Cin., 1986-89, 1991—93; assoc. counsel to Pres. The White House, Washington, 1989—91, dep. asst. to Pres., dir. Office Legis. Affairs, 1989—91; mem. US Del. to UN Subcom. on Human Rights, 1992, US Congress from 2nd Ohio Dist., 1993—2005; US Trade Rep., Office US Trade Rep. Exec. Office of the Pres., Washington, 2005—06, dir. Office Mgmt. & Budget, 2006—07; of counsel Squires Sanders & Dempsey LLP, Cin. & Washington DC, 2007—. Co-author (with Cheryl Bauer): Wisdom's Paradise: The Forgotten Shakers of Union Village, 2004. Bd. trustees Springer Sch., The United Way, Hyde Park Community United Meth. Ch.; founding trustee Cin.-China Sister City Com.; mem. advisory bd., John Glenn Sch. Pub. Affairs, The Ohio State U., 2008-; vice chmn. Hamilton County George Bush for Pres. Campaign, 1988, 92; chmn. Rep. Early Bird Campaign com., 1992; del. Rep. Nat. Conv., 1988, 92; active Hamilton County Rep. Party Exec. com., Hamilton County Rep. Party Fin. Com. Recipient Excellence in Pub. Svc. award, John Glenn Sch. Pub. Affairs, The Ohio State U., 2008, Nelson A. Rockefeller Disting. Pub. Svc. award, Nelson A. Rockefeller Ctr., Dartmouth Coll., PLANSPONSOR mag. Legend award, Nat.

Leadership award, Cmty. Anti-Drug Coalition of America, 2008, Leadership on Alcohol & Other Drug Services award, Hamilton County Mental Health & Recovery Services Bd., Albert Gallatin award, Swiss-Am. Chamber of Commerce. Mem. Cin. World Trade Assn. Republican. Methodist. Office: Squires Sanders & Dempsey LLP 221 E Fourth St Ste 2900 Cincinnati OH 45202 E-mail: rportman@ssd.com.*

PORTNEY, PAUL ROGERS, dean; BA in Econs. and Math., Alma Coll., Mich., 1967; PhD in Econs., Northwestern U., 1973. Chief economist White House Coun. on Environ. Quality, Washington, 1979-80; joined Resources for the Future, Washington, 1972—, head rsch. divisions, 1986—89, v.p., 1989-95, pres., CEO, 1995—2005; dean Eller Coll. Mgmt., U. Ariz., Tucson, 2005—, Halle chair in leadership, 2005—. Vis. prof. U. Calif., Berkeley, 1977—79, Princeton U., 1992—94. Office: U Ariz Eller Coll Mgmt McClelland Hall 1130 E Helen St Tucson AZ 85721-0108 Office Phone: 520-621-2125. Office Fax: 520-621-8105. E-mail: pportney@eller.arizona.edu.*

PORTNOY, ELLIOTT IVAN, lobbyist, lawyer; b. Morgantown, W.Va., Nov. 1, 1965; s. Donald Charles and Enid Joan (Pallant) Portnoy; m. Estee Renee Mermelstein, Sept. 6, 1992; children: Joshua Brandon, Noah Abraham, Daniela Faye. BA, Syracuse U., 1986; PhD in Politics, Oxford U., Eng., 1989; JD, Harvard U., 1992. Bar: Md. 1992, DC 1993. Staff asst., cons. dem. policy com. US Senate, Washington, 1985-88; ptnr. Arent Fox Kintner Plotkin & Kahn, Washington, 1992—2002, past head lobbying practice; ptnr. Sonnenschein Nath & Rosenthal LLP, Washington, 2002—, chair firm pub. law & policy strategies group, 2002—06, chmn., 2007—, mem. firm policy & planning com. Atty. Clinton-Gore presdl. transition, Washington, 1992-93. Author: Guide to Congress, 1991. Founder, pres. bd. dirs. Kids Enjoy Exercise Now Found., Washington, Oxford, 1987—; bd. dirs. Jewish Social Services Agy., Washington, 1996—; exec. com. Dem. Young Lawyers Com., Washington, 1996—. Recipient Rhodes scholar, Oxford U., 1986—89; named Washingtonian of Yr., Washingtonian mag., 1999; named one of 50 Top Lobbyists, 2007. Mem.: ABA (vice chair legis. process & lobbying com.). Office: Sonnenschein Nath & Rosenthal LLP Ste 600, East Tower 1301 K St NW Washington DC 20015 Office Phone: 202-408-6433. Office Fax: 202-408-6399. Business E-Mail: eportnoy@sonnenschein.com.*

PORTNOY, SARA S., lawyer; b. NYC, Jan. 11, 1926; d. Marcus and Gussie (Raphael) Spiro; m. Alexander Portnoy, Dec. 13, 1959 (dec. 1976); children: William, Lawrence. BA, Radcliffe Coll., 1946; LLB, Columbia U., 1949. Bar: N.Y. 1949, U.S. Dist. Ct. (so. dist.) N.Y. 1952, U.S. Dist. Ct. (ea. dist.) N.Y. 1975, U.S. Ct. Appeals (2d cir.) 1975, U.S. Supreme Ct. 1975. Assoc. Seligsberg, Friedman & Berliner, NYC, 1949-51; atty. AT&T, NYC, 1951-61; vol. atty. Legal Aid Soc. of Westchester, NY, 1966-74; assoc. Proskauer Rose Goetz & Mendelsohn, NYC, 1974-78, ptnr., 1978-94; ret., 1994. Mem. Commn. on Human Rights, White Plains, N.Y., 1973-78; mem. bd. visitors Columbia Law Sch., 1996-02; bd. dirs. Legal Aid Soc. of Westchester County, N.Y., 1975-83, Columbia Law Sch. Assn., 1990-94, Mosholu Montifiore Cmty. Ctr., 1998—; mem. Pres.'s Coun. Yaddo; dir. Muscular Dystrophy Assn., 2000-03. Mem. Assn. Bar City of NY (chair com. legal support staff 1994, mem. com. on homeless, sr. lawyers com., chair Pub. Svc. Network 2003-06), South Fork Country Club (dir. 1997-2006), The Children's Storefront (dir. 1998—), Legal Momentum (bd. legal advisors 2004—).

PORTOCARRERO, MELVY R., language educator; PhD, U. Iowa, Iowa City, 1993. Asst. prof. Bradley U., Peoria, Ill., 1999—. Recipient Outstanding Tchg. Asst. award, U. Iowa, 1989, Tchg. Excellence award, Knox Coll., 1996; Rassias Summer grant, Dartmouth U., 1994.

PORTOGALLO, RICHARD V., diversified financial services company executive; b. Mar. 26, 1959; m. Diane R. Portogallo. BBA, St. Francis Coll., NYC. Global head equity financing svcs. Morgan Stanley, NYC, 2005—07, co-head instl. clients and svcs., 2007—. Co-chair, Com. of Hearts Open Your Hearts to the Children Benefit, NYC, 2005. Office: Morgan Stanley 1585 Broadway New York NY 10036*

PORTOGHESE, PHILIP SALVATORE, medicinal chemist, educator; b. NYC, June 4, 1931; s. Philip A. and Constance (Antonelli) P.; m. Christine L. Phillips, June 11, 1960; children: Stephen, Stuart, Philip. BS, Columbia U., 1953, MS, 1958; PhD, U. Wis., 1961; Dr. honoris causa, U. Catania, Italy, 1986, Royal Danish Sch. Pharmacy, Copenhagen, 1992. Asst. prof. Coll. Pharmacy, U. Minn., Mpls., 1961-64, assoc. prof., 1964-69, prof. medicinal chemistry, 1969—, prof. pharmacology, 1987—, dir. grad. study in medicinal chemistry, 1974-86, head dept., 1974-83; disting. prof. medicinal chemistry, 2000; medicinal Chemistry hall of fame, 2006; div. medicinal Chemistry Am. Chem. Soc. Cons. NIMH., 1971-72; mem. med. chemistry B sect. NIH, 1972-76; mem. pharmacology, substance abuse and environ. toxicology interdisciplinary cluster President's Biomed. Research Panel, 1975; mem. expert panel of Flavor and Extract Mfrs. Assn. of U.S., 1984—. Mem. editorial adv. bd. Jour. Med. Chemistry, 1969-71; editor-in-chief, 1972—; mem. editorial adv. bd. Med. Chem. series, 1972-77. US Army, 1954—56. Recipient Ernest H. Volwiler award (oustanding contbns. to pharm. scis., Am. Assn. Colls. Pharmacy, 1984, N.B. Eddy Meml. award, Coll. on Problems of Drug Dependency-NAS NRC, 1991, Recognition award, U. Wis., 1996, Merit award, NIH, 1997, Oak and the Tulip award, European Fedn. Medicinal Chemistry, 1999, Nauta award, Internat. Fedn. Medicinal Chemistry, 2006; named Highly Cited Rschr., Inst. for Sci. Info., 2001. Fellow AAAS, Acad. Pharm. Scis., Am. Assn. Pharm. Scientists (Rsch. Achievement award 1990); mem. Am. Chem. Soc. (Medicinal Chemistry award 1990, E.E. Smissman-Bristol-Meyers-Squibb award 1991, Alfred Burger award 2000, named to Hall of Fame 2007), Am. Soc. Pharm. Exptl. Therapeutics, Internat. Union Pure and Applied Chemistry (commn. on medicinal chemistry 1978-82, internat. com. med. chemistry 1982-85), Soc. Neurosci., Sigma Xi, Rho Chi (Lectr. award 1999), Phi Lambda Upsilon. Home: 17 Oriole Ln Saint Paul MN 55127-6334 Office: U Minn Coll of Pharmacy 308 Harvard St SE Minneapolis MN 55455-0353 Office Phone: 612-624-9174. Business E-Mail: porto001@umn.edu.

PORTWAY, PATRICK STEPHEN, telecommunications consulting company executive, educator; b. June 18, 1939; s. Christopher Leo and Ceciala (King) P.; m. Malle M. Portway: children by previous marriage: Shawn, Pam, Vicki. BA, U. Cin., 1963; MA, U. Md., 1973; postgrad., Columbia U. Regional ADP coord. GSA, Washington, 1963-68; mgr. strategic mkt. planning Xerox Corp., 1969-74; mgr. plans and programs System Devel. Corp., 1974-78; fin. indsl. mktg. exec. Satellite Bus. Sys., 1978-80; western regional mgr. Am. Satellite Co., 1980-81; CEO Applied Bus. Telecomm., Livermore, Calif., 1981-98; prof., lectr. Golden Gate U. Grad. Sch., San Francisco, 1983—. Pub. Teleconference Mag., 1981-98; pub. (newspapers) Discovery Bay, Delta Clippers; prodr. Telecon & Ioccon Confs., 1981-98, CEO ET3 Internet Edn. Co., 1998—. Author: (with others) Teleconferencing and Distance Learning, 1992, 3rd edit., 1997. Presdl. elector Electoral Coll., Va., 1976; candidate Va. State Legislature from 19th Dist., 1971; mem. Discovery Bay Mcpl. Adv. Coun., 1992-96, chmn., 1992; mem. adv. com. Congl. Internet Caucus; mem. bd., corp. sec. The George C. Marshall Internat. Ctr., Leesburg, Va., 2003-06. 1st lt. US Army, 1963-65. Recipient Internat. Rotary award for Higher Edn., Bombay, India, 1999. Mem. Internat. Teleconferencing Assn. (founder, bd. dirs. 1983-88), Nat. Univ. Teleconferencing Network (mem. adv. bd., bd. dirs. 1986-89), US Distance Learning Assn. (founder, exec. dir. 1987-99), Electronic Funds Transfer Assn. (founder, bd. dirs. 1980), Satellite Profls., Internat. Internet Assn. (pres. 2001—), Internat. Higher Edn. Acad. of Sci., Global Distance Learning Assn. (founder, exec. dir., COO 1998-99), Jaycees (charter pres. Chantilly, Va., Disting. Svc. award Dale City, Va.), Commonwealth. E-mail: portwayinva@aol.com.

PORUMBESCU, DOINA ROXANA, psychologist, educator; b. Turnuseverin, Romania, Feb. 5, 1975; d. Serban Porumbescu and Doina Lungu. BS, Brigham Young U., Provo, Utah, 1997; PsyD, Ill. Sch. Profl. Psychology, Chgo., 2003; EdS, Nat. Luis U., Ill., 2004. Cert. sch. psychologist Kane County, Ill., 2004, lic. clin. prof. counselor Ill., 2005. Sch. psychologist Cusd 300, Sleepy Hollow, Ill., 2002—; psychotherapist Busch & Lawm Clin. Svcs., Naperville, Ill., 2007—. Adj. faculty Nat. Louis U., Skokie, Ill., 2001—. Office: Busch & Lawm Clin Svcs 2272 W 95th St Naperville IL 60564-8942 Office Fax: 630-753-9798. Personal E-mail: dr.porumbescu@gmail.com.

PORZAK, GLENN E., lawyer; b. Ill., Aug. 22, 1948; m. Judy Lea McGinnis, Dec. 19, 1970; children: Lindsay and Austin. BA with distinction, U. Colo., 1970, JD, 1973. Bar: Colo. 1973. Assoc. Holme Roberts & Owen, Denver, 1973-80, ptnr., 1980-85, mng. ptnr. Boulder office, 1985-95; mng. ptnr. Porzak Browning & Bushong LLP, Boulder, 1996—. Bd. dirs. Wells Fargo Bank Boulder, Ctr. of Am. West, U. Colo. Mus., U. Colo., presdl. search com., 2005-06. Contbr. articles to profl. jours. Bd. dirs. Manor Vail Resorts Condominium Assn., 2001, pres., 2003—07; bd. dirs. U. Colo. Found., 2002—09, vice chmn., 2004—06, chmn., 2006—08. Named Disting. Alumnus U. Colo., 1991, U. Colo. Sch. Law, 2006. Fellow Explorers Club (bd. dirs. 1995-96, Citation of Merit 1998); mem. Am. Alpine Club (pres. 1988-91), Colo. Mtn. Club (pres. 1983, hon. mem. 1983—), Colo. Outward Bound (trustee 1992-2002, vice chmn. 1997-99, chmn. 1999-2001), Phi Beta Kappa. Achievements include reaching summit of Mt. Everest, climbing highest peak on all seven continents. Home: 405 Baseline Rd Boulder CO 80302 Office: Porzak Browning & Bushong 929 Pearl St Ste 300 Boulder CO 80302-5108 Office Phone: 303-443-6800. Business E-Mail: gporzak@pbblaw.com.

PORZECANSKI, ARTURO CUSIEL, economist; b. Montevideo, Uruguay, Nov. 2, 1949; came to U.S., 1968; s. Bernardo and Stephanie (Kochmann) P.; m. Nina Ramondelli, May 25, 1974; children: Marc Vito, Katia Julia. BA, Whittier Coll., 1971; MA, U. Pitts., 1974, PhD, 1975. Rsch. economist Ctr. for L.Am. Monetary Studies, Mexico City, 1975-77; sr. economist Morgan Guaranty Trust Co. N.Y., NYC, 1977-89; chief economist Republic Nat. Bank N.Y., NYC, 1989-92; chief emerging-markets economist Kidder, Peabody & Co., Inc., NYC, 1992-93; Ams. chief economist ING Barings, NYC, 1994—. Mem. Nat. Assn. Bus. Economists, Coun. on Fgn. Rels. Republican. Home: 55 E 86th St # 14A New York NY 10028-1059 Office: ING Barings 55 E 52nd St New York NY 10022-5907

POSADA, JORGE RAFAEL, professional baseball player; b. Santurce, PR, Aug. 17, 1971; s. Jorge Posada, Sr.; m. Laura Posada, Jan. 21, 2000; children: Jorge Jr., Paulina. AA, Calhoon CC, Decatur, Ala., 1991. Catcher NY Yankees, 1995—. Co-founder Jorge Posada Found., 2000—. Recipient Silver Slugger award, 2000—03, 2007, Mentor of Yr. award, Kids in Distressed Situations, Inc., 2006, Thurman Munson award, 2000; co-recipient Excellence award, Puerto Rican Family Found., 2006; named NY Yankees Player of Yr., 2003; named to Am. League All-Star Team, 2000—03, 2007. Achievements include member of the World Series Championship winning New York Yankees, 1996, 1998-2000. Office: NY Yankees Yankee Stadium One E 161st St Bronx NY 10451 also: Jorge Posada Found PO Box 20541 New York NY 10021-0070 Office Phone: 866-823-8005.

POSAMENTIER, ALFRED STEVEN, retired mathematics educator, dean; b. NYC, Oct. 18, 1942; s. Ernest and Alice (Pisk) P.; children: Lisa Joan, David Richard. AB, Hunter Coll., 1964; MA, CCNY, 1966; postgrad., Yeshiva U., NYC, 1967-69; PhD, Fordham U., 1973; Nostrifizierung of Doctorate, U. Vienna, Austria, 1992. Tchr. math Theodore Roosevelt H.S., Bronx, NY, 1964-70; asst. prof. math. edn. CCNY, NYC, 1970-76, assoc. prof., 1977-80, prof., 1981—2009, prof. emeritus, 2009—, dept. chmn. dept. secondary and continuing edn. NYC, 1974-80, chmn., 1980-86, dir. select program in sci. and engring., 1978—2002, dir. Germany/CCNY Exch. Program, 1985—, dir. Austria/CCNY Exch. Program, 1987—, dir. Czech Republic/CCNY Exch. Program, 1989—, dir. sci. lectr. program, 1981-94; assoc. dean Sch. Edn., CCNY, NYC, 1986-95, dep. dean, 1995-99, dean, 1999—2009; dir. initiatives program City Coll., England, 1983—, Austria, Germany. Chmn. bd. dirs. Salvadori Ednl. Ctr. on Built Environ., 1988-99, 2005-; supr. math. and sci. Mamaroneck HS, NY, 1976-79; NSF math. devel. program for secondary sch. tchrs. math., NYC, 1978-82; project dir. numerous NSF sponsored math./sci. tchr. devel. insts., 1976-99; cons. NYC Bd. Edn., 1973-75, NYC Bd. Edn. Office of Evaluation, 1974-80, NYC Bd. Edn. Examiners, 1979-92, NYS Math Standards Comm., 2003-05, numerous others; coord. NSF NE Resource Ctr. Sci. and Engring., 1980-90; lectr. various confs.; vis. prof. U. Vienna, Austria, 1985, 87, 88, 90, Tech. U., Berlin, 1989, 95, U. Warsaw, 1988, Tech. U., Vienna, 1993-98, Pedgogical Inst., Vienna, 1993-99, Humboldt U., Berlin, 1996; dir. NYC Math. Project, 1994—, Math for the New Millennium Project, 1995-2000. Author: A Study Guide for the Scholastic Aptitude Test in Math., 1969, Challenging Problems in Geometry, 1970, 2nd edit., 1996, Challenging Problems in Algebra, 1970, Geometry, Its Elements and Structure, 1972, rev. edit., 1977, Geometric Constructions, 1973, Excursions in Advanced Euclidean Geometry, 1980, 2d edit., 1984, Teaching Secondary School Mathematics: Techniques and Enrichment Units, 1981, Uncommon Problems for Common Topics in Algebra, 1981, Unusual Problems for Usual Topics in Algebra, 1981, Math Motivators: Investigations in Pre-Algebra, 1982, Math Motivations: Investigations in Geometry, 1982, Using Computers in Mathematics, 1983, 2d edit., 1986, Math Motivators: Investigations in Algebra, 1983, Using Computers: Programming and Problem Solving, 1984, 2d edit., 1989, Advanced Geometric Constructions, 1988, Challenging Problems in Algebra, 1988, 2d edit., 1996, Arbeitsmaterialien: Mathematik, 1994, The Art of Problem Solving: A Resource for the Mathematics Teacher, 1996, Students! Get Ready for Mathematics for SAT-I: Problem Solving Strategies and Practice Tests, 1996, Teachers! Prepare Your Students for Mathematics for SAT-I: Methods and Problem-Solving Strategies, 1996, Deutsch-Englisch Mathematik Worterbuch, 1996, 2d edit., 2000, Tips for the Mathematics Teacher: Research-Based Strategies to help Students Learn, 1998, Problem-Solving Strategies for More Effective and Elegant Solutions: A Resource for the Mathematics Teacher, 1998, 2008, Making Pre-Algebra Come Alive, 2000, Making Algebra Come Alive, 2000, Making Geometry Come Alive, 2000, Advanced Euclidean Geometry: Excursions for Secondary Teachers and Students, 2002, Math Wonders: To Inspire Teachers and Students, 2003, Math Charmers: Tantalizing Tidbits for the Mind, 2003, Pi: A Biography of the World's Most Mysterious Number, 2004, What Successful Math Teachers Do, 7-12, 2005, What Successful Math Teachers Do, K-6, 2007; author: (with Dr. H.A. Hauptman Nobel Laureate) 101+ Great Ideas for Introducing Key Concepts in Mathematics, 2006; author: (series 9 textbooks) Progress in Mathematics, 2005—, Exemplary Practices for Secondary Math Teachers, 2007, The Fabulous Fibonacci Numbers, 2007, Problem Solving in Mathematics, Grades 3-6, 2009, Mathematical Amazements and Surprises, 2009; contbr. articles to profl. jours. and newspapers. Trustee Demarest Bd. Edn., 1977-80. Decorated Austrian Cross of Honor for Sci. and Art-First Class, 2004, Grand Medal of Honor, Austria, 1994; named Tchr. of Yr. CCNY Alumni Assn., 1993; hon. fellow U. South Bank, London, 1988, Ehrenbürger Vienna U. Tech., 2003; Fulbright scholar U. Vienna, 1990; recipient Medal of Distinction City of Vienna, 1996, Medal of Honor Technische Fachhochschule Berlin, 1996, 1000 Years Austria commemorative medal Govt. of Austria, 1997, Townsend Harris medal CCNY Alumni, 2006; Hon. Univ. Prof. of Austria, 1999; named to Hall of Fame, Hunter Coll., 2005. Mem. Math. Assn. Am., Nat. Coun. Tchrs. Math. (reviewer new publs., referee articles Math. Tchr. Jour.), Assn. Tchrs. Math. NY (exec. bd. 1966-67), Assn. Tchrs. Math. NY State, Assn. Tchrs. Math. NJ, Nat. Coun. Suprs. of Math. Home: 634 Caruso Ln Rivervale NJ 07675-6210 Home Phone: 201-664-1331; Office Phone: 212-650-6262. Personal E-mail: asp2@juno.com.

POSEN, ZAC, apparel designer; b. NYC, Oct. 24, 1980; s. Stephen and Susan. Grad., Parsons Sch. Design, 1999, Ctrl. St. Martins Coll. Art and Design, London, 1999—2001. Intern NY Costume Inst., Met. Mus. Art, Nicole Miller, Tocca; founder, designer Outspoke LLC, NYC, 2001—. Named to, Crain's NY Bus. "40 under 40", 2004. Office: Outspoke LLC 13-17 Laight St New York NY 10013 Office Fax: 212-925-1264. Business E-Mail: info@zacposen.com.

POSER, ERNEST GEORGE, psychologist, educator; b. Vienna, Mar. 2, 1921; emigrated to Can., 1942, naturalized, 1946; s. Paul and Blanche (Furst) P.; m. Maria Jutta Cahn, July 3, 1953; children: Yvonne, Carol, Michael. BA, Queen's U., Kingston, Ont., 1946, MA, 1949; PhD, U. London, 1952. Diplomate: Am. Bd. Profl. Psychologists; registered psychologist, B.C. Asst. prof. U. N.B., 1946-48; chief psychologist N.B. Dept. Health, 1952-54; prof. psychology McGill U., Montreal, 1954-83, assoc. prof. psychiatry Faculty Medicine, 1963-83; adj. prof. dept. psychology U. B.C., 1984-95; dir. behavior therapy unit Douglas Hosp. Center, Montreal, 1966-83. Author: Adaptive Learning: Behavior Modification with Children, 1973, Behavior Therapy in Clinical Practice, 1977. Chair World Views Collaborative, Vancouver, BC, 2004—. Hon. fellow Middlesex Hosp., London, 1964 Fellow Canadian Psychol. Assn., Am. Psychol. Assn. Home Phone: 604-222-4748. Personal E-mail: erjuposer@shaw.ca.

POSER, JOAN RAPPS, artist, writer; b. Plainfield, NJ, Apr. 10, 1940; d. Mandel Max and Marion Davidson Rapps; m. Jay Sanford Poser, Nov. 15, 1964; children: Lester Philip, Toby Anne BA, U. Conn., 1962. Self-employed travel cons., Lancaster, Pa., 1976—79; tchr. McDonogh Sch., Balt., 1982—90; artist's agt. Joan E. Poser Assocs. Agts. in the Arts, Lancaster, 1978—; co-owner, v.p. Poser's Apparel, Inc., Pa., 1990—95; co-owner Poser's Accessories Sales Reps., 1995—; polit. speech writer, 2005—; writer chldren's poetry, 2006—. Cons. Charmelle, Inc., San Francisco, 2002—. Pres. Lancaster Town Fair, 1974, Temple Beth El Sisterhood, Lancaster, 1973—77, donor chmn., 2000—03; pres. and devel. chmn. Md. Assocs. for Dyslexic Adults and Youth, Inc., 1989—91; campaign chair Bus. and Profl. Women, Assoc. Jewish Charities, Balt., 1985; spl. events chair Cultural Arts Inst. Chizuk Amuno Congregation, 1986—90, trustee, 1986—90; chmn. Lancaster Jewish Cmty. Ctr. 50th Anniversary Gala, 1994, Temple Beth El 50th Anniversary Gala, 1995; bd. dirs. Temple Beth El, 1991—92, Janus Sch., Lancaster, 1991—94, Lancaster Jewish Cmty. Ctr., 1991—93. Mem. Hadassah Democrat. Avocations: opera, sports, architecture, travel, writing. Home: 119 Greenview Dr Lancaster PA 17601-4988 Office Phone: 717-560-7976.

POSER, NORMAN STANLEY, law educator; b. London, May 28, 1928; came to U.S., 1939, naturalized, 1946; s. Jack and Margaret (Salomon) P.; m. Miriam Kugelman, Sept. 1, 1957 (div. 1979); children: Samuel Marc, Susan; m. Judith Eiseman Cohn, Aug. 11, 1985. AB cum laude, Harvard U., 1948, LLB cum laude, 1958. Bar: N.Y. 1958. Asso. Greenbaum, Wolff & Ernst, NYC, 1958-61; atty. SEC, Washington, 1961-64, asst. dir. div. trading and markets, 1964-67; asso. Rosenman, Colin, Kaye, Petschek, Freund & Emil, NYC, 1967-68; v.p. Am. Stock Exchange, NYC, 1968-72, sr. v.p., 1972-75, exec. v.p., 1975-80; adj. prof. law NYU, 1975-80; prof. law Bklyn. Law Sch., 1980—2007; prof. law emeritus, 2007—. Cons. World Bank, SEC, OAS, various stock exchs.; spl. counsel N.Y. Stock Exch., 1987—. Mem. adv. bd.: Regulation and Law Report, 1979-03, Rev. Securities and Commodities Regulation, 1975—; author: International Securities Regulation: London's "Big Bang" and the European Securities Markets, 1991, Broker-Dealer Law and Regulation, 1995, 2d edit., 1997, 3d edit. 2000, (with James A. Fanto) 4th edit., 2007, supplimentary, 2009, Escape: A Jewish Scandinavian Family in the Second World War, 2006. Served with U.S. Army, 1951-53. Mem. Am. Law Inst., ABA, N.Y.C. Bar Assn., Nat. Futures Assn. (arbitrator 1987—). Clubs: Harvard (N.Y.C.). Office: 250 Joralemon St Brooklyn NY 11201-3700 E-mail: norman.poser@brooklaw.edu.

POSES, FREDERIC M., manufacturing executive, former engineering company executive; b. 1942; BBA in Fin., NYU, 1965. Vol. Peace Corps, 1967-69; various positions Allied Corp., 1969-85; fin. analyst Allied Signal, Inc., 1969; pres. plastics and engineered materials divsn. AlliedSignal Inc., Morristown, NJ, 1985-86, pres. fibers divsn., 1986-88, exec. v.p., pres. engineered materials, 1988-98, pres. and COO, 1998-99; chmn., CEO Trane Inc. (formerly Am. Std. Companies Inc.), Piscataway, NJ, 2000; chmn. Tyco Electronics Ltd. Bd. dirs. Allied Signal, Inc., 1997—99, Trane Inc. (formerly Am. Std. Companies Inc.), 1999—2008, Raytheon Co., Centex Corp., 2001—. Office: Tyco Electronics Ltd Rheinstrasse 20 Ch-8200 Schaffhausen Switzerland Office Phone: 011-41 (0) 52 633 66 00.*

POSEY, BILL (WILLIAM J. POSEY), United States Representative from Florida; b. Washington, Dec. 18, 1947; s. Walter J. and Beatrice (Tohl) P.; m. Mary Ingram, Nov. 23, 1987; children: Pamela J., Catherine L. AA, Brevard Community Coll., 1969; student, Stetson U., 1978. Quality assurance rep. McDonnell-Douglas, Cape Kennedy, Fla., 1966-69; pres., CEO Mid Fla. Racing Inc., Melbourne, 1969-71; mgr. Gay & Taylor Inc., St. Petersburg, Fla., 1971-74; broker Sherwood Realty Inc., Cocoa, Fla., 1974-78; pres., CEO Posey & Co., Rockledge, Fla., 1978—; mem. Fla. House of Reps. from 32nd dist., Tallahassee, 1992-2000, Fla. State Senate from 15th Dist., Tallahassee, 2001—08, US Congress from 15th Fla. Dist., 2009—. Bd. dirs. Rockledge Land Co., Indian Oaks Corp., Rockledge, Rockledge Realty Corp., Nat. Racetrack Clearing House, Rockledge; founder Fla. Motorsports Hall Fame, 1986. Author: Race Track Promotters Handbook, 1971. Mem. Rockledge Planning Commn., 1974-76, Rockledge City Coun., 1976-86,

Rockledge Econ. Devel. Commn., 1985—, Bus. and Indsl. Task Force, 1985—. Mem. Fla. Assn. Realtors (bd. dirs. 1986—), Cape Kennedy Area Bd. Realtors (pres. 1987—), Cocoa Beach C. of C. (com. 100 1974—). Clubs: Country Brevard. Lodges: Kiwanis, Masons. Republican. Methodist. Office: US Congress 132 Cannon House Office Bldg Washington DC 20515 also: 2725 Judge Fran Jamieson Way Bldg C Melbourne FL 32940 Office Phone: 202-225-3671, 321-632-1776. Office Fax: 202-225-3516, 321-639-8595.*

POSEY, CAROLYN ANN, secondary school educator; b. Hobbs, N.Mex., Jan. 26, 1941; d. Ulman Garrett and Ruby Lee (Worley) Montgomery; m. Lawrence Dare Posey Jr., Dec. 23, 1983; children: James Keith, Carla Ann, Laura Ruth, Paula Lynn. BS, Ea. N.Mex. U., 1962. Apprentice embalmer Wheeler Mortuary, Portales, N.Mex., 1960-62; tchr. Houston Pub. Schs., 1962-63; sec. Baylor Med. Sch., 1963; office mgr. Albuquerque Civ. Light Opera, 1977-78; tchr. Albuquerque Pub. Schs., 1979—97; ret., 1998; producer of musicals Carlaw Enterprises, Albuquerque, 1984—; travel agt. Bolack Total Travel, 1987-88. Mem. Wool Warehouse Dinner Theatre, Albuquerque, 1987-88. Producer: George M at the Kimo Theatre, 1986, On The Town, 1987. Office asst. Rep. Party Pete Domenici's, Albuquerque, 1986; alumni bd. Eastern N.Mex. U., Portales, 1988-94; high sch. reunion com., Highland HS., Albuquerque, 1989-1999. Recipient Service award Albuquerque Civic Light Opera, 1985, Crystal Apple award Albuquerque Pub. Schs., 1993, 95, Best in Show Porcelain Dollmaking State Fair, 2005, 06. Mem. Amigos ACLOA (pres. 1975, chmn. edn. com.). Avocations: painting, tennis, ceramics, writing, travel. Home: 15947 Bridle Ridge Dr Monument CO 80132-6096 Personal E-mail: carlaw49@att.net.

POSEY, CLYDE LEE, business administration and accounting educator; b. Tucumcari, N.Mex., Dec. 27, 1940; s. Rollah P. and Opal (Patterson) P.; m. Dora Diane Vassar; children: Amanda Bennett, Julia Forsyth, Rebecca; m. Judith James Jerry, July 31, 1991; stepchildren: David Jerry, Georgia Kenyan. BBA, U. Tex., El Paso, 1963; MBA, U. Tex., 1965; postgrad., U. So. Calif., 1968; PhD, Okla. State U., 1978. Registered investment advisor. Lab. aide FBI, Washington, 1959-60; acct. Lipson, Cox & Colton (now Deloitte & Touche), El Paso, Tex., 1962; auditor Main & Co. (now KPMG), El Paso, 1963; tchg. asst. U. Tex., Austin, 1963-65; tax cons. Peat, Marwick, Mitchell & Co. (now KPMG), Dallas, 1965-66; cons. Roberson, Martin, Horg and Ryckman, Fresno, Calif., 1967; pvt. practice acctg. Fresno, 1966—78, Ruston, La., 1978—; asst. prof. Calif. State U., Fresno, Ruston, La., 1966—78; assoc. prof. La. Tech. U., Ruston, 1978-84, prof., 1984—2005; prof. MBA program Alcorn State U., Natchez, 2005—. Vis. asst. prof. Ctrl. State U., Edmond, Okla., 1971-72, U. Okla., Norman, 1976-78; cons. J. David Spence Accountancy Corp., Fresno, 1974-76; many coms. at La. Tech. U. including acad. senator, new faculty welcoming com., acctg. scholarship chmn.; faculty senate rep.; Faculty Consortium, St. Charles, Ill., 1993; expert witness Superior Ct. Calif. and Dist. Ct., La. Contbr. numerous articles to profl. jours., bus. mags., newspapers, also book reviews; presentations to profl. meetings. Past bd. dirs. Goodwill, Inc., Ctrl. Calif.; ch. deacon and mem. many coms.; pres., treas., state scripture coord. Gideons Internat. Ruston Camp; rep. United Way La. Tech. U., Ruston; deacon 1st Bapt. Ch., Ruston With USCG, 1965. Recipient El Paso CPA's Outstanding Jr. scholarship, Standard Oil scholarship, Price Waterhouse scholarship, Outstanding Educator award Gamma Beta Phi, 1986. Mem. AICPA (life), Am. Acctg. Assn. (La. membership com. chmn.), Am. Inst. for Decision Scis. (program com. chmn. acctg. track), La. Soc. CPAs, Am. Tax Assn. (internat. tax policy subcom.), Beta Gamma Sigma (pres.), Beta Alpha Psi, Delta Sigma Pi. Baptist. Avocations: triathlons, bicycle racing, golf, tennis, gardening. Home: 2700 Foxxwood Dr Ruston LA 71270-2509 Office: 9 Campus Dr Natchez MS 39120 Office Phone: 601-304-4367.

POSEY, GARRY LEE, theater educator; b. Chattanooga, Tenn., Jan. 22, 1976; s. Thomas Edward and Linda Simmons Posey. BA in Theatre with honors, Catawba Coll., Salisbury, NC, 1998; MFA in Theatre and Directing, U. Miss., Oxford, 2006. Youth theatre dir. Chattanooga Theatre Ctr., 2000—03; instr., profl. staff Chattanooga State Tech. Com. Coll., 2006—. Artistic dir., founder (theatre) Ensemble Theatre of Chattanooga (Arts Move grant, 2006); dir.: (theatre) Chattanooga State Repertory Theatre Summer Festival, Chattanooga Youth Theatre (Leighton F. Ballew MFA Directing award, Southeastern Theatre Conf., 2003). Home: 915 Central Ave Chattanooga TN 37403 Office: Chattanooga State Tech Com Coll 4501 Amnicola Hwy Chattanooga TN 37406 Office Fax: 423-697-4400. Personal E-mail: garryposey@yahoo.com. Business E-Mail: garry.posey@chattanogastate.edu.

POSEY, PAMELA GAYLE, special education educator; b. Wagoner, Okla., Feb. 2, 1958; d. Wesley and Oleta Christine Vandever; m. Terry Gene Posey, Mar. 18, 1977; children: Joshua Lee, Kerry Gene. BS in Interdisciplinary Studies, Tex. A&M, Texarkana, 2003. Tchr.'s aide Mt. Pleasant Ind. Sch. Dist., Tex., 1992—2002, spl. edn. tchr., 2003—; lead tchr. Sims Elem. Spl. Edn., 2007—09; lang. tchr. LINC, 2008—09. Sec. Ch. God Prophecy, Sugar Hill, Tex., 1985—. Recipient CitiCorp Fin. Future Tchr., 2003; named Employee of the Yr., Sims Elem., 2001—02. Mem.: Coun. Exceptional Children, Tex. Classroom Tchrs. Assn. Avocations: reading, music. Home: 2238 County Rd 3925 Mount Pleasant TX 75455 Office Phone: 903-575-2062 ext. 7149. Business E-Mail: pposey@mpisd.net.

POSEY, PARKER, actress; b. Balt., Nov. 8, 1968; d. Chris Posey. Student, SUNY, Purchase. Actor (films) Joey Breaker, 1993, Description of a Struggle, 1993, The Wake, 1993, Sleepless in Seattle, 1993, Dazed & Confused, 1993, Coneheads, 1993, Flirt, 1993, Dead Connection, 1994, Opera No. 1, 1994, Iris, 1994, Mixed Nuts, 1994, Amateur, 1994, Sleep With Me, 1994, Drunks, 1995, Frisk, 1995, An Eviction Notice, 1995, Party Girl, 1995, Kicking and Screaming, 1995, The doom Generation, 1995, The Daytrippers, 1996, Basquiat, 1996, Waiting for Guffman, 1996, SubUrbia, 1997, The House of Yes, 1997, Clockwatchers, 1997, Henry Fool, 1997, What Rats Won't Do, 1998, You've Got Mail, 1998, The Misadventures of Margaret, 1998, The Venice Project, 1999, Dinner at Fred's, 1999, Scream 3, 2000, Best in Show, 2000, Josie and the Pussycats, 2001, The Anniversary Party, 2001, Personal Velocity: Three Portraits, 2002, The Sweetest Thing, 2002, The Event, 2003, A Mighty Wind, 2003, Laws of Attraction, 2004, The Sisters of Mercy, 2004, Blade: Trinity, The OH in Ohio, 2006, Superman Returns, 2006, For Your Consideration, 2006, Fay Grim, 2006, Broken English, 2007, Broken English, 2007, The Eye, 2008; (TV series) As The World Turns, 1991-92; (TV films) First Love, Fatal Love, 1991, Tracey Takes on New York, 1993, Hell on Heels: The Battle of Mary Kay, 2002, Frankenstein, 2004; (TV miniseries) Armistead Maupin's Tales of the City, 1993, More Tales of the City, 1998, Further Tales of the City, 2001; (TV appearances) (voice only) Futurama, 2000, (voice only) The Simpsons, 2000, Will & Grace, 2001, Boston Legal, 2006; (stage) Hurlyburly, 2005, (Lucille Lortel awards, outstanding featured acress, 2005); screenwriter (with Rory Kelly) Dumb in Love, 1995; contributing editor, Open City literary mag. Recipient Spl. Jury prize Sundance Film Festival, 1997; named Queen of Indies by TIME Mag. Office: William Morris Agy 151 S El Camino Dr Beverly Hills CA 90212-2775

POSHARD, GLENN (GLENDAL W. POSHARD), academic administrator, former congressman; b. Herald, Ill., Oct. 31, 1945; BA, Southern Ill. U., 1970, MS, 1974, PhD, 1984. Tchr. high sch., 1970—74; asst. dir. then dir. Ill. State Regional Edn. Svc. Ctr., 1974—84; mem. Ill. State Senate, 1984-88, 101st-105th Congresses from 22nd (now 19th) Ill. Dist., 1989-98; tchr., adminstr. John A. Logan Coll., Carterville, Ill.; vice chancellor for adminstrn. So. Ill. U., Carbondale, Ill., 1999—2003, chmn. bd. trustees, 2004—05, pres., 2006—. Founder Poshard Found. for Abused Children. Served in US Army, 1962—65. Democrat. Office: So Ill U 1400 Douglas Dr Carbondale IL 62901 E-mail: poshard@notes.siu.edu.

POSIN, KATHRYN OLIVE, choreographer; b. Butte, Mont, Mar. 23, 1943; d. Daniel Q. and Frances (Schweitzer) P. BA in Dance, Bennington Coll., 1965; MFA in Interdisciplinary and World Dance, NYU, 1994; studies in composition, 1965-78, studies in ballet, 1965-90, studies in modern dance, 1967-80. Mem. dance co. Am. Dance Theater at Lincoln Ctr., 1965; dancer Anna Sokolow Dance Co., 1965-73; artistic dir. Kathryn Posin Dance Co., NYC, 1972-91; choreographer Eliot Feld Ballet, NYC, 1978, Netherlands Dance Theater, Den Hague, Switzerland, 1980, Alvin Ailey Am. Dance Theater, NYC, 1980; mem. dance faculty U. Wis., Milw., 1984-86, choreographer, 1984-88; tchr., choreographer UCLA, 1988-90, Trinity Coll., Hartford, Conn., 1990-91; tchr. world dance Gallatin Sch. of NYU, 2006—. Mem. dance faculty, choreographer U. Calif., Santa Barbara, 1986; tchr. dance technique and performance Tchr.'s Coll. Columbia U., spring 1990; tchr. composition and technique Nat. Inst. of Arts, Taiwan, 1991; tchr. world dance Gallatin Sch. NYU; founding chair Joffrey Ballet Sch., New Sch. U. BFA in Dance, 1998. Choreographer (performing cos./orgns.) Cherry Orchard, Lincoln Ctr., NYC, 1978, Alvin Ailey Am. Dance Theater, 1981, Netherlands Dans Theater 84182, Extemporary Dance Co. London, Balletmet, Columbus, Ohio, Milw. Ballet, 1991, 1993, 1995, 1996, Cin. Ballet, 1997, Kansas City Ballet, 2004, Louisville Ballet, 2004, (prin. works) Salvation, Off-Broadway, NYC, 1969, Waves, 1975 (Am. Dance Festival commn.), The Cherry Orchard, NY Shakespeare Festival, 1979, Mary Stuart, Acting Co., 1980, Shady Grove (grantee jt. program of Ohio Arts and Humanities Couns., 1991), The Tempest, Am. Shakespeare Festival, Stratford, Conn., 1982, Midsummer Night's Dream, Arena Stage, Washington, 1982, Boys From Syracuse, Am. Repertory Theater, Harvard U., 1983, The Paper Gramophone, Hartford Stage, 1989, Of Rage and Remembrance, 1990 (Premiere of Yr. in Music and Dance, Milw. Jour.), Stepping Stones, 1993 (co-recipient Meet the Composer/Choreographer award Milw. Ballet, 1993), many others; subject of documentary Kathy's Dance. Grantee Guggenheim Found., 1978, NY State Coun. on Arts, 1977, 79, 80, Jerome Robbins Found., 1972; grantee Nat. Endowment for Arts 1981, 82, 85-87, choreography fellow, 1995-96; Doris Humphrey fellow Am. Dance Festival, New London, Conn., 1968. Office: Kathryn Posin Dance Co 20 Bond St New York NY 10012-2406 Office Phone: 212-777-1515. Personal E-mail: Pozndance@aol.com.

POSINASETTI, NAGESWARA RAO, manufacturing engineering educator; b. Palakol, Andhra, India, June 15, 1947; permanent resident, 2004; s. Kondaiah and Suramma P.; m. Venkata Rama Lakshmi, Aug. 18, 1976; children: Prasant, Praveen. BSc in Physics, Chemistry, Math, Narsapur (India) Coll., 1967; BE in Mech. Engring., Govt. Engring. Coll., Anantapur, India, 1970; M in Engring., Birla Inst. Tech. & Sci., Pilani, India, 1973; PhD, Indian Inst. Tech., New Delhi, 1981. Asst. lectr. Birla Inst. Tech. & Sci., Pilani, India, 1973-75; lectr. Indian Inst. Tech., New Delhi, 1975-81, asst. prof., 1981-90, prof., 1990-97; vis. faculty MARA U. Tech., Shah Alam, Malaysia, 1997—2001; assoc. prof. U. No. Iowa, Cedar Falls, Iowa, 2001—06, prof., 2006—. Vis. faculty Asian Inst. Tech., Bangkok, Thailand, 1993. Author: Numerical Control and Computer Aided Manufacturing, 1985, Manufacturing Technology Foundry, Forming & Welding, 1987, Computer Aided Manufacturing, 1993, AutoCAD 14 for Engineering Drawing Made Easy, 1999, Manufacturing Technology Metal Cutting and Machine Tools, 2000, CAD/CAM Principles and Application, 2002; editor: Emerging Trends in Manufacturing, 1986; contbr. numerous articles to profl. jours. Mem.: ASME, Nat. Assoc. of Indsl. Tech., Am. Soc. Engring. Edn., Soc. Mfg. Engr., Indian Soc. Mech. Engrs. Hindu. Office: U No Iowa Dept Indsl Tech Cedar Falls IA 50614-0178 Home: 1720 Waterloo Rd Apt 3 Cedar Falls IA 50613 Office Phone: 319-273-6429. Personal E-mail: pnageswara@hotmail.com. Business E-Mail: rao@uni.edu.

POSITAN, WAYNE JOHN, lawyer; b. Newark, Sept. 11, 1948; BA in Govt. magna cum laude, Boston U., 1970; JD, NYU, 1974. Bar: NJ 1974, US Dist. Ct. NJ 1974, US Dist. Ct. (ea. dist.) NY 1987, US Dist. Ct. (so. dist.) NY 1989, US Ct. Appeals (3d cir.) 1981, US Supreme Ct. 1989. Assoc. Lum, Biunno & Tompkins, Newark, 1974-82; ptnr. Lum, Drasco & Positan, Roseland, NJ, 1982—; mng. ptnr. Lum Danzis, Roseland, NJ, 1990—. Author: (with others) Business Torts Litigation, 2005, Employment Litigation Handbook, 1998, Jury Instructions in Employment Litigation, 1994, 2d edit., 2005; assoc. editor Annual Survey of American Law, 1972-73; editor-in-chief N.J. Labor and Employment Law, 1998, 2d edit., 2005. Trustee Montclair State U., 1999-2006. Staff sgt. USAR, 1970-76. Mem. ABA (house dels. 2003—, chmn. employment and labor law com. sect. litig. 1990-93, chmn. sect. litig. ann. meeting 1995-96, co-chair task force on merit selection of judges 1996-97, coun. mem. sect. litig. 1997-2000, chmn. commn. multijurisdictional practice 2000-02, dir. divsn. 2001-05, bd. govs. 2006-2009), NJ Bar Assn. (labor and employment sect. chmn. 1995-97, pres. 2006-07), Am. Inns of Ct. (master Sidney Reitman Laborand Employment 1993-2005), Confrerie de la Chaine des Rotisseurs (vice conseiller gastronomique Saddle River Valley chpt. 1987—), Essex Fells Country Club, Phi Sigma Delta. Republican. Presbyterian. Avocations: golf, photography, fishing. Office: Lum Drasco Positan LLC 103 Eisenhower Pky Roseland NJ 07068-1049 Office Phone: 973-228-6730. E-mail: wpositan@lumlaw.com.

POSKANZER, STEVEN GARY, academic administrator, lawyer; b. Cortland, NY, Sept. 1, 1958; s. Charles Newton and Joan Rae (Mamolen) P.; m. Jane Anne Nofer; children: Jill Madeline, Craig Robert. BA, Princeton U., 1980; JD, Harvard U., 1983. Assoc. Arent, Fox, Kintner, Plotkin & Kahn, Washington, 1983-85; asst. gen. counsel U. Penn., Philadelphia, Pa., 1985—88; assoc. gen. counsel U. Penn, Philadelphia, Pa., 1988—93; spl. asst. to provost Princeton U., 1991—92; exec. asst. to pres. U. Chgo., 1993-97; assoc. provost SUNY, Albany, 1997—98, sr. assoc. provost, 1998—2000, vice provost, 2000—01, interim pres. New Paltz, 2001—03, pres., 2003—. Author: Higher Education Law: The Faculty, 2001. Mem. Phi Beta Kappa, 1980. Office: SUNY New Paltz 75 S Manheim Blvd New Paltz NY 12561 Home: 29 Cedar Ridge Rd New Paltz NY 12561-2728 Office Phone: 845-257-3288.

POSLIGUA-SINNOTT, KETTY, psychologist; d. Carmen J. Azon; 1 child, Sean Alexander Sinnott. MA in Psychology, CCNY, 1996. Cert. teacher U. State NY, 2000. Psychologist Horace Mann Pub. Sch. 90, Richmond Hill, NY, 1997—, Rosa Pks. Pub. Sch. 254, Richmond Hill, 2004—08. Office: Horace Mann Pub Sch 86-50 109 St Richmond Hill NY 11418

POSNER, ETHAN M., lawyer; b. Dec. 17, 1962; BA with high honors, Wesleyan U., 1984; JD magna cum laude, U. Mich., 1989. Bar: NY 1990, DC 1991. Adj. prof. law Georgetown U., Washington, 2001; health care mgmt. cons. APM, Inc.; law clk. for Judge Harrison L. Winter US Ct. Appeals (4th cir.); ptnr. Covington & Burling, Washington, chmn., Health Care Practice Group; dep. assoc. atty. gen. US Dept. Justice, 1999—2001. Named one of Best Lawyers in Am., 2006, Litigation's Rising Stars, The Am. Lawyer, 2007. Mem.: ABA Litig. Sect. (co-chmn., antitrust class actions com.). Office: Covington & Burling 1201 Pennsylvania Ave NW Washington DC 20004-2401 Office Phone: 202-662-5317. Office Fax: 202-662-6291. Business E-Mail: eposner@cov.com.

POSNER, GARY HERBERT, chemist, educator; b. NYC, June 2, 1943; s. Joseph M. and Rose (Klein) P.; children: Joseph, Michael. BA, Brandeis U., 1965; MA, Harvard U., 1965, PhD, 1968. Asst. prof. Johns Hopkins U., Balt., 1969-74, assoc. prof., 1974-79, prof. dept. chemistry, 1979—, Scowe prof. chemistry, 1989—, prof. dept. environ. chemistry, 1982—, chmn. dept. of chemistry, 1987-90. Mem. medicinal chemistry study sect. NIH, 1986-89; cons. Batelle Meml. Inst., Columbus, Ohio, 1983, S.W. Rsch. Inst., San Antonio, Nova Pharm. Co., Balt.; mem. Fulbright-Hays Adv. Screening Com. in Chemistry, 1978-81; Michael vis. prof. Weizmann Inst. Sci., Rehovot, Israel, 1983; leader Round Table discussion Welch Found. Conf. Chem. Rsch., Houston, 1973, 83; Novartis Chemistry lectr., 2004-2005; lectr. in field. Author: Introduction to Organic Synthesis Using Organocopper Reagents, 1980; mem. editl. bd. Organic Reactions, 1976-89; exec. editor Tetrahedron Reports, 1996-2006. Named Chemist of Yr., State of Md., 1987; fellow Japan Soc. for Promotion Sci., 1991; recipient Johns Hopkins U. Disting. Tchng. award, 1994, merit award NIH, 2006. Mem. AAAS, AAUP, AAUP, Am. Chem. Soc. (A.C. Cope Sr. Scholar award 2004), Phi Beta Kappa Office: Johns Hopkins U Dept Chemistry 3300 N Charles St Baltimore MD 21218 E-mail: ghp@jhu.edu.

POSNER, HELAINE J., museum curator; b. NYC, Nov. 17, 1953; d. Abraham and Sheila (Ferkauf) P. BA, Georgetown U., 1975; MA, George Washington U., 1978. Asst. curator Chase Manhattan Bank Art Collection, NYC, 1978-80; curator U. Gallery, U. Mass., Amherst, Mass., 1981-84, dir., 1984-88; curator contemporary art, chief curator Nat. Mus. of Women in the Arts, Washington, 1988-90; dir. Josh Baer Gallery, NYC, 1990; curator List Visual Arts Ctr., Cambridge, Mass., 1991—98; dir. exhibitions Independent Ctr. Photography, NYC, 1998; adj. curator Am. Fedn. Arts, NYC, 2003—08; chief curator, dep. dir. curatorial affairs Neuberger Mus. Art, Purchase, NY, 2008—. Co-commr. US Pavilion Venice Biennale, 1999. Co-author: Kiki Smith: Telling Tales, 2001, After the Revolution: Women Who Transformed Contemporary Art, 2007. Mem. Am. Assn. Mus. Office: Neuberger Mus Art Purchase Coll SUNY 735 Anderson Hill Rd Purchase NY 10577 Office Phone: 914-251-6106. Office Fax: 914-251-6101. E-mail: helaine.posner@puchase.edu.*

POSNER, JEROME BEEBE, neurologist, educator; b. Cin., Mar. 20, 1932; s. Philip and Rose (Goldberg) Posner; m. Gerta Grunen, Aug. 29, 1954; children: Roslyn, Joel, P.J. BS, U. Wash., 1951, MD, 1955. Internship King County Hosp., Seattle, 1955—56; asst. resident in neurology U. Wash. Affiliated Hosps., Seattle, 1956—59, fellow in neurology, 1958—59; spl. fellow NIH, U. Wash., 1961—63; instr. medicine U. Louisville Sch. Medicine, 1959—61; attending neurologist King County Hosp., 1962—63; asst. prof. neurology Cornell U. Med. Coll., NYC, 1963—67, assoc. prof., 1967—70, prof., 1970—, vice chmn. dept. neurology, 1978—87; asst. attending neurologist N.Y. Hosp., 1963—67, assoc. attending neurologist, 1967—70, attending neurologist, 1970—; assoc. Cotzias Lab. of Neuro-Oncology, Sloan Kettering Inst. Cancer Research, NYC, 1967—76, mem., 1976—; chief neuropsychiat. service, attending physician dept. medicine Meml. Hosp. for Cancer and Allied Diseases, 1967—75, attending physician, 1975—, chmn. dept. neurology, 1975—87, 1989—97, Cotzias chair neuro-oncology, 1986—; Evelyn Frew clin. rsch. prof. Am. Cancer Soc., 1996—2006. Mem. med. adv. bd. Burke Rehab. Ctr., White Plains, NY, 1973—2005; adj. prof., vis. physician Rockefeller U. and Hosp., NYC, 1973—75; mem. neurology B study sect. NIH, 1972—76; coun. mem. NINDS, 1998—2001. Author (with F. Plum): Diagnosis of Stupor and Coma, 3d edit., 1980; author: (with H. Gilbert and L. Weiss) Brain Metastasis, 1980, Neurologic Complications of Cancer, 1995; author: (with DeAngeles) Intracranial Tumor, 2002; mem. editl. bd.: Archives of Neurology, 1971—76, Annals of Neurology, 1976—80, Am. Jour. Medicine, 1978—93, Neurology, 1992—96; contbr. articles to profl. jours. Served with M.C. US Army, 1959—61. Fellow: AAAS; mem.: AMA, Am. Acad. Arts and Scis., Soc. Neuroscis., Inst. Medicine N.Y. Acad. Scis., Harvey Soc., Assn. Am. Physicians, Am. Physiol. Soc., Am. Neurol. Assn. (pres. 1997—99), Am. Fedn. Clin. Rsch., Am. Assn. Cancer Rsch., Am. Acad. Neurology (Farber Brain Tumor award 1988), Can. Neurol. Soc. (hon.), Alpha Omega Alpha. Office: Meml Sloan-Kettering Cancer 1275 York Ave New York NY 10021-6094 Home Phone: 212-753-7359; Office Phone: 212-639-7047. Business E-Mail: posnerj@mskcc.org.

POSNER, KATHY ROBIN, retired communications executive; b. Oceanside, NY, Nov. 3, 1952; d. Melvyn and Davonne Hope (Hansen) P. BA in Journalism, Econs., Manhattanville Coll., 1974. Corp. liaison Gulf States Mortgage, Atlanta, 1980-82; dir. promotion Gammon's of Chgo., 1982-83; coordinator trade show mktg. Destron, Chgo., 1983-84; pres. Postronics, Chgo., 1984-87; v.p. Martin E. Janis & Co., Inc., Chgo., 1987-90; chmn. Comm 2 Inc., Chgo., 1990—2005, ret., 2005. Editor: How to Maximize Your Profits, 1983; contbg. editor Internat. Backgammon Guide, 1974-84, Backgammon Times, 1981-84, Chgo. Advt. and Media; columnist Food Industry News. Bd. dirs. Chgo. Beautification Com., 1987, Concerned Citizens for Action, Chgo., 1987, Midwest Bd. Shaare Zedek, Med. Ctr. Jerusalem; mem. steering com. Better Boys Found.; campaign mgr. Brown for Alderman, Chgo., 1987; mem. bd. cons. Little City Found.; mem. benefit bd. C.A.U.S.E.S. Mem. NATAS, Soc. Profl. Journalists, Mensa, Chgo. Acad. for Arts (bd. mem.), Chgo. Area Pub. Affairs Group, City Club Chgo. (bd. dirs.), Chgo. Legal Clinic (bd. dirs.), Kup Purple Heart Found. (bd. dirs.), Jesse White Tumblers, (bd. dirs), Chgo. Commn. on Human Rels. Adv. Coun. on Women, Ill. State Treas. Women's Affairs Coun., 18th Dist. Police Adv. Coun., Midwest Region of the Am. Com. for Shaare Zedek Med. Ctr. Jerusalem. (bd. dirs.), The Heartland Group. Republican. Jewish. Avocations: politics, reading. Home: 100 E Huron # 3505 Chicago IL 60611 Personal E-mail: kathyposner@aol.com.

POSNER, KENNETH, lighting designer; Ed., SUNY Purchase. Lighting design (Broadway plays) The Rose Tattoo, 1995, The Father, 1996, Getting Away with Murder, 1996, The Rehearsal, 1996, The Last Night of Ballyhoo, 1997, The Little Foxes, 1997, A View From the Bridge, 1997, Side Man, 1998 (Lucille Lortel award), Little Me, 1998, You're a Good Man, Charlie Brown, 1999, The Lion in Winter, 1999, Swing!, 1999, Uncle Vanya, 2000, The Adventures of Tom Sawyer, 2001, The Goat, or Who Is Sylvia?, 2002, The Smell of the Kill, 2002, The Man Who Had All the Luck, 2002, Hairspray, 2002, Imaginary Friends, 2002, Wicked, 2003, Oldest Living Confederate Widow Tells All, 2003, The

Frogs, 2004, Little Women, 2005, Dirty Rotten Scoundrels, 2005, Glengarry Glen Ross, 2005, The Odd Couple, 2005, Lestat, 2006, The Coast of Utopia, 2006 (Drama Desk award outstanding lighting design, 2007, Tony award best lighting design of a play, 2007), The Pirate Queen, 2007, Legally Blonde, 2007, Grease, 2007, (Off-Broadway) The Wild Party, The Play About the Baby, tick, tick...BOOM!, The Waverly Gallery, Pride's Crossing, As Bees in Honey Drown, Cowgirls, The Food Chain, subUrbia.

POSNER, MICHAEL HOFFMAN, lawyer; b. Chgo., Nov. 19, 1950; s. Harry Randolph and Elizabeth (Hoffman) Posner; m. Deborah Korzenik, Dec. 12, 1986. Children: Alexander Posner, Hannah Posner, Daniel Posner. BA with honors, U. Mich., 1972; JD, U. Calif., Berkeley, 1975. Bar: Calif. 1975, Ill. 1976, US Dist Ct. No. Dist. Ill. 1976. Rsch. asst. Internat. Commn. Jurists, Geneva, 1974; assoc. Sonnenschein, Nath & Rosenthal, Chgo., 1975-78; exec. dir. Human Rights First, NYC, 1978—2005, pres., 2005—. Vis. lectr. Yale Law Sch., New Haven, 1981-84, Columbia Law Sch., NYC, 1984—; bd. dirs. Fair Labor Assn. Contbr. articles to profl. journals Mem.: Coun. Fgn. Rels., ABA. Democratic. Jewish. Avocations: tennis, skiing, hiking. Office: Human Rights First 333 7th Ave New York NY 10001-5004

POSNER, RICHARD ALLEN, federal judge; b. NYC, Jan. 11, 1939; s. Max and Blanche Posner; m. Charlene Ruth Horn, Aug. 13, 1962; children: Kenneth A., Eric A. AB, Yale U., 1959, LLD (hon.), 1996; LLB, Harvard U., 1962; LLD (hon.), Syracuse U., 1986; LLD (hon.), Georgetown U., 1992, U. Pa., 1997; LLD (hon.), Northwestern, 2001, Aristotle Univ. Thessaloniki, 2002; PhD (hon.), U. Ghent, 1995, Univ. Athens, 2002. Bar: NY 1963, US Supreme Ct. 1966. Law clk. to Hon. William J. Brennan Jr. US Supreme Ct., Washington, 1962—63; asst. to commr. FTC, Washington, 1963—65; asst. to solicitor gen. US Dept. Justice, Washington, 1965—67; gen. counsel Pres.'s Task Force on Comm. Policy, Washington, 1967—68; assoc. prof. Stanford U. Law Sch., Calif., 1968—69; prof. U. Chgo. Law Sch., 1969—78, Lee and Brena Freeman prof., 1978—81, sr. lectr., 1981—; judge US Ct. Appeals (7th cir.), Chgo., 1981—, chief judge, 1993—2000. Rsch. assoc. Nat. Bur. Econ. Rsch., Cambridge, Mass., 1971—81; pres. Lexecon Inc., Chgo., 1977—81. Author: Antitrust Law: An Economic Perspective, 1976, The Economics of Justice, 1981, The Problems of Jurisprudence, 1990, Cardozo: A Study in Reputation, 1990, Sex and Reason, 1992, The Essential Holmes, 1992, Overcoming Law, 1995, Aging and Old Age, 1995, The Federal Courts: Challenge and Reform, 1996, Law and Legal Theory in England and America, 1996, The Problematics of Moral and Legal Theory, 1999, An Affair of State: The Investigation, Impeachment, and Trial of President Clinton, 1999, Frontiers of Legal Theory, 2001, Breaking the Deadlock: The 2000 Election, The Constitution, and the Courts, 2001, Antitrust Law, 2d edit., 2001, Public Intellectuals, 2001, Law, Pragmatism and Democracy, 2003, Catastrophe: Risk and Response, 2004, Preventing Surprise Attacks: Intelligence Reform in the Wake of 9/11, 2005, Uncertain Shield: The U.S. Intelligence System in the Throes of Reform, 2006—, Not a Suicide Pact: The Constitution in a Time of National Emergency, 2006—, Countering Terrorism: Blurred Focus, Halting Steps, 2007, How Judges Think, 2008, A Failure of Capitalism: The Crisis of '08 and the Descent into Depression, 2009, Law and Literature, 3rd edit., 2009; author: (with William M. Landes) The Economic Structure of Tort Law, 1987, Little Book of Plagianism, 2007, The Economic Structure of Intellectual Property Law, 2003; author: (with Tomas J. Philipson) Private Choices and Public Health: The AIDS Epidemic in an Economic Perspective, 1993; pres. Harvard Law Rev., 1961—62; editor: Jour. Legal Studies, 1972—81, Am. Law and Econs. Rev., 1999—2005; author: A Failure of Capitalism: The Crisis, 2008, The Desert into Depression, 2009. Fellow: AAAS, Brit. Acad., Am. Law Inst.; mem.: Am. Law and Econ. Assn. (pres. 1995—96), Am. Econ. Assn., Century Assn. Office: US Ct Appeals 7th Cir 219 S Dearborn St Chicago IL 60604-1702*

POSNER, SYLVIE PÉREZ, lawyer; d. Carlos Miguel Pérez and Emilia Inés Amezaga; m. Michael J. Posner, Aug. 23, 1987; 1 child, Christopher Barrett. BS, Fla. State U., Tallahassee, 1980; JD, U. Miami, Coral Gables, 1988. Bar: Fla. 1989, Fla. So. Dist. 1989, US Ct. Appeals, 11th Cir. 1989. Legislative aide Fla. Senate, Tallahassee, 1981—84; cert. legal intern Dade County Pub. Defender, Miami, 1986—87; rsch. asst. U. Miami Sch. Law, Coral Gables, Fla., 1987—88; law clk. Frumkes and Greene, P.A., Miami, Fla., 1987—88, U.S. Ct. Appeal (4th dist.) Fla., West Palm Beach, 1990—94; asst. atty. gen. Office Atty. Gen., 1994—2000; sr. staff atty. U.S. Ct. Appeals (4th dist.) Fla., West Palm Beach, 2000—05. Mem. Phi Alpha Delta Legal Frat., Coral Gables, Fla., 1985—88, Health and Law Soc., Coral Gables, Fla., 1985—88; participant Trial Advocacy Program, Nat. Inst. of Trial Advocacy, Coral Gables, Fla., 1987; mem. Appellate Law Sect., Fla. Bar, Fla., 1994—, Govt. Law Sect., Fla. Bar, Fla., Broward County Hispanic Bar Assn., Fort Lauderdale, Fla., 1998—2000, Fla. Assn. of Police Attorneys, Fla., 1994—2000; mem. appellate law clk. edn. com. Fla. Supreme Ct., 2002—05. Vol. lawyers program Fla. Bar, Miami, 1989—90; vol. tel. crisis counselor Switchboard of Miami, Inc., Miami, 1981—83; supporting mem. Norton Art Mus., West Palm Beach, Fla., 2003; mem. leadership coun. So. Poverty Law Ctr., 1999—; mem. Emily's List, Washington, DC, 2002; apptd. mem. Dade County Dem. Exec. Com., Miami, 1982—84; exec. v.p. Dade County Young Democrats, Miami, 1988—89; del., fla. dem. conv. Fla. Dem. Party, Orlando, Fla., 1988, del., state dem. conv. Miami, 1984. Nominee Outstanding Young Women of Am., Nat. Fedn. of Dem. Women, 1985, Assoc. Ed., Inter-American Law Review, U. Miami, 1985—88. Independent. Roman Catholic. Avocations: swimming, travel, reading, hiking, dancing. Personal E-mail: sylvieposner@yahoo.com.

POSNY, ALEXA EMILY, state official, school system administrator; b. Two Rivers, Wis., Mar. 24, 1952; d. Louis Joseph and Virginia Ruth (Strope) Posny; 1 child, Alek BS in Sociology and Psychology, U. Wis., 1974; MS in Behavioral Disabilities, U. Wis., Madison, 1976, PhD in Ednl. Adminstrn., 1988. Cert. adminstr., Wis., Kans., Ill. Learning disabled tchr. Middleton Pub. Schs., Wis., 1976-79; emotionally disturbed tchr. Neenah Pub. Schs., Wis., 1979-80; human rels. instr. Fox Valley Tech. Inst., Appleton, Wis., 1980; coord. Coop. Edn. Svc. Agy., Stevens Point, 1980-81, dir. spl. edn. Gillett, Wis., 1981-85, regional svc. network coord., 1983-85; staff devel. coord., spl. edn. supr. S.W. Cook County Coop., Oak Forest, Ill., 1985-88; sr. rsch. assoc. Rsch. and Tng. Assoc. Inc., Overland Park, Kans., 1988-91, dir. curriculum and instrn. specialty option, 1991-97; dir. spl. edn. Shawnee Mission Sch. Dist., Kans., 1997—99; state dir. spl. edn. Kans. State Dept. Edn., 1999—2001, asst. commr. edn. Topeka, 2001—05, dep. commr. edn., 2005—07, commr. edn., 2007—; dir. Office of Spl. Edn. Programs US Dept. Edn., Washington, 2006—07. Adj. prof. U. Kans., Lawrence, 1997—, mem. ednl. rsch. and pub. svc. adv. coun., 1998—; mem. sch.-based leadership coun. Oxford Mid. Sch., 1996-98; chmn. Oak Hill sch.-based leadership, Overland Park, 1992-95, enrichment design team coun., 1992-94; mem. adv. coun. Blue Valley Sch. Bd., Overland Park, 1994-96; mem. quality performance accreditation design team, Overland Park, 1992-94; mem. inst. urban edn. U. Mo.; commr. states Mo. Dept. Edn., ctr. alternates assessment; mid-continent regional adv. coun. U.S. Dept. Edn., state accountability plan oversight com., negotiated rule-making; participant numerous forums; presenter in field Contbr. articles to profl. publs. Chairperson YMCA Child Care Adv. Coun., Johnson County, Kans., 1990-92; bd. dirs. Johnson County YMCA Bd., 1990-92; mem. Christian bd. edn. Colonial Ch., Prarie Village, Kans., 1992-94, mem. Christian youth adv. bd., 1992-93. Recipient Friends of Children award KAEOP, 2000, Outstanding Contbr. award CEC, 2001, Adminstr. of Yr. award KASEA, 2004; scholar Portage County Assn. for Mental Health, 1974, Elks, 1970, Wis. Honor scholarship, 1970. Mem. ASTD, Coun. Adminstrs. Spl. Edn., Ill. Coun. Adminstrs. Spl. Edn. (program com. 1987-88), Nat. Coun. Tchrs. English, Coun. for Exceptional Children, Coun. Adminstrs. Spl. Edn., Phi Delta Kappa (life), Pi Lambda Theta (life), Alpha Delta Kappa (Gov.'s award 2005, H.S. Kid's First award 2004). Democrat. Avocations: antiques, refinishing furniture, reading, travel. Office: Kans State Dept Edn 120 SE 10th Ave Topeka KS 66612 Home: 1112 Dubs Ct Lawrence KS 66049-3878 Home Phone: 785-830-9761; Office Phone: 785-296-2303. Business E-Mail: aposny@ksde.org.*

POSPISIL, JOANN, historian, archivist; b. Schulenburg, Tex., Dec. 10, 1947; d. Edwin James and Jossie Annie (Mica) Krametbauer; m. Gerald Joseph Pospisil, Nov. 19, 1966; 1 child, Ryan Joseph. BA summa cum laude, U. Houston, 1992, MA, 1994. Cert. archivist Acad. Cert. Archivists, 2001, Acad. Cert. Archivists, 2007. Sec. to v.p. Bohler Bros. of Am., Inc., Houston, 1972-75, asst. corp. sec., 1975-77; archival intern Sul Ross State U. Archives of the Big Bend, Alpine, Tex., 1993; rsch. asst. U. Houston Recovering U.S.-Hispanic Literary Heritage, 1993-94; archival technician Houston Acad. Medicine-Tex. Med. Ctr. Jesse H. Jones Libr., 1995-98; asst. archivist Baylor Coll. Medicine Archive, Houston, 1997—2004, archivist, 2004—07; dir. archives, 2008—. Task force mem., rsch. cons. Houston Urban Coun., 1993; contbg. historian Candelilla Wax Industry, Tex. Archeol. Rsch. Lab., 2004. Contbr. articles to profl. jours. Sec. handbook com. Clay Road Bapt. Parent-Tchr. Orgn., Houston, 1980-81; coord. Houston Police Dept., Houstonians on Watch, 1982-91; sec., membership chair, libr. aide Spring Branch Ind. Sch. Dist. Parent-Tchr. Assn., Houston, 1983-89; presenter geographical and cultural topics to classrooms in Spring Br. Elem. Sch., Northbrook H.S., Houston, 1985-95; interviewer oral history program Alliance Am. Quilts, 1999-; pres., pub. chair, sec. Spring Branch Addition Civic Assn. Inc., pres., 2005-07. treas. 2007-09, sec. 2009-. Recipient Spanish award Houston C.C., 1985, Josephine Del Barto scholar U. Houston, 1989-90, Helen M. Douthitt scholarship in history, 1990-91; named Sadie Iola Daniels scholar Assn. for Study of African Am. Life and History, Washington, 1990. Mem. Ctr. for Big Bend Studies, Soc. Am. Archivists, Tex. Czech Geneal. Soc. (charter and life), Archvists Houston Area (charter), Soc. Southwest Archivists, Tex. Hist. Assn., West Tex. Hist. Assn. (life, bd. dirs. 2006-09, local arrangements com., 2006, nominating com., 2007, chair, student scholarship com. 2009), Tex. Oral History Assn. (bd. dirs. 2005—, v.p. 2005-06, Cmty. award com. 2005—, pres. 2006-07, Lifetime Achievement award com., 2007—), Phi Kappa Phi (life), Phi Alpha Theta. Avocations: hiking, genealogy, whitewater rafting, reading non-fiction.

POSPISIL, LEOPOLD JAROSLAV, anthropologist, law educator; b. Olomouc, Czechoslovakia, Apr. 26, 1923; came to U.S., 1949, naturalized, 1954; s. Leopold and Ludmila (Petrlak) P.; m. Zdenka Smyd, Jan. 31, 1945; children: Zdenka, Mira. Juris Universae Candidatus, Charles U., Prague, Czechoslovakia, 1947, JD, 1991; BA in Sociology, Willamette U., Salem, Oreg., 1950; MA in Anthropology, U. Oreg., 1952; PhD, Yale U., 1956; ScD (hon.), Willamette U., 1969; PhD (hon.), Charles U., Prague, Czech Rep., 1994. Instr. Yale U., New Haven, 1956-57, asst. prof., 1957-60; asst. curator Peabody Mus., 1956-65, assoc. prof., 1960-65, prof., curator, 1965-93, dir. divsn. anthropology, 1966-93; prof. anthropology, 1965-93; prof. and curator emeritus, 1993—. Dir. Peabody Mus. Anthropology divsn. Yale U., New Haven, 1966—93; Robert Merton Prof. Law U. Munich, Germany, 1978—79; vis. prof. Anthropology Charles U., Prague, Czech Republic, 1991—; vis. prof. Law Capetown U., South Africa, 1989; DFC prof. Law U. Munich, 1982. Author: Kapauku Papuans and Their Law, 1958, Kapauku Papuan Economy, 1963, Kapauku Papuans of West New Guinea, 1963, Anthropology of Law, 1971, Ethnology of Law, 1972, Anthropologie des Rechts, 1981, Sprache, Symbole und Symbolverwendungen in Ethnologie, Kulturanthropologie, Politik, Religion und Recht, 1993, Obernberg: Quantitative Analysis of a Tyrolean Economy, 1996, Etnologie Prava, 1997, Sociocultural Anthropology, 2004; contbr. articles to profl. jours. Guggenheim fellow, 1962, NSF fellow, 1962, 64-65, 67-71, NIMH fellow, 1973-79; Social Sci. Rsch. Coun. grantee, 1966. Fellow AAAS, N.Y. Acad. Scis., Am. Anthrop. Assn.; mem. NAS, Conn. Acad. Arts and Scis., Explorers Club, Czechoslovakian Acad. Arts and Scis. (past pres.), Coun. Free Czechoslovakia, Assn. for Polit. and Legal Anthropology (pres.-at-large), Assn. for Social Anthropology in Oceania, Soc. for Econ. Anthropology, Sigma Xi. Independent. Avocations: gardening, mountain climbing. Home: 554 Orange St New Haven CT 06511-3819 Office: 51 Hillhouse Ave New Haven CT 06520-3703 Home Phone: 203-562-0661; Office Phone: 203-432-3771. Personal E-mail: pospisil@sbcglobal.net. Business E-Mail: anthropology@yale.edu.

POSS, C. THOMAS, ancient language educator; b. Atlanta, Mar. 4, 1945; s. Carl Walter and Anne Wilkinson Poss; m. Brenda Arrington, Dec. 27, 1979; children: Charlotte Poss Chromiak, Geoffrey Carl W. AB in Philosophy, Comparitive Lit., U. Ga., Athens, 1966, MA in Philosophy, 1972. Instr. Spelman Coll., Atlanta, 1984—85; lectr. dept. classics U. Ga., Athens, 1985—. German-Am. tchr. exch. program State of Ga., Athens, 1993—94. Home: 176 Catawba Ave Athens GA 30606-4304 Office: Dept Classics Univ Georgia Athens GA 30612 Business E-Mail: ctposs@uga.edu.

POSS, JEFFERY SCOTT, architect, educator; b. Harvey, Ill., May 20, 1956; m. Barbara Young Cook, May 1, 1999. BAS, U. Ill., 1978, MArch, 1980. Intern architect Charles Kober Assocs., Chgo., 1980-81, Skidmore, Owings and Merrill, Chgo., 1981; designer Newman/Lustig and Assocs., Chgo., 1983-84; design assoc. Kevin Roche John Dinkeloo and Assocs., Hamden, Conn., 1985-87; project architect and designer Tai Soo Kim Assocs., Hartford, Conn., 1987-89; pvt. practice Urbana, Ill., 1989—; prof. U. Ill. Sch. Arch., Champaign-Urbana, Ill., 1989—. Vis. prof. Glasgow Sch. Art, 1999, 2001; design cons. Isaksen Glerum Wachter Archs., P.C., Urbana, 2001—05; invited juror, lectr. in field. Contbr. articles to profl. jours. Recipient 1st Alt. Paris prize, Nat. Inst. for Archtl. Edn., 1981, 1st pl., Champaign Pk. Dist./AIA, 1989, Nat. Design award, Concrete Steel Reinforcing Inst., 1992, 2d pl. WWII Meml., State of Md., 1996, Merit award, Saluda Shoals Amphitheater, State of N.C., 2001, Silver award, Assn. Lic. Architects, 2007, Platinum award for Design Excellence (ADEX), Design Journal, 2009; 1st Pl. Francis J. Plym Traveling fellow, U. Ill., 2004. Mem. AIA (Excellence in Edn. Honors award 1993, Ctrl. Ill. award for design excellence, 1993, 97, 2000, 06, 08, Small Project award 2007), Am. Soc. Archtl. Perspectives (Excellence in Graphic Representation Architecture award 1990, 93). Business E-Mail: info@jefferyspossarchitect.net.

POST, ALAN RICHARD, lawyer; b. Milw., Feb. 6, 1948; s. John Wesley and Catherine Frances (Eviston) Post; children: Andrew, Lisa, Dana Michael. BBA, U. Wis., 1970; JD, 1972. Bar: Md. 1973, DC 1975, Nebr. 1976, (US Supreme Ct.) 1980, Ill. 1983, Kans. 1992. Atty. ICC, Washington, 1972—76; asst. gen. atty. Union Pacific R.R. Co., Omaha, 1976—78; asst. gen. solicitor BNRR Co., St. Paul, 1978—83; atty. Ill. Bell Telephone Co., Chgo., 1983—86; assoc. Sorling, Northrup, Hanna, Cullen and Cochran, Ltd., Springfield, Ill., 1986—90; atty. Kans. Gas & Electric Co., Wichita, 1990—92; pvt. practice Wichita, 1992—. With Lexis Nexis Customer Svc., Dayton, Ohio, 2001; past pres. Deaf and Hard of Hearing Svcs., Wichita, 1990—96; mem. Kans. Com. Deaf and Hard of Hearing, 1992—93. Home and Office: 841 Magnolia Dr Chatham IL 62629-1131 Home Phone: 217-483-9404; Office Phone: 217-483-9404. E-mail: arpost1@juno.com.

POST, ANTHONY BENJAMIN, gastroenterologist, director; b. Cleve., Aug. 29, 1957; s. Stanley and Gladys Post; m. Marjorie Greenfield, July 23, 1983; 1 child, Daniel. AB, Oberlin Coll., Ohio, 1979; MS, Case Western Res. U., Cleve., MD, 1983. Cert. Am. Bd. Internal Medicine, 1989, gastroenterologist 1994, transplant hepatologist 2006. Med. dir. hepatology and liver transplantation U. Hosp. Case Med. Ctr., Cleve., 1994—. Contbr. articles to profl. jour. Office: Univ Hosp Case Med Ctr 11100 Euclid Ave Cleveland OH 44106 Office Fax: 216-844-7480. Business E-Mail: anthony.post@uhhospitals.org.

POST, AVERY DENISON, retired church official; b. Norwich, Conn., July 29, 1924; s. John Palmer and Dorothy (Church) P.; m. Margaret Jane Rowland, June 8, 1946; children: Susan Post Ross, Jennifer C., Elizabeth Post Elliott, Anne Post Roy. BA, Ohio Wesleyan U., 1946; B.D., Yale U., 1949, S.T.M., 1952; L.H.D. (hon.), Lakeland Coll., Sheboygan, Wis., 1977; D.D. (hon.), Chgo. Theol. Sem., 1978, Middlebury Coll., Vt., 1978, Defiance Coll., Ohio, 1979; LL.D. (hon.), Heidelberg Coll., Ohio, 1982, Chapman Coll.; Litt.D. (hon.), Elmhurst Coll. Ordained to ministry, 1949; pastor chs. in Vt., Ohio, Conn. and N.Y., 1946-63; sr. minister Scarsdale (N.Y.) Congl. Ch., 1963-70; minister, pres. Mass. conf. United Ch. Christ, 1970-77; pres. United Ch. Christ, NYC, 1977-89; mem. central com. World Council Chs., 1978-91; exec. com., bd. govs. Nat. Council Chs., 1977-89. Moderator, planning com. 7th Gen. Assembly World Coun. Chs.; lectr. Bible Adelphi Coll., Garden City, N.Y., 1958-59; Luccock lectr. Yale U. Div. Sch., 1961; lectr. homiletics Union Sem., N.Y.C., 1967-69, bd. dirs., 1967-77; trustee Andover Newton Theol. Sem., 1970-80; del. numerous internat. ch. meetings; sr. fellow Hartford Sem., 1989-93. Bd. dirs. Bridges for Peace, 1990-94; exec. dir. Bangor Theol. Sem., Hanover, N.H., 1991-93. With USNR, 1943-45. Decorated Comdr.'s Cross (Federal Republic Germany), 1990; recipient 1st Ecumenical award Mass. Coun. Chs., 1976; Disting. Achievement award Ohio Wesleyan U., 1983 Mem. PTA (life), Randolph Mountain Club (N.H.), Phi Beta Kappa, Omicron Delta Kappa. Democrat. E-mail: avemarg@verizon.net.

POST, BARBARA J., retired mathematics educator; b. Burbank, Calif., Feb. 16, 1944; d. Carl W. and Lois C. Harris; m. Ted Post, Feb. 10, 1968; 1 child, Michael. BA, Chapman U., Orange, Calif., 1965; MA in Math., Calif. State U., Fullerton, 1992. Cert. tchg. credential Chapman U., 1966. Math tchr. Luther Burbank JHS, Calif., 1966—68, Brookhurst JHS, Anaheim, Calif., 1968—71; substitute tchr. Orange USD, Anaheim UHSD, Calif., 1972—75, Jurupa USD, Calif., 1975—78, Orange USD, 1978—84, Orange and Garden Grove, Calif., 1984—85; math tchr. and dept chair Santaigo HS, Garden Grove, 1985—2006; part time lectr. and supr. CSU Fullerton, 2006—. Elder and bd. mem. First Christian Ch., Orange, 1961—2008. Mem.: ASCD, Orange County Maths. Coun. (membership chair), NCTM, Calif. Math. Coun. (registrar 2008). Home: 1219 E Rose Ave Orange CA 92867 Personal E-mail: barbpost@aol.com.

POST, DENNY MARIE, telecommunications industry executive, marketing professional; BA in Journalism and Social Scis., cum laude, Trinity U.; student, So. Meth. U. Cox Sch. Bus. Chief mktg. officer Tricon Global Restaurants Inc., 2000—02; chief food innovation officer KFC USA, Yum! Brands Inc., 2002; sr. v.p. global food/beverage Starbucks Corp.; sr. v.p., chief mktg. officer T-Mobile USA Inc., 2008—. Chief concept officer, sr. v.p., mem. exec. leadership team Burger King Holdings Inc., 2004—. Named a Power Player, Advt. Age, 2008. Office: T Mobile USA Inc Hdqs 12920 SE 38th St Bellevue WA 98006 Office Phone: 425-378-4000. Office Fax: 425-378-4040.*

POST, DIANE, biology professor; b. Russell, Kans., Dec. 2, 1948; d. Dan and MaryAnna McClenny; m. Gail Post; children: Catherine, Christopher. BS, Kans. State U., Manhattan, 1985, PhD, 1991. Instr., divsn. biology Kans. State U., 1991—97; asst. prof. U. Tex. Permian Basin, Odessa, 1997—2003, assoc. prof., 2003—, chair, dept. biology, 2007—. Mem.: AAAS, Southwestern Assn. Naturalists, Am. Soc. Mammalogists (bd. dirs. 2007—), Sigma Xi (Full Membership 1996). Office: Univ Tex Permian Basin 4901 E University Odessa TX 79762

POST, GAINES, JR., retired history professor, dean, academic administrator; b. Madison, Wis., Sept. 22, 1937; s. Gaines and Katherine (Rike) P.; m. Jean Wetherbee Bowers, July 19, 1969; children: Katherine Doris, Daniel Lawrence. BA, Cornell U., 1959, Oxford U., 1963; MA, Stanford U., 1964, PhD, 1969. Instr. Stanford U., 1966-69; asst. prof. history U. Tex., Austin, 1969-74, assoc. prof., 1974-83; dean faculty, sr. v.p. Claremont McKenna Coll., Calif., 1983-88, prof., 1988—99, emeritus prof., 1999—. Exec dir. Rockefeller Found. Commn. on Humanities, 1978-81. Author: The Civil Military Fabric of Weimar Foreign Policy, 1973, Dilemmas of Appeasement: British Deterrence and Defense, 1934-37, 1993, Memoirs of a Cold War Son, 2000, Blue Bug, Red Road, 2008; co-author The Humanities in American Life, 1980; editor: German Unification: Problems and Prospects, 1992. Mem. exec. com. Forming the Future Project, Austin Ind. Sch. Dist., 1982; mem. Tex. Com. for Humanities, 1981-83; mem. coun. Calif. Congl. Recognition Program, 1984-88, Calif. Coun. Humanities, 1995-2003. Rhodes scholar, 1961-63; Am. Coun. Learned Socs. fellow, 1982-83; Am. Philos. Soc. grantee, 1974.

POST, GERALD V., business educator; b. Chippewa Falls, Wis., Nov. 27, 1955; s. Vernon Otto and Doris Post; m. Sarah S. Post, Aug. 14, 1982. BA, U. Wis., Eau Claire, 1978; PhD, Iowa State U., 1983. Asst. prof. Oakland U., Rochester Hills, Mich., 1982-89; prof. Western Ky. U., Bowling Green, 1989-99; prof. dept. bus. U. of the Pacific, Stockton, Calif., 1999—. Cons. analyst/programmer The Wala Group, Arden Hills, Minn., 1985-99. Author: Management Information Systems, 2009, Database Management Systems, 2007; contbr. articles to profl. jours. Office: Univ of the Pacific 3601 Pacific Ave Stockton CA 95211-0197

POST, GLEN FLEMING, III, telecommunications industry executive; b. El Dorado, Ark., Oct. 4, 1952; s. Glen F. Jr. and Mary L. (Tubberville) P.; children: Brad, Luke, Matt. BS in Acctg., La. Tech. U., 1974, MBA, 1976. Pvt. practice tax acctg., 1974-76; with CenturyTel Inc., Monroe, La., 1976—, v.p., 1982—84, sr. v.p., treas., 1984-86, sr. v.p., CFO, 1986—88, exec. v.p. & COO, 1988—90, pres. & COO, 1990—92, vice chmn., pres., CEO, 1992—2003, chmn., CEO, 2003—. Bd. dir. Yelcot Telephone Co., No. La. Regions Bank. Mem. exec. cabinet Coll. Adminstrn. & Bus., La. Tech. Univ.; bd. dir. La. Tech. Univ. Found., La.

Tech. Univ. Rsch. Found. Recipient Tower Medallion award, La. Tech. Univ., 1997, Lifetime Achievement award in bus., DeGree Enterprises, 2003. Mem. Am. Mgmt. Assn., STICC (subcom. acctg.), Beta Alpha Psi. Office: CenturyTel Inc 100 Century Tel Dr Monroe LA 71203

POST, JEFFREY H., insurance company executive; BBA, Univ. Wis., Madison. Chief actuary Fireman's Fund Ins. Co., 1994—96, CFO, 1996—2001, pres., CEO, 2001—04; pres., CEO, dir. CUNA Mutual Group, Madison, Wis., 2005—. Dir. Am. Ins. Assn. Fellow: Casualty Actuarial Soc.; mem.: Am. Acad. Actuaries. Office: CUNA Mutual Group 5910 Mineral Point Rd Madison WI 53705

POST, JOHN N., lawyer; b. 1940; BS, St. Peter's Coll., 1962; JD, Georgetown U., 1965. Bar: NJ, Dist. of Columbia. Co-founder, mng ptnr. Post, Polak, Goodsell, MacNeill & Strauchler, P.A. Jag Officer US Marine Corps. Office: Post Polak Goodsell MacNeill & Strauchler PA 425 Eagle Rock Ave Ste Roseland NJ 07068-1717 Office Phone: 973-228-9900. Office Fax: 973-994-1705. E-mail: jnp@ppgms.com.

POST, MARTIN ROGER, cardiologist; b. Bklyn, NY, Apr. 11, 1943; BA, Univ. Pa., 1963; MD, SUNY, Syracuse, 1967. Diplomate Am. Bd. Internal Med., 1974, Am. Bd. Internal Med., Cardiovascular Disease, 1974. Intern Ohio State Univ. Hosp., 1967—68, resident in cardiology, 1968—70; fellow NY Hosp. Cornell Med. Ctr., 1970—72; clinical asst. prof. med. NY Hosp. Cornell Univ. Med. Ctr., 1976—; ptnr., cardiologist NY Cardiology Associates; attending physician NY Presbyterian Hosp. Cardiologist World Wrestling Entertainment Wellness Program, 2006. Contbr. articles to profl. jours. Named one of America's Top Doctors, Castle Connolly. Fellow: Am. Coll. Cardiology, Am. Heart Assoc. (Scientific Council). Office: NY Cardiology Associates 425 E 61st St New York NY 10021 Office Phone: 212-734-3545. Office Fax: 212-752-3281.

POST, PETER DAVID, lawyer; b. Reading, Pa., Jan. 2, 1947; s. Carl B. and Frances (Gaughan) P.; children: Michael, Elizabeth. BS, Pa. State U., 1968; JD, Harvard U., 1971. Bar: Pa. 1971, La. 1974, US. Ct. of Appeals (3rd, 4th, 6th, 10th 11th & dc cirs), US Supreme Ct., All State and Fed. Cts. in Pa. Assoc. Reed, Smith, Shaw & McClay, Pitts., 1975-81, ptnr., 1982—, dept. head, 1992—2000; ptnr. Reed Smith LLP, Pitts., Ogletree Deakins, 2007—. Commr. Upper St. Clair Township, Pa., 1991—94; editor-in-chief The Pa. Labor Letter, 1998—2002. Contbr. articles to profl. jour. With JAGC USN, 1971—75. Named The Best Lawyers in Am., Pa. Super Lawyers, Who's Who in America. Avocations: golf, skiing, fishing, cycling. Office: Ogletree Deakins PC 444 Liberty Ave Ste 400 Pittsburgh PA 15222-1207 Office Phone: 412-394-3343. Office Fax: 412-232-1799. Business E-Mail: peter.post@ogletreedeakins.com.

POST, RICHARD BENNETT, retired human resources executive; b. Clyde, Ohio, July 5, 1936; s. Robert Irving and Elinor May (Bennett) P.; m. Nancy Jane Wardlow, Aug. 31, 1956; children: David Bennett, Todd McKinley, Amy Ellen, Brett Richard, Brina Marie. BS in Psychology, Iowa State U., Ames, 1958; student, Ohio U., Athens, 1954-56; postgrad., George Washington U., Washington, DC, 1959-60, So. Ill. U., Edwardsville, 1972-74. With US Civil Svc. Commn., 1958-79, chief evaluation divsn. St. Louis, 1967-71, chief staffing divsn., 1971-74, dep. reg. dir., 1974-79; dep. assoc. dir. staffing US Office Pers. Mgmt., Washington, 1979-81, assoc. dir. staffing, 1982-86, dir. Washington area svc. ctr., 1986-94; ret., 1994. Cert. lay spkr. United Meth. Ch., 1973—; treas. Meadows Homeowners Assn., 2000-07. Recipient Dirs.' Disting. Svc. award US Office Pers. Mgmt., 1986, Dirs.' citation for Exemplary Pub. Svc., 1994. Mem. AARP (pres. King George Area chpt. 2003-04, treas., 2005-08), Sr. Execs. Assn. (life), Fed. Exec. Inst. Alumni Assn., Vienna Choral Soc. (pres. 1987-89), Masterworks Chorus, King George, Va. Avocations: woodworking, singing, gardening. Business E-Mail: richard@mypostrn.com.

POST, ROBERT CHARLES, dean, law educator; b. Bklyn., Oct. 17, 1947; s. Ted and Thelma (Feifel) P.; m. Fran Layton, Jan. 22, 1981; children: Alexander, Amelia. AB, Harvard U., 1969, PhD, 1980; JD, Yale U., 1977; LLD (hon.), Chgo.-Kent U., 1998. Bar: D.C. 1979, Calif. 1983. Law clk. to Chief Judge David L. Bazelon US Ct. Appeals (D.C. cir.), 1977-78; law clk. to Justice William Brennen Jr. US Supreme Ct., 1978-79; assoc. Williams & Connelly LLP, Washington, 1980-82; acting prof. law U. Calif., Berkeley, 1983-87, prof. law, 1987-94, Alexander F. & May T. Morrison prof. law, 1994—2003; David Boies prof. law Yale U. Law Sch., New Haven, 2003—09, Sol & Lillian Goldman prof. law, 2009—, dean, 2009—. John H. Watson vis. prof. law Harvard Law Sch., 2006. Author: Constitutional Domains: Democracy, Community Management, 1995; author: (with K. Anthony Appiah, Judith Butler, Thomas C. Grey, & Rev) Prejudicial Appearances: the Logic of America Antidiscrimination Law, 2001; co-author (with Matthew M. Finkin): For the Common Good: Principles of American Academic Freedom, 2009; editor: Law and the Order of Culture, 1991, Censorship and Silencing: Practices of Cultural Regulation, 1998; co-editor (with Michael Rogin): Race and Representation: Affirmative Action, 1998; co-editor: (with Carla Hesse) Human Rights in Political Transitions: Gettysburg to Bosnia, 1999; co-editor: (with Nancy Rosenblum) Civil Society and Government, 2001; co-editor: (with Selya Benhabib) Another Cosmopolitan, 2006. Bd. editors, Representations, 1987-2003; chair, U. Calif. Humanities Rsch. Inst., 1993-97; mem. advisory bd., Julius Stone Inst. Jurisprudence, U. Sydney, 2001-; bd. trustees Nat. Humanities Ctr., 2005- Fellow Guggenheim Found., 1990-91, Am. Coun. Gen. Socs., 1990-91; recipient Koret Israel prize, 1994 Mem. Am. Assn. Univ. Professors (gen. counsel, 1992-94); fellow Am. Acad. Arts & Sciences (councilor, 2001-05, librarian, 2005-), Am. Law Inst. Office: Yale Law Sch PO Box 208215 New Haven CT 06520 Office Phone: 203-432-4946. Office Fax: 203-432-1040. E-mail: robert.post@yale.edu.*

POST, STEVEN M., lawyer, communications systems company executive; BA, U. Dayton, Ohio; JD with honors, Ind. U., 1977. Contract and fiscal law advisor, sr. trial counsel Office the Staff Judge Advocate, Ft. Dix, NJ; trial atty., litig. divsn. Judge Advocate Gen., the Pentagon, Arlington; instr., contract law dept. Judge Advocate General's Sch., Charlottesville, NC; assoc. counsel, group counsel L-3 Comm. Corp., NYC, sr. v.p. contracts, gen. counsel, integrated systems group Greenville, Tex., sr. v.p., gen. counsel, corp. sec. NYC, 2008—. Office: L-3 Comm Corp 600 Third Ave New York NY 10016 Office Phone: 212-697-1111. Office Fax: 212-682-9553.*

POSTE, GEORGE HENRY, biology professor, former pharmaceutical company executive; b. Polegate, Sussex, Eng., Apr. 30, 1944; came to U.S., 1972; s. John H. and Kathleen B. (Brooke) P.; 1 child, Eleanor Kathy; m. Linda C. Suhler Lopez, Nov. 21, 1992; stepchildren: John Robert, Lisa Carolyn. DVM, U. Bristol, 1966, PhD, 1969, DSc, 1987, LLD (hon.), 1995. Lectr. U. London, 1969-72; assoc. prof. SUNY, Buffalo, 1972-76; prof. pathology Roswell Park Meml. Inst., Buffalo, 1976-80; v.p. rsch. SmithKline Beckman, Phila., 1980-82, v.p. R & D, 1982-86, v.p. worldwide rsch. and pre-clin. devel., 1987-88, pres. R & D, 1988-89; pres. R & D techs. SmithKline Beecham, King of Prussia, Pa., 1989-90, vice-chmn., exec. v.p. R & D, 1990-91, pres. and chmn. R & D, 1992-97; chief sci. and tech. officer SmithKline Beecham Corp. PLC, King of Prussia, Pa., 1997-99; CEO Health Tech. Networks, Scottsdale, Ariz., 2000—; non-exec. chmn. OrchidBioSciences Inc., Princeton, NJ, 2002—; Del E. Webb Disting. prof biology Ariz. State U., Tempe, 2003—, dir. Biodesign Inst., 2003—. Mem. pathology B study sect. NIH, Bethesda, Md., 1978-82; chmn. Gordon Conf., N.H., 1985-86, diaDeXus, 1997-2003, Cerebrus, 1997; pres. coun. U. Tex. M.D. Anderson Cancer Ctr.; bd. dirs. Monsanto, Exelixis, SmithKline Beecham Corp. PLC, Orchid BioSciences Inc., 2000-; mem. adv. coun. Beckman Ctr. for Molecular and Genetic Medicine, Stanford U.; mem. coun. Oxford Internat. Biomedical Centre; chmn. task force on bioterrorism, U.S. Dept. of Defense, 2001-04. Editor: Cell Surface Revs., New Horizons in Therapeutics, Cancer Metastasis Revs., Advanced Drug Delivery Revs., 15 books; contbr. articles to profl. jours. Mem. governing bd. UCLA Symposia, Life Sci. Rsch. Found.; mem. bd. Overseers Sch. Vet. Medicine, U. Penn., Gov.'s adv. com. Sci. and Tech., Pa.; mem. adv. bd. Natural Sci. Assn., U. Pa. Fleming fellow U. Oxford, Eng., 1995, Pitt fellow U. Cambridge, Eng., 1995; named Comdr. of British for svcs. in devel. of bioscis., 1999, Scientist of the Year, R&D mag., 2004. Fellow Royal Soc., Royal Coll. Vet. Surgeons, Royal Coll. Pathologists, Ins. Biology (London), Acad. Med. Scis. (London); mem. AAAS, Am. Soc. Cell Biology, Pathol. Soc., Nat. Assn. Biomed. Rsch. (bd. govs. 1984), Univ. Assn. Space Rsch. (mem. coun. 1984), Pharm. Mfrs. Assn. (former chmn. rsch. and devel. section 1988). Avocations: military history, foreign affairs, photography, auto racing. Office: Biodesign Inst Ariz State Univ PO Box 875001 Tempe AZ 85287-5001 Office Phone: 480-727-8662. Business E-Mail: george.poste@asu.edu.

POSTELL, CINDY DEBORAH, secondary school educator; b. Savannah, Ga., Aug. 14, 1954; d. George Robert and Sallie Walker Postell. BA in Journalism, U. Ga., 1976; M in Edn., Ga. Southern U., 1980. Sub. tchr. Chatham County Bd. Edn., 1991—. Singer: Savannah Symphony Orch. Choir Cathedral of St. John, 1982—. Recipient Cert. of Appreciation, Pope John Paul II Cultural Ctr., DC, 2005, Jimmy Carter Ctr., Atlanta, 2006, Basilica of the Nat. Shrine for the Immaculate Conception, DC, 2006. Mem.: Order Eastern Star, Electa Chapter. Home: 128 W 51stSt Savannah GA 31405

POSTEMA, BETH E., librarian, director; d. Adrian W. and Charlotte A. (Ribbens) Kaashoek; m. James A. Postema; children: Gerrit J., Cees A. BA, Calvin Coll., Grand Rapids, Mich., 1987; MA in Libr. and Info. Sci., U. Ill., Urbana Champaign, 1989. Dep. dir. Fargo Pub. Libr., ND, 2002—, pub. svc. coord., 1992—2002. Singer: (songs) (chorus) Fargo-Moorhead Opera, 2002—. Bd. mem. Fargo-Moorhead Opera, 2008—. Mem.: ALA, Pub. Libr. Assn., ND Libr. Assn. (pres. 2006—07). Mem. Presbyterian Ch. Avocation: singing. Office: Fargo Pub Libr 102 3 St N Fargo ND 58102

POSTIER, RUSSELL GLEN, surgeon; b. Cushing, Okla., Nov. 21, 1949; s. Cecil Glen and Myrtle Ann Postier; m. Ruthann Fortner, Sept. 24, 1977; 1 child, Lee Allen. MD, U. Okla., 1975. Diplomate Am. Bd. Surgery, 1982. Resident in surgery Johns Hopkins U., Balt., 1975—80, asst. chief surgery svc., 1980—81; faculty mem. dept. surgery U. Okla., Oklahoma City, 1981—, chmn. dept. surgery, 1997—. Pres. Southwestern Surg. Congress, Chgo., 2001—02. Fellow: Am. Coll. Surgeons (pres.), Am. Surg. Assn., So. Surg. Assn., Soc. U. Surgeons; mem.: American Bd. Surgery (dir. 2001—, pres. 2008—09). Office: Dept Surgery Univ Okla PO Box 26910 WP 2140 Oklahoma City OK 73190*

POSTIGLIONE, COREY M., artist, critic, educator; b. Chgo., July 25, 1942; BA, U. Ill. Circle Campus; also with Martin Hurtig & Roland Ginzel; MA in 20th Century Art History, Sch. Art Inst. Chgo. Instr. painting Evanston Art Ctr., Ill., 1971—79, Ill. Inst. Tech., 1975—83, Columbia Coll., Chgo., 1979—89, Art Inst. Chgo., 1981—83, U. Ill., Chgo., 1983; instr. art history and criticism Columbia Coll., Chgo., 1990—, tenured prof., 1996—, instr., 2D design studio, 1999—. Asst. dir. Jan Cicero Gallery, Chgo., 1975—76; juror 38th Ann. Old Orchard Art Festival, 1995, 19th Elkhardt Regional, Midwest Mus. Am. Art, Elkhardt, Ind., 1997; judge Riverside Artfair '97, Riverside Art Ctr., Riverside, Ill., 1997; bd. dir. White Walls, 1992. Contbr. editor of reviews and articles The New Art Examiner, 1976—83, Dialogue mag., 1989—, Contbr. reviews and articles New Art Assn., 1975—76, C mag., contbr. editor ArtForum, 2003; contbr. catalogue essay for Liz Langer Retrospective, Artemisia Gallery, Chgo., catalogue essay for Alexandra Domowska for the Pougialis Exhbn., Columbia Coll. Chgo. Hokin Annex Gallery, catalogue essay for Karen Lebergott one-person exhbn., Columbia Gallery, catalogue essay for John Pillips, 2005; collections curated, Art in Chgo., 1996, 1998, 2000, 2002, one-man shows include Evanston Art Ctr., Ill., 1972, Mayer Kaplan JCC, Skokie, Ill., 1973, Jan Cicero Gallery, Chgo., Ill., 1976, 1978, 1983, 1985, 1995, 1997, Columbia Coll. Gallery, Chgo., 1981, 1997—98, Passages, Oakton Cmty. Coll., 1998, A&D Gallery, Columbia Coll., Rivereast Art Ctr., Chgo., 2005, exhibitions include New Works on Paper, Jan Cicero Gallery, 1993, Labyrinth Series, Jan Cicero Gallery, 1993, Exquisite Corpse, Transmission Gallery, Glasgow, Scotland, 1994, Lakeside Views, Evanston Art Ctr., 1994, Brad Cooper Gallery, Tampa, Fla., 2003, and others, installation work, Blink, No. Ill. U. Gallery, Chgo., 2000, exhibitions include Retrospective of Works on Paper, 1972—2007, Evanston Art Ctr., Ill., 2008, installation, Art & Design Gallery, Columbia Coll. Chgo., 2008. Recipient Third Prize (all show), Italian Am. Exhibit, 1981, Merit award, Evanston & Vicinity Exhbn., 1998. Mem.: Am. Abstracts Artists, NY, Chgo. Art Critics Assn. Home: 4508 N Monticello Chicago IL 60625 Office: Columbia Coll Dept Art & Design 623 S Wabash Rm 1004 Chicago IL 60625 Office Phone: 312-369-7190. Business E-Mail: cpostiglione@colum.edu, cpostiglione@popmail.colum.edu.

POSTMAN, ROBERT DEREK, dean, mathematics professor, writer; s. Benjamin and Edith Postman; m. Elizabeth Ann DelCorso, Aug. 6, 1965; children: Chad, Blaire, Ryan. BA, Kean Coll., 1966; MA, Columbia U., 1967, EdD, 1971. Faculty Hunter Coll., NYC, 1970—76, Tchrs. Coll. Columbia U., NYC, 1977—81; prof. math. and edn. Mercy Coll., Dobbs Ferry, NY, 1976—, chair dept., 1978—, dean grad. edn. programs, 1988—. Founder, head Urban Tchg. Acad.; math. cons. sch. dists. and state edn. depts.; cons. Psychol. Corp. Devel. of Calif.; bd. dirs. Westchester Com. Tech. and Disabled; presenter in field; lectr. in field. Author: SAT Math., 2006, GRE Math., 2008, numerous other books, Mathematics on the Geoboard, 1974, Intermediate Mathematics, 1976, Growth in Mathematics, 1980, 1982, Collegiate Reading, 1985, High School Mathematics, 2 vols., 1988, Macmillian Mathematics, 1990, Mathematics Today, 1991, Consumer Mathematics, 1993, (series) Enrichment Mathematics, 1978, Computer Programming, 1983, Mathematics Unlimited, 1986, others, books on ACT, SAT and GRE; contbr. articles to profl. jours. Mem. Closter Bd. Edn., NJ, 1973—79; del. NJ Sch. Bds. Assn., NJ, 1974—77; coach, organizer Closter Recreation Commn.; coach Closter Comets soccer team, 1984—. With USAF, 1959—63. Full Grad. Doctoral fellow, Columbia U., 1966—71, NDEA fellow, 1966—70. Mem.: Assn. Mentally Ill Children Westchester (bd. dirs.), Assnq. Tchr. Educators (exec. bd.), NY Acad. Scis., Soc. Applied Learning Tech., Nat. Coun. Tchrs. Math., Phi Delta Kappa, Kappa Delta Pi. Roman Catholic. Home: 33 Julia St Closter NJ 07624-2417 Office: Mercy Coll 555 Broadway Dobbs Ferry NY 10522-1134 Business E-Mail: bobderek@earthlink.net.

POSTOL, LAWRENCE PHILIP, lawyer; b. Bridgeport, Conn., Oct. 18, 1951; s. Sidney Samuel and Eunice Ruth (Schine) P.; m. Ellen Margaret Russell, Mar. 22, 1975; children: Raymond Russell, Stephan Russell, Carolyn Russell. BS, Cornell U., 1973, JD, 1976. Bar: Conn. 1976, D.C. 1977, U.S. Dist. Ct. D.C. 1977, U.S. Ct. Appeals (D.C. cir.) 1977, U.S. Supreme Ct. 1980, Va. 1982, U.S. Ct. Appeals (4th cir.) 1982, U.S. Dist. Ct. (ea. dist.) Va. 1985, U.S. Dist. Ct. Md. 1989, U.S. Dist. Ct. Conn. 1990. Assoc. Arent, Fox, Washington, 1976-80, Seyfarth, Shaw LLP, Washington, 1980-83, ptnr., 1985—; assoc. Jones, Day, Washington, 1983-85. Lectr. Loyola U., New Orleans, U. Cin., 1987-93; bd. advisers The Environ. Counselor Jour.; spl. counsel Greater Washington Bd. Trade, 1991-93. Author: Legal Guide to Handling Toxic Substances in the Workplace, 1990, Americans with Disabilities Act - A Compliance Manual for Employers, 1993. Jewish. Avocations: sports, soccer. Home: 6340 Chowning Pl Mc Lean VA 22101-4129 Office: Seyfarth Shaw LLP 975 F St NW Washington DC 20004-1454 Office Phone: 202-828-5385. Office Fax: 202-828-5393. Business E-Mail: lpostol@seyfarth.com.

POSTON, ANITA OWINGS, lawyer; b. Sylacauga, Ala., Sept. 24, 1949; d. John T. and Margaret Owings; m. Charles E. Poston, June 9, 1973; children: Charles Evans Jr., John W., Margaret Elizabeth. BA, U. Md., 1971; JD, Coll. William & Mary, 1974. Bar: Va. 1974. Atty. Vandeventer Black LLP, Norfolk, Va., 1974—. Substitute judge Norfolk (Va.) Gen. Dist. Cts., 1982-90; mem. Bar Examiners Bd.; mem. bd. visitors Coll. William and Mary. Mem. State Bd. C.C.s, Richmond, 1985-90, chmn. 1988-89; mem. Norfolk Sch. Bd., 1990-2002, chmn. 1998-2002; bd. dirs. WHRO Pub. Broadcasting, chair, 2002-04; bd. dirs. Access Coll. Found., Va. Symphony Orch., Towne Bank, Norfolk. Mem. ABA (law fellows), Va. Bar Assn. (pres. 2000), Norfolk-Portsmouth Bar Assn. (pres. 1998-99), Va. Law Fellows, Am. Inn of Ct. Office: Vandeventer Black LLP 500 World Trade Ctr Norfolk VA 23510-1679 Office Phone: 757-446-8600. Office Fax: 757-446-8670. Business E-Mail: aposton@vanblk.com.

POSTON, DANIEL T., bank executive; BBA, U. Cin. Auditor, partner Arthur Andersen, LLP; sr. v.p., dir. internal audit Fifth Third Bancorp, 2001—03, exec. v.p., 2003—, contr., 2007—, interim CFO, 2008. Past treas. Jr. Achievement Greater Cin. Mem.: Inst. Internal Auditors. Office: Fifth Third Bancorp 38 Fountain Sq Plz Cincinnati OH 45202-3102*

POSTON, REBEKAH JANE, lawyer; b. Wabash, Ind., Apr. 20, 1948; d. Bob E. and April (Ogle) P. BS, U. Miami, 1970, JD, 1974. Bar: Fla. 1974, Ohio 1977, U.S. Dist. Ct. (so. and mid. dists.) Fla., U.S. Ct. Appeals (11th cir.). Asst. U.S. atty. U.S. Atty.'s Office, Miami, Fla., 1974—76; spl. atty. organized crime and racketeering sect. Strike Force, Cleve., 1976—78; ptnr. Fine, Jacobson, Schwartz, Nash & Block, Miami, 1978—94, Steel Hector & Davis, Miami, 1994—2006, Squire, Sanders & Dempsey LLP, Miami, 2006—. Adj. prof. U. Miami Law Sch., Coral Gables; mem. U.S. sentencing guidelines com. So. Dist. of Fla., Miami. Contbr. articles to profl. jours. Recipient Fla.'s Super Lawyer, Law and Politics, 2006—09; named Top Lawyer, South Fla. Legal Guide, 2007—08, Fla. Top Lawyers, 2008; named one of Best Lawyers in Am., 2003—08, Fla.'s Elite Lawyers, Fla. Trend mag., 2004—06. Mem. Fla. Bar Assn., Nat. Assn. Criminal Def. Attys., Nat. Directory Criminal Lawyers, Am. Immigration Lawyers Assn., Dade County Bar Assn. Democrat. Lutheran. Avocations: power boat racing, swimming. Home: 1541 Brickell Ave Apt 3706 Miami FL 33129-1229 Office: 200 SE 2nd St Miami FL 33131 Office Phone: 305-577-7022. Business E-Mail: rposton@ssd.com.

POTAPOVA, IRINA A., cell biologist, educator; d. Anatolii F. Kuzmin and Tamara P. Kuzmina; m. Sergey V. Doronin, July 4, 1996; 1 child, Tamara M. PhD, Novosibirsk Inst. Bioorganic Chemistry, Russia, 1990. Rsch. scientist Stony Brook U., NY, 1997—2003, rsch. asst. prof., 2003—. Contbr. articles to sci. jours. Achievements include patents for human mesenchymal stem cells. Office: Stony Brook Univ Bst 5-131 Stony Brook NY 11794-8661 Office Fax: 631-444-3432. Business E-Mail: irina.potapova@stonybrook.edu.

POTASEK, MARY JOYCE, physicist, researcher; b. Mpls., Oct. 27, 1945; d. Chester and Millie Potasek. BA in Math., Coll. St. Catherine, 1967; MS in Physics, U. Ill., 1970, PhD, 1974. Research asst. U. Ill., Urbana, 1970-74; rsch. scientist IBM, Watson Rsch. Ctr., Yorktown Heights, NY, 1974-75; NSF, AAUW postdoctoral fellow Princeton (N.J.) U., 1975-78; NATO postdoctoral fellow Max Planck Inst., Gottingen, West Germany, 1978-80; mem. tech. staff AT&T, Princeton, 1980-86, AT&T Bell Labs., Murray Hill, N.J., 1986-90, Columbia U., NYC, 1990-99; mem. tech. staff Brooks AFB USAF, San Antonio, 1994-2001; physicist NYU, NYC, 2001—. Contbr. articles to profl. jours. Mem. IEEE (sr., lasers and electrooptics), SPIE, Optical Soc. Am., Women in Optics, Am. Phys. Soc., Phi Beta Kappa, Pi Mu Epsilon. Avocation: horseback riding. Home: 269 Christopher Dr Princeton NJ 08540-2323

POTASH, CHARLES, lawyer; b. May 31, 1932; BA in History with honors, U. Pa., 1953; JD, Temple U. Sch. Law, 1959. Bar: Pa. 1960, US Dist. Ct. (ea. dist.) 1972, US Ct. Appeals (3d cir.) 1981, Superior Ct. Pa. 1960, Supreme Ct. Pa. 1960, US Supreme Ct. 1982. Law clerk Justice Benjamin R. Jones, Supreme Ct. Pa., 1959—60; ptnr. Wisler, Pearlstine, Talone, Craig, Garrity & Potash, LLP, Blue Bell, Pa., 1960—2004, of counsel, 2004—08; solicitor Methacton Sch. Dist. Authority, 1960—2004, Methacton Sch. Dist., 1960—94, North Penn Sch. Dist., 1960—96, Upper Perkiomen Sch. Dist., 1960—2008, Lower Providence Twp. Sewer Authority, 1962—85, North Penn Sch. Authority, 1967—2007, Lower Merion Sch. Dist., 1970—2001, Cheltenham Twp. Sch. Dist., 1970—2008, Springfield Twp. Sch. Dist., 1973—2004, Upper Dublin Sch. Dist., 1974—2000, Jenkintown Sch. Dist., 1983—2005, Norristown Area Sch. Dist., 1988—99, Abington Sch. Dist., 1992—2008, Upper Perkiomen Sch. Authority, 1967—2004, Cheltenham Sch. Dist. Authority, 1970—96. Rsch. editor Temple Law Quarterly, 1958—59. Bd. trustees Congregation Rodeph Shalom, Phila., 1980—87; mem. Selective Svc. Adminstrn., 1985—95; mem. bd. overseers Gratz Coll., 1994—98, mem. bd. regents, 1998—; mem. selection bd. 13th Congressional Dist. Svc. Acad., 1995—2004. 1st lt. US Army, 1953—56, Korea. Named solicitor emeritus, Jenkintown Sch. Dist. Bd. Dir., 2005. Mem.: ABA, Pa. Bar Assn., Phila. Bar Assn., Montgomery Bar Assn. (bd. dirs. 1971—75, chmn. jr. bar com., chmn. Am. citizenship com., chmn. mcpl. law com., mem. judiciary com.), Military Order Fgn. Wars.

POTASH, STEPHEN JON, public relations executive; b. Houston, Feb. 25, 1945; s. Melvin L. and Petrice (Edelstein) P.; m. Jeremy Warner, Oct. 19, 1969; 1 child, Aaron Warner. BA in Internat. Rels., Pomona Coll., 1967. Account exec. Charles von Loewenfeldt, Inc., San Francisco, 1969-74, v.p., 1974-80; founder, pres. Potash & Co., Pub. Rels., Oakland, Calif., 1980-87, 1990—. Exec. dir. Calif. Coun. Internat.

Trade, 1970-87; v.p. corp. communications APL Ltd., Oakland, 1987-90; chmn. Potash & Co., Oakland, 1990-2007, dir., 1990-. Co-author (with Robert J. Chandler): Gold, Silk, Pioneers & Mail: The Story of Pacific Mail Steamship Company, 2007. Bd. dir. Calif. Coun. Internat. Trade, 1987-94, Calif.-Asia Bus. Coun., 1992—, Temple Sinai, Oakland, 1979-81; Clampers-Yerba Buena. Mem.: Pub. Rels. Soc. Am.

POTEETE, ANTHONY R., molecular biologist, educator; b. NYC, Oct. 13, 1952; AB, Harvard U., 1973; PhD, MIT, 1977. Postdoctoral fellow Harvard U., Cambridge, Mass., 1977-80; asst. prof. dept. molecular genetics and microbiology U. Mass., Worcester, 1980-84, assoc. prof., 1984-90, prof., 1991—, acting chmn. dept. molecular genetics and microbiology, 1990-91. Cons. NIH, Bethesda, Md., 1990-91. Contbr. articles to profl. jours. Helen Hay Whitney Found. fellow Harvard U., 1977-80; NIH grantee U. Mass., 1981—. Mem. Am. Soc. for Microbiology. Achievements include research in fields of bacteriophage genetics, protein chemistry and x-ray crystallography.

POTEMPA, KATHLEEN M., dean, nursing educator; b. Oct. 3, 1948; Diploma in Nursing, Providence Hosp. Sch. Nursing, Southfield, Mich., 1970; BA in Psychology summa cum laude, U. Detroit, 1974; MS in Nursing, Rush U., 1978, D in Nursing Sci., 1986. Charge nurse coronary ICU Holy Cross Hosp., Ft. Lauderdale, Fla., 1970-71; staff nurse, charge nurse cardiovasc. ICU Henry Ford Hosp., Detroit, 1971-74; nurse practitioner Rush-Presbyn.-St. Luke's Med. Ctr., Chgo., 1974-75; nursing edn. coord. dept. nursing Michael Reese Hosp. and Med. Ctr., Chgo., 1975-77, nursing supr., 1977-78; asst. unit leader dept. gerontol. nursing Rush U. Coll. Nursing, Chgo., 1978-79, asst. chmn., 1979-80, assoc. chmn., asst. prof. gerontol. nursing, 1980-85, asst. prof. gerontol. nursing, 1985-86; asst. prof. nursing, dept. internal medicine, practitioner Rush Med. Coll., Rush U., 1987-88; asst. then assoc. prof. dept. med.-surg. nursing Coll. Nursing, U. Ill., Chgo., 1988—96, dir. tng., pre and postdoctoral fellowship instnl. rsch., 1992—94, exec. assoc. dean Coll. Nursing, 1994-95, interim dean Coll. Nursing, 1995-96; prof., dean Sch. Nursing Oreg. Health Scis. U., Portland, 1996—2006, v.p., 2002—06; dean, prof. nursing, Sch. Nursing U. Mich., Ann Arbor, 2006—. Rsch. assoc. Robert Wood Johnson Tchg. Nursing Home Project, VA Edward Hines Jr. Hosp., Hines, Ill., 1985-86, co-dir. Exercise Rsch. Lab., 1985-86; dir. nursing Johnston R. Bowman Health Ctr. for Elderly, Rush Presbyn. St. Luke's Med. Ctr., Chgo., 1980-85. Contbr. articles to profl. jours. Recipient Oreg. Med. Rsch. Found. Mentor award, 2002, Disting. Alumni award, Rush U., 2003. Fellow Am. Acad. Nursing; mem. ANA (coun. nurse rschrs.), Am. Soc. Hypertension, Gerontol. Soc. Am., Midwest Nursing Rsch. Soc., Heart Assn. Met. Chgo., Am. Heart Assn. Oreg., Ill. Coun. Nurse Rschrs., Am. Heart Assn. (coun. cardiovasc. nursing, coun. hypertension, coun. on strokes), Am. Assn. Coll. Nursing Bd. (sec. 2004), Sigma Theta Tau. Office: U Mich Sch Nursing 400 N Ingalls Rm 1320 Ann Arbor MI 48109 Office Phone: 734-764-7185. Office Fax: 734-764-7186.*

POTEMPA, PHILIP MATTHEW, journalist, columnist, communications educator; b. San Pierre, Ind., Aug. 13, 1970; s. Chester John and Peggy Louise Potempa. BA, Valparaiso U., 1992. Arts and entertainment reporter Vidette-Messenger Newspaper, Valparaiso, Ind., 1991-95, Times Newspaper N.W. Ind., Munster, 1995—; adj. prof. comms. Valparaiso U., 1997—. Arts and entertainment corr. South Bend (Ind.) Tribune, 1993—; prof. comm. Purdue U., Westville, Ind., 1998—; radio commentator WLJE-FM, Ind., 2002—; corr. Indpls. Star Newspaper, 2003—; contbg. commentator WYIN-PBS TV, 2007—, WMAQ-NBC TV, 2007—. Co-author: It's a Wonderful Life: A Memory Book, 2003; author: From the Farm, 2004, More From the Farm, 2007; actor: (films) Public Enemies. Bd. dirs. Ind. Journalism Hall of Fame, Ind. Performing Arts Hall of Fame. Recipient Reporting award, Hoosier State Press Assn., 1995, AP Mng. Editors, 1997. Mem.: Ind. Hist. Soc., Soc. Profl. Journalists (award 1996), Chgo. Headline Club (bd. dirs.). Republican. Roman Catholic. Avocation: collecting historical autographs. Office: Times Newspaper 601 W 45th St Munster IN 46321 Office Phone: 800-837-3232 3247. E-mail: ppotempa@NWITimes.com.

POTENTE, EUGENE, JR., interior designer; b. Kenosha, Wis., July 24, 1921; s. Eugene and Suzanne Marie (Schmit) P.; m. Joan Cioffe, Jan. 29, 1946; children: Eugene J., Peter Michael, John Francis, Suzanne Marie. PhB, Marquette U., 1943; postgrad., Stanford U., 1943, NY Sch. Interior Design, 1948; DFA, Carthage Coll., 1997; DLitt (hon.), Concordia U., 1997. Cert. lighting Nat. Coun. on Lighting Qualification. Founder, chmn. Studios of Potente, Inc., Kenosha, Wis., 1949—; pres., founder Archtl. Svcs. Assocs., Kenosha, 1978—, Bus. Leasing Svcs. of Wis. Inc., 1978—. Past nat. pres. Inter-Faith Forum on Religion, Art and Architecture; vice chm. Wis. State Capitol and Exec. Residence Bd., 1981—. Sec. Kenosha Symphony Assn., 1968-74; bd. dirs. Ctr. for Religion and the Arts, Wesley Theol. Sem., Washington, 1983-84. With US Army, 1943—46, WWII, ETO. Recipient Disting. Alumni award Marquette U., 1999; named to St. Catherine's HS Hall of Fame, 2002. Fellow Am. Soc. Interior Designers; Mem. Am. Soc. Interior Designers (treas., pres. Wis. chpt. 1985-86, 94-95, chmn. nat. pub. svc. 1986, Gold medal Wis. chpt. 2003), Interior Design Coalition Wis (pres 2003-04), Illuminating Engring. Soc. N.Am., Internat. Interior Design Assn., Elks, Am. Legion (life), Sigma Delta Chi. Roman Catholic. Home: 8609 2nd Ave Pleasant Prairie WI 53158-4720 Office: 914 60th St Kenosha WI 53140-4041 Office Phone: 262-654-3535. Personal E-mail: gpotente@wi.rr.com. Business E-Mail: eugene@potenteinc.com.

POTENZA, JOSEPH MICHAEL, lawyer; b. Stamford, Conn., June 27, 1947; s. Michael Joseph Sr. and Rose Elizabeth (Coppola) P.; m. Karen Louise Yankee, Jan. 28, 1978; children: Wendy Lynn, Chiara Micol. BSEE cum laude, Rochester Inst. Tech., 1970; JD, Georgetown U., 1975. Bar: Va. 1975, D.C. 1976, U.S. Dist. Ct. D.C., U.S. Ct. Appeals (fed. cir.), U.S. Ct. Appeals (6th cir.), U.S. Supreme Ct. Patent examiner U.S. Patent and Trademark Office, Arlington, Va., 1970-74, law clk. bd. appeals, 1974-75, law clk. to presiding judge 6th cir. U.S. Ct. Appeals, 1975-76; assoc. Banner, Birch, McKie & Beckett, Washington, 1976-80, ptnr., 1980—, Banner & Witcoff, Washington, 1995. Adj. prof. Georgetown U. Law Ctr., Washington, 1985—; faculty Nat. Inst. Trial Advocacy-Patent Inst., 1996—; task force on intangibles. Brookings Inst. Editor (monographs) Sorting Out Ownership Rights in Intellectual Property, 1980, Recent Developments in Licensing, 1981; co-author: Patent Trial Advocacy Casebook, 2006; contbg. author Patent Litigaton Strategies Handbook, Patent Misuse-The Critical Balance, A Patent Lawyer's View, Fed. Cir. Bar Jour., Vol. 15, 2005. Bd. dirs. Found. for a Creative Am., 1991—. Recipient Patent and Trademark Office Superior Performance award Dept. Commerce, 1973-75. Fellow Am. Bar Found.; mem. ABA (young lawyers divsn. exec. coun. 1979—, chmn. legis. action com. 1980—, chmn. patent trademark and copyright com. 1977—, house of dels. 1984-86, sci. and tech. sect., coun. mem. 1985—, membership chmn. 1985—, budget co-chmn. 1987—, budget officer 1988—, vice chmn. 1991—, chmn.-elect 1992-93, chmn. 1993, chmn. standing com. on pub. oversight, 1996-2005, spl. adv. on pub. oversight 2005-, fed. practice and procedure com. intellectual property law sect. 1995-96, spring CLE program 1997-98, chmn. summer CLE 1999, 2001, chair fed. practice and procedure com. div. chmn., divsn. VI IP law sec. 1995-97, sec. 2001-04, chmn. divsn. 108 patent sys. policy 2005-), IEEE, AAAS (nat. conf. lawyers and scientists), Am. Intellectual Property Law Assn. (chmn. unfair competition com. 1980-81), DC Bar Assn. (sec. patent, trademark, copyright sect.), Va. Bar Assn., Wash. Patent Lawyers Club (pres. 1988-89), Am. Inns of Ct. (founding mem. and exec. com. Giles S. Rich 1991—, v.p. 1997, pres. 1998-99), Phi Sigma Kappa, Alpha Sigma (pres. 1979-80), Tau Beta Pi. Office: Banner & Witcoff 1100 13th St Ste 1200 Washington DC 20005-4051 Home: 11990 Market St Reston VA 20190 Office Phone: 202-824-3000. Business E-Mail: jpotenza@bannerwitcoff.com.

POTERBA, JAMES MICHAEL, economist, educator; b. Flushing, NY, July 13, 1958; s. William Samuel and Margaret Mary (Toale) P.; m. Nancy Lin Rose, June 23, 1984; children: Matthew Robert, Timothy James, Margaret Rose. AB, Harvard U., 1980; MPhil, Oxford U., Eng., 1982, DPhil, 1983. Asst. prof. economics MIT, Cambridge, Mass., 1983—86, assoc. prof., 1986—88, prof. Cambridge, Mass., 1988—, Mitsui prof. economics, 1996—, chair economics dept., 2006—08; pres., CEO Nat. Bur. Econ. Rsch., 2008—. Dir. pub. econs. rsch. program Nat. Bur. Econ. Rsch., Cambridge, 1990-2008; fellow Ctr. Advanced Study in Behavioral Scis., 1993-94, Hoover Instn. Stanford U., 2000-01, mem. Pres. Adv. Panel on Fed. Tax Reform, 2005; trustee Coll. Retirement Equity Fund, 2006-, Alfred P. Solan Found., 2009-. Editor: Economic Policy Responses to Global Warning, 1991, International Comparisons of Household Saving, 1994, Housing Markets in the United States and Japan, 1994, Empirical Foundations of Household Taxation, 1996, Fiscal Institutions and Fiscal Performance, 1999, Jour. Pub. Econs., 1998-2006; contbr. articles to profl. jours. Recipient award for Excellence in Sci. Reviewing NAS, 1999; Marshall scholar, 1980-83, Batterymarch fellow, 1986. Fellow: Ctr. Advanced Study in Behavioral Scis., Econometric Soc., Am. Acad. Arts and Scis.; mem.: Am. Fin. Assn. (dir. 1993—95), Nat. Tax Assn. (pres. 2009), Am. Econ. Assn. (exec. com. 2001—03, v.p. 2009), Phi Beta Kappa. Office: MIT 50 Memorial Dr Rm E52-350A Cambridge MA 02142-1347 Home Phone: 617-489-4580; Office Phone: 617-868-3907. Business E-Mail: poterba@mit.edu.

POTERO, VALERIE JANE, elementary school educator; b. Phila., Apr. 21, 1968; d. Richard George and Joanne Nancy Potero. Degree in early childhood edn., West Chester U., Pa., 1990; degree in ednl. tech., Chestnut Hill Coll., Phila., 2002. 1st grade tchr. Maternity BVM Sch., Phila., 1991—2000, 4th grade tchr., 2000—06; kindergarten tchr. Rising Horizons Quest Charter Sch., Phila., 2005—06; substitute tchr. MaST Cmty. Charter Sch., Phila., 2006—. Avocations: music, reading, theater. Home: 10014 Bridle Rd 1st Fl Philadelphia PA 19116

POTH, STEFAN MICHAEL, retired diversified financial services company executive; b. Detroit, Dec. 9, 1933; s. Stefan and Anna (Mayer) P.; m. Eileen T. McClimon, May 28, 1966; 1 child, Stefan Michael Jr. Cert. in acctg., Walsh Inst., Detroit, 1959. CPA Mich., cert. consumer credit exec. Sr. acct. Lybrand, Ross Bros. & Montgomery, Detroit, 1953-56, 58-61; with Ford Motor Credit Co., Dearborn, Mich., 1961-91, v.p. leasing truck and recreational products and tractor financing, 1973-77, v.p. cen. and western U.S. ops., 1977—79, v.p. mktg. and ops. svcs., 1979-85, v.p. bus. planning, 1985-90, v.p. credit policy, 1990-91. Bd. dirs. GE Credit Auto Resale Svcs., Inc.; adv. coun. Credit Rsch. Ctr., Krannert Grad. Sch. Mgmt., Purdue U., 1984—91. Chmn. adv. coun. Credit Rsch. Ctr. Krannert Grad. Sch. Mgmt., Purdue U., 1989-90; mem. bd. dirs. Internat. Credit Assoc., 1989-91. With AUS, 1956-58. Roman Catholic. Home: 7230 Mohansic Dr Bloomfield Hills MI 48301-3550

POTLURI, VENKATESWARA RAO, medical facility administrator; b. Krishna Dist., India, Jan. 1, 1955; came to U.S., 1983; s. Venkata Krishnaiah and Bulli Ademma (Koduru) P.; m. Padma Sree Peddu, Dec. 4, 1986; children: Vani, Vamsee Krishna, Varun. BSc, ANR Coll., Gudivada, India, 1975; MSc, AU Coll. Sci. and Tech., Waltair, India, 1977; MPhil, Delhi U., India, 1979, PhD, 1982. Diplomate Am. Bd. Med. Genetics, 1984. Postdoctoral fellow Mt. Sinai Med. Ctr., NYC, 1983-85, vis. asst. prof., 1985-87; lab. dir., adj. mem. med. staff Norwalk (Conn.) Hosp., 1987-98; lab. dir. Lab. Diagnostics (divsn. Cytogenetics), Norwalk, 1998—2001; lab dir. Ctr. for Genetic Svcs. Inc. (divsn. Lab. Corp. of Am.), Corpus Christi, Tex., 2001—03, Dynagene divsn. Lab. Corp. Am., Houston, 2003—. Fellow: Am. Coll. Med. Genetics (founding); mem.: Am. Soc. Human Genetics. Avocations: classical music, Telugu literature, home improvement. Home: 4018 Blue Bonnet Blvd Apt D Houston TX 77025 Office: Dynagene 7400 Fannin Ste 1200 Houston TX 77054

POTMESIL, PETR, pharmacologist; b. Pilsen, Czech Republic, Apr. 15, 1974; s. Jaroslav Potmesil and Hana Potmesilova. MD, Charles U., Prague, Czech Republic, 1999; PhD in Pharmacology, 1st Faculty Medicine Charles U., Prague, 2007—. Rschr. Inst. Clin. and Exptl. Medicine, Prague, 2000—02, Inst. Exptl. Medicine, Acad. Sci. Czech Republic, Prague, 2002—07, Ctr. New Antivirals and Antineoplastics, Prague, 2005—07; regulatory affairs mgr. Unicorn Mgmt., Prague, 2007—. Contbr. scientific papers to profl. jours.; translator: Jour. Postgrad. Medicine, 2000—03. Mem.: Assn. Medecins Francophones Tcheques, Czech Soc. Clin. and Exptl. Pharmacology. Avocations: cross country skiing, jogging, bicycling, wrestling, fitness. Home: Castkova 1824/15 Plzen 32600 Czech Republic Office: Unicorn Mgmt Jaromirova 37 Prague 128 00 Czech Republic Personal E-mail: ppotmesil@hotmail.com.

POTOKA, KAREN, psychologist; b. Mt. Pleasant, Pa., Aug. 3, 1952; d. Virginia and James Jacobs; m. Bruce Potoka, Nov. 13, 1976; children: Mark, Christian, Kathryn. BS, Pa. State U., University Pk., 1974; MEd, U. Pitts., 1981; MS, Miami U. Ohio, Oxford, 1998. Cert. sch. psychologist NASP, 2002, Am. Bd. Sch. Neuropsychologists, 2008. Ednl. liaison UC and Children's Hosp., Cin., 1993—97; sch. psychologist Pub. Sch. Sys., Cin., 1999—. Spl. edn. tchr. Pub. Sch. Sys., 1975—84. Mem.: Am. Bd. Sch. Neuropsychologists, NASP. Office: Mariemont City Sch 6750 Wooster Pike Cincinnati OH 45227 Business E-Mail: kpotoka@mariemontschools.org.

POTRA, FLORIAN ALEXANDER, mathematics professor; b. Cluj, Romania, Dec. 7, 1950; came to the U.S., 1982; s. Ioan and Ana (Popa) P.; m. ELena Lavric, Nov. 15, 1973; 1 child, Valentin. MS, Babes-Bolyai U., Cluj, 1973; PhD, U. Bucharest, 1980. Analyst IPGGH, Bucharest, Romania, 1974-78; researcher INCREST, Bucharest, 1978-82; postdoctoral researcher U. Pitts., 1982-83, asst. prof., 1983-84; assoc. prof. U. Iowa, Iowa City, 1984-90, prof., 1990-98, U. Md. Baltimore County, 1998—; Royden B. Davis chair interdisciplinary studies Georgetown U., 2008—09. Vis. rschr. Lawrence Livermore Nat. Lab., Rice U., U. Catania, Italy, Konrad Zuse Zentrum, Berlin, U. Darmstadt, Germany, 1990, U. Karlsruhe, Germany, 1987-91, Argonne Nat. Lab., 1991, U. Geneva, 1993, U. NSW, Sydney, 1995, U. Rome, 1996, INRIA, France, 1996, City U. Hong Kong, 1999; program dir. NSF, 1997-98; prof. U. Md., 1998—; adv. Nat. Inst. Stds. and Tech., 2003-. Assoc. editor: SIAM Jour. on Optimization, 1991-99, Jour. Optimization Theory and Applications, 1991—, Jour. Optimization Methods and Software, 1997—, Numerical Functional Analysis and Optimization, 1999—, Optimization and Engineering, 1999—; co-author: Research Notes in Mathematics 103, 1984; contbr. articles to profl. jours. Andrew Mellon fellow, 1982, Old Gold fellow, 1984, James Van Allen fellow in natural scis., 1991; NSF grantee, 1985-87., 94-96, 97—. Mem.: Math. Programming Soc., Inst. Ops. Rsch. and Mgmt. Scis., Soc. Indsl. and Applied Math., NY Acad. Scis. Home: 13 Brian Daniel Ct Reisterstown MD 21136 Office: U Md Baltimore County Dept Math 1000 Hilltop Cir Baltimore MD 21250-0001 Business E-Mail: potra@math.umbc.edu.

POTREPKA, DANIEL M., electronics engineer; b. Meriden, Conn., Feb. 3, 1955; s. Mary Gloria Niemiec - Potrepka and Czeslaw (Chester) Andrew Potrepka. BA, U. of Conn., 1977, PhD, 1998; MS, La. State U., 1979. Electronics engr. Army Rsch. Lab, Adelphi, Md., 2002—. Process engr. Mostek Corp., Carrollton, Tex., 1979—81; assoc. mem. tech. staff David Sarnoff Rsch. Ctr., Princeton, NJ, 1981—82; rsch. and tchg. asst. Rutgers U., New Brunswick, NJ, 1982—84, U. of Conn., Storrs, 1992—98; assoc. rsch. scientist United Technologies Rsch. Ctr., East Hartford, Conn. Officer Knights of Columbus St. Joseph Manyanet Coun., Silver Spring, Md., 2001—09; vice exec. St. Joseph Manyanet Coun., Silver Spring, Md., 2004—05, exec., 2005—09, trustee, 2006—, Knights of Columbus Isabella Coun., Southington, Conn., 1999; leader Cub Scout, Silver Spring, Md., 2003—09; counselor Columbian Squires, Manyanet Cir., Silver Spring, Md., 2005—09; treas. U. of Conn. Alumni Hartford Chpt., Conn., 1987—88. Recipient Eagle Scout, Boy Scouts of Am., 1970, Harvard Book prize, Harvard Club for Hartford Conn. Area, 1973; fellow Postdoctoral Rsch. Fellow, U. of Conn., 1998—99, Postdoctoral Associateship, NRC, 1999—2002. Mem.: Sigma Xi (chpt. pres. 2006—09), Am. Phys. Soc. (life). Roman Catholic. Achievements include patents for novel compositions of electronic materials; electromagnetic measurement system; electromagnetic detection technique.

POTSIC, AMIE SHARON, photographer, artist, educator; b. Chgo., Dec. 11, 1971; d. William P. and Roberta K. Potsic. BA in Photojournalism and English Lit. with disting. honors, Ind. U., 1993; MFA in Photography, San Francisco Art Inst., 1999. Cert. Teaching English as a Foreign Language to Adults U. Cambridge, 1996. Program coord., development asst. Shooting Back, Washington, 1993—94; freelance photographer and writer, 1996—; cons. Amie Potsic Fine Art Consulting, San Francisco, 2002—05, Phila., 2002—05; dir. Gallery 339, Phila., 2006—07; dir. career devel. program Ctr. for Emerging Visual Artists, Phila., 2007—. Acting dir. studies, tchr. Ctr. for English Studies, NYC, 1996—2002, San Francisco, 1996—2002; vis. faculty San Francisco Art Inst., 1999—2005; art/photography cons. Amie Potsic Photography, San Francisco, 2004—; adj. and ext. faculty U. Calif., Berkely, 2001—04; adj. faculty Ohlone Coll., Fremont, Calif., 2003—04. One-woman shows include Quotidian Gallery, San Francisco, 2000, 2002, Cinema and Photography Gallery 1101, So. Ill. U., Carbondale, 2001, The Painted Bride Art Ctr., Phila., 2003, 626 Gallery, LA, 2005, Sol Mednick Gallery, U. of the Arts, Phila., 2007, exhibited in group shows at Herbst Pavilion, Ft. Mason Ctr., San Francisco, 1999, The Stage Gallery, Merrick, NY, 2000, Sebastopol Ctr. for the Arts, Calif., 2000, New Langton Arts, San Francisco, 2000, Pentimenti Gallery, Phila., 2001, Mediterranean Found. for Art, Cagliari, Italy, 2001, Mus. New Art, Detroit, 2001, Artoconecto/Nat. Endowment for the Arts, Washington, 2002, DaVinci Art Alliance, Phila., 2002, Soc. for Photographic Edn. Conf., San Francisco Art Inst., 2002, Museo de Arte Moderna de Bogota, Columbia, 2002, Gallery Tonantzin, San Juan Bautista, Calif., 2003, Icebox Gallery, Mpls., 2003, Athens Inst. Contemporary Art, Ga., 2004, Mission 17, San Francisco, 2004, New Langton Arts, 2004, ATROM Gallery, Rome, 2006, Nat. Constn. Ctr. Mus., Phila., 2006, Woodmere Art Mus., 2006, Meml. Art Gallery, Rochester U., NY, 2007, publication, exhbn., Ritual and Resilience (Second Pl. Photoessay award, San Francisco Bay Guardian, 1998), publication, Prayer - Jerusalem, Israel (Jerusalem 3000 First pl. award Jewish Exponent, 1996), Casa do Vaticano, Graficos Burti Brazil. Program coord., instr. Shooting Back, Washington, 1993—94. Recipient Award of Excellence, Manhattan Arts Internat. Mag., 1996, Award of Excellence, Coll. Photography Ann., Photographer's Forum, 1999, winner Photo Alliance Slide Competition, San Francisco Art Inst., 2004. Mem.: Coll. Art Assn., Golden Key Honor Soc., Sigma Eta Phi, Phi Beta Kappa. Personal E-mail: apotsic@yahoo.com.

POTSIC, WILLIAM PAUL, otolaryngologist, educator; b. Berwyn, Ill., May 22, 1943; s. Andrew M. and Estella (Buschak) P.; m. Roberta I. Kite; children: Amie, Jordan. BS, U. Ill., 1965; MD cum laude, Emory U., 1969; postgrad., U. Pa.; M in Med. Mgmt., Tulane U., 1998. Intern, resident U. Chgo., 1969-74; practice medicine specializing in pediatric otolaryngology Phila., 1974—; staff Presbyn. Hosp., U. Pa. Hosp., Phila., Children's Seashore House, Phila.; prof. otorhinolaryngology and human comm. U. Pa., Phila., 1974—, E. Mortimer Newlin prof., 1994—2008; dir. div. otorhinolaryngology and human comm. Children's Hosp., Phila., 1975—2007, med. staff, 1982-84, med. dir. Cochlear Implant Program, 1991—, vice-chmn. clin. affairs dept. surgery, 1995—, dir. ambulatory surg. svcs., 1997—, med. dir. ctr. for childhood comm., 1999—2007. Author: Surgical Pediatric Otolaryngology, 1997; contbr. articles to profl. jours. Recipient 1st prize for clin. rsch. Am. Acad. Ophthalmology and Otolaryngology, 1977, Sylvan E. Stool award for outstanding lifetime contbns. in ear nose and throat advances in children, Presdl. award Soc. Otorhinolaryngology and Head and Neck Nurses, 2002; NIH grantee. Mem. AMA, Am. Acad. Otolaryngology Head and Neck Surgery, Am. Laryngology, Otolgy and Rhinology Soc., Am. Coll. Physician Execs., Internat. Acad. Cosmetic Surgery, Pa. Med. Soc., Phila. Coll. Physicians, Phila. County Med. Soc., Phila. Laryngol. Soc. (treas. 1983), Phila. Pediatric Soc., Am. Laryngol. Assn. (Gabriel Tucker award 2005), Phila Laryngol. Soc. (pres. 1984), Phila. Soc. Facial Plastic Surgeons, Politzer Soc., Soc. Ear, Nose and Throat Advances in Children (pres. 1983), Am. Soc. Pediatric Otolaryngology (pres. 1991, Potsic Ann. award for basic sci. rsch.), Soc. Univ. Otolaryngologists, Am. Acad. Pediat., Alpha Omega Alpha, Phi Chi. Home: 1057 Beaumont Rd Berwyn PA 19312-2007 Office: Children's Hosp Phila 34th And Civic Center Blvd Philadelphia PA 19104 Office Phone: 215-590-3450. E-mail: potsic@email.chop.edu.

POTTASH, A. CARTER, psychiatrist, hospital executive; b. Phila., Nov. 30, 1948; s. R. Robert and Elizabeth (Braunschweig) P. BS with high honors, Trinity Coll., Hartford, Conn., 1970; MD, Yale U., 1974. Intern Tufts U. Sch. Medicine, Springfield, Mass., 1974-75; clin. fellow Yale-New Haven Hosp., 1977-78; fellow Yale U., New Haven, 1975-78; med. dir. Psychiatric Diagnostic Labs. Am., Summit, NJ, 1979-83. Lectr., cons. in field; vis. prof. St. Elizabeth Med. Ctr., Northeastern Ohio U. Coll Medicine, 1979; clin. prof. NYU, 1989—; pres. Fla. Consultation Svcs., P.A., West Palm Beach, 1992—, Psychiatric Assocs. N.J., P.A., Summit, N.J., 1978-93, Met. Med. Group P.C., N.Y.C., 1981-92, So. Fla. Med. Group P.A., Delray Beach, 1984-93, Stony Lodge Hosp., Inc. and Stony Lodge Med. Group P.C., Briarcliff Manor, N.Y., 1985—, Hampton Med. Group, P.A., Rancocas and Summit, N.J., 1986—; exec. med. dir. Fair Oaks Hosp., Summit, 1978-92, The Regent Hosp., N.Y.C., 1981-92, Lake Hosp of the Palm Beaches, Lake Worth, Fla., 1984-92, Fair Oaks Hosp. at Boca/Delray, Fla., 1984-92, Hampton Hosp., Rancocas, N.J., 1986-95—; chmn. Stony Lodge Hosp., Briarcliff Manor, N.Y., 1985—. Editor Psychiatry Letter, 1980-91; mem. editl. bd.

Internat. Jour. Psychiatry in Medicine, 1978-87, The Psychiatric Hosp., 1982—, Jour. Nat. Assn. Pvt. Psychiatric Hosps., 1980-81, Fla. Psychiatry Newsletter, 1992—; reviewer Jour. Nervous and Mental Disorders, Alcoholism, Clin. and Exptl. Rsch., JAMA, Hosp. and Cmty. Psychiatry; contbr. articles to profl. jours. Mem. adv. bd. Mothers for More Halfway Houses, N.Y.C., 1986—; cons. com. on women and alcoholism Jr. League of N.Y.C., 1987; bd. dirs. Met. Soc. Arts, N.Y.C., 1984-87. Fellow Am. Coll. Clin. Pharmacology, Assn. Clin. Scientists, Nat. Acad. Clin. Biochemistry, Am. Psychiat. Assn. (disting. fellow), The Acad. Medicine N.J.; mem. AMA, Soc. Neurosci., Nat. Acad. Clin. Biochemistry, Palm Beach County Med. Soc., Am. Acad. Clin. Psychiatrists, Brit. Brain Rsch. Assn. (hon.), European Brain and Behavioral Soc. (hon.), Am. Soc. Addiction Medicine, Am. Academy of Addiction Psychiatry (founding mem. 1987), Fla. Med. Soc., Palm Beach County Psychiat. Soc., Med. Soc. State N.Y., Med. Soc. N.J., Union County Med. Soc., N.Y. Athletic Club, Canoe Brook Country Club, Beacon Hill Club, Phi Beta Kappa, Delta Phi Alpha. Office: PO Box 511 West Palm Beach FL 33402-0511 Office Phone: 561-837-2215.

POTTEBAUM, SHARON MITCHELL, farm manager, retired health educator; b. Champaign, Ill., Jan. 7, 1948; d. Robert D. and Louise M. (Straits) Mitchell; m. Joseph R. Pottebaum; children: Pamela, Nicholas. BS in Secondary Health Edn., Ohio State U., 1969, MA in Health Edn., 1978. Cert. occupl. hearing conservationist 1984, health edn. 7-12 Ohio Dept. Edn., 1969, health edn. K-12 Ohio Dept. Edn., 1978. Health edn. supr. Ctr. Sci. and Industry, Columbus, Ohio, 1970—72; jr. h.s. health tchr., dist. health coord. Scioto-Darby City Bd. Edn., Hilliard, Ohio, 1972—74; Drug, Alcohol, Tobacco & Human Behavior Project coord. Ohio State U., Columbus, 1974—75, instr. health edn., 1975—76; pub. health edn. cons. child health unit Ohio Dept. Health, Columbus, 1978—79; dir. edn. and tng. Family Hosp., Milw., 1980—85; instr. health edn. U. Wis.-Whitewater, 2000—03; agt. Mitchell-Pottebaum Farms LP, Wis., 2003—. Health edn. cons., tchrs. aide Hillside Elem. Sch., Brookfield, Wis., 1988—97; ind. sales rep. World Book-Childcraft, Brookfield, 1985—88; Head Start tng. tech. assistance project cons. Westinghouse Health Systems, 1979—82; profl. continuing edn. coord. Gtr. Milw. Assn. Hosp. Staff Devel. Dirs. and Wis. Soc. Health Edn. and Tng., 1980—85; adv. mem. geriatric edn. planning com. and indsl. medicine task force coms. Family Hosp., Milw., 1981—84. Co-author (textbook): Teaching Health Science in Middle and Secondary Schools, 1981, Toward A Healthy Lifestyle Through Elementary Health Education, 1980; editor: (monthly newsletter) The Post Graduate, 1990—92 (Wisconsin's "Nellie Bly" First Place Award for Outstanding Branch Newsletter, category of 100+ members, 1992). Recipient cert. of leadership, YWCA Gtr. Milw., 1984. Mem.: AAUW (editor bull. West Suburban-Milw. br. 1990—92, fundraiser 1990—, treas. 1992—94, pres.-elect 1995—96, pres. 1996—97, chair travel group 1997—2000, state historian Wis. chpt. 1998—2000, bd. dirs. Wis. chpt. 1999—2001, historian 1999—2001, chair Women's History Month 1999—2001, co-v.p. program 2006—08, scholarship honoree, 5-star br. award 1997), Champaign County Farm Bur. Avocations: travel, photography, painting, scrapbooks. Home: 2815 Almesbury Ave Brookfield WI 53045 Home Phone: 262-784-0270. Personal E-mail: s_pottebaum@hotmail.com.

POTTEKAT, ANITA, cell biologist; b. New Delhi, May 31, 1976; d. Narayanan Kutty Koloth Veettil and Pushpalatha Pottekat; m. Pillai Harish Parameswaran. PhD in Biochemistry, U. Wis., Madison, 2005. Rsch. assoc. Scripps Rsch. Inst., La Jolla, Calif., 2005—. Contbr. articles to profl. jours. Fellow, Scripps Rsch. Inst., 2007; scholar, Dept. Biotech., Govt. of India, 1996—98; Coun. Sci. & Indsl. Rsch. fellow, Govt. of India, 1998.

POTTER, ALLAN L., lawyer; b. Corpus Christi, Tex., Apr. 27, 1947; s. C. Burtt and Marion J. Potter. Student, U. Tex., 1965-67; BA, Baylor U., 1969, JD, 1971. Bar: Tex. 1971, U.S. Ct. Appeals (5th cir.) 1972, U.S. Ct. Appeals (6th and 11th cirs.), U.S. Supreme Ct. 1975; cert. in bus. and consumer bankruptcy Tex. Bd. Legal Specialization. Law clk. 13th Ct. Appeals Tex., Corpus Christi, 1972-73; ptnr. Potter & Potter, Corpus Christi, 1973-91. Pvt. trustee U.S. Bankruptcy Ct., Corpus Christi, 1975-91. Chmn. Nueces County Dem. Com., Corpus Christi, 1982-86. Mem. Corpus Christi Bankruptcy Bar Assn. (pres. 1992-93). Baptist. Office: PO Box 3159 606 N Carancahua Ste 820 Corpus Christi TX 78463-3159

POTTER, BLAIR BURNS, editor; b. Spartanburg, SC, Mar. 11, 1946; d. Leonard Hill and Nancy Milner (Vaughan) Burns; m. Robert Arthur Potter, May 24, 1974; children: Lillian Howard, Gordon Leonard. BA, Hollins Coll., Roanoke, Va., 1968; MA, U. N.C., Chapel Hill, 1971. Manuscript editor Science, Washington, 1970—74; freelance editor, 1974—85; assoc. editor Health Adminstrn. Press/U. Mich., Ann Arbor, 1985—87; freelance editor NAS, Inst. Medicine, Office Tech. Assessment, Washington, 1987—92; assoc. editor Science News, Washington, 1992, mng. editor, 1992—98; dir. Urban Inst. Press, Washington, 1998—2000, dir. acquisitions, 2000—01; freelance editor, 2000—. Editl. cons. nat. campaign prevent team pregnancy In Search of Memory, 2004-05; surgeon White House Commn. on Complementary & Alternative Medicine Policy, Washington, 2002, Gen.'s Report on Youth Violence, Washington, 2000-2001, White House Task Force on Infant Mortality, Washington, 1990, Nat. Commn. on Orphan Diseases, Washington, 1988-89, Nat. Comm. on Children, Washington, 1992-93; lay mem. protocol com. Nat. Heart, Lung and Blood Inst., Bethesda, Md., 1973. Whittaker fellow, 1969-70; Hollins Coll. scholar, 1964-68, English-Speaking Union scholar, 1967. Mem.: Affordable Housing Coalition Talbot County, Md. Obama (steering com. mem.), Democratic Ctrl. Com. Talbot County. Avocations: gardening, historic preservation, antique american furniture, sailing. Address: 8607 North Bend Circle Easton MD 21601-7327 Home and Office: 8607 Northbend Cir Easton MD 21601-7327

POTTER, CYNTHIA M., art educator, artist; b. Balt., July 15, 1950; d. Percel Celon and Nancy Jane (Williams) Harris; m. Willis M. Potter, Oct. 11, 1975; 1 child, Shomaree. BA, Norfolk State U., 1973, MA, 1983; postgrad., Old Dominion U., 1979, Hampton U., 1984, Va. Commonwealth U. Cert. designated gifted alternative, inservice tng. program for mainstreaming, leadership skills. Summer enrichment art tchr. African Am. art Norfolk (Va.) Pub. Schs., photojournalist tchr., art tchr. Contbr. articles to profl. newsletters. Chair planning com. Ruth Winstead Diggs Scholarship Fund, Inc., 1988—; dir. minority concerns com., 1990—. Recipient Cert. of Recognition, Superior Art Instrn. of Appreciation, 1989; fellow for travel study in West Africa; named Tidewater Elem. Art Tchr. of Yr., for Outstanding Svc., 1988. Mem. Nat. Art Edn. Assn., Nat. Conf. of Artists (exec. sec. 1991-93). Home: 1433 Flintfield Cres Chesapeake VA 23321-2824

POTTER, DAVID, sales executive; b. Kokomo, Ind., Dec. 3, 1961; m. Annette Potter; children: Stephen, Karen, Rachel. BS in Mktg., Polit. Sci., Ball State U., Muncie, Ind., 1984. Salesman Proctor & Gamble; sales mgr. Johnson & Johnson, Boston Scientific, Medtronic, VNUS Med. Technologies, Sulzer Spine Tech., Cardiva Med., 2006—08. Mem. Strongsville Rep. Club, First Luth. Ch., Strongsville, Ohio, co-chair. Mem.: Sigma Chi. Republican. Mailing: 13916 Maple Cir Strongsville OH 44136 Office Phone: 440-572-2675.

POTTER, EMMA JOSEPHINE HILL, language educator; b. Hackensack, NJ, July 18, 1921; d. James Silas and Martha Loretta (Pyle) Hill; m. James H. Potter, Mar. 26, 1949. AB cum laude with honors in classics, Alfred U., 1943; AM, Johns Hopkins U., 1946. Tchr. Latin, Balt. County Pub. Schs., 1943-44; instr. French and Spanish, Balt. Poly. Inst., 1950-83, instr. Spanish adult edn. classes, 1946-48; treas. Bruno-Potter, Inc. Trustee James Harry Potter Gold Medal award of ASME. Donor commemorative plaque in honor of Martha Pyle Hill to Chenango County Coun. Arts, 1996. Mem. Clan Hay Soc. Scotland (Am. br.), John Hopkins U. Faculty Club, Colonial Williamsburg Duke of Gloucester Soc. Democrat. Home: 419 3d Ave Avon By The Sea NJ 07717-1244

POTTER, EVERETT, travel writer; BA in English Lit., Boston U.; MA in English Lit., U. Wis., Madison. Weekly columnist NY Times Syndicate, 1988—, USA Weekend mag., 2004—; creator, editor web blog Everett Potter's Travel Report, 2005—. Founding contbg. editor SmartMoney Mag. Wall St. Jour., 1993—97; monthly columnist Diversion mag. Hearst Bus. Pub., Inc.; cons. various orgns. including Am. Express, Butterfield & Robinson, Four Seasons Hotels & Resorts, Greater Vancouver Convention & Visitors Bureau. Author: Cave Pictures, 1981, The Best of Brazil, 1989; contbr. articles to National Geographic Traveler and Washington Post; travel columnist Snow Country; contbg. editor: Ski mag.; contbr. (mags.) Endless Vacation, Conde Nast Traveller UK, Outside, Money, Forbes FYI, Bride's; guest appearances include NBC's Today Show, CNN, CNN-FN, CNBC, CBS, Fox, Bloomberg Radio, NPR's All Thing Considered. Mem.: NY Travel Writers (past pres.), Nat. Writers Union, Soc. Am. Travel Writers (Lowell Thomas Gold award 1993, 1994, 1995, Bronze award 1998). Personal E-mail: EvPotter@AOL.com.*

POTTER, FRED LEON, lawyer, retired insurance company executive; b. Kansas City, Dec. 15, 1948; s. Donald Warren and Olive Lucile (Ater) P.; m. Mertie Lorraine Scribner, June 13, 1970; children: Mark, Amy, Joy. BA, Harvard U., 1970, MBA, 1972; JD, U. Mich., 1975. Bar: N.H. 1975, U.S. Dist. Ct. N.H. 1975. Atty. Sulloway, Hollis & Soden, Concord, NH, 1975-80, 96—; pres., gen. counsel Christian Mut. Life Ins. Co., Concord, NH, 1980-96. Ptnr., mgmt. cons. Potter-Brock Assn., Tucson, 1969-82; trustee Gordon-Conwell Theol. Seminar, South Hamilton, Mass., 1983—; bd. dirs. N.H. Savs. Bank Corp., Concord, 1987-90; exec. dir. N.H. Health Plan, 2002—, N.H. Vaccine Assn., 2002—. Clk. Concord Union Sch. Dist., 1978-84; deacon 1st Bapt. Ch., Concord, 1978-85; elder Grace Bible Fellowship, 1993—; coach Concord Little League, 1985-87, 90-93. Mem. ABA, N.H. Bar Assn. (treas. 1980-84, v.p. 1984-85, pres. 1986-87, Pres. Disting. Service award 1983), Merrimack County Bar Assn. (sec. 1976-80), Christian Legal Soc., Computer Law Assn., Order of Coif. Evangelical. Home: 4 Pond Place Ln Concord NH 03301-3033 Office: 9 Capitol St Concord NH 03301-6310 Home Phone: 603-228-1272; Office Phone: 603-223-2816. Business E-Mail: FPotter@sulloway.com.

POTTER, GEORGE KENNETH, artist; b. Bakersfield, Calif., Feb. 26, 1926; s. Howard Eugene and Edythe (Keast) P.; m. Heliodora Carneiro de Mendonca, July 30, 1954 (div. July 1956); 1 child, Helen Marcia Pessoa; m. Ruth Mary Griffen, Aug. 4, 1962 (div. July 1989); children: Katherine Anne Klein, Claire Lorraine, Cynthia Ann. Student, Acad. Art U., San Francisco, 1947—48, Jean Metzinger Acad. Frochot, Paris, 1950—52, Inst. Statale dei Belli Arti, Florence, Italy, 1951; BA magna cum laude, San Francisco State U., 1974. Tchr. pvt. watercolor workshops, San Francisco, Santa Fe, Hawaii, Italy, Adriatic, Sacramento Fine Arts Ctr., others; lectr. San Francisco State U.; instr. Acad. Art U., San Francisco; judge Vacaville 28th Ann., 2005, Calif. State Fair Art Exhbn., 1968. Solo shows include Rotunda Gallery, San Francisco, 1949, 52, Gallerie 8, Paris, 1952, Brazilian-Am. Inst., Rio de Janeiro, 1955, U. Santa Clara, Calif., 1958, Maxwell Galleries, San Francisco, 1958, 62, Rosacrucian Mus., San Jose, Calif., 1959, U. Calif.-Berkeley, 1959, Palo Alto Cultural Ctr., 1977, Marin County Civic Ctr., San Rafael, Calif., 1985, NutTree Gallery, Vacaville, Calif., 1987, Foundry Gallery, Sacramento, 2003, 20th St. Gallery, Sacramento, 2005, New Artworks Fair Oaks, 2007, Blue Moon Gallery Sacramanto, 2008, Vacaville Art Gallery, 2009, Am. Watercolor Soc., NYC, 1961, 74, 76, 79, 03, Calif. Watercolor Assn., 2004-09, Phelan Awards Competition San Francisco Mus. Art, 1949, Calif. Palace Legion Honor, 1958, 60, San Francisco, Springville (Utah) Invitational, 1963, Calif. State Fair (awards 1958, 72, award of excellence 2006, two Merit awards, 2007) 1957-58, 61-68, 70-74, 76, 79, 86, 2006, 2007, 2008 (Kay Boron Memorial award & award of Merit Calif. Star State Fair, 2008, Merit award Calif. State Fair, 2009), Oakland Watercolor Ann., 1948, 52, Oakland Mus. Art, Kingsley Ann., E.B. Crocker Art Mus., Sacramento, Kigsley award 1948, 58, 61, 62, 64, 65, Western Assn. Mus. Shows, 1964, 67, 74, No. Calif. Arts Ann., 1961, 68, 88, 97, 98, 03-06, 07, 08, 09, Soc. Western Artists Ann. at M.H. De Young Mus., San Francisco, 1956-64, Statewide Watercolor Show (award), Santa Cruz, 1958, Watercolor U.S.A., Springfield, Mo., 1973, 74, Fukuoka (Japan) Invitational Exchange Show with Oakland, 1964, Royal Watercolor Soc. Invitational Exhbn., London, 1975, From London to Leeds Mus. Art, Eng., 1975, Palace of the Legion of Honor, San Francisco, A City Buys Art Invitational, 1967, Regional Watercolors, 1930-60, Calif. Heritage Mus., Santa Monica, Ca., 2004, Cities Of Promise Orange County Mus. Art, Irvine Calif, 2004, Calif. Modernist Watercolors of 1950's, Pasadena Mus. Calif. Art, 2006; Jack London Invitational (award 1958), Oakland, Calif., 1957-65, Mother Lode Ann., Sonora, Calif., 1957-58, 63, 65, Marin Soc. Artists Ann., 1948-49, 58, 61, 65-73, 75, 77, 95-98, 04-08, Marin County Ann. (awards 1966, 67), 1962, 65-67, 70, 71, 76, San Francisco Art Festival (Exhbn. award), 1975; Pi Commn. executed murals Moore Bus. Forms, Inc., Oakland, 1963, Town Hall, Corte Madera, Calif., Macy's of Calif., Sacramento, 1963, San Mateo, 1964, Stockton, 1965, stained glass dome for Hale Meml., Soc. Calif. Pioneers, San Francisco, 1974, Calif. Dept. Motor Vehicles, Oakland, 1975; stained glass and resin triptych U. Calif. at San Francisco Moffitt Hosp., 1976, Embassy Stes. Hotel, Sacramento (watercolor commn.), 2001, W. Robert Griswold, Jr., Tiburon, Calif. (sculpture commn.), 2002, 100 Watercolors Switzerland Robert Suter, Basel, Switzerland; represented in permanent collections including HUD San Francisco regional office, San Francisco Art Commn., U. San Francisco, San Diego Mus. Art, position held art dir. McCann-Erickson Advt. Inc., Rio de Janeiro, 1954-55, Johnson and Lewis Advt., San Francisco, 1957, Michelson Advt., Palo Alto, Calif., 1959-60, Christian Sci. Monitor Color Out of the West - 02/26/1949 Cover and Spread, Mag. Sect.; contbr. The Calif. Style-Watercolor Artists 1925-55 (McClelland and Last), 1985, The NY Art Rev., 1988, Watercolors Editions Limited, San Francisco, Calif., 1990, California Watercolors 1850-1970, McClelland and Last, 2002. Served with USMCR, 1944-46, PTO. Recipient Macy's Art award, San Francisco, 1958, 1st award Watercolor Delta Ann., Antioch, Calif., 1969, 1st award Alameda County Fair, 1974, 79, 85, Santa Rosa 12th Ann., 1975, Best of Show Calif. Arts League Open Exhibition, 1988, 98, First Popular award Calif. Arts League Open, 1989, 2d award Calif. Art League, 1997, 1st place award, 1997, 1st place award Marin Soc. Artists Ann. Open, 1997, Watercolor Artists Sacramento Horizons, 19th ann. Grumbacher award, 1997, Valley Sculpture Artists 1st Ann. Exhbn. Merit award, 1998-99, award of excellence Opus Magnum XI, 1998, Wash. 20th Ann. Exhbn., 1998, First award sculpture, 1997, First award 1999, Award of Merit No. Calif. Arts Annual Open, 1999, Florence Ferrario Meml. award, 1998, Award of Excellence League of Carmichael Artists Annual Open, 1999, Merit award 1998, 2d Sculpture award, 1st Mixed award Calif. Art League, 2000, First award Valley Sculpture Artists Members Show, 2000, 1st Watercolor award Watercolor Artists Sacramento Open, 2000, 1st Watercolor award, 1st Mixed award Calif. Arts. League Ann. Open, 2001, Merit award Sacramento, 1st Ann. Meml. award Valley Sculpture, 2003, No. Calif. Arts Open, 2003, 1st award, 1st Watercolor award, Best of Show, Northern Calif. Arts Mem. Show, 2008, First prize 2009, Calif. Art League Open, 2004, Richeson Golden Watercolor award Calif. Art League, 2005, First Watercolor award, 2005, Best of Color Open Show, 2006, First Watercolor award No. Calif. Arts Member Show, 2005, Judge's award Magnum Opus, Best of Color Sacramento Fine Arts Ctr., 2006, Best of Show, Magnum Opus, 2008, Magnum Opus award 2009, Hale Meml. award, 2005, Best of Show, Watercolor Artists Sacramento Open, 2005, 06, Best of Show, Watercolor Artists Sacramento Wash. Mem.'s Show, 2006, award of Excellence Watercolor Artists Sacramento Members Show, 2007, Past Pres. award, Wash. Mem. Show, 2008, Best of Show Vacaville Art Fest, 2005, First award Marin Soc. Artists, 2006, Best of Show, First Exhibition of Environ. Arts, 2008, Sacramento Fine Art Ctr., 2008, First Place in Painting Environ. Arts, 3d prize Vacaville Ann., 2006, First prize Vacaville Ann, 2009, Best of Show Northern Calif. Mem. Show, 2008, 2nd Best of Show U. Art Show, 2008, Merit award Bold Expressions Northern Calif. Open, 2008, 2nd prize Calif. Watercolor Assn. Concord, 2008, First award Northern Calif. Mems. Show, 2009, Popular award, Carmichael award, CaliColor award Sacramento Bus. Show, 2009. Mem. Am. Watercolor Soc. (signature mem.), Calif. Watercolor Assn. (signature mem.), Marin Soc. Artists (life). Address: 4824 Skyway Dr Fair Oaks CA 95628-6520 Office Phone: 916-966-8248.

POTTER, GEORGE WILLIAM, JR., mining executive; b. St. Louis, Aug. 5, 1930; s. George William and Fay Marguerite (Finch) P.; m. Emily Louise Withers, Feb. 11, 1956; 1 child, Anne Finch Russ. BA, U. Mo., Kansas City, 1952. Pres. Oritz Mines, Inc., Joplin, Mo., 1962—64, chmn. bd. dirs., 1964—87, Nancy Oil & Royalty Co., Joplin, 1981—86; pres., chmn. bd. dirs. Potter Industries, Inc., Joplin, 1981—90; chmn. bd. dirs. Cresset Corp., Joplin, 1986. One-man shows include Barn Gallery, Kansas City, Mo., 1974, Fountain Valley Sch., Colorado Springs, Colo., 1974, U. Leyden, The Netherlands, 1977, others; author books (under pseudonym E.L. Withers): The House on the Beach, 1957, The Salazar Grant, 1959, Diminishing Returns, 1960, Heir Apparent, 1961, The Birthday, 1962, Royal Blood, 1964; fgn. edits. include Brit., French, Italian, German, Scandinavian, Japanese. Founding bd. dirs. Winfred L. and Elizabeth C. Post Meml. Art Reference Libr., 1977-82, Kansas City Ballet, 1976-79; trustee Conservatory of Music, Kansas City, 1988-2001. Recipient Mo. Writers award, U. Mo., Columbia, 1967. Mem. Authors Guild, Nat. Trust for Hist. Preservation, Soc. Fellows Nelson Gallery Found. (coun. 1988-91), Kansas City Country Club. Home: 1239 W 61st Terr Kansas City MO 64113-1327

POTTER, JACK (JOHN E. POTTER), federal agency administrator; b. NYC, 1955; m. Maureen Potter; 2 children. B in Econs., Fordham U.; M in Mgmt., MIT. With US Postal Svc., 1977—, mgr. of Capital Metro ops., 1998—2000, sr. v.p. labor rels., 1998—99, sr. v.p. ops., 1999—2000, COO, 2000—01, postmaster gen., CEO, 2001—. Recipient Bd. Governors award, US Postal Svc., 1999, Elmo R. Zumwalt Legacy award, Marrow Found., 2003, J. Edward Day award, Assn. Postal Commerce, 2003, Tom Tully award, Am. Bus. Media, 2006. Office: US Postal Svc 475 L'Enfant Plz Rm 10022 Washington DC 20260-0010 Business E-Mail: pmgceo@usps.gov.*

POTTER, JAMES EARL, retired international hotel management company executive; b. Utica, NY, July 25, 1933; s. Earl Moses and Helen May Potter. BS in Hotel Mgmt. with distinction, Cornell U., 1954, postgrad., 1955-56. Owner, propr. Old Drovers Inn, Dover Plains, NY, 1956-89; various acctg. positions Inter-Continental Hotels Corp., NYC, 1960-62, fin. dir. for Asia and Pacific, 1963-69; v.p. Overseas Nat. Airways Hotels, NYC, 1969-71; sr. v.p. Inter-Continental Hotels Corp., NYC, 1972-89, London, 1990-92. Instr. acctg. Cornell U., Ithaca, N.Y., 1957-59. Author: A Room with a World View, 1996. Trustee Opera Co. Boston, 1978-85; mem. Cornell U. Coun., 1988-91; mem. patron com. Met. Opera, NYC; bd. dirs. Santa Fe Opera, 2001-06, 2008-09, treas., 2003-06, mem. investment com.,2004-06, 2008-09. Mem.: Culinary Inst. Am. (trustees com. on acad. policy 1980—90), Santa Fe Opera Found. (trustee), Cornell Hotel Soc., Santa Fe Opera Club (bd. dirs.), Cornell Club (N.Y.C.), Met. Opera Club (bd. dirs. 2003—08, pres. 2006—08). Presbyterian. Avocation: opera.

POTTER, JOE W., dentist; m. Sylvia Potter; children: Clayton, Claire. BA, U. North Tex., 1969; DDS, Baylor Dental Coll., 1973; post-grad., Baylor Coll. Dentistry, 1993. Mem.: ADA, Am. Acad. Cosmetic Dentistry, Acad. Gen. Dentistry, Tex. Dental Assn., Dallas County Dental Soc. Office: 207 W Belt Line Rd Cedar Hill TX 75104 Office Phone: 972-291-1501. Office Fax: 972-291-1503. E-mail: joewpotterdds@sbcglobal.net.

POTTER, JOHN FRANCIS, oncologist, surgeon; b. NYC, July 26, 1925; s. John Albert and Isabelle Cecelia (Sullivan) P.; m. Tanya Agnes Kristof, Nov. 19, 1955; children: Tanya Jean, Miriam Isabelle, John Mark. MD, Georgetown Med. Sch., 1949. Intern Grasslands Hosp., Valhalla, NY, 1949-50, resident in surgery, 1949-50, Georgetown U. Hosp., Washington, 1953-56; sr. investigator Nat. Cancer Inst., Bethesda, Md., 1957-60; chief divsn. surg. oncology Georgetown Med. Ctr., Washington, 1960-85; instr, asst.prof., then assoc. prof. surgery Georgetown U. Sch. Medicine, 1957-64, prof., 1969—2000; dir. Vincent T. Lombardi Cancer Rsch. Ctr., Washington, 1967-87, U.S. Mil. Cancer Inst., Bethesda, Md., 2000—. Mem. presdl. apptd. mem. bd. regents Uniformed Svcs. U. of the Health Scis., 1999. Hon. prof. Universidad Cayetano Heredia, Lima, Peru, 1980. Lt. (j.g.) USNR, 1951-53. Recipient Pres.'s medal Georgetown U., 1991. Mem. Soc. Surg. Oncology (rep. adv. bd.), ACS, Assn. Am. Cancer Insts. (v.p. 1985-86, pres. 1986-87, bd. dirs. 1982, chmn. bd. dirs. 1987-88), So. Surg. Assn., Peruvian Cancer Soc. (hon.). Office: US Mil Cancer Inst Walter Reed Army Med Ctr Bldg # A109 6900 Georgia Ave NW Washington DC 20307

POTTER, JOHN LEITH, retired mechanical and aerospace engineer, educator, consultant; b. Metz, Mo., Feb. 5, 1923; s. Jay Francis Lee and Pearl Delores (Leeth) P.; m. Dorothy Jean Williams, Dec. 15, 1957; children: Stephen, Anne, Carol. BS in Aerospace Engring., U. Ala., Tuscaloosa, 1944, MS in Engring., 1949; MS in Engring. Mgmt., Vanderbilt U., 1976, PhD in Mech. Engring., 1974. Engr., educator various indsl., ednl. and govt. orgns., 1944-52; chief, flight and aerodyns. lab. Redstone Arsenal, Ala., 1952-56; mgr., div. chief, dep. tech. dir., sr. staff scientist Sverdrup Tech., Inc., Tullahoma, Tenn., 1956-83;

research prof. Vanderbilt U., Nashville, 1983-92, prof. emeritus, 1992—; cons. engr. Nashville, 1983—. Convener NATO-AGARD, U.S. and Eng., 1980-82, mem. working group, 1984-88; mem. adv. com. Internat. Symposium on Rarefied Gasdynamics, 1970—; invited lectr. USSR Acad. Scis., 1967; mem. NRC com. on assessment nat. aeronautical wind tunnel facilities, 1987-88; mem. NASA working groups, 1987—; mem. Engring. Accreditation Commn., 1985-90. Editor: Rarefied Gas Dynamics, 1977. Contbr. articles to profl. publs., chpts. to books Chmn. bd. dirs. Coffee County Hist. Soc., Tenn., 1971-72; bd. dirs. Southeastern Amateur Athletic Union, 1972-73; pres. Tullahoma Swim Club, 1972-73. Recipient Outstanding Fellow award U. Ala. Aerospace Engring. Dept., 1987; elected 150th Anniversary Disting. Engring. Fellow U. Ala. Coll. Engring., 1988; USAF Arnold Engring. Devel. Ctr. fellow, 1993. Fellow AIAA (assoc. editor jour. 1970-73, publs. com. 1973-78, assoc. editor Progress in Astronautics and Aeronautics 1981-85, Gen. H.H. Arnold award Tenn. chpt. 1964); mem. U. Ala. Capstone Engring. Soc. (regional bd. dirs. 1972-77), Sigma Xi, Tau Beta Pi, Theta Tau, Pi Tau Sigma, Sigma Gamma Tau. Home: 400 University Park Dr Apt 394 Birmingham AL 35209

POTTER, JOHN WILLIAM, federal judge; b. Toledo, Ohio, Oct. 25, 1918; s. Charles and Mary Elizabeth (Baker) P.; m. Phyllis May Bihn, Apr. 14, 1944; children: John William, Carolyn Diane, Kathryn Susan. PhB cum laude, U. Toledo, 1940; JD, U. Mich., 1946. Bar: Ohio 1947. Assoc. Zachman, Boxell, Schroeder & Torbet, Toledo, 1946-51; ptnr. Boxell, Bebout, Torbet & Potter, Toledo, 1951-69; mayor City of Toledo, 1961-67; asst. atty. gen. State of Ohio, 1968-69; judge 6th Dist. Ct. Appeals, 1969-82, U.S. Dist. Ct., Toledo, 1982—, sr. judge, 1992—. Presenter in field, inactive sr. judge, 2004-. Sr. editor U. Mich. Law Rev., 1946. Pres. Ohio Mcpl. League, 1965; past assoc. pub. mem. Toledo Labor Mgmt. Commn.; past pres., bd. dirs. Commn. on Rels. with Toledo (Spain); past bd. dirs. Cummings Sch. Toledo Opera Assn., Conlon Ctr.; past trustee Epworth United Meth. Ch.; hon. chmn. Toledo Festival Arts, 1980. Capt. F.A., U.S. Army, 1942-46. Decorated Bronze Star; recipient Leadership award Toledo Bldg. Congress, 1965, Merit award Toledo Bd. Realtors, 1967, Resolution of Recognition award Ohio Ho. of Reps., 1982, Outstanding Alumnus award U. Toledo, 1966, conf. rm. named in his honor, U.S. Courthouse, Toledo, 1998; named to Field Arty. Officer Candidate Sch. Hall of Fame, 1999. Fellow Am. Bar Found., Am. Judicature Soc., 6th Jud. Cir. Dist. Judges Assn., Fed. Judges Assn.; mem. ABA, Ohio Bar Assn. (Found. Outstanding Rsch. award 1995), Toledo Bar Assn. (exec. com. 1962-64, award 1992), Lucas County Bar Assn., U. Toledo Alumni Assn. (past pres.), Toledo Zool. Soc. (past bd. dirs.), Old Newsboys Club, Toledo Club, Kiwanis (past pres.), Phi Kappa Phi. Home: 5916 Cresthaven Ln OH 10 Apt 428B Toledo OH 43614

POTTER, MYRTLE STEPHENS, healthcare consulting company executive, retired pharmaceutical executive; b. Las Cruces, N Mex., Sept. 28, 1958; d. Albert and Allene (Baker) Stephens; m. James Potter; children: Jamison, Lauren Elizabeth. BA in Polit. Sci., U. Chgo., 1980. Mktg. intern IBM, 1979—80; sales rep. Proctor & Gamble, 1980—81, dist. sales training mgr., 1981—82; sales rep. Merck and Co., 1982—84, mktg. analyst, 1984—85, training & planning mgr., 1985—86, field meeting svc. mgr., 1986—87, dist. sales mgr., 1987—89, product mgr., 1989—90, dir. Astra/Merck affairs, 1990—92, sr. dir market planning, 1992—93, v.p. N.E. Region Bus. Group, 1993—96; v.p. strategy and econ. US Pharmaceuticals Group Bristol-Myers Squibb, 1996—97, group v.p. Worldwide Medicine Group, 1997—98, sr. v.p. sales, US Cardiovascular/Metabolics, 1998, pres. US Cardiovascular/Metabolics, 1998—2000; exec. v.p. Genetech, Inc., South San Francisco, 2000—01, exec. v.p. comml. ops., COO, 2001, pres., comml. ops., co-chmn., product portfolio com., cons., 2004—; founder Myrtle Potter Consulting, LLC, Woodside, Calif., 2005—. Bd. dirs. Calif. Healthcare Inst., 2001—, Amazon.com, 2004—, Medco Health Solutions Inc., 2007—. Mem. Phila. Urban League, 1988—96; mem. bd. trustees Del. Valley Boys & Girls Club, 1996—2000; co-founder Chapman Devel. Group; mem. adv. bd. Healthcare Bus. Women's Assn., 2003—. Recipient National Woman of Distinction award, Girl Scouts of the USA, 2004; named Woman of Yr., Healthcare Bus. Women's Assn., 2000, Top 50 Most Powerful Women In Business, Fortune mag., 2003, Most Powerful Black Executives in America, 15 Young Global Business Influentials, TIME mag.; named one of 50 Women to Watch, Wall St. Jour., 2005. One of the architects of the Astra/Merck joint venture and led the work that set Prilosec on pace to be one of the biggest pharmaceutical products in the world; Won the Merck Chairman's Award for work on the Astra/Merck joint venture. Office: Myrtle Potter Consulting LLC 2995 Woodside Rd Ste 400 Woodside CA 94062 E-mail: myrtle@myrtlepotter.com.

POTTER, PAUL EUGENE, communications educator, consultant; b. Long Beach, Calif., May 14, 1938; s. Paul and Mae Eugenia Potter; m. Tanya Gregory, Dec. 21, 1974; children: Anthony Eugene, Mark Andrew, Jonathan Criswell. BFA in Broadcasting and Film, So. Meth. U., Dallas, 1969, MFA in Broadcasting and Film, 1970; PhD in Edn. and Speech-Drama, U. North Tex., Denton, 1978. News reporter, announcer KBOX-AM and FM, Dallas, 1966—69; prof. comm., dept. chair Thiel Coll., Greenville, Pa., 2000; prof. comm., dept. head Hardin-Simmons U., Abilene, Tex., 2000—02; instr., tchg. fellow N.Tex. State U.; asst. prof., mgr. campus radio sta. and SFA-TV2 Stephen F. Austin State U., Nacogdoches, Tex.; assoc. prof., TV dir. Xavier U., Cin.; assoc. prof., asst. dir., exec. prodr. OU TV news U. Okla., Norman; regional v.p. A. L. Williams Assocs., Okla. City; prof. comm., dept. head Angelo State U., San Angelo, Tex. Exec. prodr. QUBE programming Warner Amex Cable TV, Cin., 1980; exec. dir. Joseph Inst., Maryville, Tenn., 1997—98; cons. Pub. Speaking Made Easy, Abilene, Tex., 2004—; guest spkr. Tex. Assn. Conv. and Visitors Bur., Abilene, 2006. Prodr., interviewer (radio program) Top of the Mountain, WMEN Radio, prodr., editor, interviewer (syndicated radio program) Faith in Action, NBC, actor, on-screen narrator (TV Christmas spl.) The Messiah, ABC. Ministry team mem., united christian fellowship Phila. Freedom, Philadelphia, Pa., 1996; adminstr. Door of Hope Ch., Fairbanks, Alaska; dir. adminstrn. and ops. Bingle Camp Ministries, Inc. Yukon Presbytery, Harding Lake, Alaska. A2c USAF, 1956—60, Waco, Tex. Tchg. fellow, U. N.Tex., 1970—71. Mem.: Sigma Delta Chi, Phi Delta Kappa. Avocations: reading, travel, art, coin collecting/numismatics. Office: Hardin-Simmons Univ HSU Box 16146 Abilene TX 79698 Business E-Mail: ppotter@hsutx.edu.

POTTER, ROBERT JOSEPH, technical and business executive; b. NYC, Oct. 29, 1932; s Mack and Ida (Bernstein) P.; married; children: Diane Gail, Suzanne Lee, David Craig. BS cum laude, Lafayette Coll., 1954; MA in Physics, U. Rochester, 1957, PhD in Optics, 1960. Cons. ANPA Rsch. Inst., AEC Brookhaven Nat. Lab., RCA Labs., US Naval Rsch. Labs., 1952-60; mgr. optical physics and optical pattern recognition IBM Thomas J. Watson Research Center, Yorktown Heights, NY, 1960-65; assoc. dir. Applied Rsch. Lab., Xerox Corp., Rochester, NY, 1965-67; v.p. advanced engring. Xerox Corp., 1967-68, v.p. devel. and engring., 1968-69, v.p., gen. mgr. Spl. Products and Systems divsn. Stamford, Conn., Pasadena, Calif., 1969-71, v.p. info. tech. group Rochester, 1971-73, Dallas, 1973-75, pres. Office Sys. divsn., 1975-78; sr. v.p., chief tech. officer Internat. Harvester Co., Chgo., 1978-82; group v.p. integrated office sys. Nortel Networks, Richardson, Tex., 1984—87; pres., CEO Datapoint Corp., San Antonio, 1987—90, R.J. Potter Co., Dallas, 1990—. Bd. govs., vice chmn. IIT Rsch. Inst., 1999—2002; chmn. Tatum CIO Ptnrs., LLP, 2000—02; adv. dir. Am. Nat. Bank, 2002—05; mem. rsch. adv. bd. U. Tex., Dallas, 2003—07; bd. dirs. Zebra Techs., Cree, Inc., Molex Inc., 1981—, Bradshaw Group, Speed FC. Contbr. articles to profl. jours. Life trustee Ill. Inst. Tech.; trustee Alliance Higher Edn. Recipient IBM Outstanding Tech. Contbn. award, 1964, Disting. Achievement award Soc. Mfg. Engrs., 1981; Kroner scholar Lafayette Coll., 1954; Disting. Rochester scholar U. Rochester, 1995. Fellow Optical Soc. Am., Am. Phys. Soc.; mem. Phi Beta Kappa, Sigma Xi. Office: R J Potter Co 5215 N O Connor Blvd Ste 360 Irving TX 75039-3739 Office Phone: 972-869-8270. Office Fax: 972-869-6593. Business E-Mail: RJPotter@RJPotter.com.*

POTTER, SHARON LYNN, prosecutor; b. 1959; JD, Calif. We. Sch. Law, 1985. Bar: W. Va. 1985, US Dist. Ct. (so. dist.) W. Va. 1985, Pa. 1987. With W.Va. Pub. Svc. Comm., 1985—87; asst. dist. atty. Cenre County, Pa., 1987—89, W.Va., 1990; assoc. Martin & Seibert, Martinsburg, W.Va., 1990—92; asst. prosecuting atty. Berkeley County, W.Va.; asst. US atty. US Dept. Justice, Wheeling, W.Va., 1992, US atty. (no. dist.) W.Va., 2006—. Office: US Attys Office PO Box 591 Wheeling WV 26003-0011 Office Phone: 304-234-0100. Office Fax: 304-234-0110.*

POTTER, WILLIAM BARTLETT, diversified financial services company executive; b. Washington, Jan. 4, 1938; s. George Holland and Virginia (Bartlett) P.; m. Simone Robert, June 6, 1964; children: Eva Simone, William Bartlett. AB, Princeton U., 1960; MBA, Emory U., 1962. With Merc.-Safe Deposit & Trust Co., Balt., 1962—, asst. sec., asst. treas., 1964-66, asst. v.p., 1966-68, v.p., 1968-69, sr. v.p., 1969-76, exec. v.p., 1976, Preston Trucking Co., 1976-77, pres., 1977-86; chmn., pres. Preston Trucking, 1986-92; Preston Corp., 1986-93, chmn., 1994—. Home: 41880 RCR 44 Steamboat Springs CO 80487 Personal E-mail: will@wbpotter_family.com.

POTTER, WILLIAM GRAY, JR., university librarian; b. Duluth, Minn., Feb. 18, 1950; s. William Gray and Kathryn Martha (Scheuer) P.; m. Marsha Ann Munie, Sept. 23, 1982. BA in English, So. Ill. U., Edwardsville, 1973; MLS, U. Ill., Urbana-Champaign, 1975; MA in English, U. Ill., 1976, PhD in Libr. and Info. Sci., 1984. Libr. U. Wis.-Whitewater, 1975-78; asst. dir. gen. svcs. U. Ill.-Urbana, 1978-85; assoc. dean librs. Ariz. State U., Tempe, 1985-89; univ. libr., assoc. provost U. Ga., Athens, 1989—. Editor: Serials Automation, 1980, Libr. Trends, 1981, Info. Tech. and Librs., 1984-89; Coll. and Rsch. Libr., 2002-08. Contbr. articles to profl. jours. Bd. dirs. Richard B. Russell Found., 1989— (sec., 1990—), ARL, 1996-99, SOLINET, 2001-03; trustee OCLC, 1994-2000. Recipient Hugh Atkinson Meml. award, 1997; Nix-Jones Outstanding Libr. Ga., 1998; LITA/Gaylord Award 2000; named Disting. Alumnus of Yr. So. Ill. U., Edwardsville, 2001. Office: U Ga Librs U Ga Athens GA 30602-1641 Office Phone: 706-542-0621. Office Fax: 706-542-4144. Business E-Mail: wpotter@uga.edu.

POTTER, WILLIAM JAMES, investment banker; b. Toronto, Aug. 11, 1948; s. William Wakely and Ruby Loretta (Skidmore) P.; m. Linda Lee, Nov. 25, 1972; children: Lisa Michelle, Meredith Lee, Andrew David. AB, Colgate U., 1970; MBA, Harvard U., 1974. With White Weld & Co., Inc., NYC, 1974-75, Toronto Dominion Bank, Toronto (Can.) and NY, 1975-78, group mgr. Toronto, 1979-82; 1st v.p. Barclays Bank PLC, NYC, 1982-84; mng. dir. Prudential-Bache Securities, Inc., NYC, 1984-89; pres. Ridgewood Capital Funding Inc., NYC, 1989—, Ridgewood Group Internat. Ltd., NYC, 1989—2004, Kingsdale Capital, Inc., 2004—06; chmn. R. Meredith & Co., Inc., 2004—. Advisor Ladenberg Thalman Internat., 1990—92, Laidlaw Holdings, Inc., 1992—93, Centennial Fund LLP, Canada; bd. dirs. Aberdeen Australian Equity Fund Inc., Md., Aberdeen Asia Pacific Income Fund Inc., Md., Aberdeen Asia Pacific Income Fund Ltd., New Zealand, Alexandria Bancorp, Canada, E.C. Power Inc., Aberdeen Commonwealth Fund Inc., Md., Voicenet Inc., Del., Power Air Corp., Simberi Gold Corp., Canada. Author: Finance for the Minerals Industry, 1985. Trustee Glen Ridge Ednl. Found, 1994—; advisor Nat. Cancer Resources Found., 2003—; bd. dirs. Glen Ridge (N.J.) Cmty. Fund, 1985—94. Mem.: St. Andrews Soc. NY (bd. dir. 2007—), Nat. Fgn. Trade Coun. (exec. com. 1983—, Washington, bd. dirs., chmn. fin. com.), New England Club N.Y., Econ. Club N.Y., Buck Hill Country Club (Pa.), Glen Ridge Country Club (NJ), Nat. Club (Toronto), Williams Club (N.Y.C.), Harvard Club (N.Y.C.). Congregationalist. Avocations: golf, tennis. Office: Ridgewood Group Internat Inc 236 W 27th St Fl 3 New York NY 10001-5906 E-mail: wpottergi@aol.com.

POTTINGER, RONALD WAYNE, food products executive; b. Eugene A. and Reba R. Pottinger; m. Tamara Pottinger, July 16, 1985; 1 child, Nicole E. BA, Bellarmine, Louisville, 1980. Mem. sales/svc. staff IBM, Louisville, 1977—85; sales v.p. Blendex Co., Louisville, 1985—97, CEO, 1997—; pres. Pottinger Enterprises, Louisville, 2001—, HPP, Simpsonville, Ky., 2005—. Mem. Jeffersontown Chamber, Ky., 2006—, Custom Quality Svcs., Louisville, 2006—. Mem.: Inst. Food Technicians (assoc.). Avocation: boating. Office: Blendex Co 11208 Electron Dr Louisville KY 40299 Office Fax: 502-657-4352. E-mail: rpottinger@blendex.com.

POTTLE, STEVEN L., lawyer; b. Anchorage, Nov. 3, 1960; Student, Univ. of London, Japanese Bus. and Soc. Program, Tokyo; BBA, Univ. Wash., 1983; JD, Vanderbilt Univ., 1987. CPA; bar: Ga. 1987. Acct. Ernst & Whinney; ptnr., chmn., corp. health care group Alston & Bird LLP, Atlanta. Office: Alston & Bird LLP One Atlantic Ctr 1201 W Peachtree St NW Atlanta GA 30309-3424 Office Phone: 404-881-7554. Office Fax: 404-881-7777. Business E-Mail: spottle@alston.com.

POTTORFF, JO ANN, state legislator; b. Wichita, Kans., Mar. 7, 1936; d. John Edward McCluggage and Helen Elizabeth; m. Gary Pottorff; 2 children. BA in Elem. Edn., Kansas State U., 1957; MA in Urban Edn., St. Louis U., 1969. Elem. tchr. Pub. Sch., Keats and St. George, 1957-59; cons., elem. specialist Mid Continent Regional Edn. Lab., Kansas City, Mo., 1971-73; cons. Poindexter Assocs., Wichita, 1975; campaign mgr. Garner Shriver Congl. Camp, Wichita, 1976; interim dir. Wichita Area Rape Ctr., 1977; conf. coord. Biomedical Synergistics Inst., Wichita, 1977-79; real estate sales asst. Chester Kappelman Group, Wichita, 1979-98, J.P. Weigard & Sons, Wichita, 1998—; mem. Dist. 83 Kans. House of Reps., 1985—; regional dir. Women in Govt. Mem. exec. com. Nat. Conf. State Legis. Com. Mem. sch. bd. Wichita Pub. Schs., 1977-85; bd. dirs. Edn. Consol. and Improvement Act Adv. com., Kans. Found. for the Handicapped; mem. Children and Youth Adv. com. (bd. dirs.); active Leadership Kans.; chairperson women's network Nat. Conf., State Legislators; mem. Wichita Children's Home Bd.; vice chmn. Nat. Assessment Governing Bd.; chair edn. com. assembly on state issues Nat. Conf. State legislators. Recipient Disting. Svc. award Kans. Assn. Sch. Bds., 1983, Outstanding Svc. to Sch. Children of Nation award Coun. Urban Bds., 1984, awards Gov.'s Conf. for Prevention of Child Abuse and Neglect, Kans. Assn. Reading. Mem. Leadership Am. Alumnae (bd. dirs., sec) Found. for Agr. in Classroom (bd. dirs.), Jr. League, Vet. Aux. (pres.), Bd. Nat. State Art Agys., Rotary, Ky. Assn. Rehab. Facilities (Ann. award), Nat. Order Women in Legislature (past bd. dirs.), Nat. Conf. State Legislatures (chmn. edn. assembly state issues, exec. com.), Rotary, Chi Omega (pres.). Republican. Avocations: politics, travel. Office: Weigard 6530 E 13th St N Wichita KS 67206-1247 also: 300 SW 10th St Rm 122-W Topeka KS 66612 Office Phone: 316-686-7281, 785-296-7501. Business E-Mail: joann.pottorff@house.ks.gov.*

POTTRUCK, DAVID STEVEN, private equity firm executive; b. 1948; m. Emily Pottruck; 2 children. BA, U. Pa., 1970, MBA with honors, 1972. With Arthur Young & Co., 1974-76, sr. cons.; with Citibank N.Am., 1976-81, v.p.; with Shearson/American Express, 1981-84, sr. v.p. consumer mktg. & advt.; with Charles Schwab & Co., San Francisco, 1984—; exec. v.p. mktg., br. adminstr. Charles Schwab and Co., Inc.; pres. Charles Schwab & Co., 1992—94; pres., COO The Charles Schwab Corp., 1994—98, pres., co-CEO, 1998—2003, pres., CEO, 2003—04; chmn., CEO Red Eagle Ventures Inc. (formerly Pottruck Group), 2004—. Apptd. commr. by Congress The Advisory Commn. on Internet Commerce; bd. dirs. Intel Corp., 1998—, US Trust Co., N.A., DoveBid, Inc.; chmn. Eos Airlines. Co-author: Clicks and Mortar: Passion Driven Growth in an Internet Driven World. Bd.dirs. US Ski and Snowboard Team Found.; pres. Pottruck Family Found.; trustee U. Penn. Recipient Torch of Liberty award, Anti-Defamation League, 2000; named Exec. of the Year, San Francisco Bus. Times, CEO of the Year, Morningstar; named one of The Top 15 CEOs, Worth mag. Office: Red Eagle Ventures Inc 201 Spear St San Francisco CA 94105 also: Pottruck Family Foundation 1016 Lincoln Blvd #221 San Francisco CA 94129*

POTTS, BARBARA JOYCE, retired historic site director; b. LA, Feb. 18, 1932; d. Theodore Thomas and Helen Mae (Kelley) Elledge; m. Donald A. Potts, Dec. 27, 1953; children: Tedd, Douglas, Dwight, Laura. AA, Graceland Coll., 1951; grad., Radiol. Tech. Sch., 1953; grad. program for sr. execs. in state and local govt., Harvard U., 1989. Radiol. technician Independence (Mo.) Sanitarium and Hosp., 1953, 58-59, Mercy Hosp., Balt., 1954-55; city coun. mem.-at-large City of Independence, 1978-82, mayor, 1982-90; exec. dir. Jackson County Hist. Soc., 1991-97; ret., 1997. Chmn. Mid-Am. Regional Coun., Kansas City, Mo., 1984-85; bd. dirs. Mo. Mcpl. League, Jefferson City, 1982-90, v.p., 1986-87, pres., 1987, 88; chmn. Mo. Commn. on Local Govt. Cooperation, 1985-90; bd. dirs., Mercantile Bank, 1989-98, chair ind. adv. bd., 1997-99; bd. dirs. Women's Found. of Greater Kansas City, 1997-2003; mem. chancellor's adv. bd. UMKC Women's Ctr., 1996-; mem. adv. bd. Comprehensive Mental Health Svcs., 1997-. Author: Independence, 1985. Mem. Mo. Gov.'s Conf. Edn., 1976, Independence Charter Rev. Bd., 1977; bd. dirs. Hope House Shelter Abused Women, Independence, 1982—, Vis. Nurses Assn., 1990-93, Truman Heartland Cmty. Found., 1990-2003, bd. chmn., 1997-99, Mid-Continent coun. U.S. Girl Scouts, 1991-95, Harry S. Truman Libr. Inst., 1995—2008, Truman Med. Ctr., 2001—, Coun. on Philanthropy, 2001-03, Leadership 20/20 Vision; adv. bd. Ewing M. Kauffman Fund, 2002-06, Greater Kansas City Cmty. Found., 1999-02, Salvation Army, 1999—; pres. Child Placement Svcs., Independence, 1972-89, Greater Kansas City region NCCJ, 1990-2004; bd. vis. UMKC Sch. Medicine, 2002—; trustee Independence Regional Health Ctr., 1982-90, 94-2001, Park Coll., 1989-99, 2004-07, chmn. bd. trustees, 1995-99. Eye Found. Kansas City, 1997-99; mem. Nat. Women's Polit. Caucus, 1978—; mem. adv. bd. Greater Mo. Focus on Leadership, mem. steering com., 1989—. Recipient George Lehr Meml. award for cmty. svc., 1989, Woman of Achievement award Mid-Continent coun. Girl Scouts U.S.A., 1983, 75th Anniversary Women of Achievement award Mid-Continent coun. Girl Scouts, 1987, Jane Adams award Hope House, 1984, Cmty. Leadership award Comprehensive Mental Health Svcs., Inc., 1984, 90, Graceland Coll. Alumni Disting. Svc. award 1991, Disting. Citizen award Independence C. of C., 1993, Outstanding Cmty. Svc. award Jackson County Inter-Agy. Coun., 1994, Outstanding Cmty. Svc. award Cmty. Svcs. League, 1996, Jackson County Humanitarian of Yr. award, 1997, Disting. Citizen award, 1997, Paul Harris award Ind. Rotary Club, 1997, Outstanding Svc. award City of Independence Human Rels. Commn., 1999, Greater Kans. City Coun. Philanthropy Vol. of Yr. award, 2000; named Friend of Edn. Indpendence NEA, 1990. Mem.: LWV (Cmty. Svc. award 1990), Jackson County Hist. Soc., Nat. Trust for Hist. Preservation. Mem. Rlds Ch. Home: 18508 E 30th Ter S Independence MO 64057-1904

POTTS, CHRISTOPHER GERARD, language educator; b. Conn. s. Arthur Gerard and Alexandra Tenney Potts; m. Kathryn Flack Potts. PhD, U. Calif., Santa Cruz, 2003. Assoc. prof. linguistics dept. U. Mass., Amherst, 2003—. Contbr. articles to profl. jour. Grant, NSF, 2007—. Mem.: Linguistic Soc. America. Business E-Mail: potts@linguist.umass.edu.

POTTS, DENNIS WALKER, lawyer; b. Santa Monica, Calif., Dec. 17, 1945; s. James Longworth and Donna (Neely) P.; children: Brandon Earl Woodward, Trevor Shipley. BA, U. Calif., Santa Barbara, 1967; JD, U. Calif., 1970. Bar: Hawaii 1971, Calif. 1971, U.S. Dist. Ct. Hawaii 1971, U.S. Ct. Appeals (9th cir.) 1973, U.S. Supreme Ct. 1978, U.S. Dist. Ct. (cen. dist.) Calif. 1983. Assoc. Chuck Mau, Honolulu, 1971-74; sole practice Honolulu, 1974—. Mem. litigation com. ACLU Hawaii, 1977-82; former mem. Hawaii Acad. Plaintiff's Attys. Disting. Svc. Cert. ACLU Hawaii. Fellow Internat. Napoleonic Soc.; mem. AAJ (sustaining), Consumer Lawyers Hawaii (treas., bd. govs., Outstanding Lawyers in America). Office: 2755 ASB Tower 1001 Bishop St Honolulu HI 96813-3429 Office Phone: 808-537-4575. Business E-Mail: dennispotts@hawaii.rr.com.

POTTS, GERALD NEAL, manufacturing executive; b. Franklin, NC, Apr. 10, 1933; s. Joseph Thomas and Virgie (Bryant) Potts; m. Ann Eliza Underwood, Dec. 21, 1956 (div. 1991); children: Catherine, Thomas, Alice. BS, U. N.C., 1954; grad., Advanced Mgmt. Program, Harvard, 1973. With Vulcan Mold & Iron Co., Chgo., 1957-59, sales engr., 1959-62, gen. sales mgr. Latrobe, Pa., 1963-65, v.p. sales, 1965-68; v.p. Vulcan, Inc., Latrobe, 1968-72, exec. v.p., 1972-73, pres., 1973-85, CEO, 1977-85, chmn., 1981-85; group exec. Teledyne Inc., 1985-92; pres. Woodings Verona Tool Works Inc., 1993-97; ret. Trustee Greater Latrobe Cmty. Chest, 1970—87, pres., 1978—79; bd. dirs. Latrobe Area Hosp., chmn., 1985—88; mem. adv. bd. U. Pitts., Greensburg, Pa., 1974—80; trustee Seton Hill Coll., Greensburg, 1974—80. With US Army, 1954—56. Mem.: Duquesne Club (Pa.), Chi Phi. Personal E-mail: jpotts1120@comcast.net.

POTTS, JAMES B., III, literature and language professor; b. Spartanburg, SC, July 2, 1956; s. James B. and Jean E. Potts; m. Roxanne Marie Marlowe, Sept. 13, 1991. PhD, U. SC, Columbia, 2001. Adj. prof. English U. SC, 2001; asst. prof. English Miss. Coll., Clinton, 2002—. Sponsor Sigma Tau Delta, Clinton, Miss., 2003—, Tribesman, Clinton, 2005—; pres. Miss. Philol. Assn., Jackson, POMPA editor, Clinton, 2007—. Preacher, leader religious svcs. county jail Meadowbrook Ch.

Christ, Jackson, 2006—08. Named Disting. Lectr., Miss. Humanities Coun., 2008, William Winter Scholar, 2008. Avocations: writing, guitar. Office: Miss Coll PO Box 4022 Dept English Clinton MS 39058 Business E-Mail: potts@mc.edu.

POTTS, JOHN THOMAS, JR., physician, educator; b. Phila., Jan. 19, 1932; married; 3 children. BA, LaSalle Coll, Phila., 1953; MD, U. Pa., Phila., 1957; DSc, LaSalle U. From intern to asst. resident in medicine Mass. Gen. Hosp., Boston, 1957—59; resident Nat. Heart Inst., 1959—60; rsch. fellow in medicine Mass. Gen. Hosp., Boston, 1960—63; sr. research staff Nat. Heart Inst., 1963—66, head sect. polypeptide hormones, 1968—81; from asst. to assoc. prof. medicine Harvard U. Med. Sch., Boston, 1968—75, prof., 1975—; prof. medicine Harvard-MIT Divsn. Health Sci. and Tech., 1978—, Jackson prof. Clin. Medicine, 1981—96, disting. Jackson prof. clin. medicine, 1996—; chief endocrine unit Mass. Gen. Hosp., Boston, 1968—81, physician-in-chief, 1981—96, dir. rsch., 1995—2003. Recipient Andre Lichwitz prize, Endocrine Soc., 1968. Mem.: AAAS, Am. Soc. Bone and Mineral Rsch. (William F. Neumann award 1987), Am. Soc. Clin. Investigation, Assn. Am. Physicians, Endocrine Soc. (pres. 1987, Ernest Oppenheimer award 1968, Fred Konrad Koch award 1991), Inst. Medicine NAS. Office: Mass Gen Hosp 149 13th St Charlestown MA 02129-2020 Office Phone: 617-724-2167.

POTTS, REBECCA, literature and language professor; BS in Philosophy, U. SD, Vermillion, 1984, MA in English, 1986. English, philosophy instr. Minn. West Cmty. & Tech. Coll., Worthington, 1985—. Avocation: art collector.

POTTS, SANDRA, library director; d. Robert and Marilyn Canute; m. David Potts, June 26, 1983. Bachelor's degree, Coe Coll., 1969; MEd, Ctrl. Mich. U., 1975; MLS, Wayne State U., 1993. Elem. sch. tchr., Mich., 1970—74; libr. White Pine Libr. Coop., Saginaw, Mich., 1975—95; libr. dir. Northwood U., Midland, Mich., 1995—. Mem.: ALA, Midwest Archives, Mich. Libr. Assn., Alpha Xi Delta. Sentinal Party. Office: Northwood Univ Strosacker Library 4000 Whiting Dr Midland MI 48640

POTTS, TIMOTHY F., former museum director; b. Australia; Dir. media and telecommunications, corp. fin. dept. Lehman Brothers, NYC, London; prof. U. Melbourne; dir. Nat. Gallery of Victoria, Australia, Kimbell Art Mus., Fort Worth, Tex., 1998—2007; with Fitzwilliam Mus., Cambridge, England. Adj. prof. La Trobe U., Melbourne. Author: (monograph) Mesopotamia and the East: An Archaeological & Historical Study of Foreign Relations 3400-2000 BC, 1995; editor: Kimbell Art Museum: Handbook of the Collection, 2003; co-editor: Culture Through Objects: Ancient Near Eastern Studies in Honour of P. R. S. Moorey, 2003.

POTVIN, ALFRED RAOUL, retired engineering executive; m. Janet Holm, Mar. 20, 1965 BEE, Worcester Poly. Inst., 1964; MSEE, Stanford U., 1965, Engr. in EE, 1967; MS in Bioengring., U. Mich., 1970, MS in Psychology, 1970, PhD in Bioengring., 1971. Registered profl. engr., Tex. Asst. prof. elec. engring. U. Tex., Arlington, 1966—68, assoc. prof. biomed. engring. and elec. engring., 1971—76, prof., 1976—84, chmn. biomed. engring., 1972—84; dir. med. instrumentation sys. rsch. divsn. Eli Lilly & Co., Indpls., 1984—90, dir. tech. assessment and project mgmt., 1990—92, dir. engring., med. devices and diagnostics divsn., 1992—93; prof. elec. engring. Purdue Sch. Engring. and Tech., Ind. U.-Purdue U., Indpls., 1993—96; dean engring. and tech. Ind. U.-Purdue U., Indpls., 1993—95; pres. MEECO, Melbourne, Fla., 1996—2005; ret., 2005. Clin. prof. biophysics U. Tex. Health Sci. Ctr., Dallas, 1967-84; faculty fellow NASA, Houston, 1972-73; life scientist NASA and Moffett Field, 1974-75; founder grad. level biomed. engring. program with U. Tex., Arlington and U. Tex. Health Sci. Ctr., Dallas, 1974, med. devices rsch. divsn. Eli Lilly, Indpls., 1984; mem. phys. med. device panel FDA, Washington, 1978-84; developer NIH Rehab. Engring. Rsch. Ctr., Arlington, 1982; mem. adv. bd., reviewer Biomed. Engring. NSF, Washington, 1984-90, 93-97; founding dir. Ctr. Advanced Rehab. Engring., 1983-84, mem. adv. bd., 1984-88; mem. adv. bd. Engring. Rsch. Ctrs. NSF, Washington, 1988-92, Biomed. Engr. Worcester Polytech. Inst., Mass., 1987—, Coll. Engrs. Duke U., Durham, N.C., 1987-94, U. Calif., Berkeley, 1989-92, Coll. Engrs. U. Denver, 1990-93, Sch. Engr. and Tech. Ind. U.-Purdue U., Indpls, 1992-93, med. engring. Jet Propulsion Lab., Pasadena, Calif., 1989; chmn. NIH Resource Ctr. Case Western Res. U., Cleve., 1988-96; bd. advisors Sch. of Health and Rehab. Sci., U. Pitts., 1993-97; mem. adv. com. NIH, 1987-92, 93-95; bd. dirs. Biomed. Engring. Alliance for Engring. in Medicine and Biology; initiator grad. level biomed. engring. program Ind. U. and Purdue U., Indpls., 1995. Author two vol. book: (with W.W. Tourtellotte) Quantitative Examination of Neurologic Functions, 1985; co-editor: spl. issue on biosensors IEEE Trans. on Biomed. Engring., 1986, spl. issue on status and future directions in biomed. engring. Medicine and Biol. Mag., 1989; mem. editl. bd IEEE Spectrum, 1987-90, 92-95, Biomed. Sci. and Tech., 1990-93, mem. adv. bd. Biomed. Engring. Handbook, 1995, 2000; contbr. papers to profl. jours. Mem., fin. donor Worcester Poly. Inst. Founders Club, Ind. U. Found., U. Tex. Arlington 1895 Soc., Dana Farber Cancer Inst., Chancellors Coun., U. Tex. Sys., 2009—; life mem. Repub. Nat. Com., 1994—. Recipient Life Scientist award NASA, 1974, Hall of Achievement award U. Tex. at Arlington, 2006; spl. fellow NIH, 1968. Fellow: IEEE (life; gen. chmn. annual conf. 1982, pres. Engring. in Medicine and Biology Soc. 1983, re-elected 1984, chmn. health care engring. policy com. 1986, editl. bd. spectrum 1987—89, founding mem. steering com. symposium on computer based med. systems 1988—94, co-editor spl. issue Medicine and Biology 1989, editl. bd. Spectrum 1992—94, internat. conf. com. 1993—95, Centennial award 1984, Life Fellow award 2008), Biomed. Engring. Soc. (chmn. edn. and pub. affairs com. 1979—83), Assn. Advancement Med. Instrumentation, Am. Inst. Med. and Biol. Engring. (bd. dirs. 1991—94, founding fellow 1992, v.p. pub. awareness 1993—94, co-pres. world congress on med. biol. engring. in Chgo. 1993—99, devel. com. 1996—99), Houston Soc. Engrs. in Medicine and Biology (Career Achievement award 1993); mem.: Ind. Elec. Mfg. Assn. (bd. dirs. 1993—96, Svc. to Industry award 1996), Assn. Advancement of Med. Instrumentation, Alliance Engrs. in Medicine and Biology (v.p. nat. affairs 1987—89, pres. 1989—92), Am. Soc. Engring. Edn. (chmn. biomed. engring. divsn. 1979—80). Avocations: boating, hiking, travel, gourmet dining, skiing. Personal E-mail: arpotvin@gmail.com, arpotvin@yahoo.com.

POTVIN, PIERRE, physiologist, educator; b. Quebec City, Can., Jan. 5, 1932; s. Rosario and Eva (Montreuil) P.; m. Louise Dube, Aug. 31, 1963; children: Aline, Bernard. BA, Laval U., 1950, MD, 1955; PhD, U. Toronto, 1962. Asst. prof. Faculty of Medicine Laval U., Quebec City, 1956-63, assoc. prof., 1963-68, prof., 1968-98, prof. emeritus, 1998—, vice dean exec., 1977-86, dean, 1986-94. V.p. Internat. Conf. of Deans of French-Speaking Faculties of Medicine, 1990-96, pres. evaluation coun., 1994—2006; hon. prof. Norman Bethune U. Med. Sci., Changchun, China, 1992. Assoc. editor Modern Medicine Can., 1958-61, Laval Med., 1962-70. Fellow Royal Coll. Physicians and Surgeons Can. (hon.), Ordre Nat. du Lion (officer), Senegal, Sahamatrei Order, Cambodia, Order Can., Ordre Nat. des Palmes académiques, Légion d'Honneur, France. Roman Catholic. Avocation: painting. Office: Laval U Faculty of Medicine Dept Anat & Physiology Quebec City PQ Canada G1K 7P4 Business E-Mail: pierre.potvin@phs.ulaval.ca.

POTVIN, WILLIAM TRACEY, management consultant; b. Milw., June 20, 1951; s. William John and Joan (Wach) P.; m. Louisa I. Vorosmarty, July 23, 1983. BS in Internat. Econs., Georgetown U., 1973; MBA, Am. U., 1975. Investment mgr. GEICO, Washington, 1973-78; mgmt. cons. Touche Ross & Co. (now Deloitte & Touch LLP), NYC, 1978-85, ptnr., 1985-2000; nat. dir. Fin. Inst. Cons., NYC, 1987-90; mng. ptnr., CEO Deloitte & Touche CIS, Moscow, 1990-96; nat. dir. Deloitte & Touche Actuarial and Ins. Cons. Group, NYC, 1996-99; ret. ptnr. Deloitte & Touche, 2000—; pres., CEO The ESP Group LLC, Arlington, Va., 1999—2007; pres. Tracy Assocs. Inc., 2007—. Chmn. adv. group to Russian govt. on mass privatization World Bank, 1992-94, acting CFO Russian Privitization Ctr., 1996; speaker to ins. groups, N.Y.C., 1985—. Contbr. articles to profl. jours. Bd. dirs. Am. Russian Youth Orch., 1996—. Mem. Coll. of Ins. (mem. fin. industries task force 1985-90, lectr. 1985-90). Roman Catholic. Office: The ESP Group LLC Ste 1103 1225 Jeff Davis Hwy Arlington VA 22202 also: The ESP Group LLC 76 Chestnut Ridge Rd Armonk NY 10504-3001 E-mail: william@potvin.net, potvin@msn.com.

POU, NELIDA (NELLIE), state legislator; Attended, Kean Coll., Rutgers U., U. Va. Asst. bus. adminstr. City of Paterson, chmn. Dept. Human Resources, 1983—87; mem. Dist. 35 NJ State Assembly, 1997—, asst. minority leader, 2000—01, dep. spkr., 2002—05. Mem. Passaic-Bergen County HIV Health Svcs. Adv. Coun., 1993—97, NJ Task Force on Child Abuse & Neglect, 1997—. Democrat. Office: 100 Hamilton Plaza Ste 1403-05 Paterson NJ 07505 also: State House PO Box 098 Trenton NJ 08625-0098 Office Phone: 973-247-1555.*

POUCHARD, LINE CATHERINE, research scientist, educator; b. Caudebec-Elbeuf, Normandy, France, Aug. 5, 1958; arrived in U.S., 1983; d. Jean-Claude Louis Arsene Pouchard and Alice Maria Laisney; m. William A. Thomas, Sept. 16, 2005. Lic., U. Haute-Normandie, Rouen, France, 1982; PhD, CUNY, 1993; MS, U. Tenn., Knoxville, 1998. Adj. lectr. Hunter Coll., NYC, 1987—90, Queens Coll., NYC, 1989—91; instr. Reading U., England, 1993—95; rsch. assoc. U. Tenn., Knoxville, 1998; postdoctoral rschr. Oak Ridge (Tenn.) Nat. Lab., 1999—2001, rsch. assoc., 2001—03, staff scientist, 2003—. Mem. program com. Internat. Semantic Web Conf. Contbr. articles to profl. jours. Mem.: IEEE, Divers Alert Network, Sierra Club. Avocations: scuba diving, boating, athletics. Office: Oak Ridge Nat Lab 1 Bethel Valley Rd Oak Ridge TN 37831 Home: 11134 Sonja Dr Knoxville TN 37934

POULET, ANNE LITLE, museum director, art historian; b. Washington, Pa., Mar. 20, 1942; d. John Francis and Ruth Virginia (Kurtz) Litle; m. Francois Poulet, May 20, 1967. BA cum laude, Sweet Briar Coll., Va., 1964; MA Inst. Fine Arts, NYU, 1970. Curator Dept. European Decorative Arts and Sculpture Mus. Fine Arts, Boston, 1980—99; curator European Decorative Arts and Sculpture emerita Russell B. & Andrée Beauchamp Stearns, 1999—; dir. Frick Collection, NYC, 2003—. Catalogue, vol. 5, Wrightsman Collection, Met. Mus. Art., NYC, 1967—72, exhibitions include Corot to Braque, Mus. Fine Arts, Boston, 1978—80; author: (exhibit catalogue) Corot to Braque, 1978—80; editor-in-chief Jour. Mus. Fine Arts, Boston, 1989—93; co-author: (catalogue) Clodion (1738-1814), 1992; author, guest curator Jean-Antoine Houdon (1741-1828): Sculptor of the Enlightenment, Nat. Gallery Art, Washington, DC, 2003; contbr. articles to profl. jours. Recipient Iris Fedn. award for decorative arts, 2000, Chevalier dans l'order des arts et des letres, France; grantee, Ford Found., 1965, Lamb Mellon, 1990, 1998, 2000—01; Kress fellowship, 1976. Fellow: Am. Acad. Arts & Sciences; mem.: Assn. Art Mus. Dir., Am. Fedn. Arts, Am. Assn. Mus., French Heritage Soc. (co-founder, former vice chmn. bd.). Office: The Frick Collection 1 E 70th St New York NY 10021-4967 Office Phone: 212-288-0700. Office Fax: 212-628-4417.

POULOS, ANDREW, JR., protective services official, director; s. Andrew Poulos, Sr. and Susan Marie Poulos; m. Danielle Catherine Loblein, Mar. 5, 2005. Cert.: NJ Police Tng. Commn. (police officer), Del. Coun. Police Tng. 2001, Am. Coll. Forensic Examiners (in homeland security) 2006. Police officer first class Del. Dept. Pub. Safety, Dover, 2000—02; patrolman New Castle Police Dept., New Castle, Del., 2002—03; capt. Ft. Monmouth Police Dept., NJ, 2003—. Dir. Law Enforcement Tng. Solutions, Beachwood, NJ, 2005; exec. dir. Nat. Law Enforcement and Corrections Adv. Coun., Beachwood, 2006—07. Recipient J. Edgar Hoover Meml. Gold medal, Nat. Assn. Chiefs of Police, 2006. Mem.: Internat. Law Enforcement Educators and Trainers Assn., FBI Law Enforcement Exec. Devel. Assn., Internat. Assn. Chiefs of Police. Office: Fort Monmouth Police Dept 977 Murphy Dr Fort Monmouth NJ 08722 Office Fax: 732-532-5684; Home Fax: 877-892-6314. Personal E-mail: info@le-training.com. Business E-Mail: apoulos@fmpd.org.

POULOS, CHRISTOPHER, literature and language educator; s. Chris and Betty P. BA in Leadership Studies, Univ. Richmond; MA in Spanish Tchg., Columbia Univ. With Peace Corps, Honduras; Spanish tchr. Joel Barlow HS, Redding, Conn., 2000—. Adj. prof. Spanish Fairfield U. Named Conn. Tchr. of Yr., 2007. Office: Joel Barlow High Sch 100 Black Rock Turnpike Redding CT 06896 Business E-Mail: cpoulos@region9ps.org.

POULOS, CLARA JEAN, retired nutritionist; b. LA, Jan. 1, 1941; d. James P. and Clara Georgie (Creighton) Hill; m. Themis Poulos, Jan. 31, 1960. PhD in Biol., Fla. State Christian U., 1974; PhD in Nutrition, Lafayette U., 1984; D in Nutritional Medicine, Hearts of Jesus and Mary Coll., 1986. Registered nutritionist, cert. hypnotherapist, clin. densitometry technician, diabetes edn. Dir. rsch. Leapou Lab., Aptos, Calif., 1973—76, Monterey Bay Rsch. Inst., Santa Cruz, Calif., 1976—2001; nutrition specialist Santa Cruz, 1975—2001; dir. nutritional svcs., health enhancement, lifestyle planning, 1983—97; chief tech. and rsch. Osteoporosis Diagnostic Ctr., Santa Cruz, 2000—04; chief tech. rsch. Osteoporosis Care Ctr., San Jose, 2001—07. Instr. Stoddard Assocs. Seminars; cons. Biol-Med. Lab., Chgo., Nutra-Med Rsch. Corp., NY, Akorn-Miller Pharmacal, Chgo.; cons. Threshold Lab. Monterey Bay Aquaculture Farms, Calif.; cons. Resurrection Lab., Calif. Author: Alcoholism-Stress-Hypoglycemia, 1976, The Relationship of Stress to Alcoholism and Hypoglycemia, 1979; assoc. editor: Internat. Jour. Bio-Social Research, Health Promotion Features; editor: Nutrition and Dietary Consultant Jour.; columnist: The Connection Newspaper; contbr. articles to profl. jours. Recipient Najulander Internat. Rsch. award, 1971, Wainwright Found. award, 1979, various state and local awards. Fellow: Internat. Acad. Nutritional Consultants, Am. Nutritionist Assn., Internat. Coll. Applied Nutrition; mem.: AAAS, Internat. Fishery Assn. (health assoc.), Calif. Acad. Sci., Am. Public Health Assn., Am. Heart Assn. (pres. Santa Cruz br. 1990—91), Internat. Platform Soc., Am. Diabetes Assn. (profl., pres. Santa Cruz chpt., editor newsletter The Daily Balance Santa Cruz chpt., sec. No. Calif. chpt.), MUSE-Computer Users Group, Am. Women's Bowling Assn., Quota, Toastmistress. Business E-Mail: cjp1918@netscape.net.

POULOS, JAMES THOMAS, endocrinologist, educator; b. Lynn, Mass., Apr. 11, 1938; s. Thomas Dimitrios and Christine Julia (Zorzy) Poulos; m. Mary Margaret White, June 22, 1963; 1 child, Christopher Kreag. BS, Tufts U., 1959, MD, 1963. Diplomate Am. Bd. Internal Medicine, Am. Bd. Endocrinology and Metabolism. Intern New Eng. Med. Ctr., Boston, 1963—64, resident, 1964—65; resident and fellow in endocrinology U. Chgo., 1967—70; practice medicine specializing in endocrinology Lafayette, Ind., 1970—2004. Adj. prof. clin. pharmacology Purdue U., West Lafayette, Ind., 1976—95, pres. coun., 1995—, adv. commn. Sch. Liberal Arts, 2008—; chmn. therapeutics com. Ind. Dept. Medicaid, 2002—; clin. faculty Ind. U. Sch. Medicine, mem. dean's search com., 1998; with Friend Convocation Purdue, 1970—; mem. therapeutics com. Ind. U. Sch. Medicine, 2002—04; dir., pres. med. staff Lafayette Home Hosp., 1978—79; pres. Arnett HMO, 1986—97; bd. dirs. North Ctrl. Health Svc.; chmn. therapeutics com. State of Ind. Family and Social Svc. Adminstrn., 2002—; dir. regional diabetes ctr. Sisters of St. Francis Health Systems Inc., 1985—, Greater Lafayette Health Svc., 1985—, mem. mission com., 2005—; bd. dirs. GLHS Inc., 2005; mem. mission com. Sisters St. Francis Health Sys. Co-author: The Metabolic Influence of Progestins Advances in Metabolis Disorders, 1971; contbr. articles to profl. publ. Mem. Nat. Rep. Senatorial Com., Nat. Rep. Congrl. Com.; bd. dirs. Coalition Living Well After 50, 2007—. With M.C., US Army, 1965-67. Fellow ACP (councilor-at-large Ind. chpt.), Am. Coll. Endocrinology, Am. Assn. Clin. Endocrinologists; mem. AMA, Am. Diabetes Assn. (dir. Ind. chpt. 1980—, pres. 1986-88, 96-98, bd. dirs., com. profl. practice 1987-88, pres. 1994—), Endocrine Soc., Internat. Diabetes Fedn., Am. Lung Assn. (pres. West Ctrl. Ind. 1982-83), Lafayette C. of C, Nat. Lipid Assn., Ind. Endocrine Soc., Ind. Lipid Working Group, John Purdue Club. Home and Office: 1000 Windwood Ln West Lafayette IN 47906-4737 Office Phone: 765-743-1741. Personal E-mail: jpoulos@insightbb.com.

POULOS, JOAN GRAHAM, lawyer; d. Gilbert W. and Opal Z. Graham; m. John W. Poulos (div. 1978); children: John S., Alexandra J. Poulos Fullerton; m. David C. Lewis. BS, U. Kans., 1958; JD, U. Calif. Hastings Coll. of Law, 1962; MA, U. Calif., Riverside, 1978. Bar: Calif. 1963, US Supreme Ct., US Ct. Appeals (9th cir.), US Dist. Ct. (so., ea. and no. dists.) Calif. Pvt. practice, Davis, Calif., 1978—. Dir. People Resources Inc., Yolo County, Calif., 1994-96. City coun. mem. City Davis, 1972-74, mayor, 1974-76; chmn. juvenile justice com. Mendo County, Ukiah, Calif.; commr. Nat. Commn. Uniform State Law, 1978-86; mem. Davis Chorale; musician Fisherman's Chapel Bodega Bay; past pres. Mental Health Assn. Yolo County. Mem. ABA, LWV, Am. Women Internat. Understanding (nat. vice pres.), Grange. Avocation: music. Office: Poulos & Fullerton 1723 Oak Ave Davis CA 95616-1004 Home: PO Box 1241 Bodega Bay CA 94923-1241 Office Phone: 530-753-4450. Fax: 530-753-9457. Business E-Mail: poulosfullerton@sbcglobal.net.

POULOS, MICHAEL JAMES, insurance company executive; b. Glens Falls, NY, Feb. 13, 1931; s. James A. and Mary Poulos; m. Mary Kay Leslie; children: Denise, Peter. BA, Colgate U., 1953; MBA, NYU, 1963. CLU, 1970. With sales and mgmt. U.S. Life Ins. Co., NYC, 1958-70, dir., 1968, mem. exec. com., 1970; with Calif.-Western States Life Ins. Co., Sacramento, 1970-79, pres., chief exec. officer, 1975-79, dir., 1975; with Am. Gen. Corp., Houston, 1979-93, pres., 1981-91, mem. exec. com., dir., 1981-93, vice chmn., 1991-93; chmn., CEO, pres. Western Nat. Corp., Houston, 1993-98, now bd. dirs., 1998; ret., 1998. Mem. Sam Houston Area coun. Boy Scouts Am. Mem. River Oaks Country Club, Univ. Club of N.Y.C., Caston Woods County Club, Houston, Balboa Bay Club, Newport Beach Club Greek Orthodox. Home: 2121 Kirby Dr Unit 73 Houston TX 77019-6066 Office: 2727 Allen Pky Ste 450 Houston TX 77019

POULOS, STANLEY, plastic surgeon; BA in Chemistry, So. Meth. Univ., Dallas, Tex., 1970; MD, Univ. Tex., San Antonio, 1974. Cert. Am. Bd. Plastic Surgery, 1982. Intern in gen. surgery Univ. Calif., San Francisco, 1974—75, resident in gen. surgery, 1974—77; fellow in plastic surgery St. Francis Meml. Hosp. Plastic and Reconstructive Surgery Ctr., 1977—80; clin. prof., divsn. plastic surgery Greenbrae Surgery Ctr., Calif., 2004; co-dir., chief Plastic Surgery Ctr. Marin, Calif.; clin. prof., former asst. chmn., past chief., divsn. plastic surgery Marin Gen. Hosp., Greenbrae; former chief surgery and plastic surgery Ross Gen. Hosp., Calif.; co-founder Plastic Surgery Specialists, Greenbrae. Mem.: Marin Med. Soc., Am. Soc. Plastic Surgeons, Calif. Soc. Plastic Surgeons, Calif. Med. Assn. Office: Plastic Surgery Specialists 350 Bon Air Rd Ste 300 Greenbrae CA 94904 Office Fax: 866-398-4480.*

POULSEN, HENRIK NØRSKOV, research scientist; b. Glostrup, Gm, Denmark, June 29, 1969; s. Poul Christian and Asta Poulsen; m. Gulcan Demirci; 1 child, Selin Demirci. MEE, Tech. U. Denmark, 1995. Rsch. assoc. Tech. U. Denmark, Lyngby, 1995—2000, assoc. prof., 2000—01; sr. optical engr. Calient Networks, Santa Barbara, Calif., 2001—02; project scientist U. Calif., Santa Barbara, 2002—. Pres. Packet Photonics, LLC, Santa Barbara, 2006—. Contbr. articles to profl. jours. Achievements include patents for l-band optical amplification. Home: 2129 Vina St Santa Barbara CA 93105 Office: Dept Elec and Comp Eng Univ Calif Santa Barbara CA 93106

POULSON, RICHARD JASPER METCALFE, lawyer; b. Elizabeth City, NC, Sept. 4, 1938; s. Richard Jasper and Dorothy (Morse) P.; m. Anne Keenan, Dec. 21, 1963 (div. 1976); m. Anne Dare Wrenn, Sept. 25, 1993; children: Richard Hugh Hundley, Anna Blair Masters. BA, U. Va., 1960; JD, Am. U., 1968; ML in Taxation, Georgetown U., 1970. Bar: Va. 1968, D.C. 1969, U.S. Supreme Ct. 1976. V.p. Am. Security & Trust Co., Washington, 1968-70; assoc. Hogan & Hartson, Washington, 1970-73, ptnr., 1973-94, sr. ptnr. London, 1990-93; chmn. Rapidan Capital Ptnrs., 1994—; sr. mng. dir. The Appian Group, Washington, 1995-98; chmn. The Animex Group, Warsaw, 1998—; exec. v.p., sr. advisor to chmn. Smithfield Foods, Inc., NYC, 1998—. Adj. prof. Georgetown U. Law Ctr., 1971-76; lectr. Law and Fgn. Svc. Schs. Georgetown U.; internat. advisor in field; active Euro-Arab Conciliation and Arbitration Sys. Trustee, bd. mgrs. U. Va., Charlottesville, 1992—98, v.p., 1994—95, pres., 1995—97; dir., chmn. exec. com. Mary & Daniel Loughran Found., Washington, 1976—, pres., 2002—; chmn., dir. Montpelier Steeplechase Found., Orange, Va., 1991—98; chmn., trustee U.S. Rugby Football Found., Boston, 1988—2001. Mem. Law Soc. of Eng. and Wales, Metro. Club, Keswick Country Club, Columbia Country Club, Saratoga Golf and Polo Club, Commonwealth Club. Republican. Episcopalian. Avocations: horseback riding, hunting, steeplechase racing, thoroughbred breeding. Home: Hare Forest Farm PO Box 287 Orange VA 22960 Office: Smithfield Foods Inc 499 Park Ave 6th Fl New York NY 10022 Office Phone: 212-758-2100. Business E-Mail: dickpoulson@smithfieldfoods.com.

POUMELE, CLAIRE TUIA, state official, school system administrator; MA, U. Portland; PhD, Brigham Young U. Tchr. Leone HS, 1977—78; vice prin. Samoana HS, 1980—82, prin., 1987—88; established Tafuna HS, 1982—87; dep. dir. Secondary Div. Am. Samoa Dept. Edn., 1989, dep. dir. instructional svcs., 2005—07, acting dir. edn., 2006—07, dir. edn., 2007—. Office: Am Samoa Dept Edn Edn Bldg PO Box 186 Pago Pago AS 96799*

POUNCEY, PETER RICHARD, academic administrator, classics educator; b. Tsingtao, Shantung, China, Oct. 1, 1937; came to U.S., 1964; s. Cecil Alan and Eugenie Marde (Lintilhac) P.; m. Bethanne McNally, June 25, 1966; 1 son, Christian; m. Susan Rieger, Mar. 21, 1973; 1 dau., Margaret; m. Katherine Dalsimer, June 9, 1990. Lic. Phil., Heythrop Coll., Eng., 1960; BA, Oxford U., Eng., 1964, MA, 1967; PhD, Columbia U., 1969; AM (hon.), Amherst Coll., 1985; LLD (hon.), Williams Coll., 1985; LHD (hon.), Doshisha U., 1987; LLD (hon.), Wesleyan U., 1989, Amherst Coll., Mass., 1995; LHD (hon.), Trinity Coll., 1990. Instr. classics Fordham U., Bronx, N.Y., 1964-67; asst. prof. Columbia U., NYC, 1969-71, dean Columbia Coll., 1972-76, assoc. prof., 1977-83, prof. classics, 1983-84; pres. Amherst (Mass.) Coll., Mass., 1984-94, pres. emeritus, 1994—, prof. classics, 1994—, Fobes prof. Greek, 1995—. Cons. classical lit. Columbia Ency., 1970-73; trustee Columbia Univ. Press, 1972-75 Author: The Necessities of War: A Study of Thucydides' Pessimism, 1980 (Lionel Trilling award 1981), (novel) Rules for Old Men Waiting, 2005. Trustee Brit.-Am. Edn. Found., N.Y.C., 1971-75. Recipient Great Tchr. award Soc. Columbia Grads., 1983 Mem. Am. Philol. Assn., Phi Beta Kappa Mailing: Author Mail Random House Inc 1745 Broadway New York NY 10019

POUND, FRANK R., JR., lawyer; b. Mayo, Fla., Nov. 3, 1933; s. Frank Reese and Elizabeth (Hart) P.; m. Betty Armstrong, Aug. 31, 1957; children: Tamara, Susan, Tracy, Brittain. BS, U. Fla., 1959, JD, 1961. Bar: Fla. 1962, U.S. Dist. Ct. (mid. dist.) Fla. 1962, U.S. Supreme Ct. 1969; cert. civil trial advocate; cert. civil trial lawyer; cert. mediator. Asst. county solicitor, Orlando, Fla., 1962-64; trial assoc. Crofton, et.al., Titusville, Fla., 1964-66; assoc. Howell, et.al., Rockledge, Fla., 1966-71; ptnr., pres. Lovering, Pound & Clifton, Cocoa, Fla., 1971—90; cir. judge 18th Jud. Cir. of Fla., 1991—98. Bd. dirs. Wuesthoff Health Sys., Inc., 2000—06. Chmn. Titusville Airport Authority, 1972, Sheriff's Civil Service Bd., Titusville, 1983-86, Coll. Leadership, Brevard 2000-02. Served to col. USMC res., 1952-84. Mem. Acad. Fla. Trial Lawyers, Fla. Bar Assn. (bd. govs. 1979-82), Brevard County Bar Assn. (pres. 1972-73). Lodges: Rotary (Cocoa) (pres. 1982-83), Carlton Am. Inn of Ct. (pres. 2005-06). Office Phone: 321-639-0505.

POUND, GLENN SIMPSON, university dean; b. Hector, Ark., Mar. 7, 1914; s. Leroy and Maude (Bullock) P.; m. Daisy Cole; children: Robert Arthur, Elizabeth Jane. BA magna cum laude, U. Ark., 1940; PhD, U. Wis., 1943. Mem. faculty U. Wis., 1946-79, dept. chmn., 1954-64, prof. plant pathology, 1954-79, now also dean emeritus agrl. and life scis., acting chancellor, 1977. Assoc. in pathology U.S. Dept. Agr., 1943-46, collaborator, 1952—. Author tech. publs. vegetable diseases and plant virology. Rockefeller traveling fellow in Europe, 1959 Mem. Am. Phytopathol. Soc. (sec. 1953-56, pres. 1959, chmn. golden jubilee anniversary celebration 1958), Am. Inst. Biol. Scis., A.A.A.S., Phi Beta Kappa, Sigma Xi, Phi Eta Sigma, Phi Kappa Phi. Clubs: Kiwanian (past lt. gov.). Presbyterian. Home: 7450 Olivetas Ave Apt B143 La Jolla CA 92037-4937

POUND, JOHN BENNETT, lawyer; b. Champaign, Ill., Nov. 17, 1946; s. William R. and Louise Catherine (Kelly) P.; m. Mary Ann Hanson, June 19, 1971; children: Meghan Elizabeth, Matthew Fitzgerald. BA, U. N. Mex., 1968; JD, Boston Coll., 1971. Bar: N. Mex. 1971, U.S. Dist. Ct. N. Mex. 1971, U.S. Ct. Appeals (10th cir.) 1972, U.S. Supreme Ct., 1993. Law clk. to Hon. Oliver Seth, US Ct. Appeals, 10th Cir., Santa Fe, 1971-72. Asst. counsel Supreme Ct. Disciplinary Bd., 1977-83, dist. rev. officer, 1984—; mem. Supreme Ct. Com. on Jud. Performance Evaluation, 1983-85; bd. dirs. Archdiocese Santa Fe Cath. Social Svcs., 1995—. Contbr. articles to profl. jours. Pres. bd. dirs. N.Mex. Ind. Coll. Fund, Santa Fe; chmn. N.Mex. Dem. Leadership Coun., 1991—2000; bd. dirs. Santa Fe Boys Club, 1989-92; rules com. N.Mex. Dem. Party, 1982—; v.p. Los Alamos Nat. Lab. Comm. Coun., 1985-90; fin. chmn. N.Mex. Clinton for Pres. campaign, 1992; co-chmn. Clinton-Gore Re-election Campaign, N.Mex., 1996, 2000; co-chmn. Gore for Pres., N.Mex., 2000; co-chmn. Kerry for Pres., N.Mex., 2004, Obama for Pres., N.Mex., 2008. Fellow Am. Bar Found., Am. Coll. Trial Lawyers, N.Mex. Bar Found.; mem. ABA, Am. Bd. Trial Advocates, N.Mex. Bar Assn. (health law sect. 1987—), Santa Fe County Bar Assn. Democrat. Roman Catholic. Avocations: history, languages, literature, swimming, baseball. Office: Long Pound Komer PA PO Box 5098 2200 Brothers Rd Santa Fe NM 87505-6903 Office Phone: 505-982-8405. Personal E-mail: lpk@nm.net, jmpound@comcast.net.

POUND, KATHLEEN LAST, elementary school educator; b. Jerome, Idaho, Sept. 5, 1953; d. William Dane and Jacqueline Mitchell Last; m. Vernon Forest Pound, Feb. 18, 1989; children: Kali Janine Kennison, MacKenzie Pound Peterson, Casey Robert. BA in Edn., U. Idaho, Moscow, BEd in Child Devel., 1975; MS in Health Edn., Idaho State U., Pocatello, 1987. Cert. tchr. Idaho, 1975. Elem. tchr. St. Paul's Cath. Sch., Nampa, Idaho, 1976—79, Jerome Sch. Dist., Idaho, 1980—87, Boise Sch. Dist., Idaho, 1987—. Mentoring cadre Boise Sch. Dist., 2003—05, curriculum adoption com. mem., 2005—06. Mem. Cath. Womens' League, Jerome, 1980—87, diocsean officer, 1985—86. Mem.: Idaho Assn. Health, Phys. Edn., Recreation and Dance (assoc.), Idaho Reading Coun. (assoc.), Philanthropic Edn. Orgn. (life), Delta Delta Delta (life; ho. mgr. 1973—74, Miss Campua Chest award 1972). Non-Partisan. Roman Catholic. Avocations: reading, travel. Home: 905 Balsam Boise ID 83706 Office: Valley View Elem 3555 N Milwaukee Boise ID 83704

POUND, RICHARD WILLIAM DUNCAN, lawyer, accountant, former academic administrator; b. St. Catharines, Ont., Can., Mar. 22, 1942; s. William Thomas and Jessie Edith Duncan (Thom) Pound; m. Julie Houghton Keith, Nov. 4, 1977. B in Commerce, McGill U., Montreal, 1962, B in Civil Law, 1967; BA, Sir George Williams U. (now Concordia U.), Montreal, 1963; PhD (hon.), U.S. Sports Acad., 1989; LLD (hon.), U. Windsor, Can., 1997, U. We. Ont., 2004; D in Sports Adminstrn. (hon.), Laurentian U., 2005; D (hon.), Beijing Sports U., 2006; LLD (hon.), Lakehead U., Can., 2007; Dlitt, Loughborough U., 2008; LLD, U. Quebec, 2008, Mcgin U., 2009. Bar: Que. 1968, Ont. 1980. Auditor Riddell, Stead, Graham & Hutchinson, Montreal, 1963-65; law clk., then atty. Laing, Weldon, Courtois, Clarkson, Parsons, Gonthier & Tétrault, Montreal, 1965-71; ptnr., mem. Tax Group Stikeman Elliott LLP, Montreal, 1972—. Sec. Can. Olympic Assn., 1968—76, dir., 1968—, pres., 1977—82; mem. Internat. Olympic Com., 1978—, exec. bd., 1983—87, 1992—2000, v.p., 1987—91, 1996—2000; bd. govs. McGill U., 1986—2009, chmn. bd. govs., 1994—99, lectr. taxation Faculty Law, chancellor, 1999—2009, gov. emeritus, 2009—, chancellor emeritus, 2009—; lectr. Que. Real Estate Assn.; mem. Ct. of Arbitration of Sport, Lausanne, 1991—; founding chmn., pres. World Anti-Doping Agy., 1999—2007; mem. Internat. Coun. Arbitration Sport, 2007—. Author: Five Rings Over Korea, 1994, Chief Justice W.R. Jackett: By the Law of the Land, 1999, Stikeman Elliott The First Fifty Years, 2002, High Impact Quotations, 2004, Canadian Facts and Dates, 2004, Inside the Olympics, 2004, Inside Dope, 2006, Unlucky to the End, The Story of Janise Marie Gamble, 2007, Rocke Robertson: Surgeon and Shepherd of Change, 2008; editor-in-chief Doing Business in Canada, 1987—, Canada Tax Cases, 1993—. Gov. Martlet Found.; former trustee Stanstead Wesleyan Coll.; dir. Canada's Nat. History Soc., 2007—, RCMP Heritage Ctr., 2007—. Decorated Knight Mil. and Hospitaler Order of St. Lazarus of Jerusalem; recipient Gold Medallion award, Internat. Swimming Hall of Fame, 2002, Laureus Spirit of Sport Prize, 2008; named Hon. Lt.-Col., Can. Grenadier Guards, 2008; named one of 100 Most Influential People of 2005, Time mag., The Most Influential People in the World of Sports, Bus. Week, 2007, BC Swimming Hall of Fame, 2005; named to Can. Swimming Hall of Fame, 1969, Sports Fedn. Can. Hall of Fame, 1976, Can. Olympic Order Gold, 1995, Quebec Sports Hall of Fame, 2001; Chubb Fellow, Timothy Dwight Coll., Yale U., 2004. Fellow: Order of Chartered Accountants; mem.: Alumni Assn. McGill U. (former pres.), Internat. Assn. Practicing Lawyers, Internat. Fiscal Assn., Can. Tax Found., Can. Bar Assn., Can. Squash Racquets Assn., Mt. Bruno Country, Jesters, Club Atwater, Montreal Amateur Athletic Assn. (pres. 1987—89). Home: 87 Arlington Ave Westmount PQ Canada H3Y 2W5 Office: Ste 4000 1155 Rene Levesque Blvd W Montreal PQ Canada H3B 3V2 Office Phone: 514-397-3037. Office Fax: 514-397-3063. Business E-Mail: rpound@stikeman.com.

POUNDERS, STEPHEN C., music educator; b. Waukegan, Ill., July 2, 1964; s. Roy Lee and Virginia Ann Pounders. AA, NE Miss. Jr. Coll., Booneville, 1984; MusB in Edn., Miss. State U., Starkville, 1988; MA in Edn., U. North Ala., Florence, 1994. Dir. band Thorsby H.S. Band, Ala., 2003—. Mem.: NEA, Nat. Assn. Christian Music Educators, Am. Fedns. Tchrs., Nat. Band Assn., Music Educators Nat. Conf., Ala. Bandmasters Assn., Miss. State U. Bulldog Club, Kappa Kappa Psi, Phi Mu Alpha (sec. 1986—88). Liberal. Presbyterian. Office: Thorsby High School 54 Opportunity Dr Thorsby AL 35171 Home: 100 Reese Dr Alabaster AL 35007 Personal E-mail: spounders@aol.com. Business E-Mail: spounders@chilton.k12.al.us.

POUNDS, KEVIN D., social studies educator; b. Lincoln, Nebr., Apr. 25, 1956; s. Darrell D. and Janice I. Pounds; m. Deanna L. Pounds, July 16, 1977; children: Chris, Mike, Jordon, Joshua, Kaleb. AA, Cloud County CC, Concordia,Kans., 1977; BA, Marymount Coll., Salinu,Kans., 1979; Grad with Honors, Liberty U., 1980; MLS, Fort Hays State U., Kans., 2000. Instr. Cloud County CC, 1979—. Bd. mem. Pawnee Mental Health Regional, Kans., 2009—, USD 333. Recipient award, NISOD. Mem.: NEA, KNEA. Avocations: sports, hunting, music, farming, reading. Business E-Mail: kpounds@cloud.edu.

POUNDS, REGINA DOROTHEA, writer; arrived in U.S., 1980; d. Friedrich and Herta Klein; m. Wayne C. Pounds, June 21, 1968; 1 child, Louis C. Author: Theo's Ghost, 2000, Lord Eaglebeak, 2000, Leonora, 2002, Wild Violets, 2005; contbr. articles to publs. Mem.: Defenders of Wildlife, World Wildlife Fund. Avocations: history, languages, poetry, art. Mailing: PO Box 414 Belleville IL 62222 Personal E-mail: oldberliner@yahoo.com.

POUNDS, WILLIAM FRANK, management educator; b. Fayette County, Pa., Apr. 9, 1928; s. Joseph Frank and Helen (Fry) P.; m. Helen Anne Means, Mar. 6, 1954; children: Thomas Mcclure, Julia Elizabeth. BSChemE, Carnegie Inst. Tech., 1950, MS in Math. Econs., 1959, PhD in Indsl. Adminstrn., 1964. Indsl. engr. Eastman Kodak Co., 1950-51, 55-57; cons. Pitts. Plate Glass Co., 1958-59, asst. to gen. mgr. Forbes finishes divsn., 1960—61; faculty Sloan Sch. Mgmt., MIT, 1966-98, prof. mgmt., 1966-98, dean, 1966-80; sr. adv. Rockefeller Family and Assocs., 1981-91. Bd. dirs. Idexx Labs., Inc., Mgmt. Scis. for Health, Inc.; bd. dir. Sunoco, Inc., 1973—2000, General Mills, Inc., 1979—91; trustee/vice chmn. Putnum Funds, 1974—2000. Chmn. bd. trustees Boston Mus. Fine Arts, 2000-03; trustee WGBH Ednl. Found., 2002—. Served as aviator lt. (j.g.) USNR, 1951-55. Fellow Am. Acad. Arts and Scis. Home: 83 Cambridge Pkwy # W1205 Cambridge MA 02142-1241

POUNDSTONE, SALLY HILL, library director; m. Robert Bruce Poundstone; children: Nancy Katrina, Holly Megan, Angus Bruce, Alice Heather. BA, U. Ky., 1954, MA in Libr. Sci., 1955. Asst. head ref. dept. Louisville Free Pub. Libr., 1955-59; libr. Folger Shakespeare Libr., Washington, 1959-60; chief acquisition dept. White Plains (N.Y.) Pub. Libr., 1960-62; libr. Bedford Hills (N.Y.) Pub. Elem. Sch., 1965-66; dir. Mamaroneck (N.Y.) Free Libr. and Emelin Theatre, 1966-87, Westport (Conn.) Pub. Libr., 1987-98; prin. SHP Libr. Consultants, 1998—. Instr. libr. sci. N.Y. U., 1968-69, Coll. of New Rochelle (N.Y.), 1970-71; adv. coun. mem. Pratt Inst. Grad Sch. of Libr. and Info. Sci., 1978-87; adminstrv. svcs. comm. N.Y. Met. Ref. and Res. Libr. Agy., 1977-79, bd. trustees, 1979-88, 2d v.p. and chair, 1984-85, pres., 1985-88; planning and devel. com. mem. Bibliomation, Inc., 1988-90; chair Conn. State Adv. Coun. for Libr. Planning and Devel., 1988-90. Pres. Garden Club of Mamaroneck, 1969-70, Larchmont-Mamaroneck Film Coun., 1971-72; bd. dirs. Mamaroneck Hist. Soc., 1976-87, pres., 1976-77; vice chmn. Village of Upper Nyack Planning Bd., 1988-89; mem. leadership com. and task force Westchester 2,000, 1984-87; com. mem. Rotary Club of Westport, 1987—; active Downtown Westport Adv. Com., 1989-90, Rep. Town. Com., Weston, Conn., 1990-93, Westport Bridge and Traffic Com., 1990-97, Honorable Order of Ky. Cols., 1995—, United Way Profl. Adv. Com., 1994-97, Westport Telecomm. Com., 1994-96, and others; v.p., dir. Woodcock Nature Ctr., 1998—, pres., 2001—06; mem. Wilton Rep. Town Com., 2000—; mem. Planning and Zoning Bd. Commns., 2000—, sec., 2004-05, vice chair 2005-06, chair, 2006—. Mem. ALA, Conn. Libr. Assn., Fairfield Libr. Adminstrs. Group, Archons of Colophon, Pub. Libr. Dirs. Assn. Westchester County (various offices and chairs), N.Y. Libr. Assn. (sec. treas. adult librs. assn. 1970-72, pres. pub. librs. sect. 1981-82, chair planning com. 1984-85). Home and Office: 48 Sharp Hill Rd Wilton CT 06897-3531

POUNDSTONE, WILLIAM NICHOLAS, JR., writer; b. Morgantown, W.Va., Sept. 29, 1955; s. William Nicholas and Doris Mae (Jamison) P. Critic NY Times, NYC, 1992—, The Economist, London, 1996—. Author: Big Secrets, 1983, The Recursive Universe, 1984, Labyrinths of Reason, 1988, Prisoner's Dilemma, 1992, Carl Sagan: A Life in the Cosmos, 1999, How Would You Move Mount Fuji?, 2003, Fortune's Formula: The Untold Story of the Scientific Betting System that Beat the Casinos and Wall Street, 2005, Gaming the Vote: Why Elections Aren't Fair (And What We Can Do About It), 2008; co-producer Dave Bell Assocs., LA, 1993-94, producer, 1994-95. Mem. PEN, Writers Guild.

POUPARD, PAUL CARDINAL, cardinal, archbishop; b. Anjou, France, Aug. 30, 1930; PhD in Theology, Sorbonne; D honoris causa (hon.), Lublin Aix-en-Provence U., U. Louvain, U. Santiago, Chile. Ordained priest Archdiocese of Paris, 1954, aux. bishop, 1979—80; official Secretariat of State of Vatican City, 1959—71; chaplain San Domenico Inst., Rome, 1959—71; rector Cath. Inst., Paris, 1971—80; ordained bishop, 1979; archbishop, pro-pres. Secretariat for Non-Believers, Rome, 1980—85; elevated to cardinal, 1985; cardinal-priest S. Prassede, 1985—; pres. Secretariat for Non-Believers, Rome, 1985—93, Pontifical Coun. Culture, Rome, 1980—2007, Pontifical Coun. Inter-religious Dialogue, Rome, 2005—07. Mem. Pontifical Councils for the Laity & for Promoting Christian Unity, Congregations for Divine Worship & Discipline of the Sacraments, for Evangelization of Peoples, & for Cath. Edn. Recipient Cardinal Grente award, French Acad.; named Comdr., Legion of Honor. Roman Catholic. Address: Piazza San Calisto 16 00153 Rome Italy Home: Vatican City 00120 Vatican City Italy Personal E-mail: cardinalpoupard@org.va.

POURBEIK, POUYAN, power engineering consultant and researcher; b. Apr. 17, 1972; B in Engrng. with honors, U. Adelaide, Australia, 1992, PhD in Elec. Engrng., 1997. Application engr. GE CO., Schenectady, NY, 1997—2000; cons. engr. ABB Inc., Raleigh, NC, 2000—01, prin. cons., 2001—05, exec. cons., 2005—06; tech. exec. EPRI, Knoxville, Tenn., 2006—. Mem.: Internat. des Grands Réseaux Electriques (CIGRE), IEEE (chmn., power sys. stability sub-com. 2006—, chair CIGRE WG C4.6.01, sec. CIGRE SG C4).

POURCHOT, GEORGETA VALENTINA, political science educator; b. Ploiesti, Romania; married. BA, U. Timisoara, Romania, 1980; MA in Polit. Sci., Va. Tech, Blacksburg, 1993; PhD in Internat. Rels., Old Dominion U., Norfolk, Va., 1997. Elected rep. Romanian Parliament, Lower House, Bucharest, 1990; dep. dir. internat. action commns. CSIS, Washington, 1997—2003; sr. assoc. Ctr. Strategic and Internat. Studies, Washington, 2003—06, adj. fellow, non-resident, 2006—; dir. on-line MA, northern capital region Va. Tech, Alexandria, 2005—. Cons. Fluor Govt. Group, Rosslyn, Va., 2004—. Author: (book) Eurasia Rising: Democracy and Independence in the Post-Soviet Space. Orgnl. liaison United Cmty. Ministries, Alexandria, 2005—08; founder Romanian Green Party, Ploiesti, 1989—90; social justice program coord. Mt. Vernon Unitarian Ch., Alexandria, 2003—08. Recipient Life-Time Achievement award, Mt. Vernon Unitarian Ch., 2008. Independent. Unitarian Universalist. Avocations: gardening, cooking, tennis, travel, reading.

POURCIAU, LESTER JOHN, JR., retired librarian; b. Baton Rouge, Sept. 6, 1936; s. Lester John and Pearlie M. (Hogan) Pourciau; 1 child, Lester John III. BA, La. State U., 1962, MS, 1964; PhD, Ind. U., 1975. Asst. ref. libr. U. S.C., Columbia, 1963—64; ref. libr. Florence County Pub. Libr., SC, 1964—65; coord. ref. svcs. U. Fla., Gainesville, 1966—67; dir. librs. U. Memphis, 1970—99, assoc. v.p. for acad. affairs, dir. librs., 1987—91. Chmn. coun. of head librarians State Univ. and C.C. System Tenn., 1980, 87, 97; acad. assoc. Atlantic Coun. of U.S., U. Memphis; fgn. expert, vis. lectr. Beijing U. of Posts & Telecomms., Beijing Normal U., Peking U., Renmen U., Qinghua U., Chingqing Inst. Posts & Telcomms., Guizhou Normal U., Republic of China, 1993, Beijing U. Posts and Telecom, 1993, Nanjing U. Posts and Telecom., Anhui Normal U., Beijing U. Posts and Telecom., 1994, People's Republic of China, 1994; cons. prof. Beijing U. Posts and Telecom., 1996—; participant 2d Internat. Conf. Crimea 95, Librs. and Assn. in the Transient World, Republic of Crimea; participant, dep. chair organizing com., 1996—; Peking U. Internat. Conf., Beijing, 1998. Contbr. articles to profl. jours. With USAF, 1955-59. Recipient Adminstrv. Staff award Memphis State U., 1981, Commendation Boy Scouts Am., 1985, Commendation Tenn. Sec. State, 1989, Honor award Tenn. Libr. Assn., 1990, Allen J. Hammond award for Disting. Svc. U. Memphis, 1999, SLIS Disting. Alumni award Ind. U., 1999, TRACES award U. Memphis Assn. Retirees, 2003; named Outstanding Alumnus, La. State U., 1988; named Libr. of Yr., Memphis Libr. Coun., 1989; fellow Higher Edn. Act Ind. U.; named to 30th Ann. Honor Roll. ALA Office Intellectual Freedom and Freedom to Read Found. U. Memphis, 1999. Mem.: ALA, Memphis Old Time Car Club (sec. 1981, pres. 1982, 1989), Mid-Am. Old Time Automobile Assn., Antique Automobile Club Am., Nat. Assn. Watch and Clock Collectors (chpt. pres. 1983, sec.-treas. 1988—89). Office: Memphis State U U Libr Memphis TN 38152-0001

POURGOL-MOHAMMAD, MOHAMMAD, manufacturing executive; b. Tabriz, East Azarbayjan, Iran; married. PhD in Reliability Engrng, U. Md., Coll. Pk., 2007. Cert. profl. engr., State Md., 2008. Rsch. asst. U. Md., 2001—07; reliability mgr. Goodman Mfg. Co., Houston, 2006—. Rsch. fellow MIT, Cambridge, 2001. Achievements include research in thermal hydraulics uncertainty assessment. Office: Goodman Mfg Co 1440 Greengrass Dr Houston TX 77008 Personal E-mail: mpourgol@gmail.com. Business E-Mail: pourgol.mohammad@goodmanmfg.com.

POUSADA, LIDIA, physician; b. Mt. Kisco, NY, July 21, 1957; d. Manuel and Maria Nieves (Mejuto) P.; m. Andrew Kemper Goodman, June 26, 1983 (div. Sept. 1986); 1 child, Sara Pousada Goodman; m. Wayne William Maibaum, Apr. 11, 1987 (div. July 1993); 1 child, Anna Pousada Maibaum; m. James Paul Kreindler, Mar. 2, 1996; 1 child, Victoria Pousada Kreindler. BS, CUNY, NYC, 1978; MD, N.Y. Med. Coll., 1980. Diplomate Am. Bd. Internal Medicine, Am. Bd. Geriatric Medicine. Student geriatric fellowship NYU Med. Sch., NYC, 1978-80; resident in internal medicine Montefiore Med. Ctr., Bronx, NY, 1980-83, dir. geriatric unit, 1986-89; with nat. health svc. North Cent. Bronx Hosp., 1983-84, Morris Heights Health Ctr., Bronx, 1985; instr. City Coll. Med. Sch., NYC, 1982-85, Albert Einstein Coll. Medicine, Bronx, 1983-84, 86-89, asst. prof. medicine, 1988-89; assoc. prof. clin. medicine N.Y. Med. Coll., 1993—; pvt. practice geriatric medicine, 2002—. Dir. geriatric cons. svc. Montefiore Med. Ctr., 1987—89, assoc. chief divsn. geriatrics, 1988—92; chief divsn. geriatrics and gerontology Sound Shore Med. Ctr., 1992—2002. Author: Geriatric Diagnostics, 1983, Emergency Medicine for the House Officer, 1986, 2d edit., 1995, Emergency Medicine for Nurses, 1989, Perioperative Medical Care of the Geriatric Patient, 1989, Case Studies in Emergency Medicine for the House Officer, 1993. Physician scholar Nat. Health Svc., 1978-80. Fellow ACP, Gerontol. Soc. Am., Am. Geriatric Soc.; mem. Physicians for Social Responsibility. Office: 141 North State Rd Briarcliff Manor NY 10510 Office Phone: 914-762-2900.

POUSCHINE, JOHN LAURENCE, private equity investment executive; b. Glen Cove, NY, Jan. 28, 1957; s. Ivan and Helen (Carlson) P.; m. Catherine Dana, Nov. 16, 1991; children: Alexander, Anna. BA, Princeton U., 1979; MBA, Harvard U., 1983. Officer's asst. JP Morgan, NYC, 1979-81; assoc. Prudential Securities, Inc., NYC, 1983-85; v.p. Bradford Ventures Ltd., NYC, 1985-88; sr. v.p. Electra Inc., NYC, 1989-96; mng. dir. Pouschine Cook Capital Mgmt., LLC, 1997—. Chmn. bd. dirs. Doe & Ingalls Mgmt., Durham, NC, Latex Internat., Shelton, Conn., Great Lakes Home Health Svcs., Jackson, Mich., IGI Holdings, Inc., South Plainfield, NJ. Bd. dirs. Russian Children's Welfare Soc., N.Y.C. Mem. Bridgehampton Club, Nassau Club, Princeton Club of N.Y., Union Club. Avocation: sports. Office: Pouschine Cook Capital Mgmt 375 Park Ave Ste 3408 New York NY 10152 E-mail: jpouschine@pouschinecook.com.

POUSSAINT, ALVIN FRANCIS, psychiatrist, educator; b. NYC, May 15, 1934; s. Christopher Thomas and Harriet (Johnston) P. BA, Columbia U., 1956; MD, Cornell U., 1960; MS, UCLA, 1964. Intern UCLA

Ctr. for Health Sci., 1960-61, resident in psychiatry Neuropsychiat. Inst., 1961-64, chief resident, 1964-65; So. field dir. Med. Com. Human Rights, Jackson, Miss., 1965-66; asst. prof. psychiatry Tufts U. Med. Sch., 1966-69; assoc. prof. psychiatry, assoc. dean students Harvard Med. Sch., 1969-75, 78—, prof. psychiatry, 1993—, dean students, 1975-78. Cons. HEW, 1969-73. Author numerous articles in field. Nat. treas. Black Acad. Arts and Letters, 1969-70, Med. Com. Human Rights, 1966—. Recipient Michael Schwerner award, 1968, Am. Black Achievement award in Bus. and the Professions Johnson Pub. Co., Inc., 1986, John Jay award for Disting. Profl. Achievement Columbia Coll., N.Y., 1987, Medgar Evers Medal of Honor Beverly Hills/Hollywood chpt. NAACP, Hollywood, Calif., 1988, and numerous hon. degrees. Fellow AAAS, Am. Orthopsychiatric Assn., Am. Psychiat. Assn. (mem. com. on Black Psychiatrists 1970-75); mem. Nat. Med. Assn., Am. Acad. of Child Psychiatry, Children's Longwood. Office: Judge Baker Ctr 53 Parker Hill Ave Boston MA 02120-3225

POUSSOT, BERNARD JEAN, pharmaceutical executive; m. Delphine Cecile Poussot, May 15, 1976; children: Rodolphe, Eve, Juliette. Grad., Ecole Superieure de Commerce de Paris, 1975. Sec. gen. to gov. City of Casablanca, Morocco, 1976—77; dir. pharm. divsn. Merck Sharp & Dohme-Chibret SNC Labs., 1980—81; dir. mktg. & sales G.D. Searle & Co., France, 1981—84, dir. worldwide mktg. & sales, 1984—86; deputy gen. mgr. Wyeth, France, 1986—87, pres., gen. mgr., 1987—91; group v.p. Europe Wyeth-Ayerst Internat., Collegeville, Pa., 1991, exec. v.p., 1991—96, pres., 1996—97, pres. worldwide pharm. bus., 1997—2002; sr. v.p. Wyeth, Madison, NJ, 2001—02, exec. v.p., 2002—06, pres., 2006—, vice chmn., 2006—07, COO, 2007, chmn., CEO, 2008—. Bd. dirs. Wyeth, 2007—. Bd. overseers U. Pa. Sch. Dental Medicine; bd. trustees Eisenhower Fellowships; bd. dirs. Opera Co. Phila. Named a Power Player, Advt. Age, 2008. Mem.: PhRMA (chmn. internat. section 1999). Office: Wyeth Five Giralda Farms Madison NJ 07940-0874 E-mail: pr@wyeth.com.*

POUTSMA, MARVIN L., retired chemical research administrator; b. Grand Rapids, Mich., Aug. 7, 1937; m. Yolanda Arco, July 20, 1968; children: John C., Julie A. BS, Calvin Coll., 1958; PhD, U. Ill., 1962. Staff scientist corp. rsch. Union Carbide, Tarrytown, N.Y., 1961-65, group leader corp. rsch., 1965-68, sr. scientist corp. rsch., 1968-73, sr. group leader corp. rsch., 1972-78; group leader chemistry divsn. Oak Ridge (Tenn.) Nat. Lab., 1978-80, sect. head chemistry divsn., 1980-83, dir. chemistry divsn., 1984-93, dir. chem. & analytical scis. divsn., 1994-2000, ret., 2000. Contbr. chpts. to books and articles to profl. jours. Fellow AAAS; mem. Am. Chem. Soc. Office: Oak Ridge Nat Lab PO Box 2008 Oak Ridge TN 37831-6197 Office Phone: 865-576-8339. Business E-Mail: poutsmaml@ornl.gov.

POUW, KING T., food products executive; MSE, Ruhr U., Bochum, Germany. With Kellogg Co., 1978, dir. ops. and tech. L.Am., 1995—98, v.p. global supply chain, ops. effectiveness, 1998—99, supply chain dir. Europe, 1999, v.p. supply chain Europe, sr. v.p. ops., 2000—01, exec. v.p. ops. and tech. Battle Creek, Mich., 2001; sr. v.p. bus. transformation ConAgra Foods, Inc., Omaha, 2006—. Office: ConAgra Foods Inc 1 ConAgra Dr Omaha NE 68102-5001 Office Phone: 402-595-4000. Office Fax: 402-595-4709.

POUZILHAC, ALAIN DUPLESSIS DE, advertising executive; b. Sète, Herault, France, June 11, 1945; s. Pierre and Jeanine (Caffarel) de P.; m. Carole de Pouzilhac, Sept. 6, 1969; children: Edouard, Cedric, Philippine. Asst. account exec. Publicis, Paris, 1968; account supr. DDB, Paris, 1969—75; COO Havas Conseil, Neuilly, France, 1976-82, chmn., CEO, 1982-87, HDM, Neuilly and Puteaux, France, 1987-89, Eurocom, Neuilly, 1989—, EURO RSCG Worldwide, Neuilly, France, 1991, Havas Advt., 1996—2005, Havas, 2001—05, France 24, 2005—. Avocations: soccer, rugby. Home: 21 rue de Miromesnil 75008 Paris France Office: France 24 5 rue des Nations Unies 92455 Issy Les Moulineaux France Office Phone: 33 1 73 01 24 12. Business E-Mail: adepouzilhac@france24.com.

POVICH, DAVID, lawyer; b. Washington, June 8, 1935; s. Shirley Lewis and Ethyl (Friedman) Povich; m. Constance Enid Tobriner, June 14, 1959; children: Douglas, Johanna, Judtih, Andrew. BA, Yale U., 1958; LLB, Columbia U., 1962. Bar: D.C. 1962, U.S. Ct. Appeals (4th cir.) 1980, U.S. Tax Ct. 1981, U.S. Ct. Appeals (5th and 11th cirs.) 1984, U.S. Dist. Ct. Md., U.S. Ct. Appeals (3d cir.) 1997. Law clk. to assoc. judge D.C. Ct. Appeals, Washington, 1962-63; exec. com. Williams & Connolly, 1986-87, ptnr., 1963—2005, of counsel, 2006—. Mem.: ABA, Barristers (exec. com. 1992—93), Bar Assn. D.C., D.C. Bar Assn. Office: Williams & Connolly 725 12th St NW Washington DC 20005-5901 Office Phone: 202-434-5071. E-mail: dpovich@wc.com.

POVICH, LON F., wholesale distribution executive; m. Ilissa Povich; 2 children. Grad., Dartmouth Coll.; JD, Harvard U. Deputy chief legal counsel to Gov. William Weld, Mass.; prosecutor Dist. Mass. US Dept. Justice; atty. Goodwin Proctor, Boston; v.p., gen. counsel The Boston Cons. Group, Inc., 1996—2007; sr. v.p., gen. counsel, sec. BJ's Wholesale Club Inc., Natick, Mass., 2007, exec. v.p., gen. counsel, sec., 2007—. Office: BJ's Wholesale Club Inc One Mercer Rd Natick MA 01760*

POVICH, LYNN, journalist, Internet executive, editor; b. Washington, June 4, 1943; d. Shirley and Ethyl P.; m. Stephen B. Shepard, Sept. 16, 1979; children: Sarah, Ned. AB, Vassar Coll., 1965. Rschr., reporter, writer, editor, sr. editor Newsweek mag., NYC, 1965—91; editor-in-chief Working Woman mag., NYC, 1991—96; mng. editor, sr. exec. prodr. East coast programming MSNBC Interactive, Secaucus, NJ, 1996—2001. Editor: All Those Mornings at the Post, 2005. Bd. mem. Internat. Women's Media Found., 1998—, co-chair, 2002—05; vice chair, adv. com. women's rights divsn. Human Rights Watch, 2003—. Recipient Matrix award N.Y. Women in Comms., 1976; named to Acad. of Women Achievers YWCA, 1993. Mem.: Online News Assn. (founder).

POWDEN, MARK E., legislative staff member; b. Peacham, Vt. s. Russell Powden; m. Wendy Frances Lawrence, Sept. 7, 1985; 2 children. Grad., Harvard U. Staff dir. House Edn. and Labor Com., Washington, 1985—88; legis. dir. Senator James M. Jeffords, Washington, 1988—96; staff dir. Senate Health, Edn., Labor and Pensions Com., Washington, 1996—2001; pres. Edn. Finance Coun., Washington, 2001—04; sr. policy advisor Senator James M. Jeffords, Washington, 2004—06, Senator Sherrod Brown, Washington, 2007—09, chief of staff, 2009—. Office: Office of Senator Sherrod Brown 455 Senate Russell Office Bldg Washington DC 20510-3505 Office Phone: 202-224-2315. E-mail: mark_powden@brown.senate.gov.*

POWEL, JANE C., educational consultant; d. John Samuel and Norma Dillemuth Powel; m. Peter John Conigliaro (div.); children: Michael, Andrea, Thomas, Stephen. BS magna cum laude in Elem. Edn., Syracuse U., 1974; MS in Edn., Adelphi U., 1979. Tchr. Garden City Park (N.Y.) Sch., 1974—77; tchr. gifted children New Hyde Park (N.Y.) Sch., 1980; program dir. Roslyn (N.Y.) Pub. Sch., 1982—; pres. Omni Learn Corp., NYC, 2004—. With gate program Point Arena (Calif.) Sch., 1991—2002; dir. edn. Cold Spring Harbor Lab. (N.Y.) DNALC, 1992—97; pres. Cold Spring Harbor Acad. Inc., 1996—2004; dir. advanced learning programs East Woods Sch., Oyster Bay, NY, 1998; spkr. Adelphi U., Garden City, NY, 1998—99. Asst. minister St. Peter's Luth. Ch., Huntington, NY, 2001—03. Mem.: NY Acad. Sci., Assn. Sch. Curriculum and Devel., Kappa Delta Pi. Democrat. Lutheran. Avocations: reading, theater, travel. Home: 90 William St #15A New York NY 10038 Office Phone: 646-964-4059. Business E-Mail: jane@omnilearncorp.com.

POWELL, ALAN, engineering educator, research scientist; b. Buxton, Derbyshire, Eng., Feb. 17, 1928; arrived in U.S., 1956; s. Frank and Gwendolen Marie P.; m. June Sinclair, Mar. 28, 1956. Student, Buxton Coll., 1939-45; diploma in aeros., Loughborough Coll., 1948; BSc in Engring. (hon.), London U., 1949; honours diploma 1st class, Loughborough Coll., 1949; DTech (hon.), Loughborough U. Tech., 1980; PhD, U. Southampton, 1953. Chartered engr. Engr. Percival Aircraft Co., Luton, Eng., 1949-51; from rsch. asst. to lectr. U. Southampton, Eng., 1951-56; rsch. fellow Calif. Inst. Tech., Pasadena, 1956-57; engr. Douglas Aircraft Co., 1956; assoc. prof. UCLA, 1957-62, prof. engring., 1962-65, head Aerosonics lab., 1957-65; assoc. tech. dir., head acoustics and vibration lab. David Taylor Model Basin, Dept. Navy, Washington, 1965-66, tech. dir., 1966-67, David Taylor Naval Ship Research & Devel. Center, Bethesda, Md., 1967-85; mem. Undersea Warfare Research & Devel. Council, 1966-76, chmn., 1971-72; mem. council on Fed. Labs., 1972-85; prof. mech. engring. U. Houston, 1985-2000, chmn., 1985-87, prof. emeritus, 2000—. Com. on hearing bioacoustics and biomechs. NAS-NRC, 1961-85, exec. coun., 1963-65, chmn., 1965-66, advisor, 1985-95, mem. naval studies bd. 1990-95; mem. various coms. Naval Studies Bd. and Marine Bd., 1990-96; advisor Chinese U. Devel. Project, 1989-91; cons. Douglas Aircraft Co., 1956-65, others; adv. coun. Internat. Towing Tank Conf., 1981-85; mem. advisor U.S.-Japan Program Natural Resources, 1987-90, mem. Marine Facilities Panel; gen. chmn. 3d advanced vehicles conf. AIAA and Soc. Naval Archs. and Marine Engrs., 1976; chmn. internat. conf. Computer Aided Design, Manufacture and Ops. in Marine and Offshore Industries, 1987-88; cons. Sci. Applications Internat., Inc., 1987-90; governing bd. Am. Inst. Physics, 1995-97; mem. editl. bd. Internat. Jour. Aeroacoustics, 2007-. Contbr. articles to profl. jours. Recipient Navy Meritorious Civilian Service award, 1970; Brit. Empire scholar, 1945; named Meritorious Exec. Pres. of U.S., 1982; Capt. Robert Dexter Conrad gold medal for sci. achievement Sec. Navy, 1984; dedication spl. issue Internat. Jour. Aeroacoustics vol. 2 nos. 3/4, 2003. Fellow Royal Aero. Soc. London (Baden-Powell prize 1948, Wilbur Wright prize 1953), Acoustical Soc. Am. (biennial award 1962, assoc. editor Jour. 1962-67, chmn. edn. com. 1964-66, exec. coun. 1966-69, chmn. medals and awards com. 1978-81, v.p. elect 1981-82, v.p. 1982-83, pres. elect 1989-90, pres. 1990-91, past pres. 1991-92, Silver medal in engring. acoustics 1992, designated Nat. Spkr. in Engring. Acoustics 1994-98), Inst. Mech. Engrs., Inst. Acoustics (U.K.); mem. AIAA (assoc. fellow, Aeroacoustics award 1980), ASME (Rayleigh lectr. 1988, Per Brüel Gold medal 1991), Inst. Noise Control Engrs. (initial mem., dir. 1974-77, Disting. lectr. 1975, 83, v.p. 1981-84, bd. cert. 1993), Acoustics, Speech and Signal Processing Soc. (exec. com. 1969-72, awards com. 1971-73, bylaws com. chmn. 1973-75), Am. Soc. Naval Engrs. (life), Am. Acad. Mechanics, Tau Beta Pi (hon. life). Office: 6619 Prairie Dunes Dr Houston TX 77069-1743

POWELL, ALMA JOHNSON, writer, advocate, foundation administrator; b. Birmingham, Al., Oct. 27, 1937; d. Robert and Mildred Johnson; m. Colin L. Powell, Aug. 1962; children: Michael, Linda, Annemarie. BA, Fisk U., 1957; LHD (hon.), Emerson Coll., 1996. Audiologist Boston Guild Hard of Hearing, 1959—62. Author: (children's books) America's Promise, 2003, My Little Wagon, 2003. Chair nat. coun. Best Friends Found., 1989—2001; chair Alliance for Youth, 2004—. Named one of 100 Most Powerful Women in Wash., Washingtonian mag., 2001.

POWELL, AMY RUTH, film company executive; d. William T. and Phyllis Powell; m. Douglas Keith Chernack, June 12, 2004. BA in Art Hist. and Lit., Emory U., Atlanta; MBA, UCLA. With CNN, Sony Pictures, LA; v.p. interactive mktg. Paramount Studios, LA, 2004—. Recipient Key Art award, 2005, London Internat. award, 2005; named Media Maven, Ad Age, 2006; named a Next Gen Exec., Hollywood Reporter, 2005; named one of 50 Smartest People in Hollywood, Entertainment Weekly, 2007. Office: Paramount Pictures Corp 5555 Melrose Ave Ste 121 West Hollywood CA 90038

POWELL, ANNE ELIZABETH, editor-in-chief; b. Cheverly, Md., Nov. 11, 1951; d. Arthur Gorman and Barbara Anne (MacAran) P.; m. John Alan Ebeling Jr., 1972 (div. 1983). BS, U. Md., 1972. Reporter Fayetteville (N.C.) Times, 1973-75; home editor Columbus (Ga.) Ledger-Enquirer, 1976; assoc. editor Builder mag., Washington, 1977-78; architecture editor House Beautiful's Spl. Publs., NYC, 1979-81; editor Traditional Home mag., Des Moines, 1982-87, Mid-Atlantic Country mag., Alexandria, Va., 1987-89; editor in chief publs. Nat. Trust for Hist. Preservation, Washington, 1989-95; editor-in-chief Landscape Architecture Mag., Washington, 1995-98, Civil Engring. Mag., Washington, 1998—. Author: The New England Colonial, 1988. Mem. Nat. Press Club, Am. Soc. Mag. Editors. Office: American Society of Civil Engrs Civil Engring Mag 1801 Alexander Bell Dr Reston VA 20191-4344 Home: 4500 S Four Mile Run Dr Apt 803 Arlington VA 22204 Office Phone: 703-295-6213.

POWELL, ARDAL, music company executive, editor; b. Bournemouth, Dorset, England, Apr. 22, 1958; BA with honors, U. Cambridge, 1980, MA, 1989, PhD, 2004. Cert. Koninklijk Conservatorium, Den Haag, 1983. Pres. Folkers & Powell, Makers Hist. Flutes, Hudson, NY, 1983—; ops. dir. gen. editor Organologia & Sociology Music Series Pendragon Press, 2007—. Editor: Traverso, Hist. Flute Newsletter, 1989—; translator: The Virtuoso Flute-Player by Johann George Tromlitz; author: (monograph) The Flute, The Keyed Flute by Johann George Tromlitz (; editor: The Baroque Flute Fingering Book by Margaret N. Neuhaus, (periodical collected reprint) Traverso: Historical Flute Newsletter, Volumes 1—10, 1989—98. Fellow, NEH, 1993—94. Mem.: Am. Musical Instrument Soc. (bd. govs. 2001—07, Bessaraboff prize 2005), Nat. Flute Assn. (com. 1987), Juggler Meadow Morris Men. Avocation: sailing.

POWELL, BARRY BRUCE, classicist, educator; b. Sacramento, Apr. 30, 1942; s. Barrett Robert and Anita Louise (Burns) Powell; m. Patricia Ann Cox; children: Elena Melissa, Adam Vincent. BA in Classics, U. Calif., Berkeley, 1963, PhD, 1971; MA, Harvard U., 1965. Asst. prof. Northern Ariz. U., Flagstaff, 1970-73; from asst. prof. to prof. U. Wis., Madison, 1973—, chmn. dept. classics, 1985-92, chmn. program integrated liberal studies. Author: Composition by Theme in the Odyssey, 1973, Homer and the Origin of the Greek Alphabet, 1991, Classical Myth, 1995, 6th edit., 2008, New Companion to Homer, 1997, A Short Introduction to Classical Myth, 2001, Writing and the Origins of Greek Literature, 2002, Homer, 2003, 2d edit., 2007, Ramses in Nighttown, 2006, The War at Troy: A True History, 2006; author: (with Ian Morris) The Greeks: Society, Culture, History, 2004, numerous poems; writer screenplays; contbr. articles to profl. jours.; author (writing): Theory and History: The Technology of Civilization. Woodrow Wilson fellow, 1965. Mem.: Am. Acad. in Rome, Classical Assn. Midwest and South, Archeol. Inst. Am., Am. Sch. Classical Studies at Athens (mng. com.), Am. Philol. Assn., Phi Beta Kappa (former pres. Madison chpt.). Home: 1210 Sweetbriar Rd Madison WI 53705-2228 Office: Univ Wis Dept Classics Madison WI 53707 Home Phone: 608-233-5991; Office Phone: 608-262-2041. E-mail: bbpowell@wisc.edu.

POWELL, BAYARD LOWERY, oncologist, educator; b. Raleigh, NC, June 22, 1954; MD, U. N.C., 1980. Diplomate Am. Bd. Internal Medicine, Am. Bd. Med. Oncology. Intern, then resident in internal medicine N.C. Bapt. Hosp., Winston-Salem, 1980-83, mem. staff; fellow hematologic oncology Bowman Gray Sch. Medicine, Winston-Salem, 1983-86, prof. hematologic oncology, sect. chief hematologic oncology, dir. leukemia svc. Named one of NC's Best Doctors, Bus. NC mag., 2002. Mem. ACP, Am. Assn. for Cancer Rsch., Am. Soc. Hematology, Am. Soc. Clin. Oncology. Office: Cancer Ctr Wake Forest Univ Sch Med Med Ctr Blvd Winston Salem NC 27157-0001 also: 2707 Buena Vista RD Winston Salem NC 27106 Office Phone: 336-713-5440, 336-716-4354. Business E-Mail: bpowell@wfubmc.edu.

POWELL, BENJAMIN, economics professor; b. Haverhill, Mass., May 22, 1978; s. Eric Powell and Ruthanne Bergholm; m. Lisa Frye, July 5, 2003. BS, U. Mass., Lowell, 2000; PhD, George Mason U., Fairfax, Va., 2003. Sr. economist Beacon Hill Inst., Boston, 2007; asst. prof., economics Suffolk U., Boston, 2007—. Editor: (book) Making Poor Nations Rich: Entrepreneurship and the Process of Development. Exec. bd. mem. Assn. Pvt. Enterprise Edn., 2006—. Named Paper of Yr., Soc. Devel. Austrian Economics, 2007. Office: Suffolk Univ 8 Ashburton Pl Boston MA 02108 Business E-Mail: bpowell@suffolk.edu.

POWELL, BENJAMIN ALBOND, lawyer, former federal agency administrator; b. Apr. 1967; BSE in Fin., U. Pa., 1989, BAS in Applied Sci., 1989; JD, Columbia U., 1996. Bar: 1999. Law clk. to Hon. John M. Walker US Ct. Appeals (2nd Cir.), 1996—97; law clk. to Justice John Paul Stevens & Justice Byron R. White US Supreme Ct., 1997—98; assoc. Kellogg, Huber, Hansen, Todd and Evans LLP; corp. counsel Vitria Tech., Inc.; program examiner State and USIA Branch Office Mgmt. & Budget, Exec. Office of the Pres., Washington; spl. asst. & assoc. counsel to Pres. The White House, Washington, 2002—06; gen. counsel Office Nat. Intelligence, Washington, 2006—09; ptnr. Wilmer Cutler Pickering Hale & Dorr LLP, Washington, 2009—. Co-author: Adaptive Networks for Fault Diagnosis and Process Control, 1990. Captain USAF, 1989—93. Recipient Edmund J. Randolph award, US Dept. Justoce, 2009, Nat. Intelligence Disting. Svc. medal, Office Nat. Intelligence, 2009, Intelligence Under Law award, Nat. Security Agy., 2009, Bronze medallion, 2009, Seal medallion, CIA, 2009. Office: Wilmer Cutler Pickering Hale & Dorr LLP 1875 Pennsylvania Ave Washington DC 20006 Office Phone: 202-663-6770. Office Fax: 202-663-6363. E-mail: ben.powell@wilmerhale.com.*

POWELL, BRADFORD SCOTT, research scientist, educator; s. Robert Lee Powell and Joan Margaret Cline; m. Maria A. Powell; 1 child, Thais Cavalcante Guimaraes. BA magna cum laude, U. Colo., Boulder, 1983; PhD, U. Calif., Davis, 1989. Cert. regulatory affairs Hood Coll. Asst. scientist Abbott Labs., Abbott Park, Ill., 1983—85; vis. scientist U. Calif., Davis, 1989—90; postdoctoral rschr. Frederick Cancer Rsch. and Devel. Ctr. Nat. Cancer Inst., Md., 1990—97; chemist/molecular biologist Exponential Biotherapies, Inc. and NIH, Rockville, 1997—99; lab head and prin. investigator US Army Med. Rsch. Inst. Infectious Diseases, Frederick, 1999—. Postdoctoral adviser rsch. associateship programs NRC, Washington, 2000; adj. prof. Johns Hopkins U., Balt., 2006—. Contbr. scientific papers to profl. jours., chapters to books. Recipient Excellence in Fed. Career, Outstanding Profl. Tech., Sci. and Program Support., Balt. Fed. Exec. Bd., 2002; vis. scholar, Ministry of Edn. and Sci., Japan, Tokyo U. Med. Inst., 1991—93; Internat. Rsch. fellow, NSF, 1991. Mem.: Am. Peptide Soc., Am. Soc. Microbiology, Nature Conservancy (life). Achievements include patents for methods of screening for agents that delay a cell cycle; patents pending for prophylactic and therapeutic monoclonal antibodies against plague; research in methods for protein production and analysis; methods for analysis of essential bacterial genes; specific molecular mechanisms of pathogenesis; spectroscopic analysis of protein structure and stability; pharmaceutical product development. Avocations: hiking, travel, bicycling, kayaking, mountain climbing. Business E-Mail: bradford.powell@amedd.army.mil.

POWELL, COLIN LUTHER, former United States Secretary of State, former chairman of the Joint Chiefs of Staff; b. NYC, Apr. 5, 1937; s. Luther and Maud Ariel (McKoy) P.; m. Alma Vivian Johnson, Aug. 25, 1962; children: Michael, Linda, Annemarie. BS in Geology, CUNY, 1958; MBA, George Washington U., 1971; Grad., Nat. War Coll., 1976. Commd. 2d lt. U.S. Army, 1958; advanced through grades to gen., 1989; ret., 1993; asst. to dep. dir. Office Mgmt. & Budget, Washington, 1972—73; battalion comdr. Republic of Korea, 1973—74; comdr. 2d Brigade, 101st Airborne Div., Ft. Campbell, Ky., 1976—77; exec. asst. to sec. US Dept. Energy, Washington, 1979; sr. mil. asst. to dep. sec. US Dept. Def., Washington, 1979—81, asst. div. comdr. 4th Inf. Div. Ft. Carson, Colo., 1981—83, mil. asst. to sec. def. Washington, 1983—86; assigned to U.S. V Corps, Europe, 1986—87; dep. asst. to the Pres. for nat. security affairs NSC, Washington, 1987, asst. to Pres. for nat. security affairs, 1987—89; comdr.-in-chief US Army Forces Command (FORSCOM), Ft. McPherson, Ga., 1989; chmn. Joint Chiefs of Staff US Dept. Def., Washington, 1989—93; sec. US Dept. State, Washington, 2001—05; strategic limited ptnr. Kleiner Perkins Caufield & Byers, Menlo Park, Calif., 2005—. Pub. spkr. addressing audiences across the country and abroad; founding chair America's Promise Allliance, 1997—; mem. Wash. Baseball Club, 2005—. Author: (with Joseph E. Persico) My American Journey (autobiography), 1995. Decorated Legion of Merit (2), Bronze Star, Air medal, Purple Heart; recipient Presdl. Medal of Freedom (2), Ronald Reagan Freedom award, 1993, President's Citizens Medal, Congressional Gold Medal, Sec. of State Disting. Svc. Medal, Sec. of Energy Disting. Svc. Medal, Ellis Island Family Heritage award in Govt. Svc., Statue of Liberty-Ellis Island Found., Inc, 2005, Legion of Honor, France, 2006, several sch. and other inst. have been named in his honor; named hon. knight comdr. Most Honorable Order of the Bath Queen Elizabeth II, 1993; The White House fellow, 1972—73. Mem. Assn. U.S. Army, Am. Acad. Arts & Sciences Republican. Episcopalian. Office: Kleiner Perkins Caufield & Byers 909 N Washington St Ste 700 Alexandria VA 22314*

POWELL, COURTNEY DAVIS, lawyer; b. Joplin, Mo., Jan. 3, 1977; d. Richard Charles and Tandi Jo Davis; m. Robert Parrish Powell, Aug. 2, 2003; 1 child. Degree in Polit. Sci., U. Ark., Fayetteville, 1999; JD, Okla. City U., 2002. Bar: Okla. 2002, US Dist. Ct. (no., we., and ea. dists.) Okla., US Ct. Appeals (10th cir.) 2002. Law clk. dept. justice Immigration Ct., Balt., 2001; law clk., atty. Britton, Ramsey & Gray,

Okla. City, 2001—04; atty. Lester, Loving & Davies, Edmond, Okla., 2004—; extenship judge Vicki Miles-LaGrange Western Dist. Okla., 2001. Mem. Youth Leadership Edmond, Okla., 2005—06; vol. Citizens Caring Children Edmond Mobile Meals, 2005—06, Okla City U. Law Sch. Jessup Team, Citizens Caring Children, Okla. Dem. Party, Okla. City, 1999—2006. Scholar, The Hatton Sumner Found., 1999—2002. Mem.: ABA, Grad. Leadership Edmond, Okla. Bar Assn. (mem. moot ct. com. 2002—03, mem. legis. com. 2003—09), Okla. County Bar Assn., Okla. Pub. Employees Assn. (polit. dir. 2000), Prevent Blindness. Democrat. Avocations: travel, reading. Office: Lester Loving & Davies PC 1701 South Kelly Ave Edmond OK 73013 Office Fax: 405-844-9958. Business E-Mail: cpowell@lldlaw.com.

POWELL, DARREN D., medical educator; b. Ellensburg, Wash., Nov. 22, 1960; s. Dan H. Powell and Jan E. Kerr; m. Marlene I. Koler, May 21, 1988; children: Rachel M, Dan D, Mary J. AAS, Spokane Cmty. Coll., 1982. Cert. RCIS Cardiovasc. Credentialling Internat., NC, 1994. Mgr. cardiology Highline Cmty. Hosp., Seattle, 1986—93; tenured faculty Spokane Cmty. Coll., 1993—. Spkrs. bur. HMP Comm., Malverne, Pa., 1995—. Co-author: (book) Invasive Cardiology A manual for Cath Lab Personnel. Treas. Soc. Invasive Cardiovasc. Professionals, Raliegh, NC, 1996—2004. Fellow: SICP (chair edn. com. 2004—09). D-Liberal. Achievements include SICP Presidents award for time and efforts donated. Office: Spokane Cmty Coll 1810 N Greene St Spokane WA 99217

POWELL, DEBORAH ELIZABETH, pathologist, dean; b. Lynn, Mass., Nov. 28, 1939; MD, Tufts U., 1965. Diplomate Am. Bd. Pathology. Intern Georgetown Med. Ctr., Washington, 1965-66; resident in pathology NIH, Bethesda, Md., 1966-69; exec. dean, vice-chancellor clin. affairs U. Kans. Sch. Medicine, Kansas City, 1997—2002; dean, asst. v.p. for clin. scis. U. Minn. Med. Sch., Mpls., 2002—. Past pres. U.S. & Can. Acad. Pathology, Inc.; trustee Am. Bd. Pathology. Mem.: Am. Soc. Investigative Pathologists, Inst. Medicine, Coll. Am. Pathologists. Office: U Minn Med Sch Dean's Office MMC 293 Mayo 8293 420 Delaware St SE Minneapolis MN 55455 Home Phone: 952-546-1215. Business E-Mail: dpowell@umn.edu.*

POWELL, DINA HABIB, diversified financial services company executive, former federal agency administrator; b. Cairo, 1973; d. Onsi Habib and Hoda Soliman; m. Richard C. Powell; 2 children. BA, U. Tex., 1995. Mem. rels. coord. to Rep. Dick Army US Congress, Washington; dir. congl. affairs, sr. adv. to chmn. Rep. Nat. Com., Washington, 1999—2001; spl. asst. to Pres. for presdl. pers. Exec. Office of the Pres., Washington, 2001—03, asst. to Pres. for presdl. personnel, 2003—05; asst. sec. for ednl. & cultural affairs US Dept. State, Washington, 2005—07; mng. dir. dir. global corp. engagement The Goldman Sachs Group, Inc., NYC, 2007—; bd. dirs. Am. U.; chair Vital Voices Global Partnership. Recipient Outstanding Young Tex. Executive award, U. Tex., 2006, Outstanding Am. by Choice, US Citizenship and Immigration Svcs., 2007. Office: The Goldman Sachs Group Inc 85 Broad St New York NY 10004

POWELL, DONALD ASHMORE, clinical research psychologist; b. Spartanburg, SC, Oct. 29, 1938; s. Russell Kermit Powell and Mignon Kathlene Cox; m. Palmyra Langston, 1961 (div. 1972); children: Donald Langston, Donetta Plamyra, Ashley Preston, Stephanie Anne; m. Shirley L. Buchanan, Aug. 17, 1992 (dec. June 1998); m. Trisha Pope, May 18, 2002. BS, U. S.C., 1960, MA, 1962; PhD, Fla. State U., 1967. Rsch. pychologist Dorn VA Med. Ctr., Columbia, S.C., 1969—, acting dir. R&D, 1996-2000; prof. U. S.C. Sch. Medicine, Columbia, 1979—. Adj. prof. U. S.C., Columbia, 1969—; cons. U.S. Heart, Lung and Blood Inst., Bethesda, 1986—; program specialist VA Mental Health and Behavioral Scis., Washington, 1984-88. Author: (with others) Eyeblink Conditioning, 1999. Rsch. fellowship NIH, 1967-69; vis. scholar NIH, 1974; recipient Merit Rsch. award Dept. of Vet. Affairs, 1996—. Mem. Soc. for Neurosci., Am. Psychol. Soc., Pavlovian Soc. (Pavlovian Rsch. award 1991), Soc. for Neurosci. (pres. S.C. chpt. 1980-81, councilor 1982-85). Democrat. Avocations: running, reading. Office: Dorn VA Med Ctr 6439 Garners Ferry Rd Columbia SC 29209-1638 Office Phone: 803-695-6821. Business E-Mail: donnie.powell@med.va.gov.

POWELL, DONALD E., former federal official; b. Perryton, Tex., May 2, 1941; m. Twanna C. Powell; 2 children. BS in Econs., West Tex. State U.; grad., Southwestern Sch. Banking, So. Meth. U. Loan officer, sec. First Fed. Savings & Loan, Amarillo, Tex., 1963—71; with Boatmen's First Nat. Bank, Amarillo, Tex., 1971—97; pres., CEO First Nat. Bank Amarillo, Tex., 1997—2001; chmn. FDIC, Washington, 2001—05; coord. Recovery & Rebuilding in the Gulf Coast Region US Dept. Homeland Security, 2005—08. Bd. dirs. Stone Energy Corp., 2008—, Bank of America Corp., 2009—. Active City of Amarillo Housing Bd., Franklin Lindsay Student Aid Fund, Cal Farley's Boys Ranch; adv. bd. mem. George Bush Sch. Govt. & Public Svc.; chmn. Amarillo C. of C.; chmn. bd. regents Tex. A&M U. Sys.; past bd. dirs. High Plains Bapt. Hosp., Harrington Regional Med. Ctr.*

POWELL, EARL ALEXANDER, III, art museum director; b. Spartanburg, SC, Oct. 24, 1943; s. Earl Alexander and Elizabeth (Duckworth) P.; m. Nancy Landry Powell, July 17, 1971; children: Cortney, Channing, Sumner. AB with honors, Williams Coll., 1966; AM, Harvard U., 1970, PhD, 1974; DFA (hon.), Williams Coll., 1993, Otis Parson Art Inst. Tchg. fellow in fine arts Harvard U., 1970-74; curator Michener Collection U. Tex., Austin, 1974-76, asst. prof. art history, 1974-76; mus. curator, sr. staff asst. to asst. dir. and chief curator Nat. Gallery Art, Washington, 1976-78, exec. curator, 1979-80; dir. L.A. County Mus. Art, 1980-92, Nat. Gallery Art, Washington, 1992—. Chmn. US Commn. Fine Arts; trustee Am. Fedn. Arts, Morris and Gwendolyn Cafritz Found., White House Hist. Assn., Nat. Trust Hist. Preservation, John F. Kennedy Ctr. for Performing Arts; mem. com. for preservation The White House; fed. coun. Arts and Humanities; fine arts adv. panel Fed. Res. Bd., Friends of Art and Preservation in Embassies; mem. Nat. Portrait Gallery Com.; mem. Pres.'s Com. on Arts and Humanities; mem. vis. com. Williams Coll. Mus. Art. Author: American Art at Harvard, 1973, Selections from the James Michener Collection, 1975, Abstract Expressionists and Imagists: A Retrospective View, 1976, Milton Avery, 1976, The James A. Michener Collection: Twentieth Century American Painting, catalogue raisonne, 1978, Thomas Cole monograph, 1990. Mem. Nat. Coun. on the Arts; mem. Pres.'s Com. on the Arts and Humanities. With U.S. Navy, 1966-69, comdr. Res., 1976-80. Decorated officier Arts and Letters, chevalier Legion of Honor; grand ofcl. Order of the Infante D. Henrique medal, 1995, Mexican Order the Aztec Eagle Mexican Govt., 2007; recipient King Olav medal, 1978, Bicentennial medal Williams Coll., 1995; Harvard U. travelling fellow, 1973-74, Mexican Cultural award, 1996, commendatore dell'Ordine al Merito della Republica Italiana, 1998. Mem. Am. Acad. Arts and Scis., Walpole Soc., Assn. Art Mus. Dirs., Am. Philos. Soc., Friends of Art and Preservation in Embassies. Office: Casva National Gallery Of Art 1 E 78th St New York NY 10075-0119 Office Phone: 202-842-6001.*

POWELL, J. BRAXTON, retired state treasurer; b. Suffolk, Va. m. Judy Scott; 2 children. BSBA in Fin., Va. Tech., 1967. With Va. Dept. Treas., 1983—2008, dep. state treas., state treas., 2006—08. Bd. dir. Commonwealth Va. Treas. Bd., Va. Housing Devel. Authority. Mem.: Nat. Assn. State Treas. (so. regional v.p.).

POWELL, JAMES BOBBITT, health facility administrator, pathologist; b. Burlington, NC, Aug. 28, 1938; s. Thomas Edward and Sophia (Sharpe) P.; m. Pamela Oughton, Sept. 12, 1969 (div. Sept. 1979); 1 child, Daphne P. Markcrow; m. Anne Ellington, Oct. 20, 1984; children: James Bobbitt (dec.), John Banks, James Rosser, Helen Bobbitt. BA, Va. Mil. Inst., 1960; MD, Duke U., 1964. Diplomate Am. Bd. Pathology. Intern Duke U. Med. Ctr., Durham, NC, 1964-65; resident Cornell Med. Ctr., NYC, 1965-67, Englewood (N.J.) Hosp., 1967-69; founder Biomed Labs, Burlington, NC, 1969—; pres. Roche Biomed. Labs., 1982-95; pres., CEO Lab. Corp. Am. Holdings, 1995-97; CEO Tripath Imaging, Burlington, NC, 1997—2000. Bd. dirs. Mid-Carolina Bank; bd. dirs. vis. Internat. Faculty. Contbr. articles to sci. publs. Trustee Elon U., NC, 1979—; bd. dirs. Alamance Found. Maj. M.C. US Army, 1969—72. Mem. Alamance Country Club. Republican. Methodist. Avocations: tennis, US military history. Office: 1573 York Pl Burlington NC 27215-3355

POWELL, JAMES L., economics professor; BA, U. Calif., Berkeley, 1977; MS, Stanford U., 1980, AM, 1981, PhD, 1982. Asst. prof. economics MIT, 1982—85, U. Wis., Madison, 1986—87, assoc. prof. economics, 1987—90, prof. economics, 1990—91, Princeton U., 1991—96, U. Calif., Berkeley, 1993—. Vis. asst. prof. economics Carnegie-Mellon U., 1985; vis. assoc. prof. economics Princeton U., 1988; vis. prof. economics U. Chgo., 1990—91. Grantee NSF, 1983, 1985, 1987, 1990, 1992; fellow Econometric Soc., 1991, Jour. Econometrics, 1993, Ctr. Advanced Study in the Behavioral Sciences, 2000—01; H.I. Romnes faculty fellowship, U. Wis. Madison, 1988. Fellow: Am. Acad. Arts and Sciences. Office: Dept Economics 549 Evans Hall #3880 U Calif Berkeley Berkeley CA 94720-3880

POWELL, JAMES LAWRENCE, educational association administrator, museum director, geologist; b. Berea, Ky., July 17, 1936; s. Robert Lain and Lizena (Davis) P.; m. Joan Hartmann; children: Marla, Dirk, Joanna. AB, Berea Coll., 1958; PhD, MIT, 1962; DSc (hon.), Oberlin Coll., 1983; LHD (hon.), Tohoku Gakuin U., 1986; DSc (hon.), Beaver Coll., 1992. Asst. prof., assoc. prof., prof. Oberlin Coll., Ohio, 1962-83, chmn. geol. dept., 1965—73, v.p., provost, 1975—81, assoc. dean, 1973—75, acting pres., 1981—83; pres. Franklin and Marshall Coll., Lancaster, Pa., 1983-88, Reed Coll., Portland, Oreg., 1988-91; pres., chief exec. officer The Franklin Inst., Phila., 1991-94; pres., dir. Los Angeles County Mus. Natural History, LA, 1994—2001; exec. dir. Nat. Physical Sci. Consortium, LA, 2001—. Mem. Nat. Sci. Bd., 1986-98; adj. prof. Univ. So. Calif., 1995-2001 Author: Strontium Isotope Geology, 1972, Pathways to Leadership: Achieving and Sustaining Success: A Guide for Nonprofit Executives, 1995, Night Comes to the Coctzcems; Dinosaur Extinction and the Transformation of Modern Geology, 1998; Mysteries of Terra Firma: Age and Evolution of the Earth, 2001, Grand Canyon: Solving Earth's Grandest Puzzle, 2005. Fellow: Geol. Soc. Am.; mem.: Phi Beta Kappa, Phi Kappa Phi, Sigma Xi. Office: Nat Physical Science Consortium Ste 348 3716 S Hope Los Angeles CA 90007-4344 Business E-Mail: jpowell@usc.edu.

POWELL, JAMES MATTHEW, history professor; b. Cin., June 9, 1930; s. Matthew James and Mary Loretta (Weaver) P.; m. Judith Catherine Davidorf, May 29, 1954 (dec. 1992); children: James, Michael, Mark, Mary Helen, Miriam, John BA, Xavier U., Cin., 1953, MA, 1955; postgrad., U. Cin., 1955-57; PhD, Ind. U., 1960. Instr. Kent State U., Ohio, 1959-61; asst. prof. U. Ill., Urbana, 1961-65, Syracuse U., NY, 1965-67, assoc. prof. NY, 1967-72, prof. history NY, 1972—, dir. Ranke Cataloging Project NY, 1977—. Disting. vis. prof. medieval history Rutgers U., New Brunswick, 1996—97. Author: Medieval Monarchy and Trade, 1962, Civilization of the West, 1967, Anatomy of a Crusade, 1213-1221, 1986, 2d edit., 1990, Albertanus of Brescia: The Pursuit of Happiness in the Early Thirteenth Century, 1992, The Crusades, the Kingdom of Sicily, and the Mediterranean, 2007; translator: Liber Augustalis, 1971, The Deeds of Pope Innocent III, 2004, paperback edit., 2007; editor: Innocent III: Vicar of Christ or Lord of the World, 1963, revised and enlarged 2d edit., 1994, Medieval Studies, 1976, 2d edit., 1992; (with George G. Iggers) Leopold von Ranke and the Shaping of the Historical Discipline, 1989, Muslims Under Latin Rule, 1100-1300, 1990, (with Michael Gervers) Tolerance and Intolerance: Social Conflict in the Age of the Crusades, 2001; contbg. editor: New Catholic Encyclopedia, 2000—; cons. Ency. of the Crusades, 2000-06; contbr. articles to profl. jours. Grantee NEH, 1977-84, 84, Inst. for Advanced Study, Princeton, N.J., 1989-90, Progetto Radici, Brescia, Italy, 1994-95; Fritz Thyssen Stiftung, 1986, 89; recipient John Gilmary Shea prize Am. Cath. Hist. Assn., 1987. Fellow Royal Hist. Soc. (corr.); mem. Am. Hist. Assn., Am. Cath. Hist. Assn. (1st v.p. 2005, pres. 2006), Medieval Acad. Am., Soc. Italian Hist. Studies (coun. 1976-79, v.p. 1991-92, pres. 1993-95), Midwest Medieval Conf. (pres. 1965-66), Soc. Study of the Crusades and the Latin East (sec. 1989-95), Haskins Soc. Democrat. Roman Catholic. Office: Syracuse U Maxwell Sch Syracuse NY 13244-0001

POWELL, JEFFREY SCOTT, endocrinologist; s. Norman Emory and Barbara Ellen Powell; m. Ellen Lynn Rothbaum, June 11, 1995; children: Abigail, Ryan. BA cum laude in Biology, Harvard U., Cambridge, Mass., 1991; MD, Albert Einstein Coll., Bronx, NY, 1995. Diplomate Am. Bd. Internal Medicine. Intern to resident in internal medicine Columbia Med. Ctr., NYC, 1995—98; fellow in endocrinology Colubmia U., Coll. Physicians and Surgeons, NYC, 1998—2001; endocrinologist Mt. Kisco (N.Y.) Med. Group, 2001—. Chief divsn. endocrinology No. Westchester Hosp., Mt. Kisco, 2006—. Contbr. articles to profl. jours. Fellow: Am. Coll. Endocrinology; mem.: Am. Assn. Clin. Endocrinology, Alpha Omega Alpha. Office: Mt Kisco Med Group 90 S Bedford Rd Mount Kisco NY 10549 Office Phone: 914-241-1050. Office Fax: 914-242-2915. Personal E-mail: jpowell@mkmg.com.

POWELL, JERRY W., lawyer; b. Montgomery, Ala., Jan. 6, 1950; m. Carolyn Powell; children: Jennifer, Jeffrey. BA cum laude, Birmingham-So. Coll., 1972; JD, U. Ala., 1975. Bar: Ala. 1975, U.S. Dist. Ct. Ala. (No. and Mid. dist), U.S. Ct. Appeals (11th cir.). Law clk. No. Dist. Ala., 1975—76; gen. counsel, sec. Compass Bancshares, Inc., Birmingham, Ala. Mem. editl. bd.: Alabama Law Review, 1973—75. Mem.: ABA, Am. Soc. Corp. Secretaries, Am. Corp. Counsel Assn. (pres. Ala. chpt. 1984—85), Ala. State Bar Assn., Birmingham Bar Assn., Order of Coif (bench and bar). Office: Compass Bancshares Inc 15 S 20th St Birmingham AL 35233 Office Phone: 205-297-3960. Office Fax: 205-297-3043. Business E-Mail: jerry.powell@compassbank.com.

POWELL, JOHN, composer; b. Eng., Sept. 18, 1963; arrived in US, 1997; m. Melinda Lerner; 1 child. Student, Trinity Coll. Music, London. Band mem. The Fabulists; co-founder Independently Thinking Music, London, 1995; former mem. Media Ventures. Composer: (TV series) Stay Lucky, 1989, (TV films) High Incident, 1996, Human Bomb, 1998, (films) The Wild Heels, 1994, Mondokino, 1996, Face/Off, 1997 (ASCAP award), With Friends Like These..., 1998, Antz, 1998 (ASCAP award), Endurance, 1999, Forces of Nature, 1999, Chill Factor, 1999, The Road to El Dorado, 2000, Chicken Run, 2000 (ASCAP award), Just Visiting, 2001, Shrek, 2001 (Annie award for Music Score, 2001, ASCAP award), Evolution, 2001, Rat Race, 2001, I Am Sam, 2001, D-Tox, 2002, The Bourne Identity, 2002 (ASCAP award), Drumline, 2002, The Adventures of Pluto Nash, 2002, Two Weeks Notice, 2002, Stealing Sinatra, 2003, Agent Cody Banks, 2003, The Italian Job, 2003 (ASCAP award), Gigli, 2003, Paycheck, 2003, The Bourne Supremacy, 2004 (ASCAP award), Mr. 3000, 2004, Alfie, 2004, Be Cool, 2005, Robots, 2005 (ASCAP award), Mr. & Mrs. Smith, 2005 (ASCAP award), Ice Age: The Meltdown, 2006 (ASCAP award, Ivor Novello award, Brit. Acad. Composers & Songwriters, 2007), United 93, 2006, X-Men: The Last Stand, 2006 (ASCAP award), Happy Feet, 2006 (ASCAP award), Stop Loss, 2007.

POWELL, JOHN LIVINGSTON, retired obstetrician and gynecologist; b. Balt., Apr. 7, 1942; s. Julius Benjamen and Jean (Paul) P.; m. Caroline Walker, Apr. 11, 1967; children: John Bingham, Sarah Elizabeth. BS, Davidson Coll., 1964; MD, U. N.C., 1968. Diplomate in ob-gyn. and gynecol. oncology Am. Bd. Ob-Gyn. Intern Tripler Gen. Hosp., Honolulu, 1968-69; resident in ob-gyn. Fitzsimons Gen. Hosp., Denver, 1969-72; fellow in gynecol. oncology Crawford Long Meml. Hosp., Atlanta, 1976-78; mem. staff Baystate Med. Ctr., Springfield, Mass., 1984-94; dir. gynecologic oncology New Hanover Regional Med. Ctr., Wilmington, NC, 1995—2009. Prof. ob-gyn. Tufts U. Med. Sch., Boston, 1991, U.N.C. Sch. Med., 1994 Contbr. chpts. to books, articles to profl. jours. Mem. AMA, ACS, Am. Coll. Ob-Gyn., Soc. Gynecol. Oncology, So. Med. Assn., Gynecol. Laser Soc., Am. Soc. for Laser Medicine and Surgery, Assn. Profs. Gynecology and Obstetrics, N.C. Med. Soc., Kappa Sigma, others. Republican. Presyterian.

POWELL, JULIE, writer; b. Austin, Tex., 1973; BA in Theater and Creative Writing, Amherst Coll., Mass., 1995. Author: (books) Julie and Julia: 365 Days, 524 Recipes, 1 Tiny Apartment Kitchen, 2005 (Quill award for Debut Author of Yr., 2006, Publishers Weekly bestseller), (web log) The Julie/Julia Project, 2002—03; contbr. articles on food to numerous profl. jours. (James Beard award for food journalism, 2004). Office: c/o Author Mall Little Brown & Co 1271 Ave of Americas New York NY 10020*

POWELL, KEN (KENDALL J. POWELL), consumer products company executive; b. 1954; BA, Harvard U., 1976; MBA, Stanford U., 1979. Mktg. & mgmt. positions Gen. Mills, Inc., Mpls., 1979—90; v.p. mktg. dir. Cereal Partners Worldwide, 1990—96; pres. Yoplait USA divsn. Gen. Mills, Inc., Mpls., 1996—97, pres. Big G Cereals divsn., 1997—99, sr. v.p., 1998—2004; CEO CPW, S.A. (Cereal Partners Worldwide), Morges, Switzerland, 1999—2004; exec. v.p. Meals, Pillsbury USA, Bakeries & Foodservice Gen. Mills, Inc., Mpls., 2004—05, exec. v.p., COO U.S. retail, 2005—06, pres., COO, 2006—07, CEO, 2007—08, chmn., CEO, 2008—. Bd. dirs. Gen. Mills, Inc., 2006—, Medtronic, Inc., 2007—. Bd. mem. Twin Cities United Way, Cereal Partners Worldwide, Minn. Historical Soc. Office: General Mills Inc 1 General Mills Blvd Minneapolis MN 55426

POWELL, KENNETH GRANT, aerospace engineering educator; b. Euclid, Ohio, July 3, 1960; s. Thomas Edward and Mary Catherine (Byrum) P.; m. Susanne Maria Krummel, Aug. 31, 1991; children: Jasmine Tara, Ryan Grant, Nicole Maia. SB in Math., MIT, 1982, SB in Aeronautics, 1982, SM in Aeronautics, 1984, ScD in Aeronautics, 1987. Asst. prof. dept. aerospace engrng. U. Mich., Ann Arbor, 1987-93, assoc. prof. dept. aerospace engrng., 1993-2000, prof. dept. aerospace engrng., 2000—02, Arthur F. Thurnau prof., 2002—. Lectr. Von Karman Inst. for Fluid Dynamics, Brussels, 1990, 96; cons. Ford Motors, Dearborn, Mich., 1992-95; cons. Detroit Edison, 1996-98; exec. dir. Francois-Xavier Bagnoud Prize Bd., 1998-2000. Named Presdl. Young investigator NSF, 1988; recipient Tchg. Excellence award U. Mich. Coll. Engrng., 1992, Outstanding Tchg. award Tau Beta Pi, 1988, 99, 2005, Tchg. Excellence award Sigma Gamma Tau, 1989, 95. Fellow AIAA (assoc.); mem. Tau Beta Pi, Sigma Xi, Sigma Gamma Tau. Home: 5531 Spring Hill Dr Ann Arbor MI 48105-9552 Office: U Mich Dept of Aerospace Engrng Ann Arbor MI 48109

POWELL, LARRY, communications educator; b. Greenville, Ala., May 14, 1948; s. A. Harold Powell and Virginia Brown; m. Clarine Thrower, Dec. 19, 1970. BA, Auburn U., Ala., 1970; MA, Auburn U., 1971; PhD, U. Fla., 1975. From asst. prof. to prof. Miss. State U., Starkvill, 1975—86; vcons. Kitchens, Powell & Kitchens, Orlando, Fla., 1987—96; owner Powell Cons., Orlando, 1996—98; prof., former chair U. Ala., Birmingham, 1998—. Vis. prof. Meisei U., Hino, Japan, 1984—85; adj. prof. Ctrl. Fla. U., Orlando, 1996—98; media pollster Birmingham News, Birmingham, 2001—; cons. in field. Co-author: Political Campaign Communication, 2003, Interviewing: Situations and Content, 2005; contbr. articles to profl. jours.; co-author: Holy Murder: Abraham, Isaac, and the Rhetoric of Sacrifice, 2006. Polit. advisor Bus. Coun. of Ala., Montgomery, 1994—96, WVTM-TV/WBRC-TV, Birmingham, 2001—02. Recipient Miss. Jaycee Gov. award, 1986; named one of Top 100 Comm. Rschrs., Assn. of Comm. Adminstrs., 1998; Ala. Dept. Pub. Health grantee, 1999—2000. Master: So. States Comm. Assn. (life; chair polit. com. 1999—2000); mem.: Nat. Comm. Assn., Religious Comm. Assn. (life). Home: 328 Shadeswood Dr Hoover AL 35226 Office: Univ of Alabama Comm Studies Dept 901 S 15th St Birmingham AL 35294 Office Phone: 205-934-8784. Business E-Mail: lpowell@uab.edu.

POWELL, LEANNE, legislative staff member; Campaign mgr. Rep. Bill Hefner's Congl. Campaign, 1994; dir. women's programs USDA, 1995—99; polit. cons.; prin. Southern Campaign; campaign mgr. Larry Kissell Congl. Campaign, 2006—08; chief of staff to Rep. Larry Kissell US House of Reps., NC, 2008—. Democrat. Office: 12 Cannon House Office Bldg Washington DC 20515 Office Phone: 202-225-3715. Office Fax: 202-225-4036.*

POWELL, LEWIS FRANKLIN, III, lawyer; b. Richmond, Va., Sept. 14, 1952; s. Lewis F. Jr. and Josephine (Rucker) P.; m. Lisa T. LaFata; children: Emily, Hannah, Luke. BA, Washington & Lee U., 1974; JD, U. Va., 1978. Bar: Va. 1978, U.S. Dist. Ct. (ea. and we. dists.) Va. 1979, U.S. Ct. Appeals (4th cir.) 1979, U.S. Ct. Appeals (2d cir.) 1983, U.S. Ct. Appeals (11th cir.) 1992, U.S. Supreme Ct. 1985. Law clk. to judge U.S. Dist. Ct. (ea. dist.), Richmond, 1978-79; assoc. Hunton & Williams, Richmond, 1979—86, ptnr., 1986—. Pres. young lawyers conf. Va. State Bar, 1986-87. Bd. dirs. William Byrd Cmty. Ho., Richmond, 1982-87, Boys Club of Richmond, 1984-90, Maymont Found., Richmond, 1987-92, St. Christopher's Sch., Richmond, 1989-96. Mem. Richmond Bar Assn. (chmn. improvement justice com. 1982-83), 4th Cir. Jud. Conf., Am. Law Inst. Avocations: fly fishing, mountaineering, hiking. Office: Hunton & Williams Riverfront Plz East Tower 951 E Bird St Richmond VA 23219

POWELL, MARSHA, director, educator; BS in Math., SUNY, Cortland, 1978, MS in Math., 1992. Applications programmer Cornell U., Ithaca, NY, 1978—80; sr. systems analyst Cbord Group, Inc., Ithaca, 1980—82; prof., program chmn. Tompkins Cortland CC, Dryden, NY, 1982—; computer forensic examiner Broome County Govt. Security, Binghamton, NY, 2003—. Pres., chmn. Cayuga Chamber Orch., Ithaca, 1993—2003; patroller Nat. Ski Patrol, Cortland, 1993—2006. Recipient Incentive award for classroom rsch., Tompkins Cortland C.C., Coll. Tchg. Ctr., 1996, NY State Chancellor's award for excellence in tchg., NY State Dept. Edn., 2004. Mem.: High Tech. Crime Investigation Assn., Internat. Assn. Computer Investigative Specialists (cert.). Office: Tompkins Cortland CC 170 North St Dryden NY 13053

POWELL, MATTHEW, oncologist, educator; BS in Biochemistry, Wash. State U., Pullman, 1990; MD, Mich. State U., East Lansing, 1995. Cert. subspecialist Am. Bd. Ob-Gyn., 2003. Asst. prof. Wash. U., St. Louis, 1999—. Mem.: Soc. Gynecologic Oncologists.

POWELL, MELCHIOR DANIEL, educational administrator, lawyer; b. NYC, July 7, 1935; children: Anthony, Vanessa, Nycole. BS, NJ State U., 1957; MA, George Washington U., 1963; JD, U. Balt., 1966; PhD, U. Md., 1968. Bar: Md. 1966. City atty. City Greenbelt, Md., 1966-67; dir. contract rsch. Nat. Assn. Counties, 1967-71; assoc. prof. urban affairs U. No. Colo., Greeley, 1971-72; dir. Appalachian region com. Office of Rsch. Mgmt., Washington, 1972-73; dean Grad. Ctr. Pub. Policy and Adminstrn. Calif. State U., Long Beach, 1973-92, prof. emeritus, 1992—. Exec. sect. We. Govtl. Rsch. Assn., 1992-95; vis. prof. Fla. Atlantic U., 1995-96; exec. dir., pres. So. Md. Higher Edn. Ctr., 1997—; cons. in field. Author: Education for the Future Pub. Svc., 1981, Achieving Closer Ties, 1984; contbr. articles to profl. jours. Mem. Mayor's Task Force City of Long Beach, 1978, mem. charter comm., 1979, bd. dirs. poverty program, 1980; mem. Calif. workers compensation rate setting commn., 1991, So. Md. Workforce Infrastructure Bd., 2006-; Served to lt. (j.g.), U.S. Navy, 1959-63. Mem. Western Govt. Rsch. Assn. (pres. 1980-82, exec. sec. 1982-95), Am. Soc. Pub. Adminstrn. (pres. Md. chpt. 1972-73, program chmn. Nat. Conf. 1980, 93, conf. chmn. 1986, 93, pres. L.A. Metro chpt. 1976-77, Dykstra award 1977, Will Baughman award 1982), Urban Affairs Assn. (pres. 1986-87), Internat. Assn. Schs. and Insts. of Adminstrn. (v.p. N.Am. 1989—, mem. bd. mgmt., 2001—, chair working group accountability, culture and trust, 2006-). Democrat. Roman Catholic. Home: 422 Overlook Dr Lusby MD 20657-3202 Office: SMHEC 44219 Airport Rd California MD 20619 Office Phone: 301-737-2500.

POWELL, MICHAEL KEVIN, investment company executive, former federal official; b. Birmingham, Ala., Mar. 23, 1963; s. Colin Luther and Alma Vivian (Johnson) Powell; m. Jane Knott; children: Bryan, Jeffrey. BA, Coll. William and Mary, 1985; JD, Georgetown U., 1993. Policy adv. to asst. sec. for internat. security affairs US Dept. Def., Washington, 1988—90; law clk. to Hon. Harry T. Edwards US Ct. Appeals (D.C. Cir.), Washington, 1993—94; assoc. O'Melveny & Myers LLP, 1994—96; chief of staff antitrust divsn. US Dept. Justice, Washington, 1996—97; commr. FCC, Washington, 1997—2001, chmn., 2001—05; sr. adv. Providence Equity Partners, Washington, 2005—; chmn. MK Powell Group, 2005—. Bd. dirs. ObjectVideo Inc., 2005—, Cisco Systems, Inc., 2007—, CMWare, Inc., 2007—. Bd. visitors Georgetown U. Law Ctr.; bd. dirs. U.S. Telecomm. Tng. Inst.; bd. trustees The RAND Corp., The Aspen Inst. Cavalry platoon leader, troop exec. US Army, 1985—88, Amberg, Germany. Recipient Freedom of Speech medal, Media Inst., 1999; Henry Crown fellow, Aspen Inst., 1999. Office: Providence Equity Partners Inc 1050 Connecticut Ave NW Ste 1250 Washington DC 20036*

POWELL, MICHAEL VANCE, lawyer; b. San Diego, Sept. 30, 1946; s. Jesse Vance and Mable Louise (Cagle) P.; m. Sarada Marie Hughes, Dec. 23, 1967; children: Marilyn Jean, Michael Benjamin. AB, Davidson Coll., NC, 1968; MA, U. Tex., 1972, JD with honors, 1974. Bd. cert. civil appellate law Tex. Bd. Legal Specialization. Law clk. to judge US Ct. Appeals (9th cir.), 1974—75; assoc. Rain Harrell Emery Young & Doke, Dallas, 1975-80, ptnr., 1980-87; mem. Locke Purnell Rain Harrell, Dallas, 1987-98; ptnr. Locke Liddell & Sapp, Dallas, 1999—2007, Locke Lord Bissell & Liddell, Dallas, 2007—. Elder St. Barnabas Presbyn. Ch., Richardson, Tex. Fellow: Am. Bar Found. Avocations: music, travel. Home: 7312 Tophill Ln Dallas TX 75248-5642 Office: Locke Lord Bissell & Liddell 2200 Ross Ave Ste 2200 Dallas TX 75201-6776 Office Phone: 214-740-8520. Business E-Mail: mpowell@lockelord.com.

POWELL, NANCY JO, federal agency administrator, former ambassador; b. Cedar Falls, Iowa, 1947; BA, No. Iowa U., 1970. Dep. chief of mission US Embassy, Lome, Togo, 1990—92, consul gen. New Delhi, 1993—95, dep. chief of mission Khaka, Bangladesh, 1995—97; US amb. to Uganda US Dept. State, Kampala, 1997—99, prin. dep. asst. sec. for African affairs, 1999—2001, acting asst. sec. African affairs, 2001, US amb. to Ghana Accra, 2001—02, US amb. to Pakistan Islamabad, 2002—04, prin. dep. asst. sec. & acting asst. sec. for legis. affairs Washington, 2004—05, acting asst. sec. Bur. Internat. Narcotics and Law Enforcement Affairs, 2005, sr. coord. for Avian & Pandemic Influenza, 2005—06, US amb. to Nepal Kathmandu, 2007—09, dir. gen. Fgn. Svc. Washington, 2009—; nat. intelligence officer for South Asia, Nat. Intelligence Coun. Office Nat. Intelligence, Washington, 2006—07. Recipient Arnold L. Raphel award, US Dept. State, 2003, Homeland Security Svc. to America medal, 2006. Office: US Dept State 2201 C St NW Washington DC 20520*

POWELL, NICHOLE LARAI, chemistry professor, researcher; arrived in US, 1999, permanent resident, 2002; d. Ripton Roy Powell and Grace Monica Clarke-Powell; 1 child, Maria-Cristina Pascoe. BS in Biochemistry with honors, U. West Indies, Mona, Jamaica, 1995; PhD in Chemistry, Ga. State U., Atlanta, 2003. Instr. Ga. State U., Atlanta, 2001—03; adj. instr. Ga. Perimeter Coll., Lawrenceville, Ga., 2003—05; asst. prof. Tuskegee U., Ala., 2004—. Chmn. academic affairs com. faculty senate Tuskegee U., 2005—. Mem.: Am. Chem. Soc. (sec. Auburn local sect. 2005, chmn. elect Auburn local sect. 2006, chair Auburn local sect. 2007), Am. Soc. Microbiology, Phi Beta Delta. Office: Tuskegee University 102 Armstrong Hall Tuskegee AL 36088 Business E-Mail: nlpowell@tuskegee.edu.

POWELL, PAMELA BAKER, education educator, minister; b. Cin., Feb. 22, 1945; d. Earl Milton Baker, Jr. and LaMoine Thompson Baker; m. John Paul Powell, Aug. 20, 1977; children: Stewart Baker Jefferson, Jennifer Powell McNutt, Elliott Hamilton Jefferson. BA, Miami U., Oxford, Ohio, 1967; MDiv, Fuller Theol. Sem., Pasadena, Calif., 1982; DD, Pitts. Theol. Sem., Pitts., Pa., 2000. Ordained Minister Word and Sacrament Presbyn. Ch., 1983. Co-pastor First Presbyn. Ch. of Sherman Oaks, Sherman Oaks, Calif., 1983—88; campus pastor Tex. Tech U., Lubbock, Tex., 1989—91; interim assoc. pastor Westminster Presbyn. Ch., Lubbock, Tex., 1991—92; stated supply pastor Messiah Presbyn. Ch., Lubbock, Tex., 1994—96; pastor First Presbyn. Ch. of Finleyville, Finleyville, 1997—99; assoc. prof. pastoral theology Trinity Episcopal Sch. for Ministry, Ambridge, Pa., 1999—. Pastoral counseling practice Pvt., Lubbock, Tex., 1993—96. Contbr. articles pub. to profl. jour., chapters to books. Judge Young Mothers of Am., LA, 1984—85; pres. Lubbock Ballet Theatre, Lubbock, Tex., 1995—96; treas. Indpls. Symphony Jr. Group, Indpls., 1975—76; pres. Young Officers' Wives, Eglin AFB, Fla., 1970—71. Recipient Christian Worker's Award, Fuller Theol. Sem., 1979; nominee Outstanding Young Women of Am., Officers Wives Club -Eglin AFB, 1971. Mem.: Nat. Covenant Group, Pitts. Presbytery (com. on ministry 2001—05), Kappa Kappa Gamma (sec. 1966—67). Office: Trinity Episcopal Sch for Ministry 311 Eleventh St Ambridge PA 15243 Home: 2726 Laning Rd San Diego CA 92106-6430 Office Fax: 724-266-4617. Business E-Mail: pamelapowell@tesm.edu.

POWELL, PATRICIA LYNN, education and special education educator; b. Columbus, Jan. 4, 1954; d. Roger Lee and Geraldine (Porter) Triemstra; m. Richard Wayne Powell, Apr. 5, 1980; children: Joshua, Aaron, Kaitlyn. AB in Music and Elem. Edn., Calvin Coll., Grand Rapids, Mich., 1975; EdM in Hearing Impairments, U. Ariz., Tucson, 1976; PhD, U. Ill., Chgo., 2004. Tchr. hearing impaired Ariz. State Sch. for the Deaf and Blind, Tucson, 1976—81; music tchr. disabled students Elim Christian Sch., Palos Heights, Ill., 1986—2001; asst. prof. edn. and spl. edn. Trinity Christian Coll., Palos Heights, 1999—. Mem. com. on disabilities Reformed Ch. in Am., NJ, 2002—03. Recipient Open Hearts award, Pathways Awareness Found., 2001, Ill. Humanities award, Studs Terkel, 2001. Mem.: ASCD, Coun. for Exceptional Children, Am. Ednl. Rsch. Assn. Avocations: flute, quilting, reading, boating, gardening. Home: 12300 Nagle Ave Palos Heights IL 60463 Office: Trinity Christian Coll 6601 W College Dr Palos Heights IL 60463 Personal E-mail: patti_powell@hotmail.com. Business E-Mail: patti.powell@trnty.edu.

POWELL, RAYMOND WILLIAM, financial planner, school administrator; b. Waterbury, Conn., June 17, 1944; s. Don C. and Kathryn (Linhard) P.; m. Janet Yasinski, June 24, 1967; 1 child, Raymond Joseph. BS, So. Conn. State Coll., New Haven, 1966, MS, 1969; postgrad., U. Bridgeport, Conn. CFP; enrolled agt. CEO R.W. Powell Enterprises, Inc., fin. and tax cons., Prospect, Conn., 1972—; dir.-owner Powells Income Tax Svc., Watertown, 1972—, Powell's Acctg. Svc., 1975—, Powell's Fin. Planning Svc., 1977—; supt. of schs. Winchester, Conn., 1995—2001. Contbr. articles to profl. jours. Vice chmn. Watertown Town Coun., 1975-76. Mem. Nat. Assn. Enrolled Agts., Internat. Assn. Fin. Planners, Am. Soc. Tax Cons., Conn. Assn. Enrolled Agts. Democrat. Office: PO Box 7077 42 Waterbury Rd Prospect CT 06712-1238 Home Phone: 860-274-5880; Office Phone: 203-758-5700. Business E-Mail: powells.financial@snet.net, rwpowell@woodburyfinancial.com, rqyw@rwpenterprises.com.

POWELL, RICHARD LYNN, lawyer; b. Marietta, Ga., June 10, 1936; s. Guy Arlington and Florine (Dobbins) Powell; m. Paula Irene Hosea, Aug. 30, 1969; 1 child, Richele Anderson. LLB, John Marshall Law Sch., Atlanta, 1963, postgrad., 1964. Bar: Ga. 1966, US Dist. Ct. (no. dist.) Ga. 1966. Asst. D.A. Fulton Co., Ga., 1954—59, Ga. State U., 1958—59; assoc. Grubbs, Prosser & Burke, Marietta, 1966—67; pvt. practice Marietta, 1967—. Lectr., criminal law and criminal procedure John Marshall Law Sch., 1972—73. Richele L. Anderson sr. asst. dist. atty., Fulton, Calif.; campaign mgr. George W. Darden Dist. Atty. Cobb County, Ga., 1972; campaign worker George W. Darden Congress Cobb County, 1983—84. With US Army, 1955—58. Mem.: Cobb County Trial Lawyers Assn. (pres. 1983—84), Cobb County Bar Assn. (pres. 1973—74, Disting. Svc. award 1974), Am. Soc. Law and Medicine, Assn. Trial Lawyers America, Ga. Trial Lawyers, State Bar Ga. (bd. govs. 1974—78), Marietta Country Club. Democrat. Office: 142 Forest Ave Marietta GA 30060-1614 Office Phone: 770-427-0266. Business E-Mail: rpowell157@aol.com.

POWELL, ROBERT ELLIS, mathematics professor, dean; b. Lansing, Mich., Mar. 16, 1936; s. James Ellis and Mary Frances (Deming) P.; children: Carl Robert, Glenn Arthur, Charles Addison; m. Lisbeth Nilsen, Nov. 21, 1992. BA, Mich. State U., 1958, MA, 1959; PhD, Lehigh U., 1966. Instr. math. Lehigh U., 1964-66; asst. prof. math. U. Kans., Lawrence, 1966-69; vis. asst. research prof. U. Ky., Lexington, 1967-68; vis. asst. prof. math. Ind. U., Bloomington, summer 1969; assoc. prof. math. Kent State U., Ohio, 1969-74, prof. math., 1974-95, dean grad. coll., 1980-92, prof. math emeritus, dean emeritus grad. coll., 1995—; prof. math., dean grad. sch., dir. rsch. U. Scranton, Pa., 1995-2000. Mem. Ohio Bd. Regents' Adv. Com. on Grad. Study, 1980-92, chmn., 1983-84. Co-author: Summability Theory, 1973, rev. edit., 1988, Intuitive Calculus, 1973; contbr. numerous articles to profl. jours. Bd. dirs. Kent State U. Found., 1981-91. NSF summer grantee, 1964, 65; recipient Fulbright award, 1988. Mem. Midwestern Assn. Grad. Schs. (bd. dirs. 1988-92, chmn. 1990-91), Coun. Grad. Schs. (bd. dirs. 1990-91), Northea. Assn. Grad. Schs. (bd. dirs. 1998-2000). Home: 24300 Sandpiper Isle Way Unit 103 Bonita Springs FL 34134-3002

POWELL, RONALD ROWE, retired library science educator; b. Columbia, Mo., May 24, 1944; s. Hampstead Rowe and Elizabeth Floris (Sapp) P.; m. Jeanne Ann Branstetter, Jan. 28, 1967; children: Rebecca Lynn, Angela Leigh. AB, U. Mo., 1967; MS, Western Mich. U., 1968; PhD, U. Ill., 1976. Bibliographer U. Ill., Urbana, 1968-69, asst. circulation libr., 1969-71, rsch. asst., 1971-74, rsch. assoc., 1974-75; libr. dir. U. Charleston, W.Va., 1976-79; asst. prof. U. Mich., Ann Arbor, 1979-86; assoc. prof. U. Mo., Columbia, 1986-92, dir. grad. studies, 1987-90, chmn. Dept. Libr. Sci., 1990-92; prof. Wayne State U., Detroit, 1993—2008, interim dir., 1999; ret., 2008. Dir. Assn. Libr. & Info. Sci. Edn., Raleigh, 1984-88; vis. prof. Universidade de Brasilia, Brazil, 1985; sec. Coll. Libr. Sect., Assn. for Coll. and Rsch. Libr., Chgo., 1982; sr. fellow Coun. Libr. Resources, Wash., 1982; guest lectr. Moscow State U. of Culture, 1996. Author: Basic Research Methods for Librarians, 1997, 4th edit., 2004; co-author: Success in Answering Reference Questions, 1987, Basic Reference Sources, 1990, The Next Library Leadership, 2003; co-editor: Topics in Library and Information Studies, 1989-2000, Convergence and Collaboration Campus Information Svcs., 2008 Qualitive Research in Information Management, 1992; co-editor Jour. Edn. for Libr. and Info. Sci., 1995-2001, Research Methods in Library and Information Studies, 2000—; mem. editl. bd. Jour. Academic Librarianship, 2000-02, Jour. Edn. for Libr. and Info. Sci., 1984-88, Libr. and Info. Sci. Rsch., 2002-08. Recipient Curator's scholarship U. Mo., Columbia, 1962. Mem. ALA (chmn. standing com. libr. edn. 1992-93, chair libr. rsch. round table 1996-1998), Assn. Coll. and Rsch. Libr., Assn. for Libr. and Info. Sci. Edn., Mich. Libr. Assn., Internat. Info. Acad., Beta Phi Mu. Avocations: music, reading, movies. Home: 21529 Garrison St Dearborn MI 48124-2301 Office Phone: 313-577-6199. Business E-Mail: ad5328@wayne.edu.

POWELL, SARAH E., lawyer, automotive executive; b. Rocky Mount, Va., Apr. 2, 1966; BA magna cum laude, Univ. Va., 1988; JD cum laude, Washington & Lee Univ., 1993. Bar: Va. 1993, NC 2000. Asst. gen. counsel Food Lion LLC, Salisbury, NC; sr. atty. to v.p. & real estate counsel Advance Auto Parts, Roanoke, Va., 2002—07, acting gen. counsel, 2007—09, sr. v.p., corp. sec., gen. counsel, 2009—. Mem.: ABA, State Bar NC, State Bar Va., Va. Bar Assn., Roanoke Bar Assn., Phi Beta Kappa, Phi Alpha Delta, Sigma Tau Delta. Office: Advance Auto Parts 5008 Airport Rd Roanoke VA 24012 Office Phone: 540-561-1186. Office Fax: 540-561-1145.*

POWELL, SCOTT E., diversified financial services company executive; b. 1962; With Comml. Credit Co., 1988; dir. credit risk mgmt. Global Consumer Group, Citigroup, Inc.; chief risk officer consumer bus. Bank One Corp., 2002—03, head retail lending, 2003—05; co-CEO home fin. J.P. Morgan Chase & Co., 2005—07, CEO consumer banking, 2007—. Bd. trustees Phipps Houses. Office: JP Morgan Chase & Co 270 Park Ave New York NY 10017-2070*

POWELL, SIMON N., medical researcher; b. Manchester, England, Feb. 13, 1955; m. Naomi Joshi, June 28, 1985. BA, Oxford U., England, 1976; MBBS, U. Coll., London, 1981; PhD, U. London, 1990. Cert. in MRCP Royal Coll. Physicians, 1985. Trainee clin. oncology Royal Marsden Hosp., London, 1984—91; radiation oncologist Mass. Gen. Hosp., Boston, 1991—2004; prof. and chair Wash. U. St. Louis, St. Louis, 2004—08; chmn. attending Meml. Sloan-Kettering Cancer Ctr., New York, 2008—. Recipient Corpus Christi Coll. award, Oxford U., 1976, Rosenheim, U. Coll. London, 1981. Fellow: FRCR, Royal Coll. Physicians. Achievements include research in cancer biology and genetics. Office: Meml Sloan-Kettering Cancer Ctr 1275 York Ave New York NY 10065

POWELL, THOMAS EDWARD, III, biological supply company executive, physician; b. Elon College, N.C., Aug. 1, 1936; s. Thomas Edward, Jr., and Sophia Maude (Sharpe) P.; m. Betty Durham Yeager, June 19, 1965; children: Frances Powell Barnes, Thomas Edward IV, Caroline Powell Rogers. AB in Biology, Va. Mil. Inst., 1957; MD, Duke U., 1961; MA, Harvard U., 1966. Surgeon USPHS, 1966-68; co-founder Biomed. Reference Labs., Inc., Burlington, N.C., 1969, exec. v.p., 1969-75, chmn. exec. com., 1979-82, also dir.; exec. v.p. Carolina Biol. Supply Co., Burlington, N.C., 1968-80, chmn., 1977-80, 94—, pres., 1980-94; pres. Wolfe Sales Corp., Burlington, 1980-84, Waubun Labs. Inc., Schriever, La., 1980—, Bobbitt Labs., Inc., Burlington, 1983-94; bd. mgrs. Wachovia Bank and Trust Co. N.A., Burlington. Contbr. articles to profl. jours. Bd. dirs. United Way Alamance County, Burlington, 1968—; bd. dirs. Elon Coll., N.C., 1968—, sec., 1975—; bd. dirs. Am. Cancer Soc., Burlington, 1971-81; bd. dirs. Burlington Day Sch., 1973—, pres., 1974-78, 80-84; bd. dirs. N.C. Citizens for Bus. and Industry, Raleigh, 1983-87, Nat. Found. for Study of Religion and Econs., Greensboro, 1984-88, Blue Ridge Sch., Dyke, Va., 1985-90. Served to capt. USAR, 1957-66. Recipient Citizens Service award Elon Coll. Alumni Assn., 1980. Mem. Assn. Biology Lab. Edn., N.C. Acad. Sci., Alamance-Caswell Med. Soc., N.C. Med. Soc., Assn. Venture Founders, Newcomen Soc. Democrat. Mem. United Ch. of Christ. Clubs: Alamance Country (Burlington); Capital City (Raleigh, N.C.); Congl. Country (Washington); N.C. Country (Pinchurst); Hope Valley Country (Durham, N.C.); Greensboro City.

POWELL, THOMAS WILLIAM, speech and language pathology educator; b. Piqua, Ohio, Dec. 27, 1956; s. William G. and Lois J. Powell. BA, Ind. U., 1979, MA, 1982, PhD, 1989. Speech-lang. pathologist Western Carolina Ctr., Morganton, N.C., 1982-83, St. Vincent Hosp., Indpls., 1983-85; rsch. assoc. Ind. U., Bloomington, 1985-87; asst. prof. speech pathology Ball State U., Muncie, Ind., 1987-91; prof. comm. disorders La. State U. Med. Ctr., New Orleans, 1992—99; prof. rehab. sci. La. State U. Health Sci. Ctr., Shreveport, 2000—. Mem. Am. Speech, Lang. and Hearing Assn. (award 1986, 89, 96), Internat. Clin. Phonetics and Linguistics Assn. (treas.; editor Clin. Linguistics and Phonetics Jour.). Office: Mollie Webb Spc Hear Ctr Lsuhsc S 3735 Blair Dr Shreveport LA 71103-4601

POWELL, TIMOTHY WOOD, information executive, consultant; b. Phila., June 22, 1949; s. James Rennie and Elizabeth Clay (Thurman) P.; children: Michael Ross, David Alexander. BA, Yale U., 1971, MBA, 1979. V.p. tech. Yale Coll., 1971; field psychologist LEAP, Inc., 1971-73; outreach mgr. State of Conn., 1973-74; contracts and systems analyst State of N.J., Trenton, 1975-76; sr. fin. analyst State of N.Y., NYC, 1976-77; sr. cons. KPMG, NYC, 1979-83; mgr. nat. mktg. PricewaterhouseCoopers, NYC, 1983-89; rsch. dir. FIND/SVP, NYC, 1989-95; pres. TW Powell Co. The Knowledge Agy., mng. dir., 1995—. Author: The High Tech Marketing Machine, 1993, Analyzing Your Competition, 1993, The Knowledge Value Chain Workbook, 2007; contbr. numerous articles to profl. jours. Fellow Soc. Competitive Intelligence Profls. (bd. dirs. 1994-97, chair, coun. fellows 2006-, Catalyst award 1994); mem. ASCAP, Am. Soc. Indsl. Security, Bus. Threat Awareness Coun. (corp. sec. 2004-). Avocation: music. Office: 548 W 28th St New York NY 10001 Office Phone: 212-243-1200. Business E-Mail: tim.powell@knowledgeagency.com.

POWELL, WARREN B., engineering educator; b. Balt., Apr. 11, 1955; m. Shari Glassman; children: Elyse, Daniel. PhD, MIT, Cambridge, 1981. Prof. Princeton U., 1981—. Author: (book) Approximate Dynamic Programming: Solving the curses of dimensionality. Numerous rsch. grants, NSF, Air Force Office Sci. Rsch., 1981—2008. Fellow: INFORMS (Award 2004). Achievements include research in solving large scale resource allocation problems under uncertainty. Office: Princeton Univ Olden St Princeton NJ 08544 Business E-Mail: powell@princeton.edu.

POWELL, WILLIAM ARNOLD, JR., retired bank executive; b. Verbena, Ala., July 7, 1929; s. William Arnold and Sarah Frances (Baxter) Powell; m. Barbara Ann O'Donnell, June 16, 1956; children: William Arnold III, Barbara Calhoun, Susan Thomas, Patricia Crain. BSBA, U. Ala., 1953; grad., La. State U. Sch. Banking of South, 1966. With Am. South Bank, N.A., Birmingham, Ala., 1953—93, asst. v.p., 1966, v.p., 1967, v.p., br. supr., 1968—72, sr. v.p., br. supr., 1972—73, exec. v.p., 1973—79, pres., 1979—83, vice chmn. bd., 1983—93; pres. AmSouth Bancorp., 1979—93; ret., 1993. Bd. dirs. AmSouth Bank, Fla. Bd. dirs. United Way Found.; past pres. United Way, campaign chmn., 1987; life mem. Birmingham Met. Devel. Bd.; bd. dirs. Warrior-Tombigbee Devel. Assn.; life trustee Ala. Ind. Colls.; pres.'s coun. U. Ala., Birmingham, life bd. visitors. Lt. US Army, 1954—56. Named William A. Powell, Jr. Endowed Professorship in his honor, U. Ala. Mem.: Met. Devel. Assn. (life; bd. dirs.), Birmingham Area C. of C. (life; bd. dirs.), Birmingham Country Club, The Club, Mountain Brook. Home: Birmingham, Ala. Died Aug. 22, 2009.

POWELL, WILLIAM COUNCIL, SR., service company executive; b. Burlington, NC, Nov. 5, 1948; s. Thomas Edward Jr. and Annabelle (Council) P.; m. Jacqueline Garrison, July 3, 1976; children: William C. Jr., Ashley C. Student, U. S.C., 1968-69; BS, Va. Mil. Inst., 1971; MBA, Wake Forest U., 1974; postgrad., Elon Coll., 1972. Lic. pilot, real estate broker. NC adminstrv. assoc. Carolina Biol. Supply Co., Inc., Burlington, 1971—91; v.p. Bobbitt Labs., Burlington, 1974-77, pres., 1977—82; owner HEADS, Inc., Elon, NC, 1978—, pres., 1984—; owner Ashwil Acres Farm, Mebane, NC, 1981—2005. Pres. Granite

Diagnostics, Inc., Burlington, 1981-84, UST Specialists Inc., 1991-2000, Burlington, Warren Land Co., 1994-2005, Merrymount Property Owners Assn., Inc., 1996-2000, Merrymount Boat Slip Assn., Inc., 1996-2005, Stratonet Inc., 1996-2001, Forest Realm, Inc., 2001—, Goat Island Maritime Inc., 2001—, Powell Realm Inc., 2001—, Poignard Compact Inc., 2001-; owner Powell Real Estate, Burlington, 1979-2001; bd. dirs. Excalibur Lock Co., Inc., Waubun Labs, Inc., Schriever, La.; v.p. fin. Environ. Responsible Bus. Inc., 1992-97; mem. Babcock Sch. Alumni Coun. Wake Forest U., 1981-85; mgr. Macon Farm, 1992-95; chmn. bd. Ensci Corp., Inc., 1991-95, ptnr. Port Assocs., 1987-2002, Port Assocs. II, 1992-2002; chmn. bd. Netpath Inc., 1995-96, bd. dirs.; filed for election N.C. Senate, 2000, 02. Bd. advisors Elon Coll., NC, 1984-86, bd. visitors, 1987-92; bd. advisors Duke U. Marine Lab., Beaufort, NC, 1985-92; nat. adv. coun. Baruch Marine Inst., 1998-2006; adv. panel Air Quality Compliance Panel State of NC Dept. Environ. Health and Natural Resources, 1994-2006; guardian Boy Scouts Am., Burlington, 1985; trustee Dr. T.E. Powell Jr. Trust, 1989-95; v.p. fin. Cherokee coun. Boy Scouts of Am., 1990-92, exec. bd., 1990-94, exec. bd. Old N. State coun., 1994-95; active Front St. United Meth. Ch., Burlington, NC. Capt. USAR, 1971-79. Recipient Bill Fish Cert. State of S.C., 1983, 2 Bill Fish Certs. State of N.C., 1990, Sower's award Duke U., 1985, N.C. Gov.'s Cup for Billfishing, 1991, 3rd Pl., Big Rock Blue Marlin Tourn, 1998. Mem. NRA (life), Newcomen Soc. N.Am. (life), Billiard Congress Am., Am. Angus Assn., Billiard and Bowling Inst. Assn., NC Forestry Assn. (legis. affairs com. 1994-2007), N.C. Wildlife Habitat Found. (life), Ducks Unltd. (life sponsor, area chmn. 1985-87, 1997-2005), Safari Club Internat. (state pres. 1985-88, life), Aircraft Owners and Pilots Assn., Cessna Pilots Orgn., Atlantic Coast Conservation Assn. (life), Alamance Wildlife Club (bd. dirs. 1992-95, 2000-03, pres. 1999-2000), Rolls Royce Owners Club (life), N.Am. Hunting Club (life), Found. N.Am. Wild Sheep (life), Chaine des Rotisseurs (chevalier 1991), Brotherhood of the Knights of the Vine (master knight 1991), 10 Point Hunt Club, Am. Angus Assn., Nat. Wild Turkey Fedn., Quail Unltd. (life), NC Cattlemans Assn. (life), Nat. Cattlemans Assn., Inc., Ocean Green Assn., Debordieu Club, Nat. Soc. SAR, Sons Confederate Vets., Alamance County Cattleman's Assn., Citation Fishing Team (capt. 1979—), Alamance Country Club, Debordieu Beach Club. Home: 1109 W Front St Burlington NC 27215-3610 Office: Home Entertainment and Decor Sys Inc 945 E Haggard Ave Elon NC 27244 Office Phone: 336-584-0835, 800-275-4520.

POWELL, WILLIAM E., automotive executive; BA in Edn., Ind. U., 1969; MA, Pacific Luth. U., 1975. Joined Buick GM Corp., 1977, dist. mgr. LA, gen. mgr. Dealer Network Investment Devel. Group, 1993, regional gen. mgr. GM VSSM S.E. Region Atlanta, 1999—2004, v.p. industry-dealer affairs GM N.Am., 2004—. Office: GM Corp PO Box 33170 Detroit MI 48232-5170*

POWELL, WINONA, music educator; b. Harrisonville, Mo., Feb. 1, 1928; d. Robert James and Naomi Noell Powell; m. Carlos Aguirre, Nov. 14, 1974 (div. Sept. 5, 1975). BA, U. Kansas City, Mo., 1956; MA, Vanderbilt U., Nashville, 1958; MusM, Northwestern U., Evanston, Ill., 1963; MEd, U. Ariz., Tucson, 1977. Tchr. music Kennett H.S., Mo., 1958—59, Kansas City Pub. Sch., 1959—62, Tucson Unified Sch. Dist., 1963—90. Family planning Peace Corps, Barahona, Dominican Republic, 1966—69; airline stewardess TWA, Kansas City, Mo., 1949—55. Vol. Project Hospitality/Salvation Army, Tucson, Neighborhood Watch, Tucson, 1984—86, Tucson Bot. Gardens, 1991—95; trustor U. Ariz. Music Dept. Scholarships; publicity chair Hemlock Soc., 1985—98. R-Consevative. Methodist. Avocations: exercise, swimming, dance, travel. Home: 602 N Avenida Alegre Tucson AZ 85745 Personal E-mail: winonapowell@juno.com.

POWELL GEBHARD, JOY LEE (BOK SIN LEE), small business owner; b. Jan. 29, 1936; arrived in U.S., 1956, naturalized, 1962; d. Yong Joon and Chun Jal Lee; m. Jimmy Wayne Powell, Sept. 24, 1960; children: Chun Jal Lee, Miran Victoria, D. Gebhard; m. Karl Ten Eyck Gebhard, Oct. 15, 1995. Grad., Internat. Speech Acad., Pusan, Korea, 1952, Nat. U. Pusan, 1953—55, McMurry Coll., Abilene, Tex., 1956—58; BA, Wayland Bapt. U., Plainview, Tex., 1966; postgrad., Cen. State U., Okla., 1967—68. Cert. antique appraiser and cons. Nurse Rok Med. Sch., Pusan, 1950—53; news anchor Pusan Radio Sta., 1953; sec., ret. choir organizer chaplain's office U.N. Army divsn. 8069, Pusan, 1954—56, Meth. Mission, Pusan, 1955—56, U.S. A.S.C. Office, Ploydada, Tex., 1958, Am. U., Washington, 1958—60; with Washington Post, U.S. Acad. Sci., 1960; with spl. study of prejudice among children grades 1 to 12 Pub. Opinion and Propaganda, 1965—66; tchr. Oklahoma City Sch. Sys., 1968—70; head social studies dept. Dunjee H.S., 1968; tchr. Spanish Carl Albert H.S., 1969; owner Internat. Antiques, Upperville, Va.; founder Healing Inc., 1997. Co-founder Washington Korean Writers Assn., Fairfax, Va., 2008; charter mem. lit. mag. Hiang. Contbr. articles to profl. jours., poetry New Voices in American Poetry, 1978, poems and essays to Korean periodicals. Bd. mem. Buchanan Hall, Upperville, Va., Korean Schs. US. Mem.: World Affairs Coun. Washington, Nat. History Preservation, Smithsonian Assocs., Sigma Tau Delta (Writers award, McMurry Coll., Abilene, Tex. 1957). Avocations: music, writing, swimming, collecting, travel. Home and Office: PO Box 221 Upperville VA 20185-0221

POWELL-HUNT, SUE ROSE, art educator; b. Erie, Pa., Mar. 22, 1928; d. Arthur John and Mayme (Marshall) Hoffman; m. Robert Gramberg (div.); 1 child, Cathy Rhea Gramberg (dec.); m. Russell Rea Powell (dec.); 1 stepchild, Lenora Powell Crundwell. Degree, Am. Acad. Art, 1950; student, Palos Hills C.C., 1978—80. Tchr. oil and porcelin paintings Palos Hills CC, 1981—. Vol. Cystic Fibrosis Found., Chgo., 1957—80. Independent. Baptist. Avocation: art.

POWER, A. KATHRYN, federal agency administrator; m. Brian Power; children: Matthew, Brendan. EdB, St. Joseph's Coll., Md.; MEd, Western Md. Coll.; postgrad. Harvard U. Tchr. various pub. schs.; computer sys. analyst US Dept. Def.; exec. dir. RI Coun. Cmty. Mental Health Centers, 1985—90; dir. RI Anti Drug Coalition, Gov.'s Drug Program, RI Office Substance Abuse, RI Dept. Mental Health, Retardation and Hospitals, 1993—2003, Ctr. for Mental Health Services, Substance Abuse and Mental Health Adminstrn., HHS, Rockville, Md., 2003—. Pres. Nat. Assn. State Mental Health Program Directors, 1997. Capt. USNR. Recipient Award for Disting. Svc., Sec. US HHS, 2005; fellow Toll fellow, Coun. State Legislators, 1991. Office: Ctr for Mental Health Services 5600 Fishers Ln Rockville MD 20857*

POWER, DANIEL JOSEPH, business educator; b. Waterloo, Iowa, Feb. 9, 1950; s. LaVern Joseph and Maxine Mae (Jindrich) P.; m. Carol Esther Pokodner, Jan. 12, 1985; children: Alexander Phillip, Benjamin Jeremy, Gregory Louis. BA, U. Iowa, 1974, MA, 1977; MBA, U. Wis., 1981, PhD, 1982. Lectr. U. Wis., Madison, 1978-82; asst. prof. bus. and mgmt. U. Md., College Park, 1982-87, assoc. prof., 1987-89. Dir. computing Coll. Bus., U. Md., College Park, 1988-89; prof., head mgmt. dept. U. No. Iowa, 1989—96. Author: Decision Support Systems, 2002; co-author: Strategic Management Skills, 1986; contbr. articles to profl. jours. Editor DSSResources.com & DSS Mews. Mem.: Assn. Info. Sys. Jewish. Home: 906 Barnett Dr Cedar Falls IA 50613-6623 Office: U No Iowa Coll Bus Adminstrn Cedar Falls IA 50614-0001

POWER, FRANCIS WILLIAM, newspaper publisher; b. Webster, SD, Aug. 12, 1925; s. Frank B. and Esther C. (Fowler) P.; m. Margaret Jean Atkinson, Mar. 24, 1951; children: Patricia Ann, John Michael, Kerry Jean. BBA, U. N.Mex., 1948. Display advt. sales rep. The Register, Santa Ana, Calif., 1948-51; advt. mgr. Valley Morning Star, Harlingen, Tex., 1951-62; gen. mgr. Pampa (Tex.) Daily News, 1962-69; bus. mgr. Brownsville (Tex.) Herald, 1969-75; pub. The Lima (Ohio) News, 1975-91; v.p. Freedom Comm., Inc., until 1991; ret., 1991. Served with USNR, 1943-46. Mem.: Shawnee Country Club, Elks, Rotary. Roman Catholic. Office: Freedom Comm Inc 17666 Fitch Irvine CA 92614-6022

POWER, J.D., III, (JAMES DAVID POWER III), marketing executive; b. Worcester, Mass., May 30, 1931; m. Julie Power (dec. 2002); 4 children; m. Joan Power, 2003. BA in English, Coll. of the Holy Cross, Worcester, Mass., 1953; MBA, U. Penn., 1959; PhD (hon.), Coll. of the Holy Cross, Calif. Lutheran U., Calif. State U. Northridge, Coll. Misericordia. Financial analyst Ford; mktg. rsch. cons. Marplan GM; mktg. rsch. exec. J.I. Case; dir. corp. planning McCulloch Motors Inc., Los Angeles, Calif.; founder, pres. J.D. Power & Assocs., Calif., 1968—, chmn., 1996—. Adj. prof. mktg. Calif. State U. Northridge. Line officer duty U.S. Coast Guard, Arctic and Antarctica. Recipient Disting. Service Citation, Automotive Hall of Fame, 1992. Office: J D Power & Assocs 2625 Townsgate Rd Westlake Village CA 91361

POWER, JOHN BRUCE, lawyer; b. Glendale, Calif., Nov. 11, 1936; m. Sandra Garfield, Apr. 27, 1998; children by previous marriage: Grant, Mark, Boyd. AB magna cum laude, Occidental Coll., 1958; JD, NYU, 1961; postdoctoral, Columbia U., 1972. Bar: Calif. 1962. Assoc. O'Melveny & Myers, LA, 1961—70, ptnr., 1970—97, resident ptnr. Paris, 1973—75; Sheffelman disting. lectr. Sch. Law, U. Wash., Seattle, 1997. Mem. Social Svcs. Commn. City of L.A., 1993, pres., 1993; pres. circle, exec. com. Occidental Coll., 1979-82, 91-94, chair, 1993-94; adj. prof. UCLA Sch. Law, 1999; mem. Tri-Bar Opinion Com., 2005-. Contbr. articles to jours. Bd. dirs. Met. L.A. YMCA, 1988—, treas., 1998-2001; steering com. Working Group Legal Opinions, 2005-; bd. mgrs. Stuart Ketchum Downtown YMCA, 1985-92, pres., 1989-90; mem. L.A. County Rep. Ctrl. Com., 1962-63; trustee Occidental Coll., 1992—, chmn., 2001-03, acting gen. counsel, 1998-2000. Recipient YMCA Golden Book of Disting. Svc. award, 2002, Alumni Seal award Occidental Coll., 2003; Root Tilden scholar. Fellow Am. Coll. Comml. Fin. Lawyers (bd. regents 1999-03); mem. ABA (comml. fin. svcs. com., com. legal opinions, vice chair 2005-07, chair 2007—, UCC com., bus. law sect.), Am. Bar Found., Calif. Bar Assn. (chmn. partnerships and unincorporated assns. com. 1982-83, chmn. uniform commn. code com. 1984-85, chmn. opinions com. 2000-05, exec. com. 1987-91, chmn. bus. law sect. 1990-91, chmn. coun. sect. chairs 1992-93, liaison to state bar commn. on future of legal profession and state bar 1993-95, advisor to exec. com. 1997—, Bus. Law Sect. Lifetime Achievement award 2004), LA County Bar Assn. (exec. com. comml. law and bankruptcy sect. 1970-73, 86-89), Fin. Lawyers Conf. (bd. govs. 1982—, pres. 1984-85), Exec. Svc. Corps (sec. 1985-00, dir. 1994-2007, vice-chmn. 2000-07), Occidental Coll. Alumni Assn. (bd. govs. 1965-68, pres. 1967-68), Phi Beta Kappa (councilor 1982-2007, pres. 1990-92). Office: O Melveny & Myers 400 S Hope St Los Angeles CA 90071-2899 Personal E-mail: johnpower@earthlink.net.

POWER, JOSEPH ALOYSIUS, JR., lawyer; b. Oct. 15, 1952; s. Joseph Aloysius and Mary Ellen (Cavenaugh) Power; m. Susan Vohs, Apr. 26, 1980; children: Joseph Aloysius III, Michael Anthony, Ryan Patrick, James Ian. BA, U. Notre Dame, 1974; JD, Loyola U., Chgo., Ill., 1977. Bar: Ill. 1977, U.S. Dist. Ct. (no. dist.) Ill. 1977, U.S. Ct. Appeals (7th cir.) 1994, U.S. Supreme Ct. 1992. Assoc. John D. Hayes & Assocs., Chgo., 1977—84; ptnr. Hayes & Power, Chgo., 1984—91, Power, Rogers & Lavin, Chgo., 1991—93, Power, Rogers & Smith, Chgo., 1993—. Chmn. bd. dirs. Assn. of Trial Lawyers Assurance a mutual risk retention group, 1988—2000; author, lectr. Ill. Inst. Contg. Legal Edn., Springfield, Ill., 1983—89; bd. mgrs. Trial Lawyers for Pub. Justice, 1994—, v.p., 1996—97, pres.-elect, 1997—98, pres., 1998—99. Trustee Loyola U., Chgo., 2004—; bd. dir. Ill. Pub. Action, Chgo., 1987—93. Fellow: Inner Cir. of Advocates, Internat. Acad. Trial Lawyers, Am. Coll. Trial Lawyers; mem.: U.S. Sen. Judiciary Com. (chmn.'s adv. coun. 1994, Ill. Supreme Ct. rules com. 1995—2004, chmn. 1996—2001), ATLA, Ill. Bar Assn., Ill. Trial Lawyers Assn. (author, lectr. 1984—, bd. mgrs. 1984—, chmn. membership com. 1985—87, chmn. legis. com. 1987—89, 3d v.p. 1989—90, 2d v.p. 1990—91, pres. elect 1991—92, pres. 1992—93), Chgo. Bar Assn. (chmn. young lawyers sect. fed. trial bar advocacy program No. dist. Il 1984), ABA, Union League Club. Democrat. Roman Catholic. Home: 344 W Wellington Ave Chicago IL 60657-5637 Office: Power Rogers & Smith Three First National Plaza 70 West Madison St Suite 5500 Chicago IL 60602 Office Phone: 312-236-9381. Business E-Mail: joepower@prslaw.com.

POWER, JOSEPH EDWARD, lawyer; b. Peoria, Ill., Dec. 2, 1938; s. Joseph Edward and Margaret Elizabeth (Birkett) P.; m. Camille June Repass, Aug. 1, 1964; children— Joseph Edward, David William, James Repass Student, Knox Coll., Galesburg, Ill., 1956-58; BA, U. Iowa, 1960, JD, 1964; CAP, The Am. Coll., Bryn Mawr, Pa., 2004. Bar: Iowa 1964. Law clk. to judge U.S. Dist. Ct., 1964-65; mem. Bradshaw, Fowler, Proctor & Fairgrave, P.C., Des Moines, 1965—2005, of counsel, 2005—. Trustee Am. Inst. Bus., 1987-2002, chmn., 1992-2002; bd. dir. Iowa Law Sch. Found., 1992-2004, Plymouth Ch. Found., 1991-99; bd. dir. Des Moines Cmty. Found., 1996-2007, sec.-treas., 2001-07; bd. dir. Iowa Natural Heritage Found., 1995—, chmn., 2003-05; mem. Des Moines Civil War Roundtable. Fellow Am. Coll. Trust and Estate Counsel (state chair 1994-2000); mem. Iowa Bar Assn. (chmn. probate, property and trust law com. 1983-87), Polk County Bar Assn., Des Moines Estate Planners Forum (pres. 1982-83), Rotary Club. Mem.United Ch. Of Christ. Home: 1928 Elm Cr West Des Moines IA 50265 E-mail: jedwardpower@aol.com.

POWER, JUNE LYNN LAVOIE, librarian; b. New London, Conn., July 15, 1977; d. Kathryn G. LaVoie; m. Raymond Christopher Power, June 26, 1999; 1 child, Kathryn Taylor. BA in Elem. Edn., Coll. William & Mary, Williamsburg, Va., 1999, BA in Biol. Anthropology; MLIS, U. NC, Greensboro, 2003. Cert. tchg. profl. Commonwealth Va., 1999. Tchr. Pittsylvania County Pub. Schs., Mount Airy, Va., 1999—2000; circulation svc. supr. Averett U., Danville, Va., 2000—03, access svc. libr., 2003; reference libr. Meth. U., Fayetteville, NC, 2003—04; access svc. & reference libr. U. NC, Mary Livermore Libr., Pembroke, 2004—. Actor: (play) Robeson Little Theatre - The Odd Couple, Robeson Little Theatre - Mornings at Seven, Gilbert Theatre - Blue Room, Gilbert Theatre - Anton in Show Business (named Best Supporting Actress, Up and Coming Mag., 2004), Averett University - The Good Doctor; contbr. articles to profl. jours. Mem. Robeson Little Theatre, Lumberton, NC, 2007—08. Mem.: NC Libr. Assn. Episcopalian. Avocations: hiking, theater, travel, kayaking. Office: UNCP - Mary Livermore Libr PO Box 1510 Pembroke NC 28372 Office Phone: 910-521-6369. Business E-Mail: june.power@uncp.edu.

POWER, KATHERINE, Internet company executive; Dir. promotions Brent Bolthouse Productions, LA; west coast ed. ELLE, 2004—06, ELLEgirl, 2004—06; co-founder, creative dir. WhoWhatWear.com, 2006—. Judge Project Runway, 2005.*

POWER, MARY ELEANOR, biology professor; BA magna cum laude, Brown Univ., 1971; MS, Boston Univ. Marine Biology Program, Woods Hole, Mass., 1974; PhD in Zoology, Univ. WAshington, Seattle, 1981. Asst. prof., zoology, integrative biology Univ. Calif., Berkeley, 1987—92, assoc. prof., integrative biology, 1992—96, prof., 1996—; faculty mgr. Angelo Coast Range Reserve, 1989—. Peer adv. bd. Inst. Ecosystem Studies, Millbrook, NY, 1996—99; sci. adv. bd. Nat. Ctr. for Ecological Analysis and Synthesis, 1996—98; peer rev. panel Grand Canyon Monitoring and Rsch. Ctr., 1998—99; group leader Presdl. Adv. Commn. Western Water Policy, 1997; bd. dir. Nature Conservancy, 1997—; dir. Calif. Biodiversity Ctr., 2001—. Fellow: Am. Acad. Arts & Scis.; mem.: Ecological Soc. Am. (chair, aquatic ecology sect. 1995—97), Phi Beta Kappa, Sigma Xi. Office: Dept Integrative Biology Univ Calif Berkeley CA 94720-3140 Office Phone: 510-643-7776. Business E-Mail: mepower@socrates.berkeley.edu, mepower@berkeley.edu.

POWER, PEGGY ANN, elementary school educator; b. Chgo., Sept. 17, 1973; d. Edward and Lois Power. BA, U. Ill., Chgo., 1994, MEd, 1996, postgrad., 2004—. Cert. elem. sch. tchr., Ill. Rsch. asst. U. Ill., Chgo., 1991-96; sales asst. Chgo. Bd. Trade, 1991-96; spl. edn. tchr. Gladstone Elem. Sch. Chgo. Bd. Edn., 1995—. Poet: Outstanding Poets of 1994, Best Poems of the 90's, 1992, Distinguished Poets of America, 1993. Active Wis. Dairy Coun., 1996—, Lawry's Menu for Success, Chgo., 1996—, After-Sch. Acad. Ctr., Chgo., 1996—; rep. Chgo. Tchr.'s Union, 1997—, bd. dirs., elem. v.p., 2004—, IFT/AFT del., 2004—. Recipient Gwendolyn Brookes Poet Laureat award, 1990; Baer-Darfler scholar Morgan Park Women's Assn., 1994-96; Marilyn Mucha fellow U. Ill., Chgo., 1995. Mem. ASCD, Coun. Exceptional Children, Nat. Coun. Tchrs. English, U. Ill. Chgo. Alumni Club, Pi Lambda Theta. Democrat. Roman Catholic. Avocations: Karate, poetry, pottery, kayaking. Home: Apt 407 710 Oakton St Evanston IL 60202-2927 Personal E-mail: peggypower@juno.com.

POWER, SAMANTHA J., public policy educator, writer; b. Dungarvan, Ireland, Sept. 21, 1970; arrived in US, 1979; m. Cass Sunstein, July 4, 2008. BA, Yale U., 1993; JD, Harvard U. Law Sch., 1999. Reporter covering wars in former Yugoslavia US News & World Report and Economist, 1993—96; polit. analyst Internat. Crisis Group; prof. John F. Kennedy Sch. Govt., Harvard U., Cambridge, 2000—, founding exec. dir. Carr Ctr. for Human Rights Policy, 1998—2002, Anna Lindh prof. practice of global leadership and pub. policy; fgn. policy fellow to Senator Barack Obama US Senate, 2005—06; fgn. policy columnist Time mag., 2007—; sr. fgn. policy adviser Barack Obama Presdl. Campaign, 2008; fgn. policy adviser Obama-Biden Presdl. Transition Team, 2008—. Author: A Problem from Hell: America and the Age of Genocide, 2003 (Pulitzer prize for gen. nonfiction, 2003, Nat. Book Critics Cir. award for gen. nonfiction, 2003, Artur Ross prize for best book in US fgn. policy, 2003), Chasing the Flame: Sergio Vieira de Mello and the Fight to Save the World, 2008; co-editor (with Graham Allison): Realizing Human Rights: Moving from Inspiration to Impact, 2000; contbr. articles to pubs. such as The New Yorker, NY Rev. Books, Washington Post, NY Times. Recipient Nat. Mag. award for best reporting, 2005. Democrat. Office: John F Kennedy Sch Govt Mailbox 14 79 JFK St Cambridge MA 02138 Office Phone: 617-495-3140. Office Fax: 617-495-4297. E-mail: samantha_power@harvard.edu.*

POWER, WILL, writer, composer, rap artist; Attended, San Francisco State U., NYU. Actor: (films) Drylongso, 1998; author, performer: (plays) The Gathering, 1999; Flow, 2003; writer, composer The Seven, 2006 (San Francisco Bay Area Theatre Critics Circle award for Best Book, 2001, Lucille Lortel award for Best Musical). Recipient Pathfinder award, Black Theater Network, 2002, Joyce award, 2005, Peter Zeisler Meml. award, 2006; fellow NY Found. Arts, 2005, US Artists, 2008. Office: c/o Thomas Pearson Internat Creative Mgmt 825 Eighth Ave New York NY 10019*

POWERS, ANTHONY RICHARD, JR., educational sales professional; b. Chgo., June 14, 1942; s. Anthony Richard and Bernadine Rene (Schwenke) P.; m. Marianne Fugiel, Mar. 15, 1980; children: Kathleen Mary, Anthony Richard III. BA, Quincy Coll., 1964; MS, U. Notre Dame, 1974. Cert. tchr., Ill. Sci. tchr. St. Rene Sch., Chgo., 1964-70; sci. coord. Queen of All Saints Sch., Chgo., 1970-76; sci. and math. product mgr. Ideal Sch. Supply Co., Oak Lawn, Ill., 1976-79, customer svc. mgr., 1980-83, Midwest sales mgr., 1983-85; nat. sales mgr. Ednl. Teaching Aids, Vernon Hills, Ill., 1985-89, v.p., 1989-97; accounts mgr. Numerical Algorithms Group, Downers Grove, Ill., 1997-2001; midwest acct. mgr. Freedom Sci., Vernon Hills, Ill., 2001—, midwest regional mgr., 2001—04, Texthelp Sys., 2004—; exec. dir., ptnr. Am. Coll. Edn., 2007—. Lectr., De Lourdes Coll., Des Plaines, Ill., 1970-78; sci. adviser, Archdiocese of Chgo., 1969-76. Author sci. edn. materials. Pres. Orchard Estates Condominium Assn., 1986-87; chmn. Vernon Hills Fire and Police Commn., 1995—. Mem. Northeastern Ill. Sci. Assn. (pres. 1970-75), U.S. Golf Assn., Internat. Brotherhood Magicians, K.C. Roman Catholic. Avocations: magic, music, golf. Home: 241 Tally Ho Dr Vernon Hills IL 60061-2900 Office: Texthelp Sys 241 Tally Ho Dr Vernon Hills IL 60061 Office Phone: 847-549-0344. Personal E-mail: arpnd74@aol.com. Business E-Mail: dpowers@texthelp.com.

POWERS, CHRISTOPHER SHERIDAN, science educator, web site designer; b. Denver, Aug. 10, 1971; s. Philip Stefan Powers and Janine Marie Harp; m. Mary Theresa Ciganek, July 28, 1994; 1 child, Myrrh Curie. BS, Oral Roberts U., Tulsa, Okla., 2007. Cert. tchr. State of Colo., 2009; Assn. Christian Schs. Internat., 2007. Sci. tchr. Christian Fellowship Sch., Lakewood, Colo., 1994—2007; tchr. Faith Christian Acad., Arvada, Colo., 2007—. Sci. tchr. adv. bd. mem. Current Sci. Mag., Lakewood, 2004—; presenter Colo. Sci. Conv., Denver, 2003. Author of poems, (dialogue) A Cost So Great (1st Pl. Nat. Original Dialogue Competition, 2006). Recipient Second Mile award, Christian Fellowship Sch., 1998, Exemplary Sch. Program award, Assn. Christian Schs. Internat., 2003. Mem.: Am. Inst. Biol. Scis. Conservative. Achievements include introduced a new type of volleyball serving style which has been widely adopted; design of volleyball coaching equipment made from PVC pipe; new junior volleyball cheer that has been widely adopted. Avocations: writing, volleyball, movies, chess, reading. Office: Faith Christian HS 4890 Carr St Arvada CO 80002 Personal E-mail: xrosein3@yahoo.com.

POWERS, CLAUDIA MCKENNA, state legislator; b. Key West, Fla., May 28, 1950; d. James Edward and Claudia (Antrim) McKenna; children: Gregory, Theodore, Matthew, Thurston. BA in Edn., U. Hawaii, 1972; MA, Columbia U., 1975. Cert. tchr., N.Y. Mem. Greenwich Rep. Town Meeting, Conn., 1979-93, sec. bldg. com., 1982-84, sec. legis. com., 1986—88, 1990—93; mem. Conn. Ho. of Reps., Hartford, 1993—2008, ranking mem. govt. adminstrn. and elections com., 1995-96, asst. minority leader, 1997-98, vice chmn. Rep. bill rev. com., 1997—2004, chmn., 2007—08, house minority whip, 1999—2003, dep. minority leader, 2003—06, mem. spl. com. of inquiry into impeachment of the gov., 2004, dep. minority leader at large, 2007—08; columnist Hearst Newspapers, 2009—. Mem. editl. bd. Greenwich Mag., 1995-98. Conn. commr. Edn. Commn. of the States, 2000—, also mem. steering com.; campaign chmn. Greenwich Rep. Town Com., 1984, 85, chmn., 1986-90; sec. Rep. Round Table, Greenwich, 1988-90; bd. govs. Riverside Assn., Greenwich, 1987-91, sec., 1991-92; class mother Riverside Sch., Greenwich, 1984-90; mem. altar guild Christ Ch., Greenwich, 1990—, lay eucharistic min., 2004—; adminstrv. coord. Greenwich Teen Ctr., 1990-91; alt. del. Rep. Nat. Conv., New Orleans, 1984—, San Diego, 1996; v.p. LWV of Greenwich, 1990-91; bd. trustees Norwalk Maritime Ctr., 2001-07; bd. dirs. Gov.'s Prevention Partnership, 2004-07. Episcopalian. Home and Office: 15 Hendrie Ave Riverside CT 06878-1808

POWERS, DAVID LOUIS, lawyer; b. Bay City, Mich., Mar. 18, 1961; s. Earl Louis and Norma Beatrice (Ashcraft) P.; m. Cheryl Denise Wixson, June 1, 1991; children: Matthew Jacob, Michael Jonathan. BA, Alma Coll., 1983; JD, U. Detroit, 1986. Bar: Mich. 1986, US Dist. Ct. (ea. dist.) Mich. 1986, US Dist. Ct. (we. dist. 1987), US Ct. Appeals (6th cir.) 1990, US Supreme Ct. 2002. Ptnr. Lambert, Leser, Cook, Giunta & Smith, P.C., Bay City, Mich., 1986—2000, Smith, Martin, Powers & Knier, PC, Bay City, 2001—. Contbr. articles to profl. publs. Del. Bay County Rep. Conv., 1996-97; Vol. Action Ctr. of Bay County, Inc., dir. 1990-92. Named Superlawyer, Law and Politics Mag., 2006, Leader in Law; finalist Lawyer of Yr., Mich. Lawyers Weekly Newspaper, 2009. Mem. Bay County Bar Assn. (pres. 2000-01), Bay Area Landlords and Bus. Owners Assn. (v.p. 1988-90, dir. 1990-97), Bay Area C. of C. (dir. 2005), Bay City Downtown Mgmt. Bd. (chmn. 2002-03), Save Our Shoreline (v.p. 2001-08), Pub. Interest Adv. Group Internat. Upper-Great Lakes Study, Internat. Joint Commn. Lutheran. Home: 861 S Linwood Beach Rd Linwood MI 48634-9511 Office: Smith Martin Powers & Knier PC 900 Washington Ave Bay City MI 48708 Office Phone: 989-892-3924.

POWERS, DAVID RICHARD, educational administrator; b. Cambridge Springs, Pa., Apr. 5, 1939; s. William Herman and Elouise Fancheon (Fink) Powers; m. Mary Julia Ferguson, June 11, 1960. Student, Pa. State U., 1957-60; BA, U. Pitts., 1963, MA, 1965, PhD, 1971. Dir. CAS advising ctr. U. Pitts., 1966-68, asst. dean faculty, 1968-70, asst. to chancellor, 1970-76, assoc. provost, 1976-78, vice provost, 1978-79; v.p. for acad. affairs George Mason U., Fairfax, Va., 1979-82; vice chancellor for acad. affairs W.Va. Bd. Regents, Charleston, 1982-88; exec. dir. Minn. Higher Edn. Coord. Bd., St. Paul, 1989-94, Nebr. Coord. Commn. Post-secondary Edn., Lincoln, 1994—2005, exec. dir. emeritus, 2005. Prin. author: Making Participatory Management Work, 1983, Higher Education in Partnership with Industry, 1988; contbr. articles to Ednl. Record, Adult Learning, Forum for Applied Rsch. on Pub. Policy. Mem. bd. dirs. North Wfs Inst. Libr. Arts, founder mem. bd. trustees Western Govs. U. Grantee USOE Faculty Seminar, Taiwan, 1967, ARC Ctr. for Edn. & Rsch. with Industry Appalachian Regional Commn., 1983, Republic of China Sino-Am. Seminar, 1985; recipient Award for Acad. Quality W.Va. Coun. Faculty, 1986. Mem. State Higher Edn. Exec. Officers (past mem.), Western Coop. Ednl. Telecomm., Civil Air Patrol. Avocation: boating. Home: 6513 Spencer Ln Clinton WA 98236 Office Phone: 360-341-1533. Personal E-mail: davidpowers@whidbey.com.

POWERS, DAVID V., psychology professor, department chairman; 1 child, Hershfield. BS, La. State U., Baton Rouge, 1989; MA, Wash. U., St. Louis, 1993, PhD, 1995. Cert. clin. psychology Md., 1998. Asst. prof. Loyola Coll. Md., Balt., 1997—2003, assoc. prof., 2003—. Chair Loyola Psychology Dept., 2003—05, interim chair, 2008—. Mem.: APA, Psychologists Long Term Care, Soc. Clin. Geropsychology (pres. elect 2009). Achievements include research in clinical psychology of older adulthood. Office: Loyola Coll Md 4501 N Charles St Baltimore MD 21210 Business E-Mail: dpowers@loyola.edu.

POWERS, EDWARD ALTON, minister, educator; b. Jamestown, NY, Oct. 26, 1927; s. Leslie Edgar and Mabelle Florence (Alton) P.; children: Randall Edward, Christopher Alan, Ann Lynn. BA, Coll. of Wooster, 1948; MDiv, Yale U., 1952; EdD, Columbia U., 1973. Ordained to ministry Congl. Ch., 1951. Pastor, Hamden, Conn., 1949-53, Pleasant Hill, Ohio, 1953-56; sec. dept. youth work Congl. Christian Ch. Bd. Home Missions, 1956-60; gen. sec. divsn. Christian edn., bd. home missions Congl. and Christian Chs., 1960-61; divsn. Christian edn., bd. homeland ministries United Ch. of Christ, 1962-73; gen. sec., divsn. evangelism, edn., ch. ext. United Ch. Bd. Homeland Ministries, 1973-79; mem. faculty Inst. Mgmt. Competency, Am. Mgmt. Assn., NYC, 1980-87; affiliate faculty Milano, New Sch. Mgmt. and Urban Policy, 1981—. Mem. program bd. divsn. edn. and ministry Nat. Coun. Chs., 1963-80; mem. edn. working group World Coun. Chs.; chmn. Peace Priority Team, United Ch. of Christ, 1970-75, adminstr., editor sexuality study, 1977; ptnr. Cane Powers Cons., and Powers, Wayno & Assocs., 1987-2003. Author: Journey Into Faith, 1964, Signs of Shalom, 1973, (with Rey O'Day) Theatre of the Spirit, 1980, In Essentials Unity, 1982, Youth in the Global Village, 1982; also articles. Home: 7 Gramercy Park W Apt 5B New York NY 10003-1759 Home Phone: 212-529-4081; Office Phone: 212-229-5400 ext. 1520. Personal E-mail: powersea@aol.com.

POWERS, EDWARD LEWIS, theater educator; b. Clarksville, Tenn., May 23, 1956; s. Vester and Cecille Powers. MFA, U. Memphis, 1986. Drama dir. Waynesburg U., Pa., 2000—. Mem.: Christians Theatre Arts, Southeastern Theatre Conf. Democrat. Methodist. Avocations: history, theater, travel. Office: Waynesburg Univ 51 W College St Waynesburg PA 15370 Business E-Mail: epowers@waynesburg.edu.

POWERS, ELIZABETH WHITMEL, lawyer; b. Charleston, SC, Dec. 16, 1949; d. Francis and Jane Coleman P.; m. Henry C. B. Lindh, June 16, 2000. AB, Mt. Holyoke Coll., 1971; JD, U. S.C., 1978. Bar: SC 1978, NY 1979. Law clk. to justice S.C. Cir. Ct., Columbia; with Reid & Priest, NYC, 1978—87, Dewey & LeBoeu LLP, NYC, 1997—; ptnr. Dewey & LeBoeuf, LLP, NYC, 2004—, exec. com., 2007—; chmn. Womens Initiatives Com., 2007—, mem., leadership com., corp. dept. policy com., diversity com. Exec. editor S.C. Law Rev., Columbia, 1977-78. Vol. N.Y. Jr. League, NYC, 1983—; bd. dirs. The Seamen's Ch. Inst., 1996—2006, sec., 1999—2006. Recipient Caandall Close Bowles award, Ashley Hall Sch., 2009. Mem.: ABA.

POWERS, JAMES MATTHEW, neuropathologist, educator, researcher; b. Cleve., Sept. 15, 1943; s. Alfred Patrick and Margaret Anne (Gunther) P.; m. Karen P. Smith, 1983; children: Kristin, Scott, Conor. BS in Biology, Manhattan Coll., 1965; MD, Med. U. SC, Charleston, 1969. Diplomate in anatomic pathology and neuropathology Am. Bd. Pathology. Dir. electron micros. lab. VA Hosp., Charleston, 1973-76; asst. prof. pathology Med. U. SC, Charleston, 1973-76, assoc. prof. pathology, 1976-80, prof. pathology, 1980-88; vice chmn. dept. pathology Columbia Coll. Physicians and Surgeons, NYC, 1989-92; prof., dir. neuropathology U. Rochester, 1992—2005, assoc. chair of edn., 1994-97, dir. residency tng. program, 1994—2003, prof. pathology and lab. medicine. Sec. Biol. Stain Commn., 1994—2001. Author: (practice guidelines) Archives Pathology and Laboratory Medicine, 1995, Greenfield's Neuropathology, 2002; mem. editl. bd.: Human Pathology, 1991—2005, Brain Pathology, 1995—2000, Acta Neuropathologica, 1995—2005, Biotech. and Histochemistry, 1994—2001, Modern Pathology, 1996—2004, Neurology, 1999—2004, Am. Jour. Surg. Pathology, 1999—2005, Jour. Neuropath. Exptl. Neurology, 2000—06; contbr. chpt. to book, articles to profl. jours. Mem. Internat. Soc. Neuropathology (v.p. 1994-97), Am. Assn. Neuropathologists (pres. 1993, Moore award 1975, 76, 77, 81, Lifetime Achievement award for Meritorious Contbns. to Neuropathology 2007), US-Can. Acad. Pathology. Office: U Rochester Sch Medicine and Dentistry Box 626 601 Elmwood Ave Rochester NY 14642 Office Phone: 585-275-3201. Office Fax: 585-273-1027. E-mail: james_powers@urmc.rochester.edu.

POWERS, JOAN, artist, photographer, educator; d. Charles Edward Mattingley and Doris Kathleen Turnell; children: Jacqueline, Julie, Michael Dotter, Peter Dotter. MFA, CUNY Bklyn. Coll., 1976. Dir. photography C. W. Post Long Island U., Brookville, NY, 1981—, sr. prof., 2008; edn. editor Photoworkshop.com, 2004—05. Photography exhbns., Off Wall, Souvenirs, Heart Gallery Nat. Exhbn., Texas Revisited, More Than Still Life, 21 one person and 55 group person exhbns., Japan, Russia, Italy, Korea, US, 1980—2008. Recipient David Newton award, Long Island U., 1993; Heart grant, Union County, NJ, 1998. Mem.: Profl. Women Photographers, Nat. Assn. Photoshop Profl., Soc. Photog. Edn. Avocations: travel, woodworking. Personal E-mail: joanpowersphoto@aol.com.

POWERS, LINDA SUE, biophysicist, educator, biomedical engineer; b. Pitts., Feb. 8, 1948; d. Luther Thurston and Helen Grace (Currence) Powers. BS in Physics and Chemistry, Va. Poly. Inst. and State U., 1970; MA in Physics, Harvard U., 1972, PhD in Biophysics, 1976. Mem. tech. staff AT&T Bell Labs., Murray Hill, N.J., 1976-88; dir. bio-catalysis sci. ctr., prof. chemistry & biochemistry Utah State U., Logan, 1988-91, prof. elec. engring., biol. & irrigation engring., 1991—2006; dir. Nat. Ctr. for the Design of Molecular Function, 1991—; Thomas R. Brown prof. bioengring., prof. elec. and computer engring. U. Ariz., Tucson, 2007—. Adj. prof. U. Pa. Med. Sch., Phila., 1978-2000; vis. fellow Princeton U., 1981-82. Mem. editl. corr. Comments Molecular Cellular Biophysics, 1980-89; editl. bd. Biophysics Jour., 1989-96, editl. bd. Am. Inst. of Physics Internat. Series Basic and Applied Biol. Physics, 1993—, Wiley Encyclopedia of Biomedical Engineering, 2002-05; contbr. numerous articles to profl. jours. and books. Recipient 1st U.S. Bioenergetics award, 1982, State of Utah Gov.'s medal for sci. and tech., 1994. Fellow Am. Phys. Soc. (divsn. biol. physics 1988-92, exec. bd. 1977-83, chmn. 1984-85, fellow com. mem.), Am. Inst. Chemists, IEEE (steering com. 2002-03), AAAS, NAS (com. chem. and biol. terrorism, 1997-98, com. countering agr. bioterrorism 2001-02), Biophys. Soc., Soc. Applied Spectroscopy, Sigma Pi Sigma, Phi Lambda Upsilon. Avocations: breeding and showing horses, writing music, windsurfing, snowboarding. Office: Univ Ariz Dept Elec and Computer Engring PO Box 210104 Tucson AZ 85721-0104 Business E-Mail: lsp@ece.arizona.edu.

POWERS, MARY ELLEN, lawyer; b. Cleve., 1955; AB, Oberlin Coll., 1977; JD, Univ. Va., 1980. Bar: DC 1980, admitted to practice: US Dist. Ct. for DC 1981, US Ct. of Appeals, DC Cir. 1982, US Ct. of Appeals, Fifth Cir. 1987, US Supreme Ct. 1996. Ptnr.-in-charge DC office Jones Day, Washington. Mem.: DC Bar Assn. (pro bono com.). Office: Jones Day 51 Louisiana Ave Washington DC 20001-2113 Office Phone: 202-879-3870. Office Fax: 202-626-1700. Business E-Mail: mepowers@jonesday.com.

POWERS, MATTHEW DOUGLAS, lawyer; b. San Francisco, July 7, 1959; BS, Northwestern U., 1979; JD cum laude, Harvard Law Sch., 1982. Bar: Calif. 1982, Dist. Ariz., US Dist. Ct. (no. dist. Calif.) 1982, US Dist. Ct. (ctrl. dist. Calif.) 1983, US Ct. Appeals (9th cir.) 1983, US Dist. Ct. (ea. dist. Calif.) 1985, US Ct. Appeals (fed. cir.) 1986, US Supreme Ct. 1988, US Ct. Internat. Trade 1990, US Dist. Ct. (so. dist. Tex.) 1990, US Dist. Ct. (no. dist. Ind.) 1991, US Dist. Ct. (ea. dist. Mich.) 2003, US Ct. Appeals (2nd, 5th, and 7th cirs.) 1991, US Dist. Ct. (ea. dist. Mich.) 2003. Head, mng. ptnr., global patent litig. grp. Weil, Gotshal & Manges, LLP, Redwood City, Calif., mem. mgmt. com. Lectr. in field; tchr. patent litig. U. Calif. Boalt Hall Sch. Law, Berkeley; lectr. patent law Stanford U., Santa Clara U.; mem. adv. bd. Inst. Transitional Arbitration; mem. exec. com. Boalt Hall, Berkeley Ctr. for Law & Tech., Santa Clara U. Sch. Law, High Tech. Law Inst.; mem. No. Dist. Calif. Patent Rules Com., No. Dist. Calif. Patent Jury Instrn. Com.; chmn. Internat. Patent Law Subcommittee, 1989; mem. ICC Commn. on Intellectual and Indsl. Property, 1990. Editor-in-chief Intellectual Property & Tech. Law Jour., co-editor-in-chief Jour. of Propriety Rights, mem. editl. bd. Mealey's Litig. Reports: Intellectual Property, Internat. Litig. Quarterly, 1991, published (numerous articles). Mem. leadership coun. Am. Diabetes Assn., San Francisco; bd. dirs. Greater Bay Area Make-A-Wish Found.; mem. exec. com. Orientation in In USA Law Prog., U. Calif. Named The "Go To" Patent Litigator in No. Calif., The Recorder, 2003, Father of Yr., Father's Day Coun. San Francisco, 2004, Trial Lawyer of Yr., Santa Clara County Trial Lawyers Assn., 2005, Calif. Lawyer Atty. of Yr. in Intellectual Property, Calif. Lawyer mag., 2005; named a Leading Lawyer, PLC Which Lawyer?, 2006; named one of The 8 Star Attys. in all fields in the US, Chambers Global Guide, 2001, The Top 10 Attys. in Silicon Valley, The Lawyer (London), 2001, The Top 100 Attorneys in the World, 2001, The 7 Top IP Trial Lawyers in the Country, IP Worldwide, 2002, The Top 25 IP Lawyers in Calif., San Francisco Daily Jour., 2003, The Top 25 Attorneys in All Fields in the San Francisco Bay Area, San Francisco Chronicle, 2003, The Top 45 Attorneys Under 45, The Am. Lawyer mag., 2003, The Nation's Top Litigators, The Nat. Law Jour., 2006. Mem.: ABA. Office: Weil Gothal & Manges LLP 201 Redwood Shores Pky Redwood City CA 94065 Office Phone: 650-802-3200. Office Fax: 650-802-3100. E-mail: matthew.powers@weil.com.

POWERS, PAUL J., manufacturing executive; b. Boston, Feb. 5, 1935; s. Joseph W. and Mary T. Powers; m. Barbara Ross, June 3, 1961; children: Briana, Gregory, Jeffrey. BA in Econs., Merrimack Coll., 1956; MBA, George Washington U., 1962. Various mfg. and fin. positions with Chrysler Corp., Detroit and overseas, 1963-69; v.p., gen. mgr. Am. Standard, Dearborn, Mich., 1970-78; pres. Abex-Dennison, Columbus, Ohio, 1978-82; group v.p. Comml. Intertech Corp., Youngstown, Ohio, 1982-84, pres., chief ops. officer, 1984-87, chmn., pres., CEO, 1987-00, Chairman of the Compensation Committee Chairman of the Compensation Committee and member of the Executive Committee., Chairman of the Compensation Committee and member of the Executive Committee and Nominating and Governance Committee. Bd. dirs. 1st Energy Corp., Twin Disc, Inc., Global Marine Inc., CUNO, Inc., 19 96—. Bd. dirs. Youngstown Symphony, 1984-88. Lt. USNR, 1957-63. Mem. NAM (bd. dirs. 1986-93, 95—), Nat. Fluid Power Assn. (bd. dirs. 1984-87), Mfrs. Alliance (bd. dirs. 1995—), Youngstown Area C. of C. (bd. dirs. 1990—). Office: Commercial Intertech Corp PO Box 239 Youngstown OH 44501-0239

POWERS, PAULINE SMITH, psychiatrist, educator, researcher; b. Sept. 23, 1941; m. Henry P. Powers; children: Jessica, Samantha. AB in Math., Washington U., 1963; MD, U. Iowa, Iowa City, 1971. Med. intern Emanuel Hosp., Portland, Oreg., 1971-72; psychiatry resident U. Iowa, Iowa City, 1972-74, U. Calif., Santa Barbara, 1974-75; from asst. prof. to assoc. prof. psychiatry Coll. Medicine U. So. Fla., Tampa, 1975-85, prof., 1985—, dir. eating disorder program, 1979—, dir. psychosomatic medicine divsn., 1979—. Author: Obesity: The Regulation of Weight, 1980; editor: The Current Treatment of Anorexia Nervosa and Bulimia, 1984; co-editor: (with J. Yager and P. Powers) Clinical Manual of Eating Disorders, 2007. Fellow: Am. Psychiat. Assn. (Rush Gold Outstanding Exhibit medal 1976, Dorfman Jour. Paper award 1987); mem.: Nat. Eating Disorders Assn. (pres.-elect 2003—05, pres. 2005—06, Lifetime Achievement award 2006), Acad. Eating Disorders (founding pres., Women Helping Women award 1995, Profl. Excellence award 1997, Outstanding Clinician award 2000). Office: U So Fla Coll Medicine Dept Psychiatry 3515 E Fletcher Ave Tampa FL 33613-4706 Home Phone: 813-971-5804; Office Phone: 813-974-2926. Business E-Mail: ppowers@health.usf.edu.

POWERS, RICHARD EDWARD, JR., lawyer; b. Evanston, Ill., July 20, 1952; s. Richard Edward and Helen Lufen Powers; m. Diane Wojda, Aug. 12, 1978. BS, Gonzaga U., 1974; JD, U. Notre Dame, 1977. Bar: Tex. 1977, DC 1979. Ptnr. Butler & Binion LLP, Washington, 1977-99, Dorsey & Whitney LLP, Washington, 1999—2005, Venable LLP, Washington, 2005—. Bd. regents Gonzaga Univ.; mem. Bretton Woods Com. Mem.: ABA, Internat. Bar Assn., Energy Bar Assn., DC Bar Assn., Tex. Bar Assn. Home: 5233 Elliott Rd Bethesda MD 20816-2910 Office: Venable LLP 575 7th St NW Washington DC 20004 Office Phone: 202-344-4360. Office Fax: 202-344-8300. Business E-Mail: repowers@venable.com.

POWERS, RICHARD GERARD, history educator; b. Rochester, NY, Jan. 26, 1949; s. Albert Dominic and Evelyn Rogers Powers; m. Patricia Marie Maslyn, May 29, 1971. BA in History, SUNY, Brockport, NY, 1971, postgrad., 1971—75. Tchr. US history, govt. and European history H.W. Schroeder H.S., Webster, NY, 1971—. Recipient Excellence Secondary Sch. Tchg. award, U. Rochester, 2000, Spl. Recognition award Excellence Tchg., Tufts U., 2000. Office: Webster Central School District 875 Ridge Road Webster NY 14580 Personal E-mail: gems158@aol.com. E-mail: dick_powers@websterschools.org.

POWERS, ROBERT P., electric power industry executive; B in Biology, Tufts U., Medford, Mass., 1975; M in Radiol. Hygiene, U. NC, 1976. Cert. sr. reactor operator 1991. Radiation protection engr. Pacific Gas & Electric Co., San Francisco, 1982; sr. engr. radiation protection Diablo Canyon Nuc. Generating Sta., 1984, radiation protection mgr., 1987, dir. mech. maintenance, 1991, mgr. site svcs., 1992, mgr. quality svcs., 1993, mgr. ops. svcs., 1996, v.p., 1996; sr. v.p. nuc. generation Am. Electric Power Svc. Corp., 1998, exec. v.p. nuc. and tech. svcs., 2001—03, exec. v.p. generation, 2003—06, exec. v.p. AEP Utilities - East, 2004—07, pres. AEP Utilities, 2008—. Office: Am Electric Power Svc Corp 1 Riverside Plz Columbus OH 43215-2373 Office Phone: 614-716-1000.

POWERS, RONALD GEORGE, management consultant; s. Lee Whitney and R. Anne Powers; m. Elizabeth Braislin McClellan, July 24, 1980. Chmn. Boardroom Advisors, Inc., Winter Park and Tampa, Fla., The Strategic Mgmt. Adv. Group, Inc., Winter Park and Tampa, Fla., CEO Adv. Group LLC, Chandler, Ariz. Adviser to chief execs. of banks, corps. and govts. on strategic mgmt. issues, 1971—. Mem. Interlachen C. of C. Republican. Office: 3800 S Cantabria Circle Ste 1048 Chandler AZ 85248 Office Phone: 480-306-8595. Personal E-mail: theceoadvisor@mindspring.com. E-mail: boardroomadvisor@mindspring.com.

POWERS, ROSS, Olympic athlete; b. Bennington, Vt., Feb. 10, 1979; Mem. U.S. Snowboard Team; olympic gold medalist in halfpipe, 2002; founder Ross Powers Found., 2001. Recipient 2nd pl., 1992, 3rd pl., 1993, 1st pl., World Cup, 1995, 1996, 2nd pl., 1995, 3rd pl., 1995, 2nd pl., 1996, 3rd pl., 1996, 1st pl., World Championship, 1996, 2nd pl., World Cup, 1997, Bronze medal in Snowboarding (Halfpipe), Nagano Olympics, Japan, 1998, 1st pl., World Championship, 2000, Gold medal, NBC Gravity Games, 2000, TNT Winter Goodwill Games, 2000, Silver medal, ESPN X Games, 2000, Bronze medal, 2001, Gold medal in Snowboarding (Halfpipe), Olympic games, 2002; named Nat. Champion, 1993, 1994, 1997, Grand Prix Champion, FIS World and Overall Champion, 1998, US Open title, 1998. Home: PO Box 186 Londonderry VT 05148-0186

POWERS, ROY DARYL, JR., engineering educator; b. Abingdon, Va., May 4, 1939; s. Roy Daryl Powers, Sr. and Lillian Gladys Powers; m. Carole Lee Shiflett, Feb. 10, 1962; children: Lisa Carole, Susan Lynn. BS in Physics, Va. Poly. Inst., Blacksburg, 1967. Cert. fiber optics technician, Miss. State U., 1997. Gen. sci. tchr. Washington County Sch. Sys., Va., 1962—63; inspector Va. Dept. Hwys., 1963—66; process engr. Radford Army Ammunition Plant, Va., 1966—70; pvt. practice consumer electronic bus. ptnr., 1970—73; instr. electronic engring. tech. NE Cmty. Coll., Blountville, Tenn., 1973—76; asst. prof. indsl. and engring. tech. Mountain Empire Cmty. Coll., Big Stone Gap, Va., 1976—2008; ret., 2008. Contbr. scientific papers in field. Conservation supr. Am. Cave Conservation Assn., Horse Cave, Ky., 1982—2008; mem., chmn. Va. Cave Bd., Richmond, 1982—96. Recipient Jane Whitson award, Tenn. Nature Conservancy, 1990, Pres. award, Nature Conservancy, 1991; named Conservationist of Yr., Va. Nature Conservancy, 1992, Hon. Citizenship of Louisville, City of Louisville, 1997, Hon. Life Dir., Am. Cave Conservation, 2005. Mem.: Am. Cave Conservation Assn. (pres. 1997—2001), Nat. Speleological Soc. (va. region conservation chmn. 1977—78), Mountain Empire Grotto (life; vice-chmn. 1975—76). Achievements include design of first workable cave gates that protect endangered species of bats; discovery of why the endangered gray bat would not use bat gates and designed a type that they would use. Avocation: woodworking. Home: Rt 1 Box 153 Duffield VA 24244 Office: Mountain Empire Cmty Coll 3441 Mountain Empire Rd Big Stone Gap VA 24244 Business E-Mail: rpowers@me.vccs.edu.

POWERS, SCOTT, television producer, actor; b. Chgo., Aug. 23, 1948; s. Raymond Alford and Ruby Marilyn (Ivacko) P. BS, Ithaca Coll., 1970; MBA, Fairleigh Dickinson U., 1971. Producer Young & Rubicam, Inc.,

NYC; account exec. Kelly, Nason, Inc., NYC; sr. account exec. Bozell & Jacobs, Inc., NYC; account supr. Foote, Cone & Belding, Inc., NYC; actor NYC, LA, 1982—; pres. Scott Powers Prodns., Inc., NYC, 1988—. Pres. CaribCom, Inc., NYC, 1996—. Author: Here's Looking At You!, 1997; contbr. articles to publs.; cartoonist Thankyounext, 1990—. Mem. Better Bus. Bur. NYC, 1991—, Knickerbocker Rep. Club, NYC, 1971—; bd. dirs. Profl. Comedians Assn., NYC, 1988-91, v.p., 1989-91; bd. dirs. One World Arts Found., 1992—; judge Internat. Film and TV Festivals, NYC, 1991—. Mem. AFTRA (bd. dirs. 1989-91), SAG, Actor's Equity Assn., NATAS (judge Emmys 1985—), NYC C.of C., Met. Club, NY Athletic Club, Players Club, Mensa, Intertel. Republican. Congregationalist. Avocations: skiing, sailing, tennis, squash, international river running. Home: 180 Central Park S New York NY 10019-1562 Office: Scott Powers Studios Inc 135 W 29th St Ste 404 New York NY 10001

POWERS, SCOTT, medical association administrator; PhD, Columiba U., NYC, 1983. CSO, dir. rsch. Amplicon Cancer Genomics, Greenlawn, 1995—2004; dir. human cancer genome ctr. Cold Spring Harbor Lab., Woodbury, 2004—. Democrat.

POWERS, THOMAS MOORE, writer; b. NYC, Dec. 12, 1940; s. Joshua Bryant and Susan (Moore) P.; m. Candace Molloy, Aug. 21, 1965; children: Amanda, Susan, Cassandra. BA, Yale U., 1964. Reporter Rome (Italy) Daily American, 1965-67, U.P.I., NYC, 1967-70; freelance writer, 1970—; contbg. editor The Atlantic mag.; editor, founding ptnr. Steerforth Press, Hanover, NH, 1993—. Author: Diana: The Making of a Terrorist, 1971, The War at Home, 1973, The Man Who Kept the Secrets: Richard Helms and the CIA, 1979, Thinking About the Next War, 1982, Total War: What It Is, How It Got That Way, 1988, Heisenberg's War: The Secret History of the German Bomb, 1993, The Confirmation, 2000, Intelligence Wars: American Secret History from Hitler to Al Qaeda, 2002, The Military Error: BagHad & Beyond in America's War of Choice, 2008. Recipient Pulitzer prize for nat. reporting, 1971 Mem. PEN Am. Center, Council on Fgn. Relations. Address: 206 Chelsea St South Royalton VT 05068-9800 also: Lit Rep Lynn Nesbit 445 Park Ave New York NY 10022-2606 Office Phone: 802-763-8585. E-mail: tom@steerforth.com.

POWERS, TIMOTHY H., electric power industry executive; Sr. positions ABB, Inc., BBC Brown Boveri, Inc.; sr. v.p., CFO Hubbell Inc., 1998—2001, pres., CEO, 2001—04, bd. dir., 2001—, chmn., pres., CEO, 2004—. Office: c/o Hubbell 584 Derby Milford Rd Orange CT 06477

POWERS, WILLIAM CHARLES, JR., academic administrator, law educator; b. 1946; BA, U. Calif., Berkeley, 1967; JD, Harvard U., 1973. Bar: Wash. 1974, Tex. 1980. Law clk. to Hon. E. A. Wright U.S. Ct. Appeals (9th cir.), Seattle, 1973-74; asst. prof. Wash. U., Seattle, 1974-77, assoc. prof., 1977-78; prof. law U. Tex., Austin, 1978—, assoc. dean acad. affairs, 1984—87, 1994—95, univ. disting. prof. and Hines H. Baker and Thelma Kelly Baker chair in law, 1997—, John Jeffers Rsch. Chair in law, 2000—, dean Sch. Law, 2000—06, pres., 2006—. Chair Spl. Investigation Com. Enron Corp. Author: Texas Products Liability Law, 1992; co-author: Cases and Materials in Torts, 1998, Cases and Materials in Products Liability, 2002. Mem.: Am. Law Inst. Office: U Tex at Austin Office of Pres PO Box T Austin TX 78713-8920 Home: 3600 Murillo Cir Austin TX 78703 Home Phone: 512-472-7831; Office Phone: 512-232-1120. Office Fax: 512-471-6987. E-mail: wpowers@law.utexas.edu.*

POWLES, TREVOR JAMES, physician, oncologist; b. London, Mar. 8, 1938; s. Leonard William David and Florence Irene (Conolly) P.; m. Penelope Margaret Meyers, July 27, 1968; children: James Watson, Thomas Bartholomew, Lucy Alexandra. BSc, St. Bartholomews Med. Coll., London, 1961, MB, BS, 1964; PhD, Inst. Cancer Rsch., London, 1975. House physician, registrar Royal Postgrad. Med. Sch., London, 1967-68; registrar St. Bartholomews Hosp., London, 1969-70; rsch. fellow Med. Rsch. Coun., London, 1971-72; sr. lectr. Inst. Cancer Rsch., London, 1973-75; cons. physician Royal Marsden Hosp., London, 1975—2003; head of breast cancer unit, 1993—2003; prof. breast oncology Inst. Cancer Rsch., London, 1998—; cons. breast oncologist St. Anthony's Hosp., London, 2002—, Parkside Hosp., London, 2002—, The Liste Hosp., London, 2002—. Vis. prof. MD Anderson Cancer Ctr., Houston, 1993, Dana Farber Cancer Ctr., Harvard, Boston, 1996, Tom Baker Cancer Ctr., Calgary, Can., 1998; dir. Advance Cytometrix Inc., San Francisco, 1993-96, Oncotech Inc., Irvine, 1996—, Neothermia Inc., Dublin, Ohio, 1998—. Co-author, editor: (books) Breast Cancer Management, 1981, Prostaglandins and Cancer, 1982, Medical Management of Breast Cancer, 1991; contbr. articles to profl. jours. Recipient All Parties Parliamentary award for outstanding achievement in Breast Cancer, 2003, Brinker award, Susan G. Komen Found., 2005. Mem. Internat. Assn. Cancer Prevention (v.p. 1995—), Breast Cancer Rsch. Trust (trustee 1975—), U.K. Breast Cancer Coordinating Com. Avocations: horse riding, skiing, reading. Office: The Parkside Oncology Clinic 49 Parkside Wimbledon London Sw19 5NB England*

POWLEY, EDWARD HARRISON, III, music educator; s. Edward Harrison and Elizabeth Frances (Malinowski) P.; m. Ellen Mildred Lockwood, June 12, 1967; children: William, Barrett, Martha, Edward, Philip, Julianne, Sarah. MusB, Eastman Sch. Music, Rochester, NY, 1965, MA, 1968, PhD, 1969. Percussionist Rochester Philharm. Orch., NY, 1966—68; asst. prof. Sch. Music, Brigham Young U., Provo, Utah, 1969—75, assoc. prof., 1975—82, prof. music, 1982—, chair, 1986—. Editor: Symphonies of Druschetzky, 1985, Il Trionfo di Dori, 1990; contbr. articles to profl. jours. Pres. Am. Musical Instrument Soc., 1999—2003. Grantee NDEA, 1966, Fulbright, Vienna, Austria, 1965-66; Alcuin fellowship gen. edn., 2001-03, Karl G. Maeser gen. edn. professorship, 2004- Brigham Young U. Mem. Am. Musicol. Soc. (chmn. local chpt. 1986-87, 94-95, nat. coun. 1985-87), Percussive Arts Soc. (chmn. rsch. com. 1977-87), Internat. Musicol. Soc, Soc. Am. Music, Coll. Music Soc., Am. Musical Instrument Soc. (v.p. 1995-99, pres. 1999-2003). Mem. Lds Ch. Avocations: hiking, camping, genealogy. Office: Sch Music Brigham Young Univ C-550 HFAC Provo UT 84602

POWLEY, SUSAN ELIZABETH, lawyer; b. Schenectady, NY, Sept. 19, 1952; BA magna cum laude, Stetson U., DeLand, Fla., 1989; JD, Vanderbilt U., Nashville, 1992. Bar: Tex., U.S. Dist. Ct. (no., ea., so. dists.) Tex., U.S. Ct. Appeals (5th and fed. cirs.), U.S. Supreme Ct. Assoc. Johnson & Gibbs, PC, Dallas, 1992—95; assoc. counsel, spl. counsel Jenkens & Gilchrist, PC, Dallas, 1995—2005; of counsel Morgan, Lewis & Bockius, LLP, Dallas, 2005—08, Patterson & Sheridan LLP, Dallas, 2008—. Fellow: Dallas Bar Found. (life), Tex. Bar Found. (life); mem.: ABA, Am. Intellectual Property Law Assn., Copyright Soc. USA, Order of Coif, Phi Beta Kappa. Office: Patterson & Sheridan LLP 1700 Pacific Ave Ste 2650 Dallas TX 75201 Office Phone: 214-296-0156. Business E-Mail: spowley@pattersonsheridan.com.

POWSNER, EDWARD RAPHAEL, physician; b. NYC, Mar. 17, 1926; m. Rhoda Lee Moscovitz, June 8, 1950; children: Seth, Rachel, Ethan, David. SB in Elec. Engring., MIT, 1948, SM in Biology, 1949; MD, Yale U., 1953; MS in Internal Medicine, Wayne State U., 1957; MHSA, U. Mich. Diplomate Am. Bd. Nuclear Medicine, Am. Bd. Pathology in clin. pathology and anatomic pathology, Am. Bd. Internal Medicine; lic. physician, Mich. Intern Wayne County Gen. Hosp., Eloise, Mich., 1953-54, resident internal medicine, 1954-55, Detroit Receiving Hosp., 1955-56; fellow in hematology Wayne State U. and Detroit Receiving Hosp., 1957-58; clin. investigator VA Hosp., Allen Park, Mich., 1958-61, chief nuclear medicine svc., 1961-78; dir. clin. labs. Mich. State U., East Lansing, 1978-81; staff pathologist Ingham Med. Ctr., Lansing, Mich., 1978-81; dir. nuclear medicine St. John Hosp., Detroit, 1982-95. Rsch. asst. biology MIT, 1948-49, 50; asst. instr. medicine Wayne State U. Coll. Medicine, 1954-56, instr., 1959-61; assoc. prof. pathology Wayne State U. Sch. Medicine, 1961-68, assoc. medicine, 1961, prof. pathology, 1968-78; prof. pathology Mich. State U., 1978-81, assoc. chairperson, 1980-81, clin. prof., 1981-82; chief clin. labs. Detroit Gen. Hosp., 1969-73; chief lab. svcs. Health Care Inst., Wayne State U., 1976-78; mem. adv. coun. Nuclear Medicine Tech. Cert. Bd., 1990-91. Bd. editors Am. Jour. Clin. Pathology, 1963-76, 83-88; author 2 textbooks, 11 chpts., 50 peer reviewed papers, 17 abstracts and other publs. With U.S. Army, 1944-47. Mem. AMA (sect. coun. on pathology), Am. Soc. Clin. Pathologists (rep. 1987-89, 93-2000, govt. rels. com. 1993-95, mem. coun. nuclear medicine 1978-82, chmn. 1982-84), Am. Coll. Nuclear Physicians, Am. Soc. Nuclear Cardiology, Coll. Am. Pathologists, Detroit Acad. Medicine, Mich. Soc. Pathologists, Mich. State Med. Soc., Soc. Nuclear Medicine, Washtenaw County Med. Soc., Sigma Xi, Tau Beta Pi. Office: Eastside Nuclear Medicine 2370 E Stadium Blvd #315 Ann Arbor MI 48104-4810

POYADUE, FLORENE STEWART, nurse, foundation administrator; b. Lovejoy, Ill., Nov. 17, 1934; d. Charles Archibald and Florene (Walker) Stewart; m. Octave Anthony Poyadue, Sept. 30, 1956; children: Turhan Michael, Keith Matthew, Jill Alexandria, Dean Archibald. Diploma in nursing, St. Mary's Infirmary, St. Louis, 1955; BVE, San Jose State U., Calif., 1975; MA in Marriage, Family and Child Counseling, Santa Clara U., Calif., 1983, PhD (hon.) in Cmty. Svc., 1993. RN Calif. Staff nurse Charity Hosp., New Orleans, 1955—56; staff nurse, asst. head nurse, head nurse Providence Hosp., El Paso, Tex., 1957—65; staff nurse, supr. Muenchweiller Hosp., Germany, 1965—67; dir. nursing Rivera's Eastside Hosp., San Jose, 1968—69; program coord. Cubberly Adult Sch., Palo Alto, Calif., 1970—85; founder, CEO Parents Helping Parents, Inc., San Jose, 1976—98. Cons. FSP Enterprise, San Jose, 1998—2005; spkr., cons., presenter workshops in field. Co-author: The Parent to Parent Handbook, 2001; contbr. articles to profl. jours., chpts. to books; author: tng. manuals, course study materials, (poems) Moods in Poetry. Mem. adv. bd. Bridge Sch.; mem. PHP Cmty. Assocs. Bd. Recipient Earle Williams award, St. Mary's Infirmary, 1955, Golden Rule award, J. C. Penney, 1982, 1991, Citizen of Achievement award, AAUW, 1984, Svc. to Spl. Needs Families award, San Andreas Regional Ctr., 1984, Commendation, Bishop Diocese San Jose, 1985, Sen. Lloyd Bentson award, Surgeon Gen.'s Conf., 1987, Outstanding award, Santa Clara U., 1987, Ignatian award, 1988, Letter of Commendation, Calif. Gov. Deukmejian, 1989, Woman of Achievement award, San Jose Mercury News, Women's Fund, 1990, Inclusion award, State of Calif., 2000, Pope John 23d award, Italian Cath. Fedn., 2001, Infant Devel. Assn. State of Calif. award, 2003, numerous others; named Doer, San Jose Mercury News, 1985; named to Hall of Fame, South Bay Black Cmty., 1999; grantee Family of Achievement award, Joseph P. Kennedy Jr. Found., 1990. Mem.: South Bay Black Nurses Assn. (long range planning com. 1990—2003, Nurse of Yr.), Nat. Black Nurses Assn., St. John Vianney Sr. Club (mem. hospitality com.). Democrat. Roman Catholic. Avocations: bowling, dance, writing poetry, Scrabble. Office: Php Parents Helping Parents 1400 Parkmoor Ave Ste 100 San Jose CA 95126-3797

POYDASHEFF, ROBERT STEPHEN, lawyer; b. NYC, Feb. 13, 1930; s. Stephen Alexander Poydasheff and Pauline M. Miller; m. Anastasia Catherine Latto, Aug. 29, 1954; children: Catherine Alexandra, Robert Stephen Jr. BA in Polit. Sci., The Citadel, 1954; JD, Tulane U., 1957; MA, Boston U., 1966; diploma, Command and Gen. Staff Coll., 1969, Army War Coll., 1976; PhD (hon.), ITEP. Bar: S.C. 1958, Ga. 1979, US Supreme Ct. 1964, US Ct. Mil. Appeals, US Ct. Mil. Rev. 1964, US Dist. Ct. (fed. dist.) S.C. 1988, US Dist. Ct. (fed. and mid. dists.) Ga. 1987. Commd. 2d lt. U.S. Army, 1955, advanced through grades to col., 1975, ret., 1979; sr. v.p. SunTrust Bank of West Ga., Columbus, 1979-95; pvt. practice Columbus, 1995—. Instr. bus. law Am. U. Ext. Divsn., Ft. Benning, 1961-63; adj. prof. internat. law, Am. govt., and bus. law U. Md. Ext. Divsn., Berlin, 1964-67, Vietnam, 1967-68; adj. prof. Troy State U., Ft. Benning, Ga., 1976—; cons., exec. v.p. ATI-Allied Tech. Internat. Inc., Columbus, 1995—; past legal advisor to Sec. of Army and Sec. of Def. on mil. dependent sch. and labor rels. Contbr. commentaries, papers, and analyses to profl. jours. City councilor City of Columbus, 1996-2002; mayor of Columbus, Ga., 2003-07; bd. dir. Springer Opera House Assn., 1998—; trustee Ga. Coun. of Humanities, exec. com., 1998—; bd. edn. Ft. Benning Sch., 1976-79, chmn. pers. actions com., 1976-79; trustee Dr. Hosp., Columbia; bd. dirs. Columbus United Way, River Ctr. Performing Arts; past pres. Chattahoochee coun. Boy Scouts Am., Columbus; past pres. Chattahoochee Valley, Assn. of US Army, Anne Elizabeth Shepherd Home, Columbus Symphony, ARC; chmn. bd. dir. Leadership Morality Inst.; chmn. Civilian Mil. Coun., Ga. Govs. Commn. on Transp; bd. trustees Hughston Rehab. Hosp.; bd. visitor Brookstone Sch., Notable Citadel Alumnus. Decorated Legion of Merit with 2 oak leaf clusters, Bronze Star, Commendation medal with oak leaf cluster, Vietnam Svc. medal with four bronze stars, Order of St. George, Episcopal Ch., Inf. Order of St. Maurice; paratrooper badge; badge of The Army secretariet; recipient Ga. Govs. medal for the humanities, Outstanding Civilian Svc. medal U.S. Army, 2004; St. Michael the Anchangel medal G. Orthodox Metropolis, Red Cross Clara Barton award. Fellow Leadership Morality Inst.(chair of bd.); mem. Ga. Mcpl. Assn. (bd. dirs.), Columbus Bar Assn., C. of C. (mil. affairs com., bd. dirs.), Kiwanis, Masons (32 deg.), Sertoma Club Columbus (Svc. Mankind award), Phi Delta Phi, Pi Sigma Alpha. Republican. Avocations: walking, reading. Home: 6349 Mountainview Dr Columbus GA 31904-2213 Office: 944 2d Ave Columbus GA 31902 Office Phone: 706-317-3224. Personal E-mail: bobpoydasheff@bellsouth.net, bobnstacy5@aol.com.

POZA, ERNESTO, management consultant, educator; b. Havana, Cuba, Mar. 27, 1950; arrived in U.S., 1961; s. Hugo Ernesto and Carmen (Valle) Poza; m. Karen Elizabeth Saum, Oct. 14, 1978; 1 child, Kali Jennette. BS in Adminstrv. Sci., Yale U., New Haven, Conn., 1972; MS in Mgmt., MIT, Cambridge, 1974. Personnel mgr. rsch. Sherwin Williams Co., Chgo., 1974-75, orgn. specialist Cleve., 1975-77, dir. orgn. planning, 1977-79; pres., sr. mgmt. cons. E.J. Poza Assoc., Cleve., 1979—; prof. Weatherhead Sch. Mgmt. Case Western Res. U., Cleve., 1996—2006; prof. Thunderbird Sch. Global Mgmt., 2006—. Advisor Family Firm Inst., 1986; vis. lectr. Yale U., U. Chile, MIT, Sloan Sch. Mgmt.; mem. editl. bd. Family Bus. Rev., 1997—, Jour. Small Bus. Mgmt., 1997—; bd. dirs. Sky Fin. NE Ohio; mem. adv. bd. Mack Industries. Author: A la Sombra del Roble: La Empresa Privada Familiar y Su Continuidad, 1995, Smart Growth: Critical Choices for Business Continuity and Prosperity, 1997, La Empresa Familiar Por Dentro, 1998, Family Business, 2004, 2d edit., 2007, 3rd edit., 2009, Empresas Familiares, 2005; contbg. editor: Family Bus. Mag.; mem. editl. rev. bd. Family Bus. Rev. & Family Bus. Strategy; contbr. articles to profl. jours. Bd. dirs. Neighborhood Health Care, 1980, Family Firm Inst., 1990; mem. program com. United Way, Cleve., 1985, Hispanic Leadership, 1986. Fellow: Family Firm Inst. (sr.; founding mem. 1985, Richard Beckhard Practice award 1996); mem.: Acad. Mgmt. (entrepreneurship divsn. 1980—). Office Phone: 480-538-2120. Business E-Mail: poza@family-business.com, ernesto.poza@thunderbird.edu.

POZEN, ROBERT CHARLES, investment company executive; b. NYC, Aug. 8, 1946; s. Morris and Miriam Pozen; m. Elizabeth Kelner, Apr. 11, 1976; children: Joanna, David. BA, Harvard U., 1968; JD, Yale U., 1972, JSD, 1973. Bar: NY 1977, DC 1978, US Supreme Ct., US Ct. Appeals (4th, 5th, 7th, DC cirs.). Assoc. prof. law NYU, 1974-77; assoc. gen. counsel SEC, Washington, 1978-80; ptnr. Caplin & Drysdale, Washington, 1981-86; sr. v.p., gen. counsel, mng. dir. FMR Corp./Fidelity Investments, Boston, 1987—96; pres. Fidelity Mgmt. and Rsch. Co., Boston, 1997—2001; vice chmn. Fidelity Investments, Boston, 2001—02; sec. econ. affairs Commonwealth Mass., 2003; non-exec. chmn. Mass. Fin. Svcs. Investment Mgmt., Boston, 2004—. Mem. adv. bd., Securities Regulation Law Reporter Bur. Nat. Affairs, Washington, 1981; vis. lectr. Harvard Law Sch., Cambridge, Mass., 1986, John Olin Vis. Prof., 2002-03. mem. legal adv. com. NY Stock Exch., 1987; appt. mem. Commn. to Strengthen Social Security, 2001-02; bd. dirs. Bell Can. Enterprises., Medtronics, 2004- Author: Financial Institutions: Investment Mgmt. Cases, Materials and Problems, 1977; contbr. articles to profl. jours. Founder Fidelity Charitable Gift Fund, 1991. Mem. ABA (securities com. 1981—, employee retirement income security act 1985-86). Office: Medtronic Inc 710 Medtronic Pky Minneapolis MN 55432 Office Phone: 763-514-4000, 763-514-6272.*

POZNANSKI, ANDREW KAROL, pediatric radiologist; b. Czestochowa, Poland, Oct. 11, 1931; came to U.S., 1957, naturalized, 1964; s. Edmund Maurycy and Hanna Maria (Ceranka) P.; children: Diana Jean, Suzanne Christine. BSc, McGill U., 1952, MD CM, 1956. Diplomate: Am. Bd. Radiology, Royal Coll. Physicians and Surgeons Can. Intern Montreal (Que., Can.) Hosp., 1956-57; resident Henry Ford Hosp., Detroit, 1957-60, staff radiologist, 1960-68, U. Mich. Med. Center, Ann Arbor, 1968-79; co.-dir. pediatric radiology C.S. Mott Children's Hosp., Ann Arbor, 1971-79; radiologist-in-chief Children's Meml. Hosp., Chgo., 1979-99; prof. radiology U. Mich., 1971-79, Northwestern U. Med. Sch., 1979—. Bd. dirs. Nat. Coun. on Radiation Protection, 1983-90; mem. Internat. Commn. on Radiologic Protection, 1981-89; mem. adv. panel on radiologic devices FDA, 1975-77, chmn., 1976-77; trustee Am. Bd. Radiology, 1993-2003. Author: The Hand in Radiologic Diagnosis, 1974, 2d edit., 1983, Practical Approaches to Pediatric Radiology, 1976; co-author: Bone Displasias, An Atlas of Genetic Disorders of Skeletal Development, 2002 bd. editors: Skeletal Radiology, 1975-95, Radiographics, 1980-84, Pediatric Radiology, 1986-91. Mem.: AMA, Internat. Skeletal Soc. (founder, pres. 1992—94), John Caffey Soc., Radiol. Soc. N.Am., Soc. Pediatric Radiology (pres. 1980—81), Am. Roentgen Ray Soc. (pres. 1993—94), Polish Radiol. Soc. (hon.), Can. Assn. Radiologists (hon.), European Soc. Radiology (hon.), Alpha Omega Alpha. Home: 2400 N Lakeview Ave Chicago IL 60614-2747 Office: Childrens Meml Hosp 2300 N Childrens Plz Chicago IL 60614-3394 Office Phone: 773-880-3521. Business E-Mail: apoznanski@ameritech.net.

POZNER, LARRY S., lawyer, educator; b. Indpls., Nov. 13, 1947; BS in Bus. Adminstrn., U. Colo., 1969; JD, U. Calif., 1973. Bar: Colo. 1973. Dep. state pub. defender, 1973—77; pub. defender Colo. Springs, 1973—77, Denver, 1973—77; former lead counsel Broncos Football Club; ptnr. Reilly Pozner & Connelly, Denver. Adj. prof. law U. Denver, 1983—92, lectr., 1981—82, adj. asst. prof., 1982—85; with faculty Nat. Criminal Def. Coll., 1985—95; legal analyst NBC News, 1998—2000; lectr. on cross examination more than 200 times in 47 states & Canada. TV appearances include: NBC Nightly News; The Today Show; Fox News; CNN; NPR; Court TV; co-author (with Roger Dodd): Cross Examination: Science & Techniques, 2nd edit., 2005; contbr. articles to profl. jours. Mem.: Criminal Def. Bar (pres. 1985—86), Nat. Assn. Criminal Def. Lawyers (officer 1992, pres. 1998—99, immediate past pres. 1999—2000). Office: Reilly Pozner & Connelly The Kittredge Bldg 511 16th St Ste 700 Denver CO 80202 Office Phone: 303-893-6100. Office Fax: 303-893-6110. E-mail: lpozner@litigationcoloradox.com.

POZZATTI, RUDY OTTO, artist; b. Telluride, Colo., Jan. 14, 1925; s. Innocente and Mary L. (Mimiolla) P.; m. Dorothy I. Pozzatti, May 20, 1946; children: Valri Marie, Rudy Otto, Gina Maria, Mia Ines, Illica Lara. BFA, U. Colo., 1948, MFA, 1950, DHL, 1973. Mem. faculty dept. art U. Nebr., Lincoln, 1950-52, 53-56, Ind. U., Bloomington, 1956-91, prof. fine arts, 1964-91, disting. prof., 1975-91; ret., 1991; artist-in-residence Roswell Mus. and Art Ctr. One-man exhbns. include Cleve. Mus. Art, 1955, Whitney Mus. Am. Arts, NYC, 1961, Tyler Sch. Art, Rome, 1969, Sheldon Meml. Art Gallery U. Nebr., 1969, Mitchell Mus. Art, Mt. Vernon, Ill., 4 other sites, 1992-93, Ind. U. Art Mus., Bloomington, 2002, Evansville Mus. ARt, 2002; represented in permanent collections, Mus. Modern Art, NYC, Libr. Congress, Washington, Art Inst. Chgo., Cleve. Mus. Art. Served with AUS, 1943-46. Recipient George Norlin silver medal U. Colo., 1974; finalist Robert Foster Cherry award Baylor U., 2007; Fulbright grantee, 1952-53, 63-64, grantee US Dept. State, USSR, 1961, Yugoslavia, 1965, Brazil, 1974, Hungary, 1986; grantee Rockefeller Found., Bellagio, Italy, 1995; Guggenheim fellow, 1963-64; Fellow Ford Found., 1963, grantee, Japan, 1981. Mem. Soc. Am. Graphic Artists, Am. Color Print Soc., Coll. Art Assn. (bd. dirs.), Artists Equity Assn., Ind. Acad. (elected). Roman Catholic. Home Phone: 812-336-5645. Personal E-mail: rpozzatt@indiana.edu.

POZZO, RICCARDO, philosophy educator; b. Milan, June 7, 1959; s. Giancarlo and Carla (Rizzani) Pozzo; m. Annette Popel, Sept. 4, 1992; 1 child, Carlo. Laurea in Philosophy, U. Milan, 1983; Promotion in Philosophy, U. Saarland, Saarbrücken, 1988; Habilitation in Philosophy, U. Trier, 1995. Rsch. assoc. U. Saarland, 1984-85; fellow Deutscher akademischer Austauschdienst, 1985-97, Herzog August Bibliothek Wolfenbüttel, 1988-90, Alexander von Humboldt-Stiftung, 1990—98; h.s. tchr. Sch. Superintendency Lombardy, Milan, 1994-96; tchr. Cath. U. Am., Washington, 1996—2003, U. Verona, 2003—. Lectr. U. Trier, 1991—96. Author: Hegel: Introductio in Philosophiam, 1989, Kant und das Problem elner Einleitung, 1989, El giro kantiano, 1998, Georg Friedrich Meiers Verhunftlehre, 2000; editor: The Impact of Aristotelianism on Modern Philosophy, 2004, L'autore e i juoi diritti, 2005, Aristotele nella società contemporanea, 2006; editor: (with Karl-Otto Apel) Zur Rekonstruktion der praktischen Philosophie, 1990; editor: (with Michael Oberhausen) Vorlesungsverzeichnisse der Universität Königsberg 1720-1804, 1999; editor: (with Michael Oberhausen and Heinrich P. Delfosse) Vernunftkritik und Aufklärung, 2001; editor: (with

Heinrich P. Delfosse and Clemens Schwaiger) Meier-Index: Vernunftlehre, 2005; editor: (with Gregorio Piaia) Identika Nat., 2008; cons. editor: Longanesi Editore, 1988—89, Feltrinelli Editore, 1989—. Recipient 6th Study Tour of Japan, Japanese Ministry of Fgn. Affairs, 1984; named Amb. of Alexander von Humbolt Found., 2008. Mem.: Fedn. Internat. Socs. Philosophy (bd. dirs. 2008—), Soc. Filosofica Italiana (bd. dirs. 2005—), Soc. Medieval and Renaissance Philosophy, Hegel Soc. N.Am., Italian Soc. Kant Studies, N.Am. Kant Soc., Alexander von Humboldt Assn. Italy (sec., bd. dirs. 2003—), Alexander von Humboldt Assn. Am. (bd. dirs. 2002—03), Am. Philos. Assn., Villa Vigoni (bd. dirs. 2008—), Rotary Internat. (internat. dist. 2040 Milano Ovest). Roman Catholic. Avocation: contemporary literature. Office: via San Francesco 22 I-37129 Verona Italy Office Phone: +39/045/8028143. Business E-Mail: riccardo.pozzo@univr.it.

PRABHA, KARAN, lab administrator; b. Sirkali, Tamil Nadu, India, Feb. 25, 1949; s. Muthu Chidambaram and Rajeswari Muthu Pillai; m. Thenmozhi Prabha Pichayan; children: Vivek Prabha Karan, Vidhya Prabha Karan. PhD, U. Madras, India, 1980. V.p. Verne Medal Corp., La Jolla, Calif., 2003—07; chief sci. officer Am. Labs., Charlotte, NC, 2007—. Adj. prof. Fla. Internat. U., Miami, 2003—. Sponsor Indian Spelling Bee, Washington, 1991—96. Grant, Indian Govt, 1967—77. Mem.: Am. Chem. Soc. R-Liberal. Hindu. Avocations: photography, writing. Home: 4980 SW 133rd Ave Charlotte NC 28269 Office: Am Labs 9300 Harris Corners Pky Charlotte NC 28269 Office Fax: 704-254-6984. Personal E-mail: mprabha2@yahoo.com. Business E-Mail: prabha@poridigymeter.com.

PRABHAKAR, KUMKUM, biology professor; naturalized, US, 1999; d. Dalip Singh and Meena Rani Cheema; m. Sunil Prabhakar, Mar. 1, 1979; children: Pankaj, Rahul. BSc with honors in Botany, U. Delhi, India, 1973, MSc in Botany, 1975, PhD in Botany, 1980. Rsch. assoc., dept. botany U. Delhi, 1981, sr. lectr. botany Maitreyi Coll., 1982—93; instr. biology Nassau CC, Garden City, NY, 1995—2000, asst. prof. biology, 2000—05, assoc. prof. biology, 2005—. Overseas councillor, dept. botany The Botanica, Delhi, 1998—; advisor, reviewer biology program Kingsborough CC, Bklyn., 2005—; chmn. gen. edn. natural sci. assessment com. Nassau CC, 2001—; vis. prof. La Suerte Tropical Biology Sta.; cons. in field; treas. Women's Faculty Assn., Nassau CC, 2008—. Author: The Botany Notebook, Investigative Introductory Botany, 1st edit.; contbr. chapters to books, articles to profl. jours. Chmn. cmty. svc. com. Nassau C.C., 2005—06, presenter sr. ctrs. Spkrs. Bur., 1999. Recipient Excellence in Tchg. award, SUNY, Albany, 2002, Excellence award, Nat. Inst. Staff and Orgnl. Devel., 2007, cert. of recognition, CARES, Nassau CC Fedn. Tchrs.; grantee, NSF, 2005—. Mem.: NSTA (assoc.; presenter conf., San Diego 2002), ASCD (assoc.), Met. Assn. Coll. and U. Biologists (archivist 2000—, presenter 2008 ann. conf.), Bot. Soc. Am. (conf. presenter 2007, exec. bd. 2008—), Nat. Assn. Biology Tchrs. (assoc.; Otto Burgdorf apprenticeship NY chpt. 2001—03, presenter 2007 and 2008 ann. confs., nominee Biology Tchr. award 2006), Internat. Soc. Plant Morphologists (life; councillor 2005—), Women's Faculty Assn. at Nassau CC (pres. 2006—08), Friends Hempstead Plains (sec. 1995—2005), Delta Kappa Gamma (assoc.; v.p. elect 2006—, pres. 2008—, Ruth and Williams scholarship 2006). Hindu. Avocations: yoga, cooking, gardening, travel. Office: Nassau Community College One Education Dr Garden City NY 11530 Business E-Mail: prabhak@ncc.edu.

PRABHAKAR, SWAROOP, medical educator; married. MBBS, AIIMS, New Delhi, 1993. Asst. prof. St. Louis U. Hosp., 2002—07, UTSW, Dallas, 2007.

PRABHU, KRISH ANANT, former telecommunications industry executive, educator; b. Ankola, India, Aug. 2, 1954; came to U.S., 1975; s. Anant K. and Indira (Mahale) P.; m. Shuba George, June 14, 1980; 3 children. BSc with honors, Bangalore U., India, 1973; MSc, Indian Inst. Tech., Bombay, 1975; MSEE, U. Pitts., 1977, PhD, 1980. Mem. tech. staff Bell Labs., Holmdel, NJ, 1980-84; mem. tech. staff, also mgmt. positions Rockwell Internat., Richardson, Tex., 1984-92; v.p. R & D, Alcatel Network Systems, Richardson, 1992—95; pres. Alcatel Broadband Products, 1995—97; CEO Alcatel USA, Inc., 1997—99; COO Alcatel S.A., 1999—2001; venture ptnr. Morgenthaler Ventures, 2001—04; pres., CEO Tellabs, Inc., Naperville, Ill., 2004—08. Adj. prof. U. Tex. at Dallas, Richardson, 1988—; mem. adv. coun. U. Tex., Arlington, 1992—. Contbr. articles to tech. jours. Mem. IEEE (sr.), NMA. Avocations: tennis, chess, reading.

PRABHU, NAGABHUSHANA, industrial engineer, educator; BTech in Computer Sci., Indian Inst. Tech., Mumbai, 1991; PhD in Computer Sci., NYU, NYC; PhD in Physics, MIT, Boston. Prof. indsl. engring. Purdue U., West Lafayette, Ind., 2004—, James J. Solberg head, sch. indsl. engring., 2006—08, Vincent P. Reilly prof. indsl. engring., 2008—. Office: Purdue Univ 315 N Grant St West Lafayette IN 47907

PRABHU, VASANT M., corporate financial executive; Grad., Indian Inst. Tech., Bombay, India; MBA, U. Chgo. V.p., ptnr. N.Y. office Booz, Allen & Hamilton; with Pepsico Inc., U.S., Europe, Latin Am.; sr. v.p., CFO Pepsico Internat.; pres. info. and media group McGraw-Hill Cos., Inc., 1998—2000; exec. v.p., CFO Safeway Inc., 2000—03, Starwood Hotels & Resorts Worldwide Inc., 2003—. Office: Starwood Hotels & Resorts Worldwide Inc 1111 Westchester Ave White Plains NY 10604

PRABHU, VIKRAM CLIFFORD, physician; b. Bangalore, Karnataka, India, Dec. 20, 1967; s. Clifford George Alloysius and Aurelia Pais; m. Caroline Aranha, May 24, 1994; children: David Gerard, Michael Clifford. MD, St. John's Med. Ctr., Bangalore, India, 1991; MS, U. Nebr. Med. Ctr., Omaha, 1994. Cert. Ednl. Commn. for Fgn. Med. Grads., Fed. Licensing Exam. Surg. intern W.Va. U., Morgantown, 1994-95, resident in neurosurgery, 1995-99, chief resident in neurosurgery, 1999—. Contbr. articles, chaps. to profl. jours. Recipient W. Va. Neurosurgical Soc. Rsch. award, 1995, Annual Junior Surgical Resident Rsch. award, 1995; named Best Naval Cadet Nat. Cadet Corp, Republic of India, 1985; named to Prime Ministers Task Force for Evaluation of Nat. Cadet Corps, India, 1990. Mem. AANS, CNS, AMA, W.Va. Neurol. Soc., Am. Assn. Neurol. Surgeons, Congress of Neurol. Surgeons. Office: Dept Neurosurgery Health Scis Ctr West Virginia U PO Box 9183 Morgantown WV 26506-9183 Fax: 304-293-4819. E-mail: VPrabhu@hsc.wvu.edu.

PRABHU, VRUNDA P., mathematics professor; b. Bombay, Oct. 10, 1961; d. Sumati Prabhu; m. Shailesh Vengurlekar; 1 child, Sagar; 1 child, Natasha. BSc in Math. and Stats., U. Bombay, 1981, MSc in Math., 1983; PhD, U. Kans., Lawrence, 1993. Assoc. prof. William Woods U., Fulton, Mo., 1993—2002; assoc. prof. Bronx C.C. CUNY, NYC, 2002—. Active cmty. devel. tsunami affected regions, Tamil Nadu, India, 2005—06. Recipient award, War Trauma Found., 2005; grantee, NSF, 2002—06. Mem.: Am. Math. Soc. Achievements include design of FractionsGrid. Office: Bronx CC CUNY W181 University Ave Bronx NY 10453

PRABHUDESAI, MUKUND M., physician, educator, health facility and academic administrator, researcher; b. Lolyem, Goa, India, Mar. 17, 1942; came to U.S., 1967; s. Madhav R. and Kusum M. Prabhudesai; m. Sarita Mukund Usha, Feb. 1, 1972; 1 child, Nitin M. MB, BS (MD), G.S. Med., Bombay, 1967, postgrad., 1973-75. Diplomate Am. Bd. Pathology. Asst. pathologist Fordham Hosp., Bronx, NY, 1973-74, assoc. pathologist, 1974-76; assoc. dir. clin. pathology Lincoln Med., Bronx, 1976, dep. dir. pathology, 1977-79; chief pathology and lab. medicine svc., coord. R&D Illiana Med. Ctr., Danville, Ill., 1979—, dir. electron microscopy lab., 1987—. Senator U. Ill. Chgo.; co-investigator U. Ill. Coll. Medicine, Urbana-Champaign, clin. prof. pathology and internal medicine, 1982—. Contbr. articles to Am. Jour. Clin. Nutrition, Jour. AMA, Am. Jour. Clin. Pathology. Member Gifted Student Adv. Bd., Danville, 1984-86; v.p. Am. Cancer Soc. Vermilion County chpt., 1982, pres., 1986-88. VA rsch. grantee, 1980-82, 82-85, 83. Fellow Coll. Am. Pathology (inspector 1981-, Ill. state del. to C.A.P. Ho. Dels. 1992-, mem. reference com. 1993, chair, standard and integration com., 2000-); mem. AAAS, Am. Coll. Physician Execs., Ill. State Soc. Pathologists (bd. dirs. 1990-, chmn. membership com. 1990-). Achievements include development of cancer of bladder following portocarval shunting; research in adverse effects of alcohol on lung structure and metabolism; on effects of soy and bran on cholesterol, fish and coronary artery disease, endocrine response to soy protein, in induction and reversibility of atherosclerosis in trout, effects of ethanol on Vitamin A, lymphatics in atherosclerosis, iron in atherosclerosis, development of dermofluorometer for detection of P.V.D. Office: PO Box 3583 Placida FL 33946 Office Phone: 217-748-6272. Personal E-mail: mdesaih@aol.com. E-mail: sarita@soltec.net.

PRADA, MIUCCIA BIANCA, fashion designer; b. 1949; m. Patrizio Bertelli. PhD in Polit. sci.; student, mime performer, Teatro Piccolo, Milan, 1973—78. With family business Prada, Milan, 1978—. Introduced the following product lines to Prada: handbags, 1985, women's ready-to-wear, 1989, Miu Miu line, 1992, men's wear 1995; showed product line in NYC for the first time in 1994; opened boutique in London, 1994. Founder PradaMilanoarte (now Prada Found.), Milan, 1993—. Named one of Time Mag. 100 Most Influential People, 2005, the 30 Most Powerful Women in Europe, Wall St. Jour., 50 Women to Watch, 2005, Top 200 Collectors, ARTnews mag., 2005—08. Office: Prada SpA 2 Via Andrea Maffei 20154 Milan Italy Address: Prada ApA 30 Via Melzi D'Eril 20100 Milan Italy Office Phone: 02 54 67 01.

PRADO, EDWARD CHARLES, federal judge; b. San Antonio, June 7, 1947; s. Edward L. and Bertha (Cadena) P.; m. Maria Anita Jung, Nov. 10, 1973; 1 child, Edward C. AA, San Antonio Coll., 1967; BA, U. Tex., 1969, JD, 1972. Bar: Tex. 1972. Asst. dist. atty. Bexar County Dist. Atty.'s Office, San Antonio, 1972-76; asst. pub. defender US Pub. Defender's Office, San Antonio, 1976-80; judge US Dist. Ct. Tex., San Antonio, 1980; U.S. atty. US Dept. Justice, San Antonio, 1981—84; judge US Dist. Ct. (we. dist.) Tex., San Antonio, 1984—2003, US Ct. Appeals (5th cir.), San Antonio, 2003—. Served to capt. U.S. Army. Named Outstanding Young Lawyer of Bexar County, 1980. Mem. ABA, Tex. Bar Assn., San Antonio Bar Assn., San Antonio Young Lawyers Assn., Fed. Bar Assn. Republican. Roman Catholic.*

PRADO, WILLIAM MANUEL, psychologist, educator; b. NYC, Oct. 20, 1927; s. Manuel Fernando and Amor Maria (Bango) P.; m. Elizabeth Ann Avery, Aug. 16, 1953; children: Cheryl, Stuart, Mark. BA, Johns Hopkins U., 1950; MA, U. Ala., 1953; PhD, U. Okla., 1958. Staff psychologist VA Hosp., Little Rock, 1958-85, asst. chief psychologist svcs., 1961-82; asst., assoc. and adj. prof. psychology Philander Smith Coll., Little Rock, 1967-85; instr. Little Rock U., 1959-69, U. Ark. Grad. Ctr., Little Rock, 1963—67, St. Johns Sem., Little Rock, 1963—67; clin. psychologist in pvt. practice Little Rock, 1961—2003. Cons. in field. Contbr. articles to profl. jours. Served with U.S. Army, 1946-47. Recipient Math and Sci. Gold medal Rensselaer Poly. Inst., 1944. Mem. Am. Psychol. Assn., Ark. Assn. Profl. Psychologists, Ark. Psychol. Assn. Democrat. Roman Catholic. Avocations: music, art, movies, travel.

PRADOS, JOHN WILLIAM, retired engineering educator; b. Spring Hill, Tenn., Oct. 12, 1929; s. Gustave Olivier and Elizabeth Branham Prados; m. Ruth Lynn Baird, Sept. 2, 1951; children: Elizabeth Pauline Bowman, Laura Lynn, Anne Caroline Lynch. BS in Chem. engring., U. Miss., Oxford, Miss., 1947—51; PhD, U. Tenn., Knoxville, 1954—57, MS, 1953—54. Registered Profl. Engr., State Bd. of Archtl. and Engring. Examiners/Tenn., 1964. Asst. prof. chem. engring. U. Tenn., Knoxville, 1956—59, assoc. prof. chem. engring., 1959—64, prof. chem. engring., 1964—2001, assoc. dean engring., 1969—71, dean of admissions and records, 1971—73, acting chancellor, 1973—73, v.p. academic affairs, statewide sys., 1973—81, acting chancellor, martin campus Martin, 1979, v.p. academic affairs and rsch., statewide sys., 1981—88, v.p. emeritus, 1989—, univ. prof., 1989—2001, head, chem. engring. dept., 1990—93, univ. prof. emeritus, 2001. Cons. Nuc. Divsn., Union Carbide Corp., Oak Ridge, 1957—84, Martin Marietta Energy Sys., 1984—86; vice chmn. Engring. Accreditation Commn., Accreditation Bd. for Engring. and Tech., Inc., Baltimore, Md., 1981—84, chmn., 1984—85; commr. Commn. on Colleges, So. Assn. of Colleges and Schools, Decatur, Ga., 1986—92, exec. councillor, 1986—89; dir. Accrediation Bd. for Engring. and Tech., Inc., Baltimore, Md., 1988—93; sec. Accreditation Bd. for Engring. and Tech., Inc., Baltimore, Md., 1989—90, pres., 1991—92; trustee So. Assn. of Colleges and Schools, Decatur, Ga., 1995—98; editor, jour. of engring. edn. Am. Soc. for Engring. Edn., Washington, 1996—2001; trustee F. W. Olin Coll. of Engring., Needham, Mass., 2002—; sr. edn. assoc. NSF, Arlington, Va., 1994—97. First lt. USAF, 1951—53, Biloxi, Miss.; Albuquerque, N.Mex.; Limestone, Maine. Recipient L. E. Grinter Award for Contributions to Engring. Edn., Accreditation Bd. for Engring. and Tech., Inc., 1993, Alumni Outstanding Tchr., U. Tenn., 1967, Outstanding Engring. Alumnus, 1975, Faculty Macebearer, 1997—98, James T. Rogers Disting. Leadership award, So. Assn. Colls. and Schs., 2004, Benjamin Garver Lamme award, 2009. Fellow: Am. Inst. Chem. Engrs. (dir. 1975—77, treas. 1996—2001, Knoxville-Oak Ridge Chem. Engr. of Yr. 1977, Knoxville-Oak Ridge Chmn. Engr. of Yr. 1999), Am. Inst. of Chemists (life), Am. Soc. for Engring. Edn. (life Lifetime Achievement award 2007, Benjamin Garver Lamme award 2009); mem.: Am. Chem. Soc., Tech. Soc. of Knoxville, Torch Club, Phi Kappa Phi (Disting. Mem. 1974), Tau Beta Pi (exec. coun. 1986—90), Sigma Xi, Sci. Rsch. Soc. (pres. 1983—84, treas. 1990—2002), Alpha Tau Omega. Roman Catholic. Home: 7021 Stagecoach Trail Knoxville TN 37909-1112 Business E-Mail: jprados@utk.edu.

PRAETORIUS, WILLIAM ALBERT, SR., artist, retired real estate company officer, retired advertising executive; b. Forty-Fort, Pa., Oct. 7, 1924; s. George Albert and Elizabeth (Madden) Praetorius; m. Theresa M. Barnes, June 25, 1949; children: Kathleen Ann, William Albert, Gregg Douglas. Student, Biarittz Am. U., France, 1945-46, NY U., 1947-48. With L.W. Frohlich Intercon Internat., Inc., NYC, 1946—72, sr. v.p., dir. ops., 1969—71, chmn. operating com., 1972; sr. v.p., dir. ops. Deltakos div. J. Walter Thompson Co., NYC, 1972-73; sr. v.p. adminstrn. J.W.T. Affiliated Cos., NYC, 1973-75; pres. Healthmark Communications, Inc., NYC, 1975-77; dir. Clause Comml. div. Donald J. Clause, Southampton, 1977-78; dir. comml. div. Meadow Real Estate, Southampton, 1978-86; artist, 1987—. Author (pub.): (book) Concepts in Leadership, 1982; contbr. column to East End Bus. Rev., articles to profl. jours.; exhibitions include paintings East Hampton Town Hall, Guild Hall, East Hampton. Served AUS, 1943—46. Mem.: Artist Mem. Guild Hall, Barnes Landing Assn. Democrat. Roman Cath. Home: 30 Captains Walk East Hampton NY 11937-3169

PRAETZEL, GARY D., dean; b. Buffalo, Nov. 20, 1952; PhD, SUNY, Buffalo, 1980. Dean Coll. Hospitality & Tourism Mgmt., Niagara U., NY, 1999—. Office: Niagara Univ Coll Hospitality and Tourism Mgt Niagara University NY 14109-2012

PRAGER, DENNIS, radio talk show host; b. NYC, Aug. 2, 1948; m. Janice Adelstein, Jan. 15, 1981 (div. Aug. 1986); 1 child, David; m. Francine Stone, Sept. 4, 1988 (div. Mar. 2006); 1 adopted child, Aaron Henry; m. Susan Reed, Dec. 31, 2008. Grad. in Anthropology and Hist., CUNY Bklyn. Coll., 1970; student, U. Leeds, Eng., Columbia U. Sch. Internat. Affairs. Dir. Brandeis-Bardin Inst., Simi Valley, Calif., 1976—83; moderator weekly radio program Religion on the Line, Sta. KABC-AM, LA, 1982—92; host (nationally syndicated) The Dennis Prager Show, Sta, KRLA-870AM, 1992—99, 1999—. Weekly columnist Townhall.com. Author: Think a Second Time, 1996, Happiness Is a Serious Problem: A Human Nature Repair Manual, 1999; co-author (with Joseph Telushkin): Nine Questions People Ask About Judaism, 1986, Why the Jews? The Reason for Antisemitism, 2003. Apptd. mem. US Holocaust Meml. Coun., 2006. Jewish. Office: KRLA 701 Brand Blvd #550 Glendale CA 91203 Business E-Mail: dennis@pragerradio.com.

PRAGER, SUSAN WESTERBERG, educational association administrator, law educator, former academic administrator; b. Sacramento, Dec. 14, 1942; d. Percy Foster Westerberg and Aileen M. (McKinley) P.; m. James Martin Prager, Dec. 14, 1973; children: McKinley Ann, Case Mahone. AB, Stanford U., 1964, MA, 1967; JD, UCLA, 1971. Bar: N.C. 1971, Calif. 1972. Atty. Powe, Porter & Alphin, Durham, NC, 1971-72; acting prof. law UCLA, 1972-77, prof. Sch. Law, 1977, Arjay and Frances Fearing Miller prof. law, 1992-99, 2001—06, prof. emeritus, 2006—, assoc. dean Sch. Law, 1979-82, dean, 1982-98, rschr., prof. wills and trusts, 2001—; provost Dartmouth Coll., Hanover, NH, 1999—2001; pres. Occidental Coll., 2006—07, prof. history; exec. dir., CEO Assn. Am. Law Schs. (AALS), 2008—. Bd. dirs. Pacific Mut. Life Holding Co., Newport Beach, Calif. Editor-in-chief, UCLA Law Rev., 1970-71. Trustee Stanford U., 1976-80, 87-97. Mem. ABA (council of sect. on legal edn. and admissions to the bar 1983-85), Assn. Am. Law Schs. (pres. 1986), Order of Coif. Office: Assn Am Law Sch 1201 Connecticut Ave NW Ste 800 Washington DC 20036-2717 Office Phone: 202-296-2717. Office Fax: 202-296-8869. E-mail: prager@law.ucla.edu, sprager@aals.org.

PRAHALAD, C.K., finance educator, corporate strategist; b. India, Aug. 08; m. Gayatri Prahalad. BS, U. Madras, 1960. Harvey C. Fruehauf prof. bus. adminstrn. & prof. corp. strategy and internat. bus. Stephen M. Ross Sch. Bus., U. Mich. Co-author: Competing for the Future, 1994, The Future of Competition: Co-Creating Unique Value with Customers, 2004, The Fortune at the Bottom of the Pyramid: Eradicating Poverty Through Profits, 2004; contbr. articles to profl. jours. Office: Stephen M Ross Sch Bus U Mich 701 Tappan St Ann Arbor MI 48109-1234 Office Phone: 734-763-5573. Office Fax: 734-936-8715. E-mail: ckp@umich.edu.

PRAITIS, IRENA, literature and language professor; d. Al and Dana Praitis. PhD, Ariz. State U., Tempe, MFA, 2001. Prof. Calif. State U., Fullerton, 2001—. Author: (poetry collection) Branches, Touch. Scholarship, Lithuania Fulbright Assn., 2005. Office: CSU Fullerton English Dept 800 N State Coll Blvd Fullerton CA 92834-6848 Business E-Mail: ipraitis@fullerton.edu.

PRAKASH, CHANDRA, chemistry educator; b. Delhi, India, Sept. 20, 1952; came to U.S., 1979; s. Deep C. and Ramvati (Goel) Agarwal; m. Usha Goel, June 4, 1979; children: Seema, Sushant. BS, NRCC Coll., 1971; MS, Delhi U., 1973, PhD, 1977. Asst. prof. Delhi U., 1977-79; rsch. asst. prof. Vanderbilt U., Nashville, 1985-90, rsch. assoc. prof., 1990-92; sr. rsch. investigator Pfizer, Inc., Groton, Conn., 1992-95, prin. rsch. investigator, 1996—99, rsch. advisor, 2000—. Faculty Biomed. Rsch. Grant, College Park, 1989. Contbr. articles to profl. jours. Nat. merit scholarship Govt. of India, 1965-71; Md. Cancer grant State of Md., 1982. Office: Pfizer Inc Eastern Point Rd Groton CT 06340 Home: 41 Garnet Cir North Andover MA 01845-3373

PRAKASH, SURYA G.K., chemistry educator; b. Bangalore, India, Oct. 7, 1953; came to U.S., 1974; s. Krishnamurthy Gubbi and Anasuya Hebbur; m. Rama S. Prakash, Dec. 20, 1981; children: Archana, Arjun. BSc with honors, Bangalore U., 1972; MSc, Indian Inst. Tech., Madras, 1974; PhD, U. So. Calif., 1978. Jr. fellow U. So. Calif., Los Angeles, 1978-81, asst. prof. research, 1981-84, assoc. prof. research, 1984-90, assoc. prof. LA, 1990-94, prof., 1994—; olah nobel laureate chair in hydrocarbon chemistry, 1997; sci. co-dir. Loker Hydrocarbon res. Inst. Cons. corps. in Calif., 1984—. Author: Superacids, 1985, Hypercarbon Chemistry, 1987, Synthetic Fluorine Chemistry, 1992, Onium Ions, 1998, Beyond Oil and Gas: The Methanol Economy, 2006, Superacid Chemistry, 2009; contbr. articles to profl. jours. Recipient award Am. Chem. Soc., 2004, 2006, fellowship Am. Assn. Advancement Sci., 2006 Mem. Am. Chem. Soc., Internat. Soc. Magnetic Resonance. Avocations: music, reading. Home: 3412 Casco Ct Hacienda Heights CA 91745-6606 Office: U So Calif Hydrocarbon Rsch Inst University Park Los Angeles CA 90089-0001 Home Phone: 626-333-3734; Office Phone: 213-740-5984. Business E-Mail: gprakash@usc.edu.

PRAKASH, THAZHA PURATHIYATH, research scientist, chemist; b. Menapram, Kerala, India, May 4, 1964; came to the U.S., 1994; s. Raghavan and Janu Kunhi Parambath; m. Smitha Prakash, Mar. 21, 1993; 1 child, Piyush. BS in Chemistry, Calicut U., India, 1984; MS in Chemistry, Cochin U., India, 1986; PhD in Chemistry, Nat. Chem. Lab., Pune, Maharashtra, India, 1993. Postdoctoral rschr. U. Calif., Riverside, 1994-96, ISIS Pharms., Carlsbad, Calif., 1996-99, sr. scientist, 1999—. Contbr. articles to profl. jours. Mem. Am. Chem. Soc. Avocations: reading, tennis, volleyball, chess, ping pong/table tennis. Office: Isis Pharmaceuticals 1896 Rutherford Rd Carlsbad CA 92008-7326

PRAMMANASUDH, STACY, professional golfer; b. Enid, Okla., Sept. 23, 1979; m. Pete Upton, Jan. 24, 2004. Grad. in Exercise & Sports Sci., U. Tulsa, 2002. Mem. Futures Tour, 2002—03, LPGA, 2003—. Named Futures Tour Player of Yr., 2003; named a First-Team All-Am., 1999—2002; named an Acad. All-Am., 2000—02. Achievements include winning the 2005 Franklin American Mortgage Championship and the 2007 Fields Open in Hawaii on the LPGA Tour; winner, Frye Chevrolet Classic, 2003, and Lincoln Financial Futures Golf Classic,

2005, on the Futures Tour; winner, Stanford Pepsi Intercollegiate, 1999-2001. Avocations: yoga, gardening. Mailing: c/o LPGA 100 International Golf Dr Daytona Beach FL 32124-1092

PRANCE, SIR GHILLEAN TOLMIE, botanical gardens administrator, botanist; b. Brandeston, Suffolk, Eng., July 13, 1937; s. Basil Camden and Margaret Hope (Tolmie) P.; m. Anne Elizabeth Hay, July 13, 1961; children: Rachel Julia, Sarah Elizabeth. BA, Oxford U., 1960, DPhil, 1963, MA, 1965; Fil Dr (hon.), Goteborg U., 1983; DSc (hon.), Portsmouth U., 1994, U. Kent, 1994, Kingston U., 1994, St. Andrews U., 1995, Bergen U., 1996, Sheffield U., 1997, Fla. Internat. U., 1997, CUNY, 1998, Liverpool U., 1998, Glasgow U., 1999, Plymouth U., 1999, Keele U., 2000, Exeter U., 2000; DSc, Gloucestershire U., 2009. Rsch. asst. NY Bot. Garden, Bronx, 1963-66, assoc. curator, 1966-68, curator Amazonian botany, 1968-75, dir. rsch., v.p., 1975-81, sr. v.p., dir. Inst. Econ. Botany, 1981-88; dir. Royal Bot. Gardens, Kew, Eng., 1988-99; sci. dir. The Eden Project, 1999—; McBryde prof. Nat. Tropical Bot. Garden, 2000—02, McBryde sr. fellow, 2006—. Adj. prof. CUNY, NYC, 1968-99; vis. prof. Yale U., New Haven, 1983-88, Reading U., Eng., 1988—; dir. grad. studies Inst. Nac. Pesquisas Amazonia, Manaus, Brazil, 1973-75. Author more than 20 books and monographs; editor 11 books; contbr. more than 520 articles to sci. jours. and popular publs. Mem. White Plains Cable TV Commn., NY, 1981-88; trustee Au Sable Inst. Environ, Mancelona, Mich., 1984-2006, Bd. Rainforest Alliance, 1988-97, Margaret Mee Amazon Trust, Richmond, Eng., 1988-96, Worldwide Fund for Nature Internat., 1989-93, Horniman Mus., 1990-99, Lovaine Trust Co. Ltd., 1990-99; trustee, chmn. Bentham Moxon Trust, Richmond, 1988-99; chmn. Brazilian Atlantic Rainforest Trust, 2000—; chmn. Global Diversity Found., 2000—. Created knight bachelor, 1995; decorated grand cross Ordem de Merito Cientifico, Brazil, 1995, Comendador da Ordem Nacional do Cruzeiro do Sul, Brazil, 2000; recipient hon. diploma of merit Inst. Nat. Pesquisas Amazonia, 1978, Disting. Svc. award NY Bot. Garden, 1986, Henry Shaw medal Mo. Bot. Garden, 1988, Linnean medal, 1990, Internat. Cosmos prize Expo '90 Found., Japan, 1993, Janaki Ammal medal Internat. Soc. Ethnobotany, 1996, Internat. award excellence Botanical Rsch. Inst. Tex., 1998, Asa Gray award Am. Soc. Plant Taxonomists, 1998, Victoria medal of honour Royal Hort. Soc., 1999, Lifetime Discovery award, 1999, Fairchild medal for plant exploration, 2000, Graziela Maciel Barroso prize, Brazil, 2004, Allerton award Nat. Tropical Bot. Garden, 2005, NY Bot. Garden Gold medal, 2008; named hon. citizen Ft. Worth; hon. fellow Keble Coll., Oxford U., 1993—. Fellow AAAS, Linnean Soc. London (pres. 1997-2000), Royal Geog. Soc. (Patron's medal 1994), Inst. Biology (pres. 2000-02), Explorers Club, Royal Soc. of London for Improving Natural Knowledge, Perak Acad., Assn. for Tropical Biology and Conservation (hon., pres. 1979-80); mem. Internat. Assn. Plant Taxonomists (pres. 1999-2005), Systematics Assn. (pres. 1988-91), Royal Danish Acad. Scis. and Letters (fgn.), Royal Swedish Acad. Scis. (fgn.), Brazilian Acad. Scis. (corr.), Bot. Soc. Am. (corr.), Soc. Econ. Botany (pres. 1996-97, Disting. Econ. Botanist award 2002), Brit. Ecol. Soc. (hon.). Anglican. Avocation: stamp collecting/philately. Personal E-mail: gtolmiep@aol.com. Business E-Mail: gprance@edenproject.com.

PRANDI, JULIE DIANE, retired literature and language professor; b. San Jose, Calif., Feb. 16, 1951; d. Dante F. and Emma Kathryn (Borzone) Prandi; m. James Herbert Reid, May 22, 2005; m. Fred Safier, Jan. 2, 1984 (dec. Aug. 11, 2004). PhD, U. Calif., Berkeley, 1979. Asst. prof. German Columbia U., NYC, 1981—84; prof. German Ill. Wesleyan U., Bloomington, 1984—. Author: (lit. criticism) Spirited Women Heroes, Dare to Be Happy, a Study of Goethe's Ethics, The Poetry of the Self-Taught; co-editor: (music criticism) The Mendelssohns, Their Music in History. Bd. mem., study leader LWV, Bloomington, 2007—. Named League of Yr., McLean County LWV, 2002; grantee Academic Exch., German Govt., DAAD, 1990. Mem.: Phi Beta Kappa. Unitarian Universalist. Achievements include research in German literature, 18th and 19th century. Avocation: singing. Home: 905 N Evans St Bloomington IL 61701

PRANEVICIUS, MINDAUGAS, anesthesiologist, educator; s. Henrikas Pranevicius and Irena Praneviciene; m. Sigita Rucinskaite; children: Ausra, Ula, Ona. MD, Kaunas Med. U., Lithuania, 1994. Diplomate Am. Bd. Anesthesiology, 2004, Am. Bd. Anesthesia Pain Medicine, 2004. Surgery intern St. Luke's Roosevelt Hosp. Ctr., NYC, 1997—98, anesthesiology resident, 1998—2001, pain fellow, 2001—02; asst. prof. anesthesiology, dir. pain mgmt. Albert Einstein Coll. Medicine, Jacobi Med. Ctr., Bronx, NY, 2002—. Contbr. articles to profl. jours. Mem.: Am. Soc. Anesthesia. Achievements include patents pending for noninvasive effective cerebral outfow pressure measurement; noninvasive blood pressure measurement; noninvasive central blood pressure measurement; infusion patient controlled Analgesia; venous modulation of cerebral ischaemia; patents for cerebral blood flow maintenance during intracranial hypertensin; first to discovered cerebral venous steal-treatable cause of perifocal ischaemia. Office: Albert Einstein Coll Medicine 1400 Pelham Pk S Bronx NY 10461 Office Fax: 718-918-7902. Personal E-mail: pranevicius@gmail.com.

PRANGE, ARTHUR JERGEN, JR., psychology and psychiatry professor, neuroscientist; b. Grand Rapids, Mich., Sept. 19, 1926; s. Arthur Jergen and Martha Frances (Elliott) P.; m. Sarah Elizabeth Bowen, Feb. 4, 1950; children— Christine Anne, Martha Louise, Laura Beth, David Elliott. BS, U. Mich., 1947, MD, 1950. Intern Wayne County Gen. Hosp., Eloise, Mich., 1950-51; resident in psychiatry U. NC, Chapel Hill, 1954-57, instr., 1957-60, asst. prof., 1960-64, asso. prof., 1964-68, prof. psychiatry, 1968-83, Boshamer prof. psychiatry, 1983—, acting chmn. dept. psychiatry, 1983-85, dir. NIMH Clin. Rsch. Ctr., 1979—. Vis. scientist Med. Rsch. Coun. Unit, Epson, Surrey, Eng., 1968-69; chmn. clin. projects rsch. rev. com. HEW, NIMH, 1975-76, chmn. bd. sci. counselors, 1986-87; mem. psychopharmacologic drugs adv. com. HEW, FDA, 1979-82. Editor: The Thyroid Axis, Drugs and Behavior, 74; Contbr. articles to med. jours. Recipient NIMH Career Devel. award 1961-69, Career Scientist award, 1969-95, Gold Medal award Soc. of Biol. Psychiatry, 1992, Exemplary Psychiatrist award Nat. Alliance for the Mentally Ill, 1997, Selo prize Nat. Alliance for Rsch. in Schizophrenia and Affective Disorders, 1997. Fellow Am. Psychiat. Assn. (life, Rsch. in Psychiatry award 1996), Am. Coll. Neuropsychopharmacology (life, pres. 1987, Hoch award 1995); mem. Internat. Soc. Psychoneuroendocrinology (founding mem.), NC Neuropsychiat. Assn., Collegium Internationale Neuropsychopharmacologicum, Royal Coll. Psychiatrists (London). Home: 6503 Meadowview Rd Hillsborough NC 27278-8314 Office: Univ NC Sch Medicine Dept Psychiatry Chapel Hill NC 27599-0001

PRANGE, HILMAR WALTER, neurology educator; b. Reichenbach, Germany, Aug. 4, 1944; s. Georg Friedrich Reinhold and Gertrud Wilhelmine (Mueller) P.; m. Carin Juliane Schroeter, Mar. 14, 1970; children: Klaus Richard, Juliane. MD, U. Rostock, Germany, 1969, lic. specialist neurology and psychiatry, 1974; Habilitation, Georg-August U., Goettingen, Germany, 1982. Medical diplomate; lic. in intensive care medicine, 1997. Med. resident Regional Hosp., Stralsund, Germany, 1969-71; med. asst. then psychiatrist Univ. Hosp., Rostock, 1971-75; asst. med. dir. Ev. Johannes Hosp., Bielefeld, Germany, 1975-76; head neurologic out-patient clinic Univ. Hosp., Goettingen, Germany, 1976-78, asst. med. dir. dept. neurology, 1979—87, dir. neurol. intensive care unit, 1987—2007. Mem. expert group German Ministry of Health. Author: Neurosyphilis, 1987, Infectious Diseases of the Central Nervous System, 1995; editor: CNS Barriers and Modern CSF Diagnostics, 1993, Systemic Infections Causing Bacterial CNS Diseases, 1997, Infectious Diseases of the Central Nervous System, 2001, Emergencies in Neurology, 2002, Neurological Intensive Medicine, 2004; contbr. articles to profl. jours. Grantee German Forschungsgemeinschaft, German Tech. Cooperation, German MS Soc. Mem.: EMEA, German Med. Assn. (mem. commn. drug security), European Neurol. Soc., Neurol. Soc. Cyprus (hon.). Lutheran. Avocation: Cultural history, sports, jogging (marathons), swimming. Office Phone: 0049 551 392740. Business E-Mail: hprange@gwdg.de.

PRANGE, ROY LEONARD, JR., lawyer; b. Chgo., Sept. 12, 1945; s. Roy Leonard and Marjorie Rose P.; m. Carol Lynn Poels, June 5, 1971; children: David, Ellen, Susan. BA, U. Iowa, 1967; MA, Ohio State U., 1968; JD, U. Wis.-Madison, 1975. Bar: Wis. 1975, U.S. Dist. Ct. (we. and ea. dists.) Wis. 1975, U.S. Ct. Appeals (7th cir.) 1978, U.S. Supreme Ct. 1978. Assoc. Ross & Stevens, S.C., Madison, Wis., 1975—79, ptnr., 1979—90, Quarles & Brady, LLP, Madison, 1990—. Lectr. bankruptcy, debtor-creditor rights, U. Wis., Madison, 1982--. Contbr. Wis. Lawyer's Desk Reference Manual, 1987, Comml. Litigation in Wis. Practice Handbook, 1995, West's Bankruptcy Exemption Manual, 1997—. 1st lt. U.S. Army, 1969-72. Fellow Am. Coll. Bankruptcy; mem. ABA, Wis. State Bar (dir. bankruptcy, insolvency, creditors rights sect. 1985-91, chair 1990-92, mem. continuing legal edn. com. 1990-95), Am. Bankruptcy Inst., Dickens Fellowship (v.p. 1980-84). Avocations: swimming, bicycling, scuba diving. Office: Quarles & Brady LLP PO Box 2113 33 E Main St Ste 900 Madison WI 53701-2113 Office Phone: 608-283-2485. Business E-Mail: rlp@quarles.com.

PRANSES, ANTHONY LOUIS, retired electric power industry executive; b. Claracq, France, May 3, 1920; s. Anthony Kasimer and Georgette (Pilon) F.; m. Margaret Louise Hamill, July 24, 1948; children— Anthony Randolph, Terry Jay, Renee Louise. Student, Sorbonne, Paris, France, 1937-39; BS in Metall. Engring, Carnegie Inst. Tech., 1942, grad. student, 1946-48. With Westinghouse Electric Corp., 1945-86, mgr. mfg. planning Lima, Ohio, 1954-57, plant mgr., 1958-59, mgr. mfg. services, 1959-72, mgr. mfg., 1972-80, cons., 1980-86. Joined Am. Youth Hostels, 1935, founder Pitts. council, 1947, pres. council, 1947-50, mem. nat. bd. dirs., 1954-72, Midwest regional v.p., 1957-59, nat. pres., 1959-62, pres. Lima council, 1962-75, 87-91, chmn. nat. bd. dirs., 1963-67. Served to capt., C.E. AUS, 1942- 45. Home: 6005 Poling Rd Lima OH 45807-9492 E-mail: pranses@wcoil.com.

PRANTIL, VINCENT CARL, science educator; b. Bklyn., Apr. 20, 1959; s. Joseph V. and Dolores M. Prantil; m. Laurna Jane Hansen, Oct. 3, 1998; children: Carmen Bianca, Lorin Carl. BS, Cornell U., Ithaca, NY, 1981, MS, 1983, PhD, 1993. Mem. tech. staff Sandia Nat. Labs., Livermore, Calif., 1983—87, sr. mem. tech. staff, 1993—2000. Contbr. articles (R&D 100 award, 2000). Fellow Otto Maha fellowship, Milw. Sch. Engring., 2006—07; Andrew Dickson White fellowship, Cornell U., 1981—83. Achievements include patents for braze system and method for reducing strain in a braze joint. Office: Milw Sch Engring 1025 N Broadway Milwaukee WI 53202-3109 Office Fax: 424-277-2222.

PRASAD, ANANDA SHIVA, medical educator; b. Buxar, Bihar, India, Jan. 1, 1928; came to U.S., 1952, naturalized, 1968. s. Radha Krishna and Mahesha (Kaur) Lall; m. Aryabala Ray, Jan. 6, 1952; children: Rita, Sheila, Ashok, Audrey. BSc, Patna Sci. Coll., India, 1946, MB, BChir, 1951; PhD, U. Minn., 1957; doctorate honoris causa, U. Claude Bernard of Lyon, 1999. Intern Patna Med. Coll. Hosp., 1951-52; resident St. Paul's Hosp., Dallas, 1952-53, U. Minn., 1953-56, VA Hosp., Mpls., 1956; instr. dept. medicine Univ. Hosp., U. Minn., Mpls., 1957-58; vis. assoc. prof. medicine Shiraz Med. Faculty, Nemazee Hosp., Shiraz, Iran, 1960; asst. prof. medicine and nutrition Vanderbilt U., 1961-63; mem. faculty, dir. div. hematology dept. medicine Wayne State U., Detroit, 1963-84, assoc. prof., 1964-68, prof., 1968-2000, dir. research dept. medicine, 1984-97, disting. prof., 2000—. Mem. staff Harper-Grace Hosp., VA Hosp., Allen Park, Mich.; mem. trace elements subcom. Food and Nutrition Bd., NRC-Nat. Acad. Scis., 1965-68; chmn. trace elements com. Internat. Union Nutritional Scis.; mem. Am. Bd. Nutrition; pres. Am. Coll. Nutrition, 1991-93. Author: Zinc Metabolism, 1966, Trace Elements in Human Health and Disease, 1976, Trace Elements and Iron in Human Metabolism, 1978, Zinc in Human Nutrition, 1979, Biochemistry of Zinc, 1993; editor: Clinical, Biochemical and Nutritional Aspects of Trace Elements, 1982, Am. Jour. Hematology, Jour. Trace Elements in Exptl. Medicine; editor: Zinc Metabolism, Current Aspects in Health and Disease, 1977; co-editor: Clinical Applications of Recent Advances in Zinc Metabolism, 1982, Zinc Deficiency in Human Subjects, 1983, Essential and Toxic Trace Elements in Human Health and Disease, 1988, Essential and Toxic Trace Elements in Human Health and Disease: An Update, 1993; Jour. Am. Coll. Nutrition; contbr. articles to profl. jours., also reviewer. Trustee Detroit Internat. Inst., Detroit Gen. Hosp. Rsch. Corp., 1969—72. Recipient Rsch. Recognition award Wayne State U., 1964, award Am. Coll. Nutrition, 1976, Disting. Faculty Fellowship award Wayne State U., 1986, Medal of Honor, City of Lyon, France, 1989, Pioneer in Sickle Cell Disease Rsch. award Nat. Heart Lung Blood Inst./NIH, 1997; Pfizer scholar, 1955-56, WCMS Spl. Recognition award for Profl. Ach., 1998, Klaus Schwartz medal Internat. Assn. Bioinorganic Scientists, 2001, Spl. Recognition award Am. Assn. Physicians India, 2001; inducted Heritage Hall Fame, Mich., 2003, Asian Acad. Hall Fame, 2007. Master ACP (Outstanding Rsch. Related to Medicine award 2007), Am. Coll. Nutrition; fellow AAAS, Am. Inst. Nutrition (trace elements panel), Internat. Soc. Hematology; mem. AMA (Goldberger award 1975), Internat. Soc. Trace Element Rsch. in Humans (pres. 1986-92, chmn. steering com. 1985-86, Raulin award 1989), Am. Soc. Clin. Nutrition (awards com. 1969-70), Am. Fedn. Clin. Rsch. (pres. Mich. 1969-70), Am. Physiol. Soc., Am. Soc. Clin. Investigation, Am. Soc. Hematology, Assn. Am. Physicians, European Acad. Scis., Arts and Humanities (corr.), Ctrl. Soc. Clin. Rsch., Soc. Exptl. Biology and Medicine (councillor Mich. 1967-71), Wayne State U. Acad. Scholars (pres.-elect 1997-98, pres. 1998-99), Wayne County Med. Soc., Internat. Soc. Internal Medicine, Am. Soc. Clin. Nutrition (Robert H. Herman award 1984), Nutrition Soc. India (Gopalan oration award 1988), Nat. Heart, Lung, Blood Inst. NIH (mem. coun. 2002-2004), Cosmos Club (Washington), Sigma Xi. Home: 4710 Cove Rd Orchard Lake MI 48323-3604 Office: Univ Health Ctr 5-C 4201 Saint Antoine St Detroit MI 48201-2153 Business E-Mail: prasada@karmanos.org.

PRASAD, ASHOK, science educator; s. Priyaranjan and Leela Prasad; m. Ramaa Vasudevan, Nov. 14, 1991. PhD, Brandeis U., Waltham, 2006. Lectr., economics Khalsa Coll., Delhi U., Delhi, 1987—2001; grad. fellow, physics dept. Brandeis U., Mass., 2001—06; postdoc. assoc. MIT, Cambridge, 2006—08; asst. prof., chem. & biol. engring. Colo. State U., Fort Collins, 2009—.

PRASAD, MANIKA, geophysicist, researcher; PhD, Kiel U., Germany, 1988. Rschr. Stanford U., Calif., 1996—. Mem.: Assn. Women in Geosciences (assoc.), Am Assn. Petroleum Geologists (assoc.), Am. Geophysical Union (assoc.), Soc. Exploration Geophysicists (assoc.). Office: Stanford Univ Geophysics Dept 397 Panama Mall Stanford CA 94305-2215

PRASAD, MUKESH, otolaryngologist; b. Kolkata, India, Jan. 8, 1971; m. Chandni Prasad. MD, Johns Hopkins Med. Sch., Balt., 1997. Otorhinolaryngologist Weill Cornell Med. Coll., NYC, 2002—. Office: Weill Cornell Med Coll 1305 York Ave 5th Fl New York NY 10021

PRASAD, NAVIN, ophthalmologist; MD, Darbhanga Med. Coll., India, 1990. Bd. Cert. Ophthalmology All India Inst. of Med. Scis., New Delhi, 1995, cert. U.S. Med. Lic. Exam Ednl. Commn. of Fgn. Med. Grads., 2004. Med. intern Darbhanga Med. Coll., Laheriasarai, India, 1990—91, sr. ho. officer, 1991—92; resident physician All India Inst. of Med. Scis., New Delhi, 1992—95, registrar, sr. resident, 1995—98; sr. ho. officer, ophthalmology James Cook U. Hosp., Middlesbrough, England, 2000—03; glaucoma fellow Mass. Eye & Ear Infirmary, Harvard Med. Sch., Boston, 2005—. Author: (internat. jour. article) Jour. of Cataract Refract Surgery, Eyenews, Eye, (poster in internat. conf.) Longterm intervisit intraocular pressure fluctuation following selective laser trabeculoplasty as primary therapy in open angle glaucoma. Perform cataract eye surgeries in eye camps Second Sight of UK, Bisalpur, India, 2002. Merit Scholarship, Govt. of India, 1981, 1983. Fellow: The Royal Coll. of Physicians and Surgeons of Glasgow (assoc.); mem.: The Assn. for Rsch. in Vision and Ophthalmology (assoc.), All India Ophthal. Soc. (life), Am. Acad. Ophthalmology (assoc.). Achievements include research in Study of corneal endothelial loss due to phacoemulsification in different types of anterior capsulotomies. Personal E-mail: india12@gmail.com.

PRASAD, NEIL A., telecommunications industry executive, computer company executive; arrived in US, 1988, naturalized, 2000; s. Ayilliyath and Annie Prasad; m. Caroline George, Dec. 27, 1992; children: Jake Joseph, Anya Joseph, Gino Joseph. BEE, Gujarat U., India, 1987; MSEE, U. Houston, 1991. Cert. profl. engr., Instn. Engrs., India, 1987, Nat. Soc. Profl. Engrs., Va., 1990, Tex. Soc. Profl. Engrs., 1991; in leadership excellence Toastmasters Internat., 2004. Software engr. Software Interfaces, Inc., Houston, 1991; sr. design engr. WilTel, Inc. Advanced Tech. Group, The Woodlands, Tex., 1991—95; sr. engr. MCI Telecom. Corp., Richardson, Tex., 1995—96; sr. mgr. Stratacom, Inc., San Jose, Calif., 1996, Cisco Sys., Inc., San Jose, Calif., 1996—; dir. IPDR.org, Nantucket, Mass., 2005—07; pres. CEO Abaeca Solutions, 2006—. Amb. ATM Forum, Mountain View, Calif., 1994—99; chmn., internet protocol network mgmt. group TeleManagement Forum, Morristown, NJ, 2000—06, dir., 2006—; divsn. gov. Toastmasters Internat., Mission Viejo, Calif., 2004—05; spkr., presenter in field. Contbr. articles to profl. jours. Vol. Cisco Emergency Response Team; coun. mem. Ascension Parish, San Jose, 2006—. Recipient Project Mgmt. and Tng. Excellence award, Wiltel Inc., 1995. Mem.: IEEE, Planetary Soc., Am. Physical Soc., Assn. Computing Mahinery, Instn. Engrs. (assoc.), Mensa, Toastmasters Internat. (named Disting. Toastmaster 2006, Humorous Speech Contest winner 2006). Roman Catholic. Achievements include development and industry demonstration of network management systems for data, voice, and video telecommunications services; leading strategic industry initiatives in the network management area; patents pending for innovations in network performance management. Avocations: marathon running, travel, literature, swimming, ice skating. Home: 822 Daffodil Way San Jose CA 95117 Office: Cisco Systems Inc 170 W Tasman Dr San Jose CA 95134 Personal E-mail: ap4411@yahoo.com.

PRASAD, SHALINI, electrical and communications engineer; d. Prasad Seetha Lakshman and Vathsala Diwakarla. Grad., U. Madras, India, 2000; PhD, U. Calif., Riverside, 2004. Test engr. Motorola India Electronics Ltd., Bangalore, Karnataka, India, 2000—01; rsch. asst. U. Calif., Riverside, 2001—04; asst. prof. Portland (Oreg.) State U., 2005—. Asst. prof. dept. biomedical engring. Oreg. Grad. Inst. Contbr. articles to profl. jours.; presenter poster papers at numerous confs. Advisor Oreg. Math. Engring. Sci. Achievement, Portland, 2005. Grantee, Portland State U., 2005—. Mem.: IEEE, Internat. Soc. Optical Engring., Assn. Lab Automation (grantee 2003—), Biomed. Engring. Soc., Materials Rsch. Soc. Achievements include patents for cellular biosensors, protein biosensors and their applications; patents pending for hybrid optical biochemical sensors; micro cavity based biochemical sensors. Avocations: book collections, classical dance, violin, debates, creative writing. Office: Portland State Univ 160-11 FAB 1900 SW 4th Ave Portland OR 97201 Personal E-mail: prasads@cecs.pdx.edu.

PRASAD, VIBHA, computer engineer; d. Rajendra and Mamta Prasad. MS, U. Va., Charlottesville, 2005—. Summer intern Indian Inst. Tech., Kanpur, U.P., India, 2004; tchg. asst. U. Va., 2005—06, rsch. asst., 2006—; software engr. Raytheon, Portsmouth, RI, 2008—. Mem.: Raytheon Asian Pacific Assn. (sec. 2008—).

PRASAD, VINOD K., bone marrow transplantation physician, researcher; b. Jabalpur, India, June 30, 1960; came to U.S., 1994; s. Radha Krishna and Radha Devi P.; m. Suman Singh; children: Shreya, Varun. BS, SGTB Khalsa Coll., U. of Delhi, 1977; MBBS, Maulana Azad Med. Coll., U. of Delhi, 1977; MD, Lady Hardinge Med. Coll., U. of Delhi, 1986; MRCP, Royal Coll. of Physicians, London, 1990. Diplomate in pediatrics and pediatric hematology-oncology Am. Bd. Pediatrics. Sr. house officer in Pediatrics Hosp. for Sick Children, London, 1989-91; lecturer U. of Leeds (Eng.), 1991-93, rsch. fellow, 1993; fellow Sloan Kettering and Cornell U., NYC, 1994-96, chief fellow, 1996—; PGY III N.Y. Hosp.and Cornell U., NYC, 1995-96. Instr. BMT svc. Meml. Sloan Kettering Cancer Ctr., N.Y.C., 1999—. Recipient of Merit award Am. Soc. of Hematology, 1997, George Santos award Am. Soc. Bone Marrow Transplants, 2000. Mem. Am. Soc. Hematology, Royal Coll. Physicians, Am. Soc. Clin. Oncology assoc., Indian Acad. Pediatrics (life). Office: Memorial Sloan Kettering Hosp 1275 York Ave New York NY 10021-6094 Home: 108 Harrison CT Chapel Hill NC 27516-1183 Fax: 212-717-3239.

PRATER, EMMA LOU, retired academic administrator; b. Tyler, Tex., July 22, 1929; d. Roy Andrew and Alice Gay Wyatt; m. Kenneth L. Prater; children: Sherry S., Sandra C. AA, Tyler Jr. Coll., Tex., 1967; BS, Tex. A&M U., 1971, MS, 1982. With advt. sales and promotion Gen. Electric, Tyler, 1957—64; acct. Tyler (Tex.) Jr. Coll., 1964—77, dir. student activities, 1980—89; dir. acctg. Spring Ind. Sch. Dist., Houston, 1977—80; ret., 1989. Adv. Tex. State Govt. 600 Assn. Tex. Jr. Colls., 1989—2006; former pres. alumni bd. Nat. Jr. Coll. Cheerleader Assn., 1984; coach cheerleading Tyler Jr. Coll., 1969—89. Author: Cheerleading, 1984. Dir. adult 55+ Westwood Bapt. Ch. Recipient Black and Gold award, Tyler Jr. Coll., 1991. Mem.: Tyler Jr. Coll. Alumni Assn. Achievements include Emma Lou Prater Presdl. scolarship named in honor at Tyler Jr. Coll. Home: 509 Elmridge Tyler TX 75703 Business E-Mail: ret-epra@tjc.edu.

PRATER, MARY ANNE, special education educator, researcher; d. Herman Bates and Barbara M. Prater. MusB, U. Utah, Salt Lake City, 1975, MS, 1982; PhD, Utah State U., Logan, 1987. Asst. prof. So. Ill. U., Carbondale, 1987—90; prof., dept. chair, assoc. dean U. Hawaii at Manoa, Honolulu, 1990—2001; prof., dept. chair Brigham Young U., Provo, Utah, 2001—. Author: Developmental Disabilities in Children's Literature: Issues and Annotated Bibliography, 2000, Teaching Strategies for Students with Mild to Moderate Disabilities, 2007, Teaching About Disabilities Through Children's Literature, 2008, Making Accommodations and Adaptations for Students with Mild to Moderate Disabilities, 2009. Active Ch. of Jesus Christ of Latter-day Saints. Recipient Disting. Paper award, Hawaii Edn. Rsch. Assn., 1996, 2002, 2009, Spl. Recognition award, Devel. Disabilities Divsn. of the Coun. for Exceptional Children, 2000; Rsch. grantee, U.S. Dept. Edn., 1986—87, 2000—01, Pers. Preparation grantee, 1987—90, 2004—08, Leadership Preparation grantee, 1996—2001, Post-Doctoral fellow, U. Ky., 1997. Mem.: ASCD, Coun. for Learning Disabilities, Am. Assn. Colls. Tchr. Edn., Coun. for Exceptional Children (various coms.). Office: Brigham Young Univ 340 MCKB Provo UT 84602

PRATHER, DONNA LYNN, psychiatrist; b. Charlotte, NC, Nov. 4, 1946; d. James Boyd and Ann (Joyner) P. BA, Queens Coll., Charlotte, 1968; MD, U. N.C., 1978. Supr. Meckenburg County Dept. Social Svcs., Charlotte, 1971-74; family practice intern Charlotte Meml. Hosp., 1978-79, resident in family practice, 1979-81; fellow in family medicine U. N.C., Chapel Hill, 1981-82; resident in psychiatry N.C. Meml. Hosp., Chapel Hill, 1982-85; pvt. practice psychiatry Chapel Hill, NC, 1985—. Psychiatrist Person Counceling Ctr., Roxboro, N.C., 1983-92; med. dir. Orange-person-Chatam Mental Health Ctr., Chapel Hill, 1992—; clin. assoc. prof. U. N.C., Chapel Hill, 1985—. Mem. N.C. Psychiat. Assn., N.C. Med. Soc., Am. Psychiat. Assn., N.C. Psychiat. Assn. (chmn., com. for women 1990-91, ethics com. 1997-99). Avocation: music. Office: 200 N Greensboro St Ste D-7 Carrboro NC 27510 Office Phone: 919-929-6519.

PRATHER, GERALD LUTHER, management consultant, retired judge, military officer; b. LaGrange, Ga., Apr. 7, 1935; s. Luther Pate and Hazel Belle (McCullough) P.; m. Carolyn Pearson, Nov. 22, 1956; children: Dean Allen, Bryan Pate, Jeri Lynn, Angela BSE.E., Auburn U., 1966; MS in Mgmt., Air Force Inst. Tech., 1972; postgrad. advanced mgmt., U. Houston, 1978; grad., SQ Officer Sch., Maxwell AFB, 1963, ICAF, Washington, 1974, Ecumenical Ctr. Religion and Health, San Antonio, Tex., 2000. Enlisted USAF, 1954-56, commd. 2d lt., 1956, advanced through grades to maj. gen., 1981, various assignments as pilot, 1956-68, served in Vietnam, 1967-68, commdr. 1963d Comm. Squadron Chanute AFB, Ill., 1968-69, comdr. 1918th Comm. Squadron Scott AFB, Ill., 1969-70, dep. dir. comm.-electronics for 15th Air Force March AFB, Calif., 1970-72, chief comm. ops. div. hdqrs. Washington, 1972-75, comdr. strategic comm. div. Offutt AFB, Nebr., 1975-77, comdr. European Comm. Div. Ramstein AFB, W. Ger., 1977-80; dir. Command Control, Comm. & Computer Systems, Hdqrs. U.S. Readiness Command MacDill AFB, Fla., 1980-81; asst. chief of staff of Info. Systems Hdqrs. USAF, Washington, 1981-84, comdr. Air Force Comm. Command Scott AFB, Ill., 1984-86, ret., 1986; pvt. practice mgmt. cons. Del Rio, Tex., 1986-1997; Justice of the Peace Val Verde County, Tex., 1987-97. Lectr. in field; also air traffic controller, parachutist; bd. dir. Del Rio Internat. Airport. Speech writer: Team America, 1983 (Freedom Found. nat. award, 1984). Scoutmaster Eagle Scout, 1952, Boy Scouts Am., Sacramento, 1963, chmn. com., 1964, cub master Auburn, Ala.; sponsor Explorer Troop, Boy Scouts Am., Scott AFB, Ill., 1969; chmn. Amistad Dist. Boy Scouts Am., 1988, BSA Coun. Exec. Com., 2005—08, v.p., program, 2005—07; chmn. Eagle Scout advancement, 1994—, Val Verde County United Way campaign, 1989, pres., bd. dirs., 1990; pastoral counselor St. James Ch., 2002, pastoral care specialist, 2002—; chaplain Val Verde Regional Hosp., 2002—, Juvenile Detention Ctr., 1998—2006. Decorated DSM with oak leaf cluster, Legion of Merit with one oak leaf cluster, DFC, Bronze Star with V device, Air medal with two oak leaf clusters, Republic of Vietnam Gallantry Cross with Palm; recipient Gen. Edwin W. Rawlings award Air Force Inst. Tech., 1972, Comdt.'s award, 1972, Order of the Sword, 1986, Silver Beaver award Boy Scouts Am., 2003, Eagle Scout award, 2006; Wilma E. West fellow Boy Scouts Am., 2005, Named to Hall of Fame, Com. Info, 2008. Mem.: VFW (life), Mil. Affairs Assn. (v.p., bd. dir. 1990—2006, life dir., masonic citizen of yr.), Del Rio C. of C. (v.p. 1989—90, bd. dir. 1990—99, v.p. 1991—92, pres. 1995—96, bd. dir. 1999—, life dir. 2005—, chamber mem. of yr.), Air Force Assn. (Jimmy Doolittle award 1984, Ira Eaker award), Telephone Pioneers of Am., Soc. Logistics Engrs., Justice of the Peace and Constables Assn., Soc. Am. Mil. Engrs., Air Traffic Control Assn., Armed Forces Comm.-Electronics Assn. (mem. com. 1981—82, chmn. ethics com. 1982—83, internat. v.p. 1982—84, assoc. dir. 1984—96, bd. dirs. 1999, Meritorious Gold medal 1976, 1983), Non-Commd. Officers Assn. (hon.), Air Force Sgts. Assn. (hon.), Army Airways Comm. Svc. Alumni Assn. (life; dir. 2000—, Hall of Honor 2002, Life Achievement award 2003, 2007), Disabled Am. Vets. (life), Ret. Officers Assn. (life), Vietnam Vets. Am. (life), Del Rio Club, Lions (dir. 1989—94, v.p. 1994, Svc. award 1992—93, 2002—03, Helen Keller fellow 2004, Dist. Chaplain 2008—09), Civitan, Am. Legion, Order of Daedalians (life). Avocations: singing, gardening, sketching, automotive mechanics, private pilot. Address: HC 1 Box 7 Del Rio TX 78840-9720 Office Phone: 830-774-4483.

PRATHER, KIMBERLY ANN, chemistry professor; b. Santa Rosa, Calif., Aug. 25, 1962; d. John Harvey and Marjorie Hazel Prather; m. Joseph Ellis Mayer, Aug. 8, 1992; children: Joseph Tanner, Nickolas John. PhD, U. Calif., Davis, 1990. Prof. U. Calif., Riverside, 1992—2001, San Diego, 2001—. Mem. Bd. Atmospheric Sci. and Climate, Nat. Acad., Washington, 2008—. Recipient Smoluchowski award, GaEF, 1998, Creativity award, NSF, 2001; Rsch. grant, Am. Soc. Mass Spectrometry, 1994. Mem.: Am. Assn. Aerosol Rsch., Am. Geophys. Union, Am. Chem. Soc. (Findeis award 1996). Achievements include real-time measurements of aerosol chemistry and impacts on climate; patents for aerosol time-of-flight mass spectrometry; research in studies of the impacts of air pollution on human health and climate. Avocations: cooking, gardening, hiking.

PRATHER, LENORE LOVING, former state supreme court chief justice; b. West Point, Miss., Sept. 17, 1931; d. Byron Herald and Hattie Hearn (Morris) Loving; m. Robert Brooks Prather, May 30, 1957; children: Pamela, Valerie Jo, Malinda Wayne. BS, Miss. Univ. Women, 1953; JD, U. Miss., 1955; D (hon.), Miss. Univ. Women, 2003. Bar: Miss. 1955. Practice with B. H. Loving, West Point, 1955-60; sole practice, 1960-62, 65-71; assoc. practice, 1962-65; mcpl. judge City of West Point, 1965-71; chancery ct. judge 14th dist. State of Miss., Columbus, 1971-82, supreme ct. justice Jackson, 1982-92, presiding justice, 1993-97, chief justice, 1998-2001; interim pres. Miss. U. for Women, Columbus, Miss., 2001—02. V.p. Conf. Local Bar Assn., 1956-58; sec. Clay County Bar Assn., 1956-71 1st woman in Miss. to become chancery judge, 1971, and supreme ct. justice, 1982, and chief justice, 1998-2000; recipient Miss. Bar Found. Professionalism award, 2005; named Outstanding Miss. Woman, Pres.'s Commn. on Status of Women, 1986-87. Mem. Miss. State Bar Assn. (Jud. Excellence award 2000-01), DAR, Rotary, Pilot Club, Jr. Aux. Columbus Club. Episcopalian. Achievements include becoming the first female chancellor in Mississippi; the first female supreme court justice; the first female chief justice in Mississippi.

PRATHER, MARLA, curator; b. 1956; d. John and Jane Prather; m. Mortimer Benjamin Zuckerman, Sept. 27, 1996 (div. 2001); 1 child. MA in art history, Phi Beta Kappa, U. Kans. Curator, head of 20th-century art dept. Nat. Gallery Art, Washington, 1996—99; curator Postwar art Whitney Mus. Am. Art, NYC, 1999—2004; curator Am. art Tate Modern, London, 2005—07; sr. cons. modern and contemporary art Met. Mus. Art, NYC, 2008—. Trustee Archives Am. Art. Office: Met Mus Art 1000 Fifth Ave New York NY 10028-0198*

PRATHER, WILLIAM C., III, lawyer, writer; b. Toledo, Ill., Feb. 20, 1921; s. Hollie Cartmill and Effie Fern (Deppen) P. BA, U. Ill., 1942, JD, 1947. Bar: Ill. 1947, U.S. Supreme Ct. 1978. Co-pres. student govt. U. Ill., 1942, asst. dean, 1942-43; atty. First Nat. Bank Chgo., 1947-51; asst. gen. counsel U.S. Savs. and Loan League, Chgo., 1951-59; gen. counsel U.S. League of Savs. Instns., Chgo., 1959-82, gen. counsel emeritus, 1982—; sole practice Cumberland County, Ill., 1981—. Sem. lectr. in law, banking. Editor: The Legal Bulletin, 1951-81, The Federal Guide, 1954-81; author: Savings Accounts, 8th edit., 1981; contbr. articles to publs. Served to lt. US Army, ASTP, D-3 mil. govt. France, Germany, 1943—45. Decorated Bronze Star. Mem. ABA, FBA, Internat. Bar Assn., Ill. Bar Assn., Chgo. Bar Assn., Union Internat. des Avocats, Nat. Lawyers Club Washington, Cosmos Club, Univ. Club Chgo., Kiwanis, Mattoon Golf and Country Club, Exeter and County Club (Eng.), Am. Club Riviera (France), Tennis Club de Beaulieu (France), Soc. Colonial Wars, St. Andrew's Soc., Am. Legion, Phi Delta Phi, Phi Gamma Delta, Phi Eta Sigma, Phi Alpha Chi. Home: Applewood Farm PO Box 157 Toledo IL 62468-0157 Office: 142 Courthouse Sq Toledo IL 62468 Office Phone: 217-849-2144.

PRATHER, WILLIAM RONALD, medical association administrator; s. James Lowell and Elizabeth Ann Prather; m. Judith Ann Pressy, Dec. 6, 1985. MD, U. Mo., Kansas City, 1973. Diplomate Am. Bd. Internal Medicine, 1977. Portfolio mgr. Manning & Napier, Rochester, NY, 1995—96; sr. health care analyst Roth Capital Partners, Irvine, Calif., 1996—2000; co-founder Panacos Pharmaceuticals, Gaithersburg, Md., 2000—04; sr. v.p. corp. devel. Pluristem Therapeutics, Inc., Haifa, Israel, 2004—. Dir. Boston Biomed. Inc., West Bridgewater, Mass., 1998—2001. Office: Imprimatur Group Inc PO Box 997 Edwards CO 81632 Business E-Mail: skiingdoc@comcast.net.

PRATS, MICHAEL, petroleum engineer, educator; b. Tampa, Fla., Dec. 18, 1925; s. Miguel and Maria (Carbó) P.; m. Mary Blanche Flaherty, Apr. 7, 1951; children: Delicia Anne, Barbara Eileen, Teresa Kaye, Steven Michael. BS in Physics, U. Tex., 1949, MA in Physics, 1951. With Shell Devel. Co., Houston, 1950—, cons. rsch. engr., then sr. rsch. assoc., 1972-89; pres. Michael Prats & Assocs., Houston, 1989—. Cons. prof. petroleum engring. dept. Stanford U., 1997—99; adj. prof. dept. geosystems petroleum engring. U. Tex., Austin, 1991—2001; participant scientist exch. Royal/Dutch Shell Lab., Amsterdam, Netherlands, 1954, 55, Shell Internat. Petroleum, The Hague, Netherlands, 1981, Maraven, S.A., Caracas, Venezuela, 1981-83. Author: Thermal Recovery, 1982, Spanish transl., 1987; contbr. articles to profl. jours.; 23 patents in field. Served to staff sgt. USAAF, 1944-46, PTO. Recipient Disting. Svc. award Rep. Honduras, 1989, KAPITSA medal Acad. Natural Scis. (Moscow), 1995; named to Internat. Hall of Fame, 1989. Mem.: NAE, AIME (hon.), Russian Acad. Nat. Scis. (fgn.), Acad. Engring. Armenia (fgn.), Assn. Petroleum Engrs. Mex., Can. Inst. Mining, Acad. Medicine, Engring. and Sci. of Tex., Mex. Nat. Acad. Engring. (corr.), Soc. Petroleum Engrs. (hon.; bd. dirs. 1976—79, sr. tech. editor 1987—90, Uren award 1974, Disting. Mem. award 1983, Enhanced Oil Recovery Pioneer 1986, Thermal Recovery Disting. Achievement award Thermal Ops. Symposium 1991, Anthony F. Lucas Gold medal 1993, Legend of Hydraulic Fracturing 2006), Pi Epsilon Tau (hon. diploma of honor 1986). Avocation: travel. Address: 2834 Bellefontaine St Houston TX 77025-1610 Personal E-mail: mikep@mprats.com.

PRATS PALERM, ROBERT L., political organization administrator; b. San Juan, 1966; m. Heddle Fernandez; 2 children. Degree, Cornell U., 1990; postgrad., Georgetown U., 1991—92; JD, Inter-Am. U. P.R., 1994. Notary pub. Aux. advisor Gov. Rafael Hernandez Columbus, 1990—91; mem. staff US Congress, Washington, 1991—92; econ. advisor, minority spokesman PR Senate, 1993—94, at-large senator, 2000—04, pres. commn. govt. and pub. security; atty. Goldman, Antonetti & Córdova, 1995—97; advisor, coords. pub. rels. Municipality of San Juan, 1997—99; pvt. practice atty., 2000; chmn. PR Dem. Party, 2003—. Host Speakout, WOSO Radio. Fundraising participant Alzheimer's Assn., PR, 2002; mem. adv. bd. Cornell U., Ithaca, NY. Democrat. Office: PR Dem Party PO Box 19328 San Juan PR 00910-3939 Office Phone: 787-274-2921. Office Fax: 787-759-9075.*

PRATT, BONNIE, science educator; b. Durham, NC, Jan. 2, 1961; d. Gerald Jordan and Roselyn Bowen Woolard; m. William A. Pratt, Oct. 2, 1957; children: Cameron Gile, Parker Jordan. BS in Zoology and Microbiology, NC State U., Raleigh, 1983. Tchr. sci. Northview H.S., Duluth, Ga., 2002—. Dir. Project 2011 Northview H.S., Duluth, Ga., 2004—06. Scholar, St. George's U. Med. Sch., 2006. Achievements include developement and implementation of a schoolwide program for incoming freshmen to help them transition into high school; develop and hold seminar, teaching evolution, created project 2011 and Project 2013, a uniqe educational opportunity for students interested in medicine from economically disadvantaged backgound. Home: 5620 Timson Lane Alpharetta GA 30022 Office: Northview High School 10695 Parsons Road Duluth GA 30097

PRATT, DANA JOSEPH, publishing consultant; b. Cambridge, Mass., Dec. 9, 1926; s. Carroll Cornelius and Marjory (Bates) P.; m. Therese Louis, July 14, 1957; children: Joseph Caldwell, Michael Louis, Benjamin Lyon B.Naval Sci., Tufts U., 1946, BA, 1948. Mgmt. trainee N.J. Bell Telephone Co., Newark, 1948-50; sales asst. Princeton U. Press, NJ, 1950-53; sales mgr. U. Ill. Press, Urbana, 1953-55; field cons. Franklin Book Programs, NYC, 1955-59; staff assoc. Am. Book Pubs. Council, NYC, 1959-62; exec. sec. Assn. Am. Univ. Presses, NYC, 1962-66; asst. dir. Yale U. Press, New Haven, 1966-78; dir. pub. Library of Congress, Washington, 1978-93. Co-founder Internat. Group Pub. Librs. Contbr. articles to profl. jours. Served as ensign USNR, comdg. officer PC 566, 1946-47 Recipient Award for Superior Svc. Libr. of Congress, 1993. Mem. Washington Book Pubs. (pres. 1984-85), Soc. for Scholarly Pub. (bd. dirs. 1982-86), Washington Map Soc., Washington Rare Book Group. Home and Office: The Towers 514E 4201 Cathedral Ave NW Washington DC 20016-4901 Office Phone: 202-237-1380. E-mail: danajpratt@yahoo.com.

PRATT, DAVID M., education educator; b. Santa Maria, Calif., July 2, 1968; s. Robert Allen and Susan Pratt; children: Tyler, Catalina, Alexander. BA in liberal arts, Pepperdine U., 1990; MA, Chapman U., 1995; PhD, U. Calif, 2002. Tchr. Calif. Commn. Tchr. Credentialling, Calif., 1990—. Recipient Connecting Math. for Elem. Tchr.s, NSF, Purdue U., 2003. Mem.: Soc. for Info. Tech. and Tchr. Edn., Internat. Soc. for Tech. in Edn., Am. Ednl. Rsch. Assn. Office Phone: 219-785-5578. E-mail: dpratt@pnc.edu.

PRATT, DAVID TERRY, engineering consultant; b. Shelley, Idaho, Sept. 14, 1934; s. Eugene Francis and Bernice (Montague) P.; m. Marilyn Jean Thackston, Dec. 22, 1956; children: Douglas Montague, Elizabeth Joann, Brian Stephens. BSc in Mech. Engring., U. Wash., 1956; MSc, U. Calif., Berkeley, 1962, PhD, 1968. Asst. prof. marine engring. U.S. Naval Acad., Annapolis, Md., 1961-64; prof. mech. engring., asst. dean Wash. State U., Pullman, 1968-76; prof. mech. engring. U. Utah, Salt Lake City, 1976-78; prof., chmn. mech. engring. and applied mechanics U. Mich., Ann Arbor, 1978-81; prof., chmn. mech. engring. U. Wash., Seattle, 1981-86, prof. mech. engring., 1987-96, prof. emeritus; engring. cons. Rsch. dir. supercomputing Aerojet Propulsion Rsch. Inst., Sacramento, 1986-87. Author (with W.H. Heiser) Hypersonic Airbreathing Propulsion, 1994, (with J.D. Mattingly and W.H. Heiser) Aircraft Engine Design, 2002; editor (with L.D. Smoot) Combustion and Gasification of Pulverized Coal, 1976; contbr. articles to profl. jours. Served to 1st lt. USMC, 1956-60. NSF sci. faculty fellow, 1965-66; Fulbright-Hays sr. research fellow Imperial Coll., 1974-75; David Pierpont Gardner faculty fellow U. Utah, 1976. Fellow AIAA (assoc., Summerfield award 1999, 2005); mem. ASME, Combustion Inst. Lutheran. Home and Office: 2304 Cascade Ct Anacortes WA 98221 Personal E-mail: pratt@combustion.com.

PRATT, GEORGE CHENEY, law educator, retired judge; b. Corning, NY, May 22, 1928; s. George Wollage and Muriel (Cheney) Pratt; m. Carol June Hoffman, Aug. 16, 1952; children: George W., Lise M., Marcia Pratt Burke, William T. BA, Yale U., 1950, JD, 1953. Bar: N.Y. 1953, U.S. Supreme Ct. 1964, U.S. Ct. Appeals 1974. Law clk. to Charles W. Froessel (Judge of N.Y. Ct. Appeals), 1953—55; assoc. then ptnr. Sprague & Stern, Mineola, NY, 1956—60; ptnr. Andromidas, Pratt & Pitcher, Mineola, 1960—65, Pratt, Caemmerer & Cleary, Mineola, 1965—75; partner Farrell, Fritz, Pratt, Caemmerer & Cleary, 1975—76; judge U.S. Dist. Ct. (Ea. Dist. of N.Y.), 1976—82, U.S. Cir. Ct. Appeals for 2d cir. (Uniondale), NY, 1982—93; sr. circ. judge U.S. Cir. of Appeals for 2d Cir., NY, 1993—95; counsel Parnon & Pratt L.L.P., NYC, 1995—2000, Farrell Fritz PC, 2001—. Prof. Touro Law Sch., Huntington, NY, 1993—2003. Fellow: Coll. Comml. Arbitrators; mem.: ABA, Reins. and Ins. Arbitration Soc., Nassau County Bar Assn., N.Y. State Bar Assn. United Ch. Of Christ. Office: Farrell Fritz PC 1320 Reckson Plz Uniondale NY 11556 Office Phone: 516-227-0604. Business E-Mail: gpratt@farrellfritz.com.

PRATT, GEORGE JANES, JR., psychologist author; b. Mpls., May 3, 1948; s. George Janes and Sally Elvina (Hanson) P.; m. Vonda Pratt; 1 child, Whitney Beth. BA cum laude, U. Minn., 1970, MA, 1973; PhD with spl. commendation, Calif. Sch. Profl. Psychology, San Diego, 1976. Diplomate Am. Acad. Pain Mgmt., Assn. Comprehensive Energy Psychology; lic. psychologist, Calif., 1976. Psychology trainee Ctr. for Behavior Modification, Mpls., 1971—72, U.Minn. Student Counseling Bur., 1972—73; predoctoral clin. psychology intern San Bernardino County Mental Health Svcs., Calif., 1973—74, San Diego County Mental Health Services, 1974—76; mem. staff San Louis Rey Hosp., 1977—78; postdoctoral clin. psychology intern Mesa Vista Hosp., San Diego, 1976; clin psychologist, dir. Psychology and Cons. Assocs. of San Diego, 1976—90; chmn. Psychology and Cons. Assocs. Press, 1977—94. Bd. dirs. Optimax, Inc., 1985-94; pres. George Pratt Ph.D., Psychol. Corp., 1979—; chmn. Pratt, Korn & Assocs., Inc., 1984-94; mem. staff Scripps Meml. Hosp., La Jolla, Calif., 1986—, chmn. psychology, 1993-95, 2000—; founder La Jolla Profl. Workshops, 1977-81; clin. psychologist El Camino Psychology Ctr., San Clemente, Calif., 1977-78; grad. teaching asst. U. Minn. Psychology and Family Studies divsn., 1971; teaching assoc. U. Minn. Psychology and Family Studies divsn., Mpls., 1972-73; instr. U. Minn. Extension divsn., Mpls., 1971-73; faculty Calif. Sch. Profl. Psychology, 1974-83, San Diego Evening Coll., 1975-77, Nat. U., 1978-79, Chapman Coll., 1978, San Diego State U., 1979-80; vis. prof. Pepperdine U., L.A., 1976-78; cons. U. Calif. at San Diego Med. Sch., 1976-78, also instr. univ., 1978—; psychology chmn. Workshops in Clin. Hypnosis, 1980-84; cons. Calif. Health Dept., 1974, Naval Regional Med. Ctr., 1978-82, ABC-TV; also speaker. Author: Sensory/Progressive Relaxation, 1979, Effective Stress Management, 1979, Clinical Hypnosis: Techniques and Applications, 1985, Rx for Stress, 1994; co-author: A Clinical Hypnosis Primer, 1984, 88, 2009, HyperPerformance, 1987, 2009, Release Your Business Potential, 1988, Instant Emotional Healing, 2000, Emotional Self-Management, 2000; contbr.: Hypnosis: Questions and Answers, 1986, Handbook for Hypnotic Suggestions and Metaphors, 1990, Imagery in Sports and Physical Performance, 1994. With USAR, 1970-76. Fellow Am. Soc. Clin. Hypnosis (cert., approved cons.); mem. APA, Nat. Register of Health Svc. Providers in Psychology, San Diego Soc. Sex. Therapy and Edn. (past pres.), San Diego Soc. Clin. Hypnosis (past pres.), San Diego Psychol. Assn., Grammy (voting mem.), U. Minn. Alumni Assn., Beta Theta Pi. Office: Scripps Meml Hosp Campus 9834 Genesee Ave Ste 321 La Jolla CA 92037-1216 Home: 1127 Muirlands Vista Way La Jolla CA 92037-6210 Office Phone: 858-457-3900.

PRATT, HARRY DAVIS, retired entomologist; b. North Adams, Mass., Apr. 13, 1915; s. Harry Edward and Ethel Mae (Davis) P.; m. Caroline Georgine Kreiss, Apr. 13, 1944 (dec. May 1951); children: Harry Davis Jr., Katherine Maria Pratt Garrison, George Kreiss; m. Dora Belle Ford, Nov. 29, 1952 (dec. July 1998). BS, Mass. State Coll., 1936, MS, 1938; PhD, U. Minn., St. Paul, 1941. Registered profl. entomologist. Asst. entomologist USPHS Malaria Control War Areas, San Juan, 1942-46; chief med. entomol. lab. USPHS Communicable Disease Ctr., Atlanta, 1946-53, chief insect rodent tr., 1953-63, chief Aedes aegypti control tng., 1964-68; chief insect rodent control tng. Environ. Control Agy., Atlanta, 1968-72; cons., tchr., writer Atlanta, 1972—. Spl. cons. Econ. Coop. Administrn., Saigon, Vietnam, 1950, WHO, Geneva, 1966, Kuala Lumpur, Malaysia, 1969. United meth. South Carolina, 2003—08. Fellow Entomol. Soc. Am. (life); mem. Am. Mosquito Control Assn. (pres. 1967), Entol. Soc. Washington, Ga. Entomol. Soc. Mem. Christian Ch. (Disciples Of Christ). Home: 104 So Almond Dr Simpsonville SC 29681

PRATT, JACK, legislative staff member; b. New Haven, Jan. 20, 1976; BA cum laude, Kenyon Coll., Gambier, Ohio, 1998; MS, London Sch. Economics, 1999. Staff asst. for Rep. Ken R. Lucas, US House of Reps., Washington; dep. press sec., legis. asst. for Rep. Steve Israel, 2001—02, press sec., legis. asst., 2002—03, dep. chief of staff, 2003—04, chief of staff, 2004—. Office: Office of Congressman Steve Israel 2457 Rayburn House Office Bldg Washington DC 20515 Office Phone: 202-225-3335. Business E-Mail: jack.pratt@mail.house.gov.*

PRATT, JOHN PATRICK, lawyer; b. Managua, Nicaragua, Nov. 19, 1967; s. Alfred Sidney Pratt and Thelma Reyes; 1 child, Patrick Alexander. BA in Philosophy, Fla. State U., 1994; JD, Tulane U., 1997. Bar: Fla. 1998, D.C. 1999, U.S. Dist. Ct. (so. dist.) Fla. 1998, U.S. Ct. Appeals (11th cir.) 1998, U.S. Supreme Ct. 2001, U.S. Ct. Appeals (9th cir.) 2002, cert.: Fla. Bar Certification Com. (immigration and nationality law) 2009. Law clk. Office of Dist. Counsel IRS, St. Paul, 1995; law clk. Office of Asst. Chief Counsel U.S. Customs Svc., New Orleans, 1996-97; assoc. Zyne, Saleeby & Saleh, P.A., Miami, 1997-98, Montiel Davis & Woodward Kimber, P.A., Miami, 1998-2000, Leaf & Assocs., P.A., Miami, 2000-01, Kurzban, Kurzban, Weinger & Tetzeli, P.A., 2001—. Recipient AV Rated by Martindale Hubbell. Mem. ABA, Am. Immigration Lawyers Assn., Hispanic Nat. Bar Assn., Aila South Fla. Chpt. (pres. elect). Roman Catholic. Avocations: reading, tennis. Office: Kurzban Kurzban Weinger & Tetzeli PA 2650 SW 27 Ave Ste 200 Miami FL 33133 Office Phone: 305-444-0060. Personal E-mail: jpatrickpratt@aol.com. Business E-Mail: jpratt@kkwtlaw.com.

PRATT, JOHN S., lawyer; b. Chaffee, Mo., Oct. 19, 1942; s. John S. and Mary M. Pratt; m. Virginia Fry, Sept. 27, 1980; children: Stephanie, Kristin, Brennan, Jordan. BA in Polit. Sci., History, S.E. Mo. State U., Cape Girardeau, 1963; JD, Washington U., Saint Louis, Mo/, 1966. City prosecutor City of Springfield, Mo., 1972—74, Mayor Pro Tem Mo., 1974—77, city councilman Mo., 1974—78; atty. Pratt, Fossard Jensen, Masters LLC, Springfield, Mo., 1978—2000. Named Mo. Super Lawyer, 2002—08; named to Best Lawyers in Am., 1994—2009. Fellow: Am. Acad. Matrimonial Lawyers (pres. Mo. chpt. 2006); mem.: ABA, Mo. and Greene Co. Bar. Office: Pratt Fossard Jensen Masters 3432 Culpepper Ct Springfield MO 65804 Business E-Mail: aowens@pfjmlaw.com.

PRATT, JON, not-for-profit executive; JD, Antioch Sch. Law; MPA, Harvard U. Atty., lobbyist Minn. Pub. Interest Rsch. Group; regional dir. Youth Project; dir. Philanthropy Project; founder, exec. dir. Minn. Coun. Nonprofits, Saint Paul, 1987—. Adv. com. mem. Nat. Ctr. for Charitable Statistics, Johns Hopkins U. State of Sector Project. Contbg. editor Nonprofit Quarterly; contbr. articles to profl. jours. Mem.: Nat. Coun. Nonprofit Assns. (co-chair Pub. Policy Com.). Office: Minn Coun Nonprofits 2314 University Ave W #20 Saint Paul MN 55114 Office Phone: 651-642-1904. Office Fax: 651-642-1517.

PRATT, MARY LOUISE, librarian, writer; b. Iowa City, Iowa, May 31, 1953; d. William Winston and Helen Virginia Pratt. BA in Eng., Pa. State U., 1977; MLS, Clarion U. Pa., 1987. Dir. written comm. The Fine Arts Connection, State College, Pa., 1980—81; mgr. Unimarts, Inc., State College, 1981—84; reference libr. Evansville-Vanderburgh County Pub. Libr., Ind., 1987—88; ref. libr. Cabell County Pub. Libr., Huntington, W.Va., 1989—96, adult svcs. coord., 1996—. Cons. br. libr. Cabell County Pub. Libr., Huntington, 1989—, pub. computer instr., 1998—; English instr. Marshall Cmty. & Tech. Coll. Actor: (plays) A Christmas Carol, Deathtrap, The Boys Next Door, Ransom of Red Chief; editor: Rural Libraries; columnist: Who Said it?; author: (poem) Mr. Lonely in the City (1st pl. Ctrl. Pa. Festival of Arts Poetry Competition., 1977, 1st pl. Calamity Cafe Poetry Slam, 1999); contbr. articles to profl. jours. Active Cabell-Huntington Coalition for the Homeless, W.Va., 1998—. Mem.: W.Va. Libr. Assn., ALA, Guyandotte Poets, Acad. Am. Poets (assoc.). Democrat. Presbyterian. Avocations: acting, autograph collecting, hiking, travel. Home: 1368 13th St Huntington WV 25701 Office: Cabell County Pub Libr 455 9th St Plaza Huntington WV 25701 Personal E-mail: mlpratt007@aol.com. E-mail: mpratt@cabell.lib.wv.us.

PRATT, ROBERT CRANFORD, political scientist, educator; b. Montreal, Que., Can., Oct. 8, 1926; s. Robert Goodwin and Henrietta (Freeman) P.; m. Renate Hecht, July 15, 1956; children: Gerhard, Marcus, Anna. BA, McGill U., Montreal, 1947; postgrad., Inst. Science Politique, Paris, 1948; MPhil, Oxford U., Eng., 1952. Lectr. McGill U., 1952-54, 56-58, Makerere U., Uganda, 1954-56; rsch. officer Oxford Inst. Commonwealth Studies, 1958-60; prin. Univ. Coll., Dar-es-Salaam, Tanzania, 1961-65; chmn. internat. studies program U. Toronto, Ont., Can., 1966-71, prof. polit. sci., 1966—. Spl. asst. to pres., Tanzania, 1965, 69; rsch. fellow Internat. Devel. Rsch. Ctr., 1978; commonwealth vis. prof. U. London, 1979-80; dir. Rsch. Project on Western Mid. Powers and Global Poverty, 1985-89; vis. fellow Devel. Ctr. Orgn. for Econ. Cooperation and Devel., Paris, 1986-87. Author: (with Anthony Low) Buganda and British Overrule, 1960, The Critical Phase in Tanzania, Nyerere and the Emergence of a Socialist Strategy, 1976, Towards Socialism in Tanzania, 1979, (with Robert Matthews) Human Rights in Canadian Foreign Policy, 1988, Internationalism Under Strain: The North-South Policies of Canada, The Netherlands, Norway and Sweden, 1989; (with Roger Hutchinson) Christian Faith and Economic Justice: A Canadian Perspective, 1989); Middle Power Internationalism: The North-South Dimension, 1990, Canadian International Development Assistance Policies: An Appraisal, 1994, 2nd edit., 1996. Decorated officer Order of Can.; recipient Killam award Can. Coun., 1968, Ludwik and Estelle Jus Meml. Human Rights award, 1995; Rhodes scholar Oxford U., 1950. Fellow Royal Soc. Can.; mem. Can. Polit. Sci. Assn., Can. African Studies Assn. (past pres.), Can. Assn. for Study of Internat. Devel. (mem. exec. coun.), Ecumenical Forum Can. (past chmn.). New Democrat. Home: 205 Cottingham St Toronto ON Canada M4V 1C4 Business E-Mail: cranford.pratt@sympatico.ca.

PRATT, ROBERT WINDSOR, lawyer; b. Findlay, Ohio, Mar. 6, 1950; s. John Windsor and Isabelle (Vance) P.; m. Catherine Camak Baker, Sept. 3, 1977; children: Andrew Windsor, David Camak, James Robert. AB, Wittenberg U., Springfield, Ohio, 1972; JD, Yale U., 1975. Bar: Ill. 1975, U.S. Dist. Ct. (no. dist.) Ill. 1976, U.S. Dist. Ct. (we. dist.) Mich. 1995, U.S. Ct. Appeals (fed. cir.) 1984, U.S. Ct. Appeals (7th cir.) 1996, U.S. Ct. Appeals (D.C. cir.) 2004. Assoc. Keck, Mahin & Cate, Chgo., 1975—81, ptnr., 1981—97; pvt. practice Wilmette, Ill., 1998—99; sr. asst. atty. gen. Office Ill. Atty. Gen., 1999—2001, chief antitrust bur., 2001—. Bd. dirs. Chgo. region ARC, 1985-96, vice chmn., 1988-92, chmn., 1992-96, bd. dirs. Mid-Am. chpt., 1992-96. Mem. ABA, Yale Club (Chgo.). Office Phone: 312-814-3722. Business E-Mail: rpratt@atg.state.il.us.

PRATT, TIMOTHY, lawyer; Grad., Drake U. Law Sch. Law clerk Chief Judge Floyd R. Gibson, US Ct. Appeals; joined Shook, Hardy and Bacon LLP, Kans. City, Mo., 1977, ptnr., 1981—2008, co-chair Pharm. and Med. Def. Litig. Divsn.; exec. v.p., sec., gen. counsel Boston Sci. Corp., Natick, Mass., 2008—. Lead outside counsel, Cardiac Rhythm Mgmt. Guidant Corp. Mem. editl. bd. Medical Devices Law and Industry Report. Named a Leading Nat. Products Liability Lawyer, Chambers USA, 2006—07; named one of The Best Lawyers in America, 2006—08; named to Lawdragon 3000 Leading Lawyers in America, 2006, Lawdragon 500 Leading Litigators in America, 2006, Top 100 Mo. and Kans. Superlawyers, Chambers USA, 2006—07, Guide to the World's Leading Product Liability Lawyers, 2007, BTI Client Svc. All-Star Team for Law Firms, 2008, Definitive Guide to America's Leading Litig. Firms and Attys., 2008. Mem.: ABA, Nat. Inst. Trial Advocacy (mem. faculty), Def. Rsch. Inst. (spkr., chair Corp. Coun. Roundtable), Fedn. Def. Corp. Counsel (bd. dirs., dir., chair Corp. Coun. Symposium, chair Trial Masters Program). Office: Boston Sci Corp 1 Boston Sci Pl Natick MA 01760-1537

PRATT, WALTER F., JR., dean, law educator; BA in History magna cum laude, Vanderbilt U., 1968; D.Phil in Politics, Oxford U., 1974; JD, Yale U., 1977. Law clk. to Judge Charles Clark US Ct. Appeals (5th cir.), 1977—78; law clk. to Chief Justice Warren E. Burger US Supreme Ct., 1978—79; asst. prof. law Duke U., 1979—82, assoc. prof., 1982—86; assoc. prof. law The Law Sch., U. Notre Dame, 1986—98, co-dir. Notre Dame London Law Ctr., 1988—89, assoc. dean academic affairs, 1991—98, exec. assoc. dean, 1998—2006; dean, Ednl. Found. disting. prof. law U. SC Sch. Law, 2006—. Vis. assoc. prof. law J. Reuben Clark Law Sch., Brigham Young U., 1984—85; vis. scholar law dept. Nat. U. Ireland, Galway, 1998—99. Author: Privacy in Britain, 1979, The Supreme Court Under Edward Douglass White, 1910-1921, 1999; contbr. articles to law jours. First lt. US Army, 1968—71. Recipient Spl. Presdl. Award, U. Notre Dame; grantee Rhodes Scholarship. Mem.: ABA, Am. Soc. Legal History, Assn. Am. Law Schs. Office: U SC Sch Law Office of Dean 701 S Main St Columbia SC 29208 Office Phone: 803-777-6857. E-mail: wpratt@law.sc.edu.*

PRATT, WILLIAM, lawyer; BA magna cum laude, Tulane U., 1974; JD with honors, Columbia U., 1977. Bar: Ill. 1977, NY 1990. Named one of Am. Leading Bus. Lawyers Litig./Gen. Cmml., Chambers USA, 2004—05. Fellow: Am. Coll. Trial Lawyers; mem.: Bd. Visitors Columbia Sch. Law, Phi Beta Kappa. Office: Kirkland & Ellis LLP Citigroup Ctr 153 E 53rd St New York NY 10022-4611 Office Phone: 212-446-4862. Office Fax: 212-446-4900. Business E-Mail: wpratt@kirkland.com.

PRATT, WILLIAM CROUCH, JR., literature and language professor, writer; b. Shawnee, Okla., Oct. 5, 1927; s. William Crouch and Irene (Johnston) P.; m. Anne Cullen Rich, Oct. 2, 1954; children: Catherine Cullen, William Stuart, Randall Johnston. BA, U. Okla., 1949; MA, Vanderbilt U., 1951, PhD, 1957. Rotary Internat. fellow U. Glasgow, Scotland, 1951-52; instr. English Vanderbilt U., 1955-57, Miami U., Oxford, Ohio, 1957-59, asst. prof., 1959-64, assoc. prof., dir. freshman English, 1964-68, prof., 1968—98; prof. emeritus Mami U., 1998—. Fulbright-Hays lectr. Am. lit., prof. Am. lit. Univ. Coll., Dublin, Ireland, 1975-76; resident scholar Miami U. European Ctr., Luxembourg, fall 1976; lectr. Yeats Internat. Summer Sch., Sligo, Ireland, 1979, 81, 82, 83, James Joyce Summer Sch., Dublin, 1996; writer-in-residence Tyrone Guthrie Ctr., County Monaghan, Ireland, summer 1992, 96; lectr. in mod. lit., Lifelong Learning at Vanderbilt, Nashville, fall 2004-. Author: The Imagist Poem, 1963, rev. edit., 2001, 3rd rev. edit., 2009, The Fugitive Poets, 1965, rev. edit., 1991, The College Writer, 1969, College Days at Old Miami, 1984, The Influence of French Symbolism on Modern American Poetry, 1985, Miami Poets, 1988, Homage to Imagism, 1992, The Big Ballad Jamboree, 1996, Singing the Chaos: Madness and Wisdom in Modern Poetry, 1996, Miami University: A Personal History, 1998, Ezra Pound, Nature and Myth, 2002, Ezra Pound and the Making of Modernism, 2007, Ezra Pound, Language and Persona, 2008; contbr. essays, translations, poems, revs. to lit. jours., books. Served to lt. USNR, 1953-55. Mem.: Internat. Contemporary Lit. and Theatre Soc., Ezra Pound Internat. Conf. (sec. 1991—2005), Cin. Lit. Club, Univ. Club, Omicron Delta Kappa, Sigma Alpha Epsilon, Phi Beta Kappa. Republican. Anglican. Avocation: birdwatching. Home: 212 Oakhill Dr Oxford OH 45056-2710 Personal E-mail: wmcpratt@aol.com. *True happiness is to live in the understanding of what we love, the pursuit of what we believe in.*

PRATT-DANNALS, ED, school system administrator; B, Ga. State U., Atlanta; EdM, U. North Fla., Jacksonville. Math. tchr. John Gorrie Jr. HS Duval County Pub. Schs., Jacksonville, Fla., 1976, prin., regional supt., assoc. supt. for curriculum and instrn., chief academic officer, supt., 2007—. Recipient Commr.'s Award for Outstanding Principals Among HS Principals in North Fla., 1995, J.J. McCranie Svc. Above Self Award, West Jacksonville Rotary, 1997; named Outstanding Alumnus, U. North Fla. Coll. Edn., 2005. Mem.: Duval County Secondary Sch. Vice Principals' Assn. (past pres.), Duval County Secondary Sch. Principals (past pres.), Nat. Assn. Secondary Sch. Adminstrs., Assn. Suprs. and Curriculum Devel., Fla. Assn. Sch. Adminstrs., Duval County Assn. Secondary Sch. Adminstrs. (Asst. Adminstr. of Yr. 1984), Westside Rotary Club Jacksonville. Office: Duval County Pub Schs 1701 Prudential Dr Jacksonville FL 32207 Office Phone: 904-390-2115. Office Fax: 904-390-2586.*

PRATTE, ROBERT JOHN, lawyer; b. Victoria, BC, Can., Feb. 14, 1948; s. Arthur Louis Jr. and Marie Bertha (Latremouille) P.; children: Merie Elise, Jessica Louise, Allison Adele, Chelsea Nicole. BA, Northwestern U., 1970; JD, Tulane U., 1976. Bar: Minn. 1976, Ariz. 1997. Ptnr. Best & Flanagan, Mpls., 1976-84, Briggs & Morgan, Mpls., 1985—2007, head mortgage banking group; ptnr. DLA Piper LLP (US), Mpls., 2007—. Editor: Mortgage Lending in Minnesota—A Desktop Reference Guide, 1990. Ex-officio mem. Wilderness Inquiry, Minn.; pres. Twin Cities Northwestern U. Alumni Assn., 1978; active Wayzata Cmty. Ch., Mpls. With US Coast Guard, 1971—73. Fellow Am. Coll. Mortgage Attys. (regent); mem. ABA, Minn. State Bar Assn., Hennepin County Bar Assn., Mortgage Bankers Assn. (mem. Legal Issues and Regulatory Compliance Com.) Avocations: fly fishing, wine collecting, cooking. Office: DLA Piper US LLP 90 S Seventh St Minneapolis MN 55402-3903 Office Phone: 612-524-3030. Business E-Mail: robert.pratte@dlapiper.co. *Undertake with enthusiasm and pursue to completion the tasks that others are unwilling or unable to do. Never be satisfied with mediocrity. Surround yourself with those who are smarter than you; have the patience and judgement to let them succeed. Success can be measured by the hours you spend with your children--reading, fishing, and playing.*

PRATT-JOHNSON, YVONNE KAREN, education professor; b. Bklyn., Feb. 20, 1954; d. Cyril and Jennie Pratt; m. Raphael Nathaniel Johnson, Feb. 15, 1949; children: Jonathan Leslie Johnson, Michael Raphael Johnson. BA, Stony Brook U., NY, 1975; MS, Georgetown U., Washington, DC, 1977; MA, Columbia U., NYC, 1978, MEd, 1980, Ed.D, 1986. Prof. Borough of Manhattan CC of CUNY, NYC, 1978—2003; prof. edn. St. John's U., Queens, NY, 2003—. Tchr. trainer Hunter Coll. the CUNY, NYC, 1991—94. Recipient Excellence Award for Tchg. and Rsch., Nat. Inst. for Staff and Orgnl. Devel. Excellence; grantee The Rockefeller Fellow Award, Rockefeller Rsch. Found. Mem.: ASCD, Internat. Assn. Tchrs. English as a Fgn. Lang., Am. Ednl. Rsch. Assn. Avocation: travel. Home: 90 La Salle St 12F New York NY 10027 Office: St John's Univ 8000 Utopia Pky Jamaica NY 11439 Home Fax: 212-222-1823. Personal E-mail: yypj15@aol.com. E-mail: prattjoy@stjohns.edu.

PRAUSNITZ, JOHN MICHAEL, chemical engineer, educator; b. Berlin, Jan. 7, 1928; arrived in U.S., 1937, naturalized, 1944; s. Paul Georg and Susi Prausnitz; m. Susan Prausnitz, June 10, 1956; children: Stephanie, Mark Robert. B Chem. Engring., Cornell U., 1950; MS, U. Rochester, 1951; PhD, Princeton, 1955; Dr. Ing., U. L'Aquila, 1983, Tech. U. Berlin, 1989, U. Padova, 2004; DSc, Princeton U., 1995. Mem. faculty U. Calif., Berkeley, 1955—, prof. chem. engring., 1963—. Cons. to cyrogenic, polymer, petroleum and petrochem. industries; Miller rsch. prof., 1966, 78; sr. investigator Lawrence Berkeley Nat. Lab., Berkeley; Wilhelm lectr. Princeton U., 1980; W.K. Lewis lectr. MIT, 1993; Edward Mason lectr. Brown U., 1999; Danckwerts lectr. Royal Acad. Engring., London, 2000; hon. prof. Tech. U. Shanghai, 2001; Dodge lectr. Yale U., 2004. Author: (with others) Computer Calculations for Multicomponent Vapor-Liquid Equilibria, 1967, (Computer Calculations for High-Pressure Vapor-Liquid Equilibria, 1968, Molecular Thermodynamics of Fluid-Phase Equilibria, 1969, 2d edit., 1986, 3d edit., 1999, Regular and Related Solutions, 1970, Properties of Gases and Liquids, 3d edit., 1977, 4th edit., 1987, 5th edit., 2000, Computer Calculations for Multicomponent Vapor-Liquid and Liquid-Liquid Equilibria, 1980; contbr. to profl. jours. Recipient Alexander von Humboldt Sr. Scientist award, 1976, Carl von Linde Gold Meml. medal, German Inst. for Cryogenics, 1987, Solvay prize, Solvay Found. for Chem. Scis., 1990, Corcoran award, Am. Soc. for Engring. Edn., 1991, 1999, D.L. Katz award, Gas Processors Assn., 1992, Waterman award, Tech. U. Delft, 1998, Rossini award, Internat. Union of Pure and Applied Chemistry, 2002, Nat. medal of Sci., 2005; Guggenheim fellow, 1962, 1973, fellow, Inst. Advanced Study, Berlin, 1985, Christensen fellow, St. Catherine's Coll. Oxford U., 1994, Erskine fellow, U. Canterbury, Christchurch, New Zealand, 1996. Mem.: NAS, NAE, AIChE (Colburn award 1962, Walker award 1967, Inst. Lectr. award 1994), Am. Acad. Arts and Scis., Am. Chem. Soc. (E.V. Murphee award 1979, Petroleum Chemistry Rsch. award 1995). Office: U Calif 308 Gilman Hl Berkeley CA 94720-1462 Office Phone: 510-642-3592. Business E-Mail: prausnit@cchem.berkeley.edu.

PRAVICA, MICHAEL GOJKO, education educator; s. Walter John and Mira Pravica; m. Maria Jerinic, Aug. 2, 1998; children: Nicholas Mitchell, Natalia Mira, Luka Marko. BSc, Calif. Inst. Tech., Pasadena, 1988; PhD, AM, Harvard U., Cambridge, Mass., 1998. Staff scientist Nanodynamics, NY, 1998—99; asst. prof. N.Mex Highlands U., 1999—2003, chair math. sciences, 2002—03; asst. prof. U. Nev., 2003—08, assoc. prof., 2008—. Subject matter expert McGraw-Hill publishers, Dubuque, Iowa. Contbr. scientific papers to profl. pubs. including 30 peer-reviewed, others. Recipient George Green Meml. Prize, Caltech, 1987; PhD Fellowship grant, AT&T Bell Laboratories, 1988—92. Mem.: Am. Phys. Soc. Eastern Orthodox Christian. Achievements include discovery of ALTADENA effect. Avocations: writing, public speaking, hiking, bicycling. Home: 1471 Lodgepole Dr Henderson NV 89014 Office: Univ NV Las Vegas 4505 S MD Pky Las Vegas NV 89154-4002 Personal E-mail: pravica@yahoo.com. Business E-Mail: pravica@physics.unlv.edu.

PRAWOTO, YUNAN, materials scientist; m. Anita P. Prawoto, Dec. 28, 1992; children: Almas N., Alya N. PhD, U. Mo., Columbia, 2000. Rsch. faculty U. Tokyo, 2000—02; materials scientist NHK Internat., Wixom, Mich., 2002—. Contbr. articles to profl. jours. Mem.: Materials Info. Soc. (hon.). Achievements include patents pending for fatigue resistant steel based on fracture mechanics.

PRAY, RALPH EMERSON, metallurgical engineer; b. Troy, NY, May 12, 1926; s. George Emerson and Jansje Cornelius (Owejan) P.; m. Beverley Margaret Ramsey, May 10, 1959; children: Maxwell, Ross, Leslie, Marlene. Student, N.Mex. Inst. Mining & Tech., Socorro, 1953-56, U. N.Mex., Albuquerque, 1956; BS, U. Alaska, Fairbanks, 1961; DSc, Colo. Sch. Mines, Golden, 1966. Electrician, miner, 1944—47; chief party, field cartographer planning survey dept. N.Mex State Hwy., 1949—50; engr.-in-charge Dept. Mines and Minerals, Ketchikan, Alaska, 1957-61; asst. mgr. mfg. rsch. Universal Atlas Cement div. U.S. Steel Corp., Gary, Ind., 1965-66; rsch. metallurgist Inland Steel Co., Hammond, Ind., 1966-67; owner, dir. Mineral Rsch. Lab., Monrovia, Calif., 1968—. Pres., Keystone Canyon Mining Co., Inc., Pasadena, Calif., 1972-79, U.S. Western Mines, 1973—, Silveroil Rsch. Inc., 1980-85, v.p. Mineral Drill Inc., 1981-90; pres., CEO Copper de Mex. S.A. de C.V.; prime contractor def. logistics agy. U.S. Dept. def., 1989-92; designer Vanavara Electrolytic Gold Refinery, Krasnoyarsk, Russia, 1995; owner Precision Plastics, 1973-82; bd. dirs. Bagdad-Chase Inc., 1972-75; ptnr. Mineral R&D Co., 1981-86; lectr. Purdue U., Hammond, Ind., 1966-67, Nat. Mining Seminar, Barstow (Calif.) Coll., 1969-70; guest lectr. Calif. State Poly. U., 1977-81, Western Placer Mining Conf., Reno, Nev., 1983, Dredging and Miner Conf., Reno, 1985, others; v.p. dir. Wilbur Foote Plastics, Pasadena, 1968-72; strategic minerals del. People to People, Rep. South Africa, 1983; expert witness, cons. Bur. Land Mgmt., U.S. Dept. of Interior, 2000-2002, cons. US Dept. Justice, 2006-07; hist. cons. gold mining History TV Channel, 1999; guest spkr. Greater L.A. County Svc. Clubs, 1980-81; workshop condr. King Abdullaziz U., Jeddah, Saudi Arabia, 2002; v.p., tech. dir. U.S. Mining and Minerals Corp., 2006-. Author: Jingu, The Hidden Princess, 2002; guest editor Calif. Mining Jour., 1978—; contbr. articles to profl. jours.; contbr. author Bre-x Gold Today, Gone Tomorrow, 1997. Vol. Monrovia Police Dept.; city coord. Neighborhood Watch., 1990-99, Citizen Patrol, 1997-99. Radar technician, U.S. Army, 1950-52. Recipient Disting. Svc. medal Monrovia Police Dept., 1998. Fellow Geol. Mining and Metall. Soc. India (life), Am. Inst. Chemists, South African Inst. Mining and Metallurgy; mem. Soc. Mining Engrs., Am. Chem. Soc., Am. Inst. Mining, Metall. and Petroleum Engrs., NSPE, Can. Inst. Mining and Metallurgy, Geol. Soc. South Africa, Soc. Mineral Analysts, Sigma Xi, Sigma Mu. Achievements include research on recovery of metals from refractory ores, benefication plant design, construction and operation, underground and surface mine development and operation, mine and process plant management; syndication of natural resource assets with finance sources; freelance fiction and nonfiction writer; patents for chemical processing and steel manufacture; measurement of residual mercury in ancient and modern mine wastes of Chile. Office: 650 W Harrison Claremont CA 91711 Office Phone: 626-357-6511.

PRAY, RALPH MARBLE, III, lawyer; b. San Diego, June 7, 1938; s. Ralph Marble, Jr. and Doris (Thomson) Pray; m. Karen L. Pray (div. May 1988); children: Matthew Thomson, Kristen Leigh; m. Sandra Anne Shaw, June 7, 1988. BS, U. Redlands, 1960; JD, U. Calif., San Francisco, 1967. Bar: Calif. 1967, US Dist. Ct. (so. dist.) Calif. 1968, US Supreme Ct. 1972, US Dist. Ct. (ea. dist.) Calif. 1985, US Dist. Ct. (ctrl. dist.) Calif. 1989, US Dist. Ct. (no. dist.) Calif. 1992. Assoc. Gray, Cary, Ware & Friedenrich and predecessor, San Diego, 1967-73, ptnr., 1973—; mem. mgmt. com. Gary, Cary, Ames & Frye, San Diego, 1975-80. Arbiter Superior Ct., San Diego, 1984—. Lt. USN, 1960—64. Mem.: NRA, SAR, ABA, Am. Arbitration Soc. (arbiter), Calif. Bar Assn., Thurston Soc., San Diego Zool. Soc., Ducks Unltd., Club of Coronado, Rotary, Order of Coif. Republican. Episcopalian. Home: 535 C Ave Coronado CA 92118-1824 Office: DLA Piper US LLP 4365 Exec Dr Ste 1100 San Diego CA 92121-2133 Office Phone: 858-638-6890.

PRAYAGA, CHANDRA S., physics professor; b. Visakhapatnam, Andhra pradesh, India, Nov. 13, 1948; s. Suryanarayana Murthy and Sarada Prayaga; m. Lakshmi Suri, Feb. 23, 1975. PhD, Indian Inst. Sci., Bangalore, 1975. Assoc. prof., physics U. West Fla., Pensacola, 1991—, chair, dept. physics, 2003—. Mem.: Am. Assn. Physics Tchrs. Office: Physics Dept Univ West Fla 11000 Univ Pky Pensacola FL 32514 Business E-Mail: cprayaga@uwf.edu.

PRCHAL, JOSEF TOMAS, hematologist, researcher; b. Prague, Czech Republic, June 4, 1945; s. Ferdinand L. Prchal and Jaroslava Prchalova; m. Xylina T. Gregg, Sept. 30, 2001. MD, Charles U., Prague, 1968. Prof. Univ. of Ala at Birmingham, 1976—2000, Baylor Coll. of Medicine, Houston, 2000—. Dir. Tex. Comprehensive Sickle Cell Ctr., Houston, 2000—. Contbr. articles to profl. jours. Fellow: ACP; mem.: AAP.

PRECE, PAUL M., theater educator, department chairman; BA, Cath. U., Washington, DC, 1972; MFA, Fla. State U., Tallahassee, 1975; PhD, U. Kans., Lawrence, 2008. Tour mgr., dir., stage mgr., actor Asolo State theatre, Sarasota, Fla., 1975—77; artistic dir. Topeka Civic Theatre, 1981—82; chair, prof. dept. theatre Washburn U., Topeka, 1982—. Dir.: (plays); editor: (plays) The Woman Who Fell from the Sky. Democrat-Npl. Avocations: reading, travel. Office: Washburn Univ 1700 College Ave Topeka KS 66621 Business E-Mail: paul.prece@washburn.edu.

PRECIADO, PAMELA, artist; b. Evanston, Ill., Aug. 30, 1944; d. John James and Lena Day (Stevenson) Wills; m. Harold Prediado, June 1969 (div. July 1984). Student, U. Kans., U. Ill., San Francisco Acad. Fine Art, Am. Acad. Art Chgo., Art Inst. Chg. Comml. portrait artist. Year of the Woman, Dem. and Rep. women of 104th Congress, Black Caucus of 104th Congress, portrait montage Dem. women running for office State of Ill., 1994, exhibitions include Wells Fargo Bank, San Francisco, Godfrey Gallery, Mark Hopkins Hotel, Joseph Alioto Gallery, Macy's Dept. Store, San Francisco, Represented in permanent collections Booth Fisheries of Consol. Foods Corp., DeKalb AgResearch Corp. Mem.: NAFE, LWV, Womens Caucas Art Found., Portrait Soc. Am., Am. Soc. Portrait Artists, Chgo. Artists Coalition, Palette and Chisel Acad. Fine Art. Democrat. Avocations: travel, teaching art, tennis. Office Phone: 312-664-2506. Personal E-mail: vincel88@jiuo.com.

PRECKWINKLE, TONI, alderwoman; married; 2 children. BA, MA, U. Chgo. HS history tchr.; devel. officer Hyde Pk. Neighborhood Club, Ancona Sch.; coord. econ. devel. City of Chgo.; exec. dir. Chgo. Jobs Coun.; alderwoman, 4th ward Chgo. City Coun., 1991—. Polit. action dir. Near South Chpt. the Ind. Voters of Ill. Mem. Harold Washington Mayoral Campaign, 1977, 83, 87; pres. Disabled Adult Residential Enterprises, 1985, 86; bd. dirs. Ill. Coun. Against Handgun Violence; active Harvard Sch. Bd., Hyde Pk. Kenwood Cmty. Health Ctr., Coalition Athletic Facilities for Kenwood Acad., Friends of Murray Sch. Lot. Recipient Outstanding Alderman award, Near South Chpt. the Ind. Voters of Ill., 1993, 1995, 1997, 1999, Leon Despres award, 1997. Office: 4659 S Cottage Grove Ave Ste 203 Chicago IL 60653 also: City Hall 121 N LaSalle St Chicago IL 60602 Office Phone: 773-536-8103, 312-744-2690. Office Fax: 773-536-7296. Business E-Mail: tpreckwinkle@cityofchicago.org.*

PREDDY, RAYMOND RANDALL, retired newspaper publisher, educator; b. Texarkana, Ark., Feb. 1, 1940; s. Raymond Watson and Dorothy Belle (Long) P.; m. Sarah Elizabeth Mitchell, Nov. 20, 1965; children: Lewis, Tiffany. BS, Northwestern U., 1961, MS in Journalism, 1962. Copy editor Louisville Courier-Jour., 1965-69; with Dayton (Ohio) Daily News, 1969-74, asst. city editor, 1971, met. editor, 1971-74; systems mgr. Dayton Newspapers, Inc., 1974-76; bus. mgr. Waco (Tex.) Tribune-Herald, 1976-77, asst. pub., 1977-78; pub. Waco Tribune-Herald, 1978-96. Part time journalism instr. Baylor U., Waco. Pres. Waco United Way, 1986, Waco Found., 1984-86, Waco Symphony Assn., 1985-86; moderator Grace Presbytery, 2005. Served with USN, 1962-65; capt. Res. (ret.) Named Tex. Newspaper Leader of 1994; recipient Pat Taggart award from Tex. Daily Newspaper Assn. Mem.: Rotary. Presbyterian. Personal E-mail: rrpreddy@aol.com.

PREECE, BETTY P., electrical engineer, educator; b. Decatur, Ill. d. George A. and Margaret (Stock) Peters; m. Raymond G. Preece; children: Eric, George. BSEE, U. Ky., 1947; MS in Sci. Edn., Fla. Inst. Tech. Cert. Master Gardener, U. Fla. Engr. GE, various cities, 1947-50; project engr. Air Force Missle Test Ctr., Patrick AFB, Fla., 1951-54; tchr., faculty physics, math., phys. sci. Melbourne HS, Fla., 1972-90; exec. sec. Fla. Acad. Sci., Indialantic, 1991-96; accessibility coord. 45th Civil Engring. Sqd., Patrick AFB, Fla., 1990—; dir., engring. edn. cons. Jr. Engring. Tech. Soc., 2002—; dir., sec. Space Coast Ctr. for Ind. Living. Joined adj. faculty Fla. Inst. Tech., 1964; ret.; US del. Interam. Conf. on Physics Edn., 1987, 89, 91, 93; presenter Internat. Conf. Women Engrs. and Scientists. Contbr. articles over 100 pub. to profl. jour. Mem. Indialantic Code Enforcement Bd., 1987—; Chair bd. and local history editor So. Brevard Hist. Soc., 1975—. Recipient Fla. Found. for Future Scientists award, 1994; named Outstanding Sci. Tchr., Sigma Xi; named to Alumni Hall of Distinction, Coll. Engring. U. Ky., 2002 Fellow Soc. Women Engrs. (sr. life mem., chartered 1st sect. at Fla. Inst. Tech., counselor, chartered U. Ctrl. Fla. Collegiate sect., past counselor U. Ctrl. Fla., Miami U., chartered Space Coast Sect., past. pres., sect. rep., career guidance com. chair., nat. conv. program chair 1992, career guidance com. chair, region D dir. 1992-94, mem. leadership coach, local past pres., liaison coord. for NSTA 1994-, editl. bd. SWE Mag. 1998-, Disting. Svc. award 2007); mem. AIAA, NSTA, IEEE (life), Sci. Ed. for Students with Disabilities, Third World Orgn. for Women in Sci., Women in Engring. Programs and Advocates Network Comm. Chairs, Assn. for Women in Sci., Am. Assn. Physics Tchr. (women in physics com. 1993—, chair 2002-04, Disting. Svc. award 1997), Fla. Hist. Soc., Missile Space and Range Pioneers, Women's Engring. Soc. UK, DAR, Daus. Am. Colonists, Daus. of War of 1812, Delta Kappa Gamma, Phi Delta Kappa, Etta Kappa Nu. Achievements include being the first female electrical engineering graduate at the University of Kentucky. Office: 615 N Riverside Dr Indialantic FL 32903-4254

PREECE, JOHN EARL, plant and soil science educator; b. Woodsville, NH, Mar. 4, 1952; s. Daniel Platt and Jean (Page) P.; m. Barbara Joan Grondin, June 2, 1973; children: Ellen Platt, Molly Jean. BS, U. N.H., 1974; MS, U. Minn., 1977, PhD, 1980. Instr. U. Minn., St. Paul, 1978-79; from asst. prof. to prof. plant and soil sci. So. Ill. U., Carbondale, 1980—, asst. dept. chariperson, 1986-89, 90—. Assoc. agrl. exptl. sta. U. Calif., Davis, 1988-90. Co-author: Micropropagation, 1991, The Biology of Horticulture: An Introductory Textbook, 1993; assoc. editor: HortSci.; mng. editor: Plant Cell, Tissue and Organ Culture; contbr. articles to profl. jours. including Jour. Am. Soc. Hort. Sci. and others. Recipient Teaching Merit award Nat. Assn. Coll. Tchrs. Agriculture, 1989; grantee Martin Marietta Energy System, 1986—, Am. Rhodedendron Soc., 1988, Abbott Labs., 1988-90. Mem. AAAS, Am. Soc. Hort. Sci. (chmn. plant propagation working group 1983-85, co-chmn. plant biotech. working group 1989-90), Internat. Plant Propagators Soc., Internat. Assn. Plant Tissue Culture, Soc. for In Vitro Biology, Sigma Xi (pres. So. Ill. U. chpt. 1992-93). Achievements include first to micropropagate clonally white ash (Fraxinus Americana); first to achieve somatic embryogenesis from white ash and eastern black walnut; first to micropropagate silver maple; made major gains in adventitious shoot production from Rhododendron. Home: 3102 W Kent Dr Carbondale IL 62901-1919 Office: So Ill U Dept Plant and Soil Sci Carbondale IL 62901

PREEDOM, BARRY MASON, physicist, researcher; b. Stamford, Conn., Dec. 31, 1940; children: Bonnie Marie, Richard Lawrence. BS, Spring Hill Coll., 1962; MS, U. Tenn., 1964, PhD, 1967. Grad. fellow Oak Ridge (Tenn.) Nat. Lab., 1964-67; rsch. assoc. Mich. State U., East Lansing, 1967-70; asst. prof., then assoc. prof. U. S.C., Columbia, 1970-76, prof. physics, 1976—2006, Carolina rsch. prof., 1986-95, Carolina Disting. prof., 1995—2006, Carolina Disting. prof. emeritus, 2006—, assoc. dean for rsch., 2002—06. Vis. prof. Swiss Inst. Nuclear Rsch., Villigen, 1976; vis. staff Los Alamos (N.Mex.) Nat. Lab., 1972-91, tech. adv. panel, 1982-85; guest scientist Brookhaven Nat. Lab., Upton, N.Y., 1987—. Contbr. rsch. articles to sci. publs. Sr. teaching fellow Lilly Found., 1994-95; grantee Rsch. Corp., 1971, Office Naval Rsch., 1972-75, NSF, 1975—; recipient Mortar Bd. award for Excellence in Teaching, 1993. Mem. Am. Phys. Soc., Sigma Xi, Alpha Sigma Nu. Achievements include research and study of nuclear reaction mechanisms and nuclear structure, reaction probes including gamma rays, mesons, protons, deuterons and light ions. Office: Univ SC Dept Physics Columbia SC 29208-0001 Home Phone: 803-732-9228; Office Phone: 803-777-4121. E-mail: preedom@sc.edu.

PREER, JOAN C., retired assistant principal, science educator; d. Clarence Norman and Mary Katherine Casey; m. Andrew Stephen Preer, Sr., May 14, 1965; 1 child, Andrew Stephen Jr. BS in Chemistry, Tenn. A&I State U., Nashville, 1964; M in Adminstrn., Roosevelt U., Chgo., 1980. Ill. tchg. cert. Type 03 Chgo. Pub. Schs., 1969, tchg. cert. grades 3-8 Chgo. Pub. Schs., 1973, gen. sci. endorsement Chgo. Pub. Schs., 1987, sci. tchr. leadership workshop cert. Ill. State Bd. Edn., 1992, adminstrv. cert. Type 75 Ill. State Bd. Edn., 1995. Sci. tchr. Beasley Academic Magnet Ctr., Chgo., 1979—90; sci. coord. Beasley Academic Magnet Sch., Chgo., 1990—96, asst. prin., 1995—2001; ret., 2001. Curriculum writer Bill Kurtis Prodns., Chgo., 1986—2000, Mus. Sci. and Industry, Chgo., 1993—94, Field Mus. Natural History, Chgo., 1995, Brookfield Zoo, Chgo., Argonne Nat. Labs., Chgo., Chgo. Bur. Sci., Chgo., Chgo. Zool. Soc., Chgo.; integrated math., sci. and tech. design team Ill. State U., Normal; middle level childhood sci. stds. com. Nat. Bd. for Profl. Tchg. Stds., 1991—93. Contbg. mem. Nat. Com. to Preserve Social Security and Medicare, 2003—06, Northshore Animal League, Chgo., 2000—06, S.W. Indian Children, 2000—06; active Habitat for Humanity, 2001—06; contbg ptnr. Trinity Broadcasting Network Ministries, Calif., 2001—06. Recipient Golden Apple award, Golden Apple Found., 1988, Cert. Recognition For Excellence In Sci. and Math Tchg., Sigma Xi, 1989, Cert. Recognition For Excellence In Tchg., Ill. Fedn. Tchrs., 1989, Cert. Recognition For Contbns. To Leadership In Sci. Edn., Ill. State Bd. Edn., 1990, Cert. Recognition, Nat. Assn. Precollege Dirs. in Assn. with the AMOCO Corp.; named Honors Sci. Tchr., Ill. State Bd. Edn. Mem.: Chgo. Prins. and Adminstrs. Assn., Ret. Tchrs. Chgo. (life). Achievements include development of a school-level assessment system. Avocations: designing computer programs, travel, designing clothing, designing educational games, writing stories for children.

PREGERSON, HARRY, federal judge; b. LA, Oct. 13, 1923; s. Abraham and Bessie (Rubin) P.; m. Bernardine Seyma Chapkis, June 28, 1947; children: Dean Douglas, Kathryn Ann. BA, UCLA, 1947; LL.B., U. Calif.-Berkeley, 1950. Bar: Calif. 1951. Pvt. practice, Los Angeles, 1951—53; Assoc. Morris D. Coppersmith, 1952; ptnr. Pregerson & Costley, Van Nuys, 1953—65; judge Los Angeles Mcpl. Ct., 1965—66, Los Angeles Superior Ct., 1966—67, US Dist. Ct. Central Dist. Calif., 1967—79, US Ct. Appeals (9th cir.), Woodland Hills, 1979—. Faculty mem., seminar for newly appointed distr. Judges Fed. Jud. Center, Washington, 1970—72; mem. faculty Am. Soc. Pub. Adminstrn., Inst. for Ct. Mgmt., Denver, 1973—; panelist LA chpt. FBA, 1989, Calif. Continuing Edn. of Bar, 9th Ann. Fed. Practice Inst., San Francisco, 1986, Internat. Acad. Trial Lawyers, LA, 1983; lectr. seminars for newly-appointed Fed. judges, 1970—71. Author: over 450 published legal opinions. Mem. Community Rels. Com., Jewish Fedn. Coun., 1984—, Temple Judea, Encino, 1955—; bd. trustees Devil Pups Inc., 1988—; adv. bd. Internat. Orphans Inc., 1966—, Jewish Big Brothers Assn., 1970, Salvation Army, LA Met. area, 1988—; worked with US Govt. Gen. Svcs. to establish the Bell Shelter for the homeless Child Day Care Ctr., the Food Partnership and Westwood Transitional Village; bd. dirs. Marine Corps Res. Toys for Tots Program, 1965—, Greater LA Partnership for the Homeless, 1988—. 1st lt. USMCR, 1944—46. Decorated Purple Heart, Medal of Valor Apache Tribe; recipient Promotion of Justice Civic award, City of San Fernando, 1965, award, San Fernando Valley Jewish Fedn. Coun., 1966, Profl. Achievement award, Los Angeles Athletic Club, 1980, Profl. Achievement award UCLA Alumni Assn., 1985, Louis D. Brandeis award, Am. Friends of Hebrew U., 1987, award of merit, Inner City Law Ctr., 1987, Appreciation award, Navajo Nation and USMC for Toys for Tots program, 1987, Humanitarian award, Los Angeles Fed. Exec. Bd., 1987—88, Grateful Acknowledgement award, Bet Tzedek Legal Svcs., 1988, Commendation award, Bd. Suprs. Los Angeles County, 1988, Others award, Salvation Army, 1988. Mem.: ABA, Marines Corps Res. Officers Assn., State Bar Calif., San Fernando Valley Bar Assn., L.A. County Bar Assn., Am. Legion (Van Nuys Post), DAV (Birmingham chpt.). Office: US Ct Appeals 9th Cir 21800 Oxnard St Ste 1140 Woodland Hills CA 91367-7919*

PREISER, WOLFGANG FRIEDRICH ERNST, retired architect, educator, consultant, researcher; b. Freiburg, Germany, June 26, 1941; came to U.S., 1967; s. Gerhard Friedrich and Ursula Helene (von Huelsen) P.; m. Cecilia M. Fenoglio, Feb. 16, 1985; children: Johanna, Timothy, Andreas, Nicholas. Student, Vienna Tech. U., 1963; diploma in Engring., Architecture, Inst. of Tech., 1967; M.Arch., Va. Poly. Inst. and State U., 1969; PhD in Man-Environ. Relations, Pa. State U., 1973. Architect, Germany, Austria, Eng., 1960-66; prof. architecture Va. Poly. Inst. and State U., Pa. State U., U. Ill., U. N.Mex., U. Cin., 1970—2008; research architect constrn. engring. research lab. U.S. Army, 1973-76; co-dir. Inst. Environ. Edn., U. N.Mex., 1976-86; dir. Ctr. for R & D, U. N.Mex., Albuquerque, 1986-90; dir. research Archtl. Research Cons. Inc., 1976—2008; pres. Planning Rsch. Inst., Albuquerque, 1980—90; prin. Preiser Cons., Cin., 1990—2008. Lectr. ednl., profl. and civic groups worldwide; v.p. faculty club U. N.Mex., 1976-78; pres. Internat. Club, Va. Poly. Inst. and State U., 1968-69; rschr. in field. Author: Improving Building Performance, 2003; co-author: Post-Occupancy Evaluation, 1988; contbr. articles to profl. jours., chapters to books; editor: Facility Programming, 1982, Programming the Built Environment, 1985, Building Evaluation, 1989, Pueblo Style and Regional Architecture, 1989, Design Intervention: Toward A More Humane Architecture, 1991, Professional Practice in Facility Programming, 1993, Design Review: Challenging Urban Aesthetic Control, 1994, New Direction in Urban Public Housing, 1998, Directions in Person-Environment Research and Practice, 1999, Universal Design Handbook, 2001, Japanese transl., 2001, Assessing Building Performance, 2005, Designing for Designers: Learning From Sch. of Architecture, 2007. Trustee Cin. Chamber Orch., 1992-98, v.p., 1995-98. Recipient Outstanding Svc. award Coll. Design, Arch., Art, and Planning U. Cinn., 2005, Career award Environ. Design Rsch. Assn., 1999, Ann. Rieveschl award, U. Cin., 1999, MCB Univ. Press (UK) award excellence, 1998, Faculty Devel. award rsch. U. Cin., 1992, Faculty Achievement award, 1995, Pogue/Wheeler Traveling award, 1993, Dean's Spl. award, 1994, Finland's Inst. Tech. award, 1966, awards Am. Iron and Steel Inst., 1968, Progressive Arch. Ann., 1985, 89, undergrad. teaching award U. Ill., 1976, hon. mention 1st Kyoto award Internat. Coun. of Soc. Indsl. Design, 1979; Fulbright fellow, 1967, 87, Ford Found. fellow, 1968, Nat. Endowment Arts fellow, 1979, 82; grad. fellow U. Cin., 1996 Mem.: NAS (bldg. rsch. bd. 1985—86, chmn. com. on programming and post-occupancy evaluation), Environ. Design Rsch. Assn. (vice chmn. 1974—76, Lifetime Achievement award 2007), Soc. Human Ecology (pres. 1980—86), Prof. Emeritus of Architecture (life), U. Cin. Grad. Fellows (sec. 1973—74), Phi Kappa Phi.

PREISS, JACK, biochemistry professor; b. Bklyn., June 2, 1932; s. Erool and Gilda (Friedman) P.; m. Karen Sue; children: Jennifer Ellen, Jeremy Oscar, Jessica Michelle. BS in Chemistry, CCNY, 1953; PhD in Biochemistry, Duke U., 1957. Scientist NIH, Bethesda, Md., 1960-62; asst. prof. dept. biochemistry, biophysics U. Calif., Davis, 1962-65, assoc. prof., 1965-68, prof., 1968-85, chair dept. biochemistry, 1971-74, 77-81; prof. dept. biochemistry Mich. State U., East Lansing, 1985-2000, chair dept., 1985-89, disting. prof., 2001—09; emeritus disting. prof., 2009. 16th loomis lectr. Iowa State U., 1997—98. Mem. editl. bd.: Jour. Bacteriology, 1969—74, Arch. Biochem. Biophysics, 1969—, Plant Physiology, 1969—74, 1977—80, assoc. editor:, 1980—92; editor, 1993—95, Jour. Biol. Chemistry, 1971—76, 1978—83, 1994—99, 2000—05, Plant Physiol. Biochemistry, 1997—2003. Recipient Camille and Henry Dreyfus Disting. scholar award Calif. State U., 1983, Alexander von Humboldt Stiftung Sr. US Scientist award, 1984, Merit award, Japanese Soc. Starch Sci., 1992, Disting. Faculty Mem. award Mich. Assn. Governing Bds. State Univ., 1997, Mich. Sci. of Yr. award Impressions 5 Mus., 1997, Pan-Am. Biochemistry and Molecular Biology award lectr. Spanish Biochem. Soc., 2000; Alsberg-Schoch Meml. lectr. Am. Assn. Cereal Chemists, 1990, Nat. Sci. Coun. lectr. Republic of China, 1988; Guggenheim Meml. fellow, 1969-70, Japan Soc. for Promotion of Sci. fellow, 1992-93; grantee NIH, 1963-97, NSF, 1978-89, Dept. Energy, 1993-2005, USDA, 1988-2008, US-Isreal Binat. Agrl. R & D Fund., 2005-09. Mem. AAAS (elected fellow 2007), Am. Chem. Soc. (Charles Pfizer award in enzyme chemistry 1971), Biochem. Soc., Am. Soc. Biol. Chemists and Molecular Biology, Am. Soc. Microbiologists, Soc. for Complex Carbohydrates, Protein Soc., Pan Am. Soc. Biochemistry and Molecular Biology (sec. gen., 1994-96, vice chmn. 1997-99, chmn. 2000-02, past chmn. 2003-05). Fellow Am. Soc. Plant Biology 2008. Office: Mich State Univ Dept Of Biochemistry & Molecular Biology East Lansing MI 48824 Office Phone: 517-353-3137. Business E-Mail: preiss@msu.edu.

PREKER, ALEXANDER S., economist; b. Odder, Denmark, Mar. 27, 1951; s. Salo and Frida Preker; m. Susan C. Hulton. MD, U. BC, 1978; PhD, London Sch. Economics and Polit. Sci., 1987. Chief economist World Bank Group, Washington, 2000—03, lead economist, 2003—08, head health investment policy, 2008—. Contbr. articles and books. Recipient Academic award, Performance award, Innovation Marketplace award, World Bank; fellow Medicine, U. Coll. London. Mem.: Ont. Coll. Physicians and Surgeons, Que. Coll. Physicians and Surgeons, Internat. Health Economics Assn., Met. Mus. Art. Achievements include development of economic policy. Office: World Bank 1818 H St NW Washington DC 20008 Office Fax: 1 212 348-2866. Business E-Mail: apreker@worldbank.org, apreker@Hifcorp.com, apreker@healthfinance.org.

PREM, F. HERBERT, JR., retired lawyer; b. NYC, Jan. 14, 1932; s. F. Herbert Prem Sr. and Sybil Gertrude (Nichols) Prem; m. Patricia Ryan, Nov. 18, 1978; children from previous marriage: Julia Nichols, F. Herbert III(dec.). AB, Yale U., 1953; JD, Harvard U., 1959. Bar: NY 1960. Assoc. Whitman and Ransom, NYC, 1959-66, ptnr., 1967-93, co-chmn. exec. com., 1988-92, chmn., 1993, Whitman Breed Abbott & Morgan LLP, NYC, 1993-99, of counsel, 2000; ret., 2000. Bd. dirs. Scoville Meml. Libr., treas., 2007—; bd. dirs. Salisbury Visiting Nurse Assn., sec., 2007—; pres. Crescendo, Inc., 2005—06. Vol. atty. The Legal Aid Soc., NYC, 2000—03; vol. chaplain Sharon Hosp., Conn., 2003—05; bd. dirs. Bagaduce Music Lending Libr., Inc., 1988—95, pres., 1989—93; bd. dirs. The Health Care Chaplaincy, Inc., 1998—2004, Inter Faith Neighbors, Inc., 2001—03, Legal Aid Soc., NYC, 1969—73, Cmty. Action for Legal Svc., Inc., 1967—70, treas. Lt. j.g. USNR, 1953—56. Mem. ABA, Assn. Bar City NY (sec. 1967-69), NY State Bar Assn., Am. Law Inst. (life), Union Club, Yale Club. Episcopalian.

PREMA, NITYA, marriage and family therapist, artist; b. LA, June 15, 1941; d. James Nicholson and Phyllis Wickersham; children: Fritjof Swenson, Derek Swenson, Krista Mills. AS, Santa Rosa Jr. Coll., Calif., 1977; BA, Sonoma State U., Rohnert Park, Calif., 1980; MA, Profl. Sch. of Psychology, San Francisco, 1983. Lic. marriage and family therapist Bd. of Behavioral Sci., Calif., 1982; psychiat. technician, Bd. of Vocat. Nursing, 1979. Owner, designer and mfr. Nitya Visionary Designs and Gallery, Forestville and Sebastopol, Calif., 1982—92; therapist/social worker O'Connor Hosp. Vista's Program, San Jose, Calif., 1997—99; psychotherapist San Jose Jails/Mental Healtlh, Calif., 1998—2000; pvt. practice family therapist and military cons. San Andreas and Visalia, Calif., 2000—. Spkr. Internat. Transpersonal Conf., Ireland, 1994; spkr.'s bur. Calif. Assn. of Marriage and Family Therapists, Santa Rosa, 1996, Found. for Mythological Studies, 2008. Author: The Spiral Labyrinth Journey: A Pilgrimage into Sacred Space. Activist Rainbow Labyrinth Journey. Named one of Am.'s Top Mental Health Profls. Mem.: Ebbets Pass Forest Watch, Brewster Kaleidoscope Soc. Achievements include design of jeweled magic wands, kaleidoscopes. Business E-Mail: artglasscopes@yahoo.com.

PREMACK, DAVID, psychologist; b. Aberdeen, SD, Oct. 26, 1925; s. Leonard B. and Sonja (Liese) P.; m. Ann M. James, Oct. 26, 1951; children: Ben, Lisa, Timothy. BA magna cum laude, U. Minn., 1949, PhD, 1955. Rsch. assoc. Yerkes Labs. Primate Biology, Orange Park, Fla., 1955; rsch. assoc., asst. prof. psychology U. Mo., Columbia, 1956-58, assoc. prof., 1959-62, prof., 1963-64, U. Calif., Santa Barbara, 1965-75; vis. prof. Harvard U., 1970-71; prof. U. Pa., 1975—. Artist-in-residence Yaddo, Saratoga Springs, N.Y., 1955; fellow Van Leer Jerusalem Inst., 1980, Inst. for Advanced Study, Berlin, 1985-86; vis. scientist Japan Soc. for Promotion Sci., 1980; univ. rsch. lectr. U. Calif., Santa Barbara, 1973; mem. sci. gov. bd. Fyssen Found., Paris, 1989—; assoc. neurosci. rsch. program, La. Jolla, Calif., 1991—. Author: Intelligence in Ape and Man, 1976, (with Ann James Premack) The Mind of an Ape, 1983, Gavagai! Or the Future History of the Animal Language Controversy, 1986 (with Dan Sperber and Ann James Premack) Causal Cognition: A Multidisciplinary Debate, 1995, (with Ann James Premack) Original Intelligence: Unlocking the Mystery of Who We Are, 2003, French translation, 2003, Japanese translation, 2005; mem. editl. bd. Jour. Exptl. Psychology: Animal Processes, 1976—, Cognition, 1977—, Brain and Behavior Sci., 1978—, Jour. Cognitive

Neurosci. Served with U.S. Army, 1943-46. Ford Found. tchg. intern, 1954; USPHS postdoctoral fellow, 1956-59; Social Sci. Rsch. Coun. fellow, summer 1963; Ctr. for Advanced Study in Behavioral Scis. fellow, 1972-73; Guggenheim fellow, 1979-80; grantee NSF, 1961—, USPHS, 1960-80; recipient Kenneth Craik Resch. award St. John's Coll.-Cambridge U., 1987, Internat. Sci. prize Fyssen Found., Paris, 1987. Fellow AAAS; mem. Am. Psychol. Soc. (William James fellow 2005), Soc. Exptl. Psychologists. Personal E-mail: davidpremack@msn.com.

PREMINGER, GLENN MICHAEL, urologist, surgeon; b. NYC, Apr. 4, 1952; m. Jodi Sue Lieberstein; children: Seth, Sally. MD, N.Y. Med. Coll., 1977. Diplomate Am. Bd. Urology. Prof. urologic surgery Duke U. Med. Ctr., Durham, NC, 1993—. Office: Duke U Med Ctr Divsn Urology 3167 Rm 1572 Durham NC 27710 Business E-Mail: glenn.preminger@duke.edu.

PREMO, PAUL MARK, oil industry executive; b. Syracuse, NY, Nov. 20, 1942; s. Matthias George and Kathryn (Whitbread) P.; m. Mary Catherine Hennessy, June 19, 1965; children: Deborah, Mark. BSChemE, Manhattan Coll., Riverdale, NY, 1964; MS in Chem. Engring., MIT, 1965. Chem. engr. Chevron Rsch., Richmond, Calif., 1965-69; fin. analyst Chevron Corp., San Francisco, 1969-72, coord., mgr. supply and distbn., 1972-79; mgr. petroleum regulations Chevron USA, San Francisco, 1979-81, sec.-treas., 1981-85, mgr. property tax adminstrn., 1985-86, mgr. natural gas regulatory affairs, 1986-92; exec. cons. Resource Mgmt. Internat., San Rafael, Calif., 1992-95; v.p. Foster Assoc., Inc., San Francisco, 1995—98; prin. Energy Econs. Consulting, Mill Valley, Calif., 1998—. Dir. Ky. Agrl. Energy Corp., Franklin. Trustee Calif. Tax Found., 1985-. Mem. Calif. State C. of C. (tax com.), Western Oil and Gas Assn., Am. Petroleum Inst. (property tax com.), Natural Gas Supply Assn., Inst. Property Taxation, Calif. Taxpayers Assn. (bd. dirs. 1985-), MIT Alumni Assn., Commonwealth (San Francisco), Sigma Xi, Tau Beta Pi. Avocations: investments, carpentry, travel. Home: 310 Hazel Ave Mill Valley CA 94941-5054 Personal E-mail: paulpremo@msn.com.

PRENDERGAST, BRIAN, psychologist, educator; BA in Psychology, Williams Coll., 1993; PhD in Psychology, U. Calif., Berkeley, 1998. Fellow Johns Hopkins U., Ohio State U.; assoc. prof. psychology U. Chgo., mem. Inst. for Mind & Biology. Office: University of Chicago Dept of Psychology 5848 S University Ave Chicago IL 60637 Office Phone: 773-702-2895. Office Fax: 773-702-6898.*

PRENDERGAST, ROBERT ANTHONY, pathologist educator; b. Bklyn., Nov. 6, 1931; BA, Columbia U., 1953; MD, Boston U., 1957. Intern Bellevue Hosp., 1957-58; resident Boston City Hosp., 1958-59, Meml. Sloan-Kettering Hosp., 1959-61; vis. physician Rockefeller U., 1963-65, asst. prof., 1965-70, assoc. prof. opthamology, 1970-99; prof. ophthalmology and pathology Johns Hopkins U. Sch. Medicine, 1999—, prof. emeritus, 2002. Bd. dirs. Marine Biol. Lab., Woods Hole, Mass., 2001—08, adj. sr. scientist, 2006—. Mem. Am. Assn. Immunology, Am. Soc. Exp. Pathology, H.G. Kunkel Soc., Assn. Vision & Ophthal., Pluto Club. Achievements include research in cellular immunology, ontogeny of the immune response, transplantation immunology, viral immunopathology, immunopathology of ocular inflammatory diseases. Office: Marine Biol Lab Woods Hole MA 02543 Home Phone: 508-457-1375. Business E-Mail: rprender@mbl.edu.

PRENSKY, ARTHUR LAWRENCE, pediatric neurologist, educator; b. NYC, Aug. 31, 1930; s. Herman and Pearl (Newman) P.; m. Sheila Carr, Nov. 13, 1969. AB, Cornell U., 1951; MD, N.Y. U., 1955. Diplomate: Am. Bd. Psychiatry and Neurology. Intern Barnes Hosp., St. Louis, 1955-56; resident and research fellow in neurology Harvard U., Mass. Gen. Hosp., Boston, 1959-66; instr. neurology Harvard Med. Sch., 1966-67; mem. faculty Washington U. Sch. Medicine, St. Louis, 1967—, prof. pediatrics and neurology, to 1975, Allen P. and Josephine B. Green prof. pediatric neurology, 1975-2000, prof. emeritus of neurology, 2000—; pediatrician St. Louis Children's Hosp.; neurologist Barnes and Allied Hosps., Jewish Hosp., St. Louis. Author: (with others) Nutrition and the Developing Nervous System, 1975; editor: (with others) Neurological Pathophysiology, 2d edit, 1978, Advances in Neurology, 1976; mem. editorial bd. Pediatric Neurology, 1984-90, Jour. Child Neurology, 1985—. Served with USAF, 1957-59. Fellow Am. Acad. Neurology; mem. Am. Neurol. Assn., Am. Soc. Neurochemistry (mem. council 1973-77), Central Soc. Neurol. Rsch. (pres. 1977-78), Child Neurology Soc. (pres. 1979-80, Hower award 2000), Am. Pediatric Soc., Internat. Child Neurology Assn., Japanese Soc. Child Neurology, Profs. Child Neurology (pres. 1984-86) Office: 1 Children's Pl Saint Louis MO 63110-1014 Home: 40 North Kinshigway Apt 12F Saint Louis MO 63108 Office Phone: 314-454-6120. Business E-Mail: prenskya@neuro.wustl.edu.

PRENTICE, HOWARD MALCOLM, research scientist, educator; s. Roy and Doris Harvey Prentice; m. Linda Elizabeth McGrath, Mar. 31, 1978; children: Sarah Elizabeth, Christopher Andrew. MA, U. Aberdeen, Scotland, 1980; DEA, L'INSERM, Paris, 1981; MS, U. London, 1984, PhD, 1987. Fellow Stanford U. Sch. Medicine, Palo Alto, Calif., 1987—89, U. So. Calif., LA, 1989—93; lectr. U. Glasgow, Scotland, 1993—98, sr. lectr., 1998—2000; assoc. prof. biomedical sci. Fla. Atlantic U., Boca Raton, 2000—. Grant rev. com. Am. Heart Assn., Dallas, 2006—, Tampa, Fla., 2006—. Co-author (Lutz, P.L., Nilsson, G.E., Prentice H.M.): (book) The Brain Without Oxygen.; contbr. to numerous profl. jours. Team leader Am. Heart Assn. Ann. Sponsored Walk, Boca Raton, Fla., 2006—07. Grant Aid, Am. Heart Assn., 2005—08, Large Equipment grant, Fla. Dept. Health, Bankhead Coley., 2007—08, Project grant, Brit. Heart Found., 1993—95, Med. Rsch. Coun., UK., 1994—97, Brit. Heart Found., UK., 1995—99, Nat. Heart Rsch. Fund, UK., 1998—2000, Wellcome Trust, UK., 1998—99, Internat. Travel grant, 1995—99. Achievements include research in determination of regulatory characteristics of specific gene/promoter elements in normal and disease-stressed myocardial tissue, examination of the effects on altered cardiac contractility in cardiac muscle cells; investigation of mitochondria function and oxidative stress in age related disorders and in analysis of mechanisms of hypoxia and anoxia tolerance in brain. Business E-Mail: hprentic@fau.edu.

PRENTKE, RICHARD OTTESEN, lawyer; b. Cleve., Sept. 8, 1945; s. Herbert E. and Melva B. P.; m. Susan Ottesen, June 9, 1974; children: Catherine, Elizabeth. BSE, Princeton U., 1967; JD, Harvard U., 1974. Assoc. Perkins Coie, Seattle, 1974-80, ptnr., 1981—, CFO, 1989-94. Author: School Construction Law Deskbook, 1989, rev. 2d edit. 1998; contbr. articles to profl. jours. Pres., trustee Seattle County Day Sch., 1990-95; trustee Pocock Rowing Found., 1996-02. Lt. USN, 1967—70. Fellow Leadership Tomorrow, Seattle, 1985-86. Mem. ABA, Wash. State Bar Assn. (mem. jud. screening com. 1985-91, chmn. 1987-91), Seattle-King County Bar Assn. (chmn. jud. task force 1990-93), Am. Arbitration Assn. (arbitrator 1988—2000), Princeton U. Rowing Assn. (pres. 1993-02, trustee 1976—), Rainier Club, Princeton Varsity Club (trustee 2003-), Princeton Club Wash. (trustee 1986-95, pres. 1990-92), Seattle Tennis Club. Avocations: art, carpentry, travel, rowing, sports. Office: Perkins Coie 1201 3rd Ave Fl 40 Seattle WA 98101-3029 Office Phone: 206-359-8000. Business E-Mail: rprentke@perkinscoie.com.

PRENZLOW, ELMER JOHN-CHARLES, JR., minister; b. Norfolk, Nebr., Apr. 4, 1929; s. Elmer Edward and Alvina C. (Henning) P.; m. Karen McHarg DeMoss, July 4, 1980; 1 child, Elmer Carl III. BA, Northwestern Coll., Watertown, Wis., 1950; BD in Theology, WELS Luth. Sem., Mequon, Wis., 1953; MA in English and Philosophy, U. Minn., 1961; MS in Edn. Psychology, U. Wis., 1969; PhD in Psychology and Criminal Justice, Walden U., 1975. Pastor St Paul's Lutheran Ch., Bloomer, Wis., 1953-62; chaplain, instr. U. Wis., Milw., 1962-79; dir. devel. and pub. relations Luth. Ch.-Mo. Synod, Southern Wis. Dist., Milw., 1979-82; major gifts counselor Luth. Ch.-Mo. Synod Internat. Hdqrs., St. Louis, 1982-88; dir. devel. and fin. resources Adult Christian Edn. Found. Bethel Series, Madison, Wis., 1988-89; world relief devel. counselor Luth. Ch.-Mo. Synod Internat. Hdqrs., St. Louis, 1989-94; v.p. major gifts Luth. Ch.-Mo. Synod Found., St. Louis, 1994-98; spl. asst. to pres. Luth. World Relief, NYC, 1998—. Vice chmn. Standing Com. Dept. Campus Ministry Luth. Coun. U.S.A., N.Y., 1964-83; chmn. Milw. Religious Counselors, 1965-72, dept. humanities Spencerian Bus. Coll., 1967-77; v.p. Patricia Stevens Career Coll., bd. dirs. 1978-91; spkr., lectr. in field. Contbr. articles to profl. jours. Mem. Wis. State Legis. Com for Kerner Report, Madison, 1968-69, Nat. Adv. Commn.U.S. Justice Dept. on Law Enforcement standards and goals, Washington, 1971-73, ad hoc com. for establishing U.S. Bur. Prisons Nat. Inst. for Corrections, Washington, 1973-75, 19th congr. dist. Wis. svc. acad. review bd., Milw., 1975-82; sub. pastor for vacations in North dist. of Lutheran Ch.-Mo. Synod, 1998-2004. Named Outstanding Prof. Spencerian Bus. Coll., Milw., 1972. Mem. Assn. of Luth. Devel. Execs., Optimists, Wis. Club, Lions Club. Republican. Avocations: travel, music, auto racing, golf, fishing. Home and Office: 15794 225th Ave Bloomer WI 54724-4741 Business E-Mail: revkaren@bloomer.net. *Nothing communicates to others what we believe more loudly and effectively than the measure of those principles they witness being personally carried out in our own lives!.*

PRESCOTT, ANNE LAKE, English language educator; b. NYC, Jan. 19, 1936; d. Gerard Kirsopp and Eleanor (Hard) Lake; m. Peter Sherwin Prescott, June 22, 1957; children: David Sherwin, Antonia Courthope. BA, Barnard Coll., 1959; MA, Columbia U., 1961, PhD, 1967. Instr. English Barnard Coll., NYC, 1961-67, asst. prof., 1967-73, assoc. prof. NYC, 1973-80, prof., 1980—, chmn. English dept., 1988—92. Author: French Poets and the English Renaissance, 1978, Imagining Rabelais in the English Renaissance, 1998; contbr. articles and revs. to profl. jours. V. p. New Caanan Caucus Conn. Dems., 1968-72; trustee New Canaan Libr., 1971-74; mem. Environment Commn. New Canaan, 1985-89. Mem. MLA, Renaissance Soc. Am. (bd. dirs. 1986—), Spenser Soc. (pres. 1986), Amici Thomae Mori, Sixteenth Century Soc. (pres. 2008), Club: Century, Harvard Club. Episcopalian. Office: Barnard Coll Dept English New York NY 10027 Office Phone: 212-854-2116. Business E-Mail: aprescot@barnard.edu.

PRESCOTT, BARBARA LODWICH, educational association administrator; b. Chgo., Aug. 15, 1951; d. Edward and Eugenia Lodwich; m. Warren Paul Prescott, Dec. 2, 1979; children: Warren Paul Jr., Ashley Elizabeth. BA, U. Ill., Chgo., 1973, MEd, 1981; MA, U. Wis., 1978; postgrad., Stanford U., 1983-87. Cert. tchr., learning handicapped specialist, cmty. coll. instr., Calif. Grad. rschr. U. Ill., Chgo., 1979-81; learning handicapped specialist St. Paulus Luth. Sch., San Francisco, 1981-83; grad. rsch. asst. Sch. Edn. Stanford (Calif.) U., 1983-87; learning handicapped specialist/lead therapist Gilroy Clinic Speech-Hearing-Learning Ctr., Crippled Children's Soc., Santa Clara, Calif., 1988-89; ednl. dir. Adolescent Intensive Resdl. Svc. Calif. Pacific Med. Ctr., San Francisco, 1989-95; exec. dir. Learning Profiles, South Lake Tahoe, Calif., 1995—. Instr. evening San Jose City Coll., 1988-92. Contbr. articles to profl. jours.; author: Proceedings of Internat. Congress of Linguistics, 1987; editor: Proceedings - Forum for Research on Language Issues, 1986; author videotape: Making a Difference in Language and Learning, 1989; pub. and exec. editor August Moon Books Inc., Wheaton, Ill., 2008-. Recipient Frederick Bork Teaching Trainee award San Francisco State U., 1983; Ill. State scholar, 1973. Mem. Calif. Assn. Pvt. Specialized Edn. and Svcs., Phi Delta Kappa (v.p. 1984-86), Pi Lambda Theta (sec. 1982-83), Phi Kappa Phi, Alpha Lambda Theta. Office Phone: 630-924-8052. E-mail: prescott4@netscape.com, augustmoonbooks@usc.com.

PRESCOTT, DAVID L. C., JR., music educator; s. David L. C. Prescott, Sr. and Lavina Hall Prescott. BS in Bus. Adminstrn., Old Dominion U., 1981, MusB in Music Edn., 1992, MS in Secondary Edn., Choral Conducting, 2002. Acct. W. E. Moulton, Jr. & Assocs., Portsmouth, Va., 1981—90; music specialist Tanners Creek Elem. Sch., Norfolk, Va., 1992—93; dir. choral activities Ocean Lakes H.S., Virginia Beach, Va., 1993—97, Kempsville H.S., Virginia Beach, Va., 1997—. Guest clinician, condr. Various Churches And Civic Choirs, Va., 1992—; dir. music Holland Rd. Bapt. Ch., Virginia Beach, 1983—97, Faith Wesleyan Ch., Norfolk, 1995—2005, Thalia United Meth. Ch., Virginia Beach, 2005—. King herod: (musical theatre) Jesus Christ Superstar; costumer (dramas and musical theatre works) A Man for All Seasons, Christ and St. Luke's Arts Guild, 2000, Our Town, Christ and St. Luke's Art Guild, 1999, Jesus Christ Superstar, Christ and St. Luke's Art Guild, 2001, Guys and Dolls, Wizard of Oz, Annie Get Your Gun, Mame, Pippin, Carousel Cinderella, Kempsville H.S., 1999—2005. Mem. bd. dirs. Virginia Beach Ballet, 1990—93. Recipient Award of Distinction - Choral Conducting, Fest. Music Competitions, 1999; named Kempsville H.S. Tchr. of Yr., 2007. Mem.: Music Educators Nat. Conf., Va. Music Educators Assn., Am. Choral Dir.'s Assn., Phi Mu Alpha Sinfonia. Wesleyan. Avocations: antiques, flower arranging. Office: Kempsville High School 5194 Chief Trail Virginia Beach VA 23464 E-mail: dlpresco@vbschools.com.

PRESCOTT, EDWARD C., economist, educator; b. 1940; BA in Math., Swarthmore Coll., 1962; MS in Ops. Rsch., Case Western Res. U., 1963; PhD in Econs., Carnegie Mellon U., 1967. Lectr. U. Penn, 1966—67; asst. prof. econs. dept. U. Penn., 1967—71; asst. prof. Grad. Sch. Indsl. Admin., Carnegie Mellon U., 1971—72, assoc. prof., 1972—75, prof. econs., 1975—80, U. Minn., 1980—98, 1999—2003; vis. prof. econs. Norweigan Sch. Bus. and Econs., 1974—75, Northwestern U., 1979—80, vis. prof. fin., Kellogg Grad. Sch. Mgmt., 1980—82; Ford vis. rsch. prof. U. Chgo., 1978—79, prof. econs., 1998—99; sr. advisor rsch. dept. Fed. Reserve Bank, Mpls., 1980—2003; prof. dept. econs. Ariz. State U., 2003—; sr. monetary advisor Fed. Res. Bank, Mpls., 2003—. Leader NBER/NSF Workshop in Indsl. Orgn., 1977—84; rsch. assoc. Nat. Bureau of Economic Rsch., 1988—; spkr. in field. Author (with S.L. Parente): Barriers to Riches, 2000; co-editor: Economic Theory, 1991; assoc. editor: Jour. Econometrics, 1976—82, Internat. Economic Review, 1980—90, Jour. Economic Theory, 1990—92; contbr. articles to profl. jours. Recipient Erwin Plein Nemmers prize in Econ., Northwestern U., 2002, Laurea Honoris Causa in Economica, U. Rome, 2002, Nobel Prize for Econ. Sciences, 2004; named Regents' Prof., U. Minn., 1996, McKnight Presidential Chair in Economics, 2003, W.P. Carey Chair, U. Ariz., 2003; fellow, Econometric Society, 1980, Am. Acad. Arts & Scis., 1992; Brookings Economic Policy Fellow, 1969—70, Guggenheim Fellow, 1974—75. Mem.: Soc. Advancement of Econ. Theory (pres. 1992—94), Soc. Econ. Dynamics and Control (pres. 1992—95). Office: Ariz State U Dept Econs Tempe AZ 85287-3806*

PRESCOTT, JOHN BARRY, resource industry executive; b. Oct. 22, 1940; M. Jennifer Mary Louise Cahill; 4 children (1 dec.) BComm in Indsl. Rels., U. NSW, Australia, 1961, DSc (hon.), 1995; LLD (hon.), Monash U., 1994. With Broken Hill Proprietary Co. Ltd. (BHP), 1958-98; various indsl. rels. positions BHP, Newcastle and Whyalla, supt. indsl. rels., shipping and stevedoring Newcastle and Sydney, 1969-74, asst. mgr. fleet ops. Newcastle, 1974-79, exec. asst. to gen. mgr. transport, 1979-80, mgr. ops. transport, 1980-82, gen. mgr. transport, 1982-87; exec. gen. mgr., CEO BHP Steel, 1987-91; mng. dir., CEO BHP Melbourne, Victoria, Australia, 1991—98; exec. chmn. Horizon Pvt. Equity Party, Ltd, 1998—2005; dir. Normandy Mining Ltd., 1999—2002, Newmont Mining Corp., 2002—; chmn. ASC Pty. Ltd. (formerly Australian Submarine Corp. Pty. Ltd.), 2000—09, QR Ltd., 2006—, Patron Sunshine Coast Bus. Coun., 2007—09. Mem. adv. bd. Booz Allen & Hamilton Inc., 1991-2003; mem. internat. coun. J.P. Morgan Chase, 1994-2003; mem. Asia Pacific adv. com. N.Y. Stock Exch., Inc., 1995-2005; mem. Australian Shipping Defence Coun., 1983-87, Defence Industry Com., 1988-93, Stevedoring Industry Consultative Coun., 1983-85; chmn. Australian Mfg. Coun., 1990-95; mem. exec. com. Australian Mining Industry Coun., 1991-95; mem. Transport Industries Adv. Coun., 1982-87, dep. chmn., 1986-87; mem. Maritime Industry Coun. Australia, 1983-87; mem. exec. coun. Asia Soc. AustralAsia Ctr., 2000-03; trustee The Conf. Bd., 1993-2001, global counseller, 2001—; bd. dirs. Newmont Mining Corp. Bd. dirs. Bus. Coun. Australia, 1995-97, Walter and Eliza Hall Inst. Med. Rsch., 1994-98; mem. internat. coun. Asia Soc.; patron Australian Quality Coun., 1990-99, Australian Am. C. of C., Hawaii, 1995-98, Sunshine Coast Bus. Coun, 2007—, chmn. 2004-07; mem. Australia-Japan Bus. Cooperation Com., 1991-98. Decorated companion Order of Australia. Fellow Australian Inst. Mgmt., Australian Acad. Technol. Scis. and Engring., Australian Inst. Co. Dirs., Conf. Bd. (trustee 1995-2001), Inst. of Pub. Affairs (pres. 1999-2001). Avocations: tennis, golf. Office: 140 William St Level 39 Melbourne Victoria 3000 Australia Office Phone: 61 3 96422518. Personal E-mail: jbp@jbprescott.com.

PRESCOTT, RICHARD CHAMBERS, writer; b. Houston, Apr. 1, 1952; s. Chambers Richard and Dorothy Mae (Bashara) P.; m. Sarah Elisabeth Grace, Oct. 13, 1981. Author: The Sage, 1975, Moonstar, 1975, Neuf Songes (Nine Dreams), 1976, 2d edit., 1991, The Carouse of Soma, 1977, Lions and Kings, 1977, Allah Wake Up, 1978, 2d edit., 1994, Night Reaper, 1979, Dragon Tales, 1983, Dragon Dreams, 1986, 2d edit., 1990, Dragon Prayers, 1988, 2d edit., 1990, Dragon Songs, 1988, 2nd edit., 1990, Dragon Maker, 1989, 2d edit., 1990, Dragon Thoughts, 1990, Tales of Recognition, 1991, Kings and Sages, 1991, Dragon Sight: A Cremation Poem, 1992, Three Waves, 1992, Years of Wonder, 1992, Dream Appearances, 1992, Remembrance Recognition and Return, 1992, Spare Advice, 1992, The Imperishable, 1993, The Dark Deitess, 1993, Disturbing Delights: Waves of The Great Goddess, 1993, The Immortal: Racopa and the Rooms of Light, 1993, Hanging Baskets, 1993, Writer's Block and Other Gray Matters, 1993, The Resurrection of Quantum Joe, 1993, The Horse and the Carriage, 1993, Kalee Bhava: The Goddess and Her Moods, 1995, The Skills of Kalee, 1995, Because of Atma, 1995, Measuring Sky Without Ground, 1996, The Goddess And The God Man, 1996, Kalee: The Allayer of Sorrows, 1996, Living Sakti, 1997, The Mirage and the Mirror, 1998, Inherent Solutions to Spiritual Obscurations, 1999, The Ancient Method, 1999, Quantum Kamakala, 2000, Mortal Grounding: Cosmology and Consciousness, 2008; contbr. articles to profl. jours.

PRESLAR, LEN BROUGHTON, JR., hospital administrator; b. Concord, NC, Aug. 13, 1947; s. Len B. and Billie M. (James) P.; m. Joyce W. Whittington, July 11, 1971; children: Bradley E., Whitney A., Andrew C. BA, Wake Forest U., 1971; MBA, U. N.C., Greensboro, 1980. Admissions clk. N.C. Bapt. Hosp., Winston-Salem, 1969-71, systems analyst, 1971-72, budget mgr., 1973, contr., 1973-75, v.p. fin. mgmt., 1975-88, pres., chief exec. officer, 1988—. Bd. dirs. Univ. Healthsystem Consortium; bd. mgrs. Wachovia Bank; mem. owners and affiliate rels. com. Premier, Inc. Deacon local Bapt. ch. Fellow Hosp. Fin. Mgmt. Assn.; mem. N.C. Hosp. Assn. (bd. dirs.). Republican. Baptist. Avocations: gardening, golf. Office: NC Bapt Hosp Medical Center Blvd Winston Salem NC 27157-0001

PRESLEY, BRIAN, investment company executive; b. Evansville, Ind., Dec. 28, 1941; s. Harry and Ruth P.; m. Mary Nell Minyard, Aug. 17, 1972; children: Debra, Cynthia, David, Jeffrey, Clark, Gregory, Steven. BSBA, U. Evansville, 1963; MBA, Mich. State U., 1964; diploma, Wharton Sch., U. Pa., 1995. Market rsch. analyst Stanley Works, New Britain, Conn., 1964-68; tax shelter coord. F.I. Dupont, Memphis, 1968-73; v.p. Bullington Schas, Memphis, 1973-75; pres., mng. ptnr. Presley Assocs., Memphis, 1965-93; pres., CFO CSG, Inc., Memphis, 1975—. Gen. ptnr. various real estate and oil and gas partnerships, 1974-1986; pres. Cooper St. Group Securities, Inc., 1983-86; divsn. mgr. Advantage Capital Corp. (divsn. AIG Advisors, Inc.), 1986-89, reg. v.p., 1989, CEO 1990-94, mng. dir., mktg. strategist, 1995; pres. Presley Adv. Inc., 1995—, pub. Presley Adv. Letter; instr. fin. divsn. continuing edn. Memphis U. Bd. dirs. Apt. Coun. Tenn., 1980-86, sec.-treas., 1982-83; pres. Memphis Apt. Coun., 1983; mem., U. Evansville Nat. Alumni Bd., 1988-91; prodr. 2 daily radio stock market commentary shows, 1988; fin. commentator Sta. WEVU-TV (ABC), Ft. Myers/Naples, 1988-89; host syndicated radio show for sr. citizens, 1979-81; mem. found. bd. and fin. com. Fla. Gulf Coast U., 2001-09. Mem. Leadership Charlotte; chmn. Charlotte County Econ. Devel. Coun., 1999-2002; pres. Enterprise Charlotte Found., 2002-06; chmn. Angels Found. Charlotte County, 2002-05; fin. advisor Charlotte Symphony Orch., 2002-; bd. dirs. Charlotte County Cmty. Found., 2005—; vice chmn. Charlotte Cmty. Found., 2007—; advisor Visual Arts Ctr. Endowment Fund, 2007-. Recipient Richard L. McLaughlin award, Econ. Devel. Coun., Fla., 2002. Mem. Internat. Assn. Fin. Planners (broker dealer adv. coun. 1993-97), Admirals Club (life, bd. dirs.), Naples Jazz Soc. (chmn. bd. dirs. 1993-96), Naples Sailing and Yacht Club (bd. dirs.1991-96), Pi Sigma Epsilon, Beta Gamma Sigma, Tau Kappa Epsilon Alumni Assn. (pres. Memphis area 1979-80), Isles Yacht Club (bd. dirs. 2001-04). Presbyterian. Home and Office: Acorn Ranch 5161 Acorn Ranch Rd Punta Gorda FL 33982-9511 Office Phone: 941-505-9017. Business E-Mail: brian@presleyadvisoryinc.com.

PRESLEY, LISA MARIE, singer; b. Memphis, Feb. 1, 1968; d. Elvis and Priscilla Beaulieu Presley; m. Danny Keough, Oct. 3, 1988 (div. 1994); children: Danielle Riley Keough, Benjamin Storm Keough; m. Michael Jackson, May 18, 1994 (div. Jan. 18, 1996); m. Nicholas Cage, Aug. 10, 2002 (div. May 16, 2004); m. Michael Lockwood, Jan. 22, 2006; children: Finley Michaela Lockwood, Harper Lisette Lockwood. Mgmt. Elvis Presley Trust; owner, chmn. bd. Elvis Presley Enterprises, Inc.; co-owner with mother Priscilla Elvis Presley's Memphis nightclub, operated by Presley Estate, 1997—2003. Singer: (albums) To Whom It May Concern, 2003 (cert. Gold), Lights Out, 2003, Now What, 2005; actor: (music video) You Are Not Alone, Michael Jackson, (car commercial), 1989; appeared on (cover of Vogue mag.), 1996, (cover of Vogue mag. with mother and daughter), 2004, featured in (TV) Elvis by the Presleys, 2005. Internat. spokesperson Citizens Commn. on Human Rights; co-founder (with Isaac Hayes) LEAP (Literacy, Edn., and Ability Program); involved with Fight for Kids. Office: Elvis Presley Enterprises Inc PO Box 16508 3734 Elvis Presley Blvd Memphis TN 38186-0508

PRESLEY, PRISCILLA (PRICILLA ANN WAGNER, PRISCILLA BEAULIEU PRESLEY), actress; b. Bklyn., May 24, 1945; m. Elvis Presley, 1967 (div. 1973); 1 child, Lisa Marie; 1 child (with Marco Garibaldi), Navarone. Studied with Milton Katselas; student, Steven Peck Theatre Art Sch., Chuck Norris Karate Sch.; HHD (hon.), Rhodes Coll., Memphis, 1998. Co-owner Bis and Beau Boutique, 1973—76; co-executor, pres. Elvis Presley Enterprise, Inc. (acquired by CKX, Inc.), Memphis, 1979—2005, founder, 1980—2005, exec. cons., 2005—; bd. dir. CKX, Inc., Las Vegas, Nev., 2005—. Launched & developed internat. fragrance line, 1988—, Moments, 1990, Experiences, 1994, Indian Summer, 1996; designer of jewelry line; launched website, 2005—; bd. dir. Metro-Goldwyn-Mayer Inc., 2000—; lectr. SMART TALK. Appearances include (films) The Naked Gun: From the Files of Police Squad!, 1988, The Adventures of Ford Fairlaine, 1990, The Naked Gun 2 1/2, 1991, The Naked Gun 33 1/3: The Final Insult, 1994, (TV series) Those Amazing Animals, 1980-81, Dallas, 1983-88, Melrose Place, 1996, (TV movies) Love Is Forever, 1983, Breakfast With Einstein, 1998 (also exec. prodr.), Hayley Wagner, Star, 1999, After Dallas, 2002; performer (TV series) Dancing with the Stars, 2008; exec. prodr. (TV movie) Elvis and Me, 1988, The Road to Graceland, 1998, Finding Graceland, 1998; co-prodr.(TV mini series) Elvis, 1990; host, Elvis: The Great Performances, 1992; featured in (TV) Elvis 85, 1984, Elvis: Life and Times, 1997, After Dallas, 2002, Elvis by the Presleys, 2005, (TV mini series) Between the Lines, 2004; guest appearances include The Fall Guy, 1983, Tales from the Crypt, 1993, Touched by an Angel, 1997, Spin City, 1999, After They Were Famous, 2002, Oprah Winfrey Show, 2005; author: Elvis and Me, 1987. Amb. Dream Found., 2000—; mem. Citizen's Commn. on Human Rights. Named one of 50 Most Beautiful People in the World, People Mag., 1992. Office: Paul Bloch & Michelle Bega c/o Rogers & Cowan 8687 Melrose Ave 7th Fl West Hollywood CA 90069 Address: Norman Brokaw c/o William Morris Agency 151 El Camino Beverly Hills CA 90212 Office Phone: 310-850-4206, 310-854-8100.

PRESLEY, VIVIAN MATHEWS, junior college administrator; b. West Point, Miss., Oct. 12, 1952; d. Beatrus and Lula (Butler) Mathews; m. Dwight Presley, Sept. 12, 1971; 1 child, Julian. BA, Miss. State U., 1973, MA, 1975, Cert. Edn. Specialist, 1978, EdD, 1983. Counselor Coahoma Jr. Coll. (named changed to Coahoma Community Coll.), Clarksdale, Miss., 1975-80; title III coordinator Coahoma Jr. Coll., Clarksdale, Miss., 1981-82, asst. to pres., 1982-83, v.p., 1983—. Vice chairperson Miss. State Council on Vocat. Edn., Jackson, Miss., 1984. Named One of Outstanding Young Woman of Am., 1981, 84, 85, 88. Mem. Nat. Assn. Female Execs., Assn. Univ. Women, Nat. Council for Resource Devel., Psi Kappa Psi, Delta Sigma Theta. Democrat. Methodist. Avocations: reading, biking. Home: 3240 Friars Point Rd Clarksdale MS 38614-9359 Office: Coahoma Community Coll RR 1 Box 616 Clarksdale MS 38614-9801

PRESNIAKOV, ALEXANDER, artist, sculptor, inventor, writer; b. San Francisco, June 28, 1963; s. Alexander Alexandervich and Nina (Hanova) P. Student, Acad. of Art Coll., San Francisco, 1979-82. Curator Gen. Svcs. Adminstrn., Washington, 1983; artist Washington, 1984-85, San Francisco, 1986—; pres. Multimedia Global Arts Inc., St. Petersburg, Russia, 2007—. Songwriter Hilltop Records, LA, 1996—, Amerecord, LA, 1996—, Premier Melodies, NYC Commd. to paint life-size portraits of Prince Charles, Princess Diana, Miss Dame Barbara Cartland, Amb. Gerald Posner Carmen, presdl. candidates for 1985 Polit. Conservative Action Conf., Sheraton Hotel, Washington, Pres. Ronald Reagan, San Francisco mayor Willie Brown; series Women in Love Cycle, 1986—; author: Eagle's Nest, 2001, Lords of Death, 2005, 8 others; screenwriter. Recipient Literary Excellence award Iliad Press, 1995; named Prof. and Corr. Academician Dept. Arts Accademia Internazionale, Italy. Mem. Internat. Soc. Poets (disting. mem., Hall of Fame 1997-98), Legion of Honor Mus., De Young Mus., Gallery Marabella (hon.). Republican. Russian Orthodox. Achievements include invention of Manshield Deflector; the Scrubber glove; artistic ideal ultrafictionilization used in all US govt. agencies. Avocations: tennis, golf, equestrian.

PRESS, CHARLES, retired political science professor; b. St. Louis, Sept. 12, 1922; s. Otto Ernst and Laura (Irion) P.; m. Nancy Miller, June 10, 1950; children: Edward Paul, William David, Thomas Leigh, Laura Mary. Student, Elmhurst Coll., Ill.; B of Journalism, U. Mo., 1948; MA, U. Minn., 1951, PhD, 1953. Faculty N.D. Agrl. Coll., 1954-56; dir. Grand Rapids Area Study, 1956-57; with Bur. Govt., U. Wis., 1957-58; faculty Mich. State U., East Lansing, 1958-91, prof. polit. sci., 1964-91; emeritus, 1991—; chmn. dept. Mich. State U., 1966-73. Cons. Mich. Constl. Conv., 1962-63; supr. Ingham County, 1966-72; tchr. summers, London; tchr. U. N.S.W., Sydney, Mich. State U. Author: Main Street Politics, 1962, (with Charles Adrian) The American Government Process, 1965, Governing Urban America, 1968, 5th edit., 1977, American Politics Reappraised, 1974, States and Community Governments in a Federal System, 1979, 3d edit., 1991, American Policy Studies, 1981, The Political Cartoon, 1982, (with others) Michigan Political Atlas 1984, (with Kenneth VerBurg) American Politicians and Journalists, 1988, (with Kenneth VerBurg) Looking Over Sir Arthur's Shoulder, How Doyle Turned the Trick, 2004, with Kenneth VerBurg)Parodies and Pastiches Buzzing Around Sir Arthur Conan Doyle, 2006; (weekly newspaper column) The Pros and Cons of Politics. Sec. Ingham County Bd. Health, 1983-93; chmn., mem. East Lansing Bd. Rev., 1966-86; bd. dirs. Urban League, 1971-73; mem. East Lansing Housing and Urban Devel. Commn., 1988-93. Served with AUS, 1943-45. Recipient Disting. Prof. award Mich. State U., 1980, Alumni Merit award Elmhurst (Ill.) Coll., 1995; grantee, Ford Foundation, 1953-54. Mem. Am. Polit. Sci. Assn., Midwest Polit. Sci. Assn. (pres. 1974-75), So. Polit. Sci. Assn., Mich. Conf. Polit. Scientists (pres. 1972-73), Nat. Municipal League, B.S.I., Greek Interpreters East Lansing. Democrat. Home: 987 Lantern Hill Dr East Lansing MI 48823-2831 also: Cottage 6291 S Whiskey Creek New Era MI 49446 Personal E-mail: pressc@msu.edu.

PRESS, FRANK, geophysicist; b. Bklyn., Dec. 4, 1924; s. Solomon and Dora (Steinholz) Press; m. Billie Kallick, June 9, 1946; children: William Henry, Paula Evelyn. BS, CCNY, 1944, LLD (hon.), 1972; MA, Columbia U., 1946, PhD, 1949; DSc (hon.), 28 univs. Rsch. assoc. Columbia U., 1946—49, instr. geology, 1949—51, asst. prof. geology, 1951—52, assoc. prof., 1952—55; prof. geophysics Calif. Inst. Tech., 1955—65, dir. seismol. lab., 1957—65; prof. geophysics, chmn. dept. earth and planetary scis. MIT, Cambridge, 1965—77, inst. prof., 1981; sci. advisor to pres., dir. Office Sci. and Tech. Policy, Washington, 1977—81; pres. NAS, 1981—93, pres. emeritus, 2000—; Cecil & Ida Green sr. fellow Carnegie Inst. of Washington, 1993—97; ptnr. Washington Adv. Group, 1996—. Mem. Pres.'s Sci. Adv. Com., 1961—64, Com. on Anticipated Advances in Sci. and Tech., 1974—76, Nat. Sci. Bd., 1970—76; mem. lunar and planetary missions bd. NASA; participant bilateral scis. agreement with Peoples Republic of China and USSR; mem. U.S. delegation to Nuc. Test Ban Negotiations, Geneva and Moscow; prof. emeritus MIT, 2000—. Author (with M. Ewing, W.s. Jardetsky): Propagation of Elastic Waves in Layered Media, 1957; author: (with R. Siever) Earth, 1986; author: Understanding Earth, 2003; author: (contbr.) articles to over 160 publs. Decorated cross of Merit Germany, Legion of Honor France; recipient Columbia medal for Excellence, 1960, Pub. Svc. award, U.S. Dept. Interior, 1972, Gold medal, Royal Astron. Soc., 1972, Pub. Svc. medal, NASA, 1973, Japan prize, Sci. and Tech. Found. Japan, 1993, Pupin medal, Columbia U., 1993, Nat. medal of Sci., Pres. U.S., 1994, Philip Hauge Abelson prize, AAAS, 1995, Lomonosov Gold medal, Russian Acad. Sci., 1998; named Sherman Fairchild Disting. scholar, Calif. Inst. Tech., 1994, A.D. White prof., Cornell U. Mem.: NAS, Engring. Acad. Japan (fgn. assoc.), Acad.Scis. Russia (fgn. mem.), Royal Soc. U.K., French Acad. Scis., Am. Philos. Soc., Seismol. Soc. Am. (pres. 1963), Soc. Exploration Geophysicists, Am. Geophys. Union, Geol. Soc. Am. (councilor), Am. Acad. Arts and Scis. Office: Ste 616 South 2500 Virginia Ave Washington DC 20037-1901 Office Phone: 202-682-0164. Business E-Mail: fpress@nas.edu.

PRESS, JIM (JAMES E. PRESS), automotive executive; b. L.A., Oct. 4, 1946; BA in Bus. Adminstrn., Kans. State U., 1968. With Ford Motor Co., 1968—70; joined Toyota Motor Corp., Torrance, Calif., 1970; exec. v.p. Toyota Motor Sales, U.S.A., Inc., 1999—2005, COO, 1999—2005, pres., 2005—07; mng. officer Toyota Motor Corp., 2003—07, pres. Toyota N. Am., 2006—07; vice chmn., pres., sales, mktg. & product strategy Chrysler LLC, Auburn Hills, Mich., 2007—09; dep. CEO Chrysler Group LLC, Auburn Hills, Mich., 2009—, spl. adv. to CEO, 2009—; vice chmn. Cerberus Operating & Advisory Co. LLC, 2007—09. Bd. dirs. Toyota Motor Corp., 2007, Chrysler LLC, 2007—09, Assn. Internat. Automobile Manufacturers. Bd. dirs. Automotive Youth Ednl. Systems, Detroit Area Coun. Boy Scouts America; mem. advisory bd. Pitts. State U.; bd. trustees Coll. Creative Studies, Detroit, Chadwick Sch., Rolling Hills, Calif. Recipient Disting. Svc. Citation award, Automotive Hall of Fame, 2004. Avocations: boating, motorcycling, auto racing, skiing, scuba diving. Office: Chrysler Group LLC PO Box 21-8004 Auburn Hills MI 48321*

PRESSEL, MORGAN, professional golfer; b. Tampa, Fla., May 23, 1988; d. Kathy (Krickstein) and Mike Pressel. Profl. golfer LPGA, 2006—. Mem. US Team PING Jr. Solheim Cup, 2002, 03, 05; mem. East Team Cannon Cup, 2002—04. Recipient Nancy Lopez award, 2006, CoURagE award, Birdies for Breast Cancer, 2006; named Player of Yr., Am. Jr. Golf Assn., 2005. Achievements include winning the North and South Women's Amateur, 2004, US Women's Amateur, 2005; became youngest (18 years, 10 months, 9 days) major champion in LPGA history on April 1, 2007 at the Kraft Nabisco Championship; youngest (12) to qualify for the US Women's Open, 2001; won 11 events on the American Junior Golf Association circuit. Avocations: photography, computers. Mailing: LPGA 100 International Golf Dr Daytona Beach FL 32124-1092

PRESSER, HARRIET BETTY, social studies educator; b. Bklyn., Aug. 29, 1936; d. Phillip Rubinoff and Rose (Gudowitz) Jabish; m. Neil Nathan Presser, Dec. 16, 1956 (div.); 1 child, Sheryl Lynn. BA, George Washington U., 1959; MA, U. N.C., 1962; PhD, U. Calif., Berkeley, 1969. Statistician Bur. Census, Washington, 1959; research assoc. Inst. Life Ins., NYC, 1962-64; lectr. demography U. Sussex, Brighton, England, 1967-68; staff assoc. Population Council, NYC, 1968-69; asst. prof. sociomed. scis. Columbia U., NYC, 1969-73, assoc. prof. sociomed. scis., 1973-76; prof. sociology U. Md., College Park, 1976—99, dir. Ctr. on Population, Gender, and Social Inequality, 1988—2001, disting. faculty rsch. fellow, 1993-94, disting. univ. prof., 1999—; fellow in residence Netherlands Inst. for Advanced Study in Humanities & Social Sci., Wassenaar, The Netherlands, 1994-95. Fellow-in-residence Ctr. for Advanced Study in the Behavioral Scis., Stanford, Calif., 1986-87, 91-92, 2003-04; scholar-in-residence Russell Sage Found., NYC, 1998, 99, 2000; resident scholar Bellagio Study and Conf. Ctr., Rockefeller Found., 2000; acad. visitor Gender Inst. London Sch. Econs and Polit. Scis., 2000; vis. scholar Max Planck Inst. for Demographic Rsch., Rostock, Germany, 2007. Editl. bd. Time and Soc., 1991-95, Social Forces, 1984-87, Signs, 1975-85, Applied Population and Policy, 2002-, Rose Monograph Series, 2003-05, Jour. of Marriage and the Family, 2003, editl. advisor: Romanian Jour. Population Studies, 2007-; assoc. editor Jour. Health and Social Behavior, 1975-78; co-editor (with Gita Sen) Women's Empowerment and Demographic Processes: Moving Beyond Cairo, 2000; author: Working in a 24/7 Economy: Challenges for Am. Families, 2003; editor: Population Studies and Demographic Change, Transaction Pubs., 2005-. Grantee NICHD, 1972-78, 83-88, Population Coun., 1976-79, NSF, 1982-83, 90-94, 2000-03, Rockefeller Found., 1983-85, 88-94, William and Flora Hewlett Found., 1989—06, Andrew W. Mellon Found., 1994-95, W.T. Grant Found., 1996-99, Russell Sage Found., 1976-79, 2003-04, Alfred P. Sloan Found., 2007—08; recipient Rosabeth Moss Kanter award for excellence in work-family rsch., 2001, Lawrence R. Klein award, 2003, Disting. Sr. Scholar award AAUW Edn. Found., 2007, Disting. Career award, Am. Sociol. Assn. Family Sect, 2009, Stuart A Rici award, DC Sociol. Soc., Disting. Alumni Schdar award, Wash. U., 1992, named Outstanding Women, U. Md., 1999. Fellow AAAS, Sociol. Rsch. Assn.; mem. APHA (coun. mem. population sect. 1976-79), Population Assn. Am. (bd. dirs. 1972-75, 2nd v.p. 1983, 1st v.p. 1985, pres.-elect 1988, pres. 1989), Am. Sociol. Assn. (coun. mem. at large 1990-93, chmn., coun. mem. population sect. 1978-83). Office: U Maryland Dept Sociology College Park MD 20742-0001

PRESSER, STANLEY, social sciences educator, researcher; b. Bklyn., Feb. 18, 1950; s. Sidney and Sydonia (Cohen) P.; m. Yan Yu; 1 child, Solomon Zhi-Qian. AB, Brown U., 1971; PhD, U. Mich., 1977. Rsch. investigator Survey Rsch. Ctr., U. Mich., 1977-78, head field office, 1981-83; rsch. assoc. Inst. Rsch. Social Sci., U. N.C., 1978-81; dir. Detroit Area Study, U. Mich., 1983-85; assoc. dir. sociology program NSF, 1985-87, dir., 1987-88; prof. sociology U. Md., 1989—; dir. Survey Rsch. Ctr., 1989-2000. Vis. prof. sociology U. Md., 1988-89; dir. joint U. Md. and U. Mich. program in Survey Methodology, 1992-96; bd. overseers Nat. Opinion Rsch. Ctr. Gen. Social Survey, 1984-85, 93-97; spl. cons. Nat. Econ. Rsch. Assocs., 1986-89; cons. U.S. Dept. Justice, 1995, Dept. Commerce, 1991, GAO, 1988-89, EEO Commn., 1985, NOAA, 1991-94, State of Alaska Atty. Gen., 1989-92; bd. dirs. Roper Ctr., 2006-08, Consortium Social Sci. Assns., 2007-08. Co-author: Questions and Answers in Attitude surveys, 1981, Survey Questions: Handcrafting the Standardized Questionaire, 1986, Valuing Oil Spill Prevention, 2004; editor Pub. Opinion Quar., 1993-97; co-editor: Sourcebook of Harris National Surveys, 1981, Survey Rsch. Methods, 1989, Methods for Testing and Evaluating Survey Questions, 2004; mem. editl. bd. Pub. Opinion Quar., 1983-87, Sociol. Methods and Rsch., 1980-83, Social Psychology Quar., 1979-82; contbr. articles to profl. jours. Fulbright Scholar, 2008—09. Fellow: Am. Statis. Assn.; mem.: Sociol. Rsch. Assn., Am. Sociol. Assn. (chair profl. ethics com. 1999—2001), Am. Assn. Pub. Opinion Rsch. (pres. 1993—94). Office: U of Md Sociology Dept College Park MD 20742-1315

PRESSER, STEPHEN BRUCE, lawyer, educator; b. Chattanooga, Aug. 10, 1946; s. Sidney and Estelle (Shapiro) P.; m. Carole Smith, June 18, 1968 (div. 1987); children: David Carter, Elisabeth Catherine; m. ArLynn Leiber, Dec. 13, 1987; children: Joseph Leiber, Eastman Leiber. AB, Harvard U., 1968, JD, 1971. Bar: Mass. 1971, DC 1972. Law clk. to Judge Malcolm Richard Wilkey U.S. Ct. Appeals (D.C. cir.), 1971-72; assoc. Wilmer, Cutler & Pickering, Washington, 1972-74; asst. prof. law Rutgers U., Camden, NJ, 1974-76; vis. assoc. prof. U. Va., 1976-77; prof. Northwestern U., Chgo., 1977—, class 1940 rsch. prof., 1992-93, Raoul Berger prof. legal history, 1992—, assoc. dean acad. affairs Sch. Law, 1982-85. Prof. bus. law Kellogg Sch. Mgmt., Northwestern U., Chgo., 1992—. Author: (with Jamil S. Zainaldin) Law and Jurisprudence in American History, 1980, 7th edit., 2009, Studies in the History of the United States Courts of the Third Circuit, 1983, The Original Misunderstanding: The English, The Americans and the Dialectic of Federalist Jurisprudence, 1991, Piercing the Corporate Veil, 1991, revised ann., (with Ralph Ferrara and Meredith Brown) Takeovers: A Strategist's Manual, 2d edit., 1993, Recapturing the Constitution, 1994, (with Douglas W. Kmiec, John Eastman and Raymond Marcin) The American Constitutional Order: History, Cases, and Philosophy, 1998, 3rd edit., 2009, An Introduction to the Law of Business Organizations, 2005, 2nd edit., 2008; assoc. articles editor Guide to American Law, 1985. Trustee Village Winnetka, Ill., 2000-04, police and fire commr., 2004-, chair 2007-; mem. acad. adv. bd. Washington Legal Found. Recipient summer stipend NEH, 1975; Fulbright Sr. scholar Univ. Coll., London Sch. Econs. and Polit. Sci., 1983-84, Inst. Advanced Legal Studies, 1996; Adams fellow Inst. U.S. Studies, London, 1996; assoc. rsch. fellow Inst. U.S. Studies, 1999—. Mem. Am. Soc. Legal History (bd. dirs. 1979-82), Am. Law Inst., Univ. Club Chgo. (bd. dirs. 1997-99, sec. 1999), Legal Club Chgo., Reform Club (London), Mich. Shores Club (Wilmette). Office: Northwestern U Law Sch 357 E Chicago Ave Chicago IL 60611-3069 E-mail: s-presser@law.northwestern.edu.

PRESSLER, LARRY, former senator, lawyer; b. Humboldt, SD, Mar. 29, 1942; s. Antoine Lewis and Loretta Geneive (Claussen) P.; m. Harriet Dent, 1982; 1 child, Laura. BA, U. S.D., 1964; diploma (Rhodes scholar), Oxford U., Eng., 1965; MA in Govt., Harvard U., 1971, JD, 1971. Bar: N.Y., D.C. Fgn. svc. officer, 1971—74; mem. 94th-95th Congresses from 1st S.D. Dist., 1974-78, U.S. Senate from S.D., 1979-97; pres. Pressler and Assocs.; U.S. del. Inter-Parliamentary Union for 97th Congress; mem. bd. visitors all mil. svc. academies; chmn. commerce, sci. and transp. coms, U.S. Senate, 1995-96; founder telecomm. group Pressler & Assocs., Washington, 1997—. Prin. sponsor Telecomm. Act of 1996, Pressler Telecomm. Act; mem. fgn. rels. com., 1980-95; congl. del. to UN Gen. Assembly, 1986, 92; former bus. cons. McKinsey & Co.; former atty. U.S. State Dept. Legal Advisor's Office; sr. fellow U. Calif., L.A., 2000—; sr. ptnr. O'Connor and Hannan, 1997-2002; sr. advisor Solomon, Smith, Barney and Monitcello Capital; vis. prof. Fudan U., Shanghai, 2005; lectr. Am. govt. U.S. Naval Acad., 2005; vis. prof., Thomas Hawkins Johnson vis. scholar West Point Mil. Acad., 2006; disting. prof. St. John's U., Queens, NY, 2007; bd. mem., corp. exec. Infosys Techs., Bangalore, India; bd. dirs. Phila. Stock Exch. Author: U.S. Senators from the Prairie, 1982, Star Wars: The SDI Debates in Congress, 1986. 1st lt. U.S. Army, 1966-69, Vietnam. Mem. Am Assn. Rhodes Scholars, D.C. Bar Assn., N.Y. State Bar Assn., VFW, ABA, Century Club (N.Y.), Met. Club (Washington), St. Albans Tennis Club, Cosmos Club, 25th Infantry Divsn. Assn., Phi Beta Kappa. Avocations: golf, tennis, rowing. Home Phone: 202-210-5330; Office Phone: 202-333-5856.

PRESSLEY, DELORIS N., retired literacy educator; b. Nesmith, SC, Aug. 14, 1950; d. Murray Vanderbilt Nesmith, Sr. and Blanche Lamar Nesmith; m. Booker Theodore Pressley, Mar. 5, 1976; children: Malcolm L., Marquis B. B in Elem. Edn., Allen U., 1972; MEd, U. S.C., 1976; postgrad., U. S.C., Francis Marion U., 1995. Cert. elem. edn. Part-time curriculum and instrn. facilitator Battery Park Elem. Sch., Nesmith, 2003—04, literacy coach, 2004—07, elem. edn. tchr., 2005; writer Newspaper. Chairperson Williamsburg County Sch. Dist. Tchr. Forum, Kingstree, SC, 2000—02; rep. Pee Dee Edn. Tchr. Forum, Florence, SC, 2000—02. Recipient mini grant, Pee Dee Edn. Found., 1990, 1994; named Tchr. of Yr., Battery Pk. Elem. Sch., 1986, 2000, Williamsburg County Dist. Tchr. of Yr., 2000; grantee, Ednl. Improvement Act, 1999. Mem.: NEA, S.C. Internat. Reading Assn., Nat. Coun. Tchrs. English, Internat. Reading Assn. Democrat. United Methodist. Avocations: reading, gardening. Home: 721 Nesmith Corner Rd Nesmith SC 29580 Office Phone: 843-558-5233, 843-382-2689.

PRESSLY, JAIME ELIZABETH, actress; b. Kinston, NC, July 30, 1977; m. Eric Cubiche; 1 child, Dezzi James. Spokesmodel Liz Claiborne Cosmetics, 2000. Actress (films) Against the Law, 1997, The Journey: Absolution, 1997, Poison Ivy: The New Seduction, 1997, Can't Hardly Wait, 1998, Ringmaster, 1998, Trash, 1999, Inferno, 1999, Poor White Trash, 2000, 100 Girls, 2000, Tomcats, 2001, Joe Dirt, 2001, Ticker, 2001, Not Another Teen Movie, 2001, Footprints, 2002, Demon Island, 2002, Torque, 2004, The Karate Dog, 2004, Cruel World, 2005, Death to the Supermodels, 2005, DOA, 2006, I Love You, Man, 2009, Venus & Vegas, 2007, actress (voice) Horton Hears a Who!, 2008, actress (TV films) Mercenary, 1997, Best Actress, 2000, The Johnny Chronicles, 2002, Alligator Point, 2003, (TV series) Push, 1998, Mortal Kombat: Conquest, 1998—99, Jack & Jill, 1999—2001, My Name Is Earl, 2005— (Primetime Emmy for Outstanding Supporting Actress in a Comedy Series, Acad. TV Arts and Scis., 2007), guest appreances include Silk Stalkings, 1998, Going to California, 2001, Charmed, 2002, The Twilight Zone, 2002, Fastlane, 2003, Becker, 2003, Happy Family, 2004, Las Vegas, 2006. Avocations: hiking, horseback riding, swimming, kickboxing, dance. Office: c/o Dar Rollins Internat Creative Mgmt 10250 Constellation Blvd Los Angeles CA 90067

PRESSLY, THOMAS JAMES, history professor; b. Troy, Tenn., Jan. 18, 1919; s. James Wallace and Martha Belle (Bittick) P.; m. Lillian Cameron, Apr. 30, 1943; children: Thomas James II, Stephanie Suzuki. AB, Harvard U., 1940, AM, 1941, PhD, 1950; LLD (hon.), Whitman Coll., 1981. Instr. history Princeton (NJ) U., 1946-49; asst. prof. U. Wash., 1949-54, assoc. prof., 1954-60, prof., 1960-87, prof. emeritus, 1987—. Vis. assoc. prof. Princeton U., 1953-54, Johns Hopkins U., 1969-70. Author: Americans Interpret Their Civil War, 1954; editor: (with W. H. Scofield) Farm Real Estate Values in the United States, 1965, (with others) American Political Behavior, 1974, Diary of George Templeton Strong (abridged), 1988, (with Glenn M. Linden) Voices From the House Divided, 1995, (with Maclyn P. Burg) The Great War At Home and Abroad, 1999; contr. articles to profl. jours., Free Black Shareholders, Journal of African American History, 2006. With US Army, 1941—45. Ford Found. Faculty fellow, 1951-52; Ctr. for Advanced Study in Behavioral Scis. fellow, 1955-56. Mem. Am. Hist.

Assn., So. Hist. Assn. (editl. bd. Jour. So. History 1973-77), Orgn. Am. Historians. Home and Office: 4545 E Laurel Dr NE Seattle WA 98105-3838 Home Phone: 206-525-4655.

PRESSMAN, GABE STANLEY, reporter; b. NYC, Feb. 14, 1924; s. Benjamin and Lena (Rifkin) P.; m. Emma Mae Kracht, Nov. 8, 1953 (div. 1967); children: Mark, Elizabeth, Margaret; m. Vera Elisabeth Olsen, Apr. 1, 1972; 1 child, Michael. BA in History magna cum laude, NYU, 1946; MS in Journalism, Columbia U., 1947; degree (hon.), Marist Coll., 2002, Coll. S.I., 2003. Reporter Peekskill (NY) Star, 1941-42, Newark Evening News, 1947; corr. Overseas News Agy., NYC, 1948-49; reporter World-Telegram Sun, NYC, 1949-54, WRCA and WRCA-TV, NBC, NYC, 1954-72, WNEW-TV, NYC, 1972-80, WNBC-TV, NYC, 1980—; anchor News Forum, NYC. Served to lt. (j.g.) USN, 1943-46, PTO. Mem. N.Y. Press Club (1st v.p. 1988-97, pres. 1997-00), Inner Cir. (pres. 1990). Office: WNBC 30 Rockefeller Plz 7th Fl New York NY 10112-0036

PRESSMAN, JACOB, retired rabbi; b. Phila., Oct. 26, 1919; s. Solomon David and Dora (Levin) P.; m. Marjorie Steinberg, June 14, 1942; children: Daniel Joseph, Joel David, Judith Sharon. BA, U. Pa., 1940; MHL, Jewish Theol. Sem., 1944, Dr.Hebrew Letters, 1960, Dr. Humane Letters, 1979. Ordained rabbi, 1945. Rabbi Forest Hills Jewish Ctr., NYC, 1944-46, Congregation Sinai, LA, 1946-50, Temple Beth Am, LA, 1950—85; ret. Dir. Bonds of Israel, L.A., 1988-90, city chmn., 1990-91; vice chmn. bd. govs. L.A. Jewish Fedn. Coun., 1988—; founder U. Judaism, L.A. Hebrew High Sch., Herzl Sch., Camp Ramah at Ojai, Akiba Acad., Rabbi Jacob Pressman Acad. Author: Dear Friends, 2001, This Wild and Crazy World, 2001. Recipient Simon Greenberg award for Outstanding Achievement in Rabbinate, Ziegler Sch. Rabbinic Studies, U. Judaism, L.A., 2004. Mem. Rabbinical Assembly Western Region (pres. 1954-56), Bd. Rabbis So. Calif. (pres. 1958-61). Office Phone: 310-652-7353. E-mail: jpress6511@aol.com. *God is. God is good. His creation is good, and so, mankind, being of His creation is good. As an act of grace, God gives man the power to choose between good and evil in his ways, and with even greater grace gives man the awareness that he has this choice. Man is perfectible. His perfect stage, the Messianic era, is coming; but it will always be coming, never at a moment in time to arrive, but always inviting us to progress to newer and higher goals personally and as a society, each new mountaintop of human progress toward that nobler future merely opens our eyes to visions of even greater and more God-like human life.*

PRESSMAN, RONALD R., manufacturing executive; b. NYC, Apr. 11, 1958; m. Mary Pressman; 3 children. Grad., Hamilton College, NY, 1980. Gen. mgr. ctr. and ea. Europe GE, London, 1990—92; CEO GE Power Sys. Europe, 1992—95, CEO Power Sys. global mktg., 1995—96; pres., CEO GE Capital Real Estate, 1997—2000; sr. v.p. GE Co., 2000—; pres., CEO GE Employers Reinsurance Co., 2000—06, GE Real Estate, 2006—. Mem. Corp. Exec. Coun.; dir. GE Cap. Svcs. Inc., GE Cap. Corp. Boards. Chmn. Nat. Bd. A Better Chance; bd. dirs. Kansas City Civic Coun.; mem. exec. bd. Nat. Realty Com., Wharton Real Estate Bus. Sch.; dir. Pathways to Coll. Recipient Crown American Golden Crown award, 1998, Fin. Svcs. Exec. of Yr., Comml. Property News. Office: GE 3135 Easton Turnpike Fairfield CT 06828-0001*

PRESTAGE, JAMES JORDAN, consultant; b. Deweyville, Tex., Apr. 29, 1926; s. James J. and Mona (Wilkins) P.; m. Jewel Limar, Aug. 12, 1953; children— Terri, James Grady, Eric, Karen, Jay BS cum laude, So. U., Baton Rouge, 1950; MS, U. Iowa, 1955, PhD, 1959. Instr. biology Prairie View Coll., Tex., 1955-56; asst. prof. So. U., Baton Rouge, 1959, assoc. prof. biology, 1959-61, prof. biology, 1961—, dir. computer sci. ctr., 1968-71, 72-73, dean acad. affairs, v.p. acad. affairs, 1973-81, exec. v.p., 1981-82, chancellor, 1982-85, univ. disting. prof. emeritus, 1985—; univ. disting. prof. biology Dillard U., New Orleans, 1987—. Chair divsn. natural scis. Dillard U., 1990—97; asst. dir. La. Coordinating Council for Higher Edn., Baton Rouge, 1971—72; mem. commn. on scholars Ill. Bd. Higher Edn., 1975—82; mem. com. on off-campus instrn. La. Bd. Regents, 1975—; mem. La. Data Processing Coun., Baton Rouge, 1979—82; vis. prof. biology Dillard U., New Orleans; trustee Am. Coll. Testing Program, 1983—86; faculty assoc. Danforth Found., 1966—70; cons. in field. Mem. exec. bd. Istrouma council Boy Scouts Am.; vice chmn. bd. trustees Greater Mt. Carmel Baptist Ch., Baton Rouge; bd. dirs. Capital Area United Way, Baton Rouge. Served with USN, 1944-46, 50-52; ETO, Korea Named Most Outstanding Faculty Mem., So. U., 1966-67; Nat. Med. Fellowships fellow U. Iowa, Iowa City, 1956-59; NIH grantee, 1960-65 Mem. Conf. Acad. Deans So. States. NAACP, Sigma Xi, Alpha Chi, Alpha Phi Alpha (chpt. pres.), Sigma Pi Phi Democrat. Avocations: fishing, reading, gardening. Office: So Br PO Box 9222 Baton Rouge LA 70813 Home: 2144 Wortham Blvd Houston TX 77065

PRESTAGE, JEWEL LIMAR, political scientist, educational consultant; b. Hutton, La., Aug. 12, 1931; d. Brudis L. and Sallie Bell (Johnson) Limar; m. James J. Prestage, Aug. 12, 1953; children— Terri, James, Eric, Karen, Jay. BA, So. U., Baton Rouge, 1951; MA, U. Iowa, 1952, PhD, 1954; LHD (hon.), U. D.C., 1994, Loyola U., Chgo., 1999; LLD (hon.), Spelman Coll., 1999. Assoc. prof. polit. sci. Prairie View (Tex.) Coll., 1954-55, 56; assoc. prof. polit. sci. So. U., 1956-57, 58-62, prof., 1962—, chairperson dept., 1965-83, dean pub. policy and urban affairs, 1983-89, dist. prof. emeritus, dean emeritus pub. policy, 1989—; prof. polit. sci. Prairie View U., 1989-90; dean Benjamin Banneker Honors Coll., Prairie View (Tex.) Coll., 1990-98, prof. political sci., 1998—, disting. prof. Prairie View, 2000—02. Chmn. La. adv. com. to U.S. Commn. on Civil Rights, 1975-85; mem., chmn. nat. adv. coun. on women's ednl. programs U.S. Dept. Edn., 1980-82; dist. vis. prof. U. Iowa, 1987-88. Author: (with M. Githens) A Portrait of Marginality: Political Behavior of the American Woman, 1976; contbr. articles to profl. jours. Rockefeller fellow, 1951-52; NSF fellow, 1964; Ford Found. postdoctoral fellow, 1969-70; Hon. Thurgood Marshal Scholarship Fund, 2005. Mem. NAACP, Am. Polit. Sci. Assn. (v.p. 1974-75, Frank Goodnow award 1998), So. Polit. Sci. Assn. (pres. 1975-76, Manning Dauer award 1998), Nat. Conf. Black Polit. Scientists (pres. 1976-77), Nat. Assn. African Am. Honors Programs (pres. 1993-94), Am. Soc. for Pub. Adminstrn. (pres. La. chpt. 1988-89, nat. exec. coun. 1989-90), Policy Studies Orgn. (exec. coun. 2000), Links Inc., Alpha Kappa Alpha, Congl. Black Caucus Found. (chair faculty adv. coun., 2003-04) Home: 11114 Wortham Blvd Houston TX 77065 Office: PO Box 125 Prairie View TX 77446-0125 *Commitments which guide my life are: (1) maximum development of personal potential through pursuit of excellence in all endeavors; (2) fair play, respect, compassion and quest of community in relations with fellow human beings; (3) utilization of personal talents in the interest of removing impediments to the good life "for all persons"; (4) pursuit of truth as the pervasive concern in academia; and (5) transmission of the above as priority goals to all with whom I have contact.*

PRESTBO, JOHN ANDREW, editor, writer, journalist; b. Northwood, ND, Sept. 26, 1941; s. Oscar Bernt and Jeanne (Schol) P.; m. Darlene Parrish, Aug. 14, 1965; children: Bradford Jonathan, Laura Christine. BS, Northwestern U., 1963, MS, 1964. Reporter, writer Wall Street Jour., Chgo., 1964-74, staff editor, Page 1 NYC, 1974-75, commodities editor, 1975-77, bur. chief Cleve., 1977-81, markets editor NYC, 1984—, editor Dow Jones Indexes, 1993—; v.p. editorial Dow Jones Radio 2, Inc., Princeton, NJ, 1981-83; exec. dir. Dow Jones Indexes, Princeton, 2006—. Author: Sleuthing, 1976; co-author: (with Frederick C. Klein) News and the Market, 1974, (with Douglas R. Sease) Barron's Guide to Making Investment Decisions, 1994, 2nd edit., 1998, The Wall Street Jour. Book of Internat. Investing, 1997; editor: This Abundant Land, 1975, Dow Jones Commodities Handbook, 1976-79, The Dow Jones Guide to the World Stock Market, 1994-98, The Market's Measure, 1999, Dow Jones Indexes, 2006—. Served with USAFR, 1966-73. Recipient Econ. Reporting award Ind. Natural Gas Assn., U. Mo., 1967; recipient Achievement-bur. writing award G.M. Loeb, 1968 Home: 14 Charleston Dr Skillman NJ 08558-1801 Office: 4300 Rte 1 Monmouth Junction NJ 08852 Home Phone: 908-874-6780; Office Phone: 609-520-7079. Business E-Mail: john.prestbo@dowjones.com.

PRESTEL, DAVID KIRK, literature and language professor, department chairman; m. Lillian Elaine Wilson, Dec. 30, 1971; children: Margot Louise, Carl. MA, PhD, U. Mich., Ann Arbor, 1983. Prof., chairperson Mich. State U., East Lansing, 1983—. Co-director Ctr. Support Lang. Tchg. MSU, East Lansing, Mich., 2008—. Contbr. articles. With Germany Army, 1970—73. Recipient Tchg. Excellence award, Mich. State U., 1991. Mem.: Early Slavic Studies Assn. (pres. 2000—02). Avocation: travel. Office: Mich State Univ Linguistics & Lang A614 Wells Hall East Lansing MI 48824-1027 Business E-Mail: prestel@msu.edu.

PRESTI, SAM, professional sports team executive; b. Concord, Mass. Student, Va. Wesleyan Coll., Norfolk; BA in Comm., Politics and Law, Emerson Coll., Boston, 2000. Intern San Antonio Spurs, 2000—01, basketball spl. asst., 2001—02, asst. dir. scouting, 2002—03, dir. player pers., 2003—05, asst. gen. mgr., 2005—07, v.p., 2006—07; gen. mgr. Seattle SuperSonics, 2007—08; exec. v.p., gen. mgr. Oklahoma City Thunder, 2008—. Recipient Young Alumnus award, Emerson Coll., 2005. Office: Oklahoma City Thunder Two Leadership Sq 211 N Robinson Ave Ste 300 Oklahoma City OK 73102*

PRESTIGIACOMO, CHARLES JOSEPH, neurosurgeon, educator; b. NYC, Feb. 14, 1967; s. Franco and Francesa Paola (Calderone) P.; m. Cynthia M. Rinker, June 22, 1991; children: Rachel Diane, Laura Marie, Michelle Elizabeth. BS in Biology, Georgetown U.; MD, Columbia U., 1993. Resident in neurosurg. surgery Columbia-Presbyn. Med. Ctr., NYC, 1993-2000; endovascular fellow Beth Israel Med. Ctr., NYC, 2000; asst. prof. dept. neurol. surgery and radiology U. Medicine and Dentistry NJ, Newark. Contbr. articles to med. jours. Mem. ACS (candidate), Am. Acad. Neurol. Surgeons, Congress Neurol. Surgeons. Roman Catholic. Avocations: building wooden ship models, photography, military technology, books, collecting wine, astronomy. Office: Neurol Inst NJ U Med and Dentistry NJ 90 Bergen St Ste 8100 Newark NJ 07107 E-mail: cjp9@optonline.net.

PRESTIGIACOMO, ROBERTO, theater educator, art director; MFA, U. Calif., Irvine, 2003. Artistic dir. Potlatch Theater Lab., Miami, Theater With Your Coffee, Miami, Fla., 1995—2000, AtticRep Theater, San Antonio, 2005—, organizer, 2005—08; prof. theater Trinity U., San Antonio, 2005—. Author: (plays) The Reason of the Insane Ones, Undertones, Pastiche, Girogio; dir.: (plays) Julius Caesar, Lincolnesque, Fat Pig, As you Like It. Grantee, Artist Found. San Antonio, 2008. Mem.: Soc. Stage Dirs. and Choreographers. Achievements include development of three different theater organizations, one theater arts program. Office: AtticRep One Trinity Pl San Antonio TX 78212 Business E-Mail: rprestigiacomo@atticrep.org.

PRESTINE, JOAN SINGLETON, writer, editor, educator; b. Salt Lake City, Mar. 11, 1944; d. Herbert William and Frances Bowdidge Singleton; m. Douglas C. Prestine, Apr. 5, 1963; children: Scott, Deb, Jeffrey. BA, U. So. Calif., LA, 1965. Author, lectr., freelance editor Children's Picture Book, 1987—. Pub. cons., 1987—; lectr. Santa Monica Coll., Pierce Coll., West LA Coll., Ventura Coll., Coll. of Canyons, Moorpark Coll., Oxnard Coll., Learning Tree U., Arapahoe Coll., Colo. State U. Denver, U. Colo., Denver U., 1987—. Author: (picture books My Special Feelings series) I Want This and This and This, 1987, Love Me Anyway, 1987, My Parents Go On a Trip, 1987, Someone Special Died, 1987, Me First, 1987, Sometimes I'm Afraid, 1987, Match Who You Are With What You Do, 1987, How to Write Picture Books for Fun and Profit, 1987, Chipper Chipmunk Cruises, 1989, (picture books Kids Have Feelings Too series) Someone Special Died, 1993, 2003, Sometimes I Feel Awful, 1993, 2003, It's Hard to Share My Teacher, 1994, 2003, Mom and Dad Break Up, 1996, 2003, Moving Is Hard, 1997, 2003, (resource guides) Family Day Care Activities from A to Z, 1989, Earthquake Preparedness, 1990, Helping Children Cope with Death, 1993, Helping Children Understand Their Feelings, 1993, Helping Children Share Their Teacher, 1994, Helping Children Understand Divorce, 1996, Helping Children Cope With Moving, 1997, Easy Activities for Every Kid, 2001. Mem Jr. League LA, 1976—; chair St. Joseph Ctr., 1991—, vol. cir., 1996; pres. JLLA Sustainer, 2004—09; founder Investments Plus, 1983, pres., 1983—1986, Rec. Sec., 1986—; Benefactor Huntington Libr.; bd. mem. Parrots Internat., 2005-07; Leader Boy Scouts Am., 1972—1984, Girl Scouts Am., 1975—1980, Peterson Automotive Mus., 2003—, Nat. Charity League, 1955—, Checkered Flag 200, 2003—, Pres. Cir. Orthop. Hosp., 2004—; 11-99 Found., 2002—; mem. Coronets 1961—, LA Conservancy, 2003—, LACMA Costume Coun., 2007. Recipient Parenting Shelf, Parents Choice Mag., 1994, Dir.'s award, Early Childhood News, 1997, Carolyn Helman Lichtenberg Crest award, 2002; named PTA Parent of Yr., Bellagio Rd. Sch., 1977, Parent of Yr., Parent Tchr. Student Assn., U. High Sch., 1983. Mem.: FOCAL, Westside Writer's Guild, Pubs. Mktg. Assn., Soc. Children's Book Writers and Illustrators, So. Calif. Children's Book Writers and Illustrators, Internat. Reading Assn., Childrens Author Network, Book Publicists of So. Calif., Authors Guild, Nat. Assn. Edn. of Young Children (life), Pi Beta Phi (alumni bd., pres. 1996—99, program chair 1993—96). Avocations: car rallies, reading, travel, walking. Personal E-mail: joanprestine@msn.com.

PRESTON, CHARLES MICHAEL, lawyer; b. Balt., Oct. 11, 1945; s. Carlton Edward and Jeannette Thorn (Baker) P.; m. Carol Ann Armacost, June 21, 1969 (div. Dec. 1978), Barbara Jean Brown (Redmer), Feb. 12, 2008. BA, Western Md. Coll., 1967; JD, U. Balt., 1970. Bar: Md. 1970, U.S. Dist. Ct. Md. 1972, U.S. Supreme Ct. 1974, U.S. Dist. Ct. (trial bar) 1984. Law clk. to Hon. E.O. Weant, Jr., Westminster, Md., 1970-71; assoc. Hoffman & Hoffman, Westminster, 1972-75; ptnr. Hoffman, Hoffman & Preston, Westminster, 1976-77, Hoffman, Stoner & Preston, Westminster, 1978-79; of counsel Stoner, Preston & Boswell Chartered, Westminster, 1980—. Rev. bd., panel mem. Atty. Grievance Commn., Annapolis, Md., 1978-95; mem. Md. Ct. Appeals Commn. on alternate dispute resolution, 1998-2000, adv. bd., Md. Mediation and Conflict Resolution Office, co-chair, Circuit Courts Com., 2001-03, Md. Ct. of Appeals Task Force on Professionalism, 2002-04, Md. Ct. of Appeals Professionalism Commn., 2004-. Contbr. articles to profl. jours. Mem. Carroll County Gen. Hosp., Westminster, 1983—; trustee Raymond I. Richardson Found., Middleburg, Md., 1979-93; bd. dirs. Carroll County Agrl. Ctr., Westminster, 1975—; dir. N.W. dist. ARC, Balt., 1987-95; trustee Balt. Opera Co., 1998-2001. With U.S. Army, 1970-71. Fellow (life) Md. Bar Found. (dir. 1998-, sec., treas. 2005-07, v.p. 2007-09, pres. 2009-), Am. Bar Found.; mem. ABA (del. ho. of dels. 1997-00), Md. State Bar Assn. (treas. 1991-96, bd. govs. 1985-86, 91-00, pres.-elect 1997, pres. 98), Carroll County Bar Assn. (pres. 1985), Pro Bono Resource Ctr. Md. (bd. dirs. 1997-00), Elks, Am. Legion. Presbyterian. Avocations: skiing, ice skating, woodworking, music, travel, sailing. Office: Stoner Preston & Boswell PO Box 389 188 E Main St Westminster MD 21157-5017

PRESTON, ELIZABETH A., psychologist; b. Missoula, Mont., May 9, 1957; d. Jay William and Elizabeth (Cummings) P.; children, Katherine Jennifer Lee, Jayson Douglas Lee. BA summa cum laude, U. Minn., 1979; PhD, Princeton U., 1984; Postdoctoral Cert., Calif. Sch. Profl. Psychology, 1988. Postdoctoral intern El Dorado County, Placerville, Calif., 1984-85, San Mateo (Calif.) County, 1985-87; adj. faculty Calif. Sch. Profl. Psychology, Berkeley, 1987; postdoctoral intern Kaiser Permanent, Santa Rosa, Calif., 1988-89; therapist Waldenhouse, Inc., San Francisco, 1989; clin. dir. Alinda Youth Svcs., Fairfield, Calif., 1990; therapist Kairos Unltd., Oakland, Calif.; pvt. practice Oakland, Calif., 1994—. NSF fellow, 1980-83; U. Mont. scholar, 1975-76, 77-78. Mem. Am. Psychol. Assn., Calif. Psychol. Assn., Phi Beta Kappa, Phi Kappa Phi. Office: 4100-10 Redwood Rd 126 Oakland CA 94619 Office Phone: 510-482-5344. Business E-Mail: bethpreston@sbcglobal.net.

PRESTON, JEROME, JR., retired lawyer; b. SI, NY, Nov. 15, 1922; s. Jerome and Iva (Stone) P.; m. Dorothy Greeno McCann, Oct. 3, 1953; children: Richard M., Douglas J., David G. AB, Harvard U., 1947; LL.B., Yale U., 1950. Bar: Mass. 1951. Ptnr. Foley Hoag LLP, Boston, 1956—92, ret. sr. ptnr., 1992—. Trustee Eaton-Vance Income Fund of Boston, Inc., 1976-95. Trustee Univ. Hosp., 1956-96, overseer, 1996—; bd. dirs. Cambridge Sch. of Weston, 1973-78, pres., 1975-77; mem. Wellesley (Mass.) Planning Bd., 1962-70, chmn., 1966-68. Served to 1st lt. Signal Corps AUS, 1943-46. Mem. ABA, Mass. Bar Assn., Boston Bar Assn., Am. Law Inst., Handel and Haydn Soc. (pres. 1988-92, pres. emeritus 1992-, gov. 1988-92), Tavern Club. Democrat. Home: 1010 Memorial Dr Apt 2G Cambridge MA 02138-4853 Office: Foley Hoag LLP 155 Seaport Blvd Ste 1600 Boston MA 02210-4853 Home: 1083 State Ste 32 Round Pond ME 04564 Home Phone: 617-661-9115; Office Phone: 617-832-1149. Personal E-mail: jpreston@aol.com.

PRESTON, MALCOLM, artist, art critic; b. NJ, May 25, 1919; s. Frank and Anniece (Landau) P.; m. Mary Alice Bales, Nov. 27, 1942; children: Jennifer, Amanda. BS, U. Wis., Madison, 1940; MA, Columbia U., NYC, 1945, PhD, 1951; student, New Sch. Social Rsch., NYC, 1940-42. Display artist and designer, free lance artist, 1939-41; fellow, asst. instr. painting New Sch. Social Research, 1940-41; high sch. tchr., 1944-49; art supr. Manhasset pub. schs., 1945; part-time instr. Adelphi Coll., 1947; chmn. dept. fine arts Hofstra Coll., 1949-74, prof. fine arts, 1954-74, chmn. div. humanities, 1959-74, coordinator arts, 1961-74; dir. Inst. Arts, 1962-74; art critic Newsday, 1968-86, Boston Herald Traveler, 1970-72. Contbr. articles to newspapers and mags.; radio, television shows Met. area; developed and carried out television series Ford Found. grant, Nat. Ednl. Radio and Television Center, Arts Around Us, Am. Art Today, 1956; one-man shows include Ward Eggleston Gallery, N.Y.C., 1950-51, 54, 56, A.C.A. Gallery, 1959, S.A.G., 1962, Palm Beach, 1968, St. Mary's Coll., 1978, Benson Gallery, 1979, The Gallery, Truro, Mass., 1980, 81, 82, Customs House Gallery, 1984, Country Art Gallery, 1986, Wenniger Gallery, 1988, Elaine Benson Gallery, 1991, Galerie Mourlot, Boston, 1992; group shows include New Art Gallery, 1948-49, Ward Eggleston Gallery, 1949-50, also, L.I. Artists Exhibit, Nat. Water Color Exhibit, San Diego, Am. Artists Assn. Gallery, 1951, Roosevelt Field Art Center, 1957, Art U.S.A., 1958, Hansa Gallery Group Show, 1958, Shore Studio Gallery, Provincetown, 1957-58, Kendall Art Gallery, Wellfleet, Mass., 1974, 75, 76, 77, 78, Roko Gallery, 1978, Himelfarb Gallery, 1978, Linden Gallery, 1981-82, Tower Gallery, 1983, Customs House Gallery, 1983, 84, 85, Grand Central Art Gallery, 1984, 85; work represented in permanent collections: Queens's Mus., Guild Hall Mus., Portland Mus., Cape Cod Mus. Fine Arts, Hofstra U., Living Arts Found., N.Y.C., Islip Art Mus. Served as 2d lt. F.A. AUS, World War II. Lowe Found. research grantee, 1950; Ford Found. grantee, 1958; recipient Emily Lowe award, 1949, 50, 52, 54, 56; 1st prize oil Utica, N.Y.; Shell Research award, 1963 Home: PO Box 182 Truro MA 02666-0182 Address: C/O Julie Heller Gallery Provincetown MA 02657 Home Phone: 508-349-3352; Office Phone: 508-349-3375.

PRESTON, MARGARET MARY V., bank executive; b. 1958; BA, Trinity Coll., 1979; MBA, Harvard U., 1983. Fin. mgmt. positions through mng. dir. & CFO global pvt. bank Deutsche Bank Alex Brown Inc., Balt.; exec. v.p. Mercantile Safe Deposit & Trust Co., 2002—06; sr. v.p., US Trust, Pvt. Wealth Mgmt. Bank of America, 2006—08, mng. dir., market exec. Metro NY Pvt. Bank, 2008—. Bd. dir. McCormick & Co. Inc., 2003—, Gateway Investment Advisors. Active Girl Scouts, Huntington's Disease Soc. America; bd. dir. Harvard Sch. Pub. Health, Trinity Coll., Alex Brown & Sons Charitable Found., Balt. Symphony Orch., United Way Ctrl. Md., Roland Park Country Sch. Named one of Md. Top 100 Women, Balt. Bus. Jour., 2000—02. Mailing: Bank of America 100 N Tryon St Charlotte NC 28255*

PRESTON, MICHAEL JAMES, social studies educator; b. Carlsbad, N.Mex., May 18, 1945; s. Ronald James and Rogene Preston; 1 child, Carter James. BA in History, U. Tex., Arlington, 1969; MA in Sociology, U. North Tex., Denton, 1992. Cert. spl. olympics coach Tex., 1986, leader Boy Scouts Am., Denton, Tex., 2004. Tchg. fellow U. North Tex., 1987—97, adj. instr., 1997—. Pvt. practice, Dallas, 1974—86. Dist. camping commr. Boy Scouts Am., 2008—09; campaign organizer Dallas County Young Dems., 1974—86, Denton County Young Dems., Tex., 1986—2009. Cpl. USMC, 1963—69. Recipient Charter Pres. award, Lambda Pi Sigma, 1968—69, Chpt. Pres. award, Sociology Nat. Honor Soc., 1988—99, Lady Eagles Basketball Hon. Coach award, 2003; named one of Top Prof., Morter Bd., 1997. Avocation: golf. Office: Univ North Tex Denton TX 76203

PRESTON, RICHARD MCKIM, lawyer; b. Balt., June 2, 1947; s. Wilbur Day Jr. and May Virginia (Honemann) P.; m. Trisa Jean Thompson, Apr. 28, 1961. BA, Washington & Lee U., 1969, JD cum laude, 1976; MA cum laude, Fairleigh Dickinson U., 1973. Assoc. vomBaur, Coburn, Simmons & Turtle, Washington, 1976-79, Seyfarth, Shaw, Washington, 1979-82, ptnr., 1982—. Mng. ptnr. Constrn. Group, 1987—; bd. govs. Washington Bldg. Congress, 1997—. Contbr. articles to profl. publs., chpt. to book. Bd. advisors Jubilee Support Found., Washington, 1989—; mem. Washington & Lee Law Coun., Lexington, Va., 1986-93. Mem. River Bend Golf and Country Club, Sankaty Head Golf Club, Metro. Club (D.C.). Office: Seyfarth Shaw 975 F St Washington DC 20004 Home Phone: 703-450-5140.

PRESTON, ROB, editor-in-chief; BA in Journalism, St. Bonaventure U., NY; MA in Econs., SUNY, Binghamton. Past editl. mgmt. positions CommunicationsWeek Internat.; editor-in-chief Network Computing mag., 2002—06; sr. mgmt. editor InformationWeek mag. CMP Media Inc., editor-in-chief, 2006—. Named a Top Innovator in bus. pub., BtoB Media Bus. mag., 2008. Office: InfoWeek 600 Community Dr Manhasset NY 11030 Office Phone: 516-562-5692. Fax: 516-562-5036. E-mail: rpreston@cmp.com.*

PRESTON, SEYMOUR STOTLER, III, chemicals executive; b. Media, Pa., Sept. 11, 1933; s. Seymour Stotler and Mary Alicia (Harper) P.; m. Jean Ellen Holman, Sept. 8, 1956; children: Courtney J., Katherine E., Alicia D., Shelley S. BA, Williams Coll., 1956; MBA, Harvard Coll., 1958. With Pennwalt Corp., Phila., 1961-89, exec. v.p. in charge of chems. and equipment ops., worldwide, 1975-77, pres., COO, 1977-89; pres., CEO Elf Atochem N.Am., Inc. (formerly Atochem N.Am.), Phila., 1990-93. Chmn. AAC Engineered Sys. Inc., 1994-2003; bd. dirs., Albermarle Corp., 1996-2008, dir., Tufco Techs., Inc., 1999-2008, Ocean Power Tech. Inc., 2004-; vice chmn., Ind. Publs., Inc., 2004-, bd. dir., 2008, lead dir., 2009-. Trustee Shipley Sch., Bryn Mawr, Pa., 1976-88, Phila. Orch. Assn., 1992-95; trustee Acad. Natural Scis., 1980—, chmn., 1995-2000, pres., CEO, 2000-02; bd. mgrs. Franklin Inst., Phila., 1980-92; bd. dirs. Lawrenceville (NJ) Sch., 1982-99, Wistar Inst., 1997—, Barra Found., 1998—, chmn., 2004—. 1st lt. USAF, 1958-61. Mem. Soc. for Chem. Industry, Greater Phila. C. of C. (bd. dirs. 1979-94), Radnor Hunt Club (Malvern, Pa.). Home Phone: 610-644-5317; Office Phone: 610-889-3980. Personal E-mail: spmillrace@aol.com.

PRESTON, STEPHEN WOOLMAN, lawyer; b. May 30, 1957; BA summa cum laude, Yale U., 1979; diploma with first class honors, Trinity Coll., Univ. Dublin, 1980; JD magna cum laude, Harvard U., 1983. Bar: DC 1983. Law clk. to Hon. Phyllis A. Kravitch U.S. Ct. Appeals (11th cir.), 1983—84; vis. fellow Ctr. for Law in Pub. Interest, Washington, 1984—85; ptnr. Wilmer, Cutler & Pickering, Washington, 1986—93; prin. dep. gen. counsel, acting gen. counsel US Dept. Def., 1993—95, gen. counsel Dept. Navy, 1998—2000; dep. asst. atty. gen. US Dept. Justice, 1995—98; ptnr., co-chair, Def. Nat. Security & Govt. Practice Group Wilmer Cutler Pickering Hale & Dorr, Washington, 2001—09; gen. counsel CIA, Washington, 2009—. Editor: Harvard Law Rev. Recipient Disting. Pub. Svc. medal US Dept. Def., 1995, 2000, Dept. Navy, 2000. Fellow: Am. Bar Found.; mem.: ABA (mem. standing com. on law, nat. security adv. com.), Council on Fgn. Rels., Phi Beta Kappa. Office: Office Gen Counsel CIA Washington DC 20505

PRESTON, STEVEN C., former United States Secretary of Housing and Urban Development; b. Aug. 4, 1960; m. Molly Preston; 5 children. BA in Polit. Sci. with highest distinction, Northwestern U., 1982; MBA, U. Chgo., 1985; student, Ludwig Maximillian U., Munich, Germany. Sr. v.p. investment banking Lehman Brothers Inc., 1985-93; sr. v.p., corp. treas. First Data Corp.; CFO The ServiceMaster Co., Downers Grove, Ill., 1997—2003, exec. v.p., 2003—06; adminstr. US Small Bus. Adminstrn., Washington, 2006—08; sec. US Dept. Housing & Urban Devel., Washington, 2008—09. Vice chmn. bd. visitors Northwestern U. Weinberg Coll. Arts & Sciences; bd. dirs. Hinsdale Hosp. Found; mem. adv. bd. Tri-Artisan Partners, Concentric Equity Partners. Republican.*

PRESTWICH, ROGER, educator; b. Oldham, Lancashire, Eng., Sept. 25, 1942; s. Walter Orlando Prestwich and Elsie Bradbury; m. Cherie Mary Rollings; children: Andrew Thomas, Natalie Katerina Eschenbaum. BA in Economics Geography, U. Sheffield, Eng., 1964, Dip. Ed., 1965; MA, U. Minn., Mpls., 1968, PhD, 1971; MPhil, U. Cambridge, Eng., 1984. Lectr. Macalester Coll., St. Paul, 1968—71; sr. lectr. Anglia Poly. U., Cambridge, 1971—87; edn. program dir. Minn. Trade Office, St. Paul, 1988—2000; dir. Minn. World Trade Ctr., St. Paul, 1999—2000; prof. Metro State U., Mpls., 2001—. Contbr. articles to profl. jours. Mem. Minn. Dist. Export Coun., Mpls., Minn. World Trade Assn., Mpls., 1995—2003, Minn. Internat. Ctr., Mpls., 2001—07, Midwest Global Trade Assn., Mpls., 2003—06, UN Assn. Minn., Mpls., 2006—07; chair St. Paul Mpls. Com. Fgn. Rels., 2002—08, Brit. Am. Coun. Minn., Mpls., 2002—. Recipient Spl. Svc. award, World Trade Week Inc., 1999. Mem.: Acad. Internat. Bus., Am. Coms. Fgn. Rels. (chpt. rep. 2002—). Avocations: travel, soccer. Office: Metro State Univ 1501 Hennepin Ave Minneapolis MN 55403 Office Fax: 612-659-7268. Business E-Mail: roger.prestwich@metrostate.edu.

PRETTYMAN, ELIJAH BARRETT, JR., lawyer; b. Washington, June 1, 1925; s. Elijah Barrett and Lucy Courtney (Hill) P.; m. Noreen Prettyman; children by previous marriage: Elijah Barrett III, Jill Savage Lukoschek. BA, Yale U., 1949; LLB, U. Va., 1953. Bar: Wash., D.C. 1954, U.S. Supreme Ct. 1957. Pvt. practice, Washington, 1955—; law clk. to Hon. Justices Jackson, Frankfurter and Harlan US Supreme Ct., Washington, 1953-55; assoc. Hogan & Hartson, Washington, 1955—63, ptnr., 1964—2001, of counsel, 2002—; spl. asst. to atty. gen. US Dept. Justice, 1963; spl. asst. to Pres. for transp. mergers The White House, 1963—64; inspector gen. DC, Washington, 1998—99. Spl. cons. subcom. to investigate problems connected with refugees and escapees, U.S. Senate Judiciary Com., Vietnam, 1967-68; outside cons. to subcom. on oversight and investigations, Ho. of Reps. com. on internal and fgn. commerce, 1978; spl. cons. for ABSCAM investigation to Com. on Standards of Ofcl. Conduct, U.S. Ho. of Reps., 1980-81; trustee emeritus, past exec com. Am. U., Washington; past trustee, mem. exec. com. Washington Journalism Ctr.; past adv. com., Media Law Reporter. Author: Death and the Supreme Court, 1961 (Edgar Allan Poe award); Editor: (with William E. Jackson) The Supreme Court in the American System of Government (Justice Robert H. Jackson), 1955; contbr. articles to profl. jours. Past corp. mem. Salvation Army; past mem. adv. com. Procedures of Jud. Coun., DC; past mem. adv. bd. Inst. Comm. Law Studies, Cath. U.; bd. govs., St. Albans Sch., 1957-63, 65-72, chmn., 1965-67; past mem. nat. adv. com., Nat. Inst. for Citizen Edn. in Law; bd. dirs., past pres., exec. com. PEN/Faulkner Found.; v.p., past chmn. publ. com., exec. com. Supreme Ct. Hist. Soc.; bd. dirs. Robert H. Jackson Ctr., Jamestown, NY, 2006-; past internat. adv. group Toshiba Corp.; past commr. Supreme Ct. Jud. Fellows Commn., chmn., 2003-05. With AUS, 1943—45. Recipient Pub. Svc. Achievement award Common Cause, 1999, Disting. Pub. Svc. award DC, 1999, Justice Potter Stewart award Coun. for Ct. Excellence, 2000, Lifetime Achievement award, The Am. Lawyer mag., 2007, named 90 Gratest Wash. Lawyers, 2008 Fellow: ABA; mem.: D.C. Cir. Hist. Soc. (pres. 2000—02, chmn. 2003—07), Am. Acad. Appellate Lawyers (past pres.), Am. Judicature Soc. (past vice chair, exec. com.), Met. Washington Bd. Trade, DC Bar Assn. (bd. govs., Lawyer of Yr. award 1998), DC Bar (1st pres. 1972—73, bd. govs. 1973—74, past jud. evaluation com.), DC Bar Found. (pres. 1983—84), Jud. Conf. DC Cir., Am. Coll. Trial Lawyers, Chevy Chase Club, Met. Club, Alfalfa Club, Barristers Club, Lawyers Club (past pres.). Methodist. Home: 2737 Devonshire Pl NW # 424 Washington DC 20008-5148 Office: Hogan & Hartson Columbia Sq 555 13th St NW Washington DC 20004-1109 Home Phone: 202-483-8853; Office Phone: 202-637-5685. Business E-Mail: ebprettyman@hhlaw.com.

PRETTYMAN, JOHN A., language educator; BA in English, Syracuse U., NY, 1984; MS in Edn., SUNY, Oswego, 1996. Adj. instr., tutor Onondaga CC, Syracuse, 1985—89, asst. prof., 1990—; English instr. Ednl. Opportunity Ctr. SUNY Morrisville, 1986—90; instr. Job Tng. Partnership Agy. Program, Syracuse, 1989—90. Recipient Employee Appreciation award, Onondaga CC, 2006. Mem.: Martin Luther King, Jr. Nat. Meml. Project Found., Inc. (founding sponsor), Assn. Supervision and Curriculum Devel., Am. Civil Liberties Union, N.Y. State United Tchrs., Nat. Coun. Tchrs. English, Schomberg Ctr. for Rsch. in Black Culture, So. Poverty Law Ctr., Jazz Lincoln Ctr. Office: 4585 West Seneca Turnpike Syracuse NY 13215

PRETZAT, JULIE, academic administrator, conductor; b. Tarrytown, NY, Oct. 25, 1957; d. Walter and Anne Oglesby Pretzat; m. Benjamin Ralph Merchant, May 21, 1988; children: Emily Mihaela Merchant, Stefan Bradley Merchant. BA, Smith Coll., Northampton, Mass., 1979; MMus, U. Mich., Ann Arbor, 1981; PhD in Musical Arts, Cin. Coll. Conservatory Music, 1988. Music prof. and condr. SUNY, Oswego, 1985—2008, chmn. music dept., 2002—08, interim assoc. dean, 2008—; dir. chapel choir Syracuse U., NY, 1993—95. Musician (conductor): (multi-media music performance) The Origin, Voices of Light, (300 voice choir) Internat. Presbyterian Conf., (opera productions) 8 different operas with Oswego Opera Theatre. Vol. Samaritan Ctr. Pk. Ctrl. Presbyn. Ch., Syracuse, 1995, music dir., 1995—. Recipient Chancellor's Excellence Tchg. award, SUNY, 2006, Philip Martin Educator Excellence award, CNY Edn. Consortium, 2006; Origin Commn. and Premiere grant, NY State Fund Music, 2007—. Mem.: Am. Choral Dirs. Assn., Phi Kappa Phi, Pi Kappa Lambda. Home: 27 North St Baldwinsville NY 13027

PREUCIL, DORIS BOGEN, music educator; b. Milw., Dec. 10, 1932; d. Walter Leopold and Adele Anne (Jarvis) Bogen; m. William Warren Preucil, Sept. 4, 1954; children: William, Jr., Walter, Anne, Jeanne. MusB with distinction, Eastman Sch. Music, Rochester, NY, 1954; MusM, U. Iowa, 1968; studied with Shinichi Suzuki, Talent Edn. Inst., Japan, 1982. Violinist Rochester Philharm. Orch., 1952—54, Nat. Symphony Orch., Washington, 1954—56; freelance violinist & tchr. Iowa City, 1956—72; asst. prof. Western Ill. U., Macomb, 1972—76; founder, dir., master tchr. Preucil Sch. Music, Iowa City, 1975—97, dir. emerita, tchr., 1997—. Suzuki Professorial chair U. Wis., Stevens Point, 1986; hon. bd. mgrs. Eastman Sch. Music, Rochester, 2005—. Musician (1st violinist): Milw. Symphony, 1948—50, Rochester Philharm., 1952—54, Tri-City Symphony, 1958—72; concertmaster:, 1971—72; musician: Eastman Faculty Quartet, 1951—54, Lydian Trio, 1972—75, Preucil Family Players, 1975—84; author, editor: The Suzuki Viola Sch., 1976—, arranger: The Solo with Orchestra series 2004-. Trustee Nat. Guild Cmty. Schs. Arts, 1988—91; bd. dirs. Amateur Chamber Music Found., 1998—; elder, deacon 1st Presbyn. Ch., Iowa City, 1964—. Recipient Lifetime Achievement award, Eastman Sch. Music, 2004; named Tchr. of the Yr., Iowa State Music Tchrs. Assn., 2005. Mem.: Internat. Suzuki Assn. (founding bd. mem. 1983—95), Suzuki Assn. Am. (cert. tchr., trainer 1980—, pres. 1982—84, Disting. Svc. award 1992), Rotary (mem. music commn. 1989—). Avocations: music, reading, travel. Home: 317 Windsor Dr Iowa City IA 52245 Personal E-mail: wdpreucil@mchsi.com.

PREUDHOMME, MARCIA DENRIQUE, marketing executive, writer; b. San Fernando, Trinidad, West Indies, Nov. 12, 1966; d. Ronald and Sarah Preudhomme. Diploma in gen. draftsmanship, San Fernando Tech. Inst., Trinidad, 1991; cert. in stage mgmt., U. West Indies, Trinidad, 1992; student, Montgomery Coll., 1995. Draftsman San Fernando City Hall, 1994; mgr., team developer Brinker Internat., Inc., Washington, 1997—99; referral coord. Washington Hosp. Ctr., 1999—2001; assoc. BDO Seidman, LLP, Bethesda, Md., 2001—05. Author: Reflections of Realism, 2003, Stranger Than Fiction, 2004 (Urban Spectrum Newspaper award, 2006). Recipient Editor's Choice, Internat. Libr. Poetry, 2003. Avocations: reading, board games, philosophy, exercise. Office Phone: 202-546-1708.

PREUSS, DAPHNE, geneticist, biology professor; BS in Chemistry, U. Denver, 1985, BS in Natural Scis., 1985; PhD in Genetics, MIT, 1990. Albert D. Lasker prof. molecular genetics & cell biology U. Chgo., 1995—; prin. investigator Howard Hughes Med. Inst., Chgo., 2000—06; co-founder Chromatin, Inc., Chgo., 2000, sr. v.p., 2007, chief sci. officer, 2007—, pres., 2007—. Bd. gov. Argonne Nat. Lab. Contbr. articles to profl. jours. Bd. govs. Argonne Nat. Labs., Chgo., 2003—. Recipient Ammi Hyde award for Young Alumni Achievement, U. Denver, Women in Cell Biology Jr. award, Am. Soc. Cell Biology, Promega Early Career Life Scientist award, 2001; named one of Discover 20 (List of 20 Promising Young Scientists), Discover Mag., 2000, 40 under 40, Chgo. Crain's Bus. Review, 2001; David and Lucille Packard fellow, Packard Found., 1997-2004, Searle Scholar. Mem.: NAS (lifetime nat. assoc.). Achievements include invention of chromosomes for plants; Chromatin's patented mini-chromosome technology. Office: Dept Molecular Genetics and Cell Biology U Chgo Ctr for Integrative Sci 929 E 57th St CIS W519 Chicago IL 60637 Office Fax: 773-702-6648, 312-563-9120. E-mail: dpreuss@midway.uchicago.edu.

PREVEDOUROS, PANOS D., engineering educator, consultant; s. Dimitrios P. and Toula G. Prevedouros; life ptnr. Katie Lynn O'Donel; children: Lesna O'Donel, Endie. Diploma, Aristotle U., Thesaloniki, Greece, 1984; MS, PhD, Northwestern U., Evanston, Ill., 1990. Cert. Chamber Profl. Engrs., 1984. Prof. U. Hawaii Manoa, Honolulu, 1990—. Profl. cons. ATTRA, Honolulu, 1992—. Mayor candidate City and County of Honolulu, 2008. Recipient Van Wagoner award, Inst. Transp. Engrs., 2005. Mem.: Transp. Rsch. Bd. (subcom. chair 2005—08). Office: Univ Hawaii Manoa 2540 Dole St 383 Honolulu HI 96822 Office Fax: 808-956-5014. Business E-Mail: pdp@hawaii.edu.

PREVOST, JEAN HERVE, civil engineer, educator; b. Fez, Morocco, Sept. 10, 1947; came to U.S., 1971; s. Jean and Brigitte (Castelnau) P.; m. Carol W. Wilcox, June 18, 1975; children: Christopher, Ian, Olivia. BSCE, ETP, Paris, 1971; MS, Stanford U., 1972, PhD, 1974. Rsch. fellow NGI, Oslo, Norway, 1974-76; rsch. fellow, lectr. Cal Tech., Pasadena, 1976-78; asst. prof., assoc. prof. Princeton (N.J.) U., 1978-86, prof., 1986—. Cons. Lawrence Livermore Lab., Livermore, Calif., 1990-906, Kajima Co., Tokyo, 1992-94, Geodynamique, Paris, 1990-96. Programmer engrng. software; contbr. articles to profl. jours. Avocation: golf. Home: 76 Prince William Ct Princeton NJ 08540-4005 Office: Princeton Univ Olden St Princeton NJ 08544-0001

PREVOST, PATRICK M., chemicals executive; b. 1955; BS in Chemistry, U. Geneva; MBA, U. Chgo., 1991. V.p. chemical intermediates Amoco, Geneva, 1994—97, chmn. supervisory bd. Amoco Fabrics Germany, 1995—98, v.p. global bus. mgmt. Lisle, Ill., 1997—98; chief exec. terephthalic acid bus. BP Chemicals, Naperville, Ill., 1999, BP exec. com. London, v.p. strategy & devel., 2001—03; exec. v.p. chemicals and plastics N.Am., pres. regional divsn. BASF, 2003—05, pres. performance chemicals, 2005—07; pres., CEO Cabot Corp., Boston, 2008—. Bd. dirs. Cabot Corp., 2008—. Office: Cabot Corp 2 Seaport Ln Ste 1300 Boston MA 02210-2019 Office Phone: 617-345-0100. Office Fax: 617-345-6103.

PREVOZNIK, MICHAEL E., lawyer; BS, U. Notre Dame, 1983; MBA, U. Chgo., 1985, JD magna cum laude, 1988. With Dechert, Price & Rhodes; chief legal compliance officer SBCL, 1994—96; v.p., chief legal compliance officer SmithKline Beecham Healthcare Svcs., 1996—98, v.p. compliance, 1998—99; v.p. legal Quest Diagnostics, NJ, 1999—2003, gen. counsel, 1999—, sr. v.p. legal & compliance, 2003—. Office: Quest Diagnostics 1290 Wall St W Lyndhurst NJ 07071 E-mail: Michael.E.Prevoznik@questdiagnostics.com.

PREWETT, MATTHEW SCOTT, research scientist; b. Macon, Ga., Oct. 30, 1980; s. Michael Jon and Patricia McKibben Prewett. Attending, U. South Fla., Tampa, 2003—. Rschr. U. South Fla., 2003—; cons. U. South Fla. Med. Sch., 2008—. Office: Univ South Fla 4202 E Fowler Ave Tampa FL 33620 Personal E-mail: mprewett1027@gmail.com.

PREWITT, CHARLES THOMPSON, geochemist; b. Lexington, Ky., Mar. 3, 1933; s. John Burton and Margaret (Thompson) P.; m. Gretchen B. Hansen, Jan. 31, 1958; children: Daniel Hansen. SB, MIT, 1955, SM, 1960, PhD, 1962. Rsch. scientist E.I. DuPont De Nemours & Co. Inc., Wilmington, Del., 1962-69; assoc. prof. SUNY, Stony Brook, 1969-71, prof., 1971-86, chmn. dept. earth and space scis., 1977-80; dir. Geophys. Lab., Carnegie Inst. of Washington, 1986-98, mem. rsch. staff, 1998—2003; adj. prof. Dept. Geoscis. U. Ariz., Tucson, 2003—. Sec.-treas. U.S. Nat. Com. for Crystallography, Washington, 1983-85, 99—; gen. chmn. 14th Meeting of Internat. Mineral Assn., Stanford, Calif., 1986; chmn. NRC/NAS com. on physics and chemistry of earth materials, 1985-87; mem. bd. govs. Consortium for Advanced Radiation Svcs.; co-dir. NSF Ctr. for High Pressure Rsch., 1991—; disting. vis. prof. chemistry Ariz. State U., 1983. Editor: (jour.) Physics and Chemistry of Minerals, 1976-85; contbr. more than 190 articles to profl. jours. Bd. dirs. Internat. Ctr. for Diffraction Data, 1998-2002. Capt. USAR, 1956-65. NATO sr. postdoctoral fellow, 1975, Churchill overseas fellow, 1975, Japan Soc. for Promotion of Sci. fellow, 1983, Ernst Cloos Meml. scholar Johns Hopkins U., 2002-; recipient: medal for Excellence Internat. Mineral. Assn., 2008. Fellow AAAS, Mineral. Soc. Am. (pres. 1983-84, Roebling medal 2003), Am. Geophys. Union, Internat. Centre Diffraction Data; mem. Geol. Soc. Am., Am. Crystallographic Assn., Materials Rsch. Soc., Mineral. Soc. Gt. Britain and Ireland, Cosmos Club. Office: Dept Geoscis Univ Arizona Tucson AZ 85721-0077 Office Phone: 520-621-9993.

PREWITT, DEZZIE ALLEN, economics professor; married. BA in Economics, U. Southern Calif., LA, 1998; MS, Cal Poly Pomona, Calif., 2000. Prof., economics Moorpark Coll., Calif., 2007—, Rio Hondo Coll., Whittier, Calif., 2008—. Economist US Dept. Labor Bur. Labor Stats., San Francisco, 2000—04. Office: Rio Hondo Coll 3600 Workman Mill Rd Whittier CA 90601 Business E-Mail: dprewitt@riohondo.edu.

PREWITT, JEAN, not-for-profit organization executive; b. Oklahoma City; Degree, Harvard U.; degree in law, Georgetown U. Formerly lawyer Donovan Leisure Newton & Irvine; sr. v.p., gen. counsel United Internat. Pictures, 1982—89; with Nat. Telecomm. and Info. Adminstrn. U.S. Dept. Commerce, 1989—94; prin. Podesta Assocs., Washington DC, 1994—99; pres. Ind. Film & TV Alliance, LA, 2000—01, CEO, 2001—; bd. mem. Film LA, 2004—. Pres. Casa De Los Amigos, LA, 2003—. Adv. bd. Friends of Cancer Rsch., Washington DC, 2003—. Named one of The 100 Most Powerful Women in Entertainment, Hollywood Reporter, 2007—08. Office: Ind Film and TV Alliance 10850 Wilshire Blvd 9th Fl Los Angeles CA 90024-4321 Business E-Mail: jprewitt@ifta-online.org.

PREWITT, KEITH L., federal agency administrator; B in Psychology/Criminal Justice, Memphis State U. Police officer, Memphis; spl. agent Memphis field office US Secret Svc., 1983, served in vice presdl. protective divsn., served in liaison divsn., asst. to spl. agent in charge of Chgo. field office, asst. spl. agent in charge of candidate nominee ops., spl. agent in charge of major events divsn., dep. asst. dir. office protective ops., dep. asst. dir. office govt. and pub. affairs, asst. dir. govt. and pub. affairs, asst. dir. office human resources and tng., asst. dir. office protective rsch., dep. dir., 2008—. Bd. mem. Fed. Law Enforcement Tng. Accreditation Bd. Recipient Secretary's award for Outstanding Achievement in Diversity Mgmt., US Secret Svc., 2005. Office: US Secret Svc 245 Murray Dr Bldg 410 Washington DC 20223*

PREWITT, LENA VONCILLE BURRELL, educator; b. Feb. 17, 1932; m. Sept. 5, 1959; 1 child. B.S., Stillman Coll., 1954; M.S., Ind. U., 1955, Ph.D., 1961. Asst. prof. Stillman Coll., Tuscaloosa, Ala., 1955-57, assoc. prof., 1958, prof., 1960-67; assoc. prof., dept. chmn. Tex. So. U., Houston, 1967-69; assoc. prof. Florence (Ala.) State U., 1969-70; assoc. prof. human resource mgmt. U. Ala.-Tuscaloosa, 1970-74, prof., 1974—. Mem. Internat. Personnel Mgmt. Assn., European Found. for Mgmt. Devel., World Future Soc., AAUW, Acad. Mgmt., So. Mgmt. Assn., European Found. for Mgmt. Devel., Alpha Kappa Mu. Personal E-mail: ltrzwiho@netzero.net.

PREWITT DIAZ, JOSEPH O., psychologist, educator; b. San Juan, Nov. 23, 1943; came to U.S., 1973; s. Joe C. and Leonor (Diaz) Prewitt; m. Maria D. Rodriguez, Nov. 3, 1968 (div. 1991); children: Joseph O., Maria D., Ana J., Victoria S.; m. Milagros O. Quendo, July 12, 1997. BA, U. P.R., 1966, BEd, 1970, MEd, 1972; PhD, U. Conn., 1979. Lic. sch. psychologist Conn., Pa.; lic. principal Conn., Pa. Prof. U. P.R., Cayey, P.R., 1968-73; vice prin. Hartford (Conn.) Bd. Edn., 1973-79; assoc. prof. psychology Pa. State U., University Park, 1979-91; sch. psychologist Chester-Upland Sch. Dist., Pa., 1992-95. Adj. prof. psychology Alvernia Coll., Reading, Pa., 1992-95; adj. prof. edn. Neumonon Coll., Aston, Pa., 1994-97. Contbr. articles to profl. jours. Vol. ARC, Loncosta, Pa., 1991— (Vol. Yr. award 1994); dir. legis. affairs CAP, Pa., 1991— (Disting. Svc. award 1993). Mem. APA. Methodist. Office: Chester-Upland Sch Dist 10th & Fulton Sts Chester PA 19013

PREWOZNIK, JEROME FRANK, retired lawyer; b. Detroit, July 15, 1934; s. Frank Joseph and Loretta Ann (Parzych) Prewoznik; m. Marilyn Ruth Johnson, 1970; 1 child, Frank Joseph II. AB cum laude, U. Detroit, 1955; JD with distinction, U. Mich., 1958. Bar: Calif. 1959. Pvt. practice, Calif., 1960-91. Served in US Army, 1958—60. Mem.: State Bar Calif. Republican.

PREY, BARBARA ERNST, artist; b. NYC, Apr. 17, 1957; d. Herbert Henry and Margaret (Joubert) Ernst; m. Jeffrey Drew Prey, Jan. 11, 1986; children: Austin William Ernst Prey, Emily Elizabeth Prey. BA with honors, Williams Coll., 1979; MDiv, Harvard U., 1986. Sales staff Tiffany and Co., NYC, summer 1977; intern Met. Mus. Art, NYC, summer 1979; pers. asst. Prince Albrecht Castell, Castell, Germany, 1980-81; with modern painting dept. Sotheby's Auction House, NYC, 1981-82; sales asst. Marlborough Gallery, NYC, 1982; tchg. asst. Boston

Coll., 1984, Harvard U., Cambridge, Mass., 1984-85; vis. lectr. Tainan (Taiwan) Coll. and Sem., 1986-87; artist Oyster Bay, NY, 1987—; with Nat. Coun. Arts. Art juror Washington and Jefferson Coll., Washington, 1990; artist-in-residence Westminster Sch., Simsbury, Conn., 1998; lectr. Nat. Gallery Art, Washington, 2005; mem. chmn.'s coun. Heckscher Mus.; presenter in field. Exhibited in group shows at Mus. Fine Arts, Mus. Southwest, Midland, Tex., Nassau County, N.Y., 1988, Nat. Arts Club, NYC, 1988, Gallery One, Rockland, Maine, 1992, Williams Coll., Williamstown, Mass., 1993, Johnstown Art Mus., Pa., 1993, Blair Art Mus., Holidaysburg, Pa., 1993, Phila. Mus. Art Gallery, 1995, Westmoreland Mus. Am. Art, Greensburg, Pa., 1996 (Best in Show award), Farnsworth Mus. Art, Rockland, Maine, 1997, Guild Hall Mus., East Hampton, NY, 1998, Portland Mus. Art, Md., 1998, US Embassy, Prague, 2002, Heckscher Mus. Art, Huntington, NY, 2002, Guild Hall Mus., East Hampton, NY, 2002, 2004, Gilcrease Mus., Tulsa, 2002, Internat. Space Station, 2003, The White House, Collection of Pres. and Mrs. George Bush, 2003, 2004, Kennedy Space Ctr., 2003—06, 2008—09, US Embassy, Oslo, Prague, Liberia, Belarus, 2003, 2004, 2005, Minsk, 2004, Madrid, 2006, 2007, Paris, 2006, 2007, 2008, Vilnius, 2006, 2007, 2008—09, NASA Commn: Shuttle Discovery Relaunch, US Embassy, Paris, 2005, Mona Bismarck Found., 2007, Picturing Long Island, The Heckscher Mus., 2007, Kennedy Space Ctr., 2007, An American View: Barbara Ernst Pray, Mona Bismarck Found., 2007, one-woman shows include Harvard-Yale-Princeton Club, Pitts., 1991, Jensen Fine Arts, NYC, 1999, 2001, Represented in permanent collections Pres. and Mrs. George Bush Farnsworth Mus. Art The White House, Kennedy Space Ctr.; illustrator Boys Harbor Cookbook, 1988, A Dream Became You, A City Grows Up, 1991, (covers) NY Daily News, Am. Artist Mag., 1994, Barbara Ernst Prey: Watercolors, 1998, Internat. Art Newspaper, 2001, NY Post, 2001, (PBS) True North, 2001, (PBS) Metro Section, 2001, Arts and Antiques Mag., 2001, 2003, Barbara Ernst Prey: A Trace in the Mind, 2002, NY Times, 2002, 2003, 2004, 2005, 2007, Artwork in the American Embassy Prague, 2002, Artwork in the American Embassy Oslo, 2003, The Robb Report, 2003, White House Christmas Card, 2003, LA Times, 2004, The New Yorker, 2004, Larry King Live CNN, 2004, (PBS) WLIW-NY, 2005, 2006, Style Sect., Washington Post, 2005, NPR, 2005, Wall St. Jour., 2006, NY Sun, 2006, WWD, 2007, USA Today Mag., 2007, displayed 1997 Holiday Card on 80,000 screens worldwide Bloomberg Bus. News, featured on Fox TV News, 1999; contbr. to popular mags., local newspapers. Class agt. Williams Coll., Williamstown, Mass., 1981—91; active 1st Presby. Ch., Oyster Bay, NY. Fulbright scholar, Germany, 1979-80; grantee Roothbert Fund, Chataugua, N.Y., 1982-84; recipient Ch. History award Gordan-Conwell Sem., S. Hamilton, Mass., 1984, Henry Luce Found., Taiwan, 1986-87, Jean Thoburn award, 1994, Women of Distinction award, N.Y. State Senate, 2004, Women of Distinction award, Distinction Mag., 2005. Mem. Pitts. Watercolor Soc. (Jean Thoburn award 1994), Nat. Mus. Women in the Arts. Avocations: tennis, skiing, birdwatching, reading, squash. Home and Office: 22 Pearl St Oyster Bay NY 11771-2305 E-mail: bprey@optonline.net.

PREY, YVONNE MARY, real estate broker; b. Milw., Mar. 14, 1945; d. Irvin Raymond Reindl and Viola Rose Schneider Maresh; m. John V. Prey, Sept. 2, 1967 (div. Dec. 1984); children: James Carter, Jacquelyn Rue. BS in Sociology, U. Wis., Oshkosh, 1967, postgrad., 1967-69. Lic. real estate broker, Wis.; cert. residential specialist, relocation profl. Social worker Winnebago State Hosp., Oshkosh, 1967-69, Div. Family Svcs., State of Wis., Fond du Lac, 1969-72, Green Bay, 1972-75; real estate broker Action Realty, Inc., Wausau, Wis., 1975-81, Williams Realty, Inc., Wausau, 1982-92, RE/MAX of Wausau, 1992—. Active Habitat for Humanity, Friends of Wausau Hist. Landmarks; sponsor Wis. River Valley Jour. Mem. NAFE, LWV, Wausau Area C. of C. (bd. dirs. Coun. Women Bus. Owners 1990—, Amb. 1975-89, edn. com.), Marathon County Hist. Soc., Wausau Bd. Realtors, Wis. Realtors Assn., Realtors Nat. Mktg. Inst. Roman Catholic. Avocations: reading, gardening, gourmet food preservation. Office: RE/MAX of Wausau 1314 Grand Ave Wausau WI 54403-6672

PREZELIN, BARBARA BERNTSEN, science association director, educator; b. Portland, Oreg., Apr. 13, 1948; d. Walter Stanley Berentsen and Doreen Yvonne Mugford; m. Louis Marie Prezelin, Jan. 22, 1972 (div. Aug. 15, 1994); 1 child, Christine Marie-Louise Sieburg. BS in Biology, U. Calif., Eugene, Oreg., 1970; PhD in Marine Biology, Scripps Inst. Oceanography, U. Calif., San Diego, 1975. NSF postdoc. rschr. U. Calif., Santa Barbara, 1975—77, prof., marine scis., 1977—, asst. to chancellor, 1996—2004; study ctr. dir., edn. abroad program U. Calif. Paris, 2008—, U. Calif. Bordeaux, 2008—. Contbr. articles to numerous sci. profl. pubs. Elected mem. Am. Soc. Limnology & Oceanography. 27 Fed. grant, NSF, 1978—2005. Democrat. Avocations: travel, languages, writing, swimming, dance. Office: Univ Calif Santa Barbara Biological Scis II Santa Barbara CA 93106 Business E-Mail: prezelin@lifesci.ucsb.edu.

PREZIOSO, GIOVANNI P., lawyer; b. Boston, 1957; AB in Hist. and Lit. magna cum laude, Harvard U., 1979, JD magna cum laude. Bar: DC 1982. Assoc. Cleary, Gottlieb, Steen & Hamilton, LLP, Washington, 1982—91, ptnr., 1991—2002, 2006—; gen. counsel, chief legal officer SEC, Washington, 2002—06. Mem.: ABA (chmn. fed. securities law subcommittee on mcpl. and govtl. obligations). Office: Cleary Gottlieb Steen & Hamilton LLP 2000 Pennsylvania Ave NW Washington DC 20006 E-mail: gprezioso@cgsh.com.

PRIBAZ, JULIAN JOSEPH, plastic surgeon, medical educator; b. Trieste, Italy, June 3, 1948; MD, U. Melbourne, Australia, 1972. Diplomate Am. Bd. Plastic Surgery, 1986, registered in Medicine Mass., 1987, cert. added qualification in hand surgery 1990. Intern in gen. surgery St. Vincent's Hosp., Melbourne, 1973, resident in gen. surgery, 1974—76; resident in plastic surgery Southern Ill. U., Spingfield, 1980—82; resident in surgery Geelong Hosp.; resident in gen. surgery Salisbury Gen. Infirmary; clinical instr. plastic surgery U. Melbourne, 1982—87; clinical instr. surgery Harvard Med. Sch., Boston, 1987—89, asst. prof. surgery, 1989—94, assoc. prof. surgery, 1994—2002, prof. surgery, 2002—; with Children's Hosp. Boston, Brigham and Women's Hosp., Boston, 1987—, dir. Harvard plastic surgery residency tng. program, 1999—. Reviewer editl. bd. Microsurgery, 1987—, Jour. Reconstructive Microsurgery, 1992—, Annals of Plastic Surgery, 1992—; vis. prof. Plastic Surgery Ednl. Found.; BK rank traveling prof. Royal Australian Coll. Surgeons, 2000. Recipient Faculty Tchg. award, Harvard/Brigham/Children's, 1994, 1996, Faculty award, Harvard Med. Sch. Mem.: Assn. Academic Chmn. Plastic Surgery, Plastic Surgery Rsch. Coun., New England Soc. Plastic and Reconstructive Surgeons, Mass. Soc. Plastic Surgery, Mass. Med. Soc., Boston Hand Soc., Am. Soc. Plastic and Reconstructive Surgery, Am. Soc. Reconstructive Microsurgery (chmn. sci. program com.), Am. Soc. Surgery of Hand, AMA, Am. Assn. Hand Surgery (mem. sci. program com.). Office: Brigham and Womens Hosp Divsn Plastic Surgery 75 Francis St Boston MA 02115 Office Phone: 617-732-6390. Office Fax: 617-732-6387. Business E-Mail: jjpribaz@bics.bwh.harvard.edu, jpribaz@partners.org.

PRIBRAM, KARL HARRY, neuroscience and psychology educator, brain researcher; b. Feb. 25, 1919; BS, U. Chgo., 1938, MD, 1941; PhD in Psychology (hon.), U. Montreal, Can., 1992; PhD in Philosophy (hon.), U. Bremen, 1996. Diplomate Am. Bd. Neurol. Surgery, Am. Bd. Med. Psychotherapists. Lectr. Yale U., New Haven, 1951-58; dir. psychology Inst. of Living, Hartford, Conn., 1958; fellow Ctr. Advanced Studies Behavioral Sci., Stanford U., Calif., 1958—59, prof. Dept. Psychology and Psychiatry, 1959—89, NIH lifetime rsch. career prof. Calif., 1962—89, prof. emeritus Calif., 1989—; eminent scholar Radford U., Va., 1989—2002, prof. emeritus Va., 2002—; disting. rsch. prof. dept. psychology Georgetown U., George Mason U., 2002—. Vis. scholar, hon. lectr. MIT, 1954, Clark U., 1956, Harvard, 1956, Haverford Coll., 1961, U. So. Calif., 1961, U. Leningrad, 1962, U. Moscow, 1962, U. Alta., Can., 1968, Ctr. for Study Dem. Insts., 1967-75, U. Coll., London, 1972, U. Chgo., 1973, Menninger Sch. Psychiatry, 1973-76, Ohio State U., 1975; vis. lectr. Grass Found., 1977; Phillips lectr., Haverford Coll., 1979; Lashley lectr., Queens Coll., 1979; Hubert Humphrey lectr. Macalester Coll., 1981; lectr. Internat. Mgmt. Inst., Geneva, Switzerland, 1987, Inst. Med. Psychology, Naples, 1988; disting. lectr. Second Annual Symposium of the Mind, Arlington, Tex., 1988; hon. lectr. Sirius Seminaries, Paris, 1988, Bielfeld, Germany, 1990-1991, numerous others. Author: Brain and Behavior, vol. 1-4, 1969, What Makes Man Human, 1971, Languages of the Brain: Experimental Paradoxes and Principles in Neuropsychology, 1971; The Neurosciences: Third Study Program, 1971, Brain and Perception: Holonomy and Structure in Figural Processing, 1991, Rethinging Neural Networks: Quantum Fields and Biological Data, 1993, Origins: Brain and Self Organization, 1994, Scale in Conscious Experience: Is the Brain Too Important to be Left to Specialists to Study?, 1995, Freud's Project Reassessed, 1976; editor, mem. consulting bd. Neuropsychologia, Jour. Math. Biology, Internat. Jour. Neurosci., Behavioral and Brain Scis., Jour. Mental Imagery, Jour. Human Movement Studies, Jour. Social and Biol. Structures, ReVision, STSM Quar., Indian Jour. Psychophysiology, Internat. Jour. Psychophysiology, Cognition and Brain Theory; contbr. over 400 articles to profl. jours. Recipient Lifetime Rsch. Career award in neurosci. NIH, 1962-89, Humanitarian award INTA, 1980, Realia honor Inst. Advanced Philosophic Rsch., 1986, 93, Outstanding Contbns. award Am. Bd. Med. Psychotherapists, Neural Network Leadership award Internat. Neural Network, 1996, Dagmar and Vaclev Havel prize, 1989. Fellow Am. Acad. Arts and Scis., NY Acad. Scis. (hon. life); mem. AAUP, AMA, AAAS, APA (pres. div. physiol. and comparative psychology 1967-68, pres. div. theoretical and philos. psychology 1979-80), Internat. Neuropsychol. Soc. (founding pres. 1967-69), Internat. Assn. Study of Pain, Soc. Exptl. Psychologists (Anderson Lifetime Achievement award 2005), Am. Psychol. Soc., Am. Psychopathological Assn. (Paul Hoch award 1975), Am. Acad. Psychoanalysis, Soc. Biol. psychiatry (Manfred Sakel award 1976), Soc. Clin. and Exptl. Hypnosis (Henry Guze award 1991), Soc. Neurosci., Sigma Xi. Home: PO Box 679 Warrenton VA 20188-0679 Home Phone: 540-428-8788; Office Phone: 202-333-3763. Business E-Mail: pribramk@georgetown.edu.

PRIBYL, RICK R., English language educator; b. Omaha, Nebr., Jan. 5, 1948; s. Cecil and Mary Ann Pribyl; m. Linda Pribyl; children: Skip, Scott, Sean, Sean, Shea, David, Jamie, Patrick. BA in English, St. Louis U., Mo., 1970; degree in aeronautics, Regents U., N.Y.C., 1972; MEd, S.D. State U., Brookings, 1974; writing courses, U. Mo., Kansas City, 1988—98; PhD, Walden U., 1998. Nat. cert. bd. tchr. secondary adolescence lang. arts. Nat. presenter, cons. Success Motivation Inst., 1977—79; mgr. Edwards Co., Kansas City, 1979—85; career counselor, writing instr. Career Dynamics, Overland Park, Kans., 1985—87; tchr. English advanced placement, varsity boys and girls soccer coach Blue Valley North H.S., Overland Park, 1987—93, tchr. English advanced placement, chair English dept., varsity boys and girls soccer coach, 1993—. Tchr. summer Nat. Writing Project grad. courses U. Mo., Kansas City, 1988—2005; mem. adv. bd. Kans. State U. Sch. Edn.; rep. for Kans. U.S. Merchant Marine Acad.; tchg. excellence mentor Avila U. Contbr. articles to profl. jours. and newspapers; author: (coll. textbook) Alternatives of Assessing Student Writing, 1998. Adult leader Mic-O-Say, Order of the Arros Boy Scouts of Am. With USAF, 1970—77. Recipient Outstanding Educator Recognition award, U. Kans., 1989, 1991, 1994, 1996, 1999, 2001, 2003, 2004, Blue Valley Sch. Dist. Excellence in Edn. award, 1992, Judith C. Gilbert Nat. Writing Tchr. of Yr. award, 1998; named Kans. H.S. Coach of Yr., 1989, 1992, 1996, Blue Valley N.W. H.S. Tchr. of Yr., 1995, 2006, Tchr. of Yr., Teenink, 2000; named one of Nat. Honor Roll's Outstanding Am. Tchrs., 2004, 2005, 2006. Mem.: NEA, Nat. Fedn. Interscholastic Coaches Assn., Nat. Pks. and Conservation Assn., USAF Assn., Nat. Soccer Coaches Assn. Am., Kans. Assn. English Tchrs., Nat. Coun. for Accreditation of Tchr. Edn., Nat. Writing Project, Nat. Coun. English Tchrs., Eta Sigma Phi, Phi Delta Kappa. Office: Blue Valley NW H S 13260 Switzer Rd Overland Park KS 66213-3306 Office Phone: 913-239-3400.

PRICE, ALAN THOMAS, business and estate planner; b. Balt., Nov. 11, 1949; s. Alvah Thompson and Doris Elaine (Cole) P.; m. Page Angela Jennings, Sept. 1978 (div. 1980); m. Lauren Ann St. Clare, Aug. 12, 1983 (div. 1992); m. Melissa Renee Ballistreri, Nov. 1997. BS, U. N.C., 1972. CLU; chartered fin. cons.; cert. estate and bus. analyst, fin. planner; registered fin. planner. Mgmt. trainee Sears, Atlanta, 1972-73; ins. agt. Aetna Life & Casualty, Atlanta, 1973-76, Pilot Life/New Eng. Life, Virginia Beach, Va., 1976-81; owner, pres. Page II Prodns., Inc., Norfolk, Va., 1981—. Founding prin. 1s Fin. Resources, 1989; veteran judge Miss U.S.A. Pageant System. Fin. columnist News-Herald, 1985-86. Active Mus. Marine Scis., Virginia Beach, 1986—, Hope Found., Windsor, N.C., 1987—, Va. Stage Co., Va. Pops Orch. Named Man of Yr., Pilot Life, Tidewater, Va., 1978, 79, 80. Fellow Life Underwriter Tng. Coun.; mem. Million Dollar Roundtable (life and qualifying), Internat. Assn. Registered Fin. Planners, Am. Coun. Ind. Life Underwriters, Am. Soc. CLU's, Internat. Assn. Fin. Planning (dir. 1987-88), Inst. Cert. Fin. Planners, Nat. Assn. Life Underwriters, Sales and Mktg. Execs., Ct. of the Table, Tidewater Estate Planning Coun., Tidewater Builders Assn., Cen. Bus. Dist. Assn., Hampton Roads C. of C. Methodist. Avocations: painting, fishing, reading, interior decorating, sports. Home: 2645 River Rd Virginia Beach VA 23454-1224 Office: First Fin Resources Page II Prodns 2645 River Rd Virginia Beach VA 23454-1224 Office Phone: 757-481-3443. E-mail: first.financial.reserves@verizon.net.

PRICE, ALFRED LEE, lawyer, mining executive; b. Little Rock, May 19, 1935; s. Dewey Ernest and Dorothy Ava (Cooper) P.; m. Magdalena Torres, June 20, 1958; children: Gregory L., Ana Maria. BA, Hendrix Coll., 1956; JD, Tulane U., 1967. Bar: La. 1967, Miss. 1974, D.C., U.S. Supreme Ct., 1980, U.S. Tax Ct., 1977, cert. arbitrator, mediator, Am. Arbitration Assn. and Better Bus. Bur., Nat. Arbitration Forum. Office mgr., dir. personnel Petroleum Helicopters Co., Lafayette, La. and New Orleans, 1956-67; atty. Offshore Navigation and Petroleum Helicopters Co., New Orleans, 1967-74; gen. counsel First Miss. Corp., Jackson, 1974-93, corp. sec., 1988-93; commr. Miss. Employment Commn., Jackson, 1994—2002. Arbitrator Am. Arbitration Assn., 1998—. Mem. Jackson C.of C., chmn. legislative com., 1991-94. Recipient Arbitrator of Yr., Better Bus. Bureau, 1998. Mem. ABA, La. Bar Assn., Miss. Bar Assn., Hinds County Bar Assn., Miss. Mfrs. Assn. (bd. dirs.), Miss. Econ. Coun. (chmn. tort reform com.), River Hills Club. Methodist.

PRICE, AMELIA RUTH, not-for-profit foundation president, artist, small business owner; b. Bklyn., Sept. 4, 1942; d. Dr. Alphonse Frederick Pagano and Adele Marie Savarese; 1 child, Ean James. BA, Georgian Ct. Coll., Lakewood, NJ, 1964; MA in Art Hist., Cath. U. of Am., Washington, DC, 1968. Cert. Permanent Certificate, Art State of NY Edn. Dept., 1971. Art tchr. Bd. Coop. Ednl. Svcs., Patchogue, NY, 1967—68; art director Roland Advt. Co., NYC, 1968—69; art dept. chair Bd. Coop. Ednl. Svcs. II, Deer Park, NY, 1969—78; v.p. Delicious Selections Ltd, White Plains, NY, 1991—95; pres., owner Parker Commodities Ltd, Kings Park, NY, 1995—; owner Bubbling Oaks Samoyeds, Commack, NY, 1974—. Co-founder bubbling oaks samoyeds kennels Bubbling Oaks Samoyeds, Commack, NY, 1974—2002. Samoyed Newsletter and other publs.featuring Samoyeds, 1999—; contbr. articles on Samoyeds and their care to various publs., 1999. Pres. Samoyed Club of Am. Edn. and Rsch. Found., Inc., Madison, Wis., 2001—, v.p., 1997—2001. Recipient #1 Samoyed Bitch, Kennel Rev., 1974, 1975, 1976, 1977, 1978, 1983, 1984, #3 Samoyed, Dogs in Canada, 1976, Top Winning Team, Orgn. for the Working Samoyed Inc., 1986, 1988. Mem.: Habour Lights Painter, Decorative Artists LI, Soc. Decorative Painters, Nat. Assn. Woman Bus. Owners (pub. affairs com. 2003—), Primitive and Aboriginal Dog Soc., Russia Primitive and Aboriginal Dog Soc., Suffolk County Kennel Club Inc. (chmn. hospitality 1989—99, bd. dirs. 1996—99), Westbury Kennel Assn. (chmn. of trophies 1985, chmn. judges' transport. 2000), Samoyed Club of America Inc. (pres. 1997—99, Top Winning Bitch 1975, 1976, 1985, Top Winning Team 1985, Top Winning Bitch 1986, Top Winning Team 1987). Home: 128 Cowie Rd Commack NY 11725

PRICE, ARDYTHE BERNADEANE, registered nurse; b. Two Hills, Alta., Can., Sept. 27, 1948; d. Peter Cecil and Doris Eunice Tym; children: Shelley, Steven. AS, Pacific Union Coll., 1972; BA in English, Loma Linda U., 1973. RN Calif., 1972. RN Agnews State Hosp., Santa Clara, Calif., 1975—80, Kaiser, San Jose, Calif., 1980—90, Fremont Rideout, 1991—92, Sierra Nursing Registry, various cities, Calif., 1992—2002, Res-Care/Sierra Nurses, Yuba City, Calif., 1995—2002. Rep. Calif. Nursing Assn., San Jose, Calif., 1974; various coms. and bds. Agnews State Hosp., San Jose, Calif., 1979—80; pvt. nurse, Yuba City, Calif. Vol. Salvation Army, Marysville, Calif., 1996; sec. Yuba Sutter Dem. Club, Yuba City, 2001—; bd. dirs. comms. Samaritan Village, Yuba City, Calif., 1996—. Mem.: Sutter County Dem. Women's Club, Women of the Moose (chmn. ednl. advancement 2004—05, mem., Sutter-Yuba Mental Health Bd. 2007—). Democrat. Seventh Day Adventist. Avocations: reading, movies. Home: 1445 Stabler Ln # 4 Yuba City CA 95993 Home Phone: 530-671-4965. Personal E-mail: ardytheprice@aol.com.

PRICE, BETTY JEANNE, chimes musician; b. Long Beach, Calif., June 12, 1942; d. Grant E. and Miriam A. (Francis) Sickles; m. Harvey H. Price, Aug. 6, 1975; children: Thomas Neil Gering, Timothy Ray(dec.), Pamela Kay(dec.). Degree in Acctg., Northland Pioneer Coll., Show Low, Ariz., 1977. Youth missionary Open Bible Standard Missions, Trinidad, 1958-59; typographer Joel H. Weldon & Assocs., Scottsdale, Ariz., 1980-89; exec. chief acct. Pubs. Devel. Corp., San Diego, 1991-93; coord. music and worship College Ave. Bapt. Ch., San Diego, 1994-95; ChoirChime soloist, 1986—; exec. acct. Advance Reprographics, San Diego, 1996—2003. Chime musician and writer. Author: 101 Ways to Fix Broccoli, 1994, ABC's of Abundant Living, 1995; contbg. author God's Vitamin C for the Spirit, 1995, BounceBook, 1997, You Can Bounce Back Too, 1998, Pathway of Love, One Man's Remarkable Journey, 2002, Breaking Free from Financial Bondage: A Guide to Living Debt Free, 2004; musical arranger: handbell/chime Classical Sounds, 2005, A Musical Tour Around the World, 2005, Music for Special Occasions, 2005, Sounds of Christmas, 2005, A Musical Christmas Story, 2005, Hymns of Faith, 2005; musician: (CD) Classical Chimes, 2005, Chimes of Faith, 2005, Christmas Chimes, 2005. Mem.: ASCAP, Am. Guild English Handbell Ringers. Business E-Mail: chimesoloist@aol.com.

PRICE, CAREY, professional hockey player; b. Vancouver, BC, Can., Aug. 16, 1987; Goaltender Hamilton Bulldogs (Am. Hockey League), 2007, Montreal Canadiens, 2007—. Recipient Jack Butterfield Trophy (playoff MVP), Am. Hockey League, 2007, NHL All-Star Game, 2009; named to All-Rookie Team, NHL, 2008. Office: Montreal Canadiens 1275 St Antoine St W Montreal PQ Canada H3C 5L2*

PRICE, CAROL LEAH, mathematics educator; BS in Secondary Math. Edn., La. State Univ.; MS, Univ. So. Miss., PhD In Ednl. Leadership. Tchr., 1986—; elem. sch. tchr. E. Baton Rouge Parish; math. tchr. Zachary (La.) H.S. Recipient Presdl. Award for Excellence in Mathematics Tchg., 1998; named La. Tchr. of Yr., 2007. Office: Zachary High Sch, 4100 Bronco Lane Zachary LA 70791 Business E-Mail: carol.price@zacharyschools.org.

PRICE, CHARLES H., II, former ambassador; b. Kansas City, Mo., Apr. 1, 1931; s. Charles Harry and Virginia (Ogden) P.; m. Carol Ann Swanson, Jan. 10, 1969; children: Caroline Lee, Melissa Marie, Charles H., C. B., Pickette. Student, U. Mo., 1951-53; LLD (hon.), Westminster Coll., 1984, U. Mo., 1988; LHD (hon.), Baker U., 1991; DSc (hon.), U. Buckingham, Eng., 1993. Chmn. bd., dir. Price Candy Co., Kansas City, 1969-81, Am. Bancorp., Kansas City, 1973-81; chmn., chief exec. officer Am. Bank & Trust Co., Kansas City, 1973-81; Am. ambassador to Belgium Brussels, 1981-83; Am. ambassador to U.K. London, 1983-89. Chmn. bd. Americanc, Inc., St. Joseph, Mo., 1989—92, pres., CEO, 1990—92; chmn. bd. Merc. Bank Kansas City, Mo., 1992—96; bd. dirs. Palmer Capital Assocs., Ltd., London. Trustee Midwest Rsch. Inst., Kansas City, chmn., 1990-93. Hon. fellow Regent's Coll., London, 1986; recipient William Booth award Salvation Army, 1985, World Citizen of Yr. award Mayor of Kansas City, 1985, Trustee Citation award Midwest Rsch. Inst., 1987, Disting. Svc. award Internat. Rels. Coun., 1989, Mankind award Cystic Fibrosis Found., 1990, Gold Good Citizenship award SAR, 1991, Chancellor's medal U. Mo. Kansas City, 1992, William F. Yates medallion William Jewell Coll., 1996. Mem.: The Vintage Country Club, White's Club, Swinley Forest Club, Kansas City Country Club, Eldorado Country Club, Brook Club, Cypress Point Club, Los Angeles Country Club, River Club, Sigma Alpha Epsilon. Republican. Episcopalian. Office: 1 W Armour Blvd Ste 300 Kansas City MO 64111-2087 Office Phone: 816-360-6175.

PRICE, CHARLES STEVEN, lawyer; b. Inglewood, Calif., June 10, 1955; s. Frank Dean Price and Ann (Rounds) Bolling; m. Sandra Helen Laney, Feb. 26, 1983; children: Katherine Laney, Courtney Ann, Diana Emily. BA, U. Calif., Santa Barbara, 1976; JD, U. Chgo., 1979. Bar: Ariz. 1980, U.S. Dist. Ariz. 1980, U.S. Ct. Appeals (9th cir.) 1982. Assoc. Brown & Bain P.A., Phoenix, 1979-85, ptnr., 1985-96, Allen & Price P.L.C., Phoenix, 1996-2000, Allen, Price, Padden & Sanders, PC, Phoenix, 2000—04, Mariscal Weeks McIntyre & Friedlander, Phoenix,

2005—. Office: Mariscal Weeks McIntyre & Friedlander 2901 N Central Ave Ste 200 Phoenix AZ 85012 Office Phone: 602-285-5042. Business E-Mail: Charles.price@mwmf.com.

PRICE, CHARLES T., lawyer; b. Lansing, Mich., Feb. 11, 1944; BA, Ohio Wesleyan U., 1966; JD, Harvard U., 1969. Bar: Ohio 1969, U.S. Dist. Ct. (no. dist.) Ohio 1974, U.S. Ct. Appeals (6th cir) 1981, U.S. Supreme Ct. 1982, Ill. 1989. Former ptnr. Baker & Hostetler, Cleve.; pres., pub. Chgo. Sun-Times, 1987-88; exec. v.p. Sun-Times Co., 1989-92; ptnr. Foley & Lardner, Chgo., 2000—04, Bell, Boyd & Lloyd LLC, Chgo., 2004—. Mem. bd. govs. Sch. of Art Inst. of Chgo., former chmn.; mem. bd. trustees LaRabida Children;s Hosp. Mem.: Econ. Club, Phi Beta Kappa. Office: Bell Boyd & Lloyd 70 W Madison St Chicago IL 60602 Home Phone: 847-256-3640; Office Phone: 312-807-4431. E-mail: cprice@bellboyd.com.

PRICE, CHARLES TURNER, surgeon; b. Atlanta, Jan. 2, 1946; s. Dave and Fran Price; m. Pamela O. Price, June 24, 1967; children: Travis, Janet. BA, Emory U., 1967; MD, Baylor U., 1971. Diplomate Am. Bd. Ortho Surgery. Intern U. Fla., 1971—72, resident, 1972—76; fellow Scottish Rite Hosp. for Crippled Children, 1976—77; physician Jewett Ortho Clinic, Orlando, Fla., 1977—80, Matthews Ortho Clinic, Orlando, 1980—92; assoc. dir. med. edn. ortho Orlando Regional Healthcare Sys., 1993—96; surgeon in chief Nemours Children's Clinic, Orlando, 1997—. Cons. EBI, Inc., Parsippany, NJ, 1984—; Wilson vis. prof. Children's Hosp., UCLA, 2001; vis. prof. U. Hong Kong, 2001; disting. prof. Washington U., St. Louis, 2000; Leon Kruger guest lectr. Shriners Hosp., Springfield, Mass., 2001. Author: (book) Child With a Limb Deficiency, 1998, Lovell and Winters Ped Ortho, 5th edit., 2000, Essence of Pediatrics, 2000; editor: Instructional Course Lectures, 2000. Chmn. Scoliosis Rsch. Soc., Rosemont, Ill., 1999—2000. Mem.: AMA, Fla. Ortho Soc., So. Ortho Assn. (program chair 1994), Am. Acad. Ortho Surgeons (mem. instrnl. course com. 1998—2000), Pediat. Ortho Soc. N.Am. (sec. 1998—2001, 2d v.p. 2001—), Am. Orthopaedic Assn. Avocation: golf. Office: ORHS Med Ed Peds Ortho 89 W Copeland Dr Orlando FL 32806

PRICE, CLEMENT ALEXANDER, historian, educator; BA, MA, U. Bridgeport; PhD, Rutgers U.; PhD (hon.), William Paterson U. Co-founder Marion Thompson Wright Series, 1981; bd. govs. disting. svc. prof., prof. history Rutgers U., Newark, dir. Inst. on Ethnicity, Culture, and the Modern Experience, 1996—. Sr. trustee Newark Pub. Libr.; trustee Urban Librs. Coun.; mem. scholars adv. com. African Am. Mus. on the Mall, Smithsonian Inst. Editor: Freedom Not Far Distant: A Documentary History of Afro-Americans in New Jersey, 1980; author: Many Voices, Many Opportunities: Cultural Pluralism & American Arts Policy, 1994; co-author: Freedom Not Far Distant: A Documentary History of Afro-Americans in New Jersey, 2003, Encyclopedia of the Harlem Renaissance, 2003; contbr. articles to profl. jours. Co-recipient President's Award, Newark Pub. Libr., 2005; named Prof. of Yr. for NJ, Coun. for Advancement and Support of Edn., 1999. Fellow: NJ Hist. Soc.; mem.: Woodrow Wilson Nat. Fellowship Found. (Inaugural Scholar in Residence), NJ Hist. Commn. (Richard J. Hughes award), NJ Coun. on Arts (past chmn.), Urban League of Essex County, Save Ellis Island Found., Geraldine R. Dodge Found. Office: Inst on Ethnicity, Culture, and Modern Experience 175 University Ave Conklin Hall Rm 337 Newark NJ 07102 Office Phone: 973-353-5414. Office Fax: 973-353-5218. E-mail: caprice@andromeda.rutgers.edu.

PRICE, DANIEL MARTIN, federal official, lawyer; b. St. Louis, Aug. 23, 1955; s. Albert and Edith S. (Werner) Price; m. Kim Ellen Heebner, July 15, 1984; children: Emma Rachel, Joseph Armin, Joshua Simon. BA, Haverford Coll., Pa., 1977; diploma in law, Cambridge U., 1979; JD, Harvard U., 1981. Bar: DC 1981, Pa. 1986, US Supreme Ct. 1999. Assoc. Drinker, Biddle & Reath, Phila., 1981-82, 86-89; atty., adv. US Dept. State, Washington, 1982—84; dep. agt. US Iran-US Tribunal, Hague, Netherlands, 1984—86; dep. gen. counsel Office US Trade Rep., Washington, 1989-92; ptnr. Powell, Goldstein, Frazer & Murphy, Washington, 1992—2002; ptnr., mem. exec. com., chair Internat. Trade & Dispute Resolution practice Sidley Austin Brown & Wood LLP, Washington, 2002—07; asst. to pres. & dep. nat. security advisor Internat. Econ. Affairs, The White House, 2007—09; sr. ptnr. Global Issues, Trade & Dispute Resolution Practice Sidley Austin Brown & Wood LLP, Washington, 2009—. Lectr. Haverford Coll., 1982; legal adv. bd. mem. Internat. Bus. Forum, 1987—89; mem. adv. bd. Can.-US Law Inst., British Inst. Internat. & Comparative Law, Georgetown U. Law Ctr., Inst. Internat. Econ. Law; apptd. panel arbitrators Internat. Ctr. Settlement of Investment Disputes, 2002—07, 2009—. Editor: Harvard Law Rev., 1980—81; contbr. articles to profl. jours. Mem. Bush-Cheney Transition Team, 1999—2000. Named an Am. Keasbey scholar, Cambridge U., 1977—78. Mem.: ABA, Coun. Fgn. Rels., Internat. C. of C., Am. Arbitration Assn., Phi Beta Kappa. Republican. Office Phone: 202-736-8226. Business E-Mail: dprice@sidley.com.

PRICE, DAVID CECIL LONG, physicist, researcher; b. London, Jan. 17, 1940; came to U.S., 1966; s. Cecil Long and Freda (Salusbury) P.; m. Marie-Louise Sabougni, Nov. 24, 1989; children: Morgan, Alkes. BA, Cambridge U., 1961, MA, 1962, PhD, 1966. Rsch. assoc. Brookhaven Nat. Lab., Upton, NY, 1966-68; mem. staff Argonne (Ill.) Nat. Lab., 1968—2001, dir. solid state sci. divsn., 1974-79, dir. intense pulsed neutron source program, 1979-81, sr. physicist, 1981—2001; exec. dir. high-flux isotope reactor Oak Ridge (Tenn.) Nat. Lab., 2004—05; dir. rsch. CRMHT, Orleans, France, 2001—04, 2005—. Vis. prof. Japanese Soc. Promotion Sci., 1977; disting. vis. prof.Grad. U. for Adv. Studies, Hayama, Japan, 2000; mem. panel research opportunities with low energy neutrons Nat. Acad. Scis., 1976-77; sr. sci. advisor physics panel Energy Research Adv. Bd., Dept. Energy, 1986-87. Editor: Neutron Scattering (Methods of Experimental Physics, vols. 23 A, B, C), 1986-87. Recipient U. Chgo. award for disting. performance at Argonne Nat. Lab., 1988, Warren prize Am. Cryst. Assn., 1997, Alexander von Humboldt Rsch. award, 1998. Fellow Am. Phys. Soc., Inst. Physics (U.K.). Office: CRMHT 45071 Orleans France Home Phone: 773-752-8283; Office Phone: 33-238-255531. E-mail: price@cnrs-orleans.fr.

PRICE, DAVID EUGENE, United States Representative from North Carolina, education educator; b. Johnson City, Tenn., Aug. 17, 1940; s. Albert Lee and Elna (Harrell) Price; m. Lisa Beth Kanwit, July 27, 1968; children: Karen Elizabeth, Michael Edmond. Student, Mars Hill Coll., NC, 1957—59; BA in Am. Hist. and Math., U. NC, 1961; BD in Theology, Yale U., 1964, PhD in Polit. Sci., 1969. Legis. aide Staff of US Senator Edward Lewis Bartlett of Alaska, 1963-67; prof. polit. sci. and pub. policy Duke U., Durham, NC, 1973-86; mem. US Congress from 4th NC dist., 1987—95, 1997—, mem. appropriations com., chmn. homeland security subcommittee, mem. democracy assistance commn., co-chair Dem. budget grp. Exec. dir. NC Dem. Party, Raleigh, 1979-80, chmn., 1983-84, mem. 1983—; staff dir. nat. com. on presdl. nomination Dem. Party, 1981-82 Author: Who Makes the Laws, 1972, Bringing Back the Parties, 1984, Policymaking in Congl. Coms., 1979, The Congressional Experience: A View From the Hill, 2000. Recipient Engrng. Deans Coun. award, Am. Soc. Engrng. Edn., 2003, Charles Dick Medal of Merit, NC Nat Guard, Hubert H. Humphrey Pub. Svc. award, Am. Polit. Sci. Assn.; named a Champion of Sci., Sci. Coalition, 2002, 2004. Mem. Am. Polit. Sci. Assn., Soc. Values in Higher Edn., Phi Beta Kappa, Kiwanis. Democrat. Baptist. Avocations: jogging, music. Office: US House Reps 2162 Rayburn House Office Bldg Washington DC 20515-3304 Office Phone: 202-225-1784. Office Fax: 202-225-2014.*

PRICE, DAVID W., physician, educator, reseachrer; MD, Rutgers U., 1985. Diplomate Am. Bd. Family Medicine. Dir. edn., clinician rschr. Colo. Permanente Med. Group, Denver, 1998—; prof. family medicine U Colo. Health Sciences Ctr., Denver, 1999; clin. lead, profl. edn. and depression Kaiser Permanente Care Mgmt. Inst., Oakland, 2001—; chair Am. Bd. Family Medicine, Lexington, 2007—08. Named Tchr. of Yr., Colo. Acad. Family Physicians, 1991, Superhero Colo. Family Medicine, 1998. Fellow: Am. Acad. Family Physicians. Achievements include design of multiple physician and health professional training curricula. Avocation: running. Office: Colorado Permanente Medical Group 10065 East Harvard Ave Denver CO 80231

PRICE, DAVID WILLIAM, physician, educator, researcher; MD, U. Medicine and Denistry NJ, Piscataway, 1985. Diplomate Am. Bd. of Family Medicine, 1988, Fellow Am. Acad. of Family Physicians, 1992. Dir. med. edn. Kaiser Permanente, Denver, 1997—, clin. lead, edn. and depression Care Mgmt. Inst. Oakland, Calif., 2001—; prof. family medicine Denver Health Scis. Ctr. U. Colo., 2007—. Bd. chair Am. Bd. Family Medicine, Lexington, Ky., 2007—08. Recipient Colo. Family Medicine Tchr. of the Yr., Colo. Acad. Family Physicians, 1991; co-recipient Superhero of Family Medicine, 1998. Fellow: Am. Acad. Family Physicians (life). Office: Kaiser Permanente Colo 10065 E Harvard Ave Denver CO 80231 Business E-Mail: david.price@ucdenver.edu.

PRICE, DEBORAH A., federal agency administrator; b. St. Louis; BA, U. Mo. Dir. Nat. Prayer Breakfast, 1984—85; scheduler for Sen. William L. Armstrong US Congress, dir. rsch. and adminstrn., Senate Rep. Com., policy adv. to Sen. Don Nickles; exec. dir., Sec. Commn. on Opportunity in Athletics US Dept. Edn., sr. adv. to dep. sec., chief of staff, Office of Fed. Student Aid, asst. dep. sec., Office of Safe and Drug-Free Schs., 2004—09. Republican. Office: Office Safe and Drug-Free Schools US Dept Edn 400 Maryland Ave SW Rm 1E110 Washington DC 20202 Office Phone: 202-205-4169. E-mail: deborah.price@ed.gov.*

PRICE, DENNIS LEE, industrial engineer, educator; b. Taber, Alberta, Can., Oct. 24, 1930; s. Walter and Wilma Harlan (Nance) P.; m. Barbara Ann Shelton; children: Denice Lynn Price Tsugawa, Philip Walter. BA, Bob Jones U., 1952; BD, MA, Am. Bapt. Sem. of the West, Berkeley, Calif., 1955; MA, Calif. State U., Long Beach, 1967; PhD in Indsl. Engring., Tex. A&M U., 1974. Cert. product safety mgr., hazard control mgr., human factors profl. Clergyman Am. Bapt. Conv., Calif., 1953-66; tech. staff autonetics divsn. Rockwell Internat., Anaheim, Calif., 1966-69; sr. engr. Martin Marietta Aerospace, Orlando, Fla., 1969-72; rsch. assoc. Tex. A&M U., College Station, 1972-74; tchg. asst. Calif. State U., Long Beach, 1963-66; asst. prof. dept. indsl. engring. and ops. rsch. Va. Poly. Inst. and State U., Blacksburg, 1974-78, assoc. prof. dept. indsl. and systems engring., 1979—83, prof., 1984-95, prof. emeritus, 1996—, dir. safety projects office, 1975-95, coord. Human Factors Engring. Ctr., 1986-95. Expert witness in safety engring. and human factors, 1978—; mem. U.S. Nuclear Waste Tech. Rev. Bd., 1989-95; U.S. tech. adv. group Internat. Stds. Tech. Com. 159 Ergonomics, 1987-94; chmn. com. on transp. of hazardous materials NRC, 1981-87; chmn. group 3 coun. emerging issues subcom. Transp. Rsch. Bd., 1987-89; chmn. task force on pipeline safety NAS, 1986 Mem. editorial bd. Human Factors, Santa Monica, Calif., 1989-95; author: (with K.B. Johns, J.W. Bain) Transportation of Hazardous Materials, 1983, (with W. Hammer) Occupational Safety Management and Engineering, 2000; author: Why Christ is the Only Way, 2003, Death, That's Life, 2005,(novel) Chasing the Fourth House, 2009; contbr. chpts. to books, articles to profl. jours.; reviewer in field. Recipient Disting. Svc. award Nat. Rsch. Coun. NAS, 1987, 89, Outstanding Svc. commendation Transp. Rsch. Bd. NAS, 1981, Jack A. Kraft Innovator award Human Factors and Ergonomics Soc., 1996, Best Book award San Diego Christian Writers Guild, 2004; grantee NIOSH, Va. Dept. Transp. and Safety, 1977-82, 86-87, IBM, 1981-84, USN Office of Naval Rsch., 1978-80, USN Naval Systems Weapons Command, 1978-79. Mem. Inst. Indsl. Engrs. (sr.), Am. Soc. Safety Engrs. (profl.), Human Factors Soc. (rep. to rev. panel Guideline for the Preparation of Material Safety Data Sheets), System Safety Soc. (Educator of Yr. 1993), Alpha Pi Mu. Avocation: flying. Home: 15204 Moonglow Dr Ramona CA 92065-4529 Office: Va Poly Inst and State Univ Dept Indsl and Sys Engring Blacksburg VA 24061

PRICE, DOUGLAS ARMSTRONG, chiropractor; b. Pitts., Feb. 17, 1950; s. Walter Coachman and Janet (Armstrong) P.; m. Ann Georgette Martino, Jan. 31, 1989; 4 children. BA, Brown U., 1972; D Chiropractic, Life Chiropractic Coll., Atlanta, 1983. Diplomate Am. Bd. Chiropractic Examiners; cert. rehab. doctor; life extension physician; ind. med. examiner, Fla. Owner, CEO Applied Biomech. and Musculoskeletal Rehab., Tampa, 1989—, All Am. Chiropractic Clinic; pvt. practice Tampa, 1984—, Manalapan, Fla., 1994-96; clin. dir. Camber Clinics, South Tampa, Haines City, Fla., 1999—2001, Fla. Pain, Trauma, and Injury Clinics, Tampa, 2001—. Dir. Myofascial Therapy Found. Author: Protocols for Practioners Utilizing Myofascial Trigger Point Treatment, 1998; prodr. therapeutic exercise video for cervical and lumbar rehab.; contbr. articles to profl. jours. Magnetic Resonance Imaging fellow; named to Brown U. Athletic Hall of Fame; Southeastern Masters Champion Shotput, Discus, 1990-91. Fellow: Am. Gerontology Assn., Chiropractic Rehab. Assn., Am. Coll. Sports Medicine; mem.: APHA, Hillsborough County Chiropractic Soc. (bd. dirs. 1990—93, pres. 1992—93), Fla. Chiropractic Assn., Am. Chiropractic Assn., KC (trustee). Democrat. Roman Catholic. Achievements include research in Russian stimulation applications in low back rehabilitation; application of micro and interferential currents with utilization of manual travel myofascial release techniques, use of micro and interferential currents with manual treatment of myofascial pain syndromes. Home: 90 W Davis Blvd Tampa FL 33606-3535 Office Phone: 813-849-2459. Personal E-mail: douglasmyodoc@aol.com.

PRICE, EDGAR HILLEARY, JR., manufacturing executive, consultant; b. Jacksonville, Fla., Jan. 1, 1918; s. Edgar Hilleary and Mary Williams (Phillips) P.; m. Elise Ingram, May 24, 1947; 1 son, Jerald Steven. Student, U. Fla., 1937-38. Mgr. comml. flower farm, 1945-49, Fla. Gladiolus Growers Assn., 1949-55; exec. v.p. Tropicana Products, Inc., Bradenton, Fla., 1955-73, dir. div. govt. and industry regulations, to 1979; dir.; exec. v.p. Indsl. Glass Co., Inc., Bradenton, 1963-73; pres., chmn. bd. Price Co., Inc., Bradenton, cons., 1973—2001. Dir. emeritus F.P.L. Group, Inc.; past chmn. Fla. Citrus Commn., Fla. Gov.'s Freeze Damage Survey Team, Spl. Commn. for Study Abolition Death Penalty; bd. dirs. Fla. Power and Light Co., Fla. Fair Assn., Fla. Citrus Expn., Fla. Fruit and Vegetable Assn., G.T.E. Fla., Fla. Cyprus Gardens, Ellis Bank Co.; past chmn. Joint Citrus Legis. Com.; past mem. Fla. Plant Bd., Fla. Bd. Control, Fla. Legis. Coun.; exec. com. Growers and Shippers League Fla., Fla. Agrl. Council, Spl. Health Agrl. Research and Edn.; past pres., chmn. bd. Fla. Hort. Soc; past dir. Bank of Palmetto, CrossLand Savings FSLA, First City Federal Savings and Loan Assn., First Federal Savings and Loan Assn. Bradenton; non paid agrl. & bus. advisor to farmer governor Reubin O'D. Askew. Past chmn., commr. census 12th Jud. Circuit; mem. Gov. Fla. Com. Rehab. Handicapped, Fla. Commn. on Ethics, 1976-77, Pres. Carter Inaugural Fin. com., 1977, Ea. 5th Circuit U.S. Jud. Nominating Commn., 1977—, Fla. Senate from 36th Dist., 1958-66; past chmn. Manatee County Bd. Sch. Dist. Trustees, Local Housing Authority Bradenton, Bradenton Sub. Std. Housing Bd., Bradenton Charter Adv. Com.; del. Dem. Nat. Conv., 1960, dist. del., 1964; past trustee, mem. exec. com. Stetson U.; former trustee New Coll., Aurora Found. Served to 1st lt. USAAF, 1941-45. Named Boss of Yr., Nat. Secs. Assn., 1959, Man of Yr. for Fla. agr. Progressive Farmer mag., 1959; recipient Allen Morris award as Outstanding Freshman Senator, 1959, merit award Am. Flag Assn., 1962, Gamma Sigma Delta, 1965, leadership award Fla. Agrl. Ext. Svc., 1963, Outstanding Senator award Fla. Radio Broadcasters, 1965, Allen Morris award s most valuable mem. Fla. Legislature, 1965, Most Valuable Mem. award Fla. Senate, St. Petersburg Times, 1965, Brotherhood award Sarasota chpt. NCCJ, 1966, Disting. Citizen award Manatee County, 1970, Disting. Alumnus award U. Fla., 1972, Svc. to Mankind award Sertoma Internat., 1976, Goodwill Disting. Citizen award, 1979, Crystal Shield award Salvation Army, 1996; inducted into Fla. Agrl. Hall of Fame, 1992, Tampa Bay Bus. Hall of Fame, 1992, Outstanding Service awmrd Fla. Agrl. Council, Good Govt. award Fla. State Junior C. of C., 1961, Disting. Service award Manatee County Dem. Exec. Com., 1966, Agrl. Disting. Service award Manatee County, 1966, Manatee County Agrl. Hall of Fame, Manatee County Citizen of Yr. Bradenton Civitan Club's, 1969, Mankind award Bradenton Noon Sertoma Club's, 1976, Statesmanship in Human Affairs/Laureate in Human Rights Manatee County Branch, NAACP, 1978, Humanitarian award Palmetto Youth Ctr., 1995, Lifetime Spirit of Manatee award Manatte Cmty. Found., 2006, Leadership Legend award Grassroots Leadership Initiative, 2006, Lifetime Achievement award, Family Health Care Ctr. Manatee Found., 2008. Mem. Fla. C. of C. (bd. dirs. emeritus and past chmn.), Manatee C. of C. (past pres.), Fla. Hort. Soc. (past pres., chmn. bd.), Fla. Flower Assn., ARC Clara Barton Soc., Blue Key (hon.), Omicron Delta Kappa (hon.), Kiwanis (pres. 1955), Sigma Alpha Epsilon, Nat. Assoc. Mfrs. (dir. 1961-63, 1971-73), Manatee County Agriculture Museum (dir.), Bd. Regents Adv. Com. for Selection Chancellor (chmn.), Govs Transp. Policy Study Commn., I-75 Now Task Force (co-chmn.), Boys Club Manatee County (dir.), Manatee County Cmty. Chest (chmn.), Manatee Red Cross (chmn.), Pathfinders' Club (founder), United Way Manatee County (founder), Palmetto Hist. Commn. Home: 3009 Riverview Blvd W Bradenton FL 34205-3420 Office: PO Box 9270 Bradenton FL 34206-9270 *The turning point in my life came at the age of 32 when I accepted Jesus Christ as my personal Lord and Saviour. I believe every person should live his life up to the fullest extent of his God-given talents and ability. I think we have a responsibility to "pay our dues" for the privilege of living in a free land by being actively involved in our government.*

PRICE, EDWARD WARREN, retired aerospace engineer; b. Detroit, Dec. 6, 1920; s. Frank E. and Elizabeth Alleyne (Rattray) P.; m. Mary Kate Howard, June 21, 1952; children: Douglas Brian, Alison Tamara, Carolyn Louise. BA in Physics, Math, UCLA, 1948. Ballistician Calif. Inst. Tech., Pasadena, 1941-44; physicist U.S. Naval Weapons Ctr., China Lake, Calif., 1946-74; prof. aerospace engring. Ga. Inst. Tech., Atlanta, 1967—68, 1974—91; regents prof. emeritus, 1991—. Mem. Nat. Acad. Scis.-Nat. Rsch. Coun. Space Shuttle Booster Redesign Rev. Panel, 1986-89; cons. in field. Contbr. articles to profl. jours. With USNR, 1944—46. Recipient LTE Thompson award, 1960, US Navy, Superior Civilian Svc. medal, 1974, Pub. Svc. award, NASA, 1987, Astronauts award, 1987. Fellow AIAA (dir., v.p. tech., 1966-69, Rsch., Pendrary, Goddard awards 1966, 71, 76); mem. AAAS, NAE, Combustion Inst., Sigma Xi. Achievements include numerous contributions to science in areas of rocket propulsion and combustion. Home: 5058 Highpoint Rd NE Atlanta GA 30342-2313

PRICE, ELY, dermatologist; b. NYC, Aug. 9, 1932; s. Jacob and Mary P.; m. Joan Savitt, Jan. 18, 2009; children from previous marriage: Jeremy, Andrew. BS cum laude, CCNY, 1953; AM, Ind. U., 1956; MD, U. Lausanne, Switzerland, 1964. Diplomate Am. Bd. Dermatology. Intern Brookdale Hosp. Med. Ctr., Bklyn., 1964-65, resident internal medicine, 1965-66; fellow Mt. Sinai Hosp., NYC, 1965-66; resident in dermatology Kings County Hosp., Bklyn., 1966-69; practice dermatology Bay Ridge Skin and Cancer Dermatology, P.C., Bklyn., 1969—; attending-in-charge, head dermatology Maimonides Med. Ctr., Bklyn., 1985—; clin. assoc. prof. dermatology SUNY Sci. Ctr., Bklyn., 1985—. Cons. in medicine Luth. Med. Ctr., Bklyn., 1988—; cons. in dermatology Victory Med. Hosp., Bklyn., 1989—. Fellow ACP, Am. Acad. Dermatology, Am. Soc. Dermatol. Surgery, N.Y. Acad. Medicine. Avocation: golf. Office: Bay Ridge Skin & Cancer Dermatology PC 9921 4th Ave Brooklyn NY 11209-8347 Home: 5598 Vista Del Mando S Unit B Laguna Woods CA 92637-6923

PRICE, ERICA HIGHTOWER, psychologist; b. Madisonville, Ky., Oct. 17, 1979; d. Marvin and Marsha Hightower; m. Christopher Price, Nov. 2, 2008; children: Christopher Jr., Destiny Whitsell. EdS, Western Ky. U., Bowling Green, 2006. Sch. psychologist Hopkins County Sch. Dist., Madisonville, 2005—. Youth bible studies leader Word of Faith Christian Ctr., Madisonville, 2006—08. Mem.: KY Assn. Psychologists in Schs. Office: Hopkins County Sch Dist 320 S Seminary St Madisonville KY 42431 Business E-Mail: erica.hightower@hopkins.kyschools.us.

PRICE, FRANK, motion picture and television company executive; b. Decatur, Ill., May 17, 1930; s. William F. and Winifred A. (Moran) P.; m. Katherine Huggins, May 15, 1965; children: Stephen, David, Roy, William. Student, Mich. State U., 1949-51, HHD (hon.), 2003. Writer, story editor CBS-TV, NYC, 1951-53, Columbia Pictures, Hollywood, Calif., 1953-57, NBC-TV, Hollywood, Calif., 1957-58; producer, writer ZIV-TV, Hollywood, Calif., 1958, Universal Television, Universal City, Calif., 1959-64, v.p., 1964-71, sr. v.p., 1971-73, exec. v.p. in charge of production, 1973-74, pres., 1974-78; v.p., dir. MCA, Inc., 1976-78; pres. Columbia Pictures Prodn., 1978-79; chmn., chief exec. officer Columbia Pictures, 1979-84, also bd. dirs.; chmn. MCA Motion Picture Group, 1984-86; chmn., chief exec. officer Price Entertainment Inc., 1987-90; chmn. Columbia Pictures, 1990-91; chmn., chief exec. officer Price Entertainment, 1991—; prodr. The Tuskegee Airmen, 1996. Trustee U. So. Calif., 1996—, chmn. bd. counselors Sch. of Cinema-TV, 1990—; mem. Nat. Coun. on the Arts, 2006—. With USN, 1948-49. Recipient Peabody award, 1996, NAACP Image award, 1996. Mem. Writers Guild Am. West, NY State Soc. Cin. (pres. 2008-), NY Geneal. and Biog. Soc. (chmn., bd. trustees 2008-). Office: Price Entertainment 620 Park Ave New York NY 10021

PRICE, FREDERICK KENNETH CERCIE, minister; b. Santa Monica, Calif., Jan. 3, 1932; s. Fred Cercie and Winifred Bernice (Ammons) P.; m. Betty Ruth Scott, Mar. 29, 1953; children: Angela

Marie Price Evans, Cheryl Ann Price, Stephanie Pauline Price Buchanan, Frederick Kenneth Jr. AA, LA City Coll.; diploma (hon.), Rhema Bible Tng. Ctr., Tulsa, 1976; DD (hon.), Oral Roberts U., 1982; student (hon.), Pepperdine U., 1990. Ordained to ministry Bapt. Ch., 1955, African Meth. Episcopal Ch., 1957, Kenneth Hagin Ministries, 1975. Asst. pastor Mt. Sinai Bapt. Ch., Los Angeles, 1955-57; pastor African Meth. Episcopal Ch., Val Verde, Calif., 1957-59; pastor, Christian Missionary Alliance W. Washington Community Ch., Los Angeles, 1965-73; pastor Crenshaw Christian Ctr., Los Angeles, 1973—, Crenshaw Christian Ctr. East, NYC, 2001. Founding mem. bd. trustees Internat. Conv. Faith Ministers, Inc., Tulsa, 1979—; chmn. bd., pres. Fellowship of Internat. Christian Word of Faith Ministries, 1990. Author: How Faith Works, 1976, How to Obtain Strong Faith, 1977, Thank God for Everything, 1977, Ingredient, 1978, Faith: Foolishness or Presumption, 1979, Explanation to Receiving Your Healing by the Laying on of Hands, 1980, Now Faith Is, 1983, High Finance, God's Financial Plan, Tithes and Offerings, 1984, How to Believe God for a Mate, 1987, Marriage and the Family, Practical Insight for Family Living, 1988, The Origin of Satan, 1988, Living in the Realm of the Spirit, 1989, Concerning Them Which are Asleep, 1989, Homosexuality: State of Birth or State of Mind, 1989, Prosperity on God's Terms, 1990, Practical Suggestions for a Successful Ministry, 1991, Race, Religion & Racism, Volume 1: A Bold Encounter with Racism in The Church, 1999, Race, Religion & Racism, Volume 2: Perverting the Gospel to Subjugate a People, 2003, Race, Religion & Racism: Volume 3: Jesus, Christianity and Islam, 2002, Answered Prayer Guaranteed 2006, Prosperity Good News for Gods People Among Others 2008. Recipient Horatio Alger award, 1998, Kelly Miller Smith Interfaith award, Southern Christian Leadership Conf., 1998. Democrat. Avocation: scuba diving. Office: Crenshaw Christian Ctr Attention Angela Evans Mailing PO Box 90000 Los Angeles CA 90009-9201

PRICE, GARY, librarian; m. Lisa Cohen, May 2007. BA, U. Kansas, Lawrence, Kansas, 1988; M in Libr. and Info. Sciences, Wayne State U., Detroit, Mich., 1996. Reference libr. George Washington U. (Va. campus), 1995—2001; founder, chief editor, compiler ResourceShelf, 2001—; news editor Search Engine Watch, 2004—06; founder, contbr., editor Docuticker, 2004—; libr., dir. online info. resources Ask.com (formerly called Ask Jeeves, Inc.), 2006—. Faculty mem. WebSearch U.; frequent spkr. at Search Engines Strategies, WebSearch U., Computers in Libraries, Internet Librarian and other industry conferences; info. rsch. cons. Co-author (with Chris Sherman): The Invisible Web, 2001; contbr. articles to Washington Post, Guardian & Chronicle of Higher Edn., Fast Facts, Speech and Transcript Ctr., News Ctr., Audio/Video News on World Wide Web, Congl. Rsch. Svc. Reports, Virtual Acquisition Shelf, & News Desk, others. Recipient Innovations in tech. award, Spl. Libraries Assn., 2002, Anges Henry award, Spl. Libraries Assn. (News Divsn.), 2004, Alumnus of Yr., Wayne State U., 2004; named one of Top Librarian Personalities on the Web, 2002. Achievements include being a renowned expert in search, particularly structured data search. Office: Ask.com 555 12th St Ste 500 Oakland CA 94607 E-mail: gary.price@resourceshelf.com.

PRICE, GRIFFITH BALEY, JR., lawyer; b. Lawrence, Kans., Aug. 15, 1942; s. Griffith Baley and Cora Lee (Beers) P.; m. Maria Helena Martin, June 29, 1968 (div.); children: Andrew Griffith, Alexandra Helena; m. Nancy Culver Rhodes, Aug. 17, 1997; children: Carolyn Rhodes, Sarah Culver. AB cum laude, Harvard U., Cambridge, Mass., 1964; LLB, NYU, 1967. Bar: NY 1967, DC 1991, US Ct. Appeals (6th cir.) 1975, US Ct. Appeals (2nd cir.) 1978, US Ct. Appeals (3d, 5th and 11th cirs.) 1981, US Ct. Appeals (1st cir.) 2002, US Ct. Appeals (fed. cir.) 1984, US Supreme Ct. 2001. Assoc. Dewey, Ballantine, Bushby, Palmer & Wood, NYC, 1967-75; ptnr. Milgrim Thomajan & Lee, NYC, 1976-86; of counsel, ptnr. Finnegan, Henderson, Farabow, Garrett & Dunner, LLP, Washington, 1987—. Adj. prof., lectr. George Washington U. Law Ctr., Washington, 1989—93; mem., chair pub. adv. com. US Patent and Trademark Office, 1999—2004; lectr., spkr. in field. Author: (with others, treatise) Milgrim on Trade Secrets, 1986; contbr. articles to profl. jours. Root-Tilden scholar NYU Law Sch., 1964-67. Fellow: Am. Intellectual Property Law Assn. (bd. dirs., com. chmn.); mem.: ABA (intellectual property sec., com. chmn.), Assn. Interamerican Indsl. Property, Fed. Cir. Bar Assn., Licensing Execs. Soc., Internat. Trademark Assn. (bd. dirs., com. chmn., bd. editors, The Trademark Reporter 2006—), Cosmos Club, Nat. Press Club, Harvard Club (Washington), NY Athletic Club. Unitarian Universalist. Office: Finnegan Henderson Farabow Garrett & Dunner LLP 901 New York Ave NW Washington DC 20001-4413 Home Phone: 301-263-0853; Office Phone: 202-408-4000. Business E-Mail: gbprice@finnegan.com.

PRICE, HENRY ESCOE, broadcast executive; b. Jackson, Miss., Oct. 13, 1947; s. Henry E. Price Sr. and Alma Kate (Merrill) Noto; m. Maria Diane Harper, Apr. 8, 1972; children: Henry E. III, Norman Harper. BS in Radio, TV, Film, Journalism, U. So. Miss., 1972. Announcer, news dir. Sta. WROA Radio, Gulfport, Miss., 1967-69; comml. producer Sta. WJTV-TV, Jackson, Miss., 1969-73; prodn. mgr. Sta. WAAY-TV, Huntsville, Ala., 1973-77, Sta. WPEC-TV, West Palm Beach, Fla., 1977-79; dir. promotion Sta. WPTV-TV, Palm Beach, Fla., 1979-81; TV cons. Frank Magid Assoc., Marion, Iowa, 1981-83; dir. advt. and promotion Sta. WJLA-TV, Washington, 1983-84; v.p., dir. programming Sta. WUSA-TV, Gannett TV, Washington, 1984-88; pres., gen. mgr. Sta. WFMY-TV, Gannett TV, Greensboro, N.C., 1988-91, Sta. KARE-TV, Mpls., 1991-96; v.p., gen. mgr. Sta. WBBM-TV, CBS TV Stas., Chgo., 1996—2000; pres., gen. mgr. Sta. WXII-TV, Winston-Salem, NC, 2000—; sr. dir. in TV, Northwestern U. Media Mgmt. Ctr. Pres. Carolina News Network, 1988-91; sr. dir. media mgmt. Ctr. Northwestern U., 2000—. Avocations: furniture design and construction, reading, walking, bicycling. Address: 700 Coliseum Dr Winston Salem NC 27106

PRICE, ILENE ROSENBERG, lawyer; b. Jersey City, July 2, 1951; d. Irwin Daniel and Mildred (Riesberg) Rosenberg; m. Jeffrey Paul Price, Feb. 18, 1973. AB, U. Mich., 1972; JD, U. Pa., 1977. Bar: Pa. 1977, DC 1978, U.S. Dist. Ct. DC 1979, U.S. Ct. Appeals (D.C. cir.) 1979. Assoc. Haley, Bader & Potts, Washington, 1977-80; staff atty. Mut. Broadcasting System Inc., Arlington, Va., 1980-82, asst. gen. counsel, 1982-85; gen. counsel MultiComm Telecommunications Corp., Arlington, 1985-88; east coast counsel Westwood One, Inc., Arlington, 1988-91; gen. counsel Resource Dynamics Corp., Vienna, Va., 1991—2001; legal search cons. The McCormick Group, Arlington, 2001—03; gen. counsel Bluewave Resources, LLC, McLean, Va., 2003—. Mem. Fed. Communications Bar Assn., Wash. Met. Area Corp. Counsel Assn., Women's Bar Assn. D.C. (bd. dirs. 1984-87). Office: Bluewave Resources LLC Ste 310 6830 Elm St Mc Lean VA 22101 Home Phone: 703-893-6079; Office Phone: 703-448-3400. Business E-Mail: ileneprice@bwres.com.

PRICE, JACK F., cardiologist; b. Miami, Okla., Feb. 20, 1967; s. Ronald and Nancy Price. MD, U. Okla., 1994. Lic. physician Tex., 2002. Postdoc. fellow Baylor Coll. Medicine, Houston, 1998—2002, pediat. cardiologist, 2002—; postdoc. fellow Tex. Children's Hosp., Houston, 1998—2002, pediat. cardiologist, 2002—, co-dir. cardiac critical care rsch., 2006—. Recipient Outstanding Rsch. award, Am. Heart Assn., 2001. Mem.: Am. Heart Assn. (Outstanding Rsch. award 2001), Heart Failure Soc. Am., Internat. Soc. Heart and Lung Transplantation. Presbyterian.

PRICE, JAMES GORDON, physician, educator; b. Brush, Colo., June 20, 1926; s. John Hoover and Rachel Laurette (Dodds) Price; m. Janet Alice McSween, June 19, 1949; children: James Gordon II, Richard Christian, Mary Laurette, Janet Lynn. BA, U. Colo., 1948, MD, 1951. Diplomate charter Am. Bd. Family Practice. Intern Denver Gen. Hosp., 1951—52; practice medicine specializing in family medicine Brush Co., 1952—78; prof. family practice U. Kans. Med. Ctr., 1978—93; chmn. dept. U. Kans. Med. Center, 1982—90, exec. dean, 1990—93, prof. emeritus in family practice, 1993—. Dir., pres. Am. Bd. Family Practice, 1979; mem. Inst. Medicine of NAS, 1973—. Med. editor: Gen. Learning Corp., 1973—92, mem. editl. bd.: Med. World News, 1969—79; editor: Am. Acad. Family Physician Home Study Self Assessment Program, 1978—83; columnist: Your Family Physician, 1973—90. Trustee Family Health Found. Am., 1970—82; vol. physician St. Jude's Hosp., St. Lucia, West Indies, 1998—99. With USNR, 1943—46. Fellow: Am. Acad. Family Physicians (charter, pres. 1973); mem.: Phi Beta Kappa, Alpha Omega Alpha. Home: 12205 Mohawk Rd Shawnee Mission KS 66209-2137 Business E-Mail: jimtad@sbcglobal.net.

PRICE, JAMES MICHAEL, oceanographer; PhD, U. Hawaii, Honolulu, 1981. Oceanographer US Minerals Mgmt. Svc., Herndon, Va., 1990—. Office: US Minerals Mgmt Svc 381 Elden St MS 4041 Herndon VA 20170 Office Fax: 703-787-1053. Business E-Mail: pricej@mms.gov.

PRICE, JAMES TUCKER, lawyer; b. Springfield, Mo., June 22, 1955; s. Billy L. and Jeanne Adele Price; m. Francine Beth Warkow, June 8, 1980; children: Rachel Leah, Ashley Elizabeth. BJ, U. Mo., 1977; JD, Harvard U., 1980. Bar: Mo. 1980. Assoc. firm Spencer Fane Britt & Browne, Kansas City, 1980-86; ptnr. Spencer Fane Britt & Browne LLP, Kansas City, 1987—, chair environ. practice group, 1994—, mem. exec. com., 1997—2009. Mem. Brownfields Commn., Kansas City, 1999—; mem. steering com. Kansas City Bi-State Brownfields Initiative, 1997—. Contbr. to monographs, other legal publs. Mem. ABA (coun. sect. environ, energy and resources 1992-95, vice chmn. solid and hazardous waste com. 1985-90, chmn. 1990-92, chmn. brownfields task force 1995-97, vice chmn. environ. transactions and brownfield com. 1998-2000, vice-chmn. state & regional cooperation com., 2007-), Mo. Bar Assn., Kansas City Met. Bar Assn. (chmn. environ. law com. 1985-86, 2007-08), Greater Kansas City C. of C. (co-chair Brownfields Working Group, 1996-98, chmn. energy and environ. com. 1987-89). Office: Spencer Fane Britt & Browne LLP 1000 Walnut St Ste 1400 Kansas City MO 64106-2140 Office Phone: 816-292-8228. Business E-Mail: jprice@spencerfane.com.

PRICE, JENNIFER LEIGH, social studies educator; b. Savannah, Ga., Mar. 16, 1979; d. William Leon and Emily Jean Jones; m. Robert Clayton Price, Sept. 4, 1998. BS in Mid. Grades Edn., Ga. So. U., Statesboro, 2001; M in Elem. Reading & Literacy, Walden U., Online, 2005. Tchr. Claxton Elem. Sch., Ga., 2001—05; tchr. social studies Claxton Mid. Sch., 2005—. Mem.: Ga. Assn. Educators, Delta Kappa Gamma Soc. Internat. Conservative. Baptist. Home: 542 Sam Greene Rd Claxton GA 30417 Office: Claxton Middle School 4 N Coll St Claxton GA 30417 Personal E-mail: jenniferprice@hughes.net.

PRICE, JOE L., bank executive; B in Acctg., U. NC, Charlotte, 1983. With PriceWaterhouse; mgmt. positions Bank of Am. Corp., Charlotte, NC, 1992—95, contr., 1995—97, gen. auditor, 1997—99, pres. consumer fin. group, 1999—2002, corp. strategy & consumer spl. assets exec., 2002—03, risk mgmt. exec. global corp. and investment banking, 2003—06, CFO, 2006—. Bd. dirs. Habitat for Humanity; mem. adv. bd. Belk Sch. Bus. U. NC. Office: Bank of Am Corp 100 N Tryon St Corp Ctr Charlotte NC 28255*

PRICE, JOHN R., lawyer, educator; b. Indpls., Nov. 28, 1934; s. Carl Lee and Agnes I. P.; m. Suzanne A. Leslie, June 22, 1963; children: John D., Steven V. BA with high honors, U. Fla., 1958; LL.B. with honors, NYU, 1961. Bar: Wash. 1977, U.S. Ct. Appeals (9th cir.), U.S. Dist. Ct. (we. dist.) Wash. Assoc. McCutchen, Doyle, Brown & Enersen, San Francisco, 1961-69; prof. law U. Wash., Seattle, 1969-97, dean, 1982-88; of counsel Perkins Coie, Seattle, 1976—2004. Author: Contemporary Estate Planning, 1983, Price on Contemporary Estate Planning, 1992, 2d edit., 2000, (with Samuel A. Donaldson), 2007, 2008, 2009, Conflicts, Confidentiality and Other Ethical Issues, 2000, 2d edit., 2007. Served with U.S. Army, 1953-55 Root-Tilden fellow NYU Sch. Law, 1958-61 Fellow Am. Coll. Trust and Estate Counsel (former regent); mem. ABA, Am. Law Inst., Order of Coif, Phi Beta Kappa. Congregationalist. Home: 3794 NE 97th St Seattle WA 98115-2564 Office: 1201 3rd Ave Ste 4800 Seattle WA 98101-3099 E-mail: jprice@perkinscoie.com.

PRICE, JOHN RANDOLPH, writer; b. Alice, Tex., Feb. 12, 1932; s. John Randolph and Eva Mae (Boney) P.; m. Janis Bryant Price, June 20, 1953; children: Susan Lynn, Leslie Anne. BS, U. Houston, 1957; PhD (hon.), Emerson Inst., 2001; DHL (hon.), Holmes Inst., 2003. Dir. advt. Gates Radio Corp., Quincy, Ill., 1957-62; v.p. Sander Rodkin, Ltd., Chgo., 1962-64; exec. v.p. Stewart, Price, Tomlin, Inc., Chgo., 1964-67; v.p. Goodwin, Dannenbaum, Littman & Wingfield, Inc., Houston, 1967-70; pres. O'Neill, Price, Anderson, Fouchard, Inc., Houston, 1970-74, John Price & Co., Houston, 1974-79, Arnan, Inc., Austin, 1979-81; chmn. bd. The Quartus Found. Inc., Boerne, Tex., 1981—. Author: The Superbeings, 1981, The Manifestation Process, 1983, The Planetary Commission, 1984, Practical Spirituality, 1985, With Wings as Eagles, 1987, The Abundance Book, 1987, Prayer, Principles & Power, 1987, A Spiritual Philosophy for the New World, 1990, Empowerment, 1992, The Angels Within Us, 1993, Angel Energy, 1995, Living a Life of Joy, 1997, The Success Book, 1998, The Wellness Book, 1998, The Meditation Book, 1998, The Love Book, 1998, The Jesus Code, 2000, The Alchemist's Handbook, 2000, Removing the Masks That Bind Us, 2001, Nothing Is Too Good to Be True, 2003, Staff sgt. USAF, 1952-56. Recipient Joseph S. Cullinan award U. Houston, 1956, Grand Prix Best Consumer Mag. Advt. award, 1970. Mem. Internat. New Thought Alliance (Humanitarian award 1992, Joseph Murphy award 1994). Achievements include organizer of first annual World Peace day on December 31, 1986. Office: The Quartus Found Inc PO Box 1768 Boerne TX 78006-6768 Office Phone: 830-249-3985. Business E-Mail: quartus@quartus.org.

PRICE, JOHN ROY, JR., financial executive; b. NYC, Dec. 20, 1938; s. John Roy and Pauline Bernice (Milnes) P.; m. Victoria Scott Pohle, Dec. 19, 1970 (div. 1982); 1 child, Matthew Roy; m. Marion Cobb Hardie, Oct. 1, 1988 (div. 1996); m. Svetlana Sergeyeva, July 11, 1999. BA, Grinnell Coll., 1960, Queens Coll., Oxford U., Eng., 1962, MA, 1965; JD, Harvard U., 1965. Assoc. Casey, Lane & Mittendorf, NYC, 1965-67; v.p. Bedford-Stuyvesant D & S Corp., NYC, 1967-68; spl. asst. to Pres. U.S., Washington, 1969-71; assoc. Donaldson, Lufkin & Jenrette, NYC, 1971-72; v.p. Mfrs. Hanover Trust, NYC, 1972-75, Mfrs. Hanover Corp., NYC, 1975-80, sr. v.p. non-bank subs., 1980-83, sr. v.p., sec., 1983-87; mng. dir. Mfrs. Hanover Trust Co., 1987-88, Mfrs. Hanover Securities Corp., 1988-92; mng. dir. govt. affairs Chem. Bank, 1992-96, Chase Manhattan, 1996—. Bd. dirs. Am. Trust for Oxford, 1990-94; chmn. Bklyn. Acad. Music Cmty. Devel. Corp.; dir. Prin. Fin. Group (formerly Bankers Life Co.), Bankers Assn. for Fgn. Trade, 1990-97, pres., 1994-95, Nat. Fgn. Trade Coun., 1991—; pres. Am. for Oxford, 1987-99, chmn., 1999—. Nat. chmn. Ripon Soc., 1967-68; trustee Grinnell Coll., 1970—; bd. dirs. New Communities Corp., 1976-77; mem. exec. panel Chief of Naval Ops., 1972-79. Rhodes scholar; named Disting. Friend of Oxford, 2000. Mem. Council Fgn. Relations, Phi Beta Kappa. Clubs: Harvard (N.Y.C.). Home: 1041 S Negley Ave Pittsburgh PA 15217-1045

PRICE, JOSEPH HUBBARD, lawyer; b. Montgomery, Ala., Jan. 31, 1939; s. Aaron Joseph and Minnie Jule (Reynolds) P.; m. Cynthia Winant Ramsey, Sept. 14, 1963 (div. 1980); children: Victoria Reynolds, Ramsey Winant; m. Courtney McFadden, Apr. 25, 1980. AB, U. Ala., 1961; LLB, Harvard U., 1964; postgrad., London Sch. Econs., 1964-65. Bar: Ala. 1964, D.C. 1968. Law clk. to justice Hugo L. Black U.S. Supreme Ct., Washington, 1967-68; assoc. Leva, Hawes, Symington, Martin & Oppenheimer, Washington, 1968-71; v.p. Overseas Pvt. Investment Corp., Washington, 1971-73; ptnr. Leva, Hawes, et. al., Washington, 1973-83; ptnr., internat. law Gibson, Dunn & Crutcher, Washington, 1983—2005. Capt. US Army, 1966—67, Vietnam. Decorated Bronze Star; Frank Knox Meml. fellow London Sch. Econs., 1964-65. Mem. ABA, Am. Soc. Internat. Law, Supreme Ct. Hist. Soc., Phi Beta Kappa, Met. Club. Office: Gibson Dunn & Crutcher 1050 Connecticut Ave NW Ste 900 Washington DC 20036-5306

PRICE, JOSEPH LEVERING, neuroscientist, educator; b. Mobile, Ala., Oct. 17, 1942; s. Benjamin Joseph and Virginia (Levering) P.; m. Elisabeth Uttenthal, June 23, 1967; children: Anna Elise, Virginia Sigrid, Poul Joseph. BA in Chemistry, U. of the South, 1963; BA in Physiology, U. Oxford, Eng., 1966, PhD in Anatomy, 1969. Instr. Washington U. Sch. Medicine, St. Louis, 1969-71, asst. prof., 1971-76, assoc. prof., 1976-83, prof., 1983—. Mem. editorial bd. Jour. of Comparative Neurology, 1983—; contbr. articles to profl. jours. Jr. warden Christ Ch. Cathedral, St. Louis, 1985-87. Rhodes scholar Oxford U., 1963-66; USPHS predoctoral fellow, 1966-68; recipient C.J. Herrick award Am. Assn. Anatomoists, 1973, Javits Neurosci. Investigator award NIH, 1987. Mem. Soc. for Neurosci., Phi Beta Kappa. Democrat. Episcopalian. Office: Washington U Sch Medicine Dept Anatomy and Neurobiology Saint Louis MO 63110

PRICE, JOSEPH MICHAEL, lawyer; b. St. Paul, Dec. 2, 1947; s. Leon and Rose (Kaufman) P.; m. Louise Rebecca Braunstein, Dec. 19, 1971; children: Lisa, Laurie, Julie. BA, U. Minn., 1969, JD, 1972. Bar: Minn. 1972, U.S. Dist. Ct. Minn. 1974. Ptnr. Faegre & Benson, Mpls., 1972—. Mem. Minn. Bar Assn., Hennepin County Bar Assn. Home: 4407 Country Club Rd Minneapolis MN 55424-1148 Office: Faegre & Benson 2200 Wells Fargo Ctr 90 S 7th St Ste 2200 Minneapolis MN 55402-3901 Office Phone: 612-766-8617. Business E-Mail: Jprice@faegre.com.

PRICE, JUDITH HOLM, educational psychologist; b. Milw., Nov. 6, 1937; d. Paul James and Dorothy Ruth (Munton) Holm; m. Thomas Munro Price, Aug. 8, 1959; children: Scott Michael, Andrea Lynn. BA, Carroll Coll., 1959; MA, U. Iowa, 1973; PhD, U. Wyo., 1980. Nat. cert. sch. psychologist. Tchr. Waukesha Pub. Sch., Wis., 1959, Madison Pub. Sch., 1959-63; preschool assessment specialist Grant Wood Area Edn. Agy. 10, Cedar Rapids, Iowa, 1976-78; Ednl. Resource Ctr. facilitator Albany County Sch. Dist. 1, Laramie, Wyo., 1980-89, dir. spl. svc., 1989—93; acad. dean Brush Ranch Sch., Tererro, N.Mex., 1993—96; hist. home renovator Yerington, Nev., 1997—. Substitute tchr. Melbourne (Australia) Sch., 1978; temporary prof. U. Wyo., Laramie, 1981, 84; mem. computer conf. com. Wyo. Dept. Edn., Casper, 1984-85, com. for devel. spl. edn. database, 1987, task force cert. standards for early childhood spl. edn. tchr., 1988; speaker Wyo. Fedn. CEC, Riverton, 1986, task force on specific learning disability criteria, 1988; conf. mem. Council for Exceptional Children Software Conf., Washington, 1986; provider state-wide inservice Specific Learning Disability Criteria, 1988. Spl. edn. rules and regulations task force Wyo. Dept. Edn., 1990—92; mem. Wyo. gov. Early Intervention Coun., 1990—93; governing bd. pres. South Lyon Health Ctr.Inc., 2003—07; chmn. South Lyon Healthcare Found., Inc., 2007—. Mem. Nat. Assn. Sch. Psychologists (alt. del. 1983), Wyo. Sch. Psychoednl. Assn., Council for Exceptional Children (com. specific learning disability 1987-88, speaker 1988, pres. Frontier chpt. 1989), Assn. Curriculum Devel., N.Mex. Assn. Non-Pub. Sch., Rotary Internat. Yerington Club (co-pres. 2008-), Phi Kappa Phi, Phi Delta Kappa, 2003. Avocations: computers, skiing, camping, travel. Office: The Nordyke House 727 State Route 339 Yerington NV 89447-9553

PRICE, JUSTINE D., art educator; AB, Bryn Mawr Coll., Pa., 1992; PhD, U. Tex., Austin, 2007. Rschr. Roy Lichtenstein Found., NYC, 2001—08; asst. prof. Canisius Coll., Buffalo, 2005—. Contbr. essay. Mem.: Coll. Art Assn. Office: Canisius Coll Dept Fine Art 2001 Main St Buffalo NY 14208

PRICE, KATHLEEN MCCORMICK, editor, writer; b. Topeka, Dec. 25, 1932; d. Raymond Chesley and Kathleen (Shoffner) McCormick; m. William Faulkner Black, Aug. 25, 1956 (div. 1961); 1 child, Kathleen Serena; m. William Hillard Price, Aug. 13, 1976. BA, U. Colo., Denver, 1971. Book reviewer Denver Post, 1971-78; book editor San Diego Mag., 1978-92. Cons. editor St. John's Cathedral, Denver, 1985-95. Author: There's a Dactyl Under My Foot, 1986, The Lady and the Unicorn, 1994, From Vision to Vestment, 2001. Dir. Colo. Episcopal Vestment Guild, 1991-2008. Fellow Phi Beta Kappa; mem. Denver County Club, La Garita Club, Nat. Soc. Colonial Dames America. Episcopalian. Home: 27 Crestmoor Dr Denver CO 80220-5853 Personal E-mail: kmccp@msn.com.

PRICE, KIM DENISE, counselor; b. Pontiac, Mich., June 29, 1974; d. Priscilla Ann Newell; m. Ethan A. Price, Apr. 20, 1999; children: Destine Zion, Trinitee Davine, Jairahel Zoriah. BS in Orgnl. Comm., Western Mich. U., 1997. Asst. sec. English dept. Western Mich. U., Kalamazoo, 1992—95, orientation leader, 1996; credit adjustor 1st of Am., Kalamazoo, 1997; supr. for abused women Gospel Mission, Kalamazoo, 1998; health mgmt. technician Bronson Meth. Hosp., Kalamazoo, 1999—2000; customer svc. rep. Indy Mac Bank Loan Dept., Kalamazoo, 2000—01; youth treatment provider Lakeside Learning and Treatment Ctr., Kalamazoo, 2001—; psychiatric care specialist Havenwyck Hosp., Auburn Hills, Mich., 2004—06. V.p. of gospel chair Western Mich. U., Kalamazoo, 1996. Contbr. poetry International Book of Poetry, 1999—2000, poetry Anthology Book of Poetry. Orgnl. leader divsn. minority affairs Western Mich. U., 1997. Avocations: poetry, creating unique hairstyles, bowling, singing, camping. Home: 600 Westbury Ln Kalamazoo MI 49006-2662 Home Phone: 269-365-9293.

PRICE, LARA, professional sports team executive; Grad., Colo. State U., Ft. Collins. Dir. team svcs. Continental Basketball Assn.; mgr. team svcs. NBA; dir. mktg. Phila. 76ers, 1996—98, v.p. mktg., 1998—2001, sr. v.p. mktg., 2001—03, sr. v.p. bus. ops., 2003—. Mem. Phila. chpt. steering com. Nat. Sports Mktg. Network. Bd. dirs. Found. Melanoma Rsch. Office: Phila 76ers Wachovia Ctr 3601 S Broad St Philadelphia PA 19148*

PRICE, LARRY R., statistician, educator; b. Dallas, June 13, 1958; s. Ben T. and Pat L. Price; m. Maria Y. Young, June 14, 1997. PhD, Ga. State U., Atlanta, 1997. Sr. lectr.-biostatistician Emory U., Atlanta, 1986—99; sr. psychometrician Psychol. Corp., San Antonio, 1999—; prof. Tex. State U., San Marcos, 2001—. Author: (textbook) Psychometric Methods: Theory into Practice. Mem.: APA, Psychometric Soc., Am. Statis. Assn., Am. Ednl. Rsch. Assn. Achievements include research in new statistical method for modeling in neuroimaging; new undelying 6-Factor structure of human intelligence based on the Wechler Intelligence Scales. Office: Texas State Univ 601 University Dr San Marcos TX 78666 Personal E-mail: lrprice@mindspring.com. Business E-Mail: lprice@txstate.edu.

PRICE, LEON R., elementary school educator; s. Leon and Anna Price; m. Constance M. Ringgold, Mar. 1, 1996; 1 child, Joseph Ringgold;children from previous marriage: Kiijuana Cann, Leon R. Jr., Darius R. BS in Elem. Edn., Del. State Coll., Dover, 1977; MA in Edn. Curriculum and Instrn., Del. State U., Dover, 1993. Elem. tchr. Christina Sch. Dist., Newark, Del., 1978—. With USAF, 1965—68. Mem.: Nat. Coun. Tchrs. Math., Omega Psi Phi. Democrat. Baptist. Avocations: gardening, internet surfing. Home: 78 Bunker Hill Rd New Castle DE 19720

PRICE, (MARY VIOLET) LEONTYNE, retired concert and opera singer, soprano; b. Laurel, Miss., Feb. 10, 1927; d. James A. and Kate (Baker) Price; m. William Warfield, Aug. 31, 1952 (div. 1973). BA, Central State Coll., Wilberforce, Ohio, 1949, DMus, 1968; student, Juilliard Sch. Music, 1949-52; pupil, Florence Page Kimball; LHD, Dartmouth Coll., 1962, Fordham U., 1969, Yale U., 1979; MusD, Howard U., 1962; Dr. Humanities, Rust Coll., 1968. Singer: (Operas) (debut) in 4 Saints in 3 Acts, 1952, (appeared) Bess in Porgy and Bess, Vienna, Berlin, Paris, London, under auspices U.S. State Dept., N.Y.C. and U.S. tour, 1952—54; recitalist, soloist (symphonies) U.S., Can., Australia, Europe, 1954—, appeared concerts in India, 1956, 1964, soloist Hollywood Bowl, 1955—59, 1966, Berlin Festival, 1960, role as Mme. Lidoine in Dialogues des Carmelites, San Francisco Opera, 1957; singer: (Operas) NBC-TV, 1955—58, 1960, 1962, 1964, San Francisco Opera Co., 1957—59, 1960—61, 1963, 1965, 1967, 1968, 1971, as Aida at La Scala, 1957;: (Operas) Vienna Staatsoper, 1958, 1959—60, 1961, Berlin Opera, 1964, Rome Opera, 1966, 1968, (recital) Brussels Internat. Fair, auspices State Dept., 1958, Verona Opera Arena, 1958—59, Yugoslavia for, State Dept., 1958; rec. artist RCA-Victor, 1958—, appeared Covent Garden, London, 1958-59, 70, Chgo. Lyric Theatre, 1959, 60, 65, Oakland (Calif.) Symphony, 1980, soloist Salzburg Festival, 1959—63, appeared Tetro alla Scala, Milano, 1960-61, 63, 67, Met. Opera, N.Y.C., 1961-62, 64, 66, 75, 76, since resident mem., until 1985, soloist Salzburg Festival, 1950, 60, debut Teatre Dell'Opera, Rome, 1967, Teatro Colon, Buenos Aires, Argentina, 1969, Hamburg Opera, 1970, recordings A Christmas Offering with Karajani, God Bless America with Charles Gerhardt, Arias from Don Giovanni, Turandot, Aida, Emani, Messa di Requiem, Trovatore, Live at Ordway, The Prima Donna Collection, A Program of Song with D. Garvey, Right as the Rain with André Previn. Co-chmn. Rust Coll. Upward Thrust Campaign; trustee Internat. House.; hon. vice-chmn. U.S. com. UNESCO; Hon. bd. dirs. Campfire Girls. Decorated Order at Ment Italy; recipient Merit award for role of Tosca in NBC-TV Opera, Mademoiselle mag., 1955, 20 Grammy awards for classical vocal recs. Nat. Acad. Rec. Arts and Scis., citation YWCA, 1961, Spirit of Achievement award Albert Einstein Coll. Medicine, 1962, Presdl. medal of freedom, 1964, Springarn medal NAACP, 1965, Schwann Catalog award, 1968, Nat. Medal of Arts, 1985, Essence award, 1991, others; named Musician of Year, Mus. Am. mag., 1961. Fellow: Am. Acad. Arts and Sci.; mem.: AFTRA, Actors Equity Assn., Am. Guild Mus. Artists, Delta Sigma Theta, Sigma Alpha Iota. Inducted into Am. Classical Music Hall of Fame, 1998. Office: Price Enterprises 1133 Broadway Ste 920 New York NY 10010-7901

PRICE, MARK (WILLIAM MARK PRICE), professional basketball coach, retired professional basketball player; b. Bartlesville, Okla., Feb. 15, 1964; Attended, Ga. Inst. Tech., Atlanta. Guard Cleve. Cavaliers, 1986-95, Washington Bullets, 1995-96, Golden State Warriors, 1996-97, Orlando Magic, 1997—98; trainer & coach, Mark Price Basketball Sch. Suwanee Sports Acad.; head basketball coach South Dragons, Nat. Basketball League, Australia, 2006; shooting cons. Memphis Grizzlies, 2007—08, Atlanta Hawks, 2008—. Mem. US nat. team FIBA World Championships, Canada, 1994. Winner NBA Long Distance Shootout, 1993, 94; named to Eastern Conf. All-Star Team NBA, 1989, 1992-94; named First Team All-NBA, 1993. Achievements include leading the NBA in: free throw percentage, 1992, 1993, 1997. Office: c/o Atlanta Hawks Centennial Tower 101 Marietta St NW Ste 1900 Atlanta GA 30303*

PRICE, MARY KATHLEEN, law librarian, educator; b. Buffalo, Feb. 28, 1942; d. Donn Dale and Mary Elizabeth (Domedion) P. BA with honors, U. Fla., 1963; MS, Fla. State U., 1967; postgrad., Ala. Law Sch., Tuscaloosa, 1967-70; JD with honors, U. Ill., Champaign, 1973. Bar: Ill. 1973, U.S. Dist. Ct. (no. dist.) Ill. 1973. Tchr. Duval and Brevard County Schs., Jacksonville and Titusville, Fla., 1960-63; asst. law libr. U. Ala. Law Sch., Tuscaloosa, 1967-70, U. Ill., Champaign, 1970-73; assoc. Ross, Hardies & O'Keefe, Chgo., 1973-75; law libr., prof. law Duke U. Law Sch., Durham, NC, 1975-80; dir. law libr., prof. law U. Minn., Mpls., 1980-90, acting asst. v.p. acad. affairs, 1985-86; law libr. Libr. of Congress, 1988—94; dir. law libr., prof. law NYU Sch. Law, 1994—2003; assoc. dean libr. & tech., Clarence J. TeSelle prof. law Levin Coll. Law, U. Fla., Gainesville, 2003—. Mem. acad. adv. bd. Westlaw, St. Paul, 1984-87; vis. prof. law Uppsala U., 1987, 89. Recipient Law Librarianship award Minn. Assn. Law Libraries, 1984, Disting. Alumni award Fla. State U., 1987. Mem. Am. Assn. Law Librs. (pres. 1983-84), Commn. Legal Edn. Exchange with PRC (chmn. libr. subcom. 1984—), Assn. Am. Law Schs. (mem. accreditation com. 1983-87, exec. bd. 1988-90), Order of Coif. Democrat. Roman Catholic. Office: Levin Coll Law U Fla Box 117628 Gainesville FL 32611 Home: 415 NW 32nd St Gainesville FL 32607 Office Phone: 352-273-0706. Office Fax: 352-392-5093. Business E-Mail: pricek@law.ufl.edu.

PRICE, MARY SUE SWEENEY, museum director; d. William Robert Sweeney; m. Clement A. Price, 1988. BA in English, Allegheny Coll., 1973; D.H.C. (hon.), Caldwell Coll. With textbook pub. co., NYC; supr. pub. rels. Newark Mus., 1975, dep. dir., 1990—93, dir., 1993—, also pres., CEO. Past pres. ArtTable Inc.; v.p. ArtPrice NJ Inc.; bd. dirs. St. Vincent Acad., Newark Arts Coun. Mem.: Assn. Art Mus. Dirs., Am. Assn. Mus., NJ Assn. Mus. (bd. dirs.). Office: Newark Mus 49 Washington St Newark NJ 07102 Office Phone: 973-596-6550.

PRICE, MICHAEL F., money management executive; b. 1952; div., 3 sons. Grad., U. Okla., 1975. Rsch. asst., mgr., to CEO Heine Securities, Short Hills, NJ, 1975-97; CEO Franklin Mutual Advs. Inc. (formerly Heine Securities), Short Hills, NJ, 1997; pvt. investor, 1998—. Pres., chmn. bd. dirs. Franklin Mutual Series Fund Inc. Named one of Forbes' Richest Americans, 2006. Office: Franklin Mutual Advisers Llc 101 John F Kennedy Pkwy Ste 5 Short Hills NJ 07078-2716

PRICE, MICHAEL J., investment banker; BS in Econs., U. Pa.; MBA, Harvard U. Mng. dir., telecom, tech. group Lazard, NYC, 1994—2005; sr. mng. dir., corp. adv. bus. Evercore Ptnrs., NYC, 2005—. Bd. overseers, Coll. Arts & Sci. Univ. Pa.; bd. dir. Rockefeller Univ. Coun. Recipient Rainmaker award, Dealmaker mag., 2006. Office: Evercore Ptnrs 43rd Fl 55 E 52nd St New York NY 10055 Office Phone: 212-857-3100. Office Fax: 212-857-3101.

PRICE, NICOLE DENISE, literature and language professor; BA, Northwestern U., Evanston, Ill., 1992; MA, U. Tenn., Knoxville, 1997; PhD, U. Mo., Columbia, 2005. Vis. asst. prof. Denison U., Granville, Ohio, 2005—07, Muskingum Coll., New Concord, Ohio, 2007—08; asst. prof. No. Ariz. U., Flagstaff, 2008—. Recipient Master Tchr. award, NEH Summer Inst., 2008; Dissertation fellowship, J. William Fulbright, 2003—04. Mem.: MLA, Afro Latin Am. Rsch. Assn., Am. Assn. Tchrs. Spanish & Portuguese, Coll. Lang. Assn. Office: Northern Ariz Univ PO Box 6004 Flagstaff AZ 86011 Business E-Mail: nicole.price@nau.edu.

PRICE, PAUL, marketing and communications company executive; Various positions DDB Worldwide Comm. Group Inc., mng. dir. DDB Melbourne Australia, 1997—2001, global bus. dir. ExxonMobil acct. NYC, 2001—07, chief partnership officer, 2007—08; global pres. Rapp (formerly Rapp Collins Worldwide), NYC, 2008—. Office: Rapp 437 Madison Ave 3rd Fl New York NY 10022 Business E-Mail: paul.price@rapp.com.*

PRICE, PAUL L., lawyer; b. Chgo., Apr. 21, 1945; s. Walter S. and Lillian (Czerepkowski) L.; m. Dianne L. Olech, June 3, 1967; children: Kristen, Kathryn. BBA, Loyola U., Chgo., 1967; JD with honors, Chgo. Kent IIT, 1971. Bar: Ill. 1971, U.S. Dist. Ct. (no. dist.) Ill., U.S. Ct. Appeals (7th cir.). Tax acct. Arthur Anderson & Co., Chgo., 1970—71; assoc. Doyle & Tarpey, Chgo., 1971—75, Gordon & Assocs., Chgo., 1975—76; from assoc. to ptnr. Pretzel & Stouffer, Chartered, Chgo., 1976—96; ptnr. Price, Tunney, Reiter, Chgo., 1996—2007, Hepler Broom LLC, 2007—. With USMC, 1969—70. Fellow: Am. Coll. Trial Lawyers; mem.: Ill. Inst. Tech.-Chgo. Kent Coll. Law Alumni Assn. (pres. 1989—90), Assn. Def. Trial Attys., Lawyers for Civil Justice (bd. dirs. 1999—2001), Def. Rsch. Inst. (bd. dirs. 1999—2001), Fedn. Def. and Corp. Counsel (pres. 1999—2000), Ill. Assn. Def. Trial Counsel (pres. 1990—91), Soc. Trial Lawyers, Ill. Bar Assn. Roman Catholic. Office: Hepler Bloom LLC 150 N Wacker Dr Ste 3100 Chicago IL 60606 Home Phone: 847-253-3896; Office Phone: 312-230-9100. Business E-Mail: plprice@heplerbroom.com.

PRICE, PENRY, advertising executive; BA, Hobart Coll., Geneva, NY. Various advt. sales positions including ea. advt. dir. Rolling Stone mag.; advt. dir. US Weekly mag.; v.p. advt. sales N.Am. Google Inc., 2004—. Bd. dirs. Boston Ad Club. Bd. advs. Outward Bound USA. Named to Advt. Hall of Achievement, Am. Advt. Fedn., 2008. Office: Google Inc 1600 Amphitheatre Pky Mountain View CA 94043 Office Phone: 650-253-0000. Office Fax: 650-253-0001.*

PRICE, PETER WILFRID, ecology educator, researcher; b. London, Apr. 17, 1938; arrived in U.S., 1966; BSc with honors, U. Wales, Bangor, 1958-62; MSc, U. New Brunswick, Fredericton, 1964; PhD, Cornell U., 1970. Asst. prof. U. Ill., Urbana, 1971-75, assoc. prof., 1975-79; research ecologist Mus. No. Ariz., Flagstaff, 1979-80; assoc. prof. No. Ariz. U., 1980-85, prof. ecology, 1985-94, Regents' prof., 1994—2002, Regents' prof. emeritus, 2002—. Author: Evolutionary Biology of Parasites, 1980, Biological Evolution, 1996, Insect Ecology, 3d edit., 1997, Macroevolutionary Theory on Macroecological Patterns, 2003; editor: Evolutionary Strategies of Parasitic Insects, 1975, A New Ecology, 1984, Plant-Animal Interactions, 1991, Effects of Resource Distribution on Plant-Animal Interactions, 1992, The Ecology and Evolution of Gall-Forming Insects, 1994, Population Dynamics, 1995, Population Dynamics: New Approaches and Synthesis, 1995. Guggenheim fellow, 1977—78, Fulbright Sr. scholar, 1993—94. Fellow: NSF (panel mem. 1978—81, 1991—93), Entomol. Soc. Am. (Founders award 1993), Brit. Ecol. Soc., Ecol. Soc. Am. (bd. editors 1973—76), Royal Entomol. Soc. (hon.). Office: No Ariz U PO Box 5640 Flagstaff AZ 86011-5640

PRICE, RICHARD, writer; b. NYC, Oct. 12, 1949; s. Milton and Harriet (Rosenbaum) Price; m. Judith Hudson; children: Anne, Genevieve. BA, Cornell U., NYC, 1971; MFA, Columbia U., NYC, 1976. Urban studies instr. NYU, 1973; English instr. Hostos Coll., Bronx, 1973, fiction writing instr., 1975, SUNY, Stony Brook, 1974, Binghamton, 1976-77, Hofstra U., 1978-79, Yale U., New Haven, 1979, NYU, 1980-81, Columbia U., 1981. Author: (novels) The Wanderers, 1974, Bloodbrothers, 1976, Ladies Man, 1978, The Breaks, 1983, Clockers, 1992, Freedomland, 1998, Samaritan, 2003, Lush Life, 2008, (screenplays) The Color of Money, 1986, Night and the City, 1989, Kiss of Death, 1995, Clockers, 1995, Ransom, 1996, Shaft, 2000, Freedomland, 2006; writer (TV series) The Wire, 2003—08; exec. prodr.: (films) Mad Dog & Glory, 1993, Ethan Frome, 1993; co-prodr.: Kiss of Death, 1995, Clockers, 1995; contbr. articles to profl. jours. Recipient Lit. award, AAAL, 1999; fellow Mary Roberts Rinehart Found., 1973, NEA, 1981. Mem.: PEN (exec. com. 1979—81), Authors Guild. Jewish. Mailing: c/o Farrar Straus & Giroux 18 W 18th St New York NY 10011*

PRICE, RICHARD EDWARD, lawyer; b. Stanford, Calif., Apr. 30, 1969; s. Richard Maxwell and Mary Frances Price; m. Brook Renee Gauntz, Sept. 14, 2002. BA, U. Mass., 1991; JD, George Washington U., 1994; LLM, Cambridge U., England, 1995. Bar: N.Y. 1995, Mass. 1995, D.C. 1996, U.S. Ct. Appeals (D.C. cir.) 1997. Atty. Koteen & Naftalin LLP, Washington, 1996—99, Vinson & Elkins LLP, Washington, 1999—2005; assoc. gen. counsel One Comm. Corp., Rochester, NY, 2005—08; sr. counsel Global Crossing Telecom. Inc., Rochester, NY, 2008—. Mem.: Genesee Valley Club. Office: Global Crossing Telecom Inc 225 Kenneth Dr Rochester NY 14623

PRICE, RICHARD H., physics professor; b. NYC, Mar. 1, 1943; m. Betsy Mitchell, Sept. 13, 1993; 1 child, Gavrielle M. MS in Engring., Cornell U., Ithaca, NY, 1965; PhD, Caltech, Pasadena, Calif., 1971. Prof. Dept Physics, U. Utah, Salt Lake City, 1971—2004, CGWA, U.Tex., Brownsville, 2004—. Contbr. articles to profl. jours., chapters to books. Grant, NSF, 1971—2009, NASA, 2003—08. Fellow: APS. Home: 13 Creekbend Dr Brownsville TX 78521 Office: Ctr Gravitational Wave Astronomy UT Brownsville 80 Fort Brown Brownsville TX 78520

PRICE, ROBERT, media and communications executive, investment banker, lawyer; b. NYC, Aug. 27, 1932; s. Solomon and Frances (Berger) P.; m. Margery Beth Wiener, Dec. 18, 1955 (div.); children: Eileen Marcia, Steven. AB, NYU, 1953; LLD, Columbia U., 1958. Bar: NY 1958, U.S. Dist. Ct. 1958, U.S. Ct. Appeals 1958, U.S. Supreme Ct. 1958, ICC: 1958, FCC: 1958, IRS: 1958. With R.H. Macy & Co., Inc., 1955-58; practiced in NYC, 1958—; law clk. to judge U.S. Dist. Ct. (so. dist.) N.Y., 1958-59; asst. U.S. atty. So. Dist. N.Y., 1959-60; ptnr. Kupferman & Price, 1960-65; dep. mayor NYC, 1965-66; exec. v.p., dir. Dreyfus Corp., NYC, 1966-69; v.p., investment officer Dreyfus Fund, until 1969; gen. ptnr. Lazard, Freres & Co., 1972-82; pres. N.Y. Law Jour., Nat. Law Jour.; pres., treas., dir. Price Comm. Corp., 1979—; chmn., pres., dir. PriCellular Corp., 1988-95; pres., dir. TLM Corp., 1989—2000. Mem. adv. com. Bankers Trust Co. N.Y.; chmn. N.Y.C. Port Authority Negotiating Com. for World Trade Ctr., 1965-66; spl. counsel N.Y. State Joint Legis. Com. on Ct. Reorgn.; asst. counsel N.Y. State Joint Legis. Com. on N.Y. Banking Laws; mem. The N.Y. State Mcpl. Assistance Corp., 1996-2000; commr. N.Y. State Commn. of Investigations, N.Y.C., 2000—. Contbr. articles to profl. publs. Trustee CUNY, 1996-98; chmn. govt. and civil svc. divsn. United Jewish Appeal Greater NY, 1966; co-chmn. met. NY blood drive ARC, 1966; campaign mgr. John V. Lindsay, Campaigns for Congressman, NYC, 1958, 60, 62, 64, for Nelson A. Rockefeller Oreg. Rep. presdl. primary campaign, 1964, Lindsay campaign for mayor, NYC, 1965; del. NY Rep. State Conv., 1962, 66; del. Rep. Nat. Conv., 1988, 92, 96; lectr. Rep. Nat. Com., 1966; bd. dirs. Am. Friends Hebrew U.; past trustee Columbia U. Sch. Pharm. Scis. With US Army, 1953-55. Recipient Yeshiva U. Heritage award, Pub. Svc. award, Queens Catholic War Vets. Mem. ABA, FCC Bar Assn., Assn. Bar City NY, NY State Dist. Attys. Assn., Coun. Fgn. Rels., Columbia Law Sch. Alumni Assn. (dir.). Home: 25 E 86th St New York NY 10028-0553 Office: Price Communications Corp 25 E 86th St New York NY 10028-0553 Office Phone: 212-427-4242.

PRICE, ROBERT EBEN, judge; b. Waco, Tex., Jan. 13, 1931; s. Robert Eben and Mary Hamilton (Barnett) P.; m. Ann Hodges, June 4, 1954; children— Eben, Mary, Ann, Emily. BA, So. Methodist U., 1952, JD, 1954, LL.M., 1972; postgrad., Air War Coll., 1976. Bar: Tex. 1954, U.S. Supreme Ct., U.S. Ct. Mil. Appeals, U.S. Ct. Claims, U.S. Dist. Ct. (no. dist.) Tex. 1954. Mem. firm Taylor, Mizell, Price, Corrigan & Smith, Dallas, 1956-86; judge Dallas County Probate Ct. No. 2, 1986—. Lectr. continuing legal edn. program U. Houston Law Found., 1993—; lectr. law So. Meth. U. Law Sch., 1973-74, faculty paralegal cert. program Sch. Continuing Edn., 1987-89; lectr. practice skills program State Bar Tex., 1974-78. Editor-in-chief: Southwestern Law Jour., 1953-54. Trustee and sec. St. Michael and All Angels Found., 1984-88; bd. dirs. Downtown Ministry, Diocese of Dallas Episcopal, 1986-88; chmn. legis. and legal awareness subcom., vice chmn. Tex. Gov.'s Com. on Employment of Handicapped, 1978-82. Served as legal officer USAF, 1954-56; col. JAGC Res. ret. Fellow: Tex. Bar Found., Am. Coll. Trust and Estate Counsel; mem.: ABA (nat. conf. spl. ct. judges com. on probate and surrogates cts. 1992—), Tex. Coll. Probate Judges (mem. faculty), State Bar Tex. (lectr. profl. devel. program 1988—), Dallas Bar Assn., Coll. State Bar Tex., Nat. Coll. Probate Judges, Phi Delta Theta, Phi Eta Sigma, Phi Alpha Delta. Episcopalian. Home: 4300 Arcady Ave Dallas TX 75205-3704 Office: Probate Ct 2 ste 211 509 Main St Dallas TX 75202-3508 Home Phone: 214-528-9518; Office Phone: 214-653-7138.

PRICE, ROBERT F., lawyer; BS in Acctg., Loyola Coll., 1969; JD, U. NC, 1974. Bar: Md. 1974. Asst. gen. counsel USF&G; mng. dir., gen. counsel Alex Brown & Sons, Inc.; sr. v.p., gen. counsel Legg Mason, Inc., Boston, 1998—. Mem. exec. com. compliance and legal divisn. Securities Industry Assn., mem. fed. regulation com.; mem. legal adv. bd. NASD; bd. dirs. St. Ignatious Loyola Acad. Office: Legg Mason Cds Inv Serv PO Box 55214 Boston MA 02205-5214 Office Phone: 410-539-0000. E-mail: rfprice@leggmason.com.

PRICE, ROBERT IRA, coast guard officer; b. NYC, Sept. 22, 1921; s. Alfred and Mary Edna (Schweitzer) P.; m. Virginia Louise Miller, June 20, 1946; children: Andrea Jean, Keven Virginia. BBA, CCNY, 1942; BS, U.S. Coast Guard Acad., 1945; postgrad., M.I.T., 1950-53. Registered profl. engr., D.C. Commd. ensign U.S. Coast Guard, 1945, advanced through grades to vice adm., 1978; asst. chief Mcht. Marine Tech. Div., Washington, 1965-67; chief planning staff Office Mcht. Marine Safety, 1967-71; capt. Port of Phila., 1971-73; chief Office Marine Environ. Washington, 1974-76; comdr. 11th Coast Guard Dist. Long Beach, Calif., 1976-78; comdr. Atlantic Area and 3d Coast Guard Dist. NYC, 1978-81; ret., 1981; sr. v.p. J.J. Henry Co. (marine engrs.), NYC, 1981-86; maritime cons., 1986—. Prin. U.S. negotiator to tech. programs Intergovtl. Maritime Consultative Orgn., UN, 1962-71 Contbg. author: Ship Design and Construction, 1980; Contbr. articles to profl. jours. Decorated D.S.M. with gold star, Legion of Merit with gold star, Meritorious Service medal with gold star, Coast Guard Commendation medal. Fellow Royal Instn. Naval Architects, Soc. Naval Architects (Land medalist 1982); mem. Sigma Xi. Clubs: Propeller, Army Navy, N.Y. Yacht. Office Phone: 321-751-4666.

PRICE, ROBERT STANLEY, lawyer; b. Phila., Jan. 21, 1937; s. Benjamin and Estelle B. (Muchnick) P.; m. Emilie W. Kirschbaum, June 27, 1965 (dec. Mar. 1998); children: Louise P. Kelly, Marianna R. BA, Kenyon Coll., 1958; LLB, Yale U., 1961. Bar: Pa. 1963, U.S. Dist. Ct. (ea. dist.) Pa. 1963, U.S. Ct. Appeals (3d cir.) 1963, N.Y. 1993. Assoc. Dechert, Price & Rhoads, Phila., 1961-63; asst tax atty. Smith, Kline & French, Phila., 1963-67; tax atty. Pa. Ctrl. Transp. Co., Phila., 1967-70; tax counsel IU Internat., Phila., 1970-72; ptnr. Townsend, Elliott & Munson, Phila., 1972-76, Pepper, Hamilton & Scheetz, Phila., 1977-86, Saul, Ewing, Remick & Saul, Phila., 1986-93; spl. cons. Saul, Ewing, Remick & Saul (now Saul Ewing LLP), Phila., 1994—2001. Ind. tax cons. Fischbein-Badillo-Wagner-Harding, NYC, 1998—2001, Mintz, Levin, Cohn, Ferris, Glovsky and Popeo, P.C., NYC, 2001—. Author: ABCs of Industrial Development Bonds, 1981, 5th edit., 1990; contbr. articles to profl. jours. Pres. Samuel Eells Lit. and Ednl. Found., 1980—2007. With US Army, 1961—62. Mem. ABA (tax exempt fin. com.), Pa. Bar, Phila. Bar Assn., N.Y. Bar, Racquet Club Phila. (v.p. 1987-88), Alpha Delta Phi (pres. 1975-78). Office: 3800 Centre Sq W Philadelphia PA 19102-2186 E-mail: rpricedj@verizon.net.

PRICE, SIMANI MOHAPATRA, research scientist, director; d. Manindra and Urmila Mohapatra; m. Jeffrey L. Price, May 16, 1987; children: George M., Sydney S. PhD, Va. Tech, Blacksburg, 1996. Sr. study dir. Westat, Rockville, 2005—. Office: Westat 1650 Rsch Blvd Rockville MD 20850 Business E-Mail: simaniprice@westat.com.

PRICE, STEVEN, venture capitalist, communications executive, lawyer; b. NYC, Feb. 14, 1962; s. Robert and Margery Price; m. Tina Gitlin, Mar. 16, 1991. BS magna cum laude, Brown U., 1984; JD, Columbia U. Sch. Law, 1989. Spl. asst. to US Amb. to the START Talks in Geneva US Dept. State, 1989—90; assoc. Davis Polk & Wardell, 1991; with mergers and acquisitions group Goldman, Sachs & Co.; COO PriCellular Corp., 1994—97, bd. dirs., 1996, pres., CEO, 1997—2001; deputy asst. sec. def. spectrum and command, control and communications policy US Dept. Def., 2001—03; pres., CEO LiveWire Capital, 2003—04; gen.

partner Spectrum Equity Investors, 2004—. Dir. Met. Coun. Poverty, 1999—, UJA Fedn. NY, 2000—, US Nat. Archives Bd., 2003—; advisory bd. for computing and IT Brown U., 2003—; cons. Office Sec. Def. and Def. Sci. Bd., 2003—. Co-founder Brown U. Ctr. for Combat Casualty Recovery. Mem.: ABA, Bar Assn. Wash., DC, Assn. Bar NY, Phi Beta Kappa.

PRICE, THEODORA HADZISTELIOU, mental health services professional; b. Athens, Greece, Oct. 1, 1938; arrived in U.S., 1967; d. Ioannis and Evangelia (Emmanuel) Hadzisteliou; m. David C. Long Price, Dec. 26, 1966 (div. 1989); children: Morgan N., Alkes D. L. Diploma in piano tchg., Nat. Conservatory, Athens, 1958; BA in History/Archaeology, U. Athens, 1961; DPhil, U. Oxford, Eng., 1966; MA in Clin. Social Work, U. Chgo., 1988. LCSW, bd. cert. diplomate in clin. social work. Mus. asst., resident tutor U. Sydney, 1966-67; instr. anthropology Adelphi U., NYC, 1967-68; archaeologist Hebrew Union Coll., Gezer, Israel, 1968; asst. prof. classical archaeology/art U. Chgo., 1968-70; jr. rsch. fellow Harvard Ctr. Hellenic Studies, Washington, 1970-71; clin. social worker Harbor Light Ctr., Salvation Army, Chgo., 1988-89; therapist Inst. Motivational Devel., Lombard, Ill., 1989-90; caseworker & therapist Jewish Family & Cmty. Svc., Chgo., 1989—90; staff therapist Family Svc. Ctrs. of South Cook County, Chicago Heights, 1990-91; pvt. practice child, adolescent, family therapy Bolingbrook, Ill., 1991—; dir. counseling svcs., clin. supr., psychotherapist Family Link, Inc., Chgo., 1993; staff therapist Cen. Bapt. Family Svcs., Gracell Rehab., Chgo., 1991, 91-92; casework supr., counselor Epilepsy Found. Greater Chgo., Chgo., 1992-93; therapist children, adolescents and families dept. foster care Cath. Charities, Chgo., 1993-94; individual and family therapist South Ctrl. Cmty. Svcs. Individual-Family Counseling Svcs., Chgo. Heights, 1994-97. Bd. dirs., counselor Naperville Sch. Gifted and Talented, 1982—84; lectr. in field. Author: (monograph) Kourotrophos, Cults and Representations of the Greek Nursing Deities, 1978; contbr. articles to profl. jours. Eleutherios Venizelos scholar, 1962—65, Meyerstein Traveling grantee, Oxford, Eng., 1963, 1964. Mem.: NASW, Am. Bd. Clin. Soc. Workers, Ill. Clin. Social Workers, Nat. Acad. Clin. Social Workers. Avocations: piano, Byzantine chanting, writing. Home and Office: 10 Pebble Ct Bolingbrook IL 60440-1557 Office Phone: 630-378-1187. *Nobody stands alone, for each of us partakes and contributes to universal energy and creation. Every thought or action has progressively timeless impact. Therefore, working in helping people is influencing the flow of creation.*

PRICE, THOMAS E., United States Representative from Georgia; b. Lansing, Mich., Oct. 8, 1954; m. Elizabeth; 1 child, Robert. Bachelor's, MD, U. Mich. Intern in surgery Emory U. Affiliated Hosps., resident in orthop. surgery; founder Compass Orthop. (formerly North Fulton Orthop. Clinic); mem. Ga. Senate, Atlanta, 1996—2004, majority leader, 2002—03; mem. US Congress from 6th Ga. dist., 2005—; mem. Edn. and Workforce com., Fin. Svcs. com. Rep. health care task force Am. Legis. Enterprise Coun.; bd. dirs. Northside Bank. Mem. bd. dirs. North Metro YMCA; active Roswell Presbyn. Ch., Ga. Ensemble Theatre, Chattahoochee Nature Ctr. Mem. Rotary (bd. dirs.). Republican. Presbyterian. Office: US Ho Reps 506 Cannon Ho Office Bldg Washington DC 20515-1006 also: Dist Office Ste 50 3750 Roswell Rd Marietta GA 30062 Office Phone: 202-225-4501. Office Fax: 202-225-4656.*

PRICE, THOMAS MUNRO, computer consultant, retired; b. Madison, Wis., Oct. 2, 1937; s. John Edward and Georgia Winifred (Day) P.; m. Judith Ann Holm, Aug. 8, 1959; children: Scott Michael, Andrea Lynn. BS, Carroll Coll., Waukesha, Wis., 1959; MS, U. Wis., 1961, PhD, 1964. Prof. math. U. Iowa, 1964-77, U. Wyo., Laramie, 1978-79, computer user cons., 1979-85, MIS prof., 1985-89; computer cons., 1989—; home rebuilder Pecos, N.Mex., 1994-97; historic home renovator Yerington, Nev., 1997—. Contbr. articles to profl. jours. Mem.: Yerington Rotary (pres. 2006—07, co-pres. 2008—). Home: Nordyke House 727 State Rt 339 Yerington NV 89447

PRICE, TIMOTHY R., accountant; b. Reigate, Eng., Jan. 26, 1943; m. Frances Baird; 4 children. BA, U. Victoria, Can., 1964. Chartered acct. Touche Ross & Co., Montreal, 1965-69; pres., COO Mico Enterprises Ltd., 1970-80; pres., CEO Hees Internat. Bancorp Inc., Toronto, 1980-88, mng. ptnr., chmn., 1988—96; chmn. The Edper Group Ltd., Toronto, 1997, Trilon Fin. Corp., Toronto, 1997—2002, Brascan Fin. Corp., Toronto, 2002—04, Funds Mgmt. Brookfield Asset Mgmt. Inc., Toronto, 2005—. Bd. dirs. Astral Media Inc., Brookfield Homes Corp., HSBC Bank Can., Can. Tire Corp. Ltd.; chmn. York U. Found., 1997—. Bd. dirs. St. Michael's Hosp. Found., Ctr. for Addiction and Mental Health Found. Office: Brookfield Asset Mgmt Inc 51 Yonge St Ste 400 Toronto ON M5E 1J1 Canada Office Phone: 416-363-9491.

PRICE, TOM, journalist; b. Pitts., May 26, 1946; s. H. Samuel and Anna Mae (Nicholson) P.; m. Susan Crites; 1 child, Julianna Margaret. BS in Journalism, Ohio U., 1968. Writer, editor Athens (Ohio) Messenger, 1968-73; freelance writer, 1973-75; politics writer Dayton (Ohio) Jour. Herald, 1975-82; corr. Washington bur. Cox Newspapers, Washington, 1982-96; freelance writer politics, govt., tech., bus. and edn., 1996—; Washington columnist Optics and Photonics News, 2002—; contbg. writer Congl. Quar. Rschr., 2004—. Author: Frommer's Washington, D.C. for Dummies, 2003, 4th edit., 2007, The Irreverent Guide to Washington, DC, 2005, 6th edit., 2007; co-author: (with Susan Crites Price) The Working Parents Help Book, 1994 (Parent's Choice award, Scholastic Book Club selection), rev. edit., 1996, (with Tony Hall) Changing the Face of Hunger, 2006, paperback edit., 2007; co-author Working Solutions Internet Column; nat. newspaper columnist Working Parents Lifeline, 1996-98. Mem.: Washington Ind. Writers, Am. Soc. Journalists and Authors. Avocations: photography, hiking, travel, reading.

PRICE, TRAVIS L., III, architectural firm executive, educator; BA in Western Philosophy & Polit. Econs., St. John's Coll., Annapolis, Md., U. N.Mex., Albuquerque, MArch, Ga. Inst. Tech., Atlanta. Registered architect, NCARB, NY, Fla., Tenn., DC, Mass., Ariz., Va., Md., Colo., N.Mex. Founding prin. Travis Price Architects, Washington; dir., lectr., Spirit of Place/Spirit of Design program Cath. U. Sch. Architecture; co-founder Nat. Ctr. for Appropriate Tech. Lectr. Aix-en-Provence, Sicily, Italy, The Smithsonian, Nat. Geographic Soc., Am. Inst. Architects, ACSA, U. Md., Pratt Inst., Princeton U., Cath. U., Yale U., Carnegie Mellon U., U. N.Mex.; past pres. Am. Inst. Architects, Potomac Valley Chpt.; bd. mem. Md. Am. Inst. Architects, treas.; founding bd. mem., pres. Spirit of Place/Spirit of Design. Contbg. editor: Nat. Geographic TRAVELER Mag.; author: The Archaeology of Tomorrow, 2006; co-author: (with M. Crosbie) Green Architecture, (with P.L. Rao, J. Mahoney) Nature on View, (with J. Naar, N. Skurka) Design for a Limited Planet, (with W.A. Schurcliff) Solar Heated Buildings, (with W. Clark) Energy for Survival, (with J. Trulove, N.R. Green) Hot Dirt Cool Straw, (with J. Trulove) Tree Houses by Architects, Planning & Designing for Innovative Houses-Arid Zones, Golany, Energy Guidelines for Nantucket, Nantucket Hist. Commn.; contbr. articles to profl. jours., newspapers, mags. including Architectural Record, Cosmopolitan, Washington Post, Washingtonian, Progressive Architecture, National Geographic, NY Times, Metropolitan Home, Washington Museum & Arts, others. Mem. Montgomery County Energy Adv. Com.; past pres. Takoma Old Town Bus. Assn.; bd. trustees Washington Adventist Hosp. Recipient numerous design awards, Am. Inst. Architects, 1977—2001, Progressive Architecture Design Citation, 1977, Progressive Architecture Rsch. award, 1986, Disting. Svc. award, Energy Seminars; named Alumnae of Yr., St. John's Coll., 1996. Office: Travis Price Architects 1111 34th St NW # 320 Washington DC 20007 Office Phone: 202-965-7000. Office Fax: 202-965-6161. Business E-Mail: Travis@TravisPriceArchitects.com.*

PRICE, VERNON L., biological studies educator; b. Athens, Tex., Dec. 26, 1940; s. Thomas Harvie and Ada Price; m. Mary Fern Glover, Aug. 11, 1943; children: Danny Lynn, Tammy Renay Pruitt. AS, Henderson County Jr. Coll., Athens, Tex., 1961; BS, East Tex. State U., Commerce, Tex., 1963, MS, 1969; PhD, Tex. A&M Commerce, 1971. Rsch. and product dev. Morton Foods, Gen. Mills, Farmers Branch, Tex., 1964—67, corp. quality control mgr. Dallas, 1967—69; prof. Trinity Valley CC, Athens, Tex., 1969—. Author: (instructional pamphlet) What Every Student Should Know about Studying But Didn't Know To Ask, Candida Albicans: A Yeast Pathagen. Charter bd. mem. YMCA, Athens, Tex., 1974—78. Recipient Tchg. Excellence award, Trinity Valley CC, 2000. Conservative. Achievements include development of fermentation techniques to prevent damage from yeast activity in cucumber fermentations; pure culture fermentation of kosher dills (in Jar). Home: 210 Guadalupe Cir Athens TX 75751 Office: Trinity Valley CC 100 Cardinal Dr Athens TX 75751

PRICE, VINCENT EDWARD, academic administrator, communications and political science professor; s. Edward and Joan Price; m. Annette Newmeyer, July 23, 1983; children: Sarah, Alexander. BA magna cum laude, Santa Clara U., Calif., 1979; AM, Stanford U., 1985, PhD in Comm., 1987. Asst. dir. admissions Santa Clara U., Calif., 1981—83, adj. lectr. Dept. Theater Arts, 1982, survey cons., 1984; asst. prof. Dept. Comm. U. Mich., Ann Arbor, 1987—93, assoc. chair, 1991—95, faculty assoc. Ctr. for Polit. Studies, Inst. Social Rsch., 1987—98, assoc. prof., 1993—98, chair Dept. Comm. Studies, 1995—98; assoc. prof. Anneberg Sch. Comm., U. Pa., Phila., 1998—2004, assoc. dean undergraduate studies, 2005—07, prof., Steven H. Chaffee term chair comm. and polit. sci., 1999—; assoc. prof. Dept. Polit. Sci. U. Pa., Phila., 2001—04, prof., 2004—, assoc. provost faculty affairs, 2007—09, interim provost, 2009, provost, 2009—. Vis. scholar Faculty Comm. Sci. U. Amsterdam, Netherlands, 1995; vis. prof. Ctr. Applied Literary and Scientific Studies U. Paris Sorbonne, 2009; spkr. in field. Author: (book) Public Opinion, 1992; editor in chief Pub. Opinion Quarterly, 1998—2002; contbr. articles to profl. jours. Recipient Robert M. Worchester award, World Assn. Pub. Opinion Rsch., 1997; grantee, Pew Charitable Trusts, NSF, 1999—2006; fellow, Stanford U., 1983—87. Mem.: World Assn. Pub. Opinion Rsch., Am. Polit. Sci. Assn., Am. Assn. Pub. Opinion Rsch., Internat. Comm. Assn., Alpha Sigma Nu. Office: Annenberg Sch for Comm U Pa 3620 Walnut St Philadelphia PA 19104-6220 also: Office of Provost U Pa 122 College Hall Philadelphia PA 19104-6303 Office Phone: 215-573-1963. Business E-Mail: vprice@asc.upenn.edu.*

PRICE, WILLIAM JAMES, IV, investment banker; b. Balt., Oct. 6, 1924; s. William James 3d and Frances (Robbins) P.; m. Marjorie Beard, Dec. 6, 1952; children: Marjorie, Jonathan Robbins, William James V, Juliet Robbins. BS, Yale U., 1949. Propr. Price & Co., 1949-52; with Alex. Brown & Sons, Balt., 1952-98, gen. partner, 1959-84, mng. dir., 1984-89; vice chmn. Vanns Spices, Ltd. Chmn. Sonitrol Security Svcs., Inc., NC. Trustee Union Meml. Hosp. Found., Washington Coll., St. Paul's Sch. and St. Paul's Sch. for Girls, Eugene B. Casey Found. With inf. AUS, 1943—46, ETO. Decorated Bronze Star, Purple Heart with oak leaf cluster, Combat Infantry badge. Mem.: Nat. Assn. Securities Dealers (bd. govs. 1964—66, vice chmn. 1966).

PRICE, WILLIAM RAY, JR., state supreme court chief judge; b. Fairfield, Iowa, Jan. 30, 1952; s. William Ray and Evelyn Jean (Darnell) P.; m. Susan Marie Trainor, Jan. 4, 1975; children: Emily Margret, William Joseph Dodds. BA with distinction, U. Iowa, 1974; postgrad., Yale U., 1974-75; JD cum laude, Washington and Lee U., 1978. Bar: Mo. 1978, U.S. Dist. Ct. (we. dist.) Mo. 1978, U.S. Ct. Claims 1978, U.S. Ct. Appeals (8th cir.) 1985. Assoc. Lathrop & Norquist, Kansas City, Mo., 1978-84, ptnr., 1984-92, chmn. bus. litigation sect., 1987-88, 90-92, exec. com., 1989-92; judge Mo. Supreme Ct., Jefferson City, 1992—, chief justice, 1999—2001, 2009—. G.L.V. Zumwalt monitoring com. U.S. Dist. Ct. (we. dist.) Mo., Kansas City. Pres. Kansas City Bd. Police Commrs.; mem. Together Ctr. & Family Devel. Ctr., Kansas City; chmn. merit selection com. U.S. marshal Western Dist. of Mo., Kansas City; bd. dirs. Truman Med. Ctr., Kansas City. Rockefeller fellow, 1974-75; Burks scholar Washington & Lee U., 1976. Mem. Christian Ch. Office: Supreme Ct Mo PO Box 150 207 W High St Jefferson City MO 65102-0150*

PRICE, WILLIAM WALLEY, JR., counselor, artist; b. Providence, May 21, 1957; s. William Walley and Betty Price; m. Danijela Milicevic, July 7, 2001. BFA in Illustration, RI Sch. Design, Providence, 1979, postgrad., 1999—2000. Counselor Amos Ho., Providence, 1988—. Tchr. art Amos Ho., 1988—97, carpenter, 1988—97, dir. men's shelter, 1988—95. Poet (collection of poetry fom various poets) Songs of Honour, (collection of poetry from various poets) Labours of Love, (collection of poetry) The Colors of Life (Editor's Choice award, 2003), A Surrender to the Moon (Editor's Choice award, 2005), (collection of poetry form various poets) Great Poems of the Western World, (cd's (seven in all) The Sound Of Poetry, The League of American Poets, Centres of Expression, photographer (collection of photography) Colours of the World, photography (collection of photographers) Internat. Libr. Photography (Best Photos, 03, 2005, Editor's Choice award). Mem. ACLU, Providnce, RI, 2004—06, So. Poverty Law Ctr., Montegomery, Ala., 2002—06. Recipient First Black Eagle Scout, Boy Scouts of Am., 1975; named one of The Best Poems and Poets, 2004, 2005, 2007. Democrat. Achievements include design of public library bookmobile bus. Avocations: fishing, travel, computers. Home: 135 Providence St Providence RI 02907 Office: 415 Friendship St Providence RI 02907 Personal E-mail: williamprice388@hotmail.com.

PRICE BODAY, MARY KATHRYN, choreographer, small business owner, educator; b. Ft. Bragg, NC, May 20, 1945; d. Max Edward and Katharine Jordan Price; m. Les Boday (div. 1982); children: Shawn Leon Boday, Irmali Ferecho Boday; m. Richard A. Weil, May 1, 1986. BFA, U. Okla., 1968, MFA, 1970; studies with David Howard, 1972-74. Soloist dancer Mary Anthony Dance Co., NYC, 1971-74, Larry Richardson Dance Co., NYC, 1971-73; dancer Pearl Lang Dance Co., NYC, 1971-73, Gaku Dance Theater, NYC, 1972-74; ballet mistress and soloist dancer St. Gallen Ballet, Switzerland, 1974-75; dancer, tchr. Zurich Ballet, Switzerland, 1975-76; asst. prof. U. Ill., Champaign-Urbana, 1976-79; artist-in-residence Cornish Inst., Seattle, 1979-80; pres. The Dance Works, Inc., Seattle, 1981-90; dir. Seahurst Ballet, 1982-84; pres. The Dance Works, Inc., Erie, Pa., 1990-94; dir. dance dept., asst. prof. Mercyhurst Coll., Erie, Pa., 1990-94; dir. Peoria Ballet, 1994-99; asst. prof. Bradley U., Peoria, 1994—; dir. Ill. Ballet (formerly Ctrl. Ill. Ballet), 1999—; assoc. prof. Ann Lacy Sch. Am. Dance and Arts Mgmt., Oklahoma City U. Tchr. Harkness Ballet NY, Mary Anthony Dance Sch., Zurich Ballet, Nat. Acad. Arts Ill., Summer Dance lab., Kneeland Workshops, Port Townsend, Wash., 1968, Pa. Gov.'s Sch. of Arts, 1991, 92, 94, Dance Masters Am., 2006, Okla. Dance Masters, 2006; tchr., choreographer Jefferson HS Performing Arts, Portland; choreographer Mary K. Price Dance Co., U. Ill., Nat. Acad. Arts, Cornish Inst., Seahurst Ballet; tchr., co-dir. Kneeland Seminars, Las Vegas, Nev., Port Townsend, 1989, Port Townsend, 90, Oklahoma City U., 1990, Am. Coll. Dance Festival, 1991—93; tchr. David Howard summer workshop Mercyhurst Coll., 1992, Tulsa Ballet Theatre, 1993, 94; tchr. David Howard workshop Seattle tchrs., 1996, U. Ill., 1997, Western Mich. U., 1999; guest artist, asst. prof. Slippery Rock U., 1994; owner Dance Works, Peoria, Ill., 1994—; guest artist So. Ballet Theatre, 2000, 01, David Howard and Mary Price Boday Summer Intensives, Worcester, 2000—02, Mt. Hood Ballet Acad., 2002—03; lectr. Knox Coll., 2000—; assoc. prof. Oklahoma City U., 2005—; dir., workshop tchr. Ann Lacy Sch. Am. Dance and Arts Mgmt., 2006—07; guest tchr. Dance Master America, 2009. Choreographer (ballets) Ballet Co. St. Gallen, 1988, The Nutcracker, Warner Theater Erie, Peoria Ballet, 1995, Texarkana Ballet, 2006, Gloria, Ill. Ballet with Bradley U. Chorale, 2002, Liebeslieder Waltzes, 2003, Carmina Burana, 2005, 30 Yr. Gala, 1995, Alice in Wonderland, 1996, Little Mermaid of Lake Peoria, 1997, Rudolph the Red Nose Reindeer, Ill. Ballet, Shrine Mosque, 2000, Evanston Dance Ctr., 2004, Rock Ballet, Peoria Civic Ctr. Theatre, The Lion, Witch, and Wardrobe, 2001, Sleeping Beauty, 2003, Hansel and Gretel, 2002, Power of Dance, 2002, Coppella, 2002, Nat. Ballet Panama, 2003, Mary & Friends, Seattle, 1990, co-choreographer (ballets) The Nutcracker Ballet, 1991—93, Coppella, 1993, The Little Mermaid of Lake Erie, Warner Theater, 1994, staged Swan Lake, 1999, 2004. Recipient Outstanding Dancer award, U. Okla., 1968; named one of Outstanding Young Women of Am., 1977, 25 Women in Leadership, Week TV, 2003. Office: Ann Lacy Sch Am Dance and Arts Mgmt Okla City Univ 2501 N Blackwelder Oklahoma City OK 73106 Office Phone: 405-208-5523. Home Fax: 908-673-1179. Business E-Mail: mboday@okcu.edu.

PRICHARD, JOHN DAVID, minister; b. Burnwell, W.Va., July 19, 1948; s. Joseph and Agnes Arvada (Fisher) P.; m. Drema Kay Clark, Apr. 11, 1970; children: Angela Kay, John David II. AB, Nazarene Bible Coll., 1980; postgrad., U. Bibl. Studies, Bethany, Okla., 1989; BA in Biblical Studies, Am. Bible Coll. and Sem., 2000, postgrad., 2003, Masters Sem., Evansville, Ind., 2007. Ordained minister Ch. of the Nazarene, 1981. Pastor, zone youth dir. Dille (W.Va.) Ch. of the Nazarene, 1975-77; pastor Craigsville (W.Va.) Ch. of the Nazarene, 1980-82, Walton (W.Va.) Ch. of the Nazarene, 1982-84, Marion (Va.) Ch. of the Nazarene, 1984-88, Beckley (W.Va.) First Ch. of the Nazarene, 1988-95, Charleston (W.Va.) South Hills Ch. of the Nazarene, 1995—; rep. Nazarene Pub. House, Kansas City, Mo., 2007. Ch. planter Va. Dist., Wytheville, 1985-86; area coord. Va. Nazarene Dist., Marion, 1987-88; dist. adult dir. W.Va. South Dist., 1990-99; cafeteria mgr. W.Va. Dist. Campgrounds, 1990—2006; dist. coll. recruiter Nazarene Bible Coll., Colorado Springs, Colo., 1990-95; small ch. growth trainer W.Va. South Dist. Ch. of the Nazarene; Sunday sch. chmn. W.Va. South Dist. Ch. of the Nazarene, 1999—2007. Chmn. Libr. Commn., Walton, W.Va., 1983-84; dir. Weekday Religious Edn. Program, Marion, 1985-86; co-chair Greater Beckley Area Crusade, 1993; mem. Beckley Ministerial Assn.; vol. hospice chaplain Raleigh County Hospice Group, 1993-95. With USN, 1966-70, Vietnam. Recipient Gt. Commn. Leadership award W.Va. South Dist., 1990, Second Mile award W.Va. South Sunday Sch. Ministries, 1998, W.Va. South Dist. Disting. Svc. award, 2006; named Alumnus of Yr., W.Va. South Dist., Nazarene Bible Coll., Colorado Springs, 1990. Mem. Am. Acad. Ministry. Democrat. Office: South Hills Ch of the Nazarene 1565 Smith Rd Charleston WV 25314-2326 E-mail: johnprichard@suddenlink.net.

PRICHARD, MARK NEAL, virologist, educator; s. Neal Wayne and Patricia Ann Prichard; m. Lynn Ellis Prichard, June 18, 1988; children: Joshua Ellis, Brian Ellis. PhD in Microbiology and Immunology, U. Mich., Ann Arbor, 1992; BS, U. Minn. Rsch. scientist Hybridon Pharms., 1996—97, Iconix Pharms., 1997—99; sr. scientist MedImmune Vaccies, Mountain View, Calif., 1999—2003; assoc. prof. U. Ala., Birmingham, 2002—. Cons. in field. Contbr. articles to profl. jours. Achievements include patents for in the field of virology. Avocations: gardening, fishing, woodworking. Office: Univ Ala 1600 6th Ave S Birmingham AL 35233-1711

PRICHARD, VINCENT MARVIN, lawyer; b. Kirksville, Mo., July 16, 1946; s. George William and Mary Elizabeth (Love) P. BS, U. Colo., 1969; JD, U. Denver, 1974. Bar: Colo. 1975, U.S. Dist. Ct. Colo. 1975. Atty. Bur. Hearings and Appeals Social Security Adminstrn., Denver, 1975-79; asst. regional counsel Dept. Energy, Lakewood, Colo., 1979-82; atty. Fed. Legal Info. Through Electronics, Denver, 1982-93; info. tech. profl. U. Colo. Health Scis. Ctr., Denver, 1994-99; info. tech. mgr. Colo. Water Conservation Bd., Denver, 2000—04, ret., 2004. With U.S. Army, 1969-71. Mem. Colo. Bar Assn., 1st Jud. Dist. Bar Assn. Home: PO Box 3520 Evergreen CO 80437-3520

PRICKETT, DAVID CLINTON, physician; b. Fairmont, W.Va., Nov. 26, 1918; s. Clinton Everett and Mary Anna (Gottschalk) Prickett; m. Mary Ellen Holt, June 29, 1940 (dec. Feb. 1987); children: David C., Rebecca Ellen, William Radcliffe, Mary Anne, James Thomas, Sara Elizabeth; m. Pamela S. Blackstone, Nov. 17, 1991 (dec. Mar. 2002). Student, Fairmont State Coll., 1940—42; AB, W.Va. U., 1944; MD, U. Louisville, 1946; MPH, U. Pitts., 1955. Pres. Prickett Chem. Co., 1938-43; acct. W.Va. Conservation Commn. and Fed. Works Agy., 1941, 42; lab. asst., instr. chemistry W.Va. U., 1943; intern Louisville Gen. Hosp., 1947; surg. resident St. Joseph's Hosp., Parkersburg, W.Va., 1948-49; gen. practice W.Va., 1948-50, 55-61; mem. staff Fairmont (W.Va.) Gen. Hosp., 1955-60, Fairmont Emergency Hosp., 1955-60; physician USAF, N.Mex. and Calif., 1961-62, U.S. Army, Fort Ord, Calif., 1963-64; resident physician San Luis Obispo County Hosp., 1965-66; pvt. practice LA, 1967—; mem. staff St. Francis Hosp., LA, 1970-71; physician So. Calif. Edison Co., 1981-84. Physician Bethlehem Mines Corp., Idamay, W.Va., 1956; resident physician Sedgwick County Hosp., Wichita, Kans., 1964-65; med. dir. South Gate auto assembly plant GM, 1969-71; staff physician City of LA, 1971-76; relief med. practice Appalachia summer seasons, W.Va. and Ky., 1977, 86, 88-97. Author: The Newer Epidemiology, 1962, rev., 1990, Public Health, A Science Resolvable by Mathematics, 1965; contbr. articles to profl. jours. Sr. counsellor, US Commercial Travelers, Fairmont, W.Va., 1939-40; med. officer USPHS, Navajo Indian Reservation, Tohatchi (N.Mex.) Health Ctr., 1953-55, surgeon, res. officer, 1957-59; pres. W.Va. Pub. Health Assn., 1951-52; sec. indsl. and pub. health sect. W.Va. Med. Assn., 1956; W.Va. dist. 4 health officer; health officer Marion County, W.Va., 1951-53; dist. health officer Allegheny County, Pa., 1957; officer Aux. Civil Def. Police, W.Va., 1942; med. advisor Boy Scouts Am., W.Va., 1956-57, N.Mex., 1954; mem. Med. Rsv. Corps of LA, 2005—. 2d lt. AUS, 1943-46. Dr. Thomas Parran fellow U. Pitts. Sch. Pub. Health, 1955; named to Hon. Order Ky. Cols. Fellow APHA; mem. AMA, Am. Occupl. Med. Assn., Am. Acad. Family Physicians,

Western Occupl. Med. Assn., Calif. Med. Assn., Los Angeles County Med. Assn., SR, W.Va., Am. Legion, Elks, Sierra Club Calif., Rio Hondo Symphony Guild, Phi Chi. Avocations: photography, amateur radio, square and round dancing, history, church choir. Address: PO Box 4032 Whittier CA 90607-4032 Office Phone: 626-330-4106.

PRICKETT, STEPHEN, retired literature and language professor; b. Freetown, Sierra Leone, June 4, 1939; s. William Ewart and Barbara Browning Prickett; m. Diana Joan Mabbutt, July 20, 1957 (div.); children: Ruth Charlotte, Mark Thomas; m. Patricia Erskine-Hill Prickett, Oct. 4, 2001. Diploma, UK Ministry of Edn., 1962; BA, Trinity Hall, Cambridge, Eng., MA, 1961, PhD, 1967. Lectr., reader English U. Sussex, Brighton, England, 1967—82; prof. English Australian Nat. U., Canberra, 1982—89; regius prof. English lang. & lit. U. Glasgow, Scotland, 1990—2001; vis. prof. Duke U., Durham, 2001—03; dir. Armstrong Browning libr. & Margaret Root Brown, prof. English Baylor U., Waco; Prof. English U. Kent, Canterbury, England, 2008—. Author: (novel) Do It yourself Doom. Recipient Dr. Honoris Causa award, U. Artois, France, 2002, MLA prize, 1987; fellowship, Australian Acad. Humanities, 1984—. Fellow: English Assn. Home: 61 High St Charing Ashford Kent TN27 0LS England Home Phone: 01233-714071. Personal E-mail: stephenprickett@stephenprickett.co.uk.

PRIDGEON, ANTHONY R., science educator; m. Marlene M. Pridgeon. PhD, SUNY, Buffalo, 1982. Secondary sch. tchr. Pub. Schs., 1970—2003; adj. prof. SUNY, 1980—84, Canisius Coll., 1987—89, 2003—. Capt. US Army, Buffalo, 1973—83. Contbr. articles to ednl. jours. Mem.: STANYS. Home: 2550 N French Rd East Amherst NY 14051 Office: Canisius Coll 2001 Main St Buffalo NY 14208

PRIDHAM, THOMAS GRENVILLE, retired microbiologist; b. Chgo., Oct. 10, 1920; s. Grenville and Gladys Etheral (Sloss) P.; m. Phyllis Sue Hokamp, July 1, 1943 (dec. Feb. 1994); children: Pamela Sue, Thomas Foster, Grenville Thomas, Rolf Thomas, Montgomery Thomas; m. Edna Lee Boudreaux, Mar. 6, 1995 (dec. Apr. 2006). BS Chemistry, U. Ill., 1943, PhD Bacteriology, 1949. Instr. bacteriology U. Ill., Champaign-Urbana, 1947; rsch. microbiologist No. Regional Rsch. Lab., USDA, Peoria, Ill., 1948—51, No. Regional Rsch. Lab. USDA, Peoria, 1953—65, U.S. Indsl. Chem., Balt., 1951—52; supr. tech. ops. Acme Vitamins, Inc., Joliet, Ill., 1952—53; sr. rsch. biologist U.S. Borax Rsch. Corp., Anaheim, Calif., 1965—67; supervisory rsch. microbiologist No. Regional Rsch. Ctr. USDA, Peoria, 1967—81, head agrl. rsch. culture collection No. Regional Rsch. Lab., 1967—81; ret., 1981. Cons. Mycogen Corp., San Diego, 1985-87; U.S. sr. scientist Germany, Darmstadt, 1977 Contbg. author: Actinomycetales: The Boundary Microorganisms, 1974, Bergey's Manual of Determinative Bacteriology, 1974, Synopsis and Classification of Living Organisms, 1982; mem. editl. bd. Jour. Antibiotics, 1969-81; contbr. articles to Jour. Bacteriology, Applied Microbiology, Phytopathology, Actinomycetes, Mycologia, Devel. Indsl. Microbiology, Jour. Antibiotics, Internat. Bull. Bacteriological Nomenclature Taxonomy, Antibiotics Ann., Antimicrobial Agts., Chemotherapy, also others With USNR, 1943-45, with Rsch. Res., 1948-54, lt. ret. Fulbright scholar, Italy, 1952; grantee Soc. Am. Bacteriologists, 1957 Fellow: Am. Acad. Microbiology; mem.: Alexander von Humboldt Assn. Episcopalian. Achievements include patents in fermentative production of riboflavin and of antibiotics; research in microbial culture collection technology and management, systematics of streptomycetes, industrial microbiology. Home: Rancho Del Rey Mobile Home Estates 208 PO Box 1098 Sunset Beach CA 90742 Home Phone: 714-465-2976.

PRIDMORE, ROY DAVIS, retired federal official; b. Gaffney, SC, May 18, 1925; s. Davis Bailey and Ethel (Hughes) P.; m. Doris Hedy Glatzl, July 16, 1960 (dec. Aug. 5, 2000); children: Lisa Ann, David Michael. Cert., Columbus U., Washington, 1949, Am. Inst., 1953, U.S. Dept. Agr. Grad. Sch., 1957. Pers. asst. Dept. Army, Fort Myer, Va., 1955-58; staff asst. D.C. Hwy. Dept., Washington, 1962-67; adminstrv. asst. Dept. Transp., Washington, 1958-62, adminstrv. officer, 1967-94, ret., 1994. Vice pres. Springboard Swim Club, Springfield, Va., 1984-85. Served with U.S. Army, 1946-47; mem. Res. (ret.) Decorated Legion of Merit. Democrat. Roman Catholic. Avocations: swimming, gardening.

PRIEBE, LANCE, Internet company executive, application developer; Founder, owner RocketSnail Games, 1999—2007; with New Horizon Prodns., Kelowna, BC, New Horizons Interactive Ltd., 2005—; co-founder, chief tech. officer & lead designer ClubPenguin.com, 2005—07; sr. mgr. Club Penguin unit Walt Disney Internet Grp., Burbank, Calif., 2007—. Office: Club Penguin/NHI 410-1620 Dickson Ave Kelowna BC V1Y 9Y2 Canada E-mail: info@nhinteractive.com.

PRIEBUS, REINCE, lawyer, political organization administrator; BS cum laude, U. Wis., Whitewater, 1994; JD cum laude, U. Miami, 1998. Bar: Wis. 1998, US Dist. Ct. (we. dist.) Wis., US Dist. Ct. (ea. dist.) Wis. Ptnr. Litig. Practice Group Michael Best & Griedrich LLP. Co-chair Southeastern Wis. Am. Heart Assn. Heart Ball, 2007, chair, 2008; vice chmn. 1st dist. Rep. Party of Wis., chmn. 1st dist., treas., vice chmn., 2006—07, chmn., 2007—; exec. com. mem. Rep. Nat. Com. Named one of Milwaukee's 40 Under 40, Milw. Bus. Jour., 2008. Office: Michael Best & Griedrich LLP Ste 3300 100 E Wisconsin Ave Milwaukee WI 53202-4108 also: Rep Party of Wis 148 E Johnson St Madison WI 53703 Office Phone: 414-225-2746. Office Fax: 414-227-0656. E-mail: rrpriebus@michaelbest.com, Reince@wisgop.org.

PRIEM, RICHARD GREGORY, writer, executive; b. Munich, Sept. 18, 1949; arrived in U.S., 1953; s. Richard Stanley and Elizabeth Teresa (Thompson) Priem; m. Janice Lynne Holland, July 27, 1976; children: Michael John, Matthew Warren(dec.), Kathryn Elizabeth Guthrie. BS in Radio-TV-Film, U. Tex., 1970; MEd in Ednl. Tech., U. Ga., 1979; postgrad., Coll. William and Mary, 1981-82. Cert. fraud examiner. Radio personality, sales exec. KOKE, Inc., Austin, Tex., 1968-73; numerous positions including asst. prof. dept. behavioral scis. and leadership U.S. Mil. Acad., anti-terorism staff officer and insp. gen. U.S. Army, 1973-94; dep. divsn. mgr. Sci. Applications Internat. Corp., Vienna, Va., 1994-97; asst. v.p. SAIC, 2003—. Cons. Dallas Cowboys Football Club, 1981; scouting coord. Army Football, 1983-85; cons. in field of anti-terrorism. Contbr. articles to profl. jours. Mem. Assn. Cert. Fraud Examiners, Internat. Soc. for Performance Improvement, Phi Kappa Phi, Kappa Delta Pi, Internat. Assn. Bomb Technicians and Investigators. Home: 13505 Trail Vista Ct NE Albuquerque NM 87111-9248 Personal E-mail: rpriem@earthlink.net.

PRIESAND, SALLY J., rabbi; b. Cleve., June 27, 1946; d. Irving Theodore and Rosetta Elizabeth (Welch) P. BA in English, U. Cin., 1968; B.Hebrew Letters, Hebrew Union Coll.-Jewish Inst. Religion, 1971, MA in Hebrew Letters, 1972; D.H.L. (hon.), Fla. Internat. U., 1973; DD (hon.), Hebrew Union Coll., 1997. Ordained rabbi 1972. Student rabbi Sinai Temple, Champaign, Ill., 1968, Congregation B'nai Israel, Hattiesburg, Miss., 1969-70, Congregation Shalom, Milw., 1970, Temple Beth Israel, Jackson, Mich., 1970-71; rabbinic intern Isaac M. Wise Temple, Cin., 1971-72; asst. rabbi Stephen Wise Free Synagogue, NYC, 1972-77, assoc. rabbi, 1977-79; rabbi Temple Beth El, Elizabeth, NJ, 1979-81, Monmouth Reform Temple, Tinton Falls, 1981—2006, rabbi emerita, 2006—; chaplain Lenox Hill Hosp., NYC, 1979-81. Author: Judaism and the New Woman, 1975. Mem. commn. on synagogue rels. Fedn. Jewish Philanthropies N.Y., 1972-79, mem. com. on aged commn. synagogue rels., 1972-75; mem. task force on equality of women in Judaism pub. affairs com. N.Y. Fedn. Reform Synagogues, 1972-75; mem. com. on resolutions Ctrl. Conf. Am. Rabbis, 1975-77, com. on cults, 1976-78, admissions com., 1983-89; chmn. Task Force on Women in Rabbinate, 1977-83, chmn. 1977-79, mem. exec. bd., 1977-79, com. on resolutions, 1989-92, chmn. com. conv. program, 1993-96; mem. joint commn. on Jewish edn. Ctrl. Conf. Am. Rabbis-Union Am. Hebrew Congregations, 1974-77; mem. task force on Jewish singles Commn. Synagogue Rels., 1975-77; mem. N.Y. Bd. Rabbis, 1975—, Shore Area Bd. Rabbis, 1981—; mem. interim steering com. Clergy and Laity Concerned, 1979-81; bd. dirs. NCCJ, N.Y.C., 1980-82, Jewish Fedn. Greater Monmouth County, trustee, 1988-2000, strategic planning commn., 1996—, hon. v.p., 2000—; trustee Planned Parenthood of Monmouth County, 1982-90, 2006—; v.p. Interfaith Neighbors, 1988-96, pres., 1997—; mem. UAHC-CCAR Joint Commn. on Synagogue Affiliation, 1992-2002; bd. govs. Hebrew Union Coll.-Jewish Inst. Religion, 1993-2005; trustee Union Am. Hebrew Congregations, 1994-98; mem. nat. clergy adv. bd. Planned Parenthood Fedn. Am., 2007—; bd. dirs. Ctr. Holocaust Studies, Brookdale C.C., 2006—, Jewish Heritage Mus. Monmouth County, 2007—; editor, newsletter Ctrl. Confs. Am. Rabbis, 2008-. Cited by B'nai Brith Women, 1971; named Woman of Yr. Temple Israel, Columbus, Ohio, 1972, Woman of Yr. Ladies Aux. N.Y. chpt. Jewish War Vets., 1973, Woman for All Seasons N. L.I. region Women's Am. ORT, 1973, Extraordinary Women of Achievement NCCJ, 1978, Woman of Achievement Monmouth County Adv. Commn. on Status Women, 1988; recipient Quality of Life award Dist. One chpt. B'nai B'rith Women, 1973, Medallion Judaic Heritage Soc., 1978, Eleanor Roosevelt Humanities award Women's div. State of Israel Bonds, 1980, Rabbinical award Coun. Jewish Fedn., 1988, Woman of Leadership award Monmouth Coun. Girl Scouts U.S., 1991, The Woman Who Dares award Nat. Coun. Jewish Women, 1993, Women's Studies Disting. Alumnae award Friends of Women's Studies U. Cin., 1997, Elizabeth Blackwell award Hobart & William Smith Colls., 2009, Disting Alumni award Memicken Coll. Arts & Scis., U. Cin., 2009; named to Alumni Hall of Fame, Fairview Park H.S., 2002. Mem. Hadassah (life), Ctrl. Conf. Am. Rabbis, NOW, Am. Jewish Congress, Am. Jewish Com., Assn. Reform Zionists Am., Jewish Women Internat. (life), Nat. Coun. Jewish Women (life), Women Reform Judaism (life), Jewish Peace Fellowship, Women's Rabbinic Network, Nat. Breast Cancer Coalition, HUC-JIR Rabbinic Alumni Assn. (sec., treas. 1997-99, v.p. 1999-2001, pres. 2001-03, past pres., 2003-05). Achievements include being the first US woman rabbi. Office: 332 Hance Ave Tinton Falls NJ 07724-2730 Home: 32 Fernwood Dr Ocean NJ 07712-8713 Office Phone: 732-493-4896. Business E-Mail: rsjp@optonline.net.

PRIEST, DANA, journalist; b. 1959; married; 2 children. BA in Polit. Sci., U. Calif., Santa Cruz, 1981. Intelligence reporter, Nat. News Desk Washington Post, 1987—. Guest scholar US Inst. Peace; guest spkr., host, four-part speaking series on the U.S. Mil. and Fgn. Policy for the Secretary's Open Forum. Author: The Mission: Waging War & Keeping Peace with America's Military, 2003 (Pulitzer prize finalist for gen. non-fiction, 2004, NY Pub. Libr. Helen Bernstein Book award for Excellence in Journalism, 2004). Recipient MacArthur Found. Rsch. & Writing grant, 2001, Gerald R. Ford prize for Disting. Reporting on Nat. Def., 2001, Excellence in Journalism award, State Dept., 2001, George Polk award for nat. reporting, 2006, Pulitzer prize for beat reporting, 2006, Bob Considine award, Overseas Press Club, 2006, Disting. Alumni award, Divsn. Social Scis., U. Calif., Santa Cruz, 2006, Pulitzer prize for public service, 2008; named one of The 50 Most Powerful People in DC, GQ mag., 2007. Office: Washington Post Nat News Desk 1150 15th St Washington DC 20071-0070 Office Phone: 202-334-4490. Office Fax: 202-496-3883. E-mail: priestd@washpost.com.*

PRIEST, GEORGE L., law educator; b. 1947; BA, Yale U., 1969; JD, U. Chgo., 1973. Assoc. prof. U. Puget Sound, Tacoma, 1973-75; law and econ. fellow U. Chgo., 1975-77; prof. U. Buffalo, 1977-80, UCLA, 1980-81, Yale U., New Haven, 1981—, John M. Olin Prof. Law and Econs., 1986—2009, dir. John M. Olin Ctr. for Law, Econs. and Pub. Policy, 1986—, prof. law & economics, 2009—. Dir. program in civil liability. Mem. Pres.' Com. on Privatization, 1987-88. Office: PO Box 208215 New Haven CT 06520-8215 E-mail: george.priest@yale.edu.

PRIEST, JESSIE SHAW, media specialist; d. Shaw Wesley and Shaw McFadden (Teddie) James; m. David Priest, Dec. 27, 1972; children: David, LaDawndrea Catoria. Degree in Elem. Edn., Allen U., 1967; degree, U. SC, 1972, Appalachian State U., 1974, Coll. Charlton, 1990; MEd, Cambridge Coll., 2001. Cert. edn. tchr. SC State Dept. of Edn., 1967. Reading tchr. Chavis Elem. Sch., Hemmingway, SC, 1967—70; elem. tchr., 1967—73; media specialist Planterville Elem. Sch., Georgetown, SC, 1970—, SC Edn. Assn.

PRIEST, MICHAEL B, professional sports team executive; married; 2 children. BA cum laude, Ohio State U., 1986. Ptnr. Meade & Moore; v.p., controller JMAC, Inc., 1996—97, v.p., CFO, 1997, pres., 2001—, Columbus Blue Jackets, 2007—; alt. dir. Columbus Destroyers. Alt. gov. NHL Bd. Govs. Office: Columbus Blue Jackets Nationwide Arena 200 W Nationwide Blvd, Ste Level Columbus OH 43215

PRIESTLEY, JASON (JASON BRADFORD PRIESTLEY), actor; b. Vancouver, BC, Can., Aug. 28, 1969; m. Ashlee Petersen, Feb. 2, 1999 (div. Jan. 2, 2000); m. Naomi Lowde, May 14, 2005; 2 children. Driver Kelley Racing, 2002; co-owner Rubicon Race Team (Indy Racing League), 2008—. Actor: (TV series) Sister Kate, 1989-90, Beverly Hills 90210, 1990-1998 (Golden Globe award nominee for best actor in a drama series 1993)(also dir. 15 episodes, 1993-97, prodr., dir. episodes in 1995-96; prodr. 58 episodes 1996-97, exec. prodr. 1997-98), Eek! The Cat(voice), 1992, Tru Calling, 2004-2005; (TV movies) Teen Angel, 1989, Choice of the Heart: The Margaret Sanger Story, 1995, Vanishing Point, 1997, Kiss Tomorrow Goodbye, 2000 (also exec. prodr., dir.), Teen Angel Returns, 1990, Common Ground, 2000, Homicide: The Movie, 2000, Warning: Parental Advisory, 2002, The True Meaning of Christmas Specials, 2002, I Want to Marry Ryan Banks, 2004, Sleep Murder, 2004, Murder at the Presidio, 2005, Colditz, 2005, Snow Wonder, 2005, Shades of Black: The Conrad Black Story, 2006, Subs, 2007, Luna: Spirit of the Whale, 2007; (films) The Boy Who Could Fly, 1986, Watchers, 1988, Nowhere To Run, 1989, Calendar Girl, 1993, Tombstone, 1993, Cold-Blooded, 1995, Love and Death on Long Island, 1997, Hacks, 1997, The Thin Pink Line, 1998, Conversations in Limbo, 1998, Choose Life, 1999, Dill Scallion, 1999, Standing On Fishes, 1999, Eye of the Beholder, 1999, Barenacked in America, 1999 (also prodr., dir.), The Highwayman, 2000 (also prodr.), Lion of Oz (voice), 2000, Herschel Hopper: New York Rabbit (voice), 2000, Zigs, 2001, The Fourth Angel, 2001, Cherish, 2002, Cover Story, 2002, Darkness Falling, 2002, Time of the Wolf, 2002, Fancy Dancing, 2002, Die, Mommie Die, 2003, Chicks with Sticks, 2004, Going the Distance, 2004, Hot Tamale, 2005, Made in Brooklyn, 2006; (TV mini series) Above and Beyond, 2006; guest appearances include Airwolf, 1987, 21 Jump Street, 1987, The Outer Limits, 1997 (also dir.), MacGyver, 1988, Quantum Leap, 1989, Superman, 1998, Grosse Point, 2001 (also dir.), Spin City, 2001 & 2003, 8 Simple Rules...for Dating My Teenage Daughter, 2002, 2003, Celebrities Uncensored, 2003, 04, American Idol, 2004, Overhaulin, 2004, What I Like About You, 2005, Hockeyville, 2006, Love Monkey, 2006, Without a Trace, 2006, Masters of Horror, 2006, Medium, 2007, (several episodes) Side Order of Life, 2007 Named one of the 50 Most Beautiful People in the World, People Mag., 1991, 1992, TV's 25 Greatest Teen Idols, TV Guide, 2005; won 1998 Grand-Am race, Mid-Ohio Sports Car Course. Avocations: hockey, race car driving. Office: Rubicon Race Team 12801 Clay Center Rd Carmel IN 46032*

PRIEUR, C. JAMES, insurance company executive; BA, Coll. Militaire Royal de S. Jean, Quebec; MBA, Univ. We. Ontario, 1975. Equity analyst & portfolio mgr. Sun Life Fin. Inc., 1979—85, head Canadian private placements, 1985—88, v.p. securities investments Canada, 1988—91, v.p. investments Canada, 1991—92, v.p. investments U.S., 1992—97, sr. v.p., gen. mgr. U.S. ops., 1997—99, pres., COO, 1999—2006; CEO Conseco Inc., Carmel, Ind., 2006—. Bd. dir. LIRMA Internat. Inc. Office: Conseco Inc 11825 N Pennsylvania St Carmel IN 46032

PRIHOD, KEVIN F., museum administrator; m. Mary Zatina. BA in Sociology, Brown U.; MBA in Ops. Rsch., Case Western Reserve U. Cons. Coopers & Lybrand; indsl. engr., materials mgr. Gen. Motors; pres., COO Lincoln Brass Works; dir. quality Durakon Industries; nationwide dir. customer bus. Constellation Brands, Inc.; v.p. engring. services INCAT; adj. ops. rsch. prof. U. Detroit Sch. Bus.; mem. bd. trustees Detroit Sci. Ctr., 2003—, chief sci. officer, 2004—05, CEO, pres., 2005—. Adv. bd. mem. Inst. Mgmt. and Engring., Case Western Reserve U.; mem. bd. dirs. Space, Engring., Math., Aerospace prog. Wayne State U. Mem.: Am. Prodn. and Inventory Control Soc., Soc. Mfg. Engrs. Office: Detroit Sci Ctr 5020 John R St Detroit MI 48202

PRILIPKO, OLGA, medical researcher; MD, Med. Sch. U. Geneva, 1999. Resident, fellow Geneva Hosp., 1999—2005; postdoc. fellow Stanford U., Calif., 2005—. Author: (graphic novels) Full Circle (Rising Stars of Manga, 2008).

PRIMEAU, KEITH, professional sports team executive, retired professional hockey player; b. Toronto, Nov. 24, 1971; m. Lisa Primeau; 4 children. Center Detroit Red Wings, 1990—96, Hartford Whalers, 1996—97, Carolina Hurricanes, 1997—99, capt., 1998—99; center Phila. Flyers, 2000—06, capt., 2001—06; spl. asst. to gen. mgr., dir. player devel. Las Vegas Wranglers (East Coast Hockey League), 2009—. Mem. Team Can., Olympic Games, Nagano, Japan, 1998; co-founder, instr. Durham Hockey Inst.; co-ptnr. Whitby Fury (Ontario Provincial Jr. Hockey League). Named to NHL All-Star Game, 1999, 2004. Office: Las Vegas Wranglers Orleans Arena 4500 W Tropicana Ave Las Vegas NV 89103 also: PO Box 303 Voorhees NJ 08043*

PRIMEAUX, HENRY, III, automotive executive, author, speaker; b. New Orleans, Nov. 16, 1941; s. Henry Jr. and Ethel (Ritter) P.; m. Jane Cathrine Velcich, July 23, 1960; children: Joann Primeaux Longa, Lisa Primeaux Lotz, Henry Joseph. Student, La. State U., New Orleans, 1959-63. Compt. Jimco, New Orleans, 1965-66; owner, mgr. Picone Seafood, New Orleans, 1966-67; v.p. NADW Inc., Metairie, La., 1967-78, Am. Warranty Corp., LA, 1978-80; pres. F&I Warranty Corp., Arlington, Tex., 1980-87; exec. v.p. F&I Mgmt. Corp., Arlington, 1980-87; pres., CEO Primco Corp., Arlington, 1987-91; owner Flavors Restaurant, Tulsa, Okla., Primeaux Mktg. Mng. ptnr. Crown Auto World, Bristow; founder, Pimeaux Family Found., 1998; mgr., Primeaux Family Dealerships; mng. ptnr., Primeaux Family Realty; cons., corr. Wards Auto Dealer, Detroit, 1987-95, weekly TV program Automotive Satellite TV Network; cons. Nissan Motor Co., L.A., 1988-89, Convergent div. Unisys, Hunt Valley, Md., 1988-90; cons. Mercedes-Benz N.Am.; exec. com. Okla. Workforce Investment Bd.; chmn. Tulsa Workforce Investment Bd.; owner Tusla Talons AF2 Football, 2004. Writer Auto Age mag., Dealer mag., 2003-; author: F&I Handbook. Mem. Rep. Task Force Okla. Workforce Devel. Com.; bd. dirs. John Starks Found., Boy Scouts U.S.; mem. nat. adv. bd. Automotive Yes Sch. to Work Initiative; mem. Okla. Sch. to Work Commn.; bd. regents Okla. State U., Tulsa. With USN, 1959-61. Recipient Automotive Yes Dealer Yr., 2004. Mem. Am. Internat. Automobile Dealers Assn., Assn. of F&I Profls. (bd. dirs. 1990—, pres. 1994), Nat. Auto Dealers Assn. (pres. Tulsa chpt. 1994, Time Quality Dealer of Yr. 1994), Okla. State C. of C. (bd. dirs.), Met. Tulsa C. of C. (bd. dirs. 1998-2000). Roman Catholic. Office: Crown Bristow 901 S Roland Bristow OK 74010 Home: 6201 E 108th St Tulsa OK 74137-8903 Office Phone: 918-367-3423. E-mail: primeaux1@aol.com, crownhen@aol.com, henry@crownbristow.com.

PRIMEGGIA, SALVATORE, sociologist, educator; s. Frank and Caterina Primeggia; m. Pamela Barreto. PhD, New Sch. Social Rsch., NY, 1974. Prof. sociology Adelphi U., Garden City, NY, 1967—. Office: Adelphi Univ One S Ave Garden City NY 11530 Office Fax: 516-877-4717. Business E-Mail: primeggi@adelphi.edu.

PRIMM, EARL RUSSELL, III, publishing executive; b. Rhinelander, Wis., Oct. 24, 1958; s. Earl Russell and Betty Joan (Dennis) P. AB in Classics (hon.), Loyola U. Chgo., 1980; MA in Libr. Sci., U. Chgo., 1990. Asst. to edn. dir. J.G. Ferguson Pub. Co., Chgo., 1981-84; prodn. mgr. Joint Commn. on Accreditation of Hosps., Chgo., 1984-85; sr. editor J.G. Ferguson Pub. Co., Chgo., 1985-87; asst. editor U. Chgo. Press., 1987-88; editorial dir. J.G. Ferguson Pub. Co., Chgo., 1988-89; project mgr. Children's Press, Chgo., 1989-92; exec. editor Franklin Watts, Inc., Chgo., NYC, 1992-95; editl. dir. Grolier Children's Pub., Danbury, Conn., 1995-97; pres. Editl. Directions, Inc., Chgo., 1997—. Mem. adv. bd. U. Chgo. Pub. Program, 1990-2000; judge Lambda Lit. awards, Washington, 1994-2000; guest lectr. Sch. Edn. Harvard U., 2004. Editl. chief: Career Discovery Encyclopedia, 1990, Favorite Children's Authors and Illustrators, 2002, 2nd edit. 2006; editor: Civil Rights Movement in America, 2nd edit., 1991, Extraordinary Hispanic Americans, 1991; editl. dir. The Child's World, 2002-05, Tradition Books, 2002. Mem. crisis counselor Nat. Runaway Switchboard, Chgo., 1985-88; Horizon's hotline counselor, Chgo., 1987-88; bd. dirs. Gerber/Hart Libr. and Archives, Chgo., 1992-94. Named Honors Sr. of Yr., Loyola U. Chgo., 1980; recipient Mertz Latin Scholarship key Loyola U. Chgo., 1980. Mem. Am. Libr. Assn. Democrat. Home: 1000 W Washington Blvd #147 Chicago IL 60607-2148 Office: 1000 W Washington Blvd # 203 Chicago IL 60607 Office Phone: 312-829-5456. E-mail: russell@editorialdirections.com.

PRIMM, RICHARD KIRBY, physician; b. Thomasville, NC, May 23, 1944; s. Richard Wesley and Gertrude (Berrier) P.; m. Sharon Kay Lucas, Dec. 28, 1968; children: Heather, Lucas. BA, Duke U., 1966; postgrad., Baylor U., 1966-67; MD, U. N.C., 1970. Intern internal medicine Vanderbilt U. Hosp., Nashville, 1970-71, resident in internal medicine, 1973-75, chief resident, 1975-76; fellow cardiovascular diseases U. Ala., Birmingham, 1976-78, chief fellow, instr. medicine, 1978-79; asst. prof. medicine Vanderbilt U. Sch. Medicine, Nashville, 1979-84; staff cardiologist Wenatchee Valley Med. Ctr., 1984—. Clin. asst. prof. medicine U. Wash., Seattle, 1985-91, clin. assoc. prof. medicine, 1991-2003, clin. prof. medicine, 2003—; adminstrv. lead dept. cardiology Wenatchee Valley Clinic, 1987-91, 1997-2006. Contbr. articles to profl. jours. Capt. U.S. Army, 1971-73. Recipient Heusner Pupil award U. N.C., 1969, Hillman Teaching Excellence award Vanderbilt U., 1976. Fellow: Am. Coll. Cardiology (gov. Wash. chpt. 2002—05); mem.: AHA, Wash. Heart Assn. (trustee 1990—94), North Pacific Soc. Internal Medicine (pres. 2007), Physicians for Social Responsibility, Alpha Omega Alpha. Avocations: downhill skiing, backpacking. Office: Wenatchee Valley Med Ctr 820 N Chelan Ave Wenatchee WA 98801-2028 Home Phone: 509-662-3789; Office Phone: 509-663-8711. Business E-Mail: rprimm@wvclinic.com.

PRIMMER, LILLIAN JUANDA, science educator; d. Melvin Palmer and Amanda Severina (Olstad) Bekkum; m. Donald Gale Primmer, June 17, 1967; children: Donald Guy, Jacqueline Juanda Gruber. BS, U. Wis., 1990, MEd, 1993. Tchr. Clintonville Pub. Schs., Wis., 1990—96; part-time tchr. Christa McAulliffe Acad., Appleton, Wis., 2002, 2004. Part-time tchr. Enstein Acad., Green Bay, Wis., 1991; participant/tchr.-facilitator Sci. World, Drummond, Wis., 1994—99; pres. Wis. Elem. & Middle Level Sci. Tchrs., Wis., 1998—99. Merit badge counselor Boy Scouts/Girl Scouts, Clintonville, Wis., 1990—; hunter safety instr. Dept. Nat. Resources, Clintonville, 1994—; fundraiser, participating survivor Relay for Life, Clintonville, Viroqua. Recipient Disting. Tchr. Sci., Wis. Elem. Sci. Tchrs., 1995; grantee Earthwatch grant, Wis. Acad. Scis., Arts & Letters, 1994. Mem.: NSTA, Wis. Soc. Sci. Tchrs. (co-chair forum com., Outstanding Tchr. Sci. 1996). Avocations: hunting, fishing, camping, volleyball, knitting. Home: 69 Ninth St Clintonville WI 54929

PRIMO, DAVID MARTIN, political science professor; s. Mauro and Elda Primo; m. Neeta Primo. BA in Polit. Sci. and Econs., Brown U., Providence, 1998, MA in Polit. Sci., 1998; MA in Econs., Stanford U., Calif., 2001, PhD in Polit. Sci., 2002. Asst. prof. polit. sci. U. Rochester, NY, 2002—. Author: The Plane Truth: Airline Crashes, the Media, and Transportation Policy, 2003, Rules and Restraint: Government Spending and the Design of Institutions, 2007; contbr. articles to profl. jours. Recipient Goergen award for Disting. Artistry in Undergraduate Edn., U. Rochester, 2005; named Undergraduate Prof. of Yr., U. Rochester Students' Assn., 2005. Mem.: APSA (mem. legis. studies sect. 2008, Alan Rosenthal prize), Phi Beta Kappa, Omicron Delta Epsilon. Office: Univ Rochester Political Science Dept Harkness Hall 333 Rochester NY 14627-0146

PRIMONT, DANIEL, economics professor; PhD in Economics, U. Calif., Santa Barbara, 1970. Assoc. prof. economics Southern Ill. U. Carbondale, 1978—82, prof. economics, 1982—. Office: Southern Ill Univ Carbondale Mailcode 4515 Carbondale IL 62901 Business E-Mail: primo@siu.edu.

PRIMUS, ROBERT E., legislative staff member; Legis. coord. for Rep. Michael Capuano, US House of Reps., Washington, 2000, legis. dir., 2001—02, adminstrv. asst., 2002—07, chief of staff, 2007—; sr. policy adviser US House Adminstrn. Com., Washington, 2008—. Office: Office of Congressman Michael Capuano 1414 Longworth House Office Bldg Washington DC 20515 Office Phone: 202-225-5111. Office Fax: 202-225-9322. E-mail: robert.primus@mail.house.gov.*

PRIMUS, WENDELL, legislative staff member; b. Eldora, Iowa; BA, Iowa State U., Ames, PhD in Econs. Asst. prof. econs. Georgetown U., Washington; subcom. on human resources staff dir., ways and means com. US House of Reps., Washington, chief economist, ways and means com., minority staff dir., joint econ. com., 2003—05, sr. policy advisor budget and health, Rep. Nancy Pelosi, 2005—; dep. asst. sec. human services policy US Dept. Health and Human Services, Washington, 1993—97; dir. income and security Ctr. on Budget and Policy Priorities, Washington, 1997—2003. Vis. prof. law and pub. policy U. Md. Democrat. Office: 235 Cannon House Office Bldg Washington DC 20515 Office Phone: 202-225-4965. Office Fax: 202-225-8259.*

PRINCE, ANDREW STEVEN, lawyer, retired government agency administrator; b. Bklyn., Oct. 9, 1943; s. Milton S. and Beatrice M. (Ratkin) P.; m. Rochelle Moskowitz, July 4, 1973; children: Brett, Kenneth. BS, U.S. Naval Acad., 1965; MBA, JD, Harvard U., 1974. Bar: N.Y. 1975, U.S. Supreme Ct. 1980. Assoc. firm Shearman & Sterling, NYC, 1974-81; dep. asst. sec. Navy Dept., Washington, 1981-86; exec. v.p., gen. counsel Urquhart and Co., Inc., McLean, Va., 1986-94; mng. dir. Nat. Capital Cos. LLC, Bethesda, Md., 1997-2000; mng. dir., COO HFS Capital LLC, McLean, Va., 2000—02; CEO, pres. Bretken Enterprises, 2002—03, Prince Strategic Group LC, McLean, Va., 2003—; CEO, pres., dir. Precision Aerospace Components, Inc., 2007—. Sec. Potash Import & Chem. Corp., N.Y.C., 1979-81; mem. panel of arbitrators Am. Arbitration Assn., N.Y.C., 1979- Bd. dirs. Harvard Coop. Soc., Cambridge, Mass., 1972-74, USO, Washington, 1982-86, N.Y.C., 1979-81, Gibbs & Gx. Served with USN, 1965-70; Res., ret Mem. Harvard Bus. Sch. Club, Washington, DC (bd. dir., pres.), Mil Order World Wars (judge adv.), Naval Acad. Alumni Assn., Naval Acad. Found. (dir.). Office: 2200 Arthur Kill Rd Staten Island NY 10309

PRINCE, ANNA LOU, composer, music publisher, construction executive; b. Isabella, Tenn., May 28, 1935; d. Ulysses Gordon and Della Carrie (Hawkins) Prince; children: Sandra, Teresa, Vandi. Diploma, Carolina Sch. Broadcasting, 1966; Zion diploma, Israel Bible Sch., Jerusalem, 1970; diploma, S.W. Tech. Coll., 1970; student, United Christian Assn., 1976; MusD, London Inst. Applied Rsch., 1991; diplomatic diploma, Acad. Argentina de Diplomacia, 1993; PhD (hon.), Australian Inst. Coord. Rsch., Victoria, 1993; diploma of honors on internat. affairs, Inst. Des Affaires Internat., Paris, 1994. Lic. Bible tchr. United Christian Acad. Songwriter Hank Locklin Music Co., Nashville, 1963-70; entertainer 1982 World's Fair, Knoxville, Tenn., 1982; ptnr., owner Prince Wholesale Bait Co., Canton, NC, 1976-82, Grad Builders, Canton, 1982-86, Prince TV Co., Canton, 1986—. Music pub. Broadcast Music, Inc., Nashville, 1982—; mem. prodn. staff, talent coord. (TV series) Down Home, Down Under, 1989-90; host TV show Real Heroes of Country Music in Nashville, 1997-2003. Songs recorded on RCA: I Feel a Cry Coming On, 1965 (#1 in Eng.), Best Part of Loving You, (#1 in Eng.), Anna, 1969 (Billboard 1970, recorded in Ireland 1974, hit in Europe and New Zealand); singer, composer I'm In Love With You, 1995; over 20 songs recorded to date; appeared Grand Ole Opry, 1970; exec. prodr., host TV talk show, Real Hereos of Country Music, 1989— (Emmy nomination 1997); author: The Strange Life of Anna Prince, 2006. Candidate for county commr. Dem. Party Macon County, NC, 1984; bd. dirs. Macon County Taxpayers Assn., Inc., 1984, v.p., 1984-86; bd. dirs. Head Start, Topton, NC, 1969-73; judge Emmy Awards, Am. Registrar Ohio Valley, 2002— Nominated Disting. Women NC, NC Coun. Coun. on Status of Women, 1984, Jefferson award WYFF TV and Am. Inst. for Pub. Svc., Outstanding Bus. Woman Small Bus. Adminstrn., 1984. Mem. BMI, Internat. Parliament Safety and Peace (life, dept. fgn. affairs, dep. mem. assembly), Nashville Songwriters Assn. Internat. (moderator, tchr. 1984-86), Country Music Assn., Reunion Profl. Entertainers, Fraternal Order Police, C. of C., Order of Knight of Templars (dame) Lofsensic Order (dame), Maison Internat. des Intellectuals. Democrat. Personal E-mail: docaprince@aol.com.

PRINCE, CHARLES O., III, (CHUCK PRINCE), financial consulting firm executive, retired diversified financial services company executive; b. Lynwood, Calif., Jan. 13, 1950; s. Charles Prince Jr.; m. Margaret L. Wolff, Sept. 20, 2003. BA, U. So. Calif., 1971, MA, JD, 1975; LLM, Georgetown U., 1983. Bar: Pa. 1975, Md. 1979, Minn. 1982. Atty. U.S. Steel Corp., 1975—79; gen. counsel Commercial Credit Co., 1979—86; exec. v.p., gen. counsel, sec. Traveler's Group, NYC, 1986-98; co-gen. counsel, sec. Citigroup (merger of Traveler's Group and Citibank), NYC, 1998—2000; chief admin. officer Citigroup, Inc., NYC, 2000, COO, 2001—02, CEO, 2003—07, chmn., 2006—07, chmn., CEO, Global Corp. & Investment Bank Group, 2002—03; vice chmn. Stonebridge Internat. LLC, Washington, 2008—, chmn. bd. advisors, 2008—. Mem. Coun. Fgn. Rels.; bd. trustees Brookings Instn.; bd. dirs. Johnson & Johnson, New Brunswick, NJ, 2006—, Xerox Corp., 2008—. Bd. dirs. United Negro Coll. Fund; trustee Columbia U., Juilliard Sch. Office: Stonebridge Internat LLC 555 Thirteenth St NW Ste 300 W Columbia Sq Washington DC 20004

PRINCE, DANFORTH, publishing executive, journalist; b. Toledo, June 14, 1953; s. Edward Mitchell Prince and Elizabeth Jane Danforth. BA, Hamilton Coll., Clinton, NY, 1975. V.p., treas. Porter & Prince Corp., NYC, 1983—; pres., CEO, publ. Blood Moon Prodns. Ltd., NYC, 1997—; pres., CEO Ga. Lit. Assn., NYC, 1997—. Co-author, dir. rsch.: Europe & Caribbean Series of The Frommer Guides, 1983—; co-author: Blood Moon's Guide to Film, 2006, Hollywood Babylon, 2008. Mem.: North Am. Travel Journalists Assn. Office: Blood Moon Prodns Ltd 75 Saint Marks Pl Staten Island NY 10301 Office Phone: 718-556-9410. Office Fax: 718-816-4092. Personal E-mail: danforthprince@hotmail.com.

PRINCE, DAVID CANNON, lawyer; b. Hawkinsville, Ga., July 4, 1950; s. Carl Willis and Carobel (Cannon) Prince; m. Mary MacIntyre, June 30, 1973. BA in Econs., Clemson U., 1972; JD, St. John's U., Jamaica, NY, 1980. Bar: NY 1981, Ga. 1982, US Dist. Ct. (no. dist.) Ga. 1982. Atty. enforcement SEC, Atlanta, 1981-86; regional counsel Shearson Lehman Bros. Inc., Atlanta, 1986-92; gen. counsel Robinson-Humphrey Co., Inc., Atlanta, 1992—2001; chief legal officer SunTrust Capital Markets, Inc., 2001—06; gen. counsel Stephans Investment Mgmt. Group, LLC, Little Rock, 2006—. Capt. USAF, 1972—78. Mem.: ABA (co-chairperson young lawyers divsn. 1986—88). Democrat. Avocations: sailing, running. Office: Stephens Inc 111 Ctr St 23rd Fl Little Rock AR 72201

PRINCE, ERIK D., protective services company executive; b. Holland, Mich., June 6, 1969; s. Edgar D. and Elsa Prince; m. Joan Nicole Prince (dec. 2003); 4 children; m. Joanna Ruth Prince; 2 children. Attended, US Naval Acad.; grad., Hillsdale Coll. Intern under George H. W. Bush The White House; intern to Dana Rohrabacher Calif. Republican Rep.; co-founder Blackwater USA, 1997, chmn., CEO, 1997—, Prince Group. V.p. Edgar and Elsa Prince Found.; contbr. Rep. Campaign; bd. mem. Christian Freedom Internat. SEAL officer USN, 1993—96. Republican. Office: Blackwater USA PO Box 1029 Moyock NC 27958 Office Phone: 252-435-2488. Office Fax: 252-435-6388.

PRINCE, FAITH, actress, singer; b. Augusta, Ga., Aug. 5, 1957; m. Larry Lunetta, 1986; 1 child, Henry. Performer: (Broadway plays) Jerome Robbins' Broadway, 1989—90, Nick & Nora, 1991, Guys and Dolls, 1992 (Drama Desk award, Outstanding Actress in a Musical, Tony award, Best Actress in a Musical, 1992), What's Wrong With This Picture?, 1994, The King and I, 1996—98, 1998—99, Little Me, 1998—99, James Joyce's The Dead, 2000, Belles Are Ringing, 2001, Noises Off, 2001—02, A Catered Affair, 2008, The Little Mermaid, 2009; actor: (films) The Last Dragon, 1985, Dave, 1993, My Father, the Hero, 1994, Big Bully, 1996, Picture Perfect, 1997, It Had to Be You, 2000, Our Very Own, 2005, Material Girls, 2006; (TV series) Encyclopedia, 1986, High Society, 1995, Spin City, 1997—2000, Now and Again, 2000, Huff, 2004—06; (TV films) Friends at Last, 1995, A Season for Miracles, 1999, Sweet Potato Queens, 2003.

PRINCE, GREGORY SMITH, JR., retired college president; b. Washington, May 7, 1939; s. Gregory Smith and Margaret (Minor) P.; m. Toni Layton Brewer; children: Tara Wyndom, Gregory S. III. BA, Yale U., 1961, M in Philosophy, 1969, PhD, 1973; cert. in teaching English as a Second Language, Georgetown U., 1961; DHL (hon.), Amherst Coll., 1991. Instr. New Asia Coll., Kowloon, Hong Kong, 1961-62, Chinese U., Kowloon, 1962-63, Yale China Assn., Kowloon, 1961-63, Woodberry Forest (Va.) Sch., 1963-65; dean summer programs Dartmouth Coll., Hanover, NH, 1970-72, asst. dean faculty, 1972-78, assoc. dean faculty, 1978-89; pres. Hampshire Coll., Amherst, Mass., 1989—2005; sr. cons. Pathways to Coll., 2005—. Vice chair coun. on racial and ethnic justice ABA, 1996-2006; bd. dirs. Mass Ventures. Producer: (film) A Way of Learning, 1988; Author: Teach Them to Challenge Authority: Educating For Healthy Solutions, 2008 Trustee Montshire Mus. Sci., Hanover, 1973-89, Washington Campus, 1978—; trustee, chmn. Univ. Press New England, Hanover, 1983-84; trustee, pres. Yale-China Assn., New Haven, 1969-84, 2005-; bd. dirs. Five Colls., Inc., Amherst, 1989-2005; bd. dirs. Mass. Internat. Festival for Arts, 1994-98; chmn. bd. dirs. Assn. Ind. Colls. and Univs. Mass., 1994-95; chair commn. on accreditation Am. Coun. Edn.; bd. dirs. Mass. Nature Conservancy, 1996—2004; bd. dirs. Nat. Assn. Ind. Colls. and Univs., 1999-2001, Friendship Pub. Charter Sch., 2005-, Vermount Inst. Natural Scis., 2006-. Coe fellow Stanford U., 1965, Woodrow Wilson fellow Yale U., 1966, NDEA fellow, 1967-70. Mem. Internat. Assn. of Chiefs Police Found. (bd. dirs. 1991-95), Nat. Assn. of Ind. Colls. and Univs. Democrat. Episcopalian. Office: Hampshire Coll 893 West St Amherst MA 01002-3372 Home: 24 Academy Rd Norwich VT 05055-9480

PRINCE, KENNETH STEPHEN, lawyer; b. Newton, Mass., Jan. 28, 1950; s. Samuel and Edna L. Prince; m. Patricia Denning, Jan. 15, 1977 (dec. Nov. 1985); 1 child, Kenneth Stephen Jr.; m. Jane M. McCabe, Sept. 5, 1987; 1 child, Allison Pamela. BA, U. Pa., 1972; JD, Boston Coll., 1975. Bar: N.Y. 1976, Mass. 1975, U.S. Dist. Ct. (so. and ea. dists.) N.Y. 1978. Assoc. Shearman & Sterling, NYC, 1975-83, ptnr., 1984—, antitrust group practice leader, 1992—2003, 2005—. Mem. N.Y. Law Inst. (exec. com. 1984-96), Order of Coif. Home: 15 Dellwood Rd Darien CT 06820-2915 Office Phone: 212-848-4139. Business E-Mail: kprince@shearman.com.

PRINCE, LAWRENCE, science educator; BS, U. Miami, Coral Gables, Fla., 1989; MD, PhD, U. Ala., Birmngham, 1996. Diplomate in neonatal-perinatal medicine Am. Bd. Pediat., 2005. Asst. prof. U. Ala., Birminghama, 2003—07, Vanderbilt U., Nashville, 2007—. Office: Vanderbilt Univ 9435-A MRBIV 2213 Garland Ave Nashville TN 37232

PRINCE, LEAH FANCHON, lab administrator, executive secretary; b. Hartford, Conn., Aug. 12, 1939; d. Meyer and Annie (Forman) Berman; m. Herbert N. Prince, Jan. 30, 1955; children: Daniel L., Richard N., Robert G. Student, U. Conn., 1957—59, Rutgers U., 1962; BFA, Fairleigh Dickinson U., 1970; postgrad., Caldwell Coll. for Women, 1973—75, Parsons Sch. of Design, NYC, 1978. Cert. tchr. art, N.J. Tchr. art Caldwell-West Caldwell Pub. Schs., NJ, 1970—75; pres. Britannia Imports Ltd., Fairfield, NJ, 1979—89; tchr. religious studies Bohrer-Kaufman Hebrew Acad., Randolph, NJ, 1981—82; co-founder, corp. sec. Gibraltar Biol. Labs., Inc., Fairfield, 1970—; dir., co-founder Gibraltar Inst. for Rsch. and Tng., Fairfield, 1984—. Cons. Internat. Antiques and Fine Arts Industries, U.K., 1979-89; cons. in art exhibitry Passaic County Coll., Paterson, N.J., 1989-93; art curator Fairleigh Dickinson U., Rutherford, N.J., 1972-74; curator history of nursing 20th century Bloomfield (N.J.) Coll., 1990-91; lectr. Am. Soc. Microbiology, New Orleans, 1989; spkr. in field. Exhibited in group shows at Bloomfield Coll., NJ, 1990, Caldwell Women's Club, NJ, 1991, State Fedn. Women's Clubs Ann. Show, 1992 (1st pl. award 1992), Newark Art Mus., 1992, West Essex Art Assn., NJ, 1990, Somerset Art Assn., NJ, 1994, Mortimer Gallery, Gladstone, NJ, 1994 (1st pl. award 1998, 2008), Tewksbury Hist. Soc., 1994, 98, 2004 (1st pl. award 1994, 98, 2004), Tewksbury Hist. Soc., 2001-02, 04-08, (Juried Art award 2001-02, 04-06, 07), Nat. Meeting Am. Pen Women, Calif., 2002, Washington, 2004 (1st pl. award); one-woman shows include Passaic County Coll., NJ, 1990, Caldwell Coll., 1990; author children's stories. Chair ann. juried art awards Arts Coun. of Essex Bd. Trustees, Montclair, N.J., 1984-90; chair fundraising Arts Coun. Essex County, N.J., 1989. Mem. AAUW, Soc. Childrens Book Writers and Illustrators, Somerset Art Assn., Nat. League Am. Pen Women (pres. N.J. br., Juried Art award 2001, 2004), Barnegat Light Yacht Club. Republican. Avocations: boating, tennis, opera, painting, travel. Home: 5 Standish Dr Mendham Twp Morristown NJ 07960-3224 Home Phone: 973-267-4594.

PRINCE, MARTIN RAYMOND, radiologist; b. Deland, Fla., July 23, 1958; SB in Mech. Engring., MIT, 1980, SM in Mech. Engring., 1982, PhD in Med. Engring. and Physics, 1988; MD cum laude, Harvard U., 1985. Diplomate Nat. Bd. Med. Examiners. Summer fellow Inst. von Karman, Brussels, 1980; rsch. asst. George Harrison Spectroscopy Lab., MIT, 1983; intern in medicine U. Calif. Moffitt Hosp., San Francisco, 1986-87; rsch. fellow Mass. Gen. Hosp., Harvard Med. Sch., 1985-89, clin./rsch. fellow, resident in radiology, 1988-93, MRI fellow radiology, 1992-93; asst. prof. radiology Harvard Med. Sch., 1993-95, co-dir. MRI, 1994-95. Lectr. in field. Patentee nitinol blood clot filter, optical fiber catheters, selective laser angioplasty and lithotrypsy, and dynamic gadolinium enhanced MR angiography; contbr. chpts. to books and articles to profl. jours. NSF fellow, 1975, Case Western Res. U. rsch. fellow, 1976, Eloranta fellow, 1979, Deflorez/Hoist and Crane Engring. Design award, 1980, Tau Beta Pi grad. fellow, 1981, Med. Engring. Med. Physics grad. fellow, 1981-85; grantee NIH, 1992; recipient Nat. Rsch. Svc. award NIH, 1986-89, RSNA Rsch. Resident award, 1991. Recipient NSF Summer Sci. Tng. Program fellowship, 1975, Case Western Res. U. Sumemr Rsch. fellowship, 1976, Eloranta fellowship for undergrad. rsch., 1979, Deflorez/Hoist and Crane Engring. Design award, 1980, Tau Beta Pi Grad. fellowship, 1981, Med. Engring. Med. Physics grad. fellowship, 1981-85, NIH Nat. Rsch. Svc. award, 1986-89, RSNA Rsch. Resident award, 1991, grant NIH, 1992. Mem. AAAS, Radiol. Soc. N.Am., Am. Roentgen Ray Soc., Am. Soc. for Laser Medicine and Surgery, Internat. Soc. for Optical Engring., Sigma Xi.

PRINCE, SUSAN HUKILL, ancient language educator; b. Wilmington, Del., June 26, 1964; d. David Dickson and Margaret Hukill Prince; m. Matthew George Ward, July 3, 1999; children: Christopher Ward, Elissa Ward, Julia Ward. BA, Yale U., New Haven, 1986, U. Oxford, Eng., 1989; PhD, U. Mich., Ann Arbor, 1997. Asst. prof. classics U. Cin., 2007—. Democrat. Episcopalian. Achievements include research in Socratic philosophy. Office: Univ Cin 410 Blegen Libr Cincinnati OH 45221-0226 Business E-Mail: susan.prince@uc.edu.

PRINCE, TAYSHAUN DURELL, professional basketball player; b. Compton, Calif., Feb. 28, 1980; s. Thomas and Diane Prince; m. Farrah Brown, Apr. 11, 2005; 1 child. BA in Sociology, U. Ky., Lexington, 2002. Forward Detroit Pistons, 2002—. Mem. US Men's Sr. Nat. Basketball Team, 2007, Beijing, 08. Actor: Hood of Horror, 2006. Recipient Gold medal, men's basketball, Beijing Olympic Games, 2008; named to NBA All-Defensive Second Team, 2005, 2006, 2007, 2008. Achievements include being a member of the NBA Championship winning Detroit Pistons, 2004. Avocations: reading, theater. Office: Detroit Pistons The Palace of Auburn Hills 5 Championship Dr Auburn Hills MI 48326

PRINCE, THOMAS E., bank executive; b. 1947; With Security Pacific Corp., LA, 1968-92, sr. v.p., controller, 1984—92; exec. v.p., treas. Downey Savs Loan Assn., Newport Beach, Calif., 1992—2004, CFO, 1992, COO, 2004—08, interim CEO, 2008, sr. exec. v.p., CEO office, 2008—. Office: Downey Savs Loan Assn 3501 Jamboree Rd Ste 5000 Newport Beach CA 92660-2980 Mailing: Downey Savings Loan Assn PO Box 6000 Newport Beach CA 92658-6000 Office Phone: 949-509-4440. Office Fax: 949-854-8162.*

PRINCE, THOMAS RICHARD, accountant, educator; b. New Albany, Miss., Dec. 7, 1934; s. James Thompson and Callie Florence (Howell) P.; m. Eleanor Carol Polkoff, July 14, 1962; children: Thomas Andrew, John Michael, Adrienne Carol. BS, Miss. State U., 1956, MS, 1957; PhD in Accountancy, U. Ill., 1962. CPA, Ill. Instr. U. Ill., 1960—62; mem. faculty Northwestern U. Kellogg Sch. Mgmt., Evanston, Ill., 1962—, prof. acctg. info. and mgmt., 1969—, chmn. dept. acctg. info. and mgmt., 1968—75, prof. health industry mgmt., 1990—; cons. in field. Dir. Applied Rsch. Sys., Inc. Author: Extension of the Boundaries of Accounting Theory, 1962, Information Systems for Management Planning and Control, 3d edit, 1975, Financial Reporting and Cost Control for Health Care Entities, 1992, Product Life-Cycle Costing and Management of Large-Scale Medical Systems Investments, 1997, Strategic Management for Health Care Entities: Creative Frameworks for Financial and Operational Analysis, 1998. 1st lt. US Army Fin. Corps, 1957—60. Mem. AICPA, INFORMS, AHA, HFMA, HIMMS, AUPHA, Am. Accounting Assn., Am. Econ. Assn., Fin. Execs. Inst., AAAS, Ill. Soc. CPA, Inst. Mgmt. Acct., Alpha Tau Omega, Phi Kappa Phi, Omicron Delta Kappa, Delta Sigma Pi, Beta Alpha Psi. Congregationalist. Home: 303 Richmond Rd Kenilworth IL 60043-1138 Office: Northwestern U Leverone Hl Evanston IL 60208-2002 Home Phone: 847-251-4339. Business E-Mail: t-prince@sbcglobal.net.

PRINCE, (PRINCE ROGERS NELSON), musician, actor; b. Mpls., June 7, 1958; s. John L. and Mattie D. (Shaw) Nelson; m. Mayte Garcia, 1996 (div., 2000); 1 son (dec.); m. Manuela Testolini, Dec. 31, 2001 (separated, 2006) Singer, songwriter, actor. Albums include For You, 1978, Dirty Mind, 1979, Controversy, 1981, 1999, 1983, film star and soundtrack Purple Rain, 1984 (Academy Award for best original score, 1984), Around the World in a Day, 1985 (Best Soul/Rhythm and Blues Album of the Yr., Downbeat readers poll, 1985), Parade, 1986, Chaos and Disorder, 1996, Sign O' the Times, 1987, Lovesexy, 1988, Batman:

Motion Picture Soundtrack, 1989 (Soundtrack of Yr. award Playboy mag. readers' poll, Best Pop/Rock album Downbeat mag. readers' poll), (with the New Power Generation) Diamonds and Pearls, 1991, (symbol as title), 1992, Come, 1995, The Greatest Romance Ever Sold, 1999, 94 East, 2000, The Very Best of Prince, 2001, Beautiful Experience, 2001, The Rainbow Children, 2001, One Night Alone...Live!, 2002, N.E.W.S., 2003, Musicology, 2004, 3121, 2006, Planet Earth, 2007 (Grammy award for Best Male R&B Vocal Performance, 2008); films include Purple Rain, 1984, film star and soundtrack Under the Cherry Moon, 1986, film star and soundtrack Sign O' the Times, 1987; film appearance and soundtrack Graffiti Bridge, 1990 (ASCAP award for most performed songs from a motion picture, 1991); formerly mem. group Prince and the Revolution (Best Soul/Rhythm and Blues Group of Yr. Downbeat mag. readers poll 1985); composer Showgirls, 1995, Girl 6, 1996, The Gold Experience, 1995, Crystal Ball, 1998, Rave Un2 the Joy Fantastic, 1999, Bamboozled, 2000, Happy Feet, 2006 (The Song of the Heart, Best Original Song-Motion Picture, Golden Globe award, Hollywood Fgn. Press Assn., 2007). Recipient 3 Grammy awards, 1985, Am. Music Achievement award for infuence on look and sound of the 80's, NAACP Spl. Achievement award, 1997, Webby Lifetime Achievement award, Internat. Acad. Digital Arts and Sciences, 2006, Best Male R&B award, Black Entertainment TV (BET), 2006, Male Artist award, NAACP Image Awards, 2007; named Rhythm and Blues Musician of Yr. Down Beat mag. readers' poll, 1984, 1992; inducted Rock and Roll Hall of Fame, 2004. Office: Paisley Park Studios 7801 Audubon Rd Chanhassen MN 55317-8201

PRINCETON, JOY CAROL, retired nursing educator; b. St. Paul, Dec. 8, 1935; d. Eugene Russell Princeton and Margaret Edna Ehlers Princeton; children: Todd A. Myers, Michael D. Myers, Sarah C. Mooney. BSN, U. Colo., 1969, MSN, 1970, MA in Anthropology, 1975, PhD in Anthropology, 1977. RN Minn., Colo., N.C., Utah. Head nurse, obstetrics Abbott Hosp., Mpls., 1958—65; supr. obstetrics Boulder Meml. Hosp., Colo., 1965—68; asst. prof. U. Co. Sch. Nursing, Denver, 1970—73; assoc. prof. Duke U. Sch. Nursing, Durham, NC, 1978—81; prof. U. Utah Coll. Nursing, Salt Lake City, 1982—95; assoc. dir. U. Hosp., Salt Lake City, 1987—91. Mem. White House Com. on Children & Youth, Colo. Chpt., Denver, 1970—73; expert panel mem. Am. Acad. Nursing, Culturally Competent and Sensitive Health Care, Washington, 1991—93; cons. U. N.C. Med. Sch., Chapel Hill, NC, 1984—85, U. Rochester Sch. of Nursing, NY, 1988, NIH, Nat. Ctr. Nursing Rsch., 1988, U. Capetown Sch. Medicine, South Africa, 1990—91, HHS, PHS Divsn. Nursing, Rockville, Md., 1987—88, 1990—91, St. Louis U. Med. Ctr., 1990—91, Regis Coll. Sch. of Nursing, Denver, 1990—91; adv. Utah State Dept. Health, Salt Lake City, 1991—92; cons. in field, grad. student mentor, 1995—. Author: Maternity Nursing Today, 1973—77 (Am. Nurses Assn. Book of Yr., Parent/Child Nursing, 1973); mem. editl. bd.: Health Care for Women, 1984—94, Medical Anthro Quar., 1984—88, 1993—94, Scholarly Inquiry for Nursing Practice, 1985—90, Jour. Profl. Nursing, 1985—91, 1994—97, Jour. Nursing Edn., 1991—94, Nursing Outlook Jour., 1993—94; contbr. articles to profl. jours.; review panel mem. profl. jours., 1995—2006. Named Nurse of Yr., NC Nurses Assn., 1980; grantee, Dept. Health and Human Svcs., 1982—95; Ednl. grants, Dept. Health, Edn. and Welfare, U. Colo. Programs, 1970—73, grants for master's and doctoral edn., U.S. Pub. Health Svc., 1982—95. Fellow: Soc. Applied Anthropology, Am. Acad. Nursing. Democrat. Avocations: library work, hiking, camping, travel. Home: 2720 14th St Boulder CO 80304 Office Phone: 303-444-8163.

PRINCIPATO, AMY, psychologist; b. Canandaigua, NY, Oct. 1970; d. John Patrick and Roberta Bolger; m. Peter Principato, July 1, 1995; children: Marisa, Allison, Ryan. MA, Alfred U., NY, 1995. Cert. sch. psychologist NY Dept. Edn., 1995, in advanced studies Alfred U., 1995. Sch. psychologist Canandaigua Elem. Sch., 1995—. Bd. mem. YMCA, Canandaigua, 2008. Mem.: NY Assn. Sch. Psychologists. Home: 5100 Laura Ln Canandaigua NY 14424 Office: Canandaigua Elem Sch 90 W Gibson St Canandaigua NY 14424 Business E-Mail: principatoa@canandaiguaschools.org.

PRINCIPI, ANTHONY JOSEPH, pharmaceutical company executive, former United States Secretary of Veterans Affairs; b. NYC, Apr. 16, 1944; s. Antonio Joseph and Theresa (Princiotta) P.; m. Elizabeth Ann Ahlering, June 26, 1971; children: Anthony Jr., Ryan, John BS, U.S. Naval Acad., 1967; JD, Seton Hall U., 1975. Commd. 2d lt. U.S. Navy, 1967, advanced through grades to comdr., 1984, line officer Washington, 1967-72; atty. JAGC, San Diego, 1975-80; counsel Com. on Armed Service U.S. Senate, Washington, 1980-83, staff dir. Com. on Vet.'s Affairs, 1984—88; dep. adminstr. congl. & pub. affairs VA, Washington, 1983-84; dep. sec. US Dept. Veterans Affairs, Washington, 1989-90, acting sec., 1992—93; ptnr. Luce, Forward, Hamilton & Scripps, San Diego, 1990-95; sr. v.p., CEO Lockheed Martin IMS Integrated Solutions Co., Santa Clara, Calif., 1995-2001; pres. QTC Medical Services, Inc., 2001; sec. US Dept. Veterans Affairs, Washington, 2001—05; chmn. QTC Mgmt., Inc., Alexandria, Va., 2005—; v.p. govt. rels. Pfizer, Inc., Washington, 2005—. Chmn. Base Realignment & Closure (BRAC) Commn., 2005—; bd. dirs. Perot Systems Corp., 2005—. Decorated Bronze Star with combat "V", Vietnamese Cross of Gallantry, Navy Commendation medal with combat "V" (3); recipient Meritorious Service medal VA, 1983 Mem. ABA (chmn. subcom. gen. practice sect. 1985—) Republican. Roman Catholic. Avocations: gardening, skiing. Office: Pfizer Inc 325 Seveth St NW Ste 120 Washington DC 20004

PRING, ROBERT BRADFORD, banker, securities trader; b. St. Louis, July 22, 1951; s. Charles Branscombe Pring and A Helen Crosson Reim; m. Bernice Rosalyn Crisp, Oct. 25, 1975 (div. Dec. 2001); children: Robert Bradford III, Jennifer Christiane; m. Linda Colleen Mueller, Aug. 10, 2002. BS in Agr., U. Mo., Columbia, 1973, postgrad., 1973. Lic. life, accident and health ins agt; cert. fin planner, stockbroker, registered investment advisor rep. Ptnr. Prings Nursery, St. Louis, 1973-74; dist. sales mgr. Curtis Circulation Co., Nashville, 1974-75, reg. mktg. mgr. Orlando, Fla., 1975-77, West Coast account exec. West Caldwell, NJ, 1977-79, div. mktg. supr. St. Louis, 1979-81; trust mktg. officer Commerce Bank, St. Louis, 1982-84; v.p. bus. devel./comml. lending Commerce Bank St. Charles County, N.A., St. Peters, Mo., 1984—97; v.p., comml. devel. officer Commerce Bank St. Louis, St. Peters, Mo., 1991-97; mgr. Bus. Mgr. program First State Bank St. Charles, St. Charles, Mo., 1997-2001; fin. advisor, investment mgr., personal fin. planning INVEST Fin. Corp., 2001—02; ins. cons. fin. advice, mortgage banking Robert B. Pring & Assocs., 2002—04; v.p. comml. lending, br. mgr. CBC Bank, St. Peters, 2004—05; asst. v.p. Bank of Old Monroe, 2005, v.p. lending, investment svcs., 2006—, founder, program mgr., v.p. Old Monroe Investment Svcs., 2006—; sr. portfolio mgr., sr. fin. advisor, CFP registered investment advisor rep. Prodr., dir.: St. Charles County, A World of Opportunity, 1987. Pres., chmn. United Serv Handicapped, St. Charles, 1988—89; treas. bd. dirs YMCA St. Charles County, 1989—99, chmn. bd. dirs., 1991—92; treas. Citizens St. Charles County C.C., 1990, co-chmn., 1991, scholarship com., pres. search com., chair bd. devel. com., 2005—; bd. dirs. YMCA Greater Met. S.t Louis, 1991—92, Mid-Am Theatre Co., St. Charles, St. Charles YMCA, 1985—2000, St. Charles C.C. Found., 1994—2007, past chmn., treas. sec. chmn. bd., major gifts com., exec. dir. search com., chmn. nominating, devel. com., 2005—07, St. Charles C.C. Found. Bd. Emeritus, 2007—; mem. Eastern Lincoln County Economic Devel. Com. Recipient Meritorious Serv Award, United Servs Handicapped, 1989, Bell Vol Award, St Charles County Community Coun and Southwestern Bell, 1990. Mem.: Fin. Planning Assn., Inst. Cert. Fin. Planners, Greater St. Louis Soc. Cert. Fin. Planners (bd dirs 1990—91), St. Peters C. of C. (past dir, pres, chmn 1988, Disting Leadership Award 1990), Rotary (bd dirs St Charles chpt 1992). Presbyterian. Avocations: flying, soaring, water sports. Home and Office: 2163 Roselake Cir Saint Peters MO 63376-7772 Office Phone: 636-665-5601. E-mail: rbpring@charter.net.

PRINGLE, CURT, Mayor, Anaheim, California; m. Alexis Pringle; children: Katie, Kyle. BBA, MPA, Calif. State U., Long Beach. Pres. Curt Pringle and Associates, LLC, Irvine, Calif.; mem. Calif. State Assembly, 1988—90, 1992—98; mayor City of Anaheim, Calif., 2003—. Rep. leader, Rep. Caucus chair, chmn. appropriations com., chmn. rules com., vice chmn. budget com. Calif. State Assembly, spkr. house, 1996; vis. faculty mem. U. Calif., Irvine. Bd. dirs. Tiger Woods Learning Ctr. Found., John Burton Found. for Children Without Homes; bd. mem. Leadership Traq; mem. Calif. Film Commn., 1996—99; nominee Calif. State Treas., 1998; Calif. del. Nat. Rep. Conv., 1996; active Calif. Rep. Ctrl. Com.; mem. Calif. High Speed Rail Authority, 2008—, Commn. on 21st Century Economy, 2008—; served on Pub. Employees Post-Employment Benefit Commn., 2007, 2008; dir. Orange County Transportation Authority; governing bd. mem. Ukleja Ctr. for Ethical Leadership, Calif. State U. Named Best Problem Solver and as the Most Influential Leader of the Calif. State Assembly, Calif. Jour. Office: Anaheim City Hall 200 S Anaheim Blvd Anaheim CA 92805 Office Phone: 714-765-5247.*

PRINGLE, DAVID L., insurance company executive; BA in Ins. and Risk Mgmt., Miss. State U. Sales assoc. to state sales coord. AFLAC Inc., asst. agy. dir. West territory, dir. tng., sr. v.p. fed. rels. Sec., prin. fundraiser Aflac's Polit. Action Com. (Aflac PAC). Office: AFLAC Inc 1932 Wynnton Rd Columbus GA 31999 Office Phone: 706-323-3431. Office Fax: 706-324-6330.

PRINGLE, LAURENCE PATRICK, writer; b. Rochester, NY, Nov. 26, 1935; s. Laurence Erin and Marleah Elizabeth (Rosehill) P.; m. Judith Malanowicz, June 23, 1962 (div. 1970); children: Heidi Elizabeth, Jeffrey Laurence, Sean Edmund; m. Alison Newhouse, July 14, 1971 (div. 1975); m. Susan Deborah Klein, Mar. 13, 1983; children: Jesse Erin, Rebecca Anne. BS in Wildlife Biology, Cornell U., 1958; MS in Wildlife Biology, U. Mass., 1961. Tchr. sci. Lima (N.Y.) Cen. Sch., 1961-62; editor Nature and Sci. mag. Am. Mus. Natural History, NYC, 1963-70; free-lance writer, 1970—. Writer-in-residence Kean College, Union, N.J., 1985-86. Author: (children's books) Dinosaurs and Their World, 1968, The Only Earth We Have, 1969, From Field to Forest, 1970, In a Beaver Valley, 1970, One Earth, Many People, 1971, Ecology: Science of Survival, 1971, Cockroaches: Here, There, Everywhere, 1971, From Pond to Prairie, 1972, This Is a River, 1972, Pests and People: The Search for Sensible Pest Control, 1972, Estuaries: Where Rivers Meet the Sea, 1973, Into the Woods: Exploring the Forest Ecosystem, 1973, Follow a Fisher, 1973, Twist, Wiggle and Squirm: A Book about Earthworms, 1973, Recycling Resources, 1974, Energy: Power for People, 1975, City and Suburb: Exploring an Ecosystem, 1975, Chains, Webs and Pyramids: The Flow of Energy in Nature, 1975, Water Plants, 1975, The Minnow Family: Chubs, Dace, Minnows and Shiners, 1976, Listen to the Crows, 1976, Our Hungry Earth: The World Food Crisis, 1976, Death is Natural, 1977, The Hidden World: Life Under a Rock, 1977, The Controversial Coyote: Predation, Politics and Ecology, 1977, The Gentle Desert: Exploring an Ecosystem, 1977, Animals and Their Niches: How Species Share Resources, 1977, The Economic Growth Debate: Are There Limits to Growth?, 1978, Dinosaurs and People: Fossils, Facts and Fantasies, 1978, Wild Foods, 1978, Nuclear Power: From Physics to Politics, 1979, Natural Fire: Its Ecology in Forests, 1979, Lives at Stake: The Science and Politics of Environmental Health, 1980, What Shall We Do with the Land?: Choices for America, 1981, Frost Hollows and Other Microclimates, 1981, Vampire Bats, 1982, Water: The Next Great Resource Battle, 1982, Radiation: Waves and Particles/Benefits and Risks, 1983, Wolfman: Exploring the World of Wolves, 1983, Feral: Tame Animals Gone Wild, 1983, The Earth Is Flat—and Other Great Mistakes, 1983, Being a Plant, 1983, Nuclear War: From Hiroshima to Nuclear Winter, 1985, Animals at Play, 1985, Here Come the Killer Bees, 1986, Throwing Things Away: From Middens to Resource Recovery, 1986, Restoring Our Earth, 1987, Home: How Animals Find Comfort and Safety, 1987, Rain of Troubles: The Science and Politics of Acid Rain, 1988, Living in a Risky World, 1989, Nuclear Energy: Troubled Past, Uncertain Future, 1989, Bearman: Exploring the World of Black Bears, 1989, The Animal Rights Controversy, 1989, Saving Our Wildlife, 1990, Global Warming: Assessing the Greenhouse Threat, 1990, The Golden Book of Insects and Spiders, 1990, Killer Bees (rev. edit.), 1991, Batman: Exploring the World of Bats, 1991, Living Treasure: Saving Earth's Threatened Biodiversity, 1991, Antarctica: The Last Unspoiled Continent, 1992, The Golden Book of Volcanoes, Earthquakes, and Powerful Storms, 1992, Chemical and Biological Warfare: The Cruelest Weapons, 1993, revised edit., 2000, Oil Spills: Damage, Recovery, and Prevention, 1993, Jackal Woman: Exploring the World of Jackals, 1993, Scorpion Man: Exploring the World of Scorpions, 1994, Dinosaurs! Strange and Wonderful, 1995, Vanishing Ozone: Protecting Earth from Ultraviolet Radiation, 1995, Coral Reefs: Earth's Undersea Treasures, 1995, Dolphin Man: Exploring the World of Dolphins, 1995, rev. edit., 2002, Fire in the Forest: A Cycle of Growth and Renewal, 1995, Taking Care of the Earth: Kids in Action, 1996, Smoking: A Risky Business, 1996, An Extraordinary Life: The Story of a Monarch Butterfly, 1997, Nature! Wild and Wonderful, 1997, Everybody Has a Bellybutton: Your Life Before You Were Born, 1997, Elephant Woman: Cynthia Moss Explores The World of Elephants, 1997, Drinking: A Risky Business, 1997, One Room School, 1998, Explore Your Senses: SIGHT, 1999, Explore Your Senses: HEARING, 1999, Explore Your Senses: TASTE, 1999, Explore Your Senses: TOUCH, 1999, Explore Your Senses: SMELL, 1999, BATS! Strange and Wonderful, 2000, The Environmental Movement: From Its Roots to the Challenges of a New Century, 2000, Sharks! Strange and Wonderful, 2001, Global Warming: The Threat of Earth's Changing Climate, 2001, A Dragon in the Sky: The Story of a Green Darner Dragonfly, 2001, Scholastic Encyclopedia of Animals, 2001, Strange Animals, New to Science, 2002, Crows! Strange and Wonderful, 2002, Dog of Discovery: A Newfoundland's Adventures with Lewis and Clark, 2002, Whales! Strange and Wonderful, 2003, Snakes! Strange and Wonderful, 2004, American Slave, American Hero: York of the Lewis and Clark Expedition, 2006, Penguins! Strange and Wonderful, 2007, Imagine A Dragon, 2008, Alligators and Crocodiles! Strange and Wonderful, 2009, (fiction) Jesse Builds a Road, 1989, Octopus Hug, 1993, Naming the Cat, 1997, Bear Hug, 2003, (adult books) Wild River, 1972, Rivers and Lakes, 1985. Recipient Spl. Conservation award, Nat. Wildlife Fedn., 1978, Eva L. Gordon award, Am. Nature Study Soc., 1983, Orbis Pictus award, Nat. Coun. Tchrs. English, 1998, Nonfiction award, Washington Post/Children's Book Guild, 1999, Lifetime Achievement prize for excellence in sci. books, AAAS, 2005; fellow, John Simon Guggenheim Meml. Found., 2006. Mem.: The Authors Guild. Home and Office: PO Box 252 West Nyack NY 10994-0252 Office Phone: 845-623-7275.

PRINGLE, LEWIS GORDON, marketing professional, educator; b. Lansing, Mich., Feb. 13, 1941; s. Gordon Henry and Lucile Roxana (Drake) P.; children: Lewis Gordon Jr., William Davis, Thomas Benjamin. BA, Harvard U., 1963; MS, MIT, 1965, PhD, 1969. V.p., dir. mktg. sci. BBDO, Inc., NYC, 1968—73; asst. prof. mktg. Carnegie-Mellon U., Pitts., 1973—74; exec. v.p., dir. rsch. svcs., corp. dir. BBDO, Inc., NYC, 1978—91; exec. v.p. BBDO Worldwide, 1986—91; chmn., CEO BBDO Europe, 1986—91, LG Pringle and Assocs., 1992—95; Joseph C. Seibert prof. mktg. Farmer Sch. Bus. Adminstrn., Miami U., Oxford, Ohio, 1995—2000. Bd. dirs. Yorktown U., prof.; mem. vis com. Sloan Sch. Mgmt., MIT. Assoc. editor Jour. Advt. Rsch.; mem. editl. bd. Jour. Mktg. Sci.; mem. editl. bd. Jour. Market Rsch.; contbr. numerous articles to Harvard Bus. Rev., Mktg. Scis., others. Active local Boy Scouts Am. Ford Found. fellow, 1967 Fellow Royal Statis. Soc.; mem. INFORMS (chmn. mktg. strategy com.), Market Rsch. Coun., Am. Psychol. Assn., European Soc. Mktg. and Opinion Rsch., Am. Mktg. Assn., Inst. Ops. Rsch. and Mgmt. Sci. Office: Mind / Matter 2858 N Stout Rd Liberty IN 47353 Business E-Mail: lewpring@ruraltek.com.

PRINGLE, ORAN ALLAN, mechanical and aerospace engineering educator; b. Lawrence, Kans., Sept. 14, 1923; s. Oran Allan and Mae (McClell) Pringle; m. Billie Hansen, June 25, 1947; children: Allan, Billie, James, Rebecca. BSME, U. Kan., 1947; MS, U. Wis., 1948, PhD, 1967. Registered profl. engr., Mo. Mech. engr. Black and Veatch (cons. engrs.), Kansas City, Mo., 1947-48; engr. Boeing Airplane Co., Wichita, 1952—; prof. U. Mo., Columbia, 1948—90, prof. emeritus, 1991—. Co-author: Engineering Metallurgy, 1957; contbr. articles to profl. lit. Bd. dirs. Untied Cerebral Palsy Boone County, Mo. With US Army, 1943—45. Ford Found. grantee. Mem.: ASME (chmn. fastening and joining com. design engring. divsn.), Sigma Xi. Home: 1820 University Ave Columbia MO 65201-6004 Office: Dept Mech and Aerospace Engring U Mo Columbia MO 65201 Home Phone: 573-449-5035.

PRINGLE, PAUL C., lawyer; b. 1943; AB, Dartmouth Coll., 1965; JD, U. Mich., 1968. Bar: NY 1969, Calif. 1972. Ptnr. corp. securities Sidley Austin Brown & Wood LLP, San Francisco and LA. Office: Sidley Austin Brown & Wood Ste 2000 555 California St San Francisco CA 94104-1715 Office Phone: 415-772-1249. Office Fax: 415-772-7400. Business E-Mail: ppringle@sidley.com.

PRINGLE, ROBERT BERNARD, lawyer; b. Summit, NJ, Jan. 2, 1944; s. Edward Harvey and Caroline (Mazuco) P.; m. Rebecca Winslow, June 29, 1974; children: Robin Stevens, Parker Winslow, Edward Sterling. BS, U. NC, 1966; JD, Duke U., 1969. Bar: Pa. 1970, Calif. 1971, US Dist. Ct. (no. dist.) Calif. 1971, US Ct. Appeals (9th cir.) Calif. 1970, US Dist. Ct. (cen. dist.) Calif. 1975, Supreme Ct. of US, US Ct. of Appeals (fed. cir.), bar assn. of City & County of San Francisco. Assoc. Thelen, Marrin, Johnson & Bridges, San Francisco, 1971-77, ptnr., 1978—2004, Thelen Reid Brown Raysman & Steiner LLP, San Francisco, 2004—08, Winston & Strawn LLP, San Francisco, 2008—. Spl. litig. coun. to bd. dir. of major software co. Contbr. articles to prof. journs., co-author numerous books on law. Mem. Tiburon Planning Commn., 1980-83, chmn., 1984; mem. bd. visitors Duke U. Sch. Law. Best Lawyers in US, Chambers USA's America's Leading Lawyers for Bus., Super Lawyer (San Francisco magazine). Mem. ABA (anti-trust sect., civil practice and procedure com. 1977—, litigation sect., past chair intellectual property litigation com.), Olympic Club (San Francisco), San Francisco Yacht Club (Belvedere, Calif.), litig. sect. (past chair of various com. chair ann. meeting) 1992, State Bar Calif., mem. exec. com. Unfair Competition & Antitrust sect. 2001-2003, bd. of advisors 2003-, ABA Pub. Utility, Communications & Transp. Law (chair, antitrust com., coun. mem.), Tiburon Peninsula Club. Avocations: sailing, skiing, fly fishing, golf. Office: Winston & Strawn LLP 101 California St San Francisco CA 94111 Office Phone: 415-591-1420. Office Fax: 415-591-4000. Business E-Mail: rpringle@winston.com.

PRINN, RONALD G., atmospheric science educator; b. Hamilton, New Zealand, June 11, 1945; BSc, U. Auckland, New Zealand, 1967, MSc with 1st honors, 1968; ScD, MIT, 1971. Asst. prof. MIT, Cambridge, Mass., 1971-76, assoc. prof., 1976-82, prof., 1982-93, Tepco prof., 1993—, head dept. earth, atmospheric and planetary scis., 1998—2003. Chair com. on earth sci. NAS, Washington, 1982-84; chair Internat. Global Atmospheric Chemistry Project, Stockholm, 1988-95. Recipient Vernadsky Meml. lectr. Russian Acad. Sci., Moscow, 1984. Fellow Am. Geophys. Union (Macelwane medal 1981), AAAS (chmn. atmospheric and hydrospheric scis. 1999). Office: MIT Bldg 54-1312 Cambridge MA 02139 Business E-Mail: rprinn@mit.edu.

PRINS, HARALD EDWARD LAMBERT, anthropologist, educator; b. Alphen aan de Rijn, The Netherlands, Sept. 7, 1951; came to US, 1978; s. Adriaan Hendrik Johan and Pietertje Anna Catharina (Poorter) P.; m. Bunny McBride, Sept. 29, 1985. Doctorandus, Radboud U. Nijmegen, The Netherlands, 1976; cert. in advanced 16 mm filmmaking, Parsons Sch., NYC, 1980; PhD, New Sch. Social Rsch., NYC, 1988. Asst. prof. comparative hist. Radboud U. Nijmegen, 1976—78; dir. R & D Assn. Aroostook Indians, Houlton, Maine, 1981—82; staff anthropologist Aroostook Band of Micmacs, Presque Isle, Maine, 1982—90; mem. grad. faculty Kans State U., Manhattan, 1990—, prof. anthropology, 1996—, Coffman chair Univ. Disting. Tchg. Scholars, 2004—05, Univ. Disting. prof., 2005—. Vis. lectr. anthropology Bowdoin Coll., Brunswick, Maine, 1986—88; vis. asst. prof. Colby Coll., Waterville, Maine, 1988—89; adj. prof. U. Maine, Orono, 1989; expert witness on Indian rights US Congress, Washington, 1990; faculty adv. AISES, 1992—97, Native Am. Student Body, 1997—2001; internat. observer presdl. elections, Paraguay, 1993; expert witness Nfld. aboriginal landclaims Nfld. Fed. and Provincial Ct., Canada, 1998—; disting. lectr. U. Maine, Presque Isle, 2002; keynote spkr. High Plains Soc. Applied Anthropology, 2002, Northeastern Anthrop. Assn., 2003; plenary spkr. U. Nijmegen, Netherlands, 2003; prin. investigator Acadia Nat. Pk. Ethnohistory Project, Nat. Pks. Svc., 2003—07; invited speaker UNESCO Symposium, Paris, 2005; guest curator mus. exhibit Smithsonian Instn., 2003—07; invited spkr. Ecole des Hautes Etudes, Paris, 2008; rsch. assoc. Nat. Mus. Nat. History, Smithsanran Inst., 2008—. Co-prodr.: (documentaries) Our Lives in Our Hands, 1986, Oh, What a Blow that Phantom Gave Me!, 2003, Among Xavante Friends, 2008; mem. editl. bd. Maine Hist., 1992—, Am. Anthropologist, 1998—2002, Explorations in Media Ecology, 2005—; co-editor: American Beginnings, 1994; author: The Mi'kmaq: Resistance, Accommodation and Cultural Survival, 1996; editor: Am. Anthropologist, 1998—2002, Visual Anthropology Rev., 2000—04; co-author: Cultural Anthropology: The Human Challenge, 2005, Asticou's Island Domain: Wabanaki Peoples at Mount Desert Island, 1500-2000, 12th edit., 2007, Evolution and Prehistory: The Human Challenge, 2005; co-editor: 8th edit., 2007; co-author: The Essence of Anthropology, 2006, 2009, Kulturel Antropoloji, 2008, Indians in Eden: Wabanakis and Rusticators at Mount Desert Islands, 2009; contbr. chapters to books, articles to profl. jours. Mem adv. bd. Salt Inst. Documentary Field Studies, Maine, 1990—;

adv./rschr. land claims Miawpukek Band of Mikmaq, Conne River, Nfld., 1996—; cultural preservation adv. Plains Apache Tribe, Anadarko, Okla., 1993-97; fed. recognition and landclaims adv./rschr. Aroostook Band of Micmacs, Presque Isle, 1981-91. Recipient Conoco Prize Outstanding Tchg., Kans. State U., 1993, Presdl. award Outstanding Tchg., 1999, John Culkin award Outstanding Practice in Media, 2004, Profl. Performance award; named Kans. Prof. of Yr., Carnegie Found. for Advancement of Tchg. and Coun. for Advancement and Support of Edn., 2006, McNair Outstanding Mentor, 2008; grantee, NEH, 1989; Vera List fellow, 1978. Mem.: NY Acad. Scis., Soc. Anthropology of Lowland S.Am., Maine Hist. Soc., Soc. L.Am. Anthropology, Soc. Visual Anthropology (prog. editor 1995, bd. dirs. 1995—2002, pres. 2000—02), Am. Anthrop. Assn. (jury Ethnographic Film Festival 1998). Avocations: hiking, sailing, drawing, photography, wildlife. Office: Dept Anthropology Kans State U 207 Waters Hall Manhattan KS 66506 Office Phone: 785-532-4966. E-mail: prins@ksu.edu.

PRINS, RICHARD T., lawyer; b. Grand Rapids, Mich., 1950; BA summa cum laude, Calvin Coll., 1972; JD cum laude, U. Mich., 1977. Bar: NY 1979. Ptnr., heads investment mgmt. group Skadden, Arps, Slate, Meagher & Flom LLP, NYC. Office: Skadden Arps Slate Meagher & Flom LLP 4 Times Sq New York NY 10036 Office Phone: 212-735-2790. Office Fax: 917-777-2790. Business E-Mail: rprins@skadden.com.

PRINS, ROBERT JACK, retired academic administrator; b. Grand Rapids, Mich., Oct. 12, 1932; s. Jacob and Marie (Vanden Brink) P.; m. Ruth Ellen John, Oct. 10, 1950; children: Linda, Douglas, Debra, Nancy, Eric, Sarah. BA, Hope Coll., 1954; DBA, Coll. Emporia, 1974; DHL, Iowa Wesleyan U., 1999. With Mich. Bell Tel. Co., Detroit area, 1954—63; asst. pres. Hope Coll., 1964; with Chesapeake and Potomac Tel. Co., 1965—66; dir. devel. Bethesda Hosp., Denver, 1966-68; v.p. planning and devel. Park Coll., Parkville, Mo., 1969-70; chief adminstrv. officer Coll. of Emporia, Kans., 1970-75; dir. fin. and devel. The Abbey Sch., Canon City, Colo., 1975-79; dir. devel. Kirksville Coll. Osteo. Medicine, Mo., 1979-84; v.p. devel. McKendree Coll., Lebanon, Ill., 1984-86; pres. Iowa Weslyan Coll., Mt. Pleasant, 1986-99, pres. emeritus, 1999—; exec. dir. Internat. Student Svcs., Canon City, Colo., 1999—2008. Bd. dirs. Iowa Coll. Found., Iowa Commn. on Vol. Svc.; mem. Iowa Assn. Ind. Colls. and Univs.; former chmn., mem. bd. Potomak Worldwide, Taipei, Taiwan, bd. trustees Hillbodde Group, 2008 Mem. Nat. Assn. Ind. Colls. and Univs., Coun. for Advancement and Support Edn.

PRINS, ROBERT MICHAEL, medical educator; b. Balt., Jan. 11, 1969; s. Robert Peter and Mary Elizabeth Prins; m. Mayumi Lynn Smith; children: Madeline Jade, Ainsley Akane. PhD, Med. Coll. Va., Richmond, 2001. Postdoc. fellow Cedars-Sinai Neurosurgical Inst., LA, 2001—02; asst. rschr. UCLA, Dept. Neurosurgery, 2002—06, asst. prof., 2006—. Recipient Howard Temin award, Nat. Cancer Inst., 2006—. Mem.: Am. Assn. Immunologists, Soc. Neuro-Oncology, Am. Assn. Cancer Rsch. Liberal. Achievements include research in brain tumor immunotherapy. Office: UCLA Dept Neurosurgery 10833 Le-Conte CHS 74-145 PO Box 956901 Los Angeles CA 90095 Office Fax: 310-206-2093.

PRINZ, RICHARD ALLEN, surgeon; MD, Loyola U., Chgo., 1972. Diplomate Am. Bd. Surgery, bd. dirs., 1994—. Intern Barnes Hosp., St. Louis, 1972-73, resident in surgery, 1973-74, Loyola U., Chgo., 1974-77, attending surgeon, 1980-93; staff Rush Presbyn.-St. Luke's Med. Ctr., Chgo., 1993—; Helen Shedd Keith prof., chmn. dept. gen. surgery Rush U., Chgo., 1993—. Mem. Am. Surg. Assn., Am. Assn. Endocrine Surgeons (pres. 1996), Midwest Surg. Assn. (pres. 1997), Western Surg. Assn. (treas. 1993-97, pres. 2002-), Chgo. Surg. Soc. (pres.-elect 2002-, pres. 2003). Office: Rush U 818 Profl Bldg 1725 W Harrison St Chicago IL 60612-3828 Office Phone: 312-942-6511. Business E-Mail: rprinz@rush.edu.

PRINZE, FREDDIE, JR., actor; b. LA, Mar. 8, 1976; m. Sarah Michelle Gellar, Sept. 1, 2002. Grad., La Cueva H.S., 1994. Actor: (TV series) Family Matters, 1994, ABC Afterschool Spl., 1996, Freddie, 2005—06; (films) To Gillian on Her 37th Birthday, 1996, The House of Yes, 1997, I Know What You Did Last Summer, 1997, I Still Know What You Did Last Summer, 1998, She's All That, 1999, Wing Commander, 1999, Boys and Girls, 2000, Head Over Heels, 2001, Summer Catch, 2001, Scooby-Doo, 2002, Scooby-Doo 2: Monsters Unleashed, 2004, (voice) Shark Bait, 2006, Brooklyn Rules, 2006, (voice) Happily N'Ever After, 2007, Delgo, 2008. Office: c/o BWR Pub Rels 6th Fl West Tower 9100 Wilshire Blvd Beverly Hills CA 90212*

PRIOLEAU, FLORENCE W., lobbyist, lawyer; BA, Goucher Coll., 1974; JD, Georgetown U., 1979. Bar: DC. Sr. legis. asst. to Congressman Charles B. Rangel, 1975—76; prof. staff House Ways and Means Com., 1976—79; asst. dir. domestic policy staff The White House; ptnr. Pillsbury Winthrop Shaw Pittman LLP, Washington, Crowell & Moring LLP, Washington, 2008—. Former pres., mem. bd. dirs. Children's Inn at the Nat. Insts. Health; former mem. DC Cts. of Appeals Com. on Unauthorized Practice of Law. Contbr. articles to law jours. Named one of Top Lobbyists in Washington, Washingtonian mag., 1998, 50 Top Lobbyists, 2007. Office: Crowell & Moring LLP 1001 Pennsylvania Ave, NW Washington DC 20004-2595 Office Phone: 202-624-2965. Office Fax: 202-628-5116. E-mail: fprioleau@crowell.com.*

PRIOR, CORNELIUS BERNARD, JR., utilities executive, financial consultant; b. Hartford, Conn., Feb. 26, 1934; s. Cornelius B. Sr. and Katherine (Daly) P.; m. Trudie Yolleck, 1993; children: Elizabeth, Michael, Sarah. AB, Holy Cross Coll., Worcester, Mass., 1956; LLB, Harvard U., Cambridge, Mass., 1962. Bar: NY 1963. Assoc. atty. Sullivan and Cromwell, NYC, 1963-68; gen. counsel Private Investment Co. for Asia, Tokyo, 1969-71; v.p. Drexel Firestone, NYC, 1971-75; sr. v.p. Blythe Eastman Dillon, NYC, 1975—78; mng. dir. Paine Webber, NYC, 1978—80, Kidder, Peabody and Co., NYC, 1980-87; chmn. & CEO Atlantic Tele-Network, Inc., St. Thomas, V.I. Bd. dirs. Atlantic Telenetwork Co., St. Thomas. Bd. dirs., trustee Holy Cross Coll.; mem. vis. com. Harvard Law Sch., dean's adv. coun.; trustee, chair capital campaigns Antilles Sch.; chmn. Caribbean Assn. of Nat. Telephone Orgns.; mem. adv. bd. Peter Gruber Found.; chmn. Caribbean and C.Am. Action; dir. Kneisel Hall Music Sch. Served to lt (j.g.) USN, 1956-59. Fulbright scholar, 1962—63. Mem.: Bar Assn. of NY, Univ. Club (NYC). Roman Catholic. Office: Atlantic TeleNetwork Inc PO Box 12030 St Thomas VI 00801 Office Phone: 340-774-2260. Business E-Mail: cbpriorjr@atni.com.

PRIOR, MARK WILLIAM, professional baseball player; b. San Diego, Sept. 7, 1980; s. Jerry Prior; m. Heather Gora, Nov. 15, 2003; 1 child, Amanda Grace. Attended, Vanderbilt U., 1998—99; B in Bus., U. Southern Calif., 2004. Pitcher Chgo. Cubs, 2002—06, San Diego Padres, 2008—. Recipient Golden Spikes award, USA Baseball, 2001; named to Nat. League All-Star Team, 2003. Mailing: c/o San Diego Padres PETCO Pk 100 Park Blvd San Diego CA 92112*

PRISANT, LOUIS MICHAEL, cardiologist, educator; b. Albany, Ga., Dec. 25, 1949; s. Bennie Martin and Mozelle Cosper Prisant; m. Rose Corinth Trincher, June 28, 1975 (dec. Nov. 7, 2008); children: Michelle Elizabeth Underwood, Louis Michael. BA, Emory U., Atlanta, 1971; MD, Med. Coll. Ga., Augusta, 1977. Diplomate Nat. Bd. Med. Examiners, 1978, Am. Bd. Internal Medicine, 1980, in cardiovascular diseases 1984, Am. Bd. Clin. Pharmacology, 1991, Am. Bd. Forensic Examiners, 1996, Am. Bd. Forensic Medicine, 1996, cert. specialist in clin. hypertension Am. Soc. Hypertension, 1999, diplomate Am. Bd. Clin. Lipidology, 2005. Internship: straight medicine Med. Coll. Ga., Augusta, Ga., 1977—78, residency: internal medicine, 1978—80, cardiology fellow, 1980—82, instr. medicine, 1982—83, asst. prof. medicine, 1983—89, assoc. prof. medicine, 1989—94, prof. medicine, 1994—, dir. hypertension & clin. pharmacology unit, 2002—; chpt. pres. Am. Coll. Clin. Pharmacology Ahlquist Soc., 1992—95; nominating com. Am. Soc. Hypertension, NYC, 2001—04, CME com., 2007—; co-chmn., Sphygmomanometer Com. Assn. Advancement Med. Instrumentation, Arlington, Va., 2003—08. Editl. bd. mem. Heart Disease, 1999—2004, Blood Pressure Monitoring, 1995—, Jour. Clin. Hypertension, 1999—, Jour. Clin. Radiology, 2006—, Am. Jour. Therapeutics, 2000—. Editor: (textbook) Hypertension in the Elderly; contbr. articles to profl. jours. Recipient Physicians Recognition award, AMA, 1982—, Disting. Faculty award, Med. Coll. Ga., 2006; fellowship, Am. Heart Assn., 1992. Fellow: Am. Coll. Cardiology; mem.: AMA, Am. Assn. U. Pre, Southeast Lipid Assn., Nat. Lipid Assn. (Physicians Recognition award 1982—2005), Am. Soc. Echocardiography, Am. Coll. Clin. Pharmacology, Am. Coll. Chest Physicians, Am. Soc. Hypertension (pres. Carolinas & Ga. chpt. 2005—07). Jewish. Avocations: science fiction, computers, scuba diving. Home: 617 Brae Burn Martinez GA 30907 Office: Med Coll Ga 1467 Harper St HB-201- Augusta GA 30912 Office Fax: 706-854-0025; Home Fax: 706-854-0255. Personal E-mail: lprisant@comcast.net. Business E-Mail: mprisant@mcg.edu.

PRISCHMANN GRYNIEWICZ, DEBORAH ANNE, vocalist, educator; d. Richard D. Prischmann and Carole Anne Frascone; m. Ronald Joseph Gryniewicz, Mar. 13, 1962. B in Music Edn., U. Ariz., 1979; MusM in Opera/Vocal Pedagogy, Temple U., 1985. Cert. N.J. Dept. Edn., 1984. Vocal solo artist Jubilant Voice Ministry, Doylestown, Pa., 1990—; dir., instr. Meadow Lark Vocal Studio, Doylestown, 1990—; vocalist in Voices of Pops Peter Nero and the Philly Pops, Phila., 2001—07; prof. voice U. of the Arts, Phila., 2005—07. Gen. music tchr. Lebanon (N.J.) Boro Sch., 1987—91; dir. music Washington's Crossing (Pa.) United Meth. Ch., 1987—88; youth chorus dir. Musical Arts Acad., Doylestown, 1997—99; musical vocal dir. Ctrl. Bucks West H.S., Doylestown, 1998—99; worship leader Doylestown United Meth. Ch., 1999—2001; vocal worship cons. Calvary Chapel, Chalfont, Pa., 2001—03; vocal clinician William Penn H.S., Newark, 2004—04. Composer: (solo debut vocal album) Light My Way, (vocal solo album) Deborah - Christmas at America's Keswick - live!, (solo vocal contemporary christian album) The Me God Sees, (solo contemporary christian album) The Way, The Truth, The Life. Dir. music Ctrl. Schwenkfelder Ch., Worcester, Pa., 1979—82. Recipient Ruby Sword of Honor for outstanding leadership, Sigma Alpha Iota, 1979, Grad. Tchg. Assistantship, Temple U., 1980; finalist Outstanding Sr. award, U. Ariz., 1979; Full Gen. Music scholar, 1976. Mem.: ASCAP, Nat. Assn. Tchrs. Singing (vocal adjudicator 1992—93). Republican. Avocations: travel, equestrian, gardening, birdwatching. Office: University of the Arts 320 South Broad St Philadelphia PA 19102

PRISING, JONAS, employment services executive; MBA, Stockholm Sch. Econs. Asia-Pacific regional mgr. AB Electrolux, Singapore, 1989—93, mng. dir. comml. cleaning equipment divsn. Paris, 1993—95, mng. dir. comml. cleaning equipment divsn., head global sales and mktg. for divsn. London, 1995—99; dir. global accounts Europe, Mid. East and Africa Manpower, Inc., London, 1999—2002, mng. dir. Italy Milan, 2002—05, exec. v.p., pres. N.Am. Milw., 2006—.

PRISINZANO, THOMAS EDWARD, chemistry professor, researcher; b. NYC, July 19, 1973; s. Paul Robert and Eileen Gilleece Prisinzano; m. Deanna Olech Olech, Sept. 30, 1973; children: Sara Marie, Joseph Paul. BS, U. Del., Newark, 1995; PhD, Va. Commonwealth U., Richmond, 2000. Grad. asst. Va. Commonwealth U., 1995—2000; asst. prof. U. Iowa, Iowa City, 2003—. Faculty mem. Ctr. Biocatalysis and Bioprocessing, Iowa City, 2003—, U. Iowa Pain Rsch. Program, 2003—. Co-author: (textbook) Comprehensive Medicinal Chemistry Second Edition. Recipient J. Doyle Smith award, Va. Commonwealth U., Sch. Pharmacy, 1998, Early Career Investigator award, Coll. Problems Drug Dependence, 2003, D. John Faulkner award, Am. Soc. Pharmacognosy, 2005, Travel award, Internat. Narcotics Rsch. Conf., 2005; grantee, Nat. Inst. Drug Abuse, 2005; fellow, Nat. Inst. Diabetes and Digestive and Kidney Diseases, 2000—03. Mem.: Internat. Narcotics Rsch. Conf., Soc. Neurosci., Am. Assn. Pharm. Scientists, Coll. Problems Drug Dependence, Am. Soc. Pharmacognosy, Am. Chem. Soc., Theta Xi (life). Roman Catholic. Achievements include patents pending for Novel Opioid Receptor Ligands; discovery of Novel Scaffold for Mu Opioid Receptor Ligands; Mu Opioid with Altered Receptor Regulation; research in Method for the Detection of Salvinorin A in Biological Fluids; patents pending for Novel Opiate Agonists That Do Not Promote Receptor Regulation as Analgesics with Limited Tolerance Liability. Office: U Iowa 115 S Grand Ave Iowa City IA 52242 Office Fax: 319-335-8766. E-mail: thomas-prisinzano@uiowa.edu.

PRISTOOP, SIMON MORRIS, retired physicist, systems engineer, consultant; b. Balt., Mar. 8, 1933; s. Leon Pristoop and Gladys Marner; m. Maria del Carmen Carmona Santana, Nov. 29, 1986; children from previous marriage: Flora Gee, Robert Erich, Gina Springmann, Steven. BS in Physics and Math., U. Md., College Park, 1954. Physicist Naval Ordnance Lab., White Oak, Md., 1954—56, Vitro Corp., Silver Spring, Md., 1956—58; engr. Melpar Corp., Falls Church, Va., 1958—60, Northrop Corp., Arlington, Va.; electronic systems engr. Westinghouse Corp., Friendship Airport, Md., 1960—64; cons. NASA, Greenbelt, Md., 1964; sr. engr., program mgr. Tracor Corp., Rockville, Md., 1965—69; program mgr. Litton Sys., College Park, Md., 1970—74; program mgr., sys. engr. Syscon Corp., Washington, 1975—89; program mgr. software Colsa Corp. Naval Base, PR, 1989—95; cons. Dynecorp, United Def., RI, 1995—96, Pa., 1996—98; ret. Contbr. scientific papers to profl. jours. Co-chair Home Rule Charter Campaign, Prince George County, 1960—62; chmn. Prince George Bd. Appeals, Md., 1971—74; candidate fed. congress Dem. Congl. Dist. 15, Fla., 2004; vice chair Brevard County Dem. Exec. Com., Fla., 2002—03, com. chair, 1999—2008. Mem.: Am. Civil Liberties Union, Moose Lodge. Democrat. Avocations: politics, jogging, weightlifting.

PRITCHARD, CLAUDIUS HORNBY, JR., retired university president; b. Charleston, W.Va., June 28, 1927; s. Claudius Hornby and Katherine (Ellison) P.; m. Marjorie Walker Pullen, Aug. 9, 1952; children: Virginia Aiken, Katherine Winston, Olivia Reynolds, Claudius V. BA, Hampden-Sydney Coll., 1950; MA, Longwood U., 1965; PhD, Fla. State U., 1971; LLD, Maryville U., 1992. Comml. loan teller Am. Nat. Bank and Trust Co., Danville, Va., 1950-53; asst. cashier Planters Bank & Trust Co., Farmville, Va., 1953-55; asst. to pres. Hampden-Sydney (Va.) Coll., 1955-57, bus. mgr. and treas., 1957-67, v.p. devel., 1967-71; sr. budget analyst-edn. State of Fla., Tallahassee, 1971-72; pres. Sullins Coll., Bristol, Va., 1972-76; v.p. adminstrn. Maryville U., St. Louis, 1976-77, pres., 1977-92, pres. emeritus, 1992—. Adv. dir. Commerce Bank of St. Louis, 1982—92. Author: Col. D. Wyatt Aiken (1828-1887) South Carolina's Militant Agrarian, 1970; contbr. articles to profl. jours. Mem. bd. visitors Charleston So. U., 1993—2005; chmn. Summerville Comml. Design Rev. Bd., 1999—; bd. dirs. West St. Louis County YMCA, Chesterfield, Mo., 1985—92. With USNR, 1945—46. Fla. State U. fellow, 1969-70, Arthur Vining Davis fellow Am. Council on Edn., 1974; recipient Disting. Svc. award Charleston Southern U., 2000; named Citizen of Year Chesterfield, Mo., 1986. Mem. AAUP, SCV, Am. Assn. Higher Edn., So. Hist. Assn., S.C. Hist. Soc., Mo. Colls. Fund (bd. dirs., chmn. 1987-88), Mil. Order of the Stars and Bars, Ind. Colls. and Univs. Mo., Chesterfield C. of C. (pres. 1987, Chesterfield Citizen of Yr. award 1986), Rotary. Republican. Presbyterian.

PRITCHARD, ELSIE TOMLINSON, librarian; b. Dothan, Ala., Nov. 14, 1947; d. Eugene and Merle (Coleman) Tomlinson; m. Robert Donald Pritchard II, Dec. 23, 1966; children: Claire, Alison. BS, Old Dominion U., 1969; MLS, U. Pitts., 1972; MusM, Morehead State U., 1990. Tech. svcs. libr. Boston Conservatory, 1978-79; music cataloger Morehead (Ky.) State U., 1972-78, 82-86, acquisitions libr., 1986-92, asst. dir. Tech. Svcs., 1993—2005, dean libr. svc., 2005—. Elder Morehead Presbyn. Ch., 1982—. Mem. ALA, Ky. Libr. Assn., Assn. Coll. and Rsch. Librs. Office: Camden Carroll Libr Morehead St # U Morehead KY 40351

PRITCHARD, HUW OWEN, chemist, educator; b. Bangor, Wales, July 23, 1928; s. Owen and Lilian Venetia P.; m. Margaret Ramsden, Nov. 3, 1956; children— Karen, David. B.Sc., U. Manchester, 1948, M.Sc., 1949, PhD, 1951, D.Sc., 1964. Asst. lectr. chemistry Manchester (Eng.) U., 1951-54, lectr., 1954-65; prof. chemistry York U., Ont., Can., 1965-97, prof. emeritus Can., 1997—. Contbr. articles to profl. jours. Fellow: Royal Soc. Can. Office: Chemistry Dept York Univ Toronto ON Canada M3J 1P3 Business E-Mail: huw@yorku.ca.

PRITCHARD, KEVIN, professional sports team executive; b. Bloomington, Ind., July 17, 1967; Grad., U. Kans., 1990. Player Golden State Warriors, 1990—91, Boston Celtics, 1991—92, Phila. 76ers, 1994, Miami Heat, 1995, Washington Bullets, 1995—96; scout San Antonio Spurs; coach, gen. mgr., dir. player pers. Am. Basketball Assn. Kans. City Knights; dir. player pers. Portland Trail Blazers, 2004—05, interim head coach, 2005, asst. gen. mgr., 2006—07, gen. mgr., 2007—. Office: Portland Trail Blazers Rose Garden One Center Ct Portland OR 97227*

PRITCHARD, LLEWELYN GEORGE, lawyer; b. NYC, Aug. 13, 1937; s. Llewelyn and Anne Mary (Streib) P.; m. Joan Ashby, June 20, 1959; children: David Ashby, Jennifer Pritchard Vick, Andrew Harrison, William Llewellyn. AB with honors, Drew U., 1958; LLB, Duke U., 1961. Ptnr. Helsell & Fetterman, Seattle. Trustee Allied Arts Found., pres. 2005-07; pres., trustee, corp. counsel Allied Arts Seattle, 1973-76; dir. Fifth Ave. Theatre, 2005-; trustee Meth. Ednl. Found., 1970-85, pres., 1991-92; life trustee PONCHO Patrons of Pacific N.W. Civil, Cultural and Charitable Orgns., pres., 1972-73; bd. dirs. Planned Parenthood of Western Wash., 1972-78, 2007-; trustee Seattle Symphony Orch., 1979-83, chmn. bd., 1980-82, life trustee; trustee U. Puget Sound., 1972-99, exec. com., 1973-96, chmn. bd. visitors to Law Sch., 1984-88; trustee Mus. of Glass, 2000-07, Betty Bowen com. Seattle Art Mus., 2007; chancellor Pacific N.W. Ann. conf. United Meth. Ch., 1969—. Fellow Am. Bar Found. (life, state chmn. 1988-98); mem. ABA (state del. 1982-86, bd. govs. 1986-89, chmn. program com. 1988-89, exec. com. 1988-89, Ho. of Dels. 1979—, nat. dir. young lawyers divsn. 1971, chmn. sect. of individual rights and responsibilities 1975-76, exec. coun. family law sect. 2002-05, chair standing com. on legal aid and indigent defendants 1973-75, chair legal needs study 1995-98, chair adv. com. to pro bono immigration project 1991-01, dir. Ctr. for Human Rights 2001-), Commn. Rule of Law Initiatives, World Justice Project Commn., Wash. State Bar Assn. (chair young lawyers com., bd. govs. King County 1972-75), King County Bar Assn. (chair young lawyers sect. 1970). Avocations: reading, art collector. Home: 5229 140th Ave NE Bellevue WA 98005-1024 Office: Helsell & Fetterman 1001 Fourth Ave Ste 4200 Seattle WA 98154 Office Phone: 206-292-1144.

PRITCHARD, MARC S., consumer products company executive; b. Oakland, Calif., May 14, 1960; BS in Fin., Ind. U., Bloomington, 1982. Cost analyst paper divsn. Proctor & Gamble Co., 1982, mgr. acctg. Mehoopany, Pa., 1982—84, profit forecaster paper divsn., 1984—85, sr. fin. analyst paper divsn., 1985—86, corp. fin. analyst comptroller's divsn., 1986—88, assoc. dir. comptroller's divsn., 1988, asst. brand mgr., 1988—89, brand mgr., 1989—90, assoc. advt. mgr. hair care products, 1990—92, assoc. advt. mgr. oral care products, 1992—93, mktg. dir. oral care products, 1993—94, gen. mgr. skin care products, 1994—96, v.p., gen. mgr. cosmetic, fragrance products N. Am., 1996—99, v.p. cosmetics N. Am., L.Am., 1999, v.p. cosmetics, global design, 2000—02, v.p. global cosmetics, personal care, 2002—03, pres. global cosmetics, personal care, 2003—04, pres. global cosmetics, deodorants, retail hair colorants, 2004, pres. global cosmetics, hair colorants, 2004—06, pres. global strategy, productivity & growth, 2006—08, global mktg. officer, 2008—09, global brand building officer, 2009—. Named a Power Player, Advt. Age, 2008. Mem.: Cosmetic, Toiletries & Fragrance Assn. Office: Hdqs 1 Procter & Gamble Plz Cincinnati OH 45202 Office Phone: 513-983-1100. Office Fax: 513-983-6369.*

PRITCHARD, MARY D'ERCOLE, elementary school educator; b. Seneca Falls, NY, Jan. 8, 1940; d. Pasquale Anthony and Italia Marie (DeRousi) D'Ercole; m. Alun Pritchard, Aug. 8, 1965; children: Michael Arthur, Amy Marie. Student, Mynderse Acad., Seneca Falls, 1957; BS, SUNY at Cortland, 1961; student, SUNY at Albany, 1983. Cert. tchr., N.Y., Iowa, S.D. Tchr. Ballston Spa Sch. System, N.Y., 1961-62; tchr. Sioux City (Iowa) Sch. System, 1962-63, Vermillion Sch. System, S.D., 1963-64, Shenenedowa Cen. Sch., Elnora, N.Y., 1964-65; sub. tchr. Schenectady Sch. System, N.Y., 1968-78; dir. teen pregnancy network Human Svc. Planning Coun., N.Y., 1978-80; ednl. coord. Refreshing Spring Day Care Ctr., Schenectady, 1980-83; asst. dir. day care Campus Children Ctr., Albany, 1983-85; dir. Carol A. Dunigan Day Care Ctr., Albany, 1985—2001; tchr. Schenectady Sch. System, 1987. Campaign worker Dem. Party, Schenectady, 1988-2001; chmn. allocation panel United Way, Schenectady, 1988-93, mem. bd., 1993-99; rels. chmn. Cancer Soc., Schenectady, 1989; sec. YWCA, 1983-84; treas. Coop. Ext., 1986-92; deacon Presbyn. Ch., 1988-92, elder, 1994; vol. usher Saratoga Performing Arts Ctr., 1969, Capital Repertory Theater, 1984—, Empire Ctr. Performing Arts, 1989—, Troy Music Hall, 1991—; mem. NY State Met. Adv. Com. Cornell Coop. Ext., 1990-95; vice moderator Assn. Presbyn. Ch., 1991-95. Recipient Woman of Vision award, 1992-93, YWCA United Way Vol. of Yr. award, 1993. Mem. AAUW (pres., 1985-86, LWV, 2007-, leader spark coord., 2006-, NYSUTRC12 2nd v.p., 2002-). Democrat. Avocations: sewing, golf, water sports, swimming, camping. Home: 1670 Wendell Ave Schenectady NY 12308-2029 E-mail: apritchard@nycap.rr.com.

PRITCHARD, SARAH MARGARET, library director; b. Boston, Feb. 8, 1955; d. Wilbur Louis and Kathleen Hunton (Moss) P.; m. Timothy John Brennan, Aug. 20, 1977 (div. 1993); m. Neal Edward Blair, July 15, 2005. BA, U. Md., 1975; MA in French, U. Wis., 1976, MLS, 1977. Intern Libr. Congress, Washington, 1977-78, reference specialist in women's studies, 1978-88, head microform reading rm., 1988-90; sr. program officer Assn. Rsch. Librs., Washington, 1990-91, assoc. exec. dir., 1991-92; acad. libr. mgmt. intern Coun on Libr. Resources Princeton U., NJ, 1988-89; dir. librs. Smith Coll., Northampton, Mass., 1992-99; univ. libr. U. Calif., Santa Barbara, 1999—2006, Northwestern U., Evanston, Ill., 2006—. Editl. advisor Women's Rsch. and Edn. Inst., Washington, 1987-92; bd. dirs. Western Mass. Regional Libr. Sys., 1997-98; bd. dirs. U. Calif. So. Regional Libr. Facility, Gold Coast Libr. Network, Libr. Calif.; mem. steering com. Scholarly Pub. and Academic Resources Coalition, 2006-08; Charles Deering McCormick disting. chair rsch. libr. Northwestern U., 2006-; editl. bd. mem. Jour. Acad. Librarianship, 1993-99, Portal: Libr. and The Acad., 2000-08. Editor: The Women's Annual, 1984, Portal: Librs. and the Acad., 2009-; compiler ARL Stats., 1990-92; contbr. articles to profl. jours.; contbg. editor Libr. Issues, 1994-99. Trustee Leroy C. Merritt Humanitarian Fund, 1991-94. Named Wis. Alumni Rsch. Found. fellow, 1975-77, Outstanding Alumna U. Wis. Sch. of Libr. and Info. Studies, 1997. Mem. ALA (chair machine assisted reference sect. 1986-87, chair women's studies sect. 1989-90, coun. 1990-98, 2000-04, 2008-, chair stds. com. 1998-2002, chair ethics com. 2002-06, Equality award 1997), Nat. Women's Studies Assn., Cosmos Club, Phi Beta Kappa. Democrat. Office: Northwestern Univ Libr Evanston IL 60208

PRITCHARD, WILLIAM ROY, former university systems administrator; b. Portage, Wis., Nov. 15, 1924; s. William Roy and Lillian Edith (Roberts) P.; m. Deanna Elaine Pritchard; children: Rosan June, William Roy, Caryl Jean, Alyn Evan, Cynthia Bedeau. Student, U. Wis., 1942-43; DVM, Kans. State U., 1946; PhD, U. Minn., 1953; JD, Ind. U., 1957; DSc (hon.), Kans. State U., 1970, Tufts U., 1988, Purdue U., 1977, U. Guelph, 1998. Asst. prof. U. Wis., 1946-49; assoc. prof. U. Minn., 1949-53; prof. Purdue U., 1953-57; prof., head vet. sci. U. Fla., 1957-61; assoc. dir. Vet. Med. Rsch. Inst., Ia. State U., 1961-62; prof. U. Calif., Davis, 1962—, dean Sch. Vet Medicine, 1962-82; assoc. dir. Agrl. Expt. Sta., 1962-72; coord. internat. agrl. programs U. Calif. system, 1977-81. Vis. fellow Woodrow Wilson Sch. Pub and Internat. Affairs, Princeton, 1968-69; John Thomson lectr. U. Queensland, 1966; co-dir. nat. vet. edn. program Duke U., 1987-92; spl. research hemmorrhagic diseases animals. Cons. Dept. Agr., Def. Dept., USPHS, VA, Calif. Dept. Health, FDA, 1962-97; bd. cons. agr. Rockefeller Found., 1962-66; nat. med. cons. surgeon gen. USAF, 1962-64; mem. FAO/WHO Expert Panel Vet. Edn., Pres.'s Sci. Adv. Com. Panel World Food Supply, 1966-67, President's Sci. Adv. Com. Panel Biology and Med. Sci., 1969-70, Joint Rsch. Com. Bd. Internat. Food and Agr. AID, 1977-81; Recognition lectr. Assn. Am. Vet. Med. Colls., 2005. With U.S. Army, 1942-44. Recipient Gov. Fla. award, 1961, Disting. Svc. award Kans. State U., 1963, Outstanding Achievement award U. Minn., 1976, Disting. Pub. Svc. award U. Calif., Davis, 1991, Gold Headed Cane award Am. Soc. Vet. Epidemiology, 1992. Mem. AAAS, APHA, Am. Vet. Med. Assn. (Internat. Vet. Congress award 1988), Nat. Acad. of Practice in Vet. Medicine (elected 1986), Am. Soc. Vet. Epidemiologists, Conf. of Pub. Health Vets. (hon. life), U.S. Animal Health Assn., Nat. Assn. State Univs. and Land-Grant Colls. (internat. affairs com. 1965-70), Order of Coif, Sigma Xi, Phi Zeta, Gamma Alpha. Achievements include california davis veterinary teaching hospital named after him. Home: 2409 Madrid Ct Davis CA 95616-0141

PRITCHETT, PHILIP LENTNER, physicist, researcher; b. Chgo., Jan. 29, 1944; s. Charles Herman and Marguerite Almira (Lentner) P. AB, Oberlin Coll., 1965; MS, Stanford U., 1966, PhD, 1970. Postdoctoral fellow NATO/DESY, Hamburg, Fed. Republic of Germany, 1970-71; rsch. assoc. Northwestern U., Evanston, Ill., 1971-73, vis. asst. prof. physics, 1973-75; NSF energy fellow UCLA, 1975-76, asst. rsch. physicist, 1976-81, assoc. rsch. physicist, 1981-86, rsch. physicist, 1986—. Adj. prof. UCLA, 1987—. Contbr. articles to profl. jours. Grantee NSF, 1965-69, 1975-76, Woodrow Wilson Found., 1965-66. Mem. Am. Phys. Soc., Am. Geophys. Union, Sigma Xi. Office: UCLA Dept Physics 405 Hilgard Ave Los Angeles CA 90095-1547 Office Phone: 310-825-3637. Business E-Mail: pritchet@physics.ucla.edu.

PRITCHETT, SAMUEL TRAVIS, finance and insurance educator, researcher, consultant; s. Harvey Eugene and Mary (Brown) P.; m. Bertha Yates, Feb. 20, 1960; children: John Travis, Meri Katherine. BSBA, Va. Poly. Inst. and State U., 1960, MSBA, 1967; DBA, Ind. U., 1969. CLU, ChFC, CPCU. Claim rep. Equitable Life Assurance Soc., Richmond, Va., 1960-64, asst. div. claim mgr., 1964-65; asst. prof. bus. adminstrn. U. Richmond, 1969-70; asst. prof. ins. Va. Commonwealth U., Richmond, 1970-72, assoc. prof. ins., 1972-73; assoc. prof. fin. and ins. U. S.C., Columbia, 1973-76, prof. fin. and ins., 1976-99, J.H. Fellers prof., 1981-83, W.F. Hipp prof. ins., 1983-2000, program dir., chair banking, fin., ins. and real estate, 1977-83, 99-00, acad. dir. MBA program, 1993-95, disting. prof. finance and ins., 1999-2000, disting. prof. emeritus, 2000—. Vis. prof. ins. Ind. U., Bloomington, 1995-96; chmn. Risk Theory Soc., Columbus, Ohio, 1987-88; acad. dir. internat. exec. devel. program Bamerindus Seguros, Curtiba, Brazil, 1995; mem., investment commr. S.C. Retirement Sys., 2005—. Author: Risk Management and Insurance, 7th edit., 1996, Stock Life Insurance Company Profitability, 1986, Individual Annuities as a Source of Retirement Income, 2d edit., 1982, An Economic Analysis of Workers' Compensation in South Carolina, 1994; assoc. editor Jour. Risk and Ins., 1982-86, editor, 1987-91; assoc. editor Fin. Svcs. Rev., 1989-95, 97-99; asst. editor Jour. Am. Soc. CLU and ChFC, 1993-98; mem. acad. rev. bd. Jour. Fin. Planning, 1990-91; mem. editl. bd. Jour. Bus. Rsch., 1976-83, Am. Jour. Small Bus., 1975-79; contbr. articles to profl. jours. Active S.C. Joint Ins. Study Com., 1981-86, 89-95; commr. S.C. Retirement Systems Investment Commn., 2005—, SC Treas.'s Task Force COLAs, 2007-08. Recipient Disting. Svc. award, Moore Sch. Bus. USC, 2009. Mem. Am. Risk and Ins. Assn. (pres. 1980-81), Acad. Fin. Svcs. (pres. 1987-88), So. Risk and Ins. Assn. (pres. 1977-78), Profl. Ins. Agts. Found. (named Ins. Educator of Yr. 1989), Beta Gamma Sigma (pres. chpt. 1980-81), Gamma Iota Sigma (nat. trustee 1976-92), State Retirees Assn., (bd. mem., 2004—). Independent. Mem. Christian Ch. (Disciples Of Christ). Home: 709 Marlin Ln Charleston SC 29412-5039 Home Phone: 843-762-2645; Office Phone: 843-762-2645. Personal E-mail: tpritch@comcast.net. *Apply to others religious values such as honesty, humility, respect, and service. Cultivate a strong work ethic and select admirable mentors.*

PRITCHETT, TIMOTHY MICHAEL, physicist; PhD, U. Calif., Berkeley, 1990. Vis. asst. prof. physics Pomona Coll., Claremont, Calif., 1992—94; assoc. prof. physics US Mil. Acad., West Point, NY, 1994—2002; physicist US Army Rsch. Lab., Adelphi, Md., 2002—. Office: US Army Research Laboratory 2800 Powder Mill Rd Hyattsville MD 20783-1197

PRITT, STACY L., veterinarian; b. Charleston, W.Va., Mar. 17, 1971; d. Ken and Betty Pritt; m. Daniel Ray Hanson, Dec. 30, 1995. BS, Calif. State Poly. U., Pomona, 1993; DVM, Wash. State U., Pullman, 1997; MBA, U. Phoenix, Ariz., 2004. Cert. in bus. adminstrn. Clark Coll., Vacounver, Wass., 2000. Mgr., vet. svcs. Toxikon Corp., Bedford, Mass., 2001—03; dir., animal resources facility Joslin Diabetes Ctr., Boston, 2003—04; assoc. dir., animal care, tng. & ops. Harvard Med. Sch., Boston, 2004—05; dir., animal welfare & regulatory compliance Covance, Denver, 2005—. Chair, bd. dirs. Assn.Women Vet., LA, 2007—. Mem.: AVMA (com. mem. 2006—), Lab. Animal Welfare Tng. Exch. (pres. 2006—07), Am. Assn. Lab. Animal Sci. (com. chair 2004—). Office: Biological Test Center B Braun Medical 2525 McGaw Ave Irvine CA 92614 Office Phone: 949-660-2412. Personal E-mail: stacy_pritt@yahoo.com.

PRITTIE, JENNIFER E., veterinarian; b. Silver Spring, Md., Sept. 9, 1969; d. Howard C. Bowman and Jane E. Prittie. DVM, Va.-Md. Regional Coll. Vet. Medicine, Blacksbury, 1997. Cert. ACVIM NYC, 2002, ACVECC. Resident, staff criticalist Animal Med. Ctr., 2002—. Contbr. articles to profl. jour. Office: Animal Med Ctr 510 E 62nd St New York NY 10065 Business E-Mail: jennifer.prittie@amcny.org.

PRITZKER, JOHN A., leisure services executive; s. Robert Pritzker; m. Lisa S. Pritzker; 3 children. Grad., Menlo Coll., U. Denver Coll. Hotel and Restaurant Mgmt. Various positions to divisional v.p. Calif. Hyatt; pres. Hyatt Ventures, Inc.; founder, pres. Red Sail Sports, Inc., 1988—. Exec. v.p. bus. devel. Key3Media Events, Inc., 2000; bd. dirs. Zoomedia Inc. Trustee San Francisco Mus. Modern Art; dir. Pritzker Found., Pritzker Cousins Found., Children Now; bd. dirs. U. Calif. San Francisco Found. Named one of Forbes Richest Americans, 2006, Top 200 Collectors, ARTnews mag., 2005—08. Office: Red Sail Sports 5 Pier 102 San Francisco CA 94111-2027

PRITZKER, PENNY SUE, investor; b. Chgo., May 2, 1959; d. Donald N. and Sue Ann (Sandel) Pritzker; m. Bryan Traubert, Sept. 10, 1988; children: Donald Pritzker Traubert, Rose Pritzker Traubert. B in Econs., Harvard U., 1981; JD, MBA, Stanford U., 1985. Bar: Ill. 1985. Mgr. Hyatt Devel. Corp., Chgo., 1985-87; pres., chmn. Classic Residence by Hyatt, Chgo., 1987—; ptnr. Pritzker & Pritzker, Chgo., 1987—; pres., chmn. Pritzker Realty Grp. (formerly Penguin Group, L.P.), Chgo., 1990—; co-founder, chmn. The Parking Spot, 1998—; chmn. TransUnion Corp., 2005—. Chmn. exec. com. Encore Sr. Living, Portland, Oreg.; corp. adv. bd. mem. Mayor Daley's Exec. Fellows Prog., Chgo.; mem. Mayor Daley's fin. com.; bd. dirs. Global Hyatt Corp., William Wrigley, Jr. Co., Chgo., Coast-to-Coast Fin. Corp., NYC, Nat. Investment Conf., Washington.; nat. fin. chair Barack Obama Presdl. Campaign, 2008; co-chair Presdl. Inaugural Com., 2009; mem. President's Econ. Recovery Adv. Bd., 2009-. Chair Mus. Contemporary Art, Chgo.; adv. bd. dirs. Chgo. Cares; mem. dean's coun. Harvard U.; mem. Women's Issues Network, Chgo., 1991—, The Chgo. Network, 1992—, Internat. Women's Forum, Chgo., Coun. Fgn. Rels., NY. Recipient Brick & Mortar award, Chgo. Equity Fund, 1991, Disting. Svc. award, REIA Kellogg, 1995; named a Woman to Watch, Crain's Chgo. Bus., 2007; named one of 50 Women to Watch, Wall St. Jour., 2005, 100 Most Powerful Women, Forbes mag., 2005, 2009, 400 Richest Ams., 2006. Mem. Nat. Assn. Sr. Living Industry Execs. (bd. dirs. 1989-91), Urban Land Inst., Young Pres.'s Orgn. Office: Classic Residence By Hyatt 71 S Wacker Dr Ste 900 Chicago IL 60606-4637*

PRITZKER, THOMAS JAY, hotel executive; b. Chgo., June 6, 1950; s. Jay Arthur and Marian (Friend) P.; m. Margot Lyn Barrow-Sicree, Sept. 4, 1977; 3 children. BA, Claremont Men's Coll., Calif., 1971; MBA, U. Chgo., 1976, JD, 1976. Assoc. Katten, Muchin, Zavis, Pearl and Galler, Chgo., 1976-77; exec. v.p. Hyatt Corp., Chgo., 1977-80, pres., 1980—2002, chmn., CEO, 1999—2004; chmn. Hyatt Hotels Corp., 1980—2002, Hyatt Internat. Corp., 1999—2004; ptnr. Pritzker & Pritzker, Chgo., 1980—; CEO Hyatt Hotels Corp., Chgo., 2005—06, chmn., 2005—. Chmn. bd. dirs. The Pritzker Orgn., 1998—; bd. dirs. Royal Caribbean Cruises Ltd. Bd. trustees, chmn. Art Inst. Chgo., 1988—; bd. trustees U. Chgo. Named one of Forbes' Richest Americans, 2006. Mem. ABA, Ill. Bar Assn., Chgo. Bar Assn., Standard Club, Lake Shore Country Club. Office: Hyatt Ctr 71 S Wacker Dr Ste 4700 Chicago IL 60606 Office Phone: 312-873-4901.

PRIVETT, RONNA, literature and language professor; married. PhD in Am. Lit., Tex. Tech U., Lubbock, 1999. Assoc. prof. English Lubbock Christian U., 1999—.

PRIVETT, STEPHEN A., academic administrator, priest; b. San Francisco; BA in Philosophy and Classics, Gonzaga U., 1966; MDiv, U. Calif., Berkeley, 1972; postgrad., U. Calif., Santa Barbara, 1973—74; MA in Catechetics/Religious Edn., Cath. U. Am., 1982, PhD in Catechetics, 1985. Entered Soc. of Jesus, 1960. Instr. Latin, western civilization and religion Jesuit H.S., Sacramento, 1966—69; dir. Project 50 Santa Clara U., 1970—71; asst. dir. novices Coll. Queen of Peace, Santa Barbara, 1972—73; instr. modern European history, Latin and English Bellarmine Coll. Preparatory, San Jose, Calif., 1974—80, prin., 1975—80; asst. prof. religious studies dept. Santa Clara U., 1985—90, assoc. prof. religious studies dept., 1990—2000, co-dir. The Eastside Project, 1985—91, dir. Voice of the Voiceless: Inst. on Human Rights and Social Justice, 1989—91, v.p. acad. affairs, 1991—97, provost, v.p. acad. affairs, 1997—2000; pres. U. San Francisco, 2000—. Mem. U.S. Cath. Conf. on Certification and Accreditation, 1990—99; mem. Strategic Planning Commn. Calif. Province of the Soc. of Jesus, 1996—2002; mem. Nat. Seminar on Jesuit Higher Edn. U. Scranton, 1999—. Contbr. articles to profl. jours.; author: The U.S. Catholic Church and Its Hispanic Members: The Pastoral Vision of Robert E. Lucey, 1988. Vol. pastoral worker Jesuit Refugee Svc., El Salvador, 1988; bd. dirs. Jesuit Vol. Corps S.W., 1987—95, chair, 1988—91; bd. dirs. Christians for Peace in El Salvador, 1997—2000, Fromm Inst. for Lifelong Learning, U. San Francisco, 2000—; trustee Brophy Coll. Preparatory, Phoenix, 1996—, Seattle U., 2000—, U. Iberoamericana, Mexico City, 2001—; hon. mem. San Francisco Host Com., 2000—. Mem.: Assn. Grad. Programs in Ministry, Assn. Profs. and Rschrs. in Religious Edn. (mem. Cath. Assembly), Religious Edn. Assn., Assn. Cath. Colls. and Univs. (bd. dirs. 2002—), Assn. Jesuit Colls. and Univs. (bd. dirs. 2000—), Commonwealth Club Calif. (bd. govs.). Office: U San Francisco Office of Pres 2130 Fulton St San Francisco CA 94117 Office Phone: 415-422-6762. E-mail: president@usfca.edu.*

PRIVETTE, JANET BROWN, elementary school educator; b. Raleigh, NC, Mar. 5, 1958; d. Dwight Dale and Peggy Hurt Brown; m. Randy Lee Privette, Dec. 21, 1980; children: Andrew Scott, Todd McLean. BS in Elem. Edn., East Carolina U., Greenville, NC, 1980; MEd in Elem. Edn., N.C. Ctrl. U., Durham, NC, 2000. Cert. tchr. Nat. Bd. Edn., 2000. Tchr. kindergarten Franklin County Schs., Louisburg, NC; reading specialist Wake County Pub. Schs., Zebulon, NC. Mem.: Internat. Reading Assn., Internat. Soc. Women Educators, Delta Kappa Gamma. Baptist. Home: 8409 Halifax Rd Youngsville NC 27596 Office: Zebulon Elem Sch 700 Proctor St Zebulon NC 27597

PRIVETTE, LOUISE JUDITH, school psychologist; b. Chgo., May 12; d. Sidney Paul and Mary Goldstein; m. John Joseph Privette, Nov. 18, 2002; 1 stepchild, John Edward. BA in Psychology, Ariz. State U., 1976, M in Counseling, 1978. Nat. cert. sch. psychologist Md., cert. guidance counselor K-12 Ariz., secondary tchr. Ariz., nat. cert. reality therapist Calif. Dir. guidance, tchr. Seton H.S.; sch. psychologist Mesa Pub. Sch. Dist., Ariz., 1985—2003, Buckeye Union HS Dist., 2003—07, Agua Fria Union HS Dist., Goodyear, 2007—. Amb. for edn. Motorola, Ariz., 1996—98; therapist Dobson Bay Psychol. Ctr.; prodr. guidance materials. Luke air force officers' wives club; nat. honor soc. sponsor. Named Sch. Psychologist of Yr., Mesa Assn. Sch. Psychologists, 2000. Mem.: Nat. Assn. Sch. Psychologists (assoc.), Ariz. Assn. Sch. Psychologists (assoc.; regional dir. 2006, psychologist of yr. 2001), Pi Lamda Theta, Psi Chi. Office: Agua Fria Union HS Dist 14802 W Wigwam Blvd Goodyear AZ 85338 Business E-Mail: lprivetta@aquafria.org.

PRIVITERA, GREGORY JOSEPH, neuroscientist, educator; b. Amherst, NY, Mar. 30, 1977; s. James Edwards and Donna Marie Privitera; m. Alisha Ann McHenry, May 24, 2003; 1 child, Grace Ann; 1 child, Aiden Andrew. BA summa cum laude, U. Buffalo, NY, 2002, MA, 2004, PhD, 2006—. Grad. instr. U. Buffalo, SUNY, 2003—06; asst. prof. D'Youville Coll., Buffalo, 2005—06; postdoctoral rsch. assoc. Ariz. State U., 2006—, faculty assoc., 2007—08; instr. Glendale CC, 2007—. Rsch. asst. Rsch. Inst. on Addictions, Buffalo, 2004; adj. prof. D'Youville Coll., Buffalo, 2004—05, Daemen Coll., Buffalo, 2005. Contbr. articles to profl. jours. Vol. mediator BBB, Buffalo, 2000—02. Sgt. USMC, 1995—99. Decorated Nat. Def. Svc. medal USMC, Good Conduct medal; recipient Extra Mile Tchg. award, U. Buffalo, SUNY, 2004; scholar, 2002—06. Mem.: Soc. Neurosci., APA, Assn. Psychol. Sci., Psi Chi. Office: Univ Buffalo SUNY 206 Park Hall Buffalo NY 14260 Home: 1463 E Sargosa St Chandler AZ 85225 Office Phone: 623-845-4778. Business E-Mail: gjp@asu.edu.

PRO, PHILIP MARTIN, judge; b. Richmond, Calif., Dec. 12, 1946; s. Leo Martin and Mildred Louise (Beck) P.; m. Dori Sue Hallas, Nov. 13, 1982; 1 child, Brenda Kay. BA, San Francisco State U., 1968; JD, Golden Gate U., 1972. Bar: Calif. 1972, Nev. 1973, U.S. Ct. Appeals (9th cir.) 1973, U.S. Dist. Ct. Nev. 1973, U.S. Supreme Ct. 1976. Pub. defender, Las Vegas, 1973-75; asst. U.S. atty. Dist. Nev., Las Vegas, 1975-78; dep. atty. gen. State of Nev., Carson City, 1979-80; magistrate US Dist. Ct. Nev., Las Vegas, 1980-87, judge, 1987—, chief judge, 2002—07. Instr. Atty. Gen.'s Advocacy Inst., Nat. Inst. Trial Advocacy, 1992; chmn. com. adminstrn. of magistrate judge system Jud. Conf. U.S., 1993—; bd. dirs. Fed. Jud. Cts. Program com. and issues in justice com. NCCJ, Las Vegas, 1982—. Mem. ABA, Fed. Judges Assn. (bd. dirs. 1992—, v.p. 1997-2001), Nev. State Bar Assn., Calif. State Bar Assn., Nev. Judges Assn. (instr.), Assn. Trial Lawyers Am., Nev. Am. Inn Ct. (pres. 1989-91), Ninth Cir. Jury (instructions com.), Nat. Conf. U.S. Magistrates (sec.). Republican. Office: US Dist Ct 7015 Fed Bldg 333 Las Vegas Blvd S Ste 7015 Las Vegas NV 89101-5883 Office Phone: 702-464-5510. Business E-Mail: philip_pro@nvd.uscourts.gov.

PROBERT, TIM, oil industry executive; BS in Geology, Geography, U. London, 1972. Field geologist Exploration Logging Inc.; v.p. mktg. Baker Sand Control; pres. Milpark Drilling Fluids, Eastman Teleco, Baker Hughes INTEQ, 2000—03; pres., CEO Input/Output Inc., Houston; sr. v.p. drilling and evaluation divsn. Halliburton, Houston, 2003—08, exec. v.p. strategy, corp. devel., 2008—09, pres. drilling & evaluation divsn. & corp. develop., 2009—, acting v.p. tech., 2009. Mem. exec. com. Halliburton. Office: Halliburton 5 Houston Ctr 1401 McKinney Ste 2400 Houston TX 77010-4008 Office Phone: 713-759-2600.*

PROBERT, WALTER, retired law educator; b. Portland, Oreg., Jan. 13, 1925; s. Raymond and Mildred Marie (Pyburn) P.; m. Barbara Louise Stevenson, Mar. 22, 1952; children: Richard Walter, James Stevenson. Student, Alfred U., 1944; BS, U. Oreg., 1948, JD, 1951; JSD (Grad. fellow), Yale U., 1957. Bar: Oreg. 1951. Practiced in Portland, 1951-52; asst. prof. Western Res. U., 1953-57, asso. prof., 1957-59; prof. U. Fla., Gainesville, 1959—85, endowed prof. law, 1985—96, titled prof. emeritus, 1996—2002; ret. Vis. prof. Northwestern U., 1960-61, U. Tex., summer 1970, U. Wash., 1972-73; vis. research prof. U. Denver, 1966-67; lectr. Balliol Coll., Oxford U., 1968; dir. law and social sci. program NSF, 1973-74. Author: Law, Language, and Communication, 1972; faculty editor Western Res. U. Law Rev., 1953-59; contbr. articles to profl. jours. Served with AUS, 1943-47. Recipient grants for law-communication research. Mem. ATLA, Internat. Assn. Philosophy of Law and Social Philosophy, Phi Beta Kappa, Order of Coif, Order of St. Ives, Delta Theta Phi. Home: 1522 SW 35th Pl Gainesville FL 32608-3530 Home Phone: 352-376-9059. Business E-Mail: probertw@ufl.edu.

PROBST, LAWRENCE F., III, interactive software/gaming executive; b. 1950; BS, U. Del., 1972. Dist. sales mgr. Johnson & Johnson, 1972-80; nat. accounts mgr. The Clorox Co., 1980-82, Mediagenic (formerly Activision Inc.), 1982-84; v.p. sales Electronic Arts, Inc., 1984—86, sr. v.p., distbn., 1987—91, pres., 1991—98, CEO Redwood City, Calif., 1991—2007, exec. chmn., 1994—. Bd. dirs. Electronic Arts, Inc., 1991—, MP3.com, Inc., 1999—. Office: Electronic Arts Inc 209 Redwood Shores Pkwy Redwood City CA 94065

PROBST, TAHIRA M., psychology professor; PhD, U. Ill., Urbana-Champaign, 1998. Assoc. prof. Wash. State U., Vancouver, 1998—. Contbr. articles to profl. publs. (SHRM Rsch. award, 2002). Recipient Tchg. Assistantship award, Fulbright Commn., Austria, 1994—95. Office: Wash State Univ 14204 NE Salmon Creek Ave Vancouver WA 98686 Business E-Mail: probst@vancouver.wsu.edu.

PROBSTEIN, RONALD FILMORE, mechanical engineering educator; b. NYC, Mar. 11, 1928; s. Sidney and Sally (Rosenstein) P.; m. Irene Weindling, July 30, 1950; 1 child, Sidney. BME, NYU, 1948; MSE, Princeton U., NJ, 1950, AM, 1951, PhD, 1952; ScD (hon.), Brown U., 1997. Rsch. asst. physics NYU, 1946-48, instr. engring. mechanics, 1947-48; rsch. asst. dept. aero. engring. Princeton U., 1948-52, rsch. assoc., 1952-53, asst. prof., 1953-54; asst. prof. divs. engring., applied math. Brown U., 1954-55, assoc. prof., 1955-59, prof., 1959-62; prof. mech. engring. MIT, Cambridge, 1962—89, Ford prof. engring., 1989-96, prof. mech. engring., 1996—2001, Ford prof. engring. emeritus, 1996—; Disting. prof. engring. U. Utah, 1973; sr. ptnr. Water Purification Assoc., Cambridge, 1974-82; chmn. bd. Water Gen. Corp., Cambridge, 1982-83; sr. corp. tech. advisor Foster-Miller, Inc., 1983-91. Commr. commn. on engring. and tech. systems NRC, 1980-83, mem. space studies bd., 2004-07; sci. advisor to bd. Corrpro Cos., 1993-2001. Author: Hypersonic Flow Theory, 1959, Hypersonic Flow, Inviscid Flows, 1966, 03, Water in Synthetic Fuel Production, 1978, Synthetic Fuels, 1982, 2006, Physicochemical Hydrodynamics, 1989, 03, Honest Sid, 2009; editor: Introduction to Hypersonic Flow, 1961, Physics of Shock Waves, 1966, 02, Jour. PhysicoChem. Hydrodynamics, 1987-89; contbr. articles to profl. jours.; patentee in field. Guggenheim fellow, 1960-61; R.F. Probstein Lecture Series in Engring. Sci., MIT, established 1999. Fellow AAAS, AIAA, Am. Acad. Arts and Sci. (councilor 1975-79), Am. Phys. Soc., ASME (Freeman award 1971); mem. AIChE, NAS (chmn. engring. sci. sect. 2005-08), NAE (com. membership 2001-05, chmn. 2005), Internat. Acad. Astronautics. Home: 5 Seaver St Brookline MA 02445-5714 Office: 77 Massachusetts Ave Cambridge MA 02139-4301 Office Phone: 617-253-2240. Business E-Mail: rfprobst@mit.edu.

PROCHASKA, ALICE, historian, librarian; m. Franklyn Kimmel Prochaska, June 25, 1971; children: Elizabeth, William. BA in Modern History, Somerville Coll., U. Oxford, 1968; MA in History, U. Oxford, 1973, DPhil in Modern History, 1975. Asst. keeper Pub. Record Office, England, 1975—84; sec. & libr. Inst. Hist. Rsch. U. London, 1984—92; dir. spl. collections Brit. Libr., 1992—2001; univ. libr. Yale U., New Haven, 2001—. Mem. dept. edn. sci. history working group, Nat. Curriculum, 1989-90; trusteeSir Winston Churchill Archive Trust, 1995-2001; chair Nat. Coun. Archives, UK, 1992-95; gov. London Guildhall U. (now London Metro. U.), 1995-2001; commr. Royal Commn. Hist. Manuscripts, 1998-2001; mem. Rare Books and Manuscripts Standing com. Internat. Fed. Libr. Assn., 1997-, chair 1999-2003; chair collection and access issues com., Assn. Rsch. Libr., 2003-05, spl. collections working group, 2007-; mem. adv. com. for global resources network Assn. Am. Univs.2003-; bd. mem. Ctr. Rsch. Libr., 2003-, vice chair 2005-07, chair 2007-; bd. mem. Yale U. Press 2004. Author: History of the General Federation of Trade Unions, 1982, Irish History from 1700: A Guide to Sources in the Public Record Office, 1986; co-editor (with Frank Prochaska): Margaretta Acworth's Georgian Cookery Book, 1987; contbr. numerous articles in scholarly and profl. jours. Recipient JJ Astor prize in Libr. Sci., Checkpoint Charlie Found., Berlin, 2006; named an Hon. Fellow, Royal Holloway U. of London, 2002, Inst. Hist. Rsch. U. London, 2001. Fellow: Royal Hist. Soc. (v.p. 1995—99). Avocations: history, theater, collecting watercolors, gardening. Office: Libr Adminstrv Services Sterling Meml Libr Yale U 130 Wall St PO Box 208240 New Haven CT 06520-8240 Home Phone: 203-624-3683; Office Phone: 203-432-1818. Business E-Mail: alice.prochaska@yale.edu.

PROCHNOW, DOUGLAS LEE, lawyer; b. Omaha, Jan. 9, 1952; s. Albert Delmer and Betty Jean (Wood) Prochnow. BA with high distinction, U. Nebr., 1974; JD, Northwestern U., 1977. Bar: Ill. 1977, U.S. Dist. Ct. (no. dist.) Ill. 1977, U.S. Ct. Appeals (7th cir.) 1989, U.S. Supreme Ct. 2000. Assoc. Wildman, Harrold, Allen & Dixon, Chgo., 1977-84, ptnr., 1985—. Spl. asst. corp. counsel City of Chgo., 1986—87; adj. prof. law Northwestern U. Sch. Law, 2005—. Pres. Chgo. bd. Prevent Child Abuse Am., 2003—08. Mem. ABA, ATLA (assoc.), Ill. Bar Assn., Chgo. Bar Assn., Soc. Trial Lawyers, Def. Rsch. Inst., Am. Health Lawyers Assn., Phi Beta Kappa, Phi Eta Sigma. Office: Wildman Harrold Allen & Dixon 225 W Wacker Dr Ste 2700 Chicago IL 60606-1224 Home: 159 E Walton St Unit 12B Chicago IL 60611 Home Phone: 312-951-8975; Office Phone: 312-201-2526. Business E-Mail: prochnow@wildman.com.

PROCKOP, DARWIN JOHNSON, biochemist, medical educator; b. Palmerton, Pa., Aug. 31, 1929; s. John and Sophie (Gurski) Prockop; m. Elinor Sacks, Apr. 15, 1961; children: Susan Elizabeth, David John. AB, Haverford Coll., 1951; MA, Oxford U., 1953; MD, U. Pa., 1956; PhD, George Washington U., 1962; DSc (hon.) (hon.), U. Oulu, Finland, 1983, U. So. Fla., 1993. Investigator NIH, 1957—61; assoc., asst. prof., asso. prof., prof. medicine and biochemistry U. Pa., Phila., 1961—72; prof., chmn. dept. biochemistry U. Medicine and Dentistry of N.J. (Rutgers Med. Sch.), Piscataway, NJ, 1972—86; prof., chmn. dept. biochemistry and molecular biology Jefferson Med. Coll., Phila., 1986—96, dir. Jefferson Inst. Molecular Medicine, 1986—96; prof., dir. Ctr. for Gene Therapy, MCP/Hahnemann Med. Coll., Phila., 1996—2000; prof., dir. Ctr. Gene Therapy Tulane U. Med. Ctr., New Orleans, 2000—08; dir. Tex. A & M Health Sci. Ctr. Inst. Regenerative Med., Scott & White Temple, 2008—. Contbr. Served with USPHS, 1958—61. Recipient Disting. Alumnus award, George Washington U., 1991, U. Pa., 1994, Hopkins Meml. medal., Brit. Biochem. Soc, 1998; named hon. companion, U. Manchester, 1999; grantee, NIH, 1961—; fellow Fulbright Found., 1951—53. Mem.: NAS, Am. Assn. Physicians, Am. Soc. Clin. Investigation, Am. Soc. Biol. Chemists, Acad. Finland, Inst. Medicine, Alpha Omega Alpha, Phi Beta Kappa. Achievements include research in on collagen and gene therapy. Home: 291 Locust St Philadelphia PA 19106-3913 Office: Ctr Gene Therapy Tulane U Med Ctr 1430 Tulane Ave New Orleans LA 70112-2699 E-mail: dprocko@tulane.edu.

PROCOP, GARY W., microbiologist, educator, physician; BS in Biology and Microbiology, Ea. Mich. U., Ypsilanti, 1987; MD in Microbiology, Marshall U. Sch. Medicine, Huntington, W.Va., 1992; MS in Microbiology, Marshall U., 1992. Cert. anatomic and clin. pathology Am. Bd. Pathology. Resident anatomic and clin. pathology Duke U. Med. Ctr., Durham, NC, 1996; fellow clin. microbiology Mayo Clinic, Rochester, Minn., 1997; physician Hillcrest Med. Ctr., Tulsa, Okla.; sect. head clin. microbiology Cleve. Clinic; prof. pathology U. Miami Miller Sch. Medicine, Fla., 2006—; dir. clin. microbiology Jackson Meml. Hosp., Miami, 2006—. Trustee Am. Bd. Pathology; designate chair Microbiology Test Devel. and Adv. Com.; mem. subcommittee microbial identification by gene sequencing Clin. and Lab. Stds. Inst. Recipient Quest for Quality award, Cleve. Clinic. Fellow: Am. Acad. Microbiology; mem.: Internat. Acad. Pathology, Coll. Am. Pathologists (mem. pub. affairs com.), Am. Soc. Microbiology (BD award for Rsch. in Clin. Microbiology 2007). Office: Dept Pathology U Miami Miller Sch Medicine 1611 NW 12th Ave Miami FL 33136 Office Phone: 305-585-6303. Office Fax: 305-326-9363.

PROCOPE, ERNESTA GERTRUDE, insurance company executive; b. Bklyn. d. Clarence and Elvira Forster; m. Albin Bowman (dec. 1952); m. John L. Procope, July 3, 1954. Student, Bklyn. Coll., Coll. Ins., Pohs Inst. Ins.; LLD (hon.), Adelphi U., Marymount Manhattan Coll., 1987, Howard U., 1989; HHD (hon.), Morgan State U., 1978. Founder, pres., CEO E.G. Bowman Co. Inc., NYC, 1953—. Panelist corp. governance and advancement of women US Dept. Labor, 1981; former bd. dir. Avon Products, Inc., Chubb Corp., Columbia Gas Sys. Amb. 10th anniversary independence celebration Republic of Gambia, 1975; trustee NY Zool. Soc., Cornell U., Adelphi U. Recipient Achievement award, Thelma T. Johnson Meml. Scholarship Fund, 1972, Interracial Coun. for Bus. Opportunity, 1973, Women of the Yr. award, presented at White House by First Lady Patricia Nixon, 1972, Cmty. Svc. award, F & M Schaefer Brewing Co., 1974, Sojourner Truth award, Negro Bus. and Profl. Women's Club, Inc., 1974, Bus. Achievement award, Nat. Bus. League, 1976, Catalyst award, Women Dirs. of Corps., 1977, Torch of Liberty award, Anti-Defammation League, 1990, Disting. Svc. award, NAACP, 1991, Entrepreneurial Excellence award, Dow Jones/Wall Street Jour., 1992, Whitney M. Young, Jr. award, 1992, Trumpet award, Turner Broadcasting Sys., 2002, Essence Power award, 2004, Women of Power Legacy award, Black Enterprise Mag., 2006, Support Network's Pres.'s award, 24th Ann. New Year's Eve Gala, 2006, Lifetime Achievement award, Nat. African-Am. Ins. Assn., 2008—09, Alice Hall Dowling and Jane D. Edwards Trailblazer's award, Harlem Dowling Westside Ctr., 2008, Excellence award, CPCU Soc. NY, 2008; named Disting. Black Woman in Corp. Role, Nat. Coun. Negro Women, Inc., 1981, Bus. Person of Yr., Urban Bankers Coalition, 1990, Legend, Barnes Hist. Soc., 2007; named to African Am. Bus. Hall of Fame & Mus., 2003, Minority Bus. Hall of Fame and Mus., 2006. Mem.: Nat. Assn. Ins. Women, Nat. Assn. Ins. Brokers, Cosmopolitan Club, Women's Forum, Alpha Kappa Alpha (hon.). Presbyterian. Office: EG Bowman Co Inc 97 Wall St New York NY 10005-4302 Office Phone: 212-425-8150. Business E-Mail: procope@egbowman.com.

PROCTER, EMILY MALLORY, actress; b. Raleigh, NC, Oct. 8, 1968; d. William Procter and Barbara. Grad., East Carolina U. Weather girl CBS affiliate, Greenville. Actress (TV films) Fast Company, 1995, The Dukes of Hazzard: Reunion!, 1997, Submerged, 2001, (films) Leaving Las Vegas, 1995, Crosscut, 1996, Jerry Maguire, 1996, The Girl Gets Moe, 1997, Breast Men, 1997, Family Plan, 1998, Kingdom Come, 1999, Guinevere, 1999, Forever Fabulous, 1999, Body Shots, 1999, The Big Tease, 1999, Big Momma's House 2, 2006, (TV series) The West Wing, 2000—06, CSI: Miami, 2002—07. Vol. All Saints' Episcopal Ch. soup kitchen, Beverly Hills. Office: c/o William Morris Agy 1 William Morris Pl Beverly Hills CA 90212

PROCTER, ROBERT J., economics professor, consultant; s. Robert F. and Charlotte D. Procter. AB in Economics, U.Calif., Berkeley, 1976; MS in Agrl. Economics, Purdue U., West Lafayette, Ind., 1979; PhD in Agrl. Economics, Mich. State U., East Lansing, 1984. Cert. in fine arts, painting & drawing Pacific NW Coll. Art, Portland, Oreg., 2004. Prof. economics Mt. Hood CC and Portland CC, Gresham, Oreg., 2007—; pvt. practice Gresham, Oreg., 2007—; economist Bonneville Power Adminstrn., Portland, GAO, Wash. Numerous painting and printmaking, exhibitions include chinese calligraphy Shenzhen Fine Art Mus., China, 2005 (awards); contbr. articles to profl. jours. Pres. Oreg. Nordic Club, Portland, 1990—91; rescue team leader, bd. dir. Portland Mountain Rescue, 1993—97; vol. mentor Mazamas Mountaineering Club, Portland; water safety instr. ARC, San Diego. Named to Dean's List, U. Calif, Berkeley, 1973—75. Liberal. Achievements include design of economically efficient solar collector for single family residences; developed methodologies to adjust power rates in the Pacific Northwest; method to determine the potential costs of transmission line outages and regional economic impacts; led economic analysis of the first energy code adopted throughout the Pacific Northwest. Avocations: skiing, painting, calligraphy, hiking, mountain climbing.

PROCTOR, CLAUDE OLIVER, Russian language educator; b. Ahoskie, NC, June 9, 1938; s. Claude Oliver and Helen Louise (Lassiter) P.; m. Doris Merle Stricker, July 7, 1962; children: Christopher Michael, Gabriel Marcus. Student, Davidson Coll., 1956-58, Syracuse U., 1962-63; BGE, U. Nebr., Omaha, 1966; MA, U. Notre Dame, 1974; Tchr.'s cert. with distinction, Southwestern U., 1981; PhD, U. Tex., 1990. Commd. 2d lt. USAF, 1966, advanced through grades to maj., 1977, Russian linguist Tex., Alaska and Turkey, 1958-67, intelligence officer West Germany, 1968-70, chief fgn. lang. dept. Air Force Sch. Applied Cryptol. Scis. Tex., 1971-72, Soviet area specialist Def. Lang. Inst. Calif., 1974-77, asst. prof. Russian, chmn. strategic langs. USAF Acad. Colo., 1977-80, ret., 1980; legal edn. officer Prosecutor Coun., Austin, Tex., 1980-83; dir. S.W. Lang. Svc., Georgetown, Tex., 1983-86; asst. instr. U. Tex., Austin, 1986-88; prof. Russian Ctrl. Tex. Coll., Killeen, 1989—; faculty of sr. U. of Greater Georgetown, 1998—. Comml. Russian translator; lang. cons. Internat. Space Sta., 1998-2004. Author: Soviet Press Translation, 1980, The Analysis of Soviet Press Propaganda: A Case Study of Soviet Polemics in the Sino-Soviet Conflict, 1960-69, 73, Illustrated International Dictionary, 1990, Evaluation of Quality in a Russian-English Machine Translation System, 1990, Multilingual Dictionary of American Sign Language, 1994, Signing in Fourteen Languages, 2000. Merit badge counselor Lone Star coun. Boy Scouts Am., 1980—; booth chmn. Colorado Springs Intercultural Festival, 1979; mem. Interagy. Task Force for Indochina Refugees, 1975-76; mem. Georgetown City Charter com., 1995; commr. planning and zoning, 1996—; mem. bd. dirs. Sr. Univ. Greater Georgetown, 1997—, Georgetown Area Cmty. Found., 1996—; mem. Hist. Preservation Commn., 1998—. Mem. Am. Coun. for Tchrs. Russian, Tex. Fgn. Lang. Assn., Air Force Assn., Assn. Former Intelligence Officers, Lions, Sertoma, Rotary Internat. (dir. internat. svc. com. 1987-89, mem. world community svc. com. 1988, Paul Harris fellow 1993), Gamma Theta Upsilon, Sigma Phi Epsilon, Literacy Coun. Williamson County (instr. ESL 2007-), Nat. Lang. Svc. Corps. Lutheran. Avocations: translating, travel, relocating russian emigrees. Office: SW Lang Svcs PO Box 1131 Georgetown TX 78627-1131 Home: 106 Brazos Dr Georgetown TX 78628-2655 Personal E-mail: ProctorC@att.net, c-dproctor@suddenlink.net.

PROCTOR, GEORGANNE C., investment company executive; b. 1956; m. Robert Proctor. BS in Bus. Mgmt., U. S.D.; MBA in Fin., Calif. State U., Hayward. From fin. analyst Bechtel Financing Svcs. (now part of Bechtel Enterprises), 1982-89; mgr. Bechtel Info. Tech. Group., 1989-91, mgr. project cost controls for Disney MGM Studio project Paris, 1991; dir. fin. & acctg. Buena Vista Home Video Internat., 1991-93; dir. project & divsn. fin. Walt Disney Imagineering, 1993-94; CFO Bechtel Enterprises, 1994-97; sr. v.p., CFO Bechtel Group, Inc., San Francisco, 1997—2002; exec. v.p., CFO Golden West Fin. Corp., 2002—06, Teachers Ins. & Annuity Found. Coll. Retirement Equities Fund (TIAA-CREF), NYC, 2006—. Bd. dirs. The Bechtel Group, 1994—2002. Amb. Calif. State. U., Hayward. Office: TIAA-CREF 730 3rd Ave New York NY 10017*

PROCTOR, KENNETH DONALD, lawyer; b. Balt., Apr. 28, 1944; s. Kenneth Chauncey and Sarah Elizabeth (Kent) P.; m. Judith Danner Harris, Aug. 2, 1969; children: Kenneth Scott, Kent Harris, Janet Cameron BS, Lehigh U., 1966; JD, U. Md., 1969. Bar: Md. 1969, U.S. Dist. Ct. Md. 1970, U.S. Supreme Ct. 1974, U.S. Ct. Appeals (4th cir.) 1980. Law clk. to judge Md. Ct. Appeals, 1969-70; assoc. Miles & Stockbridge, Balt., 1970-73, 74-76, ptnr., 1976-81, Towson, Md., 1981-96; asst. atty. gen. State of Md., Balt., 1973-74. Trustee Gilman Sch., Balt., 1982-85. Mem. ABA, Md. Bar Assn., Baltimore County Bar Assn. Democrat. Episcopalian. Office: Proctor & McKee PA 102 W Pennsylvania Ave Ste 505 Towson MD 21204-4542 Office Phone: 410-823-2258. E-mail: kdproctor@proctorlaw.com.

PROCTOR, KENNETH GORDON, physiology educator; b. LA, Aug. 6, 1952; s. Peter Edward and Helen Phyllis Proctor; m. Marcia Eugenie Culbertson, Dec. 26, 1976; children: Andrea Michelle, Matthew Scott. BA, Calif. State U., Fullerton, 1974; PhD, Ind. U., 1979. Prof. U. Tenn. Coll. Medicine, Memphis, 1982—. Rsch. grantee NIH, 1983, Office of Naval Rsch., 1995, various pharm. cos., 1994—.

PROCTOR, PAUL WAINWRIGHT, retired psychologist; b. Sept. 14, 1915; s. Paul Bullard and Jessie Elizabeth (Wainwright) P.; m. Shizu Asahi, Nov. 23, 1944. BSBA, Wash. U., 1936; MA, Columbia U., 1945; postgrad., Johns Hopkins U., 1947, Claremont Coll., 1948; PhD, NYU, 1952. Cert. psychologist, sch. psychologist, N.Y. Tchr. social studies and remedial reading Friends Sch., Balt., 1945—47; asst. psychologist U. Md. Hosp., Balt., 1947; tchr. remedial reading Slade Sch., Olney, Md., 1947—48; psychologist, tchr. NYU Reading Inst., 1948—50; asst. dir., sr. psychologist Testing and Advisement Ctr. NYU Testing & Advisement Ctr., 1950—70; instr. psychol. tests and measurements Bank St. Coll. of Edn., 1970; psychologist, dir. Internat. Sch. Psychol. Svc., 1964—65, 1970—71; assoc. prof., counselor Kingsborough C.C., Bklyn., 1971—2000. Exec. bd. Metro. Coll. Mental Health Assn., 1980-82. Kansas City Honor scholar, 1932-33, 34-36. Mem. APA, Am. Counseling Assn., Nat. Career Devel. Assn., NY State Psychol. Assn., Soc. Personality Assessment, Nat. Assn. Sch. Psychologists, Internat. Coun. Psychologists, Soc. Friends. Home: 44 W 10th St New York NY 10011-8762

PROCTOR, RICHARD JAMES, geologist, consultant; b. LA, Aug. 2, 1931; s. George Arthur and Margaret Y. (Goodman) P.; m. Ena McLaren, Feb. 12, 1955; children: Mitchell, Jill, Randall. BA, Calif. State U., LA, 1954; MA, UCLA, 1958. Engring. geologist, Calif.; cert. profl. geologist Am. Inst. Profl. Geologists. Chief geologist Met. Water Dist., LA, 1958-80; pres., cons. geologist Richard J. Proctor, Inc., Arcadia, Calif., 1980-95. Vis. assoc. prof. Calif. Inst. Tech., Pasadena, 1975-78. Author: History of AIPG, 2003; co-author: Citizens Guide to Geologic Hazards, 1993; editor: Professional Practice Guidelines, 1985, Engineering Geology Practice in Southern California, 1992, (screenplays) My Friend Tom Horn, 2005, Stopping by Woods, 2006. Pres., dir. Arcadia Hist. Soc., 1993-96. Fellow Geol. Soc. Am. (Burwell Meml. award 1972); mem. Assn. Engring. Geologists (hon., pres. 1979), Am. Inst. Profl. Geologists (hon., pres. 1989, Van Couvering Meml. award 1990, Parker Meml. medal 2003), Am. Geol. Inst. (sec.-treas. 1979-83), Conf. Calif. Hist. Socs. (pres. 2004-06).

PROCTOR, WILLIAM LEE, state legislator, academic administrator; b. Atlanta, Jan. 27, 1933; s. Samuel Cook and Rose Elizabeth (Nottingham) P.; m. Pamela Evans Duke; children: Samuel Matthews (dec.), Priscilla Nottingham. BS, Fla. State U., 1956, MS, 1964, PhD, 1968; DHL (hon.), Nova Southeastern U., 2003; LLD (hon.), Flagler Coll., 2004. Tchr. Seminole County Pub. Schs., Longwood, Fla., 1956-57, 58-62, Orange County Fla. Pub. Schs., Orlando, 1957-58; athletic coach Fla. State U., Tallahassee, 1962-65, asst. dean men, 1965-67, grad. fellow, 1967-68; supt. of schs. Rock Hill (S.C.) Sch. Dist. #3, 1968-69; dean of men U. Ctrl. Fla., Orlando, 1969-71; pres. Flagler Coll., St. Augustine, Fla., 1971-2001, chancellor, 2001—; mem. Dist. 20 Fla. House of Reps., Tallahassee, 2004—. Cons. on higher edn. policy Heritage Found., Washington, 1983—, Fla. Bd. Edn., 2001-03, State Bd. Edn., 2003-2004; mem. Commn. on Colls., So. Assn. Colls. and Schs., 1995-2000; dir. Tchr. Edn. Accreditation Coun. Vice-chmn. Fla. Edn. Stds. Commn., 1995-2001; bd. dirs. Penney Retirement Cmty., chmn., 1991-2004; bd. dirs. Vicar's Landing Retirement Cmty., chmn., 1992-95, bd., 1990-96; trustee, chmn. Fla. Sch. for Deaf and Blind, St. Augustine, 1984-2001; adv. coun. Salvation Army, St. Johns County; devel. coun. First Coast Work Force, 1998-2001; mem. Bus./Higher Edn. Partnership, 2000-01; chmn. Cmtys. in Schs., St. Johns County, Fla., 2002-04. Recipient Disting. Educator award Fla. State U. Coll. Edn., 1989, Phil Carrol award Soc. for Advancement Mgmt., 1990, Disting. Svc. award Fla. Sch. for Deaf and Blind, 1990, Patrick Henry Medallion patriotic achievement Mil. Order of World Wars, 1991, Stetson S Club Achievement award, 1993, Order of the South So. Acad. Letters, Arts, and Scis., Excellence in Mgmt. award Soc. for Advancement of Mgmt., 2000, Lifetime Edn. Achievement award, 2001, Disting. Svc. award Fla. Assn. Colls. and Univs., 2002, Sec. Jim Horne's Life Edn. Leadership award; named to Fla. State U. Athletic Hall of Fame, 1988, Order of La Florida, 2001. Mem. Am. Assn. Pres. of Ind. Colls., State Hist. Assn., Ind. Colls. and Univs. of Fla. (legis. chmn. 1974-77, vice chmn. 1976-77, chmn. 1978-79, Liberty Bell award 2003), Rotary (pres. 1978-79, bd. govs. dist. 697 1988-89). Republican. Presbyterian. Avocations: history, jogging, Karate. Office: Flagler Coll Office of the Chancellor PO Box 1027 Saint Augustine FL 32085-1027 Office Phone: 904-819-6210 ext. 210. Business E-Mail: proctorw@flagler.edu.

PRODAN, EMIL, physics professor; b. Romania; m. Camelia Prodan. PhD, Rice U., Houston, 2003. Rsch. assoc. dept. Physics U. Calif., Santa Barbara, 2003—05; fellow Princeton Ctr. for Complex Materials, NJ, 2005—07; asst. prof. Yeshiva U., NYC, 2007—. Contbr. scientific papers. Grant, Rsch. Corp. Sci. Advancement, 2008—. Office: Yeshiva Univ 245 Lexington Ave Rm 510 New York NY 10016 Office Fax: 212-340-7831. Business E-Mail: prodan@yu.edu.

PROEBSTING, EDWARD LOUIS, JR., retired horticulturist; b. Woodland, Calif., Mar. 2, 1926; s. Edward Louis and Dorothy (Critzer) P.; m. Patricia Jean Connolly, June 28, 1947; children: William Martin, Patricia Louise, Thomas Alan (dec.). BS, U. Calif., Davis, 1948; PhD, Mich. State U., 1951. Asst. horticulturist Wash. State U., Prosser, 1951-57, assoc. horticulturist, 1957-63, horticulturist, 1963-93, supt. Irrigated Agrl. Rsch. and Ext. Ctr., 1990-93; ret., 1993. Vis. prof. Cornell U., Ithaca, N.Y., 1966; vis. scientist Hokkaido U., Sapporo, Japan, 1978, Victoria Dept. Agr., Tatura, Australia, 1986—. Contbr. numerous articles to profl. jours. Scoutmaster Boy Scouts Am., Prosser, 1963-76, dist. chmn., 1976-78. Served to lt. USNR, 1943-46, 52-54. Recipient Silver Beaver award Boy Scouts Am.; fellow Japan Soc. Promotion Sci., Sapporo, 1978, Res. Bank. Australia, 1986. Fellow AAAS, Am. Soc. Hort. Sci. (pres. 1983-84, sci. editor jour. 1993-98). Methodist. Avocations: backpacking, native plants. Home: 1929 Miller Ave Prosser WA 99350-1532

PROEFROCK, CARL KENNETH, academic medical administrator; b. Curtis, Ill., Mar. 30, 1928; s. Carl Robert and Anna Lorraine (Hagel) Proefrock; m. Margaret Muntz (dec. Apr. 1984); 3 children; m. Janelle Dillon, Sept. 8, 1988 (dec. Sept. 2001). BA, Carthage Coll., Kenosha, Wis., 1949; MDiv, Chgo. Luth. Theol. Sem., 1953. Pastor Evang. Luth. Ch. Am., 1953—66; sr. com. orgn. specialist N.Y.C. Housing and Devel. Adminstrn., 1966-68; exec. dir. Model Cities Program, Manchester, NH, 1968-70, Health Assn. Rochester and Monroe, NY, 1970-73, Mahoning Shenango Area Health Edn. Network, Youngstown, Ohio, 1973-78; spl. asst. to dean Northeastern Ohio Univs. Coll. Medicine, Rootstown, 1978-79; v.p. Med. Coll. Ohio, Toledo, 1979-88, sr. v.p. govtl. affairs, 1988-93; pres. KPA Assocs., Inc., 1993—. V.p. Found. for Applied Rsch., Washington, 1976; chmn. adv. bd. Ohio AHEC, Columbus, 1976; program adminstr. Ohio Statewide Area Health Edn. Ctr., Toledo, 1988-93. Chmn. Toledo Area Coun. Tech., 1986; spl. asst. to clergy All Saints Parish, Pawleys Island, S.C., 1998-2000. Mem. Nat. Area Health Edn. Ctrs. Assn. (bd. dir. 1988-95), Nat. Assn. Univ. Rsch. Adminstrs., Soc. Rsch. Adminstrs., Internat. Assn. Univ. Rsch. Parks, Soc. Univ. Patent Adminstrs., Nat. Assn. Health Manpower Edn. Systems, Northeastern Ohio Med. Educators Assn. (bd. dir.), Rotary. Anglican. Home: 46 Pawleys Pl Dr Pawleys Island SC 29585-7254 Office: KPA Assocs PO Box 194 Pawleys Island SC 29585-0194 E-mail: kenkpa@cornellbox.com.

PROENZA, BILL (XAVIER WILLIAM PROENZA), meteorologist, former federal agency administrator; b. Oct. 30, 1944; Grad. in Meteorology, Fla. State U. With NOAA/Nat. Weather Svc., Miami, Fla., 1963—, Huntsville, Ala., 1968, Columbus, Ga., 1969—, NOAA Nat. Weather Svc., Atlanta, 1970; asst. and acting nat. prog. leader Pub. Weather Br. Air Pollution and Fire NOAA/Nat. Weather Svc., Silver

Spring, Md., 1970—72, mgr. regional pub., marine, forestry, agrl. and air pollution progs. Ctrl. Region Kansas City, Mo., 1973—75, forecaster regional warning coordination ctr. Ctrl. Region, 1974, exec. officer so. region Ft. Worth, 1976, acting dep. dir. so. region, 1986—87, dep. dir. so. region, 1987—97, acting dir. so. region, 1990, 1998—99, dir. so. region, 1999—2007, dir. Nat. Hurricane Ctr., 2007. Fellow: Am. Meteorol. Soc. (Francis W. Reichelderfer award 2001); mem.: Nat. Weather Assn.

PROENZA-COLES, CHRISTINA, history professor; b. Miami, Aug. 19, 1970; d. Morris Christopher and Catherine Comer Proenza; m. George Minor Coles, Feb. 16, 2003; children: George Morris, Mercedes Catherine. PhD in Hist. Studies & Sociology, New Sch. for Social Rsh., New York, 2004. Asst. prof. history Va. State U., Petersburg, 2004—. Contbr. academic jour. Grant, Nat. Endowment for the Humanities, 2008. Office: Va State Univ Colson Hall 101-H Petersburg VA 23804

PROFFIT, WILLIAM ROBERT, orthodontics educator; b. Harnett County, NC, Apr. 19, 1936; s. Glenn Theodore and Edna Marie (Queener) P.; m. Sara Thomas, Sept. 20, 1953; children: Lola Ann, Edward Thomas, Glenn Theodore. BS, U. N.C., 1956, DDS, 1959; student, Campbell Coll., Buies Creek, NC, 1952-53; PhD, Med. Coll. Va., 1962; MS, U. Wash., 1963; FDS, Royal Coll. Surgeons, 1990. Cert. Am. Bd. Orthodontics. Investigator Nat. Inst. Dental Research, Bethesda, Md., 1963-65; asst. prof. orthodontics U. Ky., Lexington, 1965-68, assoc. prof., 1968-71; prof. U.Ky., Lexington, 1971-73; prof. orthodontics U. Fla., Gainesville, 1973-75; prof., chmn. dept. orthodontics U. NC, Chapel Hill, 1975—, Kenan prof., 1992. Cons. NIH, Bethesda, 1974, 76— Author: Contemporary Orthodontics, 1986, 4th edit., 2006; co-author: Surgical Correction of Dentofacial Deformity, 1980, Surgical-Orthodontic Treatment, 1990, Contemporary Treatment of Dentofacial Deformity, 2003; contbr. articles to sci. jours. Served to lt. comdr. USPHS, 1963-65. Fulbright research scholar U. Adelaide, Australia, 1972 Mem. ADA, Am. Assn. Orthodontists (coun. on rsch. 1970-76), Internat. Assn. Dental Rsch., Phi Beta Kappa. Democrat. Presbyterian. Home: 620 Rock Creek Rd Chapel Hill NC 27514-6716 Office: UNC Sch Dentistry Dept Orthodontics Chapel Hill NC 27599-7450 E-mail: william_proffit@dentistry.unc.edu.

PROFFITT, DENNIS R., psychology professor, department chairman; BS in Psychology, Pa. State U., 1970, MS in Psychology, 1973, PhD in Psychology, 1976. Asst. prof. psychology Wesleyan U., Middletown, Conn., 1976—79, U. Va., Charlottesville, 1979—85, assoc. prof. psychology, 1985—91, prof. psychology, 1991—, founding dir. cognitive sci. program, 1992—, Cavalier disting. tchg. prof., 1999—2001, Commonwealth prof. psychology, 2004—, chmn. dept. psychology. Cons. editor: Perception & Psychophysics, 1983—93, Jour. Exptl. Psychology: Human Perception and Performance, 1988—99, Psychol. Rev., 1990—96, Psychol. Sci., 2003—, Perception, 2003—; contbr. articles to profl. jours. Recipient James McKean Cattell Sabbatical award, 1988—89; grantee, NSF, 2005—09, NIH, 2007—, US Army, 2007—08. Fellow: Am. Psychol. Soc. Office: Dept Psychology Univ Va PO Box 400400 Charlottesville VA 22904-4400 Office Phone: 434-924-0655. Business E-Mail: drp@virginia.edu.*

PROFFITT, JOHN RICHARD, information technology executive, educator, public official; b. Grand Junction, Colo., Sept. 12, 1930; s. Hillus D. and Joy Elaine (Lindsay) P.; m. Claire Boyer Miller, May 8, 1965 (div. 1992); children: Cameron Lindsay Taylor, William Boyer. BA in Edn., U. Ky., 1953, MA in Polit. Sci., 1961; postgrad., U. Mich., 1959-65. Asst. dean of men, instr. polit. sci. dept. U. Ky., Lexington, 1957-59; teaching fellow U. Mich., Ann Arbor, 1961-63, 63-65; asst. dir. Nat. Commn. on Accrediting, Washington, 1966-68; dir. accreditation and eligibility staff U.S. Dept. HEW, Washington, 1968-75; dir. divsn. eligibility and agy. evaluation U.S. Dept. Edn., Washington, 1975-80, dir. divsn. instnl. and state incentive programs, 1980-82; pres. The Clairion Corp., Bethesda, Md., 1982-84, Nat. Asbestos Removal, Inc., Beltsville, Md., 1985-90, Commonwealth Environ. Svcs., Inc., Alexandria, Va., 1987-91, also chmn. bd. dirs.; chmn. Internat. Environ. Engrs., Inc., Alexandria, Va., 1991-92; pres. Canterbury Internat., Vienna, Va., 1992-95; cons., 1995-99; v.p. E-Pass Techs., Inc., McLean, Va., 1999—. Cons. Conn. State Commn. Higher Edn., Hartford, 1967, Am. Coun. Edn., Washington, 1970; cons. U.S. Dept. Hew, 1967, 68; mem. study steering com. Am. Vocat. Assn., Washington, 1968; exec. sec. Nat. Adv. Com. on Accreditation and Instnl. Eligibility, Washington, 1968-80; mem. gen. com. Nat. Study Sch. evaluation, Alexandria, 1970-78; mem. task force Edn. Commn. of the States, Denver, 1972; subcom. chmn. Fed. Interagy. Com. on Edn., Washington, 1974-76; lectr., presenter profl. confs.; chmn. Commn. Accrediting. Co-author: Accreditation and Certification in Relation to Allied Health Manpower, 1971; contbg. author: Health Manpower: Adapting in the Seventies, 1971, Accreditation in Teacher Education, 1975, Transferring Experiential Credit, 1979; contbr. articles to profl. and govtl. agy. publs., 1968-79. Bd. dirs. and chmn. accrediting commn. Nat. Accreditation Coun. for Agys. Serving the Blind, N.Y.C., 1983-89, v.p. and bd. dirs., 1985-89; pres., chmn. bd. dirs. Found. for Advancement of Quality Svcs. for the Blind, Alexandria, 1988. Capt. USAFR. Decorated Korean War UN and Nat. Defense Svc. medals; Higher edn. fellow, Univ. Mich., 1959. Mem. YMCA, Optimist Club (Lexington, Ky.), Club Internat. (Chgo.), Island Club (Hobe Sound, Fla.), Thoroughbred Club Am. (Lexington), Tower Club (Vienna, Va.), Sigma Nu, Omicron Delta Kappa. Democrat. Episcopalian Ymca. Avocations: travel, antiques, art, animal welfare, conservation. Home: 515 Beall Ave Rockville MD 20850-2106 E-mail: johnproff@aol.com.

PROFFITT, WALDO, JR., newspaper editor; b. Plainview, Tex., Oct. 8, 1924; s. Waldo and Susan Ann (Smith) P.; m. Marjorie Baltzegar, Sept. 14, 1946 (div. 1963); children: Ann Herbert, Deborah, Geoffrey Harrison, Laurence Scott; m. Anne Collier Greene, Feb. 6, 1966; 1 child, Robert Waldo. BA cum laude, Harvard U., 1948. Reporter Bangor (Maine) Cochran Commercial, 1948—50; assoc. dir. Harvard News Office, Cambridge, Mass., 1952-54; city editor Charlotte (N.C.) News, 1954-58; mng. editor Journal, Lorain, Ohio, 1958-61; editorial dir. Sarasota (Fla.) Herald-Tribune, 1961-84; editor, 1984-98; columnist Sarasota-Herald Tribune, 1998—. Author: A View From Sarasota Published, 2007. Lt. U.S. Army, 1943-46, ETO, lt. USAF, 1950-52. Recipient Global Media Lifetime Achievement award, Population Inst., 2003. Mem. Am. Soc. Newspaper Editors, Fla. Soc. Newspaper Editors (pres. 1978). Democrat. Unitarian Universalist. Home: 1581 Hillview Dr Sarasota FL 34239-2047 Office: Sarasota Herald-Tribune PO Box 1719 Sarasota FL 34230-1719 Personal E-mail: wproffitt@comcast.net.

PROFIT, LORETHA SPURS, retired elementary school educator; b. Monroe, La., Aug. 15, 1947; d. James and Willie Mae (Kiper) Spurs; m. Simon Profit Jr., June 6, 1966; children: Anthony Simeon, Adriane Sirena, Simon III. BA, N.E. La. U., 1976. From sst. mgr. to co-owner Nelsons Drive In and Motel, Monroe, 1966—84; tchr. 2d grade Woodlawn Elem. Sch., West Monroe, La., 1976—90, Lincoln Elem. Sch., Monroe, 1990—2005; ret., 2005. Substitute tchr., vol. tutor Ouachita Parish Sch. Bd., Monroe, 1968—69; paraprofl. Swayze Elem. Sch., Monroe, 1973—76. Ptnr. Spl. Olympics, La. Named Hon. Citizen, Girls and Boys Town. Mem.: NEA, Self-Employed Bus. Women's Club Dallas, Internat. Platform Assn., La. Assn. Educators Black Caucus (lead tchr. La. challange grant), Monroe City Assn. Educators (faculty rep.), La. Assn. Educators, ULM Alumni Assn., Nat. Coun. Negro Women, Inc., Smithsonian Nat. Assoc., Breeze Gospel Group, PPW Club, Order Eastern Star, Delta Sigma Theta. Home: 4005 Gaston St Monroe LA 71203-5819 Mailing: PO Box 5059 Monroe LA 71211-5059 Office: 2120 Ticheli Rd Monroe LA 71202

PROFITT, DONALD RALPH, secondary school educator; b. Dayton, Jan. 23, 1949; s. Everett Ralph and Mary Francis Profitt; m. Karen Sue Freeman, Feb. 16, 1998; m. Karen Sue McDermott; children: Chad McDermott, Mathew McDermott, Shelly McDermott. BS, Bowling Green State U., Ohio, 1972; MA, Mich. State U., Mich., 1976; EdD, Nova Southeastern U., Fla., 1996. Profl. Educator Fla. Dept. of Edn., 2004. Prin. Elem. Sch., Edinburg, Tex., 1982—92, Elem. Prin., Pasadena, Fla., 1992—95; tchr. Orange County Pub. Schs., Orlando, Fla., 1998—. Author: (book on edn.) Teaching: A Survival Manual for the First Year Teacher (Sam's Club Tchr. Yr. in Fla., 1999). Recipient Excellence In Tchg., Sci. Am., 2002. Mem.: Orange County Classroom Tchrs. Assn. (assoc. Tchr. of the Yr. 2005). Home: 10624 Denali Dr Clermont FL 34711-9127 Office: Colonial 9th Grade Ctr 7775 Valencia College Ln Orlando FL Personal E-mail: dprofitt@cfl.rr.com. Business E-Mail: profitd@ocps.net.

PROFUSEK, ROBERT ALAN, lawyer; b. Cleve., Jan. 14, 1950; s. George John and Geraldine (Hobl) Profusek; life ptnr. Linda Gail Schmidt, May 7, 1972; children: Robert Charles, Kathryn Anne. BA, Cornell U., 1972; JD, NYU, 1975. Bar: Ohio 1975, Tex. 1981, NY 1994. Assoc. Jones Day, Cleve., 1975—81, Dallas, 1981—82, ptnr., 1982—, NY, 1993. Bd. dirs. CTS Corporcitum and Valero, LP; spkr. in field. Contbr. articles to profl. jours. Mem.: ABA, Tex. Bar Assn., Assn. Bar City NY, NY Bar Assn., Greenwich Country Club. Republican. Episcopalian. Home: 541 North St Greenwich CT 06830-3424 Office: Jones Day 222 E 41st St 15th Fl New York NY 10017 Office Phone: 212-326-3800. Office Fax: 212-755-7306. E-mail: raprofusek@jonesday.com.

PROGER, PHILLIP A., lawyer; b. NYC, Apr. 8, 1948; BA, Univ. Maryland, 1969, JD with honors, 1973. Bar: Ohio 1973, D.C. 1978, U.S. Supreme Ct. 1978. Head Antitrust Divsn. Jones Day, Washington. Adj. prof. Georgetown Univ. Law Ctr., 1983-84; adv. bds. BNA (antitrust & trade regulation report), M&A Lawyer; mem., bd. visitors, U. Md. Sch. of Law. Mem. editl. bd. Law Rev. Moot Ct., 1973; contbr. articles to profl. jours. Fellow Am. Bar Found.; mem. ABA (chmn. Antitrust Law sect. 1998-99, bd. gov. 2003-2006), Am. Law Inst., Ohio State Bar Assn., D.C. Bar Assn., Am. Acad. Hosp. Attys. (pres. 1994-95). Office: Jones Day 5th Fl 51 Louisiana Ave Washington DC 20001-2113 Office Phone: 202-879-4668. Office Fax: 202-626-1700. Business E-Mail: paproger@jonesday.com.

PROKASY, WILLIAM FREDERICK, academic administrator; b. Cleve., Nov. 27, 1930; s. William Frederick and Margaret Lovinia (Chapman) P.; m. Pamela Pearson; children: Kathi Lynn, Cheryl Anne; stepchildren: Lisa Wier Cauthen, Kevin Wier. BA, Baldwin-Wallace Coll., 1952; MA, Kent State U., 1954; PhD, U. Wis., 1957. Grad. asst. Kent State U., 1953-54; W.A.R.F. fellow U. Wis., 1954-55, teaching asst., 1955-57; asst. prof., then asso. prof. Pa. State U., 1957-66; prof. psychology, chmn. dept. U. Utah, 1966-69, Disting. rsch. prof., 1971-72, dean social and behavioral sci., 1968-70; dean U. Utah (Coll. Social and Behavioral Sci.), 1970-79; acting dean U. Utah (Grad. Sch. Social Work), 1979-80; prof. psychology dean Coll. Liberal Arts and Scis., U. Ill., Champaign-Urbana, 1980-88; prof., v.p. for acad. affairs U. Ga., 1988-98. Cons. in field. Editor: Classical Conditioning, 1965, (with A.H. Black) Classical Conditioning II, 1971, (with D. Raskin) Electrodermal Responding in Psychological Research, 1973, Psychophysiology, 1974-77; editor (with I. Gormezano and R. Thompson) Classical Conditioning III, 1986; assoc. editor Learning and Motivation, 1969-76; cons. editor Jour. Exptl. Psychology, 1968-80. Trustee Utah Planned Parenthood Assn., 1977—80; Utah bd. dirs. ACLU, 1978—80; v.p., bd. dirs. Champaign-Urbana Symphony, 1986—88; mem. bd. advisors Ga. Mus. Art, 1989—, U. Ga. Performing Arts Ctr., 1998—2003; mem. bd. visitors U. Ga. Librs., 1998—2007; mem. Athens-Clarke County Libr. Bd., 1999—; treas. Athens Opera Co. Guild, 2001—06; pres. Friends Ga. Mus. Art, 2002—03, Athens-Clarke County Libr. Bd., 2003—04, Friends of Dance, 2003—04; v.p. Athens-Clarke County Libr. Endowment Bd., 2003—07; mem. Classic Ctr. Cultural Found., 2003—, treas., 2006—07; mem. adv. bd. Franklin Coll. Arts and Scis., 2003—06; chmn. Athens chapt., Am. Wine Soc., 2007—; del. Utah Dem. Conv., 1968—70, 1972—74; mem. Athens Regional Libr., 2002—, chmn., 2006—. Recipient Alumni Merit award Baldwin Wallace Coll., 1992, Disting. Alumni award Piedmont Coll., 1998, U. Ga. Alumni award of excellence, 1998; NSF sr. postdoctoral fellow, 1963-64. Fellow AAAS, Am. Psychol. Assn. (chmn. bd. sci. affairs 1977-78, coun. of reps. 1980-86, bd. dirs. 1983-86, bd. ednl. affairs 1993-96); mem. Fedn. Behavioral, Pyschol. and Cognitive Scis. (v.p. 1984-85, pres. 1985-87), coun. of Sci. Soc. Pres.'s (exec. bd. 1987-91, chmn. 1990), Psychonomic Soc., Coun. Rsch. Librs. (bd. dirs. 1990-96), NASULGC (exec. com. coun. on acad. affairs 1995-96), Am. Assn. Higher Edn., Soc. Psychophysiol. Rsch. (bd. dirs. 1978-84, pres. 1982-83), Utah Psychol. Assn. (exec. bd. 1968-70, pres. 1971-72), Assn. Advancement Psychology (bd. dirs. 1982-83), Sigma Xi (pres. U. Utah chpt. 1972-73), Phi Kappa Phi. Avocations: genealogy, wine tasting, reading, photography. Personal E-mail: wfp@charter.net.

PROKHOROVA, ELENA V., language educator; d. Valentina Shemonaeva; m. Alexander Prokhorov; 1 child, Daria A. PhD, U. Pitts., 2003. Vis. asst. prof. Russian U. Richmond, Va., Coll. William and Mary, Williamsburg, Va., 2006—08. Mem.: AAASS. Office: Coll William and Mary Washington Hall 232 PO Box 8795 Williamsburg VA 23187

PROKOPANKO, JAMES T., agricultural products executive; b. 1953; BS, U. Manitoba; MBA, U. We. Ontario. V.p. N.Am. crop inputs bus. Cargill Inc., with, 1978—2006; platform leader Cargill, 1999—2006; corp. v.p. procurement Cargill Inc., 2002—06; corp. v.p. Cargill, 2002—06; exec. v.p., CEO The Mosaic Co., Plymouth, Minn., 2006—07, pres., CEO, 2007—. Bd. dirs. The Mosaic Co., 2004—. Office: The Mosaic Co Atria Corp Ctr 3033 Campus Dr Ste E490 Plymouth MN 55441 Office Phone: 800-918-8270. Office Fax: 763-559-2960.

PROKOPOVICH, PETR, federal official; Past dep. prime minister Govt. of Belarus; chmn. bd Nat. Bank Rep. Belarus, Minsk. Office: Nat Bank Rep Belarus 20 Nezavisimosty Ave 220008 Minsk Belarus Office Phone: +375 17 219-22-01.

PROMAULAYKO, MICHELE, editor-in-chief; Degree in Journalism, Rutgers U., New Brunswick, NJ, 1993. With YM Mag.; editor Teen People Mag.; dep. editor Cosmopolitan Mag., exec. editor, 2000—08; v.p., editor-in-chief Women's Health Mag., 2008—. Office: Womens Health Mag Rodale Inc 733 Third Ave New York NY 10017*

PROMISLO, DANIEL, lawyer, small business owner; b. Bryn Mawr, Pa., Nov. 15, 1932; s. Charles and Pearl (Backman) Promislo; m. Estelle Carasso, June 10, 1961 (dec. Apr. 2006); children: Mark, Jacqueline, Steven. BSBA, Drexel U., 1955; JD magna cum laude, U. Pa., 1966. Bar: Pa. 1966. Pres., owner Hist. Souvenir Co., Phila., 1957—; assoc. Wolf, Block, Schorr & Solis-Cohen, Phila., 1966-70, ptnr., 1977-94, exec. com., 1987-89, mng. dir., 1997-2001, of counsel, 1994—; founder, pres. dir. Inst. Paralegal Tng., Phila., 1970-75, cons., 1975-77; pres., owner Hist. Documents Co., 1992—. Editor: Corporate Law, 1970, Real Estate Law, 1971, Estates and Trusts, 1971, Civil Litigation, 1972, Employee Benefit Plans, 1973, Criminal Law, 1974; contbr. articles to profl. jours. Bd. dirs. Phila. Drama Guild, 1977—95, chmn., 1982—86; bd. dirs. Phila. Israel Econ. Devel. Program, 1983—88, Inst. Arts in Edn., 1990—93, WHYY, Inc., 1994—2003, vice-chmn., 1995—96, chmn., 1996—97; bd. dirs. U.S. Physicians, Inc., 1995—98; chmn. Phila. Jewish Sports Hall Fame, 2006—08; trustee RAIT Fin. Trust, 1997—; bd. advisors Drexel U. Coll. Arts and Scis., 2001—; bd. dirs. Jewish Cmty. Ctrs. Greater Phila., 2006—09. Mem.: Drexel U. 100, Blue Key, Order of Coif, Phi Kappa Phi. Democrat. Jewish. Avocations: movies, basketball, tennis, golf. Office: Wolf Block Schorr & Solis-Cohen 1650 Arch St Fl 22 Philadelphia PA 19103-2097 E-mail: dpromislo@comcast.net.

PROMOD KUMAR, RAMACHANDRAN PILLAI, neurosurgeon, educator; s. Ramachandran Pillai and Sarojani Amma; m. Rashmi Vandse; 1 child, Shravan Pillai. MD, NIMHANS, Bangalore, 2003. Intern Kottayam Med. Coll., Kerala, 1994—95; instr. Sch. Med. Edn., Kottayam, 1996, resident physician, 1996—97, NIMHANS, 1997—2003; asst. prof. Amrita Inst. Med. Scis., Kochi, 2004—05; fellow U. Pitts., 2005, Ohio State U., Columbus, 2006—08; assoc., rsch. LSUHSC, Shreveport, La., 2005—06; clin. instr. OSUMC, Columbus, 2008—. Nat. Merit scholarship, Govt. India. Business E-Mail: promod.pillai@osumc.edu.

PRONGER, CHRIS, professional hockey player; b. Dryden, Ont., Can., Oct. 10, 1974; m. Lauren Pronger, 2001; children: Jack, George, Lilah. Defenseman Hartford Whalers, 1993—95, St. Louis Blues, 1995—2005, Edmonton Oilers, 2005—06, Anaheim Ducks, 2006—09, capt., 2007—08; defenseman Phila. Flyers, 2009—. Mem. Team Canada, Olympic Games, Nagnao, Japan, 1998, Salt Lake City, 2002, Torino, Italy, 06. Recipient Bud Ice Plus-Minus award, 1997—98, Norris Trophy, 2000, Hart Meml. Trophy, 2000; named to All-Rookie Team, NHL, 1994, Second All-Star Team, 2007, NHL All-Star Game, 1999, 2000, 2002, 2004, 2008; finalist Lester B. Pearson Award, 2000. Achievements include being a member of gold medal Canadian Hockey team, Salt Lake City Olympic Games, 2002; being a member of Stanley Cup Champion Anaheim Ducks, 2007. Office: Philadelphia Flyers Wachovia Ctr 3601 S Broad St Philadelphia PA 19148*

PRONOVOST, AMY LYNNE, dancer, educator; b. Royal Oak, Mich., Aug. 5, 1976; d. Gerald and MaryAnn Pronovost. BA in Dance and English, Western Mich. U., Kalamazoo, 1998. Cert. Stott Pilates, Gyrotonic and pilates for golf. Ballet dir., tchr. Dance Dynamics, Walled Lake, Mich., 2000—. Pilates and gyrotonic instr. Equilibrium, Bloomfield Hills, Mich., 2000—, Stottpilates instr. trainer. Home: 7073 Magnolia Ln Waterford MI 48327-4419 Personal E-mail: amypronovost@sbcglobal.net.

PRONOVOST, PETER J., anesthesiologist, health facility administrator, medical educator; b. Waterbury, Conn., Feb. 22, 1965; s. Henry and Ann Pronovost; m. Marlene Rosemary Miller, Oct. 5, 1996; children: Ethan, Emma. BS, Fairfield U., 1987; MD, Johns Hopkins U., 1991, PhD, 1999. Lic. Md., diplomate Am. Bd. Anesthesiology, Md., cert. spl. cert. competency in critical care medicine Md. Intern John Hopkins Hosp., Balt., 1991—92; resident Johns Hopkins U., Balt., 1992—95, fellow, 1994—96, instr., 1997—98, core faculty program for med. tech. and practice assessment, 1998—, asst. prof., 1998—2001, assoc. prof. to prof., 2001—; faculty Inst. for Healthcare Improvement, Boston, 2001—; med. dir. Ctr. for Innovations and Quality Care, Balt., 2001—. Co-chair patient safety com. Johns Hopkins Hosp., Balt., 2001—, dir. performance improvement, 1998—, dir. inpatient care, 1997—; chair adv. panel for ICU core measures Joint Commn. on Accreditation of Healthcare Organizations, Oakbrook Terrace, Ill., 2002—; med. advisor The Leapfrog Group, Washington, 2000—; cons. Vol. Hosps. of Am., Irving, Tex., 2000—; adv. bd. mem. grad. tng. program in clin. investigation Johns Hopkins Bloomberg Sch. of Pub. Health, Balt., 1999—; bd. mem. instl. rev. bd. Johns Hopkins U., Sch. of Medicine, Balt., 1999—2002; chair strategic planning com. Soc. of Critical Care Medicine, Chgo., 2002—; presenter Internat. AIDS Conf.; med. advisor purchasing std. for leapfrog group ICU Physician Staffing Std. Contbr. articles pub. to over 100 profl. jours. Recipient Rsch. scholarship in Preventive Cardiology, 1987, MAP-Reader's Digest Internat. fellowship for work in Nigeria, 1991, Ctr. for AIDA Rsch. (CFAR) scholarship, 1991; named a MacArthur Fellow, The John D. and Catherine T. MacArthur Found., 2008; named one of the 100 Most Influential People in the World, TIME mag., 2008; grantee Impact of Critical Pathways on Reportable Adverse Events and Liability Claims Experience, MCIC Vt., Inc., 1999—2000, Reducing the rate of failed extubation in the ICU, 1998-1999, Assn. between surg. critical pathways and complications and liability claims experience, MCIC, 1998-1999, Intensive Care Unit Safety Reporting Sys., Evaluating the Impact of the Leapfrog Group's Std. for ICU Physician Staffing. Mem.: Soc. of Critical Care Medicine Patient Safety Found. (founding mem., bd. of trustees), Soc. of Critical Care Medicine (chmn. 2002—02, Presdl. citation 2002, Rsch. award 2001), Assn. for Health Svcs. Rsch. (assoc.), Anesthesia Rsch. Soc. (assoc.), Am. Soc. of Critical Care Anesthesiologist (assoc.), Am. Soc. of Anesthesiologists (assoc.), AMA (assoc.), Delta Omega, Alpha Epsilon Delta, Alpha Sigma Nu. Democrat. Achievements include research in Leapfrog Group adopted Health Care Purchasing Standard based on my research; Reducing Catheter Related Blood Stream Infection in the ICU. Office: Johns Hopkins U Meyer 295 600 N Wolfe St Baltimore MD 21287-7294 Office Fax: 410-502-3235. E-mail: ppronovo@jhmi.edu.

PRONZINI, BILL JOHN (WILLIAM PRONZINI), writer; b. Petaluma, Calif., Apr. 13, 1943; s. Joseph and Helene (Guder) P.; m. Marcia Muller. Author: 71 novels (including under pseudonyms), 4 books of non-fiction, 20 collections of short stories, 1971—; first novel, The Stalker, 1971, novel, Hoodwink, 1981 (Best Novel), Boobytrap, 1998 (Best Novel); editor 80 anthologies; contbr. numerous short stories to publs. Recipient 6 scroll awards Mystery Writers Am., Named Grand Master, 2008; recipient Life Achievement award Pvt. Eye Writers Am., 1987. Office: PO Box 2536 Petaluma CA 94953-2536 E-mail: pronhack@comcast.net.

PROPERZIO, PAUL J., classicist, educator; b. Keene, NH, May 20, 1947; s. Joseph M. and Virginia T. Properzio; m. Deborah E. Jewett, Jan. 31, 1970; 1 child, Lucy A. BA in Latin and Greek, U. NH, 1969; PhD in Classical Studies, Loyola U., Chgo., 1982. Lic. educator Mass. Chair, assoc. prof. classics Drew U., Madison, NJ, 1975—87; tchr. Latin Hanover HS, NH, 1987—88; tchr. Latin, history, mythology Reading Meml. HS, Mass., 1988—93; assoc. prof. classics and humanities St.

Anselm Coll., Manchester, NH, 1993—97; tchr. Latin and Greek Boston Latin Acad., 1997—. V.p. Archaeol. Inst. of Am. (Boston Soc.), Boston, 2002—. Editor: (jour.) Am. Classical League Newsletter, 2003—; contbr. presentation,; author: (book chpt.) Heroic Epithets in Early Greek and Han Chinese Literature, New Light on the Cults of Apollo and Artemis in Marseilles, Heroic Honor and Responsibility: The Iliad as a Reflection of Global Conflict, Social Values, and Human Interaction in the Modern World; contbr. presentations, presentation, articles to profl. jours. Lector St. Joseph's Ch., Andover, Mass., 1988—. Capt. M.I. US Army, 1971—79. Recipient Rome and China Participant grant, NEH, 2000—02, Elaine G. Batting Meml. scholarship, Mass. Fgn. Lang. Assn., 2003, Arthur P. McKinley scholarship, Am. Classical League, 2002, FIPSE (Fund for Improvement of Post Secondary Edn.) fellowship, Woodrow Wilson Found., Princeton U., 1985; Fulbright scholar, Italy, 1969. Mem.: Classical Assn. of the Atlantic States (pres. 1984—85), Classical Assn. of New Eng. (pres. 1993—94), Am. Philol Assn. (minority students scholarship com. 2002—05), Prof. John C. Rouman Classical Lecture Series, U. of N.H. (adv. bd. 1997—). Independent. Roman Catholic. Avocations: travel, cooking, tennis, theater, walking. Home: 15 Ballardvale Rd Andover MA 01810 Office: Boston Latin Acad 205 Townsend St Boston MA 02121 Office Fax: 617-635-6696; Home Fax: 603-864-2496. Personal E-mail: pjpropertius@comcast.net.

PROPST, CHRISTOPHER M., literature and language professor; MFA in English, Tex. State U., San Marcos, 1998. Cert. TESOL Seattle U., 2005. Asst. prof English and ESL Western Wyo. C.C., Rock Springs, 1999—. Film discussion facilitator Wyo. Coun. Humanities, Rock Springs, 2006—07. Achievements include development of WWCC poetry slam.

PROPST, MICHAEL TRUMAN, pathologist; b. Lebanon, Oreg., July 3, 1940; s. Lynn Edward and Vera Ruth (Forbes) P.; m. Susan Jean Joesting, Dec. 26, 1974; children: Christopher M., Andrew J., Matthew A., Michael Jonathan, Edwin Cam. BS, Oreg. State U., 1962; MD, U. Oreg., 1966. Diplomate Am. Bd. Pathology. Pathologist Humana Hosp., Anchorage, 1974—84; med. examiner State of Alaska, Anchorage, 1975—94; med. dir. Physicians Med. Lab., Anchorage, 1984—94; chief med. examiner State of Alaska, Anchorage, 1994—2001; cons. forensic pathology, 2001—. Served to maj. USAF, 1971-74. Fellow Coll. Am. Pathologists, Am. Soc. Clin. Pathologists, Am. Acad. Forensic Scientists, Royal Soc. Medicine (Gr. Britain),; mem. Nat. Assn. Med. Examiners. Lutheran. Office Phone: 541-469-2317, 541-207-3788. Personal E-mail: mpropstmd@charter.net.

PROSE, NEIL STUART, pediatric dermatologist; b. NYC, 1949; MD, NYU, 1975. Cert. Am. Bd. Dermatology, 1983. Intern in pediat. San Francisco Gen. Hosp., 1975—76; resident in dermatology SUNY, 1980—83, asst. prof. pediat., 1983—84; dermatologist Duke U. Med. Ctr., Durham, NC, assoc. prof. medicine. Office: Duke U Med Ctr PO Box 3252 Durham NC 27710 Office Phone: 919-684-5146. Office Fax: 919-681-8073. Business E-Mail: prose001@mc.duke.edu.

PROSIENSKI, LISA, legislative staff member; Exec. dir. They Work for Us; campaign mgr. Chellie Pingree's Congl. Campaign; chief of staff to Rep. Chellie Pingree US House of Reps., Washington, 2008—. Democrat. Office: 1037 Longworth House Office Bldg Washington DC 20515 Office Phone: 202-225-6116. Office Fax: 202-225-5590.*

PROSPERI, DAVID C., social sciences educator; b. NYC, Sept. 10, 1948; s. David C. Prosperi Jr and Alma R. Prosperi; life ptnr. Karen Ann Esteves; 1 child, Jenifer R. PhD, Ind. U., Bloomington, 1978. Prof. U. Cin., 1980—89; Henry D. Epstein prof., urban and regional planning Fla. Atlantic U., Fort Lauderdale, 1989—. Author: (book) Large-Scale 3D Data Integration. Challenges and Opportunities.; contbr. articles to profl. jour. (Best Paper Recognition award, 1990). Founding mem. Met. Form Rsch. Group, Fort Lauderdale-Seattle-Delft, Fla., 2004—09; dir. Riverwalk, Fort Lauderdale, Fla., 1997—2003. Mem.: Urban Data Mgmt. Soc. (nat. rep. 2006—09), Salzburg Congress Urban Planning and Devel., Internat. Soc. City and Regional Planners, Assn. Collegiate Schs. Planning (Cert. Appreciation award 1986). Avocation: classical music. Office: FL Atlantic Univ 111 E Las Olas Blvd Fort Lauderdale FL 33301 Business E-Mail: prosperi@fau.edu.

PROSPERO, MOISES, social studies educator, director; b. El Paso, Tex., Apr. 26, 1964; s. Moises and Magdalena Prospero; m. Trinh Tuyet Mai, Mar. 22, 2003; 1 child, May Linh. PhD, U. Houston, 2006. Asst. prof. U. UT Coll. Social Work, Salt Lake City, 2006—; rsch. dir. UT Criminal Justice Ctr., Salt Lake City, 2007—. Bd. vice chair UT Domestic Violence Coun., Salt Lake City, 2008—. Contbr. articles to profl. jour. Bd. mem. Dual Immersion Acad., Salt Lake City, 2008—08; chair assessment subcom. UT Gov. Task Force Board, Salt Lake City, 2008—. Mem.: Coun. on Social Work Edn. Achievements include development of dating violence prevention program for youth. Avocation: travel. Office: Univ UT Coll Social Work 395 S 1500 E Salt Lake City UT 84112 Office Fax: 801-585-3219. Business E-Mail: moises.prospero@socwk.utah.edu.

PROSSER, DAVID THOMAS, JR., state supreme court justice, former state legislator; b. Chgo., Dec. 24, 1942; s. David Thomas, Sr. and Elizabeth Averell (Patterson) Prosser. BA, DePauw U., 1965; JD, U. Wis., 1968. Bar: Wis. 1968. Lectr. Ind. U., Indpls., 1968-69; advisor U.S. Dept. Justice, Washington, 1969-72; adminstrv. asst. to U.S. Rep. Harold V. Froehlich, Washington, 1973-74; pvt. practice Washington, 1975, Appleton, Wis., 1976; dist. atty. Outagamie County Wis., Appleton, 1977-78; state rep. State of Wis., Madison, 1979-96; commr. Tax Appeals Commn., 1997-98; justice Supreme Ct. Wis., 1998—, Jud. Coun., 2002—06. Commr. Nat. Conf. Commrs. Uniform State Laws, 1982—96, 2005—07; mem. Wis. Sesquicentennial Commn., Madison, 1993—99; minority leader Wis. Assembly, 1989—94, spkr., 1995—96. Mem.: Outagamie Bar Assn., Milw. Bar Assn., Dane Bar Assn., Wis. Bar Assn. Presbyterian. Avocation: art collector of American prints. Office: Supreme Ct Wis PO Box 1688 Madison WI 53701-1688 Office Phone: 608-266-1882.*

PROSSER, FRANKLIN PIERCE, computer scientist; b. Atlanta, July 4, 1935; s. Edward Theron and Eunice (McDaniel) P.; m. Brenda Mary Lau, June 16, 1960; children: Edward, Andrea. BS, Ga. Inst. Tech., 1956, MS, 1958; PhD, Pa. State U., 1961. Prof. computer sci. Ind. U., Bloomington, 1969-99; asso. dir. Wrubel Computing Center, 1969-81, chmn. dept. computer sci., 1971-77, 87-93, spl. asst. for acad. computing, 1979-81; v.p. Logic Design, Inc., 1982-92. Cons. Lockheed Theoretical Physics Lab., Palo Alto, Calif., 1967 Home: 1200 S Longwood Dr Bloomington IN 47401-6072 Office: Ind U Dept Computer Sci Bloomington IN 47405

PROSSER, MICHAEL HUBERT, communications educator; b. Indpls., Mar. 29, 1936; arrived in China, 2001; s. Marshall Herbert and Clydia Catharine (O'Dea) P.; m. Carol Mary Hogle, Nov. 27, 1958 (div. 1983); children: Michelle Ann, Leo Michael, Louis Mark; m. Joan Ann Kirkeby, Dec. 6, 1986 (div. 2001). BA, Ball State U., 1958, MA, 1959; PhD, U. Ill., 1964. Tchr. Latin Urbana Jr. HS, Ill., 1960-63; asst. prof. speech SUNY, Buffalo, 1963-69; assoc. prof. speech Ind. U., Bloomington, 1969-72; prof. rhetoric and comm. U. Va., Charlottesville, 1972-2001, chair, 1972-77, prof. emeritus, 2001—; William A. Kern prof. in comm. Rochester Inst. Tech., 1994—98; chair internat. adv. bd. Coll. English Shanghai Internat. Studies U. Intercultural Inst., 1998—2001, disting. prof., 2006—. Vis. lectr. comm. CUNY Queens Coll., 1966—67; vis. assoc. prof. speech Calif. State U., Hayward, 1971; vis. prof. curriculum Meml. U., Newfoundland, St. John's U., 1972, St. Paul U., 1975, U. Ottawa, Canada, 1975; cons. U.S. Info. Agy., Washington, 1977; disting. vis. prof. speech Kent State U., Ohio, 1978; Fullbright prof. English U. Swaziland, Kwalusene, 1990—91; disting. vis. prof. comm. Rochester Inst. Tech., 1998—2001; adj prof. SUNY, Brockport, 1998—99; prof. English Yangzhou U., 2001—02; disting. prof. English Beijing Lang. and Culture U., China, 2002—05, Shanghai Internat. Studies U., China, 2005—; keynote spkr. various Chinese comm. confs., India, Russia. Author: The Cultural Dialogue, 1978 (translated into Japanese 1982); co-author: Diplomatic Discourse: International Conflict at the United Nations: Addresses and Analysis, 1997; editor: An Ethic for Survival: Adlai Stevenson Speaks on International Affairs, 1936-65, 1969, Sow the Wind, Reap the Whirlwind: Heads of State Address the United Nations (2 vols.), 1970, Intercommunication Among Nations and Peoples, 1973; co-editor: Readings in Classical Rhetoric, 1969, Readings in Medieval Rhetoric, 1973, Civic Discourse: Multiculturalism, Cultural Diversity, and Global Communication, 1998, Civic Discourse: Intercultural, International and Global Media, 1999, Sino-American Compositions of Shared Topics, 2003, Intercultural Perspectives on Chinese Communication, 2007; series editor Civic Discourse for the Third Millennium, 1998-2004, Ablex Pub. Co., Praeger, Greenwood Pub. Co., 2005; featured in China Talent Semi-monthly, Chinese edit.; numerous interviews on China Radio Internat., 2007-08. Chair AFS Global Awareness Day, U. Va., 1983-90, RIT Global Awareness Day, 1995-98; bd. dirs., v.p. Assn. Rochester UN, 1996-97, pres., 1997-98; pres. Rochester Area Fulbright chpt., 1995-97; mem. Nat. Comm. Assn., Internat. Comm. Assn. Recipient Disting. Alumnus award Ball State U., 1978, Citizen of World award, SIETAR Internat., 1986, Prosser-Sitaram award, 2000. Mem. Internat. Soc. for Intercultural Edn., Tng. and Rsch. (pres. 1984-86, Citizen of World 1986, Outstanding Sr. Interculturalist 1990), Internat. Comm. Assn. (v.p., Disting. Svc. award 1978), UN Assn. U.S.A., Fulbright Assn., Nat. Comm. Assn., UN Assn. of Rochester (bd. dirs., v.p., pres.), Am. Field Svc. (pres. intercultural programs 1982-86, Charlottesville). Democrat. Roman Catholic. Avocation: travel. Office: Shanghai Internat Studies U Intercultural Inst Coll Journalism and Comm 121 Guanglingyilu Shanghai 200083 China Home Phone: 086 21 6542 3070; Office Phone: 086 21 6542 3070 ext. 1303. Office Fax: 86 21 6544 8852. Personal E-mail: michaelhprosser@yahoo.com.

PROST, SHARON, federal judge; b. Newburyport, Mass., May 24, 1951; m. Kenneth F. Greene, June 24, 1984; 1 child, Matthew Prost-Greene. BS, Cornell U., 1973; MBA, George Washington U., 1975, LLM in Taxation, 1984; JD, Am. U., 1979. Bar: D.C. Labor rels. specialist Office of Personnel Mgmt., 1973-76; with Gen. Acctg. Office, 1976-79; trial atty. Fed. Labor Rels. Authority, 1980-83; atty. chief counsel's office Dept. of Treasury, 1983-84; assoc. solicitor Nat. Labor Rels. Bd., 1984-89; chief minority labor counsel Senate Com. on Labor and Human Resources, 1989-93; minority chief counsel Senate Com. on the Judiciary, 1993—2001; judge US Ct. Appeals, (Fed. cir.), 2001—. Office: US Court Appeals Fed Cir 717 Madison Pl NW Washington DC 20439*

PROTAS, ELIZABETH J., physical therapist, academic administrator; m. Eugene D. Protas, Mar. 6, 1950; 1 child, Mark Jason. PhD, SUNY, Buffalo, 1974—80. Cert. phys. therapist Tex., 1980. Assoc. dean, sch. phys. therapy Tex. Woman's U., Houston, 1980—2002; chair, dept. phys. therapy U. Tex. Med. Br., Galveston, 2002—06, interim dean, 2006—08, dean, 2008—. Bd. trustees Am. Coll. Sports Medicine, Indpls., 2002—04. Recipient Joseph Valley Gerontologica Profl. of Yr. award, U. Tex. Health Sci. Ctr., 2000; grantee Support Rsch. and Tng. Grad. Students, Dept. of Veterans; fellow Founding Fellow, Am. Assn. Cardiovasc. and Pulmonary Rehab. Mem.: Am. Phys. Therapy Assn. (Worthingham fellow 2008). Achievements include research in Rehabilitation outcomes for persons with chronic disabilities. Office: U Tex Med Branch 301 U Blvd Galveston TX 77555-1144

PROTHRO, JERRY ROBERT, lawyer; b. Midland, Tex., Dec. 22, 1946; s. Jack William Prothro and Nita Marie (Stovall) Milligan; m. Leslie Joan Lepar, Aug. 15, 1970 (div. 1994); ptnr. David Majeau; children: Laura Kay, Evan Jackson. BA, Southwestern U., 1969; JD, U. Tex. Sch. Law, 1972. Lawyer, capt. U.S. Army, JAGC, 1972-76; ptnr. Turpin, Smith & Dyer, Midland, 1975-85, Boyd, Sanders, Wade, Cropper & Prothro, Midland, 1985-91; pvt. practice Dallas and Midland, Tex., 1991—95. Mem. admissions com. M/O div. U.S. Dist. Ct. for Western Dist. Tex., 1987-2000; staff atty. Dallas Legal Hospice, 2000-06; spkr. in field, real estate appraisals. Treas., v.p. Southwestern U. Alumni Bd., Georgetown, Tex., 1980-90, pres.-elect, 1991, pres., 1992-94; trustee, Southwestern U., 1992-94; adminstrv. bd. First United Meth. Ch., Midland, 1989-96; vice chmn. Permian Basin AIDS Coalition Bd., 1994; active Midland County Hist. Commn., 1980-85. Named Univ. scholar Southwestern U., 1969; recipient Disting. Svc. medal U.S. Army, 1974. Mem. Midland County Young Lawyers (pres. 1979-80), Midland County Bar Assn., 5th Cir. Bar Assn., Pi Kappa Alpha Social Frat., Blue Key Leadership Frat., Pi Gamma Mu Social Sci. Frat. Methodist. Avocations: antiques, camping. Office: 9 Rue Lavel No 1 Quebec City PQ Canada Personal E-mail: prothro@swbell.net.

PROTIC, PAUL B., legislative staff member; m. Caroline Protic; 6 children. MA, Harvard U. Spl. asst. to pres. US Dept. of Health and Human Svcs., Washington, 1983—85; dir. Capitol Hill ministry Campus Crusade for Christ, Washington; prof., dir. apprenticeship program in govt. Patrick Henry Coll., Purcellville, Va.; chief of staff for Rep. Todd Akin US House of Reps., Washington, 2006—. Avocations: tennis, jogging. Office: Office of Congressman Todd Akin 117 Cannon House Office Bldg Washington DC 20515 Office Phone: 202-225-2561. Business E-Mail: paul.protic@mail.house.gov.*

PROUD, DAYNA, public relations executive; Grad., London Sch. Pub. Rels. Retail team leader Carlman Booker Reis Pub. Rels., Orlando, Fla.; account supr. GolinHarris, Chgo.; with media rels. dept. McDonald's USA, 2006—07, sr. mgr. media rels. & comm., 2007—. Named a Woman to Watch, Advt. Age, 2009. Office: McDonalds Corp 2111 McDonalds Dr Oak Brook IL 60523*

PROULX, (EDNA) ANNIE, writer; b. Norwich, Conn., Aug. 22, 1935; d. George Napolean and Lois Nellie (Gill) Proulx; m. James Hamilton Lang, June 22, 1969 (div. 1990); children: Sylvia Marion, Jonathan Edward, Gillis Crowell, Morgan Hamilton. BA cum laude, U. Vt., 1969; MA, Sir George Williams U., Montreal, Can., 1973; DHL (hon.), U. Maine, 1994; DLitt (hon.), U. Toronto, 2000; LLD, Concordia U., Montreal, 2002. Author: Sweet and Hard Cider: Making It, Using It and Enjoying It, 1980, Heart Songs and Other Stories, 1988, Postcards, 1991 (PEN/Faulkner award for fiction, 1993), The Shipping News, 1993 (Irish Times Internat. Fiction award, 1993, Nat. Book award for fiction, 1994, Pulitzer Prize for fiction, 1994), Accordion Crimes, 1996 (Dos Passos prize for lit., 1996), Brokeback Mountain (later adapted to film), 1998 (Nat. Mag. award, 1998), Close Range: Wyoming Stories, 1999, That Old Ace in the Hole, 2002, Bad Dirt: Wyoming Stories 2, 2004, Fine Just the Way It Is: Wyoming Stories 3, 2008; editor: Best American Short Stories, 1997; contbr. articles to mags. Recipient Amb. Book award, English Speaking Union, 2000. Mem.: PEN Am. Ctr., Phi Alpha Theta, Phi Beta Kappa. Avocations: canoeing, reading, fishing.*

PROUST, JOYCELYN ANN, retired librarian; d. Merry Aylor and Alice Wilhelmina (Morgan); m. George Edward Proust (dec.); children: Gabrielle Cynara, Bertrand Gerard. BA, U. Denver, 1950, MA, 1955; cert., U. Paris Sorbonne, 1953. Lifetime French tchg. credential Calif. C.C., lifetime libr. credential C.C. Libr. Colo. Sch. Mines, Golden, 1955—62; prof. libr. sci. Long Beach (Calif.) City Coll., 1962—92, prof. emerita, 1992—. Chair Calif. C.C. Libr. Cooperative, 1968—75; exec. dir., pres. Libr./Learning Resources Assn., Calif., 1985—86. Bd. mem. Long Beach Mozart Festival, 1975—95, chair; active 1976 Bicentennial Com., LA, 1976. Mem.: Alpha Gamma Delta, Phi Sigma Iota, Alpha Lambda Delta. Unitarian. Home: 5249 Village Rd Long Beach CA 90808

PROUT, CURTIS, internist, educator; b. Swampscott, Mass., Oct. 13, 1915; s. Henry Byrd and Eloise (Willett) P.; m. Daphne Brooks, June 27, 1939 (div. 1985); children: Diana P. Cherot, Daphne P. Cook, Rosamond P. Warren, Phyllis P.; m. Diane Neal Emmons, Dec. 7, 1985. AB, Harvard U., 1937, MD, 1941. Diplomate Am. Bd. Internal Medicine. Intern Peter Bent Brigham Hosp., Boston, 1942; resident in internal medicine Johns Hopkins Hosp., Balt., 1943; research fellow Mass. Gen. Hosp., Boston, 1944—45; practice medicine specializing in internal medicine, 1945—; asst. dir. Univ. Health Services Harvard U., Cambridge, Mass., 1961-72; dir. prison health project Office of Econ. Opportunity, 1972-74; asst. dean Harvard Med. Sch., Boston, 1980-94, asst. clin. prof. medicine, 1975-82. Trustee Humane Soc. Mass., Boston, 1975-2005, pres., 2004; bd. dirs. Nat. Commn. on Correctional Health Care, 1980-98, chmn., 1990; dir., treas. The Med. Found., Boston, 1980-98. Chmn. Bd. Health, Dover, Mass., 1960-75. Fellow ACP, Mass. Med. Soc.; mem. AMA, Am. Clin. and Climatol. Assn., Tavern Club of Boston (pres. 1980-82). Avocations: sailing, writing. Home and Office: 115 School St Manchester MA 01944-1232 Personal E-mail: dr.curtisprout@adelphia.net.

PROUT, ROBERT STEPHEN, higher education consultant, law enforcement consultant; b. June 24, 1944; Degree in law, LaSalle Ext. U., Chgo., 1967; BA, Muskingum Coll., New Concord, Ohio, 1969; MEd, Ohio U., Athens, 1970; PhD, Ohio State U., Columbus, 1972. State trooper Ohio Hwy. Patrol, Akron, Ohio, 1965-68; coord. Zane State Coll., Zanesville, Ohio, 1969—72; dept. chair criminal justice St. Cloud State U., Minn., 1972—96, 2002—, dir. grad. program criminal justice, 1988—. Adj. faculty St. John's U., Coll. St. Thomas, U. Louisville, Alexandria Tech. Coll.; chmn. Govs. Com. on Crime Prevention-Region D, Minn., 1976-77. Author: Meeting Ohio's Law Enforcement Needs, 1973; contbr. articles to profl. jours. Recipient Tchr. of Yr. award, 1988. Office: St Cloud State Univ 245 Stewart Hall Saint Cloud MN 56301 Office Phone: 320-308-5541. Business E-Mail: prout@stcloudstate.edu.

PROVDA, LOIS M., psychologist, educator; BS in Social Studies, Boston U., BS in English, 1962; MA in Spl. Edn., NYU, 1964, PhD in Ednl. Psychology, 1983. Cert. marriage, family and child counselor, learning handicapped specialist, reading specialist, advanced study in edn. 1976. Ednl. dir. Payne Whitney Psychiat. Clinic NY Hosp., NYC, 1964—68; dir. reading Buckingham Sch., Bklyn., 1968—73; instr. CUNY, Bklyn., 1973—76, UCLA, 1996—2003; ednl. psychologist LA, 1976—. Ednl. cons. NY Assn. Blind, NYC, 1974—76; ednl. specialist psychol. svcs. dept. Bur. Jewish Edn., LA, 1982—. Fellow: Orthopsychiatric Assn.; mem.: NY Acad. Sci., Internat. Reading Assn., Am. Assn. Sch. Psychology, Assn. Ednl. Therapists. Home and Office: 9911 W Pico Blvd Ste 675 Los Angeles CA 90035 Office Phone: 310-277-5551. Personal E-mail: lprovda@aol.com.

PROVENCHER, CATHERINE A., state treasurer; b. Merrimack, NH; married; 2 children. BS in Acctg., Bentley Coll.; MBA, South NH Univ. CPA. With NH Office Legis. Budget, 1985—2006, dir. audits, 1997—2006; state treas. State of NH, 2007—. Chmn. New England Govtl. Forum. Grantee Caroline Gross Fellowship, 2006. Mem.: NH Soc. CPA, AICPA. Office: State Treas 25 Capitol St Rm 121 Concord NH 03301 Office Phone: 603-271-2621. Office Fax: 603-271-3922. Business E-Mail: treasury@treasury.state.nh.us.*

PROVENCIO, MARLA, marketing executive; b. Calif. married; 1 child. BA in English, UCLA. Production coord. ABC Entertainment, LA, 1979, prodr., sr. prodr, exec. dir. daytime, children's promotion, v.p. drama, long-form programming, sr. v.p. mktg., exec. v.p. mktg., 2007—. Named an Entertainment Marketer of the Yr. 2005, 2007, Advt. Age mag.; named one of top Hispanic Marketers of the Yr., AdWeek's Marketing y Medios Mag. Office: ABC Entertainment Ctr 2040 Ave of the Stars Los Angeles CA 90067 Office Phone: 310-557-7777.

PROVENCIO, ROBERTO ENRIQUE, music educator and minister; b. El Paso, Tex., July 14, 1957; s. Jesus Roberto and Velia Rivero Provencio; m. Linda Kay Johnson, Aug. 18, 1984; children: Robert Phillip, Charles Raymond, Elizabeth Anne, Victoria Lynn. MusB, U. Ariz., 1980; MusM, Tex. State U., 1986; D Musical Arts, U. Colo., 1993. Prof. music Calif. State U., Bakersfield, 1988—; academic senate Senate Exec. Com., 2004—; min. music First Presbyn. Ch., Bakersfield, 1995—; chair Academic Support & Student Svcs. Com., 2006—. Pvt. practice cons., Bakersfield, 1980—. Mem. editl. bd. The Choral Jour.; translator: History of the Choral Movement of Venezuela; author: Releasing the Artist Within: Mnemonics for Achieving Artistic Choral Performance. Mem. Adult Rehab. Ctr. Salvation Army, Bakersfield, 1999; bd. dirs. The Beethoven Festival, Bakersfield, 1992—95. Named Outstanding Hispanic Alumnus, Tex. State U., 1994, Outstanding Music Educator, Calif. Music Educators Assn., 1994, Outstanding Prof., 2001;, Calif. State U. fellow, 1988—92, Choral Rsch. fellow, U. of Colo., Boulder, 1986—88. Mem.: Nat. Assn. Ch. Musicians (bd. govs. 1998—, chair publs. com. jour.), Internat. Fedn. Choral Music, Am. Choral Directors Assn. (life; chair multicultural perspectives western divsn. 1992—96, mem. editl. bd. 1995—), Rotary (dir., scholarship chair 1994, Bakersfield East), Pi Kappa Lambda (life). Conservative. Avocations: motorcycle touring, fly fishing, tennis, photography, tobacciana. Home: 101 Camino del Oeste Bakersfield CA 93309 Office: Calif State U 9001 Stockdale Hwy Bakersfield CA 93311 Business E-Mail: rprovencio@csub.edu.

PROVENSEN, ALICE, artist, writer; b. Chgo. d. Jay Horace and Kathryn (Zelanis) Twitchell; m. Martin Provensen, Apr. 17, 1944 (dec.); 1 child, Karen Anna. Student, Art Inst. of Chgo., 1930-31, U. Calif., LA, 1939, Art Student League, NYC, 1940-41; D.H.L. (hon.), Marist Coll., 1986. With Walter Lanz Studios, Los Angeles, 1942-43; OSS, 1944-45. Author, illustrator Karen's Opposites, 1963, Karen's Curiosity, 1963, What is a Color?, 1967, author, illustrator (with Martin Provensen) Who's in the Egg?, 1970, author, illustrator The Provensen Book of Fairy Tales, 1971, Play on Words, 1972, My Little Hen, 1973, Roses are Red, 1973, Our Animal Friends, 1974, The Year at Maple Hill Farm, 1978, A Horse and a Hound, A Goat and a Gander, 1979, The Owl and Three Pussycats, 1981, Town and Country, 1984, Shaker Lane, 1987, The Buck Stops Here, 1990, Punch in New York, 1991 (Best Books N.Y. Times, 1991), My Fellow Americans, 1995, Count on Me, 1998 (Book of Yr. Parenting Mag., 1998), The Master Swordsman, 2001, The Magic Doorway, 2001, A Day in the Life of Murphy, 2003 (named One of the Three Best Childrens Books, 2003), Klondike Gold, 2005 (Spur award Western Writers Am., 2006), illustrator (with Martin Provensen) Mother Goose Book, 1976, illustrator Old Mother Hubbard, 1977, A Peaceable Kingdom, 1978, The Golden Serpent, 1980, A Visit to William Blake's Inn, 1981 (Caldecott honor book, 1981), Birds, Beasts and the Third Thing, 1982, The Glorious Flight, 1984 (Caldecott medal, 1984), The Voyage of Ludgate Hill, 1987, also textbooks; exhibitions include with Martin Provensen Balt. Mus., 1954, exhibitions include Am. Inst. Graphic Arts, NYC, 1959, Botolph Group, Boston, 1964, Eric Carle Mus., Amherst, Mass., 2005—06, one-woman shows include Henry Feiwel Gallery, NYC, 1991, Children's Mus., Washington, 1991, Moscarelle Mus. Art, Williamsburg, Va., 1991, Eric Carle Mus. Picture Book Art, Amherst, Mass., 2005—06; books represented Fifty Book of Yr. selections Am. Inst. Graphic Arts, 1947, 1948, 1952 (The Charge of the Light Brigade named Best Illustrated Children's Book of Yr. N.Y. Times, 1964, co-recipient medal Soc. Illustrators, 1960), In Progress: Murppy in the City, 2009. Recipient Empire State award, Youth Svcs. sect. NY Libr. Assn., 2004; named to Soc. Illustrators Hall of Fame, 2000. Office Phone: 949-276-8744, 949-492-2856.

PROVINCE, DENNIS, chemistry professor; PhD, Okla. State U., Stillwater, 1999. Chemistry prof. Harding U., Searcy, Ark., 1999—. Office: Harding Univ 915 Market Ave Searcy AR 72149-2272

PROVORNY, FREDERICK ALAN, lawyer, educator; b. Bklyn., Sept. 7, 1946; s. Daniel and Anna (Wurm) P.; m. Nancy Ileene Wilkins, Nov. 21, 1971; children: Michelle C., Cheryl A., Lisa T., Robert D. BS summa cum laude, NYU, 1966; JD magna cum laude, Columbia U., 1969. Bar: NY 1970, US Supreme Ct. 1973, DC 1975, Mo. 1977, Md. 1987, Calif. 1989; CPA, Md., Mo. Law clk. to Judge Harold R. Medina U.S. Ct. Appeals (2d cir.), NYC, 1969-70; asst. prof. law Syracuse (NY) U., 1970-72; assoc. Debevoise, Plimpton, Lyons & Gates, NYC, 1972-75, Cole & Groner PC, Washington, 1975-76; with Monsanto Co., St. Louis, 1976-86, asst. co. counsel, 1978-86; pvt. practice Washington, 1986-89; ptnr. Provorny & Jacoby, Washington, 1989-91; counsel Shaw, Pittman, Potts & Trowbridge, Washington, 1991-93; ptnr. Tydings & Rosenberg, Balt., 1993-94; pvt. practice Balt., 1994—98; Harold R. Tyler prof. law and tech. Sci. and Tech. Law Ctr., Albany (NY) Law Sch., 1998—2004, dir., 1998—2003; pres. Empire State Venture Group, Inc., 2001—03; dir. Md. Intellectual Property Legal Resource Ctr., Rockville, 2004—07. Vis. prof. U. Md. Sch. Law, 2004-07; lectr. Bklyn Law Sch., 1973-74; adj. prof. U. Balt. Sch. of Law, 1996-98, Rensselaer Poly Inst., 2004; pres. Sci. and Tech. Assocs., Inc., 1986-91; founder, dir. Ctr. for New Tech. Enterprise, rockville, Md., 2007-. Contbr. articles to profl. jours. Trustee Christian Woman's Benevolent Assn. Youth Home, 1979-83, Jewish Family Svcs. of N.E. NY, 1999—2004. Mem. ABA, Am. Law Inst., Am. Arbitration Assn. (panel comml. abitrators), Am. Intellectual Property Lawyers Assn., Licensing Execs. Soc. (U.S., Can.), Assn. Univ. Tech. Mgrs., Philo-Mt. Sinai Lodge 968, Masons, Beta Gamma Sigma. Jewish. Home: 11803 Kemp Mill Rd Silver Spring MD 20902-1511 Office: Ctr for New Tech Enterprise 9601 Med Ctr Dr Rockville MD 20850 Home Phone: 301-593-9115; Office Phone: 301-793-1618. Business E-Mail: fprovorny@newtechenterprise.org.

PROVOST, GLEN JOHN, bishop; b. Lafayette, La., Aug. 9, 1949; s. Cyrus and Sadie Marie (Blanchet) Provost. BA in English Lit., St. Joseph Sem. Coll., St. Benedict, La., 1971; BST, St. Thomas U., Rome, 1974, STL, 1975; MA in English Lit., U. La., Lafayette, 1981. Ordained priest Diocese of Lafayette, La., 1975; assoc. pastor St. Mary Magdalene, Abbeville, La., 1975—83; pastor St. Leo, Roberts Cove, La., 1983—85, St. John Cathedral, 1985—98, Our Lady of Fatima, 1998—2007; ordained bishop, 2007; bishop Diocese of Lake Charles, La., 2007—. Mem.: KC, SAR (mem. nat. chaplains com.), Equestrian Order of Knights of and Ladies of Holy Sepulchre Jerusalem (knight), Phi Eta Sigma. Roman Catholic. Office: Diocese of Lake Charles PO Box 3223 414 Iris St Lake Charles LA 70602 Office Phone: 337-439-7400. Office Fax: 337-439-7413.

PROWN, JULES DAVID, art historian, educator; b. Freehold, NJ, Mar. 14, 1930; s. Max and Matilda (Cassileth) P.; m. Shirley Ann Martin, June 23, 1956; children: Elizabeth Anderson, David Martin, Jonathan, Peter Cassileth, Sarah Peiter. AB, Lafayette Coll., 1951, DFA (hon.), 1979; AM, U. Del., 1956, Harvard U., 1953, PhD, 1961. Dir. Hist. Soc. Old Newbury, Newburyport, Mass., 1957-58, Old Gaol Mus., York, Maine, 1958-59; asst. to dir. Harvard U., Fogg Art Mus., Cambridge, Mass., 1959-61; instr. to Paul Mellon prof. history of art Yale U., New Haven, 1961-99, Paul Mellon prof. emeritus history of art, 1999—; curator Am. art Yale U. Art Gallery, New Haven, 1963-68; vis. lectr. Smith Coll., Northampton, Mass., 1966-67; dir. Yale Ctr. for Brit. Art, New Haven, 1968-76, sr. rsch. fellow, 1999—; assoc. dir. Nat. Humanities Inst., New Haven, 1977. Trustee Whitney Mus., N.Y.C., 1975-94; mem. editorial adv. bd. Am. Art-Smithsonian, Washington, 1986-2001, On Common Ground, 1993—; mem. vis. com. Harvard U. Art Museums, 1993-98. Author: John Singleton Copley, 2 Vols., 1966, American Painting from Its Beginnings to the Armory Show, 1969, The Architecture of the Yale Center for British Art, 1977; Art as Evidence: Writings on Art and Material Culture, 2002, (catalogue) American Art from Alumni Collections, 1968; editor (with Kenneth Haltman) American Artifacts: Essays in Material Culture, 2000. Recipient George Washington Kidd award Lafayette Coll., 1986, recipient Iris Found. award outstanding contbns. to the decorative arts, 2001, Lawrence A. Fleischman award Scholarly Excellence Am. Art History, 2001, William Clyde DeVane award Scholarship and Tchg. Phi Beta Kappa, Yale U., 2005. Fellow The Athenaeum of Phila. (hon.); mem. Am. Antiquarian Soc., Coll. Art Assn. (Disting. Tchg. of Art History award 1996), Conn. Acad. Arts & Scis., Walpole Soc., Royal Soc. Arts. Office: Yale Ctr for Brit Art PO Box 208280 New Haven CT 06520-8280 Business E-Mail: jules.prown@yale.edu.

PRUCHA, JOHN JAMES, geologist, educator; b. River Falls, Wis., Sept. 22, 1924; s. Edward Joseph and Katharine (Schladweiler) P.; m. Mary Elizabeth Helfrich, June 12, 1948; children: David, Stephen, Katharine, Carol, Mark, Barbara, Margaret, Christopher, Anne, Andrew. Student, Wis. State U., River Falls, 1941—43; PhB, U. Wis., 1945, PhM, 1946; MA, Princeton U., 1948, PhD, 1950. Asst. prof. geology Rutgers U., 1948-51; sr. geologist NY State Geol. Survey, 1951-56; rsch. geologist Shell Devel. Co., 1956-63; prof. geology Syracuse (NY) U., 1963-90, prof. emeritus, 1990—, chmn. dept., 1963-70, 88-89, dean Coll. Arts and Scis., 1970-72, vice chancellor acad. affairs, 1972-85; pres. Syracuse U. Press, 1973-85, bd. dirs., 1985-90. Author: Basement Tectonics of Rocky Mountains, 1965, Structural Behavior of Salt, 1967, Stratigraphy and Structure of Southeastern New York, 1959, Fracture Patterns, 1979, Zones of Structural Weakness, 1992; (with Norman A. Foss) Kinnickinnic Years, 1993. Trustee Le Moyne Coll., 1971-78; bd. dirs. Cultural Resources Coun., Syracuse, 1974—, pres., 1978-80; bd. dirs. Everson Mus. Art, Syracuse, 1977-83, v.p., 1980-81; regents vis. com. NY State Mus., 1993-96. Recipient John Mason Clarke medal NY State Geol. Survey, 1990. Fellow AAAS, Geol. Soc. Am.; mem. Am. Assn. Petroleum Geologists, Am. Geophys. Union, NY State Coun. Profl. Geologists. Home: 112 Ardsley Dr Syracuse NY 13214-2110 Office: Syracuse Univ 204 Heroy Geology Lab Syracuse NY 13244-0001

PRUDEN, WESLEY (JAMES PRUDEN), retired editor; b. Jackson, Miss., Dec. 18, 1935; s. James Wesley and Anne (Wilder) P.; m. Ann Fontaine Rice, Oct. 15, 1960 (div. 1961). Student, U. Ark., Little Rock, 1954—55. Sportswriter Ark. Gazette, Little Rock, 1953, asst. state editor, 1954-56; reporter The Comml. Appeal, Memphis, 1956-63; fgn. corr. The Nat. Observer, Washington, 1963-77; free-lance journalist, 1977-82; chief polit. corr. The Washington Times, 1982-84, dep. mng. editor, 1984-87, mng. editor, 1987-92, editor-in-chief, 1992—2008, nat. polit. columnist, 1982. Author: Vietnam: The War, 1965. Ark. del. to Dem. Nat. Conv., L.A., 1960. With USAF, 1957-58, Ark. Air Nat. Guard, 1954-63. Recipient H.L. Mencken prize Balt. Sun, 1991. Mem. Am. Soc. Newspaper Editors, Sigma Delta Chi. So. Bapt.

PRUETT, JAMES WORRELL, librarian, educator, musicologist; b. Mt. Airy, NC, Dec. 23, 1932; s. Samuel Richard and Gladys Dorne (Worrell) P.; m. Lilian Maria-Irene Pibernik, July 20, 1957; children—Mark, Ellen. BA, U. N.C., Chapel Hill, 1955, MA, 1957, PhD, 1962. Mem. faculty U. N.C., Chapel Hill., 1961-87, prof. music, 1974-87, music librarian, 1961-76, chmn. dept. music, 1976-86; chief music div. Library of Congress, Washington, 1987-95. Vis. prof. U. Toronto, 1976; cons. in music, 1995—. Editor: Studies in the History, Style and Bibliography of Music in Memory of Glen Haydon, 1969; author: Research Guide to Musicology, 1985. Contbr. profl. jours., encys. Newberry Libr. fellow, 1966. Mem. Internat. Musicol. Soc., Am. Musicol. Soc. (chpt. chmn. 1964-66, mem. coun. 1974-77), Music Libr. Assn. (pres. 1973-75, editor jour. 1974-77), Cosmos Club (Washington). Home: 343 Wesley Dr Chapel Hill NC 27516-1520 Home Phone: 919-942-4322.

PRUETZ, ADRIAN MARY, lawyer; Student, U. Wis., 1966—69; BA, Loyola U., Chgo., 1972, postgrad., 1972—73; JD magna cum laude, Marquette U., 1982. Bar: Wis. 1982, Calif. 1985. Assoc. Whyte and Hirschboeck, SC, 1982—84, Morrison and Foerster, 1984—88, ptnr., 1988—94, Quinn Emanuel Urquhart Oliver & Hedges, LLP, LA, 1994—2007, co-chair intellectual property litigation group; with Pruetz Law Group LLP, El Segundo, Calif., 2007—. Spkr., lectr. Price Waterhouse Intellectual Property Forum, Licensing Execs. Soc., Am. Soc. Indsl. Security. Named Top Patent, Corp. Counsel, 2007—08, Rank 1 in Copyright, Trademark and Trade Secret, Chambers USA, 2008; named one of Calif. Top 50 Litigators, LA Daily Jour., 2001—07, Most Influential Trial Lawyers in Calif., 2002—07, State's Top 25 Intellectual Property Lawyers, 2003—05, Calif.'s Most Successful Lawyers, Calif. Law Bus., Top 10 trademark Litigators, Chambers USA, 2008. Mem.: ABA (past chair com. U.S. lit. affecting internat. patent problems, past chair com. impact 1991 amendments), LA County Bar, State Bar Calif., Fed. Bar Assn. (spkr., lectr.). Office: Pruetz Law Group LLP 200 N Sepulveda Blvd Ste 1525 El Segundo CA 90245-4399 Office Phone: 310-765-7655. Business E-Mail: ampruetz@pruetzlaw.com.

PRUGH, WILLIAM BYRON, lawyer; b. Kansas City, Mo., Jan. 3, 1945; s. Byron E. and Helen Prugh; m. Linda Stuart, Aug. 12, 1968; 1 child, K. Niccole. BA, U. Mo., Kansas City, 1966, JD, 1969, LLM in Taxation, 1971. Bar: Mo. 1969, U.S. Tax Ct. 1975, U.S. Supreme Ct. 1975, Kans. 1982. Mem. Shughart Thomson & Kilroy, P.C., Kansas City, 1969—2009; sr. ptnr. Polsinelli Shughart PC, Kans. City, 2009—. Author, editor: Missouri Corporation Law and Practice, 1985, Missouri Taxation Law and Practice, 1987, 3d edit., 1996. Mem.: ABA, Kansas City Met. Bar Assn. (chmn. tax com. 1989—90, chmn. computer law com. 1989—91, Pres. award 1988), Mo. Bar Assn. (chmn. taxation com. 1988—90, chmn. computer tech. com. 1989—90). Republican. Methodist. Office: Polsinelli Shughart PC 700 W 47 St Kansas City MO 64112 Home Phone: 913-492-6987; Office Phone: 816-374-0570. Business E-Mail: wprugh@polsinelli.com.

PRUIS, JOHN J., manufacturing executive; b. Borculo, Mich., Dec. 13, 1923; s. Ties J. and Trientje (Koop) P.; m. Angeline Rosemary Zull, Sept. 14, 1944; children: David Lofton, Daniel J., Dirk Thomas. BS, Western Mich. U., 1947; MA, Northwestern U., 1949, PhD, 1951; Litt.D. (hon.), Yeungnam U., Taegu, Korea, Ind. State U.; LL.D. (hon.), Ball State U., U. So. Ind.; DHL (hon.), Keuka Coll. Tchr. pub. schs., Mich., 1942-43; supervising tchr. Campus Sch., Western Mich. U., 1947-48; instr. speech U. No Ia., 1951-52; from asst. prof. to assoc. prof. speech So. Ill. U., 1952-55; mem. faculty Western Mich. U., 1955-68, sec. bd. trustees, 1964-68, v.p. adminstrn., 1966-68; pres. Ball State U., 1968-78; v.p. corp. rels. Ball Corp., 1978-88. Cons., examiner North Central Assn., 1959-78; also bd. dirs. N. Central Assn. V.p. Country dr. chmn. Kalamazoo Cmty. Chest, 1964; bd. dirs. Kalamazoo chpt. Am. Cancer Soc., 1963-68, Del. County United Way, Muncie Symphony Assn., Ball Meml. Hosp., Big Bros./Big Sisters, Ind. Legal Found.; trustee U. So. Ind., 1985-90; exec. v.p. George and Frances Ball Found. With USNR, 1943-46; capt. Res., ret. Mem. Am. Assn. Higher Edn., Speech Communication Assn., Muncie C. of C., Blue Key, Rotary, Phi Delta Kappa, Omicron Delta Kappa, Beta Gamma Sigma Presbyterian. Personal E-mail: jjpruis@iquest.net.

PRUITT, BASIL ARTHUR, JR., surgeon, retired military officer; b. Nyack, NY, Aug. 21, 1930; s. Basil Arthur and Myrtle Flo (Knowles) P.; m. Mary Sessions Gibson, Sept. 4, 1954; children: Scott Knowles, Laura Sessions, Jeffrey Hamilton. AB, Harvard U., 1952, postgrad., 1952—53; MD, Tufts U., 1957. Diplomate Am. Bd. Surgery. Intern Boston City Hosp., 1957—58, resident surgery, 1958—59, 1961—62; commd. capt., M.C. U.S. Army, 1959, advanced through grades to col., 1972; resident Brooke Gen. Hosp., Ft. Sam Houston, Tex., 1962—64; chief clin. divsn. Inst. Surg. Rsch., Ft. Sam Houston, 1965—67; chief profl. svcs. 12th Evacuation Hosp., Vietnam, 1967—68; comdr., dir. U.S. Army Inst. Surg. Rsch., Brooke Army Med. Ctr., Ft. Sam Houston, 1968—95, ret., 1995; clin. prof. gen. surgery U. Tex. Health Sci. Ctr., San Antonio, 1975—, Dr. Ferdinand P. Herff chair surgery, 2009—; prof. surgery Uniformed Svcs. U. Health Scis., Bethesda, Md., 1978—. Mem. surgery, anaesthesiology and trauma study sect. NIH, 1978—82; mem. Shriners Burns Adv. Bd., 1985—92, Shriners Med. Adv. Bd., 1992—95, Shriners Rsch. Adv. Bd., 1996—2006, Shriners Clin. Outcomes Studies Adv. Bd., 1999—2007; merit rev. bd. for surgery VA, 1990—93; bd. dirs. Am. Bd. Surgery, 1982—88, sr. mem., 1989—. Author med. books; contbr. chpts. to textbooks, articles to profl. jours.; mem. editl. bd. Jour. Trauma, 1975-94, editor, 1995—; mem. edit. bd.: Archives Surgery, 1981-93, Consultations in Surgery, Correspondence Society of Surgeons, Collected Letters, 1978-2000, Circulatory Shock, 1985-93, Jour. Burn Care and Rehab., 1984-87, Jour. Investigative Surgery, 1987-97, Shock, 1993—, Current Opinion in Surg. Infections, 1993-2001, Sepsis, 1996-2002, Injury, 1998-2003, Turkish Jour. Trauma, 2002—, English edit. Chinese Jour. Traumatology, 1998—, Med. Jour. Chinese People's Liberation Army, 2005—. Decorated Bronze Star, Legion of Merit, DSM; recipient ISS/SIC Danis prize, 1995, G. Whitaker Internat. Burns prize, 2000, Tanner-Vandeput-Boswick Burn prize, 2006, Roswell Park medal, 2007, King Faisal Internat. prize, 2008. Fellow: ACS (pre and postoperative care com. 1969—79, vice chmn. 1973—75, gov. 1973—79, com. on trauma 1974—84, internat. rels. com. 1983—93, chmn. 1987—89), Am. Coll. Critical Care Medicine (Disting. Investigator award 2000); mem.: We. Trauma Assn., Ea. Assn. Surgery Trauma, N.Am. Burn Soc. (pres. 1993—94), Shock Soc. (clin. counselor 1995—98, pres. 2007—08, chmn. 2005 program com.), Internat. Surg. Group, Surg. Infection Soc. (recorder 1980—84, pres. 1985—86), Assn. Acad. Surgery, Internat. Soc. Surgery, Surg. Biol. Club III, Am. Assn. Surgery Trauma (recorder 1976—80, bd. mgr. 1976—80, pres. 1982—83, bd. mgr. 1982—86, 1995—), Halsted Soc. (pres. 1985—86), So. Surg. Assn. (pres. 2004—05), We. Surg. Assn. (dist. rep. 1984—88, pres. 1993—94), Tex. Surg. Assn., Am. Surg. Assn. (2d v.p. 1980—81, pres. 1999—2000, Medallion 1998), Soc. Univ. Surgeons (Lifetime Achievement award 2007), Am. Trauma Soc. (pres. Tex. divsn. 1974—75, dir. 1974—, sec. 1986—88, v.p. 1988—90, pres.-elect 1990—92, pres. 1992—94), Smoke Burn and Fire Assn. (adv. coun. 1976—2008), Internat. Soc. Burn Injuries (nat. rep. 1974—82, co-chmn. disaster planning com. 1982—86, pres.-elect 1990—94, pres. 1994—98), Am. Burn Assn. (program com. chmn. 1971—73, bd. trustees 1974—79, pres. 1975—76, chmn. archives com. 1991—), Mediterranean Club Burns and Fire Disasters (regional rep. Ams. 1999—), Surgeons' Travel Club (pres. 2002—03). Home: 402 Tidecrest Dr San Antonio TX 78239-2517 Office: U Tex Health Sci Ctr Dept Surgery 7703 Floyd Curl Dr San Antonio TX 78229-3900 also: Editl Office Jour Trauma 7330 San Pedro Ste 654 San Antonio TX 78216-6236 Home Phone: 210-655-4769; Office Phone: 210-342-7903. Business E-Mail: pruitt@uthscsa.edu.

PRUITT, DEAN GARNER, psychologist, educator; b. Phila., Dec. 26, 1930; s. Dudley McConnell and Grace (Garner) P.; m. France Juliard, Dec. 27, 1959; children: Andre Juliard, Paul Dudley, Charles Alexandre. AB, Oberlin Coll., 1952; MS, Yale U., 1954, PhD, 1957. Postdoctoral fellow U. Mich., 1957-59; rsch. assoc. Northwestern U., 1959-61; asst. prof., then assoc. prof. U. Del., 1961-66; assoc. prof. to prof. SUNY, Buffalo, 1966—96, disting. prof., 1996—2001, disting. prof. emeritus, 2001—, dir. grad. program in social psychology, 1969—73, 1976—77, 1985—88, 1998—2001; disting. scholar in residence George Mason U., 2001—. Author: Negotiation Behavior, 1981, (with J. Z. Rubin and S.H. Kim) Social Conflict, 1986, 94, 2004, (with P.J. Carnevale) Negotiation in Social Conflict, 1993; editor: (with R.C. Snyder) Theory and Research on the Causes of War, 1969, (with K. Kressel) Mediation Research, 1989. Grantee Office Naval Rsch., 1965, NIMH, 1969, NSF, 1969, 74, 76, 80, 83, 86, 88, 93, Guggenheim Found., 1978-79. Fellow APA, Am. Psychol. Soc., Soc. for Psychol. Study Social Issues; mem. Internat. Assn. for Conflict Mgmt. (pres. 1990-92, Lifetime Achievement award 1997), Internat. Soc. Polit. Psychology (v.p. 1984-85, Harold D. Lasswell award 1992), Phi Beta Kappa, Sigma Xi. Home: 9006 Friars Rd Bethesda MD 20817-3320 Office: George Mason U Inst Conflict Analysis and Resolution Fairfax VA 22030-4444 Business E-Mail: dean@pruittfamily.com.

PRUITT, GARY B., publishing company executive; b. 1957; m. Abby Pruitt; children: Katherine, Allison. BA summa cum laude, U. Fla., 1978; MA in Pub. Policy, U. Calif. Berkeley, 1981, JD, 1982. Counsel The McClatchy Co., 1984—87, gen. counsel, corp. sec., 1987—91, v.p. ops. & tech., 1994-95, pres., 1995—, COO, 1995—96, CEO, 1996—, chmn., 2001—; pub. The Fresno Bee, 1991-94. Bd. dirs. The McClatchy Co., 1995—. Mem. chancellors com. U. Calif., Berkeley, mem. bd. advisors Goldman Sch. Pub. Policy. Mem.: James Irvine Found. (bd. dirs. 1999—, vice chmn. 2003—05, chmn. 2006—), Newspaper Assn. Am, Phi Betta Kappa. Office: The McClatchy Co 2100 Q St Sacramento CA 95816-6816

PRUITT, GEORGE ALBERT, academic administrator; b. Canton, Miss., July 9, 1946; s. Joseph Henry and Lillie Irene (Carmichael) P.; m. Pamela Young; 1 child, Shayla Nicole. BS, Ill. State U., 1968, MS, 1970, DHL (hon.), 1994; PhD, Union Grad. Sch., Cin., 1974; D Pub. Svc. (hon.), Bridgewater State Coll., 1990, MA (hon.), 1990; LLD (hon.), Ill. State U., 1994; DHL (hon.), SUNY Empire State Coll., 1996. Asst. to v.p. for acad. affairs Ill. State U., Normal, 1968-70, dir. high potential students program, 1968-70; dean students Towson State U., 1970-72; v.p., exec. asst. to pres., assoc. prof. urban affairs Morgan State U., 1972-75; v.p., prof. Tenn. State U., 1975-81; exec. v.p. Council for Advancement Experiential Learning, Columbia, Md., 1981-82; pres. Thomas A. Edison State Coll., Trenton, 1982—. Commn. on ednl. credit and credentials, labor/higher edn. coun. Am. Coun. on Edn.; advisor group XII, Nat. Fellowship program W.K. Kellogg Found., 1990-94, advisor group XV, 1995-99; chair SEEDCO, bd. dirs. Sun Nat. Bank, Vineland, N.J., Capital City Partnership Inc., 2008-; nat. adv. com. on instnl. quality and integrity U.S. Dept. Edn., 1994-2008; mem., chmn. N.J. Pres. Coun., 2004-2006; chair N.J. Capital Region Conv. and Vis. Bur., 2004-2006, bd. dirs. Trenton Savs. Bank, bd. dirs. Structured Employment Econ. Devel. Corp., bd. dirs. Sun Bank, bd. dirs. Sun Bancorp, Inc., 2002-; mem. RWJ Found.-Nurses in Bd. Rm. Nat. Adv. Commn., 2008-. Past chair Mercer County C. of C., 1999—2001; mem. Govs. Edn. Cabinet, 2002—05, N.J. State Planning Commn., 2002—07; trustee Union Inst., Cin., 1988—, Rider U., Lawrenceville, NJ, 2001—, Econ. Devel. Corp., Trenton, 2001—07; bd. dirs. N.J. Assn. Colls. and Univs. Recipient Resolution of Commendation Bd., Trustees Morgan State U., 1975, Outstanding Svc. to Edn. award Tenn. State U., 1981, Gubernatorial citation Gov. of Tenn., 1981, Good Guy award George Washington coun. Boy Scouts Am., 1991, Humanitarian award NCCJ, 1992, Educator of Yr. award Black N.J. Mag., 1993, Disting. Alumni award Ill. State U., 1996; apptd. hon. mem. Gen. Assembly Tenn., 1981, hon. mem. U.S. Congress from 5th Tenn. dist., 1981; named ofcr. of the Most Effective Coll. Pres. in U.S., Exxon Edn. Found. Study, 1986; named to Coll. of Edn. Hall of Fame, Ill. State U., 1995; named Mercer Co. N.J. Citizen of Yr., Mercer Co. C. of C., 1997; Inducted to Hall of Fame, Ill. State U., 2005. Mem. Coun. for Advancement Exptl. Learning, Am. Assn. State Colls. and U. (bd. dirs. 2008-), Coun. for Advancement and Support of Edn., Am. Coun. Edn., Mid. States Assn. Colls. and Schs. (accreditation evaluator commn. on higher edn.). Office: Thomas Edison Coll 101 W State St Trenton NJ 08608-1176 Office Phone: 609-984-1105. Business E-Mail: gpruitt@tesc.edu.

PRUITT, JONATHAN NEAL, research scientist; b. Winterhaven, Fla., Dec. 11, 1985; BS, U. South Fla., Tampa, 2006; attending in progress, U. Tenn., Knoxville, 2009. Contbr. scientific papers. Home: 1539 Highland Ave Knoxville TN 37916 Office: Univ Tenn Knoxville 569 Dabney Hall Knoxville TN 37996-1610 Personal E-mail: jpruitt6@utk.edu.

PRUITT, NANCY LOUISE, educator; b. Phila., Feb. 24, 1953; d. Walter E. and Dorothy (Barnes) P.; m. Jonathan Jacobs, Dec. 17, 1990. BA, Gettysburg Coll., 1975; MA, Wake Forest U., 1977; PhD, Ariz. State U., 1983. Assoc. prof. biology Colgate U., Hamilton, NY, 1983—2005, prof. biology, 2000—. Program dir. divsn. undergrad. edn. NSF, 2005. Author: BioInquiry, 2000, 2003, 2005; contbr. articles to profl. jours. Grantee Rsch. Corp., Hamilton, 1986-87, NSF, Hamilton, 1987, 92, 96. Mem. Am. Physiol. Soc., AAAS, Soc. for Integrative and Comparative Biology. Avocations: running, squash. Office: Colgate Univ Dept Biology Hamilton NY 13346 Office Phone: 315-228-7398. Business E-Mail: npruitt@mail.colgate.edu.

PRUITT, ROBERT E., geneticist, educator; b. Palo Alto, Calif., Jan. 25, 1959; s. William E. and Parsla K. Pruitt; m. Madeline A. Crosby, 1983 (div. 1997); children: Laura, Liese; m. Amanda J. Deering, 2007. BS, U. Minn., St. Paul, 2008; PhD, Calif. Inst. Tech., Pasadena, 1986. Asst. prof. U. Minn., 1988—92, Harvard U., Cambridge, Mass., 1992—97, assoc. prof., 1997—2000, Purdue U., W.Lafayette, Ind., 2000—06, prof., 2006—. Grantee Predoctoral fellowship, NSF, 1980—83, fellow, Achievement Rewards Coll. Scientists, 1984—85, NSF Postdoctoral fellowship, NSF, 1986—87; Rsch. grant. in molecular genetics of pollen stigma interactions, 1988—91, Rsch. grant. in molecular genetics of fertilization in arabidopsis, 1991—94, Rsch. grant in genetic & molecular analysis of cellular interactions in arabidopsis, 1994—95, Rsch. grant in analysis of molecular mechanisms regulating epidermal cell interactions in arabidopsis fiddlehead Mutants, 1994—97, Rsch. grant in molecular genetic characterization of epidermal cell interaction mutants of arabidopsis, 1997—2000, Rsch. grant in genetic & molecular analysis of organ fusion in arabidopsis, 2000—02, Rsch. grant. in analysis of novel mechanism of genetic reversion in arabidopsis, 2003—. Achievements include research in arabidopsis molecular genetics; discovery of non-mendelian inheritance in arabidopsis. Avocations: cooking, travel, bicycling, gardening.

PRUITT, ROSALYN JOLENA, science educator; b. Denville, NJ, Sept. 7, 1977; d. John Henry Jr. and Arlena Cobb Pruitt. BS, U. Memphis, 2001. Lab. technician GTW Analytical Svcs., Memphis, 2000—03; sci. educator Memphis City Schs., 2003. Head softball coach Kirby HS, Memphis, 2005. Profl. Devel. grantee, Exxon/Mobil, 2005. Office: Kirby HS 4080 Kirby Pkwy Memphis TN 38115

PRUITT, STEPHEN WALLACE, finance educator; b. Indpls., Feb. 3, 1957; s. Harry Wallace and Dorothy (Thorp) P.; m. Mary Melinda Settle, Dec. 19, 1981; children: Rebecca Elizabeth, Victoria Barrick. BS in Mgmt., Purdue U., 1979; MBA in Fin., Ohio State U., 1980; PhD in Fin., Fla. State U., 1987. Internat. cash mgr. Marathon Oil Co., Findlay, Ohio, 1980-81; fin. analyst Nat. Svc. Industries, Crawfordsville, Ind., 1981-83; asst. prof. fin. U. Miss., Oxford, 1986-88, Ind. U., Bloomington, 1988-93; assoc. prof. fin. U. Memphis, 1993-96, prof. fin., 1996-2000; Arvin Gottlieb/Mo. chmn. in bus. econs. and fin. U. Mo., Kansas City, 2005—. Cons. in field. Contbr. articles to profl. jours. Bd. dirs. Art Mus. U. Memphis, 1995-2000; founder, pres. Memphis Print Club, 1995-2000. Mem. So. Fin. Assn., Fin. Mgmt. Assn. Avocations: collecting art and antiques, recording original music, producer/director original feature films including works in progress. Office: U Mo Henry W Bloch Sch Bus & Pub 5100 Rockhill Rd Kansas City MO 64110-2481 Home: 5316 W 140th St Overland Park KS 66224 Office Phone: 816-235-2334. E-mail: pruittst@umkc.edu.

PRUITT, VIRGINIA DIANE, literature and language professor; b. Rochester, Minn., May 8, 1943; d. Raymond Donald and Lillian Elaine Pruitt. BA, St. Olaf Coll., Minn., 1965; MA, U. NC, Chapel Hill, 1966; PhD, U. Va., Charlottville, 1974. English tchr. Hutchison Sch., Memphis, 1966—68; English instr. U. Memphis, 1968—71; asst. prof. English Washburn U., Topeka, 1974—78, assoc. prof. English, 1978—83, prof., 1983—. Co-editor: (book) Women's Voices from the Thirties, 1997; contbr. chapters to books, articles to profl. jours.; co-editor (with Karl A Arennigia): The Selected Professional Correspondance, 1965. Dean Dr. Menninger: Women's Vioce From the Thirties. Recipient Excellence Tchr. award, Washburn U., 2006. Mem.: Popular Cultural Assn. Democrat. Home: 3518 SW Skyline Pky Topeka KS 66614 Office: Washburn Univ Dept English 1700 SW College Ave Topeka KS 66621

PRUSHA, JEFFREY A., elementary school educator; b. Cleve., Apr. 4, 1955; s. Richard A. and Shirley A. Prusha; 1 child, Jennifer A. Lourenco. MLS, Ball State U., Muncie, Ind., 1978. Cert. in K-12 instrnl. media Ohio, 1978. Tchr. grade seven and eight Louisville Mid. Sch., Ohio, 1979—. Mem.: Ohio Edn. Assn. Independent. Avocations: gardening, reading. Home: 91580 Kilgore Ridge Rd Scio OH 43988

PRUSINER, STANLEY BEN, neurologist, educator, biochemist; b. Des Moines, May 28, 1942; s. Lawrence Albert and Miriam (Spigel) Prusiner; children: Helen Chloe, Leah Anne. AB cum laude, U. Pa., Phila., 1964, MD, 1968, DSc (hon.), 1998; PhD (hon.), Hebrew U., Jerusalem, 1995, René Descartes U., Paris, 1996, Claremont Grad. U., Calif., 2007; DSc (hon.), Dartmouth Coll., Hanover, NH, 1999, U. Liege, Belgium, 2000, Pa. State U., 2001; MD (hon.), U. Bologna, Italy, 2000. Diplomate Am. Bd. Neurology. Intern medicine U. Calif., San Francisco, 1968—69, resident neurology, 1972—74, asst. prof. neurology, 1974—80, assoc. prof., 1980—84, prof., 1984—, prof. biochemistry, 1988—2008, dir. Inst. Neurodegenerative Diseases, 1999—. Mem. neurology rev. com. Nat. Inst. Neurodegenerative Diseases (NIND), NIH, Bethesda, Md., 1982—86, Bethesda, 1990—92; mem. sci. adv. bd. French Found., LA, 1985—, chmn. sci. adv. bd., 1996—; mem. sci. rev. com. Alzheimer's Disease Diagnosic Ctr. & Rsch Grant Program, Calif., 1985—89; chmn. sci. adv. bd. Am. Health Assistance Found., Rockville, Md., 1986—2000, hon. mem. bd. dirs., 2001—; mem. adv. bd. Alzheimer's Disease and Related Disorders Found., San Francisco, 1985—91; mem. spongiform encephalopathy adv. com. FDA, 1997—2001; bd. govs. Found. Biomed. Rsch., Washington, 2002—; bd. dirs. Fromm Inst. Lifelong Learning, San Francisco, 2002—, Internat. Longevity Ctr., NYC, 2003—; chmn. bd. dirs. InPro Biotech. Inc., San Francisco, 2001—08; dir. Inst. Neurodegenerative Diseases, Imperial Coll., London, 2007—08. Editor: The Enzymes of Glutamine Metabolism, 1973, Slow Transmissible Diseases of the Nervous System, 2 vols., 1979, Prions--Novel Infectious Pathogens Causing Scrapie and CJD, 1987, Prion Diseases of Humans and Animals, 1992, Prions Prions Prions, 1996, Molecular and Genetic Basis of Neurologic Disease, 3d edit., 2003, Prion Biology and Diseases, 2d edit., 2004; contbr. articles to profl. jours. Trustee U. Pa., 2000—05, Congregation Sherith Israel, San Francisco, 1999—2002. Lt. comdr. USPHS, 1969—72. Recipient Potamkin prize for Alzheimer's Disease rsch., NIH, 1991, Disting. Med. Grad. award, U. Pa. Sch. Medicine, 1991, Med. Rsch. award, Met. Life Found., 1992, Christopher Columbus Discovery award, NIH/Med. Soc. Genoa, Italy, 1992, Charles A. Dana award, 1992, Dickson prize, U. Pitts., 1992, Max Planck Rsch. award, Alexander von Humboldt Found./Max Planck Soc., 1992, Gairdner Found. Internat. award, 1993, Albert Lasker award for basic med. rsch., 1994, Caledonian Rsch. Found. prize, Royal Soc. Edinburgh, 1995, Paul Ehrlich & Ludwig Darmstaedter award, Germany, 1995, Paul Hoch award, Am. Psychopath. Assn., 1995, Wolf Found. prize in medicine, Israel, 1996, ICN Virology prize, 1996, Victor & Clara Soriano award, World Fedn. Neurology, 1996, Pasarow Found. prize, 1996, Charles Leopole Mayer prize, French Acad. Scis., 1996, Keio Internat. prize, 1996, Baxter award, Am. Assn. Med. Colleges, 1996, Louisa Gross Horwitz prize, Columbia U., 1997, Nobel prize in medicine, 1997, K.J. Zulch prize, Gertrude Reemtsma Found., 1997, Benjamin Franklin medal, Franklin Inst., 1998, Jubilee medal, Swedish Med. Soc., 1998, Sir Hans Krebs medal, Fedn. European Biochem. Socs., 1999, Ellen Browning Scripps medal, 2000, Disting. Alumni award, U. Pa. Coll. Arts & Scis., 2003, Commonwealth award, 2004, William Beaumont medal, 2005; grantee, Howard Hughes Med. Inst., 1976—81; Alfred P. Sloan Rsch. fellow, U. Calif., 1976—78. Fellow: AAAS, Royal Coll. Physicians, Am. Acad. Arts & Scis., Am. Soc. Microbiology; mem.: NAS (councilor 2007—, Inst. Medicine, Richard Lounsbery award extraordinary achievements biology and medicine 1993), NRC (governing bd. mem. 2008—), World Jewish Acad. Scis., Serbian Acad. Scis., Protein Soc. (Amgen award 1997), Royal Soc. London, Am. Philos. Soc., Am. Soc. Molecular Biol. & Biochemistry, Am. Soc. Cellular Biology, Am. Soc. Cell Biology, Genetics Soc. Am., Am. Soc. Human Genetics, Soc. Neurosci., Am. Chem. Soc., Am. Soc. Biochemistry & Molecular Biology, Am. Soc. Clin. Investigation, Am. Neurol. Assn., Am. Soc. Virology, Am. Soc. Neurochemistry, Am. Assn. Physicians, Am. Acad. Neurology (George Cotzias award outstanding rsch. 1987, Presdl. award 1993, Disting. Achievement award 1998), Bohemian Club, Concordia Argonaut Club (bd. dirs. 1997—2005). Office: U Calif Inst Neurodegenerative Diseases 513 Parnassus Ave Box 0518 San Francisco CA 94143-0518 Office Phone: 415-476-4482. Business E-Mail: stanley@ind.ucsf.edu.

PRUSSING, LAUREL LUNT, mayor, economist; b. NYC, Feb. 21, 1941; d. Richard Valentine and Maria (Rinaldi) Lunt; m. John Edward Prussing, May 29, 1965; children: Heidi Elizabeth, Erica Stephanie, Victoria Nicole Johanna. AB, Wellesley Coll., 1962; MA, Boston U., 1964; postgrad., U. Calif., San Diego, 1968-69, U. Ill., 1970-76. Economist Arthur D. Little, Cambridge, Mass., 1963-67, U. Ill., Urbana, 1971-72; mem. county bd. Champaign County, Urbana, 1972-76, county auditor, 1976-92; legis. dir. ERA Ill., 2002—03; founder ERA Yes!, 2003. Mem. local audit adv. bd. Office Ill. Compt., Chgo., 1984-92. Contbr. to Illinois Local Government: A Handbook, 1990. Founding mem. Citizens Forum on Gambling and Campaign Fin. Reform, 1999; downstate program dir. Citizen Action/Ill., 1999; legis. dir. AAUW, Ill., Inc., 2001; with Champaign-Urbana Mass Transit Dist. Bd., 2004—05; state rep. 103d dist. Ill. Gen. Assembly, 1993—95; Dem. nominee Ill. 15th dist. U.S. Congress, 1996—98; mayor Urbana, 2005—. Named Best Freshman Legislator Ind. Voters Ill., 1994; recipient Friend of Agriculture award Ill. Farm Bur., 1994; named to Legis. Honor Roll Ill. Environ. Coun., 1994. Mem. AAUW, NAACP, LWV, Govt. Fin. Officers Assn., U.S. and Can. (com. on acctg., auditing and fin. reporting 1980-88, Fin. Reporting award 1981-91, Disting. Budget award 1986), Nat. Assn. Local Govt. Auditors (charter), Ill. Assn. County Auditors (pres. 1984-85), US Conf. Mayors, Mayors Water Council. Democrat. Home: 2106 Grange Dr Urbana IL 61801-6609 Office Phone: 217-328-2071.

PRUTEANU-MALINICI, IULIAN, research scientist; b. Galati, Romania, Mar. 20, 1979; s. Corneliu and Silvia Pruteanu-Malinici. PhD, Duke U., Durham, NC, 2008. Tchg. asst. Duke U., 2002—03, rsch. asst., 2003—. Rsch. fellowship, Duke U., 2002—03. Achievements include research in topic modeling of the State of the Union Addresses from 1780. Home: 135 Erlwood Way Apt 201 Durham NC 27704 Office: Duke Univ Research Dr Durham NC 27708 Personal E-mail: ip6@ee.duke.edu.

PRUTER, MARGARET FRANSON, editor; b. Oak Park, Ill., Jan. 16; d. Frederick G. and Margaret K. (Svoboda) Franson; m. Robert D. Pruter, July 22, 1972; 1 child, Robin. AB, Dominican U., River Forest, Ill., 1961; MA, Northwestern U., Evanston, Ill., 1965. Asst. editor Am. People's Ency., Chgo., 1961-62; rsch. assoc. AMA, Chgo., 1962-63; asst. editor New Standard Ency., Chgo., 1964-66, assoc. editor, 1966-75, sr. editor, 1975-96; editl. dir. Elmhurst Editl. Svcs., Ill., 1996—2005; editor McDougal Littell, Evanston, Ill., 1997—2004; sr. editor The Book Edit Group, 2005—. Exec. dir. Militaria Archives, Elmhurst, Ill., 1972—. Co-author: DuPage Roots, 1985 (Ill. State Hist. Publ. award 1986); contbr. Encyclopedia of Chgo., 2004. Mem. Elmhurst Hist. Commn., 1981—2007, v.p., 1995—2000, pres., 2000—01; mem. Friends of Elmhurst Pub. Libr., Elmhurst Art Mus. Found.; exec. bd. North Ctrl. Coll. Parents Assn., 1995—98; mem. Elmhurst Heritage Found., 2007—; bd. dirs. DuPage County Hist. Soc., Wheaton, Ill., 1982—, 1st v.p., 2004—; bd. dirs. DuPage County Sesquicentennial Com., Wheaton, Ill., 1988—89. Mem.: AAUW (bd. dirs. Elmhurst br. 1995—99), Ocean Conservancy, Nature Conservancy, Arch. Conservancy, Am. Studies Assn., Nat. Women's History Mus., Nat. Trust Historic Preservation, Orgn. Am. Historians, Am. Philat. Soc., Ill. Hist. Soc., Elmhurst Hist. Soc., Chgo. Hist. Soc., Chgo. Architecture Found., Nat. Parks and Conservation Assn., World Wildlife Fedn., Chgo. Women in Pub., Byrd's Nest Chapel Questers (pres. 1992—94, 2003—07), Sisters in Crime, Nat. Wildlife Fedn., Sierra Club. Office: The Book Edit Group PO Box 245 Elmhurst IL 60126-0768 Business E-Mail: bookedit1@yahoo.com.

PRUTHI, TARUN, research scientist; married. BTech, Indian Inst. Tech., Guwahati, India, 1999; MS, U. Md., College Park, 2003, PhD, 2007. Software engr. Hughes Software Systems, Delhi, 1999—2001; r&d engr. Cybernetics Infotech Inc., Rockville, Md., 2001; rsch. asst. Speech Comm. Lab, U. Md., 2001—07; sr. rsch. engr. Think A Move, Ltd, Beachwood, Ohio, 2007—. Recipient Inst. Silver Medal at IIT Guwahati, IIT Guwahati, 1999, Best student Paper, Acoustical Soc. of Am., 2005; co-recipient Team award, Hughes Software Systems, 2000. Mem.: Internat. Speech Comm.Assn., Acoustical Soc. Am., IEEE. Office: Think A Move Ltd 23715 Mercantile Rd Ste 100 Beachwood OH 44122 Personal E-mail: t.pruthi@ieee.org.

PRUZAN, ROBERT ALAN, diversified financial services company executive; b. 1963; s. Joseph and Linda Pruzan; m. Tracey Sheryl Winn, Aug. 17, 1989. BA in Mathematical-Economics, Wesleyan U., 1985; MBA, Harvard U. Head investment banking, CEO DrKW N.Am.; assoc. to pres. Wasserstein Perella & Co., NYC; CEO N.Am. Dresdner Kleinwort Wasserstein; co-founder, prin. Centerview Ptnrs. LLC, NYC, 2006—. Exec. com. bd. trustees Ethical Culture Fieldston Sch., The Jewish Mus., ArtsConnection. Office: Centerview Ptnrs LLC 640 Fifth Ave, 19th Fl New York NY 10019 Office Phone: 212-380-2660. Office Fax: 212-380-2651.

PRUZANSKY, JOSHUA MURDOCK, lawyer; b. NYC, Mar. 16, 1940; s. Louis and Rose (Murdock) P.; m. Susan R. Bernstein, Aug. 31, 1980; 1 child, Dina Gabrielle. BA, Columbia Coll., 1960, JD, 1965. Bar: NY, 1965, US Dist. Ct. (ea. and so. dists.) NY, 1968, US Supreme Ct., 1980. Ptnr. Scheinberg, DePetris & Pruzansky, Riverhead, NY, 1965-85, Greshin, Ziegler & Pruzansky, Smithtown, NY, 1985-2000, Pruzansky & Besunder, LLP, Islandia, NY, 2001—06; spl. counsel Bracken & Margolin, LLP, 2006—. Pres. NY State Bar Assn., house of dels. 1982-, exec. com. 1992-99, spl. com. women and law 1986-91, chmn. spl. com., fiduciary appts., 2003—, trusts and estates sect., gen. practice, elder law sects., 1997-98, chmn. spl. com. solo and small firm practices, 2006-; exec. coun. NY State Conf. Bar Leaders, 1984—, chmn., 1988-89; grievance com. Appellate Divsn. 10th Judicial Dist., 1992-96; LI adv. bd. HSBC Bank, 1995-2007. Mem. bd. visitors Columbia Law Sch., 1998—; chair bd. visitors Touro Law Sch., 1998-2004; dir., sec. L.I. Mus., 1998-2004. Fellow ABA Found., NY State Bar Found. (bd. dir. 1994-03); mem. ABA (house of dels. 1997-03, standing com. on solo and small firm practitioners 1998-00, NY state del. Caucus State Bar Assns.), Suffolk County Bar Assn. (bd. dir. 1979-89, pres. 1985-86), Nassau County Bar Assn. Office: Bracken & Margolin LLP Ste 300 One Suffolk Sq Islandia NY 11749 Office Phone: 631-234-8585. Business E-Mail: jmp@pruzlaw.com.

PRY, CARL G., bank executive; b. Tiffin, Ohio, Jan. 14, 1967; m. Angel M. Jones, Sept. 28, 2002; children: Ryan J., Jason R. JD, U. Toledo Coll. Law, Ohio, 1993; MBA, U. Toledo Coll., Ohio, 1993; BSBA, Bowling Green State U., Ohio, 1989. Cert. CRCM ABA, Wash., 2006, CRP BAI, Mo., 2006. Mgr. Accenture, Chgo., 2001—03; v.p., compliance mgr. KeyBank, N.A., Cleve., 2003—. Home: 5061 Terrell Ln Sheffield Village OH 44054 Office: KeyBank NA 2025 Ontario St Cleveland OH 44115 Office Fax: 216-689-8673. Personal E-mail: carl_pry@hotmail.com. Business E-Mail: carl_g_pry@keybank.com.

PRY, GEORGE LAWRENCE, art institute administrator; b. Denver, Mar. 23, 1952; s. James Russell and Flavia Elizabeth (Bridge) P.; m. Barbara Irene Bodnar, Oct. 20, 1979; children: Jessica Lee, Gregory Richard. BA with honors, St. Fidelis Coll., Herman, Pa., 1975; MA in Clin./Cmty. Psychology, Indiana U. Pa., 1977. Assoc. prof. psychology St. Fidelis Coll., 1977-80; dir. counselling svcs. Art Inst. Pitts., 1977-80, dir. student svcs., 1980-81; pres. Art Inst. Houston, 1981-84, Art Inst. Seattle, 1984-89, Art Inst. Pitts., 1999—; sr. v.p. Edn. Mgmt. Corp., Pitts., 1989—99; exec. dir. Art Inst. and Internat. Coord. Bd., 1990-94. Appointed Pa. State Bd. Private Lic. Schs., Harrisburg, 2000-05, elect chmn., 2002-05; commr. Accrediting Coun. Ind. Colls. and Schs., Washington, 2002-08, bd. dirs., 2005-, chair elect, 2006, chmn., 2007; mem. exec. com. Nat. Postsecondary Edn. Cooperative, Washington, 2004-06; bd. trustees Carlow U., Pitts., 2006-; elected to Sch. Bd. for Baldwin-Whitehall Sch. Dist., 2005-. Trustee Art Inst. Seattle, 1991-99, Art Inst. Phila., 1991-99. Mem. Accreditation Commn. Career Schs. and Colls. Tech., Wash. Fedn. Pvt. Vocat. Schs. (bd. dirs.-at-large 1984-88, pres. 1987-88). Roman Catholic. Avocations: skiing, reading, hunting. Personal E-mail: pryg@earthlink.net. Business E-Mail: gpry@aii.edu.

PRYCE, DEBORAH DENINE, former United States Representative from Ohio; b. Warren, Ohio, July 29, 1951; m. Randy Walker (div.); 1 child. BA cum laude, Ohio State U., 1973; JD with honors, Capital U. Law Sch., 1976. Bar: Ohio 1976. Adminstrv. law judge Ohio State Dept. Ins., 1976—78; first asst. city prosecutor, sr. asst. city atty., asst. city mgr. Columbus City Atty.'s Office, Ohio, 1978—85; judge Franklin County Mcpl. Ct., Columbus, 1989, 1990, 1992; mem. US Congress from 15th Ohio dist., 1993—2009, chair Ho. Rep. Conf., 2003—09, mem. fin. svcs. com., ranking mem. subcommittee on capital markets, ins. and govt. sponsored enterprises, 2007—09, dep. whip, co-chair cancer caucus. Republican. Presbyterian. Avocation: skiing.*

PRYCE, JONATHAN, actor; b. Flintshire, North Wales, June 1, 1947; Appearences include (stage) Liverpool Everyman, 1972, Nottingham Playhouse, Comedians, 1977 (Tony award, Theatre World award), 1980, Hamlet (Olivier award), 1986, Macbeth, The Caretaker, 1981, Accidental Death of an Anarchist, 1984, The Seagull, 1986, Uncle Vanya, 1989, Miss Saigon, 1991 (Tony award, Olivier award), Oliver, 1995, My Fair Lady, 2001-02, A Reckoning, 2003, The Goat or Who Is Sylvia, 2004, Dirty Rotten Scoundrels, N.Y.C., 2006, Glengarry Glen Ross, 2007; (films) Voyage of the Damned, 1976, Breaking Glass, 1980, Loophole, 1981, Praying Mantis, 1982, The Plowman's Lunch, 1983, Something Wicked This Way Comes, 1983, Brazil, 1985, The Doctor and the Devils, 1985, Haunted Honeymoon, 1986, Jumpin Jack Flash, 1986, Hotel London, 1987, Man On Fire, 1987, The Adventures of Baron Munchausen, 1988, Consuming Passions, 1988, The Rachel Papers, 1989, Glengarry Glen Ross, 1992, The Age of Innocence, 1993, Shopping, 1994, A Business Affair, 1994, Carrington, 1996 (Best Actor award Cannes Film Festival 1995), Evita, 1996, Tomorrow Never Dies, 1997, Regeneration, 1997, Ronin, 1998, Stigmata, 1999, Very Annie Mary, 2001, Unconditional Love, 2001, Bride of the Wind, 2002, The Affair of the Necklace, 2002, What a Girl Wants, 2003, Pirates of the Caribbean, 2003, De Lovely, 2004, The Brothers Grimm, 2004, The New World, 2005, Pirates of the Caribbean 2: Dead Man's Chest, 2006, The Moon and The Stars, 2007, Pirates of the Carribean 3: At World's End, 2007, Leatherheads, 2007, Bedtime Stories, 2008; (TV movie) Barbarians at the Gate, HBO, 1993 (Emmy nomination, Supporting Actor - Miniseries or Special, 1993), David, 1997, Confessions of an Ugly Stepsister, 2002, The Baker Street Irregulars, 2007, HR, 2007, Clone, 2008. Recipient BAFTA Cymru spl. award, 2002. Address: UTA 9560 Wilshire Blvd Beverly Hills CA 90212 Mailing: Julian Belfrage Assocs ADAM House 16 New Burlington St London W1S 3BQ England*

PRYER, MARY JANE, retired lawyer; b. Dayton, Ohio, Dec. 20, 1920; d. Warren A. Plumer and Agnes L. Mott; m. Vernon Pryer, June 27, 1953; children: Patricia, Thomas, Ronald, Terry. BA, U. Mich., Ann Arbor, 1943, JD, 1945. Mng. editor Mich. Law Review, Ann Arbor, 1945—49; atty. Thrun & Sidwell, Lansing, Mich., 1949—54; ret., 1954. Trustee Santa Ana Unified Sch. Dist., Calif., 1973—89. Avocation: genealogy. Personal E-mail: mamep@roadrunner.com.

PRYHUBER, GLORIA SALVINI, pediatrician, educator; b. Stamford, NY, Aug. 10, 1959; m. Keith Pryhuber, July 2, 1986. MD, SUNY, Syracuse, 1985. Cert. in neonatal perinatal medicine Am. Bd. Pediat., 1991. Assoc. prof., dept. pediat. and environ. medicine, strong children's rsch. ctr. U. Rochester, NY, 2000—, assoc. dir. neonatal perinatal medicine fellowship program, 2000—. Contbr. articles to profl. jour. Chair Boy Scouts Am., Local Troop, Rochester, 2005—08; bd. mem. Rochester Area Performing Arts, 2008. Rsch. grant, Nat. Inst. Health, 1994—. Mem.: Am. Acad. Pediat., Am. Thoracic Soc. Office: Univ Rochester 601 Elmwood Ave Rochester NY 14618 Business E-Mail: gloria_pryhuber@urmc.rochester.edu.

PRYOR, BETTY JO, biology professor; b. Carlton, Ga., Nov. 30, 1940; d. Wilson Gilbert Veal and Flora Pass; m. Kenneth Rodney Veal, Aug. 7, 1967; 1 child, Dawn Elizabeth. MS, U. Ga., Athens, 1966. Biology tchr. Oglethorpe County HS, Lexington, Ga., 1962—67; assoc.

prof. biology Anderson U., SC, 1967—. Home: 109 Partridge Ln Anderson SC 29621 Office: Anderson Univ 316 Blvd Anderson SC 29621 Business E-Mail: bpryor@ac.edu.

PRYOR, CAROL GRAHAM, retired obstetrician, gynecologist; b. Savannah, Ga. m. Louis O.J. Manganiello, June 11, 1950; children: Carol Helen, Victoria Manganiello Mudano. AB, Ga. Coll., 1943; MD, Med. Coll. Ga., 1947. Rotating intern City Hosps., Balt., 1947-48; asst. resident pathology Baroness Erlanger Hosp., Chattanooga, 1948; intern. obstetrics City Colls., Balt., 1949; coll. physician Ga. State Coll. for Women, Milledgeville, Ga., 1949-50; resident obstetrics City Hosps., Balt., 1950-51; asst. resident gynecology Univ. Hosp., Balt., 1951-52, sr. resident ob-gyn. Augusta, Ga., 1952; pvt. practice ob-gyn. Augusta, 1952—; chmn. ob-gyn. St. Joseph Hosp., Augusta, 1998—2008. Chair ob-gyn. dept. St. Joseph Hosp., Augusta. Mem., former pres. Iris Garden Club, Augusta; mem. coun. on maternal and infant health State of Ga., Atlanta, 1981-90; mem. edn. found. AAUW, 1961-63, state v.p., state pres., 1963-65. Recipient Cert. of Achievement-Community Leadersip, Ga. div. AAUW, 1982; named Med. Woman of Yr., Ga. br. 51 Am. Med. Women's Assn., 1961; Heritage award Ga. Coll. and State U., 2001, Achievement award, Ga. Coll. U., 1982. Fellow ACS (1st woman mem. Ga. chpt.); mem. ACOG, AMA, Richmond County Med. Soc., So. Med. Assn., So. Surg. Congress, Delta Kappa Gamma. Democrat. Methodist. Office Phone: 766-733-8140. Personal E-mail: cpryor@bellsouth.net.

PRYOR, DAVID BRAM, health science association administrator; b. Charleston, SC, Oct. 18, 1951; s. Sydney and Grace Prystowsky; m. Christin Marie Kennedy; children: Rebecca Whitaker, Rachel Celia, Grace Eileen. Attended, U. Mich., Ann Arbor, 1969—72; MD, U. Mich. Med. Sch., 1972—76. Cert. Am. Bd. Internal Medicine, 1979, bd. cert. cardiovascular diseases 1983, lic. Pa., 1976, NC, 1979, Mass., 1994, Minn., 1996, Mo., 2004. Intern in medicine Pa. Hosp., Phila., 1976—77, resident in medicine, 1977—79; fellow in cardiology Duke U. Med. Ctr., Durham, NC, 1979—81, asst. prof. medicine, 1983—89, assoc. prof. medicine, 1989—94; sr. staff mem. cardiovascular divsn. Duke U., Durham, NC, 1981—94, dir. section clinical epidemiology and biostatistics, 1984—89, dir. clinical program devel., 1993—94; pres. New England Med. Ctr. Hosp., Boston, 1994—95; prof. medicine Tufts U. Sch. Medicine, 1994—97; sr. v.p./chief info. officer Allina Health Sys., Mpls., 1995—2001; chief med. officer Ascension Health, St. Louis, 2001—. Program com. and biometry track chair 11th Symposium on Computer Applications in Med. Care, 1987; bd. dir. Clinical Rsch. Internat., Inc., 1989—90, PatientKeeper (Virtmed) Inc., 2001—06; chmn. task force reducing med. uncertainty Joint Commn. Accreditation Healthcare Orgn., 1989—91, adv. coun. performance measurement, 1995—, chmn. adv. coun. performance measurement, 1998—2003, mem. performance measurement coord. com., 1998—2000; chmn. epidemiology and prevention track Am. Coll. Cardiology Sci. Session Com., 1991—92, chmn. health svc. delivery track, 1991—92; mem. exec. com. and steering com. Health Care Financing Adminstrn., Coop. Cardiovascular Project, 1992—94; chmn. ops. com. Acad. Med. Ctr. Consortium, 1992—94; mem. sci. session program com. Am. Heart Assn., 1994—96; chmn. bd. dir. Strategicare, Inc., 1996—99; bd. gov. Bioengineering Inst., U. Minn., Mpls., 1996—2002; mem. 2000 Spring Congress Sci. Program com. Am. Med. Informatics Assn. (AMIA), 1999—2000; mem. IT expert adv. panel Nat. Quality Forum (NQF) Nat. Forum for Health Care Quality Measurement and Reporting, 2001—02; mem. adv. bd. Ctr. Info. Tech. Leadership (CITL), 2001—; cons. prof. Cardiovascular Inst., Favaloro Found., Buenos Aires, 1994—97; cons. assoc. prof. medicine Duke U. Med. Ctr., 1994—; adj. prof. epidemiology U. Minn. Sch. Pub. Health, Mpls., 1996—2002; pres. New England Med. Ctr., Boston, 1994—95; adj. prof. St. Louis U. Sch. Pub. Health; numerous positions with Allina Health Sys., Mpls., 1995—2001; reviewer numerous jour. and rsch. grants; presenter in field; mem. numerous nat. and internat. com.; cons. in field. Contbr. articles to jour., chapters to books. Recipient Innovations in IT awards, 2nd place, HIMMS and Deloitte and Touche (Allina Health Sys.), 1998, Tng. for Future, 3rd place, Allina Health Sys., 1998, Quest for Best award, 2000, Silver award, 2001, CareScience Exec. Leadership award, 2006; named Laureate, Computerworld Smithsonian award, Allina Health Sys., 1999, Lifetime Scholar, Barton Haynes Soc., Duke U., 2005; named one of 100 Most Powerful People in Healthcare, Modern Healthcare, 2002, 2005, 50 Most Powerful Physician Execs., Modern Physician, 2005, Modern Healthcare, 2006; fellow, Am. Coll. Med. Informatics, 1986, Am. Soc. Clinical Investigation, 1992. Fellow: Am. Coll. Med. Informatics, Am. Coll. Physicians, Am. Coll. Cardiology; mem.: Am. Med. Informatics Assn., Am. Heart Assn. (fellow coun. on clinical cardiology), Am. Soc. Clinical Investigation, Am. Fedn. Clinical Rsch. Office: Ascension Health 4600 Edmundson Rd Saint Louis MO 63134 Office Phone: 314-733-8192, 314-733-8196. Business E-Mail: dpryor@ascensionhealth.org.

PRYOR, FREDERIC L., economist, educator; b. Apr. 23, 1933; s. Millard H. and Mary S. Pryor; m. Zora Prochazka, Mar. 26, 1964; 1 child, Daniel. BA, Oberlin Coll., Ohio, 1955; PhD, Yale U., 1962. Prof. econs. Swarthmore (Pa.) Coll., 1967—2002, sr. rsch. scholar, 2003—. Author: The Political Economy of Poverty, Equity and Growth: Malawi and Madagascar, 1990, The Red and the Green: The Rise and Fall of Collective Agriculture, 1992, Economic Evolution and Structure, 1995, The Future of U.S. Capitalism, 2002, Economic Systems of Foraging, Agricultural and Industrial Societies, 2005; co-author: Who's Not Working and Why, 1999. Trustee Tougoloo Coll., 1981-2008. Office: Swarthmore College Ave Swarthmore PA 19081-1390 Business E-Mail: fpryor1@swarthmore.edu.

PRYOR, HAROLD S., retired college president; b. Overton County, Tenn., Oct. 3, 1920; s. Hubert S. and Ethel (Stockton) P.; m. LaRue Vaughn, June 26, 1946. BS, Austin Peay State U., 1946; MA, George Peabody Coll., 1947; Ed.D., U. Tenn., 1951. Instr. George Peabody Coll., Vanderbilt U., 1946-47, E. Tenn. State U., 1947-49, U. Tenn., Knoxville, 1949-51; head dept. edn. Austin Peay State U., 1952, dir. tchr. edn., 1954-68; pres. Columbia (Tenn.) State Community Coll., 1968-84, now pres. emeritus, 1984—. Dir. First Farmers and Merchants Nat. Bank, Columbia, 1970—, First Farmers and Mchts. Corp., 1982—; Columbia State Found., 1971—. Contbr. articles to profl. jours. With U.S. Army, 1943-46. Grantee Dept. Labor; Grantee HEW. Mem. NEA, Tenn. Coll. Assn. (past pres.), Tenn. Edn. Assn., Am. Assn. Higher Edn., Comparative Edn. Soc., Graymere Country Club, Kiwanis, Kappa Delta Pi, Phi Delta Kappa. Democrat. Presbyterian.

PRYOR, JAY R., oil industry executive; b. Miss. BSc in Petroleum Engring., Miss. State U., 1979. Petroleum engr. to mgmt. positions with increasing responsibilities in Asia, US, Europe and the former Soviet Union Chevron USA Prodn. Co., 1979—92; mgr. petroleum engring. Chevron Overseas Petroleum Inc., Kazakhstan, 1992—96; sponsor career devel. for ops. pers., gen. mgr. human resources, worldwide ops. Chevron Corp., San Ramon, Calif., 1996—99; mng. dir. Chevron Offshore Ltd., Thailand, 1999—2002, Chevron Nigeria Ltd., 2002—06; v.p. corp. bus. devel. Chevron Corp., 2006—. Co-chair Nigerian Bus. Coalition Against HIV/AIDS. Mem.: Soc. Petroleum Engrs., Kazakhstan Br. Office: Chevron Corp Hdqs 6001 Bollinger Canyon Rd San Ramon CA 94583*

PRYOR, LANDON SCOTT, plastic surgeon; b. Chgo., Mar. 31, 1976; s. Robert Morrow and April Lynn Pryor. MD, Loyola U. Chgo. Stritch Sch. Medicine, Maywood, Ill., 2002. Gen. surgery resident Akron Gen. Med. Ctr., Ohio, 2002—05; plastic surgery resident Summa Health Sys., Akron, 2005—07; pediat. craniofacial fellow UCSD Med. Ctr., 2007—08; aesthetic surgery fellow Cleve. Clinic, 2008—. Vol. surgeon Fresh Start Surg. Gifts, San Diego, 2008—. Contbr. articles to profl. jours. Interface vol. surgeon Interface, San Diego, 2007—08. Home: 3736 Fairway Pk Dr Apt 213 Copley OH 44321 Office: 1451 Stony Creek Way Apt 3 Rockford IL 61108 Home Phone: 330-284-9633; Office Phone: 815-964-3333. Office Fax: 216-444-9419, 815-964-3333. Personal E-mail: landonpryor98@hotmail.com.

PRYOR, MARK LUNSFORD, United States Senator from Arkansas; b. Fayetteville, Ark., Jan. 10, 1963; s. David H. Pryor; m. Jill Pryor; children: Adams, Porter. BA in History, U. Ark., 1985, JD, 1988. Pvt. practice Wright, Lindsey & Jennings, Little Rock, 1988—97; mem. Ark. Ho. of Reps., 1990—98, chmn. Freshman Caucus, mem. judiciary com., com. on aging and legis. affairs; atty. gen. State of Ark., 1999—2002; US Senator from Ark., 2003—. Mem. com. commerce, sci. and transp. US Senate, com. homeland security and govt. affairs, com. small bus. and entrepreneurship, spl. com. ethics, armed svcs. com., com. rules and adminstrn. Contbr. articles to profl. jours. Chmn. Alliance to Save Energy; mem. cardiovascular cabinet Ark. Heart Assn.; mem. Friends of Carousel. Recipient Spirit of Enterprise award, US C. of C., 2005; named Big Brother of Yr., 1992. Democrat. Presbyterian. Office: US Senate 257 Dirksen Senate Office Bldg Washington DC 20510 also: The River Market Ste 401 500 President Clinton Ave Little Rock AR 72201-1745 Office Phone: 202-224-2353, 501-324-6336. Office Fax: 202-228-0908, 501-324-5320.

PRYOR, RICHARD WALTER, telecommunications executive, retired air force officer; b. Poplar Bluff, Mo., Nov. 6, 1932; s. Walter V. and Mary (Clifford) P.; m. Barbara LeCompte, Feb. 19, 1955; children: Richard, Susan Davis, Robert, William. B in Gen. Studies, U. Nebr., Omaha, 1972; MA, Webster Coll., St. Louis, 1975. Commd. 2d lt. USAF, 1953, advanced through grades to maj. gen., 1982, ret., 1982; instr. U.S. Air Force Acad.; DVMT engr. space and missile systems USAF, chief of staff Comm. Svcs.; dir. worldwide def. comm. sys. Def. Comm. Agy., 1980-81; pres. ITT World Comm., NYC, 1982-84, ITT Indsl. Transmission Co., NYC; sr. v.p. engring. ops. ITT Comm. Svcs. GP; pres., gen. mgr. ITT Christian Rovsing-Copenhagen DK, 1984-86; chmn. Christian-Rovsing Inc., Tulsa; exec. v.p. Electronic Data Sys. (EDS) Comm. Corp., Dallas, 1986-89; pres., COO IMM Corp.-Interdigital AMEX, Phila., 1989-92; chmn., CEO. officer Ultranav Corp, Dallas, 1992—; chmn. Prism Video, Dallas, 1994—; pres. Trans-Tech Holdings Corp., Dallas, 1996—; pres., CEO Unison Corp., Dallas, 1998—, Video Net, Addison, Tex.; chmn., CEO Mega Link Tech., LA, 2003—, MIUSA, LA, 2003—; ptnr. BOR Assoc., 2005—. Dir. RPost, LA, 2000—. Contbr. articles to tech. publs. Assoc. dir. Boy Soucts Am., N.Y.C., 1983. Recipient Cert. of Appreciation Okla. Mental Health Assn., 1979, Kansas City Lions Club, 1974. Mem. Armed Forces Communications and Electronics Assn. (pres. N.Y.C. 1983, nat. dir.), Air Force Assn., Oklahoma City Soc. Profl. Engrs., Canoe Brook Country Club, Army-Navy Club, Phi Alpha Theta. Republican. Roman Catholic. E-mail: dick1955@tx.rr.com.

PRYOR, STEFAN I., city manager, real estate developer; b. NYC, Jan. 14, 1972; JD, Yale U., 1998. Policy adv. to mayor City of New Haven; v.p. Partnership for NYC, exec. dir. sch. reform program; sr. v.p. policy and programs Lower Manhattan Devel. Corp., NYC, 2001—05, pres., 2005—06; dep. mayor for econ. devel. City of Newark, NJ, 2006—. Founder ReStart Ctrl., NYC, Achievement First; co-founder Amistad Acad., New Haven. Grantee John V. Lindsay Pub. Svc. Fellowship, Yale U., 2000. Office: City Hall 920 Broad St Ste 200 Newark NJ 07102

PRYOR, STEPHEN D., oil industry executive; b. NYC; B in Biology, Lafayette Coll., Easton, Pa., 1971; MBA, Harvard U. Mktg. rep. Mobil Oil Corp., NYC, 1971, gen. mgr. Cyprus, New Zealand, v.p. Mobil Chem. Co., gen. mgr. plastics divsn., 1993, pres. Mobil Asia Pacific, 1996—98, exec. v.p. internat. downstream bus., 1998; pres. Lubricants & Specialties Co. Exxon Mobil Corp., 1999—2002, exec. v.p. Exxon-Mobil Chem. Co., 2002—04, pres., 2004—, pres. ExxonMobil Refining & Supply Co., 2004—. Chmn. downstream com. Am. Petroleum Inst. Trustee Lafayette Coll. Mem.: NAM (mem. bd. dirs., chmn. energy/environ. policy group). Office: Exxon Mobil Corp Hdqs 5959 Las Colinas Blvd Irving TX 75039-2298*

PRYOR, VIKKI LYNN, insurance company executive; b. Great Lakes, Ill., Aug. 22, 1953; d. Karl Eugene and Mary Dorothy (Nesbitt) Pryor. BA magna cum laude, SUNY-Buffalo, 1975, JD, 1978, MBA, U. Ill., Chgo. C.P.A. Sec. Bonwit Teller, NYC, 1972-73; office mgr. Ops. Mgmt., Buffalo, 1973-75; law clk. Corp. Counsel, Buffalo, 1976-78; sr. trial atty. Office of Chief Counsel, IRS, Chgo., 1978-86; product devel. mgr., All State Ins. Co., 1986-87, cons. services mgr., 1987; sr. v.p. Oxford Health Plans; Blue Cross Blue Shield, Mass.; bd. dirs., pres., CEO SBLI USA Mutual Life Ins. Co., Inc., 1999-. Named one of The 100 Most Influential Women in NYC Bus., Crain's NY Bus., 2007. Mem. ABA, Cook County Bar Assn., Erie County Bar Assn., Chgo. Bar Assn., Federally Employed Women (sec. 1980—), Minn. Legal Edn. Resources (dir. 1980-82), Women's Bar Assn. Ill., Women in Mgmt., League Black Women. Home: 180 Park Rd Park Forest IL 60466-1737

PRYOR, WAYNE DAVID, social sciences educator; b. Washington, Nov. 23, 1945; s. Arthur and Leona M. Pryor; m. Beverly J. Shefts, Dec. 18, 1976; 1 child, Wayne David Jr. BS, Tex. A&M U. Commerce, MS, 1973. Prof. Brazosport Coll., Lake Jackson, Tex., 1975—, chair, divsn. social scis., 1996—. Elder Bethel Presbyn. Ch., West Columbia, Tex., 1997—2001. Mem.: Tex. CC Tchrs. Assn. Independent. Presbyterian. Avocations: travel, fantasy football, photography. Home: 425 N Amherst Dr West Columbia TX 77486 Office: Brazosport Coll 500 Coll Dr Lake Jackson TX 77566 Business E-Mail: wayne.pryor@brazosport.edu.

PRYOR, WILLIAM C., Senior Judge, DC Court of Appeals; b. Washington, May 29, 1932; BA, Dartmouth Coll., 1954; LLB with honors, Georgetown U., 1959. Bar: D.C. 1959, Ohio 1964, U.S. Supreme Ct. 1965. With U.S. Dept. Justice, Washington, 1959-68; judge D.C. Dist. Ct., Washington, 1968—; former chief judge; now sr. judge DC Ct. of Appeals, Washington, 1993—. Instr. Georgetown U., Washington, 1969, 71, Potomac Law Sch., 1976—; now disting. prof. of law, resident scholar, D.C. U. David A. Clarke Sch. of Law. Bd. dirs. YMCA, St. Albans Sch., Opportunities Industrialization Ctr., Am. Cancer Soc. Lt. USAS, 1955-56. Mem. ABA, Washington Bar Assn., D.C. Bar, Washington Athletic Club. Office: Dist of Columbia Ct of Appeals 500 Indiana Ave NW Washington DC 20001-2131 also: David Clarke Sch of Law DC U 4200 Conn Ave NW Washington DC 20008*

PRYOR, WILLIAM DANIEL LEE, humanities educator; b. Lakeland, Fla., Oct. 29, 1926; s. Dahl and Lottie Mae (Merchant) P. AB, Fla. So. Coll., 1949; MA, Fla. State U., Tallahassee, 1950, PhD, 1959; postgrad., U. NC, Chapel Hill, 1952—53; pvt. art studies with Florence Wilde; pvt. voice studies with Colin O'More, Anna Kaskas; pvt. piano studies with Waldemar Hille and audited piano master classes of Ernst von Dohnányi. Asst. prof. English, dir. drama Bridgewater Coll., Va., 1950-52; grad. tchg. fellow humanities Fla. State U., Tallahassee, 1953-55, 57-58; instr. English U. Houston, University Park, Houston, 1955-59, asst. prof. University Park, 1959-62, assoc. prof., 1962-71, prof., 1971-97, prof. emeritus, 1997. Vis. instr. English, Fla. So. Coll., Lakeland, MacDill Army Air Base, Tampa, Fla., summer 1951, Tex. So. U., 1961-63, humanities, govt. U. Tex. Dental Br., Houston, 1962-63; lectr. The Women's Inst., Houston, 1967-72, humanities series Jewish Cmty. Ctr., Houston, 1972-73; originator, moderator TV and radio program The Arts in Houston Stas. KUHT-TV and KUHF-FM, 1956-57, 58-63. Author: An Examination of the Southern Milieu in Representative Plays by Southern Dramatists, 1963; contbg. author: National Poetry Anthology, 1952, Panorama das Literaturas das Americas, vol. 2, 1958-60, Perspectives on Ernst von Dohnányi, 2005, Dohnányi Evkönyu 2005, 2006; assoc. editor Forum, 1967, editor, 1967-82; contbr. articles to profl. jours.; dir. Murder in the Cathedral (T.S. Elliot), U. Houston, 1965; performed in opera as Sir Edgar in Der Junge Lord (Henze), Houston Grand Opera Assn., 1967; played the title role in Aella (Chatterton), Am. premiere, U. Houston, 1970. Bd. dir., founding mem. Contemporary Music Soc., Houston, 1958-63, Houston Shakespeare Soc., 1964-67; bd. dirs., founding mem., program annotator Houston Chamber Orch. Soc., 1964-76; narrator Houston Symphony Orch., Houston Summer Symphony Orch., Houston Chamber Orch. (with Charles Rosekrans), U. Houston Symphony Orch., St. Stephen's Music Festival Symphony Orch., New Harmony, Ind.; narrator world premier of The Bells (Jerry McCathern), 1969, U. Houston Symphony Orch., 1969, Am. premier Symphony No. Seven, Antartica (Vaughn-Williams), Houston Symphony Orch. (with Andre Previn), 1967, L'Histoire du Soldat (Stravinski), U. Houston Symphony Orch., 1957, Am. premier Babar the Elephant (Poulenc-Francais), Houston Chamber Orch. (with Charles Rosekrans), 1967, Le Roi David (Honegger), 1979, Voice of God in opera Noye's Fludde (Britten), St. Stephen's Music Festival, New Harmony, Ind. 1981; bd. dir., program annotator Music Guild, Houston, 1960-67, v.p., 1963-67, adv. bd., 1967-70; mem.-at-large, bd. dir. Houston Grand Opera Guild, 1966-67; repertory com. Houston Grand Opera Assn., 1967-70; bd. dir. Houston Grand Opera, 1970-75, adv. bd. 1978-79; cultural adv. com. Jewish Cmty. Ctr., 1960-66; bd. dir. Houston Friends Pub. Libr., 1962-67, 73-75, 1st v.p., 1963-67; adv. mem. cultural affairs com. Houston C. of C., 1972-75; adv. bd. dir. The Wilhelm Schole, 1980-98, Buffalo Bayou Support Com., 1985-87, bd. dir. Moores Sch. Music Soc., 1998—, trustee, 2002-04, advisory bd. dir., 2004—; bd. dir. U. Houston Retiree Assn., 1999-2001, v.p., 2000-2001; founding bd. dir. Internat. Dohnányi Rsch. Ctr., Inc., 2002-. Recipient Master Tchg. award Coll. Humanities and Fine Arts U., Houston, 1980, Favorite Prof. award Bapt. Student Union, U. Houston, 1991. Mem. MLA, AAUP, Coll. English Assn., L'Alliance Francaise, English-Speaking Union, Alumni Assn. Fla. So. Coll., Fla. State U., South Ctrl. MLA, Conf. Editors Learned Jours., Coll. Conf. Tchrs. English, Nat. Coun. Tchrs. English, Am. Studies Assn., Shepard Soc. Rice U., Nature Conservancy, Nat. Trust for Hist. Preservation, Inst. Internat. Edn., Century Club, Fla. So. Coll., President's Club, James D. Westcott Legacy Soc., Fla. State U., Tex. Ret. Tchrs. Assn., Phi Beta (patron), Phi Mu Alpha Sinfonia, Alpha Psi Omega, Pi Kappa Alpha, Sigma Tau Delta (Outstanding Prof. English U. Houston chpt. 1990), 1927 Soc. U. Houston, Houston Philos. Soc., Caledonian Club (London), Tau Kappa Alpha, Phi Kappa Phi. Episcopalian. Avocations: tennis, racquetball, swimming, travel. Home: 2625 Arbuckle St West University Place TX 77005-3929 Office: U Houston Dept English Univ Park 3801 Cullen Blvd Houston TX 77004-2602 Home Phone: 713-665-2401. *My commitment is to the humanities. I believe that the most important thing that a teacher can do is to help a student to stand on his/her own intellectual hind legs; to help him/her to learn how to aquire facts; to help him/her to learn how to organize and utilize these facts in intelligent, responsible ways.*

PRYOR, WILLIAM HOLCOMBE, JR., federal judge, former state attorney general, educator; b. Mobile, Ala., Apr. 26, 1962; s. William Holcombe Sr. and Laura Louise (Bowles) Pryor; m. Kristan Camille Wilson, Aug. 15, 1987; children: Caroline Elizabeth, Victoria Camille. BA in Legal Studies with honors, N.E. La. U., 1984; JD with honors, Tulane U., 1987. Law clk. US Ct. Appeals (5th cir.), Judge John Minor Wisdom, New Orleans, 1987—88; assoc. Cabaniss, Johnston, Gardner, Dumas & O'Neil, Birmingham, Ala., 1988—91, Walston, Stabler, Wells, Anderson & Bains, Birmingham, 1991—95; dep. atty. gen. State of Ala., Montgomery, 1995—97, atty. gen., 1997—2004; judge US Ct. Appeals (11th cir.), 2004—. Adj. prof. Samford U. Cumberland Sch. Law, Birmingham, 1989—94, U. Ala. Sch. Law, 2006—. Bd. student editors: Tulane Law Rev., 1985—86, editor-in-chief:, 1986—87, bd. adv. editors:, 1995—. La. nat. com. Young Rep. Nat. Fedn., 1984—86; mem. Ala. Rep. Exec. Com., 1994—95. Mem.: Federalist Soc. (assoc.), Amer. Law Inst. (assoc.), Order of Coif, Omicron Delta Kappa, Phi Kappa Phi. Republican. Roman Catholic. Office: US Court of Appeals 900 Federal Courthouse 1729 5th Ave N Birmingham AL 35203 Business E-Mail: william_h_pryor_jr@calluscourts.gov.*

PRYPCHAN, LIDA D., psychiatrist; b. Caracas, DF, Venezuela, July 8, 1960; arrived in USA, 1989; d. Roman Orestes Prypchan Hryculak and Edel Sayagues Sanchez. MD, U. Carabobo, Venezuela, 1986. Cert. physician Ednl. Commn. Fgn. Med. Grads., USA, Venezuela, adult psychiatrist U. Ctrl. Venezuela, Venezuelan Psychiatric Assn. Physician Clinica Residencia Carabobo, Valencia, Venezuela, 1986—89; rsch. assoc., the Schizophrenia Project at We. Psychiatric Inst. and Clinic U. Pitts. Med. Ctr., 1989—90, rsch. assoc., the Anxiety Disorders Project at Pitts. Adolescent Alcohol Rsch. Ctr., 1990—92, sr. rsch. assoc. World Psychiatric Assn., 1990—94; adult psychiatric resident Hosp. U. Caracas, U. Ctrl. de Venezuela, 1996—99, Elmhurst Hosp. Ctr., NY, 2001—05; fellow Child and Adolescent Psychiatry Elmhurst Hosp. Ctr., Mt. Sinai Sch. Medicine, 2005—07; attending adult, child and adolescent psychiatrist Wyo. Behavioral Inst., 2007—. Sr. rsch. assoc. Elmhurst Hosp. Ctr./World Psychiatric Assn., 2003—05; founder ppplus-a.org, 2008. Contbr. articles to profl. jours. Active mem. Soka Gakkai Internat.-USA, 1989—. Recipient Nat. Sci. Journalism award, Venezuela, 1987, 1988, 1989. Mem.: AMA, Nat. Assn. Mental Illness, Wyo. Psychiatric Assn., Wyo. Med. Assn., Acad. Child and Adolescent Psychiatry, Am. Psychiatric Assn. Democrat. Buddhist. Avocations: movies, theater, travel, walking, reading. Home: 2661 East 15th St Unit 204 Casper WY 82609 Office: Wyo Behavioral Inst 2417 East 15th St Casper WY 82609 Office Phone: 307-472-2271.

PRYSTAUK, ELISSA, artist; b. 1953; BFA, Rutgers U., Newark; postgrad., Urbino U., Newark Sch. Find and Ind. Advisor NJ Pastel Soc., 2005—. Work included in book, Best of Oil Painting, 1996, The Art of Pastel, 2005, North American Pastel Artists, 2007. Recipient Best of Show award, Avila Arts, NJ, 2003, Excellence award, Internat. Pastel Exhgn., Giverny, France, 2006. Fellow: Am. Artists Profl. League (medal of honor 2005); mem.: Hudson Valley Art Assn., Millburn Short Hills Art (treas. 2002—04), Pastel Soc. Am. (treas. 2004—). Home: 20 Knox Hill Rd Morristown NJ 07960-3502

PSARRAS, MARY AUTEN, language educator, tax specialist; b. Bridgeport, Conn., Dec. 26, 1945; d. James Ernest and Mary Dillon Auten; m. Georgios Psarras, Dec. 21, 1974 (dec.); children: Demetrios, Patrick. BA in Modern Spanish and Am. Lit., Brown U., Providence, RI, 1967; MS in Elem. Edn., U. Bridgeport, Conn., 1973. Cert. tchr. pre-K-8, Spanish grades 7-12, ESL pre-K-12 Conn. Cmty. vol. Peace Corps, Itapuranga, Goias, Brazil, 1967—69; tchr. ESL Bridgeport Bd. Edn., Conn., 1970—78, 1984—97, tchr., English lang. learner assessment and data specialist, 1997—. Pres., v.p. and treas. Bridgeport Assn. for Childhood Edn.; pres. and v.p. Conn. Assn. Childhood Edn., 1972—79; mem. steering com. Stratford Tchrs. Applying Whole Lang., 1992—97; mem. election com. Bridgeport Edn. Assn.; del. rep. assy. Conn. Edn. Assn. Grantee, Bridgeport Pub. Edn. Fund, Am. Brands. Mem.: Bridgeport Edn. Assn. (bldg. del. 1997—), Alpha Delta Kappa. Home: 106 Bridgeview Pl Stratford CT 06614 Office: Bridgeport Bd Edn Bilingual Dept 948 Main St Bridgeport CT 06606 Personal E-mail: mpsarras@optonline.net.

PSATHAS, GEORGE, sociologist, educator; b. New Haven, Feb. 22, 1929; s. Milton Emanuel and Melpa (Joannides) P.; m. Irma M. Amatruda, Feb. 5, 1951; children: Christine Ann, David George, Anthony Paul. BA, Yale U., 1950, PhD, 1956; MA, U. Mich., 1951; diploma, N.E. Sch. Photography, 1979. Instr. to asst. prof. Ind. U., Bloomington, 1955-63; lectr. Harvard U., Cambridge, Mass., 1961-62; assoc. prof. Washington U., St. Louis, 1963-68, rsch. assoc. Social Sci. Inst., 1963-68; program dir. cmty. mental health tng. program NIMH/Washington U., St. Louis, 1966-68; prof. sociology Boston U., 1968—97, prof. emeritus, 1997—, acting chair, 1968-69, assoc. chair, 1969-70, 76-78, chair, 1984-85, dir. Ctr. for Applied Social Sci., 1970-73, co-dir. post-doctoral rsch. tng. program in sociology and mental health NIMH, 1976-79; co-dir. Sociology and Health Svcs. Rsch. Tng. Program NCHSR and Boston U., 1970-78. Vis. lectr. MRC Med. Sociology-U. Aberdeen, Scotland, 1974, U. Colo., 1963, U. London, 1973, U. Bologna, 1996; vis. prof. Panteios Sch. Polit. Sci., Athens, 1982, Internat. U. Japan, Yamato-Machi, 1988, Doshisha U., Kyoto, Japan, 1989; Brit. Acad. vis. prof. U. Manchester, Eng., 1996; guest prof. Inst. for Human Scis., Vienna, Austria, 1996, 03; adj. prof. Bentley Coll., 2003-07; chair Mass. Interdisciplinary Discourse Analysis seminar, 1989-00; cons. NSF, 1978, 79, 89, 94, 95, Rsch. Coun. Can., 1983-84, Social Sci. Rsch. Coun. Eng., 1981-82; active Ctr. Advanced Rsch. in Phenomenology, 1980—; Alfred Schutz Meml. lectr. Soc. Phenomenology and the Human Scis., 2000; bd. dirs. Soc. Ret. Faculty and Staff, Boston U., 2001—, v.p., 2001-03, pres., 2004-07; co-chair Lang. and Social Interaction Seminar, 2004—; presenter in field. Author: Student Nurse in Diploma School of Nursing, 1968, Phenomenology & Sociology, 1989, Conversation Analysis, 1995, 2000 Outstanding Intellectuals of the 21st Century, 2001; editor: Phenomenological Sociology, 1973, Everyday Language, 1979, Interaction Competence, 1990; co-editor: Situated Order, 1994, Alfred Schutz Collected Papers, IV, 1996, Explorations of the Life-World, 2005, The Sociology of Radical Commitment: Kurt H. Wolff's Existential Turn, 2007, Alfred Schutz and his Intellectual Partners, 2009; editor-in-chief: Human Studies, Boston, 1978—; assoc. editor: Social Problems, 1958-61, Visual Sociology, 1993-2001; hon. bd. mem. Visual Studies, 2000—; mem. internat. editl. bd. Culture and Soc., 2000—07; cons. editor: Temple Univ. Press, Kluwer Acad. Pubs., Qualitative Sociology; contbr. numerous presentations, 13 chpts. to books, over 60 articles to profl. jours. Cons. Human Rels. Lab., Boston, Bethel, St. Louis, 1967, 69, Sch. for the Blind, Kallithea, Athens, Greece, 1982; tng. dirs. com. Nat. Ctr. for Health Svcs. Rsch., Washington, 1971-73; bd. dirs. Carroll Ctr. for the Blind, Newton, Mass., 1974-79. Recipient Sci. Faculty Devel. award NSF, 1978-79; grantee Fulbright Commn., Greece and Turkey, 1982, Brit. Acad., 1996; Post-Doctoral fellow NIMH Dept. Social Rels., Harvard U., Cambridge, 1961-62, Contemporary Authors, 1969, Am. Men of Science, 1962. Mem. AAUP (sec. 1977-79, v.p. Boston U. chpt. 1979-80, pres. 1997—), Am. Sociol. Assn., Ea. Sociol. Soc., Internat. Sociology Assn., Internat. Visual Sociology Assn., Internat. Inst. Ethnomethodology and Conversation Analysis (chair 1990-2001, hon. chair 2001—), Soc. Phenomenology and Existential Philosophy, Soc. Phenomenology and Human Scis. (co-chair 1981-85, exec. com. 1993-98, 2004-2006, hon. mem., 2006-), Soc. Study Social Problems (treas., bus. mgr. 1959-61). Home: 150 Mount Vernon St Newton MA 02465-2517 Office: Sociology Dept Boston Univ Boston MA 02215

PSOMIADES, HARRY JOHN, political science professor; b. Boston, Sept. 8, 1928; s. John and Koula (Yalmanides) P.; m. Dorothy Smith, Aug. 18, 1962 (dec. Aug. 27, 1984); children— Kathy Alexis, Christine Anne. BA, Boston U., 1953; M.Internat. Affairs, Columbia U., 1955; cert., Middle East Inst., 1956, PhD (Ford Found. fellow), 1962; Litt.D. (hon.), Holy Cross/Hellenic Coll., 1985. Lectr. govt. Columbia U., 1959-65, asst. dean Grad. Sch. Internat. Affairs, 1959-65, dir. Carnegie Endowment Fellowships in Diplomacy, 1959-71; assoc. prof. polit. sci. Queens Coll., City U. N.Y., 1965-69, prof., 1970—2003, chmn. dept. polit. sci., 1967-71, dep. exec. officer Ph.D. program in polit. sci., 1975-76, program dir. seminar on the modern Greek state, 1976—2004; dir. Ctr. Byzantine and Modern Greek Studies, 1976—2004. Cons. faculty U.S. Army Command and Gen. Staff Coll., 1968-86; U.S. Dept. State Fgn. Service Inst., 1968-71; mem. screening com. Fgn. Area Fellowships Program for Asia and Middle East Joint Com., Social Sci. Research Council and Am. Council Learned Socs., 1967-69 Author: Greece and Turkey: Mutual Economic Interests, 1964, (with Thomas Spelios) A Pictorial History of the Greeks, 1967, The Eastern Question: The Last Phase, 1968, 2d edition, 2000, Greek edit., 2004, (with T.A. Couloumbis) Foreign Interference in Greek Polics: An Historical Perspective, 1976, (with A. Scourby) The Greek American Community in Transition, 1982, (with R.S. Orfanos) Education and Greek Americans: Proccess and Prospects, 1987, (with S. Thomadakes) Greece, The New Europe and the Changing International Order, 1993, (with Van Coufoudakis) Greece and the New Balkans: Challenges and Opportunities, 1999, (with Sam Tsemberis) Greek American Families: Traditions and Transformations, 1999; editor: Jour. Modern Hellenism, 1984—; contbr, articles to profl. jours. Served with U.S. Army, 1946-50; to col. AUS, 1950-83. Hon. fellow Soc. Macedonian Studies, Thessaloniki, Greece, 1970—; named Comdr. Order of Honor The Republic of Greece, 1996. Fellow Middle East Studies Assn. N.Am.; mem. Am. Polit. Sci. Assn., Middle East Inst., Modern Greek Studies Assn. (mem. exec. com. 1972-76), Phi Beta Kappa. Greek Orthodox. Home: 440 Riverside Dr New York NY 10027-6828

PSORAS, ANDREA MARIE, financial analyst; BA in Bus. Mgmt., Franklin & Marshall Coll., Lancaster, Pa. Fin. instn. and fin. sector analyst; founder & principal, consulting and counseling firm Strategic Advisory, NYC. US vice-presdl. candidate Vote Here Party, 2008. Mem.: NY Soc. Security Analysts (mem. improved corp. reporting com., mem. corp. governance/shareholder rights com., mem. socially responsible investments com., author, Corp. Governance Handbook). Independent. Office: 201 W 117th St #2b New York NY 10026 Office Phone: 212-666-2569. Business E-Mail: andreapsoras@earthlink.net.*

PSOTKA, JOSEPH, psychologist; b. Krnjaja, Yugoslavia, Oct. 12, 1942; came to U.S., 1970; s. Karl and Elizabeth (Schaffer) P.; m. Barbara Schwartz, Nov. 9, 1971; children: Mitchell, Jonathan. BA, Toronot U., Can., 1969; MA, Harvard U., 1971; PhD, Yale U., 1975. Lectr. Douglas Coll., Burnaby, B.C., Can., 1971-72; asst. prof. Waterloo U., Ont., 1975-78; ednl. researcher Nat. Inst. of Edn., Washington, 1979-81; rsch. psychologist Army Rsch. Inst., Alexandria, Va., 1981—. Author: Hypertext, 1990; editor: Intelligent Tutors, 1978, Intelligent Instruction, 1991. Trustee Green Acres Sch., Rockville, Md., 1990. Fellow NIE, 1980, U.S. Army, 1990. Mem. Cognitive Sci. Soc., Artificial Intelligence and Edn. (chair 1989). Home: 1436 Fallsmead Way Rockville MD 20854-5535

PSUTY, NORBERT PHILLIP, marine sciences educator; b. Hamtramck, Mich., June 13, 1937; s. Phillip and Jessie (Proszkowski) P.; m. Sylvia Helen Zurinsky, June 13, 1959; children: Eric Anthony, Scott Patrick, Ross Phillip. BS, Wayne State U., 1959; MS, Miami U., Oxford, Ohio, 1960; PhD, La. State U., 1966. Rsch. assoc. Coastal Studies Inst., La. State U., Baton Rouge, 1962-64; instr. dept. geography and dept. geology U. Miami, Coral Gables, Fla., 1964-65; asst. prof. geography U. Wis., Madison, 1965-69; assoc. prof. geography and geol. scis. Rutgers U., New Brunswick, NJ, 1969-73, prof., 1973—2002, chmn. dept. marine and coastal scis., 1991-99, prof. marine and coastal scis., geog., geol. scis., 1989—2002, dir. Marine Scis. Ctr., 1972-76, dir. Ctr. for Coastal and Environ. Studies, 1976-90; assoc. dir. Inst. Marine and Coastal Scis., New Brunswick, 1990—2002; prof. emeritus Rutgers U., 2002—; dir. Sandy Hook Coop. Programs, 2002—. Mem. sci. com. Thalassas, Vigo, Spain, 1985—; mem. geog. scis. com. US NRC, 2007—. Co-author: Living with the New Jersey Shore, 1986, Coastal Dunes, 1990, Coastal Hazard Management, 2002, Coastal Dune Ecology, 2004; mem. editl. bd. Coastal Mgmt., 1981—, Jour. Coastal Rsch., 1987—, Jour. of Coastal Conservation, 1996—; contbr. numerous articles to scholarly jours., chapters to books, monographs. Mem. Water Policy Bd., East Brunswick, NJ, 1981—83, N.J. Shoreline Adv. Bd., Trenton, 1984—86; chmn. N.J. Gov.'s Sea Level Rise Com., Trenton, 1987—90; mem. N.J. State Beach Erosion Commn., 1994—99. Recipient Disting. Pub. Svc. award Pres. Rutgers U. 1988, Mel Marcus Disting. Career award, 2003, Natural Resources Rsch. award North Atlantic Region, US Nat. Park Svc., 2006; named Natural Resources Scientist of Yr., US Nat. Pk. Svc., 2006; grantee NSF, Nat. Park Svc., EPA, Office Naval Rsch., Nat. Sea Grant Program, NOAA, 1961—, others. Mem.: AAAS, N.J. Acad. Sci. (pres. 1982), Internat. Geog. Union (editor newsletter 1984—96, vice chair commn. on coastal environment 1988—92, chmn. commn. on coastal systems 1992—96, editor newsletter 2002—), Coastal Soc. (pres. 1980—82), Assn. Am. Geographers (Honors award 1993), Profl. Assn. Volleyball Ofcls. (chair N.J. bd. 2000—08). Avocations: gardening, reading. Office: Rutgers U Inst Marine & Coastal Scis 74 Magruder Rd Highlands NJ 07732 Office Phone: 732-708-1462.

PSZOTA, GABOR, physics educator; b. Miskolc, Hungary, Aug. 19, 1977; s. Gabor Pal Pszota and Margit Farkas. PhD in Astrophysics, Purdue U., West Lafayette, Ind., 2008. English translator U. Debrecen, Hungary, 1995—2000, physicist, 1995—2000; grad. tchg. rsch. asst. Purdue U., 2001—08; upper sch. physics tchr. Wooster Sch., Danbury, Conn., 2008—. Contbr. scientific papers. Recipient Grodzin's Summer Rsch. award, 2007. Mem.: Am. Astron. Soc. Office: Wooster Sch 91 Miry Brook Rd Danbury CT 06810 Office Fax: 203-790-7147. Business E-Mail: gabor.pszota@woosterschool.org.

PTACEK, LOUIS JOHN, medical educator, medical researcher; b. Madison, Wis., May 14, 1961; married. BS in Math., U. Wis., Madison, 1982, MD, 1986. Lic. Utah, 1987, cert. Am. Bd. Neurology and Psychiatry, 1993, lic. Calif., 2005. Intern in medicine U. Wash., 1986—87; resident in neurology U. Utah, 1987—90, chief neurology resident, 1989—90, Muscular Dystrophy Assn. neuromuscular fellow, 1990—91, postdoc in molecular biology, 1991—94, instr. neurology, 1990—92, asst. prof. neurology, 1992—96, assoc. prof. neurology and human genetics, 1996—2002, dir. neurogenetics divsn., 2000—03, prof. neurology and human genetics, 2002—03; prof. neurology U. Calif., San Francisco, 2003—, dir. neurogenetics divsn., 2003—, John C. Coleman disting. prof. neurogenerative diseases, 2004—. Assoc. investigator Howard Hughes Med. Inst., 1997—2003, investigator, 2003—. Assoc. editor Annals of Neurology, 1997—, Neurogenetics, 1997—, Neuromuscular Disorders, 2000—04, Jour. Neuroscience, 2005—. Fellow: Am. Acad. Arts and Sciences, Am. Soc. for Clin. Investigation; mem.: Am. Acad. Neurology, NAS Inst. Medicine. Office: U Calif San Francisco Fu & Ptacek Labs 1550 4th St San Francisco CA 94158-2324 Office Phone: 415-502-5614. Office Fax: 415-502-5641. E-mail: ljp@ucsf.edu.*

PTACEK, WILLIAM H., library director; BA in English and Psychology, U. Ill., 1972; MLS, SUNY, Geneseo, 1974; cert. of advanced study, U. Ill., Chgo., 1979. Reference libr. South Br. Chgo. Pub. Libr., 1974-75, head libr. Mt. Greenwood br., 1975-76, head system-wide circulation, 1976-77, asst. dir. pers., 1977-78, chief NE dist., 1978-79; dir. Idaho Falls Pub. Libr., 1979-83, Louisville Free Pub. Libr., 1984-89, King County Libr. Sys., Wash., 1989—. Co-author: (with Peggy Sullivan) Public Libraries: Smart Practices in Personnel, 1982; contbr. articles to profl. jours. Mem.: Pub. Libr. Assn., Bellevue Rotary Club (pres. 2002—03). Office: King County Libr Sys 960 Newport Way NW Issaquah WA 98027-2702 Office Phone: 425-369-3232. E-mail: billp@kcls.org.

PTASHNE, MARK STEVEN, molecular biology professor; b. Chgo., June 5, 1940; s. Fred and Mildred P.; m. Lucy Gordon, 1994. BA, Reed Coll., 1961; PhD, Harvard U., 1968. Lectr. biochemistry Harvard U., Cambridge, Mass., 1968-71, prof., 1971—73, chmn. dept. biochemistry and molecular biology, 1980-83, Herchel Smith prof. of molecular biology, 1993-97; Ludwig prof. molecular biology Sloan Kettering Cancer Rsch. Ctr., NYC, 1997—. Feodor Lynen lectr. U. Miami, Fla., 1988. Author: A Genetic Switch, 1986; contbr. numerous articles to sci. jours. Recipient Eli Lilly award, 1975, prix. Charles-Leopold Mayer Acad. des Scis., Inst. de France, 1977, Louisa Gross Horwitz prize Bd. Trustees Columbia U., 1985, Gairdner Found. Internat. award, 1985, Albert Lasker award for Basic Med. Rsch., Lasker Found., 1997; co-recipient Ledle award Harvard U., 1986, GM Sloan prize, 1990. Fellow N.Y. Acad. Sci., Am. Acad. Sci.; mem. NAS, Fedn. Am. Scis. (bd. sponsors 1981). Avocations: opera, classical music, violin. Office: Sloan Kettering Cancer Rsch Ctr 1275 York Ave # New York NY 10021-6094*

PTASYNSKI, HARRY, geologist, oil industry executive; b. Milw., May 26, 1926; s. Stanley S. and Frances V. (Stawicki) Ptasynski; m. Nola G. Whitestine, Sept. 15, 1951; children: Ross F., Lisa Joy. BS, Stanford U., 1950. Cert. profl. geologist, petroleum geologist. Dist. geologist Pure Oil Co., Amarillo, Tex., 1951-55, Casper, Wyo., 1955-58; ind. geologist, oil prodr. Casper, 1958—. With USN, 1943—46, PTO. Mem.: Soc. Petroleum Engrs., Rocky Mountain Oil and Gas Assn. (bd. dirs., mem. exec. com. 1980—96), Ind. Petroleum Assn. Mountain States (v.p., bd. dirs. 1976—80), Ind. Petroleum Assn. Am. (v.p., bd. dirs. 1976—85), Am. Inst. Profl. Geologists, Am. Assn. Petroleum Geologists. Republican. Episcopalian. Avocations: trout and salmon fishing, western history, golf. Home: 1515 Brookview Dr Casper WY 82604-4895 Office: 123 W 1st St Ste 560 Casper WY 82601-2483 Office Phone: 307-234-8392. Business E-Mail: hptasyn@tribcsp.com.

PU, CALTON, computer scientist; BS in Physics, U. Sao Paulo, Brazil, 1978, BS in Computer Sci., 1979; MS, U. Wash., 1983, PhD, 1986. From asst. to assoc. prof. dept. computer sci. Columbia U., 1986-92; assoc. prof. dept. computer sci. and engring. Oreg. Grad. Inst. Sci. and Tech., Portland, 1993-96, prof. dept. computer sci. and engring., 1996-99; prof., John P. Imlay Jr. chair in software Ga. Inst. Tech., Atlanta, 1999—. Vis. rsch. scientist IBM T.J. Watson Rsch. Ctr., summer 1990-91; co-gen. chair Internat. Conf. on Data Engring., 1997, co-PC chair, 1999; vice-chair Heterogeneous Sys. Interoperability, 1995, program com. 1993-95; program. com. Internat. Conf. on Partial Evaluation and Program Manipulation, 1997, Internat. Conf. on Distributed Computing Sys., 1989, 91, 93, 97; co-chair program com. Am. and Pacific Rim Internat. Symposium on Reliable Distributed Sys., 1995, 2003; presenter in field. Mem. editl. bd. Internat. Jour. Digital Libr., 1995—, Jour. Brazilian Computer Soc.; patentee apparatus and method for certifying the delivery of information. Grantee NSF, 1991—, DARPA, 1994—. Mem. ACM; sr. mem. IEEE; fellow AAAS. Office: Ga Inst Tech Coll of Computing 801 Atlantic Dr Atlanta GA 30332-0280 Office Phone: 404-385-1106. Business E-Mail: calton.pu@cc.gatech.edu.

PUANGSUVAN, SOMPORN, surgeon, consultant; b. Rajburi, Thailand, 1941; arrived in US, 1967; s. Boon and Sanguan P.; m. Chintana Chanvitayapongs, Mar. 18, 1978; children: Nick, Neesann. MD, Chiengmai U., Thailand, 1966. Diplomate Am. Bd. Surgery. Intern St. Clares Hosp., NYC, 1967—68; resident Aultman Hosp., Canton, Ohio, 1968—69, Tuskegee VA Hosp., Ala., 1969—73; pvt. practice Caruthersville, Mo., 1979—. Attending physician Pemiscot County Meml. Hosp., Hayti, Mo., chief surgery 1994, surg. cons. 1979—. Fellow ACS. Office: Doctors Clinic PO Box 201 Caruthersville MO 63830-0201 Home Phone: 573-333-5644; Office Phone: 573-333-1124.

PUCCIO, THOMAS PHILLIP, lawyer; b. Bklyn., Sept. 12, 1944; s. Matthew and Jeanette Puccio; m. Carol L. Ziegler (div.); m. Kathy Puccio. BA, Fordham U., 1966, JD, 1969. Bar: N.Y. 1969, U.S. Ct. Appeals (2d cir.) 1970, D.C. 1982, U.S. Supreme Ct. 1982, U.S. Ct. Appeals (4th and 9th cirs.) 1993. Lawyer Office U.S. Atty. Ea. Dist. N.Y., 1969—76, chief criminal divsn., 1973—75; exec. asst. U.S. atty., 1975—76; chief U.S. Dept. Justice Organized Crime Strike Force (ea. dist.) NY, 1976—82; atty. Booth, Lipton & Lipton, NYC, 1982—83; ptnr. Fisher, Puccio & Wilker, 1983—85, Stroock & Stroock & Lavan, 1985—87, Milbank, Tweed, Hadley & McCloy, 1987—92; mem. Law Offices of Thomas P. Puccio, NYC, 1992—. Co-author (with Dan Collins): In the Name of the Law: Confessions of a Trial Lawyer, 1995. Named NY Super Lawyer, 2007, 2008. Mem.: Assn. Bar City N.Y., D.C. Bar, Fed. Bar Coun. Office: Law Offices of Thomas P Puccio 230 Park Ave Ste 301 New York NY 10169 E-mail: tpuccio@lotpp.com.*

PUCHALA, LINDA A., federal agency administrator; b. 1949; BA in Bus. Adminstrn., Cleary U. Pres. Assn. Flight Attendants-CWA (AFA-CWA), 1979—86; staff dir. Mich. State Employees Assn.; mediator than sr. mediator, assoc. dir. alternative dispute resolution svcs. Nat. Mediation Bd., 1999—2009, chmn., 2009—. Office: Nat Mediation Bd 1301 K St NW, #250e Washington DC 20005*

PUCIATO, KATHLEEN, education educator; b. Yonkers, NY, June 21, 1954; d. Vincent and Jean Tompkins; m. Thomas Puciato, Aug. 14, 1982; children: Clair, Julia. MEd, SUNY Oneonta, 2003. Cert. Pub. Sch. Tchr. NY, 2004. Tchg. asst. BOCES, Stamford, NY, 1988—94; assoc. prof. SUNY Cobleskill, 1998—. V.p., bd. dirs. Cobleskill Campus Child Care Ctr., NY, 2007—. Photography & art. Mem.: NAEYC. Home: PO Box 115 Summit NY 12175 Office: SUNY Cobleskill Rt 7 Cobleskill NY 12043 Office Fax: 518-255-5021. Business E-Mail: puciatka@cobleskill.edu.

PUCINO, CARRIE, critical care nurse; b. Pa. married. MS in Nursing, York Coll. Pa. RN Am. Assn. Critical Care Nurses, 2006. Clin. nurse Wellspan Health, York, Pa., 2001—03; nursing faculty, baccalaureate nursing program York Coll. Pa., 2004—; clin. nurse Holy Spirit Health Sys., Camp Hill, 2004—. Health and wellness program Camp Hill United Meth. Ch., Pa., 2005—. Grantee, United Meth. Conf., 2005. Mem.: Sigma Theta Tau, Nat. Honor Soc. Nursing. Avocation: yoga. Office: York Coll PA 441 Country Club Rd York PA 17403-3651 Office Fax: 717-849-1651.

PUCK, WOLFGANG, chef; b. St. Veit, Austria, July 8, 1949; m. Marie France, 1976 (div. 1979); m. Barbara Lazaroff, 1984 (div. Nov. 27, 2002); children: Cameron, Bryon; m. Gelila Assefa, July 2008; children: Oliver Wolfgang, Alexander. Doctor of Culinary Arts (hon.), Johnson & Wales U., Providence, RI, 1998. Former chef Hotel de Paris, Monaco, Maxim's, Paris, L'Oustau de Baumanière, Provence; chef, part owner Ma Maison, LA, 1975—; exec. chef, ptnr. Spago, 1982—, Chinois on Main, Santa Monica, 1983—, Postrio, San Francisco, 1989—, Trattoria del Lupo, Las Vegas, 1989—, Granita, Malibu, Calif., 1991—, Spago Las Vegas, 1992—, Chinois Las Vegas, 1998—, Postrio Las Vegas, 1998—, Wolfgang Puck Bar & Grill, Las Vegas, 2004—, 20 21, Mpls., 2005—, Vert, Hollywood, Calif., CUT, Beverly Hills, Calif., 2006—; owner Wolfgang Puck Express, Wolfgang Puck Cafes, 1993—; owner, chef Wolfgang Puck Catering, 1998—; ptnr. Wolfgang Puck Worldwide, Inc., 2000—. Fund raising Meals on Wheels, A. Cancer Soc. LA; exec. chef Governor's Ball, The Oscars, 1995-, ptnr. with Humane Soc. US, factory farming animal welfare prog., 2007- Author: (cookbooks) Modern French Cooking for the American Kitchen, 1982, The Wolfgang Puck Cookbook: Recipes from Spago and Chinois, 1986, Adventures in the Kitchen with Wolfgang Puck, 1991, Pizza, Pasta and More!, 2000, Live, Love, Eat! The Best of Wolfgang Puck, 2002, Wolfgang Puck Makes It Easy, 2004, (newspaper columns) Wolfgang Puck's Kitchen, 2003-; producer (instructional cooking video) Spago Cooking with Wolfgang Puck; appeared in TV series Wolfgang Puck, 2001 (Daytime Emmy for Outstanding Service Show, 2004), Wolfgang Puck's Cooking Class, 2003-; actor: (guest appareances) (films) The Weather Man, 2005, (TV series) Who's the Boss?, 1987, Blossom, 1991, Tales from the Crypt, 1992, Ellen, 1996, Frasier, 2000, 2002, Good Morning Am., Late Night with David Letterman, Tonight Show with Jay Leno, Entertainment Tonight, Hollywood Squares, Wheel of Fortune, ABC News, CBS News, Politically Incorrect with Bill Maher, Las Vegas, 2006, (voice) The Simpsons, 2002. Founder Puck-Lazaroff Charitable Found.,

1982—. Recipient Humanitarian of Yr. award, James Beard Found., 1994, Bus. Statesman of Yr. award, Harvard Bus. Sch. of So. Calif., 2001, Smithfield Foods Outstanding Service award, James Beard Found., 2005; named Outstanding Chef of the Yr., 1991; named one of The 100 Most Powerful Celebrities, Forbes.com, 2008.

PUCKETT, ELIZABETH ANN, law librarian, educator; b. Evansville, Ind., Nov. 10, 1943; d. Buell Charles and Lula Ruth (Gray) P.; m. Joel E. Hendricks, June 1, 1964 (div. June 1973); 1 child, Andrew Charles; m. Thomas A. Wilson, July 19, 1985. BS in Edn., Eastern Ill. U., 1964; JD, U. Ill., 1977, MS in L.S., 1977. Bar: Kans. 1978, Ill. 1979. Acquisitions/reader services librarian U. Kans. Law Library, Lawrence, 1978-79; asst. reader services librarian So. Ill. U. Law Library, Carbondale, 1979-81, reader services librarian, 1981-83; assoc. dir. Northwestern U. Law Library, Chgo., 1983-86, co-acting dir., 1986-87; dir./assoc. prof. South Tex. Coll. Law Library, Houston, 1987-89; dir./prof. South Tex. Coll. Law Libr., Houston, 1990-94, U. Ga. Law Libr., Athens, 1994—. Co-author: Evaluation of System-Provided Library Services to State Correctional Centers in Illinois, 1983; co-editor Uniform Commercial Code: Confidential Drafts, 1993. Mem. ABA, Am. Assn. Law Librs. (mem. exec. bd. 1993-96). Avocations: reading, antiques. Office: U Georgia Law Libr Athens GA 30602-6018 Office Phone: 706-542-5078. E-mail: apuckett@uga.edu.

PUCKETT, RICHARD EDWARD, artist, former recreation executive; b. Klamath Falls, Oreg., Sept. 9, 1932; s. Vernon Elijah P., Leona Bell (Clevenger) P.; m. Velma Faye Hamrick, Apr. 14, 1957 (dec. 1985); children: Katherine Michelle Briggs, Deborah Alison Bolinger, Susan Lin Rowland, Gregory Richard. Student, So. Oreg. Coll. Edn., 1951—56, Lake Forest Coll., 1957—58, Hartnell Jr. Coll., 1960—70; BA, U. San Francisco, 1978. Acting arts and crafts dir., Ft. Leonard Wood, Mo., 1956-57; arts and crafts dir., asst. spl. svcs. officer, mus. dir. Ft. Sheridan, Ill., 1957-59; arts and crafts dir. Ft. Irwin, Calif., 1959-60, Ft. Ord, Calif., 1960-86; dir. arts and crafts br. Art Gallery, Arts and Crafts Ctr. Materials Sales Store, 1960; opening dir. Presidio Monterey Army Mus., 1968; dir. Model Army Arts and Crafts Program. One-man shows include Seaside City Hall, 1967—86, 2002, Ft. Ord Arts and Crafts Ctr. Gallery, 1967, 1973, 1979, 1981, 1984, 1986, Presidio of Monterey Art Gallery, Del Messa Gallery, Carmel, Calif., 1998, So. Oreg. Art Gallery, Medford, 2000, Country Rose Gallery, Hollister, Calif., 2001—03, Walter Avery Gallery Seaside City Hall, 2002, Sasoontsi Gallery, Salinas, Calif., 2004, juried show, 2006, one-man shows include U. Monterey Bay and Richard Puckett, Calif., 2008, also pvt. collections, designed and opened first Ft. Sheridan Army Mus., Presidio of Monterey Mus., exhibited in group shows at 2nd and 3rd Annual Nat. Glass Exhibition, Gatlinburg, Tenn., 1981—82, Glass on Holiday, 1981—82, City Hall Avery Gallery, Seaside, Calif., 1987—2001, Salinas Valley Art Gallery, Calif., 1990—98, Del Messa Gallery, Carmel, Calif., 1990—2007, Internat. Congress on Arts and Comm., 1997, City Hall Avery Gallery, Seaside, Calif., 2003—08, Steinbeck Mus., 2009, miniature show, Monterey Art Museum, 2004—08, Monterey Govt. Bldg. Art Gallery, Salinas, Calif., 2007—08. Donated over 8000-10000 photographs, slides, paintings, arts and crafts to U. Monterey Bay; donated photo collection, art slides and books to Hartnell Jr. Coll. Recipient 1st pl. Dept. Army and US Army Forces Command awards for programming and publicity, 1979-81, 83-85 (exhibited in Smithsonian), Juried Show 1st pl., Flower Art Show Steinbeck Mus., Salinas, Calif., 2009, 1st and 3d pl. sculpture awards Monterey County Fair Fine Arts Exhibit, 1979, Fort Ord Arts and Crafts Exhibit, Montterey Airport, 2008, Fort Ord, Comdrs. medal civilian svcs., 1986, Golden Acad. award, Internat. Man of Yr. award, 1991-92, Champion of Arts-Friend of Arts Spl. Tribute award Art Coun. Monterey County, 2007, Spl. Congl. Recognition cert. Salimas City Coun., 2007, others. Mem.: Internat. Soc. Acrylic Painters, Ft. Ord Alumni Assn., Salinas Valley Art Assn. (pres. 2000—09), Monterey Peninsula Art Mus. Assn. Home: 210 San Miguel Ave Salinas CA 93901-3021 Home Phone: 831-424-8904. Personal E-mail: puckettart@comcast.net.

PUCKETT, RUBY PARKER, food service executive, writer, dietician; b. Dora, Ala., Nov. 26, 1932; d. John Franklin Parker and Ethel V. (Short) Tuggle; m. Larry Willard Puckett, July 2, 1955; children: Laurel Lynn Puckett Brown, Hollie Kristina Puckett Walker. BS in Food and Nutrition, Auburn U., Ala., 1954; postgrad. in vocat. edn., U. Fla., 1970-80; MA in Health Sci. Edn., Cen. Mich. U., 1976. Registered dietitian, foodservice adminstr., food svc. exec., military traveller. Dietetic intern Henry Ford Hosp., Detroit, 1955; staff dietitian VA Hosp., Houston, 1955-56; dietitian Matty Hersee Hosp., Meridian, Miss., 1957-58; asst. dir. U. Miss. Med. Ctr., Jackson, 1960-61; dir. dietetics Ft. Sanders Presbyn. Hosp., Knoxville, Tenn., 1961-63, Waterman Meml. Hosp., Eustis, Fla., 1963-68; dir. food and nutrition U. Fla. Shands Hosp., Gainesville, 1968-95; pres. Square One Cons. Service, Gainesville, 1979-85; pres., owner Food Svc. Mgmt. Cons., 1995—. Adv. com. on jr. coll. dietetic programs Fla. Dept. Edn., 1967-69; nominating com. Southeastern Hosp. Conf. for Dietitians, 1969, sec., 1974-75; pres. Field Agy. Nutrition, 1970; instr. U. Fla., 1972-73, 82-85, clin. and cmty. coordinated undergrad. dietetic program adv. bd., 1974-89; instr. Santa Fe Jr. Coll., Gainesville, 1977-81; adv. com. Marquis Libr. Soc., Inc., 1974; health project rev. com. North Ctrl. Fla. Planning Coun., 1974-76; named to White House Conf. on Food and Nutrition, 1976, Senate Select Com. on Food and Nutrition, 1976; com. on animal products NRC Adv. Bd. on Mil. Pers. Supplies, 1978-81; site evaluator dietetic programs in colls and univs., 1998-2008; mem. Commn. on Accrediation Dietetic Edn., 1997-2008, program reviewer for dietary mgr. tng., 2003-06; reviewer abstracts, articles Jour. Am. Dietetic Assn.; spkr. in field.; content advisor position papers ADA. Author: Food Service Manual for Health Care Institutions, 1988 (Jim Rose Pub.award, 2005, 2009), 3d edit., 2004, Basic Nutrition and Diet Modification Shands Hospital, 1992, revised edit., 2002, Managing Foodservice Operations, 1992, HACCP The Future Challenge, 4th edit., Basic Food, Nutrition & Medical Nutrition Therapy Through the Life Cycle, 4th edit., 2009, Disaster and Emergency Preparedness for Food Service Operations, 2003, Dietary Managers Course by Correspondence, 12th edit., 2009, Nutrition for the Elderly, Safety, Sanitation and Security for Food Services Operation, Topics in Practice: Productivity Measures for Food Service Operations, 2005, Standards of Professional Performance; mem. editl. adv. com.: Stokes Report, 1980—84, editl. advisor: Food Management, 1986—, Topics in Clinical Nutrition, 1988—, Aspen's Focus, 1984—91, Aspen's Hosp. Nutrition and Foodservice Forms; editl. advisor Marketlink, 2006; contbr. articles to profl. jours.; developer nutrition and older adult distance edn.course. V.p. Campus USA Credit Union, 1980—81, pres.-elect, 1981—82; chmn. Shands Hosp. chpt. United Way, 1978, mem. speakers bur., 1985—86; profl. adv. bd. Shands Home Care; vol. Mothers Supporting Daus. with Breast Cancer, 2000—; mem. Sexual Phys. Abuse Bd.; courtesy faculty appt. Divsn Youth, Family and Ext.; election clk., inspector Alachua County (Fla.) Elections, 2000—06; bd. dir. Campus USA Credit Union, 1978—, chmn. bd., 1998—2000; mem. budget and allocations com. United Way, 1983—2005; mem. adv. bd. Harvest Gainesville, 1991—93, Children's Miracle Telethon, 1992—95; adv. bd. Sta. WRUF Pub. Radio, 1992; bd. dir. Fla. 4-H Found., 2000—04, North Fla. Regional Vocat. Sch. Recipient Community Leader award, Sta. WRUF-FM, 1972, Ivy award, Restauranteurs of Distinction, 1980, Disting. Pace Setter award, Roundtable for Women in Foodservice, 1984, Award of Distinction, Sch. Human Svc., Auburn U., 1991, Outstanding Dietitian, Fla.; named Alumni of Yr., Auburn U. Sch. Home Econs., 1985, Disting. Woman, Alachua County, Fla., 1992; named to Woodlawn H.S. Hall of Fame, 1982, Fla. Women's Hall of Fame, 1986. Mem.: IFMA (Silver Plate award 1978), Food Svc. Consultants Internat. Soc. (N.Am. divsn. bd. trustees 2006—, program planning com. 2007, code of ethics chair task force 2007, governance task force 2007—09, chair publ. com. 2009), Fla. Coun. on Aging (sec. nutrition sect. 1974—76, chmn. 1974—76, adv. bd. 1974—76), Nat. U. Continuing Edn. Assn. (disting. ind. study course 1986, 1989), Nutrition Edn. Soc. (liaison with industry com. 1974, legis. com. 1974, charter), Dietary Mgr. Assn. Found. Fla. (steering com., Disting. Svc. award 2005, 2006), Am. Soc. Hosp. Food Service Adminstrs. (edn. com. 1968—71, nomination com. 1978, chmn. publ. com. 1981—82, chmn. legis. com. 1984, adv. bd. Trends 2006—09, task force HACCP cert., Jim Rose Pub. award 2005, Editl. Excellence award 2007, Jim Rose Pub. award 2009, 2009), Gainesville Dietetic Assn. (v.p. 1969, pres. 1970, 1976), Fla. Dietetic Assn. (sec. 1968—70, pres. 1973—74, del. 1980—87, chmn. by-laws com. 1985, numerous other offices), Am. Dietetic Assn. (house of delegates 1981—85, pres. practice group 41 1982—84, area III coord. 1985—88, chair DPG41 Area III Found. 1988—91, chair practice group mgmt. in food and nutrition svc. 2001, hons. award com. 2005, emergency task force 2006—07, chmn. stds. of profl. performance, profl. performer 2007—09, Excellence in Mgmt. Practice award 1994, Medallion for Profl. Cmty. and Career Achievement 1996, Marjorie Hulsizer Copher award 2003), The Athenaeum Soc., Internat. Gold and Silver Plate Soc. (sec. bd. trustees 1983—85), Ivy Soc., Altrusa, Pi Lambda Beta, Kappa Sigma Phi. Republican. Mem. Lds Ch. Avocations: whitewater rafting, hiking, gardening. Office: 5200 NW 43d St Ste 102-302 Gainesville FL 32606 Office Phone: 352-371-6160. Personal E-mail: puckerp@juno.com.

PUDAS, TERRY J., federal agency administrator, retired military officer; BS, Univ. Wash., 1969; MA in Nat. Security & Strategic Studies, Naval War Coll.; MA in mgmt., Webster Univ.; grad., Def. Language Inst. Naval aviator, fighter squadrons US Navy, 1977—2001; exchange pilot Deutsche Marine (German Navy); air officer, Persian Gulf for Operations Desert Shield & Desert Storm USS Midway (CV-41); dep. & exec asst. to pres. Naval War Coll., Newport, RI; dep. dir. Force Transformation US Dept. of Def., Washington, 2001—, acting dir. Force Transformation, 2005—. Office: Dir Force Transformation 2500 Defense Pentagon Washington DC 20301-2500*

PUDDY, WILLIAM CURTISS, retired military officer, not-for-profit developer; s. Harry Curtiss and Lee Puddy; m. Laryn Gail Puddy, Oct. 7, 1972; children: Karel Marie Decker, Steffany Lyn, Alan Curtiss. BS, US Mil. Acad., West Point, NY, 1972; MS in Systems Mgmt., U. So. Calif., LA, 1982; Resident Grad. Diploma, US Army War Coll., Carlisle Barracks, Pa., 1994. Lic. Life, Health, Annuities, Property and Casualty, Long Term Care ins. Va. Bur. Ins., 2005; cert. investment advisor Series 65 Nat. Securities Administrators Assn., 2004. Commd. 2d lt. US Army, 1972, advanced through grades to col., 1995, comdr. Co. B 9th Tng. Bn. Ft. Lewis, Wash., 1976, comdr. Co. A 1st Bn. 7th Inf. Aschaffenburg, Germany, 1977—79, com. chief and comdr. light weapons com. Co. C infantry tng. group Ft. Benning, Ga., 1984—85, comdr. 5th Bn. 10th Inf. Regiment Ft. Leonard Wood, Mo., 1990—92, comdt. Inst. for Profl. Devel., Tng. Support Ctr. Ft. Eustis, Va., 1996—2000, chief of staff mil. dist. Washington Washington, 2000—02, ret., 2002; registered rep. and agt. First Command Fin. Planning, Woodbridge, 2002—05; exec. dir., sec., treas. Emmanuel Farms Outreach, Inc., Lonaconing, Md., 2005—08; vice chmn. Savage River Dog Rescue, Inc., 2008—09, exec. dir., 2008—09. Sound ministry Cornerstone Bapt. Ch., Cumberland, Md., 2007; youth soccer and baseball coach Army Dependent Youth Activities, Forts Benning, Detrick, Leonard Wood, 1986—92. Decorated Nat. Defense medal with two stars Dept. Defense, Ga. Commendation medal Ga. Dept. of Def., Legion of Merit Hdqs., Tng. and Doctrine Command, US Army Mil. Dist. Wash.; recipient Primicerius level, Order of St. Maurice medal, Nat. Inf. Assn., 1972—2002, Army Commendation medal, 9th Infantry divsn., 1976, Meritorious Svc. medal, US Army Europe, 3rd Infantry divsn., 1980, Combined Arms Ctr., 1983, Infantry Sch. Ft. Benning, 1986, Army Staff, DCS Ops., 1988, Engr. Sch., Ft. Leonard Wood, 1992, 24th Infantry divsn., 1993, Army Tng. Support Ctr., 2000, Army Achievement medal, 29th Infantry Regiment, 1985, Bronze level, Order of de Fleury medal, US Army Engr. Rgt., 1990—92, Defense Meritorious Svc. medal, Joint Staff, 1990, Distance Learning XXI Contract award, Joint Svc. Commendation medal, HQ NATO Stabilization Force, Bosnia, 1999, Svc. medal, Dept. Army, 1980, Armed Forces Expeditionary medal, 1999, Global War on Terrorism Svc. medal, 2001, Overseas Ribbon, 1980, NATO medal, 1999, Army Superior Unit medal, 2000, Expert Infantry badge, Joint Staff Badge, Army Staff badge, Cold War cert., Dept. Defense, 2000, Ga. Commendation medal, State Ga., Dept. Defense, Mil. divsn., HQ 48th Brigade, Ga. Nat. Guard, 1993, Joint Meritorious medal, Joint Staff, Pentagon, 1990. Mem.: Nat. Soccer Coaches Assn. Am., 1814 Soc., U. So. Calif. Trojan Family Assn., Non-Commd. Officers Assn. Am. (hon.), Assn. Grads. US Mil. Acad. (life), Nat. Inf. Assn. (life), Army War Coll. Alumni Assn. (life), Mil. Officers' Assn. Am. (life). Independent. Achievements include development of National Training Center Instrumentation System. Avocations: soccer, leadership and management science, music, martial arts, history.

PUDLIN, HELEN POMERANTZ, lawyer; d. George and Claire Pomerantz; m. David B. Pudlin, Dec. 23, 1973; children: Alexander R., Julia H. BA cum laude, U. Pa., 1970, MS, 1971, JD, 1974. Bar: Pa. 1974. Lectr. U. Pa. Law Sch., 1983-87; asssoc. Ballard, Spahr, Andreas & Ingersoll, Phila., 1974-81, ptnr., 1981-89; gen. counsel Provident Nat. Bank, Phila., 1989-93; sr. v.p., dep. gen. counsel PNC Fin. Corp., Pitts., 1992-93; sr. v.p., mng. gen. counsel PNC Bank Corp., Pitts., 1993; sr. v.p., gen. counsel The PNC Fin. Svc. Group, Pitts., 1993—. Speaker in field. Author: (with others) Review of Antitrust Laws and Procedures, 1983, Criminal Antitrust Litigation Manual, 1983, Pennsylvania Medical Society Handbook, 1989; co-author: Joint Ventures in Healthcare. Former mem. Bd. of Ethics City of Phila.; former mem. bd. dirs. Phila. Facilities Mgmt. Corp.; bd. advisors Pub. Interest Law Ctr. Phila.; former mem. bd. overseers U. Pa.; bd. trustees Wistar Inst. Mem. ABA (antitrust sect., litigation sect., bus. law sect.), Pa. Bar Assn. (former mem. ho. of dels., judiciary com.), Phila. Bar Assn. (bd. govs. 1989-91, fed. cts. com., bus. law sect.), Acad. Natural Scis. (former bd. dirs., trustee), Duquesne Club. Office: The PNC Fin Svc Group 249 5th Ave Pittsburgh PA 15222-2709

PUDLO, STEVEN EDWARD, computer technician; s. Chester Joseph and Mary Ann Pudlo; life ptnr. Linda Sue Jacobsen; 1 child, Julia Briggs. AS in Data Processing, Thames Valley State Tech. Coll., Norwich, Conn., 1982; BS in Computer Sci., Ea. Conn. State U., Willimantic, Conn., 1985—86; AS in Indsl. Mgmt., Three Rivers CC, Norwich, 1986—87; MBA, Rensselaer Polytech, Hartford, Conn., 1992—95. Asst dir. IT Three Rivers CC, 1985—. Contbr. book. Sec. Ancient Accepted Scottich Rite, Preston, Conn., 1998—2006; mem. Norwich Rep. Town Com., 1990—94; master Somerset-St. James Lodge #34, Preston, 2000—03. Mem.: Masonic Motorcycle Assn. Australia, Patriot Guard Riders, Masonic Motorcycle Club, Internat. R-Consevative. Avocations: motorcycling, travel. Home: 59 Saint Regis Ave Norwich CT 06360 Office: Three Rivers CC 574 New London Turnpike Norwich CT 06360 Office Fax: 860-886-4960. Business E-Mail: spudlo@trcc.commnet.edu.

PUENTE, ANTONIO E., psychologist, educator, scientist; b. Habana, Cuba, Feb. 14, 1952; s. Antonio A. and Sylvia (Llanso) P.; m. Linda Newman, June 11, 1977; children: Kirsta, Antonio, Lucas. AA, Fla. Jr. Coll., Jacksonville, 1971; BA, U. Fla., 1973; PhD, U. Ga., 1978. Diplomate Am. Bd. Profl. Neuropsychology. Asst. prof. neuroanatomy St. George's U. Sch. Medicine, Grenada, W.I., 1978-79; clin. psychologist N.E. Fla. State Hosp., Macclenny, Fla., 1979-81; clin. neuropsychologist Wilmington, NC, 1982—; prof. psychology U. N.C., Wilmington, 1981—. Author: Neuropsychological Assessment of the Spanish Speaker, Handbook of Neuropsychological Assessment, others; editor: Neuropsychology Review. Mem. AMA (current procedural terminology panel 1994—, Ctr. Medicare and Medicade Svcs. medicare coverage adv. com. 1999-2003), APA (coun. of reps. 1994-2000, pres. divsn. neuropsychology 2002, Karl Heiser award 1995), Nat. Acad. Neuropsychology (pres. 1991, disting. svc. award 2000), N.C. Psychol. Assn. (pres. 1990), N.C. Psychol. Found. (founding pres. 1991), Hispanic Neuropsychological Soc. Republican. Roman Catholic. Avocations: surfing, tennis. Home: 1916 Lunar Ln Wilmington NC 28405-4211 Office: U NC Wilmington Dept Psychology Wilmington NC 28403 Office Phone: 910-962-3812. Business E-Mail: puente@uncw.edu.

PUENTE, HENRY, communications educator; s. Rosa Ruelas Puente. PhD, U. Tex., Austin, 2004. Sales dir. Arenas Entertainment, Beverly Hills, Calif., 2004—05; account exec. Hoy, LA, 2005—06; asst. prof. Calif. State U., Fullerton, 2006—. Author: (book) US Latino Films: A Goldmine or Fool's Gold. Office: Calif State Univ 800 N State College CP400 Fullerton CA 92831 Business E-Mail: hpuente@fullerton.edu.

PUENTE, MARIA LUZ, bilingual educator; b. Bilbao, Spain, Feb. 8, 1964; came to U.S., 1990; d. Jose L. and Luz (Ordonez) P. BA in History and Arts, U. Complutense, Madrid, 1987; Superior Degree in Classical Piano, Royal Conservatory of Music, Madrid, 1988, Superior Degree in Chamber Music, 1990; MBA, U. Redlands, Calif., 2000. Solfeggio tchr. Royal Conservatory of Music, Madrid, 1988; h.s. tchr. Ministry of Edn., Madrid, 1988-90; bilingual tchr. in elem. sch. Desert Sands Unified Sch. Dist., Indio, Calif., 1990—. Instr. Practising Sch. of Archeology, U. Deusto, Bilbao, 1983. Pianist, performing in concerts, 1974-89; contbr. articles to profl. jours. Mem. La Quinta (Calif.) Hist. Preservatin Commn., 1994—. Roman Catholic. Avocations: photography, piano, collecting, travel, music. Home: 78-620 Forbes Cir La Quinta CA 92253 E-mail: mlpuente@aol.com.

PUENTE, TAMAGARY, psychologist; b. Hoboken, NJ, Nov. 18, 1980; d. Santa and Gerardo Puente. MS in Psychology, Fairleigh Dickinson U., Teaneck, NJ, 2006. Tchr.'s asst. South Bergen Jointure Commn., Lodi, NJ, 2003—06. Psychologist cons. Paterson Charter Sch. Sci. and Tech., NJ, 2007—08. Mem.: Nat. Assn. Sch. Psychologists. Office: Englewood Pub Sch 12 Tenafly Rd Englewood NJ 07631 Business E-Mail: tpuente@epsd.org.

PUESCHEL, SIEGFRIED M., pediatrician, educator; b. Waldenburg, Germany, July 28, 1931; came to U.S., 1961; naturalized, 1971; widowed. Student, Braunschweig Coll., Germany, 1953-55, Leibniz Coll., Tubingen, Germany, 1955-56, U. Tubingen, Germany, 1955-57, Free U., Berlin, 1957-58, U. Freiburg, Germany, 1958; MD summa cum laude, Med. Acad., Dusseldorf, Germany, 1960; MPH, Harvard U., 1967; PhD, U. R.I., 1985; JD, So. New Eng. Sch. Law, 1996. Diplomate Am. Bd. Pediatrics, Am. Bd. Med. Genetics. Intern Mercer Hosp., Trenton, NJ, 1961-62; jr. resident in pediatrics Children's Hosp., Honolulu, 1962-63; asst. resident in pediatrics Children's Hosp. Med. Ctr., Boston, 1963-64, asst. in mental retardation, 1967-68, assoc. in mental retardation, 1968-75, dir. Down Syndrome Program, 1970-75, dir. PKU Clinic, 1972-75; sr. resident in pediatrics Montreal Children's Hosp., 1964-65, fellow in biochemical genetics/metabolism, 1965-66; assoc. physician R.I. Hosp., Providence, 1975-79, dir. child devel. ctr., 1975-94, dir. PKU and Amino Acid Program, 1975—, dir. Down Syndrome Program, 1978—, physician, 1979—. Instr. pediatrics Harvard U., Cambridge, Mass., 1968-74, asst. prof. in pediatrics, 1974-75, lectr. in pediatrics, 1975—; asst. prof. in pediatrics Brown U., Providence, 1975-77, assoc. prof. in pediatrics, 1977-85, prof. in pediatrics, 1985—; consulting pediatrician Waltham (Mass.) Hosp., 1968-75; cons. in genetics Lying in Hosp., Boston, 1969-75, Women and Infants Hosp., Providence, 1975—; cons. Devel. Evaluation Clinic Children's Hosp. Med. Ctr., Boston, 1975—; mem. prevention of mental retardation com. Internat. League of Socs. for Persons with Mental Handicaps; mem. rsch., prevention and program svc. com. Assn. for Retarded Citizens U.S.; mem. nat. conf. on rsch. perspectives in down syndrome Nat. Inst. Child Health and Rehab. Svcs.; mem. state-of-the-art conf. on down syndrome Office Spl. Edn. and Rehab. Svcs. U.S. Dept. Edn.; mem. nat. adv. child health and human devel. coun. NIH, Washington; mem. sub-com. on tng., edn. and quality assurance-tech. assistance Devel. Disabilities Coun., R.I.; mem. med. adv. com. Spl. Olympics. Author chpts. to books; mem. editl. bd. Down Syndrome Papers and Abstracts for Profls., Exceptional Parents, Down's Syndrome: Rsch. and Practice; reviewer numerous jours.; contbr. articles to profl. jours. Grantee Mass. Dept. Health, 1968, Vigneron Meml. Fund, 1984-85, Charlotte Taylor Fund, 1985-86, Dept. Health and Human Svcs., 1982-86, March of Dimes Nat. Found., 1987-89, Sigma-Tau Pharm., Inc., 1990-93; recipient Recongnition award March of Dimes, 1976, Recognition award Blackstone Valley chpt. R.I. Assn. for Retarded Citizens, 1979, Fogarty Founders award, 1988, Edn. award Muscular Dystrophy Assn., 1985, 86, Muscular Dystrophy Tchg. award, 1988, Recognition award Devel. Ctr. for Handicapped Personsn-Utah State U., 1986, Down Syndrome Assn. of Greater Cin. award, 1986, Colegion John Langdown Down award Mexico City, 1987, Disting. Rsch. award Assn. for Retarded Citizens of U.S., 1990, Conn. Down Syndrome Assn. award, 1991, Sindrome de Down award Asociación Down de Monterrey (Mexico), 1994. Fellow Am. Acad. Pediatrics, Am. Coll. Med. Genetics (founder); mem. AAAS, Am. Assn. Mental Retardation (Profl. Contbn. award 1991), Am. Acad. Cerebral Palsy and Devel. Medicine, Am. Pediatric Soc., Am. Soc. Human Genetics, Nat. Down Syndrome Congress (past pres., Recognition for Disting. Svc. award 1980, Mid-Hudson Valley award 1983, Achievement in Rsch. award 1988, Outstanding Physician award 1991), N.Y. Acad. Sci., R.I. Med. Soc., New Eng. Regional Genetics Group, Soc. Inherited Metabolic Disorders, Down Syndrome Soc. R.I. (award 1985), Assn. for Children with Down Syndrome (bd. dirs.). Office: RI Hosp Child Devel Ctr 593 Eddy St Providence RI 02903-4923 Office Phone: 401-444-8477.

PUFFER, JAMES C., sports medicine physician, educator, medical association administrator; married. BS, UCLA, MD, 1976. Prof., chief, divsn. family medicine UCLA; prof., family medicine Univ. Ky., Lexington; exec. dir., sec. Am. Bd. Family Medicine, Lexington, Ky., 2003—05, pres., CEO, 2005—. Physician US Winter Olympic Team,

Sarajevo, 1984; head team physician US Summer Olympic Team, Seoul, 1988; mem., sports medicine, sports sci. coun. US Olympic Com., 1985—92; com. mem. NCAA Com. on Competitive Safeguards and Med. Aspects of Sports, 1983—90; cons. Pres. Coun. on Physical Fitness and Sports, 1988—90. Assoc. editor Medicine and Science in Sports and Exercise, 1989—98, editor-in-chief Sports Medicine Digest, 1992—, editl. bd. mem., peer reviewer numerous profl. jours. Recipient Duke Paoa Kahanamoku award, USA Water Polo, 2004. Fellow: Am. Coll. Sports Medicine; mem.: US Olympic Sports Medicine Soc. (bd. dir. 1993—96), Am. Med. Soc. for Sports Medicine (pres. 1996—97, founding mem.), Am. Bd. Family Medicine (bd. dir. 1989—94, exec. com. mem.-at-large 1993—94, v.p. bd. dir. 1993—94). Avocation: water polo. Office: ABFM 2228 Young Dr Lexington KY 40505-4294 Office Phone: 859-269-5626. Business E-Mail: jpuffer@theabfm.org.*

PUFFER, KEITH ANDREW, psychology professor; b. Detriot, Apr. 14, 1957; s. Herbert John and Mary Ellen Puffer; m. Wendy Lynn Willock, May 22, 1987; children: Brittany Lauren, Kaity Brooke, Benjamin John. Grad. cum laude, Trinity Internat. U., Deerfield, Ill., MA in Counseling Psychology; PhD in Counseling, Purdue U., West Lafayette, Ind., 1998; grad., Internat. Sch. Theology, San Bernardino, Calif., MA in Theological Studies. Cert. Nat. Bd. Cert. Counselors, Inc, 1997, lic. mental health counselor, marriage & family therapist State Of Ind., Ind. Profl. Lic. Agy., social worker MFT, Mental Health Counselors Bd. Prof. psychology Ind. Wesleyan U., Marion, 1991—; therapist Wabash Friends Ch. Counseling Ctr., Ind., 1995—2007, Puffer Counseling, Converse, Ind., 2007—. Contbr. articles to profl. jours. including Pastoral Psychology, Jour. Psychology and Christianity, jours. Psychology & Theology. Asst. girls varsity soccer coach Oak Hill HS, Meir, Ind.; bd. mem. Oak Hill Soccer Assn., Swayzee, Ind. Mem.: ACA (assoc.), Christian Assn. Psychol. Studies, Evang. Ch. Alliance (assoc.), Psi Chi (life). Republican. Avocations: running, travel. Office: Ind Wesleyan Univ 4201 S Washington Marion IN 46953 Office Fax: 765-677-2487. E-mail: keith.puffer@indws.edu.

PUFFER, RICHARD JUDSON, retired college chancellor; b. Chgo., Aug. 20, 1931; s. Noble Judson and Lillian Katherine (Olson) P.; m. Alison Foster Cope, June 28, 1952; children— Lynn, Mark, Andrew. Ph.B., Ill. Wesleyan U., 1953; MS in Edn, Ill. State U., 1962; PhD (Roy Clark Meml. scholar), Northwestern U., 1967. Asst. plant supt. J.A. Olson Co., Winona, Miss., 1957-59; tchr. Leroy Community Unit Dist. (Ill.), 1959-60; tchr., prin. Community Unit, Dist. 7, Lexington, Ill., 1960-62; asst. county supt. schs. Cook County, Ill., 1962-65; dean arts and scis. Kirkwood Community Coll., Cedar Rapids, Iowa, 1967-69; v.p. Black Hawk Coll., Moline, Ill., 1969-77, pres., 1977-82, chancellor, 1982-87; pres. The Ark Computer Ctr., 1989-92. Dir. W. Ctrl. Ill. Ednl. TV Corp., Springfield, Ill., 1977-87; cons. examiner North Central Assn., 1978-87. Editor: Cook County Ednl. Digest, 1962-65. Bd. dirs. Cedar Rapids Symphony, 1967-69, United Way of Rock Island and Scott Counties, Ill., 1978-80, Unitarian Universalist Dist. of Mich., 1995-98; bd. dirs., sec. West Shore Unitarian Universalist Congregation, 1996-99; sec., treas. Ill. Ednl. Retirement Cts., 1987-91; vice-chmn. Illini Hosp. Bd., 1988-93, chmn., 1993-95; bd. dirs. Illowa coun. Boy Scouts Am., 1979-83, v.p., 1981-83. With USNR, 1953-57. Mem. Rotary (pres. 1975-76, East Moline, Ill.), Green Medallion, Blue Key, Phi Delta Kappa, Pi Gamma Mu. Home and Office: 6191 Grace Ave Ludington MI 49431-8629

PUGESEK, BRUCE H., statistician; b. Chgo., Aug. 28, 1951; s. Harry John and Jean Pugesek; m. Yolanda Ysasi, Nov. 23, 1988; children: Genevieve, Harrison Bruce. BA in Environ. Biology, U. Mont., Missoula, BS in Zoology, 1973; MS in Zoology & Physiology, U. Wyo., Laramie, 1976; PhD, Bowling Green State U., Ohio, 1982. Rsch. statistician biology USGS Nat. Wetlands Rsch. Ctr., Lafayette, La., 1990—2000, USGS Northern Rocky Moutain Sci. Ctr., Bozeman, Mont., 2000—; postdoc. fellow NIH Pa. State U., State Coll., 1987—90; asst. prof. Dept. Biology, Purdue U., West Lafayette, Ind., 1984—87; postdoc. assoc. Bowling Green State U., 1982—84. Author: (book) Structural Equation Modeling: Applications in ecological and evolutionary biology (Superior Svc. award, 1991, 1992, additional Superior Svc. awards, 1993, 1994, 1995, 1997, 1999); contbr. articles to profl. jours. Recipient Rsch. support awards, Nat. Inst. Aging, 1987—90; Doctoral Dissertation Improvement grant, NSF, 1979—80, Paul Stewart grant, Wilson Ornitholgical Soc., 1979—80, grant, Sigma Xi, 1979—80, Frank N. Chapman meml. grant, Am. Mus. Natural History, 1984, Internal funding grant, Dept. Interior, 1990—. Achievements include discovery of fractal nature of climate patterns, disease pandemics. Avocations: hiking, fishing, baseball. Office: Northern Rocky Mountain Sci Ctr 1648 S 7th Ave MSU Bozeman MT 59717 Office Fax: 406-994-6416. Business E-Mail: bpugesek@usgs.gov.

PUGH, ARTHUR JAMES (JAY PUGH), retired retail executive; b. Glen Morrison, W.Va., Sept. 24, 1937; s. Arthur James and Mary Pugh; m. Sharon Hubacher, Sept. 26, 1961; children: James Gregory, Mary Elizabeth. BSBA, W.Va. U., 1959; Master of Retailing, U. Pitts., 1960. Mgmt. trainee, buyer Woodward & Lothrop, Washington, 1960-71, v.p., 1971-77, sr. v.p., 1977-80, exec. v.p., 1980-87, Coun. of Better Bus. Bur., Arlington, Va., 1987-90, bd. dir.; cons., bd. dir. Fairfax, Va., 1990—. Trustee, chmn. audit com. Calvert Mut. Funds, Washington, 1983—; bd. dirs. Acacia Capital Corp., Washington; bd. dirs., exec. com. compensation com., chmn. investment com. Acacia Fed. Savs. Bank, Falls Church, Va. Chmn. bd. dirs. Better Bus. Bur. Met. Washington, 1987. Mem. Rotary Found. of Washington (pres. 1990-91), Nat. Retail Mchts. Assn. (bd. dirs. 1986), W.Va. U. Alumni Assn. (bd. dirs. 1993-98), Fairfax Country Club (bd. dirs. 1990-92), Rotary Club of Washington (Rotarian of Yr. 1982, pres. 1984). Republican. Presbyterian. Avocations: golf, skiing, swimming. Home and Office: 4823 Prestwick Dr Fairfax VA 22030-4533 Office Phone: 703-385-1312. Personal E-mail: jaypugh@prodigy.net.

PUGH, BRYAN, retail company marketing executive; Mgr., mktg. Arkansas State U.; asst. store mgr., Sam's Club divsn. Wal-Mart Stores Inc., v.p., membership mktg.; purchasing CP Group of Asia, 1993—99; with Tesco Thailand; worked with fresh & easy neighborhood markets Tesco USA, co. v.p., fresh & easy neighborhood markets, 2005—08; v.p., format devel. & merchandising Walgreen Co., 2009—. Office: Walgreen Co 200 Wilmot Rd Deerfield IL 60015 Office Phone: 847-914-2500. Office Fax: 847-914-2804.*

PUGH, CARLA M., surgeon, educator; b. Oakland, Calif., Feb. 3, 1966; d. Tillman and Helen (Abram) Pugh; m. Joseph D. Towles, Aug. 16. BA, U. Calif., Berkeley, 1988; MD, Howard U., Washington, 1992; PhD, Stanford U., Calif., 2001. Surg. intern Howard U. Hosp., 1992—93, resident in surgery, 1993—97; staff surgeon Kaiser Med. Group, Redwood City, Calif., 1998—2003; rsch. assoc. Stanford U. Sch. Med., 2002—03; assoc. dir., asst. prof. edn. and surgery Northwestern U., Chgo., 2003—; staff surgeon Chgo. VA Westside, 2004—. Office: Ste 650 676 N St Clair Chicago IL 60611-3197 Office Phone: 312-695-0641, 312-695-1414.

PUGH, DAVID L., manufacturing executive; b. Lynchburg, Va. m. Barbara Pugh; 2 children. BSEE, Duke U. Former chief mktg. officer, v.p. and gen. mgr. power equipment bus. unit Square D Co.; former plant mgr., v.p. constrn. sales Westinghouse Electric Corp.; sr. v.p. indsl control group Rockwell Automation, 1994-99; pres., COO Applied Indsl. Technologies, Cleve., 1999-2000, chmn., CEO, 2000—. Bd. dir. J.L.G. Industries, R.W. Beckett Corp. Office: Applied Indsl Technologies 1 Applied Plz 3301 Euclid Ave Cleveland OH 44115

PUGH, DOROTHY GUNTHER, performing company executive; b. Memphis, May 8, 1951; Grad. magna cum laude, Vanderbilt U., 1973; studied with Raymond Clay, studied with Donna Carver, studied with David Howard; student, Royal Acad. Dancing, London. Founder Ballet Memphis, 1985, also artistic dir., 1985—. Panelist Nat. Endowment for the Arts. Recipient Woman of Achievement award for Initiative, 1987, Gordon Holl Artistic Adminstr. of Yr. award, State of Tenn., 1999; named one of city's influential citizens, Memphis Mag.; fellowship Ctr. Social Innovation, STanford U. Office: Ballet Memphis 7950 Trinity Cordova TN 38018 E-mail: info@balletmemphis.com.*

PUGH, EMERSON WILLIAM, electrical engineer; b. Pasadena, Calif., May 1, 1929; s. Emerson Martindale and Ruth Hazel (Edgin) P.; m. Elizabeth Burnam Russell; children: William Russell, Sarah Elizabeth, David Emerson. BS in Physics, Carnegie Mellon U., 1951, PhD in Physics, 1956. Asst. prof. physics Carnegie Mellon U., Pitts., 1956-57; with IBM, 1957-93, rsch. staff mem. rsch. div., Poughkeepsie, N.Y., 1957-61, engring. mgr. components div., 1962-65, group dir. data processing group, Harrison, N.Y., 1965-66, dir. tech. planning rsch. div., Yorktown Heights, N.Y., 1966-68, asst. to v.p. IBM Corp., Armonk, N.Y., 1968-71, rsch. mgr. rsch. div., Yorktown Heights, 1971-85, mgr. tech. history, 1985-93. Vis. scientist IBM Lab., Zurich, Switzerland, 1961-62; mem. United Engring. Trustees Bd., N.Y.C., 1986-92; mem. Engring. Soc. Libr. Bd., N.Y.C., 1986-89; trustee Charles Babbage Found., 1990-2006, Samuel Morse Hist. Site, 1998-99. Author: Principles of Electricity and Magnetism, 1960, Memories That Shaped an Industry, 1984, IBM's Early Computers, 1986, IBM's 360 and Early 370 Systems, 1991, Building IBM, 1995; also articles; 10 patents. Fellow IEEE (v.p. 1986-87, pres. 1989, chmn. friends com. Ctr. for History Elec. Engring. 1991-94, chmn. history com. 1995-98, dir. found. 1996-2005, pres. found. 2000-04 treas. trustees History Ctr., 2006—), AAAS, Am. Phys. Soc. Home: 3 Rock St Cold Spring NY 10516-2911

PUGH, GEORGE WILLARD, law educator; b. Napoleonville, La., Aug. 17, 1925; s. William Whitmell and Evelyn (Foley) P.; m. Jean Earle Hemphill, Sept. 6, 1952; children: William Whitmell III, George Willard Jr., David Nicholls, James Hemphill. BA, La. State U., Baton Rouge, 1947, JD, 1950; J.S.D., Yale U., New Haven, Conn., 1952; Dr. h.c., U. Aix-Marseille III, France, 1984. Bar: La. 1950. Instr. La. State U. Law Sch., 1950, mem. faculty, 1952-94, prof. law, 1959-94, Julius B. Nachman prof. law, 1984-94; prof. law emeritus, 1994—. Faculty U. Thessaloniki Greece 1974, Aix-en-Provence, France, 1985, 91; faculty U. San Diego, Paris, 1977; rsch. cons. La. State Law Inst., 1953-54; 1st jud. adminstr. Jud. Coun. Supreme Ct. La., 1954-56; vis. prof. U. Tex., 1961; vis. Doherty prof. law U. Va., 1966-67; faculty orientation program in Am. law Assn. Am. Law Schs., 1968, law teaching clinic, 1969; vis. prof. U. Aix-Marseille III, France, 1983, 1987, U. Catholique de Louvain, Belgium, 1987; cons. La. State U.S. Vietnam Legal Adminstrn. Project, 1969; coord., reporter Code of Evidence for La., 1981-95. Author: Louisiana Evidence Law, 1974, supplement, 1978; co-author: Cases and Materials on the Adminstration of Criminal Justice, 2d edit., 1969, Handbook on Louisiana Evidence Law, 1989, 21th edit., 2009. Bd. dirs. Legal Aid Soc. Baton Rouge, 1965-89, chmn., 1963-64; adv. bd. St. Alban's Episcopal Student Ctr., La. State U., 1965-68, 70-72. Served with AUS, World War II. Named George W. and Jean H. Pugh Inst. for Justice in his honor, La. State U. Law Ctr., 1997; fellow, Comparative Study Adminstrn. Justice, 1962—65. Mem. Am., La., Baton Rouge bar assns., Order of Coif, Omicron Delta Kappa, Lambda Chi Alpha. Democrat. Episcopalian. Home: 167 Sunset Blvd Baton Rouge LA 70808-5073

PUGH, RICHARD CRAWFORD, lawyer, educator; b. Phila., Apr. 28, 1929; s. William and Myrtle P.; m. Nanette Bannen, Feb. 27, 1954; children: Richard Crawford, Andrew Lembert, Catherine Elizabeth. AB summa cum laude, Dartmouth Coll., 1951; BA in Jurisprudence, Oxford U., Eng., 1953; LLB, Columbia U., 1958. Bar: N.Y. 1958. Assoc. firm Cleary, Gottlieb, Steen & Hamilton, NYC, 1958—61, ptnr., 1969—89; disting. prof. law U. San Diego, 1989—2009, univ. prof., 1998—99. Mem. faculty Law Sch. Columbia U., 1961-89, prof., 1964-69, adj. prof., 1969-89; lectr. Columbia-Amsterdam-Leyden (Netherlands) summer program Am. law, 1963, 79; dep. asst. atty. gen. tax div. U.S. Dept. Justice, 1966-68; Cons. fiscal and fin. br. UN Secretariat, 1962, 64. Editor: Columbia Law Rev., 1957—58; co-editor: Legal Aspects of Foreign Investment, 1959; co-author: International Law, 2001, Taxation of Business Enterprises, 2002, Taxation of International Transactions, 2006. With USNR, 1954—56. Rhodes scholar, 1951-53. Mem. ABA, Am. Law Inst., Am. Coll. Tax Counsel, Internat. Fiscal Assn. (pres. U.S. br. 1978-79). Home: 7335 Encelia Dr La Jolla CA 92037-5729 Office: U San Diego Sch Law Alcala Park San Diego CA 92110-2429 Office Phone: 619-260-2322. Business E-Mail: rpugh@sandiego.edu.

PUGH, THOMAS WILFRED, lawyer; b. St. Paul, Aug. 3, 1949; s. Thomas Leslie and Joann Marie (Tauer) P.; m. Susan Elizabeth Beattie, Sept. 12, 1971; children: Aimee Elizabeth, Douglas Thomas. AB cum laude, Dartmouth Coll., 1971; JD cum laude, U. Minn., 1976. Assoc. Thuet & Lynch, South St. Paul, 1976-79; ptnr. Thuet, Lynch & Pugh, South St. Paul, 1980-85; atty., pres. Thuet, Pugh, Rogosheske & Atkins, Ltd., South St. Paul, 1986—2007; mem. Minn. Ho. of Reps., St. Paul, 1989—2004, Dem. leader, 1999—2002; commr. Minn. Pub. Utilities Commn., 2004—. Mem. Supreme Ct. Task Force Conciliation Ct., St. Paul, 1992, Dakota County Tech. Coll. Adv. Bd., 1991-96. Bd. dirs. Wakota Arena, South St. Paul, 1984-87; pres. Luther Meml. Ch., South St. Paul, 1983-84. Daniel Webster scholar Dartmouth Coll., 1970, Rufus Choate scholar, 1971. Mem. Minn. State Bar Assn., 1st Dist. Bar Assn., Ducks Unltd., Pheasants Forever, South St. Paul C. of C. (local issues chair 1982, Dedicated Svc. award 1983), South St. Paul Jaycees (pres. 1978-79, Key award 1979), Lions. Lutheran. Avocations: tennis, golf, hunting, fishing, reading. Office: 121-7th Place E Saint Paul MN 55101

PUGSLEY, MICHAEL KENNETH, cardiac pharmacologist, research scientist; b. Burnaby, BC, Can., Aug. 28, 1967; came to U.S., 1995; s. Kenneth Richard and Mary Agnes Pugsley; m. Suzanne Pugsley, Aug. 23, 1997. BSc, U. B.C., Vancouver, 1989, MSc, 1992, PhD, 1995. Postdoctoral rsch. fellow U. Calif., Irvine, 1995-98; rsch. scientist II Xoma (US) LLC, Berkeley, Calif., 1998-2000, sr. scientist, 2001—. Cons. Nortran Pharms., Vancouver, 1995-98, Chem. Works of Gedeon Richter, 1994-98; vis. rsch. fellow Australian Nat. U., Canberra, 1993. Editor, author: Methods in Cardiac Electrophysiology, 1997, Methods in Vascular Pharmacology, 2000; mem. editl. bd. Jour. Pharmacology and Toxicology Methods, Cardiovasc. Toxicology; contbr. articles to profl. jours. including Circulatory Shock, Brit. Jour. Pharmacology, European Jour. Pharmacology, Jour. Pharmacol. & Toxicol. Methods, Cardiovasc. Rsch., Cardiovasc. Drug Revs., Biochemica Biophysica Acta, Life Scis., Clin. and Exptl. Cardiology, Pharmacol. Rsch. Grantee Heart & Stroke Found. (Can.), 1992, 93, 94; recipient scholarship B.C. Med. Svcs. Found,. 1994, Sci. Coun. B.C., 1994; postdoctoral fellow Med. Rsch. Coun. Can, 1995-98. Mem.: Internat. Complement Soc., Internat. Soc. for Heart Rsch., Western Pharmacology Soc. (pres.-elect), Brit. Pharmacol. Soc., Cardiac Electrophysiology Soc., Am. Assn. for Lab. Animal Sci., Safety Pharmacol. Soc., Am. Heart Assn. Avocations: walking, ice hockey, reading, skiing, golf. Office: Xoma (US) LLC Dept Pharmacol & Toxicol 2910 7th St Berkeley CA 94710-2700 Home: 40 Churchhill Downs Dr Tinton Falls NJ 07724-3804 Fax: 510-841-7805.

PUGSLEY, ROBERT ADRIAN, law educator; b. Mineola, NY, Dec. 27, 1946; s. Irvin Harold and Mary Catherine P. BA, SUNY-Stony Brook, 1968; JD, NYU, 1975, LLM in Criminal Justice, 1977. Instr. sociology New Sch. Social Rsch., NYC, 1969-71; coord. Peace Edn. programs The Christophers, NYC, 1971-78; assoc. prof. law Southwestern U., LA, 1978-81, prof., 1981—, Paul E. Treusch prof. law, 2000-01. Adj. asst. prof. criminology and criminal justice Southampton Coll.-Long Island U., 1975-76; acting dep. dir. Criminal Law Edn. and Rsch. Ctr., NYU, 1983-86; bd. advisors Ctr. Legal Edn. CCNY-CUNY, 1978, Sta. KPFK-FM, 1985-86; founder, coord. The Wednesday Evening Soc., L.A., 1979-86; vis. prof. Jacob D. Fuchsberg Law Ctr. Touro Coll., L.I., N.Y., summers, 1988, 89; lectr. in criminal law and procedure Legal Edn. Conf. Ctr., L.A., 1982-96; prof., dir. Comparative Criminal Law and Procedure Program U. B.C., Vancouver, summers, 1994, 98-2003; chair pub. interest law com. Southwestern U., 1990-2001; lectr. legal profl. responsibility West Bar Rev. Faculty, Calif., 1996-98; legal analyst/commentator for print and electronic media, 1992—. Creative advisor (syndicated TV program) Christopher Closeup, 1975-83; host (cable TV) Earth Alert, 1983-87; prodr., moderator (TV program) Inside L.A., Sta. KPFK-FM, 1979-86, Open Jour. program, Sta. KPFK-FM, 1991-94; contbr. articles to profl. jours. Founding mem. Southwestern U. Pub. Interest Law com., 1992—; mem. L.A. County Bar Assn. Adv. Com. on Alcohol & Drug Abuse, 1991-95, co-chair, 1993-95; mem. exec. com. non-govtl. orgns. UN Office Pub. Info., 1977; mem. issues task force L.A. Conservancy, 1980-81, seminar for law tchrs. NEH UCLA, 1979; co-convenor So. Calif. Coalition Against Death Penalty, 1981-83, convener, 1983-84; mem. death penalty com. Lawyer's Support Group, Amnesty Internat., U.S.A.; founding mem. Ch.-State Coun., L.A., 1984-88; bd. dirs. Equal Rights Sentencing Found., 1983-85, Earth Alert, Inc., 1984-87; mem. adv. bd. First Amendment Info. Resources Ctr., Grad. Sch. Libr. and Info. Scis., UCLA, 1990—; mem. coun. Friends UCLA Libr., 1993—, pres., 1996-2002; mem. adv. bd. Project Prevention, 1998-. Robert Marshall fellow Criminal Law Edn. and Rsch. Ctr., NYU Sch. Law, 1976-78. Mem. ABA (sect. criminal justice 1978-, Ctr. Profl. Responsibility 1995-), Am. Legal Studies Assn., Am. Soc. Polit. and Legal Philosophy, Assn. Am. Law Schs., Inst. Soc. Ethics and Life Scis., Soc. Am. Law Tchrs., Internat. Platform Assn., Internat. Soc. Reform of Criminal Law, The Scribes. Democrat. Roman Catholic. Office: Southwestern U Sch Law 675 S Westmoreland Ave Los Angeles CA 90005-3905 Office Phone: 213-738-6757. Business E-Mail: rpugsley@swlaw.edu.

PUIG, CARLOS J., plastic surgeon; b. Camden, NJ, July 21, 1946; married. DO, Chgo. Coll. Osteo. Medicine, 1972. Diplomate Am. Bd. Emergency Medicine, 1996, Am. Bd. Hair Restoration Surgery, 1998. Med. dir. Puig Med. Group, Hosuton, 1976—2000; assoc. med. dir. Med. Hair Restoration, Maitland, Fla., 2002—08; med. dir. Physician Hair Restoration Ctr., Katy, Tex., 2008—. Pres. Am. Hair Loss Coun., Chgo., 1996—97, Am. Bd. Hair Restoration Surgery, Lansing, Ill., 2001—02; chair, physician tng. task force ISHRS, Geneva, 2005—07; Govs. bd. Internat. Soc. Hair Restoraiton Surgery, Geneva, 2007—. Author: Core Competencies in Hair Restoration Surgery, Scalp Reduction: The Key to Optimizing Donor Area, Planned Decompression., Hairline with Ridge Line, New Instrumentation for Scalp Reduction, Hair Transplantation for Congenital Alopecia, Hairline Sculpting with Integrated Line grafting and Single; contbr. chapters to books to profl. jours. Bd. mem. & spl. projects team leader Living Water Internat., Houston, 1996—2005. Maj. US Army, 1968—76. Mem.: ISHRS (bd. Govs. 2007). Avocations: jazz, music, horseback riding. Office: Physician's Hair Restoration Ctr 23501 Cinco Ranch Blvd Suite G205 Katy TX 77494 Office Fax: 281-34734250. Personal E-mail: cpuig@jazzperformances.com. Business E-Mail: cpuig@hairdoctexas.com.

PUIG, STEVE, ancient language educator; MA, UNC-Chapel Hill, NC, 2004. Tchg. fellow UNC-Chapel Hill, 2001—04; adj. lectr. Hunter Coll., New York, 2005—. Business E-Mail: spuig@gc.cuny.edu.

PUJOLS, ALBERT (JOSE ALBERTO PUJOLS), professional baseball player; b. Santo Domingo, Dominican Republic, Jan. 16, 1980; naturalized, US, 2007; m. Deidre Pujols, Jan. 1, 2000; children: Isabella, Albert Jr., Sophia. Attended, Maple Woods CC, Kansas City, Mo., 1999. First baseman St. Louis Cardinals, 2001—. First baseman, Dominican Republic nat. team World Baseball Classic, 2006; co-owner Patrick's Restaurant, Maryland Heights, Mo. Founder Pujols Family Found., 2005. Recipient Silver Slugger award, Maj. League Baseball, 2001, 2003, 2004, 2008, Hank Aaron award, 2003, Gold Glove award, 2006, Roberto Clemente award, 2008; named Nat. League Rookie of Yr., 2001, Maj. League Player of Yr., 2003, Nat. League Championship Series MVP, 2004, Nat. League MVP, 2005, 2008, Best Maj. League Baseball Player, ESPY awards, 2005, 2006, Best Internat. Player, 2006, Man of Yr., Players Choice awards, 2006; named to Nat. League All-Star Team, Maj. League Baseball, 2001, 2003—09. Achievements include leading the National League in: batting average, hits, doubles, 2003; runs, 2003, 2004, 2005; member of the World Series Champion St. Louis Cardinals, 2006; becoming the first player in Major League Baseball history to hit 30 or more home runs in first nine seasons, 2009. Mailing: c/o St Louis Cardinals Busch Stadium 250 Stadium Plz Saint Louis MO 63102*

PULEO, FRANK CHARLES, lawyer; b. Montclair, NJ, Nov. 25, 1945; s. Frank and Kathren (Despenzerie) Puleo; m. Alice Kathren Leek, June 1, 1968; children: Frank C., Richard James. BSE cum laude, Princeton U., 1967; JD, NYU, 1970. Bar: NY 1971. Assoc. Milbank, Tweed, Hadley & McCloy, NYC, 1970—76, ptnr., 1976—, mem. exec. com., 1982—91, 1996—2002. Co-chmn. Global Fin. Group; bd. dirs. Capital Markets Engring. and Trading Holdings LLC., SLM Corp., Comml. Indsl. Fin. Corp., Apollo Investment Corp., 2008—. Lectr. Columbia U. Sch. of Law, 1997—2001. Mem.: ABA (mem. com. on fed. regulation securities), NY State Bar Assn. Office: Apollo Investment Corp 9 W 57th St New York NY 10019 Office Phone: 212-515-3450. Business E-Mail: fpuleo@milbank.com.

PULGRAM, WILLIAM LEOPOLD, architect, space designer; b. Vienna, Jan. 1, 1921; came to U.S., 1940; s. Sigmund and Gisela (Bauer) P.; married, Jan. 12, 1952; children: Deirdre, Laurence, Anthony, Christopher. BS, Ga. Inst. Tech., 1949, BArch, 1950; postgrad., Ecole des Beaux Arts, Fontainebleau, France, 1951. Archtl. designer various firms, Atlanta, 1951-58; assoc., chief interior design FABR&P, Atlanta, 1958-63; exec. v.p., gen. mgr. Associated Space Design Inc., Atlanta,

1963-70, pres., CEO, 1971-85, chmn., CEO, 1985-86, chmn. emeritus, 1986-88; arch., cons. Atlanta, 1988—. Cons. UN, 1986; com. mem. NAS, 1980-84; lectr. at colls., univs., U.S. and abroad. Author: Designing the Automated Office, 1984, Japanese transl., 1985; contbr. articles to jours. in field. Mem., lectr. High Mus. Art, Atlanta, 1970—. With U.S. Army, 1943-46. Named to Hall of Fame Interior Design mag., 1986. Fellow AIA (chmn. interiors 1978-84, archtl. res. coun. AIA Found. 1983-85); mem. Archs., Designers and Planners for Social Responsibility (nat. bd. dirs. 1989-93), Am. Soc. Interior Designers, Atlanta C. of C., Atlanta City Club, Lake Lanier Sailing Club. Mem. Unitarian Universalist Ch. Home and Office: W L Pulgram FAIA Cons 4317 E Conway Dr NW Atlanta GA 30327-3528 Office Phone: 404-255-8514. Business E-Mail: pulgramga@mindspring.com.

PULHAMUS, MARLENE LOUISE, retired elementary school educator; b. Paterson, NJ, Sept. 11, 1937; d. David Weeder and Elfrieda (Ehler) Wemmell; m. Aaron R. Pulhamus, Aug. 20, 1960; children: Steven, Thomas, Nancy. Student, Trenton State U., 1957; BS, William Paterson U., 1959; postgrad., Rutgers U., 1992. Cert. elem. tchr., NJ. Kindergarten tchr. Wayne Bd. Edn., NJ, 1959-63, Paterson Bd. Edn., 1974-75, 2d grade tchr., 1975-81; basic skills instr. Paterson Pub. Schs., 1981—, tchr. accelerated program 1st grade, 1992—; cons. lang. arts, literacy Kendall Hunt Pegasus, Wayne; ret., 1997. Trainer for insvc. groups of learning ctrs. and math. with manipulatives for local pub. schs., trainer for local pub. schs, exec. bd. mem. Quilts ASP & Habitat Appalachian Svc. Project Habitat Humanity, Salisbury, Md. Contbr. Lessons 4Mat in Action, 3d edit., 4Mat: A Quest for Wholeness, 1977—. Pres. Friends of Eisenhower Libr., Totowa, NJ, 1975-77; coord. ch. sch. Preakness Reformed Ch., Wayne, 1990-93, Elder, chair outreach commn.; sec. VTTC Homeowners Assn., Salisbury, Md. Recipient Gov.'s award for tchg. excellence State of NJ Commn. Edn., 1991, 4Mation program award, 1994; named Woman of Yr., 2007, Salisbury, 2008. Mem. ASCD, NEA, AAUW, Nat. Coun. Tchrs. Math., Nat. Assn. for Edn. Young Children, NJ Edn. Assn., Passaic County Edn. Assn., Paterson Edn. Assn. (mem. exec. bd., 1985-89, legis. chmn. 1986-89), Altar Guild (v.p., 2007-), VMW (v.p. 2007-2008). Personal E-mail: mylilycat@verizon.net.

PULIAFITO, CARMEN ANTHONY, dean, ophthalmologist, healthcare executive; b. Buffalo, Jan. 5, 1951; s. Dominic F. and Marie A. (Nigro) P.; m. Janet H. Pine, May 19, 1979 AB cum laude, Harvard Coll., 1973, MD magna cum laude, 1978; MBA, U. Pa., 1997. Diplomate Am. Bd. Ophthalmology. Intern Faulkner Hosp., Tufts U. Sch. Medicine, 1978-79; resident Mass. Eye and Ear Infirmary, Boston, 1979-82, retina fellow, 1982-83; instr. Harvard Med. Sch., Boston, 1983-85, asst. prof., 1985-89, assoc. prof., 1989-91, dir. divsn. continuing edn. dept. ophthalmology, 1989-91; dir. Bascon Palmer Eye Inst., Miami, 2001—07; dean Keck Sch. Medicine, U. So. Calif., LA, 2007—. Vis. scientist MIT Regional Laser Ctr., Cambridge, 1982—, asst. prof. health scis. and tech. program, 1987-89, assoc. prof., 1989-91; mem. staff Mass. Eye and Ear Infirmary, Boston, 1983; dir. Morse Laser Ctr., Mass. Eye and Ear Infirmary, 1986-91, dir. New Eng. Eye Ctr., 1991-2001; prof., chmn. dept. ophthalmology Tufts U. Sch. Medicine, 1991-2001, prof. ophthalmology and health mgmt., 1997-2001; adj. prof. biomed. engring. Tufts U., 1991—; chmn. med. bd. New Eng. Med. Ctr. Hosps., 1994-95, ophthalmologist in chief, 1991-2001; assoc. examiner Am. Bd. Ophthalmology, 1990—; sr. v.p. for network devel. Lifespan, 1997-2001; prof., chmn. dept. ophthalmology U. Miami Sch. Medicine, 2001—; med. dir. Anne Bates Leach Eye Hosp., 2001—. Author: (with D. Albert) Foundations of Ophthalmic Pathology, 1979, (with R. Steinert) Principles and Practice of Ophthalmic YAG Laser Surgery, 1984, Lasers in Surgery and Medicine: Principles and Practice, 1996, (with M.R. Hee, J.S. Schuman and J.G. Fujimoto) Optical Coherence Tomography of Ocular Diseases, 1996, (with E. Reichel) Atlas of Indocyanine Green Angiography, 1996; editor-in-chief Lasers in Surgery and Medicine, 1987-95, Ophthalmic Surgery and Lasers, 1995—; contbr. about 120 articles to profl. jours. Pres. Am. Soc. for Laser Medicine and Surgery, 1994-95; v.p. Mass. Soc. Eye Physicians and Surgeons, 1994-96; assoc. examiner Am. Bd. Ophthalmology, 1990—; retina trustee Assn. Rsch. in Vision and Ophthalmology, 1995-99, pres., 2000-01. Recipient Richard and Hinda Rosenthal award in visual scis., 1994, Man of Vision award Boston Aid to the Blind, 1993, Leon Goldman award Biomed. Optics Soc., 1993, I Migliori award Pirandello Lyceum of Mass., 1994. Fellow Am. Acad. Ophthalmology, Am. Soc. for Laser Medicine and Surgery (pres. 1994-95); mem. Assn. Rsch. in Vision and Ophthalmology (pres.-elect 1998-99, pres. 1999-2000, immediate past pres. 2000-2001), Mass. Soc. Eye Physicians and Surgeons (v.p. 1994-96). Roman Catholic. Office: Keck Sch Medicine U So Calif 1975 Zonal Ave Los Angeles CA 90033 Office Phone: 323-442-1900. Office Fax: 323-442-2724. Business E-Mail: deanksom@usc.edu, cpuliafito@usc.edu.

PULIDO, MIGUEL ANGEL, Mayor, Santa Ana, California; b. Mex. City, 1956; m. Laura Pulido; children: Miguel Robert, David Andrew, Isabel. BSME, Calif. State U., Fullerton. V.p. McCaughey & Smith Energy Assocs., dir. computer program; mayor City of Santa Ana, Calif., 1986—. Mem. Santa Ana Redevel. Agy.; bd. dirs. Orange County Transp. Authority, mem. 1st dist. Santa Ana rep. Orange County Transp. Authority; bd. dir. Calif. Workforce Investment, Bowers Mus., Discovery Sci. Ctr. Orange County, Pacific Symphony Orch., UCI Found., Fed. Inter-Govtl. Policy Adv. Com. Trade, Fullerton Cmty. Bank, Great Park Corp., South Coast Air Quality Mgmt. Dist. Achievements include becoming the first Latino mayor in the city's history; development of the Mayor's Task Force on Arts and Culture. Avocations: chess, backgammon, tennis, music, guitar. Office: Office Mayor & City Coun 20 Civic Ctr Plaza PO Box 1988 M31 Santa Ana CA 92702-1988 Address: Pulido for Mayor 401 E 1st St Santa Ana CA 92701 Fax: 714-647-6954. Business E-Mail: mpulido@santa-ana.org. E-mail: mpulido@ci.santa-ana.ca.us, pulidoformayor@gmail.com.

PULIKOLLU, RAJASEKHAR VENKATA, materials engineer, researcher; b. Nidubrollu, Andhra Pradesh, India, Oct. 13, 1977; s. Subbarayudu and Nagavardhani Pulikollu; life ptnr. Lavanya Pulikollu, June 29, 2007. BS in Mech. Engring., Osmania U., Hyderabad, India, 2000; MS in Materials Sci., Wright State U., Dayton, Ohio, 2001, PhD in Engring., 2005. Rsch. asst. Wright State U., 2000—05, tchg. asst., 2001—02; lead engr. VEXTEC, Brentwood, Tenn., 2005—. Contbr. articles to profl. jours. Scholarship, Dayton Area Grad. Studies Inst., 2003—05, Am. Soc. for Metals, 2004, 2005. Mem.: Internat. Profl. Hon. Soc. for Materials Sci. and Engring., Am. Ceramic Soc., Am. Soc. Metals and Materials, Materials and Metals Soc., Alpha Sigma Mu (Ohio Epsilon chpt.). Achievements include development of probabilistic microstructural based fatigue simulation software; nanoscale coatings for control of nanotube growth; nanoscale coatings for masking or patterning of metal interconnects in the fabrication industry; a new technique for the measurement of intergranular stress fields in ceramics; research in the modification of interfaces in lightweight composites; high temperature superconductors; design and certification of structural components. Office: Vextec 750 Old Hickory Blvd Bldg #2 Brentwood TN 37027 Home: 1709 Enclave Cir Nashville TN 37211 Personal E-mail: psnraja@yahoo.com. Business E-Mail: rpulikollu@vextec.com.

PULITZER, EMILY RAUH (MRS. JOSEPH PULITZER JR.), art historian, consultant; b. Cin., July 23, 1933; d. Frederick and Harriet (Frank) Rauh; m. Joseph Pulitzer Jr., 1973 (dec. 1993). AB, Bryn Mawr Coll., Pa., 1955; student, Ecole du Louvre, Paris, 1955-56; MA, Harvard U., Cambridge, Mass., 1963; LHD honoris causa (hon.), U. Mo., St. Louis, 1989; DFA honoris causa (hon.), Aquinas Inst., St. Louis, 2002, St. Louis U., 2003; HHD honoris causa (hon.), Washington U., St. Louis, 2005. Mem. staff Cin. Art Mus., 1956-57; asst. curator drawings Harvard U. Fogg Art Mus., 1957-64, asst. to dir., 1962-63; curator City Art Mus., St. Louis, 1964-73; mem. painting and sculpture com. Mus. Modern Art, 1985—, trustee, 1994—, vice chair paintings and sculpture com., 1996—, mem. drawings com., 2003—; chmn. visual arts com. Mo. Arts Coun., 1976-81; bd. mem. Inst. Mus. Svcs., 1979-84; commr. St. Louis Art Mus., 1981-88, vice chmn., 1988, chair, collection com., 2007—; bd. dir. Pulitzer, Inc., 1993—2005; founder, chmn. of bd. dirs. Pulitzer Found. for the Arts, 2001—. Bd. dirs. Contemporary Art Mus., St. Louis, 1980-83, 2004-, pres., 1990-95; bd. dirs. Mark Rothko Found., 1980-89, Grand Ctr., 1993-95, 99—, arts strategy com. chair, 2003—; bd. trustees St. Louis Symphony Orch., 1994-2004, bd. overseers, 2005—; bd. dirs. arts in transit com. Bi-State Devel. Agy., vice-chmn. and co-founder, 1987-98; mem. Leadership St. Louis, 1990-91; trustee Mus. Modern Art, 1994—; mem. overseer's com. to visit the art mus. Harvard U., 1990—, chair, 2004—, mem. collections com., 1992—, chair, 1992-2004, mem. Fogg Fellows, 1978—, co-chair, 1978-94, bd. overseers, 2006—, pres.'s adv. com. on Allston Initiative, 2005—. Recipient St. Louis award, Contbn. to Arts Cmty., 2003, MacDowell Colony, 2005, Gertrude Vanderbilt Whitney award, Skowhegan, 2006; named one of Top 200 Collectors, ARTnews Mag., 2003—. Mem. Am. Fedn. Arts (dir. 1976-89), St. Louis Mercantile Libr. Assn. (bd. dirs. 1987-93), Mo. Women's Forum.

PULLEN, DAVID JOHN, physicist, researcher; b. Merton, Surrey, Eng., June 28, 1936; came to U.S. 1963; s. Arthur Lester and Alexandra Q. (Griffiths) P.; m. Heather Morgan, Aug. 6, 1960; children: Katrina, Adrian, Lester, Andrew. BSc first class, London U., 1958; DPhil, Oxford U., Eng., 1963. "1851" rsch. fellow Oxford U., 1961-63; instr. MIT, 1963-65; asst. prof. physics U. Pa., Phila., 1965-70; assoc. prof. Lowell (Mass.) Tech. Inst., 1970-73; prof. physics U. Mass. Lowell, 1973—2002, prof. emeritus, 2002—. Ptnr. CPS Nuc., 1990—; cons. Internat. Atomic Energy Agy., Vienna, 1991—99. Author: Physics Laboratory Experiments, 1975, 7th edit., 2008; inducted in Mass. Hall of Fame, Sci. Educators, 2003, contbr. over 70 articles to profl. jours. Royal Commn. for Exhbn. of 1851 rsch. fellowship, 1961-63. Mem. Am. Phys. Soc., Am. Assn. Physics Tchrs., Sigma Xi. Home: 2 Reeves Rd Bedford MA 01730-1335 Office: U Mass Lowell 1 University Ave Lowell MA 01854-5009 Office Phone: 978-934-3765. Business E-Mail: david_pullen@uml.edu.

PULLEN, PENNY LYNNE, non-profit organization administrator, state legislator; b. Buffalo, Mar. 2, 1947; d. John William and Alice Nettie (McConkey) P. BA in Speech, U. Ill., 1969. Tv technician Office Instnl. Resources, U. Ill., 1966-68; cmty. newspaper reporter Des Plaines (Ill.) Pub. Co., 1967-72; legis. asst. to Ill. legislators, 1968-77; mem. Ill. Ho. of Reps., 1977-93, chmn. ho. exec. com., 1981-82, minority whip, 1983-87, asst. minority leader, 1987-93; pres., founder Life Advocacy Resource Project, Arlington Heights, Ill., 1992—. Exec. dir. Ill. Family Inst., 1993-94; dir. Legal Svcs. Corp., 1989-93; mem. Pres.'s Commn. on AIDS Epidemic, 1987-88; mem. Ill. Goodwill Del. to Republic of China, 1987. Summit conf. observer as mem. adhoc Women for SDI, Geneva, 1985; active Nat. Coun. Ednl. Rsch., 1983—88; dir. Eagle Forum of Ill., 1999—2003, pres., 2003—; del. Rep. Nat. Conv., 1984; mem. Rep. Nat. Com., 1984—88; del. Atlantic Alliance Young Polit. Leaders, Brussels, 1977; pres. Maine Twp. Rep. Women's Club, 1997—99, Rep. Women of Park Ridge, Ill., 2001—03, Rep. Women of Wheeling Twp., Ill., 2004—. Recipient George Washington Honor medal Freedoms Found., 1978, Dwight Eisenhower Freedom medal Chgo. Captive Nations Com., 1977, Outstanding Legislator awards Ill. Press Assn., Ill. Podiatry Soc., Ill. Coroners Assn., Ill. County Clks. Assn., Ill. Hosp. Assn., Ill. Health Care Assn.; named Ill. Young Republican, 1968, Outstanding Young Person, Park Ridge Jaycees, 1981, One of 10 Outstanding Young Persons, Ill. Jaycees, 1981. Mem. DAR, Am. Legis. Exch. Coun. (dir. 1977-91, exec. com. 1978-83, 2d vice chmn. 1980-83), Com. on the Status of Women (sec. 1997—).

PULLEN, RANDY, political organization administrator; MBA, Ariz. State U. CPA Calif., Ariz. Founder Charleston Marina and Shipbuilding, 1979—88; ptnr. Deloitte & Touche, 1988—92; pres. ILX Resorts, Inc., 1992—99; dir. Oasis Partners, LLC; chmn, CEO WageWatch, Inc., 1999—. Co-founder Ariz. Pachyderm Coalition; pres. Rosie's House Music Acad. for Children; chmn. First Class Edn. for Ariz.; bd. dirs. ePropety Tax, Inc. Chmn. Yes On Proposition 200; mem.-at-large Maricopa County Rep. Com.; co-chair fin. com. Ariz. Rep. Party, 2000, chmn., 2007—; nat. committeeman Ariz. Rep. Assembly. Republican. Office: Ariz Rep Party 3501 N 24th St Phoenix AZ 85061 Office Phone: 602-957-7770. Office Fax: 602-224-0932.*

PULLEN, ROBERT W., telecommunications industry executive; BSEE, BS, U. Ill.; MBA, Northwestern U. Elec. engr. Tallabs, Inc., Naperville, Ill., 1985, dir. product mgmt. and mktg. Digital Sys. Divsn., 1993—97, v.p., 1997—2000, sr. v.p. optical networking group, 2000—02, sr. v.p. N.Am. mktg. and sales, 2002—05, sr. v.p. global svcs., 2005—08, pres., CEO, dir., 2008—. Mem.: Electronics Industries Alliance (bd. govs.), Telecom. Industry Assn. (TIA) (chmn. exec. bd.). Office: Tellabs Inc One Tellabs Ctr 1415 W Diehl Rd Naperville IL 60563 Office Phone: 630-798-8800.

PULLEY, LARRY (LAWRENCE B. PULLEY), dean, economics professor; Grad., Coll. William & Mary, 1974; PhD in Econs., U. Va. Asst. prof. econs. Brandeis U.; faculty mem. Mason Sch. Bus., Coll. of William & Mary, 1985—, assoc. dean, 1993—96, dean, T.C. and Elizabeth Clarke prof., 1998—. Contbr. articles to profl. jours. Office: Mason Sch Bus Miller Hall 2039-H PO Box 8795 Williamsburg VA 23187 Office Phone: 757-221-2891. E-mail: Larry.Pulley@mason.wm.edu.*

PULLEY, (J.) WAVERLY. (III), lawyer; b. Franklin, Va., May 19, 1946; BA in English, Univ. Richmond, 1968, JD, 1972. Bar: Va. 1972. Ptnr., capital fin., real estate Hunton & Williams LLP, Richmond, Va. Editor-in-chief Univ. Richmond Law Rev., 1971—72. Fellow: Am. Bar Found.; mem.: ABA, Va. State Bar Assn., McNeill Law Soc., Phi Delta Phi, Omicron Delta Kappa. Office: Hunton & Williams LLP Riverfront Plz East Tower 951 E Byrd St Richmond VA 23219-4074 Office Phone: 804-788-8783. Office Fax: 804-788-8218. Business E-Mail: wpulley@hunton.com.

PULLIAM, KESHIA KNIGHT, actress; b. Newark, Apr. 9, 1979; d. James and Denise P. Pulliam. Degree in Sociology, Spelman Coll., 2001. Actor: (TV series) The Cosby Show, 1984-92, House of Payne, 2007- (Best Supporting Actress in a Comedy Series, NAACP Image award, 2009), (TV films) The Little Match Girl, 1987, Polly, 1989, A Connecticut Yankee in King Arthur's Court, 1989, Polly: Comin' Home!, 1990, What About Your Friends: Weekend Getaway, 2002, Christmas at Water's Edge, 2004, (films) The Last Dragon, 1985, Motives, 2004, Beauty Shop, 2005, The Gospel, 2005, Cuttin Da Mustard, 2008, Death Toll, 2008, Madea Goes to Jail, 2009; TV guest appearances include A Different World, 1987, 1988, Cosby, 1997, Fear Factor, 2002. Office: c/o Endeavor Agency 9601 Wilshire Blvd, 3rd Fl Beverly Hills CA 90212*

PULLIAM, LARRY G., food products executive; b. Grapevine, Tex. m. Cynthia Pulliam; 2 children. With a regional food svc. co., Ft. Worth, 1974—87, Sysco Corp., LA, 1987—91, v.p. ops., 1991—95, exec. v.p., CEO Balt., 1995—97, v.p., chief info. officer Houston, 1997—2000; pres., CEO Sysco Food Services Houston, 2000—02; sr. v.p. mdse. services Sysco Corp., 2002—05, exec. v.p. mdse. services, 2005—07, exec. v.p. sales & global supply chain, 2007—. Mem. dirs. coun. Sysco Corp.; bd. dirs. Capital Bank. Bd. dirs. End Hunger Network. Office: Sysco Corp 1390 Enclave Pky Houston TX 77077-2099*

PULLIKUTH, ASHOK K., research scientist; s. Vasudevan Nambuthodi and Devaki Pullikuth. PhD, U. Calif., Riverside, 1997, postdoc, 1998, St. Louis U. Sch. Medicine, 2001, La. State U., 2007. Rsch. assoc. ICRISAT, Patancheru, Andhra Pradesh, India, 1988—90; rsch. asst. prof. U. Calif., 2001—03; rsch. instr. La. State U., New Orleans, 2008—. Reviewer FASEB Jour., EMBO Jour., Biochem. Pharmacology, Jour. Cell Sci. Contbr. articles to jour. publs. Recipient Reviewer grant, NSERC, Can. Discovery Grant Program, 2007—; Internat. Rotary Predoc fellowship, Rotary Internat., Ill., 1990—93. Mem.: AAAS, Am. Assn. Cell Biology, NY Acad. Scis., Sigma Xi(Calif. Chpt.). Office: LA State Univ HSC 1901 Perdido St New Orleans LA 70112

PULLMAN, BILL, actor; b. Hornell, NY, Dec. 17, 1953; m. Tamara Hurwitz, 1987; children: Maesa, Jack, Louis. BFA, SUNY, Oneonta; MFA, U. Mass., Amherst. Theatre instr. Mont. State U., Bozeman. Actor: (plays) The Rover, 1981, Ah, Wilderness!, 1983, The Old Flag, 1983, Dramathon '84, 1984, Curse of the Starving Class, 1985, All My Sons, 1986, Barabbas, 1986, Nanawatai, 1986, Demon Wine, 1988, Control Freaks, 1993, The Subject Was Roses, 2006, Peter and Jerry, 2007; (Broadway plays) The Goat, or Who Is Sylvia?, 2002; (films) Ruthless People, 1986, Spaceballs, 1987, The Serpent and the Rainbow, 1988, Rocket Gibraltar, 1988, The Accidental Tourist, 1989, Cold Feet, 1989, Brain Dead, 1989, Sibling Rivalry, 1990, Going Under, 1991, Bright Angel, 1991, Newsies, 1992, A League of Their Own, 1992, Singles, 1992, Sommersby, 1993, Sleepless in Seattle, 1993, Malice, 1993, Mr. Jones, 1993, The Favor, 1994, Wyatt Earp, 1994, While You Were Sleeping, 1995, Casper, 1995, Mr. Wrong, 1996, Independence Day, 1996, Lost Highway, 1997, The End of Violence, 1997, The Thin Red Line, 1998, Brokedown Palace, 1998, Zero Effect, 1998, A Man is Mostly Water, 1999, History Is Made at Night, 1999, The Guilt, 1999, Brokedown Palace, 1999, Lake Placid, 1999, (voice) Coming to Light: Edward S. Curtis and the North American Indians, 2000, (voice) Titan A.E., 2000, Numbers, 2000, Ignition, 2001, Igby Goes Down, 2002, 29 Palms, 2002, Rick, 2003, The Grudge, 2004, The Orphan King, 2005, Dear Wendy, 2005, Scary Movie 4, 2006, You Kill Me, 2007, Nobel Son, 2007, Bottle Shock, 2008, Phoebe in Wonderland, 2008, Surveillance, 2008; (TV movies) Home Fires Burning, 1989, Crazy in Love, 1992, The Last Seduction, 1994, Mistrial, 1996, Merry Christmas George Bailey, 1997, The Virginian, 2000, Tiger Cruise, 2004; (TV series) Revelations, 2005-. Office: Big Town Prodns Ste 80 6201 Sunset Blvd Los Angeles CA 90028-8704

PULLMAN, JENNIFER KING, artist, educator; d. John Lindsay King, Jr. and Leila Luening King; 1 child, Ian Thomas. BA, Stockton Coll. N.J., 1978; MA in Tchg., Marygrove Coll., 1999; PhD, Walden U., 2007. Cert. elem. educator N.J., art edn. N.J. Artist, interior designer, 1978—, Egg Harbor, 1978—, McKee City, 1978—; tchr. kindergarten Our Lady of Sea Sch., Atlantic City, 1985—89; tchr. 3d grade Atlantic City Pub. Schs., 1989—93, educator art, 1993—. Leader curriculum task force Atlantic City Pub. Schs., 2001—02, new tchr. mentor, 1992—, advisor art club, 1993—. Contbg. editor: Jour. of Educational Practice for Social Change, 2006—. Mem. bd. dirs. Jan-ai Scholarship Fund, 2009—. Recipient Govs. Recognition award, NJ Edn. Dept., 1998, Recognition award, Atlantic City Edn. Found., 2006. Mem.: Jan-Ai Scholarship Fund (bd. dirs. 2009—), Asoc. Bd. Supr. and Am. Devel., NJ Art Educators Assn., Nat. Art Educators Assn., Noyes Mus. Art, Atlantic City Art Ctr., Phi Delta Kappa (v.p. programs 2004—07). Avocations: interior decorating, singing, guitar, gardening, yoga. Office Phone: 609-343-7300. Personal E-mail: cyberhen@verizon.net.

PULLMAN, MAYNARD EDWARD, biochemist; b. Chgo., Oct. 26, 1927; s. Harry and Gertrude (Atlas) P.; m. E. Phyllis Light, Sept. 12, 1948; children: H. Cydney, B. Valerie, Jacky Leigh. BS, U. Ill., 1948, MS, 1950; PhD (NIH fellow), Johns Hopkins U., 1953. Fellow in pediatrics Johns Hopkins Hosp., 1953-54; asst. Pub. Health Rsch. Inst., NYC, 1954-56, assoc., 1956-61, assoc. mem., 1961-65, mem., 1965-89, chief, 1973-87, assoc. dir., 1983-89; sr. rsch. scientist Coll. Physicians and Surgeons Columbia U., 1989-92. Vis. prof. biochemistry U. São Paulo (Brazil) Sch. Medicine, 1963-64; research assoc. prof. biochemistry Sch. Medicine NYU, 1966-76, research prof., 1976-90; biochemistry study section mem. NIH, 1969-73. Editorial bd.: Jour. Biol. Chemistry, 1967-71, 78-80. NIH grantee, 1956-85; Shubert Found. grantee, 1972-74. Fellow N.Y. Acad. Scis.; mem. AAAS, Am. Soc. Biol. Chemistry and Molecular Biology, Brit. Biochem. Soc., Am. Chem. Soc. Home and Office: 338 Archer St Freeport NY 11520-4233 Home Phone: 516-378-7442; Office Phone: 516-378-7442. Personal E-mail: mep2658@aol.com.

PULOS, WILLIAM WHITAKER, lawyer; b. Hornell, NY, Aug. 29, 1955; s. William Leroy and Juanita (Whitaker) P. BA in Econs. magna cum laude, Alfred U., 1977; JD, Union U., 1980. Bar: N.Y. 1982, U.S. Supreme Ct. 1987, sr. prize trial first team. Pvt. practice, Alfred, NY, 1982—92, Hornell, NY, 1992—. Adj. prof. law Alfred U., 1981-90; prof. bus. adminstrn. SUNY-Alfred, 1982-84; tutor Empire State Coll., 1982-85; atty. Town of Alfred, 1982-99, Village of Almond (N.Y.), 1983-97, Town of West Almond (N.Y.), 1987-97, Town of Jasper, N.Y., 1988-91, Town of Almond, 1990-97, Town of West Union (N.Y.), 1992-98, Town of Birdsall (N.Y.), 1993-97; mem. Allegany County and Steuben County Assigned Counsel Program for Indigent Defendants, 1982-85; asst. counsel N.Y. State Assembly, 1980; hearing officer NY State Small Claims Assessment Rev., 1983-87, NY State Bd. Equalization and Assessment, 1988-91; tax atty. NY State Dept. Tax and Fin., 1983-91; pres. Alfred Dombec, Ltd., 1985-99, Maple City Way, Inc., 1990-97, Saxon Properties, Ltd., 1984-92. Active Alfred Sta. Vol. Fireman's Assn., Inc., 1985-98, 2d chief, 1988-92, pres. 1994-96, life mem; pres. Alfred Lions Club Inc., 1982-94. Recipient Outstanding Young Man Am. award U.S. Jaycees, 1982, 86, Internat. Humanitarian award Lions Club Internat., 1991, Lions Club Leadership award, Dist. 20 E-1, NYC and Bermuda. Mem. ABA, N.Y. State Bar Assn. (lawyer referral program 1983-90, 98—), Steuben County Bar Assn., NYS Acad. Trial Lawyers, Phi Kappa Phi, Pi GAmma Mu, Delta Mu Delta, Alpha Iota Delta, Am. Assn. Justice Office: PO Box 337 70 Main St Hornell NY 14843-0337 Home Phone: 607-587-8403; Office Phone: 607-324-7333. Business E-Mail: wpulos@stny.rr.com.

PULS, SARAH, marketing executive; MBA, Krannert Sch. Mgmt., Purdue U., 1989. Dir. laundry product devel. Whirlpool Corp., 1997—99; gen. mgr. Evenflo Co., 1999—2004; v.p. brand mktg. Hobart Corp., Troy, Ohio, 2005—. Named one of Best Marketers, BtoB Mag., 2007, 2008. Office: Hobart Corp 701 S Ridge Ave Troy OH 45374 Office Phone: 973-332-3000. Office Fax: 973-332-2852.*

PULTE, WILLIAM J., retired construction executive; married; 14 children. Founder, pres. William J. Pulte, Inc., 1950—69; pres. Pulte Homes Corp. (formerly William J. Pulte, Inc.), 1969—, chmn. of exec. com. of bd., 1972—90, chmn., 1991—99, 2001—09. Named one of Forbes' Richest Ams., 2005—06. Avocations: golf, art. Office: Pulte Homes 100 Bloomfield Hills Pky Ste 300 Bloomfield Hills MI 48304*

PULWERS, JACK EDWARD, public affairs specialist, news executive, writer, historian, journalism educator, lecturer, broadcaster; b. NYC, July 2, 1924; s. Leon and Frances Pulwers; m. Florence Jeanette Prisaznick, Apr. 29, 1989; children: George Conlon, Christina Carter, Marilyn Smith, John Pulwers, Mary Komm, Peter Conlon, Paul Conlon, Jack E. Pulwers Jr., Therese Conlon, Clare Conlon, David Pulwers, Patrick Conlon, Gerard Conlon, Abbe Pulwers, Anne Johnson. Student, Centenary Coll., Shreveport, La., La. State U., Baton Rouge, BA, 1948; Masters in Polit. Sci. and History, La. State U., 1955; graduate, USAF Air War Coll., 1972; Doctorate in History with distinction, Catholic U. Am., 1983. News and pub. affairs dir. leading stations in US and on major networks; news and pub. affairs chief WABC NY; head Armed Forces Radio and Television; broadcast and news chief US Armed Forces Radio and Television, 1966—82; PA action officer Sec. Weinberger's Defense Pub. Affairs News Br., Washington, 1982—89; head depts. history and journalism Inst. Arts and Design, Bklyn., Washington Hall Coll., Penn Media Ctr., Washington; assoc. prof., co-founder journalism dept. Bowie State U. Among the first disc jockeys in Am.; vis. prof. various institutions; expert in WWII history and military journalism; advisor to several TV networks on special documentaries; writer, rschr., lectr., narrator; acchor Press Panels Hurricane Katrina WWII. Author: The Press of Battle: The GI Reporter and the American People, My Sons Wore Gray, Mr. Smith Comes to Washington, Jefferson's Newsman, The Biggest Bang: The U.S. Army's Information Explosion of World War II, A History of the U.S. Army Public Affairs, 1783-1983; exhibitions include Meet the Artists & Artisans Spring Art Festival, Milford, CT; contbr. numerous manuscripts, tapes, narrative documentaries, interviews, special events broadcasts, and essays to archives, libraries, and universities. Pvt. US Army, 1943—45. Recipient Mayor's award, Detroit, 1957, Mich. Constitution award, former Gov. George Romney, 1958, Citizen's Budget Com. award, NYC, 1962, Documentary award, Ohio State U., 1963, Equitable Savings award, NYC, 1964, Governor's award, NJ Gov. Richard Hughes, 1964, Mayor's award, Mayor Robert Wagner, NYC, 1964, DuPont Journalism award, 1965, Dept. Defense Quality awards, 1978, 1980, 1982, 1984, Medal award for WWII rsch. and writings, Stars and Stripes Newspaper, 2005, Hall of Fame, Byrd HS, Shreveport La., 2005, Alumni Achievement award, Catholic U. Am., 2006; named one of Nationally Humorist. Mem.: KC (Fourth Degree as Sir Knight), Oral History Com., Diplomatic and Consular Orgn. Retired, Aviation and Space Writers Soc. (founding mem.), Nat. Hist. Soc. (founding mem.), Orgn. Am. Historians, Am. Hist. Assn., Nat. Radio-TV News Dir. Assn., Soc. Profl. Journalists, European and Pacific Stars and Stripes Assn., Internat. Combat Camera Assn., Assn. US Army, USAF Assn., Nat. Fed. Retired and Active Govt. Employees, USAF Pub. Affairs Assn., US Marine Combat Correspondents Assn., Am. Legion, Uniformed Firemen's Assn. of NY (life), Catholic U. Am. Alumni Assn., La. State U. Alumni Assn., Loyal Order of the Moose (Legionaire mem.), NYU Alumni Assn., Overseas Press Club. Am., Nat. Press Club, Phi Alpha Theta (Theta Omricon br., life), Sigma Delta Chi. Achievements include among the first radio documentarians; produced 365 documentaries and social commentaries for both individual radio stations and networks, 1945-1982; introduced the world to the first around-the-clock 24-hours a day worldwide news broadcasting service on cable and shortwave; organized and supervised the broadcast; interviewed notable individuals such as the Beatles (exclusive interview on their first trip to America, 1964), Malcolm X, Elvis Presley, Eleanor Roosevelt, Harry Truman, Bob Hope, and others; first to record, produce and narrate a documentary on vinyl records, on the first trip to America by a Pope of the Catholic Church (Pope Paul VI); first in America to offer 24-hour news coverage from a news street patrol; a founding member of one of the first post-WWII American Legion and Amvets Posts, Shreveport, Louisiana. Avocations: travel, history. Personal E-mail: jpnews@cox.net.

PUMARIEGA, ANDRES JULIO, medical administrator, educator, researcher; b. Matanzas, Cuba, Jan. 25, 1953; came to U.S., 1962; s. Andrès Augustin and America Maria (Mechoso) P.; m. JoAnne Buttacavoli, Dec. 26, 1975; children: Christina Marie, Nicole Marie. BS, U. Miami, Coral Gables, Fla., 1973; MD, U. Miami, Fla., 1976. Resident in psychiatry Duke U., Durham, N.C., 1976-78, fellow in child psychiatry, 1978-80; dir. child psychiatry consultation/liaison svc. Vanderbilt U., Nashville, 1980-83; clin. asst. prof. psychol. Meharry Coll. Med., 1981—89; dir. pediat. psychiatry consultation/liaison svc. Tex. Children's Hosp. Baylor Coll. Medicine, Houston, 1983-86; dir. divsn. child adolescent psychiatry U. Tex. Med. Bd., Galveston, 1986-91, dir. residency program, 1987-92; prof. neuropsychiatry and behavioral scis. U. S.C., Columbia, 1992-96, dir. divsn. child and adolescent psychiatry, 1992-96, vice-chmn. dept. neuropsychiatry and behavior sci., 1994-96; assoc. dir. William S. Hall Psychiat. Inst., Columbia, 1992-96; prof. psychiatry and behavioral scis. East Tenn. State U., Johnson City, 1996—2006, chmn. dept. psychiatry and behavioral scis., 1996-2001, dir. divsn. child and adolescent psychiatry, 1996—2006, dir. Ctr. of Excellence Children in Custody, 2002—06; chmn. dept. psychiatry Reading Hosp. and Med. Ctr., Pa., 2006—; prof. psychiatry Temple U., Phila., 2006—; clin. prof. psychiatry U. Medicine and Dentistry NJ, Camden, 2006—, Phila. Coll. Osteopathic Medicare, 2007—. Examiner in child psychiatry and gen. psychiatry Am. Bd. Psychiatry and Neurology, Chgo., 1983—; co-investigator, mem. exec. com. Ctr. Cross-Cultural Rsch., Galveston, 1989-91; chmn. rsch. com. and exec. bd. S.C. Pub. Acad. Mental Health Consortium, 1994-96; chair Nat. Latino Behavioral Health Work Group, 1995—2000; chair Hispanic panel managed care initiative Ctr. for Mental Health Svcs. Substance Abuse and Mental Health Adminstrn., 1996—2000; cons. Ctr. for Substance Abuse Treatment USPHS, 1995-96; mem. nat. adv. coun. Ctr. Mental Health Svcs., Substance Abuse and Mental Health Adminstrn. U.S. Dept. HHS, 1997-2001. Editor: (with H. Vance) Clinical Assessment of Child and Adolescent Behavior, 2001; (with N. Winters) Handbook of Child and Adolescent Systems of Care: The New Community Psychiatry, 2003; japanese translation, Y. Ono, 2007, Chinese Translation, 2008; editor Psychline Jour. Hispanic Am. Psychiatry, 2005-06; assoc. editor Jour. Child and Family Studies, 1996-2002, Am. Jour. Orthopsychiatry, 2005-; contbr. over 160 articles, chpts., monographs, and over 190 abstracts to profl. jours. Bd. dirs. Tex. Network for Children, Austin, 1986-88, Ctrl. Hispanic David Torres, Reading, Pa., 2007—; mem. adv. coun. Ptnrs. Advocacy Network, 1990-92. Recipient Exemplary Psychiatrist award, Nat. Alliance for Mentally Ill, 1993, 1997, cert. of merit for beneficiary svc., Health Care Fin. Adminstrn., U.S. Dept. HHS, 1996, Jasper Chen See MD Healthcare Profl. award, Caron Found., 2009, Cmty. Svc. award, Regional Coun. Child & Adult Psychiatry SE-Pa., 2009; named to Alumni Hall of Fame, U. Miami Sch. Medicine, 1999; grantee, Ctr. for Cross-Cultural Rsch., NIMH, Bethesda, Md., 1988—92, Fullerton Found., 1993—95; Minority Child Psychiatrist Tng. grant, NIMH, 1988—92, site coord., grantee, Nat. Assn. State Mental Health Dir. Rsch. Fellowship, 1993—, Forest Pharm., 2000. Fellow: Coll. Physicians Phila., Am. Orthopsychiat. Assn. (bd. dir. 2004—, pres. elect 2007—09), Tenn. Coun. Child and Adolescent Psychiatry (pres. 2001—06), Am. Psychiat. Assn. (chair Hispanic com. 2006—09, disting. fellow, Simon Bolivar award 2004, Silver award outstanding svcs. 2004), Am. Acad. Child Psychiatry (chmn. work group on sys. of care 1994—2001, chmn. cmty. psych. com. 2001—07, chmn. diversity and culture com. 2007—, Outstanding Mentor award 1994, Catchers in the Rye award 2001, Jeanne Spurlock Diversity and Culture award and lectr. 2007), Am. Acad. Pediat., Acad. Psychosomatic Medicine, Am. Coll. Psychiatrists; mem.: S.C. Soc. Child and Adolescent Psychiatry (founding pres. 1996—97), Tex. Mental Health Assn. (mem. children's adv. com. 1991—92), Tenn. Soc. Child Psychiatry (sec. 1982—83, pres. 2001—06), Bay Area Pediat. Soc. (pres. 1990—91), Soc. Profs. of Child Psychiatry, Am. Assn. Cmty. Psychiatrists (bd. dir. 1996—2006, Ethics in Pub. Managed Care award 2000), Nat. Mental Health Assn. (bd. dir. 1999). Roman Catholic. Avocations: swimming, political history, public affairs. Home: 27 Linree Ave Reading PA 19606-9075 Office: Reading Hosp & Med Ctr Dept Psychiatry Sixth Ave and Spruce St Reading PA 19611 Office Phone: 610-988-9318. Personal E-mail: pumarieg@verizon.net. Business E-Mail: pumariegaa@readinghospital.org.

PUMARIEGA, JOANNE BUTTACAVOLI, mathematics educator; b. Coral Gables, Fla., May 27, 1952; d. Ciro Charles and Rosaria Frances (Calabrese) Buttacavoli; m. Andres Julio Pumariega, Dec. 26, 1975; children: Christina Marie, Nicole Marie. BA in Math. and Edn. magna cum laude, U. Miami, 1973, MA in Math., 1974; postgrad., U. Houston, 1991-92. Cert. secondary math. tchr., Tex., Fla., Tenn., N.C. Grad. tchg. asst. U. Miami, Coral Gables, 1973-74; substitute tchr. Dade County Pub. Schs., Miami, 1975; math. instr. Miami Dade C.C., 1975-76; math. and G.E.D. instr. Durham (N.C.) Tech. Inst., 1976-77; math. instr. Durham H.S., 1977-78, Durham Acad., 1978-80, Univ. Sch. of Nashville, 1980-83; pvt. practice math. instr. Houston, 1984-86; tutor Clear Lake Tutoring Svc., Houston, 1987-90; pvt. practice, S.A.T, lang. instr. League City, Tex., 1990-92; pvt. practice math. and S.A.T. instr. Johnson City, Tenn., 1996—; lang. instr. Nelson Elem. Sch., Columbia, 1993-96. Instr. fgn. langs. and math. Lonnie B. Nelson Elem. Sch., Columbia, SC; faculty math. East Tenn. State U., 1999-2006, Pa. State-Berks., 2006—. Author (with F. Rodriguez and A. Pumariega): HIV/AIDS in Children and Adolescents, 1999; co-author (with A. Pumariega): Risk Factors of Mental Illness and Addiction Amongst Hispanic Immigrant Youth, 2002; contbr. articles to profl. jours. Chair bd. edn. St. Mary Parish, League City, 1988-90, lector, 1992, v.p. coun. Cath. Women, Johnson City, 1997-99; C.C.E. tchr. St. John Neumann Cath. Ch., Columbia, SC, Johnson City, Tenn., 1993-95, lector, 1992-96; lector St. Mary's Ch., Johnson City, 1996-2006, St. Catharine of Siena Ch., Reading, Pa., 2006—; treas. St. Thomas More Women's Club, Houston, 1985-86; v.p., then pres. housestaff med. wives Duke U., Durham, NC, 1978-80; mem. Wash./Unicoi/Johnson County Med. Alliance, 1999-2004, chair pub. rels. com., 1999-2002, asst. treas., 2002-03, membership chair, 2003-04, co-chair caring com., 2004-05, corr. sec., 2005-06; co-chair Am. Med. Assn., 2004-05. Recipient Above and Beyond award, East Tenn. State U., 2002. Mem. Berks County Med. Alliance, Newcomers of Greater Columbia (chmn. pub. rels. chpt. 1993,95), Newcomers of Greater Colo. (com. chair coord. 1994-95), Welcome Neighbors of Bay Area (v.p., program chmn. 1991-92), Tex. Med. Aux., Bay Area Med. Wives, East Tenn. State U. Women's Club (v.p. 1997-98, pres. 1998-99, parliamentarian 1999-2000), U. S.C. Faculty Women's Club (v.p. 1993-94, pres. 1994-95, parliamentarian, advisor 1995-96), Phi Kappa Phi, Kappa Delta Pi, Delta Kappa Gamma (corr. sec. Gamma chpt. 2004-06), Alpha Lamba Delta (Woman of Yr. 1972). Roman Catholic. Avocations: reading, travel. Home: 27 Linree Ave Reading PA 19606-9075 Home Phone: 610-779-8707; Office Phone: 610-396-6007. Personal E-mail: pumarieg@verizon.net. Business E-Mail: jbp12@psu.edu.

PUMPHREY, JANET KAY, editor, publishing executive; b. Balt., June 18, 1946; d. John Henry and Elsie May (Keefer) P. AA in Secondary Edn., Anne Arundel C.C., Arnold, Md., 1967, AA in Bus. and Pub. Adminstrn., 1976. Libr. office mgr. Anne Arundel C.C., 1964—2002; mng. editor Am. Polygraph Assn., Severna Park, Md., 1973—98; owner JKP Publ. Svcs., 1990—; dir. Am. Polygraph Assn. Reference Svc., 1995—98; owner Brooke Keefer Ltd.Editions, 1999—. Editor: (with Albert D. Snyder) Ten Years of Polygraph, 1984, (with Norman Ansley) Justice and the Polygraph, 1985, 2d edit., 1998, A House Full of Love, 1990, Mama, There's A Mouse in My House, 1996; pub. Vergennes, Vermont and The War of 1812, 1999; pub.: (with Vickie T. Murphy-Carr) An Investigator's Guide to Non-Verbal Communication, 3d edit., 2007. Mem. Rep. Nat. Sustaining Com. Mem. Am. Polygraph Assn. (hon.), Md. Polygraph Assn., Anne Arundel County Hist. Soc.(mem. bd. dirs., 2008), Alumni Assn. Anne Arundel Community Coll. Republican. Methodist. Avocations: travel, poetry, gardening, mystery writer. Home: 3 Kimberly Ct Severna Park MD 21146-3703 Office: JKP Pub Svcs Brooke Keefer Ltd Edits 3 Kimberly Ct Severna Park MD 21146-3703 Personal E-mail: brookekle@worldnet.att.net.

PUNGOR, ERNÖ, chemist, educator; b. Vasszécsény, Hungary, Oct. 30, 1923; s. Jozsef and Franciska (Faller) P.; m. Elisabeth Lang, Oct. 26, 1950; children: Ernó, Andras, Katalin; m. Tünde Horváth, Sept. 8, 1984. Diploma of chemistry, Pazmany Peter U., Budapest, 1948; Dr.h.c., Tech. U. Vienna, 1983; Consejo cultural mondial diploma, Heidelberg, 1987; doctorate (hon.), Tech. U. Bratislava, 1988, U. Bucharest, 1993, Tech. U. Budapest, 1993, Lomonosov U., Moscow, 1999, U. Miskolc, 1999, U. Veszprém, 1999, Babes-Bolyai U., 2000. Asst. prof. Inst. Inorganic and Analytic Chemistry, Eotvos Lorand U., Budapest, 1948-51, reader, 1951-53, assoc. prof., 1953-62; prof. Inst. Analytical Chemistry, U. of Chem. Industry, Veszprém, 1962-70, Inst. for Gen. and Analytical Chemistry, Tech. U. Budapest, 1970-90; dir. Bay Zoltán Inst. Applied Rsch., 1994—2001; prof. emeritus Budapest U. Tech. & Econ., 1993—. Minister without portfolio, pres. Hungarian Nat. Comm. Technol. Devel., 1990-94; mem. nat. environ. com. Com. for Nat. Tech. Devel. of Hungary; redwood lectr. English Soc. for Analytic Chemistry, 1979; hon. prof. Agrl. U. Lima, 1973, Shanghai Tchrs. U., 1987, Árpád Acad., 1989; mem. sci. adv. bd. Orgn. Prohibition Chem. Weapons, 1998—; mem. sci. adv. bd. Hungarian Govt., 1999-2002. Author: Oscillometry and Conductometry, 1965, Flame Photometry Theory, 1962, Ion Selective Electrodes, 1973, 5th edit., 1989, Lab Manual, 1974, Coulometric Analysis, 1979, Medizinische und Biologische Bedeutund der Thiocyante, 1982, Modern Trend in Analytical Chemistry, 1984, Bioelectroanalysis I, 1987, A Practical Guide to Instrumental Analysis, 1994, For the Development of Hungary, 1996, My Years, My Researches, 1998, The Theory of Ion Selective Electrodes, 1998, (with K. Toth) Indicator Electrode, 1973, (with E. Lindner, K. Toth) CRC Book series: Dynamic Characters of Ion Selective Electrodes, 1988, Profession and Creed/For the Development of Hungary, 1998; mem. editl. bd. Acta Chimica Hungarica, 1967—, Periodica Polytech., 1972, Mikrochimica Acta, 1964; gen. editor Magyar Kémiai Folyóirat Kémiai Közlemények, 1970-2002, Talanta, 1968, Analyst, 1970, Analitica Chimica Acta, 1966, Analytical Letters, 1967, Bull. des Soc. Chimiques Belges, 1974, Bunseki Kagaku, 1981; mem. adv. bd. Analytical Chemistry, 1985-88; contbr. over 500 articles to profl. jours., chpts. to books. Recipient Talanta Gold medal, 1986, gold medal, Tech. U. Vienna Inst. for Analytical and Microchemistry, 1988, medal, R7. Mem. Internat. Union Pure and Applied Chemistry (titular mem. electroanalytical commn. 1979-87, dep. chmn. electroanalytical commn. 1985-87, pres. nat. Adhering Orgn. 1985—), European Sci. Acad., Fedn. European Chem. Socs. (chmn. working group of European analysts 1981-87), Hungarian Chem. Soc. (head analytical group), Hungarian Acad. Sci. (head analytical divsn., gold medal 1988), Indian Acad. Scis. (hon.), Czechoslovakian Acad. Scis. (hon. mem. chemistry divsn.), Austrian Analytical and Microanalytical Soc. (hon.), Finnish Chem. Soc. Tech. (hon.), Finnish Tech. Soc. (hon.), Chem. Soc. Finland (hon.), Austrian Analytical and Microanalytical Soc. (hon.), Japanese Analytical Chem. Soc. (hon.), Royal Soc. Chemistry (hon.), Acad. Sci. India (hon.), Egyptian Pharm. Soc. (hon.). Home: Meredek u 4 H-1112 Budapest Hungary Office: Bay Zoltan Inst Appl Rsch Kondorfa u 1 H-1116 Budapest Hungary Personal E-mail: pungor@t-online.hu. E-mail: pungor@tki.aak.bme.hu.

PUNNOOSE, A. JOHN, hospital administrator; BSc in Chemistry, Dehli U., New Dehli, 1989; MBA, Nagpur U., India, 1991; MPhil in Health and Health Sys. Mgmt., Birla Inst. Tech. and Scis., Pilani, India, 1997; student, Indian Inst. Mgmt., Ahmedabad, India, 2007—. CEO Apollo Hosps. Enterprises Ltd., India, 2003—05, Madras Med. Mission, India, 2005—07; healthcare advisor Kapico Holding Co., Kuwait, 2007—. Grantee Ctr. Social Innovation fellowship, Stanford U. Grad. Sch. Bus., 2007. Office: Madras Med Mission 4A Dr J Jayalalitha Nagar Mogappair Chennai 600 037 India Office Phone: 914426565901 ext. 2006. E-mail: pearlyjohn@rediffmail.com.

PUNYON, ELLEN, principal; d. Herbert and Gloria Punyon; m. Rick Saling, Dec. 28, 1980; 1 child, Bryan Marti Saling. BS in edn., Syracuse U., 1973; MEd, U. Wash., 1976. Cert. ednl. adminstr. Office of Supt. Pub. Instrn., 1993. Tchr. Syracuse (NY) Pub. Schs., 1973—75, Issaquah (Wash.) Pub. Schools, 1975—76; spl. edn. tchr. Seattle Pub. Schs., 1984—92, elem. prin., 1992. Mem.: Prin. Assn. Seattle (bd. mem.), Seattle Assn. Elem. Sch. Prins. (pres., Seattle Disting. Prin. award 2009), Wash. State Legis. Action Com. (v.p. 2003—05), Assn. Wash. Sch. Prins., Internat. Reading Assn. Avocations: hiking, bicycling, cross country skiing, international travel. Office: Dearborn Pk Elem 2820 S Orcas St Seattle WA 98108 Personal E-mail: epunyon@yahoo.com.

PUPPALA, ANAND JAGADEESH, engineering educator; s. Prasad and Devi Puppala; m. Padmaja Puppala; children: Aneesha, Rishik. PhD, La. State U., Baton Rouge, 1993. Lic. civil engr., La., 1993. Assoc. prof. engrng. U. Tex., Arlington, 2001—05, prof. engrng., 2005—. Named Outstanding Rschr., U. Tex. Coll. Engrng., 2003—04. Mem.: ASCE (com. chair 2004—07). Achievements include research in expansive soil modification methods. Office: Univ Tex 408 Yates St Arlington TX 76019 Business E-Mail: anand@uta.edu.

PURAO, SANDEEP, engineering educator; PhD, U. Wis.-Milw., 1995. Cert. chartered acct., Inst. Chartered Accts. India, 1984. Assoc. prof. Pa. State U., Coll. IST, Univ. Pk. Grantee, NSF, 2007—. Mem.: IEEE, AIS, ACM. Office: Penn State Univ Coll IST Bldg University Park PA 16802 Business E-Mail: sandeep-purao@psu.edu.

PURCELL, ALEXANDER HOLMES, entomologist, educator; b. Summit, Miss., Oct. 12, 1942; s. Alexander H. and Dorothy (Adams) P.; m. Rita Hall, Oct. 14, 1946. BS, USAF Acad., 1964; PhD, U. Calif., Davis, 1974. Commd. capt. USAF, 1964, officer, pilot, 1964-70, resigned, 1970; grad. rsch. asst. U. Calif., Davis, 1971-74, prof. entomology Berkeley, 1974—, dept. chair, 1993, head div. entomology and plant and soil microbiology, 1994, head divsn. environ. biology dept. environ. sci., policy and mgmt. Cons. FAO (UN), 1981. Contbr. articles to profl. jours. Fellow Calif. Acad. Sci.; mem. AAAS, Am. Soc. for Microbiology, Entomological Soc. Am., Am. Phytopath. Soc. Avocations: flying, fishing. Office: U Calif Dept Environ Sci and Policy and Mgmt 137 Mulford Hall MC 3114 Berkeley CA 94720-3114

PURCELL, ANN RUSHING, state legislator, human services manager; b. Reidsville, Ga., May 12, 1945; d. William Robert and Katie (Dasher) Rushing; m. Dent Wiley Purcell, May 26, 1966; children: Edwin Wiley, Mieke Ann, Mikki Marie. BS in Edn., Ga. So. Coll., 1966; degree (hon.), Ga. Future Farmers Am., 1999. Cert. secondary tchr. Tchr. math. Evans H.S., Ga., 1966-68; tchr. math., earth and sci. Beaumont Jr. H.S., Lexington, Ky., 1969-70; substitute tchr. Tallahassee, 1970's; agt. Noblin Realty, Tallahassee, 1970's; office mgr. Radiation Therapy Assocs., PC, Savannah, Ga., 1979—2008; state legislator Ho. of Reps. Ga. Gen. Assembly, Atlanta, 1991—2005. Author: Purcells of South Georgia and Other Related Families, 1976, Purcell Family History 1777-2006. Bd. dirs. Med. Assn. Ga. Polit. Action Com., Atlanta, 1988-89, Girl Scout Coun. Savannah, 1991-93, Effingham YMCA, 1999-, New Ebenezer Retreat Ctr., 2006—; Effingham County fin. chmn. State YMCA, 1991-05, vice chmn. steering com., 1999, bd. dirs., 1999; trustee Ga. So. U. Found., 1992-2009, Armstrong Atlantic U. Found., 2004-05, 06, 07, 08, sec., 2005, 06, 07, Vice Chmn. Bd., 2007, 08, chmn. bd. 2008-; mem. adv. com. Effingham County Extension Svc., 1992-2006; chmn. steering com. Effingham YMCA Bd., 2004, 05, 06, 07, chmn. fin. devel., 2005-07; mem. adv. com. Treutlin Home, 1999-04; bd. adv. Claxton Youth Detention Ctr. Hon. comdr. 165th Ga. Air Guard Airlift, 1997-04; hon. mem. Civil Air Patrol, 2001-05, Ga. State Patrol, 2001; state bd. mem. Ga. Dept. Tech. and Adult Edn., Tech. Coll. Sys. Ga., 2005-; co-chmn. Ga. Edn. Joint Edn. Com., 2006, 07, 08, 09; Effingham Campus of Savannah Tech. Coll., 2007, 2008, 09; mem. adv. bd. Ga. Pacific, 2006—; bd. dirs. New Ebenezer Retreat Ctr., 2006-09, chmn. bd. trustees Armstrong Atlantic, 2008-09. Decorated WA-PO-HE award Ga. Nat. Air Guard, Minuteman award, Dept. Def. Commendation medal; recipient Friend of Medicine award, Med. Assn. Ga., 1991, 1993, 1994, 1996, Ga. Vet. award, 2003, Guardian of Small Bus. award, Nat. Fedn. Ind. Bus., 1992, 1994, 1996, Commendation cert., Ga. Emergency Mgmt. Agy., 1995, Vol. of Yr. award, Effingham 4-H, 1998, Nat. Am. hon. degree, Future Farmers Am., 1999, Friend of State 4-H award, 1999, Svc. award, Effingham Recreation Dept., 2000, Cmty. Svc. award, Guyton Masonic Lodge, 2000, Hon. Family Consumer Cmty. Leaders of Ga. award, 2001, Ga. Pub. Health award, 2003, Effingham Jr. Adv. Family Connection award, 2003, 2004, Environ. Leadership award, Ga. Conservation Voters, 2003, 2004, Pub. Rels. award, Ga. Ext. Assn. of Family and Consumer Scis., 2003, Leadership award, Ga. Water Coalition, 2003, 2004, Charles Dick award, U.S. Nat. Guard, 2003, Air Nat. Guardsmen award, Savannah Assn. Flying, 2003, City of Pembroke award, 2004, Bryan County Svc. award, 2004, Friend of Effingham 4-H award, 2005, Friends award, Ga. Med. Soc., 2005, Vol. Yr., Coastal Ga. YMCA, 2007; named Ga.'s Legislator of Yr., Ga. Sch. Counselors Assn., 1996, Ga. Legislator of Yr., Coastal Conservation Assn. Ga., 1998, Vol. of Yr., Effingham YMCA, 2006; named to Hon. Ga. State

Patrol, 2001. Mem. Aux. to the Med. Assn. Ga. (pres. 1985), Aux. to the Ga. Med. Soc. (pres. 1981-82), Ga. Salzburger Soc. (bd. dirs. 2005, v.p. 2005, 06, 07, pres., 2007—09), Effingham County Pub. Ofcls. Assn., Rotary Internat. (Effingham bd. dirs., 2007-08, 2008-09, Paul Harris fellow 2003), Ga. Peace Officers Assn. (hon.), Rincon Noon Lions Club, Exch. Club. Republican. Methodist. Avocations: painting, genealogy, fishing. Home: 410 Willowpeg Way Rincon GA 31326-9157

PURCELL, BILL, academic administrator, former mayor; b. Phila., Oct. 25, 1953; s. William Paxson, Jr. and Mary (Hamilton) Purcell; m. Deborah Lee Miller, Aug. 9, 1986; 1 child, Jesse Miller. AB, Hamilton Coll., 1976; JD, Vanderbilt U., 1979. Bar: Tenn. 1979, U.S. Ct. Appeals (6th cir.) 1985, U.S. Supreme Ct. 1988. Staff atty. W. Tenn. Legal Svcs., Jackson, 1979—81; asst. pub. defender Metro Pub. Defender, Nashville, 1981—84, sr. asst. pub. defender, 1984—85; assoc. Lionel R. Barrett, P.C., Nashville, 1985—86; ptnr. Farmer, Berry & Purcell, Nashville, 1986—90; mem. Tenn. Ho. of Reps., Nashville, 1986—96, majority leader, 1990—96; dir. child and family policy ctr. Inst. Pub. Policy Studies, Vanderbilt U., Nashville, 1996—99; mayor Met. Govt. of Nashville and Davidson County, 1999—2007; dean Coll. Pub. Svc. and Urban Affairs, Tenn. State U., 2008; dir. Harvard Inst. Politics, John F. Kennedy Sch. Govt., Cambridge, 2008—. Chmn. select com. on children and youth Tenn. Gen. Assembly, 1989—96; exec. dir. Vanderbilt Legal Aid Soc., 1978—79; chmn. NCSL Assembly State Issues, 1995; chmn. policy makers' program adv. bd. Danforth Found., 1993—2002; mem. adv. bd. U.S. Conf. Mayors, 2001—02, trustee, 2002—07, chmn. task force hunger and homelessness, 2001—05; fellow Inst. Politics Kennedy Sch. Govt., Harvard U., 2007. With Nat. League Cities, 2000—02, chmn. coun. youth, edn. and families, 2003; chmn. human svcs. com. Nat. Conf. State Legislatures, Washington, 1993; mem. exec. com. Dem. Nat. Com., 1994—97; exec. com. 6th Dist. Dems., Nashville, 1986—88; mem. Tenn. State Gen. Assembly, Nashville, 1986—96, majority leader, 1990—96; chmn. Dem. Legis. Campaign Com., 1994—96. Recipient Disting. Alumnus award, Vanderbilt Law Sch., 2004, Pub. Ofcl. of Yr., Governing mag., 2006; named Legislator of Yr., Dist. Atty.'s Gen. Conf., 1989, Tenn. Conservation League, 1991; Toll fellow, Coun. State Govts., 1988. Mem.: ABA, Nashville Bar Assn., Tenn. Bar Assn. Methodist. Office: Inst Politics Kennedy Sch Govt 79 John F Kennedy St Cambridge MA 02138 Office Phone: 617-495-1363. Office Fax: 617-495-8957. Business E-Mail: bill_purcell@harvard.edu.

PURCELL, BRADFORD MOORE, publishing company executive; b. Garden City, NY, Oct. 1, 1929; s. William Lawrence and Margaret (Moore) P.; m. Louise Rauth, July 10, 1954; children: Margaret, Philip, Mark, Louisa, Christopher. BA, Williams Coll., 1951; MBA, Columbia U., 1957. Sr. v.p. devel. McGraw Hill, Inc., 1976-79, sr. v.p., 1979-81, group v.p. tng. systems, 1981-83, sr. v.p. mktg., 1983-85; pres. W.H. Smith Pubs Inc., NYC, 1985-91; v.p. admin. and fin. Rsch. Books Inc., 1992. Served to 1st lt. USAF, 1951-53. Home and Office: 106 Tantumorantum Rd Lyme CT 06371-3137 E-mail: bradfordpurcell@yahoo.com.

PURCELL, CHRISTINE M., music educator, music company executive; d. John William and Eleanor B. Purcell. MusB, Berklee Coll. Music, Boston, 1983; MA, Duquesne U., Pitts., 2004. Music edn. Cath. Diocese Harrisburg, 1987. V.p. creative svc. Ken Chandler Prodn., Harrisburg, Pa., 1984—87; music instr. Holy Name of Jesus Elem. Sch., Harrisburg, 1987—98; founder Anevon Music Prodn., Lemoyne, Pa., 1990—, pres., 1990—; music composer Funimals Inc., Lancaster, Pa., 1995—98, performer, 1995; prof. music Harrisburg Area C.C., 1998—; music instr. State St. Klassical Kids, Harrisburg, 2003—05, curriculum developer, 2003—05; artistic cons. Ctrl. Pa. Women's Chorus, Harrisburg, 2006—, vocalist, 2006—. Radio announcer KNDI Radio, Honolulu, 1983—84; curriculum advisor Music Industry Dept., Harrisburg Area CC, Pa., 2003—. Composer: (jazz tune) I Remember You, (musical) Into The Desert, (theme music) Strangers: A One Act Play; prodr.: (cd) The Seven Sorrows, A Kid's Christmas in Story & Song, Suffer the Children; musician: (cd) Children Pray the Rosary. Music liturgist Cath. Diocese, Harrisburg, Pa., 1984; fundraising chair ALS Assn., Harrisburg, Pa., 2001. Recipient First Pl. Nat. Proclaim award, 2002; named in Harrisburg Mag. as Mover and Shaper in Creativity for Ctrl. Pa. Region, 2002; finalist in writing contest for composing original score, New Century, 2002, in jazz category, USA Internat. Song Writing Competition, 2006. Democrat. Roman Catholic. Avocations: travel, golf, bicycling, volunteering. Business E-Mail: anevon2000@comcast.net.

PURCELL, CYNTHIA D., bank executive; married; 4 children. Controller First Am. Banking Co.; sr. v.p. pres., CFO Inland Empire Bank; exec. v.p., COO Banner Bank, Walla Walla, Wash., 2000—; chmn. BancSource, Inc. Mgmt. asset com. Inland Empire Bank, chair, asset and liability mgmt. com.; mem. exec. com. Banner Bank; prof. Am. Banker's Assn. Grad. Sch. Bank Investments and Fin. Mgmt.; bd. dirs. Oregon Bankers Assn., 2009—. Active YWCA, Walla Walla; chair, bd. dirs. BancSource, 2005—. Named one of 25 Women to Watch, US Banker, 2007. Mem.: Oreg. Banker's Assn., Am. Banker's Assn. (bd. advisors, exec. com., funds mgmt. and capital markets divsn., exec. acctg. com.). Office: Banner Corp 10 S First Ave PO Box 907 Walla Walla WA 99362-0265 also: Banner Corp 10 S Ist Ave Walla Walla WA 99362 Office Phone: 509-527-3636. Office Fax: 509-526-8898.*

PURCELL, JAMES NELSON, JR., international organization administrator; b. Nashville, July 16, 1938; s. James Nelson and Mary Helen P.; m. Walda Jean Primm, July 16, 1961; children: Deirdre Ann, Carole Elizabeth. BA in Polit. Sci., Furman U., 1961; M.P.A. (Maxwell Grad. Sch. fellow), Syracuse U., 1962. Mgmt. intern U.S. AEC, NYC, Washington, Oak Ridge, 1962, budget analyst Oak Ridge, Washington, 1962-66; mgmt. analyst AID, State Dept., Washington, 1966-68; budget preparation specialist Office Mgmt. and Budget/Exec. Office of the Pres., 1968-69, dept. chief budget preparation, 1969-72, sr. budget examiner Internat. Ednl. Exch. program, 1972-74, chief Justice-Treasury br., 1974-76; chief resources programming and mgmt. div. Bur. Ednl. and Cultural Affairs, Dept. State, Washington, 1976-77; exec. dir. Bur. Adminstrn., Dept. State, Washington, 1978-79; dep. asst. sec. Bur. Refugee Programs, Dept. State, Washington, 1979-82, dir., 1982-87; dir. gen. Internat. Orgn. for Migration, Geneva, 1988-98; internat. cons., 1998—; CEO Opine Pub., Columbia, Md., 2002—. Bd. dirs. Coun. for Cmty. of Democracies; sr. adv. Inst. for Study of Internat. Migration, Georgetown U. Mem. Am. Soc. Pub. Adminstrn., Cosmos Club, Washington. Home: 5113 W Running Brook Rd Columbia MD 21044 Office Phone: 443-745-2380. Personal E-mail: jpurcell7@verizon.net.

PURCELL, MARY HAMILTON, speech educator; b. Ft. Worth; d. Josseph Hants and Letha (Gibson) Hamilton; m. William Paxson Purcell, Jr., Dec. 28, 1950; children: William Paxson III, David Hamilton. BA, Mary Hardin-Baylor Coll., 1947, HHD (hon.), 1986; MA, La. State U., 1948; HHD (hon.), U. New Eng., 2000. Instr. dept speech and dramatic arts Temple U., Phila., 1948-53, 60-61; part-time instr. speech Cushing Jr. Coll., Bryn Mawr, Pa., 1966-78. Pres. Pa. Program for Women and Girl Offend, 1968—73, Nether Providence Parent Tchr. Orgn., 1975—76; treas. Virginia Gildersleeve Internat. Fund U. Women, 1975—81, bd. dirs., 1987—93; US del. UN Commn. on Status of Women, 1996; co-chmn. NGO Com. for UNICEF, 1994—2000, mem. global forum, 2001—; bd. dirs. Wallingford-Swarthmore Sch. Dist., 1977—83, Ministers and Missionaries Fund Am. Bapt. Conv., 1985—94, pres., 1995—2003, Internat. Devel. Conf., 1986—; bd. dirs. Nat. Peace Inst. Found., 1983—86; active Big Bros./Big Sisters of Am., 1985—90; bd. dirs. Citizens Crime Commn. of Phila., 1976—, Pa. Women's Campaign Fund, 1985—88, 1993—. Recipient Eleanor Schnurr award, UNA/USA, 2000; named Outstanding Alumna, Mary Hardin-Baylor Coll., 1972, Disting. Dau. Pa., 1982, v.p., 1994—95, pres., 1995—97, Woman of Yr., DECO Women's Conf., 1998. Mem. AAUW (Pa. state pres. 1968-70, v.p. mid. Atlantic region, 1973-77, program v.p. 1979-81, pres. 1981-85, rep. to UN 1985-89), Internat. Fedn. Univ. Women (1st v.p. 1986-89, pres. 1989-92, rep. to UN 1992-2005; pres. UN Dept. Pub. Info. Non Govt. Orgn. ann. conf. 1993), Speech Assn. Am. (Zeta Phi Eta award for excellence in comm. 1983), Pi Kappa Delta, Pi Gamma Mu, Delta Sigma Rho, Alpha Psi Omega, Alpha Chi. Democrat. Baptist. Home: 10 Willowbrook Ave Lansdowne PA 19050 Personal E-mail: mjd1926@verizon.net.

PURCELL, MARY LOUISE GERLINGER, retired adult education educator; b. Thief River Falls, Minn., July 17, 1923; d. Charles and Lajla (Dale) Gerlinger; m. Walter A. Kuyawski, June 9, 1950 (dec. July 1954); children: Amelia Allerton, Jon Allerton; m. Dale Purcell, Aug. 26, 1962 (dec. Nov. 2005). Student, Yankton Coll., 1941-45, Yale Div. Sch., 1949-50, NYU, 1949; MA, Columbia U., 1959, EdD, 1963. Teenage program dir. YWCA, New Haven, 1945-52; dir. program in family rels. Earlham Coll., Richmond, Ind., 1959-62, asst. prof. sociology and psychology, 1959-62, conf. coord. undergrad. edn. for women, 1962; chmn. divsn. home and cmty. Stephens Coll., Columbia, Mo., 1962-73, chmn. family and cmty. studies, 1962-78; dir. continuing edn. women Learning Unltd., 1974-78; prof. Auburn (Ala.) U., 1978-88, head dept. family and child devel., 1978-84, chmn. search com. for v.p. acad. affairs, 1984, spl. asst. to v.p. acad. affairs, 1985-86, prof. emerita, 1988—. Developer course, cons. Contemporary Am. Woman, 1962; vis. prof. Ind. U. Summer Sch., 1970; cons. student pers. svcs. Trenton (N.J.) State Coll., 1958—59, 1961. Contbr. articles to coll. bulls., jours. V.p. Falls Villate-Canaan Hist. Soc., 1998—2001, pres., 2002—07. Recipient Alumni Achievement award, Yankton Coll., 1975; Alumni fellow, Tchrs. Coll. Columbia U., 1959. Mem.: AAUW, Nat. Coun. Family Rels., Groves Conf. Family (nat. program chmn. 1977, dir., chmn.-elect affiliated couns. 1981—82, chmn. 1982—84, chmn. film awards com., chmn. spl. emphases sect., bd. dirs.), Am. Home Econs. Assn. (bd. dirs. 1967—69, chair 1st subject matter unit 1969, family rels. and child devel. sect. 1986—89), Falls Village Can. Hist. Soc. (v.p. 1998—2001, pres. 2002—07), Litchfield County Univ. Club (mem. scholarship com. 2001—, bd. dirs. 2001—06), Housatonic Camera Club (co-pres. 1996—2000), Delta Kappa Gamma. Congregationalist. Home: 120 Belden St Falls Village CT 06031-1124

PURCELL, PATRICK JOSEPH, publishing executive; b. NYC, Nov. 9, 1947; s. Patrick Joseph and Sarah (Muller) P.; m. Maureen T. Shuart, Aug. 8, 1970; children: Kathleen, Erin, Patrick, Kerry. BBA, St. John's U., 1969; MBA, Hofstra U., 1977. Various supr. positions N.Y. Daily News, NYC, 1969-80; assoc. pub. Village Voice, NYC, 1980-82; v.p. advt. N.Y. Post, NYC, 1982-83; v.p. sales and mktg. Skyband Inc., NYC, 1983; pres., pub. Boston Herald, 1984—, owner, 1994—; pub. The N.Y. Post, 1986-88; exec. v.p. News Am./Newspapers, 1986-90, pres., 1990-93, CEO, 1993-94; East Coast pres. Am. Ireland Fund, 1996—; exec. chmn. Ottaway Newspapers, Inc., Campbell Hall, NY, 2009—. Bd. dirs. Bay Bank, MetroWest Sub. Regional Bd., The Genesis Fund. Bd. dirs. NCCJ, Boston, 1984-86, Boy Scouts Am., Boston, 1984-85, Cath. Charitable Bur., Boston, 1984-86, John F. Kennedy Found.; mem. Greater Boston Assn. Retarded Citizens, 1984-86; chmn. Boston Against Drugs, 1988—; mem. White House Conf. for a Drug Free Am., 1987. Mem. Boston Better Bus. Bur., Am. Newspaper Pub. Assn., New Eng. Newspaper Assn., Boston C. of C. (bd. dirs. 1984-86), Downtown Crossing Assn. (bd. dirs.) Clubs: Publicity, Ad (Boston). Roman Catholic. Avocations: jogging, skiing. Office: Boston Herald PO Box 55843 Boston MA 02205-5843*

PURCELL, PHILIP JAMES, investment company executive; b. Salt Lake City, Sept. 5, 1943; m. Anne Marie Mc Namara, Apr. 2, 1964; 7 children. BBA, U. Notre Dame, 1964; M.Sc. in Econs., London Sch. Econs. and Polit. Sci., U. London, 1966; MBA, U. Chgo., 1967. Mng. dir., cons. McKinsey & Co., Inc., Chgo., 1967-78; sr. v.p. corp. planning and adminstrn. Sears, Roebuck and Co., Chgo., 1978-82; pres., COO Dean Witter Reynolds, 1982—86; chmn., CEO Dean Witter, Discover & Co., NYC, 1986—97, Morgan Stanley, NYC, 1997—2005; founder, pres. Continental Investors, LLC, Chgo., 2006—. Bd. dirs. NY Stock Exch., 1995-96, AMR Corp., 2000-; mem. coun. U. Chgo. Grad. Sch. Bus. Trustee U. Notre Dame. With USNR. Mem. Econ. Club Chgo., Chgo. Club, Links. Roman Catholic. Office: Continental Investors LLC 227 W Monroe St Ste 5045 Chicago IL 60606

PURCELL, ROBERT HARRY, virologist, researcher; b. Keokuk, Iowa, Dec. 19, 1935; s. Edward Harold and Elsie Thelma (Melzl) P.; children: David Edward, John Leslie. BA in Chemistry, Okla. State U., 1957; MS Biochemistry, Baylor U., 1960; MD, Duke U., 1962. Intern in pediatrics Duke U. Hosp., Durham, NC, 1962-63; officer USPHS, 1963; with Epidemic Intelligence Svc., Communicable Disease Ctr. Atlanta; assigned to vaccine br. Nat. Inst. Allergy and Infectious Diseases, Bethesda, Md., 1963-65; sr. surgeon Lab. Infectious Diseases, NIH, Bethesda, Md., 1965-69, med. officer, 1969-72, med. dir., 1972-74, head hepatitis viruses sect., 1974-2001, co-chief, 2001—; dist. investigator NIH, 2007. Organizer, invited participant, speaker numerous nat. and internat. symposia, confs., workshops, meetings; temporary advisor WHO, 1967—; expert cons. in hepatitis U.S.—China, U.S.—Taiwan, U.S.—Japan, U.S.—Russia, U.S.—India, U.S.—Pakistan Bilateral Sci. Agreements; lectr. various virology classes. Reviewer numerous sci. jours.; contbr. 700 articles to profl. jours., chpts. to books; 40 patents in field. Recipient Superior Svc. award USPHS, 1972, Meritorious Svc. medal USPHS, 1974, Gorgas medal, 1977, Disting. Svc. medal USPHS, 1978, Disting. Alumni award Duke U. Sch. Medicine, 1978, Eppinger prize 5th Internat. FALK Symposium on Virus and Liver, Switzerland, 1979, Medal of City of Turin, Italy, 1983, Gold medal Can. Liver Found., 1984, Nat. Acad. Scis., 1988, King Faisal Internat. prize for Medicine, 1998, Rsch. Sci. award Hepatitis Found. Internats., 1999; named to Alumni Hall of Fame East Okla. State Coll., 1996, Dist. Alumni award Okla State U., 2009 Fellow AAAS, Washington Acad. Scis., Am. Acad. Microbiology, Molecular Medicine Soc., Ind. Nat. Sci. Acad.; mem. Am. Epidemiology Soc., Am. Soc. Microbiology, Am. Soc. Virology, Soc. Epidemiol. Rsch., Infectious Diseases Soc. Am. (Squibb award 1980), N.Y. Acad. Scis., Am. Soc. Clin. Investigation, Assn. Am. Physicians, Am. Coll. Epidemiology, Am. Assn. Study of Liver Diseases (Disting. Achievement award 2000), Internat. Assn. Study and Prevention Virus Associated Cancers, Internat. Assn. Biol. Standardization, Internat. Assn. Study Liver, Soc. Exptl. Biology and Medicine (Disting. Scientist award 1986), Nat. Acad. Scis. (Washington chpt. 1988). Office: NIH Lab Infectious Diseases 50 S Dr MSC 8009 Rm 6523 Bethesda MD 20892-8009 Office Phone: 301-496-5090. Business E-Mail: rpurcell@niaid.nih.gov.

PURCELL, SCOTT, Internet company executive, publishing executive; b. Deerfield, Mass., Feb. 8, 1967; married. Grad., Univ. So. Calif., Sloan Sch. Bus., MIT. Founder, pres., CEO Epoch Networks, Irvine, Calif., 1994—99; pres., CEO OnAir Streaming Networks Inc. (originally www.com), 1999; pres. Browsercast, 2002—; founder, pres. WebBiographies, Denver, 2005—; publisher Kasidie Mag., 2007—. Mem.: Big Brothers. Office: WebBiographies PO Box 17409 Denver CO 80217

PURCELL, STEVEN RICHARD, international management consultant, engineer, economist; B in Mech. and Indsl. Engring., NYU Coll. Engring., 1950; MS in Indsl. Engring., Columbia U., 1951; EdM, Harvard U., 1968. Registered profl. engr., Can. Lectr. engring. NYU Coll. Engring., NYC, 1948-50; gen. mgr. Dapol Plastics Co., Inc., Boston, 1956-58; gen. div. mgr. Am. Cyanamid Co., Sanford, Maine, 1958-61; sr. prin., mgmt. cons. investment banking Purcell & Assocs., NYC, 1961-66; prof., chmn. Bristol Coll., Fall River, Mass., 1966-68; assoc. dean grad. faculty adminstrv. studies York U., Toronto, Ont., Can., 1969-71; chief economist Dept. Manpower and Immigration, Ottawa, Ont., Can., 1970-71; cons. Treasury Bd., Ottawa, 1971-72; dir. urban and internat. environ. policy Ministry of State for Urban Affairs Internat. Activities, Ottawa, 1973-74; mem. com. on challenges of modern soc. NATO, Ottawa, 1973-74; mem. sci., econ. policy com. OECD UN, Ottawa, 1973-74; prof. Grad. Sch. Bus. Adminstrn. and Econs. Algonquin Coll., Ottawa, 1974-76; advisor, cons. House of Commons, 1976-77; sr. prin. Purcell & Assocs., Internat. Mgmt. Cons., Washington, 1977-80, chmn., CEO, 1981—, Phoenix Internat. Capital Associates, Washington, 1981—; exec. dir. nat. coastal zone mgmt. adv. com. NOAA U.S. Dept. Commerce, Washington, 1980-81. Profl. lectr. Northeastern U. Grad. Sch. Bus. Adminstrn., Boston, 1953-56, U. Toronto, 1968-69, George Washington U. Grad. Sch. Bus. Adminstrn., Washington, 1979; vis. prof. Rensselaer Poly. Inst. Advanced Mgmt. Program, 1967, U. Ottawa Grad. Sch. Bus. Adminstrn., 1971-74; lectr. Council for Internat. Progress in Mgmt., N.Y.C., 1960, Royal Bank Can. Mgmt. Assn., Toronto, Ont., 1970; corp. appointment cons. Harvard U., Cambridge, Mass., 1967-68; cons. Govt. Venezuela, 1967-68, Can. Inst. Bankers, Toronto, 1969-70; internat. sr. adviser NASA, 1985-86, mem. nat. adv. bd. Ctr. for Nat. Policy; dir. Rental Resource Corp., 1986-89. Contbr. articles on indsl. orgn., sci. policy and fin. to profl. jours. Lt. AC, USNR, 1943-46. Mem. UN Assn., Soc. for Advancement of Mgmt. (pres. 1949-50, leadership award 1950), Tau Beta Pi, Alpha Pi Mu (v.p. 1949-50), Columbia Univ. Club (Washington, trustee 1982-84, chmn., sr. trustee 1984-85), Harvard Univ. Club.

PURCHASE-OWENS, FRANCENA, marketing professional, consultant, educator, scholar; b. Milw., Nov. 14, 1960; d. Johnny Purchase Sr. and Arlene (Roberts) Pleas Brown. Student, Grand Rapids CC, Mich., 1978—79, Ga. State U., Atlanta, 1980; degree, Patricia Stevens Coll., Atlanta, 1980; student, Milw. Area Tech. Coll., 1982; AA cum laude, Bryant Stratton Coll., 1982; student, Cardinal Stritch Coll., Milw., 1982—83, Mount Mary Coll., 1984, U. Wis., 1987—88, Grand Valley state U., Grand Rapids, 1996; BS in Applied Liberal Studies, Western Mich. U., Kalamazoo, 1997, M in Ednl. Leadership cum laude, 2004; student, U. Phoenix, Grand Rapids, Mich., 2006—, Capella U., Grand Rapids, 2006—. Cert. Mich. Profl. Sch. Modeling, 1980. Various office, clerical positions, 1972—84; sec. internat. mktg. dept. Am. Seating, Grand Rapids, 1980—81; adminstrv. asst. to Elizabeth Kubler-Ross Ga. State U., 1980; investment mgmt. sec. M&I Bank, Milw., 1984-85; cons. United Devel. Corp., Milw., 1986-88; sales Weathermasters Industries, Milw., 1989; paraprofessional Grand Rapids Pub. Schs., Mich., 1990-92; temp. helper Dayton Hudson, Grand Rapids, 1990; customer svc. rep. Kent County Conv. and Visitors Bur., Grand Rapids, 1995; customer svc. rep. children's dept. Meijers, Inc., 1995; mktg. rschr. Wirthlin Worldwide, Grand Rapids, 1996-98; pres. Creative Works, Grand Rapids, 1988—, Francena Purchase Internat. Honors & Awards Soc., Grand Rapids, 1999—, Francena Purchase Internat. Applied Studies, 1999—, Francena Purchase Internat. Applied Profl. Studies Soc., 2000—, Purchase Bus. Inst., Grand Rapids, 1999—; rsch. specialist Directions in Rsch., Grand Rapids, 2004—05, 2008—; mktg. rschr. Francena Purchase Cons. Svcs., Grand Rapids, 2006—. Sec. Mich. Nat. Bank, Grand Rapids, 1980-81, Volt. Tech. Svcs., Milw, 1980, United Devel. Corp. Access, Milw., 1988; asst. to pres. Alissia Cosmetics, Miss Black Pageant, 1980; legal sec. to atty. David Clowers, Milw., 1980; asst. exec. sec. Manpower Internat. Inc., Milw., 1982-84; human resource asst., computer programmer, sec., Patricia Stevens Coll., Milw., 1985-86; sales First Home Fin., Grand Rapids, 1998; activities asst. Olds Manor Grand Rapids, Mich., 1998; grad. student adv. bd. Western Mich. U., 2000; cons. in field. Co-editor: Smoke Signal, 1975; contbr. articles to profl. jours. Miss J. fashion bd. Jacobson's Dept. Store, East Grand Rapids, Mich., 1979, mem. pub. com., refreshment com., model; bd. mem. adminstrv. profls. Bryant & Stratton Coll., Milw., 1981-82; tutor Kent County Literacy Coun., Grand Rapids, 1988; host Grad. Rapids Cmty. Media Ctr., 2007-; intake asst. Baxter Cmty. Ctr., Grand Rapids, 1989; vol. Jerry's Kids, Jerry Lewis Muscular Dystrophy Telethon, Patricia Stevens Coll., 1985-86, Grand Valley State U., United Way, Grand Rapids, 1990, co-chair, 2006-, TV fundraiser vol., chair cmty. investment coun., 2006—, basic needs investment com., 2006-, agy. impact com., United Way, Grand Rapids, 2007—; reading condr. SE Neighborhood Assn., Grand Rapids, 1990, reading program asst. 1993, mem. exec. bd. dirs, 2006; rehab. asst. Kent Comty. Hosp. Complex, Grand Rapids, 1991; mem. literacy coun. Kent County Literacy Coun., Grand Rapids, 1991—; vol. Kent Cmty. Hosp., Grand Rapids, 1992, Metro Health (formerly Met. Hosp.), Grand Rapids, 1992; mem. task force First Call Help United Way, Grand Rapids, 1992, Herkimer Apt. Projects, Weston Apts. Dwelling Place, Grand Rapids, 1999; facilitator trainer Employers Coalition for Healing Racism, Grand Rapids, 1997, Citizens Cirs. Resource Ctr., Grand Rapids, 1998, Ptnrs. in Pub. Edn., Grand Rapids, 1999, United Way Champions of Diversity, 1999; bd. dirs.program and quality com., pers. com., fin. com., Adhoc Com., Touchstone Innovaré Mental Health, Grand Rapids, 2006-09, consumer adv. bd., Grand Rapids, 2000—, mem. nominating com., 2000-01, Kent County Cmty. Mental Health, 1999—; com. mem. Cherry St. Health Svcs., Grand Rapids, 2003; cons. Children King Day Care Ctr., Together Faith Ministries, Grand Rapids, 1998; asst. sec. First Missionary Bapt. Ch., Grand Rapids, 2005—, fin. asst., 2005-, program com., 2006-, exec. bd. dirs., 2006-07; pastors asst. First Missionary Bapt. Ch., Grand Rapids, 2005—, adult usher bd., kitchen com., 2007—; program com. First Vol. Cancer Soc. Finalist Miss Black Milw. Pageant, 1979, Internat. Faces, Milw., 1985, Internat. Theatre Arts, Milw., 1986; recipient Typist award Edn. Assn., 1981, Leadership award Milw. Area Tech. Coll. Office Edn. Assn., 1977, 78, 1st Pl. extemporaneous speaking, 1979, 1st Pl. extemporaneous speaking with Letter of Recognition from Wis. Sen. Berger, 1981, Shorthand awards Bryant Stratton Coll., 1981-82, Machine Transcription award, 1981, Century award, 1982, cert. recognition, Kiwanis Club Internat., 1998, 2007, Am. Soc. Training & devel., 2002, Kent County Literacy Coun, 1991, Kent County Literacy Coun., 1991,

Personal Svc. and Sales Accomplishment cert. Manpower, Inc., 1982, Appreciation cert. Touchstone Innovare Bd. Mem., Grand Rapids, 1998-2007, SE End Neighborhood Assn., Grand Rapids, 1993, 2006-07, Recognition Appreciation Cert., 2007; Touchstone Ins., 1999, 2007, Leadership Recognition, Profl. Bus. Leaders, Milw., 1981-82, Recognition Appreciation cert. United Way, Impact Com., Grand Rapids, 2007-09, Mark Kistler's Summer Art Camp, Grand Rapids, 2006, SE End Neighborhood Assn., 2006, 07, recognition appreciation cert. SE & Neylbmland Assn., Grand Rapids, 2008, Mpls. & Minn. Cmty. Spotlight recognition, Capella U., 2006-07, Young Alumni Student Spotlight recognition Western Mich. U., Bryant and Stratton Coll., 2007, other honors and awards; Phillip Morris scholar Alverno Coll., 1981, Thurgood Marshall Assistantship scholar Western Mich. U., 1989, 1998, Nontraditional Student grantee 1994, 2000, Thurgood Marshall Tuition grantee, 2000. Mem.: West Mich. Postal Customer Coun., Office Edn Assn., Profl. Bus. Leaders, Econ. Club Grand Rapids, Internat. Econ. Assn., Cmty. Media Ctr. (scholarships com.), Soc. Human Resource Mgmt., Am. Mgmt. Assn., Am. Soc. Tng. and Devel. (Cert. Recognition 1991), Parkinson's Assn., Alzheimer's Assn., Rotary Internat., Paraprofessional Assn., Western Mich. U. Alumni, Internat. Jaycees, Networking and Leads (mem. networking and leads com., com.), Phi Beta Lambda (sec. elect 1981—82), Phi Lambda Theta (Cert. Recognition 2002—). Avocations: modern dancing, reading, tennis, writing. Address: PO Box 88304 Kentwood MI 49518 E-mail: francenapurchase@peoplepc.com, embree.mclemore@peoplepc.com.

PURCIFULL, DAN ELWOOD, retired plant virologist, educator; b. Woodland, Calif., July 1, 1935; s. Ernest Lee and Virginia (Margaroli) P.; m. Marcia Ann Weatherby, Sept. 7, 1966; children: Scott, Douglas. BS, U. Calif., Davis, 1957, MS, 1959, PhD, 1964. Asst. prof. plant pathology U. Fla., Gainesville, 1964-69, assoc. prof., 1969-75, prof., 1975-99, prof. emeritus, 2000—; ret., 2000. Plant virus subcom. Internat. Com. for Taxonomy of Viruses, 1973-75, mem. potyvirus study group, 1987-93; mem. plant virology adv. com. Am. Type Culture Collection, 1993-99; mem. Internat. Legume Virus Working Group, 1999. Assoc. editor Phytopathology, 1971-73, Plant Disease, 1987-89; contbr. articles to profl. jours. Mem. Morningside Nature Center Commn., City of Gainesville, 1978-81, treas., 1981. With US Army, 1957. Fellow AAAS, Am. Phytopathol Soc. (Lee Hutchins award 1981, Ruth Allen award 1992); mem. Fla. State Hort. Soc., N.Y. Acad. Sci., Am. Soc. Virology, Phytopathol. Soc. Japan, Australasian Plant Pathology Soc., Brazilian Phytopath. Soc., U.S. Golf Assn., Nat. Wildlife Fedn. (assoc.), Nature Conservancy, Nat. Geographic Soc., Smithsonian Instn. (assoc.), Sigma Xi, Gamma Sigma Delta. Home: 3106 NW 1st Ave Gainesville FL 32607-2504 Home Phone: 352-376-9926. Personal E-mail: depurc@aol.com.*

PURDOM, THOMAS JAMES, lawyer; b. Seymour, Tex., Apr. 7, 1937; s. Thomas Exer and Juanita Florida (Kuykendall) P.; m. Betty Marie Shoemaker, May 31, 1969; 1 son, James Robert. Student, U. Syracuse, 1956—57, U. Md., 1958—59; BA, Tex. Tech. Coll., 1962; JD, Georgetown U., 1966. Bar: Tex. 1966, U.S. Supreme Ct. 1978, U.S. Ct. Appeals (5th cir.) 1983. Ptnr. Griffith & Purdom, Lubbock, Tex., 1966-67; asst. dist. atty. 72d Jud. Dist., Lubbock, 1967-68; county atty. Lubbock County, Tex., 1968-72; pres. Purdom Law Offices, P.C., Lubbock, 1972—. Mem. com. for Vol. 5 pattern jury charges, 1988-97. Author: West's Texas Forms Vols. 16, 17, 18, 1984-96, Family Law, Texas Practice and Procedure, 1981. Served with USAF, 1956-60. Recipient Sam Emison award Tex. Acad. Family Law Specialists, 2000. Fellow Tex. Bar Found.; mem ABA, Lubbock County Bar Assn. (bd. dirs. 1970, Disting. Sr. Lawyer award 2000, Justice James G. Denton Disting. Lawyer award 2008), State Bar Assn. Tex. (sec. family law sect. 1974-75, chmn. family law sect. 1975-76, mem. examining commn. for family law specialization), Am. Acad. Matrimonial Lawyers (cert. family law, Tex. bd. legal specialization), Delta Theta Phi. Democrat. Baptist. Home: 3619 55th St Lubbock TX 79413-4713 Office: Purdom Law Offices PC 3619 55th St Lubbock TX 79413-5713 Business E-Mail: purdom6@aol.com.

PURDY, ALAN HARRIS, biomedical engineer; b. Mt. Clemens, Mich., Dec. 13, 1923; s. Harry Martin and Elinor (Harris) P.; m. Anna Elizabeth Sohn, Aug. 16, 1968 (dec.); children: Catherine, Charles, Susan, Harry; m. Margaret Josephine Kelley, Mar. 5, 1997. BSME, U. Miami, 1954; MS in Physiology, UCLA, 1967; PhD in Engring., U. Mo., 1970. Cert. clin. engr., Washington. Project engr. in acoustics Arvin Industries, Columbus, Ind., 1954-56, AC Spark Plug Co., Flint, Mich., 1956-60; asst. prof. engring. Calif. Poly. U., Pomona, 1960-62; assoc. dir. biomed. engring. U. Mo., Columbia, 1967-71; dep. assoc. dir., assoc. dir. Nat. Inst. for Occupational Safety and Health, Rockville, Md., 1971-81, scientist, biomed. engr. Cin., 1983-86; asst. dir. Fla. Inst. Oceanography, St. Petersburg, 1981-83; pres. Alpha Beta R & D Corp., San Marcos, Calif., 1986—. Cons. Smithy Muffler Corp., L.A., 1961-62, Statham Instruments, L.A., 1966; cons. faculty, Tex. Tech. U., Lubbock, 1972-73; lectr. U. Cin., 1980. Patentee in diving, acoustical and occupational safety fields. Pilot CG Aux., 1989-98. With USAF, 1942-43. Nat. Heart Inst. spl. fellow, 1963-67; Fulbright scholar, Yugoslavia, 1984. Mem. Acoustical Soc. Am., Biomed. Engring. Soc., Am. Inst. Physics, Exptl. Aircraft Assn., Aircraft Owners and Pilots Assn., DAV, FAA (Inspection Authorization 1983, Designated airaworthiness Rep., 2003). Democrat. Home and Office: 941 Cycad Dr San Marcos CA 92078-5013 E-mail: ahpurdy@nethere.com.

PURDY, ALAN MACGREGOR, financial executive; b. Iowa City, Apr. 23, 1940; s. Rob Roy MacGregor and Frances (Edwards) P.; m. Sarah Lane Robins, June 13, 1964; children— William Wallace, John Alan, Tammi Ann. AB, Duke U., 1962; MBA, Wharton Sch. Fin. and Commerce, U. Pa., 1968. Bus. analyst Gen. Mills, Inc., Mpls., 1968-71; sr. fin. analyst Dayton Hudson Corp. (now Target Corp.), Mpls., 1972-73; mgr. capital expenditure analysis Dayton Hudson Corp., Mpls., 1973, dir. corp. analysis, 1973-75, dir. planning and analysis, 1975-77; v.p., treas. Fleming Cos., Inc., Oklahoma City, 1977-81; v.p. fin., chief fin. officer John A. Brown Co. (subs. Target Corp.), Oklahoma City, 1981-83; sr. v.p., chief fin. officer B. Dalton Co. (subs. Target Corp.), Mpls., 1983-86, Robinson's of Fla.(subs. May Co.), St. Petersburg, 1986-87, Miller's Outpost (subs. Am. Retail Group), Ontario, Calif., 1988-92, Builders Emporium (subs. Collins and Aikman Group), Irvine, Calif., 1993, RemedyTemp, Aliso Viejo, Calif., 1994—2002. Served with USN, 1962-66. Office: Remedy Temp 101 Enterprise Aliso Viejo CA 92656-2604 Home: 93 Ambroise Newport Coast CA 92657-0122 also: 31111 Almara Ln Laguna Niguel CA 92677 Home Phone: 949-376-9604. Personal E-mail: sallyalan@gmail.com.

PURDY, DAVID LAWRENCE, medical products executive; b. NYC, Sept. 18, 1928; s. Earl and Mabel (Roberts) Purdy; m. Margaret Helen Rye, July 7, 1951; children: Susan Lee, John F.(dec.), Ross David(dec.), Thomas Griffith. BME, Cornell U., 1951; degree in advanced & creative engring., GE, 1955, degree in profl. bus. mgmt., 1956. Devel. engr. GE, Valley Forge, Pa., 1953—64; mgr. energy conversion divsn. Nuc. Materials and Equipment Corp. (acquired by ARCO), Apollo, Pa., 1964—69, Atlantic Richfield Corp., Apollo, 1969—72; founder, pres., chmn. Biocontrol Tech., Inc., Indiana, Pa., 1972—2000; chmn., treas. Diasense, Inc. Biomedical Engring., Indiana, 1989—2000; pres., founder Purdy Tech., Inc., Marion Center, Pa., 2000—. Contbr. articles to profl. jours. 1st lt. USAF, 1961—63. Fellow: ASME (life); mem.: AAAS. Achievements include 32 patents in field; patents for generator of electrical energy by radioisotope thermoelectric conversion; radioisotope powered cardiac pacemaker; radioisotope powered artificial heart; thermoelectric apparatus for high thermoelectric efficiency by cascading materials; method of metals joining and articles produced by such method including brazing copper to tungsten; rate responsive pacemaker; artificial pancreas; noninvasive glucose sensor; multi-leaflet heart valve. Office: Purdy Tech Inc 1482 Ambrose Rd Marion Center PA 15759 Personal E-mail: penllwyn@yourinter.net.

PURDY, G. MICHAEL, observatory director; Student, London U.; PhD in Marine Geophysics, Cambridge U., Eng., 1974. Postdoctoral scholar Woods Hole Oceanographic Instn., Mass., 1974, chmn. dept. geology and geophysics Mass., 1991-95; dir. divsn. ocean scis. Geoscis. Directorate NSF, 1995-2000; dir. Lamont-Doherty Earth Obs. Columbia U., Palisades, NY, 2000—. Participated in several rsch. cruises. Contbr. rsch. articles in peer reviewed jours.;, author (of several conf. abstracts). Recipient Maurice Ewing medal, Am. Geophysical Union, 2006. Office: Lamont-Doherty Earth Obs PO Box 1000 61 Rt 9W Palisades NY 10964-1000

PURDY, JAMES AARON, medical physics professor; b. Tyler, Tex., July 16, 1941; s. Walter Bethel and Florence (Hardy) P.; m. Marilyn Janette Coers, Jan. 29, 1965; children: Katherine, Laura. BS, Lamar U., 1967, MA, U. Tex., 1968, PhD, 1971. Asst. rsch. scientist U. Tex., Austin, 1969-71; rsch. asst. M.D. Anderson Hosp. and Tumor Inst., Houston, 1968-69, fellow in med. physics, 1972-73; from instr. physics to prof. Sch. of Medicine, Washington U., St. Louis, 1973—83, chief physics sect., 1976—2004, prof., 1983—2004, assoc. dir. Radiation Oncology Ctr., 1987—2004; prof., vice chmn. Med. Ctr. Dept. Radiology Oncology U. Calif., Davis, 2004—. Mem. NIH Radiaton Study sect. Divsn. Rsch. Grantes, 1991-95; Landauer lectr., Oakland, Calif., 1991. Editor: Three Dimensional Treatment Planning, 1991, Advances in Radiation Oncology, 1992, 3D Radiation Treatment Planning and Conformal Therapy, 1995, A Practical Guide to 3D Planning and Conformal Radiation Therapy, 1999, 3-D Conformal and Intensity Modulated Radiation Therapy: Physics and Clinical Applications, 2001, Technical Basis of Radiation Therapy, 2006; sr. physics editor: Internat. Jour. Radiation Oncology, Biology, and Physics, 1996—2003. With USMC, 1961-64. Fellow Am. Assn. Physicists in Medicine (pres. 1985, William D. Coolidge award 1997), Am. Coll. Radiology (ACR Gold Medal 2002), Am. Coll. Med. Physics (chmn. bd. chancellors 1990, Marvin M.D. Williams award 1996); mem. Am. Inst. Physics, Am. Bd. Med. Physics (vice chmn. 1988-92), Am. Bd. Radiology, Am. Soc. Therapeutic Radiology and Oncology (ASTRO Gold medal 2000). Methodist. Avocation: travel. Home: 918 Eucalyptus St Davis CA 95616 Office: Univ Calif Davis Med Ctr Dept Rad Oncology 4501 X St Ste G126 Sacramento CA 95817 Home Phone: 530-758-9149; Office Phone: 916-734-3932. Business E-Mail: james.purdy@ucdmc.ucdavis.edu.

PURDY, JAN RAE, music educator; b. Detroit, July 11, 1937; d. Fred B. and Irma B. Purdy; m. Norman R. Rapp (div.); children: Lisa Ann Rapp, Lynda Rae Rapp. BA in music, Madonna U., Livonia, Mich., 1992. Tchr. voice and piano Mich. Conservatory, Detroit, Birmingham Conservatory, Mich., Plymouth Music Acad., Mich.; tchr. voice Marion HS, Birmingham, Immaculata HS, Detroit, Art Ctr. Music Sch., Detroit, Orchard Lake Sch. Music, West Bloomfield, Mich., 2007—; tchr. voice and piano from home, 1988—2008; pvt. practice, 2008—. Performed with Mt. Clemens Symphony, Dearborn Symphony, Pontiac Symphony, Clarion Symphony Orch., Sarnia, Ont., Cambodia, 2001, Mich. Opera Co., Mich. Opera Theatre Outreach Program, Detroit Lyric Opera, Dearborn Opera Group, Boris Goldovsky Opera Workshop and Performance Co., Verdi Opera Theatre, Oakway Symphony, Warren Symphony, Little Detroit Symphony. Soloist: Mich. Rep. Coun., Pres. Gerald Ford, Sen. Griffin, Detroit Mayor J. Cavanagh, astronaut James A. McDivitt, Detroit Symphony, 1955, 1969, Ctrl. Meth. Ch., Detroit, various area chs. Former mem. Birmingham Musicale; mem. Tuesday Musicale, 2005—08. Recipient Belle Isle award, Detroit Symphony, 1955. Mem.: Sigma Alpha IOta. Republican. Avocations: movies, theater, concerts. Home and Office: 23235 Canfield Farmington Hills MI 48336 Office Phone: 248-471-1604.

PURDY, JESSE E., psychology professor; b. Denver, Colo., Sept. 7, 1952; s. Howard E. and Mary F. Purdy; m. Karen L. Culp, June 10, 1972; children: Kristopher L., Matthew A. BS, Colo. State U., Ft. Collins, 1974, MS, 1976, PhD, 1978. Prof. psychology Southwestern U., Georgetown, Tex., 1978—. Assoc. nat. resource coun. Nat. Marine Fisheries Svc., Seattle, 1984—85. Author: (book) Learning and Memory, 2001; contbr. chapters to books, articles to profl. jours.; contr. to documentaries World of Wonder Discovery Channel, 1996, Kings of Camouflage Kaufmann Prodn. Inc., 2006. Grantee, NSF, 1981, 2002; fellow, Nat. Resource Coun., 1984. Mem.: Southwestern Psychol. Assn. (pres. 1998—99), Internat. Soc. Behavioral Ecology, Animal Behavior Soc., Psi Chi (pres. 2000—01). Democrat. Office: Southwestern Univ 1001 E Univ and Maple Sts Georgetown TX 78626 Office Fax: 512-863-1846. Business E-Mail: purdy@southwestern.edu.

PURE, PAMELA J., former health products executive; B in Health Adminstrn., U. NC. Various mgmt., product devel. and mktg. positions Shared Med. Sys. (now divsn. Siemens); COO Channel Health Subs. IDX Systems, 1999—2001; grp. pres. product devel. and support McKesson Corp., San Francisco, 2001—02, COO McKesson Info. Solutions, 2002—04, exec. v.p., pres. McKesson Technology Solutions, 2004—09. Named Woman of Yr. Tech. (enterprise bus.), (WIT) Women in Tech., 2005.*

PURI, MADAN LAL, mathematics professor; b. Sialkot, Feb. 20, 1929; came to U.S., 1957, naturalized, 1973; s. Ganesh Das and S. W. P.; m. Uma Kapur, Aug. 24, 1962; 3 children. BA, Punjab U., India, 1948, MA, 1950, DSc, 1975; PhD, U. Calif., Berkeley, 1962. Head dept. math. D.A.V. Coll., Punjab U., 1955-57; instr. U. Colo., 1957-58; tchg. asst., rsch. asst., jr. rsch. statistician U. Calif. at Berkeley, 1958-62; asst. prof., assoc. prof. math. Courant Inst., NYU, 1962-68; prof. math. Ind. U., Bloomington, 1968—, Coll. Arts and Scis. Disting. Rsch. scholar, 2004—. Vis. rsch. assoc. prof. U. NC., 1966, 1967; guest prof. stats. U. Gottingen, West Germany, 1972, Alexander von Humboldt guest prof., 1974-75; guest prof. U. Dortmund, West Germany, 1972, Technische Hochschule Aachen, West Germany, 1973, U. Goteborg, Chalmers U. Tech., both Sweden, 1976; vis. prof. U. Auckland, N.Z., 1977, U. Calif., Irvine, 1978, U. Wash., Seattle, 1978-79, U. Bern, Switzerland, 1982, Va. Poly. Inst., 1988, U. Tex. Arlington, 2008-09; disting. vis. London Sch. Econs. and Polit. Sci., 1991; vis. prof. U. Göttingen, Germany, 1991-92; rsch. fellow Katholieke U., Nijmegen, The Netherlands, 1992; vis. prof. U. Des Scis. et Tech. de Lille, France, 1994, U. Basel, Switzerland, 1995—, U. NSW, Australia, 1996; vis. fellow Australian Nat. U., Canberra, Australia, 1999; guest prof. U. Konstanz, Germany, 2000, U. Gottingen, 2001. Co-author: Non Parametric Methods in Multivariate Analysis, 1971, Non Parametric Methods in General Linear Models, 1985. Editor Stochastic Process and Related Topics, 1975, Statistical Inference and Related Topics, 1975, Non Parametric Techniques in Statistical Inference, 1970-2008; co-editor: Nonparametric Statistical Inference, Vols. I and II, 1982, New Perspectives in Theoretical and Applied Statistics, 1987, Mathematical Statistics and Probability Theory, Vol. A, 1987, Statistical Sciences and Data Analysis, 1993, Recent Advances in Statistics and Probability, 1994, Asymptotics in Statistics and Probability, 2000, Probability, Statistics and their Applications, 2003. Recipient Sr. U.S. Scientist award, Humboldt Preis, 1974-75, 83, Rsch. award Humboldt Found., U. Göttingen, 2001; disting. vis. scholar Inst. for Advanced Study, Ind. U., 2007. Fellow Royal Statis. Soc. (adv. editor statistics book series Taylor and Francis Book Group Inc., 2005), Inst. Math. Statistics, Am. Statis. Assn., Internat. Indian Statis. Assn. (hon.); mem. Internat. Statis. Inst. Office: Ind U Dept Math Rawles Hall Bloomington IN 47405 Office Phone: 812-855-9537. Business E-Mail: puri@indiana.edu.

PURI, RAJ K., medical researcher, director; s. Sita R. and Radha D. Puri; m. Mara R. Micic, Sept. 24, 1982; 1 child, Rada A. MS, Lucknow U., India, 1976; PhD, Ctrl. Drug Rsch. Inst., Lucknow, 1980; MD, U. Juarez Sch. Medicine, Cd. Juarez, Mex., 1986. Postdoc. scientist Mayo Clinic, Rochester, Minn., 1980—84; sr. staff fellow Nat. Cancer Inst., Bethesda, Md., 1986—88, FDA, Ctr. Biologics Evaluation & Rsch., Bethesda, 1988—92, chief lab. molecular tumor biology, 1993—2002, dir. divsn. cellular and gene therapies, 2002—. Contbr. articles to profl. jour. Achievements include patents in field. Office: FDA Ctr Biologics Evaluation & Rsch 29 Lincoln Dr Bethesda MD 20892-4555 Office Fax: 301-827-0449. Business E-Mail: raj.puri@fda.hhs.gov.

PURI, RAJENDRA KUMAR, business and tax specialist, consultant; b. Hoshiarpur, Punjab, India, Dec. 22, 1932; came to the U.S., 1965, naturalized, 1969; s. Harbans Lal and Satya Vati (Jerath) P.; children: Neena, Veena, Ram. BS, Agra U., 1952; diploma in Russian lang. and lit., U. Dehli, 1958; BA, U. Wash., 1968, MBA, 1969; MS in Taxation, Golden Gate U., 1982. Customs officer Govt. of India, New Delhi, 1955-60; asst. treas. Merc. Bank Ltd., New Delhi, 1960-65; mem. staff Peat, Marwick, Mitchell & Co., CPAs, Seattle, 1969-70; state examiner State of Wash., Seattle, 1970-72, asst. supervising state examiner, 1972-74, supervising state examiner, 1974-77; sr. internal auditor Lockheed Corp., Sunnyvale, Calif., 1977-79; sci. programming analyst Lockheed Missile and Space Co., Sunnyvale, 1979-80, data processing specialist, 1980-84, sci. programming specialist, 1984-88; chief acct. Tex. Dept. Health, Austin, 1989-90; dir. internal audit, internal auditor Tex. Workers' Compensation Commn., Austin, 1990-95; bus. and tax cons., 1996—2003. Del. Wash. State Rep. Conv., 1976, Snohomish County Rep. Conv., 1976; Rep. nominee for state auditor, Wash., 1976; spl. advisor U.S. Congl. Adv. Bd., 1982-83. Home: 2608 Hunlac Cove Round Rock TX 78681-7107 E-mail: rkpi_2000@yahoo.com.

PURI, VANDANA, linguist, educator; b. New Delhi, Sept. 22, 1978; d. Lalit Kumar and Late Mrs. Meenakshi Puri; m. Mohit Sharma, Apr. 4, 2003; 1 child, Eva Sharma. BA, St. Stephens Coll., Delhi, 1998; MA in Linguistics, U. Delhi, 2000, MPhil in Linguistics, 2002; MA in Linguistics, U. Ill. Urbana Champaign, 2009. Rsch. assoc. IBM, New Delhi, 2005; tchg. asst. U. Ill., 2006—, fellow, 2008—09. Rsch. assoc. Hoshangabad Sci. Tchg. Programme, India, 2001—02; freelance copy-editor, New Delhi, 2000—03; tchg. asst. U. York, Heslington, 2002—03; student editor Ctrl. Inst. Indian Langs., Mysore, 2002; cons., core team Edn. Coun., Ministry Human Resource Devel., Govt. India, New Delhi; rsch. asst. Deshkal Pubs., New Delhi, 2002. Exhibitions include oil painting. Achievements include research in bilingual phonology, socio-linguistics, ladakhi morphology, silence and power. Office: Univ IL Urbana-Champaign 4080 FLB 707 S Mathews Urbana IL 61801 Business E-Mail: vpuri2@illinois.edu.

PURIS, MARTIN FORD, media company executive; b. Chgo., Feb. 22, 1939; s. Martin and Virginia Lee (Farmer) Puris; m. Mary M. Herrmann; children: Kimberly Mayo, Jason Patterson, Mary Elizabeth. Student, DePauw U., 1961. With Campbell-Ewald Co., Detroit, 1962—64, Young & Rubicam, Inc., NYC, 1964-66; v.p. Carl Ally, Inc., NYC, 1966-74; pres., CEO Ammirati & Puris, Inc., NYC, 1974-94; chmn., CEO, chief creative officer Ammirati, Puris, Lintas, NYC, 1995—99; chmn., CEO Not Traditional Media, NYC, 2004—. Media advisor Pres. George Bush; dir. IPG Group, 1995—99; vice chmn. Sheltering Arms; mng. dir. New Things Investment Group; treasurer Hampton Classic; exec. com The Quills. Author: Comeback: How Seven Straight-Shooting CEO's Turned Around Troubled Companies, 1999. Recipient awards Art Dir. Club, Copy Club, N.Y.C., Cannes Film Festival. Mem.: Devon Yacht Club, Union Club, Am. Yacht Club, Nantucket Yacht Club, N.Y. Yacht Club. Republican. Roman Catholic. Avocations: sailing, tennis, horseback riding, hunting. Office Fax: 212-371-8884.

PURKERSON, MABEL LOUISE, physician, physiologist, educator; b. Goldville, SC, Apr. 3, 1931; d. James Clifton and Louise (Smith) P. AB, Erskine Coll., 1951; MD, M.U.S.C., Charleston, 1956. Diplomate Am. Bd. Pediat. Instr. pediat. Washington U. Sch. Medicine, St. Louis, 1961-67, instr. medicine, 1966-67, asst. prof. pediat., 1967-98, asst. prof. medicine, 1967-76, assoc. prof. medicine, 1976-89, prof., 1989-98, prof. emerita, 1998—, assoc. dean curriculum, 1976-94, assoc. dean acad. projects, 1994-98. Cons. in field. Editl. bd. Am. Jour. Kidney Diseases, 1981-87; contbr. articles to profl. jours. Mem. bd. counselors Erskine Coll., 1971—87, trustee, 2000—06, The Mabel Dorn Reeder Found., 2007—; historian St. Louis Symphony Orch., trustee; bd. dir. St. Louis Symphony Orchesta, 1999—2008, hon. trustee, 2008—; bd. dirs. Trailnet, 2008—, St. Louis Acad. Sci., 2008—, Erskine Coll. Alumni Assn., 2008—, Opera Theatre, St. Louis, 2009—. USPHS spl. fellow, 1971-72. Mem. Am. Heart Assn. Coun. on the Kidney (exec. com. 1973-81), Am. Physiol. Soc., Am. Soc. Nephrology, Internat. Soc. Nephrology, Ctrl. Soc. Clin. Rsch., Am. Soc. Renal Biochemistry and Metabolism, Internat. Assn. History Nephrology, Am. Osler Soc., Explorer's Club (chair St. Louis chpt., 2005-), Sigma Xi (chpt. sec. 1974-76), Alpha Omega Alpha. Home: 20 Haven View Dr Saint Louis MO 63141-7902 Home Phone: 314-994-1649.

PURL, O. THOMAS, retired electronics company executive; b. East St. Louis, Ill., June 5, 1924; s. Ruthford Keith and Muriel Agnes (Thompson) P.; m. Martha Elaine Smalley, Feb. 21, 1948; children— Thomas Keith, Jeanne Marie Purl Elder. BS, U. Ill., 1948, BS, 1951, MS, 1952, PhD, 1955. Head high-power traveling wave tube sect., mem. tech. staff Hughes Research Lab., Culver City, Calif., 1955-58; sect. head, dept. mgr., group v.p., v.p. shareholder relations and planning coordination Watkins-Johnson Co., Palo Alto, Calif., 1958-86. Contbr. articles to profl. jours.; patentee in field. Chmn. career guidance com. Santa Clara Valley Joint Engring. Council, 1971-73; bd. dirs. Jr. Achievement of Santa Clara County, 1975-79. Served to 1st lt. USAAF, 1943-46. Fellow IEEE (chmn. Santa Clara Valley subsect. 1972); mem. Sigma Xi, Eta Kappa Nu, Phi Kappa Phi, Sigma Tau. Clubs: Commonwealth of Calif. Home: 300 Hot Springs Rd K220 Montecito CA 93108

PURNELL, MAURICE EUGENE, JR., lawyer; b. Dallas, Feb. 17, 1940; s. Maurice Eugene Sr. and Marjorie (Maillot) P.; m. Diane Blake, Aug. 19, 1966; children: Maurice Eugene III, Blake Maillot. BA, Washington and Lee U., 1961; MBA, U. Pa., 1963; LLB, So. Meth. U., 1966. Bar: Tex. 1966. Ptnr. Locke, Purnell, Boren, Laney & Neely, Dallas, 1966-87; shareholder Locke Purnell Rain Harrell PC, Dallas, 1987-99; ptnr. Locke Lord Bissell & Liddell LLP, Dallas, 1999—2002, of counsel, 2002—. Bd. dirs. Leggett & Platt, Inc. Bd. dirs. Dallas Summer Musicals. Mem. ABA, Tex. Bar Assn., Tex. Bar Found., Dallas Bar Assn. Am. Judicature Soc., Dallas C. of C, Brook Hollow Golf Club. Home: 4409 S Versailles Ave Dallas TX 75205-3044 Office: Locke Lord Bissell & Liddell LLP 2200 Ross Ave Ste 2200 Dallas TX 75201-6776 Office Phone: 214-740-8444.

PURNELL, OLIVER GORDON, JR., men's college basketball coach; b. Berlin, Md., May 19, 1953; m. Vicky Purnell; children: Olivia, Lindsay. BS in Health and Phys. Edn., Old Dominion U., 1975, MA in Phys. Edn. and Adminstrn., 1978. Draft pick Milw. Bucks, 1975; grad. asst. Old Dominion U., 1975—77, asst. coach, 1978—85, head coach, 1991—94; asst. coach U. Md., 1985—88; head coach Radford U., 1988—91, U. Dayton, Ohio, 1994—2003, Clemson U., SC, 2003—. Head coach US Olympic Festival, 1994; asst. coach World U. Games, 1995, head coach, 99; mem. USA Basketball Men's Collegiate Com., 2000; asst. coach Goodwill Games, 2001, Olympic Qualifying, 2003, US Olympic Team, Athens, Greece, 2004. Recipient Devel. Coach of Yr. award, USA Basketball, 1999; named Big South Conf. Coach of Yr., 1991, Colonial Athletic Assn. Coach of Yr., 1993, Coach of Yr. in State of Va., 1993, Atlantic 10 Coach of Yr., 1998; named to Old Dominion Athletic Hall of Fame, 1988, All-Time Old Dominion U. Basketball Squard, 2006. Mem.: Nat. Assn. Basketball Coaches (pres. 2006—, bd. dirs. 1998, Dist. Coach of Yr. 1998, Dist. IV Coach of Yr. 1993). Avocations: jogging, cooking. Office: Clemson U Mens Basketball Jervey Athletic Ctr 100 Perimeter Rd Clemson SC 29633 Office Phone: 864-656-1954. E-mail: opurnel@clemson.edu.*

PURSCELL, HELEN DUNCAN, sociologist, educator; b. Cottonwood County, Minn., Jan. 8, 1926; d. Arthur Albert Frenzen and Pearl Blanche Pope; m. Boyd Alvah Duncan (dec.); children: Bruce Howard-(dec.), Stuart Lachlan(dec.), Scott Boyd; m. Keith William Purscell, June 17, 1994. BA, Mankato State U., 1963, postgrad., 1981—84; MA, U. Iowa, 1967; postgrad., U. Minn., 1969—73. Cert. sex educator Am. Assn. Sex Educators, Counselors and Therapists. Elem. sch. tchr., Redwood County, Minn., 1944—45, Cottonwood County, 1945—46; English tutor Parsons Coll., Fairfield, Iowa, 1964—65; asst. instr. Mankato (Minn.) State U., 1965—66, instr., 1966—68, asst. prof., 1968—90, assoc. prof., 1990—94; ret. Home: PO Box 3639 Mankato MN 56002 Home Phone: 507-625-3309. Personal E-mail: kwpurscell@charter.net.

PURSCELL, KEITH WILLIAM, minister; b. Council Bluffs, Iowa, Feb. 12, 1931; s. Benjamin William and Marie Esther (Lowe) Purscell; m. Mary Louise Elliott, May 16, 1952 (dec. Jan. 22, 1993); children: Kenneth, Sally, David, Glenda; m. Helen Margaret Duncan, June 17, 1994. Student, Johnson Bible Coll., Knoxville, Tenn., 1949—51; BA in Religion, Nebr. Christian Coll., Norfolk, 1953; postgrad. studies, Lincoln Christian Coll. Sem., Ill., 1953—54; MDiv. in Ministry, with hon., Phillips Grad. Sem., Enid, Okla., 1970. Ordained Clergy The Christian Ch., 1951. Pastor Ch. Christ, Red Cloud, Nebr., 1954—58, Clay Ctr. Christian Ch., Nebr., 1958—60, First Christian Ch., Florence, Kans., 1962—67, Spencer, Iowa, 1970—79, Douglass, Kans., 1967—70, Broadway Christian Ch., Wichita, Kans., 1979—82, 1st Christian Ch., Independence, Kans., 1982—86, La Junta, Colo., 1986—90, Mankato, Minn., 1990—97; interim pastor Congl. UCC Ch., Webster City, Iowa, 1998—99, Fairmont, Minn., 2005, St. Lukes, Fairbault, Minn., 1999—2000; retired; interim pastor United Ch. Mapleton, Minn., 2005—06, UCC Ch., Gaylord, Minn., 2008—09. Chaplain NW Iowa Alcoholism & Drug Treatment Unit, Spencer, Iowa, 1971—78; vice moderator Christian Ch. Upper-Midwest Region, 1976—79, mem.; chmn. com. on scholarships for ministry Disciples of Christ, Kans., 1979—86; chmn. com. on ministry Disciples of Christ Colo., and Wyoming, 1989—90; organising pres., v.p. Living at Home Block Nurse Program, Mankato, Minn., 1991—2005; pres. Minn. State U. for Srs. Orgn., Mankato, 2005—06; chai Vital Ch. Com.; with Min.'s Inst. Planning-CCUM. Co-author: (devotional prayer) Secret Place, 1982; contbr. articles to Christian mags., 1955—95. Mem. adv. com. hospice Wesley Hosp., Wichita, Kans., 1981—82; creator sr. ctr. and county transportation for Clay County Iowa, 1976—79; pres. consumer adv. coun. Kans. Gas and Electric Co., 1984—86. Named Disting. alumus, Phillips U. Alumni, 2001. Disciples Of Christ. Achievements include design of regional policy on sexual abuse by clergy or staff for Christian Church in the Central Rockies Region. Avocation: photography. Home and Office: PO Box 3639 Mankato MN 56002 Office Phone: 507-625-3309.

PURSE, CHARLES ROE, investment banker; b. Redhill, Surrey, Eng., May 19, 1960; arrived in U.S., 1960; s. James Nathanial II and Rolande Marie-Louise (Redon) Purse; m. Carole Lynn Sadler, July 5, 1986; children: Hayley Elizabeth, Cameron James, Andrew Lang. BA, Dartmouth Coll., 1982; MBA, Northwestern U., 1985. Account officer No. Trust Bank, Chgo., 1982—85; asst. v.p. Citicorp Real Estate, Inc., Chgo., 1985—88; v.p. Citibank, Ltd., Sydney, 1988—91, Citibank Realty Investment Advisors, NYC, 1991—94; sr. v.p. Yarmouth Group, NYC, 1994—96; mng. dir. DRA Advisors, Inc., NYC, 1996—2000; mng. dir. real estate pvt. fund group Credit Suisse First Boston, NYC, 2000—05; mng. prin. Park Hill Real Estate Group, LLC, NYC, 2005—07; sr. mng. dir. The Blackstone Group (Park Hill Real Estate Group, LLC), NYC, 2007—. Mem.: Pension Real Estate Assn., Bald Peak Colony Club, Belle Haven Club, Hillsboro Club (Hillsboro Beach, Fla.), Country Club (Cleve.). Republican. Avocations: golf, photography, skiing, tennis. Office: Park Hill Real Estate Group LLC 345 Park Ave 15th Fl New York NY 10154

PURSELL, DAVID P., chemistry professor; BS in Engring., US Mil. Acad., West Point, NY, 1981; MS in Chemistry, Lehigh U., Bethlehem, Pa., 1985, MA in Sci. Edn., 1987; PhD in Chem. Physics, U. Pa., Phila., 2000. EIT Va., 1981. Engr. officer, lt. col. US Army, 1981—2006; exec. dir. dept. chemistry U. Pa., 2006—07; chemistry prof. Sch. Sci. and Tech., Ga. Gwinnett Coll., Lawrenceville, 2007—. Contbr. articles to profl. jours. Recipient numerous award, US Army, 1981—2006. Office: SST Ga Gwinnett Coll 1000 University Center Ln Lawrenceville GA 30043

PURSLEY, FRANK JAMES, retired personal development specialist; b. Durham, NC, May 5, 1927; s. James Alton and Vesta Andwers Pursley; m. Dymple Edwards (dec.); children: Cynthia, Susan, Frank Jr.; m. Barbara Jean Pursley; children: Charles, Keith, Vanessa. AA, Ctrl. Va. C.C., Lynchburg, 1978. Sales mgr. WLVA-T Inc., Lynchburg, 1953—75; pers. devel. Va. Dept. Transp., Lynchburg, 1976—98; ret., 1998. Mem. adv. bd. Va. C.C., Lynchburg, adj. instr., 1998—2002; chmn. Svc. Corps. Ret. Exec. (SCORE) 529, 2003—. Mem. adv. bd. Local Red Cross, Lynchburg; active Rep. Nat. Com.; chair adminstrv. bd. Ct. St. Meth. Ch., Lynchburg, 1978—80. 1st. lt. US Army, 1956, col. US Army, 1980. Mem.: Mil. Order World Wars, Oakwood Country Club (golf com. 2000—). Avocations: golf, music, fishing, hunting. Home: 517 Midvale St Lynchburg VA 24502 Office: Score 529 Fed bldg Ste A42 1101 Court St Lynchburg VA 24504 Personal E-mail: fpurs17868@aol.com.

PURSLEY, MARK R., philosopher, educator; b. San Diego, Feb. 1, 1955; s. James J. and Nadene Pursley; 1 child, Shane N. BA, Westmont Coll., Montecito, Calif., 1978; MA, Fuller Theol. Sem., Pasadena, Calif., 1981. Asst. prof. philosophy LA Mission Coll., Sylmar, Calif., 1993—, pace dir., 1999—. Pres. Honors Transfer Coun. Calif., 2002—03. Mem.: Alpha Gamma Sigma (faculty advisor 2000—). Democrat. Avocations: running, sports. Home: 4340 Mill Valley Rd Moorpark CA 93021 Office: LA Mission Coll 13356 Eldridge Ave Sylmar CA 91342 Office Fax: 818-833-3356. Business E-Mail: purslemr@lamission.edu.

PURSLEY, MICHAEL BADER, engineering educator, communications systems researcher, consultant; b. Winchester, Ind., Aug. 10, 1945; s. Bader E. and Evelyn L. (Bennett) P.; m. Lou Ann Hinchman, July 6, 1968; 1 child, Jessica Ann. BS, Purdue U., 1967, MS, 1968; PhD, U. So. Calif., 1974. Mem. tech. staff Hughes Aircraft Co., Los Angeles, 1967; engr. Northrop Co., Hawthorne, Calif., 1968; staff engr. Hughes Aircraft Co., Los Angeles, 1968-74; acting asst. prof. UCLA, 1974; asst. prof., then assoc. prof. elec. engring. U. Ill., Urbana, 1974-80, prof., 1980-93; Holcombe prof. elec. and computer engring. Clemson (S.C.) U., 1992—; assoc. Ctr. Advanced Study, 1980-81; vis. prof. UCLA, 1985; cons. U.S. Army, Huntsville, Ala., 1977, Ft. Monmouth, NJ, 1983-86, 91, ITT, Ft. Wayne, Ind., 1979—; pres. SIGCOM, Inc., 1986-90; prin. scientist Techno-Scis. Inc., 1990—96. Author: Random Processes in Linear Systems, 2002, Introduction to Digital Communications, 2005; contbr. chapters to books. Recipient Fred W. Ellersick award Comms. Soc., 1996, Tech. Achievement award Mil. Comm. Conf., 1999, Edwin Howard Armstrong Achievement award, 2002, Alumni award, U. So. Calif. Sch. Engrs., 2005, Purdue U. Outstanding Electrical Engr., 2008. Fellow IEEE (pres. info. theory group 1983, Centennial medal 1984, Millennium medal 2000); mem. Inst. Math. Stats. Office: Clemson U 303 Fluor Daniel Bldg Dept ECE Clemson SC 29634

PURTLE, JOHN INGRAM, lawyer, former state supreme court justice; b. Enola, Ark., Sept. 7, 1923; s. John Wesley and Edna Gertrude (Ingram) P.; m. Marian Ruth White, Dec. 31, 1951 (dec. 1995); children: Jeffrey, Lisa K.; m. Phyllis Kelly Purtle. Student, U. Ctrl. Ark., 1946—47; LLB, U. Ark., 1950. Bar: Ark. 1950, U.S. Dist. Ct. (ea. dist.) Ark. 1950. Pvt. practice, Conway, Ark., 1950-53, Little Rock, 1953—78, 1990—; mem. Ark. State Legislature, 1951-52, 69-70; assoc. justice Ark. Supreme Ct., 1979-90. Tchr., deacon Baptist Ch. Served with U.S. Army, 1940-45. Mem. ABA, Ark. Bar Assn., Am. Judicature Soc., Ark. Jud. Coun. Democrat. Home Phone: 501-450-0066.

PURVES, DENNIS PATRICK, library director; b. Elizabeth, NJ, Dec. 25, 1970; s. Dennis Patrick and Mary Theresa Purves. BA, Seton Hall U., 1993; MLS, Rutgers U., 1994. Libr. page Linden (N.J.) Pub. Libr., 1987—95, libr., 1996—2004, sr. libr., 2004—; libr. Alexander Libr. Rutgers U., New Brunswick, NJ, 1995; freelance subject cataloger Bowker-Reed Reference, New Providence, NJ, 1996—97. Mem.: ALA, Librs. of Union County Consortium (v.p. 2005, pres. 2006), N.J. Libr. Assn. Roman Catholic. Home: 38 E Elm Street Apt 3A Linden NJ 07036 Office: Linden Pub Libr 31 E Henry St Linden NJ 07036 Business E-Mail: dpurves@lindenpl.org.

PURVES, WILLIAM KIRKWOOD, biologist, educator; b. Sacramento, Oct. 28, 1934; s. William Kirkwood and Dorothy (Brandenburger) P.; m. Jean McCauley, June 9, 1959; 1 son, David William. BS, Calif. Inst. Tech., 1956; MS, Yale U., 1957, PhD, 1959. NSF postdoctoral fellow U. Tubingen, Germany, 1959-60; Nat. Cancer Inst. postdoctoral fellow UCLA, 1960-61; asst. prof. botany U. Calif., Santa Barbara, 1961-65, assoc. prof. biochemistry, 1965-70, prof. biology, 1970-73, chmn. dept. biol. scis., 1972-73; prof. biology, head biol. sci. group U. Conn., Storrs, 1973-77; Stuart Mudd prof. biology Harvey Mudd Coll., Claremont, Calif., 1977-95, prof. emeritus, 1996—, chmn. dept. biol., 1985-95, chmn. dept. computer sci., 1985-90; adj. prof. plant physiology U. Calif., Riverside, 1979-85. V.p., sci. dir. The Mona Group LLC, 1996-2004. Author: Life, the Science of Biology, 1983, 8th edit., 2007. NSF sr. postdoctoral fellow U. London, 1967, Harvard U., 1968; vis. fellow computer sci. Yale U., 1983-84; vis. scholar Northwestern U., 1991; NSF rsch. grantee, 1962-83, 97-2001. Fellow AAAS; mem. Sigma Xi. E-mail: Bill_Purves@hmc.edu.

PURVIN, JACK MITCHELL, physician; b. Bklyn., May 27, 1953; s. Saul and Sylvia (Masey) P. BA in Psychology, U. Denver, 1975; postgrad., U. Autonoma de Guadalajara, Mex., 1978-81; MD, Dominica Sch. of Medicine, 1983. Pres. P.E.C. Inc., Del. Developer diabetic food products, prelim sys. Patentee in field. Owner Jack M. Purvin Found. Mem. Am. Diabetes Assn., Montana Hist. Soc. Avocations: chess, coin collecting/numismatics, philatelic collections, rare documents, sports. Home: 1901 84th St Apt 4A Brooklyn NY 11214-3032 Office: PEC Inc PO Box 140028 Brooklyn NY 11214-0028 Home Phone: 718-759-7335; Office Phone: 718-333-9198. Personal E-mail: jackpurvin@aol.com.

PURVIS, GAIL, elementary school educator; b. Chgo., June 26, 1945; d. Arthur J. and Elaine (Herron) Hoffman; 1 child, Leo II. BFA, BS in Edn., U. Cinn., 1967; MS in Edn. with honors, U. Miami, 1982; psychology, art edn., fine arts, U. Ill., 1967, DBAE Art Specialist, 1991. Cert. K-12 art tchr., Fla. Instr., art Broward County Schs., Coral Springs, Fla.; tchr., art instr. St. Johns Coll., Nassau, Bahamas; tchr., pottery specialist Queens Coll., Nassau; youth planning specialist Broward Employment Tng. Adminstrn., Ft. Lauderdale, Fla. Adj. prof. Nova So. U., Ft. Lauderdale, Fla., Barry U., Miami Lakes, Fla. Mem. Nat. Art Edn. Assn., Fla. Art. Edn. Assn., Assn. Supervision Curriculum Devel. Home Phone: 954-344-0613. E-mail: purvis@nsu.nova.edu.

PURVIS, JOHN ANDERSON, lawyer, educator; b. Aug. 31, 1942; s. Virgil J. and Emma Lou (Anderson) P.; m. Charlotte Johnson, Apr. 3, 1976; 1 child, Whitney; children by previous marriage: Jennifer, Matt. BA cum laude, Harvard U., 1965; JD, U. Colo., 1968. Bar: Colo. 1968, U.S. Dist. Ct. Colo. 1968, U.S. Ct. Appeals (10th cir.) 1978. Dep. dist. atty., Boulder, Colo., 1968-69; asst. dir., dir. legal aid U. Colo. Sch. Law, 1969; assoc. Williams, Taussig & Trine, Boulder, 1969; head Boulder office Colo. Pub. Defender Sys., 1970-72; assoc., ptnr. Hutchinson, Black, Hill, Buchanan & Cook, Boulder, 1972-85; ptnr. Purvis, Gray, Schuetze and Gordon, 1985-98, Purvis, Gray & Gordon, LLP, 1999—2001, Purvis Gray LLP, 2001—03, 2008—, Purvis Gray & Murphy, 2003—08. Acting Colo. State Pub. Defender, 1978; adj. prof. law U. Colo., 1981, 84-88, 94, others; lectr. in field; chmn. Colo. Pub. Defender Commn., 1979-89; mem. nominating commn. Colo. Supreme Ct., 1984-90; mem. com. on conduct U.S. Dist. Ct., 1991-97, chmn., 1996-97; chmn. Boulder County Criminal Justice Com., 1975-81. Recipient Recipient Ames award, Harvard U., 1964, Outstanding Young Lawyer award, Colo. Bar Assn., 1978, Dist. Achievement award, U. Colo. Law Sch. Alumni Assn., 1997. Mem.: ATLA, Am. Bar Found., Colo. Bar Found., Trial Lawyers for Pub. Justice, Colo. Trial Lawyers Assn., Boulder County Bar Assn., Colo. Bar Assn. (chair litigation sect. 1994—95), Am. Coll. Trial Lawyers (state chmn. 1998—2000), Am. Bd. Trial Advs., Internat. Acad. Trial Lawyers (state chmn. 2002—), Internat. Soc. Barristers, Faculty of Fed. Advs. (bd. dirs. 1999—2001), Supreme Ct. Hist. Soc. (state chmn. 1998—2002). Democrat. Address: 4410 Arapahoe Ave Ste 200 Boulder CO 80303 Home Phone: 303-444-0744; Office Phone: 303-442-3366. Personal E-mail: jpurvis@purvisgray.net.

PURYEAR, EUGENE, advocate, writer; b. Charlottesville, Va., 1986; Student, Howard U., Washington, 2004—. Organizer Movement to Free the Jena 6; nat. organizer Act Now to Stop War and End Racism Coalition. Contbr., mem. editl. bd.: Socialism and Liberation mag., Liberation. US vice presdl. candidate Party for Socialism and Liberation, 2008, mem. nat. com. Party For Socialism And Liberation. Office: c/o Party for Socialism and Liberation 611 Pennsylvania Ave SE 433 Washington DC 20003 Office Phone: 202-543-4900.*

PURYEAR, MARTIN, artist, educator; b. Washington, May 23, 1941; s. Reginald Thomas and Martina Alice (Morse) P. BA, Cath. U., 1963; postgrad., Swedish Royal Acad., Stockholm, 1966-68; M.F.A., Yale U., 1971, Doctorate (hon.), 1994. Mem. Peace Corps, Sierra Leone, 1964—66; asst. prof. Fisk U., Nashville, 1971-73, U. Md., College Park, 1974-77; assoc. prof. art U. Ill., Chgo., 1978-86, prof., 1986-88; staff Calder Atelier, Saché, France, 1992—93; resident Am. Acad., Rome, 1997; represented by Donald Young Gallery, Chgo. Exhibited in group shows at Whitney Biennial Exhbn., 1979, 81, 89, Whitney Mus. Am. Art, NY, Guggenheim Mus., NYC, 1978, 85, 87, Mus. Modern Art, NYC, 1984, St. Louis Art Mus., 1988, Donald Young Gallery, Chgo., 2002, 2003, McKee Gallery, NYC, 2002, Irish Mus. Modern Art, Dublin, 2004, others; one-man shows include Corcoran Gallery Art, 1977, Joslyn Art Mus., 1980, Univ. Art Mus., 1985, Bklyn. Mus., 1988; commd. sculptures include Bodard Art, Nathan Manila Sculpture Pk., Govs. State U., University Park, Ill., Chevy Chase Garden Pla., Md.; traveling retrospective Art Inst. Chgo., Hirshorn Museum, Washington, D.C., Museum of Contemporary Art, Los Angeles, 1991-92; Documenta IX, Kassel, Germany, 1992. Recipient Purchase prize Balt. Mus. Art, 1962, award Francis J. Greenburger Found., 1988, Best Artist prize Sao Paulo Bienal, 1989, Creative Arts award for sculpture Brandeis U., 1989, medal for sculpture Skowhegan Sch. Painting & Sculpture, 1990, award Coll. Art Assn., 1993; Louis Comfort Tiffany Found. grantee, 1981; Guggenheim fellow, 1982. Mem.: Am. Acad. and Inst. Arts and Letters.

PUSCAS, VASILE LOUIS, bishop emeritus; b. Aurora, Ill., Sept. 3, 1915; Attended, Quigley Preparatory Sem., Chgo., Oradea-Mare, Romania, Propaganda Fide Sem., Rome, Benedictine Coll., Lisle, Ill. Ordained priest, 1942; ordained bishop, 1983; vicar apostolic Eparchy of Saint George's in Canton (Romanian), 1983—87, bishop, 1987—93, bishop emeritus, 1993—. Roman Catholic. Office: 1121 44th St NE Canton OH 44714-1297

PUSCHECK, ELIZABETH ELLA, physician; b. Frankfurt, Fed. Republic of Germany, Feb. 22, 1961; came to U.S., 1963; d. Herbert Charles and Elizabeth Lina (Schlecht) P. BA, U. Chgo., 1983, MS, 1985; MD, Wash. U., 1987. Resident in ob.-gyn. Wash. U., St. Louis, 1987—. Adminstrv. chief Wash. U., St. Louis, 1990-91; fellow reproductive endocrine, 1991-93; tchr. physician's asst. St. Louis U., 1990. Contbr. articles to profl. jours. Fellow Am. Coll. Ob.-Gyn.; mem. St. Louis Ob.-Gyn. Soc., Sigma Xi. Lutheran. Avocations: hiking, sailing, dance, piano, horseback riding. Home: 8106 W Boulevard Dr Alexandria VA 22308-1711

PUSEY, WILLIAM ANDERSON, lawyer; b. Richmond, Va., Mar. 17, 1936; s. Paul H. and Vernelle (Barnes) P.; m. Patricia Powell, Sept. 3, 1960; children: Patricia Brent, William A. Jr., Margaret Glen. AB, Princeton U., 1958; JD, U. Va., 1962. Bar: Va. 1964. Assoc. McCutchen, Brown, et al, San Francisco, 1962-63; dep. dist. atty. Alameda County, Oakland, Calif., 1963-64; assoc., ptnr., sr. counsel Hunton & Williams, Washington, Fairfax and Richmond, Va., 1964—. Former dir. Ea. Mineral Law Found., pres., 1987-88. Chmn. bd. dirs. Presbyn. Sch. Christian Edn., Richmond, 1984-85. Mem. Am. Hort. Soc. (bd. dirs. and sec. 1995-2002, gen. counsel 2002—06), Order of Coif, Phi Beta Kappa, Omicron Delta Kappa. Home: 57 E Square Ln Richmond VA 23238 Office: Hunton & Williams Riverfront Pk 2a East Town 951 E Byrd St Richmond VA 23219 Office Phone: 804-784-0490.

PUSHKARSKY, LOUIS PAUL, retired mathematics educator; b. Slovak Town, Ark., Aug. 17, 1922; s. Erasmm and Yadwiga (Petroczynski) P.; m. Clarice W. Pollard, Jan. 19, 1963; children: Larry, David. BS in Math. and Sci., U. Ctrl. Ark., 1951; MA in Math., U. Ark., 1953. Cert. tchr. Mo. Head math. and sci. Bradford (Ark.) Schs., 1952-55; prof. math. North Ctrl. Mo. Coll., Trenton, 1955-89, head math. and sci., 1955-89, prof. emeritus, 1989—2008. Founding mem. Mo. C.C. Assn., Jefferson City, 1963. Mem. Trenton City Coun., 1985-91. Sgt. U.S. Army Air Corp, 1942-46. Recipient Glynne E. Clark Disting. Svc. award, Mo. C.C. Assn., 2003. Mem. VFW (comdr. 1973-74, bd. dirs. Mo. dept. 1976-77, asst. insp. gen. 1980-81. mat. adc 1978, 98, comdr. ritual team 1995—, dist. adj. 1974—), DAV (comdr. 1999-2000), Am. Legion (Post 31 comdr. 2005-06), Elks (exalted ruler 1975), Alpha Chi. Avocations: observing nature, collecting music, gardening. Home: 169 E 7th St Trenton MO 64683

PUSKAS, JOHN DANIEL, cardiothoracic surgeon, medical educator; b. New Liskeard, Canada, Sept. 2, 1960; s. Alexander John and Mary Frances Puskas; m. Jane Chace Lopes, June 6, 1986; children: Caroline, John, Jillian. AB, Princeton U., 1982; MD, Harvard U., 1986; MSc, U. Toronto, 1991. Diplomate Am. Bd. Surgery, Am. Bd. Thoracic Surgery. Resident in gen. surgery Mass. Gen. Hosp., Boston, 1986; rsch. fellow, lung transportation lab. Toronto Gen. Hosp., 1989—91; resident and fellow cardiothoracic surgery Emory U. Sch. Medicine, Atlanta, 1993—96, staff surgeon, divsn. cardiothoracic surgery, 1996—, surgical dir. Emory Carlyle Fraser Ctr. for Atrial Fibrillation, 2005—, dir. Clin. Rsch. Unit, Divsn. Cardiothoracic Surgery, 2005—, prof. surgery, assoc. chief, 2005—; chief cardiac surgery Emory Crawford Long Hosp., Atlanta, 2005—. Edward D. Churchill fellowship, Mass. Gen. Hosp., 1989—91. Fellow: Am. Coll. Surgeons; mem.: Soc. Univ. Surgeons, Am. Coll. Chest Physicians, Soc. Thoracic Surgeons (mem. program com. 2003—05), Internat. Soc. for Minimally Invasive Cardiothoracic Surgery (sec. 2002, v.p.), Am. Assn. Thoracic Surgery (mem. program com. 2003—05). Avocations: piano, tennis, skiing, sailing. Office: Emory U Sch of Medicine 550 Peachtree St 6th Fl MOT Atlanta GA 30308

PUST, RONALD E., physician, educator; b. Sidney, Mont., May 5, 1941; s. Erich W. Pust and Marie Leis; m. Karen J. Blomquist, June 12, 1966; children: Joel E., Sara M. Meza, Rachel K. Durazo, Brian P. BA, Wheaton Coll., Ill., 1962; MD, U. Wash., Seattle, 1962—66. Cert. Am. Bd. Preventive Medicine, 1973, Amercan Bd. Family Medicine, 1978, qualification Am. Soc. Tropical Medicine & Hygiene, 2000. TB control physician Indian Health Svc., Window Rock, Ariz., 1969—71; med. epidemiologist CDC, USPHS, Enugu, Nigeria, 1971—73; med. officer, dir. Immanuel Luth. Hosp., Wapenamanda, Papua New Guinea, 1973—79; prof. family medicine and pub. health U. Ariz., Tucson, 1979—. Pres. Global Health Edn. Consortium, NYC, 1992—93; prof. and head family health Moi U., Eldoret, Kenya, 2004—05. Med. missionary to Papua New Guinea Luth. Ch., St Louis, 1973—79. Recipient Smallpox Target Zero, WHO, 1980, Smilkstein Internat. Family Medicine award, Soc. Tchrs. Family Medicine, 2007. Democrat. Presyterian. Avocations: travel, photography, poetry. Business E-Mail: rpust@email.arizona.edu.

PUSTAY, MELANIE ANN, federal agency administrator; b. 1957; BA summa cum laude, George Mason U., Fairfax, Va., 1979; JD, Am. U. Washington Coll. Law, 1982. Joined as atty adv. US Dept. Justice, Washington, 1983, various adv. and supr. positions dealing in litig., records disclosure and Freedom of Info. Act. compliance, dep. dir. Office Info. & Privacy (OIP), 1999—2007, acting dir., 2007, dir., 2007—. Recipient Atty. Gen.'s Disting. Svc. award, US Dept. Justice. Office: US Dept Justice Office Info & Privacy (OIP) 950 Pennsylvania Ave NW Washington DC 20530*

PUTALLAZ, MARTHA, psychologist, educator; m. Blair Hesson Sheppard, Aug. 16, 1980; children: Philip Hesson Sheppard, Christopher Shea Sheppard. AB, Smith Coll., Northampton, Mass, 1976; MS, PhD, U. Ill., Urbana-Champaign, 1981. Asst. prof. U. NC, Chapel Hill, 1981—83; asst. prof. psychology Duke U., Durham, NC, 1983—89, assoc. prof. psychology, 1989—2000, prof. psychology, 2000—; exec. dir. Duke Talent Identification Program, Durham, 2004—. Mem. Am. Assn. Gifted Children, Durham, 2005, Next Generation Venture Fund, NYC, 2005. Fellow: APA; mem.: Nat. Assn. Gifted Children, Assn. Psychol. Sci., Soc. Rsch. Children, Sigma Xi, Phi Beta Kappa. Office: Duke Talent Identification Program 1121 West Main St Durham NC 27701-2097 Office Fax: 919-668-9141. Business E-Mail: putallaz@duke.edu.

PUTHENPURAKAL, JOSEPH MATHEW, information technology executive; b. Changanacherry, India, Feb. 12, 1949; arrived in U.S., 1978; s. Mathew Joseph and Teresa Mathew P.; m. Mary Jose Shirly, Aug. 21, 1977; children: Mathew Joseph, Thomas Joseph, Sherin Jose. BS, Kerala U., India, 1976; MS, Kerala U., 1978; AA, Dupage Coll., Glen Ellyn, Ill., 1982; BA, North Cen. Coll., Naperville, Ill., 1984; MBA, Thornewood U., Amsterdam, Netherlands, 1998, PhD, 2001. Software engr. AT&T Tech., Lisle, Ill., 1983-84; mem. tech. staff AT&T Bell Labs., Naperville, Ill., 1984-87; info. systems cons. Indecon, Inc., Chicago, 1987-89; pres. Chicagoland Star Telephone Co., 1988, Global Resources Co., Chgo., 1988—; mgr. Jewel Info. Systems Group, Melrose Park, Ill., 1989—91; pres. Optimum Techs. Inc., Lisle, Ill., 1992—2005; owner Optimum Real Estate, 2003—; pres. Alert IT Solutions, Inc., Woodridge, Ill., 2006—; CEO 24/7 Computer Dr. Call, Ill., 2008—. Trustee Rep. Presdl. Task Force, Washington, 1986. Mem. Data Processing Mgmt. Assn., Am. Entrepreneurs Assn., Internat. Traders. Avocations: reading, travel, swimming, investing. Home and Office: Alert IT Solutions Inc PO Box 5433 1230 Golfview Dr Woodridge IL 60517 Office Phone: 630-854-3762. Personal E-mail: jputhen1@gmail.com. Business E-Mail: jputhen@alertitsolutions.com.

PUTHOFF, HAROLD E., physics researcher; m. Adrienne Kennedy, 1974; 5 children. BEE, U. Fla., 1958, MSE, 1960; PhD, Stanford U., 1967. Engr. Gen. Electric, Schenectady, N.Y., 1958, Sperry Electronic Tube Div., Gainesville, Fla., 1959-60; lt. USNR Nat. Security Agy., Ft. Meade, Md., 1960-63; rsch. assoc., lectr. Microwave Lab, Stanford (Calif.) U., 1963-71; sr. rsch. physicist SRI Internat., Menlo Park, Calif., 1971-85; dir. Inst. for Advanced Studies at Austin (Tex.), 1985—. Author: (with R. Pantell) Fundamentals of Quantum Electronics, 1969, (with R. Targ) Mind Reach, 1977. Mem. The Am. Physics Soc., AAAS, Soc. for Sci. Exploration, Sigma Xi.

PUTHOFF, MARK ALLEN, lawyer; b. Ft. Loramie, Ohio, Dec. 13, 1972; s. Robert Lee and Teresa Francis Puthoff; m. Jennifer Ellen Ondera, Nov. 17, 2001; children: Jordyn Taylor, Milan Isabelle, Hunter Ty. B, Hawaii Pacific U., Honolulu, 1996; JD, Thomas M. Cooley Law Sch., Lansing, Mich., 2003. Bar: Ohio 2005. Intern asst. prosecutor Montgomery County Prosecutor's Office, Dayton, Ohio, 2002—03; adminstr. contracts and real estate Pacific LightNet, Inc., Honolulu, 2003—04; atty. Dungan & LeFevre Co., L.P.A., Troy, Ohio, 2004—07, Puthoff & Assocs. LLC, Troy, Ohio, 2007—. Amb. Troy Area C. of C., Ohio, 2006; chmn. Taste of Troy, 2006; participant Leadership Troy, 2006—06; asst. Strawberry Festival, Troy, 2005; basketball ofcl. Ohio H.S. Athletic Assn., Miami Valley, 2005; mem. Mayor's Roundtable, 2007—; v.p. Troy Main St., 2006; legal advisor Troy Sr. Citizens Ctr., 2006. Scholar, Thomas M. Cooley Law Sch., 2001—03. Mem.: KC (assoc.), Miami County Bar Assn., Ohio Bar Assn., Home Builders Assn. (assoc.), Kiwanis (assoc.). Home: 514 S Plum St Troy OH 45373 Office: Puthoff & Assocs LLC 16 S Cherry St Troy OH 45373 Personal E-mail: puthoffmark@hotmail.com. Business E-Mail: mark@puthoff.us.

PUTKA, ANDREW CHARLES, lawyer; b. Cleve., Nov. 14, 1926; s. Andrew George and Lillian M. (Koryta) Putka. Student, John Carroll U., 1944, U.S. Naval Acad., 1945-46; AB, Adelbert Coll., Western Res. U., 1949, JD, 1952. Bar: Ohio 1952. Practice law, Cleve.; instr. govt. Notre Dame Coll.; v.p. Koryta Bros. Coal Co., Cleve., 1952-56; supt. divsn. bldg. and loan assns. Ohio Dept. Commerce, 1959-63; pres., chmn. bd., CEO Am. Nat. Bank, Parma, Ohio, 1963-69; dir. fin. City of Cleve., 1971-74; dir. port control, 1974-78; dir. Cleve. Hopkins Internat. Airport, 1974-78. Mem. Ohio Ho. of Reps., 1953-56, Ohio Senate, 1957-58; dep. auditor, acting sec. Cuyahoga County Bd. Revision, 1970-71; mem. exec. com. Cuyahoga County Democratic Com., 1973-81, Assn. Ind. Colls. and Univs. Ohio, 1983-89; bd. govs. Sch. Law, Western Res. U., 1953-56; mem. exec. com. World Service Student Fund, 1950-52; U.S. rep. Internat. Pax Romana Congress, Amsterdam, 1950, Toronto, 1952; mem. lay adv. bd. Notre Dame Coll., 1968-90, trustee, 1990-93, hon. trustee, 1993—, life mem., 1993—; mem. adv. bd. St. Andrew's Abbey, 1976-88; trustee Case-Western Res. U., Newman Found. No. Ohio, 1980-93, hon. trustee, life mem., 1993—; 1st v.p. First Cath. Slovak Union of U.S., 1977-80; pres. USO Council of Cuyahoga County, 1980-83. Voted an outstanding legislator Ohio Press Corrs., 1953; named to All-Star Legislative team Ohio Newspaper Corrs., 1955; named one of Fabulous Clevelanders Cleve. Plain Dealer, John Henry Newman honor Soc. Mem. DAV (life), KC (4th degree), NCCJ, Cuyahoga County, Cleve. Bar Assn., Nat. Assn. State Savs. and Loan Suprs. (past. nat. pres.), US Savs. and Loan League (mem. legis com, 1960-63), Am. Legion, Ohio Mcpl. League (bd. trustees 1973), Parma C. of C. (bd. dir., treas. 1965-67), Newman Fedn. (past nat. pres.), Cath. Lawyers Guild (treas.), Am. Ohio Bankers Assn., Am. Inst. Banking, Adelbert Alumni Assn. (exec. com.), Cathedral Latin Alumni Assn. (trustee 1952—), Internat. Order Alhambra (internat. parliamentarian 1971—, past grand comdr., supreme advocate 1973), Amvets, Pi Kappa Alpha, Delta Theta Phi (past. pres. Cleve. alumni senate, master inspector 1975). Office: 28 Pond Dr Cleveland OH 44116-1062

PUTMAN, DALE CORNELIUS, management consultant, lawyer; b. Ponca, Nebr., Apr. 29, 1927; s. Merle H. and Catherine V. (Sheahan) P.; m. Alice Anselmi, Sept. 8, 1951; children: Mark, Lee, Neil, Bruce, Kirk, Nancy, Wendy. BS, U. Nebr., 1949, LL.D., 1951. Bar: Nebr. 1951, Iowa 1951, Mo. 1977. Mgr. Interstate Assn. Credit Mgmt., Sioux City, Iowa, 1951-52; sec., legal counsel Metz Baking Co., Sioux City, 1953-66, v.p., 1966-69, exec. v.p., 1969-72, pres., 1972-76; chief operating officer Interstate Brands Corp., Kansas City, Mo., 1976-77, pres., dir., 1977-80, pres., chief exec. officer, 1980-84; chmn., chief exec. officer, pres., dir. Interstate Bakeries (formerly DPF, Inc.), 1980-84; pvt. practice mgmt. cons., 1984—. Served with U.S. Army, 1945-46. Knight, Order of the Holy Sepulchre of Jerusalem, knight Order of Malta. Mem. KC (4th degree), Serra Internat., Mensa. Republican. Roman Catholic. Home: 8405 Reinhardt Ln Shawnee Mission KS 66206-1316 Personal E-mail: putman9752@aol.com.

PUTNAM, ADAM HUGHES, United States Representative from Florida, farmer, rancher; b. Bartow, Fla., July 31, 1974; s. William Dudley and Sara Elizabeth (Hughes) Putnam; m. Melissa Putnam; children: Abbie Anna, Elizabeth Langford, Emma Katherine, Adam Jr. BS in Food and Resource Econs., U. Fla., 1995. Co-owner Dudley Putnam, Inc., Bartow, Fla., 1988—; mem. Fla. House of Reps., Tallahassee, 1996—2000, US Congress from 12th Fla. dist., Washington, 2001—, US House Financial Services; chmn. US House Republican Policy Com., 2006—07, US House Republican Conf., 2007—09. Mem. Nat. Rep. Congl. Com.; chair Rep. Policy Com.; co-chair Congl. Sportsmen's Caucus. Mem. bd. assoc. Fla. Sheriff's Youth Villa; past v.p and pres. Fla. 4-H Found. Mem.: U. Fla. Alumni Assn., Polk County Hist. Assn., Polk County Farm Bureau, Polk County Cattlemen's Assn., Bartow C. of C., Fla. Farm Bur., Fla. Blue Key, Kiwanis, Alpha Gamma Rho. Republican. Episcopalian. Avocations: hunting, fishing, reading. Office: US Congress 442 Cannon House Office Bldg Washington DC 20515-0912 also: 650 E Davidson St Bartow FL 33830 Office Phone: 863-534-3530. Office Fax: 202-226-0585, 863-534-3559.*

PUTNAM, ALFRED W., JR., lawyer; b. Phila., 1951; married; 1 child. AB summa cum laude, Harvard U., 1973; BA, U. Oxford, Eng., 1975; JD, U. Pa., 1978. Bar: Pa. 1978. Assoc. Drinker Biddle & Reath LLP, Phila., 1979—85, ptnr., civil litig., 1985—, chmn. bd., 2005—. Sec., gen. counsel People for John Heinz; southeastern fin. chmn. Rick Santorum polit. campaign. Trustee, chmn. Lankenau Hosp., Main Line Health Sys., Jefferson Health Sys., 2004—. Mem.: Univ. Pa. Law Sch. Am. Inn of Ct. (pres.). Republican. Office: Drinker Biddle & Reath LLP One Logan Sq 18th & Cherry Sts Philadelphia PA 19103-6996 Office Phone: 215-988-2907. Office Fax: 215-988-2757. E-mail: alfred.putnam@dbr.com.

PUTNAM, JAMES DEAN, secondary school educator; b. Bioling Springs, NC, Mar. 25; s. William Leo and Joyce Putnam; m. Melissa Hopper Enloe (div.); children: Kristen, Justin, Jessica. BS in Phys. Edn. magna cum laude, Appalachian State U., Boone, NC, 1982, BS in Health Edn. magna cum laude, 1983. Cert. phys. and health edn. tchr. NC, 1983. Tchr., coach Avery HS, Banner Elk, NC, 1982, Pebblebrook HS, Atlanta, 1983—86, Chase HS, Forest City, NC, 1993—95, C-STOP/Phoenix Sch., Shelby, NC, 2004—08, C-STOP/CCAP, 2008—09; co-owner, mgr. Nautilus of Shelby, 1986—; 2d and 5th grade classroom tchr. Boiling Springs Elem. Sch., NC, 1995—96; tchr. # 3 Elem. Sch., Shelby, 1996—2004. Pres. Seven Successful Steps, Inc., Shelby, 1988—96; v.p. Shout 4 Edn., Shelby, 1998—2002, pres., 2003—; spkr. in field; personal trainer, individual fitness programs, 1982—. Author: Seven Successful Steps, 1992; contbr. articles to profl. publs. Mem., coach Nautilus/Phoenix Powerlifting Team; missionary Russia, 1992. Recipient numerous gold medals, county records, 3 Best Lifter awards for powerlifting, NC State Powerlifting Records, Leadership Patron award, Friends of Children Soc., Richmond, Va., 2002—03, Patron Ptnr. award, Christian Children's Fund, Richmond, 2004—05; named Outstanding Adult Vol., Shout 4 Edn., 2000—01. Mem.: AAHPERD, NCAAHPERD (SPKR. 2008), Profl. Educators NC (rep. 2002—06), Am. Assn. Health Edn. Republican. Avocations: exercise, dance, skiing, games, movies. Home: PO Box 2606 Shelby NC 28151 Office: Cleve County Schs C-Stop/Phoenix 910 S Post Rd Shelby NC 28152 Office Phone: 704-476-8399. Office Fax: 704-476-8359. Business E-Mail: dputnam@clevelandcountyschools.org.

PUTNAM, JERRY (GERALD D. PUTNAM), stock exchange executive; b. May 21, 1958; BS, U. Pa., 1981. With Walsh Greenwood, 1983—87, Jefferies & Co., PaineWebber, Prudential, Geldermann Securities, Inc.; founder, pres. Terra Nova, 1994—99; founder, CEO Archipelago Holdings, Inc., Chgo., 1999—2006; pres., co-COO NYSE Group, Inc., NYC, 2006—07; vice chmn. NYSE Euronext, NYC, 2007, sr. advisor, 2007—. Named one of Outstanding Innovators, Time mag., 2000; named to Entrepreneurship Hall of Fame, U. Ill., 2000. Avocation: hunting. Office: NYSE Euronext 11 Wall St New York NY 10005

PUTNAM, KERI, film company executive; married; 2 children. Grad., Harvard U. Asst. HBO; with literary dept. Arena Stage, Washington; dir. develop. Devillier Donegan Enterprises, Washington; dir. devel. HBO, 1992—95; v.p. NYC Productions HBO Films, 1995—99, sr. v.p. LA, 1999—2004, exec. v.p., 2004—06; pres. prodn. Miramax Film Unit Walt Disney Co., 2006—. Recipient Excellence in Media award, Women in Film, 2005; named one of The 100 Most Powerful Women in Entertainment, Hollywood Reporter, 2006, 2007. Office: Miramax 375 Greenwich St New York NY 10013

PUTNAM, MICHAEL COURTNEY JENKINS, classics educator; b. Springfield, Mass., Sept. 20, 1933; s. Roger Lowell and Caroline (Jenkins) P. AB, Harvard U., Cambridge, Mass., 1954, AM, 1956, PhD, 1959; LLD (hon.), Lawrence U., Appleton, Wis., 1985. Instr. classics Smith Coll., Northampton, Mass., 1959-60; faculty classics Brown U., Providence, 1960—2008, prof., 1967—2008, chmn., 2000-2001, prof. comparative lit., 1980—2008, MacMillan prof. classics, 1985—2008; acting dir. Ctr. for Hellenic Studies, Harvard U., 1961-62, sr. fellow, 1971-86; Townsend prof. classics Cornell U., 1985; Mellon prof.-in-charge Am. Acad. in Rome, 1989-91; Martin classical lectr. Oberlin Coll., 2004. Scholar in residence Am. Acad. in Rome, 1969-70, classical jury, 1982-83, trustee, 1991—; assoc. univ. seminar on classical civilization Columbia U., N.Y.C., 1972—; mem. cath. Commn. on Intellectual and Cultural Affairs, 1969—; adv. coun. dept. classics Princeton U., 1981-87, chmn., 1983-87; cons. Am. Coun. Learned Socs., 1987-89; mem. Inst. for Advanced Study, 1987-88; vis. scholar Phi Beta Kappa, 1994-95; councillor Assn. of Lit. Scholars and Critics, 1996-99. Author: The Poetry of the Aeneid, 1965, Virgil's Pastoral Art, 1970, Tibullus: A Commentary, 1973, Virgil's Poem of the Earth, 1979, Essays on Latin Lyric, Elegy and Epic, 1982, Artifices of Eternity: Horace's Fourth Book of Odes, 1986, Virgil's Aeneid: Interpretation and Influence, 1995, Virgil's Epic Designs, 1998, Horace's Carmen Saeculare, 2000, Maffeo Vegio: Short Epics, 2004, Poetic Interplay: Catullus and Horace, 2006; co-editor (with Jan M. Ziolkowski): The Virgilian Tradition, 2008, Jacopo Sannazaro: The Latin Poems, 2009; contbr. articles to profl. jours. Trustee Lowell Obs., Flagstaff, Ariz., 1967-87, bd. advisors, 1987—; trustee Bay Chamber Concerts, Camden, Maine, 1972-88, incorporator, 1988-94; mem. bd. cons. Portsmouth Abbey Sch., 1985-89; hon. sec. Keats-Shelley Meml. Assn., Rome, 1989-91. Rome Prize fellow Am. Acad. in Rome, 1963-64; Guggenheim Meml., Centennial medal, 2009; fellow, 1966-67; sr. fellow NEH, 1973-74, cons. 1974-78, 87-90; Am. Council Learned Soc. fellow, 1983-84. Fellow Am. Acad. Arts and Sci. 1996—; mem. Am. Philol. Assn. (bd. dir. 1972-75, mem. com. on award of merit 1975-78, chmn. 1977-78, 1st v.p. 1981, pres. 1982, del. Am. Coun. Learned Soc. 1984-87, Charles J. Goodwin award of merit 1971, fin. trustee 1997-2004, co-chair, endowment campaign, 2006-), mem. Am. Philosophical Soc., 1998—; Archaeol. Inst. Am., Classical Assn. New Eng., Medieval Acad. Am., Vergilian Soc. Am. (trustee 1969-73, v.p. 1974-76), Accademia Nazionale Virgiliana, Art Club. Office: Brown Univ Dept Classics Providence RI 02912-1856 Home: 100 Memorial Dr Apt 11-8A Cambridge MA 02142 Business E-Mail: michael_putnam@brown.edu.

PUTNAM, PAUL ADIN, federal agency administrator; b. Springfield, Vt., July 12, 1930; s. Horace Adin and Beatrice Nellie (Baldwin) P.; m. Elsie Mae (Ramseyer) June 12, 1956; children: Pamela Ann, Penelope Jayne, Adin Tyler II, Paula Anna. BS, U. Vt., 1952; MS, Wash. State U., 1954; PhD, Cornell U., 1957. Research animal scientist Agrl. Rsch. Svc., USDA, Beltsville, Md., 1957-66, investigation leader beef cattle nutrition, 1966-68, chief beef cattle research br., 1968-72; asst. dir. Beltsville Agrl. Rsch. Ctr., 1972-80, dir., 1980-84; dir. cen. plains area Ames, Iowa, 1984-87; assoc. dir. mid. south area Stoneville, Miss., 1987-88; dir. mid south area, 1988-94; ret., 1994; selectman Town of Springfield, Vt., 1996—2002, 2004—06. Contbr. articles to profl. jours. Recipient Kidder medal U. Vt.; Outstanding Performance awards USDA, also cert. merit; Danforth fellow; Borden fellow; Purina Research fellow. Fellow AAAS (rep. sect. O), Am. Soc. Animal Sci. (pres., North Atlantic sect., chmn. various coms., N.E. sect. Disting. Service award); mem. Am. Dairy Sci. Assn., Orgn. Profl. Employees USDA (pres. Beltsville chpt.), Council for Agrl. Sci. and Tech. Home: 36 Putnam Rd Springfield VT 05156-9115 E-mail: pputnam8@vermontel.net.

PUTNAM, ROBERT D., public policy professor; m. Rosemary Werner; children: Jonathan, Lara. BA, Swarthmore Coll., Pa., 1963, LLD (hon.), 1990; Fellowship, Oxford U., Eng., 1964; MA, Yale U., New Haven, 1965, PhD with distinction, 1970; PhD (hon.), Stockholm U., 1993, Ohio State U., 2000, U. Antwerp, 2000, U. Edinburgh, 2003, John Cabot U., Rome, 2006. From lectr. to prof. polit. sci. U. Mich., Ann Arbor, 1968—79; prof. govt. Harvard U., Cambridge, Mass., 1979—, chmn. dept. govt., 1984—88, assoc. dean faculty arts and scis., 1986—88, dean, John F. Kennedy Sch. Govt., 1989—91, assoc. dean faculty arts and scis., 1992—94, dir., Ctr. Internat. Affairs, 1993—96, Stanfield prof. internat. peace, 1996—2000, Peter and Isabel Malkin prof. pub. policy, 2000—. Vis. prof. polit. sci. Stockholm U., 1974, U. Catania, Italy, 1977; mem. exec. com. Brit. Politics Group, 1974—79, Coun. on European Studies, 1983—86; pres. Conf. Group on Italian Politics, 1981—83; mem. Internat. Inst. Strategic Studies, 1986—, Trilateral Commn., 1990—98; adv. bd. Swedish Collegium for Advanced Study in the Social Sciences, 1987—89, Westchester Children's Mus., NY, Thomas C. Wales Found., Seattle; adv. coun. on environmentally sustainable devel. World Bank, 1992—96; dir., Saguaro seminar civic engagement in Am. John F. Kennedy Sch. Govt., 1995—; Leverhulme vis. prof. faculty history St. Johns Coll., Cambridge U., 2002—03; vis. prof., dir. grad. summer programme in social change U. Manchester, England; cons. in field. Author: Bowling Alone: The Collapse and Revival of American Community, Making Democracy Work, Better Together: Restoring the American Community; mem. editl. bd.: Am. Polit. Sci. Rev., 1971—76, Brit. Jour. Polit. Sci., 1975—79, Comparative Polit. Studies, 1982—2005, Legislative Studies Quar., 1983—89, Internat. Orgn., 1989, Nonprofit and Voluntary Sector Qrly., 2000—04, Am. Sociol. Rev., 2004—, Critical Rev., 2004—. Staff US NSC, Washington, 1978; active President's Coun. on Svc. & Civic Participation, Washington, 2003; pres.-elect. Am. Polit. Sci. Assn., 2000—01, pres., 2001—02, v.p., 1997—98; adv. bd. Anne E. Borghesani Cmty. Found., Lexington, Mass. Recipient Louis Brownlow Book award, Nat. Acad. Pub. Adminstrn., 1993, Gregory Luebbert award, Am. Polit. Sci. Assn., 1994, Ithiel de Sola Pool award, 1995, Charles H. Levin award, Internat. Polit. Sci. Assn., 1994, Wilbur Lucius Cross medal, Yale U. Grad. Sch. Arts & Science, 2003, Commendatore in the Order of the Star of Italian Solidarity, Pres., Italian Republic, 2004, Johan Skytte prize in Polit. Sci., Statsvetenskapliga Inst., Uppsala U., 2006; fellow, SSRC-ACLS, 1966—68, Ford Found., 1970, Ctr. for Advanced Study in the Behavioral Sciences, 1974—75, 1988—89, Woodrow Wilson Internat. Ctr. for Scholars, 1977, 1979, Coun. on Fgn. Rels., 1977—78, German Marshall Fund, 1979, SSRC-Fulbright, 1982, SSRC-Foreign Policy Studies, 1988—89, Guggenheim fellow, 1988—89; Fulbright fellow, 1964—65, 1977, Marshall Lectr. fellow, U. Cambridge, 1999. Fellow: Nat. Acad. Pub. Adminstrn., Am. Acad. Arts & Sciences, Brit. Acad. (corr.); mem.: NAS (assembly of behavioral & social sciences 1978—81), Coun. on Fgn. Rels., Am. Acad. Polit. & Social Sci., Am. Philos. Soc., Phi Beta Kappa. Office: Harvard Univ John F Kennedy Sch Govt 79 JFK St Mail Box 114 Cambridge MA 02138 Business E-Mail: robert_putnam@ksg.harvard.edu.*

PUTNAM, ROBERT ERVIN, chemist, consultant; b. Northampton, Mass., Oct. 18, 1927; s. Ervin Earl and Mary Gertrude (Connelly) P.; m. Caroline Wright, Aug. 23, 1952; children: David Earl, Mary Caroline, Robert Edward, Andrew Wright. BS in Chemistry, U. Mass., 1950; PhD in Organic Chemistry, U. Ill., 1953. Rsch. chemist E.I. du Pont de Nemours, Wilmington, Del., 1953-59, rsch. supr., 1959-65, sr. rsch. supr., 1965-67, Parkersburg, W.Va., 1967-78, rsch. lab. supt., 1978-82, rsch. mgr., 1982-85; adj. faculty Washington State C.C., Marietta, Ohio, 1985-95; pvt. practice Marietta, 1985-95. Alumni adv. coun. dept. chemistry U. Mass., Amherst, 1975-78; instr. chemistry Marietta Coll., 1982-89, adv. coun., 1989-95, dir. Inst. for Learning in Retirement, 1995-98. Editor Bull. Am. Friends of Puttenham, 1984-2000; contbr. 20 articles to profl. jours. With USNR, 1945-46. NSF fellow, U. Ill., 1952-53. Fellow AAAS; mem. Am. Chem. Soc. (chmn. Ohio Valley sect. 1976-78), Rsch. Soc. Am., Valley Renaissance Consort, Mid-Ohio Valley Aviation Assn., Sigma Xi, Gamma Alpha, Phi Lambda Upsilon. Democrat. Mem. Unitarian Ch. Achievements include patents on fluorine containing polymers and monomers, ion exchange resins; research on industrial processes for nylon, polyacetals, acrylics, rubber toughened plastics, fluorinated plastics. Address: 100 Alden Ave Marietta OH 45750-1138 Office Phone: 740-373-4510. Personal E-mail: putnamr@suddenlink.net.

PUTNAM, SUSAN K., psychology educator; b. Buffalo, Apr. 20, 1953; d. Wilford C. Gustavel and Alberta J. Schmitt; m. John S. Putnam, Jr.; children: Alyssa Marie, Nathan John. A in Gen. Studies, Erie CC, Williamsville, NY, 1993; BA, Canisius Coll., Buffalo, 1995; PhD, SUNY, Buffalo, 2000. Soccer coach Erie CC, Williamsville, NY, 1993—95; rsch. asst. SUNY, 1995—99, behavioral neurosci. postdoctoral fellow, 1999—2000, vis. asst. prof., 2000—01; assoc. prof. psychology Canisius Coll., 2001—. Mem. autism spectrum disorder rsch. consortium Inter-Institutional, Buffalo, 2004—; mem. Instl. Animal Care and Use Com. of Canisius Coll., 2002—; pres. Penn York Undergraduate Rsch. Assn., Regional, NY, 2003—04; kairos adult leader

Canisius Coll., 2005—05, advisor psychology club, 2005—, co-dir. Ctr. Study Neurodevlopmental Disorders, 2007—. Soccer coach Akron Soccer League, NY, 1983—94; mem. Music Ministry Team Surrender; Advisor Canisius Coll. Pet Rescue Soc.; vol Adopt a Boxer Rescue.; choir dir., organist First Bapt. Ch. Akron, 1983—2006, dir. music ministry, 1985—, youth group leader, 2001—06, mem. pastoral rels. com., 2001—04. Recipient Milton Plezur Excellence in Tchg. award, SUNY, 1999, Chancellor's award for grad. sch. tchg. excellence, 1999, Outstanding Instr. Recognition award, 1999, UPA/Psi Chi Excellence in Tchg. award, 2001, Lay Person of Yr. award, First Bapt. Ch. Akron, 2003, Peter Canisius Disting. Professorship award, Canisius Coll., 2007; Dean's Rsch. grants, 2002, 2004, 2005. Mem.: Soc. Neuroscience, Am. Psychology Soc., Penn York Undergrad. Rsch. Assn. (assoc.; pres. 2003—04), Internat. Brain Rsch. Orgn. (assoc.), Am. Neuroendocrine Soc. (assoc.), Soc. Behavioral Neuroendocrinology (assoc.), Alpha Sigma Lambda Hon. Soc. (pres. 1995), Phi Theta Kappa Internat. Honor Soc., Psi Chi Nat. Honor Soc., Alpha Sigma Nu Nat. SJ Honor Soc., Alpha Sigma Nu Hon. Soc. Avocations: skiing, photography, music, camping, canoeing. Office: Canisius Coll 2001 Main St Buffalo NY 14208 Business E-Mail: putnams@canisius.edu.

PUTNAM, THOMAS J., library and museum director; b. 1962; m. Phyliis Wentworth; 2 children. Grad., Bowdoin Coll., 1984; MPA, Princeton U., 1987. With Upward Bound, Maine and Conn., 1990—99; dir. edn. John F. Kennedy Libr., Boston, 1999—2003, dep. dir., 2003—06, acting. libr. dir., 2006—07; dir. John F. Kennedy Libr. & Mus., 2007—. Fulbright Scholar, Senegal, West Africa, 1987. Office: John F Kennedy Presdl Libr & Mus Columbia Point Boston MA 02125-3398 Office Phone: 617-514-1651. Office Fax: 617-514-1652. E-mail: thomas.putnam@nara.gov.

PUTNEY, MARK WILLIAM, lawyer, utilities executive; b. Marshalltown, Iowa, Jan. 25, 1929; s. Lawrence Charles and Geneva (Eldridge) P.; m. Ray Ann Bartnek, May 25, 1962 (dec. Feb. 2000); children: Andi Bartnek, William Bradford, Blake Reinhart; m. Linda Phelps, July 21, 2003. BA, U. Iowa, 1951, JD, 1957. Bar: Iowa 1957, U.S. Supreme Ct. 1960. Ptnr. Bradshaw, Fowler, Proctor & Fairgrave, Des Moines, 1961-72, of counsel, 1992-94; chmn., CEO. Bradford & Blake Ltd., Dakota Dunes, SD, 1992—; pres., chmn., chief exec. officer Iowa Resources, Inc., 1984-90; chmn., chief exec. officer Iowa Power & Light Co., 1984-90, Iowa Gas Co., 1984-85, Midwest Resources Inc., 1990-92. Civilian aide to Sec. Army Iowa, 1975-77; bd. dirs. Greater Des Moines YMCA, 1976-86, Boys' Home Iowa, 1982-86, Hoover Presdl. Libr. Assn., 1983-2008, U. Iowa Found., 1984—, Edison Electric Inst., 1986-89, Greater Des Moines Com., 1984—, pres. 1988; bd. dirs. Assoc. Edison Illuminating Cos., 1988-93, pres., 1991-92; chmn. Iowa Com. Employer Support of Guard and Res., 1979-86; bd. dirs. Des Moines Devel. Corp., 1984-92, chmn., 1989-90; bd. dirs. Iowa Law Sch. Found., 2006-. With USAF, 1951-53. Recipient Disting. Alumnus award U. Iowa, 1995. Mem. Iowa Utility Assn. (chmn. 1989, dir.), Des Moines Club (pres. 1977), Desert Forest Golf Club (Carefree, Ariz.), Masons, Shriners, Delta Chi, Phi Delta Phi. Republican. Episcopalian. Home: PO Box 1126 Carefree AZ 85377 Office Phone: 602-549-7731. Personal E-mail: markwputney@aol.com.

PUTRA, ERWINSYAH, petroleum engineer; b. P. Siantar, North Sumatra, Indonesia, Oct. 10, 1969; s. Abdul Muin and Siti Zubaidah Nasution; m. Dewi T. Hidayati, June 2, 1996; children: Faris W., Tazkia S. BS, Inst. Teknologi Bandung, Indonesia, 1993; MS, N.Mex Inst. Mining and Tech., Socorro, 1996, PhD, 1999. Asst. prof., cons. Inst. Tech. Bandung, 1993—95; rsch. assoc. Petroleum Recovery Rsch. Ctr., Socorro, N.Mex., 1999—2000; rsch. engr. iv TEES Tex. A&M U., Coll. Sta., 2000—05; staff engr. Kindermorgan CO2 Co., Houston, 2005—. Contbr. articles to profl. jours. Grant, US-DOE, 2001—05. Mem.: Soc. Petroleum Engring. (Dallas) (speree rev. chmn. editl. com. 2002—05, Best Tech. award 2005). Home: 19011 Windsor Sails Dr Houston TX 77094 Office: Kindermorgan CO2 Co 500 Dallas Ste 1000 Houston TX 77002 Office Fax: 713-369-8940. Personal E-mail: erputra@yahoo.com.

PUTTER, IRVING, retired French language educator; b. NYC, Dec. 3, 1917; s. Joseph and Anna (Schrank) P.; children— Paul Stephen, Candace Anne Putter. BA, CCNY, 1938; MA, State U. Iowa, 1941; PhD, Yale U., 1949. Mem. faculty U. Calif. at Berkeley, 1947-88, prof. French, 1961-88, chmn. dept., 1968-71, humanities research fellow, 1971-72, 78-79, 84-85; ret., 1988. Author: Leconte de Lisle and His Contemporaries, 1951, The Pessimism of Leconte de Lisle: Sources and Evolution, 1954, The Pessimism of Leconte de Lisle: The Work and The Time, 1961, La Dernière Illusion de Leconte de Lisle: Lettres Inédites a Emilie Leforestier, 1968; also numerous articles.; editor, translator: Chateaubriand: Atala, René, 1952. Guggenheim fellow, 1955-56; Fulbright fellow, 1955-56 Home: 115 Saint James Dr Piedmont CA 94611-3603

PUTTERMAN, ALLEN MICHAEL, surgeon, oculofacial plastic surgeon; b. Beloit, Wis., May 19, 1938; s. Mayer Leon and Mollie (Tankel) P.; m. Jacqueline Orner, Dec. 23, 1962 (div. 1978); 1 child, Jill Tracy; m. Lynett Solomon, Sept. 24, 1983. BS, U. Wis., 1960, MD, 1963. Cert. zumba tchr., blackbelt NIA instr. Intern Cook County Hosp., Chgo., 1963-64; resident in ophthalmology Michael Reese Hosp., Chgo., 1966-69, dir. oculoplastic surgery, 1970—, chief ophthalmology, 1996—; fellow in oculoplastic surgery Manhattan Eye, Ear and Throat Hosp., NYC, 1969-70; pvt. practice, Chgo., 1970—; prof. ophthalmology, co chief oculoplastic surgery U. Ill. Eye and Ear Infirmary, Chgo., 1970—. Editor: Cosmetic Oculoplastic Surgery, 1983, 3d edit., 1999; contbr. articles to med. jours., chpts. to textbooks. Capt., M.C., USAF, 1964-66. Named one of 350 Top Doctors, Chgo. Mag., 2004, 2006; named to America's Top Doctors, 2003, 2006, 2007, 2008, Best Doctors in America. Fellow ACS, Am. Soc. Ophthalmic Plastic and Reconstructive Surgery (pres. 1982, Wendell Hughes lectr. 1984, Baylis Lifetime Achievement in Cosmetic Plastic Surgery award, 2005), Am. Acad. Ophthalmology (sr. honor award), Chgo. Ophthal. Soc. (v.p. 1991, pres.-elect 1992, pres. 1993). Avocations: skiing, bicycling, aerobics, yoga, Nia. Home: 161 E Chicago Ave Apt 43B Chicago IL 60611-6678 Office: 111 N Wabash Ave Ste 1722 Chicago IL 60602-2007 Office Phone: 312-372-2256. Office Fax: 312-372-1762. E-mail: puttermanmd@hotmail.com.

PUTTERMAN, LOUIS G., economics professor; b. NYC, Apr. 27, 1952; s. Milton and Eileen L. (Goldstein) P.; (div.); 1 child, Laura Lee; m. Vivian Tseng, Apr. 5, 1981; children: Serena Rose, Mark Isaac. BA summa cum laude, Columbia U., 1976; MA in Internat. Relations, Yale U., 1978, PhD in Econs., 1980; MA (hon.), Brown U., 1983. From asst. prof. to prof. econs. Brown U., R.I., 1980—; rsch. assoc., Ctr. for East Asian Rsch. Harvard U., Cambridge, Mass., 1987-93. Dir. devel. studies program Brown U., Providence. Author: Peasants, Collectives and Choice, 1986, Division of Labor and Welfare, 1990, Continuity and Change in China's Rural Development: Collective and Reform Eras in Perspective, 1993, Dollars and Change: Economics in Context, 2001; co-author: Economics of Cooperation and the Labor-Managed Economy, 1987; editor: The Economic Nature of the Firm, 1986, (with Randall Kroszner) 2d edit., 1996, (with Dietrich Rueschemeyer) State and Market in Development: Synergy or Rivalry, (with Avner Ben-Ner) Economics, Values and Organization, 1998; mem. editl. bd. Modern China, 1990—, Comparative Economic Studies, 1991-93, Annals of Public and Cooperative Economics, 1992—, Jour. Comparative Econs., 1989-91, 97-99, China Econ. Rev., 2001—; assoc. editor Pacific Econ. Rev., 1996-2004. Recipient Sloan Rsch. fellow, Alfred P. Sloan Found., 1983, Fellow in Chinese Studies, Wang Inst., 1986, Am. Coun. Learned Socs., 1997. Mem. Am. Economic Assn., Assn. for Comparative Economic Studies, Econ. Sci. Assn., Phi Beta Kappa. Office: Brown U Dept Econs 64 Waterman St Providence RI 02912-9029 Home Phone: 978-287-4491. Business E-Mail: Louis_Putterman@brown.edu.

PUTTLITZ, KARL JOSEPH, SR., metallurgist; b. Kingston, NY, Aug. 4, 1941; s. Adalbert and Elizabeth Anges (Barthel) P.; m. Dianne Elizabeth Markle, Sept. 16, 1967; children: Kirk, Christian, Karl Joseph Jr., Sara Ann. BS, Mich. State U., East Lansing, 1965, MS, 1967, PhD, 1971. Chem. technician IBM Corp., Poughkeepsie, NY, 1961—62, assoc. metallurgist, 1965—66, sr. assoc. metallurgist East Fishkill, NY, 1967, staff metallurgist, 1971—72, adv. metallurgist, 1972—84, sr. engr., 1984—99, sr. tech. staff mem., 1999—2004; Pres. Puttlitz Engring. Consultancy LLC, Wappingers Falls, NY, 2004—. Pvt. practice cons., Wappingers Falls, 1975—. Contbr. over 15 articles to profl. jours. Team mgr. Little League, Wappingers Falls, 1982, Sr. League, Wappingers Falls, 1984-88; pres. Lake Oniad Lot Owners Assn., Wappingers Falls, 1974-76. IBM Corp. scholar Mich. State U., 1968-71. Mem. IEEE, ASM (pres. Mich. State U. chpt. 1964-65), Nat. Assn. Corrosion Engrs., N.Y. Acad. Scis., Internat. Soc. Hybrid Microelectronics, Am. Welding Soc., Sigma Xi, Phi Lambda Tau. Conservative. Roman Catholic. Achievements include over 30 published inventions including U.S. and foreign patents in microelectronic interconnection technology. Home: 21 Central Ave Wappingers Falls NY 12590 Office: Puttlitz Engineering Consultancy LLC 21 Central Ave Wappingers Falls NY 12590 Business E-Mail: kjputtlitz@aol.com.

PUTTNAM, LORD DAVID TERENCE, film producer; b. London, Feb. 25, 1941; s. Leonard Arthur and Marie Beatrix Puttnam; m. Patricia Mary Jones, 1961; two children. LLD (hon.), Bristol U., Eng., 1983; DLitt (hon.), Leicester U., 1986, Leeds U., 1992, U. Bradford, 1993. With advt. firms, 1958-66; photographer's agt., 1966-68; film prodr., 1968—; chmn., CEO Columbia Pictures, 1986-88. Vis. prof. films Bristol U.; dir. Anglia TV Survival Anglia; chancellor, U. Sunderland, 1998-. Prodr. films including Melody, 1971, That'll Be the Day, 1973, Mahler, 1973, Bugsy Malone, 1976, The Duellists (Spl. Jury prize Cannes 1977), 1977, Midnight Express, 1977 (2 Acad. awards), Chariots of Fire (4 Acad. awards and 3 BAFTA awards including Best Film award 1981, 4 Oscars including Best Picture), Local Hero, 1983, The Killing Fields, 1984 (3 Am. Acad. awards, 8 Brit. Acad. awards, BAFTA award for Best Picture), Cal, 1984, The Mission, 1986 (Palme d'Or 1986, Acad. award), Memphis Belle, 1990, Meeting Venus, 1991, Being Human, 1992, War of the Buttons, 1993, The Burning Season, 1994 (Golden Globe award best film for TV), Le Confessional, 1995, The World of Moss, 1998, My Life So Far, 1999. Chmn. ITEL; founder, pres. Atelier du Cinema European; trustee Nat. Energy Found., Sci. Mus., 1996; hon. fellow The Chartered Soc. Designers, Manchester Poly.; chmn. Nat. Mus. Photography, film and TV com. Knighted, 1995; made life peer, 1997; decorated Officier dans l'Ordre des Artes et des Lettres, 1986, comdr. of the Most Excellent Order of the Brit. Empire, 1982; recipient Michael Balcon award for Outstanding Contbn. Brit. Film Industry, BAFTA, 1982, Benjamin Franklin award, 1996, Crystal award World Econ. Forum, 1997, acad. fellowship, British Acad. Film and TV Arts, 2006. Fellow Royal Soc. Arts, Royal Photographic Soc., Royal Geog. Soc. Office: U Sunderland Edinburgh Bldg Chester Rd Sunderland SR1 35D England

PUTUKIAN, MARGOT, sports medicine physician; b. Newton, Mass., Aug. 15, 1962; d. John Harry and Elissa Ann (Bedrosian) P. BS in Biology, Yale U., 1984; MD, Boston U., 1989. Cert. internal medicine; cert. additional qualifications sports medicine. Intern Strong Meml. Hosp. Primary Care, Rochester, N.Y., 1989-92; fellow in internal medicine Mich. State U., East Lansing, 1992-93, fellow in sports medicine, 1992-93; dir. athletic medicine, assoc. clin. prof. Robert Wood Johnson UMDNJ. Asst. prof. orthopedic rehab. Hershey (Pa.) Med. Ctr., 1993—. Fellow Am. Coll. Sports Medicine; mem. Am. Med. Soc. Sports Medicine (bd. dirs. 1992—, charter), ACP. Democrat. Office: Princeton U Health Scis Washington Rd Princeton NJ 08544 Office Phone: 609-258-8471. Business E-Mail: putukian@princeton.edu.

PUTZ, J.J. (JOSEPH JASON PUTZ), professional baseball player; b. Trenton, Mich., Feb. 22, 1977; m. Kelsey Putz; children: Lauren, Kaelyn. Attended, U. Mich., Ann Arbor. Pitcher Seattle Mariners, 2003—08, NY Mets, 2008—. Mem. US nat. team World Baseball Classic, 2009. Recipient Rolaids Relief Man of Yr. award, 2007; named to Am. League All-Star Team, Maj. League Baseball, 2007. Office: NY Mets Citi Field 126th St & Roosevelt Ave Flushing NY 11368*

PUTZEL, CONSTANCE KELLNER, retired lawyer; b. Balt., Sept. 5, 1922; d. William Stummer and Corinne (Strauss) Kellner; m. William L. Putzel, Aug. 28, 1945; 1 son, Arthur William. AB, Goucher Coll., 1942; LLB, U. Md., 1945, JD, 1969. Bar: Md. 1945. Social worker Balt. Dept. Pub. Welfare, 1945-46; atty. New Amsterdam Casualty Co., Balt., 1947; staff atty. Legal Aid Bur., Balt., 1947-49; mem. Putzel & Putzel, P.A., Balt., 1950-89; pvt. practice Balt., 1989—; instr. U. Balt. Sch. Law, 1975-77, Goucher Coll., 1976-77. Chair character com. Ct. Appeals for 3d Cir., 1976-97. Author: A Practice Guide to Divorce, 1999, Representing the Older Client in Divorce, 1992. Commr. Md. Com. on Status of Women, 1972-76, Com. to Implement ERA, 1973-76; Pres. U. Md. Law Alumni Assn., 1978; bd. dirs. Legal Aid Bur., 1951-52, 71-73. Fellow Am. Acad. Matrimonial Lawyers (chair elder issues com. 1996); mem. ABA (co-chair elder issues com., mem. coun. sr. lawyers divsn. 1996-2000, editl. bd. 1996-99, family law sect.), Md. Bar Assn. (bd. govs. 1972-73, chmn. family law sect. 1978-79, chair sr. lawyers divsn. 2001-03). Home: 7121 Park Heights Ave Unit 401 Baltimore MD 21215-1610 Home Phone: 410-358-4099. Personal E-mail: lawtowson@aol.com.

PUTZEL, MICHAEL, journalist, editor; b. Washington, Sept. 16, 1942; s. Max and Nell (Converse) P.; m. Ann Blackman, Feb. 23, 1974; children: Leila Elizabeth, Christof Blackman. BA, UNC in Polit. Sci., 1967. Reporter Charleston (W.Va.) Gazette, 1963-66; newsman AP, Raleigh, NC, 1967-68, NYC, 1968-69, war corr. Vietnam, 1969-72, reporter Washington, 1972-79; asst. metro editor Washington Post, Washington, 1979; White House corr. AP, Washington, 1979-84, chief White House corr., 1984-87, chief of bur. Moscow, 1987—90, diplomatic corr. Washington, 1990-91; Washington bureau chief Boston Globe, 1991-92, White House corr. Washington, 1993-94; columnist "Plugged In", 1994-95; founder, CEO Trysail, Inc., Washington, 1996—; founder, pres. Milestones Inc., Washington, 1999—2000; v.p. Continental Computer Corp., Washington, 2000; freelance writer, book doctor Washington, 2003—. Lectr. Georgetown U., Washington, 1999—. With USAR, 1964-65. Recipient AP Mgn. Editors citation, 1975, 81, Merriman Smith Meml. award White House Corr. Assn., 1986. Home: 4938 Quebec St NW Washington DC 20016-3231 Office Phone: 202-362-3133. Personal E-mail: mputzel@trysail.com.

PUTZY, KARRY ANN, secondary school educator; MA, U. Iowa, Iowa City. Cert. k-12 tchr. U. Iowa. Tchr. Solon Cmty. Sch. Dist., Iowa, 2001—; adj. faculty Kirkwood CC, Cedar Rapids, Iowa. Mem.: NEA, SEA (pres. chief negotiator), AATSP, ISEA, Sigma Delta Pi, Phi Lamba Theta.

PUYAU, FRANCIS ALBERT, retired radiology educator, physician; b. New Orleans, Dec. 1, 1928; s. Frank Albert and Rose Sue (Jones) P.; m. Geraldine Sally diBenedetto, June 6, 1951; children: Michael, Stephen, Jeanne Marie, Julie, Melissa. BS, Notre Dame U., 1948; MD, La. State U., 1952. Diplomate Am. Bd. Pediat., Am. Bd. Pediat. Cardiology, Am. Bd. Radiology. Intern Charity Hosp., New Orleans, 1952-53, resident in pediat., 1955-57; from instr. pediat. to prof. radiology and pediat. La. State U. Sch. Medicine, New Orleans, 1957-74, acting head dept. radiology, 1971-72, head dept., 1972-74; asst. prof. pediat. Vanderbilt U., 1961-68; fellow dept. diagnostic radiology Charity Hosp., New Orleans, 1968-70; prof. radiology and pediat. Tulane U. Sch. Medicine, New Orleans, 1974-97, prof. medicine, 1974-95, acting chmn. dept. pediat., 1976-78; cons. St. Tammany Hosps., Covington, La., 1968-81; dir. cardiac catherization lab. dept. cardiology Charity Hosp., New Orleans, 1970-85; staff radiologist Our Lady of the Lake Regional Med. Ctr., Baton Rouge, 1986-93, ret., 1997. Mem. staff Hotel Dieu, New Orleans, 1973-80; head x-ray dept. Children's Hosp. of New Orleans, 1976-82. Contbr. articles to profl. jours. With USPHS, 1953-55. Fellow Am. Coll. Cardiology, Am. Coll. Radiology; mem. East Baton Rouge Med. Soc., So. Soc. Pediatric Research, Am. Coll. Radiology, La. Radiology Soc., New Orleans Radiology Soc. (pres. 1985), New Orleans Pediatric Soc., Soc. Chmn. Acad. Radiology Depts., Radiol. Soc. N.Am., Am. Roentgen Ray Soc., Assn. Univ. Radiologists, Southern Yacht Club (New Orleans), Alpha Omega Alpha. Roman Catholic. Home: 458 Shady Lake Pkwy Baton Rouge LA 70810-4322

PUZIO, BONNIE JEAN, special education educator; b. Paterson, NJ, Sept. 13, 1950; d. John and Agnes Eleanor Murray; m. Gregory Edwin Puzio, Aug. 26, 1972; children: Kristin, Matthew. BA in Biologi. Sci., Montclair State U., NJ, 1972; MS in Edn. Curriculum, Instrn. and Assessment, Walden U., Balt., Md., 2006. Sci. tchr. Dumont H.S., Dumont, NJ, 1972—79, Pope John XXIII H.S., Sparta, NJ, 1987—92; bio. tchr., spl. edn. tchr. High Point Regional H.S., Wantage, NJ, 1992—. Youth min. coord. St. Monica's Parish, 1999—2006. Recipient Tchr. of the Yr., High Point Regional H.S., 1999, Sussex County, 1999. Office: High Point Regional HS 299 Pidgeon Hill Rd Sussex NJ 07461-2733

PUZZO, JOSEPH ANTHONY, JR., middle school educator; b. Red Bank, NJ, May 7, 1959; s. Joseph Anthony Puzzo, Sr. and Rita Ann (Scala) Puzzo. BA, Rutgers U., 1981; MA, Nova Southeastern U., 2003. Lic. English tchr. N.J. Fitness instr. Matawan Athletic Club, NJ, 1989—90; fitness instr., personal trainer The Racquetplace, Matawan, 1990—95, Powerhouse Gym, Matawan, 1995—96; full-time substitute tchr. Middletown Twp. Schs., NJ, 1996—97; tchr. lang. arts Thorne Mid. Sch., Port Monmouth, NJ, 1997—. Ednl. advisor Jr. Nat. Young Leaders Conf., Washington, 2003—. Author: (monthly fitness column) Shape Up, 1990—92. Mem.: Middletown Twp. Ednl. Assn., N.J. Ednl. Assn. Roman Catholic. Avocations: writing, films, music, sports, fitness. Personal E-mail: joepuzzo@comcast.net.

PYATT, EVERETT ARNO, federal official; b. Kansas City, Mo., July 22, 1939; s. Arno Doyne and Myrl Elizabeth (Osborn) P.; m. Susan Evelyn Kristal, Sept. 28, 1968; children: Jennifer, Laura, Jeffrey. B.E., BS, Yale U., 1962; MBA, U. Pa., 1977. Staff engr. office dir. def. research and devel. Office Sec. Def., Dept. Def., Washington, 1962-72; dir. acquisition planning Office Asst. Sec. Def. for Program Analysis and Evaluation, 1972-75; dir. logistics resources Office Asst. Sec. Def. for Installations and Logistics, 1975-77; prin. dep. asst. sec. for logistics Dept. Navy, Washington, 1977-79, prin. dep. asst. sec. for shipbldg. and logistics, 1981-84, asst. sec. for shipbldg. and logistics, 1984-89; exec. advisor Coopers & Lybrand, 1989—; pres. EV Ventures; dep. chief fin. officer Dept. Energy, 1979-81; dir. Dept. Energy (Office of Alcohol Fuels), 1980. Recipient Disting. Civilian Svc. medal USN, 1980-81, 87, Superior Civilian Svc. medal, 1981, Outstanding Svc. medal Dept. Energy, 1981, Pres.'s award of meritorious excellence, 1983, Disting. Civilian Pub. Svc. award Dept. Def., 1989; Office of Sec. Def. fellow, 1975-77. Mem.: IEEE, Yale Club. Home: 4560 25th Rd N Arlington VA 22207-4147 Home Phone: 703-528-5828; Office Phone: 703-841-8318. Personal E-mail: epyatt1@comcast.net.

PYATT, KEDAR DAVIS, JR., research and development company executive; b. Wadesboro, NC, May 20, 1933; s. Kedar D. and Frances (Hales) P.; m. Mary Mackenzie, June 2, 1956; children: Geoffrey, Kira, David, Rebecca. BS in Physics, Duke U., 1955; PhD in Physics, Yale U., 1960. With Gen. Atomic, San Diego, 1959-67; sr. v.p. Fed. sys. divsn. Maxwell Techs., San Diego, 1967—2001; chief scientist SAIC, San Diego, 2001—. Recipient Exceptional Pub. Svc. medal Dept. Def., 1985, Lifetime Achievement medal DSWA, 1997. Office Phone: 858-826-1629. Personal E-mail: bud-mary@att.net. Business E-Mail: kedar.d.pyatt@saic.com.

PYATT, LEO ANTHONY, retired real estate broker; b. Key Port, NJ, Oct. 20, 1925; s. Ralph James and Anna Regina (Kussmaul) Pyatt; m. Geraldine Genevive Gibb, May 31, 1947; children: Steven Lee, Rebecca Lynn. Student, Franklin U., 1947-49. Salesperson Standard Oil Co., Columbus, Ohio, 1947-49, Borden Dairy Co., Columbus, 1950-57, Frito-Lay, Inc., Columbus, 1958-74; sec., treas. Snack Time, Inc., Columbus, 1974-75; agt. N. NE Realty Co., Columbus, 1976-86; owner-broker Pyatt's Rose Realty Co., Columbus, 1986—2003; ret., 2003. Mem. Citizens for An Alternative Tax Sys. With U.S. Naval Air Force, 1943—46, PTO. Decorated DFC, Air medal with silver star, Philippine Liberation award; Combat Aircrew Hall of Fame. Roman Catholic. Avocations: writing, travel, reading. Home: 4400 Wanda Lane Rd Columbus OH 43224

PYBURN, KEITH MCBRIDE, JR., lawyer; b. Shreveport, La., Sept. 20, 1950; s. Keith McBride and Marjorie Owens Pyburn; m. Barbara Joan St. Romain, June 15, 1979; children: Keith McBride III, Bradford Plauche. JD, Tulane Law Sch., New Orleans, La., 1974. Law clk. La. Supreme Ct., New Orleans, 1974—75; assoc. Jones, Walker, et al, New Orleans, 1975—80; mng. ptnr. McCalla, Thompson, Pyburn & Hymowitz, New Orleans, 1980—2004; ptnr. Fisher & Phillips LLP, New Orleans, 2004—, regional mng. ptnr. Com. mem. ABA-EEO, 1976—; planning com. mem. Tulane Multi-State Labor and Employment Law Program, New Orleans, 1983—; fellow Coll. Labor and Employment Lawyers, Washington, 1999—. Contbr. articles to profl. jours., to numerous presentations. V.p. Youth Alternatives, New Orleans, 1982—84; bd. mem. St. George's Episcopal Sch., New Orleans,

1989—95. Fellow: Coll. Labor and Employment Lawyers; mem.: ABA, La. State Bar Assn. Office: Fisher & Phillips LLP 201 St Charles Ave Ste 3710 New Orleans LA 70170 Office Fax: 504-529-3850.

PYCH, RICK, professional sports team executive; b. Hartford, Conn. m. Marilou Pych; 1 child, Zach. Grad. in Acctg., Fairfield U. CPA. CFO Spurs Sports & Entertainment (parent co. of NBA Spurs, Am. Hockey League Rampage and WNBA Silver Stars), San Antonio, 1993—2000, chief devel. officer AT&T Ctr., 1999—, exec. v.p. fin. and corp. devel., 2000—08, pres. bus. ops., 2008—. San Antonio Rampage repr. Am. Hockey League Bd. Govs. Bd. trustees Via Met. Transit; bd. dirs. San Antonio Sports Found., 1989—, Boys and Girls Clubs San Antonio; bd. mem. San Antonio Tax Increment Reinvestment Zone. Office: Spurs Sports and Entertainment One AT&T Ctr San Antonio TX 78219*

PYE, GORDON BRUCE, economist; b. Oak Park, Ill., Oct. 30, 1933; s. Harold Charles and Florence Martha P BS in Chem. Engring, M.I.T., 1955, PhD in Econs, 1963. Asst. prof. bus. adminstrn. U. Calif., Berkeley, 1963-66, assoc. prof., 1966-69, prof., 1969-72; econ. cons. Standard Oil Co. Calif. (name changed to Chevron Corp.), San Francisco, 1972-74; v.p., sr. economist Irving Trust Co., NYC, 1974-78, sr. v.p., mgr. econ. research and planning div., 1978-89; prin. Gordon B. Pye Assocs., NYC, 1990—. Assoc. editor: Fin. Analysts Jour, 1972-89 Mem. Forecasters Club N.Y. (pres. 1980-81) Home: 230 E 50th St New York NY 10022-7702 Personal E-mail: GBPye@aol.com.

PYERITZ, REED EDWIN, geneticist, educator, medical researcher; b. Pitts., Nov. 2, 1947; s. Paul L. and Ida Mae (Meier) P.; m. Jane Ellen Tumpson, May 28, 1972; 2 children. SB in Chemistry, U. Del., 1968; AM, Harvard U., 1971, PhD in Biochemistry, 1972, MD, 1975. Diplomate Am. Bd. Internal Medicine, Am. Bd. Med. Genetics. Intern Peter Bent Brigham Hosp., Boston, 1975-76; resident Peter Bent Bingham Hosp., Boston, 1976-77, Johns Hopkins Hosp., Balt., 1977-78; from instr. to prof. medicine and pediatrics Sch. Medicine, John Hopkins Hosp., Balt., 1977-93, chair dept. human genetics, 1994-00, prof. human genetics, medicine and pediatrics, 1994-01, MCP Hahnemann Sch. Medicine, 1993-00; prof. medicine and genetics U. Pa. Sch. Medicine, Phila., 2001—, chief divsn. med. genetics, 2001—, vice chair, dept. med., 2008—, chair com. on appointments and promotions, 2004—08, mem. faculty senate exec. comm., 2006—; dir. Penn Ctr. Integration Genetic Healthcare Tech., 2007—, chair, senate com. faculty, 2009—. Dir. Inst. Genetics, Allegheny U. Health Sci., 1993-99; dir. Ctr. for Med. Genetics, Allegheny Gen. Hosp., 1995-00; chief physician Md. Athletic Commn., Balt., 1978-93; med. adv. bd. Nat. Marfan Found., N.Y.C., 1982—, chmn. 1982-93, clin. care adv. bd., Nat. Neurofibromatosis Found., 1985—; med. adviser Alliance of Genetic Support Groups, 1994-01; mem. rsch. adv. bd. Nat. Orgn. Rare Disorders, 1989-00; mem. rsch. adv. com. Am. Heart Assn., 1996-98; mem. genetic adv. bd. Nat. Cancer Inst., 1996-99; mem. med. adv. bd. Can. Marfan Assn., 1999-, chmn., 2003-; mem. sci. adv. bd. Hereditary Hemorrhagic Telangiectasia Found., 2003—, chair med. adv. bd., Canadian Marfan Assn., 2003-08, Can. Inst. Health Rsch., 2005-, sci. adv. bd., Coriell Inst. Med. Res., 2008-. Co-editor Principles and Practice of Medical Genetics, 1992-; mem. editl. bd. New Eng. Jour. Medicine, 1993-96, JAMA, 1997-2001, Circulation, 2002—; contbr. over 300 articles to profl. publs. Lt. col. USAR Med. Corp., 1981—91. NIH grantee. Fellow: ACP, Am. Coll. Med. Genetics (dir. 1992—94, pres.-elect 1995—96, founding fellow, pres. 1997—99, past pres. 1999—2000); mem.: AAAS (coun. 2009—), AMA, Human Med. Genetics (assoc. prof., councilor 1998—2004, pres. 2000—02), Am. Coll. Med. Genetics Fedn. (sec. treas. 2001—), Coll. Physicians Phila., Am. Med. Accred. Program (spl. adv. com. 1998—2000), Assn. Profs. Human Med. Genetics (pres. elect 1998—99, pres. 2000—02), Assn. Am. Physicians, Am. Soc. Clin. Investigation, Am. Fedn. Med. Rsch., Physician Consortium for Performance Improvement, Am. Heart Assn., Am. Soc. Human Genetics (chmn. program com. 1994—95, bd. dirs. 2005—07). Office: Divsn Med Genetics Maloney 538 U Pa Sch Medicine 3400 Spruce St Philadelphia PA 19104-4283 Office Phone: 215-662-4740. Business E-Mail: reed.pyeritz@uphs.upenn.edu.

PYKE, THOMAS NICHOLAS, JR., science administrator; b. Washington, July 16, 1942; s. Thomas Nicholas and Pauline Marie (Pingitore) Pyke; m. Carol June Renville, June 22, 1968 (dec. Oct. 2002); children: Christopher Renville, Alexander Nicholas. BS, Carnegie Inst. Tech., 1964; MS in Engring., U. Pa., 1965. Electronic engr. Nat. Bur. Standards, Gaithersburg, Md., 1964-69, chief computer networking sect., 1969-75, chief computer systems engring. div., 1975-79, dir. ctr. for computer systems engring., 1979-81, dir. ctr. programming sci. and tech., 1981-86; asst. adminstr. for satellite and info. services NOAA, Washington, 1986-92, dir. high performance computing and com., 1992-00, dir. The Globe Program, 1994—2002, chief info. officer, dir. high performance computing and comm., 2000—01; chief info. officer US Dept. Commerce, 2001—05, US Dept. Energy, 2005—. Organizer profl. computer confs., 1970-86; mem. Presdl. Adv. Com. on Networking Structure and Function, 1980, Interagy. com. on Info. Resources Mgmt., 1983-84, bd. dirs., 1984-87, vice chmn. 1986-87 (Exec. Excellence award 1991), chmn. Interagy. Working Group on Data Mgmt. for Global Change, 1987-93; speaker in field. Mem. editl. bd. Computer Networks Jour., 1976-86; contbr. articles to profl. jours. Mem. Task Force on Computers in Schs., Arlington, 1982—85; co-pres. Jamestown Elem. Sch. PTA, Arlington, 1984—85; bd. dirs. Glebe Commons Assn., Arlington, Va., 1976—79, v.p., 1977—79. Recipient silver medal Dept. Commerce, 1973, gold medal, 1995; award for exemplary achievement in pub. adminstrn. William A. Jump Found., 1975, 76, Presdl. Rank award of Meritorious Exec., 1988, 99; Westinghouse scholar Carnegie Inst. Tech., 1960-64; Ford Found. fellow U. Pa., 1964-66. Fellow Washington Acad. Scis. (Engring. Sci. award 1974); mem. IEEE (sr. mem.), Computer Soc. of IEEE (Golden Core mem., bd. govs. 1971-73, 75-77, vice chmn. tech. com. on personal computing 1982-86, chmn. 1986-87), AAAS, Assn. Computing Machinery, Sigma Xi, Eta Kappa Nu, Omicron Delta Kappa, Pi Kappa Alpha (chpt. v.p. 1963-64) Episcopalian. Office: US Dept Energy 1000 Independence Ave SW Washington DC 20585 Office Phone: 202-586-0166. Business E-Mail: tom.pyke@hq.doe.gov.

PYLANT, BETHANY S., engineering educator; d. Wilson Watkins and Jeanette Lovelace Sharman; m. Kenneth Dean II Pylant, Dec. 19, 1981 (dec.); children: Kenneth Dean III, Adam Carl, Blake MacMichael, William Sharman-Ables. EdD, Auburn U., Ala., 1996. Instr. Columbus Area Vocat. Tech. Sch., Ga., 1980—84, Southern Union State Jr. Coll., Valley, Ala., 1984—86, West Ga. Tech. Inst., LaGrange, 1987—88, Columbus Tech. Coll., 1988—2006, program mgr., instr., 2006—; grad. tchg. asst. Auburn U., Ala., 1986—87.

PYLE, GERALD FREDRIC, geographer, educator; b. Akron, Ohio, Dec. 22, 1937; s. Russell Roy and Ruth (Martin) P.; m. Carole Wood, Aug. 29, 1959; children: Eric, Frances. BA, Kent State U., 1963; MA, U. Chgo., 1968, PhD, 1970. Cartographer Rand McNally, Chgo., 1962-64; rsch. geographer Ency. Brit., Chgo., 1964-65; cartographer U. Chgo., 1965-70; from asst. prof. to prof. U. Akron, 1970-80; prof. geography and earth sci. U. N.C., Charlotte, 1980-98, prof. health promotion, 1995—2002, prof. health behavior and adminstrn., 2002—04, emeritus prof., 2004—. Vis. fellow Macquarie U., Sydney, 1988; rsch. dir. Ctr. for Urban Studies, Akron, Ohio, 1973—80; tech. dir. Akron Area Census File, 1974—80; vis. scholar U. SC, 1977; interim dir. health adminstrn. program U. NC, Charlotte, 2001—02; interim dir. Health Adminstrn. Program, 2008, Undergrad. Programs, 2009. Author: Heart Disease, Cancer and Stroke in Chicago, 1971, Spatial Dynamics of Crime, 1974, Applied Medical Geography, 1979, Diffusion of Influenza: Patterns and Paradigms, 1986, (with Shannon and Bashshur) The Geography of AIDS, 1990, (with shannon) Medical Atlas of the Twentieth Century, 1993; sr. editor Med. Geography, Social Sci. and Medicine, 1977-84; book rev. editor Social Sci. and Medicine, 1990-2005. Recipient Scholars medal First Citizens Bank, 1992; grantee Ill. Regional Med., 1969, Law Enforcement Adminstrn. Agy., 1972, 74, NSF, 1979, 82, Nat. Geog. Soc., 1988, NRC, 1995, Smart Start 1999-2001. Fellow Ohio Acad. Sci.; mem. APHA, Am. Coll. Epidemiology, Assn. Am. Geographers (Rsch. Honors S.E. divsn. 1994), Phi Kappa Phi. Democrat. Anglican. Achievements include research in spatial diffusion of infectious diseases and the location of health care delivery facilities. Home: PO Box 641 Matthews NC 28106 Office: U NC Dept Pub Health Scis 9201 University City Blvd Charlotte NC 28223-0002 Home Phone: 704-846-3227; Office Phone: 704-578-7458. Personal E-mail: gfpyle@msn.com.

PYLE, HOWARD, lawyer, consultant; b. Richmond, Va., Feb. 1, 1940; s. Wilfrid and Anne Woolston (Roller) P.; m. Victoria M. Sheffield; children: Elizabeth Roller Ross, Howard. AB, Princeton U., 1962; JD, U. Va., 1967. Bar: Va. 1967, D.C. 1969. Career trainee CIA, Washington, 1967-69; adminstrv. asst. to Congressman Odin Langen, U.S. Ho. of Reps., Washington, 1969-70, to Congressman Hastings Keith, 1971; asst. to sec. Dept. Interior, Washington, 1971-73; Washington rep. Std. Oil Co. Ind., 1973-77; mgr. fed. pub. affairs R.J. Reynolds Industries, Inc., Winston-Salem, NC, 1977-80; dir. fed. rels. Houston Industries, Washington, 1980-99; pres. HPYLE Cons., Alexandria, Va., 1999—. Mem.: SAR, NRA, Gadsbys Tavern Mus. Soc. (bd. mem.), Va. Bar, DC Bar, Order of St. John, Naval Res. Assn., Washington Assembly, Alexandria Assn., Res. Officers Assn., Delta Theta Phi. Republican. Episcopalian. Home: 125 N Lee St Alexandria VA 22314-3260 Office: HPYLE Cons PO Box 320817 Alexandria VA 22320-4817 Personal E-mail: howard@hpyle.net.

PYLE, JEAN L., economist, consultant; BA, Bucknell U., 1966; MA, U. Mich., 1967; PhD, U. Mass., 1985. Asst. prof. econ. Smith Coll., Northampton, Mass., 1986—87, U. Mass., Lowell, 1987—91, from assoc. prof. to prof., 1991—97, prof. dept. regional econ. and social devel., 1997—2002, prof. emerita, 2002—, sr. assoc. Ctr. Women and Work, 2002—. Author: The State and Women in the Economy: Lessons From Sex Discrimination in the Republic of Ireland, 1990; editor: Approaches to Sustainable Development: The Public University in the Regional Economy, 2001, Globalization, Universities, and Issues of Sustainable Human Development, 2002; mem. editl. bd.: Globalizations; contbr. chapters to books, articles to profl. jours. Grantee, U. Mass., Lowell, 1987—2002; fellow, U. Mich., 1966—67, U. Mass., Amherst, 1980—81, 1981—82. Mem.: Soc. Internat. Devel., Assn. Women's Rights in Devel., ASA Sect. Sex & Gender, Am. Sociol. Assn., Internat. Assn. Feminist Economics, Phi Beta Kappa. Office: Dept Reg Econ & Social Dev Univ Mass 61 Wilder Lowell MA 01854 Business E-Mail: jean_pyle@uml.edu.

PYLE, JEANNE, library director; b. Wichita Falls, Tex., Aug. 30, 1961; d. Barbara and Thomas Standley; m. Daniel Keith Pyle, July 5, 1987. BA in English, Midwestern State U., Wichita Falls, 1983; MS in Information Sci., North Tex. State U., Denton, 1985; MA in English, U. Tex., Tyler, 1995. Head ctrl. reference U. Tex., Arlington, 1998—2000, dir. libr., 2000—. Mem.: Tex. Libr. Assn. (chair, coll. and U. divsn. 2001—02). Office: Univ Tex Tyler 3900 Univ Blvd Tyler TX 75799 Office Fax: 903-565-5562. Business E-Mail: jpyle@uttyler.edu.

PYLE, NANCY, Councilwoman; m. Roger Pyle; 2 children. BS, LeMoyne Coll., Syracuse; M in Ednl. Adminstrn., US Internat. U., San Diego. Tchr. San José Unified Sch. Dist., cmty. rels. mgr., legis. analyst; councilwoman, Dist. 10 San José City Coun., 2005—. Bd. trustee San Jose/Evergreen Cmty. Coll. Dist., 1997—. Mem. San José Small Bus. Commn.; bd. mem. Notre Dame High Sch., YWCA. Mem.: Almaden Valley Cmty. Assn. (bd. mem.). Democrat. Office: San Jose City Coun 200 E Santa Clara St San Jose CA 95113 Office Phone: 408-535-4910. Office Fax: 408-292-6478. Business E-Mail: district10@sanjoseca.gov.*

PYLE, ROBERT MILNER, JR., financial consultant; b. Orange, NJ, Oct. 24, 1938; s. Robert M. and Dorothy (Collings) Pyle; m. C. Page Neville, May 31, 1969; children: Cynthia Neville, Laura Collings. BA, Williams Coll., 1960; JD, U. Va., 1963. Bar: N.Y. 1964. Assoc. Mudge Rose Guthrie & Alexander, NYC, 1963—68; with Studebaker-Worthington, Inc., NYC, 1968—77, sec., 1972—76, assoc. gen. counsel, 1974—77; with Singer Co., NYC, 1977—79; v.p., counsel Am. Soc. Corp. Secs., Inc., NYC, 1979—89, v.p., sec., counsel, 1989—91; v.p., sr. asst. sec. Am. Express Co., NYC, 1991—96, cons., 1997—. Career counseling rep. Williams Coll., 1977—. Trustee Pingry Sch., Martinsville, NJ, 1972—74, Arts Coun. Suburban Essex Inc., 1979—84, chmn. bd., 1981—84; trustee Suburban Cmty. Music Ctr., 1985—87; mem. Millburn-Short Hills Rep. Mcpl. Com. Essex County, 1998—2003; bd. govs. Colonial Dances, Ltd., NYC, 1970—74; bd. dirs. Millburn-Short Hills Hist. Soc., 1985—90, v.p., 1985—87. Mem.: ABA, Assn. Bar City N.Y., Am. Soc. Corp. Secs. (hon.), Pilgrims U.S., Pingry Sch. Alumni Assn. (bd. dirs. 1966—78, pres. 1972—74, cert. of merit 1968, Nelson Carr Svc. award 2006), Hillsboro Club (Fla.), Short Hills Club, Bay Head Yacht Club (N.J.), No. N.J. Squash Racquets Assn. (past sec., trustee, Disting. Svc. award 2005), Met. Squash Racquets Assn. (past treas.), Racquet and Tennis Club, Pi Delta Epsilon, Delta Theta Phi, Sigma Phi. Episcopalian. E-mail: rmpylejr@aol.com.

PYLE, ROBERT NOBLE, public relations executive; b. Wilmington, Del., Oct. 23, 1926; s. Joseph Lybr and LaVerne Ruth (Noble) Pyle; m. Patricia Carlile Pyle, Jan. 21, 2006; children: Robert Noble Jr., Mark C., Nicholas A., Louis P. Crosier, Sarah P. Moore. BA, Dickinson Coll., 1948; postgrad., Wharton Sch., U. Pa., 1949, U. Minn. Pres. Robert N. Pyle, Inc., Wilmington, 1949-52; adminstrv. asst. to US Congress, Washington, 1952-63; bus. and polit. cons. Robert N. Pyle & Assoc., Washington, 1970—2007, chmn. Sec./treas. Bulgarian Am. Bus. Ctr.; cons. in field. Contbr. numerous articles to profl. jours.; reporter covering Nurnburg Trials, Paris Peace Conf. for, Stars & Stripes, Europe, 1946. Dir. World Affairs Coun.; field man Rep. Nat. Congl. Com., 1959—74. With US Army, 1945—46, ETO. Mem.: Palm Valley Golf Club, Kenwood Country Club, La Quinta Resort and Club. Presbyterian. Home: 50255 Via Simpatico La Quinta CA 92253 Office: 1223 Potomac St NW Washington DC 20007-3212 Office Phone: 202-333-8190. Personal E-mail: carlile8@verizon.net.

PYLES, RICHARD B., medical educator; b. Carbondale, Ill., Aug. 26, 1964; s. C. Richard and Elizabeth A. Pyles; m. Tonyia D. Eaves-Pyles, Aug. 1, 1987. PhD, U. Cin., 1993. Asst. prof. Cin. Children's Hosp. Rsch. Found., 1993—2000; assoc. prof. U. Tex. Med. Br., Galveston, 2000—. Contbr. scientific papers to profl. jours. Presbyn. ch. elder West Isle Presbyn., Galveston, 2005—08. Recipient Vaccine Devel. Investigator award, UTMB Sealy Ctr., 2001—02, Student Advocacy award, UTMB Grad. Student Orgn., 2005; grantee Predoctoral fellowship, AJ Ryan Found., 1990—92; scholarship, Nat. Presbyn. Ch., 1982—86, NRSA fellowship, NIH, 1995—97. Achievements include patents for replication competent herpes simplex virus. Office: Univ TX Med Br 301 University Blvd; L22486 Galveston TX 77555-0436

PYLES, RODNEY ALLEN, archivist, county official; b. Morgantown, W.Va., June 21, 1945; s. Melford John and Luci L. (Scarcella) P.; m. Carol Louise Wrobleski, May 20, 1972; 1 child, Janessa Louise. BA, MA (Benedum scholar 1966-67, grad. research asst. 1967-68, grad. teaching fellow 1968-69), W.Va. U., 1967-69. Instr. polit. sci. Alderson-Broaddus Coll., Philippi, W.Va., 1969-71; asst. curator W.Va. U. Library, 1971-77; dir. archives and history div. W.Va. Dept. Culture and History, 1977-85; dep. chief Assessor's Office Monongalia County, 1985-88; assessor Monongalia County, 1989—. Mng. editor: W.Va. History quar, 1977-85 Mem. Morgantown (W.Va.) Dem. exec. com., 1966-69, Monongalia County (W.Va.) Dem. exec. com., 1972-76; mem. Morgantown Libr. Bd., 1988-91, Morgantown Hist. Landmarks Commn., 1986—; trustee W.Va. Pub. Theatre, 1999—, treas., 2004. Mem. Soc. Am. Archivists, W.Va. Hist. Soc. (exec. sec. 1977-90, bd. dirs. 1990—), Am. Assn. State and Local History (state awards chmn. 1980-85, state membership com. 1981-87), Monongalia Hist. Soc. (pres. 1986-88, bd. dirs. 1988—), W.Va. Polit. Sci. Assn. (treas. 1991—), W.Va. Assessors' Assn. (pres. 1992-93, bd. dirs. 2005—), KC (pres. bowling league 1995-96, 4th deg., faithful capt. 1996—, chancellor 1998-2000, dep. Grand Knight 2000-02, Grand Knight, 2002-2007), Sons of Italy (treas. 1995—). Roman Catholic. Home: 536 Harvard Ave Morgantown WV 26505-2157 Office: County Court House Rm 215 Morgantown WV 26505 Office Phone: 304-291-7222. Business E-Mail: rpyles@assessor.org.

PYLES, SELMA BROADWAY, music educator; b. Columbus, Ohio, June 7, 1955; d. Norman James and Ruth (Demarest) Broadway; m. Michael Lee Pyles, Aug. 4, 1990. MusB Edn., Ohio State U., 1977. Cert. tchr. Ohio Dept. Edn., 1977. Mid. sch. orch. tchr. South-We. City Sch. Dist., Grove City, Ohio, 1977—88; asst. h.s. orch. tchr. Hilliard City Sch. Dist., Ohio, 1988—2001, mid. sch. orch. tchr., 1988—2001, elem. orch. tchr., 2001—. Orch. condr. Columbus Symphony Cadet Youth Orch., Ohio, 1989—90; orch. tchr. Ohio String Tchrs. Assn. Mid. Sch. Orch. Summer Camp, Columbus, 1988—97. Contbr. book. Choir dir. Westgate Friends Ch., Columbus, 1980—95, Youth Musicale, Canton, Ohio, 1980—82, Sounds of Celebration, Elyria, Ohio, 1984—86; orch. dir. N.W. Bible Ch., Hilliard, Ohio, 1998—2004, interim choir dir., 2002—04. Recipient Pub. Sch. Orch. Tchr. of Yr., Ohio Orch. and String Tchrs. Assn., 2003. Mem.: NEA (assoc.), Am. String Tchr. Assn. (assoc.), Ohio Orch. and String Tchrs. Assn. (assoc. Pub. Sch. Orch. Tchr. of the Yr. 2003), Ohio Edn. Assn. (assoc.). Achievements include Middle School Large Group Contests Superior Ratings 1989-2001. Avocations: church music, bible study, violin. Home: 4266 Ongaro Dr Columbus OH 43204 Office: Hilliard City Sch Dist 4681 Leap Road Hilliard OH 43026 E-mail: selma_pyles@fclass.hilliard.k12.oh.us.

PYLIPOW, STANLEY ROSS, retired manufacturing company executive; b. Coudersport, Pa., Apr. 4, 1936; s. Stanley Edward and Helen L. (Haskins) P.; m. Phyllis Beverly Moore, Dec. 1, 1956; children— David, James, Vicky, Kenneth, Sandra BBA in Acctg. cum laude, St. Bonaventure U., 1957. Various fin. positions Chicopee Mfg., New Brunswick, NJ, 1957-65; various positions to v.p., gen. mgr. Domestic Coatings div. Mobil Chem. Co., NYC, 1965-73; asst. corp. controller Monsanto Co., St. Louis, 1974-76; controller, dir. planning Monsanto Comml. Products, St. Louis, 1976-79; sr. v.p., bd. dirs., chief fin. officer Fisher Controls Internat., Inc., St. Louis, 1979-92; ret., 1992; bd. dirs. RBA Group, 1996—2008. Treas. Ulster Project, St. Louis, 1998—2002. Treas., City of Town and Country, Mo., 1980-84; bd. dirs. Ecumenical Housing Prodn. Corp., St. Louis, 1980-90; mem. Acctg. Edn. Change Commn., 1992-96. Served to 1st lt., U.S. Army, 1958. Named Exec. of Yr., Profl. Secs. Internat., 1982 Mem. Inst. Mgmt. Accts. (pres. 1990-91, chmn. 1991-92), Fin. Execs. Inst., Winghaven Country Club. Republican. Avocations: golf, exercise, spectator sports. Office Phone: 636-625-8921. Personal E-mail: stanpylipow@centurytel.net.

PYLYSHYN, ZENON W., science educator; s. George and Anna Pylyshyn; m. Anne G. Telford, Sept. 14, 1996; children: Sonia R., Joel E. BS in Engring., McGill U., Montreal, 1959; PhD, U Sask., Saskatoon, Can., 1963. Prof. U. Western Ont., London, Ontario, Canada, 1966—94; bd. governors, prof. cognitive sci. Rutgers U., New Brunswick, NJ, 1994—, founding dir., cognitive sci., 1994—2000. Contbr. scientific papers, chapters to books. Recipient Donald Hebb award, Can. Psychol. Assn., 1992, Jean Nicod prize, CNRS, France, 2004. Fellow: Royal Soc. Can. Office: Rutgers Ctr Cognitive Sci 152 Frelinghuysen Rd Piscataway NJ 08854

PYNCHON, THOMAS RUGGLES, JR., writer; b. Glen Cove, NY, May 8, 1937; s. Thomas Ruggles Pynchon and Katherine Frances Bennett. BA in English, Cornell U., NYC, 1958. Former editl. writer Boeing Aircraft Co., Seattle. Author: (novels) V., 1963 (Best first Nover of Yr., William Faulkner Found., 1963), The Crying of Lot 49, 1966 (Rosenthal award, AAAL, 1967, named one of 100 Best English-lang. Novels from 1923 to 2005, TIME mag.), Gravity's Rainbow, 1973 (Nat. Book award, 1979), Slow Learner, 1984, Vineland, 1990, Deadly Sins, 1994, Mason & Dixon, 1997, Against the Day, 2006, Inherent Vice, 2009 (Publishers Weekly bestseller); contbr. non-fiction works NY Times Book Rev., NY Rev. of Books; contbr. numerous short stories to various publs. Served with USN, 1955—57. Recipient William Dean Howells medal, AAAL, 1975. Mailing: c/o Penguin Group Inc 375 Hudson St New York NY 10014*

PYNE, GEORGE, marketing executive; b. Milford, Mass. Grad., Brown U., 1989. With Portman Cos., exec. dir., AMC events; dir., licensing NASCAR, 1995—98, v.p., mktg., 1998—2000, sr. v.p., 2000—02, COO, bd. dirs., 2002—06; pres., bd. dirs. IMG Sports and Entertainment, 2006—. Recipient Sports and Spl. Event Licensor of Yr. award, 1998, 2002; named Exec. of Yr., Sports Mktg. Letter's; named one of Top 100 Marketers, Advt. Age, Top 10 Promoters of Decade, Top Most Influential People in Profl. Sports, The Sporting News, The Most Influential People in the World of Sports, Bus. Week, 2007, 2008; named to Forty Under Forty, Sports Bus. Jour., Sports Bus. Jour.'s Hall of Fame. Office: IMG Sports and Entertainment 825 7th Ave New York NY 10019

PYOTT, DAVID EDMUND IAN, pharmaceutical executive; b. London, Eng., Oct. 13, 1953; married; 4 children. MA, U. Edinburgh, 1975; diploma in German and European Law, U. Amsterdam, 1976; MBA, London Bus. Sch., 1980. Numerous positions Sandoz Nutrition, Barcelona, 1980-90, gen. mgr., 1990-92; pres., CEO Sandoz Nutrition Corp., Mpls., 1992-95; head divsn. nutrition Sandoz Internat. AG, 1995—97; mem., exec. com. Novartis AG (merger Sandoz and Ciba), 1995—97;

pres. Allergan, Inc., Irvine, Calif., 1998—2006, CEO, 1998—, chmn., 2001—. Bd. dirs. PhRMA, Avery Dennison Corp., Edwards Lifescis. Corp., Advanced Med. Optics, Inc.; chmn. Calif. Healthcare Inst.; mem. bd. dirs. U. Calif. (Irvine) Grad. Sch. Mgmt.; mem.LA Bus. Advisors; vice-chair Chief Exec. Roundtable for UCI Bd. dirs. Internat. Coun. of Ophthalmology Found., Eyecare Am.; pres. Pan-Am. Ophthalmological Found. Mem. Pharm. Rsch. and Mfrs. Am. (bd. dirs., Allergan rep.), Pan Am. Assn. Ophthalmology (bd. dirs.), L.A. Bus. Advisors. Achievements include transforming Botox, an obsure treatment for rare muscular diseases, into a cultural and medical phenomenon. Office: Allergan Inc 2525 Dupont Dr Irvine CA 92612-1531 Address: Allergan Inc PO Box 19534 Irvine CA 92623*

PYRGIOTIS, YANNIS N., former sports association administrator; b. Athens, Greece, 1944; married; 1 child. BArch, MArch, AS, MCP, MIT Sch. Architecture and Urban Planning. Advisor Ministries Nat. Econ. and Environ., Phys. Planning and Pub. Works, Greece, 1983—88; dir. Orgn. Urban Planning and Environ. Protection, Athens, Greece. Tech. expert in drafting the European and Hellenic Land Develop. Plan Min. Environ. and Pub. Works; tech. expert EEC Gen. Directorate REGIO; teaching staff planning and regional develop. dept. U. Thessaly; teaching staff Greek Open U., Nat. Sch. Pub. Admin. Author of numerous studies on urban and phys. planning. Bd. dirs. Athens 2004 Olympic Organising Com., 1998—2004; exec. dir. Athens 2004 Olympic Works and Tech. Divsn., 2000—04; exec. dir., chief tech. officer Olympic Games Organizing Com. "Athens 2004"; founding mem. bd. dirs. Greek Urban and Land Planners; mem. Assn. Concerned Citizens for Modernisation and Soc.; mem. exec. com. Benaki Mus.; nat. rep. Orgn. for Econ. Cooperation and Develop., Urban Affairs Com., UNEP Blue Plan for the Mediterranean.

PYRON, NONA FAYE, music educator, director; b. LA, July 20, 1933; d. Harold Hicks Pyron and Winifred Ferne Riley. MusB, Eastman Sch. Music, LA, 1955; MM, 1957; DMA, U. South Calif., LA, 1967. Asst. prof. music Willamette U., Salem, Oreg., 1957—68; founder & chief editor Grancino Edns, Santa Barbara, Calif.; adj. prof. cello Westmont Coll., Santa Barbara, 2006—. Cellist Portland Symphony, Oreg., 1957—60. Co-author (with William Pleeth): (book) Yehudi Menuhin Series, musician (performer) pablo casals master classes; musician: (solo cello concerts london) Wigmore Hall, Purcell Rm. Leader students to Germany Expt. in Internat. Living, Putney, Vt., 1966—68. Mem.: Pi Kappa Lambda. Christian Ch. Achievements include research in discovering unknown cello music & iconographical materials in Europe; first to concerts which combine later music on the modern cello with early works on period instruments; founder & editor in chief of grancino editions. Avocations: travel, gardening, horseback riding, farming, photography. Home: 616 Calle de los Amigos Santa Barbara CA 93105 Office: Westmont Coll 955 La Paz Rd Santa Barbara CA 93108-1089 Personal E-mail: pyroncello@gmail.com.

PYRSOPOULOS, NIKOLAOS T., medical educator, director; s. Theodoros and Ekaterini Pyrsopoulos; m. Giselle Monique Pyrsopoulos; children: Theodoros, Alexios. PhD, U. Athens, Greece, 2005. Diplomate U. Athens, 1991, in internal medicine Hellenic Bd. Medicine, 1999, Am. Bd. Internal Medicine, 2003, in gastroenterology 2005, in transplant hepatology 2008. Asst. prof., medicine U. Miami, Fla.; med. dir., liver transplantation Broward Gen. Hosp., Fla. Hosp., Orlando, 2007—, chiar, hepatology, 2007—; assoc. prof., medicine U. Ctrl. Fla., Orlando, 2007—. Fellow: ACP; mem.: AMA, Internat. Transplantation Soc., Internat. Liver Transplantation Soc., Am. Assn. Study of Liver Diseases, Am. Soc. Transplantation, Am. Coll. Gastroenterology, Am. Gastroent. Assn. Office: Fla Hosp 2501 N Orange Ave Ste 542 Orlando FL 32804

PYSH, JOSEPH JOHN, neurologist, neuroanatomist; b. Olyphant, Pa., Nov. 14, 1935; s. John Andrew and Anna Mary (Marusin) P.; m. Deborah Ann Prass, Dec. 15, 1991. BA in Biology, Wayne State U., 1958; DO, Midwestern U. Chgo. Coll. Osteo. Medicine, 1962; PhD in Neuroanatomy, Northwestern U., Chgo., 1967. From instr. to assoc. prof. anatomy Northwestern U., Chgo., 1966-86, acting chmn. cell biology and anatomy, 1978-81, resident physician in neurology, 1983-86; assoc. prof. neurology Mich. State U., East Lansing, 1986-95, prof. neurology, 1995—, founding mem. dept. neurology, 2000—, emeritus prof. neurology, 2008—, founding dir. neurology residency program, 2001—03. Grant referee NSF, Washington, 1974—; frequent CME neurology speaker in field. Contbr. numerous articles to profl. jours; manuscript reviewer various orgns., Washington and N.Y.C. Recipient Tchg. award Northwestern U.; NIH grantee, 1969-82. Fellow Am. Coll. Neuropsychiatrists; mem. AAAS (life), NIH (mem. rsch. grant neurology study sect. 1976-77), Am. Acad. Neurology, Am. Soc. Cell Biology, Am. Assn. Anatomists, Soc. Neurosci., Sigma Xi. Independent. Achievements include research in synaptic transmission and brain development. Avocations: rare book collecting, sailing. Office: Mich State U Coll Osteo Medicine Dept Neurology 138 Service Rd A217 Clin East Lansing MI 48824 Office Phone: 517-353-8122. Business E-Mail: pysh@msu.edu.

PYSHKIN, SERGEI L., physics professor, researcher; b. St. Petersburg, Russia, July 5, 1941; s. Lev Nikolaevich Pyshkin and Lidia Yakovlevna Pyshkina; m. Tatiana V. Krasnojon, Jan. 27, 1973; children: Kirill S., Marina S. Samarina, Tatiana S.; m. Tatiana N. Moiseiuk, Aug. 19, 1961 (div. Nov. 25, 1972). Student, St. Petersburg State Poly. U., 1958—64; postgrad., State U. Moldova, Kishinev, 1967; DSc in Physics, Moscow State U., 1978. Rschr. Inst. Applied Physics, 1967—86, head laser rsch. lab, 1986—2001, prin. investigator, 2001—; prof. Free Internat. U., Kishinev, 1998—2005; adj. prof. Clemson U., 2005—, sr. fellow Ctr. Optical Materials Sci. and Engring. Techs. Anderson, SC, 2006—. Contbr. articles to profl. jours. Grantee, USAF, 1995, 1997, 1998, 1999, US Civilian R&D Found., 2003, 2005, 2007, US Navy, 2008, UNESCO, Italy, 2007; Fulbright fellow, US Dept. State, 2005—06, Rsch. grant, Soros Found., 1991, 2001. Achievements include research in light emissive structures for optoelectronics. Home: 55/3 Shosse Hinceshti Apt 51 Kishinev MD2028 Moldova Office: Inst Applied Physics 5 Academy St Kishinev MD2028 Moldova also: Ctr for Optical Materials Sci and Engring Techs Clemson Rsch Park Technology Dr 91 Anderson SC Home Phone: (37322) 732621; Office Phone: 37322 739513. Office Fax: (37322) 738149. Business E-Mail: spyshki@clemson.edu, spyshkin@phys.asm.md.

PYTELL, ROBERT HENRY, retired lawyer, judge; b. Detroit, Sept. 27, 1926; s. Henry Carl and Helen (Zielinski) P.; m. Laurie Mazur, June 2, 1956; children: Mary Beth, Mark Henry, Robert Michael. JD, U. Detroit, 1951. Bar: Mich. 1952. Of counsel Pytell & Varchetti, P.C., Detroit, 1952-2001; asst. U.S. atty. Ea. Dist. Mich., 1962-65; judge Mcpl. Ct., Grosse Pointe Farms, Mich., 1967-85. With USNR, 1945-46. Mem. Am. Coll. Trust and Estate Counsel, State Bar Mich. (mem. probate coun. probate sect. 1998-2000), Crescent Sail Yacht Club (Grosse Pointe), Delta Theta Phi. Roman Catholic. Avocations: gardening, bicycling, photography.

PYTKA, STEPHEN MILTON, office equipment executive; b. Ludlow, Mass., Apr. 29, 1947; s. Milton Ignatius and Jean Marie (Kmiecik) P.; m. Linda Rachel Madsen, May 25, 1969; children: Jonathan Stephen, Justin Stephen, Brendan Stephen. BSEE, Worcester Poly. Inst., 1968; MBA, Dartmouth Coll., 1977. Design engr. AT&T, Whippany, N.J., 1968-69, Kwajalein, Marshall Islands, 1970-71, Greensboro, N.C., 1969-70, Langdon, N.D., 1971-73; sys. engr. GE, Pittsfield, Mass., 1973-75; planning mgr. Xerox Corp., Rochester, N.Y., 1977-81; mktg. mgr. Wang Labs., Inc., 1982-83; exec. v.p. Cap. Internat., Marshfield, Mass., 1983—; mng. ptnr. Consilium Ptnrs. LLC, Boston, 2004—. Co-founder P&R Microtech, 1982-83; exec. v.p. BIS Cap Internat., 1983-89; pres., chief ops. officer BISCOM, Inc., 1990-96; v.p. The Onstott Group, 1997-98; chmn., CEO Streamware, Inc., 1998-2000; pres., CEO eChinaLink, 2000-01; CEO Talksender, Inc., 2000-01, Hellotech, 2001-02, Gazelle Systems, Inc., 2002-03; mng dir., Consilium Ptnrs., 2004-07; chmn., Universal Mind, Inc., 2007-08; CEO, VIGIX, 2008-; mem. exec. bd. WPI Venture Forum; mem Touch Applications, HUB Angels, Common Angels; panelist MIT Enterprise Forum; trustee Andover YMCA; spkr. in field. Mem. Am. Mgmt. Assn, HubAngels, CommonAngels. Republican. Roman Catholic. Home: 9 Langley Ln Andover MA 01810-4259 Office: VI6IX 485 Massachusetts Ave Cambridge MA 02139-4081

PYTLEWSKI, LAURA JEAN, chemistry professor; b. Freeport, Ill., Aug. 26, 1959; d. James Franklin and Darlene Ann Donahue; m. James Andrew Pytlewski, Oct. 8, 1983; children: Michael Steven, Matthew John. BS in Biology, St. Xavier U., 1981; MS in Analytical Chemistry, Govs. State U., 1992; PhD student in Analytical Chemistry, Loyola U., Chgo., 2008—. Cert. med. technologist Am. Soc. Clin. Pathologists, 1983. Adj. prof. chemistry Moraine Valley C.C., Palos Hills, Ill., 1993—2003; prof. chemistry Triton Coll., River Grove, Ill., 2002—06; adj. prof. chemistry Lewis U., Romeoville, Ill., 2006—; lab. supr. natural sci. dept. U. St. Francis, Joliet, Ill., 2006—07. Mem. focus group Benjamin Cummings Publishers, San Francisco, 2004; adj. prof. Govs. State U., Univ. Pk., Ill., 2006—. Author: Biology for Life, 2001; reviewer: Chemistry: A World of Choices, 1998. Mem. com. devel. of new lab. St. Joseph's Sch., Lockport, Ill., 2005—06. Scholar, St. Xavier U., 1980—81. Democrat. Roman Catholic. Achievements include development of a visual factoring method for algebra II. Avocations: painting, reading, rollerblading, swimming, travel. E-mail: pytlewla@lewisu.edu.

PYTLINSKI, JERZY TEODOR, physicist, educator, research scientist; b. Warsaw, Apr. 1, 1938; s. Stanislaw and Natalia (Matuszewska) P.; m. Bonnie Laurie Bennett, Dec. 30, 1969; 1 child, Christine Barbara. MS, Tech. U. Warsaw, 1962; PhD Plasma Physics with distinction, U. Paris, 1967. Program mgr., acting divsn. head N.Mex. State U., Las Cruces, 1977—80; sr. scientist, divsn. head U. PR, Mayaguez, 1981—83, program dir., sr. scientist San Juan, 1983—86, sr. scientist, founding dir. Univ.-Industry Rsch. Ctr. Tampa, Fla., 1986—89; pres. Univ.-Industry Rsch. Ctr., Tampa, Fla., 1989—, prof., 1989—. Mem.adv. bd. on solar energy UNESCO, 1979-85; referee Am. Jour. Physics, 1980—, Solar Energy Jour., 1983-87, 38th Internat. Sci. and Engring. Fair, 1987; mem. U.S. tech. adv. group of ISO TC-180, 1981— Mem. editl. bd. Internat. Jour. Energy, Environ. Econs., 1990—; co-editor Procs. Internat. Conf. Energy for Ams., 1987; contbr. more than 90 articles to profl. jours. and procs. Grantee state and fed. agys., various edn. and rsch. founds.; Postdoctoral fellow U. Liverpool, Eng., 1968-69; recipient commendation State of Kans., 1977. Mem. Am. Phys. Soc., Nat. Coun. Univ. Rsch. Adminstrs., Soc. Rsch. Adminstrs., Internat. Solar Energy Soc., Internat. Energy Soc. (sci. coun. 1985—), Sigma Phi Sigma. Republican. Roman Catholic. Achievements include pioneering research in plasma physics, alternative energy sources. Avocations: reading, tennis, travel.

PYTTE, AGNAR, physicist, retired academic administrator; b. Kongsberg, Norway, Dec. 23, 1932; arrived in U.S., 1949, naturalized, 1965; s. Ole and Edith (Christiansen) Pytte; m. Anah Currie Loeb, June 18, 1955; children: Anders H., Anthony M., Alyson C. AB, Princeton U., 1953; AM, Harvard U., 1954, PhD, 1958. Faculty Dartmouth Coll., 1958—87, prof. physics, 1967—87, chmn. dept. physics and astronomy, 1971—75, assoc. dean faculty, 1975—78, dean grad. studies, 1975—78, provost, 1982—87; pres. Case Western Res. U., Cleve., 1987—99; adj. prof. physics Dartmouth Coll., 1999—. Rschr. in plasma physics; mem. Project Matterhorn Princeton U., 1959—60, 1978—79, U. Brussels, 1966—67. Bd. dirs. Goodyear Tire and Rubber Co., 1988—2004, Accreditation Coun. for Grad. Med. Edn., 2000—04, A.O. Smith Corp., 1991—2003, Sherman Fairchild Found., Inc., 1987—2006. Mem.: Am. Phys. Soc., Sigma Xi, Phi Beta Kappa.

QAZI, MUJTABA A., ophthalmologist; b. Karachi, Pakistan, Jan. 5, 1971; arrived in US, 1975; s. Asghar H. and Rehana Qazi; m. Erum Qazi, Aug. 3, 1995; children: Amaan, Rida, Ameen. BA, NYU, 1993, MD, 1997. Diplomate Am. Bd. Ophthalmology. Intern St. Vincent's Hosp., NYC, 1997—98; resident dept. ophthalmology Boston U. Med. Ctr., 1998—2001; chief resident dept. ophthalmology Boston VA Med. Ctr., 2000; fellow in corneal, anterior segment and refractive surgery Pepose Vision Inst., Chesterfield, Mo., 2001—02. Dir. clin. studies Pepose Vision Inst.; clin. instr. Washington U. Sch. Medicine, St. Louis. Author: Pupil Assessment for Refractive IOLS, 2008, Tonometry and Biomechanical Analysis, 2008; reviewer Am. Jour. Ophthalmology, Jour. of Refractive Surgery. Bd. mem. Midwest Cornea Rsch. Found. Named Best Dr's in St. Louis, 2008. Mem.: Internat. Soc. Refractive Surgeons, Am. Soc. Cataract & Refractive Surgery, Am. Acad. Ophthalmology. Office: Pepose Vision Inst PC 1815 Clarbson Rd Chesterfield MO 63017 Office Phone: 636-728-0111. E-mail: mqazi@peposevision.com.

QI, GANG, mechanical engineer, educator; b. Hohhot, China; arrived in US, 1991; s. Shaoliang Qi and Airu Wang; m. Zhihong Li, Oct. 1, 1983; 1 child, Xin. PhD, Tex. Tech U., Lubbock, 1996. Asst., assoc. prof. U. Memphis, 1998—. Author: (book) Engineering Design Communication and Modeling. Recipient Excellence in Rsch. and Svc. to Engring. Cmty. award, Memphis Area Joint Engrs. Coun., 2005, Outstanding Rsch. award, Herff Coll. Engring., 2008—. Fellow: Acoustic Emission Working Group (life). Achievements include patents for dental implant fixture; dental implant abutment; unitary dental implant. Office: The Univ Memphis 3815 Ctrl Av Memphis TN Office Fax: 901-678-5459. Business E-Mail: gangqi@memphis.edu.

QI, HUAQING, special education educator; d. Zhenhua Qi and Qingduo Sun; m. Matthew Schlecht; 1 child, Isaac Schlecht; 1 child, Peter Li. MEd, Belmont U., Nashville, 1992, Vanderbilt U., 1998, PhD, 2001. Cert. early childhood spl. edn. Nashville. Asst. prof. West Chester U., Pa., 2001—04, U. of N.Mex, Albuquerque, 2004—. Grant reviewer, jour. reviewer profl. agys. Editor: Editing for a Professional Newsletter; contbr. articles to profl. jours. (Frederick Douglass scholarship, 2000). Mem.: CEC, Autism Soc. of Am., Am. Assn. of Mental Retardation, Soc. of Rsch. and Children Devel., Am. Speech, Lang., and Hearing Assn. (travel fellowship 2002, 2003). Office: Univ NMex Dept Ednl Specialties Hokona Hall 248 Albuquerque NM 87131 Business E-Mail: hqi@unm.edu.

QI, LI, research scientist; d. Jintai Qi and Zhuying Li. PhD, Tex. A&M U., Coll. Sta., 2004. Asst. scholar scientist Fla. State U., Tallahassee, 2004—. Mem.: IEEE.

QI, XIAONING, electrical engineer, electronics engineer, research scientist; PhD, Stanford U., Calif., 2001. Mem. tech. staff R&D Sun Microsystems, Inc., Sunnyvale, Calif., 2001—05; staff engr., sr. staff engr. R&D Synopsys Inc., Mountain View, Calif., 2005—07; sr. mem. tech. staff R&D Rambus, Inc., 2007—08; sr. staff engr. R&D Intel Corp., Santa Clara, 2008—. Mem.: IEEE (sr.), Toastmaster Internat. (v.p. edn.). Achievements include technical papers and patents in field. Avocations: tai chi, reading, travel.

QI, ZHENYU, research scientist; Rsch. asst. U. Calif., Riverside, 2003—05, U. Va., Charlottesville, 2005—. Contbr. scientific papers.

QIAN, MICHAEL C., science educator, consultant; PhD, U. Minn., St Paul Mpls. Sr. scientist Land O'Lakes, Inc, St Paul, 1990—2001; prof. Oreg. State U., Corvallis, 2001—. Mem.: Am. Soc. Enology and Viticulture, Am. Soc. Dairy Sci., Inst. Food Technologist, Am. Chem. Soc., The Honor Soc. Phi Kappa Phi. Office: Oreg State Univ 100 Wiegand Hall Corvallis OR 97331 Business E-Mail: michael.qian@oregonstate.edu.

QIAN, QIN, engineering educator; arrived in US, 2000; d. Guanhua Qian and Meihua Huang; m. Qi Fu, Feb. 4, 1999; children: Cynthia X. Fu, Melissa Y. Fu. BS, Nanjing U., China, 1994; M in Software Sys., U. St. Thomas, St. Paul, 2002; MS, U. Minn., Mpls., 2004, PhD, 2008. EIT Minn. Constrn. & geotech. engr. Nanjing Constrn. Co., 1994—98; rsch. & tchng. asst. Nanjing U., 1997—2000, U. Minn., 2003—08; civil engr. HZ United, Plymouth, Minn., 2007—08; asst. prof. Lamar U., Beaumont, Tex., 2008—. Lab. asst. U. Minn., 2003, U. St. Thomas, 2002—03. Contbr. scientific papers to profl. jours. Recipient Excellent Internat. Instr., U. Minn., 2005, Advanced Sci. Prize, Edn. Dept. China, 1998. Mem.: Am. Water Resources Assoc., Am. Geophysical Union, Am. Soc. Civil Engr. Avocations: reading, sewing. Office: Lamar Univ Cherry Engring Bldg Beaumont TX 77710 Home: 2528 Oak Dale Way Seabrook TX 77586

QIAN, SUN, finance educator; b. Wuhan, Hubei, China; d. Xinhua Sun and Yunzhen Huang; m. Jia Zhu; 1 child, Shawn Zhu. MA in Economics, Old Dominion U., Norfolk, Va., 2005, PhD student in Fin., 2005—. Tchg., rsch. asst. Old Dominion U., 2003—07, instr., 2007—. Contbr. articles to profl. jours. Mem.: Fin. Mgmt. Assn. Home: 1142 Bolling Ave Apt 232B Norfolk VA 23508

QIAN, ZHAOMING, literature educator, critic; b. Shanghai, July 25, 1944; s. Shaozhong Qian and Wenjing Chen; m. May Fang Wang, Jan. 1, 1969; children: Yuyan, Yuli. BA, Beijing Fgn. Studies U., 1967, MA, 1980; PhD, Tulane U., 1991. Instr. English, Beijing Fgn. Studies U., 1981-83, lectr. English, mng. editor, 1983-86, assoc. dir. transl. studies, 1985-86; instr. English and Asian lit. Tulane U., New Orleans, 1986-91; asst. prof. English U. New Orleans, 1991-96, assoc. prof. English, 1996-2001, prof., 2001—04, univ. rsch. prof., 2004—09, chancellors rsch. prof., 2009—; Y. C. Tang chair prof. Zhejiang U., Hangzhou, China, 2008—. Author: Orientalism and Modernism: The Legacy of China in Pound and Williams, 1995, The Modernist Response to Chinese Art: Pound, Moore, Stevens, 2003, Ezra Pound's Chinese Friends, 2008; editor: 20th Century English and American Stories, 1987, Annotated Shakespeare: The Sonnets, 1990, 95, 98, Ezra Pound and China, 2003, Annotated Shakespeare: Narrative Poems, 2006; contbr. articles to profl. jours. Beinecke fellow, Yale U., 1992-93; NEH sr. fellow, 1998-99, Franklin Rsch. fellow Am. Philos. Soc., 2003-05, Comparative Lit. fellow, Yale U., 2005. Mem. MLA, Modern 1st Studies Assn., Ezra Pound Soc., William Carlos Williams Soc., Wallace Stevens Soc., Marianne Moore Soc. Office: U New Orleans Dept English New Orleans LA 70148-0001

QIAN, ZIFEN, artist, editor-in-chief; b. Shanghai, Dec. 30, 1957; came to U.S., 1987; s. Mingkong and Xuan Wu (Chen) Q.; m. Li Dai, Mar. 27, 1992; 1 child, Kristin. BA, Shanghai Normal U., 1983; MFA, Portland State U., 1989. Sr. artist Carol Wilson Fine Arts, Portland, 1992—; art instr. Pacific Northwest Coll. Art, Portland, 1989-95, Portland State U., 1987-89; art dir. Classic Clay Concept Inc., 1990-92; art editor Youth and Health mag. WHO, Shanghai, 1983-87; pres. Northwest Chinese Artists Assn., Portland, 1993-95; editor-in-chief World Arts Pub. Co., Portland, 1997—. Fine artist: (paintings, art philosophy) The Oregonian newspaper, 1987, Stepping Out Arts mag., 1988, (paintings in a book) Entertaining with Betsy Bloomingdale, 1994, (paintings prints) Carol Wilson Fine Arts, 1992—, (art experience) The Dictionary of World Chinese Artists Achievements, 1994. One-man exhbns. Denise Amato Galleries, 1989-98, Indigo Gallery, 1992, Portland State U. Gallery, 1989 (fine artist award), U.S. Nat. Bank Tower, 1987, Broderick Gallery, 2000, Internat. Artexpo, NYC, 2002, Dragon Gallery, NYC, 2002, 03, Kavanaugh Art Gallery, West Des Moines, Iowa, 2002, Art Show At Portland U., 2008; group exhbns. include Shanghai Fine Arts Acad. Shows, 1982, 84, Across East China Nat. Art Show, 1986, San Francisco World Exposition, 1987, Pacific N.W. Coll. Art, 1992, Denise Amato Galleries, 1991, 93, 94, 96, 97, Emerly Fine Arts Gallery, 1997, Portland Art Mus., 1999, Malovat Art Gallery, Chgo., 2003, Broderick Gallery, 2004, Artexpo NY, 2006; featured in The Washington Post, 1995, The Houston Chronicle, 1995, The Oregonian newspaper, 1987, (book) Always Bright (Paintings From 1970-1999), 1999; painting on cover of book Traditions and Encounters-A Global Perspective on The Past (From 1500 To The Present), 2000; oil painting Classical Meditation pub. on The Asian Reporter; represented in permanent collections at State Senate of Oreg., State House of Oreg., City Hall of Portland, Portland Christian Ctr., Portland Art Mus.; watercolors printed in art products shown in over 40,000 art galleries and gift stores, U.K., France, Finland, Italy, Germany, Denmark, Australia, N.Z., Japan, Can., U.S; author: (book) The Art of Zifen Qian. Pres. Chinese Friendship Assn. Portland, 2004—05. Recipient Outstanding Painting award Lucil S. Welch Meml. Found., 1988. Avocations: creating poetry, singing, tennis.

QIANG, MEI, biomedical researcher, educator; d. Xiaofeng Qiang and Wenlian Zhao; m. Jianping Xie; 1 child, Yi Xie. MD, PhD, Shanxi Med. U., Taiyuan, China, 1994. Instr. UTHSCSA, San Antonio, 2004—, asst. prof., 2007—. Mem.: Soc. Neurosci. Achievements include research in molecular biological mechanisms. Personal E-mail: mqiang99@yahoo.com.

QIAO, FENGXIANG, transportation engineer, educator; b. Taizhou, Jiangsu Province, China, Sept. 26, 1963; s. Deheng Qiao and Sufang Shen; m. Jinghong Ma, Sept. 28, 1988; 1 child, Yijun. Bachelor of Engring. in Automatic Control, Nanjing Inst. Tech., China, 1985; Master of Engring. in Mech. Engring., SE U., China, 1988; PhD in Civil Engring., Hong Kong U. Sci. and Tech., 2000. Asst. prof., dir. transp. lab SE U., Nanjing, 1988—97; rsch. and tchg. asst. Hong Kong U. Sci. and Tech., Hong Kong, 1997—2000; post doctoral rsch. assoc. and rsch. asst. prof. Tex. So. U., Houston, 2000—05, asst. prof., 2005—. Dir. Ctr. for Modeling and Simulation Tex. So. U., dir. Ctr. for Intelligent Transp. Sys. Recipient 2d Pl. award for transp. planning, Henan Province, China, 1992, 2d Pl. award for sci. and tech. progress, Chinese Edn. Com., 1992; Tex. So. U. Seed grantee, Tex. So. U., 2006. Master: Houston Area Nat. Summer Transp. Inst. (mentor 2002—06), United Assns. Chinese Alumni in Greater Houston Area (life; pres. 2005—07); mem.: N.Am. China Overseas Transp. Assn., Transp. Rsch. Bd., Air & Waste Mgmt. Assn., Am. Assn. Civil Engring. (assoc.), Tex. Dept. Transp. (mem. tech. adv. panel, Award for rsch. on symbols and warrants for major traffic generator guide signing), SW. Region U. Transp. Ctr. (prin. investigator 2004—07, Award for rsch. on intelligent transp. sys. data compression 2004, Award for rsch. on using GPS and ITS data to calibrate micro simulation model VISSIM 2005, Award for rsch. on computer simulation based algorithm for optimizing evacuation plans 2006). Achievements include first to develop Wavelet Transformation based approach for Intelligent Transportation System data aggregation and compression; research on collecting and evaluating on-road vehicle emission for mobile source air quality control; research in computer simulation based optimization strategy for evacuation under unexpected events in large urban areas; improving framework and systematic calibration for intersection left-turn yellow intervals including red clearance time; intelligent intersection delay estimation methogology by using Fuzzy logic theory; synthesizing warrants for major traffic generator guide signing; intelligent classification of traffic flow states using Neural Network Pattern Recognition technique; intelligent simulation and prediction of taffic flow dispersion; an equity-based model to control massive transit rail passenger flow; updating crash record data property based on new crash for improving regional air quality. Home: 5606 Bissonet St # 12 Houston TX 77081 Office: Texas Southern University Transp D 3100 Cleburne Ave Houston TX 77004 Office Fax: 713-313-1856. Personal E-mail: ceqfx@yahoo.com. Business E-Mail: qiao_fg@tsu.edu.

QIAO, JIAN-HUA, pathologist, researcher; b. Shanghai, Sept. 17, 1960; m. Mei-Qian Guan, Sept. 27, 1985; children: Mona G., George S. Qiao-Guan. MD, Shanghai Med. U., 1984. Diplomate Am. Bd. Pathology, 2003. Resident diagnostic radiology Children's Hosp., Shanghai Med. U., 1984—90, chief resident diagnostic radiology, 1988—90; rsch. fellow cardiology Cedars-Sinai Med. Ctr., LA, 1990—91, resident pathology, 1997—2002; asst. rschr. cardiologist UCLA Med. Ctr., 1991—97, fellow cardiac and pulmonary pathology, 2002—03, clin. instr., 2003—04; staff attending pathologist Mercy Hosp., Bakersfield, Calif., 2004—06, Cath. Healthcare West, 2004—, Calif. Hosp. Med. Ctr., 2006—. Contbr. articles to profl. jours. Recipient Physician Recognition award, AMA, 2001—07, Nathan B. Friedman, M.D. prize for rsch., Cedars-Sinai Med. Ctr., 2002, 1st prize, Shanghai Life Sci. Young Investigator Forum, 1998; named Am. Top Physicians, Consumer's Rsch. Coun. Am., 2007—08. Fellow: Coll. Am. Pathologists; mem.: L.A. Soc. Pathologists, US and Can. Acad. Pathology. Achievements include research in size of atherosclerotic plaque in coronary arteries in patients who died from acute myocardial infarction; rejection in cardiac transplantation; mouse models for athersclerosis; discovery of define genetic determination of arterial calcification; heart disease and HIV infection; describe cartilage cells in artery wall in human calcified diabetic peripheral vascular disease; research in imaging studies of pulmonary hypertension in Chinese children with congenital heart disease; gated MRI in diagnosis of congenital heart disease in children in Shanghai. Avocations: swimming, bicycling, stamp collecting/philately, photography. Office: Calif Hosp Med Ctr Dept Pathology 1401 S Grand Ave Los Angeles CA 90015 Office Phone: 213-742-5791. Personal E-mail: jianhuaqiao@yahoo.com. Business E-Mail: jian-hua.qiao@chw.edu.

QIN, QING-MING, agriculturist; married. PhD, China Agrl. U., Beijing. Grad. rsch. asst. China Agrl. U., 1990—93, 1999—2002, rsch. fellow & lectr., 1993—96; asst. prof. Inst. Plant Protection, Chinese Acad. Agrl. Scis., Beijing, 1996—2002; vis. postdoc. scholar U. Calif., Davis, Salinas, 2002—05; postdoc. rsch. assoc. Tex. A&M U., Coll. Station, 2005—09, asst. rsch. scientist, 2009—. Contbr. scientific papers to profl. jours. Decorated Rsch. award; recipient Achievement award, Ministry Agr., China, 1998. Mem.: Am. Soc. Microbiology. Achievements include research in plant protection, molecular plant pathology & biochemistry, host-pathogen interactions. Office: Tex A&M Univ 2132 Tamu College Station TX 77843-2132 Business E-Mail: qqin@ag.tamu.edu.

QIN, SHU, materials scientist; b. Beijing, May 21, 1950; arrived in U.S., 1986; d. Ni and Jin Zhang Qin; m. Fuping Zhai Qin, Jan. 21, 1978; 1 child, Zhen. Diploma, Beijing Poly. U., 1976; MS, Tsinghua U., Beijing, 1982; PhD, Northeastern U., Boston, 1992. Asst. prof. Tsinghua U., Beijing, 1976—82; lectr. Beijing Inst. of Posts and Telcoms., 1982—86; rsch. scientist Lehigh U., Bethlehem, Pa., 1986—87; sr. scientist Northeastern U., Boston, 1992—97; prin. scientist Silicon Genesis Corp., Campbell, Calif., 1997—2000, Axcelis Technologies, Inc., Beverly, Mass., 2000—. Cons. Eaton Corp., Beverly, 1993—97. Contbr. over 104 articles to profl. jours. Mem.: AAAS, IEEE (sr.), Materials Rsch. Soc. Achievements include patents for in field. Avocations: photography, sports, travel, classical music. Home: 47 Francis St Apt 2 Malden MA 02148 Office: Axcelis Technologies Inc 108 Cherry Hill Dr Beverly MA 01915

QIN, XIAOFA, medical educator, research scientist; b. Botou, Hebei, China, June 1, 1963; s. Hai-Quan Qin and Xiu-Qin Ma; m. Shuqin Zheng, June 19, 1991; children: Zhe Jason, Ryan. MD in Pub. Health, Beijing Med. U., 1986, MS in Toxicology, 1989, PhD in Toxicology, 1992. Lectr. Beijing Med. U., 1992—94, assoc. prof., 1994—96; postdoctoral asst. La. State U. LSU Med. Ctr., Shreveport, 1996; postdoctoral fellow U. Cin. Coll. Medicine, 1996—2004, rsch. instr., 2004—06; asst. prof. U. Medicine Dentistry NJ, Newark, 2006—. Temp. advisor WHO, Manila, 1995; com. mem. Chinese Soc. Indsl. Toxicology, 1994—96. Contbr. articles to profl. jours. Recipient 3d Advance in Scis. & Tech. award, Ministry of Health China, 1996. Achievements include research in causative role of digestive proteases in inflammatory bowel disease and some other allergic and autoimmune diseases; possible cause of the mysterious bilirubin or biliverdin predominance in animals. Personal E-mail: xiaofa_qin@yahoo.com.

QIN, YUFEN, immunologist, researcher; m. Yiping Zhang. MD (hon.), Harbin Med. U., China, 1977, MD in Immunology, 1982; PhD summa cum laude (hon.), U. Würzburg, Germany, 1990. Resident First Tchg. Hosp., Harbin Med. U., 1982—85; rsch. fellow Dept. Neurology U. Calif., Irvine, 1990—93; rsch. scientist Inst. Pathology, U. Würzburg, 1993—95, Dept. Virology, U. Quebec Inst. Armand-Frappier, Laval, 1995—96, Montreal Nuerol. Inst. Hosp., McGill U., 1996—99; asst. rschr. Dept. Neurology, U. Calif., Irvine, 1999—2003, asst. prof., 2003—. Contbr. articles to profl. jours. Recipient Rsch. award, Max-Planck Soc., 1986—90, Deutsche Forschungsgemeinschaft, 1993—95, van den Noort award, U. Calif., Dept. Neurology, 2005; grantee, Nat. Multiple Sclerosis Soc., 2000—03, NIH, 2001—06; fellow, U. Calif., 1990—93. Mem.: AAAS (assoc.), NY Acad. Sci. (assoc.), Am. Acad. Neurology (assoc.; multiple sclerosis sect.). Peace Party. Achievements include discovery of multiple sclerosis being considered as a neural and axonal autoimmune disease; glycolytic enzymes glyceraldehyde-3-phosphate dehydrogenase (GAPDH) and triosephosphate isomerase (TPI) being identified as target antigens in MS; antobodies in MS brains attack glycolytic enzymes in neuron and axon of a majoriey of MS patients; patents for B cell-mediated immune response in MS, in particular the patents at early stages of clinically isolated syndromes for the early diagnosis and treatment; patents pending for development of diagnosis kits for early detect glycolytic enzyme autoimmunoty in patients with MS and patients with other diseases. Avocations: philosophy, writing, travel, logical argumentation, photography. Office: U Calif 100 Irvine Hall Irvine CA 92697-4275 Business E-Mail: qiny@uci.edu.

QINGPING, TAO, research and development company executive; b. Hefei, Anhui, China; s. Siguo Tao and Xinlian Li. BE, Hefei U. Tech.; MA, U. Sci. & Tech. China; PhD, U. Nebr., Lincoln, 2004. V.p. R & D GC Image, LLC, Lincoln, Nebr., 2005—. Contbr. articles to profl. jours. Grant, SBIR-STTR NIH, 2008—09. Mem.: Assn. Computing Machinery. Independent. Office: GC Image LLC 201 N 8th St Ste 420 Lincoln NE 68508

QISHENG, PAN, transportation executive, educator; PhD, U. Southern Calif., LA, 2003. Assoc. prof. Dept. Urban Planning and Env. Policy, Tex. Southern U., Houston, 2003—08, interim chair, 2008. Cons., sch. policy, planning and devel. U. Southern Calif., 2003—06. Contbr. chapters to books. Grant, Tex. Dept. Transp., 2004—08. Mem.: ACSP. Office: Tex Southern Univ 3100 Cleburne St Houston TX 77004

QIU, MEIKANG, engineering educator; b. La. s. Shiqing Qiu and Longzhi Yuan; m. Diqiu Cao; 1 child, David. BS in Engring., Shanghai Jiao Tong U., 1992, MS in Engring., 1998; MS in Computer Sci., U. Tex., Dallas, Richardson, Tex., 2003, PhD, 2007. Cert. China, 1998. Engr. Chinese Helicopter Rsch. Inst., China, 1992—94; dir. engr. Rayes Electronic and Telecom. Group Co., Shenzhen, Guangdong, China, 1994—97; computer engr. IBM, Shenzhen, 1997—98; sr. computer engr. Shenzhen Quality & Tech. Supervision Bur., China, 1998—2001; editor Internat. Jour. Multimedia and Ubiquitous Engring.; asst. prof. U. New Orleans, 2007—. Contbr. scientific papers to profl. jours. V.p. SJTU Alumni Assn., Dallas; activity coord. Friendship Assn. Chinese Students and Scholars, Dallas. Grantee UNO Start Up Fund, U. New Orleans. Mem.: IEEE, ACM. Achievements include patents for minimize energy consumption using optimal voltage assignment algorithm; patents pending for parallel variable length pattern matching using hash table. Home: 2000 Lakeshore Dr UNO PMB 2728 New Orleans LA 70148 Office: Univ New Orleans Elect Eng 2000 Lakeshore Dr New Orleans LA 70148 Office Fax: 504-280-3950; Home Fax: 504-280-3950. Personal E-mail: qiumeikang@yahoo.com. Business E-Mail: mqiu@uno.edu.

QIU, PEIPEI, language educator; b. China; PhD, Columbia U., NYC, 1994. Instr. and asst. prof. Fordham U., NYC, 1992—94; assoc. prof. Vassar Coll., Poughkeepsie, NY, 1994—. Contbr. articles to profl. publs. Fellowships, Japan Found., 1984, Japan Soc. Promotion of Sci., 1998, grants, Andrew W. Mellon Found., 1999—2001, 2006. Mem.: Assn. Asian Studies. Office: Vassar Coll 124 Raymond Ave Poughkeepsie NY 12604

QIU, ROBERT CAIMING, engineering educator, consultant; s. Dafu Qiu and Shuxian Li; m. Lily Liman Li; children: Michelle Feng, David Yifeng, Jackie Linyuan. PhD, NY U., 1995. Tech. staff mem. GTE Labs., Waltham, Mass., 1995—97, Bell Labs, Lucent Techs., Whippany, NJ, 1997—2000; ceo, pres., & bd dirs. Wiscom Techs., Inc., Clark, 2000—03; prof. Tenn. Tech U., Cookeville, 2003—. Contbr. articles to profl. jour. Indsl. adv. bd. NJ. Ctr. Wireless Telecom., Newwark, 2001—03. Recipient Kinslow Rsch. award, TTU, 2006. Mem.: IEEE. Achievements include patents for doppler frequency estimation; multilayer resource management in wireless communication system; improving user access performance by adjusting power of user probe signal; long-range prediction of fading signals for WCDMA high speed downlink packet access (HSDPA); adaptive pilot/traffic channel power control for 3GPP WCDMA. Office: TN Tech Univ W 10th St Cookeville TN 38505 Business E-Mail: rqiu@tntech.edu.

QIU, ROBIN G., adult education educator; BS, MS, Beijing Inst. Tech.; PhD, Pa. State U., 1996. Prof. Pa. State U., Malvern, 1996—. Achievements include patents for radio frequencey identification. Office: Pa State U 30 E Swedesford Malvern PA 19355 Business E-Mail: robinqiu@psu.edu.

QIU, SHENFENG, medical researcher; married. MD, MPH, U. Calif., Riverside, PhD, MB, UCR, Calif, 2004. Rsch. fellow Vanderbilt U. Med. Ctr., Nashville, 2004—. Contbr. articles to sci. profl. pubs. Mem.: Soc. Neurosci. Personal E-mail: shenfeng.qiu@gmail.com.

QIU, TONG, engineering educator, consultant; s. Binghua Qiu and Jing Huang; m. Manyu Margaret Yu; children: Quantum Zexing, Ella Xiangye. PhD, U. Calif., LA, 2005. Cert. profl. engr., Ohio, 2006. Project engr. Ninyo & Moore, San Diego, 2005—07; asst. prof. Clarkson U., Potsdam, NY, 2007—. Contbr. articles to profl. jours. Office: Clarkson Univ 8 Clarkson Ave Potsdam NY 13699-5710 Personal E-mail: qiutong@ucla.edu. Business E-Mail: tqiu@clarkson.edu.

QIU, WULIN, chemist, materials scientist, materials engineer; s. Shiqing Qiu and Chengcui Xu; m. Suya Wang, June 18, 1997; 1 child, Zhiyuan. BS, East China Inst. Tech., 1989, MS, 1992; PhD, Nanjing U. Sci. and Tech., China, 1995. Guest rschr. Nat. Inst. of Advanced Indsl. Sci. and Tech., Takamatsu, Kagawa, Japan, 1999—2004; postdoctoral rsch. assoc. U. of Tenn., Knoxville, Tenn., 2004—. Contbr. more than 60 sci. papers to peer reviewed jours. Recipient Excellent Grad. award, Nanjing U. of Sci. and Tech., 1996, Sci. and Tech. Devel. award, Sci. and Tech. Com. Jiangsu Province, China, 1997, Excellent U. Student award, Jiangsu Province, 1995; grantee Sci. Funds for the Postdoctoral fellows of China, Ednl. Com., 1996, Sci. Funds for the Postdoctoral fellow, Guangdong Province, 1996. Mem.: Internat. Union Pure and Applied Chemistry, Am. Chem. Soc. Achievements include patents for novel thermal-resistance polymers; research in reversibility between glass and melting transition of polymers; observed glass transition within the polymer crystals; proved interfacial esterification between cellulose and maleated polyolefins in solid state; nanocomposites of polymer/inorganic hybrid; prepared inorganic nanoparticles with a new method; developed a novel macromolecular coupling agents, studied its effect on properties of polymer composites; synthesized novel metal-containing diamines; synthesized novel polymers (thermal-resistance, metal-containing, non-linear optical, liquid crystalline); synthesized dendrimers and hyperbranched polymer hybrids. Avocations: reading, travel, photography, badminton. Office: U Tenn Chem Dept 1420 Circle Dr Knoxville TN 37996-1600 Personal E-mail: qiuwulin@yahoo.com.

QIU, XIANGJUN, mining engineer; s. Anren Zhao and Peijin Qiu; m. Hong Lin, Jan. 17, 1961; children: Joanna Lin, Grace. BS, Nanjing U. Aeronautics and Astronautics, China, 1982, MS, 1984; PhD, U. Wis., Madison, 1990. Mgr. applied mechanics Conveyor Dynamics, Inc., Bellingham, Wash., 1990—2002; chief scientist high fidelity simulation Metso Minerals Industries, Inc., Colorado Springs, Colo., 2002—. Contbr. articles to profl. jours. Achievements include first to precisely solve equations for belt conveyor rolling resistance; development of numerical approach to madel mill linear wear.

QIU, ZHIJUN, engineer, researcher; s. Shuian Qiu and Jinxiang Du; m. Na Gao, July 18, 2003. PhD, U. Wis., Madison, 2007. Postdoc. rschr. U. Wis., 2007—08, U. Calif. Berkeley, Richmond, 2008—. Mem.: IEEE, Transp. Rsch. Bd. Office: Calif Path 1357 S 46 St Bldg 452 Richmond CA 94804

QNARDELLI, ROBERT LOUIS, private equity firm executive, former automotive executive; b. Old Forge, Pa., May 17, 1948; m. Sue QNardelli, 1971; 4 children. BS in Bus., Western Ill. U., 1971; MBA, U. Louisville, 1975; D in Bus. Adminstrn. (hon.), U. Louisville, 2001; LLD (hon.), Siena Coll., 2001; LHD (hon.), Western Ill. U., 2002. With GE, 1971-88; exec. v.p., gen. mgr. worldwide parts & components Case Corp., Racine, Wis., 1988-91; pres., CEO Can. Appliance Mfg. Co. subs. GE, Toronto, Ont., Canada, 1991-92, GE Transp. Sys., Erie, Pa., 1992-95, GE Power Sys., 1995-2000, The Home Depot, Atlanta, 2000—07, chmn., 2002—07; chmn., CEO Chrysler LLC, Auburn Hills, Mich., 2007—09; CEO, Cerberus Oper. and Adv. Co. LLC, Cerberus Capital Magmt., L.P., 2009—. Bd. dirs. The Home Depot, 2000—07, The Coca-Cola Co, 2002—05, Chrysler LLC, 2007—09. Pres. Bush's Coun. Savannah Coll., Art and Design, chmn., atlanta bd. visitors; mem. The Bus. Coun.; bd. advisors. U. Louisville Grad. Sch. Bus.; mem. advisory bd. We. Ill. U. Coll. Bus. & Tech. Recipient Disting. Pennsylvanian Award, Gannon U., 1995, Disting. Alumni Award, Western Ill. U. Coll. Bus. & Tech., 1998; named Exec. of Yr., Schenectady County C of C, 2000, Alumnus of Yr., U. Louisville, 2001. Mem.: The Bus. Coun., President's Coun. on Service and Civic Participation, 2003. Office: Cerebrus Capital Mgmt LP 299 Park Ave New York NY 10171 Office Phone: 212-891-2100. Office Fax: 212-891-1540.*

QU, DONGXIA, physicist, researcher; m. Zhi Quan, May 25, 2004. BS, Zhejiang U., Hangzhou, China, 2002; MS, Okla. State U., Stillwater, 2004; PhD student, Princeton U., NJ. Rsch. asst. Princeton U., 2005—. Contbr. articles to profl. jours. Mem.: Inst. Elec. and Electronic Engrs., Optical Soc. Am., Am. Phys. Soc. Achievements include research in the areas of solid state physics, non-linear and quantum optics, and electronic materials; invention of chaotic cavity for optical trace gas sensing systems; patents pending for asymmetric chaotic optical multi-pass cavity. Business E-Mail: dqu@princeton.edu.

QU, LIANGTI, research scientist; s. ShunXuan Qu and XueRong Cao; m. Aihua Guo, Aug. 16, 2002; 1 child, Allen. PhD, Tsinghua U., Beijing, 2004. Contbr. scientific papers to profl. jours., chapters to books. Mem.: SAMPE (Outstanding Paper award 2007). Achievements include aligning carbon nanotube mimetic gecko foot; patents for substrate enhanced electroless deposition; patents pending for super long carbon nanotubes, carbon nanotube dry adhesives. Business E-Mail: quliangz@notes.udayton.edu.

QU, QI, communications engineer; b. Chengdu, Sichuan, China; married. PhD, U. Calif. San Diego, La Jolla, 2008. Grad. rschr. U. Calif. San Diego, 2004—08; rsch. engr. NTT-DoCoMo Comm. Lab USA, Inc., Palo Alto, Calif., 2007; sr. sys. engr. SST Comm. Corp., Los Angeles, 2008—09. Contbr. articles to profl. jours. Recipient Academic Merit award, U. Miami, 2004, award, Chinese Govt., 2007; fellowship, Elec. and Computer Engring. Dept., U. Calif. San Diego, 2004. Achievements include research in significant original scientific contributions to wireless communications. Avocation: travel. Home: 3800 Parkview Ln 12D Irvine CA 92612 Office Phone: 310-577-3600.

QU, RONGHAI, electrical engineer; b. Heilongjiang, China; s. Baoshen Qu and Guilan Wang; m. Dongning Sun, Jan. 29, 1996; children: Chen, Jeffrey. BS in Elec. Engring., Tsinghua U., Beijing, China, 1993, MS in Elec. Engring., 1996; PhD, U. Wis., Madison, 2002. Faculty mem. Tsinghua U., Beijing, 1996—98; sr. devel. engr. Northland, a Scott Fetzer Co., Watertown, NY, 2002—03; elec. engr. in sr. profl. band GE Global Rsch. Ctr., Niskayuna, NY, 2003—. Com. mem. Tech. Com. Energy and Power Sys., Internat. Assn. Sci. and Tech. Devel., 2004—07. Contbr. scientific papers numerous articles to profl. jours.; presenter in field. Recipient Mgmt. award, GE Global Rsch. Ctr., 2004. Mem.: IEEE (sr.; com. mem. elec. machines com. 2002—, Best Paper award, 3rd prize 2003, 3rd prize 2005), Sigma Xi. Achievements include patents for 8 patents on electrical machines; 22 patents pending on electrical machines. Office: EP 118A GE Global Rsch Ctr 1 Research Cir Niskayuna NY 12309

QU, WEI, research scientist; PhD, U. Ill., Chgo., 2006. Sr. rsch. scientist Motorola, Schaumburg, Ill., 2004—07, Siemens, Hoffman Estates, Ill., 2007—. Mem.: IEEE (Best Paper award, Signal Processing Soc., ICIP 2006).

QUAAL, WARD LOUIS, broadcast executive; b. Ishpeming, Mich., Apr. 7, 1919; s. Sigfred Emil and Alma Charlotte (Larson) Q.; m. Dorothy J. Graham, Mar. 9, 1944; children: Graham Ward, Jennifer Anne. AB, U. Mich., 1941; LL.D. (hon.), Mundelein Coll., 1962, No. Mich. U., 1967; D.Pub.Svc., Elmhurst Coll., 1967; D.H.L. (hon.), Lincoln Coll., 1968, DePaul U., 1974. Announcer-writer Sta. WBEO (now sta. WDMJ), Marquette, Mich., 1936—37; announcer, writer, producer Sta. WJR, Detroit, 1937—41; spl. events announcer-producer WGN, Chgo., 1941—42, asst. to gen. mgr., 1945—49; exec. dir. Clear Channel Broadcasting Service, Washington, 1949—52, pres., chief exec. officer, 1964—74; v.p., asst. gen. mgr. Crosley Broadcasting Corp., Cin., 1952—56; v.p., gen. mgr., mem. bd. WGN Inc., Chgo., 1956; exec. v.p., then pres. WGN Continental Broadcasting Co. (now Tribune Broadcasting Co.), 1960—75; pres. Ward L. Quaal Co., 1975—; dir. Tribune Co., 1961—75; dir., mem. exec. com. U.S. Satellite Broadcasting Co., 1982—2000. Bd. dirs. Christine Valmy Inc.; chmn. exec. com., dir. WLW Radio Inc., Cin., 1975-81; co-founder, dir. Universal Resources Inc., 1961-86; mem. FCC Adv. Com. on Advanced TV Sys., 1988-96. Author: (with others) Broadcast Management, 1968, rev. edit., 1979, new edit. 1997; co-prodr. (Broadway play) Teddy and Alice, 1988. Mem., Hoover Commn. Exec. Br. Task Force, 1949-59; mem. U.S.-Japan Cultural Exchange Commn., 1960-70; mem. Pres.'s Council Phys. Fitness and Sports, 1983-93; bd. dirs. Farm Found., 1963-73; bd. trustees Hollywood (Calif.) Mus., 1964-78, MacCormac Jr. Coll., Chgo., 1974-80; chmn. exec. com. Council for TV Devel., 1969-72; mem. bus. adv. coun. Chgo. Urban League, 1964-74; bd. dirs. Broadcasters Found., Internat. Radio and TV Found., Sears Roebuck Found., 1970-73; trustee Mundelein Coll., 1962-72, Hillsdale Coll., 1966-72. Served as lt. USNR, 1942-45. Recipient Disting. Bd. Gov.'s award, NATAS, 1966, 1987, Inaugural Inductee Mgmt. Hall of Fame, 2003, Freedoms Found. award,

Valley Forge, 1966, 1968, 1970, Disting. Alumnus award, U. Mich., 1967, Loyola U. Key, 1970, Advt. Man of Yr. Gold medallion, Chgo. Advt. Club, 1968, Disting. Svc. award, Nat. Assn. Broadcasters, 1973, Ill. Broadcaster of Yr. award, 1973, Press Vet. of Yr. award, 1973, Comm. award of distinction, Brandeis U., 1973, Founder & Leadership award, Broadcast Pioneers Libr., 1991, 1st recipient Sterling medal, Barren Found., 1985, Lifetime Achievement award in broadcasting, Ill. Broadcasters Assn., 1989, Lifetime Achievement award, WGN TV, 1998, 1st person named to Better Bus. Bur. Hall of Fame, Coun. on Better Bus. Burs., Inc., 1975; named Radio Man of Yr., Am. Coll. Radio, Arts, Crafts & Scis., 1961, Laureate in Order of Lincoln, Lincoln Acad. Ill., 1965, Communicator of Yr., Jewish United Fund, 1969, Advt. Club Man of Yr., 1973; named one of Top 100 Mems., Delta Tau Delta, 1999, 1st 100 5th Estaters, Broadcasting 20th Century, 1999, First 50 Giants of Broadcasting, Libr. Am. Broadcasting, 2003; named to Delta Tau Delta Disting. Svc. Chpt., 1970, Broadcasting Mag. Hall of Fame, 1991, Mgmt. Hall of Fame, NATAS/TV Bur. Advt., 2003. Mem. NATAS (bd. govs. 1966-76, Silver Circle award 1993), Nat. Press Found. (bd. dirs. 1991-99), Nat. Assn. Broadcasters (bd. dirs. 1952-56), Fed. Comm. Bar Assn., Broadcast Music Inc. (bd. dirs. 1953-70), Assn. Maximum Svc. Telecasters Inc. (bd. dirs. 1952-72), Broadcast Pioneers (pres., bd. dirs. 1962-73), Broadcast Pioneers Libr. (pres. 1981-84), Broadcast Pioneers Ednl. Fund Inc., Broadcasters Found. (chmn. bd. 1996-99). Office: Ward L Quaal Co PO Box 336 Winnetka IL 60093

QUACKENBUSH, JUSTIN LOWE, federal judge; b. Spokane, Wash., Oct. 3, 1929; s. Carl Clifford and Marian Huldah (Lowe) Q.; m. Marie McAtee; children: Karl Justin, Kathleen Marie, Robert Craig. Student, U. Ill., 1947-49; BA, U. Idaho, 1951; LLB, Gonzaga U., Spokane, 1957. Bar: Wash. 1957. Dep. pros. atty., Spokane County, 1957-59; ptnr. Quackenbush, Dean, Bailey & Henderson, Spokane, 1959-80; dist. judge U.S. Dist. Ct. (ea. dist.) Wash., Spokane, 1980—, now sr. judge. Part-time instr. Gonzaga U. Law Sch., 1960-67 Chmn. Spokane County Planning Commn., 1969-73. Served with USN, 1951-54. Mem. Wash. Bar Assn., Spokane County Bar Assn. (trustee 1976-78), Internat. Footprint Assn. (nat. pres. 1967), Shriners. Episcopalian. Office: US Dist Ct PO Box 1432 Spokane WA 99210-1432 Office Phone: 509-458-5280.

QUACKENBUSH, MARGERY CLOUSER, psychoanalyst, researcher; b. Reading, Pa., Apr. 30, 1938; d. Carl Brumbach and Katherine Elvina (Althouse) Clouser; m. Robert Mead Quackenbush, July 3, 1971; 1 child, Piet Robert. BFA, Pratt Inst., 1960; MA, Calif. Grad. Inst., 1982; PhD in Psychoanalysis, Internat. U. Grad. Studies, NYC, 2001. Cert. in psychoanalysis Ctr. for Modern Psychoanalytic Studies, 1992. Instr. Pratt Inst., Bklyn., 1978-79, Fashion Inst. of Tech., NYC, 1980-81; counselor Wiltwyck, Bronx Ctr., 1981-82; exec. dir. Nat. Assn. for Advancement of Psychoanalysis, NYC, 1982—; pvt. practice in psychoanalysis NYC, 1980—. Adj. prof. Union Inst., 2007. Mem. Lenox Hill Dem. Club, N.Y.C., 1993-95; spkr. various cmty. groups, 1991—. Recipient Maison Blanche award, 1959, Miriam Berkman Spotnitz award, 1992, Am. Bd. Accreditation Profl. Svc. award, 2000-04. Mem. Nat. Assn. for Advancement of Psychoanalysis, Nat. Soc. DAR, Alumni Assn. of the Ctr. for Modern Psych. Studies (sec. 1992-94, Alumni Assn. program dir., v.p. 1995-98), Soc. Modern Psychoanalysts. Democrat. Avocations: reading, writing, golf, horseback riding. Home: 460 E 79th St Apt 14E New York NY 10075-1447 Office: Nat Assn Advancement Psychoanalysis 80 8th Ave # 1501 New York NY 10011-5126 Office Phone: 212-741-0515. Personal E-mail: margeryquackenbush@yahoo.com. Business E-Mail: mq@naap.org.

QUADE, VICKI, editor, writer, theater producer; b. Chgo., Aug. 15, 1953; d. Victor and Virginia (Uryasz) Q.; m. Charles J. White III, Feb. 15, 1986 (div. Aug. 1996); children: Michael, David, Catherine. BS in Journalism, No. Ill. U., 1974. Staff reporter news divsn. The News-Tribune, LaSalle, Ill., 1975-77; staff writer news divsn. The News-Sun, Waukegan, Ill., 1977-81; staff writer ABA Jour., Chgo., 1981-85; mng. editor ABA Press, Chgo., 1985-90, editor, 1990-2000, sr. editor, 1994-2000. Author: (poetry) Rain and Other Poems, 1976, Laughing Eyes, 1979, Two Under the Covers, 1981, (biography) I Remember Bob Collins, 2000; playwright Late Nite Catechism, 1993, Room for Advancement, 1994, Mr. Nanny, 1997, (musical) Lost in Wonderland, 1998, (musical) Here Come the Famous Brothers, 2001, Put the Nuns in Charge!, 2005, Sunday School Cinema, 2007; prodr. Late Nite Catechism, Mr. Nanny, Here Come the Famous Brothers, Christopher Carter Messes With Your Mind, Forever Plaid, Cast on a Hot Tin Roof, Verbatim Verboten, Put the Nuns in Charge; U.S. premiere of Drapes, 2005; contbr. to numerous anthologies and publs.; contbd. to: 20th Century Chicago: 100 Years, 100 Voices (contbd. the year 1953), owner/operator Crossroads Theater, Naperville, Ill Recipient numerous awards from Soc. Nat. Assn. Publs., AP, UPI, Spirit of Benedict award Benedictine Sisters Chgo., 2003, Partners in Mission award Sisters of the Living Word, 2005 Mem. Am. Soc. Bus. Press Editors (award), Chgo. Newspaper Guild (award), Am. Soc. Assn. Execs. (Gold Circle award 1989, 90). Avocations: travel, photography.

QUAEGEBEUR, JAN MODEST, pediatric thoracic surgeon; b. 1945; MS, U. Notre Dame, Namur, Belgum, 1965; MD, Catholic U. Leiden, Leuven, Belgum, 1969; PhD cum laude, State U.Leiden, Netherlands, 1986. Diplomate Am. Bd. Surgery. Resident gen. surgery St. Michel Clin., Brussels, 1969—73; fellowship cardiovasc. surgery Baylor U. Coll. Medicine, Houston, 1973—74; fellowship cardiopulmonary surgery U. Hosp. Leiden, 1974—78, staff surgeon, chief dept. thoracic surgery, 1978—86; prof. pediat. cardiac surgery Erasmus U., Rotterdam, Netherlands, 1986—90; asst. attending surgeon NY-Presbyn. Hosp./Columbia U. Med. Ctr., NYC, 1990—91, assoc. attending surgeon, 1991—98, attending surgeon, 1990—, dir. pediat. cardiac surgery, 1991—; asst. prof. surgery Columbia U. Coll. Physicians & Surgeons, NYC, 1990—91, assoc. prof. surgery, 1991—98, prof. surgery, 1998—. Spl. fellow cardiac surgery U. Ala., Birmingham, 1977, Harvard Med. Sch., Boston, 1978; pres. Surgeons of Hope Found., 2007—. Contbr. articles to profl. jours. Named one of America's Top Dr.'s, Castle Connolly Med. LTD; named to NY Mag. Best Dr.'s. Mem.: Dutch Assn. Thoracic Surgery, European Assn. Cardio-Pulmonary Surgery, NY Med. Soc., NY Soc. Thoracic Surgery, Congenital Heart Surgeons Soc., Soc. Thoracic Surgeons, Internat. Soc. Heart and Lung Transplanation, Am. Assn. Thoracic Surgery. Avocations: golf, skiing, tennis. Mailing: NY Presbyn Babies & Childrens Hosp N Rm 276 3959 Broadway New York NY 10032 Office Phone: 212-305-5975. Office Fax: 212-305-4408.

QUAID, DENNIS, actor; b. Houston, Apr. 9, 1954; s. William Rudy and Juanita B.; m. P.J. Soles, Nov. 25, 1978 (div. Jan. 23, 1983); m. Meg Ryan, Feb. 14, 1991 (div. July 16, 2001); 1 child, Jack Henry; m. Kimberly Buffington, July 4, 2004; children: Thomas Boone, Zoe Grace. Student, U. Houston, 1972-75. Actor (films) Crazy Mama, 1975, I Never Promised You A Rosegarden, 1977, Sept. 30, 1955, 1977, Our Winning Season, 1978, The Seniors, 1978, Breaking Away, 1979, G.O.R.P., 1980, The Long Riders, 1980, Caveman, 1981, All Night Long, 1981, The Night the Lights Went Out in Georgia, 1981, Tough Enough, 1983, Jaws 3-D, 1983, The Right Stuff, 1983, Dreamscape, 1984, Enemy Mine, 1985, Innerspace, 1987, The Big Easy, 1987, Suspect, 1987, D.O.A., 1988, Everybody's All-American, 1988, Great Balls of Fire, 1989, Postcards from the Edge, 1990, Come See the Paradise, 1990, Undercover Blues, 1993, Wilder Napalm, 1993, Flesh and Bone, 1993, Wyatt Earp, 1994, Something to Talk About, 1995, Dragonheart, 1996, Criminal Element, 1997, Going West, 1997, Gang Related, 1997, Savior, 1997, Switchback, 1997, The Parent Trap, 1998, On Any Given Sunday, 1999, Frequency, 2000, Traffic, 2000, The Rookie, 2002, Far From Heaven, 2002, Cold Creek Manor, 2003, The Alamo, 2004, The Day After Tomorrow, 2004, Flight of the Phoenix, 2004, In Good Company, 2004, Yours, Mine and Ours, 2005, Am. Dreamz, 2006, Vantage Point, 2008, Smart People, 2008, The Express, 2008, The Horsemen, 2009, G.I. Joe: The Rise of Cobra, 2009; (theatre) The Last of the Knucklemen, 1983, True West, 1984; (TV movies) Are You In the House Alone?, 1978, Amateur Night at the Dixie Bar and Grill, 1979, Bill, 1981, Johnny Belinda, 1982, Bill: On His Own, 1983, Everything That Rises (also dir, prod.), 1998, Dinner with Friends, 2001; (TV appearances) Baretta, 1977. Named Hollywood Walk of Fame, 2005. Office: The William Morris Agy One William Morris Pl Beverly Hills CA 90212 *An artist must take chances in performing his craft. If he is to succeed he must be willing to fall flat on his face.**

QUAINI, DUANE C., lawyer; b. Napa, Calif., Mar. 30, 1945; BA summa cum laude, Claremont Men's Coll., 1967; JD, Stanford U., 1970. Bar: Ill. 1970. Assoc. Sonnenschein Nath & Rosenthal LLP, Chgo., 1970—76, ptnr., 1976—, chmn., 1997—2007. Note editor Stanford Law Rev., 1969-70. Mem. exec. com. bd. visitors Stanford Law Sch., 1995—, chmn.; vice chmn. bd. Jane Addams Juvenile Ct. Found.; dir. emeritus Les Turner ALS Found. Office: Sonnenschein Nath & Rosenthal LLP 8000 Sears Tower 233 S Wacker Dr Chicago IL 60606 Office Phone: 312-876-8051. Office Fax: 312-876-7934. Business E-Mail: dquaini@sonnenschein.com.

QUAINOO, GEORGE KOW, physics professor, department chairman; s. Alfred Asabil Quainoo and Comfort Abayaa Arthur; m. Gertrude Aku Sika Ankrah; 1 child, Janice Obiriwa. BSc, U. Cape Coast, Ghana, 1989, MSc, 1993; PhD, U. Sask., Canada, 2004. Part-time lectr. U. Cape Coast, 1992—94, lectr., 1994—2004; sessional lectr., grad. student asst. U. Sask., 1999—2004; asst. prof. Southern Oreg. U., Ashland, 2005—08, assoc. prof. and chair, 2008—. Reviewer NSF, Washington, 2006—. V.p. Sigma Xi Southern Oreg. Chpt., 2009—; mem. Navigator Ministry, Cape Coast, 1990—99; leader African Christian Fellowship, Saskatoon, 2002—05; assoc. chaplain Saskatoon Correctional Ctr., 2003—05; mem. Ashland Christian Fellowship, Oreg., 2005—, Emmanuel Bapt. Ch., Saskatoon, 1999—2005. Scholarship, Ghana Govt., Start-up grant, Southern Oreg. U., Carpenter II grant. Mem.: Abdus-Salam Internat. Ctr. Theoretical Physics, Oreg. Nanoscience and Microtechnologies Inst., Am. Assn. Physics Tchrs., Sigma Xi (2nd v.p. 2008). Office: Southern Oreg Univ 1250 Siskiyou Blvd Ashland OR 97520 Business E-Mail: quainoog@sou.edu.

QUAINTON, ANTHONY CECIL EDEN, diplomat; b. Seattle, Apr. 4, 1934; s. Cecil Eden and Marjorie Josephine (Oates) Q.; m. Susan Long, Aug. 7, 1958; children: Katherine, Eden, Elizabeth. BA, Princeton U., 1955; BLitt, Oxford U., Eng., 1958; LHD (hon.), LaRoche Coll., Pitts., 2006. Rsch. fellow St. Antony's Coll., Oxford, 1958-59; with Fgn. Svc., State Dept., 1959-97; vice consul Sydney, Australia, 1960-62; Urdu lang. trainee, 1962-63; 2d sec., econ. officer Am. embassy, Karachi, Pakistan, 1963-64, Rawalpindi, Pakistan, 1964-66, 2d sec., polit. officer New Delhi, 1966-69; sr. polit. officer for India Dept. State, Washington, 1969-72; 1st sec. Am. embassy, Paris, 1972-73, counselor, dep. chief mission Kathmandu, Nepal, 1973-76; amb. to Ctrl. African Empire, Bangui, 1976-78, Managua, Nicaragua, 1982—84, Kuwait, 1984—87; dir. Office for Combating Terrorism, Dept. State, Washington, 1978-81; dep. insp. gen. Dept. State, 1987-89; amb. Lima, Peru, 1989-92; asst. sec. of state for diplomatic security Dept. State, Washington, 1992-95, dir. gen. fgn. svc., 1995-97. Exec. dir. Una Chapman Cox Found., 1998—99; vis. lectr. Princeton U., 1998—99; pres., CEO Nat. Policy Assn., 1999—2003; diplomat in residence Am. U., 2003—; co-dir. Ctr. N. Am. Studies, Am. U.; cons. internat. policy com. U.S. Conf. Cath. Bishops, 1999—2005; chmn. bd. dirs. Washington Theol. Consortium, 2005—08; bd. dirs. Interfaith Conf. of Washington; project dir. Am. Acad. Diplomacy, 2004—05. Pres. Washington Lions Found., 2008—09, Pub. Diplomacy Coun.; bd. trustees LaRoche Coll., Pitts. English Speaking Union fellow, 1951-52; Marshall scholar, 1955-58; recipient Rivkin award, 1972, Herter award, 1984, Disting. Honor award Dept. State, 1997. Fellow Fgn. Policy Assn.; mem. Coun. on Fgn. Rels., Am. Acad. Diplomacy, Am. Fgn. Svc. Assn., Washington Inst. Fgn. Affairs, Lions Internat., Met. Club, Phi Beta Kappa. Home: 3424 Porter St NW Washington DC 20016-3126 Office Phone: 303-885-1669. Personal E-mail: aquainton@aol.com. Business E-Mail: quainton@american.edu.

QUAKE, STEPHEN R., physics professor, researcher; BS in Physics, Stanford U., 1991, MS in Math., 1991; PhD in Physics, U. Oxford, 1994. Asst. prof. applied physics Calif. Inst. Tech., 1996—99, assoc. prof., 1999—2002, assoc. prof. applied physics and physics, 2002—03, prof., 2003—04, Thomas E. and Doris Everhard prof., 2004; prof. dept. bioengineering Stanford U. Mem. Quake Group, Calif. Inst. Tech., Pasadena, CSULA-Calif. Inst. Tech. Partnerships for Rsch. and Edn. in Materials (PREM) Collaborative, 2004—; co-founder Fluidigm Corp. Contbr. articles to profl. jours. Recipient Career award, 1997, R29 "First" award, NIH, 1997, Pioneer award, 2004; named one of Brilliant 10, Popular Sci. mag., 2003; named to TR100 "Young Innovators that will create the Future", MIT Tech. Rev., 2002; Packard fellow, 1999. Achievements include research in fundamental and applied topics in biophysics, specifically single molecule science. Office: Stanford U Dept Bioengineering James H Clark Ctr Rm E300 318 Campus Dr Stanford CA 94305 Office Phone: 650-736-7890. E-mail: quake@stanford.edu.

QUALE, ANDREW CHRISTOPHER, JR., lawyer; b. Boston, July 7, 1942; s. Andrew Christopher and Luella (Meland) Q.; m. Sally Sterling Ellis, Oct. 15, 1977; children: Andrew, Addison. BA magna cum laude, Harvard U., 1963, LLB cum laude, 1966; postgrad., Cambridge U., Eng., 1966-67. Bar: Mass. 1967, N.Y. 1971. Fellow Internat. Legal Ctr., Bogota, Colombia, 1967-68; cons. Republic of Colombia, Bogota, 1968-69; assoc. Cleary, Gottlieb, Steen and Hamilton, NYC, 1969-75; ptnr. Coudert Brothers, NYC, 1975-82, Sidley Austin, LLP, NYC, 1982—. Adj. prof. Sch. of Law U. Va., Charlottesville, 1976—88; cons. privatizations and internat. financings World Bank, Inter-Am. Devel. Bank, UN, Harvard Inst. Internat. Devel., 1982—; bd. dirs. Battell Art Found., Norfolk. Contbr. articles to profl. jours. Pres. Bronxville (NY) Sch. Bd., 1991-93; founder, bd. dirs. Bronxville Sch. Found., 1991-95, 96-2002; bd. dirs. Coun. of the Ams., Youth Orch. Am., Doolittle Lake Co. Knox fellow, 1966—67. Mem.: ABA, The Little Forum (co-chair Bronxville 2000—03), Colombian-Am. Assn. (v.p., bd. dirs.), NY State Bar Assn., Assn. Bar City NY (chmn. Inter-Am. affairs com. 1982—85), Anglers' Club, Norfolk (Conn.) Country Club, Bronxville Field Club. Office: Sidley Austin LLP 787 7th Ave New York NY 10019

QUALLEY, CHARLES ALBERT, art educator; b. Creston, Iowa, Mar. 19, 1930; s. Albert Olaf and Cleora (Dietrick) Q.; m. Betty Jean Griffith, Nov. 26, 1954; children: Janet Lynn, John Stuart. BFA, Drake U., 1952; MA, U. Iowa, 1956, MFA, 1958; EdD, Ill. State U., 1967. Art tchr. Des Moines Pub. Schs., 1952, 1954—55; critic art tchr. U. Iowa, 1955-57; prof. fine arts U. Colo., Boulder, 1958-90, prof. emeritus, 1990—, chmn. dept. fine arts, 1968-71, assoc. chmn., 1981-82. Vis. prof. Inst. for Shipboard Edn., semester at sea, 1979, vis. disting. prof. Ill. State U., 1985. Author: Safety in the Art Room, 1986, rev. edit., 2005; contbg. editor Sch. Arts, 1978-85, mem. editl. adv. bd., 1985-87; author column Safetypoint, 1981-85. Served with AUS, 1952-54, Korea. Fellow Nat. Art Edn. Assn. (v.p. 1980-82, pres. 1987-89, dir. conv. svcs. 1990-99, Art Educator of Yr. 1993); mem. Nat. Art Edn. Found. (trustee 1987—, chair bd. trustees 1996-2004), Colo. Art Edn. Assn. (editor 1965-67, 75, pres. 1976- 78), Delta Phi Delta, Omicron Delta Kappa, Pi Kappa Delta. Home: 9025 Natalie Ave NE Albuquerque NM 87111-3131

QUALLS, PAULA FONTANA, religious studies educator; b. Rochester, Pa., Aug. 13, 1964; married. PhD, U. Louisville, 1997. Asst. prof. Campbellsville U., Ky., 1997—99; religion prof. Gardner-Webb U., Boiling Springs, NC, 1999—. Tchr. Various Chs., NC, 1999—, guest spkr., 1999—. Recipient Excellence Tchg. award, Gardner-Webb U., 2007—08. Mem.: Soc. Bibl. Lit. Avocations: swimming, travel. Office: Gardner Webb Univ 110 S Main St Boiling Springs NC 28017 Business E-Mail: pqualls@gardner-webb.edu.

QUALLS, ROBERT L., manufacturing and bank executive, educator, retired state official; b. Burnsville, Miss., Nov. 6, 1933; s. Wes E. and Letha (Parker) Q.; m. Carolyn Morgan, Feb. 10, 1979 (dec. July 1996); 1 child, Stephanie Elizabeth; m. Nancy Martin, Sept. 11, 1999. BS, Miss. State U., 1954, MS, 1958; PhD, La. State U., 1962; LLD, Whitworth Coll., 1974; DBA (hon.), U. of the Ozarks, 1984. Prof., chmn. div. econs. and bus. Belhaven Coll., Jackson, Miss., 1962-66, asst. to pres., 1965-66; asst. prof. finance Miss. State U., State College, 1967-69, adj. prof., 1969-73; sr. v.p., chmn. venture com. Bancorp South, Tupelo, Miss., 1969-73; v.p. Wesleyan Coll., Macon, Ga., 1974; pres. U. of the Ozarks, Clarksville, Ark., 1974-79; mem. cabinet Bill Clinton Gov. of Ark., 1979-80; exec. v.p. Bank of America, Little Rock, 1980-85, chmn., CEO, dir. Harrison, Ark., 1985-86; pres., dir. First Bank Fin. Services, Inc., 1980-85, Advt. Assocs., Inc., 1980-85; pres., chief oper. officer Baldor Electric Co., Ft. Smith, Ark., 1986-91, CEO, 1992-97, vice chmn., 1998—2000, dir., mem. exec. com., 1987—, compensation com., presiding non-mgmt. dir., 2004—. Vice chmn. Taylor Co., 2007-; mktg. cons. Ill. Central Industries, Chgo., 1964; mem. faculty, thesis examiner Stonier Grad. Sch. Banking, Rutgers U., 1973-86; mem. faculty Miss. Sch. Banking, U. Miss., 1973-78; course coord. Sch. Banking of the South, La. State U., 1978-88, Banking Sch., Duke U., 1977; lectr. Southwestern Sch. Banking, So. Meth. U., 1983; adj. prof. bus. adminstrn. U. Central Ark., 1985-86; bd. dirs. Bank of Ozarks, 1997—, mem. audit com., chmn. corp. governance com., personal com., 2008-, presiding ind. dir., 2003—. Author: Entrepreneurial Wit and Wisdom, 1986; co-author: Strategic Planning for Colleges and Universities: A Systems Approach to Planning and Resource Allocation, 1979; mem. editorial adv. bd.: Bank Mktg. Mag., 1984-86. Chmn. cmty. svc. and continuing edn. com. Tupelo Cmty. Devel. Found., 1972-73; mem. Miss. 4-H adv. coun., 1969; active Boys Scouts Am.; mem. Lee County Dem. Exec. Com., 1973-74; trustee Walton Family Found., 1975-79, Oklahoma City U., 1990-95; trustee, mem. exec. com. U. Ozarks, 1982-88, chmn. bd., 2000-03; mem. Pres.'s Roundtable U. Ctrl. Ark., 1982-87; mem. exec. com. Coll. Bus. Adv. Bd., U. Ark., Little Rock, 1980-85; bd. dirs. U. Ark. Med. Sch. Found., 1991-97, Ark. Inst., 1991-94; chmn. bd. Petit Jean Youth Found., 2001-03; mem. Clarksville Light and Water Commn., 2000-01; elder Clarksville Presbyn. Ch., 1997-2000; bd. dirs. Vera Lloyd Presbyn. Home and Family Svcs., 2004-05, Thea Found., 2008-, Lt. AUS, 1954-56. Found. for Econ. Edn. fellow, 1964; Ford Found. faculty research fellow Vanderbilt U., 1963-64; recipient Pillar of Progress award Johnson County, 1977 Mem. Am. Bankers Assn. (mktg. planning and rsch. com. 1972-73), Ark. Coun. Ind. Colls. and Univs. (chmn. 1978-79), Johnson County C. of C. (pres. 1977), Fort Smith C. of C. (dir. 1995-98), Blue Key, Omicron Delta Kappa, Delta Sigma Pi, Sigma Phi Epsilon (citation 1977), Beta Gamma Sigma, Masons (32 deg.), Clarksville Rotary (pres. 1979). Presbyterian. Home Phone: 501-661-9095. Personal E-mail: nancy_qualls@msn.com.

QUALLS, ROXANNE, mayor; D (hon.), Cin. State Tech. and C.C., 1996. Former exec. dir. Women Helping Women; former dir. No. Ky. Rape Crisis Ctr.; former dir. Cin. office Ohio Citizen Action; councilwoman City of Cin., 1991-93, mayor, 1993-98, founder youth summer jobs program Artworks, Cin. Homeownership Partnership. Former chairperson Cin. City Council's Intergovtl. Affairs and Environment Com.; former vice chairperson Community Devel., Housing and Zoning Com.; mem. Gov.'s Commn. on Storage and Use of Toxic and Hazardous Materials, Solid Waste Adv. Com. of State of Ohio, Gov.'s Waste Minimization Task Force; former chair bd. commrs. Cin. Met. Housing Authority; bd. dirs. Shuttlesworth Housing Found. Hon. chair Friends of Women's Studies; mem. Jr. League Adv. Coun.; bd. dirs. Nat. Underground Railroad Freedom Ctr., Ctr. Voting and Democracy; past bd. didrs. No. Ky. Cath. Commn. Soc. Jusitice. Recipient Woman of Distinction award Girl Scouts U.S., 1992, Woman of Distinction award Soroptomists, 1993, Outstanding Achievement award Cin. Woman's Polit. Caucus, 1993, Women of Achievement award YWCA, 1994, Outstanding Svc. award Ohio Pub. Employees Lawyers Assn., 1996, Pub. Offcl. of Yr. award State of Cinn., 1996, Nat. Assn. Soc. Workers, 1996, Nat. Homebuilders Assn., 1997. Mem. Nat. Assn. Regional Couns. (former pres., 1st v.p., 2d v.p.), Ohio Ky. Ind. Regional Coun. Govts. (1st v.p., 2d v.p.). Fax: 513-352-5201.

QUALSET, CALVIN O., agronomist, educator; b. Newman Grove, Nebr., Apr. 24, 1937; s. Herman Qualset and Adeline (Hanson) Vakoc; m. Kathleen Boehler; children: Douglas, Cheryl, Gary. BS, U. Nebr., 1958; MS, U. Calif., Davis, 1960, PhD, 1964. Asst. prof. U. Tenn., Knoxville, 1964-67; from asst. prof. to assoc. prof. U. Calif., Davis, 1967, prof., 1973-94, prof. emeritus, 1994—, chmn. dept. agronomy and range sci., 1975-81, 91-94, assoc. dean Coll. Agrl. and Environ. Sci., 1981-86, dir. Genetic Resources Conservation Program, 1985—2002, dir., found. seed and plant materials svc., 1991—93, dir. Agrl. Sustainability Inst., 2005—06. Sci. liaison officer U.S. AID, Washington, 1985-93, rsch. adv. com., 1989-92; nat. plant genetic resources bd. USDA, Washington, 1982-88; trustee Am. Type Culture Collection, 1993-99, Internat. Rice Rsch. Inst., 1999-2004, Agronomic Sci. Found., 1999—2008, chmn., 2006—08. Contbr. over 300 articles to profl. jours. and tech. publs. Bd. dirs. Calif. Crop Improvement Assn., 1975—85, Auksuciai Found., 1999—; chair, exec. bd. generation challenge program cons. Group Internat. Agrl. Rsch., 2008—; contbr. to wheat improvement in Mex. citation, 1988. Fulbright fellow, Australia, 1976, Yugoslavia, 1984; recipient Pub. Plant Breeding award U.S. Coun. Comml. Plant Breeders, 1996, Master Alumni award U. Nebr., 1997, Charles Black award Coun. Agrl. Sci. and Tech., 2002, William L. Brown award Mo. Bot. Garden, 2002, Citation for Excellence, U. Calif., Calif. Aggie Alumni Assn., 2003, Citation for contbns. to Calif. agr. State Calif. Senate, 2003, award of excellence Coll. Agrl. and Environ. Sci., U. Calif., Davis, 2003, Citation for contbns. to agr. in Lithuania, 2004, 06. Fellow AAAS (chmn. agr. sect. 1992), Am. Soc. Agronomy (pres. 1994, agronomy honoree Calif. sect. 2001), Crop Sci. Soc. Am. (pres. 1989, editor-in-chief 1980-84, Frank N. Meyer medal for plant genetic resources 2006); mem. Soc. Conservation Biology, Soc. Econ. Botany, Genetic Soc. Am., Internat. Union Biol. Scis. (mem. U.S. nat. com. 2000-06), Am. Genetic Assn., U. Nebr. Alumni Assn. Achievements include development of more than 18 cultivars of wheat, oat, triticale. Office: Dept Plant Sci U Calif One Shields Ave Davis CA 95616 Office Phone: 530-754-8502.

QUAM, LOIS, investment company executive, former health insurance company executive; b. June 12, 1961; m. Matt Entenza; children: Ben, Steve. BA magna cum laude, Macalaster Coll., Minn.; MA in Philos., Politics, Econs., U. Oxford, 1985. Dir. rsch. and eval. UnitedHealth Group, 1989-93, v.p. pub. sector svcs., 1993, CEO AARP/United divsn. Mpls., 1996-98, exec. v.p., CEO Ovations, 2002—06, exec. v.p., pres. public & sr. markets group, 2006—07; mng. dir. alternative investments Piper Jaffray & Co., Mpls., 2007—. Bd. dirs. General Mills, 2007—, George C. Marshall Found., Coun. Fgn. Rels.; adv. com. Am. Democracy Inst.; sr. adv. The White House Task Force Nat. Health Care Reform, 1993—96. Mem. editl. bd.: British Med. Jour.; contbr. articles to profl. jours. Bd. trustees Macalester Coll. Recipient America-Norway Heritage Fund award, Nordmann-Forbundett Norway-Am. Assn.; named one of Next 20 Female CEOs, Pink Mag. & Forté Found., 2006, 50 Most Powerful Women in Bus., Fortune mag., 2006. Office: Piper Jaffray & Co 800 Nicollet Mall Ste 800 Minneapolis MN 55402

QUANDAHL, MARK C., lawyer, former political organization administrator; b. Omaha, Oct. 10, 1961; m. Stacey Quandahl, May 24, 1986; children: Sarah, Scott, R.J. Grad., U. Nebr., 1984, JD, 1987. Cert. Consumer Credit Exec.; bar: US Dist. Ct. Nebr. 1987, US Dist. Ct. Iowa 1988. Prin. Brumbaugh & Quandahl PC, Omaha, 1990—; mem. Nebr. State Legislature from 31st dist., Lincoln, 1999—2005; chmn. Nebr. Republican Party, 2005—09. Del. Rep. Nat. Conv., 2004. Mem.: Phi Delta Phi, Comml. Law League Nebr., Nat. Assn. Retail Collection Attorneys, Iowa State Bar Assn., Nebr. State Bar Assn. Republican. Office: Brumbaugh & Quandahl PC 4485 S 118th St Ste 100 Omaha NE 68137 Office Phone: 402-861-4702, 402-554-4400. E-mail: mquandahl@bqlaw.com.*

QUANDT, RICHARD EMERIC, economics professor; b. Budapest, Hungary, June 1, 1930; arrived in US, 1949, naturalized, 1954; s. Richard F. and Elisabeth Quandt; m. Jean H. Briggs, Aug. 6, 1955; 1 child, Stephen. BA, Princeton U., NJ, 1952; MA, Harvard U., 1955, PhD, 1957; Dr. Econs. (hon.), Budapest U. Econs. Scis., 1991, Kossuth Lajos U., Hungary, 1994, Gödöllö Agrl. U., 1995, Comenius U., Slovakia, 1996; DrLaws (hon.), Queens U., Can., 1996. Mem. faculty Princeton U., 1956-95, prof. econs., 1964-95, prof. emeritus, sr. rsch. economist, 1995—, Hughes-Rogers prof. econs., 1976-95, chmn. dept., 1968-71, 85-88; dir. Fin. Rsch. Ctr., 1982-95; rsch. prof. Ford Found., 1967-68. Cons. Anderson Assocs., 1959—61, Internat. Air Transport Assn., 1974—75, NY Stock Exch., 1976—77, NY State Dept. Edn., 1978; sr. cons. Mathematica, Inc., 1961—67; editl. adviser Holt, Rinehart & Winston, 1968—72; adviser Am-Hungarian Found., 1977—78; vis. prof. Birkbeck Coll., 1981, U. Leicester, 1989—92; mem. Census Adv. Com., 1983—86; fin. adviser Inst. Rsch. History, 1986; sr. advisor Andrew W. Mellon Found., 1989—2008; mem. adv. coun. Budapest U. Econ. Scis., 1992—93; mem. adv. com. Coll. Fin. and Acctg., Budapest, 1993—94; bd. dirs. Ctr. Econ. Rsch. and Grad. Edn.-Econ. Inst., Prague, 2002—05. Author (with J. M. Henderson): Microeconomic Theory: A Mathematical Approach, 1958, 3d edit., 1980; author: (with W. L. Thorp) The New Inflation, 1959; author: (with B. G. Malkiel) Strategies and Rational Decisions in the Securities Option Market, 1969; editor: The Demand for Travel: Theory and Measurement, 1970; author: The Econometrics of Disequilibrium, 1988, The Changing Landscape in Eastern Europe: A Personal Perspective on Philanthropy and Technology Transfer, 2002; author: (with P. Asch) Ractrack Betting: The Professor's Guide to Strategies, 1986; author: (with H. S. Rosen) The Conflict Between Equilibrium and Disequilibrium Theories, 1988; editor (with S.H. Goldfeld): Studies in Nonlinear Estimation, 1976; editor: (with S. M. Goldfeld) Nonlinear Methods in Econometrics, 1972; editor: (with M. Peston) Prices, Competition and Equilibrium, 1986; editor: (with R. Ekman) Technology and Scholarly Communication, 1999; editor: (with A. Lass) Library Automation in Transitional Societies, 2000, Union Catalogs at the Crossroads, 2004; assoc. editor: Econometrica, 1976—80, Jour. Am. Statis. Assn., 1974—80, Bell Jour. Econs., Jour. Comparative Econs., 1988—91, Empirica, 1988—93; mem. editl. bd. Applied Econs., Econ. Planning, Rev. Econ. and Stats., 1980—91; exec. editor: Oxford U. Press, 2001—; translator: If Dogs Could Talk (V. Csányi), 2005; contbr. articles to profl. jours. Trustee Corvina Found., 1992—2008. Recipient Merit citation, Jagiellonian U., Poland, 1991, medal Merentibus, 1998, Gold medal, Eötvös Lóránd U., 1991, Order of Merit, Govt. of Hungary, 1997, Karel Englis medal, Czech Acad. Sci., 2002; Guggenheim fellow, 1958—59, McCosh fellow, 1964, NSF Sr. Postdoctoral fellow, 1971—72. Fellow: Am. Acad. Arts and Scis., Econometric Soc. (mem. coun. 1985—88), Am. Statis. Assn.; mem.: Am. Philos. Soc., Am. Econ. Assn., Hungarian Librs. Assn. (hon.). Home: 162 Springdale Rd Princeton NJ 08540-4948 Office: Princeton U Dept Econs Princeton NJ 08544-1021

QUANN, JOAN LOUISE, French language educator, real estate broker; b. Phila., Oct. 14, 1935; d. John Joseph and Pauline Cecelia (Karpink) Q. Diploma, U. Paris, 1963; BA in French, U. Pa., 1976; grad., Temple U. Real Estate Inst., 1988; MEd, Temple U, 1994. Lic. real estate broker. Exec. sec. to chief fgn. corr. Newsweek, Inc., Paris, 1964—70, internat. editl. asst. NYC, 1971—73; exec. sec., adminstrv. asst. Richard I. Rubin & Co., Inc., Phila., 1977—91; tchr. French and English to spkrs. of other langs. The Sch. Dist. of Phila., Bd. Edn., 1991—2007. Judge of elections City of Phila., 1977-81. Mem. AAUW (2d v.p. membership 1985-87, bd. dirs., corr. sec. 1987-91, fin. com. 1993, nominating com., 2008), Alliance Francaise, La Societe Francophone Arts et Loisirs (bd. dirs. 1988—), Am. Coun. on Tchg. of Fgn. Langs., Pa. Acad. Fine Arts (docent 2006—), MLA of Phila. and Vicinity, Phila. Mus. Art (Asian adv. group 2000). Republican. Roman Catholic. Avocations: art history, reading, swimming, travel. Office: Pa Acad Fine Arts 118 N Broad St Philadelphia PA 19102 Office Phone: 215-972-7600.

QUANT, HAROLD EDWARD, retired financial services company executive, rancher; b. Aug. 21, 1948; s. Harold Atwell and Dorothy Ann Quant; m. Michelle Bumpers, June 27, 1982; children: Andrew, Angela, Emily. BSBA, San Jose State U., 1976. Account exec. Dun & Bradstreet, San Jose, Calif., 1970-81; pres. Telecredit Collection Svcs., Inc., LA, 1981-85; v.p. FCA, Arlington, Tex., 1986-90; pres., CEO Creditwatch, Inc., Arlington, 1990-2000, chmn. bd. dirs.; ret., 2000. Sgt. USMC, 1965—70, Vietnam. Mem.: City Club. Republican. Mem. United Ch. Of God. Avocation: horses.

QUARANTA, MICHAEL J., legislative staff member; Legis. asst. for Senator David Durenberger, US Senate, Washington; profl. staff mem. US Senate Govtl. Affairs Com.; with TRW; v.p. fed. and state rels. Experian; chief of staff for Rep. Michael Castle, US House of Reps., 2003—. Office: Office of Congressman Mike Castle 1233 Longworth House Office Bldg Washington DC 20515 Office Phone: 202-225-4165. Office Fax: 202-225-2291.*

QUARLES, CARROLL ADAIR, JR., physicist, researcher; b. Abilene, Tex., Nov. 24, 1938; s. Carroll Adair and Marguerite Marie (Vollmers) Q.; m. Sonja Gale Bandy, May 14, 1971; children: Jennifer Anne, John Patrick. BA, Tex. Christian U., 1960; PhD, Princeton U., 1964. Rsch. physicist Brookhaven Nat. Lab., Upton, NY, 1964-67; mem. faculty Tex. Christian U., Ft.Worth, 1967—, assoc. prof. physics Ft. Worth, 1970-76, prof. Ft.Worth, 1976—, W.A. Moncrief Jr. prof. physics, 1986—, chmn. dept. physics Ft. Worth, 1978-84, 96-99, assoc. dean Coll. Arts and Scis. Ft.Worth, 1974-78. Contbr. articles to profl. jours. Mem. AAAS, Am. Phys. Soc. (sec.-treas. Tex. sect. 1993-99, chair Tex. sect. 2003, mem. exec. com. Forum on Physics and Soc., 1999-2002), Am. Assn. Physics Tchrs. (pres. Tex. sect. 1984), Sigma Xi, Phi Beta Kappa (pres. Delta of Tex. chpt. 1982-84). Roman Catholic. Office: Tex Christian U Dept Physics Fort Worth TX 76129-0001 Home Phone: 817-926-7584. Business E-Mail: c.quarles@tcu.edu.

QUARLES, CHARLES LELAND, religious studies educator, researcher; s. Chester Leland and Dorothy Quarles; m. Julie Caryl Chesser; children: Rachael Erin, Hannah Ellen, Joshua David. PhD, Mid-America Bapt. Theol. Sem., 1994. Cert. in ordination. Rsch. prof. La. Coll., Pineville, 2005—, v.p.; assoc. prof. New Orleans Bapt. Theol. Sem. Contbr. scientific papers. Avocations: running, woodcarving. Office: La Coll LC Box 612 Pineville LA 71359 Office Fax: 318-487-7241. Business E-Mail: quarles@lacollege.edu.

QUARLES, JAMES LINWOOD, III, lawyer; b. Huntington, W.Va., Oct. 12, 1946; s. James Linwood Jr. and Beatrice (Hardwick) Q.; m. Sharon Taft, Dec. 20, 1969; children: Jessica, Matthew. BS cum laude, Denison U., 1968; JD cum laude, Harvard U., 1972. Bar: Mass. 1974, U.S. Dist. Ct. Mass. 1975, U.S. Ct. Appeals (D.C. cir.) 1975, U.S. Ct. Appeals (6th cir.) 1979, U.S. Supreme Ct. 1980, D.C. 1981, U.S. Ct. Appeals (2d cir.) 1981, U.S. Ct. Appeals (1st and 4th cirs.) 1983, Md. 1985, Va. 2000. Law clk. Judge Frank A. Kaufman, U.S. Dist. Ct. Md., Balt., 1972-73; asst. spl. prosecutor Watergate Spl. Pros. Force, Washington, 1973-75; from assoc. to sr. ptnr. Wilmer Cutler Pickering Hale & Dorr, Washington, 1975—, co-chmn. Appellate & Supreme Ct. Litigation group, mem. exec. com. Mem. Am. Law Inst., ABA, DC Bar Assn., Mass. Bar Assn., Boston Bar Assn., Phi Beta Kappa. Democrat. Home Phone: 301-229-9449; Office Phone: 202-663-6236. Business E-Mail: james.quarles@wilmerhale.com.

QUARLES, MARY JO, school librarian, educator; b. Many, La., Apr. 22, 1949; d. Basile Arthur Bell and Lucille Meredith; 1 child, Scott Wade Jackson. BA, Northwestern State U., Natchitoches, La., 1987, MEd, 1998. Cert. in secretarial sci. Sabine Valley Voc. Tech., 1972, in libr. sci. Northwestern State U., 1998. Libr. tchr. Many Elem. Sch., 2000—. Home: 110 Ann St Many LA 71449

QUARLES, RANDAL KEITH, private equity firm executive, former federal agency administrator; b. San Francisco, Sept. 5, 1957; s. Ralph Ray and Beverly Kay (Hulse) Q.; m. C. Hope Eccles, Sept. 13, 1997; children: Randal, Spencer, Hope. AB, Columbia U., 1981; JD, Yale U., 1984. Assoc. Davis Polk & Wardwell, NYC, 1984-91, ptnr., 1993—2001; spl. asst. to sec. US Dept. Treasury, Washington, 1991-92, deputy asst. sec., fin. insts. policy, 1992-93, asst. sec. internat. affairs, 2002—05, under sec. for domestic fin., 2005—06; mng. dir. The Carlyle Group, Washington, 2006—. U.S. exec. dir. IMF, 2001—02, European Bank Reconstrn. and Devel., 2002; mem. bd. dirs. Overseas Pvt. Investment Corp., 2004—05. Mem. fin. adv. com. Dole Presdl. Campaign, Washington, 1996. Mem. Yale Club, Salt Lake Country Club. Republican. Mem. Lds Ch. Avocations: aviation, skiing. Office: The Carlyle Group 1001 Pennsylvania Ave Washington DC 20004 Office Phone: 202-729-5626. Office Fax: 202-347-1818.*

QUARLES, STEVEN PRINCETON, lawyer; b. Kansas City, Mo., May 9, 1942; s. Samuel Princeton and Marianna (Platt) Q.; m. Suzanne Margaret-Mary Cleary, June 2, 1970. AB, Princeton U., 1964; JD, Yale U., 1968. Bar: NY 1980, DC 1981. Counsel Senate Com. Energy and Natural Resources, Washington, 1971-78; dir. office coal leasing U.S. Dept. Interior, Washington, 1978-79, dep. under sec. interior, 1979-81; ptnr. Nossaman, Guthner, Knox & Elliott, Washington, 1981-83, Crowell & Moring, Washington, 1983—. Mem. energy and mineral resources bd. Nat. Acad. Scis., 1985-88, abandoned mine lands com., 1985-86, oil and gas leasing com., 1988-89; mem. Bi-National Softwood Lumber Coun., 2007-; trustee Md. Environ. Trust, 2008-, Henry M. Jackson Found., 2008-, Am. Forest Found., 2009-, Catoctin Land Trust, 2009-. Chmn. Sugarloaf Citizens Assn., Dickerson, Md., 1977-81, Md. Hazardous Waste Facilities Siting Bd., Annapolis, 1985-87; mem. Md. Sewage Sludge Mgmt. Commn., Annapolis, 1984; chmn. Montgomery County Solid Waste Adv. Com., Rockville, Md., 1980-85; pres. Frederick County Civic Fedn., 1989-94. Fulbright scholar India, 1964-65. Mem. ABA (enviroment, energy and resources sect.), N.Y. State Bar Assn., D.C. Bar Assn., Fed. Wind Tunbine Guidelines (adv. com. mem. 2008-), Nat. Agrl. Rsch. Ext., Edn. and Economics (adv. bd. mem. 2008-). Independent. Episcopalian. Avocation: horse breeding. Home: Some Day Soon Farm 13549 Glissans Mill Rd Mount Airy MD 21771-8509 Office Phone: 202-624-2665. Business E-Mail: squarles@crowell.com.

QUARTARARO, PHILIP, JR., mathematics professor; s. Philip Quartararo and Laura Nicoll, Joseph Nicoll (Stepfather), Angeline S. Quartararo (Stepmother); m. Dorothy Marie Morvant; children: Philip III, Sharon Campbell, Deborah Michael, Beth Davis. B in Math., La. State U., New Orleans, 1964; M in Math., La. State U., Baton Rouge, 1966, PhD in Math., 1972. Instr, asst. prof., assoc. prof. So. U., Baton Rouge, 1967—76, prof. math., 1976—2002, asst. to vice chancellor acad. affairs, 1989—91; ret., 2002. Developer ednl. material. Co-author: (textbooks) College Algebra: The UNCPAL Approach, Elementary Applied Mathematics; contbr. rsch. pubs. in Commutative Ring Theory. Bd. dirs. Lamar YMCA, 1971—85, bd. chair, 1974—79. Recipient grants in field. Mem.: La. Goat Coop. (helped establish on bd. dirs., treas. 2007—09), Com. Math. Edn. Tchrs., Math. Edn. Reform, Nat. Coun. Tchrs. Math., Am. Math. Soc., Math. Assn. Am. (chmn. LA-MS sect. 1995—96, mem., Com. Math. Edn. Tchrs. & Com. Sects.), Kiwanis Internat. (life; bd. dirs., lt. gov., pres., cert. leadership trainer, dist. chmn. Hugh O'Brian Youth Leadership com.), Phi Delta Kappa. Presbyterian. Achievements include research in commutative ring theory; developing educational material. Avocations: swimming, home repair projects, small goat farm, golf, church choir singing. Office: So U PO Box 9261 Baton Rouge LA 70813 Personal E-mail: pquartjr@yahoo.com.

QUATE, CALVIN FORREST, engineering educator; b. Baker, Nev., Dec. 7, 1923; s. Graham Shepard and Margie (Lake) Quate; m. Dorothy Marshall, June 28, 1945 (div. 1985); children: Robin, Claudia, Holly, Rhodalee; m. Arnice Streit, Jan. 1987; children: Christine, Carol, Richard. BS in Elec. Engring, U. Utah, 1944; PhD, Stanford U., 1950. Mem. tech. staff Bell Telephone Labs., Murray Hill, NJ, 1949-58; mem. Def. Sci. Bd., 1958—60; dir. research Sandia Corp., Albuquerque, 1959—60, v.p. research, 1960-61; prof. dept. applied physics and elec. engring. Stanford U., Calif., 1961-95, chmn. applied physics Calif., 1969-72, 78-81, Leland T. Edwards prof. sch. engring. Calif., 1986—, assoc. dean Sch. Humanities and Scis. Calif., 1972-74, 82-83, rsch. prof. dept. elec. engring. Calif., 1995—. Sr. rsch. fellow Xerox Rsch. Ctr., Palo Alto, Calif., 1984—94. Contbr. several articles to profl. jours. Served as lt. (j.g.) USNR, 1944—46. Recipient Pres.'s Nat. medal of Sci., 1992; named Scientist of Yr., R&D Mag., 1995; Guggenheim Fellow and Fulbright Scholar, Faculty Sci., Montpellier, France, 1968—69. Fellow: World Tech. Network (co-recipient, World Tech. award for IT Hardware 2006), Am. Phys. Soc. (Joseph F. Keithley award for Advances in Measurement Sci. 2000), Am. Acad. Arts and Scis., Acoustical Soc. Am., IEEE (Morris N. Liebmann award 1981, IEEE medal of honor 1988, Third Millennium award 2000, Ultrasonics Rayleigh award 2002), Royal Microscop. Soc. (hon.); mem.: Royal Soc. London (fgn.) (Rank prize for Opto-electronics 1982), NAS, NAE, Tau Beta Pi, Sigma Xi. Achievements include being one of the inventors of the the scanning acoustic microscope. Avocations: skiing, hiking, jogging, kayaking, sailboarding. Office: Stanford U Ginzton Laboratory Room 12 Palo Alto CA 94305-4085 Office Phone: 650-723-0213. Business E-Mail: quate@stanford.edu.

QUATRANO, ANNE, chef, restaurant owner; Grad., Calif. Culinary Acad., San Francisco. Chef, co-owner Bacchanalia, Atlanta, Floataway Cafe, Atlanta, Star Provisions, Atlanta, Quinones; chef Grolier Club, NY, Bimini Twist, La Petit Ferme. Elected mem. James Beard Found. Named one of America's Best New Chef, Food & Wine mag., 1995. Office: 1198 Howell Mill Rd Atlanta GA 30301

QUATTRONE, FRANK P., investment company executive; b. Phila., 1955; BA in Econs. with honors, U. Pa. Wharton Sch. Bus., 1977; MBA, Stanford U., Calif., 1981. Investment banker Morgan Stanley, Deutsche Bank, Credit Suisse First Boston; co-founder, CEO Qatalyst Group, San Francisco, 2008—. Fundraiser The Innocent Project, 2004—.

QUAY, THOMAS EMERY, lawyer; b. Cleve., Apr. 3, 1934; s. Harold Emery and Esther Ann (Thomas) Q.; divorced; children: Martha Wyndham, Glynis Cobb, Eliza Emery; m. Winnifred B. Cutler, May 13, 1989. AB in Humanities magna cum laude (Univ. scholar), Princeton U., 1956; LLB (Univ. scholar), U. Pa., 1963. Bar: Pa. 1964. Assoc. Pepper, Hamilton & Scheetz, Phila., 1963-65; with William H. Rorer, Inc., Ft. Washington, Pa., 1965—, sec., counsel, 1974-79, v.p., gen. counsel, sec., 1979-88; v.p. legal planning and adminstrn. Rorer Group, 1988-90; counsel Reed Smith Shaw and McClay, Phila., 1991-93; v.p., gen. counsel Athena Inst., Chester Springs, Pa., 1993—. Bd. dirs. Main Line YMCA, Ardmore, Pa., 1971-73, chmn. bd., 1972-73; editor 10th Reunion Book Princeton Class of 1956, 1966, 25th Reunion Book, 1981—, class sec., 1966-71, class v.p., 1971-81, pres., 1981-86. Lt. (j.g.) USNR, 1957-60. Recipient Commendation award, Main Line YMCA, 1984. Mem. ABA, Pa. Bar Assn., Phila. Bar Assn., Pharm. Mfrs. Assn. (chmn. law sect. 1983), Pa. Biotech. Assn. (chmn. legis. com., mem. exec. com. 1991-93), Phila. Drug Exch. (chmn. legis. com. 1975-78), Cannon Club of Princeton U., Sharswood Law Club of U. Pa., Princeton Club of Phila. Democrat. Presbyterian.

QUAYE, SYLVIA SISSUH, lawyer; b. Accra, Ghana, Nov. 19, 1971; arrived in US, 2000, permanent resident; d. Emmanuel and Comfort Otoo Sissuh; m. Joseph Otu Quaye, June 16, 2001; children: Nediva, Attoley, Joelle Akweley. LLB, U. Ghana, Accra, 1997; JD, Ghana Sch. Law, Accra, 1999; MA in Pub. Adminstrn., U. Louisville, 2003. Bar: Ghana 1999, Ky. 2006. Grad. rsch. asst. U. Louisville, 2001—03; employment specialist Ctr. Women & Families, Louisville, 2003—05, family advocate, 2005—06; mng. atty. Gibson & Sharps, PSC, 2006—. Co-author: (book) Ghanaian Constitution, abridged edit., 2000. Facilitator, lectr. YWCA, Accra, 1999—2000. Mem.: ABA, Ghana Bar Assn., Ky. Bar Assn. Avocations: reading, writing. Office Phone: 502-454-8977. Business E-Mail: sylvia.quaye@gibson-sharpslaw.com.

QUAYLE, DAN (JAMES DANFORTH QUAYLE), former Vice President of the United States; b. Indpls., Feb. 4, 1947; s. James C. and Corinne (Pulliam) Q.; m. Marilyn Tucker, Nov. 18, 1972; children: Tucker Danforth, Benjamin Eugene, Mary Corinne Berger. BS in Polit. Sci., DePauw U., Greencastle, Ind., 1969; JD, Ind. U., 1974. Bar: Ind. 1974. Ct. reporter, pressman Huntington (Ind.) Herald-Press, 1965-69, assoc. pub., gen. mgr., 1974-76; with consumer protection divsn. Office Atty. Gen., State of Ind., 1970-71; adminstrv. asst. to Gov. State of Ind., 1971-73; dir. Ind. Inheritance Tax Div., 1973-74; tchr. bus. law Huntington Coll., 1975; mem. US Congress from 4th Ind. dist., Washington, 1977—81; US Senator from Ind. Washington, 1981-89; v.p. US, Washington, 1989-93; founder BTC, 1994; chmn. global investments Cerberus Capital Mgmt., LP, 2000—; pres. Quayle & Associates, Phoenix. Disting. vis. prof. Am. Grad. Sch. Internat. Mgmt., 1997-99; bd. mem. IAP Worldwide Svcs., Inc., K2, Inc., Aozora Bank Ltd., 2000—; cons. in field. Author: Standing Firm: A Vice-Presidential Memoir, 1994, Worth Fighting For, 1999; co-author (with Diane Medved) The American Family: Discovering the Values that Make Us Strong, 1996 Chmn. Campaign Am., 1995-99; hon. trustee emeriti Hudson Inst. With Ind. Army N.G., 1970-76. Republican. Office: Cerberus Investments 7001 N Scottsdale Rd Ste 2010 Scottsdale AZ 85253-3644

QUAYLE, MARILYN TUCKER, wife of former United States Vice President, lawyer; b. 1949; d. Warren S. and Mary Alice (Craig) Tucker; m. J. Danforth Quayle, Nov. 18, 1972; children: Tucker Danforth, Benjamin Eugene, Mary Corinne. BA in Polit. Sci., Purdue U., 1971; JD, Ind. U., 1974. Pvt. practice atty., Huntington, Ind., 1974—77; ptnr. Krieg, DeVault, Alexander & Capehart, Indpls., 1993—2001; pres. BTC Inc., Phoenix, 2001—. Author (with Nancy T. Northcott): Embrace the Serpent, 1992; author: The Campaign, 1996. Nat. adv. bd. The Salvation Army. Office: Quayle and Associates Ste 2010 7001 N Scottsdale Rd Scottsdale AZ 85253-3644

QUAZI, MOUMIN MANZOOR, literature educator, consultant; b. San Francisco, Sept. 16, 1962; s. Manzoor Quazi and Bettsy Ferrell; m. Elise Smyrl, Dec. 25, 2007; 1 child, Madeline Lopez. BFA, Tex. Christian U., Fort Worth, 1980—84; MA in Bibl. Studies, Dallas Theol. Sem., TX, 1984—90; MA in English, U. North Tex., Denton, 1989—95; PhD in English, U. North Tex., 1995—99. Tchg. fellow English U. North Tex., 1990—99; adj. prof. English Tarrant County Coll., Fort Worth, 1998—99; assoc. prof. English Wayland Bapt. U., Plainview, Tex., 2004—05; vis. prof. Lamar U., Beaumont, Tex., 2005—06; asst. prof. English U. Incarnate Word, San Antonio, 1999—2004, Tarleton State U., Stephenville, Tex., 2006—; Coord. Profl. English Educator Program TSU, Stephenville, 2008—. Contbr. columns in newspapers;, author short stories; contbr. poem, articles to profl. jours. Active Hale County Literacy Coun., Plainview, 2004—05; bd. mem. Young Pegasus Soc., San Antonio, 1999—2004. Recipient Contbn. to the Profession award, Wayland Bapt. U., 2004—05. Mem.: Conf. Coll. Tchrs. English (editor

2003—08), MLA, South Asian Lit. Assn. (editor 2004—08), Phi Kappa Phi, Alpha Epsilon Rho, Sigma Tau Delta (advisor 1999—2004). Avocations: travel, saxophone. Home: 1015 W Sloan St Stephenville TX 76401 Office: Tarleton State Univ Box T-0300 Stephenville TX 76402 Office Fax: 254-968-1931. Personal E-mail: mouminquazi@hotmail.com. Business E-Mail: quazi@tarleton.edu.

QUEEN, JAMES E., automotive executive; b. Zanesville, Ohio, Feb. 4, 1949; B in Aero. and Aerospace Engring., U.S. Naval Acad., 1971. Mgr. customer satisfaction and engring. Buick, 1985—86; sr. staff engr. Buick Car Group Powertrain Divsn., Detroit, 1986—88; asst. chief engr. GM, 1988—91, Bucik-Oldsmobile-Cadillac Lansing Automotive Divsn., 1991—95; engring. dir. N. Am. GM Tech. Ctr., Warren, Mich., 1995—97; group dir. engring. GM Small Car Group, 1997—99; v.p./group dir. engring. GM N. Am., 1999—2001; v.p. N.Am. engring. GM, 2001—05, v.p. global engring., 2005—07, group v.p. global engring., 2007—. Served USMC, 1971—77.*

QUEEN, KAY WALLACE, education educator; b. Chgo., Aug. 28, 1937; d. Frederick Lawrence and Kathryn Louise (Tabb) W.; m. Donald Reed Meyer, Jan. 23, 1960 (div. June 1975); children: Cynthia L., Daniel B., Diane Y., Patrick S.; m. Michael Lamar Queen, Dec. 20, 1983; 1 child, Tyler Glen Sherwood. BA, North Tex. State U., 1976; MA, East Tex. State U., 1984; PhD, Tex. A&M U., 1993. Cert. tchr., Tex. Tchr. Richardson (Tex.) Ind. Sch. Dist., 1976-77, 79-81; dir. Physics Instrnl. Ctr. North Tex. State U., Denton, 1977-78; tchr. McKinney (Tex.) Ind. Sch. Dist., 1978-79; adult edn. instr. Cooke County Coop., McKinney, 1978-81; fin. analyst Tex. Instruments, Dallas, 1981-83; instr. Dallas County Community Coll. Dist., 1980-91, So. Meth. U., Dallas, 1983-84; founder, dir. Esperanza Acad. for at Risk Youth, Plano, Tex., 1986-91; prof. Blinn Coll., Brenham and Bryan, Tex., 1991-93; asst. prof. Tex. A&M U., Corpus Christi, 1993—, mem. faculty senate, 1993-94. Cons. Tex. A&M U., College Station, 1991-93; chair univ. libr. com. Tex. A&M U., Corpus Christi, 1994-96; leader, facilitator discoveries project mid. sch. task force for restructuring Corpus Christi Ind. Sch. Dist.,1993-94; chair steering com. E.M. Clark grant Corpus Christi Ind. Sch. Dist., 1995—; project dir. Coastal Bend Ctr. Profl. Devel. & Tech., 1993—; prin. investigator, project dir. South Tex. Tchg. Consortium for Spl. Populations, 1995—. Bd. dirs. United Presbyn. Homes, Waxahachie, Tex., 1969-72, Trinity River Mission, Dallas, 1970-72; vol. Dallas County Juvenile Probation, 1970-72; translator Kiwanis Internat. Conv., Dallas, 1973; foster parent State of Tex., 1972-82; elder Presbyn. Ch., Dallas, 1972—; trainer Richardson (Tex.) Ind. Sch. Dist., 1976-80; leader Cub Scouts, Girl Scouts U.S.A., Dallas, 1968-75; mem. adv. coun. Head Start, Bryan, 1991-93. Recipient Scholarship and Grant, East Tex. State U., Commerce, 1980. Mem. ASCD, Am. Creativity Assn., Assn. Edn. of Gifted Underachieving Students, Tex. Assn. Gifted and Talented, Coun. for Exceptional Children, Task Force for Gifted and Talented Edn. in Tex. Republican. Avocations: reading, writing, working with at-risk youth, gardening. Office: Lon Morris College 800 College Jacksonville TX 75766 Personal E-mail: kayqueen2000@yahoo.com. Business E-Mail: kqueen@lonmorris.edu.

QUEEN, MARLA FRUDDEN, psychologist; b. Oakland, Calif., Mar. 30, 1953; d. Jon Herbert and Loretta Margaret Frudden; m. Don Mathya Rubinstein, Nov. 17, 1979 (div. Nov. 15, 1990); children: Tara Pauline Rubinstein, Alexa Rubinstein; m. Richard Frank Richardson, June 22, 1997 (div. June 4, 2002); m. Joseph Eugene Queen, Apr. 1, 2006; stepchildren: Daniel Craig, Rebekah Ann. BA, U. Calif., Santa Barbara, 1975; MA, EdS, U. Mich., Ann Arbor, 1979, PhD, 1986. Lic. psychologist Mich., 1980; cert. in intensive mediation 1994, in personalized prevention adventure edn. 1991, sch. psychologist 1984. Therapist rschr. Dept. Psychiatry, U. Mich., Ann Arbor, 1979—81; co-developer, intervention by precipitation DOE project U. Mich., Dearborn, 1979—82; ind. cons. Plymouth Canton Sch. Dist., Mich., 1982—83; project dir., high risk and devel. awareness project Wayne Intermediate Sch. Dist., Mich., 1983—84; therapist Ten Southfield Clinic, Mich., 1983; sch. psychologist Chelsea Sch. Dist., Mich., 1984—; owner, innkeeper Queen's Residence Bed and Breakfast, Ypsilanti, Mich., 2007—. Contbr. articles to profl. jours. Fund raiser Ypsilanti Heritage Found., 1999, 2007, Meals Wheels, Ypsilanti, 2007; bd. dirs. Ypsilanti Visitors Convention Bur., 2009; pres. Cmty. Dare Care, Ann Arbor, 1985—87. Named Best of Gt. Lakes Region, Bedand Breakfast Com., 2008—09. Avocations: dance, tennis, golf. Home: 220 S Huron St Ypsilanti MI 48197 Personal E-mail: innkeeper@queensresidence.com.

QUEENEY, DEBORAH ANN, special education educator; b. Allentown, Pa., Feb. 4, 1949; d. William and Jane Swartz; m. Stephen Francis Queeney, Aug. 5, 1978; children: Nicole Ellen, Jessica Elaine. BSc, Kutztown State Coll., 1972; MEd, U. Pitts., 1975. Tchr. blind, multihandicapped Lincoln Intermediate Unit 12, York, Pa., 1973—74; tchr. Monmouth Assn. Retarded Children, Shrewsbury, NJ, 1975—78; instrnl. assoc., tutor Amherst Sch. Dist. Regional Svcs. and Edn. Ctr., NH, 1988—91; spl. needs tchr. Milford Sch. Dist., NH, 1991—. Recipient Monmouth County Tchr. of Yr., Monmouth Assn. Retarded Citizens, 1977, Excellence in Edn. award, Nat. Ctr. Low Incidence Disabilities, Denver, 2004; named NH Tchr. of Yr., Assn. Retarded Citizens NH, 1994. Mem.: NH Connections. Avocations: seashell collecting, sketching. Home: 7 Roberts Rd Amherst NH 03031 Office: Milford Mid Sch 33 Osgood Rd Milford NH 03055

QUEEN LATIFAH, (DANA ELAINE OWENS), actress, musician; b. Newark, Mar. 18, 1970; d. Lance and Rita Owens. Student, Borough of Manhattan C.C. Co-founder, CEO Flavor Unit Entertainment, 1993—; spokeswoman Revlon. Model, spokesperson Covergirl. Actress: (films) House Party 2, 1991, Jungle Fever, 1991, Juice, 1992, Who's the Man, 1993, My Life, 1993, Set It Off, 1996, Hoodlum, 1997, The Wizard of Oz, 1998, Living Out Loud, 1998, Sphere, 1998, The Bone Collector, 1999, (voice only) Bringing Out the Dead, 1999, The Country Bears, 2002, Brown Sugar, 2002, (voice only) Pinocchio, 2002, Chicago, 2002 (Acad. Award Nomination for Best Supporting. Actress, 2003), Scary Movie 3, Barbershop 2: Back in Business, 2004, Taxi, 2004, Last Holiday, 2006, (voice only) Ice Age: The Meltdown, 2006, Stranger Than Fiction, 2006, (voice only) Arctic Tale, 2007, Hairspray, 2007 (voice only) Ice Age: Dawn of the Dinosaurs, 2009; actor, exec. prodr.: (films) Bringing Down the House, 2003; actor, prodr.: (films) The Cookout, 2004, Beauty Shop, 2005, The Perfect Holiday, 2007, Mad Money, 2008, The Secret Life of Bees, 2008; exec. prodr. Who's Your Caddy?, 2007; actor: (TV movies) Sister in the Name of Rap, 1992, Mama Flora's Family, 1998, Living with the Dead, 2002, (voice only) Crash Nebula, 2004, The Muppets' Wonderful Wizard of Oz, 2005, Life Support, 2007 (Best Performance by an Actress in a Mini-Series or Motion Picture Made for TV, Golden Globe award, Hollywood Fgn. Press Assn., 2008, Outstanding Performance by a Female Actor in a TV Movie or Miniseries, 2008, Outstanding Actress in a TV Movie, Miniseries or Special, NAACP Image award, 2008); exec. prodr. (TV movies) Wifey, 2007; host, exec. prodr.: The Queen Latifah Show, 1999-2001; TV appearances include In Living Color, 1991, Fresh Prince of Bel Air, 1991, Living Single, 1993, Mad TV, 1997, Living Single, 1996, 1997, Spin City, 2001, Kung Faux, 2003, The Fairly OddParents, 2004, Eve, 2004; composer (films) New Jack City, 1991, White Man Can't Jump, 1992, Girls Town, 1996; singer (albums) All Hail the Queen, 1990, The Nature of Sista, 1991, X-tra Naked, 1992, Black Reign, 1994, Order In The Court, 1998, She's the Queen: A Collection of Hits, 2002, The Dana Owens Album, 2004, Trav'lin' Light, 2007; Author: Ladies First: Revelations of a Strong Woman, 1999, Queen of the Scene, 2006 Recipient Grammy award nomination, 1990, Soul Train Music award, 1995, Sammy Davis Jr. award, 1995, Entertainer of Yr. award, 1995, Grammy award for best rap solo performance, 1995, Arist of the Yr. award, Harvard Found., 2003; named Best New Artist, New Music Seminar, 1990, Best Female Rapper, Rolling Stone Readers' Poll, 1990, Woman of the Yr. Glamour mag., 2006; named one of 50 Most Influential African-Americans, Ebony mag. 2004, named to Hollywood Walk of Fame, 2005, Power 150, Ebony mag. 2008. Achievements include becoming first hip-hop artist honored with star on the Hollywood Walk of Fame. Office: Flavor Unit Entertainment 155 Morgan St Jersey City NJ 07302-2932

QUE HEE, SHANE STEPHEN, environmental health educator; b. Sydney, Oct. 11, 1946; came to U.S., 1978; s. Robert and Beris (Byers) Que Hee. BS, U. Queensland, Brisbane, Australia, 1968, MS, 1971; PhD, U. Saskatchewan, Can., 1976. Registered profl. indsl. hygienist. Asst. prof. U. Cin., 1978-84, assoc. prof., 1984-89, U. Calif., LA, 1989-94, prof., 1994—. Mem. Hazardous Materials Data Bank Nat. Libr. Med., 1984—89; mem. biol. monitoring com. Am. Indsl. Hygiene Assn., 1993—; mem. com. on methods for water and waste water Am. Water Works Assn., Am. Pub. Health Assn., 1993—; mem. bd. sci. counsellors NIOSH, 2001—04; mem. Nat. Toxicol Program Rsch. on Carcinogens, 2006—. Author: The Phenoxyalkanoic Acids: Chemistry, Analysis and Environmental Pollution, 1981, Biological Monitoring: An Introduction, 1993, Hazardous Waste Analysis, 1999, Biological Monitoring Guide, 2004; contbr. more than 160 articles to profl. jours. and book chpts. Sec. Lesbian Gay Acad. U., Cin., 1978-87, pres. 1988-89, facilitator Gay/Lesbian March Activists, Cin., 1987-89; pres. Lesbian Gay Health and Health Policy Found., L.A., 1994—. Postdoctoral fellow McMaster U., Hamilton, Ont., Can., 1976-78. Fellow Am. Inst. Chemists, Am. Indsl. Hygiene Assn. (chmn. biol. environ exposure level project team 2008-09); mem. AAAS, Am. Indsl. Hygiene Assn. Biological Monitoring Com. (sec. 2006, vice-chmn. 2007, chmn. 2008), Am. Coll. Toxicology, Am. Indsl. Hygiene Assn., Am. Chem. Soc., Am. Conf. Indsl. Govt. Hygienists, Am. Pub. Health Assn., N.Y. Acad. Scis. Avocations: civil rights, piano, writing, tennis, bridge, chess. Home: 923 Levering Ave Unit 102 Los Angeles CA 90024-6612 Office: UCLA Sch Pub Health Dept Environ Health Sci 650 Charles Young Dr S Los Angeles CA 90095-1772 Home Phone: 310-208-1624; Office Phone: 310-206-7388. Business E-Mail: squehee@ucla.edu.

QUELLER, DAVID C., ecology and biology professor; BA in history and philosophy of sci., U. Ill., 1976; MS and PhD in biol. sciences, U. Mich., 1976—79; studied tropical ecology, U. Costa Rica, 1979. NATO postdoctoral fellow U. Sussex, 1983—84; Huxley rsch. instr. Rice U., 1984—87, rsch. assoc., 1987—88, sr. rsch. assoc., 1988—89, asst. prof., 1989—94, assoc. prof., 1994—96, prof., 1996—2005, Harry Carothers and Olga Keith Wiess prof. natural sciences, 2005—. John Simon Guggenheim fellow, 1988—89. Fellow: Am. Acad. Arts and Sciences; mem.: AAAS, Scientia, Am. Soc. Naturalists (Young Investigator award 1985), Behavioral Ecology Soc., Internat. Union Study of Social Insects, Soc. Study of Evolution (Councilor 2003—05), Sigma Xi, Phi Beta Kappa. Office: Rice U Dept Ecology & Evolutionary Biology PO Box 1892 Houston TX 77251-1892 Office Phone: 713-285-5220. Office Fax: 713-285-5232. E-mail: queller@rice.edu.

QUENCER, ROBERT MOORE, neuroradiologist, researcher; b. Jersey City, Nov. 14, 1937; s. Arthur Bauer and Isabell (Moore) Quencer; m. Christine F. Thomas, Sept. 16, 1972; children: Kevin, Keith. BS, Cornell U., 1959, MS, 1963; MD, SUNY, Syracuse, 1967. Diplomate Am. Bd. Radiology, Nat. Bd. Med. Examiners; cert. of added qualifications in neuroradiology. Intern Jackson Meml. Hosp., Miami, Fla., 1967-68; resident in radiology Columbia U., NYC, 1968-71, fellow in neuroradiology, 1971-72; asst. prof. Downstate Med. Ctr., Bklyn., 1972-76; assoc. prof. U. Miami, 1976-79, prof., 1979-92, chmn., prof., 1992—, chief sect. neuroradiology, 1976-86, dir. divsn. magnetic resonance imaging, 1986-92, Robert Shapiro MD prof. radiology. Vis. prof. U. Tenn. Coll. Medicine, Memphis, 1982, Downstate Med. Ctr. Coll. Medicine, Bklyn., 1992, U. Vt. Coll. Medicine, Burlington, 1983, NY Med. Coll., Valhalla, 1984, U. Va. Sch. Medicine, Charlottesville, 1984, U. Ky. Sch. Medicine, Lexington, 1985, Yale U. Sch. Medicine, New Haven, 1986, 2000, Columbia U. Sch. Medicine, NYC, 1986, The Mayo Clinic & Found., Rochester, Minn., 1987, Med. Coll. Va., Richmond, 1988, U. Pa. Sch. Medicine, Phila., 1988, Harvard U. Sch. Medicine/Mass. Gen. Hosp., Boston, 1989, U. Conn., Farmington, 1990, Kumamoto, Japan, 1993, U. Man., Can., 1992, Mich. State U., 1996, Mt. Sinai Med. Ctr., 1997, Cornell U. Sch. Medicine, 1998, U. Minn., 2001, U. Ky., 2002; UTMB Galveston, 2003; Dartmouth Hitchcock Med. Sch., 2003, Duke Univ. Sch. of Med., 2003, U. Calif., San Francisco, 2005, U. Mass., 2006; guest lectr. Asian Oceanic Soc. Neuroradiology, 2001, Internat. Med. Soc. Paraplegic, Lucerne, Switzerland, 2001; Phaler lectr. Phila. Roentgen Soc., 1995; dir. programs in dept. radiology U. Miami Sch. Medicine, 1984, 86, Med. Coll. Wis., 1990, 92, Kauai, Hawaii, 1991, Whistler, B.C., 1990; guest lectr. at ASEAN Congress of Radiology, Malaysia, 1992, Royal Australia Radiology Soc., Brisbane, 1993, Brazilian Congress Neurology, 1996, NY Roentgen Soc., 1997, Somerset MR course, Torquay, UK, 1998, Republic of China, 1999, Yale U., 2000, U. Minn., 2001, U. Tex., 2003, Duke U., 2003, U. Calif., San Francisco, 2005, Downstate Med. Ctr., 2007; adv. cons. NIH, 1987, 90; sci. merit reviewer V.A., 1987; presenter, lectr. in field. Author: Neurosonography, 1988; dep. editor Am. Jour. Neuroradiology, 1984-96, editor-in-chief, 1998—; assoc. editor for neuroimaging Yearbook of Neurology and Neurosurgery, 1991—; manuscript reviewer Am. Jour. Neuroradiology, 1984—, Paraplegia, 1989—, Radiographics, 1991—, Pediatrics, 1993—, Radiology, 1994—; mem. editl. bd. Jour. Clin. Neuro-Ophthalmology, 1980-90; contbr. articles to profl. jours. Pres. Am. Soc. Neuroradiology, 1994-95; prin. investigator NIH Grant on imaging/pathology of spinal cord injury; chmn. Commn. Neuroradiological Socs. World Fedn. Neuroradiology Soc., 2003-, Neuroradiology Sci. Program Com. Radiological Soc. North Am., Scientific RSNA Program, 2008-, dir. for neuroradiology, 2004-; Lt. (j.g.) USN, 1959-61. Fellow Am. Coll. Radiology, Am. Soc. Neuroradiology (pres. 1994-95, program com. 1985-89, 92, editl. com. 1984—, publs. com. 1984—, Gold medal 2007); mem. AMA, Fla. Radiology Soc. (Gold medal 2008-), Radiol. Soc. N.Am. (program subcom. on neuroradiology 1990-94, chmn. neuroradiology program 2004—, sci. program dir. 2008—), Southeastern Neuroradiol. Soc. (founder, pres. 1980-81, examiner for bd. certification in radiology and neuroradiology), Fla. Radiol. Soc. (magnetic resonance com. 1991-92, gold medal award, 2008), Alpha Omega Alpha. Avocations: golf, travel. Business E-Mail: rquencer@med.miami.edu.

QUENEAU, PAUL ETIENNE, retired metallurgical engineering educator; b. Phila., Mar. 20, 1911; s. Augustin L. and Jean (Blaisdell) Q.; m. Joan Osgood Hodges, May 20, 1939, (dec.); children: Paul Blaisdell, Josephine Downs. BA, Columbia U., 1931, BSc, 1932, M of Engring., 1933; postgrad., Cambridge U., Eng., 1934; DSc, Delft U. Tech., Netherlands, 1971. With INCO, 1934-69; rsch. supt. Internat. Nickel Co., 1940-41, 46-48, v.p., 1958-69, chief tech. officer, tech. asst. to pres., 1960-66, asst. to chmn., 1967-69; vis. scientist Delft U. Tech., 1970-71; prof. engring. Dartmouth Coll., 1971-87, prof. emeritus, 1987. Cons. engr., 1972—; vis. prof. U. Minn., 1974-75, U. Utah, 1987-91; geographer Perry River Arctic Expdn., 1949; chmn. arctic rsch. adv. com. USN, 1957; gov. Arctic Inst. N.Am., 1957-62; mem. engring. coun. Columbia U., 1965-70; mem. vis. com. MIT, Cambridge, 1967-70; mem. extractive metallurgy and mineral processing panels NAS; pres. Q-S Oxygen Processes Inc., 1974-79, also bd. dir. Author: (with Hanson) Geography, Birds and Mammals of the Perry River Region, 1956; Cobalt and the Nickeliferous Limonites, 1971; editor: Extractive Metallurgy of Copper, Nickel and Cobalt, 1961; (with Anderson) Pyrometallurgical Processes in Nonferrous Metallurgy, 1965; The Winning of Nickel, 1967; contbr. articles to profl. jours.; patentee 500 internat. patents, 36 U.S. patents including processes and apparatus employed in the pyrometallurgy, hydrometallurgy and vapometallurgy of nickel, copper, cobalt, lead, zinc, iron and steel, extractive metallurgy oxygen tech. including INCO oxygen flash smelting, oxygen top-blown rotary converter, lateritic ore matte smelting, nickel high pressure carbonyl and iron ore recovery processes; co-inventor Lurgi QSL direct lead-making, QSOP direct coppermaking and nickelmaking reactors, Lurgi direct steelmaking reactors, and Dravo oxygen sprinkle smelting copper furnaces. Bd. dir. Engring. Found., 1966-76, chmn. bd. dir., 1973-75. With C.E. US Army, 1937—45, ETO, to col. US Army, 1945—71. Decorated Bronze Star, ETO medal with 5 Battlestars, Army Commendation medal; recipient Appreciation Cert. US Army, Egleston medal Columbia U., 1965, Fletcher award Dartmouth Coll., 1991, Chem. Engring Personal Achievement McGraw Hill, 1996; Evans fellow Cambridge U., 1933-34. Fellow Metall. Soc. of AIME (dir. 1964, 68-71, pres. 1969, Extractive Metallurgy Lecture award 1977, Paul E. Queneau TMS Internat. Symposium on Extractive Metallurgy of Copper, Nickel and Cobalt 1993); mem. AIME (Douglas Gold medal 1968, v.p. 1970, dir. 1968-71, Henry Krumb lectr. 1984, keynote lectr. ann. meeting 1990, McGraw Hill award personal achievement in chem. engring.), NAE, NSPE, Can. Inst. Mining and Metallurgy, Inst. Mining and Metallurgy U.K. (overseas mem. council 1970-80, Gold medal 1980), Sigma Xi, Tau Beta Pi. Achievements include 36 U.S. patents and 500 foreign patents. Office: Dartmouth Coll Thayer Sch Engring Hanover NH 03755

QUENNELL, NICHOLAS, landscape architect, educator; b. London, Sept. 30, 1935; s. Cecil William and Beatrice Irene Quennell; m. Grace Tankersley, Apr. 30, 1983. AA, Archtl. Assn., London, 1957; MLA, Harvard U., 1969. Registered landscape architect, N.Y., N.J., Conn., Mass., N.C. Architect London County Coun., 1959-61, Jose Luis Sert, Cambridge, Mass., 1961-62, Lawrence Halprin & Assocs., San Francisco, 1962-65, Vollmer Assocs., NYC, 1965-68; prin. Nicholas Quennell Assocs., NYC, 1968-79, Quennell Rothschild Assocs., NYC, 1979-97, Quennell, Rothschild & Ptnrs., NYC, 1998—. V.p. The Mcpl. Art Soc. (dir. 1978-85), N.Y.C., 1985-92, dir. The Archtl. League, N.Y.C., 1984-89. Bd. dirs. Nat. Assn. for Olmsted Pks., Washington, 1988-90, chmn., 1990-93; mem. Art Commn. of City of N.Y., 1992-97, pres., 1993-97. Fellow Am. Soc. of Landscape Architects; mem. Century Assn. Office: Quennell Rothschild & Ptnrs 118 W 22nd St New York NY 10011-2416 E-mail: quennell@qrpartners.com.

QUENNEVILLE, JOEL, professional hockey coach; b. Windsor, Ont., Can., Sept. 15, 1958; m. Elizabeth Quenneville; children: Dylan, Lily, Anna. Defenseman Toronto Maple Leafs, 1979—80, Colorado Rockies, 1980—82, NJ Devils, 1982—83, Hartford Whalers, 1983—90, Baltimore Skipjacks (AHL), 1990—91, Washington Capitals, 1990—91; defenseman, player asst. St. John's Maple Leafs (AHL), 1991—92, asst. coach, 1992—93; head coach Springfield Indians (AHL), 1993—94; asst. coach Colo. Avalanche, 1995—96, head coach, 2004—08, St. Louis Blues, 1997—2004; scout Chgo. Blackhawks, 2008, head coach, 2008—. Recipient Jack Adams Award, NHL, 2000. Office: Chgo Blackhawks United Ctr 1901 W Madison St Chicago IL 60612

QUENON, ROBERT HAGERTY, retired mining consultant and holding company executive; b. Clarksburg, W.Va., Aug. 2, 1928; s. Ernest Leonard and Josephine (Hagerty) Q.; m. Jean Bowling, Aug. 8, 1953; children: Evan, Ann, Richard. BS in Mining Engring., W.Va. U., 1951; LL.B., George Washington U., 1964; PhD (hon.), U. Mo., 1979, Blackburn Coll., 1983, W.Va. U., 1988. Mine supt. Consol. Coal Co., Fairmont, W.Va., 1956-61; mgr. deep mines Pittston Co., Dante, Va., 1964-66; gen. mgr. Riverton Coal Co., Crown Hill, W.Va., 1966-67; mgr. ops. coal and shale oil dept. Exxon Co., Houston, 1967; pres. Monterey Coal Co., Houston, 1969-76; sr. v.p. Carter Oil Co., Houston, 1976-77; exec. v.p. Peabody Coal Co., St. Louis, 1977-78, pres., chief exec. officer, 1978-83, Peabody Holding Co., Inc., St. Louis, 1983-90, chmn., 1990-91. Bd. dirs. Newmont Mining Co., Denver, Ameren Corp., St. Louis, Laclede Steel Co., St. Louis, Miss. Lime Co., Alton, Ill.; bd. dirs., chmn. Fed. Res. Bank St. Louis, 1993-95, dep. chmn., 1990-92; mem. coal industry adv. bd. Internat. Energy Agy., 1980-97, bd. chmn., 1984-90; chmn. Bituminous Coal Operator's Assn., 1980-83, 89-91. Trustee Blackburn Coll., Carlinville, Ill., 1975-83, St. Louis U., 1981-91; pres. St. Louis Art Mus., 1985-88. Served with AUS, 1946-47. Recipient Eavenson award Soc. Mining, Metallurgy, and Exploration, 1994, Erskine Ramsay award Am. Inst. Mining, Metallurg. and Petroleum Engrs., 1985. Mem. Am. Mining Congress (vice-chmn. 1980-91), Nat. Coal Assn. (chmn. bd. 1978-80), U.S. C. of C. (dir. 1982-88).

QUENTEL, ALBERT DREW, lawyer; b. Miami, Fla., Nov. 27, 1934; s. Charles Edward Jr. and Alberta Amelia (Drew) Q.; m. Paula Staelin Hagar, Feb. 9, 1957 (dec. Mar. 1998); children: Albert D. Jr., Stephen C., Marshall Lee, Paul G., Peter E., Michael J. BA, U. Fla., 1956, JD with honors, 1959. Bar: Fla. 1959. Assoc. Mershon, Sawyer, Johnston, Dunwody & Cole, Miami, 1959-64, ptnr., 1965-71; prin., shareholder Greenberg Traurig P.A., Miami, 1971—. Editor-in-chief U. Fla. Law Rev., 1959; contbg. author: Florida Real Property Practice, 1965, Real Estate Partnerships Selected Problems and Solutions, 1991, Commercial Real Estate Finance, 1993. Mem. Gov.'s Growth Mgmt. Adv. Com., Tallahassee, 1985-87; bd. dirs. Nat. Parkinson Found., Miami, 1980-98, v.p., 1985-97. Mem. NRA (life 1989—), Am. Coll. Real Estate Lawyers, Fla. Bar Assn. (chmn. pub. rels. com. 1970-72, chmn. editorial com. jour. 1972-73), Lions (pres. Key Biscayne, Fla. club 1973), Miami Club (pres. 1991-92), Bath Club, Blue Key, Beta Theta Pi (pres. local chpt. 1954-55), Phi Eta Sigma, Phi Kappa Phi. Republican. Congregationalist. Avocations: reading, shooting, photography. Home: 825 Algeria Ave Coral Gables FL 33134-2401 Office: Greenberg Traurig 1221 Brickell Ave Miami FL 33131-3224 Home Phone: 305-442-8788; Office Phone: 305-579-0505. Business E-Mail: QuentelA@gtlaw.com.

QUERESHI, MOHAMMED YOUNUS, retired psychology professor; b. Haripur Hazara, Pakistan, Dec. 12, 1929; arrived in U.S., 1953; s. Mohammed Noor and Meryam Khatoon Quereshi; m. Nora Jane Knapp, May 27, 1958 (div. Nov. 1979); children: Ahmed, Amna, Shukria, Shawn; m. Farzana Kaukab, May 17, 1980; children: Ajmel, Sabeeha, Azem. PhD, U. Ill., 1958. Lic. psychologist Wis., diplomate Am. Bd. Psychol. Specialties. Asst. prof. psychology U. Minn., Duluth, 1960-62,

U. N.D., Grand Forks, 1962-64; assoc. prof. psychology Marquette U., Milw., 1964-70, prof., 1970—2003, prof. emeritus psychology, 2003—, chmn. dept. psychology, 1971-77. Cons. psychologist. Author: Statistics and Behavior: An Introduction, 1980, 2d edit., 1991; contbr. articles to sci. and profl. jours. Pres. 81st St. Sch. PTA, 1968—70; merit badge counselor Milwaukee County coun. Boy Scouts Am., 1973—88; pres. Islamic Assn. Greater Milw., 1978—83; chmn. bd. trustees Islamic Soc. Milw., 2004—. Grantee, NIH, 1962—69, TOPS Club, 1969—76, Office of Edn., 1970—71. Mem.: Psychometric Soc., Am. Psychol. Assn., Sigma Xi. Home: 15660 Monet Ct Brookfield WI 53005-5125 Office: Marquette U Schroeder Health Complex PO Box 1881 Milwaukee WI 53201-1881 Office Phone: 414-288-7468.

QUERY, LANCE D., dean, university librarian; EdB in History, Spanish, U. Mo., 1969; MA in Latin Am. History, Ind. U., PhD; MLS, U. Chgo. Acting univ. libr. Northwestern Univ., Chgo.; asst. univ. libr., planning and adminstrn. We. Mich. U., and faculty, history dept., to dean, univ. libraries; dean libraries and academic info. resources Tulane U., New Orleans, 2000—; interim dir. Law Libr. Tulane U. Law Sch., 2005—. Office: Dean Libr Academic Info Resources Tulane Univ 6823 St Charles Ave New Orleans LA 70118-5698 Office Phone: 504-865-5131. Office Fax: 504-865-6773. Business E-Mail: lquery@tulane.edu.

QUERY, LOIS A., elementary school educator; b. Ft. Scott, Kans., Sept. 8, 1940; d. Lawrence B. and Ida M. Query. BS in Elem. Edn., Pitts. State U., Kans., 1962, MS in Elem. Edn., 1968. Cert. tchr. Kans. Dept. Edn., 2006. Elem. tchr. Sch. Dist. #1, Hickman Mills, Mo., 1963—65, Ft. Scott Christian Heights, Kans., 1966—73; reading specialist Sch. Dist. R-4, Cabool, Mo., 1974—75; tchr., prin. Tutu Ch. of God Elem. Sch., St. Thomas, Virgin Islands, 1976—81; early childhood tchr. Barton-Dade-Jaspe County Spl. Edn. Coop., Lockwood, Mo., 1989—91; reading specialist U.S.D. #246, Arma, Kans., 1992—2006; ret., 2006. Master of ceremonies Title I Parent Meeting, Arma, 2002—06; coord. Young Author's Conf., Arma, 2004, Arma, 06. Treas. Harmony Hill Youth Camp, Fulton, Mo., 1960—68; activities dir. Harmony Hill Girls Camp, Fulton, 1968—75; twp. chmn. Am. Cancer Soc., Ft. Scott, 1974. Nominee Kans. Tchr. of Yr., U.S.D. #246, 2006; Jr. scholar, Pitts. State U., Kans., 1961, Sr. scholar, 1962. Mem.: Phi Kappa Phi, Kappa Delta Pi. Republican. Ch. Of God. Avocations: music, gardening, reading, sewing. E-mail: laqfarm@terraworld.net.

QUESENBERRY, KENNETH HAYS, agronomy educator; b. Springfield, Tenn., Feb. 28, 1947; s. James William and Cora Geneva (Moore) Quesenberry; m. Joyce Ann Kaze; children: James Kenneth, Kendra Joyce. BS, Western Ky. U., 1969; PhD, U. Ky., 1975. D.F. Jones predoctoral fellow U. Ky., Lexington, 1972—75; asst. prof. U. Fla., Gainesville, 1975—80, assoc. prof. agronomy, 1980—86, prof. agronomy, 1986—. Contbr. articles to profl. jours. With US Army, 1969—71, Vietnam. Fellow: Crop Sci. Soc. Am. (chair divsn. C-8 1993—94, bd. reps. 2005—07, pres. 2009), Am. Soc. Agronomy. Achievements include research in germplasm enhancement of forages with release of four cultivars of tropical grasses and three clovers and genetic transformation of clovers; specialist Trifolium species germplasm and forage breeding and genetics. Avocations: sports, antique furniture refinishing. Office: U Fla PO Box 110500 Gainesville FL 32611-0500 Office Phone: 351-392-1811 ext. 213. Business E-Mail: clover@ifas.ufl.edu.

QUESENBERY, ERIKA LYNN, media specialist, curator; b. Balt., Apr. 29, 1969; d. Lonnie Ray Quesenbery Jr. and Ruth Ann Pierce. Student, Harford CC, 1987—89; grad., Cecil Leadership Acad., 2006. News dir. Delmarva Broadcasting, Sta. WXCY, Havre de Grace, Md., 1989—91; editor The Rising Sun Herald and Herald County edit. Octoraro Pub. Co., Rising Sun, Md., 1995—2000; grant writer, media rels. specialist Boys & Girls Club of Cecil County, North East, Md., 2000—05; mktg. assoc. Stewart Assoc., Perryville, Md., 2005—. Curator Paw Paw Mus., Port Deposit Heritage Corp., Port Deposit, Md., 1998—. Author (researcher): (non-fiction) A Snowball's Chance: Captain Alonzo Snow's 1st Maryland Light Artillery, Battery B, 1861-1865; author: Images of America: United States Naval Training Center Bainbridge, 2007; contbr. chapters to books. Co-founder Torne Sch. clean-up vols. Naval Tng. Ctr. Bainbridge, Port Deposit, 1997—2000; vol., tour guide, first civilian mem. US Naval Tng. Ctr. Bainbridge Hist. Assn., Port Deposit, 1999—2006; chmn. event com. Capt. John Smith 400th Anniversary Am. in Port Deposit, 2007; bd. dirs., former tour com. chair, vol. Port Deposit Heritage Corp., Port Deposit, 1996—98. Recipient Non-Metro Radio Editl. Writing award, AP, Balt., 1989, Non-Metro Radio Enterprise in Reporting award, 1990, Sch. Bell award for media coverage of edn., Md. State Tchrs.' Assn., 1997, U.S. Navy Civilian Citizen Recognition for Bainbridge/NAPS and Tome Sch. Clean-Up Volunteers, USN, 2000. Mem.: Port Deposit C. of C. (v.p. 2006—07). Democrat. Presbyterian. Avocations: historic preservation, local and regional history, genealogy, Irish heritage, travel. Home: 704 Main St Delta PA 17314 Personal E-mail: historacle@verizon.net. E-mail: erikaq@stewartrealestatedev.com.

QUESTER, GEORGE HERMAN, political science professor; b. Bklyn., July 14, 1936; s. Jacob George and Elizabeth (Mattern) Q.; m. Aline Marie Olson, June 20, 1964; children: Theodore, Amanda. AB, Columbia U., 1958; MA, Harvard U., 1964, PhD, 1965. Instr., then asst. prof. govt. Harvard U., 1965-70; assoc. prof. govt. Cornell U., 1970-73, prof., 1973-82; prof. polit. sci. U. Md., College Park, 1982—. Vis. prof. U.S. Naval Acad., Annapolis, Md., 1991-93. Author: Deterrence Before Hiroshima, 1966, Nuclear Diplomacy, 1970, The Politics of Nuclear Proliferation, 1973, The Continuing Problem of International Relations, 1974, Offense and Defense in the International System, 1977, American Foreign Policy: The Lost Consensus, 1982, The Future of Nuclear Deterrence, 1986, The International Politics of Television, 1990, Nuclear Monopoly, 2000, Before And After The Cold War, 2002, Nuclear First Strike, 2006. Served with USAF, 1958-61. Fellow Center Advanced Study Behavioral Scis., 1974-75 Mem. Council Fgn. Relations, Inst. Strategic Studies, Am. Polit. Sci. Assn. Home: 5124 37th St N Arlington VA 22207-1862 Office: Univ Md 3140 Tydings College Park MD 20742-0001 Office Phone: 301-405-4146. Business E-Mail: gqueste@gvpt.umd.edu.

QUESTROM, ALLEN I., private equity firm executive, former retail executive; b. Newton, Mass., Apr. 13, 1941; s. Irving Allen and Natalie (Chadbourne) Questrom; m. Kelli Questrom. BS, Boston U., 1964. From exec. trainee to div. mdse. mgr. Abraham & Straus, Bklyn., 1965-73; v.p., gen. mdse. mgr. home store Bullock's, L.A., 1973-74, sr. v.p., gen. mdse. mgr. all stores, 1974-77; exec. v.p. Bullock's div. Federated Dept. Stores, L.A., 1977-78, pres. Rich's div. Atlanta, 1978-80, chmn. bd., chief exec. officer, 1980-84, chmn. bd., chief exec. officer Bullock's/Bullocks Wilshire div., 1984-88, corp. exec. v.p. Cin., 1987-88, vice-chmn., 1988; chmn., CEO Allied Stores Corp., Cin., 1990-97; pres., CEO Neiman Marcus Group Inc., Dallas, 1988-90; chmn., CEO Federated Dept. Stores Inc., Cin., 1990-97; chmn., pres., CEO Barneys New York, Inc., NYC, 1999—2000; chmn., CEO J.C. Penney Co., Inc., Plano, Tex., 2000—04; sr. adv. Lee Equity Partners LLC, NYC, 2006—. Bd. dirs. Federated Dept. Stores, 1990—97, J.C. Penney Co., Inc., 2000—04, Sotheby's, 2004—, Jones Apparel Group, Inc., 2005—07, Wal-Mart Stores, Inc., 2007—. Avocations: skiing, golf, travel. Office: Lee Equity Partners LLC 767 5th Ave New York NY 10153*

QUEZADA TORUÑO, RODOLFO CARDINAL, cardinal, archbishop; b. Guatemala, Mar. 8, 1932; D in Canon Law. Ordained priest Archdiocese of Guatemala, 1956, vice-chancellor, archbishop, 2001—; parochial vicar El Sagrario; rector Beatas di Belen, Nat. Maj. Sem. of Assumption; ordained bishop, 1972; aux. bishop Diocese of Zacapa, Guatemala, 1972—75, coadjutor bishop, 1975—80, bishop, 1980—86, Diocese of Zacapa y Santo Cristo de Esquipulas, 1986—2001; elevated to cardinal, 2003; cardinal-priest S. Saturnino, 2003—. Pres. Nat. Commn. for Reconciliation, Guatemala, 1987—93, Bishops Conf. Guatemala, 1988—92, 2002—06; mem. Pontifical Council for Culture, Pontifical Commn. for Latin Am. Roman Catholic.

QUIALA, MARIBEL, psychotherapist, consultant; d. Guillermo H. Quiala and Neris Aroche; m. Jesus A. Rios, Apr. 24, 1993; children: Natalie, Jesus. BA in Psychology and Music, Seton Hall U., 1985; MSW, Barry U., 1995. LCSW, bd. cert. Fla. Pvt. pracitce, Miami, Fla., 2000—. S.E. regional coord. Nat. Latina Health Network, Washington, 2000—; field instr. Barry U., Miami, Fla., 2000—, Fla. Internat. U., Miami, 2000—, Nova Southeastern U., Ft. Lauderdale, Fla., 2000—, Carlos Albizu U., Miami, 2000—; internship dir. Psychiat. Solutions Inc., Ft. Lauderdale, 2000—, Hispanic Devel., Leeza Gibbons Memory Found.; mem. Minority Tobacco Control Task Force, Dept. Health, Fla., 1999—2002; spokesperson HIV/AIDS Awareness Campaign, State Fla., Breast/Cervical Cancer Campaign, State Fla., Hispanic Heart Healthy Day Campaign, S.E. Region. Named Most Dynamic Woman, Am. Cancer Soc., 2005. Mem.: NASW (MSW Gosnell Meml. Scholarship Panel 2003—06, Nat. Com. on Women's Issues 2005—), Am. Coll. Musicians, Nat. Guild Piano Tchrs. Roman Catholic. Avocations: dance, piano, meditation. Office Phone: 305-571-9996. Personal E-mail: mquiala@bellsouth.net.

QUICK, BECKY (REBECCA QUICK), financial news correspondent; b. Ind., July 18, 1972; BA in Polit. Sci., Rutgers U., NJ, 1993. Copy editor, copyreader, rsch. asst. overseas copy desk Wall St. Jour., 1993, retail/e-commerce reporter, 1997—2001; internat. news editor Wall St. Jour. Online, 1996; co-anchor Squawk Box CNBC, 2001—. Grantee Times Mirror Fellowship, Rutgers U. Journalism Resources Inst. Office: CNBC Hdqs 900 Sylvan Ave Englewood Cliffs NJ 07632 Office Phone: 201-735-2622. Office Fax: 201-735-3200.*

QUICK, EDWARD RAYMOND, museum director, educator, curator; b. LA, Mar. 22, 1943; s. Donald Russell Quick and Gertrude Ruth (Albin) Thornbrough; m. Ruth Ann Lessig; children: Jeannette Lee, Russell Raymond. BA, U. Calif., Santa Barbara, 1970, MA, 1977. Adminstr. supr. Civil Service, Santa Ana, Calif., 1971-75; sr. computer operator Santa Barbara Rsch. Ctr., 1975-77; asst. collections curator Santa Barbara Mus. Art, 1977-78; collections mgr. Montgomery (Ala.) Mus. Fine Arts, 1978-80; asst. dir. Joslyn Art Mus., Omaha, 1980-85; dir. Sheldon Swope Art Mus., Terre Haute, Ind., 1985-95, Berman Mus., Anniston, Ala., 1995-97; mus. curator National Archives, Washington, 1998-2000, William Clinton Presdl. Libr. and Mus., 2000—04; staff curator mus. mgmt. Nat. Archives Office Presdl. Librs., Washington, 2004—, nat. safety com. mem., 2008—. Adv. Ind. Arts Commn., Indpls., 1986-91; mem. Arts in Pub. Places Commn., Terre Haute, Ind., 1986-93; pres. Friends Vigo County Pub. Libr., 1988-95, treas., 1990-93. Author: Code of Practice for Couriering Museum Objects, 1985, Gilbert Brown Wilson and Herman Melville's Moby Dick, 1993, The American West in the Berman Collections, 1997, Cattle Drive, 1997 others; co-author: Registrars on Record, 1987; contbg. author: Dante Marioni: Blown Glass, 2000. Bd. dirs. Vol. Action Ctr., Terre Haute, 1987-90, Terre Haute Cmty. Relief Effort for Environ. and Civic Spirit, 1989. With USAF, 1961-65, Air N.G., 1979-96. Mem. Am. Assn. Mus. (adv. 1994—, mgmt. and long-range planning com. 1994—), Assn. Ind. Mus., Am. Assn. State and Local History, Internat. Coun. Mus., Washington Print Club, Rotary Internat., Kiwanis Internat., English Conv. Club (leader 2007—), Alpha Gamma Sigma. Office: Nat Archives Presdl Librs 8601 Adelphi Rd Rm 1350 College Park MD 20740-6001 Office Phone: 301-837-0611. Business E-Mail: edward.quick@nara.gov.

QUICK, ELIZABETH L., lawyer; b. Izmir, Turkey, May 22, 1948; BA, Duke U., 1970; JD with honors, U. NC, 1974. Bar: NC 1974. Mem., trusts & estates Womble Carlyle Sandridge & Rice, Winston-Salem, NC, mem. mgmt. com. Vis. lectr. U. NC Sch. Law, 1977. Mem. U. NC Law Review, 1973—74, co-author, editor NC Estate Adminstrn. Manual, 1984; contbr. articles to profl. jours. Bd. dir. Cannon Found., Concord, NC, Reynolda House, inc., Winston-Salem, NC, Wake Forest U. Health Scis., Winston-Salem, NC. Fellow Am. Coll. Trust and Estate Counsel (past chmn.); mem. ABA, NC Bar Assn. (pres. 1997-98), Forsyth County Bar Assn. (treas.), Order of Coif. Mailing: Womble Carlyle Sandridge & Rice PLLC 1 W 4th St Winston Salem NC 27101 Office: Womble Carlyle Sandridge & Rice PLLC One West 4th St Winston Salem NC 27101 Office Phone: 336-721-3638. Office Fax: 336-733-8359. Business E-Mail: equick@wcsr.com.

QUICK, RENEE, mathematics professor, department chairman; m. Keith Quick; m. Keith Quick; children: K., B. MaEd, U. Ala. Birmingham, 1991. Math. instr. Wallace State CC, Hanceville, Ala., 1988—, math. dept. chairperson, 2004—. Recipient Outstanding Academic Faculty Mem. of Yr., Wallace State CC, 1996—97. Mem.: NEA, AEA, AMATYC, WSCEA.

QUICK, THOMAS CLARKSON, brokerage house executive; b. Westbury, NY, Feb. 26, 1955; s. Leslie Charles and Regina (Clarkson) Q. BS in Bus., Fairfield U., 1977. Br. mgr. Quick & Reilly Inc., Palm Beach, Fla., 1977-81; dir. The Quick & Reilly Group, NYC, 1981-85; v.p. Quick & Reilly Inc., Palm Beach, 1981-86, pres., dir. NYC, 1985-96, also bd. dirs.; pres., COO Quick & Reilly/Fleet Securities, Inc., 1996-98; also bd. dirs.; pres., COO Quick & Reilly Group Inc., 1998-2001. Trustee Security Industry Found. for Econ. Edn., Securities Industry Inst.; bd. dirs. Senesco Techs., corcoran.com., MindArrow Systems.com. Treas. Nat. Corp. Theater Fund, Alcoholism Coun. of N.Y.C; trustee U.S. Com.; bd. trustees Fairfield U.; mem. investment adv. bd. and endowment com. St. Jude Children's Rsch. Hosp., Memphis, 1986—; chmn. com. Wall Street Friends of St. Jude Children's Rsch. Hosp., 1979—, mem. endowment com.; bd. dirs. Best Buddies, Am. Ireland Fund. Mem. The Investment Assn. N.Y., N.Y. Stock Exch., Securities and Industry Assn. (econ. edn. com.), Am. Assn. of Sovereign Mil., Order of Malta, Young Pres.'s Orgn., Univ. Club, Friendly Sons of St. Patrick, Apawamis Country Club (Rye, N.Y.), The Beach Club (Palm Beach, Fla.), Chgo. Athletic Club., New York Yacht Club, Lotus Club, Lost Tree Club. Home: 291 El Vedado Way Palm Beach FL 33480 Office: 230 S County Rd Ste C Palm Beach FL 33480 E-mail: tquick@quick-reilly.com.

QUICKE, ANDREW CHARLES, cinema-television educator, consultant, writer; b. Exeter, Eng., Oct. 8, 1936; s. John and Diana Elena (Harris) Q.; m. Juliet Christina Ricketts, Jan. 2, 1971; 1 child, Matthew. BA in Modern History with honors, Oxford U., Eng., 1958, MA in Modern History, 1962. Dir., prodr. BBC, London, 1959-68; v.p. Prestel Prodns., London, 1968-71; exec. prodr. Ctrl. Office Info., London, 1972-73, Reuters Visnews, London, 1973-78; pres. Kensington Film Svcs., London, 1979-82; v.p. Clearview Internat. Cable, Hawaii, Bangkok, 1983-84; news bur. chief CBN Jerusalem Bur., 1984-86; assoc. prof. cinema-TV Regent U., Virginia Beach, Va., 1986-97, prof., 1997—, chmn. Sch. Cinema-TV, 1996—2008. Dir. United Motion Pictures, London, 1980-83, United Media Fin., London, 1981-83; pres. Fellowship Christian Writers, London, 1972-82. Author: Tomorrow's Television, 1976, Changing the Dragon, 1980, Hidden Agendas, 1992, Every Frame a Rembrandt, 2000. Prospective candidate M.P. House of Commons, Kingston on Thames, 1971, Harrow, 1980. Mem. Royal TV Soc. London, Broadcast Ednl. Assn. (Festival of Media Arts awards, Cine Coun. for Non-Theatrical Entertainment (mem. edn. com., 10 Cine Eagle awards, 6 Angel awards, 6 Aegis awards, 4 Aurora awards, 4 Wordfest Houston awards), Intercollegiate Religious Broadcasters (pres. 1991), Torch Club (pres. 1997-98), Va. Assn. Communication Arts & Scis. (pres. 2008-). Episcopalian. Avocations: shakespeare, travel in asia, restoring antique houses, sailing, movies. Office: Regent U Sch Cinema-TV 1000 Regent University Dr Virginia Beach VA 23464-5037 Office Phone: 757-226-4226. Personal E-mail: adrew-quicke@yahoo.com. E-mail: andrqui@regent.edu.

QUICKEL, KENNETH ELWOOD, JR., physician, medical center executive; b. Harrisburg, Pa., Aug. 20, 1939; s. Kenneth E. and Carolyn (Chick) Q.; m. Mary Wickersham Jennings, July 1, 1961; children: Robert Reid, Mary Elizabeth, David Blake. BA, Dartmouth Coll., 1961, B in Med. Sci., 1962; MD, Johns Hopkins U., 1964. Med. resident Johns Hopkins Hosp., Balt., 1964-66; endocrine fellow Duke U., Durham, N.C., 1966-67, 69-71; staff endocrinologist Geisinger Med. Ctr., Danville, Pa., 1971-84, pres., 1982-84; asst. dean Milton S. Hershey Med. Ctr., Hershey, Pa., 1973-77; pres. Geisinger Med. Mgmt. Corp., Danville, 1978-82, NPW Med. Ctr., Wilkes Barre, Pa., 1979-82; exec. v.p. Geisinger Found., Danville, 1981-84; pres. Ramsey Clinic, St. Paul, 1984-87, Joslin Diabetes Ctr., Boston, 1987-99. Bd. dirs. Controlled Risk Ins. Co., Barbados, 1987—. Contbr. articles to sci. jours. Trustee Deaconess Hosp., Boston, 1987—. Surgeon USPHS, 1967-69. Fellow ACP, Am. Coll. Physician Execs. (disting.); mem. Am. Diabetes Assn., Endocrine Soc., Harvard Club. Republican. Home: 435 Elliott Rd Centerville MA 02632-3666 Office: Joslin Diabetes Ctr 1 Joslin Pl Boston MA 02215-5306

QUIE, PAUL GERHARDT, pediatrician, educator; b. Dennison, Minn., Feb. 3, 1925; s. Albert Knute and Nettie Marie (Jacobson) Quie; m. Elizabeth Holmes, Aug. 10, 1951; children: Katie, Bill, Paul, David. BA, St. Olaf Coll., 1949; MD, Yale U., 1953; PhD (hon.), U. Lund, 1993. Diplomate Am. Bd. Pediat., Nat. Bd. Med. Examiners (mem.). Intern Hennepin County Hosp., 1953—54; pediatric resident U. Minn. Hosps., 1957—59; mem. faculty U. Minn. Med. Sch., 1959—, prof. pediat., 1968—99, prof. microbiology, 1974—99, assoc. dean of students, 1992—, Am. Legion meml. heart rsch. prof., 1974—91, Regents prof., 1991; Regent's prof. emeritus, 1999—; interim dir. Ctr. for Biomed. Ethics U. Minn. Med. Sch., 1985—86; attending physician Hennepin County Hosp., 1959—91. Cons. U. Minn. Nursery Sch., 1959—91; chief of staff U. Minn. Hosp., 1979—84; vis. physician Radcliffe Infirmary, Oxford, England, 1971—72; mem. Adv. Allergy and Infectious Disease Coun., 1976—80; mem. pediat. com. NRC, 1978; mem. bd. sci. counselors Gamble Inst., 1985—90; vis. prof. U. Bergen, 1991; hon. prof. U. Hong Kong Med. Sch., 1995; vis. prof. pediat. Chubu Hosp., Nagasaki, Japan, 1996; co-dir. internat. med. edn. and rsch. prog. U. Minn. Med. Sch., 1998—. Editl. bd. Pediat., 1970—76, Rev. Infectious Diseases, 1989—92. Pres. Fairview Found., 1998—2007; bd. dirs. Ctr. for Victims of Torture, Elizabeth Glaser Pediat. AIDS Found., 1998—2005. Med. officer USNR, 1954—57. Recipient E. Mead-Johnson award, Am. Acad. Pediat., 1971, Shotwell award, Hennipen Med. Soc., 2001, Gold Headed Cane award in Pediat., 2005; fellow Guggenheim, 1971—72, Alexander von Humboldt, 1986; scholar John and Mary R. Markle, 1960—65. Mem.: Minn. Acad. Medicine (pres. 1993—94), Assn. Am. Physicians, Am. Acad. Pediat., Minn. Acad. Pediat., Am. Soc. Clin. Investigation, Am. Pediatric Soc. (coun. 1976—83, pres. 1987—88), Soc. Pediatric Rsch., Infectious Diseases Soc. Am. (coun. 1977—82, pres. 1985, Bristol award 1994), Am. Soc. Microbiology, Am. Fedn. Clin. Rsch., Minn. Med. Found. (pres. 1986—88), N.W. Pediat. Soc., Inst. Medicine of NAS. Achievements include research in function of human leukocytes and internat. med. ed. and rsch. Home: 2154 Commonwealth Ave Saint Paul MN 55108 Office: PO Box 293 Minneapolis MN 55455-0374 Office Phone: 612-626-2558. Business E-Mail: quiex001@umn.edu.

QUIGLEY, AUSTIN EDMUND, literature and language professor, former dean; b. Newcastle-upon-Tyne, Eng., Dec. 31, 1942; arrived in US, 1969; s. Edmund and Marguerita Mary (Crilley) Quigley; m. Patricia Denison; children: Laura, Rebecca, Caroline, Catherine. BA with honors, U. Nottingham, Eng., 1967; MA, U. Birmingham, Eng., 1969; PhD, U. Calif., Santa Cruz, 1971. Asst. prof. U. Mass., 1971-73; from asst. prof. to prof. U. Va., 1973-90, chmn. dept. English, 1986-90; H. Gordon Garbedian prof. English and comparative lit. Columbia U., NYC, 1990, mem. Hammerstein Ctr. for Theatre Studies, dean Columbia Coll., 1995—2009, Brander Matthews prof. dramatic lit. Chmn. Lionel Trilling Seminars, 1993—; vis. prof. U. Konstanz, Germany, 1981, U. Geneva, 1982, U. Nottingham, Eng., 1983-84; lectr. at univs., convs. and theatres. Author: The Pinter Problem, 1975, The Modern Stage and Other Worlds, 1985; contbr. many articles on modern lit., drama, lit. theory to profl. jours.; mem. edit. bd. New Lit. History, Va., 1974—, Modern Drama, Toronto, 1978—, The Pinter Rev., Tampa, Fla., 1987—, Theater/Theory/Text Performance, Ann Arbor, Mich., 1988—. Recipient Alexander Hamilton Award, 2008; fellow NEH, London, 1977—78; Danforth fellow, U. Calif., 1970—71. Mem. MLA (exec. com. drama div. 1987-92), Linguistics Assn. Gt. Britain, Samuel Beckett Soc., Harold Pinter Soc., Am. Soc. Theatre Rsch., Shakespeare Assn. Am., Phi Beta Kappa, Omicron Delta Kappa. Avocations: tennis, squash, soccer, hiking. Office: Columbia Coll 208 Hamilton Hall / Mail Code 2805 1130 Amsterdam Ave New York NY 10027 Office Phone: 212-854-2441. E-mail: aeq1@columbia.edu.*

QUIGLEY, ELLEN WHITE, legislative staff member; m. Fran Quigley. Former dep. mayor City of Indpls.; chief of staff for Rep. André Carson, US House of Reps., Washington, 2008—. Office: Office of Congressman Andre Carson 425 Cannon House Office Bldg Washington DC 20515 Office Phone: 202-225-4011. Office Fax: 202-225-5633. E-mail: ellen.quigley@mail.house.gov.*

QUIGLEY, HARRY ALAN, ophthalmologist, medical professor; b. St. Louis, Sept. 17, 1945; children: David, Erica. AB with honors, Harvard Coll., Cambridge, Mass., 1967; MD, Johns Hopkins U. Sch. Medicine, Balt., 1971. Diplomate Am. Bd. Ophthalmology. Intern ophthalmology Mt. Zion Hosp., San Francisco, 1971—72; resident ophthalmology/glaucoma Wilmer Opthal. Inst., Johns Hopkins U., 1972—75; fellowship Bascom Palmer Eye Inst., U. Miami, Fla., 1975—77; asst. prof. Johns Hopkins U. Sch. Medicine, 1977—80, assoc. prof., 1980—85, prof., 1985—94, A. Edward Maumenee prof. ophthalmology, 1994—. Dir. Dana Ctr. Preventive Ophthalmology, Wilmer Inst. Glaucoma Svc.; organizer WHO-sponsored meeting World-wide Glaucoma 2000. Editor-in-chief (med. jour.) Investigative Ophthalmology & Visual Sci., 1993—97; contbr. articles to profl jours. Recipient Prix Jules Francois, European Soc. Ophthalmology, Mackenzie Medal, Ophthal. Soc. Scotland, Gregg Medal, Australian Soc. Ophthalmology, Mooney Medal, Irish Ophthal. Soc., Doyne Medal, Oxford Ophthal. Congress, Lewis Rudin prize, NY Acad. Scis.; named Best Tchr., Chgo. Ophthal. Soc.; named one of America's Top Doctors, Castle Connolly Med. Ltd., 2002—07. Mem.: Am. Glaucoma Soc. (founding mem.), Assn. Rsch. Vision & Ophthalmology (chmn. glaucoma sect. 1984—84, sec.-treas. 1987—92, trustee 1987—97, Friedenwald award 2004). Achievements include research in progenitor cells derived from adult eyes; the epidemiology of eye disease and glaucoma in American, African, Asian, and Hispanic populations; first to report long-term success with laser iridotomy. Office: Johns Hopkins Hosp Wilmer 122 600 N WolfeSt Baltimore MD 21287 Office Fax: 410-955-2542.

QUIGLEY, JAMES B., diversified financial services company executive; BS in Internat. Econs., George Washington U. Elliott Sch. Internat. Affairs. With NY Syndicate Grp. Merrill Lynch, 1983, exec. dir. London Syndicate Grp., head US High Grade Syndicate Grp., head Debt Transactions Grp., head global issuer client grp. for global debt markets, sr. v.p., head client strategies for global debt markets, vice chmn. exec. client coverage grp., 2002—, vice-chmn., head Latin Am. global markets and investment banking, 2006—08, chmn. Merrill Lynch Internat., Inc., 2007—08, pres. Latin Am. & Canada, 2008—. Office: Merrill Lynch 4 World Fin Ctr 250 Vesey St New York NY 10080

QUIGLEY, JAMES H., accounting firm executive; b. Utah, 1953; m. Bonnie Quigley; 3 children. BS, Utah State U., 1974; PhD in comml. sci. (hon.), Bentley Coll., Waltham, Mass., 2005. With Deloitte & Touche USA LLP, 1974—, asst. to chmn., sec. to bd. dirs., chief staff to office of chmn., nat. industry leader mfg. practice, vice chmn., regional mng. ptnr. N.E. practice, 1999—2003, CEO, 2003—, also bd. dirs.; bd. dirs. Deloitte Touche Tohmatsu. Bd. dirs. US C. of C., Catalyst; bd. trustees Fin. Acctg. Found. Bd. dirs. Partnership for NYC; bd. trustees Ctrl. Park Conservancy; nat. adv. coun. Brigham Young U. Marriott Sch. Mgmt.; mem leadership com. Lincoln Ctr. Corp. Fund. Mem.: Union League Club, Econ. Club NY. Office: Deloitte & Touche USA LLP 1633 Broadway New York NY 10019-6754 Office Phone: 212-489-1600. Office Fax: 212-489-1687.*

QUIGLEY, JEROME HAROLD, management consultant; b. Green Bay, Wis., Apr. 19, 1925; s. Harold D. and Mabel (Hansen) Q.; m. Lorraine A. Rocheleau, May 3, 1947; children: Kathy, Ross, Michael, Daniel, Mary Beth, Andrew, Maureen. BS, St. Norbert Coll., 1951. Pers. adminstr. Gen. Motors Corp., 1959-64; dir. indsl. rels. Raytheon Co., Santa Barbara, Calif., 1964-67; dir. pers. U. Calif., Santa Barbara, 1967-72; corp. dir. indsl. rels. Gen. Rsch. Corp., 1972-73; dir. indsl. rels. ISS Sperry Univac, 1973-75; corp. dir. indsl. rels. Four-Phase Systems, Inc., Cupertino, Calif., 1975; sr. v.p. human resources UNC, Annapolis, Md., 1975-86; pres. Profl. Guidance Assocs., Inc., 1986—. Aviator with USN, 1943-47. Mem. Am. Electronics Assn., Assn. For Intelligence Officers, Scottsdale Civilian Police Acad., Navy Intelligence Profls., Assn. Naval Aviation, Tailhook Assn., Ariz. County Attys. and Sheriffs Assn., Ret. Officers Assn., AVCAD/NAVCAD Assn., Navy Aviation Mus. Found., Navy League, LaCamarilla Racquet Club, Am. Legion, VFW. Republican. Roman Catholic. Office: Profl Guidance Assocs Inc 7789 E Joshua Tree Ln Scottsdale AZ 85250-7962 Office Phone: 480-483-0540. Personal E-mail: jerryq1@cox.net.

QUIGLEY, JOHN BERNARD, law educator; b. St. Louis, Oct. 1, 1940; s. John Bernard and Ruth Rosina (Schieber) Q. BA, Harvard U., 1962, MA, LLB, 1966. Bar: Ohio 1973, Mass. 1967, U.S. Dist. Ct. (so. dist.) Ohio 1976, U.S. Ct. Appeals (6th cir.) 1986, U.S. Supreme Ct. 1989. Research assoc. Harvard U. Law Sch., Cambridge, Mass., 1967-69; prof. law Ohio State U., Columbus, 1969—. Author: Basic Laws on the Structure of the Soviet State, 1969, The Soviet Foreign Trade Monopoly, 1974, Palestine and Israel: A Challenge to Justice, 1990, The Ruses for War: American Interventionism since World War II, 1992, 2nd edit., 2007, Flight into the Maelstrom: Soviet Immigration to Israel and Middle East Peace, 1997, Genocide in Cambodia, 2000, The Case for Palestine: An International Law Perspective, 2005, The Genocide Convention: An International Law Analysis, 2006, Soviet Legal Innovation and the Law of the Western World, 2007, Consular Law and Practise, 2008 Mem. Nat. Lawyers Guild (v.p. 1977-79), Am. Soc. Internat. Law(consular law & practise, 2008), AAUP. Avocations: tennis, speed skating, violin. Office: Ohio State U Coll of Law Coll of Law 55 W 12th Ave Columbus OH 43210-1338

QUIGLEY, JOHN MICHAEL, economist, educator; b. NYC, Feb. 12, 1942; BS with distinction, U.S. Air Force Acad., 1964; MSc with honors, U. Stockholm, Sweden, 1965; AM, Harvard U., 1971, PhD, 1972; TekndD (hon.), Royal Inst. Tech., 2007. Commd. 2d lt. USAF, 1964, advanced through grades to capt., 1968; asst. prof. econs. Yale U., 1972-74, assoc. prof., 1974-81; prof. pub. policy U. Calif., Berkeley, 1979—, prof. econs., 1981—, Chancellor's prof., 1997—, prof. bus., 1999—, I. Donald Terner disting. prof., 1999—, chmn. dept. econs., 1992-95; vis. prof. econs. and stats. U. Gothenberg, 1978. Cons. numerous govt. agys. and pvt. firms; econometrician Hdqrs. U.S. Air Force, Pentagon, 1965-68; research assoc. Nat. Bur. Econ. Research, N.Y.C., 1968-78; mem. com. on nat. urban policy NAS, 1985-93. Author, editor, contbr. articles to profl. jours.; editor in chief Reg. Sci. and Urban Econs., 1987-2003; mem. editl. bd. many sci. and scholarly jours. Fulbright scholar, 1964-65; fellow NSF, 1968-69, Woodrow Wilson, 1968-71, Harvard IBM, 1969-71, NDEA, 1969-71, Thord-Gray Am. Scandinavian Found. 1971-72, Social Sci. Research Council, 1971-72. Mem. Am. Econ. Assn., Econometric Soc., Regional Sci. Assn. (bd. dirs. 1986—), Nat. Tax Assn., Assn. for Pub. Policy and Mgmt. (bd. dirs. 1986-89, v.p. 1987-89), Am. Real Estate and Urban Econs. Assn. (bd. dirs. 1987-2001, pres. 1995-97), Royal Swedish Acad. Engrng. Scis. (fgn.). Office: U Calif 2607 Hearst Ave Berkeley CA 94720-7305 Business E-Mail: quigley@econ.berkeley.edu.

QUIGLEY, MARTIN SCHOFIELD, writer, educator; b. Chgo., Nov. 24, 1917; s. Martin Joseph and Gertrude Margaret (Schofield) Q.; m. Katherine J. Dunphy, July 2, 1946; children: Martin, Elin, William, Kevin, Karen, Patricia, John, Mary Katherine, Peter. AB magna cum laude, Georgetown U., 1939; MA, Columbia U., 1973, EdD, 1975. Reporter Motion Picture Herald, NYC and Hollywood, Calif., 1939-41; with overseas br. OWI, 1942; secret war work U.S. Govt., 1943-45; various editl. and mgmt. posts Quigley Pub. Co., Inc., NYC, 1946—2001, pres., 1964-2001, chmn., 2001—; staff, dept. higher and adult edn. Tchrs. Coll., 1974-75; prof. higher edn. grad. courses Baruch Coll. CUNY, 1977-89; prof. higher edn. grad. courses Tchrs. Coll. Columbia U., 1979-80, 90; prof. higher edn. grad. courses Seton Hall U., 1981-82. Pres. QWS, Inc., 1975-80; ednl. cons.; cons. supt. schs. N.Y. Archdiocese, 1962-70 Author: Great Gaels, 1944, 2d edit. 1997, Roman Notes, 1946, Magic Shadows--the story of the origin of motion pictures, 1948, Government Relations of Five Universities in Washington, 1975, Peace Without Hiroshima-Secret Action at the Vatican in Spring of 1945, 1991, First Century of Film, 1995, A U.S. Spy in Ireland, 1999, Community College Movement in Perspective, 2003, Martin J. Quigley and the Glory Days of American Film-1915-65, 2006; co-author: Catholic Action in Practice, 1962, Films in America, 1969; editor: New Screen Techniques, 1953. Pres. NY Christian Family Movement, 1960-62, nat. exec. com., 1960-65; founder, chmn. NY Ind. Schs. Opportunity Project, 1965-77; pres. Found. Internat. Coop., 1960-65; bd. dirs. Will Rogers Inst., Motion Picture Pioneers; treas. Religious Edn. Assn. US and Can., 1975-81, chmn., 1981-84; trustee Village of Larchmont, NY, 1977-79, mayor, 1980-84; trustee Am. Bible Soc., 1984-2008; bd. dirs. William J. Donovan Meml. Found., 1994-2001. Mem.: Larchmont Yacht. Roman Catholic. Personal E-mail: greatgaels@aol.com.

QUIGLEY, MIKE, United States Representative from Illinois, former county commissioner; b. Carol Stream, Ill., Oct. 17, 1958; m. Barbara Quigley; children: Alyson, Meghan. BA in Polit. Sci., Roosevelt U., Chgo., 1981; MA in Pub. Policy, U. Chgo., 1985; JD, Loyola U. Sch. Law, Chgo., 1989. Aide to alderman Bernie Hansen Chgo. City Coun., 1983—89; atty. Law Offices of Michael B. Quigley, 1990—2009; rep. from Dist. 10 Cook County Bd. Commrs., Chgo., 1998—2009; mem. US Congress from 5th Ill. Dist., 2009—. Instr. polit. sci. Loyola U., Chgo. Recipient Disting. Svc. award, Ill. Com. for Honest Govt., Leon Despres award, Ind. Voters of Ill./Ind. Precinct Orgn., Cmty. Advocate award, Chgo. Battered Women's Network, Chgo. Recycling Coalition award, Pub. Svc. Award, Chgo. House, 2008, Legislator award, Respiratory Health Assn., Cmty. Advocate award, Chgo. Battered Women's Network, Leon Despres award, Ind. Voters of Ill., Human Rights Campaign Equality award, Audobon Leadership award, Disting. Svc. award, Ill. Com. for Honest Govt., Chgo. Recycling Coalition award, Human Rights award, Evangelical Catholic Church. Mem.: Lakeview C. of C. (Outstanding Pub. Servant award). Democrat. Office: US Congress 1319 Longworth House Office Bldg Washington DC 20515 also: 3742 W Irving Park Rd Chicago IL 60618 Office Phone: 202-225-4061. Office Fax: 202-225-5603. E-mail: mquigle@luc.edu.*

QUIGLEY, THOMAS JOHN, lawyer; b. NYC, July 26, 1957; s. Thomas Armour and Joan Martina Quigley; m. Norma Marie Quigley; children: Rachel, Neil. BA, Fairfield U., Conn., 1979; JD, St. John's U., Jamaica, NY, 1983. Bar: NY 1994, U.S. Dist. Ct. (so. and ea. dists.) NY 1984, U.S. Dist. Ct. (we. dist.) NY 1998. Assoc. Winston & Strawn LLP, NYC, 1983—91, ptnr., 1991—. Named NY Super Lawyer, 2006; named one of Best Lawyers in Am., 2005, 2006, Best Lawyers in NY, 05, 2006. Mem.: ABA, Fed. Bar Coun. 2d Cir., NY State Bar Assn., St. John's U. Law Sch. Alumni Assn. (bd. dirs. 2004—, v.p. 2006—, pres. Manhattah chpt. 2006—). Office: Winston & Strawn LLP 200 Park Ave New York NY 10166

QUIGLEY, WILLIAM G., automotive supplier company executive; BA in Acctg., Mich. State U. CPA Mich. Audit mgr. Deloitte & Touche USA LLP; asst. corp. controller rsch. and devel. Nissan Motor Corp.; fin. dir. after market bus. ops. Fed.-Mogul Corp., 1995—2000, fin. dir. Americas and Asia Pacific, 2000—01, v.p., corp. controller, 2001—05; v.p., corp. controller, chief acct. officer Visteon Corp., 2005—07, sr. v.p., CFO, 2007, exec. v.p., CFO, 2007—. Mem.: Mich. Assn. CPA's, Am. Inst. CPA's. Office: Visteon Corp Hdqs 1 Village Ctr Dr Belleville MI 48111 Office Phone: 734-710-2000. Office Fax: 734-736-5560.

QUIGNEY, THERESA ANN, special education educator; b. East Cleveland, Ohio, June 19, 1952; d. James and Lenora Mary (McDonald) Q.; m. Joseph Carl Lang, July 23, 1983. BA, Notre Dame Coll., 1974; MEd, Cleve. State U., 1980; PhD, Kent State U., 1992. Cert. tchr. handicapped K-12; cert. ednl. adminstrv. specialist edn. of exceptional pupils; cert. ednl. supr.; cert. elem. prin.; cert. h.s. prin. cert. tchr. French K-12, Ohio. Spl. edn. tchr. Newbury (Ohio) Local Schs., 1974—80; county supr., specific learning disabilities and behavior handicaps Geauga County Bd. Edn., Chardon, Ohio, 1980—86, 1987—88; asst. prof. spl. edn. West Chester (Pa.) U., 1992—93; asst. prof. edn. Heidelberg Coll., Tiffin, Ohio, 1993—94; assoc. prof. spl. edn. Cleve. State U., 1994—, coord. spl. edn. program Coll. Edn., 2000—02. Ednl. rschr.; presenter in field. Contbr. articles to profl. jours., chapters to books. Vol. cons. Tchrs. for Action Rsch. South Euclid/Lyndhurst (Ohio) Sch. Dist. 1996—; past participant issues task force Ohio Coun. for Exceptional Children; presenter, participant Oxford Round Table, Oxford U., England; past bd. mem. Camp Sue Osborne, Lake County, Ohio; mem. steering com. State Improvement Grant (Edn.), 2000—02. Grantee Ohio State Supt.'s Task Force on Spl. Edn., 1997, Cleve. State U. Coll. Edn., 1997, Am. Sch. Counselor's Assn.; recipient achievement recognition Assn. for Children and Adults with Learning Disabilities, Ohio, 1980. Mem. CEC, Am. Ednl. Rsch. Assn., Learning Disabilities Assn., Kappa Delta Pi, Phi Delta Kappa, Pi Lambda Theta. Avocations: travel, writing, reading, sketching. Office: Cleveland State Univ Euclid Ave at E 24th St Cleveland OH 44115 Business E-Mail: t.quigney@csuohio.edu.

QUILES, ESTHER, art educator; b. Bklyn., Nov. 1, 1957; children: John Rivera, Ashley Rivera. BA with honors, Sch. Visual Arts, NYC, 1980; MS, Adelphi U., NYC, 1985. Tchr. art Boys Club N.Y., NYC, 1979—92, West Side H.S., NYC, 1981—2004; tchr. for student tchrs. Sch. Visual Arts, NYC, 1994—97. Vol. tchr. Lehigh U. STAR Acad., Bethlehem, Pa., 2005—06; advisor Aspira N.Y. S.I., 1996—98. Mem. Lation Civic Assn. Inc., SI, NY, 1995—2006, Calvary Temple Ch., 2002—06; bd. dirs., mem. steering com. Lation Civic Assn. Inc., SI, NY, 2004—05; art dir. Girls Club N.Y.; mem. sch. bd. Allentown Christian Sch., Pa., 2004—05. Recipient Appreciation, Recognition, Contbn., and Cmty. Svc. award, Latino Civic Assn., Inc., Cert. Mem. Congress Recognition Svc. to the Cmty. award, 1998, Proclamation award, City Coun. N.Y., 1998, Recognition of Achievement, N.Y. State Assembly, 1998, Bd. of Edn. award, 8th Ann. Hostos award gala, 1998; named Outstanding Dedicated Art Tchr., Sch. Art League, Met. Mus. Art, 1997, Tchr. of Yr., N.Y. City Pub. Schs., 1991—93, N.Y.C. Pub. Schs., 1992. Avocations: crafts, interior decorating, singing, horseback riding. Office: West Side HS 140 West 102 St New York NY 10025 Office Phone: 212-678-7300. Office Fax: 212-678-7380.

QUILLEN, CECIL DYER, JR., engineer, lawyer, consultant; b. Kingsport, Tenn., Jan. 21, 1937; s. Cecil and Mary Louise (Carter) Q.; m. Vicey Ann Childress, Apr. 1, 1961; children: Cecil III, Ann C. Macaulay. BS, Va. Poly. Inst., Blacksburg, 1958; LLB, U. Va., Charlottesville, 1962. Bar: Va. 1962, NY 1963, Tenn. 1974; cert. in exec. devel., U. Tenn., Knoxville, 1976. Atty. patent dept. Eastman Kodak Co., Rochester, NY, 1962—65; atty. patent sect. Tenn. Eastman Co. (divsn. Eastman Kodak), Kingsport, 1965—69, mgr. patent sect., 1969—72, mgr. licensing, 1972—74, sec. and asst. chief counsel, 1974—76, v.p., chief counsel, 1983—85; dir. patent litigation Eastman Kodak, 1976—82, dir. antitrust litigation, 1978—82, v.p., assoc. gen. counsel, 1986, sr. v.p., gen. counsel, dir., 1986—92; sr. advisor Putnam, Hayes, Bartlett and PHB Hagler Bailly, Washington, 1992—2000, Cornerstone Rsch., Washington, 2000—. Contbr. articles to profl. jours. Bd. dirs. Pub. Patent Found., 2006—; former mem. law alumni adv. coun. U. Va. Law Sch. Mem. ABA, Va. State Bar, Am. Intellectual Property Law Assn., Va. Poly. Inst. Com. of 100, Assn. Gen. Counsel, Phi Kappa Phi, Omicron Delta Kappa, Tau Beta Pi, Phi Lambda Upsilon. Office Phone: 202-912-8930. Personal E-mail: cecilquillen@comcast.net. Business E-Mail: cquillen@cornerstone.com.

QUILLEN, CECIL DYER, III, lawyer; b. Rochester, NY, Aug. 15, 1963; s. Cecil Dyer, Jr. and Vicey Ann (Childress) Q.; m. Mary Stuart Humes, Oct. 20, 1990; children: Caroline, James C.D., George, Elizabeth. AB magna cum laude, Harvard U., 1985; JD, U. Va., 1988. Bar: NY 1989, DC 1991, US Ct. Appeals (4th cir.) 1989. Law clk., Sr. Cir. Judge US Ct. Appeals (4th cir.), Richmond, Va., 1988-89; assoc. Sullivan & Cromwell, NYC, 1989-95, Linklaters, NYC, 1995-96, ptnr., 1996—, ptnr. London office, 2000—. Bd. dirs. European High Yield Assn.; spkr. various profl. confs. Notes editor Va. Law Rev., 1987-88. Mem. ABA, NY State Bar Assn., Assn. Bar City of NY, Raven Soc., Order of Coif, Phi Beta Kappa. Office: Linklaters One Silk St London EC2Y 8HQ England

QUILLEN, MICHAEL DUANE, biology professor; b. Jenkins, Ky., Dec. 9, 1967; married. BS in Biology, Morehead State U., Ky., 1989; MS in Biology, Morehead State U.2, Ky., 1992. Prof. biology Maysville Cmty. & Tech. Coll., Ky., 2004—, chair math, sci. & agr., 2007—. Faculty regent KCTCS, Versailles, Ky., 2006—. Office: Maysville Cmty & Tech Coll 1755 US 68 Maysville KY 41056

QUILLEN, MICHAEL J., energy executive; Grad., Va. Tech. U. Chmn., CEO Addington Inc.; v.p. ops. NERCO Coal Corp.; v.p. AMVEST Corp.; pres. Pittston Coal Sales Corp.; v.p. ops. Pittston Coal Co.; exec. v.p. ops. Am. Metals & Coal Internat., 1998—2002; pres. Alpha Natural Resources LLC, Abingdon, Va., 2002—, CEO, 2003—; pres. ANR Holdings Inc., Abingdon, Va., 2002—, CEO, 2003—; pres., CEO Alpha Natural Resources Inc., Abingdon, Va., 2004—06, chmn., CEO, 2006—. Office: Alpha Natural Resources 1 Alpha Pl PO Box 2345 Abingdon VA 24212 Office Phone: 276-719-4410.

QUILLEN, WILLIAM TATEM, retired judge, lawyer, educator; b. Camden, NJ, Jan. 15, 1935; s. Robert James and Gladys Collings (Tatem) Quillen; m. Marcia Everhart Stirling, June 27, 1959; children: Carol Everhart, Tracey Tatem. BA, Williams Coll., 1956; LLB, Harvard U., 1959; LLM, U. Va., 1982; LLD (hon.), Widener U. Sch. Law, 2002. Bar: Del. 1959. Assoc. Richards, Layton & Finger, Wilmington, Del., 1963—64; adminstrv. asst. to Gov. of Del., 1965; assoc. judge Superior Ct. of Del., 1966—73; chancellor State of Del., 1973—76; sr. v.p. Wilmington Trust Co., 1976—78; justice Supreme Ct. of Del., 1978—83; ptnr. Potter Anderson & Corroon, Wilmington, 1983—86; gen. counsel, v.p. Howard Hughes Med. Inst., 1986—91; sec. of state State of Del., Dover, 1993—94; assoc. judge Superior Ct. Del., Wilmington, 1994—2000; of counsel Drinker Biddle & Reath, Wilmington, 2003—. Mem. adj. faculty Widener U. Sch. Law, Wilmington, 1976—83, 1985—86, 1995—2000, 2002—, disting. vis. prof. law, 1992—94, 2001—02. Trustee Widener U., 1979—91; Dem. candidate for gov. Del., 1984. With JAGC USAF, 1959—62. Mem.: ABA, Del. State Bar Assn., Wilmington Club, Phi Beta Kappa. Democrat. Presbyterian. Office Phone: 302-467-4219. Business E-Mail: william.quillen@dbr.com.

QUILLEY, JOHN, medical educator, researcher; s. Denis Frank and Molly Quilley; m. Elisa Babilonia, Apr. 14, 2007; children: Sean James, Michelle Juliette Delfiacco, Ryan Gavin; m. Caroline Patricia Bell, Jan. 13, 1979 (div. 2000). PhD, Bath U., Eng., 1979. Asst. prof. NY Med. Coll., Valhalla, 1981—89, assoc. prof., 1989—. Assoc. prof. U. Medicine and Dentistry NJ, Sch. Osteopathic Medicine, Stratford, 1997—2000. Contbr. articles to numerous profl. jours., chapters to books. Recipient Young Scholar's award, Am. Soc. Hypertension; grantee, NIH, 1990, 1996—2001, 2004—07; Rsch. grant, Am. Diabetes Assn., 1985—88, 2001—08. Fellow: Coun. High Blood Pressure Rsch.; mem.: Eastern Hypertension Soc., Brit. Pharm. Soc. Independent. Avocations: tennis, hiking, travel, reading. Office: NY Med Coll Grasslands Rd Valhalla NY 10595 Office Fax: 914-347-4956. Business E-Mail: john_quilley@nymc.edu.

QUILLIAN, WARREN WILSON, II, pediatrician, educator; b. Miami, Fla., Jan. 21, 1936; s. Warren Wilson and Rosabel (Brown) Q.; m. Sallie Ruth Creel, July 26, 1958; children: Rutledge, Ruth, Warren C., Frances. MD, Emory U., 1961. Diplomate Am. Bd. Pediat. (examiner 1966—, bd. dirs. 1974-80, 1992-98, treas. 1978, v.p. 1979, pres. 1980). Intern in pediat. Vanderbilt U., Nashville, 1961-62; resident Children's Hosp. Med. Ctr., Harvard U., Boston, 1962-63; chief resident Grady Meml. Hosp., Emory U., Atlanta, 1963-64; pvt. practice Coral Gables, Fla., 1966. Instr., asst. clin. prof., assoc. clin. prof., now clin. prof. pediat. U. Miami Med. Sch., 1966—; emeritus staff, bd. dirs. Miami Children's Hosp.; emeritus staff Jackson Meml. Hosp.; past chief pediat. Doctors' Hosp.; mem. hon. staff Mercy Hosp., Bapt. Hosp., South Miami Hosp.; chmn. health adv. com. Dade County Schs.; bd. dirs., v.p. Am. Bd. Pediat. Found., 1991-98; mem. adv. bd. McGlannon Sch.; cons. Fla. Divsn. Med. Svcs.; bd. dirs. Bank Coral Gables. Contbr. articles to med. jours. Hon. bd. dirs. Soc. Abused Children of Children's Home Soc., Miami, 1980-84; mem. Coral Gables Code Enforcement Bd., 1986-88; team-sch. physician Coral Gables Sr. H.G., 1980-88; bd. dirs. Dade County March of Dimes, Miami, 1968-72; bd. advisors Dade County Assn. Retarded Children, 1968-76; trustee Emory U., 1991-97; mem. coun. ministries, youth coord., mem. fin. com., Sunday Sch. tchr. United Meth. Ch. Coral Gables, 1966—; chair staff parish rels. com.; mem. bd. advisors The Growing Place; mem. Citizens Bd. U. Miami, 1997—; v.p. bd. Good Hope Equestrian Tng. Ctr. for the Handicapped, 1999-. Capt. M.C., U.S. Army, 1964-66. Recipient citation of merit Emory U., 1980, Alumni Commendation, Miami Children's Hosp., 1983, Tchg. award U. Miami Sch. Medicine, 1995, 2002, 06, Winston Churchhill medal, 1999, Commendation Key to City, City of Coral Gables, 2007, Lifetime Achievement award Miami Children's Hosp., 2007; named to CGHS Athletic Hall of Fame, 1996, Wisdom Hall of Fame, 1998. Fellow Am. Acad. Pediat.; mem. AMA, Fla. Med. Assn. (sch. health com.), Fla. Pediat. Soc. (past chmn. sch. health com.), So. Med. Assn., Dade County Med. Assn. (sch. health com., continuing edn. com.), Empirical Soc. (past pres.), Soc. for Pediat. Rsch., So. Perinatal Soc., Greater Miami Pediat. Soc. (past pres., chmn. legis. and sch. health com., Hall of Fame), Miami Med. Forum (past pres., Haverfield Cup 1985, Mansfield Trophy 1983, 88, 98), Sr. Soc. Emory U., Biscayne Bay Yacht Club (commodore, bd. govs.), DVS Sr. Honor Soc., Alpha Omega Alpha, Omicron Delta Kappa, Alpha Epsilon Upsilon, Phi Delta Theta. Democrat. Avocations: fishing, golf, boating.

QUILLIGAN, EDWARD JAMES, retired obstetrician, gynecologist, educator; b. Cleve., June 18, 1925; s. James Joseph and Maude Elvira (Ryan) Q.; m. Betty Jane Cleaton, Dec. 14, 1946; children: Bruce, Jay, Carol, Christopher, Linda, Ted. BA, MD, Ohio State U., 1951; MA (hon.), Yale, 1967. Intern Ohio State U. Hosp., 1951-52, resident, 1952-54, Western Res. U. Hosps., 1954-56; asst. prof. obstetrics and gynecology Western Res. U., 1957-63, prof., 1963-65; prof. obstetrics and gynecology UCLA, 1965-66; prof., chmn. dept. Ob-Gyn Yale U., 1966-69, U. So. Calif., 1969-78, asso. v.p. med. affairs, 1978-79; prof. Ob-Gyn. U. Calif., Irvine, 1980-83, vice chancellor health affairs, dean Sch. Medicine, 1987-89; prof., chmn. ob.-gyn. dept. U. Wis., 1983-85; prof., chmn. Ob-Gyn Davis Med. Ctr. U. Calif., Sacramento, 1985-87, vice chancellor Health Scis., dean Coll. Med. Irvine, 1987-89, prof. ob-gyn, 1987-94, prof. emeritus ob-gyn., 1994; exec. dir. med. edn. Long Beach (Calif.) Meml. Health Svcs., 1995—2005; ret., 2005. Contbr. articles to med. jours.; editor-in-chief emeritus: Am. Jour. Obstetrics and Gynecology. Served to 2d lt. AUS, 1944—46. Recipient Centennial award Ohio State U., 1970 Mem. Soc. Gynecologic Investigation, Am. Gynecol. Soc., Am. Coll. Ob-Gyn., Sigma Xi. Home: 1 Goldenglow Irvine CA 92612-4077 E-mail: equilligan@cox.net.

QUIMBY, FRED WILLIAM, retired pathology educator, veterinarian; b. Providence, Sept. 19, 1945; s. Edward Harold and Isabel (Barber) Q.; m. Cynthia Claire Connelly, Aug. 21, 1965; children: Kelly Ann, Cynthia Jane. VMD, U. Pa., 1970, PhD, 1974. Diplomate Am. Coll. Lab. Animal Medicine. Hematology fellow New Eng. Med. Ctr., Boston, 1974-75, instr. pathology, 1975-76, asst. prof., 1976-79; assoc. prof. pathology Cornell Med. Coll., NYC, 1979—92, prof. pathology, 1993—2000; assoc. v.p., sr. dir. Lab. Animal Rsch. Ctr. Rockefeller U., 2001—07; ret., 2007. Dir. lab. animal medicine Tufts-New Eng. Med. Ctr., Boston, 1975—79; dir. Ctr. Rsch. Animal Resources Cornell U., Ithaca, 1979—2001. Editor Animal Welfare, 1992, Lab. Animal Sci., 1992-93, consulting editor, 1993-95; editor: Clinical Chemistry of Laboratory Animals, 2d edit., 1999, Laboratory Animal Medicine, 2d edit., 2002, The Mouse in Biomedical Research, 2d edit., 2006; guest editor Applied Animal Behavior Sci., 1997; chmn. editl. bd. ILAr News, 1988-91; contbr. articles to profl. jours. Trustee NH Pub. Libr., New Durham, 2008—; chmn. Rochester Opera House Devel. Com., NH, 2009—. Recipient Focused Giving award, Johnson and Johnson, 1987—90; Greenfield Trust scholar, 1966—70, N.H. Rural Rehab. Corp. scholar, 1966—70, U. Pa. scholar, 1969—70. Mem. Am. Vet. Med. Assn. (Charles River prize 1995), Am. Assn. Lab. Animal Sci. (pres. N.E. br. 1978-79, bd. trustees Metro NY br. 2003-05, N.E. br. Trum award 1979, Metro br. Veterinarian of Yr. award (now Fred W. Quimby award), 2007), Am. Soc. Lab. Animal Practitioners (Rsch. award 2004), World Vet. Assn. (sec. exec. com. animal welfare 1990-96). Roman Catholic. Home: 46 South Shore Rd New Durham NH 03855 Home Phone: 603-859-4280. Business E-Mail: quimby@rockefeller.edu.

QUIMBY, JANICE ANN, minister; b. Brunswick, Maine, May 6, 1944; d. Kenneth Blakney Libby and Charlotte Rachel Hill; m. Melvin David Cole Willis (dec.); m. Herbert Leslie Quimby, May 22, 1993. BS in Music Edn., U. So. Maine, Gorham, 1966. Music tchr. SAD 50, Thomaston, Maine, 1966—67, Bingor Pub. Schs., Okla., 1967—69; exec. program dir. YWCA, Bar Harbor, Maine, 1971—72; music tchr. Woolwich Pub. Schs., 1976—77; accounts receivable clk. L.L. Bean, Freeport, Maine, 1977—88; computer operator Maine Motor Transport, Augusta, 1988—91; pastor Sandy River Chapel, Starks, Maine, 1995—. With USCGR, 1973—87. Republican. Pentecostal Church. Avocations: music, knitting, writing, crocheting. Home and Office: 565 Sandy River Rd Anson ME 04911

QUIN, LOUIS DUBOSE, chemist, educator; b. Charleston, SC, Mar. 5, 1928; s. Louis DuBose and Olga vonOven (Jatho) Q.; children: Gordon, Howard, Carol. BS, The Citadel, 1947; MA, U. N.C., 1949, PhD, 1952. Research chemist Am. Cyanamid Co., Stamford, Conn., 1949-50; research project leader FMC Corp., South Charleston, W.Va., 1952-54, 56; mem. faculty dept. chemistry Duke U., Durham, NC, 1956-86, prof., 1967-81, James B. Duke prof. chemistry, 1981-86, prof. emeritus, 1986, chmn. dept., 1970-76; prof. chemistry U. Mass., Amherst, 1986-96, prof. emeritus, 1996—, head dept., 1986-94; adj. prof., disting. vis. prof. chemistry U. N.C., Wilmington, 1996—. Mem. Durham Human Relations Commn., 1978-81 Author: Heterocyclic Chemistry of Phosphorus, 1981, (with J.G. Verkade) Phosphorus-31 NMR Spectroscopy in Stereochemical Analysis, 1987, Phosphorus-31 NMR Spectral Properties in Compound Characterization and Structural Analysis, 1994, Practical Interpretation of P-31 NMR Spectra and Computer Assisted Structure Verification, 2004; co-author: (with A. Williams) A Guide to Organophosphorus Chemistry, 2000. Served to 1st lt. U.S. Army, 1954-56. Recipient Arbusovs award in phosphorus chemistry, 1997. Fellow AAAS; mem. Am. Chem. Soc. Office: 15 Aldersgate Ct Durham NC 27705 Office Phone: 919-384-2412.

QUINBY, WILLIAM ALBERT, lawyer, arbitrator, mediator; b. Oakland, Calif., May 28, 1941; s. George W. and Marge (Diaz) Q.; m. Marion Bach, Nov. 27, 1964; 1 child, Michelle Kathleen. BA, Harvard U., 1963; JD, U. Calif., San Francisco, 1967. Bar: Calif. 1967. V.p., dir., shareholder Crosby, Heafey, Roach & May, Oakland, 1967-96; mediator, arbitrator Am. Arbitration Assn. and AAA Ctr. for Mediation, San Francisco, 1996—; ptnr. Wulff, Quinby & Sochynsky, 2001—. Past bd. dirs. Haws Drinking Faucet Co., Berkeley, Calif.; mem. faculty Hastings Coll. Advocacy, San Francisco, 1980, instr. Boalt Hall Sch. Law, 1997; co-moderator Counsel Connect's Calif. ADR Discussion Group; lectr. currents devels. in banking arbitration and mediation; mem. fellowship rev. com. HEW; past trustee Nat. Pre-Suit Mediation Program; adj. prof. Hastings Coll. of the Law, U. Calif., 1998, 99. Author: Six Reasons--Besides Time and Money--to Mediate Rather Than Litigate, Why Health Care Parties Should Mediate Rather Than Litigate, Starting an ADR Practice Group in a Law Firm, Mediation Process Can Amicably Solve Business Disputes and Not a Gold Rush (But Silver, Maybe), ADR Practice in a Large Law Firm Produces No Overnight Bonanzas, Making The Most of Mediation (Effective Mediation Advocacy). Bd. dirs. Big Bros. East Bay, Oakland, 1983-87, Easter Seals Soc. East Bay, 1973; past bd. dirs. Oakland East Bay Symphony, Oakland Pub. Libr. Found.;past chmn. bd. dirs. Bay Area Tumor Inst. Scholar Harvard U., 1962-63. Fellow Coll. Comml. Arbitrators; mem. ABA (sect. on dispute resolution, chair programs, mediation coms.), Calif. Bar Assn., Alameda County Bar Assn., San Francisco Bar Assn., Contra Costa County Bar Assn., Calif. Bus. Trial Lawyers Assn., Am. Arbitration Assn. (large, complex case panel, internat., employment, constrn., and comml. mediation and arbitration panels), Oakland C. of C. (past bd. dirs., exec. com.), Alameda County Barristers Club (bd. dirs., pres. 1972), Harvard Club, San Francisco Calimari Club, Am. Coll. Civil Trial Mediators, Mediation Soc. Republican. Avocations: running, skiing, tennis, travel, gardening. Office: Wulff Quinby & Sochynsky Dispute Resolution 1901 Harrison St Ste 1420 Oakland CA 94612-3582 Office Phone: 510-663-5220. Personal E-mail: wquinby@aol.com.

QUINCE, PEGGY A., state supreme court chief justice; b. Norfolk, Va., Jan. 3, 1948; m. Fred L. Buckine; children: Peggy LaVerne, Laura LaVerne. BS in Zoology, Howard U., 1970; JD, Cath. U. of Am., 1975; LLD (hon.), Stetson U., 1999, St. Thomas U., 2004. Hearing officer Rental Accomodations Office, Washington; pvt. practice Norfolk, 1977-78, Bradenton, Fla., 1978-80; asst. atty. gen. criminal divsn. Atty. Gen.'s Office, 1980; apptd. 2d Dist. Ct. of Appeals, 1994-98; justice Fla. Supreme Ct., 1998—, chief justice, 2008—. Lectr. in field. Former asst. Sunday sch. tchr., former mem. #3 usher bd. New Hope Missionary Bapt. Ch.; active Jack and Jill of Am., Inc., Urban League, NAACP, Tampa Orgn. for Black Affairs. Recipient award Cath.'s Neighborhood Legal Svcs. Clinic, Margaret Brent Women Lawyers Achievement award, 2007, Fla. Women's Hall Of Fame. Mem. Nat. Bar Assn., Fla. Bar, Va. State Bar, George Edgecomb Bar Assn., Fla. Assn. Women Lawyers, Tallahassee Women Lawyers, William H. Stafford Inn. Ct., Alpha Kappa Alpha. Office: Fla Supreme Ct 500 S Duval St Tallahassee FL 32399-1925 Office Phone: 850-922-5624. Business E-Mail: Larryg@flcourts.org.*

QUINDLEN, ANNA, journalist, writer; b. Phila., July 8, 1952; d. Robert V. and Prudence Quindlen; m. Gerald Krovatin; children: Quindlen, Christopher, Maria. BA, Barnard Coll., 1974. Reporter New York Post, NYC, 1974-77; gen. assignment, city hall reporter New York Times, NYC, 1977-81, columnist About New York, 1981-83, dep. met. editor, 1983-85, columnist Life in the 30's syndicated, 1986-89, columnist Public and Private, 1990-94; full-time novelist, 1995—; columnist, "Last Word" Newsweek mag. Author: (novels) Object Lessons, 1991, One True Thing, 1994, Black and Blue, 1998, Blessings, 2000, Rise and Shine, 2006, (non-fiction) A Short Guide to a Happy Life, 2000, Being Perfect, 2005 (Publishers Weekly Bestseller non-fiction list, 2005), Good Dog. Stay, 2007, (children's books) The Tree That Came to Stay, 1992, Happily Ever After, 1997, (compilation) Living Out Loud, 1988, Thinking Out Loud, 1993, Loud and Clear, 2004; wrote text for: coffee table pictorial Naked Babies, 1996, Siblings, 1998. Bd. mem. Nightingale-Bamford Sch., NYC, NARAL Found. Recipient Mike Berger award for disting. reporting, 1983, Pulitzer Prize for commentary, 1992, Amelia Earhart award, Crittenton Women's Union, 2006; named Woman of Yr., Glamour Mag., 1991. Mem.: Planned Parenthood Fedn. of Am. (bd. adv.), Author's Guild (coun. mem.), Bd Trustees, Barnard Coll. (chmn. 2003—). Achievements include being first writer to ever appear on fiction, nonfiction & self-help NewYork Times Best Seller lists. Office: c/o ICM 40 W 57th St New York NY 10019-4001

QUINET, ELAINE MARIE, molecular biologist, researcher; b. NYC, Feb. 28, 1955; d. James J. and Josephine M. Quinet; life ptnr. David J. Shuey. BS, Rutgers U., Douglass Coll., NB, NJ, 1977; PhD, George Wash. U., Washington, 1986. Postdoc. fellow, dept. medicine Columbia U., Coll. Physicians and Surgeons, NYC, 1987—90; prin. rsch. scientist II Wyeth Rsch., Dept. Cardiovasc., Metabolic Diseases, Collegeville, Pa., 1992—. Contbr. articles to sci. publs. Mem.: NY Lipid Rsch. Club, Rockefeller U. (NYC) (pres. elect 1998—99), Am. Heart Assn., Coun. Arteriosclerosis. Achievements include patents for nucleic acid molecule encoding a novel estrogen receptor beta variant; methods and reagents for identifying inhibitors of proteolysis of membrane-associated proteins; patents pending for lipoxygenase modulation; quinolines useful in treating cardiovascular disease. Office: Wyeth Rsch 500 Arcola Rd RN 2226 Collegeville PA 19426 Business E-Mail: quinete@wyeth.com.

QUINLAN, CATHERINE, library director; MusB, Queens U.; MLS, Dalhousie U.; MBA, Meml. U. Newfoundland. Dir. librs., chief libr. U. Western Ontario; univ. libr. U. BC, 1997—2007, dir. Irving K. Barber Learning Ctr., 2004—07; dean librs. U. So. Calif., 2007—. Mem.: Harry Hawthorne Found., Canadian Libr. Assn., Canadian Assn. Rsch. Libraries, Assn. Rsch. Libraries, Golden Key Soc., Coalition for Networked Info. Avocations: playing chamber music, opera, queuing theory, running. Office: U So Calif Dean Libr Los Angeles CA 90089 Office Phone: 213-821-2344. Business E-Mail: cquinlan@usc.edu.

QUINLAN, GUY CHRISTIAN, lawyer; b. Cambridge, Mass., Oct. 28, 1939; m. Mary-Ella Holst, Apr. 18, 1987. AB, Harvard Coll., Cambridge, Mass., 1960; JD, Harvard U., Cambridge, 1963. Bar: NY 1964, US Dist. Ct. (so. and ea. dists.) NY 1965, US Ct. Appeals (2d cir.) 1967, US Supreme Ct. 1969, US Ct. Appeals (8th cir.) 1973, (10th cir.) 1977, (4th cir.) 1993, (11th cir.) 1995, US Tax Ct. 1977. Assoc. Clifford Chance, NYC, 1963-70, ptnr., 1970—90, of counsel, 1991—2007, cons., 2007—. Past pres. Unitarian Universalist Svc. Com., Yorkville Common Pantry; Unitarian Universalist Dist. of Met. N.Y.; mem. Adv. Coun. Ministerial Studies, Harvard U. Div. Sch., NGO Com. Disarmament Peace and Security; chair nuclear disarmament task force All Souls Unitarian Ch. Mem.: ABA, Lawyers Com. on Nuclear Policy (bd. mem.), Amnesty Internat., Arm Control Assn., Harvard Club. Democrat. Office: Clifford Chance US LLP 31 W 52d St New York NY 10019-6131 Office Phone: 212-878-8219. Business E-Mail: guy.quinlan@cliffordchance.com.

QUINLAN, J(OSEPH) MICHAEL, lawyer; b. Rockville Centre, NY, Nov. 2, 1941; s. Joseph Charles Quinlan and Harriet Veronica (Gorman) Greene; m. Agnes Mary Quinlan, May 5, 1973; children: Kara Quinlan Davis, Kristen Quinlan Calder. BS in Social Sci., Fairfield U., Conn., 1963; JD, Fordham U., Bronx, NY, 1966; LLM, George Washington U., Washington, DC, 1970. Bar: NY 1966, DC 1967, Va. 1993, US Ct. Mil. Appeals 1967, US Supreme Ct. 1970. Exec. asst. to warden US Penitentiary, Leavenworth, Kans., 1973-74; of counsel N.E. region US Bur. Prisons, Phila., 1974-75, exec. asst. to dir. Washington, 1975-78, from dep. asst. dir. to dir., 1985-92; supt. Fed. Prison Camp, Eglin AFB, Fla., 1978-80; warden Fed. Correctional Inst., Otisville, NY, 1980-85; dir. strategic planning Corrections Corp. Am., 1993-97; dir., bd. dirs. UK Detention Svcs., London, 1993-97; vice-chmn., bd. trustees Prison Realty Trust, 1997-99. 1st vice-chmn. bd. dirs. Horton Meml. Hosp., Middletown, NY, 1982-85; CEO Prison Realty Trust, 1997-99; pres. Corrections Corp of Am., 1999-2000, exec. v.p., COO, 2000-02, sr. v.p., 2002—. Lt. col. USAFR, 1966—93. Recipient SES Presdl. Disting. Rank award, 1988, SES Presdl. Meritorious Rank award, 1991, Exceptional Leadership award US Atty. Gen., 1991, Nat. Pub. Svc. award Nat. Acad. Pub. Adminstrn./Am. Soc. Pub. Adminstrn., 1992, John Marshall award Dept. Justice, 1993, E.R. Cass award ACA, 2003. Fellow Nat. Acad. Pub. Adminstrn. (chair prisons com.); mem. ABA (corrections and sentencing com. 1985—), Am. Correctional Assn., Nat. Com. Comm. Corrections, NY Bar Assn., DC Bar Assn., Va. Bar Assn. Roman Catholic. Avocation: reading. Home: 1462 Evans Farm Dr Mc Lean VA 22101-5652 E-mail: mike.quinlan@correctionscorp.com.

QUINLAN, THOMAS J., III, printing company executive; b. Feb. 3, 1963; m. Diane Quinlan; 4 children. BS, Pace U. Sr. v.p., treas. World Color Press Inc.; exec. v.p., treas. Walter Industries, Inc., 2000, Moore Wallace Inc., 2000—02, exec. v.p., bus. integration, 2003—04; exec. v.p. ops. R.R. Donnelley & Sons Co., Chgo., 2004—06, group pres. glob. services, CFO, 2006—07, pres., CEO, 2007. Office: RR Donnelley & Sons Co 111 S Wacker Dr Chicago IL 60606-4301

QUINLIVAN, GARY M., dean, educator; b. NY; s. Quinlivan and Bolster; m. Sandra Sue Scheumann; 1 child, Vanessa Repasi. PhD, U. Albany (SUNY), NY, 1981. Dean McKenna Sch. St. Vincent Coll., Latrobe, Pa., 1981—2008. Contbr. articles to profl. jours. Editl. exec. bd. markets & morality Acton Inst., Grand Rapids, Mich., 2002—08. Recipient Fulbright award, CIES US govt., 1988—89, award, U. Albany, 1975—81, Carnegie Melon U., 2000, Prof. of the Yr., St. Vincent Coll., 1993, Thoburn award, 2007, Hon. Full Prof., Shandong U. PR China, 1997, Tchg. award, CMU & SVC; grant, Acton Inst., 2002—08, CIBER fellowship, U. Pitts., 2005. Mem.: Am. Econ. Assn., Nat. Assn. of Scholars, Omicron Delta Epsilon, Delta Mu Delta, Fulbright Assn. Roman Cath. Avocations: reading, travel. Office: Saint Vincent Coll 300 Fraser Purchase Rd Latrobe PA 15650 Office Fax: 724-537-4599.

QUINLY, SCOTT ANDERSON, secondary school educator; s. Mike K. and Karen Jean Quinly; m. Cynthia Annett Kinnear, Dec. 15, 2007; 1 child, Ashlyn Nichole. BS in Edn., Pittsburg State U., Kans., 2001. Cert. tchg. Kans. and Mo., 2001. Coach Carthage Sch. Dist., Mo., 1998—2008, tchr., 2001—08; coach Columbus Unified Sch. Dist., Kans., 1998—2008, tchr., 2008—. Mem. Abu Ben Adem Shrine Club, Springfield, Mo., 2005—08. Mem.: Kans. State HS Football Coaches Assn. Conservative.

QUINN, ALEXANDER JAMES, bishop; b. Cleve., Apr. 8, 1932; Attended, St. Charles Coll., Catonsville, Md., St. Mary Sem., Cleve., Lateran Sem., Rome, Cleve. State U. Ordained priest Diocese of Cleve., 1958; ordained bishop, 1983; aux. bishop Diocese of Cleve., 1983—2008, vicar western region, aux. bishop emeritus, 2008—. Roman Catholic. Office: 2500 Elyria Ave Lorain OH 44055-1367 E-mail: ajquinn@dioceseofcleveland.org.

QUINN, ANDREW PETER, JR., lawyer, retired insurance company executive; b. Providence, Oct. 22, 1923; s. Andrew Peter and Margaret (Canning) Q.; m. Sara G. Bullard, May 30, 1952 (dec. Feb. 2004); 1 child, Emily H. AB, Brown U., 1945; LLB, Yale U., 1950. Bar: R.I. 1949, Mass. 1960, U.S. Tax Ct. 1960, U.S. Supreme Ct. 1986. Pvt. practice, Providence, 1950-59; ptnr. Letts & Quinn, 1950-59; with Mass. Mut. Life Ins. Co., Springfield, 1959—88, exec. v.p., gen. counsel, 1971-88; of counsel Day, Berry & Howard, Hartford, Conn. and Boston, 1988-99; retired, 1999. Pres., trustee MML Series Investment Fund, 1971-88; pres. Sargasso Mut. Ins. Co., Ltd., 1986-89, chmn. bd. dirs., 1989-93. Trustee, MacDuffie Sch., 1974-87, chmn. bd., 1978-85; trustee Baystate Med., Springfield, 1977-80. Lt. (j.g.) USNR, 1944-46. Mem. ABA (co-chmn. nat. conf. lawyers and life ins. cos. 1973), Assn. Life Ins. Counsel (pres. 1983-84, Anderson Disting. Svc. award 1998), Am. Coun. Life Ins. (chmn. legal sect. 1971), Life Ins. Assn. Mass. (chmn. exec. com. 1975-77), Brown U. Alumni Assn. (bd. dirs. 1969-72), NY Yacht Club, Dunes Club(Fla.), Hillsboro Club(Fla.). Home (Winter): 1205 Meadow Ridge Redding CT 06896 Home (Summer): 130 Shadow Farm Way Unit 31 Wakefield RI 02879

QUINN, ANDREW THOMAS, urban planner; b. Balt., Sept. 11, 1984; s. Thomas Charles and Kliphardt Joan Quinn. BA, Columbia U., NYC, 2006. Coord. NY Acad. Medicine, NYC, 2006—. Office: NY Acad Medicine 1216 5th Ave New York NY 10029 Business E-Mail: aquinn@nyam.org.

QUINN, ART JAY, retired veterinarian, educator; b. Bennington, Kans., Aug. 2, 1936; s. Arthur Jess and Edith Mae (Reigle) Q. BS, Kans. State U., 1959, DVM, 1961. Diplomate Am. Coll. Vet. Ophthalmologists. Pvt. practice, Albuquerque, 1961-75; field rep. Am. Animal Hosp. Assn., Denver, 1968-69; prof. Coll. Vet. Medicine, Okla. State U., Stillwater, 1975-95, prof. emeritus, 1995—. Contbr. articles to profl. jours. Capt. U.S. Army, 1962-64. Recipient Small Animal Proficiency award, Kans. Vet. Med. Assn., 1961, Upjohn award, 1961, Western Region Practitioner award, AAHA, 1993, Meritorious Svc. award, Western Vet. Conf., 2002; named to Hall of Fame, Vet. Ophthalmology, Am. Biog. Inst., 2009; grant, Sarkey Found., 1981. Mem.: AVMA, Am. Coll. Vet. Ophthalmologists, Am. Animal Hosp. Assn. Democrat. Home: 210 Cedar Ln Diamond Head Sand Springs OK 74063-5309

QUINN, BRADY (BRADY TYLER QUINN), professional football player; b. Dublin, Ohio, Oct. 27, 1984; s. Ty and Robin Quinn. BBA in Fin. Admin., U. Notre Dame, South Bend, Ind., 2006, BA in Polit. Sci., 2007. Quarterback Cleve. Browns, 2007—. Recipient Sammy Baugh trophy, 2005, College Football Player of Yr. award (Maxwell award), Maxwell Football Club, 2006, Johnny Unitas Golden Arm award, 2006; named Cingular All-Am. Player of Yr., 2006, Second Team All-American, AP, 2006. Achievements include holding 30 University of Notre Dame Fighting Irish passing records including: career yardage, single season yardage, single game yardage & touchdown passes. Office: Cleveland Browns 76 Lou Groza Blvd Berea OH 44017*.

QUINN, BRIAN PATRICK, physics professor; m. Carol Couvrette; 1 child, Michael Ray. PhD, MIT, Cambridge, Mass., 1984. Rsch. assoc. MIT, 1978—84; postdoc. assoc. Carnegie Mellon U., Pitts., 1984—88, prof. physics, 1988—. Rschr. Jefferson Lab, CERN, Brookhaven Nat. Lab. Achievements include research in medium energy nuclear, particle physics. Office: Carnegie Mellon Univ Physics Dept Pittsburgh PA 15213

QUINN, CHARLES NICHOLAS, journalist; b. Utica, NY, July 28, 1930; s. Charles Dunaway and Elsa (Zarth) Q.; children— Diana David, Ben, Jane. BA, Cornell U., 1951; MS, Columbia U. Sch. Journalism, 1954. Reporter Providence Jour., 1954-56, N.Y. Herald Tribune, 1956-62; corr. NBC News, NYC, 1962-66, Washington, 1966-71, Rome, 1971-74; mng. editor, chief corr. NBC Radio News, Washington, 1978-80; corr. Ind. Network News, Washington, 1980-81; electronic media rep. Am. Petroleum Inst., Washington, 1981-91. Reported on hunger in U.S. on: Huntley-Brinkley Report, (co-recipient Emmy 1969). Served with arty. U.S. Army, 1951-53. Mem. Nat. Press Club (bd. govs. 1990-91).

QUINN, CHRISTINE CALLAGHAN, city councilwoman; b. Glen Cove, NY, July 25, 1966; d. Mary and Lawrence Quinn; life ptnr. Kim Catullo. BA in Urban Studies and Edn., Trinity Coll., Hartford, Conn., 1988. With Assn. Neighborhood and Housing Development, 1989—91; chief staff Councilman Thomas K. Duane, 1992—96; exec. dir. NYC Gay and Lesbian Anti-Violence Project, 1996—98; city councilwoman Dist. 3 NY City Coun., 1999—, spkr., 2006—. Mem. NYC Police/Community Relations Task Force; del. DNC, 2000, mem. platform com., 04. Named one of Fifty Most Powerful Women in NYC, NY Post, Forty Under Forty, Gotham Mag., The 50 Most Powerful Women in NYC, NY Post, 2007, 2008. Avocation: reading. Office: Dist Office Christine Quinn 224 W 30th St Ste 1206 New York NY 10001*

QUINN, DONAL, diagnostic equipment company executive; BS in Econs., Cork U., Ireland. Exec. positions with Mallinckrodt Med., Abbott Labs.; group pres. Biology products divsn. Dade Behring, Deerfield, Ill., 1998-99, pres. Europe, Mid. East and Africa divsn., 1999—2000, pres. internat., 2000—02, pres. global customer mgmt., 2002—07, COO, 2007; exec. v.p., chief customer officer Siemens Healthcare Diagnostics, 2007—08, CEO, 2008—. Fellow: Inst. Chartered Mgmt. Accountants. Office: Siemens Healthcare Diagnostics 1717 Deerfield Rd Deerfield IL 60015-0778*

QUINN, EUGENE FREDERICK, diplomat, minister; b. Oil City, Pa., Sept. 16, 1935; s. Eugene Frederick and Wilma (Scott) Q.; m. Charlotte Alison Smith, Aug. 25, 1965 (dec. June 2000); children: Christopher Edward Vermilye, Alison Moore; m. Carolyn Tanner Irish, June 14, 2001. AB, Allegheny Coll., 1957; MA in African studies, UCLA, 1966, MA in History, 1969, PhD in History, 1970; diploma in theol. studies, Va. Theol. Sem., 1974. Ordained to ministry Episcopal Ch., 1975. Info. officer Am. Embassy, Rabat, Morocco, 1958-59, cultural affairs officer Port-au-Prince, Haiti, 1959-61; country pub. affairs officer Ouagadougou, Upper Volta, 1961-63; field rep. Joint U.S. Affairs Office, Saigon, Vietnam, 1964-66; country pub. affairs officer Am. embassy, Yaounde, Cameroon, 1966-68, counselor embassy for press and cultural affairs Prague, Czechoslovakia, 1975-78; apptd. career mem. Sr. Fgn. Service with class of counselor, 1981, minister-counselor, 1986; dir. fgn. service personnel Voice of Am., Washington, 1981-83; dep. asst. sec. pub. affairs Dept. Transp., 1983-85; dir. Office Pub. Affairs Voice of Am., 1985-86; internat. coord. for Bicentennial U.S. Constn., dir.'s office U.S. Info. Agy., 1986-91; cons. internat. affairs, 1992—. Dir. rule of law programs, conf. on security and cooperation in Europe, Office of Dem. Instns. and Human Rights, Warsaw, 1993-95. Author: Federalist Papers' Reader, 1992, To Heal the Earth, 1994, Democracy at Dawn, Notes from Poland and Points East, 1998, Human Rights and You, 1998, French Overseas Empire, 2000, To Be A Pilgrim, The Anglican Ethos in History, 2001, African Saints, Martyrs and Holy People, 2002, Courthouse at Indian Creek, 2002; co-author: Pride, Faith and Fear: Islam in Africa, 2003, Building the Goodly Fellowship of Faith, and History of the Episcopal Church in Utah 1867-1996, 2004, In Search of Salt, a History of the Beti People 1970-1960, 2006, The Sum of All Heresies, The Image of Islam in Western Thought, 2008; editor: Diplomacy for the Seventies, 1969; mem. editl. bd. Fgn. Svc. Jour., 1972—75, Dept. State Open Forum Jour., 1982—83; contbr. articles to profl. jours., chapters to books. Trustee N.J. Ednl. Consortium, 1970-72; coord. USIA Yorktown Bicentennial Activities, 1981; assisting clergyman St. Columba's Ch., Washington, 1973-75, 78-81, Nat. Cathedral, Washington, 1981-82, 95-2001, Grace Ch., Silver Spring, Md., 1981-82, Epiphany Ch., Washington, 1983, 86-92; chaplain Anglo-Am. Diplomatic Cmty., Prague, 1975-78, Warsaw, 1993-95; vicar St. James Ch., Bowie, Md., 1983-84; rector Christ Ch., Accokeek, Md., 1985, St. John's Ch., Pomonkey, Md.; assisting clergyman All Saints Ch., Chevy Chase, Md., 1981-82, 86-90; interim pastor Ch. of Holy Communion, Washington, 1992-93, St. Andrew's Leonardtown, Md., 1998-99; chair environ. com. Episcopal Diocese of Washington Peace Commn., 1991-92; mem. Environ. Stewardship Team, Episcopal Ch., 1992-95. Recipient Meritorious Honor award USIA, 1964, 66, 85; Merit medal Republic of Vietnam, 1965, medal of honor 2d class, 1966 Personal E-mail: frederickquinn@hotmail.com.

QUINN, FRANCIS ANTHONY, bishop emeritus; b. LA, Sept. 11, 1921; Attended, St. Joseph's Coll., Mountain View, Calif., St. Patrick's Sem., Menlo Park, Calif., Cath. U., Washington, U. Calif., Berkeley. Ordained priest Archdiocese of San Francisco, 1946, aux. bishop, 1978—79; ordained bishop, 1978; bishop Diocese of Sacramento, 1979—94, bishop emeritus, 1994—. Roman Catholic. Office: 2110 Broadway Sacramento CA 95818-2518 Office Phone: 916-733-0200.

QUINN, FRANCIS FLAHERTY, lawyer; b. Phila., Jan. 22, 1946; AB with honors, St. Joseph's U., 1967; JD, U. Pa., 1971. Bar: Pa. 1972, N.J. 1993, N.Y. 1995, U.S. Supreme Ct. 1985. Law clk. to Hon. Daniel H. Huyett III U.S. Dist. Ct. (ea. dist.) Pa., 1971-73; ptnr. Lavin, O'Neill, Ricci, Cedrone & DiSipio, NYC, 1973—. Lectr. in field. Mem. Phila. Bar Assn., Def. Rsch. and Trial Lawyers Assn., NY Assn. Def. Counsel, Bar Assn. City of NY, NY State Bar Assn., Alpha Sigma Nu. Office: Lavin O'Neil Ricci Cedrone & DiSipio 420 Lexington Ave Ste 2900 New York NY 10170 Office Phone: 212-415-8201. Business E-Mail: fquinn@lavin-law.com.

QUINN, FRANCIS XAVIER, arbitrator, mediator, writer, law educator; b. Dunmore, Pa., June 9, 1932; s. Frank T. and Alice B. (Maher) Q.; m. Marlene Stoker Quinn; children: Kimberly, Catherine, Cameron, Lindsay, Megan, Savannah, Jackson Blair. BA, Fordham U., NYC, 1956, MA, 1958; STB, Woodstock Coll., Md., 1964; MS in Indsl. Rels., Loyola U., Chgo., 1966; PhD in Indsl. Rels., Calif. Western U., LA, 1976. Assoc. dir. Inst. Indsl. Rels. St. Joseph's Coll., Phila., 1966-68; Manpower fellow Temple U., Phila., 1969-74, asst. to dean Sch. Bus. Adminstrn., 1972-78. Arbitrator Fed. Mediation and Conciliation Svc., Nat. Mediation Bd., Am. Arbitration Assn., Nat. Assn. Railroad Referees, Dem. Nat. Steering Com.; apptd. to Presdl. Emergency Bd., 1975, to Fgn. Svc. Grievance Bd., 1976, 78, 80. Author: The Ethical Aftermath of Automation, 1963, Ethics and Advertising, 1965, Population Ethics, 1968, The Evolving Role of Women in the World of Work, 1969, Developing Community Responsibility, 1970; editor: The Ethical Aftermath Series; contbr. articles to profl. jours. Chmn. Tulsa City-County Mayor's Task Force to Combat Homelessness, 1991-92; mem. exec. bd. Tulsa Met. Ministries, 1990-92, Labor-Religion Coun. Okla., 1990-98; pres. pastoral coun. Ft. Worth Holy Family Roman Cath. Ch., 2000-03, formation adv. bd., 2002-05. Named Tchr. of Yr. Freedom Found., 1959; recipient Human Rels. award City of Phila., 1970; inducted into Hall of Fame, Internat. Police Assn., 2000. Fellow Coll. of Labor and Employment Lawyers; mem. Nat. Acad. Arbitrators (v.p. 1999-2001), Indsl. Rels. Rsch. Assn., Assn. for Social Econs., Soc. for Dispute Resolution, Am. Arbitration Assn. (arbitrator), Nat. Assn. Railroad Refs. (pres. 2000-04), Internat. Soc. Labor Law and Social Security. Democrat. Home: 4213 Blackhaw Ave Fort Worth TX 76109-1618 Office Phone: 817-924-7372. Personal E-mail: Quinnfrank@msn.com.

QUINN, JACK (JOHN M. QUINN), lobbyist, lawyer; b. NYC, Aug. 16, 1949; m. Susan Monroney; children from previous marriage: Jonathan, Megan, Caitlin, Brendan 1 stepchild, Jocelyn. AB, Georgetown U., 1971, JD, 1975. Bar: D.C. 1975. Staff mem. US Senate Select Com. on Nutrition & Human Needs, Washington, 1969-73, Democratic Nat. Com., 1973; chief legis. asst. to Senator Floyd Haskell US Senate, Washington, 1974—75; campaign mgr. Morris Udall Presdl. Campaign, 1975—76; ptnr. Arnold & Porter LLP, Washington, 1976—93; dep. chief of staff, counsel to V.P. The White House, Washington, 1993—95, counsel to Pres., 1995—97; co-founder, co-chmn. Quinn Gillespie & Assocs., LLC, Washington, 2000—. Adj. prof. law Georgetown U., 1990-91; bd. dirs. Fannie Mae (Fed. Nat. Mortgage Assn.), 1997-2000 Editor: Georgetown Law Jour., 1974-75. Named one of The Top 50 Lobbyists, Washingtonian mag., 2007. Mem. ABA (mem. adv. commn., standing com. on eletion law, adminstrv. law sect., com. on election law). Democrat. Office: Quinn Gillespie & Associates LLC 133 Connecticut Ave NW 5th Fl Washington DC 20036*

QUINN, JACK (JOHN FRANCIS QUINN), former congressman, English language educator; b. South Buffalo, NY, Apr. 13, 1951; s. Jack Sr. and Norma Ide Q.; m. Mary Beth McAndrews, 1974; children: Jack III, Kara. BA, Siena Coll.; MA in Edn., SUNY, Buffalo. English language tchr. Orchard Park (N.Y.) Schs., 1973—83; town councilman Town of Hamburg, 1982—84, also town supv.; mem. U.S. Congress from 30th N.Y. Dist., 1993—2002, U.S. Congress from 27th N.Y. Dist., 2003—05; mem. transp. and infrastructure com., chmn. subcom. on railroads, mem. vet. affairs com.; pres. Cassidy & Associates, Washington, 2005—. Recipient Humanitarian award Erie County for the Disabled, Pub. Svc. award Niagara Frontier Parks and Recreation Soc., Disting. Grad. award Nat. Cath. Elem. Schs. Assn., Bronze Good Citizen medal SAR, New Horizons award Drug Edn. of Internat. Assn. of Lions Club, Red, White and Blue award Am. Legion of N.Y., Honor medal Hilbert Coll., Fin. Reporting award Govt. Fin. Officer's Assn., Disting. Career Svc. award Siena Coll., 1995. Mem. Hamburg C. of C., Greater Buffalo C. of C., Buffalo KC, Hamburg Kiwanis Club. Republican. Roman Catholic. Office: Cassidy & Associates 700 13th St NW Washington DC 20005

QUINN, JANE BRYANT, journalist, writer; b. Niagara Falls, NY, Feb. 5, 1939; d. Frank Leonard and Ada (Laurie) Bryant; m. David Conrad Quinn, June 10, 1967; children: Matthew Alexander, Justin Bryant. BA magna cum laude, Middlebury Coll., 1960. Assoc. editor Insiders Newsletter, NYC, 1962-65, co-editor, 1966-67; sr. editor Cowles Book Co., NYC, 1968; editor-in-chief Bus. Week Letter, NYC, 1969-73, gen. mgr., 1973-74; syndicated fin. columnist Wash. Post Writers Group, 1974—2001; contbr. fin. column to Women's Day mag., 1974-95, Good Housekeeping, 1995—2007; contbr. NBC News and Info. Service, 1976-77; bus. corr. WCBS-TV, NYC, 1979, CBS-TV News, 1980-87, ABC-TV Home Show, 1991-93; contbg. editor Newsweek mag., 1978—; columnist Bloomberg Com., 2007—. Host PBS personal fin. series Take Charge!, 1988; bd. dirs. Bloomberg LP., GSE Systems Inc., 2008- Author: Everyone's Money Book, 1979, 2d edit., 1980, Making the Most of Your Money, 1991, 2d edit., 1997, A Hole in the Market, 1994, Smart and Simple Financial Strategies for Busy People, 2006; contbr. (software program) Quicken Financial Planner, 1995. Dean's coun. Harvard Sch. Pub. Health; mem. bd. advisors Jerome Levy Econs. Inst. Bard Coll. Recipient Emmy award for outstanding coverage fin. on TV, Gerald Loeb award for lifetime achievement and disting. bus. and fin. journalism, John Hancock award for excellence in bus. and fin. journalism, Janus award for excellence in TV and bus. reporting, Journalism award for excellence in personal fin. reporting, ICI-Am. U., three-time winner Nat. Press Club award for consumer journalism, two-time winner Nat. Headliner award, honored for outstanding consumer media svc., Consumer Fedn. Am.; named one of 25 Most Influential Women in US, World Almanac. Mem. Phi Beta Kappa. Office: Newsweek Inc 251 W 57th St New York NY 10019-1802 Office Phone: 212-445-4000.*

QUINN, JARUS WILLIAM, physicist, former association executive; b. West Grove, Pa., Aug. 25, 1930; s. William G. and Ellen C. (DuRoss) Q.; m. Margaret M. McNerney, June 27, 1953; children: J. Kevin, Megan, Jennifer, Colin, Kristin. BS, St. Joseph's Coll., 1952; postgrad., Johns Hopkins U., 1952-55; PhD, Cath. U. Am., 1964. Rsch. assoc. physics Johns Hopkins U., 1954-55; staff scientist Rsch. Inst. Advanced Study, 1956-57; rsch. assoc. physics Cath. U. Am., 1958-60, instr., 1961-64, asst. prof., 1965-69; exec. dir. Optical Soc. Am., Washington, 1969-93; governing bd. Am. Inst. Physics, 1973-94; pres. Stellar Focus, Sunnyvale, Calif., 1994-95. Bd. govs. Am. Assn. Engring. Socs., 1990-93. Fellow Optical Soc. Am. (Distinguished Service Award, 1993), mem. Am. Phys. Soc., Coun. Engring. and Sci. Soc. Execs. Home: 15 Forsythia Ct Durham NC 27705 E-mail: optics2010@yahoo.com.

QUINN, JEFFRY N., chemicals executive, lawyer; BS, Univ. Ky., 1981, JD, 1984. Sr. v.p. sec., gen. counsel Arch Coal Inc.; exec. v.p., chief adminstrv. officer, sec., gen. counsel Premcor Inc.; sr. v.p., gen. counsel, chief restructuring officer Solutia Inc., St. Louis, 2004—04, pres., CEO, 2004—06, chmn., pres., CEO, 2006—. Office: Solutia Inc 575 Maryville Centre Dr Saint Louis MO 63166 Business E-Mail: jnquin@solutia.com.

QUINN, JOHN ALBERT, chemical engineering professor; b. Springfield, Ill., Sept. 3, 1932; s. Edward Joseph and Marie (Von De Bur) Q.; m. Frances Wilkie Daly, June 22, 1957; children: Sarah D., Rebecca V., John E. BSChemE, U. Ill., 1954; PhDChemE, Princeton U., 1959. Mem. faculty chem. engring. U. Ill., Urbana, 1958-70; prof. U. Pa., Phila., 1971—, Robert D. Bent prof., 1978—, chmn. dept. chem. engring., 1980-85. Vis. prof. Imperial Coll. U. London, 1965-66; vis. scientist MIT, 1980; vis. prof. U. Rome/La Sapienza, 1992; mem. sci. adv. bds. Sepracor, Inc., Marlborough, Mass., 1984—, Whitaker Found., Mechanicsburg, Pa., 1987—; Mason lectr. Stanford U., 1981; Katz lectr. U. Mich., 1985; Reilly lectr. U. Notre Dame, 1987; Michael's lectr. MIT, 2001. Contbr. articles to profl. publs.; editl. advisor Jour. Membrane Sci., 1975—, Indsl. and Chem. Engring. Rsch., 1987-88, Revs. in Chem. Engring., 1980—; pioneer rschr. on mass transfer and interfacial phenomena. Sr. postdoctoral fellow NSF, 1965-66; Sherman Fairchild scholar Calif. Inst. Tech., 1985. Fellow AAAS, Am. Inst. Med. and Biol. Engring.; mem. NAE, AIChE (Allan P. Colburn award 1966, Alpha Chi Sigma award 1978), Am. Acad. Arts and Scis., Am. Chem. Soc., Internat. Soc. Oxygen Transport to Tissue, Sigma X, Phi Lambda Upsilon, Tau Beta Pi. Home: 275 E Wynnewood Rd Merion Station PA 19066-1627 Office: Univ Pa Towne Bldg 220 S 33rd St Philadelphia PA 19104-6393 Office Phone: 215-898-8503.

QUINN, JOHN B., lawyer; b. Ft. Belvoir, Va., June 20, 1951; BA magna cum laude, Claremont Men's Coll., 1973; JD cum laude, Harvard U., 1976. Bar: NY 1978, Calif. 1979. Assoc. Cravath, Swaine & Moore, 1976—79; founding ptnr. Quinn Emanual Urquhart Oliver & Hedges, LLP, 1979—. Gen. counsel Acad. Motion Picture Arts and Scis., 1987—; instr. Brigham Young U. Sch. Law, 1977; lectr. fed. practice Calif. Continuing Ed. of Bar; mem. Fed. Courts and Practice Com., Com. on Fed. Courts, Million Dollar Advocates Forum; dir. Rose Bowl Operating Co. Fellow: Internat. Acad. Trial Lawyers; mem.: ABA, Calif. Bar Assn., NY Bar Assn., Union Internationale Des Avocats, LA County Bar Assn. Office: Quinn Emanuel Urquhart Oliver & Hedges LLP 865 South Figueroa St 10th Fl Los Angeles CA 90017 Office Phone: 213-443-3000. Office Fax: 213-443-3100. E-mail: johnquinn@quinnemanuel.com.

QUINN, JOHN COLLINS, publishing executive, editor; b. Providence, Oct. 24, 1925; s. John A. and Kathryn H. (Collins) Q.; m. Lois R. Richardson, June 20, 1953; children: John Collins, Lo-anne, Richard B., Christopher A. AB, Providence Coll., 1945; MS, Columbia U. Sch. Journalism, 1946. Successively copy boy, reporter, asst. city editor, Washington corr., asst. mng. editor, day mng. editor Providence Jour.-Bull., 1943-66; with Gannett Co. Inc., Rochester, NY, 1966-90; exec. editor Rochester Democrat & Chronicle, Times-Union, 1966-71; gen. mgr. Gannett News Service, 1967-80, pres., 1980-88, v.p. parent co., 1971-75, sr. v.p. news and info., 1975-80, sr. v.p., chief news exec. parent co., editor USA TODAY, 1983-89; exec. v.p. Gannett Co., Arlington, Va., 1983-90; trustee Gannett Found., Arlington, 1988-91; dep. chmn. Freedom Forum, Arlington, 1991-97, trustee, 1991—. Named to R.I. Hall of Fame, 1975, Editor of Yr. Nat. Press Found., 1986; recipient William Allen White citation, 1987, Women in Communications Headliner award, 1986, Paul Miller/Okla. State U. medallion, 1988 Al Neuharth award for Excellence in the Media, 2007. Mem. AP Mng. Editors (past dir., nat. pres. 1973-74), Am. Soc. Newspaper Editors (dir., chmn. editorial bd., chmn. conv. program, nat. pres. 1982-83) Roman Catholic. Home: 365 S Atlantic Ave Cocoa Beach FL 32931-2719 Home Phone: 321-784-6165, 401-364-7726; Office Phone: 401-364-9282.

QUINN, JOHN J., lawyer; b. Sept. 19, 1932; BA, Univ. So. Calif., 1954, JD, 1959. Bar: Calif. 1959, US Supreme Ct. 1965. Ptnr., LA Office Mgmt. Arnold & Porter, LA. Past chmn. US Senator Barbara Boxer Fed. Judicial Selection Com.; chmn., Disciplinary Com. US Dist. Ct., Ctrl. Calif., 1995—2001. Recipient Learned Hand award, Am. Jewish Com., Disting. Svc. award, U.S. Ct. Appeals, Ninth Cir. Fellow: Am. Col. Trial Lawyers; mem.: ABA (mem. Ho. of Dels. 1977—82), L.A. County Bar Assn. (pres. 1976—77, Shattuck-Price award), Am. Bd. Trial Advocates, Order of the Coif. Office: Arnold & Porter 777 S Figueroa St Los Angeles CA 90017-2513 Office Phone: 213-243-4080. Office Fax: 213-243-4199. Business E-Mail: john.j.quinn@aporter.com.

QUINN, JOHN JAMES, political science professor; s. Dennis P. and Joan C. Quinn; m. Renuka Srikitja, June 30, 2008; 1 child, John James Jack Jr. BA, St. Vincent Coll., Latrobe, Pa., 1981, BA, 1983; MA, UCLA, 1992, PhD, 1995. Cert. profl. tchr. Commonwealth, Pa., 1983, in social studies, English State Calif., 1987. Assoc. prof. polit. sci. Truman State U., Kirksville, Mo., 1996—. Vis. prof. polit. sci. U. Ghana-Legon, 2001. Contbr. chapters to books, articles to profl. publs. Vol. tchr. Peace Corps, Kisangani, 1983—85, regional rep., 1985—86. Office: Truman State Univ 100 E Normal St Kirksville MO 63501 Business E-Mail: jquinn@truman.edu.

QUINN, JOHN MICHAEL, bishop; b. Detroit, Dec. 17, 1945; s. George and Mary Quinn. BA, Sacred Heart Sem., Detroit; MDiv, St. John's Provincial Sem., Plymouth; M in Religious Studies, U. Detroit/Mercy, M in Systemic Theology. Ordained priest Archdiocese of Detroit, 1972, assoc. dir. justice & peace, assoc. dir. religious edn., dir. edn. dept., 1990—2003; ordained bishop, 2003; aux. bishop for ctrl. region Archdiocese of Detroit, 2003—08; coadjutor bishop Diocese of Winona, Minn., 2008—09, bishop, 2009—. Cardinal's del. Sacred Heart Major Sem., Detroit, adj. faculty, also bd. trustees; bd. trustees Madonna U., Livonia, Mich., Loyola HS, Detroit. Bd. mem. New Detroit, Salvation Army, Habitat for Humanity. Mem.: Internat. Order of Alhambra, Equestrian Order of the Holy Sepulchre of Jerusalem (chaplain), US Conf. Cath. Bishops (African Am. Catholics com., Cath. Campus Ministry com., episcopal advisor Commn. on Accreditation & Certification). Roman Catholic. Office: Diocese of Winona PO Box 588 55 W Sanborn St Winona MN 55987 Office Phone: 507-454-4643. Office Fax: 507-454-8106.*

QUINN, JOHN RAPHAEL, archbishop emeritus; b. Riverside, Calif., Mar. 28, 1929; s. Ralph J. and Elizabeth (Carroll) Q. Student, St. Francis Sem., Immaculate Heart Sem., San Diego, 1947-48; Ph.B., Gregorian U., Rome, 1950, Licentiate in Sacred Theology, 1954, S.T.L., 1954. Ordained priest Diocese of San Diego, Calif., 1953; assoc. pastor St. George Ch., Ontario, Calif., 1954-55; prof. theology Immaculate Heart Sem., San Diego, 1955-62, vice rector, 1960-62; pres. St. Francis Coll. Sem., El Cajon, Calif., 1962-64; rector Immaculate Heart Sem., 1964-68; ordained bishop, 1967; aux. bishop, vicar gen. Diocese of San Diego, 1967-72; bishop Diocese of Okla. City-Tulsa, 1971—72; archbishop Archdiocese of Okla. City, 1972—77, Archdiocese of San Francisco, Calif., 1977—95, archbishop emeritus, 1995—. Provost U. San Diego, 1968-72; pastor St. Therese Parish, San Diego, 1969; apptd. consultor to Sacred Congregation for the Clergy in Rome, 1971; pres. Nat. Conf. Cath. Bishops, 1977-80, chmn. Com. of Liturgy; chmn. com. on Family Life U.S. Cath. Conf.; chmn. Bishops' Com. on Pastoral Rsch. and Practices, Bishops' Com. on Doctrine; mem. Bishops' Com. on Sems., Pontifical Commn., Seattle, 1987-88, Bishops' Com. for Pro-Life Activities, 1989—; apptd. pontifical del. for religious in U.S., 1983; pres. Calif. Cath. Conf., 1985; mem. Synod of Bishops, Rome, 1994; chmn. Nat. Conf. Cath. Bishops Com. on Doctrine, 1994—; vis. fellow Campion Hall, U. Oxford, 1996. Trustee U. San Diego, 1991-93. Mem. Cath. Theol. Soc. Am., Canon Law Soc. Am., Am. Cath. Hist. Soc. Roman Catholic. Address: 445 Church St San Francisco CA 94114-1720 Home: 2140 Santa Cruz Ave Apt A103 Menlo Park CA 94025-6331

QUINN, KATHERINE SARAH, psychologist; d. George and Esther Blank; m. Ed Quinn (div. 1994); children: Adam(dec.), Molly Quinn Panepinto. BA in Psychology, U. Nev., 1982, MA in Psychology, 1987; PhD in Psychology (hon.), Calif. Sch. Profl. Psychology, 1999. Intern Children's Behavioral Svcs., Las Vegas, 1980—83, child devel. specialist, 1984—85; rsch. devel. coord. San Diego County Mental Health, 1988—97; intern Southwood Hosp., San Diego, 1991—92; therapist Child Sexual Abuse Treatment Ctr., San Diego, 1992—93; post-doctoral intern Neuropsychological Assessment and Psychotherapy, Solana Beach, Calif., 1999—2002; pvt. practice Solana Beach, 2002—04, Del Mar, Calif., 2004—. Mem.: APA, San Diego Psychol. Assn. Roman Catholic. Avocations: reading, music, opera, theater, hiking. Home: 721 Genter St La Jolla CA 92037 Office: 240 9th St Del Mar CA 92014 Office Phone: 858-720-0682. Business E-Mail: quinnphd@san.rr.com.

QUINN, KEVIN ANTHOMY, investment banker; b. 1964; m. Jane Katherine Zoidis, Aug. 28, 1993; 3 children. BS, Columbia Coll., NYC; MBA, Columbia U., NYC. Mng. dir., mergers and acquisitions Goldman Sachs & Co., Menlo Park, Calif. Named a Top Dealmaker, Dealmaker mag., 2006.

QUINN, KEVIN J., utilities executive; BCE, U. Dayton, Ohio; MBA, Columbia U., NYC. Engr. Exxon Rsch. and Engring. Co.; mgmt. cons. McKinsey and Co., Inc.; dir. enterprise strategy PSEG, bus. strategy mgr. corp. planning, 1991; pres. PSEG Energy Resources & Trade, 2006—08; v.p. corp. planning PSEG, 2008—. Mem. parish fin. com. St. Patrick's Sch., Chatham, NJ. Office: PSEG Energy Resources & Trade PO Box 570 Newark NJ 07101 Office Phone: 973-430-7000.

QUINN, LARRY (LAWRENCE QUINN), professional sports team executive; Grad., U. Notre Dame, 1974. Dir. devel. City of Buffalo, commr. devel.; pres., CEO Buffalo Sabres, 1996—98, mng. ptnr., 2003—, minority owner, 2008—; vice chmn. Erie Canal Harbor Devel. Corp., 2005. Alt. gov. NHL Bd. Govs. Office: Buffalo Sabres Hockey Western NY Hockey LLC One Seymour H Knox III Plaza Buffalo NY 14203-3096

QUINN, LEBRIS SMITH, cell biologist; b. Norwalk, Conn., Apr. 13, 1954; s. James Edward and Jean Marie (Kuzenski) Smith; m. Thomas Peter Quinn, Aug. 25, 1979 (div. 1983); m. Travis C. Gamble, June 8, 1985. BA in Biology with distinction, Swarthmore Coll., 1976; PhD in Anatomy and Cell Biology, U. Wash., 1982. Rsch. asst. prof. Dept. Biol. Structure, U. Wash., Seattle, 1986—. Contbr. articles to profl. jours. Rsch. grantee USDA, ACS and others. Mem. AAAS, Women in Sci., Women in Cell Biology, Am. Soc. for Cell Biology, Am. Soc. of Animal Sci., Sigma Xi. Avocations: cross country skiing, sea kayaking, hiking. Office: U Wash # Sm-20 Seattle WA 98195-0001

QUINN, LOIS MARIE, health service innovator; b. Boston, Sept. 8, 1933; d. Charles Edward and Grace Marie (Lowder) Seabrook; m. Richard Edward Quinn (div.); children: Deborah Marie, Christopher Edward, Erin Elizabeth, Patrick Richard. RN, Boston City Hosp.; BA, Glassboro State Coll., 1977; MA, Ctrl. Mich. U., 1982. Pediatric staff nurse Boston City Hosp.; staff nurse, coronary care nurse, supr., patient edn. coord.dir. nursing svc. Rancocas Valley Hosp., Willingboro, NJ, 1967—78; nursing mgmt. cons. Am. Medicorp., Bala Cynwyd, Pa., 1977-78; asst. adminstr. Washington Meml. Hosp., Turnersville, N.J., 1978-80; pres. Lois Quinn Assocs. Nursing Mgmt. Cons., Willingboro, 1980—83; mgr. nursing svcs. Universal Health Svcs., Inc., King of Prussia, Pa., 1983-84, dir. mgmt. svcs. and profl. stds., 1984-90; dir. profl. svcs. Am. Healthcare Mgmt. Inc., 1990-93, v.p. profl. affairs, 1993-94; sr. v.p. profl. affairs Primary Health Sys., Inc., 1994-97; founder Touch Ministry Compassionate Massage, Devon, Pa., 1998—. Mem. Assoc. Bodywork and Massage Profls., Common Cause, Amnesty Internat., Green America, Phila. Mus. Art, Bryn Mawr Film Inst., Bread for World, Surrey Svc. Srs.(bd. dir., 2009-, vol. exec. com. 2009-), Sigma Iota Epsilon. Roman Catholic. Address: 360 Old Forge Crossing Devon PA 19333-1123

QUINN, NIGEL WILLIAM TREVELYAN, research scientist; b. Belfast, Northern Ireland, Dec. 28, 1955; arrived in U.S., 1978; s. Stanley Quinn and Elaine Elizabeth Hayes. BSc with honors, Cranfield U., 1977; MS, Iowa State U., 1981; PhD, Cornell U., 1987. Registered profl. engr., Calif. GE fellow Cornell U., 1984—86, sr. rsch. assoc., 1987—90; lead groundwater modeler San Joaquin Valley Drainage Program, 1987—90; geol. scientist, group leader Hydro Ecol. Engring. Advanced Decision Support Berkeley (Calif.) Nat. Lab., 1990—. Convener Calif. Water and Environ. Modeling Forum, Sacramento, 2002—; bd. dirs. Internat. Symposium on Environ. Software Sys., Germany; adj. prof. Calif. Water Inst.; assoc. rsch. prof. Calif. State U., Fresno; rsch. engr. U. Calif., Merced. Contbr. chapters to books, articles to profl. jours. Dir. UN Assn., Ames, 1978—81. Recipient Hunting Challenge Cup, Cranfield U., 1977. Mem.: ASCE, Calif. Water Inst., Water Environment Fedn., Am. Water Resources Assn., Am. Geophysical Union, Berkeley Yacht Club, Wine Country Polo. Unitarian. Avocations: sailing, travel, polo. Home: 1123 Lochbrae Rd Sacramento CA 95815 Office: Berkeley Nat Lab 70A-3317H 1 Cyclotron Rd Berkeley CA 95815 Office Phone: 510-486-7056. Business E-Mail: nwquinn@lbl.gov.

QUINN, PAT (JOHN BRIAN PATRICK QUINN), professional hockey coach; b. Hamilton, Ont., Can., Jan. 29, 1943; s. John Ernest and Jean (Ireland) Quinn; m. Sandra Gergia Baker, May 1, 1963; children: Valerie, Kathleen. BA in Econs., York U., 1972; LLB, Widener U. Sch. Law, 1987; LLD (hon.), McMaster U., 2008. Defenseman Toronto Maple Leafs, 1968—70, Vancouver Canucks, 1970—72, Atlanta Flames, 1972—77; asst. coach Phila. Flyers, 1977—78, head coach, 1979—82, LA Kings, 1984—86; pres., gen. mgr. Vancouver Canucks, 1987—97, head coach, 1991—95, Toronto Maple Leafs, 1998—2006, Edmonton Oilers, 2009—. Player rep. NHL, Atlanta, 1973—77; mem. NHL Bd. Govs., 1987; head coach Team Canada, Olympic Games, Salt Lake City, 2002, Torino, 06, Team Canada, World Cup of Hockey, 2004, Team Canada, Spengler Cup, 2006, Team Canada, IIHF World 18 & Under Championships, 2008; co-owner Vancouver Giants (Western Hockey League). Recipient Jack Adams Award, 1980, 1992, Coach of Yr., Hockey News, 1980, 1982, Jake Milford Award, 1994, Jack Diamond Award, 1994; named Coach of Yr., Sporting News, 1980, 1992. Roman Catholic. Achievements include being the head coach of gold medal Canadian Hockey Team, Salt Lake City Olympic Games, 2002; being the head coach of World Cup Champion Team Canada, 2004. Avocations: sports, reading. Office: Edmonton Oilers Hockey Club 11230 - 110 St Edmonton AB T5G 3H7 Canada*

QUINN, PATRICIA K., international television consultant, co-producer; b. Chico, Calif. d. Donald Joseph and Kathleen (Alexander) Q. BA, Bennington Coll.; MFA in Drama, Yale U. Prodr., devel. exec. various Off-Broadway and regional theatres, 1976-84; devel. cons. Sundance Film Inst., Utah, 1983—85; theatrical agt. I.C.M., LA, 1985-90; v.p. comedy devel. Warner Bros. TV, Burbank, Calif., 1990-92; lit. and packaging agt. various agys. LA, 1995—2006; cons., ptnr., mgr. Quinn Media Mgmt., 2006—. Lectr. Nat. Assn. of TV Programming Execs., Fla. Bar, NATAS; mem. TV com. Brit. Acad. Film and TV Arts, 2002-; adj. faculty Dodge Coll. Film and Media Arts, Chapman U., 2007-; ptnr., mgr. Quinn Media Mgmt., 2006-. Founding mem. N.Y. Theatre Workshop, NYC, 1980—86. Mem.: Women in Film (v.p. 1995—2001, bd. dirs. 2005—). Office: 330 S Spalding Dr #403 Beverly Hills CA 90212 Office Phone: 310-228-8720.

QUINN, PATRICK, Governor of Illinois; b. Chgo., Sept. 22, 1948; children: Patrick, David. BS, Georgetown U., 1971; JD Northwestern U. Sch. of Law. Commr. Cook County Bd. of Tax Appeal, 1982; treas. State of Ill., Springfield, 1990—94, lt. gov., 2003—09, gov., 2009—. Chmn. Ill. River Coordinating Counc., Ill. Rural Affairs Counc., Ill. Rural Bond Bank. Author: How to Appeal Your Illinois Property Taxes Without a Lawyer, 1988. Democrat. Catholic. Office: Office of the Governor 207 State House Springfield IL 62706 Office Phone: 217-782-0244.*

QUINN, PATRICK, transportation executive; BA, U. Nebr., 1968, JD, 1971. From assoc. to ptnr. Nelson & Harding, Lincoln, Nebr., 1971-77; gen. counsel S.W. Motor Freight, Chattanooga, 1977-85; pres., co-chmn. U.S Xpress Enterprises, Inc., Chattanooga, Tenn., 1985—. Office: US Xpress Enterprises Inc 4080 Jenkins Rd Chattanooga TN 37421-1174 Office Phone: 423-510-3000.

QUINN, STEPHEN F., marketing executive; m. Linda Quinn; 3 children. BA in Econs., Queens U., Can.; MBA, U. Western Ont. Ivey Sch. Bus., Can. Various mktg., sales and fin. positions The Quaker Oats Co., Johnson & Johnson, Procter & Gamble Co., Nortel Networks Corp.; various mktg. positions PepsiCo Inc., 1992—2005, including gen. mgr. convenience foods, head mktg. Frito-Lay Can., chief mktg. officer Frito-Lay N.Am.; sr. v.p. mktg. Wal-Mart Stores, Inc., Bentonville, Ark., 2005—07, exec. v.p., chief mktg. officer, 2007—. Bd. dirs. Assn. Nat. Advertisers. Bd. dirs. Give Kids the World. Named a Power Player, Advt. Age, 2008. Office: Wal-Mart Stores Inc 702 SW 8th St Bentonville AR 72716-8611*

QUINN, THOMAS CHARLES, medical researcher, educator; BS, U. Notre Dame, 1969, MS, 1970; MD, Northwestern U., 1974. Diplomate Am. Bd. Internal Med, 1977, Am. Bd. Infectious Disease, 1981. Intern, resident in internal medicine Albany (NY) Med. Ctr., 1974—77; prof. medicine, internat. health, epidemiology, molecular microbiology, immunology and pathology Johns Hopkins U., Balt., 1981—; dir. Johns Hopkins Ctr. Global Health, Balt.; sr. investigator, dir. internat. STD/HIV lab. Nat. Inst. Allergy & Infectious Diseases, Balt., 1982—. Med. cons. Academic Alliance, Washington, 2001—03. Capt. USPHS, 1977—. Decorated Disting. Svc. award USPHS. Fellow: Infectious Diseases Soc. Am. (bd. dirs. 2002—03); mem.: Inst. Medicine. Office: Johns Hopkins Univ Ross 1159 720 Rutland Ave Baltimore MD 21205 E-mail: tquinn@jhmi.edu.

QUINN, THOMAS H., lawyer, lobbyist; b. Pawtucket, RI, 1937; AB, Providence Coll., 1959; LLB, Georgetown Univ., 1963. Bar: RI 1963, DC 1964. Atty., legis. counsel, Office Comptroller Currency US Treasury Dept., 1963—66; ptnr. legis. and regulatory practice O'Connor & Hannan, Washington; ptnr., legis. affairs group Venable LLP, Washington, 2001—. Apptd. mem. US Govt. Bd Internat. Broadcasting, 1974—82; alt. US observer Internat. Fund for Ireland, 1993; trustee Dem. Senatorial Campaign Com., House Dem. Congl. Campaign Com. Mem.: ABA, RI Bar Assn., DC Bar Assn. Democrat. Office: Venable LLP 575 Seventh St NW Washington DC 20004 Office Phone: 202-344-4701. Office Fax: 202-344-8300. Business E-Mail: thquinn@venable.com.*

QUINN, TOM, communications executive; b. LA, Mar. 14, 1944; s. Joseph Martin and Grace (Cooper) Quinn; children: Douglas, Lori, Shelby. BS, Northwestern U., 1965. Reporter, newswriter ABC Radio, Chgo. and L.A., 1965; reporter, prodr. Sta. KXTV, Sacramento, 1966; day editor City News Svc., LA, 1966-68, chmn., 1980-85; pres. Americom Broadcasting, Inc., LA, 1985—. Pres. Radio News West, LA, 1968—70, Reno Radio Reps., 1998—, KFSO Radio, Fresno, 1995—98; dir. Southland News, LA. Mem. governing bd. Tahoe Regional Planning Agy., 2002—05; campaign mgr. Jerry Brown for Sec. State, LA, 1970; dep. sec. state Calif. Sacramento, 1971—74; campaign mgr. Brown for Gov., LA, 1974; sec. Calif. Dept. Environ. Affairs, Sacramento, 1975—79; chmn. Calif. Air Resources Bd., Sacramento, 1975—79, Tom Bradley Mayoral Campaign, 1985. Recipient Headliner of Yr. award Greater L.A. Press Club, 1978, Environ. Protection award Calif. Trial Lawyers Assn., 1979. Democrat. Office: Ste 780 11400 W Olympic Blvd Los Angeles CA 90064-1541 Office Phone: 310-481-0440.

QUINN, YVONNE SUSAN, lawyer; b. Spring Valley, Ill., May 13, 1951; d. Robert Leslie and Shirley Eilene (Morse) Quinn. BA, U. Ill., 1973; JD, U. Mich., 1976, MA in Econs., 1977. Bar: NY 1978, US Dist. Ct. (ea. and so. dists.) NY 1978,US Ct. Appeals (3d, 5th, 9th, 10th and DC cirs.) 1982, US Ct. Appeals (2d cir.) 1992, US Ct. Appeals (4th cir.) 1994, US Supreme Ct. 1982. Assoc. Cravath, Swaine & Moore, NYC, 1977-80, Sullivan & Cromwell, NYC, 1980-84, ptnr. litig., 1984—, and coord. antitrust practice area. Mem. ABA, Assn. of Bar of City of NY Office: Sullivan & Cromwell 125 Broad St New York NY 10004-2489 Office Phone: 212-558-3736. Office Fax: 212-558-3588. Business E-Mail: quinny@sullcrom.com.

QUINNAN, GERALD VINCENT, JR., medical educator; b. Boston, Sept. 7, 1947; s. Gerald Vincent and Mary (Lally) Q.; children: Kevin, Kylie, Kathleen, John, Gerald; m. Leigh A. Sawyer. AB in Chemistry, Coll. Holy Cross, 1969; MD cum laude, St. Louis U., 1973. Diplomate Am. Bd. Internal Medicine. Intern, resident, fellow Boston U. Med. Ctr., 1973-77; med. officer Bur. Biologics, USPHS, Bethesda, Md., 1977; advanced through grades to asst. surgeon gen. RADM USPHS, 1992; dir. herpes virus br., dep. dir. div. virology Bur. Biologics, Bethesda, 1980-81; dir. div. virology Ctr. for Drugs and Biologics, Bethesda, 1981-88; dep. dir. Ctr. Biologics Evaluation and Rsch., Bethesda, 1988-93, acting dir., 1990-92; prof. Uniformed Svcs. U. Health Scis., Bethesda, 1993—, chair preventive medicine, 2002—. Contbr. chpts. to books, numerous articles to profl. jours.; editl. bd./reviewer several jours. Fellow Infectious Diseases Soc. Am.; mem. AAAS, Am. Soc. for Microbiology, Am. Soc. for Clin. Investigation, Sigma Xi, Alpha Omega Alpha. Roman Catholic. Office: Uniformed Svcs U Hlth Scis Dept Preventive Medicine & Biometrics 4301 Jones Bridge Rd Bethesda MD 20814-4712 Home Phone: 301-460-6625; Office Phone: 301-295-3173. Business E-Mail: gquinnan@usuhs.mil.

QUIÑONES-HINOJOSA, ALFREDO, neurosurgeon, educator; b. Mexico, Mexico, Jan. 2, 1968; m. Anna Quiñones; children: Gabriella, David, Olivia. BA, Escuela Normal Urbana Fed. Fronteriza, Mexicali, Mexico, 1986; Transfer core curriculum to the U. Calif., San Joaquin Delta Cmty. Coll., Stockton, Calif., 1991; BA in Psychology (highest honors), U. Calif., Berkeley, 1994; MD (cum laude), Harvard Med. Sch., Boston, 1999. Basic Life Support Calif., 1999, Advanced Cardiac Life Support Cert. Calif., 1999, Advanced Trauma Life Support Cert. Calif., 1999, lic. Calif., 2001, Md., 2005. Migrant worker San Joaquin Valley, Frenso, Calif., 1987—88; crew leader Calif. Railcar Repair, Stockton, Calif., 1988—91, 1990—91; statistics tutor, Tutor Learning Ctr. San Joaquin Delta Coll., Stockton, Calif., 1990—91; calculus & physics asst. profl. develop. program U. Calif., Berkeley, 1992—94, lab. asst., neuroscience dept., 1994, intern, gen. surgery San Francisco, 2000, tng. in clin. rsch., dept. epidemiology and biostatistics, 2003, NIH postdoctoral fellowship, dept. develop. and stem cell biology, 2004, resident, neurosurgery, 2005; house officer, internal medicine St. Francis Hosp., San Francisco, 2002—04; asst. prof. neurosurgery & oncology John Hopkins U. Sch. Medicine and Sidney Kimmel Comprehensive Cancer Ctr., 2005—07; asst. prof., cellular and molecular medicine John Hopkins U. Sch. Medicine, 2007—, assoc. prof. neurosurgery, 2007—; clin. dir., Brain Tumor Surgery Program John Hopkins Bayview Hosp., 2005—; attending neurosurgeon John Hopkins Hosp., 2005—, John Hopkins Bayview Hosp., 2005—. Invited spkr. in field; cons. Revolution Health Group, 2006—; Alpha Omega Alpha vis. prof. Mt. Sinai Sch. Medicine, 2008; vis. prof. U. Utah, Dept. Neurosurgery, 2008. Editl. bd. mem. Self Assessment in Neurosurgery, Topic Editor, Cerbrovascar, 2004, Journal Neurosurgery, 2004—, Journal Neursurgery: Neurosurgical Focus. Topic Editor, Stem cells opportunities in Neursurgery, 2005—, Journal Neurosurgery Clinics of NAm., 2007—, jour. peer review activitities Neurosurgery, 2004—, ad hoc reviewer Cancer Research Journal, 2007—, Journal National Cancer Institute, 2007—, Journal Neurology, 2007—, Journal Experimental Neurology, 2007—, Stem Cells Journal, 2007—, Journal Neurology (India), 2007—, Journal Comparative Neurology, 2007—, Journal Neurosurgicall Review, 2007—, Journal Rejuvenation Research, 2007—, Journal Neuro-Oncology, 2007—; contbr. chapters to books, several articles to profl. jours. Mem. adv. bd. Cord Found., 2007—, Angels of the Operating Room Organization, 2007—; bd. dirs. Hispanic Scholarship Fund, 2007—. Recipient San Francisco Police Dept. Commendation award, 2003, City of San Francisco Appreciation award, 2003, Edwin Boldrey Sci. award, 55th Ann. Meeting San Francisco Neurological Soc., 2003, 57th Ann, Meeting San Francisco Neurological Soc., 2005, Howard Hughes Med. Inst. Physician-Scientist Career award, 2006, Herbert W. Nickens award, Assn. Am. Med. Colleges, 2006, Robert Wood Johnson Found. award, 2007, Popular Sci. Mag. Brilliant 10 Scientists award, 2007, Internat. Hispanics award Sol Azteca, 2008, Merage Found. Nat. Leadership in Sci. and Medicine award, 2008; named one of Balt. Mag. US Top Docs, 2007, Hispanic Bus. Jour. Top 100 Most Influential Hispanics in the US, 2007; grantee Robert Wood Johnson Found., 2008—, NIH/NINDS, 2006—. Mem.: AMA, Am. Soc. for Clin. Oncology (Found. Career Develop. award 2006), Am. Brain Tumor Assn., Am. Assn. for Cancer Rsch., ACS (First Pl., Region IX Resident Paper Competition 2003, Franklin Martin Faculty Rsch. award 2006), Congress of Neurological Surgeons (Blue Ribbon award for Poster Presentation 2002), Am. Assn. Neurological Surgeons (Ronald Bittner award 2004, Jour. Neurooncology award 2004, Lorenz Surgical Young Clinician Investigator award 2006), Soc. for Exptl. Biology and Medicine, AAAS, Assn. for Ethnic Diversity in the Neurosciences, Boston Area Neuroscience Group, Mass. Med. Soc., Pfeiffer Fellow, Hinton-Wright Soc., Harvard Med. Sch., Soc. for the Advancement of Chicanos and Native Americans in Sci., Soc. for Neuroscience, Am. Assn. Neurological (mem. exec. com. 2007—), Nat. Chicano Health Organization and Latin American Student Assn., Harvard Med. Sch., Sigma Xi (Honorable mention award 1999). Office: Dept Neurosurgery Cancer Research Bldg II 1550 Orleans St Rm 247 Baltimore MD 21231-1044 Address: John Hopkins Bayview Medical Ctr Dept Neurosurgery 4940 Eastern Ave B-121 Baltimore MD 21224-2780 Office Phone: 410-502-2906, 410-550-3367. Office Fax: 410-502-7995, 410-550-0748. Business E-Mail: aquinon2@jhmi.edu.*

QUIÑONES KEBER, ELOISE, art historian, educator; b. LA; d. Rudy Jr. and Margaret Q. BA, Immaculate Heart Coll., 1966; MA, UCLA, 1967, Columbia U., 1979, PhD, 1984. Lectr. Columbia U., NYC, 1984-86; prof. art history Baruch Coll., The Grad. Ctr., CUNY, 1986—. Author: Codex Telleriano Remensis: Ritual, Divination, and History in a Pictorial Aztec Manuscript, 1995 (Getty Grant Program Publ. Subvention award, 1992); co-author: Art of Aztec Mexico: Treasures of Tenochtitlan, 1983; editor: Chipping Away on Earth: Studies in Prehispanic and Colonial Mexico in Honor of Arthur J.O. Anderson and Charles E. Dibble, 1995, In Chalchihuitl in Quetzalli: Mesoamerican Studies in Honor of Doris Heyden, 2000, Representing Aztec Ritual: Performance, Text, and Image in the Work of Sahaqún, 2002; co-editor: The Work of Bernardino de Sahagun: Pioneed Ethnographer of 16th-Century Aztec Mexico, 1988, Mixteca-Puebla: Discoveries and Research in Mesoamerican Archaeology and Art, 1994; contbr. articles to profl. jours. Mellon postdoctoral fellow Columbia U., 1984-86, fellow Ford Found./NRC, 1986-87, Am. Coun. of Learned Socs. fellow, 1987-88, 93-94, grantee, 1985, 95, NEH fellow, 1993-94, grantee, 1986, 91; grantee Am. Philos. Soc., 1986; fellow Guggenheim Found., 1998; recipient Ralph Waldo Emerson award Phi Beta Kappa Soc., 1996. Mem. Coll. Art Assn., Assn. Latin Am. Art, Am. Soc. for Ethnohistory. Office: CUNY Grad Ctr Art History Program 365 Fifth Ave New York NY 10016 also: CUNY Baruch Coll Dept Fine and Performing Arts 1 Bernard Baruch Way New York NY 10010-1703 Office Phone: 646-312-4052. Business E-Mail: EQuinones-Keber@gc.cuny.edu. E-mail: Eloise_Quinones-Keber@baruch.cuny.edu.

QUIÑONES-SÁNCHEZ, MARIA D., councilwoman; m. Tomas Sánchez; children: Edgar, Tomasito. B, Temple U., Phila.; M in Human Services, Lincoln U., Pa., 1992. Various positions including dep. commr. elections and city coun. legis. asst. City of Phila., 1988—96; exec. dir. ASPIRA, 1996—2000; regional dir. PR Fed. Affairs Adminstrn., 2001—07; councilwoman, dist. 7 Phila. City Coun., 2008—. Chmn. licenses & inspections com. Phila. City Coun., vice chmn. streets com. Founding mem., co-chair bd. dirs. Pa. Statewide Latino Coalition, 2001; bd. dirs. Pa. Women's Campaign Fund, Phila. Cultural Fund. Democrat. Office: Phila City Coun City Hall Rm 592 Philadelphia PA 19107-3290 Office Phone: 215-686-3448. Office Fax: 215-686-1936.*

QUINOY, MELISA, marketing and advertising executive; b. Puerto Rico, 1963; Grad., Cornell U., NYC, 1984. With EURO RSCG Worldwide, Australia, FCB Worldwide, Lowe & Ptnrs. Worldwide, NY; regional dir. client svcs. Ammiratti Puris Lintas; sr. v.p. internat. mktg. partnerships MTV Networks Latin America, Miami, Fla., 1999—2006; exec. v.p. Viacom Brand Solutions MTV Networks Internat., London, 2006—08; CEO Dieste Harmel & Ptnrs., Dallas, 2008—. Named a Woman to Watch, Advt. Age, 2008. Office: 1999 Bryan St Ste 2700 Dallas TX 75201 Office Phone: 214-259-8000. Office Fax: 214-259-8040. Business E-Mail: CEO@dieste.com.*

QUINSON, BRUNO ANDRE, painter, retired publishing executive; b. Norwich, Conn., Jan. 1, 1938; s. Louis Jean and Suzanne Marie (Richard) Q.; m. Mary Ann Goodman, May 3, 1980; children by previous marriage: Timothy Bruno, Marc Albert (dec.), Christopher Louis; stepchildren: J. Geoffrey Taylor, Luke J. Taylor (dec.), Adam J. Taylor, Joshua P. Taylor. BA, Williams Coll., 1958; postgrad., NYU, 1960-61. Product mgr. Simon & Schuster, NYC, 1960-65; pub., gen. mgr. Golden Press (div. Western Pub. Co., Inc.), 1965-70; pres. Larousse & Co., Inc., NYC, 1970-82, also bd. dirs.; pres. trade and reference div. Macmillan Pub. Co., NYC, 1982-88; pres., chief exec. officer Henry Holt & Co. Inc., NYC, 1988-96, ret., 1996. Bd. dirs. Nat. Book Found., chmn., 1993-96; treas. Columbia U. Press, 1994-03, vice chmn., 1997-03; exec. bd. Macmillan Ltd., 1995-96; nat. coun. Graywolf Press, 2005— Exhibitions include Nat. Acad. Art, Century Assn., NYC, Meeting House, Southfield, Mass., IS 183, Interlaken, Mass., Norfolk Libr.Conn., Frost Pl., Franconia, N.H. Bd. dirs. Rye (NY) Art Ctr., treas., 1973-74; bd. dirs. Northside Ctr. for Child Devel., 1981-89, chmn., 1987-89, adv. bd., 1990—; bd. dirs. 1115 Fifth Ave. Corp., 1983-94, 96-04, pres., 1998-03; bd. dirs. Mus. of the City of NY, 1999—, Lycee Francais NY, 1994-96, Vol. Cons. Group, 1997, Each Child a Reader Found., 1996; founding mem. Barrington Stage Co.; founding mem., bd. dirs. Interlaken Sch. Art, 1998-01; nat. adv. bd. Eudora Welty Found., 2002—; trustee Leopold Schepp Found., 2001—, PEN Am. Ctr., 2003-07; bd. dirs. Manhattan Theater Club, 1991-97, emeritus 1997—Decorated chevalier Des Arts et Lettres (France). Mem. Am. Assn. Pubs. (bd. dirs. 1991-95), Pubs.' Lunch Club (pres. 1990-93), Century Assn., Norfolk Country Club, The River Club. Office: 2 E 93rd St New York NY 10128-0610

QUINT, ARNOLD HARRIS, lawyer; b. Boston, Jan. 3, 1942; s. Milton and Esther Quint; m. Susan Arenson, July 23, 1967; children: Edward, Michael. AB, Haverford Coll., Pa., 1963; LLB, Yale U., 1966. Bar: D.C. 1967. Supervisory atty. Power Commn., Washington, 1967-70; assoc. Hunton & Williams, Washington, 1970-74, ptnr., 1974—2007, sr. counsel, 2007—. Mem. ABA. Office: Hunton & Williams 1900 K St NW Washington DC 20006-1110 Office Phone: 202-955-1542. E-mail: aquint@hunton.com.

QUINT, DAVID LOUIS, literature and language professor; BA, Yale U., 1971, PhD, 1976. From lectr. to full prof. Princeton U., 1976—91; prof. English and comparative lit. Yale U., 1991—96, George M. Bodman prof. English and comparative lit., 1996—2006, Sterling prof. English and comparative lit., 2006—, chair comparative lit. dept., 2003—. Translator: The Stanze of Poliziano, 1978, Ariosto's Cinque Canti, 1996; author: Origin and Originality in Renaissance Literature, 1983, Epic and Empire, 1993, Montaigne and the Quality of Mercy, 1998, Cervantes's Novel of Modern Times, 2003; co-editor: Renaissance Theory/Renaissance Texts, 1986. Recipient William Nelson prize, Renaissance Quarterly, 1984, James Holly Hanford award, Milton Soc. America, 2005; fellow Harvard Ctr. Renaissance Studies; Danforth grad. fellow, Fulbright-Hays traveling fellowship. Fellow: Am. Acad. Arts and Sciences. Office: Yale U Dept Comparative Lit 451 College St Rm 102 PO Box 208299 New Haven CT 06520-8299 Office Phone: 203-432-4750. E-mail: david.quint@yale.edu.

QUINT, DAVID PAUL, investment banking executive; b. Independence, Iowa, July 24, 1950; s. Paul Theodore and Mary Ann (Connolly) Q.; m. Kathleen Mary Stern, May 25, 1973; children: Jennifer, Angela, David, Geoffrey. BA in Modern Langs., U. Notre Dame, 1972, JD, 1975.

Assoc. Arter & Hadden, Cleve., 1975-82; mng. dir. Belden & Blake, London, 1983-92; pres., CEO RP&C Internat., London, 1992—. Mem. Notre Dame Law Rev., 1974. Rotary Internat. fellow, 1978. Mem. Ohio State Bar Assn. Republican. Roman Catholic. Avocation: travel. Home: Avallon East Rd KT1 30LF Weybridge Surrey England Office: RP&C Internat 31A St James Square SW1Y 4JR London England Office Phone: 011 44 207 766 7000. E-mail: dquint@rpcint.co.uk.

QUINT, IRA, retail executive; b. NYC, May 29, 1930; s. Theodore Isaac and Rebecca (Ginandes) Q.; m. Carol Ann Goldsmith (div. Feb. 1984); children: Susan Amy, Stephanie Ann. BS, NYU, 1951; MBA, Harvard U., 1954. Group nat. mdse. mgr. Sears Roebuck & Co., Chgo., 1954-78; pres. Colonial Corp. Am., NYC, 1978-79; pres., CEO Venture Stores, St. Louis, 1979-81; exec. v.p. Montgomery Ward, Chgo., 1981-85; pres. Lane Bryant Stores, NYC, 1985-90; pres., chief exec. officer Conston Corp., Phila., 1990-92; pres. Quint Consultancy, NYC. Mem.: Harvard (N.Y.C.). Home and Office: 130 E 67th St New York NY 10021-6136

QUINTANA-ALLENSON, ANA M., government agency executive; b. Chgo., Oct. 16, 1967; d. Sergio Antonio (Tony) Quintana and Ana Ilia Gonzalez; m. James M. Allenson, May 5, 2006. BA in Comm. cum laude, Loyola U. Chgo., 1989. Cert. Media Rels. Cmty. Media Workshop, 2001, U. of S.C., 2001. Claims rep. Social Security Adminstrn., Chgo., 1993—99, mgmt. support specialist, 2000—01, pub. affairs specialist, 2001—02, acting asst. dist. mgr., 2003, exec. staff asst., 2003—. President-Hispanic task force Gift of Hope Organ and Tissue Donation Network, Elmhurst, Ill., 2002—03. Mem.: Nat. Assn. Hispanic Journalists (mem. Chgo. region Hispanic action com. 1995—, Ill. vice chair 2003—04). D-Liberal. Avocations: photography, reading, drawing, art shows. E-mail: ana.quintana-allenson@ssa.gov.

QUINTANA-ALSINA, MYRIAM, chemistry professor; d. Roman Quintana and Milagros Alsina; m. Andres Vidarte, May 19, 1991; children: Mayrim Andrea Vidarte, Fabian Andres Vidarte. MS, Pontifical Cath. U. PR. Lic. chemist Colegio de Quimicos de PR, 1996. Instr. Pontifical Cath. U. PR, Ponce, PR, 1992—2000, asst. prof., 2000—. Mem. expert faculty, collaborative excellence in tchr. preparation program Pontifical Cath. U. PR, 1998—2000, mem. expert faculty title V program, chemistry component, 2001—04, dir. tutoring and mentoring component, title V program, 2003—04, expert faculty USDA program, 2004—05, mem. expert faculty, minority sci. and engring. improvement program, 2006—07, coord. minority sci. and engring. improvement program, 2008—09. Juror regional sci. fairs; catechism tchr. Pontifical Cath. U. PR, 2000—01. Patricia Robert Harris fellow, 1988—90. Mem.: Am. Chem. Soc., Cath. Dau. Am. and Colegio Quimicos de P.R. Achievements include incorporation of technology in the general chemistry courses; development of general chemistry laboratory manual in Spanish using the MeasureNet technology; blended of a general chemistry blended course. Office: Pontifical Catholic University of PR 2250 Las Americas Ave Ste 569 Ponce PR 00717-0777 Business E-Mail: mquintana@email.pucpr.edu.

QUINTANILLA, ANTONIO PAULET, retired physician, educator; b. Feb. 8, 1927; came to U.S., 1963, naturalized, 1974; s. Leandro Marino and Edel Paulet Quintanilla; m. Mary Parker Rodriguez, May 2, 1958; children: Antonio Paulet, Angela, Francis, Cecilia, John. PhD, San Marcos U., 1948, MD, 1957. Assoc. prof. physiology U. Arequipa, Peru, 1960-63; assoc. in physiology Cornell U., N.Y., 1963-64; prof. physiology U. Arequipa, 1964-68; assoc. prof. medicine Northwestern U., 1969-80, prof., 1980-2000; ret., 2000. Chief renal sect. VA Lakeside Hosp., 1976-90; cons. nephrologist Northwestern Meml. Hosp., Evanston Hosp., 1990-98, sr. attending emeritus; lectr. nat. Ctr. Advanced Med. Edn., Chgo.; mem. adv. bd. Am. Fedn. Clin. Rsch. Contbr. articles on renal disease to med. jours.; author books in English, French and Spanish, poetry, short stories. Fellow ACP; mem. Ctrl. Soc. Clin. Rsch., Internat. Soc. Nephrology, Am. Soc. Nephrology, Am. Physiol. Soc. Home: 820 Graceland Ave #303 Des Plaines IL 60016

QUINTERO, ELIAS MATTHEW, biomedical researcher; s. Elias and Delia Quintero; m. Cheryl Ann Byham, July 11, 1992. BS in Biology, Midwestern State U., Wichita Falls, Tex., 1988; MS in Anatomy, Baylor U., Dallas, 1994; PhD, Tex. A&M Health Sci. Ctr., Dallas, 2000; MS in Clin. Rsch., Med. U. SC., Charleston, 2005. Rsch. technician Baylor Coll. Dentistry, Dallas, 1988—91; asst. prof. Parker Coll. of Chiropractic, Dallas, 1992—99; rsch. assoc. U. Tex. Southwestern Med. Ctr., Dallas, 1993—94; instr. El Centro Coll., Dallas, 1995—97; postdoctoral fellow Med. U. SC., Charleston, 2000—06; scholar Inst. Rsch. Minority Mental Health and Aging, Charleston, 2003—06. Vol. KidSport Inc., Dallas, 1995—96; pub. spkr. Soc. Neurosci, Brain Awareness Week, Charleston, 2002—05; vol. venue head Spl. Olympics, Charleston, 2002—06. Recipient Paul McFarland Resident Rsch. award, U. Tex., Houston Health Sci. Ctr., 1999, Travel award, Internat. Stereology Workshop, 2002, Internat. Conf. on Neural Transplantation and Repair, 2003; grantee, SC. Coop. Healthy Aging in Minority Populations, 2005—06; fellow, Nat. Inst. on Aging, NIH, 2003—06. Mem.: Soc. Neuroscience (assoc.), Am. Soc. Neural Transplantation and Repair (assoc.), Am. Assn. Geriatric Psychiatry (assoc.). Achievements include research in characterized the therapeutic potential of tetracylines in Parkinson's Disease Pathology. Office Fax: 214-456-6199. Personal E-mail: tb4@att.net.

QUINTO, ZACHARY JOHN, actor; b. Pitts., June 2, 1977; Grad., Carnegie Mellon U., Pitts., 1999. Appearances in (TV series) The Others, 2000, Touched by an Angel, 2001, CSI: Crime Scene Investigation, 2002, Off Centre, 2002, Lizzie McGuire, 2002, Haunted, 2002, The Agency, 2002, Six Feet Under, 2003, Charmed, 2003, Miracles, 2003, Dragnet, 2004, Hawaii, 2004, Joan of Arcadia, 2004, Blind Justice, 2005, Crossing Jordan, 2006, Twins, 2006; actor: (TV films) An American Town, 2001; (TV series) 24, 2003—04, So noTORIous, 2006, Heroes, 2006— (Future Classic award, TV Land Awards, 2007); (films) Boutonniere, 2009, Star Trek, 2009. Office: c/o Tailwind Productions 100 Universal City Plz Bldg 5225 Universal City CA 91608*

QUINTON, PAUL MARQUIS, physiologist, educator; b. Houston, Sept. 17, 1944; s. Curtis Lincoln and Mercedes Genale (Danley) Quinton; m. Liesbet Joris Quinton, Dec. 31, 1992; 1 child, Marquis. BA, U. Tex., 1967; PhD, Rice U., 1971. Asst. prof. physiology & medicine UCLA Med. Sch., 1975—79; asst. prof. biomed. scis. U. Calif., Riverside, 1979—81, assoc. prof., 1981—84, prof., 1984—, Pediatrics, UCSD, 1997—; assoc. prof. physiology UCLA, 1981—91. Assoc. educator Journal Physiology: Cell Biology (Bethesda), Exptl. Physiology (Cambridge). Recipient Rsch. Career Devel. award, NIH, 1978, Paul di Sant'Agnese Disting. Sci. Achievement award, Nat. Cystic Fibrosis Found, 1991, Joseph Levy Meml. award, Cystic Fibrosis (Mucovisidosis) Assn., 1994. Office: UCSD School of Medicine 9500 Gilman Dr La Jolla CA 92093-0830

QUINTUS, JOHN ALLEN, English professor; b. Wash., DC, Jan. 10, 1943; s. Paul Elmer and Vivienne Willson Quintus. BA with honors, U. NC; MA, U. Va.; MEd, Harvard U., 1966; PhD in English Lit., U. Del., Newark, 1974. Fgn. svc. officer US Info. Agy., DC, 1980—99, US Dept. State, DC, 1999—2005; adj. prof. fgn. policy and victorian prose U. Del., 2005—. Cultural affairs and public affairs officer, Canberra, Bonn, Port Louis, Yerevan, Belgrade, Leipzig and Vienna. Contbr. articles to profl. jours. County rep. Del. Stonewall Democrats, Wilmington, 2006—. Recipient Career Achievement award, US Dept. State, 2005. Mem.: Libr. Assocs. (assoc.; bd. mem. 2007—). D-Liberal. Episcopalian. Avocations: music, reading, cooking. Office: U Del Dept English Memorial Hall Newark DE 19716 Business E-Mail: jquintus@udel.edu.

QUIRK, FRANK JOSEPH, management consulting company executive; b. NYC, Feb. 27, 1941; s. Frank J. and Madeline B. Quirk; m. Betty Josephine Mauldin, Jan. 7, 1967; children: Laura Josephine, Katherine Elizabeth. BA, Cornell U., 1962, MBA, 1964. Assoc. Booz, Allen & Hamilton, Inc., Chgo. and Washington, 1967-72; exec. v.p. Macro Internat., Inc., Calverton, Md., 1972-79, pres., CEO, 1980-98, CEO, 1998—2006, chmn., 1998—2006, ret., 2006; exec. v.p. Opinion Rsch. Corp., Princeton, NJ, 1999—2003, pres., 2003—05, ret., 2006; chmn. Alexandria Buick Pontiac GMC, 2005—. Bd. dirs. Smithsonian Inst. Libr. Capt. US Army, 1964—66. Mem.: Belle Haven Country Club. Home: 2110 Foresthill Rd Alexandria VA 22307-1128

QUIRK, JAMES, museum director; BA, Carroll Coll., 1972. Pres., CEO Milw. Envelope, Oconomowoc, Wis.; owner Quirk Reality, Watertown, Wis.; exec. dir. Charles Allis and Villa Terrace Art Mus., Milw., 2007—. Former bd. mem. Internat. Folk Art Mus.; former treas. Friends of Folk Art, Santa Fe; bd. dirs. Earlier European Art Acquisitions, Milw. Art Mus., 2003—, Santa Fe Film Festival, 2006—. Office: Charles Allis Art Mus 1801 N Prospect Ave Milwaukee WI 53202 also: Villa Terrace Decorative Arts Mus 2220 N Terrace Ave Milwaukee WI 53202

QUIRK, JOHN JAMES, investment company executive; b. NYC, July 10, 1943; s. Francis J. and Madeline A. (Meizinger) Q.; m. Kathryn Anne O'Brien, Mar. 21, 1963; children: John James, Ashlin Carter, Merritt Andrew. BA, Georgetown U., 1965; MBA, U. Va., 1967. Asst. treas., mgr. corp. fin. dept. W.R. Grace & Co., NYC, 1967-74; asst. v.p., asst. treas. City Investing Co., NYC, 1974-77, v.p., treas., 1978-81, sr. v.p., treas., 1982-85; chmn. bd. Quirk Carson Peppet Inc., 1985-98; prin. Churchill Capital, Inc., 1999—2001; mng. dir. Morgan, Joseph & Co. Inc., 2001—09, Bonjon Morinc Co., 2009—. Bd. dirs. Environ. Opportunities Fund., Ltd., City Investing Co. Liquidating Trust. Mem.: Racquet and Tennis; Wee Burn (Conn.). Home: 445 Hollow Tree Ridge Rd Darien CT 06820-3030 Office: 600 5th Ave Fl 19 New York NY 10020-2302 Business E-Mail: john.quirk@donjon.com.

QUIRK, KATHLEEN L., mining executive; BS in Acctg., La. State U. With Mobil Oil Corp., Dallas; from mem. staff to treas. Freeport-McMoRan Copper & Gold Inc., New Orleans, 1989—2000, v.p., treas., 2000—03, sr. v.p., CFO, treas., 2003—07, exec. v.p., CFO, treas., 2007—. Office: Freeport McMoRan 1 N Central Ave Phoenix AZ 85004-4414*

QUIRK, RAYMOND R. (RANDY QUIRK), insurance company executive; b. 1946; m. Linda J. Quirk; 3 children. Pres. Fidelity Nat. Fin., Inc., Jacksonville, Fla., 2002—05, CEO Fidelity Nat. Title Group, Inc., 2005—, co-pres., 2007—. Mem. bd. dirs. Fidelity Nat. Title, Alamo Title, Chgo. Title, Home Warranty subsidiaries of Fidelity Nat. Fin. Avocation: golf. Office: Fidelity Nat Fin Inc 601 Riverside Ave Jacksonville FL 32204 Office Phone: 888-934-3354.

QUIRMBACH, HERMAN CHARLES, state legislator; b. St. Paul, Oct. 6, 1950; s. William and Elizabeth. AB in Govt. cum laude, Harvard U., 1972; MA in Econs., Princeton U., 1980, PhD in Econs., 1983. Assoc. economist, cons. Rand Corp., Santa Monica, Calif., 1981—; assoc. prof. econs. Iowa State U., Ames, 1990—; councilman Ames City Coun., 1995—2003; mayor pro-tem Ames, 2002; mem. Dist. 23 Iowa State Senate, 2003—. Vis. asst. prof. econs. U. Wis., Madison, 1983—84; mem. numerous coms. Iowa State Senate. Contbr. articles to profl. jours. Treas. Story County Dem. Party, Ames, 1992-94; pres. Iowa Civil Liberties Union, 2001-02, bd. dirs., 1996-02; bd. dirs. Ames Mcpl. Utility Retirement Sys., 1996-03, Ames Conv. and Visitors Bur., 1997-99; mem. Iowa Coll. Student Aid Commn., 2003-, Iowa Property Tax Implementation Com., 2003-04, Gov's Task Force on Local Governance, 2005, Iowa Tobacco Use Prevention and Control Commn., 2005—, Iowa Local Govt. Innovation Commn., 2007-; chair, senate local govt. com., 2005—; vice chair Senate Edn. Appropriation Sub Com., 2009-; co-chair Ames Vets. Meml. Com., 2001—07. Recipient Don Biggs award for polit. leadership, 1998-99, Stick Your Neck Out award Nat. Assn. for Mentally Ill Ctrl. Iowa, 2005, Outstanding Contbns. to Tobacco Control Appreciation cert. Clean Air for Everyone of Iowa, 2006, Pub. Health award, Story County Tobacco Task Force, 2008. Mem. AAUP, ACLU, Ames LWV, Am. Econ. Assn., Econometric Soc., Ames C. of C., Appalachian Mountain Club, White Mountain Four Thousand Footer Club, Ames Kiwanis Club, Ames Patriotic Coun. Democrat. Office: State Capitol E 12th & Grand Des Moines IA 50319 Office Phone: 515-281-3371. Business E-Mail: herman.quirmbach@legis.state.ia.us.

QUIROS-TEJEIRA, RUBEN ELOY, pediatrician, educator, researcher; b. Panama, July 5, 1962; s. Felix A. Quiros and Olimpia Tejeira de Quiros; m. Nubia Noemi Navarrete, Nov. 12, 1994; children: Ruben Eloy Quiros Jr., Jonathan Elias Quiros, Jacob Eli Quiros. MD, Nat. U. Panama, 1986. Cert. Am. Bd. Pediat., 1995, diplomate Am. Bd. Hosp. Physicians, 2005, Am. Coll. Ethical Physicians, 2005. Resident Children's Hosp. Panama, 1988—91; sci. rschr. duPont Hosp. Children, Thomas Jefferson U., Wilmington, Del., 1992; resident Thomas Jefferson U., Phila., 1993—95; asst. prof. pediat. U. Rochester, NY, 2000—01, dir. pediatric hepatology, 2000—01; asst. prof. pediat. and surgery Baylor Coll. Medicine, Houston, 2001—04, med. dir. pediatric liver transplantation, 2001—04; assoc. prof. pediat. and surgery U. Tex., 2004—, med. dir. pediatric liver, intestinal transplantation, 2004—, dir. pediatric hepatology, 2004—; assoc. prof. pediat. U.T. M.D. Anderson Cancer Ctr., Houston, 2005—. Chmn. med. adv. com. Am. Liver Found., South Tex. Chpt., Houston, 2004—, bd. dirs.; reviewer peer rev. jour. Am. Jour. Transplantation, Edmonton, Canada, 2004—, Jour. Pediatric Gastroent. and Nutrition, Denver, 2004—, Archives Med. Rsch., Mexico D.F., 2003—, Bone Marrow Transplantation Jour., London, 2002—, Jour. Pediat., Cin., 2004—; med. adv. bd. mem. Life Gift Organ Donation Ctr., Houston, 2002—, Alagille Syndrome Alliance, Tualatin, Oreg., 2004—, Hepatitis Mag., Houston, 2005—07, Liver Health Mag., Houston, 2007—; chmn. internat. com. N.Am. Soc. Pediatric Gastroent., Hepatology and Nutrition, Flourtown, Pa., 2007—. Contbr. articles to profl. jours. Mem. focus group Tex. Gulf Digestive Disease Ctr., 2004—. Recipient Herman Roseblum award, Thomas Jefferson U., 1994—95; grantee, NIH; fellow, UCLA, 1995—98, 1998—2000. Fellow: AMA (assoc.), Am. Acad. Pediatric (assoc.); mem.: AAAS (assoc.), Assn. Med. Students U. Panama (hon.), Nat. Med. Assn. Panama (hon.), Panamanian Pediatric Soc. (hon.), Internat. Liver Transplantation Soc. (assoc.), Am. Gastroent. Assn. (assoc.), Am. Assn. Study Liver Disease (assoc.), Am. Soc. Transplantation (assoc.; mem. diversity and minority affairs com. 2006—), N.Am. Soc. Pediatric Gastroent., Hepatology and Nutrition (assoc.), Internat. Pediatric Transplant Assn. (assoc.), Am. Liver Found. (assoc.), Jefferson Med. Coll. Alumni Assn. (hon.). Roman Catholic. Office: U Tex 6431 Fannin St MSB 3140A Houston TX 77030 Office Fax: 713-500-5750.

QUIROZ, ALFONSO WALTER, history professor; b. Lima, Peru, Oct. 4, 1956; s. Alfonso Carlos Quiroz Munoz and Edith Cristina Norris Zanelli; m. Monica Ricketts; 1 child, Daniela. PhD, Columbia U., NYC, 1986. Asst. prof. Bowdoin Coll., Brunswick, Maine, 1985—86; prof. Baruch Coll. and Grad. Ctr., CUNY, 1986—. Author: (history books) Corrupt Circles, 2008. Grantee John Simon Guggenheim Found. fellowship; fellow, Woodrow Wilson Ctr. for Internat. Scholars; Fulbright; Humboldt; McNamara-World Bank, 1989—2008. Mem.: Swimming Red Tide. Office: Baruch Coll and Graduate Ctr CUNY 55 Lexington Ave New York NY 10010 Office Fax: 646-312-4311. Business E-Mail: alfonso.quiroz@baruch.cuny.edu.

QUIROZ ROBLES, FERNANDO, bank executive; With Banamex, 1979, former chief economist, dep. pres., head of specialized banking, pres. Accival; CEO Latin Am. markets and banking Citigroup. Sr. leadership com. Citigroup, corporate client steering com.; mgmt. com. Citigroup Institutional Clients Group, bus. com., bus. practices com.; adv. coun. Citgroup Latin Am. Diversity Com.; bd. dirs. Banchile Asesorias Financieras S.A., Banchile Factoring S.A., Banchile Corredora de Bolsa S.A. Office: Banamex Isabel la Católica 44 CP 06000 Districto Federal Mexico Mexico also: Citigroup 399 Park Ave New York NY 10043*

QUIST, GORDON JAY, federal judge; b. Grand Rapids, Mich., Nov. 12, 1937; s. George J. and Ida F. (Hoekstra) Q.; m. Martha Jane Capito, Mar. 10, 1962; children: Scot D., George J., Susan E., Martha J., Peter K. BA, Mich. State U., 1959; JD with honors, George Washington U., 1962. Bar: DC 1962, Ill. 1964, US Dist. Ct. (no. dist.) Ill. 1964, US Supreme Ct. 1965, Mich. 1967, US Dist. Ct. (we. dist.) Mich. 1967, US Ct. Appeals (6th cir.) 1967. Assoc. Hollabaugh & Jacobs, Washington, 1962-64, Sonnenschein, Levinson, Carlin, Nath & Rosenthal, Chgo., 1964-66, Miller, Johnson, Snell & Cummiskey, Grand Rapids, 1967-72, ptnr., 1972-92, mng. ptnr., 1986-92; judge US Dist. Ct. (we. dist.) Mich., Grand Rapids, 1992—2006, sr. judge, 2006—. Mem. Code of Conduct com. US Cts., 2000—08, chmn., 2004—08. Bd. dirs. Wedgewood Acres-Ch. Youth Home, 1968-74, Mary Free Bed Hosp., 1979-88, Christian Ref. Publs., 1968-78, 82-88, Opera Grand Rapids, 1986-92, Mary Free Bed Brace Shop, 1988-92, Better Bus. Bur., 1972-80, Calvin Theol. Sem., 1992-93; bd. dirs. Indian Trails Camp, 1970-78, 82-88, pres., 1978, 88. Recipient Disting. Alumnus award George Washington U. Law Sch. 1998 Mem. Fed. Bar Assn., Am. Judicature Soc., Mich. State Bar Found., Univ. Club Grand Rapids, Order of Coif. Avocations: reading, travel. Office: 482 Ford Fed Courthouse 110 Michigan St NW Grand Rapids MI 49503-2313 Business E-Mail: Gordon_J_Quist@miwd.uscourts.gov.

QUITORIANO, NATHANIEL J., research scientist; b. Calif., May 8, 1978; PhD, MIT, Cambridge, 2006. Rsch. scientist Hewlett-Packard Labs., Palo Alto, Calif., 2006—. Achievements include patents for nanowire photonic apparatus.

QUITTMEYER, PETER CHARLES, lawyer; b. Charlottesville, Va., Oct. 9, 1957; s. Charles L. and Maureen (Rankin) Q.; children: Charles Lake, Laura Slater. BA with high distinction, U. Va., Charlottesville, 1979, JD, 1982. Bar: Ga. 1985. Assoc. King & Spalding, Atlanta, 1982-87; shareholder Trotter, Smith & Jacobs, Atlanta, 1987-91; ptnr. Nelson Mullins Riley & Scarborough, Atlanta, 1991—2001, Sutherland Asbill & Brennan, Atlanta, 2001—. Adj. prof. computer law Emory U. Sch. Law, Atlanta, 1996, 98, 2000; spl. asst. atty. gen. State Ga., 2002; vice chmn. Ga. chpt. Arthritis Found. Author: Computer Software Agreements, 1985—; mem. editl. bd. Va. Law Rev., 1981-82; contbr. articles to profl. jours. Recipient Vol. award, Ga. chpt. Arthritis Found., 2005; Nat. Merit scholar semifinalist, Westinghouse Sci. Talent Contest. Mem. ABA, Ga. Bar Assn., Raven Soc., Order of Coif, Phi Beta Kappa. Office: Sutherland Asbill & Brennan 999 Peachtree St NE Ste 2300 Atlanta GA 30309 Office Phone: 404-853-8186. Business E-Mail: peter.quittmeyer@sablaw.com.

QUOCK, RAYMOND MARK, pharmacologist, biomedical researcher, health sciences educator; b. San Francisco, June 9, 1948; s. Dick Gar and Madge (Mak) Q.; m. Lina Yen Chiu, Jan. 25, 1975; children: Lauren Rae, Daniel Grant, Lindsay Paige. B.S., U. San Francisco, 1970; Ph.D., U. Wash., 1974. Research lab. asst. U. Calif., San Francisco, 1964-70; USPHS predoctoral fellow U. Wash., Seattle, 1970-74, instr., 1974-75; asst. prof. U. Pacific, Stockton, Calif., 1975-79; asst. prof. Marquette U., Milw., 1979-82, assoc. prof., 1982-87, prof. 1987-89; vis. res fellow USAF Sch Aerospace Med., Brooks AFB, Tex., 1989; assoc. prof. U. Ill. Coll. Medicine, Rockford, 1989-93, prof., 1993—98, Wash. State U., 1999-, affiliated prof. neurosci., 1998-, chair pharm. sci. 1999-2002, 2007, Allen I. White prof., 2007-; cons. Calif. State Bd. Pharmacy, San Francisco, 1976-79; asst. adj. prof. Medical Coll. Wis., 1980-89, research assoc. in toxicology VA Med. Ctr., Wood, Wis., 1981-89, cons. dentistry, 1982-89; prof. pharm. anesthesiol. U. Ill. Coll. Medicine, Chgo., 1993-98. Winsor C. Cutting Disting. vis. prof. U. Hawaii, 2002. Contbr. articles to profl. jours. Exec. v.p. Wis. chpt. Orgn. Chinese-Ams., Milw., 1982-83; mem. research com. Am. Heart Assn. Wis., Milw., 1984—; bd. dirs. Asian Community Health Clinic, Seattle, 1971-75; dir. Rockford Regional Acad. Industrial Consortium, Ill., 1992-95. Recipient Dr. Elwood Molseed award U. San Francisco, 1970, Dr. Leo Pinsky award Marquette U., 1983, 86, Raymond B. Allen Instructorship award U. Ill. Coll. Medicine, 1990-94, 96-98; named One of Outstanding Young Men of Am., U.S. Jaycees, 1978, Tchr. of Yr. award Wash. State U., Coll. Pharmacy, 2002, 08, 09, Pres.'s Tchg. Acad., 2004. Mem. Am. Assn. Coll. Pharmacy, Western Pharmacology Soc., Am. Soc. Pharmacology and Exptl. Therapeutics (v.p. Gt. Lakes chpt. 1994-95), Soc. Neurosci., (councillor Greater Milw. chpt. 1985, pres., 1987), Internat. Behaviorial Neurosci. Soc. Office Phone: 509-335-5956. Business E-Mail: quock@wsu.edu.

QUREISHI, A. SALAM, computer company executive; b. Aligarh, India, July 1, 1936; s. M.A. Jabbar and Saira (Sattar) Q.; m. Naheed Fatima; children: Lubna, Leila. BS in Physics and Math., Aligarh U., India, 1954; MS in Stats., Patna U., India, 1957. Mgr. applications IBM Corp., Palo Alto, Calif., 1961-67; founder, pres., chmn. bd. Optimum Sys., Inc., Palo Alto, Calif., 1967-71; CEO Sysorex Internat., Inc., Mountain View, Calif., 1972—. Republican. Home: 925 Mountain Home Rd Woodside CA 94062-2519 Office: A Salam Qureishi 506 Clyde Ave Mountain View CA 94043-2212

QURESHI, HALIMA AKHTAR, economics professor; d. Shaifiqur and Sharafatunnessa Rahman; m. Mohammed Humayun Aziz Qureshi, Dec. 1; children: Hasina Akhtar Mohyuddin, Tamanna, Taaseen, Tihami,

Maahin. PhD, Vanderbilt U., Nashville, 1987. Online faculty U. Phoenix, 2004—05; assoc. prof. Ala. A&M U., Normal, 2005—. Econ. cons. Learning Link, Nashville, 2001—04. Contbr. articles to profl. jours. Organizer Hasina Islamic Ctr., Chittagong, Bangladesh, 1990—. Named one of Top Rschr., 2008. Mem.: Am. Econ. Assn. Office: Ala A&M Univ 4900 Meridian St Normal AL 35762 Business E-Mail: halima.qureshi@aamu.edu.

QURESHI, IQBAL HUSSAIN, nuclear chemist; b. Ajmer, India, Sept. 27, 1936; arrived in Pakistan, 1950; s. Ashiq Hussain and Hasina Begum Q.; m. Zeenat, Sept. 21, 1965 (wid. July 1984); children: Adnan Iqbal, Imran Iqbal; m. Khurshid, June 9, 1987. BSc, Govt. Coll., Hyderabad, Pakistan, 1956; MSc, U. Sind, Hyderabad, Pakistan, 1958; MS, U. Mich., 1962; PhD, Tokyo U., 1963. Lectr. Govt. Coll., 1956-60; officer on spl. tng. Pakistan Atomic Energy Commn., Karachi, 1960-63, sr. scientific officer Lahore, 1963-68; prin. scientific officer Pakistan Atomic Energy Comm., Lahore, 1969-76; rsch. chemist U.S. Nat. Bur. Standards, Washington, 1967-68; vis. scientist AEC, Roskilde, Denmark, 1970-72; chief scientific officer Pakistan Atomic Energy Comm., Islamabad, 1976-88; chief scientist Pakistan Atomic Energy Commn., Islamabad, 1988-96. Dir. Pakistan Inst. Nuclear Sci. and Tech., Islamabad, 1984-91; tech. mem. Pakistan AEC, Islamabad, 1991-95, sr. mem., 1995-96, scientist emeritus, 1996. Contbr. more than 160 articles to sci. jours. Recipient Chancellor's Gold Medal for scis. U. Sind, 1958, Gold Medal for phys. scis. Pakistan Acad. Scis., 1988, Star of Distinction Sci. award Gov. Pakistan, 1992, Spl. award for sci. Govt. Coll. Hyderabad, 1995, Kharazmi Internat. award Iranian Rsch. Orgn. for Sci. and Tech., 1997, Shield of Hon. Awd., Pak. Nuclear Soc., 1999. Fellow Pakistan Acad. Scis. (Gold medal), Chem. Soc. Pakistan, Pakistan Nuc. Soc. (chmn. adv. com. reactor safety, chmn. adv. com. on uses of radiation in agriculture, medicine and industry, pres. 2001-05); mem. Internat. Union Elementologists, Nat. Com. on Internat. Geosphere-biosphere Program, Nat. Accrediation Com. Avocations: poetry, music. Home: House No 211 St No 18 F-10/2 Islamabad Pakistan Office: Pakistan Inst Nuc Sci and Tech PO Nilore Islamabad Pakistan Office Phone: (051)2207254. Personal E-mail: driqbalqureshi@yahoo.com.

QURESHI, SAJDA, information scientist, educator; children: Peter, Shiraz. BBA, John Cabot U., Rome, 1988; Postgrad. Diploma in Mgmt. Info. Sys., London Sch. Economics & Polit. Sci., 1989, MS in Analysis, Design & Mgmt. Info. Sys., 1991, PhD, 1995. Assoc. prof., dept. info. sys. & quantitative analysis U. Nebr. Omaha, Coll. Info. Sci. & Tech., grad. faculty fellow, 2002—; mgr., libr. John Cabot U., Rome, 1986—87; cons., fin. dept. ITALSTAT, 1988; IT cons., designed acctg. sys. F.S. Tyabji Chartered Accountants, London, 1988—89; rsch. asst. London Sch. Economics & Polit. Sci., 1990—92; coord., commonwealth network info. tech. Commonwealth Secretariat, 1992—95; rsch. fellow Erasmus U., Rotterdam Sch. Mgmt., Netherlands, 1996, asst. prof., dept. Info. & decision scis., 1997—2004, vis. prof.; fellow Erasmus Rsch. Mgmt.; vis. prof., MIS dept. U. Ariz., Sch. Bus. & Pub. Adminstrn., Tucson, 1996; dir., collaborative work consulting V.O.F. Innovative Group Support, Delft, Netherlands, 2001—07; vis. scholar, dept. bus. info. mgmt. & operations Westminster Bus. Sch., London, 2005; vis. scholar, info. sch. U. Washington, Seattle, 2009. Editor-in-chief Jour. Info. Tech. Devel.; sr. editor Electronic Commerce Rsch. & Applications; assoc. editor Electronic Jour. Info. Sys., 1999—2004, ACM SigGroup, 2001, ICIS, 2002—03; editl. bd. mem. Internat. Jour. Mobile Computing & Commerce, ECollaboration, Jour. Info. Tech.; adv. bd. mem. IEEE Conf. Hawaii Internat., AIS Special Interest Group; co-founder, IS specialist group London Sch. Economics; programme com. mem., group decision & negotiation ACM SigGroup, CIKM. Contbr. articles to sci. jours., chapters to books. Grant, Ctrl. Rsch. Fund U. London, 1993, GOVERNET, Adminstrv. Reform Network, 1994, Bldg. Trust Inter-Orgnl. Sys., 1996, Computer Support Collaborative Work Lab., 1998, Commonwealth Secretariat, ICT Strategies Decision Making, 2000, Commonwealth Secretariat Info. Tech., 2003, John Wiley & Sons Info. Tech., 2005—07, Nebr. U. Found., 2008. Mem.: IEEE Profl., IEEE Comm., IEEE Transactions Engring. Mgmt., IFIP Working Groups, Acad. Info. Sys., Operational Rsch. Soc., Brit. Computer Soc. Office: Univ Nebr Coll Info Sci & Tech Dept Info Sys & Quantitative Analysis Omaha NE 68182-0392 Office Fax: 402-554-3400. Business E-Mail: squreshi@mail.unomaha.edu.

QURESHI, TASLEEM ELAHI See ZULFI, TASLEEM

QURESHI, WAQAR A., medical educator; MD, Royal Free Hosp. Sch. Medicine, London, 1983. Diplomate in med. U. London, 1984, Am. Bd. Internal Medicine, 1990, in gastroenterology 1993. Chief endoscopy Baylor Coll. Medicine, Houston, 1997—, assoc. prof. medicine, 2002—. Fellow: ACP, Am. Soc. Gastrointestinal Endoscopy (mem. stds. practice guidelines), Am. Coll. Gastroenterology (mem. edn. com.). Office: Baylor Coll Medicine 1709 Dryden St Ste 800 Houston TX 77030 Office Fax: 713-798-0951.

QUTUB, MUSA YACUB, hydrogeologist, educator, consultant; b. Jerusalem, June 2, 1940; came to U.S., 1960; s. Yacub and Sarah Qutub; married; children: Hanhia, Jennan, Sarmad, Muntaser, Aya, Saif, Tasneem. BA in Geology, Simpson Coll., Indianola, Iowa, 1964; MS in Hydrogeology, Colo. State U., 1966; PhD in Water Resources, Iowa State U. Sci. and Tech., 1969. Instr. earth sci. Iowa State U., Ames, 1966-69; from asst. prof. to prof. Northeastern Ill., Chgo., 1969-80, prof. geography and environ. studies, 1980—. Cons. hydrogeology, Des Plaines, Ill., 1970—; sr. adviser Saudi Arabian Ministry Planning, Riyadh, 1977-78; leader U.S. environ. sci. del. to People's Republic of China, 1984; pres., founder Islamic Info. Ctr. Am. Author: Secondarty Environmental Science Methods, 1973; contbr. numerous articles to profl. jours.; editor Environ. Resource, Directory Environ. Educators and Cons. World. NSF grantee, 1970-71, 71-72, 72-73, 75, 76, New grantee, 1974, grantee Ill. Dept. Edn., 1970. Mem. AAAS, NSF (cons.), Am. Waterworks Assn., Am. Men and Women Sci., Nat. Assn. Geology Tchrs. (pres. central sect. 1974), Environ. Sci. Inst. (edn. com.), Internat. Assn. Advancement of Earth and Environ Sci. (pres. 1975—, founder), Ill. Earth Sci. Edn. (pres. 1971-73, founder), Phi Delta Kappa. Muslim. Avocations: tennis, track, cross country, soccer.

RA, HYUNGSHIM YOO, biologist, researcher; b. Kimje, Cheonrabook-Do, Republic of Korea, Jan. 12, 1964; d. Okdol Ra and Bokdong Seo; m. Sunhee Yoo, June 10, 1989; children: Suran Yoo, Aran Yoo, Daeyeon Yoo. B, Paichai U., Republic of Korea, 1986; M, Sungshin Women's U., Republic of Korea, 1991; PhD, U. Ill., 2002. Cert. Achieve. U. Ill., in bus. mgmt. U. Ill., grad. tchr. U. Ill. Rschr. U. Ill., Urbana-Champaign, 2002—. Contbr. articles to profl. jours. Tchr. Korean Lang. Sch., Champaign, 2005—06; group leader summer Christian youth conf. Mountain Top, 2003—04; group leader New Year Christian Youth Conf., 2003—05, Camp Grow, 2004; organizer Ch. Blending Week, 2004; treas. Ch. Champaign, Ill., 2004—05; bridge builder Korean Presbyn. Ch., 2006, pres. women's club, 2007; vol. Empty Tomb, 2007; pres. women's club Korean Presbyn. Ch., Champaign, 2007—; bd. dirs. Nat. Women's Hist. Mus., DC, 2005; rsch. bd. adv. Am. Biog. Inst., Inc., Raleigh, NC, 2005. Recipient Internat. Peace prize, United Cultural Conv., 2005, Lifetime Achievement award, World Congress Arts, Scis. & Comms., 2006. Mem.: AAUW (assoc.), Am. Bryological and Lichenological Soc. (assoc.), Habitat for Humanity (assoc.), Nat. Com. to Preserve Social Security and Medicare (assoc.), The Nature Conservancy (assoc.), Sierra Club (assoc.). Consumer. Office: U Illinois 265 Morrill Hall 505 S Goodwin Ave Urbana IL 61801 Home: 3906 Turnberry Dr Champaign IL 61822 Business E-Mail: hs-yoo@life.uiuc.edu.

RAAB, JENNIFER J., academic administrator; b. NYC, June 12, 1956; m. Michael Goodwin; children: Scott, Miranda. AB with distinction, Cornell U., 1977; MPA, Princeton U., 1979; JD cum laude, Harvard U., 1985. Spl. projects mgr. South Bronx Devel. Org., 1979-81; dir. pub. affairs NYC Planning Commn., 1981-82; litigation assoc. Cravath, Swaine & Moore, NYC, 1985-90; campaign dir. Rose State Senate Campaign, 1988; issues dir. Giuliani Mayorial Campaign, 1989; litigation assoc. Paul, Weiss, Rifkind, Wharton & Garrison, NYC, 1990-94; chair NYC Landmarks Preservation Commn., 1994—2001; pres. Hunter Coll., 2001—. Bd. dirs. Argus Cmty., Inc., Bronx, NY, 1987-94, City Vol. Corps, 1994; active Manhattan Cmty. Bd. 5, 1990-94; pres. E. 154-155th St. Housing Corp., Bronx, 1992-94; vol. arbitrator Small Claims divsn. Bronx Civil Ct., 1993-94; mem. citizen's adv. coun., Mid-Town Cmty. Ct., 1994. Recipient Benjamin E. Mays award, A Better Chance, 2006; named one of The 100 Most Influential Women in NYC Bus., Crain's NY Bus., 2007. Mem. Phi Beta Kappa. Office: Hunter College Room E1700 695 Park Ave New York NY 10021 Office Phone: 212-772-4242. E-mail: president@hunter.cuny.edu.*

RAAB, SHELDON, lawyer; b. Bklyn., Nov. 30, 1937; s. Morris and Eva (Shereshevsky) Raab; m. Judith Deutsch, Dec. 15, 1963; children: Michael Kenneth, Elisabeth Louise, Andrew John. AB, Columbia U., 1958; LLB cum laude, Harvard U., 1961. Bar: N.Y. 1961, U.S. Ct. Appeals (2d cir.) 1963, U.S. Dist. Ct. (so. and ea. dists.) 1967, US Supreme Ct. 2000. Dep. asst. atty. gen. State of N.Y., 1961—63, asst. atty. gen., 1963—64; assoc. Frank, Harris, Shriver & Jacobson LLP (and predecessor firm), NYC, 1964—69, ptnr., 1970—81, inc. ptnr., 1981—2003, gen. counsel, of counsel, 2003—09. Bd. dirs. lawyers com. Civil Rights Under Law, 1998—2008. Mem. exec. com. lawyers' divsn. United Jewish Appeal, 1982—93. Mem.: ABA, Assn. of Bar of City of N.Y. (adminstrv. law com. 1968—71, spl. com. electric power and environment 1971—73, chmn. energy com. 1974—79, fed. cts. com. 1981—84, state superior cts. juris. com. 1985—88), N.Y. State Bar Assn. (trial lawyers sect. 1968—), Am. Law Inst. Democrat. Office: Fried Frank Harris Shriver & Jacobson LLP 1 New York Plz New York NY 10004-1980 Office Phone: 212-859-8090. Business E-Mail: raabsh@ffhsj.com.

RAABE, GERHARD KARL, epidemiologist; b. Flushing, NY, Feb. 24, 1948; s. Oscar Albert and Eugenie (Loehr) R.; m. Barbara Irene Douglas, Nov. 27, 1969; children: Andrew John, Emily Jean. BA in Biology, Hofstra U., 1969; MS in Computer Sci., Pratt Inst., 1971; DrPH, Columbia U., 1987. Sr. rsch. scientist N.Y. State Dept. Mental Hygiene, NYC, 1970-77; med. systems analyst Mobil Oil Corp., NYC, 1977-79, indsl. med. advisor, 1979-81, mgr. epidemiology and med. info. svcs., 1982-89, dir. epidemiology and med. info. svcs. Princeton, N.J., 1990-97; dir. med. info. and health risk assessment Global Med. Svcs., Mobil Bus. Resources Corp., 1997-99; pres., prin. scientist occupl. and environ. health Health Risk Scis., Inc., New Hope, Pa., 1999—. Cons. spl. studies Cornell U. Med. Ctr., NYC, 1973-77; cons. NYC Health Systems Agy., 1976; chmn. occupational health com. Fla. Phosphate Coun., Lakeland, 1979-85; reviewer profl. jours.; expert panelist WHO, IARC, U.S. EPA. Contbr. articles to profl. jours., chpts. to books. Fellow Am. Coll. Epidemiology; mem. AAAS, Soc. for Epidemiologic Rsch., Internat. Soc. for Environ. Epidemiology, Am. Petroleum Inst. (chmn. epidemiology 1985-88, chmn. health and product stewardship 1996-2000), NY Acad. Scis., Soc. for Risk Analysis, Indsl. Epidemiology Forum (chmn. 1991), Internat. Commn. on Occupl. Health. Republican. Lutheran. Avocations: science fiction, tennis. Home: 2215 Aquetong Rd New Hope PA 18938-1149 Office: Health Risk Scis Inc PO Box 189 New Hope PA 18938-0189 Office Phone: 215-862-5718. Personal E-mail: gkraabe@cs.com.

RAABE, WILLIAM ALAN, tax writer, business educator; b. Milw., Dec. 14, 1953; s. William Arthur and Shirley R.; m. Nancy Elizabeth Miller, Mar. 1989; children: Margaret Elisabeth, Martin William. BS, Carroll Coll., 1975; MAS, U. Ill., Urbana, 1976, PhD, 1979. Wis. Disting. prof. U. Wis., Milw., 1979-96; tax edn. cons. Price Waterhouse Coopers, NYC, 1985—; prof., dir. acctg. programs Samford U., Birmingham, Ala., 1997-2001; founding dean Sch. Mgmt., disting. prof. Capital U., Columbus, Ohio, 2001—02; tax faculty Fisher Coll. Bus. Ohio State U., Columbus, 2002—. Vis. assoc. prof. Ariz. State U., Tempe, 1985; vis. faculty Ernst & Young, NYC, 1990—, Deloitte & Touche, NYC, 1998—, KPMG, NYC, 2008-, Calif. CPA Found., 1986, AICPA, 1984-94, Wis. Bar Assn., 1992, Capital U. Law Sch., 2002-04; developer Estate Tax Planner, McGraw Hill Software, NYC, 1980-88; expert witness, 1985—; cons. corp. income tax State Ala., 1997-01, State of Wis., 1995, 99; dir. Fisher/Ohio State U. Tax Clinic, 2003—. Author Federal Taxation, 1983—, Federal Tax Research, 1986—, Income Shifting After Tax Reform, 1987, Multistate Corporate Tax Guide, 1985-96, California Income Taxation, 1999-2006, Schedule M-3, 2006, 2008, Tax Law Analysis, 2005-; Price Waterhouse Coopers Tax Case Studies, 2005-; contbr. articles to profl. & academic jours. Bd. dirs., Nat. Luth. Choir, 2008-, Luth. High Sch. Assn. Milw., 1991-96, pres., 1993-96, Bethesda Luth. Home and Found., Watertown, Wis., 1989-91, Luth. Counseling and Family Svcs., 1982-88, Concord Chamber Orch., Milw., 1983-88, Nat. Luth. Choir, 2008-; mem. Econ. Devel. Com., Wauwatosa, Wis., 1986-89; faculty athletic rep. to NCAA from U. Wis. Milw., 1990-96; mem. Milw. Symphony Chorus, Master Singers of Milw., Samford Master Singers, 1985-2000; vice chair faculty senate Samford U., 2000-01. Named to Alumni Hall Fame, Milw. Luth. H.S., 1995, Carroll Coll., 2005; fellow, U. Ill., 1978; fellowship, Earnst & Young, 1979, Nat. Ctr. Tax Edn. and Rsch., 1982. Mem. Am. Acctg. Assn., Am. Taxation Assn., Wis. Inst. CPAs (Educator of Yr. 1987), Ala. Acctg. Educators Assn. (pres. 1999-2000). Office: Fisher Coll Bus 2100 Neil Ave Columbus OH 43210-1144 Office Phone: 614-292-4023. Business E-Mail: raabe.12@osu.edu.

RAAD, ISSAM I., medical educator, researcher; s. Inaam Raad and Loulou Dagher; m. Lamia Raad; children: Sammy, Nayla, Ted. MD, Am. U. Beirut, 1982. Medical License Tex. State Bd. of Med. Examiners, 1989, cert. in internal medicine Am. Bd. Internal Medicine, 1988, infectious diseases sub-specialist 1990. Prof. medicine U. Tex. M. D. Anderson Cancer Ctr., Houston, 1999—, chmn., dept. infectious diseases, infection control and employee health, 2005—. Pres. Health Outreach to Mid. East, Houston, Worldwide Inst. Med. Edn., Houston. Recipient Order of Cedars medal, Pres. Lebanon, 2005, Med. Leadership award, Am. U. Beirut Alumni Assn., 2007, Sci. Achievement award, Am. Lebanese Med. Assn., 2007, Ben Qurrah award, Arab AMA - Houston Chpt., 2008, Otis W. and Pearl L. Walters Faculty Achievement award, U. Tex. M.D. Anderson Cancer Ctr., 2006; named Outstanding Inventor of Yr., Houston Intellectual Property Lawyers Assn., 2004; named one of America's Top Physicians, Consumer's Rsch. Coun., 2004—05. Fellow: ACP, Infectious Diseases Soc. America; mem.: Am. Lebanese Med. Assn., Internat. Immunocompromised Host Soc., Multinational Assn. Supportive Care in Cancer, Soc. Healthcare Epidemiology America, Lebanese Soc. Infectious Disease, AMA, Tex. Infectiuos Diseases Soc., Harris County Med. Soc., Tex. Med. Assn., Nat. Arab AMA, Am. Soc. Microbiology. Achievements include patents for antimicrobial coated medical implants; EDTA with other chelators with or without antifungal antimicrobial agents for the prevention and treatment of fungal infections; patents in field. Office: M D Anderson Cancer Ctr 1515 Holcombe Blvd Houston TX 77030 Office Fax: 713-792-8233. Business E-Mail: iraad@mdanderson.org.

RAAD, VIRGINIA, pianist, educator; b. Salem, W.Va., Aug. 13, 1925; d. Joseph M. and Martha (Joseph) R. BA in Art History, Wellesley Coll., 1947; spl. student, New Eng. Conservatory Music, 1947-48; student, Berthe Bert, 1949—55, Jeanne Blancard, 1949—55, student, 1968—70, Alfred Cortot, 1950—51, Jacques Chailley, 1953—55; PhD with honors, U. Paris, 1955; diplôme, Ecole Normale de Musique, Paris, 1950. Artist in residence Salem Coll., W.Va., 1957-70; ind. concert pianist, 1960—; musician in residence at cmty. colls. NC Arts Coun., 1971—. Adjudicator Nat. Guild Piano Tchrs., Nat. Fedn. Music Clubs; panelist, grant reviewer NEH, 1978-84, 92—; mem. com. Nat. Endowment Arts, 1978; Am. rep. Debussy Centennial Colloque, Paris, 1962. Perfomances, concerts, lectrs. master classes at West Ga. Coll., Carrollton, La Grange Coll., Ga., Columbus Coll., Ga., Young Harris Coll., Ga., U. Fla., Gainesville, Norton Gallery, Palm Beach, Fla., Alliance Française de Rollins Coll., Winter Park, Fla., Dixon Gallery and Gardens, Memphis, St. Jude Children's Rsch. Hosp., Memphis, Cleveland State CC, Tenn., Sampson Tech. Inst., Clinton, NC, Wayne CC, Goldsboro, NC, Brevard Coll., NC, Ctrl. Wesleyan Coll., SC, Ky. Wesleyan Coll., Owensboro, Berea Ky., Coll., Alice Lloyd Coll., Pippa Passes, Ky., Coll. of William and Mary, Williamsburg, Va., Eastern Mennonite Coll., Harrisonburg, Va., The Phillips Gallery, Washington, Trinity Coll., Washington, Manhattanville Coll., Purchase, NY, Elmira Coll., NY, Fordham U., NYC, The Piano Tchrs. Congress of NY, Middlebury Coll., Vt., St. Anselm's Coll., Manchester, N.H., Mount St. Mary's Coll., Hooksett, NH, Wellesley Coll., Mass., Curry Coll., Milton, Mass., So. Conn. State U., New Haven, Slippery Rock U., Pa., Seton Hill Coll., Greensboro, Pa., Alliance Française de Pitts. and U. Pitts., Channel 13 WQED (PBS) Pitts., Lincoln U., Oxford, Pa., The Grier Sch., Tyrone, Pa., Mount de Chantal Acad., Wheeling W.Va., Wheeling Jesuit U., among other colls. and univs.; contbg. author: Debussy et l'Evolution de la Musique au XX Siècle, 1965, l'Influenc Debussy Amerique; author: The Piano Sonority of Claude Debussy, 1994; recording artist: EDUCO, 1995—; contbr. articles to profl. jours. Active Amnesty Internat. Urgent Action Network; alumna regional rep. Wellesley Coll.; mem bd. visitors New Eng. Conservatory of Music, 2004—. Named Outstanding W.Va. Woman Educator Delta Kappa Gamma, 1965; presented biography to Schlesinger Library on History of Women in Am. Radcliffe Coll., 1967; grantee Govt. France, Am. Coun. Learned Socs. Mem. Soc. Française de Musicologie, Am. Musicol. Soc. (regional officer 1960-65), Am. Coll. Musicians, Internat. Musicol. Soc., Music Tchrs. Nat. Assn. (adjudicator, musicology program chair 1983-87), W.Va. Music Tchrs. Assn., Audubon Activist, Alpha Delta Kappa (hon.). Roman Catholic. Avocations: hiking, gardening, birding. Home and Office: 60 Terrace Ave Salem WV 26426-1116 Office Phone: 304-782-2274. Personal E-mail: virginiaraad@aol.com.

RAAF, JOHN HART, retired surgeon, educator, health facility administrator; b. Portland, Oreg., Aug. 10, 1941; s. John E. and Lorene (Rardin) R.; m. Heather Neilson, June 15, 1965; children— Jennifer, John, Sabrina AB magna cum laude, Harvard U., 1963, MD cum laude, 1970; D.Phil., Oxford U., 1966. Diplomate Am. Bd. Surgery. Intern Mass. Gen. Hosp., Boston, 1970-71, resident in surgery, 1971-73, 75-77; research fellow Sloan-Kettering Inst., NYC, 1973-75; fellow in immunology Meml. Hosp., NYC, 1973-74; faculty assoc. in surgery M.D. Anderson Hosp. and Tumor Inst., Houston, 1977-78, asst. prof. surgery, 1978-79, Cornell U. Med. Coll., NYC, 1979-81; assoc. prof. surgery Meml. Sloan-Kettering Cancer Ctr., NYC, 1981-85; dir. Cleve. Clinic Cancer Ctr., 1985-90; chmn. dept. surgery Meridia Huron Hosp., Cleve., 1991-94; chief surg. svc. VA Med. Ctr. Cleve., 1994-2001; prof. surgery Case Western Res. U., 1994—2009, vice chmn. dept. surgery, 1994-2001. Mem. selection coms. for Rhodes scholarships, Vt., 1969-71, New Eng., 1969-71, La., 1977, Tex., 1978, Ohio, 1989-94; mem. soft tissue sarcoma discussion group Nat. Cancer Inst., 1980; mem. clin. trials com. Nat. Cancer Inst., NIH, 1984-88 Co-author Meml. Sloan-Kettering Cancer Ctr. publs., 1980; also numerous articles, chpts., abstracts, letters, short papers, movies, med. photographs; editor: Diagnosis and Treatment of Soft Tissue Sarcomas, 1993; editor-in-chief Primary Care and Cancer, 1981-92; mem. editorial bd. Meml. Sloan-Kettering Cancer Ctr. Clin. Bull., 1979-82; assoc. editor Oncology mag., 1987-92; mem. editorial com. Cleve Clinic Jour. Medicine, 1987-90. Rhodes scholar Oxford U., Eng., 1963; nat. scholar Harvard U. Med. Sch., 1966-70; Am. Cancer Soc. postdoctoral scholar Harvard U. Med. Sch., 1969-70; ACS scholar Mass. Gen. Hosp., Boston, 1975-77; Am. Cancer Soc. jr. faculty clin. fellow, 1980-83. Fellow ACS; mem. Am. Assn. Cancer Research, Am. Assn. Endocrine Surgeons, Am. Soc. Clin. Oncology, Assn. Acad. Surgery, Assn. Am. Rhodes Scholars, Cen. Surg. Assn., Soc. Surg. Oncology (publs. com. 1981-84, working group on edn. 1982, membership com. 2000), Meml. Hosp. Alumni Soc. (chmn. program com. 1982), Cleve. Skating Club, Charaka Club (N.Y.C.). Home: 12501 Fairhill Rd Cleveland OH 44120-1017

RAAFLAUB, KURT ARNOLD, classics educator; b. Buea, Cameroon, Feb. 15, 1941; s. Fritz and Heidi (Ninck) R.; m. Deborah Dickmann Boedeker, July 14, 1978. MA, U. Basel, Switzerland, 1967, PhD, 1970. Asst. prof. ancient history Free U. Berlin, 1972-78, Brown U., Providence, 1978-80, assoc. prof. classics and history, 1980-83, prof., 1983—, John Rowe Workman Disting. prof. classics and humanistic tradition, 1989-92, David Herlihy Univ. prof., 2001—, Royce Family prof. excellence in tchg., 2005—, chmn. dept. classics, 1984-89; co-dir. Ctr. for Hellenic Studies, Washington, 1992-2000, chmn. program in ancient studies, 2000—. Author: Dignitatis Contentio, 1974, Die Entdeckung der Freiheit, 1985, The Discovery of Freedom in Ancient Greece, 2004; co-author: Studien zum Attischen Seebund, 1984, Aspects of Athenian Democracy, 1990, Ancient History: Recent Work and New Directions, 1997, Origins of Democracy in Ancient Greece, 2007; editor or co-editor: Social Struggles in Archaic Rome, 1986, 2d edit., 2005, Between Republic and Empire: Interpretations of Augustus and His Principate, 1990, Athens and Rome, Florence and Venice: City-States in Classical Antiquity and Medieval Italy, 1991, Anfänge politischen Denkens in der Antike: Die nahöstlichen Kulturen und die Griechen, 1993, Studies in the Ancient Greek Polis, 1995, More Studies in the Ancient Greek Polis, 1996, Democracy 2500: Questions and Challenges, 1998, Democracy, Empire and the Arts in Fifth-Century Athens, 1998, War and Society in the Ancient and Medieval Worlds, 1999, War and Peace in the Ancient World, 2007, A Companion to Archaic Greece, 2009; contbr. articles to profl. jours. Mem. Historisches Kolleg Munich, 1989-90. Am. Coun. Learned Socs. fellow, 1983-84, Ctr. for Hellenic Studies fellow, 1976-77, NEH fellow, 1989; faculty fellow U. New England, Armidale, Australia, 1996. Mem. Philol. Assn., Assn. Ancient

Historians, Am. Inst. Archaeology, German Archaeol. Inst. (corr.). Avocation: music. Home: 495 Lloyd Ave Providence RI 02906-4547 Office: Brown U Dept Classics Providence RI 02912-1856 Office Phone: 401-863-2123. Business E-Mail: kurt_raaflaub@brown.edu.

RAB, GEORGE T., pediatric orthopedic surgeon; b. Cleve., Nov. 11, 1946; s. Thomas P. and Patricia S. Rab; m. Wendy Andereson Rab, Aug. 31, 1968; children: Geoffrey W., Nicholas A. BS, Northwestern U., Chgo., 1968; MD, Northwestern U., 1970; MS, U. Minn., Mpls., 1975. Lic. physician Calif., diplomate Am. Bd. Orthop. Surgery, Nat. Bd. Med. Examiners. Intern in surgery Chgo. Wesley Meml. Hosp., 1970—71; resident in orthop surgery Mayo Clinic, Rochester, Minn., 1971—75; resident in pediat. orthop. surgery Gillette Children's Hosp., St. Paul, 1974; asst. prof. dept. orthop. surgery Sch. Medicine, U. Calif., Davis, 1977—82, assoc. prof. dept. orthop. surgery, 1982—88, prof. dept. orthop., 1988—, Ben Ali chair in pediat. orthop., 1998—, chair dept. orthop. surgery, 2000—06. Guest lectr. Shriners Hosp. for Crippled Children and Sch. Medicine Oreg. Health Scis. U., Portland, 1985, Duncan Seminar Children's Orthop. Hosp. and Med. Ctr., Seattle, 1987; vis. prof., guest lectr. dept. orthop. Children's Hosp. Med. Ctr., Cin., 1986; vis. prof., guest lectr. Carrie Tingley Hosp. Annual Meeting, Albuquerque, 1992; vis. prof., guest lectr., Robert Samilson lectr., San Francisco, 96; vis. prof. U. Calif., Irvine, 1998, U. Colo., 1999, New Eng. Med. Ctr., 1999, Children's Hosp. Med. Ctr. of Akron, Ohio, 2001; Arthur A. Thibodeau vis. prof. Tufts U. Sch. Medicine, 1999; John M. Roberts vis. prof. Children's Hosp. of New Orleans, 2000; vis. prof., Leslie Meyers lectr. Shriners Hosp., Greenville, SC, 2001; Charles LeRoy Lowman vis. prof. Orthop. Hosp., LA, 2002; orthop. surgeon, med. dir. motion analysis lab. Shriners Hosp. for Children, 1995—; pediat. orthop. specialist Sutter Cmty. Hosps., Sacramento, 1987—; vis. assoc. prof. dept. orthop. Harvard Med. Sch., Boston, 1983—84; rsch. fellow gait lab. Children's Hosp., Boston, 1983—84; editl. cons. Am. Jour. Diseases of Children, 1990—93; cons., rev. com. Orthop. Rsch. and Edn. Found., 1994—99; civilian cons. med. specialist in pediat. orthop. surgery Oakland Naval Hosp., Calif., 1990—95; pediat. orthop. cons. Kaiser Permanente Hosp., Sacramento, 1977—98. Mem. editl. bd. Gait and Posture, 1992—97, bd. editors Jour. Pediat. Orthopedics, 1992—, Jour. Children's Orthopedics, 2006—. Bd. dirs. Sacramento Make-A-Wish Found., Inc., 1988—92. Maj. US Army, 1975—77. Recipient Goldsmith Intern Humanitarian award, Chgo. Wesley Meml. Hosp., 1971, Frank Stitchfield award, Hip Soc., 1976, annual award for excellence in tchg. clin. scis., Kaiser Found. Hosp., 1978, Best Poster award, Gait and Clin. Analysis Soc. Meeting, 2000; named Outstanding Clin. Instr., U. Calif. Davis Sch. Medicine, 1980, Outstanding Tchr. of Yr. in Orthop. Surgery, 1991, 1996; named one of Best Drs. in Am., 2005—06; Berg-Sloat Traveling fellow, 1977. Fellow: Am. Acad. Pediat., Am. Acad. Orthop. Surgeons (com. on biomed. engring. 1980—82, com. on psychomotor skills 1980—87, com. ednl. content 1981—82, sec. com. on biomed. engring. 1982—85, subcom. on pediat. of com. on exams. and evaluations 1985—91, chmn. com. on biomed. engring. 1986—87); mem.: Sierra Sacramento Valley Med. Soc., Sacramento Pediat. Soc., Paul R. Lipscomb Soc., West Coast Gait Lab. Group, Western Orthop. Assn., Calif. Med. Assn., Am. Orthop. Assn., Pediat. Orthop. Soc. N.Am. (com. on computer applications in pediat. orthop. 1985—90), Orthop. Rsch. Soc., Internat. Soc. Electrophysiol. Kinesiology, Internat. Pediat. Orthop. Think Tank (site selection com. 1998—2000), Gait and Clin. Movement Analysis Soc. (awards com. 2001—02), Am. Soc. Biomechanics (arrangements com. annual meeting 1987, pres.-elect 1989—90, exec. com. 1989—93, pres. 1990—91), Am. Bd. Orthop. Surgery (certifying examiner 1984—92), Am. Acad. Cerebral Palsy and Devel. Medicine (nominating com. 1990—94). Avocations: bicycling, sailing, hiking, cooking. Office: Dept Orthop Surgery U Calif-Davis 4860 Y St # 3800 Sacramento CA 95817 Office Phone: 916-734-5770. Office Fax: 916-734-7904. E-mail: george.rab@ucdmc.ucdavis.edu.

RABABAAH, HAROUN R., engineering educator, researcher; s. Rasheed and Amenah Rababaah; m. Alaa M. Rababah. BSc in Indsl. Engring., 1995, MS in Applied Math. and Computer Sci., 2005. Plant mgr. design engr. Almajd Engring. Industries, Amman, Jordan, 1995—97; quality mgr. MRQ CST, Ramtha, Irbid, Jordan, 1997—2000; adj. faculty and rsch. asst. Ind. U. South Bend, 2002—05; lectr. and rsch. asst. Tenn. State U., Nashville, 2005—. Achievements include invention of new multi sensor data fusion engine. Office: Tenn State Univ 3500 John A Merritt Blvd Nashville TN 37209 Office Fax: 615-963-5094. Business E-Mail: haroun01@gmail.com.

RABADAN, RAUL, physics professor; Fellow CERN, Geneva, 2001—03; mem. Inst. Advanced Study, Princeton, NJ, 2003—08; prof. Columbia U., NYC, 2008—. Contbr. articles to profl. jours. Office: Columbia Univ ICRC Bldg 1130 St Nicholas Ave New York NY 10032 Business E-Mail: rabadan@dbmi.columbia.edu.

RABADI, MEHEROZ HOSHANG, neurologist, consultant; s. Hoshang Hormusji and Rhoda Hoshang Rabadi; m. Freny Meheroz Wadiwalla, June 28, 1998. MBBS, Dow Med. Coll., Karachi, 1982. Cert. Am. Bd. Psychiatry and Neurology, 2002. Neurology fellow Burke Rehab. Hosp. affiliate Weill Med. Coll. Cornell U., White Plains, NY, 1998—2000, attending neurologist, 2000—. Co-dir. stroke unit Burke Rehab. Hosp., White Plains, 2000—05. Contbr. articles to profl. jours. Priest Zoroastrian Assn. Greater N.Y., Sonoma, NY, 1998—2005. Mem.: Royal Coll.Physicians Ireland (licentiate). Office: VA Med Ctr 921 NE 13th St Oklahoma City OK 73104 Home: 1919 E 2nd St Apt 152 Edmond OK 73034 Home Phone: 405-216-5081; Office Phone: 405-456-5298. Office Fax: 914-597-2774. Personal E-mail: mhrabadi@gmail.com. Business E-Mail: meheroz.rabadi@va.gov.

RABAK, DAVID WILLIAM, retired family practice physician, educator, consultant; b. Washington, Sept. 3, 1919; s. William Rabak and Jessie Garnet Hastings; m. Barbara Jean Rabak, Mar. 25, 1943 (dec. Mar. 6, 2005); children: Martha Jean Tatum, Thomas William, Judith Ann Wagoner. Degree, Edison Vocat. Coll., Seattle, 1938; BS, U. Wash., Seattle, 1942; MD, U. Calif., San Francisco, 1949. Diplomate Am. Bd. Family Practice, 1971, lic. physician Calif., 1949, Wash., 1950. Platoon leader, instr. US Army 10th Mountain Divsn., Ft. Lewis, Wash. and Denver, 1942—49; intern San Joaquin County Hosp., French Camp, Calif., 1949—50; resident The Dr.'s Hosp., Seattle, 1950—51; pvt. practice gen. and family medicine Seattle, 1951—73; pvt. practice FAA-United Airlines, Seattle and Washington, 1951—84; clin. asst. prof. U. Wash., Seattle, 1972—74, clin. assoc. prof., 1974—77; family physician, chief primary care and clinic svcs. USAF Clinic Ramstein, Germany, 1975—76, dir. base med. svcs., 1976, chief clinic svcs., 1976—78; assoc. prof. Uniformed Svcs. Med. Sch., Bethesda, Md., 1978—84; chief primary care clinic Malcolm Grow USAF Med. Ctr., Andrews AFB, Md., 1978—79, chmn. dept. primary care, 1979—80, chmn. dept. family practice, 1980—84. Cons. United Airlines, Seattle, 1955—73; aviation med. examiner FAA, 1960—75; med. dir., physician Alaska Airlines, Seattle, 1966; staff physician Sound Health Assocs., Tacoma, 1973—74; family practice cons. Surgeon Gen. USAF, 1980—84; program dir. family practice residency Malcolm Grow USAF Med. Ctr., 1980—84; preceptor dept. familly medicine Swedish Hosp., Seattle, 1984—85; tutor U. Wash. Sch. Medicine, Seattle, 1992. Contbr. articles to profl. jours. Col. USAF, 1942—84. Recipient Meritorious Svc. medal, US Govt., Washington, 1978—84. Fellow: Am. Acad. Family Physicians (pres. Seattle 1954—92, del. to state 1969—71, pres. King County chpt. 1970); mem.: AMA (pres. Wash. state 1972—73), Wash. Acad. Family Physicians (v.p. 1971—72, pres. 1973—74, chmn. liaison com. 1967—73, former del.), Soc. Tchrs. Family Medicine, King County Med. Soc. (past del. to state, formerly univ. com., program com.), Wash. State Med. Assn. (past mental health and liaison com.), Mountain Rescue Coun. Presbyterian. Avocations: skiing, mountaineering, golf, hiking. Home: 720 Seneca St # 909 Seattle WA 98101-2766 Personal E-mail: drabak@sprynet.com.

RABASSA, CLEMENTINE CHRISTOS, humanities educator, translator; b. NYC, July 31, 1932; d. Sotter and Mary (Legatos) Christos; m. Gregory Rabassa; 1 child, Clara C. BA cum laude, Hunter Coll., 1953, MA, 1958; PhD with distinction, Columbia U., 1971. Preceptor, instr. Spanish Columbia U., NYC, 1963-66, instr. Spanish, 1964-66; from asst. prof. to assoc. prof. humanities Medgar Evers Coll., CUNY, 1973-79, prof. humanities, 1979-90, prof. humanities emerita, 1990—, coord. fgn. langs., 1976-79. Author: Demetrio Aguilera - Malta and Social Justice, 1980, En Torno a Aguilera - Malta, 1981, Summer II, a novella, 1999, (poetry) Pollock's Polka, 2004; co-editor Studies in Afro-Hispanic Lit., 1977-79; translator: Canticle for a Memory (Francisco Arriví), 1993, Emotions (Julio Ortega), 1999. Fellow Fulbright-Hays, 1963, NEH, 1971-72, Rockefeller Found., 1979-80, Gulbenkian Found., 1989; named to Hunter Coll. Hall of Fame, 1982. Mem. MLA, Am. Lit. Translators Assn., Alliance Française, PEN Am. Ctr., Phi Beta Kappa, Sigma Delta Pi. Democrat. Greek Orthodox. Avocations: music, painting, writing. Home and Office: 140 E 72d St Apt 10B New York NY 10021-4268

RABASSA, GREGORY, language educator, translator, poet; b. Yonkers, NY, Mar. 9, 1922; m. Clementine Christos, 1966; children: Kate, Clara. AB, Dartmouth Coll., 1945, Litt.D. hon., 1982; MA, Columbia U., 1947, PhD in Portuguese, 1954; Litt.D. (hon.), U. Hartford, 2005; LHD, U. Mass., 2008. Instr. Spanish Columbia U., 1947-52, assoc., 1952-58, asst. prof., 1958-63, assoc. prof. Spanish and Portuguese, 1963-68; prof. Romance langs. Queens Coll., CUNY Grad. Sch., Flushing, NY, 1968-86, Disting. prof., 1986—2008. Assoc. editor Odyssey Rev., 1961-64 Contbr. articles to profl. jours.; author If This Be Treason: Translation and Its Dyscontents, 2005, A Cloudy Day in Gray Minor, Early Poems, 1945-1948, 1992. Staff sgt. OSS, 1942-45. Decorated Croce al Merito di Guerra Italy, Order of San Carlos Colombia, Order Rio Branco Brazil; recipient Nat. Book award for transl., 1967, Transl. prize, PEN Am. Ctr., 1977, Transl. medal, 1982, Gregory Kolovakos award, 2001, Martha Albrand award Art of Memoir, 2006, Transl. prize, Wheatland Found., 1988, Gode award, Am. Transl. Assn., 1980, Arts award, N.Y. Gov., 1985, Lit. award, Am. Acad. and Inst. Arts and Letters, 1989, Presdl. medal, Dartmouth Coll., 1991, Ivan Sandrof award, The Nat. Book Critics Cir., 1993, Lit. Lion award, N.Y. Pub. Libr., 1993, Mellon Humanities award, Loyola U., Chgo., 1995, Gabriela Mistral prize, Chile, 1996, John Steinbeck Writers award, Southampton Coll., 2002, Machado de Assis medal, Union Brazilian Writers, NY, 2005, Aurora Borealis award, Internat. Fedn. Translators, 2005, Nat. Medal of Arts, Nat. Endowment Arts, 2006, Lifetime Achievement award, Brazilian Studies Assoc., 2008, Thornton Wilder Translation prize, Am. Acad. Arts & Letters, 2009; fellow Fulbright-Hays fellow, 1965—66, NEH fellow, 1979—80, Guggenheim fellow, 1988—89. Mem. Renaissance Soc. Am., MLA, Am. Assn. Tchrs. Spanish and Portuguese, Latin Am. Studies Assn., Am. Lit. Translators Assn., Hispanic Soc. Am., Century Assoc., PEN Club, Phi Beta Kappa. Office: Dept Hispanic Langs & Lits CUNY Queens Coll Flushing NY 11367 Office Phone: 212-439-6636.

RABATÉ, JEAN-MICHEL, literature and language professor; MA in English lit., Sorbonne Paris-VIII, 1970, PhD summa cum laude, 1980. Prof. English and comparative lit. U. Pa., Phila., 1992—, Vartan Gregorian prof. humanities, 2008—. Dir. Coll. Internat. de Philosophie, Paris, 1992—97; sr. curator Slought Found., Phila., 2002—. Author: The Ghosts of Modernity, 1996, Joyce and the Politics of Egoism, 2001, Jacques Lacan and Literature, 2001, Given: 1) Art, 2) Crime, 2006, The Cradle of Modernism, 2007, The Ethic of the Lie, 2008; editor: Writing the Image After Roland Barthes, 1997, Jacques Lacan in America, 2000, The Cambridge Companion to Jacques Lacan, 2002, The Future of Theory, 2002, Advances to James Joyce, 2004, Architecture Against Death: On Arakwa and Gins, 2005; co-editor (with Aaron Levy): On the Diagram: The Art of Marjorie Welish, 2004; co-editor: William Anastasi's Pataphysical Society, 2005, Helene Cixous: On Cities, 2006. Fellow: Am. Acad. Arts and Sciences. Office: U Pa Dept English Fisher-Bennett Hall 339 3340 Walnut St Philadelphia PA 19104-6273 Office Phone: 215-989-5870. E-mail: jnrabate@english.upenn.edu.

RABB, BRUCE, lawyer; b. Cambridge, Mass., Oct. 4, 1941; s. Maxwell M. and Ruth (Criedenberg) R.; m. Harriet Rachel Schaffer, Jan. 4, 1970; children: Alexander Charles, Katherine Anne. AB, Harvard U., 1962; Cert. d'Etudes Politiques, Institut d'Etudes Politiques, Paris, 1963; LLB, Columbia U., 1966. Bar: NY 1966. Law clk. to judge U.S. Ct. Appeals (5th cir.), 1966-67; assoc. Stroock & Stroock & Lavan, NYC, 1967-68, 71-75, ptnr., 1976-91, Kramer Levin Naftalis & Frankel LLP, NYC, 1991—2003, counsel, 2003—09. Staff asst. to Pres. U.S., 1969-70; supr. bd. dir. Agora-Gazeta, sp.zo.o., 1993-98, Agora-Druk, sp.zo.o., 1995-98, Agora, SA, 2006-09; pub. mem. Adminstrv. Conf. U.S., 1982-86, 89-92, spl. counsel, 1986-88; bd. dir. Helicor, Inc. 2005-. Bd. dirs. Human Rights First (formerly Lawyers Com. Human Rights, 1977-95), nat. coun., 1996—; sec. Lehrman Inst., 1978-88; bd. dirs. Citizens Union of NY, 1981-87, 88-94, 95-01, 02—09, treas., 2002-05; mem. Human Rights Watch Ams., 1982-, Human Rights Watch Helsinki, 1985-97, Fund for Free Expression, 1987-97, Am. Friends Alliance Israelite Universelle, 1987-01; bd. dirs. Human Rights Watch Middle East No. Africa, 1989-, vice chmn., 1990-, Nat. Ctr. Law and Econ. Justice (formerly Welfare Law Ctr.), 1997-, Sabre Found., 2003—, Human Rights Watch Asia, 2003—, Nat. Com. Am. Fgn. Policy, 2004-05, Human Rights Watch, 2004—, Human Rights Watch, LGBT, 2005—, co-chair, 2006-, Cinereach, 2007-; mem. internat. adv. com. Internat. Parliamentary Group Human Rights in the Soviet Union, 1984-88; dir. Human Rights Watch Internat. Bd., 1988-03, dir. emeritus, 2003—,sec., 2003—;08, sec. & gen. council Youth Outreach-CapeVerde,2006- prin. Coun. Excellence in Govt., 1990—; mem. adv. coun. Drs. of World USA, 1996-, FilmAid Internat., 2000-03, dir., sec., 2003-; dir. Nat. Econ. and Social Rights Initiative, 2007-, Sustainable South Bronx, 2007-, dir. Rwanda Cmty. Works, 2007-, mem. adv. bd. BNA Antitrust, Trade Repulation Report, 2008- With USCGR, 1967—72. Mem. ABA (adv. panel Internat. Human Rights Trial Observer project), Am. Law Inst., Assn. of Bar of City of N.Y. (fed. legis., internat. law chair 1992-95, internat. human rights, civil rights, legal edn. and admission to bar, internat. trade coms., coun. fgn. affairs, energy), Coun. Fgn. Rels., Harvard Club N.Y.C., Met. Club of Washington.; Fellow NY Inst. Humanities NY U. Business E-Mail: brabb@colrainassociates.com.

RABB, GEORGE BERNARD, zoologist, conservationist; b. Charleston, SC, Jan. 2, 1930; s. Joseph and Teresa C. (Redmond) R.; m. Mary Sughrue, June 10, 1953. BS, Coll. Charleston, 1951, LHD (hon.), 1995; MA, U. Mich., 1952, PhD, 1957. Teaching fellow zoology U. Mich., 1954-56; curator, coord. rsch. Chgo. Zool. Park, Brookfield., Ill., 1956-64, assoc. dir. rsch. and edn., 1964-75, dep. dir., 1969-75, dir., 1976—2003, dir. emeritus, 2003—. Rsch. assoc. Field Mus., 1965—; lectr. dept. biology U. Chgo., 1965-89; mem. Com. on Evolutionary Biology, 1969—; pres. Chgo. Zool. Soc., 1976-2003, pres. emeritus, 2004—; mem. steering com. Species Survival Commn., Internat. Union Conservation of Nature/World Conservation Union, 1983-2003, vice-chmn. N.Am., 1986-88, dep. chmn., 1987-89, chmn., 1989-96, vice-chmn. comms., 1997-2003; chmn. policy adv. group Internat. Species Info. System, 1974-89, chmn. bd., 1989-92; pres. bd. dirs. Chgo. Wilderness Mag., 1999—2008; v.p. Fauna and Flora Internat., 1998—; chmn. bd. Ill. State Mus., 1999—2009; bd. dirs. Ctr. Humans and Nature. Bd. dirs. Defenders of Wildlife, 2002—. Recipient Lifetime Achievement award, Nat. Coun. Sci. & Environment, 2008. Fellow AAAS; mem. Am. Soc. Ichthyologists and Herpetologists (pres. 1978), Herpetologists League, Soc. Systematic Zoology, Am. Soc. Mammalogists, Soc. Study Evolution, Ecol. Soc. Am., Soc. Conservation Biology (council mem. 1986), Soc. for Integrative and Comparative Zoology, Soc. Study Animal Behavior, Am. Assn. Museums (named to Centennial Honor Roll, 2006), Am. Soc. Naturalists, Am. Assn. Zool. Parks and Aquariums (dir. 1979-80), World Assn. Zoos and Aquariums, World Conservation Union (hon. mem.), Sigma Xi. Office: 9236 Broadway Brookfield IL 60513 Personal E-mail: georgerabb@sbcglobal.net.

RABB, HARRIET SCHAFFER, academic administrator, lawyer; b. Houston, Sept. 12, 1941; d. Samuel S. and Helen G. Schaffer; m. Bruce Rabb, Jan. 4, 1970; children: Alexander, Katherine. BA in Govt., Barnard Coll., 1963; JD, Columbia U., 1966. Bar: N.Y. 1966, U.S. Supreme Ct. 1969, D.C. 1970. Instr. seminar on constl. litig. Rutgers Law Sch., 1966-67; staff atty. Ctr. for Constl. Rights, 1966-69; spl. counsel to commr. consumer affairs NYC Dept. Consumer Affairs, 1969-70; sr. staff atty. Stern Cmty. Law Firm, Washington, 1970-71; asst. dean urban affairs Law Sch., Columbia U., NYC, 1971-84, prof. law, dir. clin. edn., 1984-99, George M. Jaffen prof. law and social responsibility, 1991-99, vice dean, 1992-93; gen. counsel Dept. Health and Human Svcs., Washington, 1993—2001; v.p., gen. counsel Rockefeller U., NYC, 2001—. Mem. faculty employment and tng. policy Harvard Summer Inst., Cambridge, Mass., 1975-79. Author: (with Agid, Cooper and Rubin) Fair Employment Litigation Manual, 1975, (with Cooper and Rubin) Fair Employment Litigation, 1975. Bd. dirs. Ford Found., 1977-89, NY Civil Liberties Union, 1972-83, Lawyers Com. for Civil Rights Under Law, 1978-86, Legal Def. Fund NAACP, 1978-93, Mex. Am. Legal Def. and Edn. Fund, 1986-90, Legal Aid Soc., 1990-93, The Hastings Ctr., 2004-; mem. exec. com. Human Rights Watch, 1991-93; trustee Trinity Episcopal Sch. Corp., 1991-93; mem. external adv. bd. Columbia U. Ctr. Bioethics, 2002-; mem. adv. bd. Howard Hughes Med. Inst. Bioethics, 2007—. Mem.: NAS (com. on sci., tech. and law 2007—). Office: Rockefeller U 1230 York Ave New York NY 10021 Office Phone: 212-327-8070. Business E-Mail: hrabb@rockefeller.edu.

RABBAT, GUY, electronics executive, consultant; b. Cairo, Jan. 30, 1943; arrived in U.S., 1972; s. Victor and Alice R.; m. Elfriede Freitag, Aug. 3, 1968; children: Ralph, Shirley; m. Nadia Kobinger, Feb. 8, 1992; children: Richard, Jacques, Laurent. Baccalaureate, France; BS, Queens U., Eng., 1967; MS, Queens U., 1969, PhD Elec. Engring. honors, 1971. Design supr. Siemens AG, Germany, 1964—68; asst. lectr. Queens U., England, 1968—72; dir. ops. IBM, 1972—84; v.p. Austin ops., CAE sys. divsn. Tektronix, 1984—86; head elec. engring. GM Corp., Mich., 1986—87; pres., CEO Modular Computer Sys., Inc., Ft. Lauderdale, Fla., 1987—92; mng. dir., exec. bd. dirs. Rank Xerox, Ltd., Welwyn Garden City, Herts, England, 1992—96; corp. v.p. GE, Milw., 1996—98; chief tech. officer, chief info. officer Gen. Elec. Med. Sys., Milw., 1996—98; sr. v.p. Solectron Corp., 1998—2004; chmn., gen. ptnr. Corcica Tech. Ventures, 2001—05; pres., CEO HTC Corp., Sunnyvale, Calif., 2004—; CEO Nest Group Cos., Foster City, Calif.; chmn. Auriga-Nest, Dubai, 2005—. Chmn. Internat. IEEE Conf. on Circuits and Computers, 1980, Internat. IEEE Conf. on Computer Design, 1983; bd. dirs. indsl. affiliates Mich. State U., 1986-88; pres. Am. Automation Assn., 1984-86; chmn., founder High Tech. Consortium Yr. 2000 and Beyond, 1998-02 Author: Hardware and Software Concepts in VLSI, 1983, Advanced Semiconductor Technology and Computer Systems, 1988; contbr. numerous scis. tech. papers; patentee in field Fellow: IEEE (Eng. chpt., editor-in-chief, chmn. editl. bd. Circuits and Devices Mag. 1984—86, invention and outstanding contbn. awards), Royal Engring. Coun. (London). Avocations: history, archaeology, poetry, jogging. Home: 360 Saint Andrews Ln Half Moon Bay CA 94019 Office: Nest Group Cos Dubai United Arab Emirates Office Phone: 408-218-4393. Personal E-mail: rabbat@corcica.com. Business E-Mail: guy.rabbat@nestgroup.net.

RABBITT, LINDA D., construction executive; b. 1948; BA, U. Mich., Ann Arbor; MA, George Wash. U. With KPMG (formerly Peat Marwick), 1981—85, dir. mktg., 1982—85; co-founder, co-owner, exec. v.p. Hart Construction Co., Inc.; founder, CEO Rand Construction Corp., 1989—. Bd. dirs. Watson Wyatt Worldwide, Inc., 2002—, Watson Wyatt & Co., 2002—, Brookfield Properties, 2005—; bd. governors Fed. Reserve Bank of Richmond, 2009—. Bd. trustees George Wash. U., Federal City Coun. Recipient Working Woman 500, 2001; named Person of Vision, Arlington C. of C., 1995, Bus. Woman Yr., United Cerebral Palsy, 1996, Wash. Woman of Genius, Trinity Coll., 2002, Washingtonian Yr., Washingtonian mag., 2004; named one of 100 Most Powerful Women, 2001. Mem.: Wash. Bd. Trade (past chair), Comml. Real Estate Women (past pres., Annual Achievement award 2003). Office: Watson Wyatt Worldwide Inc 901 N Glebe Rd Arlington VA 22203 Office Phone: 703-703-8000.*

RABCHENUK, PAUL THOMAS, lawyer; b. Salem, Mass. s. Nicholas and Apolonia Pauline (Napierski) R. BA, Suffolk U., 1962; MPA, U. Pitts., 1964; JD, New Eng. Law Sch., 1981; postgrad., Tufts U. Bar: Mass. 1981, U.S. Dist. Ct. 1982, U.S. Ct. Appeals 1982, U.S. Supreme Ct. 1986, U.S. Ct. Internat. Trade, 1999. Clk. Essex Superior Ct, Salem, Mass., 1958-61; negotiator Commonwealth of Mass., Boston, 1962-63; realty specialist D.C. Redevel. Agy., Washington, 1964-65; rsch. assoc. Boston Mcpl. Rsch. Bur., 1966-67; urban renewal dir. City of Nashua, N.H., 1967-68, City of Haverhill, Mass., 1969-73; town adminstr. North Reading, Mass., 1973-78; town mgr. Town of Saugus, Mass., 1982-87; pvt. practice law Salem, Mass., 1981—. Cons. numerous pub. entities, 1966-85; vis. prof. civil rights Salem (Mass.) State Coll., 2001—. Chmn. Topsfield (Mass.) Housing Authority, 1978-83, Mass. Bay Tranportation Authority, Boston, 1973-86. Mem. ATLA, Mass. Bar Assn. Avocation: Eastern European history. Home: 37 Glendale Rd Marblehead MA 01945-1804 Office: Rabchenuk Law Offices 81 Washington St Ste 305 Salem MA 01970-3514 Office Phone: 978-741-1163. Business E-Mail: rablaw@verizon.net.

RABEJA, IRINA RODICA OLGA, electronics engineer, computer scientist, writer; b. Tirgoviste, Romania, Feb. 7, 1946; d. Iacob and Elena (Varonidis) Rabeja. Diploma in Electronics Engring., Poly. Inst., Bucharest, 1968; diploma in Computer Sci., U. Auckland, New Zealand, 1999, MEE, 1996. Electronics engr. Enterprise Maintenance and Repair of Calculus Devices, Bucharest, 1968—72, Physics-Chemistry Ctr., Bucharest, 1972—77; chief electronics engr. Inst. Rsch. Chemistry, Bucharest, 1977—90; cons. Electronics & Computers Consultancy, Sydney, 2000—. Author: (book) Diodes and Transistors, 1987; author, editor, pub.: rev. edit., 2007, Earth & Space, 2004, poetry, 2008; author, editor, pub. (classical music book) 175 Musical Programmes, 2005, Paintings of Flowers, 2008. Recipient Classical Music Piano Player, Diploma Singing Romania Festival, 1978—79, 1981. Mem.: IEEE. Achievements include invention of facility for visualization of impulses from calculator with monitor screen; potentiostat; temperature stabilizer for filament in vacuum; stabilized current generator; temperature stabilizer with thermocouple; digital clock; digital frequency-meter/voltmeter; corrosometer. Avocations: astronomy, swimming, music, painting.

RABEN, ROBERT, lobbyist, lawyer; s. Murray and June Raben; m. Carol Raben; 1 child, Madeline. BA, Wharton Coll.; JD, NYU. Clk. to Hon. James Robertson Supreme Ct. Miss.; assoc. Arnold & Porter, 1990; counsel to Congressman Barney Frank, Washington; Dem. counsel Subcommittee on Courts and Intellectual Property, Washington; asst. atty. gen. Office Legis. Affairs US Dept. Justice, Washington, 1999—2001; founder The Raben Group, LLC, Washington; exec. dir. American Task Force Argentina, Arlington, 2006—. Former adj. prof. Georgetown U. Law Sch. Named one of 50 Top Lobbyists, Washingtonian mag., 2007. Mem.: Am. Constitution Soc. and Alliance for Justice (bd. mem.), Hispanic Bar Found. (bd. mem.), Hispanic Bar Assn. of DC (past pres.). Office: Raben Group 1640 Rhode Island Ave, NW, Ste 600 Washington DC 20036 Office Phone: 202-466-6630. Office Fax: 202-463-4803. E-mail: robertraben@rabengroup.com.*

RABENSTEIN, DALLAS LEROY, chemistry professor; b. Portland, Oreg., June 13, 1942; s. Melvin Leroy and Rose Marie (Nelson) R.; m. Gloria Carolyn Duncan, Aug. 30, 1964; children: Mark, Lisa. BS, U. Wash., 1964; PhD, U. Wis., 1968. Lectr. U. Wis., Madison, 1967-68; research chemist Chevron Research Co., Richmond, Calif., 1968-69; from asst. prof. to prof. chemistry U. Alta., Edmonton, Can., 1969-85; prof. U. Calif., Riverside, 1985-97, chmn. dept. chemistry, 1989—92, 1998—2000, 2002—03, dean Coll. Natural and Agrl. Scis., 1993-94, disting. prof. chemistry, 1997—, dean, grad. divsn., 2003—08, exec. vice chancellor & provost, 2009—. Vis. prof. U. Oxford, 1976-77, U. Western Ont., 1982; McElvain lectr. U. Wis., 1981; Dow lectr. U. B.C., 1988; Eli Lilly lectr., Ind. U., 1993; faculty rsch. lectr. U. Calif., Riverside, 2000; cons. in field. Contbr. articles to profl. jours. NIH and NSF grantee. Fellow AAAS, Chem. Inst. Can. (Fisher Sci. Lecture award 1984); mem. Am. Chem. Soc., Internat. Soc. Magnetic Resource. Avocations: reading, gardening, music. Home: 5162 Palisade Cir Riverside CA 92506-1521 Office: U Calif Dept Chemistry Riverside CA 92521-0001 Office Phone: 951-827-5649. Business E-Mail: dallas.rabenstein@ucr.edu.

RABIDEAU, PETER WAYNE, dean, chemistry professor, educator; b. Johnstown, Pa., Mar. 4, 1940; s. Peter Nelson and Monica (Smalley) R.; m. Therese Charlene Newquist, Sept. 1, 1962 (div.); children: Steven, Michael, Christine, Susan; m. Jennifer Lee Mooney, Nov. 15, 1986; children: Mark, Leah. BS, Loyola U., Chgo., 1964; MS, Case Inst. Tech., Cleve., 1967; PhD, Case Western Res. U., Cleve., 1968. Postdoctoral asst. U. Chgo., 1968-69, instr., 1969-70; asst. prof. Ind. U.-Purdue U., Indpls., 1970-73, assoc. prof., 1973-76, prof., 1976-90, chmn. dept. chemistry, 1985-90; dean Coll. Basic Scis. La. State U., Baton Rouge, 1990-99; dean Coll. Liberal Arts and Scis. Iowa State U., Ames, 1999—2003; provost, v.p. acad. affairs Miss. State U., 2003—. Program officer NSF, 1988-89. Contbr. numerous articles to profl. jours. Recipient rsch. award Purdue Sch. Sci. at Indpls., 1982, Outstanding Alumnus award chemistry dept. Case Western U., 2001. Fellow AAAS; mem. Am. Chem. Soc. (chmn. Ind. sect. 1974, councilor 1981-90). Home: 105 Derbyshire Rd Starkville MS 39759 Office: Miss State U PO Box BQ Mississippi State MS 39762 Home Phone: 662-324-7778. E-mail: prabideau@provost.msstate.edu.

RABIL, ALBERT, JR., humanities educator; b. Rocky Mount, NC, May 8, 1934; s. Albert and Sophie Mae (Safy) R.; m. Janet Spain, Aug. 29, 1956; children: Albert III, J. Alison. BA, Duke U., 1957; MDiv, Union Theol. Sem., 1960; PhD, Columbia U., 1964. Instr. religion Trinity Coll., Hartford, Conn., 1964-65, asst. prof., 1965-68; asst. prof. hist. theology Chgo. Theol. Sem., 1969-71; assoc. prof. SUNY-Old Westbury, 1971-74, prof., 1974-77, disting. tchg. prof. humanities, 1977-98, emeritus prof., 1998. Program dir. NEH Summer Inst., 1992, 94, 95, 96, 98, 2000, 01, 03, 04, 05. Author: Merleau-Ponty, 1967 (Ansley award 1964), Erasmus and the New Testament, 1972, Laura Cereta, 1981, (with others) Her Immaculate Hand, 1983, Erasmus' Paraphrases of Romans and Galatians, 1983, Erasmus' Annotations on Romans, 1994, Teaching Other Voices: Women and Religion in Early Modern Europe, 2006; editor: Renaissance Humanism (3 vols.), 1988; editor, translator: Knowledge, Goodness, and Power, 1991, Henricus Cornelius Agrippa Declamation on the Nobility and Preeminence of the Female Sex, 1996; co-editor Renaissance Quarterly, 1992-97; series co-editor The Other Voice in Early Modern Europe, 1993—; mem. editl. bd. Soundings: An Interdisciplinary Jour., 1992-94. Travelling fellow Union Theol. Sem., 1960, Soc. for Values in Higher Edn., 1961; grantee Fulbright Found., 1961, NEH, 1974, 81, 94, 2002, 03, 04. Mem. Erasmus Rotterdam Soc. (mem. editl. bd. 1980—2007), Soc. for Values in Higher Edn. (bd. dirs. 1981-90), Renaissance Soc. Am. (bd. dirs. 1991-97). Democrat. Home and Office: 2305 Honeysuckle Rd Chapel Hill NC 27514-1716 Office Phone: 919-967-0231. Personal E-mail: arabil@nc.rr.com.

RABIL, MITCHELL JOSEPH, lawyer; b. Smithfield, NC, Sept. 19, 1931; s. Albert G. and Eva (Nassif) R.; m. Antoinette M. Olivry, Nov. 25, 1956 (div. Oct. 1986); children: Elizabeth, Nathalie, Marcus, Gregory; m. Dolores E. Bleam, Jan. 21, 1989; children: Susan Starr Vermes, Scott Starr. BS, Wake Forest Coll., 1953; LLB, Georgetown U., 1961. Bar: N.C. 1961, N.J. 1967, D.C. 1980, Pa. 1981, U.S. Tax Ct. 1962, U.S. Supreme Ct. 1979; CPA, N.J., N.C. Supervisory acct. GAO, Washington, 1956—60; fin. analyst, staff acct. SEC, Washington, 1960—62; tax atty. Office of Chief Counsel, IRS, Phila. and NYC, 1962—66; assoc. Archer, Greiner, Hunter & Read, Camden, NJ, 1966—71; ptnr. Myers, Matteo, Rabil, Norcross & Landgraf, Cherry Hill, NJ, 1971—89, Montgomery, McCracken, Walker and Rhoads, Cherry Hill, 1989—95; sole stockholder, pres. Mitchell J. Rabil & Assocs., P.A., Cherry Hill, 1995—2000; mem. Rabil & Harris LLC, Cherry Hill, 1998—2000, Rabil & Ropka, LLC, Cherry Hill, 2000—02, Rabil, Ropka, Kingett & Hatzell LLC, Cherry Hill, 2002—04, Rabil, Ropka, Kingett & Stewart LLC, 2005—08, Rabil, Kingett & Stewart LLC, 2008—; tax counsel Cureton Clark, Pa., 2008—. Mcpl. chmn. Riverton (N.J.) Rep. Com., 1976-83; chmn. area 2 Burlington County Rep. Com., 1976-82; bd. dirs. West Jersey Chamber Music Soc., 1990-91, Zurbrugg Meml. Hosp., 1991-93; mem. N.J. New Capital Sources Bd., 1996-2000. With AUS, 1953-55 Mem. AICPA, N.J. Bar Assn., N.J. Soc. CPA, Phila. Bar Assn., Am. Assoc. Atty. CPA (bd. dirs., past pres.) Cherry Hill C. of C. (bd. dirs. 1990-94), World Affairs Coun. Phila., Union League (Phila.), Riverton Country Club, Rotary (pres. Cherry Hill chpt. 1980-81, past dir.). Roman Catholic. Home: 107 Wayside Ct Delran NJ 08075-2000 Office: 524 Main St Riverton NJ 08077

RABIN, ALAN A., economics professor; b. NYC, June 16, 1947; s. Sidney and Claire Rabin. BA, Hamilton Coll., 1969; PhD, U. Va., 1977. NSF trainee U. Va., 1970—71, 1971—72; intern Coun. Econ. Advisors, 1971; instr. Calif. State U., Northridge, 1973-74, Georgetown U., Washington, 1975; asst. prof. econs. U. Tenn., Chattanooga, 1977-81, assoc. prof., 1981-86, prof., 1986—. Author: Monetary Theory, 2004; contbr. articles to profl. jours. NDEA fellow, 1969-70; U. Tenn.-Chattanooga faculty rsch. grantee, 1982. Mem. Am. Econs. Assn., So. Econs. Assn., Atlantic Econs. Soc., We. Econs. Assn., U. Tenn. Chattanooga Coun. Scholars, Omicron Delta Epsilon. Avocations: sports, stamp collecting/philately, theater. Home: 1175 Pineville Rd Apt 161 Chattanooga TN 37405-2653 Office: U Tenn-Chattanooga Dept Economics Chattanooga TN 37403 Office Phone: 423-425-4360. Business E-Mail: alan-rabin@utc.edu.

RABIN, BERNARD M., psychology professor; married. PhD, SUNY, Buffalo, 1968. Prof. psychology UMBC, Balt., 1970—. Office: UMBC 1000 Hilltop Cir Baltimore MD 21250 Business E-Mail: rabin@umbc.edu.

RABIN, ETHAN M., legislative staff member; B in Polit. Sci., Syracuse U., NY, 2004. Field dir. Eric Massa's Congl. Campaign, 2005—06; legis. asst., press sec. to Rep. Gene Taylor US House of Reps., Washington, 2006—. Democrat. Office: 2269 Rayburn House Office Bldg Washington DC 20515 Office Phone: 202-225-5772. Office Fax: 202-225-7074. Business E-Mail: ethan.rabin@mail.house.gov.*

RABIN, HERBERT, physicist, educator, dean; b. Milw., Nov. 14, 1928; 2 children. BS, U. Wis., 1950; MS, U. Ill., 1951; PhD in Physics, U. Md., 1959. Physicist elec. divsn. U.S. Naval Rsch. Lab., 1952-54, physicist solid state physics divsn., 1954-62, head radiation effects sect. optical materials br., 1962-67, head quantum optics sect., applied optics br., 1967-68, head quantum optics br., 1968-71, assoc. dir. rsch. for space sci. and tech., 1971-77, assoc. dir. rsch. for space and comm. sci. and tech., 1977-79; dep. asst. sec. for rsch., applied and space tech. Office of Navy Secretariat, Washington, 1979-83; dir. engring. rsch. ctr., prof. elec. engring., assoc. dean Coll. Engring., U. Md., College Park, 1983—, interim dean coll. engring., 1999-2000, 2007—08. Dir. GRC Internat., 1988—98, Washington Aluminum Co., 1992—95, Yurie Sys. Inc., 1995—98, VT Linx Multimedia Sys., Inc., 2000—02; vis. scientist Technisch Hochschule, Stuttgart, Germany, 1960—61; mem. staff physics dept. George Washington U., 1955—73; cons. Sch. Engring. Sao Carlos U., Sao Paulo, Brazil, 1964, Sao Paulo, 70; trustee Nat. Technol. U., 1984—2000, life trustee, 2000—03; vis. fellow SEEDA, England, 2003. Contbr. articles to tech. jours. Recipient Meritorious Civilian Svc. award, USN, 1969, Disting. Civilian Svc. award, 1976, 1993, Dept. Def., 1979, Cert. of Commendation, NASA, 1986, Centennial medal, U. Md. Coll. Engring., 1994. Fellow: AIAA, AAAS, Optical Soc. Am., Am. Phys. Soc.; mem.: IEEE (sr.), Brazilian Acad. Scis. (corr.). Achievements include patents in field. Home: 7109 Radnor Rd Bethesda MD 20817-6332 Office: U Md Engring Rsch Ctr College Park MD 20742-0001 Office Phone: 301-405-3906. Business E-Mail: hrabin@umd.edu.

RABIN, JACK, lawyer; b. Aug. 19, 1930; s. Leo and Bertha Rabin; m. Roberta Edith Libson, Oct. 25, 1953; children: Keith Warren, Michael Jay, Adam Douglas. Student, Bklyn. Coll., 1948-50; LLB, Bklyn. Law Sch., 1953. Bar: N.Y. 1953, U.S. Tax Ct. 1960, U.S. Ct. Claims 1964, U.S. Supreme Ct. 1964, U.S. Ct. Appeals (2d cir.) 1968. Ptnr. Hoffberg, Rabin & Engler and predecessor firms, NYC, 1968-82, Javits, Hinckley, Rabin & Engler, NYC, 1982-84, Phillips, Nizer, Benjamin, Krim & Ballon, NYC, 1984-94, counsel, 1994—. Arbitrator gen. comml. and constrn. panel Am. Arbitration Assn., 1968—; instr. Real Estate Inst., NYU, 1976-78; ct. apptd. mediator U.S. Dist. Ct. (so. dist.), N.Y., 1994—, N.Y. Supreme Ct., N.Y. County, 1999. Assoc. editor Bklyn. Law Rev., 1952, editor-in-chief, 1953, also author law rev. note. 1st lt. JAGC, U.S. Army, 1954-57, col. res., ret., 1983. Mem. N.Y. State Bar Assn., Res. Officers Assn. U.S. (pres. Rockland County chpt. 1967-68), B'nai B'rith (pres. New City, N.Y. 1965-66). Jewish. Office: 10 W 66th St Ste 8G New York NY 10023 Office Phone: 212-724-1050. E-mail: sutleg@earthlink.net.

RABIN, JOSEPH HARRY, marketing research company executive; b. Chgo., Dec. 12, 1927; s. Morris and Libby (Broder) Rabinovitz; m. Barbara E. Leader, Oct. 31, 1954; children: Marc Jay, Michelle Ann, Deborah Susan. BSc, Roosevelt U., 1950; MBA, DePaul U., 1951. Account exec. Gould, Gleiss & Benn, 1951-56; asst. dir. mktg. rsch. Paper Mate Co., Chgo., 1956-63; pres. Rabin Rsch. Co., Chgo., 1963—. Pres. Mather HS Coun., 1972-74; mem. adv. coun. U. Toledo, 1976-77, Kellstadt Ctr. DePaul U., 1986-93; mem. adv. com. Bur. of the Census, 1978-83; bd. dirs. Market Rsch. Inst., 1973-75, Ner Tamid Synagogue, 1976-2007, Jewish Vocat. Svc., 1977-80. With AUS, 1946-47. Mem. Am. Mktg. Assn. (pres. Chgo. chpt. 1961-62, nat. dir. 1973-75, nat. v.p. mktg. rsch. 1978-79, nat. pres. 1981-82), Assn. Consumer Rsch., Am. Statis. Assn. (pres. Chgo. chpt. 1962-63), Am. Assn. Pub. Opinion Rsch. Home: 7061 N Kedzie Ave Chicago IL 60645-2846 Office: Rabin Rsch Co 150 E Huron St Chicago IL 60611-2999 Home Phone: 773-465-6661; Office Phone: 312-482-8500. Business E-Mail: jrabin@rabin-research.com.

RABIN, MONROE STEPHEN ZANE, physicist; b. Bklyn., Dec. 19, 1939; s. Louis and Helen (Haspel) R.; m. Joan Greenblatt, Feb. 27, 1965; children: Elaine Judith, Carolyn Sandra. AB, Columbia Coll., 1961; PhD, Rutgers U., 1967. Physicist Lawrence Berkeley (Calif.) Lab., 1967-72; assoc. prof. physics U. Mass., Amherst, 1972-81, prof. physics, 1981—; vis. physicist Stanford Linear Accelerator Ctr., Palo Alto, Calif., 1979-80; vis. scholar Physics Dept. Harvard U., Cambridge, Mass., 1986-87; Soriano scholar in radiol. physics, radiation therapy dept. Mass. Gen. Hosp., Boston, 1986-87. Mem. oversight panel Proton Therapy Med. Facility, Mass. Gen. Hosp., Boston, 1991-96. Contbr. articles to Physical Rev., Physical Rev. Letters, Physics Letters, Nuclear Instruments and Methods. Mem. Am. Phys. Soc., Sigma Xi. Achievements include research in experimental particle physics, medical physics, cancer therapy using accelerated protons, ductal carcinoma in situ and heavy-ion physics. Home: 21 Atwater Cir Amherst MA 01002-3205 Office: U Mass Dept Physics Amherst MA 01003 Office Phone: 413-545-0424. Business E-Mail: rabin@physics.umass.edu.

RABINEAU, PHYLLIS, museum administrator; AB in Anthropology, Cornell U., 1970, MA in Anthropology, 1973. Collections mgr., dept. anthropology Field Mus., 1974—85, project direction staff, 1986—96; sr. mgmt., v.p. interpretation and edn. Chgo. Hist. Soc., 1997—. Exhibit curator Field Mus., 1981—85, dep. chair, program devel., 1991—94; cons. in field. Contbr. articles to profl. jours. Mem.: Am. Assn. Mus. (mem. nat. program com. 2005, 2006, 2008, mem. nominations com. 2007, Curators' Com. award 1991), QM2 Dep. Dirs. Roundtable, Nat. Assn. Mus. Exhbn. (bd. dirs. 1994—96, pres. 2004—, mem. standing profl. com. for exhbns. 2005—). Office: Chgo History Mus 1601 N Clark Chicago IL 60614 Office Phone: 312-799-2130. Office Fax: 312-799-2430. Business E-Mail: rabineau@chicagohistory.org.

RABINOVICH, REGINA, pediatrician, epidemiologist, director; married; 3 children. MD, Southern Ill. U.; MPH, U. NC, Chapel Hill. Pediat. intern U. NC, chief resident; fellow epidemiology tng. program Nat. Inst. Allergy and Infectious Diseases, 1988—91, various positions including chief clin. and regulatory affairs divsn. microbiology and infectious diseases, 1991—99; dir. malaria vaccine initiative Program for Appropriate Tech. in Health; dir. infectious diseases program Bill & Melinda Gates Found., 2003—. Mem. vaccine adv. com. Nat. Vaccine Program Office, Am. Acad. Pediat., Inst. Medicine, WHO. Recipient Merit award, NIH, 1993, Dir.'s award, 1995. Office: Bill and Melinda Gates Found PO Box 23350 Seattle WA 98102 Office Phone: 206-709-3100.

RABINOVITCH, BENTON SEYMOUR, chemist, educator emeritus; b. Montreal, Que., Can., Feb. 19, 1919; came to U.S., 1946; s. Samuel and Rachel (Schachter) R.; m. Marilyn Werby, Sept. 18, 1949; children: Peter Samuel, Ruth Anne, Judith Nancy, Frank Benjamin; m. Flora Reitman, 1980. BSc, McGill U., 1939, PhD, 1942; DSc (hon.), Technion Inst., Haifa, 1991. Postdoctoral fellow Harvard, 1946-48; Milton fellow, 1949—50; mem. faculty U. Wash., Seattle, 1948—, prof. chemistry, 1957—, prof. chemistry emeritus, 1985—. Cons. and/or mem. sci. adv. panels, coms. NSF, Nat. Acad. Scis.-NRC; adv. com. phys. chemistry Nat. Bur. Standards. Author Antique Silver Servers, 1991, Contemporary Silver, 2000, Contemporary Silver Part II, 2005; co-author: Physical Chemistry, 1964; former editor: Ann. Rev. Phys. Chemistry; mem. editorial bd.: Internat. Jour. Chem. Kinetics, Rev. of Chem. Intermediates, Jour. Phys. Chemistry, Jour. Am. Chem. Soc. Served to capt. Canadian Army, 1942-46, ETO. Nat. Research Council Can. fellow, 1940-42; Royal Soc. Can. Research fellow, 1946-47; Milton Research fellow Harvard, 1948; Guggenheim fellow, 1961; vis. fellow Trinity Coll., Oxford, 1971; recipient Sigma Xi award for original research, Debye award in phys. chemistry, 1984, Polanyi medal Royal Soc. Chemistry; named hon. liveryman Worshipful Co. of Goldsmiths, London, 2000. Fellow Am. Phys. Soc., Am. Acad. Arts and Scis., Royal Soc. London; mem. Am. Chem. Soc. (past chmn. Puget Sound sect., past chmn. phys. chemistry divsn., assoc. editor jour.), Faraday Soc. Achievements include rsch. in Unimolecular gas phase reaction and history and design of silver implements. Home: 12530 42nd Ave NE Seattle WA 98125-4621 Office: Univ Washington Chemistry Box 351700 Seattle WA 98195 Office Fax: 206-285-8665.

RABINOWITZ, DAVID LINCOLN, research scientist; b. New Haven, Nov. 13, 1960; s. Harold Wolf and Madeline Virginia Rabinowitz; m. Anne Sommer. PhD, U. Chgo., 1988. Rsch. assoc. U. Ariz., Tucson, 1989—93, Carnegie Instn., Dept Terrestrial Magnetism, Washington, 1994—96; rsch. scientist Jet Propulsion Lab., Calif. Inst. Tech., Pasadena, 1996—99, Yale U., Ctr. Astronomy & Astrophysics, New Haven, 1999—. Achievements include discovery of many near-Earth asteroids and distant Kuiper belt objects, including Pholus, Sedna, and Eris; design of large mosaic CCD camera that was used to detect the first dwarf planet larger than Pluto.

RABINOWITZ, JACK GRANT, radiologist, educator; b. Monticello, NY, July 9, 1927; s. Abraham and Bessie (Sussman) R.; m. Rica Gedalia Arnon, Oct. 19, 1972; children— Antoine, Anne, Pierre, Yaron, Tal. BA, UCLA, 1949; MD, U. Berne, Switzerland, 1955. Diplomate: Am. Bd. Radiology. Intern Kings County Hosp., Bklyn., 1955-56, resident, 1956-59; instr. radiology Downstate Med. Center, Bklyn., 1960-61, assoc. prof. radiology, 1967-70, prof. radiology, 1970-73; asst. radiologist Mt. Sinai Sch. Medicine, NYC, 1962-65, asst. prof. radiology, 1965-66, asso. prof. radiology, 1966-67, prof., chmn. dept. radiology, 1978-95, prof., 1995—. Asso. attending radiologist Mt. Sinai Hosp., N.Y.C., 1965-67, dir. radiology, 1978—; radiologist-in-chief Bklyn.-Cumberland Med. Center, Bklyn., 1967-70; dir. diagnostic radiology Kings County Hosp. Center, Bklyn., 1970-73; prof., chmn. dept. diagnostic radiology U. Tenn., Memphis, 1973-78; cons. in radiology VA Hosp., Bronx, N.Y. Author: Pediatric Radiology, 1978, Radiology for the Primary and Emergency Care of Physicians, 1981. Fellow Am. Coll. Radiology; mem. Radiol. Soc. N. Am., Am. Roentgen Ray Soc., Assn. Univ. Radiologists, AMA, Soc. Chmn. Acad. Radiology Depts. Office: Mt Sinai Hosp 1 Gustave L Levy Pl New York NY 10029-6500 Home Phone: 201-501-8190. Business E-Mail: jack-rabinowitz@msnyu.health.org.

RABINOWITZ, YARON GIL, psychologist, educator, military officer; b. Memphis, Dec. 21, 1973; s. Jack Grant and Rica Rabinowitz; m. Bethany Lee Washington, June 7, 2008; 1 child, Mia Jaden. AB in Govt., Harvard U., Cambridge, Mass., 1996; MA in History, Stanford U., Calif., 2000; PhD in Clin. Psychology, Pacific Grad. Sch. Psychology, Palo Alto, Calif., 2005. Cert. psychologist Ala. History tchr. Blair Acad., Blairstown, NJ, 1996—98; clin. rschr. Stanford U. Sch. Medicine, 2000—04; commd. 2d lt. US Army, 2004, advanced through grades to capt., 2004; clin. psychology resident Walter Reed Army Med. Ctr., Washington, 2004—05; dep. command psychologist JFK Spl. Warfare Ctr. and Sch., Fort Bragg, NC, 2005—06; command psychologist Spl. Forces Assessment and Selection Program, JFK Spl. Warfare Ctr. and Sch., Fort Bragg, NC, 2006—; asst. prof. psychology Tex. A&M U., Corpus Christi. Contbr. articles to profl. publs. Decorated Nat. Svc. ribbon, Army Parachutist badge, Army Commendation medal, Global War on Terrorism ribbon; recipient Student Award for Excellence in Alzheimer's Rsch., California-Nevada Alzheimer's Assn., 2004, STAR award for achievement, Palo Alto VA Health Care Sys., 2004; Health Profession scholar, US Army Med. Dept., 2002—04, Jared and Mae Tincklenberg fellow, Pacific Grad. Sch. Psychology, 2002—03, Rabbi Stephen S. Pearce fellow, 2003—04. Mem.: APA (chmn. grad. students 2004—05, chmn. advocacy coord. team 2003—04), Divsn. Mil. Psychology. Avocations: triathlons, wrestling, music, travel, accordion. Office: Dept of Psychology Tex 16M Univ 6300 Ocean Dr Corpus Christi TX 78412 Office Phone: 361-825-2719, 361-825-2350. Personal E-mail: rubes0509@gmail.com.

RABKIN, ERIC S., English educator; b. Queens, NY, Mar. 8, 1946; s. Joseph and Annette (Schwartz) R.; m. Elizabeth J. Backer, July 1, 1967; children: David Ivan, Rachel Ann. AB in English, Cornell U., 1967; PhD in English, U. Iowa, 1970. Asst. prof. dept. English U. Mich., Ann Arbor, 1970-74, assoc. prof. dept. English, 1974-77, dir. Collegiate Inst. Values and Sci., 1976-82, assoc. dean long-range planning Coll. Lit., Sci. and Arts, 1979-83, interim dir. English Lang. Inst., 1982-84, interim chmn. dept. linguistics, 1982-84, prof. dept. English, 1977—, Arthur F. Thurnau prof., 1990-93. Author: Narrative Suspense, 1973, The Fantastic in Literature, 1976, co-author: Science Fiction: History, Science,

Vision, 1977, Teaching Writing that Works, 1990, It'a a Gas: A Study of Flatulence, 1991. Am. Coun. Learned Socs. fellow, 1973. Office: Univ Mich Dept English Ann Arbor MI 48109 Home: 1330 Glendaloch Cir Ann Arbor MI 48104-2830

RABKIN, MITCHELL THORNTON, physician, educator, hospital administrator; b. Boston, Nov. 27, 1930; s. Morris Aaron and Esther (Quint) Rabkin; m. Adrienne M. Najarian, June 24, 1956; children: Julia Margaret, David Gregory. AB magna cum laude, Harvard U., 1951, MD cum laude, 1955; DSc (hon.), Brandeis U., 1983; DPharm (hon.), Mass. Coll. Pharmacy, 1983; DSc (hon.), Curry Coll., 1989, Northeastern U., 1994; DHumLet (hon.), Salem State Coll., Mass., 1995. Cert. Am. Bd. Internal Medicine. Intern Mass. Gen. Hosp., Boston, 1955—56, resident in internal medicine, 1956—57, 1959—60, chief resident, 1962, mem. staff, 1963—72, bd. consultation, 1972—80, hon. physician, 1981—; clin. fellow NIH, Bethesda, Md., 1957—59; gen. dir. Beth Israel Hosp., Boston, 1966—80, pres., 1980—96; CEO CareGroup, Boston, 1996—98; now disting. inst. scholar Carl J. Shapiro Inst. for Edn. and Rsch. Harvard Med. Sch. and Beth Israel Deaconess Med. Ctr., Boston, 1996—; dir. Washington Adv. Group LECG, 1999—. Asst. prof. medicine Harvard U., 1969—70, assoc. prof., 1971—83, prof., 1983—, pres. med. alumni coun., 2002—03; chmn. Albert Schweitzer Fellowship, 2005—, chair. bd. dirs., 2007—08. With USPHS, 1957—59. Fellow: AAAS, ACP, Am. Acad. Arts and Scis.; mem.: Inst. Medicine of NAS, Assn. Am. Med. Colls. (chmn. 1996—97), Soc. Med. Adminstrs., Mass. Med. Soc., Tavern Club Boston, Harvard Club of Boston. Jewish. Office: Beth Israel Deaconess Med Ctr/Harvard U Shapiro Inst Edn and Rsch 330 Brookline Ave Boston MA 02215-5400 Office Phone: 617-667-9400. Personal E-mail: mtrabkin@mindspring.com. Business E-Mail: mrabkin@theadvisorygroup.com.

RABNER, STUART, state supreme court chief justice, former state attorney general; b. Passaic, NJ, June 30, 1960; s. George and Stella (Litwok) Rabner; m. Deborah Wiener, July 2, 1989; children: Erica, Carly, Jacob. AB, Princeton U., 1982; JD, Harvard U., 1985. Bar: NJ 1986, NY 1986, US Dist. Ct. NJ 1986, US Ct. Appeals (3rd cir.) 1986. Law clk. to Hon. Dickinson R. Debevoise US Dist. Ct. NJ, 1985-86; asst. U.S. atty. US Dept. Justice, Newark, 1st asst. US atty., dep. chief spl. prosecutions divsn., exec. asst. U.S. atty., chief criminal divsn., dep. chief criminal divsn., 1986—2005; chief counsel to gov. State of NJ, Trenton, 2006, atty. gen., 2006—07; chief justice NJ Supreme Ct., Trenton, NJ, 2007—. Chmn. Holocaust Resource Ctr., Clifton, NJ, 1986—. Office: NJ Supreme Ct PO Box 023 Trenton NJ 08625*

RABSON, ALAN SAUL, federal agency administrator, pathologist, educator; b. NYC, July 1, 1926; s. Abraham and Florence (Shulman) Rabson; m. Ruth L. Kirschstein, June 11, 1950; 1 child, Arnold. BA, U. Rochester, 1948; MD, SUNY, Bklyn., 1950. Intern Mass. Meml. Hosp., Boston, 1951—52; resident in pathology NYU Hosp., 1952—54, USPHS Hosp., New Orleans, 1954—55; pathologist Nat. Cancer Inst., Bethesda, Md., 1955—; prof. pathology Georgetown U. Med. Sch., 1974—, Uniformed Services U. Health Scis., 1978—, George Washington U., 1978—; dep. dir. Nat. Cancer Inst., NIH, Bethesda, 1995—, acting dir., 2001—02. Contbr. articles to med. jours. Mem.: Am. Assn. Pathologists, Alpha Omega Alpha, Sigma Xi, Phi Beta Kappa. Address: NIH-Nat Cancer Inst 9000 Rockville Pike Bldg 31 Bethesda MD 20892-0001

RABSTEJNEK, GEORGE JOHN, healthcare executive; b. Queens, NY, June 14, 1932; s. George John and Rose Anna (Krasa) R.; m. Patsy Kidd, July 17, 1964; 1 child, Marley Ann. B in Indsl. Engring., Ga. Inst. Tech., 1954; postgrad., U. Conn. Sch. Law, 1960, NYU Sch. Bus., 1965-69; advanced mgmt. program, Harvard U., 1975. Dir. material mgmt. svcs. divsn. Harbridge House, Inc., Boston, 1965-69, v.p., group head, 1969-75, exec. v.p., 1975-76, pres., 1976-83, CEO, 1983-92, chmn., 1983-93, ret., 1993. Chmn. bd. dirs. R.P.W., Inc., Bluelight, Inc.; chmn. bd. dirs. C.T.C., Inc. (Ctr. for Tech. Commercialization), 2002; founder, mem. exec. com. Keck Neural Prothesis Rsch. Ctr.; chmn. emeritus Mass. Eye and Ear Infirmary. Contbr. articles to profl. jours. Vice chmn. World Affairs Coun. Boston, 1988, pres., 1984-87; trustee Internat. Coord. Coun., Boston, 1984-2003; trustee, chmn. bd. dirs. Mass. Eye and Ear Infirmary, Boston, 1984—, vice chmn. bd. dirs., chmn. emeritus, 2006—; bd. emeritus Draper Labs. Corp., 1994, chmn. bd. dirs., 2002; mem. adv. bd. Town of Cohasset, Mass., 1975; chmn. nat. adv. bd. Ga. Inst. Tech., 1991-92; mem. exec. adv. bd. Ivan Allen Coll.; mem. bd. visitors Northeastern U. Comdr. USNR, 1954-75, ret. Recipient Disting. Alumni award Sch. Indsl. and Sys. Engring., Ga. Inst. Tech., named to Acad. Disting. Engring. Alumni. Mem. Am. Inst. Indsl. Engrs., Nat. Security Indsl. Assn. (v.p. 1987—), Nat. Def. Transp. Assn. (Def. Transp. award 1980), Assn. Naval Aviators, Navy League, Reynolds Soc. (chmn.), Nat. Security Industry Assn. (trustee 1990-93), Harvard Club, Algonquin Club (Boston), Cohasset Golf Club (Mass.), Cohasset Yacht Club, Cohasset Tennis and Squash Club, Mill Reef Club, Antigua, B.W.I., Comml. Club, F St. Club (Washington), Phi Kappa Sigma, Economics Club Boston. Republican. Unitarian Universalist. Home: 181 Border St Cohasset MA 02025-2043

RABUCK, DONNA FONTANAROSE, English writing educator; b. Edison, NJ, Aug. 2, 1954; d. Arthur Thomas and Shirley Gertrude (Golub) Fontanarose; m. John Frederick Rabuck, July, 28, 1973; 1 child, Miranda Rose. BA in Eng., Rutgers U., 1976, MA in Eng. Lit., 1980, PhD in Eng. Lit., 1990. Prof. writing Pima C. C., Tucson, 1981-86; asst. dir. writing skills program U. Ariz., Tucson, 1983—. Asst. dir. summer inst. writing U. Ariz., Tucson, 1985—, dir. grad. writing inst., 1996—; adj. faculty Pima C. C., Tucson, 1992-95. Author: The Other Side of Silence: Performing Heroinism in the Victorian Novel, 1990, Writing Ctr. Perspectives, 1995; editor: Writing is Thinking: Collected Writings of the Summer Inst., 1985—. Founder, pres. Miles East-West Neighborhood Assn., Tucson, 1983—; dir. Ctr. for Sacred Feminine, Tucson, 1995—; program coord. U. Ariz. Arts and Scis. Minority Retention Program, 1988-93. Rutgers Alumni scholar, 1972-76; Bevier fellow Rutgers U., 1976-78. Mem. Intercollegiate Writing Com. (task force), Commn. Cultural Thinking (task force), Nat. Coun. Tchrs. Eng. Avocations: feminist scholarship, women's rituals, yoga, hiking, meditation. Home: 1115 N Camino Miraflores Tucson AZ 85745-1612 Office: Univ Ariz Writing Skills Program 1201 E Helen St Tucson AZ 85719-4407 E-mail: drabuck@u.arizona.edu.

RABUKA, SITIVENI LIGAMAMADA, Fijian government official, army officer; b. Nakobo, Fiji, Sept. 13, 1948; s. Kolinio E.V. and Salote Lomaloma R.; m. Suluweti Camaivuna Tuiloma, 1975; 3 children. Student, New Zealand Army Schs., 1972-73; postgrad., Indian Def. Svcs. Staff Coll., 1979, Australian Joint Svcs. Staff Coll., 1982. Sr. operational plans officer UNIFIL, Lebanon, 1980-81; chief staff Fiji, 1981; ops. and tng. officer Fiji Army, 1982-83, 85-87; comd. Fiji Bn., Sinai, 1983-85; staged coup, May 1987; adviser on home affairs, head security, 1987; staged 2d coup, declared a republic, Oct. 1987; comdr., head interim mil. govt. Fiji, 1987; comdr. Fiji Security Forces, 1987; min. for home affairs, nat. youth svc. and aux. army svcs., 1987-91; 1st pres. Fijian polit. party Min. Home Affairs, Suva, from 1991; prime min. Fiji, 1992-99. With Commonwealth Sec. Gen.'s Spl. Envoy for Peace, Solomon Islands, 1999—; chmn. Great Coun. of Chiefs, Govt. Bldgs. Box. Author: No Other Way, 1988; subject of biography: Rabuka of Fiji (John Sharpham), 1999. Avocations: golf, rugby. Office: Govt Bldgs Box 2437 Suva Fiji

RABUN, DANIEL W., oil and gas industry executive; BBA in Acctg., U. Houston; JD, So. Meth. U., Dallas. CPA 1976. Positions up to ptnr. Baker & McKenzie, 1986—2001, ptnr., 2001—06; v.p., gen. counsel, sec. Chorum Techs. Inc., 2000—01; pres., bd. dirs. ENSCO Internat. Inc., 2006—, CEO, 2007—, chmn., 2007—. Office: ENSCO Internat Inc 500 N Akard St Ste 4300 Dallas TX 75201-3331 Office Phone: 214-397-3000.

RABUN, JOHN BREWTON, JR., criminal justice agency administrator; b. Augusta, Ga., Nov. 16, 1946; s. John Brewton and Alsie Imor (Bateman) R.; m. Anna Betsy Park, Dec. 27, 1967; children: Kerry Kristin, John Candler. BA, Mercer U., 1967; postgrad., So. Bapt. Theol. Sem., 1967—70; MSW, U. Louisville, 1971. Cert. social worker Ky., DC. Exec. dir. Ky. Civil Liberties Union, Louisville, 1971—72; dir. Cmty. Residential Treatment Svcs., Louisville, 1973—78; program mgr. Field Svcs., Louisville, 1978—80, Exploited and Missing Child Unit, Louisville, 1980—84; exec. v.p., COO Nat. Ctr. for Missing and Exploited Children, Washington, 1984—2006, COO, 1984—, exec. v.p., 2006—. Mem. Alderman's Task Force on Social Svcs., Louisville, 1982, Mayor's City Youth Commn., Louisville, 1983-84; trainer and/or cons. to numerous agys. in U.S., U.K., Can., Mex., Belgium, Germany, Austria, Netherlands. Author: (book) Healthcare Guideslines Infant Abduction, 2009; contbr. articles to profl. jours., chapters to books. Recipient Key to City of Louisville, 1983, Disting. Alumnus award U. Louisville, 1985, 2003, Russell L. Colling Lit. award Internat. Assn. for Healthcare Security and Safety, 1991; named hon. chief of police City of Louisville, 1982; Alumni fellow U. Louisville, 1999. Mem. ACLU, NASW, Nat. Sheriff's Assn., Internat. Juvenile Officers Assn., Acad. Cert. Social Workers, Internat. Assn. Healthcare Safety and Security, Am. Soc. Indsl. Security, Internat. Assn. Chiefs of Police. Baptist (deacon). Avocations: photography, hunting, fishing, internet. Home: 13519 Oak Ivy Ln Fairfax VA 22033-1230 Office: Nat Ctr for Missing and Exploited Children 699 Prince St Alexandria VA 22314-3117 Office Phone: 703-837-6216. Business E-Mail: jrabun@ncmec.org.

RABURN, VERN L., air transportation executive, former Internet company executive; b. Okla., 1950; m. Dottie Raburn. Student in Aeronautical Engring., Calif. Polytechnical Inst., San Luis Obispo; BS in Indsl. Tech., Long Beach State Univ., 1976. With 3M Corp.; pres., consumer products divsn., to corp. v.p. Microsoft Corp., 1979—82; exec. v.p., gen. mgr. Lotus Devel. Corp.; chmn., CEO Symantec Corp., Slate Corp.; pres. Paul Allen Group; founder Eclipse Aviation, Albuquerque, 1998—. Bd. dir. Experimental Aircraft Assn.; exec. coun., Rsch., Engring, Devel. Adv. Com. FAA; presdl. adv. bd. Embry-Riddle Aeronautical Univ. Recipient Michael A. Chowdry Aviation Entrepreneur of Yr. award, Airport Jour., 2005; named a Time 100 Innovator, 2001; named one of 50 Who Matter Now, Business 2.0, 2007. Office: Eclipse Aviation 2503 Clark Carr Loop SE Albuquerque NM 87106 Office Phone: 505-245-7555.

RABUSE, LYNNE MARIE, language educator; b. Minn. d. William and Shirley Rabuse; m. Paul Kohner; 1 child, E. J. Kohner. MAT, Sch. Internat. Tng., Brattleboro, Vt., 1990. Vol. US Peace Corps., Pretoria, Ecuador, 1882—85; tchr. Spanish St. Bernard's HS, St. Paul, 1985—90, Melrose-Mindoro HS, Wis., 1990—2002; instr. Spanish Minn. SE Tech. Coll., Winona, 2002—. Vol. Winona Health, 2004—08. Recipient Cultural Diversity Recognition, Winona State U., 2008; scholarship, State of Yucatan, Mex., 1991. Mem.: Minn. Coun. Tchrs. Lang. and Culture (presenter 1985—2008, Best of Minn. 1995). Avocations: hiking, camping, cooking, knitting, yoga. Home: 203 East Wabasha St Winona MN 55987 Office: MN SE Tech Coll 1250 Homer Rd Winona MN 55987

RABUZZI, DANIEL D., medical association administrator; b. Pitts., June 19, 1935; s. Daniel Ralph and Victoria (Bruni) R.; m. Kathryn Allen, June 11, 1958; children: Daniel, Matthew, Douglas. AB, Harvard Coll., 1957; MD, U. Pa., 1961. Diplomate Am. Bd. Otolaryngology. Instr. otolaryngology U. Md., Balt., 1967-68; asst. prof. SUNY, Syracuse, 1968-71, assoc. prof., 1971-77, prof., 1977-81, clin. prof. otolaryngology, 1984-97, emeritus prof., 1997—; prof., chmn. N.Y. Med. Coll. and N.Y. Eye & Ear Infirmary, NYC, 1981-84. Pres. St. Joseph's Hops. Med. Staff, Syracuse, 1990-92; med. dir. Harrison Surgery Ctr., 1996—. Contbr. 55 articles to profl. jours., chpts. to books. Capt. U.S. Army, 1966-68. Fellow ACS; mem. Am. Soc. Head and Neck Surgery, Am. Acad. Otoloaryngology, Am. Cancer Soc. (pres. County unit 1978-80), Onondaga County Med. Soc. (pres. 1987-88). Avocations: roman archeology, european travel, golf, historical readings. Office: Harrison Outpatient Surgery Ctr 550 Harrison St Ste 230 Syracuse NY 13202-3064 Home Phone: 315-446-5225; Office Phone: 315-472-4424. Personal E-mail: buzdoc@verizon.net.

RABY, JOHN CORNELIUS, secondary school educator; b. NYC, May 18, 1944; s. John Cornelius and Adele Lambrose Raby; m. Betty Louise Hays, July 31, 1971; 1 child, John Hays. BA in History, Stanford U, 1966; MA in History, Columbia U Tchr. Coll., 1968. Cert. teach social studies N.Y., N.J., Calif. History tchr. Mountain HS, West Orange, NJ, 1968—71; faculty mem. The. Gov. Sch. of N.J. for Pub. Issues, West Long Branch, 1983—88, 1990, 1992—93, 1995; history tchr. James Caldwell HS, West Caldwell, NJ, 1973—89, The Pingry Sch., Martinsville, NJ, 1989—. Cross-country coach The Pingry Sch., Martinsville, NJ, 1993—. Mem. Dem. Com., Warren, NJ, 1995—, treas., 2002—03. Recipient U.S. Presdl. Tchr. award, NEA, 1986, Nat. Tchr. award Finalist, The Disney Corp., 1994; fellow, Soc. For Values In Higher Edn., 1994—. Mem.: Organization of Am. Historians, Soc. For Values In Higher Edn. (Nat. Bd. Mem. 2003), Am. Historical Assoc. (assoc.). Democrat. Avocations: running, travel, gardening, reading. Office: The Pingry School Box 366 Martinsville Rd Martinsville NJ 08836

RABY, JULIAN, art gallery director; b. London, Eng., 1950; m. Lorna Raby. PhD in Oriental Stdues, Univ. Oxford, 1981. Lectr. in Islamic Art & Architecture Univ. Oxford, England, 1979—2002; chmn. of curators Oriental Inst., 1991—93, 1995—2000, chmn. of bd, faculty of Oriental Studies, 1993—95; dir. Freer Gallery of Art and Arthur M. Sackler Gallery, Smithsonian Instn., Washington, 2002—. Founder, former co-owner Azimuth Editors publisher. Series founder and editor Oxford Studies in Islamic Art; author: Venice, Durer, and the Oriental Mode, 1982, IZNIK: The Pottery of Ottoman Turkey, 1989, Turkish Bookbinding in the 15th Century, The foundation of a Court Style, 1993, Qajar Portraits, 1999. Fellow: Soc. of Antiquaries; mem.: Coun. of Britis Inst. of Archaeology and History, Amman, Jordan. Office: Freer Gallery of Art Smithsonian Instn MCR707 PO Box 37012 Washington DC 20013-7012 Office Phone: 202-633-4880. Office Fax: 202-357-4911.

RABY, KENNETH ALAN, lawyer, retired military officer; b. Dec. 29, 1935; s. Carl George and Helen Josette (Milne) R.; m. Shirley Rae Nelson, June 2, 1957; children: Randolph Carlton, Shelly Ann. BA, U. S.D., 1957, JD, 1960; grad. with honors, Command and Gen. Staff Coll., 1975, U.S. Army War Coll., 1981. Bar: US Ct. Mil. Appeals 1961, Supreme Ct. SD 1960, US Supreme Ct. 1968, US Ct. Mil. Review 1983, DC Ct. Appeals 1983, Ga. 1988, Ga. Ct. Appeals 1988, Supreme Ct. Ga. 1988. Commd. 2d lt. U.S. Army, 1957, chief mil. def. counsel U.S. vs. Calley (My Lai Massacre), 1969—71, chief legal team Inf. Sch. Ft. Benning, Ga., 1969-71, advanced through grades to col. JAGC, 1979, staff judge adv. Armor Ctr. Ft. Knox, Ky., 1979—80, ret., 1987; dep. staff judge adv. Am. Divsn., Chu Lai, Vietnam, 1968-69; team chief, acting divsn. chief adminstrv. law divsn. Dept. Army, TJAG, 1971—74, chief criminal law divsn., 1981—84; staff judge adv. Hdqs. 24th Inf. Divsn., Ft. Stewart, Ga., 1974-79; sr. judge Army Ct. Mil. Rev., Falls Church, Va., 1984-87; staff atty. Ga. Ct. Appeals, 1987—2005; ret., 2006. Former chmn., mem. Joint Svc. Com. on Mil. Justice, 1981-84; mem. Mil. Justice Act of 1983 Adv. Commn., 1984-87; army liaison to criminal law sect. ABA, 1981-84. Eagle Scout Boy Scouts Am., 1951. Decorated Legion of Merit, Bronze Star with oak leaf cluster, Meritorious Svc. medal with 2 oak leaf clusters, Joint Svc. Commendation medal, Air medal, Army Commendation medal with oak leaf cluster, Army Achievement medal. Mem.: FBA (chmn. law enforcement liaison com. 1986—87), Ga. Bar Assn., Masons (32d degree, KCCH), Order Ea. Star (grand chpt. Ga. 1999—2000, worthy grand patron 1999—2000, gen. grand chpt. parliamentarian 2003—06, 2006—09), KCCH, Arturo Reghine Lodge (Italy) (hon.), Royal Order Scotland (hon.), Scottish Rite, Theta Xi, Delta Theta Phi. Home: 575 Spender Trace Atlanta GA 30350-5017 Home Phone: 770-393-3293. Personal E-mail: alanraby@bellsouth.net.

RABY, THERI GREIGO, health facility administrator, internist; b. N.Mex. MD, U. N.Mex., Albuquerque, 1992. Cert. Internal Medicine. Resident Rush Presbyn. St. Luke's Med. Ctr., Chgo., chief resident, internal medicine; clin. instr. internal medicine Northwestern U. Feinberg Sch. Medicine; internist & med. dir., Ctr. Integrative Medicine Northwestern Meml. Hosp., Chgo., 1996—, founder, pres., Raby Inst. Integrative Medicine. Office: Northwestern Meml Hosp 680 N Lake Shore Dr Chicago IL 60611 also: Raby Inst Integrative Medicine 233 E Erie Ste 500 Chicago IL 60611 Office Phone: 312-276-1212. Office Fax: 312-276-1213.*

RABY, WILLIAM LOUIS, writer, consultant; b. Chgo., July 16, 1927; s. Gustave E. and Helen (Burgess) R.; m. Norma Claire Schreiner, Sept. 8, 1956 (dec. Feb. 2006); children: Burgess, Marianne, Marlene. BSBA, Northwestern U., 1949; MBA, U. Ariz., 1961, PhD, 1971. Ptnr. VAR CPA Firms, 1950-76, Touche Ross & Co., NYC, 1977-87; ret. ptnr. Deloitte & Touche, NYC. Pres. Ariz. State Bd. Accountancy, 1993-94; mem. Ariz. State Bd. Tax Appeals, 1994-2006, chmn., 1997-99, 2003-05; prof. acctg. emeritus Ariz. State U.; columnist Tax Notes mag., Arlington, Va., 1990-2008; cons. on video and audio tax edn. tapes Bisk Pub. Co., 1992—. Author: The Income Tax and Business Decisions, 1964, Building and Maintaining a Successful Tax Practice, 1964, The Reluctant Taxpayer, 1970, Tax Practice Management, 1974, Introduction to Federal Taxation, annually, 1980-91, Tax Practice Management: Client Servicing, 1986; editor: Raby Report on Tax Practice, 1986-96, PPC Guide To Successful Tax Practice, 1991; mem. editorial adv. bd. Practical Tax Strategies; contbr. articles to profl. jours. Mem. AICPA (chmn. fed. tax divsn. 1980-83, v.p. 1983-84, coun. 1983-90), Tax Ct. Bar. Presbyterian (elder, United Presbyn. Ch. chmn. adv. coun. on ch. and soc. 1979-81). Office: PO Box 26846 Tempe AZ 85285-6846 Home Phone: 480-756-4333; Office Phone: 480-967-1501. Personal E-mail: rabyw@aol.com.

RACALTO, JOSEPH, legislative staff member; Legis. asst. to congressman Barney Frank US House of Reps., Washington, 1996—2007, sr. policy adv., 2007—08, chief of staff to congressman Eric Massa, 2009—. Democrat. Mailing: US House Reps 1208 Longworth House Office Bldg Washington DC 20515 Office Phone: 202-225-3161. Office Fax: 202-225-6599.*

RACE, GEORGE JUSTICE, pathology educator; b. Everman, Tex., Mar. 2, 1926; s. Claude Ernest and Lila Eunice (Bunch) R.; m. Annette Isabelle Rinker, Dec. 21, 1946; children: George William Daryl, Jonathan Clark, Mark Christopher, Jennifer Anne (dec.), Elizabeth Margaret Rinker. MD, U. Tex., Southwestern Med. Sch., 1947; MS in Pub. Health, U. N.C., 1953; PhD in Ultrastructural Anatomy and Microbiology, Baylor U., 1969. Intern Duke Hosp., 1947-48, asst. resident pathology, 1951-53; intern Boston City Hosp., 1948-49; asst. pathologist Peter Bent Brigham Hosp., Boston, 1953-54; pathologist St. Anthony's Hosp., St. Petersburg, Fla., 1954-55; staff pathologist Children's Med. Center, Dallas, 1955-59; dir. labs. Baylor U. Med. Center, Dallas, 1959-86, chief dept. pathology, 1959-86, vice chmn. exec. com. med. bd., 1970-72; cons. pathologist VA Hosp., Dallas, 1955-71; adj. prof. anthropology and biology So. Meth. U., Dallas, 1969; instr. pathology Duke, 1951-53, Harvard Med. Sch., 1953-54; asst. prof. pathology U. Tex. Southwestern Med. Sch., 1955-58, clin. assoc. prof., 1958-64, clin. prof., 1964-72, prof., 1973-94, prof. emeritus, 1994—, dir. Cancer Center, 1973-76, assoc. dean for continuing edn., 1973-94, emeritus assoc. dean, 1994—. Pathologist-in-chief Baylor U. Med. Ctr., 1959-86, prof. biomed. studies Baylor Grad. sch., 1989-94; chmn. Baylor Rsch. Found., 1986-89; prof. microbiology Baylor Coll. Dentistry, 1962-68, prof. pathology, 1964-68, prof., chmn. dept. pathology 1969-73, dean A. Webb Roberts Continuing Edn., 1973-94; spl. advisor on human and animal diseases to gov. State of Tex., 1979-83. Editor: Laboratory Medicine (4 vols.), 1973, 10th edit., 1983; Contbr. articles to profl. jours., chpts. to textbooks. Pres., Tex. div. Am. Cancer Soc., 1970; chmn. Gov.'s Task Force on Higher Edn., 1981. Served with AUS, 1944-46; flight surgeon USAF, 1948-51, Korea. Decorated Air medal. Fellow AAAS, Coll. Am. Pathologists, Am. Soc. Clin. Pathologists; mem. AMA (chmn. multiple discipline research forum 1969), Am. Assn. Pathologists, Internat. Acad. Pathology, Am. Assn. Med. Colls., Explorers Club (dir., v.p. 1993-2000), Sigma Xi, Alpha Omega Alpha. Office Phone: 214-528-7501. Office Fax: 214-526-8607. Personal E-mail: georgejrace@yahoo.com.

RACE, TIM, editor; BA, Miami Univ., 1978; MA, Bowling Green State Univ., 1980; MS in journalism, Am. Univ., 1983. Editor CMP Publications; exec. editor Comm. Week; editor, Bus. World sect. New York Times, 1989—91, info. tech. & media editor, 1991—97, founding editor, Circuits sect., 1997—98, editor, Monday Bus. sect., 1998—2004, tech. & health care editor, 2004—. Mem.: Assn. Healthcare Journalists. Office: New York Times 620 8th Ave New York NY 10018 Office Phone: 212-556-1526. Office Fax: 212-556-1448. Business E-Mail: timrace@nytimes.com.

RACHELEFSKY, GARY STUART, medical educator; b. NYC, 1942; BS, Columbia Coll., 1963. Intern Bellevue Hosp. Ctr., NYC, 1967-68; resident in pediatrics Johns Hopkins Hosp., 1968-70, Ctr. Disease Control, 1970-72; fellow UCLA Med. Ctr., 1972-74; prof. allergy and immunology, dir. exec. care UCLA, Ctr. Asthma, Allergy and Immunology. Fellow Am. Acad. Allergy, Asthma and Immunology (bd. dirs., past pres.). Mailing: 14933 Alva Dr Pacific Palisades CA 90272 Personal E-mail: rachruss@ix.netcom.com. Business E-Mail: grachelefsky@mednet.ucla.edu.

RACHLIN, HARVEY BRANT, writer; b. Phila., June 23, 1951; s. Philip and Mazie (Drucker) R.; m. Marla Sivak Goldwert, June 28, 1987; 1 child, Glenn. BA in Biology, Hofstra U., Hempstead, NY, 1973. With music pub. cos., 1973—; owner Western Hemisphere Music Co., Ellipsis Music Mgmt. Co., Manhasset Hills, NY, 1975—, pres., 1982-92; mem. faculty Five Towns Coll., Seaford, NY, 1978-84, Manhattanville Coll., Purchase, NY, 1995—. Author: The Songwriter's Handbook, 1977 (NY Pub. Libr. Book for Teen Age 1979-82); The Encyclopedia of the Music Business, 1981 (Outstanding Music Reference Source ALA 1981, ASCAP-Deems Taylor award 1982, Writer's Digest Book Club Spl. Selection, included in Selected Bibliography for Musicians Libr. of Congress); Love Grams, 1983; The Money Encyclopedia, 1984 (Outstanding Fin. Reference Book, Libr. Jour., 1984, Ency. Britannica Home Libr. selection); The Kennedys: A Chronological History 1823--, 1986; The Songwriter's and Musician's Guide to Making Great Demos, 1988 (NY Pub. Libr. Book for Teen Age 1989); The Making of a Cop, 1991 (NY Pub. Libr. Book for Teen Age, 1992); The Songwriter's Workshop, 1991; The TV and Movie Business: An Encyclopedia of Careers, Technologies, and Practices, 1991 (Fireside Theatre Book Club main selection); The Making of a Detective, 1995 (featured on Good Morning America, NYPD Retired Detectives Assn. award); Lucy's Bones, Sacred Stones, and Einstein's Brain, 1996 (History Book Club selection, named one of best books in print The Reader's Catalog 1997, Best Books Young Adult Readers Grades 7-12, 1997, Pub. Libr Catalog, 1999, Sr. HS Libr. Catalog, 1997-02); co-writer, cons. adapted as three-part TV mini-series History's Lost and Found (daily series on The History Channel, CineGold Eagle award 2000); Jumbo's Hide, Elvis's Ride, and the Tooth of Buddha, 2000 (Book-of-the-Month Club's Quality Paperback Book Club selection); Scandals, Vandals, and Da Vincis: A Gallery of Remarkable Art Tales, 2007; free-lance music journalist; contbr. Songwriter Mag., 1978—, Law and Order Mag., 1992—, Songwriter's Market, 1979-80, 87, 92, The Writer, 2005, 08, 09, Sch. Arts, 2009, Wall St. Jour., 2007; guest on The Joe Franklin Show, 1977, 81, The Dinah Shore Show, 1978, Nine Broadcast Plaza, 1991, The Sally Jessy Raphael Show, 1993, The Late Late Show with Tom Snyder, 1996; compositions performed L.I. Mandolin and Guitar Orch., 1988; featured in NY Times, 1982, 96, Pro-Music, 1982, Something About the Author, 1987, Valley Stream Herald, 1995-96, 98, Writer's Market, 1994, Newsday, 1996, 99, 07, Sarasota Herald-Tribune, 1996, Coral Springs Forum, 1997, L.I. Lifestyles, 2000, City Line News, 2001, Recess for Tchrs., 2005, Northwest Herald, 2007, The Windsor Star, 2007, The Times(London), 2007, Sch. Arts, 2009 Recipient Outstanding Reference Book of Yr. award, ALA, 1981, award, Libr. Jour., 1984. Mem.: Am. Soc. Journalists and Authors. Home: 125 Lake St Apt 8h S White Plains NY 10604 Office: Manhattanville Coll Music Dept 2900 Purchase St Purchase NY 10577 Home Phone: 516-568-1795; Office Phone: 914-323-7204. Personal E-mail: hbrachlin@msn.com.

RACHLIN, JEANNE-MARIE, mathematics educator; b. Baton Rouge, Nov. 10, 1948; m. Neal Rachlin, May 18, 1969; children: Sean, Aron. BA Math, San Jose State Univ., Calif., 1971. Standard Secondary Credential Calif. Math tchr. R.J. Fisher Sch., Los Gatos, Calif., 1971—81, v.p., 1981—85; math tchr. Los Gatos/Saratoga High, 1985—. Math dept. chair R.J. Fisher Sch., 1978—81, Los Gatos High, 2002—. Recipient Educator of the Yr., Home & Sch. Club, 2000, Tchr. of the Yr., Los Gatos/Saratoga High, 2005. Avocations: reading, travel, yoga, photography. Office: Los Gatos high 20 High Sch Ct Los Gatos CA 95030

RACHLIN, LAUREN DAVID, lawyer; b. Buffalo, Feb. 6, 1929; s. Harry A. and Thelma (Goldberg) R.; m. Jean K. Rachlin, June 27, 1954; children: Laura Gail, Ellen Joan, James N. BS, U. Buffalo, 1948; JD, Harvard U., 1951. Bar: NY 1952, U.S. Dist. Ct. (no. and we. dists.) NY 1952, U.S. Tax Ct. 1952, U.S. Supreme Ct. 1958, U.S. Ct. Appeals (2d cir.) 1967, U.S. Ct. Internat. Trade 1978. Ptnr. Rachlin & Rachlin, Buffalo, 1952—81; sr. ptnr. Kavinoky & Cook, Buffalo, 1981—2003; ptnr. Hodgson Russ, LLP, Buffalo and Toronto, 2003—. U.S. appointee to Bi-nat. Dispute Settlement Panel created under U.S.-Can. Free Trade Agreement, 1989-93; U.S. appointee N.Am. Free Trade Agreement Bi-Nat. Dispute Settlement Panel, 1994-96, 2004-; arbitrator Internat. C. of C., Internat. Dispute Resolution Panel, Am. Arbitration Assn.; founder and dir. Can./U.S. Border Alliance regionalizing the bi-national trade corridor linking Toronto, Hamilton, Buffalo, Syracuse and Rochester, 1996—; founder, past pres., dir. World Trade Ctr.-Buffalo Niagara, 1986—; lectr. in field. U.S. del. to UN Human Rights Commn., 1970; cons. to temporary commn. NY State Constl. Conv.; mem. Erie County Charter Rev. Commn.; mem.-at-large U.S. Nat. Commn. for UNESCO, 1972-76, chmn. human rights task force; mem. industry functional adv. com. Customs for Trade Policy Matters of U.S. Dept. Commerce, Office U.S. Trade Rep., 1987—. Mem. ABA (fgn. investment in U.S. real estate com., internat. bus. law com., subcom. on trade import), NY State Bar Assn. (founding chmn. internat. sect. 1987-89, chmn. internat. divsn. 1989-94, chair legal edn. and admission to bar com. 1999-2002, ADR com. 2005—, award for distinction in internat. law and affairs Internat. Law and Practice sect. 2005), World Arbitration Inst. (adv. bd., bd. dirs.), Am. Assn. Exporters & Importers (trade policy com.), Interpacific Bar Assn., Interam. Bar Assn., Customs and Internat. Trade Bar Assn., Erie County Bar Assn, Industry Trade Adv. Commn. on Customs and Trade Facilitation, US Dept. Commerce. Office: Hodgson Russ LLP Ste 2000 1 M & T Plz Buffalo NY 14203-2391 Address: Ste 2309 150 King St W Toronto ON M5H 1J9 Canada Office Phone: 716-848-1460.

RACHLIN, NATHALIE, language educator; m. Stephen Rachlin; children: Julian, Anna. PhD, Princeton U., NJ. Prof. French Scripps Coll., Claremont, Calif., 1989—. Office: Scripps Coll 1030 Columbia Ave Claremont CA 91711 Business E-Mail: nrachlin@scrippscollege.edu.

RACHOFSKY, DAVID J., lawyer; b. Oceanside, NY, Nov. 17, 1936; s. Lester M. and Marjorie A.; m. Faith Allen; children: Robert, Patricia, Edward. BSEE, MIT, 1958; JD, Temple U., 1968. Bar: Pa., U.S. Dist. Ct. (ea. dist.) Pa., U.S. Tax. Ct., U.S. Ct. Fed. Claims, Pa. Supreme Ct. 1968. Of counsel Dechert LLP, Phila., 1968—. Lectr. law Temple U. Law Sch., 1976-95. Contbr. articles to profl. jours. With USAF, 1969-72. Mem. Phila. Bar Assn., Internat. Fiscal Assn. (chmn. mid-Atlantic region 1985-87, mem. coun. 1986-2008, mem. exec. com. 1992—, v.p., sec. 1992-96, exec. v.p. 1996-98, pres. 1998-2000). Office: Dechert LLP 2929 Arch St Philadelphia PA 19104-2808

RACHOFSKY, HOWARD, retired investor, art collector, patron; m. Cindy Rachofsky, 2000; children: Meghan, Matthew. Former bd. chmn. Regal Securities Investment, L.P. Bd. dirs. Dallas Symphony Assn., Dallas Mus. Art, NYC Dia Ctr. for the Arts, East Dallas Cmty. Sch., Tate Lecture Series, So. Methodist U.; adv. dir. Booker T. Washington Magnet HS for the Performing and Visual Arts, Dallas Theater Ctr., Dallas Archtl. Found., U. Tex. Sch. Architecture; founder, bd. dirs. Dallas Ctr. for the Performing Arts Found., chair, site design com.; mem. adv. bd. Wharton Club, Dallas/Ft. Worth, Dallas Bus. Com. for the Arts; founder Howard Earl Rachofsky Found.; mem. investment com. St. Phillips Acad. Named one of Top 200 Collectors, ARTnews mag., 2003—08. Avocation: Collector of Contemporary Art. Office: Dallas Center For The Performing Arts 2100 Ross Ave Ste 650 Dallas TX 75201-6709

RACHOR, JEFFREY C., former automotive supplies company executive; Region v.p. mid-south Sonic Automotive, Inc., Charlotte, NC, 1997—98, v.p. retail ops., 1998—99, exec. v.p. retail ops., 1999—2002, exec. v.p., COO, 2002—04, pres., COO, 2004—07; pres., CEO The Pep Boys-Manny, Moe & Jack, Phila., 2007—08.

RACHOW, LOUIS A(UGUST), librarian; b. Shickley, Nebr., Jan. 21, 1927; s. John Louis and Mable (Dondlinger) R. BS, York Coll., 1948; MS in L.S., Columbia U., 1959. Librarian York Coll., Nebr., 1949-54; instr. library asst. Queens Coll., NYC, 1956-57; serials acquisition asst. Columbia U. Law Library, NYC, 1957-58; asst. librarian Univ. Club, NYC, 1958-62; librarian Hampden-Booth Theatre Library at the Players, NYC, 1962-86, curator, 1986-88; library dir. Internat. Theatre Inst. U.S., NYC, 1989—2002. Cons. theatre sect. U. Calif., San Diego, new campuses program, 1964, Music Ctr. Operating Archives, Los Angeles, 1985; mem. library adv. bd. Eugene O'Neill Meml. Theatre Center, 1966— Editor, compiler: Guide to Performing Arts, 1968; assoc. editor Am. Notes and Queries, 1971-74, asst. editor, 1967-71; mem. editorial adv. bd. Nat. Dir. for Performing Arts and Civic Ctrs.; editor Performing Arts series Gale Info. Guide, 1976-83, Theatre and Performing Arts Collections, 1981; contbr. articles and revs. to profl. jours. Mem. adv. bd. Am. Theatre Co., OKC Theatre Prodns. Served with AUS, 1954-56 Mem. Theatre Libr. Assn. (rec. sec. 1966-67, pres. 1967-72, 81-83, v.p. 1976-80, editor Broadside 1973-81), ALA, Spl. Librs. Assn. (sec.-treas. mus. group N.Y.C. chpt. 1964-66), N.Y. Libr. Club (pres. 1979-80), Am. Theatre Assn., New Drama Forum Assn. (pres. 1983-86), Am. Soc. Theatre Rsch., N.Y. Tech. Svcs. Librs., Archons of Colophon (convener 1982-83), Episcopal Actors Guild Am. (bd. dirs. 1976-2002, v.p. 2002—), Drama Desk, Broadway Theatre Inst. Outer Critics Circle (treas. 1998—), Players Club, The Lambs Club. Home: 528 W 114th St New York NY 10025-7841

RACHOW, SHARON DIANNE, realtor; b. St. Joseph, Mo., Apr. 12, 1939; d. Norman DeLos Zancker and Sylvia Lavina (Hawkins) Trouel; m. Thomas Eugene Rachow, Oct. 22, 1968; children: Todd A., Tiffany K. Student, So. Ill. U., 1969-72. Sec. Westab, Inc. (now Mead), St. Joseph, 1957-60, Seitz Packing Co. (now Sara Lee), St. Joseph, 1960-66; exec. asst. to v.p., gen. mgr. Kansas City (Mo.) Chiefs, 1972; co-owner, mgr. Pool 'N Patio Plus, St. Joseph, 1973-84; realtor Coldwell Banker Gen. Realtors, St. Joseph, 1984-93, RE/MAX, 1993—2004, Evans Realty, 2004—. Trustee Nat. Multiple Sclerosis Soc., Mid Am. chpt., Midland M.S. Express Br., 1993-98. Mem.: Real Estate Buyers Agt. Coun. (accredited buyers rep. 1996—), St. Joseph Regional Bd. Realtors (residential specialist 1987—, Multi-List com. 1993—2002, bd. dirs. 1994, forms com. 1994—2002, Top Residential Sales award 1986—, Top 10), Multi Million Dollar Club (quality svc. cert. 2001, quality svc. cert. 2003). Republican. Lutheran. Home: 4211 Country Ln Saint Joseph MO 64506-2454 Office: Reece & Nichols Ide Capital Realty 3827 Beck Rd Saint Joseph MO 64506 Office Phone: 816-262-0022.

RACIC, STANKO, finance educator; b. Karlovac, Croatia, May 2, 1962; s. Kresimir and Branka Racic; m. Maja Stefanovic-Racic; children: Sandra, Andrea, Tamara. PhD, U. Pitts., 2005. Asst. prof. fin. Robert Morris U., Moon Township, Pa., 2005—. Contbr. articles to porfl. jours. Named Disting. Prof., Exec. MBA, Katz Grad. Sch. Bus., U. Pitts., 1999. Mem.: Am. Assn. Bus. and Behavioral Scis. Home: 59 Moffett St Pittsburgh PA 15243 Office: Robert Morris Univ 6001 University Blvd Moon Township PA 15108 Business E-Mail: racic@rmu.edu.

RACINE, KARL A., lawyer; b. Port au Prince, Haiti, Dec. 14, 1962; Student French, French civilization, Sorbonne, Paris; BA in Economics, U. Pa., 1985; JD, U. Va., 1989. Bar: Md. 1989, DC 1992. Litig. assoc. Venable LLP, Washington, 1989—92, ptnr., corp. and civil litig. groups, 2002—, dep. mng. ptnr., 2005—06, mng. ptnr., 2006—; staff atty. Pub. Defender Svc., Washington, 1992—94; ptnr. Cacheris & Treanor, Washington, 1994—97; assoc. counsel The White House, Washington, 1997—2000. Named one of 50 Most Influential Minority Lawyers in America, Nat. Law Jour., 2008. Achievements include co-producing the first Haitian/Creole/English legal dictionary, 1994. Office: Venable LLP 575 Seventh St NW Washington DC 20004 Office Phone: 202-344-8322. Office Fax: 202-344-8300. E-mail: karacine@venable.com.*

RACINE, PHILIP NOEL, retired history educator; b. Brunswick, Maine, Dec. 25, 1941; s. Russell Adelard and Rebecca Yvonne Racine; m. Frances Melton, Aug. 31, 1968; children: Russell Marcoux, Alawee Howard. AB, Bowdoin Coll., Brunswick, 1964; PhD, Emory U., Atlanta, Ga., 1969. Kenan prof. history Wofford Coll., Spartanburg, SC, 1991—2008. Contbr. articles to jour. (Founder's award, Mus. Confederacy, 1986); author: (photographic history) Seeing Spartanburg: A History in Images. Mem Hist. and Archtl. Rev. Bd., Spartanburg, SC, 2001—07. Mem.: Southern Hist. Assn. Home: 200 Pineville Rd Spartanburg SC 29307 Office: Wofford Coll 429 N Church St Spartanburg SC 29303 Personal E-mail: pracine@charter.net. Business E-Mail: racinepn@wofford.edu.

RACINE, RICHARD B., lawyer; b. Cleve., Mar. 20, 1956; BS in chem., Georgetown U., 1978; JD, Case Western Reserve U., 1981. Bar: Ohio 1981, DC 1984, registered: US Patent & Trademark Office. Ptnr. Finnegan, Henderson, Farabow, Garrett & Dunner LLP, Washington, mng. ptnr., leader, chem. practice group, mem. mgmt. com., mem. compensation com. Mem.: ABA (subcom. chmn. atty. opinions com. 1993—94), Rd. Patent Resources Group (lectr. 2005—), Intellectual Property Owners Assn. (lectr. 2006), Southwestern Legal Found. (lectr. 1993—94), Fed. Cir. Bar Assn., Am. Chem. Soc. (program chmn. 1991—93, divsn. chmn. elect 1993, divsn. chmn. 1994), Am. Intellectual Property Law Assn., Bar Assn. DC, DC Bar. Office: Finnegan Henderson Farabow Garrett Dunner LLP 901 New York Ave NW Washington DC 20001-3315 Office Phone: 202-408-4038. Office Fax: 202-408-4400. Business E-Mail: rich.racine@finnegan.com.

RACINE, SCOTT H., lawyer; b. Chgo. BA, Bradley U., 1972; JD cum laude, Pepperdine U., 1978; LLM in Tax., NYU, 1979. Bar: Calif. 1978, US Dist. Ct. (ctrl., so. districts) Calif., US Ct. of Appeals (9th cir.), US Tax Ct., US Ct. of Claims. Law clk. Judge William M. Drennen US Tax Ct., 1979—80; shareholder tax specialty firm, LA; ptnr., chair, tax practice group LA Akin Gump Strauss Hauer & Feld LLP, LA. Adj. prof. law Pepperdine Univ., 1980—, Univ. San Diego, 1983—87, Loyola Univ., 2000—. Student writings editor Pepperdine Law Rev., 1976—78; author: numerous articles for profl. publs. Bd. visitors Pepperdine Univ. Sch. Law; bd. adv. Loyola Univ. Sch. Law; planning com. Univ. So. Calif. Tax Inst. Mem.: ABA (sect. on tax.), Calif. Bar Assn. (sect. on tax.), LA County Bar Assn. (sect. on tax.). Office: Akin Gump Strauss Hauer & Feld LLP Ste 2400 2029 Century Pk E Los Angeles CA 90067-3012 Office Phone: 310-229-1059. Office Fax: 310-229-1001. Business E-Mail: sracine@akingump.com.

RACKER, DARLENE KATIE, cardiovascular anatomist, electrophysiologist; b. Chgo., Dec. 8, 1937; d. George Oliver and Katie Venoy (Gibson) Cameron; m. Lester Eugene Racker, Nov. 1, 1959; children: Lester Keith Van Racker, Victoria Venice Racker Finney. Cert. Histologist, U. Chgo., 1962; BSc in Cell Biology, Ill. State U., Chgo., 1976; PhD in Physiology, Chgo. Med. Sch., 1988. Histology technician Northwestern U., Chgo., 1959-60; histology and TEM technician U. Chgo., 1959-60; TEM technologist VA Lakeside Hosp., Chgo., 1965-81; postdoctoral fellow Coll. Phys. & Surgs., Columbia U., NYC, 1988-90; rsch. assoc. prof. Northwestern U. Med. Sch., Chgo., 1990—. Presenter in field. Author: Transmission Electron Microscopy Methods of Application, 1983; contbr. articles to profl. jours. APS and Procter & Gamble fellow, 1983-88. Mem. Am. Soc. Clin. Pathology, Am. Physiol. Soc., N.Am. Soc. Pacing and Electrophysiology, Am. Heart Assn. Democrat. Roman Catholic. Achievements include rsch. in seminal demonstrations by TEM of membrane channels, of the sinoventricular conducting system in dog heart, of sinoventricular conduction system with discover of the missing links: atrionodal bundles and proximal AV bundle, discovery of the muscular valvular apparatus, transmembrane and extracellular potentials evoked by the sinoventricular conduction sys. and muscular valvular apparatis tissues; development of new tissue culture techniques for investigation of neuronal development in slice cultures. Home: PO Box 6104 Wilmette IL 60091-6104 Office: Northwestern U Med Sch Medicine Cardiology Dept/CH233 303 E Chicago Ave Chicago IL 60611-3072 E-mail: d.racker@northwestern.edu.

RACKOW, ERIC C., health care company executive; Grad., Franklin and Marshall Coll.; MD, SUNY, Downstate Med. Ctr., Brooklyn, 1971. Bd. cert. internal medicine, cardiovasc. diseases, critical care medicine, internal medicine, 1975, cardiology, 1977, critical care, 1987. Residency Kings County Hosp. Ctr., 1970—72, chief residency, 1972—73, clin. fellow, 1973—75; dir. clin. trials NYU Hosp. Ctr.; prof. heath care mgmt. NYU Med. Ctr., Sch. Medicine; sr. v.p., chief med. officer NYU Hosp. Ctr., NYC, 2000—04, pres., 2004—07; pres., CEO SeniorBridge, NYC, 2007—. Adj. prof. medicine NY Med. Coll.; chmn. emeritus St. Vincent's Hosp. & Med. Ctr. of NY, Dept. Medicine; hon. role, Physician-in-Chief Inst. Critical Care Medicine; past pres. Soc. Critical Care Medicine; past chair Am. Bd. Internal Medicine, Critical Care Medicine Subspecialty Bd. Contbr. articles to profl. jours. Office: 845 Third Ave New York NY 10022 Office Phone: 212-263-2606, 212-994-6100. Business E-Mail: eric.rackow@nyumc.org.*

RACKOW, JULIAN PAUL, lawyer; b. Phila., Dec. 16, 1941; s. Lawrence Lionel and Blanche (Wachman) R.; m. Paulette Schorr, June 23, 1963; children: Jeffrey A., Andrea B. AB, Cornell U., 1963; JD, Harvard U., 1966. Bar: Pa. 1966, US Dist. Ct. (ea. dist.) Pa. 1966. Assoc. atty. Goodis, Greenfield, Narin & Mann, Phila., 1966-69; ptnr., co-chmn. dept. real estate Blank, Rome LLP, Phila., 1970—. Exec. com., bd. dirs. Ctrl. Phila. Devel. Corp., 1990—, pres. 1996-2000, chmn., 2000—; bd. dirs. Ave of the Arts, Inc., 2000—, Parkway Coun. Found., 2004—. Mem. Phila. Bar Assn., Harvard Law Sch. Assn. Phila, Am. Coll. Real Estate Lawyers, Anglo-Am. Real Property Inst., Ave. of the Arts, Inc. Avocations: tennis, travel, piano. Office: Blank Rome LLP One Logan Sq Philadelphia PA 19103-6998 Office Phone: 215-569-5671. Business E-Mail: rackow@blankrome.com.

RACLIN, GRIER C., lawyer, telecommunications industry executive; BA, JD, Northwestern U. Vice chmn., mng. ptnr. Gardner, Carton & Douglas; exec. v.p., chief adminstrv. office, gen. counsel, corp. sec. Global TeleSystems, Inc.; chief legal officer, corp. sec. SAVVIS, Inc., St. Louis; exec. v.p., sec. gen. counsel Charter Comm., St. Louis, 2005—09, exec. v.p., chief adminstrv. officer, 2009—. Office: Charter Comms 12405 Powerscourt Dr Saint Louis MO 63131 Office Phone: 314-543-2308. Office Fax: 314-965-0555.*

RADA, DAVID CHARLES, dermatologist; b. Chgo., Apr. 8, 1954; s. Irwin C. and Mary A. Rada; m. Christina Lynne Fogle, Mar. 27, 1981; children: Matthew D., Megan E., Rebecca C. BS in Microbiology, U. Nebr., Omaha, 1976, MD, 1980. Diplomate Am. Bd. Dermatology. Resident in dermatology U. Kans. Med. Ctr., 1982—85; pvt. practice Kansas City, Mo., 1985—; pres. CryoHist, Inc., Kansas City, 1995—. Inventor (in field). Fellow: Am. Soc. Dermatologic Surgery, Am. Acad. Dermatology; mem.: Kansas City Dermatologic Soc., Mo. Dermatologic Soc. Achievements include invention of technology to get the surface cut by the surgeon's knife onto glass slides for histologic margins, a technique applicable for cancer resection margins using frozen sections. Office: 4320 Wornall Rd Ste 728 Kansas City MO 64111 Office Phone: 816-561-3641. Personal E-mail: cryohist@aol.com. Business E-Mail: camargin@cryohist.com.

RADA, MIHAI CATALIN, application developer; b. Bucharest, Romania, Aug. 14, 1974; s. Mircea and Dora Rada; m. Catalina Kopetz, Aug. 9, 2004; 1 child, Mara. PhD, U. Md., Coll. Pk., 2004. Programmer analyst Ceresoft Inc., Silver Spring, Md., 2004—06; software developer Mooring Fin. Corp, Vienna, 2006—.

RADA, RUTH BYERS, retired dean; b. LA, Oct. 3, 1923; d. George and Gerda Marie (Lihm) Byers; children: Kaaren Ruth, Georgene Melanie. AB, U. So. Calif., LA, 1944, MA, 1945; EdD, Nova South Eastern U., Davie, Fla., 1976. Asst. dean instrn. and evening East L.A. Coll., 1964-69, dean instrn., 1969-70; dean student personnel L.A. Harbor Coll., 1970-73, East L.A. Coll., 1973-77, L.A. Mission Coll., 1977-83; prof. biol. sci. East L.A. C.C., 1945-69, ret., 1983. Author: Water Biology, 1950, (with others) Human Body in Health and Disease, 1969, Structure and Function of Human Body, 1970, Laboratory Manual for Introductory Microbiology, 1963. Mem. Calif. Cmty. and Jr. Coll. Assn. (area pres. 1973-74), Calif. Woman Adminstrs. Assn., Los Angeles Coll. Adminstrs. Assn. (sec. 1973-74), Phi Beta Kappa, Phi Kappa Phi, Pi Lambda Theta, Phi Sigma. Republican. Mem. Ch. of Religious Sci.

RADAKOVICH, DANIEL I., communications executive, consultant; b. Easton, Pa., Sept. 27, 1958; s. Daniel L. and Nancy A. Radakovich. BA in History, Pa. State U., University Park, 1979. Overseas mktg. mgr. Investment and Income-Producing Properties Internat., Inc., Denver, 1983—84, exec. v.p. LA, 1984—85; substitute tchr. Philipsburg Sch. Dist., NJ, 1985—87; asst. warehouse mgr. Steelcrete, North Royalton, Ohio, 1991—93; v.p. Swing-Sling Inc., Strongsville, Ohio, 1994—96; ptnr. with Matthew W. Fluck Cleve. Shock Expansion Team Project '96, Strongsville, Ohio, 1996; rschr. DesertSun Films LLC, Garfield, NJ, 2003—04; sr. exec. v.p. prodn. DesertSun Films, LLC, Garfield, NJ, 2004—07; chief rsch. officer, 2005—07; pres. Radfilmz, Pittsburgh, Pa., 2008. Cons. Strategicon, Inc., Fullerton, Calif., 1981—85, Diverse Talents Inc., LA, 1985, New Universe Project SF Convs., Fullerton, 1986—88, GuardTower Games, Brunswick, Ohio, 1999—2005; spl. cons. HollyDanWorks, Belgrade, 2003—04, Ontario, 2003—04, lead specialist cons., 2005—08; staff mem. Alpha Young Writer's Workshop,

Greensburg, Pa., 2003—08. Actor: (films) Darkest Days (NY Ind. Film Festival Best thriller award, 2005); contbr. articles to profl. jours. Mem. Cleve. Ams. Mid. Ea. Origin, 1997—2001, Polish-Ams., Inc., Cleve., 1997—2001; exec. com. mem. Cuyahoga County Dems., Cleve., 1994—2000; mem. Cosmopolitan Dem. League, Cleve., 1997—2001, Ward 15 Dem. Club, Cleve., 1998—2001; Dem. candidate 2000 US senate primary, Ohio. Mem.: PARSEC, KC. Democrat. Roman Catholic. Avocations: reading, writing, strategic gaming, acting, politics. Office: c/o Pittsburgh Film Workers Association PO Box 97761 Pittsburgh PA 15227 Business E-Mail: radfilmz@aol.com.

RADANOVICH, GEORGE P., United States Representative from California; b. Mariposa, Calif., June 20, 1955; s. George F. and Joan Radanovich; m. Ethie Weaver; 1 child, George King. BS in Agr. Bus. Mgmt., Calif. State Polytechnic U., San Luis Obispo, 1978. Owner Radanovich Winery, 1986—2004; mem. Mariposa County Bd. Suprs., 1989—92, US Congress from 19th Calif. dist., Washington, 1994—, asst. whip, 1994—, mem. energy & commerce com., chmn. natural parks subcom., water/power subcom. Vice chair Congl. Competitiveness Caucus; mem. Scouting Caucus, Nat. Guard & Reserve Components Caucus, Nat. Environment Policy Act Task Force, Methamphetamine Caucus, Ho. Energy Action Team, Horticulture Caucus, Heart & Stroke Caucus, Forest Task Force, Forest Caucus, Fire Services Caucus, Diabetes Caucus, Courthouse Caucus, Armenian Caucus, Western Caucus, 1997—2005; co-chair Congl. Wine Caucus, 1997—2005, Congl. Croatian Caucus, 2005. Mem. Calif. Agrl. Leadership Found., 1990—92. Mem.: Mariposa C. of C., Calif. Farm Bureau, Calif. Assn. Wine Grape Growers, Wine Inst., Mariposa Rotary. Republican. Roman Catholic. Office: US Ho Reps 438 Cannon Ho Office Bldg Washington DC 20515-0519 Office Phone: 202-225-4540.*

RADCLIFF, JOYCE B., librarian; d. Robert and Rosanna Bullard; m. Doc Radcliff, June 24, 1968; children: Nicole Lynn, Rasheda Asia. BA, U. South Ala., Mobile, 1973, MLS, 1996. Tech. asst. U. S. Ala., Mobile, 1974—99; cataloging libr. U. So. Miss., Hattisburg, 1999—2001; serials libr. Tenn. State U., Nashville, 2001—; cons. Libr. of Congress, Washington, 1996; mem. exec. bd. Reading Is Fundamental, Nashville, 2004—06. Exec. bd. Libr. Sch. Assn. U. Ala., 1997—2002. Contbr. articles to profl. jours. Advisor ABeneefuo KUO Honor Soc., 1989—99; greeter Frist Mus., Nashville, 2002—; advisor Girl Scouts Am., Mobile, 1982—86. Recipient Award of Appreciation, Libr. Congress, Washington, 1996, Congress award, Congressman Sonny Callahan, 2000; named Staff of Yr., U. S. Ala., 1999. Mem.: ALA, Tenn. Libr. Assn., Delta Sigma Theta. Avocations: walking, reading, travel, computers. Office: Tenn State Univ 330 10th Ave N Nashville TN 37203 Home Phone: 615-754-1848; Office Phone: 615-963-7383. Personal E-mail: jardcliff@tds.net. Business E-Mail: jradcliff@tnstate.edu.

RADCLIFFE, DANIEL (DANIEL JACOB RADCLIFFE), actor; b. London, July 23, 1989; s. Alan Radcliffe and Marcia Gresham. Actor: (films) Tailor of Panama, 2001, Harry Potter and the Sorcerer's Stone, 2001, Harry Potter and the Chamber of Secret's, 2002, Harry Potter and the Prisoner of Azkaban, 2004, Harry Potter and the Goblet of Fire, 2005, Harry Potter and the Order of the Phoenix, 2007, December Boys, 2007, Harry Potter and the Half-Blood Prince, 2009; (TV films) David Copperfield, 1999, My Boy Jack, 2008; appearances (TV) The Today Show, 2001, The Oprah Winfrey Show, 2001, Late Night with Conan O'Brien, 2004, (TV special) David Copperfield, 1999; actor: (plays) Equus, 2007; (Broadway plays), 2008. Named one of The 100 Most Powerful Celebrities, Forbes.com, 2008. Office: c/o Artists Rights Group Talent 4 Great Portland St London W1W 8PA England*

RADCLIFFE, MARK FLOHN, lawyer; b. Dayton, Ohio, Mar. 11, 1952; Cert. of completion, Sorbonne, Paris, 1972; BS in Chem. magna cum laude, U. Mich., 1974; JD, Harvard U., 1981. Bar: Calif. 1982. Law clk. to chief judge U.S. Dist. Ct. (so. dist.) Calif., San Diego, 1981-82; assoc. Brobeck, Phleger & Harrison, San Francisco, 1982-86; assoc. to ptnr. Gray Cary Ware & Freidenrich, Palo Alto, Calif., 1986—2004; ptnr. DLA Piper, 2004—, co-chmn. Technology and Sourcing Group Ea. Palo Alto, Calif., 2005—. Gen. counsel The Open Source Initiative; chair com. C for reviewing GPLv3. Mem. editorial bd.: Computer Lawyer, 1988—, Cyberspace Lawyer; mem. adv. bd. BNA Electronic Commerce & Law Report, Global Intellectual Property Asset Mgmt. Report; country corr. European Intellectual Property Rev.; editor-in-chief Jour. Internet Law; co-author Multimedia Law, Internet Law and Business; contbr. articles to profl. law jours. Lt. (j.g.) USNR, 1974-77. Recipient Disting. Alumni award, Harvard Univ., 1998; named one of Am. 100 Most Influential Lawyers, Nat. Law Jour., 1997, World's Leading Trademark Lawyers, Expert Guide, 2003, No. Calif Super Lawyer & one of Top 100 No. Calif. IP Lawyers, San Francisco mag., 2004, Best Lawyers in Am., 2005—06, Am. Leading Lawyers for Bus., Chanbers USA, 2006. Mem. ABA (chmn. subcom. 1985-88), Am. Intellectual Property Law Assn., Internat. Trademark Assn., San Francisco Bar Assn. (chmn. computer law sect. 1985-86), Computer Law Assn. (dir.), Licensing Exec. Soc., South Bay Trademark Lawyers Assn. (founder), Harvard Club. Office: DLA Piper 2000 University Ave Palo Alto CA 94303 Office Phone: 650-833-2266. Office Fax: 650-833-2001. Business E-Mail: mark.radcliffe@dlapiper.com.

RADDE-GALLWITZ, ANDREW, theology studies educator; b. Newark, Ohio, Mar. 16, 1979; s. David and Ruth Ann Gallwitz; m. Kristen Radde, June 15, 2002. BA, Lipscomb U., Nashville, 2000; PhD, Emory U., Atlanta, 2007; MTS, Duke U., Durham, NC, 2002. Asst. prof. theology Loyola U. Chgo., 2007—. Mem.: Soc. Bibl. Lit., North Am. Patristics Soc. Roman Catholic.

RADDING, ANDREW, lawyer; b. NYC, Nov. 30, 1944; m. Bonnie A. Levinson, Oct. 7, 1972; children: Judith Lynne, Joshua David. BBA, CCNY-Baruch Sch., 1965; JD, Boston U., 1969. Bar: N.Y. 1968, Md. 1977, D.C. 1977, U.S. Supreme Ct. Grad. fellow Northwestern U. Sch. Law, 1968-69; asst. counsel U.S. Ho. of Reps. Select Com. on Crime, 1969-72; asst. U.S. atty. for Dist. Md., 1972-77; ptnr. Francomano, Radding & Mannes, Balt., 1977-80, Burke, Gerber, Wilen, Francomano & Radding, Balt., 1980-85, Blades & Rosenfeld P.A., Balt., 1985-97, Adelberg, Rudow, Dorf and Hendler LLC, Balt., 1997—. Mem. adj. faculty clin. practice skills, criminal law, fed. criminal practice U. Balt. Sch. Law, 1980—; mem. trial experience com. U.S. Dist. ct., 1986-88; apptd. by gov. State Adminstrv. Bd. of Election Laws, 1995-96; instr. professionalism course Md. State Bar Assn., 1999—; mem. inquiry panel and peer rev. panel Atty. Grievance Commn., 1991—. Bd. dirs. Copper Hill Condominium, 1979-82, pres., 1981-82; vice chair Lawyers for Erlich for Gov. Com., 2002; mem. subcom. Md. Republican Conv., 1981; sen. C.M. Mathias Jud. Selection com., 1986; chmn. U.S. Dist. Ct. Bicentennial Program, 1989-90; mem. Mayor's Domestic Violence Coord. com., 2001—. Mem.: ABA, Simon Sobeloff Law Soc. (pres. 2008—), Nat. Arbitration Forum (arbitrator), U.S. Arbitration and Mediation, Md. Inst. Continuing Profl. Edn. for Lawyers (bd. govs. 1987—92), U.S. Atty. Alumni Assn. Md. (pres. 1978—), Fed. Bar Assn. (Balt. chpt. pres. 1986—87), Balt. City Bar Assn. (jud. selection com. 1990—92, co-chmn. membership com. 1999—2000, exec. coun. 2000—, chmn. fee arbitration com. 2001—02, chmn. 2004—, 2004—, jud. selection com. 2008—09, sec. 2008—09, treas. 2009—, 2009—), Md. Bar Assn. (CLE com. 2002—, bd. govs. 2005—07, chair program com. 2005—). Jewish. Office: Adelberg Rudow et al LLC 7 St Paul St Ste 600 Baltimore MD 21202 Home Phone: 410-486-1229; Office Phone: 410-986-0824. Business E-Mail: aradding@adelbergrudow.com.

RADDING, CYNTHIA, historian, educator; d. Benjamin Irving and Dorothy Lowman Radding; m. Ramon Xicotencatl Murrieta, May 22, 1970; children: Daniel Murrieta, David Murrieta. PhD, U. Calif., 1990. Prof. history U. N.Mex, Albuquerque, 2004—08, dir. Latin Am. and libr. inst., 2004—07; gussenhoven disting. prof. Latin Am. Studies U. NC, Chapel Hill, 2008—. Author: (scholarly book) Wandering Peoples. Colonialism, Ethnic Spaces and Ecological Frontiers in Northwestern Mexico (Erminie Wheeler Voegelin prize, 1998), Landscapes of Power and Identity. Comparative Histories in the Sonoran Desert and the Forests of Amazonia from Colony to Republic. Recipient Wheeler prize for Best Book in Ethnohistory, Am. Soc. Ethnohistory, 1998. Mem.: Am. Soc. Ethnohistory (nominating com. 2008—09), Latin Am. Studies Assn., Conf. Latin Am. History (v.p. 2008—), Am. Hist. Assn. Office: Univ NC Chapel Hil History Dept CB 3195 Chapel Hill NC 27599 Office Fax: 919-962-1403.

RADEL, EVA, pediatrician, hematologist; b. Vienna, Apr. 10, 1934; came to U.S., 1939; d. Ernest O. and Marian (Feiks) Grossman; m. Stanley Robert Radel, May 31, 1954; children: Carol, Laura. AB, N.Y. U., 1954, MD, 1958. Pediatric intern, resident Bronx Mcpl. Hosp. Ctr., 1958-61; pediatric hematology rsch. fellow Albert Einstein Coll. Medicine, Bronx, 1961-63; pediatrician, head pediatric hematology Morrisania city Hosp., Bronx, 1963-76; assoc. dir. pediatrics North Cen. Bronx Hosp., 1978-82; attending physician pediatric hemetology out patients Montefiore Med. Ctr., Bronx, 1965-79, svc. head pediatric hematology-oncology, 1979—2004; head pediatric hematology North Cen. Bronx Hosp., 1976-97. Responsible investigator Children's Cancer Study Group, 1980-2001; dir. pediatric hematology-oncology Albert Einstein Coll. Medicine, Bronx, 1980-2004; prin. investigator Children's Oncology Group, 2001-05 Fellow Am. Acad Pediatrics; mem. Am. Soc. Hematology, Am. Soc. Pediatric Hematology-Oncology, Soc. for the Study of Blood. Office: Childrens Hosp at Montefiore Sect Pediat Hematology-Oncology 3415 Bainbridge Ave Bronx NY 10467-2401 Office Phone: 718-741-2342. Business E-Mail: eradel@montefiore.org.

RADEMACHER, DANA ELLIS, urologist; b. Denver, Sept. 25, 1964; s. James Dennis and Barbara Jane Rademacher; m. Jonella Gross, Sept. 5, 1987; children: Ryan John, Erin Janelle, Connor Jacob. MD, U. Colo., Denver, 1992. Diplomate Wis., Minn., 1998, cert. bd. cert. urologist Am. Bd. Urology, 2003. Intern in gen. surgery U. Calif. Davis Med. Ctr., Sacramento, 1992—94, resident in urology, 1994—98; urologist FranciscanSkemp Mayo Healthcare, LaCrosse, Wis., 1998—. Chmn. fin. com. FranciscanSkemp Mayo Healthcare, 2001—07. Recipient Am. Outstanding Dr. award, 2006; named Americas Outstanding Drs., 2006—08, Americas Outstanding Urologist, 2008. Mem.: N.Ctrl. Cancer Treatment Grp. (assoc.), N.Ctrl. Urol. Assn. (assoc.), Am. Urol. Assn. (assoc.). Office: FranciscanSkemp Mayo Healthcare 800 West Ave S La Crosse WI 54601

RADEMAKER, STEPHEN GEOFFREY, lobbyist, former federal agency administrator; b. Balt., July 18, 1959; s. Thomas Joseph and Ruth Virginia (Wentz) R.; m. Danielle Pletka; children: Andrew, Olivia, Sophia, Nicola. BA with highest distinction, U. Va., 1981, JD, 1984, MA in Fgn. Affairs, 1985. Bar: Va. 1984, D.C. 1985. Assoc. Covington & Burling LLP, Washington, 1984-86; law clk. to Hon. James L. Buckley US Ct. Appeals (DC Cir.), Washington, 1986; counsel to vice chmn. US Internat. Trade Commn., Washington, 1986-87; spl. asst. to asst. sec. for Inter-Am. affairs US Dept. State, Washington, 1987-89; dep. legal adv., assoc. counsel to Pres. NSC, Washington, 1989-92; gen. counsel Peace Corps, Washington, 1992-93; minority chief counsel US House Com. on Fgn. Affairs, Washington, 1993-95; chief counsel US House Com. on Internat. Rels., Washington, 1995—2001, dep. staff dir., chief counsel, 2001—02; chief counsel US House Select Com. on Homeland Security, Washington, 2002; asst. sec. for arms control US Dept. State, Washington, 2002—05, acting asst. sec. for internat. security & nonproliferation, 2005—06; dir. nat. security & sr. counsel to Senator Bill Frist US Senate, Washington, 2006—07; v.p. BGR International, 2007—. Mem. US Commn. on the Prevention of Proliferation of weapons of Mass Destruction & Terrorism, 2008. Recipient Raven award U. Va., 1984; S. Philip Heiner scholar U. Va., 1983. Mem. Va. Bar Assn., D.C. Bar Assn., Phi Beta Kappa, Omicron Delta Kappa. Republican. Lutheran. Avocations: skiing, bicycling, scuba diving. Office: BGR Group The Homer Bldg Eleventh Fl S 601 Thirteenth St NW Washington DC 20005 E-mail: srademaker@bgrdc.com.*

RADER, ANGELA NICHOLE, music educator; b. Buckhannon, W.Va., Dec. 28, 1974; d. Paul Douglass and Leda Linette Koon; m. Brent David Rader, July 5, 1997; 1 child, Jordan McKenzie. B in Music Edn., W.Va. Wesleyan Coll., 1997. Tchr. Waynesboro City Schs., Va., 1997—98; tchr., band dir. Lexington City Schs., Va., 1998—; girls' basketball coach; music tchr. Fine Arts Rockbridge, 2006—; dir. handbell choir Trinity Methodist Ch., 2006—. Advisor Waddell Svc. Club, 2004—. Mem. Trinity United Meth. Handbell Choir, 2000—. Mem.: Music Educators Nat. Conf., Va. Music Edn. Assn. Republican. Methodist. Avocations: flute, handbells, coaching girls basketball. Office: Waddell Elem Sch 100 Pendleton Pl Lexington VA 24450

RADER, BENJAMIN GENE, history educator; b. Delaware, Mo., Aug. 25, 1935; s. Lowell Leslie and Lydia Eddings Rader; m. Barbara Anne Koch, June 10, 1961; children: Anne Elizabeth, Stephen Lowell. Student, U. Wichita, 1953-56; BA, S.W. Mo. State Coll., 1958; MA, Okla. State U., 1959; PhD, U. Md., 1964. Tool and die maker Boeing Aircraft Co., Wichita, 1953-56; instr. Okla. State U., Stillwater, 1961-62; from instr. to asst. prof. U. Mont., Missoula, 1962-66; from assoc. prof. to prof. U. Nebr., Lincoln, 1966-96, James L. Sellers prof. history, 1996—. Joint editor sport and soc. series U. Ill. Press, Urbana, 1985—. Author: (books) American Sports, 1983, In Its Own Image, 1985, Baseball, 1992; bd. editors: Jour. Sport History, 1979-96, Internat. Jour. History of Sport, 1983—. Mem. Pk. and Recreation Bd., Lincoln, 1981-87. NEH jr. fellow, 1969, Am. Coun. Learned Socs. fellow, 1985. Mem. N.Am. Assn. Sport Historians (Betts Hon. Address 1976—), Orgn. of Am. Historians. Avocations: tennis, travel. Office: U Nebr Lincoln NE 68588-0327

RADER, DANIEL J., cardiologist, educator; BA, Lehigh U., 1981; MD, Pa. Med. Coll., 1984. Intern Yale-New Haven Hosp., resident; fellow NIH; prof. dept. medicine, pharmacology & pathology U. Pa. Sch. Medicine; dir. Preventive Cardiovascular Medicine & Lipid Clinic Penn Heart & Vascular Ctr. Office: University of Pennsylvania 654 Biomedical Rsch Bldg 421 Curie Blvd Philadelphia PA 19104-6160 Office Phone: 215-573-4176. Office Fax: 215-573-8606. E-mail: rader@mail.med.upenn.edu.*

RADER, DOTSON CARLYLE, writer, journalist; b. Minn., July 25, 1941; s. Paul Carlyle and Lois (Schacht) R. Student, Columbia, 1962-68. Editor Defiance: A Radical Rev. (Warner Communications, Inc.), 1969-71; contbg. editor Evergreen Rev., 1969-73, Esquire, NYC, 1973-77, N.Y. mag., 1977-80; cons. Nat. Com. for Lit. Arts at Lincoln Center, NYC, 1980—. Mem. sponsoring bd. New Politics, 1972—; host Free Time Show, WNET-TV, N.Y.C., 1972-73 Author: I Ain't Marchin' Anymore!, 1969, Government Inspected Meat and Other Fun Summer Things, 1971, Blood Dues, 1973, Tennessee: Cry of the Heart; An Intimate Memoir of Tennessee Williams, 1985; screenplay The Bronze Lily, 1974, The Dream's on Me: A Love Story, 1976, Miracle, 1978; novel Beau Monde, 1981; play (with Mike Miller) Shattered Glass, 1990; contbg. editor Parade Mag., 1984—, Why Are we at War?, 2003 Mem. Student Peace Union, 1961-63, Students for a Democratic Soc., 1964-69, War Resisters League, 1970—; pres. Humanitas, Columbia, 1963-67; vice chmn. Peoples Coalition for Peace and Justice, 1972. Named hon. ambassador State of W. Va., 1982; recipient award for nat. journalism Odyssey Inst., 1982, Spl. Olympics award for nat. journalism Joseph P. Kennedy Found., 1985 Mem. PEN, Overseas Press Club, The Dramatists Guild.

RADER, KAREN A., director; PhD, Ind. U., Bloomington, 1995. Marilyn Simpson chair, sci. & soc. Sarah Lawrence Coll., Bronxville, NY, 1998—2006; dir., STS initiative Va. Commonwealth U., Richmond, 2006—. Author: (book) Making Mice Princeton UP. Mem.: AAAS (sect. 2007—), History Sci. Soc. (coun. mem. 2007—). Office: Va Commonwealth Univ Box 842001 Richmond VA 23284 Business E-Mail: karader@vcu.edu.

RADER, NANCY LOUISE DE VILLIERS, psychology professor, consultant; b. Danbury, Conn., May 21, 1948; d. Martin Anthony and Elsie Concetta (Lauricella) R.; m. David Strutt de Villiers, Sept. 6, 1975; 1 child, Alyssa Jane. AB magna cum laude, Smith Coll., 1970; PhD, Cornell U., 1976. Asst. prof. psychology UCLA, 1974-82, dir. Infant and Child Lab., 1979-82, scholar Found. for Child Devel., 1982-83, postdoctoral fellow, rsch. psychologist Neuropsychiat. Inst., 1983-84; vis. scholar Cornell U., Ithaca, N.Y., 1979, rsch. assoc., 1984-85; asst. prof. Ithaca Coll., 1985-90, assoc. prof., 1990—2004, prof., 2004—, chair psychology dept., 2000—03. Contbr. articles to profl. jours., chpts. to books. Bd. dirs. Coddington Community Ctr., Ithaca, 1991-94, Family and Children Svcs., 1999-2002. Fellow NDEA, 1968, 71-74, Ford Found., 1970-74; grantee NIMH, 1982, NSF, 2001—. Mem. APA, Am. Psychol. Soc., Soc. for Rsch. in Child Devel., Internat. Soc. for Study Behavioral Devel., Internat. Soc. for Ecol. Psychology, Ea. Psychol. Assn., Sigma Xi (pres. Ithaca Coll. chpt. 1988-89), Phi Kappa Phi. Avocations: gardening, mystery. Home: 201 Eastman Hill Rd Willseyville NY 13864-1229 Office: Ithaca Coll Psychology Dept Ithaca NY 14850 Office Phone: 607-274-3510. E-mail: rader@ithaca.edu.

RADER, PAMELA J., literature and language professor; d. Frank J. and Carol A. Rader; m. Stephen L. Christopher, July 28, 2007. BA, U. Del., Newark, 1991; MA, U. Colo., Boulder, 1996, PhD, 2002. Honorarium instr. U. Colo., 2002—03; asst. prof. English Georgian Ct. U., Lakewood, NJ, 2003—. Mentor Minority Acad. Careers, Morristown, NJ, 2008—. Contbr. articles to profl. jours. Recipient Tchg. Excellence award, Georgian Ct. U., 2007, Advising award, 2008, 2009; Rsch. Grant, 2006. Mem.: MLA, NJ. Coll. English Assn., Rocky Mountain MLA, MELUS. Avocations: writing, gardening, hiking, travel, photography. Office: Georgian Ct Univ 900 Lakewood Ave Lakewood NJ 08701 Business E-Mail: raderp@georgian.edu.

RADER, RALPH TERRANCE, lawyer; b. Clarksburg, W.Va., Dec. 5, 1947; s. Ralph Coolidge and Jeanne (Cover) R.; m. Rebecca Jo Vorderman, Mar. 22, 1969; children: Melissa Michelle, Allison Suzanne. BSME, Va. Poly. Inst., 1970; JD, Am. U., 1974. Bar: Va. 1975, U.S. Ct. Customs and Patent Appeals, 1977, U.S. Dist. Ct. (ea. dist.) Mich. 1978, Mich. 1979, U.S. Ct. Appeals (6th cir.) 1979, U.S. Dist. Ct. (we. dist.) Mich. 1981, U.S. Ct. Appeals (fed. cir.) 1983. Supervisory patent examiner U.S. Patent Office, Washington, 1970-77; patent atty., ptnr. Cullen, Sloman, Cantor, Grauer, Scott & Rutherford, Detroit, 1977-88; ptnr. Dykema, Gossett, Detroit, 1989-96; founder, ptnr. Rader, Fishman & Grauer, Bloomfield Hills, Mich., 1996—. Contbr. articles to profl. jours. Mem. adminstrv. bd. 1st United Meth. Ch., Birmingham, Mich., 1980—. With U.S. Army, 1970-76. Mem. ABA, Am. Patent Law Assn., Mich. Patent Law Assn., Mich. Bar (governing coun. patent, trademark and copyright law sect. 1981-84), Engring. Soc. Detroit, Masons, Tau Beta Pi, Pi Tau Sigma, Phi Kappa Phi. Methodist. Home: 4713 Riverchase Dr Troy MI 48098-4186 Office: Rader Fishman & Grauer 39533 Woodward Ave Ste 140 Bloomfield Hills MI 48304-5098 Office Phone: 248-594-0620. Business E-Mail: rtr@raderfishman.com.

RADER, RANDALL RAY, federal judge; b. Hastings, Nebr., Apr. 21, 1949; BA magna cum laude, BYU, 1974; JD with honors, George Washington U., 1978. Bar: DC, US Ct. Appeals (fed. cir.) 1990, US Claims Ct., US Supreme Ct. Legis. asst. to Congresswoman Virginia Smith US Ho. of Reps., 1975—78, mem. staff Ways and Means Com., 1978—81; chief counsel subcom. on Constn. US Senate Judiciary Com., 1981—86, chief counsel, staff dir. subcom. on patents, copyrights and trademarks, 1987—88; counsel to Senator Orrin Hatch, 1981—88; judge US Ct. Claims, Washington, 1988—90, US Ct. Appeals (Fed. cir.), Washington, 1990—. Lectr. patent law U. Va. Sch. Law, 1993—99; lectr. trial advocacy, lectr. George Washington U. Nat. Law Ctr., Washington, 1993—97; lectr. comparative patent law Georgetown U. Law Ctr., Washington, 1998—99. Co-author: Patent Law, 1997; co-editor: Criminal Justice Reform, 1983; contbr. articles to profl. jours. Mem.: FBA. Office: US Ct Appeals Fed Cir 717 Madison Pl NW Ste 913 Washington DC 20439-0002*

RADEST, HOWARD BERNARD, clergyman, educator; b. NYC, June 29, 1928; s. Louis and Gussie (Permison) R.; m. Rita Stollman, Dec. 22, 1951; children: Robert, Michael. AB, Columbia U., 1949, PhD, 1971; MA (Hillman fellow 1950), New Sch. Social Research, 1951. Dir. youth activities N.Y. Soc. Ethical Culture, 1955-56; leader Ethical Culture Soc. Bergen County, Teaneck, N.J., 1956-64, Ethical Culture Movement, 1956—; mem. Coun. Ethical Leaders, 1958—; exec. dir. Am. Ethical Union, NYC, 1964-70; asso. prof. philosophy Ramapo Coll., N.J., 1971-73, prof., 1973-79; dir. Ethical Culture Schs., 1979-91. Adj. prof. philosophy U. S.C., Beaufort, 1991—2008; co-chmn., sec. gen. Internat. Humanist and Ethical Union, 1970-86, bd. trustees, 1986-97; assoc. Am. Civilization Seminar Columbia U., chmn. moral edn. seminar, 1983-91; adv. bd. NBC, 1988-94; dir. Camp Elliott, Jeffersonville, N.Y., 1963, 64; dean Humanist Inst., 1982-92; dean emeritus; cons. state based programs NEH, co-chair ethics com., Beaufort Meml. Hosp., 1994-97, chair ethics com., Hilton Head Hosp., 1994—2008; mem. assessment com. Vols. in Medicine, 1994-97; adv. council Human Svcs. Program Univ. S.C., 2005—2008; cons. Ctr. Pub. Health Preparedness, S.C. Author: Understanding Ethical Religion, 1958, On Life and Meaning, 1963, Toward Common Ground, 1969, To Seek a Humane World, 1971, Can We Teach Ethics, 1989, The Devil and Secular Humanism, 1990, Community Service Encounter with Strangers, 1992, Humanism with a Human Face, 1996, Felix Adler: An Ethical Culture, 1998, From Clinic to Classroom,

2000, Biomedical Ethics, 2007, Ethics and Public Health Preparedness in the Time of Terrorism, 2007, Bioethics: Catastrophes in a Time of Terror, 2009; also articles; editor: Ramapo Papers, 1976-79, International Humanism 1981-1986; mem. editl. bd. Religious Humanism, Free Inquiry, 1981-2000, The Humanist. Mem. bd. Encampment for Citizenship, 1963-71, Mental Health Assn. Bergen County, Bergen Co. Mental Health Bd., 1964-67, Assn. Moral Edn., 1986-94; mem. bd. past treas., v.p. N.J. Welfare Conf., 1958-64; mem. bd., past pres. Health and Welfare Coun. Bergen County, 1956-64; bd. mgrs. Bergen Pines County Hosp., 1966-70; mem.Bergen County (N.J.) Democratic Com., 1970-71; mem. human svcs. leadership coun. Beaufort County Alliance, 2003—2008. Served with AUS, 1953-55. Mem. AAUP (treas. N.J. coun. 1973-74), Com. Sane Nuclear Policy (sponsor N.J.), Am. Assn. UN, Am. Philos. Assn., Soc. Advancement Am. Philosophy, N.Am. Com. Humanism (trustee 1985—), S.C. Philos. Assn., Grad. Faculties Alumni Columbia U. (trustee 1989-91), Network Progressive Educators (steering com. 1988-91), Highlands Inst. for Am. Religious Thought, SC Med. Assn., (ethics com., 1997—), Phi Beta Kappa; fellow: Ctr.Inquiry (chair, bd. trustees, ethical cmty. charter sch. 2008-). Home: 459 Passaic Ave Apt 255 West Caldwell NJ 07006-7472

RADEV, IVAN, electronics engineer, educator; b. Samokov, Sofia County, Bulgaria, Dec. 16, 1958; s. Stephan Radev and Simeonka Pavlova Todorov; m. Ana Kubarelova; 1 child, Simeon. MSc, Tech. U., Sofia, Bulgaria, 1983; postgrad., Cen Inst. Computing Technique and Tech., Sofia, 1985—87, Inst. for Instrumentation and Computer Tech., 1987—88; postgrad. entrepreneurship & mgmt., U. Natl. & World Economy, Sofia, 1992; MSc, U. S.W. La., 1996, PhD, 1998. Computer design engr. Ctrl. Inst. Computing Technique and Tech., Sofia, 1983-85; rsch. assoc. Inst. for Instrumentation and Computer Tech., Sofia, 1990-91; part-time instr. U. Sofia, 1991-93; instr. Tech. U., Sofia, 1992-94; asst. prof. Ga. S.W. State U., 1998-99, Merrimack Coll., 1999-2000, William Paterson U., NJ, 2000—04; assoc. prof. S.C. State U., 2005—. Contbr. articles to profl. jours. Mem. Program Com. Profl. Confs., IEEE (sr., mem. program com. profl. confs.), IEEE Computer Soc.

RADEVIC, MIROSLAV RADE, pathologist; s. Rade and Nives Radevic; m. Tatjana Kovacevic; children: Stefan, Andreja. MD, Sch. Medicine, U. Belgrade, Serbia, 1993. Diplomate in combined anatomic Am. Bd. Pathology, cert. ACGME, 2005, Ednl. Commn. Fgn. Med. Grads., 1999. Med. doc., gastrointestinal, liver pathology Weill Med. Coll. Cornell U., NY Presbyn. Hosp., NYC, 2005—06; med. doc., resident anatomic clin. pathology Lenox Hill Hosp., NY U. Med. Ctr., NYC, 2000—05; med. doc., resident gen. surgery, Zemun Med. Ctr., U. Belgrade, Montenegro, 1994—94, med. internship, 1993—94; pathologist Pathology Solutions LLC, Eatontown, NJ, 2009—; instr. pathology Dept. Pathology, Beth Israel Med. Ctr., NYC, 2008—. Chief resident, anatomic pathology Lenox Hill Hosp., NY U. Med. Ctr., 2002—03. Contbr. articles to profl. jours. Home: 500A E 87th St #7G New York NY 10128 Personal E-mail: radevic1@hotmail.com.

RADFORD, JAMES H., retired military officer, political science professor; b. Portland, Oreg., Mar. 18, 1947; s. Edwin Smith and Miriam Elizabeth Bentley Radford; m. Carole L. Seyfrit, Apr. 7, 1991. BS in Occupl. Edn., So. Ill. U., Carbondale, 1976; MPA, Shippensburg U., Pa., 1995; PhD in Internat. Studies, Old Dominion U., Norfolk, Va., 2005. Instr. Christopher Newport U., Newport News, Va., 1998—2001, Radford U., Va., 2003—. Lt. col. Signal Corps US Army, 1968—98, US, Vietnam, Germany. Independent. Avocations: bookbinding, clockmaking. Home: 412 Vista Ridge Radford VA 24141 Office: Radford Univ Dept Polit Sci Box 6945 Radford VA 24142 Personal E-mail: radfordj1@earthlink.net. Business E-Mail: jradford2@radford.edu.

RADFORD, R. S., lawyer, law educator; b. Independence, Kans., July 30, 1945; s. Lloyd Raymond and Arlene (Bacon) R.; m. Sharon L. Browne, Nov. 24, 1992; children: Jessica Siegel, Jacob Siegel. BS in Bus. Adminstrn., Rockhurst Coll., 1974; MA in Econs., U. So. Calif., 1976; JD, 1988. Bar: Calif. 1988, Supreme Ct. 1992. Prin. atty. Pacific Legal Found., Sacramento, Calif., 1988—; dir. progrm for jud. awareness, 1999—. Adj. prof. law U. Pacific McGeorge Sch. Law, Sacramento, 2001—. Contbr. numerous articles to profl. jours. Named Laywer of Yr. Calif. Lawyer, 1997 Office Fax: (916) 362-2932. Business E-Mail: rsr@pacificlegal.org.

RADHAKRISHNAN, MALATHI, biologist, educator; arrived in USA, 2001; d. Sundarrajan Chakravarthy and Shanbagam Sundarrajan; m. Radhakrishnan Palaniswamy, Nov. 11, 1983; children: Deepa, Veena. BSc in Botany, U. Madras, Queen Mary's Coll., Marina, India, 1978; MSc in Botany, U. Madras, Presidency Coll., Chepauk, India, 1980, PhD in Botany, 1996; MPhil in Botany, U. Madras, Pachaiyappa Coll., Chetput, India, 1981; BEd, Kamaraj U., Madurai, India, 1981; MEd, Annamalai U., Chidambaram, India, 1983. Prof. biology Balt. City C.C., 2002—. Contbr. articles to profl. jours. Mem.: Nat. Sci. Tchrs. Assn., Am. Jour. Botany, Paleobotanical Soc. (life). Achievements include research in medicinal plants; discovery of the presence of hydropoten cells in the land plant; pharmacological evaluation-drug efficacy of compounds present in some polygonaceae and malpighiaceae. Avocations: drawing, painting, doll making, music. Office: Balt City Cmty Coll 2901 Liberty Heights Ave Baltimore MD 21215

RADHAKRISHNAN, RAJESH, architect; b. London, Sept. 14, 1968; s. Tevangudi Radhakrishnan and Radha Radhakrishnan; m. Anandhi Rajesh Thiagarajan, Apr. 4, 1999; 1 child, Shankar Rajesh. BA, Loyola Coll., Chennai, India, 1990; MS, U. Va., Charlottesville, 2004; MBA, Old Dominion U., Norfolk, Va., 1999. Cert. storage arch., Sun Microsys., 1998, ITIL masters, itSMF, 2007, in togaf 8, Open Group, 2008, sr. IT arch., IBM, 2008. IT arch. Zygous, Reston, Va., 2004—06; sr. mng. cons. & sr. ITA IBM, Reston, 2006—. Engagement Deliverable (Svc. Excellence Award, 2006); contbr. articles to profl. publs. Vol. AIDS Marathon, Washington, 2005—06. Recipient award, AISSCE, 1986, Svc. Excellence award, IBM, 2006. Mem.: itSMF, Open Group. Home: 12174 Chancery Station Cir Reston VA 20190

RADHAKRISHNAN, SURESH, finance educator; s. Vaitheeswaran and Seetha Radhakrishnan; m. Uma Suresh, Dec. 1, 1991; children: Rajiv Suresh, Rajat Ram Suresh. B in Commerce, Vivekananda Coll. Madras U., India, 1980; MS in Stats., Stern Sch. NY U., NYC, 1988, PhD, 1991. Cert. assoc. chartered acct., Indian Inst. Chartered Accountants, 1983, Inst. Cost and Mgmt. Accountants India, 1983. Mgmt. acct. Larsen and Toubro Bangalore Works, Karnataka, India, 1983—84; sr. cons. A F Ferguson & Co., New Delhi, 1984—96; asst. prof., acctg. Grad. Sch. Mgt. Rutgers U., Newark, 1992—95, Stern Sch. Bus. NY U., 1995—99; vis. asst. prof., acctg. Grad. Sch. Ind. Adminstrn. Carnegie Mellon U., Pitts., 1997—98; assoc. prof., acctg. and info. mgmt. Sch. Mgmt. U. Tex., Richardson, 1999—2002, prof., acctg. and info. mgmt., 2002—. Vis. rsch. scholar City U. Hong Kong, 2002—03; vis. rsch. fellow Hong Kong Poly. U., 2005—08; internat. vis. scholar Nat. Taiwan U., Taipei, 2007—08. Contbr. scientific papers (Runner-up Moskowitz prize, 2006). Achievements include first to measure organization capital; research in valuation of intangibles; employee, executive stock options. Office: Sch Mgmt Univ Tex Mail Stop SM 41 800 W Campbell Rd Richardson TX 75080 Business E-Mail: sradhakr@utdallas.edu.

RADHAKRISHNAN, T., engineering educator, educator; PhD, U. Wis., Madison, 1980. Faculty, mech. engg. Villanova U., Pa., 1984—; asst. prof. U. RI, Kingston. Mem.: ASME, ASEE, SAE, SME. Office: Villanova Univ 800 E Lancaster Av Villanova PA 19085 Business E-Mail: t.radhakrishnan@villanova.edu.

RADICE, ANNE-IMELDA MARINO, federal agency administrator, museum director; b. Buffalo, Feb. 29, 1948; d. Lawrence and Anne (Marino) R. AB, Wheaton Coll., 1969; MA, Villa SchiFanoia, Florence, Italy, 1971; PhD, U. N.C., 1976; MBA, Am. U., 1984. Asst. curator, staff lectr. Nat. Gallery of Art, Washington, 1972-76; archtl. historian US Capitol, Washington, 1976—81, curator Office of Architect, 1981—85; dir. Nat. Mus. Women in the Arts, 1985-89; chief divsn. of creative arts USIA, 1989-91; sr. dep. chmn. Nat. Endowment for Arts, Washington, 1991-92, acting chmn., 1992-93; exec. v.p. Gray & Co. II, Miami, Fla., 1993; prodr. World Affairs TV Prodn., 1994; assoc. producer Think Tank, 1994; chief spl. projects, confidential adviser Courtney Sale Ross, 1994-96; v.p., COO ICL Internat., 1996; exec. dir. Friends of Dresden Inc., 1998—2001; exec. dir. appeal Conscience Found., NYC, 2001—03; chief staff to sec. US Dept. Edn., Washington, 2003—05; acting asst. chmn. for programs Nat. Endowment Humanities, Washington, 2005—06; dir. Inst. Mus. and Libr. Services, Washington, 2006—. Cons. in pub. rels. and TV, 1994—. Contbr. articles to profl. jours. Recipient Forbes medal for disting. contbn. to conservation, Am. Inst. for Conservation of Hist. and Artistic Works, 2008, Presdl. Citizens medal, 2008. Office: Inst Mus and Libr Services 1800 M St NW 9th Fl Washington DC 20036

RADICE, FRANK J., communications executive; b. Washington, Dec. 13, 1949; m. Vida S. Radice, July 4, 1995. Student, U. Md., 1968-72. Film editor WRC/NBC-TV, Washington, 1971-72, ABC News, Washington, 1972, assignment editor, 1976, assoc. prodr. Good Morning Am., 1978, ops. prodr. World News Tonight, 1979—82; prodr. Nightline NYC, 1982—83; program prodr. The Last Word ABC News, NYC, 1983; field dir. Entertainment Tonight Paramount Motion Pictures, NYC, 1984; prodr., developer Live At 5:00 WRC/NBC-TV, Washington, 1985; exec. prodr. Entertainment News, Cable News Network, NYC, 1987-89; InterActive sr. producer/product devel., producer advt. and promotion ABC News, NYC, 1989-91; advt. mgr. WCBS-TV, NYC, 1991; v.p. advt. and promotion NBC Entertainment, NYC, 1996; sr. v.p. The NBC Agy., NYC, 2000—07, exec. v.p., 2007—09. Exec. prodr. NBC on Ted, 2004—05, NBC Inflight on United Airlines, 1993—2005; v.p. Vida F.R. Co., 1999; chmn. mktg. Nat. Acad. TV Arts and Sci., 2005—08, pres. CMO, 2009—. Author: (with Vida Radice) Sam Katz On The Loose, 2005; prodr. A Line in the Sand, War of Peace, War in the Gulf; writer, prodr., 1992; co-exec. prodr. (CD): The Best of The Today Show Summer Concerts, Vols. 1 and 2, 2000. Bd. govs. N.Y. Festivals, 2003—. Recipient award Coll. Emergency Physicians, 1983, Emmy award NATAS, 1984, 1990, 7 NY Festival awards, 2000-03; Alfred I Dupont grantee Columbia U., NYC, 1984, 91, Mobius award, 1998, 2005, Cine Golden Eagle award 2002-04; Brand Builder award, B & C, 2003; inductee Promax Hall of Fame, 2004; Emmy nomination for Outstanding Original Song, 2006. Mem. Broadcast Music Inc. (writer affiliate), AFTRA, Nat. Assn. Broadcast Employees and Technicians, Internat. Alliance Theatrical and Stage Employees, Writers Guild Am., Dirs. Guild Am., Congressional Country Club, Friars (N.Y.C.). Democrat. Roman Catholic. Office: Natas 111W 57th St 6th Fl New York NY 10019 Office Phone: 212-484-9434. Personal E-mail: fradice@enmyovl.ne.tv. Business E-Mail: frank.radice@nbc.com.

RADIN, ALAN MERVYN, physician; b. NYC, Aug. 6, 1948; m. Barbarea Shaffer Radin, June 9, 1983; 1 child, Shara Faith. BA, U. Rochester, NY, 1970; MD, Pa. State U., Hershey, 1974. Diplomate Am. Bd. Internal Medicine, 1977. Intern, resident U. Vt., Burlington, 1974—77, chief med. resident & clin. instr., 1977—78; asst. prof. medicine Yale U., New Haven, 1978—82; fellow ACP, 1981; pvt. practice Wilton, Conn., 1982—. Med. dir. Wilton Meadows Health Care Ctr., Conn., 1988—. Office: Arbor Med Group LLC 195 Danbury Rd Whitlock Bldg Ste 210 Wilton CT 06897 Business E-Mail: amradin@pol.net.

RADIN, ALEX, former association executive, consultant; b. Chattanooga, June 14, 1921; s. Joseph and Mollie (Pernat) R.; m. Sara Leah Gordon, Sept. 6, 1943 (dec. Nov. 20, 1964); children— Jay Jacob, William Gordon m. Carol Nita Schuman, Sept. 21, 1979 BA, U. Chattanooga, 1947. Reporter Chattanooga Times, Chattanooga, 1938-42; adminstrv. asst. Office of Price Adminstrn., Washington, 1942-43; adminstrv. analyst Dept. of State, Washington, 1945-48; asst. to gen. mgr. Am. Pub. Power Assn., Washington, 1948-51, exec. dir., 1951-86; pres. Radin & Assocs. Inc., 1986—. Cons. U.S. Senate Com. on Interior and Insular Affairs, Washington, 1959; mem. exec. com. Am. Nuclear Energy Coun., Washington, 1973-88; v.p. Consumer Fedn. Am., Washington, 1978-86; mem. So. States Energy Bd.'s Adv. Com. on TVA, 1986-87; chmn. Monitored Retrievable Storage Rev. Commn., 1988-89; rep., sec. U.S. Dept. Energy, Independent Mgmt. and Fin. Rev. of Yucca Mt. (Nev.) Project, 1994-95; mem. adv. bd. Ford Found. Energy Policy Project, 1973-74; bd. dirs. Consumer Energy Coun. Am., 1999—2006. Columnist, Pub. Power Mag.; contbr. articles to newspapers and mags.; author Public Power, Private Life, 2003. Mem. adv. bd. Dance Theatre of Harlem, N.Y.C., 1985—. Recipient Leland Olds award Western States Water and Power Consumers Conf., 1970, Philip Hart Disting. Consumer Svc. award Consumer Fedn. Am., 1985, Alex Radin Disting. Svc. award Am. Pub. Power Assn., 1986, named Disting. Alumnus of 2001 U. Tenn. Chattanooga, 2001, Lifetime Achievement award Energy Daily, 2003. Mem. Alpha Soc. Clubs: Nat. Press. Democrat. Jewish. Avocations: photography, music, art, hiking. Home: 2510 Virginia Ave NW Apt 610N Washington DC 20037-1904 Office: Radin & Assocs Inc Ste 609 2510 Virginia Ave NW Washington DC 20037-1904

RADIN, AMY JANINE, marketing executive, publishing executive; b. Mar. 30, 1958; d. Harold I. and Selma M. Friedman; m. Mitchell E. Radin, Nov. 1984; 3 children. BA magna cum laude, Coll. Letters and Spanish, Wesleyan U.; MBA, Wharton Sch., U. Pa. Mktg. develop. mgr. KMG Main Hurdman, NY; various positions in mgmt., customer loyalty, new product develop. and channel mgmt. American Express; exec. v.p., chief mktg. officer Dime Savings Bank of NY; exec. v.p., Citi cards e-bus. Citigroup, Inc., 2000, exec. v.p., customer engagement, 2005, chief innovation officer, global consumer group, 2005—07, exec. v.p. global direct banking, 2007—09; sr. v.p., chief mktg. officer Reader's Digest Assn., Inc., Pleasantville, NY, 2009—. Spkr. in field. Trustee The Healthcare Chaplaincy, 2006—; founder, pres. The Small Acts of Kindness Found., Inc. Named one of 25 Masters of Innovation, BusinessWeek, 25 Women to Watch, US Banking, 2007. Office: Readers Digest Assn Pleasantville NY 10570*

RADIN, BERYL AVIS, public administration and policy educator; b. Aberdeen, SD, Nov. 15, 1936; d. Norman and Sophie (Edelman) R. BA, Antioch Coll., 1958; MA, U. Minn., 1963; PhD, U. Calif., Berkeley, 1973. Asst. prof. LBJ Sch. of Pub. affairs U. Tex., Austin, 1973—77; prof. pub. adminstrn. Washington Pub. Affairs Ctr., U. So. Calif., 1978—94, dir., 1982—85; prof. pub. adminstrn. and policy SUNY, Albany, 1994—2001; prof. govt. and pub. adminstrn. Univ. Balt., 2002—05; scholar-in-residence Am. U., 2005—. Vis. prof. Fudan U., Shanghai, China, 1985; vis. fellow pub. policy program The Australian Nat. U., Canberra, 1985, 86, 88, 93; vis. prof. Grad. Sch. Pub. Policy, U. Calif., Berkeley, 1987, visitor Hong Kong U., 2009; Fulbright lectr. to India, Indian Inst. Pub. Adminstrn., New Delhi, 1990; speaker, presenter, cons. in field Author: Implementation, Change and The Federal Bureaucracy: School Desegretation Policy in HEW (1964-68), 1977, Linkages Between Civil Rights Enforcement and Operating Programs, 1980, Evaluation of the Planning Requirements Reform Demonstration Project, 1981; co-author: New Governance For Rural America: Creating Intergovernmental Partnerships, 1996, The Politics of Federal Reorganization: Creating the U.S. Department of Education, 1988, Serving Children and Families Effectively: How the Past Can Help Chart the Future, 1991, Beyond Machiavelli: Policy Analysis Comes of Age, 2000, The Accountable Juggler, 2002, Challenging the Performance Movement, 2006, Fed. Govt. Reorganization a Policy and Mgmt. Perspective, 2009; mng. editor Jour. Pub. Adminstrn. Rsch. and Theory, 2000-05; contbr. chpts. to books and articles to profl. jours. Asst. info. officer U.S. Commn. on Civil Right, 1963-65; policy analyst SSI Study Group, Social Security Adminstrn., 1975; sr. policy analyst Office of Asst. Sec. for Planning and Evaluation, 1977-78, Pres.'s Reorgn. Project, OMB, 1978, advisor, Office Asst. Sec. Mgmt. and Budget, HHS, 1996-2000; asst. edn. dir. Phila. Joint Bd., Amalgamated Clothing Workers of Am., 1960-62; cons. Nat. Urban League, Ford Found., The Urban Inst., Nat. Urban Coalition, Civil Rights Dept., Survey of Race Rels. in Britain, The World Bank; bd. dirs. Human Svcs. Rsch. Inst. Fellow Nat. Assn. Schs. Pub. Affairs and Adminstrn. (mem. stds. com., 1982-85), Nat. Acad. Pub. Adminstrn.; mem. ASPA (program com. 1993, bd. dirs. Nat. Capital Area chpt. 1983-85, Donald Stone award), Assn. Pub. Policy Analysis and Mgmt. (program com. 1991, vice chair program com. 1992, pres. 1995-97), Am. Polit. Sci. Assn. (chair pub. adminstrn. program com. 1992, chair Gaus lecture com. 1994), Pub. Mgmt. Rsch. Assn. (bd. dirs.), Ctr. for Women Policy Studies. Office: American Univ Sch Pub Affairs Ward 327 4400 Massachusetts Ave NW Washington DC 20016-8070 Office Phone: 202-885-3258. Business E-Mail: radin@american.edu.

RADIN, MARGARET JANE, law educator; b. 1941; AB, Stanford U., 1963; MFA in Music, Brandeis U., 1965; doctoral studies in Music History, U. Calif., Berkeley, 1965—68; JD, U. So. Calif. Law Ctr., 1976; LLD (hon.), Ill. Inst. Tech. Chgo.-Kent Sch. Law, 1993. Bar: Calif. 1977. Asst. prof. law U. Oreg. Sch. Law, 1976—78; assoc. prof. law U. So. Calif. Law Ctr., 1979—82, prof. law, 1982—87, Carolyn Craig Franklin prof. law, 1987—89; prof. law Stanford Law Sch., 1989—96, William Benjamin Scott & Luna M. Scott prof. law, 1996—2007, founder & co-dir. Ctr. for E-Commerce, 2002, co-dir. program in law, science and tech., 1997—2001, dir. program in law, science and tech., 2001, dir. LLM program in law, science and tech., 2001—04; prof. law U. Mich. Law Sch., 2007—. Vis. prof. law UCLA Law Sch., 1978—79, Harvard Law Sch., 1984—85, U. So. Calif. Law Ctr., 1989—90, U. Mich. Law Sch., 2004—05; of counsel Heller, Ehrman, White & McAuliffe, Palo Alto, Calif.; presenter in field. Author: Reinterpreting Property, 1993, Contested Commodities, 1996; co-author: Internet Commerce: The Emerging Legal Framework, 2002; series editor with Robert Gordon New Perspectives on Law, Culture and Society. Fellow: Am. Acad. Arts & Scis.; mem.: State Bar Calif., Order of Coif, Law Professors for the Rule of Law (co-founder), The Copyright Soc. of USA, Computer Law Soc., Am. Intellectual Property Lawyers Assn., Am. Soc. Polit. and Legal Philosophy, Assn. Computing Machinery (law and tech. policy com.), Cyberspace Law Inst. (co-founder), Phi Beta Kappa. Office: U Mich Law Sch 332 HH 625 S State St Ann Arbor MI 48109-1215 Office Phone: 650-725-3803, 734-763-4861. Business E-Mail: mjradin@stanford.edu, mjradin@umich.edu.

RADISKY, DEREK CHARLES, biomedical researcher, educator; b. San Francisco, Calif., Feb. 29, 1968; s. Robert Charles and Karen Rice Radisky; m. Evette Sanborn Radisky, Dec. 26, 1987; 1 child, Abigail Karen. PhD, U. Utah, Salt Lake City, 1999. Postdoctoral rschr. Lawrence Berkeley Nat. Lab., Berkeley, Calif., 1999—2005; asst. prof. Mayo Clinic Cancer Ctr., Jacksonville, Fla., 2005—. Achievements include discovery of microenvironmental influences on breast cancer development. Home: 13439 Ellsworth Lane Jacksonville FL 32225 Office: Mayo Clinic Cancer Center 4500 San Pablo Road Jacksonville FL 32224 Business E-Mail: radisky.derek@mayo.edu.

RADKE, KIRK AUGUST, lawyer; b. Mar. 21, 1958; m. Erin M. Radke. BA, Stanford U., 1980; JD, MBA, U. Va., 1984. Bar: Ill. 1985, NY 1991. Ptnr. Kirkland & Ellis LLP. Adj. prof. Columbia Law Sch., 1998—99. Bd. trustees Second Stage Theatre Co., Liz Gerring Dance Co.; pres. Trisha Brown Dance Co. Named The Best Private Equity Lawyer: USA, World Finance, 2009; named one of America's Leading Lawyers for Bus. in Private Equity & Fund Formation, Chambers USA, 2003, 2004, 2005, America's Leading Lawyers in Private Equity: Buyouts and Venture Capital Investment, 2006, 2007, 2008. Mem.: Tate Modern America Acquisitions Com., NY State Democratic Com. Office: Kirkland & Ellis LLP Citigroup Ctr 153 E 53rd St New York NY 10022-4675 Home Phone: 212-874-0455; Office Phone: 212-446-4940. Office Fax: 212-446-4900. Business E-Mail: kradke@kirkland.com.*

RADLO, EDWARD JOHN, lawyer, mathematician; b. Pawtucket, RI, Mar. 7, 1946; s. Edward Zygmund and Sue Mary (Borek) Radlo; m. Patricia Jackson, Feb. 22, 1989; children: Heather Sue, Graeme Michael, Connor Andrew. BS, MIT, 1967; JD, Harvard U., 1972. Bar: Calif. 1972, U.S. Dist. Ct. (no. dist.) Calif. 1972, R.I. 1973, U.S. Patent Office 1973, Can. Patent Office 1974. Staff. dir. Atty. Gen.'s Adv. Commn. on Juvenile Code Revision, Boston, 1970—72; law clk. R.I. Supreme Ct., 1972—73; patent atty. Honeywell Info. Systems, Waltham, Mass., 1973—74, Varian Assoc., Palo Alto, Calif., 1974—78, Ford Aerospace Corp., 1978—83, patent counsel, 1983—90; ptnr. Fenwick & West LLP, Mountain View, Calif., 1991—2004, Sonnenschein Nath & Rosenthal LLP, San Francisco, 2004—09, Glenn Patent Group, 2009—. Lectr. U. Calif., San Jose State U., U. Santa Clara, 1975—78. Organizer So. Peninsula Emergency Comm. Sys., 1970; mem. Los Altos Hills (Calif.) Emergency Comm. Com, Lawyers' Alliance for Nuclear Arms Control, 1982—83; Environ. Def. Fund, 1979—; bd. dir. Tomahawks Lacrosse Club, Menlo Park, Calif., 2002—05; bd. dirs. No. Calif. Jr. Lacrosse Assn., Corte Madera, Calif., 2004—05. Lt. (jg.) USPHS, 1967—69. Mem.: ABA, Calif. Bar (intellectual property sect.), Silicon Valley Intellectual Property Law Assn., Assn. Radio Amateurs of So. New England Inc. (sec. 1962—63), No. Calif. Contest Club (pres. 1984—85), Sigma Xi. Home: 28040 Elena Rd Los Altos Hills CA 94022-2454 Office: Glenn Patent Group 3475 Edison Way Ste Menlo Park CA 94025

RADMANESH, ALIREZA, medical researcher; s. Ramezan Radmanesh and Esmat Pourbafrani. MD, Tehran U. Med. Scis., Iran, 2005. Rschr. Digestive Disease Rsch. Ctr., Tehran, Iran, 2001—03, Pharm. Scis. Rsch. Ctr., Tehran, 2002—03, Children's Hosp. Imaging Ctr., Tehran U. Med. Scis., 2003—05; rsch. fellow Med. Imaging Ctr., Tehran U. Med. Scis., 2005—07; postdoc. rsch. fellow Brigham & Women's Hosp., Harvard Med. Sch., Boston, 2007—, consulting rschr, Dpt. Neurosurgery, 2007—; Consulting rschr., Dept. Surgery Brigham & Women's Hosp, 2008—. Tutor slicer software Surg. Planning Lab., Boston, 2008—. Contbr. chapters to books. Vol. Tobin Sch., Roxbury, Mass., 2008—09. Recipient Rsch. Excellence award, Biomed. Rsch. Inst., 2008, Chemistry Olympiad Silver medal, Ministry Edn., 1996, Mil. Exemption, Iranian govt., 2005; Travel grant, Tehran U. Med. Scis., 2003, Brigham & Women's Hosp., Harvard Med. Sch., 2008. Fellow: Nat. Ctr. Image Guided-Therapy (Rsch. Excellence award 2008), Johns Hopkins CME office; mem.: Nat. Postdoc. Assn., Am. Soc. Neuroradiology, Am. Roentgen Ray Soc., Am. Coll. Radiology, Radiol. Soc. North America. Achievements include development of two-tensor tractography method to optimally delineate the corticospinal tracts in brain; research in optimizing seeding methods to visualize the hand & face motor tracts in brain, MR-guided procedure data-mining project, important factors on the diagnostic yield and complication rate of MR-guided brain biopsy; brain imaging findings of methylmalonic acidemia. Office: Brigham & Women's Hosp Harvard Med Sch 75 Francis St Boston MA 02115

RADMER, MICHAEL JOHN, lawyer, educator; b. Wisconsin Rapids, Apr. 28, 1945; s. Donald Richard and Thelma Loretta (Donahue) R.; children from previous marriage: Christina Nicole, Ryan Michael; m. Laurie J. Anshus, Dec. 22, 1983; 1 child, Michael John BS, Northwestern U., 1967; JD, Harvard U., 1970. Bar: Minn. 1970. Assoc. Dorsey & Whitney, Mpls., 1970-75, ptnr., corp. practice group, 1976—, chmn., funds practice. Lectr. law Hamline U. Law Sch., St. Paul, 1981-84; gen. counsel, rep., sec. 59 federally registered investment cos., Mpls. and St. Paul, 1977—. Contbr. articles to legal jours. Active legal work Hennepin County Legal Advice Clinic, Mpls., 1971—. Mem. ABA, Minn. Bar Assn., Hennepin County Bar Assn., Mpls. Athletic Club. Office: Dorsey & Whitney 50 South 6th St Ste 1500 Minneapolis MN 55402 Office Phone: 612-340-2724. Office Fax: 612-340-8738. Business E-Mail: radmer.michael@dorsey.com. *A key to a successful and happy life is achieving a balance. Intellectual, academic and vocational goals are important, but their pursuit should be balanced with ample time spent with family and friends, travel and enjoying reading, music, art and sports. Don't be afraid to try something new; realize that education should be a lifelong pursuit. Much frustration can be avoided by realizing that life is full of trade-offs. You can't experience the joy of raising children and have the complete freedom of the child-free. Finally, while you should strive for perfection, be content with less. We are only human, and live in an imperfect, yet wonderful, world.*

RADNER, ROY, economist, educator, researcher; b. Chgo., June 29, 1927; s. Samuel and Ella (Kulansky) R.; m. Virginia L. Honoski, July 26, 1949 (dec. Apr. 1976); children: Hilary A., Erica H. (dec.), Amy E., Ephraim L.; m. Charlotte Virginia Kuh, Jan. 22, 1978. PhB with honors, U. Chgo, 1945, BS in Math., 1950, MS in Math., 1951, PhD in Math. Stats., 1956. Rsch. asst. Cowles Commn. for Rsch. in Econs. U. Chgo., 1951, rsch. assoc., 1951-54, asst. prof., 1954-55; mem. Cowles Found. for Rsch. in Econs. Yale U., New Haven, 1955-57, asst. prof. econs., 1955-57; assoc. prof. econs. and stats. U. Calif., Berkeley, 1957-61, prof. econs. and stats., 1961-79, chmn. dept. econs., 1966-69; Taussig prof. econs. Harvard U., Cambridge, Mass., 1977-78, vis. prof. Kennedy Sch. Govt., 1978-79; mem. tech. staff AT&T Bell Labs, Murray Hill, NJ, 1979-84, disting. mem. tech. staff, 1985-95; rsch. prof. econs. NYU, NYC, 1983—95, prof. econs. and info. sys., 1995, L.N. Stern Sch. prof. bus., 1996—, prof. environ. studies, 2006—. Mem. tech. adv. com. Carnegie Commn. on Future of Higher Edn., 1967-73; com. on fundamental rsch. relevant to edn. NRC-NAS, 1976-77, commn. on human resources, 1976-79; assembly of behavioral and social scis. NRC, 1979-82, com. on risk and decision making, 1980-81, working group on basic rsch. in behavioral and social scis., 1985-86, com. on info. tech. workforce, 1999-2000, com. on geophys. and environ. data, 2001-05; panel on contingent valuation methology NOAA, U.S. Dept. Commerce, 1992-93; steering com. Enjeux et Procedures de Decentralization Commisariat du Plan, Paris, 1992-95; mem. Com. on Prevention of Nuc. War. Author: Notes on Theory of Econ. Planning, 1963; co-author (with D. Jorgensen and J.J. McCall): Optimal Replacement Policy, 1967; co-author: (with J. Marshack) Econ. Theory of Teams, 1972; co-author: (with L.S. Miller) Demand and Supply in U.S. Higher Edn., 1975; co-author: (with C.V.Kuh) Mathematicians in Academia, 1980; co-editor: Decision and Orgn., 1972, Edn. as an Industry, 1976, Info., Incentives and Econ. Mechanisms, 1987, Perspectives on Deterrence, 1989, Bargaining with Incomplete Info., 1992; mem. editl. bd.: Mgmt. Sci., 1959—70, Econometricia, 1961—68, Jour. Econ. Theory, 1968—2005, Am. Econ. Review, 1979—82, Games and Econ. Behavior, 1989—2005, Econ. Theory, 1991—2003, Econ. Design, 1993—, Info. Sys. Frontiers, 2000—, Theoretical Econ., 2005—; prodr.: Nat. Acad. Sci.; contbr. articles to profl. jours. 2d lt. U.S. Army, 1945-48, PTO. William Cook scholar U. Chgo., 1944-45; fellow Ctr. Advanced Study in Behavioral Scis., Stanford, Calif., 1955-56, Guggenheim Found. fellow, 1961-62, 65-66, overseas fellow Churchill Coll., Cambridge U., Eng., 1969-70, 89. Fellow AAAS (disting. fellow), Econometric Soc. (v.p. 1970-72, pres. 1972-73), Am. Acad. Arts and Scis., Am. Econ. Assn. (disting. fellow); mem. NAS (chair econ. sect. 1994-97, sec. class 5 2004—07, chair class 5 2007-09), Inst. Math. Stats. Avocations: music, hiking, cross country skiing. Home: 3203 Davenport St NW Washington DC 20008-2211 Business E-Mail: rradner@stern.nyu.edu.

RADNER, SIDNEY HOLLIS, retired retail executive; b. Holyoke, Mass., Dec. 8, 1919; s. William I. Radner; m. Helen Jane Cohen, Dec. 12, 1946; children: William Marc, Richard Scott. Student, Yale U., 1941. Ret. pres. Am. Rug Co., Holyoke. Lectr., cons., investigator on crooked gambling U.S. Armed Forces, Govt. of Can., state and mcpl. police squads; dir. Houdini Magical Hall of Fame, Niagara Falls, Ont., Canada; dir., organizer Ann. Ofcl. Houdini Seance. Author: Radner on Poker, Radner on Dice, Radner on Roulette and Casino Games, How to Detect Card Sharks; contbr. articles to profl. jours.; appeared in (TV series) Turn of a Card, 1953, Tonight Show, 1956, BBC Omnibus: Houdini, 1971, CNN, 1993—94, Today Show, Merv Griffin Show, CNBC, PBS, CBC, In Search Of..., Can. Discovery on magic, 1998, History Channel on Houdini, 2000, Ripley's Believe It or Not, History Channel, 2000, (TV series) Today Show, 2004, BBC History of Magic, 2004, cons. (TV films) Houdini, 1998, cons., participant (TV Spl.) A&E Houdini, 1996, appeared in (TV spl.) E Network Houdini documentary, 1998; cons., participant: (TV spl.) History Channel show on the world's largest Houdini collection, 2005; cons., participant (TV films) Discovery Channel documentary, 1997. Past pres. Holyoke C. of C.; co-founder Volleyball Hall of Fame; past bd. dirs. Greater Springfield (Mass.) Better Bus. Bur.; hon. curator, dir. Houdini Hist. Ctr., Appleton, Wis. With criminal investigation divsn. US Army, 1942—46. Named to Volleyball Hall of Fame, 1999. Mem.: Acad. Magical Arts, Nat. Assn. Bunco Investigators, Magicians Guild (charter), Magic Cir. London (mem. Inner Magic Cir.), Internat. Brotherhood Magicians, Soc. Am. Magicians (mem. occult investigation com.), Profls. Against Confidence Crime, China-Burma-India Vets. Assn. (life), Magic Collector's Assn. (charter, Honor award 1992), Houdini Club Wis. (hon.), Shriners, Masons, Rotary, Soc. Osaris (hon.). Jewish. Home (Summer): 3200 S Ocean Blvd Apt C203 Palm Beach FL 33480-6670

RADNOR, ALAN T., lawyer; b. Cleve., Mar. 10, 1946; s. Robert Clark and Rose (Chester) R.; m. Carol Sue Hirsch, June 22, 1969; children: Melanie, Joshua, Joanna. BA, Kenyon Coll., 1967; MS in Anatomy, Ohio State U., 1969, JD, 1972. Bar: Ohio 1972. Ptnr. Vorys, Sater, Seymour & Pease, Columbus, Ohio, 1972—. Adj. prof. law Ohio State U., Columbus, 1979-99. Author: Cross-Examining Doctors: A Practical Guide, 1999; contbr. articles to profl. jours. Bd. dirs., trustee Congregation Tifereth Israel, Columbus, 1975—, pres., 1985-87; trustee Columbus Mus. Art, 1995-98; pres. The Thurber House., 2004. Named Boss or Yr., Columbus Assn. Legal Secs., 1983. Fellow Am. Coll. Trial Lawyers; mem. ABA, Ohio State Bar Assn., Columbus Bar Assn. Avocations: reading, sculpture. Home: 400 S Columbia Ave Columbus OH 43209-1629 Office: Vorys Sater Seymour & Pease 52 E Gay St PO Box 1008 Columbus OH 43216-1008

RADO, PATRICIA A., stock exchange executive, retired electric power industry executive; b. May 28, 1942; BS in Acctg., Ctrl. Conn. State; MBA in Computer Info. Systems, U. New Haven. V.p., contr. Pub. Svc. Electric & Gas Co. (PSEG), Newark, 1999—2007; pres., COO The Am. Stock Exch. LLC, NYC, 2007—. Bd. trustees Coll. NJ, 1998—2006. Office: Am Stock Exch LLC 86 Trinity Pl New York NY 10006

RADO, PETER THOMAS, lawyer; b. Berlin, Nov. 12, 1928; came to U.S., 1931; naturalized, 1937; s. Sandor and Emmy (Chrisler) R.; m. Jacqueline Danenberg, Sept. 11, 1977. AB, HArvard U., 1949, LLB, 1952, LLM, 1953. Bar: N.Y. 1952. Assoc. Ide, Haigney & Rado, NYC, 1956-61, ptnr., 1961—. With U.S. Army, 1953-55. Mem. ABA, N.Y. State Bar Assn., Assn. of Bar of City of N.Y., Harvard Club (N.Y.C.). Home: 176 E 71st St New York NY 10021-5159 Office: Ide Haigney & Rado 176 E 71st St New York NY 10021-5159 E-mail: radopandj@aol.com.

RADOFF, LEONARD IRVING, retired librarian, consultant; b. Houston, Jan. 9, 1927; s. Morris Aaron and Jenny (Goldberg) R.; m. Lisel Ruth Ephraim, July 25, 1953; 1 child, Lesley Radoff Rappaport BA, Rice U., Houston, 1949; M.L.S., U. Tex., Austin, 1965. Cert. secondary sch. tchr., Tex. Tchr. math Aldine Ind. Sch. Dist., Houston, 1959-61, sch. librarian, 1961-63; head pub. services Abilene Pub. Library, Tex., 1964-65; library dir. Pasadena Pub. Library, Tex., 1966-70; chief br. services Houston Pub. Library, 1971-92, ret., 1992; library bldg. cons. Houston, 1975—. Treas. Literacy Vol. Am., Houston, 1984-85; mem. Northside Interests, Houston, 1982-85. Served with USN, 1945-46 Hoenthal scholar, 1948 Mem. Tex. Library Assn., ALA, Freedom to Read Found., Houston Great Books Council (leader trainer 1953-59, pres. 1967-69) Avocations: tutoring, music, stamp collecting/philately. Home: 4013 Gano St Houston TX 77009-4119

RADON, JENIK RICHARD, lawyer; b. Berlin, Jan. 14, 1946; arrived in U.S., 1951, naturalized, 1956; s. Louis and Irmgard (Hinz) R.; m. Heidi B. Duerbeck, June 10, 1971 (dec. Sept. 1999); 1 child, Kaara H.D. BA, Columbia Coll., 1967; MCP, U. Calif., Berkeley, 1971; JD, Stanford U., 1971. Bar: Calif. 1972, NY 1975, US Ct. Appeals (2d cir.) 1975, US Dist. Ct. (so. dist.) NY 1975. Atty. Radon & Ishizumi, NYC, 1981—. Bd. dirs. Gland Pharma Ltd., India, 1997-2007; pub. Baltic Rev., 1993-04, City Paper (Baltic), 1993-03; trustee, executor Vetter Pharma, Germany, 1999-2007; adj. faculty Sch. Law Stanford U., 2000-02, Bus. Sch., 2000-01, Sch. Internat. Pub. Affairs Columbia U., 2002-; vis. prof. Indira Gandhi Inst. Devel. Rsch., Mumbai, 2004—; disting. prof. Monterrey Tech. Queretaro U., Mex., 2008-; constitution drafting advisor Nepal Govt. and Civil Soc., 2006-2007. Editor-in-chief Stanford Jour. Internat. Studies, 1970-71; contbr. The Internat. Acquisitions Handbook, 1987, Negotiating and Financing Joint Ventures Abroad, 1989, How to Form and Manage Successful Strategic Alliances, 1990, Risks Mgmt. in Internat. Bus. 1991, Investing in Reform, 1991, Comrade Goes Pvt., 1992, Covering Energy and Development. A Reporter's Handbook, 2005, Escaping The Natural Resource Course, 2004; contbr. articles to profl. jours. Active Am. Coun. on Germany, NYC, 1978—2009; vice-chmn. US.-Polish Econ. Coun., 1989-93; mem. exec. com. Afghanistan Relief Com., NYC, 1980-95; bd. dirs. Columbia Coll. Alumni Assn., 1988-92, nat. coun., 1996-98, Freedom Medicine, 1987-94, chmn., 1989-94; trustee Direct Relief Internat., Santa Barbara, Calif., 1987-89; founder, dir. Eesti and Eurasian Fellowship of Columbia U., 1990—; profl. advisor Estonian Ministry Economy, Reform and Justice, 1991-95, Harriman Inst., 1993-2004; advisor to Parliament Republic of Georgia, 1996-98, to Pres. of Georgia, 1999-03; advisor Min. of Fin. of Georgia, 1998-00, Georgian Internat. Oil Corp., 1998-04; chmn. Estonian-Am. C. of C., 1990-93, Deutsche Stiftung for internat. rechtliche Zusammenarbeit, Estonia Commn., Beirat, 1992-94, Ctr. for Global Change and Governance Rutgers U., 2004-. Recipient Order of Honor award Republic of Georgia, 2000. Mem. ABA, German-Am. Law Assn. Roman Catholic. Office: Radon & Ishizumi 269 W 71st St New York NY 10023-3701

RADOSH, RONALD, history professor; b. NYC, Nov. 1, 1937; s. Reuben and Ida (Kreichman) R.; divorced 1970; children: Laura, Daniel; m. Allis W.; 1 child, Michael. BA, U. Wis., 1959; MA, State U. Iowa, 1960; PhD, U. Wis., 1967. Prof. emeritus history Queensborough C.C., CUNY Grad. Ctr., 1964—92; Olin prof. Adelphi U., Garden City, NY, 1994—96; sr. fellow Hudson Inst., Washington, 1996, adj. sr. fellow, 2003—; sr. rsch. assoc. Ctr. Comm. Policy Studies George Washington U., Washington, 1997—2002. Author: A Safe Heaven: Harry S. Truman And The Founding Of Israel, 2009, Am. Labor and U.S. Foreign Policy, 1969, Prophets on the Right: Profiles of Conservative Critics of American Globalism, 1975, The Rosenberg File: A Search for the Truth, 1983, 2d edit., 1997, Divided They Fell: The Demise of the Democratic Party, 1964-96, 1996, The Amerasia Spy Case: Prelude to McCarthyism, 1996, Spain Betrayed: The Soviet Union in the Spanish civil War, 2001, Commies, 2002, Red Star Over Hollywood, 2005; editor in field; co-author of chpts.; contbr. articles to profl. jours.; numerous book revs. Rsch. grantee John M. Olin Found., 1996-99, Smith Richard Fedn., N.Y.C., 1987-88, L&M Bradley Found., Milw., 1988-89, 1999-00, The Earhart Found., 1999-00. Mem.: Nat. Assn. Scholars. Jewish. Home: 51 Castlerock Ln Martinsburg WV 25405-5766 E-mail: rradosh@comcast.net.

RADOVIC, MILADIN, engineering educator, researcher; s. Nedeljko and Milica Radovic. BSME, U. Belgrade, Serbia, 1992, MSME, 1997; PhD in Materials Engring., Drexel U., Phila., 2001. Tchg. asst., rsch. assoc. U. Belgrade, 1992—98; rsch. asst., assoc. dept. materials engring. Drexel U., Phila., 1998—2001; postdoctoral fellow Oak Ridge Nat. Lab., Tenn., 2001—06; asst. prof. dept. mech. engring. Tex. A&M U., College Station, 2006—. Guest scientist Nat. Inst. Stds. and Tech., Gaithersburg, Md., 1991—2001. Recipient A.W. Grosvenor award Acad. Performance, Drexel U., 2001; scholar, Ministry Sci. and Tech. Republic of Serbia, 1993, Gordon Rsch. Conf., Solid State Studies Ceramics, 2001. Mem.: ASM, European Structural Integrity Soc., Am. Ceramic Soc. Achievements include research in processing and characterization of nano-laminated MAX phases; reliability and durability of materials and components for solid oxide fuel cells; processing and characterization of the high-tempera. Office: Texas A&M Univ 3123 Tamu College Station TX 77843-3123 Home: 425 Chimney Hill Dr College Station TX 77840-1833 Office Fax: 979-845-3081. Business E-Mail: mradovic@tamu.edu.

RADOVICH, DONALD, painter, illustrator, retired art educator; b. Nazareth, Pa., Jan. 3, 1932; s. Zivan and Angeline (Trumich) R.; m. Sheryl Ann Nash; children: Steven Michael, Nicholas Daniel. BFA, U. N.Mex., 1956, MA in Painting, 1960; postgrad., San Miguél Allende, Gto, Mex., 1970. Instr. of art to prof. of art Western State Coll., Gunnison, Colo., 1964-88, prof. emeritus, 1988—. Illustrator U. N.Mex. Press, 1963, Western State Press, 1980, Reader's Digest Corp., 1990, Phil. Acad. of Sci., 1990, Denver Colo. Sci., 1990, Nat. Wildlife Fedn., 1990, Birds of West Indies, 1998, Birds of Western Colorado, 2004, Wilson Jour. Ornithology, 2005-06, 2008-09, many others; invitational exhibit Wave Hill Mus., 1982; one person exhibit Nat. Wildlife Fedn., 1988, two person, Tohono Chul Pk. Gallery, Tucson, 2003. With US Army, 1956-58. Avocation: gardening. Home: 17232 Woodgate Rd Montrose CO 81403-7722

RADOVICH PIPER, DANIELLE, legislative staff member; BA, Colo. State U., Fort Collins, 1994. Caucus dir. Colo. Dem. Senate Campaign Fund; Dem. chief of staff Colo. State Senate; campaign mgr. Ed Perlmutter's Congl. Campaign; chief of staff to Rep. Ed Perlmutter US House of Reps., Washington, 2007—. Democrat. Office: 415 Cannon House Office Bldg Washington DC 20515 Office Phone: 202-225-2645. Office Fax: 202-225-5278.*

RADTKE, DEREK PAUL, lawyer; b. Edmonds, Wash., May 5, 1970; AA in Audio Engring., Shoreline C.C., Seattle, 1990; BA in English Composition, U. Wash., 1993; JD, Gonzaga U., 1997. Bar: Wash. 97, U.S. Ct. Appeals (9th cir.) 98, U.S. Dist. Ct. (we. dist.) Wash. 99, U.S. Supreme Ct. 02. Assoc. Buckley & Assocs., Seattle, 1998—2009, Phillips & Webster Assocs., 2009—. Mem.: Wash. State Trial Lawyers. Office: Phillips & Webster 13303 NE 175th St Woodinville WA 98072

RADU, BOGDAN, aerospace engineer; b. Bucharest, Romania, Jan. 29, 1957; arrived in USA, 1991; s. Ionel and Maria Radu; m. Doina Radu, Jan. 17, 1981; 1 child, Ana Maria Radu. MS in Aerospace Engring., Poly. Inst., Bucharest, 1981. Cert. Airframe and Powerplant engr., Romanian Aero. Civil Authority, 1982, profl. engr., ASME, 1993, AIAA, 1993, Airframe and Powerplant engr., Airframe and Powerplant Fed. Aviation Adminstrn., 1993, profl. engring. maintenance engr., Profl. Airframe Maintainence Assn., 1994, aerospace engr., Seattle Profl. Engring. Assn., 1994, profl. engr., Seattle Profl. Engring. Assn., 1995. Mgr. engr. Tarom, Bucharest, 1981—91; sr. mgr. engr. Tower Air, NYC, 1991—94; sr. engr. design devel. Boeing, Seattle, 1994—96; sr. lead engr. design devel., project engr. Pratt & Whitney Can., Toronto, Ont., 1996—99; mng. engr. R&D Keykert, Detroit, 1999—2001; mgr. project door sys. Lear Corp., 2001—04; CEO Advanced Sys. Tech., 2004—05; gen. mgr. country MGI Coutier Romania, Timisoara, 2005—06; sr. lead engr. ops. project design fabrication Sikorsky Helicopters, Stratford, Conn., 2006—, bd. dirs. advanced sys. engring., 2008—. Achievements include 24 patents in field; 49 patents pending. Home: 5 7th Ave Garden City Park NY 11040 Personal E-mail: bogdanradu@yahoo.com.

RADULOVIĆ, NOVAK ALEKSANDAR, economist, composer; b. Apače, Slovenia, Sept. 7, 1951; s. Aleksandar Novak Radulović and Mileva Kosta Trninić; m. Divna Bogoljub Popović, Nov. 29, 1981; children: Milica, Miloš. Degree in econs., NIS, Serbia, 1976. Guitar tchr. Scout's Ctr., Niš, Serbia and Montenegro, 1976—80; newspaper reporter Zbivanja, Niš, 1975—79; economist ZTP-Beograd, Niš, 1978—83; chief of mktg. ZTP-BGD, Niš, 1984—87; coord. Fin. Sector ZTP-BGD, Niš, 1987—2001, contr., 2001—. Composer: Children's Dreams, 1986, Let's Learn Music, 1988, Chanson My Way, 1989, Tram for Ice-Cream, 1989, Children's Dreams 2, 1990, Ode to Saint Tzar Constantine, 2007, Guitar for the Young, 2008. Art dir. summer children's festival Cultural Ctr. Josip Kolumbo, Niš, 1995—96; mem. internat. profl. jury Festival Million Miracles, Sofia, Bulgaria, 2001; pres. profl. jury Romany Children's Festival, Niš, 2004, 2008, 8th Romany Children's Festival, Niš, 2008; mem. internat. profl. jury Festival Golden Fish, Varna, Bulgaria, 2004. Recipient 2nd prize, Internat. Festival La Voce del Lago, Italy, 1986, Italy Golden Heart 1st prize, Festival Children Sing with Heart, Pucarevo, Bosnia and Herzegovina, 1988—89, 1st prize for composition, Naša radost '88 children's song festival, Podgorica, Montenegro, Gold commendation and diploma, Festival Ugola d'Oro, Avellino, Italy, 1988, Bronze commendation, Festival Castello d'Oro, Mirandola, Italy, 1988, Silver Banjo, Golden Banjo '90, Novi Sad, Serbia, Golden Key, Festival Mali Šlager, Sarajevo, Bosnia and Herzegovina, 1991, diploma and medal, Festival Bimbo '91, Venice, Italy, 1st prize for composition, Freedom Children's Song Festival, Donji Milanovac, Serbia, 1991, 1994. Eastern Orthodox. Avocations: ethnomusicology, playing old string instruments. Personal E-mail: nokymus@gmail.com.

RADY, ERNEST S., thrift and loan association executive; b. Winnipeg, Canada, Aug. 28, 1937; s. Max and Rose Rady; m. Evelyn Rady; 3 children. B in Commerce (U. Gold Medal), U. Manitoba, JD. Founder, chmn. Am. Assets Inc., San Diego, 1967—; chmn. Ins. Co. West (ICW Group), 1972—; chmn. bd., CEO, founder Westcorp as the holding company for Western Thrift & Loan Assn. (sold to Wachovia in 2005 for $3.42 billion), Irvine, Calif., 1974—2005; acquired Amfac Thrift & Loan Assn. Westcorp, 1977, acquired Evergreen Savings and Loan Assn. (name changed to Western Financial Savings Bank), 1982; bd. dirs. Wachovia, 2006—, chmn. consumer fin. divsn. and Calif. bank, 2006—. Principal shareholder Coast Distributing, a distributor of Anheuser-Busch products in San Diego, PAR Broadcasting; purchased with Leon Parma KIOZ/FM 105.3, KOGO/AM 600, KLNV/FM 106.5 (then known as Q106), and KCBQ/AM 1170 (Sold to Clear Channel for $75 million in 1998); past part owner San Diego Sockers, San Diego Padres, 1990—94. Chmn. bd. trustees Children's Hosp. and Health Ctr. San Diego, 1990—93; chmn. Dean's Advisory Bd. Univ. Calif. San Diego Rady Sch. Mgmt.; trustee Salk Inst. Biological Sciences, Scripps Health; founder Rady Family Found.; pres. United Jewish Fedn., 1980—81; past chmn. Nat. Conf. Christians and Jews; involved Congregation Beth Israel Synagogue, San Diego. Recipient Thomas F. Carter Leadership award, Children's Hosp. and Health Ctr. San Diego, 2003; named one of Forbes' Richest Americans, 2004—06. Mem.: World Presidents Orgn., The Exec. Com. Achievements include $30 million contribution to UC San Diego's new School of Management in 2004 - renamed Rady School of Management; $60 million contribution to Children's Hosp. and Health Ctr. San Diego in 2006 - renamed Rady Children's Hosp. and Health Ctr. Office: Insurance Co West 11455 El Camino Real San Diego CA 92130

RADZELY, HOWARD MARC, lawyer, former federal agency administrator; b. 1970; m. Lisa B. Radzely; 2 children. BS summa cum laude, U. Pa. Wharton Sch. Bus., 1992; JD magna cum laude, Harvard Law Sch., 1995. Law clk. to Hon. J. Michael Luttig US Ct. Appeals (4th Cir.), 1995—96; law clk. to Justice Antonin Scalla US Supreme Ct., 1996—97; sr. assoc. Wiley Rein & Fielding, Washington, 1997—2001; dep. solicitor labor US Dept. Labor, Washington, 2001, dep. solicitor, 2001—03, acting solicitor, 2001—02, 2003, solicitor, 2003—07, acting dep. sec., 2007, dep. sec., 2007—09, acting sec., 2009; ptnr. Morgan, Lewis & Bockius LLP, Washington, 2009—. Bd. dirs. Overseas Pvt. Investment Corp., 2007—09; commr. Congressional-Exec. Commn. on the People's Republic of China, 2007—09. Office: Morgan Lewis & Bockius LLP 1111 Pennsylvania Ave NW Washington DC 20004 Office Phone: 202-739-5996. Office Fax: 202-739-3001. E-mail: hradzely@morganlewis.com.*

RADZEVICH, STEPAN PAVLOVICH, mechanical engineering educator; b. Bila Tserkva, Kiev, Ukraine, Feb. 19, 1953; s. Pavlo Stepanovich and Anna Pavlivna (Oblomiy) R.; m. Natalia Ivanivna Starikova, Oct. 22, 1982; children: Irina, Andrey. MS, Kyiv Polytech. Inst., 1976, PhD, 1982; D of Engring. Sci., Tula Poly. Inst., 1991; D (hon.), Dieprodzerzhinsk State Tech U., 1995. Asst. prof. Kiev Polytech. Inst., 1976—82, assoc. prof., 1982—91, prof., 1991—2000; dean mech. engring. faculty Dnieprodzerzhinsk State Tech. U., Ukraine, 1993—96; sr. engr. gear design Daimler/Chrysler Corp., NVG Divsn., East Syracuse, NY, 2000—01; sr. product engr. Eaton Corp., 2002—; pvt. cons. engr., 2002—. Vis. scholar Mich. State U., Ea. Lansing, Mich., 1993—98; prof. Kyiv Polytech. Inst., Ukraine, 1996—2000. Author: Hobbing of Hardened Gears, 1985, Cutting Tools for NC Machine, 1987, NC Machining of Sculptured Surfaces, 1991, Fundamentals of Surface Machining, 2001, Kinematic Geometry of Surface Machining, 2008, CAD/CAM of Sculptured Surfaces on Multi-Axis NC Machine: The DG/K-Based Approach, 2008, numerous others; co-author: Drilling of Plastics, 1980; contbr. over 400 articles to profl. jours.; patentee in field. Hon. inventor of Ukraine, 1989; recipient State prize by V.K. Seminsky, Pres. of Ukraine, 1990. Avocations: winter swimming, history of science and engineering, arts and culture, military history, classical music. Home: 38679 Filly Dr Sterling Heights MI 48310-1781 Office Phone: 248-226-6831. Personal E-mail: radzevich@hotmail.com. Business E-Mail: stephenpradzevich@eaton.com, dephenpradzerie@eaton.com.

RADZIK, ALBIN F., federal analyst, military consultant; b. Berwyn, Ill., Oct. 21, 1947; s. Albin F. and Evelyn Clara Radzik; children: Melanie Rose, Amy Marie. BS, Northwestern U.; MBA, Georgetown U., 1994; HHD (hon.), Kalinin U., St. Petersburg, 1995. Analyst U.S. Govt., Washington, 1976—, mil. cons., 1978—2001. Author: (poetry) Love and Distance, 1967 (Hole Creative Writing award, 1967). Mem. and vol. Cambodian Land Mine Relief Org.; vol. Chechnya Refugee Org.; open space com. City of Redlands, Calif., 1985—86. Served to capt. US Army, 1966—82. Decorated Bronze Star for Valor, Purple Heart, Disting. Svc. Cross, Army Commendation medal for valor, Air medal for valor, Combat Inf. badge, Rnager badge Spl. Forces Grad., Parachutist badge, hon. capt. Russian Army; recipient Cold War Recognition cert., U.S. Sec. Def., 2003, cert. Special Merit, City Police Dept., Redwood City, Calif., Cert. Appreciation, Belmont, Calif., Police Dept. Mem.: MENSA, VFW, Royal Order of the Purple Heart. Roman Catholic. Personal E-mail: aradzik@netzero.net.

RADZINOWICZ, MARY ANN, language educator; b. Champaign, Ill., Apr. 18, 1925; d. Arthur Seymour and Ann (Stacy) Nevins; m. Leon Radzinowicz, June 16, 1958 (div. 1978); children: Ann Stacy Radzinowicz Prior, William Francis Henry. BA, Radcliffe Coll., 1945; MA, Columbia U., 1947, PhD, 1953; MA (hon.), U. Cambridge, Eng., 1960. Prof. Vassar Coll., Poughkeepsie, NY, 1947-50, 52-59, Girton Coll., Cambridge, England, 1960-80, U. Cambridge, 1973-80, Cornell U., Ithaca, NY, 1980-90, Jacob Gould Schurman prof. English emeritus, 1990—. Mem. adv. bd. 2d, 3d, 4th Internat. Milton Symposia, 1985—. Author: Toward Samson Agonistes, 1978 (Hanford prize 1979), Milton's Epics and Psalms, 1989, Milton and the Tragic Women of Genesis, 1995 (Hanford prize); editor American Colonial Prose, 1984, Paradise Lost, Book VIII, 1974; mem. editl. bd. Milton Quar., 1981-2005, Christianity and Lit., 1989—. Mem. MLA, Renaissance Soc. Am., Milton Soc. Am. (honored scholar 1987), John Donne Soc. Home: Ballycorny House Ballyvaughan County Clare Ireland Office: Cornell U Dept English Lit Ithaca NY 14850 Home Phone: 353-65-7077085; Office Phone: 353-65-7077-085. E-mail: manr@eircom.net.

RAE, BARBARA JOYCE, staging company; b. Prince George, BC, Can., May 17, 1930; d. Alfred and Lottie Kathleen (Davis) Holmwood; m. George Suart, Feb. 14, 1984; children: James, Glenn, John. MBA, Simon Fraser U., Burnaby, B.C., 1975, LLD (hon.), 1998. Chmn., CEO Adia Can., Ltd., Vancouver, 1953-95; exec. chmn., CEO Dekora Staging Inc., Vancouver, B.C., 2003—. Bd. dirs. emeritus Can. Imperial Bank Commerce, Grosvenor Internat. Ltd., Noranda, Inc., Telus, Xerox Can.; dir. VLINX.Com., Can. Inst. Adv. Rsch., 1995-2001, KTCS Pub. Broadcasting; bd. govs. Multiple Sclerosis Soc., 1995—; mem. Fed. Task Force on Future of Can. Fin. Svcs. Sector, 1997-98; past chmn. B.C. Women's Hosp. Found., 1994-97. Chancellor Simon Fraser U., 1987—93; mem. Jud. Appts. Com., B.C., 1988—90; commr. Triennial Commn. Judges Salaries and Benefits; mem. Premier's Econ. Adv. Coun., B.C., 1987—91, Prime Minister's Com. on Sci. and Tech., 1989—94; gen. chmn. United Way Lower Mainland, 1987; chair Salvation Army Red Shield Vancouver Campaign, 1986; bd. dirs. Vancouver Bd. Trade, 1972—76; dir. Royal B.C. Mus.; patron Can. Coun. Christians and Jews; mem. adv. bd. Salvation Army, 1985—2004. Decorated Order of Can., Order of B.C.; recipient Outstanding Alumnae award Simon Fraser U., 1985, Disting. Alumni Svc. award, 1995, Bus. Women of Yr. award Vancouver YWCA, 1986, West Vancouver Achievers award, 1987, B.C. Entrepreneur of Yr. award, 1987, Nat. Vol. award, 1990, Can. Woman Entrepreneur B.C. award, 1992, Queen's Jubilee medal, 2003, Clan Leader award Simon Fraser U., 2004, BC Woman of Distinction, Lifetime Achievement, 2008. Home: 3355 Osprey Box 508 Whistler Canada V0N 1B3 Personal E-mail: brae@dekora.com.

RAE, MATTHEW SANDERSON, JR., lawyer; b. Pitts., Sept. 12, 1922; s. Matthew Sanderson and Olive (Waite) R.; m. Janet Hettman, May 2, 1953; children: Mary-Anna, Margaret Rae Mallory, Janet S. Rae Dupree. AB, Duke, 1946, LLB, 1947; postgrad., Stanford U., 1951. Bar: Md. 1948, Calif. 1951. Asst. to dean Duke Sch. Law, Durham, NC, 1947-48; assoc. Karl F. Steinmann, Balt., 1948-49, Guthrie, Darling & Shattuck, LA, 1953-54; nat. field rep. Phi Alpha Delta Law Frat., LA, 1949-51; research atty. Calif. Supreme Ct., San Francisco, 1951-52; ptnr. Darling, Hall & Rae (and predecessor firms), LA, 1955—. Mem. Calif. Commn. Uniform State Laws, 1985—, chmn., 1993-94; chmn. drafting com. for revision Uniform Prin. and Income Act of Nat. Conf., 1991-97, Probate and Mental Health Task Force, Jud. Coun. Calif., 1996-2000. Vice pres. L.A. County Rep. Assembly, 1959-64; mem. L.A. County Rep. Ctrl. Com., 1960-64, 77-90, 2000—, exec. com., 1977-90; vice chmn. 17th Congl. Dist., 1960-62, 28th Congl. Dist., 1962-64; chmn. 46th Assy. Dist., 1962-64, 27th Senatorial Dist., 1977-85, 29th Senatorial Dist., 1985-90, sec. 53d Assembly Dist., 2000-; mem. Calif. Rep. State Ctrl. Com., 1966—, exec. com., 1966-67; pres. Calif. Rep. League, 1966-67; trustee Rep. Assocs., 1979-94, pres., 1983-85, chmn. bd. dirs., 1985-87. 2d lt. USAAF, WWII. Fellow Am. Coll. Trust and Estate Counsel; academician Internat. Acad. Estate and Trust Law (exec. coun. 1974-78); mem. ABA, L.A. County Bar Assn. (chmn. probate and trust law com. 1964-66, chmn. legis. com. 1980-86, chmn. program com. 1981-82, chmn. membership retention com. 1982-83, trustee 1983-85, dir. Bar Found., 1987-93, Arthur K. Marshall award probate and trust law sect. 1984, Shattuck-Price Meml. award 1990), South Bay Bar Assn., State Bar of Calif. (chmn. state bar jour. com. 1970-71, probate com. 1974-75; exec. com. estate planning trust and probate law sect. 1977-83, chmn. legis. com. 1977-89; co-chmn. 1991-92; probate law cons. group Calif. Bd. Legal Specialization 1977-88; chmn. conf. dels. resolutions com. 1987, exec. com. conf. dels. 1987-90), Lawyers Club L.A. (bd. govs. 1981-87, 1st v.p. 1982-83), Am. Legion (comdr. Allied post 1969-70), Legion Lex (bd. dirs. 1964-99, pres. 1969-71), Air Force Assn., Aircraft Owners and Pilots Assn., Town Hall (gov. 1970-78, pres. 1975), World Affairs Coun., Internat. Platform Assn., Breakfast Club (law, pres. 1989-90), Commonwealth Club, Chancery Club (pres. 1996-97), Rotary, Phi Beta Kappa (councilor Alpha Assn. 1983—, pres. 1996), Omicron Delta Kappa, Phi Alpha Delta (supreme justice 1972-74, elected to Disting. Svc. chpt. 1978), Sigma Nu. Presbyterian. Home: 600 John St Manhattan Beach CA 90266-5837

RAE, NANCY ANN, automotive executive; b. 1956; 1 child. BS in Bus. Adminstrn., Ea. Mich. U., MA in Indsl. Rels. Interviewer Chrysler Corp., Warren, Mich., 1978, various positions Auburn Hills, Mich., 1978—92, group personnel exec., procurement and supply and product strategy and regulatory affairs, 1992—94, mgr. workforce diversity and econ. equality, 1994, group personnel mgr., Chrysler Tech. Ctr., 1994—96; group human resources mgr. tech. ops. DaimlerChrysler Corp., Auburn Hills, Mich., 1996—98, mgr. health ins. and disability, 1998, v.p. compensation and benefits, 1998—2000, sr. v.p. human resources, 2000—07; sr. v.p. human resources & corp. communication Chrysler LLC, Auburn Hills, Mich., 2007—08, exec. v.p. human resources & communication, 2008—09; exec. v.p. human resources Chrysler Group LLC, 2009—. Office: Chrysler Group LLC PO Box 21-8004 Auburn Hills MI 48321*

RAEBURN, ANDREW HARVEY, performing arts consultant; b. London, July 22, 1933; arrived in Canada, 1993, permanent resident, 2007; s. Walter Augustus Leopold and Dora Adelaide Harvey (Williams) Raeburn. BA in History, King's Coll., Cambridge U., 1958, MA, 1962; diploma in music performance (hon.), Mt. Royal Coll., 1998; LLD (hon.), U. Calgary, 2005. Mus. dir. Argo Record Co., London, 1959—64; asst. to music dir., program editor Boston Symphony Orch., 1964—73; dir. artists and repertory New World Records, NYC, 1975—79; artistic adminstr. Detroit Symphony Orch., 1979—82; exec. dir. Van Cliburn Found. Inc., Ft. Worth, 1982—85; performing arts cons., 1985—93; exec. v.p. The Peter Pan Children's Fund, 1990—91; exec. dir. Esther Honens Internat. Piano Competition Found., 1993—95, pres., 1995—99, vice chmn., artistic dir., 1999—2001, pres., artistic dir., 2001—04; freelance cons., recording prodr. Calgary, Canada, 2004—. Cons. music; radio and TV commentator; mem. faculty Boston U., 1966-67; condr. New World String Orch., 1978; v.p. World Fedn. Internat. Music Competitions, 2003-06. Author record liner notes, Argo, RCA, Time-Life records, 1960-79, program notes, Boston Symphony Orch., 1968-73. Served with Royal Arty. Brit. Army, 1952-55; founding dean Prague Mozart Acad. 1992-93. Recipient Lifetime Achievement award, World Fedn. Internat. Music Competitions, 2006. Home and Office: 702 235 15th Ave SW Calgary AB Canada T2R 0P6 Office Phone: 403-263-9939. Personal E-mail: araeburn@telus.net, ar@andrewraeburn.com.

RAEBURN, JOHN HAY, language educator; b. Indpls., July 18, 1941; s. Gordon Maurice and Katherine (Calwell) R.; m. Gillian Kimble, Aug. 18, 1963 (div. July 1979); children— Daniel Kennedy, Nicholas Kimble; m. Kathleen Kamerick, July 5, 1986. AB with honors, Ind. U., 1963; A.M., U. Pa., 1964, PhD, 1969. Asst. prof. U. Mich., Ann Arbor, 1967-74; vis. lectr. U. Iowa, Iowa City, 1974-75, assoc. prof., 1976-83, prof. English, 1983—; chmn. Am. Studies dept., 1983-85, 94-2000; chmn. English dept. U. Iowa, Iowa City, 1985-91; assoc. prof. U. Louisville, 1975-76. Author: Fame Became of Him: Hemingway as Public Writer, 1984, A Staggering Revolution: A Cultural History of Thirties Photography, 2006; editor: (with others) Frank Capra: The Man and His Films, 1975. Mem.: Am. Studies Assn., Orgn. Am. Historians. Democrat. Home: 321 Hutchinson Ave Iowa City IA 52246-2407 Office: U Iowa Dept Am Studies 210 Jefferson Bldg Iowa City IA 52242-1418 Home Phone: 319-338-5590; Office Phone: 319-335-0320. Business E-Mail: john-raeburn@iowa.edu.

RAEDER, JOACHIM, geophysicist; b. Cologne, Germany, June 7, 1956; s. Hans and Edith Raeder; m. Renate Kraus; children: Rebecca, Timothy. Diploma in Geophysics, U. Cologne, Germany, 1984, PhD in Geophysics, 1989. Rsch. geophysicist UCLA, LA, 1990—. Contbr. articles to numerous profl. jours. Decadal rev. panel mem. NRC, Washington, 2001—02. Sgt. US Army, 1975—77, Germany. Recipient Group Achievement award, NASA, 1998. Mem.: Am. Geophys. Union. Office: IGPP/UCLA 405 Hilgard Ave Los Angeles CA 90095 Home: 26 Ross Rd Durham NH 03824-4219 Home Phone: 310-391-0193; Office Phone: 310-267-2338. Office Fax: 310-206-3051. Business E-Mail: jraeder@igpp.ucla.edu.

RAEL, HENRY SYLVESTER, SR., retired health administrator, financial and management consultant; b. Pueblo, Colo., Oct. 2, 1928; s. Daniel and Grace (Abeyta) R.; m. Helen Warner Loring Brace, June 30, 1956 (dec. Aug. 1980); children: Henry Sylvester Jr., Loring Victoria, Thomas Warner Bush. AB, U. So. Colo., 1955; BA in Bus. Adminstrn., U. Denver, 1957, MBA, 1958. Sr. boys counselor Denver Juvenile Hall, 1955-58; adminstrv. asst. to pres. Stanley Aviation Corp., Denver, 1958-61; Titan III budget and fin. control supr. Martin Marietta Corp., Denver, 1961-65; mgmt. adv. services officer U. Colo. Med. Center, Denver, 1965-72; v.p. fin., treas. Loretto Heights Coll., Denver, 1972-73; dir. fin. and adminstrn. Colo. Found. for Med. Care, 1973-86, Tri-County Health Dept., 1987—96; ret., 1996. Instr. fin. mgmt., mem. fin. com. am. Assn. Profl. Standards Rev. orgn., 1980-85; speaker systems devel., design assns., univs., 1967-71. Mem. budget lay adv. com. Park Hill Elem. Sch., Denver, 1967-68, chmn., 1968-69; vol. worker Boy and Girl Scouts, 1967-73; bd. dirs. Community Arts Symphony, 1981-83, 85-87; controller St. John's Episcopal Cathedral, 1982-83; charter mem. Pueblo (Colo.) Coll. Young Democrats and Reps., 1954-55, founder; block worker Republican Party, Denver, 1965-68, precinct committeeman, 1978-84; trustee Van Nattan astron. Scholarship Fund, 1974-96; bd. dirs. Vis. Nurse Assn., 1977-84, treas., 1982-84; cons. to dir. Clayton Found., 1996; cons. Colo. Dept. Health Contr., 1997. Served with USAF, 1947-53, res., 1954-61. Recipient Disting. Service award Denver Astron. Soc., 1968, Citation Chamberlin Obs., 1985; Stanley Aviation masters scholar, 1957; Ballard scholar, 1956. Mem.: Nat. Astronomers Assn. (exec. bd. 1965—97), Am. Assn. Founds. for Med. Care (fin. com. 1981—82), Denver Astron. Soc. (pres. 1965—66, bd. dirs. 1982—94), Colo. Pub. Employees Retirement Assn. (bd. dirs. 1993), Budget Execs. Inst. (sec. 1963—64, v.p. chpt. 1964—65), Hosp. Systems Mgmt. Soc., Assn. Systems. Mgmt. (pres. 1971—72), Whispering Pines of Denver Homeowners Assn. (dir.-at-large 2001, pres. bd. dirs. 1998, 2000), Brandy Chase Homeowners Assn. (bd. dirs. 1997), Delta Psi Omega, Epsilon Xi. Home: 7755 E Quincy Ave Apt 57 Denver CO 80237-2312 Personal E-mail: barkleythemightydog@msn.com.

RAESE, DAVID SENNA, aerospace and mass properties engineer, consultant; b. Morgantown, W.Va. s. John Thomas and Joan Marie (Keeney) Raese. BSCE, Washington State U., Pullman, 1981, BS in Gen. Sci., 1981; attended, U. Bonn, Germany, 1978—79. Cert. profl. engr., Wash., 1995. Engr. Boeing Comml. Airplanes, Everett, Wash., 1981—85, Renton, 1981—85, Boeing Space and Comm., Huntsville, Ala., 1985—87; engring. team leader Boeing Missile Sys. Divsn., Kent, Wash., 1987—91, Boeing Comml. Space Co., Tukwila, 1997—99; engr., auditor, cons. Boeing Helicopters Divsn., Ridley Park, Pa., 1991—93; engring. team leader, cons. Boeing Def. and Space Divsn., Kent, Wash., 1993—97, Boeing Integrated Def. Sys., Kent, 1999—. Mass properties engring. mentor Boeing Ed Wells Mentoring Program NW Region, 2005—; tech. focal cons., Boeing assoc. tech. fellow N.W. Region, 2006. Contbr. chapters to books. Mem.: SAR, Soc. Automotive Engrs., Soc. Allied Weight Engrs., Inc., Am. Inst. Aeronautics and Astronautics (sr.), Descendants of Knights of Garter, Friends of St. George's, Nat. Hugenot Soc. Wash., Nat. Soc. Magna Charta Dames and Barons. Independent. Presbyterian. Avocations: travel, hiking, art, history. Office: The Boeing Co PO Box 3999 Seattle WA 98124-2499 Business E-Mail: david.s.raese@boeing.com.

RAEZ, LUIS ESTUARDO, physician; b. June 29, 1967; MD, Cayetano Heredia U., Lima, Peru, 1992. Diplomate Am. Bd. Internal Medicine, Am. Bd. Med. Oncology, Am. Bd. Ctr. Geriatric Medicine, 2009. Resident in internal medicine U. Miami, Fla., 1993-96, resident in hematology and clin. oncology, 1996-99; practice hematology and oncology Sylvester Comprehensive Cancer Ctr., 1999—, co-chair thoracic oncology group, 2001—; asst. prof. medicine U. Miami, 1999—, asst. prof. epidemiology and pub. health, 2002—06, assoc. prof., 2007—; dir. chemotherapy oncology clin. Sylvester Cancer Ctr., 2004—, cheif med. svcs., 2005—. Mem. thoracic com. Ea. Coop. Oncology Group, mem. head and neck com.; mem. North Ctrl. Cancer Treatment Group. Contbr. articles to med. and profl. jours.; author 4 books on med. ethics; contbr. chpts. to books; presenter in field. Med. advisor Am. Cancer Soc. Fla. Keys. Recipient Award for Lung Cancer Vaccine Rsch., Fla. Dept. Health, 2005. Fellow: ACP, Am. Coll. Specialists Geriatrics, Am. Coll. Chest Physicians; mem.: Internat. Assn. Lung Cancer, Am. Assn. of Cancer Rsch., Am. Soc. Hematology, Peruvian Med. Assn., Am. Soc. Clin. Oncology (Clin. Career Devel. award). Address: 1475 NW 12th Ave #3510 Miami FL 33136 Office Phone: 305-243-4909.

RAFAJKO, ROBERT RICHARD, science administrator; b. Chgo., Sept. 3, 1931; s. Edward Michael and Mildred Eleanor (Simo) R.; m. Mary Ann Filipi, June 24, 1954 (div. 1979); children: Rorie Rae, Ronald Raymond, Robin Rene, Rod Richard, Rebecca Rae.; m. Anne Thorne Sloan, Jan. 26, 1982; 1 son, Andrew Sloan. BA, Coe Coll., Cedar Rapids, Iowa, 1953; MS, U. Iowa, Iowa City, 1958, PhD, 1960. Rsch. assoc. Merck Sharp and Dohme, West Point, Pa., 1960-61; rsch. scientist Microbiol. Assos., Bethesda, Md., 1961-66; v.p., gen. mgr. Med. Rsch. Cons., Rockville, Md., 1966-69; v.p R & D, N.Am. Biols., Rockville, 1969-74; pres. Biofluids, Inc., Rockville, 1974-99, Bonheur Inc., Keswick, Va., 1999—. Pres. Tysan Serum, Inc., Rockville, 1974-2000, Kytaron Inc, Rockville, 1987-99; breeder thoroughbred horses, 1980—. Contbr. 23 articles to profl. jours. Chmn. PVAAU Swimming Program, Washington, Md. and Va., 1973-76; bd. dirs. Montgomery County Swim League, Montgomery County, Md., 1968-76. Served with USAF, 1954-55. Mem. AAAS, NY Acad. Scis., Am. Soc. Microbiology, Tissue Culture Assn., Am. Horse Council, Horsemans Benevolent and Protective Assn. Republican. Presbyterian. Avocations: scuba diving, photography, collecting stamps, travel. Home and Office: 1349 Queenscroft Keswick VA 22947-2731 Personal E-mail: bonheur421@aol.com, rafajko421@gmail.com.

RAFALSKI, BRIAN, professional hockey player; b. Dearborn, Mich., Sept. 28, 1973; m. Felicity Rafalski; children: Danny, Evan James, Matthew. Grad., U. Wis., 1995. Defenseman NJ Devils, 1999—2007, Detroit Red Wings, 2007—. Mem. USA Olympic Hockey Team, Salt Lake City, 2002, Torino, Italy, 06. Named to All-Rookie Team, NHL, 2000, NHL All-Star Game, 2002, 2004, 2007. Achievements include being a member of Stanley Cup Champion New Jersey Devils, 2000, 2003, Detroit Red Wings, 2008; being a member of silver medal winning USA Hockey Team, Salt Lake City Olympics, 2002. Office: Detroit Red Wings Joe Louis Arena 600 Civic Center Dr Detroit MI 48226

RAFEYAN, ROUEEN, psychiatrist, educator; b. Tehran, Iran, Oct. 1, 1961; came to U.S., 1979; s. Majid Rafeyan and Nezhat Babanoury; m. Helena Linda Hernandez, Feb. 15, 1991; 1 child, Ryan Michael. BA, Knox Coll., 1981; MD, U. Istanbul, Turkey, 1989. Cert. Am. Bd. Psychiatry & Neurology, 2001; Am. Bd. Psychiatry and Neurology. Resident U. Ill. Chgo., 1996; dir. outpatient clin. svcs., dir. med. student edn. Michael Reese Hosp., Chgo., 1996-99; med. dir. Rush Presbyn., Chgo., 1997—; asst. clin. prof. psychiatry U. Ill., Chgo., 1996—; asst. prof psychiatry Rush U., 2005—. Cons. Threshold Cmty. Mental Health Ctr., Chgo., 1996—. Mem. AMA, Am. Psychiatric Assn., Ill. Psychiatric Soc., Chgo. Med. Soc. Avocations: tennis, music, world history. Office: Michael Reese Hosp 2959 S Cottage Grove Ave Chicago IL 60616 Office Phone: 312-791-3930. Personal E-mail: roueen@msn.com.

RAFFAELLI, JOHN D., lobbyist, lawyer; BS, Am. U.; JD, U. Ark.; LLM in Taxation, NYU. Atty. advisor to Chief Judge Samuel Sterrett, US Tax Ct., Washington; counsel tax and internat. trade to Senator Lloyd Bentsen; ptnr. Bishop, Cook, Purcell, and Reynolds, Raffaelli, Spees, Springer, and Smith; founder former chmn. Washington Group; founding ptnr. Capitol Counsel LLC, 2007—. Mng. trustee Dem. Nat. Com.; mem. Clinton-Gore Nat. Fin. Com., 1996; vice chair Kerry for Pres. campaign. Mem. Pres. adv. com. on arts John F. Kennedy Ctr., Washington. Named one of 50 Top Lobbyists, Washingtonian mag., 2007. Office: Capitol Counsel LLC 900 19th St NW, Ste 800 Washington DC 20006 Office Phone: 202-861-3207. Office Fax: 202-861-3219. E-mail: jraffaelli@capitolcounsel.com.*

RAFFAY, STEPHEN JOSEPH, manufacturing executive, director; b. McAdoo, Pa., Oct. 25, 1927; s. Stephen John and Stephanie (Severa) R.; m. Audree Eugenia Kuehne, Sept. 12, 1953; children: Andrea, Stephen, Leslie. BA, Columbia U., NYC, 1950, MS, 1951. C.P.A., N.Y. Sr. accountant Arthur Andersen & Co., NYC, 1951-56; asst. controller Emhart Corp., Farmington, Conn., 1956-61, asst. treas., 1961-63, treas., 1963-67, v.p. internat., 1967-72, v.p., group pres., 1972-79, exec. v.p., 1979-84, vice chmn., chief adminstrv. officer, 1984-87, dir., 1980-87; sr. v.p. Dexter Corp., Windsor Locks, Conn., 1987-90. Bd. dirs. United Plumbing Tech., Inc., EDAC Techs. Inc. Bd. dirs. Hartford Symphony Soc. With AUS, 1946-47. Mem. AICPA, Conn. Soc. CPAs. Home: 93 Westmont St West Hartford CT 06117-2929

RAFFEGEAU, JEAN MICHEL, audit and consulting company executive; b. St. Germain en Laye, Yvelines, France, Sept. 24, 1930; s. Louis and Irene (Pithon) R.; m. Nicole Laporte, Jan. 19, 1962; children: Catherine, Brigitte. Diploma in law, Sorbonne U., Paris, 1954; diploma in bus. adminstrn., H.E.C., Paris, 1954. Chartered acct. Commissaire aux Comptes, 1966. Asst. mgr. Banque de Paris et des Pays-Bas, Paris, 1955-57; adminstrv. and fin. mgr. Société Industrielle de Transmissions, 1958-66; chmn., mng. dir. Befec, Paris, 1966-89, Befec-Price Waterhouse, 1989-94; regional mng. pntr. French-speaking Europe and Africa Price Waterhouse, Paris, 1994-96, hon. pres., 1995—. Legal expert Court Appeal, Paris, 1979, adminstv. court, Paris, 1982. Co-author: L'Audit Opérationnel, 1993; co-author, editor: Les Comptes Consolidés, 1989, Guide du Financement des Entreprises, 1993, Le Mémento Comptable, 1997, Evaluation of Enterprise, 4th edit., 2003. Recipient silver medal Order of Experts Comptables, Paris, 1979, Chevalier de la Légion d'Honneur, Govt. France, Paris, 1995, Mem. Chartered Accountancy Exams. Jury, Rotary (Paris) (treas. 1987-88), Cercle Union Interalliée. Avocations: reading, cinema, photography. Office Phone: 33-1-47-47-80-45. E-mail: j.raffegeau@free.fr.

RAFFEL, BURTON NATHAN, novelist, poet, translator; b. NYC, 1928; married, six children. BA cum laude, Bklyn. Coll., 1948; MA, Ohio State U., 1949; JD, Yale U., 1958. Lawyer Milbank, Tweed, Hadley & McCloy, NYC, 1958-60; editor Foundation News, 1960-63; instr. English SUNY, Stony Brook, 1964-65, asst. prof. of English, 1965-66, assoc. prof. English Buffalo, 1966-68; prof. English and Classics U. Tex., Austin, 1969-71; sr. tutor, dean Ont. Coll. Art, Toronto, Can., 1971-72; prof. English U. Denver, 1975-87; dir. Adirondack Mountain Found., 1987-89; Disting. prof. arts and humanitites, prof. English U. La., Lafayette, 1989—2003; assoc. prof. English U. Haifa, 1968—69. Lectr. English dept. Bklyn. Coll., 1950-51; instr. Ford Found. English Lang. Tchr. Tng. program in Indonesia, resident in Makassar, 1953-55; vis. prof. Humanities York U., Toronto, 1972-75, vis. prof. English Emory U., 1974; sr. editor, cons. McDonnell Douglas Computer-Based Systems Tng. Group, Denver, 1985-87; lectr. in law U. Denver, 1986-87. Author: The Development of Modern Indonesian Poetry, 1967, Mia Poems, 1968, The Forked Tongue: A Study of the Translation Process, 1971, Why Re-Create?, 1973, Four Humours, 1979, (film) The Legend of Alfred Packer, 1979, Robert Lowell, 1981, T.S. Eliot, 1982, Changing the Angle of the Sun-Dial, 1984, Grice, 1985, Evenly Distributed Rubble, 1985, Ezra Pound: The Prime Minister of Poetry, 1985, The Art of Translating Poetry, 1988, American Victorians: Exploration in Emotional History, 1984, Possum and Ole Ez in the Public Eye, 1985, After Such Ignorance, 1986, Man as a Social Animal, 1986, Artists All, 1986, Politicians, Poets, and Con Men, 1986, Founder's Fury, 1988, The Art of Translating Poetry, 1988, Founder's Fortune, 1989, From Stress to Stress: An Autobiography of English Prosody, 1992, The Art of Translating Prose, 1994, The Annotated Milton, 1999, Beethoven in Denver and Other Poems, 1999, The Annotated Hamlet, 2003, The Annotated Romeo and Juliet, 2004, Macbeth, 2005, Midsummer Night's Dream, 2005, Othello, 2005, Taming of the Shrew, 2005, The Tempest, 2006, Henry IV, Part One, 2006, The Merchant of Venice, 2006, Julius Ceasar, 2006, Twelfth Night, 2007, King Lear, 2007, Richard III, 2007, Antony and Cleopatra, 2007, Yankee Doric: America Before the Civil War, 2009; mem. editl. bd. Oral Tradition, 1983—, Literature East and West, 1967-70; adv. editor The Lit. Rev., 1987-03; reviewer/writer Asian Wall St. Jour., 1978-85; contbr. articles to profl. jours. Mem. Bar of the State of N.Y., The Nat. Faculty. Home: 203 S Mannering Ave Lafayette LA 70508-4829 Business E-Mail: bnraffel@cox.net.

RAFFEL, LEROY B., real estate developer; b. Zanesville, Ohio, Mar. 13, 1927; s. Jacob E. and Anne M. (Oliker) R.; m. Shirley Balbot, Sept. 11, 1949; children: Kenneth, Janet, James, Nancy. BS, U. Pa., 1949. Pres. Raffel Bros., Inc., Youngstown, Ohio, 1949-78, York Mahoning Co., Youngstown, 1950-64, Arby's, Inc., Youngstown, 1964-70, chmn. bd., 1971-79; pres. Brom Equity Devel., Inc., Miami, Fla., 1979—. Served with USNR, 1945-46. Home: 2141 NE 190th Ter North Miami Beach FL 33179-4352 Office: Brom Equity Devel Inc 16375 NE 18 Ave Ste 206 Miami FL 33162 Home Phone: 305-935-2187; Office Phone: 305-949-6445.

RAFFERTY, CATHERINE MARY, lawyer; b. Washington, Aug. 20, 1966; d. Joseph Patrick and Angene George Rafferty. BA in Pub. Policy Studies, U. Chgo., 1988, MA in Internat. Rels., 1988; JD, Cath. U., 1991; LLM in Tax, Georgetown U., 1994. Bar: D.C. 1991, U.S. Tax Ct. 1992, U.S. Dist. Ct. D.C. 1992, U.S. Ct. Appeals (D.C. cir.) 1992, Md. 1994. Atty. Office Assoc. Chief Counsel (Internat.) IRS, Washington, 1991-92; atty. Kelly & Nicolaides, Chevy Chase, Md., 1992-94; pvt. practice Chevy Chase, 1994-95; mem. Rafferty & Farmakides, LLC, Washington, 1995; mng. mem. Rafferty & Rafferty, PLLC, Washington, 1995-2000; atty. Law Offices of Catherine Mary Rafferty, Washington, 2001—. Chairwoman Montgomery/Prince George's County Tax Study Group, Md., 1998-2001. Chair various events Philoptochos Soc. St. Sophia Greek Orthodox Cathedral, Washington, 1994—, mem. Perish Coun., 2009-, asst. treas., 1999-2001, treas. 2001-2003, pres. 2003-2005, advisor 2005—07, v.p. 2009-; mem. Leadership 100 Greek Orthodox Archdiocese America, NYC, 2001-. Mem. Md. State Bar Assn. (sec. coun., vice chair tech. 2001-2002, asst. editor Tax Talk 2002-2003, editor Tax Talk 2003-05, co-chair mem. svcs. 2004-05, treas. 2008-09), D.C. Estate Planning Coun., Holton-Arms Alumnae Bd. (chair nominating com. 2003-05, v.p. 2005—07, pres. 2007-08), DC Bar Estates, (trust and probate law section, steering com., 2006—, secy 06-07, treas. 07-08, co-chair 08-). Office: Law Offices of Catherine Mary Rafferty 4801 Yuma St NW Washington DC 20016 Personal E-mail: cm.rafferty@verizon.net. Business E-Mail: c-rafferty-11@alumni.uchicago.edu.

RAFFERTY, EMILY KERNAN, museum administrator; b. NYC, Mar. 13, 1949; m. John Rafferty; children: Nicholas, Sara. BA cum laude, Boston U., 1971. Arts and philanthropy asst. to David Rockefeller, Jr., Boston, 1971; deputy dir. edn. Inst. Contemporary Art, Boston, 1973—75; adminstr. corp., found. and individual fundraising Met. Mus. of Art, NYC, 1976—81, mgr. devel., 1981—84, v.p. devel. and membership, 1984—96, sr. v.p. devel. and membership, 1996—99, sr. v.p. external affairs, 1999—2005, pres., 2005—. Mem. blue ribbon com Am. Cancer Soc. Found., 1999—2000; lifetime honorary trustee Convent of the Sacred Heart; v.p. bd. Independent Sch. Chmn. Assn.; pres. Blue Hill Troupe, 1998—99; mem. bd. dirs. Nat. Sept. 11 Meml. & Mus. at World Trade Ctr. Recipient ArtTable award for disting. svc. to visual arts, 2007; named one of The 100 Most Influential Women in NYC Bus., Crain's NY Bus., 2007, 25 Leaders Reshaping NY, Crain's NY mag., 2008. Mem.: Independent Sector (Met. Mus. rep.), Am. Assn. Museums (devel. com. 1984—94), Women in Financial Devel., Assn. Fundraising Professionals, ArtTable (bd. dirs. 1991—94). Office: Met Museum of Art 1000 Fifth Ave New York NY 10028-1098

RAFFERTY, GENEVIEVE KENNEDY, social service agency administrator; b. Davenport, Iowa, Jan. 21, 1922; d. Thomas Cyril and Mabel Veronica (Finefield) Kennedy; B.A., St. Ambrose Coll., 1942; postgrad. U. Iowa, 1972; m. Daniel J. Rafferty, Aug. 22, 1942 (dec. 1984); children— Daniel D., Michele M., Genevieve, Thomas K., Eileen M., Margaret M., Sheila M. Real estate saleswoman Manhard Realty, Moline, Ill., 1950-59; substitute tchr., Rock Island, Ill., 1963-67; head start tchr. Rock Island-Scott County Dept. Social Services, 1966; public welfare worker Scott County Dept. Social Services, Davenport, Iowa, 1967-72; exec. dir. Info. and Referral of the Quad-Cities, Rock Island, 1972—92, ret.; mem. Travelers Aid Internat.; chair Rock Island Housing Authority; mem. Quad-City Council on Crime and Delinquency, 1977-80; mem. Rock Island County Council on Alcoholism, 1976-82; chairperson CETA Adv. Bd., 1982-84, bi state regional commn. 1986—; steering com., Quad-City Vision for the Future, 1987; bd. dirs. Quint-City Drug Abuse; chair Just Kids Day Care, 1991—; with United Way Bay Area, 1992-94; Peace Corps vol., Uzbekistan, 1994-96. Named Social Worker of Yr. Quad-City, Nat Assn. Social Workers, 1973, Jefferson award for Cmty. Svc., 2003, Key to The City award, 2008, Queen of Mardi Gras, Quad City Cmty., 2009, Jr. Svc. League, 2009; Mem. Nat. Assn. Social Workers, Iowa Council Info. and Referral Providers, Nat. Conf. Social Welfare, Ill. Welfare Assn., NOW, Ill. Alliance Info. and Referral Services (dir.). Democrat. Roman Catholic. Office: 1818 3rd Ave Ste 202 Rock Island IL 61201-8030 Office Phone: 309-737-6931.

RAFFI, See CAVOUKIAN, RAFFI

RAFFIN, THOMAS ALFRED, physician, educator, venture capitalist; b. San Francisco, Jan. 25, 1947; s. Bennett L. and Carolyn M. Raffin; m. Michele Raffin, June 19, 1987; children: Ross Daniel, Jason Bennett, Nicholas Ethan; m. Margaret Raffin, June 23, 1969; 1 child, Elizabeth S. AB in Biol. Sci., Stanford Med. Sch., 1968, MD, 1973. Cert. Am. Bd. Internal Medicine, diplomate Am. Bd. Pulmonary Medicine, Am. Bd. Critical Care Medicine. Med. resident Peter Bent Brigham Hosp., 1973-75; fellow in respiratory medicine sch. medicine Stanford U., Stanford, Calif., 1975-78, med. fiberoptic bronchoscopy service dir. med. ctr., 1978—, acting asst. prof. sch. medicine, 1978-80, assoc. dir. med. ctr. intensive care units, med. dir. dept. respiratory therapy hosp., 1978—, assoc. prof. medicine sch. medicine, 1986-95, chief divsn. pulmonary and critical care, 1990—2004, prof. medicine sch. of medicine, 1995—, Colleen and Robert Haas emeritus prof. medicine/biomed. ethics, 1999—; dir. emeritus Stanford U. Ctr. for Biomed. Ethics, 1989—; co-founder Rigel Pharms., Inc. Co-founder, gen. ptnr. Telegraph Hill Ptnrs., San Francisco, 2002—; bd. dirs. New Link Genetics, BioProtection Sys., AngioScore, Pneum Rx, LDR Holding, Confirma, Freedom Innovations. Author: Intensive Care: Facing the Critical Choices, 1988; contbr. articles to profl. jours.; watercolor show, Thomas Reynolds Gallery, San Fransisco, 2009. V.p. lung cancer com. No. Calif. Oncology Group, 1983—85; com. mem. NIH Workshop, 1984; pres. Raffin Family Found., San Francisco. Recipient award, Henry J. Kaiser Found., 1981, 1984, 1988, 1997, Arthur L. Bloomfield award, 1981. Fellow: ACP (rep. coun. subspecialty socs. 1986), Am. Coll. Chest Physicians (program com. mem. 1985—86); mem.: AAAS, Calif. Thoracic Soc., Soc. Critical Care Medicine, Calif. Med. Assn. (chmn. sect. chest diseases 1984—85), Santa Clara County Med. Soc., Santa Clara County Lung Assn., Am. Thoracic Soc., Am. Fedn. Clin. Rsch. Independent. Jewish. Avocations: painting, gardening, raising miniature donkeys, Nigerian dwarf goats. Office: Telegraph Hill Ptnrs 360 Post Ste 601 San Francisco CA 94108 also: Ctr Biomed Ethics Stanford U 701 Welch Rd Ste A1105 Palo Alto CA 94304-1709 Office Phone: 415-765-6980, 415-765-6985. Business E-Mail: tar@stanford.edu.

RAFFO, KRISTIN L., elementary school educator; d. Alan L. Austin and Debra A. Thompson, Larry D. Thompson (Stepmother); m. John-Edward Raffo, Sept. 30, 2005; 1 child, Hayden T. BA, Fla. Atlantic U., Boca Raton, 2004. Cert. in gen. edn. Fla., 2004, English spkrs. other langs. Fla., 2004. Gymnastics coach, camp dir. Twisters Gymnastics, Boca Raton, Fla., 2001—04; elem. educator Palm Beach County Schs., Lake Worth, Fla., 2004—05, Flagler County Schs., Bunnell, Fla., 2005—. Office: Belle Terre Elem 5545 Belle Terre Pky Palm Coast FL 33431 Personal E-mail: ka5218@msn.com.

RAFI, MOSTAFA, ophthalmologist; b. Oujda, Morocco, May 20, 1947; s. Miloud Rafi and Fatna (Hemri) R.; m. Amina Samir Rafi, Aug. 5, 1973; children: Fedoua, Nada. PhD in Medicine, U. Rabat, 1974; diploma in Ophthalmology, U. Paris, 1976. Cert. ophthalmologist Paris. Asst. prof., Sale, 1976; prof. Avicenne's Hosp., Rabat, 1980-86, Specialty Hosp., Rabat, 1986-97; head dept., 1990—; pvt. practice Clinique d'Ophthalmologie, Rabat. Dir. Sale's Hosp., 1983-85; head of OTO-Neuro-Ophthalmology Dept., 1990—; pres. 1982-85, v.p., 1986-89, Moroccan Ophthalmological Soc., pres. Qualification's Commn. in Ophthalmology, 1987-93. Mem. Direction of the Social Assn. Anjoad, 1983—; pres. Assn. Against Blindness, 1993—. Recipient Gov.'s award, Oujda, 1989, Settat, 1995, Honor award Moroccan Soc. of Ophthalmology, 2004. Avocations: golf, hunting, tennis. Home: 252 rue Beni Garfat Rabat Morocco Office: Specialty Hosp Afdal Rabat Morocco Home Phone: 21237751805; Office Phone: 212 37660389/90.

RAFTERY, ANDREW STEIN, printmaker; b. Goldsboro, NY, 1962; BFA, Boston U., 1984; MFA, Yale U., 1988. Represented in permanent collections Yale U. Art Gallery, Jane Voorhees Zimmerli Art Mus., New Brunswick, NJ, Met. Mus. Art, NYC, Princeton U. Art Mus., Whitney Mus. Am. Art, NYC, one-man shows include Narrative Paintings and Prints, Contemporary Realist Gallery, San Francisco, 1994, Narrative Impulse, Frye Art Mus., Seattle, 1998, Drawings and Prints, Lenore Gray Gallery, Providence, RI, 1998, Real Estate Chiaroscuros, 2002, A Shopper's Paradise, Hackett-Freedman Gallery, San Francisco, 1998, exhibited in group shows at Objects and Everyday Life, Montserrat Coll. Art, Beverly, Mass., 1993, RISD Collects RISD, RI Sch. Design Mus., Providence, 1996, Chiaroscuro, 2004, South Coast New Eng. Printmaking, U. Mass., North Adams, 2003, Newer Genres, Jane Voorhees Zimmerli Art Mus., New Brunswick, NJ, 2003, Drawn to Representation, Corcoran Gallery Art, Washington, 2005, Invitational Exhbn., AAAL, 2006 (Purchase award, AAAL, 2006), Portfolios and Series, NY Pub. Libr., NYC, 2007, 60 Years of N.Am. Prints, Boston U. Art Gallery, 2007, Ann. Invitational Exhbn. Contemporary Am. Art, Nat. Acad. Mus., NYC, 2008. Recipient Louis Comfort Tiffany award, 2003; Fritz Eichenberg Printmaking fellow, RI State Coun. Arts, 2001, John. S. Guggenheim Meml. Found. fellow, 2008. Studio: 76 8th St Providence RI 02906 Office: Mary Ryan Gallery 527 W 26th St New York NY 10001*

RAFTERY, LAUREL A., research biologist, educator; b. Hilo, HI, Oct. 8, 1956; d. John Cornwell and Helga Ruth (Isakson) R.; m. Jeffrey Allen Casey, Apr. 10, 1982; 1 child, Bret W.R. Casey. AB, U. Calif., Berkeley, 1979; PhD, U. Colo., 1986; postdoctoral, Harvard U., 1986-92. Teaching fellow Harvard Univ., 1988; asst. prof. dept. dermatology Cutaneous Biology Rsch Ctr. Mass. Gen. Hosp. and Harvard Med. Sch., Charlestown, Mass., 1993—; asst. biologist Mass. Gen. Hosp.; instr. Harvard Med. Sch., asst. prof., 1995—2003, assoc. prof., 2003—. Speaker in field. Postdoctoral fellowship NIH, 1986-89, Charles A. King Trust, 1989-91; scholar Am. Cancer Soc., 1996-2004. Mem. AAAS, Soc. for Devel. Biology, Genetics Soc. Am. Office: Cutaneous Biology Rsch Ctr MGH-East 13th St Bldg 149 Charlestown MA 02129-2000 Business E-Mail: laurel.raftery@cbrc2.mgh.harvard.edu.

RAFUSE, NANCY E., lawyer, director; b. Columbia, SC, Dec. 14, 1966; m. Mark Rafuse; 2 children. BBA cum laude, U. Ga., 1988, JD magna cum laude, 1991. Ptnr., chair dept. employment law Paul, Hastings, Janofsky & Walker, Atlanta, 1991—2003; co-founder, mng. ptnr. Ashe, Rafuse & Hill, Atlanta, 2003—. Spkr. in field; mem. bar coun. and disciplinary com. No. Dist. Ga., 2002—05. Contbr. articles to profl. jours. Bd. dirs. Atlanta Urban League, Zoo Atlanta; mem. Atlanta United Way Women's Leadership Coun. Named one of Georgia's Legal Elite, Georgia Trend mag., 2003—04, Top 40 Lawyers Under 40, Nat. Law Jour., 2005. Mem.: ABA (mem. labor and employment law sect.), Atlanta Bar Assn. (mem. labor and employment law sect.), State Bar Ga. (mem. labor and employment law sect.). Office: Ashe Rafuse & Hill LLP 1355 Peachtree St Ste 500 Atlanta GA 30309 Office Phone: 404-253-6002. Office Fax: 404-253-6060. E-mail: nancyrafuse@asherafuse.com.

RAGAN, ANN TALMADGE, media and production consultant, actor; b. Raleigh, NC, July 6, 1951; d. Samuel Talmadge and Marjorie Lois (Usher) R.; m. L. Worth Keeter III, Aug. 22, 1992. Student, U. NC, Chapel Hill, 1969-71, Finch Coll., 1972-73, New Sch. Social Rsch., 1973-74, Western Wash. U., 1978. Acct. estimator Benton & Bowles Inc., NYC, 1971-72, media buyer, 1974-77; speechwriter, press aide Senator Robert Morgan, Washington, 1978-79; asst. prodr., casting dir. John F. Murray Inc., NYC, 1979—80; prod., sales dir. Grand St. Films, NYC, 1980-84; ind. prod. for various clients NYC, 1984-86; asst. pub. The Pilot, Inc., Southern Pines, NC, 1986-96, bd. dirs. Prodn. mgr. Anglo Am. Media Workshops, London, 1988—90; dir. SAG Conservatory Am. Film Inst., LA, 2003—07, coach Film Camp, 2005—07, cons.; mgr., exec. prodr. films, commercials, audio books Blue Kiss, LLC, 2000—; prodn. mgr., coach Directing Workshop for Women; workshop leader in field. Contbr. articles to newspapers and jours.; prodr.: (narrator) Sign of the Salamander. Life mem. Roanoke Island Hist. Assn.; mem. Moore County Arts Coun., 1986-89; mem. adv. bd. Art & Soul 2006-; Lost Colony Alumni Com., 2007-, Voice Advance Team 2008-. Mem.: SAG (conservatory com., rec. sec. 1997—2006, cons., vice-chair 2003—), AFTRA, Audio Pubs. Assn., Women in Film, Women in Theatre (adminstrv. dir. 1995—97, treas. 1997—99, bd. dirs. 1997—99, pres. 2004—), Actors Equity Assn., Kings and Clowns Ednl. Shakespeare Alliance (treas. bd. dirs. 1999—2002, adv. bd. 2003—), Pi Beta Phi. Democrat. Methodist. Home and Office: 10542 Bloomfield St Toluca Lake CA 91602-2813 Home Phone: 818-762-1926; Office Phone: 818-762-6339. Business E-Mail: bluekissllc@aol.com.

RAGAN, CHARLES RANSOM, lawyer; b. NYC, Aug. 13, 1947; s. Charles Alexander Jr.; children: Alexandra Watson, Madeline McCue. AB, Princeton U., 1969; JD, Fordham U., 1974. Bar: N.Y. 1975, U.S. Ct. Appeals (3d cir.) 1975, Calif. 1976, U.S. Ct. Appeals (9th cir.) 1976, U.S. Dist. Ct. (no. dist.) Calif. 1976, U.S. Supreme Ct. 1981, U.S. Dist. Ct. (so. dist.) N.Y. 1982, U.S. Ct. Appeals (2d cir.) 1984. Law clk. to Hon. R.J. Aldisert U.S. Ct. Appeals (3rd cir.), 1974-76; assoc. Pillsbury, Madison & Sutro, San Francisco, 1976-81, ptnr., 1982-97, Palo Alto, 1997-2000, Pillsbury Winthrop, Palo Alto, San Francisco, 2001—05; founder, ptnr. Redgrave Daley Ragan & Wagner, 2005—09; mng. dir. Huron Consulting Group, 2009—. Mem. exec. com. 9th Cir. Judicial Conf., 1987-91. Avocations: bicycling, swimming, sports. Office: Huron Consulting Group 550 W van Buren St Chicago IL 60607 Home Phone: 415-264-1319; Office Phone: 312-880-0535, 415-954-7113. Business E-Mail: cragan@huronconsultinggroup.com.

RAGAN, CHARLOTTE ANN, music educator; b. Elberton, Ga., May 4, 1929; d. Harry Sanders and Pauline Melissa (Edwards) Bell; m. Gordon Billy Ragan (dec.); children: Gordon Billy Jr., Evelyn Melissa Swanson. BFA, U. Ga., 1950; MA, Columbia U., 1954. Pvt. piano tchr. Dir. hand bells First Bapt. Ch., Milledgeville, Ga., pianist for Merri Maker Choir. Mem.: DAR (state curator 1994—96, state treas. 1996—98, state chorus dir. 2002—), Music Tchrs. Nat. Assn., C. of C., U. Ga. (Sigma Lamda chpt., treas. mortar bd.), Milledgeville Music Club (pres. 1968—70), Alpha Omicron Pi, Sigma Alpha Iota. Baptist. Avocations: dance, bridge, reading. Home: 330 Doles Blvd Milledgeville GA 31061 Office Phone: 478-452-1674.

RAGAN, JAMES THOMAS, communications executive; b. San Diego, Mar. 15, 1929; m. Susan Held, Nov. 9, 1957; children: James, Maria, Carey, Andrew. BA, Oxford U., Eng., 1951, MA, 1955; elect. engring. vocat. cert., U. State of N.Y., 1954. With Gen. Electric Co., 1954-69; pres., chief operating officer Athena Communications Corp. subs. Gulf & Western Industries, Inc., NYC, 1969-74; v.p. broadcast services Western Union Telegraph Co., 1974-76, v.p. satellite services, 1976-82, pres. Western Union personal communications corp., v.p. communication systems group, 1982-85; pres. Associated Info. Services Corp., 1985-86; pres., dir. Bunting, Inc., 1985-88; ptnr. Pierce Kennedy Hearth, 1988-91; CEO Nat. Lang. Assocs. Lanarea Pub., Green Valley, Ariz., 1990—. Patentee recreational sports equipment; author: The Ultimate Diet, The First Alaskans, A Guide to the Geography of the Native Languages, Cultures, Their Communities, and Populations, 1996. Pres. Wilton Pop Warner Football League, Wilton, Conn., 1972—73. Maj. USMCR, 1952—54, Korea. Home: PO Box 1112 Green Valley AZ 85622 Office: Nat Lang Assocs PO Box 1112 Green Valley AZ 85622 Office Phone: 520-399-2294. Personal E-mail: jtragan@gmail.com.

RAGAN, JOHN W., energy executive; BA, W.Va. U.; MBA, Tulane U. With Mirant Corp., 1996—2004, sr. v.p., CEO internat. group, 2003—04; gen. mgr. containerboard and packaging Ga. Pacific Corp., 2004—05; v.p. bus. mgmt. N.E. region FPL Energy, 2005—06, v.p. trading, transmission, and ops., 2006; exec. v.p., regional pres. N.E. NRG Energy, Inc., Princeton, NJ, 2006—09, exec. v.p., COO, 2009—. Office: NRG Energy, Inc 211 Carnegie Center Princeton NJ 08540*

RAGAN, ROBERT ALLISON, private investment executive, financial consultant; b. Gastonia, NC, Aug. 21, 1938; s. Caldwell and Jocelyn (Sikes) R. BS in Bus. Adminstrn., U. NC, 1961; postgrad., Rutgers U., 1968. V.p. N.C. Nat. Bank (now Bank of Am.), Charlotte, 1961-81; pres., treas. R.A. Ragan & Co., Inc., Charlotte, 1981—. Dir. Carolina Mills, Inc., Maiden, N.C., 1977—. Author, pub.: The Ragans of Gastonia (1790-1995), 1995, The Textile Heritage of Gaston County, N.C. (1848-2000), 2000. Founder, pres. bd. govs. The Gaston Soc. of Mecklenburg County, Charlotte, NC, 1999—; trustee, bd. visitors Darlington Sch., Rome, Ga., 1981—; mem. bd. visitors Daniel Stowe Bot. Gardens, Belmont, NC, 2001—; pres. bd. trustees Gaston County Mus. Art and History, Dallas, NC, 1978—81, 1997—99. Mem. Charlotte City Club, DeBordieu Colony Country Club (Georgetown, S.C.), Linville (N.C.) Ridge Country Club. Republican. Presbyn. Avocations: preservation and recording of local and North Carolina history, travel. Home: 227 Fenton Pl Charlotte NC 28207-1913 also: 407 DeBordieu Blvd Georgetown SC 29440 Home: R A Ragan & Co 227 Fenton Pl Charlotte NC 28207-1913 Personal E-mail: robertragan1@aol.com.

RAGAUSS, PETER A., oil industry executive; B. in mech. engring., Mich. State U., 1980; MBA, Harvard U., 1987. V.p. corp. devel. Tenneco Energy Inc.; v.p. fin. El Paso Energy Internat. Corp.; v.p. fin. & portfolio mgmt. Amoco Energy Internat.; asst to grp. chief exec. BP plc, 1998; CEO Air BP; segment contr. refining & mktg. BP plc, London, 2003—06; sr. v.p. & CFO Baker Hughes Inc., Houston, 2006—. Office: Baker Hughes Inc 3900 Essex Ln Houston TX 77027-5177 Office Phone: 713-439-8600. Office Fax: 713-439-8699.

RAGAVAN, ANPALAKI JEYABALASINKHAM, software developer, researcher; arrived in U.S., 1992; d. George Nagularajah and Thangaranee Veluppillai Jeyabalasingham; m. Ragavan Vinasithamby, July 1, 1993; 1 child, Muhundhan. BS (hon.), U. Sri Lanka, 1985, MPhil (hon.) in Hydrology, 1989; MS in Hydrogeology (hon.), U. Nev., 1996, MS in Civil Engring., 2003, MS in Hydrology, 2005, MS in Math., 2008, postgrad., 2000—, postgrad., 2005—. Cert. BASIC computer programmer, geographic info. sys., Visual Basic programmer, GIS and web design, SAS programmer, well drilling with LS 100. Asst. prof. U. Sri Lanka, Kilinochchi, Jaffna, 1989—92; rsch. asst. Ind. State U., Tere Haute, 1992—93; rsch./tchg. asst. U. Nev., Reno, 1993—96, rsch. asst., 1999—; software developer Bur. Labor Stats., Washington, 1996—99. Grad. fellow U. Nev., Reno, 1993—96, grad. asst., 1999—; student amb. SAS Inst., 2008; presenter in field. Contbr. articles to profl. jours.; author: Introductory Statistics, Lab-Guide - SAS, 1st edition., 1993. Recipient Cert. of Appreciation, Nev. State Mental Health and Devel. Services, 2000, Excellence in Abstract Submission award, APHA, HIV/AIDS Sect., 2001, Am. Jour. Pub. Health, 2001, Poster award, SAS Inst., Inc., 2007, 2008; grantee, State of Nev., 2002; scholar, Asian Inst. Of Tech. in Thailand, 1991, Ind. State U., 1992—93, U. Nev., Reno, 1993—, Soroptimist Internat. of Reno, Sierra Nev. Region, 2000, Water Resources Assn., 2005, Grad. Student Assn., 2005—06; Overseas Devel. Adminstrn. scholar, Govt. of UK, 1986—89, Conf. scholar, Western Users Stats. Analysis Sys., 2007, 2008. Mem.: AAAS (Travel award 2007, Joshua Nemark Travel award 2008), Nature Pub. Group, Am. Geophys. Union, Nat. Ground Water Assn., Nev. Water Resources Assn., Am. Math. Soc., Am. Statis. Assn., Geol. Soc. Am., Great Woman of the 21st Century (profl. women's adv. bd.), Alumni Assn. U. Nev. (mem. profl. women's adv. bd.), Sigma Xi. Mem. Lds Ch. Avocations: dance, music, guitar, swimming, sports. Office: U Nev Dept Internal Med Reno NV 89512 Home: 1215 Beech St Apt 26 Reno NV 89512-2209 Business E-Mail: ragavan@unr.edu.

RAGENT, BORIS, physicist; b. Cleve., Mar. 2, 1924; s. Samuel and Bertha (Lev) R.; m. Dorothy Kohn, Sept. 11, 1949; children: David Stefan, Lawrence Stanton, Jesse Ron. Student, Ohio State U., 1941—44; BSEE, Marquette U., 1944; PhD in Physics, U. Calif., Berkeley, 1953. Registered profl. engr., Calif. Engr. Victoreen Instrument Co., Cleve., 1946-48; engr., physicist Radiation Lab., U. Calif., Berkeley, 1948-53; physicist Livermore, Calif., 1953-56, Broadview Rsch. Corp., Burlingame, Calif., 1956-59, Vidya divsn. Itek Corp., Palo Alto, Calif., 1959-66, Ames Rsch. Ctr., NASA, Moffett Field, Calif., 1966-87, San Jose (Calif.) State U. Found., 1987-98. Lectr. Stanford U., U. Calif. Ext. Served in USNR, 1944-46. Mem. AAAS, Am. Phys. Soc., Optical Soc. Am., Am. Geophys. Union, Sigma Xi.

RAGER, RUDOLPH RUSSELL, retired lawyer; b. Miles City, Mont., Jan. 15, 1932; s. Harry E. and Esther (Anderson) R.; m. Sharon E. Keeling, Dec. 30, 1959; children: Sean, Kurt, Quita, Elani, Valari, Jordan. BBA, U. ND, Grand Forks, 1956; JD, U. N.Mex., Albuquerque, 1958. Bar: N.Mex. 1958, US Dist. Ct. N.Mex. 1959. Sole practice, Albuquerque, 1958—60, 1970—2003; ptnr. Grantham, Spann, Sanchez & Rager, 1961—69. Atty. Village of Corrales, 1971-81; bd. dirs. Anderson Devel. Corp., Albuquerque, Anderson Western Corp., Albuquerque. Pres., bd. dirs. Albuquerque Tutoring Assn., 1967; co-founder, bd. dirs., sec. Security Escrow Corp., 1974-80, Intermountain Conservation Trust, 1996-2005; bd. dirs. Luth. Coordinating Coun., Albuquerque, 1975, Corrales Hist. Soc., 1988-94; bd. dirs., sec. Anderson Charitable Found., 1994-, Anderson Abruzzo, Internat. Balloon Mus., Albuquerque, 1984-2006; adv. bd. dirs. Albuquerque City Balloon Mus., 1991-2006; bd. dirs., treas. San Pedro Creek Homeowners Assn., 1996-2000. Gold Seal scholar, 1949. Mem. N.Mex. Bar Assn., Albuquerque Bar Assn. Lodges: Kiwanis (pres. Albuquerque chpt. 1966). Republican. Lutheran. Home: 20 Canada Vista Dr Sandia Park NM 87047-9645 Personal E-mail: rrager@msn.com.

RAGGI, REENA, federal judge; b. Jersey City, May 11, 1951; BA, Wellesley Coll., 1973; JD cum laude, Harvard U., 1976. Bar: NY 1977, US Dist. Ct. (ea. dist.) NY 1987, US Ct. Appeals (2d cir.) 2002. Law clerk US Ct. of Appeals, 7th Circuit, 1976—77; assoc. Cahill, Gordon & Reindel, NY, 1977—79; asst. U.S. atty. Dept. Justice, Bklyn., 1979—86; ptnr. Windels, Marx, Davies & Ives, NYC, 1986—87; judge US Dist. Ct. (ea. dist.) NY, 1987—2002, US Ct. Appeals (2nd cir.), NYC, 2002—. Office: US Courthouse 225 Cadman Plz E Brooklyn NY 11201*

RAGGIO, LOUISE BALLERSTEDT, lawyer; b. Austin, Tex., June 15, 1919; d. Louis F. and Hilma (Lindgren) Ballerstedt; m. Grier H. Raggio, Apr. 19, 1941; children: Grier, Thomas, Kenneth. BA, U. Tex., 1939; student, Am. U. Washington, 1939-40; JD, So. Methodist U., 1952. Bar: Tex. 1952, U.S. Dist. Ct. (no. dist.) Tex. 1958. Intern Nat. Inst. Pub. Affairs, Washington, 1939-40; asst. dist. atty. Dallas County, Tex., 1954-56; shareholder Raggio and Raggio, 1956—. Sec. Gov.'s Commn. on Status of Women, 1970-71; trustee Tex. Bar Found., 1982-86, chmn., 1984-85, chmn. fellows, 1993—, Dallas Women's Found., 1993—, Nat. Conf. Bar Founds., 1986-92. Recipient Zonta award, Bus. and Profl. Women's Club award, So. Meth. U. Alumni award, Woman of Yr. award Tex. Fedn. Bus. and Profl. Women's Clubs, 1985, award Internat. Women's Forum, 1990, Disting. Law Alumni award So. Meth. U., 1992, Disting. Trial Lawyer award, 1993, Outstanding Trial Lawyer award Dallas Bar Assn., 1993, Pacemaker award Nat. Bus. Women Owners Assn., 1994, Thomas Jefferson award ACLU, 1994, Courage award Women Journalists North Tex., 1995, Tex. Lawyer award 1999, Entrepreneur award Fortune Sm. Bus. Mag., 2000, Gillian award 2000, Professionalism award Dallas (Tex.) Bar, 2003; named to Tex. Women's Hall of Fame, 1985; named one of Heroes of Sm. Bus., Fortune Sm. Bus. Mag., 2000. Fellow Am. Bar Found.; mem. ABA (chmn. family sect. 1975-76, Best Woman Lawyer award 1995, Lifetime Achievement award 2002), LWV (pres. Austin 1945-46), State Bar Tex. (chmn. family law sect. 1965-67, dir. 1979-82, citation for law reform 1967, Pres.'s award 1987, Sarah T. Hughes award 1993, named one of 100 Tex. Lawyers of Century, 1999, 50 Yr. Lawyer award 2003), Dallas Bar Found. (pres. fellow com. 1991), Am. Acad. Matrimonial Lawyers (gov. 1973-81, trustee found. 1992—), Bus. and Profl. Women's Club (pres. Town North 1958-59), Phi Beta Kappa (pres. Dallas chpt. 1970-71, 90-92). Unitarian Universalist. Office: Raggio and Raggio 3316 Oak Grove Ave Ste 100 Dallas TX 75204-2338 Home: 3316 Oak Grove Ave Ste 100 Dallas TX 75204-2340 Office Phone: 214-880-7500. E-mail: louise@raggiolaw.com. *All things are possible in our expanding universe if we can tune in to the infinite power available to all of us. Our ancestors concentrated on the problems— let us be a part of the solutions so desperately needed in our complex and troubled world.*

RAGGIO, THOMAS LOUIS, lawyer; b. Dallas, Sept. 11, 1946; s. Grier H. and Louise (Ballerstadt) R.; m. Janice B. Savage, May 23, 1970; children: Stephen, Kristen. BA, U. Tex., 1968; JD, So. Meth. U., 1971. Bar: US Dist. Ct. (no. dist. Tex.) 1971; cert. family law specialist. Atty. Raggio & Raggio, PLLC, Dallas, 1971—, mng. ptnr., 1985—. Author, spkr. in field of family law. Named one of Best Lawyers in Dallas, D Mag., 2001—09, Best Lawyers in America, 2002—09, Tex. Super Lawyers, Tex. Top 100 Super Lawyers, 2005. Mem. Am. Acad. Matrimonial Lawyers, Tex. Bar Found. Office: Raggio and Raggio PLLC 3316 Oak Grove Ave Ste 100 Dallas TX 75204-2338 Office Phone: 214-880-7500. E-mail: tom@raggiolaw.com.

RAGGIO, WILLIAM JOHN, state legislator, lawyer; b. Reno, Oct. 30, 1926; s. William John and Clara M. (Cardelli) R.; m. Dorothy Brigman, August 15, 1948 (dec. Apr. 1998); children: Leslie Ann, Tracy Lynn, Mark William (dec.); m. Dale Checket, Apr. 27, 2003. Student, La. Poly. Inst., 1944-45, U. Okla., 1945-46; BA, U. Nev., 1948; grad., U. Calif., Berkeley, 1951; JD, U. Calif., San Francisco. Bar: Nev. 1951, U.S. Supreme Ct. 1959. Atty., Reno and Las Vegas; asst. dist. atty. Washoe County, Nev., 1952-58; dist. atty., 1958—70; ptnr. Wiener, Goldwater, Galatz & Raggio, Ltd., 1971-72, Raggio, Walker & Wooster, Reno and Las Vegas, 1974-78, Raggio, Wooster & Lindell, 1978-92; sr. ptnr. Vargas & Bartlett, 1992-98, Jones-Vargas (formerly Vargas & Bartlett), 1998—. Coun. State Govts., 1972-75; v.p., dir. Archon Corp.; mem. legis. commn., Nev. State Senate, vice chmn. criminal law and adminstrn. com., majority fl. leader, 1987-07, minority fl. leader, 1977-81, 82-87, 91, 2009, mem. Dist. Washoe 3, 1973—. Mem. Nev. Am. Revolutionary Bicentennial Commn., 1975-81; mem. Republican State Cen. Com.; past nat. chmn., current dir. Am. Legislative Exchange Council, dir. Sierra Health Svcs., 1983-2006; rep. candidate U.S. Senate, 1970. Served with USNR, 1944-46; to 2d lt. USMCR, 1946-47. Named Young Man of Yr., Reno-Sparks Jr. C. of C., 1959, Alumnus of Yr., U. Nev. Reno, 1999, Civic Leader of Yr., Greater Reno C. of C., Disting. Eagle Scout, 1989; named to Jr. Achievement of Nev. Hall of Fame, 1999, Reg. Trans. Commn. Hall of Fame; recipient Disting. Nevadan award, 1968, Fellows award The Salvation Army, Torch of Liberty award The Anti-Defamation League, SIR award Assoc. Gen. Contractors, 1995, Outstanding Svc. award Airport Authority of Washoe County, Pres.'s medal UNLV, 2000. Fellow Am. Bd. Criminal Lawyers; mem. ABA (state chmn. jr. bar conf. 1957-60, ho. dels.) Am. Judicature Soc., Am. Coll. Trail Lawyers, Am. Bd. Trial Advocates, Am. Inns of Ct., Nat. (nat. pres. 1967-68; named Outstanding Prosecutor 1965), Nev. State (sec. 1959, pres. 1960-63) Dist. Attys. Assn., NCJ (Brotherhood award 1965), Nev. Peace Officers Assn., Internat. Assn. Chiefs Police, Am. Leg. Exch. Coun. (nat. chmn. 1991-92, The William J. Raggio Excellence in Leadership Outstanding award 2007), Coll. of Edn. U. Nev. (life), Am. Legion, Elks, Lion Club, Prospectors Club, Alpha Tau Omega, Phi Alpha Delta. Republican. Roman Catholic. Office: Nevada State Senate 401 South Carson St Rm 2160 Carson City NV 89701 Home Phone: 775-786-5000; Office Phone: 775-684-1419, 7757865000. Office Fax: 775-786-1177. Business E-Mail: wraggio@sen.state.nv.us. E-mail: wjr@jonesvargas.com, wraggio@jonesvargas.com.

RAGHAVENDRA, AMAR, systems engineer; b. Bangalore, Karnataka, India; BEE, Nat. Inst. Tech., Surathkal, India, 1991; MEE, La. State U., Baton Rouge, 1996. Cert. Java programmer Sun Microsys., Inc., 2000; lic. profl. engr., LA, 2007. Rsch. assoc. LSU-La. Transp. Rsch. Ctr., Baton Rouge, 1996—2008, applications engring. mgr., 2008—. Contbr. scientific papers to conf. pubs. Mem.: IEEE, Assn. Computing Machinery, Am. Mensa. Office: LSU - LA Trans Rsch Ctr 4101 Gourrier Ave Baton Rouge LA 70810

RAGHUPATHI, RAMESH, neuroscientist, educator; s. Raghupathi Varadachar; m. Revathi Krishnaswamy Raghupathi, June 2, 1988; children: Varun, Vikram. BSc, U. Madras, Chennai, India, 1985; PhD, Va. Commonwealth U., Richmond, 1991. Postdoc. fellow U. Conn. Health Ctr., Farmington, 1991—92, U. Pa. Sch. Medicine, Phila., 1992—95, rsch. asst. prof., 1995—2003; asst. prof. Drexel U. Coll. Medicine, Phila., 2003—07, assoc. prof., 2007—. Treas. Treddyfrin Easttown Soccer Assn., Berwyn, Pa., 2008; dir. and player agt. Berwyn Paoli Area Little League, Berywn, 2008. Recipient Prof S Rengachari Oration award, Neurotrauma Soc. India, 2003. Mem.: Nat. Neurotrauma Soc., Soc. Neurosci. Office: Drexel Univ Coll Medicine 2900 Queen Ln Philadelphia PA 19129 Business E-Mail: rramesh@drexelmed.edu.

RAGHUVEER, GEETHA, pediatrician, educator; b. Mysore, India, Dec. 11, 1959; MBBS, Mysore U., India, 1983. Cert. Pediat., Pediat. Cardiology. Intern pediat. Govt. Med. Coll., Mysore, India, 1981—92; residency pediat. Montefiore Med. Ctr., Albert Einstein Coll. Medicine, NY, 1995—97; fellow pediat. cardiology U. Iowa Hospitals and Clinics; assoc. prof. pediat. U. Mo.-Kansas City Sch. Medicine. Office: Children's Mercy Hosp and Clinics KCM05 2401 Gillham Rd Kansas City MO 64108

RAGINS, HERZL, retired surgeon; b. Tel Aviv, July 27, 1929; arrived in US, 1929; s. Aaron and Ida (Kraus) R.; m. Karen Anderson, Sept. 16, 1979; 1 child, Jonathan Daly. BS, U. Ill., 1949; MS, MD, U. Ill., Chgo., 1951; PhD, U. Chgo., 1956. Intern Cook County Hosp., Chgo., 1951-52; surg. resident U. Chgo. Clinics, 1952-53, 55-60; gastrointestinal endoscopy fellowship Beth Israel Hosp., NYC, 1972-73; clin. prof. surgery A. Einstein Coll. Medicine, Bronx, NY, 1973—2007, ret., 2007. Contbr. articles to profl. jours. Capt. USAF, 1953-55, Korea. Mem. ACS, Am. Soc. Gastrointestinal Endoscopy, Am. Gastroent. Assn., Am. Physiol. Soc., Soc. Surgery Alimentary Tract, Soc. Am. Gastrointestinal Endoscopic Surgeons, Am. Soc. Colorectal Surgeons. Avocations: gardening, tennis. Personal E-mail: herzl.raqins@gamil.com.

RAGINSKY, NINA, artist; d. Bernard Boris and Helen Theresa R.; 1 child, Sofya Katrina. BA, Rutgers U., 1962; studied painting with, Roy Lichtenstein; studied sculpture with, George Segal; studied Art History with Allan Kaprow, Rutgers U. Freelance photographer Nat. Film Bd., Ottawa, Ont., Canada, 1963-81; instr. metaphysics Emily Car Coll. Art, Vancouver, B.C., Canada, 1973-81; painter Salt Spring Island, B.C., 1989—. Sr. artist, jury Can. Coun.; selected Can. rep. in Sweden for Sweden Now Mag., 1979; tchr., lectr. in field, 1973—. One woman shows include Vancouver Art Gallery, Victoria Art Gallery, Edmonton Art Gallery, Art Gallery Ont., San Francisco Mus. Art, Acadia U., Nancy Hoffman Gallery, N.Y.C., Meml. U. Newfoundland Art Gallery; exhibited in group shows at Rutgers U., 1962, Montreal Mus. Fine Arts, 1963, Nat. Film Bd., Ottawa, 1964, 65, 67, 70, 71, 76, 77, Internat. Salon Photography, Bordeaux, France, 1968, Nat. Gallery Ottawa, 1968, Eastman House, Rochester, N.Y., 1969, Vancouver Art Gallery, 1973, 80, Mural for Conf. Ctr. Ottawa, 1973, Field Mus., Chgo., 1976, Edmonton Art Gallery, 1978, 79, Walter Philips Gallery, 1979, Glenbow Mus. Gallery, 1979, Harbour Front Community Gallery, 1980, Hamilton Art Gallery, 1980, Musée Maisil de St. Lambert, 1981, Mendel Art Gallery, 1981, Dunlop Art Gallery, Regina, Can., 1981, Vancouver Art Gallery, 2001; represented in permanent collections Nat. Film Bd. Stills divsn., Ottawa, Ont., Banff (Alta.) Sch. Fine Arts, Nat Gallery Ottawa, Can., George Eastman House, Rochester, NY, Wadsworth Atheneum, Conn., Edmonton Art Gallery, U. Victoria, B.C., various pvt. collections. Bd. dirs. Island Watch, Salt Spring Island, B.C., 1993; founder, coord. Salt Spring Island Ecosys. Stewardship Project, 1993; founder, coord. Salt Spring Island Waterbird Watch Collective, 1994—. Decorated officer Order of Can., 1984; recipient Kees Vermeer award for edn. and conservation Simon Fraser U., 1997, Burns Bog award for environ. excellence, Vancouver, 2005. Mem.: Soc. for Advancement of Slow, Royal Can. Acad. Arts. Avocations: gardening, birding, subject of numerous publs. Home and Office: 272 Beddis Rd Salt Spring Island BC Canada V8K 2J1

RAGLAND, JACK WHITNEY, artist; b. El Monte, Calif., Feb. 25, 1938; s. Jack Rider and Dorsey (Whitney) R.; m. Marilee J. Weaver, July 31, 1969; children— Roxanne, Natasha. BA, Ariz. State U., Tempe, 1960, MA, 1964; postgrad., UCLA, 1961-64. Grad. asst. tchr. Ariz. State U., 1960-61; grad. teaching asst. UCLA, 1961-64; head art dept. Simpson Coll., Indianola, Iowa, 1964-76. Demonstrator Nat. Art Materials Trade Assn., Denver, 1993, Pasadena Conv. Ctr., 1994 One-man shows include Kleine Gallery, Vienna, Austria, Simpson Coll., Internat. Art Svc., Pan Paciific Hotel, San Diego, Lakes Art Ctr., Okaboji, Iowa, Hilltop Ctr., Fallbrook, 1996-98, Desert Art Source Gallery, 1999-2007, published painting book Land of Sunlight, San Diego Flora, 2007, in top 100 and 2nd mini 50 of Nat. Paint Am. Competition, 2007; exhibited in group shows, Lyn Kottler Gallery, NYC, Phoenix Art Mus., Tucson Festival Art, Talisman Gallery, Bartlesville, Okla., Exhibiting Artists Fedn., Poultney, Vt., Des Moines Art Center, Joslyn Mus. Art, Omaha, Lagerquist Gallery, Atlanta, Desert Art Source Gallery, Palm Desert, Calif., Desert Pleine Air Show, La Quinta, Calif., San Diego, NAMTA Art Show, San Francisco, 1995, Christian Art Show Jubilee 2000, 04, Fallbrook, Calif., Pleine Air San Diego/Calif. Art Club, La Quinta Festival, 2000, Eagle Gallery, La Jolla, Calif., Encouragment Gallery, Fallbrook, Calif., Show Case Houses, Pasadena, Rancho Santa Fe, Calif., 1995, 96, Palm Springs Paradise, 2000, San Diego, 97, 98, 99, French Gallery, Fallbrook, 2005, 07, Insides Open Art Studio Tour, Fallbrook, 2008, Reflection Gallery, Santa Fe, N.Max., 2009; represented in permanent collections, Albertina Museum, Vienna, Kunstmus., Basel, Switzerland, Bibliothèque National, Paris, Los Angeles County Mus., Simpson Coll., Phoenix Art Mus., Ariz. State collection, Graphische Bundes Versuchsanstalt, Vienna, Austria, Equitable ns. Co., Des Moines, also pvt. collections, works include stained glass windows, Meth. Ch., Perry, Iowa.; works reproduced Applause mag, 1971, New Woman mag, 1974, Artists of Cen. and No. Calif., Vol. II, San Diego Better Homes and Gardens Lifestyles mag., 1995, San Diego Decorating mag., 1995, 98, Pasadena Showcase House Design Mag., 1995, San Diego Decor and Style, 1996, 97, 98, Sci. of Mind Mag., 1997, Desert Art Scene Mag., 1999-2008; poster artist Vintage Car Show, Fallbrook, 2002-04, Stop Granite Quarry, Rainbow and Temecula, Calif.; signature artist Malabar Homes, 2007; commd. J.D. Properties, Stockton, Calif., 2007. Recipient 1st prize So. Calif. Expn. Art, Del Mar, 1984, 1st Prize San Diego State Fair, Best of Show, selected for Sacramento State Fair, 2005, 1st Prize, 3rd Prize, Hon. Ment., 2006, 2nd Prize, 3rd Prize, 2 Hon. Merit. 2007, 1 2nd prize, 1 Hon. Merit, 2009, 1st Prize, 2 3rd Prizes, 4 Hon. Ment. 2008, Fallbrook Art Assoc. Expn. 1st Prize 2000, 1st Prize, Best of Show 2003, 2na Prize 2006, Internat. Invit. Grand Nat. Art Show, Cow Palace, San Francisco, Calif. Best of Show, 2008. others; featured in Am. Artist mag. Oct. 1993, San Diego Decor and Style mag. June 2005; named Paint America 2nd Mini 50 Paint The Pks. Nat. Show, 2007, Top Mini 50, 2009 Mem. Calif. Art Club, Oil Painters Am. Home and Office: 5555 8th St Fallbrook CA 92028-9619 Personal E-mail: jackragland@sbcglobal.net.

RAGLAND, KATHRYN MARIE, dancer, educator; b. Lakewood, Ohio, Nov. 22, 1948; d. Earl Albert and Alice Maxine (Outzs) R.; m. Donald Glen Rubright, Sept. 1, 1973 (div. 1977); m. Jack Victor Rutberg, Mar. 9, 1980 (div. 1988); 1 child, Jessica Erin; m. Johnny Anthony Vergona, Oct. 9, 1988; 1 child, David Sean; stepchildren: Danielle Evelyn Vergona, Jonathan Chaunch Vergona. AA, L.A. Valley Coll., 1971; BFA cum laude, U. Utah, 1973, MFA in Dance, 1975; MA in Marriage, Family and Child Counseling/Clin. Child Devel., Pacific Oaks Coll., 1993; EdD in Ednl. Leadership and Change, Fielding Grad. U., 2005. Lic. marriage and family therapist; cert. ednl. specialist, Calif. With Momentum Dance Co., LA, 1975-77; dance spl. pub. sch. LA, 1975-76; instr. Scripps Coll., Claremont, Calif., 1976-77; dir. dance Cypress Coll., 1978-85, instr. dance Calif., 1978—85, Calif., 1986—2002; owner, operator Gymboree, 1985-88. Adj. faculty Antioch U., 1998—, Pacific Oaks Coll., 2006—; faculty facilitator MA-CEL program Fielding Grad. U.; dance instr. Hollywood Little Red Sch. Ho., 1985—89, sch. coun., 1997—, asst. head of sch., 2000—02, Hollywood Schoohouse prin., 2002—04; inclusion specialist Milagro Charter Sch., 2004—; spl. products coord. Learning Ctr., 2004—05; dance instr. McGroarty Arts Ctr., 1992—97, bd. dirs., 1991—92, 1997—2002, LA Odyssey of the Mind, 2002—, coach, 1998—, LA regional dir., 2002, bd. dirs. LA Basin, 2002—07; mem. arts assistance team LA Spt. Schs.; curriculum coun. LA HS Performing Arts, adv. bd., 1986—88, Dance Resource Ctr., 1991—92; intern Julie Ann Singer Ctr. Therapeutic Sch., 1991—92; coord. infant devel. program Santa Clara Valley Child and Family Devel. Ctr., 1992—93; therapist Julia Ann Singer Ctr. Family Stress Program, 1994—95, Verdugo Mental Health Ctr., 1994—; crisis counselor Verdugo Disaster Recovery Program, 1994—95; trainer Project COPE, 1995—96; co-dir. Verdugo Creative Arts Group, 1995—2002; program coord. Atwater Park Ctr., 1996—97; bd. dirs. Highlander Schs., 2007—; bd. mem. Highlander Charter Sch., 2007—. Author/choreographer Kitty Kats, 1986; choreographer: Man of La Mancha, 1976-80, Pippin, 1981, Fiddler on the Roof, 1982, Music Man, 1983, Spanish Suite, 1983, A Funny Thing Happened on the Way to the Forum, 1984, Skaters Edge, 1984, Cartoon, 1984, Urban Primitive, 1985, Cabaret, 1985, Healings, 1987, Cloud Reveries, 1988, Guys and Dolls, 1988, The Lottery, 1988, Cabaret, 1989, Atmos, 1990, Damn Yankees, 1990, Conflict of Interest, 1990; author, dir., choreographer We Saved the Day, 1987, The Visit, 1988, Where the Wild Things Are, 1991, Evening's After Image, 1992, Hair, 1992, South Pacific, 1993, Hello Dolly, 1993, In Search of Quieter Times and Places, 1993, Fiddler on the Roof, 1994, Pajama Game, 1994, Nine, 1994, Testosteroni Baloney, 1994, Guys and Dolls, 1995, Into the Woods, 1995, Alice in Wonderland, 1996, Pirates of Penzance, 1997, Rags, 1997; dir. Courage of the Heart, 1998; dir./choreographer Bye Bye Birdie, 1998; choreographer Mikado, 1998, Sweeney Todd, 1999, Funny Thing Happened on the Way to the Forum, 1999, Jesus Christ Superstar, 1999, Oklahoma, 2000, Rocky Horror Show, 2000, Man of La Mancha, 2001, Joseph and the Amazing Technicolor Dreamcoat, 2001, Cabaret, 2002, Fiddler on the Roof, 2005, Nightmare Before Christmas, 2005. Mem. So. Calif. steering com. Legis. Action Coalition Arts Edn.; den leader Cub Scouts, 1996-2000. Mem. AAHPERD, ASCD, AARP, AERA, ASCD, Dance Resource Ctr., Calif. Dance Educators Assn. (v.p. 1980-82, legis. rep. 1982-86), Calif. Music Educators (legis. com. 1982-86), LA Area Dance Alliance, Faculty Assn. CC, Calif. Assn. Health, Phys. Edn., Recreation and Dance, Calif. Assn. Marriage and Family Therapists, So. Calif. Assn. Edn. Young Children (bd. dirs. South Bay chpt.), Calif. Confedn. Arts, Calif. Learning Disabilities Assn., Calif. Elem. Edn. Assn., Assn. Ednl. Therapists, Learning Disabilities Assn. LA, Calif. Elem. Edn. Assn., Coun, for Exceptional Children, Assn. for Supervision and Curriculum Devel., Phi Delta Kappa. Democrat. Personal E-mail: kmragland@verizon.net. Business E-Mail: k.ragland@pucschools.org.

RAGLAND, ROBERT ALLEN, lawyer; b. Bartlesville, Okla., Apr. 18, 1954; s. Thomas Martin and Joan Ethel (Murphy) R. BA, U. Md., 1976; JD, George Mason Sch. of Law, 1980. Dir. regulatory reform and govt. orgn. Nat. Assn. Mfrs., Washington, 1979-82, asst. v.p. taxation, 1983-86; mgr. congl. rels. The Clorox Co., Oakland, Calif., 1982-83; dir. tax rsch. U.S. C. of C., Washington, 1988-93; v.p., officer Wachovia Bank, 1995—2004; v.p. SunTrust Bank, Orlando, Fla., 2004—05, Fifth Third Bank, Cin., 2006; ptnr. The Ragland Law Firm, Orlando, Fla., 2006—. Chief tax counsel, mng. dir. Nat. Chamber Found., Washington, 1989-93. Author: Transportation Reform, 1980, Employee Stock Ownership Plans, 1989, Taxation of Foreign Source Income, Distributional Impact of Excise Taxes, 1990; editor Taxation of Intercorporate Profits, 1990, Jour. Regulation and Social Costs, 1992-93, Jour. Regulation, 1992-93. Active Boy Scouts Am., Washington, 1967—, bd. dirs. nat. capital area coun.; dep. dir. duPont for Pres., 1987-88; v.p. Nat. Chamber Found. U.S. C. of C., 1989-93, dir., Liz Lerman Dance Exchange, 1993-2001, dir. Our House, Inc., 1988-2000. Republican. Roman Catholic. Home: The Waverly 803 322 E Central Blvd Orlando FL 32801

RAGNARSSON, KRISTJAN TOMAS, physiatrist; b. Reykjavik, Iceland, Nov. 15, 1943; s. Ragnar T. and Vigdis (Schram) Arnason; m. Hrafnhildur Agustsdottir; children: Hildur Schmidt, Vigdis Boulton, Thorunn Zimmermann, Kristin. BA, U. of Iceland, Reykjavik, 1963; MD, U. Iceland, Reykjavik, 1966. Diplomate Am. Bd. Phys. Medicine and Rehab. 1976. Gen. practitioner Dist. Pub. Health, Reykjavik, Iceland, 1969—70; instr. NYU, New York, 1973—79; lectr. rehab. medicine U. Iceland, Reykjavik, Iceland, 1976; instr. NYU Med. Ctr., New York, 1973—79, asst. prof. rehab. medicine, 1976—82, assoc. prof., 1982—86; Lucy G. Moses prof., chmn. dept. rehab. medicine Mt. Sinai Sch. Medicine, New York, 1986—. Bd. dirs. World Rehab. Fund, NYC, 1993—; pres. Med. Bd. Mt. Sinai Hosp., 1995—97; chair, Bd. Govs. Faculty Practice Assn. Mt. Sinai Sch. Medicine, 1997—2003; chmn. NIH Consensus Devel. Conf. Panel on Rehab. of Persons with Traumatic Brain Injury, 1997—99. Contbr. articles to profl. jours., chpts. to books. Pres. bd. trustees Am. Scandinavian Found., NYC, 2000—03; bd. dirs. Icelandic Am. Soc. N.Y., NYC, 1977—85. Decorated Knights Cross of the Icelandic Order of the Falcon Pres. of Iceland; recipient Dr. Howard A. Rusk Humanitarian award, World Rehab. Fund, 1995, Outstanding Faculty award, Com. of 1000 Mt. Sinai Med. Ctr., 1997, The Jacobi Medallion, Alumni Ass. of Mt. Sinai Hosp., 1998, Lifetime Achievement award, ASIA, 2002, Excellence in Tchg. award, N.J. Med. Sch., 2002, Ellis Island medal of honor, 2004; grantee Mt. Sinai Spinal Cord Injury Model System grantee, Nat. Inst. on Disability and Rehab. Rsch., 1990—. Mem.: Am. Acad. Phys. Medicine and Rehab. (chmn. mktg. task force 1995—98), Assn. of Acad. Physiatrists (chmn. legis. affairs com. 1995—2003, sec. 2003), Am. Paraplegia Soc. (bd. dirs. 1997—99), Am. Spinal Injury Assn. (pres. 1993—95, Disting. Svc. award 1995), Am. Congress of Rehab. Medicine (Disting. Mem. Svc. award 1993), Icelandic Am. C. of C. (N.Y.C.), Am. Scandinavian Soc. N.Y. Office: Mt Sinai Med Ctr Box 1240 1425 Madison Ave New York NY 10029 Office Phone: 212-659-9340.*

RAGO, DOROTHY ASHTON, retired elementary school educator; b. NYC, Oct. 10, 1925; d. Thomas Percy and Isabel (Seddon) Ashton; divorced, 1958; 1 child, Thomas Ashton. BA, Wellesley Coll., 1946; MA, Columbia U., 1964. Cert. early childhood edn. tchr., N.Y. Editor Alford Baby Group mags., NYC, 1948-52; kindergarten tchr. N.Y.C. Bd. Edn., 1964-86, ret., 1986. Mem. vestry Chapel of St. John, Saunderstown, R.I., 1988-91; mem. Human Rights Com., North Kingstown, R.I., 1988-94; treas. Pettaquamscutt Hist. Soc., 1991-98; mem. exec. bd. Friends of Oceanography/GSO-URI, 1997-2001. Mem. South County Mus., Gilbert Stuart Mus., South County Women's Club, Saunderstown Yacht Club, R.I. Wellesley Club. Episcopalian. Avocations: local history, hand bell ringing.

RAGON, ROBERT RONALD, clergyman; b. Flintstone, Ga., Sept. 10, 1939; s. Robert Emmett and Frances Cora (Stoner) R.; m. Judith Ann Ward, Apr. 27, 1962; children: Ronald Russell, Regina Renee. BS, U. Chattanooga, 1962; BDiv, MDiv, Columbia Theol. Sem., Decatur, Ga., 1967. Ordained to ministry Presbyn. Ch., 1967. Pastor Trion (Ga.) Presbyn. Ch., 1967-72; dir., pastor Chattooga County Presbyn. Ministries, Trion, 1971-72; pastor Brainerd Presbyn. Ch., Chattanooga, 1972—2007. Moderator Knoxville Presbytery, 1979-80; founder An Order of Slaves of Christ, Chattanooga, 1970; stated clk. Presbytery of S.E., 1990-93, moderator, 1995-96, founding bishop Christian Family Ch., 2009. Author: Covenant Agreement: O.S.C., 1970, The Journey, 1990. Trustee King Coll., Bristol, Tenn., 1983-86. Mem. Masons (Ga. chaplain 1980), KT (sec. 1991), Shriners. Republican. Presbyterian. Avocation: investments. Home: 4229 Happy Valley Rd Flintstone GA 30725-2222 Personal E-mail: ragonr@bellsouth.net.

RAGONE, CAROL DIANE, horticulturist, ethnobotanist; b. Roanoke, Va., Dec. 28, 1953; d. Peter Joseph and Drucilla F. (Romine). BS, Va. Poly. Inst., 1977; MS, U. Hawaii, Honolulu, 1984, PhD, 1991. Dir. Breadfruit Inst. Nat. Tropical Bot. Garden, Kalaheo, Hawaii, 2003—. Author: (booklet) Breadfruit Varieties Pacific Atolls, 1988, Breadfruit: Promoting the Conservation and Use of Underutilized and Neglected Crops, 1997. Pres. grad. student orgn. U. Hawaii, 1982, treas. Soc. Econ. Botant, 2003-08. East West Ctr. fellow, 1988; named Scholar of Yr., Coll. Tropical Agriculture, U. Hawaii/ARC Found., 1987. Mem. Am. Inst. Biol. Sci., Am. Soc. Horticultural Sci., Soc. Econ. Botany (Fulling award 1989), Pacific Sci. Assn., Sigma Xi. Achievements include research in collection and evaluation of breadfruit in the Pacific Islands, conservation of native Hawaiian plants, horticultural uses of native Hawaiian plants. Office: Nat Tropical Bot Garden 3530 Papalina Rd Kalaheo HI 96741 Office Phone: 808-332-7324.

RAGONE, DAVID VINCENT, former university president; b. NYC, May 16, 1930; s. Armando Frederick and Mary (Napier) R.; m. Katherine H. Spaulding, Dec. 18, 1954; children: Christine M., Peter V. BS, MIT, 1951, MS, 1952, DSc, 1953. Asst. prof. chem. and metall. engring. U. Mich., Ann Arbor, 1953-57, assoc. prof., 1957-61, prof., 1961-62; asst. dir. John J. Hopkins Lab. for Pure and Applied Sci., also chmn. metallurgy dept. Gen. Atomic divsn. Gen. Dynamics, La Jolla, 1962-67; Alcoa prof. metallurgy Carnegie-Mellon U., Pitts., 1967-69, assoc. dean Sch. Urban and Pub. Affairs, 1969-70; dean Thayer Sch. Engring. Dartmouth Coll., 1970-72; dean Coll. Engring. U. Mich., 1972-80; pres. Case Western Res. U., Cleve., 1980-87; vis. prof., dept. materials sci. and engring. MIT, Cambridge, 1987-88, sr. lectr. dept. materials sci. and engring., 1988-98; gen. ptnr. Ampersand Ventures, 1988-92, ptnr., 1992—2005. Mem. Nat. Sci. Bd., 1978-84; mem. tech adv. bd. US Dept. Commerce, 1967-75; chmn. adv. com. advanced auto power systems Coun. on Environ. Quality, 1971-75; trustee Henry Luce Found. Named Outstanding Young Engr., Engring. Soc. Detroit, 1957. Mem. Univ. Club (NYC), Longwood Cricket Club (Boston), Sigma Xi, Tau Beta Pi. Home: 10 Longwood Dr Apt 368 Westwood MA 02090-1144 Home Phone: 781-326-4866. Business E-Mail: ragone@mit.edu.

RAGOSTA, MICHAEL, cardiologist; b. Providence, Nov. 10, 1959; s. Michele and Angela E. Ragosta; m. Kiyoko Asao-Ragosta, Apr. 16, 1988; children: Nicholas Hiroshi, Anthony Takashi, Sachiko Angela. BS, U. RI, Kingston, 1981; MD, Brown U., Providence, 1985. Cert. in internal medicine ABIM, 1988, in cardiovascular diseases 1991, in interventional cardiology 2000. Asst. prof. medicine U. Pitts., 1993—94; assoc. prof. medicine U. Va., Charlottesville, 1994—, dir. cardiac catheterization labs. Health Sys., 2005—08. Author: (textbook) Clinical Hemodynamics. Mem. SSJ Judo, Charlottesville, 2006—08. Office: Univ Va Cardiology Divsn Hospital Dr Charlottesville VA 22908

RAHAL, JAMES JOSEPH, JR., medical educator; b. Boston, Oct. 14, 1933; AB cum laude, Harvard Coll., 1955; MD cum laude, Tufts U., 1959. Bd. cert. Am. Bd. Internal Medicine, Am. Bd. Infectious Diseases. Intern, asst. resident in medicine 2d (Cornell) med. divsn. Bellevue Hosp., NYC, 1959-61; sr. resident in medicine New Eng. Med. Ctr. Hosps., 1961-62, chief resident in infectious diseases, 1963-64, USPHS trainee in infectious diseases, 1962-63, 64-65, asst. physician dept. medicine and infectious disease svc., 1965-69; from instr. to sr. instr. to asst. prof. medicine Tufts U. Sch. Medicine, 1965-69; from asst. prof. medicine to assoc. prof. medicine NYU Sch. Medicine, 1969-89; chief divsn. infectious disease Manhattan VA Med. Ctr., 1969-86; chief infectious diseases sect. N.Y. Infirmary Beekman Downtown Hosp., 1986-88; dir. infectious disease sect. N.Y. Hosp. Med. Ctr. Queens (formerly Booth Meml. Med. Ctr.), 1988—; from assoc. prof. to prof. medicine Albert Einstein Coll. Medicine, 1988-94; from clin. prof. medicine to prof. medicine Weill Coll. Medicine, Cornell U., 1994—. Vis. investigator dept. biochemistry Pub. Health Rsch. Inst. of City of N.Y., 1969-70; mem. adv. expert com. on infectious disease control N.Y.C. Dept. Health, 1974-85; mem. VA adv. com. on infectious disease VA Cen. Office, Washington, 1976-81; mem. subcom. on access to therapeutic trials N.Y. State AIDS Inst., 1987-88; mem. data and safety monitoring bd. for AIDS treatment evaluation units NIH, 1988-96; chmn. med. adv. coun. N.Y. State Dept. of Health AIDS Inst.: AIDS Drug Assistance Program, 1991-93; mem. steering com. and chmn. clin. subcom. N.Y. State Dept. of Health AIDS Inst.: HIV Uninsured Care Programs, 1993—; lectr. in field. Mem. editl. bd. Microbial Drug Resistance, Current Treatment Options in Infectious Diseases, Infectious Disease News; editl. reviewer: New Eng. Jour. Medicine, Jour. AMA, Annals of Internal Medicine, Archives of Internal Medicine, Jour. Infectious Diseases, Clin. Infectious Diseases, The Med. Letter; contbr. numerous articles to profl. publs., including New Eng. Jour. Medicine, Sci., Current Therapy. Rsch. fellow Med. Found. Boston, 1966-68. Fellow ACP (mem. AIDS subcom. of health and pub. policy com. N.Y. state chpt. 1988), Infectious Disease Soc. Am.; mem. AAAS, Am. Soc. for Microbiology, Am. Fedn. for Clin. Rsch., N.Y. Soc. Infectious Diseases (pres. 1996-97), Alpha Omega Alpha. Address: 314 W 77th St Apt 8B New York NY 10024-6868 Office: New York Hosp Med Ctr Queens 56-45 Main St Flushing NY 11355 Home Phone: 212-799-0711; Office Phone: 718-670-1525. Business E-Mail: jjr9002@nyp.org.

RAHAL, ROBERT WOODWARD (BOBBY RAHAL), automotive company and race car team executive, retired professional race car driver; b. Medina, Ohio, Jan. 10, 1953; s. Michael G. and Barbara (Woodward) R.; m. Deborah Ann Kuhl, Nov. 16, 1980; children: Michaela, Jarrad, Graham, Samantha. BA in History, Denison U., Granville, Ohio, 1975. Profl. race car driver Truesports, 1982—88, Kraco, 1989, Galles-Kraco, 1990—91, Rahal-Hogan Racing, 1992—95, Team Rahal, 1996—98; ret., 1998; co-owner Rahal/Hogan Racing, 1992—96, Rahal Letterman Racing (formerly Team Rahal), Dublin, Ohio, 1996—; CEO Jaguar Racing, Ford Motor Co., Europe, 2000; interim pres., CEO Championship Auto Racing Teams (CART), 2000, bd. dirs., Road America; owner Bobby Rahal Automotive Group. 1st pl. Indpls. 500 Indpls. Motor Speedway, 1986. Hon. chmn. Easter Seals Ctrl. Ohio, Columbus; chmn. Children's Hosp., Columbus; trustee Columbus Zoo; bd. dirs. Huntington Nat. Bank, Bobby Rahal Found. Named CART Rookie or Yr., 1982, CART Series Champion, 1986—87, 1992; named to Internat. Motorsports Hall of Fame, 1994, Motor Sports Hall of Fame America, 2004. Achievements include being the third man to win the Indy 500 as a driver (1986) and an owner (2004), along with Parnelli Jones and A.J. Foyt. Avocations: golf, antiques, antique cars, reading. Office: Rahal Letterman Racing PO Box 39 Hilliard OH 43026-0039

RAHALL, NICK JOE, II, (NICK RAHALL), United States Representative from West Virginia; b. Beckley, W.Va., May 20, 1949; s. Joe and Alice Rahall; m. Melinda Ross; children: Rebecca Ashley, Nick Joe III, Suzanne Nicole. BA, Duke U., Durham, NC, 1971. Asst. to Senator Robert C. Byrd US Senate, 1971-74; sales rep. Sta. WWNR, Beckley, 1974; pres. Mountaineer Travel Co., Beckley, 1975-77, W.Va. Broadcasting, 1980; mem. US Congress from 4th W.Va. dist., 1977—93, US Congress from 3rd W.Va. dist., 1993—, US House Transp. & Infrastructure Com.; chmn. US House Nat. Resources Com., 2007—. Bd. dirs. Rahall Comm. Corp.; mem. US Constn. Bicentennial Commn., Mo. Mem. profl. adv. bd. Alsac-St. Jude Children's Rsch. Hosp.; chmn. March of Dimes, W.Va., 1979; del. Dem. Nat. Conv., 1972, 1974, 1978, 1980, 1984, 1988, 1992, 1996. Recipient Achievement award, Logan Cripple Children Soc., 1978, Citizenship award, KC, 1978, Disting. Svc. award, Am. Fedn. Govt. Employees W.Va., 1984, Seneca award, Sierra Club, 1988, River Conservation award, Am. River Assn., 1988; named Young Man of Yr., Beckley Jaycees, 1972, Coal Man of Yr., Coal Industry News, 1979, Young Dem. of Yr., Dem. Nat. Conv., 1980, Outfitter of Yr., Profl. Outfitters, 1987, Son of Yr., W.Va. Soc. of Washington, 1996; named an Outstanding Young Man in W.Va., W.Va. Jaycees, 1977. Mem.: NAACP, NRA (life), Shriners, Elks, Masons (33rd degree), Moose. Democrat. Presbyterian. Office: US Congress 2307 Rayburn House Office Bldg Washington DC 20515-4803 also: 220 Dingess St Logan WV 25601 Office Phone: 202-225-3452. Business E-Mail: nrahall@mail.house.gov.*

RAHARINAIVO, ANDRÉ LÉON, research scientist, educator; b. Tananarive, Madagascar, Sept. 1, 1940; arrived in France, 1954; s. Ignace Léon and Marthe (Rasoazanamalala) R.; m. Christiane Martine Laurent, May 7, 1966 (div. June 1994); 1 child, Jacques Yves. Engr. mining and metallurgy, Ecole des Mines, Nancy, France, 1964; degree superior scientific studies, U. Nancy, France, 1964; PhD, U. Compiegne, France, 1982. Cert. engr. Head sect. Lab. Ctrl. Ponts et Chaussées, Paris, 1971-80, dep. head dept., 1980-83, sec. sci. coun., 1983-91, rsch. mgr., 1991—2005; cons. Cefracor, 2005—. Author: Fracture Mechanics and Mechanisms, 1990; patentee in field. Capt. Equipment, 1967-69, France. Mem. Ctr. Français Anticorrosion, Nat. Assn. Corrosion Engrs. Avocation: singing gospel music. Home: 378 rue de Vaugirard F-75015 Paris France

RAHER, PATRICK MICHAEL, lawyer; b. Kalamazoo, June 15, 1947; BBA, U. Notre Dame, 1969; JD, Georgetown U., 1972. Bar: Va. 1972, D.C. 1973. Prof. legal rsch. and creditors rights Internat. Sch. Law, Washington, 1972-75; law clk. to Hon. Roger Robb U.S. Ct. Appeals, Washington, 1972-73; ptnr. Hogan & Hartson LLP, Washington, environ. practice group dir. Vice chair DC Jud. Disabilities and Tenure Commn., 1986-92; mem. EPA Clean Air Act Adv. Com., 1994—. Mem. ABA, DC Bar. Office: Hogan & Hartson LLP Columbia Sq 555 13th St NW 13E-300 Washington DC 20004-1161 Office Phone: 202-637-5682. Office Fax: 202-637-5910. Business E-Mail: pmraher@hhlaw.com.

RAHIMI, BABAK, literature and language professor; s. Gholam Hussainn Rahimi and Nasrin Katuzim; m. Nasi Eizady, Aug. 29, 2006. PhD, European U. Inst., Florence, Italy, 2004. Asst. prof. U. Calif. San Diego, La Jolla, 2005—08. Sr. fellow US Inst. Peace, Washington, 2005—06. Educator Cmty. Orgns., San Diego, 2005—08. Independent. Avocations: poetry, travel, reading. Office: Univ Calif San Diego 9500 Gilman Dr La Jolla CA 92093-0410 Office Fax: 858-534-2147. Personal E-mail: brahimi77@yahoo.com.

RAHMAN, ABDUR, neuroscientist, educator; married. PhD, Cornell U., Ithaca, NY, 1995. Rsch. scientist NYS IBR, Staten Island, 2001—05; asst. prof. Kuwait U., 2005—. Mem.: Soc. Neuroscience. Achievements include research in kynurinine pathway for alzherimer's disease. Avocations: travel, field hockey, swimming. Office: Kuwait Univ Coll Women Dept Family Sci Kuwait 13060 Kuwait Office Fax: 965 2251 3929. Business E-Mail: abdur_rahman31@hotmail.com.

RAHMAN, AHMAD A., history professor, writer; s. James Douglass and Catherine Ann Irwin; m. Tammy Latrice Armstrong; children: Khalil Smith, Sundiata Hamadi, Askia Ahmad children: Saidah Thandiwe. PhD, U. Mich., Ann Arbor, 1999. History prof. U. Mich., Dearborn, 2003—; mem. Mich. Coun. Humanities, Mich., 2006—. Mem. Com. Against Police Brutality, Detroit, 2003. Author: (book) The Regime Change of Kwame Nkrumah: Epic Heroism in Africa and the Diaspora. Student advisor Amnesty Internat., Dearborn, Mich., 2007. King-Chavez-Parks fellowship, U. Mich., 2001. Master: Prince Hall Masons. Independent. Achievements include research in history of the black panther party. Avocations: yoga, meditation. Office: Univ Mich-Dearborn 4901 Evergreen Rd Dearborn MI 48128 Personal E-mail: ahmrah@msn.com.

RAHMAN, ATEEQUR, pharmacist, educator; MBA, Nebr. La. U., 1999; PhD, U. La., Monroe, 2000. Cert. pharmacist Bd. Pharmacy, 2008. Prof. Shenandoah U., Winchester, Va., 2004—. Mem.: Bus. and Health Adminstrn. Assn. (Outstanding Leadership award 2007). Office: Pharmacy Sch Shenandoah Univ 1460 University Dr Winchester VA 22602 Business E-Mail: arahman@su.edu.

RAHMAN, GAZIUR, finance educator; b. Comilla, Bangladesh, Dec. 9, 1951; s. Fazlur and Rezia Rahman; m. Diana Sue Vaughn, July 5, 1984; children: Penny Jean Hutchens, Carrie Lynn Simpson. BA with honors, U. Dhaka, Bangladesh, 1972, MA with honors, 1974; MBA, U. Maine, Orono, 1977. Mgr. negotiator HOQSONS Export-Import, Dhaka, 1972—74; instr. bus., economics Lincoln Trail Coll., Robinson, Ill., 1977—. Chairperson, higher edn. coun. Ill. Edn. Assn., Springfield, 2001—07, bd. dirs., 2001—07, Midwest Inst. Intercultural Internat. Edn., Kalamazoo, 2002—04. Grassroots activist NEA, Washington, 2001—08. Mem.: Midwest Economics Assn., Acient Free and Accepted Masons. Avocations: travel, sports. Office: Lincoln Trail Coll 11220 State Hwy 1 Robinson IL 62454 Business E-Mail: rahmang@iecc.edu.

RAHMAN, JACQUELYN, language educator, researcher, director; PhD in Linguistics, Stanford U., Palo Alto, Calif., 2004. Prof., dir. linguistics program Miami U., Oxford, Ohio, 2004—. Contbr. chapters to books, articles to numerous profl. jours. Fellow, AAUW, 2002, fellowship, Spencer Found., 2003, Heanon Wilkins fellowship, Miami U., 2004—06. Mem.: Internat. Soc. Humor Studies, Am. Dialect Soc., Linguistic Soc. America (mem, com. ethnic diversity linguistics exec. bd. 2009—). Achievements include research in first linguistic studies of stand-up comedy, language of the African American middle-class and Caribbean Creole Language. Office: Miami Univ 327 Bachelor Hall Oxford OH 45056 Business E-Mail: rahmanj@muohio.edu.

RAHMAN, MUHAMMAD ABDUR, mechanical engineer; b. Sylhet, Assam, India, Mar. 1, 1930; came to U.S., 1950; s. Haji Sajjad Ali Khan and Momotaj Khanom. BSME, U. Toledo, 1953, MSME, 1968; PhD in Engring., Calif. Coast U., 1985. Registered profl. engr., Calif. Mech. design engr. various cons. firms, LA, 1955-61; aerospace engr. Douglas Aircraft Co., Santa Monica, Calif., 1962-63, N.Am. Aviation, Inc., LA, 1963-64, NASA Manned Spacecraft Ctr. Gemini & Apollo Program Office, Houston, 1964-70; safety engr. U.S. Dept. Labor, OSHA, Washington, 1975-86; invention researcher Arlington, Va., 1987—. Contbr. articles to profl. jours. Mem. N.Y. Acad. Scis. Democrat. Muslim. Achievements include patent for solar energy collector, supersonic MHD generator system; copyrights for hypothesis on unified field theory and creation of the universe, on the gravitoenergy in the creation of cosmic matters in the space, on the mechanism of superconductivity, a note of caution for superconductivity in reference to permeability and permitivity, concentration on suggesting methods to build superconductors and biomedical engineering instrumentation for cancer in particular, others. Home and Office: 1805 Crystal Dr Apt 1013 Arlington VA 22202-4407

RAHMAN, NURUR, astrophysicist; s. J. K. M. Waliur and Nurjahan Rahman. PhD, U. Kans., Lawrence, 2004. NASA postdoc. fellow JPL, Caltech, Pasadena, Calif., 2005—07; postdoc rsch. fellow U. Sussex, Brighton, England, 2007—08; postdoc. rsch. assoc. U. Md., Coll. Pk., 2008—. Mem.: Am. Astron. Soc. Office: Dept Astronomy Univ Md College Park MD 20742 Office Fax: 301-314-9067. Business E-Mail: nurur@astro.umd.edu.

RAHMAN, RAFIQ UR, oncologist, educator; b. Mirali, Pakistan, Mar. 3, 1957; came to U.S., 1985; s. Rakhman and Bibi (Sana) Gul; m. Shamim Ara Bangash; children: Maryam, Hassan, Haider. BS, MB, U. Peshawar, Pakistan, 1980. Bd. cert. internal medicine, med. oncology, hematology; lic. physician Pa., Ala., Ky. House officer in internal medicine Khyber Tchg. Hosp.-U. Peshawar, 1980-81, house officer in gen. surgery, 1981, jr. registrar med. ICU, 1983-84; jr. registrar internal medicine Khyber Tchg. Hosp., 1981-82; sr. registrar internal medicine Khyber Tchg. Hosp.-Lady Reading Hosp. & Postgrad. Inst., Peshawar, 1984-85; Audrey Meyer Mars fellow in med. oncology Roswell Park Cancer Inst., Buffalo, 1985-86; resident in internal medicine SUNY-Buffalo Gen. Hosp.-Erie County Med. Ctr.-VA Med. Ctr., 1986-88; chief resident in internal medicine SUNY-Buffalo-Erie County Med. Ctr., 1988; fellow in hematology and med. oncology SUNY-Buffalo-Roswell Park Cancer Inst., 1989-90; hematologist, med. oncologist Daniel Boone Clinic and Harlan A.R.H., 1991-92; clin. asst. prof. medicine U. Ky., 1991—; attending physician, hematology, med. oncologist Hardin Meml. Hosp., Elizabethtown, Ky., 1993—, chief medicine, 1996, pres.-elect med. staff, 2001—02, pres. med. staff, 2002—03. Tchr. med. students Med. Sch., SUNY; participant CALGB protocol studies Roswell Park Cancer Inst., investigator. Editor English sect. Cenna mag.; contbr. articles to profl. jours. Founder Cmty. Uplift Program, Pakistan; founding dir. Pakistan Human Devel. Fund, Pakistan Am. Leadership Ctr., Washington. Mem.: Assn. Pakistan Physicians Ky. and Ind. (pres. 2002—03), Ky. Med. Assn. Avocations: travel, aeromodeling, swimming, studying political science and history. Home: 400 Briarwood Cir Elizabethtown KY 42701-6915 Office: 1107 Woodland Dr Ste 105 Elizabethtown KY 42701-2789 Home Phone: 270-769-2003; Office Phone: 270-769-6665. Personal E-mail: rahmanrafiq@hotmail.com.

RAHMAN, SALEH MAHMUDUR, medical educator; s. Afaz Uddin Sarkar and Feroza Begum; m. Selina Rahman, Dec. 10, 1992; children: Tishian Mahmud, Renoa Mahmud. MBBS, Sir Salimullah Med. Coll., Dhaka, Bangladesh, 1992; MPH, Harvard U., Boston, 1997; PhD, U. Ala., Birmingham, 2001. Lic. Joslin Health Behavior Diabetes Ctr., Harvard Med. Sch., 1995. Cons. ACIPCO, Birmingham, Ala., 1999—2000; asst. prof. NW Ohio Consortium Pub. Health, Bowling Green, Ohio, 2000—04; adj. asst. prof. Med. U. Ohio, Toledo, 2000—04, cons., co-investigator, 2001—02; asst. prof. Fla. A&M U., Tallahassee, 2004—. Author: (books) Social Marketing and Community Based Participatory Research, 2002; reviewer Jour. Behavioral Services & Research, 2003—, Ethnicity and Diseases, 2003—, Cancer Causes and Control, 2004—, Jour. Health Disparities Research & Practice, 2006; contbr. articles to profl. jours. Recipient Nat. Acad. Children award, Nat. Acad. for Children, Bangladesh, 1989, Our Pride award, Bangladesh Am. Found. Inc., 2005, Outstanding Achievement award, Alabama Power Found., B award, ENHR; grantee Rsch. grant, Bowling Green State U., 2003, NIH-NCMHD, 2004—, 2005—. Mem.: APHA (pub. health edn. & health promotion workgrp. 2006, Early Career award 2006), Bangladesh Med. Assn. N.Am., Am. Assn. Diabetes Educators, European Assn. Study Diabetes, Internat. Diabetes Fedn., South Asian HIV Network (steering com. 2000—05). Office: Fla A&M Univ COPPS IPH 209-A FSH Sci Rsch Ctr Tallahassee FL 32307 Office Fax: 850-599-8830; Home Fax: 850-599-8830. Business E-Mail: saleh_rahman_97@post.harvard.edu, saleh.rahman@famu.edu.

RAHMAN, SHAFIQUR, neuropharmacologist, scientist, professor, editor; b. Faridgonj, Chandpur, Bangladesh, Jan. 1, 1963; d. Mohammad Ali and Momotaj Begum; m. Moursheda Rahman, May 24, 1993; 2 children, Zarin and Kashfia. BSc with honors, Dhaka U., Bangladesh, 1985, MSc, 1987; PhD, Meml. U., Newfoundland, Can., 1995. Lectr. Jahangirnagar U., Dhaka, 1988—93, asst. prof., 1993—97, assoc. prof., 1997—98; rsch. assoc. Ind. U. Sch. Medicine, Indpls., 1998—2001; scientist Ctr. Addiction Mental Health, 2001—04; asst. prof. dept. psychiatry and neurosci. U. Toronto, Canada, 2002—04; sr. rsch. sci. Ctr. Drug Abuse Rsch. Translation, U. Ky., 2005—07; assoc. prof., scientist Coll. Pharmacy, SD State U., Brookings, SD, 2008—. Cons. Inst. Psychiat. Rsch., Indpls., 1998—; rschr., investigator in field.editor Neurosci. Pharmacology Jours., Jour. Drug Discovery Therapeutics, Jour. CNS Neurol. Disorder, Drug Targets. Contbr. articles to profl. jours.; investigator, rschr. for profl. jour. articles. Active Lions Club Dhaka Topekhana, 1984-88, ADHUNIK, Dhaka, 1989-98. Recipient Chancellor and Pres. Bangladesh, Dhaka, 1987, rsch. grant, Ctr. Drug Addiction and Mental Health, Toronto, Can., 2001, U. Toronto, Can., 2001, Nat. Inst. on Drug Abuse, US, 2002, Canadian Inst. Health Rsch., 2003; vis. scientist rsch. grantee Ind. U. Sch. Medicine, 1998; Meml. Rsch. fellow Meml. U., Newfoundland, 1990, Clark Found. Postdoctoral fellow Clarke Inst. Psychiatry, U. Toronto, Can., 1995. Mem. Internat. Brain Rsch. Orgn., Soc. for Neurosci., Am. Soc. Pharmacology Expert Therpeutics, Soc. Rsch. Nicotine and Tobacco, Canadian Ctr. of Substance Abuse, Am. ASSO Coll. Pharmacy, Am. ASSO Pharmacist Scientist, Am. Soc. Neurochemistry. Avocations: writing, reading, travel. Office: SD State Univ Coll Pharmacy Dept Pharm Scis 1 Administration Ln Box 2202C Brookings SD 57007 Office Phone: 605-688-4239. Business E-Mail: shafiqur.rahman@sdstate.edu.

RAHMAN, YUEH-ERH, biologist; b. Kwangtung, China, June 10, 1928; came to U.S., 1960; d. Khon and Kwei-Phan (Chan) Li; m. Aneesur Rahman, Nov. 3, 1956; 1 dau., Aneesa. BS, U. Paris, 1950; MD magna cum laude, U. Louvain, Belgium, 1956. Clin. and postdoctoral research fellow Louvain U., 1956-60; mem. staff Argonne (Ill.) Nat. Lab., 1960-72, biologist, 1972-81, sr. biologist, 1981-85; prof. pharmaceutics Coll. Pharmacy, U. Minn., Mpls., 1985—2002, prof. emeritus, 2002—, dir. grad. studies, pharmaceutics, 1989-92, head dept. pharmaceutics, 1991-96, 97-98. Vis. scientist State U. Utrecht, Netherlands, 1968-69; adj. prof. No. Ill. U., DeKalb, 1971-85; cons. NIH.; Mem. com. of rev. group, div. research grants NIH, 1979-83 Author; patentee in field. Recipient IR-100 award, 1976; grantee Nat. Cancer Inst., Nat. Inst. Arthritis, Metabolic and Digestive Diseases. Fellow Am. Assn. Pharm. Scientists; mem. AAAS, Am. Soc. Cell Biology, N.Y. Acad. Scis., Radiation Rsch. Soc., Assn. for Women in Sci. (1st pres. Chgo. area chpt. 1978-79). Unitarian Universalist. Home: 939 Coast Blvd Unit 6G La Jolla CA 92037-4115

RAHMAN, ZIA-UR, research scientist; b. Karachi, Pakistan, Jan. 19, 1962; came to the U.S., 1981; s. Abdul Rahman and Arifa (Khatoon) Siddiqi; m. Katherine Irene Miner, June 23, 1988; children: Haroun Aaron, Kamran Patrick Miner, Noor Joseph Miner. AB in Physics and Math, Ripon Coll., 1984; MSEE, U. Va., 1986, PhD in Elec. Engring., 1989. Rsch. scientist Sci. and Tech. Corp., NASA Langley, Hampton, Va., 1989-96; rsch. asst. prof. Coll. William and Mary, Williamsburg, Va., 1996—. V.p. R&D TruView Imaging Co., Hampton, 1996—. Author: Visual Communication: An Information, 1997. Active PTA, Williamsburg, 1996. Named Outstanding Young Alumnus, Ripon Coll., 1994. Mem. IEEE, SPIE, Phi Beta Kappa, Sigma Pi Sigma, Tau Beta Pi. Achievements include discovery of a new method for digital image enhancement (patent pending). Office: Coll William and Mary Dept Computer Sci PO Box 8795 Williamsburg VA 23187-8795

RAHMANDAD, HAZHIR, engineering educator; b. Tehran, Iran, Sept. 9, 1977; s. Ahmad Rahmandad and Mahin Moradi. BS in Indsl. Engring., Sharif U. Tech., Tehran, Iran, 2000; PhD, MIT, Cambridge, Mass., 2005. Post-doctoral assoc. MIT, Cambridge, 2005—06; asst prof. indsl. sys. engring. Va. Tech. U., 2006—. Founding mem., mem. of exec. bd. Farsi Teach Net, Cambridge, Mass., 2005—; mgmt. cons. Hadi Bargh Co., Tehran, 1999. Mem. of coun. Iranian Assn. of Boston, 2004—05. Recipient Gold Medal in Chemistry Olympiad, Internat. Chemistry Olympiad, 1996, Best Paper award, Iranian Indsl. Engring. Conf., 1999; fellow Wilson Fund fellow, MIT, 2000—05, Presdl. Grad. fellow, 2000—01; scholar Bridges of Hope award and scholar, Iranian Am. Tech. Coun., 2005. Mem.: Internat. Assn. Iranian Mgrs. (founding mem., bd. dirs.), Iranian Studies Group (founding mem., exec. bd.), INFORMS, Acad. of Mgmt., Sys. Dynamics Soc. (assoc.). Achievements include research in Effect of time delays on organizational learning. Explores how organizations fail to learn useful lessons from their experiences because of the delays inherent between actions and results; Dynamics of multiple release product develoment: analysis of traps that hinder successful product development; Examining the effects of network structure and heterogeneity in the dynamics of disease diffusion; design of Design of an online community to produce and use teaching material. Office: Va Tech No Va Ctr Rm 403 7054 Haycock Rd Falls Church VA 22043 Personal E-mail: hazhir@sloan.mit.edu.

RAHMANI, AMIR R., research scientist; s. Ali Rahmani and Mansoureh Ebrahim. PhD, U. Wash., Seattle, 2008. Grad. rsch. asst. U. Wash., 2003—08; postdoc. fellow Ga. Inst. Tech., Atlanta, 2008—. Pres. Found. Internat. Understanding Through Students, Seattle, 2005—08. Office: GA Inst Tech Sch Elec & Computer Engring Atlanta GA 30332 Business E-Mail: amir@teamrahmani.com.

RAHMANI, CAROL HIPP, retired school system administrator, psychologist; b. Loris, SC, May 4, 1950; d. James Chester and Edith Bedenbaugh Hipp; m. Abdul Manan Rahmani, May 18, 1985. BA, NC State U., 1972, MS, 1976, PhD, 1981. Lic. psychologist NC, sch. psychologist NC, cert. health svcs. provider-psychologist NC. Sch. psychologist Wake County Pub. Sch. Sys., Raleigh, NC, 1978—80, coord. psychol. svcs., 1980—90, sr. dir. related svcs., 1990—2003, sr. dir. counseling and student svcs., 2003—07; ret., 2007. Mem.: Nat. Assn. Sch. Psychologists, NC Sch. Psychology Assn. (Practitioner of Yr. 1998). Democrat. Methodist. Avocations: beach-combing, tennis, reading, sports, walking. Home: 819 Running Brook Trl Raleigh NC 27609-6974 Personal E-mail: acrahmani@bellsouth.net.

RAHMANI, RAMIN KHOSRAVI, mechanical engineer, researcher; s. Rasoul Khosravi Rahmani and Nayereh Lajevardi Qamsari; m. Anahita Ayasoufi, May 5, 1997; children: Darivs Khosravi children: Cyrus Khosravi. BS in Mech. Engring., Sharif U. Tech., 1994, MS in Mech. Engring., 1997; PhD in Mech. Engring., U. Toledo, 2004. Project mgr. and rschr. Niroo Rsch. Inst., Tehran, 1997—99; computational fluid dynamics engr. Ill. Tool Works, Maumee, Ohio, 2001—04; postdoctoral rschr. U. Ala., Birmingham, 2005—06; applied rsch. engr. A.O. Smith, 2006—. Mem.: AIAA, ASME. Achievements include research in new grid generation algorithm; new algorithm to solve heat conduction. Office: 1100 E Fairview Johnson City TN 37601 Personal E-mail: rrahmani@uab.edu.

RAHMATI, AHMAD, electrical engineer, researcher; b. Tehran, Iran, June 11, 1982; s. Abdolreza Rahmati and Fariba Khashehchi. BSc, Sharif U., Tehran, 2004; MSc, Rice U., Houston, 2008. Rsch. asst. Rice U., 2005—; summer intern AT&T Labs Rsch., Florham Pk., NJ, 2006, Motorola Labs., Schaumburg, Ill., 2008.

RAHMING, ETTA LORRAINE, social worker, psychotherapist, school psychologist, consultant; b. Bronx, Mar. 6, 1957; d. Henry Lewis and Irene (Linen) R. BA in Sociology, CCNY, 1979; MSW, Howard U., 1981; EdS, U. VI, 2006. Lic. social worker, N.Y.; lic. counselor, N.Y., alchohol and substance abuse counselor. Investigative probation officer N.Y.C. Dept. Probation, 1981-85; social worker E.N.T.E.R. Alcoholism O.P.D., 1985-86; psychiat. social worker Bronx Lebanon Alcoholism O.P.D., 1986-88; clin. supr. residential treatment program E.N.T.E.R. Inc., 1988-89; supr. Comprehensive Employment Opportunity Support Ctr. Fedn. Employment Guidance Ctr., 1989-92; therapist Our Lady of Mercy Mental Health Clinic, Bronx, 1994—96; sch. psychologist intern Dept. of Svcs. Virgin Islands Dist., 1997—. Dist. mgr. Dept. Human Svc., 1997—. Mem. APA, NASW, Nat. Assn. Black Social Workers, Inc., N.Y. Fedn. Alcoholism Counselors. Home Phone: 813-435-8876. Personal E-mail: ettarahming@yahoo.com.

RAHNAVARD, NAZANIN, engineering educator; b. Tehran, Iran, Dec. 31, 1976; d. Ahmad Rahnavard and Farideh Haj Hosseinkhan; m. Reza Abdolvand, Jan. 1, 2004. BS, Sharif U. Tech., Tehran, 1999, MS, 2001; PhD, Ga. Inst. Tech., Atlanta, 2007. Rsch. asst. Ga. Inst. Tech., 2002—07; asst. prof. Okla. State U., Stillwater, 2008—. Contbr. numerous articles to profl. jours. Recipient Outstanding Rsch. award, Ctr. Signal & Image Processing Ga. Inst. Tech., 2007. Mem.: IEEE. Achievements include research in modern error-control coding schemes and their applications; wireless ad-hoc and sensor networks; first to unequal error protection rateless codes; design of efficient video-on-demand scheme using UEP-rateless codes. Office: Okla State Univ 202 Eng S Stillwater OK 74078 Office Phone: 405-744-1402. Business E-Mail: nazanin.rahnavard@okstate.edu.

RAI, ALEXANDER K., international affairs executive; s. K. and M. Roy. Degree, U. Pa., Wharton Sch. Bus., 2007; degree in Fin., Psychology, Engring., Camden County Coll., 2004; MIT, Sloan Sch. Mgmt., 2008. CEO Alternative Pathway Program Found., Voorhees, NJ, 2004—06; prin. to dir. Astarin LLC, 2005—; dir. Zivylin LLC, Phila., 2006—; exec. mng. ptnr. Guru Connector Consultancy, LLC, 2006—; dir. Green Therapy Global, Oslo, 2007—. Hon. chmn. Bus. Adv. Coun., Wash., DC, 2005—; CEO to dir. West Phila. Found., 2008, Internat. Libertarian Taskforce, 2008; CEO Future to Facebook, 0208, Macedonia Found., 2008. Contbr. nearly 50 articles to profl. jours. Hon. chmn. Nat. Republican Congressional Com.; mem to keynote advocate Am. Libertarian Party; CEO Zivylin Small Bus. Devel. Commune, Phila., 2005—. Recipient Congl. medal, Distinction, 2006; named Bus. Leader of Yr., 2005, Businessman of Yr., 2006. Master: F & Am; fellow: Melita Lodge 295; mem.: Psi Beta Soc., Mensa, Phi Theta Kappa Internat., Bus. Adv. Coun. (hon. Rep. of Yr. 2006). Libertarian. Avocation: interior decorating. Business E-Mail: alex@zivylin.com.

RAI, AMITABH SHAMBHU, humanities educator; b. Bhopal, Madhya Pradesh, India, Feb. 17, 1968; s. Shambhu Kumar and Meera Rai; 1 child, As'sia-Thara. PhD, Stanford U., Palo Alto, Calif., 1995. Assoc. prof. Fla. State U., Tallahassee, 2003—. Advisor Human Rights Orgn., 2008—. Green Party. Home: 6547 Man O War Trail Tallahassee FL 32309 Business E-Mail: asrai@fsu.edu.

RAI, BHARATENDRA K., statistician, educator; married; children: Shivam, Shreya. PhD, Wayne State U., Detroit, 2004. Cert. Six-Sigma Blackbelt, Am. Soc. Quality, 2004. Reliability, quality engr. Ford Motor Co., Detroit, 2002—06; asst. prof. bus. stats. U. Mass., North Dartmouth, 2006—. SQC specialist Indian Statis. Inst., Pune, Maharastra, India, 1994—2000. Author: (book) Reliability Analysis and Prediction with Warranty Data; contbr. articles to profl. jour. Recipient Presenters award, ASI's Robust Engring. Symposium, 2002, 2004, Powertrain Tech. Innovation award, Ford Motor Co. 'Warranty Forecasting Model', 2006. Mem.: ICDF (Coimbatore, India) (internat. adv. com. mem. 2008), ICDM (Ghaziabad, India) (internat. adv. com. mem. 2008), ICIRBH (Ghaziabad, India) (internat. adv. com. mem. 2008), IMETI (Orlando, Fla.) (mem. program com. 2008). Office: Charlton Coll Bus UMASS-D 285 Old Westport Rd North Dartmouth MA 02747 Office Fax: 508-910-6434; Home Fax: 508-999-8646. Business E-Mail: brai@umassd.edu.

RAI, RAM C., physics professor; b. Dharan, Nepal; s. Ratna B. and Amrita K. Rai; m. Meena Rai; 1 child, Ryan. PhD, U. Ky., Lexington, 2004. Lectr. Kathmandu U., Dhulikhel, 1994—97, Tribhuvan U., Kathmandu, 1997—98; postdoc. rsch. assoc. U. Tenn., Knoxville, 2004—07; asst. prof. SUNY Coll., Buffalo, 2007—. Contbr. to numerous profl. jours. Mem.: Am. Phys. Soc. Achievements include research in Studies on advanced electronic and magnetic materials. Office: SUNY Coll at Buffalo 1300 Elmwood Ave Buffalo NY 14222

RAI, SANJIV, research and development company executive, educator; s. Sri-Kusheshwar and Rukmini Rai; m. Arpana Rawat; children: Rushat, Kushagra. Grad. with honors, Calcutta U., 1995; postgrad. in elec. engring., UCL. Cert. project mgmt., strategic mgmt. and leadership. Rsch. exec. ORG-MARG, Calcutta, 1992—94; ednl. cons. Lotus Learning, India, 1993—94; CEO, chief architect Malth Solutions, Calcutta, India, 1994—99; CEO Advanced Radio Engring., Bombay, 2000—, NYC, 2004—06, 2007, UNIRF, Princeton, NJ, 2007—. Adj. prof., hon. lectr. U. Bridgeport, Conn., 2007; dir. Advanced Radio Engring., NYC; telecom. tech. advisor Gerson Lehrman Group Tech. Coun. Advisors; wireless industry leader Standard Poor's Soc. Industry Leaders; principal investigator on CHANDRA project for NASA UNIRF, Princeton, NJ. Assoc. editor: Internat. Jour. Telecomm. and Networking, Internat. Jour. on SCSS; editor: ACS; author: Location Based Services: Applications Over Cellular Networks, 2004, iMode Wireless: Network Architecture and Applications, 2004, Wireless Project Management Basics for RF Engineers, Network Engineers and Application Engineers, 2004, GPS and Satellite Technologies in Communications, 2005, SS7 and GSM: Signaling Protocols and Networking, 2005, CDMA IS95 Communication: Signaling and Network Architecture, 2005, CDMA 2000: Technology, Network Architecture and Signaling, 2005, 2.5G and 3G: GPRS, UMTS and EDGE Architectures, Protocols and Signaling, 2005, Wireless Security: WLAN Security and IEEE 802.11i, 2005, Wireless Personal Area Networks-Bluetooth and IEEE 802.15x: Network Architectures and Implementation, 2005, Enterprise-wide Wireless LAN IEEE 802.11 a,b and g: Standards Network Architectures, Large Scale Implementations and Managing QoS Issues, 2005, RF Front-end and Antennas for Wireless Communication, 2006, DSP and Modulation Techniques in Wireless: PSKs, QAM, OFDM and Beyond, 2006, Wi-Max: Standards, Technologies and Architectures, 2006; contbr. articles to profl. jours. Vol. UN, NYC, 2006—. Recipient Spl. Recognition award for contbns. to engring and entreprenuership, ASEI, 2006, Outstanding Chapter award, IEEE Computer Soc, 2007—08, Outstanding Leadership and Service award, IEEE CT, 2008, Appreciation cert. for leadership contributions, ASQ, 2008; named Top 100 Disruptive Innovators, Red Herring, 2006, Top 10 Asian Visionaries, ZDNET, 2006, Young Inventor's Hall of Fame, 2007; named a Top 10 Emerging Stars in ICT Industry, 2003. Mem.: IEEE (chair NOKIA conf. 2004, chair Conn. Computer Soc., chair Man and Cybernetics Soc., chair Radio and Convergence Techs., Tech. Com. Computer Comms., tech. program com. Internat Conf. SCSS, founding chair Nanotech. Com., tech. program com. Internat. Conf. Telecom. Networking, working group mem., contbg. author and reviewer Comm. Taxonomy), Nat. Assn. Software and Svcs. Companies, Brit. Computer Soc. Wireless IT Security Group, Project Mgmt. Inst., IEEE Comm. Soc., IEEE Computer Soc. (chair radio and convergence techs. 2000—, chair CT sect. 2006—), Am. Soc. Quality (sr.; chair-elect electronics and comm. divsn. 2006—, founding chair nanotech. com. 2006—, sec. Elec. Comm. Divsn.), Search Extra Terrestrial Intelligence. Hindu. Achievements include development of a universal theory of communication, signaling simulation, D5, AceWP product, AceWP launch contract for 142 countries; founded three companies; helped launch India's first mobile network; development of CHANDRA (Compact, High-performance, Agile, Nano, Digital RAdio) for NASA towards creating the 1st communication infrastructure on the moon for making first home in space. Avocations: golf, sailing, skyjumping, ice skating. Office: uniRF Technologies Inc Four Winds Corporate Campus 2nd Fl 88 Orchard Rd Skillman NJ 08558 Personal E-mail: s.r@ieee.org.

RAICHLE, MARCUS EDWARD, radiology and neurology educator; b. Hoquiam, Wash., Mar. 15, 1937; m. Mary Elizabeth Rupert, 1964; children: Marcus Edward, Timothy Stephen, Sarah Elizabeth, Katherine Ann. BS, U. Wash., 1960, MD, 1964. Diplomate Am. Bd. Psychiatry and Neurology. Intern Balt. City Hosps., 1964—65, resident, 1965—66; asst. neurologist N.Y. Hosp. Cornell Med. Ctr., NYC, 1966—68, neurologist, chief resident, 1968—69; clin. instr. dept. medicine divsn. neurosci. U. Tex. Med. Sch., San Antonio, 1969—70; rsch. instr. Washington U. Sch. Med., St. Louis, 1971—72, from asst. prof. neurology to assoc. prof. neurology, 1972—78, from asst. prof. radiology (radiation scis.) to assoc. prof. radiology Edward Mallinckrodt Inst. Radiology, 1972—79, from asst. prof. to assoc. prof. biomedical engring., 1974-79, prof. neurology, 1978—, prof. radiology Edward Mallinckrodt Inst. Radiology, 1979—, prof. biomedical engring., 1979—; and prof. psychology Washington Univ., St. Louis, 2000—. Instr. dept. neurology Cornell U. Med. Coll., NYC, 1968—69; asst. neurologist Barnes Hosp., St. Louis, 1971—75, assoc. neurologist, 1975—78, neurologist, 1978—; cons. neurologist St. Louis Children's Hosp., 1975—; neurologist Jewish Hosp., St. Louis, 1984—, St. Louis Regional Hosp., St. Louis, 1984—; mem. neurology study sect. A NIH, 1975—79; mem. com. cerebrovascular diseases Nat. Inst. Neurol. Diseases and Stroke, long range planning effort, 1978, basic sci. task force, 78; mem ad hoc adv. panel Nat. Inst. Neurol. Diseases and Stroke, 1983, chmn. PET grants spl. rev. com., 83, chmn. brain imaging ctrs. spl. rev. com., 85; mem. adv. bd. McDonnell-Pew Program cognitive neuroscience, 1989; other coms. Mem. editl. bd.: Stroke, 1982, Neurology, 1976—82, Annals of Neurology, 1979—86, Brain, 1985—90, Journal Cerebral Blood Flow and Metabolism, 1983—86, dep. chief editor:, 1981—83, mem. editl. bd.: Human Neurobiology, 1985—87, Brain Rsch., 1985—90, Synapse, 1987—90, Jour. Neurosci., 1989—95, Jour. Cognitive Neurosci., 1989—, Cerebral Cortex, 1990—, Jour. Nuclear Medicine, 1990—96. Maj. USAF, 1969—71. Recipient umerous awards, lectrs., fellows including Charles A. Dana award for pioneering achievements in health and edn., Dana Found., 1996. Fellow: Am. Assn. Advancement of Sci.; mem.: NAS, Inst. Medicine of NAS.

RAIFFA, HOWARD, economics educator; Faculty mem. Harvard U., 1957—; Frank Plumpton Ramsey prof. managerial econs. Harvard Bus. Sch. and Kennedy Sch. Govt.; prof. emeritus Harvard U.; first dir. Internat. Inst. Applied Sys. Analysis, Vienna, 1973—75. Co-author: Games and Decisions, 1959, Decisions with Multiple Objectives: Preferences and Value Trade-offs, 1993, Introduction to Statistical Decision Theory, 2000, Negotiation Analysis: The Science and Art of Collaborative Decision Making, 2003. Mem.: NAE. Mailing: 175 Somerset St Belmont MA 02478 Office Phone: 617-495-6289. E-mail: hraiffa@hbs.edu.

RAIJMAN, ISAAC, gastroenterologist, educator; b. Empalme, Sonora, Mex., July 6, 1959; arrived in US, 1985, naturalized, 2000; s. Jose and Amalia (Langsam) R. MD, Nat. Autonomous U., Mexico City, 1985; postgrad., U. Wis., Milw., 1985—89, U. Tex., Houston, 1989—92. Diplomate Am. Bd. Internal Medicine, Am. Bd. Gastroenterology. Resident in medicine Mt. Sinai Hosp., Milw., 1986-88, chief resident, 1989; fellow in therapeutic endoscopy Wellesley Hosp., U. Toronto, 1992—93; rsch. fellow in gastroenterology U. Tex., Houston, 1989-90, clin. fellow, 1990-92, asst. prof. medicine, 1993-97, dir. therapeutic endoscopy, 1993-97, asst. prof. M.D. Anderson Cancer Ctr., 1993—2000, dir. ann. therapeutic endoscopy course, 1995-97, dir. therapeutic endoscopy, 2002—, assoc. prof. Houston, 2002—, Baylor Coll. Medicine, Houston, 2005—, U. Houston, 2005—. Chair Ann. Therapeutic Endoscopy Meeting; chair gastroenterology and endoscopy sub. com., GI subcom. on endoscopic credentialing and quality assurance Hermann Hosp., Houston. Author: Pancreas, 1993, Bockus Textbook of Gastroenterology, 1993; also numerous articles; reviewer jours. in field. Fellow Am. Gastroenterology Assn.; mem. Am. Coll. Gastroenterology, Internat. Assn. Pancreatology, Am. Soc. Gastrointestinal Endoscopy, Am. Soc. Internal Medicine. Jewish. Avocation: painting. Office: 6620 Main Ste 1510 Houston TX 77030 Office Phone: 713-795-4444.

RAIKES, JEFFREY SCOTT, foundation administrator, former computer software company executive; b. Nebr., May 29, 1958; m. Tricia McGinnis; children: Michaela, Conner, Gillian. BS in Engring. & Econ. Systems, Stanford U., Calif., 1980. Software devel. mgr. Apple Computer Inc., 1980—81; product mgr. Microsoft Corp., Redmond, Wash., 1981—84, dir. applications mktg., 1984, chief strategist, v.p. office sys., then sr. v.p., Microsoft N.Am., 1993—98, group v.p. worldwide sales and support group, 1998—2000, group v.p. productivity & bus. services, 2000—04, group v.p., information worker bus., 2004—05, pres. bus. software divsn., 2005—08; CEO Bill & Melinda Gates Found., Seattle, 2008—. Ptnr. Seattle Mariners Baseball Club, 1992—; bd. dirs. Software Pubs. Assn., 1987—93, Costco Wholesale Corp., 2008—, XO Comm. Inc., Washington Tech. Ctr.; co-founder Raikes Family Found., 1997—. Trustee U. Nebr. Found., Wash. State U. Found.; active United Way; co-chair ann. campaign United Way King County, 2006—07; founder Lincoln J. D. Edwards Honors Prog. (now Jeffrey S. Raikes Sch. Computer Sci. & Mgmt.) U. Nebr.; mem. exec. com. Nat. Found. Tchg. Entrepreneurship. Named to Computer Industry Hall of Fame, Computer Reseller News Mag., 2003. Office: The Bill & Melinda Gates Found PO Box 23350 Seattle WA 98102*

RAILSBACK, SHERRIE LEE, management consultant, educator; b. Phila., Mar. 12, 1942; children: Ricky, Cindy. BBA, U. Ky., 1981. Sales mgr. Marjo Cosmetics, Ft. Wayne, Ind.; asst. dir. patient fin. svcs. Riverside Meth. Hosp., Columbus, Ohio; cons. Railsback and Assocs., Long Beach, Calif.; adoption search/reunion cons., educator Spirited Comm., LA. Mem.: ASTD, NAFE, Book Publicists So. Calif., Nat. Spkrs. Assn. Office Phone: 562-822-3671. Personal E-mail: sherrie_railsback@yahoo.com.

RAILTON, W(ILLIAM) SCOTT, retired commissioner; b. Newark, July 30, 1935; s. William Scott and Carolyn Elizabeth (Guiberson) R.; m. Karen Elizabeth Walsh, Mar. 31, 1979; 1 son, William August; children by previous marriage: William Scott, Anne Greenwood. BSEE, U. Wash., 1962; JD with honors, George Washington U., 1965. Bar: D.C. 1966, Md. 1966, Va. 1993, U.S. Patent Office 1966. Assoc., then ptnr. Kemon, Palmer & Estabrook, Washington, 1966-70; sr. trial atty. Dept. Labor, Washington, 1970-71, asst. counsel for trial litigation, 1971-72; chief counsel U.S. Occupational Safety and Health Rev. Commn., Washington, 1972-77, acting gen. counsel, 1975-77; ptnr. Reed Smith LLP, Pitts., 1977—2002, ret., 2002; commr., chmn. U.S. Occupl. Safety and Health Rev. Commn., 2002—07, ret., 2007. Lectr. George Washington U. Law Sch., 1977-79, seminar chmn. Occupational Safety and Health Act, Govt. Inst., 1979-96; lectr. Practicing Law Inst., 1976-79. Author: (legal handbooks) The Examination System and the Backlog, 1965, The OSHA General Duty Clause, 1977, The OSHA Health Standards, 1977; OSHA Compliance Handbook, 1992; contbg. author: Occupational Safety and Health Law, 1988, 93. Regional chmn. Montgomery County (Md.) Republican party, 1968-70; pres. Montgomery Sq. Citizens Assn., 1970-71; bd. dirs., pres. Foxvale Farms Homeowners Assn., 1979-82; pres. Orchards on the Potomac Homeowners Assn., 1990-92; dir. Great Falls Hist. Soc., 1991-94; scoutmaster Troop 55 Boy Scouts Am., 1993-98. With USMC, 1953-58. Recipient Meritorious Achievement med Dept. Labor, 1972, Outstanding Service award OSHA Rev. Commn., 1977, elected fell. Coll. Labor and Employment Lawyers, 1998. Fellow Coll. Labor and Employment Lawyers; mem. ABA (mgmt. co-chmn. occupational safety and health law com. 1995-98), Md. Bar Assn., Va. Bar Assn., Bar Assn. D.C. (vice chmn. young lawyers sect. 1971), Order of Coif, Sigma Phi Epsilon, Phi Delta Phi. Home: 10102 Walker Lake Dr Great Falls VA 22066-3502 Personal E-mail: fysh4it@aol.com. *Lawsuits are won by pre-trial preparation. A litigator should be candid with his clients and honest in his dealings with associates, opponents and the courts; an attorney should also volunteer his service to the community of which he is a part.*

RAIMAN, ROSEMARY A., advocate; d. Claude and Emma Butch; m. John L. Davidson (div.); children: Jennifer Lynne Davidson, Jacqueline Rose Davidson; m. Irwin Raiman, Aug. 29, 1981. Cert. nat. victims acad. Am. U., 1998, victim assistance specialist Greenville, SC, 2000, trauma svcs. specialist Irmo, SC, 2001, domestic violence counselor Am. Coll. Cert. Forensic Counselors, 2001, advanced care advocate Nat. Advocate Credential, Washington, 2004, roper victim asst. U. Balt., 2004. Program coord. Del. Opportunities Inc., Delhi, NY, 1977—81; dir. Title IIIC Nutrition/Supportive Svcs. for Elderly, Delhi, 1981—85; office coord. Psychol. Svcs. Inc., Annapolis, Md., 1986—91; office mgr. Reliance Comm., Inc., Latham, Md., 1991—94; agy. receptionist Sanders Ins. Agy., LaPiata, Md., 1994—96; cert. victim advocate/admin. dep. Ctr. for Abused Persons, Waldorf, Md., 1996—. Chairperson Charles County Dept. Social Svcs., 1996—2005, bd. mem., 1996—2005; mem. Md. Divsn. Parole and Probation Victim's Adv. Bd., 1998—2001; bd. mem. Md. Assn. Social Svc., 1999—2003; founder Silent Witness Program for Charles County, 1999—, co-coord., 1999—; bd. mem. Md. Network Against Domestic Violence, Bowie, Md., 2000—; crisis respondent Charles County Sheriff's Victim Svc. Unit, LaPlata, 2001—06; bd. chair Md. Assn. Social Svc., 2002—03; mem. Family Violence Coord. Coun. Charles County, 2003—, mem. pro bono legal svcs. com., 2003—; co-chairperson Legal Advocates Task Force, Bowie, Md., 2004—; chair Charles County Commn. for Women, 2004—05. Recipient Silver Tray of Appointment, Del. Opportunities Inc., Outstanding Svc. award, Psychol. Svcs. Inc., Cert. Appreciation, Ctr. for Abused Persons, Charles County Commn. Women, 1999—2007, Md. Most Beautiful Nominee and 1st Runner-Up, Charles County Commissioners, Silent Witness Plaque award, Charles County Co-Coord., Cmty. Svc. award, Commn. for Women, Gov. Victim Assistance award, Crime Control and Prevention Bd. Victims Svc., Bd. Mem. of Yr., Dept. Social Svc., Cmty. Svc. award, Dept. Social Svcs., Appreciation Plaque, Md. State Bd. Mem., Svc. award, Ctr. for Abused Persons, Plaque of Appreciation, Charles County Sheriff's Dept., Achievement award, Md. Coalition Against Sexal Assault, 2006; nominee Spirit of Cmty. award, Med. Ctr., Svc. award, Charles County Comm. for Women, 2007. Mem.: Assn. Traumatic Stress Specialist. Republican. Methodist. Office: Ctr for Abused Persons 2670 Crain Hwy Ste 303 Waldorf MD 20601

RAIMI, BURTON LOUIS, lawyer; b. Detroit, May 5, 1938; s. Irving and Rae (Abel) R.; m. Judith Morse, Mar. 31, 1963 (div. Mar. 1985); children: Diane L., and Matthew. BA, Brandeis U., 1960; JD with honors, U. Mich., 1963; LLM, George Washington U., 1964. Bar: Mich. 1963, D.C. 1964, Fla. 1991, U.S. Ct. Appeals (4th, 7th, 8th, 9th, 10th, 11th and DC cirs.), U.S. Ct. of Fed. Claims, U.S. Supreme Ct. Atty. appelate ct. sect. NLRB, Washington, 1964-69; assoc. Morgan, Lewis & Bockius, Washington, 1969-71; dep. gen. counsel FDIC, Washington, 1971-78; ptnr. Rosenman and Colin, Washington, 1978-86, Dechert Price & Rhoads, Washington, 1986-93; shareholder McCaffrey & Raimi, P.A., Naples and Sarasota, Fla., 1994—2002, Law Offices of Burton L. Raimi PA, Sarasota, Fla., 2003—05; gen. counsel Washington Mgmt. Corp., 2005—07, Law Offices Burtow L. Raimi, Pa., 2007—. Spkr. various insts. Mem. ABA (past chmn. bank receiverships subcom. of banking com.), D.C. Bar Assn. (past chmn. banking law com., com. on interest on lawyers trust accounts), Fla. Bar (bus. law com.), Am. Arbitration Assn. (panel of arbitrators), Nat. Arbitration Forum (arbitrator). Avocations: travel, golf, fishing. Office: 8499 S Tamiami Trail No 266 Sarasota FL 34238 Office Phone: 941-927-1603. Office Fax: 941-927-1703. Business E-Mail: burt@moneylaw.com.

RAIMI, RALPH ALEXIS, mathematics professor; b. Detroit, July 25, 1924; s. Jacob and Sylvia (Krusner) R.; m. Sonya Lenore Drews, June 29, 1947; children: Jessica, Diana. BS in Physics, U. Mich., 1947, MS in Math, 1948, PhD, 1954. Faculty U. Rochester, 1952—, prof. math., 1966—95, chmn. dept. sociology, 1983—86, assoc. dean for grad. studies Coll. Arts and Sci., 1967—75, prof. emeritus math., 1995—. Cons. in Math. Edn. State of Calif. Bd. Edn. and private ednl. founds. Author: Vested Interests, 1982, The Philomathic Debating Club, 1991; contbr. articles to mags., jours., newspapers. Served to 1st lt. USAAF, 1943-46. Fulbright Grad. fellow Paris, 1949-50; Lloyd postdoctoral fellow U. Mich., 1955-56; NSF grantee; Office of Naval Rsch. grantee. Mem.: Nat. Assn. Scholars, Am. Math. Soc., Math. Assn. Am., Philomathic Debating Club, Nat. Coun. Tchrs. Maths. Home: 46 Glen Ellyn Way Rochester NY 14618-1502 Office Phone: 585-275-4429. Business E-Mail: rarm@math.rochester.edu. *In my childhood I was told to be like everyone else, and not to take on airs. My relatives and teachers doubtless had a democratic virtue in mind, but their egalitarianism slowed my ambition. Books came from the library and not from the likes of me, I thought, and wealth was theft from the poor. Now I know better, but it is mostly too late.*

RAIMI, SAMUEL M., film director; b. Royal Oak, Mich., Oct. 23, 1959; s. Leonard Ronald and Celia Barbara (Abrams) R.; m. Gillian Greene, 1993; 5 children. Student in humanities study, Mich. State U., East Lansing, 1977-79. V.p. Renaissance Pictures, Ferndale, Mich., 1979—. Writer, dir. (films) Crimewave, 1985 (Best Dir. award 1986), Evil Dead II, 1986, Darkman, 1990, Army of Darkness: Evil Dead 3, 1993, Drag Me to Hell, 2009; co-writer: (screenplay) The Hudsucker Proxy, 1994; prodr. Hard Target, 1993, Timecop, 1994, Boogeyman, 2005; dir. (films) The Quick and the Dead, 1995, A Simple Plan, 1998, For Love of the Game, 1999, The Gift, 2000, Spider-Man, 2002, Spider-Man 2, 2004, Boogeyman, 2005, The Messengers, 2007, Spider-Man 3, 2007; appeared in films Spies Like Us, 1985, Thou Shall Not Kill...Except, 1987, Maniac Cop, 1988, Miller's Crossing, 1990, Innocent Blood, 1992, Intruder, 1994, Terminal Force, 1995, others; exec. prodr., writer, dir.: (films) The Evil Dead, 1981; exec. prodr., writer (films) Easy Wheels, 1989, (TV films) M.A.N.T.I.S., 1994; exec. prodr. (films) Lunatics: A love Story, 1991, Hard Target, 1993, The Grudge, 2004, The Grudge 2, 2006, (TV series) Hercules: The Legendary Journeys, 1995-99, Xena: Warrior Princess, 1995-2001, American Gothic, 1995-96, Spy Game, 1997, Young Hercules, 1998, Jack of All Trades, 2000, Cleopatra 2525, 2000-2001. Recipient Best Horror Film, Knokke'heist Film Festival Belgium, 1982, Best Horror Film and Best Spl. Effects, Sitges Film Festival, Spain, 1982, 1st Prize of the Critics, 1st Prize of the Pub., Paris Festival Sci. Fiction, Fantasy and Horror, 1983, Best Horror Film of Yr., Fangoria Mag., 1983; named one of 50 Most Powerful People in Hollywood Premiere mag., 2004-06. Mem. Mich. State U. Soc. for Creative Film Making (founder, pres. 1978, 79), Calif. Rare Fruit Growers.*

RAIMONDI, RUGGERO, opera singer; b. Bologna, Italy, Oct. 3, 1941; m. Isabel Maier, 1987. Studies with, Teresa Pediconi, Armando Piervenanzi. Debut in La Boheme, Spoleto, Italy, 1964; singer in major houses, Europe and US; Met. debut in Ernani, NYC, 1970; favorite roles include Don Giovanni, Philip II, Boris and Don Quichotte; recorded Verdi Requiem, Vespri Siciliani, La Boheme, Aida, Attila, Don Carlos, Macbeth, Simon Boccanegra, Don Giovanni, Boris Godunov, Tosca, Turandot, Barbiere di Siviglia, Mosè, Nozze di Figaro, Italiana in Algieri, Cenerentola, Il Viaggio a Reims, Don Pasquale, Murder in the Cathedral and others; appeared in films Don Giovanni (Joseph Losey), 1979, Six Characters in Search of a Singer (Maurice Bejart), 1983, Carmen (Francesco Rosi), 1986, Tosca (B. Jaquot), 2001, others; opera prodn. since, 1986—. Decorated Comdr. Arts et Lettres, Officier de la Légion d'Honneur (France), chevalier Ordre de Malte, Grand Ufficiale della Repubblica Italiana, comdr. Mérite Culturel (Monaco), others; named Citizen of Honor, City of Athens, Greece. Office: 140 bis rue Lecourbe F-75015 Paris France

RAIN, DAVID RICKTER, social sciences educator; b. Lansing, Mich., Nov. 18, 1962; s. Donald Oscar and Phyllis Carlson Rickter; m. Anna Caroline Reedy, Sept. 3, 1988; children: Avery Caroline, Lydia Wealthy, Callen Oliver, Jasper Carlson. BA, U. Mich., Ann Arbor, 1984; MS, Pa. State U., Coll. Pk., 1993, PhD, 1997. Cert. in project mgmt. George Wash. U., 2002. Statistician US Census Bur., Suitland, Md., 1997—2004; asst. prof. George Washington U., 2004—. Co-dir. Ctr. Urban and Environ. Rsch., Washington, 2005—08. Author: (book) Eaters of the Dry Season. Home: 4107 Oliver St Hyattsville MD 20782 Office: George Washington Univ 1922 F St NW Rm 221 Washington DC 20052 Office Fax: 202-994-2481. Business E-Mail: drain@gwu.edu.

RAINER, REX KELLY, civil engineer, educator; b. Montgomery, Ala., July 17, 1924; s. Kelly Kenyon and Pearl (Jones) R.; m. Betty Ann Page, Aug. 28, 1945; children: Rex Kelly, John Kenyon. BS, Auburn U., Ala., 1944, MS, 1946; PhD, Okla. State U., 1967. Asst. engr. L. & N. R.R. Co., Cin., 1944-45; design engr. Polglaze & Basenberg, Birmingham, Ala., 1945-51; pres., chmn. Rainer Co., Inc., Orlando, Fla., 1951-62; prof. civil engring. Auburn U., 1962-67, head civil engring. dept., 1967; exec. v.p., 1980; hwy. dir. State of Ala., 1979-80, fin. dir., 1981-82; spl. asst. to gov. of Ala., 1981-82; dir. Office for Advancement Devel. Industry U. Ala., Birmingham, 1982-86; pres., cons. engr. Rex K. Rainer, Inc., 1982-98, ret., 1998. Cons. to ins. cos., constrn. engring. firms; mem. Ala. Bd. Registration Profl. Engrs. and Land Surveyors, 1977-89. Contbr. articles to profl. jours Mem. Municipal Planning Bd., 1963-65, Indsl. Park Devel. Bd., 1969-71, So. Regional Edn. Bd., 1982-86. Served with AUS, 1943. Fellow ASCE (sec., treas. 1970, pres. Ala. chpt. 1976-77, chmn. Constrn. Rsch. Coun., chmn. hwy. div. publs. com.; Civil Govt. award 1981); mem. Assn. Gen. Contractors Am. (bd. dirs. 1955), Am. Soc. for Engring. Edn. (chmn. constrn. engring. com.), Am. Pub. Works Assn., Phi Kappa Phi, Tau Beta Pi, Chi Epsilon.

RAINER, WILLIAM GERALD, cardiac surgeon; b. Gordo, Ala., Nov. 13, 1927; s. Jamie Flournoy and Lula (Davis) R.; m. Lois Sayre, Oct. 7, 1950; children: Vickie, Bill, Julia, Leslie. Student, Emory U., Atlanta, Ga., 1943-44, U. Ala., 1944-45; MD, U. Tenn., Memphis, 1948; MS in Surgery, U. Colo., Denver, 1958. Diplomate Am. Bd. Surgery, Am. Bd. Thoracic Surgery. Intern Wesley Hosp., Chgo., 1949; gen. practice medicine Blue Island, Ill., 1950-52; resident Denver VA Hosp., 1954-59; practice medicine specializing in cardiac surgery Denver, 1960—. Bd. dirs. St. Joseph Hosp. Found., Denver; disting. clin. prof. surgery U. Colo. Health Sci. Ctr. Contbr. articles to profl. jours. Active Colo. Symphony Assn.; dir. emeritus St. Joseph Hosp. Found. Bd. Lt. U.S. Army, 1952-54. Decorated Bronze Star; recipient Disting. Alumnus award U. Tenn. Health Sci. Ctr., 1992, Florence Sabin award U. Colo. Health Sci. Ctr., 1998, Disting. Svc. award U. Colo., 2004, Outstanding Clin. Vol., U. Colo. Health Sci. Ctr., 2006, Disting. Svc. award We. Thoracic Surg. Assn., 2007. Mem. Soc. Thoracic Surgeons (sec. 1980-85, pres. 1989, historian 1992—, Disting. Svc. award 1998), Colo. Med. Soc. (pres. 1984-85), Denver Med. Soc. (pres. 1984), Denver Clin. and Pathology Soc. (pres. 1997), Am. Coll. Chest Physicians (pres. 1984), Am. Bd. Thoracic Surgeons (bd. dirs. 1982-88), Am. Surg. Assn., Am. Assn. Thoracic Surgery, Societé Internationale de Chirugie, Cactus Club. Avocations: photography, travel. Office: 2552 E Alameda 48 Denver CO 80209 Office Phone: 303-601-0532. Personal E-mail: wrainer@qwest.net.

RAINER, YVONNE, choreographer, filmmaker; b. San Francisco, Nov. 24, 1934; Choreographer US, Scandinavia, London, Germany, and Italy, 1964—72; co-founder Judson Dance Theater, 1962; disting. prof., Claire Trevor Sch. of Arts Univ. Calif., Irvine. Dir.: (films) Film About a Woman, 1974, Christina Taking Pictures, 1976, (also actor, editor) Journeys from Berlin, 1980, (also editor, screenwriter) The Man Who Envied Women, 1985,: Privilege, 1990 (Filmmaker's Trophy Sundance Film Fest., 1990), (also editor, prodr., screenwriter): (films) Murder and Murder, 1996 (Teddy award Berlin Film Fest., 1996, Spl. Jury award Miami Lesbian and Gay Film Fest., 1999), Many a Summer Dies the Swan, 2002; actor: Underground and Emigrants, 1976, Rainer Variations, 2002. Grantee MacArthur Fellow, 1995. Fellow: NY Found. Arts, Am. Acad. Arts & Scis. Office: NY Found for Arts 155 Ave Americas New York NY 10013-1507 also: Arts-Studio Art 2231 ACT Univ Calif Irvine CA 92697-2775 Office Phone: 949-824-0350. Office Fax: 949-834-5297. Business E-Mail: yrainer@uci.edu.

RAINES, C. FAY, medical association administrator, dean; BS & MS in Nursing, U. Va.; PhD in Nursing, U. Md. Assoc. dean for acad. programs U. Va. Sch. Nursing, interim dean; assoc. provost for inst. effectiveness U. Ala. Coll. Nursing, dean & prof., 1990—. Ed. bd. Jour. Profl. Edn. Mem.: Am. Assn. Colleges Nursing (pres.). Office: One Dupont Cir NW Ste 530 Washington DC 20036 Office Phone: 202-463-6930. Office Fax: 202-785-8320.*

RAINES, DEBORAH A., neonatal/perinatal nurse specialist, educator, nursing researcher, consultant; BSN, Syracuse U., NY, 1978; MSN, U. Pa., Phila., 1982; PhD, Med. Coll. Va. at Va. Commonwealth U., Richmond, 1992. Disting. practitioner, Nat. Acads. Practice, 2004. Nursing edn. coord., perinatal nurse specialist George Wash. U. Med. Ctr., Washington, 1984—89; nurse, maternal infant nurse Med. Coll. Va. Hosps., Richmond, 1992—98; asst. to assoc. prof. Va. Commonwealth U., Richmond, 1992—2000; prof. Fla. Atlantic U., Boca Raton, Fla., 2000—. Cmty. svc. assoc. Va. Commonwealth U., 1997—99; online tchg. liaision Fla. Atlantic U., 2001—04, dir., principle investigator, 2003—06, dir. accelerated second degree program, 2003—06, freshman reading program leader, 2007—; cons. Palm Healthcare Found., West Palm Beach, Fla., 2004—. Editor: (book) Perinatal Secrets, 2004; author: The Quick Study for Nursing, 2007; contbr. articles to profl. jours. Bd. mem. Karen Slattery Early Edn. Devel. Rsch. Ctr., Boca Raton, Fla., 2003—07. Recipient Excellence in Edn. award, Soc. Pediat. Nurses, 2002, Disting. Tchr. the Yr., Fla. Atlantic U., 2004, Excellence in Undergraduate Tchg. award, 2005, Cmty. Ptnr. award, Palm Health Care Found., 2006, Excellence in Online Tchg. award, e-College Internat., 2007, Faculty Svc. award, TIAA/CREF, 2007, Outstanding Alumni award, Med. Coll. Va., 2007. Mem.: Nat. League for Nursing, Assn. Women's Health Obstet. and Neonatal Nurses (Medialllion of Excellence 2000), Sigma Theta Tau (Evidence Based Practice award 2007). Avocations: travel, reading, theater, music. Office: Fla Atlantic Univ 777 Glades Rd Boca Raton FL 33431 Business E-Mail: draines@fau.edu.

RAINES, EDGAR FRANK, JR., historian; b. Murphysboro, Ill., Aug. 17, 1944; s. Edgar Frank and Mary Bernice (Mohlenbrock) R.; m. Gretchen Rose Beuscher, Aug. 9, 1975 (div. Dec. 1982); 1 child, Edgar Jacob; m. Rebecca Celia Robbins, June 20, 1987. BA, So. Ill. U., 1966, MA, 1968; PhD, U. Wis., 1976. Asst. acad. dean Silver Lake Coll., Manitowoc, Wis., 1976-79; historian Office of Air Force History, Washington, 1979-80, U.S. Army Ctr. of Mil. History, Washington, 1980—. Chmn. book selection com. Mil. Classics Seminar, Washington, 1984-86, 89-92; ad hoc com. on Dept. of Def. Reform, Dept. of Army, 1985, historian Directorate of Roles and Missions, Office of Dep. Chief of Staff for Ops. and Plans, 1994-95, historian sec. Army Realignment Task Force, 2001-02; pres. Mil. Classics Seminar, Washington, 2001-02. Co-author: The Army and the Joint Chiefs of Staff, 1986; author: Eyes of Artillery, 2000. Sec. of the Army fellow Dept. of the Army, 1987. Mem. Am. Hist. Assn., Orgn. Am. Historians, Soc. Mil. History, Soc. History in the Fed. Govt., Wis. Hist. Soc., Soc. Historians Am. Fgn. Rels. Office: US Army Ctr of Mil History 103 3d Ave Fort McNair DC 20319-5058 Office Phone: 202-685-2094. E-mail: edgar.raines@us.army.mil.

RAINES, FRANKLIN DELANO, former mortgage company executive; b. Seattle, Jan. 14, 1949; s. Delno Thomas and Ida Mae Raines; m. Wendy Farrow. BA magna cum laude, Harvard U., 1971, JD cum laude, 1976; postgrad., Oxford U., 1971-73. Assoc. dir. Seattle Model Cities Prog., 1972-73; assoc. Preston, Thorgrimson, Ellis, Holman & Fletcher, Seattle, 1976-77; asst. dir. White House Domestic Policy Staff, Washington DC, 1977-78; assoc. dir. Office Mgmt. & Budget Exec. Office of the Pres., Washington DC, 1978-79; v.p. Lazard, Freres & Co., NYC, 1979-82, sr. v.p., 1983-84, ptnr., 1985—91; dir. Office Mgmt. & Budget Exec. Office of the Pres., Washington DC, 1996-98; vice-chmn. Fannie Mae (Fed. Nat. Mortgage Assn.), Washington DC, 1991-96, chmn., CEO, 1999—2004. Vice chmn. bd. dirs. Revolution Health Group LLC. Vice-chmn. bus. council Nat. Urban League; Enterprise Found.; Black Student Fund. Rhodes scholar, 1971. Mem. AAAS, Coun. Fgn. Rels., Nat. Acad. Social Ins., Wash. State Bar Assn., D.C. Bar Assn. Avocations: running, golf.*

RAINES, HOWELL HIRAM, columnist, former newspaper editor; b. Birmingham, Ala., Feb. 5, 1943; s. W.S. and Bertha Estelle (Walker) R.; m. Laure Susan Woodley, Mar. 22, 1969 (div.); children: Ben Hayes, Jeffrey Howell; m. Krystyna Anna Stachowiak, March 8, 2003 BA, Birmingham So. Coll., 1964; MA, U. Ala., 1973. Reporter Birmingham Post-Herald, 1964-65, Sta. WBRC-TV, Birmingham, 1965-67, Tuscaloosa News, Ala., 1968-69, Birmingham News, 1970-71; polit. editor Atlanta Constitution, 1971-74, St. Petersburg (Fla.) Times, 1976-78; Atlanta bur. chief New York Times, 1978-80, White Ho. corr., 1980-82, nat. polit. corr., 1982-84, dep. Washington editor, 1985-86, London bur. chief, 1987-88, Washington editor, 1988-92, editl. page editor, 1993—2001, exec. editor, 2001—03; polit. commentator The Guardian, 2004—; contbg. editor, media columnist Condé Nast Portfolio, 2008—. Author: Whiskey Man, 1977, My Soul is Rested: Movement Days in the Deep South Remembered, 1977, Fly Fishing Through the Midlife Crisis, 1993, The One That Got Away: A Memoir, 2006. Recipient Pulitzer Prize for feature writing, 1992. Office: Condé Nast Portfolio 4 Times Sq 17th Fl New York NY 10036

RAINES, J. PAUL, computer company executive; Staff consumer products group Kurt Salmon Associates, 1986—96; global sourcing positions L.L. Bean, 1996—2000; various retail ops. mgmt. positions including exec. v.p. US stores and pres. Southern divsn, Home Depot

Inc., 2000—08; COO GameStop Corp., 2008—. Office: GameStop Corp 625 Westport Pky Grapevine TX 76051 Office Phone: 817-424-2000. Office Fax: 817-424-2002. Business E-Mail: paulraines@gamestop.com.*

RAINES, JEFF, biomedical scientist, medical research director; b. NYC, Sept. 5, 1943; s. Otis J. and Mildred C. (Wetzler) Raines; children: Gretchen Christena, Victoria Jean. BSME, Clemson U., 1965; MME, U. Fla., 1967; PhD in Biomed. Engring., MIT, 1972. Mem. staff MIT, Cambridge, 1968—70; biophysicist dept. surgery Mass. Gen. Hosp., Boston, 1972—77, dir. Vascular Lab., 1972—77; instr. surgery Harvard Med. Sch., Boston, 1973—77; preceptor Harvard/MIT Sch. Health Scis., 1976—77; rsch. dir., dir. Vascular Lab. Miami (Fla.) Heart Inst., Miami Beach, 1977—88; adj. prof. bioengring. U. Miami, Coral Gables, 1977—; prof. surgery U. Miami (Fla.) Sch. Medicine, 1977—; with Miami Vein Ctr., 2004—. Prin. investigator series NIH programs and pharm. firms, 1977—; Harvard Travelling fellow lectr. in Europe, 1975. Contbr. numerous articles on biomechanics, cardiovasc. diagnosis, dynamics and instrumentation to sci. jours. Recipient Apollo Achievement award, NASA, 1969; fellow, NIH, 1972. Fellow: Am. Assn. Physicists in Medicine, Am. Coll. Radiology, Am. Coll. Cardiology; mem.: ASME, AAAS, Cardiovasc. Sys. Dynamics Soc. (founding mem., editor 1976—, pres. 1980—82), Internat. Cardiovasc. Soc., Instrument Soc. Am., Biomed. Engring. Soc., New Eng. Cardiovasc. Soc., Am. Heart Assn., MIT Club, Harvard Club, Coral Gables Club, Kiwanis, Sigma Xi, Tau Beta Pi. Republican. Presbyterian. Achievements include patents for medical devices; development of mathematical models of arterial hemodynamics and clinical use of autotransfusion. Home Phone: 305-246-0333. Personal E-mail: drjraines@yahoo.com.

RAINES, KEN S., literature and language professor; s. Clyde and Betty Raines; m. Patricia C. Clark, Aug. 23, 1985; children: Jefferson, Taylor. BA, Brigham Young U., Provo, UT, 1989; MA, Utah State U., Logan, 1992. Faculty mem. Mohave CC, Lake Havasu, Ariz., 1997—2004, Ea. Ariz. Coll., Thatcher, 2004—. Dept. chair Dept. English, MCC, Lake Havasu, 2000—04. Mem.: Nat. Orgn. Scholars. Avocation: guitar. Office: Eastern Arizona Coll 615 N Stadium Ave Thatcher AZ 85552

RAINES, MARJORIE D., insurance company executive; BA, Fla. State U., Tallahassee; MBA in Internat. Fin., Fordham U., Bronx, NY. Chartered fin. analyst. Investment and trust mgmt. assoc. Atlantic Nat. Bank, Jacksonville, Fla.; equity investment mgr. State Bd. of Adminstrn. Fla.; investment analyst The Chubb Corp., NYC, mng. dir., exec. v.p., chief internat. investment officer, 2003—08. Trustee The Chubb Found. Fellow: Fin. Analyst Fedn.; mem.: NY Soc. Security Analysts. Office: Chubb Group Ins Companies 15 Mountain View Rd Warren NJ 07059 Office Phone: 908-903-2000. Office Fax: 908-903-2027.

RAINES, SHIRLEY CAROL, academic administrator; b. Jackson, Tenn., Apr. 15, 1945; m. Robert J. Canady; 1 stepchild, Brian Scott Smith. BS, U. Tenn., Martin; MS, EdD, U. Tenn., Knoxville; grad. mgmt. program, Harvard Grad. Sch. of Edn. Dept. head Northeastern State U, 1983—87; assoc. prof. edn. George Mason U., Fairfax, Va., 1987—92; prof. and chmn. dept. of childhood/ lang. arts/ reading U. South Fla., 1992—95; prof. U. Ky. Coll. of Edn., 1995—2001, vice chancellor academic svcs. and dean of coll., 1998—2001; pres. U. Memphis, 2001—. Author books; contbr. articles to profl. jours. Recipient Dist. Svc. to Edn., Phi Delta Kappa, Dist. Paper awards, Ednl. Rsch. Assn. Office: U Memphis 341 Adminstrn Bldg Memphis TN 38152 Office Phone: 901-678-2234. E-mail: sraines@memphis.edu.

RAINES, TIM (TIMOTHY RAINES), baseball coach, retired professional baseball player; b. Sanford, Fla., Sept. 16, 1959; m. Virginia Hilton (div.); children: Tim Jr., André Darrell; m. Shannon Watson, 2007. Outfielder, second baseman Montreal Expos, 1977-90, 2001; outfielder Chgo. White Sox, 1990-95; outfielder, designated hitter NY Yankees, 1996-99, Oakland Athletics, 1999, Balt. Orioles, 2001, Fla. Marlins, 2002; ret., 2002; mgr. Class A Brevard County Manatees, 2003; coach Chgo. White Sox, 2004, first base coach, 2005, bench coach, 2006; hitting coach Class AA Harrisburg Senators, 2007; mgr. Newark Bears, Atlantic League, 2008—. Recipient Sporting News Gold Shoe award, 1984, Silver Slugger award 1986; named Minor League Player of Yr. The Sporting News, 1980, Nat. League Rookie of Yr., 1981, All-Star Game MVP, 1987; named to Nat. League All-Star Team, 1981-87. Achievements include leading the National League in: stolen bases, 1981-84; runs, 1983, 1987; doubles, 1984; batting average, on-base percentage, 1986; member of the World Series Championship winning New York Yankees, 1996, 1998, Chicago White Sox, 2005. Office: Newark Bears Bears & Eagles Riverfront Stadium 450 Broad St Newark NJ 07102*

RAINEY, BARBARA WHITE, insurance company executive; d. Harry Jennings and Grace Frances White; m. James Pugh Gillmore (div.); children: James C., Cheryl, Katherine, Barbara C.; m. Frank Cobb Rainey, July 11, 1974. BA in TV and Speech, U. Ala., Tuscaloosa, 1953; postgrad., U. Nev., Reno, 1965. Cert. life, accident, health, property and casualty ins. agt. Calif., Colo.; tchr. Nev., Calif., Colo. Spokesperson WDSU TV, New Orleans, 1954—59; fashion model, model Motion Picture Adv., New Orleans, 1954—59; ski instr. Vail Resort Assn., Colo., 1965—70, coord. ctrl. reservations and info., 1967—68; tchr. grades K-4 Vail Country Day Sch., 1966—67; tchr. grade 5 Minturn Grade Sch., Colo., 1968—69; counselor Best Agy., San Francisco, 1970—71; ins. agt. Met. Life, San Francisco, 1971—72; ins. agt., asst. Strong & Co., Barry O'Neill & Diercks, San Francisco, 1972—75; v.p., pres., owner Vail Ins. Agy., 1977—82; real estate agt. Mich. Homes, Priscilla Murphy, Ft. Myers, Fla., 1983—93; v.p., sec., co-owner Rainey Ins. Cons., Inc., Ft. Myers and Bonita Springs, Fla., 1994—. Mem.: Mensa, Alpha Chi Omega. Avocations: skiing, dance, art collecting, swimming, exercise. Home and Office: Rainey Ins Cons Inc 9650 Village Vw Blvd #201 Bonita Springs FL 34135

RAINEY, GORDON FRYER, JR., lawyer; b. Oklahoma City, Apr. 26, 1940; s. Gordon F. and Esther (Bliss) R.; m. Selina Norman, Aug. 3, 1968; children: Kate, Melissa, Gordon III. BA in English, U. Va., 1962, LLB, 1967. Bar: Okla. 1967, Va. 1968. Assoc. Rainey, Flynn, Wallace, Ross & Cooper, Oklahoma City, 1967-68, Hunton & Williams LLP, Richmond, Va., 1968-75, ptnr., 1975—, chmn. exec. com., 1994—2006, chmn. emeritus, 2006—. Chmn. emeritus Hunton & Williams; denior trustees, Colonial Williamsburg Found., denior. dir., Colonial Williamsburg Co.; dir., Brown Adv. Holdings Inc., Brown Investment Adv. & Trust Co.; bd. visitors, past rector U. Va. Past pres. U. Va. Alumni Assn.; lifetime trustee, Va. Found. Ind. Colls.; mem. Gov.'s Blue Ribbon Commn. on Higher Edn.; campaign chmn. United Way of Greater Richmond, 1982, trustee, 1981-84; bd. dirs., past pres. Sheltering Arms Hosp., 1984; trustee Sheltering Arms Found.; chmn. Gov.'s Econ. Devel. Adv. Coun. Dist. 12; mem. Gov.'s Adv. Com. for Va. Strategy on Econ. Devel.; mem. Bd. Housing and Cmty. Devel.; past mem. bd. govs. St. Catherine's Sch.; past chmn. bd. dirs. Leadership Met. Richmond.; past pres., bd. dirs. Met. Bus. Found. 1st lt. U.S. Army, 1962-64, Korea. Recipient Disting. Grad. award Casady Sch., Humanitarian award Nat. Conf. Cmty. and Justice, 2003, Disting. Alumni award U. Va. Coll. Found., 2005, Ukrop Cmty. Vision award, 2006, Samuel Crockett award, U. Va. Coll., Wise, Svc. award Young Alumni Coun. U. VA. Mem. ABA (sect. on bus. law, banking law com., com. on devel. in investment svcs.), Richmond Metro C. of C. (bd. dirs., past chmn.), Commonwealth Club, Country Club of Va., The Brook (NYC), Forum Club (Richmond). Republican. Episcopalian. Office: Hunton & Williams Riverfront Plz East Tower PO Box 1535 Richmond VA 23219-4074 Home Phone: 804-353-3004; Office Phone: 804-788-8275. Office Fax: 804-788-8218. Business E-Mail: grainey@hunton.com.

RAINEY, JEAN OSGOOD, public relations executive; b. Lansing, Mich., Apr. 5, 1925; d. Earle Victor and Blanche Mae (Eberly) Osgood; m. John Larimer Rainey, Nov. 29, 1957 (dec. Oct. 1991); children: Cynthia, John Larimer, Ruth. Grad., Lansing Bus. U., 1942. Pub. rels. dir. Nat. Assn. Food Chains, Washington, 1954-59; v.p. pub. rels. Manchester Orgns., Washington, 1959-61; ptnr. Rainey, McEnroe & Manning, Washington, 1962-73; v.p. Manning, Selvage & Lee, Washington, 1973-79, pres. Washington divsn., 1979-84, sr. counsellor, 1985; owner Jean Rainey Assocs., Washington, 1986-87; sr. v.p. Daniel J. Edelman Inc., 1987-96; owner Jean Rainey Assocs., Washington, 1996—. Chmn. bd. Windward Mortgage, 1997—2001. Author: How to Shop for Food, 1972. Pres. Hyde Home and Sch. Assn., Washington, 1969-71; co-chmn. Nat. Adv. Com. for Reelection of the Pres., 1972; chmn. bd. trustees St. John's Presch., 1996-99, vice chair, 2003-04; pres. Sherwood Forest Endowment Fund, 1995-97; adminstr. A Few Good Women-Advancing the Cause of Women in Govt., 1969-74, 97-; bd. dirs. Westchester Corp., 2001-04. Mem. Internat. Women's Forum, Pub. Rels. Soc. Am. (accredited, Hall of Fame 1999), Am. Women in Radio and TV (pres. Washington chpt. 1962-63, mem. nat. bd. 1963-65), Am. News Women's Club (pres. 1973-75), City Tavern Club. Democrat. Episcopalian. Personal E-mail: jorainey@aol.com.

RAINEY, SUSAN J., school system administrator; m. Jack Rainey; 1 child, Jordan. BA, MA, U. Redlands; PhD, U. So. Calif. Tchr. Moore Jr. H.S., Redlands Unified Sch. Dist.; tchr. Palo Alto, Calif., Yucaipa H.S., 1972—76, dir. activities, 1976—78; asst. prin. Monrovia H.S.; h.s. prin. Brea-Olinda High, Brea, Calif.; asst. supt. for adminstrv. svcs. Helmet Unified Sch. Dist., asst. supt. for personnel svcs., assoc. supt.; supt. Charter Oak Unified Sch. Dist., Covina, Calif., 1991—98; sutp. Riverside Unified Sch. Dist., 1998—. Avocations: travel, reading detective novels, golf. Office: Riverside Unified Sch Dist 3380 14th St Riverside CA 92501 Office Phone: 951-788-7134. Business E-Mail: srainey@rusd.k12.ca.us.

RAINEY, TIMOTHY J., air transportation executive; married. Grad. in Bus. Adminstrn., U. Minn. With NW Airlines Corp., Minn., 1977—, various mgmt. positions in systems ops. control and ground ops., mng. dir. ops. control, with sys. ops. control ctr., v.p. sys. ops. control, 1999, sr. v.p. flight ops. and sys. ops. control, 2001—. Office: NW Airlines Corp 2700 Lone Oak Pky Eagan MN 55121 Office Phone: 612-726-2111.

RAINEY, WILLIAM JOEL, lawyer; b. Flint, Mich., Oct. 11, 1946; s. Ralph Jefferson and Elsie Matilda (Erickson) R.; m. Cynthia Hetsko, June 15, 1968; children: Joel Michael, Allison Elizabeth. AB, Harvard U., 1968; JD, U. Mich., 1971. Bar: NY 1973, Wash. 1977, Ariz. 1987, Mass. 1992, Oreg. 2007, US Dist. Ct. (so. and ea. dists.) NY 1973, US Ct. Appeals (2nd cir.) NY 1973, US Dist. Ct. (we. dist.) Wash. 1977, US Supreme Ct. 1976, US Ct. Appeals (9th cir.) Wash. 1978, US Dist. Ct. Ariz. 1987, US Dist. Ct. Mass. 1992; registered in-house counsel, Calif., 2005. Assoc. atty. Curtis, Mallet-Prevost, Colt & Mosle, NYC, 1971-76; atty., asst. corp. sec. Weyerhaeuser Co., Tacoma, 1976-85; v.p., corp. sec., gen. counsel Southwest Forest Industries Inc., Phoenix, 1985-87; sr. v.p., corp. sec., gen. counsel Valley Nat. Corp. and Valley Nat. Bank, Phoenix, 1987-91; v.p., gen. counsel Cabot Corp., Boston, 1991-93; exec. v.p., gen. counsel, corp. sec. Fourth Fin. Corp., Wichita, Kans., 1994-96; sr. v.p., gen. counsel, corp. sec. Payless ShoeSource, Inc., Topeka, 1996—2003, Longs Drug Stores Corp., Walnut Creek, Calif., 2003—08. Editor U. Mich. Jour. Law Reform, 1970-71. Bd. dirs. Big Bros./Big Sisters, 1994—96. Maj. USAR, 1970—91. Mem. ABA (chmn. task force 1984-91, com. of corp. gen. counsel, 1993—), Wash. State Bar Assn., State Bar of Ariz., Assn. Bank Holding Cos. (steering com. 1989-91, chmn. lawyers com. 1990-91), Assn. Corp. Coun., Soc. Corp. Secs. and Governance Profls., Harvard Club of Phoenix (bd. dirs. 1989-91). Avocations: hiking, running, bicycling. Home: 1208 Bridlewood Ct Clayton CA 94517 Office Phone: 925-210-6720. Business E-Mail: brainey@longs.com.

RAINIER, ROBERT PAUL, publisher, consultant; b. Adrian, Mich., Oct. 19, 1940; s. Paul Leslie and Mildred Sofia (Magdefrau) R.; m. Dorothy Krauss, May 28, 1966; children: Michele Carole, Kenneth Charles. BA, Northwestern U., 1962, MA, 1964. From mem. staff to editor-in-chief McGraw Hill Book Co., NYC, 1964—74, editor-in-chief humanities, 1974—79; edit. exec. CBS Coll. Pub., NYC, 1979—86, v.p., editor in chief, 1984-86; dir. publs. AICPA, NYC, 1986-97, dir. prof. devel., 1997-99, sr. cons. strategic devel., 1999—2003; pres. Rainier Assocs., 2003—. Vestryman St. Johns Episcopal Ch., Larchmont, NY, 1987-90, treas., 2007-. Staff sgt. NY Nat. Guard, 1964-70. Mem. The Dessoff Choirs (pres. 2000-04), Soc. Nat. Assn. Publs. (pres. 1992-93). Democrat. Episcopalian. Avocations: music, sports. Home: 21 Summit Ave Larchmont NY 10538-2913 Office Phone: 914-643-0994. Personal E-mail: rainierinc@optonline.net.

RAINIS, EUGENE CHARLES, bank executive; b. NYC, Sept. 24, 1940; s. Charles William and Louise Theresa (Nold) Rainis; m. Jane Margaret Micucci, Nov. 28, 1964; children: Ellen, David, Mark. BS, Fordham U., 1962; MBA, U. Pa., 1964. Security analyst trainee Merrill, Lynch Pierce Fenner & Smith, NYC, 1963-65; ptnr. Brown Bros. Harriman & Co., NYC, 1965—. Bd. dirs. Bio-Brite, Inc. Trustee Robert Brunner Found., Gregorian U. Found., St. Vincents Cath. Med. Ctrs., Cristo Rey NY HS, NYC, NY Med. Coll.; trustee fellow Fordham U. Mem.: Inst. Chartered Fin. Analysts, Knights of Malta, Down Town Assn. (N.Y.C.), Harbour Ridge Golf Club (Palm City, Fla.). Republican. Roman Catholic. Avocations: fishing, golf. Office: Brown Bros Harriman & Co 140 Broadway New York NY 10005 Office Phone: 212-493-7830.

RAINS, CAMERON JAY, lawyer; BA cum laude, Coll. Holy Cross, 1978; JD summa cum laude, Notre Dame U., 1981. Bar: Calif. 1981, US Dist. Ct. (so. dist. Calif.) 1981. Ptnr., co-chmn. Corp. & Securities practice group DLA Piper US LLP, San Diego, 1981—. Editor (assoc.): Notre Dame Lawyer. Mem.: State Bar Calif., San Diego County Bar Assn., US Golf Assn. (mem. exec. com., chmn. 2008 US Open Com., v.p.), Century Club San Diego (past pres., gen. chmn. 2000 Buick Invitational), Phi Alpha Delta. Office: DLA Piper US LLP 4365 Executive Dr Ste 1100 San Diego CA 92121 Office Phone: 858-677-1476. Office Fax: 858-677-1401. Business E-Mail: jay.rains@dlapiper.com.

RAINS, M. NEAL, lawyer; b. Burlington, Iowa, July 26, 1943; s. Merritt and Lucille Rains; children: Robert Baldwin, Kathleen Kellogg. BA in Polit. Sci. with honors, U. Iowa, 1965; JD, Northwestern U., 1968. Bar: Ohio 1968. Assoc. Arter & Hadden, Cleve., 1968-76, ptnr., 1976—2001, mem. exec. com., 1981-90, Cleve. mng. ptnr., 1990-92; ptnr. Frantz Ward LLP, Cleve., 2001—. Lectr. on profl. topics, including alternative dispute resolution, distbn. law, litigation practice and procedure, and antitrust. Contbr. articles to profl. jours. With U.S. Army, 1968-70 Named one of Best Lawyers in America. Fellow: Am. Bar Found.; mem.: ABA, William K. Thomas Am. Inn Ct. (pres. 1999—2000), Cleve. Bar Found. (pres. 2005—07), Cleve. Bar Assn. (v.p. 2007—08, Outstanding Svc. award 2008), Ohio State Bar Assn., Rowfant Club, Union Club, City Club, Print Club, Phi Delta Phi, Omicron Delta Kappa, Phi Beta Kappa. Office: Frantz Ward LLP 2500 Key Ctr 127 Public Sq Cleveland OH 44114 Home: 1783 Bur Oak Dr Westlake OH 44145 Office Phone: 216-515-1660. Business E-Mail: nrains@frantzward.com.

RAINS, MARY JO, banker; b. Konawa, Okla., Oct. 27, 1935; d. Albert Wood and Mary Leona (Winfield) Starns; m. Billy Z. Rains, June 17, 1956; one child, Nicky Z. Student, Okla. Sch. Banking, 1969, Seminole Jr. Coll., 1970—72, East Ctrl. State U., 1978—79; diploma, Am. Inst. Banking, 1981—83; student, Okla. State U., 1987, Adult Vocat. Tech. Ctr., Pontotoc County, 1987. With acctg. divsn. Universal C.I.T., Okla. City, 1953—56; cashier Okla. State Bank (now Bancfirst), Konawa, 1957—89, sr. v.p., 1989—95; sr. v.p., br. mgr. Bancfirst, Konawa, 1995—2002; bd. sec. Seminole County Election Bd., Okla., 2003—. Mem. cmty. bd. dirs. Bancfist, Konawa, 2006—. Sec. First Bapt. Ch., Konawa, Okla. 1969-79, budgeting com., 1982-92, 2006-, chmn. fin. com., 1994-2004, 06-, lectureship adminstr.; fin. bd. Kennedy Libr., 1997—; bd. dir. Sacred Heart Mission Hist. Soc.; mem. exec. bd. Ctrl. Okla. Family Med. Ctr., 2004-2008, fin. com., 2004-. Mem. Okla. Bankers Assn. (dir. women's divsn. 1974-76), Konawa C. of C., Am. Legion, Wewoka C. of C. Office: Courthouse Ste 101 Wewoka OK 74884 Home: 35204 EW 1410 Rd Konawa OK 74849-5508 Office Phone: 405-257-2786.

RAINTREE, SHAWN, museum administrator, former insurance company executive; m. Jes Raintree. Grad., USAF Acad., 1970; MS in Health Adminstrn., U. Colo., Denver. Sr. v.p. no. divsn. VHA, Inc.; founder, exec. dir. Kaiser Permanente Colo. Springs Health Plan, 1997—2007; interim pres., CEO Colo. Springs Fine Arts Ctr., 2007—. Former bd. mem. Colorado Springs C. of C., Colo. Springs Symphony; chmn. bd. dirs. Goodwill Industries, 2004, mem. found. bd. Bd. mem. YMCA of Pikes Peak Region. Office: Fine Arts Ctr 30 W Dale St Colorado Springs CO 80903 Office Phone: 719-634-5583.

RAINWATER, CAROL JEAN, psychology communication professor; d. Robert and Charlie Sullivan; m. Gary Earl Carol Jean Sullivan, Apr. 9, 1966 (div. Sept. 17, 1988); children: Darren Scott, Stephanie Dawn Nunes, Jason Brent. BA in Communication Disorders, CA State U., Fresno; MS in Psychology & Counseling, CA State U., Northridge, 1992; EdD in Higher Edn. and Human Svcs., Nova Southeastern U., North Miami Beach, Fla., 2007. Cert. in strong interest inventory Nat. Bd. Career Counselors, 1999, Am. Bd. Disability Analysts, 2000, svc.-learning instr. Coll. Canyons - State Calif., 2000, in alcohol,drugs Nat. Bd. Cognitive Behavioral Therapist, Calif., 2001, in forensic therapist, counselor Nat. Assn. Forensic Counselors State Calif., 2001. Dir. coll. career ctr. Coll. Canyons, Santa Clarita, Calif., 1996—2005; core faculty social sci. grad. & undergrad. programs - academic & career advisor Chapman U. Coll., Palmdale, Calif., 2002—08; adjunt prof. communication and psychology Woodbury U., Burbank, Calif., 2002—. Online faculty mem., prof., mentor grad. sch. psychology World U. Ojai, Calif., 2004—. Chmn. bd. dirs. grant programs Coll. Canyons, 1997—2002. Mem.: Calif. Assn. Marriage & Family Therapists, Calif. Career Devel. Assn. Pres. (pres. 1996—98, Honor award 1996—97), Alpha Sigma Lambda, Phi Gamma Sigma. Conservative. Baptist. Avocations: travel, flying, hiking, sewing, cooking. Office: Woodbury Univ 7500 Glenoaks Blvd Burbank CA 91510-7846 Personal E-mail: cjrainwater@earthlink.net. Business E-Mail: carol.rainwater@woodbury.edu.

RAINWATER, ERIC, composer, music educator; b. Long Beach, Calif., July 23, 1955; s. Paul Eugene Rainwater and Billye Ree Wallace; m. Candy Marie Layne, Mar. 29, 1980; children: Autumn, Crescent, Shiloh. BA in Music Composition, Azusa Pacific U., Calif., 1988. Dir. 5 home sch. choirs, Sacramento, 1992—; owner Rainwater Music Co., Sacramento, 1995—; dir. 3 home sch. bands Sacramento, 1997—. Music dir. River Ridge Neighborhood Ch., Elk Grove, Calif., 2004—; children's dir., seminar spkr. various music conventions, 1993—. Author, songwriter, arranger: children's musical The Not-So-Silent Night!, 1998 (Top Best Selling Musical award), Samson, The Day God Brought Down the House, 1997 (Top Best Selling Musical award), composer 25 adult, teen and children's musicals; author, songwriter, arranger: children's musical Check Out That Star!, 1995 (Top Best Selling Musical award), arranger: I've Been Working on the Railroad, Sacramento Light Rail Assn. Recipient Hall of Fame award, Azusa Pacific U., 2000, 1st Pl. Novelty Song award, Christian Artists Sem. in Rockies, Estes Park, Colo., 1989. Mem.: Yellowstone Assn. Socialist. Avocations: hiking, swimming. Home and Office: 10 Springmist Ct Sacramento CA 95831-3817 Office Phone: 866-428-2056. Personal E-mail: rainh2omusic@sbcglobal.net.

RAINWATER, GARY L., electric power industry executive; BSEE, U. Mo., Columbia; M of Systems Mgmt., U. So. Calif. Engr. electric transmission and distbn. Union Electric Co. (now Ameren Corp.), v.p. corp. planning, 1993—97; exec. v.p. Ameren CIPS, 1997, pres., CEO, 1997—2001, Ameren CILCO, 2000—01; pres., COO Ameren Corp., St. Louis, 2001—04, chmn., pres., CEO, 2004—09, exec. chmn., 2009—. Mem. dean's adv. coun. U. Mo. Sch. Engring.; mem. adv. coun. engring. mgmt. and engring. tech. Washington U.; bd. dirs. AmerenUE, Ameren CILCO, Ameren CIPS and other Ameren subs., Mo. Hist. Soc., St. Louis USO, Ill. Energy Assn., Urban League Met. St. Louis, US Bank. Recipient Mo. Honor award for disting. svc. in engring., U. Mo.-Columbia Coll. Engring., 2000. Mem.: Engrs.' Club (Knight of St. Patrick 2000). Office: Ameren 1901 Chouteau Saint Louis MO 63166-6149*

RAIRDON, JAMES LEE, paralegal, educator; b. Marion, Ohio, Oct. 25, 1947; s. James Russell and Eleanor Jane (Gandert) Rairdon; m. Ellen Kathryn Findley, Feb. 6, 1977; children: Devin Michael, Patrick Alex. BA in Internat. Studies, Ohio State U., Columbus, 1976; MA in Mgmt., Webster U., Denver, 1993; D in Mgmt., Colo. Tech. U., Colorado Springs, 2006. Regional mgr. group sales Hartford Ins. Group, Denver, 1979—89; paralegal Dept. Justice, Denver, 1989—90; sr. paralegal Great West Life and Annuity Ins. Co., Greenwood Village, Colo., 1990—. Adj. faculty Nat Am. U, Denver, 1993—. 1st. lt. US Army, 1976—79, Ft. Carson, Colo. Fellow: Life Mgmt. Inst.; mem.: Front Range Fly Fishing, Acad. Mgmt. Avocations: fly fishing, hiking. Office: Great West Life adn Annuity Ins Co 8525 E Orchard Rd Greenwood Village CO 80111

RAISH, DAVID LANGDON, lawyer; b. Cleve., Mar. 12, 1947; s. John E. Raish and Roslyn V. (Skeels) Pettibone; m. Roslyn Anne Dinnick, Sept. 12, 1969; children: David Jr., Anne, Julia. BA, Yale U., 1969; JD, Harvard U., 1973. Bar: Mass. 1975, DC 1981. Law clk. to hon. James R. Browning U.S. Ct. Appeals-9th Cir., San Francisco, 1973-74; assoc. Ropes & Gray LLP, Boston, 1974-82, ptnr., 1982—. Mem. ABA Tax sect. 1991—, mem. Employee Benefits Com., 1993—, mem. coun., 1999-2004, vice chair, 2002-04. Author: Cafeteria Plans, 2000, Cash or Deferred Arrangements, 1997, Compensation and Benefits for Key Employees of Tax-Exempt Organizations, 1995; bd. advisors Jour. Taxation of Employee Benefits, 1990-2000. Tenor Tanglewood Festival Chorus; mem. bd. overseers New Eng. Conservatory. Office: Ropes & Gray One International Pl Boston MA 02110 Business E-Mail: david.raish@ropesgray.com.

RAISIAN, JOHN, think-tank executive, economist; b. Conneaut, Ohio, July 30, 1949; s. Ernest James and Ruby Lee (Owens) Raisian; m. Joyce Ann Klak, Aug. 17, 1984; children: Alison Kathleen, Sarah Elizabeth. BA, Ohio U., 1971; PhD, UCLA, 1978; LLD (hon.), Albertson Coll. Idaho, 1995. Rsch. assoc. Human Resources Rsch. Ctr., U. So. Calif., LA, 1972—73; cons. Rand Corp., Santa Monica, Calif., 1974—75; vis. asst. prof. econs. U. Wash., Seattle, 1975—76; asst. prof. econs. U. Houston, 1976—80; sr. economist Office Rsch. and Evaluation, US Bur. Labor Stats., Washington, 1980—81; spl. asst. for econ. policy Office Asst. Sc. for Policy, US Dept. Labor, Washington, 1981—83, dir. rsch. and tech. support, 1981—84; pres. Unicon Rsch. Corp., LA, 1984-86; sr. fellow Hoover Instn., Stanford, Calif., 1986—, assoc. dir., dep. dir., 1986—90, dir., 1989—. Advisor Nat. Coun. on Handicapped, Washington, 1985—86, Nat. Commn. on Employment Policy, Washington, 1987—88; chmn. minimum wage bd. Calif. Indsl. Welfare Commn., 1987; mem. nat. adv. com. Student Fin. Assistance, Washington, 1987—89; corp. mem. Blue Shield Calif., 1994—96; bd. dirs. Sentinel Groups Fund, Inc., 1997—; mem. Pacific Coun. Internat. Policy; nat. adv. bd. City Innovation. Editor (editl. bd.): (jour.) Jour. Labor Rsch., 1983—; contbr. articles to profl. jours. Exec. dir. Presdl. Task Force on Food Assistance, Washington, 1983—84. Recipient Best Publ. of Yr. award, Econ. Inquiry, Western Econ. Assn., 1979, Disting. Tchg. award, U. Houston Coll. Social Scis., 1980, Disting. Svc. award, U.S. Dept. Labor, 1983; fellow predoctoral fellow, Rand Corp., 1976. Mem.: Nat. Assn. Scholars, Coun. on Fgn. Rels., Mont Pelerin Soc., World Affairs Coun., Commonwealth Club of Calif., We. Econs. Assn., Am. Econs. Assn., Phi Beta Kappa. Republican. Avocation: wine collecting, sports enthusiast. Office: Hoover Instn Stanford Univ 434 Galvez Mall Stanford CA 94305-6010 Office Phone: 650-723-1198. Office Fax: 650-725-8990.*

RAISLER, KENNETH MARK, lawyer; b. New Rochelle, NY, May 15, 1951; s. Herbert A. and Norma (Glaubach) Raisler; children: Caroline Elisabeth, Katharine Kelsey, David Mark. BSBA, Yale Coll., 1973; JD, NYU, 1976. Bar: NY 1977, DC 1977, US Dist. Ct. (so. dist.) NY 1977, US Dist. Ct. DC 1977, US Ct. Appeals (2d and DC cirs.) 1977, US Ct. Appeals (10th cir.) 1983, US Supreme Ct. 1985. Law clk. US Dist. Ct. (so. dist.) NY, NYC, 1976—77; asst. US atty. Dept. Justice, Washington, 1977—82; dep. gen. counsel Commodity Futures Trading Commn., 1982—83, gen. counsel, 1983—87; ptnr. Roger & Wells, NYC, 1987—92; ptnr., coord. commodities, futures and derivatives practice area Sullivan & Cromwell, 1992—. Mem.: Assn. Bar City of NY (chair futures regulation com. 1988—91). Office: Sullivan & Cromwell 125 Broad St 33d Fl New York NY 10004-2498 Office Phone: 212-558-4675. Office Fax: 212-558-3588. Business E-Mail: raislerk@sullcrom.com.

RAIS-ROHANI, MASOUD, aerospace and engineering mechanics educator; b. Tehran, Iran, Mar. 8, 1960; came to U.S., 1979; s. Mohammad and Ehteram Rais-Rohani; m. Grace Regino, June 5, 1989. BS magna cum laude, Miss. State U., 1983, MS, 1985; PhD, Va. Polytech Inst. & State U., 1991. Registered profl. engr., Miss. Instr. Miss. State U., Starkville, 1984-87, asst. prof., 1991-96, assoc. prof., 1996—; rsch. assoc. NASA Langley Rsch. Ctr., Hampton, Va., 1990. Summer faculty fellow NASA-ASEE, 1993-94. Va. Space Grant Consortium co-investigator grantee, 1992, NASA Langley Rsch. Ctr. Prin. investigator grantee, 1994, 95, 96, 97, 98, 99. Mem. AIAA (sr.), Am. Soc. Engring. Edn., Ctr. for Composite Materials and Structures, Tau Beta Pi, Phi Kappa Phi, Sigma Gamma Tau, Gamma Beta Phi, Sigma Xi. Muslim. Achievements include research in multidisciplinary design optimization, aerospace structures with emphasis on composites. Office: Miss State U Aerospace Dept PO Drawer A Mississippi State MS 39762

RAJ, MADHWA HG, healthcare educator; married. MSc, Indian Inst. Sci., Bangalore, PhD, 1969. Prof. LSU Health Sci. Ctr, New Orleans, 1984—. Mem.: Amer.Assos.Reprod.Med. Office: LSU Health Sci Ctr 533 Boliver St New Orleans LA 70112

RAJ, TILAK D., anesthesiologist, educator; arrived in US, 1999; s. Premavathy Dharmaraj; m. Catherine C. O'Donovan, June 12, 1994; children: Vijay M., Anushka M., Kieran T., Roshan A. MB, BChir, Madras U., Chennai, 1982. Diplomate Am. Bd. Anesthesiology, 1996. Resident St. Mary's Hosp., London, 1990—92; assoc. prof. dept. anesthesiology Okla. U. Health Scis. Ctr., Oklahoma City, 2000—, dir. rsch. dept. anesthesiology, 2003—. Contbr. articles to profl. jours. Fellow: Royal Coll. Anaesthetists; mem.: Obstetric Anaesthetists Assn., Soc. Cardiovasc. Anesthesiologist, Internat. Anesthesia Rsch. Soc., Am. Soc. Anesthesiology. Home: 2008 Morning Star Edmond OK 73034 Office: Oklahoma Univ Health Sciences Ctr Rm WP 2530 920 Stanton L Young Blvd Oklahoma City OK 73104 Office Phone: 405-271-4351. Business E-Mail: tilak.raj@unhsc.edu.

RAJA, DAYAL DAVIS, endocrinologist; b. Paravur, Kerala, India, Mar. 7, 1973; s. Rajagopal Davis and Bella Januvina Raja; m. Suji Ann Alexander, May 15, 2004; 1 child, Sarah Neha. BS in Biology/Pre-Med summa cum laude, York Coll., NY, 1996; MD with hightest honors, Mercer U. Sch. Medicine, George U., Ga., 2001. Cert. in internal medicine Am. Bd. of Internal Medicine, 2006, endocrinologist Am. Coll. Endocrinologists, 2008, in ultrasound guided thyroid biopsy Am. Coll. of Endocrinologists, 2008. Internal medicine Mercer U., Med. Ctr. of Ctrl. Ga., Macon, Ga., 2002—07, emergency medicine, 2002—07; endocrinologist Med. Coll. Ga., Augusta, endocrine cancer specialist, assoc. prof. of endocrinology, endocrinology specialist attending, Veterans Adminstrn. Med. Ctr. Endocrinology specialist Ga. Dept. of Corrections/Prison Hosp., Augusta, Ga. Author: (book) Endocrinology; contbr. articles to profl. pubs. Recipient SIGMA Xi, Sci. Rsch. Soc., 1996, Outstanding Rsch., York Coll./Biomedical Rsch. Support Group, 1996, Excellence in Biology, York Coll., Dept. Natural Sci., 1996, Resident of Yr., Mercer U. / Med. Ctr. of Ctrl. Ga., 2006, 2007, America's Top Physicians, Consumer Rsch. Group, 2007, Fellow of Yr., Med. Coll. of Ga., 2008; scholar Full Tuition Merit scholarship, York Coll., 1992—96. Fellow: ACP (life), Am. Coll. of Clin. Endocrinologists (life), AMA (life). Achievements include development of ultrasound guided fine needle aspiration; research in endocrinology, diabetes and metabolism; endocrine cancer specialist; endocrinology specialist attending. Avocations: reading, exercise, sewing. Office: Med Coll Ga 1467 Harper St HB-5025 Augusta GA 30912 Personal E-mail: dayal_raja@juno.com. Business E-Mail: draja@mail.mcg.edu.

RAJA, RAJALINGAM, immunologist, educator; b. Nallampalli, Dharmapuri District, Tamil Nadu, India, Apr. 15, 1963; s. Raja Manickam and Rakshmi Ramagounder; m. Victoria Rajalingam; children: Karan Rajalingam, Kavi Rajalingam. PhD, All India Inst. Med. Scis., New Delhi, 1996. Diplomate Am. Bd. Histocompatibility and Immunogenetics, 2008. Postdoc. rsch. affiliate Stanford U., 1997—2001; asst. clin. prof. dir. molecular immunogenetics UCLA, 2002—. Contbr. scientific papers (Shakuntala Amir Chand prize, 1996). Mem.: Indian Immunology Soc., Am. Soc. Transplantation, Am. Soc. Histocompatibility and Immunogenetics, Soc. Natural Immunity, Am. Assn. Immunologists. Achievements include research in diversity of KIR-HLA gene combinations, and their role in human health and disease. Office: Univ Calif LA 1000 Veteran Ave Rm 1-536 Los Angeles CA 90095-1652 Office Fax: 310-206-3216. Business E-Mail: rrajalingam@mednet.ucla.edu.

RAJA, RAJENDRAN, physicist; b. Guruvayur, Kerala, India, July 14, 1948; arrived in US, 1974; s. P.K. Sreeveerarayan and Chandramathi Raja; m. Selitha Barbara Freundorfer, 1976; 1 child, Anjali. BA with honors, Cambridge U., Eng., 1970, MA with honors, 1974, PhD, 1974. Rsch. assoc. Fermilab, Batavia, Ill., 1975—78, assoc. scientist, 1978—83, scientist I, 1983—88, scientist II, 1988—. Monte Carlo convenor DO Expt., 1986—97, top quark physics convenor, 1990—94; head DO Software Support Group, 1986—93, DO Electron ID Group, 1989—94; head emittance exch./ring coolers group Muon Collider/Neutrino Factory Collaboration, 2001—03; spokesman Mipp Expt. Fermilab, Batavia, 2001—; fellow Trinity Coll. Cambridge U., 1973. Contbr. over 300 articles to profl. jours. Pres. Cambridge U. India Soc., 1969—70. Mem.: AAAS, Planetary Soc., Am. Phys. Soc. Achievements include discovery of top quark. Home: 1304 Margate Ct Naperville IL 60540 Office: Fermi Nat Accelerator Lab PO Box 500 Batavia IL 60510 Office Phone: 630-840-4092. Business E-Mail: raja@fnal.gov.

RAJAGOPALAN, RAGHAVAN, medical researcher; b. Tiruvarur, Tamil Nadu, India, May 6, 1954; s. Parthasarathi and Vasantha Rajagopalan; m. Vaidehi Raghavan Rangaswamy; children: Desikan Raghavan, Kiran. PhD, Columbia U., NYC, 1980. Cert.: US Patent and Trademark Office (patent agent). Rsch. fellow Ricerca Bioscis., Concord, Ohio, 2002—03; prin. rsch. scientist Covidien, Hazelwood, Mo., 2004—. Contbr. articles to profl. jours. Cons. Abhinaya, St. Louis. Achievements include patents for diagostic and therapeutic pharmacetuicals. Avocations: philosophy, classical music. Home: 204 City Gate Ln Saint Charles MO 63303 Office: Covidien 675 McDonnell Blvd Hazelwood MO 63042 Business E-Mail: raghavan.rajagopalan@covidien.com.

RAJAMOHAN, KALLURU R., science educator, researcher; married. PhD, Srivenkateswara U., Tirupati, India, 1998. Rsch. scientist Miss. Ethanol LLC, Winona, Miss., 2005—07; asst. prof. Jackson State U., Miss., 2007—. Contbr. scientific papers to profl. jours. Office: Jackson State Univ 1400 JRLynch St Jackson MS 39217 Office Fax: 601-979-3630.

RAJAN, RAGHURAM, economist, educator; s. R and M Govindarajan; m. Radhika Puri, Aug. 21, 1989; children: Naintara, Akhil. BTech, Indian Inst. Tech., New Delhi, 1985; PGDM, Indian Inst. Mgmt., Ahmedabad, 1987; PhD, MIT, Mass., 1991. Prof. U. Chgo., 1991—; chief economist IMF, Washington, 2003—06. Econ. advisor to prime min. India, 2008—. Author: (non-fiction book) Saving Capitalism from the Capitalists. Bd. Chgo. Coun. Global Affairs, 2008. Recipient Fischer Black prize, Am. Fin. Assn., 2003. Avocations: squash, tennis, skiing.

RAJAN, RAMKISHEN S., economist, educator; m. Harminder K. Chyle, Jan. 30, 2000. MA, Claremont U., 1996, U. Mich., 1998; PhD, Claremont U., 1999. Sr. lectr. U. Adelaide, South Australia, Australia, 1999—; vis. freeman scholar Claremont McKenna Coll., Calif., 2003—04; assoc. prof. pub. policy George Mason U., Arlington, Va., 2004—. Vis. fellow Inst. Policy Studies, Singapore, 2001—. Author: (book) Economic Globalization and Asia: Essays on Finance, Trade and Taxation; editor, author (book) Sustaining Competitiveness in the New Global Economy: The Experience of Singapore. Guest columnist Bus. Times, Singapore, 2003—04. Fellow Bradley Found. award, 1999. Office: George Mason Univ MSN 3B1 3401 N Fairfax Dr Arlington VA 22201

RAJAPAKSE, NIHAL, horticulturist, educator; b. Colombo, Sri Lanka, Sept. 13, 1955; s. RPK and Daya Rajapakse; m. Sriyani Amunugama, Aug. 6, 1981; 1 child, Dilani. BS, U. Peradeniya, Sri Lanka, 1980; MS, Tex. A & M, Coll. Sta., PhD, 1986. Lectr. U. Peradeniya, 1987—88; prof. Clemson U., SC, 1989—. Office: Clemson Univ RM E 143 Poole Ag Ctr Clemson SC 29634 Home Phone: 864-654-9035; Office Phone: 864-656-4970. Office Fax: 864-656-4960. Business E-Mail: nrjpks@clemson.edu.

RAJARAM, SRI-SUJANTHY, internist, educator; arrived in US, 1993, permanent resident, 1998; d. Vel and Sribalasaras Veluppillai; m. K. Rajaram, June 4, 1989; children: Sanjev, Sankavi, Sweda. MBBS, U. Jaffna, Srilanka, 1989. Diplomate Am. Bd. of Internal Medicine 1996, Critical Care 1998, Am. Acad. Sleep Medicine 2003. Asst. prof. medicine Albert Einstein Sch. Medicine, Bronx, NY, 1998—2003; med. dir. Cardio Sleep Ctr., Oldbridge, NJ, 2003—04; intensivist Robertwood Johnson U. Hosp., New Brunswick, NJ, 2003—05; asst. prof. medicine Robertwood Johnson Med. Sch. UMDNJ, NJ, 2003—05; asst. prof. medicine Cooper U. Hosp., NJ, 2005—, intensivist, 2005—. Intern, pediats. ob-gyn. U. Colombo, Sri Lanka, 1991—92, sr. house officer, anesthesiology, 1992; residency, internal medicine LI Coll. Hosp., NY, 1993—96; fellowship, critical care medicine Mt. Siani Sch. Medicine, 1996—98; sleep medicine NJ Neuro-Sleep Inst., JFK Med. Ctr., Edison, NJ, 2001—02. Contbr. chapters to books, articles to profl. jours., abstracts to profl. jours. Cmty. svc. project, primary health care svcs. to Sri Lanka, 2004, 2005; bd. dir. Internat. Med. Health Orgn. USA, 2003—; dir., continuous med. edn. Internat. Med. Health Orgn., 2004—; NJ coordinator Internat. Med. Health Orgn. USA, 2003—. Fellow: Am. Acad. Sleep Medicine, American Coll. Chest Physicians (Gov.'s Cmty. Svc. award 2004); mem.: Soc. Critical Care Medicine. Hindu. Home: 5 Rushton Ct West Windsor NJ 08550 Office: Cooper U Hosp One Cooper Plaza Camden NJ 08103 Business E-Mail: rajaram-sri-sujanthy@cooperhealth.edu.

RAJASEKAR, ARCOT, computer scientist; s. Kuppuswamy and Sakunthala Arcot; m. Malini Govindaraj Purasawalkam, Aug. 21, 1989; children: Rupak, Bhairavi. B with honors in engring., Coll. of Engring., U. of Madras, India, 1979; MS, Indian Inst. of Tech., India, 1982; PhD, U. Md., 1984. Post doctoral rsch. assoc. U. Md. Inst. for Advanced Computer Studies, Coll. Pk., Md., 1989—90; asst. prof. U. Ky., Lexington, 1990—96; scientist to principle scientist San Diego Supercomputer Ctr., La Jolla, Calif., 1996—2001, dir., data grid technologies group, 2001—08. Vice thrust area liaison Nat. Partnership for Advanced Computational Infrastructure, La Jolla, Calif., 1997—2003; reviewer NSF, Washington, 2000—02; prof. U. NC, Chapel Hill, 2008—; chief scientist Renaissance Computing Inst., Chapel Hill, 2008—; co-dir. Ctr. Data Intensive Cyber Environments UNC. Author: (research monograph) Foundations of Disjunctive Logic Programming; guest editor Annals of Mathematics and Artificial Intelligence; contbr. articles various profl. jours., chapters to books various profl. text. Founder, dir. South India Heritage Found. Various scientific grants, NSF, 1991—, Storage Resource Broker Performance Optimization grant, Dept. of Def., 2000—01, Biomedical Imaging Rsch. Network Coordinating Ctr. grant, NIH, 2001—, Nat. Archives and Records Agency, Persistent Archive Testbed, 2001—, Libr. of Congress Digital Archives Project, 2005—07, Portal Web Services: Support of DOE SciDAC Collaborations grant, Dept. of Energy, 2002-2005, Rsch. in String-oriented Databases grant, Dept. of Def., 1996, grant, Data Grids For Cmty. Driven Applications, 2007—. Mem.: Global Grid Forum. Hindu. Achievements include development of storage resource broker; patents for collection-based persistent digital archive; development of MCAT - a metadata catalog, iRODS - integrated Rule Oriented Data System; research in data grid technology; logic programming. Avocations: reading, fish-breeding, web-surfing, camping, hiking, numismatics. Office: San Diego Supercomputer Ctr UCSD 9500 Gilman Dr La Jolla CA 92014-0505 Business E-Mail: sekar@diceresearch.org.

RAJASEKARAN, SANGUTHEVAR, computer science educator; b. Andipatty, India, June 7, 1957; came to U.S., 1983; s. Subbiah and Ponnuthayammal (Sonai Servai) Sanguthevar; m. Krishnavadhana Ramaswami, Feb. 4, 1988; 1 child, Keeran. BSc in Spl. Physics, Madurai Kamaraj U., 1977; BE in Elec. Tech., Indian Inst. Sci., 1981, ME in Automation, 1983; PhD in Computer Sci., Harvard U., 1988. Teaching asst. Aiken Computing Lab., Harvard U., Cambridge, Mass., 1983-86; assoc. in rsch. dept. computer sci. Duke U., Durham, N.C., 1986-88; asst. prof. computer and info. sci. U. Pa., Phila., 1988-94; assoc. prof. computer and info. sci. U. Fla., Gainesville, 1994-99, prof., 1999—2000; chief scientist ARCoT Sys., 2000—02; United Tech. Corp. chair, prof. Computer Sci. and Engring. U. Conn., Storrs, 2002—, dir. Booth Eng. Ctr. for Advanced Techs., 2006—. Vis. scientist U. Saarlandes, Saarbrücken, Germany, 1991; vis. scholar U. Md. Inst. for Advanced Computer Studies, 1993; mem. program com. Internat. Parallel Processing Symposium, 1996-97; chmn. workshop on randomized parallel computing, 1996, 97; lectr., presenter numerous seminars; referee numerous profl. jours., including Jour. Computer and Systems Sci., IEEE Trans. on Computers, Parallel Processing Letters, Soc. Indsl. and Applied Math. Jour. on Computing. Contbg. author: Advances in Parallel Algorithms, 1992, Synthesis of Parallel Algorithms, 1993, Parallel Algorithm Derivation and Program Transformation, 1993, Computer Algorithms/C++, 1997; contbr. numerous articles to profl. jours. Rsch. grantee NSF, 1989—, Army Rsch. Office, 1989-93, NSF, 1992. Mem. Assn. Computing Machinery, Conn. Acad. Sci. and Engring. (elected mem.); fellow IEEE Office: Univ Conn 257 ITE Bldg CSE Storrs Mansfield CT 06269-2155

RAJENDRA, ANAND LAXMIKANTRAO, electrical engineer; b. Parbhani, Maharashtra, India, Dec. 4, 1980; s. Laxmikant V. and Manorama L. Rajendra; m. Amruta Anand Brahmanathkar, July 6, 2008. Diploma in Elec. Engring., Govt. Poly., Aurangabad, Maharashtra, 1999; BEE, Govt. Coll. Engring., Pune U., Maharashtra, 2002; MEE, U. Ala., Birmingham, 2006. EIT Ala., 2008. Sandwich trainee engr. Tata Motors Co. Ltd., Pimpri, Pune, 2001—02; elec. engr., officer Tata Power Co. Ltd., Mumbai, 2002—04; project engr.-instrumentation and controls Malcolm Pirnie Inc., Birmingham, Ala., 2006—. Participant U. Ala., 2004. Mem.: IEEE. Hindu. Achievements include design of PLC/SCADA based controls and monitoring systems; phisical security and access control systems. Avocations: music, sports, travel. Office: Malcolm Pirnie Inc 2170 Highland Ave S Ste 250 Birmingham AL 35205 Personal E-mail: anandrajendra@yahoo.com.

RAJENDRA, KUNWAR, retired engineering educator, consultant; PhD, Mich. State U., 1980. Cert. prof. engr., Mich., 1976. Engr. Sarvajanik Nirman Vibhag, Lucknow, Uttar Paradesh, India, 1962—71; project engr. high energy physics Mich. State U., East Lansing, Mich., 1972—76; transp. planning dir. City of Lansing, Mich., 1976—88; engr. transp. sys. State of Mich., 1991—2002; adj. prof. Mich. State U., East Lansing, 2003—. Program dir. Intelligent Transportation Sys., Mich. Fellow, ASCE, 2002, Inst. of Transp. Engrs., 2002. Office Fax: 517-353-1980.

RAJFER, JACOB, urologist, educator; b. Trinidad, W.I., Nov. 16, 1948; M. Susan. BS honors, U. Ill., Chgo., 1964-68; MD, Northwestern U., 1968-72. Cert. Am. Bd. Urology, Calif., Colo., Md., Wash. Intern U. So. Calif. Med. Ctr., Los Angeles, 1972-73; resident in surgery St. Joseph's Hosp., Denver, 1973-74; jr. asst. resident in urology Johns Hopkins Hosp., Balt., 1974-75, sr. asst. resident; research fellow Johns Hopkins U. Sch. Med., Balt., 1975-76; chief resident Johns Hopkins Hosp., Balt., 1977-78; chief urology Wash. Med. Ctr., Seattle, 1978-80, Harbor UCLA Med. Ctr., Torrance, Calif., 1980—; asst. prof. dept. urology U. Wash., Seattle, 1978-80; asst. prof. div. urology, dept. surgery UCLA, 1980-83, assoc. prof., 1983—. Asst. prof. urology, U. Wash., 1978-80, urology, UCLA, 1980—. Contbr. articles to profl. jours. Fellow Am. Coll. of Surgeons; mem. Am. Fertility Soc., Kidney Found. of So. Calif., Soc. for the Study of Reproduction, Los Angeles Urol. Soc., So. Calif. Transplant Soc., Soc. of Univ. Urologists, Pacific Coast Fertility Soc., Am. Urol. Assn., Calif. Urol. Soc. (3rd prize lab. research Grayson Carroll Essay 1977, 1st prize Grayson Carroll Essay 1978, 1st prize Joseph F. McCarthy Essay 1984, 85, Am. Soc. Andrology, Urol. Soc. Transplantation and Vascular surgery, Soc. Univ. Urology Residents (chmn. 1977-78). Office: Harbor UCLA Med Ctr PO Box 2910 Torrance CA 90509-2910

RAJKOWSKI, E. MARK, corporate financial executive; BS, Lehigh Univ. CPA NY, NJ, Pa. Positions through mng. ptnr. Pricewaterhouse Coopers LLP, 1981—98; corp. contr. Eastman Kodak Co., 1998—2001, v.p. fin., 2001—03, COO consumer digital bus., 2003, v.p., gen. mgr. worldwide ops imaging systems, 2004; sr. v.p., CFO MeadWestvaco Corp., Glen Allen, Va., 2004—. Bd. dir. Performance Technologies Inc. Mem.: Fin. Executives Inst., Am. Inst. CPAs. Office: MeadWestvaco Corp 11013 W Broad St Glen Allen VA 23060

RAJLICH, VACLAV THOMAS, computer science educator, researcher, consultant; b. Prague, Czech Republic, May 3, 1939; came to U.S., 1980; s. Vaclav and Marie Rajlich; m. Ivana M., Aug. 6, 1968; children: Vasik, Paul, John, Luke. MS, Czech Tech. U., Prague, 1962; PhD, Case Western Res. U., 1971. Rsch. engr. Rsch. Inst. for Math. Machines, Prague, 1963-67, scientist, 1971-75, mgr., 1975-79; vis. assoc. prof. computer sci. Calif. State U., Fullerton, 1980-81; assoc. prof. computer and communication sci. U. Mich., Ann Arbor, 1982-85; prof. Wayne State U., Detroit, 1985—, chair dept. computer sci., 1985-90. Vis. scientist Carnegie-Mellon U., Pitts., 1987, Harvard U., Cambridge, Mass., 1988. Contbr. articles to profl. jours. Recipient Chrysler Challenge Fund, 1988. Mem. Computer Soc. of IEEE, Assn. for Computing Machinery. Roman Catholic. Achievements include development of tools for software maintenance, program comprehension, software design methods, parallel grammars, graph rewriting, abstract state machines. Office: Wayne State U Dept Computer Sci Detroit MI 48202 Office Phone: 313-577-5423. Business E-Mail: rajlich@cs.wayne.edu.

RAJU, MINNIE M., application analyst, critical care nurse; arrived in U.S., 1974; d. Pazhavilla I. and Mary Raju. BS in Biology, Albany State U., 1994; ADN, Rockland CC, Suffern, NY, 1997; BSN, U. Md., 2003, MS in Nursing Informatics, 2005. RN N.Y., Md., DC. Clin. nurse Nyack Hosp., NY, 1997—99, Washington Hosp. Ctr., 1999—, clin. mgr., 2004—05; applications devel. mgr. Computer Scis. Corp., 2005—08; clin. nurse informaticist NIH, 2008—. Mem.: Am. Assn. Critical Care Nurses, Health Info. Mgmt. Sys. Soc., Am. Med. Informatics Assn., Greater Washington Area Chamber Am. Assn. Critical Care Nurses, Sigma Theta Tau. Seventh Day Adventist.

RAJU, T. SHANTHA, medical researcher; s. Thimme and Nagamma Thimme Gowda; m. Savitha Raju; 1 child, Sudesh. PhD, U. Mysore, 1988. Scientist Genentech Inc., South San Francisco, 1995—2001; asst. dir. Centocor, Radnor, Pa., 2004—05; rsch. fellow Centocor R&D Inc., Radnor, 2005—. Mng. ptnr. CarboWorld, San Mateo, Calif., 2001—04. Fundriser United Way, Radnor, 2004—08. Mem.: ASBMB, Am. Chem. Soc. Office: Centocor R&D Inc 145 King Prussia Rd Radnor PA 19087 Office Fax: 610-993-7817. E-mail: traju@its.jnj.com.

RAJUK, VENUGOPAL KUPPANNA, computer engineer, educator; b. Bangalore, Karnataka, India, Mar. 26, 1956; s. Kuppanna and Muniamma (Narayanappa) Muniswamappa; m. Karthyayini Venkappa, June 15, 1989; 1 child, Tejaswi Venugopal. B in Electronics, U. Visvesvaraya Coll. Engring., Bangalore, 1979; MA in Econs., Karnatak U., 1982; B in Comm., Bangalore U., 1984, B in Law, MA in Bus. Fin., 1986, PhD in Economics, 1989, M. Bus. Fin., 1990; M in Computer Sci., Indian Inst. Sci., 1992, postgrd. diploma in journalism, 1985, postgrad. diploma in pub. rels., 1986, postgrad. diploma in indsl. rels., 1987; PhD in Comp. Sci., Indian Inst. Tech., 1999. Engr. Hindustan Machine Tools, Bangalore, 1980-82; prof. computer sci., chmn. dept. computer sci., electronics and info. sci., prin. Evening Coll., U. Visvesvaraya Coll. Engring., Bangalore, 1982—, prin., dean faculty of engring., 2007—. Convenor Indian Econs. Forum, Bangalore, 1990-91; founder Alpha Coll. Engirng., Bangalore; mem. acad. coun. Bangalore U. Author: Petrodollar and the World Economy, 1990, Programming with Fortran, 1993, Programming with Pascal and C, 1994, Microprocessors, 1995, Programming with C, 1997, Programming with Pascal, 1997, Programming with C++, 1997, Finite Automata and Formal Languages, 2005, Data Structures Using C, 2005, Mastering-C, 2006, Mastering Java, 2006, Test Your C Aptitude, 2006, C++ Aptitude, 2006, File Structures, 2007, Data Mining and Algorithms, 2007, Wavelength Converters in Optical Networks, 2007, Growth Imbalance and Indian Economy, 2007, Fiscal and Monetary Reforms in India, 2007, Digital Electronics, 2008, Soft Computing and Data Mining, 2008. Pres. St. Joseph's Coll., Bangalore, 1974, Bharatiya Vidya Bhavan, Bangalore, 1988; chmn. Alpha Ednl. and Charitable Trust, 2001—. Nat. Merit scholar Govt. India, 1973-79, Nat. Hindi scholar, 1973-75; recipient Kulapathi Gold medal Bharatiya Vidya Bhavan, 1988, Kulapathi Silver medal, 1989, Outstanding Br. Counsellor award IEEE, 2005. Mem. Aryabhata Edn. Soc. (pres. 1991—), Cotton Sports Assn. (v.p. 1983—, chmn. alpha ednl. and chariable trust), Soc. for Promotion of Indian Classical Music and Culture Among Youth (sec. 1985-86), Sun Club (founder), Lions, Jaycees (v.p. Cosmos chpt. 1986-87). Avocations: cricket, social work, film appreciation, photography. Home: 109 4th Main 2d Cross HAL III Stage Bangalore 560 075 India Office: U Visvesvaraya Coll Engring K R Circle Bangalore 560 001 India Personal E-mail: venugopalkr@gmail.com.

RAKER, IRMA S., retired Judge, Maryland Court of Appeals; b. Bklyn. m. Samuel K. Raker. BA, Syracuse U., 1959; cert. of attendance (hon.), Hague (The Netherlands) Acad. Internat. Law, 1959; JD, Am. U., 1972. Bar: Md. 1973, D.C. 1974, U.S. Dist. Ct. Md. 1977, U.S. Ct. Appeals (4th cir.) 1977. Asst. state's atty. State's Atty.'s Office Montgomery County, Md., 1973-79; ptnr. Sachs, Greenebaum & Tayler, Washington, 1979-80; judge Dist. Ct. Md., Rockville, 1980-82, Cir. Ct. for Montgomery County, Md., 1982-94, Md. Ct. of Appeals, 1994—2008. Adj. prof. Washington Coll. Law, Am. U., 1980—; mem. faculty Md. Jud. Inst., Nat. Criminal Def. Inst., 1980, 81, 82; mem. legis. com. Md. Jud. Conf., mem. exec. com., 1985-89, mem. commn. to study bail bond and surety industry in Md.; mem. spl. com. to revise article 27 on crimes and punishment State of Md., 1991—; mem. inquiry com. atty. Grievance Commn. Md., 1978-81; chair jud. compensation com. Md. Jud. Conf., 1997—. Treas., v.p. West Bradley Citizens Assn., 1964-68; mem. adv. com. to county exec. on child abuse Montgomery County, 1976-77, mem. adv. com. to county exec. on battered spouses, 1977-78, mem. adv. com. on environ. protection, 1980; mem. citizens adv. bd. Montgomery County Crisis Ctr., 1980. Recipient Robert C. Heeney award Md. State Bar Assn., 1993, Dorothy Beatty Meml. award Women's Law Ctr., 1994, Rita Davidson award Women's Bar Md., 1995, Margaret Brent Trailblazers award ABA Commn. on Women in the Profession/Women's Bar Assn. Md., 1995, Elizabeth Dole Woman of Achievement award ARC, 1998, Leadership in Law award The Daily Record, 2001, Nat. Assn. Social Workers' Pub. Citizen of Yr. award, 2001, others; named of Md.'s Top 10 Women Warfield's Bus. Record, 1997, 99, 2001. Fellow Md. Bar Found.; mem. ABA (chair criminal justice stds. com. 1995-96, mem. coun. criminal law sect. 1997—, del. nat. conf. state trial judges, active various coms.), Am. Law Rev., Md. State Bar Assn. (chair coun. criminal law and practice sect., mem. bd. govs. 1981, 82, 85, 86, 90, mem. coun. litigation sect., active coms., chair com. to draft pattern jury instrns. in civil and criminal cases 1980—), Nat. Assn. Women Judges, Internat. Acad. Trial Judges, Am. Law Inst., Montgomery County Bar Assn. (chair criminal law sect. 1978-79, mem. exec. com. 1979-80, active other coms., Outstanding Jurist award 2000), Montgomery County Bar Leaders, Women's Bar Assn. Md., Women's Bar Assn. D.C., Hadassah Women's Orgn. (life), Pioneer Women Na'amat (Celebration of Women award 1985), Pi Sigma Alpha.

RAKES, GANAS KAYE, retired finance and banking educator; b. Floyd, Va., May 2, 1938; s. Samuel D. and Ocie J. (Peters) R.; m. Mary Ann Simmons, Oct. 1, 1961; 1 child, Sabrina Darrow. BS, Va. Tech., 1960, MS, 1964; D of Bus. Adminstrn., Washington U., St. Louis, 1971. Assoc. prof. commerce U. Va., Charlottesville, 1968-80; O'Bleness prof. fin. and banking Ohio U., Athens, 1980—2003, chmn. fin. dept. Coll. of Bus. Adminstrn., 1983—2003, O'Bleness prof. emeritus fin., 2003—. Contbr. articles to profl. jours. Served to 1st lt. U.S. Army, 1961-63. Mem. Fin. Mgmt. Assn., Eastern Fin. Assn., Two Rivers Country Club. Republican. Episcopalian. Avocations: golf, sailing. E-mail: rakes1@verizon.net.

RAKHNO, IGOR, physicist; s. Leonid and Elena Rakhno; m. Olga Kopeliovich, Nov. 24, 1984; 1 child, Eugenia. MS in Physics, Belarusian State U., Minsk, Belarus, 1981; postgrad. in nuc. engring., Nuc. Power Engring. Inst., Minsk, 1988. PhD Diploma Supreme Exam. Bd., Moscow, 1991. Jr. scientist Nuc. Power Engring. Inst., Minsk, 1981—91; scientist Radiation Physics and Chemistry Problems Inst., Minsk, 1991—93, sr. scientist, 1993—2000; rsch. assoc. Fermi Nat. Accelerator Lab., Batavia, Ill., 2000—03, guest scientist, 2004—; rsch. assoc. U. Ill., Urbana-Champaign, 2003—04. Fellow, Matsumae Internat. Found., Tokyo, 1994. Achievements include research in theoretical and experimental research on nuclear waste transmutation with low-energy neutrons and high-energy hadrons; theoretical research on radiation environment in high-luminosity regions in the Large Hadron Collider to be built at CERN (Geneva, Switzerland) to study proton-proton collisions at 14 TeV. Office: Fermi National Accelerator Lab MS 220 PO Box 500 Batavia IL 60510-0500 Office Fax: 630-840-6039. Business E-Mail: rakhno@fnal.gov.

RAKIC, PASKO, neuroscientist, educator; b. Ruma, Yugoslavia, May 15, 1933; came to U.S., 1969; m. Patricia Goldman, 1969. MD, U. Belgrade, 1959, PhD in Devel. Biology and Genetics, 1969. With inst. path. physiology Med. Sch. U. Belgrade, 1959-61, resident in neurosurgery, 1961-62; NIH research fellow neuropathology Harvard Med. Sch., Boston, 1962-66; asst. prof. Inst. Biol. Rsch., Belgrade, 1967-68; from asst. prof. to assoc. prof. neuropathology and neuroscience Harvard Med. Sch., 1969-77; prof. neurosci. Yale Med. Sch., New Haven, 1977-78, Dorys McConnell Duberg prof. neurosci., 1978—, also chmn. neurobiology dept. Author of 300 sci. papers and gen. books on brain orgn. and devel. Co-recipient Kavli prize for neurosci., Norwegian Acad. Sci. and Letters in partnership with the Kavli Found. and the Norwegian Ministry of Edn. and Rsch., 2008. Mem.: AAAS, NAS, Inst. Med., Am. Phys. Soc. (Lashley award, Fyssen Internat. Sci. prize, Gerard prize, Pasarw award, Henry Gray award, Bristol Myers Squibb award), Soc. Neurosci. (pres. 1996). Office: Yale U Neurosci Program L200 SHM PO Box 208074 New Haven CT 06520 Office Phone: 203-785-4330.

RAKIP, ANNE MARIE, psychology professor; b. Lowell, Mass., Apr. 09; d. George Thomas Johnson and Ruth Madeline Jones-Johnson; m. Michael Albert Rakip, Feb. 22; children: Thomas Michael, Madeline Anne. BA, Western New Eng. Coll., Springfield, Mass., 1992; MS, Fitchburg State Coll. Grad. Sch., Mass., 1994; EdD, U. Mass. Grad. Sch. Edn., Lowell, 2003. Cert. in psychometrics Durham VAMC Duke U., 2005; GRI Fla. Assn. Realtors, 2009. Adj. prof. Palm Beach CC, Lake Worth, Fla., 2004—; asst. prof. SC State U., Orangeburg, 2008—. Disaster team mem. ARC, West Palm Beach, Fla., 2004—08. Recipient Coburn award, U. Mass. Faculty, 2003. Mem.: ASCD. Democrat. Roman Catholic. Home: 953 39th Ct West Palm Beach FL 33407 Personal E-mail: anne.rakip@gmail.com. Business E-Mail: arakip@scsu.edu.

RAKKOLAINEN, ISMO, research scientist; s. Erkki Rakkolainen and Sinikka Svanström; m. Kaarina Havia, Apr. 25, 1992; 1 child, Mikael. MSc, U. Helsinki, 1990; PhD in Tech., Tampere U. Tech., Finland, 2002. Lic. tech. Tampere U. Tech, 2000. Sr. rschr. Tampere U. Tech., 1994—2007; vis. rschr. U. Calif., Santa Barbara, 2005, 2008—. CTO FogScreen, Inc., Helsinki, Finland, 2003—07. Recipient 1st prize award, Finnish New Tech. Found., 2003, InnoSuomi Nat. Innovation Contest award, Pres. Finland, 2003, 2005 European IST prize, European Union, 2004, 1st prize, Laval Virtual, France, 2004, Innovation award, Profl. Lighting and Sound Assn., 2005, The Event Svcs. Assn. UK, 2006, Bottom Line Design award, Bus. 2.0 Mag., 2007, Best Effects Product award, Club World, 2007. Mem.: Mensa, IEEE, Soc. for Info. Display, Assn. Computer Machine. Achievements include patents for fog screen; patents pending in field. Avocations: mountaineering, travel, photography. Business E-Mail: ira@cs.ucsb.edu.

RAKO, SUSAN, psychiatrist, writer, producer, filmmaker; b. Springfield, Mass., Sept. 4, 1939; d. Robert and Ann (Melnikoff) Mandell; 1 child, Jennifer Sarah. Student, Wellesley Coll., 1957-60; BS, U. Cin., 1961; MS in Film, Boston U., 1988; MD, Albert Einstein Coll. Medicine, 1966. Med. rsch. asst. neuroendocrinology Worcester Found. Exptl. Biology, Shrewsbury, Mass., 1959; med. rsch. asst. May Inst., Cin., 1961-62; intern in medicine, surgery Mt. Auburn Hosp., Cambridge, Mass., 1966-67; resident in adult psychiatry Mass. Mental Health Ctr., Boston, 1967-69; tchg. fellow in psychiatry Harvard Med. Sch., Boston, 1967-69, clin. fellow in psychiatry, 1969-70; pvt. practice Newton, Mass., 1970—; clin. instr. psychiatry Harvard Med. Sch., Boston, 1970-75; resident in child and adult psychiatry Beth Israel Hosp., Boston, 1969-70; psychiatrist Mass. Mental Health Ctr., Boston, 1970-77, Newton-Wellesley Hosp., 1982. Cons. Cutler Counseling Ctr., Norwood, Mass., 1983, VA Hosp., San Juan, 1990—94; founder, pres. Women's Health on Alert, Inc., 2003—; spkr. in field. Author: No More Periods? The Risks of Menstrual Suppression, 2003, The Hormone of Desire: The Truth About Testosterone, Sexuality, and Menopause, 1996, 2d edit., 1999, That's How the Light Gets In: Memoir of a Psychiatrist, 2005, The Blessings of the Curse, 2006; co-editor: Semrad: The Heart of a Therapist, 1980, (paperback) 2004; film maker: Susan and Jenni, 1987, (documentary) Alexandra Almost Three, 2007; (documentary) exec. prodr. play Hysterics, 2005. Business E-Mail: susanrako@aol.com.

RAKOFF, JED SAUL, federal judge, author; b. Phila., Aug. 1, 1943; s. Abraham Edward and Doris Tobiah (Michell) R.; m. Ann Rosenberg, Aug. 4, 1974; children: Jena Lynn, Elana Beth, Keira Jan. BA, Swarthmore Coll., 1964, LLD (hon.), 2003; MPhil, Balliol Coll., Oxford U., Eng., 1966; JD, Harvard U., 1969; LLD (hon.), St. Francis U., 2005. Bar: N.Y. 1971, D.C. 1983, U.S. Supreme Ct. 1986. Law clk. U.S. Ct. Appeals (3rd cir.), Phila., 1969-70; assoc. Debevoise, Plimpton, Lyons & Gates, NYC, 1970-73; asst. U.S. atty. So. Dist. N.Y., NYC, 1973-80, chief bus. and securities fraud prosecutions U.S. Atty.'s Office, 1978-80; ptnr. Mudge Rose Guthrie Alexander & Ferdon, NYC, 1980-90, Fried Frank Harris Shriver & Jacobson, NYC, 1990-96; judge U.S. Dist. Ct. (So. Dist.), 1996—. Lectr. in law Columbia Law Sch., 1988-; mem. bd. mgrs. Swarthmore Coll., 2003-08; mem. governing bd. project law and neuroscience MacArthur Found., 2007—. Author: (with S. Arkin et al) Business Crime, 6 vols., 1982, Criminal Defense Techniques, 6 vols., 1982, (with H. Goldstein) RICO: Civil and Criminal Law and Strategy, 1989, (with J. Sack) Corporate Sentencing Guidelines,: Compliance and Mitigation (with L. Sand et al), 1993, Modern Federal Jury Instructions, 2007; editor-in-chief Bus. Crimes Bull., 1994-95; columnist N.Y. Law Jour., 1985-95; contbr. numerous articles to law revs. Mem. exec. bd. N.Y. chpt. Am. Jewish Com., 1971-95. Fellow Am. Coll. Trial Lawyers (chmn. N.Y. State 1993-94), Am. Bd. Criminal Lawyers; mem. ABA, N.Y. State Bar Assn., Assn. of Bar of City of N.Y. (chmn. criminal law com. 1986-89), Fed. Bar Coun., N.Y. Coun. Def. Lawyers (dir. 1990-94). Democrat. Jewish. Office: US Courthouse 500 Pearl St Rm 1340 New York NY 10007-1316 Office Phone: 212-805-0401. Business E-Mail: Jed_S_Rakoff@nysd.uscourts.gov.

RAKOTOBE-JOEL, THIERRY, engineering educator, researcher, executive director; s. Max Hoambinintsoa Rakotobe and Lydia Nicole Rajoely; m. Andoveloniaina Rasolofo, Jan. 8, 2000. MS in Engring., U. Madagascar, Antananarivo, 1994; PhD, U. Cin., 2000. Rsch. assoc. U. of Sheffield, England, 1998—2000; rsch. fellow U. of Warwick, Coventry, England, 1999—2001; asst. prof. mgmt. Ramapo Coll. of N.J., Mahwah, NJ, 2001—03, assoc. prof. mgmt., 2003—, chmn. dept. mgmt., 2005—08; exec. dir. Sabrin Ctr. Bus. Excellence, 2008—. Editor: (book) Complex Systems and Complexity in Industry; newsletter editor divsn. internat. mgmt. Acad. Mgmt., 1999—2003; contbr. articles to profl. jours. (Highly Commended award, MCB Univ. Press, 2001). Fellow Sam Walton fellow, WalMart Found., 2001; scholar Fulbright scholar, Inst. of Internat. Edn. Mem.: Acad. of Mgmt. (newsletter editor 2000—03), Decision Sci. Inst. (assoc.), Am. Coun. for Que. Studies (assoc.), Inst. for Ops. Rsch. and Mgmt. Sci. (assoc.), Phi Beta Delta. Office: Ramapo College of New Jersey 505 Ramapo Valley Rd Mahwah NJ 07430 Personal E-mail: trakotobe@aol.com.

RALEIGH, CECIL BARING, geophysicist; b. Little Rock, Aug. 11, 1934; s. Cecil Baring and Lucile Nell (Stewart) R.; m. Diane Lauster, July 17, 1982; children: Alison, Marianne, Lawrence, David. BA, Pomona Coll., Calif., 1956; MA, Claremont Grad. Sch., Calif., 1958; PhD, UCLA, 1963. Fellow Research Sch. Phys. Sci., Australian Nat. U., Canberra, 1963-66; geophysicist U.S. Geol. Survey, Menlo Park, Calif., 1966-80, program mgr. for earthquake prediction research program, 1980-81; dir. Lamont-Doherty Geol. Obs. and prof. geol. scis. Columbia U., Palisades, NY, 1981-89; dean Sch. Ocean and Earth Sci. and Tech. U. Hawaii, Honolulu, 1989—2003; rschr. Hawaii Nat. Energy Inst. U. Hawaii, 2003—. CEO Ctr. for a Sustainable Future, Inc., 1996-2005, pres., chmn., HR Biopetroleum, 2004—; mem. Gov.'s Task Force on Sci. Tech., 1996-98; mem. NAS/NRC Ocean Studies Bd.; chmn. NAS/NRC Yucca Mountain Panel. Author papers control earthquakes, rheology of the mantle, mechanics of faulting, crystal plasticity. Trustee Bishop Mus., 1997—2003. Recipient Interdisciplinary award U.S. Nat. Com. Rock Mechanics, 1969, 74; Meritorious Service award Dept. Interior, 1974; Barrows Centennial Dist. Alumnus award Pomona Coll. Fellow Am. Geophys. Union, Geol. Soc. Am. Democrat. Inventor formation fracturing method. Business E-Mail: cbraleigh@att.net.

RALES, MITCHELL P., automotive parts company executive; b. 1956; married; 2 children. B, DePauw U.; grad., Miami U., Ohio, 1978. Ptnr. Equity Grp. Holdings, Washington, 1979—; pres. Danaher Corp., Washington, 1984—, bd. dirs., chmn. exec. com., 1990—; founder, dir. Colfax Corp., 1995—. Chmn. Capital Campaign for Hosp. Sick Children; treas., trustee, chmn. Capital Campaign of Norwood Sch.; mem. adv. coun. Miami U., Ohio; bd. trustees Hirshorn Mus. and Sculpture Garden; mem. trustees coun. Nat. Gallery Art. Named one of Top 200 Collectors, ARTnews mag., 2003—08, Forbes' Richest Americans, 2006. Avocation: Collector of Modern and Contemporary Art. Office: Danaher Corpn 2099 Pennsylvania Ave NW 12th Fl Washington DC 20006-6800

RALES, STEVEN M., automotive parts company executive; b. Pitts., Mar. 31, 1951; m. Christine Plank Rales (div. 2002). BA, DePauw U., 1973; JD, America U., 1978. Ptnr. Equity Grp. Holdings, Washington, 1979—; chmn., CEO Danaher Corp., Washington, 1984—2001, chmn., 2001—. Named one of Top 200 Collectors, ARTnews mag., 2003—08, Forbes' Richest Americans, 2006. Avocation: Collector of Impressionism, Modern and Contemporary Art. Office: Danaher Corpn 2099 Pennsylvania Ave NW 12th Fl Washington DC 20006

RALEY, BEVERLY SPICKELMIER, retired systems administrator, writer; b. Lawton, Okla., Aug. 13; d. Ted and Audry Spradlin; m. Richard Raley, Sept. 5, 1981; children: Ray Spickelmier, Lori Spickelmier, Robin Moye, Rolinda Smoak. BS in Bus. Edn., Okla. State U., 1970; Master's degree in Curriculum and Instn., U. South Fla., 1981. Cert. Bus. Edn. Tchr. Fla., vocat. dir. Tchr. Hillsborough County Pub. Sch., Tampa, 1970—2005, cons., 1975—94. Spkr. Houghton-Mifflin's Spkrs.' Bur., Nation-Wide, 1978—89; adj. prof. U. South Fla., Tampa, 1989—91. Editor: (accounting editor) Business Education Forum, 1984—85, author articles to profl. jours. Sec. Meadowood Condominium Assn., Tampa, 1985—89, pres., 1985—89. Recipient Outstanding Secondary Bus. Educator, Fla. Bus. Edn. Assn., 1982, Nat. Bus. Edn. Assn., 1983.

RALEY, JOHN WESLEY, JR., lawyer; b. May 23, 1932; s. John Wesley and Helen Thames; children: John Wesley III, Robert Thames. AB, Okla. Baptist U., 1954; JD, U. Okla., 1959. Bar: Okla. 1959, U.S. Supreme Ct. 1973, U.S. Ct. Appeals (10th cir.), 1962, U.S. Dist. Ct. (we. dist.) Okla. 1961, U.S. Dist. Ct. (no. dist.) Okla. 1988, U.S. Dist. Ct. (ea. dist.) Okla. 1989. Asst. U.S. atty. We. Dist. Okla. U.S. Dept. Justice, 1961-69; ptnr. Northcutt, Raley, Clark and Gardner, Ponca City, Okla., 1969-90; U.S. atty. Ea. Dist. Okla. U.S. Dept. Justice, 1990-97; of counsel Northcutt, Clark, Gardner & Hron, Ponca City, 1997—; mcpl. ct. judge Ponca City, 2001—05. Mayor of Ponca City, Okla., 1980-83; mem. Okla. Ethics Commn., 2002—, chmn., 2005-06, 2008-09. Capt. USNR, 1950-84, ret., Surface Warfare Officer. Recipient George Washington Honor medal Freedoms Found. at Valley Forge, 1971, Meritorious Achievement award, U.S. Dept. Justice, 1993, Spl. Initiative award, 1994, Outstanding Alumni Achievement award Okla. Bapt. U., 1981, Outstanding Citizen award Ponca City, 1984. Fellow Am. Coll. Trial Lawyers; mem. ABA, Am. Bd. Trial Advs. (pres. Okla. chpt. 2005), Okla. Bar Assn. (bd. govs. 1988-90), Kay County Bar Assn. (pres. 1980), Am. Legion, Masons, Res. Officers Assn., Naval Res. Assn., VFW. Republican. Southern Baptist. Office: 400 E Central Ave Ste 401 Ponca City OK 74601-5428 Address: PO Box 1412 Ponca City OK 74602-1412 Office Phone: 580-762-1655.

RALL, WILFRID, neuroscientist, sculptor; b. LA, Aug. 29, 1922; s. Udo and Doris (Keiser) R.; m. Ava Lou Freed, 1946 (dec.); children: Sarah E., Madelyn Rall Badger; m. Mary Ellen Condon, 1983. BS summa cum laude, Yale U., 1943; MS, U. Chgo., 1948; PhD, U. N.Z., 1953. Jr. physicist Manhattan Project U. Chgo., 1943-46, biophysics fellow, 1946-48; lectr., sr. lectr. physiology, biophysics U. Otago, Dunedin, N.Z., 1949-56; head biophysics divsn. Naval Med. Rsch. Inst., Bethesda, Md., 1956-57; biophysicist, office math. rsch. Nat. Inst. Arthritis and Metabolic Diseases, Bethesda, 1957-67; sr. rsch. physicist math. rsch. br. Nat. Inst. Diabetes and Digestive and Kidney Diseases, 1967-94; scientist emeritus Nat. Insts. Health, 1994—. Mem. NRC Com. on Brain Scis., 1968-73. Contbr. articles to profl. jours. Fellow: Am. Acad. Arts and Sciences; mem.: Soc. Neurosci. (Swartz prize 2008). Achievements include being an amateur sculptor.

RALLI, CONSTANTINE PANDIA, lawyer; b. Bronxville, NY, Apr. 6, 1948; s. Pandia C. and Mary (Motter) R.; m. Alison Rhoads, Aug. 11, 1973; children: Pandia C., Christopher A. BA, Middlebury Coll., 1970; JD, Fordham U., 1973; LLM in Taxation, NYU, 1986. Bar: NY 1974, US Ct. Appeals (2nd cir.) 1974, US Dist. Ct. (so. and ea. dists.) NY 1975, US Tax Ct. 1977, Fla. 1985, Conn. 1985, US Dist. Ct. Conn. 1987. Assoc. Davis Polk & Wardwell, NYC, 1973-81; ptnr. Hall, McNicol, Hamilton & Clark, NYC, 1981-88, Dewey & LeBoeuf, NYC, 1988—2009; chmn. trust & estates dept. Sullivan & Worcester LLP, NYC, 2009—. Sec., bd. dirs. Fairfield-Maxwell Ltd., Campo Tankers SA, NYC, 1987—95. Bd. dirs. Samaritan Counseling Ctr., Rye, NY, 1987-90, Rye Free Reading Room, 1990-93, Rye Presbyn. Ch., 1986-89. Mem. Union Club, Am. Yacht Club, Ekwanok Country Club (Manchester, Vt.). Republican. Presbyterian. Office: Sullivan & Worcester LLP 1290 Ave of the Americas New York NY 10104 Office Phone: 212-660-3089, 203-259-8383. Office Fax: 212-660-3001. Business E-Mail: cralli@sandco.com.

RALLO, JAMES GILBERT, retired management company executive; b. Balt., Mar. 1, 1942; s. James Vincent and Thelma Mary (Hannahs) R.; m. Frances Elaine Petro, June 13, 1965; children: James Michael, Robert Francis. BS, U. Md., 1965; postgrad., George Washington U., 1967—. Mktg. trainee Chessie Sys., Balt., 1965—66; market analyst Bendix Corp., Balt., 1966—68, contract adminstr. NYC, 1968—70; account exec. Peterson, Howell & Heather, Inc. (name changed to PHH Arval) PHH Vehicle Mgmt. Svcs., Hunt Valley, Md., 1970—75; regional mgr. Peterson, Howell & Heather, Inc., Hunt Valley, 1975—80, v.p. sales, 1980—83, v.p. sales and client rels., 1983—87, sr. v.p. sales and client rels., 1987—91, sr. v.p. client and industry rels., 1991—94, v.p. industry rels., 1994—2003, v.p. strategic partnership, 2003—08. Bd. dirs., mem. fin. com. Towson YMCA, Md., 1981-93, mem. fundraising com., mem. budget com.; coach Cockeysville-Springlake Recreation Coun., 1973-82; advisor Jr. Achievement, 1975-76; fund solicitor United Way, 1983-84; v.p. NAFA Found., 1995—. Mem.: Balt. County C. of C. (legis. com. mem.), Am. Automotive Leasing Assn. (sponsor Industry Standards project 1990—2008), Automotive Fleet and Leasing Assn. (dir. lessors 1993—95, conf. com. 1993—2001, v.p. 1999—2000, exec. v.p. 2000—01, pres. 2001—02, bd. dirs., ednl. com.), Nat. Assn. Fleet Adminstrs. (affiliate chmn. intercounty chpt. 1978—80, nat. affiliate com. 1990—2000, editl. com. 1992—96, mem. conf./program com. 1993—98, bd. govs. 1993—, chmn. affiliates com. 1995—97, co-chair edn. com. 1999—2001, affiliate trustee 2000—03, bd. trustees 2001—03, Hon. award for disting. svc. 1997), Optimists Club (v.p. Springdale-Cockeysville 1982—84, chmn. fundraising com.). Avocations: skiing, sports, classic cars, reading, golf.

RALLS, W. MATTHEW, gas and oil industry drilling executive; BME, MBA, U. Tex., Austin. Various positiions including exec. v.p. Nations Bank, San Antonio, until 1990; exec. v.p., CFO, dir. Kelley Oil Corp., 1990-96; v.p. calital markets & corp. devel. Meridian Resource Corp., 1996-97; v.p., treas. Global Marine, Inc., Houston, 1997-99; sr. v.p., chief fin. officer, treas. Global Marine, Inc (merged in 2001 to become GlobalSantaFe.), Houston, 1999; exec. v.p., COO GlobalSantaFe Corp., 2005—07; CEO, pres., bd. mem. Rowan Companies, Inc., 2009—. Office: Rowan Companies Inc 2800 Post Oak Blvd Ste 5450 Houston TX 77056*

RALPH, NANCYJO, retired music educator; d. Alfred M. and Phyllis L. Niles; m. Dwight G. Ralph, Mar. 28, 1970; children: Victoria L. Fortna, Erik C. MusB in Edn., Grove City Coll., Pa., 1969; M in Elem. Edn., Edinboro U. Pa., 1974; postgrad. in Music Edn., Kent State U., Ohio, 1989. Registered music educator. Elem. music tchr. Lakeview Sch. Dist., Sandy Lake, Pa., 1969; h.s. music tchr. Cambridge Springs H.S., Penncrest Sch. Dist., Pa., 1970—2000, elem. music tchr., 2000—05; pvt. piano tchr. Vol. music tchr. Cornerstone Day Care and Penncrest Day Care Ctrs.; with Tool City Bell Ringers, 2005—. Choir mem., pianist, various com. Saegertown (Pa.) United Meth. Ch., 1970—; dir. Justified By Faith, Saegertown, 2002—. Named to Nat. Honor Roll for Am. Outstanding Tchrs., 2005—06. Mem.: Pa. Music Educators Assn. (curriculum and instrn. chair dist. 2 1993—2003), Pa. State Edn. Assn. (alt. profl. rights and responsibilities commn. 2001—05), Penncrest Area Edn. Assn. (assoc.; v.p. 1982—84, negotiator 1982—86, pres. 1984—86, negotiator 2000—01, v.p. 2001—02, pres. 2001—03), Tool City Ringers. Methodist. Avocations: music, reading, painting, knitting. Home: 17768 Grange Center Rd Saegertown PA 16433-4506 Personal E-mail: schoolmarm@zoominternet.net.

RALPH, ROBERT ALAN, ophthalmologist, educator; b. New Haven, Jan. 29, 1941; s. Joseph S. and Elsie S. Ralph; m. Jan Eden; children: Alison, Stephanie. AB, Harvard U., Cambridge, Mass., 1961; MD, Tufts U., Boston, 1965. Diplomate Am. Bd. Ophthalmology. Intern, then resident in surgery Yale Med. Ctr., New Haven, 1965—67; clin. assoc. Nat. Cancer Inst., Bethesda, Md., 1967—69; resident in ophthalmology Georgetown U., Washington, 1969—72, clin. prof. ophthalmology, 1995—2007; fellow in cornea rsch. Mass. Eye and Ear Infirmary, Boston, 1972—74; pvt. practice ophthalmology Washington and Rockville, Md., 1974—; asst. prof. ophthalmology Wilmer Eye Inst., Johns Hopkins U., Balt., 1995—2008. With USPHS, 1967—69. Fellow: ACS, Am. Acad. Ophthalmology; mem.: Photographic Soc. Am., Cosmos Club. Avocations: photography, art, creative writing. Home: 11400 Grundy Ct Potomac MD 20854 Office: 6212 Montrose Rd Rockville MD 20852

RALSTIN, MONTE ROBERT, musician, director; MA in Music, Okla. City U., 1976. Musical dir. Sch. Theatre Arts, Tucson, 1999—. Office: University Arizona Tucson AZ 85721 Business E-Mail: mralstin@email.arizona.eud.

RALSTON, ANTHONY, computer scientist, mathematician, educator; b. NYC, Dec. 24, 1930; s. Alfred Joseph and Ruth (Bien) R.; m. Jayne Madeleine Rosenthal, Feb. 14, 1958; children: Jonathan, Geoffrey, Steven, Elizabeth. BS, MIT, 1952, PhD, 1956. Mem. tech. staff Bell Tel. Labs., 1956-59; lectr. U. Leeds, 1959-60; mgr. tech. computing Am. Cyanamid Co., 1960-61; assoc. prof. math. Stevens Inst. Tech., 1961-64, prof., 1964-65; dir. computer svcs. SUNY, Buffalo, 1965-70, prof., 1965-95, chmn. dept. computer sci., 1967-80, prof. emeritus, 1995—. Bd. examiners Grad. Record Exam in Computer Sci., 1976-82; mem. computer sci. and tech. bd. NRC, 1976-79, math. sci. edn. bd., 1985-89; acad. visitor Imperial Coll., London, 1995-2003. Author: A First Course in Numerical Analysis, 1965, 2d edit., 1978, Introduction to Programming and Computer Science, 1971, Discrete Algorithmic Mathematics, 1991, 3d edit., 2004, Algorithms, 1997; editor: Ency. of Computer Science, 1976, 2d edit., 1982, 3d edit., 1992, 4th edit., 2000, concise edit., 2004, ABACUS, 1983-88; co-editor: Mathematical Methods for Digital Computers, Vol. 1, 1960, Vol. 2, 1967, Vol. 3, 1977, The Influence of Computers and Informatics in Mathematics and Its Teaching, 1993. 2d lt. U.S. Army, 1957. Fellow AAAS, Royal Soc. of Arts, Assn. Computing Machinery (pres. 1972-74, mem. coun. 1968-76, Disting. Svc. award 1982); mem. Math. Assn. Am. (bd. govs. 1984-87), Am. Fedn. Info. Processing Soc. (pres. 1975-76), Com. Concerned Scientists (bd. dirs.). Home: Flat 4 58 Prince Consort Rd London SW7 2BA England Office Phone: 44-20-75892195. E-mail: ar9@doc.ic.ac.uk.

RALSTON, JOANNE SMOOT, public relations executive; b. Phoenix, May 13, 1939; d. A. Glen and Virignia (Lee) Smoot; m. W. Hamilton Weigelt, Aug. 15, 1991 (dec.). BA in Journalism, Ariz. State U., 1960. Reporter The Ariz. Rep., Phoenix, 1960-62; co-owner, pub. rels. dir. The Patton Agy., Phoenix, 1962-71; founder, pres., owner Joanne Ralston & Assocs., Inc., Phoenix, 1971-87, 92—. Pres. Nelson Ralston Robb Comm., Phoenix, 1987—91, Joanne Ralston & Assocs., Inc., Scottsdale, 1991—, Kapaau, Hawaii, 2000—. Contbr. articles to profl. jours. Bd. dirs. Ariz. Parklands Found., 1984-86, Gov.'s Coun. on Health, Phys. Fitness and Sports, 1984-86; mem. task force Water and Natural Resources Coun., Phoenix, 1984-86; mem. Hawaii Gov.'s Adv. Bd., 2003-05, Hawaii Gov.'s Coun. Advisors, 2005—, others. Recipient Lulu awards (36) L.A. Advt. Women, 1964—, Gold Quill (2) Internat. Assn. Bus. Communicators, Excellence awards Fin. World mag., 1982-93, others; named to Walter Cronkite Sch. Journalism Hall of Fame, Coll. Pub. Programs Ariz. State U., 1987; named one of 25 Most Influential Arizonians, Phoenix Mag., 1991. Mem. Pub. Rels. Soc. Am. (counselor sect.), Internat. Assn. Bus. Communicators, Phoenix Press Club (pres. bd.), Investor Rels. Inst., Phoenix Met. C. of C. (bd. dirs. 1977-84, 85-91), Governor's Adv. Coun., Rotary Internat. Republican. Avocations: horses, dog training. Address: PO Box 808 Kapaau HI 96755-0808 Office Phone: 808-889-6433. Personal E-mail: joanne-ralston@juno.com.

RALSTON, JOSEPH W., retired military officer; b. Hopkinsville, Ky., Nov. 4, 1943; m. Diane Dougherty; children: Christopher, Paige, David, Sarah. BA in Chemistry, Miami U., Ohio, 1965; MA in Pers. Mgmt., Ctrl. Mich. U., 1976; student, Army Command and Gen. Staff Coll., Ft. Leavenworth, Kans., 1975—76, Nat. War Coll., Ft. McNair, Wash. DC, 1983—84, Harvard U., 1989. Commd. 2d lt. res. officer tng. corps. program USAF, 1965, advanced through grades to gen., 1995, ret., 2003, student pilot training Laughlin AFB, Tex., 1965—66, student, F-105 combat crew training sch. Nellis AFB, Nev., 1966—67, F-105 combat crew mem. 67th Tactical Fighter Squadron later 12th Tactical Fighter Squadron Kadena AFB, Japan, 1967—69, student, F-105 combat crew training sch. Nellis AFB, Nev., 1969, F-105 Wild Weasel instr. pilot 66th Fighter Weapons Squandron, 1970—71, F-105 Wild Weasel pilot, 354th Tactical Fighter Takhli Royal Thai AFB, Thailand, 1970, fighter requirements officer & project officer for F-15 & lightweight fighter programs, Office of the Dep. Chief of Staff for requirements Langley AFB, 1971—73, asst. ops. officer, 335th Tactical Fighter Squandron, the chief Standardization & Evaluation, 4th Tactical Fighter Wing Seymour Johnson AFB, NC, 1973—75, tactical fighter requirements officer, Office of the Dep. Chief of Staff for Rsch. & Devel. Washington, 1976—79, ops. officer later comdr. 68th Tactical fighter Squandron Moody AFB, Ga., 1979—80, spl. asst. later exec. officer to the comdr. Hdqs. Tactical Air Command Langley AFB, 1980—83, spl. asst. for low observables tech., Office of Dep. Chief of Staff for Rsch., Devel., & Acquisition Washington, 1984—86, comdr., 56th tactical training wing MacDill AFB, Fla., 1986—87, asst. dep. chief of staff for ops., later dep. chief of staff for requirements, Hdqs. Tactical Air Command Langley AFB, Va., 1987—90, dir. tactical programs Office of the Asst. Sec. for acquisition Washington, 1990—91, dir. operational requirements, Office of the Dep. Chief of Staff for plans & ops., 1991—92, comdr. Alaskan Command, Alaskan N. Am. Aerospace Def. Command Region, 11th Air Force & Joint Task Force Elmendorff AFB, Alaska, 1992—94, dep. chief of staff plans & ops., 1994—95, comdr., Hdqs. Air Combat Command Langley AFB, Va., 1995—96; vice chmn. Joint Chiefs of Staff The Pentagon, Washington, 1996—2000; comdr. US European Command (USEUCOM), Mons, Belgium, 2000—03; supreme allied comdr. NATO, Europe (SACEUR), Brussels, 2000—03; vice chmn. The Cohen Group, Washington, 2003—; spl. envoy for Countering the Kurdistan Worker's Party (PKK) US Dept. State, 2006—07. Bd. dirs. Lockheed Martin Corp., 2003—, The Timken Co., 2003—, URS Corp., 2003—. Recipient: Def. Disting. Svc. medal with oak leaf cluster, Disting. Svc. medal, Legion of Merit with two oak leaf cluster, Disting. Flying Cross with three oak leaf cluster, Meritorious Svc. medal with two oak leaf cluster, Air medal with 19 oak leaf cluster, Air Force Commendation medal with four oak leaf cluster Office: The Cohen Group 500 8th St NW Ste 200 Washington DC 20004 Office Phone: 202-863-7200. E-mail: jralston@cohengroup.net.

RALSTON, MARTHA JANE, retired medical/surgical nurse; b. Chgo., May 23, 1928; d. Joseph D. and Pheobe Josephine (Furguson) Salato; m. Paul R. Ralston, Mar. 10, 1956; children: Craig, Donna, Paula, Barbara. Diploma, Little Company of Mary Hosp., Evergreen Park, Ill., 1950. Cert. in oper. rm. procedures and techniques. Oper. rm. supr. Meml. Hosp., Woodstock, Ill., 1952-62; staff nurse oper. rm. Boulder Community Hosp., 1962-67; staff nurse oper. rm., asst. supr. Boulder (Colo.) Meml. Hosp., 1967-83; ophthalmology recovery rm. staff nurse Rocky Mountain Eye Found. Surgery Ctr., Boulder, 1983-92. Mem. Assn. Oper. Rm. Nurses.

RALSTON, RONALD LEE, retired manufacturing tradesman; b. Vincennes, Ind., May 22, 1942; s. Joe Franklin and Anna Lee Ralston. Student, Purdue U., 1963—66; degree in indsl. mgmt., Ivy Tech., Indpls., 1980. Machinist Allison Aircraft & Transmission, Indpls., 1962—78; skilled tradesman Allison Transmission Plants, Indpls., 1978—2005; ret., 2005. Sgt./tank comdr. US Army, 1966—68. Mem.: Shriners, Scottish Rite, Masons. Republican. Methodist. Avocation: woodworking. Home: 1814 Inisheer Ct Indianapolis IN 46217 Personal E-mail: mrronralston@aol.com.

RAM, CHITTA VENKATA, physician; b. Machilipatnam, India, Oct. 24, 1948; s. Chitta M. Row and Chitta (Cheruvu) Sarojini; m. Ashalata Ram, Feb. 17, 1979; children: Gita, Radha. B.Sci, Marathwada U., Aurangabad, India, 1966; MD, Osmania U., Hyderabad, India, 1972. Diplomate Am. Bd. Internal Medicine. Resident in internal medicine Brown U., R.I. Hosp., Providence, 1974-76; fellow in hypertension Hosp. U. Pa., Phila., 1976-77; faculty assoc. U. Tex. Southwestern Med. Ctr., Dallas, 1977-78, asst. prof., 1978-83, assoc. prof., 1983-89, prof. internal medicine, 1989—. Dir. Tex. Blood Pressure Inst., Dallas; dir. rsch. and edn. Dallas Nephrology Assocs.; dir. hypertension clinic Parkland Meml. Hosp., Dallas, hypertension unit St. Paul Med. Ctr., Dallas, dir. continuing med. edn. dept., 1996-98, chmn. instnl. rev. com., 1996-98, pres. med. staff, 1997-98; dir. Tex. Blood Pressure Inst., Dallas. Contbr. numerous articles to profl. jours. and chpts. to textbooks; editl. cons., reviewer numerous nat. and internat. jours. and pubs. Pres. Tex. IndoAm. Physician Soc., Dallas, 1988; trustee Dallas/Ft. Worth Hindu Temple Soc., Dallas, 1988. Named Outstanding Tchr. St. Paul Med. Ctr., 1982; recipient Mother of India award, 1992. Master ACP; fellow Am. Coll. Cardiology, Am. Coll. Chest Physicians (regent), Am. Coll. Clin. Pharmacology; mem. Am. Assn. Physicians from India (pres.-elect 1994-95, pres. 1995-96), Tex. Indo-Am. Physicians Soc. Office Phone: 214-358-2300. E-mail: ramv@dneph.com.

RAMACHANDRAN, VENKATANARAYANA DEEKSHIT, electrical engineering educator; b. Mysore, India, May 3, 1934; s. K.C. Venkatanarayana Deekshit and Subbamma Deekshit R.; m. Kamala Visweswaraiya, June 12, 1960; 1 child, Ravi P. BS, U. Mysore, 1953; B in Engring., Indian Inst. Sci., Bangalore, 1956, M in Electronics, 1958, PhD, 1965. Registered profl. engr. Sr. research asst. Indian Inst. Sci., 1958-59, lectr., 1959-66; asst. prof. N.S. Tech. Coll., Halifax, Can., 1966-69; prof. elec. engring. Concordia U. (formerly Sir George Williams Univ.), Halifax, Can., 1971—; acting chmn. dept. elec. and computer engring. Montreal, various times; grad. program dir. dept., 1969-84. Adj. prof. U. Windsor, Ont., Can., 1983—, Ecole Tech. Superieure U. Quebec, Montreal, 1989—; mem. program com. Internat. Symposium on Operator Theory of Networks and Systems, 1975; vice chmn. Internat. Symposium on Circuits and Systems IEEE, Montreal, 1984, mem. tech. program com., 1987; internat. coordinator Internat. Conf. on Computers, Systems and Signal Processing, Indian Inst. Sci., 1984. Author papers in profl. jours., over 125 papers presented to confs., others. Named to Order of Engrs. of Que.; recipient Merit award Concordia Council on Student Life, 1981-82, Outstanding Contbn. award Engring. and Computer Sci. Assn., Concordia U., 1996. Fellow Inst. Electronics and Telecomms. India (edit. bd. jour. 1986), Inst. Engrs. India, Inst. Elec. Engrs. Eng., Engring. Inst. Can. (sec. Montreal chpt. 1979-80, centennial bd. 1983-84), IEEE (Outstanding Engring. Educator award IEEE Can. 2003); mem. Circuits and Systems chpt. IEEE (chmn. Montreal sect. 1978-84), Can. Soc. Elec. Engrs. (editor jour. 1983-85, editor bull. 1981-83), Am. Soc. Engring. Edn. (chmn. awards com. St. Lawrence chpt. 1987-88, Western Elec. Fund award 1983, Myril B. Reed Best Rsch. Paper award 1984, Outstanding Svc. 1993) Office: Concordia U Faculty of Engring 1455 de Maisonneuve Blvd W Montreal PQ Canada H3G 1M8 Office Phone: 514-848-2424 ext. 3078, 514-848-2424 ext 3078. Business E-Mail: kamala@ece.concordia.ca.

RAMADAN, MOHAMED IBRAHIM, psychiatrist; b. Alexandria, Egypt, Jan. 25, 1967; s. Ibrahim Abd Alla and Zainab Shaban Ramadan; m. Mariam Mohamed Gad, Dec. 9, 2001; children: Amira Mohamed children: Zainab Mohamed, Ibrahim Mohamed. MD in Medicine and Surgery, U. Alexandria, Egypt, 1990; MS, Benha Sch. Medicine Zagazig U., Benha, Egypt, 1996. Lic. Ednl. Commn. Fgn. Med. Graduates, 1998, Fedn. of State Med. Bds. US, 1998, Kans. State Bd. Healing Arts, 2003, Ariz. Med. Bd., 2004, bd. cert. psychiactrist Am. bd. Psychiatry Neurology, 2007. Psychiatry resident U. Wis., Madison, 2000—01, U. Kans., Wichita, 2001—04; psychophrmacology fellow Clin. Rsch. Inst., 2004—05; chief resident dept. psychiatry U. Kans., Kans., 2004—05; staff psychiatrist Mohave Mental Health Clinic, Kingman, Ariz., 2005—. Co-leader group therapy chronic pain patients Shadyside Hosp., U. Pitts, 1999—2000; study physician Psychirat. Rsch. Inst., Wichita, Kans., 2002—05; residents rep. med. students psychiatry interest group U. Kans., examiner neuropsychiatry clerkship, 2003—05, dept. psychiatry rep. residents coun., 2004—05; residents' rep. residency com. Wichita Ctr. Grad. Med. Edn., 2004—05. Contbr. articles to profl. jours. Mem. and spkr. UN Dane county Chpt., Madison, Wis., 2000—01; bd. mem. Alexandria Students Sci. Assn., Egypt, 1984—92. Recipient prize of Exellence, Ministry Edn. Egypt, 1984, Medal of Honor, U. Alexandria Sch. of Medicine, 1992, Star of the Moment award, Via Christi Med. Ctr., 2002, Ralph Bharati award, U. Kans., 2003, Excellence in Rsch., 2004, 2005, Resident of Yr., Dept. Psychiatry U. Kans., 2005, Master Psychopharmacologist awrad, Neuroscince Edn. Inst., 2005; fellow, Am. Soc. Clin. Psychopharmacology, 2005. Mem.: Psychiat. Rsch. Network, Am. Soc. Clin. Psychopharmacology, Kans. Psychiat. Soc., Am. Assn. Psychiat. Medicine, Am. Psychiat. Assn. (Lilly Chief resident exec. leadership program 2004). Achievements include research in assessment of gustatory perception in schizophrinic patients; development of mentor system for residents; design of new resolving conflicts mechanism between residents; research in cost analysis of tonsillectomy, septoplasty and Typampanoplasty; sequenced treatment alternatives to relieve depression; treatment of somatization disorders; comparison of the formal published human clinical trials for the six seretonin selective reuptake inhibitors; effect of escitalopram versus sertraline versus duloxetine on liver enzymes. Office: Mohave Mental Health Clinic 1743 Sycamore Kingman AZ 86401 Home: 2830 Ft Mojave Bullhead City AZ 86429 Personal E-mail: ibramadan@yahoo.com.

RAMADANOVIC, PETAR, literature and language professor, writer; b. Belgrade, Yugoslavia, Jan. 3, 1964; m. Catherine Peebles; children: Georgia Peebles, Iliya Peebles. PhD, Binghamton U., 1997. Postdoc. fellow Cornell U., Ithaca, NY, 1997—98; assoc. prof. English U. NH, Durham, 1999—. Fellow Ctr. Humanities, Va. Found. Humanities, UVA, Charlottesville. Contbr. rsch. papers. Home: 212 Miller Ave Apt A3 Portsmouth NH 03801 Office: Univ NH Durham NH 03824 Business E-Mail: petarr@unh.edu.

RAMAKER, DAVID E., chemistry professor, researcher; s. Alma Ramaker; m. Beverly A. Back, Sept. 3, 1966; children: Julie Ann, Jacqueline Marie, Jan David, Jason Allen. PhD, U. Iowa, Iowa City, 1971. Postdoc. Sandia Laboratories, Albuquerque, 1970—72; res assoc. instr. U. Utah, Salt Lake City, 1972—74; vis. asst. prof. Calvin Coll., Grand Rapids, Mich., 1974—75; prof. chemistry George Washington U., 1975—. Rsch. chemist Naval Rsch. Lab., Wash., 1976—. Contbr. articles to profl. jours. Fellow: Wash. Acadecy of Sciences, Am. Vacuum Soc.; mem.: Chem. Soc. Wash. (Hillebrand 1988). Achievements include development of delta XANES technique in X ray absorption spectroscopy. Avocation: travel. Office: George Wash Univ Chemistry Dept Washington DC 20052 Office Fax: 202-994-5873. Business E-Mail: ramaker@gwu.edu.

RAMAKRISHNAN, VENKATASWAMY, civil engineer, educator; b. Coimbatore, India, Feb. 27, 1929; came to U.S., 1969, naturalized, 1981; s. Venkataswamy and Kondammal (Krishnaswamy) R.; m. Vijayalakshmi Unnava, Nov. 7, 1962; children: Aravind, Anand. BEng, U. Madras, India, 1952, DSS, 1953; Diploma in Hydropower and Concrete Tech, Imperial Coll., London, 1957; PhD, Univ. Coll., London, 1960. From lectr. to prof. civil engring., head dept. P.S.G. Coll. Tech., U. Madras, 1952-69; vis. prof. S.D. Sch. Mines and Tech., Rapid City, 1969-70, prof. civil engring., 1970—, dir. concrete tech. research, 1970-71, head grad. div. structural mechanic and concrete tech., 1971—, program coordinator materials engring. and sci. Ph.D. program, 1985-86, disting. prof., 1996—. Emeritus mem. TRB. Author: Ultimate Strength Design for Structural Concrete, 1969; contbr. over 350 articles to profl. jours. Recipient Outstanding Prof. award, S.D. Sch. Mines and Tech., 1980, 1st Rsch. award, 1994; Colombo Plan fellow, 1955—60. Mem. ASCE (vice chmn. constrn. divsn. publs. com. 1974), NSPE, Internat. Assn. Bridge and Structural Engring., Am. Concrete Inst. (chmn. subcom. gen. considerations for founds., chmn. com. 214 on evaluation of strength test results, sec.-treas. Dakota chpt. 1974-79, v.p. 1980, pres. 1981, Robert Philio Rsch. Excellence award), Instn. Hwy. Engrs., Transp. Rsch. Bd. (chmn. com. on admixtures and curing, chmn. com. on mech. properties concrete), Am. Soc. Engring. Edn., Internat. Coun. Gap-Graded Concrete Rsch. and Application, Sigma Xi. Address: 5260 Autumn Place Rapid City SD 57702 Home Phone: 605-721-0242; Office Phone: 605-394-2403. Personal E-mail: vramakrishnan@rushmore.com. *To me, success is a coin with hard work on one side and perseverance with devotion on the other. No matter what—head or tails—the message is the same: keep on working. Goals in my life were pursuit of truth and beauty. The structures I have created, and my writings based on research have given me greater satisfaction than any wealth, position, or power.*

RAMALHO-AHRNDT, MARIA GABRIELA, art educator; b. Foz Do Arelho, Portugal, June 14, 1965; arrived in Can., 1967, arrived in U.S., 1991; d. Bernardino Maria and Maria Gabriela (Da Silva) Ramalho; m. Timothy James Ahrndt, Aug. 26, 1995; children: Vincent J. Ahrndt, Alexandra Maria Ahrndt. BA, U. Toronto, Can., 1988; MA in Edn., Mankato State U., 1993. Printing asst. Art Svcs. Agy., Toronto, 1988; gallery asst. Wynick/Tuck Gallery, Toronto, 1988, Odon Wagner Gallery, Toronto, 1989-91, Art Gallery Ont., Toronto, 1990-91; art tchr. Washington Elem. Sch., Mankato, Minn., 1993, Spring Lake Park (Minn.) HS, 1994—. Author, illustrator: Bedtime Stories about Zany

Creatures, 2002. Mem.: Am. Arts Crafts Coun., Nat. Art Edn. Assn., Nat. Mus. Women in the Arts. Roman Catholic. Avocations: sculpting, stamp-collecting, art history. Office: Spring Lake Park HS 8001 Able St NE Minneapolis MN 55432-2059

RAMALINGAM, MURUGAN, researcher; s. Govindaraju and Narayanasamy; married. MS, Annamalai U., Chidambaram; PhD, U. Madras, 2002. Cert. NRC US Nat. Acads., 2007. Smf assoc. Nat. U. Singapore, 2002—06; rsch. assoc. U. Ctrl. Fla., Orlando, 2006—07; joint nist to NIH assoc. US NRC, Washington, 2007—; sr. rsch. fellow Ctrl. Leather Rsch. Inst., Chennai, India. Author: (book) Biomaterials (Best Paper award, 2007). Vol. NIST, Gaithersburg, Md., 2008—. Cadet NCC/Naval, 1990—92. Recipient award, NRC, 2007; fellowship, Counsil Sci. and Indsl. Rsch. India, 1997. Fellow: Singapore Millenium Found.; mem.: Am. Vacuum Soc., Biomaterials Soc. (life). Office: US Nat Inst Stds & Tech 100 Bureau Dr Gaithersburg MD 20899 Business E-Mail: murugan.ramalingam@nist.gov.

RAMALINGAM, SURESH S, oncologist; s. Ramalingam and Saraswathi Sakkaraiappan; m. Tamilselvi Subramanian; 1 child, Rohan. MD, Kilpauk Med. Coll., Chennai, 1992. Diplomate in medical oncology U. Madras, 1992, Am. Bd. Internal Medicine, 2003. Asst. prof. U. Pitts., 2003—07; chief thoracic oncology Emory U., Winship Cancer Inst., Atlanta, 2007—. Mem. editl. bd. Clin. Lung Cancer, Dallas, 2005—; co chair Lung Cancer Working Group, Ga. Cancer Coalition, Atlanta, 2008—. Recipient Clin. Rsch. Career Devel. award, Am. Soc. Clin. Oncology, 2006—09, James Eckman award, Emory U., UPCI Leadership award, Clin. Trials Program Devel., Paul Ruble award, Wayne State U. Mem.: Internat. Assn. Study Lung Cancer, Ea. Coop. Oncology Group, Am. Soc. Clin. Oncology. Office: Emory Univ 1365 Clifton Rd NE Rm - C-3090 Atlanta GA 30345 Office Fax: 494-778-5520. Business E-Mail: suresh.ramalingam@emory.edu.

RAMAN, BARANIDHARAN, research scientist; b. Chennai, Tamil Nadu, India, June 20, 1979; s. Raman Raghavan and Sundaralakshmy Raman; m. Ranjani Muralidharan, June 5, 2008. BS in Engring. with distinction, U. Madras, 2000; MS, Tex. A&M U., Coll. Sta., 2003, PhD, 2005. Rsch. asst. Tex. A&M U., 2000—05; joint postdoc. fellow NIH, NIST, NRC, Washington, 2006—. Recipient IJCNN Travel award, IEEE Computational Intelligence Soc., 2005; Internat. Edn. Study grant, Tex. A&M U., 2005. Mem.: Soc. Neurosci. Achievements include research in theoretical and electro-physiological approaches to study principles of neural computation, machine learning, sensor-based machine olfaction, biomedical intelligent and dynamical systems. Business E-Mail: ramanbar@mail.nih.gov.

RAMAN, SHANKAR, surgeon; b. Thirukoilur, India, Apr. 2, 1977; s. L. and Vidya Raman; m. Nivedita Krishnan, May 28, 2007; 1 child, Sahaana. MBBS, JIPMER, Pondicherry, India, 2000, MS, 2003; DNB, Nat. Bd. Examiners, New Delhi, 2003; MD, ECFMG, Phila., USA, 2006. Md ECFMG, 2006, Ms Pondicherry U., Pondicherry, India, 2003, Diplomate of National Board Nat. Bd. of Med. examiners, New Delhi, India, 2003. Sr. resident surgery Jipmer, 2003—04; resident surgery Bronx Lebanon Hosp. ctr., NY, 2006—; registrar surgery Kent & Canterbury Hosp., England, 2006; sr. ho. officer William Harvey Hosp., Ashford, England, 2005—06; jr. resident surgery JIPMER, 2000—03. Contbr. chapters to books. Recipient MOH Hassan Kuthoos Maricar Endowment prize, JIPMER, 2000, Dr SC Mitra award, 2004, SB SEN award, Pondicherry U., 2004. Mem.: Am. Tamil Med. assn., JIPMER Alumni Assn., Med. Soc. NY, Royal Coll. Surgeons Edinburgh, ACS, SAGES. Achievements include research in helicobacter pylori and association to erosive gastroduodenitis, venous ulcers; REM sleep deprivation and its association with hypothalamic self stimulation. Office: Bronx Lebanon Hosp Ctr Selwyn Ave Bronx NY 10457 Personal E-mail: shankarrraman@gmail.com.

RAMANAN, SUNDARAM V., internist, hematologist, oncologist; s. Tarakad Appadoraier Sundaram. MD, MS, Vellore Christian Med. Coll., India, 1959. Prof. medicine U. Conn., Farmington, 1976—; emeritus attending physician St. Francis Hosp., Hartford, Conn., 1993—; assoc. prof. medicine West Va. U. Fellow: ACP (corr.), Royal Soc. Medicine (London), Royal Coll. Physicians (Edinburgh). Office: St Francis Hosp 1000 Asylum Ave Ste # 1004 Hartford CT 06105 Office Phone: 860-714-4152.

RAMANATHAN, GEETHA, literature and language professor; b. Madras, Tamil Nadu, India, July 31, 1956; d. K.V. and Radha Ramanathan; m. Valerian DeSousa, Jan. 29, 1982; children: Kehan DeSousa, Dhario Walter DeSousa. MA, U. Bombay, India, 1978; AM, U. Ill., Urbana, 1982; PhD, 1987. Disting. chair Fulbright, Klagenfurt, Austria, 2002; prof. West Chester U. of PA, 2008—. Author: (criticism) Sexual Politics and the Male Playwright, Feminist Auteurs; editor: Third World Women's Inscriptions, (special issue) Third World Women's Films. Mem. West Chester Human Rels. Coun., Pa., 2006—08. Office: W Chester Univ High St West Chester PA 19383 Business E-Mail: gramanathan@wcupa.edu.

RAMANATHAN, RANGASAMY, pediatrician; arrived in US, 1982; s. Rangaswamy Naidu and Gunavathi Rangaswamy; m. Prema Naidu, July 12, 1978; children: Anusha, Vinitha. MBBS, Stanley Med. Coll., Chennai, India, 1975; D, Madras Med. Coll., Chennai, India, 1978, MD in Pediat., 1981, NY Med. Coll., NY, 1984. Diplomate Am. Bd. Pediat., 1987, neonatal-perinatal medicine Am. Bd. Pediat., 1987. Intern Lincoln Med. Ctr., NY, 1982—83, resident, 1983—84; clin. instr. pediat. U. So. Calif., LA, 1984—86; rsch. fellow Harbor U. Calif. Med. Ctr., LA, 1987—88; asst. prof. pediat. sch. medicine Olive View med. ctr. U. Calif., Sylmar, Calif., 1988; asst. prof. of pediat. Keck sch. medicine U. So. Calif., LA, 1988—98, assoc. prof. of pediat. Keck sch. medicine, 1998—2002, prof. pediat. Keck sch. medicine, 2003—, assoc. divsn. chief divsn. neonatology Keck sch. medicine, 2003—. Program dir, neonatal-perinatal medicine fellowship Keck sch. medicine U. So. Calif., 2002—; med. dir. newborn icu Women's and Chlidren's Hosp., LA, 1988—; sect. head divsn. neonatology Women's and Children's Hosp., 2001—, med. dir. respiratory therapy dept., 1991—; assoc. med. dir. Good Smaritan Hosp., LA, 1989—; dir. high risk infant follow-up program Good Samaritan Hosp., 1990—, chief neonatolgy sect., 2003—; lectr. in field. Contbr. articles to profl. jours. Recipient Outstanding Tchr. award, Dept. Pediat., U. So. Calif., 2004, Richard H. Paul Disting. Tchg. award, U. So. Calif., 2005; named Physician of Yr., Good Samaritan Hosp., LA, 2004; named one of Best Doctors in Am., Best Doctors, Inc., Boston, 2005. Mem.: Am. Acad. Pediat. (regional trainer 1991—). Achievements include research in molecular basis of lung injury and oxgen radical mediated disorders in newborn infants. Avocation: travel. Office: Women's & Children's Hosp LAC+USC 1240 North Mission Rd Room L-919 Los Angeles CA 90033 Office Phone: 323-226-3406. Business E-Mail: ramanath@usc.edu.

RAMANI, GIRISH, marketing educator, researcher; s. Venkateswaran and Jayalakshmi Ramani; m. Jayanthi Rajan, Aug. 9, 1990; 1 child, Neharika Girish. BSc in Mech. Engring., Regional Engring. Coll., Kurukshetra, India, 1984; MBA, Indian Inst. Mgmt., Ahmedabad, 1988; PhD in Mktg., U. Conn., Storrs, 2006. V.p. Lowe Lintas & Ptnrs., Bangalore, India, 1989—2001; rsch. asst., instr. U. Conn., 2002—06; asst. prof. mktg. Drexel U., Phila., 2006—. Mem. academic adv. bd. Chief Mktr. Officers' Coun., 2007—. Contbr. chapter to book, articles to profl. jours. Recipient Best Paper award, Interactive Mktg., 2006; grantee Rsch. grant, Mktg. Sci. Inst., 2006. Mem.: Academic Adv. Bd. (chief mktg. officers' coun. 2007), Beta Gamma Sigma (life). Avocation: kayaking. Office: Drexel Univ Mktg Dept Matheson 502E 3141 Chestnut St Philadelphia PA 19104-2875 Business E-Mail: girish.ramani@drexel.edu.

RAMAPRABHU, PRAVEEN, engineering educator; b. Chennai, Tamil Nadu, India, May 20, 1975; s. Ramaprabhu Rajagopalan and Deepalakshmi Ramaprabhu; m. Vidya Parthasarathy. PhD, Tex. A&M U., Coll. Station, 2003. Postdoc. rsch. assoc. Los Alamos Nat. Lab., N.Mex., 2004—07; asst. prof. U. NC Charlotte, 2007—. Contbr. conf. pubs. to profl. jours. Nominee Award, Am. Phys. Soc., 2004; grantee, Los Alamos Nat. Lab., 2008. Mem.: AIAA, ASME, Am. Phys. Soc. Achievements include discovery of limits of potential theory to rayleigh-taylor flows. Office: Univ NC Charlotte 9201 Univ City Blvd Charlotte NC 28223

RAMASAMY, SHAKER GNANASEKARAN, science educator; PhD, Okla. State U., Stillwater, OK, 1984. Asst. prof. Mansfield U., 1984—90, assoc. prof., 1990—94, prof., 1994—2008, chair, 2002—. Chairperson Am. Chem. Soc., Local Sect., Corning, NY, 1997—98. Contbr. articles to profl.jours. (Chemically Modified Surfaces award, 1992, Surface Interface Analysis award, 1992, Jour. Vacuum Sci. & Tech. award, 1991, Surface & Interface Analysis award, 1990, Analytical Chemistry award, 1985, Modern Trends Analytical Chemistry award, 1984). Mem.: Am. Chem. Soc. (Cert. Excellence award 1997).

RAMASWAMY, BHUVANESWARI, medical educator, researcher; MD, Kilpauk Med. Coll., Chennai, India, 1987. Registrar The Cardiff U., Wales, 1993—95; resident Mt. Carmel Med. Ctr., Columbus, Ohio, 2000—02; breast cancer rsch. fellow Ohio State U., Columbus, 2002—04, med. oncology fellow, 2004—06, asst. prof., 2006—. Editor med. jourl.; contbr. articles to peer review publ. K 12, NIH, 2008, Pilot grant, Clin. Translational Sci. assn., 2008, rsch. grant. Mem.: MRCP, Am. Assn. Cancer Rsch., Am. Soc. Clin. Oncologist. Office: Ohio State Univ 320 W 10th Ave Columbus OH 43210 Office Phone: 614-293-6401. Office Fax: 614-293-7529. Business E-Mail: bhuvaneswari.ramaswamy@osumc.edu.

RAMAYYA, EDWIN BOSCO, engineer, researcher; b. Kanyakumari, Tamilnadu, India, Nov. 27, 1977; s. Appavoo Ramayya and Mary Louise. MS, Ariz. State U., Tempe; PhD student, U. Wis., Madison, 2005—. Software engr. Siri Tech., Bangalore, 2000—03; rsch. asst. Ariz. State U., Tempe, 2004, U. Wis., Madison, 2005—. Mem. Nat. Social Svc., Tiruchirappalli, Tamilnadu, 1996—2000. Recipient YIP award, Air Force, 2008—. Mem.: IEEE (student mem. 2006—08, reviewer, transactions nanotech. 2008—). Office: Univ Wis 1415 Engring Dr #4620 Madison WI 53706 Business E-Mail: ramayya@wisc.edu.

RAMBERG, WALTER DODD, architect; b. Charlotte, NC, Feb. 17, 1932; s. Walter Gustav Charles and Julia Elisabeth (Lineberger) R.; m. Lucinda Jenifer Ballard, Nov. 25, 1961 (dec. 1989); children: Lucinda E.G., Jenny S.F., Julia E.L.; m. Seska Peck Dunne, Sept. 14, 1996. BA, Yale U., 1953, M.Arch., 1956. Fulbright fellow Kyoto (Japan) U., 1956-58; apprentice architect Paul Rudolph, New Haven, 1958-61; project designer Meyer & Ayers, Balt., 1961-63; partner Howe & Ramberg, Washington, 1963-65; prin. Walter Dodd Ramberg (Architect), Washington, 1965—. Prof. architecture Cath. U. Am., 1977-2006, prof. emeritus, 2006—; mem. design adv. panel Balt. Dept. Housing and Cmty., 1973—; mem. bd. architecture rev. Baltimore County, 1986-89. Designer: N.W. Balt. High Sch, 1963 (P.A. Excellence in Design award); architect: Bridge for Washington Cathedral, 1965 (Excellence in Design award Washington Bd. Trade, AIA), Kidder Guest House, 1965 (1st Honor award Balt. AIA), Azrael House, 1969 (Honor award Balt. AIA), Cutts House, 1973 (Honor award Balt. AIA), Woody House, 1975 (Merit award Balt. AIA), Lineberger Meml. Library, 1976 (Merit award Nat. AIA, ALA); contbr. articles to profl. publs. Served to lt. USCGR, 1958-59. Mem. AIA (corp.), AAUP, Soc. Archtl. Historians. Clubs: Met. (Washington). Episcopalian. Home: 1651 Belfast Rd Sparks MD 21152-9788 Office: 1830 T St NW Washington DC 20009-7138

RAMBIS, KURT (DARRELL KURT RAMBIS), professional basketball coach, retired professional basketball player; b. Cupertino, Calif., Feb. 25, 1958; B, Santa Clara U., Calif., 1980. Forward AEK Athens BC, Greece, 1980—81, LA Lakers, 1981—88, 1993—95, interim head coach, 1998—99, asst. gen. mgr., asst. coach, 1999—2009; forward Charlotte Hornets, 1988—89, Phoenix Suns, 1989—92, Sacramento Kings, 1992—93; ret., 1995; head coach Minn. Timberwolves, 2009—. Actor: (TV series) 7th Heaven; (films) Forget Paris, 1995, Johnny Mnemonic: The Interactive Action Movie, 1995, Eddie, 1996, The Lovemaster, 1997. Named Player of Yr., West Coast Conf., 1980. Achievements include member of the NBA Finals championship winning Los Angeles Lakers, 1982, 1985, 1987, 1988. Office: Minn Timberwolves 600 1st Ave N Minneapolis MN 55403*

RAMBO, KELLY CLIFFORD, lawyer; b. Easton, Pa., Apr. 26, 1961; d. Brian D. and Roslyn Clifford; m. William K. Rambo, Apr. 11, 1987; children: William Clifford, Grace Caroline, Luke Evan. BS cum laude, Pa. State U., University Park, 1983; JD with high distinction, Temple U. Sch. Law, Phila., 1986. Bar: Pa. 1986. Assoc. atty. White & Williams, Phila., 1986—87, Cohen & Feeley, Easton, 1987—91; prin. atty. Kelly Clifford Rambo, Atty. at Law, Easton, 1991—95; atty./mng. atty. worker's compensation dept. Post & Schell, Allentown, Pa., 1995—97; ptnr. Cohen & Feeley, Bethlehem, Pa., 1997—. Author: (article) The Legal Field and the Health Care Professional: Weathering Involvement. Fellow Rotary Club, Easton, 2005; mem. Third St. Alliance for Women and Children, Easton, 1994. Mem.: Pa. Trial Lawyers Assn. (assoc.), Pa. Bar Assn. (assoc.), Northampton County Bar Assn. (assoc.). Avocations: travel, reading. Office: Cohen & Feeley 2851 Baglyos Cir Ste 200 Bethlehem PA 18020 Office Fax: 610-332-2722. Business E-Mail: krambo@cohenfeeley.com.

RAMER, BRUCE M., lawyer; b. Teaneck, NJ, Aug. 2, 1933; s. Sidney and Anne S. (Strassman) R.; children: Gregg B., Marc K., Neal I. BA, Princeton U., 1955; LLB, Harvard U., 1958. Bar: Calif. 1963, NJ 1958. Assoc., Morrison, Lloyd & Griggs, Hackensack, NJ, 1959-60; ptnr. Gang, Tyre, Ramer & Brown, Inc., LA, 1963—. Exec. dir. Entertainment Law Inst., Law Ctr. U. So. Calif., bd. councilors; chmn., nat. bd. govs. Am. Jewish Com., 1995-98, nat. v.p., 1982-88, pres., 1998—, LA chpt., 1980-83, chair Western region, 1984-86, Cmty. Svc. award, 1987, nat. pres., 1998—, adv. bd. Skirball Inst. on Am. Values, 1998—; chmn. Asia Pacific Rim Inst., 1989-98; trustee Loyola Marymount U., LA Children's Mus., 1986-89; vice chair United Way, 1991-93, corp. bd. dirs., 1981-93, chair coun. pres. 1989-90, mem. cmty. issues coun., 1989-90, chair discretionary fund distbn. com., 1987-89; bd. dirs., chair Geffen Playhouse, 1995-98, founding chair, 1998—; bd. dirs. LA Urban League, 1987-93, 96—, Jewish Fedn. Coun. of Greater LA (mem. Cmty. Rels. com., bd. dirs., exec. com.), Jewish TV Network, Sta. KCET-TV; mem., bd. dirs. Rebuild LA, 1992-96; mem. bd. govs. Calif. Cmty. Found., 1988-98; recipient Ann. Brotherhood award NCCJs, 1990; mem. Fellows of Am. Bar Found.; mem. econ. strategy panel State Calif., 1997—; bd. dirs. Shoah Visual History Found., Righteous Persons Found., LA 2012 Bid Com. for So. Calif. Olympic Games; bd. dirs. Jewish Fedn. Coun. Greater LA, mem. exec. com., cmty. rels. com. Pvt. US Army, 1958-59, 2d lt., 1961-62. Mem. ABA (mem. spl. com. jud. ind.), LA County Bar Assn., Calif. Bar Assn., Beverly Hills Bar Assn. (Exec. Dirs. award 1988, Entertainment Lawyer of Yr. award 1996), LA Copyright Soc. (pres. 1974-75), Calif. Copyright Conf. (pres. 1973-74), Princeton Club (pres. 1975-78). Office: Gang Tyre Ramer & Brown Inc 132 S Rodeo Dr Beverly Hills CA 90212-2415

RAMER, DEBORAH LYNNE, special education educator; married. BA in English, Secondary Edn., James Madison U., Harrisonburg, Va., 1991; MEd in Spl. Edn., U. Va., Charlottesville, 1994, Degree in Spl. Edn., 2002. Spl. edn. tchr. Verona Elem. Sch., Augusta County Pub. Schs., Va., 1993—96; adj. instr. U. Va., Richmond Ctr., 1997—2001; ednl. cons. Hosp. Edn. Program, Richmond Pub. Schs., 1997—2001; supr. James Madison U., Harrisonburg, Va., 2004—05, Coll. William & Mary, Williamsburg, Va., 2006—, vis. instr. spl. edn., 2007—. Mem. Va.'s Early Reading Initiative Task Force, Richmond, 1997; ednl. cons. Va. Dept. Edn., Divsns. Elem. Edn., Richmond, 1997; pres. Epilepsy Assn. Va., Ctrl. Va. Chpt., Richmond, 1998—2001, bd. mem., 1998—2001, Learning Disabilities Coun. Va., 1998—2008, Epilepsy Found. Va., Charlottesville, 1998—2001; guest reviewer Kids Block, Inc., Va., 2001. Mem., chair com. Jr. Woman's Club Williamsburg, 2002—07. Recipient Tchr. of Yr., Verona Elem. Sch., Augusta County Pub. Schs., 1995—96. Mem.: Coun. Exceptional Children. Avocation: photography. Office: Coll William & Mary Jones Hall Williamsburg VA 23187 Home Phone: 757-564-7796. Business E-Mail: dlrame@wm.edu.

RAMER, JAMES LEROY, civil engineer; b. Marshalltown, Iowa, Dec. 7, 1935; s. LeRoy Frederick and Irene (Wengert) Ramer; m. Jacqueline L. Orr, Dec. 15, 1957; children: Sarah T., Robert H., Eric A., Susan L. Student, U. Iowa, Iowa City, 1953-57; MCE, Washington U., St. Louis, 1976, MA in Polit. Sci., 1978; postgrad., U. Mo., Columbia, 1984—. Registered profl. engr., land surveyor. Civil and constrn. engr. US Army C.E., Tulsa, 1960-63; civil and relocations engr. US State Dept., Del Rio, Tex., 1964; project engr. H.B. Zachary Co., San Antonio, 1965-66; civil and constrn. engr. US Army C.E., St. Louis, 1967-76, tech. advisor for planning and nat. hydropower coord., 1976-78; project mgr. for EPA constrn. grants Milw., 1978-80; chief arch. and engring. HUD, Indpls., 1980-81; civil design and pavements engr. Whiteman AFB, Mo., 1982-86; project mgr. maintenance, 1993—; soil and pavements engr. Hdqrs. Mil. Airlift Command, Scott AFB, Ill., 1986-88. Project mgr. AF-1 maintenance hangar; cattle and grain farmer, 1982—; pvt. practice civil-mech. engr., constrn. mgmt., estimating, cost analysis, cash flow, project scheduling, expert witness, profl. land surveying, Fortuna, Mo., 1988—2001; chief constrn. inspector divsn. design and constrn. State of Mo., 1992—93; project engr. Mil. Housing, 2001—; adj. faculty civil engring. Washington U., 1968—78, U. Wis., Milw., 1978—80, Ga. Mil. Coll., Whiteman AFB, Longview Coll., Kansas City; adj. rsch. engr. U. Mo., Columbia, 1985—86; project engr., quality control officer Korte Constrn. Co. Mem.: AAUP, NSPE, ASCE, Soc. Am. Mil. Engrs., Optimists Internat. Lutheran. Achievements include patents for in diverse art, 9 copyrights; development of solar waterstill, deep shaft hydropower concept. Home Phone: 660-882-0054; Office Phone: 660-882-9444. Business E-Mail: jlramer1@yahoo.com.

RAMER, LAWRENCE JEROME, corporation executive; b. Bayonne, NJ; s. Sidney and Anne (Strassman) R.; m. Ina Lee Brown, June 30, 1957; children: Stephanie Beryl, Susan Meredith, Douglas Strassman. BA in Econs, Lafayette Coll., 1950; MBA, Harvard U., 1957; LLD (hon.), Lafayette Coll., 1992. Sales rep., then v.p. United Sheet Metal Co., Bayonne, 1953-55; with Am. Cement Corp., 1957-64; v.p. mktg. div. Riverside Cement Co., 1960-62, v.p. mktg. parent co., 1962-64; vice chmn. bd., chief exec. officer Clavier Corp., NYC, 1965-66; exec. v.p., vice chmn. bd. Pacific Western Industries, LA, 1966-70; pres., chief exec. officer Nat. Portland Cement Co. Fla., 1975-89; chmn. bd. Sutro Partners, Inc., LA, 1977-89, Somerset Mgmt. Group, 1975-92, Luminall Paints Inc., LA, 1972-95; chmn. bd., CEO Bruning Paint Co., Balt., 1979—2000; chmn. bd., chief exec. officer Pacific Coast Cement Co., LA, 1979-90; pres., CEO Ramer Equities, Inc., 1990—2000, chmn., 2000—; chmn. bd. Scott Paint Co., Sarasota, Fla., 2000—. Chmn. Lee and Lawrence J. Ramer Family Found., 1986—; bd. dirs. The Music Ctr., LA, Canyon Ranch, Tucson; bd. dirs. Ctr. Theatre Group-Mark Taper Ahmanson Theatres, LA, pres. and chmn., 1987-97. Mem. Coun. on Fgn. Rels., NYC; chmn. bd. trustees Lafayette Coll., Easton, Pa., 1992—2001, bd. trustees, 1976—2001, Helen Keller Internat., NYC, Calif. Inst. Arts, Valencia, 1990—, chmn. bd. trustees, 1995—2006; nat. bd. govs. Am. Jewish Com., NY, treas. NY; bd. dirs. LA World Affairs Coun., Pacific Coun. Internat. Policy; trustee Leo Baeck Inst., NY. Mem.: Geffen Theatre (bd. dirs.). Office: Ramer Equities Inc 10900 Wilshire Blvd Ste 550 Los Angeles CA 90024-6501 Office Phone: 310-209-0442.

RAMESH, BALASUBRAMANIAM, science educator; s. Balasubramanian Modikondan Srinivasa and Vasantha Balasubramanian; m. Meera Ramesh; children: Pranav, Nikhil. BE with honors, U. Madras, Trichy, India, 1981; MBA, Indian Inst. Mgmt., Kolkata, 1983; MPhil, NYU, 1988, PhD, 1991. Cons. A. F. Ferguson & Co., Madras, Tamil Nadu, 1983—85; asst. prof. Naval Postgrad. Sch., Monterey, Calif., 1990—95, assoc. prof., 1995—97, Ga. State U., Atlanta, 1997—2004, prof., 2004—, bd. advisors prof. info. sys., 2007—. Dir. M. S. Program Info Sys. Audit and Control, Atlanta, 2006—. Contbr. articles to profl. sci. jours. Adv. bd. mem. Gwinnett Sch. Math, Sci. and Tech., Duluth, Ga., 2007—08. Recipient Regents Tchg. Excellence award, State Ga., Outstanding Rsch. Achievement award, Naval Postgrad. Sch., 1995, Outstanding Instructional Achievement award, 1997, Outstanding Faculty Achievement award, 2002, Bd. Advisors Excellence award, 2007; named Top Faculty award, Robinson Coll. Bus., 2002, 2007; grants, NSF, DARPA, ONR, ARL, AFRL, 1991—2008. Mem.: ACM, IEEE, Assn. Info. Sys. Home: 5704 Orchard Pl Crossing Lilburn GA 30047 Office: Ga State Univ Coll Bus 35 Broad St Atlanta GA 30303 Business E-Mail: bramesh@gsu.edu, bramesh@ieee.org.

RAMEY, DAVID, legislative staff member; Chief of staff for Rep. Ken Calvert, US House of Reps., Washington, 2000—; asst. US House Sci. Com., 2006, US House Appropriations Com., 2007—. Office: Office of Congressman Ken Calvert 2201 Rayburn Office Bldg Washington DC 20515 Office Phone: 202-225-1986. Office Fax: 202-225-2004. E-mail: dave.ramey@mail.house.gov.*

RAMEY, DENNY L., bar association executive director; b. Portsmouth, Ohio, Feb. 22, 1947; s. Howard Leroy and Norma Wylodine (Richards) R.; m. Jeannine Gayle Dunmyer, Sept. 24, 1971 (div. Nov.

1991); children: Elizabeth Michelle, Brian Michael. BBA, Ohio U., 1970; MBA, Capital U., 1976. Cert. assn. exec. Adminstrv. mgr. Transit Warehouse div. Elston Richards Storage Co., Columbus, Ohio, 1970-73; mgr. continuing profl. edn. Ohio Soc. CPA's, Columbus, 1973-79; exec. dir. Engrs. Found. of Ohio, Columbus, 1979-80; asst. exec. Ohio State Bar Assn., Columbus, 1980-86, exec. dir., sec., treas., 1986—. Treas., exec. com., bd. dirs. Ohio Bar Liability Ins. Co., Columbus, 1986—; treas. Ohio State Bar Found., 1986—; treas. Ohio Legal Ctr. Ins., Columbus, 1988-91; sec. Ohio Printing Co., Ltd., 1991; v.p. Osbanet, Inc., 1993—; chmn. Lawriter LLC, 2000-08; bd. dirs. OSBA.com, LLC. Mem.: Ohio Soc. Assn. Execs., Am. Soc. Assn. Execs., Nat. Assn. Bar Execs., Scioto Country Club. Methodist. Avocations: golf, sports, music, art. Office: Ohio State Bar Assn 1700 Lake Shore Dr PO Box 16562 Columbus OH 43216-6562 Office Phone: 614-487-4405. Business E-Mail: dramey@ohiobar.org.

RAMEY, EUDORA MALOIS, minister; b. Maywood, Ill., Oct. 26, 1923; d. Cleonus and Ora Helen Garner; m. Edward F Ramey, July 27, 1947; children: Jonathan, RoseMary, Paul. Student, Herzl Jr. Coll., Chgo., Peter's Bus. Coll., Master's Sewing Coll., Vennard Bible Coll., Moody Bible Inst. Ordained minister African Episcopal Ch., 1951. Mem. Dist. 9 Bd. Edn., McKinley Sch., Chgo., 1966—75; counselor aide Bd. Edn./Whitney Young Magnet Sch., Chgo., 1975—80; implementor Job Club/Pres.'s Office/Employment Tng., Chgo., 1980—92. Advisor Garfield Pk. Conservatory, Chgo., 1991—, bd. dirs., 1996—. Mem. Chgo. Urban League, 1943—68, PUSH (People United to Serve Humanity), Chgo., 1970—91; ordained local elder/min. St. Stephen AME Ch., Chgo., 1951—; mem. NAACP, Chgo., 1943—68. Recipient Chgo. Sr. Citizen's Hall of Fame, 1997, Svc. award, North Dist. Sunday Schs. Chgo. Conf., 1990, Garfield Pk. Conservatory Alliance, Chgo., 1998, Unsung Heroes award, Christian Edn. Commn., 1998, Cert. of Honor, Internat. Way of Life /City of Chgo., 1999, Trailblazer for Women in Ministry award, 4th Dist. of the AME Ch., 2001; named Sr. of Yr., Christian Edn. Commn., 2005. Avocations: Scrabble, Bingo, reading, checkers, crossword puzzles. Personal E-mail: rev.eudora1026@sbc.global.net.

RAMGOOLAM, NAVINCHANDRA, Prime Minister of the Republic of Mauritius; b. July 14, 1947; s. Late Sir Seewoosagur and late Lady Sushill R.; m. Veena Brizmonun, 1979. Degree, Royal Coll. Surgeons, Dublin, LRCP, LRCSI; London Sch. Econs.; LLB with honors, Inns of Ct. Sch. of Law; D (hon.), U. Mauritius, 1998, Aligarh Muslim U., 1998. Bar: Inner Temple, 1993. Leader Mauritius Labour Party, 1991—, pres., 1991-92, Member of Parliment, leader of opposition, 1991-95; min. def. and home affairs, min. external comm. Republic of Mauritius, prime min., 1995—2000, 2005—. Mem. internat. adv. bd. Ctr. for Internat. Devel. Harvard U., 1999. Hon. Fellow Inner Temple, 1998. Mem. internat. adv. bd. Centre for Internat. Devel., Harvard U., 1999. Avocations: reading, music, water-skiing, chess. Home: 37 Riverwalk Vacoas Mauritius Office: Govt House Port Louis Mauritius

RAMIREZ, AMELIE G., health facility administrator, director; b. Laredo, Tex., Oct. 17, 1951; m. David Gutierrez. MPH, U. Tex., Houston; DPH, U. Tex. Asst. dir. adminstrn. and cmty. health promotion S.Tex. Health Rsch. Ctr., U. Tex. Health Sci. Ctr., San Antonio, 1989—94, assoc. dir. cmty. health promotion, 1994—97; assoc. dir., Ctr. Cancer Control Rsch. Baylor Coll. Medicine, Houston, 1997—99, dep. dir., Chronic Disease Prevention and Control Rsch. Ctr., 1999—2006; dir., Inst. Health Promotion Rsch. U. Tex. Health Sci. Ctr., 2006—, prof. epidemiology and biostatistics, Dielmann chair in health disparities and cmty. outreach rsch. Mem. Lance Armstrong Found., Austin, Tex., 2007; mem. selection com. Am. Cancer Soc., 2004; mem. external adv. com. to NIH grant Sch. Pub. Health, U. Medicine and Dentistry of NJ, 2005; mem. Nat. Childrens Study Adv. Com., Md., 2006; chair Social Mktg. and Cancer Genetics Among Hispanics, Tex., 2007; mem. Susan G. Komen Sci. Adv. Bd., Tex., 2007, Inst. Medicine and Divsn. Earth and Life Studies Roundtable on Translating Genomic Based Rsch. Health, Tex., 2007—; adv. bd. mem. Avon Found. Breast Cancer Crusade, Tex., 2007—; chair fed. adv. bd. Cervical Cancer Early Detection Program, Ctrs. Disease Control, Tex., 2007—. Recipient First Pl. award, Women in Comm., 1997, Bronze Telly award, Nat. Hispanic/Latino Cancer Network, 2002, Silver, Platinum and Bronze Quill award, 2005, Prof. Survivorship award, Susan G. Komen for Cure, 2007. Mem.: APHA, Inst. Medicine Nat. Academies, Internat. Union Health Promotion Edn., Soc. Pub. Edn., Soc. Behavioral Medicine, Am. Acad. Health Behavior, Am. Soc. Preventive Oncology. Office: Univ Tex Health Sci Ctr 8207 Callaghan Rd Ste 353 San Antonio TX 78230*

RAMIREZ, ANGELA, legislative staff member; b. Sacramento; B in Polit. Economy, Princeton U., NJ, 1997. Cert. in Spanish Princeton U. Trial preparation asst. NY Dist. Attorney's Office; healthcare cons. Adv. Bd. Co., Washington; legis. asst., Rep. Joseph Crowley US House of Reps., Washington, 2002—03, sr. legis. asst., Rep. Joseph Crowley, 2003—06, exec. dir., Congl. Hispanic Caucus, 2006—08, chief of staff to Rep. Ben Luján, 2008—. Fellow, Calif. State Senate. Democrat. Office: 502 Cannon House Office Bldg Washington DC 20515 Office Phone: 202-225-6190. Office Fax: 202-226-1528.*

RAMIREZ, HANLEY, professional baseball player; b. Samana, Dominican Republic, Dec. 23, 1983; s. Toribio and Isabel Ramirez; 1 child, Hanley Jr. Shortstop Fla. Marlins, 2005—. Mem. Dominican Republican nat. team World Baseball Classic, 2009. Recipient Silver Slugger award, 2008; named Nat. League Rookie Yr., 2006; named to All-Stars Future Game, 2005, Nat. League All-Star Team, Maj. League Baseball, 2008, 2009. Achievements include hitting 7 leadoff home runs in 2006, a franchise first; being the first Marlin ever to post double digits in triples (11), home runs (17) and stolen bases (51) in 2006. Avocations: pool, video games. Mailing: c/o Fla Marlins Dolphin Stadium 2267 Dan Marino Blvd Miami FL 33056*

RAMIREZ, LEO ARMANDO, SR., mathematics educator; Math. tchr. McAllen HS, Tex., 1985—; founder, owner Ram Materials, Inc., McAllen, Tex. Recipient Denius Univ. Interscholastic League Sponsors Excellence award, 1991, Tandy Corp. Scholar award, 1995; named Hero in Edn., Reader's Digest, 1992, Tex. State Math. Tchr. of Yr., 1993, Disney's Am. Teacher award finalist, 1994, Teacher award Honorable Mention, USA Today, 1999, HEB Excellence award finalist, 2004. Mem.: Tex. Math and Sci. Coaches Assn. (Numerous Coach of Yr. award), Univ. Interscholastic League. Achievements include has written more Number Sense, Calculator, and Mathematics tests for invitational tournaments and more workbooks/practice tests than any person in the history of University Interscholastic League. Office: Ram Inc Materials 2908 Flamingo Mcallen TX 78504 Office Phone: 956-682-5185. Office Fax: 956-682-7281. Business E-Mail: toywiz127@aol.com.

RAMIREZ, MANNY (MANUEL ARISTIDES RAMIREZ), professional baseball player; b. Santo Domingo, Dominican Republic, May 30, 1972; m. Juliana Ramirez. Outfielder Cleve. Indians, 1993—2000, Boston Red Sox, 2000—08, LA Dodgers, 2008—. Recipient Players Choice award for Am. League Outstanding Player, 1999, Silver Slugger award, 1995, 1999—2006, Hank Aaron award, 1999, 2004, Am. League Batting Title, 2002; named World Series MVP, 2004; named to Am. League All-Star Team, 1995, 1998—2008. Achievements include led the American League in RBIs (165), 1999, home runs (43), 2004; being a member of World Series Champion Boston Red Sox, 2004, 2007; hitting his 500th career home run, May 31, 2008. Office: LA Dodgers 1000 Elysian Park Ave Los Angeles CA 90012*

RAMIREZ, MARY CATHERINE, retired secondary school educator; b. McLeansboro, Ill., Feb. 16, 1921; d. George Washington and Mary Margaret (Lane) Tousley; m. John Ramirez, Oct. 30, 1948 (dec. 1975). BS, Ctrl. U., Edmond, Okla., 1942; MA, U. Okla., 1945. Tchr. Bradley (Okla.) High Sch., 1942-43, McLeansboro (Ill.) High Sch., 1943-46, No. Okla. Jr. Coll., Tonkawa, Okla., 1946-47, Draughon Bus. Coll., Springfield, Mo., 1947-48, VA Hosp., Springfield, Mo., 1948-52, Madison, Wis., 1952-63, Madison pub. sch., 1963-85; tchr. ESL Poland, 1995. Tchr. English (summer), Poland, 1994. Mem. AAUW (publicity chmn. Madison br. 1954-60)., NEA, Madison Civics Club. Avocations: travel, photography, coin and stamp collecting, needlecrafts.

RAMIREZ, MICHAEL P., editorial cartoonist; b. Tokyo; s. Ireneo Edward and Fumiko Maria R. Degree, Univ. Calif., Irvine. Cartoonist Baker Comm./Palos Verdes Peninsula News, Calif., 1982—89, The Daily Sun/Post, San Clemente, Calif., 1989—90, The Comml. Appeal, Memphis, 1990—97, LA Times, 1997—2005; syndicated cartoonist Copley News Svc., 1986—; sr. editor, cartoonist Investor's Bus. Daily, 2005—. Recipient Pulitzer prize for editorial cartooning, 1994, Soc. Profl.Journalism award for editorial cartooning, 1996, Nat. Journalism award for editorial cartooning, Scripps Howard Found., 2006, Pulitzer prize for editorial cartooning, 2008. Office: Copley News Service 7776 Ivanhoe Ave La Jolla CA 92037-4520

RAMIREZ, MONICA E., science educator, dean; b. NYC, Nov. 27, 1952; d. Luis Ramirez de Arellano and Margarete Brendel; m. Neil Allen, Aug. 17, 2002; children: Luis Preiss, Suellen Melzer-Drinnen. BA, MS, U. Munich, 1979; EdS, Novasout Eastern, 1989; PhD, Columbia Pacific U., 1992; EdD, U. Wyoming, 2007. Assoc. prof. Fla. Atlantic U., Boca Raton, 1994—97; prof. geology Aims Coll., Greeley, Colo., 1997—2004; assoc. prof. Colo. State U. at Pueblo, 2004—07. Geology state chmn. Aims Coll., 2001—04; stormwater adv. bd. City of Greeley, 2003—06; vice pres. Pueblo Nature Ctr., 2004—07. Contbr. articles to jours.; lang. editor Ctrl. European Sci. Jour., 2002—; editor: (jour.) The Earth Scientist, 2006—. Recipient grant, NSF, 2000—04; nominee Fla. Governor's award, Fla. Dept. Environ. Edn., 1993; grant, Math and Sci. Initiative, Colo. Commn., 2004—05. Avocations: rock climbing, kayaking. Office: 1000 Coconut Creek Blvd Coconut Creek FL 33066 Business E-Mail: mramirez@broward.edu.

RAMIREZ, NOLA MARIE, librarian; b. Painesville, Ohio, July 25, 1953; d. Ruth Alice Young; m. Robert Cisneros Ramirez, Dec. 20, 1983; 1 child, Geoffrey Michael Ross. Attended, West Valley Jr. Coll., San Jose, Calif. Vol. Merced County Libr., Gustine, Calif., 1988—90, libr. asst., 1990—92, branch mgr., 1992—. Co-leader Girl Scouts Am., 1998—. Mem.: Assn. Rural Small Libr. Avocation: reading. Home: 263 Laurel Ave Gustine CA 95322 Office: Merced County Libr Gustine Branch 205 Sixth St Gustine CA 95322 Office Phone: 209-854-3013. Personal E-mail: nolar55@hotmail.com.

RAMIREZ, RAMON SANTO, professional baseball player; b. Puerto Plata, Dominican Republic, Aug. 31, 1981; Pitcher Colo. Rockies, 2006—08, Kansas City Royals, 2008, Boston Red Sox, 2008—. Office: Boston Red Sox Fenway Pk 4 Yawkey Way Boston MA 02215

RAMIREZ, RICARDO, bishop; b. Bay City, Tex., Sept. 12, 1936; s. Natividad and Maria (Espinosa) R. BA, U. St. Thomas, Houston, 1959; MA, U. Detroit, 1968; Diploma in Pastoral Studies, East Asian Pastoral Inst., Manila, 1973-74. Ordained priest Congregation of St. Basil, 1966; missionary Basilian Fathers, Mex., 1968-76; exec. v.p. Mexican Am. Cultural Ctr., San Antonio, 1976-81; ordained bishop, 1981; cons. US Bishop's Com. on Liturgy, 1981—; advisor US Bishop's Com. on Hispanic Affairs, 1981—; aux. bishop Archdiocese of San Antonio, 1981-82; bishop Diocese of Las Cruces, N.Mex., 1982—. Author: Fiesta, Worship and Family, 1981. Mem. N.Am. Acad. on Liturgy, Hispanic Liturgical Inst., Padres Asociada Derechos Religiosos Educativos y Sociales Lodges: K.C; Holy Order Knights of Holy Sepulcher. Roman Catholic. Office: Diocese Las Cruces 1280 Med Park Dr Las Cruces NM 88005-3239

RAMIREZ, SAUL N., JR., housing association executive; b. Oct. 22, 1958; m. Maria Agnes Ramirez; children: Saul, Joaquin, Alexis Nicole. City councilman City of Laredo, Tex., 1982—90, mayor Tex., 1990—97; asst. sec. for cmty. planning & devel. US Dept. Housing & Urban Devel., Washington, 1997—98, dep. sec., 1998—2001; exec. dir. Nat. Assn. Housing & Redevelopment Officials (NAHRO), Washington, 2002—. Named Disting. Citizen of Yr., Boy Scouts America, Mayor of Yr., Tex. Mcpl. Library Dir. Assn., 1995, The Laredoan of the Yr., Laredo Morning Times, 1997; named one of The Nation's 35 Most Dynamic Mayors, Newsweek mag., 1996. Democrat. Office: Nat Assn Housing & Redevelopment Officials 630 Eye St NW Washington DC 20001

RAMIREZ, TINA, performing company executive; b. Caracas, Venezuela; d. Gloria Maria Cestero and Jose Ramirez Gaonita. Studied dance with Lola Bravo, Alexandra Danilova, Anna Sokolow. Toured with Federico Rey Dance Co.; founder, artistic dir. Ballet Hispanico, NYC, 1970—2009. Panelist NEA N.Y. Sate Coun. on Arts; mem. advisory panel N.Y.C. Dept. Cultural Affairs; bd. dirs Dance Theater Workshop. Appearances (Broadway plays) Kismet, Lute Song, (TV series) Man of La Mancha. Bd. mem. The New 42nd Street, Inc. Recipient Arts and Culture Honor award, Mayor of NYC, 1983, Ethnic New Yorker award, NYC, 1986, Gov.'s Arts award, NY State Gov. Mario Cuomo, 1987, honoree Nat. Puerto Rican Forum, Hispanic Inst. for Performing Arts., Hispanic Heritage Award, 1999, Dance Magazine Award, 2002, Nat. Medal of Arts, Nat. Endowment for the Arts, 2005; named one of ten people of yr., AARP Mag., 2004.*

RAMIREZ GARZA, ELIZABETH ANN, biology professor, researcher; d. Joe E. Ramirez Sr. and Diamantina Ramirez; m. Simon Garza, Jr., Sept. 18, 1982; children: Jonathan David Garza, Aaron Zachary Garza, Joshua Joseph Garza, Caleb Daniel Garza. BS in Biology, U. Tex., San Antonio, 1981, MS in Biology, 1986. Cert. radiology Tex. State Bd. Dental Examiners, 1989, dental practice mgmt. asst. Tex., 1990. Rsch. asst. U. Tex. Health Sci. Ctr., San Antonio, 1981—82, 1985—86; student intern genetics lab U. Tex., San Antonio, 1984—85; biology tutor St. Edward's U., Austin, Tex., 1991; lectr. Incarnate Word Coll., San Antonio, 1991—92; adj. faculty biology Austin C.C., 1993—2004, asst. prof. biology, 2004—06; adj. faculty biology Concordia U., Austin, 2002—03. Coll. assistance migrant program mentor St. Edward's U., Austin, 1991—92; biology faculty mentor Dept. Biology, Austin, 1999, biology 1408 com. chmn., 2005. Mem. campus adv. coun. Lyndon Baines Johnson H.S., Austin, 2002—04; active City Charter Commn., Yoakum, Tex., 1987; pres. Bailey Mid. Sch. PTA, Austin, 1999—2000. Nat. Hispanic scholar, Nat. Hispanic Scholarship Com., 1984. Mem.: Tex. C.C. Tchr. Assn. (assoc.). Avocations: hiking, camping, swimming, bicycling. Office: Austin Community College 1212 Rio Grande Austin TX 78701 Personal E-mail: lramlgarz@msn.com. Business E-Mail: lramirez@austincc.edu.

RAMIREZ GELPI, ANA SOFIA, language educator, consultant; b. Zaragoza, Spain, Aug. 29; life ptnr. Nathan William Deack. PhD, U. Southern Calif., LA, 1995. Tenured Spanish lang. prof. Allan Hancock Coll., Santa Maria, Calif., 1999—2008. Consulting Gelpi Consulting, Inc., Santa Maria, 1998—. Recipient Tchr. Yr. award, Allan Hancock Coll., 2007. Office: Allan Hancock Coll 800 S Coll Dr Randsburg CA 93554 Business E-Mail: sgelpi@hancockcollege.edu.

RAMIREZ-MIRELES, FERNANDO, electronics engineer, consultant; s. Fernando Ramirez Matuk and Maria Elia Mireles Tabares; m. Gina Miroslava Guerrero Barja; children: Tania Fernanda Ramirez Guerrero, Thalia Miroslava Ramirez Guerrero. BSc in Electronics Comm., Met. Autonomous U., Mex. City, 1986; MScEE, Ctr. Rsch. and Advanced Studies Nat. Politechnic Inst., Mex. City, 1988; PhDEE, U. Southern Calif., LA, 1998. Diplomate in fin. and acctg., 2008; diplomate in bus. adminstrn., ITAM, 2005; diplomate in legal aspects it and telecom.: 2005, cert.: (diplomate in intellectual property) 2007; diplomate in human devel. 2009. Rschr. comm. group Cinvestav, Mex. City, 1988—92; mem. tech. staff Glenayre/Wireless Access, Santa Clara, Calif., 1998—2000; comm. sys. engr. Aware, Inc., Lafayette, Calif., 2000—01; sr. comm. sys. engr. Ikanos Comms., Fremont, Calif., 2001—03; prof. Inst. Tech Autonomo, Mex. City, 2003—. Cons. Banamex Bank, Mex. City, 1991, Tecgram, Mex. City, 2005; rsch. asst. U. Southern Calif., LA, 1996—98; intern Torrey Sci. Corp., San Diego, 1997, Telmex Ctr. Rsch. and Devel., Mex. City, 1986—87; organist Frenctlmexican Telecom Summer Schs., ITAM-LAFMI-ENSTB-GET, Mex. City, Mexico, 2006—07; vis. rschr. San Francisco State U., San Francisco, 2007, Comm. Rsch. Ctr., Ottawa, Ont., Canada, 2008. Contbr. articles to profl. jours. Spkr. Cofetel's Symposium On Regulation Mobile TV, Mex. City, 2008; jury First Lego League, 2008. Recipient Fulbright Scholarship, Fulbright-Garcia Robles Commn., 1992—97, U. Merit medal, Met. Autonomous Univ., Mex., 1987, Honorific Mention, IV Ericsson's Nat. Prize of Sci. and Tech., Mex., 1990; named Nat. Rschr., Nat. Sys. Rschrs., Mex., 2007—; named one of Best Students of Mex., Best Students of Mex. Orgn., 1989. Mem.: IEEE (sr.; student br. counsellor 2008—09), Tech. Mgmt. Coun. (chpt. chair 2008—09), Soc. Hispanic Profl. Engrs., Tau Beta Pi. Independent. Roman Catholic. Achievements include patents in field of DSL communications. Avocations: travel, music. Office: Inst Tech Autonomo Rio Hondo 1 Mexico City Mexico Office Phone: 525 55 628 4000 ext. 362. Office Fax: 52 555 490 4663. Personal E-mail: fernandomireles@yahoo.com. Business E-Mail: ramirezm@ieee.org.

RAMÍREZ-MONTAGUT, MÓNICA, curator; MA in art and architecture, PhD in theory and history of architecture. Dir. Carlos Taché Gallery, Barcelona; curator Price Tower Art Ctr., Bartlesville, Ohio; asst. curator architecture and design Solomon R. Guggenheim Mus., NYC, 2006—08; curator Aldrich Contemporary Art Mus., Ridgefield, Conn., 2008—. Art cons. Arts Internat., NYC. Curator (exhibitions) Dennis Oppenheim: Indoors/Outdoors, Price Tower Arts Ctr., 2005, Bruce Goff: The Drunken Boat, 2005, Prairie Skyscraper: Frank Lloyd Wright's Price Tower, traveling, 2006, Zaha Hadid, Solomon R. Guggenheim Mus., NYC, 2006 (2nd place award for Best Architecture or Design Show, Internat. Assn. Art Critics), Cai Guo Qiang: I Want to Believe, 2008. Office: Aldrich Contemporary Art Mus 258 Main St Ridgefield CT 06877 Office Phone: 203-438-4519. Office Fax: 203-438-0198.*

RAMIREZ QUINTANA, JOSE LUIS, research scientist; s. Jesus Ramirez Gonzales and Alicia Quintana Martinez. BS, Idaho State U., Pocatello, 2002; MS, U. Calif. Riverside, 2006; PhD student, Johns Hopkins U., Baltimore, 2006—. A. Ralph & Sylvia E. Barr fellowship, Johns Hopkins Sch. Pub. Health, 2007, fellowship, NIH, NIAID, 2009—. Mem.: Am. Assn. Advancement Sci., Am. Mosquito Control Assn., Am. Soc. Tropical Medicine, Am. Soc. Microbiology (Robert D. Watkins Grad. fellowship 2008—), Entomol. Soc. Am. Avocations: travel, dance, music, hiking, mountain climbing, photography. Office: Johns Hopkins Univ 615 N Wolfe St Rm E 5132 Baltimore MD 21205 Personal E-mail: luisjosera@gmail.com. Business E-Mail: jramirez@jhsph.edu.

RAMIREZ-RIVERA, JOSE, physician; b. Mayaguez, PR, June 26, 1929; s. Jesus Ramirez and Nieves Rivera; m. Leila Suner, May 14, 1971; children: Frederico, Steven, Sally, Juliette, Natasha, Leila. BA, Johns Hopkins U., 1949; MD, Yale U., 1953. Diplomate Am Bd Internal Med, re-certified 1974. Intern U. Md. Hosp., 1953-54; resident in medicine Univ. Hosp., Balt., 1954-55, fellow in hematology, 1958-59, resident, 1959; staff physician VA Hosp., Balt., 1960-67, assoc. chief of staff, 1962-68; asst. in medicine Johns Hopkins U., 1960-67, instr. in medicine, 1967-68; asst. prof. medicine U. Md., 1961-68; assoc. prof. Duke U., Durham, NC, 1968-70; dir. med. edn. and clin. investigation Western Region P.R., 1970-80; chief medicine Mayaguez (P.R.) Med. Ctr., 1971-82. Prof med Univ PR, San Juan, 1974—, dir univ med servs Med Sci Campus, 1982—86; prof med Univ Cent del Caribe, 1998—; dir Rincon Rural Health Project, 1975—82; assoc chief staff educ VA Med Ctr, San Juan, 1990—92; dir clin investigation La Concepcion Hosp, San German, 1996—. Contbr. articles to med. jours.;, author books of Puerto Rican Legends. Bd dirs Soc Educ Suroeste. With USPHS, 1955—57. Decorated Comendador Imperial Orden Hispanica de Carlos V; named Man of Yr., PR Med. Soc. Western Sect., 1975, 1981. Master: ACP (pres. PR chpt. 1986—88, Blaine Brower Traveling Scholar 1967, Laureate award 2005); fellow: Coll. Chest Physicians, Royal Soc. Med (London); mem.: Imperial Orden Hispanica de Carlos V, Puerto Rican Fedn. Bioethics (bd. dirs. 1999—2002, pres. 2002—), Soc. Autores Puertorriguenos, PR Lung Assn. (bd. dirs. 1975—80), Casa Espanã (bd. dirs. 1998—2009), Alliance Francaise PR (v.p. 1995—96, pres. 1996—2000, bd. dirs. 2006—09), PEN Club. Roman Catholic. Achievements include creating a technique of lung lavage for alveolar proteinosis. Avocations: classical music, literature. Office Phone: 787-793-6576. Personal E-mail: raramirez.r629@gmail.com.

RAMIREZ RUBIO, DEBORAH, school librarian; d. Arturo Ramirez and Avilda Salinas Ramirez; m. Sergio Rubio; children: Sergio Rubio Jr., Rubio Diego Andres, Marco Antonio Rubio. MLS, Sam Houston State U., Huntsville, Tex., 2001. Cert. sch. libr. Tex., 2007. Tchr. Psja Isd, Pharr, Tex., 2001—03, Edcouch-Elsa ISD, Tex., 2002—05; libr. W. A Todd 9th Grade Campus, Donna, Tex., 2005—. Libr. W. A Todd 9th Grade Campus, Donna, Tex., 2005—. Office Fax: 956-464-1824. Personal E-mail: drubio@donnaisd.net.

RAMIS, HAROLD ALLEN, film director, screenwriter, actor; b. Chgo., Nov. 21, 1944; s. Nathan and Ruth (Cokee) R.; m. Anne Jean Plotkin, July 2, 1987 (div.) 1984; 1 child, Violet; m. Erica Mann May 7, 1989; children: Julian, Daniel. BA, Washington U., St. Louis, 1966, ArtsD (hon.), 1993. Assoc. editor Playboy mag., 1968-70; actor, writer

Second City, Chgo., 1970-73, Nat. Lampoon Radio Hour, Lampoon Show, 1974-75; actor, head writer SCTV, 1977-78; producer, head writer Rodney Dangerfield Show, ABC-TV, 1982. Screenwriter (with Douglas Kenny and Chris Miller) National Lampoon's Animal House, 1978, (with Janice Allen, Len Blum and Dan Goldberg) Meatballs, 1979, (with Douglas Kenny, Brian Doyle-Murray) Caddyshack, 1980, (with Len Blum and Dan Goldberg) Stripes, 1981, (with Dan Aykroyd) Ghostbusters, 1984, (with Brian Doyle-Murray) Club Paradise, 1986; co-screenwriter (with Peter Torokvei) Armed and Dangerous, 1986; writer (with Dan Akroyd) Ghostbusters II, 1989, Rover Dangerfield, 1991; dir. Stuart Saves His Family, 1995, The Ice Harvest, 2005; dir., prodr. Multiplicity, 1996, Bedazzled, 2000; dir., writer: Caddyshack, 1980, National Lampoon's Vacation, 1983, Club Paradise, 1986, Analyze This, 1999, Analyze That, 2002; writer, dir. prodr. Groundhog Day, 1993, Year One, 2009; exec. prodr. The First $20 Million is Always the Hardest, 2002; exec. prodr., co-screenwriter (with Rodney Dangerfield) Back to School, 1986; film appearances include: Stripes, 1981, Ghostbusters, 1984, Baby Boom, 1987, Stealing Home, 1988, Ghostbusters II, 1989, As Good As It Gets, 1997, Orange County. Mem. AFTRA, SAG, Writers Guild Am., Dirs. Guild Am.*

RAMLAL, DEREK, history professor, personal trainer; m. Priya Amy Kim Ramlal, Dec. 12, 2007; 1 child, Kelly Akira Nirvana. BA, St. John's U., Queens, NY, 2001, MA, 2003, ArtsD, 2007. Cert. health fitness instr. Internat. Sports Sci. Assn., 2008, personal trainer Am. Coll. Sports Medicine, 2008. Tchr. Martin Luther HS, Maspeth, NY, 2001—04; personal trainer Comprehensive Body Conditioning, Queens, 2005—; adj. asst. prof. St. John's U., Queens, 2006—. Fitness trainer Laurelton Cmty. Assn. Martial Arts Exhbn. Mem. St. Vincent Ferrer Cath. Ch., Bklyn., 1984—. Mem.: Phi Alpha Theta. Achievements include research in qigong and the modernization of China. Office: St John's Univ 8000 Utopia Pky Jamaica NY 11439 Office Fax: 718-990-2644. Personal E-mail: derek979@gmail.com. Business E-Mail: ramlald@stjohns.edu.

RAMLER, SIEGFRIED, foundation administrator, researcher; b. Vienna, Oct. 30, 1924; s. Lazar and Eugenia Ramler; m. Piilani A. Ahuna, Dec. 1948 (dec. July 2003); children: David K., Dita L., Laurence K., Malia R.; m. Kiyoko Koizumi, Dec. 1, 2003. Diplôme supérieur, U. Paris, 1958; MA, U. Hawaii, 1961. Interpreter Internat. Mil. Tribunal, Nuremberg, Germany, 1945—46, chief interpreting br., 1946—49; chair fgn. lang. dept. Punahou Sch., Honolulu, 1951-71, dir. instnl. svcs., 1971-91, dir. Wo Internat. Ctr., 1990-95; exec. dir. Found. Study in Hawaii and Abroad, Honolulu, 1969-90. Sr. adj. fellow East-West Ctr., 1995—; pres. adv. bd. Pacific Basin Consortium, Hawaii, 1997-02. Author: Nuremberg and Beyond: The Memoirs of Siegfried Ramler; contbr. articles to profl. publs. Vice chair, sec., bd. dir. Crown Prince Akihito Scholarship Found., 1989—2008; trustee St. Francis Sch., Honolulu, 1996-07 Decorated Order of the Palmes Académiques, Ordre National du Mérite (France); Order of the Sacred Treasure (Japan); recipient medal Freedom Found., 1958. Mem. ASCD, Internat./Global Edn. Com. (chair nat. adv. com. 1987-93), Japan-Am. Soc. Hawaii (pres. 1986-87, program chmn. 1975-94, Alliance Française Hawaii (pres. and founder 1961, bd. dir. 1992-2001, regent 2001-), World Assn. Internat. Studies (bd. dir. 2000—). Avocations: running, travel, swimming. Home: 921 Maunawili Cir Kailua HI 96734-4620 Office: East West Ctr 1777 E West Rd Honolulu HI 96848 Home Phone: 808-261-0225; Office Phone: 808-944-7609. Personal E-mail: ramlers001@hawaii.rr.com.

RAMM, DOUGLAS ROBERT, psychologist; b. New Haven, Dec. 11, 1949; s. Robert Frederick and Gladys (Torgrimson) R.; m. Barbara Stephens, Aug. 10, 1974; children: Jennifer, Jessica. BA, Ithaca Coll., 1972; MA, Duquesne U., 1974, PhD, 1979. Diplomate Am. Bd. Profl. Psychology; bd. cert. clin. psychologist Am. Bd. Profl. Psychology. Staff psychologist Westmoreland Hosp., Greensburg, Pa., 1976-79, chief clin. psychologist, dir. child & adolescent psychiat., 1979-82; pvt. practice Greensburg, Pa., 1980—. Pres. Ethics, Inc., Ctr. for Sci. Study of Values and Morality, 1995-98; cons. U. Pitts., Pa. Bur. Vocat. Rehab., Westmoreland County Ct. of Common Pleas; past pres. Mental Health Assn. Westmoreland County. Author: Clinically Formulated Principles of Morality, 1996, Consider the Scientific Study of Morality, 1998, The Formula for Happiness, 2004, Principles for Achieving Emotional Well-Being, 2005, Motivating Juvenile Offenders Toward Making Responsible Revision in Daily Life. Mem. APA, ASCD, Am. Philos. Assn., Pa. Psychol. Assn., Acad. Clin. Psychology, Soc. Personality Assessment, Nat. Acad. Neuropsychologists, Nat. Register Health Svc. Providers in Psychology, Am. Coll. Forensic Examiners (diplomate), Soc. Bus. Ethics, Rotary Club. Methodist. Office: 225 Humphrey Rd Ste 4 Greensburg PA 15601-4571 Office Phone: 724-832-9096. Personal E-mail: rammpsychsvcs@aol.com.

RAMME, TINA M., biology professor, director; b. Ashland, Wis. BS in Biology, Northland Coll., Ashland, 1998; MS in Conservation Biology, U. Minn., Mpls., 2002; MS in Biol. Scis., Harvard U., Cambridge, Mass., 2004; degree in Conservation and Wildlife Vet. Medicine, Tufts U. Cunningham Coll. Vet. Medicine, Grafton, Mass., 2006. Cert. in secondary edn. Mich., Wis., Minn., 1995. Rsch. assoc. Jane Goodall Ctr. Primate Studies U. Minn., St. Paul; wildlife rsch. specialist Hoedspruit Cheetah Rsch. Ctr., Hoedspruit, South Africa; wildlife rsch. assoc. Serengeti Lion Project, Serengeti Nat. Pk., Tanzania; biol. rsch. assoc. US Fish & Wildlife Svc., Ashland, Wis., USGS Gt. Lakes Ctr., Ann Arbor, Mich., Russian Acad. Sci., Ulan Ude, Siberia, US Geol. Survey Biol. Divsn., Ann Arbor, Wis.; NSF long term ecol. rsch. asst. Cedar Creek Natural History Area, U. Minn.; field biology program dir. Itasca Field Sta., U. Minn.; conservation edn. dir. Minn. Dept. Natural Resources, St. Paul; project engr. IWP, Ironwood, Mich.; biol. rsch. asst. Rainforest Assessment Program, Jatun Sasha Biol. Rsch. Sta., Mischushaulli, Ecuador, Migratory Bird Program Northland Coll., Monte Verde, Costa Rica; curatorial specialist & staff biologist. Harvard U., Cambridge, program coord., vis. scientist fellowship rsch. program, asst. dean, Radcliffe sci. dept.; curatorial specialist & staff biologist. Harvard U. Peabody Mus., Cambridge; prof., biol. scis. Mass. Bay CC, Wellesley, 2009—, Cambridge Coll., 2009—, Framingham State U., Mass., 2009—, Harvard U., Cambridge, 2009—; roundtable discussions evolution participant & presenter Oxford U., 2009. Biol. rsch. expdn. leader Harvard U. Mus. Comparative Zoology, Cambridge; v.p. Harvard U. Marine Sci. Rev., Cambridge; pres. Lion Conservation Fund, Cambridge, dir., 2009—, Ctr. Lion Conservation & Rsch., Nairobi, Samburu, Kenya, 2009—, pres. & CEO; consulting biologist, ecology working group Kenya Wildlife Svc., Nairobi, 2009—; CEO & dir. Conservation-KARES, Nanyuki, Kenya, 2009—; co-founder, v.p. & directorship New Eng. Seacoast Inst. & Biol. Rsch. Ctr., Nahant, Mass., 2009—. Contbr. articles and sci. papers to profl. jours. (Harvard Marine Sci. Rev. Honors award, 2001). CEO KARE, Cambridge; v.p. New Eng. Seacoast Inst., Cambridge. Recipient Tchg. Excellence award, State Mich. Gov.'s Office, 1995, Sci. Faculty award, Northland Coll., 1996, Dean's Hall of Recognition award, 1996, Sci. Achievemant award, Russian Acad. Sci. Internat. Symposium, 2000; named to Nat. Dean's List, Northland Coll., 1997; grant, NSF U. Minn., 2001, NSF fellowship, U. Minn., 2002, Rsch. grant, Nat. Geog. Soc., 2005. Mem.: Africa Sect. Soc. Conservation Biology, African Wildlife Soc., Soc. Conservation Biology, Phi Kappa Phi. Achievements include research in species designation omul, coregonus autumnalis; biology, ageing technique and social structure of coalitions in African lions. Avocations: travel, art, photography. Home and Office: Lion Conservation Fund PO Box 380 170 Cambridge MA 02138 Business E-Mail: tina@kenyalions.org.

RAMMOHAN, KOTTIL WALAPPIL, neurologist, educator; s. Balakrishnan and Subhadra Marar; m. Bindu Rammohan; children: Kalyani, Jayan. MD, Madras Med. Coll., Chennai, 1967, BS in Medicine, 1969, BS in Surgery, 1969. Dir., Multiple Sclerosis Ctr. Ohio State U., Columbus, 1982—, assoc. prof., 1988—2002, prof., 2002—. Chair, profl. adv. com. Nat. Multiple Sclerosis Soc., NYC, 2000—04, vol. Named to Nat. Hall of Fame, Nat. Multiple Sclerosis Soc., 2003. Home Fax: 614-293-3445.

RAMO, ROBERTA COOPER, lawyer; b. Denver, Aug. 8, 1942; d. David D. and Martha L. (Rosenblum) Cooper; m. Barry W. Ramo, June 17, 1964. BA magna cum laude, U. Colo., 1964; JD, U. Chgo., 1967; LLD (hon.), U. Mo., 1995; LLD, U. Denver, 1995; LHD (hon.), U. Colo., 1995; JD (hon.), Golden Gate U., 1996; LLD (hon.), U. S.C., 2001. Bar: N.Mex. 1967, Tex. 1971. With NC. Fund, Durham, 1967-68; nat. tchg. fellow Shaw U., Raleigh, N.C., 1968-70; mem. Sawtelle, Goode, Davidson & Troilo, San Antonio, 1970-72, Rodey, Dickason, Sloan, Akin & Robb, Albuquerque, 1972-74; sole practice law Albuquerque, 1974-77; dir., shareholder Poole, Kelly & Ramo, Albuquerque, 1977-93; shareholder Modrall, Sperling, Roehl, Harris & Sisk, Albuquerque, 1993—. Lectr. in field., bd. dirs. Black Rock Mutual Funds, Ednl. Credit Mgmt. Corp. Co-author: New Mexico Estate Administration System, 1980; editor: How to Create a System for the Law Office, 1975; contbg. editor: Tex. Probate Sys., 1974; contbr. articles to profl. jours., chpts. to books. Mem. steering com. World Conf. Domestic Violence, 1996—99; mem. Am. Law Inst. Coun., 1997—, exec. com., 2000—, exec. v.p., 2003—; mem. Martindale-Hubbell Legal Adv. Bd., 1996—2000; bd. dirs., past pres. N.Mex. Symphony Orch., 1977—86; bd. dirs. Albuquerque Cmty. Found., N.Mex. First, 1987—90, Santa Fe Opera, Santa Fe, 2001—08; bd. regents U. N.Mex., 1989—94, pres., 1991—93; founding bd. mem. Think N.Mex., 1998—; mem. Civitas Initiative, 1997—2008; pres. Am. Law Inst. Coun., 2008—; chmn. bd. Cooper's Inc., 1999—. Recipient Disting. Pub. Svc. award Gov. of N.Mex., 1993. Fellow: Am. Bar Found.; mem.: ABA (bd. govs. 1994—97, pres. 1995, Asia Law Initiatives Coun. 1999—2005, chmn. London 2000 com., others), Albuquerque Economic Devel. Com. (exec.com. mem. 2001—), Am. Arbitration Assn. (bd. dirs. 1997—2004, 2004—), Law Inst. Coun., Am. Judicature Soc. (bd. dirs. 1988—91), Am. Bar Retirement Assn. (bd. dirs. 1990—94), N.Mex. Bar Assn. (Outstanding Contbn. award 1981, 1984), Albuquerque Bar Assn. (pres. 1980—81, bd. dirs.). Address: Modrall Sperling Roehl Harris & Sisk PO Box 2168 Albuquerque NM 87103-2168

RAMO, SIMON, retired engineering executive; b. Salt Lake City, May 7, 1913; s. Benjamin and Clara (Trestman) Ramo; m. Virgina Smith, July 25, 1937 (dec. Aug. 19, 2009); children: James Brian, Alan Martin. BS, U. Utah, 1933, DSc (hon.), 1961; PhD, Calif. Inst. Tech., 1936; DEng (hon.), Case Western Res. U., 1960, U. Mich., 1966, Poly. Inst. NY, 1971; DSc (hon.), Union Coll., 1963, Worcester Polytechnic Inst., 1968, U. Akron, 1969, Cleve. State U., 1976; LLD (hon.), Carnegie-Mellon U., 1970, U. So. Calif., 1972, Gonzaga U., 1983, Occidental Coll., 1984, Claremont U., 1985. With Gen. Electric Co., 1936—46; v.p. ops. Hughes Aircraft Co., 1946—53; with Ramo-Woolridge Corp., 1953—58; dir. U.S. Intercontinental Ballistic Missile Program, 1954—58, TRW Inc., 1954—85, exec. v.p., 1958—61, vice chmn. bd., 1961—78, chmn. exec. com., 1969—78, cons., 1978—; pres. The Bunker-Ramo Corp., 1964—66; chmn. bd. TRW-Fujitsu Co., 1980—83. Vis. prof. mgmt. sci. Calif. Inst. Tech., 1978—; Regents lectr. UCLA, 1981—82, U. Calif. at Santa Cruz, 1978—79; chmn. Ctr. for Study Am. Experience, U. So. Calif., 1978—80; Faculty fellow John F. Kennedy Sch. Govt., Harvard U., 1980—84; mem. White House Energy Rsch. and Devel. Adv. Coun., 1973—75; chmn. Pres.'s Com. on Sci. and Tech., 1976—77; bd. advisors for sci. and tech. Repu. of China, 1981—84; chmn. bd. Aetna, Jacobs & Ramo Venture Capital, 1987—90, Allenwood Ventures, Inc., 1987—. Author: The Business of Science, 1988, other sci., engring. and mgmt. books, (non-fiction) Meetings, Meetings and More Meetings, 2005. Life trustee Calif. Inst. Tech., Nat. Symphony Orch. Assn., 1973—83; trustee emeritus Calif. State U.; bd. govs., pres. Performing Arts Coun. Mus. Ctr. LA, 1976—77; co-chair bd. overseers Keck Sch. Medicine, U. So. Calif., 1999—; bd. dirs. W. M. Keck Found., 1983—, LA World Affairs Coun., 1973—85, Mus. Ctr. Found., LA, LA Philharm. Assn., 1981—84. Recipient IAS, 1956, award, Am. Inst. Elec. Engrs., 1959, Am. Iron and Steel Inst., 1968, Medal of Achievement, AEA, 1970, DSM, Armed Forces Comm. and Electronics Assn., 1970, medal of achievement, WEMA, 1970, Kayan medal, Columbia U., 1972, award, Am. Cons. Engrs. Coun., 1974, Nat. Medal of Sci., Pres. of US, 1976, 1979, medal, Franklin Inst., 1978, awards, U. So. Calif., 1979, Pres. medal Sci., 1981, UCLA medal, 1982, Presdl. Medal of Freedom, Pres. of US, 1983, Aesculapian award, UCLA, 1984, Durand medal, AAIA, 1984, John Fritz medal, 1986, Henry Townley Heald award, Ill. Inst. Tech., 1988, Nat. Engring. award, Am. Assn. Engring. Socs., 1988, Franklin-Jefferson medal, 1988, Howard Hughes meml. award, 1989, Air Force Space and Missile Pioneers award, 1989, Pioneer award, Internat. Coun. on Sys. Engring., 1997, Disting. pub. Svc. medal, NASA, 1999, Lifetime Achievement trophy, Smithsonian Inst., 1999, John F. Kennedy Astronautics award, Am. Astronautical Soc., 2000, John R. Alison award for indsl. leadership, Air Force Assn., 2000, Presdl. Medallion, U. So. Calif., 2002, Founders award, USC Thornton Sch. of Music, 2003, Lifetime Space Achievement award, Space Found., 2007; named to Bus. Hall of Fame, 1984. Fellow: IEEE (Electronic Achievement award 1953, Golden Omega award 1975, Founders medal 1980, Centennial medal 1984), Am. Acad. Polit. Sci., Am. Acad. Arts and Scis.; mem.: NAS, Nat. Acad. Engring. (founder, coun. mem. Bueche award), Internat. Acad. Astronautics, Pacific Coun. Internat. Policy, Coun. Fgn. Rels., Inst. advancement Engring., Am. Philos. Soc., Am. Phys. Soc., NY Acad. Scis., Theta Tau (Hall of Fame laureate), Eta Kappa Nu (eminent mem. award 1966). Office: 9200 W Sunset Blvd Ste 801 Los Angeles CA 90069-3603

RAMONI, RACHEL BADOVINAC, medical educator; b. Chgo, Oct. 29, 1973; d. John Frank and Pamela Lyn Badovinac; m. Marco Francesco Ramoni, May 26, 2007. BA, Johns Hopkins U., Balt., 1994; DMD, Harvard Sch. Dental Medicine, Boston, 1999; DSc, Harvard Sch. Pub. Health, Boston, 2006. Instr. Harvard Sch. Dental Medicine, 2006—. Mem.: Nat. Birth Defects Prevention Network, Am. Dental Edn. Assn., Am. Med. Informatics Assn. Office: Harvard Sch Dental Medicine 188 Longwood Ave Boston MA 02115

RAMOS, ALBERT A., electrical engineer; b. LA, Feb. 28, 1927; s. Jesus D. and Carmen F. (Fontes) Ramos; m. Joan C. Pailing, Sept. 23, 1950; children: Albert A., Richard R., James J., Katherine. BS in Elec. Engring., U. So. Calif., 1950, MS in Sys. Mgmt., 1972; PhD, US Internat. U., 1975. Registered profl. engr., Calif. With guided missile test group Hughes Aircraft Co., 1950—60; with TRW DSG, 1960—91; sr. staff engr. Norton AFB, San Bernardino, Calif., 1969—91; ret., 1991. Served USNR, 1945—46. Mem.: NSPE, IEEE, Mexican-Am. Profl. Mgmt. Assn. (mem. administering commn. dept. community svcs.), Mexican-Am. Engring. Soc., Air Force Assn., Tau Beta Pi, Eta Kappa Nu, Sigma Phi Delta. Home: 8937 Napoli Dr Las Vegas NV 89117-1182

RAMOS, CARLOS F., physics educator; b. Buenaventura, Camaguey, Cuba, May 26, 1959; s. Rolando Andres Ramos and Isabel Florinda Gonzalez; m. Yamina I. Perdomo, Dec. 24, 1982; 1 child, Carlos N. MS in Tchg., Physics, Fla. Atlantic U., Boca Raton, Fla., 2001. Undergrad. instr., physics Higher Pedagogic Inst. Manzanillo, Las Tunas, Cuba, 1980—82; province methodological advisor, physics Ednl. Bd. Las Tunas Province, 1982—82; physics dept. chair Adult Edn. Ctr. Julio A. Mella, Amancio Rodriguez, Las Tunas Province, 1982—85; physics instr. Higher Poly. Inst. Jose Antonio Echeverria, Havana City, 1985—92; v.p. JCR Trucking Corp., West Palm Beach, Fla., 1993—98; adj. instr., physics Palm Beach CC, Lake Worth, Fla., 1998—2000, math. learning specialist, 2001—06, assoc. prof., physics, 2006—. Office: Palm Beach CC 4200 Congress Ave Lake Worth FL 33461 Business E-Mail: ramoscarlos@bellsouth.edu, ramosc@pbcc.edu.

RAMOS, CHARLES JOSEPH (JOE RAMOS), wealth management consultant; b. Orinda, Calif., July 29, 1960; s. Charles Pimentel Ramos Jr. and Louise Antoinette Troja; children: Summer Erica, Drake Joseph, Andrew Joseph. BS, U. Calif., Berkeley, 1982. CPA, Calif.; CFP; SEC Registered Investment Advisor. CPA Arthur Andersen, San Francisco, 1982-85; sr. analyst Montgomery Securities, San Francisco, 1985-87; pres. Ramos Fin. Group, San Francisco, 1987—2001; CEO Ramos Fin. Corp., DBA, Pvt. Capital Mgmt., Inc., Larkspur, Calif., 2002—; sr. mng. dir. The Pvt. Cons. Group., Inc., Larkspur, 2002—. Nat. adv. bd. Empowered Wealth, LLC; mem. Fidelity Instl. Adv. Coun. Mem. AICPA, Internat. Bd. CFP, The Fin. Planning Assn., Nat. Assn. Securities Dealers, Marin Estate Planning Coun., San Francisco Estate Planning Coun., Olympic Club, Meadow Club. Republican. Office: Pvt Capital Mgmt Inc 900 Larkspur Landing Cir Ste 240 Larkspur CA 94939-1757 Office Fax: 415-464-9755.

RAMOS, DENISE L., corporate financial executive; MBA, Univ. Chgo., 1979. Fin. mgmt. positions through asst. treas. Atlantic Richfield Co., LA; sr. v.p., treas., CFO KFC Yum! Brands, 2000—05; CFO Furniture Brands Internat., 2005—07; sr. v.p., CFO ITT Corp., White Plains, NY, 2007—. Office: Itt 1133 Westchester Ave Ste N100 West Harrison NY 10604-3543

RAMOS, ELMO, JR., music company executive; b. Bridgeport, Conn., Mar. 9, 1977; s. Elmo and Noemi Ramos. Chief music prodr. Hitmen Productions LLC, Orlando, 1992—; ceo Oasis Records Inc, 1997—2007, Lord & Oasis, Orlando, Fla., 1998—; founder & mgr. DJ Flexx, LLC, Orlando, 1988—, Benny Blanco, LLC., Aguadilla, PR, 1990—, Tickle Me Productions, LLC., Orlando, 1990—, Chica Power, LLC, Orlando, 1999—, Benny Blanco Clothiers, LLC., NYC, 1999—, Oasis Records LLC, 2008—, Extreme Youth Ministries, Orlando, 2008—, Lord & Oasis Telecom. LLC, 2008—, Hope Ministries, Orlando, 2008—; author & founding dir. Lord & Oasis Pub. LLC, 2005—. Mentor Audio Engrs. Soc., NYC, 2004—. Office: Lord & Oasis PO Box 620003 Orlando FL 32862 Business E-Mail: bb9east247@aol.com.

RAMOS, FIDEL V. (EDDIE RAMOS), former president of The Philippines; b. Lingayen, Pangasinan, Philippines, Mar. 18, 1928; s. Narciso Ramos and Angela Valdez; m. Amelita Martinez; 5 children. BS, U.S. Mil. Acad., 1950; MSCE, U. Ill., 1951; M in Nat. Security Adminstrn., Nat. Def. Coll. Philippines, 1969; MBA, Ateneo de Manila U., 1980; HHD (hon.), Mindanao State U., 1983; LLD (hon.), Lyceum U., 1986, Centro Escolar U., 1987; PhD (hon.), U. Philippines, Fordham U., Georgetown U., Waseda U., U. Sydney, others. With Philippines Armed Forces, 1950-91, 2nd lt. infantry platoon leader Philippine Expeditionary Force Korea, 1952, chief of staff Philippine Civil Action Group Vietnam, 1966-68, comdr. 3rd infantry brigade, 1970-71, dep. chief of staff home def., 1971-72, chief Philippine constabulary, 1972-86, vice chief of staff, 1981-86, chief of staff, 1986-88, sec. nat. def., 1988-91; past chmn. Nat. Disaster Coordinating Coun., vice chmn. Nat. Peace and Order Coun., cabinet officer Regional Devel. Region 9, southwest Philippines; pres. The Philippines, 1992-98. Decorated Philippine Legion of Honor, U.S. Legion of Merit; recipient Peace Prize award UNESCO, 1997; Govt. scholar, 1946. Home: 120 Maria Cristina St AAVA Muntinlupa Philippines Office: 37/F UrbanBank Plz Urban Ave Makati Philippines E-mail: fvr@urbanbank.com.

RAMOS, FRANCISCO, language educator; b. Soria, Spain, June 24, 1961; Diploma in Ensenanza Gen. Basica, Escuela Formacion del Prof., Soria, 1982; MA in TESOL, Calif. State U., LA, 1995; PhD in Lang., Literacy, and Learning, U. Southern Calif., LA, 2000. Lic. in filologia inglesa U. Zaragoza, Spain, 1985. Asst. prof. Fla. Internat. U., Miami, 2001—03; assoc. prof. Loyola Marymount U., LA, 2003—. Contbr. articles to profl. jours. Recipient Dissertation award, 2001; grant, Spencer Found., 2008. Mem.: CABE, TESOL, Inst. Lang. and Edn. Policy. Office: Loyola Marymount Univ 1 LMU Dr Ste 2649 Los Angeles CA 90045 Business E-Mail: framos@lmu.edu.

RAMOS, JENNIFER V., Councilwoman; Attended, San Antonio Coll.; BBA, U. Incarnate Word, MA in Org. Devel., 2004. Owner El Torero Mexican Restaurant; councilwoman, Dist. 3 San Antonio City Coun., 2008—. Rep. Dist. 3 Alamo Cmty. Colleges Bd. Trustees, 2004—. Former mem. Habitat for Humanity, Caesar Chavez Org., Casa Amparo in Reynosa, Mexico; vol. Presa Real, Presa Cmty. Ctr., St. Cecilia's Ch. Office: City Hall PO Box 839966 San Antonio TX 78283 also: 3319 Sidney Brooks Bldg 510 San Antonio TX 78235 Office Phone: 210-207-7064, 210-534-1300. Business E-Mail: district3@sanantonio.gov.*

RAMOS, JORGE, newscaster; b. Mex. City, Mar. 16, 1958; arrived in U.S., 1983; 2 children. Grad. in Comm., Ibero-Am. U., Mex. City; M in Internat. Studies, U. Miami. News reporter Univision, LA, 1984—86; host Mundo Latino, Univision TV prog., 1986; anchorman Noticiero Univision, 1986—. Founder Wake Up Reading book club, 2002—. Author: (autobiography) No Borders: a Journalist's Search for Home, Behind the Mask, The Other Face of America, What I Saw, Hunting the Lion, The Latino Wave, Dying to Cross; contbr. weekly column, NY Times Syndicate. Recipient Maria Moors Cabot award, Columbia Univ., 2001, Ruben Salazar award, Nat. Council La Raza, 2002, Ron Brown award, Nat. Child Labor Com., 2002, David Brinkley award for Journalistic Excellence, Barry Univ., 2003, 8 Emmy awards, Nat. Acad. Television Arts & Sci.; named one of Ten Most Admired Latinos, Latino Leaders mag., 2004, 25 Most Influential Hispanics, Time Mag., 2005. Office: Univision Communications Ste 3050 1999 Ave of the Stars Los Angeles CA 90067 Studio: WNJU-TV Noticiero 47 6th Fl 2200 Fletcher Ave Fort Lee NJ 07024 Office Phone: 201-969-4247. Office Fax: 201-969-4120. E-mail: jramos@univision.net, jorge.ramos@nbcuni.com.

RAMOS, JORGE RAFAEL, computer scientist, researcher; s. Jorge Rafael Ramos and Trudy Rinze; m. Maria del Pilar del Busto; 1 child, Isabella del Pilar. MSc in Computer Sci., Purdue U., West Lafayette, Ind., 2003, PhD, 2007. Rsch. asst. Purdue U., 2003—07, postdoc. rsch. assoc., 2007—08, Microsoft Corp., 2008—. Recipient Gold medal, Nat. Sci. Olympics, Guatemala, 1998, Halstead Software Engring. award, Purdue U., 2007; Grad. fellowship, 2003—05. Mem.: Assn. Computer Machinery, Upsilon Pi Epsilon (treas. 2003—05).

RAMOS, MARTA, language educator; d. Juan Ramos and Benny Silva; m. Manuel Granda; 1 child, Monica Granda. PhD, U. PR, Rio Piedras. Spanish instr. Fla. Gulf Coast U., Ft. Myers, 2005—. Advisor Global Cmty. Engagement, Ft. Myers, 2006—08. Avocation: travel.

RAMOS-CANO, HAZEL BALATERO, caterer, chef, innkeeper, restaurateur, entrepreneur; b. Davao City, Mindanao, Philippines, Sept. 2, 1936; came to U. S., 1960. d. Mauricio C. and Felicidad (Balatero) Ramos; m. William Harold Snyder, Feb. 17, 1964 (div. 1981); children: John Byron, Snyder, Jennifer Ruth; m. Nelson Allen Blue, May 30, 1986 (div. 1990); m. A. Richard Cano, June 25, 1994. BA in Social Work, U. Philippines, Quezon City, 1958; MA in Sociology, Pa. State U., 1963, postgrad., 1966—67. Cert. exec. chef, Am. Culinary Fedn. Faculty, tng. staff Peace Corps Philippine Project, University Park, Pa., 1961-63; sociology instr. Albright Coll., Reading, Pa., 1963-64; rsch. asst. Meth. Ch. U.S.A., State College, Pa., 1965-66; rsch. asst. dept. child devel. & family rels. Pa. State U., University Park, 1966-67; exec. dir. Presbyn. Urban Coun. Raleigh Halifax Ct. Child Care and Family Svc. Ctr., 1973-79; early childhood educator Learning Together, Inc., Raleigh, NC, 1982-83; loan mortgage specialist Raleigh Savs. & Loan, 1983-84; restaurant owner, mgr. Hazel's on Hargett, Raleigh, 1985-86; admissions coord., social worker Brian Corp. Nursing Home, Raleigh, 1986-88, food svc. dir., 1989-90; regional dir. La Petite Acad., Raleigh, 1989-90; asst. food svc. mgr. Granville Towers, Chapel Hill, NC, 1990-92; mgr. trainee Child Nutrition Svcs. Wake County Pub. Sch. Sys., Raleigh, 1993-94; food svc. dir. S.W. Va. 4-H Ednl. Conf. Ctr., Abingdon, 1994-95; caterer, owner The Eclectic Chef's Catering, 1995—; innkeeper, owner Love House Bed and Breakfast, 1996—; pres. Ramos-Cano Inc., 1996—, Ramos-Cano Mgmt. Svcs., LLC, 2002—; owner Withers Hardware Restaurant, Abingdon, 2002—, The Frame Shop, Abingdon, 2004—, The Victoria and Albert Inn, 2000—, Sunshine Sewing and Screen Printing, Abingdon. Cooking instr. Wake Cmty. Tech. Coll., Raleigh, 1986-92; freelance caterer, 1964-95; chair Internat. Cooking Demonstrations Raleigh Internat. Festival, 1990-93. Pres. Wake County Day Care United Coun., 1974-75, NC Assn. Edn. Young Children (Raleigh chpt.), 1975-76; bd. dirs. Project Enlightenment Wake County Pub. Schs., 1976-77; active Pines of Carolina coun. Girl Scout USA, 1976-85; chmn. Philippine Health and Medical Aid Com., Phil-Am Assn. Raleigh 1985-88 (publicity chmn.); elder Trinity Presbyn. Ch., Raleigh, 1979-81, bd. deacons, 1993-94; elder, session mem. Sinking Spring Presbyn. Ch., 1997-99, 2008—, Sinking Spring, Presby Ch., Abingdon, 2008-; treas. Abingdon Newcomers Club, 1997—, Presbyn. Women, Sinking Spring Presbyn. Ch., Abingdon, 1999—; master gardener Va. Tech. Master Gardeners Program, 1998—. Rockefeller grant Rockefeller Found., 1958-59; recipient Ramon Magsaysay Presdl. award Philippine Leadership Youth Movement, 1957; Gov.'s Cert. Appreciation State NC, 1990, Raleigh Mayor's award Quality Childcare Svcs., 1990, award for keeping hist. Abington beautiful Abington Kiwanis Club, 1997 Mem. Am. Culinary Fedn., Presby. Women, Raleigh, (historian 1975-76), Penn State Dames (pres. 1968-69). Democrat. Office: Victoria & Albert Inn 224 Oak Hill St Abingdon VA 24210 also: The Love House Bed and Breakfast 210 E Valley St Abingdon VA 24210 also: Withers Hardware Restaurant 260 W Main St Abingdon VA 24210 also: The Frame Shop 115 Charwood Dr Abingdon VA 24210 also: Somethyme Bistro 115 Charwood Dr Abingdon VA 24210 Home Phone: 276-623-1281; Office Phone: 276-628-1111, 276-628-8172. E-mail: v&ainn@naxs.com, rcano@naxs.com.

RAMOS-PELLICIA, MICHELLE FRANCES, linguist, educator; d. Jose Miguel Ramos Colon and Mirta Maritza Pellicia Hilversum; 1 child, Antonio Jose Rodriguez Ramos. PhD, Ohio State U., Columbus, 2004. Asst. prof. George Mason U., Fairfax, Va., 2005—. Mem. S.E.R., Rio Piedras, PR, 1993—95. Office: George Mason Univ MCL 4400 University Dr MS 3E5 233 Thompson Fairfax VA 22030 Business E-Mail: mrampose@gmu.edu.

RAMPACHER, HERMANN HANS, writer, consultant; b. Ulm, Germany, Dec. 29, 1934; s. Hermann Alexander and Pauline Katharine (Milch) R.; m. Ursel Hanna Brand; 1 child, Carsten. BS, Coll. Stuttgart, 1954, MSc in Physics, 1962; Dr.rer.nat., U. Munich, 1968. Charter IT profl. Brit. Computer Soc. Rsch. asst. Max Planck Gesellschaft, Munich, 1965-68; asst. prof. U. Tuebingen, 1968-70; systems engr. IBM Deutschland, Stuttgart, 1970-79; rschr. GMD German Nat. Rsch. Ctr. for Info. Tech., Bonn, 1979-81; chief exec. German Informatics Soc., Bonn, 1982-99; mng. dir. German Info. Acad. GmbH (DIA), 1997-2000; ptnr. DLGI Ltd. Bd. dirs. Internat. Conf. and Rsch. Ctr. for Computer Sci., Castle Dagstuhl, 1995-99; founder Coun. European Profl. Informatics Socs Fellow Brit. Computer Soc. (chartered info. tech. profl.); mem. Max-Planck Gesellschaft, German Soc. Philosophy, Gesellschaft Deutscher Naturforscher und Aerzte. Avocations: normative theories, history, classical music. Office: DLGI Am Brrner Bogen 6 D-53 227 Bonn Germany Office Fax: 49 0 228 688 448 99. Business E-Mail: hrampacher@dlgi.de.

RAMPE, KEVIN M., real estate developer; b. 1966; m. Christine Rampe; children: William, Matthew. BA cum laude, Union Coll.; JD magna cum laude, Albany U.; grad. in Sr. Exec. Program, Harvard U.; LLD (hon.), Union Coll., 2004. Litig. assoc. Shearman & Stearling, 1992—96; first asst. counsel Gov. Pataki's Office, 1996—99; from dep. supt. and gen. counsel to first dep. supt. Ins. Dept. N.Y. State Ins. Dept., 1999—2004, first dep. supt., COO, 2004—05; exec. v.p., gen. counsel Lower Manhattan Devel. Corp, NYC, 2002—03; pres. Lower Manhattan Devel. Corp., NYC, 2003—05, chmn., 2006—. Named one of 40 Under 40, Crain's NY Bus., 2005. Office: Lower Manhattan Development Corp One Liberty Plaza 20th Fl New York NY 10006

RAMPERSAD, ARNOLD, writer, literature educator; b. Trinidad, W.I., Nov. 13, 1941; BA, MA, PhD, Harvard U. Prof. English Stanford (Calif.) U., 1974-83, Rutgers U., New Brunswick, N.J., 1983-88; Zora Neale Hurston prof. English Columbia U., NYC, 1988-90; Woodrow Wilson prof. literature Princeton (N.J.) U., 1990—. Author: Melville's Israel Potter: A Pilgrimage and Progress, 1969, The Art and Imagination of W.E.B. DuBois, 1976, The Life of Langston Hughes, Vol. I: 1902-41: I, Too, Sing America, 1986 (Nat. Book Critics Cir. award nomination for biography 1986, Anisfield-Wolf Book award in race rels. Cleve. Found. 1987, Clarence L. Holte prize Phelps Stokes Fund 1988), The Life of Langston Hughes, Vol. II: 1941-67: I Dream a World, 1988 (Pulitzer Prize nomination in biography 1989, Am. Book award Before Columbus Found. 1990), (with Arthur Ashe) Days of Grace: A Memoir, 1993; co-editor: Slavery and the Literary Imagination, 1989, The Collected Poems of Langston Hughes, 1994; editor: Richard Wright's Works (2 vols.), 1991, Richard Wright: A Collection of Critical Essays, 1994. Recipient Literary Lion award N.Y. Pub. Libr., 1993. Office: Princeton Univ Dept of English McCosh Hall Princeton NJ 08544-1016

RAMPERSAD, SALLY ELIZABETH, anesthesiologist; d. Gerald Richard and Bridget Parker; m. Carlyle Rampersad; children: Indira Grace children: Isabella Anjali. MB, Southampton U., Eng., 1986. Diplomate Am. Soc. Anesthesiologists, 2004, cert. in pediat. advanced life support instructor Am. Heart Assn., 2008. Fellows pediat. anesthesia Hosp. Sick Children, Toronto, Ont., Canada, 1995—96; attending anesthesiologist Seattle Children's Hosp., 1996—98, 2003—, interim edn. dir. Anesthesiology Dept, 2004—05, co-chair operative services quality improvement and patient safety coun., 2007—; resident in anesthesiology Va. Mason Med. Ctr., Seattle, 1999—2003. Contbr. articles, chapters to books. Mem.: Royal Coll. Physicians (London), Assn. Anaesthetists Gt. Britain, No. Ireland, Am. Soc. Regional Anesthesia, Am. Soc. Anesthesiologists, Soc. Pediat. Anesthesia.

RAMPERSAUD LUNDY, SHERYLL, special education educator; b. Portsmouth, Va., Dec. 30, 1947; d. Rebecca Greene and Freddie Lee Drake; children: Vincent Earle Rampersaud, Sean Derrik Rampersaud, Sharon Antoinette Rampersaud. BS in Acctg., Norfolk State U., 1971—74, Advanced Studies Tchr. Certification, 2000—01; MS in Gen. Edn., 2007. Lic. postgrad. professional Va., 2007; Spl. Educator Emotional Disturbance and Specific Learning Disabilities Va. Bd. Edn., 2002. Fire rates clk. Geico, Friendship Heights, Md., 1968—70; staff acct. Peat, Marwick, Mitchell CPAs, Washington, 1974—76; asst. internal auditor Howard U., Washington, 1976—80; pension acct./ cons. Qualified Pension Consultants/ Compdesign Inc., Bethesda, Md., 1983—98, Thomas F. Barrett, Inc., Bethesda, 1998—99; spl. edn. tchr. The Pines Residential Treatment Ctr., Portsmouth, Va., 2000—. Dir. Sankofa Cultural and Learning Ctr., Inc., Portsmouth, 1999—. Chief officer John F. Kennedy Poling Sta., Portsmouth, 1999—2001. Mem. Christian Ch. Home: 3204 Gwin St Portsmouth VA 23704 Office: The Pines Residential Treatment Center 825 Crawford Pky Portsmouth VA 23070 Personal E-mail: srampersaud@cox.net. E-mail: sheryl.rampersaud@absfirst.com.

RAMPHAL, JULIE FRANCES, retired secondary school educator; b. Sioux Falls, SD, Jan. 31, 1944; d. Shelton Russell and Frances Pauline (Hospers) Tilgner; m. Cecil Edward Ramphal, Aug. 29, 1976 (dec. Apr. 2000); stepchildren: Richard Andre, Rani. BA in English, Macalester Coll., 1966; MS in Ednl. Computing, Pepperdine U., 1985. Secondary tchr. Glendora Unified Sch. Dist., Calif., 1966—69, Tustin Unified Sch. Dist., Calif., 1969—2000. Coll. instr. Nat. U., Irvine, Calif., 1987; mentor tchr. Tustin Unified Sch. Dist., Calif., 1995—97; workshop leader Orange County Dept. of Edn., Costa Mesa, Calif., 1998. Workshop presenter Computer Using Educators (CUE) State Confs., Palm Springs, Calif., 1988—95. Recipient Exemplary Achievement in the field of Ednl. Tech., Ednl. Computing Alumni of Pepperdine U., 1992, grant, Women's Action Alliance of NYC, 1991—93, Mentor Tchr. in Tech., Tustin Unified Sch. Dist., 1995—97; grant, Calif. Academic Partnership Program, 1992. Mem.: AAUW (v.p. membership 2004—06, legal advocacy fund chair 2006—08, pres. 2008—). Avocations: swimming, singing, gardening, piano, travel. Home: 20141 Crown Reef Lane Huntington Beach CA 92646 Personal E-mail: julieps23@aol.com.

RAMSAUR, MICHAEL F., lighting designer; s. Hal S. and Carol L. Ramsaur; m. Pauline K. Ellis; children: Jeremy M., Kirsten E. McMullen. MFA, Carnegie Mellon U., Pitts., 1971. Chmn. oistat edn. commn. Internat. Orgn. Scenographers, Theatre Architects and Technicians, Taipei, Taiwan, 1997—2005, pres., 2005—. Lighting designer Broadway Bay, San Mateo, Calif., 2008—. Lighting designer (theatre prodn.) Miss Saigon (Outstanding Lighting Design award, 2006). Rsch. fellowship, US Inst. Theatre Tech., 2008. Mem.: Internat. Assn. Lighting Designers, Illumination Engring. Soc. North Am., US Inst. Theatre Tech., Internat. Alliance Theatrical Stage Employees, United Scenic Artist Assn. Achievements include design of argus, lighting design software. Office: Stanford Univ 551 Serra Mall Stanford CA 94305-5010 E-mail: mram@stanford.edu.

RAMSAY, DAVID LESLIE, physician, dermatologist, educator; b. Rochester, NY, Apr. 25, 1943; s. Joseph Walter and Jean (Eastwood) R. AB in English with honors, Ind. U., 1965, MD, 1969; MEd, U. Ill., 1973. Diplomate Am. Bd. Dermatology. Assoc. faculty mem. Ind. U., Indpls., 1965-69; intern in medicine George Washington U. Med. Ctr., 1969-70; resident in dermatology NYU Med. Ctr., 1970-73; dir. dermatology residency tng. Nat. Naval Med. Ctr., Bethesda, Md., 1973-75; asst. prof. medicine Georgetown U., Washington, 1974-75; asst. prof. dermatology NYU, 1974-78, assoc. prof. dermatology, 1978-95, prof. dermatology, 1995—2003, clin. prof. dermatology, 2003—, senator, 1986-94, pres. faculty coun., 1988-90, dir. ednl. affairs dermatology, 1975—2002, dir. cutaneous lymphoma sect., 1975—. Author: Simulations in Dermatology, 1974; contbg. author: Adolescent Dermatology, Basic Mechanisms of Physiologic and Aberrant Lymphoproliferation in the Skin, Hematology and Oncology Clinics in North America; sr. editor: Jour. of Drugs in Dermatology, 2003-; contbr. more than 25 articles to profl. jours. Pres., bd. dirs. One Fifth Ave. Apt. Corp., N.Y.C., 1978-80; trustee Bklyn. Acad. Music, 1989—, chmn. visual arts com., chmn. edn. com; bd. dirs. Cutaneous Lymphoma Found., 2003—. Lt. comdr. USN, 1973-75. NIH fellow U. Ill., 1972-73. Fellow ACP, Internat. Soc. Cutaneous Lymphomas, Am. Acad. Dermatology; mem. Am. Dermatologic Assn. Roman Catholic. Avocations: collecting visual art, swimming, reading. Home: One Fifth Ave New York NY 10003 Office: NYU Med Ctr 530 5th Ave New York NY 10036-5101 E-mail: DRamsay1@nuc.rr.com.

RAMSAY, HAMISH ANDREW, aerospace scientist; s. Robert James and Charlotte Anne Ramsay. PhD in Meteorology, U. Okla., Norman, 2008. Rsch. scientist Ctr. Australian Weather & Climate Rsch., Melbourne, 2008—; postdoc. fellow NASA Goddard Inst. Space Studies, NYC, 2009—. Office: NASA Goddard Inst Space Studies 2880 Broadway New York NY 10025

RAMSAY, J. RUSSELL, psychologist; 2 children. BA in Psychology, U. Miami, 1988; MS in Clin. Psychology, Pacific Grad. Sch. Psychology, 1994, PhD in Clin. Psychology, 1995. Instr. U. Pa. Sch. Medicine, Phila., 1997—2000, asst. prof. psychology in psychiatry, 2001—. Mem. editl. bd. Jour. Attention Disorders, 2005—, Jour. Psychotherapy Integration, 2005—; author: Cognitive Behavioral Therapy for Adult ADHD, 2008; contbr. articles to profl. jours., chapters to books. Fellow, Ctr. Cognitive Therapy, Phila., 1995—96; Henry King Stanford scholar, U. Miami, 1984—88. Fellow: Pa. Psychol. Assn.; mem.: APA, Internat. Assn. Cognitive Psychotherapy, Psi Chi, Golden Key Honor Soc. Avocations: soccer, exercise, reading.

RAMSAY, WILLIAM CHARLES, writer, composer; b. NYC, Nov. 6, 1930; s. Claude Barnett and Myrtle Marie (Scott) Ramsay; m. Jane Coutant Evans, July 7, 1997; children from previous marriage: Alice, John, Carol Ramsay Scott, David. BA in English Lit., U. Colo., 1952; MA in Physics, UCLA, 1957, PhD in Physics, 1962. NFS postdoctoral fellow U. Calif., San Diego, 1962-64, asst. prof. Santa Barbara, 1964-67; tech. mgr. Sys. Assocs., Inc., Long Beach, Calif., 1967-72; sr. environ. economist U.S. AEC, Bethesda, Md., 1972-75; tech. adviser U.S. Nuc. Regulatory Agy., Washington, 1975-76; sr. fellow Resources for the Future, Washington, 1976-83, Ctr. Strategic and Internat. Studies, Washington, 1983-85; sr. staff officer NAS, Washington, 1985-86; freelance writer, editor, publ. Washington, Santa Barbara, 1986—. Cons. Vols. Tech. Assistance, Arlington, Va., 1987—90, Arlington, 1998—, Internat. Resources Group, Washington, 1991. Author: (book) Bioenergy and Economic Development, 1985, (plays) Agamemnon, 2000; co-author: (book) Managing the Environment, 1972, Energy in America's Future, 1979; composer: Glory Road, The Hawk, Cities, Spring Dawn, Golden Fortresses; author: Me and King John, 2008; composer: CD Genesis, 2008. Bd. dirs. Opera Santa Barbara. Buenos Aires Conv. fellow, 1952, NSF fellow, 1962, NATO scholar, 1960, 1962. Mem.: Am. Phys. Soc. Avocation: piano. Home and Office: 115 Summit Ln Santa Barbara CA 93108-2323 E-mail: ram556@cox.net.

RAMSDELL, HEATHER L., speech pathology/audiology services professional, researcher; b. Plattsburgh, NY, Apr. 23, 1979; d. Robert H. and Donna L. Ramsdell. PhD student, U. Memphis, AUSP, 2003—. Cert. in clin. competence Am. Speech-Lang. Hearing Assn., 2008. Speech-lang. pathologist Invo Health Care Assn., Memphis City Schs., 2006—. Mem.: Am. Speech-Lang. Hearing Assn. Home: 2107 Heather Ridge Southaven MS 38672 Office: Univ Memphis AUSP 807 Jefferson Ave Memphis TN 38105

RAMSDEN, MARY CATHERINE, substance abuse specialist; Diploma, St. Joseph Mercy Hosp., 1966; postgrad., Mason City Jr. Coll., Kirkwood Community Coll. Cert. alcohol and drug counselor; RN Iowa, cert. chem. dependency nurse. Nursing supr. children's unit State Mental Health Inst., Cherokee, Iowa, 1966-69, Iowa Security Med. Facility, Oakdale, 1969; staff nurse psychiatry St. Luke's Meth. Hosp., Cedar Rapids, Iowa, 1969-74, asst. psychiat. nursing instr., 1970-74; mem. staff Sedlacek Treatment Ctr. Mercy Hosp., Cedar Rapids, 1974-85; cons. drug and alcohol CareUnit, Jacksonville Beach, Fla., 1985-86; nursing mgr. adolescent chem. dependency unit Broadlawns Med. Ctr., Des Moines, 1987-88; tng. mgr. Div. Substance Abuse and Heath Promotion Iowa Dept. Pub. Health, 1988-91; clin. program dir. Forest City (Iowa) Treatment Ctr., 1991-92; facilitator Employee & Family Resources Enhancement Women Pr Iowa Correctional Instn. for Women, Mitchellville, 1992-97; cast mgmt. tng. coord. Employee & Family Resources, Des Moines, 1998-99; substance abuse cons., trainer Des Moines, 1999—; sr. counselor Powell Chem. Dependency Ctr. Iowa Luth Hosp., Des Moines, 1999—2003; case mgr., substance abuse counselor drug ct. 5th Jud. Dist., Employee & Family Resources, 2003—08; pvt. cons., vol. Enduring project Freedom, CISM Tng. Mem. licensing rev. com. Iowa Bd. of Nursing. Author: (with others) Nurses Quick Reference, 1989. Vol. Project Enduring Families, 2004—. Lt. comdr. Nurse Corps USNR. Named Nurse Expert Coll. Nursing U. Iowa., 1985. Mem.: Consortium Behavioral Health Nurses and Assoc., Res. Officers Assn. Home: 1519 Idaho St Des Moines IA 50316-2425 Office: 65 Gruber Des Moines IA 50315 Office Phone: 515-242-6982. Personal E-mail: mrrncd@yahoo.com.

RAMSEUR, DAVID, legislative staff member; BA in Polit. Sci., U. NC-Asheville; M in Journalism, U. Mo. Columnist Fairbanks Daily News-Miner, Washington; press. sec. Gov. Steve Cowper, Alaska, 1986—90; dep. chief of staff Gov. Tony Knowles, Alaska, 1994—2002, chief of staff, 2002—03; sr. advisor, chief of staff Mayor Mark Begich, Anchorage, 2003—08; chief of staff to Senator Mark Begich US Senate, Washington, 2008—. Democrat. Office: 825C Hart Senate Office Bldg Washington DC 20510 Office Phone: 202-224-3004.*

RAMSEY, CHARLES, retired government agency administrator; b. Pineapple, Ala., Aug. 2, 1937; s. James Augustus and Ophelia Ramsey; m. Maratha Ann Reed, Aug. 31, 1968; children: Charles Jr., Kevin. Master degree, U. Pitts., 1974. Cert. draftsman, Cleve. Engring. Soc., 1970. Commr. divsn. of rehab. and conservation City of Cleve., 1980—88; dep. dir. Ohio Dept. of Transp. State of Ohio, Columbus, 1990—92. Organizer and campaign dir. 21 Congl. Dist. Caucus, Cleve. With USAF, 1955—63. Mem.: Paralyzed Vets. of Am. (assoc.; bd. dirs. 2000—06), Legion Honor. Independent. Achievements include Past imperial potentate (1992) of the Ancient Egyptian Arabic order of the Mystic Shrine of North and South America and it's jurisdiction. Home: 25801 Lake Shore Blvd Apt 61 Euclid OH 44132-1124 Personal E-mail: cramsey37@yahoo.com.

RAMSEY, CHARLES EUGENE, sociologist, educator; b. Paragon, Ind., Apr. 24, 1923; s. Sarcefield Dodson and Stella (Goss) R.; m. Alberta Mae Jordan, July 19, 1943; children— James D., Charles W., Jane E., Suzanne. BS, Ind. State Tchrs. Coll., 1947; MS, U. Wis., 1950, PhD, 1952. Faculty U. Wis., 1951-52, U. Minn., 1952-54, Cornell U., 1954-62, Colo. State U., 1962-65; prof. sociology U. Minn., Mpls., 1965-77; chmn. dept. sociology U. Tex., Arlington, 1977-83. Vis. prof. Inter-Am. Instn. Agrl. Sci., Costa Rica, 1961, Exptl. Sta., U. P.R., 1961-62; research cons. to various univs., agys. Author: (with Lowry Nelson and Cooley Verner) Community Structure and Change, 1960, (with David Gottlieb) The American Adolescent, 1965, Understanding the Deprived Child, S.R.A, 1967, Problems of Youth, 1967, (with D.J. McCarty) The School Managers: Power and Conflict in American Public Education, 1971, (with William A. Stacey) Social Statistics, 1992; also articles. Achievements include developing and testing theory of variations in community power structure, types of sch. bds., and roles of sch. supt., developed method of comparative measurement of level of living for different countries. Home: 1102 De Pauw Dr Arlington TX 76012-5339 Office: U Tex Dept Sociology Arlington TX 76004

RAMSEY, CHARLES H., police commissioner; b. Chgo., 1950; BA in Criminal Justice, Lewis U., 1990, MS in Criminal Justice, 1991; grad., FBI Nat. Acad., 1986, Intergovernmental Exec. Devel. Program, 1989, Electronic Criminal Surveillance Officer Training, 1990. Cadet Chgo. Police Dept., 1968—71, patrolman, 1975—77, sergeant, 1977—84, lt., 1984—88, captain, 1988—92, commdg. officer Area 1 detetctive divsn., 1986—87, comdr. Area 1 detective divsn., 1987—88, comdr. patrol divsn. 11th dist., 1988—89, comdr. narcotics units, 1989—92, dep. chief, patrol divsn., 1992—94, dep. supt., 1994—98; chief of police Met. Police Dept., Washington, 1998—2007; commr. Phila. Police Dept., 2008—. Spkr. in field; adj. prof. Lewis U., 1992—96, Northwestern U. Traffic Inst. Sch. Police & Command, 1993—97. Co-founder, pres. Ill. Drug Enforcement Officer's Assn., 1990, Recipient Gary P. Hayes award, Police Exec. Rsch. Forum, 1994, Good Scout award, Boy Scouts Am., 1995, Disting. Police Cooperation medal, Korean Nat. Police, 1995, Robert Lamb Humanitarian award, Nat. Orgn. Black Law Enforcement Exec., 2001, Civil Rights award, Internat. Assn. Chiefs of Police, 2001. Office: Phila Police Dept One Franklin Sq Philadelphia PA 19106

RAMSEY, DAVID SELMER, retired health facility administrator; b. Mpls., Feb. 19, 1931; s. Selmer A. and Esther D. (Dahl) R.; m. Betty Seiler, May 15, 1953; children— Scott, Stewart, Thomas BS, U. Mich.,

1953, MS in Microbiology, 1954, M.H.A., 1962. Research asst. Detroit Inst. Cancer Research, 1954-60; asst. adminstr. Harper Hosp., Detroit, 1962-68, assoc. adminstr., 1968-72; exec. v.p. Iowa Meth. Med. Ctr., Des Moines, 1972-83, pres., 1983-93, Iowa Health Sys., 1993-95, Fine Wood Designs, 1996—. Avocations: golf, tennis, photography. Home: 18710 Poco Rio Dr Rio Verde AZ 85263-7108

RAMSEY, FRANK ALLEN, veterinarian, retired army officer; b. Rocksprings, Tex., May 1, 1929; s. Reynolds Allen and June (Burdette) R.; m. Lucette C. Reboul, Jan. 1958; children: Randal R., Ramsay A.; m. 2d, Mary Lou Cain, June 1991. D.V.M., Tex. A & M U., 1954; grad., U.S. Army Command and Gen. Staff Coll., 1965, U.S. Army War Coll., 1972. Commd. 1st. lt. U.S. Army Vet. Corps, 1955, advanced through grades to brig. gen., 1980; chief vet. service Ft. Leonard Wood, Mo., 1958-61; acad. vet. U.S. Mil. Acad., West Point, NY, 1962-64; vet. staff officer U.S. Army Combat Devel. Command Med. Service, Ft. Sam Houston, Tex., 1965-67; asst. chief profl. programming and planning br. Office Surgeon Gen., Washington, 1967-68, chief profl. programming and planning br., 1968-71, chief food inspection policy office, 1972-73, sr. vet. staff officer, 1973-77; asst. chief of staff Vet. Service, 7th Med. Command, Army Europe and 7th Army, Heidelberg, W. Ger., 1977-80; asst. for vet. services to surgeon gen. and chief U.S. Army Vet. Corps, Hdqrs. Dept. Army, Washington, 1980-85; ret., 1985. Decorated Army Commendation medal, Legion of Merit with oak leaf cluster, D.S.M. Mem. AVMA, Assn. Fed. Veterinarians, Assn. Mil. Surgeons U.S., Assn. Equine Practitioners, Am. Assn. Food Hygiene Veterinarians, Conf. Pub. Health Veterinarians, Tex. Vet. Med. Assn. Lodges: Masons (32 degree). Presbyterian. Home: 8 El Norte Cir Uvalde TX 78801-4021 Home Phone: 830-278-2088; Office Phone: 830-591-3736.

RAMSEY, GEORGE BERNARD, retired financial planner; b. Phila., Nov. 24, 1931; m. Josephine Marie Martinelli, Sept. 24, 1960; children: G. Christopher, J. Timothy. AS, Valley Forge Mil. Acad., 1950; BA, U. Pa., 1954. With IDS Fin. Svcs. Inc. (now Am. Express Fin. Advisors, Inc.), 1963—; tng. mgr. IDS Fin. Svcs. Inc., 1964-66, divsn. v.p., 1969-87; pers. and bus. fin. planner Am. Express Fin. Advisors, Inc., Sea Isle City, NJ, 1987—2002; ret., 2002. Contbr. numerous articles to profl. publs. Pres. Levy Civic Assn., Naples, Fla. Mem. Nat. Assn. Securities Dealers, Internat. Assn. for Fin. Planning, Sea Isle C. of C., Cape May County C. of C., South Jersey C. of C., Valley Forge Mil. Acad. Alumni Assn., Sea Isle City Civic Clubs, Sigma Phi Epsilon. Avocations: fishing, golf, boating, music. Home (Summer): 52nd and Atlantic Ocean Sea Isle City NJ 08243 E-mail: gbr1931@aol.com.

RAMSEY, IRA CLAYTON, retired petroleum industry executive; b. Quitman, Ga., May 13, 1931; s. James Redding and Ruth Frances (Treadaway) R.; m. Marianne Vinzant, Dec. 23, 1962; children: Clayton Hamilton, Robin Leigh. BBA, U. Ga., Atlanta, 1954; LLB, Atlanta Law Sch., 1950; postgrad., U. Tex., 1968, U. Pitts., 1973. With Plantation Pipe Line Co., Atlanta, 1948-96, asst. sec., 1967-70, treas., contr., 1970-90, v.p. fin., 1990-96. Life trustee Ga. Found. for Ind. Colls.; trustee emeritus KingsBridge Retirement Ctr., Inc. Baptist. Home: 780 Wesley Oak Rd NW Atlanta GA 30328-4738

RAMSEY, JAROLD WILLIAM, literature and language professor, writer; b. Bend, Oreg., Sept. 1, 1937; s. Augustus S. and Wilma E. Ramsey; m. Dorothy Ann Quinn, Aug. 16, 1959; children: Kate, Sophia, John. BA with honors, U. Oreg., 1959; Ph. D., U. Wash., 1966. Acting instr. U. Wash., Seattle, 1963-65; asst. prof. English U. Rochester, NY, 1965-70, assoc. prof. NY, 1970-81, prof. NY, 1981-97; prof. emeritus, 1997—; dir. undergrad. rsch. U. Rochester, NY, 1990-96. Vis. prof. English U. Victoria, B.C., Can., 1974, 75-76; dir. NEH summer seminars on Indian lit., 1985, 88. Author: The Space Between Us, 1970, Love in an Earthquake, 1973 (Lillian Fairchild award 1973), Dermographia, 1982, Reading the Fire, 1983, rev. edit., 1999, Hand-shadows, 1989, (play) Coyote Goes Upriver, premier 1985, (cantata) (with Samuel Adler) The Lodge of Shadows, premiere 1988; editor: Coyote Was Going There, 1977, Nehalem Tillamook Tales, 1990, The Stories We Tell: Oregon Folk Literature (with Suzi Jones), 1994, New Era: Reflections on the Human and Natural History of Central Oregon, 2003, (with Dorothy Ramsey) The Piper of Cloone: Father Keegan and the Early Gaelic Revival, 2005, (with Lori Burlingame) In Beauty I Walk: The Literary Roots of Native American Writing, 2008. Recipient Don Walker award Western Am. Lit., 1979, Borestone Mount Found. Best Poems award, 1972, 75, 76; Helen Bullis prize, 1984, Poetry prize Quar. Rev., 1989; Alumni Achievement award U. Oreg. Alumni Assn, 1990; Nat. Endowment Arts writing grantee, 1974, 76; Ingram Merrill Found. writing grantee, 1976 Mem.: MLA (chair com. on lits. and langs. of Am. 1991—92), Assn. Study Am. Indian Lit. (pres. 1981), Phi Beta Kappa. Democrat. Home: 5884 NW Highway 26 Madras OR 97741-9543 E-mail: jwr1937@madras.net.

RAMSEY, JOHN ARTHUR, lawyer; b. Apr. 1, 1942; s. Wilbert Lewis and Lillian (Anderson) R.; m. Nikki Ann Ramsey, Feb. 9, 1943; children: John William, Bret Anderson, Heather Nichole. AB, San Diego State U., 1965; JD, Calif. Western Sch. Law, 1969. Bar: Colo. 1969, Tex. 1978. Assoc. Henry, Cockrell, Quinn & Creighton, 1969-72; atty. Texaco Inc., 1972-80; asst. to pres. Texaco U.S.A., 1980-81, asst. to divsn. v.p. Houston, 1981-82, divsn. atty. Denver, 1982-88; ptnr. Holland & Hart, 1989—. Editor-in-chief: Calif. Western Law Rev., 1969. Bd. dirs. Selective Svc., Englewood, Colo., 1972-76; chmn. coun. Bethany Luth. Ch., Englewood, 1976; mem. exec. bd. Denver Area coun. Boy Scouts Am., 1999—. Mem. ABA (vice-chmn. oil, natural gas exploration and prodn. com. sect. natural resource law 1983-88, chmn. 1989, coun. sect. natural resources, energy and environ. law 1990-93). Republican. Office: Holland & Hart 8390 E Crescent Pkwy Ste 400 Greenwood Village CO 80111-2822 Office Phone: 303-290-1600.

RAMSEY, JOHN MICHAEL, chemistry professor, researcher; b. Mansfield, Ohio, May 9, 1952; BS, Bowling Green State U., Ohio, 1974; PhD, Ind. U., 1979. Rsch. assoc. Ind. U., Bloomington, Ind., 1974—79, assoc. instr., 1974—79; Eugene P. Wigner Fellow Oak Ridge Nat. Lab., Tenn., 1979—81, rsch. assoc. III Tenn., 1981—82, rsch. staff I Tenn., 1982—85, R&D group leader II Tenn., 1985—86, group leader, rsch. staff II Tenn., 1986—89, group leader, sr. rsch. staff I Tenn., 1989—92, group leader, sr. staff scientist II Tenn., 1992—96, group leader, corp. rsch. fellow Tenn., 1997—2004; co-founder, scientific adv. bd. mem. Caliper Technologies, Inc., Mountain View, Calif., 1995—2003; Minnie N. Goldby Disting. prof. chemistry U. NC, Chapel Hill, 2004—. Invited lectr. in field; vis. scientist Lawrence Livermore Lab., Calif., 1977—78; mem. permanent scientific com., High Performance Capillary Electrophoresis, 1996—; mem. steering com. μTAS, 1998—. Contbr. articles to peer-reviewed jours.; assoc. editor Journal of Microcolumn Separations, 2001, mem. editl. adv. bd. Journal of Proteome Research, 2001—, mem. editl. bd. Biomedical Microdevices, 1997—, Chromotographia, 1999—, Assay and Drug Development Technologies, 2002—, Combinatorial Chemistry & High Throughput Screening, 2004—. Recipient Merck Index award, 1971, Am. Inst. Chemists award, 1974, Martin Marietta Energy Systems, Publications award, 1985, 1994, Martin Marietta Energy Systems, Significant Achievement award, 1987, 1992, Lockheed Martin Energy Systems, Publication award, R&D Accomplishments award & Scientist of Yr. award, 1996, Lockheed Martin NOVA award, 1996, Lockheed Martin Energy Systems, Publication award, 1998, Discover Mag. Annual Tech. award, 1996, R&D 100 award Lab-on-a-Clip Technology, 1996, Alexander von Humboldt award for Sr. Scientist, 1999, Frederick Conf. Capillary Electrophoresis award, 2000, R&D 100 Top 40, Lab-on-a-Chip Technology, 2001, Energy@23 award, 2001, A.J.P. Martin Gold medal for Separation Sci., 2001, Jacob Heskel Gabbay award in Biotechnology and Medicine, 2001, Battelle Disting. Inventor award, 2003, Marcel J.E. Golay award in Capillary Chromatography, 2003, R&D 100 award μTrapMS, 2003, Southeast Region Fed. Lab. Consortium Tech. Transfer award, 2003, Fed. Lab. Consortium Excellence in Tech. Transfer award, 2004; Lockheed Martin Corp. Rsch. Fellow, 1997. Fellow: Optical Soc. Am.; mem.: Sigma Xi, Delta Phi Alpha, AAAS, Analytical Divsn. Am. Chem. Soc. (mem. program adv. com. 1986—88, chmn. program adv. com. 1989—91, mem. award selection com. 1991—94, mem. program adv. com. 1992, chair 1999, undergraduate award in analytical chemisty 1974, award in chem. instrumentation 2003, summer fellowship 1977), Am. Chem. Soc. (mem. award selection com. 1994—96, Toledo sect. graduating sr. award 1974, award in chromatography 2007), Sigma Pi Sigma, Kappa Mu Epsilon. Achievements include patents in field; patents pending in field. Office: Univ NC UNC-CH Dept Chemistry CB# 3290 Chapel Hill NC 27599-3290 Office Phone: 919-962-7492. Office Fax: 919-962-4952. Business E-Mail: jmramsey@unc.edu.

RAMSEY, LLOYD BRINKLEY, retired savings and loan executive, retired army officer; b. Somerset, Ky., May 29, 1918; s. William Harold and Mary Ella (Barnett) R.; m. Glenda Burton, Feb. 22, 1941 (dec. Oct. 20, 2000); children: Lloyd Ann (Mrs. Kyle D. Wallace), Larry Burton, Judi Ramsey (Mrs. David E. Derr). AB, U. Ky., 1940; postgrad., Yale U., 1946, Command and Gen. Staff Coll., Ft. Leavenworth, Kans., 1949-50, U.S. Army War Coll., Carlisle Barracks, Pa., 1953-54, Harvard, 1961. ADC HRLG Alexander, 1943; Commd. 2d lt. U.S. Army, 1940, advanced through grades to maj. gen., 1968; bn. comdr. 7th Inf., 3d Inf. Div., 1944-45; instr. Inf. Sch., Ft. Benning, Ga., 1946-49; assigned Office G-2 Dept. Army Gen. Staff, 1950-53; sec. joint staff UN Far East Command, 1954-57; comdg. officer 1st Inf. Brigade, Ft. Benning, Ga., 1957-58; adv. Korean Army War Coll., 1959-60; with Office Chief Legis. Liaison, Dept. Army Gen. Staff, 1960-63, Office Asst. Chief Staff Force Devel., 1963-64; dep. comdr. Ft. Leonard Wood, Mo., 1964—65; dep. chief information, 1966-67; chief of staff Third Army, Ft. McPherson, Ga., 1967-68; div. comdr. Americal 23d Div., Vietnam, 1969-70; provost marshall gen. Army, Washington, 1970-74, ret., 1974; chmn. bd. McLean Savs. & Loan Assn., Va., 1974-88. Decorated D.S.M. with oak leaf cluster, Silver Star with two oak leaf clusters, Legion of Merit with oak leaf cluster, D.F.C., Bronze Star medal with V and three oak leaf clusters, Air medal with 16 oak leaf clusters, Purple Heart with four oak leaf clusters, Combat Inf. badge; mem. Order Brit. Empire; Croix de Guerre France; Vietnamese Nat. Order; Vietnamese Armed Forces Honor medal; Vietnamese Gallantry Cross with palm. Mem. Sigma Chi, Omicron Delta Kappa. Baptist. Home Phone: 540-776-2100. *Accept a man for what he is, not for what you want him to be.*

RAMSEY, MARGIE, librarian; b. Bay City, Tex., Aug. 29, 1921; d. Cyrus Otis Lansford and Myra Lenore Ferrell; m. Joe Bryan Ramsey, July 29, 1945 (dec. 2003); children: Ronald Lansford, Kevin Bryan. BA in Libr. Sci., Tex. State U., 1942. Cert. tchr., Tex. Libr. Talco (Tex.) Ind. Sch. Dist., 1942-44; sec. Consolidated Aircraft, San Diego, summer 1943; bookkeeper Lockheed Aircraft, Dallas, 1944; libr. Dallas Pub. Libr., 1944-45; sec. Steck Co., Austin, Tex., 1946-48; libr. U. Tex., Austin, 1948-51. Author, poet:. Vol. libr. Hyde Park United Meth., Austin, 1963-2002, Leander (Tex.) Ind. Sch. Dist., 1982-92, Aspen Ridge Lodge, Los Alamos, N.Mex.; mem. The Internat. Libr. of Poetry. Named Outstanding Vol., Nat. Assn. Ptnrs. in Edn., Kraft-Disney, 1989. Fellow AAUW. Democrat. Avocations: teaching, camping, computers, reading, collecting rare books. Home: 1010 Sombrillo Ct 313 Los Alamos NM 87544 Personal E-mail: laraishere8321@aol.com.

RAMSEY, MICHAEL W., lawyer; b. Galveston, Tex., Feb. 18, 1940; s. V.V. Ramsey; married; 2 children. BA, So. Meth. U., 1962, JD, 1965. Bar: 1965. With Richard Haynes & Assoc., 1965—72; ptnr. Ramsey & Tyson, 1972—85; pvt. practice, 1985—. Named Criminal Def. Lawyer of the Year, Tex. State Bar Assn., 1999. Office: Law Office of Michael Ramsey 2120 Welch St Houston TX 77019*

RAMSEY, NATALIE D., lawyer; b. Greeneville, Tenn., Dec. 6, 1959; d. William Trent and Nancy (Maupin) Ramsey. BS, U. Del., 1981; JD, Villanova U., 1984. Bar: Pa. 1984, US Dist. Ct. (ea. dist.) Pa., US Ct. Appeals (3d and 11th cirs.), US Supreme Ct. 2004. Assoc. Montgomery, McCracken, Walker & Rhoads, LLP, Phila., 1985-93; ptnr. Montgomery, McCracken, Walker & Rhoads, Phila., 1993—, chair bankruptcy and reorgn. group, 1997—. Dir. Consumer Bankruptcy Advocacy Project, 1998—; chair Ea. Dist. Pa. Bankruptcy Conf., 2005—06. Contbr. articles to profl. jours. Pres. bd. dirs. Delaware County Habitat for Humanity, 1997—2002. Mem.: Turnaround Mgmt. Assn., Comml. Law League. Presbyterian. Avocations: travel, reading. Office: Montgomery McCracken Walker & Rhoads LLP 123 S Broad St Ste 2538 Philadelphia PA 19109-1099 Office Phone: 215-772-7354.

RAMSEY, NORMAN F., physicist, researcher; b. Washington, Aug. 27, 1915; s. Norman F. and Minna (Bauer) Ramsey; m. Elinor Jameson, June 3, 1940 (dec. Dec. 1983); children: Margaret, Patricia, Janet, Winifred; m. Ellie Welch, May 11, 1985. AB, Columbia U., NYC, 1935, PhD, 1940; BA, Cambridge U., Eng., 1937, MA, 1941, DSc, 1954; DSc (hon.), Harvard U., Cambridge, Mass., 2006, MA (hon.), 1947; DSc (hon.), Case Western Res. U., Cleve., 1968, Middlebury Coll., Vt., 1969, Oxford U., Eng., 1973, DCL (hon.), 1990; DSc (hon.), Rockefeller U., 1986, U. Chgo., 1989, U. Sussex, 1990, U. Houston, 1991, Carleton Coll., Northfield, Minn., 1991, Lake Forest Coll., Ill., 1992, U. Mich., 1993, Phila. Coll. Pharmacy & Sci., 1995, Colby Coll., Waterville, Maine, 1998, U. Stony, Brook, 2008. Kellett fellow Columbia U., 1935—37, Tyndall fellow, 1938—39; Carnegie fellow Carnegie Inst. Washington, 1939—40; assoc. U. Ill., 1940—42; asst. prof. Columbia U., 1942—46; assoc. MIT Radiation Lab., 1940—43; cons. Nat. Def. Rsch. Com., 1940—45; expert cons. sec. of war, 1942—45; group leader, asso. div. head Los Alamos Lab., 1943—45; assoc. prof. Columbia U., 1945—47; head physics dept. Brookhaven Nat. Lab. of AEC, 1946—47; assoc. prof. physics Harvard U., 1947—50, prof. physics, 1950—66, Higgins prof. physics, 1966—86, Higgins prof. emeritus, 1986—. Sr. fellow Harvard Soc. Fellows, 1970—; Eastman prof. Oxford U., 1973—74; Luce prof. cosmology Mt. Holyoke Coll., 1982—83; prof. U. Va., 1983—84; dir. Harvard Nuc. Lab., 1948—50, 1952—53, Varlan Assocs., 1963—66; mem. Air Forces Sci. Adv. Com., 1947—54; sci. advisor NATO, 1958—59; mem. Dept. Def. Panel Atomic Energy; exec. com. Cambridge Electron Accelerator; gen. adv. com. AEC. Author: Nuclear Moments and Statistics, 1953, Nuclear Two Body Problems, 1953, Molecular Beams, 1956, 2d edit., 1985, Quick Calculus, 1965, Spectroscopy with Coherent Radiation, 1998; contbr. articles to profl. jours. Trustee Assoc. Univs., Inc., Brookhaven Nat. Lab., Carnegie Endowment Internat. Peace, 1962—85, Rockefeller U., 1977—90; pres. Univs. Rsch. Assocs., Inc., 1966—72, 1973—81, pres. emeritus, 1981—. Recipient Presdl. Order of Merit for radar devel. work, 1947, award, E.O. Lawrence and AEC, 1960, Columbia award for excellence in sci., 1980, medal of honor, IEEE, 1983, Rabi prize, 1985, Monte Ferst award, 1985, Compton medal, 1985, Rumford premium, 1985, Oersted medal, 1988, Nat. medal of Sci., 1988, Nobel prize for Physics, 1989, Pupin medal, Columbia Engring. Sch. Alumni Assn., 1992, Sci. for Peace prize, 1992, Einstein medal, 1993, Vannevar Bush award, 1995, Svc. award, PTTL, 2005; fellow Guggenheim, Oxford U., 1954—55. Fellow: Am. Phys. Soc. (coun. 1956—60, pres. 1978—79, Davisson-Germer prize 1974), Am. Acad. Sci.; mem.: AAAS (chmn. physics sect. 1977), NAS, Am. Inst. Physics (chmn. bd. govs. 1980—87), Am. Philos. Assn., French Acad. Sci., Sigma Xi, Phi Beta Kappa (senator 1979—88, v.p. 1982—85). Achievements include research in nuc. physics, molecular beam experiments, radar, nuc. magnetic moments, radiofrequency spectroscopy, masers, nucleon scattering. Home: 24 Monmouth Ct Brookline MA 02446-5634 Office: Harvard U Lyman Physics Lab Cambridge MA 02138 Office Phone: 617-495-2864.*

RAMSEY, PAUL GLENN, dean, internist; b. Pitts., 1949; MD, Harvard U., 1975. Diplomate Am. Bd. Internal Medicine. Intern Cambridge Hosp., 1975-76; resident in medicine Mass. Gen. Hosp., Boston, 1976-78, Univ. Wash., Seattle, 1980-81, fellow infectious diseases, 1978-80, prof., 1991—, chmn. dept. medicine, 1992-97, dean Sch. Med., 1997—; physician-in-chief Univ. Wash. Medicine, 1992-97, v.p., med. affairs, 1997—2006, CEO, exec. v.p. med. affairs, 2006—. Mem.: Inst. Medicine, AAAS, Assn. Am. Physicians, Am. Fedn. Clin. Rsch., ACP. Office: U Wash Sch Medicine PO Box 356350 Seattle WA 98195-6350

RAMSEY, RONALD L., Lieutenant Governor of Tennessee; b. Johnson City, Tenn., Nov. 20, 1955; married; three children. BS in Indsl. Tech., East Tenn. State U., 1978. Real estate broker/auctioneer; mem. Tenn. House of Reps., 1993—97, Tenn. State Senate, 1997—, spkr., 2007—; lt. gov. State of Tenn., Nashville, 2007—. Mem. Elizabeth Chapel United Meth. Ch.; mem. adv. bd. Farm Credit Assn. Mem. Bristol Tenn.-Va. Assn. Realtors (past pres.), Blountville Ruritan, Blountville Bus. Assn. (past pres.). Republican. Methodist. Office: Office Lt Gov 1 Legislative Plaza Nashville TN 37243 also: Tenn State Senate 2132 Feathers Chapel Rd Blountville TN 37617 also: 3311 Hwy 126 Blountville TN 37617 Office Phone: 615-741-4524. Office Fax: 615-253-0197. E-mail: sen.ron.ramsey@legislature.state.tn.us.*

RAMSEY, SALLY JUDITH WEINE, chemist, research and development company executive; married; 2 children. B in Chemistry, Hiram Coll.; attended grad. study in chemistry, Iowa State U. Founder, v.p. new product devel. Ecology Coatings, Inc., Akron, Ohio, 1990—. Recipient Silver winner and Materials and other Base Technologies winner, Wall Street Jour. Technology Innovation award, 2005; named Best Inventions 2005: Thin Skins, Time Mag. Achievements include 7 patents in field and others pending. Office: Ecology Coating 1238 Brittain Rd Akron OH 44310 Office Phone: 330-633-3500. Office Fax: 330-633-3464. Business E-Mail: sally@ecologycoatings.com, sally.ramsey@ecologycoatings.com.

RAMSEY, SCOTT D., researcher, educator; BS, u. Iowa, 1983; MD, U. Iowa, 1990; PhD, U. Pa., 1994. Intern, internal medicine U. Wash., 1990—93, acting asst. prof., health sciences, 1995—97, asst. prof., Sch. Pub. Health and Cmty. Medicine, health services, 1997—2000; fellow, medicine, gen. internal medicine U. Wash. Sch. Medicine, 1993—94, acting instr., medicine, 1994—95, acting asst. prof., medicine, gen. internal medicine, 1995—97, asst. prof., medicine, gen. internal medicine, 1997—2000, assoc. prof., medicine, gen. internal medicine, 2001—06, prof., medicine, 2006—; chief med. resident, medicine U. Wash. Med. Ctr., 1994—95; joint asst. mem. Fred Hutchinson Cancer Rsch. Ctr., Pub. Health Sciences, 1997—2000; assoc. mem. Fred Hutchinson Cancer Rsch. Ctr., Cancer Prevention Rsch. Program, Pub. Health Sciences, 2000—05, mem., 2005—; dir. Seattle Cancer Care Alliance Cancer Prevention Clinic, 2006—. Dir., Ctr. for Cost and Outcome Rsch., Clin. Economics U. Wash., 1995—2000; staff physician VA Puget Sound Health Care System, Seattle Divsn., 1995—98. Contbr. several articles to profl. publications, abstracts. Recipient Cecile Lehman Mayer Rsch. award, Am. Coll. Chest Physicians, 1994—95, Robert H. Williams award, Am. Fedn. for Clin. Rsch., 1995—96, Howard Temin Career Develop. award, NCI, 1997—98; Kellogg Washington Health Policy Fellowship, Wharton Sch. U. Pa., 1986—87. Mem.: Soc. for Med. Decision Making, Internat. Soc. for Pharmacoeconomic and Outcomes Rsch., Internat. Health Economics Assn., Cancer Intervention and Surveillance Network, Am. Soc. Clin. Oncology, ACP, Omicron Delta Kappa, Beta Gamma Sigma, BeBeta Gamma Sigma. Office: Fred Hutchinson Cancer Research Ctr 1100 Fairview Ave North M3-B232 Seattle WA 98109-1024 Office Phone: 206-667-7846. Office Fax: 205-667-7597. Business E-Mail: sramsey@fhcrc.org.*

RAMSEY-COOK, HEATHER, legislative staff member; Chief of staff to Rep. Ted Poe US House of Reps., Washington, 2005—. Republican. Office: 430 Cannon House Office Bldg Washington DC 20515 Office Phone: 202-225-6565. Office Fax: 202-225-5547.*

RAMSEYER, CHRIS CHARLES EMIL, engineering educator; s. Albert Charles Ramseyer and Elsbeth Rutschi; m. Karen Catherine Barker, Dec. 30, 1995. PhD, U. Okla., Norman, 2006. Cert. profl. engr., Calif., 2001, Okla., 2002. Adj. faculty U. Okla., 2000—05, asst. prof., 2006—. Engineer: SkyDance Bridg, Okla. City. Recipient Engring. Achievement award, Okla. Soc. Profl. Engrs., 1998, Alumni Tchg. award, OU Coll. Engring., 2007. Mem.: Am. Soc. Engring. Educators, ASCE, Am. Iron and Steel Inst. (mem. com. specification, base test and anchorage task group 2005—08), Structural Stability Rsch. Coun. (mem. task groups on axial columns, frames and rsch. methods 2005—08), Chi Epsilon. Home: 700 Highland Hills Dr Norman OK 73026 Office: Univ Okla 202 W Boyd Rm 334 Norman OK 73019

RAMSEY-GOLDMAN, ROSALIND, physician; b. NYC, Mar. 22, 1954; d. Abraham L. and Miriam (Colen) Goldman; m. Glenn Ramsey, June 29,1 975; children: Ethan Ramsey, Caitlin Ramsey. BA, Case We. Res. U., 1975, MD, 1978; MPH, U. Pitts., 1988, DPH, 1992. Med. resident U. Rochester, NY, 1978—81; chief resident Rochester Gen. Hosp., 1981—82; staff physician U. Health Svc., Rochester, 1982—83; rheumatology fellow U. Pitts., 1983—86, instr. medicine, 1986—87, asst. prof., 1987—91, co-dir. Lupus Treatment and Diagnostic Ctr., 1987—91; asst. prof. medicine Northwestern U., Chgo., 1991—96, assoc. prof. medicine, 1996—2001, prof. medicine, 2001—; soc. rsch. prof. Solovy Arthritis Rsch. Dir. Chgo. Lupus Registry, Northwestern U., Chgo., 1991—, chairperson Systemic Lupus Internat. Collaborating Clinics Group, 2003-08; program dir. Gen. Clin. Rsch. Ctr. at NCRR/NIH, 2005-08; dir. Clin. Rsch. Unit, NUCATS, NCRR/NIH, 2008- Contbr. rsch. articles to profl. jours. Recipient Finkelstein award Hershey (Pa.) Med. Ctr., 1986. Fellow ACP, Am. Coll. Rheumatology; mem. Soc. for Epidemiologic Rsch., Ctrl. Soc. Clin. Rsch. Office: Northwestern U Feinberg Sch Medicine McGaw Pavilion 240 E Huron Ste M-300 Chicago IL 60611 Office Phone: 312-503-8003. Business E-Mail: rgramsey@northwestern.edu.

RAMSINGHANI, SUSHMA, medical educator; d. Gauri Shankar and Sushila Devi Baderia; m. Pradeep Ramsinghani, Feb. 21, 1985; 1 child, Arjun. PhD, U. Toledo, Ohio, 1998. Asst., assoc. prof. Hampton U., Va., 2001—08; assoc. prof., rschr. U. Incarnate Word, San Antonio, 2008—. Vol. local sch. and univs. Recipient G.P. Nair award, Indian Drug Mfg. Assn., 1985; Rsch. grants, NIH, 2003—07. Mem.: Am. Chem. Soc. Achievements include research in improve cancer therapy outcome through designing, synthesizing and testing inhibitors of the enzyme, PARG. Office: Univ Incarnate Word 4301 Broadway PO Box 99 San Antonio TX 78209 Business E-Mail: ramsingh@uiwtx.edu.

RAMSTAD, JAMES MARVIN (JIM RAMSTAD), former United States Representative from Minnesota, lawyer; b. Jamestown, ND, May 6, 1946; s. Marvin Joseph and Della Mae (Fode) Ramstad. BA, U. Minn., 1968; JD with honors, George Washington U., 1973. Bar: ND 1973, DC 1973, Minn. 1979, admitted to practice: US Supreme Ct. 1976. Adminstrv. asst. to LL Duxbury Minn. House Reps., 1969; spl. asst. to Congressman Tom Kleppe US Congress, 1970; pvt. practice law Jamestown, 1973, Washington, 1974—78, Mpls., 1978—90; asst. campaign mgr. for Congressman William E. Frenzel US Congress, 1978; mem. Minn. State Senate, 1981—90, asst. minority leader, 1983—87; mem. US Congress from 3rd Minn. dist., 1991—2009. Adj. prof. Am. U., Washington, 1975—78. Bd. dirs. D.A.R.E., Minn., Children's Heart Fund, Lake Country Food Bank, The Nat. Ctr. on Addiction & Substance Abuse, Columbia U., 2008—; mem. C. of C., Twin West, Wayzata, North Metro. 1st lt. USAR, 1968—74. Recipient Fulbright Disting. Pub. Service award; named Rep. of Yr., Nat. Assn. Police Orgns., 1997, 2000, Legislator of Yr., Nat. Assn. Alcoholism and Drug Addiction Counselors, 1998, Nat. Mental Health Assn., 1999. Mem.: U. Minn. Alumni Assn., Hennepin County Bar Assn., ND Bar Assn., DC Bar Assn., Minn. Bar Assn., Minn. Prayer Breakfast Com., Plymouth Lions Club, Am. Legion, Phi Delta Theta, Phi Beta Kappa. Republican.*

RAMZY, IBRAHIM, medical educator; came to U.S., 1978; m. Faye Ramzy; children: Joseph I., Peter I. MD, MBBCh, Cairo U., 1958. Diplomate Am. Bd. Pathology. Prof. U. Tex. Health Scis. Ctr., San Antonio, 1978—86; chief, anatomic pathology Meth. Hosp., Houston, 1989—2003; prof. pathology & ob-gyn. Baylor Coll. Medicine, Houston, 1986—2003, U. Calif., Irvine, 2003—, chief anatomic pathology, Irvine Med. Ctr. Orange, 2003—06. Cons. in gynecol. oncology various hosps., 1976—; pathologist, dir. cytopathology Victoria Hosp., London, 1970-78; vis. prof. dept. ob-gyn. U. Western Ontario, London, dept. pathology U. Cairo, 1980, med. sch. Iowa U., 1993; dir. cytopathology Med. Ctr. and VA Hosps., San Antonio, 1978-86, cytotech. sch. Med. Ctr. Hosp., San Antonio, 1978-86; attending pathologist, dir. cytopathology The Meth. Hosp., Houston, 1986-89; attending pathologist Harris County Hosp. Dist., Houston, 1986—; editl. bd. mem. Acta Cytol Jour., Cancer Cytopathology Jour., Diagnostic Cytopathology Jour., Human Cytopathology Jour. Author: Testicular Disorders, 1974, Essentials of Gynecologic and Obstetric Pathology, 1983, Clinical Cytopathology and Aspiration Biopsy: Fundamental Principles and Practice, 1990, 2nd edit., 2001, Pulmonary Cytopathology, 2009; contbr. chpts. to books, articles to profl. jours. Recipient John J Andujar Lifetime Achievement award, Tex. Soc. Pathologists, 2006, Mvp Outstanding Svc. award, U. Calif. Irvine Sch. Medicine, 2008, Alberto Manetta Tchg. award, 2008. Fellow Coll. Am. Pathologists; mem. AMA, Internat. Acad. of Cytology, Internat. Soc. Gynecol. Pathologists, Internat. Acad. of Pathology, Royal Coll. Physicians and Surgeons of Can., Papanicolaou Soc. of Cytopathology, Am. Soc. Clin. Pathologists, Am. Soc. Cytopathology (v.p. 1992-93, pres.-elect 1993-94, pres. 1994-95), Can. Soc. Cytology (pres. 1974-75), Can. Med. Assn., Tex. Soc. Cytology (pres. 1982, 83), Tex. Soc. Pathologists (pres. 1994-95), Tex. Med. Assn., Harris County Med. Soc., Ont. Med. Assn. Office: Univ Calif Med Sci Bldg #1 Rm D440 Irvine CA 92697 Business E-Mail: iramzy@uci.edu.

RANA, PASHUPATI S.J.B., legislator; b. Laxmi Niwas, Kathmandu, Nepal, May 7, 1941; s. Bijaya Shumsher Jung Bahadur and Rani Sarla Devi Rana; m. Rani Usha Raje (Princess of Gwalior); children: Urrashi R. L., Deryani R. L. Attended, Haileybury and ISC, England, New Coll., Oxford. Mem. Parliament, 1973—2008; Min. Edn., Transport, Civil Aviation, and Tourism, 1977—79, Water Resources, 1983—86, 1997—98, Panchayat and Local Devel., 1986—88, Fgn. Affairs, Fin., Water Resources, and Comm., 1990; gen. sec. Rashtriya Prajatantra Party, Nat. Dem. Party, 1991—2002, chmn., 2003—; leader Parl. Party, 2006—. Mem. India Internat. Ctr.; pres. Alliance-Francaise Nepal. Mem.: Internat. Coun. Asia Soc. Avocations: reading, classical music, writing, mountain climbing. Office: Ctrl Secretariat Rashtriya Prajatantra Party Charumati Bahal Chahabhil Kathmandu Nepal Home: Bijaya Bas POB 271 Maharajgunj Kathmandu Nepal Office Phone: 4471071. Office Fax: 4460324; Home Fax: 4423384. Personal E-mail: p-rana@ntc.net.np.

RANALLO, FRANK N., medical researcher; b. Chgo., Sept. 26, 1951; s. Nunzio F. and Betty Ranallo; 1 child, Sarah Ann. BS in Physics & Math., DePaul U., Chgo., 1973; MS in Physics, U. Wis., Madison, 1976, PhD in Physics, 1993. Cert. in diagnostic radiol. physics Am. Bd. Radiology, 1994. Rschr. U. Wis. Dept. Med. Physics, 1980—94, clin. asst. prof., 1994—97, asst. prof., 1998—2004, assoc. prof., 2005—. Mem. diagnostic radiologic physics item writing task force Am. Bd. Radiology Written Exam., 2006—. Vol. tchr. and storyteller Madison Met. Sch. Dist., Wis., 1997—2008. Mem.: Soc. Physics Students, Am. Coll. Med. Physics, Am. Assn. Physicists Medicine, Delta Epsilon Sigma, Phi Eta Sigma, Sigma Pi Sigma, Sigma Xi. Achievements include patents for instrument for the measurement of x-ray beam characteristics and x-ray sources; invention of RMI model 230 digital kVp Meter, RMI model 232 mammographic kVp Meter; research in development of optimized protocols for use in ct scanning to improve image quality and reduce radiation dose and also test tools and methods for performance testing of radiographic equipment. Avocations: astronomy, photography. Home: 5102 Buffalo Trl Madison WI 53705-4751 Office: UW Dept Med Physics 1111 Highland Ave 1161 WIMR Madison WI 53705-2275 Business E-Mail: ranallo@wisc.edu.

RANCK, EDNA RUNNELS, academic administrator, researcher; b. Waterville, Maine, Aug. 24, 1935; d. Everett Elias and Edna May (King) Runnels; m. James Gilmour Ranck, June 30, 1971 (dec. May 1979); children: Matthew, Christopher, Joshua Duggan; m. Martin Fleischer, Apr. 19, 1982; stepchildren: Christina, Laura. BA cum laude, Fla. State U., Tallahassee, 1957; MDiv magna cum laude, Drew U. Theol. Sch., Madison, NJ, 1971, MEd in Edn. Adminstrn., 1978; EdD in Curriculum and Tchg., Columbia U., NYC, 1986. Dir. Collinsville Child Care Ctr., Morristown, NJ, 1971-78; exec. dir. Children's Svcs. Morris County, Morristown, 1980-84; co-mgr. NJ Child Care Clearinghouse, Trenton, NJ; coord. NJ Child Care Adv. Coun., Trenton, 1987-92; dir. NJ Office Child Care Devel., Trenton, 1992; child care coord. NJ Dept. Human Svcs., Trenton, 1992-98, Nat. Assn. Child Care Resource & Referral Agys., Washington, 1998—2002, Westover Consultants, Inc., Bethesda, Md., 2002—07, Washington (DC) Child Devel. Coun., 2009—. Adj. faculty Kean U. NJ, Union, 1983; bd. dir. Sprout House Presch., Chatham, NJ, 1984-87; mem. Morris County Human Svcs. Adv. Coun., Morristown, NJ, 1986-87, spkr. in field. Author: Dodge Foundation Project, 1984, Young Children, 1987, Our History, Our Vision: A History of the National Association of Child Care Rsource and Referral Agencies, 1997, NAFCC@25: 1982-2007, 2007, Early Childhood Education: An International Encyclopedia, 2007; writer monthly Policy Perspectives column, 2000-02; contbr. chapters to books, articles to profl. jours. Exec. bd. Drew U. Alumni Assn. Theol. Sch., 1986-92; active Drew U. Alumni Study Commn., 1993, Non-Govt. Orgn. rep. to UN Internat. Fedn. Educative Cmtys., 1992-99; mem. history/archives panel Nat. Assn. for Edn. of Young Children, 1999-2001. Recipient Volpe Commitment in Child Care award, NJ Child Care Assn., 1991, Essex C.C. Early Childhood award, 1997, Aletha Wright award for Excellence in Early Edn., 1998. Mem. Internat. Assn. Presch. Edn. N.Am. (bd. dirs.), Child Care Action Campaign Panel, Acad. Child and Youth Care Workers, Nat. Assn. Regulatory Adminstrn. (bd. dirs. 2000-05), World Orgn. Presch. Edn. USA (bd. dirs. 2000—, pres. 2006—), Reel Fathers (Nat. Adv. bd.), Nat. Assn. Edn. Young Children (moderator history seminar 2002—, co-editor ECE history column, contbr. Exch. Everyday 2004—), Tchrs. Coll. Columbia U. Washington Alumni Assn. (co-chmn.), Fla. State U. Emeritus Alumni Soc., DC PlayBlocks, Inc. (sec./treas. bd. dirs. 2004—), Phi Beta Kappa, Pi Sigma Alpha, Sigma Delta Pi. Republican. United Methodist. Avocations: writing, travel, clothing design, art collecting, walking. Home: 4447 MacArthur Blvd NW Washington DC 20007-2564 Personal E-mail: edna.ranck@verizon.net.

RANCK, JAMES BYRNE, JR., neuroscience researcher, educator; b. Frederick, Md., Aug. 17, 1930; s. James Byrne and Dorothy Irene (Schwieger) R.; m. Helen Haukeness, June 9, 1961; 1 child, Mary Haukeness. BA, Haverford Coll., 1952; MD, Columbia U., 1955. Intern U. Chgo. Clinics, 1955-56; scientist NIH, Bethesda, Md., 1956-58; postdoctoral fellow Dept. Physiology U. Washington, Seattle, 1959-61, instr., 1961-62; from asst. prof. to prof. U. Mich., Ann Arbor, 1962-75; prof. SUNY Health Sci. Ctr., Bklyn., 1975—2005, disting. tchg. prof., 2005—. Home: 100 Bank St New York NY 10014-2123 Office: SUNY Dept Physiology 450 Clarkson Ave Brooklyn NY 11203-2056 Home Phone: 212-989-9487; Office Phone: 718-270-1600. E-mail: jranck@downstate.edu.

RAND, A. BARRY (ADDISON BARRY RAND), retirement association executive; b. Washington, Nov. 5, 1944; s. Addison Penrod and Helen (Matthews) Rand; m. Donna Rand, 1990; 1 child, Allison 1 stepchild, Christopher. Student, Rutgers U., NJ; BS in Mktg., Am. U., Washington, 1968; MBA, Stanford U., Calif., 1972, MA in Mgmt. Sci., 1973. Sales rep. Xerox Corp., 1968—70, regional sales rep., 1970—80, corp. dir. major account mktg., 1980—81, v.p. major account mktg. ops., 1981—82, v.p. field ops., 1983—84, v.p. Ea. ops., 1984—85, corp. v.p., 1985—86, sr. v.p., v.p. US mktg. group, 1986—92, exec. v.p. worldwide ops., 1992—99; chmn., CEO Avis Group Holdings, Inc., Garden City, NY, 1999—2001; non-exec. chmn. Aspect Comm., 2001—03; chmn., CEO Equitant Corp., 2003—05; CEO Am. Assn. Retired Persons (AARP), Washington, 2009—. Bd. dirs. AT&T Wireless, 2001—03, Campbell Soup Co., 2005—. Chmn. bd. dirs. Howard U., Washington. Recipient NAACP Image award, 1993; named to Nat. Sales Hall of Fame, 1993. Democrat. Office: AARP 601 E St NW Washington DC 20049*

RAND, ANTHONY EDEN, state legislator, lawyer; b. Panther Branch, NC, Sept. 1, 1939; s. Walter and Geneva; m. Karen Rand; 2 children. BA in Polit. Sci., UNC, 1961; LLD (hon.), UNC, Chapel Hill, 2008; JD, UNC Law Sch., Chapel Hill, 1964; LLD (hon.), Fayetteville State U., 2000; HHD (hon.), Meth. U., 2008. Ptnr. Mitchiner, Andrews, Rand, Raleigh, NC, 1965-68, Rose, Thorp, Rand & Ray, Fayetteville, NC, 1968-81, Rose, Rand, Winfrey & Gregory, Fayetteville, 1982-89, Rand, Finch & Gregory, Fayetteville, 1989-93, Rand and Gregory, Fayetteville, 1993—; mem. Dist. 12 NC State Senate, 1982—88, mem. Dist. 24, 1995—2002, mem. Dist. 19, 2003—, majority leader, 1987—88, 2001—. Sec., legal counsel, cons. Lithotripters, Inc.1989-96; cons. Prime Med. Svcs., 1996-2000, Sonorex, Inc., 2001—. Mem. N.C. State Dem. Exec. Com., 1975-77; chmn. exec. com. Cumberland County Dem. party (N.C.), 1977-81; bd. visitors U. N.C.-Chapel Hill, Meth. Coll.; bd. dirs., founding mem. Pub. Sch. Forum; bd. dirs. Fayetteville Area Sentencing, 1985; mem. adv. bd. Mus. Cape Fear, 1989-95; mem. nat. adv. panel Child Care Action Com., 1989—; pres. Med-Tech Investments, 1989-97. Recipient William Davie award, U. N.C. Chapel Hill, 1995, DSM, U. N.C. Chapel Hill Gen. Alumni Assn., 1998, Disting. Alumnus award, U. N.C. Chapel Hill, 2001, Legis. Leadership award, N.C. Coun. Cmty. Programs, 2000, Fayetteville C. of C. Realtors Cup, 2000, Chancellor's medallion, Fayetteville State U., 2001, Law Disting. Alumni award, U. N.C. Chapel Hill, 2001, Disting. Svc. award, N.C. State, 2002, Hon. Trustee award, Fayetteville Tech. C.C., 2003, N.C. Gun Violence Prevention Citizen of Yr. award, 2003, Legis. award, ARC of N.C., 2003, William N. Martin award, Covenant with N.C. Children, 2005, Pub. Leadership in Tech. award, N.C. Tech. Assn., 2005, 2007, MOVE award, Nat. MS Soc. NC, 2007, Leadership award, NC Housing Trust Fund, 2007, Dir. award, NC Alcohol Law Enforcement, Charles Dick medal of Merit, NC Nat. Guard, 2007, NC Pub. Lib. Champion award, 2008, Legislative Supporters of Foster and Adoptive Parents award, Childrens & Family Svcs. Assn., 2008; named Legis. of Yr., N.C. Nurses' Assn., 2003, Autism Soc., 2004, Legislator of Yr., Disabled Am. Vet. NC, 2008. Mem. ABA, ATLA (state commiteeman 1968-72), N.C. Bar Assn., Alpha Tau Omega, Delta Theta Phi, State Legislative Leadership Found. (bd. dirs.), Senete Pres. Forum (bd. dir.). Democrat. Episcopalian. Office: 2014 Litho Pl Fayetteville NC 28304 also: NC Senate Legislature Bldg 300 N Salisbury St Room 300C Raleigh NC 27603-5925 Office Phone: 919-733-9892, 910-222-8096. Office Fax: 919-715-8346, 910-222-4420. Business E-Mail: tony.r@ncleg.net.

RAND, CALVIN GORDON, art educator, consultant; b. Buffalo, May 15, 1929; s. George Franklin and Isabel (Williams) R.; m. Patricia Clemens Andrew, Aug. 18, 1951; children: Robin, Melissa, Jennifer, Lucinda, Elizabeth BA, Princeton U., 1951; MA, Columbia U., 1954; LHD (hon.), York U., Can., 1984. Head history dept. Riverdale Sch., NYC, 1955-60; lectr. philosophy SUNY-Buffalo, 1961-68, acting dir. cultural affairs, 1968-71; founder, pres. The Niagara Inst., Niagara-on-the-Lake, Canada, 1971-79; pres. Am. Acad. in Rome, NYC, 1980-84; ind. producer, theatre and film cons., NYC, 1985-90. Founding chmn., dir. Shaw Festival Theatre, Niagara-on-the-Lake, 1964-78,. bd. govs., 1979—; trustee Playwrights Horizons Theatre, N.Y.C., 1982-92; bd. dirs. Arts in Edn. Inst.; mem. N.Y. State Coun. on Arts, 1978-82, Arts Coun. Western N.Y., 1987-93; chmn. World Ency. Contemporary Theater; chmn. arts coun. SUNY, Buffalo, 1987-94, adj. prof. theater, 1988—. Contbr. articles to profl. jours. Bd. dirs. Burchfield-Penney Art Ctr., Buffalo, 1991—, vice-chair, 1999—; bd. dirs. Irish Classical Theater, 1993—, pres., 1998-2004; trustee Albright-Knox Gallery, Buffalo, 1976-80, 84-88, 90-94. Recipient spl. citation Ont. Arts Coun., 1976, Fellowship Fund award Niagara Inst., 1980, Centennial Arts award Nichols Sch., 1992, Red Jacket award, Erie County Hist. Soc., 2000, Arts award Nat. Conf. Cmty. and Justice, 2007; named Man of Yr., Coun. World Affairs, 1976, Buffalo Courier Express, 1976, Arts Patron of Yr., Western N.Y. Arts Coun. and C. of C., 1989, Disting Non-Alumni, SUNY, Buffalo, Man of Yr., 1997, YMCA of Western NY, 1999; Vanier Coll. fellow York U. Mem. Princeton Club, Saturn Club. Home Phone: 716-883-7238; Office Phone: 716-883-2942.

RAND, ELIZABETH HARTMANN, psychiatrist; b. Morristown, NJ, Apr. 17, 1941; d. Henry Fredrick and Virginia Lawther Hartmann; m. Richard Aldrich Rand, May 20, 1967; children: Ilona Theodora Dotson, Sebastian Gerard, Paul Hartmann. BA in Govt., Smith Coll., 1963; MA in Econs., NYU, 1968; MD, Yeshiva U., Bronx, NY, 1980; student, U. Conn., 1983—85. Diplomate Nat. Bd. Psychiatry and Neurology, 1987, lic. psychiatrist N.Y., 1980, Conn., 1983, Ala., 1985. Asst. project dir. Sperry & Hutchinson Co., NYC, 1964—65, project dir., 1965—67; rsch. analyst Nat. Bur. Econ. Rsch., NYC, 1968—70, sr. rsch. analyst, 1972—73; freelance editor NYC, 1970—72; attending Newington (Conn.) V.A. Hosp., 1983; in-house physician Nalchaug Hosp., Willimantic, Conn., 1983—85; chief resident Outpatient Psychiatry Clinic, 1984; chief resident Inpatient Psychiatry Clinic, 1985; from asst. prof. psychiatry to prof. Sch. Medicine U. Ala., Tuscaloosa, Ala., 1985—99; technician Neurol. Inst. Columbia Coll. Physicians and Surgeons, NYC, 1996; prof. psychiatry Sch. Medicine U. Ala., 1999—2005, chmn. Dept. Psychiatry and Neurology, 1990—2005, assoc. dean Academic Affairs, 1999—2000, prof. emeritus, 2005—. Prof. Dept. Psychiatry Sch. Medicine U. Ala., Birmingham, Ala., 2004—05, clinician, 2004—05, mem. numerous coms., Tuscalooosa, 1987—; cons. in field. Contbr. articles to profl. jours., chapters to books. Vol. Am. Red Cross, Tuscaloosa, 2000—; pres. bd. dirs. Ala. Bay Choir, Tuscaloosa, 1996. Recipient The Sandoz award, Sandoz Pharm., 1985; grantee, NIMH, 1985, 1990—93, U. Ala., 1987, 1989, CCHS, 1994, 1998—2000, SmithKline Beecham Pharms., 1999, Eli Lilly and Co., 2000, Parke-Davis Pharm. Rsch., 2000. Mem.: Ala. Psychiatric Soc. (bd. dirs. 1990—91), Tuscaloosa (Ala.) Psychiatric Soc. (pres. 1990—91, sec. 1997—98, treas. 1997—98), Am. Psychiatric Inst. Rsch. and Edn. (sci. adv. panel 1999—), Am. Assn. Suicidology, Am. Coll. Psychiatrists, Am. Assn. Gen. Hosp. Psychiatrists, Am. Psychiatric Assn. (sci. program com. 1988—94, advertisers and exhibitors component 1990—94), Assn. Academic Psychiatry (pres. 1996, exec. coun. 1990—99, treas. 1994—96, assoc. editor bull. 1989—90, editor bull. 1991—94, coord. region VII 1987—90, task force recruiting and retaining women in academic psychiatry 1989—90), Phi Kappa Phi, Alpha Omega Alpha. Avocations: cooking, cello, skiing. Home: 1612 Deaning Place Tuscaloosa AL 35401 Office: Univ Ala University Med Ctr Tuscaloosa AL 35401 Address: 2-4 Rue du Sabot 75006 Paris French Guinea

RAND, JIM FRANCIS, science educator; b. Milw., July 18, 1941; s. Florence Rand; m. Jama Allyn Zubal, Nov. 6, 1980; children: James Paul, John Charles, Joe Nmi, Ryan James, Mellissa Joyce. BS, Marquette U., Milw., 1963; LLB, LaSalle U., chgo., 1972; PhD, Calif. Western U., Santa Monica, 1976. Cert. SHRM Alexandra Va., 1972, in Cpt ISPI, Wash. DC, 2003. Prof. Seattle Pacific U., 1993—; cons., founding ptnr. Seattle Rsch. Ptnrs., 1993—. Pres. Marquette U., 2002—; chmn. Swedish Home Health, Seattle, 2005. With Arty., 1963—67, Germany, RVN. Home: 5614 107th Pl SW Mukilteo WA 98275 Office: Seattle Pacific Univ 3307 Third Ave West Seattle WA 98119 Business E-Mail: jfrand@spu.edu.

RAND, JOELLA MAE, retired nursing educator, counselor; b. Akron, Ohio, July 9, 1932; d. Harry S. and Elizabeth May (Miller) Halberg; m. Martin Rand (dec.); children: Craig, Debbi Stark. BSN, U. Akron, 1961, MEd in Guidance, 1968; PhD in Higher Edn. Adminstrn., Syracuse U., 1981. Lic. mental health counselor 2006. Staff nurse Akron Gen. Hosp., 1953-54; staff-head nurse-instr. Summit County Receiving, Cuyahoga Falls, Ohio, 1954-56; head nurse psychiat. unit Akron Gen. Hosp., 1956-57; instr. psychiatric nursing Summit County Receiving, Cuyahoga Falls, 1957-61; head nurse, in-service instr. Willard (N.Y.) State Hosp., 1961-62; asst. prof. Alfred (N.Y.) U., 1962-76, assoc. prof., assoc. dean, 1976-78, acting dean, 1978-79, dean, 1979-90, dean coll. profl. studies, 1990-91, prof. counseling, 1991-2000; ret., 2000. Cons. N.Y. State Regents Program for Non-Collegiate Sponsored Instrn., 1984; cons. collegiate programs N.Y. State Dept. Edn., 1985, Elmira Coll., 1991, U. Rochester, 1992-93; accreditation visitor Nat. League for Nursing, 1984-92; ednl. cons. Willard Psychiat. Hosp., 1992-93; mem. profl. practice exam. subcom. Regents Coll., 1990-95. Vol. Willard Drug Treatment Ctr., 1997—; bd. dirs. Williard Drug Treatment Ctr., Romulus Zoning Bd., 2002—; vol. Red Cross, 2003—, co-capt. disaster team, 2004—05; bd. dirs. Five Point Correctional Facility, Willard Drug Treatment Ctr. Recipient Tchg. Excellence award Alfred U., 1977, Mary E. Gladwin Outstanding Alumni award Akron U. Coll. Nursing, 1983, Alfred Alumni Friends award, 1989, Grand Marshall commencement Alfred U., 1993, Vol. of Yr. award Willard Drug Treatment Ctr., 1999, Cert. Appreciation, Seneca County Cmty. Svcs. Bd., 2005. Mem.: ACA (NAR rep. 2000—04, co-capt. disaster team Red Cross-Finger Lakes chpt. 2003—05, pres. NYCA 2005, Seneca County Med. Reserve Corps. 2005—), Genesee Valley Edn. Com. (chair 1984—86), Western N.Y. League Nursing (bd. dirs. 1991—93), Genesee Regional Consortium (v.p.), N.Y. State Coun. of Deans (treas. 1984—88), N.Y. State Counseling Assn. (v.p.-elect profl. svcs. 1995—96, v.p. profl. svcs. 1996—98, 1999—2000, pres. 2005—06), Sigma Theta Tau (treas. Alfred chpt. 1984—85). Avocations: boating, fishing, public speaking in areas of family and child abuse. Personal E-mail: drand@rochester.rr.com.

RAND, LAWRENCE ANTHONY, investor, finance company executive; b. Bklyn., Nov. 19, 1942; s. Gerald M. and Elaine Shirley Rand; m. Madelon L., July 4, 1942; children: Allan, Joshua, Emily. AB with honors, Brown U., 1964; MA, NYU, 1965, PhD, 1998. Lectr. NYU, 1967, CUNY, 1968; analyst CIA, Langley, Va., 1967-68; account supr. Ruder & Finn Inc., NYC, 1968-71; co-founder, sr. v.p. Kekst & Co., NYC, 1971—, also bd. dirs. Chmn., bd. dirs. ALS Assn., L.A., 1987-92; adj. prof. NYU Grad. Sch. Bus., 2008-. Ethics bd. mem. West County, NY, 2008—; chmn. ethics com. Village Rye Brook, NY, 1993—2000, village trustee, 2000—02, mayor, 2004—08; bd. dirs. USTA and Edn. Found., West County Bd. of Ethics, 2008—. Mem. Brown U. Club, Bailiwick Club (Greenwich, Conn.). Office: Kekst & Co 437 Madison Ave 19th Fl New York NY 10022-7195 Home Phone: 914-939-4762; Office Phone: 212-521-4800. Personal E-mail: lar@kekst.com.

RAND, LEON, academic administrator; b. Boston, Oct. 8, 1930; s. Max B. and Ricka (Muscanto) Rakisky; m. Marian L. Newton, Aug. 29, 1959; children: Debra Ruth, Paul Martin, Marta Leah. BS, Northeastern U., 1953; MA, U. Tex., 1956, PhD, 1958. Postdoctoral fellow Purdue U., 1958-59; asst. prof. to prof. U. Detroit, 1959-68; prof., chmn. dept. chemistry Youngstown (Ohio) State U., 1968-74, dean grad. studies and research, 1974-81, acting acad. v.p., 1980; vice chancellor acad. affairs U. N.C., Pembroke, 1981—85; chancellor Ind. U.-S.E., New Albany, 1986-96; chancellor emeritus Ind. U., 1996—, prof. emeritus, 1999—; spl. asst. to chancellor IUPUI, 1996-98. Bd. dirs. Floyd Meml. Hosp., New Albany, 1987—90, Jewish Hosp., Louisville, 1991—96. Bd. dirs., mem. exec. com. Louisville (Ind.) area chpt. ARC; docent Indpls. Mus. Art, 1998—. Mem.: Metroverity (bd. dirs.), Am. Inst. Chemists, Am. Chem. Soc., Sigma Xi, Phi Kappa Phi. Home: 1785 Arrowwood Dr Carmel IN 46033-9019 E-mail: LRand7658@sbcglobal.net.

RAND, RICHARD PIERCE, plastic surgeon; b. San Diego, Mar. 25, 1955; AB, Stanford U.; MD, U. Mich., 1981. Cert. Am. Bd. Plastic Surgery, Am. Bd. Surgery, Nat. Bd. Med. Examiners. Resident in surgery Tufts-New Eng. Med. Ctr., Boston, 1981—86; resident in plastic reconstructive surgery Emory U., 1986—89; fellow in craniofacial surgery fellow U. Miami, 1989; chief of plastic surgery U. Wash. Med. Ctr., 1990—2000; owner, dir. Northwest Ctr. Aesthetic Plastic Surgery, Bellevue, Wash. Examiner Am. Bd. Plastic Surgery. Recipient Sr. Resident Chmn.'s award in Gen. Surgery, Tufts-New Eng. Med. Ctr.; named one of Top100 Golf Doctors in Am., Golf Digest, 2006; named to Best Doctors in America, Seattle's Best Doctors, America's Top Doctors, America's Top Surgeons, America's Top Physicians, America 's Top Cosmetic Doctors and Dentists. Fellow: Am. Coll. Surgeons; mem.: Wash. State Med. Assn., Ralph A. Deterling Surg. Soc., Maurice J. Jurkiewicz Soc., King County Med. Soc., Royal & Ancient Assn. Plastic Surgeons, Seattle Surg. Soc., Wash. Soc. Plastic Surgeons (Golden Hands/Golden Scalpel award), Northwest Soc. Plastic Surgeons, Am. Soc. Maxillofacial Surgeons, Am. Soc. Plastic Surgeons, Am. Soc. Aesthetic Plastic Surgery, Am. Soc. Plastic Surgeons, Phi Beta Kappa. Office: Northwest Ctr for Aesthetic Plastic Surgery Ste 630 1135 116th Ave NE Bellevue WA 98004 Office Phone: 866-616-6183. Office Fax: 425-455-0921.

RANDALL, CHANDLER CORYDON, theologian; b. Ann Arbor, Mich., Jan. 22, 1935; s. Frederick Stewart and Madeline Leta (Snow) R.; m. Marian Archias Montgomery, July 2, 1960; children: Sarah Archais, Elizabeth Leggett, Rebekah Stewart. AB in History, U. Mich., 1957; STB in Theology, Berkeley Div. Sch., Yale, 1960, DD with honoris causa, 1985; PhD in Hebraic Studies, Hebrew Union Coll., 1969. Rector St. Paul's Episcopal Ch., Richmond, Ind., 1967-71; rector Trinity Episcopal Ch., Ft. Wayne, Ind., 1971-88, St. Peter's Episcopal Ch., Del Mar, Calif., 1988—2000; theologian-in-residence Christ Ch. Cranbrook, Bloomfield Hills, Mich., 2000—08. Bd. dirs. Living Ch. Found., Milw.; bibl. theologian Episcopal Ch. Stewardship, N.Y.C., 1985; alumni coun. Berkeley Divinity at Yale, New Haven, Conn., 1981-87; bishop's cabinet Diocese of No. Ind., South Bend, 1983-87. Author: Satire in the Bible, 1969, An Approach to Biblical Satire, 1990; contbr. articles to profl. jours. Founder Canterbury Sch., Ft. Wayne, 1977; commr. Ind. Jud. Qualifications Commn., Indpls., 1981-87; pres. Ft. Wayne Plan Commn., 1977; bd. dirs. Ft. Wayne Park Found., 1983-88; platform com. Ind. Republican Party, Indpls., 1974. Recipient Disting. Svc. medal U. Mich., 1981, Scheuer scholar Hebrew Union Coll., 1963-66, Liberty Bell award Ft. Wayne Bar Assn., 1988; named Sagamore of the Wabash, Gov. Ind., 1987. Mem. Am. Schs. Oriental Research, Yale U. Alumni Club (pres. 1982-88), Quest Club (pres.), Mayflower Soc. in Mich. (historian 2001-, gov. 2007-), Detroit Soc. Geneal. Rsch. (pres. 2000-), Oakland County Geneal. Soc. (pres.), Rotary Club, Chi Psi (nat. chaplain 1982). Republican. Episcopalian. Avocation: genealogy. Office: Christ Ch Cranbrook 470 Church Rd Bloomfield Hills MI 48304 Office Fax: 248-644-0148. Personal E-mail: umpadre@aol.com.

RANDALL, CLIFFORD WENDELL, civil engineer, educator; b. Somerset, Ky., May 1, 1936; s. William Lesbert and Geneva (James) R.; m. Phyllis Amis, Aug. 15, 1959; children: Andrew Amis, William Otis. BSCE, U. Ky., 1959, MS in Sanitary Engring., 1963; PhD in Environ. Health Engring., U. Tex., 1966. Asst. prof. civil engring. U. Tex., Arlington, 1965-68; mem. faculty Va. Poly. Inst. and State U., 1968—2001, prof. civil engring., 1972-81, Charles Lunsford prof., 1981—2001; vis. prof. U. Cape Town, South Africa, 1983; chmn. environ. engring. and scis. program Va. Poly. Inst. and State U., 1979-97, Charles Lunsford prof. emeritus, 2001—. Lectr. Shanghai Archtl. and Mcpl. Engring. Inst., Wuhan Tech. U., 1987; dir. Occoquan Watershed Monitoring Program, 1971-2001; mem. Occoquan watershed monitoring subcom. Va. State Water Control Bd., 1971—, chair, 1971-85, 2001-, vice chair, 1986-2001; US nat. com. Internat. Water Quality, 1976-88, chair 1986-88, mem. 1992 IAWQ Biennial Conf. Com., chair conf. arrangements, Washington; tng. grant cons. EPA, 1970-71; cons. to industry, 1969—; WHO cons. to Nat. Environ. Engring. Rsch. Inst. India, 1983-84; Va. gov. appointee sci. and tech. adv. com. Chesapeake Bay Program, 1984; mem. sci. and tech. adv. com. Chesapeake Bay Program, 1984-2006, chmn. 1993-97; nitrogen tech. adv. com. NYC Dept. Environ. Protection, 1994-2006; blue ribbon panel wastewater treatment City of Atlanta, 1997-2001; nitrogen removal tech. adv. com. mem., Water and Sewage Authority, Washington, 2006-2008. Author tech. papers in field; co-author: Biological Process Design for Wastewater Treatment, 1980, Stormwater Management in Urbanizing Areas, 1983, Design and Retrofit of Wastewater Treatment Plants for Biological Nutrient Removal, 1992. Troop com. chmn. Boy Scouts Am., 1978-82, chmn. dist. Camporee com., 1977; camp pres. Gideons Internat., 1976-78, 80, 95-97, 2008-, v.p., 2005-2008, state cabinet mem., 1985-88; vice moderator Highlands Bapt. Assn., 1980-81, moderator, 1982-83; bd. deacons Blacksburg Bapt. Ch., 1971-74, 79-82, chmn., 1974. Lt. U.S. Coast and Godetic Survey, 1959-62. Ford Found. fellow, 1964-65; recipient citation Engring. News-Record, 1988, Disting. Svc. award US nat. com. Internat. Assn. Water Quality, 1989, Salute to Excellence Gov. of Md., 1994, Alumni Pub. Svc. award Va. Tech., 1996, Mathias medal for sci. excellence Chesapeake Rsch. Consortium and the Sea Grant Offices of Md. and Va., 1996, Dean's award Excellence Pub. Svc., Va. Tech. Engring., 1997, Disting. Svc. award Assn. Environ. Engrs. and Scientists Profs., 1997; Lifetime Achievement award Va. Water Resources Ctr., 2006, Leadership award Va. Water Rsch. Ctr., 2006; named Conservationist of Yr. Chesapeake Bay Found., 1986; AEC trainee U. Tex., 1963-65. Mem. ASCE (elected disting. mem. 2008,; chmn. water resources mgmt. com. 1977, chmn. environ. engring. rsch. coun. 1989-90, svc. award 1978, 80, meritorious tech. paper award 1969), Am. Water Works Assn. (cert. recognition for acad. excellence 1980, 89), Water Environ. Fedn. (bd. dirs. 1981-84, Morgan cert. of merit for full scale rsch. 1982, Bedell award 1983, svc. award 1984, Gordon M. Fair medal for excellence in engring. edn. 1998), Internat. Water Assn. (nat. com., 1978-88, chair, 1986-88, governing bd. 1986-88, USA rep. on sci. and tech. com. 1994-98, mem. nutrient removal specialist group mgmt. com. 1990-2002, chmn. 1994-98), Va. Water Environment Assn. (v.p. 1974-75, pres. 1975-76), Assn. Environ. Engring. Profs. (sec.-treas. 1979-80, bd. dirs. 1978-80, 93-97, v.p. 1994-95, pres. 1995-96, past pres. 1996-97, Founders award, 2008, Lifetime Achievement award 2005). Home: 1302 Crestview Dr Blacksburg VA 24060-5609 Office: Va Tech Dept Civil and Environ Engring 418 Durham Hall Blacksburg VA 24061-0246 Office Phone: 540-231-6018. Business E-Mail: cliff@vt.edu.

RANDALL, DALE BERTRAND JONAS, English language educator; b. Cleveland Heights, Ohio, Mar. 18, 1929; s. Myron Welcome and Lettie Jane (Perrin) R.; m. Phyllis Rosanna Link, June 25, 1955; children: Lettie Rosanna, Kenneth Dale. BA, Western Res. U., 1951; MA, Rutgers U., 1953; PhD, U. Pa., 1958. Teaching asst. Rutgers U., New Brunswick, NJ, 1951-53, U. Pa., Phila., 1953-57; instr. Duke U., Durham, NC, 1957-60, asst. prof. of English, 1960-65, assoc. prof., 1965-70, prof., 1970—99, prof. dramatic lit., 1991-94, prof. practice theater arts, 1994—99, prof. emeritus English, theater studies, 1999—; interim dir. Duke Drama, 1991-92. Chmn. Southeastern Inst. of Medieval and Renaissance Studies, 1969-74, 75-76; chmn. Duke Ctr. for Medieval and Renaissance Studies, Durham, 1971-72, governing com., 1969-89, 93-97; mem. ctrl. exec. com. Folger Inst., Washington, 1983-92; assoc. trustee Chi Psi Ednl. Trust, 1994-96, trustee, 1996-2002. Author: The Golden Tapestry: A Critical Survey of Non-Chivalric Spanish Fiction in English Translation, 1963, Gentle Flame: The Life and Verse of Dudley, Fourth Lord North, 1983, Joseph Conrad and Warrington Dawson, 1968, Jonson's Gypsies Unmasked, 1975, Theatres of Greatness, 1986, Winter Fruit: English Drama 1642-1660, 1995, Soliloquy of a Farmer's Wife, 1999, Cervantes In Seventeenth-Century England, 2009; editor: Studies in the Continental Background of Renaissance English Literature, 1977, Medieval and Renaissance Studies, 1976-79, Renaissance Papers, 1984-91; also articles. Active Friends of Duke U. Libr., Friends of the Bodleian Libr. Recipient award Am. Philos. Soc., 1986, Alumni award Chi Psi, 1993; Guggenheim fellow, 1970-71, sr. fellow Folger Libr., 1978, 86, Southeastern Inst., 1978. Mem. MLA, Gypsy Lore Soc., Southeastern Renaissance Conf. (adv. coun. 1984-95, v.p. 1992-93, pres. 1993-94, chair adv. coun. 1994-95), Cervantes Soc. Am., Sixteenth Century Soc, Am. Culture Assn. Avocations: gardening, playreaders, antiques. Office: Duke U Dept English Box 90015 Durham NC 27708-0015 Business E-Mail: dbjandpr@duke.edu.

RANDALL, DAVID CLARK, medical educator, researcher; b. St. Louis, Apr. 23, 1945; s. Walter Clark and Gwendolyn Ruth (Niebel) R.; m. Lea Carol Wylder, Sept. 1, 1985; children: Christopher C., Matthew F., Benjamin W. BA, Taylor U., 1967; PhD, U. Wash., 1971. Asst. prof. divsn. behavioral biology Johns Hopkins U. Sch. Medicine, Balt., 1972-75; asst. prof. dept. physiology U. Ky., Lexington, 1975-78, assoc. prof., 1978-85, prof., 1985—2007, Donald T. Frazier endowed prof., 2007—. Instr. Asbury Coll., Wilmore, Ky., 1979—; vis. assoc. prof. dept. neurobiology and behavior SUNY, Stony Brook, 1981; dir. grad. studies dept. physiology and biophysics U. Ky., 1981-84, joint prof. grad. ctr. biomed. engring. 1987—, exec. com., 1990-92, chair faculty senate, 2008—. Co-author: Cardiopulmonary Physiology, 1998, 2005, ECG Interpretation, 2004. Active behavioral medicine br. NIH, Nat. Heart, Lung and Blood Inst., 1982—. Mem. Am. Heart Assn. (various coms., bd. chmn. Ky. affiliate 1994-96), Am. Physiol. Soc., Am. Sci. Affiliation, Fedn. Am. Socs. Exptl. Biology, Internat. Autonomic Soc., Internat. Soc. Gravitational Physiology, Christian Med. Dental Soc., Pavlovian Soc. Am. (exec. com. 1983—, pres. 1983), Soc. Neurosci. Avocations: amateur radio, orchard and bee keeping, regional history, horseback riding. Office: U Ky Coll Medicine Dept Physiology Lexington KY 40536-0298

RANDALL, DOUGLAS D., biochemist, educator; b. Cheyenne, Wyo. BS, SD State U., 1965; PhD, Mich. State U., 1970. With U. Mo.-Columbia, 1971—, prof. emeritus biochemistry, dir. interdisciplinary program on plant biochemistry-physiology, 1981—. Bd. dirs. Nat. Sci. Bd., 2002—; mem. Great Barrier Reef Photorespiration Expdn. Nat. Sci. Found., 1973. Mem. editl. bd. Plant Physiology, Annual Reviews Plant Physiology and Plant Molecular Biology, Protein Expression and Purification, Biochemical Archives, Current Topics in Plant Biochemistry and Physiology; contbr. articles to profl. jours. Recipient William H. Byler Disting. Prof. Award, U. Mo.-Columbia, Faculty/Alumni Award, Gold Chalk Teaching Award, Disting. Alumni Award, SD State U., Biochemistry Dept.'s Alumni Award, Mich. State. Fellow: Am. Soc. Plant Biologists (chmn. bd. trustees 1996—99); mem.: Am. Soc. of Plant Physiologists (sec. 1991—93, chmn. bd. trustess), Am. Chemical Soc., Am. Soc. Biol. Chemistry. Achievements include research in plant metabolism, signal transduction, regulation of plant enzymes and understanding the metabolic interations between photosynthesis, photorespiration and respiration. Office: U Mo Columbia Biochemistry Dept 117 Schweitzer Hall Office 213 Columbia MO 65211 Office Phone: 573-882-4847. Office Fax: 573-882-5635. Business E-Mail: randalld@missouri.edu.

RANDALL, FRANCES, technical writer; b. Frederick, Md., Oct. 6, 1924; d. George Birely and Ruth Carty Delaplaine; m. Myron William Randall, Apr. 10, 1949; children: George Elliott, Myron William Jr., Ruth Ann Randall, Eleanor Jane Randall Luttrell. BA, Hood Coll., 1945; MS, Johns Hopkins U., 1947; DHL (hon.), Hood Coll., 2006. Chemist U.S. Army Lab., Frederick, Md., 1947—49; writer-historian Frederick News-Post, 1965—. Chmn. bd. dirs. The Randall Family LLC, 2001—. Author: Mirror on Frederick, 1998, More Reflections on the History of Frederick, 2005 Bd. dir. Cmty. Found. Frederick County, 1988-96, Braddock Hts. Cmty. Assn.; past bd. dirs. Penn Laurel coun. Girl Scouts US. Recipient Cmty. Svc. award Ch. Transfiguration, Braddock Heights, Md., 1999, Thanks Badge, Penn Laurel Girl Scout Coun., 1988, Alumnae Achievement award Hood Coll., 1998, Woman of Distinction award Penn Laurel coun. Girl Scouts US, 2000, Families Plus! Cmty. Svc. award, 2004. Mem. DAR (Woman of Yr. in History, 2005), Hood Coll. Alumnae Assn. (pres., sec.), Frederick Woman's Civic Club (publicity chair, pres.), bd. trustees,Hood Coll, 1988-2000, Hist Soc. Frederick County (bd. dirs. 2005-, v.p. 2007—) Avocations: swimming, photography, travel, music. Home: 6301 Jefferson Blvd Frederick MD 21703-5809

RANDALL, FRANCIS BALLARD, retired historian, educator, writer; b. NYC, Dec. 17, 1931; s. John Herman, Jr. and Mercedes (Moritz) R.; m. Laura Regina Rosenbaum, June 11, 1957; children: David R., Ariane R. BA, Amherst Coll., 1952; MA, Columbia, 1954, PhD, 1960. Instr. history Amherst Coll., 1956-59; from instr. to asst. prof. history Columbia, 1959-61, vis. prof., 1967-68; humanities faculty Sarah Lawrence Coll., Bronxville, NY, 1961—2002, chmn., 1985—89, 1998—2001, trustee, 1971-76. Author: (with others) Essays in Russian and Soviet History, 1963, Stalin's Russia, an Historical Reconsideration, 1965, N.G. Chernyshevskii, 1967, Vissarion Belinskii, 1987, History Papers: A Teaching Life, 2000. Freedom rider civil disobedience to racism, 1961, war draft resistance arrests, 1967, 70. Fulbright fellow for study in India, 1965, Wye fellow, 1986. Mem.: AAUP (chpt. chmn. 1966—69), Am. Assn. for Advancement Slavic Studies, Am. Hist. Assn., Sigma Xi, Phi Beta Kappa. Home: 425 Riverside Dr Apt 10I New York NY 10025-7730

RANDALL, JANET ANN, biology professor, researcher; b. Twin Falls, Idaho, July 3, 1943; d. William Franklin and Bertha Silvia Orr; m. Bruce H. MacEvoy. BS, U. Idaho, Moscow, 1965; MEd, U. Wash., Seattle, 1969; PhD, Wash. State U., Pullman, 1977. Postdoctoral fellow U. Texas, Austin, 1977-79; from asst. to assoc. prof. biology Ctrl. Mo. State U., Warrensburg, 1979-87; assoc. prof. biology San Francisco State U., 1987-92, prof., 1992—2004, emeritus, 2004—. Vis. prof. Cornell U., Ithaca, N.Y., 1984-85. Contbr. articles to profl. jours. Rsch. grantee Nat. Geog. Soc., 1982, 86, 94, 96, NSF, 1984, 87, 88-89, 89-91, 91-93, 93-95, 97-00; Civilian R&D Found., 2000, 02, Alumni Achieve. award U. Idaho. Fellow Calif. Acad. Sci.; mem. Animal Behavior Soc. (mem. at large 1986-89, sec. 2005-08, editor 2008-), Am. Soc. Zoologists (program officer), Am. Soc. Mammalogists, Internat. Soc. Behavioral Ecology, Soc. Behavioral Neurobiology, Endangered Species Coalition (bd. mem.). Avocations: opera, travel, hiking. Office: San Francisco State U Dept Biology San Francisco CA 94132 Home: 862 Jonive Rd Sebastopol CA 95472-9567 Business E-Mail: jrandall@sfsu.edu.

RANDALL, KARL W., air transportation executive, lawyer; b. Mount Pleasant, Mich., Feb. 12, 1951; s. Herbert J. and Wilma E. (Worstell) R.; m. Natalie Kilmer Randall, Dec. 17, 1971; children: Adam B., Kara J. AA, Mich. Christian Coll., Rochester, 1971; BA, Oakland U., Rochester, 1977; JD, Wayne State U. Law Sch., Detroit, 1981. Bar: Mich., 1981, U.S. Dist. Ct., 1981, U.S. Ct. Appeals, 1983; cert. airport mgr., Mich., 1993. Quality contr. Staley SNO BOL Corp., Pontiac, Mich., 1971-72; engring. tech. Oakland Co. Drain Comm., Pontiac, 1972-83; sr. asst. corp. counsel Oakland County Corp. Counsel, Pontiac, 1983-93; mgr. aviation Oakland County Internat. Airport, Waterford, Mich., 1993—. Dir. Integrity Jour., Mt. Pleasant, 1980-98, Oakland County Coord. Child Care Coun., Waterford, 1992-97. Author, editor: (religious jour.) Integrity, 1982, 94-95. Mem. Rep. Com. Oakland County, 1988—, Exec. Club Oakland County, 1993—. Mem. Mich. Assn. Airport Execs. (exec., pres., 2005-2006), Langsford Men's Chorus. Republican. Mem. Ch. of Christ. Avocations: physical fitness, motorcycling, jogging, golf, piano. Office: Oakland County Internat Airport 6500 Highland Rd Waterford MI 48327-1607 Office Phone: 248-666-3900.

RANDALL, KAY TEMPLE, accountant, retired real estate agent; b. Chattanooga, Sept. 23, 1952; d. James H. Temple and Hortense N. (Dailey) Goodner; m. Gary F. Goodner, Feb. 9, 1968 (div. July 1972); 1 child, Jeffrey F. Goodner; m. Rodney B. Randall, Oct. 3, 1987. Student, Chattanooga State Coll., 1970-77, 82-83, Am. Inst. Banking, 1977-79. Lic. real estate agt., Tenn., ret.; notary public, Tenn. Ins. rep. Colonial Life Accident and Health, Columbia, SC, 1980-82; real estate appraiser, agt. Chattanooga, 1983-88; acct. Mr. Transmission of Chattanooga, Inc., 1987—; real estate agt. Chattanooga, 1989—. Adminstrv. asst. to legal profession, Chattanooga, 1972-75. Adv. bd. United Meth. Ch., Chattanooga, 1979-82, tchr., 1979-83; fellow cen. br. YMCA, Chattanooga, 1977-97. Fellow Walden's Club. Republican. Episcopalian. Avocation: collecting art. Home: 1858 Rivergate Ter Soddy Daisy TN 37379-5947 Office: Mr Transmission of Chattanooga Inc PO Box 1395 Soddy Daisy TN 37384-1395 E-mail: rodkayj@aol.com.

RANDALL, KENNETH C., dean, law educator; JD, Hofstra U., 1981; MA, Yale U., 1982, Columbia U., 1985, PhD, 1988. Practice law Simpson Thacher & Bartlett, NYC, 1982-84; faculty mem. U. Ala. Sch. Law, Tuscaloosa, 1985—, vice dean, 1989-93, dean, 1993—, Thomas E. McMillan prof. law, spl. counsel to the pres. Author: Federal Courts and the International Human Rights Paradigm, 1990; contbr. articles to law jours. and revs. W. Bayard Cutting Jr. fellow internat. law, Columbia U. Sch. Law, 1984—85. Office: U Ala Law Sch PO Box 870382 Tuscaloosa AL 35487-0001 Office Phone: 205-348-5117. E-mail: krandall@law.ua.edu.*

RANDALL, LILIAN MARIA CHARLOTTE, museum curator; b. Berlin, Feb. 1, 1931; came to U.S., 1938; d. Frederick Henry and Elizabeth Agnes (Ziegler) Cramer; m. Richard Harding Randall, Apr. 11, 1953; children: Christopher, Julia, Katharine. BA cum laude, Mount Holyoke Coll., 1950; MA, Radcliffe Coll., 1951, PhD, 1955; LHD (hon.), Towson State U., 1993; D of Arts (hon.), Mt. Holyoke Coll., 1998. Asst. dir. Md. State Arts Coun., 1972-73; curator manuscripts and rare books Walters Art Gallery, Balt., 1974-85, rsch. curator manuscripts, 1985-95; rsch. cons., 1995-97. Vis. lectr. dept. art history Johns Hopkins U., 1964-68; hon. vis. lectr. U. Mich., Ann Arbor; lectr. in field; bd. dirs. Digital Scriptorium: Electronic Access to Medieval Manuscripts; advisor Union Manuscript Computer Catalogue, 1996—. Author: Images in the Margins of Gothic Manuscripts, 1966; co-editor: Gatherings in Honor of Dorothy Miner, 1974, The Diary of George A. Lucas: An American Art Agent in Paris, 1909-1957, 1979, Illuminated Manuscripts: Masterpieces in Miniature, 1984, Medieval and Renaissance Manuscripts in the Walters Art Gallery, Vol. I, France, 875-1420, 1989, Vol. II, France, 1420-1540, 1992, Vol. III, Belgium, 1250-1530, 1997; contbr. articles to profl. jours. Mem. Williston Libr. com., 1988-89; reviewer, panelist NEH, 1980. Grantee AAUW, 1953-54, ACLS, 1960, 65, Bunting Inst., 1961-63, Ford Found., 1967-69, Am. Philos. Soc., 1971, NEA, 1975, Samuel H. Kress Found., 1979, 81-84, NEH, 1977-84, 89-95; grantee publ. subsidy Md. State Arts Coun., 1972, Mcpl. Art Soc. Balt., 1972, Andrew W. Mellon Found., 1988, Getty Grant program, 1990-92, NEA Mus. program, 1992-93; recipient Festschrift, Walters Art Gallery, ed. Elizabeth Burin, 1996, Sesquicentennial award Mount Holyoke Coll., 1987. Fellow Medieval Acad. Am. (libr. preservation com., various coms. 1985-87, 90-93, 2004—); mem. Internat. Ctr. Medieval Art (bd. dir. 1978-82, 96-99, mem. com. 2004—), Coll. Art Assn. (Arthur Kingsley Porter prize 1957), Balt. Bibliophiles (bd. dir. 1966-80, pres. 1980-83), Pyramid Atlantic (bd. dir. 1985-88), Mus. Fine Arts Boston (vis. com. Art of Europe dept. 2002-, adv. bd. Manuscripta 2004—), Grolier Club, Phi Beta Kappa. Home: 370 Adams St Milton MA 02186-4233 Personal E-mail: lrandall370@comcast.net.

RANDALL, LINDA LEA, biochemist, educator; b. Montclair, NJ, Aug. 7, 1946; d. Lowell Neal and Helen (Watts) Randall; m. Gerald Lee Hazelbauer, Aug. 29, 1970. BS, Colo. State U., 1968; PhD, U. Wis., 1971. Postdoctoral fellow Inst. Pasteur, Paris, 1971—73; asst. prof. Uppsala (Sweden) U., 1975—81; assoc. prof. Wash. State U., Pullman, 1981—83, prof. biochemistry, 1983—2000; Wurdock prof. biochemistry U. Mo., Columbia, 2000—. Guest scientist Wallenberg Lab. Uppsala U., 1973—75; mem. study sect. NIH, 1984—88. Contbr. articles to profl. jours.; co-editor: (book) Virus Receptors Part I, 1980; mem. editl. bd.: Jour. Bacteriology, 1982—96. Recipient Eli Lilly award in Microbiology and Immunology, 1984, Faculty Excellence Award in Rsch., Wash. State U., 1988, Parke-Davis award, 1995. Fellow: AAAS, Am. Acad. Arts and Scis., Am. Acad. Microbiology; mem.: NAS, Protein Soc., Am. Soc. Biol. Chemists, Am. Microbiological Soc. Avocation: dance. Office: Univ Mo Dept Biochemistry 117 Schweitzer Hall Columbia MO 65211 Home Phone: 573-449-2042; Office Phone: 573-884-4160.

RANDALL, LISA, physics professor; b. June 18, 1962; BA in Physics, Harvard U., 1983, PhD in Particle Physics, 1987. Pres.'s fellow U. Calif., Berkeley, 1987—89; postdoctoral fellow Lawrence Berkeley Lab., 1989—90; jr. fellow Harvard Soc. Fellows, 1990—91; asst. prof. physics MIT, 1991—95, assoc. prof., 1995—98, prof., 1998—2001, Princeton U., 1998—2000, Harvard U., 2001—; fellow Radcliffe Inst., 2002; chair Radcliffe Inst. Cosmology & Theoretical Astrophysics Cluster, 2003. Contbr. articles to sci. jours. and popular publs., chapters to books; editor: Jour. High Energy Physics, 1997—98, 2000—06, Ann. Rev. Nuc. and Particle Sci., 1997—2000; assoc. editor: Nuc. Physics B, 1999—; author: Warped Passages: Unraveling the Mysteries of the Universe's Hidden Dimensions, 2005; featured in Vogue Mag., 2007. Recipient Young Investigator award, NSF, 1992, Outstanding Jr. Investigator award, Dept. Energy, 1992, Premio Caterina Tomassoni e Felice Pietro Chisesi award, U. Rome, 2003, Klopsteg award, Am. Assn. Physics Tchrs., 2006, Elizabeth A. Wood award, Am. Crystallographic Assn., 2007; named a Sci. Icon, Seed Mag., 2005; named one of The World's Most Influential People, TIME mag., 2007; named to Who's Next in 2006, Newsweek; grantee Alfred P. Sloan Found. Rsch.

fellowship, 1992. Fellow: Am. Phys. Soc. (Julius Edgar Lilienfeld prize 2007), Am. Acad. Arts & Scis. Office: Dept Physics Harvard U 17 Oxford St Cambridge MA 02138 Office Phone: 617-496-8188. E-mail: randall@physics.harvard.edu.

RANDALL, MARILYN MAE, writer; d. Dice A. and Margaret L. Hartman; m. Charles D. Randall, Aug. 24, 1991; children: Philip E. Marechal, Cheryl L. Pittman. BA magna cum laude, Trinity Coll., Washington, 1988. Registrar Va. Theol. Sem., 1974—87; bus. mgr. St. Margaret's Episcopal Ch., 1987—89; bus. owner, 1989—95. Vis. author/lectr. various elem. and mid. schs. across US, 2002—; featured lectr./workshop presenter Christian Writers' Conf., Memphis, 2002, 06, Ea. Tenn. State U. Celebration Books and Authors, 2004; featured local author Fall for the Book George Mason U., 2004; workshop presenter; contest judge Life Press, 2006. Author: (children's books) Southern Christmas, 2001, Wishes for Christmas, 2002, Wellington's Windows, 2003, The Three Wives of Hero the Second, 2004, The Meanie, 2006, Razzle Dazzler, 2007, Sweetwater Village, 2008, Bears Don't Snore, 2009, A Marine Salute (endorsed by USMC and Young Marine Orgn.); editor: The Forty Days of Lent; composer, lyricist: Angel with an Attitude, 2004. Pres. Good Samaritan chpt. Daus. of the King, Knoxville, 1998—2004; spkr. DAR Meeting, Lawrenceburg, Tenn., 2006. Mem.: Alpha Sigma Lambda, Phi Beta Kappa. Episcopalian. Avocations: composing, poetry. Home: 1550 Scenic View Dr Loudon TN 37774 Personal E-mail: mmrandall@hughesnet.com.

RANDALL, NEIL WARREN, gastroenterologist; b. White Plains, NY, Mar. 24, 1957; s. Leroy Bruce and Libby Cynthia (Brandt) R.; m. Linda Ilene Zell, Oct. 31, 1992. BA, U. Va., 1978; MD, U. Md., 1983. Diplomate Am. Bd. Internal Medicine with subspecialty in gastroenterology, geriat. Resident in internal medicine Ochsner Clinic, New Orleans, 1983-86; fellow in gastroenterology Tufts U., Boston, 1986-88; staff gastroenterologist Cleve. Clinic Fla., Fort Lauderdale, 1988-92, Geisinger Clinic, Danville, Pa., 1992-97, Pa. State Geisinger Health Sys., Danville, 1997-98; med. dir. gastrointestinal endoscopy Geisinger Health Sys., 1999-2000; gastroenterologist Gastroenterology Group of Naples, 2001—. Fellow ACP, Am. Coll. Gastroenterology; mem. Am. Soc for Gastroent. Endoscopy. Avocations: theater, travel, wine. Office: Gasterenterology Group of Naples 1064 Goodlette-Frank Rd Naples FL 34102-5449 Office Phone: 239-649-1186.

RANDALL, PETER, retired plastic surgeon; b. Phila., Mar. 29, 1923; s. Alexander and Edith Tilghman (Kneedler) R.; m. Rose Gordon Johnson, May 1, 1948; children: Deborah K., Peter G., Julia B., Susanna T. BA, Princeton U., 1944; MD, Johns Hopkins U., 1946; MS (hon.), U. Pa., 1969. Diplomate Am. Bd. Plastic Surgery. Intern Union Meml. Hosp., Balt., 1946—47; asst. resident in surgery Hosp. of U. of Pa., Phila., 1949—50; fellow in plastic surgery Barnes Hosp.-St. Louis Childrens Hosp., 1950—52, resident in plastic surgery, 1952—53; asst. instr. plastic surgery Washington U., St. Louis, 1950—53; from asst. prof. to assoc. prof. plastic surgery U. Pa. Hosp., Phila., 1953—69, prof. plastic surgery, 1969—, emeritus prof. plastic surgery; chief div. plastic surgery sch. medicine U. Pa., Phila., 1979—87; ret., 1994. Sr. surgeon Children's Hosp. Phila., 1965—. Contbr. articles to profl. jours. Pres. Plastic Surgery Edn. Found., 1972-73. Lt. (j.g.) USNR, 1947-49. Fellow: ACS (bd. govs., chmn. 1982—84, 1st v.p. 1985—86), Am. Assn. Plastic Surgeons (hon. Clinician of Yr. award 1987, disting. fellow 1994); mem.: AMA, Am. Cleft Palate Assn. (pres. 1965—66, Honors award 1986), Plastic Surgery Rsch. Coun. (founder, chmn. 1964—65), Phila. Acad. Surgery, Phila. County Med. Soc., Northea. Soc. Plastic Surgery (founder), Am. Surg. Assn., Coll. Physicians of Phila., Am. Soc. Plastic Surgeons (pres. 1978—79, Spl. Achievement award 1987), Am. Bd. Plastic Surgery (vice-chmn. 1976—77), Am. Cleft Palate Ednl. Found. (founder, pres. 1972—73), Robert H. Ivy Soc. (founder, pres. 1966—67), Halsted Soc., Sigma Xi.

RANDALL, RICHARD J., academic administrator; BA, U. Maine, 1966, MA, 1967, LLD, 2004. Instr. sociology U. Maine at Augusta, 1967, asst. prof., assoc. prof., prof., dir. student affairs, 1968—71, dean student affairs and ednl. svcs., 1971—78, acting dean, 1984—85, dean, 1985—87, provost, 1989—93, provost, v.p. academic affairs, 1993—2001, interim assoc. provost, 2005, interim pres., 2005—06, pres., 2006—. Office: U Maine at Augusta Off of Pres 46 University Dr Augusta ME 04330-9410 Office Phone: 207-621-3403. Office Fax: 207-621-3496. E-mail: rrandall@maine.edu.

RANDALL, RICHARD RAINIER, geographer; b. Toledo, July 21, 1925; s. Robert Henry and Maree (Gard) R.; m. Patricia Lee Spencer, June 9, 1962; children: Allison Maree, Susan Rebecca, Richard Rainier Jr. BA, George Washington U., 1949, MA, 1950; PhD, Clark U., 1955. Fulbright scholar Graz U., Austria, 1953—54; Geog. analyst CIA, Washington, 1955-61; Washington rep. Rand McNally & Co., Washington, 1961-72; owner Randall Assocs., Washington, 1972-73; exec. sec. U.S. Bd. Geog. Names, Washington, 1973-93; geographer Def. Mapping Agy., Washington, 1973-93; ret., 1993; cons. on geog. names, 1993—. Convenor UN Working Group on Undersea and Maritime Feature Names, 1975-84; mem., prin. U.S. tech. advisor U.S. and U.K. Conf. on Geog. Names, 1976, 79, 81, 84, 86, 88, 92; dep. head U.S. del. UN Conf. on Geog. Names, 1977, head, 1982, 87, 92; 1st v.p. of 6th UN Conf. 92; prin. U.S. expert UN Group Experts on Geog. Names, 1975, 77, 79, 82, 84, 86, 87, 89, 92; pres. com. on geog. terminology Pan Am. Inst. Geography and History, 1973-77, pres. working group on geog. names and gazetters, 1981-94. Author: Place Names: How they Define the World—And More, 2001; contbr. articles to profl. jours.; inventor flexible fishhook. V.p. North Cleveland Park Citizens Assn., Washington, 1968. With U.S. Army, 1943-46, ETO. Decorated ETO ribbon with 4 battle stars, Bronze Star, Combat Infantryman's badge; recipient Pioneer Achievement award United Black Christians Region III United Ch. Christ, 1994, Named to Hall Fame Nat. Geospatial Intelligence Agency, 2009. Mem. Am. Congress on Surveying and Mapping (dir. cartography divsn. 1973-75, dir. press rels. 1961-72, program dir. cartography divsn. ann. meeting 1967), Am. Geog. Soc., Assn. Am. Geographers (chmn. Mid-Atlantic divsn. 1978, dir. press rels. ann. conf. 1968), Am. Names Soc., Am. Austrian Soc. (v.p. 1955-57), Explorers Club (Washington group steering com., 2001-2008), Nat. Press Club, Cosmos Club. Republican. Home Phone: 202-966-8354.

RANDALL, ROBERT L(EE), ecological economist; b. Aberdeen, SD, Dec. 28, 1936; s. Harry Eugene and Juanita Alice (Barstow) Randall. MS in Phys. Chemistry, U. Chgo., 1960, MBA, 1963. Market devel. chemist E.I. du Pont de Nemours & Co., Inc., Wilmington, Del., 1963-65; chem. economist Battelle Meml. Inst., Columbus, Ohio, 1965-68; mgr. market and econ. rsch. Kennecott Copper Corp., NYC, 1968-74, economist, 1974-79, dir. new bus. venture devel., 1979-81; pres., mng. dir. R.L. Randall Assocs., Inc., 1981—; economist U.S. Internat. Trade Commn., Washington, 1983—. Founder, pres., exec. dir. RainForest ReGeneration Inst., 1986—, ind. internat. press corr., 1997—, indsl. panel policy rev. of effect of regulation on innovation and U.S.-internat. competition U.S. Dept. Commerce, 1980-81; participant preparatory com. UN Conf. on Environ. and Devel., Rio de Janeiro, 1991; del. observer internat. negotiating com. UN Framework Conv. on Climate Change, 1991—. Contbg. author: Computer Methods for the 80's; sect. lead author, editor: World Energy Assessment, 2000; pub. reviewer intergovtl. panel on climate change Third Assessment Report; addresser 4th Internat. Greenhouse Gas Tech. conf., Interlaken, Switzerland, 1998; contbr. articles to profl. jours. Mem. Gay Activists Alliance, N.Y.C., 1971-75, chmn. state and fed. legislation com., 1975. Mem. AAAS (organizer ann. meeting, Tropical Forest Regeneration Symposium), AIME (econ. coun., mineral econ. subsect.), Internat. Soc. Ecol. Health, Internat. Soc. Ecol. Economists, Am. Econ. Assn., Am. Statis. Assn., Am. Chem. Soc., Soc. Mining Engrs., Chemists Club of N.Y.C., Metall. Soc., N.Y. Acad. Scis., Nat. Econs. Club Washington (sec., reporter), Assn. Environ. and Resource Economists, Marine Biol. Assn. (Plymouth, Eng.), Wanderbirds Hiking Club (hike leader, treas.), Capital Hiking Club (hike leader, Washington). Home: 1727 Massachusetts Ave NW Washington DC 20036-2153 Office: US Internat Trade Com 500 E St SW Washington DC 20436-0003 E-mail: randall@usitc.gov. *Like thousands of organizations around the world, The RainForest ReGeneration Institute is trying to find a practical and effective way forward, through United Nations-sponsored treaty negotiations, appropriate national actions, and imaginative project work, on the ground, in local communities. Tropical rainforests must have recognizable community value if they are to be viable. Global value is not enough for the conservation of the tropical rainforests. Ultimate wisdom does not reside in any individual or organization. All must work together through every available forum and mechanism, and to create new modalities where those presently in existence are inadequate or ineffective.*

RANDALL, WILLARD STERNE, biographer, historian; b. Phila., Mar. 13, 1942; s. Leslie Fairbanks and Joan (Shepherd) R.; BA, Thomas Edison Coll., 1982; MA in History, Princeton U., 1984; m. Mary Anne Hogan, Jan. 23, 1965 (div.); children: Christopher Fairbanks, Maryann, Alice Amanda; m. Nancy A. Nahra, Oct. 19, 1985; 1 child, Lucy. Reporter, Pottstown (Pa.) Mercury, 1960-61; reporter Mainland Jour., Pleasantville, N.J., 1966; editor, feature writer Phila. Evening and Sunday Bulletin, 1966-71; investigative reporter Phila. mag., 1971-72; corr. Time-Life News Service, Phila., 1972-73; freelance writer, Ocean City, N.J., 1973-80; lectr. in history U. Vt., 1984-94, vis. prof. history, John Cabot U., Rome, 1994—; prof. history Champlain Coll., Burlington, Vt., 1998-. Mem. Ocean City Bd. Edn., 1978-80, Burlington (Vt.) Library Bd., 1985-92. Recipient Nat. Mag. award public service Columbia Grad. Sch. Journalism, 1972, Best Story of Year award Standard Gravure Assn., also Sidney Hillman Found. award, John Hancock award and Gerald Loeb award, 1976, research prize U. Mo. Grad. Sch. Journalism, 1985, medal Soc. Colonial Wars, 1986, Fraunces Tavern Book award, Colonial Dames Best Book, Am. Rev. Round Table Best Book, 1990, Award of Merit, 2002. Mem. N.Y. Acad. Sci., N.Y. Authors Guild. Author: Journalist, 1975; (with others, also sr. editor) The Founding City, 1976; The Proprietary House in Amboy, 1975, rev. edit., 1990; (with others) Building 6, 1977; A Little Revenge: Benjamin Franklin and his Son, 1985, Benedict Arnold: Patriot and Traitor, 1990, Thomas Jefferson, A Life, 1993, George Washington, A Life, 1997, Alexander Hamilton: A Life, 2003, (with others) American Lives, 1996, Forgotten Americans, 1998,; contbg. author various books; contbr. articles to profl. publs. Office: Deborah Grosvenor Kneerim and Williams Lit Agy 1425 K St NW Ste 1100 Washington DC 20005 Office Phone: 802-922-0088. Business E-Mail: randall@champlain.edu.

RANDAZZO, BEVERLY PAULINA, retired assistant principal; b. New Orleans, Sept. 5, 1933; d. Simon James and Mildred Ary Paulina; m. Michael Randazzo, Feb. 9, 1994 (dec.); m. Ronald Jones, Apr. 19, 1953 (dec.); 1 child, Bethany Jones Gonski; m. Anthony Gambino, July 14, 1965 (dec.); 1 child, Toni Gambino Hanson. B in Elem. Edn., U. New Orleans, 1964, M in Ednl. Adminstrn., 1974. Tchr. New Orleans Pub. Schs., 1964—82, asst. principal, 1982—95; ret., 1995. Supr. coll. student tchrs. U. New Orleans, 1978, grad. asst., 79; adminstrv. cons. New Orleans Pub. Schs., 1980. Contbr. parent newsletters, flyers on child mgmt. techniques. Planner in-svc. programs New Orleans Pub. Schs., mem. superintendent's leadership team, coord. Chpt. I parent workshops, 1981; dir. Bicentennial program, 1976. Recipient Outstanding Woman award, AARP Chpt. 4417, Outstanding Svc. and Leadership award, La. Ret. Tchrs. Assn., 2004. Mem.: New Orleans Ret. Tchrs. Assn. (pres. 2002—05, Mem. of the Yr. award 2005), East Jefferson Hosp. Aux. (bd. dirs. 2007—), Republican Woman's Club of Jefferson Parish (bd. dirs. 2002—08, Betty Heitman award 2005, 2007). Republican. Avocations: reading, dance, travel.

RANDAZZO, MARISA R., psychologist; d. Hilary Phillip and Susan Hilborn Reddy; m. Robert Salvatore Randazzo, May 15, 2004. BA in Psychology and Religion, Williams Coll., 1989; MA in Psychology, Princeton U., 1993, PhD in Psychology, 1995. Chief rsch. psychologist US Secret Svc., Washington, 1996—2004; sr. expert Bus. Intelligence Advisors, Boston, 2004—06; pres. Threat Assessment Resources Internat., Reno, 2006—. Editl. bd. Jour. Threat Assessment, 2001—. Recipient Recognition award, US Secret Svc., 1998—2004, Bicentennial Medal Recipient, Williams Coll., 2005; fellow, Soc. Psychol. Study Social Issues, Washington, 1995—96. Mem.: APA, Am. Psychology-Law Soc. (program chair 1998—2000). Achievements include research in American school shooters; preventing violence in schools; co-authoring a federal model of school threat assessment credited in the media and law enforcement with preventing school attacks. Office Fax: 775-424-6687. Business E-Mail: mrr@threatresources.com.

RANDEL, DON MICHAEL, foundation administrator, former academic administrator, musicologist; b. Dec. 9, 1940; m. Carol Randel; children: Amy Elizabeth Keating, Julia, Emily Catherine Pershing, Sally Randel Eggert. AB magna cum laude, Princeton U., NJ, 1962, MFA in Music, 1964, PhD in Music, 1967. Asst. prof., dept. fine arts Syracuse U., NY, 1966—68; asst. prof. music Cornell U., Ithaca, NY, 1968—71, assoc. prof. music, 1971—75, prof. music, 1975—90, Given Found. prof. musicology, 1990—2000, chair dept. music, 1971—76, vice provost, 1978—79, assoc. dean Coll. Arts & Scis., 1989—91, Harold Tanner dean Coll. Arts & Scis., 1991—95, provost, 1995—2000; pres. U. Chgo., 2000—06, Andrew W. Mellon Found., NYC, 2006—. V.p. Am. Musicological Soc., 1977—78; mem. adv. com., dept. music Princeton U., 1987—99; mem. Penn Nat. Commn. Soc., Culture & Cmty., 1996—99; bd. govs. Argonne Nat. Lab., Ill., 2000—; bd. dirs. Chgo. Coun. Fgn. Rels., 2001, CNA Fin. Corp., 2002—. Editor: New Harvard Dictionary of Music, 1986, Harvard Biographical Dictionary of Music, 1996, Harvard Concise Dictionary of Music and Musicians, 1999, The Harvard Dictionary of Music, 2003; editor-in-chief Jour. Am. Musicological Soc., 1972—74, mem. editl. bd. Ency. Britannica. Bd. trustees Chgo. Symphony Orch. Assn., 2001—06; bd. dirs. Lyric Opera Chgo., 2004—06. Recipient Academic Leadership award, Carnegie Corp. NY, 2005; Danforth Grad. fellow, 1962—66. Fellow: Am. Acad. Arts & Scis.; mem.: AAAS, Modern Language Assn., Am. Musicological Soc., Am. Philos. Soc. Office: Andrew W Mellon Found 140 E 62nd St New York NY 10021 Office Phone: 212-838-8400. Office Fax: 212-500-2302.*

RANDELL, CORTES W., news service executive; b. Washington, 1935; m. Joan. V. (Wirz) 1968; children: Cortes John, Christina Alexis. BSME, U. Va., 1959; student, Darden Sch., U. Va., 1962. Engr. Gen. Electric, N.Y., 1959-61, Internat. Telephone & Telegraph, Chgo., 1962-64; pres. Nat. Student Mktg., N.Y., 1964-71; cons. and trustee Washington Trust, 1972-84; pres. Federal News Svc., Washington, 1985—2002; mcht. banker, 2002—. Author: Taking the Stand, Testimony of Oliver North, 1987, The National Press Club's Best Contemporary Speakers, 1995. Mem. Nat. Press Club. Avocations: boating, ballooning. Office: 9017 Swift Creek Rd Fairfax Station VA 22039-2815 E-mail: cort.randell@cox.net.

RANDI, JAMES (RANDALL JAMES HAMILTON ZWINGE), magician, educator; b. Toronto, Aug. 7, 1928; naturalized U.S. citizen, 1987; s. George Randall and Marie Alice (Paradis) Zwinge. Student, Oakwood Collegiate Inst., Toronto, 1940-45; LittD (hon.), U. Indpls., 1995. Internationally known conjuror, lectr., author, investigator. Regent's lectr. UCLA, 1984; skeptical lectr. on paranormal subjects. Author: The Magic of Uri Geller, 1975 (with Bert Sugar) Houdini, His Life and Art, 1978, Flim-Flam, 1982, Test Your ESP Potential, 1983, The Faith Healers, 1987, The Magic World of the Amazing Randi, 1989, The Mask of Nostradamus, 1990, James Randi: Psychic Investigator, 1991, Conjuring, 1992, An Encyclopedia of Claims, Frauds, and Hoaxes of the Occult and Supernatural, 1995 (English, Chinese, French, Italian, German, Japanese, Korean, Norwegian, Punjabi, Polish and Spanish edits.); host TV spls. Japan, Korea, UK. Recipient Blackstone award Internat. Platform Assn., 1983, 87, Forum award Am. Phys. Soc., 1988, Nat. Consumer Svc. award Nat. Coun. Against Health Fraud, 1988, Gold medal U. Ghent, Belgium, 1989, Humanist Disting. Svc. award Am. Humanist Assn., 1990, medal with golden wreath Hungarian Soc. for Dissemination of Scientific Knowledge, 1992; MacArthur Found. fellow Inner Magic Cir., London 1986, Spl. fellow Acad. Magical Arts and Scis., 1987; inducted into Soc. Am. Magicians Hall of Fame, 1988. Founding fellow Com. for Scientific Investigation of Claims of the Paranormal (exec. bd. dirs. 1973-91). Achievements include performing at White House, 1974. Home: 12000 NW 8th St Fort Lauderdale FL 33325-1406 Office: James Randi Ednl Found 201 SE 12th St Fort Lauderdale FL 33316-1815 Office Phone: 954-467-1112. Personal E-mail: randi@randi.org. *Well into the third millennium, we still have "Creation Science," "faith healing," and other such mythological notions embraced and promoted by the media- and thus accepted by the uncritical public. Charlatans who claim to "speak to the dead" have become TV stars, promoters of quack medicine and spurious "Ponzi-style" financial scams have firm control of late-night broadcasting, and yet state and federal agencies sit by and watch the American dream turning into a multidimensional nightmare- and they just don't care.Our media feed on the grief and vulnerability of citizens who are deceived and swindled by con artists; whether what they present to viewers/readers is true, matters not at all. Their bottom line is sponsor satisfaction and the resultant approval of Upstairs executives. The naive notions of research and fact-checking are - to them- old-fashioned and no-longer-needed principles from long-forgotten classroom days. Money speaks louder to them; compassion, truth, and ethics are unheard. The acceptance of medieval notions and the increasingly popular sport of science bashing threaten our intellectual survival and our place in world society. Reaching out to our youth and developing in them a renewed respect and understanding for real science and rationality must take place before we slide further down the evolutionary scale. Acceptance of "politically correct" and "faith-based" standards, and of unquestioning belief in obviously crackpot theories, have brought us to this crisis in education. We need to adopt higher standards for our young people in respect to critical thinking, and encourage them to question the claims of the quacks and the scam artists. A one-million dollar prize offered by our Foundation for the last 10 years now, for evidence of any paranormal power, for any supernatural phenomenon and for any "occult" or "magical" event, is still unclaimed Why? Because the charlatans who bend spoons (?) talk to ghosts, and prescribe useless remedies, flourish unchecked- though hardly unchallenged. We invite them to take the prize.*

RANDIC, MILAN, retired chemistry professor; b. Belgrade, Serbia, Oct. 1, 1930; s. Dinko and Olga Randic; m. Mirjana Jovic, Oct. 8, 1960; 1 child, Velimir. PhD, Cambridge U., Eng., 1958. Rsch. scientist Inst. Rudjer Boskovic, Zagreb, Croatia, 1959—64; prof. U. Zagreb, 1964—71. Disting. prof. Drake U., Des Moines, 1980—2000. Contbr. articles to profl. publs. (City of Zagreb Sci. award, 1966, Govt. of Iowa Sci. award, 1990, Skolnik award Am. Chem. Soc., 1996). Compulsory regrut Atomic Biology Chem. warfare Yugoslav Army, 1958—59. Fellow: Inst. Acad. Math. Chemistry (v.p. 2005—07), Croatian Chem. Soc.; mem.: Croatian Acad. Scis. and Arts. Achievements include research in application of mathematics to chemistry. Home: 3225 Kingman Rd Ames IA 50014 Home Fax: 515-292-8629. Personal E-mail: mrandic@msn.com.

RANDIC, MIRJANA, retired neurologist; b. Ogulin, Croatia, Oct. 12, 1934; d. Stevan Jovic and Mileva Vujnovic; m. Milan Randic; 1 child, Velimir. MD, U. Zagreb, Croatia, PhD, 1959. Rschr. Inst. Rudjer Boskovic, Zagreb, 1959—62; vis. scholar Inst. Animal Physiology, Cambridge, England, 1962—64; asst. prof. Sch. Medicine, McGill U., Montreal, Canada, 1964—65; vis. lectr. Med. Sch., U. Edinburgh, 1968; assoc. prof. Tufts U. Sch. Medicine, Boston, 1972—75; prof. Iowa State U., Ames, 1977—2007; vis. prof. U. Heidelberg, Germany, 1978; sr. internat. fellow fogarty ctr. NIH U. London, 1985, Nat. Inst. Physiol. Sci., Okazaki, Japan, 1986; vis. scientist Med. Coll., U. Utah, Salt Lake City. Grant, NSF, 1973—2005, NIH, 1973—96, Merck Inst. Therapeutic Rsch., 1973, Tafts U., 1973—75, Multiple Sclerosis, 1974, Iowa State U. Rsch. Found., 1977—2003, USDA, 1979—89, Spinal Cord Rsch. Found., 1997—2001, Christopher Reeve Paralysis Found., 2001—03. Office: Retired Iowa State Univ Ames IA 50011 Personal E-mail: mrandic@iastate.edu.

RANDINELLI, TRACEY ANNE, magazine editor; b. Morristown, NJ, Apr. 6, 1963; d. Andrew R. and Patricia Ann (Brenner) Randinelli. BA in Comm., U. Del., 1985. Copywriter Macy's N.J., Newark, 1985-86; editl. asst. Globe Comms. Corp., NYC, 1986-87; from asst. editor to assoc. editor Scholastic Math and DynaMath Mags. Scholastic, Inc., NYC, 1987-89, editor Scholastic Math Mag., 1989-95; mng. editor Zig Zag Mag. Games Pub. Group, NYC, 1995; sr. editor Contact Kids Mag./Sesame Workshop, NYC, 1996-2001; freelance writer, 2001—02; sr. editor Pearson Learning Group, 2002—04, supervising editor, 2004—07; project mgr. Tighe Publishing Svcs., 2007—. Mem. Soc. Children's Book Writers, Ednl. Press Assn. Am. (Disting. Achievement award feature articles divsn. 1991, 95, coverdesign 1996, how-to feature divsn. 1998, 99). Personal E-mail: pen4kidz@aol.com.

RANDLE, BERNADETTE, musician, composer, graphics designer; b. St. Louis, Jan. 8, 1947; d. William George Randle and Louise Robinmae Randle-Ware. BA summa cum laude, Concordia U. Wis., 1993; MA, Lindenwood U., 1994. Dir. employment programs YMCA of Greater St. Louis, 1980—83; freelance studio musician Platinum Chess Record, Englewood, NJ, 1983—86; office clk. Def. Contract Audit Agy. & HUD,

St. Louis, 1986—87; mktg. specialist Tailored Software Corp., Maryland Heights, Mo., 1987—89; graphic illustrator The Bionetics Corp., St. Louis, 1989—97; concept developer/tech. writer Bus. Blueprints, St. Louis, 1997—2000; composer, arranger ReMembered/The Gozz Ensemble; creative dir. Prosit Media Group; min. music Third United Presbyn. Ch., St. Louis. Mktg. cons. The Enterprise Found., St. Louis, 2002—03. Author: (short story) Chicken Soup for the Surviving Soul; pianist, arranger, composer numerous recs., 1974—. Vol. counselor CanSurmount, St. Louis, 1991—96; vol. visitor Am. Heartland Hospice, St. Louis, 1994. Grantee, Mo. Arts Coun., 1991. Mem.: Broadcast Music Inc., Mensa, Sigma Phi Omega. Avocations: reading religious histories, surfing the web, collecting baseball caps and kaleidoscopes. Office: Prosit Media Group 11621 Olive Street Rd Creve Coeur MO 63141 Personal E-mail: bernadettrandle@sbcglobal.net.

RANDLE, JONATHAN THOMAS, language educator; b. New Orleans, June 14, 1972; s. Thomas Albert and Beverly Bobitt Randle; m. Lauren Elizabeth Brown, July 11, 2004; children: Myles Tucker Little, Fiona Margaret. BA, Miss. Coll., Clinton, 1994; MA, Emmanuel Coll., Cambridge, 1996; PhD, U. Cambridge, 1999. Asst. prof. English Miss. Coll., 1999—. Office: Miss Coll P O Box 4022 200 S Capitol St Clinton MS 39058 Business E-Mail: randle@mc.edu.

RANDLETT, MARY WILLIS, photographer; b. Seattle, May 5, 1924; d. Cecil Durand and Elizabeth (Bayley) Willis; m. Herbert B. Randlett, Oct. 19, 1950 (div.); children: Robert, Mary Ann, Peter, Susan. BA, Whitman Coll., Walla Walla, Wash., 1947. Freelance photographer, 1949—. One-woman shows include Seattle Sci. Ctr., 1971, Western Wash. State U., 1971, Seattle Art Mus., 1971, Art Gallery Greater Victoria, 1972, Alaska State Mus., 1972, State Capitol Mus., 1983, Whatcom Mus. History and Art, Bellingham, Wash., 1986, Janet Huston Gallery, LaConner, Wash., 1990, Gov.'s Gallery, Office of Gov., Olympia, Wash., 1991, Stonington Gallery, Seattle, 1992, Valley Mus. Art, LaConner, 1992, Grad. Sch. Design Dept. Landscape Arch. Harvard U., Cambridge, Mass., 1996, Mus. N.W. Art, LaConner, 1998, Mary Randlett Portraits in the Arts Cmty., Wright Exhbn. Space, Seattle, 2002—03, Safco Plaza, Seattle and Richmond, Wash., 2003, Seattle's One Percent for Art, 2004, Walla Walla CC, 2004, Wash. State Libr., Olympia, 2005, Tacoma Art Mus., 2007—, others, exhibited in group shows at Am. Soc. Mag. Photographers, 1970, Whatcom Mus., Bellingham, Henry Gallery, Seattle, 1971, 1974, Royal Photg. Soc., 1979, Heard Mus., Phoenix, 1979, State Capital Mus., Olympia, Wash., 1983, 1984, 1988, 1989, 1993, Santa Fe Ctr. for Photography, 1987, Tacoma Art Mus., 1989, Helen Day Art Ctr., Stowe, Vt., 1989, Valley Mus. N.W. Art, LaConner, 1991, 1994, 1996—98, Allen Libr. U. Wash., Seattle, 1991, Wing Luke Asian Mus., 1991, Cheney Cowles Mus., Spokane, 1991, 1998, Security Pacific Gallery, Seattle, 1992, Benham Gallery, 1993, Stonington Gallery, 1993, 1998, Rainier Club, Seattle, 1994, Port Angeles (Wash.) Fine Arts Ctr., 1994, Mus. History and Industry, Seattle, 1994, Whatcom Mus., Bellingham, 1994, Pacific N.W. Annual Bellevue Art Mus., Wash., 1995, Skagit Valley Hist. Mus., LaConner, 1995, Seattle Art Mus., 1996—98, Kirkland (Wash.) Arts Ctr., 1997, Bainbridge Arts and Crafts, Bainbridge Island, Wash., 1997, Lucia Douglas Gallery, Bellingham, 1997, Anchorage Mus. History & Art, 1997, Burke Mus. Natural History and Culture, Seattle, 1998, Henderson House, Turnwater, Wash., 1998, Whatcom Arco Exhibit Gallery, Bellingham, 1998, Sea First Gallery, Seattle, 1998, 1999, Citizens Cultural Ctr., Fujinomita, Japan, 1999, Mus. Am. Indian, N.Y.C., 1999, Cheney Cowels Mus., Spokane, 1999, J. Paul Horiuchi Seattle Asian Art Mus., 2000, Mus. NW Art, 2000, Seattle Art Mus., 2002, Whitney Mus. Am. Art, N.Y.C., 2002, High Mus., Atlanta, 2002, Mus. NW Art, 2003, Seattle Art Mus., 2003, Tacoma Art Mus., 2003, Whatcom Mus., 2003, MONA, La Conner, Wash., 2004, Lucia Douglas Gallery, Bellingham, Wash., 2005, U. Wash. Press, Seattle, 2005, U. Portland, Oreg., 2006, Whatcom Mus., Bellingham, 2006—07, Stonington Gallery, Seattle, 2007, Grays Harbor Coll., 2007, Mary Randlett: Artist's Portraits, Hallie Ford Mus. Art, Salem, Oreg., 2009, Harry Widman: Image, Myth and Modernism, Hallie Ford Mus. Art, Salem, 2009, and numerous others, Represented in permanent collections Met. Mus., Nat. Collection of Fine Arts, Nat. Portrait Gallery, Washington State Libr., Manuscript divsn. U. Wash., Pacific Northwest Bell, Seattle, Swedish Med. Ctr., Whatcom Mus., Bellingham, Henry Gallery, Seattle, Wash. State Capitol Mus., Olympia, Phillips Collection, Wash.; works appeared in books The Master and His Fish (Roderick Haig-Brown), 1982, Theodore Roethke: The Journey to I and Otherwide (Neal Bowers), 1982, Mountain in the Clouds (Bruce Brown), 1982, Masonry in Architecture (Louis Redstone), 1982, Writings and Reflections from the World of Roderick Haig-Brown, 1982, Pike Place Market (Alice Shorett and Murray Morgan), 1982, The Dancing Blanket, (Cheryl Samuel), 1982, Collected Poems of Theodore Roethke, 1982, Spires of Form (Victor Scheffer), 1983, Assault on Mount Helicon (Mary Barnard), 1983, New as a Wave (Eve Triem), 1983, Sketchbook: A Memoir of the '30's and the Northwest School (William Cumming), 1983, Good Intentions (Jane Adams), 1985, Blackbirds of the Americas (Gordon Orians and Tony Angell), 1985, Historic Preservation in Seattle (Larry Kreisman), 1985, Down Town Seattle Walking Tours (Mary Randlett and Carol Tobin), 1986, Seattle, the Seattle Book, 1986, When Orchids Were Flowers (Kate Knap Johnson), 1986, Jacob Lawrence, American Painter, (Ellen Wheat), 1986, Manic Power: Robert Lowell and His Circle (Jeffrey Meyers), 1987, The Isamu Noguchi Garden Museum (Isamu Noguchi), 1987, Washington's Audacious State Capitol an its Builders (Norman Johnston), 1988, The Bloedel Reserve: Gardens in the Forest (Lawrence Kreisman), 1988, Washingtonians: A Biographical Portrait of the State on the Occasion of its Centennial, 1988, Directory of Literary Biography: Canadian Writers 1920-59, 2d series, 1989, Crafts of America, 1989, The Lone Tree Tragedy (Bruce Brown), 1989, Northwest Coast Handbook of North American Indians, 1990, Dancing on the Rim of the World, 1990, Openings, Original Essays by Contemporary Soviet and American Writers (eds. Robert Atwan, Valeri Vinokurov), 1990, George Tsutakawa (Martha Kingsbury), 1990, Contemporary American Poetry (ed. Al Polin Jr.), 1991, Natural History of Puget Sound Country (Arthur Kruckberg), 1991, Bones (Joyce Thompson), 1991, Cebu (Peter Basho), 1991, Catalogue of Historic Preservation Publications, 1992, Art in Seattle's Public Places (James Rupp), 1992, The Olympic Rainforest (Ruth Kirk with Jerry Franklin), 1992, Steelhead Fly Fishing (Trey Combs), 1992, Illustrated Guidelines for Rehabilitation Historic Buildings, 1993, A History of African American Artists (Bearden and Henderson), 1994, Childrens Literature Review Vol. 1, 1994, Invisible Gardens: The Search for Modernism the American Landscape (Walker and Simo), 1994, Seeing Seattle (Roger Sale), 1994, Reaching Home (Jay and Matson), 1994, Redesigning the American Lawn: A Search for Environmental Harmony (Gordone Geballe, Diana Balmari and F. Herbert Bormann), 1995, Reaching Home: Pacific Salmon, Pacific People (Foves, Jay and Matson), 1995, Carl F. Gould: A Life in Architecture and the Arts (T. William Booth and William H. Wuksib), 1995, Destination Zero (Sam Hamill), 1996, Market Sketchbook, 25th Anniversary Edition, 1996, Spirits of the Ordinary, 1997, Instrument of Change: Jim Schoppert 1947-1992, 1997, Looking for Eulabee Dix (JoAnn Ridley), 1997, Jack Lenor Larsen: A Memoir, 1998, Museo Nacional Centro de Arte Reina (Mark Tobey), 1998, Fountains Splash, and Spectacle: Water and Design from the Renaissance to Present (ed. Marilyn Symmes), 1998, Ghost Dancing (Anna Linzer), 1998, The Flower in the Skull (Kathleen Alcala), 1998, This Great Unknowing: Last Poems (Denise Levertov), 1999, Building Washington (Paul Dorpat, Genevier McCoy), 1999, The Wright Collection, Seattle Art Museum, 1999, Made to Last: Historic Preservation in Seattle and King County (Larry Kreisman), 1999, Isamu Noguchi: A Study of Space (Ana Maria Torres), 2000, The Tiger Iris (Joan Swift), 2000, The Eighth Lively Art (Wesley Wehr), 2000, All Powers Necessary and Convenient (Mark F. Jenkins), 2000, Ice Breakers: Alaska's Most Innovative Artists (Julie Decker), 2000, Over the Line: The Life and Art of Jacob Lawrence (Peter Nesbett and Michelle Dubois), 2000, Iridescent Light: The Emergence of Northwest Art (Delores Tarzan Ament), 2001, Messages from Frank's Landing, 2000, Leo Kenney: A Retrospective, 2000, Building for Learning: Seattle Public Schools History 1860-2000, 2001, Geology and Plant Life, 2001, and numerous others; works also appeared in newspapers and mags., book, Maritime Seattle, 2002, Picture Bainbridge Island: A Pictorial History, Distant Corner, 2003, Child of the Oemulgee, Passing the Three Gates, 2003, Northwest Mythologies, The Interactions of Mark Tobey, Morris Graves, Kenneth Callahan and Guy Anderson, 2003, The Accidental Collector, Art, Fossils, Friendships, 2004, Isamu Noguchi and Sky Viewing Sculpture, 2004, A San Juan Island's Journal, 2004, Poems From Ish River Country, 2004, American Knees, 2005, Groundswell: Constructing the Contemporary Landscape, 2005, Vanishing Seattle, Archaeology in Washington, 2007, Mary Randlett: Landscapes, Tacoma Art Mus. Washington, 2007—08; author: (book) Mark Di Suvero: Dreambook, 2008, Joe Feddersen: Vital Signs, 2009, Puget Sound Through an Artist's Eye, 2009, Harry Widman: Image, Myth and Modernism, 2009, Robert B. Heilman: His Life In Letters, 2009, Henry Klein, Architect: Pilgrim On a Journey; one-woman shows include Portraits of Writers, U. Washington, Mary Randlett Photographs, Laura Russo Gallery, Portland, Oreg., 2008, over 40 permanent collections nationwide & over 90 exhbns., numerous others.; contbr. articles to profl. publs. Recipient Wash. State Gov.'s award for spl. commendation for contbns. in field of photography, 1983, Individual Artist award, King County Arts Commn., 1989, Lifetime Achievement award, Artist Trust, 2001, Matrix Table, Seattle Women of Achievement, 1999, Nancy Blankenship Pryor award, 2001, Alumnus of Merit award, Whitman Coll, 2003, History Maker's award, Mus. History and Industry, 2003, Betty Bowen award, Seattle Art Mus.; grantee, Nat. Endowment for Arts, 1976, Allied Arts Found., 2000. Mem. AIA (hon.), Am. Soc. Mag. Photographers. Home: PO Box 11238 Olympia WA 98508-1238 Office Phone: 360-352-1716.

RANDOLPH, A(RTHUR) RAYMOND, federal judge; b. Riverside, NJ, Nov. 1, 1943; m. Eileen J. O'Connor, May 18, 1984; children: John Trevor, Cynthia Lee. BS, Drexel U., 1966; JD summa cum laude, U. Pa., 1969. Bar: Calif. 1970, DC 1973, US Supreme Ct. 1973. Law clk. to Hon. Henry J. Friendly US Ct. Appeals (2d cir.), NYC, 1969—70; asst. to solicitor gen. US Dept. Justice, Washington, 1970—73, dep. solicitor gen., 1975—77; ptnr. Sharp, Randolph & Green, Washington, 1977—83, Randolph & Truitt, Washington, 1983—87, Pepper, Hamilton & Scheetz, Washington, 1987—90; judge US Ct. Appeals (DC cir.), Washington, 1990—. Spl. asst. atty. gen. State of Mont., 1983—90, State of N.Mex., 1985—90, State of Utah, 1986—90; adv. panel Fed. Cts. Study Com., 1989—90; spl. counsel Com. on Stds. Ofcl. Conduct, US Ho. of Reps., 1979—80; adj. prof. Georgetown U. Law Ctr., 1974—78; exec. sec. Atty. Gen.'s Com. on Reform of Fed. Jud. Sys., 1975—77; com. on fed. rules evidence US Justice Dept., 1972; chmn. Com. on Govtl. Structures, McLean, Va., 1973—74; adj. prof. law sch. George Mason U., 1992, disting. prof., 1998—; com. codes conduct Jud. Conf. US, 1992—95, chmn., 1995—98. Recipient Spl. Achievement award, U.S. Dept. Justice, 1971, James Wilson Disting. Alumnus award, U. Pa. Law Sch., 2004, Drexel 100 award, Drexel U., 2005. Mem.: DC Bar Assn., Calif. Bar Assn., Am. Law Inst., Order of Coif. Office: US Court of Appeals 333 Constitution Ave NW Washington DC 20001-2866*

RANDOLPH, DAVID, conductor; b. NYC, Dec. 21, 1914; s. Morris and Elsie (Goodman) R.; m. Mildred Greenberg, July 18, 1948. BS, CCNY, 1936; MA, Tchrs. Coll., Columbia U., 1942; LHD (hon.), Saint Peter's Coll., Jersey City, 2006; DFA (hon.), CUNY, 2006. Music specialist OWI, NYC, 1943-47. Adj. prof. music NYU, 1948-85, Mostly Mozart course, 1976-85; lectr. Town Hall, N.Y.C., 1955-60, Columbia U., 1957, Cosmopolitan Club, N.Y.C., 1962-63; pre-concert lectr. N.Y. Philharm., Avery Fisher Hall, 1964-86,Cleve. Orch., 1981, Vienna Symphony Orch., 1988; tchr. conducting Dalcroze Sch., 1948-49; music commentator Little Orch. Soc. Concerts and Broadcasts, 1950-62, Met. Opera Intermission Broadcasts, 1951, 52; intermission commentator Lewisohn Stadium Concert Broadcasts, 1952-58; vis. prof. music SUNY, New Paltz, 1970-72, Fordham U., 1972-73; lectr. New Sch. for Social Rsch., 1973-90, IBM, N.Y.C., 1978-86, Beethoven Soc., 1977, 83; prof. music Montclair State Coll., Upper Montclair, N.J., 1973-87; guest condr. Rockland County (N.Y.) Ann. Choral Festival, 1972, 73; adviser film Music to Live By, mem. N.J. Arts Coun., 1967-70; mem. music com. Gov. N.J.'s Commn. to Study Arts, 1965; honored guest Handel Festival, Halle, Germany, 1991. Condr. Randolph Singers, 1944-62 (appeared on NBC Today, and Tonight Shows), concerts Town Hall, NYC, Carnegie Recital Hall, recs. for Columbia, Concert Hall Soc., Esoteric Records, Vanguard, Westminster Records, The Triumphs of Oriana, 1953, Monteverdi's Lagrime d'amante, Beethoven's Elegischer Gesang, Satie's Mass for the Poor, CRI, 13 Modern American Madrigals composed for the Randolph Singers, condr. United Choral Soc., LI, NY, 1961-86, Masterwork Chamber Orch., 1982-83, Philharmonia Orch. in Brahms' Requiem, Barbican Ctr., London, 1988, Barge Concert, NYC, 1987, 89, NJ Ballet Orch., 1977, 83, guest condr., Conn. Symphony Orch., 1961; condr. concert tour Spain with Am. choruses and Radio TV Orch. of Moscow, 1992; music annotator, CBS, NYC, 1947-48; choral seminar leader Mohonk Mountain House, 1986-95; music dir., condr. Masterwork Chorus and Orch., 1955-93, St. Cecilia Chorus and Orch., NYC, 1965—; performances at Carnegie Hall, Avery Fisher Hall, Lincoln Ctr., Kennedy Ctr. including Brahms' Requiem, Schicksalslied, Nänie, Gesang der Parzen, Mozart's Requiem, C Minor Mass, Vesperae de Confessore, Beethoven's Missa Solemnis, Symphony No. 3 (Eroica), Symphony No. 9, Mass in C Major, Choral Fantasy, Bach's Mass in B Minor, St. John Passion, St. Matthew Passion, Christmas Oratorio, Magnificat, C.P.E. Bach's Magnificat, Haydn's St. Cecilia Mass, Theresienmesse, Paukenmesse, Lord Nelson Mass, The Creation, Heiligmesse, Schöpfungsmesse, Michael Haydn's Requiem, Bruckner's Mass in E Minor, Requiem, Vaughan Williams' A Sea Symphony, Dona Nobis Pacem, Mass in G Minor, Hodie, Verdi's Requiem, Four Sacred Pieces, Honegger's King David, Elgar's The Music Makers, Corigliano's Fern Hill, Salieri's Mass in D, Purcell's The Fairy Queen, Mendelssohn's Elijah, Die erste Walpurgisnacht, Lobgesang, Lauda Sion, Poulenc's Gloria, Rutter's Gloria, Dvorak's Requiem, Te Deum, Kodaly's Te Deum, Berlioz' Requiem, Messe solennelle, Cherubini's Requiem, Schubert's Masses 5 and 6, Stabat Mater, Vivaldi's Gloria, Dixit Dominus, Zelenka's Missa Dei Patris, Gounod's St. Cecilia Mass, Handel's Solomon, Israel in Egypt, Judas Maccabaeus, Dixit Dominus and 173 complete performances of Handel's Messiah, Orff's Carmina Burana, Saint-Saëns' Requiem, Puccini's Messa di Gloria, Zimmermann's Psalmkonzert, Finzi's For St. Cecilia, In Terra Pax, Rachmaninoff's The Bells, others; broadcaster: David Randolph Concerts, WNYC and radio stas. of Nat. Assn. Ednl. Broadcasters, 1946-79, Young Audience telecasts, CBS-TV, 1958-59, series of candid rehearsals of Bach's Mass in B minor, PBS, 1967; host: weekly broadcasts Lincoln Ctr. Spotlight, Sta. WQXR, NYC, 1966-67; regular guest critic First Hearing program Sta. WQXR, NYC, and 68 other stas., 1986-95; author: This Is Music, 1964, 98, numerous album jacket notes; A New Music Made with a Machine, Horizon Magazine, 1959; editor: David Randolph Choral Series; writer, narrator: Instruments of the Orchestra, 1958, compact disc 1995, Stereo Review's Guide to Understanding Music, 1973; music critic, High Fidelity Mag., 1952-57; composer: A Song for Humanity, 1968, Andante for Strings, 1937, Edward, 1937, three anti-war choruses, 1937; contbg. author: NY Times Guide to Listening Pleasure, 1968; analyzed Mendelssohn's Symphony No. 3 on records for Book of Month Club. Recipient 1st award for edn. by radio Ohio State Inst., 1948, 50, 51, Sylvania TV award, 1959, Disting. Alumni award Columbia U., 1982, cert. of appreciation Mayor of City of N.Y. at Carnegie Hall, 1991, Townsend Harris medal CCNY, 1996, Lifetime Achievement award Carnegie Hall, MidAmerica Prodns., 2000; St. Cecilia Chorus endowed David Randolph Disting. Artist-in-Residence Program at New Sch. in N.Y., 1996. Home: 420 E 86th St Apt 4-c New York NY 10028-6456 Home Phone: 212-744-1444; Office Phone: 212-744-1444.

RANDOLPH, JENNINGS, JR., (JAY RANDOLPH), sportscaster; b. Cumberland, Md., Sept. 19, 1934; s. Jennings and Mary Katherine (Babb) R.; m. Sue Henderson, May 28, 1966; children: Jennings, Brian Robert, Rebecca Sue. Student, George Washington U., 1952—54, student, 1957—58; BA, Salem Coll., W.Va., 1963. Sports and promotion dir. Sta. WHAR, Clarksburg, W.Va., 1958-61; sportscaster Sta. KLIF, Dallas, 1963-66; Sta. KMOX, St. Louis, 1966-68; with Sta. KSDK-TV, St. Louis, 1968—, sports dir., 1968-88, spl. sports corr., 1988—, also on nationally televised broadcasts for various sports events including Sr. PGA tour; TV announcer Fla. Marlins Baseball Club, Ft. Lauderdale, 1993—2002; announcer PGA Tour Classic on Golf Channel, 2002—06; staff KFNS Radio, St. Louis, 2002—06; St. Louis Cardinals announcer Sta. KSDK-TV, 2007—. Interviewer analyst Champions Tour on Golf Channel and CNBC; broadcaster coll. basketball ESPN regional TV; TV announcer St. Louis Cardinals, 1970-87, Cin. Reds., 1988; mem. NBC's broadcast staff for 1988 Olympics, Seoul, Korea and 1992 Summer Games, Barcelona, Spain; host The Golf Show. Trustee Salem Coll., 1976-89. With U.S. Army, 1954-56. Named to Boys and Girls Clubs of Am. Hall of Fame, 1990, Tex. Radio Hall Fame, 2005, Mo. Sports Hall of Fame, 2007, Champion, So. Conf. Golf, 1958 Mem. Nat. Assn. Sportscasters, Delta Tau Delta (Disting. Alumni award 2006) Achievements include being an amateur golf champion. Home: 12021 Charter Oakpky Saint Louis MO 63146

RANDOLPH, JESSE See CASTILE, RAND

RANDOLPH, LEONARD MCELROY, JR., career officer; b. Washington, Sept. 22, 1943; s. Leonard McElRoy and Jessie Marshall (Stockton) R.; m. Linda Fleming Raney, Aug. 1, 1987; children: Nathaniel Randolph, Brion Randolph, Holly Tocknell, Chad Muterspaw, Judd Muterspaw. BS in Biology, Marietta Coll., Ohio, 1965; MS in Microbiology, Howard U., Washington, 1967; MD, Meharry Med. Coll., Nashville, 1972; DHL (hon.), Meharry Med. Coll., 2001. Diplomate Am. Bd. Surgery, Am. Bd. Med. Mgmt., Am. Coll. Physician Execs.; cert. physician exec. Grad. tchg. asst. Howard U., Washington, 1966-67; rsch. microbiologist Georgetown U., Washington, 1966-67; chemistry tchr. Ballou H.S., Washington, 1967-68; commd. 2d lt. USAF, 1978, advanced through grades to maj. gen., 1998, ret., 2003, intern Keesler AFB, Miss., 1972-73, resident, 1973-77, gen. surgeon Bergstrom AFB, Tex., 1977-78, chief gen. surgery, 1978-80, chief surg. svcs., 1980-83, attending surgeon Wright-Patterson AFB, Ohio, 1983-84, dir. med. edn., 1984-85, chief med. officer Minot AFB, ND, 1985-86, hosp. cmdr. George AFB, Calif., 1988-90, dep. command surgeon HQ Tactical Air Command Langley AFB, Va., 1990-91, forward command surgeon Desert Storm Riyahd, Saudi Arabia, 1990-91, med. ctr. comdr. Travis AFB, Calif., 1994-97; asst. prof. surgery Wright State U. Sch. Medicine, Dayton, Ohio, 1983-88; command surgeon U.S. Ctrl. Command, MacDill AFB, Fla., 1991-94, U.S. Transp. Command and Air Mobility Command, Scott AFB, Ill., 1997-99. Lead agt. DOD Health Svc. Region 10, 1994-97; spec. asst. to USAF Surg. Gen., 1999, dep. surgeon gen., 1999-2001; dep. exec. dir. Tricare Mgmt. Activity, Office of Under Sec. Def., Washington, 2001-03; assoc. prof. surgery U. Calif. Davis Sch. Medicine, 1995-97; assoc. prof. mil. medicine and emergency medicine Uniformed Svcs. U. of Health Scis., 1995—; acting dep. asst. sec. def. Health Plan Adminstrn., TRICARE Mgmt. Activity, 2003—04, COO, 2003-04; v.p. med. ops. Cath. Healthcare West, 2003-05; sr. v.p. and chief med. officer, Mercy Health Ptnrs., 2005-. Contbr. articles to profl. jours. Bd. trustees Marietta Coll., 2001—, Cin. Hills Chistian Acad., 2008-; bd. dirs. Health Found. Greater Cin. 2006-, Tri State Trauma Coalition, 2006-, HealthEast Care Sys., 2008-. Decorated Def. Superior Svc. medal for Operation Restore Hope, Legion of Merit Operation Desert Storm, Disting. Svc. medal USAF; selected for Boys State (Georgetown U.); recipient Excellence award Fed. Healthcare Execs., 1997, Disting. Alumni of Yr. award Nat. Assn. for Equal Opportunity in Higher Edn., 1999, Disting. Alumnus award Marietta Coll. Alumni Assn., 2000, Exceptional Svc. award Uniformed Svcs. U. of the Health Scis., 2003; named to Hall of Excellence, Ohio Found. Ind. Colls., 2003. Fellow ACS (bd. govs. 1996—2002), Am. Coll. Physician Execs. (disting. pres. 2000-2001), Am. Acad. Med. Adminstrs. (hon.); mem. Soc. Air Force Clin. Surgeons (bd. govs. 1996-2002), Soc. Med. Adminstrs., Soc. Med. Cons to Armed Forces, Assn. Mil. Surgeons of the U.S., Air Force Assn. (life), Christian Med. Assn., Aerospace Med. Assn., Cincinanatus Assn., Alpha Omega Alpha, Beta Kappa Chi, Beta Beta Beta. Avocations: reading, sports, writing. Office: Mercy Health Partners 4600 McAuley Pl 6th Fl Cincinnati OH 45242-4745 Office Phone: 513-981-6347. Office Fax: 513-981-6133. Business E-Mail: lmrandolph@health-partners.org. E-mail: caprand@aol.com.

RANDOLPH, LINDA A., medical association administrator; b. Washington, Mar. 3, 1941; d. Oscar Horace Randolph and Marie Louise Fernandez. BS in zoology, Howard U., 1962, MD, 1967; MPH in maternal and child health, U. Calif., Berkeley, 1971; DHL (hon.), SUNY, Albany, 2009. Intern in internal medicine and pediat. Harlem Hosp. Ctr., NYC, 1967—78, resident in pediat., 1968—70; dir. health services, Project Head Start Dept. Health and Human Services, Washington, 1972—79; assoc. state health commr. for NYC affairs NY State Dept. Health, 1980—83, dir. office of pub. health, 1983—91; faculty SUNY Albany Sch. Pub. Health; exec. dir. Task Force on Meeting the Needs of Young Children Carnegie Corp. of NY, 1991—94; clin. prof. cmty. medicine, pediat. and psychiatry Mt. Sinai Sch. Medicine, NYC, 1991; dir. Nat. Women's Resource Ctr. Substance Abuse and Mental Health, 1995—99; co-chief exec. officer DC Developing Families Ctr., Washington, 1999—2002, pres. and CEO, 2003—. Recipient Haven Emerson award for Disting. Svc., Pub. Health Assn. NYC, 1983, Leadership award, Westchester Black Women's Polit. Caucus, 1987, Disting. Svc. award, NY State Fedn. Profl. Health Educators, 1988, Cmty. Svc. award, Greater Harlem C. of C., 1994, Martha May Eliot award for Exceptional Health Services to Mothers and Children, Am. Pub. Health Assn., 2001.

Mem.: Inst. Medicine, NY Acad. Medicine, Alpha Omega Alpha. Office: DC Developing Families Ctr 801 17th St NE Washington DC 20002-7200 Office Phone: 202-398-2007. Office Fax: 202-398-2027.*

RANDOLPH, MICHAEL K., state supreme court justice; b. 1946; m. Kathy Webb; 3 children. BA in Bus. Administration, Rollins Coll., Winter Park, Fla., 1972; JD, U. Miss. Sch. of Law, 1974. Atty. Ross, King and Randolph, Biloxi, 1975—76, Bryan, Nelson, Allen, Schroder and Randolph, Hattiesburg, 1976—2004; justice Miss. Supreme Ct., 2004—. Former mem. Nat. Coal Council. Mem. adv. bd. Hattiesburg Salvation Army; former pres. Hattiesburg Civic Assn.; mem. Hattiesburg Area Development Partnership; mem. bd. dirs. William Carey Coll., Boys and Girls Club of Hattiesburg, Hattiesburg Girls Shelter. Air traffic controller US Army, atty., Judge Advocate General Corps USN. Mem.: ABA, Miss. Bar Assn. (Com. on Continuing Legal Ed. 1975—76), S. Central Miss. Bar Assn. (pres. 1986). Office: Miss Supreme Ct PO Box 117 Jackson MS 39205*

RANDOLPH, ROBERT DEWITT, lawyer; b. Sligo, Pa., Mar. 6, 1929; s. DeWitt Lyman and Hazel Irene (McCall) R.; m. Betty Ann McElhattan, May 8, 1953 (dec. Aug. 1979); children: Douglas, Andrew; m. Susan Denise Hopkins, Oct. 15, 1988 BA, Westminster Coll., 1951; LLB, Harvard U., 1957. Bar: Ohio 1958, Pa. 1960, U.S. Supreme Ct. 1981. Assoc. Buckingham, Doolittle & Burroughs, Akron, Ohio, 1957-59, Rose, Houston, Cooper & Schmidt, Pitts., 1959-60, 61-65; fgn. svc. officer U.S. Dept. State, Washintgon, 1960-61; ptnr. Houston, Cooper, Spear & German, Pitts., 1965-70, Randolph & O'Connor, Pitts., 1970-74, Buchanan Ingersoll P.C., Pitts., 1974-93. With US Army, 1951—54. Mem. St. Clair Country Club. Democrat. Presbyterian. Avocations: golf, skiing. Home: 750 Washington Rd Pittsburgh PA 15228-2051 Personal E-mail: randolrobert@hotmail.com.

RANDOLPH, VIRGELLA, retired federal official; d. Russell and Catherine (Smith) Snowden; m. Alphonso L. Randolph, 1960; children: Victor, Pebble, Deborah. At, D.C. C.C., 1976, Georgetown U. Clk. typist census bur. U.S. Dept. Commerce, Suitland, Md., 1955—56; clk. typist to dep. chief fed. acquisition and assistance divsn. Nat. Bur. Stds. (now Nat. Inst. Sci. Tech.) U.S. Dept. Commerce, Gaithersburg, 1956—87; ret. Vol. Providence Hosp., 1987; past mem., pres. We Chick, Inc.; past mem. The Musical Choraleers; past mem., v.p. The Stereophonic Chorale; deaconess Greater First Baptist Ch., Washington, 2004—; mem. Gospel Chorus, Pres., v.p., fin. sec.; mem. Fellowship Choir; co-chair Elevator Ministry. Recipient Bronze medal, U.S. Dept. Commerce, 1974. Mem.: Choir Dirs. and Organists Guils, Hampton U. Annual Minister's Conf. Democrat. Baptist. Achievements include development of in-house procurement training program for Nat. Bur. Stds; subject of Black History Week at Nat. Bur. Stds. for accomplishments. Avocations: flower arranging, singing, writing. Personal E-mail: virgella7@aol.com.

RANDOLPH, WILLIE (WILLIE LARRY RANDOLPH JR.), professional baseball coach, retired professional baseball player; b. Holy Hill, SC, July 6, 1954; m. Gretchen Foster; children: Taniesha, Chantre, Ciara, Andre. DHL (hon.), Fordham U., 2007. Second baseman Pitts. Pirates, 1975—76, NY Yankees, 1976—88, L.A. Dodgers, 1989—90, Oakland A's, 1990, Milw. Brewers, 1991, NY Mets, 1992; asst. gen. mgr. NY Yankees, 1993, third base coach, 1993—2003, bench coach, 2004, Milw. Brewers, 2008—; mgr. NY Mets, 2004—08. Named Dodgers' MVP Anaheim/L.A. chpt. BBWAA, 1989; named to Am. League All-Star Team 1976-77, 1980-81, 1987, Nat. League All-Star Team, 1989; recipient James P. Dawson award, 1976 Office: Milw Brewers Miller Pk One Brewers Way Milwaukee WI 53214*

RANDOLPH, ZACH, professional basketball player; b. Marion, Ind., July 16, 1981; Attended, Mich. State U., East Lansing, 2000—01. Forward Portland Trailblazers, 2001—07, NY Knicks, 2007—08, LA Clippers, 2008—09, Memphis Grizzlies, 2009—. Named Most Improved Player, NBA, 2004. Office: Memphis Grizzlies 191 Beale St Memphis TN 38103*

RANDOLPH-BROUGHMAN, MARY ETTA, music educator; b. Staunton, Va., Sept. 11, 1953; d. Morris V. Randolph, Jr. and Claudine (Wimmer) Randolph; children from previous marriage: Katrina Marie Broughman, Sarah Elizabeth Broughman. BA in Music Edn., Bridgewater Coll., 1974; M in Music Edn., James Madison U., 1978; dipoma in music, Mozarteum Hoschschule für Musik und darstellende Kunst, 1980; postgrad., Shenandoah U., 2002—. Tchg. lic. Pvt. piano tchr., Va., 1974—; music tchr. Roanoke (Va.) City Schs., 1974—77, Richmond County Schs., Warsaw, Va., 1978—79, Botetourt County Schs., Fincastle, Va., 1980—81, Montgomery County Schs., Christiansburg, Va., 1981—82, Staunton (Va.) County Schs., 1982—87, Rockridge County Schs., Lexington, Va., 1987—; tchg. asst. piano James Madison U., Harrisonburg, Va., 1977—78. Adjudicator dist. and regional chorus Montgomery and Roanoke Counties, Va.; accompanist, 1974—; summer FAIR instr. Fine Arts Rockbridge, 1999—; coord. Teen Battle of Bands, Rookbridge Regional Fair, 2007, 08. Composer, arranger: Come and Worship, Spencer's Mountain. Chmn. Reflections Program Natural Bridge Dist. PTA, 2004—09; vol. 4-H; organist Buena Vista (Va.) Bapt. Ch., 1999—2003; organist, choir dir./accompanist various chs. Fellow, Rotary Internat., Salzburg, Austria, 1979—80. Mem.: Va. Choral Dirs. Assn., Nat. Guild Piano Tchrs., Am. Coll. Musicians, Am. Guild Organists, Va. Music Educators Assn. (25 Yr. Tchg. award 1999), Music Educators Nat. Conf. (25 Yr. Tchg. award 1999). Home: 3017 Forge Rd Glasgow VA 24555 Office: Natural Bridge Elem Sch 42 Natural Bridge School Rd Natural Bridge Station VA 24579 Personal E-mail: mary_broughman@rockbridge.k12.va.us.

RANDT, CLARK THORP, JR., former ambassador, lawyer; b. Cleve., Nov. 24, 1945; s. Clark Thorp and Mary-Louise (Mitchell) R.; m. Sarah Talcott, Nov. 3, 1979; children: Clark Thorp III, Paull Mitchell, Clare Talcott. BA, Yale U., 1968; JD, U. Mich., 1975; People's Republic China law diploma, U. East Asia, 1988. Bar: NY 1976, Hong Kong 1992. Assoc. Milbank, Tweed, Hadley & McCloy, NYC, Hong Kong and Tokyo, 1975-82; lst sec., comml. attache Am. Embassy, Beijing, 1982-84; ptnr. Heller, Ehrman, White & McAuliffe, San Francisco and Hong Kong, 1985-87, Gibson, Dunn and Crutcher, Hong Kong, 1987—91, Shearman & Sterling, Hong Kong, 1991—2001; US amb. to China US Dept. State, Beijing, 2001—09. Legal adv. Nat. Coun. US-China Trade, 1974; bd. dirs., Valmont Industries, Inc., 2009- With USAF, 1968-72. Recipient Disting. Svc. medal US Dept. Commerce, 1984. Mem.: Coun. Fgn. Rels. Office: PO Box 3164 Park City UT 84060-3164

RANEY, MIRIAM DAY, actress; b. Florence, SC, Sept. 30, 1922; d. Lewie Griffith and Iola Lewis (Edwards) Day; m. Robert William Raney, Mar. 31, 1946 (div. Sept. 1976); children: Robert William Jr., Miriam, Kevin Paige, Megan. BSM in Voice, Music Edn., U. NC, Greensboro, 1943; student, Julliard Sch. Music, 1942—43; BA in Music History and Lit., U. Ark., Little Rock, 1981; cert., Adam Roarke Film Actors Lab., Irving, Tex., 1989. Singing chorus NYC Ctr. Opera Co., 1943-44; understudy, singing chorus Oklahoma, Theater Guild, NYC, 1944-45; ingenue lead Connecticut Yankee, Geosan Subway Cir., NYC, 1945; understudy, singing chorus Up In Central Park, Michael Todd, NYC, 1945-46. Beauty cons. Mary Kay Cosmetics, Inc., Dallas, 1993—98. Author: Ark Women in Music, 1982; composer, lyricist: songs The Bend and the Wiillow, 1982, Ballad of Petit Jean, 1983; actor: (plays) Hedda Gabler, 1990, Time of Your Life, 1991, Our Town, 1991, Evening with Women II, 1991; (TV series) Unsolved Mysteries, 1988; (films) Killing Time with Aunt Olene, 1988, commls. and tng. films, 1987—99; reviewer: Ency of Ark. History, 2005—09; print model, Little Rock, Memphis, Ft. Worth, 1988—98. Sec. sr. adult coun. Pulaski Heights United Meth. Ch., 2004—07. Recipient Thanks Badge, Girl Scouts USA, Oachita Coun., Little Rock, 1962; named Illustrious Alumna, U. NC, Greensboro, 1945. Mem.: AAUW (mem. Little Rock br. legis. com., mem. program com. 1973—79, cultural interest rep. 1975—77, 1996—98, state rep. cultural interests 1976—78), Ctrl. Ark. Guild Organists (pres. student chpt. 1977—80). Democrat. Avocations: birdwatching, gardening, reading, movies. Home and Office: 25 Valley Forge Dr Little Rock AR 72212-2613 Office Phone: 501-225-3460. Personal E-mail: mimraney@comcast.net.

RANGANATHAN, NAGARAJAN, engineering educator; b. Tiruvaiyaru, Tamil Nadu, India; m. Radhika Ranganathan. PhD, UCF, Orlando, 1988. Contbg. editor manuscripts; contbr. articles to profl. jours. Fellow: IEEE (editor-in-chief, VLSI sys. 2003—06). Office: Univ S Fla 4202 E Fowler Ave ENB 118 Tampa FL 33620

RANGANATHAN, NATARAJAN, research and development company executive; s. S. Natarajan and Natarajan Nagalakshmi; m. Parimalam Lalitha Parimalam Thankachi, Mar. 31, 1972; children: Mahesh, Ramesh. PhD, Temple U., Phila., 1976. Med. cons. Med-Life Sys. Inc., Upper Darby; sr. vp r&d Kibow Biotech Inc., Newtown Square, Pa., 1985—. Donor Several, Broomall, Pa., 1970—2008. Achievements include invention of a oral dietary supplement product for kidney health. Avocations: travel, music. Office: Kibow Biotech Inc 4629 W Chester Pike Newtown Square PA 19073 Office Phone: 610-353-5130. Personal E-mail: natarajan.ranganathan@gmail.com. Business E-Mail: rangan@kibowbiotech.com.

RANGAPPA, SUNIL, cardiologist; Cert. in internal medicine and cardiology ABIM. Cardiologist Cedar Sinai Med. Ctr., LA, 2006—. Mem. Face Forward Organisation Battered Children and Domestic Violence. Recipient William B Kirlin award, Cardiovasc. Inst. Phila., Best Young Investigator awarded, Nat. U. Singapore and Singapore Cardiac Soc.; grantee Health Rsch. grant, Commonwealth Pa., 2001. Mem.: Am. Heart Assn., Am. Coll. Cardiology.

RANGARI, VIJAYA KUMAR, chemistry professor, researcher; s. Ranganath Rao and Chendramani Rangari; m. Vatsalya Rao, Dec. 19, 1995; children: Shivani, Shashank Kumar. BSc, Osmania U., India, 1987, PhD, 1996. Rschr. Indian Inst. Sci., Bangalore, 1996—98, Barilan U., Ramatgan, Israel, 1999—2001; rsch. asst. prof. Tuskegee U., Ala., 2001—. Fellow, Coun. Sci. Rsch. India, 1996. Mem.: Soc. for the Advancement of Material and Process Engring. (assoc.). Achievements include research in nanomaterials for structural applications. Office: Tuskegee Univ 101 James Ctr T-Cam Tuskegee AL 36088 Office Fax: 334-727-2286. Business E-Mail: rangariv@tuskegee.edu.

RANGASWAMY, PADMA, historian, director, author, interculturist; m. Krish Rangaswamy, May 25, 1966; children: Priya Playle, Anjali. PhD, U. Ill., Chgo., 1996. Cert. Intercultural Comm. Inst., 2006. Dir. South Asian Am. Policy & Rsch. Inst., Chgo., 2005—; sr. assoc. Lang. & Culture Worldwide, Chgo., 2006—. Vol. Chgo. Delhi Sister Cities, 2006—09; founding mem. Indo-Am. Heritage Mus., Chgo., 2007—09.

RANGAVAJHULA, KRISHNA, mechanical engineer, educator; s. Chalapathi Sastri and Lakshmi Rangavajhula; m. Ramani Garimella; children: Saipriya, Athreya Sastri. BTech with honors, Indian Inst. Tech., Kharagpur, 1985; MS in Mech. Engring., Va. Tech., Blacksburg, 1988; PhD in Mech. Engring., U. NB, Fredericton, Can., 1996; MBA, San Jose State U., Calif., MS in Indsl. and Sys. Engring., 2006. Cert. Six Sigma Black Belt Am. Soc. Quality, Inst. Indsl. Engrs., 2008. Adj. prof. San Jose State U., 2004—; engr. neurovascular divsn. Boston Sci. Corp., Fremont, Calif., 2006—. Postdoc. fellow U. NB, 1996—97, U. Alta., Edmonton, Canada, 1997—98; asst. prof. Lake Superior State U., Sault Ste Marie, Mich., 1998—99; cons. Cisco Sys., Bell Micro Sys., San Jose, 1999—2006. Mem.: ASME, AIAA, Am. Soc. Quality, Inst. Indsl. Engrs., Beta Gamma Sigma, Tau Beta Pi. Achievements include research in dynamical systems, bifurcation theory, vehicle dynamics. Home: 2289 Natoma Dr Virginia Beach VA 23456 Office: Boston Sci Corp 47900 Bayside Pky Fremont CA 94538 Personal E-mail: krishna_62@hotmail.com. Business E-Mail: rangavak@bsci.com.

RANGEL, CHARLIE (CHARLES BERNARD RANGEL), United States Representative from New York; b. NYC, June 11, 1930; s. Ralph and Blanche (Wharton) Rangel; m. Alma Carter, July 26, 1964; children: Steven, Alicia. BS, NYU, 1957; JD, St. John's U. Sch. Law, NY, 1960; LLD (hon.), Wagner Coll., 1982, Atlanta U., 1983, St. John's U., 1988, Mt. Sinai Sch. Medicine, 1988, NYU, 1988, Howard. U., 1988, Hofstra U., 1989. Bar: NY 1960. Counsel NYC Housing and Redevelopment Bd.; asst. US atty. (so. dist.) NY US Dept. Justice, 1961-62; mem. NY State Assembly, 1966-70, US Congress from 15th NY Dist., 1971—, US House Ways & Means Com., 1975—, ranking minority mem., 1996—2007, chmn., 2007—; vice chmn. Joint Com. on Taxation, 2007—. Co-chair African Trade and Investment Caucus, Congressional Glaucoma Caucus; mem. Congressional Human Rights Caucus. Co-author (with Leon Wynter): And I Haven't Had a Bad Day Since: From the Streets of Harlem to the Halls of Congress, 2007. Served in US Army, 1948—52, Korea. Decorated Bronze Star, Purple Heart; recipient Korean Presdl. citations, Henry F. Scheig Nat. Pub. Svc. award, Aid Assn. Luths., 1987, Pub. Svc. award for excellence, Am. Acad. Pediat., 1988, Marcus Garvey Lifetime Achievement award, Inst. Caribbean Studies, 1995, Edmund S. Muskie Disting. Pub. Svc. award, Ctr. Nat. Policy, 2002; named one of Most Influential Black Americans, Ebony mag., 2006; named to Power 150, 2008. Mem.: NAACP, NY State Bar Assn., Nat. Assn. State Legislators, 369th Vets. Assn. Democrat. Roman Catholic. Office: US Congress 2354 Rayburn House Office Bldg Washington DC 20515-0001 also: 163 W 125th St Ste #737 New York NY 10027 Office Phone: 202-225-4365. Office Fax: 202-225-0816.*

RANIERI, LEWIS S., investment company executive; b. 1946; Mem. exec. com. Salomon Bros. Inc., NYC, vice-chmn., 1986-89; founder Hyperion Capital (now Hyperion Partners LP), NYC, 1989—; chmn., pres., CEO Ranieri & Co., Inc., 1988—; chmn. Franklin Bank Corp., Houston, 2001—, CEO, 2008—. Mem. Nat. Assn. Home Builders Mortgage Roundtable, 1989—; bd. dirs. CA, Inc., 2001, lead independent dir., 2002—04, non-exec. chmn., 2004—07; chmn. Am. Fin. Realty Trust, Capital Lease Funding, Inc., Root Markets Inc. Trustee Environ. Defense, Met. Opera Assn.; chmn. bd. Am. Ballet Theatre. Recipient Lifetime Achievement Award, Fixed Income Analysts Soc., Inc., Disting. Industry Svc. Award, Am. Securitization Forum, 2005; named one of The Greatest Innovators of the Past 75 Years, BusinessWeek mag., 2004; named to Nat. Housing Hall of Fame, FIASI Hall of Fame. Office: Franklin Bank Corp 9800 Richmond Ave Ste 680 Houston TX 77042 also: Root Markets Inc 601 W 26th St, Ste 1500 New York NY 10001 Office Phone: 212-645-6320. Office Fax: 212-645-6343.

RANIS, GUSTAV, economist, educator; b. Darmstadt, Germany, Oct. 24, 1929; s. Max and Bettina (Goldschmidt) R.; m. Ray Lee Finkelstein, June 15, 1958; children: Michael Bruce, Alan Jonathan, Bettina Suzanne. BA summa cum laude, Brandeis U., 1952, hon. degree, 1982; MA, Yale U., 1953, PhD, 1956. Asst. adminstr. program and policy AID/Dept. of State, 1965-67; dir. Econ. Growth Ctr. Yale U., New Haven, 1967-75, prof. econs., 1964—81, Frank Altschul prof. internat. econs., 1981—2005, Frank Altschul prof. emeritus internat. econs., 2005—, dir. Ctr. Internat. and Area Studies, 1996—2004. Ford Found. vis. prof. U. De Los Andes, Bogota, Colombia, 1976-77; Ford Found. vis. prof. Colegio de Mex., 1971-72; fellow Inst. for Advanced Study, Berlin, 1993-94; cons. World Bank, AID, Ford Found., ILO, FAO, Inter-Am. Devel. Bank. Author: (with John Fei) Development of the Labor Surplus Economy: Theory and Policy, 1964,; (with Fei and Shirley Kuo) Growth with Equity: The Taiwan Case, 1979; (with Keijiro Otsuka and Gary Saxonhouse) Comparative Technology Choice in Development, 1988; (with F. Stewart and E. Angeles-Reyes) Linkages in Developing Economies: A Philippine Study, 1990; (with S.A. Mahmood) Political Economy of Development Policy Change, 1992; (with John C. H. Fei) Growth and Development from an Evolutionary Perspective, 1997, Globalization and the Nation State, 2006, Globalization and Self-Determination: In the Nation-State Under Siege?, 2006; editor: Taiwan: From Developing to Mature Economy, 1992, En Route to Modern Economic Growth: Latin America in the 1990s, 1994, Japan and the U.S. in the Developing World, 1997,; co-editor: The State of Development Economics, 1988, Science and Technology: Lessons for Development Policy, 1990; mem. editl. bd. Jour. Internat. Devel., 1995—, Oxford Devel. Studies, 1996—, Internat. Econ. Jour., 2005-. Trustee Brandeis U., 1967-93, chmn. acad. affairs com., 1986-93. Social Sci. Rsch. Coun. fellow, Japan, 1955-56, Carnegie scholar, 2004-06. Mem. Am. Econ. Assn., Coun. Fgn. Rels., Overseas Develop. Coun. (mem. adv. com.). Home: 7 Mulberry Rd Woodbridge CT 06525-1716 Office: Econ Growth Ctr Yale 27 Hillhouse Ave New Haven CT 06520 Office Phone: 203-432-3632. Business E-Mail: gustav.ranis@yale.edu.

RANJAN, PRIYA, research scientist; b. Dehri On Sone, Bihar, India, Nov. 1, 1975; PhD, U. Md., Coll. Pk., 2003. Rsch. assoc. U. Md., 2003—; sr. rsch. scientist Intelligent Automation Inc., Rockville, Md., 2007—. Grant, NSF, 2001—, DARPA, 2001—, Army, 2001—. Mem.: Assn. India's Devel. (bd. mem. 2006—08). Independent. Achievements include research in new criteria for global stability of network resource allocation. Home: 8316 Adelphi Rd Hyattsville MD 20783 Home Fax: 301-294-5201. Personal E-mail: pranjan@gmail.com.

RANJAN, RAHUL, engineer, researcher; b. Ranchi, Jharakhand, India, June 28, 1980; arrived in US, 2004; s. Rajendra Prasad and Asha Chaudhary. BTech, Indian Inst. Tech., Kharagpur, 2002; MS, Wayne State U., Detroit, 2006. Rsch. engr. CDOT, New Delhi, 2002—04; high speed circuit design engr. Altera Corp., San Jose, Calif., 2006—. Author (and co-author): jour. articles and conf. papers. Recipient GRA award, Wayne State U., 2004, Outstanding Grad./Profl. Leadership award, 2005; Thomas C. Rumble Fellow, 2005. Mem.: SPIE, IEEE, Asha, Sillicon Valley, Calif. Achievements include development of Video Image Fusion using Fuzzy and Neuro Fuzzy Logic; research in Image Fusion using Subtractive Clustering Approach; Fuzzy Applications. Avocations: reading, travel. Home: 3500 Granada Ave Apt 168 Santa Clara CA 95051-3318 Personal E-mail: rahulr@wayne.edu. Business E-Mail: rranjan@altera.com.

RANJAN, SRIKANT, mechanical engineer; s. Yamuna Prasad and Maya Devi; m. Garima Singal, Nov. 22, 2008. BS (hon.), Indian Inst. Tech., Kharagpur, West Bengal, India, 1999; PhD (hon.), U. Fla., Gainesville, 2005. Tchg. asst. No. Ill. U., DeKalb, 1999—2000; rsch. asst. U. Fla., 2000—05; finite element analyst Solidworks, SantaMonica, Calif., 2005—. Co-chairman Am. Soc. Mech. Engr., 2006. Contbr. scientific papers. Project coord. Asha Edn., Gainesville, 2003—05; project leader L.A. Works, LA, 2006—08; tchr. Iridescent, LA, 2007—. Recipient prize, IIT, 1998, medal, 1999. Mem.: U. of Fla. Alumnii Assn., ASME (assoc.). Personal E-mail: srikantagrawal@yahoo.com.

RANJEVA, RAYMOND, judge; b. Antananarivo, Madagascar, Aug. 31, 1942; s. René and Eugénie (Raolosoa) Ranjeva; m. Yvette Madeleine Rabetafika, June 17, 1967; 5 children. Teaching cert., U. Madagascar, LLB, 1965; student, U. Madagascar Nat. Sch. Adminstrn., 1966; diplôme, U. Madagascar, 1967, U. of Paris, 1966; doctorate (hon.), U. Limoges Strasbourg. Dir. law and polit. sci. U. Madagascar, Antananarivo, 1973-82, pres., dean, faculty law, econs., mgmt. and sociology, 1982-88, rector, 1988-90; judge Internat. Ct. of Justice, The Hague, Netherlands, 1991—, v.p., 2003—06. Atty. counsel border dispute Govt. Mali.; CEO, chmn. bd. dirs. bur. consultations JURECO, 1986—88. Editor: (monthly jour.) JURECO, 1988—90. Active Justitia & Pax, Antananarivo; mem. pub., civil, social coms. Coun. Cath. Chs. Madagascar, Antananarivo, 1978—90. Recipient Nat. Assn. Doctors in Law award, Nat. Sch. Adminstrn. Madagascar award; named Knight Grand Cross, l'Ordre Nat. Malgache, Officier Legion Honneur, Chevalier l'Ordre de Merite Madagascar, l'Ordre National Mali. Mem.: Interant. C. of C. (internat. ct. arbitration 1994—), Ct. Arbitration for Sport. Avocations: walking, traditional music. Office: Internat Ct Justice Palais de la Paix Carnegieplein 2 2517 KJ The Hague Netherlands E-mail: ry.ranjeva@icj-cij.org.

RANK, MARK ROBERT, sociologist; b. Milw., May 18, 1955; s. Robert Arthur Hallie Jean (Hughes) R.; m. Anne Elizabeth Deutch, Sept. 15, 1984. B.A. with honors, U. Wis., 1978, M.S., 1980, Ph.D., 1984. Demography trainee U. Wis., Madison, 1978-79, project asst., 1979-81, lectr., 1982, research asst., 1981-84; profl. fellow U. N.C., Chapel Hill, 1984—. Contbr. articles to profl. jours. Bush Inst. for Child Family Policy fellow, 1984; Nat. Inst. Child Health Human Devel. demography traineeship, 1978. Mem. Am. Sociol. Assn., Nat. Council Family Relations, Midwest sociol. Assn. Avocations: Tennis; music; skiing, basketball; cooking. Office: Washington University Campus Box 1196 Saint Louis MO 63130

RANK, NATHAN, biologist, educator; b. Freeport, Ill., June 19, 1961; s. John and Barbara Rank; m. Michaela Grobbel; children: Daniel Grobbel-Rank, Malia Grobbel-Rank. PhD, U. Calif., Davis, 1990. Asst. prof. Swiss Fed. Inst. Tech., Zurich, Switzerland, 1992—95; prof. Sonoma State U., Rohnert Pk., Calif., 1995—. Dir. Fairfield Osborn Preserve, Penngrove, Calif., 2000—. Recipient Merton Love award, U. Calif., 1990; Regents fellowship, 1983, 1989, Nato Postdoc. fellowship, NSF, 1991—92. Mem.: Soc. Study Evolution, Ecol. Soc. America, Bay Area Biosystematists (mem. steering com. 2006—), Orgn. Biol. Field Stas. Office: Sonoma State Univ 1801 East Cotati Rohnert Park CA 94928 Office Fax: 707-664-3012. Business E-Mail: rank@sonoma.edu.

RANKAITIS, SUSAN, artist; b. Cambridge, Mass., Sept. 10, 1949; d. Alfred Edward and Isabel (Shimkus) Rankaitis; m. Robbert Flick, June 5, 1976. BFA in Painting, U. Ill., 1971; MFA in Visual Arts, U. So. Calif., 1977. Rsch. asst., art dir. Plato Lab., U. Ill., Urbana, 1971-75; art instr. Orange Coast Coll., Costa Mesa, Calif., 1977-83; chair dept. art Chapman Coll., Orange, Calif., 1983-90; Fletcher Jones chair art Scripps Coll., Claremont, Calif., 1990—; priest, assoc. faculty mem., art dept. Claremont Grad. U., 2009—. Represented by Robert Mann Gallery, NYC; overview panelist visual arts Nat. Endowment for Arts, 1983, 84; selector Bingham Ednl. Trust, 1997—2002; scholar-in-residence Borchard Found., Missillac, France, 2004; artist-in-residence Europos Parkus, 2005. One-woman shows include LA County Mus. Art, 1983, Internat. Mus. Photography, George Eastman House, 1983, Gallery Min. Tokyo, 1988, Ruth Bloom Gallery, Santa Monica, 1989-90, 92, Schneider Mus., Portland, Ore., 1990; Ctr. Creative Photography, 1991, Robert Mann Gallery, NYC, 1994, 97, 2007, Mus. Contemporary Photography, Chgo., 1994, Mus. Photog. Arts, 2000, Europos Parkas, Vilnius, 2005; represented in permanent collections MOCA, LA, U. N.Mex Art, Ctr. Creative Photography, Mus. Contemporary Photography, Chgo., Santa Barbara Mus. Art, LA County Mus. Art, Mpls. Inst. Arts, St. Louis Art Mus., San Francisco Mus. Modern Art, Art Inst. Chgo., Mus. Modern Art, Lodz, Poland, Princeton U. Art Mus., Stanford U. Art Mus., Contemporary Art Mus., Honolulu, Mus. Contemporary Photography, Art Inst. Chgo., St. Louis Art Mus., others. Active art auction Venice Family Clinic, 1980-2005. Recipient Graves award in Humanities, 1985; fellow NEA, 1980, 88, USA/La Napoule Found. French, 1989, Agnes Bourne fellow Djerassi Found., 1989, Award in the Visual Arts, Flintridge Found., 2004; Durfee Chinese/Am. grantee, 2000-2001, Cultural Affairs grantee City L.A., 2001, grantee Mellon Found., 2005, 06; Borchard Found. scholar-in-residence, France, 2004. Mem. Mus. Photographic Arts, Coll. Art Assn., LA County Mus. Art, Mus. Contemporary Art. Office: Scripps Coll Art Dept Box 1051 1031 N Columbia Ave Claremont CA 91711-3931 Studio: Flick & Rankaitis Art Studio 1225 W 9th St Upland CA 91786-5707 Office Phone: 909-607-4439, 909-920-5969. Business E-Mail: srankait@scrippscollege.edu.

RANKIN, ALFRED MARSHALL, JR., manufacturing executive; b. Cleve., Oct. 8, 1941; s. Alfred Marshall and Clara Louise (Taplin) R.; m. Victoire Conley Griffin, June 3, 1967; children: Helen P., Clara T. BA in Econs. magna cum laude, Yale U., 1963, JD, 1966. Mgmt. cons. McKinsey & Co., Inc., Cleve., 1970-73; with Eaton Corp., Cleve., 1974-81, pres. materials handling group, 1981-83, pres. indsl. group, 1984-86, exec. v.p., 1986, vice chmn., chief oper. officer, 1986-89; pres., COO NACCO Industries, Inc., Cleve., 1989-91, pres., CEO, 1991-94, also bd. dirs., chmn., pres., CEO, 1994—. Bd. dir. Goodrich Corp., Vanguard Group. Former pres., trustee Hathaway Brown Sch.; trustee U. Hosps. Health Sys., Cleve., Mus. Arts Assn., Univ. Circle, Inc., Cleve. Mus. Art, John Huntington Art Trust, Greater Cleve. Partnership; dir., exec. com. mem. Nat. Assn. Manufacturers; past chairperson The Cleve. Found. Mem. Ohio Bar Assn. Clubs: Chagrin Valley Hunt, Union, Tavern, Pepper Pike, Kirtland Country (Cleve.); Rolling Rock (Ligonier, Pa.); Met. (Washington). Republican. Office: NACCO Industries Inc 5875 Landerbrook Dr Ste 300 Mayfield Heights OH 44124 Office Phone: 440-449-9600. Office Fax: 440-449-9607.

RANKIN, CLIFF (CLIFTON S. RANKIN), lawyer; Ptnr. Vinson & Elkins LLP, Houston, 2001—07; gen. counsel, corp. sec. The Shaw Group Inc., 2007—. Bd. dirs. Boys and Girls Clubs of Greater Houston. Office: The Shaw Group Inc 4171 Essen Lane Baton Rouge LA 70809*

RANKIN, CLYDE EVAN, III, lawyer; b. Phila., July 3, 1950; s. Clyde Evan, Jr. and Mary E. (Peluso) Rankin; m. Camille Cozzone, Aug. 24, 1997. AB, Princeton U., 1972; JD, Columbia U., 1975; postgrad., Hague Acad. Internat. Law, 1975. Bar: NY 1976, NJ 1976, DC 1978, US Supreme Ct. 1980. Law clk. to Judge Dudley B. Bonsal US Dist. Ct. So. Dist. NY, 1975—77; assoc. Debevoise, Plimpton, Lyons & Gates, NYC, 1977—79, Coudert Bros., 1979—83; ptnr. Corp. & Fin. Practice, 1984—2005, chmn., 2005; ptnr. Baker & McKenzie LLP, 2005—. Trustee Rensselaerville Inst., NY, 1989—, chmn., 2001—; mem. Coun. on Fgn. Rels., 1996—. Contbr. articles to profl. pubs. Chmn. alumni coun. Princeton U., 2003—05; bd. vis. Columbia U. Law Sch., 1991—. Stone scholar, 1974. Mem.: ABA, NJ Bar Assn., DC Bar Assn., NY State Bar Assn., Assn. Bar City NY, Amateur Comedy Club. Roman Catholic. Office: Baker & McKenzie LLP 1114 Ave of Americas New York NY 10036-7703 Office Phone: 212-626-4740. Office Fax: 212-310-1639. Business E-Mail: clyde.e.rankin@bakernet.com.

RANKIN, DANIEL F., JR., humanities educator; b. Alexandria, La., June 7, 1949; s. Daniel F. and Nettye Gertrude Rankin; m. Sherry K. Wilson. MA, Stephen F. Austin State U., Nacogdoches, Tex., 1986. Pastor Atoy Bapt. Ch., Rusk, Tex., 1989—; instr. Angelina Coll., Lufkin, Tex., 2003—. 1st lt. US Army, 1974—76, Ft. Leonard Wood, Mo. Office: Angelina Coll 7500 S First St Lufkin TX 75904 Business E-Mail: drankin@angelina.edu.

RANKIN, DON, art educator, educator; b. Fairfield, Ala., Dec. 9, 1942; s. Joseph P. and Edith Mae (Jones) R.; m. Geneal Muckleroy, Aug. 29, 1964; children: Jennifer Carol, David Rhodes/ MFA, Drawing Board Coll. Comml. and Fine Art, 1966; BA in Fine Art, Samford U., 1969; PhD in Visual Comm., Union Inst., Cin., Ohio, 1998. Staff artist Birmingham News, 1969-74; art dir. Martin White & Mickwee Advt., Birmingham, 1974-77; sr. art dir. Stiener/Bressler Advt., Birmingham, 1977-80; pres. Don Rankin, Inc., graphic design, Birmingham, 1980-92; asst. prof. art Samford U., Birmingham, 1992—. Author: Mastering Glazing Techniques in Watercolor, 1985, Painting from Sketches, Photos and Imagination, 1986, Fifty Questions About Watercolor Glazing Techniques, 1988. With U.S. Army, 1963-65. Mem. So. Watercolor Soc. (pres. 1992-94), Watercolor Soc. Ala. (v.p. 1968). Avocation: world oyama karate (2d degree black belt). Home: 3412 Wellford Cir Birmingham AL 35226-2616

RANKIN, JAMES, finance company executive; b. Morris Plains, NJ, Jan. 25, 1957; s. Bernard James and Carol Joyce (Cooper) R.; m. Rebecca R. Samuel, May 11, 1989. BS, U. Calif., Davis, 1980; postgrad., U. Calif., Berkeley, 1981-83; MBA, Harvard U., 1986. Asst. v.p. Wells Fargo Bank, San Francisco, 1979-88; v.p. T. Rowe Price, LA, 1988-93; v.p., chmn. oper. com. Founders Asset Mgmt., Denver, 1993-98; v.p. customer support FOLIOfn Investments, LLC, Vienna, Va., 1999-2000; sr. mng. dir. product mgmt. EquiServe, Jersey City, 2000—03; dir. Pacific Alternative Asset Mgmt. Co., Irvine, Calif., 2004—. Mem. Harvard Bus. Sch. Club of So. Calif. Avocations: skiing, bicycling, travel. Office: Pacific Alternative Asset Mgmt Co 1920 Main St Irvine CA 92614 Home: 120 Sidney Bay Dr Newport Coast CA 92657-2112 Office Phone: 949-261-4937. E-mail: rankinjp@yahoo.com.

RANKIN, JAMES WINTON, lawyer; b. Norfolk, Va., Sept. 9, 1943; s. Winton Blair and Edith (Griffin) R.; m. Donna Lee Carpenter, June 25, 1966 (dec.); children— Thomas James, William Joseph, Elizabeth Jeanne; m. JoAnne Katherine Murray, Feb. 11, 1978. AB magna cum laude, Oberlin Coll., 1965; JD cum laude, U. Chgo., 1968. Bar: Ill. 1968, U.S. Dist. Ct. (no. dist.) Ill. 1969, U.S. Ct. Appeals (7th cir.) 1971, U.S. Ct. Appeals (5th cir.) 1979, U.S. Supreme Ct. 1975, Calif. 1986. Law clk. U.S. Dist. Ct. (no. dist.) Ill., 1968-69; assoc. Kirkland & Ellis, Chgo., 1969-73, ptnr., 1973—. Fellow Am. Bar Found.; mem. ABA, Order of Coif, Mid-Am. Club, Univ. Club, Mich. Shores Club, Kenilworth Club, Ephriam Yacht Club. Presbyterian. Home: 633 Kenilworth Ave Kenilworth IL 60043-1070 Office: Kirkland & Ellis 300 N La Salla St Chicago IL 60654

RANKIN, KATHERINE POLLOCK, psychology professor, researcher; b. Lakewood, Ohio, Jan. 18, 1970; d. Robert Pollock and Moira Smith Rankin; m. Christopher Lorin Coon, June 19, 1999; children: Lauren Elizabeth Coon, Aaron Zachary Coon. BA in Psychology, Yale U., New Haven, 1992; MA in Theology, Fuller Sem., Pasadena, Calif., 1997; PhD, Fuller Grad. Sch. Psychology, Pasadena, 2000. Lic. psychology Calif., 2007. Neuropsychology fellow U. Calif., San Francisco, 2000—02, asst. prof., dept. neurology, 2002—08, assoc. prof., dept. neurology, 2008—. Contbr. articles to profl. sci. jours. Recipient Career Devel. award, Larry L. Hillblom Found., 2002—05, K-23 Career Devel. award, Nat. Inst. Aging, 2003—07; R-01 Fed. Rsch. grant, 2008—. Office: Univ Calif San Francisco Memory and Aging Ctr 350 Parnassus Ave Ste 905 San Francisco CA 94143-1207 Office Fax: 415-476-4800. Business E-Mail: krankin@memory.ucsf.edu.

RANKIN, KELLY HARRISON, prosecutor; b. 1967; JD, U. Wyo., 1994. County and prosecuting atty. Park County, Wyo.; asst. US atty. Dist. Wyo. US Dept. Justice, Casper, US atty. Dist. Wyo Cheyenne, 2008—. Office: US Attys Office PO Box 668 Cheyenne WY 82003-0668 Office Phone: 307-772-2124. Office Fax: 307-772-2123.

RANKIN, MARY ANN, dean, biology professor; BS in Biology and Chemistry, La. State Univ., 1966; PhD in Physiology and Behavior of Insects, Univ. Iowa, 1972; postdoctoral study, Harvard Univ., 1972—74. Asst. prof. zoology U. Tex., Austin, 1975, chmn. divsn. biol. sci., 1989—94, dean Coll. Natural Scis., 1994—, prof. zoology, 1996—. Pre-doctoral fellow Imperial Coll. Field Sta., Ascot, England. Office: Coll Natural Scis U Tex Austin 1 University Sta G2500 Austin TX 78712 Office Phone: 512-471-3285. Office Fax: 512-471-4998. E-mail: maryann.rankin@cns.utexas.edu.

RANKIN, PRESSLEY ROBINSON, JR., physician; b. Mt. Gilead, NC, Dec. 7, 1920; s. Pressley R. and Katie (McAuley) Rankin; m. Paula S. Story, Apr. 30, 1992; children: Pressley III, Susan, Rebecca. BS, Davidson Coll, NC, 1942; MD, Bowman Gray Sch. Medicine, 1947; grad., USAF Sch. Aviation Medicine, San Antonio, 1951. Rotating intern Watts Hosp., Durham, NC, 1948; family practice physician Mt. Gilead, NC, 1949; pvt. practice Ellerbe, NC, 1957—. Mem. Montgomery Meml. Hosp., 1957—87, Richmond Meml. Hosp., 1957—87, Moore Regional Hosp., 1957—87; med. examiner Richmond County Med. Examiner, NC, 1970—2000. Bd. mem. Richmond County Health Dept., 1973—95, 2005—; appointed to Govs. Waste Mgmt. Bd., 1990; dir. Town Creek Indian Mound, 1980—2000, Land Trust Ctrl. NC, 1995—99, United Mills, Mt. Gilead, 1949—56, Mt. Gilead Bldg. and Loan, NC, 1949—56, Mt. Gilead Brick Co., 1949—56; bd. dirs. Mt. Gilead Untied Carolina Bank, Southern Nat. Bank, Mt. Gilead, 1952—94; bd. mem. Richmond County Health Dept., 1973—95. With US Army, 1942—46, flight surgeon USAF, 1951—54, Europe and North Africa, capt. USAAF, 1954—72. Recipient Honor award, Smithsonian Mus. Am. Indians, 2006, Citizen of Yr. award, Richmond County, 1987. Mem.: Rankin Mus. Am. Heritage (founding mem. 1985), Richmond County Scottish Heritage Soc., Richmond County Hist. Soc. (pres. 1984—86), NC Med. Soc., Am. Acad. Family Physicians (charter mem.), Mason (Thirty Third Degree), NC Forestry Assn. (Recognition award 1983). Office: PO Box 40 Ellerbe NC 28338

RANKIN, ROBERT ARTHUR, journalist; b. Richmond, Va., May 31, 1949; s. Arthur Norton and Martha Louise (Rountree) Rankin; m. Janis Johnson, May 11, 1979 (div. May 2001); 1 child, Benjamin John; m. Judy A. Stromberg, Apr. 9, 2005. BA in Polit. Sci., Randolph Macon Coll., 1971; MA in Govt., U. Va., 1974; Walter Bagehot fellowship, Columbia U., 1978-79. Reporter Richmond News Leader, Va., 1972-75; reporter Congl. Quar., Washington, 1975-78; editorial writer Miami Herald, Fla., 1980-85, Phila. Inquirer, 1985-87; nat. corr. Washington bur. Knight Ridder Newspapers, Washington, 1987—99, govt. and politics editor, 2000—06, McClatchy Newspapers, Washington, 2006—; adj. prof., media & politics Randolph-Macon Coll., 2009. V.p. Civic Assn. Hollin Hills, Alexandria, Va., 1991—92. Recipient Olive Br. award, NYU Ctr. War, Peace and News Media, 1990, 1st prize, Va. Press Assn., 1974, Best Editl. award, Phila. chpt. Sigma Delta Chi, 1987; co-recipient Pulitzer prize for editl. writing, 1983. Mem.: Nat. Press Club, White House Corr. Assn. (bd. govs. 1996—98). Office: McClatchy Newspapers 700 12th St NW Ste 1000 Washington DC 20005-3994 Office Phone: 202-383-6017. Business E-Mail: rrankin@mcclatchydc.com.

RANKIN, SCOTT DAVID, artist, educator; b. Newark, Mar. 21, 1954; s. Clymont J. and Jean L. (Lane) R.; m. Linda K. Piemonte, Sept. 3, 1989 (div. Apr. 2000); m. Stephanie Volz, Apr. 23, 2005. BFA, Tyler Sch. of Art, Phila., 1976; MFA, UCLA, 1980. Asst. prof. U. Iowa, Iowa City, 1985-86, U. Chgo., 1986-94; assoc. prof. Ill. State U., Normal, 1994—2005, prof., 2005—. Video cons. Math. Edn. Rsch. Project, LA, 1991—93, 3d internat. math. and sci. study UCLA dept. psychology, 1994—95, 1998—99. Prodr., dir.: (videotapes) Fugue, 1985, This and that (version 1), 1987, (version 2), 1990, The Pure, 1993, Wire, 1998, Flow, 2000, Central, 2001, Path, 2003, Piccadilly, 2004, Reduced Shakes Hare Hare, 2007. Regional media arts fellow, Nat. Endowment for Arts, 1984, visual artists fellow, Ill. Arts Coun., 1989, 1990, Nat. Endowment for Arts, 1990, 1993. Business E-Mail: sdranki@ilstu.edu.

RANKINE, PATRICE D., literature and language professor; b. NYC, Sept. 25, 1971; s. George A. and Patricia E. Rankine. PhD in Classical Lit., Yale U., New Haven, 1998. Assoc. prof. Purdue U., West Lafayette, Ind., 1998—. Office: Purdue Univ 640 Oval Dr West Lafayette IN 47907 Office Fax: 765-496-2365. Business E-Mail: rankine@purdue.edu.

RANKS, ANNE ELIZABETH, retired elementary and secondary education educator; b. Omaha, July 9, 1916; d. Salvatore and Concetta (Turco) Scolla; m. Harold Eugene Ranks, Aug. 20, 1955 (dec.). B in Philosophy, Duchesne Coll., Omaha, 1937; MA, Creighton U., 1947. Tchr. Good Shepherd Parochial H.S., Omaha, 1937-38, St. Benedicts H.S., Omaha, 1938-39, Omaha Pub. Schs., 1939-81. Pres. women's divsn. Dem. Cen. Com., Nebr.; chmn. Gov.'s Profl. Practices Commn. Nebr., 1938-39; vol. Bergan-Mercy Hosp., Omaha, 1980-86, 99—, hosp. mem. aux. bd. dirs., 1985-86; vol. Saddleback Hosp., Laguna Hills, Calif., 1989-91; bd. dirs. Sylvia Tischhauser CRTA divsn. Scholarship Found., 1989-94; mem. bd. dirs. Saddleback Valley Ednl. Found., 1990-92; bd. dirs. Orange County Diocesan Coun. Cath. Women, 1989-90, 2d v.p., 1990-94; vol. Bergan Mercy Hosp., 1998-2001. Mem. AAUW (v.p. Laguna Hills br. 1988-91), Nebr. Edn. Assn. (bd. dirs. 1957-60, pres. dist. II 1960-62), Omaha Edn. Assn. (bd. dirs. 1950-55), Womens Club, Cath. Daus. Regent Omaha Ct. (rec. sec. Lake Forest, Calif. Ct. 1988-90), Coll. Club of Leisure World (v.p. 1990-95), Nat. Ret. Tchrs. Assn., Nebr. Ret. Tchrs. Assn., Local Ret. Tchrs. Assn., Cath. Daus. Home: Apt 244 9804 Nicholas St Omaha NE 68114-2180 Home Phone: 402-384-8925.

RANNALA, BRUCE, biology professor; b. New Westminster, BC, Can., Mar. 10, 1964; s. Ivar Helmer Rannala and Rayna Kinny; m. Kimberly Anne Rannala, Aug. 10, 1988; 1 child, Bruce. BSc, U. BC, Vancouver, 1989; MSc, U. Toronto, Ont., Can., 1991; PhD, Yale U., New Haven, 1995. Asst. prof. SUNY, Stony Brook, 1998—2000; assoc. prof. U. Alta., Edmonton, Canada, 2000—04; prof. U. Calif., Davis, 2004—, assoc. dir. bioinformatics Genome ctr., 2006—08. Recipient award, Can. Inst. Health Rsch. and Peter Lougheed Found., 2000—04. Home Fax: 530 754-4060.

RANNEBERGER, MICHAEL E., United States Ambassador to Kenya; BA, Towson State U.; MA, U. Va., 1973. Angola desk officer Bur. African affairs US Dept. State, spl asst. to under sec., 1984—85, dep. chief of mission Office US amb. to Mozambique, 1986—89, dep. chief of mission Office US amb. to Paraguay, 1989—92, dep. dir. Office Ctrl. Am. and Panamanian Affairs, Bur. We. Hemisphere Affairs, 1992—94, dep. chief of mission Office US amb. to Somalia, 1994, coord. Cuban affairs, 1995—99, US amb. to Mali, 1999—2002, spl adv. Office Sudan Programs Group, 2002—04, prin. dep. asst. sec. Bur. African Affairs, 2004—05, US amb. to Kenya Nairobi, 2006—. Office: 8900 Nairobi Pl Washington DC 20521*

RANNER, SHANNA, music educator; d. Gare and Shirley Kraemer; m. Christopher Ranner, May 31, 1997; 1 child, Jayson. BA with Instrumental Emphasis, Truman State U., Kirkville, Mo., 1997; MusB in Percussion Performance, Truman State U., Kirksville, Mo, 1997; MusM in Edn., U. Mo.-St. Louis, 2003. Cert. instrumental music edn. K-12 Mo., 2003, vocal music edn. K-12 Mo., 2006. Tchr. music Lincoln County R-III Sch. Dist., Troy, Mo., 2000—04, U. City Sch. Dist., University City, Mo., 2004—. Musician: (mallet keyboard competition) Percussive Arts Soc. Internat. Mallet Keyboard Competition, Music Tchrs. Nat. Assn. Competition-Percussion. Named to Nat. Dean's List, Truman State U., 1995. Mem.: Sigma Alpha Iota, Mo. Music Educators Assn., Music Educators Nat. Conf., Phi Kappa Phi. Lutheran. Avocations: water aerobics, crafts. Home: 12 Fairfield Court Saint Peters MO 63376

RANNEY, GEORGE A., JR., lawyer; b. Chgo., Apr. 11, 1940; BA magna cum laude, Harvard U., 1962; JD, U. Chgo., 1966. Bar: Ill. 1966. Law clk. to Hon. Carl McGowan U.S. Ct. Appeals, Washington, 1966-67; dep. dir. Bur. Budget, State of Ill., 1969-73; counsel, v.p. Inland Steel Co., 1973-86; now sr. counsel Mayer, Brown & Platt, Chgo.; and pres., CEO Chigo. Metropolis 2020; also chmn., CEO Prairie Holdings Corp., Grayslake, Ill. Mem. Commn. Uniform State Laws, Campaign for RTA 1969-73; chmn. State Task Force on Future Ill., 1978-80; lectr. U. Chgo., 1975-79. Editor-in-chief U. Chgo. Law Rev., 1966-67. Fellow Am. Acad. Arts & Scis.; mem. ABA, Chgo. Bar Assn.

RANNEY, HELEN MARGARET, retired internist, hematologist, educator; b. Summer Hill, NY, Apr. 12, 1920; d. Arthur C. and Alesia (Toolan) Ranney. AB, Barnard Coll., 1941; MD, Columbia U., 1947; ScD, U. S.C., 1979, SUNY, Buffalo, 1996. Diplomate Am. Bd. Internal Medicine. Intern Presbyn. Hosp., NYC, 1947—48, resident, 1948—50, asst. physician, 1954—60; practice medicine specializing in internal medicine, hematology NYC, 1954—70; instr. Coll. Phys. and Surg. Columbia, NYC, 1954—60; from assoc. prof. to prof. medicine Albert Einstein Coll. Medicine, NYC, 1960—70; prof. medicine SUNY, Buffalo, 1970—73, U. Calif., San Diego, 1973—90, chmn. dept. medicine, 1973—86, Disting. physician vet. adminstr., 1986—91; cons. Alliance Pharm. Corp., San Diego, 1991—2004; ret., 2004. Master: ACP; fellow: AAAS; mem.: NAS, Am. Acad. Arts and Scis., Am. Assn. Physicians, Harvey Soc., Am. Soc. Hematology, Am. Soc. for Clin. Investigation, Inst. Medicine, Alpha Omega Alpha, Sigma Xi, Phi Beta Kappa. Personal E-mail: hranney@ucsd.edu.

RANNEY, JOSEPH AUSTIN, lawyer; b. Urbana, Ill., May 19, 1952; s. Joseph Austin and Elizabeth (Mackay) R.; m. Rebecca S. Rice, Sept. 5, 1982; 1 child, Emily M. BA, U. Chgo., 1972; JD, Yale U., 1978. Bar: Wis. 1978, U.S. Dist. Ct. (ea. dist. 1978, we. dist. 1988) Wis., U.S. Ct. Appeals (7th cir.) 1995, U.S. Ct. Appeals (Fed. cir.) 2000. Assoc. Gibbs, Roper, Loots & Williams, Milw., 1978-81, Trowbridge, Planert & Schaefer, Green Bay, Wis., 1981-88, Ross & Stevens, S.C., Madison, Wis., 1988-90, ptnr., 1990-94, DeWitt Ross & Stevens S.C., Madison, Wis., 1995—. Dir., pres. Legal Svcs. of Northeastern Wis., Green Bay, 1982-88; adj. prof. Marquette Law Sch., Milw., Wis., 2000—. Author: Trusting Nothing to Providence: A History of Wisconsin's Legal System, 1999, In the Wake of Slavery: Civil War, Civil Rights and the Reconstruction of Southern Law, 2006, Deposition Objections; contbr. articles to profl. law refs. Chmn. Brown County Dem. Party, Green Bay, 1984-86, Wis. 8th Congl. Dist., Dem. Party, 1986-88. With U.S. Army, 1972-75. Recipient Charles Dunn Author award Wis. State Bar, 1993. Office: DeWitt Ross & Stevens SC Two E Mifflin St Madison WI 53703 Home: 595 Fargo Tr Middleton WI 53562 Home Phone: 608-827-3057; Office Phone: 608-255-8891. Business E-Mail: jar@dewittross.net.

RANNEY, RICHARD RAYMOND, periodontist educator, researcher, dean; b. Atlanta, July 11, 1939; s. Russell Ballou and Maureen Joan (Bannon) R.; m. Beverly Anne Toton, June 10, 1961 (div.); children: Christine Marie, Kathleen Anne; m. Patricia Marie DeNoto, Feb. 22, 1969; children: Maureen Frances, Russell Christopher. DDS, U. Iowa, 1963; MS, U. Rochester, 1969; D (hon.), U. Buenos Aires, 1995. Asst. prof. periodontology U. Oreg., 1969-72; assoc. prof. periodontics Va. Commonwealth U., Richmond, Va., 1972-78, prof., 1978-86, dir. grad. periodontics, 1972-76, chmn. dept. periodontics, 1974-77, asst. dean rsch. and grad. affairs, 1977-84, asst. dean rsch., 1984-86; dir. Clin. Rsch. Ctr. Periodontal Diseases, Richmond, 1978-86; prof. Sch. Dentistry U. Ala., Birmingham, 1986-91, dean, 1986-89; prof. U. Md., Balt., 1991—2005, prof. emeritus, 2005, dean, 1991—2002; Sr. Policy fellow Am. Dental Edn. Assn., 2003—04, Gies Edn. fellow, 2004—05; dir. Eastman Dental Ctr. Found., Inc., 2005—; sr. cons. Acad. for Academic Leadership, 2006—. Contbr. chpts. to books, articles to profl. jours. With USPHS, 1963-66. Nat. Inst. Dental Rsch. grantee, 1970-86. Fellow: AAAS, Am. Coll. Dentists, Internat. Coll. Dentists; mem.: ADA, Am. Dental Edn. Assn. (Presdl. citation 2005), Am. Assn. Dental Rsch. (pres. 1990—91), Internat. Assn. Dental Rsch. (pres. 1995—96, basic rsch. periodontology award 1985), Am. Acad. Periodontology, Omicron Kappa Upsilon, Sigma Xi. Home Phone: 410-923-1049. Personal E-mail: pranney3@comcast.net.

RANSEL, DAVID LORIMER, history professor; b. Gary, Ind., Feb. 20, 1939; s. Joseph A. and Patricia (Lorimer) R.; m. Therese Holma; children: Shairstin, Annaliisa. BA, Coe Coll., 1961; MA, Northwestern U., 1962; PhD, Yale U., 1969. Instr. Tollare Folkhogskola, Boo, Sweden, 1959-60; asst. instr. Yale U., New Haven, 1966-67; instr. U. Ill., Urbana, 1967-69, asst. prof., 1969-73, assoc. prof., 1973-81, prof., 1981-85, Ind.

U., Bloomington, 1985—, Robert F. Byrnes prof. history, 2001—, dir. Russian and East European Inst., 1995—2009; co-dir. European Union Ctr., 2005—08. Author: The Politics of Catherinian Russia, 1975, Mothers of Misery, 1988, Village Mothers: Three Generations of Change in Russia and Tataria, 2000, A Russian Merchant's tale: The Life And Adventures of Ivan Alekseevich Tolchënov Based on his Diary, 2008; editor: The Family in Imperial Russia, 1978, Imperial Russia: New Histories for the Empire, 1998, Polish Encounters, Russian Identity, 2005; editor/translator: Village Life in Late Tsarist Russia, 1993; editor Slavic Rev., Urbana, 1980-85, Am. Hist. Rev., Bloomington, 1985-95; bd. editors The History of the Family: An International Quarterly, Historisk Tidskrift, Forum for Anthropology and Culture, Kritika: Explorations in Russian and Eurasian History, Jour. Modern History, 2005—08. Fellow Guggenheim Found., 1989-90, Wilson Nat. Fellowship Found., 1989-90, NEH, 1998-99, Bogliasco Found., 2007; Fulbright-Hays grantee, 1979, 90, Irex grantee, 1990, 93. Mem. Am. Hist. Assn. (gov. coun. 1985-95, fin. com. 1989-95), Am. Assn. for Advancement of Slavic Studies (bd. dirs. 1979-85, mem. fin. com. 1980-85, chmn. com. on status of women 1991-93, v.p., pres.-elect 2003, pres. 2004-05, immediate past pres. 2005), Irex (program com. 1995-99). Avocations: classical guitar, sailing, swimming. Office: Ind Univ Dept History 742 Ballantine Hall Bloomington IN 47401-5017 Office Phone: 812-855-8036. Business E-Mail: ransel@indiana.edu.

RANSOM, ROGER L., retired history professor; b. Berkeley, Calif., Sept. 5, 1938; s. David H. and Dorothy Ransom; m. Connie Flint, June 18, 1960; children: Charlotte Ransom McKenzie, Leslie Flint. PhD, U. Wash., Seattle, 1963. Asst. prof. economics U. Va., Charlottesville, 1963—68; disting. prof. history and economics U. Calif., Riverside, 1968—2008. Author: (book) Coping With Capitalism: The Economic Transformation of the United States, 1776 1980, Conflict and Compromise: The Political Economy of Slavery, Emancipation, and the American Civil War., The Confederate States of America: What Might Have Been; co-author: The Academic Scribblers: American Economists in Collision, One Kind of Freedom: The Economic Consequences of Emancipation. Mem., pres. Riverside Unified Sch. Bd., Calif., 1975—83. Recipient Clio award, Cliometrics Assn., 1988, Disting. Tchg. award, U. Calif., Riverside, 2003, Disting. Humanist Achievement award, 2006; fellowship, Guggenheim Found., 1987—88. Mem.: Econ. History Assn. (pres. 2004—05, Arthur H. Cole prize 1986).

RANSOM, TASHA ELANA, perspective production field producer; d. Vincent Allen and Mary Geraldine Ransom. BS, Drake U., Des Moines, 1995; postgrad., Valparaiso U., Ind., 1996—97; MA, Columbia Coll., Chgo., 2002. Law clk. Vickie Pasley & Assocs., Chgo., 1992, 1994; product mgr. Zachs Investment & Rsch., Chgo., 1996; law clk. Hoeppner Wagner & Evans, Valparaiso, Ind., 1997—98; intern Lawyers for the Creative Arts, Chgo., 1999—2000; asst. Linda S. Mensch P.C., Chgo., 1999—2001; intern, prodn. cmty. affairs Fox News Chgo., 2000—01, asst. to news dir., 2001—05, asst. to news dir., prodr., 2005—. Bd. mem. Metro. and Family Svc., 2005—. Recipient Alumni of the Yr., Outstanding Contbn. in the African Am. Cmty., Youth Action Ministry, 2003, Portrait of Achievers award, 2009; Chuck Suber scholarship, Columbia Coll., 2001—02. Mem.: Hoffman Estates Chapt. Links Inc., Nat. Assn. Black Journalists, Phi Alpha Delta, Delta Sigma Pi.

RANSOME, RONALD D., physics professor; b. Pueblo, Colo., June 9, 1954; s. Carl and Mae Ransome; m. Kathleen Friedl, Mar. 14, 2005; 1 child, Vincent. PhD, U. Tex., Austin, 1981. Asst. prof. Rutgers U., Piscataway, NJ, 1985—91, assoc. prof., 1991—2001, prof., 2001—. Rsch. grant, NSF, 1986—2009. Mem.: Am. Phys. Soc. Achievements include research in nuclear physics, few body interactions and nucleon structure. Office: Rutgers Univ 136 Freylinghuysen Rd Piscataway NJ 08854

RANTA, RICHARD ROBERT, university dean; b. Virginia, Minn., Nov. 18, 1943; s. V. Robert and Bernice (Smith) R.; 1 child, Erick H.; m. Carol Crown. AS, Hibbing Community Coll., Minn., 1963; BS, U. Minn., 1965; MA, Cornell U., 1967; PhD, U. Iowa, 1974. Floor dir. Sta. KDAL-TV, Duluth, Minn., 1964-65; asst. prof. U. Va., Charlottesville, 1969-72, U. Memphis, 1972-75, assoc. prof., 1975-91, prof., 1991—, interim dean Univ. Coll., 1975, asst. v.p. academic affairs, 1976-78, dean Coll. Comm. and Fine Arts, 1977—; gen. mgr. High Water Records, Memphis, 1980—. Bd. dirs. Concerts Internat., Memphis, pres., 1988-90; TV cons., free-lance producer, 1973—; mem. Rec. Hall of Fame selection panel Nat. Rec. Acad., L.A., 1986-2000; vice-chmn. Gilliam Comm., 1992-. Assoc. prodr.: (TV program) Nat. Arthritis Telethon, 1985-90; Rec. Acad. graphics and prodn. coord. Grammy Awards TV program, 1983—, writer and judge Knowledge Bowl TV Show, 1986-; author articles in Communication Adminstrn. Bull., 1977-2001, editl. bd., 1991-2001, exec. com., 1996-2000. Chmn., v.p. Tenn. Humanities Coun., Nashville, 1980-82; v.p. Memphis Devel. Found., 1983-86; bd. dirs. Leadership Memphis, 1987-90, 94-97, chmn. mktg. com., 1987-90, chmn. selection com., 1994-95; bd. dirs. Life Blood, Memphis, 1984-92; treas. Memphis-Shelby County Film and TV Commn., 1986-98, chair, 1999-2002, bd. dirs., 2002--; mem. Tenn. Film, Entertainment and Music Commn., Nashville, 1987-97, chmn., 1993-95; chmn. bd. dirs. Crime Stoppers Memphis Assn., 1993-95; chmn. Memphis Arts Festival, 1992-94;bd. dirs. Tenn. Arts Commn., 2000-06. Recipient Edn. Operational Models grant Ednl. Testing Svc., 1975, Communication Lab. grant HEW, 1976, Disting. Alumnus award Minn. Cmty. Coll. System, 1984, Alumni Cmty. Svc. award Leadership Memphis, 1997. Mem. NARAS (v.p. 1986-88, 92-93, chmn. edn. com. 1983—2001, trustee 1982-86, 88-92, 93-97, pres. Memphis chpt. 1984-86, bd. govs. 1978-98), So. States Comm. Assn. (pres. 1987-88, fin. bd. 1985-87, 93-95, exec. dir. 1995—2000), Tenn. Speech Comm. Assn. (pres. 1986-87, editor Communicator 1993—), Nat. Comm. Assn. (vice chmn., then chmn. exptl. learning com. 1979-83, mem. fin. and adminstrn. coms. 1989-93, chmn. fin. com. 1991-93), So. Arts Fedn. (bd. dirs. 1994-2000, 2003-, treas.), Internat. Coun. Fine Arts Deans (parliamentarian 1996-2000), Tenn. Arts and Scis. Deans Assn. (chair 1997-98), Advt. Fedn. (bd. dirs. 2001-03), Delta Sailing Assn. Club (sec. 1984-2000), Memphis Rotary Internat. Club (pres.-elect, asst. dist. govs. 2008-), Nat. Metal Mus. (bd. dirs. 2004-, greater memphis greenways bd. mem., 2009-). Avocations: sailing, tennis, photography, fishing. Office: U Memphis Coll Communication & Fine Ar Memphis TN 38152-0001 E-mail: rranta@memphis.edu.

RANU, HARCHARAN SINGH, biomedical scientist, administrator, orthopaedic biomechanics educator; b. Lyallpur, India; came to U.S., 1976; s. Jodh Singh and Harnam Kaur R. BSc, De Montfort U., Eng., 1963; MSc, U. Surrey, Guilford, Eng., 1967, Cambridge U., Eng., 1972; PhD, Middlesex Hosp. Med. Sch. and U. Westminster, London, 1975; diploma, MIT, 1984. Chartered engr., scientist, Eng. Med. scientist Nat. Inst. Med. Rsch. of the Med. Rsch. Coun., London, 1967-70; rsch. fellow Middlesex Hosp. Med. Sch. and Poly. of Cen. London, 1971-76; rsch. scientist Plastics Rsch. Assn. of Great Britain, Shawbury, Eng., 1977; asst. prof. Wayne State U., Detroit, 1977-81; prof. biomed. engring./orthopaedic biomechanics biomaterials La. Tech. U., Ruston, 1982—; prof., chmn. dept. biomechanics N.Y. Coll. Osteo. Medicine, Old Westbury, 1989-93; dir. tng. Rehab. R&D Ctr., 1983-85; mem. La. Tech. U. Libr. Com., 1983-85; chmn. design competition Assn. Biomed. Engrs.; mem. steering com. So. Biomed. Engring. Confs., 1983—; chmn. tech. in health care conf. U. Cambridge, 1985; chmn. Internat. Symposium on Bioengring., Calcutta, India, 1985; dir. orthopaedic biomechanics rsch. labs., staff Nassau County Med. Ctr., Long Island, 1989—; prof., exec. asst. to pres., and dir. doctoral program Life U., Marietta, Ga., 1993—; pres. Am. Orthop. Biomechanics Rsch. Inst., Atlanta, 1997—. Biomed. engring. faculty com. La. Tech. U., faculty com., rsch. awards com., grad. studies com., grad. faculty, acad. bd. dirs; vis. scientist Dryburn Hosp., Durham, Eng., 1985-87, cons., 1988—; vis. prof. U. Istanbul, 1982, Lab. de Recherch Orthopediques, Paris, 1985—, Kings Coll. Med. Sch. U. London, 1989—, Indian Inst. Tech., New Delhi, Postgrad Inst. Med. Edn. and Rsch., Chandigarh, India, 1989—, Polytech. Ctrl. London, 1991—, U. Buenos Aires, Pontific Cath. U. Chile, Fed. U. Rio de Janeiro; adj. prof. Coll. Physicians and Surgeons Columbia U., NYC, 1988—, Inst. Biol. Physics USSR Acad. Sci., Moscow, 1990, NY Coll. Podiatric Medicine, 1991—, CUNY, 1992—; cons. Lincoln Gen. Hosp., Ruston, La., 1982-85, La. State U. Med. Ctr., Shreveport, 1982—, St. Luke's and Roosevelt Hosp. Ctr., NY, 1988—, Foot Clinics N., 1991—, Vets. Affairs Med. Ctr., NY, 1992—, others; media resource svc. Inst. Pub. Info., NY, 1989—; med. scientist, cons. NATO, 1982—; presenter, lectr. in field; external examiner for doctoral candidates All India Inst. Med. Scis., New Delhi, Indian Inst. Tech., New Delhi, Banaras Hindu U., Varanasi, India, 1994; prof. U. Surrey, 2009; pres. Am. Orthop. Biomechanics Rsch. Inst., Atlanta, 1997; rsch. award com. mem. Am. Coll. Sports Medicine. Author: Rheological Behavior of Articular Cartiliage Under Tensile Loads, 1967, Effects of Ionizing Radiation on the Mechanical Properties of Skin, 1975, Effects of Fractionated Doses of X-irradiation on the Mechanical Properties of Skin--A Long Term Study, 1980, Effects of Ionizing Radiation on the Structure & Physical Properties of the Skin, 1983, 3-D Model of Vertebra for Spinal Surgery, 1985, Application of Carbon Fibers in Orthopaedic Surgery, 1985, Relation Between Metal Corrision & Electrical Polarization, 1989, The Distribution of Stresses in the Human Lumbar Spine, 1989, Medical Devices & Orthopaedic Implants in the United States, 1989, Spinal Surgery by Modeling, 1989, Multipoint Determination of Pressure-Volume Curves in Human Intervertebral Discs, 1993, Evaluation of Volume-Pressure Relationship in Lumbar Discs Using Model and Experimental Studies, 1994, A Mechanism of Laser Nuclectomy, 1994, Microminiaturization in Laser Surgery in Vivo Intradiscal Pressure Measurements in Lumbar Intervertebral Discs, 1994, An Experimental and Mathematical Simulation of Fracture of Human Bone Due to Jumping, 1994; editor The Lower Extremity, 1993—; guest editor IEEE Engring. in Medicine & Biology, 1991; mem. editl. bd. Med. Instrumentation, 1988—, Jour. Biomed. Instrumentation & Tech., 1988—, Jour. Med. Engring. & Tech., 1989—, Jour. Med. Design & Material, 1990—, Jour. Long-Term Effects Med. Implants, 1991—, Biomed. Sci. & Tech., 1991—, Health & Fittness, 2007, rsch. award com. Am. Coll. Sports Medicine, 2009; reviewer Jour. Biomechanics, 1981—, Clin. Biomechanics, 1984—, Jour. Biomed. Engring., 1981, Phys. Therapy, 1990—, IEEE Biomed. Transactions, 1991—, Jour. Engring. in Medicine, 1989—; contbr. articles to profl. jours. Faculty advisor India Students Assn. Wayne State U., 1980. Recipient Edwin Tate award U. Surrey, 1968, Third Internat. Olympic Com. World Congress On Sprots Scis. award, Atlanta, 1995; numerous rsch. grants. Fellow ASME (bioengring. com. 1990—, award L.I. chpt. 1991), Biol. Engring. Soc. (London, President's prize 1984), Instn. Mech. Engrs. (chmn. revv. bd. for corp. memberships, James Clayton awards 1974-76), Inst. Physics and Engring. in Medicine; mem. AAAS, Am. Soc. Biomechanics (edn. com. 1990—), Orthopaedic Rsch. Soc., Am. Coll. Sports Medicine, Biomed. Engring. Soc., India Assn., India Assn. North La., Sci. Coun. Eng. (chartered scientist). Sikh. Achievements include research in microfracture simulation of human vertebrae under compressive loading, laserectomy of the human nucleus pulposus and its effect on the intradiscal pressure, pressure-volume relation in human intervertebral discs, in vitro and in vivo intradiscal pressure measurements before and after laserectomy of the human nucleus pulposus, gait analysis of a diabetic foot, bioengineering in the millennium, bioengineering-building the future of biology and medicine, bioengineering the cutting edge of biology and medicine in the millennium, in vivo micro-fracture simulation in Indian Olympic field hockey players, relief from low-back pain in sports by infusion of saline into the human nucleus pulposus and establishing the pressure-volume relationship, clinical applications of bioinstrumentation for better health, fifth IOC World Congress on sports sciences, micro-fracture simulation in tennis players, human gait analysis normal and pathological, simulation of micro-fracture injury in female gymnasts-an in vivo study, pattern recognition in human gait, identification of ethnicity from human gait; micro-fracture injury simulation in pole-vaulting and female gymnasts; 3-D simulation of drop in intradiscal pressure in spinal discs due to laserectomy; Ranu's principle and laserectomy to relieve low back pain; Ranu's cumulative gait effect phenomenon, invivo micro-fracture simulation in skiers; 3-D foot pressure measurements in normal and diabetic persons; normal and abnormal gait of successive steps with miniature triaxial load cells; gait analysis of amputees initally and one month later for successive steps; stress-fracture simulationi n ski jumpers, the effect of ovariectomy on antioxidant system of bone, micro-fracture simulation in vivo in human bone, amputees gait analyses for sucssessive steps. Office: Life Univ Sch Grad Studies Marietta GA 30060 Personal E-mail: profranu@yahoo.com.

RANUM, OREST ALLEN, historian, educator; b. Lyle, Minn., Feb. 18, 1933; s. Luther George and Nada (Chaffee) R.; m. Patricia McGroder, July 4, 1955; children— Kristin, Marcus BA, Macalester Coll., St. Paul, 1955; MA, U. Minn., 1957, PhD, 1961. Asst. prof. U. So. Calif., 1960-61; asst. prof. Columbia U., NYC, 1961-63, assoc. prof., 1963-69; prof. history Johns Hopkins U., Balt., 1969-99; ret., 1999. Mem., chmn. GRE Ednl. Testing Service, Princeton, 1973-78 Author: Richelieu and Councilors, 1963, Paris, Age of Absolutism, 1968, revised and expanded edit., 2002, Artisans of Glory, 1981, The Fronde, 1993, Paris in the Age of Absolutism, 2002. Recipient Bronze medal City of Tours, France, 1980. Mem. Am. Hist. Assn., Soc. French Hist. Studies, Inst. de France (corr.), Académie des Sciences Morales et Politiques (Paris; corr. 1989), Société de l'Histoire de France, Collège de France (internat. chair 1994-95). Home: 208 Ridgewood Rd Baltimore MD 21210-2539 Office: History Dept Johns Hopkins U Baltimore MD 21218 Office Phone: 410-516-7575. E-mail: orestranum@verizon.net.

RAO, AKKINEPALLI BADRI NARAYAN, physician, educator; b. Hyderabad, India, Oct. 7, 1923; arrived in Australia, 1973; s. Sita Ram and Rama Chudamma (Rangaraju) R.; m. Norah Janet Gardner, Mar. 22, 1958; children: Priti, Nandita. FSc, Osmania U., 1942, B Medicine B Surgery, 1947. House surgeon medicine, surgery and obstetrics, Hyderabad, 1948; house surgeon ear nose and throat Royal Nat. Ear Nose and Throat Hosp., London, 1951-52; registrar ear nose and throat Birmingham and Midland Ear Nose and Throat Hosp., 1952-54; ear nose and throat surgeon Osmania Gen. Hosp. and Med. Coll., Hyderabad, 1954-67, prof. ear nose and throat, 1958-73; cons. ear nose and throat surgeon Birmingham Regional Hosp., Eng., 1967-69; sr. ear, nose and throat surgeon Royal Darwin (Australia) Hosp., 1973-97, emeritus ear, nose and throat cons.; emeritus prof. ear, nose and throat Osmania Med. Coll., Hyderabad, India. Fgn. collaborant Acta Otolaryngologica, Stockholm; vis. ear, nose and throat specialist Mackay Base Hosp., Queensland, 1997—; lectr., presenter in field. Contbr. articles to profl. publs., chpts. to books. Recipient Citizen of Australia award Australian Day Coun., 1996, Order of Australia, 1997; fellow Internat. Coll. Surgeons, 1957-67. Fellow Royal Soc. Medicine; mem. Royal Commonwealth Soc. Australia (life), Australian Med. Assn. (mem. exec. coun. N.T. sect.), Neuro Equilibriomatic Soc., Prosper Meniere Soc., Assn. Otolaryngologists of India (life), Otolaryngol. Soc. Australia. Avocations: travel, teaching. Home: 57 Pamela St Mount Waverley VIC 3149 Australia Office: Royal Darwin Hosp Casuarina Darwin 0811 Australia Office Phone: 61 3 9560 8595.

RAO, ANIL VITHALA, science educator; b. Mumbai, Dec. 14, 1965; s. Rajeswara Vithala and Saroj Vithala Rao; m. Anita Badhwar, July 7, 2000; children: Vikram Vithala, Divya Vithala. PhD, Princeton U., NJ, 1996. Sr. mem. tech. staff Charles Stark Draper Lab., Inc., Cambridge, Mass., 2000—06; asst. prof. U. Fla., Gainesville, 2006—. Named Tchr. of Yr., Boston U., 2003—04. Office Fax: 352-392-7303. Personal E-mail: anilvrao@gmail.com. Business E-Mail: anilvrao@ufl.edu.

RAO, CHINTAMANI NAGESA RAMACHANDRA, science educator, Indian government official, academic administrator; b. Bangalore, Karnataka, India, June 30, 1934; s. Hanumantha Nagesa and Nagamma Nagesa R.; m. Indumati Rao, May 15, 1960; children: Suchitra, Sanjay. BSc, Mysore U., India, 1951; MSc, Banaras Hindu U., Uttar Pradesh, India, 1953; PhD, Purdue U., 1958; DSc, Mysore U., Karnataka, 1961; DSc (honoris causa), other 35 univs. Head Dept. Chemistry Indian Inst. Tech., Kanpur, Uttar Pradesh, 1963-77; chmn. Solid State and Structural Chemistry Unit and Materials Rsch. Centre Indian Inst. Sci., Bangalore, 1977-84, dir., 1984-94; chmn. sci. adv. coun. Prime Min. Rajiv Gandhi, 1985—89; chmn. sci. adv. com. Union Cabinet, 1997—98; hon. pres., Linus Pauling rsch. prof. Jawaharlal Nehru Ctr. Advanced Sci. Rsch. Indian Inst. Sci., Bangalore, 1990—99; Albert Einstein rsch. prof., 1995—99; Linnett prof. Cambridge U., 1998; Gauss prof. Germany, 2003. Blackett lectr., 1991, Centenary lectr. Royal Soc. Chemistry, London, 2000; bd. dirs. Res. Bank India; mem. exec. bd. Internat. Coun. Unions, Sci. Inst. Groups, Princeton; internat. sci. adv. bd. and internat. coun. chemistry, UNESCO; chmn. Indo-Japan Sci. Coun., Indo-Russia Long-term Programme Sci. and Tech.; Linnett vis. prof. U. Cambridge.; vis. prof. including Purdue U., Oxford U., Melbourne U., Grenoble and Cardiff; mem. AEC India; chmn. Indo-Japan Sci. Coun.; pres. Internat. Union Pure and Applied Chemistry, 1985-97, Indian Sci. Congress Assn., 1987-88, Materials Rsch. Soc. India, 1989-91; rschr. in field. Author 39 books, over 1400 rsch. publs.; mem. editl. bds. 15 leading profl. jours. Decorated comdr. Order of Rio Branco, 2002; fellow Jawajarlal Nehru Ctr., 1973, Padma Shri, 1974, Centennial Fgn. fellow Am. Chem. Soc., 1976, hon. fellow Royal Soc. Chemistry, London, 1989; recipient Marlow medal Faraday Soc., 1967, Bhatnagar prize, 1968, Sir C.V. Raman award, 1975, S.N. Bose medal Indian Nat. Sci. Acad., 1980, Padma Vibhushan award Pres. India, 1985, G.M. Modi award, 1989, Golden Jubilee prize phys. scis. Coun. Sci. and Indsl. Rsch., 1991, Sahabdeen award Sri Lanka, TWAS (The Acad. Scis. Devel. World) medal lectr., 1995, Einstein Gold medal UNESCO, 1996, Karnataka Ratna Karnataka Govt., 2001, Order Sci. Merit (Grand Cross) Pres. of Brazil, 2002, Somiya award Internat. Union Materials Rsch., 2004, India Sci. award Govt. of India, 2005, Dan David prize, 2005; named Chem. Pioneer Am. Inst. Chemists, 2005, Chevalier la Légion d'Honneur Pres. French Republic, 2005. Fellow NAS (fgn. assoc.), Indian Nat. Sci. Acad. (pres. 1985-86), Meghnad Saha medal 1990), Indian Acad. Scis. (pres. 1989-91), Royal Soc. London (Hughes medal 2000), Royal Soc. Can. (fgn.), Royal Soc. Chemistry (Centenary medal 2000), Third World Acad. Scis. (pres. 2002-2007); mem. AAAS (hon. fgn.), Russian Acad. Scis. (fgn.), French Acad. Scis., Japan Acad., Polish Acad., Czechoslovakia Acad. (Hevrovsky Gold medal 1989), Serbia Acad. Scis., Slovenia Acad. Scis., Brazil Acad. Scis., Spanish Acad. Scis., Korean Acad. Scis., African Acad. Scis., Am. Philos. Soc., Pontifical Acad. Scis., European Acad. Scis. (fgn.). Avocations: gourmet cooking, gardening, reading. Office: TWAS The Acad Scis Developing World c/o Abdus Salam ICTP Strada Costiera 11 Trieste 34014 Italy E-mail: cnrrao@jncasr.ac.in.

RAO, CV, medical educator; b. Bantumelli, Andhra Pradesh, India; m. Vijayalakshmi Rao, Oct. 10, 1971; children: Satish C. children: Naveen C. BSc, Andhra Vet. Coll., Tirupathi, India, 1964; MS in Animal Scis., Wash. State U., Pullman, 1966, PhD in Animal Scis., 1969. Rsch. asst. Wash. State U., 1964—69; rsch. fellow biochemistry Albert Einstein Coll. Medicine, Bronx, NY, 1969—70; rsch. fellow Cornell U. Med. Coll., NYC, 1970—72; asst. prof. U. Louisville Sch. Medicine, 1972—76, assoc. prof., 1976—79, prof. obstetrics, gynecology and women's health, 1979—2008; prof. cell biology, molecular & human genetics, dir. reproduction & devel. Fla. Internat. U. Coll. Medicine, Miami. Contbr. more than 275 sci. articles to profl. jours. Recipient Outstanding Alumnus award, Wash. State U., 2009; named Med. Rsch. Coun.'s Disting. Vis. Scientist, U. Cape Town, South Africa, 2005; Rsch. grant, US NIH, 1975—2008. Mem.: AAAS, Sigma Xi, Internat. Fedn. Fertility Societies, Am. Soc. Reproductive Medicine, Soc. Study Reproduction, Soc. Gynecologic Investigation, Edocrine Soc., Am. Physiol. Soc., Am. Soc. Cell Biology, Internat. Soc. Study Trophoblastic Diseases, Internat. Fedn. Placenta Assn., Am. Soc. Biochemistry and Molecular Biology. Office: FIU Coll Medicine 112 SW 8th St GL 495C Miami FL 33199 Office Fax: 305-348-1577. Business E-Mail: crao@fiu.edu.

RAO, DEVULAPALLI VENKATA, physics educator; b. Pithapuram, India, July 6, 1933; arrived in U.S., 1966; s. Janakiramayya and Suryakantham Rao; m. Lalitha Rao, May 24, 1962; children: Radhika, Sandhya, Amsu. AB, Harvard U., 1986, JD, 1990; BS, U. Calif., Berkeley, 1991; BA, U. Mass., 1997. Lectr. in physics Andhra U., Vizag, India, 1957-59, 61-63; rsch. asst. Duke U., Durham, N.C., 1959-61; sr. scientist Solid State Physics Lab., Delhi, India, 1963-66; rsch. physicist Maser Optics Inc., Boston, 1966-68; assoc. prof. U. Mass., Boston, 1968-75, prof. physics, 1975—, chair physics dept., 1978-80, dist. prof., 2007—, adj. prof. Amherst, 1991—; rsch. fellow, div. engring. & applied physics Harvard U., 1967—69. Grad. program dir. U. Mass., 1986-88, 92-95, 1997-2008. Contbr. 100 articles to profl. jours. including Phys. Rev., Phys. Rev. Letters, Applied Physics Letters, Optics Letters, Optics Comm, contbr. chptr. to books. Recipient Chancellor's award for excellence in scholarship, 1992, Nano award, 2005. Mem. Am. Phys. Soc., Optical Soc. Am., Materials Rsch. Soc., Optical Engring. Achievements include 5 patents. Office: U Mass Harbor Campus Boston MA 02125

RAO, DHANANJAI M., engineering educator; PhD, U. Cin., 2002. Sr. software engr. Elsevier, Miamisburg, Ohio, 2002—04; vis. asst. prof. Miami U., Oxford, Ohio, 2004—. Achievements include development of innovative methodology for multi-scale modeling & parallel, distributed simulation. Office: Miami Univ 205 Benton Hall Oxford OH 45056

RAO, DITTAKAVI N., law librarian; b. Gudivada, Andhra Pradesh, India, June 10, 1944; s. Subbarao and Subhadramma Dittakavi; m. Anurajyalakshmi Dittakavi, Feb. 6, 1976; 1 child, Anila Dittakavi. MLS,

U. Pitts., 1978. Assoc. dir. Duquesne U. Sch. Law, Pitts., 1986—. Exec. bd. S.V. Temple, Pitts., 1992—96. Named Outstanding Law Libr., Alert Publs., 1988. Home: 301 N Battery Dr Mc Donald PA 15057 Office: Duquesne Univ Sch Law 600 Forbes Ave Pittsburgh PA 15282 Home Fax: 412-396-6294. Business E-Mail: rao@duq.edu.

RAO, I. JOGA, mechanical engineer, educator; s. Ivatury Mrityunjaya and Meera Rao; m. Alice Wright, Aug. 16, 1999. BTech, Indian Inst. Tech., Mumbai, 1990; MS, U. Calif., Berkeley, 1994; PhD, Tex. A&M U., Coll. Sta., 1999. Asst. prof. NJ Inst. Tech., Newark, 2000—05, assoc. prof., 2005—. Mem., bd. dirs. Soc. Polymer Engrng., Brookfield, Conn., 2001—04; editl. bd. mem. Mechanics Rsch. Comm., Elsevier, Amsterdam, 2004—06, assoc. editor, 2006—. Contbr. scientific papers. Recipient Excellence Tchg. award, Newark Coll. Engring., 2005, NJ Inst. Tech., 2008; grant, Dept. Energy, 2001—05, 2006—, Nat. Sci. Found., 2003—06, fellow, Air Force Office Sponsored Rsch., 2008. Mem.: ASME (NYC) (constitutive equations com. mem. 2001—), Soc. Engrng. Sci. Achievements include research in mechanics of complex materials. Office: NJ Inst Tech Dept Mech Engring Newark NJ 07102 Office Fax: 973-642-4282.

RAO, JAGADEESH SRIDHARA, research scientist; s. Sridhara Madhavarao and Padma Rao; m. Sudha Rao; children: Srikar, Sahana. PhD, NIMHANS, Bangalore, 1998. Rsch.scientist Johnson & Johnson, Spring House, 2001—03; scientist NIH, Bethesda, Md., 2003—. Mem.: ACNP (Sanofi aventis Travel award). Home: 20104 Boxwood Pl Ashburn VA 20147

RAO, KATIKINENI MURALI KRISHNA, medical researcher; came to U.S., 1969; s. Umapathy Katikineni Rao and Jayalakshmi (Tandra) Katikineni; m. Sheela Tandra Rao, May 17, 1973; children: Shilpa, Suhale. MBBS, Gandhi Med. Coll., Hyderabad, Andhra Pradesh, India, MD, 1968. Diplomate Am. Bd. Pathology. Rsch. asst. prof. Duke U. Med. Ctr., Durham, NC, 1986—96; rsch. med. officer NIOSH, Morgantown, W.Va., 1996—. Mem. staff VA Med. Ctr., Durham, 1987—. Contbr. articles to profl. jours. Mem. Am. Assn. Immunologists, Am. Fedn. Clin. Rsch. (Henry Christian award 1992), Am. Fedn. Aging Rsch., Soc. Leukocyte Biology. Hindu. Avocations: tennis, bridge. Home: 6 Geneva Ct Durham NC 27713 Office: NIOSH 1095 Willowdale Rd Morgantown WV 26505 Office Fax: 304-285-5938. Personal E-mail: muraliwv@hotmail.com.

RAO, KORCHERLAKOTA RAMCHANDAR, mechanical engineer, consultant; b. Guntur, India, May 9, 1933; arrived in US, 1970; s. Kocherlakota Narayana Murthy and Kocherlakota Annapoorna Vimla; m. Korcherlakota Indira Tadepalli, Dec. 11, 1967; children: Uma Rohini, Ishu V. BS in Engring., Banaras U., India, 1957; M Planning, Sch. of Planning and Architecture, New Delhi, 1964; postgrad., Carnegie Mellon U., Pitts., 1982—84; PhD in Pub. and Internat. Affairs, U. Pitts., 1976. Registered profl. engr., Pa., 1977, Tex., 1978, chartered engr., India, 2006. Grad. tech. asst. Tata Engring. and Locomotive Co., Jamshedpur, India, 1957—58; regional and assoc. planner Town & Country Planning Dept., Goft. of Uttar Pradesh, Lucknow, India, 1958—69; rsch. asst., pre-doctoral fellow Grad. Sch. Pub. and Internat. Studies, U. Pitts., 1970—72; engr. planner Urban Design Assocs., Pitts., 1972—74; engr. planner, designer Peter Loftus Corp., Pitts., 1979; structural engr. planner Pullman Swindell Inc., Pitts., 1979—80; sr. engr. Westinghouse Electric Corp., Pitts., 1980—87; sr. staff engr. Entergy Ops. Inc., Jackson, Miss., 1987—2002; engring. cons., 2003—. Adj. lectr. Sch. Pub. Adminstrn., Lucknow, 1965, Indian Inst. Tech., Kanpur, 1966, Govt. Poly., Kanpur, India, 1967; cons. engring., mgmt. and spl. projects, 2002—; spkr., presenter, organizer confs. in field. Co-author: Model for Location of Service, 1973; editor: Criteria and Companion Volume, 2002, 2006; contbg. editor: numerous publs. in field; contbr. articles to profl. jours. Judge Miss. State Math. and Sci. Contest, Biloxi, 1995—. Recipient Engring. Achievement and Svc. awards, Westinghouse Elec. Corp., 1984—85, Recognition award, Andhra Pradesh C. of C., 1984, Svc. and Recognition awards, Entery Ops., Inc., 1990—97, Recognition and Appreciation award, Telugu Assn. N.Am., 1984. Fellow: Instn. Engrs. (India); mem.: ASME (mem. gen. awards com. 1995—2000, mem. southeastern regional operating bd. 1995—2004, founder, chmn. Expo'96 1996, chmn. honors and awards 1996—2000, bd. dirs. Miss. sect. 1996—, dir. Expo'98 1998, chmn. pub. rels. and code profl. ethics Miss. sect. 1998—99, advisor to so. regional v.p. 2003—05, chmn. coord. com. early career tech. conf. 2006, chmn. programs com. Miss. sect. 1994—95, mem. exec. com. 1994—95, vice chmn. divsn. codes and stds. tech. com. 1994—96, G.H. "Dick" Duncan award 1996, Valued Svcs. award 1997, Outstanding award 2001, Dedicated Svc. award 2003, Appreciation Plaque 1996, divsn. cert. recognition 1993, 1995), India Assn. Miss. (pres. 2003, bd. dirs. 2003—, Recognition and Appreciation awards 2002—03), Jackson Philatelic Club, Am. Philatelic Soc. Office Phone: 601-992-0484. Personal E-mail: kr768@bellsouth.net.

RAO, K.V.R. MOHAN See KOTTAMASU, MOHAN

RAO, NAGESWARA MADDALI, space and planetary scientist; b. Bapatla, India, July 11, 1931; arrived in US, 1989, naturalized, 1996; s. Narayana and Sitamma; m. Sita Devi; children: Radha, Prasad, Subha. MS in Chemistry, Andhra U., Waltair, India, 1954; Dr. rer. nat in Nuc. Chemistry, Max- Planck Inst., Mainz, Cologne, Germany, 1963. Cert. in nuclear chemistry U. Cologne, 1963. Alexander von Humboldt sr. scholar Max-Plank-Inst. Chemistry, 1959—63; asst. prof., rsch. assoc. U. Ark., Fayetteville, 1964—69; assoc. prof., prof. Phys. Rsch. Lab., Ahemedabad, Gujarat, India, 1974—89; vis. scientist Lunar and Planetary Inst., 1992—93; NAS sr. fellow, Nat. Rsch. Coun. NASA Johnson Space Ctr., Houston, 1989—92, 1997—2001, scientist, engring. sci. contracting group, 2002—, Jacobs NASA. Vis. scientist, adj. prof. Sam Houston State U., Huntsville, Tex., Tex. A&M U., Coll. Sta., 1973—76. Contbr. over 150 articles to prof. jours. Sr. fellow, Indian Acad. Scis., 1984—. Mem.: Meteortical Soc., Internat. Astron. Union, Sigma Xi. Hindu. Achievements include research in lunar and planetary science and Mars, regolith in SNCs; construction of nobel gas (Reynolds-type glass) masspectrometer. Avocations: tennis, jogging, music. Home: 16931 Tower Ridge Friendswood TX 77546 Office: Engring Sci Group-Jacobs Johnson Space Ctr Bldg 31 NASA Road One Houston TX 77058 Home Phone: 281-993-9191; Office Phone: 281-244-5020. Office Fax: 281-483-1573; Home Fax: 281-483-1573. Personal E-mail: sitarao@sbcglobal.net.

RAO, NANNAPANENI NARAYANA, electrical engineer; b. Kakumanu, Andhra Pradesh, India; m. Sarojini Jonnalagadda, June 10, 1955; children: Vanaja, Durgaprasad, Hariprasad. BSc in Physics, U. Madras, India, 1952; DMIT in Electronics, Madras Inst. Tech., 1955; MSEE, U. Wash., Seattle, 1960, PhD in Elec. Engring, 1965. Acting instr. elec. engring. U. Wash., 1960-64, acting asst. prof., 1964-65; asst. prof. elec. engring. U. Ill., Urbana, 1965-69, asso. prof., 1969-75, prof., 1975—2007, Edward C. Jordan prof., 2003—07, Edward C. Jordan prof. emeritus, 2007—, assoc. head elec. and computer engring., 1987—2006; disting. prof. Amrita U., India, 2006—. Cons. Fakultas Teknik, Univ. Indonesia, Jakarta, 1985-86, 87. Author: Basic Electromagnetics with Applications, 1972, Elements of Engineering Electromagnetics, 6th edit., 2004, Fundamentals of Electromagnetics for Electrical and Computer Engring, 2009; contbr. numerous articles to profl. jours. Recipient Engring. award Telugu Assn. N.Am., 1983, Excellence in Edn. award, 1999, Fakultas Teknik award Universitas Indonesia, 1986. Fellow IEEE (life; Undergrad. Teaching award 1994); mem. Am. Soc. Engring. Edn. (life; AT&T Found. award for excellence in instrn. engring. students 1991), Internat. Union Radio Sci. (life; US Commn. G). Achievements include contributions to engineering education in the United States and abroad. Home: 2509 S Lynn St Urbana IL 61801-6841 E-mail: nnrao@illinois.edu.

RAO, NARSING A., ophthalmologist, pathologist, educator; arrived in U.S., 1968; MD, Osmania U., Hyderabad, India, 1967. Cert. Am. Bd. Ophthalmology, Am. Bd. Pathology. Prof. ophthalmology and pathology U. So. Calif., LA, 1983—; dir. uveitis and ophthalmic pathology Doheny Eye Inst., LA, 1983—. Contbr. articles to profl. jours. Pres. Internat. Uveitis Soc., Bethesda, Md., 2000—05. Recipient Zimmerman Gold (Bietti) medal, Am. Acad. Ophthalmology, 2003; grantee, NIH, 1985—2008. Mem.: Am. Ophthal. Soc. Achievements include research in free radical biology. Office: Doheny Eye Inst 1450 San Pablo St Los Angeles CA 90033 Office Fax: 323-442-6634. Business E-Mail: nrao@usc.edu.

RAO, NATTI SREERAMA, small business owner, consultant; b. Pulivendla, Andhra Pradesh, India, Oct. 28, 1935; arrived in US, 2002, permanent resident; s. Natti Sreeramulu and Bhadipetla Satyanarayanamma; m. Rosemarie Ruth Dorrer, July 1, 1966; children: Steffen Schneider, Sylvia Van Ledden. B in Mech. Engring. with honors, Indian Inst. Tech. Madras, India, M in Chem. Engring.; PhD in Chem. Engring., U. Karlsruhe, Germany, 1960—64. Lic. chem. engr., U. Karlsruhe, 1964. Sr. rsch. engr. Basf Ag, Ludwigshafen/Rh, Germany, 1964—81; propr. Plastics Solutions Internat. Cons., Ghent, NY, 1987—. Vis. prof. Indian Inst. Tech. Madras, Chennai, India, 1983—84. Author: (book) Formulas for Plastics Engineers. Fellow: Soc. Plastics Engrs. USA; mem.: Tech. Assn. Paper and Pulp Industry. Achievements include research in computer aided design of plasticating screws; design of machines and dies for polymer processing with computer programs. Home and Office: Plastics Solutions Internat Cons 327 County Rte 21 C Ghent NY 12075 Office Fax: 518-672-4281; Home Fax: 518-672-7608. Business E-Mail: raonatti@aol.com.

RAO, NEOMI, law educator; b. 1973; BA cum laude, Yale U., 1995; JD, U. Chgo. Sch. Law, 1999. Bar: Va. 2001, qualified solicitor: England & Wales 2005. Reporter & correspondence editor The Weekly Standard, 1995—96; law clk. to Hon. J. Harvie Wilkinson III US Ct. Appeals (4th Cir.), 1999—2000; counsel US Senate Judiciary Com., 2000—01; law clk. to Justice Clarence Thomas US Supreme Ct., 2001—02; assoc. Clifford Chance LLP, London, 2002—05; assoc. counsel & spl. asst. to Pres. The White House, 2005—06; asst. prof. law George Mason U. Sch. Law, 2006—. Office: George Mason University School of Law 3301 Fairfax Dr Arlington VA 22201 Office Phone: 703-993-8079. Office Fax: 703-993-8202. E-mail: nrao@gmu.edu.*

RAO, POTARAZU KRISHNA, environmental consultant; b. Andhra Pradesh, India, Mar. 26, 1930; s. Satyanarayana and Annapooma (Mullapudi) Rao; m. Rukmani Krutivinti, Aug. 5, 1954; children: Ramanarayan, Sreedhar. BS, Andhra U., 1950, MS, 1952, Fla. State U., 1957; PhD, NYU, 1968. Meteorologist Can. Meteorol. Svc., Montreal, Canada, 1960-61; rsch. phys. scientist Nat. Oceanic and Atmospheric Adminstrn./Nat. Environ. Satellite Data and Info. Svc., Washington, 1961-74, chief atmospheric energetics br., acting dir., 1976-80, chief satellite applications lab., 1980-86, dir. office of rsch. and applications, 1986-96; chief scientist for satellite and info. svcs. Nat. Oceanic and Atmospheric Adminstrn., Washington, 1996—2002; program dir., weather modification NSF, Washington, 1971-72; advisor on satellite programs World Meteorological Orgn., Geneva, 1974-76; cons. TRW, ITT. Bd. dirs. Climate and Global Change Program Nat. Oceanic and Atmospheric Adminstrn., Washington; mem. adv. bd. Coop. Inst. for Rsch. in Atmospheres, Ft. Collins, 1986—. Editor: Weather Satellites, 1990; contbr. articles to profl. jours. Founder, trustee Sri Siva Vishnu Temple, Lanham, Md. Fellow: N.Y. Acad. Scis., Royal Meteorol. Soc. U.K., Am. Meteorol. Soc. Hindu. Avocations: tennis, photography. Home: 15824 Buena Vista Dr Rockville MD 20855-2658 E-mail: potarazukrao@netscape.net.

RAO, RAMA KRISHNA R., pharmaceutical company executive; b. Tanuku, Andhra Province, India, Nov. 20, 1955; came to U.S., 1998; s. R.R. and Satyavani R. (Gudipati) R.; m. Kavitha Advikolanu, May 19, 1996. B in Tech., Indian Inst. Tech., Delhi, 1977; postgrad. diploma in mgmt., Indian Inst. Mgmt., Calcutta, 1981; MBA, INSEAD, Fontainebleu, France, 1989. Asst. mgr. Metal Box India, Calcutta, 1977-84; exec. asst. to gen. mgr. Bank of Bahrain & Kuwait, Bahrain, 1985-88; fin. assoc. Eli Lilly, Geneva, credit and customer svc. mgr., 1993-94, fin. mgr. Africa, 1994-95; mgr. (global treasury) Gems Eli Lilly, Brussels, 1995-97; fin. advisor corp. fin. and investment banking Lilly Corp. Ctr., Indpls., 1998-99; CFO, fin. mgr. PC/NS Lilly USA, Indpls., 1999—2001; fin. dir. intercontinental region Novartis Oncology Bus. Unit, East Hanover, NJ, 2001—04; CFO, v.p. fin. Novartis Can., Dorval, Canada, 2004—06; exec. dir., head fin., oncology global devel. unit Novartis, 2006—. Alumni mem. panel for INSEAD interviews, Belgium, U.S., 1995-99. Contbr. journalist Students' Newsletter, IIT, Delhi, co-editor Students' Newsletter, I.I.M., Calcutta, INSEAD, Fontainebleu, France. Vol. Samaritans/Befrienders, Bahrain, 1987, 88; donor of blood Red Cross/Crescent, India, Belgium, US, Bahrain, 1974-97. Recipient First prize Nat. Young Mgrs. Competition, All India Mgmt. Assn., 1983. Mem. AMA, Assn. Investment Mgmt. and Rsch., Inst. Mgmt. Accts. Hindu. Avocations: travel, military history, foreign policy. Office Phone: 862-778-5459. Business E-Mail: rama.rao@novartis.com.

RAO, RAMACHANDRA U., aerospace scientist; b. Udipi, India, Mar. 10, 1932; BSc, Madras U., 1951; MSc, Benaras Hindu U., 1953; PhD, Gujarat U., 1960; DSc (hon.), Bologna U., 1992. Assoc. prof. U. Tex., Dallas, 1963-66; prof. Phys. Rsch. Lab., Ahmedabad, India, 1966-72; dir. ISRO Satellite Ctr., Bangalore, 1972-84; chmn. Indian Space Orgn., 1984-94; disting. prof. U. Saraghai, 1994-99. Chair UN Com. on Peaceful Uses of Outer Space, 1997-2000; pres. Unispace III conf., 1999. chair PRL coun. Author: Space and Agenda 21—Caring for Planet Earth, 1995, Space Technology for Sustainable Development, 1996; editor, author: Physics of Communication, 1987, Science & Technology for Achieving Food, Economic & Health Security, 1996. Fellow 3d World Acad. Scis.; mem. Internat. Astronautical Fedn. Home: 3367E 13 Main II Stage Indiranagar 560038 Bangalore India Office: Antariksh Bhavan Dept Space New Bel Rd 560094 Bangalore India Home Phone: (091)80-25262526; Office Phone: (080)23416406, (091)80-2 341-6406. Fax: 23410705. Personal E-mail: urrao_isro@hotmail.com.

RAO, SOWMYA R., medical educator; d. Ranganatha S. and Santha Rao; m. Morgan S. David, Mar. 7, 1999. BSc in Stats., Madras Christian Coll., Chennai, 1983; MSc, Bangalore U., Karnataka, India, 1985; MA, SUNY, Buffalo, 1992; PhD in Biostatistics, Boston U., Mass., 2001. Sr. programmer Eiko Computers Pvt. Ltd., Bangalore, 1985—89; systems exec. Grandslam Computers Pvt. Ltd., Bangalore, 1989—90; rsch. data analyst, statis. analyst Slone Epidemiology Ctr., Boston, 1992—2001; assoc. scientist Abt Assocs., Cambridge, Mass., 2004—05; asst. prof., dept. medicine Mgh & Hms, Boston, 2005—. Cons. U. Md., Balt., 2002; crta postdoc. fellow Nat. Cancer Inst., Rockville, Md., 2001—04. Recipient Recognition award, Nat. Cancer Inst., Divsn. Cancer Epidemiology & Genetics, 2002, 2003, Rsch. Excellence award, Nat. Inst. Health, 2003. Office: MGH Biostatistics Ctr 50 Staniford St Ste 560 Boston MA 02114

RAO, SUDHAKAR, aerospace engineer, researcher; b. Tenali, Andhra Pradesh, India, July 15, 1951; arrived in US, 1996, naturalized, 2004; s. Baparao and Hymavathi Krothapalli; m. Rajani Krothapalli, Apr. 30, 1978; 1 child, Neha. BE, JNT U., Warangal, India, 1974; ME, Indian Inst. Tech., Kharaghpur, 1976; PhD, Indian Inst. Tech., Madras, 1980. Tech. officer Electronic Corp. India Ltd., Hyderabad, Andhra Pradesh, India, 1976—77; sr. sci. officer Electronic and Radar Devel. Establishment, Bangalore, Karnataka, India, 1980—81; postdoctoral rsch. fellow U. Trondheim, Norway, 1981—82; rsch. assoc. U. Man., Winnipeg, Canada, 1982—83; staff scientist Spar Aerospace Ltd., Ste-Anne-de-Bellevue, Que., Canada, 1983—96; chief scientist Boeing Satellite Sys., El Segundo, Calif., 1996—2003; corp. sr. fellow Lockheed Martin Comml. Space Sys., Newtown, Pa., 2003—. Mem. intellectual property rev. bd. Lockheed Martin. Contbr. more than 120 articles to profl. jours. Sponsored eye camps Rotary Club India, Vijayawada, Andhra Pradesh, 2005—06. Recipient Boeing's Spl. Invention award, 2002, Lockheed Martin's Key Inventor award, 2005, 2007, Lockheed Martin Corp. Sr. Fellow award, 2006; NTNF Postdoctoral fellow, Norwegian Coun. Sci. and Indsl. Rsch., 1981, 1982. Fellow: IEEE (Benjamin Franklin Key award 2006, Asian Am. Engrs. of Yr. 2008, Delaware Valley Elec. Engrs. of Yr. 2008). Republican. Hindu. Achievements include 30 US patents for advanced payloads for satellite communications; development of radiation templates for interferences analysis of various satellite systems. Avocations: tennis, basketball. Home: 125 Livery Dr Churchville PA 18966 Office: Lockheed Martin Comml Space Sys 100 Campus Dr Newtown PA 18940 Personal E-mail: skraoks@yahoo.com.

RAO, SUNIL V., cardiologist, educator; MD, Ohio State U. Coll. Medicine, 1996. Resident Duke U. Med. Ctr., 1996—99, fellow, 1999—2004, cardiologist, asst. prof. medicine. Office: 508 Fulton St 111A Durham NC 27705 Office Phone: 919-286-0411 ext. 2352. Office Fax: 919-286-6821.*

RAO, VELCHERU NARAYANA, south asian professor; s. Buchi Narasinga and Venkubayamma Rao. PhD, Andhra U., Visakhapatnam, India. Prof. U. Wis., Madison. Translator: (play) Girls for Sale. Fellow, John Simon Guggenheim Found., 1991. Home: 4501 ONaway Pass Madison WI 53711 Office: Univ Wis 1220 Linden Dr Madison WI 53706 Business E-Mail: vnrao@wisc.edu.

RAOUFI, AZADEH, music educator; arrived in U.S., 1998; d. Mohammad Sadogh Raoufi and Fatemeh (Mali) Fakoor-Sevvom. B in Piano and Computer Sci., U. Iowa, 2004, postgrad., 2005—. Tchr. English Shokoh, Mashad, 1995—98; with Info. Tech. Ctr., Iowa City, 2001—02; with internal med. rsch. lab. U. Iowa, Iowa City, 2001—02; piano tchr. West Music, Iowa City, 2002—. Mem.: Iowa City Ind. Piano Tchrs. (v.p.), Iowa Music Tchr. Assn. (pub. rels. person 2004—), Music Tchr. Nat. Assn., Phi Theta Kappa. Home: 1612 Avenue Y Apt 107A Lubbock TX 79401-4404 E-mail: azadeh-raoufi@uiowa.edu.

RAPADAS, LEONARDO M., prosecutor; b. 1960; BS, Pacific Univ.; JD, Williamette Univ. Coll of Law. Pros. Guam Atty. Gen. office, 1989—97, chief pros., 1997—99; US Atty. dist. Guam & Mariana Islands US Dept. Justice, Saipan, 2003—. Office: US Attys Office Sirena Plz 108 Hernan Cortez Ste 500 Hagatna GU 96910 Office Phone: 671-472-7332. Office Fax: 671-472-7334.*

RAPAPORT, MICHAEL, actor; b. Bronx, NY, Mar. 20, 1970; m. Nichole Beattie, Jan. 2000 (separated); 2 children. Founder Release Entertainment. Actor: (films) Zebrahead, 1992, Point of No Return, 1993, Poetic Justice, 1993, Money for Nothing, 1993, True Romance, 1993, The Scout, 1994, Higher Learning, 1994, Kiss of Death, 1995, Mighty Aphrodite, 1995, The Basketball Diaries, 1995, Ill Town, 1996, Beautiful Girls, 1996, The Pallbearer, 1996, Copland, 1997, Kicked in the Head, 1997, Metro, 1997, A Brother's Kiss, 1997, Subway Stories: Tales from the Underground, 1997, The Naked Man, 1998, Men, 1998, Palmetto, 1998, King of the Jungle, 1999, Deep Blue Sea, 1999, Kiss Toledo Goodbye, 1999, Small Time Crooks, 2000, Men of Honor, 2000, Bamboozled, 2000, Chain of Fools, 2000, Lucky Numbers, 2000, The 6th Day, 2000, (voice) Dr. Doolittle 2, 2001, King of the Jungle, 2001, Paper Soldiers, 2002, Triggermen, 2002, A Good Night to Die, 2003, This Girl's Life, 2003, America Brown, 2004, Scrambled Eggs, 2004, Hitch, 2005, Special, 2006, (TV series) Boston Public, 2001-04, The War at Home, 2005, (TV films) Subway Stories: Tales from the Underground, 1997, Rescuers: Stories of Courage: Two Families, 1998; actor, exec. prodr. (films) 29 Palms, 2002; TV appearances include China Beach, 1990, Murphy Brown, 1992, The Fresh Prince of Bel-Air, 1993, NYPD Blue, 1993, ER, 1998, Rude Awakening, 1998, Friends, 1999.*

RAPAPORT, ROBERT, pediatric endocrinologist; b. Romania, Feb. 23, 1949; MD, SUNY Downstate Med. Ctr., Bklyn., 1974. Cert. in pediat. 1980, in pediatric endocrinology 1983. Internship in pediat. LI Jewish Med. Ctr., Glen Oaks, NY, 1974—75, residency in pediatric endocrinology, 1974—77; fellowship in pediatric endocrinology St. Christopher's Hosp. Children, Phila., 1977—78, NY Hosp. Cornell Med. Ctr., NYC, 1978—80; hosp. appointment Children's Hosp., Newark; assoc. prof., dept. pediat. U. Medicine & Dentistry NJ, Newark; prof. pediat. Mt. Sinai Sch. Medicine, NYC, Emma Elizabeth Sullivan prof. pediatric endocrinology and diabetes, chief, divsn. pediatric endocrinology and diabetes, dir., Hall Family Ctr. Pediatric Endocrinology and Diabetes. Contbr. articles to profl. jours. Office: Mt Sinai One Gustave L Levy Pl New York NY 10029 Office Phone: 212-241-6936. Office Fax: 212-876-4395. Business E-Mail: robert.rapaport@mssm.edu.

RAPAPORT, SAMUEL I., educator, physician; b. Los Angeles, Nov. 19, 1921; s. Hyman and Bertha (Krupnick) R.; m. Joyce Mildred Cooperman, Oct. 3, 1951; children: Susan Rapaport Braunwald, Sally Rapaport Hartinian, Mark Hyman, Bruce Allen. Student, UCLA; MD, U. So. Calif., 1945. Diplomate: Am. Bd. Internal Medicine (mem. bd. 1973-80, bd. govs. 1976-80, sec.-treas., chmn. hematology subcom. 1978-80). Intern Los Angeles County Hosp., 1945; resident medicine VA Hosp., Long Beach, Calif., 1948-50, chief hematology sect., 1950-57; asso. prof. medicine U. Calif. at Los Angeles Med. Center, 1957-58; mem. faculty U. So. Calif. Sch. Medicine, 1958-74, head hematology div. dept. medicine, 1958-74, prof. medicine, 1964-74; head hematology div. Los Angeles County-U. So. Calif. Med. Center, 1958-74; chief med. service San Diego VA Hosp., 1974-78; prof. medicine U. Calif., San Diego, 1974-96; prof. emeritus, 1996—; vice chmn. dept. medicine U.

Calif., 1974-78, co-head hematology-oncology div., 1978-87, prof. pathology, 1980-93; dir. Hematology Lab., U. Calif.-San Diego Med. Ctr., 1980-87. Cons. hematology tng. grants study sect. Nat. Inst. Arthritis and Metabolic Diseases, 1968-71; mem. med. adv. coun. Nat. Hemophilia Found., 1970, 77—; chmn. adv. com., div. blood diseases and resources Nat. Heart, Lung and Blood Inst., 1980-82, mem. adv. coun., 1989-93; mem. hematology study sect. NIH, 1984-88, chmn. study sect., 1977-88. Author: Introduction to Hematology, 1971, 2d edit., 1987; also papers in field. Chmn. coun. on thrombosis Am. Heart Assn., 1995-97. Served with USAAF, 1946-48. Spl. fellow Nat. Heart Inst., U. Oslo, 1964-65; Fulbright research scholar U. Oslo, 1953-54; fellow Sackler Inst. for Advanced Study, Tel Aviv U., 1983; recipient Disting. Sci. Achievement award Coun. on Arteriosclerosis, Thrombosis, and Vascular Biology Am. Heart Assn., 2001. Master ACP (John Phillips Meml. award for outstanding work on clin. medicine 1996); fellow Am. Acad. Arts and Sciences; mem. Assn. Am. Physicians, Am. Soc. Hematology (pres. 1977), Western Soc. Clin. Rsch. (pres. 1966), Am. Fedn. Clin. Rsch. (chmn. Western sect. 1960), Am. Soc. Clin. Investigation, Western Assn. Physicians (pres. 1973) Home: 7887 Lookout Dr La Jolla CA 92037-3951

RAPER, CHARLES ALBERT, retired management consultant; b. Charleston, W.Va., Aug. 18, 1926; s. Kenneth B. and Louise (Williams) R.; m. Margaret Ann Weers, Dec. 26, 1947; children: Kathleen, Josephine, Charles. Student, Okla. State U., 1945; BS, U. Ill., 1949. Sales mgr. Meyer Furnace Co., Peoria, Ill., 1949-54; v.p. mktg. Master Consol., Inc., Dayton, Ohio, 1954-61; mgmt. cons. McKinsey & Co., Inc., Chgo., 1961-67; v.p. mktg. Gen. Portland Inc., Dallas, 1967-69, pres., also dir., 1969-75; v.p., gen. mgr. Scholl Inc., Chgo., 1975-81; pres. Oxford Group of Sara Lee, 1981-84; mgmt. cons. McKinsey & Co., 1984—. Vice-chmn. devel. bd. U. Tex., Dallas; exec. bd. Circle 10 coun. Boy Scouts Am.; Svc. Corp. of Ret. Execs. counselor. With USN, 1944-46. Mem. Dallas C. of C. (chmn. bd. dirs. 1974—), Sales Execs. Club, Cherokee Country Club, Chattooga Club, Atlanta Mallet Club (pres.), Phi Gamma Delta. Methodist. Home: 3750 Peachtree Rd Apt 482 Atlanta GA 30319

RAPER, WILLIAM BURKETTE, retired college president; b. nr. Wilson, NC, Sept. 10, 1927; s. William Cecil and Beulah Maybelle (Davis) R.; m. Rose Mallard, Aug. 19, 1951; children: Olivia, Kristie, Burkette, Elizabeth, Stephen (dec.), Laura. AB, Duke U., 1947, MDiv, 1951; MS (Kellogg fellow), Fla. State U., 1962; LLD, Atlantic Christian Coll. (now Barton Coll.), 1960. Ordained to ministry Free Will Baptist Ch., 1946; pastor Hull Rd. Free Will Bapt. Ch., Snow Hill, NC, 1951-55; pres. Mt. Olive (N.C.) Coll., 1954-95, ret. pres. emeritus, 1995. Dir. Wachovia Bank and Trust Co., 1979-97; promotional dir. Free Will Bapt. State Conv. N.C., 1953-54; pres. council Ch.-Related Colls. N.C., 1966-67; mem. N.C. Edn. Assistance Authority, 1972-76; sec. Ind. Coll. Fund of N.C., 1976-78; Mem. N.C. Gov.'s Com. on Hwy. Traffic Safety, 1968; regional coordinator U.S. Office Edn. Program with Developing Instns., 1968-70; dir. Edn. Professions Devel. Act Grant for Strengthening Devel. in Pvt. Two-Year Colls., 1970-72; trustee N.C. Coll. Found., 1977-94; adv. com. Ind. Coll. Presidents, U. N.C. Pres. N.C. Found. Christian Ministries, 2005. Recipient Disting. Service award Mt. Olive Jr. C. of C., 1961; named N.C. Young Man of Year, 1961 Mem. Am. Assn. Community and Jr. Colls. (commn. on legislation 1963-66, cons. 1968-71, chmn. commn. on student personnel 1970-71), N.C. Assn. Ind. Colls. and Univs. (exec. com. 1967-70, 76-77, 83-85), N.C. Assn. Colls. and Univs. (pres. 1969-70), Masons. Democrat. Office: Mt Olive Coll Office of Pres Emeritus Mount Olive NC 28365 Home Phone: 919-658-3855; Office Phone: 919-658-5250. E-mail: wraper@moc.edu.

RAPER, WILLIAM CRANFORD, lawyer; b. Asheville, NC, Aug. 17, 1946; s. James Sidney and Kathryn (Cranford) R.; m. Patricia Dotson, Sept. 28, 1974; children: Kimber-leigh, Heather, James. AB, U. NC, 1968; JD, Vanderbilt U., 1972. Bar: NC 1972, US Ct. Appeals 4th Cir. 1972, US Supreme Ct. 1977, US Ct. Appeals Fed. Cir. 1985, US Dist. Ct. Ea., Mid., & We. Districts NC. Legal asst. to Senator Sam Ervin Jr. US Senate Subcom. on Constl. Rights, Washington, 1970; jud. clk. to Judge J. Braxton Craven, Jr. US Ct. Appeals 4th Cir., Richmond, Va., 1972-73; assoc. Womble, Carlyle, Sandridge & Rice PLLC, 1973—79, ptnr., 1979—, head litig. sect., 1982—92, past mng. ptnr. Charlotte office, now firm gen. counsel. Fellow Am. Coll. Trial Lawyers; mem. ABA, NC Bar Assn., Mecklenburg County Bar Assn., NC Assn. Def. Attorneys(charter). Office: Womble Carlyle Sandridge & Rice PLLC One Wachovia Ctr Ste 3500 301 S College St Charlotte NC 28202-6037 Office Phone: 704-331-4935. Office Fax: 704-338-7805. E-mail: braper@wcsr.com.

RAPHAEL, ALBERT ASH, JR., retired lawyer; b. NYC, June 4, 1925; s. Albert Ash and Clare (Schindler) R.; m. Dorothy Buck, Oct. 7, 1960; 1 child, Bruce William. AB, Yale U., 1947; LL.D., Harvard U., 1950. Bar: N.Y. 1950, Vt. 1972. Mem. firm Gallert, Hilborn & Raphael, NYC, 1950-60, Alter, Lefevre, Raphael, Lowry, and Gould, NYC, 1960-78; pvt.practice Waitsfield, Vt., 1972—86; pvt. practice, 1995—2002; ptnr. Raphael and Ware, Waitsfield, 1986-95; ret., 2002. Dir. various real estate cos. Mem. bd. zoning appeals, Waitsfield, 1974-83, selectman, 1976-82, chmn. bd. selectmen, 1981-82 Mem. Waitsfield Planning Commn., 1996-2003. Served with F.A., AUS, 1943-46. Mem. Assn. of Bar of City of N.Y. Home: PO Box 113 Warren VT 05674-0113

RAPHAEL, CAROL, health care administrator; b. NYC, Apr. 21, 1942; BA, CUNY, 1962; MEd, Boston U., 1965; MPA, Harvard U., 1979. Dir. EDP planning and contract mgmt. Human Resources Adminstrn., NYC, 1979-82, asst. dep. adminstr. office home care svcs., 1982-84, dep. commr. med. assistance program, 1984-88, exec. dep. commr. income and med. assistance adminstrn., 1988-89; dir. ops. mgmt. Mount Sinai Med. Ctr. N.Y., 1989; pres., CEO Vis. Nurse Svc. NY, 1989—. Named one of The 100 Most Influential Women in NYC Bus., Crain's NY Bus., 2007.

RAPHAEL, LOUISE ARAKELIAN, mathematician, educator; b. NYC, Oct. 24, 1937; d. Aristakes and Antionette (Sudbeaz) Arakelian; m. Robert Barnett Raphael, June 12, 1966 (div. 1985); children: Therese Denise, Marc Philippe. BS in Math., St. John's U., 1959; MS in Math., Cath. U., Washington, 1962; PhD in Math, Cath. U., 1967. Asst. prof. math. Howard U., Washington, 1966-70, vis. prof., 1981-82, assoc. prof., 1982-86, prof., 1986—; assoc. prof. Clark Coll., Atlanta, 1971-79, prof., 1979-82. Vis. assoc. prof. MIT, Cambridge, 1977-78, vis. prof., 1989-90; vis. mem. Courant Inst. Math. Scis., NYU, 1996-97; vis. scholar Cornell U., 2004. Contbr. over 40 rsch. articles to profl. jours. Program dir. NSF, Washington, 1986—88; acting adminstrv. officer Conf. Bd. Math. Scis., 1985—86. Grantee NSF, 1975-76, 79-81, 89-91, Army Rsch. Office, 1981-89, Air Force Sci. Rsch., 1981-82, 91-95, Nat. Security Agy., 1994-96. Mem.: Soc. Indsl. and Applied Math., Math. Assn. Am. (1st v.p. 1996—98, chmn. minorities in math. task force 1988), Am. Math. Soc. (coun. 2001—04, com. mem.), Sigma Xi. Democrat. Roman Catholic. Office: Howard U Dept Math Washington DC 20059-0001 Business E-Mail: lraphael@howard.edu.

RAPHAEL, MOLLY (MARY E. RAPHAEL), retired library director; b. Columbus, Ohio; d. Paul and Dorothy Osborn Horst; m. Ted Raphael. B in Psychology, Oberlin Coll., Ohio, 1967; MLS, Simmons Coll., Boston, 1969. Various positions starting with asst. children's libr. DC Pub. Libr., 1970—98, dir., 1998—2003; dir. librs. Multnomah County Libr., Portland, Oreg., 2003—09, ret., 2009. Mem. Freedom to Read Found., Friends of Librs. USA. Recipient Alumni Achievement award, Simmons Coll. Grad. Sch. Libr. and Info. Sci., 2007, Arthur Flemming Civil Rights award, 2008. Mem.: ALA (mem. governing bd.), Urban Librs. Coun.*

RAPHAEL, STEVEN P., dean, political science professor; BA in Econs., San Diego State U., 1990; PhD in Econs., U. Calif., Berkeley, 1996. Asst. prof. econs. U. Calif., San Diego, 1996—99, asst. prof. pub. policy Berkeley, 1999—2002, assoc. prof., 2002—06, chancellors prof., 2002—07, prof. pub. policy, 2006—; assoc. dean Goldman Sch. Pub. Policy, U. Calif., Berkeley, 2003—06, now interim dean. Rsch. affiliate Nat. Poverty Ctr., U. Mich., 2004—; co-dir., co-prin. investigator Berkeley Integrated Grad. Edn., Rsch., and Training (IGERT) Program in Politics, Economics, Psychology, and Public Policy, 2005—. Contbr. articles to profl. jours. Office: Richard & Rhoda Goldman Sch Pub Policy U Calif, Berkeley 2604 Hearst Ave Berkeley CA 94720-7320 Office Phone: 540-643-0536. Office Fax: 510-643-9657. E-mail: stevenraphael@berkeley.edu.*

RAPHAELSON, JOEL, retired advertising agency executive; b. NYC, Sept. 27, 1928; s. Samson and Dorothy (Wegman) R.; m. Mary Kathryn Hartigan, Aug. 20, 1960; children: Matthew, Katherine, Paul. BA, Harvard U., 1949. Copywriter Macy's, NYC, 1950-51, BBDO, NYC, 1953-58; with Ogilvy & Mather, Inc., NYC, 1958-94, sr. v.p., dir., 1966-75, mem. exec. com., 1970-75, exec. creative dir. Chgo., 1976—82; sr. v.p. internat. creative svcs. Ogilvy & Mather Worldwide, 1982-92, spl. assignments as editor, writer, speechwriter, cons., 1993-94, ret., 1995. Lectr. Am. Assn. Advt. Agys., others. Author: (with Kenneth Roman) How To Write Better, 1978, Writing That Works, 1981, rev. expanded edit., 1992, 00; editor: The Unpublished David Ogilvy, 1986, Viewpoint (co. jour.), 1983-94; contbr. Harvard Bus. Rev., Advertising Age, other bus. publs. Cons. Lyric Opera Chgo., 1983—, Exec. Svc. Corps, Chgo., 1997-2007, Art Inst. Chgo., 2007—; dir. Santa for the Very Poor, 1988— Home: 20 E Cedar St Apt 8A Chicago IL 60611-5115 Home Phone: 312-751-0987. Personal E-mail: joelr28@aol.com.

RAPINI, RONALD PETER, dermatology educator; b. Akron, Ohio, Feb. 15, 1954; s. Vincent Thomas and Joann Irene (Tufexis) R.; m. Mary Jo Beigel, June 16, 1979; children: Brianna Marie, Sarina Elizabeth. BS in Biology, U. Akron, 1975; MD, Ohio State U., 1978. Diplomate Am. Bd. Dermatology (bd. dirs. 1996-2004, pres. 2004), Am. Bd. Dermatopathology. Assoc. prof. U. Tex. Med. Sch., Houston, 1983-93; prof. and chair dermatology dept. Tex. Tech. U., Lubbock, 1994—2002; prof., chair dept. dermatology U. Tex. Med. Sch., Houston, 2002—, MD Anderson Cancer Ctr., Houston, 2002—. Author (with K.G. Gross and H.K. Steinman): Mohs Surgery, 1999; author: (with J. Bolognia and J. Jorizzo) Dermatology, 2007; author: Practical Dermatopathology, 2005, of over 150 other publications. Fellow Am. Acad. Dermatology, Am. Soc. Dermatol. Surgery (bd. dir. 1995-98), Soc. Investigative Dermatology; mem. AMA, Am. Soc. Dermatopathology (pres. 1998-99), Am. Soc. Mohs Surgery (pres. 2003), Internat. Soc. Dermatopathology, Tex. Dermatol. Soc. (pres. 2006—07). Avocations: tennis, entomology, piano. Office: U TEx Med Sch 6655 Travis St 980 Houston TX 77030-0001 Office Phone: 713-745-1113.

RAPINO, MICHAEL, music company executive; b. Can. Grad. in Bus., Lakehead U., Thunder Bay, Ont. Dir. entertainment and sports Labatt's Breweries Can., head mktg. brands; ptnr. Core Audience Entertainment (acquired by SFX in 1999), Canada; head Internat. Music divsn. Clear Channel Entertainment (formerly SFX), London; CEO, pres. Global Music Clear Channel Music Group; CEO Live Nation, 2005—. Named a Maverick, Details mag., 2008. Office: Live Nation 9348 Civic Ctr Dr Beverly Hills CA 90210 Office Phone: 310-867-7000.

RAPOLU, PRAVEEN, physician; s. KrishnaMurthy and Sujatha Rapolu; m. Samatha Eppakayala, Nov. 11, 2007. MD, Kakatiya Med. Coll., India, 2000, Maimonides Med. Ctr., Bklyn., 2006; MPH, Western Ky. U., Bowling Green, Mass., 2003. Diplomate Am. Bd. Internal Medicine, 2006. Internal medicine resident Maimonides Med. Ctr., Bklyn., 2003—06; academic hospitalist NorthShore Med. Ctr., Salem, Mass., 2006—. Pub. health profl. Western Ky. U., 2001—03. Contbr. articles to publs. Com. mem. Instl. Rev. Bd., Salem, 2006—07. Recipient Excellence award, Ptnrs. Health Care, 2007. Mem.: AMA (assoc.), Mass. Med. Soc. (assoc.), Soc. Hosp. Medicine (assoc.), Am. Gastroenterology Assn. (assoc.), Am. Coll. Physician (assoc.). Achievements include research in mortality reduction in GI bleeding.

RAPOPORT, BERNARD ROBERT, lawyer; b. NYC, Jan. 18, 1919; s. Max and Rose (Gerard) R.; m. Robyrta Wechter, May 31, 1959; 1 son: Michael. AB, Cornell U., 1939, JD, 1941. Bar: NY 1941, Fed. Ct. (so. dist.) 1946. Assoc. firm Proskauer, Rose, Goetz, Mendelsohn, NYC, 1941-50; gen. counsel M. Lowenstein Corp., NYC, 1950-86; dir., treas., sec. Leon Lowenstein Found. Capt. Signal Corps, U.S. Army, 1942-45. Mem. ABA, Assn. of Bar of City of N.Y. Address: 910 5th Ave New York NY 10021-4155

RAPOPORT, JUDITH, psychiatrist; b. NYC, July 12, 1933; d. Louis and Minna (Enteen) Livant; m. Stanley Rapoport, June 25, 1961; children: Stuart, Erik. BA, Swarthmore Coll., 1955; MD, Harvard U., 1959. Lic. psychiatrist. Cons., child psychiatrist NIMH/St. Elizabeth's Hosp., Washington, 1969—72; clin. asst. prof. Georgetown U. Med. Sch., Washington, 1972—82, clin. assoc. prof., 1982—85, clin. prof. psychiat., 1985—; med. officer biol. psychiatry br. NIMH, Bethesda, Md., 1979—82, chief, child psychiatry lab. of clin. scis., 1982—84, chief, child psychiatry div. intramural rsch. programs, 1984—; prof. psychiatry George Washington U. Sch. Med., Washington, 1979—; prof. pediat. Georgetown U., Washington, 1985—. Cons. in field. Author: (non-fiction) The Boy Who Couldn't Stop Washing, 1989 (best seller literary guild selection, 1989), Childhood Obsessive Compulsive Disorder, 1989. Recipient Scolnick award, MIT, 2005. Fellow: Am. Acad. Arts & Sci., Am. Acad. Child Psychiatry, Am. Psychiat. Assn.; mem.: Inst. Medicine, D.C. Psychiat. Assn. Home: 3010 44th Pl NW Washington DC 20016-3557 Office: NIMH Rm 3N202 10 Center Dr Bldg 10 Bethesda MD 20892-0001 Office Phone: 301-496-6081. Business E-Mail: rapoport@helix.nih.gov.

RAPOPORT, MILES S., advocate, former state official; m. Sandra Luciano; children: Jeff, Ross. BA in Polit. sci., N.Y. U., 1971. Exec. dir. Conn. Citizen Action Group, 1979-84; mem. Conn. Ho. of Reps., asst. majority leader, 1987-92, house chmn. govt. adminstrn. and elections com., mem. fin., revenue and bonding com.; sec. of state State of Conn., 1994-98; exec. dir. Democracy Works, Hartford, Conn., 1999—2001; pres. Demos, NYC, 2001—. Office: President Demos 5th Fl 220 Fifth Ave New York NY 10001*

RAPOPORT, NANCY B., law educator; m. Jeffrey D. Van Niel, Oct. 13, 1996. BA in Legal Studies, Psychology with hon., summa cum laude, Rice U., 1982; JD, Stanford Law Sch., 1985. Bar: Calif. 1987, Ohio 1993, Nebr. 1999, Calif. Supreme Ct. 1987, Ohio Supreme Ct. 1993, Nebr. Supreme Ct. 1999, US Dist. Ct. Hawaii 1988, US Dist. Ct. (no., ea., ctrl., and so. dists.) Calif. 1987, US Dist. Ct. (no. dist.) Tex. 2003, US Ct. Appeals (9th cir.) 1987, US Supreme Ct. 2000. Jud. clk. Hon. Joseph T. Sneed, U.S. Ct. Appeals (9th cir.), San Francisco, 1985—86; assoc. bus.dept. of bankruptcy and workouts group Morrison & Foerster, San Francisco, 1986—91; asst. prof. Ohio State U. Coll. Law, Columbus, 1991—95, tenured assoc. prof., 1995—98, assoc. dean student affairs, 1996—98, prof., 1998; dean, prof. law U. Nebr. Coll. Law, Lincoln, 1998—2000; dean U. Houston Law Ctr., 2000—06, prof. law, 2000—06; with Gordon & Silver Ltd., 2006—07; prof. law. William S. Boyd Sch. Law, U. Nev., Las Vegas, 2007—. Invited spkr., panelist, and presenter in field. Co-editor (with Bala G. Dharan): Enron: Corporate Fiascos and Their Implications, 2004. Bd. trustees Law Sch. Admissions Coun., 2001—04; bd. dir. ADL Southwest Regional Bd., 2001—, Houston Area Women's Ctr., 2003—; bd. mem. Mayor's Adv. Bd. of World Energy Cities Partnership, 2001—04, Houston Disaster Relief Adv. Bd., 2001—04, Houston Chpt. Tex. Gen. Counsel Forum, 2001—05, Anti-Defamation League Southwest Regional Bd., 2001—06, Advisory Coun., WWW United Inc., 2002—06, Tex. Environ. Health Inst., 2002—04, Houston Hillel, 2002—07, Vinson & Elkins Women's Initiative Adv. Bd., 2003—, Houston Area Women's Ctr., 2003—06, Tex. Ctr. for Legal Ethics, 2004—06, Tex. Supreme Ct. Hist. Soc. Adv. Bd., 2004—06, Houston World Affairs Coun., 2002—05, NALP Found. for Law Career Rsch. and Edn., 2005—, Assn. Rice Alumni Bd., 2006—, Am. Bd. Cert., 2007—. Recipient Rice U. Dist. Alumna award; named Outstanding Prof. of Yr., Ohio State U. Coll. Law., 1997, fellow, Am. Bankruptcy Law Jour., 1998. Fellow: Am. Coll. Bankruptcy, Am. Bar Found., Houston Bar Found. (selection com. 2000—, Best Article award); mem.: ABA (task force atty. discipline 2005—, commn. legal debt and forgiveness), Assn. Am. Law Sch.'s Profl. Develop. Com., Ohio State Bar Assn. (legal edn. com. 1997—98), Am. Bankruptcy Inst. (law sch. com. 1994—), Bar Assn. San Francisco, Nat. Assn. Coll. and U. Attys., Nebr. State Bar Assn. (Named Legal Pioneer for Women in Law 1999), Houston Bar Assn., Am. Law Inst. Democrat. Jewish. Avocations: dance, photography, music, movies, history. Office: Univ Nev Las Vegas William Boyd Sch Law Box 451003 4505 S Maryland Pkwy Las Vegas NV 89154-1003 Business E-Mail: nrapoport@money-law.org.

RAPOPORT, RONALD JON, journalist; b. Detroit, Aug. 14, 1940; s. Daniel B. and Shirley G.; m. Joan Zucker, Sept. 2, 1968; children—Rebecca, Julie. BA, Stanford U., 1962; MS, Columbia U., 1963. Reporter Mpls. Star, 1963-65; asso. editor Sport mag., 1965-66; sports reporter AP, NYC, San Francisco, 1966-70, Los Angeles Times, 1970-77; sports columnist Chgo. Sun-Times, 1977-88, Los Angeles Daily News, 1988-95; sports commentator Weekend Edit. Nat. Pub. Radio, 1986—2007; dep. sports editor Chgo. Sun-Times, 1996-98, sports columnist, 1998—2006. Author: (with Chip Oliver) High for the Game, 1971; (with Stan Love) Love in the NBA, 1975, (with Jim McGregor) Called for Travelling, 1979; editor: A Kind of Grace: A Treasury of Sportswriting by Women, 1994; (with Betty Garrett) Betty Garrett and Other Songs, 1998, See How She Runs: Marion Jones and the Making of a Champion, 2000, The Immortal Bobby: Bobby Jones and the Golden Age of Golf, 2005, (with Eddie Einhorn) How March Became Madness: How the NCAA Tournament Became the Greatest Sporting Event in America, 2006. Served with U.S. Army Res., 1963.

RAPOZA, ELIZABETH, theater educator, playwright, director; d. Joseph Francis and Izaura Rapoza. MA in Theater Edn., Emerson Coll., Boston, 2003. Performer King Richard's Faire, Carver, Mass., 1991—; adj. faculty Cape Cod CC, West Barnstable, Mass., 2003—. Dir. Backyard Dramatics, New Bedford, Mass., 1989—. Author: (plays) Perstephanie Goes Underground (Boston Pub. Sch. Short Play Devel. award, 2007), The Amazing Adventures of Pajamazon (Mae West Fest Ultimate Female Protagonist, 2005). Pres. Funeral Consumer Alliance, New Bedford, 1994—98. Mem.: NOW. Liberal. Avocations: dance, acting, art, music. Office: Cape Cod CC 2240 Iyanough Rd West Barnstable MA 02668 Personal E-mail: felizbinah@yahoo.com. Business E-Mail: erapoza@capecod.edu.

RAPP, EDWARD J., manufacturing executive; BA in Fin., U. Mo., Columbia; grad. exec. devel. program, U. Ill. Pricing anlayst Caterpillar, Inc., pricing and prodn. positions, mgr. planning support for the N.Am. comml. divsn., San Francisco dist. mgr., area mgr. Johannesburg, dept. mgr. bldg. constrn. products Geneva, v.p. Europe, Africa, Mid. East mktg. divsn., 2000—04, v.p. bldg. constrn. products divsn. Cary, NC, 2004—07, group pres. Peoria, Ill., 2007—. Bd. mem. Mitsubishi/Cat Forklift JV. Bd. advisors Raleigh C. of C., NC; bd. mem. NC State U. Coll. Mgmt. Office: Caterpillar Inc 100 NE Adams St Peoria IL 61629*

RAPP, GEORGE ROBERT (RIP), geology and archeology educator; b. Toledo, Sept. 19, 1930; s. George Robert and Gladys Mae (Warner) R.; m. Jeannette Messner, June 15, 1956; children: Kathryn, Karen. BA, U. Minn., 1952; PhD, Pa. State U., 1960. Asst. then assoc. prof. S.D. Sch. Mines, Rapid City, 1957-65; assoc. prof. U. Minn., Mpls., 1965-75, prof. geology and archeology Duluth, 1975-95, dean Coll. Letters and Sci., 1975-84, dean Coll. Sci. and Engring., 1984-89, dir. Archeometry Lab., 1975—2004, Regents' prof. geoarchaeology, 1995—2003, emeritus, 2003—. Prof. Ctr. for Ancient Studies, U. Minn., Mpls., 1970-93, prof. interdisciplinary archaeol. studies, 1993—; cons. USIA, Westinghouse Corp., Exxon Corp., Ford Found. Author, editor: Excavations at Nichoria, 1978, Troy: Archeological Geology, 1982, Archeological Geology, 1985, Excavations at Tel Michal, 1989, Encyclopedia of Minerals, 1989, Phytolith Systematics, 1992, Geoarchaeology, 1998, Artifact Copper Sources, 2000, Archaeomineralogy, 2002; mem. editl. bd. Jour. Field Archeology, 1976-85, Jour. Archeol. Sci., 1977-79, Geoarcheology Jour., 1984-92, Am. Jour. Archeology, 1985-92. NSF postdoctoral fellow, 1963-64, Fulbright-Hayes sr. rsch. fellow, 1972-73. Fellow AAAS (chmn. sect. E, 1987-88, nat. coun. 1992-95), Geol. Soc. Am. (Archeol. Geology award 1983), Mineral. Soc. Am.; mem. Nat. Assn. Geology Tchrs. (pres. 1986-89), Soc. for Archeol. Sci. (pres. 1983-84), Assn. Field Archeology (pres. 1979-81), Archaeol. Inst. Am. (Pomerance medal 1988), Sigma Xi (bd. dirs. 1990-98). Avocations: classical music, exercise, nutrition. Office: U Minn-Duluth Dept Geol Scis Duluth MN 55812 Home Phone: 520-825-9770; Office Phone: 218-726-7629. Business E-Mail: grapp@d.umn.edu.

RAPP, RICHARD TILDEN, economist, consultant; b. Miami, Fla., Nov. 30, 1944; s. Melville Benjamin and Rachel (Marx) R.; m. Wilma J. Levin, Aug. 20, 1967; children: Ethan, Sandra. BA cum laude, Bklyn. Coll., 1965; MA, U. Pa., 1966, PhD, 1970. Asst. prof. SUNY, Stony Brook, 1970-75, assoc. prof. econ. history, 1976-77; pres., chief exec. officer Nat. Econ. Rsch. Assocs., Inc., White Plains, NY, 1977—. Cons. on internat. trade and competition econs. Author: Industry and Economic Decline in Seventeenth-Century Venice, 1976, Trade Warfare and the New Protectionism, 1986; co-author: European Economic History, 1975. Nat. adv. bd. Santa Fe Opera, 1989—. Kent fellow Danforth found.,

1968-70; Fulbright fellow, 1968-69. Mem. Am. Econ. Assn., Inst. for Advanced Study. Home: 52 Whippoorwill Lake Rd Chappaqua NY 10514-2314 Office: Nat Econ Rsch Assocs Inc 50 Main St White Plains NY 10606-1901

RAPP, ROBERT ANTHONY, metallurgical engineering educator; s. Frank J. and Goldie M. (Royer) R.; m. Heidi B. Sartorius, June 3, 1960; children: Kathleen Rapp Raynaud, Thomas, Stephen, Stephanie Rapp Surface. BSMetE, Purdue U., 1956; MSMetE, Carnegie Inst. Tech., 1959, PhDMetE, 1960; D (hon.), Inst. Polytech., Toulouse, France, 1995. Asst. prof. metall. engring. Ohio State U., Columbus, 1963—66, assoc. prof. metall. engring., 1966—69, prof., 1969—, M.G. Fontana prof., 1988—95, prof., 1989—95, disting. univ. prof. emeritus, 1995—. Vis. prof. Ecole Nat. Superior d'Electrochimie, Grenoble, France, 1972-73, U. Paris-Sud, Orsay, 1985-86, Ecole Nat. Superior de Chimie, Toulouse, France, 1985-86, U. New South Wales, Australia, 1987; Acta/Scripta Metallurgica lectr., 1991; rsch. metallurgist WPAFB, Ohio, 1960-63. Editor: Techniques of Metals Research, vol. IV, 1982, High Temperature Corrosion, 1984; translator Metallic Corrosion (Kaesche), 1986; bd. rev. jour. Oxid. Metals; contbr. 265 publs. and numerous articles to profl. jours. First lt. USAF, 1960—63, Wright-Patterson AFB. Decorated chevalier des Palmes Academiques; recipient Disting. Engring. Alumnus award Purdue U., 1988, B.F. Goodrich Collegiate Inventor's award, 1991, 92, Ulrick Evans award Brit. Inst. Corrosion, 1992; Guggenheim fellow, 1972; Fulbright scholar Max Planck Inst. Phys. Chemistry, 1959-60, Linford award for Disting. Tchg.,The Electrochem. Soc., 1998. Fellow: Nat. Assn. Corrosion Engrs. (W.R. Whitney award 1986), Electrochem. Soc. (HTM Divsn. Outstanding Achievement award 1992, Linford Tchr. award 1998, Olin Palladium award 2005), Mining Metals and Materials Soc. (R.F. Mehl medal 2000, Educator award 2003), Am. Soc. Metals Internat. (Zay Jeffries lectr. 2006, B. Stoughton award 1968, Howe gold medal 1974, Gold medal 2000); mem.: Nat. Acad. Engring., Brit. Inst. Corrosion (hon.), Japanese Inst. Metals (hon.), French Soc. Metals and Materials (hon.). Lutheran. Achievements include about twenty patents. Avocations: gardening, golf, travel. Home: 1379 Southport Dr Columbus OH 43235-7649 E-mail: rrapp001@columbus.rr.com, rapp.4@osu.edu.

RAPP, STEPHEN JOHN, international prosecutor; b. Waterloo, Iowa, Jan. 26, 1949; s. Spurgeon John and Beverly (Leckington) R.; m. Donna J.E. Maier, 1981; children: Alexander, Stephanie. AB cum laude, Harvard U., 1971; JD with honors, Drake U., 1973. Bar: Iowa 1974, US Dist. Ct. (no. and so. dists.) Iowa 1978, US Ct. Appeals (8th cir.) 1979, US Supreme Ct. 1979. Rsch. asst. Office US Senator Birch Bayh, Ind., 1970; community program asst. HUD, Chgo., 1971; mem. Iowa Ho. Reps., 1972-74, 79-83, Coun. to Majority Caucus, Iowa Ho. Reps., 1975; staff dir., counsel subcom. on juvenile delinquency US Senate, Washington, 1977-78; ptnr. Rapp & Gilliam, Waterloo, 1979-83; pvt. practice Waterloo, 1983-93; U.S. atty. US Dist. Ct. (no. dist.) Iowa, 1993—2001; sr. prosecuting atty. UN Internat. Crime Tribunal Rwanda, 2001—05, chief prosecutions, 2005—07; prosecutor Spl. Ct. for Sierra Leone, 2007—. Del., mem. com. Dem. Nat. Conv., 1976, 80, 84, 88, 92; mem. Dem. Nat. Adv. Com. on Econ., 1982-84, chmn. Black Hawk Dem. Com., 1986-91; mem. Iowa Dem. Com., 1990-93; chair 2d C.D. Dem. Com., 1991-93. Mem. ABA, Iowa Bar Assn., Order of Coif. Methodist. Home: 219 Highland Blvd Waterloo IA 50703-4229 Office: SC52 Jomo Kenyatta Rd Freetown Sierra Leone Office Phone: 212-963-9915 ext. 1787380. E-mail: rapp@un.org.

RAPP, STEVEN M., lawyer, consumer products company executive; BA in English, SUNY, Buffalo, 1975; JD, St. John's U. Sch. Law. Atty. Willkie, Farr & Gallagher; corp. lawyer PepsiCo. Inc., 1986, divsn. counsel, 1994; v.p., dep. gen. counsel, asst. sec. Pepsi Bottling Group, Inc., Somers, NY, 1999—2004, sr. v.p., gen. counsel, sec., 2005—. Office: Pepsi Bottling Grp Inc 1 Pepsi Way Somers NY 10589-2201 Office Phone: 914-767-6000.*

RAPPAPORT, CAREY MILFORD, electrical engineering educator; b. Tokyo, Jan. 9, 1959; came to U.S., 1964; s. Paul Julian and Evelyn Rappaport; m. Ann Welke Morgenthaler, Nov. 12, 1989; children: Sarah Nason, Brian Hampton. BSEE, BS in Math., MSEE, EngEE, MIT, 1982, PhD, 1987. Asst. prof. elec. and computer engring. Northeastern U., Boston, 1987-93, assoc. prof., 1993-2000, prof., 2000—. Cons. AJ Devaney Assocs., Boston, 1987—; Dept. Homeland Security Ctr. Excellence Awareness and Localization Explosives-Related Threats, NSF Ctr. for Subsurface Sensing and Imaging Systems. Author: Progress in Electromagnetics Research, Vol. I, 1989, Alternatives for Landmine Detection, 2003, Wave Propagation, Scattering and Emission in Complex Media, 2004, Ground Penetrating Radar, 2004; contbr. articles to profl. jours.; patentee in field. Recipient MIT K.T. Compton award, 1985. Fellow: IEEE (H.A. Wheeler award 1986); mem.: Eta Kappa Nu, Sigma Xi. Avocations: skiing, bridge, backpacking, chess, swimming. Office: Northeastern U 302 Stearns Boston MA 02115 Office Phone: 617-373-5110. Business E-Mail: rappaport@neu.edu.

RAPPAPORT, CHARLES OWEN, lawyer; b. NYC, May 15, 1950; s. Edward and Edith (Novick) R.; m. Valerie B. Ackerman, Oct. 11, 1987; children: Emily Randle, Sarah Elisabeth. BA, Columbia U., 1970; JD, NYU, 1975. Bar: N.Y. 1976. Assoc. Simpson, Thacher & Bartlett LLP, NYC, 1975—82, ptnr., 1982. Office: Simpson Thacher & Bartlett LLP 425 Lexington Ave 14th Fl New York NY 10017-3954 Home: 90 Franklin St New York NY 10013 E-mail: corappaport@stblaw.com.

RAPPAPORT, IRVING S., entrepreneur, lawyer IP consultant; s. Melvin Rappaport and Minette Grober; m. Lesley Radoff; children: Steven, Matthew, Diana Robinson, David. BSEE, Wash. U., St. Louis, 1962; JD (hons.), George Wash. U. Law Sch., Washington, DC, 1966; MBA, Boston Univ. Grad. Sch. Mgmt., 1969. Bar: Mo. State Bar 1966, Ct. Appeals (fed. cir.) 1966, US Supreme Ct. 2005, registered: US Patent & Trademark Office (patent atty.) 1966, Can. Intellectual Property Office (patent agent) 1980. Patent examiner US Patent & Trademark Office, Washington, 1962—63; 1st lt. US Army, Ft. Meade, Md., 1963—65; patent agt. RCA, Washington, 1965—66, Philpitt, Steininger & Priddy, Washington, 1965; patent and trademark atty. Raytheon Co., Lexington, Mass., 1966—70, Schiller & Pandiscio, Waltham, Mass., 1970—71; asst. gen. counsel for patents, asst. sec. Medtronic, Inc., Mpls., 1971—77; corp. sec., gen. counsel Renal Sys., Inc., Mpls., 1977—78; chief patent counsel Data Gen. Corp., Westboro, Mass., 1978—82; assoc. gen. counsel for intellectual property and licensing Bally Mfg., Chgo., 1982—84, Apple Computer, Inc., Cupertino, Calif., 1984—90; intellectual property cons. Intel Corp., Santa Clara, Calif., 1990—91; v.p., assoc. gen. counsel for intellectual property and licensing Nat. Semiconductor Corp., Santa Clara, 1991—93; founder, dir. and v.p. intellectual property Aurigin Sys., Inc., Cupertino, 1993—2002; v.p. intellectual property licensing bus. Symyx Technologies, Inc., Sunnyvale, Calif., 2002—03; intellectual property lawyer and cons. Irving S. Rappaport, Palo Alto, Calif., 2003—; co-founder, mng. dir. IP Checkups, LLC, Berkeley, Calif., 2004—. Sec. Minn. Patent & Trademark Law Assoc., Mpls., 1977—78; mem. bd. dirs. Aurigin Sys., Inc., Cupertino, Calif., 1993—2002; bd. of advisors Intellectual Property Innovations, Charlotte, NC, 2004—, Altitude Capital Ptnrs., NYC, 2006—; mng. dir. Telemaze LLC, Los Altos, Calif., 2005—; cert. lic. profl. expert witness IP Litigation. Author over 60 articles and presentations on intellectual property matters; contbr. chapters to books. First lt. Army Sec. Agy. US Army, 1963—65. Recipient Svc. to U.S. Gov't. on Trade Related IP Matters, 3 U.S. Secretaries of Commerce & 3 U.S. Trade Rep., 1987—94; named one of World's 250 Leading Intellectual Property Strategists, Intellectual Asset Mgmt. Mag., 2009. Mem.: Ill. State Bar, Minn. State Bar, Mass. State Bar, Minn. Patent & Trademark Law Assn. (sec. 1977—78), Boston Patent Law Assn., Am. Intellectual Property Law Assn., Licensing Execs. Soc., ABA. Achievements include having 22 US patents & 10 pending application. Avocations: jogging, bicycling, tennis, squash. Business E-Mail: isport1@yahoo.com.

RAPPAPORT, LAWRENCE, plant physiology and horticulture educator; b. NYC, May 28, 1928; s. Aaron and Elsie R.; m. Norma, Nov. 21, 1953; children: Meryl, Debra Kramer, Craig. BS in Horticulture, U. Idaho, 1950; MS in Horticulture, Mich. State Coll., 1951; PhD in Horticulture, Mich. State U., 1956. Lectr. U. Calif., Davis, 1956-67, jr. olericulturist, dept. vegetable crops, 1956-58, asst. olericulturist, 1958-63, assoc. olericulturist, 1963-67, prof., 1968—, prof. emeritus, 1991—, dir. plant growth lab., 1975-78, chairperson dept. vegetable crops, 1978-84. Vis. scientist Calif. Inst. Tech., 1958; co-dir. Horticulture Subproject, Calif./Egypt project, 1978-82. Contbr. articles to profl. jours. 1st pres. Davis Human Rels. Coun., 1964-66; v.p. Jewish Fedn. Sacramento, 1969; pres. Jewish Fellowship, Davis, 1985-89; founder, 1st dir. Hillel Counselership at Davis, 1965-76. Decorated Bronze star; Guggenheim Found. fellow, 1963, Fulbright fellow, 1964, USPHS Spl. fellow, 1970, Am. Soc. Horticulture Sci. fellow, 1987, Sir Frederick McMaster fellow, 1991. Achievements include discovery of evidence for gibberellin-binding protein in plants; evidence for the signal hypothesis operating in plants, positive evidence for phytochrome-mediated gibberellin metabolism and stem growth; isolation of somaclonal variants of celery bearing stable resistance to Fusarium oxysporum f. sp. apii. Home: 637 Elmwood Dr Davis CA 95616-3514 Office: Dept Plant Environ Sci One Shields Ave Davis CA 95616 Business E-Mail: lrappaport@ucdavis.edu.

RAPPAPORT, LINDA ELLEN, lawyer; b. Freeport, NY, Jan. 12, 1952; d. William Jay and Marcia Ann (Wiland) Rappaport; m. Leonard Chazen, June 1, 1980; 1 child, Matthew Ross Chazen. BA, Wesleyan U., Middletown, Conn., 1974; JD, NYU, 1977. Bar: N.Y. 1977. Law clk. Chief Judge James S. Holden U.S. Dist. Ct. Vt., Rutland, 1978; assoc. Shearman & Sterling, NYC, 1979—85, ptnr., 1986—, elected mem. policy com., 1995—2005, mem. exec. group, 2005—07, sr. mgmt. team, 2008—. Adv.bd. dirs. NYC Ballet, 2006—; bd. dirs. NY Women's Found., NYC, 1995—2001, AIESEC Internat., NYC, 1994—2000; bd. govs. Mannes Coll. Music, 2004—; bd. dirs. Legal Aid Soc. N.Y., 2005—, exec. com., 2005—. Fellow: Am. Coll. Employee Benefits Coun.; mem.: Bar Assn. City of N.Y. (employee benefits com. 1986—, employment law com. 1986—). Office: Shearman & Sterling 599 Lexington Ave Fl 13 New York NY 10022-6069 Office Phone: 212-848-7004. Business E-Mail: lrappaport@shearman.com.

RAPPAPORT, MARGARET MARY WILLIAMS EWING, psychologist, physician, writer, pilot, consultant; b. Nov. 16, 1947; d. Leo J. and Marie L. (Rischle) Williams; m. Herbert Rappaport (div.); children: Amanda, Alexander. BA, U. Buffalo; MA, SUNY; PhD, MD, U. Colo. Zone Perfect cert. instr. Prof., rschr. U. Dar es Salaam, Tanzania; with Rappaport Assocs., Phila., 1974-94; exec. dir. Inst. for Parent/Child Svcs., Phila., 1978-94; pres., CEO Diabetes Edn. Ctr. Cape Cod, 2002—03. Mem. adj. faculty Temple U., Phila., 1974—94; aviation safety counselor FAA; cons., spkr. in field.; pres. Reach New Heights, Inc., 1994—2005; founder Fit to Fly. Mem. AAUP, Nat. Profl. Spkrs. Assn., Cosmopolitan Club, Orleans Yacht Club. Home: PO Box 1845 Orleans MA 02653-1845 Office Phone: 508-255-9570. Personal E-mail: rappaportmm@yahoo.com.

RAPPAPORT, MARTIN PAUL, internist, nephrologist, educator; b. Bronx, NY, Apr. 25, 1935; s. Joseph and Anne (Kramer) R.; m. Bethany Ann Mitchell; children: Karen, Steven; stepchildren: Aaron Cole, Kevin Cole. BS, Tulane U., 1957, MD, 1960. Diplomate Am. Bd. Internal Medicine, Nat. Bd. Med. Examiners. Intern Charity Hosp. of La., New Orleans, 1960-61, resident in internal medicine, 1961-64; pvt. practice internal medicine and nephrology, Seabrook, Tex., 1968-72, Webster, Tex., 1972-98; internist Univ. Med. Group, Houston, 1998; mem. courtesy staff Mainland Ctr. Hosp. (formerly Galveston County Meml. Hosp.), Texas City, 1968-96, Bapt. Meml. System, 1969-72, 88-98; mem. staff Clear Lake Regional Med. Ctr., 1972-98, cons. staff St. Mary's Hosp., 1973-79; cons. nephrology St. John's Hosp., Nassau Bay, Tex.; fellow in nephrology Northwestern U. Med. Sch., Chgo., 1967—68; clin. asst. prof. in medicine and nephrology U. Tex., Galveston, 1969—2009; part-time physician dept. family medicine outpatient clinics U. Tex. Med. Br., Galveston, 2000; locum tenens, 2000—06; ret., 2006. Lectr. emergency med. technician cours e, 1974-76; adviser on respiratory therapy program Alvin (Tex.) Jr. Coll., 1976-82; cons. nephrology USPHS, 1979-80. Served to capt. M.C. U.S. Army, 1961-67. Fellow ACP, Am. Coll. Chest Physicians; mem. Internat., Am. Socs. Nephrology, So. Med. Assn., Tex. Med. Assn., Tex. Soc. Internal Medicine (bd. govs. 1994-96), Am. Soc. Artificial Internal Organs, Tex. Acad. Internal Medicine, Harris County Med. Soc., Am. Geriatrics Soc., Bay Area Heart Assn. (bd. govs. 1969-75), Clear Lake C. of C., Conroe Rotary Club, Rotary, Phi Delta Epsilon, Alpha Epsilon Pi, Tulane Alumni Assn. Home: 15913 Malibu W Willis TX 77318-6784 Home Phone: 936-890-0673.

RAPPAPORT, NORMAN HARVEY, plastic surgeon; b. Phila., Apr. 23, 1947; s. Herbert and Ruth Rappaport; m. Deborah Ann Finn, Oct. 2, 1982; children: Jonathan David, Betsy, William. BA, LaSalle Coll., 1969; DDS, Temple U., 1972; MD, Hahnemann Med. Coll., 1975. Diplomate Am. Bd. Plastic Surgery. Resident in gen. surgery Abington (Pa.) Meml. Hosp., 1975-78; fellow in hand surgery U. Pa., Phila., 1978; resident in plastic surgery Baylor Coll. Medicine, Houston, 1978-80; clin. assoc. prof. surgery Baylor Coll. Surgery, Houston, 1994—. Contbr. articles to profl. jours. Fellow: ACS; mem.: AMA, Houston Surg. Soc. (pres. 2001), Tex. Soc. Plastic Surgeons, Tex. Med. Assn., N.Am. Burn Soc., Houston Soc. Plastic Surgeons (pres. 2002), Harris County Med. Soc., Am. Assn. Hand Surgeons, Am. Assn. Plastic Surgeons, Am. Soc. for Aesthetic Plastic Surgery, Am. Soc. Plastic Surgeons (bd. dirs. 1998—2000), Plastic Surgery Ednl. Found. (bd. dirs. 1994—2000), Am. Soc. Maxillofacial Surgeons (pres. 2000), Omicron Kappa Upsilon. Office: 6560 Fannin St Ste 1812 Houston TX 77030-2775 Office Phone: 713-790-4500. E-mail: nhr@hcps.cc.

RAPPAPORT, RICHARD J., lawyer; b. Chgo., Aug. 13, 1943; m. Roberta Rappaport; children: Michael, Barbara. BS, Loyola U., 1965, JD cum laude, 1967. Bar: Ill. 1967, Fla. 1993, US Dist. Ct. No. Dist. Ill. 1967, US Ct. Appeals 7th Cir. 1978, 10th Cir. 1978, 6th Cir. 1986, 4th Cir. 1988, 11th Cir. 1997, 8th Cir. 2000, 2d Cir. 2006, US Tax Ct. 1988, US Supreme Ct. 1979. Trial atty. antitrust divsn. US Dept. Justice, Washington, 1967-69; ptnr. Ross & Hardies (merged with McGuire-Woods LLP in 2003), Chgo., McGuireWoods LLP, Chgo., 2003—, co-mng. ptnr. Chgo. office, 2003—04. Bd. dirs. Am. Assn. for Klinefelter Syndrome Info. & Support; bd. mem. Loyola U. Sch. Law Inst. Consumer Antitrust Studies. Fellow: Am. Bar Found.; mem.: ABA, Lawyers Club of City of Chgo., Chgo. Bar Assn. Office: McGuireWoods LLP Ste 4100 77 W Wacker Dr Chicago IL 60601-1818 Office Phone: 312-750-8618. Office Fax: 312-920-3696. Business E-Mail: rrappaport@mcguirewoods.com.

RAPPAPORT, STUART RAMON, lawyer; b. Detroit, Apr. 13, 1935; s. Reuben and Zella (Golechen) R.; m. Anne M. Plotnick; children: Douglas, Erica Rappaport Witt. BA in History, U. Mich., 1956; JD, Harvard U., 1959. Bar: Calif. 1962. Trial lawyer, chief trials, bur. chief, chief. asst. pub. defender L.A. County Pub. Defender's Office, LA, 1962-87; pub. defender Santa Clara County, San Jose, Calif., 1987-95; pvt. practice, 1995—. Mem. standing adv. com. on criminal law Jud. Coun. Calif., San Francisco, 1993—; mem. discipline evaluation com. State Bar of Calif. Contbr. articles to profl. jours. Recipient Lifetime Achievement award Calif. Attys. for Criminal Justice. Mem. Calif. Pub. Defenders Asn. (pres. 1982-83, Lifetime Achievement award), L.A. County Pub. Defenders Assn. (pres.), Caljic com. Democrat. Jewish. Home: 4500 Bloomfield Rd Sebastopol CA 95472 Business E-Mail: sturap@mcn.org.

RAPPAPORT, YVONNE KINDINGER, educator; b. Crestline, Ohio, Feb. 15, 1928; d. Paul Theodore and Florence Iona (Cover) Kindinger; BS summa cum laude, Northwestern U., 1949; MA, Va. Poly. Inst. and State U., 1973, PhD, 1980; m. Norman Lewis Rappaport; children: Michael, Laura, Hilary, Stephen, Jocelyn. Pers. officer, then cons. and mgmt. analyst USAF, 1953-63; cons. mgmt. analysis, pers. and pub. rels., 1963-67; cons. program devel., instr. U. Va., 1967-70, dir. continuing edn. for women, 1970-75, dir. and faculty continuing edn. for adult, 1975-85, dir. for continuing edn., 1986-93, cons. human resources, 1993—, dir., performer theatre, children's theatre, radio and TV, 1953—; bd. dirs. Coalition Adult Edn. Orgns. U.S., 1979—, sec.-treas., 1981-83, v.p., 1983-84, pres.-elect, 1984-85, pres., 1985-87, chair internat. assocs. adult edn., 1987-89; U.S. rep. UNESCO conf., Hamburg, Germany 1983, 1997; del. Buenos Aires World Assembly, 1985, Helsinki Peace Conf., 1986, Bangkok World Assembly, 1990; cons. in field. Mem. Va. Legis. Adv. Com. Continuing Edn., 1970-71, No. Va. Adv. Com. Ednl. Telecommunications, 1971—; bd. dirs. Home and Sch. Inst., Washington, 1971—; adv. bd. Svc. League Va., 1976-78. Recipient Meritorious Svc. award USAF, 1959; Career Devel. award ASTD/TOC, 1980, Outstanding Eucator award, Va. Tech, 1998. Mem. AAUW, PTA, LWV (state dir. 1968-73, nat. pub. rels. com. 1970-75), Nat. Assn. Women Deans, Adminstrs. and Counselors (S.E. regional coord. 1973-76), Adult Edn. Assn. U.S. (nat. leadership award 1973, 74, 76, 78, 79, 82, 83, 86, 88; v.p. 1978-79; chmn. commn. status women in edn. 1972-74, dir. 1973-83, chmn. coun. affiliate orgns. 1974-75, chmn. pub. affairs 1975-78, chair program gen. session 1987), Adult Edn. Assn. Va. (pres. 1971-73; recognition of merit award 1971-73), Pers. and Guidance Assn., Nat. Univ. Extension Assn., Assn. Continuing Higher Edn., World Affairs Coun. (bd. dirs. 1987—), Am. Bus. Women Assn. (award 1960), Fairfax, Va. C. of C. (mem. edn. com. 1987—), Order Ea. Star, Phi Delta Kappa, Phi Delta Theta (v.p. programs, 1994, pres.-elect, 1994). Author handbooks and work books, also radio, TV scripts. Home: 3225 Atlanta St Fairfax VA 22030-2127 Office: Sch Continuing Edn U Va Charlottesville VA 22903

RAPPENEAU, JEAN-PAUL, film director, scriptwriter; b. Auxerre, Yonne, France, Apr. 8, 1932; s. Jean and Anne-Marie (Bornhauser) R.; m. Claude-Lise Cornély, 1971; 2 children. Works include: (screenwriter) Signé Arsène Lupin, 1959, Le Mariage (in Française et l'Amour) 1959, Zazie dans le métro, 1960, Vie privée, 1961, Le Combat dans l'île, 1961, L'Homme de Rio, 1962; (dir.) La Maison sur la place, Chronique provinciale, 1958; (screenwriter, dir.) La Vie de château, 1966, (Prix Louis Delluc), Les Mariés de l'An Deux, 1970, Le Sauvage, 1975, Tout feu, tout flamme, 1982; (dir., adaptor) Cyrano de Bergerac, 1990 (Best Picture César award 1990, Best Dir. César award 1990, Best Fgn. Film Golden Globe award 1990, Best Fgn. Film U.S. Nat. Rev. Bd., 1990), Le Hussard Sur Le Toit, 1995, Bon Voyage, 2002. Decorated officier Legion of Honor, commdr. des Arts et des Lettres, officier Ordre Nat. du Mérite (France). Home: 24 rue Henri Barbusse 75005 Paris France

RAPPLEY, MARSHA D., dean, physician, educator; BS in Nursing, U. Mich., 1980; MD, Mich. State U. Coll. Human Medicine, 1984. Cert. in gen. pediatrics and devel. & behavioral pediatrics Am. Bd. Pediatrics. Resident in pediatrics Mich. State U. Coll. Human Medicine, faculty mem., 1988—, interim assoc. dean acad. affairs, 2002, interim chair Dept. Pediatrics & Human Devel., 2001—03, divsn. dir. gen. pediatrics and dir. gen. pediatric clinics, 1991—2001, assoc. dean acad. affairs, 2003—, prof. Dept. Pediatrics and Human Devel., acting dean, 2005—06, dean, 2006—, divsn. dir. Devel. and Behavioral Pediatrics, dir. Collaborative Devel. Clinic. Office: Office of Dean Univ Mich Coll Human Medicine A118-E Fee Hall East Lansing MI 48824-1316 Office Phone: 517-353-4998. E-mail: rappley@msu.edu.*

RAPSOMANIKIS, THEMISTOKLIS THEODORE, independent electrical engineering researcher; b. Athens, Greece, Oct. 24, 1967; s. Theodore Constantine and Evangelia Ioannis Rapsomanikis. Diploma in French Studies (2d degree), U. Paris Sorbonne, 1985; BS, MS in Elec. Engring., Nat. Tech. U. Athens, 1994, PhD in High Speed Networks, 2003. Lic. elec. engr., Tech. Chamber of Greece, 1994. Rsch. assoc. Telecomm. Lab., Nat. Tech. U. Athens, 1995—96, 1998—2003; self-employed rsch., 2003—. Reviewer IEEE, Transactions on Circuits and Systems for Video Tech., NYC, 1999, IEEE/ACM, Transactions on Networking, NYC, 2001. Contbr. articles to profl. jours. and conf. procs., chapters to books. Airman Hellenic Air Force, 1996—98, Greece. Mem.: IEEE (Comm. Soc. Cert. of Appreciation 2004), Tech. Chamber of Greece. Achievements include patents in field; invention of system and method for efficient transfer of real-time traffic over scalable multiservice packet switching networks; first to create new autonomous systems paradigm for unified guarantees on quality of real-time service and resource efficiency, under generic network environmental conditions. Personal E-mail: thraps@runbox.com.

RAPSON, RICHARD (RIP RAPSON), foundation administrator; b. Bonn, Germany, Mar. 16, 1952; arrived in US, 1954; s. Ralph E. and Mary Christine (Dolan) Rapson; m. Gail M. Johnson, Aug. 19, 1989; children: Anna, Avery. BA, Pomona Coll., Claremont, Calif., 1974; JD, Columbia U., NYC, 1981. Legis. asst. to rep. Donald M. Fraser US Congress, Washington, 1974-78; assoc. Leonard, Street & Deinard, Mpls., 1981-86, ptnr., 1987-89; dep. mayor City of Mpls., 1989—93; sr. fellow Design Ctr. Am. Urban Landscape, U. Minn.; pres. McKnight Found., Mpls., 1999—2005, sr. fellow, 2005—06; pres. The Kresge Found., Troy, Mich., 2006—. Counsel Harriet Tubman Women's Shelter, Mpls., 1982—89, Coffee House Press, Mpls., 1986—89; bd. dirs. Environ. Law & Policy Ctr., Chgo., Local Initiatives Support Corp. NY, Downtown Detroit Partnership, Detroit RiverFront Conservancy. Co-author: Troubled Waters: The Fight for the Boundary Waters Canoe Area Wilderness, 1995, Ralph Rapson: Sixty Years of Modern Design, 1999. Trustee Mpls. Pub. Libr., 1983; bd. dirs. Mpls. Bd. Estimate & Taxation,

1985—88, Mpls. Youth Coordinating Bd., 1986—89. Recipient Sigurd Olsen award for outstanding vol. svc. to environment, Sierra Club. Mem.: ABA, Hennepin County Bar Assn., Minn. Bar Assn. Democrat. Avocations: art collecting, running, tennis, literature. Office: The Kresge Found 3215 W Big Beaver Rd Troy MI 48084 Office Phone: 248-643-9630. Office Fax: 248-643-0588. Business E-Mail: rrapson@kresge.org.*

RAPSON, RICHARD L., history professor; b. NYC, Mar. 8, 1937; s. Louis and Grace Lillian (Levenkind) R.; m. Susan Burns, Feb. 22, 1975 (div. June 1981); m. Elaine Catherine Hatfield, June 15, 1982; 1 child, Kim Elizabeth. BA, Amherst Coll., 1958; PhD, Columbia U., 1966. Asst. prof. Amherst (Mass.) Coll., 1960-61, Stanford (Calif.) U., 1961-65, U. Calif., Santa Barbara, 1965-66; from assoc. prof. to prof. history U. Hawaii, Honolulu, 1966—, founder, dir. New Coll., 1968-73. Bd. dirs. Semester at Sea, U. Pitts.; psychotherapist, Honolulu, 1982—. Author: Individualism and Conformity in the American Character, 1967, Britons View America, 1971, The Cult of Youth, 1972, Major Interpretations of the American Past, 1978, Denials of Doubt, 1980, Cultural Pluralism in Hawaii, 1981, American Yearnings, 1989, Amazed By Life: Confessions of a Non-Religious Believer, 2003, Magical Thinking and The Decline of America, 2007; co-author: (with Elaine Hatfield) Love, Sex and Intimacy: Their Psychology, Biology and History, 1993, Emotional Contagion, 1994, Love and Sex: Cross-Cultural Perspectives, 1995, Rosie, 2000, Recovered Memories, 2002, Darwin's Law, 2003; mem. edtl. bd. Univ. Press Am., 1981—. Woodrow Wilson fellow Wilson Found., Princeton, 1960; Edward Perkins scholar, Columbia U., 1961; Danforth tchr. Danforth Found., St. Louis, 1965; recipient E. Harris Harbison for Gifted Tchg. award Danforth Found., 1973, Outstanding Tchr. award Stanford U. 25th Reunion Class, 1992. Mem. Am. Hist. Assn., Orgn. Am. Hist., Nat. Womens Hist. Project, Phi Beta Kappa, Outrigger Canoe Club, Honolulu Club. Avocations: squash, travel, classical music. Office: U Hawaii Dept History 2530 Dole St Honolulu HI 96822-2303 Office Phone: 808-956-6801.

RARDIN, RONALD L., engineering educator; b. Kansas City, Mo., May 3, 1943; s. Eugene M. and Virginia Shepherd Rardin; m. Blanca Q Quiroga, Sept. 3, 1969; 1 child, Robert R. BA in Math. & Poli Sci., U. Kans., Lawrence, 1965, MS in Pub. Adminstrn., 1967; PhD in Indsl. & Systems Engring., Ga. Inst. Tech., Atlanta, 1974. Asst. ssoc prof. indsl. & sys. engring. Ga. Inst. Tech., 1974—82; prof. indsl. engring. Purdue U., West Lafayette, Ind., 1982—2006; disting. prof & white chair, indsl. engring. U. Ark., Fayetteville, 2007—. Program dir. NSF, Arlington, Va., 2000—03. Author: (textbook) Discrete Optimization, Optimization in Operations Research (Inst. of Indsl. Engineers Book of the Yr., 1999); contbr. scientific papers. Fellow: Inst. Indsl. Engrs.; mem.: Math. Programming Soc., Inst. Ops. Rsch. and Mgmt. Scis. Office: Indsl Engring University AR Fayetteville AR 72701 Office Fax: 479-575-8451. Business E-Mail: rrardin@uark.edu.

RARICK, PHILIP JOSEPH, lawyer, retired state supreme court justice; b. Troy, Ill., Nov. 10, 1940; s. Philip J. and Mary (Buckman) R.; m. Janet N. Arnovitz, Feb. 1, 1963; 1 child, Philip J. IV. BA, So. Ill. U., 1962; JD, St. Louis U., 1966. Bar: Ill. 1966, U.S. Dist. Ct. Ill. 1966. Twp. atty. Collinsville & Jarvis, Collinsville, Ill., 1966-75; asst. state's atty. Madison County, Edwardsville, Ill., 1966-75; city atty. City of Collinsville, 1967-75; cir. judge Third Jud. Cir., Edwardsville, 1975-88; presiding judge Criminal Div. in Madison County, Ill., 1982—85; chief cir. judge Third Jud. Cir., Edwardsville, 1985-87; presiding judge Criminal Div. in Madison County, Ill., 1987—88; elected judge Appellate Ct., Fifth Dist., Ill., 1988; judge indsl. commn. divsn. Ill. Appellate Ct., 1988—2002; elected judge, retained Appellate Ct., Fifth Dist., Ill., 1998; justice Ill. Supreme Ct., 2002—04; with Callis, Papa, Hale, Szewczyk, Rongey & Danzinger, PC, Granite City, Ill., 2004—. Mem. exec. com. Ill. Jud. Conf., Springfield, 1985—2000, chmn. complex litigation com., 1988—2000, mem. Industrial Comm. Div. of the Appellate Ct., 1992-2002, Ill. Cts. Commn. State of Ill., Springfield, 1992—99. Chmn. (manual) Illinois Manual for Complex Litigation. Mem. Ill. State Bar Assn., Ill. Judges Assn. (dir. 1977—82), Madison County Bar Assn., Tri-City Bar Assn. Office: Callis Papa Hale Szewczyk Rongey & Danzinger PC 1326 Niedringhaus Ave Granite City IL 62040 Office Phone: 618-452-1323.

RARIDON, RICHARD JAY, retired computer scientist; b. Newton, Iowa, Oct. 25, 1931; s. Jack Allison and Letha Helen (Woods) R.; m. Mona Marie Herndon, May 28, 1956; children— Susan Gayle, Ann Chaney. BA, Grinnell Coll., 1953; MA, Vanderbilt U., 1955, PhD, 1959. Assoc. prof. phys. sci. Memphis State U., 1958-62; rsch. scientist Oak Ridge Nat. Lab., 1962-92; cons. ORNL, 1992—2004. Environ. specialist Coop. Sci. Edn. Center, Oak Ridge, 1971-72 Contbr. articles to profl. jours. Radiol. Physics fellow AEC, 1953-55 Fellow AAAS, Tenn. Acad. Sci. (pres. 1971); mem. Assn. Acads. Sci. (sec.-treas. 1972-76, pres. 1977), Sigma Xi. Home: 111 Columbia Dr Oak Ridge TN 37830-7720 Personal E-mail: raridon@hotmail.com.

RASANSKY, MITCHELL, city councilman; Councilman, Dist. 13 Dallas City Coun., 2001—, chair fin., audit & accountability com., mem. econ. devel. com., pub. safety com., Trinity River Corridor Project. Mailing: Dallas City Coun 1500 Marilla St Rm 5FN Dallas TX Office Phone: 214-670-3816. Office Fax: 214-670-5117. Business E-Mail: mrasans@mail.ci.dallas.tx.us.*

RASBAND, JAMES R., dean, law educator; BA magna cum laude, Brigham Young U., Provo, Utah, 1986; JD cum laude, Harvard U. Law Sch., Mass., 1989. Bar: Wash. 1991. Law clk., hon. J. Clifford Wallace US Ct. Appeals (9th cir.), 1989—90; assoc. Perkins Coie, Seattle, 1990—95; faculty mem., Hugh W. Cotton prof. law Brigham Young U. J. Reuben Clark Law Sch., 1995—, assoc. dean rsch. and academic affairs, 2004—07, dean, 2009—; assoc. academic v.p. faculty Brigham Young U., 2008—. Vis. fellow U. Queensland T.C. Beirne Sch. Law, Brisbane, Australia, 2002; vis. prof. Murdoch U. Sch. Law, Perth, Australia, 2007. Co-author (with J. Salzman and M. Squillace): Natural Resources Law and Policy; contbr. articles to profl.jours., chapters to books. Office: Brigham Young Univ Law Sch PO Box 28000 Provo UT 84602 Office Phone: 801-422-6383. Business E-Mail: rasbandj@law.byu.edu.*

RASCHE, ROBERT HAROLD, banker, retired economics educator; b. New Haven, June 29, 1941; s. Harold A. and Elsa (Bloomquist) R.; m. Dorothy Anita Bensen, Dec. 28, 1963; children: Jeanette Dorothy, Karl Robert. BA, Yale U., 1963; A.M., U. Mich., 1965, PhD, 1966. Asst. prof. U. Pa., Phila., 1966-72; assoc. prof. econs. Mich. State U., East Lansing, 1972-75, prof., 1975-98, prof. emeritus, 1999—; sr. v.p., dir. rsch. St. Louis Fed. Res. Bank, 1999—2009, exec. v.p. sr. policy advisor, 2009—. Vis. scholar St. Louis Fed. Res., 1971-72, 76-77, 94-98, San Francisco Fed. Rsch. Bank, 1985, Bank of Japan, Tokyo, 1990; disting. vis. prof. econs. Ariz. State U., Tempe, 1986; rsch. assoc. Nat. Bur. Econ. Rsch., Cambridge, Mass., 1982-91; mem. Mich. Gov. Coun. Econ. Advisers, 1992-96; mem. Shadow Open Market Com., 1973-98 Mem. Am. Econs. Assn. Lutheran. Home: 14531 Radcliffeborough Ct Chesterfield MO 63017-5626 Office: Fed Res Bank St Louis Rsch Divsn PO Box 442 Saint Louis MO 63166-0442 Home Phone: 636-728-1918. Business E-Mail: rasche@msu.edu.

RASCHKE, JEANNE M., psychologist; EdD, Nova Southeastern U., Ft. Lauderdale, Fla., 1998. Sch. psychologist Hillsborough County Sch. Dist., Tampa, Fla., 1992—; pvt. practice Lakeland, Fla., 1995—. Cons. St. Paul Luth. Ch., Lakeland, 1992—. Lutheran.

RASCON, ALFRED V., former federal agency administrator; b. Chihuahua, Mexico, 1945; s. Alfredo and Andrea Rascon; m. Carol Lee Richardson; 2 children. Grad. US Army's Infantry Officers Candidate Sch., 1970. Commd. 2d lt. U.S. Army, ret., 1976; with Immigration & Naturalization Svc. US Dept. Justice, with Drug Enforcement Adminstrn., with internat. criminal police orgn.; insp. gen. Selective Svc. System, Arlington, Va., 1996—2001, dir., 2001—03. Served US Army, 1963—66, South Vietnam. Decorated Congl. Medal of Honor.

RASEKH, ABDI, cardiologist; b. Esfahan, Iran, July 07; m. Azita Madjidi, Dec. 28, 1998; children: Shahrzad Rose, Shewin John. MD, U. Paris 13, 1991. Diplomate ABIM, 1994, in cardiovascular diseases 1997, in interventional cardiology 1999, clinical cardiac electrophysiology 2003. Cardiologist & electrophysiologist Tex. Heart Inst., St Luke's Episcopal Hosp., Houston, 1999—; clin. asst. prof. Baylor Coll. Medicine, Houston. Recipient Bronze medal, U. Paris, 1991; fellow, Am. Coll. Cardiology, 2200. Fellow: Am. Coll. Cardiology. Achievements include research in ablation of atral fibrillation. Office: 6624 Fannin #2480 Houston TX 77030 Office Fax: 713-791-1786.

RASH, JOHN EDWARD, medical educator; s. Ralph Ray and Freddie McLarry Rash; m. Laura Lela Stach. BA, MA, U. Tex., Austin, PhD, 1969. Postdoc. fellow Johns Hopkin Med. Instn., Balt., 1969—71, Carnegie Instn. Wash., 1971—73, U. Colo., Boulder, 1973—74; asst., assoc. prof. U. Md., Balt., 1974—79; assoc. prof. Colo. State U., Ft. Collins, 1979—84, prof., 1984—. Contbr. articles to sci. jours. Rsch. grants, NIH, 1979—. Mem.: AAAS, AM. Soc. Cell Biology, Soc. Neurosci. Achievements include research in first demonstration of antibody destruction of junctional folds in myasthenia gravis; first identified aquaporin-4 in astrocyte square arrays; first demonstration of connexin-36 in ultrastructurally-defined gap junctions between neurons; development of freeze-fracture replica immungold labeling (FRIL) for visualizing, mapping, and identifying connexins, aquaporins and glutamate receptors in neurons and glia. Office: Colo State Univ Center St Fort Collins CO 80523-1617

RASH, RON, writer, educator; b. Chester Springs, SC, 1953; BA in English, Gardner-Webb Coll., Boiling Springs, NC; MA in English, Clemson U., SC. Vis. writer U. SC; John A. Parris Jr. & Dorothy Luxton Parris Disting. Prof. Appalachian cultural studies Western Carolina U., Cullowhee, NC, 2003—. Author: (novels) One Foot in Eden, 2002 (Novello Literary award, 2002, Gold medal in Lit. Fiction, ForeWord Mag., 2002, Appalachian Book of Yr., 2002), Saints at the River, 2004 (Southern Book Critics Circle Fiction Book of Yr., 2004, Southeastern Booksellers Assn. Fiction Book of Yr., 2004), The World Made Straight, 2006, Serena, 2008, (short story collections) The Night The New Jesus Fell to Earth and Other Stories from Cliffside, North Carolina, 1994, Casualties, 2000, Chemistry and Other Stories, 2007, (poetry) Eureka Mill, 1998, Among the Believers, 2000, Raising the Dead, 2002, (children's books) The Shark's Tooth, 2001; contbr. articles, short stories and poems to numerous publs. Recipient GE Younger Writers award, 1987, Sherwood Anderson prize, 1996, James Still award, Fellowship Southern Writers, 2005, O. Henry prize, 2005; grantee Arts Poetry fellowship, NEA, 1994. Office: WCU Dept English 402 Coulter Cullowhee NC 28723 Office Phone: 828-227-3917. Business E-Mail: ronrash@email.wcu.edu.*

RASH, WAYNE, JR., journalist; b. Erie, Pa., Mar. 2, 1948; s. Wayne and Elizabeth Rash; m. Carolyn Louise Hall, Nov. 25, 1972; children: Julia Leigh, Wayne III, Brittany Lynne. BA, Lynchburg Coll., Va., 1980. Dep. commr. revenue City of Lynchburg, 1976-80; prin. Am. Mgmt. Systems, Inc., Arlington, Va., 1984-92; pres. Wayne Rash & Assocs., 1990—; columnist InternetWeek, 1992—2002, mng. editor tech., 1998-2000, editor/events, 2000-01, sr. contbg. editor, 2001—02; contbg. editor CNet/ZDNet, 2001—02, SD Times, 2001—02; sr. analyst Infoworld, 2002—04, sr. contbg. editor, 2004—06. Mem. review bd. Infoworld, 1990-94, contbg. editor, 2002; Washington Bar Chief 2006-08; sr. writer 2006; sr. tech. editor 2007; exec. editor; editor, eweek Knowledge CPA 2007-2009; contbg. editor CABS 2008; contbg. editor Info. Week 2008-, Techweb Events 2008-, Ziff Davis Events and Custom Ricisting 2008-, Computercore 2009-; cons. Synaxis Consulting, Seattle 2008-. Author: The Novell Connection, 1989, The Executive Guide to Local Area Networks, 1989, WordPerfect Office 3.0: The Basics, 1991, Politics on the Nets, 1997; columnist Byte Mag., 1988-92, cons. editor, 1992-95; columnist The Star Ledger, Newark, 1996-98, OS/2 Mag., 1994-96, Windows NT Mag., 1995-96; cons. editor Byteweek, 1988-92, Computer Digest, 1986-91; editor Byte Information Exchange, 1984-2001, The Washington Post Computer Showcase, 1992-93; contbr. The Washington Post, 1994—; editor Tech Report/The Washington Post, 1996-97; sr. tech. editor, columnist InternetWeek, 1996-98; contbg. editor Plane and Pilot, 1995—, CNet.ZDNet, 2001-02, SD Times, 2001-02. Pres. Kings Park West Civic Assn., Fairfax, Va., 1986-88; active Citizens Adv. Coun. on Nat. Space Policy, Studio City, Calif., 1986—; dir. tech. policy Commonwealth Policy Inst. Network. Lt. USN, 1980-84. Mem. Nat. Press Club, Lions (program chmn. Brookville-Timberlake chpt., Lynchburg 1976-80), Aircraft Owners and Pilots Assn., Am. Flying Club, Exptl. Aircraft Assn., Am. Radio Relay League, Va. Amateur Radio Emergency Svc. Episcopalian. Avocations: amateur radio, scuba diving, writing, foreign travel, flying. E-mail: wayne@rash.org.

RASHID, FRANK DAMIAN, literature and language professor; b. Detroit, Dec. 20, 1950; m. Rebecca McKinney Stroud, May 30, 1999; 1 child, Carolina Rebecca Stroud-Rashid; m. Rosemary Margaret Bernardine, June 13, 1975 (dec. June 29, 1991); children: Anne Marie, Joseph Damian. PhD, U. Detroit, 1980. Project devel. coord. Focus Hope; English prof. Marygrove Coll., Detroit, 1980—. V.p. Mich. Assn. Depts. English, 2005—07. Founding mem. Tiger Stadium Fan Club, Detroit, 1987—97. Mem.: AAUP, MLA, Emily Dickinson Internat. Soc., Nat. Coun. Tchrs. English, Am. Studies Assn. Liberal. Roman Catholic. Office: Marygrove Coll 8425 W McNichols Rd Detroit MI 48221 Office Fax: 313-927-1345. Business E-Mail: frashid@marygrove.edu.

RASHID, KHADIJAT K., finance educator; PhD, Am. U., Washington, 2004. Prof., chair Dept. Bus., Gallaudet U., Washington, 2007—. Internat. devel. cons., South Africa, 1998—. Mem.: Am. Econ. Assn. Office: Gallaudet Univ 800 Florida Ave NE Washington DC 20002

RASHID, RICHARD F., computer software company executive; B in Math. & Comp. Lit. with hon., Stanford U., Calif., 1974; MSc in Computer Sci., U. Rochester, NY, 1977, PhD in Computer Sci., 1980. Prof. computer sci. Carnegie Mellon U., Pitts., 1979—91; with Microsoft Corp., Redmond, Wash., 1991—, from mem. staff to v.p. rsch., 1991—94, v.p. rsch., 1994—2000, sr. v.p. rsch., 2000—. Mem. computer directorate adv. com. Nat. Sci. Found.; bd. trustees Anita Borg Inst. Women and Technology, 2004—. Contbr. articles to profl. jours. Fellow: Am. Acad. Arts and Sciences; mem.: IEEE (sr. Emanuel R. Piore award 2008), Assn. Computing Machinery, Nat. Acad. Engring. Achievements include development of one of earliest networked computer games, Alto Trek. Office: One Microsoft Way Redmond WA 98052-6399*

RASI, HUMBERTO MARIO, editor, educator; b. Buenos Aires, Mar. 23, 1935; arrived in USA, 1962, naturalized, 1968; s. Mario and Gertrudis Frida (Heyde) R.; m. Julia Cuchma, Feb. 28, 1957; children: Leroy Mario, Sylvia Beatrice. BA, Instituto Superior del Profesorado, Buenos Aires, 1960; MA, San Jose State U., 1966; PhD, Stanford U., 1971; D honoris causa, U. Peruana Union, Peru, 1999, U. Adventista del Plata, Argentina, 2001, U. Montemorelos, Mex., 2003. Ordained to ministry Seventh-day Adventist Ch., 1980. Mem. faculty Instituto Florida, Buenos Aires, 1957-61; asst. editor Pacific Press Publ. Assn., Mountain View, Calif., 1962-66; asst. prof., assoc. prof. modern langs. Andrews U., 1969-76, prof., dean Sch. Grad. Studies, 1976-78; chief editor internat. publs. Pacific Press Publ. Assn., 1978-83, v.p. editorial devel., 1984-86; assoc. world dir. edn. Gen. Conf. Seventh-day Adventists, Silver Spring, Md., 1987-90, world dir. edn., 1990—2002; ret., 2002. Exec. dir. Inst. for Christian Teaching, 1987—. Author: The Life of Jesus, 3 vols., 1984—85; contbg. editor: Handbook of L.Am. Studies, Libr. of Congress, 1972—82; editor: Comentario Biblico Adventista, 7 vols., 1978—90; co-editor: Meeting the Secular Mind, 1985; founder, editor-in-chief: Coll. and Univ. Dialogue, 1989—2007, compiler: Christ in the Classroom, 38 vols., 1991—; contbr. articles on modern Hispanic lit., cultural issues, and religious trends. Exec. sec. Found. Adventist Edn., 2005-. NEH postdoctoral fellow Johns Hopkins U., 1975-76. Personal E-mail: h.rasi@roadrunner.com.

RASIH, BUU-VAN AJAREYAJEMIR, language and culture expert; b. Luangprabang, Luangprabang, Laos, Mar. 1, 1950; arrived in US, 76, naturalized, 1984; s. Duoc Thi Rasih-Nguyen and Thiem Van Nguyen; m. Vilaykhone Connie Simuong, Jan. 29, 1977; children: Bobby Amata, George Amarit, Valentina Cupid. AS, Irrigation Coll., Nonthaburi, Thailand, 1975. Irrigation engr. Ministry Agr., Vientiane, Laos, 1975—76; pres.'s asst. Agapi Tolstoy Found., Chula Vista, Calif., 1976—77; assoc. dir. Cath. Charities, San Diego, 1977—81; refugee program specialist US Cath. Conf., Washington, 1981—82; chmn., CEO Internat. Mut. Assistance Assn, San Diego, 1982—83; life and health underwriter NY Life, 1983—91; city commr. City of San Diego Human Rels., 1991—95; lang. and culture expert Global Childe, 1995—. Exec. coun. NY Life, San Diego, 1983—84; chmn. of the bd. Calif. Ct. Interpreters Assn., 1995—96; ct. interpreter/lang. specialist San Diego Superior Ct., 1995—; host / tv cmty. & govt. affairs dir. VietNam Pub. TV of San Diego, 1997—98. Author: (book) Verses of Social Thoughts (Asian Heritage Awards for Art, Philosophy &Lit., 2006), (poems) My Home Town in Immortal Verses Series (Editor's Choice Award & Best Poems and Best Poets, 2006), A Happy Marriage and A Happy Home in CD Sound of Poetry (32 Best Internat. Poets in a new CD poetry Selection, 2005). Human rels. city commr. City of San Diego, San Diego, 1991—94. Recipient AsianHeritage award for Art, Philosophy and Lit., Asia Media Inc., 2006, Proclamation for exemplary efforts in helping to improve the quality of life in cmtys. throughout the county, County San Diego,; named to Am. Immigrant Wall of Honor, Statue Liberty-Ellis Island Found., Inc. Mem.: Elite Registry USA, Nat. Lang. Svcs. Corps. (charter mem.), Asian Heritage Soc., Vietnamese Culture & Sci. Assn., Am. Acad. Poets, Asia Media Inc. (assoc.; contbr. 2006, Art, Philosophy and Lit. 2006), USA Honor Soc. Liberal. Avocations: reading, travel, art, music, poetry. Home: 16916 Hutchins Landing Ste 71 San Diego CA 92127 Office: Global Childe PO Box 178503 San Diego CA 92177 Office Phone: 858-232-5874. Office Fax: 858-312-5319; Home Fax: 858-312-5319. Personal E-mail: buuvanrasih@yahoo.com, rasih858@hotmail.com, americasnewtriumph@gmail.com. Business E-Mail: globalchilde@yahoo.com, globalculturecenter@gmail.com.

RASIO, FREDERIC ARMAND, astrophysicist; b. Brussels, Apr. 20, 1964; came to U.S., 1985; s. Eugenio Rasio and Danièle Journé; m. Anne Alberte Thoul, July 12, 1986 (div. 1997); children: Jonathan Philippe, Rebecca Thoul; m. Vassiliki Kalogera, June 16, 2001; 1 child: Stefan Geor. MS in Engring., Brussels Free U., 1985; PhD in Physics, Cornell U., 1991. Tchg. asst. physics dept. Cornell U., Ithaca, N.Y., 1986-88, rsch. asst. astronomy dept., 1988-91, rsch. assoc. astronomy dept., 1991-92; postdoctoral fellow Inst. for Advanced Study, Princeton, N.J., 1992-95; asst. prof. physics MIT, Cambridge, Mass., 1995—2001, assoc. prof., 2001—02; Joseph Cummings prof. physics Northwestern U., 2009—. Contbr. numerous articles to profl. jours. Hoover fellow Belgian Am. Ednl. Found., 1985-86, Hubble fellow NASA, 1992-95; recipient Grad. Student prize Astron. Soc. N.Y., 1991. Fellow. Am. Phys. Soc., Am. Astron. Soc. Achievements include research in astrophysical fluid dynamics, relativistic astrophysics, supercompter simulations. Office: Northwestern University Dept of Physics & Astronomy Evanston IL 60208 also: Northwestern Univ 518 Ctrl Ave Wilmette IL 60091

RASKA, KAREL FRANTISEK JULIAN, JR., pathologist, virologist, educator; b. Prague, Czech Republic, May 26, 1939; arrived in U.S., 1965; s. Karel Raska and Helena (Heller) Raskova; m. Jana Dostalova, Feb. 18, 1960; children: Karel III, Francis. MD, Charles U., Prague, 1962; PhD in Biochemistry, Czechoslovak Acad. Scis., Prague, 1965. Diplomate Am. Bd. Pathology (anatomic and clin., immunopathology). Fellow Yale U. Sch. Medicine, New Haven, 1965—66; assoc. Waksman Inst. Microbiology, New Brunswick, NJ, 1966—67; scientist Czech Acad. Sci., Prague, 1967—68; prof. microbiology and pathology Rutgers Med. Sch., Piscataway, NJ, 1968—82; profl. pathology, lab. medicine, microbiology U. Medicine and Dentistry-Robert Wood Johnson Med. Sch., New Brunswick, 1982—; prof., chmn. dept. lab medicine and pathology U. Medicine and Dentistry NJ Med. Sch., Newark, 1989—92; chmn. dept. lab medicine and pathology St. Peter's U. Hosp., New Brunswick, 1992—. Cons. Newark Beth Israel Med. Ctr., Newark, 1991—2001, E. Orange (NJ) VA Med. Ctr., 1991—; vis. prof. Charles U. Med. Sch., Prague, 1993—94; prof. path. and lab. medicine Drexel U., Coll. Medicine, Phila., 2005—. Contbr. articles to profl. jours., chapters to books. Trustee N.J. Organ Sharing Network, Springfield, 1991—2000; pres. Czechoslovak Soc. for Arts and Scis. in Am., 2006—; mem. exec. bd. Slavic Heritage Inst., 2007—. Lt. Czechoslovak Air Force, 1962—63. Grantee, NIH, 1975—93, Damon Runyon-Walter Winchell Cancer Rsch. Fund, 1975, NJ Commn. Cancer Rsch., 1985—86, 1994—95. Mem.: Learned Soc. of the Czech. Republic, Am. Soc. Cell Biologists, Am. Soc. Virology, NJ Soc. Pathology, Assn. Univ. Pathologists, Internat. Acad. Pathology, Am. Assn. Cancer Rsch., Am. Soc. Clin. Immunology, Am. Assn. Immunology, Am. Soc. Investigative

Pathology. Avocations: skiing, boating. Office: St Peters Univ Hosp Dept Lab Medicine & Pathology 254 Easton Ave New Brunswick NJ 08901 Office Phone: 732-745-8504. Personal E-mail: jkraskamd@aol.com.

RASKIN, ANNA VIKTOROVNA (ROPER RASKIN), history professor; b. Irkutsk, Irkutsk region, Russia, Sept. 25, 1975; d. Olga Alekseevna Lisichnikova and Viktor Nikolaevich Lisichnikov; m. Vladimir Alexandrovich Raskin, Jan. 9, 2008; 1 child, Helen Crystal. PhD in History (hon.), Irkutsk State U., Russia, 2001. History instr. Seminole CC, Sanford, Fla., 2003—05; history prof. mem. spkrs. bur. Montgomery CC, Blue Bell, Pa., 2005—. Lectr. Jewish Sr. Cmty. Ctr., Kline Br., Phila., 2008, Assn. Profl. Women Phila., 2006. Grantee Visual Resources in Tchg. and Rsch. in Early East Slavic Cultures, Nat. Endowment Humanities, 2006. Mem.: Am. Assn. Advancement Slavic Studies. Democrat. Avocation: travel. Office: Montgomery County CC 340 DeKalb Pike Blue Bell PA 19422 Personal E-mail: ropera@mail.com.

RASKIN, JONATHAN D., psychologist; b. Bklyn. s. Sherman and Paula Diane (Fishbach) Raskin; m. Shay A. Humphrey, Dec. 19, 1992; children: Ari Melissa, Noa Emily. AB in Psychology, Vassar Coll., Poughkeepsie, NY, 1990; MS in Counseling Psychology, U. Fla., 1992, PhD in Counseling Psychology, 1995. Lic. psychologist, N.Y. Predoctoral intern Emory U., Atlanta, 1994-95; asst. prof. psychology Tenn. State U., Nashville, 1995-96, SUNY, New Paltz, 1996—2001, assoc. prof., 2001—06, prof., 2006—. Co-editor: Constructions of Disorder, 2000, Studies in Meaning 2, 2004, Studies in Meaning 3, 2008; pres.: Constructivist Psychology Network, 2000—06, book rev. editor: Jour. Constructivist Psychology, 1999—2004; assoc. editor Jour. Constructivist Psychology, 2004—. Mem.: APA (sec. divsn. 32 1999—2002, fellow 2007), N.Am. Personal Construct Network (steering com.). Office: SUNY New Paltz 600 Hawk Dr New Paltz NY 12561-2440

RASKIN, MICHAEL A., retail executive, director; b. N.J., Feb. 26, 1925; s. Harry and Elizabeth Rose (Furstenberg) R.; m. Mary Bonetta Whalen, June 12, 1948; children: Robin Raskin Crowell, Hillary Raskin Maass, Mary Allison Sullivan. AB, Pa. State Coll., 1947; MBA, Columbia U., 1948. With Abraham & Straus, 1949-65; successively mdse. v.p., dir. stores, sr. v.p. Abercrombie & Fitch, NYC, 1966-68; exec. v.p. Dayton's div. Dayton Hudson Corp.; pres. Jos. Magnin Co., San Francisco, 1978—. Chmn., CEO, bd. dirs. Imnar Corp., San Francisco, Info. Please; chmn. More Investments; chmn. exec. com. Acajoe Internat.; bd. dirs. Fortune Almac, Canterbury Cuisine, Cultural Devel. Assocs., HELP Inc., Express Yourself Through Art, Inc., Munsingwear, Inc., B&B Acceptance Corp. Bd. dirs. Amyotrophic Lateral Sclerosis Assn.

RASKIN, RICHARD D., lawyer; b. St. Louis, Aug. 7, 1957; s. Lawrence M and Miriam S Raskin; m. Alba Alexander, July 16, 2000; children: Samuel David, Abby Rachel, Molly Rose. AB, Brown U., 1979; JD, U. Cin., 1985. Bar: Ill. 1985. Jud. clk. Hon. Hubert L. Will, Chgo., 1985—87. Bd. mem. Cmty. Counseling Centers, Chgo., 1994—98, Ill. Assn. Healthcare Attorneys, Chgo., 1995—98; feature editor Antitrust Health Care Chronicle, 1997—2001; adv. bd. mem. Health Law Reporter, Washington, 2000—. Contbr. articles to profl. jours. Mem. Cmty. Counseling Centers of Chgo., Chgo., 1994—98, Oak Park. Temple B'Nai Abraham Zion, Ill., 1993—97. Recipient William Worthington award, U. Cin. Coll. Law, 1984, Paxton & Seasongood prize, 1985; Fellow, Urban Morgan Inst. for Human Rights, 1982—84. Mem.: ABA (vice chair antitrust sect. 2002—), Order of the Coif, Am. Lawyers Assn. Jewish. Avocations: music, travel, literature. Office: Sidley Austin LLP One South Dearborn St Chicago IL 60603 Office Fax: 312-853-7036; Home Fax: 312-853-7036. Business E-Mail: rraskin@sidley.com.

RASKIN, SARAH BLOOM, state banking agency administrator, lawyer; b. Medford, Mass., Apr. 15, 1961; d. Herbert and Arlene (Perlis) Bloom; m. Jamin B. Raskin, Aug. 11, 1990; children: Hannah Grace, Thomas. BA magna cum laude in Econs., Amherst Coll., 1983; JD, Harvard U., 1986. Bar: NY 1987, DC 1989, US Dist. Ct. Md. Assoc. Mayer, Brown & Platt, NYC, 1986-88, Arnold & Porter, NYC and Washington, 1989-93; counsel US Senate Banking Com., Washington, 1993; mng. dir. Promontory Fin. Grp., Washington; commr. Md. Divsn. Fin. Regulation, 2007—. Bd. dirs. Conf. State Bank Suprs.; chair Fed. Legis. Com., Regulatory Restructuring Task Force. Recipient James R. Nelson Award in Econs.; John Woodruff Simpson fellow, Amherst Coll., 1983. Mem. Women Housing and Fin., Phi Beta Kappa. Office: Office of Commr Fin Regulation 500 N Calvert St Ste 402 Baltimore MD 21202 Office Phone: 410-230-6100. E-mail: sbloomraskin@dllr.state.md.us.*

RASKIND, LEO JOSEPH, law educator; b. Newark, Nov. 2, 1919; s. Isaac and Fannie (Michelson) R.; m. Mollie Gordon, June 14, 1948; children— Carol Inge, John Richard. AB, UCLA, 1942; MA, U. Wash., 1949; PhD, London Sch. Econs., 1952; LLB, Yale U., 1955. Faculty Stanford Law Sch., 1955-56; lectr., research asso. Yale Law Sch., 1956-58; faculty Vanderbilt Law Sch., 1958-64, Ohio State U. Coll. of Law, 1964-70, U. Minn., 1970-90, emeritus, 1991—. Counsel Am. Econ. Assn., 1979—88; vis. tchr. NYU, 1964, 83, U. Tex., 1964, U. Utah, 1967, So. Meth. U., 1973, U. N.C., 1978, Lyon III, 1984, Kiel U., 1988; vis. prof. Coll. Law, U. Tenn., Knoxville, 1994, Law Sch., U. Calif., Davis, 1995, U. Minn., 1998, Bklyn. Law Sch., 1998—2004. Co-author: Casebook Corporate Taxation, 1978, Casebook Antitrust Law, 2001; mem. adv. bd. BNA jour. Served to capt. AUS, 1942-46. Fulbright fellow, London Sch. Econs., 1952. Mem. Am. Law Inst. Office: U Minn Law Ctr 229 19th Ave S Minneapolis MN 55455 Personal E-mail: ljraskind@aol.com.

RASLEY, GEORGE, JR., legislative staff member; Grad., Hanover Coll., Ind., 1974. Lead advance rep., Pres. Ronald Reagan The White House; spl. asst. domestic policy to Dan Quayle. Office of the V.P.; staff mem. Senator Richard G. Lugar US Senate, Washington, cons., Senator Jesse Helms; polit. cons. Fla.; comm. dir. to Rep. Adam Putnam US House of Reps., Washington, 2001, dir. policy & comm., Rep. Adam Putnam, 2001—03, press sec., Rep. Mac Thornberry, 2007, comm. dir. to Rep. Mac Thornberry, 2007—; lead advance rep., Gov. Sarah Palin McCain/Palin Presdl. Campaign, 2008. Republican. Office: 2209 Rayburn House Office Bldg Washington DC 20515 Office Phone: 202-225-3706. Office Fax: 202-225-3486. Business E-Mail: george.rasley@mail.house.gov.*

RASMUS, JOHN CHARLES, retired trade association administrator, lawyer, consultant; b. Rochester, NY, Dec. 27, 1941; s. Harold Charles and Myrtle Leota (Dybevik) R.; m. Elaine Green Reeves, Mar. 19, 1982; children: Kristin, Stuart, Karin. AB, Cornell U., 1963; JD, U. Va., 1966. Bar: Va. 1970, U.S. Supreme Ct. 1974. Spl. agt. Def. Dept., Washington, 1966-70; v.p., adminstrv. officer, legis. rsch. counsel U.S. League Savs. Instns., Washington, 1970-83; asst. to exec. v.p. Nat. Assn. Fed. Credit Unions, 1983-84; sr. fed. adminstrv. counsel, mgr. regulatory & trust affairs Am. Bankers Assn., 1985—2008. Mem. ABA, FBA (disting. svc. award 1980, 82, past chmn. long range planning com., past chmn. coun. fin. instns. and economy), Univ. Club, Exchequer Club, Masons. Home: 647 Romany Rd Kansas City MO 64113 Personal E-mail: jcrasmus@gmail.com.

RASMUSON, BRENT J., photographer, small business owner; b. Logan, Utah, Nov. 28, 1950; s. Eleroy West and Fae (Jacobsen) Rasmuson; m. Tess Bullen, Sept. 30, 1981 (div. Jan. 2003); children: John, Mark, Lisa. Grad. auto repair and painting sch., Utah State U. Pre-press supr., ptnr. Herald Printing Co., Logan, 1969—80; profl. drummer, 1971-75; owner, builder auto racing engines Valley Automotive Specialties, 1971-76; exec. sec. Herald Printing Co., 1980—89; owner Brent Rasmuson Photography, Logan, 1986—, Temple Picture Classics, Logan, 1996—. Author photo prints of LDS temples: Logan, 1987, 95, 98, 2000, 04, 08, Manti, 1989, 2000, Jordan River, 1989, 96, 98, 2000, Provo, 1990, 2001, Mesa, Ariz., 1990, 96, Boise, Idaho, 1990, 96, 2000, 08, Salt Lake Temple, 1990, 96, 2001, 04, Idaho Falls, 1991, 94, 2000, St. George, 1991, 93, 2000, Portland, Oreg., 1991, 96, 97, 2000, LA, 1991, 96, 97, 2000, Las Vegas, Nev., 1991, 08, Seattle, 1992, Oakland, Calif., 1993, 94, Ogden, 1992, 2001, Bountiful, 2002, Mt. Timpanogos, 2002; author photo print: Statue of Angel Moroni, 1994; author photos used to make neckties and watch dials of LDS temples: Salt Lake, Manti, Logan, LA, Oakland, Seattle, Las Vegas, Mesa, Portland, St. George, Jordan River, scenic tie Mammoth Hot Springs in Yellowstone Park, 1995; landscape scenic photographs featured in Best of Photography Ann., 1987-89, also in calendars and book covers; author photo print of Harris Rsch., Inc. Internat. Hdqrs. (recipient 1st prize nat. archtl. photo competition); designer several bus. logos. Mem.: Internat. Freelance Photographers Orgn., Assoc. Photographers, Internat. Platform Assn., Nat. Air and Space Soc., Nat. Trust Hist. Preservation. Republican. Mem. Lds Ch. Avocations: automobile collecting, travel, reading, coin collecting/numismatics, stamp collecting/philately. Home and Office: 66 W 100 N Logan UT 84321-4506 Office Phone: 435-755-0668. Personal E-mail: brxtrxmxn@yahoo.com.

RASMUSON, EDWARD BERNARD, banker; b. Aug. 27, 1940; s. Elmer Edwin and Lile Vivian Rasmuson; m. Cathryn Elaine Robertson, Sept. 11, 1969; children: Natasha Ann, Laura Lile, David Edward. BA, Harvard U., 1962. Mgmt. trainee Brown Brothers Harriman, 1963, Chem. NY, 1964; asst. cashier Nat. Bank Alaska, Anchorage, 1964—66, asst. v.p., 1966—68, v.p., 1968—73, pres., 1973—85, chmn. bd. dirs., 1986—2001; chmn. adv. bd. Wells Fargo Bank, Anchorage, 2001—02. Bd. regents U. Alaska, 1975—89; mem. Rasmuson Found., 1973—; past trustee Sheldon Jackson Coll.; past pres. Anchorage United Way; Hon. Consul of Sweden State of Alaska. Mem.: World Bus. Coun., Young Pres.'s Orgn., Harvard Club (N.Y.C.), Rainier Club, Seattle Yacht Club, Wash. Athletic Club, Metropolitan Club, Pioneers Club Am., Explorers Club, Elks, Rotary. Office: Wells Fargo K3212-051 PO Box 196127 Anchorage AK 99519 Home Phone: 907-243-1155; Office Phone: 907-265-2927. Personal E-mail: erasmuson@gci.net.

RASMUSSEN, BRYAN PHILIP, engineering educator; s. V. Philip and Linda K. Rasmussen; m. Holly S. Stevens, Dec. 26, 1998; children: Melissa A., Amanda D., Maren C., Megan K. BS, Utah State U., Logan, 2000; MS, U. Ill., Urbana, 2002, PhD, 2005. Mech. engr. Casper's Ice Cream, Richmond, Utah, 1999—2000; grad. rschr. Air Conditioning and Refrigeration Ctr. U. Ill., 2000—05, ASME grad. tchg. fellow, 2004—05; asst. prof. Tex. A&M U., Coll. Sta., 2006—. Scoutmaster Boy Scouts America, Coll. Sta., 2006—. Recipient Career award, NSF, 2007—, John Weese Tchg. award, Pi Tau Sigma, Tex. A&M U., 2008. Mem.: ASEE, ASME, IEEE, Tau Beta Pi. Mem. Lds Ch. Office: Dept Mech Engring 3123 Tamu College Station TX 77843-3123 Business E-Mail: brasmussen@tamu.edu.

RASMUSSEN, HARRY PAUL, horticulture and landscape educator; b. Tremonton, Utah, July 18, 1939; s. Peter Y. and Lorna (Nielsen) R.; m. Mary Jane Dalley, Sept. 4, 1959; children: Randy Paul, Lorianne, Trent Dalley, Rachelle. AS, Coll. of So. Utah, 1959; BS, Utah State U., 1961; MS, Mich. State U., 1962, PhD, 1965. Rsch. scientist Conn. Agr. Expt. Sta., New Haven, 1965-66; rschr., instr. Mich. State U., East Lansing, 1966-81; chmn. dept. horticulture and landscape architecture Wash. State U., Pullman, 1981-88; dir. Utah Agrl. Expt. Sta. Utah State U., 1988—, assoc. v.p., 1992—99, 2002—06. Contbr. articles to profl. jours., chpts. to books. Mem. bd. control YMCA, Lansing, Mich., 1976; mem. coun. Boy Scouts Am., Lansing, 1980; stake pres. Ch. of Jesus Christ of Latter Day Saints, Lansing, 1973-81. NDEA fellow, 1961-65. Fellow Am. Soc. Horticulture Sci.; mem. AAAS, Scanning Electron Microscopy (chmn. plant sect. 1976-83, chmn. exptl. sta. com. on orgn. and policy 1996-97). Home: 1949 N 950 E Logan UT 84341-1813 Office: Utah State U 225 Agr Sci Bldg Logan UT 84322-0001

RASMUSSEN, JOHN OSCAR, nuclear research scientist; b. St. Petersburg, Fla., Aug. 8, 1926; s. John Oscar and Hazel R.; m. Louise Brooks, Aug. 27, 1950; children: Nancy, Jane, David, Stephen. BS, Calif. Inst. Tech., 1948; PhD, U. Calif., Berkeley, 1952; MA (hon.), Yale U., 1969. Mem. faculty dept. chemistry U. Calif., Berkeley, 1952-68, 73-91, prof. chemistry, 1971-91, ret., 1991, mem. research staff, 1952-68; sr. rsch. assoc. Lawrence Berkeley Nat. Lab., 1972—91, participating retiree, 1991—; cons., mem. panel nuclear isomer energy project U.S. Dept. Energy, 2004—06. Prof. chemistry Yale U. 1969-73; assoc. dir. Yale Heavy Ion Accelerator Lab., 1970-73; vis. research prof. Nobel Inst. Physics, Stockholm, 1953; vis. prof. Inst. Nuclear Sci. U. Tokyo, 1974, Fudan U., Shanghai, 1979, hon. prof., 1984. Contbr. articles to profl. jours. Served with USN, 1944-46. Recipient E.O. Lawrence Meml. award AEC, 1967; NSF sr. postdoctoral fellow Niels Bohr Inst., Copenhagen, 1961-62, NORDITA fellow, 1979, Guggenheim Meml. fellow, 1973, Alexander von Humboldt sr. rsch. fellow Tech. U. Munich, 1991. Fellow Am. Phys. Soc., AAAS; mem. Am. Chem. Soc. (Nuclear Applications in Chemistry award 1976), Fedn. Am. Scientists (chmn. 1969). Office: Lawrence Berkeley Nat Lab MS 70 319 Berkeley CA 94720-0001

RASMUSSEN, LISA ANNE, art educator, department chairman, gallery director; b. Walla Walla, Wash., Mar. 19, 1963; d. Richard Jens and Jo Anne Dickens Rasmussen. AA in Liberal Arts, Walla Walla CC, 1983; BA in Fine Arts, Whitman Coll., 1986; MA in Coll. Instrn. in Art, Ea. Wash. U., 1994. Dir. children's theatre Walla Walla CC, 1980—2002, drawing instr., 1987—99, art dept. chair, fine arts instr., 2000—; tech. asst. Sheehan Gallery, Whitman Coll., Walla Walla, 1986—87; drawing instr. Columbia Basin Coll., Pasco, Wash., 1993; gallery dir. Walla Walla CC Fine Arts Gallery. Sound technician Walla Walla CC Found. Summer Musical Prodns., 1985—98; lighting designer China Pavilion Theatre, Walla Walla CC, 1986—2001. Dir.: (plays) Stuart Little. Mem.: Blue Mountain Arts Alliance, Carnegie Art Ctr., Nat. Mus. Women in Arts. Home: 310 Juniper Walla Walla WA 99362 Office: Walla Walla CC 500 Tausick Way Walla Walla WA 99362 Office Phone: 509-527-1873. Personal E-mail: lisa.rasmussen@charter.net. Business E-Mail: lisa.rasmussen@wwcc.edu.

RASMUSSEN, RICHARD ROBERT, lawyer; b. Chgo., July 5, 1946; s. Robert Kersten Rasmussen and Marisa Bruna Batistoni; children: Kathryn, William. BS, U. Oreg., 1970, JD, 1973. Bar: Oreg. 1973. Atty. U.S. Bancorp, Portland, Oreg., 1973-83, 95-00, v.p. law divsn., 1983-87, mgr. law divsn., 1983-95, sr. v.p., 1987-95, mgr. corp. sec. divsn., 1990—95; exec. v.p., gen. counsel, sec. West Coast Bancorp, Lake Oswego, Oreg., 2000—. Mem. editl. bd. Oreg. Bus. Law Digest, 1979-81, Oreg. Debtor/Creditor newsletter, 1980-84; contbr. articles to profl. jours. Chmn. mgmt. com. YMCA of Columbia-Willamette, Portland, 1978-79; bd. dirs. Camp Fire, 1988-89, v.p., 1990-91; bd. dirs. Portland Repertory Theatre, 1994-96. Mem.: ABA, Am. Bankers Assn. (bank counsel com. 1996—99), Multnomah County Bar Assn., Oreg. State Bar Assn. (chmn. corp. counsel com. 1979—81, debtor/creditor sect. 1982—83, sec. com. on sects. 1982—83, award of merit, debtor/creditor sect. 2003), Beta Gamma Sigma. Avocations: mountain climbing, white-water rafting, tennis, basketball. Office: West Coast Bancorp 5335 Meadows Rd Ste 201 Lake Oswego OR 97035

RASMUSSEN, ROBERT KENNETH, dean, law educator; b. Brunswick, Ga., Mar. 13, 1960; s. Robert Edward and Marlene Joan (Kus) Rasmussen; m. Rebecca Brown. BA magna cum laude, Loyola U., Chgo., 1982; JD cum laude, U. Chgo., 1985. Bar: Calif. 1987, US Ct. Appeals (1st, 2nd, 5th, 9th cirs.) 1987, US Ct. Appeals (DC, 4th cirs.) 1988. Law clk. for Hon. John C. Godbold US Ct. Appeals (11th cir.), Montgomery, Ala., 1985-86; atty. US Dept. Justice, Washington, 1986-89; asst. prof. law Vanderbilt U. Law Sch., Nashville, 1989—92, assoc. prof., 1992—94, prof., 1994—2007, dir. law and econs. program, 1998—2006, assoc. dean academic affairs, 2002—04, Fed Ex rsch. prof., 2004—05, Milton Underwood prof. law, 2004—07, dir. Ctr. Law and Human Behavior, 2006—07; dean Gould Sch. Law, U. So. Calif., LA, 2007—. Vis. prof. law U. Mich. Law Sch., 1994, U. Chgo. Law Sch., 2004. Contbr. articles to law jours. Mem.: ABA, Order of the Coif. Democrat. Roman Catholic. Avocations: softball, astronomy, cooking. Office: Gould Sch Law U So Calif Los Angeles CA 90089-0071 Office Phone: 213-740-6473. Business E-Mail: dean@law.usc.edu.

RASMUSSEN, ROBERT L., museum director, military officer; b. Calif. m. Phyllis Colter; children: Kathryn, Eric. Joined USN, 1951, advanced through ranks to capt., ret., 1983; mem. Naval Aviation Cadet Prog., 1951—53; served aboard USS Philippine Sea, 1953—56; 1st exec. officer, commdg. officer Fighter Squadron 111, 1966; chief of staff, ops. officer Carrier Divsn. Seven; commdg. officer USS Mount Hood, Roosevelt Roads Naval Sta., PR; comdr. Bur. Navy Personnel, Aviation Officer Distbn. Divsn., Washington; commdg. officer Naval Aviation Schools Command, Pensacola, Fla.; dir. devel. Nat. Aviation Mus. Found., Pensacola, Fla., 1983—87; dir. Nat. Mus. Naval Aviation, Pensacola, Fla., 1987—. Avocations: watercolors, aviation art, sculpting. Office: Nat Mus Naval Aviation 1750 Radford Blvd Ste C Pensacola FL 32508-5400 Business E-Mail: bob.rasmussen@cnet.navy.mil.

RASMUSSEN, STEPHEN SCOTT, insurance company executive; b. 1953; BS in Bus. Adminstrn., U. Iowa. Underwriting & mktg. Allied Ins., 1974—82, regional v.p., pacific coast regional office, 1982—86, v.p., underwriting, 1986—98, exec. v.p., product mgmt., 1998—2001; pres., COO CalFarm Ins., 2001—03; pres., COO property & casualty ops. Nationwide Mutual Ins. Co., Columbus, Ohio, 2003—09, pres., CEO, 2009—. Trustee Grand View Coll.; 2002 Walk corp. chair, ctrl. Iowa chpt. Juvenile Diabetes Rsch. Found.; bd. mem. Nat. Urban League, Ins. Inst. for Highway Safety, Franklin County Convention Facilities Authority, Columbus Metropolitan Library. Office: Nationwide One Nationwide Pl Columbus OH 43215-2220*

RASMUSSEN, TERESA J., lawyer, insurance company executive; b. Fergus Falls, Minn., Oct. 9, 1956; BS magna cum laude, Moorhead State U., 1981; JD, U. ND, 1984. CPA 1981; bar: Colo. 1984, Minn. 1986. Trial atty. tax divsn. US Dept. Justice, Washington, 1984—86; assoc. Oppenheimer, Wolff & Donnelly, Mpls., 1986—89; exec. v.p., gen. counsel N.E. Securities Corp., Mpls., 1989—90; legal positions up to v.p., gen. counsel, IDS Life Ins. subs. Am. Express Fin. Corp., 1990—2005; sr. v.p., gen. counsel, sec. Thrivent Fin. for Luths., Mpls., 2005—. Mem.: ABA, Minn. State Bar Assn., Hennepin County Bar Assn. Office: Thrivent Financial for Lutherans 625 4th Ave S Minneapolis MN 55415-1624

RASMUSSEN, TODD C., hydrologist, educator; BS in Natural Resources, U. Calif., Berkeley, 1976; MS in Hydrology, U. Arizona, 1982, PhD, 1988. Watershed technican - peace corps COHDEFOR, Tegucigalpa, Francisco Morazán, Honduras, 1976—79; rsch. scientist U. Ariz., Tucson, 1988—92; prof. U. Ga., Athens, 1992—. Tech. support Water Conservation Com., Athens, 2003, Upper Oconee Watershed Network, Athens, 1998. Mem.: Ga. Assn. Water Profls., Soil Sci. Soc. America, Ga. Ground Water Assn., Assn. Ground Water Scientists & Engrs., Am. Water Resources Assn., Am. Geophys. Union, Nat. Speleological Soc. Office: Sch Forestry & Natural Resources Univ Georgia Athens GA 30602-2152

RASOCHOVA, LADA, research scientist; d. Vlastimil Rasocha and Marie Rasochova. BS, MS, Czech Agrl. U., Prague, 1986, Iowa State U., Ames, 1993, PhD, 1996. Cert. clin. trials mgmt. Calif., 2006. Scientist Biol. Rsch. Ctr., Szeged, Hungary, 1989—91; postdoctoral rsch. assoc. Iowa State U., Ames, 1996—97; scientist Inst. Genetic Engring. and Cell Biology, Kiev, Ukraine, 1988, Rsch. Inst. for Crop Prodn., Prague, Czech Republic, 1986—88; postdoctoral rsch. assoc. U. Wis., Madison, 1997—98; scientist Mycogen, San Diego, 1998—99, Dow Chem. Co., San Diego, 1999—2003, r&d group leader, 2003—06; mgr., vaccine product devel. Dowpharma, Dow Chem. Co., San Diego, 2007—. Recipient Rsch. Excellence award, Czech Acad. Scis., 1989, Spl. Recognition award, TDCC, 2001, 2005, 2006; fellow, Internat. Union Microbiol. Socs., Virology Divsn., 1996, UN, UNESCO, 1988, 1989—91; Mary J. Brinton Grad. scholar, Iowa State U., 1991—93, Profl. Travel grant, 1993, 1995, 1996. Mem.: Am. Soc. Microbiology, Americal Chem. Soc., Am. Soc. Virology (Travel Grant from the Am. Soc. for Virology 1993, 1995, 1998), Gamma Sigma Delta, Sigma Xi. Achievements include research in virology; vaccines; 15 patents pending. Office: Dowpharma Dow Chem Co 5501 Oberlin Dr San Diego CA 92121 Business E-Mail: lrasochova@dow.com.

RASOR, DINA LYNN, journalist, private investigator; b. Downey, Calif., Mar. 21, 1956; d. Ned Shaurer and Genevieve Mercia (Eads) R.; m. Thomas Taylor Lawson, Oct. 4, 1980. BA in Polit. Sci., U. Calif., Berkeley, 1978. Editorial asst. ABC News, Washington, 1978-79; researcher Pres.'s Commn. on Coal, Washington, 1979; legis. asst. Nat. Taxpayers Union, Washington, 1979-81; founder, dir. Project on Mil. Procurement, Washington, 1981-89; investigative reporter Lawson-Rasor Assocs., El Cerrito, Calif., 1990-92; pres., CEO, investigator Bauman & Rasor Group, El Cerrito, Calif., 1993—; chief investigator Follow the Money Project, 2005—. Author: The Pentagon Underground, 1985, Betraying Our Troops, 2007; editor: More Bucks, Less Bang,

1983; contbr. articles to profl. jours. Recipient Sigma Delta Chi Outstanding Leadership award Soc. Profl. Journalists, 1986; named to register Esquire Mag., 1986, Nat. Jour., 1986. Mem. United Ch. Christ. Office Phone: 510-235-5021.

RASOUL, SAM, entrepreneur; b. Warren, Ohio; s. Ralph and Jenny Rasoul; m. Layaly Rasoul, 2006. BBA, Roanoke Coll., Salem, Va.; MBA in Internat. Bus., Hawaii Pacific U., Honolulu. Founder Sunshine Entertainment 2, LLC, 2003—; gen. mgr. Provita USA LLC, 2004—; owner shopping plaza, 2005—. Democrat. Office: Provita USA LLC 8345 Moneta Rd Bedford VA 24523 also: Sunshine Entertainment 2 LLC 8347 Moneta Rd Bedford VA 24523 Office Phone: 540-297-7400, 540-297-3900.

RASPEN, JANICE ANN, librarian, educator; d. Richard and Ann Marie Raspen; life ptnr. Karen Moschetto. BA in English and Elem. Edn., Wilkes U., Wilkes-Barre, Pa., 1992; MLS, Cath. U. America, Washington, 2000. Cert. in libr. media Va., 2000. Tchr. Beaufort Acad., SC, 1992—96, Fredericksburg Acad., Va., 1996—2000; libr. media specialist Pk. Ridge Elem. Sch., Stafford, Va., 2000—05, Conway Elem. Sch., Fredericksburg, 2005—. Adj. instr. U. Va., Wise, 2008—. Mem.: ALA, Am. Assn. Sch. Librs., Va. Ednl. Media Assn. (sec. 2007—). Liberal. Avocations: reading, sewing. Home: 1607 Gayle Ter Fredericksburg VA 22401 Office: Conway Elem Sch 105 Primmer House Rd Fredericksburg VA 22405 Personal E-mail: jraspen@gmail.com. Business E-Mail: jraspen@staffordschools.net.

RASPINO, LOUIS A., energy executive; b. 1953; Various positions to sr. v.p. fin., adminstrn., CFO La. Land & Exploration Co. (merged with Burlington), 1978—97; sr. v.p. Burlington Resources, 1997—98; v.p., fin. Halliburton Co., 1999—2000; exec. v.p., CFO, COO JRL Enterprises Inc., 2000—01; sr. v.p., fin., CFO Grant Prideco. Inc., Houston, 2001—03; exec. v.p., CFO Pride Internat. Inc., Houston, 2003—05, pres., CEO, dir., 2005—. Office: Pride Internat Inc 5847 San Felipe Houston TX 77057 Office Phone: 713-789-1400.

RASSAS, GEORGE JAMES, bishop; b. Balt., May 26, 1942; BA in Philosophy, U. St. Mary of the Lake Sem., Mundelein, Ill.; MA in Counseling Psychology, Loyola U., Chgo. Deacon St. Thaddeus Parish, Chgo., 1967—68; ordained priest Archdiocese of Chgo., 1968, dir. Cath. Family Consultation Svc., 1975—84, assoc. moderator Archdiocesan Coun. Cath. Women, 1976—84, assoc. dir. Office Family Ministries, 1984—90, chmn. Presbyteral Coun., 1999—2002, vicar gen., 2004—06, aux. bishop, 2006—; assoc. pastor Queen of the Rosary Parish, Elk Grove Village, Ill., 1968—74, St. Genevieve Parish, Chgo., 1974—83, St. Norbert's Parish, Northbrook, Ill., 1983—88, Sacred Heart Parish, 1988—90; pastor St. Mary Parish, Lake Forest, Ill., 1990—2004; ordained bishop, 2006. Roman Catholic. Office: Archdiocese of Chgo 200 N Milwaukee Ave Ste 200 Libertyville IL 60048

RASSBACH, HERBERT DAVID, marketing executive; b. Glen Ridge, NJ, Mar. 23, 1944; s. Merrill Augustus and Ruth Bruce (Sims) Rassbach. BS, Del. State Coll., 1971; MBA, Drexel U., 1979. Prodn. planning mgr. Standard Brands Chem. Industries, Edison, NJ, 1971-74; order fulfillment mgr. P Q Corp., Valley Forge, Pa., 1974-77, mkt. devel. project mgr., 1977-82; market mgr. Sperian Protection, Reading, Pa., 1983-85; pres. HDR Group, mktg. and mgmt. cons., Wayne, Pa., 1986—. Guest speaker Wharton Sch. U. Pa., 1988, Temple U., Phila., 1989, Wharton Club, 1995. Media comms. bd. Upper Merion Twp., 1989, vice-chmn., 1990, 1992—2004, chmn., 1991, 2005—, ex-officio mem. Citizens Police Adv. Bd., 2005—, committeeman, 1977. With USAF, 1962—66, hon. discharged, 1968. Mem. Drexel U. Alumni Assn. (v.p. Montgomery County chpt. 1988-91), Alpha Kappa Mu, Delta Mu Delta. Avocations: golf, tennis, running, travel, american history. Home: 635 Mallard Rd Wayne PA 19087-2346 Office: HDR Group PO Box 2164 Southeastern PA 19399-2164 Office Phone: 610-964-8555. Business E-Mail: hdrassbach@hdrgroup.com.

RASSMANN, JOEL H. H., corporate financial executive; b. NYC, May 16, 1945; Grad., Bernard Baruch Coll., 1967. CPA, N.Y. Acct. S.D. Leidesdorf & Co., 1967—72; ptnr. Kenneth Leventhal & Co., 1972—84; sr. v.p., treas., CFO Toll Brothers Inc., Horsham, Pa., 1984—2002, exec. v.p., treas., CFO, 2002—. Mem. AICPA, N.Y. State Soc. CPA's. Achievements include appearing frequently as commentator on CNBC, CNN, Fox, Bloomberg TV & Radio. Office: Toll Brothers Inc 250 Gibraltar Rd Horsham PA 19044

RASSULI, ALI, economist, consultant; b. Tehran, Iran, Oct. 1, 1950; s. Mohammad and Parvin Rassouli; m. Mahtab Madani, Jan. 7, 2000; m. Kathleen M. Best, Sept. 1, 1976 (dec. Jan. 2, 1999); 1 child, Ramin Ali. MA in Polit. Sci., U. Toledo, Ohio, 1976, MA in Economics, 1976; PhD in Economics, U. Nebr., Lincoln, 1981. Dir. grad. studies bus. Ind. Purdue U. Ft. Wayne, 1993—2001, assoc. prof. economics, 1996—. Contbr. articles to profl. jours. Office: Ind Purdue Univ Ft Wayne 2101 E Coleseum Blvd Fort Wayne IN 46805 Business E-Mail: rassuli@ipfw.edu.

RASTETTER, WILLIAM H., biotechnology company executive; BS in Chemistry, MIT; MA, Harvard U., PhD in Chemistry. Faculty MIT, Cambridge, Mass., 1975—82; scientist/rschr. biocatalysis and chem. scis. groups Genentech, 1982—84, dir. corp. ventures, 1984—86; pres. & CEO IDEC Pharms. Corp., San Diego, 1986—2002, CFO, 1988—93; dir. IDEC Pharms. Corp. (now Biogen IDEC), 1986—; chmn. bd. dirs. IDEC Pharms. Corp., 1996—2002; CEO Biogen IDEC, 2002—03, exec. chmn., 2003—. Bd. dir. Argonaut Technologies, Inc., Illumina, Inc., 1998—, non-exec. chmn., 2005—; mem. Calif. Healthcare Inst.; R.B. Woodward vis. scholar, dept. chem. and chem. biology Harvard U. Office: Biogen IDEC 5200 Research Pl San Diego CA 92122 also: Biogen IDEC 14 Cambridge Ctr Cambridge MA 02142

RASTOGI, ANIL KUMAR, health products executive; b. India, July 13, 1942; came to U.S., 1969, naturalized, 1978; s. R.S. and K.V. Rastogi; m. Anjali Capur, Mar. 18, 1970; children: Priya, Sonya. BS with honors, Lucknow U., 1963, MS, 1964; PhD in Polymer Sci., McGill U., 1969. From staff to dir. corp. diversification portfolio Owens-Corning Tech. Ctr., Granville, Ohio, 1969—87; v.p. Mead Imaging, Miamisburg, Ohio, 1987-89; pres. Mead Cycolor Divsn., Dayton, Ohio, 1989-92; v.p., gen. mgr.infusion systems div. Pharmacia Deltec, Inc., St. Paul, 1992-93, exec. v.p., 1993-94; COO SIMS Deltec, Inc., St. Paul, 1994-95; pres., COO Sabratek Corp., Niles, Ill., 1995—98; pres., CEO NOMOS Corp., Sewickley, Pa., 1998—2002; v.p. entrepeneurship and tech. commercialization Drexel U., Phila., 2002—05; pvt. investor Reston, Va., 2005—. Mem. adv. bd. Central Ohio Tech. Coll.; lectr., cons. in field. Author of 15 bus. and tech. publs.; patentee in field. Bd. dirs. Licking County Family Services Assn.; bd. dirs. Tech. Alliance of Central Ohio; v.p. local United Way; bd. dirs. and treas. Columbus Bus. Tech. Ctr.; mem. Overview Adv. Com. Strategic Hwy. Research Program. Fellow NRC Can., 1966-69 Mem. AAAS, Am. Mgmt. Assn., Am. Chem. Soc., Soc. Plastics Engrs., Comml. Devel. Assn., Med. Alley (bd. dirs.), Health Ind. Mfrs. Assn., Nat. Infusion Therapy Alliance (bd. dirs.), Toastmasters (past pres.), Rotary, Sigma Xi. Home and Office: 1616 English Oak Ct Wexford PA 15090

RASTOGI, ANJALI, health care executive; b. Lucknow, Uttar Pradesh, India, Nov. 20, 1951; d. Gyan Kapoor and Sneh Capur; m. Anil Kumar Rastogi, Mar. 18, 1970; children: Ptiya, Sonya. BS in Computer Sci., Denison U., Grunville, 1982; MS in Computer Sci., Wright State U., Dayton, 1990. Cert. in profl. project mgmt. Cons. Accenture, Mpls., 1993—97, Price Water House, Chgo., 1997—2000, IBM, Pitts., 2002—04; sr. dir, Info. Tech. Sallie Mae, Reston, 2004—08; v.p., planning & analysis Coventry Health Care, Pitts., 2008—. Bd. dirs. YMCA, Newark, 1983. Mem.: Project Mgmt. Inst., Phi Beta Kappa.

RASTOGI, PRIYA, medical educator; BA in Chemistry, Miami U., Osford, Ohio, 1993; MD, Wright State U. Sch. Medicine, Dayton, Ohio, 1997. Cert. in internal medicine residency St. Joseph Hosp., Colo., 2000. Asst. prof. medicine Magee-Womens Hosp. U. Pitts. Med. Ctr. Cancer Inst., 2003—; asst. dir. Nat. Surg. Breast and Bowel Project, Pitts., 2005—06, vice chair, med. affairs, 2006—08, assoc. dir. med. affairs, 2008—. Contbr. articles to profl. publs. Recipient Achievement award, Magee-Womens Hosp., 2008; Hematology, Oncology fellowship, U. Pitts. Med. Ctr. Sch. Medicine, 2003. Mem.: Magee-Womens Hosp. (oncology team bldg. com., patient focused care com., pharmacy and therapeutics com.), Am. Soc. Clin. Oncology, Am. Assn. Cancer Rsch., Clin. Rsch. Ctr. Adv. Com. Achievements include research in effects of trastuzumab on structure and function of the heart in breast cancer patients; neurological research to explore nerve growth factor on hypertensive and normal rats. Office: Magee-Womens Hosp UPMC 300 Halket St Ste 3525 Pittsburgh PA 15213

RASU, RAFIA S., pharmacy and nursing educator researcher; married. MPharm, Dhaka U. Sch. Pharmacy, Bangladesh, 1999; MBA, Dhaka U. Inst. Bus. Adminstrn., Bangladesh, 2001; PhD, U. Tex. Sch. Pub. Health, Houston, 2005. Grad. rsch. asst. M D Anderson Cancer Ctr., Houston, 2004—05; product officer Roche Bangladesh Ltd., Dhaka; asst. prof. nursing U. Miss., Kans. City, 2008—, asst. prof. pharmacy. Rschr. pharmacy program, dept. veterans affairs Med. Ctr. Kans. City, 2008—. Office Fax: 816-235-6008. Business E-Mail: rasur@umkc.edu.

RATCHES, JAMES ARTHUR, chief scientist; b. Hartford, Conn., May 12, 1942; s. Joseph Anthony and Edith Bernadette Ratches; m. Kristina Zoe Edberg, July 14, 1973; children: Zoe Edberg, Nathaniel Edberg, Eve Edberg. PhD, Worcester Poly. Inst., Mass., 1969. Scientist US Army Cerdec Nvesd, Fort Belvoir, Va., 1969—. Mem.: OSA. Home: 9102 Chickawane Ct Alexandria VA 22309 Office: US Army Cerdec Nvesd 10221 Burbeck Rd Fort Belvoir VA 22060

RATCHEV, BORIS A., high technology executive; b. Sofia, Bulgaria, July 16, 1969; s. Anton Slavov and Blaga Borisova Ratchev; m. Leticia G. Ratchev, Mar. 22, 1996. BSc, U. of Wis., 1990—93, MSc, 1993—95, Stanford U., 2000—05. Summer intern-analyst Siemens Power Sys. Control Divsn., Mpls., 1995; sr. reliability engr. Altera Corp., San Jose, Calif., 1996—2000, sr. software engineer-arch., 2000—05; mgmt. cons. Pittiglio Rabin Todd McGrath, Mountain View, 2005—07; v.p. product strategy DJ Nitrogen, 2007—. Grad. fellowship, U. of Wisconsin-Madison, 1993. Mem.: IEEE (life). Achievements include patents for technology mapping technique for fracturable logic; novel method of using randomly generated; techniques for automated sweeping of parameters in computer aided design to achieve optimum performance and resource usage. Avocations: skiing, soccer, reading, travel. Home: 992 Belmont Terrace #9 Sunnyvale CA 94086

RATCHFORD, JOSEPH THOMAS, science and technology policy educator, consultant; b. Kingstree, SC, Sept. 30, 1935; s. Raymond Howard and Elizabeth Arabella (Senn) R.; m. Joanne Walton Causey, June 18, 1960; children: Joseph Thomas, Laura Leigh, James Raymond, David Andrew. BS, Davidson Coll., NC, 1957; MA, U. Va., 1959, PhD, 1961. Asst. prof. physics Washington and Lee U., Lexington, Va., 1961-64; physicist U.S. Air Force Office of Sci. Rsch., Arlington, Va., 1964-70; sci. cons. Com. on Sci. and Tech., U.S. Ho. of Reps., Washington, 1970-77; assoc. exec. officer AAAS, Washington, 1977-89; assoc. dir. Office of Sci. and Tech. Policy White House Office of Sci. and Tech. Policy, Washington, 1989-93; dir. Ctr. for Sci., Trade and Tech. Policy George Mason U., Arlington, Va., 1994—99, prof. internat. sci. and tech. policy, 1993-98, disting. vis. prof., 1998—; dir. sci. and trade policy program George Mason U. Sch. Law, Arlington, Va., 1999—. Cons. internat. trade and tech., Davidson, NC, 1993—, Alexandria, Va., 1993-; chair Forum on Internat. Phys. Soc., 1994-96; mem. Internat. Affairs Commn., Am. Assn. Engring. Soc., 1993—; mem. tech. task force Coun. on Competitiveness, Washington, 1987-88; chmn. adv. com. for internat. programs NSF, Washington, 1984-87; chmn. adv. panel on energy from bio processes Office Tech. Assessment, 1979-80; chmn. Rsch. Coordination Panel, Gas Rsch. Inst., Chgo., 1976-79; prin. Sci., Trade and Tech. Assocs., 1998—; co-chair U.S.-China Sci. Policy Initiative, 1999—; bd. dirs., v.p. Charlotte Area Sci. Network, 2004—; bd. mem., v.p. Charlotte Area Sci. Network, 2004—; bd. trustees, chair acad. affairs com., Lees-McRae Coll., Banner Elk, NC, 2001—. Contbr. chpts. to books, numerous articles to profl. jours. Hon. mem. World Innovation Found., 2005—. Fellow AAAS, Am. Phys. Soc.; mem. Coun. on Fgn. Rels., Phi Beta Kappa, Sigma Xi. Achievements include initiation of academic center to address policy interrelationships among science, trade, legal and technology issues; development of legislation on a variety of science-based issues including establishment of Congl. Office of Technology Assessment, innovative approaches to international technological and business alliances; at the White House developed international science policy and math. and science edn. initiatives. Office: PO Box 458 Davidson NC 28036-0458 Home Phone: 704-892-0970; Office Phone: 704-892-3025. Personal E-mail: tomratchford@bellsouth.net.

RATCHFORD MERCHANT, BETTY JO, retired elementary school educator; b. Huntsville, Ala., Feb. 9, 1937; d. Howard Clyde and Margaret (Kyle) Wikle; m. McClellan Ratchford, 1960 (div.); children: McClellan III, Margaret Lee, Rosalyn Hampton; m. Curtis Merchant, 1992. BS, Auburn U.; MEd, Ala. A&M U., 1998. Cert. tchr. elem. Tchr. elem. Gilbert Sch., Atlanta, Madison County Sch. Sys., Huntsville, Ala., Riverton Elem. Sch., Mt. Carmel Elem. Sch., 2003; choir mem. DAR. Named Tchr. of Yr. for Madison County, 1992. Mem. NEA, AAUW, Ala. Edn. Assn., Environ. Edn. Assn. Ala., Madison County Edn. Assn. Episcopalian. Avocations: poetry, singing, reading, painting, rock climbing. Home: 11033 Everest Cr Huntsville AL 35803

RATCHYE, BOYD HAVENS, lawyer; b. Helena, Mont., June 10, 1938; s. John Frederick and Leanora (Boyd) R.; m. Jean P. Cunningham, Sept. 1, 1962 (div. Oct. 1985); children: Ellen C., Stephen B.; m. Susan Light, May 21, 1994. BA cum laude, Harvard U., 1960, JD, 1963. Bar: Minn. 1964, U.S. Dist. Ct. (Minn. 1964, ND 1993), U.S. Ct. Appeals (8th cir.) 1967, U.S. Supreme Ct. 1972, U.S. Ct. Appeals (fed. cir.) 1983. Law clk. to justice J.C. Otis Supreme Ct. Minn., St. Paul, 1963-64; assoc. Erickson, Popham, Haik & Schnobrich, Mpls., 1964-65; assoc. to ptnr. Doherty, Rumble & Butler, P.A., St. Paul, 1966—99; shareholder, civil litig. Bassford Remele, Mpls., 1999—. Adj. prof. William Mitchell Coll. of Law, 1975-94. Chmn., bd. dir. Yellowstone Assn.; bd. dir. Animal Human Soc. Named a Minn. Super Lawyer, Mpls.-St. Paul Mag. and Minn. Law and Politics mag., 2000—07; named one of Best Lawyers in Am., 1986—2007. Mem. ABA, Am. Bd. Trial Advocates (pres. Minn. chpt. 1990-91), Minn. State Bar Assn., Minn. Def. Lawyers Assn., Hennepin County Bar Assn., Harvard Radcliffe Club Minn., Inns of Ct. (Warren Burger chpt., pres. 1999-2000, counselor 2000-01). Episcopalian. Avocations: rowing, running, cross country skiing, scuba diving, snorkeling. Office: Bassford Remele Ste 3800 33 S 6th St Minneapolis MN 55402 Office Phone: 612-376-1604. Office Fax: 612-333-8829. Business E-Mail: bratchye@bassford.com.

RATCLIFF, BLAIR NORMAN, physicist; s. Arnold Bufkin and Eva Geneva Ratcliff; m. Ruth Collins Cronkite, Aug. 16, 1976; children: Bryce William Cronkite-Ratcliff, Collin Norman Cronkite-Ratcliff. BA, Grinnell Coll., Iowa, 1966; MS, PhD, Stanford U., Calif., 1971. Rsch. assoc. Rutherford High Energy Lab., Chilton Didcot, Berkshire, 1971—75, SLAC, Stanford, Calif., 1975—78, exptl. staff physicist, 1978—2003; vis. scientist CERN, Geneva, 1971—75; mem. permenant sci. staff lab. SLAC Nat. Accelerator Lab., Menlo Park, Calif., 2003—. Fellow: Am. Phys. Soc. (Fellow 2002); mem.: AAAS, Phi Beta Kappa. Achievements include invention of scientific research instruments, especially the DIRC imaging cherenkov counter; design of babar detector. Office: SLAC Nat Accelerator Lab 2575 Sand Hill Rd Menlo Park CA 94025

RATCLIFFE, DAVID M., utilities executive; b. Tifton, Ga. BS in Biology, Valdosta State U., Ga., 1970; JD, Woodrow Wilson Coll. Law, 1975. Bar: Ga. Biologist Ga. Power, 1971; v.p. fuel svcs. Southern Co., 1986—89, exec. v.p., 1989—91, pres., CEO Miss. Power, 1991—95, sr. v.p. external affairs, 1995—98, exec. v.p., treas., CFO Ga. Power, 1998—99, CEO Ga. Power, 1999—2003, chmn., pres., CEO, 2004—. Bd. dirs. Edison Electric Inst., CSX Transp., Ga. Rsch. Alliance, Ctrl. Atlanta Progress, Ga. Partnership for Excellence in Edn., chair, 2001—04; bd. dirs. Fed. Res. Bank Atlanta, chair, 2004. Trustee Woodruff Arts Ctr.; mem. adv. bd. Salvation Army. Mem.: Metro Atlanta C. of C. (chair econ. devel.), Ga. Bar Assn. Office: Southern Co 30 Ivan Allen Jr Blvd NW Atlanta GA 30308 Office Phone: 404-506-5000.*

RATH, HOWARD GRANT, JR., lawyer; b. LA, Sept. 2, 1931; s. Howard Grant and Helen (Cowell) R.; m. Peyton McComb, Sept. 13, 1958 (dec. Apr. 1984); children: Parthenia Peyton, Francis Cowell; m. Dorothy Moser, Aug. 29, 1986. BS, U. Calif., 1953; JD, U. So. Calif., 1958. Bar: Calif. 1959, US Dist. Ct. (cen. dist.) Calif., 1959, US Ct. Claims 1974, US Tax Ct. 1960. Assoc. O'Melveny & Myers, LA, 1959-66; tax counsel, dir. tax adminstrn., asst. treas. Northrop Corp. LA, 1966-74; sr. tax ptnr. Macdonald, Halsted & Laybourne, LA, 1974-86, Hill & Weiss, LA, 1986-90; ptnr. Lewis Brisbois Bisgaard & Smith, LA, 1990—; dir. Rath Packing Co., Waterloo, Iowa, 1966-81. 1st lt. US Army, 1953-55. Mem. State Bar Calif., LA County Bar Assn., LA Yacht Club, The Athenaeum, Order of Coif, Phi Beta Kappa. Republican. Episcopalian. Office: Lewis Brisbois Bisgaard & Smith 221 N Figueroa St Ste 1200 Los Angeles CA 90012-2646 Business E-Mail: rath@lbbslaw.com.

RATH, MANIK K., lawyer; b. Pitts., 1969; m. Wendy Rath. BA, U. Va., 1991, JD, 1994. Admitted: State Bar of Tex., Va. State Bar, DC Bar Assn., US Dist. Ct., US Ct. of Appeals. Atty. Baker & McKenzie LLP, Dallas, McGuire Woods LLP, Richmond, Va., 1997—99, McKenna Long & Aldridge LLP, 1999; v.p., dep. gen. counsel, asst. sec. Alion Sciences and Tech. Corp., 2002—05; gen. counsel, corp. sec., v.p. adminstrn. LMI, McLean, Va., 2005—. Bd. dirs. Alion Sci. and Tech. Corp. Office: LMI Hdqs 200 Corporate Ridge Mc Lean VA 22102-7805 Office Phone: 800-213-4817. Office Fax: 703-917-9800.

RATHA, NALINI K., computer scientist, researcher; s. Satyabadi Ratho and Urmila Ratha; m. Meena Hota, July 9, 1991; 1 child, Navin Rath. B of Tech, Indian Inst. Tech., Kanpur, 1982, M of Tech, 1984; PhD, Mich. State U., East Lansing, 1996. Sys. specialist CMC R&D Ctr., Secunderabad, Andhra Pradesh, India, 1989—92; mem. rsch. staff IBM Rsch., Hawthorne, NY, 1996—. Sr. tech. office ECIL, Hyderabad, Andhra Pradesh, India, 1984—89. Co-author: (technical book) Guide to Biometrics; editor: Automatic Fingerprint Recognition Systems; assoc. editor: IEEE Tran. Systems, Man and Cybernetics Jour., Pattern Recognition Jour., IEEE Trans. Pattern Analysis and Machine Intelligence Jour. Editor Advances Biometrics: Sensors, Algorithms &Sys. Recipient Rsch. Divsn. award, IBM, Best Paper award, Ministry Home Affairs, Govt. India. Fellow: IEEE; mem.: IAPR, ACM (profl.). Achievements include patents for cancelable biometrics.

RATHBONE, PETER B., art appraiser; BA in Art History, Boston U. Dir., Am. paintings, drawings and sculpture dept. Sotheby's, NYC, 1972—. Office: Sotheby's 1334 York Ave New York NY 10021 Office Phone: 212-606-7280. Office Fax: 212-606-7039. Business E-Mail: peter.rathbone@sothebys.com.

RATHER, DAN (DANIEL IRVIN RATHER, JR.), news correspondent, former network news anchor; b. Wharton, Tex., Oct. 31, 1931; m. Jean Goebel, 1957; children: Dawn Robin, Daniel Martin. BA in Journalism, Sam Houston State Tchrs. Coll., Huntsville, Tex., 1953; student, U. Houston, South Tex. Sch. Law. Journalism instr. Sam Houston State Coll.; reporter AP, Huntsville, Tex., 1950, UPI, 1950—52, Houston Chronicle, 1954—55; news writer, reporter, news dir. KTRH Radio, Houston, 1956; dir. news & pub. affairs KHOU (CBS TV affiliate), Houston, 1959—61; chief southwestern bur. CBS, Dallas, 1961—64, White House corr., 1963, 1966—74, chief London bur., 1965—66, war corr. Vietnam, 1966; anchor, corr. CBS Reports, 1974—75; corr., co-editor 60 Minutes, 1975—81; anchor Dan Rather Reporting, CBS Radio Network, 1977—2005; anchor, mng. editor CBS Evening News with Dan Rather, 1981—2005; anchor 48 Hours, 1988—2002; corr. 60 Minutes II, 1998—2006; prodr., host, Dan Rather Reports HDNet, 2006—. Co-editor TV show Who's Who, CBS, 1977; anchored numerous CBS News spl. programs. Author (with Gary Gates): The Palace Guard, 1974; author: (with Mickey Herskowitz) The Camera Never Blinks, 1977; author: (with Peter Wyden) Memoirs, I Remember, 1991; author: The Camera Never Blinks Twice: The Further Adventures of a Television Journalist, 1994, The American Dream, 2001. Recipient seven George Foster Peabody awards, ten Emmy awards. Office: HDNet 320 S Walton St Dallas TX 75226*

RATHER, LUCIA PORCHER JOHNSON, library administrator; b. Durham, NC, Sept. 12, 1934; d. Cecil Slayton and Lucia Lockwood (Porcher) Johnson; m. John Carson Rather, July 11, 1964; children: Susan Wright, Bruce Carson. Student, Westhampton Coll., 1951-53; AB in History, U. N.C., 1955, MS in Library Sci., 1957; PhD in History, George Washington U., 1994. Cataloger Library of Congress, Washington, 1957-64, bibliographer, 1964-66, systems analyst, 1966-70; group head MARC Devel. Office, 1970-73, asst. chief, 1973-76, acting chief, 1976-77, dir. for cataloging, 1976-91. Chmn. standing com. on cataloguing Internat. Fedn. Library Assns., 1976-81; sec. Working Group on Content Designators, 1972-77; chmn. Working Group on Corp. Headings, 1978-79, Internat. ISBD Rev. Com., 1981-87. Co-author: the MARC II Format, 1968. Recipient Libr. Congress Disting. Svc. award, 1991, Disting. Alumnus award U. N.C. Sch. Libr. and Info. Sci., 1992. Mem. ALA (Margaret Mann award 1985, Melvil Dewey award 1991), Phi Beta Kappa. Democrat. Presbyterian. Home: 438 Heron Point Chestertown MD 21620-1680

RATHKE, SHEILA WELLS, strategic planning and marketing executive; b. Columbia, SC, Aug. 9, 1943; d. Walter John and Betty Marie (McLaughlin) Wells; m. David Bray Rathke, Sept. 1966 (dec. 1997); 1 child, Erinn Michele. BA summa cum laude, U. Pitts., 1976, postgrad., 1976-77. Loan coord. Equibank, Pitts., 1961-65; office mgr. U.S. Steel Corp., Pitts., 1966-70; various account and mgmt. positions Burson-Marsteller, Pitts., 1977-87, exec. v.p., gen. mgr., 1987-94, CEO Can. ops. Toronto, Montreal, Ottawa, Vancouver, 1994-95; sr. v.p., dir. corp. devel. Young and Rubicam, Inc., NYC, 1995-99, COO, 1999-2000; asst. provost strategic and program devel. U. Pitts., 2001—. Instr. Slippery Rock Coll., Pitts., 1984-85; adviser Exec. Report Mag., Pitts., 1986-88, A Better Chance, N.Y.C., 1996-2000, N.Y. Philharm., 1997-99. Trustee U. Pitts., 1976-80, mem. alumni bd. dirs., 1990-94; trustee Robert Morris Coll., 1992-95; bd. dirs. Vocat. Rehab. Ctr., 1987-93, Freewheelers, 1989-92, Pitts. Hist. Soc., River City Brass Band, Quantam Theatre, 2003-07. Named Disting. Alumnus, U. Pitts., 1992, Legacy Laureate, 2000. Mem. AAUW, Female Execs. Am., Am. Assn. Advt. Agys. (chair ea. region 1994-95), Pitts. Advt. Club (bd. dirs. 1988-91, pres. 1990), Alpha Sigma Lambda (charter). Avocations: skiing, reading, gardening, travel, photography, cooking. Home: 1819 Sarah St Apt 2 Pittsburgh PA 15203 Office: U Pitts Cathedral of Learning Pittsburgh PA 15260-E-mail: sheilarathke@msn.com.

RATHMAN, WILLIAM ERNEST, retired lawyer, minister; b. Middletown, Ohio, Jan. 10, 1927; s. Ernest Daniel and Marguerite (Sebald) R.; m. Constance Schedler, Nov. 28, 1958; children: Marchie, William E. Jr. Grad., Phillips Exeter Acad., 1944; BA, Kenyon Coll., 1948; postgrad., Harvard U., 1950, Ohio State U. Coll. of Law, 1951, United Theol. Seminary, Dayton, Ohio, 1975. Bar: Ohio 1952; ordained to ministry Episc. Ch., 1975. Pvt. practice law, Middletown, Ohio, 1952-78; sr. ptnr. Rathman, Elliott & Boyd, Middletown, 1979-84, Rathman, Combs, Schaefer, Valen & Kaup, Middletown, 1985-88, Rathman, Combs, Schaefer & Kaup, Middletown, 1989-95, ret., 1995—. Spl. counsel to County of Butler, 1956-64, City of Middletown, 1965-66, asst. Ohio Atty. Gen., 1967-69; acting judge Middletown Mcpl. Ct., 1969-74. Pres. Middletown Community Found., 1972-76, Middletown Chamber Found., 1977-80, Butler County Park Commn., 1986-90; trustee-at-large Ohio Found. of Ind. Colls., Columbus, 1972-90; trustee, mem. exec. com. Middletown United Way, 1963-90; trustee Middleton Req. Hosp. Found., 1986-90; adv. bd. Middletown campus Miami U., 1984-90. With USN, 1944-46, capt. USAF, 1959, comdr. Am. Legion, 1965. Named Exec. Yr., Middletown chpt. Nat. Secs. Assn., 1969; recipient Outstanding Community Svc. award Middletown post Am. Legion, 1975, Outstanding Svc. award Parstoral Counselling Svc., 1983, Vol. of Yr. award Middletown Area United Way, 1986. Fellow Am. Coll. Trust and Estate Counsel; mem. ABA (estate tax com. 1966-69), Ohio Bar Assn. (coun. del. 1980-93), Butler County Bar Assn. (pres. 1980), Middletown Bar Assn. (pres. 1967), Fed. Bar Assn. (pres. Cin. chpt. 1975), Ohio State Bar Found. (trustee 1992-96, Ohio Supreme Ct. bd. commrs. on grievances and discipline 1996-99), Masons (master 1959-60, 33d deg.), Scottish Rite Valley of Cin. (treas. 1986, chmn. bd. 1990), Sea Pines Country Club. Episcopalian. Home (Summer): 501 Thorn Hill Ln Middletown OH 45042-3750 Home: 1924 S Beach Club Hilton Head Island SC 29928-3750 Personal E-mail: crathman@aol.com.

RATHMELL, JAMES P., anesthesiologist, educator; MD, Wake Forest U., Winston-Salem, NC, 1988. Diplomate Am. Bd. Anesthesiology, 1993. Assoc. prof. anaesthesia Harvard U. Med. Sch., Boston, 2006—; chief, divsn. pain medicine Mass. Gen. Hosp., Boston, 2007—. Office: Mass Gen Hosp 15 Parkman St GB444 Boston MA 02114 Business E-Mail: jrathmell@partners.org.

RATHNAU, HEATHER HEARN, music educator, writer; b. San Antonio, Tex., Mar. 8, 1958; d. Claude Adam Hearn, Jr. and Mildred Ruby Damron; m. Ronald Alan Rathnau, Aug. 1, 1981; children: Alison Renee, Mallory Dawn. MusB magna cum laude, Baylor U., 1980, MusM, 1982. Pvt. music and voice tchr., Houston, 1984—; prin., owner Theory Time, Mo. City, Tex., 1996—. Guest instr. Schmitt Music Expo, 1999, Mpls., 2005; lectr. in field. Author: Theory Time, 1996, 2002. Mem.: Music Tchrs. Nat. Assn., Tex. Music Tchrs. Assn., Forum Music Tchrs. Assn. (pres. 1992—94), Nat. Piano Tchrs. Guild (adjudicator 1990—2007), Houston (Tex.) Music Tchrs. Assn. (v.p. 1989—90), Music Tchrs. Nat. Conf., Houston (Tex.) Fedn. Music Clubs, Mu Phi Epsilon. Republican. Baptist. Avocations: travel, reading, gardening. Home: 6639 Sutters Creek Trail Missouri City TX 77459

RATHOD, MULCHAND, mechanical engineering educator; b. Pathri, India, Mar. 3, 1945; came to U.S., 1970, naturalized, 1981; s. Shamjibhai Laljibhai and Ramaben Rathod; m. Damayanti Thakor, Aug. 15, 1970; children: Prerana, Falgun, Sejal. BS in Mech. Engring., Sardar Patel U., India, 1970; MS, Miss. State U., 1972, PhD, 1975. Rsch. grad. asst. Miss. State U., 1970-75; cons. engr. Bowron & Butler, Jackson, Miss., 1975-76; asst. prof. Tuskegee Inst., Ala., 1976-78; assoc. prof., coord. MET program SUNY, Binghamton, 1979-87; prof. Wayne State U., Detroit, 1987—, dir. engring. tech. divsn., 1987—2003. Cons. Interpine, Hattiesburg, Miss., 1977-79, Jet Propulsion Lab., 1980-83, IBM Corp., 1982-85; pres. Shiv-Parvati, Inc. 1982—. Contbr. articles to profl. jours.; patentee in field. Den leader Susquahanna coun. Boy Scouts Am., Vestal, N.Y., 1983-84. Recipient award NASA, 1981; grantee SUNY Found., 1984, Dept. Energy, 1978, GM, 1988-92, UAW Chrysler, 1990-91, Hudson-Webber Found., 1991-92, Ford, 1992-93, Kellogg Found., 1993-94, SME Found., 1994, Mich. Dept. Edn., 1994, NSF, 1995-2001. Fellow: ASME (cert. of appreciation 1982—89, 1991—2005, Dedicated Svc. award 1995, Ben C. Sparks medal 1998, BMW award 2001); mem.: ASHRAE, Profl. Order Engring. Tech., N.Y. State Engring. Tech. Assn., Am. Soc. Engring. Edn. (reviewer), India Assn. Miss. State U. (pres. 1972—73), Tau Beta Pi, Tau Alpha Phi (founder, faculty advisor 1989—), Pi Tau Sigma. Home: 1042 Woods Ln Grosse Pointe Woods MI 48236-1157 Office: Wayne State U Div Engring Tech Detroit MI 48202

RATHORE, JITENDRA S., chemist; s. Krishna Dayal S. and Aruna Rathore; m. Roli Singh; 1 child, Prisha. PhD, City U., NY, 2007. Co-op. GE Advanced Materials, Tarrytown, NY; postdoc. rsch. assoc. Rensselaer Poly. Inst., Troy, NY; rsch. assoc. IBM Almaden Rsch. Ctr., San Jose, Calif., 2008—, CUNY Rsch. Found., NYC. Contbr. articles to profl. sci. jours.; author: (book) Functional Polysilixanes: New Avenues, New Outcomes: Nanoparticle. Jr. Rsch. fellowship, Coun. Sci. & Indsl. Rsch., 2001. Mem.: Am. Chem. Soc., Sigma Xi. Achievements include development of new strategies using silicon polymer for synthesis of nanoparticles. Home: 600 Marathon Dr Apt 48 Campbell CA 95008 Office: IBM Almaden Rsch Ctr 650 Harry Rd K17F/E1-420 San Jose CA 95120 Personal E-mail: rathorechem@gmail.com.

RATHWELL, PETER JOHN, lawyer; b. Windsor, Ont., Can., Aug. 20, 1943; came to U.S., 1947; s. Harold Wilfred and Jean Isabel (Lucas) R.; m. Ann Wickstrom Williams, Sept. 10, 1977; 1 child, James Michael. BA, U. Ariz., 1965, JD, 1968. Bar: Ariz. 1968. Assoc. Boettcher, Crowder & Schoolitz, Scottsdale, Ariz., 1972-73; ptnr. Snell & Wilmer, Phoenix, 1978—. Lectr. in field. Mem. exec. com. Jr. Achievement Ariz., Phoenix, 1980—92, 2000—, bd. advisors, 1980—, chmn. bd. advisors, 2006—; chmn. scholarship fund St. Mary H.S., 1982—91; mem., chmn. Phoenix Pks. Bd., 1982—87; trustee Orme Sch., 1991—, chair devel. com., 1994—, mem. exec. com., 2006—; treas., trustee Smith Scholarship Trust U. Ariz. Law Sch., 1985—; bd. advisors ABI S.W. Bankruptcy Conf., 1995—, co-chair, 2003—04. Capt. JAGC USAF, 1969—72. Fellow State Bar Ariz. Found. (founding mem.), Maricopa County Bar Found. (founding mem.); mem. Am. Bankruptcy Inst., Ariz. Bar Assn. (bar counsel 1982-87, 97, chmn. discipline hearing com. 1987-93, mem. bankruptcy sect.), Maricopa County Bar Assn. (seminar lectr. 1987), Comml. Law League Am., Phoenix Zoo Wildest Club in Town (founding mem. 1972). Republican. Avocations: fishing, raising cattle. Home: 4523 E Mountain View Rd Phoenix AZ 85028-5213 Office: Snell & Wilmer 1 Arizona Ctr Phoenix AZ 85004 Home Phone: 480-948-5154; Office Phone: 602-382-6203. Business E-Mail: prathwell@swlaw.com.

RATIGAN, DYLAN, journalist, financial news correspondent; b. Saranac Lake, NY, Apr. 19, 1972; s. John and Adrienne Ratigan. BA in Polit. Economics, Union Coll., 1994. Reporter Portsmouth Herald, NH; bus. corr. Bloomberg TV; co-creator, host Morning Call Bloomberg TV & USA Network; global mng. editor for corp. fin. Bloomberg News Svc.; joined CNBC, 2003, host On the Money, 2005—07, anchor Bullseye, anchor, co-creator Fast Money, 2006—09, co-anchor The Call, co-anchor Closing Bell; host Morning Meeting with Dylan Ratigan MSNBC, 2009—. Reporter NASCAR Gold CNBC on Assignment, reporter Las Vegas, Inc.; host Fast Money MBA Challenge; spkr. World Econ. Forum, Davos, Switzerland; contbr. ABC News. Contbr. articles to NY Times, Washington Post, Miami Herald, Chgo. Tribune. Recipient Gerald Loeb Award, 2005. Office: MSNBC 1 MSNBC Pl Secaucus NJ 07094*

RATKE, DAVID C., religious studies educator; b. Edmonton, Alta., Can. BA in History with distinction, U. Alta., Edmonton, 1985; MA, Grad. Theol. Union, Berkeley, Calif., 1992; MDiv, Pacific Luth. Theol. Sem., Berkeley, 1993; PhD, Regensburg U., Germany, 1998. Religion prof. Lenoir Rhyne U., Hickory, NC, 1999. Contbr. to monograph. Mem.: Am. Acad. Religion. Office: Lenoir Rhyne Univ Box 7210 Hickory NC 28603

RATLIFF, DAN A., marriage and family therapist, educator; m. Nancy Deel, July 5, 1990; children: Camille, Kenton. PhD, Tex. Tech U., Lubbock, 1990. Min. pastoral care First Bapt. Ch., El Paso, Tex., 1981—87; prof. St. Mary's U., San Antonio, 1990—. Dir. Mil. Family Svc. Ctr., San Antonio, 2007—. Office: St Mary's Univ One Camino Santa Maria San Antonio TX 78209

RATLIFF, LOUIS JACKSON, JR., mathematics professor; b. Cedar Rapids, Iowa, Sept. 1, 1931; s. Louis Jackson and Ruth Sara (Sidlinger) R.; m. Georgia Lee Smith, May 9, 1996. BA, State U. Iowa, 1953, MA, 1958, PhD, 1961. Lectr. Ind. U., Bloomington, 1961-63, U. Calif., Riverside, 1963-64, asst. prof. math., 1964-67, assoc. prof., 1967-69, prof., 1969—. Author: Chain Conjectures in Ring Theory, 1978; assoc. editor Procs. of AMS, 1987-92, Comm. in Algebra, 1990-95; contbr. articles to profl. jours. 1st lt. USAF, 1953-57. NSF fellow, 1960-62, grantee, 1965-69, 71-88; recipient Disting. Teaching award, U. Calif.-Riverside, 1983. Mem. Am. Math. Soc., Phi Beta Kappa. Democrat. Seventh Day Adventist. Home: 26660 Ridgemoor Rd Sun City CA 92586 Office: U Calif Dept Math Riverside CA 92521-0001 Office Phone: 951-827-5020. Business E-Mail: ratliff@math.ucr.edu.

RATLIFF, RAMONA, librarian; d. Mabrey and Madge Miller; m. John Ratliff, May 27, 1972; children: Tracie, Cheryl, Crystal. AA, York Coll., Nebr., 1969; BA in Psychology & Sociology, Harding U., Searcy, Ark., 1972; MA in Info. Sci. and Learning Technologies, U. Mo., Columbia, 2008. Bus. office clk. York Coll., 1993—98, campus post office mgr., 1998—2000, circulation asst., periodicals levitt libr., 2000—. Contbr. articles to profl. jours. Mem. York Mothersingers, 1990—94, East Hill Ch. Christ, York, 1988—. Mem.: Christian Coll. Librs., Mountain Plains Libr. Assn., Nebr. Libr. Assn. Avocations: reading, travel. Office: York Coll Levitt Libr 1125 E 8th St York NE 68467

RATLIFF, THEO, professional basketball player; b. Demopolis, Ala., Apr. 17, 1973; m. Kristina Ratliff; children: Stacia, Yasmeen, Alexis, Sasha. B, U. Wyo., Laramie, 1995. Forward Detroit Pistons, 1995-97, 2008, Phila. 76ers, 1997—2001, 2008—09, Atlanta Hawks, 2001—04, Portland Trailblazers, 2004—06, Boston Celtics, 2006—07, Minn. Timberwolves, 2007—08, San Antonio Spurs, 2009—. Mem. NBA All-Star Reading Team. Named Second Team All-Defense, NBA, 1999, 2004; named to Eastern Conf. All-Star Team, 2001. Achievements include leading the NBA in: blocked shots, 2001, 2003, 2004. Avocations: playing pool, listening to music. Office: San Antonio Spurs 1 AT&T Ctr Pky San Antonio TX 78219*

RATMANSKY, ALEXEI, performing company executive, dancer, choreographer; b. St. Petersburg, Russia; Studied with A. Markeyeva, Pyotr Pestov, Moscow Bolshoi Ballet Sch.; grad. choreographer's divsn., Moscow State Inst. Theatrical Arts, 1992. Dancer Kiev Ballet, 1986-88, prin. dancer, 1988-92; soloist Royal Winnipeg (Man., Can.) Ballet, 1992-1995; dancer Royal Danish Ballet, 1997—2004; artistic dir. State Acad. Bolshoi Theatre of Russia(Bolshoi Ballet), 2004—08; artist in residence Am. Ballet Theater, NYC, 2009—. Guest artist Ballet Nat. du Québec. Dance performances include Tarantella (George Ballanchine), Spectre de la Rose (Michel Fokine), Giselle (Peter Wright), La Sylphide, Cinderella, Square Dance (Ballanchine), Tchaikovsky Pas de Deux (Ballanchine), Lilac Garden (Antony Tudor), La Bayadere Act II (Petipa), Nutcracker (John Neumeier), Romeo and Juliet (Rudi van Dantzig), Don Quixote, Pas de Dix (Ballanchine); choreographer: Stravinsky's A Fairy's Kiss, 1994, The Charms of Mannerism, 1997, Stravinsky's Capriccio, 1997, Dreams of Japan, 1998 (Golden Mask Nat. Theatre prize, 1999), A Poem of Ecstasy, 1998, Turandot's Dream, 2000, Nutcracker, 2001, Flight to Budapest, 2001, Bolero, 2001, Lea, 2001, Cinderella, 2002, The Firebird, 2002, The Bright Stream, 2003 (Golden Mask Nat. Theatre prize for Choreography, 2004, Nat. Dance Awards Critics' Cir. prize, 2007), Animal Carnival, 2003, Anna Karenina, 2004 (Benois de la danse prize, 2005), Bolt, 2005, Russian Seasons, 2006. Recipient First prize Second Nat. Ballet Competition, Donietsk, Russia, 1987, Vaslav Nijinsky prize First Internat. Diaghilev Ballet Competition, Moscow, 1992, 2nd prize for choreography Serge Lifar Ballet Competition, 1994; named Honored Artist of Ukraine, 1992, Knight, Order of the Danish Flag, 2002; Bolshoi Ballet named best fgn. dance co., Nat. Dance Awards, 2007. Office: Am Ballet Theatre 890 Broadway New York NY 10003 Office Phone: 692-08-18, 212-477-3030. Office Fax: 692-33-67, 212-254-5938. E-mail: pr@bolshoi.ru.*

RATNER, BRUCE C., professional sports team owner, real estate developer; b. Cleve., Jan. 23, 1945; children: Rebecca, Elizabeth. BA cum laude, Harvard U., 1967; JD, Columbia U., 1970. Dir. Model Cities Prog., head Consumer Protection Divsn. NYC, 1970—73, commr. consumer affairs, 1978—82; prof. law NYU, 1974—78; pres., CEO Forest City Ratner Cos., NYC, 1982—; owner NJ Nets, 2004—. Trustee Bklyn. Acad. Music, 1989, chmn., 1992—2001; bd. dirs. Mus. Jewish Heritage, Met. Mus. Art, City Pks. Found., Internat. Rescue Com., Bklyn. C. of C., NYC Partnership. Recipient NY State Gov.'s Arts award, 1994; named The Top NYC Exec., Crain's NY Bus., 1992; named one of NY's Most Influential Bus. Leaders, 2002. Office: Forest City Ratner Cos 1 Metrotech Ctr N Brooklyn NY 11201*

RATNER, BUDDY DENNIS, biomedical engineer, educator; b. Bklyn., Jan. 19, 1947; s. Philip and Ruth Ratner; m. Cheryl Cromer; 1 child, Daniel Martin. BS in Chemistry, Bklyn. Coll., 1967; PhD in Polymer Chemistry, Bklyn. Poly. U., 1972. From fellow to prof. U. Wash., Seattle, 1972—86, prof., 1986—, Darland prof. bioengring., 2005—. Dir. U. Wash. Engineered Biomaterials Engring. Ctr.; founder Asemblon, Inc., Healionics, Inc. Editor: Surface Characterization of Biomaterials, 1989, Plasmas and Polymers, 1994-99, Biomaterials Science: An Introduction to Materials in Medicine, 2d edit., 2004, Characterization of Polymeric Biomaterials, 1997; mem. editl. bds. 9 jours. and book series; editor Jour. Undergrad. Rsch. in Bioengring., 1998—; contbr. over 400 articles to profl. jours. Recipient Faculty Achievement/Outstanding Rsch. award, 1990, Perkin Elmer Phys. Electronics award for excellence in surface sci., Acta Biomaterialia Gold medal, 2009. Fellow AAAS, Internat. Acad. Med. and Biol. Engring., Am. Inst. Med. Biol. Engring. (founder, pres. 2002-03), AVS Sci. Technol. Soc. (Medard Welsh medal 2002); mem. AIChE (C.M.A. Stine award 1998), Nat. Acad. Engring., Am. Chem. Soc., Internat. Soc. Contact Lens Rsch., Materials Rsch. Soc., Soc. for Biomaterials (pres. 1991-92, Clemson award 1989, fellow 1994, Founders award 2004, C.W. Hall award 2006), Biomed. Engring. Soc. Achievements include patents in field. Home Phone: 206-286-0969; Office Phone: 206-685-1005. E-mail: ratner@uweb.engr.washington.edu.

RATNER, CARL JOSEPH, opera stage director, baritone; b. Memphis, Sept. 17, 1957; MusB, Oberlin Conservatory of Music, 1980; MA, Northeastern Ill. U., 1999; DM, Northwestern U., 2005. Intern Juilliard Sch., NYC, 1980-81, N.Y.C. Opera, 1981-82; asst. dir. Lyric Opera Chgo., 1982-84; prodn. asst. San Francisco Opera, 1985-86; asst. dir. Metropolitan Opera, NYC, 1989-90; artistic dir. Chamber Opera Chgo., 1985-93, Chgo. Opera Theater, 1994-99; opera dir. Western Mich. U., 2001—. Cons. in field. Home: 3440 N Lake Shore Dr Apt 9D Chicago IL 60657-2848 Office: Western Michigan Univ Sch Music Dalton Ctr 1903 W Michigan Ave Kalamazoo MI 49008-5434 Office Phone: 269-387-4706, 773-454-4919. Personal E-mail: carlratner@aol.com.

RATNER, DAVID LOUIS, retired law educator; b. London, Sept. 2, 1931; AB magna cum laude, Harvard U., 1952, LLB magna cum laude, 1955. Bar: N.Y. 1955. Assoc. Sullivan & Cromwell, NYC, 1955-64; assoc. prof. Cornell Law Sch., Ithaca, NY, 1964-68, prof., 1968-82; prof. law U. San Francisco Law Sch., 1982-99, dean, 1982-89, prof. emeritus, 1999—. Exec. asst. to chmn. SEC, Washington, 1966-68; chief counsel Securities Industry Study, Senate Banking Com., Washington, 1971-73; vis. prof. Stanford (Calif.) U., 1974, Ariz. State U., Tempe, 1974, U. San Francisco, 1980, Georgetown U., Washington, 1989-90, U. Calif., Hastings, San Francisco, 1992, U. Ariz., 2004; mem. Larkspur (Calif.) Planning Commn., 1992-2004. Author: Institutional Investors: Teaching Materials, 1978, Securities Regulation: Cases and Materials, 6th edit., 2002, Securities Regulation in a Nutshell, 9th edit., 2006. Fulbright scholar Monash U., Australia, 1981. Mem. Harvard Club of San Francisco (pres. 1999-2000), Phi Beta Kappa. Home and Office: 84 Polhemus Way Larkspur CA 94939-1928 E-mail: dlratner@aol.com.

RATNER, ELLEN FAITH, news analyst and correspondent, writer; b. Cleve., Aug. 28, 1951; d. Harry Ratner and Anne Spott. BA, Goddard Coll., 1974; EdM, Harvard U., 1978. Coord. women's svcs. Homophile Comty. Health Svc., Boston, 1971-73; co-dir., co-founder Boundaries Therapy Ctr., Acton, Mass., 1973-86; dir. psychiat. day treatment program South Shore Mental Health Ctr., Quincy, Mass., 1974-81; v.p. rsch., devel. and svc., dir. ARC Rsch. Found. Addiction Recovery Corp., Rockville, Mass., 1986-90; health care cons., dir. Found. for Addiction Rsch., 1990-94; White House reporter, bur. chief Talk Radio News Svc., Washington, 1991—, chief polit. corr., news analyst; polit. analyst FOX News Channel, 1997—; Washington bur. chief, polit. editor Talkers Mag., 1996—; CEO Coll. Media News Co. Tchr. Curry Coll., Milton, Mass., 1979-80; cons. program devel. Addiction Recovery Corp., 1984-86; developer, planner The Art's in Mileau Treatment of Phychiatric Outpatients, Quincy, 1980, New Eng.'s first conf. on Chem. Dependency and AIDS, 1988. Author: The Other Side of the Family: A Book for Recovery from Abuse, Incest and Neglect, 1990, 101 Ways to Get Your Progressive Issues on Talk Radio, 1997; mem. adv. bd. The Counselor Mag., 1987-90; appeared on nat. TV and radio shows including C-SPAN, The Oprah Winfrey Show, CNN, Nat. Empowerment TV, others; co-host (radio) Washington Reality Check, Good Day USA, New World Chronicle; polit. corr, Talk Radio Countdown Show; prodr. Talk Daily. Bd. trustees, mem. exec. com., vis. com. presdl. search com. Goddard Col., Plainfield, Vt. 1977-81; bd. trustees Samaritan Coll., L.A., 1988-90; bd. dirs. Nat. Lesbian and Gay Health Found., Washington, 1985-92, pres., exec. com., program com., program chair; v.p. Harry Ratner Human Svcs. Fund, Cleve., 1991—; mem. adv. bd. Women of Washington, Inc., 1992—; bd. dirs. Theater Chamber Players, Kennedy Ctr., Washington, 1988-91, An Uncommon Legacy Found., N.Y.C., 1993—, The Ctr. for Spiritual Enlightment, Falls Church, Va., 1994—. Recipient Comty. Svc. award Lesbian and Gay Counseling Svc., Boston, 1985, The Addams-Brown award Nat. Lesbian and Gay Health Found., 1993. Mem. Nat. Assn. Radio Talk Show Hosts, Mass. Assn. Day treatment Adminstrs. (chair regulations and standards com. 1979-81), Lily Dale Assembly. Democrat. Jewish. Avocation: writing works on spiritualism. Address: FOX News Channel 1211 Avenue of the Americas New York NY 10036 Home: 25 Central Park W Apt 17u New York NY 10023-7201

RATNER, GERALD, lawyer; b. Chgo., Dec. 17, 1913; s. Peter I. and Sarah (Soreson) R.; m. Eunice Payton, June 18, 1948. PhB, U. Chgo., 1935, JD cum laude, 1937. Bar: Ill. 1937. Since practiced in, Chgo.; sr. ptnr. Gould & Ratner and predecessor firm, 1949—. Officer Henry Crown & Co., CC Industries, Inc., Material Svc. Corp., Freeman United Coal Mining Co., Mineral and Land Resources Corp.; lectr., writer on real estate law. Capt. US Army, 1942—46. Gerald Ratner Athletics Ctr. named in his honor, U. Chgo.; recipient Disting. Svc. medal, 2005, Disting. Service Professorship of Law, 2007, U. Chgo., Alumni Svc. medal, 2009. Mem. ABA, Ill. Bar Assn., Chgo. Bar Assn., Order of Coif,

Phi Beta Kappa. Home: 180 E Pearson St Apt 6205 Chicago IL 60611-2191 Office: 222 N La Salle St Ste 800 Chicago IL 60601-1086 Office Phone: 312-236-3003. Business E-Mail: gratner@gouldratner.com.

RATNER, HANK J., broadcast executive; BA, Emory U., JD with distinction. Assoc. Sullivan & Cromwell; asst. gen. counsel Cablevision Sys. Corp., Bethpage, NY, 1987—88; exec. v.p. Rainbow Media, 1993—98, COO, 1998—2002, vice chmn., 2002—, Cablevision Sys. Corp., 2002—, Madison Sq. Garden, 2003—. Office: Cablevision Systems Corp 1111 Stewart Ave Bethpage NY 11714-3581*

RATNER, MICHAEL D., lawyer; b. June 13, 1943; s. Harry and Anne (Spott) Ratner. BA, Brandeis U., 1966; JD magna cum laude, Columbia U., 1971. Bar: N.Y. 1971, U.S. Supreme Ct. 1983. Law clk. U.S. Dist. Ct. (so. dist.), NYC, 1971-72; prof. NYU Law Sch., NYC, 1973-74; atty. Ctr. for Constl. Rights, NYC, 1978-85, legal dir., 1985-90, pres., 2002—. Adj. prof. Yale Law Sch., New Haven, 1990—95, lectr., 2000; spl. counsel for human rights Govt. of Haiti, 1996; lectr. Columbia Law Sch., NYC, 1999—. Author: International Human Rights Litigtion in U,S. Courts, 1997, Che Guevara and the FBI, 1997, The Pinochet Papers: The Case of Augusto Pinochet Ugarte in Spain and Britain, 2000; co-author (with Barbara Olshansky & Jennie Green): Against War with Iraq, 2003; co-author: (with Ellen Ray) Guantanamo: What the World Should Know, 2004; contbr. articles to profl. jours.; co-author: Disappeared in America, 2005, International Prosecution A Human Rights Crimes, 2006, The Trial of Donald Rumsfeld, 2008. Recipient medal of excellence, Columbia Law Sch., 2004, John Minor Wisdom pro bono award, ABA, 2006, Brandeis Alumni award, 2006, Hans Litten prize, 2006, Puffin National award, 2007; named Trial Lawyer of Yr., Trial Lawyers for the Pub. Interest; named one of 100 Most Influential Lawyers, Nat. Law Jour.; Lennon Ono Peace grantee, 2006, Skelly Wright fellow, Yale Law Sch., 2000, Hon fellow, U. Pa. Law Sch., 2005. Mem. Nat. Lawyers Guild (pres. 1982-83). Office Phone: 212-614-6429. E-mail: mratner@igc.org.

RATTERREE, JOHN ERIC, academic administrator; b. Spartanburg, SC, Feb. 20, 1962; s. Hugh Bryson and Jane Goins Ratterree; m. Allison Albee, Mar. 4, 1995. BS, Clemson U., SC, 1985; MEd, Converse Coll., Spartanburg, 1988; MS, Capella U., Mpls., 2008. Cert. energy auditor. Curriculum facilitator Byrnes Freshman Acad., Duncan, SC, 1999—; dist. energy mgr. Sch. Dist. 5 of Spartanburg County, Duncan, 2001—. Adj. prof. Converse Coll., Spartanburg, 1998—. Mem. SC Acad. Learning Environment, Duncan, 2000—. Named Spartanburg Conservation Tchr. of the Yr., Spartanburg Soil and Water Conservation Dist., 1995, Lockhart HS Tchr. of the Yr., Union County Schs., 1990. Mem.: ASCD (assoc.), Nat. Sci. Tchrs. Assn., Assn. Energy Engrs. (cert. energy auditor), SC Acad. Sci. Avocations: woodworking, natural science, cooking. Personal E-mail: cu85tiger@yahoo.com.

RATTI, RICARDO ALLEN, lawyer; b. Humacao, PR, Sept. 3, 1922; s. Augustus Peter and Gertrude Alice (Allen) Ratti; m. Ruth Anne Holland, Aug. 15, 1947; children: Carolyn, Christine, Steven, Julia; m. Jean E. Royer, May 26, 1991. BS in Marine Engring., USCG Acad., 1944; JD, George Washington U., 1956. Bar: US Ct. Appeals (DC cir.) 1956. Chief counsel US Coast Guard, Washington, 1973—76; dep. asst. chief counsel FAA, Washington, 1976—78; chief counsel subcom. Mcht. Marine, US House Reps., Washington, 1978—85. With USCG, 1972—76. Decorated Legion of Merit; recipient John Ordronaux prize, George Washington Law Sch., 1954, John B. Larner medal, 1956. Mem.: Nat. Assn. Uniformed Svcs. (dir. 1981—84), Ret. Officers Assn., Fed. Bar Assn. Republican.

RATTIE, KEITH O., gas industry executive; Sr. v.p. The Coastal Corp., 1996—2001; pres. Questar Corp., 2001—02, pres., CEO, 2002—03, chmn., pres., CEO, 2003—. Dir. Zions First Nat. Bank, Gas Technology Institute, U. Wyo. Energy Resources Coun. Mem.: Salt Lake C. of C. Office: c/o Questar 180 E 100 S Salt Lake City UT 84111*

RATTIGAN, DENISE, special education educator; MEd, Southern Ill. U., Edwardsville, 1991. Tchr., literacy coach & spl. edn. coord. Zion Elem. Sch. Dist., Ill., 1990—; instr. Carthage Coll., Kenosha, Wis., 1993—. Bd. dirs. Learning Disabilities Assn. Wis., 2007—. Contbr. articles to publs. Mem.: ASCD. Home and Office: Prestigious Ednl Group PO Box 94 Kenosha WI 53141 Business E-Mail: deniserattigan@prestigiouseducationalgroup.com.

RATTNER, STEVEN LAWRENCE, former private equity firm executive; b. Great Neck, NY, July 5, 1952; s. George Seymour and Selma Ann (Silberman) R.; m. Patricia Maureen White, June 22, 1986; children: Rebecca White, Daniel Irvin, David William, James Brennan. AB in Economics. with honors, Brown U., 1974. Asst. to James Reston, corr. The NY Times, Washington, NYC, London, 1974-82; assoc., v.p. Lehman Brothers Kuhn Loeb, NYC, 1982-84; assoc., v.p., prin., mng. dir., head communications group Morgan Stanley & Co., NYC, 1984-89; mng. dir., head comms. group Lazard Fréres & Co., LLC, NYC, 1989-97, dep. chief exec., dep. chmn., 1998—2000; co-founder, mng. prin. Quadrangle Group LLC, NYC, 2000—09; counselor to sec. on auto industry issues US Dept. Treasury, Washington, 2009. Dir. Falcon Cable Holding Group, 1993—. Contbr. articles to various publs. including NY Times, Wall St. Jour., LA Times, Fin. Times. Trustee Brookings Instn., 1998—, Met. Mus. Art, 1996—; trustee Ednl. Broadcasting Corp., 1990—, vice chmn., 1994-98, chmn., 1998-2006; fellow & chmn. budget & fin. com. Brown Univ.; adv. coun. NYC Outward Bound Ctr., 1990—; past trustee Mus. TV & Radio. Harvey Baker fellow Brown U. 1974, Poynter fellow Yale, 1979. Mem. Coun. Fgn. Rels., Royal Inst. for Internat. Affairs (assoc.). Democrat.*

RATUM, CECILIA BANGLOY, retired psychologist; b. Jones, Isabela, Philippines, Feb. 1, 1935; arrived in U.S., 1968, naturalized, 1974; d. Federico Reyes and Vivina Pastor Bangloy; m. Pablo Agpaoa Ratum, Apr. 21, 1958; children: Nympha, Locelia. Psychology program, U. San Francisco, 1980—81; MA in Elem. Counseling, San Francisco State U., 1975; grad. program, Philippine Normal U., 1963, BS in Elem. Edn., 1955. Cert. tchr. Ilocos Norte Normal Sch., Philippines, 1953, nat. cert. sch. psychologist 1989. Instr. Philippine Wesleyan Coll., Cabanatuan, Philippines, 1955—56; critic tchr. Philippine Women's U., Manila, 1956—57; head tchr., classroom tchr. Philippine Pub. Schs., Jones, 1957—60, dist. guidance coord., 1960—68; filing clk. Pacific Telephone, San Francisco, 1968—69; substitute tchr. San Francisco Unified Sch. Dist., 1969—70, counselor, 1970—78, tchr., 1978—79, counselor, 1979—81, psychologist, 1981—98; ret., 1998—2002; psychologist San Francisco Unified Sch. Dist., 2002—04; ret., 2004. Team leader for sch. pschologist San Francisco Unified Sch. Dist., 1984—86, supr. sch. psychology intern, 1993—96, cadre leader for sch. psychologists, 1997—98; advisor Jones Internat. Assn. Mem. JCC, San Francisco. Mem.: Calif. Ret. Tchrs. Assn. (San Francisco Divsn.) (exec. bd. dirs.), Sixty Plus San Francisco U. Beta Chpt., Internat. Dyslexia Assn., Calif. Assn. Sch. Psychologists, Nat. Assn. Sch. Psychologists, San Francisco State U. Alumni Assn. (life), San Francisco State U. Osher Learning Inst. (life). Avocations: reading, writing, music, writing. Home: 168 Lowell St San Francisco CA 94112-4307 Personal E-mail: ratum5f@sbcglobal.net.

RATZENBERGER, JOHN DESZO, actor, writer, film director; b. Bridgeport, Conn., Apr. 6, 1947; s. Dezso Alexander and Bertha (Grohowski) R.; m. Elizabeth Georgia Stiny, Sept. 9, 1984 (div. May 27, 2004); children: James John, Nina Katherine. Grad. high sch., Bridgeport, Conn.; PhD, Sacred Heart U., 1992, LHD (hon.), 2002. Actor, writer, dir. own theater troupe Sal's Meat Market, 1971-75; touring actor, 1971-81. Owner, pres., founder Eco-Pack Industries, Kent, Wash. Performed various one-man shows and directed, Stowe Playhouse, Vermont; appeared in plays Curse of the Starving Class, The Connection; films include The Ritz, 1974, Twilight's Last Gleaming, 1977, A Bridge Too Far, 1977, Valentino, 1977, Warlords of Atlantis, 1978, Superman, 1978, The Bitch, 1979, Arabian Adventure, 1979, Yanks, 1979, Star Wars: Episode V-The Empire Strikes Back, 1980, Motel Hell, 1980, Superman II, 1980, Outland, 1981, Ragtime, 1981, Warlords of the 21st Century, 1982, Firefox, 1982, Gandhi, 1982, House II: The Second Story, 1987, Going to the Chapel, 1988, (voice) Toy Story, 1995, That Darn Cat, 1997, One Night Stand, 1997, Bad Day on the Block, 1997, A Fare to Remember, 1998, (voice) A Bug's Life, 1998, (voice) Toy Story 2, 1999, Tic Tock, 2000, Determination of Death, 2001, Monsters, Inc., 2002, (voice) Finding Nemo,2003, (voice) The Incredibles, 2004, All In, 2005, Something New, 2006, (voice) Cars, 2006, (voice) Superman II, 2006, (voice) Ratatouille, 2007, (voice) WALL-E, 2008, (voice) Up, 2009; (TV films) The Good Soldier, 1981, Goliath Awaits, 1981, Combat High, 1986, Timestalkers, 1987, Friends in Space, 1990 (also writer), Camp Cucamonga, 1990, Dog's Best Friend, 1997, The Pennsylvania Miners' Story, 2002, Mystery Woman: Redemption, 2006; video (voice) Toy Racer, 2001, Extreme Skate Adventure, 2003, The Incredibles: Rise of the Underminer, 2005; TV performances include Songs of a Sourdough, Secret Amy, 1979, (series) Cheers, 1982-1993 (also dir. several episodes 1988-93); guest appearences include Hill Street Blues, 1982, Wizards and Warriors, 1983, Magnum P.I., 1984, St. Elsewhere, 1985, The Love Boat, 1985, The Tortellis, 1987, Mickey's 60th Birthday, 1988, Disneyland, 1990, Wings, 1990, Captain Planet and the Planeteers, 1990, Nurses, 1992, Bill Nye, the Science Guy, 1993, Moon Over Miami, 1993, (voice) The Simpsons, 1994, Murphy Brown, 1995, Caroline in the City, 1996, Sabrina, The Teenage Witch, 1997, The Detectives, 1997, Remember WENN, 1998, Touched by an Angel, 2000, (voice) Pigs Next Door, 2000, That '70's Show, 2001, Fraiser, 2002, 8 Simple Rules for Dating My Teenage Daughter, 2003; (TV mini series) Small World, 1988; dir. (TV series) Sister, Sister, 1994, (1 episode) Evening Shade, 1994, Pearl, 1996; prodr., screenwriter BBC, Paravision, Royal Court Theater, Hampstead Theater Club, Royal Acad. Dramatic Arts, and Granada TV; co-author TV plays: Friends in Space, 1978, Scalped, 1979; exec. prodr., creator, (TV) Locals, 1994; host Pixar's 20th Anniversary Special, 2006; performer Dancing with the Stars, 2007; co-author with Joel Engel We've Got It Made In America: A Common Man's Salute to an Uncommon Country, 2006. Chmn., largest internet venture connecting diabetes info. & rsch. www.childrenwithdiabetes.com; nat. walk chmn. Juvenile Diabetes Found.; actively involved with other various diabetes organizations; founder, actively involved Nuts, Bolts and Thingamajigs Found.; road trip (Travel Channel) Made in America. Recipient cash award Arts Council of Great Britain, Father of Yr. award, Father's Day Coun. Am., 1996, Outstanding Role Model award, Am. Diabetes Assn., for writing, directing and producing, awarded Cleo and 3 Aegis awards. Mem. AFTRA, SAG, Writers Guild Am., Dirs. Guild, Am. Farmland Trust, Brit. Actors Equity Assn., Greenpeace, Wilderness Soc., Nat. Resources Def. Coun., Sierra Club (San Francisco). Achievements include development of packaging alternatives in 1989 made from biodegradable and non-toxic recycled paper; rowed a boat non-stop for more than 36 miles around Vashon Island, Wash. State to raise money for Special Olympics, 1993. Holds record as only person to make this 16 hour trip non-stop; drove Harley Davidson cross-country from NY to Las Vegas to raise awareness for Juvenile Diabetes, 1998. Avocations: sailing, reading, woodworking. Mailing: c/o Schachter Entertainment 1157 S Beverly Dr Los Angeles CA 90035*

RATZLAFF, DAVID EDWARD, minister; b. Kansas City, Mo., Mar. 12, 1938; s. John Henry and Amy May (Cathcart) R.; m. Shiela Paige Hickerson, June 9, 1958; children: Perry Dean, Kevin Lee, Kalista Kay. BA in Ministry, Nebr. Christian Coll., 1961; MDiv, Memphis Theol. Sem., 1991; DMin, Lake Charles Bible Coll., 1996. Ordained to ministry Christian Ch., 1962. Min. Christian Ch., Neligh, Nebr., 1959-67; owner, mgr. Kordsman Evangelistic Assn., Hiawatha, Kans., 1967-75; sr. min. Christian Ctr., Hiawatha, Kans., 1970-72; salesman Saladmaster Co., Springfield, Mo., 1975-76; ops. coord. Blackwood Bros. Quartet, Memphis, 1976-79, 85; mgr. sales and svc. Elliot Impression Products, Memphis, 1980-85; elder, tchr. Lindewood Christion Ch., 1985—2003; min. Bethany Christian Ch., Eads, Tenn., 1986-95; owner Soma Co., 1993-96; sales cons., fleet mgr., dealership coord. Midway Ford, Collierville, Tenn., 1996-99; customer rels. mgr. Landers Ford, 1999—2001; assoc. pastor Macon Christian Ch., Collierville, Tenn., 1997-99; courtesy delivery dealer trade mgr. Hutton Chevrolet, 2001—; sr. cons. pastor Morning Star Bible Ch., Nashville, 2003—05, Kirk's Christian, 2005—. Program chair exec. commn. on ministry com. Christian Chs. (Disciples of Christ), Tenn., 1988—95, ch. cons., 1996; western area moderator, mem. gen. and exec. bds. Region of Christian Ch. of Tenn., 1991—93; small bus. founder, 1993; mem. pastoral adv. bd. Genesis Crisis Ctr., Memphis, 1994; cons. WYLT-FM Radio, Collierville, 1997—2001, WUVLL-AM Radio, Mobile, Ala., 1997—2001. Author: At the Table, 2006; co-author: (songbook) Kordsman Presents, 1966; recorded and produced 6 long play albums, 1966-74. Bd. dirs. Memphis Family Link, 1985-86; mem. United Cerebral Palsy, 1983-86; asst. police chief City of Neligh, 1962-67, coord., 1965-67. Mem. Nat. Arts and Recording Artists, Collierville Ministerial Assn., Christian Ch. Ministers Memphis. Republican. Mem. Disciples Christ. Avocations: fishing, weightlifting, basketball, coaching baseball and softball. Home: 4093 Muirfield Dr Memphis TN 38125 Home Phone: 901-861-4385; Office Phone: 901-365-9700. E-mail: drdaver2000@yahoo.com.

RAU, LEE ARTHUR, lawyer; b. Mpls., July 22, 1940; s. Arthur W. and Selma A. (Lund) R.; m. Janice R. Childress, June 27, 1964; children: Brendan D., Patrick C., Brian T. BSB, U. Minn., 1962; JD, UCLA, 1965. Bar: Calif. 1966, DC 1972, Va. 1986, US Dist. Ct. DC 1973, US Dist. Ct. (ea. dist.) Va. 1988, US Ct. Mil. Appeals 1966, US Ct. Appeals (DC cir.) 1972, US Ct. Appeals (3d cir.) 1975, US Ct. Appeals (6th cir.) 1980, US Ct. Appeals (4th cir.) 1988, US Supreme Ct. 1971. Trial atty. evaluation sect. antitrust div. US Dept. Justice, Washington, 1965-66, appellate sect., 1970-72; assoc. Reed Smith Shaw & McClay, Washington, 1972-74, ptnr., 1975—2002; commr. Fairfax County Redevel. and Housing Authority, 2002—. Former mem. constl. and adminstrv. law adv. com. Nat. Chamber Litigation Ctr. Inc.; sec., bd. dirs. Old Dominion Land Co., Inc. Contbr. articles to profl. jours. Mem. Washington Dulles Task Force, 1982—91; mem. exec. com., ops. com. Fairfax-Falls Church United Way, mem. regional coun., 1988—92; chair Fair Fairfax Cts., High Rise Panel, 2006—; sec. bd. dirs. Reston Found., 1982—93; bd. dirs. Reston Interfaith Inc., 1973—89, pres., 1984—88; bd. dirs. Greater Reston Arts Ctr., 1988—96, pres., 1989—91, sec., 1991—95. Capt. JAGC US Army, 1966—70. Named Restonian of Yr., 1990; decorated Commendation with oak leaf cluster; recipient Best of Reston award, Merit citation Washington Post and Fairfax County Fedn. Civic Assns., 2006. Mem.: D.C. Bar Assn. (past chmn. energy study group). Democrat. Lutheran. Home: 11654 Mediterranean Ct Reston VA 20190-3401 Personal E-mail: leerau@verizon.net.

RAU, MAGDA, ophthalmologist; b. Zlin, Czechoslovakia, Aug. 31, 1952; arrived in Germany, 1982; d. Jaromir Broul and Vera Broulova; m. Cestmir Mican, Dec. 20, 1975 (div. 1992); 1 child, Cestmir Mican; m. Björn Rau, Dec. 23, 1996 (div. 1998). Degree, Coll., Frydlant, Czechoslovakia, 1970; med. diploma, Palacky U., Olomouc, 1976; ophthalmologist diploma, Prag, Czechoslovakia, 1980, Munich, 1984. Intern Residency Hosp., Frydek-Mistek, Czech Republic, 1976—82; ophthalmologist Prof. Dr. Dausch Eye Dept., Amberg, Germany, 1983—85; practice owner Furth Im Wald, 1985—; day clinic owner Augenklinik, Cham, 1995—; chief ophthalmologist Hosp., 1995—; pvt. clinic owner Privatklinik Rau, 2000—. Contbr. articles to opththalmological jours.; author: (interactive CD-ROM) ICRS (Intrastromal Corneal Ring Segments), 1999, 2001; co-author: (book) Multifocal IOLS, 2008. Mem. Albert Schweizer Stiftung Lambarene, 1996. Mem.: European Soc. Cataract and Refractice Surgery, Internat. Soc. Refractive Surgery. Roman Catholic. Avocations: tennis, horseback riding, skiing, skating. Home: Aepflet 24 93437 Furth im Wald Germany Office: Ophtalmologist Practice Von Mueller Str 12 93437 Furth im Wald Germany Office Phone: 00499973-801242.

RAU, MARGARET E., writer; b. Shantou, Guangdong, China; (parents Am. citizens); d. George Wright and Mary Victoria (Wolfe) Lewis; m. Neil L. Rau, Jan. 6, 1935 (dec. Nov. 6, 1971); children: Robert, Peter, Mary Margaret Frank, Thomas. Student, U. Chgo., Columbia U.; BA, U. Redlands; student, Riverside Coll. L.S., 1932. Freelance writer. Author: (novels) Band of the Red Hand, 1939; author: (with Neil Rau) (book) My Father Charlie Chaplin, 1960, Act Your Way to Successful Living, 1966, My Dear Ones, Story of the Founding of Recovery, Inc., 1971; author: Dawn from the West, 1964, The Penguin Book, 1965, The Yellow River, The Yangtze River, 1970, Jimmy of Cherry Valley, 1973, Our World: The People's Republic of China, 1974 (notable Children's Trade Book), The People of New China, 1975, Musk Oxen, Bearded Ones of the North, 1976 (Outstanding Sci. Book for Children), The Giant Panda at Home, 1977 (Outstanding Sci. Book for Children), The Gray Kangaroo at Home, 1978, The Snow Monkey at Home, 1979 (Best Non-Fiction Book of the Yr. So. Calif. Coun. Lit. Children), Red Earth Blue Sky, 1981, Minority Peoples of China, 1983, Holding Up the Sky (China's Youth), 1983 (notable Children's Trade Book), Young Women in China, 1989 (Outstanding Book N.Y. Pub. Libr.), The World's Scariest "True" Ghost Stories, 1994, The Ordeal of Olive Oatman, 1997, Wells Fargo's Book of the Gold Rush, 2001, Belle of the West, 2001, The Mail Must Go Through (the story of the Pony Express), 2005. Fellow: So. Calif. Coun. Lit. Children; mem.: Soc. Children's Book Writers and Illustrators, Authors Guild. Avocation: travel. Home: 5700 Via Real # 97 Carpinteria CA 93013

RAU, RALPH RONALD, retired physicist; b. Tacoma, Sept. 1, 1920; s. Ralph Campbell and Ida (Montgall) R.; m. Maryjane Uhrlaub, June 2, 1944; children: Whitney Leslie, Littie Elise. BS in Physics, Coll. Puget Sound, 1941; MS in Physics, Calif. Inst. Tech., 1943, PhD in Physics, 1948; LHD (hon.), U. Puget Sound, 2002. Asst. prof. physics Princeton U., 1947-56; Fulbright research prof. physics Ecole Polytechnique, Paris, 1954-55; physicist Brookhaven Nat. Lab., Upton, NY, 1956-66, chmn. dept. physics, 1966-70, assoc. dir. for high energy physics, 1970-81. Adj. prof. U. Wyo.; vis. prof. MIT, 1984-88; staff scientist Desy Lab., Hamburg, Fed. Republic Germany, 1984-85. Trustee U. Puget Sound, 1978-84 Named Alumnus Cum Laude U. Puget Sound, 1968; recipient Alexander von Humboldt U.S. Sr. Scientist award 1988. Mem. Am. Phys. Soc. Office: Brookhaven Nat Lab Upton NY 11973 Home Phone: 631-286-4774. Business E-Mail: rau@bnl.gov.

RAU, RAVI PRAKASH, physics professor, researcher; b. Kolkata, India, Aug. 9, 1945; came to U.S., 1966; s. Mysore Anantaswamy and Vijaya Lakshmi (Rao) R.; m. Luba Marie Witer, June 28, 1969 (dec. Jan. 1981); children: Nicholas Naveen, Alexander Vikram; m. Dominique Gabrielle Homberger, May 16, 1985. PhD, U. Chgo., 1970. Vis. fellow Tata Inst. Fundamental Rsch., Mumbai, 1972—73; prof. La. State U., Baton Rouge, 1974—. Vis. assoc. prof. Yale U., New Haven, 1978-79; vis. prof. Raman Rsch. Inst., Bangalore, 1983, Australian Nat. U., Canberra, 1987-88; vis. fellow Joint Inst. for Lab. Astrophysics, Boulder, Colo., 1984. Co-author: Atomic Collisions and Spectra, 1986, Symmetimes in Quantum Physics, 1996; contbr. articles to profl. jours. Fellowship, Alexander v Humboldt Assn., 1999—2000. Fellow Am. Phys. Soc. Home: 730 Carriage Way Baton Rouge LA 70808 Office: La State Univ Nicholson Hall-Physics & Astronomy Baton Rouge LA 70803 Office Fax: 225-578-5855. Business E-Mail: arau@phys.lsu.edu.

RAUCH, ALLAN N., lawyer; BA, U. Pa., 1980, JD, 1983. Bar: NY 1983. Mgr., dir. law dept. Bed Bath & Beyond, Union, NJ, gen. counsel, 1997—. Contbr. articles to law jours. Office: Bed Bath & Beyond 650 Liberty Ave Union NJ 07083 Office Phone: 908-688-0888. Office Fax: 908-688-8385. E-mail: allan.rauch@bedbath.com.

RAUCH, ARTHUR IRVING, management consultant; b. NYC, Sept. 18, 1933; s. David and Miriam (Frankel) R.; m. Roxane M. Spiller, Aug. 19, 1962 (div. 1977); children: David S., Janine B.; m. Lynn R. Saidenberg, Oct. 11, 1987. BA magna cum laude, Dartmouth Coll., 1954, MS, 1955. Chartered fin. analyst. Security analyst Lionel D. Edie & Co., NYC, 1959-64; group dir. rsch. Eastman Dillon, Union Securities & Co., NYC, 1964-68; v.p., sr. analyst Laird, Inc., NYC, 1968-69, dir. rsch., 1969-71, sr. v.p., 1970-73; ptnr. Oppenheimer & Co., NYC, 1973-77; v.p. corp. devel. Rorer Group, Inc., Ft. Washington, Pa., 1977-84; v.p. corp. fin. Arnhold & S. Bleichroeder, Inc., NYC, 1984-88; cons. corp. devel. ICN Pharms., Inc., NYC, 1988-89. Mem. investment com. Becker Fund, 1969-73. Exec. com. Dartmouth Class of 1954, 1968-79, 94-2004. Lt. (j.g.) USNR, 1956-59. Rufus Choate scholar Dartmouth Coll., 1951. Mem. NY Soc. Security Analysts, Assn. Corp. Growth, Fin. Analysts Fedn. (corp. fin. com.), Phi Beta Kappa. Home and Office: 115 Central Park W Apt 9D New York NY 10023-4153 Personal E-mail: arauch@rcn.com.

RAUCH, BILL, performing company executive, theater director; BA, Harvard Coll. Co-founder, artistic dir. Cornerstone Theater Co., LA, 1986—2006; artistic dir. Oreg. Shakespeare Festival, Ashland, 2007—. Assoc. artist Yale Repertory Theater, South Coast Repertory Theater; bd. dirs. Theater Comm. Group, 1992—98; Claire Trevor prof. drama U. Calif., Irvine, 2005—07. US Artists Prudential fellow, 2008. Office: Oreg Shakespeare Festival 15 S Pioneer St Ashland OR 97520*

RAUCH, GEORGE WASHINGTON, lawyer, director; b. Marion, Ind., July 18, 1919; s. George W. and Emma Asenath (Nolen) R.; m. Audrey M. Cranfield, Feb. 28, 1943 (div.); children: George Washington III, Nancy Lynn, Jane Nolen; m. Dorothy D. Farlow, June 26, 1970. BS, Ind. U., 1941; LL.B., U. Va., 1947. Bar: Ind. 1948, Ill. 1957, Mass. and Fla. 1972. Practice law Batton, Harker and Rauch (and predecessor firms), Marion, Ind., 1948-57; v.p., gen. counsel The Greyhound Corp., Chgo., 1957-61; mem. firm Hubachek & Kelly Ltd. and predecessor firms, Chgo., 1961-82; pres. Hubachek & Kelly Ltd., 1972-80; of counsel firm Chapman and Cutler, Chgo., 1982-95; gen. counsel Household Internat., 1967-78, dir., 1967-92, mem. fin. com., 1969-92, exec. com., 1972-92; dir. Edwards Engring. Corp., Constrn. Materials Co., Indsl. Air & Hydraulics Co., 1976-90, Burch Co., 1972-97, pres., 1975-97; dir. 1242 Lake Shore Dr. Corp., 1971-83, pres., 1973-74. Mem. Nat. Conf. Commrs. on Uniform Laws, 1955-57. Served as aviator USNR, 1941-45; lt. comdr. Mem. Raven Soc., Sankaty Head Golf Club (Nantucket, Mass.), Casino Club (Nantucket), Masons, Shriners, Phi Delta Phi, Delta Tau Delta. Home: 40 Sherburne Commons Apt 102 Nantucket MA 02554

RAUCH, IRMENGARD, linguist, educator; b. Dayton, Ohio, Apr. 17, 1933; d. Konrad and Elsa (Knott) R.; m. Gerald F. Carr, June 12, 1965; children: Christopher, Gregory. Student, Nat. U. Mex., summer 1954; BS with honors, U. Dayton, 1955; MA, Ohio State U., 1957; postgrad. (Fulbright fellow), U. Munich, Fed. Republic Germany, 1957-58; PhD, U. Mich., 1962. Instr., German and linguistics U. Wis., Madison, 1962-63, asst. prof., 1963-66; assoc. prof. German U. Pitts., 1966-68; assoc. prof. German and linguistics U. Ill., Urbana, 1968-72, prof., 1972-79, U. Calif., Berkeley, 1979—. Author: The Old High German Diphthongization: A Description of a Phonemic Change, 1967, The Old Saxon Language: Grammar, Epic Narrative, Linguistic Interference, 1992, Semiotic Insights: The Data Do the Talking, 1998, The Gothic Language: Genetic Provenance and Typology, Readings, 2002, The Phonology/ Paraphonology Interface and the Sounds of German Across Time, 2008; editor (with others): Approaches in Linguistic Methodology, 1967; editor: Spanish edit., 1974, Der Heliand, 1974, Linguistic Method: Essays in Honor of Herbert Penzl, 1979, The Signifying Animal: The Grammar of Language and Experience, 1980, Language Change, 1983, The Semiotic Bridge: Trends from California, 1989, On Germanic Linguistics: Issues and Methods, 1992, Insights in Germanic Linguistics I: Methodology in Transition, 1995, Across the Oceans: Studies from East to West in Honor of Richard K. Seymour, 1995, Insights in Germanic Linguistics II: Classic and Contemporary, 1996, Synthesis in Diversity: Semiotics Around the World, 1997, New Insights in Germanic Linguistics I, 1999, II, 2001, III, 2002; editor of three series: Berkeley Insights in Linguistics and Semiotics, Berkeley Models of Grammars, Studies in Old Germanic Languages and Literatures; founder, co-editor Interdisciplinary Jour. for Germanic Linguistics and Semiotic Analysis; contbr. articles to profl. jours. Named outstanding woman on campus U. Ill. Sta. WILL, 1975; recipient Disting. Alumnus award U. Dayton, 1985; research grantee U. Wis., summer 1966, U. Ill., 1975-79, Eastern Ill. U., 1976, Nat. Endowment Humanities, 1978, U. Calif., Berkeley, 1979—; travel grantee NSF, Linguistics Soc. Am., 1972; Guggenheim fellow, 1982-83; IBM Distributed Acad. Computing Environment, 1986; NEH grantee, 1988; Festschrift: Interdigitations: Essays for Irmengard Rauch, 1999. Mem. Linguistics Soc. Am., MLA, Am. Assn. Tchrs. German (hon.), Society for Germanic Philogy, Philogical Assn. of the West Coast, Phonetics Assn., Semiotic Soc. Am. (pres. 1982-83), Semiotic Circle of Calif. (founder), Internat. Assn. for Semiotic Studies (pres., dir. 5th congress 1994), Alpha Sigma Tau, Delta Phi Alpha. Home: 862 Camden Ct Benicia CA 94510-3633 Office: U Calif Dept German Berkeley CA 94720-0001

RAUCH, PAULA, psychiatrist; b. Northampton, Mass., Apr. 27, 1956; d. Harold and Ruth Nelson Rauch; m. Aubrey Dickman, May 12, 1985; children: Daniel Isaac Dickman, Benjamin Michael Dickman, Laura Eve Dickman. BA, Amherst Coll., Mass., 1977; MD, U. Cin. Coll. Medicine, 1981. Cert. in child psychiatry Bd. Psychiatry and Neurology, 1991. Founding dir. Mass. Gen. Hosp. Cancer Ctr., Boston, 1995—2008, Mass. Gen. Hosp.; chief child psychiatry consultation svc. to pediat. Mass. Gen. Hosp. Children. Author: Raising an Emotionally Healthy Child When a Parent is Sick. Bd. trustees mem. Amherst Coll., 2005—. Named Compassionate Caregiver of Yr., Schwartz Ctr. Compassionate Care, 2003. Office: Mass Gen Hosp Yawkey 6A/6900 Fruit St Boston MA 02114

RAUCHER, GARY M., psychotherapist, educator; b. NYC; MA in Psychology, Calif. Inst. Integral Studies, San Francisco, 1999. Cert. instructor Radiance Technique Internat. Assn., 1994, registered dance therapist Nat. Assn. Drama Therapy, 2001, cert. bd. trainer Nat. Assn. Drama Therapy, 2008. Marriage family therapist, drama therapist Bay Area Children First, San Francisco, 2001—05; core faculty, drama therapy program Calif. Inst. Integral Studies, San Francisco, 2006—. Prin. Acts Wisdom, San Francisco; journalist Object Mag., 1996—98; prin., cons. GMR Creative, San Francisco, 1995—; v.p. Nat. Assn. Drama Therapy, Ashburn, Va., 2007—; faculty Inst. Devel. Transformations, NYC, 2007—. Actor: (theatre-stage) Minnie's Boys, Trumpets and Drums, An Object Orientation; contbr. articles to profl. jours. Achievements include development of drama therapy protocol in support of people living with HIV. Business E-Mail: graucher@ciis.edu.

RAUCHER, HERMAN, screenwriter, novelist; b. Bklyn., Apr. 13, 1928; s. Benjamin Brooks and Sophie (Weinshank) R.; m. Mary Kathryn Martinet, Apr. 20, 1960; children: Jacqueline Leigh, Jennifer Brooke. BS, NYU, 1949. Asst. trade ad mgr. 20th Century Fox Films, NYC and Los Angeles, 1950-54; copy dir. Walt Disney Studios, NYC, 1954-55; copy supr. Calkins & Holden Advt., NYC, 1955-57; copy dir., v.p., dir. Reach McClinton Advt., NYC, 1957-63; v.p., creative dir. Maxon Advt., NYC, 1963-64; creative supr. Gardner Advt., NYC, 1964-65; v.p. advt., cons. Benton & Bowles Advt., NYC, 1965-67; freelance novelist, screenwriter, 1967—; pres. Bearfilm Prodns., 1971-96. Author: (novels and screenplays) Watermelon Man, 1970, Summer of '42 (nominated Acad. award for best original screenplay 1971, Writers Guild award nomination, Photoplay award), Ode to Billy Joe, 1975, A Glimpse of Tiger, 1972, (novel) Maynard's House, 1979, (screenplays) Sweet November, 1968, The Other Side of Midnight, 1977, Class of 44, 1972, Hieronymus Merkin (Best Original Screenplay award Writers Guild of Great Britain 1969), There Should Have Been Castles, 1978, Ginger, 1995, ARA/Froom, 2001 also various dramas appearing on TV in Alcoa Hour, Studio One, Matinee Theatre, Goodyear Playhouse, (TV mini-series under pseudonym) Master of the Game, 1984, (TV pilot) Remember When, 1974; playwright: Harold, 1962, Two Weeks Somewhere Else, 1967, Red Lights and Dragons, 1996, Kitty Hawk (musical), 2000; contbg. editor: Greenwich Time; contbr. to book revs. to N.Y. Times. Served with U.S. Army, 1950-52. Mem. Writers Guild Am., Authors League Am., Am. Film Inst., Dramatists Guild, Acad. of Motion Picture Arts and Scis.

RAUE, JORG EMIL, electrical engineer; b. Stettin, Germany, June 13, 1936; came to U.S., 1952; s. Ludwig and Liselotte (Barth) R.; m. Anke Volkmann, June 29, 1957; children: Monika Kay, Jennifer Faye. BSEE, Milw. Sch. Engring., 1961; MSEE, Marquette U., 1965, PhDEE, 1968. Mem. faculty Milw. Sch. Engring., 1961-68, chmn. dept., 1968-69; research engr. TRW Systems, Redondo Beach, Calif., 1969-76, mgr. dept., 1976-79; sr. research scientist TRW Electronic Systems, Redondo Beach, advanced systems mgr., 1980-93; tech. cons. Calif., 1993—; chmn. dept. elec. engring. Calif. Poly. State U., San Luis Opispo, 1979-80. Mem. faculty Marquette U., Milw., 1968-69, Loyola U., L.A., 1970-72, U. So. Calif., L.A., 1983—. Contbr. articles to profl. jours. Served with U.S. Army, 1955-58. Recipient Disting. Tchr. award Milw. Sch. Engring., 1968; named Outstanding Alumnus Milw. Sch. Engring., 1985. Fellow IEEE; mem. Microwave Soc. of IEEE (sec. adminstrn. com. 1985—), Sigma Xi. Avocations: tennis, bicycling, flying, bridge. Home and Office: 28813 Rothrock Dr Palos Verdes Estates CA 90275-3060

RAUF, ZAMIR, energy executive; BA in Bus. & Commerce, U. Houston, MBA. Various acctg. and fin. roles, credit and lending roles Comerica Bank; various acctg. and fin. roles Dynegy Inc., Enron N.Am.; mgr. fin. Calpine Corp., 2000—01, dir. fin., 2001—02, v.p. fin., 2002—05, sr. v.p. fin., 2005—08, treas., 2007—08, interim CFO, 2008, exec. v.p., CFO, 2008—. Office: Calpine Corp Ste 1000 717 Texas Ave Houston TX 77002 Office Phone: 713-830-2000. Office Fax: 713-830-2001.*

RAUH, CARL STEPHEN, lawyer; b. Washington, Dec. 14, 1940; s. Joseph L. and Olie (Westheimer) R. AB, Columbia U., 1962; LL.B., U. Pa., 1965; LL.M., Georgetown U., 1968. Bar: D.C. 1966, U.S. Supreme Ct. 1969. Asst. U.S. atty. for D.C., 1966-69; atty. Dep. Atty Gen.'s Office Dept. Justice, Washington, 1969-71; 1st asst. atty. gen. U.S. V.I., 1971-73; prin. asst. U.S. atty. for D.C., 1974-79; U.S. atty. for D.C., 1979; ptnr. Dunnells, Duvall, Bennett & Porter, Washington, 1980-90, Skadden, Arps, Slate, Meagher & Flom, Washington, 1990—. Mem. D.C. Jud. Nomination Commn., 1985-90. Recipient Dir.'s award Dept. Justice, 1976; Atty. Gen.'s Disting. Service award, 1980 Fellow Am. Coll. Trial Lawyers; mem. ABA, D.C. Bar Assn., Nat. Assn. Former U.S. Attys., Asst. U.S. Attys. Assn. (Harold J. Sullivan award 1980). Office: 1440 New York Ave NW Washington DC 20005-2111 Office Phone: 202-371-7000.

RAUH, LINDA ANN, rehabilitation services professional, counselor; d. John Matthew and Edna Ruth Rauh. MA in Counseling Edn., Kean U., 1997. Cert. counselor Nat. Bd. for Cert. Counselors, clin. hypnotherapist Md., psychosocial rehab. practitioner Md., marriage and family therapist N.J., lic. profl. counselor. Sr. counselor Bridgeway Rehab. Svcs., Inc., Elizabeth, NJ, 1999—2001, dir. staff devel. and quality improvement, 2001—. Clinician SERV Behavioral Healthcare, Elizabeth, 1997—99. Counselor Ctr. for Hope Hospice, Linden, NJ, 1996—97. Mem.: Am. Mental Health Counselors Assn., N.J. Counseling Assn. (Grad. Student of Yr. award 1997). Avocations: guitar, reading, swimming. Office: Bridgeway Rehab Svcs Inc 615 N Broad St Elizabeth NJ 07208 Office Fax: 908-355-6668. Personal E-mail: msrauh@comcast.net. E-mail: linda.rauh@bridgewayinc.com.

RAUL, ALAN CHARLES, lawyer; b. Bronx, NY, Sept. 9, 1954; s. Eugene and Eduarda (Müller-Mañas) R.; m. Mary Tinsley, Jan. 30, 1988; children: Caroline Tinsley, William Eduardo Tinsley, Alexander Tinsley. AB magna cum laude, Harvard U., 1975, MPA, 1977; JD, Yale U., 1980. Bar: N.Y. 1982, D.C. 1982, U.S. Ct. Appeals (D.C. cir.) 1982, U.S. Supreme Ct. 1988. Law clk. to judge U.S. Ct. Appeals (D.C. cir.), Washington, 1980-81; assoc. Debevoise & Plimpton LLP, NYC, 1981-86; assoc. counsel to Pres. The White House, Washington, 1986-88; gen. counsel Office Mgmt. & Budget, Exec. Office of the Pres., Washington, 1988-89, USDA, Washington, 1989-93; prin. Beveridge & Diamond P.C., Washington, 1993-97; ptnr. Sidley Austin LLP, Washington, 1997—. Vice chmn., Pres. Oversight Bd. on Privacy and Civil Liberties, 2006-08. Author: (book) Privacy and the Digital State, 2001. Co-chair, co-founder Lawyers Have Heart; chmn. bd. USDA Grad. Sch., 1991-93; bd. dirs. Nation's Capital affiliate Am. Heart Assn., 1993-97, Greater Washington region, 2002-; bd. dir. Wash. Tennis and Edn. Found., 2007-; treas., dir. Citizens Assn. Georgetown, 1993-97; mem. adv. coun. Atlantic Legal Found., 2001—. Recipient Disting. Achievement award Am. Heart Assn., 1991, Vol. of Yr. award, 1993, Lifetime Achievement award, 1999, Outstanding Support award 2006. Mem. ABA (chmn. com. on nat. security and internat. law 1990-92, coun. sect. internat. law and practice 1992-98, standing com. on election law 1995-99, sect. internat. law and practice govt. affairs officer 1996-98, coun. sect. adminstrv. law and regulatory practice 2004-05), Assn. of Bar of City of N.Y. (chmn. subcom. on Cen. Am. issues 1985, mem. com. on inter-Am. affairs 1983), Federalist Soc. (mem. nat. practitioners adv. coun., chair environ. and property rights practice group 1996-99), Coun. on Fgn. Rels. Office: Sidley Austin LLP 1501 K St NW Washington DC 20005 Office Phone: 202-736-8477. Business E-Mail: araul@sidley.com.

RAULINAITIS, PRANAS ALGIS, electronics executive, consultant; b. Kaunas, Lithuania, May 13, 1927; came to U.S., 1954, naturalized, 1960; s. Pranas Viktoras and Paulina (Gervaite) R.; m. Angele Staugaityte, Oct. 4, 1952; 1 son, Pranas Darius. With Commonwealth Rys. of Australia, Melbourne, 1949-53; asst. to fin. acct. Kitchen & Sons, Pty. Ltd., Melbourne, 1953-54; v.p. photo divsn. Interphoto Corp., LA, 1954-71; sr. v.p. fin., sec. Craig Corp., LA, 1971-87; pres. PAR Enterprises, Burbank, Calif., 1987—. Adviser Ministry Fgn. Affairs Republic of Lithuania, 1992; asst. sec. M & F Corp. Enterprises, Ltd., Chgo., 2004-07. Former pres. Lithuanian Am. Coun., Inc. of Calif.; bd. dirs. Lithuanian-Am. Assns.; founder, former dir., v.p. Baltic Am. Freedom League; former mem. Am. Soc. Internat. Law. Home and Office: PAR Enterprises 1501 W Riverside Dr Burbank CA 91506-3027

RAUM, HANS L., librarian; b. Phila., July 26, 1940; s. Hans Leonhard and Eleonore Beatrice Raum. BA, Pa. State U., Univ. Pk., 1962; MLS, Drexel U., Phila., 1964. Edn. libr. State Libr. NJ, Trenton, 1964; asst. libr. Pa. State U., 1965—67, assoc. undergrad. libr., 1967—72; asst. libr. & head pub. svcs. Castleton State Coll., Vt., 1972—75; asst. libr. Middlebury Coll., Vt., 1975—77, assoc. coll. libr., 1977—2007, curator, Vt. collection, 2007—. Mem., fed. depository libr. coun. to pub. printer GPO, Washington, 1985—88; trustee Sheldon Mus., Middlebury, 1999—2005. Bd. dir. Cornwall Hist. Soc., Vt., 2003—07. Mem.: ALA (chair, bibliography & indexes com., reference svcs. divsn. 1970—73), Vt. Libr. Assn. (chair, intellectual freedom com. 1982—83). Avocations: photography, hiking, scuba diving. Home: 2663 West St Cornwall VT 05753 Office: Middlebury Coll 110 Storrs Ave Middlebury VT 05753 Office Fax: 802-443-5698. Business E-Mail: raum@middlebury.edu.

RAUM, MARY BETH, performing arts educator; b. Takoma Park, Md., Oct. 14, 1957; d. Lawrence Arthur and Catherine Tompkins Raum. BS cum laude, U. Md., 1979; M in Adminstrv. Sci. magna cum laude, Johns Hopkins U., 1979; PhD summa cum laude, U. Wash., 1992. Adminstr. Johns Hopkins U./APL, Laurel, Md., 1976—82; adj. faculty/tech. mgmt U. Md. Open Univ., College Park, 1980—84; cons. Lawrence A. Raum & Assocs., Inc., Tacoma, 1982—92; doctoral rsch. assoc. George Washington U., Washington, 1983; asst. prof. orgnl. leadership Chapman U., Bangor, Wash., 1984—2005; adj. grad. faculty City U., Silverdale, Wash., 1986—88; corps de ballet/instr. Pacific Regional Ballet, Bremerton, Wash., 1996—2004; doctoral rsch. assoc. U. Wash., Seattle; ballet instr. MK Ballet Studio, Bremerton, Wash.; adj. faculty Pacific U., Dept. Econs., 2005; nat. security decision making prof. Naval War Coll., 2006—, dir. effective command and staff decision making, 2007. Ballet mistress Pacific Regional Ballet, Bremerton, Wash., 2002—. Classical dance pointe, Raymonda (High Second Pl. Regional Dance Competition, 2002), character dance, Untitled (Internat. Dance Competition Sterling Silver Champion, 2001), classical ballet pointe, Raymonda (Dance Magic Regional High Score 2nd Pl., 2002), Spanish character dance, Voz de la Referencia (Regional lst Pl. & Championship High Score Adult Trophy, 2002)., NSF grantee, 1985. Mem.: Soc. Judgement and Decision Making, European Assn. Decision Making, Women in Internat. Security, Women in Aviation Internat., Phi Kappa Phi. Methodist. Avocation: free lance writer. Office: Naval War Coll 686 Cushing Rd Newport RI 02840 Home: 97 Narragansett Ave Newport RI 02840-6903 Personal E-mail: maryraumphd@aol.com. Business E-Mail: mary.raum@nwc.navy.mil.

RAUNIAR, RUPAK, management educator; b. Kathmandu, Nepal, Apr. 27, 1972; s. P.P. and Madhuri Rauniar; m. Samhita Shah, June 23, 2004; children: Aashvi, Amaani. PhD in Mfg. Mgmt. and Engring., U. Toledo, 2002. Cert. in profl. project mgmt. Project Mgmt. Inst. Product mgr. Novell Unlimited Software Inc., Kathmandu, 1995—96; mgmt. cons. PriceWaterHouse Coopers, Phila., 1998—2000; asst. prof. Jackson State U., Miss., 2002—06, U. St. Thomas, Houston, 2006—. Program com. mem. Decision Scis. Inst., Atlanta, 2006—; rsch. asst. U. Toledo, 2000. Rep. UN Global Compact, PRME, NYC, 2007; asst. sec. Nepalese Assn. Houston, 2006. Recipient Mahendra Bidhya Bhusan medal, Ministry Edn., Govt. Nepal, 2006; scholar Colombo Plan, Govt. India, 1991—95; Instl. Rsch. grant, Jackson State U., 2006, Summer Rsch. grant, 2005, Cameron Sch. Bus., 2008. Mem.: Inst. Ops. Mgmt. Soc., Prodn. and Ops. Mgmt. Soc., Acad. Mgmt., Decision Scis. Inst. (Cert. of Appreciation 2007—08), Project Mgmt. Inst. Achievements include research in in integrated product development and commerce. Avocations: fishing, camping, travel, mountain climbing. Home: 12105 Amber Creek Dr Pearland TX 77584 Office: Cameron Sch Bus 3800 Montrose Blvd Houston TX 77006 Business E-Mail: rauniar@stthom.edu.

RAUP, DAVID MALCOLM, paleontology educator; b. Boston, Apr. 24, 1933; s. Hugh Miller and Lucy (Gibson) R.; m. Susan Creer Shepard, Aug. 25, 1956; 1 son, Mitchell D.; m. Judith T. Yamamoto, May 30, 1987. BS, U. Chgo., 1953; MA, Harvard U., 1955, PhD, 1957. Instr. Calif. Inst. Tech., 1956-57; mem. faculty Johns Hopkins U., 1957-65, assoc. prof., 1963-65; mem. faculty U. Rochester, 1965-78, prof. geology, 1966-78, chmn. dept. geol. scis., 1968-71, dir. Center for Evolution and Paleobiology, 1977-78; curator geology, chmn. dept. geology Field Mus. Natural History, Chgo., 1978-80, dean of sci., 1980-82; prof. geophys. sci. U. Chgo., 1980-95, chmn. dept., 1982-85, Sewell L. Avery disting. service prof., 1984-95; prof. emeritus, Sewell L. Avery disting. svc. prof. emeritus, 1995—. Geologist U.S. Geol. Survey, part-time, 1959-77; vis. prof. U. Tubingen, Germany, 1965, 72 Author: (with S. Stanley) Principles of Paleontology, 1971, 78, The Nemesis Affair, 1986, 2d edit., 1999, Extinction: Bad Genes of Bad Luck?, 1991; editor: (with B. Kummel) Handbook of Paleontological Techniques, 1965; contbr. articles to profl. jours. Recipient Best Paper award Jour. Paleontology, 1966; Schuchert award Paleontol. Soc., 1973; grantee Calif. Rsch. Corp., 1955-56, Am. Assn. Petroleum Geologists, 1957, Am. Philos. Soc., 1957, NSF, 1960-66, 75-81, Chem. Soc., 1965-71, NASA, 1983-95. Mem. AAAS, Am. Acad. Arts and Scis., Nat. Acad. Sci., Paleontol. Soc. (pres. 1976-77, medal 1997), Am. Soc. Naturalists (v.p. 1983), Am. Philos. Soc. Home: 423 Johnson Dr Washington Island WI 54246-9753

RAUSCHENBERG, BRADFORD LEE, retired museum program director; b. Atlanta, Sept. 11, 1940; BS in Archaeology and Biology, Ga. State Coll., 1963; MA in History, Wake Forest U., 1995; PhD (hon.), Kendal Coll. Arts and Design, 2006. Archaeologist Ga. Hist. Commn., 1963-64; site supr., asst. Stanley South, State Archaeologist of N.C., 1964-66; antiquarian, asst. Dir. Restoration Old Salem, Inc., Winston-Salem, NC, 1966-73; asst. to dir. Mus. Early So. Decorative Arts, Winston-Salem, 1973-76, rsch. fellow, 1976-87, dir. rsch., 1987-93, Mus. Early So. Decorative Arts and Old Salem, Inc., Winston-Salem, 1993—, sr. fellow emeritus. Cons., lectr. in field. Author: British Regional Carving (1600-1640), and Furniture (1600-1800), 1984, Wachovia Historical Society: 1895-1995, 1995, Charleston Furniture, 1680-1820, 3 vols., 2003. With USCG, 1964-72. Recipient Halifax Resolves award, 1986; grantee NEH, 1972-81, Kaufman Americana Found., 1981-82. Mem. Am. Ceramic Circle (grantee), Orgn. Am. Historians, No. Ceramic Soc., So. Hist. Assn., Friends of Swiss Ceramic Circle, Regional Furniture Soc., Furniture History Soc., Soc. Hist. Archaeology, Soc. Post-Medieval Archaeology, Soc. Historians Early Am. Republic. Address: 221 Harmon Ct Winston Salem NC 27106-4613 Personal E-mail: k4blr@triad.rr.com.

RAUSCHENBERGER, ROBERT, psychologist, educator; s. Peter Hans and Hubertine Rauschenberger. PhD, Johns Hopkins U., Balt., 2001. Prin. rsch. scientist Siemens Corp. Rsch., Princeton, NJ, 2005—; adj. prof. Simon Fraser U., Vancouver, Bc, Canada, 2008—. Vis. scholar MIT, Cambridge, Mass., 2004—05; assoc. Harvard U., Cambridge, 2004—05; rsch. social scientist U. Ariz., 2004—05. Contbr. scientific papers. Grantee, NSF, 2004—07. Office: Siemens Corp Rsch 755 College Rd E Princeton NJ 08540

RAUSCHENBUSCH, STEPHANIE, artist, educator, poet; b. Washington, July 27, 1942; d. Stephen and Josephine Burns Raushenbush; m. Joseph Marchant Hayman, Dec. 29, 1984; m. Louis R. Rowan, June 20, 1964 (div. June 20, 1979); 1 child, Quentin Rowan. BA magna cum laude, Radcliffe Coll., Cambridge, Mass., 1964; MA summa cum laude, Columbia U., NYC, 1966. Treas. Noho Gallery, NYC, 1999—2007; docent Bklyn. Mus. Art, 2007—. One-woman shows include Noho Gallery, NYC, 1983, 1987, 1989, 1991, 1993, 1995, 1997, 1999, 2002, 2005, 2007—, exhibited in group shows at Woodstock (NY) Guild, 1986, Art and the Law traveling exhibit, 1988—1889, Biennale d'Arte Contemporanea, Florence, 2001, in pvt. collections; author: (book of poetry) The Heart's Ice Thaws, 1999; contbr. poetry to lit. jours.; exhibitions include, 1986—. Trustee Friends Sem., NYC, 1998—2001. Grantee Kent fellowship grad. studies, Danforth Found., 1966—70; fellow, Woodrow Wilson Found., 1964—65. Mem.: Nat. Assn. Women Artists, N.Y. Soc. Women Artists (pres. 2006—), Women's Caucus for Art, Catherine Lorillard Wolfe Art Club. Democrat. Mem. Soc. Of Friends. Avocation: gardening. Home: 46 Sherman St Brooklyn NY 11215 Home Phone: 718-832-0161. E-mail: srauschenbusch@earthlink.net.

RAUSCHER, BERNARD JOSEPH, astrophysicist; b. Bethesda, Md., Jan. 2, 1963; s. Bernard Joseph Rauscher and Helen Louis Morgan; life ptnr. Francesca Galbani. PhD, U. Chgo., 1993. Postdoc. rsch. assoc. U. Chgo., 1993—95; lectr. physics U. Durham, NC, 1995—99; asst. scientist Space Telescope Sci. Inst., Balt., 1999—2003; astrophysicist NASA Goddard Space Flight Ctr., Greenbelt, Md., 2003—, prin.

investigator james webb space telescope nr. infrared spectrograph detector subsystem, 2003—, dep. project scientist, james webb space telescope integrated sci. instruments module, 2003—. Recipient Congl. Space Act award, NASA, 2004. Mem.: Am. Astron. Soc. Achievements include research in part of a team that deployed a 60-cm infrared telescope to the earth's south pole. Avocations: bicycling, skiing, scuba diving, langages (french & italian), travel. Office: NASA Goddard Space Flight Ctr Mail Code 665 B21 Rm 048 Greenbelt MD 20771 Business E-Mail: bernard.j.rauscher@nasa.gov.

RAUSHENBUSH, WALTER BRANDEIS, retired law educator; b. Madison, Wis., June 13, 1928; s. Paul A. and Elizabeth (Brandeis) R.; m. Marylu de Watteville, May 3, 1956; children: Lorraine Elizabeth, Richard Walter, Carla de Watteville, Paul Brandeis. AB magna cum laude in Govt., Harvard U., 1950; JD with high honors, U. Wis., 1953. Bar: Wis. 1953. Ptnr. LaFollette, Sinykin & Doyle, Madison, 1956-58; mem. faculty U. Wis., Madison, 1958—, prof. law, 1966-95, prof. emeritus, 1995—; vis. prof. law U. San Diego, 1992—94, 1996—; project dir. real estate transfer study Am. Bar Found., 1967-72. Trustee nat. Law Sch. Admission Coun., 1968-70, 72-95, chmn. pre-law com., 1970-74, chmn. svcs. com., 1976-78, pres., 1980-82; legal advisor Madison Citizens Fair Housing, 1961-63, Wis. Citizens Family Planning, 1965-73; real property drafting com. Multistate Bar Exam., 1986-2002. Author: Wisconsin Construction Lien Law, 1974, (with others) Wisconsin Real Estate Law, 1984, 4th edit., 1994, Brown on Personal Property, 3d edit., 1975, Real Estate Transactions Cases and Materials, 1997. With USAF, 1953-56, col. Res. ret. Mem. ABA, State Bar Wis., Order of Coif, Stage Harbor Yacht Club (Chatham, Mass.), Cape Cod Nat. Golf Club (Harwich, Mass.), Phi Beta Kappa, Phi Delta Phi (province pres. 1963-75). Presbyterian (Elder). Home: Unit 908 1730 Avenida Del Mundo Coronado CA 92118-3026

RAUSSER, GORDON C(LYDE), agricultural and resource economics educator; b. Lodi, Calif., July 21, 1943; s. Elmer A. and Doyve Ester (Meyers) R.; children: Sloan, Stephanie, Paige. BS summa cum laude, Calif. State U., 1965; MS with highest honors, U. Calif., Davis, 1968, PhD with highest honors, 1971. Prof. econs. and agrl. econs. U. Calif., Davis, 1969-74; vis. prof. U. Chgo., 1972-74; prof. econs. and stats. Iowa State U., 1974-75; prof. bus. adminstrn. Harvard U., 1975-78; prof., chmn. dept. agrl. and resource econs. U. Calif., Berkeley, 1979-85, 93-94, Robert Gordon Sproul disting. prof., 1985—, dean nat. resources, 1994-2000; dir. Giannini Found., Berkeley, 1984-86. Vis. prof. Hebrew U. and Ben-Gurion U., Israel, 1978; Ford Found. vis. prof., Argentina, 72; spl. cons. and sr. economist Coun. Econ. Advisors, 1986—87; chief economist AID, 1988—90; advisor econ. rsch. svc. USDA, 1978—80, 1986—88, Agr. Can., 1977—79, Bur. Agrl. Econs., Australia, 1987, U.S. Office Mgmt. and Budget, 1986; mem., chmn. planning com. Sch. Bus. Adminstrn. U. Calif., Berkeley, 1986—87, mem. adv. com. Agrl. Issues Ctr., 1984—85, mem. planning com. Agrl. and Natural Resources Program, 1986, mem. econs. programs evaluation com., 1987—88; mem. Citrus Planning Commn., Brazil, 1984; pres. Inst. for Policy Reform, Washington, 1989—94; prin., founder Law & Econ. Cons. Group, Berkeley, Washington, Chgo., NYC, 1990—2000; sr. cons. CRA Internat., 2000—06. Author: Macroeconomic Environment for U.S. Agricultural Policy, Alternative Agricultural and Food Policies and the 1985 Farm Bill, The Emergence of Market Economies in Eastern Europe, New Directions in Econometric Modeling and Forecasting, Dynamics of Agricultural Systems: Economic Prediction and Control, Quantitative Methods in Agricultural Economics, GATT Negotiations and the Political Economy of Policy Reform; co-editor: Handbook of Agricultural Economics, Vol. 2A, 2002, Vol. 2B, 2002, Vol. 1A, 2001, Vol. 1B, 2001; editor Decision-Making in Business and Economics, 1977-79, Am. Jour. Agrl. Econs., 1983-86, Ann. Rev. Resource Econs., 2006. Mem. western nutrition ctr. coordinating com. USDA, 1980-83; mem. Arab-Am. Coun. for Cultural and Econ. Exch., 1979-81; bd. dirs. Giannini Found. Agrl. Econs., 1979-84, mem. exec. com., 1979-84; mem. planning com. Berkeley Food Coop., 1980-83, planning com. for food policy Resources for the Future, 1984-85; mem. adv. com. Calif. State Dept. Agr., 1982-84; bd. dirs. Am. Agrl. Econs. Awards. Grantee USDA, NSF, World Bank, Chgo. Merc. Exch., U.S. Bur. Mines; Fulbright scholar, Australia, 1987; Sr. fellow Resources for Future, 1984-85. Fellow: AAAS, Am. Agrl. Econs. Assn. (outstanding enduring rsch. contbn. com. 1982—84, outstanding PhD dissertation com. 1974—76, chmn. outstanding article com. 1983—86, rsch. awards of merit 1976, 1978, 1980, 1982, 1986, 1989, 1992, Pub. Enduring quality award 1993, rsch. awards of merit 1993, Disting. Policy Contbn. award 1993, rsch. awards of merit 1994, 2000, 2001), Am. Statis. Assn.; mem.: Coll. Natural Resources Citation, Western Agrl. Econ. Assn. (Best Pub. Rsch. award 1978, Outstanding Pub. Rsch. award 1994), Ops. Rsch. Soc., Math. Assn. Am., Econometric Soc., Am. Acad. Polit. and Social Sci., Am. Econ. Assn., Commonwealth Club (dir. agr. study group 1983—84), Alpha Zeta, Alpha Gamma Rho. Home: 661 San Luis Rd Berkeley CA 94707-1725 Office: U Calif Berkeley ARE 230 Giannini Hall Berkeley CA 94720-3310 Business E-Mail: rausser@are.berkeley.edu.

RAUT, USHA, physics professor; d. Sivaram and Rajalakshmi Chidambaram; m. Sanjay Sumant Raut, Dec. 7, 1979; children: Alex Vikrum, Eric Keshuv, Ryan Vittal. PhD, Indian Inst. Sci., Bangalore, 1981. Asst. prof. U. Wis. Platteville, 1987—89; instr. U. Wis. Stout, Menomonie, 2007—, prin. investigator, 2007—08. Asst. prof. Ctrl. Mich. U., Mount Pleasant, Wis., 1985—87. Contbr. scientific papers to profl. jours. Mem.: Am. Phys. Soc., Sigma Pi Sigma. Avocations: music, travel, reading. Office: Univ Wis Stout Dept Engring and Tech Fryklund Hall Menomonie WI 54751 Business E-Mail: rautu@uwstout.edu.

RAUTIOLA, NORMAN A., manufacturing executive; b. Hancock, Mich., Aug. 6, 1932; s. Arnold and Irene Rautiola; m. Sarah-Binah Rautiola, Dec. 5, 1997; children: Jeffrey, Jordan, Leijona, Niikolas, Ari. BS in Metal Engring., Mich. Tech. U., 1954; MBA, George Washington U., 1960. Engring. officer U.S. Air Force, Hamilton AFB, Calif., 1954—56; sr. patent examiner U.S. Patent Office, Washington, 1957—60; patent devel. mgr. Tex. Instruments, Dallas, 1960—65; asst. to president Bunker Ramo Corp., Canoga Park, Calif., 1965—66; dir., corp. devel. Sparton Corp., Jackson, Mich., 1966—68; pres. Nartron Corp., Reed City, Mich., 1968—; founder, chmn. Smart Power Sys. Inc., Sylvan Lake, Mich., 1986—. Dir. Smart Power Sys. Inc., Sylvan Lake, Mich., 1985—, Nartron Corp., Reed City, Mich., 1968—; chmn. Nonometal LLC, Birmingham, Mich., 2004—. Bd. of control Mich. Tech. U., Houghton, Mich., 2002—. Cpt. USAF, 1954—68. Mem.: IEEE (sr.). Achievements include patents in field. Office: Nartron Corp 5000 N US 131 Reed City MI 49677 Office Phone: 231-832-5525. Business E-Mail: hhuber@nartron.com.

RAUWERDINK, WILLIAM JAY, accountant; b. Sheboygan, Wis., Mar. 3, 1950; s. Harvard M. and Dorothy M. (Duenk) R.; m. Ann Catherine Geske, July 14, 1979; 1 child, Margaret Allene. BBA, U. Wis., 1972; MBA, Harvard U., 1974. CPA, N.Y., Mich., Mass. Ptnr. Deloitte & Touche, Detroit, 1978—93; exec. v.p., CFO, treas., sec. The MEDSTAT Group, Inc., Ann Arbor, Mich., 1994—96, Lason, Inc., Troy, Mich., 1996—2000; exec. v.p., CFO, treas. Hotwire.com, San Francisco, 2001; interim pres., CFO, Gyricon, LLC, Ann Arbor, 2002—04; mng. dir. BAM Investments, LLC, West Bloomfield, Mich., 2005—. Bd. dirs. Trinity Health Svcs., Novi, Mich. Mem. Wis. Bus. Alumni Assn. (bd. dirs. 1980-89, 92—, pres. 1984-85), Harvard Club (Boston). Mailing: 5382 Pembrooke Crossing Ct West Bloomfield MI 48322

RAVAL, MA FLORENA TENAZAS, retired pathologist; b. Philippines, June 20, 1939; arrived in U.S., 1964; d. Salvador U. Tenazas and Salvacion C. Torrefiel; m. Antonio S. Raval, Nov. 1961; children: Cynthia, Edwin, Jeffrey, Steven. MD, U. Santo Tomas, Philippines, 1962. Pathologist Detroit Med. Ctr., Harper U. Hosp., 1973—2004; asst. prof. Wayne State U., Detroit, pathology resident, 2001. Recipient Residents Faculty award; named one of Am. Top Physicians, Consumers Rsch. Coun. Am., Wash., 2004—05. Fellow: Coll. Am. Pathologists. Business E-Mail: antonflr@earthlink.net.

RAVANAS, PHILIPPE CLAUDE DOMINIQUE, management educator, consultant; b. Avignon, France, June 5, 1967; s. Pierre and Michele Ravanas; m. Suellen Beatrice Lillmars, June 19, 1999; 1 child, Isabelle Nancy. MBA, U. Wis., Madison, 1990; DESCAF, Ecole Superieure de Commerce de Marseille, Marseilles, France, 1989. Mgr., sponsorship Euro Disney, Marne la Vallee, France, 1992—96, 1996—98; dir., client devel. Christie's Auction House, London, 1998—99; tenured prof. Columbia Coll. Chgo., 2000—. Cons. Internat. Trade Ctr., Geneva, 2004—06, Nat. Geographics, Washington, 2001—. Co-author: (book) Marketing Planning for Culture and the Arts; contbr. articles to profl. jours. Mem.: Am. Mktg. Assn. Office: Columbia Coll Chgo AEMM Dept 600 S Michigan Chicago IL 60607 Business E-Mail: pravanas@colum.edu.

RAVDIN, PETER MARCUS, internist, educator, oncologist; b. June 3, 1949; MD, U. Miami Sch. Med., 1981; PhD in Neurobiology, Cornell U. Cert. Internal Medicine, Med. Oncology. Resident U. Wis., Madison, 1981—84, fellow, 1984—87; asst. prof. to clin. prof. med. oncology U. Tex. Health Sci. Ctr., San Antonio; rsch. prof. biostatistics U. Tex. MD Anderson Cancer Ctr., San Antonio; exec. officer Southwest Oncology Group. Spkr. in field. Prin. author (computer program) Adjuvant!; contbr. several articles to profl. jours.*

RAVECHÉ, HAROLD JOSEPH, academic administrator; b. NYC, Mar. 18, 1943; s. Harold Edward Raveche and Helen Patricia (DeVincent) Gravino; m. Elizabeth Marie Scott, Jan. 26, 1974; children: John Vincent, Justin Blaise, Bernice Helen, Elizabeth Ann. BA in Chemistry, Hofstra U., 1963; PhD in Phys. Chemistry, U. Calif., San Diego, 1968. NRC postdoctoral assoc. Nat. Bur. Stds., Gaithersburg, Md., 1968—70, rsch. chemist, 1970—78, chief thermophysics divsn., 1978—85; dean Sch. of Sci., prof. chemistry Rensselaer Poly. Inst., Troy, NY, 1985—88; pres. Stevens Inst. Tech., Hoboken, NJ, 1988—. Bd. dirs. Nat. West NJ and Bancorp, Atlantic Energy Inc.; commr. sci. and tech., NJ. Editor: Perspectives in Statistical Physics, 1980; contbr. articles to profl. jours. Pres. Potomac Highlands Citizens Assn., Md., 1978-80 Recipient Disting. Young Scientist of Yr. award Md. Acad. Scis., 1975, US Sr. Exec. Svc. award Nat. Bur. Stds., 1983, Equal Employment Opportunity award, 1984. Mem. AAAS (commn. sci. edn. 1972-75), Am. Phys. Soc. (adv. coun. 1975-78), Soc. Indsl. and Applied Math. (adv. bd. conf. on large-scale computational problems 1984-88), Am. Chem. Soc., Sigma Xi. Roman Catholic. Avocations: hiking, swimming, skiing, music, theater. Office: Stevens Inst Tech Office of Pres Castle Point On Hudson Hoboken NJ 07030 Office Phone: 201-216-5213. E-mail: hraveche@stevens.edu.*

RAVEN, ABBE, broadcast executive; b. NY, 1953; 1 child. BA in Theater, U. Buffalo, 1974; MA in Cinema and Theater, Hunter Coll. Prodn. mgr., stage mgr. Manhattan Theater Club, Bklyn. Acad. Music, NYC; mgr. prodn. Hearst/ABC Video Svcs.; dir. prodn. svcs. A&E TV Networks, 1984-88, sr. v.p. prodn., 1988—95; sr. v.p. programming and prodn. The History Channel and HTV Prodns., 1995-97; sr. v.p. programming The History Channel, 1997—2000, gen. mgr., exec. v.p., 2000—02, A&E Network-USA, pres., 2004—05; pres., CEO A&E TV Networks, 2005—. Instr. various edni. instns.; active competition com., chair 12 ann. ceremonies CableACE Awards. Recipient U. Buffalo Alumni award, National History Day Org. Corp. Leadership Award, 2000; named one of The 100 Most Powerful Women in Entertainment, Hollywood Reporter, 2006, 2007, The 100 Most Influential Women in NYC Bus., Crain's NY Bus., 2007; named to Hunter Coll. Hall of Fame. Mem.: NATAS, Nat. Acad. Cable Programming, Am. Women in Radio and TV, Women in Cable. Office: A&E TV Networks The Hearst Corp 235 E 45th St 9th Fl New York NY 10017-3305

RAVEN, BERTRAM H(ERBERT), psychology professor; b. Youngstown, Ohio, Sept. 26, 1926; s. Morris and Lillian R.; m. Celia Cutler, Jan. 21, 1961; children: Michelle G., Jonathan H. BA in psychology summa cum laude with great distinction, Ohio State U., 1949, MA in psychology, 1950; PhD in social psychology, U. Mich., 1953. Rsch. assoc. Rsch. Ctr. for Group Dynamics, Ann Arbor, Mich., 1952-54; lectr. psychology U. Mich., Ann Arbor, 1953-54; vis. prof. U. Nijmegen, U. Utrecht, Netherlands, 1954-55; psychologist RAND Corp., Santa Monica, Calif., 1955-56; prof. UCLA, 1956—, chair dept. psychology, 1983-88, prof. emeritus, 1991—. Vis. prof. Hebrew U., Jerusalem, 1962-63, U. Wash., Seattle, 1965, U. Hawaii, Honolulu, 1968, London Sch. Econs. and Polit. Sci., 1969-70; external examiner U. of the W.I., Trinidad and Jamaica, 1980—, rsch. assoc. Psychol. Rsch. Ctr., 1993—; participant Internat. Expert Conf. on Health Psychology, Tilburg, Netherlands, 1986; cons., expert witness in field, 1979—; mem. internat. adv. bd. Acad. Freedom, Bar-Ilan U., 2005—; mem. sci. bd. Kurt Lewin Ctr. Psychol. Rsch. Kazimierza Wielkiego U., Poland; affiliate prof. U. Haifa, 2006—. Author: (with others) People in Groups, 1976, Discovering Psychology, 1977, Social Psychology, 1983, Social Psychology: People in Groups (Chinese edit.), 1994; editor: (with others) Contemporary Health Services, 1982, Policy Studies Rev. Ann., 1980; editor: (with others) Lewinian Psychology, 2006; editor: Jour. Social Issues, 1969-74; mem. editl. bd. Jour. of Criminology and Social Psychology, 2001-, Revista de Psicologia de la Salud, 1995-; mem. adv. bd. Jour. Entrepreneurship, 2004-; contbr. articles to profl. jours. Co-dir. Tng. Program in Health Psychology, UCLA, 1979-88; cons. WHO, Manila, 1985-86; cons., expert witness various Calif. cts., 1978—; mem. bd. dir., UCLA Emeriti Assn., 2007-. Guggenheim fellow, Israel, 1962-63; Fulbright scholar Netherlands, 1954-55, Israel, 1962-63, Britain, 1969-70; recipient Citation from L.A. City Coun., 1966, 2006, Rsch. on Soc. power by Calif. Sch. of profl. psychology, L.A., 1991; NATO sr. fellow, Italy, 1989. Fellow APA (chair bd. social and ethical responsibility 1978-82, ethics com. 2003-06), Assn. Psychol. Sci., Soc. for Psychol. Study of Social Issues (pres. 1973-74, coun. 1995-97, Kurt Lewin award 1998), Soc. for Personality and Social Psychology; mem. AAAS, Am. Sociol. Assn., Internat. Assn. Applied Psychology, Soc. Exptl. Social Psychology, Assn. Advancement of Psychology (founding, bd. dirs. 1974-81), Internat. Soc. Polit. Psychology (governing coun. 1996-98), Interam. Psychol. Soc., Am. Psychology-Law Soc. Democrat. Jewish. Avocations: guitar, travel, international studies. Home: 2212 Camden Ave Los Angeles CA 90064-1906 Office: UCLA Dept Psychology Los Angeles CA 90095-1563 Office Phone: 310-825-2296.

RAVEN, FRANCIS HARVEY, mechanical engineer, educator; b. Erie, Pa., July 29, 1928; s. Frederick James and Eleanor Elizabeth (Sopp) R.; m. Therese Mary Strobel, June 21, 1952; children: Betty, Ann Raven McCarthy, Paul, John, Mary Raven Mansmann, Cathy, Linda. BS in Math., Gannon U., Erie, Pa., 1948; BSME, Pa. State U., University Park, 1950, MSME, 1951; PhD, Cornell U., Ithaca, NY, 1958. Design engr. Hamilton Standard div. United Techs., Hartford, Conn., 1951-54; instr. Cornell U., Ithaca, N.Y., 1954-58; asst. prof. mech. engring. U. Notre Dame, 1958-62, assoc. prof., 1962-66, prof., 1966—. Cons. microprocessor and computer control of robots and mech. systems; devel. Vector Loop Method (first analytical method for the design of mechanisms and cam systems.). Author: Automatic Control Engineering, 1961, 5th edit., 1995, Mathematics of Engineering Systems, 1966, Engineering Mechanics, 1973; pub. McGraw-Hill Book Co. Mem. ASME, Am. Soc. for Engring. Edn. (AT&T Teaching award 1968-69), Sigma Xi. Roman Catholic. Home Phone: 574-272-7865; Office Phone: 574-631-7381. Business E-Mail: fraven@nd.edu.

RAVEN, PATRICIA ELAINE (PENNY RAVEN), real estate broker, developer, columnist; b. Oakland, Calif., Apr. 27, 1943; d. Allen James and Patricia Elaine (McClure) Nichelini; m. Larry Joseph Raven, June 15, 1963; children: Laurence Tagge Allen, Corbyn Lance. Student, U. So. Calif., 1961—62, U. Calif., Fresno, 1962—63, Fresno City Coll., 1973. Model, Fresno, Calif., 1960—; owner, operator Del Mar Motel and apts., Fresno, 1963—64; owner R Pantry Markets, 1965—72, v.p., 1968—72; owner Holy Cow Meat Markets, Fresno, 1965—72; real estate developer, 1973; real estate broker, owner The Raven Co., Fresno, 1974—; owner Raven Alcohol Distillery, 1979—89; pres. Am. Gasohol, Inc., 1980—; spl. events cons. Royal Cruise Line, 1986. Co-author: National Handbook on Toll Roads, 1977; columnist: Party Line, Fresno Bee, 1978—87, Central Valley Homes & Lifestyles, 2003—; contbg. editor: Fresno Weekly, 2001—02, Fresno Mag. Lunch Ladies, 2006—; editor (home and gracious living editor): Fresno Mag., 2003—; actress: (TV miniseries) Fresno, 1986; (films) Pretty Woman, 1989; Princess Diaries 2, 2004. Pres. Fresno Cancer League, 1972—73, Jackson Sch. PTA, 1980—82; hon mem. Fresno Zool. Soc.; commr. Fresno County Hist. Landmarks and Records Commn., 2005—; Democratic candidate for lt. gov. Calif., 1978; Fresno County Dem. ctrl. com. alt., 1977; bd. dirs. Women's Symphony League, 1973—74; pres. Huntington Blvd. Homeowners Hist. Assn., 1987—97, officer, 1997—2008. Recipient Mayor's award, 1976, Hon. Svc. award, Jackson Sch. PTA, 1982, Appreciation award, United Cerebral Palsy Assn., 1982—86, Fresno Zool. Soc., 1982, Calif. State Senate, 1983, San Joaquin chpt. Assn. Gen. Contractors, 1983, Holland Sch., 1984, Huntington Blvd. Neighbors, 1985, proclamation in her honor, City of Fresno, 1985, others, San Joaquin Valley's Most Fashionable award, 1984, Appreciation award, Huntington Blvd. Neighbors, 1986, hon. mayor, City of Fresno, 1986; named Betty Crocker Homemaker of Tomorrow, 1961; named one of 50 Most Influential People in Fresno, 2007. Roman Catholic.

RAVEN, PETER HAMILTON, botanist, director; b. Shanghai, June 13, 1936; s. Walter Francis and Isabelle Marion (Breen) R.; children—Alice Catherine, Elizabeth Marie, Francis Clark, Kathryn Amelia. AB with highest honors, U. Calif.-Berkeley, 1957; PhD, UCLA, 1960; DSc (hon.), St. Louis U., 1982, Knox Coll., 1983, So. Ill. U., 1983, Miami U., 1986, U. Goteborg, 1987, Rutgers U., 1988, U. Mass., 1988, Leiden U., The Netherlands, 1990; HHD (hon.), Webster U., 1989; D.Sc. (hon.), Universidad Nacional de La Plata, Argentina, 1991, Westminster Coll., 1992, U. Mo., 1992, Washington U., 1993, U. Conn., 1993; DSc (hon.), U. Cordoba, Argentina, 1993. Taxonomist, curator Rancho Santa Ana Botanic Garden, Claremont, Calif., 1961-62; asst. prof., then assoc. prof. biol. scis. Stanford U., Calif., 1962-71; dir. Mo. Bot. Garden, St. Louis, 1971—; adj. prof. biology St. Louis U., 1973—; Engelmann prof. botany Washington U., St. Louis, 1971—; adj. prof. biology U. Mo., St. Louis, 1976—. Sr. rsch. fellow New Zealand Dept. Sci. and Indsl. Rsch., 1969-70; v.p. XIII Internat. Bot. Congress, Sydney, 1981; Home Sec. Nat. Acad. Scis., 1987—; chmn. report rev. com. NRC, 1989—; mem. pres. com. Adv. on Sci. and Tech., 1994—; hon. vice-chair 27th Internat. Geographical Cong., 1992; hon. v.p. XV Internt. Bot. Cong., Tokyo, 1993; mem. Nat. Sci. Bd., 1990-94; mem. jury Internat. St. Francis Prize for Environment, 1990-93; mem. exec. com. Joint Appeal by Religion and Sci. for Environment, 1991—; mem. external adv. bd. Com. on Peabody Mus., Yale U., 1992-94; mem. coun. World Resources Inst., 1992—; mem. adv. com. Africa Ctr. for Resources and Environment, 1992—, Third World Found. N.Am., 1993; mem. adv. com. to biodiversity com. Chinese Acad. Scis., 1993—; mem. Exec. Com. Round Table, St. Louis, 1993—; mem. hon. fgn. adv. bd. Botanical Garden Orgn. Thailand, 1993—. Author: Native Shrubs of Southern California, 1966, (with P.R. Ehrlich, R.W. Holm) Papers on Evolution, 1969, (with H. Curtis) Biology of Plants, 1971, 4th edit., 1986, (with R.F. Evert and S.E. Eichhorn) 5th edit., 1992, (with B. Berlin and D. Breedlove) Principles of Tzeltal Plant Classification, 1974, (with G.B. Johnson) Biology, 1986, 3d edit., 1992, Understanding Biology, 1988, 3d edit., 1995; editor: (with L.E. Gilbert) Coevolution of Animals and Plants, 1981, (with F.J. Radovsky & S.H. Sohmer) Biogeography of the Tropical Pacific, 1984, (with others) Topics in Plant Population Biology, 1979, (with K. Iwatsuki and W.J. Bock) Modern Aspects of Species, 1986; editor-in-chief Brittonia, 1963-66; mme. editorial bd. Flora Neotropica, 1965-84; editor (with D.E. Osterbrock) Origins and Extinctions, 1988, paperback, 1992, (with R.M. Polhill) Advances in Legume Systematics, 1981 (with L. Berg and G.B. Johnson) Environment, 1995; mem. editorial bd. Evolution, 1963-65, 76-79, Memoirs of N.Y. Botanical Garden, 1966-84, N.Am. Flora, 1966-84, Am. Naturalist, 1967-70, Annual Rev. Ecology and Systematics, 1971-75, Flora of Ecuador, 1974—, Evolutionary Theory, 1975—, Adansonia, 1976—, Jour. Biogeography, 1978—, Science, 1979-82, Proceedings of U.S. Nat. Acad. Scis., 1980-87, World Book, Inc., 1982-86, Diversity, 1985-90, Bothalia, 1985—, Serie Botánica of the Anales del Instituto de Biología UNAM, 1989, Ecol. Applications, 1989-92, others; mem. adv. bd. Applied Botany Abstracts, 1981—, Tropical Plant Sci. Research, 1982—, Darwiniana, 1985—; mem. internat. editl. com. Acta Botánica Mexicana, 1987—; mem. internat. editl. adv. bd. Candollea, 1995—; mem. editl. bd. Botanical Bulletin Academia Sinica, 1988—, Botanical Mag., 1988-92, Chinese Jour. of Botany, 1991—, Edinburgh Jour. of Botany, 1994—; co-chmn. editl. com. Flora of China, 1988—; advisor Plants Today, 1988-89; contbr. over 400 articles to profl. jours. Bd. curators U. Mo., 1985-90; commr. Tower Grove Park, St. Louis, 1971—; mem. Arnold Arboretum Vis. Com., 1974-81, chmn. 1976-81; bd. overseers Morris Arboretum, 1977-81; mem. sci. adv. bd. Nat. Tropical Botanical Garden, 1975—; mem. Smithsonian Council, 1985-90; chmn. St. Louis Area Mus. Collaborative, 1985-91, Commn. for Flora Neotropica, 1985—; mem. Commn. on Mus. for New Century, 1981-84; mem. sci. and engring. panel Com. on Scholarly Communication with People's Republic China, 1981-85; chmn. com. to visit dept. organismic and evolutionary biology Harvard U., 1982-84, mem. 84-85; edtl. adv. bd. John Simon Guggenheim Meml. Found., 1986—; research assoc. botany Bernice P. Bishop Mus., 1985—; hon. trustee Acad. Sci. of St. Louis, 1986—; chmn. Internat. Union for the Conservation of Nature, World Wildlife Fund, 1984-87, hon. chmn. 1987-90; mem. adv. and tech. bd. Fundación de Parques Nacionales and Fundación Neotrópica, Costa Rica, 1988—; mem. Nat. Coun. World Wildlife Fund and Conservation Foun., 1989—, U.S. bd. dirs. 1983-88, bd. dirs. Conservation Found.,

1985-88, sci. adv. com. Conservation Internat., 1988—, chmn's. coun., 1989, World Wildlife Fund, 1987-90, Conservation Found., 1989—, Found. Flora Malesianna, 1992—, Sci. Svc., 1993—; hon. scientific adv. com. XVII Pacific Sci. Congress, 1990-91; adv. bd. The Winslow Found., 1993—, The Internat. Sci. Camp The Earth We Share, 1993—; exec. bd. Internat. Sci. Found. for the Former Soviet Union, 1992—; internat. adv. bd. Fifth ICSEB Congress, Hungary, 1994—. Commn. mem. U.S. MAB, 1994-95. Recipient A.P. DeCandolle prize, Geneva, 1970; Disting. Service award Japan Am. Soc. So. Calif., 1977; award of Merit, Bot. Soc. Am., 1977; Achievement medal Garden Club Am., 1978; Willdenow medal Berlin Bot. Garden, 1979; Disting. Service award Am. Inst. Biol. Scis., 1981; Joseph Priestly medal, Dickinson Coll., 1982; Gold Seal medal Nat. Council of State Garden Clubs, 1982; Internat. Environ. Leadership medal UN Environ. Program, 1982; Spl. citiation Doña Dorís Yankelewitz de Monge, 1985, Internat. Prize for Biology, Govt. Japan, 1986, Hutchinson medal Chgo. Hort. Soc., 1986, Archie F. Carr medal, 1987, Global 500 Honor Roll UN Environ. Program, 1987, Am. Fuchsia Soc. Achievement Medal, 1987, George Robert White Medal of Honor Mass. Horticultural Soc., 1987, Robert Allerton Medal Nat. Tropical Bot. Garden, 1988, Nat. Conservation Achievement award Nat. Wildlife Fedn., 1989, Delmer S. Fahrney medal Franklin Inst., Phila., 1989, (with E.O. Wilson) Environ. prize Institut de la Vie (Paris), 1990, Order of Golden Ark (officer), The Netherlands, 1990, award for Support of Sci. Coun. Sci. Soc. Pres., 1990, (with Norman Myers) Volvo Environ. prize, 1992, Pres.'s Conservation Achievement Awd., 1993, Nature Conservancyvement award TNC, 1993, Internat. award Internat. Inst. of St. Louis, 1994, Founder's Coun. Centennial Merit award The Field Mus. of Natural History, 1994, Sword of St. Ignatius Loyola award St. Louis U., 1994, Tyler Environ. Achievement prize, 1994, and numerous other botanical awards and honors; Guggenheim fellow, 1969-70; John D. and Catherine T. MacArthur Found. fellow, 1985-90, NSF postdoctoral fellow, Brit. Mus. London, 1960-61. Fellow Am. Acad. Arts and Scis. (com. on membership 1980-82), Linnean Soc. London (fgn. mem.), Calif. Acad. Scis. (CAS Fellow, Fellows' medal 1988), AAAS, Indian Nat. Sci. Acad., Third World Acad. Scis., World Acad. Art & Sci.; mem. NSF (systematic biology panel 1973-76, chmn. adv. com. for biol. behavioral and social scis. 1984-90), NAS (com. on human rights 1984-87, home sec. 1987—), Royal Danish Acad. Scis. and Letters (fgn. hon.), Royal Swedish Acad. Scis. (fgn.), Royal Soc. New Zealand (hon.), NRC (gov. bd. 1983-86, 87-88, chmn. com. on research priorities in tropical biology 1977-79, assembly life scis. 1979-81, com. on selected research problems in humid tropics 1980-82, commn. internat. relations 1981-82), Calif. Bot. Soc. (v.p. 1968-69), Am. Soc. Plant Taxonomists (pres. 1972), Assn. Systematics Collections (pres. 1980-82, Fed. Council Arts and Humanities, Nat. Geographic Soc. (com. on research and exploration 1982—), Internat. Orgn. Plant Biosystematists (v.p. 1989-92, pres. 92-95), Internat. Assn. for Plant Taxonomy (council 1981—), Orgn. Tropical Studies (treas. 1981-84, v.p. devel. 1984-85, pres. 1985-88, past pres. 1988-90, bd. dirs. 1981-91), Am. Soc. Naturalists (pres. 1983), Miller Inst. Basic Research in Sci. (adv. bd. 1983-89), Am. Inst. Biol. Scis. (pres. 1983-84), Mo. Acad. Scis., Geol. Soc. Am., Bot. Soc. Am. (pres. 1975, chmn. com. on sci. exchange with People's Republic China 1978-84), Assn. Tropical Biology (bd. dirs. 1981-85), Am. Assn. Mus. (exec. com. 1980-83, named to Centennial Honor Roll, 2006), Assn. Sci. Mus. Dirs., Assn. Pacific Systematists, Sociedad Argentina de Botanica (socio honorario), Fundación Miguel Lillo (hon.), Soc. Systematic Zool., Sociedad Botánica de México (life), Assn. pour l'Etude Taxonomique de la Flore d'Afrique Tropicale, Orgn. for Phyto-Taxonomic Investigation of Mediterranean Area (council 1975-89), All-Union Botanical Soc. USSR (hon. fgn. mem.), Accademia Nazionale delle Scienze detta dei XL (fgn.), Am. Philosophical Soc, Russian Acad. Scis. (fgn. mem.), Nat. Acad. Scis. India (fgn. fellow 1990—), Academia de Ciencias Exactas, Físicas y Naturales, Austrian Acad. Scis., Academia Chilena de Ciencias, Academia Nacional de Ciencias, Academy Scis. Ukraine, Chinese Acad. Scis., Nature Conservancy (Pres. Conservation Achievement Awd., 1993), Phi Beta Kappa, Sigma Xi Office: Missouri Botanical Garden PO Box 299 Saint Louis MO 63166-0299 Office Phone: 314-577-5111. Office Fax: 314-577-9595. E-mail: peter.raven@mobot.org.

RAVEN, RONALD JACOB, education educator, researcher, consultant; b. San Francisco, Jan. 7, 1935; s. Jacob and Ella (O'Connor) R.; m. Cynthia Opacinch; children— Michael, Julie. B.S., U. San Francisco, 1952-56; M.A., Calif. State U. at San Francisco, 1960; Ed.D., U. Calif.-Berkeley, 1965. Physics and chemistry tchr. Campbell High Sch., Calif., 1959-62; lectr. in biology Fullerton Coll., Calif., 1962-63; prof. SUNY-Amherst, 1965—96, prof. emeritus, 1996-, dir., grad. studies, 1972-79; mem. Grad. Sch. Execs. Com., 1972-79; vis. prof. U. Calif.-Berkeley, summer 1968, Ontario Inst. for Edn. Studies, summer 1970, U. Iowa, Iowa City, summer 1973, U. Minas Gerais, Belo Horizonte, Brazil, summer 1976; cons. NSF, Sci. Curiculum Improvement Study UC Berkeley, Nat. Assessment Ednl. Progress. Author tests: Raven Test of Logical Ops., 1980; Raven Test of Sci. Reasoning, 1982. Mem. editorial bd. Sci. Edn., 1970—93, Jour. Research in Sci. Teaching, 1970-83; sect. editor Sci. Edn., 1972-75. 1st lt. US Army-Armor, 1961-64. Recipient 30 Yr. Svc. award, SUNY-Buffalo, 1996. Fellow AAAS; mem. Assn. for Edn. Tchrs. Sci. (bd. dirs. 1973-76), Assn. for Research in Sci. Teaching (exec. bd., bd. dirs. 1976-80), Nat. Sci. Tchrs. Assn., Am. Ednl. Research Assn. Roman Catholic. Avocations: piano, tennis. Home: 53 Wellingwood Dr East Amherst NY 14051-1744

RAVENAL, EARL CEDRIC, international relations educator, writer; b. NYC, Mar. 29, 1931; s. Alan M. and Mildred S.; m. Carol Bird Myers, May 26, 1956; children: Cornelia Jane, John Brodhead, Rebecca Eliza. BA, Harvard U., 1952; postgrad., U. Cambridge, Eng., 1952-53; M.M.P. diploma, Harvard Bus. Sch., 1958; MA, Johns Hopkins U., 1971, PhD, 1975. Treas. Elbe File & Binder Co., Inc., Fall River, Mass., 1955-64, pres., 1965-67; dir. Asian div. systems analysis Office Sec. Def., Washington, 1967-69; prof. internat. relations Johns Hopkins U. Sch. Advanced Internat. Studies, Washington, 1973-78, Georgetown U. Sch. Fgn. Service, Washington, 1976—. Bd. advisors Ctr. for Def. Info., Washington, 1971-97, Ctr. for Study Conflict, 1983—; bd. dirs. Critical Rev. Author: (with others) Peace with China?, 1971, (with others) Atlantis Lost, 1976, Never Again, 1979, Toward World Security, 1978, Strategic Disengagement and World Peace, 1979, NATO's Unremarked Demise, 1979, Defining Def., 1984, NATO: The Tides of Discontent, 1985, Large-Scale Foreign Policy Change, 1989, Designing Defense, 1991, Defending America in an Uncontrollable World, 2005; contbg. editor Inquiry Mag., 1976-85, Critical Rev., 1987—; contbr. articles to profl. jours. Advisor Democratic Presdl. Campaign, 1972; advisor Jerry Brown Presdl. Campaign, 1976, Libertarian Presdl. Campaigns, 1980, 84. Served with JAGC U.S. Army, 1953-55. Henry fellow U. Cambridge, 1952-53; mem. faculty Salzburg Seminar in Am. Studies, 1977; fellow Bellagio Ctr. Rockefeller Found., 1975, Woodrow Wilson Internat. Ctr. for Scholars, 1973, Washington Ctr. of Fgn. Policy Research, 1974; sr. fellow Cato Inst., 1985-91, 97—. Mem. Council Fgn. Relations, Am. Polit. Sci. Assn., Internat. Inst. Strategic Studies, Fed. Am. Scientists, Internat. Studies Assn. Clubs: Cosmos (Washington); Harvard (NYC); Signet (Cambridge, Mass.); Tred Avon Yacht (Oxford, Md.). Libertarian. Home and Office: 4439 Cathedral Ave NW Washington DC 20016-3562

RAVENEL, SHANNON, book publishing professional; b. Charlotte, NC, Aug. 13, 1938; d. Elias Prioleau and Harriett Shannon (Steedman) R.; m. Dale Purves, May 25, 1968; children: Sara Blake, Harriett. BA, Hollins Coll., 1960. Mktg. asst., sch. dept. Holt, Rinehart & Winston, Inc., NYC, 1960-61; editl. asst. Houghton Mifflin Co., Boston, 1961-64, editor, 1964—70; editl. cons. pvt. practice, St. Louis, 1973-90; sr. editor, co-founder Algonquin Books of Chapel Hill, NC, 1982-91, editl. dir., 1991—2000; dir. Algonquin imprint Shannon Ravenel Books, 2001—. Series editor: Best American Short Stories, 1978-90; editor: Best American Short Stories of the Eighties, 1990, New Stories From the South, 1986-2005 Recipient Disting. Achievement award Coun. Lit. Mags. & Presses, NYC, 1990, R. Hunt Parker Meml. award for contbns. to the lit. of N.C., 2004. Mem. PEN Am. Ctr., Fellowship Southern Writers. Democrat. Office: Algonquin Books of Chapel Hill PO Box 2225 Chapel Hill NC 27515-2225 Business E-Mail: shannonr@algonquin.com.

RAVENELL, ALMA RENA, school librarian; d. Jeffrey J. and Alma V. Flowers; m. Donald E. Ravenell, Sept. 9, 1988; 1 child, Mario J. AS, Gadsden CC, Anniston, Ala., 1994; BS, Wiley Coll., Marshall, Tex., 1999; MS, U. North Tex., Denton, 2001. Libr. elem. schs. Hallsville Ind. Schs., Tex., 2001—02; libr. East Tex. Bapt. U., Marshall, 2002—. Libr. aide Marshall HS, 1999—2001. Bd. mem. Ct. Apptd. Spl. Adv., Marshall, 2007. With US Army, 1986—92, Ft. McClellan, Desert Storm. Mem.: LOEX. Office: East Tex Bapt Univ 1209 N Grove Marshall TX 75670 Office Phone: 903-923-2263. Office Fax: 903-935-3447. Business E-Mail: aravenell@etbu.edu.

RAVENHOLT, REIMERT THOROLF, epidemiologist, researcher; b. Milltown, Wis., Mar. 9, 1925; s. Ansgar Benedikt and Kristine Henriette (Petersen) R.; divorced; children: Janna, Mark, Lisa, Dane; m. Betty Butler Howell, Sept. 26, 1981. BS, U. Minn., 1948, MB, 1951, MD, 1952; MPH, U. Calif., Berkeley, 1956. Bd. cert. preventive medicine. Intern USPHS Hosp., San Francisco, 1951-52; epidemic intelligence service officer USPHS Communicable Disease Ctr., Atlanta, 1952-54; dir. epidemiology and communicable disease div. Seattle-King County Health Dept., 1954-61; epidemiology cons. European area USPHS, Paris, 1961-63; assoc. prof. preventive medicine U. Wash. Med. Sch., Seattle, 1963-66; dir. Office of Population, AID, Washington, 1966-79, World Health Surveys, Ctrs. for Disease Control, 1980-82; asst. dir. epidemiology and research Nat. Inst. Drug Abuse, Rockville, Md., 1982-84; chief epidemiology br. FDA, Rockville, Md., 1984-87; dir. World Health Surveys, Inc., Seattle, 1987-93; pres. Population Health Imperatives, Seattle, 1993—. Author/designer website Adventures in Epidemiology. Served with USPHS, 1951-54, 61-63. Recipient Disting Honor award AID, 1973, Hugh Moore Meml. award IPPF and Population Crisis Com., 1974. Fellow Am. Coll. Epidemiology, APHA (Carl Schultz award 1978), mem. Am. Coun. on Sci. and Health (bd. dirs.); mem. Cosmos Club (Washington). Independent. Achievements include discovery of cause of Meriwether Lewis' death of progressive neurosyphilis. Home: 3156 E Laurelhurst Dr NE Seattle WA 98105-5333 Personal E-mail: ravenrt@oz.net.

RAVENSTAHL, LUKE R., Mayor, Pittsburgh; b. Pitts., Pa., Feb. 6, 1980; s. Robert P. and Cindy Ravenstahl; m. Erin Lynn Feith, July 2004; 1 child, Cooper Luke. Attended, Mercyhurst Coll., U. Pitts.; BBA with honors, Washington and Jefferson Coll., 2002. Account mgr. for courier svc.; mem., Coun. Dist. 1 Pitts. City Coun., 2004—05, pres., 2005—06; mayor City of Pitts., 2006—. Bd. mem. City of Pitts. Mcpl. Pension Fund. Bd. pres. Neighborhood Enterprises; mem. Allegheny County Democratic Com., 1998—2004; bd. mem. Fireman's Relief and Pension Fund, Comprehensive Mcpl. Pension Trust Fund., Pitts. Cultural Trust, Sports and Exhbn. Authroity, Carnegie Libr.; bd. trustee Carnegie Mellon U.; mem. adv. bd. North Catholic HS; mem. Northside Cmty. Develop. Fund, City-County Summit Com. of Pub. Works, Parks, and Facilities. Office: Rm 512 City County Bldg 414 Grant St Pittsburgh PA 15219 Office Phone: 412-255-2626. Office Fax: 412-255-2687. Business E-Mail: mayorcompl@city.pittsburgh.pa.us.*

RAVETCH, JEFFREY VICTOR, molecular biologist, immunologist, educator; s. Sylvia and Paul H. Ravetch; m. Wendy Evans Joseph, Oct. 27, 2001. Grad., Yale U., New Haven; PhD in Genetics, Rockefeller U.; MD, Cornell U. Postdoctoral rschr. NIH; mem. faculty Meml. Sloan-Kettering Cancer Ctr. and Cornell Med. Coll., 1982; guest investigator lab. cellular physiology and immunology Rockefeller U., NYC, 1984, prof., 1996—, Theresa and Eugene M. Lang prof., 1997—, head of Leonard Wagner lab. molecular genetics and immunology. Mem. sci. adv. bd. Cancer Rsch. Inst., Irvington Inst. Med. Rsch., Damon Runyon Found.; co-founder, former dir. MacroGenics, Rockville, Md., 2000. Contbr. articles to profl. jours. Recipient Burroughs Wellcome Fund award in molecular parasitology, 1986, Willam B. Coley award, Cancer Rsch. Inst., 2007; named a Pew Scholar, 1985. Fellow: Am. Acad. Arts and Sciences, NAS; mem.: NAS Inst. Medicine, Am. Assn. Immunologists (Lee J. Howley Jr. award 2004, Huang Found. Meritorious Career award 2005). Office: Leonard Wagner Lab Molecular Genetics and Immunology Rockefeller U 1230 York Ave New York NY 10021 E-mail: ravetch@rockefeller.edu.*

RAVI, R., finance educator; Prof. ops. rsch. & computer sci. Carnegie Mellon U., Pitts., 1995—. Assoc. dean intellectual strategy Tepper Sch. Bus., CMU, Pitts., 2005—. Office: Tepper Sch Bus CMU 5000 Forbes Ave Pittsburgh PA 15213

RAVI, SUJITH, environmental scientist; s. Velayudhan Ravindran and B. Savitha; m. Anjana Vidyadharan. MS, U. Va., Charlottesville, 2005, PhD, 2008. Rsch. asst., tchg. asst. U. Va., 2003—08; postdoc. rsch. assoc. U. Ariz., Tucson, 2008—. Contbr. articles to sci. profl. publs. Recipient award, U. Va., 2004, 2007, Moore Rsch. award, 2007. Mem.: ESA, AGU. Personal E-mail: sujith@virginia.edu, sujithravi@gmail.com. Business E-Mail: sr9k@virginia.edu.

RAVICHANDRAN, NADARAJAH, civil engineer, researcher; PhD, U. Okla., Norman. Postdoc. U. Okla., 2006—07; asst. prof. Clemson U., SC, 2007—. Office: Clemson Univ 320 Lowry Hall Clemson SC 29634 Business E-Mail: nravic@clemson.edu.

RAVILISETTY, PADMANABHA RAO, research scientist; b. Chirala, Andhra Pradesh, India, July 10, 1951; s. Ramulu Ravilisetty and Nagarthnama Ravailisetty; m. Rama Devi Pasupulate, Oct. 22, 1980; children: Pavan Kumar, Sai Krishna. MSc in Tech., Andhra U., Waltair, India, 1975; PhD, Indian Inst. Tech., Kharagpur, 1980. Sr. rsch. asst. Indian Inst. Tech., Kharagpur, 1981—82; scientist Electrochem. Rsch. Inst., Karaikudi, 1985—90; vis. scientist U. Waterloo, Canada, 1990—92; materials scientist Thomas Electronics Inc., Wayne, NJ, 1992—94; sr. scientist Coloray Display Corp., Fremont, Calif., 1994—96; mgr. phosphor R & D Plasmaco, Inc., Highland, NY, 1996—2005; dir. R&D, Authentix, Inc., 2005—06; dir. phosphorous engring. Intematix Corp., Fremont, Calif., 2006—07; program leder SRI Internat., Menlo Pk., Calif., 2008—. Vis. fellow U. Sci. Tech. Languedoc, Montpellier, France, 1982—84; cons. Anapurna Agro Products, Hyderabad, India, 1984—86; mem. com. on color TV devel. Govt. of India, 1987—90; editor Bull. of Electrochemistry, 1985—90. Editor: Luminescence: Phenomena, Materials and Devices, 1992; contbr. articles to profl. jours. Grantee, Dept. Sci and Tech., Govt. of India, 1987—92, 1988—93, 1990—93, Dept. Transp., Govt. of India, 1988—90; rsch. fellow, Coun. Sci. Indsl. Rsch., Govt. of India, 1976—80, 1984—85. Mem.: IEEE (sr.), SPIE, Matter Rsch. Soc., Am. Chem. Soc., The Electrochem. Soc., Assn. Med. Physicians India (life), Luminescence Soc. India (life), Instrument Soc. India (life), Soc. Info. Display (sr.; chmn. (mid-atlantic chpt. sec.) 2002, 2004). Democrat-Npl. Achievements include development of nanomaterials used medical applications in solid state lighting, LCD and plasma display panels; 18 patents; several patents pending. Avocations: photography, swimming, gardening, coin collecting/numismatics, stamp collecting/philately. Office: 333 Ravenswood Ave Menlo Park CA 94025 Office Phone: 650-859-3259. Personal E-mail: ravilisetty2000@yahoo.com. Business E-Mail: ravi.rao@sri.com.

RAVINDER, UJWALA, research scientist; d. Ravinder and Pushpalatha Balaguru. BS in Engring. and Computer Sci., Osmania U., Hyderbad, India, 2000; MS in Computer Sci., U. Minn., Mpls., 2003. Rsch. asst. U. Minn., Mpls., 2000—03; sr. rsch. assoc. NASA Ames Rsch. Ctr., Moffett Field, Calif., 2003—. Recipient Merit cert., Math. Olympiad, 1991—94, Reading List award, Behavioral Representation In Modeling & Simulation Conf., 2004, Outstanding Paper award, SAE Internat. Jour.; scholar, Govt. of India, 1994—95, Govt. of Andhra Pradesh, India, 1994—96. Mem.: IEEE Sys. Man and Cybernetics Soc. (mem. tech. com. on soft computing), Toastmaster. Home: 7712 162ND ST Fresh Meadows NY 11366-1924 Business E-Mail: ujwala.ravinder@nasa.gov.

RAVINDRA, KADIYALA V, medical educator, director; b. Vishkhapatnam, Andhra Pradesh, India, July 18, 1964; s. Vishnu Vardhana Rao Kadiyala and Varalakshmi Kadiyala; m. Anuradha Sabapathi, Nov. 25, 1988; children: Vishnu Kiran Kadiyala, Shruthi Kadiyala. MD, JIPMER, Pondicherry, India, 1988, MS in Gen. Surgery, 1992; MBBS, Madras U., 1988; CM, Pondicherry U., 1991; Magister Chirurgia in Surg. Gastroenterology, SGPGIMS, Lucknow, India, 1994. Asst. prof. St.John's Med. coll., Bangalore, Karnataka, India, 1996—2000; clin. fellow in hepatobiliary surgery & transplantation St. James's U. hosp., Leeds, 2000—03; clin. fellow in transplantation U. Nebr., Omaha, 2003—05; asst. prof. U. Louisville, 2005—. Dir. Jewish Hosp., Louisville, 2007—. Contbr. scientific papers to numerous profl. jours. Recipient Young investigator award, Indian assn. study of liver, 1999; Travel grant, Japanese surg. soc., 1995. Fellow: Am. soc. transplantation (Young Investigator award 2004); mem.: ACS, Am. soc. reconstructive transplantation, Am. soc. transplant surgeons. Achievements include research in hand & composite tissue transplantation. Office: Univ Louisville 225 Abraham Flexner Way Louisville KY 40292 Office Fax: 502-587-4140.

RAVINDRAN, CHOLAPURATH NISHAL, physician; s. Ravindran Cholapurath and Vijaya Ravindran; m. Nimitha Kumar, Jan. 27, 2003; 1 child, Jaya Lakshmi Nishal. MBBS, Calicut Med. Coll., 1996; MD in Gen. Medicine, Coimbatore Med. Coll., Tamil Nadu, India, 2002. Sr. house officer medicine elderly Luton and Dunstable Hosp., England, sr. house officer med. rotation; registrar medicine Eastbourne Hosp., England; resident internal medicine Upmc Mckeesport, Pa.; preregistration house officer Calicut Med. Coll. Hosp., 1995—96; sr. house officer surgery & medicine Ernakulam Med. Ctr., Kerala, 1996—97; sr. house officer medicine Calicut Med. Coll., 1997—98; sr. house officer surgery Ernakulam Med. Ctr., 1997, sr. house officer emergency medicine, 1998—99; residency internal medicine Coimbatore Med. Coll., 1999—2002; registrar medicine Malabar Inst. Med. Scis., Calicut, 2002—03; locum sr. house officer medicine QE II Hosp., Welwyn Garden City, England, 2003—04. Contbr. articles to profl. jours., numerous presentations. Recipient Silver, Duke Edinburgh Award Scheme, 1986. Master: RCP (Ireland), RCP (UK); mem.: ACP, Travancore Cochin Med. Coun., Tamil Nadu Med. Coun., Indian Med. Coun., Pa. Med. Bd.

RAVINES, PATRICK C., conservator, researcher; b. Kans., Calif., Oct. 13, 1955; s. Heber Tulio Ravines Valderrama and Grace Maria Clarke Ravines; m. Caroline Todd Todd; children: Grace Ana, Eli Daniel, Amos Gabriel. MLS, Columbia U., NYC, 1985. Cert. art conservation Columbia U., 1985. Chief conservation office Baha'i World Ctr., Haifa, Galilee, Israel, 1993—2005; sr. rsch. fellow George Eastman Ho. Intl Mus. Photography & Film, Rochester, NY, 2005—. Mem.: Internat. Inst. Conservation Art & Hist. Works, Am. Chem. Soc., Am. Inst. Conservation Hist. and Artistic Works. Home: 754 Hillside Ave Rochester NY 14618 Personal E-mail: ravines55@gmail.com.

RAVINSKY, ANTHONY, music educator; s. Tony and Anna Ravinsky. MusB, Crane Sch. Music, 2003; MusM, U. Conn., 2007. Carpenter N.Y. Stage and Film, Poughkeepsie, 2002—04; choral dir. Cornwall (N.Y.) Ctrl. H.S., 2003—. Mem.: Orange County Music Educators Assn. (exec. bd. mem.), N.Y. State Theater Educators Assn., Music Educators Nat. Conf., Am. Choral Dir. Assn.

RAVITCH, DIANE SILVERS, historian, writer, government official, educator; b. Houston, July 1, 1938; d. Walter Cracker and Ann Celia (Katz) Silvers; m. Richard Ravitch, June 26, 1960 (div. 1986); children: Joseph, Steven (dec.), Michael. BA, Wellesley Coll., 1960; PhD, Columbia U., 1975; LHD (hon.), Williams Coll., 1984, Reed Coll., 1985, Amherst Coll., 1986, SUNY, 1988, Ramapo Coll., 1990, St. Joseph's Coll., NYC, 1991, Middlebury Coll., 1997, Union Coll., 1998. Adj. asst. prof. Tchrs. Coll., Columbia U., NYC, 1975-78, assoc. prof., 1978-83, adj. prof., 1983-91; asst. sec. office ednl. rsch. and improvement U.S. Dept. Edn., Washington, 1991-93, counselor to the sec. edn., 1991-93. Vis. fellow Brookings Instn., Washington, 1993-94, non-resident sr. fellow, 1994-, editor papers on edn. policy, 1997-05, Brown chair in edn. policy, 1997-05; rsch. prof. NYU, 1994-; mem. Nat. Assessment Governing Bd., 1997-04; com. on edn. policy Nat. Acad. Scis., 2003-05; mem. Koret task force Hoover Instn., 1999-, sr. fellow, 2005-. Author: The Great School Wars, 1974, The Revisionists Revised, 1977, The Troubled Crusade, 1983, The Schools We Deserve, 1985, National Standards in American Education, A Citizens Guide, 1995, Left Back, 2000, The Language Police, 2003; author: (with others) Educating an Urban People, 1981; author: The School and the City, 1983, Against Mediocrity, 1984, Challenges to the Humanities, 1985, What Do Our 17 Year Olds Know?, 1987, Edspeak, 2007; editor: The American Reader, 1990; co-editor: The Democracy Reader, 1992, New Schools for a New Century, 1997, City Schools, 2000, Making Good Citizens, 2001, Kid Stuff, 2003, Forgotten Heroes of American Education, 2006, The English Reader, 2006; editor: Learning from the Past, 1995, Debating the Future of American Education, 1995. Chair Ednl. Excellence Network, 1988—91, 1994—96; trustee Nat. Humanities Ctr., 1999—2000, NY Pub. Libr., 1981—87, hon. life trustee, 1988—; trustee NY Coun. on Humanities, 1996—2004; mem. Landmarks Preservation Commn., Southold, NY, 2000—02; bd. dirs. Woodrow Wilson Nat. Fellowship Found., 1987—91, Coun. Basic Edn., 1989—91, Thomas B. Fordham Found., 1998—, New Am. Found., 2000—06, Albert Shanker

Inst., 2002—, Core Knowledge Found., 2003—, Hunt Inst. Ednl. Policy and Leadership, 2002—, Nat. History Ctr., 2007—, John Dewey Ednl. Found., 2007—. Recipient Disting. Svc. award NY Acad. Pub. Edn., 1994, Alumnae Achievement award Wellesley Coll., 1989, Uncommon Book award Hoover Instn., 2004, John Dewey award United Fedn. Tchrs., 2005, Gaudium award Breukelein Inst., 2005, Pub. Svc. award Am. Jewish Hist. Soc., 2006; Guggenheim fellow, 1977-78; Phi Beta Kappa vis. scholar. Mem. Nat. Acad. Edn., Am. Acad. Arts and Scis., Soc. Am. Historians, N.Y. Hist. Soc. (trustee 1995-98), PEN Internat. Office: NYU 82 Wash Sq E New York NY 10003-6644

RAVITCH, RICHARD, lawyer, former city official; b. NYC, July 7, 1933; s. Saul and Sylvia Ravitch; m. Diane Ravitch, 1960 (div. 1986); children: Joseph, Michael; m. Betsy F. Perry, May 7, 1994. BA in Am. Hist., Columbia U., NYC, 1955; JD, Yale U. Law Sch., 1958. Atty. US House. Govt. Ops. Com., Washington, 1959—60; chmn. HRH Constrn. Corp., 1960—77, NY State Urban Devel. Corp., 1975—79, Bowery Bank, Met. Transp. Authority (MTA), 1979—83; gen. ptnr. The Blackstone Group, NYC, 1979—83; pres. players rels. com. Major League Baseball, 1991—94; co-chmn. Millennial Housing Commn., 2000—02; chmn. Ravitch, Rice & Co., 2004—; lt. gov. State of NY, Albany, 2009. Candidate NYC mayoral race Dem. primary, 1989. Named Housing Person of the Yr., Nat. Housing Conf., 2003. Mem.: The Century Club, Coun. Fgn. Rels. Democrat. Office: Ravitch Rice & Co LLC 610 5th Ave Rm 420 New York NY 10020*

RAWITCH, ALLEN BARRY, medical educator, academic administrator; b. Chgo., Dec. 29, 1940; s. Sam and Jean Rawitch; m. Patricia Nan Karlan, July 21, 1962; children: Bruce, David. BS in Chemistry, UCLA, 1963, PhD in Biol. Chemistry, 1967. Rsch. fellow U. Ill., Urbana, 1967-69; asst. prof. Kent (Ohio) State U., 1969-73, assoc. prof., 1973-75, U. Kans. Med. Ctr., Kansas City, 1975-80, prof., 1980—, asst. dean student affairs, 1999-2000, vice chancellor acad. affairs, dean grad. studies, 2000—, chmn. biochemistry and molecular biology, 2002—03. Vice chair biochemistry U. Kans. Med. Ctr., 1977-95, chair edn. coun., 1995-99 Editor Med. Biochemistry Question Bank, 1985-94; contbr. articles to profl. jours. Res. police officer capt. Overland Park Police Dept., 1979—. Rsch. grant NIH, 1971-2000, NSF, 1970, Am. Heart Assn., 1998-2002. Mem. Am. Soc. for Biochemistry and Molecular Biology, The Protein Soc., Am. Thyroid Assn., Sigma Xi. Avocations: amateur radio, woodworking, target shooting. Office: Office Acad Affairs U Kans Med Ctr 3901 Rainbow Blvd Mail Stop 1040 Kansas City KS 66160-0001 Office Phone: 913-588-1258. Business E-Mail: arawitch@kumc.edu.

RAWL, ARTHUR JULIAN (LORD OF CURSONS), corporate director, retail executive, consultant, accountant, writer; b. Boston, July 6, 1942; s. Philip and Evelyn (Rosoff) R.; m. Karen Lee Werby, June 4, 1967; 1 child, Kristen Alexandra. BBA, Boston U., 1967, postgrad, 1974; DBA in Business (hon.), St. George's U., London, 1995. CPA, Mass., N.Y., La. Audit mgr. Touche Ross & Co., Boston, 1967-77, NYC, 1977-79, ptnr., 1979, Newark, 1980-88, NYC, 1988-89, Deloitte & Touche, NYC, 1989-90; exec. v.p., CFO Hanlin Group, Inc., Linden, NJ, 1990-94, United Auto Group, Inc., NYC, 1994-97; pres., CEO, bd. dirs. Brazil Internat. Motors, Brazil Am. Auto Group, São Paulo, Brazil, 1999—2003; chmn., CEO Auto Alliance, Englewood, NJ, 2003—, Rawl & Assocs., Miami, Fla., 2003—. Bd. dirs. BiakalInterPlast (USSR), Kuperwood Enterprises, Hanlin Group, Inc., Quipp, Inc., Ecolocap Solutions, Inc., Montreal, Can.; chmn. Tiger Ethanol, Inc., Montreal, Canada; mem. adj. faculty Boston U., 1971-75, Lectr. Practicing Law Institute, NY 2007, KPMG Audit Committee Institue 2006-. Contbr. articles to profl. journals, mags. and trade publs. Mem. Newton Upper Falls (Mass.) Hist. Commn., 1977; bd. dirs. Sherburne Scholarship Fund Boston U., 1977-80; mem. Englewood (N.J.) Planning Bd., 1981-83; trustee Englewood Bd. Edn., 1983-85, 89-93, pres., 1991-92; trustee, treas. exec. com. Englewood Econ. Devel. Corp., 1986-89; fin. and compensation com. Dwight Englewood Sch., 1985-90; mem. parent devel. com. Mt. Holyoke Coll., 1991-94; chmn. Brit. Meml. Garden Trust, NY, 2003—; chmn. British Meml. Garden Trust, London, 2007-. Served to 2d class Petty Officer, Aviation Electronics and Combat Air Crewman (hon. discharge 1967) USN, 1960—63. Decorated Naval Expeditionary medal, Armed Forces Expeditionary Medal, Good Conduct Medal, National Defense medal; named member, Her Majesty's Most Excellent Order of the British Empire. Fellow AICPA, Mass. Soc. CPAs, NY Soc. CPAs; mem. VFW, Am. Legion, Navy League U.S., N.J. Hist. Soc. (bd. govs., exec. com., nominating com., treas. 1987-99), St. George's Soc. NY (treas. exec. com. 1998-2005), Officer H.M. Sovereign Order of St. John, Coll. Arms Found. (dir. 2001—), Brit. Am. Inst., Fin. Execs. Internat. Officer of Most Venerable Order of Hosp. of St. John of Jerusalem, Univ. Club (NY), Essex Club, Sloane Club (London). Conservative. Home: 1581 Brickell Ave Ste 1003 Miami FL 33129 Business E-Mail: a.rawl@att.net.

RAWLEIGH, SARA LYNETTE, elementary school educator; b. Rochester, NY, Oct. 15, 1982; d. Robert C. and LaVaughn M. Shepard; m. Benjamin Rawleigh, July 19, 2008. BS in Edn., Keuka Coll., NY, 2004; MS in Edn., Alfred U., NY, 2005. Lic. tchr. elem. edn., children with disabilities grades 1-6 NY Dept. Edn., 2004, literacy tchr. NY Dept. Edn., 2005, elem. tchr. Commonwealth Va. Dept. Edn., 2005. First grade tchr. A.G. Richardson Elem. Sch., Culpeper, Va., 2005—06; reading specialist grade K-5 Whitesville Ctrl. Sch., NY, 2006—07; spl. edn. tchr. pre K-7 Whitesville, 2007—08; spl. edn. tchr. pre K-4th, 2008—. Mem.: NY State Tchrs. Union. Avocations: travel, reading, scrapbooks.

RAWLINGS, JENNIFER SUE, primary school educator; b. Union City, Tenn., Oct. 27, 1977; d. Johnny Lee and Susan Witherspoon; m. John Whitney Rawlings, May 30, 2003. BS, U. Tenn., Martin, 1998; EdM, Trevecca Nazarene U., Nashville, 2001; postgrad., Cumberland U., Lebanon, Tenn., 2002—03; attending, Tennessee State U., 2009; EdD, Tennessee State U., Edn. Administrn., 2009—. 2nd grade substitute tchr. Milan Elem. Sch., Tenn., 1999; tchr. Gibson County Area Wide Alternative Sch., Milan, 1999; 1st grade tchr. Martin Primary Sch., Tenn., 1999—2003, Oak Hill Sch., Nashville, 2003—, dir. summer enrichment program, 2004—. Fellow: Internat. Reading Assn., Phi Kappa Phi. Avocations: tennis, swimming, reading, piano. Home: 7113 Calderwood Dr Antioch TN 37013 Office: Oak Hill Sch 4815 Franklin Rd Nashville TN 37220

RAWLINGS, PAUL C., retired government official; b. Cave City, Ark., June 21, 1928; s. Otha A. and Leona (King) R.; m. Catherine Terral, 1951 (div. 1970); children: William A., Rebecca, Neal; m. Erma Martin, June 20, 1971 (div. Jan. 1997). Grad., Little Rock Jr. Coll.; LL.B., Ark. Law Sch., 1950. Bar: Ark. 1950. Practiced in, Little Rock, 1950, 52-73; adminstrv. law judge Office Hearings and Appeals, Social Security Adminstrn., HEW, Hattiesburg, Miss., 1973-92; ret.; ptnr. firm Terral, Rawlings, Matthews & Purtle, until 1973. Asst. atty. gen., Ark., 1955-56 Bd. dirs. Ark. Enterprises for Blind, 1964-67; del. White House Conf. on Aging, 1995. Served with AUS, 1950-52 Mem. Ark. Bar Assn., Law Sci. Acad. Methodist (past chmn. bd. adminstrn., trustee). Club: Lion (past pres.). Home: 100 # 14 Swinging Bridge Dr Heber Springs AR 72543-8717

RAWLINGS, ROBERT HOAG, newspaper publisher; b. Pueblo, Colo., Aug. 3, 1924; s. John W. and Dorothy (Hoag) R.; m. Mary Alexandra Graham, Oct. 18, 1947; children: Jane Louise, John Graham, Carolyn Anne, Robert Hoag II. Student, Colo. Coll., 1942—44, Colo. U., 1944—45; BA, Colo. Coll., 1947. Reporter Pueblo Chieftain and Pueblo Star-Jour., 1947-51, advt. rep., 1951-62, gen. mgr., 1962-79, pub., editor, 1980—. Sec. Star-Jour. Pub. Corp., 1962-84, pres., 1984—; past chmn. bd. dirs. Colo. Nat. Bank, Pueblo; mem. adv. bd. U.S. Bank. Bd. dirs. U.S. Air Force Acad. Found., Colo. State U.-Pueblo Found.; pres. Robert Hoag Rawlings Found., So. Colo. Cmty. Found., Medal of Honor Meml. Com. With USNR, 1945-47. Named Colo. Newspaper Person of Yr., 1989, Disting. Univ. Fellow Pres. Club U. So. Colo., 1993, Outstanding Citizen of Yr. Pueblo C. of C. 1994, Colo. Bus. Leader of Yr., Colo. Assn. of Commerce and Industry, 1994; recipient Outstanding Svc. to Univ. award U. So. Colo. Alumni Assn., 1993, Colo. Corp. Philanthropy award Nat. Philanthropy Assn., 1993, Louis T. Benezet award Colo. Coll. Alumni Assn., 1996, Living Legend award U. Colo., 1997, Outstanding Am. Achievement award U. So. Colo., 1997, Outstanding Svc. to Hispanic Cmty. award, U. So. Colo. and Pueblo Hispanic Edn. Found., 1999, Creative Spirit award Pueblo United Way, 1998, Lifetime Svc. award Colo. Bd. Vet. Affairs, 2000, Medal of Valur, Congl. Medal Honor Soc., 2000, Libr. Benefactor award Pueblo Libr. Assn., 2001, Vol. of Yr. award Coun. for Advancement and Support Edn., 2004, Voice award Nat. Alliance for Mentally Ill, 2002, Vol. of Yr. award Dist. VI of Coun. for Advancement and Support of Edn., 2004; named to Pueblo Hall of Fame, 1999, The Pueblo Greater Sports Assn. Hall of Fame, 1999; named Donor of Yr. Nat. Assn. Univ. Athletic Devel. dirs., 1995. Mem. Colo. Press Assn. (dir. 1963-66, 76-78, pres. 1985, chmn. bd. dirs. 1986, Golden Rule Makeup award 1998), Rocky Mountain Ad Mgrs. (past pres.), Colo. Forum (past pres.), U. So. Colo. Found. (trustee emeritus), Colo. Mental Health Inst., Rotary. Presbyterian. Home: 1401 Rancho Del Sol Pueblo CO 81008-2043 Office: The Pueblo Chieftain Star Jour Pub Corp PO Box 4040 Pueblo CO 81003-0040

RAWLINS, DONALD RAY, lawyer; b. Dyersburg, Tenn., Apr. 28, 1965; s. Dal M. and Rebecca S. Rawlins. BBA, U. Memphis, 1987; JD, Am. U., 1990. Bar: Tenn., 1990, NC, 2008. V.p., asst. gen. counsel, asst. sec. AutoZone, Inc., Memphis, 1990—2004; asst. gen. counsel Thomas & Betts Corp., Memphis, 2004—05, asst. sec., 2004—05, chief compliance officer, 2004—05, Rawlins Law Firm, PC, 2009—; counsel Alston and Bird LLP, Charlotte, NC, 2007—09. Vice chmn. Memphis Landmarks Commn., 2004—05. Recipient Best Brief award ATLA, 1990. Republican. Methodist. Office: Rawlins Law Firm PC 1115 E Morehead Rd Ste 206 Charlotte NC 28204 Office Phone: 704-307-2542.

RAWLINS, V. LANE, economics professor, retired academic administrator; b. Rigby, Idaho, Nov. 30, 1937; m. Mary Jo Rawlins, three children. BA in Economics, Brigham Young U., 1963; PhD in Economics, U of Calif., Berkeley, 1969. Faculty Wash. State U., Pullman, 1968-86, chair. economics, 1977-82, vice provost, 1982—86; vice chancellor, academic affairs U. of Alabama, 1986-91; pres. Memphis St. U., Memphis, 1991-00, Wash. State U., Pullman, 2000—07, prof. econs.; mem. William D. Ruckelshaus Ctr. Office: Washington State U Hulbert 121C Pullman WA 99164-1048 Office Phone: 509-335-6666. E-mail: rawlins@wsu.edu.

RAWLINSON, HELEN ANN, librarian; b. Columbia, SC, Mar. 30, 1948; d. Alfred Harris and Mary Taylor (Moon) R. BA, U. S.C., 1970; MLS, Emory U., 1972. Asst. children's librarian Greenville (S.C.) County Library, 1972-74, br. supr., 1974-76, asst. head extension div., 1976-78; children's room librarian Richland County Pub. Library, Columbia, 1978-81, sr. adult services librarian, 1981-82, chief adult services, 1982-85, dep. dir., 1985—. Mem. adv. com. S.C. Pre-White House Conf. on Libr. and Info. Svcs., chmn. program com. Recipient Outstanding S.C. Librarian award by S.C. Library Assn., 1998. Mem. ALA, S.E. Libr. Assn., S.C. Libr. Assn. (2d v.p. 1987-89, editl. com. 1993, chmn. pub. libr. sect. 1995), U. S.C. Thomas Cooper Soc. (bd. dirs., v.p., pres.-elect, pres.). Baptist. Home: 1316 Guignard Ave West Columbia SC 29169-6137 Office: Richland County Pub Libr 1431 Assembly St Columbia SC 29201-3101 Office Phone: 803-799-9084. Business E-Mail: harawlin@rhycpl.com. E-mail: harawlin@richland.lib.sc.us.

RAWLINSON, JOHNNIE BLAKENEY, federal judge; b. Concord, NC, Dec. 16, 1952; BS in Psychology summa cum laude, NC A&T State U., 1974; JD, U. of Pacific, 1979. Private practice, Las Vegas, 1979—80; staff atty. Nevada Legal Services, 1980; from dep. dist. atty. to asst. dist. atty. Clark County Dist. Atty.'s Office, 1980—98; judge US Dist. Ct. Nev., 1998—2000, US Ct. Appeals (9th cir.), 2000—. Office: 333 Las Vegas Blvd S Rm 7072 Las Vegas NV 89101 Office Phone: 702-464-5670.*

RAWLINSON, JOSEPH ELI, foundation administrator, lawyer; b. Delta, Utah, May 9, 1915; s. Eli Wilford and Dora Pearl (Day) Rawlinson; m. Elaine Millicent Andersen, June 2, 1947; children: James, Jolene, Nancy, Rex, Anina, Cheryl, Mark, Lisa, David. BS, U. Utah, 1936; JD, Loyola U., 1958. CPA Calif.; bar: Calif. 1959. Agt. IRS, Wichita, Kans., 1938—52; acct. Serene Koster, Barbour, Calif., 1952—62; pvt. practice Calif., 1959; pres., CEO Fritz B. Burns Found., Burbank, Calif., 1980—. Recipient Silver medal, Am. Inst. Accts., 1942. Office: Fritz B Burns Found 4001 W Alameda Ave Ste 203 Burbank CA 91505-4338 Home Phone: 818-886-3142; Office Phone: 818-840-8802. Personal E-mail: josepheli@sbcglobal.net.

RAWLINSON, KENNETH J., dentist; BS in Chem. Engring.; DDS, Case Western Reserve U. Pvt. practice, Riverside, RI. Tchr. restorative and cosmetic dentistry RI Hosp. Mem.: RI Dental Assn., Am. Acad. Cosmetic Dentistry, Tropical Fish Soc. RI (bd. dirs.). Office: 2861 Pawtucket Ave Riverside RI 02915 Office Phone: 401-434-1334. Office Fax: 401-434-7939. E-mail: DrKen@supersmiledocs.com.

RAWLS, FRANK MACKLIN, lawyer; b. Suffolk, Va., Aug. 24, 1952; s. John Lewis and Mary Helen (Macklin) R.; m. Sally Hallum Blanchard, June 26, 1976; children: Matthew Christopher, John Stephen, Michael Andrew. BA in History cum laude, Hampden Sydney Coll., 1974; JD, U. Va., 1977. Bar: Va. 1977, U.S. Dist. Ct. (ea. dist.) Va. 1977, U.S. Ct. Appeals (4th cir.) 1977. Assoc. Rawls, Habel & Rawls, Suffolk, 1977-78, ptnr., 1978-91, Ferguson & Rawls, Suffolk, 1991-96, Ferguson, Rawls, MacDonald, Overton & Grissom PC, Suffolk, 1996-98, Ferguson, Rawls, MacDonald & Overton PC, Suffolk, 1999—2002, Ferguson, Rawls & Raines, P.C., 2002—. Sec., Suffolk Title Ltd., 1986-95; bd. dirs. Secure Title, Inc. Deacon Westminster Reformed Presbyn. Ch., Suffolk, 1979-83, elder, clk. of session, 1984-91, 94-99, elder, 2004—, co-chmn. forward by faith capital campaign, 2001—; chmn. bd. dirs. Suffolk Crime Line, 1982-90, Suffolk Cheer Fund, 1982—, Covenant Christian Schs., Suffolk, 1982-84; bd. dirs. Norfolk Christian Schs., 1990-2004, v.p., 1998-99, pres., 1999-2004; pres. Parent Tchr. Fellowship, 1995-97, vice-chmn. steering com. for capital campaign, 1996-98, v.p., 1997-98; adv. bd. dirs. Salvation Army, Suffolk, 1977-95, chmn., 1989-90; chmn. Suffolk Com. on Affordable Housing, 1989-90; bd. dirs. Suffolk YMCA, 1988-90, Suffolk Youth Athletic Assn., 1999-2000. Mem. Suffolk Human Soc., Suffolk Bar Assn. (past pres.), Va. State Bar, Va. Bar Assn., Christian Legal Soc., Va. Trial Lawyers Assn., Suffolk Bar Assn. Office Phone: 757-539-2400. Business E-Mail: frawls@frrlaw.com.

RAWLS, S. WAITE, III, museum director, investment company executive; b. Norfolk, Va., July 15, 1948; s. Sol Waite Jr. and Ann Arendel (Peace) R.; m. Margaret Louise Thorn, Sept. 26, 1970. BA, Va. Mil. Inst., 1970; MBA, JD, U. Va., 1975. Mng. dir. Chem. Bank, NYC, 1975-88, with retail banking dept., 1975-77, with comml. lending dept., 1977-79, with securities trading and sales dept., 1980-88; vice chmn. Continental Bank Corp., Chgo., 1988-91; exec. v.p. Fixed Income Chgo. Corp., 1993-95; pres. Ferrell Rawls & Co., Greenwich, Conn., 1995; exec. dir. Mus. of Confederacy, Richmond, Va., 2004—. Bd. dirs. Liberty Brokerage, Inc., NYC; vice chmn., bd. dirs. Nat. Ctr. for Pub. and Pvt. Initiatives, Inc.; bd. dirs. Nevander Asset Mgmt., Inc.; mem. fin. instruments adv. com. Chgo. Merc. Exch.; vis. prof. Darden Sch., U. Va., 1991-92; mem., former chmn. com. Chgo. Risk Mgmt. Ctr. Bd. dirs. Chgo. Urban League Devel. Corp., Camp Found.; trustee Mus. Sci. and Industry, The Civil War Trust, 1994—, Va. Mil. Inst. Found., 1993—, Darden Found. of the Darden Sch., U. Va., 1991—; chmn. nat. adv. coun. The Seeing Eye, Inc.; mem. Chgo. Com. Mem. Econ. Club Chgo., Chgo. Club, Chgo. Golf Club, Farmington Country Club, Torrington Country Club. Baptist. Avocations: golf, quail hunting, art, antiques. Office: Mus of Confederacy 1201 E Clay St Richmond VA 23219 Office Phone: 804-649-1861.

RAWNSLEY, HOWARD MELODY, pathologist, educator; b. Long Branch, NJ, Nov. 20, 1925; s. Walter A. and Elizabeth (Melody) R.; m. B. Eileen Fiddes, Sept. 5, 1967; children: Virgilia Ingram, Elizabeth Sue. AB, Haverford Coll., Pa., 1949; MD, U. Pa., Phila., 1952. Diplomate Am. Bd. Pathology (trustee 1988-96). Intern Hosp. U. Pa., 1952-53, resident, 1953-57; practice medicine, specializing in pathology Phila., 1957-75; mem. Wm. Pepper Lab., U. Pa., 1957-75, asst. dir., 1960-68, dir., 1968-75; assoc. dir. Clin. Research Ctr., 1962-67, acting dir., 1969— 70, asst. prof. pathology and medicine, 1960-65, assoc. prof., 1965-69, prof., 1969—75; prof. pathology Dartmouth Hitchcock Med. Ctr., Hanover, NH, 1975-95, chmn. dept., 1980-87, sr. v.p. med. affairs, 1987-94. Cons. VA Hosp.; mem. exec. com. Am. Bd. Med. Spltys., 1998-2001. Chmn. bd. dirs. New Eng. Blood Svcs. ARC, 1996—2000, 2002—05. With US Army, 1944—46. Woodward fellow in chemistry, 1953-55 Mem. AMA, ARC (biomed. svcs. com. 1990-92), Pathology Soc. Phila. (pres.), Coll. Am. Pathologists (bd. govs. 1985-93), Coll. Am. Pathologists Found. (bd. dirs. 2003-08), Am. Soc. Clin. Pathology (Disting. Svc. award 1995).

RAWOOL-SULLIVAN, MOHINI, research scientist; d. Waman S. and Shobha W. Rawool; m. John Peter Sullivan, Mar. 24, 1989. PhD, N.Mex. State U., Las Cruces, 1988. Scientist Los Alamos Nat. Lab., N.Mex., 1992—.

RAWSON, CLAUDE JULIEN, literature and language professor; b. Shanghai, Feb. 8, 1935; came to U.S., 1985; m. Judith Ann Hammond, July 14, 1959; children: Hugh, Tim, Mark, Harriet, Annabel. BA, Oxford U., Eng., 1955, MA, BLitt, 1959; DLitt (hon.), U. Keele, Eng., 2007. English lectr. U. Newcastle, Eng., 1957-65; from lectr. to prof., chmn. dept. U. Warwick, Coventry, Eng., 1965-85, hon. prof., 1986—; George Sherburn prof. English U. Ill., Urbana, 1985-86; George M. Bodman prof. English Yale U., New Haven, Conn., 1986-96, Maynard Mack prof. English, 1996—. Vis. prof. U. Pa., Phila., 1973, U. Calif., Berkeley, 1980; chmn. Yale Boswell Papers, 1990—2001; del. for lang. and lit. Oxford U. Press, NY, 2001—05; mem. ednl. adv. bd. John Simon Guggenheim Meml. Found., 2005—. Author: Henry Fielding and the Augustan Ideal, 1972, 2d edit., 1991, Gulliver and the Gentle Reader, 1973, 2d edit., 1991, The Character of Swift's Satire, 1983, Order from Confusion Sprung, 1985, 2d edit., 1992, (with F.P. Lock) Collected Poems of Thomas Parnell, 1989, Satire and Sentiment 1660-1830, 1994, 2d edit., 2000, (with H. B. Nisbet) Cambridge History of Literary Criticism, vol. 4: The Eighteenth Century, 1997, God, Gulliver, and Genocide, 2001, 2d edit. 2002, Basic Writings of Jonathan Swift, 2002, Cambridge Companion to Henry Fielding, 2007, Henry Fielding: Playwright, Novelist, Journalist, Magistrate, 1707-1754, 2008; editor: Modern Lang. Rev. and Yearbook of English Studies, London, 1974-88; gen. editor: Cambridge (Eng.) History of Literary Criticism, 1983—, Unwin Critical Libr., London, 1974—, Blackwell Critical Biographies, 1985—, Cambridge Edition of the Works of Jonathan Swift, 2001—, (with Ian Higgins) Essential Writings of Jonathan Swift, 2009. Recipient Cert. of Merit for Disting. Svc. Conf. of Editors of Learned Jours., 1988; Andrew Mellon fellow Clark and Huntington Libr., 1980, 90, Guggenheim fellow, 1991-92, Sr. Faculty fellow Yale U., 1991-92; NEH grantee, 1991. Fellow Am. Acad. Arts and Scis.; mem. Modern Humanities Rsch. Assn. (life mem., com. mem. 1974-88), Internat. Soc. 18th Century Studies, Am. Soc. for 18th Century Studies, Brit. Soc. for 18th Century Studies (pres. 1973-74). Office: Yale U Dept English PO Box 208302 New Haven CT 06520-8302

RAWSON, HARVE E., psychologist, writer; b. Webb CIty, Mo., July 25, 1934; s. Paul Charles and Florence Landon Rawson; m. Joyce Elaine Blossom, June 9, 1961; children: Paul Gerald, Reed Harve. BA, Antioch Coll., 1957; MA, Ohio State U., 1959, PhD, 1961. Rsch. specialist N.Am. Aviation Inc., Columbus, Ohio, 1961—63; prof. psychology Hanover (Ind.) Coll., 1963—94, prof. emeritus, 1994—; dir. children's svcs. Englishton Pk., Lexington, Ind., 1969—93; dean faculty Franklin (Ind.) Coll., 1994—96; vis. prof. psychology Miss. State U., Starkville, 1998. Grant reviewer Coun. Internat. Exch. Scholars, Washington, 2000—04. Author: Webb City, 2000, Around the World in 30 Years, 2001, Purposeful Parenting, 2002, A Delightful Ordeal, 2003, Travels of an Iconoclast, 2005, Buried In The Ivy, 2008; contbr. over 40 articles to profl. jours. Pres. Lide White Boys and Girls Club, Madison, Ind., 1969, 1974, 1978, 1999—2001; v.p. Jefferson County Youth Shelter, Madison, 1992. Recipient Sagamore of the Wabash award, Gov. Ind., 1993; scholar, Fulbright Found., Bahrain, 1988—89, Fulbright Found., 1994. Mem.: Gwinnett County Sr. Leadership Coun., Ind. Psychol. Assn. (pres. 1974—76, Cmty. Svc. award 1991, Disting. Acad. Psychologist award 1986—87), Traveler's Century Club. Avocation: travel. Home: 230 Collins Industrial Way Apt #134 Lawrenceville GA 30043 Home Phone: 770-280-2241.

RAWSON, RICHARD J., telecommunications industry executive, lawyer; b. Florham Park, NJ, Nov. 22, 1952; BS, Notre Dame U.; JD, Rutgers U. Formerly with Sullivan & Cromwell, NYC and Washington; various positions with Law Divsn. AT&T, 1984—96, sr. v.p., gen. counsel, 1995, Lucent Technologies, Murray Hill, NJ, 1996—. Mem. ABA, Am. Corp. Counsel Assn.

RAWSON, ROBERT H., JR., lawyer; b. Washington, Oct. 18, 1944; AB, Princeton U., 1966; MA, Oxford U., Eng., 1968; JD, Harvard U., 1971. Bar: Ohio 1971, D.C. 1972. Ptnr. Jones, Day, Cleve.; ptnr.-in-charge Jones Day, Cleve. Rhodes scholar. Mem.: ABA, Bar Assn. of DC,

Cleve. Bar Assn., Ohio State Bar Assn., Phi Beta Kappa. Office: Jones Day North Point 901 Lakeside Ave E Cleveland OH 44114-1190 Office Phone: 216-586-3939. Office Fax: 216-579-0212. Business E-Mail: rrawson@jonesday.com.

RAY, ALBERT, physician, educator; b. NYC, Aug. 8, 1948; s. Herman and Stella (Meritz) R.; m. Cheryl Antecol, Oct. 8, 1977; children: Heather, Erin, Samantha. BA, Bklyn. Coll., 1969; MD, Cath. U. Louvain, Belgium, 1976. Diplomate Am. Bd. Family Practice, Can. Coll. Family Physicians, cert. profl. coder AAPC. Intern Meml. U. of Nfld., St. John's, Can., 1976; resident McGill U., Montreal, 1978; family physician SCPMG, San Diego, 1978—. Clin. prof. U. Calif., San Diego, 1978—; cmty. faculty UCLA, USD, U. Calif., Davis, USC; clerkship cmty. adv. bd. U. Calif., San Diego, 1995—; pres. profl. staff Kaiser Found. Hosp.; bd. dirs. So. Calif. Permanente Med Group; asst. chief family medicine Kaiser Permanente, San Diego; physician dir, patient edn. & health promotion Kaiser Permanente, regional asst., med. dir bus. mgmt, physician dir. doc. choice wellness ctr. Author: Lecons d'Histologie, 1973; contbr. to profl. jours. Program chair adult edn. Congregation Beth Israel, 1995; bd. dirs. Temple Emanuel, San Diego, 1990, Agy. for Jewish Edn.; expert reviewer Med. Bd. Calif., 1995; spl. med. cons. Calif. Dept. of Corps., 1996; hon. chmn. physician's adv. bd. Nat. Rep. Congl. Com. Named Family Physician of Yr., Calif. Acad. Family Physicians, 2002. Fellow: Am. Acad. Family Physicians; mem.: Calif. Acad. Family Physicians, San Diego Acad. Family Physicians, San Diego County Med. Soc. (councilor 2002—03, treas. 2004—06, pres.-elect 2006—07, pres. 2007—08), Calif. Med. Assn. (ho. of dels.), AMA (alt. del.). Avocations: golf, tennis, travel, antiques, gardening. Home: 7035 Convoy Ct San Diego CA 92111 Office Phone: 619-516-7400.

RAY, ASOK KUMAR, physicist, researcher; s. Chittaranjan and Anita Roy; m. Swati Ray. BS in Physics, Calcutta U., 1967, B of Tech. in Radio-Physics and Elecs., 1969; MS in Physics, Okla. State U., Stillwater, 1973; MS in Math., Tex. Tech. U., 1975, PhD in Physics, 1977. Postdoctoral rsch. fellow U. Fla., 1979—81; asst. prof. physics Mich. Tech. U., 1981—82; vis. asst. prof. physics U. Tex, Arlington, 1982—84; asst. prof. physics U. Tex., Arlington, 1984—88, assoc. prof. physics, 1988—92, prof. physics, 1992—. Grantee, U. S. Dept. Energy, Welch Found., 2003—. Mem.: Materials Rsch. Soc., Am. Phys. Soc. Achievements include research in Over 130 Publications in Peer-Reviewed Journals; computational condensed matt. Office: Physics Univ of Texas 502 Yates St Arlington TX 76019 Office Fax: 817-272-3637. Business E-Mail: akr@uta.edu.

RAY, BRITTANY E., literature and language educator; m. Ronald Smith; 3 children. BA, Colby Coll., Maine, 1990; student Grad. Edn. Program, Univ. Maine. English tchr. Narraguagus H.S., Harrington, Maine, 1995—. Named Maine Tchr. of Yr., 2007. Office: Narraguagus High Sch RR 1 Box 489 Harrington ME 04643 Business E-Mail: bray@sad37.com.

RAY, CARINA, history professor; PhD, Cornell U., Ithaca, NY, 2007. Asst. prof. Fordham U., Bronx, NY, 2008—. Columnist New African Mag., London, 2005—. Post doc. fellow, Penn. State U., 2006—07, Fullbright fellow, Ghana, 2002. Mem.: Ghana Studies Coun., African Studies Assn., Am. Hist. Assn. Office: Fordham Univ History Dept 441 E Fordham Rd Bronx NY 10458 Business E-Mail: caray@fordham.edu.

RAY, CARLOS See NORRIS, CHUCK

RAY, CHARLES, sculptor; b. Chgo., 1953; BFA cum laude, U. Iowa, 1975; MFA, Rutgers U., 1979. One-man shows include 64 Market St., Venice, Calif., 1983, Mercer Union, Toronto, 1985, Feature, Chgo., 1987, NYC, 1989, 1990, 1991, 1992, Burnett Miller, LA, 1988, The Mattress Factory, Pitts., 1989, Galerie Claire Burrus, Paris, 1990, Donald Young Gallery, Seattle, 1992, Galerie Metropol, Vienna, 1993, Rooseum Ctr. Contemporary Art, Malmo, Sweden, 1994, Kunsthalle Bern, Switzerland, 1994, Kunsthalle Zurich, 1994, Studio Guenzani, Milan, 1996, Regen Projects, LA, 1997, Whitney Mus. Am. Art, NYC, 1998, Mus. Contemporary Art, LA, 1998, Chgo., 1998, Matthew Marks Gallery, NYC, 2006, 2007, Regen Projects II, LA, 2007, exhibited in group shows at Recent Drawings, Whitney Mus. Am. Art, NYC, 1990, Whitney Biennial, 1997, The American Century: Art and Culture 1900-2000, 1999, Pollock to Today: Highlights from the Permanent Collection, 2002, Helter Skelter: LA Art in the 1990's, Mus. Contemporary Art, Calif., 1992, Regarding Beauty: A View of the Late 20th Century, Hirshhorn Mus. and Sculpture Garden, Washington, 1999, Let's Entertain, Walker Art Ctr, Minn., 2000, Walk Around Time, 2002—04, Mythologies, 2005—08, Barbara Gladstone Gallery, NYC, 2000, Made in California: Art, Image and Identity 1900-2000, LA County Mus. Art, 2000, Au-dela du Spectacle, Ctr. George Pompidou, Paris, 2001, Open Ends: Art Since 1960, MoMA, NYC, 2001, Take Two-Worlds and Views, 2005—06, A Room of Their Own, Mus. Contemporary Art, LA, 2001, After Cezanne, 2005, Collecting Collections, 2008, Venice Biennale, 2003, Singular Forms (Sometimes Repeated), Guggenheim Mus., NYC, 2004, Yes Bruce Nauman, Zwirner & Wirth, NYC, 2006, The Lath Picture Show, Friedrich Petzel Gallery, NYC, 2007, Represented in permanent collections MoMA. Recipient Larry Aldrich Found. award, 1997; grantee NJ Coun. Arts, 1980, Louis Comfort Tiffany Found., 1987, Art Matters, Inc., 1987; fellow Rutgers U., 1978—79, Can. Art Coun., 1985, Nat. Endowment Arts, 1988. Fellow: Am. Acad. Arts and Sciences. Office: c/o Regen Projects 629 N Almont Dr Los Angeles CA 90069 Office Phone: 310-276-5424.

RAY, CHARLES AARON, ambassador; b. Center, Tex., July 5, 1945; m. Myung Wook Soe, Nov. 3, 1973; children: David Edward, Denise Ellen, Gayle Denene, Jason Andre. BSBA, Benedictine Coll., 1972; MS in Sys. Mgmt., U. So. Calif., 1981; MS in Nat. Security Strategy, Nat. War Coll., 1997. Commd. 2nd lt. US Army, 1965, advanced through grades to maj., ret., 1982; consular officer US Consulate Gen., Guangzhou, China, 1983-84, chief consular sect. Shenyang, China, 1985-87, chief adminstrv. sect. Chiangmai, Thailand, 1988-91; spl. asst. to dir. Office Def. Trade Controls, Washington, 1991-93; dep. chief of mission Am. Embassy, Freetown, Sierra Leone, 1993-96; detailed to Nat. War Coll., Washington, 1996-97, Nat. Fgn. Affairs Tng. Ctr., Arlington, Va., 1997-98; consul gen. US Consulate Gen., Ho Chi Minh City, Vietnam, 1998-2001; sr. seminar Nat. Fgn. Affairs Tng. Ctr., 2001—02; US amb. to Cambodia US Dept. State, Phnom Penh, Cambodia, 2002—05; diplomat in residence U. Houston, 2005—06; dep. asst. sec. for POW/missing persons affairs US Dept Def., 2006—09. Editl. cartoonist Spring Lake News, 1975-79; contbr. articles to Asia Mag., 1974-79, Things Learned From My Grandmother About Leadership And Life, Balt., 2008, Taking Charge: Offence Leadership for the Twenty-First Century, Balt., 2009; editor mag. Psyop Digest, 1976-78; exec. editor Def. Trade News, 1992-93. Avocations: golf, taekwondo, softball, tennis, painting, poetry. Office: 1416 Saddle River Dr Gaithersburg MD 20878 Home Phone: (855) 23 218 932; Office Phone: 703-699-1101. E-mail: rayca@state.gov.

RAY, CHARLES DEAN, neurosurgeon, spine surgeon, bioengineer, inventor; b. Americus, Ga., Aug. 1, 1927; s. Oliver Tinsley and Katherine (Broadfield) Ray; children: Bruce, Marlene. AB, Emory U., Atlanta, 1950; MS, U. Miami, Coral Gables, 1952; MD, Med. Coll. Ga., 1956. Diplomate Am. Bd. Neurol. Surgery, Am. Bd. Spine Surgery, Internat. Cert. Commn. Cert. Clin. Engr. Intern Bapt. Meml. Hosp., Memphis, 1956-57; resident, rsch. assoc. neurosurgery U. Tenn. Hosp., Memphis, 1957-62; fellow, rsch. asst. Mayo Clinic and Found., Rochester, Minn., 1962-64; asst. prof. neurosurgery, lectr. bioengring. Johns Hopkins U. Med. Sch., Balt., 1964-68; chief dept. engring. F. Hoffmann-LaRoche, Basel, Switzerland, 1968-73; clin. assoc. prof. medicine U. Minn., Mpls., 1973—83; practice medicine specializing in spinal neurosurgery Mpls., 1982—96, Norfolk, Williamsburg, Va., 1996—2000. Lectr. U. Basel, Switzerland, 1968—73; dir. emeritus Inst. Low Back and Neck Care, 1982—96; med. dir. The Spine Fellowship Program Ea. Va. Med. Sch., Norfolk, Va.; pres. Am. Coll. Spine Surgery; mem. staff Sentara Hosps., Norfolk, Abbott-Northwestern Hosp., Mpls.; chmn. bd. pres. Cedar Devel. Corp., Cedar Surg., Inc., 1985—92; v.p. med. rsch. Medtronic, Inc., Mpls., 1972—79; bd. dirs. Herman Miller, Inc., 1987—97; chmn. emeritus, med. dir. Raymedia, Inc., Mpls.; cons. in field; adj. prof. orthopedics Ain Shams U., Cairo, 2002—, U. Colo., Denver, 2002—04; pres. N.Am. Spine Soc., Internat. Spine Arthroplasty Soc.; vis. prof. Ain Shams U., Cairo. Author: Principles of Engineering Applied to Medicine, 1964, Medical Engineering, 1974, Lumbar Spine Surgery, 1988; contbr. over 360 articles to profl. publs. Chmn. com. materials and devices World Fedn. Neurosurg. Socs., 1977—, Cosmos Club, 1976—; vestry St. Martin's Episcopal Ch., Wayzata, Minn., 1976-79. With USN, 1945-49. Named Disting. Alumnus, Med. Coll. Ga., 1999; recipient Gold award for Best Med. Device Design of Yr. R&D 100, 2000, Leon Wiltse award for Contbns. to Spine Science and Mgmt., 1999. Fellow: ACS, Royal Soc. Health, Am. Coll. Spine Surgery (pres.); mem.: ASTM, AMA (sr.), IEEE (sr.), Internat. Spine Arthroplasty Soc. (pres.), N.Am. Spine Soc. (past pres., chmn., Wiltse award 1999), Internat. Orgn. Standardization, Pan-Am. Med. Assn. (life), Am. Assn. Neurol. Surgeons (sr.), Internat. Soc. Stereotaxic and Functional Neurosurgery, Internat. Fedn. Med. Biol. Engring., West Germany Armed Forces Med. Soc., Congress Neurol. Surgeons, Mpls. Club, Sigma Xi. Achievements include over 54 US patents and over 100 foreign patents. Home and Office: 4320 Via Presada Santa Barbara CA 93110 Office Phone: 805-964-7026. Personal E-mail: inveray@gmail.com.

RAY, CHARLES KENDALL, retired dean; b. Boise City, Okla., Mar. 15, 1928; s. Volney Holt and Mamie (Burton) R.; m. Doris Derby, Aug. 26, 1951. BA, U. Colo., 1951; MA, Columbia, 1955, Ed.D., 1959. Teaching prin. Bur. Indian Affairs, Savoonga, Alaska, 1951-54; mem. faculty U. Alaska, 1957-93, prof. edn., 1960-93, dean Sch. Behavioral Scis. and Edn., 1961-80, dir. summer sessions, 1980-93. Author: A Program of Education for Alaska Natives, 1959, Alaskan Native Secondary School Dropouts, 1961. Mem. N.E.A., Phi Delta Kappa. Home: 900 Univ St 1405 Seattle WA 98101-3726 Personal E-mail: ckddray@comcast.net.

RAY, CLYDE HOSEA, retired educator, writer; b. Waynesville, NC, Aug. 30, 1938; s. Clyde Hosea and Caroline Pafford Ray; m. Dorothy Lea Pennington, July 9, 1982; 1 child, Clyde Hosea IV. MA, East Tenn. State U., Johnson City, 1974. Instr. Haywood CC, Clyde, NC, 1994—, Southwestern CC, Sylva, NC, 1994—. Author: (novel) Across The Dark River: The Odyssey of the 56th North Carolina Infantry in the American Civil War. Bd. mem. Haywood County Bd. Edn., Waynesville, NC, 1976—80. Capt., commdg. officer, 3rd bn., 83rd rgt. NC State Def. Militia, 1991—2008, Asheville. Decorated Courage Govt. State; recipient Tchg. Excellence award, Haywood CC, 2005. Liberal. Roman Catholic.

RAY, CREAD L., JR., retired judge; b. Waskom, Tex., Mar. 10, 1931; s. Cread L. and Antonia (Hardesty) Ray; m. Janet Watson Keller, Aug. 12, 1977; children: Sue Ann(dec.), Robert E., Glenn L., David B., Marcie Lynn, Anne Marie. BBA, Tex. A&M U., 1952; JD, U. Tex., 1957; LHD (hon.), Wiley Coll., Marshall, Tex., 1980. Bar: Tex. 1957. Pvt. practice law, Marshall, 1957-59; judge Harrison County, 1959-61; justice 6th dist. Ct. Civil Appeals, Texarkana, 1970-80, Supreme Ct. Tex., Austin, 1980-90; ret., 1990; prin. C.L Ray, Austin, 1991—. Prin. C. L. Ray, Austin, 1991—; pres., CEO White Oil, Inc. Past pres. Marshall Jaycees, Marshall C. of C.; active Boy Scouts Am.; mem. Tex. Ho. of Reps., 1966—70; trustee Wiley Coll. Lt. col. USAF, 1952—54, Korea. Recipient awards, Boy Scouts Am. Mem.: N.E. Tex. Bar Assn. (past pres.), State Bar Tex., Tex. Aggies, Rotary. Democrat. Methodist. Home and Office: 604 Beardsley Ln Austin TX 78746-4929 Home Phone: 512-327-6137; Office Phone: 512-328-9238. Personal E-mail: clray4523@hotmail.com. E-mail: judgeclray@aol.com, judgeclray@msn.com.

RAY, DIPAN B., director; s. Birendra Chandra and Juthika Ray; m. Anuradha Bose, Nov. 24, 1988. PhD, St. Johns U., NY, 1995. Cert. RPH NY, 1988. Sect. mgr., r & d Internat. Splty. Products, Wayne, NJ, 2001—08; dir., exptl. edn. Touro Coll. Pharmacy, NYC, 2008—. Owner Yonkers Pharmacy, NY, 2002—08. Prodr.(founder): South Asian Theater Festival (Felicitation, 2008). Pres. Epic Actors Workshop, Old Bridge, NJ, 1988—2008. Grantee, Middlesex County Culture & Heritage Commn., 2007—08. Mem.: Am. Assn. Pharm. Scientists. Achievements include patents for novel excipient of pharmaceutical industry.

RAY, DOUGLAS ELLSWORTH, dean, law educator; b. Mpls., July 7, 1947; s. Henry E. and Hazel O. (Tollefson) R.; m. Caroline Sue Logan, July 25, 1970; children: Kathleen Susan, Michael David. Ba, U. Minn., 1971; JD, Harvard U., 1975. Bar: Minn. 1975, U.S. Dist. Ct. Minn. 1975. Economist U.S. Dept. Labor, Washington, 1971-72; assoc. Dorsey & Whitney, Mpls., 1975-78; assoc. prof. law U. Richmond, Va., 1978-81; prof. U. Toledo Coll. Law, 1981—98, assoc. dean, 1984—86, 1988—89, dean, 2006—; v.p., dean Widener U. Sch. Law, 1999—2005. Labor arbitrator Fed. Mediation & Conciliation Svc., Toledo, 1981-, taught & pub. fields of labor law, employment discrimination law, torts and labor arbitration, spkr. in field. Co-author: Labor Management Relations: Strikes, Lockouts and Boycotts, 1992, Understanding Labor Law, 1999, 2d edit., 2005; contbr. articles to profl. jours. Bd. dirs. Luther Home Mercy, Williston, Ohio, 1985-88. Sgt. U.S. Army, 1966-70. With US Army, 1966—70. Mem. ABA (labor law sect.), Am. Arbitration Assn., Assn. of Am. Law Schs. (chmn. labor and employment law sect.), Nat. Acad. Arbitrators (chmn. seminar Labor Law & Labor Arbitration 1999, 2005). Lutheran. Office: Univ Toledo Coll Law 2801 W Bancroft Mail Stop 507 Toledo OH 43606-3328 Office Phone: 419-530-2379. Office Fax: 419-530-4526. Business E-Mail: douglas.ray@utoledo.edu.*

RAY, FRANK ALLEN, lawyer; b. Lafayette, Ind., Jan. 30, 1949; s. Dale Allen and Merry Ann (Fleming) R.; m. Carol Ann Olmutz, Oct. 1, 1982; children: Erica Fleming, Robert Allen. BA, Ohio State U., 1970, JD, 1973. Bar: Ohio 1973, U.S. Dist. Ct. (so. dist.) Ohio 1975, U.S. Supreme Ct. 1976, U.S. Tax Ct. 1977, U.S. Ct. Appeals (6th cir.) 1977, U.S. Dist. Ct. (no. dist.) Ohio 1980, U.S. Dist. Ct. (ea. dist.) Mich. 1983, U.S. Ct. Appeals (1st cir.) 1986; cert. civil trial adv. Nat. Bd. Trial Advocacy. Asst. pros. atty. Franklin County, Ohio, 1973-75, chief civil counsel, 1976-78; dir. econ. crime project Nat. Dist. Attys. Assn., Washington, 1975-76; assoc. Brownfield, Kosydar, Bowen, Bally & Sturtz, Columbus, Ohio, 1978, Michael F. Colley Co., L.P.A., Columbus, 1979-83; pres. Frank A. Ray Co., L.P.A., Columbus, 1983—93, 2000—05, Ray & Todaro Co., LPA, Columbus, 1993-94, Ray, Todaro & Alton Co., L.P.A., Columbus, 1994-96, Ray, Todaro, Alton & Kirstein Co., L.P.A., Columbus, 1996, Ray, Alton & Kirstein Co., L.P.A., Columbus, 1996—98; sr. ptnr. Ray & Alton, L.L.P., Columbus, 1998—2000; ptnr. Chester, Willcox & Saxbe, LLP, 2006—; adj. prof. Moritz Coll. of Law, Ohio State U., 2003—. Mem. seminar faculty Nat. Coll. Dist. Attys., Houston, 1975-77; mem. nat. conf. faculty Fed. Jud. Ctr., Washington, 1976-77; bd. editors Man. for Complex Litigation, Fed. Jud. Ctr., 1999—2004; bd. mem. bar examiners Ohio Supreme Ct., 1992-95, mem. rules adv. com., 1995-99. Editor: Economic Crime Digest, 1975-76; co-author: Personal Injury Litigation Practice in Ohio, 1988, 91. Fin. com. Franklin County Rep. Orgn., Columbus, 1979-84, 2005—; trustee Ohio State U. Coll. Humanities Alumni Soc., 1991-93, Nat. Coun. Ohio State U., Moritz Coll. Law Alumni Soc., 1998-2008; capital campaign fund cabinet Legal Aid Soc. of Columbus, 1998. Capt. inf. U.S. Army, 1976. Named to Ten Outstanding Young Citizens of Columbus, Columbus Jaycees, 1976; recipient Nat. award of Distinctive Svc., Nat. Dist. Attys. Assn., 1977, Worthy Adversary award Ohio Assn. Civil Trial Attys., 2005, Disting. Alumnus award Ohio State U. Moritz Coll. Law, 2006. Fellow: Ohio Acad. Trial Lawyers (pres. 1989—90, Pres.'s award 1986), Ohio State Bar Found., Roscoe Pound Found., Am. Coll. Trial Lawyers, Internat. Soc. Barristers, Columbus Bar Found. (pres. 2009—); mem.: ATLA (state del. 1990—92), Franklin County Trial Lawyers Assn. (pres. 1987—88, Pres.'s award 1990), Ohio State Bar Assn. (com. negligence law 1990—97, mem. com. jury instrns. 2002—06, coun. del. 2008—, Friend of Legal Edn. award 2005), Million Dollar Advs. Forum, Columbus Bar Assn. (pres. 2001—02, Profl. award 1987), Am. Bd. Trial Advs. (pres., Ohio Chpt. 2004), Inns of Ct. (pres. Judge Robert M. Duncan chpt. 1993—94). Presbyterian. Home: 2030 Tremont Rd Columbus OH 43221-4330 Office: 65 E State St Ste 1000 Columbus OH 43215-4216 Office Phone: 614-221-4000. Business E-Mail: fray@cwslaw.com.

RAY, GILBERT T., lawyer; b. Mansfield, Ohio, Sept. 18, 1944; s. Robert Lee Ray and Renatha (Goldie) Washington; m. Valerie J. Reynolds, June 14, 1969; children: Tanika, Tarlin. BA, Ashland Coll., 1966; MBA, U. Toledo, 1968; JD, Howard U., 1972. Assoc. O'Melveny & Myers, LA, 1972-79, ptnr., 1980-2000, ret. ptnr., 2000—. Bd. dirs. Sierra Monolithics, Inc., IHOP Corp., Advance Auto Parts, Automobile Club of So. Calif., Haynes Found., DiamondRock Hospitality, Inc., Seasons Series Fund, SunAmerica Series Trust, Watson, Wyatt & Co., 2000—. Mem. The Calif. Club, L.A. Country Club. Democrat. Office: Watson Wyatt Worldwide Inc 901 N Glebe Rd Arlington VA 22203 Office Phone: 703-258-8000.*

RAY, HILLOL KUMAR, environmental engineer, poet; arrived in US, 1975, permanent resident, 1986; s. Nibaran Chandra and Angur Lata Ray; m. Seema Ray; children: Brian Kumar, Ryan Kumar Ray. BS in Civil Engring., U. Calcutta, India, 1973; MS in Environ. Engring., ND State U., Fargo, 1977. Environ. engr. Brown & Root Inc., Houston, 1978—80; civil/structural engr. PLACON Ltd., Calcutta, India, 1973—75; rsch. asst. N. Dakota State U., Fargo, 1975—77; sr. environ. engr. Ecology and Environment Inc., Dallas, 1980—92; program mgr., environ. engr. US EPA, Dallas, 1992—. Author poetry. Chmn., editor North Tex. Bengali Assn., Dallas, 1992—99. Recipient Bronze medal, US EPA, 2001, Excellence in Customer Svc. award, 2002, Nat. Liberal & Fine Arts award, Nat. Fedn. Indian Am. Assn., 2006. Hindu. Avocations: creative writing, poetry, watch repair, antique cars, stamp collecting/philately. Home: Milestone 2723 Riviera Ct Garland TX 75040 Office: US EPA 1445 Ross Ave Dallas TX 75202-2733 Personal E-mail: mukhosh@verizon.net. Business E-Mail: ray.hillol@epa.gov.

RAY, HUGH MASSEY, JR., lawyer; b. Vicksburg, Miss., Feb. 1, 1943; s. Hugh Massey and Lollie Landon (Powell) R.; m. Carroll Robertson, Sept. 7, 2002; children: Hugh, Hallie. BA, Vanderbilt U., 1965, JD, 1967. Bar: Tex. 1967, U.S. Dist. Ct. (so. dist.) Tex. 1967, U.S. Dist.Ct. (we. dist.) La. 1979, U.S. Dist. Ct. (we. dist.) Tex. 1979, U.S. Dist Ct. (no. dist.) Tex. 1980, U.S. Ct. Appeals 1st, 5th, 9th, 11th cirs.) 1982, U.S. Dist. Ct. (no. dist.) Calif. 1989, N.Y. 1992; cert. Tex. Bd. Legal Specialization. Asst. U.S. atty. So. Dist. Tex., 1967-68; assoc. Andrews & Kurth, Houston, 1968-77, ptnr., Bankruptcy Dept., 1977—; ct. appointed examiner Asbestos Billings Mutters Dist. Coun. Lectr. Ctrl. and Ea. European Law Initiative, Vilnius, Lithuania, 1996. Co-author: Bankruptcy Investing, 1992, Creditor's Rights in Texas, vol. 1 & 2, 1998, Last Rights--Liquidating a company, 2007; contbr. articles to profl. jours. Mem.: ABA (chmn. real property practice com. 1975—77, chmn. cont. legal edn. com. young lawyers divsn. 1976—78, vice-chmn. 1979, chmn. oil and gas subcom. bus. bankruptcy com. 1985—89, chmn. executory contracts subcom. 1989—93, chmn. bus. bankruptcy com. 1993—96, chmn. com. on trust indentures and indenture trustees 1995—97, mem. standing com. on jud. selection, tenure and compensation 1996—97, chmn. ad hoc com. on bankruptcy ct. structure 1996—2001, mem. bus. law sect. 1997—2001, chair energy com. 2001—06), South Tex. Coll. Law (trustee 2003—), Houston Symphony Orch. (governing trustee 2004—06), Am. Coll. Bankruptcy., Am. Law Inst., Tex. Bar Assn. (chmn. bankruptcy com. 1985—88), Houston Bar Assn., River Oaks Country Club, Houston Country Club. Episcopalian. Office: Andrews & Kurth 600 Travis St Ste 4200 Houston TX 77002-2910 Office Fax: 713-238-7225. Business E-Mail: hray@andrewskurth.com.

RAY, HUGH MASSEY, III, lawyer; b. Houston, June 25, 1970; s. Hugh Massey and Florence Hargrove Ray; m. Katheryn Elaine Shaffer, June 19, 1993; children: James Henry, Mary Carol, John William. BA, Vanderbilt U., Nashville, 1992; MDiv, JD, Vanderbilt U., 1996. Cert.: Tex. Bd. Legal Specialization (bus. bankruptcy law) 2005, bar: Tex. 1998, US Ct. Appeals (5th cir.) 2001, US Ct. Appeals (11th cir.) 2001, US Supreme Ct. 2001. Shareholder Weycer, Kaplan, Pulaski & Zuber, P.C., Houston, 2001—. Barrister of Davis-Foltz Inn of Ct. Am. Inns of Ct., Houston, 2004—, barrister of Garland Walker, 2006—. Patron Houston Symphony, 2004; mem. St. Martin's Episc. Ch., Houston, 1993—. Mem.: ABA (editl. bd. young lawyers mag. 2004—05, young lawyer divsn. profl. devel. team 2005—06), State Bar Tex. (mem. disciplinary rules com. 2000—), Am. Law Inst., Houston Bar Assn. (disting. spkr. 2004—, disting. faculty 2005—, CLE com. 2006—, chair CLE seminar com. 2008—09, mem. bankruptcy sect., chair CLE com. 2009—), Coll. of State Bar Tex., Houston Livestock Show and Rodeo (life), Ritz Club (London), Houston Club, Briar Club, Phi Alpha Delta, Lambda Chi Alpha. Episcopalian. Avocations: running, hunting, triathlon. Office: Weycer Kaplan Pulaski & Zuber PC 11 Greenway Plz Ste 1400 Houston TX 77046 Office Fax: 713-961-5341.

RAY, JANE ZIMRUDE, retired machine shop executive; b. Strawn, Tex., May 9, 1937; d. M.A. and Susie Matilda (Kitchens) Wooton; m. Earl Vernon Ray, Oct. 19, 1956; children: Marcus Vernon, Martha Ruth Ray O'Grady, Douglas Wayne, Patricia Ann. Grad., Stephenville (Tex.)

High Sch., 1955. Bookkeeper Ray's Texaco Svc. Ctr., Ft. Worth, Tex., 1967-74, Ray's Repair & Mfg., Ft. Worth, Tex., 1974-79, pres., 1979-80, Cisco, Tex., 1980-92. Sunday sch. tchr., Cisco, Tex., 1983-92, sub. tchr., 1992—; mem. Civic League of Cisco, 1990—; instr. Community Svc. course Cisco Jr. Coll., 1991.

RAY, JOHN WALLACE, III, political science professor; b. New Iberia, La., Feb. 1, 1948; s. John Wallace and Ruth Rita Ray; m. Roberta K. Turnbull, Dec. 23, 1970. BA, U. Southwestern La., Lafayette; MA, U. Wis., Madison, PhD, 1975. Prof. Mont. Tech U., Butte, 1975—. Cons. and tng. Ray Comm. Consultants, Butte, 1980—. Contbr. articles to profl. jours. Mem. Butte Restoration Alliance, 2007—, Citizens Tech. Environ. Com., Butte, 1992—99; bd. mem. and pres. MT Environ. Info. Ctr., Helena, 1985—2007; mem. Clark Fork Coalition, Missoula, Mont., 1995—98. Recipient Lynn and Sandy Sargent award, Mont. Environ. Info. Ctr., 2004. Mem.: Commn. Am. Parliamentary Practice (Phifer award 1997), Am. Inst. Parliamentarians, Nat. Comm. Assn. Avocations: travel, hiking. Office: Mont Tech Univ 1300 West Park St Butte MT 59701 Office Fax: 406-496-4510.

RAY, LARRY L., language educator; s. Thomas E. and Bernice Ray. MA in Spanish, U. Miss., Oxford, 1999. Cert. Internat. TESOL Tng. Ctr. Ont., Can., 2000. Mail handler US Postal Svcs., Jackson, Miss., 1976—84, 1985—97, tng. supr., 1986—87; study abroad coord. Jackson State U., 1999—2003; english instr. Guangxi U., Nanning, China, 2000—01; MFLA instr. Tougaloo Coll., Miss., 2004—, MFLA coord. & dir., 2004—. Contbr. articles. With USAF, 1971—75. Home: 3601 JFK Blvd Jackson MS 39213 Office: Tougaloo Coll 500 W County Line Rd Tougaloo MS 39174 Personal E-mail: larrylray@bellsouth.net. Business E-Mail: lray@tougaloo.edu.

RAY, MARILYN ANNE, nursing educator, researcher; b. Hamilton, Ont., Can., Jan. 24, 1938; d. Arthur William Anthony and Elvera Caroline (Montag) Ray; m. James L. Droesbeke, Aug. 18, 1979 (dec. Nov. 2001). Diploma, St. Joseph's Hosp. Sch. Nursing, Hamilton, 1958; BSN, U. Colo. Denver, 1968, MSN, 1969; MA in Anthropology, McMaster U, 1978; PhD of Nursing, U. Utah, 1981; HD (hon.), Nev. State Coll., 2005. RN Fla., cert. transcultural nurse, CTN. Instr. sch. nursing U. San Francisco, 1970—72; asst. prof. sch. nursing McMaster U., 1973—76; asst. prof. U. Colo., 1984—89; Christine E. Lynn eminent scholar Coll. Nursing Fla. Atlantic U., Boca Raton, 1989—94, prof. Coll. Nursing, 1995—2004, adj. prof., 2004—05, prof. emeritus, 2006—. Vis. prof. U. Colo., 1989—2004; Yingling vis. scholar Va. Commonwealth U., Richmond, 1994—95; vis. prof. Alta. Heritage Found., U. Alberta, 2005. Contbr. articles to profl. jours. Col. USAF, 1967—99. Recipient Leininger award, 1989, Disting. Alumni award, U. Utah Coll. Nursing, 2007; Transcultural Nursing scholar, 2005. Fellow: Soc. Applied Anthropology; mem.: ANA, Soc. Med. Anthropology, Soc. Applied Anthropology, Internat. Assn. Human Caring (charter), Space Nursing Soc. (charter), Aerospace Human Factors Assn. (charter), Coll. Nurses Ont., Transcultural Nursing Soc. (cert., mem. editl. bd. jour.), Am. Anthrop. Assn., Sigma Theta Tau. Avocations: travel, music. Home Phone: 561-470-8109; Office Phone: 561-297-4055. Business E-Mail: mray@fau.edu.

RAY, MARJORIE, retired financial planner; b. Hemingway, SC, Mar. 6, 1927; d. James Earl Ray and Maybelle Jordan; divorced; 2 children, Debra Boyd and Roberta Jill Sharp. AB in English and History, U. Calif., Berkeley, 1962, MLS, 1965; teaching degree, U. Ill., 1966. Lic. real estate agt., Conn. Dir. libr. program Sch. Dist. 57, Westmont, Ill., 1965—67; instr. English coll. edn. Evanston, Ill., 1966—67; coord. children's and adult svcs. Tampa Pub. Libr., Fla., 1967; dir. profl. svcs. Weston (Conn.) Woods Film Studios, 1968-69; asst. dir. Danbury (Conn.) Pub. Libr., 1970-73, Westport (Conn.) Pub. Libr., 1973-74; cons. Conn. State Libr., Hartford, 1974-76, assoc. state libr., 1977-79; broker rep. P&I Equities, White Plains, N.Y., 1980-82, MHA Fin. Corp., Braintree, Mass., 1983-84, Townsley Assocs., Corning, N.Y., 1984-89, v.p. corp. devel., 1985-89; v.p. Planned Mgmt. Co. Savs. Bank Rockville, Conn., 1989-90; sr. v.p. Specialized Investments, 1991-92; investment officer FSC Securities Corp., 1993—97, Conn. regional sales mgr., 1995—; investment officer and asst. treas. Rockville (Conn.) Bank, 1998—2002, ret., 2002. Cons., propr. Colmar, Glastonbury, Conn., l985—; instr. grad. English West Conn. Star Coll., 1971. Mem. Internat. Assn. Fin. Planning (bd. dirs. Hartford 1983-84, Disting. Svc. award 1984), Glastonbury Bus. and Profl. Women. Republican. Congregationalist. Avocations: travel, theater, literature, tennis, golf, ballroom dancing.

RAY, MICHAEL EDWIN, lawyer; b. Charlotte, NC, Dec. 13, 1949; s. Daniel Shaw Ray and Jane (Horne) Keziah; m. Janet Langston Jones, July 14, 1973; children: John Daniel, Jennifer Marjory. BA, Furman U., 1972; JD, U. S.C., 1978. Bar: N.C. 1978, S.C. 1978, U.S. Dist. Ct. (ea., mid. and we. dists.) N.C. 1978, U.S. Ct. Appeals (4th cir.) 1981, U.S. Ct. Appeals (Fed. cir.) 1989. Legal adminstr. Wyche Burgess Freeman & Parham, Greenville, S.C., 1973-75; assoc. Womble Carlyle Sandridge & Rice, PLLC, Winston-Salem, N.C., 1978-85, mem., 1985—. Editor-in-chief S.C. Law Rev., 1977-78. Bd. dirs. Piedmont Opera Theatre, Inc., 1997-98; S.C. Manpower Planning Coun., Columbia, 1971-72. T.B. Clarkson scholar Furman U., 1971-72. Mem. ABA, Internat. Bar Assn., N.C. Bar Assn., S.C. Bar Assn., Fed. Cir. Bar Assn. (bd. govs. 1994-97), Am. Intellectual Property Law Assn., Forsyth County Bar Assn., Furman U. Alumni Assn. (bd. govs. 1995-2000), Lex Mundi, Ltd. (dir. 1995-99, sec. 1996-97, chair-elect 1997-98, chair 1998-99, chair emeritus 1999-2000). Democrat. Presbyterian. Avocations: sailing, woodworking, music. Home: 4269 Stonehenge Ln Winston Salem NC 27106-3535 Office: Womble Carlyle Sandridge & Rice PLLC One W Fourth St Winston Salem NC 27101 E-mail: mray@wcsr.com.

RAY, NELDA HOWTON, financial consultant; Grad., U. Montevallo, Ala., 1962. Fin. cons. Merrill Lynch, Tuscaloosa, Ala. Mem.: Rotary Internat. (local and dist. officer). Home: 4704 Oneida Ave Northport AL 35473-1431 Office: Merrill Lynch 302 Merchants Walk Ste 100 Tuscaloosa AL 35406-2214

RAY, PAUL RICHARD, JR., executive recruiter, consultant; b. Columbus, Ga., Nov. 6, 1943; s. Paul Richard and Sarah (Campbell) R.; m. Elizabeth Richards, June 29, 1968; children: Paul Richard III, John Ray, Alice Ray. BSBA, U. Ark., 1966; JD, U. Tex., 1969. Bar: Tex. 1970. Dir. mktg., various mktg. positions tobacco divsn. R.J. Reynolds Tobacco Co., Winston-Salem, N.C., 1969-78; cons. Paul R. Ray & Co., Ft. Worth, 1978, v.p., 1978-79, sr. v.p., 1979-83, exec. v.p., 1983-84, pres., 1984—, COO, 1984-86; CEO Ray & Berndtson, Ft. Worth, 1986-98, chmn. bd., CEO, 1998—. Chmn. bd. CEO Rays Beradtson, Ft. Worth, 1998—2002; vice chmn. Keavney Exec. Search, 2002—06; mng. dir. EWKP, 2006—07; with Paul Ray & Co., 2007—. Bd. dirs. Cook-Ft. Worth Children's Med. Ctr., United Way Met. Tarrant County; liberal arts adv. bd. U. Tex.; dean's exec. adv. bd. U. Ark. Recipient Brite Divinity Sch. Exec. Com. Bd. Mem. ABA, Assn. Exec. Search Cons. (chmn. 1995-98), Tex. Bar Assn., Young Pres.' Orgn., World Pres. Orgn., River Crest Country Club, City Club, Ft. Worth club. Personal E-mail: pray@poulrayco.com.

RAY, PAUL SUKHAMAY, engineering educator, researcher; b. Bengal, India, Feb. 1, 1933; arrived in U.S., 1974; s. Suresh Chandra and Radha Rani Ray; m. Sudha Karmakar, Apr. 29, 1961; children: Steve S., Sumit S. B in Mech. Engring. with first class honors, Jadavpur U., Calcutta, India, 1956; M in Mech. Engring., Indian Inst. Tech., Kharagpur, India, 1961; MBA in Mgmt., Golden Gate U., 1978; PhD in Indsl. Engring., U. Okla., 1988. Registered profl. engr., Tex., chartered engr., Engring. Coun., London; cert. safety profl. Bd. Cert. Safety Profls. Sr. indsl. engr. Hindustan Motors Ltd., India, 1960—63; sr. asst. Union Carbide (I) Ltd., India, 1963—72; mgr. mgmt. svcs. Hindustan Copper Ltd., India, 1972—74; project plan-scheduling engr. Bechtel Corp., San Francisco, 1974—87; asst. prof. U. Ala., Tuscaloosa, 1989—95, assoc. prof., 1995—2005, prof., 2005—. Presenter in field. Mem. editl. bd. Internat. Jour. Indsl. Engring., Theory, Applications and Practice; contbr. chapters to books, articles to profl. jours. Recipient Outstanding advisor Departmental Hon. award Ala. chpt. Alpha Pi Mu, Coordinating Coun. Student Orgns. U. Ala., 2004—05, Outstanding Faculty Mem. award, Dept. Indsl. Engring., U. Ala., 2009; Gordon fellow, U. Okla., 1985, recipient numerous rsch. grants. Fellow: Inst. Indsl. Engrs. (sr.; v.p. publ. Okla. chpt. 1988—89, 2d v.p. Birmingham chpt. 1992—93, sec. 1994—95, bd. dirs. 1995—96, v.p. Region 3 2006—, Tech. Brief award 2008); mem.: Nat. Safety Coun., Sys. Safety Soc. (Educator of the Yr.), Human Factors and Ergonomics Soc. (newsletter editor indsl. ergonomics tech. group 1990—91), Internat. Soc. Occupl. Ergonomics & Safety (pres. elect 2002—03, pres. 2003—04), Am. Soc. Safety Engrs. (Safety Rsch. award 1999), Alpha Pi Mu. Achievements include patents pending for. Avocations: travel, TV, reading. Home: 3 Highland Manor Dr Tuscaloosa AL 35406 Office: Univ Ala Tuscaloosa Dept Constrn Engring & Mgmt PO Box 870288 Tuscaloosa AL 35487 Office Phone: 205-348-1603. Personal E-mail: rpl9825@aol.com. Business E-Mail: pray@eng.ua.edu.

RAY, PRIYADIP, research scientist; s. Pradip Kumar and Mahua Ray. MTech, Indian Inst. Tech., New Delhi, 2004. Grad. rsch. asst., dept elec. engring. and computer sci. Syracuse U., NY, 2004—. DAAD scholar, Germany Academic Excellence Svc., 2003. Mem.: IEEE (Best Student Paper award 2007), Phi Kappa Phi Internat. Honor Soc. Achievements include research in statistical signal processing. Personal E-mail: priyadipr@gmail.com.

RAY, RACHAEL DOMENICA, chef, television personality; b. Cape Cod, Mass., Aug. 25, 1968; m. John Cusimano, Sept. 24, 2005. Student, Pace U. Mgr. fresh foods dept. Macy's Marketplace, NY; store mgr., buyer Agata & Valentina, NY; mgr., pub and rest. Sagamore Resort, Lake George, NY; food buyer Cowan & Lobel, Albany; editor-in-chief Everyday with Rachael Ray mag., 2005—. Spokesperson Dunkin Donuts, 2007—; founder Rachael's Rescue; creator Rachael Ray Nutrish pet food, 2008. Author: 30-Minute Meals, 1999, Veggie Meals, 2001, Comfort Foods, 2001, 30-Minute Meals 2, 2003, Get Togethers: Rachael Ray 30 Minute Meals, 2003, $40 a Day: Best Eats in Town, 2004, Cooking 'Round the Clock: Rachael Ray's 30-Minute Meals, 2004, Cooking Rocks!: Rachael Ray's 30-Minute Meals for Kids, 2004, 30-Minute Get Real Meals: Eat Healthy Without Going to Extremes, 2005 (Quills award cookbook The Quills Literacy Found., 2005), Comfort Food: Rachael Ray's Top 30 30-Minute Meals, 2005, Rachael Ray 365: No Repeats, 2005 (Quills award cookbook The Quills Literacy Found., 2006), Kid Food, 2005, Guy Food, 2005, Classic 30-Minute Meals, 2006, Express Lane Meals, 2006, 2, 4, 6, 8: Great Meals for Couples or Crowds, 2006, Just in Time, 2007, Yum-O! The Family Cookbook, 2008, Rachel Ray's Big Orange Book, 2008; host (TV series) 30 Minute Meals, Food Network, 2002— (Emmy award for outstanding svc. show, 2006), $40 A Day, 2004—, Inside Dish, 2004—, Rachael Ray's Tasty Travels, 2005—, The Rachel Ray Show, 2006—, Rachael's Vacation, 2008—; prodr.: (TV series) Viva Daisy!, 2009—; guest appearances Pyramid, 2003, The Tony Danza Show, 2004, 2005, Live With Regis and Kelly, 2004, 2005, Sidewalks Entertainment, 2004, Good Day Live, 2004, The View, 2005, Isaac Mizrahi, 2005, Tonight Show with Jay Leno, 2005, Late Show with David Letterman, 2005, Oprah Winfrey Show, 2005, 2006. Named one of 100 Sexiest Women, FHM-US Mag., 2004, 100 Most Influential People, TIME mag., 2006, The 100 Most Influential Women in NYC Bus., Crain's NY Bus., 2007, The 50 Most Powerful Women in NYC, NY Post, 2007, 2008, The 100 Most Powerful Celebrities, Forbes.com, 2008. Office: c/o Everyday with Rachael Ray Fifth Floor 260 Madison Ave New York NY 10016-2402*

RAY, RAM LAKHAN, civil engineer; s. Bahuru Ray and Rashwati Devi; m. Alpana Lakshmi, Apr. 22, 1996; children: Samiksha, Shawn. PhD student in Civil Engring., U. NH, Durham, 2005—. Civil engr. TAEC Consult P. Ltd., Kathmandu, Nepal, 1993—95, Govt. of Nepal, Kathmandu, 1996—2002. Contbr. articles to profl. jour. Fellowship, NASA, 2005—08. Mem.: IEEE, Am. Geophys. Union, Nepal Engrs.' Assn. (Kathmandu), Nepal Engring. Coun. (Kathmandu). Achievements include research in satellite soil moisture data in landslide analysis. Home: Thalaha Kataha VDC-8 Siraha Nepal Office: Univf NH 218 Forest Pk Durham NH 03824 Office Fax: 603-862-3957. Personal E-mail: ramlakhan36@yahoo.com. Business E-Mail: rlj3@unh.edu.

RAY, RAYMOND B., federal judge; b. 1943; BA, U. South Fla., 1965; JD, U. Fla., 1971. Bar: Fla. 1971. Asst. U.S. atty. Dept. Justice, So. Dist. Fla., Miami, 1971-74; bankruptcy judge U.S. Bankruptcy Ct. (so. dist.) Fla., Ft. Lauderdale, 1993—. Comdr. USNR, 1961—85, ret. Office: US Courthouse Rm 306 299 E Broward Blvd Fort Lauderdale FL 33301-1944 Business E-Mail: raymond_ray@flsb.uscourts.gov, betty_robaina@flsb.uscourts.gov.

RAY, ROSABELL HARRIET See BATTIN, R.

RAY, RUTH ALICE YANCEY, retired rancher, real estate developer; b. Birmingham, Ala., July 26, 1931; d. John Grayson and Ruth Ethel (Lutman) Yancey; (div. July 1986); children: Virginia Ruth, John Edward, William Arthur. Student, Fla. State U., 1949-50; BS, Appalachian State U., 1954; postgrad., Stetson U., 1966-67, Appalachian State U., 1962-63, Stetson U., 1964-67; grad., Miami Sr. HS. Tchr. pub. schs., Nenana, Alaska, 1955-56; tchr. 1st Christian Ch., Clermont, Fla., 1965-67, Lake County Sch. Bd., Clermont, 1969-70; rancher Rays' Ranch, Clermont, 1963-97; pvt. real estate developer Clermont, 1990—; substitute tchr. Buncombe County Asheville City Sch. Sys., 1999—; tchr. Marion County Sch. Bd., 2006—. Chmn. Clermont Planning and Zoning Commn., 1973-81; mem. Heart of Fla. Girl Scout Coun., 1988—, life mem. Ctr. Fla. Gir. Scout Coun.; life mem. Friends of Cooper Mem. Libr., South Lake Art League; assoc. Sisters of St. Mary. Named Conservation Farmer of Yr., State of Fla., 1982. Mem. Lake County Farm Bur. (bd. dirs. 1977-81), Lake County Cattlemen's Assn. (v.p. 1979-81), Lake County Farmer's Home Adminstrn. (bd. dirs. 1984-88, 1990—, chmn. 1985, 88, 90-91), Nat. Cutting Horse Assn. (life), Am. Quarter Horse Assn., Am. Paint Horse Assn., E.S.A. Internat., Daus. of King (pres., sec.), St. Bridcats Guild, Order St. Luke, Sigma Kappa. Republican. Episcopalian (sr. warden, eucharistic min.). Avocations: needlepoint, fishing, hiking, reading. Home: 3001 SE Weir Ave Apt 1106 Ocala FL 34471-6778 Home Phone: 352-857-7234. Personal E-mail: raray415@aol.com.

RAY, SIBA PRASAD, materials scientist, ceramics scientist; b. Dinhata, India, Jan. 4, 1944; came to U.S., 1969; s. Nilmony P. and Bina Pani Ray; m. Liplka Ray, May 28, 1977; children: Sourav, Leena. B in Engring., Calcutta U., India, 1964; MS, Columbia U., NYC, 1970, D in Engring. Sci., 1974. Sci. officer Bhabha Atomic Rsch. Ctr., Bombay, 1964-68; rsch. assoc. Pa. State U., University Park, 1974-76; scientist Alcoa Labs., Alcoa Ctr., Pa., 1977-78, sr. scientist, 1978-82, sci. assoc. Alcoa Center, Pa., 1982-91, sr. sci. assoc., 1991-98; program mgr. materials devel. NGAP, Alcoa, Alcoa Center, 1999—. Cons. Alcoa Separations Tech., Warrendale, Pa., 1991, Electro Metallurgy and Electrochemistry Cons., New Kensington, Pa., 1992. Contbr. articles to Jour. Solid State Chemistry, J. Am. Ceramic Soc., Light Metals, Bull. Am. Ceramic Soc. Pres. Bengali Assn. Pitts., 1988. Mem. The Metall. Soc., Am. Ceramic Soc., Sigma Xi. Achievements include 52 patents in the area of inert elctrodes, ceramic composites and reaction sintering. Home: 6007 Pilgrim Ct Murrysville PA 15668-8533 Office: Alcoa Labs Alcoa Tech Ctr New Kensington PA 15069 Office Phone: 724-337-2803. Business E-Mail: siba.ray@alcoa.com.

RAY, STEVEN BILLY, lawyer; b. Sidney, Nebr., June 23, 1948; BA, Colo. State U., Ft. Collins, 1971; JD, U. Tulsa, 1973; grad., Nat. Inst. Trial Advocacy, 1985, Gerry Spence Trial Lawyers Coll., 2001. Bar: Nebr. 1974, Colo. 1974, U.S. Ct. Mil. Appeals 1975, Wyo. 1997, cert.: Nat. Bd. Trial Advocacy (civil). Judge advocate, mil. judge USMC, 1974—2005, chief of staff marine forces Offutt AFB, Nebr., 2002—03; mem. judicial performance commn. Colo. Ho. Reps., Denver, 1994—97; pvt. practice Fort Collins, 2006—. Spkr. in field. Co-author: Colorado Water Law, 1985. Chmn. Ft. Collins/Loveland Airport Authority, Colo., 1990—92; mem. found. adv. coun. Front Range CC, Ft. Collins, 1998—; mem. Crossroads Safehouse Bd., 2006—; mem. vestry St. Luke Episcopal Ch., Ft. Collins, 1998. Col. USMC, 1974—2005. Mem.: Wyo. Bar Assn., Nebr. Bar Assn., Colo. Bar Assn., Colo. Trial Lawyers Assn. (mem. exec. com., other coms. 1986—98), Fox Acres Country Club (bd. dirs. 2004—06). Avocations: flying, horseback riding, hiking, camping, fishing. Office: 2038 Caribou Dr Ste 100 Fort Collins CO 80525

RAY, SUSAN ELAINE, principal; b. Huntington, W.Va. d. Emory Joseph and Frances Fulkerson Ray. BS, Fla. State U., Tallahassee, 1974, MS in Edn., 1976; MS in Edn. Adminstrn., Coll. New Rochelle, NYC, 2003; post grad., St. Johns U. Cert. tchr. N.Y., Fla., admistr. N.Y., Fla. Tchr. Longwood Ctrl. Schs., Middle Island, NY, 1979—85; instr. Elon Coll., NC, 1986—87; tchr. Riverside H.S., Durham, 1988—2000; instr. edn. Kamuzu Coll., Lilogwe, Malawi, 2000; asst. prin. Lake Grove (N.Y.) Sch., 2001—02, Copiague Mid. Sch., 2003—04; prin. The Broach Sch., St. Petersburg, Fla., 2005—. Staff developer Tchg. Children of Poverty and Tng. New Tchrs., Copiague, NY, 2003—04; dir. The Broach Sch., St. Petersburg, Fla., 2005—. Youth coach U.S. Volleyball Assn., Durham, NC, 1988—99; site dir. Internat. Spl. Olympics, 1999; active Tchrs. Africa Fellowship, 2000—01. Recipient Outstanding Achievement in Edn award, Duke U., 1998; named Durham County Tchr. of Yr., 1998, State Volleyball Coach of Yr., N.C. H.S. Athletic Assn., 1998. Mem.: ASCD, Phi Delta Kappa.

RAY, THOMAS M., history professor; b. Tulsa, Okla., July 25, 1952; s. John R. and Jeanne M. Ray; m. Linda W. Ray, Aug. 19, 1972; children: Christy Jolly, Nathan Thomas. BA, Okla. City U., 1974; MA, Tex. Christian U., Fort Worth, 1977. Tchg. asst. Tex. Christian U., Fort Worth, Tex., 1977—80; instr. History James Madison U., Harrisonburg, Va., 1980—83; instr. history, Wayland Bapt. U., Plainview, Tex., 1983—85, asst. prof. history, 1985—97, Chair, honors coun., 1992—97, assoc. prof. history, 1997—. Contbr. to numerous profl. jours. Deacon First Bapt. Ch., Plainview, 1998—. Recipient Faculty Svc. award, Wayland Bapt. U., 1991, Disting. Faculty Svc. Alumni award, Assn. former Students, WBU, 2005; named Outstanding Sr. Man, Coll. Arts and Sci. Okla. City U., 1974. Mem.: Southwestern Hist. Assn., Soc. Historians Early Am. Republic, Phi Alpha Theta. Southern Baptist. Avocation: travel. Home: 1214 Amarillo St Plainview TX 79072 Office: Wayland Baptist Univ 1900 W 7th St Plainview TX 79072 Office Fax: 806-291-1972. Business E-Mail: tomray@wbu.edu.

RAY, WAYNE ALLEN, epidemiologist, educator; b. Yakima, Wash., July 2, 1949; s. Allen and Patsy (McKay) R.; m. Janine Elise Thorson, June 11, 1972; children: Lily Amelia, Lea Camille. BS, U. Washington, 1971; MS, Vanderbilt U., 1974, PhD, 1981. Research assoc. Vanderbilt U. Sch. Medicine, Nashville, 1974-75, research instr., 1975-78, research asst. prof., 1979-83, asst. prof., 1984-85, dir. div. pharmacoepidemiology, 1984—, assoc. prof., 1985-90, prof., 1991—. Contbr. articles to profl. jours. Recipient Burroughs Wellcome scholar in Pharmacoepidemiology Am. Coll. Preventive Medicine, 1984. Mem. Am. Statis. Assn., Assn. Computing Machinery, Computer Soc. of IEEE, Soc. Epidemiologic Research, Am. Pub. Health Assn., Phi Beta Kappa. Avocation: gardening. Office: Vanderbilt U A-1124 Medical Ctr N 1211 22d Ave S Nashville TN 37232-2637*

RAY, WILLIAM JACKSON, psychologist; b. Birmingham, Ala., Sept. 3, 1945; s. William J. and Mary K. Ray; m. Judith Mebane, Aug. 22, 1987; children from previous marriage: Adam, Lauren. BA, Eckerd Coll., 1967; MA, Vanderbilt U., 1969, PhD, 1971; Fellow in med. psychology, Langley Porter Neuropsychiat. Inst., U. Calif. Med. Center, San Francisco, 1971-72. Prof., dir. clin. psychology tng. program Pa. State U., 1972—, dir. clin. trng., 1991-97, dir. scan program specialization cognitive & effective neurosci., 2007—. Author: (with R.M. Stern) Biofeedback, 1977, (with others) Evaluation of Clinical Biofeedback, 1979, (with R.M. Stern and C.M. Davis) Psychophysiological Recording, 1980, 2d edit. (with R.M. Stern and K. Quigley), 2000, Methods Toward a Science of Behavior and Experience, 1981, 9th edit., 2009, (with E. Susman & L. Feajous) Emotion, Cognition, Health and Development in Children and Adolescents, 1992, (with L. Michelson) Handbook of Dissociation, 1996 (Cornelia Wilbur award ISSD); series editor: Plenum Series in Behavioral Psychophysiology and Medicine. Recipient Nat. Media award Am. Psychol. Found., 1976, 78, Rsch. award Best Empirical Paper, Soc. Clin. Experimental Hypnosis. Mem. AAAS, APA, APS, Soc. Psychophysiol. Rsch. Office: Dept Psychology Pa State U University Park PA 16802 Home Phone: 814-234-3402; Office Phone: 814-863-1726. Business E-Mail: wjr@psu.edu.

RAYBACK, CYNTHIA ANN, educational association administrator; b. Washington; d. Myrtle Ruth and Thomas Benjamin Smith; m. James Randall Rayback; 1 child, Randall Benjamin. BS, U. Nebr., Kearney. Cert. in vocat. credential Colo. State, 2009. Academic advisor Front Range CC, Longmont, Colo., 2006—, instr. Westminster, Colo., coord. tutor svcs. Recipient Tchg. & Leadership Excellence award, NISOD, U. Tex., Austin, 1998. Mem.: Nat. Bus. Educators. Avocations: travel, swimming, yoga. Office: 2190 Miller Dr Longmont CO 80501 Office Phone: 303-678-3722. Business E-Mail: cindy.rayback@frontrange.edu.

RAYBURN, CAROLE ANN (MARY AIDA), psychologist, researcher, writer, consultant; b. Washington, Feb. 14, 1938; d. Carl Frederick and Mary Helen (Milkie) Miller; m. Ronald Allen Rayburn (dec. Apr. 1970). BA in Psychology, Am. U., 1961; MA in Clin. Psychology, George Washington U., 1965; PhD in Ednl. Psychology, Cath. U. Am., 1969;

MDiv in Ministry, Andrews U., 1980. Lic. psychologist, Md. Psychometrician Columbian Prep. Sch., Washington, 1963; clin. psychologist Spring Grove State Hosp., Catonsville, Md., 1966—68; pvt. practice, 1969, 1971—; staff clin. psychologist Instl. Care Svcs. Divsn. D.C. Children's Ctr., Laurel, Md., 1970—78; psychologist Md. Dept. Vocat. Rehab., 1973—74; psychometrician Montgomery County Pub. Schs., 1981—85. Lectr. Strayer Coll., Washington, 1969-70; forensic psychology expert witness, 1973—; guest lectr. Andrews U., Berrien Springs, Mich., 1979, Hood Coll, Frederick, Md., 1986-88; instr. Johns Hopkins U., 1986, 88-89; adj. faculty Profl. Sch. Psychology Studies, San Diego, 1987; adj. asst. prof. Loyola Coll., Columbia, Md., 1987; cons. Julia Brown Montessori Schs., 1972, 78, 82—, VA Ctr., 1978, 91-93; adv. grad. psychol. students Cardinal Strich U., Milw., 2005-. Author (copyrighted inventories); Religious Occupational and Stress Questionnaire, 1986, Organizational Relationships Survey, 1987, Attitudes Toward Children Inventory, 1987, State-Trait Morality Inventory, 1987, Body Awareness and Sexual Intimacy Comfort Scale (BASICS), 1993, Inventory on Religiousness, 1996, Inventory on Spirituality, 1996, Sports, Exercise, Leadership and Friendship Questionnaire, 1997, Peacefulness Inventory, Life Choices Inventory, 1998, Inventory on the Supreme and Work, 1999, Children's and Adolescents' Peace Inventory, 2002, Inventory on Well-Being, 2004, TEACH: Traumatic Experiences and Children's and Adolescents' Health, 2005, Creative Personality Inventory, 2005, Intuition Inventory, 2005, Health and Traumatic Experiences in Adults, 2005, Inventory on Religiousness, Children's Version, 2005; Co-editor: (with M.J. Meadow) A Time to Weep and a Time to Sing, 1985, (with Violet Franks) Springer Pub Focus on Women Series Co-ed, 2005, (with Lillian Comas-Diaz) Woman Soul: Inner Life of Women's Spirituality, 2008, Psychology of Women Series, 2008, (with E. Gavin, A. Clamar, M.A. Siderits) Women of Vision, 2007; contbg. author: Montessori: Her Method and the Movement (What You Need to Know), 1973, Drugs, Alcohol and Women: A National Forum Source Book, 1975, The Other Side of the Couch: Faith of the Psychotherapist, 1981, Clinical Handbook of Pastoral Counseling, 1985, An Encyclopedic Dictionary of Pastoral Care and Counseling, 1990, Religion Personality and Mental Health, 1993; co-editor (with Violet Franks) Springer Focus on Women series; cons. editor Profl. Psychology, 1980-83; assoc. editor: Jour. Pastoral Counseling, 1985-90, guest editor, 1988; coproposer: (with Lee Richmond) The Theory and Field of Theobiology: interfacing of theology and the sciences, 1998; mem. editl. bd.: Internat. Jour. Ethics (Nova Sci.), 2004—; contbr. numerous articles to profl. jours. Bd. dirs. Psychologists Ethical Treatment of Animals, 1998-2000; spkrs. Task Force Mont County NOW, 2002-07, treas., 2005-07, chair Task Force Women's Spirituality, pres., 2007-. Recipient Svc. award Coun. for Advancement Psychol. Professions and Scis., 1975, cert. D.C. Dept. Human Resources, 1975, 76, cert. recognition D.C. Psychol. Assn., 1976, 1985; AAUW rsch. grantee, 1983. Fellow: APA (editl. bd. Jour. Child Clin. Psychology 1978—82, divsn. psychology women chair task force on women and religion 1980—81, chair equal opportunity affirmative action divsn. clin. psychology 1980—82, clin. psychology women's sect. 1984—86, divsn. psychology issues in grad. edn. and clin. tng. 1988—, program chair 1991—94, pres. divsn. psychology of religion 1995—96, gen. psych. divsn. liaison to commn. internat. rels. 2004—, fellow com. mem. clin. psychology divsn. 2006, fellows chair, clin. psychology divsn. 2007—, fellow, divsn. on internat. psychology, divsn. psychology of religion, psychology of women, clin. psychology, cons. psychology, gen. psychology, psychotherapy, state assn. affairs, divsn. media psychology, divsn. family psychology, soc. psychol., study social issues, div. child youth & family svcs., health psychology, edn. psychology, sch. coun. psychology, psychology ethnic minority affairs, ednl. psychology, Sch. Psychology, Mentoring award divsn. clin. psychology, sect. of clin. psychology of women 1997, divsn. psychology of religion 1997, William C. Bier rsch. award divsn. psychology of religion 2000), APA Soc. Clin. Psychology (chair 2005—09), Md. Psychol. Assn. (editor newsletter 1975—76, chair ins. com. 1981—83, pres. 1984—85, exec. adv. com. 1985—, chpt. recognition 1978), Am. Assn. Applied & Preventive Psychology (sec. 1992—93, chair fellows com. 1992—93), Am. Orthopsychiat. Assn.; mem.: NOW (treas. 2005—07, pres. Montgomery County, Md. chpt. 2007—09), Md. Assn. Counseling and Devel., Md. Assn. Measurement and Evaluation (pres. 2005—07), Balt. Assn. Cons. Psychologists (pres. 1991—92), Assn. Practicing Psychologists Montgomery-Prince George's Counties (pres. 1986—88, editor newsletter 1990—, treas. 1996—98), Internat. Soc. Polit. Psychology, Psi Chi (hon.). Achievements include research in stress in religious professionals, women and stress, women and religion, pastoral counseling, state-trait morality inventory, leadership, mentoring, clergy stress, psychotherapy, children, body image; intimacy, peacefulness, spirituality, life choices, religiousness, well-being, work, traumatic experiences and health, creative personality, intuition. Address: 1200 Morningside Dr Silver Spring MD 20904-3149 Personal E-mail: valentinecarole@copper.net.

RAYBURN, WILLIAM FRAZIER, obstetrician, gynecologist, educator; b. Lexington, Ky., Aug. 19, 1950; s. Charles Calvin and Charlotte Elizabeth (Ballard) R.; m. Pamela Rae Gilleland, Nov. 27, 1976; children: Lindsay Ann, Britany Beth, Drake Tanner. BS, Hampden Sydney Coll., 1971; MD, U. Ky., 1975; MBA in Healthcare Bus. Adminstrn., U. Tex., 2007. Diplomate Nat. Bd. Med. Examiners, Am. Bd. Ob.-Gyn. (examiner), Divsn. Maternal-Fetal Medicine. Intern family medicine U. Iowa Hosps. and Clinics, Iowa City, Iowa, 1975-76; resident ob.-gyn. U. Ky. Med. Ctr., Lexington, 1976-79; fellow in maternal-fetal medicine dept. ob.-gyn. Ohio State U. Hosps., Columbus, 1979-81; asst. prof. ob.-gyn. U. Mich. Med. Sch., Ann Arbor, 1981-83, assoc. prof. ob.-gyn., 1983-86; assoc. prof. dept. ob.-gyn. and pharmacology U. Nebr. Coll. of Medicine, Omaha, 1985-88, prof. dept. ob-gyn. and pharmacology, 1988-92, U. Okla. Coll. Medicine, Oklahoma City, 1992-98, John W. Records endowed chair, 1992-98; prof. dept. ob/gyn U. N.Mex. Sch. Medicine, Albuquerque, 1998—, chair dept. ob/gyn, 1998—. Prof., chair dept. ob-gyn. U. N.Mex. Sch. Medicine, Albuquerque, 1998—, Randolph V. Seligman endowed prof., 1999—; chief obstetrics U. Okla. Coll. Medicine, Oklahoma City, 1992-98; dir. maternal fetal medicine dept. ob-gyn. U. Mich. Med. Ctr., 1981-85; reviewer for various jours.; mem. staff U. Nebr. Med. Ctr., 1985-92, U. Okla. Health Sci. Ctr., 1992-98, Presbyn. Hosp., Oklahoma City, 1992-98, Univ. Hosp., Albuquerque, 1998—; chief staff U. N.Mex. Hosps., 2006-08, bd. regents U. N.Mex., 2006-; bd. trustees U. N.Mex. Hosp., 2006-. Author: Obstetrics/Gynecology: Pre Test Self Assessment and Review, 1982; (with others) Every Woman's Pharmacy: A Guide to Safe Drug Use, 1983, Obstetrics for the House Officer, 1984, 2d rev. edit., 1988, Every Woman's Pharmacy, 1984, The Women's Health and Drug Reference, 1993, Oklahoma Notes: Obstetrics and Gynecology, 1994, 2d rev. edit., 1996, Obstetrics and Gynecology for the House Officer, 1996, 2d rev. edit., 2001; editor: (with F.P. Zuspan) Drug Therapy in Obstetrics and Gynecology, 1982, 3d rev. edit., 1992; symposia editor Diagnosis and Management of the Malformed Fetus, Jour. Reprod. Medicine, 1982, Operative Obstetrics, Clinics in Perinatology, 1983, Controversies in Fetal Drug Therapy, Clin. Obstetrics and Gynecology, 1991, Drugs in Pregnancy, Clinical Obstetrics and Gynecology, 2002, Substance Use Disorders in Women, 2003; editor-in-chief Jour. Reproductive Medicine, 2002-03; contbr. more than 50 chpts. to books, more than 250 articles to profl. jours., delivered more than 185 abstract papers at sci. meetings. Dir. maternal and infant care programs U. Nebr. Med. Ctr., Omaha, 1986-92; U.S. Pharmacopeia Conv. field reviewer, 1983—. Recipient Residents' prize paper award Ky. Ob.-Gyn. Soc., 1978, 79, Faculty Teaching award for Excellence, 1993, 94, 96, 03, 04, 05, Rsch. Excellence award Soc. Perinatal Obstetricians, 1998, Nat. Tchg. award Assn. Profs. in Gynecology & Obstetrics, 2005, Disting. Alumnus award, U. Ky. Coll. Medicine, 2005. Fellow Am. Coll. Ob-Gyn. (Ephraim McDowell prize paper award 2d pl. 1978, 1st pl. 1979, Searle-Donald F. Richardson Prize Paper award 1980, Best Doctors in Am., 1998, 2000); mem. Am. Gynecol. and Obstet. Soc., Coun. Univ. Chairs in Ob-Gyn., Soc. Maternal Fetal Medicine, Assn. Profs. in Gynecology and Obstetrics (Faculty Excellence in Tchg 2005), Soc. for Gynecol. Investigation, Teratology Soc. Achievements include contributions to the knowledge of drug effcts on developing fetus and of principals about induction of labor and to the influence he has had on peers not only through teaching and patient care but through his extensive writing. Office: U New Mex Health Sci Ctr 2211 Lomas Blvd NE # Acc-4 Albuquerque NM 87106-2745 Office Phone: 505-272-6372.

RAY CHAUDHURI, SAMIT, civil engineer, researcher; married. PhD, U. Calif., Irvine, 2005. Cert. in EIT, Calif., 2008. Postdoc. rschr. U. Calif., 2006—. Recipient award, Calif. Inst. Telecom. and Info. Tech., 2002; Regent's fellowship, U. Calif., 2001—02. Office: Univ Calif Irvine Dept Civil and Environ Engring Irvine CA 92697-2175

RAYCHOWDHURY, SUBHENDU, research scientist; b. Kirnahar, West Bengal, India, Mar. 29, 1971; s. Sibshankar and Anjali Roychowdhury; m. Oli Chattoraj; 1 child, Sheelon Roychowdhury. PhD, Indian Inst. Tech., Kharagpur, 2001. Cert. scientist, NJIT, 2006. Vis. scientist Pusan Nat. U., Republic of Korea, 2001—01; postdoc. assoc. Cornell U., Ithaca, NY, 2001—05, Pa. State U., State Coll., 2005—06; rsch. scientist NJ. Inst. Tech., Newark, 2006—08; scientist NFTDC, Hyderabad, Andrapredesh, India, 2009—. Contbr. scientific papers to numerous publs. Cultural Sec. B. C. Roy Hall. Recipient Best Cultural Sec. award, 2000; Fellowship, CSIR, 1995. Mem.: ACS. Home: Plot 77 Vinay nagar Apt 502 Hyderabad Andrapradesh 500059 India Office: NFTDC Kanchanbagh Hyderabad Andhrapradesh 500058 India Personal E-mail: rcsubhendu@gmail.com. Business E-Mail: rcsubhen@njit.edu.

RAYKOV, IVAN L., mathematics professor; s. Lyuben I. Raykov and Kamelia V. Raykova. PhD, Inst. Math., BAS, Sofia, 2000. Diploma Ministry Sci. and Edn., Bulgaria, 2000. Vis. prof. Ohio U., Athens, 2005—08; lectr. Ohio State U. Newark, Ohio, 2008—. Vis. prof. U. Toledo, 2002—05. Contbr. scientific papers. Activist Dem. Party, UDF, Varna, Bulgaria. Mem.: UMB, EMS, SIAM, MS. Home: 1370 Residence Dr Newark OH 43055 Office: Ohio State Univ Newark Dept Math Newark OH 43055 Business E-Mail: raykov.1@osu.edu.

RAYLE, HEATHER LYNNETTE, chemist; b. Greensboro, NC, June 10, 1968; d. Donald Lee and Sharon Sue R. BS in Chemistry with high distinction, Pa. State U., 1989; PhD in Chemistry, UCLA, 1994; MBA, Lehigh U., 2001. Sr. scientist Rohm & Haas Co., Spring House, Pa., 1994-98, rsch. sect. mgr., 1998-99, mgr. tech. planning, 1999-2000, bus. devel. mgr., 2001—03, mktg. dir., 2003—05, dir. slurry technology, 2006—; pres. Advanced Materials, 2008—09; global gen. mgr. Optical and Ceramic Techs., 2009—. Bd. dirs. Rohm & Haas Tech. Comty. Orgn., Spring House, Pa., 1997-2000, chair 1999; alumni bd. Pa. State U. Coll. Sci., 2001—, treas., 2005—, v.p., 2007—; exec. mem. com. SEMI Chems. and Gas Mfrs. Group, 2005-07. Braddock scholarship, Pa. State U. Coll. of Sci., 1985-89; fellow NSF, 1989-92, fellow UCLA, 1989-94; recipient Otto Haas award for Scientific Achievement, 1998. Mem. Am. Chem. Soc., Phi Beta Kappa. Achievements include development of commerical processes to manufacture agricultural chemicals and their intermediates; commercial marketing and technology management of materials for semiconductor processing. Office: Dow Electronics Materials 455 Forest St Marlborough MA 01752

RAYLESBERG, ALAN IRA, lawyer; b. NYC, Dec. 6, 1950; s. Daniel David and Sally Doris (Mantell) Raylesberg; m. Caren Thea Coven, Nov. 20, 1983; children: Lisa Maris, Jason Todd. BA in Polit. Sci., NYU, 1972; JD cum laude, Boston U., 1975. Bar: NY 1976, US Dist. Ct. (so. dist.) NY 1976, US Dist. Ct. (ea. dist.) NY 1978, US Tax Ct. 1981, US Ct. Appeals (2d and 5th cirs.) 1982, US Ct. Appeals (1st cir.) 1986, US Ct. Appeals (9th cir.) 1996, US Ct. Appeals (fed. cir.) 2004. Assoc. Orans, Elsen & Polstein, NYC, 1975-77; from assoc. to ptnr. Guggenheimer & Untermyer, NYC, 1977—85; ptnr. Rosenman & Colin, NYC, 1985—2002, co-chmn. litig. dept., 1998—99, chmn. litig. dept., 1999—2002; ptnr., sect. head litig. group Vinson & Elkins, NYC, 2002—04; ptnr. Chadbourne & Parke, NYC, 2004—, co-head comml. litig. group, 2006—. Adj. instr. NY Law Sch., 1980—83; instr. Nat. Inst. Trial Advocacy; mem. adv. group comml. divsn., mem. mediation panel NY State Supreme Ct.; mem. arbitration panel US Dist. Ct. (ea. dist.) NY; mem. CPR Inst. Dispute Resolution Panel Disting. Neutrals, NYC; judge Nat. Moot Ct. Competition, 1980—. Author: Case Evaluation, Commercial Litigation in New York State Courts, 2005; editor: Boston U. Law Rev., 1974—75. Bd. dirs. Fund Modern Cts., 1994—. Recipient Humanitarian award, Award of Courage Found., 2006. Fellow: NY Bar Found.; mem.: ABA, NY Coun. Def. Lawyers, Securities Industry Assn. Legal and Compliance Divsn., NY State Bar Assn. (house of dels. 1996—2000), NY County Lawyers Assn. Found. (bd. dirs. 1998—2003), NY County Lawyers Assn. (mem. fed. ct. com. 1988—, mem. appellate ct. com. 1990—, co-chmn. appellate ct. com. 1992—93, chair appellate ct. com. 1993—96, bd. dirs. 1995—98, 1999—2002), Assn. Bar City NY, Fed. Bar Coun., Town Club New Castle (mem. exec. com. 1987—91). Democrat. Jewish. Office: Chadbourne & Parke LLP 30 Rockefeller Plz New York NY 10112 Office Phone: 212-408-5198. Business E-Mail: araylesberg@chadbourne.com.

RAYMAN, RUSSELL BARRY, physician; b. Toledo, Ohio, Jan. 13, 1936; m. Ludy Rayman; children; Joseph, David, Ariel. MD, U. Mich., 1961. Diplomate Am. Bd. Family Practice, Am. Bd. Aerospace Medicine. Intern Jackson Meml. Hosp., Miami, Fla., 1961-62; commd. 2d lt. USAF, 1962, advanced through grades to col., 1989; resident in aerospace medicine Brooks AFB, Tex., 1969-72; mgr. operational medicine Lockheed, Washington, 1989-92; exec. dir. Aerospace Med. Assn., Alexandria, Va., 1992—. Author: Clinical Aviation Medicine, 1982, 4th edit., 2006. Decorated numerous mil. awards. Office: Aerospace Med Assn 320 S Henry St Alexandria VA 22314-3524

RAYMER, JAMES HOWARD, chemist, researcher; b. Lyons, NY; life ptnr. Evan J. Ellis-Raymer. BA, SUNY Coll., Brockport, 1979; PhD, Ind. U., Bloomington, 1984. Sr. rsch. chemist RTI Internat., Rsch. Triangle Pk., NC, 1984—. Mem.: Am. Chem. Soc., Internat. Soc. Exposure Sci. Liberal. Office: RTI Internat 3040 Cornwallis Rd Research Triangle Park NC 27709 Office Phone: 919-541-5924. E-mail: jraymer@rti.org.

RAYMER, JOHN DAVID, literature and language professor; b. Elkhart, Ind., July 9, 1948; m. Kathleen Russell, June 24, 2006; children: Carolyn Mary McEachran, Janet Theresa, Thomas Joseph, Mariah Trench. BA, Wittenberg U., Springfield, Ohio, 1970; MA, Nat. U. Ireland, Dublin, 1971; PhD, Ohio U., Athens, 1975; postdoctoral, Purdue U., West Lafayette, Ind. Asst. prof. English Purdue U., Hammond, Ind., 1976—80; ins. agt. C.M. Alliance Group Inc., South Bend, Ind., 1980—90; adj. asst. prof. Ind. U., South Bend, 1989—94; adj. tchr. Saint Mary's Coll., Norte Dame, Ind., 2007—08; assoc. prof. English Holy Cross Coll., Notre Dame, Ind., 1990—; lectr. Purdue U. North Ctrl. Campus, Westville, Ind., 2008—. Chair faculty forum Holy Cross Coll., Notre Dame, 1991—93, homework tutoring campus coord., 1994—2006, co-founder, dir. homework tutoring program, 1995—, acad. affairs faculty rep., 1997—98, chair promotions and retention com., 2005—, chair, dept. English, 2008—; mem. Ind. Middle Grades Reading Network, 1993—, Nat. Scholastic Hon.; adv. editor Collegiate Press, 1995—2004; mentee Midwest Tech. Tchg. Acad., Chgo., 2000—01; book reviewer Salem Press, Pasadena, Calif., 2007—. Contbg. editor: The Hole in Me Since the Day You Died, 2005 (Reader of June 2008 AP English Lang. Examination, Daytona Beach, Fla.). Leader student groups South Bend Walk for Hospice; founding mem. English Connection; former bd. mem., pres. Big Brothers/Big Sisters, South Bend; lectr. St. Michael and All Angels Episcopal Ch., South Bend, Ind., 1996—, sr. warden, 2004—; bd. mem. Dismas House, South Bend, Ind., 2007. Recipient Outstanding Cmty.-Coll. Collaboration award, Coll. Compact, Miami Beach, Fla., 1998, Attendance award, Kiwanis Internat., 2003, 2004, George Hixson award, 2004, Outstanding Young Men of Am. award; named Outstanding Mentoree of U. Notre Dame bound students, 2005. Mem.: Internat. Reading Assn., Knute Rockne Kiwanis Club, Phi Kappa Phi. Democrat. Episcopalian. Avocations: travel, swimming, canoeing, hiking, reading, painting. Home: 1613 E Madison St South Bend IN 46617 Office: Holy Cross Coll 54515 State Rd 933 Notre Dame IN 46556-0308

RAYMOND, BRUCE ALLEN, retired surgeon, medical association administrator; b. Aberdeen, SD, Dec. 8, 1924; s. Samuel A. and Pearl (Blackstone) R.; m. Virginia Stratton, Apr. 2, 1948 (div. 1969); children: Judith Ann, Jaqueline Marie, Bruce Allen Jr., Brian Andrew; m. Jane Molnar, Nov. 15, 1969; children: Douglas A., Andrew D., Colin K. BS, Leland Stanford U., U. S.D., 1945; MD, Washington U., St. Louis, 1949. Diplomate Am. Bd. Surgery, Am. Bd. Thoracic Surgery. Intern U. Ored. Med. Sch. Hosps., Portland, 1949-50; resident Walter Reed Gen. Hosp., Washington, 1953—60, asst. chief thoracic surgery, 1959-60; chief thoracic and cardiovascular surgery Letterman Gen. Hosp., San Francisco, 1960-64, Fitzsimmons Gen. Hosp., Denver, 1967-69, chief dept. surgery, 1969-71; pvt. practice surgery Warwick, RI, 1975-86; sr. med. dir. various insurance co.; med. dir. The Health Plan of the Upper Ohio Valley, 1996—2003. Asst. clin. prof. U. Colo., 1967-71; assoc. clin. prof. surgery Northwestern U., Chgo., 1973-80; mem. staff Kent County Med. Mem. Hosp., Warwick, 1975-86, Miriam hosp., Providence, 1975-86; cons. in field. Contbr. articles to profl. jours. Col. MC US Army, 1949—72. Decorated Legion of Merit. Fellow ACS, Am. Coll. Cardiology, Am. Coll. Chest Physicians; mem. Soc. Thoracic Surgeons. Avocation: downhill skiing. Home: 218 Salem Dr Upper Saint Clair PA 15241-2226 Personal E-mail: braymond66@adelphia.net.

RAYMOND, DAVID ALAN, business executive, former government official; b. Frankfurt, Apr. 30, 1948; s. Jack and Gertrude Raymond; m. Dorothy (Molly) C. Dillon; children: Sam, Anna. BA with honors, Princeton U., 1969; MA, Tufts U., 1970; JD, Georgetown U., 1977. Asst. dean. Sch. Fgn. Service, Georgetown U., 1970-74; sr. legis. and fgn. policy aide U.S. Senator Stuart Symington, Armed Services Com. and Fgn. Relations Com., 1974-77; exec. asst. to adminstr. of AID, U.S. Dept. State, 1977-79; dep. dir. U.S. reimbursable devel. program, 1979-80; founding dir. U.S. Trade and Devel. Agy., 1980-81; internat. v.p. TAMS Engrs., Inc., 1981-85; dir. internat. programs ENSERCH Corp., 1985-89; pres. Ebasco Svcs. Internat., NYC, 1989-93; internat. v.p. Raytheon Engrs. and Constructors, 1994—99; pres., CEO Am. Coun. of Engring. Cos., 1999—. Mem. Coun. Fgn. Rels., NYC; Com. of 100, US C. of C.; former bd. dirs. USA-ROC Bus. Coun., Washington, Ebasco-ECEPDI, Shanghai, China, Gibsin Engrs., Taiwan; former chmn. US C. of C. US Romania Bus. Coun., Washington, US-ASEAN Coun. Vietnam Bus. Com. Office: ACEC 1015 15th St 8th Fl Washington DC 20005-2605 Business E-Mail: draymond@acec.org.

RAYMOND, DAVID WALKER, lawyer; b. Chelsea, Mass., Aug. 23, 1945; s. John Walker and Jane (Beck) R.; m. Sandra Sue Broadwater, Aug. 12, 1967 (div.); m. Margaret Byrd Payne, May 25, 1974; children: Pamela Payne, Russell Wyatt. BA, Gettysburg Coll., 1967; JD, Temple U., 1970. Bar: Pa. 1970, D.C. 1971, Ill. 1975, U.S. Dist. Ct. (no. dist.) Ill. 1981, U.S. Supreme Ct. 1974. Govtl. affairs atty. Sears, Roebuck and Co., Washington, 1970-74, atty. Sears Hdqrs. law dept. Chgo., 1974-80, asst. gen. counsel advt., trademarks and customs, 1981-84, asst. gen. counsel adminstrn., 1984-86, mgr. planning and analysis corp. planning dept., 1986-89, sr. corp. counsel pub. policy corp. law dept., 1989-90; assoc. gen. counsel litigation and adminstrn. law dept. Sears Mdse. Group, 1990-92, dep. gen. counsel, 1992-93, v.p., gen. counsel, 1993-95; v.p. law Sears Roebuck and Co., 1996; of counsel Winston & Strawn, Washington, 1996-2001; v.p., gen. counsel C-NAV Systems, Inc., Gettysburg, Pa., 2001—03. Mem. staff Temple Law Quar., 1968—69; editor: Temple Law Quar., 1969—70. Trustee No. Ill. U., 1996—98; bd. vis. Christopher Newport U., 1999—2003; bd. fellows Gettysburg Coll., 1999—2003; bd. dirs. ATO Chpt. House Corp., 1997—, pres., 2004—. Mem.: ABA, Phi Alpha Delta. Presbyterian. Personal E-mail: dwraymond74@cox.net.

RAYMOND, FRED DOUGLAS, III, lawyer; b. Phila., May 12, 1958; s. F. Douglas Jr. and Carolyn Sue (MacReynolds) R.; m. Elizabeth Tuan Partridge, June 28, 1980; children: Peter Randolph, Alexander Partridge, Louisa Woodward. AB cum laude, Harvard U., 1980; JD magna cum laude, U. Pa., 1985. Bar: Pa. 1985, U.S. Ct. Appeals (3d cir.) 1986. Comml. banker Fidelity Bank, Phila., 1980-82; jud. clk. U.S. Ct. Appeals (3d cir.), Phila., 1985-86; ptnr. Drinker, Biddle & Reath LLP, Phila., 1996-99, mng. ptnr., 2000—, mktg. ptnr., 1996—99, head corp. securities, 1996—. Contbr. articles to law jours. Bd. dirs. Children's Aid Soc., Pa., 1992—. Mem. Independence Hall Assn. (bd. dirs., sec. 1984—). Home: 605 Winsford Rd Bryn Mawr PA 19010-2603 Office: Drinker Biddle & Reath LLP 1100 PNB Bldg 1 Logan Sq 18th & Cherry St Philadelphia PA 19103-6996 Office Phone: 215-988-2548. Office Fax: 215-988-2757. Business E-Mail: doug.raymond@dbr.com, fdr@dbr.com.

RAYMOND, GEORGE MARC, city planner, educator; b. Odessa, Russia, Jan. 1, 1919; came to U.S., 1937, naturalized, 1942; s. Mark J. and Rachelle (Schneiderman) R.; m. Kathleen E. Waid, Oct. 3, 1942 (div. Mar. 1978); 1 dau., Valerie M.; m. Lois Jean Gainsboro, Mar. 26, 1979. BArch, Columbia, 1946. Planning dir. Harrison, Ballard & Allen, Inc., NYC, 1952-54; founder, pres. Raymond, Parish, Pine & Weiner, Inc., 1954-83; pres. George M. Raymond Assocs., 1983—2006; prof. planning, chmn. dept. city and regional planning Pratt Inst., Bklyn., 1959-75; founder, dir. Pratt Ctr. for Community Improvement, Bklyn., 1963-70. Lectr. planning Columbia U., 1955-58; lectr. planning and urban renewal New Sch. Social Rsch., 1967-72; pres. Assn. Collegiate Sch. Planning, 1968-69; chmn. Westchester County Housing Implementation Commn., 1992-93. Editor: Pratt Planning Papers, 1963-73, (with

Astrid Monson) Pratt Guide to Housing, Planning and Urban Renewal for New Yorkers, 1965. V.p. Citizens Housing and Planning Coun. N.Y.C., 1967-86, N.Y. Assn. Environ. Profls., 1977-79; pres. Westchester Citizens Housing Coun., 1964-66, Met. Com. on Planning, 1950-51; founder, pres. Friends of Music Concerts, 1954-57, Spoken Arts Soc., 1966-67; past 1st v.p. Federated Conservationists Westchester County; past dir. Nat. Housing Conf., Phipps Houses, Wave Hill, Settlement Housing Fund; chmn. Westchester County Housing Opportunity Commn., 1994—; land use adv. com. N.Y. State Legis. Commn. on Rural Resources, 1992-98. Fellow: Am. Inst. Cert. Planners; mem.: Am. Planning Assn. (pres. NY met. chpt. 1983—85), Am. Soc. Cons. Planners (pres. 1968—70). Home: 192 Locust Ln Irvington NY 10533-2315 Office: 101 Executive Blvd Elmsford NY 10523-1316

RAYMOND, JILL M., microbiologist, educator; d. Joseph M and Judith R Turchany; m. Andrew V Raymond, May 16, 1998. BS in Biology cum laude, Northern Ill. U., 1990; PhD in Microbiology, U. of Calif., Davis California, 1993. Postdoctoral rschr. U. of Calif., San Diego, 1993—95; prof. of life sci. Rock Valley Coll., Rockford, Ill., 1995—. Author: (text book) Hands On Biology, Modern Biology, 2005, Human Diseases: A Systemic Approach, 6th edit., 2005. Office: Rock Valley College 3301 N Mulford Rd Rockford IL 61114 Office Fax: 815-921-3469. Business E-Mail: j.raymond@rockvalleycollege.edu.

RAYMOND, JOSHUA H., legislative staff member; b. NYC; m. Lisa Raymond, July 25, 1998; 2 children. BA, Boston U., 1993; MPA, Columbia U. NY, 1997; JD, Georgetown U., Washington, 2002. Bar: NY 2002, DC 2004. Staff Office Mgmt. & Budget The White House, Washington, 1997—99; sr. legis. asst. for Rep. Darlene Hooley US House of Reps., 1999—2001, chief of staff for Rep. Chris Murphy, 2007—; atty. Skadden, Arps, Slate, Meagher and Flom, LLP, 2002—04, DLA Piper, LLP, 2004—07. Office: Office of Congressman Chris Murphy 2439 Rayburn House Office Bldg Washington DC 20515 Office Phone: 220-225-4476. Business E-Mail: joshua.raymond@mail.house.gov.*

RAYMOND, KENNETH NORMAN, chemistry professor, researcher; b. Astoria, Oreg., Jan. 7, 1942; s. George Norman and Helen May (Dunn) R.; m. Jane Galbraith Shell, June 19, 1965 (div. 1976); children: Mary Katherine, Alan Norman; m. Barbara Gabriele Sternitzke, June 17, 1977; children: Gabriella Petra, Christopher Norman. BA, Reed Coll., 1964; PhD, Northwestern U., 1968. Asst. prof. chemistry U. Calif.-Berkeley, 1967-74, assoc. prof., 1974-78, prof., 1978—; vice chmn. dept. U. Calif. Berkeley, 1982-84, 1999—2000, chmn., 1993-96; faculty sr. scientist Lawrence Berkeley Lab., 1996—; dir. Seaborg Ctr., 2002—. Mem. study sect. NIH, 1983—86, 2006—; adv. com. NSF, 1985—87; co-chmn. bd. chem. scis. & tech. NRC, 2000—; co-founder Lumiphore, Inc., 2001; Chancellor's prof. U. Calif., Berkeley, 2007—. Editor: Bioinorganic Chemistry II, 1977; assoc. editor Biology of Metals, 1987-91; editl. bd. Inorganic Chemistry, 1976-86, Accounts Chem. Rsch., 1982-90, Inorganica Chemica Acta f-Block Elements, 1984-90, Jour. Coordination Chemistry, 1981-2003, Jour. Inorganic and Nuclear Chemistry, 1974-81, Jour. Am. Chem. Soc., 1983-95, Topics in Current Chemistry, 1981-97, Metals in Biology, 1993—, Jour. Supramolecular Chemistry, 1992—, Jour. Biol. Inorganic Chemistry, 1996-2004, Procs. NAS USA, 2002-04, Accts. Chem. Rsch., 1982-88, 2005—; US editl. advisor Springer-Verlag in Chemistry, 1972-91; contbr. articles to profl. jours.; author more than 400 papers. Alfred P. Sloan rsch. fellow, 1971-73; Miller rsch. prof., 1977-78, 96, 2004; Guggenheim fellow, 1980-81; recipient E.O. Lawrence award Dept. Energy, 1984, Humboldt Rsch. award for U.S. Scientists, 1992, 2000, Alfred R. Bader award Am. Chem. Soc., 1994, Vollum award Reed Coll., 2002, Izatt/Christensen award, 2005. Mem. NAS, Am. Acad. Arts and Scis., Am. Chem. Soc. (chair divsn. inorganic chemistry 1996, Inorganic Chemistry award, 2008), Am. Crystallographic Soc., Sigma Xi. Democrat. Achievements include 15 patents in field. Office: U Calif Berkeley Dept Chemistry Berkeley CA 94720-1460 E-mail: raymond@socrates.berkeley.edu.

RAYMOND, KRISTY LYNN, language educator; b. Moore, Okla. d. Joseph and Patricia LoVecchio; m. Jason Raymond. BA in English, Southwestern Okla. State U., Weatherford, 1998. Cert. in clad Calif., 2004. English, social sci. tchr. Mohave Mid. Sch., Scottsdale, Ariz., 2002—04; English tchr. Livermore HS, Calif., 2004—. Grant, Livermore Valley Edn. Found., 2008. Office: Livermore High Sch 600 Maple St Livermore CA 94550

RAYMOND, LEE R., retired oil company executive; b. Watertown, SD, Aug. 13, 1938; m. Charlene Raymond, 1960. BSChemE, U. Wis., 1960; PhD ChemE, U. Minn., 1963, LLD (hon.), 2001. Joined Exxon Corp., Tulsa, Okla., 1963; various positions Exxon Co. USA and Creole Petroleum Corp., Houston and Caracas, Venezuela, 1963—72; mgr. planning Exxon Internat. Co., NYC, 1972—75; v.p. Lago Oil, Aruba, 1975—76, pres., 1976—79, Exxon Nuclear Co., Inc., Bellevue, Wash., 1979—81; exec. v.p. Exxon Enterprises Inc., NYC, 1981—83; pres. Esso Inter-Am. Inc., Coral Gables, Fla., 1983—84; sr. v.p. Exxon Corp., NYC, 1984—86, pres., 1987—93, 1996—99, chmn., CEO, 1993—99, Exxon Mobil Corp., Irving, Tex., 1999—2006; chmn. Nat. Petroleum Coun., Washington, 2006—. Bd. dirs. Exxon Corp., 1984—99, Exxon-Mobil Corp., 1999—2005, J.P. Morgan & Co., Inc., 1987—2000, J.P. Morgan Chase & Co., 2000—, Morgan Guaranty Trust Co. NY, Am. Petroleum Inst., 1987—; mem. Emergency Com. for Am. Trade, President's Export Coun.; vice chmn. bd. trustees Am. Enterprise Inst. Bd. dirs. United Negro Coll. Fund, 1991—; mem. adv. bd. Project Shelter Pro-Am, Sect. Energy; trustee Wis. Alumni Rsch. Found., 1987—; bd. dirs., hon. trustee bus. coun. Internat. Understanding, Inc.; mem. innovations in medicine leadership coun. U. Tex. Southwestern Med. Ctr.; ptnr. emeritus N.Y.C. Partnership; vice chmn., bd. trustee Am. Enterprise Inst., Washington; mem. Dallas Citizens Coun., U. Wis. Found., Am. Coun. on Germany, Dallas Com. Fgn. Rels., Coun. on Fgn. Rels., Emergency Com. for Am. Trade, Singapore-US Bus. Coun., Trilateral Commn. Mem.: Am. Inst. Chem. Engrs. (mem. exec. com. of the 21st Century Campaign), Trilateral Commn., Occupl. Physicians Scholarship Fund (chmn. fundraising campaign 1995), Am. Soc. Engring. Edn. (nat. adv. coun.), Singapore-U.S. Bus. Coun., Coun. Fgn. Rels., Nat. Petroleum Coun. (mem. nom. and natural gas coms.), Bus. Roundtable (mem. policy com., security task force, taxation task force, govt. rels. working group), Bus. Coun., NAE. Office: The Nat Petroleum Coun 1625 K St NW Ste 600 Washington DC 20006

RAYMOND, LISA, professional tennis player; b. Norristown, Pa., Aug. 10, 1973; d. Ted and Nancy Raymond. Student, U. Fla. Profl. tennis player WTA Tour, 1993—. Mem. US Fed Cup Team, 1997—98, 2000, 2002—03. Recipient 4 Career singles title, 67 Career Doubles Titles, WTA Tour, 1 career doubles title, ITF; winner US Open, 1996, 2002, Wimbledon, 1999, Australian Open Grand Slam doubles, 2000, Wimbledon, 2001, US Open Grand Slam doubles, 2001, WTA Doubles Championship, 2001, Mixed Doubles Roland Garros, 2003; named NCAA Singles Champion, 1992, 1993; named Doubles Team of Yr., WTA 2006 Player Awards. Avocations: shopping, hanging out with friends, watching television, football, volleyball. Office: WTA Corp Hdqs 1 Progress Plz Ste 1500 Saint Petersburg FL 33701

RAYMOND, MEGAN FREELAND, lawyer; b. Poughkeepsie, NY, Nov. 27, 1980; d. Torrance Crawford and Caroline Freeland Raymond. AB in Biochem. Scis., cum laude, Harvard U., Cambridge, Mass., 2001; JD, U. Va., Charlottesville, 2005. Bar: Mass. 2005, US Ct. Appeals (fed. cir.) 2006, DC 2007. Fellow US FDA Lab. Immunoregulation NIH, Bethesda, Md., 2001—02; law clk. US Ct. Appeals (fed. cir.), Washington, 2005—06; assoc. Ropes & Gray, Washington, 2006—. Contbr. articles to profl. jours. Judge US Figure Skating, 1998—. Mem.: ABA, Giles S. Rich Inn Ct. Avocations: figure skating, ballroom dancing, travel, running. Office: Ropes & Gray 700 12th St NW Ste 900 Washington DC 20005 Business E-Mail: megan.raymond@ropesgray.com.

RAYMOND, RICHARD GERARD, JR., lawyer; b. Detroit, Jan. 1, 1959; s. Richard G. Raymond Sr. and Mary Jo (Bradley) Raymond; m. Holly Lyn Russell, Aug. 4, 1984; 3 children. BS in chemistry, U. Mich., 1981; JD, U. Detroit, 1986. Bar: Mich. 1986, US Dist. Ct. Ea. Dist. Mich. 1986. Indsl. chemist Product-Sol Inc., Birmingham, Mich., 1982-83; assoc. Johnson & Valentine, Detroit, 1986—89; asst. gen. counsel Fruehauf Trailer Corp., 1989; assoc. gen. counsel, asst. sec. Gen. Automotive Corp.; corp. counsel Am. Axle & Mfg. Holdings Inc., 1995—2000, gen. counsel, 2000—. Mem. ABA, Mich. Bar Assn., Detroit Bar Assn., Am. Chem. Soc. Roman Catholic. Office: Am Axle & Mfg Holdings Inc 1840 Holbrook Ave Detroit MI 48212

RAYMOND, URAL WAYNE, retired retail executive; b. Missoula, Mont., May 20, 1944; s. Ural Daniel and Fayetta Arilla Raymond. Student, U. NC, 1969-70, U. Mont., 1962-66, 93-94. Enlisted man U.S. Army, 1966-69, 70-89; advanced through grades to master sgt. U.S. Army, 1985; ret., 1989; advt. mgr. Sears & Roebuck, Missoula, 1993—2000; ret., 2001. Chmn. western dist. Am. Legion Baseball, Missoula, 1997—; pres. Friends of the Libr., Missoula, 1997-99. With U.S. Army, 1966-69. Decorated Bronze Star. Mem. Aubrey Merle Darnielle Meml. Collectors Assn. (treas. state br. 1998—). Democrat. Evangelical. Avocations: collecting license plates, collecting flags, baseball, collecting stamps, collecting coins.

RAYMOND, USHER, IV, (USHER), singer, actor; b. Chattanooga, Tenn., Oct. 14, 1978; s. Jonnetta Patton and Usher Raymond; m. Tameka Foster, Aug. 3, 2007; children: Usher, Naviyd Ely; 3 stepchildren. Co-owner Cleve. Cavaliers NBA team. Singer: (albums) Usher, 1994, My Way, 1997, Live, 1999 (Grammy award Best Male R&B Vocal Performance, 2001), All About U, 2000, 8701, 2001 (Grammy award Best Male R&B Vocal Performance, 2002, Platinum 7 times), Confessions, 2004 (Favorite Pop Album, Favorite R&B Album, Am. Music Awards, 2004, Billboard 200 Album of Yr., 2004, R&B/Hip Hop Album of Yr., Billboard Music Awards, 2004), Here I Stand, 2008, (songs) You Make Me Wanna, 1997 (Soul Train award Best R&B/Soul Single, 1998), Yeah!, 2004 (Best Dance Video, Best Male Video, MTV Video Music Awards, 2004, Hot 100 Single of the Yr., Hot 100 Airplay Single of Yr., Mainstream Top 40 Single of Yr., Billboard Music Awards, 2004); actor: (films) The Faculty, 1998, She's All That, 1999, Light It Up, 1999, Texas Rangers, 2001, In the Mix, 2005; (TV films) Gepetto, 2000; (TV series) Moesha, 1997—98, The Bold and the Beautiful, 1998, (TV guest appearances) The Famous Jett Jackson, 2000, Sabrina the Teenage Witch, 2002, The Twilight Zone, 2002, American Dreams, 2002, 7th Heaven, 2002, Soul Food, 2003; (Broadway plays) Chicago, 2006. Recipient Pop Music award, ASCAP, 2003, Favorite Male Artist award Pop or Rock, Am. Music Awards, 2004, Favorite Male Artist award Soul/Rhythm & Blues Music, 2004, R&B/Hip Hop Artist of Yr., Billboard Music Awards, 2004, R&B/Hip-Hop Albums Artist of Yr., 2004, Male Entertainer of Yr., World Music Awards, 2005; named Artist of Yr., Billboard Music Awards, 1998, 2004, Mainstream Top 40 Artist of Yr., 2004, Hot 100 Artist of Yr., 2004, Billboard 200 Artist of Yr., 2004, Artist of Yr., Radio Music Awards, 2004; named to Boys & Girls Clubs of America Alumni Hall of Fame, 2009. Achievements include finishing first place on the Star Search TV talent series, 1992. Mailing: c/o JPat Mgmt 3996 Pleasantdale Rd # 104A Atlanta GA 30340*

RAYMOND, VALERIE, psychologist; PhD, Columbia U., NYC. Cert. in spl. edn. NY, 1973, lic. psychologist NY, 1991. Learning specialist Dalton Sch., NYC, 1975—86; psychologist Valerie M. Raymond, NYC, 1984—; sch. psychologist Little Red Sch. House, NYC, 1986—89, Friends Sem., NYC, 1989—. Cons. Banana Splits, NYC, 1991—; founding mem. Assn. Psychoeducational Consultants Ind. Schs., NYC. Mem.: APA, Gateway Sch. Adv. Bd., Assn. Orton-Gillingham Practitioners and Educators, Internat. Dyslexia Assn. Office: Valerie M Raymond 510 East 86 St New York NY 10028 Personal E-mail: vmrny@aol.com.

RAYMS-KELLER, ALFREDO, molecular biologist; s. Gustavo O. Ramos and Ligia B. Yepez; m. Diane Marie Keller, Sept. 27, 1987; children: Roderick K., William A., Gabrielle M. PhD, Case Western Res. U., 1990; MA, Naval War Coll., 2005. Cert. Acquisition, Tech. Workforce, Dept. of Navy. Head, chem. biol. sci., tech. br. Naval Surface Warfare Ctr. Dalgren Divsn., Va., 2002—04, sr. scientist, 2005—. Rsch. prof. molecular microbiology, toxicology Colo. State U., Fort Collins, 1990—2000; scientist Naval Surface Warfare Ctr. Dalgren Divsn., 2000—01, head, biotechnology sect., 2001—02. Contbr. articles various profl. jours. Grantee Rsch. Funds, Epa, Darpa, Onr, 2000, 2001, 2002, 2003, 2004, 2005, 2006. Mem.: USA Moodok Kwan Karate (assoc.). Achievements include patents for method of producing dimethyl dinitro butane and products; patents pending for microtags for detection and identification of materials. Office: Naval Surface Warfare Ctr Dahlgren Divsn 17320 Dahlgren Rd Dahlgren VA Personal E-mail: raymskeller@adelphia.net.

RAYMUND, STEVEN A., computer company executive; b. Van Nuys, Calif., Nov. 16, 1955; s. Edward C. and Annette Leah Raymund. BS in Economics, U. Oreg., 1978; MA in Internat. Polit., Georgetown U. Sch. Fgn. Svc., 1980. With Manufacturers Hanover Corp., NYC, 1980—81; ops. mgr. Tech Data Corp., 1981—84, COO, 1984—86, CEO, 1986—2006, chmn., 1991—2006, non-exec. chmn., 2006—. Bd. Dir. Jabil Circuit. Named Entrepreneur of the Yr., Arthur Young Entrepreneurial Services, 1988; named one of 25 Most Influential Executives in the PC Industry, Computer Reseller News, 1989—2004; named to Industry Hall of Fame, 1999. Office: Tech Data Corp 5350 Tech Data Dr Clearwater FL 33760-3122

RAYNER, ARNO ALFRED, investment company executive, consultant; b. San Francisco, Sept. 23, 1928; BS in Econs., U. Calif., Berkeley, 1949, MBA, 1954. Security analyst Bank of Calif., San Francisco, 1950—54; various positions to sr. v.p. Indsl. Indemnity, San Francisco, 1954—74; v.p. internat. svcs. Bechtel Group, San Francisco, 1975—76; pres. Rayner & Haynor, Mill Valley, Calif., 1977—99, chmn. bd., 1999—; pres. Raynor Found. Recipient Investment prof. of the yr., San Francisco Bond Club, 1999, Disting. Citizen of the Yr., Marin Coun. Boy Scouts of Am., 2000. Mem.: Security Analysts (San Francisco) (life). Home: 7 Venado Dr Belvedere Tiburon CA 94920-1625 E-mail: arnorayner@aol.com.

RAYNER, VICTORIA LEIGH, medical educator, consultant; b. Sacramento, Mar. 6, 1954; d. Harold Edward Rayner and Angela Jane Allitore; m. Vallucci Rayner, July 20, 1997. BA, Coll. of Marin, 1974; AA in Bus. Studies, Highline CC, Seattle, 1976. Lic. post-secondary instr. Calif., 1995, continuing edn. instr. Calif. Bd. of Registered Nursing, 1996. Founder and pres. Bay Area Skin Assn., San Francisco, 1981; founder and dir. Ctr. Appearance and Esteem, 1987; founder Camouflage Therapy Clinic, dept. dermatology San Francisco Gen. Hosp., 1987, clin. assoc. Camouflage Therapy Clinic, 1986—; clin. assoc. Alta Bates Hosp., Berkeley; founder Rayner Inst. Career Advancement, Washington; owner Creative Career Bldg. Inst. Contbg. mem. and presenter U. Calif. Arts and Lectrs., San Francisco, 1988—; adv. bd. Dermascope, Sunnyvale, Tex., 1990—, Les Nouvelle Esthetique, Coral Gables, Fla., 1990—; adv. com. rsch. divsn. Almay Cosmetics, Oxford, NC, 1992—93; cons. and rep. Nat. Assn. Women in Bus., mem. public rels. com., 1993—95; founder Women's Forum for Discussion Group, San Francisco, 1996; spokesperson Fibroid Ctr. Wash. Med. Ctr.; lectr. on med. esthetics; presenter in field. Author: Clin. Cosmetology; A Med. Approach to Aesthetic Procedures, 1993, A Survival Guide for Today's Career Woman, 1994; columnist Skin Inc. Mag.; contbr. articles to profl. jours., chapters to books. Hon. chmn. Bus. Adv. Coun., Washington, 2005; leader medical esthetics trng. and care Task Force Legis. Reform of Patients' Rights, Sacramento, 1993—95; bd. dirs. Alissa Ann Ruch Burn Found., San Francisco, 1991—93. Recipient For Those Who Care Vol. award, KRON-TV, 1989, Merit award, Commn. on Status of Women of City and County of San Francisco, 1993, Contribn. to Cosmetology, Internat. Congress of Esthetics, 2003. Mem.: NAFE, Am. Med. Women Assn. (author online distance edn. course 2006), Nat. Cosmetology Esthetic Assn., Am. Soc. Plastic Surgery Skin Care Specialists, Dermatology Nursing Assn. Independent. Roman Catholic. Achievements include development of long distance learning programs in esthetic procedures; women over forty, reentry career devel. programs; four outpatient cosmetic rehabilitation clinics for women and children. Avocations: interior design, cooking, reading, painting. Office: Rayner Inst for Career Advancement #300 1201 Penn Ave NW Washington DC 20004 Home: 450 Massachusetts AVE NW APT 150 Washington DC 20001-6202 Office Phone: 202-667-6272. Office Fax: 202-667-6297. Personal E-mail: victoriarayner@hotmail.com.

RAYNER, WILLIAM ALEXANDER, retired newspaper editor, author; b. Winnipeg, Man., Can., Nov. 7, 1929; s. William and Annie Mitchell (McDonald) R.; divorced; 1 child, Robert William. Student Can. schs. Sports editor Trail Times, B.C., 1954-55; sportswriter Victoria (B.C.) Times, 1955-57, Vancouver (B.C.) Herald, 1957; copy editor, reporter Montreal (Que.) Star, 1957-58; asst. sports editor Vancouver Sun, 1958-62, copy editor, then slotman, 1962-74, news editor, 1974-83, systems mgr., 1983-88, ret., 1988; copy editor Toronto Globe & Mail, 1962. Author: Vancouver Sun Style Guide, 1976, Images of History - Twentieth Century British Columbia Through the Front Pages, 1997, British Columbia's Premiers in Profile-The Good, The Bad and the Transient, 2000, Scandal! 130 Years of Damnable Deeds in Canada's Lotus Land, 2001, The Canadian Journey - Provocative Glimpses into Canada's Past, 2006. Dir. B.C. Newspaper Found. Mem. Writers Union Can. Personal E-mail: wrayner@telus.net.

RAYNES, JEFFRY, science association director; b. 1954; BS, Univ. Maine. Dir. mktg. Association Management Corporation, Springfield, NJ; pres., CEO Better Home Heat Council of Boston; exec. v.p., CEO North American Die Casting Association, Wheeling, Ill.; exec. dir., COO Assn. for Operations Mgmt. (APICS), Alexandria, Va., 1995—2005; exec. dir. IEEE, 2005—. Mem.: Am. Soc. Assn. Execs. (chmn. 2000—01). Office: IEEE 17th Fl 3 Park Ave New York NY 10016-5997

RAYNOLDS, DAVID ROBERT, buffalo breeder, writer; b. NY, Feb. 15, 1928; s. Robert Frederick and Marguerite Evelyn (Gerdau) R.; m. May (Kean) Raynolds, May 12, 1951; children: Robert, Linda, Martha, Laura, David A.F. AB, Dartmouth Coll., 1949; MA, Wesleyan U., Middletown, Conn., 1955; predoctoral, Johns Hopkins Sch. Advanced Internat. Studies, Washington, 1956; grad., Nat. War Coll., Washington, 1973. Account exec. R.H. Morris Assoc., Newtown, Conn., 1949-50; fgn. svc. officer Dept. of State, Washington, 1956-76; pres. Ranch Rangers, Inc., Lander, Wyo., 1976—. Pres. Nat. Buffalo Assn., Ft. Pierre, S.D., 1987-88. Author: Rapid Development in Small Economies (Praeger); contbr. articles to profl. jours. Trustee, bd. dirs. Liberty Hall Found.; dir. Leader Corp.; mem. steering com. Wyo. Bus. Alliance; chmn. bd. govs. Mus. of the Am. West. With US Army, 1950—53. Recipient Meritorious Svc. Award, Dept. of State, Washington, 1966. Mem. The Explorers Club, Dacor Assn., Fremont County Farm Bur., Fgn. Svc. Assn., Am. Legion, Rotary, Elks. Republican. Episcopalian. Avocation: travel. Office: Table Mountain Group PO Box 1310 Lander WY 82520-1310

RAYNOLDS, ELAINE SPALDING, sales executive, photojournalist; b. Flushing, NY, June 26, 1940; d. John Arpad and Thelma Smith Rado; m. Arthur Reginald Raynolds, Nov. 21, 1992; m. Larry Lee Spalding (div.); children: Timothy A. Spalding, Linda Spalding Morrison. Student, Coll. Wooster, Ohio, 1959—60, NYU, NYC, 1961—62. Administrv. asst. Bus. Internat., NYC, 1960—64; pub. rels. staff Duke Med. Ctr., Durham, NC, 1967—70; sales exec. Seyforth Labs., Clearwater, 1975—95; adminstrv. aide Pinellas County, Clearwater, Fla., 1980—90; sales exec. Herbalife Internat., Lake Toxaway, NC, 1995—. Photojournalist Mountain Voice, Lake Toxaway, 2004—. Musician: Brevard (N.C.) Cmty. Band, 2003—04; co-author: Art on a Shoestring. Mem. Brevard C. of C., NC. Mem.: Nat. Mus. Women in the Arts, Friends Libr., Transylvania Arts Coun., Transylvania Choral Soc. (treas. 2003—). Avocations: travel, photography, music, nature, wildlife. Home: PO Box 334 Lake Toxaway NC 28747 Personal E-mail: eraynolds@citcom.net.

RAYNOR, EILEEN MARGOLIES, otolaryngologist, educator; b. NYC, Feb. 11, 1965; d. Allan Fred and Noemi (Schmerz) Margolies; m. Dewey Lee Raynor, Jr., Nov. 9, 1991; children: Stephanie Dianne, Logan Foster. AB in Chemistry, Duke U., 1987; MD, U. N.C., 1993. Cert. Am. Bd. Otolaryngology. Resident otolaryngology Med. Coll. Ga., Augusta, 1993—98; asst. prof. otolaryngology U. Fla., Jacksonville, 1998—2006, assoc. prof., 2006—. Cons. Medimetrics Corp., Jacksonville, Fla., 1999—; med. dir. Pediat. Hearing Program, Jacksonville, 2000—; mem. Cleft Palate Team Childrens Med. Svcs., Jacksonville, 2000—. Contbr. articles to profl. jours., chapters to books. Recipient Nat. Leadership award, Rep. Nat. Com., 2003; Deafness Rsch. Found. rsch. grantee, 1991. Fellow: Am. Coll. Surgeons, AAO-HNS (bd. governors 2007—), Am. Acad. Otolaryngology (cmty., acad. rels. com. 2002—); mem.: AMA, Assn. for Rsch. in Otolaryngology, Triological Soc. (James Harrell award So. sect. 1997), Am. Acad. Facial Plastic Surgery, Duke Alumni Club (bd. dirs. 2000—). Avocations: cooking, skiing, photography, jewelry design. Mailing: 8 Brookside Pl Durham NC 27705-1971 E-mail: eileen.raynor@duke.edu.

RAYNOR, RICHARD BENJAMIN, neurosurgeon, educator; b. NYC, Aug. 16, 1928; s. Murray and Mildred (Pitt) R.; m. Barbara Golob; children: Geoffrey, Michele. BSME, U. Mich., 1950; MD, U. Vt., 1955. Diplomate Am. Bd. Neurol. Surgery. Intern Mt. Sinai, NYC, 1955-56; residency Neurol. Inst. Presbyn. Hosp., NYC, 1956-57, Nat. Hosp., London, 1957; residency neurosurgery Neurol. Inst. Presbyn. Hosp., 1958-62; assoc. in neurosurgery Coll. Physicians and Surgeons Columbia U., NYC, 1965-77; clin. assoc. prof. NYU, NYC, 1977-2000, clin. prof., 1984—. Pvt. practice neurosurgery, N.Y.C., 1965—. Cons. editor Spine; contbr. over 50 articles to profl. jours., chpts. to books. Served as capt. U.S. Army, 1962-64. Fellow Am. Coll. Surgeons; mem. Cervical Spine Research Soc. (pres. 1986-87), Am. Assn. Neurol. Surgeons, Congress Neurol. Surgeons. Clubs: University (N.Y.C.). Avocation: skiing. Office: 870 United Nation Plaza New York NY 10017 Office Phone: 212-535-1255.

RAYNOVICH, GEORGE, JR., retired lawyer; b. Pitts., Dec. 30, 1931; s. George Sr. and Zora (Mamula) R.; m. Mary Ann Senay, July 11, 1953; children: George III, Andrew. BS, U. Pitts., 1957; JD, Duquesne U., 1961. Bar: Pa. 1962, U.S. Dist. Ct. (we. dist.) Pa. 1962, U.S. Patent and Trademark Office 1962, U.S. Supreme Ct. 1966, U.S. Ct. Appeals (fed. cir.) 1986. Patent agt. Consolidation Coal Co., Library, Pa., 1959-62; ptnr. Stone & Raynovich, Pitts., 1962-75; atty. Wheeling-Pitts. Steel Corp., Pitts., 1975-77, gen. counsel, sec., 1978-85, v.p., 1980-85; sr. atty. Buchanan Ingersol P.C., Pitts., 1986-88, 89-96; ptnr. Price & Raynovich, Pitts., 1988-89; of counsel Gorr Moser Dell and Loughney, Pitts., 1997-2000, Paul A. Beck and Assocs., Pitts., 2001—04; ret., 2004. Councilman Borough of Baldwin, Allegheny County, Pa., 1972-75, govt. study commr., 1973. 1st lt. USAF, 1952-56. Mem. Allegheny County Bar Assn., Pitts. Intellectual Property Law Assn., Acad. Trial Lawyers Allegheny County. Democrat. Mem. Serbian Orthodox Ch. Home: 335 Jean Dr Pittsburgh PA 15236-2511

RAYOR, DIANE JILL, classics educator; b. Cheyenne, Wyo., Apr. 18, 1958; d. Harold Arthur and Connie Pearl (Shidler) R.; m. David Jay Hast, Oct. 6, 1986; 1 child, Daniel. BA in Classics, Colo. Coll., 1980; PhD in Comparative Lit., U. Calif., Santa Cruz, 1987. Lectr. U. Chgo., 1987-88; vis. asst. prof. Northwestern U., Evanston, Ill., 1988-91; asst. prof., English dept. Grand Valley State U., Allendale, Mich., 1991—96, assoc. prof., English dept., 1996—2000, assoc. prof., classic dept., 2000—04, prof. classic dept., 2004—. Author/translator: Sappho's Lyre: Archaic Lyric and Women Poets of Ancient Greece, 1991, Homeric Hymns, 2004; co-translator: Callimachus, 1988; co-editor: Latin Lyric and Elegiac Poetry, 1995; contbr. articles to profl. jours. Mem. Am. Philol. Assn., Women's Classical Caucus, Classical Assn. of Midwest and South, Phi Beta Kappa. Democrat. Jewish. Office: Grand Valley State U Classics Dept Allendale MI 49401 Office Phone: 616-331-3284.

RAYSON, GLENDON ENNES, internist, preventive medicine specialist, writer; b. Oak Park, Ill., Dec. 2, 1915; s. Ennes Charles and Beatrice Margaret (Rowland) R.; m. Sarah Weida. AB, U. Rochester, NY, 1939; MD, U. Ill., Chgo., 1948; MPH, Johns Hopkins U., Balt., 1965; MA, Northwestern U., Evanston, Ill., 1965. Diplomate Am. Bd. Internal Medicine, Am. Bd. Preventive Medicine, Am. Bd. Forensic Medicine, Am. Bd. Forensic Examiners. Resident in internal medicine Presbyn.-St. Luke's Hosp., Chgo., 1953-56; physician-in-charge Contagious Disease Hosp., Chgo., 1956-58, asst. med. supt., 1958-64; rsch. assoc. Sch. Hygiene and Pub. Health Johns Hopkins U., Balt., 1966-71; internist Johns Hopkins Hosp., 1971-82, Columbia Free State Health Plan, Balt., 1984-91; pvt. practice Balt., 1984—; with Neurodiagnostics Assocs., 1990—2001. Attending internist emergency rm. South Balt. Gen. Hosp., 1982-84; asst. prof. health sci. U. Ill., Chgo., 1958-64; fellow in gastroenterology and endocrinology Presbyn.-St. Luke's Hosp., 1956-58. Contbr. articles to med. jours., chpt. to book. Vol. physician, Vietnam, 1968, 71, 72, 73; mem. Citizens Amb. Program Delegation to Vietnam, 1993. Capt. M.C., USAF, 1951-53. Master: Am. Acad. Cardiology; fellow: Am. Coll. Forensic Examiners Inst., Am. Geriatrics Soc., Am. Col. Preventive Medicine; mem.: APHA, ACP-Am. Soc. Internal Medicine, AMA. Avocations: poetry, writing, composing songs. Office: 218 N Charles St Apt 1407 Baltimore MD 21201-4024 Home: 8218 Maidencene Pl Port Saint Lucie FL 34952

RAYWARD, WARDEN BOYD, librarian, educator; b. Inverell, NSW, Australia, June 24, 1939; s. Warden and Ellie Rayward. BA, U. Sydney, 1960; diploma in libr., U. NSW, 1964; MS in L.S, U. Ill., 1965; PhD, U. Chgo., 1973. Asst. state library, NSW, 1961-64; research librarian planning and devel. NSW, 1970; lectr. Sch. Librarianship U. NSW, Sydney, 1971-72, head sch. Info., Libr. and Archive Studies, 1986-92, prof., 1986-00, dean Faculty Profl. Studies, 1993-96, prof. emeritus, 2000—; asst. prof. U. Western Ont., 1973-74, Grad. Library Sch. U. Chgo., 1975-77, assoc. prof., 1978-80, prof., 1980-86; dean U. Chgo. Grad. Library Sch., 1980-86; rsch. prof. U. Ill., Champaign, 2000—04, prof., 2004—08, prof. emeritus, 2008—. Cons. NEH, 1976-79, U.S. Dept. Edn., 1981; bd. govs. Charles Stuart U., 1994-96; bd. dirs. Internat. House-U. NSW, 1992-97; George A. Miller vis. prof. U. Ill., 1997-98; Leverhulme Trust vis. prof. Leed Met. U., 2002; vis. prof. Leeds Met. U., 2004-08. Author: The Universe of Information: The Work of Paul Otlet for Documentation and International Organization, 1975 (also transl. Russian and Spanish), Hasta la documentacion electronica, 2002; editor: The Variety of Librarianship: Essays in Honour of John Wallace Metcalfe, 1976, The Public Library: Circumstances and Prospects, 1978, Library Quar., 1975-79, Library History in Context, 1988, Libraries and Life in a Changing World: the Metcalfe Years 1920-1970, 1993; editor, translator: International Organization and the Dissemination of Knowledge: Selected Papers of Paul Otlet, 1990; editor Confronting the Future, University Libraries in the Next Decade, 1992, Developing a Profession in Librarianship in Australia: Travel Diaries and Other Papers of John Wallace Metcalfe, 1996, Aware and Responsible: Papers of The Nordic-International Colloquium (Scarlid), 2004, Pioneers in Library Info Science, 2005; (with Christine Jenkins) Libraries in Time of War Revolution and Social Change, 2007, European Modernism & The Information Society, 2008, mem. editl. bd., World Book Encyclopedia, 1990-97; co-editor: History and Heritage of Scientiful and Technological Information Systems, 2004, Library Trnds, 2007-; contbr. articles to profl. jours. Coun. on Library Resources fellow, 1978, vis. fellow U. Coll. London, 1986, 90, Mortenson fellow U. Ill., 1992-93, Garfield fellow in hist. sci. lit., 2000, vis. scholar U. Ghent, 2007-09. Mem.: ALA, Union Interant. Assns., Am. Soc. Info. Sci. (Rsch. award 2004), Australian Libr. and Info. Assn. (hon.). Business E-Mail: wrayward@illinois.edu.

RAZ, JOSEPH, philosophy and law educator; b. Haifa, Israel, Mar. 21, 1939; arrived in Great Britain, 1970; M in Juris summa cum laude, Hebrew U., Jerusalem, 1963; PhD, Oxford U., Eng., 1967; Doctorate (hon.), Cath. U., Brussels, 1993; LLD (hon.), King's Coll., London, 2009. Lectr. then sr. lectr. depts. law and philosophy Hebrew U., Jerusalem, 1967-72; fellow, tutor in law Balliol Coll., Oxford, 1972-85, fellow, 1985—2006; prof. philosophy of law Oxford U., 1985—2006, rsch. prof., 2006—09. Author: (book) Practical Reason and Norms, 1975, The Authority of Law, 1979, The Concept of a Legal Sys., 1970—80, The Morality of Freedom, 1986, Practical Reason and Norms, 2d edit., 1990, Ethics in the Pub. Domain, 1995, Engaging Reason, 2000, Value, Respect and Attachment, 2001, The Practice of Value, 2003, Between Authority and Interpretation, 2009. Recipient The W.J.M. Mackenzie Book prize The Polit. Studies Assn. of the U.K., 1987, The Elaine and David Spitz Book prize The Conf. for the Study of Political Though, 1988, Internat. Hector Fix-Zamndio prize Legal Rsch. UNAM, Mexico City, 2005. Fellow Brit. Acad.; mem. Am. Acad. Arts and Scis. (fgn. hon.). Office: Balliol Coll Broad St Oxford OX1 3BJ England also: Columbia Law Sch 435 W 116th St New York NY 10027 Office Phone: 212-845-5191. E-mail: raz@law.columbia.edu.

RAZA, ASIM, psychiatrist; b. Rawalpindi, Pakistan, Apr. 27, 1958; s. Kamal and Sughra Raza. FSc, Sir Syed Sch. and Coll., Rawalpindi, 1975; BSc, B Medicine and Surgery, Rawalpindi Med. Coll., 1983. Diplomate Am. Bd. Psychiatry and Neurology. Intern dept. medicine Rawalpindi Gen. Hosp., 1983; med. officer dept. medicine Cantonment Gen. Hosp., Rawalpindi, 1984—91, med. officer outpatient dept., 1991—92; resident dept. psychiatry U. Mo. Sch. Medicine, Kansas City, 1993—97, chief resident dept. psychiatry, 1996—97; mem. staff Counseling Assocs., Inc., Conway, Ark., 1998—. Cons. in field; mem. spkrs. bur. Pfizer Inc., Wyeth Pharms., Sanofi-Aventis Pharms., Sepracor Inc.; adv., cons. Pfizer Inc. Treas. Residents Assn. Western Mo., Kansas City, 1994—95, v.p., 1995—96, pres., 1996—97. Recipient Psychiatry Resident of Yr. award, Pfizer, 1997; fellow, Eli Lilly, 1994. Fellow: Am. Psychiat. Assn. (Wyeth Ayerst Resident Reporter 1996, mem.-in-tng. rep. Western Mo. br. 1996—97); mem.: Ark. Psychiat. Soc. Home: 1801 Champlin Dr 112 Little Rock AR 72223 Office Phone: 501-336-8300. Personal E-mail: selfless@sbcglobal.net.

RAZAK, ARISIKA, social studies educator, department chairman; b. NYC, Nov. 2, 1948; d. Deavera Boston; m. Thomas Osha Neumann, Nov. 8, 1993; 1 child, Diallo Imani McLinn. MPH, U. Calif., Berkeley, 1978. Cert. nurse midwife, Calif., 1979. Nurse midwife Alameda County Med. Ctr., Oakland, Calif., 1980—2000; assoc. prof. Calif. Inst. Integral Studies, San Francisco, 2001—, program chair, womens spirituality. Choreographer spiritual dancer, leader (workshops) Ishe Oluwa; Stay on the Battlefield, The Vulva Dance, Birth Dance. V.p., program chair Am. Acad. Religion, Western Region, Santa Clara, Calif., 2008—, pres., 2009—. Recipient Dreamspeaker award, CA Legislature, 2007; named to Hall of Fame. Home: 514 62nd St Oakland CA 94609 Office: Calif Inst Integral Studies 1453 Mission St San Francisco CA 94103 Business E-Mail: arazak@ciis.edu.

RAZZAGHI, HAMID, molecular biologist, researcher; b. Tehran, Iran, Mar. 21, 1962; s. Mohsen Razzaghi and Khadijeh Pedram; m. Mitra Arjmandi, Dec. 31, 1993; children: Raud, Mehraud. BS cum laude, Wash. State U., 1989; MS, U. of Toronto, 1993; PhD, U. of Pitts., 1999. From lab. technician to tchg. asst. Wash. State U., Pullman, Wash., 1987—89, tchg. asst., 1989; rsch. assoc. Mount Sinai Hosp. Rsch. Inst., Toronto, Ontario, Canada, 1990—93; graduate student rschr. U. of Pitts., Pitts., 1994—99, postdoc. fellow, 1999—2002; asst. prof. dept. medicine U. Colo. Health Sci. Ctr., Denver, 2003—. Fellow: Am. Heart Assn.; mem.: Am. Soc. of Human Genetics. Avocations: long distance running, swimming, camping, scuba diving, travel. Home: 10888 E Colorado Dr Aurora CO 80012-5058 Office: UCD Rsch Complex II P15-8025 12700 E 19th Ave Aurora CO 80045 Office Phone: 303-724-1667. Business E-Mail: hamid.razzaghi@cdenver.edu.

RAZZANO, FRANK CHARLES, lawyer; b. Bklyn., Feb. 25, 1948; s. Pasquale Anthony and Agnes Mary (Borgia) R.; m. Stephanie Anne Lucas, Jan. 10, 1970; children: Joseph, Francis, Catherine. BA, St. Louis U., 1969; JD, Georgetown U., 1972. Bar: NY 1973, US Dist. Ct. (so. and ea. dists.) NY 1973, NJ 1976, DC 1981, Va. 1984, US Dist. Ct. NJ 1976, US Dist. Ct. Md. 1977, US Dist. Ct. (no. dist.) Calif. 1981, US Dist. Ct. DC 1982, US Dist. Ct. (ea. dist.) Va. 1989, US Dist. Ct. (we. dist.) Va. 1990, US Ct. Appeals (2d cir.) 1973, US Ct. Appeals (3d cir.) 1975, US Ct. Appeals (DC and 5th cirs.) 1983, US Ct. Appeals (4th cir.) 1984, US Ct. Appeals (6th cir.) 1990, US Ct. Appeals (8th and 9th cirs.) 2000, US Supreme Ct. 1976. Assoc. Shea & Gould, NYC, 1972-75; asst. US atty. Dist. of NJ, Newark, 1975-78; asst. chief trial atty. SEC, Washington, 1978-82; ptnr. Shea & Gould, Washington, 1982-94, mng. ptnr., 1991-92; ptnr. Camhy Karlinsky Stein Razzano & Rubin, Washington, 1994-96, Dickstein, Shapiro LLP, Washington, 1996—2008, Pepper Hamilton, LLP, Washington, 2008—. Lectr. in field; adv. bd. Securities Litigation Reform Act Reporter, Securities Regulation Law Jour.; adj. prof. law U. Md. Sch. Law; bd. dirs. Fin. Fraud Law Report. Civil law editor Rico Law Reporter; hon. adv. com. Jour. Internat. Law and Practice, Detroit Coll. Law; contbr. articles to legal jours. Scoutmaster Vienna coun. Boy Scouts Am., 1984. Recipient spl. achievement award Justice Dept., 1977, spl. commendation, 1978, Outstanding Achievement award Detroit Coll. of Law, 1993. Mem. ABA (chmn. criminal law com., sect. bus. law 1996-98), Va. Bar, D.C. Bar (chmn. litigation sect. 1987-89, vice-chmn. coun. sects. 1988-89), Assn. Securities & Exch. Commn. Alumni (pres. 1993-95), Phi Beta Kappa, Eta Sigma Phi. Roman Catholic. Home: 2425 L St NW Apt 623 Washington DC 20037 Office Phone: 202-220-1286. Business E-Mail: razzanof@pepperlaw.com.

RAZZANO, PASQUALE ANGELO, lawyer; b. Bklyn., Apr. 3, 1943; s. Pasquale Anthony and Agnes Mary (Borgia) R.; m. Maryann Walker, Jan. 29, 1966; children: Elizabeth, Pasquale, Susan, ChristyAnn. BSCE, Poly. Inst. Bklyn., 1964; student law, NYU, 1964-66; JD, Georgetown U., 1969. Bar: Va. 1969, N.Y. 1970, U.S. Ct. Appeals (2d, 3d, 7th, 9th and fed. cirs.), U.S. Supreme Ct., U.S. Dist. Ct. (so., ea. and western dists.) N.Y., U.S. Dist. Ct. (we. dist.) Tex., U.S. Dist. Ct. Hawaii, U.S. Dist. Ct. Conn. Examiner U.S. Patent Office, 1966-69; assoc. Curtis, Morris & Safford, P.C., 1969-71, ptnr., 1971-91, Fitzpatrick, Cella, Harper & Scinto, 1991—. Guest lectr. U.S. Trademark Assn., Am. Intellectual Property Law Assn., Practicing Law Inst., NYU Law Ctr., ABA, N.Y. Intellectual Property Law Assn. Mem. bd. editors Licensing Jour., 1986—; mem. bd. editors Trademark Reporter, 1987—, book rev. editor, 1989-91, pub. articles editor, 1991-94, domestic articles editor, 1992-93, 95, editor-in-chief 1996-98. Rep. committeeman Rockland County. Recipient Robert Ridgeway award, 1964. Mem.: FBA (chmn. patent law com. 1999—2002, bd. govs. 2002—06), ABA (guest lectr.), Columban Laws Assn., Bar Assn. City N.Y., Italian Am. Bar Assn., Va. Bar Assn., N.Y. Coun. Bar Leaders (exec. coun. 1993—94), N.Y. Bar Assn., Am. Intellectual Property Law Assn., Internat. Trademark Assn. (bd. dirs. 1996—99), Licensing Exec. Soc. (chmn. N.Y. chpt. 1996—99), N.Y. Intellectual Property Law Assn. (bd. dirs. 1985—93, sec. 1988—91, pres. 1994—95), Shorehaven Golf Club (bd. dirs. 2005—09, pres. 2007—09), Minute Man Yacht Club, N.Y. Athletic Club. Republican. Roman Catholic. Address: 21 Covlee Dr Westport CT 06880-6407 also: 14 Deerwood Trl Lake Placid NY 12946-1834 Office Phone: 212-218-2253. Business E-Mail: prazzano@fchs.com.

RAZZE, DENNIS, theater educator, director; b. Wilmington, Del., Jan. 10, 1953; s. Anthony and Edith Razze. BA, DeSales U., Ctr. Valley, Pa., 1975; MFA in Directing, Wayne State U., Detroit, 1977. Dir. theatre DeSales U., 2005—; assoc. artistic dir. Pa. Shakespeare Festival, Ctr. Valley, 2005—. Office: DeSales Univ 2755 Station Ave Center Valley PA 18034

RAZZOUK, BASSEM IBRAHIM, hematologist, oncologist; b. Afisdeek, Lebanon, Aug. 13, 1964; US, 1990; s. Ibrahim M. and Lamia C. Razzouk; m. Jacky F. Farah, Sept. 7, 1997; children: Lamya Celina, Ralph Bassem, Carla Janet, Nour Grace. BSc, Am. U. Beirut, Lebanon, 1983, MD, 1987. Diplomate in pediat. Am. Bd. Pediat., 1992, in hematology and oncology Am. Bd. of Pediat., 1996. Internship, residency Am. U. Beirut, 1987—90; resident to chief resident SUNY Health Sci. Ctr., Syracuse, 1990—92; fellowship in pediat. St. Jude Children's Rsch. Hosp., Memphis, 1992—95; attending pediatrician Boaz-Albertville Med. Ctr., Ala., 1995—98; asst. St. Jude Children's Rsch. Hosp., 1998—2004, assoc., 2004—. Med. dir., Mid. East and Telemedicine Programs St. Jude Children's Rsch. Hosp., 1998—, chmn. clin. protocol sci. rev. and monitoring com., 2004—. Contbr. articles to profl. jours. Fellow: Am. Acad. Pediat.; mem.: Am. Soc. Hematology. Achievements include research in new agents for relapsed leukemia, prognostic factors in pediatric leukemia. Office: St Jude Children's Research Hospital 332 North Lauderdale Memphis TN 38105 Home: 7416 Fox Hollow Rdg Zionsville IN 46077-8339 Office Fax: 901-495-3122. Business E-Mail: bassem.razzouk@stjude.org.

RE, EDWARD DOMENIC, JR., construction executive; b. Bklyn., Aug. 11, 1955; s. Edward Domenic Sr. and Margaret (Corcoran) R.; m. Eileen Frances McMahon, Jan. 14, 1989; children: Edward, Joseph, Michael. AAS in Construction Mgmt., NYC Tech. Coll., 1978; BS, Pratt Inst., 1981, MS, 1997; Postgrad. in Land Use Planning & Structural Tech., Inst. Design & constrn., Pratt Inst. Cert. environ. inspector, real estate appraiser, profl. constructor; registered architect, N.Y. Chief exec. officer, pres. Con-Solid Contracting, NYC, 1994—, Re Bros., Constrn. Mgmt., Inc., 1972—94; arch. Internat. Facilities Mgmt. Assoc.; adj. assoc. prof. NYU, 2005. Prof. constrn. mgmt. Pratt Inst., 1992—, prof. facility mgmt., 1993—; cons. in field. Inventor in field. Mem. N.Y.C. Cmty. Bd. 14 Zoning Com., 1985-87, bd. dirs., chmn.; v.p. Belle Harbor Property Owners Assn., Inc. Recipient Design/Build Civic award City of Long Beach, N.Y. Mem. United Inventor Assn., Constrn. Mgmt. Assn. Am. (founder), Am. Inst. Constructors (trustee, question formulator for nat. exam.), AIA, Am. Arbitration Assn., N.Y.C. Tech. Coll. Alumni Assn. (hon. life), IFMA (metro NY/NJ chpt. Disting. Educator award), Pratt Inst. Constrn. Mgmt. Alumni Assn. (founder constrn. mgmt. scholarship fund, Golden Hammer award). Conservative. Roman Catholic. Avocation: architecture. Office: Con-Solid Contracting Inc 436 Beach 129th St Belle Harbor NY 11694 Home: 186 Beach 137 th St Belle Harbor NY 11694 Office Phone: 718-634-8800. Office Fax: 718-634-8909. Personal E-mail: rebros@aol.com. E-mail: consolid@aol.com.

RE, JOSEPH R., lawyer; BS in Civil Engring., Rutgers U. Coll. Engring., NJ, 1982; JD, St. John's U. Sch. Law, NYC, 1985. Bar: NY, Calif., U.S. Supreme Ct., U.S. Ct. of Appeals for the Federal, Fourth and Ninth Circuits, U.S. Ct. of Federal Claims, U.S. Ct. of Internat.Trade. Clk. Hon. Howard T. Markey, Chief Judge of the U.S. Ct. of Appeals for Federal Cir., 1985—87; assoc. Knobbe Martens Olson & Bear LLP, Irvine, Calif., 1987—90, ptnr., 1990—. Recipient 20th Annual Rossman Meml. Award, U.S. Patent and Trademark Office, 1993, Calif. Lawyer Atty. of Yr. for Intellectual Property, 2004; named one of 100 Leading Lawyers in Calif., Daily Jour., 2006, 100 Most Influential Lawyers, Nat. Law Jour., 2006. Mem.: U.S. Ct. of Appeals for Fed. Cir. (adv. coun. 2005—), Am. Intellectual Property Law Assn. (bd. dirs. 2003—06), Fed. Cir. Bar Assn. (pres. 2008—), Amicus Comm. (chmn. 1997—99), Chi Epsilon. Office: Knobbe Martens Olson & Bear LLP 2040 Main St 14th Floor Irvine CA 92614-3641 Business E-Mail: jre@kmob.com.

RÉ, PAUL BARTLETT, artist, writer, peace worker; b. Albuquerque, Apr. 18, 1950; s. Ernest Ré and Helen Alice Bartlett. BSc in Physics with honors, Calif. Inst. Tech., Pasadena, 1972. Artist and writer, N.Mex., 1972—; dir. Paul Ré Collection and Archives, Albuquerque, 1994—. Mem. artist adv. bd. Mus. Am. Folk Art Access to Art Program, NYC, 1987—94. *Critically acclaimed as a virtuoso of the pencil for art of quiet greatness and noble simplicity, the aim of such artwork is to harmonize the world. The Dance of the Pencil was cited in The Journal of the Print World as one of the outstanding art books of the year. Touchable Art exhibit has been shown 18 times. Blind person responses included comments like "made my skin and bones real excited" and "feeling a human experience come to life". Georgia O'Keeffe, Raymond Jonson, Nobel Laureates and other notables have highly regarded such work.* Permanent exhibit in rotation, Paul Ré Gallery and Sculpture Garden, Jonson Gallery, U. N.Mex., one-man shows include Triangle Gallery, San Francisco, 1974, 1975, Jonson Gallery, U. N.Mex. Art Mus., 1978, J.B. Speed Mus., 1985, Albuquerque Mus., 1986, Wichita Mus., 1986, ABEC Ctr., Can., 1989, Sumter Gallery, S.C., 1990, Colo. Springs Mus., 1990, Jonson Gallery, U. N.Mex., 2001, Karpeles Mus., 2002, 22 one-man shows in 13 states and provinces; subject: (documentaries) Touchable Art by Paul Ré, 1990; author: Touchable Art: A Book for the Blind and Sighted, 1983, The Dance of the Pencil: Serene Art by Paul Ré, 1993; contbr. chapters to books (Rolex award, Geneva, 1990), articles on art to profl. jours.; traveling exhibit, Touchable Art, 1981—. Recipient World Lifetime Achievement award, ABI, 2004, Legion of Honor, United Cultural Convention, 2005; named to The Paul Bartlett Ré Peace prize, U. N.Mex.; grantee, Wurlitzer Found., 1982, 1984, Popejoy Soc. U. N.Mex., 2008; Torchbearers Caltech, Calif. Inst. Tech., 2002. Mem.: Order of Am. Ambs., Nature Conservancy (life), Caltech Alumni Assn. (life). Avocations: guitar, bicycling, Escherian puns, walking. Office: Paul Ré Archives 10533 Sierra Bonita Ave NE Albuquerque NM 87111 Office Phone: 505-298-0290.

REA, ANN W., librarian; b. Jefferson City, Mo., Aug. 3, 1944; d. William H. and Ruby (Fogleman) Webb; m. Glen N. Rea, Sept. 28, 1974; children: Sarah, Rebecca. BA, U. Mo., 1966; MLS, U. So. Calif., 1968. Libr. St. Charles (Mo.) County Libr., 1967-71; libr. adult svcs. Paterson (N.J.) Free Pub. Libr., 1971-74; libr. Beal Coll. Libr., Bangor, Maine, 1983—. Mem ALA, Maine Libr. Assn.(scholarship and loan com.). Office: Beal Coll Libr 99 Farm Rd Bangor ME 04401 Office Phone: 207-947-4591.

REA, ANNE E., lawyer; b. 1959; AB, Brown U., 1981; JD, U. Cgho., 1984. Bar: Ill. 1984. With Sidley Austin Brown & Wood, Chgo., 1984—, ptnr., 1992—. Selected as one of 15 Rising Stars You Won't Want to Oppose in Ct., Ill. Legal Times. Mem.: ABA, Leadership Greater Chgo., Chgo. Bar Assn., Ill. State Bar Assn.

REA, PATRICK SHAW, secondary school educator; b. Evansville, Ind., Aug. 30, 1948; s. Ernest Arthur and Mary Carolyn (Steen) R.; m. Linda Joyce Gaisser, Aug. 1, 1970; children: Jason Christopher, Erin Rebecca. BS in Geography, Ind. State U., 1970; MS in Secondary Edn., Ind. U. S.E., 1974, postgrad., 1983. Lic tchr., Ind. Tchr. New Albany

(Ind.)-Floyd County Schs., 1970—; mem. adj. faculty Ind. U. S.E., New Albany, 1975-78, 91-92, Jefferson C.C., Louisville, 1983. Mem. state planning com. Geography Awareness Week, Indpls., 1989—; tchr. rep. Project Marco Polo, Nat. Geog. Soc. and USN, 1991; geography test analyst Ind. Dept. Edn., Indpls., 1991. Author: (textbook) Realm of Physical Geography, 1988. Co-pres. New Albany High Sch. Band Boosters, 1992; leader ministry team Northside Christian Ch., New Albany, 1988—. Mem. NEA, Ind. State Tchrs. Assn., Nat. Coun. for Geog. Edn. (Disting. Tchr. award 1993), Geography Educators Network Ind. (tchr. cons., bd. dirs. 1991—, mid. sch. State Geography Tchr. of Yr. 1991), New Albany-Floyd County Edn. Assn. Avocation: travel. Home: 1108 Woodfield Dr New Albany IN 47150-2067 Office: Nathaniel Scribner Jr High 910 Old Vincennes Rd New Albany IN 47150-5401

READ, BILL (WILLIAM L. READ), meteorologist; b. 1949; With USN, on-bd. meteorologist Hurricane Hunters; staff test and evaluation divsn. NOAA Nat. Weather Svc., Sterling, Va., 1977, forecaster Ft. Worth, San Antonio, leader severe thunderstorm and flash flood program Silver Spring, Md., meteorologist-in-charge Houston/Gaveston weather forecast office, 1992, acting dep. dir. Tropical Predication Ctr., 2007—08, dir. Tropical Prediction Ctr., 2008—, dir. Nat. Hurricane Ctr., 2008—. Mem. Hurricane Liasion Team Nat. Hurricane Ctr., Miami, 2003. Recipient Spl. award for Pub. Edn., Nat. Hurricane Conf., 2004. Office: NOAA 1401 Constitution Ave NW Washington DC 20230 Office Phone: 202-482-6090. Office Fax: 202-482-3154. Business E-Mail: bill.read@noaa.gov.

READ, IAN C., pharmaceutical executive; BSChemE, London U. Imperial Coll., 1974. Cert. Inst. Chartered Accts. Eng. & Wales, 1978. Operational auditor Pfizer, Inc., 1978, CFO Mexico, country mgr. Brazil, pres. Internat. Pharms. Group L.Am./Can., 1996, exec. v.p. Europe/Can., 2000, v.p. Pfizer, 2001—06, exec. v.p. Africa/Mid. East, 2004, exec. v.p. L.Am., 2006, sr. v.p. Pfizer, 2006—, pres. worldwide pharm. ops., 2006—09. Bd. dirs. Kimberly-Clark Corp., 2007—; exec. com. rep. internat. sect. Pharm. Rsch. & Mfrs. America. Named Power Player, Advt. Age mag., 2008. Office: Pfizer Inc 235 E 42nd St New York NY 10017 Office Phone: 212-573-2323. Business E-Mail: ian.c.read@pfizer.com.*

READ, JOHN CONYERS, non-profit company executive; b. NYC, May 21, 1947; s. Edward Cameron Kirk and Louise (Geary) R.; m. Alexandra Gould, Mar. 30, 1968; children: Cameron Kirk, Trevor Conyers, Alexandra. AB, Harvard, 1969, MBA, 1971; LHD (hon.), Centenary Coll., 2004. Ops. rsch. analyst HEW, Washington, 1971-72; exec. asst. to dir. Cost of Living Council, Washington, 1973; chief econ. adviser to Gov. Mass., 1974; exec. asst., counselor to sec. labor Washington, 1975; asst. sec. labor for employment standards, 1976—77; dir. corp. employee rels., pers. Cummins Engine Co., Columbus, Ind., 1977-80, plant mgr., 1980-85; v.p. Midrange Engines, 1986-90; v.p., gen. mgr. engine group Donaldson Co., Inc., Mpls., 1990-92; exec. v.p., 1992-94; ptnr. Hidden Creek Industries, Mpls., 1996—2000; pres., CEO Heavy Duty Holdings, Mpls., 1997-2000; pres. Read Ptnrs. Inc., Mpls., 2001—02; pres., CEO Outward Bound USA, Garrison, NY, 2002—. Cons. nat. productivity and energy policies; chmn. NAM Task Force on Wage and Price Policies, 1978-80; bd. dirs. MAC Equipment Co., Active Leasing Co., Summer Search. Contbr. articles to newspapers and mags. Trustee Summer Search, Nat. Ctr. Occupl. Readjustment, 1984-87; trustee NC Outward Bound Sch., dir., 1995—, chmn., 1997-2000; chmn. Charleston Pvt. Industry Coun., 1985; plant closing task force US Dept. Labor, 1986, mfg. task force NRC, 1989, critical industries task force Def. Dept., 1989 Mem. Nat. Assn. Mfrs. (bd. dirs., chair employee rels. com. 1993-95). Home: 111 Marlborough Rd Briarcliff Manor NY 10510

READ, KENNETH FRANCIS, JR., physics professor, researcher; married. BS with distinction, Stanford U., Calif., 1981; MS, Cornell U., Ithaca, NY, 1984; PhD, 1987. Rsch. assoc. Princeton U., NJ, 1987—90, rsch. staff mem., 1990, Oak Ridge Nat. Lab., Tenn., 1991—2003, sr. rsch. staff mem., 2003—; joint faculty mem. Oak Ridge Nat. Lab. U. Tenn., Knoxville, 1993—; asst. prof. U. Tenn., 1991—99, assoc. prof., 1999—2005, prof., 2005—. Contbr. articles to profl. jours. Recipient David Levine award, Stanford U., 1980; grantee Andrew D. White fellowship, Cornell U., 1981; fellow, Nat. Merit Scholar Corp., 1977, NSF, 1981. Mem.: Am. Phys. Soc., Phi Beta Kappa, Sigma Xi. Office: Oak Ridge Nat Lab Bldg 6010 MS 6356 PO Box 2008 Oak Ridge TN 37831

READ, MICHAEL OSCAR, editor, consultant; b. Amarillo, Tex., July 11, 1942; s. Harold Eugene and Madeline (Welch) R.; m. Jill Kay Vanderby, July 6, 1963 (div. Apr. 1967); 1 child, Rebecca Anne; m. Fawn Dale Barby, Apr. 10, 1977; 1 child, Nathan Michael. AA in Chemistry, Amarillo Coll., 1962; BA in Journalism, Tex. Tech. U., 1965. News editor Olton Enterprise, Tex., 1963—64; reporter, photographer Lubbock Avalanche-Jour., Tex., 1964—67, copy editor, 1967—70, city editor, 1970—72; copy editor Houston Post, 1972—74, sys. editor, 1974—89, dir. news tech., 1989—95; coord. electronic media content Houston Chronicle, 1995—2000, editor web ops. and devel., 2000—07; dir. online devel. ASP Westward LP, 2008—. Bd. dirs. People's Trust Fed. Credit Union, Houston, vice chmn., 2002—, supervisory com., 1996-2001; tchr. Let's Compute!, Stafford, Tex., 1985—; cons. Newspaper Pub. Sys., Stafford, 1989—; mem. joint Newspaper Assn. Am.-Internat. Press, Telecomm. Coun. Com. Wire Svc. Stds.; mem. adv. bd. Found. for Am. Comms. FACSNET; mem. adv. com. Sch. of Mass Comm., Tex. Tech U., chmn., 2001-04 Author weekly newspaper column, 1977—. Vol. United Way, Houston, 1973—; bd. dirs. Meadows (Tex.) Cmty. Improvement Assn., 1985-95, Meadows Utility Dist., 1988-93, Meadows Econ. Devel. Corp., 1994-99. Named among Outstanding Alumni, Tex. Tech U. Sch. Mass Comms., 2001; Eldon Durrett scholar, 1961-65. Mem. Am. MENSA, Am. Philatelic Soc., Am. 1st Day Cov. Soc. (life), U.S. Chess Fedn. (life), Soc. Profl. Journalists (conv. com. 1989-90), Press Club of Houston. Avocations: stamp collecting/philately, photography, gardening. Office: ASP Westward LP 523 N Sam Houston Parkway E (500) Houston TX 77060 Office Phone: 281-674-1279. Business E-Mail: mread@aspwestward.com.

READ, RICHARD EATON, newspaper reporter; b. St. Andrews, Scotland, Sept. 3, 1957; s. Arthur H. and Katharine (Eaton) R.; m. Kim R. Kunkle, July 26, 1986; 1 child, Nehalem Kunkle-Read. BA in English, Amherst Coll., 1980; postgrad., Harvard U., 1996—97; LHD (hon.), Williamette U., 2003. Press sec. Mass. Commn. on State and County Bldgs., 1980; staff writer The Oregonian, 1981-86; fellow The Henry Luce Found./The Nation, Bangkok, 1986-87; freelance writer Tokyo, 1987-89; Asia bur. chief The Oregonian, Tokyo, 1989-94; sec., 1st dir., 1st v.p. Fgn. Corrs. Club of Japan, 1990-93; internat. bus. writer The Oregonian, Portland, 1994-99, sr. writer internat. affairs, 1999—. V.p., pres., bd. dirs. The Internat. Sch., Portland, 2007—08. Recipient Pulitzer prize for explanatory reporting, 1999, Finalist, 2008, Overseas Press Club award for bus. reporting from abroad, 1999, Scripps Howard Found. award for bus. reporting, 1999, Blethen award for enterprise reporting Pacific Northwest Newspaper Assn., 1999, 2001, Pacific Northwest Soc. Prof. Journalists first place award for social issues, 2001, 05, bus. 1998, 2004, spot news 1997, edn. 1990, Oreg. Gov.'s award for achievement in internat. bus., 2000, Pulitzer prize for pub. svc., 2001, Unity award in media investigative reporting, Lincoln U., 2001, Blethen award, 2001, Bruce Baer award, 2001, Media Leadership award Am. Immigration Lawyers Assn., 2001; named Internat. Citizen of Yr. 1999 World Affairs Coun. Oreg., named Internat. Citizen of Yr. 2002 Oreg. Assn. Consuls Gen. Eisenhower Exch. fellow, Peru, 1997; Nieman fellow, 1996-97; U. Md. CASE fellow, 2002.

READ, ROBERT RICHARD, mathematical statistics educator; b. Columbus, Ohio, Oct. 5, 1929; s. Ira Jay and Pearl V. (Scott) R.; m. Dagmar Ann Ruud, Dec. 19, 1963 (div. Sept. 1974); children: Christopher, Steven, Darren. BSc, Ohio State U., 1951; PhD, U. Calif., Berkeley, 1958. Lectr., rsch. statistician U. Calif., Berkeley, 1957—60; asst. prof. U. Chgo., 1961; prof. USN Postgrad. Sch., Monterey, Calif., 1961—. Cons. Maritime Cargo Transp. Conf., San Francisco, 1959, United Tech. Ctr., Sunnyvale, Calif., 1962-65. Contbr. rsch. articles to profl. jours Mem. Inst. Math. Statistics, Am. Stats. Assn., Sigma Xi Home: PO Box 6191 Carmel CA 93921-6191 Office: USN Postgrad Sch Monterey CA 93943 Home Phone: 831-624-1859; Office Phone: 831-656-2382. E-mail: rread@nps.edu.

READ, RUSSELL, investment company executive; b. Chgo., May 22, 1963; s. Ralph Clarence and Grace (Jachim) R.; m. Andrea Judith Ballou, Dec. 13, 1986; children: Hannah Catherine, Alexander Winston. BA in Statistics, U. Chgo., 1984, MBA in Fin., 1987; MA in Econ., Stanford U., 1990, PhD. in Pol. Sci., 1993. Cert. CFA, ChFC. Assoc. econ. First Nat. Bank of Chgo., 1983-85; sr. fin. analyst CNA Ins., Chgo., 1985-86; investment mgr. The Prudential, Newark, 1987-89; internat. fin. cons. Dow Chem. Co., Midland, Mich., 1990; dir. quantitative rsch. Oppenheimer Funds, Inc., NYC, 1993-96, v.p., portfolio mgr., 1996-98, sr. v.p., 1997—2000; global head quantitative investment & rsch. Zurich Scudder Investments, 2000—02; ind. cons., 2002—04; dep. chief investment officer Deutsche Asset Mgmt., 2004—06; chief investment officer The Calif. Pub. Employees' Retirement Sys. (CalPERS), 2006—08; CEO C Change Investments, LLC, Cambridge, Mass., 2008—. Bd. dirs. The Future of Life, Inc., 2007—. Author: Politics & Policies of National Economic Growth, 1993. H.S. mentor Seward Park H.S., N.Y.C., 1996—. Named one of The 30 Most Influential People in Bus. & Fin., SmartMoney, 2007, The 75 Most Effective Chief Executives, Institutional Investor, 2008. Mem. Am. Fin. Assn., Assn. Investment Mgmt. & Rsch. Avocation: trombone. Office: C Change Investments LLC One Main St 14th Fl Cambridge MA 02142*

READ, SUSAN PHILLIPS, state appeals court judge; b. Gallipolis, Ohio, June 27, 1947; d. Gomer Wesley and Elizabeth Molineaux Phillips; m. Howard John Read. BA summa cum laude, Ohio Wesleyan U., 1969; JD Floyd R. Mechem Prize Scholar, U. Chgo., 1972. Bar: NY 1974. Legal intern US Atomic Energy Commn., 1972—73; asst. counsel SUNY, 1974—77; in-house counsel GE Co., 1977—88, chief environ. counsel, 1980—85; ptnr. Bond, Schoeneck & King, Albany, NY, 1988—94; dep. counsel to Gov. Pataki State of NY, Albany, 1995—97; judge (confirmed for an unexpired term in 1998 and full term in 1999) NY Ct. of Claims, 1998—2003, presiding judge, 1999; assoc. judge NY State Ct. Appeals, Schenectady, 2003—. Mem.: Phi Beta Kappa. Office: NY State Ct Appeals 20 Eagle St Albany NY 12207-1095*

READ, VIRGINIA HALL, retired biochemistry professor; b. Louisville, Miss., Oct. 15, 1937; d. Angus R. and Hassie (Bowie) Hall; m. Dale Gilbert Read Sr., Mar. 5, 1960; children: Laura Read Sprabery, Dale Gilbert Jr., Eva Read Warden. BS, U. Miss., 1959; MS, U. Miss., Jackson, 1962, PhD, 1964. Instr. biochemistry U. Miss., Jackson, 1965-66, asst. prof. biochemistry, 1966-68, 70-74, assoc. prof. biochemistry, 1974-2000, assoc prof. pathology, 1979-2000; asst. prof. medicine U. Ala., Birmingham, 1968-70. Contbr. articles to Jour. Clin. Investigation, Jour. Clin. Endocrinology and Metabolism, Nature, Biochem. Pharmacology. Grantee U.S. Pub. Health Svc., 1960-62, fellow, 1968-70. Mem. Am. Assn. Clin. Chemistry, Acad. Clin. Biochemistry, Endocrine Soc., Sigma Xi. United Methodist. Home Phone: 601-992-1890. Personal E-mail: vh44424@bellsouth.net.

READ, WILLIAM L. See READ, BILL

READE, CLAIRE ELIZABETH, lawyer; m. Earl Phillip Steinberg, Nov. 22, 1980; children: Evan Samuel, Emma Miriam. BA, Conn. Wesleyan U., 1973; JD, Harvard U., 1979; MA in Law and Diplomacy, Tufts U., 1979. Bar: Mass. 1980, D.C. 1983. Sheldon fellow Harvard U., Cambridge, Mass. and, Republic of China, 1979-80; assoc. Ropes & Gray, Boston, 1980-82, Arnold & Porter, Washington, 1982-86, ptnr. internat. law, chmn. Hiring Com., 1987—2006; chief counsel China trade enforcement Office U.S. Trade Rep., Washington, 2006—. Exec. editor: International Trade Policy: The Lawyer's Perspective, 1985; contbr. articles to profl. jours. Mem. ABA (co-chair internat. trade com.), DC Bar Assn., Coun. on Foreign Rels. Office: Office of the US Trade Rep 600 17th St NW Washington DC 20508 Office Phone: 202-395-9625. Office Fax: 202-395-3639. Business E-Mail: creade@ustr.eop.gov.

READE, KATHLEEN MARGARET, legal consultant, author, educator; d. Ralph S. and Margaret Catherine (Stark) R.; 1 child, Kathryn Michelle Walters. BA in English and Polit. Sci., Tex. Christian U., 1978; student, El Centro Coll.; postgrad., Tex. Christian U., Tex. Tech. Asst. land and legal dept. Am. Quasar Petroleum, Ft. Worth, 1971-74; paralegal and office mgr. Law Offices of George Sims, Ft. Worth, 1974-81; asst. Criminal Cts. #2 and #3 Tarrant County Dist. Atty., Ft. Worth, 1981; ind. paralegal Ft. Worth, 1982-84; paralegal Law Offices of Brent Burford, Ft. Worth, 1982-85; sr. paralegal/litigation Law Offices of Windle Turley, Dallas, 1985-90; major case supr. The Dent Law Firm, Ft. Worth, 1990-96, Whitaker, Chalk, Swindle & Sawyer, LLP, Ft. Worth, 1996—. Internat. corp., ind. legal cons.; jury selection, expert witness cons.; instr. paralegal program, U. Tex., Arlington, 1996—; active Tex. Christian U. Writer's Continuous Workshop. Author: Plaintiff's Personal Injury Handbook, 1995; contbg. author: Legal Assistant's Letter Book, 1995; editl. com. Tex. Paralegal Jour.; advisor, editor Law and Policy Institutions Guide; reviewer texbook proposals and manuscripts; contbr. articles to profl. jours. Recipient scholarship Tex. Christian U., Ft. Worth. Mem. Am. Assn. Paralegal Edn., Assn. Trial Lawyers, State Bar Tex. (paralegal divsn.), Nat. Paralegal Assn., Writer's League Tex., Text and Acad. Authors. Home: PO box 101641 Fort Worth TX 76185-1641 E-mail: kmrparal@aol.com.

READER, JOSEPH, physicist; b. Chgo., Dec. 1, 1934; BS, Purdue U., 1956, MS, 1957; PhD in Physics, U. Calif., 1962. Rsch. assoc. physics Argonne Nat. Lab., 1962-63; staff physicist Nat. Inst. Standards and Tech., Gaithersburg, Md., 1963—, group leader atomic spectroscopy group, 1999—2008. Recipient Gold medal Dept. Commerce, 1989. Fellow Am. Phys. Soc., Optical Soc. Am. (William F. Meggers award 1992). Achievements include research in experimental atomic physics, optical spectroscopy, hyperfine structure, electronic structure of highly ionized atoms, wavelength standards, and ionization energies of atoms and ions. Office: Natl Inst Of Stds & Tech Gaithersburg MD 20899-8422

READING, ANTHONY JOHN, retired psychiatrist, educator; b. Sydney, Sept. 10, 1933; s. Abe Stanley and Esma Daisy R.; m. Elisabeth Ann Hoffman, July 27, 1975; children— Wendy Virginia Elisabeth, Sarah Alexandra Jane. MBBS, U. Sydney, 1956; MPH, Johns Hopkins U., Balt., 1961, DSc, 1964. Intern Sydney Hosp., 1957-58; resident in psychiatry Johns Hopkins Hosp., Balt., 1965-68; asst. prof. psychiatry and medicine Johns Hopkins U. Sch. Medicine, Balt., 1968-73, assoc. prof. psychiatry, 1973-75, dir. psychiat. liaison service, 1974-75; dir. comprehensive alcoholism program Johns Hopkins Hosp., 1972-75; prof. U. South Fla. Coll. Medicine, 1975—2006, chmn. dept. psychiatry and behavioral medicine, 1975—2002, assoc. dean, 1993-96; med. dir. Bay Med. Behavioral Health Ctr., Panama City, Fla., 2004—05; ret., 2006. Mem.: AAAS. Home: 3202 Magnolia Islands Blvd Panama City Beach FL 32408-7176 Personal E-mail: tonytoo@comcast.net.

READING, MARGERY SCHROCK, psychology professor, artist; b. Pitts., Pa., Oct. 5, 1935; d. Archy Toy and Isabelle Adams Schrock; m. George Paul Reading, Dec. 29, 1984; m. Roger Kenneth Brown (div.); 1 child, Kathryn Lynn. BA cum laude in Art, We. Coll. Women, 1957; MEd in Tchr. Edn., Springfield Coll., Mass., 1961; MA in Clin. and Sch. Psychology, SUNY, Plattsburgh, NY, 1972; PhD in Clin. Psychology, SUNY, Albany, NY, 1976. Lic. psychologist N.Y., 1977, cert. sch. psychologist Nat. Bd. Certification, 1988, N.Y., 1989. Psychologist Faculty and Counseling Ctr. Siena Coll., Loudonville, NY, 1975—84; from asst. prof. psychology to assoc. prof. emerita Rochester Inst. Tech., NY, 1985—95, assoc. prof. emerita, 1995—. Vis. prof. Shanghai (China) Inst. Tech., 1990. Exhibitions include U. N.Mex., 1999 (Pres. Choice award, 1999), Taos Open, N.Mex., 1996—2004, Chautauqua National Exhibition, 2007, 2008, Small Works, Millicent Rogers Museum, 2006—08, Amazing Women of Taos, 2006. Adv. coun. spl. edn. BOCES, Rochester, 1989—92; active Kerry Campaign Dem. Party, Taos, N.Mex., 2004; active Obama Campaign, 2008. Scholar, We. Coll. Women, 1953—57. Mem.: Taos (N.Mex.) Soc. Portrait Artists (sec. 2003—05). Democrat. Unitarian. Avocations: archaeology, travel, reading. Home: HCR 74 Box 22624 El Prado NM 87529 Studio: 291 Hondo Seco Rd Arroyo Seco NM 87514

READY, ROBERT JAMES, finance company executive; b. Bridgeport, Conn., June 26, 1952; s. John Edward and Anne (Salata) R.; m. Margaret S. Neale, Aug. 23, 1975; children: Carolyn, Christopher and Steven (twins). AS, Housatonic Community Coll., 1972; BS, Babson Coll., 1974. CLU; chartered fin. cons.; registered fin. cons.; cert. ins. cons; cert. retirement cons.; cert. retirement adminstr. Agt. John Hancock Mut. Life Ins. Co., Hamden, Conn., 1975-77; broker Beardsley, Brown & Bassett Inc., Bridgeport, Conn., 1977-80; agt. Aetna Life and Casualty Ins. Co., Trumbull, Conn., 1980-83; v.p. Crestview Fin. Services Inc., Westport, Conn., 1983-2000, Crestview Securities Inc., Westport, Conn., 1983-2000, Crestview Investment Advisors Inc., Westport, Conn., 1983-2000; sr. v.p. ins. RDM Ins. Svcs. Inc., Westport, Conn., 2000—. Mem. Nat. Assn. Life Underwriters, Conn. Assn. Life Underwriters, Bridgeport Life Underwriters (bd. dirs. 1977), New Haven County CLU and Chartered Fin. Cons., Soc. of Fin. Svc. Profls. (Fairfield county chpt.). Roman Catholic. Avocations: golf, tennis, softball. Office: RDM Financial Group Inc 1555 Post Rd E Westport CT 06880-5602 Office Phone: 203-255-0222. E-mail: bready@rdmfinancial.com.

REAGAN, GARY DON, state legislator, lawyer; b. Amarillo, Tex., Aug. 23, 1941; s. Hester and Lois Irene (Marcum) R.; m. Nedra Ann Nash, Sept. 12, 1964; children: Marc Kristi, Kari, Brent. BA, Stanford U., 1963, JD, 1965. Bar: N.Mex. 1965, US Dist. Ct. N.Mex. 1965, US Supreme Ct. 1986. Assoc. Smith & Ransom, Albuquerque, 1965—67; ptnr. Smith, Ransom, Deaton & Reagan, Albuquerque, 1967—68, Williams, Johnson, Houston, Reagan & Porter, Hobbs, N.Mex., 1968—77, Williams, Johnson, Reagan, Porter & Love, Hobbs, 1977—82; pvt. practice Hobbs, 1982—; city atty. City of Hobbs, 1978—80, 1997—2004, City of Eunice, N.Mex., 1980—2004; mem. N.Mex. State Senate, 1993—96. Instr. N.Mex. Jr. Coll. and Coll. of S.W., Hobbs, 1978-84; N.Mex. commr. Nat. Conf. Commrs. Uniform State Laws, 1993-96; adv. mem. N.Mex. Constl. Revision Commn., 1993-95. Mayor City of Hobbs, 1972-73, 76-77, 2008-, city commr., 1970-78; pres., dir. Jr. Achievement of Hobbs, 1974-85; pres., trustee Landsun Homes, Inc., Carlsbad, N.Mex., 1972-84; trustee Lydia Patterson Inst., El Paso, Tex., 1972-84, N.Mex. Conf. United Meth. Ch., 1988—, Coll. SW Hobbs, 1989-2001. Mem. ABA, State Bar N.Mex. (coms. 1989-96, v.p. 1992-93, pres. 1994-95), Lea County Bar Assn. (pres. 1976-77), Hobbs C. of C. (pres. 1989-90), Rotary (pres. Hobbs 1985-86), Hobbs Tennis Club (pres. 1974-75). Home: 200 E Eagle Dr Hobbs NM 88240-5323 Office: 1819 N Turner Ste G Hobbs NM 88240-3834 Home Phone: 575-393-9072; Office Phone: 575-397-6551. Business E-Mail: lglregan@nm.net.

REAGAN, HARRY EDWIN, III, lawyer; b. Wichita, Kans., Sept. 9, 1940; s. Harry E. II and Mary Elizabeth (O'Steen) R.; m. Marvene R. Rogers, June 17, 1965; children: Kathleen, Leigh, Mairen. BS, U. Pa., 1962, JD, 1965. Bar: Pa. 1965, U.S. Dist. Ct. (ea. dist.) Pa. 1965, U.S. Ct. Appeals (3d cir.) 1965. From assoc. to ptnr. Morgan, Lewis & Bockius, Phila., 1965-98. Chmn. Northhampton Twp. Planning Commn., Bucks County, Pa., 1974-79; mem. Warwick Twp. Planning Commn., 1980-95, chmn., 1994; supr. Warwick Twp., 1996-98; mem. San Miguel County (Colo.) Open Space Commn., 1998—, chmn., 2001-05, 08-09; mem. Town of Telluride Open Space Commn., 1999-2002, San Miguel County Planning Commn., 2002—. Mem. ABA (labor sect.), Pa. Bar Assn. (labor sect.), Phila. Bar Assn. (labor sect.), Indsl. Rels. Assn. (pres. Phila. chpt. 1990-91). Republican. Presbyterian. Avocations: rugby, skiing, raising horses, bicycling. Home and Office: Box 190 Norwood CO 81423

REAGAN, JANET THOMPSON, psychologist, educator; b. Sept. 15, 1945; d. Virgil Joe and Carrie (Alexander) Thompson; children: Natalia Alexandria, Robert Barry. BA in Psychology, Berea Coll., 1967; PhD in Psychology, Vanderbilt U., 1972. Mgr. rsch. and eval. Nashville Mental Health Ctr., 1971-72; mgr. eval. Family Health Found., New Orleans, 1973-74; asst. prof. dept. health systems mgmt. Tulane U., New Orleans, 1974-77; dir. eval. Project Heavy West, LA, 1977-78; asst. prof. health adminstrn. Calif. State U.-Northridge, 1978-83; assoc. prof., dir. health adminstrn., 1983-87; prof., dir. health adminstrn., 1987—. Cons. in field. Contbr. articles to profl. jours., chpts. to books; mem. editl. bd. Jour. Long Term Care Adminstrn., Healthcare Papers. Mem. Am. Pub. Health Assn., Am. Coll. Health Care Adminstrn., Am. Coll. Health Care Execs. (com. on higher edn. 1987, chmn. 1991), Assn. Univ. Programs in Health Adminstrn. (task force on undergrad. edn. 1985-90, chmn. 1988-90, mem. bd. dirs. 1995, chmn. bd. dirs. 1998-99), Psi Chi, Phi Kappa Phi. Office: Calif State U Dept Health Sci Northridge CA 91330-0001 Office Phone: 818-677-2298. Business E-Mail: janet.reagan@csun.edu.

REAGAN, JOSEPH BERNARD, retired aerospace executive, management consultant; b. Somerville, Mass., Nov. 26, 1934; s. Joseph B. and Helen Lowry R.; m. Dorothy Hughes; children: Patrick, Michael, Kevin, Kathleen, Brian, John, Maureen. BS in Physics, Boston Coll., 1956, MS in Physics, 1959; PhD in Space Sci., Stanford U., 1975;

postgrad. exec. mgmt., Pa. State U., State College, 1981. Staff scientist, rsch. scientist, sr. scientist, scientist Lockheed Rsch. & Devel. Div., Palo Alto, Calif., 1959-75, mgr., 1975-84, dir., 1984-86, dep. gen. mgr., 1986-88, v.p., asst. gen. mgr., 1988-90; v.p. gen. mgr. Lockheed Missle and Space Co., 1991-96. Contbr. articles to profl. jours. Capt. U.S. Army, 1956-64. Recipient Career Achievement in Sci. award Boston Coll. Alumni Assn., 1993. Fellow AIAA (outstanding engr. San Francisco chpt. 1988); mem. Am. Geophys. Union, Nat. Acad. of Engring., Nat. Rsch. Coun. Republican. Roman Catholic. Avocation: computer and woodworking hobbies. Home and Office: 13554 Mandarin Way Saratoga CA 95070-4847 Home Phone: 408-867-0557. Personal E-mail: jbr733@comcast.net.

REAGAN, LESLIE JEAN, history professor, writer; d. Philip Reagan and Susan Harris Gardner, Laurie Edwards (Stepfather) and Anne Hunter Hamilton (Stepmother); m. Daniel Walters Schneider; children: Jacob William Schneider, Rose Jasmine Schneider. BA, U. Calif., Davis, 1981; MA, PhD, U. Wis., Madison, 1991. Postdoc. rschr. Johns Hopkins U., Balt., 1991—92; asst. prof. U. Ill., Urbana-Champaign, 1992—97, assoc. prof., 1997—. Sabbatical vis. scholar U. Calif., Berkeley, 1999—2000, 2006—07. Contbr. articles to profl. publs. (Willard Hurst Book award, 1997, Louis Pelzer Meml. award, 1990, Social Sci. History Assn. Pres.'s award, Choice). Recipient Willard Hurst prize, Law and Soc. Assn., 1997; fellow, UCLA; Nat. Libr. Medicine Publ. grant, NIH, Rsch. grants, U. Ill. Rsch. Bd., fellowship, ACOG-McNeil, Mellon and Coll. LAS, UIUC. Mem.: Am. Assn. U. Women, Am. Hist. Assn., Orgn. Am. Historians (Louis Pelzer Meml. award 1990), Berkshire Conf. Women's Historians, Am. Assn. History of Medicine (coun. 2008—). Avocations: hiking, biking. Office: Univ Ill Urbana-Champaign 810 S Wright St Urbana IL 61801 Business E-Mail: lreagan@illinois.edu.

REAGAN, NANCY DAVIS (ANNE FRANCIS ROBBINS), former First Lady of the United States, volunteer; b. NYC, July 6, 1921; d. Kenneth and Edith (Luckett) Robbins, Loyal Davis (Stepfather); m. Ronald Reagan, Mar. 4, 1952 (dec. June 5, 2004); children: Patricia Ann, Ronald Prescott stepchildren: Maureen(dec.), Michael. BA in Theatre, Smith Coll., 1943; LLD (hon.), Pepperdine U., 1983; LHD (hon.), Georgetown U., 1987. Sales clk. Marshall Fields Dept. Store, Chgo.; First Lady of the US Washington, 1981—89. Contract actress, MGM, 1949-56; films include Portrait of Jennie, 1948, East Side, West Side, 1949, Doctor and the Girl, 1949, Shadow on the Wall, 1950, The Next Voice You Hear, 1950, Night into Morning, 1951, It's a Big Country, 1951, Shadow in the Sky, 1952, Talk About a Stranger, 1952, Donovan's Brain, 1953, Hellcats of the Navy, 1957, Crash Landing, 1958, You Can't Hurry Love, 1988, Lunar: Silver Star Story, 1992; TV credits include Schlitz Playhouse of Stars, 1951, Climax, 1954, General Electric Theater, 1953, Zane Grey Theater, 1956, The Tall Man, 1960, 87th Precint, 1961, Wagon Train, 1957, Different Strokes, 1978, Dynasty, 1981; Broadway: Lute Song, 1946; formerly author syndicated column on prisoner-of-war and missing-in-action soldiers and their families; author: Nancy, 1980; (with Jane Wilkie) To Love a Child, 1982, (with William Novak) My Turn: The Memoirs of Nancy Reagan, 1989. Civic worker, visited wounded Viet Nam vets., sr. citizens, hosps. and schs. for physically and emotionally handicapped children, active in furthering foster grandparents for handicapped children program; hon. nat. chmn. Aid to Adoption of Spl. Kids, 1977; spl. interest in fighting alcohol and drug abuse among youth: hosted first ladies from around the world for 2d Internat. Drug Conf., 1985; hon. chmn. Just Say No Found., Nat. Fedn. of Parents for Drug-Free Youth, Nat. Child Watch Campaign, President's Com. on the Arts and Humanities, Wolf Trap Found. bd. of trustees, Nat. Trust for Historic Preservation, Cystic Fibrosis Found., Nat. Republican Women's Club; hon. pres. Girl Scouts of Am. Named one of Ten Most Admired Am. Women, Good Housekeeping mag., ranking #1 in poll, 1984, 85, 86; Woman of Yr. Los Angeles Times, 1977; permanent mem. Hall of Fame of Ten Best Dressed Women in U.S.; recipient humanitarian awards from Am. Camping Assn., Nat. Council on Alcoholism, United Cerebral Palsy Assn., Internat. Ctr. for Disabled; Boys Town Father Flanagan award; 1986 Kiwanis World Service medal; Variety Clubs Internat. Lifeline award; numerous awards for her role in fight against drug abuse. Republican. Presbyterian.

REAGAN, PAUL, legislative staff member; Bachelor's, Coll. William and Mary, 1982; JD, George Mason U., 1991. Legis. asst. Office of Rep. Rick Boucher, 1982—87; press sec. Office of Rep. Owen B. Pickett, 1987—94; comm. dir. Office of Rep. L.V. Payne, 1994—96; chief of staff Office of Rep. Jim Moran, 1996—2002; comm. dir. Office of Gov. Mark R. Warner, Va., 2002—05; sr. v.p. McGuire Woods Consulting, 2005—06; chief of staff Office of Senator James H. Webb, 2007—. Office: Office of Senator James H Webb 114 Senate Russell Office Bldg Washington DC 20510-4605 Office Phone: 202-224-4024. E-mail: paul_reagan@webb.senate.gov.*

REAGINS, TONY, professional baseball team executive; b. Indio, Calif., Mar. 11, 1967; m. Colleen Reagins; children: Kennedy, Luke. AA in Bus. Adminstrn., Coll. of the Desert, 1988; degree in Mktg., Calif. State U., Fullerton, 1991. Intern, baseball ops. Calif. Angels, 1992, intern, mktg. and sales, 1993, mktg. asst., 1994—96, sponsorship svcs. rep., 1996—98; mgr., baseball ops. LA Angels of Anaheim (formerly Anaheim Angels), 1999—2002, dir. player devel., 2002—07, gen. mgr., 2007—. Active supporter Boy's and Girls Clubs of Am.; bd. dirs. Boys Girls Clubs Coachella Valley; active supporter Major League Baseball's Urban Youth Acad. Mem.: Buck O'Neil Scout Assn. Mailing: c/o LA Angels of Anaheim Angel Stadium 2000 Gene Autry Way Anaheim CA 92806 Office Phone: 714-940-2000.

REAM, JAMES B. (JIM REAM), air transportation executive; married; 1 child. MBA, Northwestern Univ. Mng. dir. fin. planning Am. Airlines Inc.; v.p. fin. Continental Airlines, 1994—96; exec. v.p., COO Continental Micronesia Inc., Guam, 1996, pres., COO Guam, 1996—98; sr. v.p. Asia Continental Airlines, 1998—99; pres. ExpressJet Holdings, Houston, 1999—, CEO, 2002—. Office: ExpressJet Holdings Ste 200 700 N Sam Houston Pkwy W Houston TX 77067 Office Phone: 713-324-4722. Office Fax: 713-324-4716.

REAMAN, GREGORY HAROLD, pediatric hematologist, oncologist; b. Akron, Ohio, Sept. 9, 1947; s. Harold J. and Margaret U. (D'Alfonso) R.; m. Susan J. Pristo, Sept. 7, 1974; children: Emily Margaret, Sarah Elizabeth. BS in Biology, U. Detroit, 1969; MD, Loyola U., Chgo., 1973. Diplomate Nat. Bd. Med. Examiners, Am. Bd. Pediats. with subspecialty in pediat. hematology and oncology. Pediatric intern Loyola U. Med. Ctr., 1973-74; resident in pediatrics Montreal Children's Hosp., McGill U., 1974-76; clin. assoc. pediatric oncology br. Nat. Cancer Inst., NIH, Bethesda, Md., 1976-78, investigator pediatric oncology br., 1978-79; assoc. dept. hematology/oncology, attending physician Children's Nat. Med. Ctr., Washington, 1979—, chmn. dept. hematology/oncology, 1985—2003, dir. med. spl. svcs., 1995—99, exec. dir. Ctr. for Cancer and Blood Disorders, 1999—2002; asst. prof. pediats. Sch. Medicine and Health Scis. George Washington U., 1979—82, assoc. prof. pediats., 1982—87, prof. pediats., 1987—. Assoc. chmn. Children's Cancer Group; strategic planning com. Children's Oncology Svcs. of Met. Washington; exec. v.p. for sci. and med. affairs Nat. Childhood Cancer Found./Children's Oncology Group, chmn., 2000-; mem. oncologic drugs adv. com., FDA, 2002-06; chmn. Pediat. sub-com., bd. dir. Am. Soc. Clin. Oncology. Mem. editl. bd. Cancer Data Query, Nat. Cancer Inst., Jour. Clin. Oncology, Am. Jour. Pediat. Hematology Oncology, Cancer, Pediatric Blood and Cancer, Leukemia and Lymphoma, The Oncologist; reviewer Blood, Jour. Clin. Oncology; assoc. editor: Cancer, 1990-2000; contbr. articles to profl. publs. Trustee Nat. Childhood Cancer Found., Arcadia, Calif.; bd. dirs. Am. Cancer Soc., Atlanta; trustee, chmn. patient care and profl. edn. coms. Leukemia Soc. Am. Lt. comdr. USPHS, 1976-79, Res., 1979—. With US Pub. Health Svc., 1976—80, with active reserves, 1980—99. Folger Summer scholar Am. Cancer Soc.; recipient Spl. Fellowship Rsch. award Leukemia Soc. Am., 1980-82, Tree of Life award, Leukemia and Lymphoma Soc.; grantee DHHS, Nat. Cancer Inst., 1987—. Mem. Soc. Pediat. Rsch., Am. Soc. Hematology, Am. Pediat. Soc., Am. Fedn. Clin. Rsch., Am. Soc. Clin. Oncology, Am. Assn. Cancer Rsch., Am. Soc. Pediat. Hematology/Oncology, Children's Oncology Group, Washington Blood Club, Alpha Omega Alpha. Democrat. Roman Catholic. Home: 7306 Brennon Ln Chevy Chase MD 20815-4064 Office: Children's Nat Med Ctr 111 Michigan Ave NW Washington DC 20010-2916 Office Phone: 240-235-2220. Business E-Mail: greaman@childrensoncologygroup.org.*

REAMS, BERNARD DINSMORE, JR., law educator; b. Lynchburg, Va., Aug. 17, 1943; s. Bernard Dinsmore and Martha Eloise (Hickman) Reams; m. Rosemarie Bridget Boyle, Oct. 26, 1968 (dec. Oct. 1996); children: Andrew Dennet, Adriane Bevin; m. Lee Anne Oberhofer, Apr. 19, 2003. BA, Lynchburg Coll., 1965; MS, Drexel U., 1966; JD, U. Kans., 1972; PhD, St. Louis U., 1983. Bar: Kans. 1973, Mo. 1986, N.Y. 1996, Tex. 2002. Instr., asst. libr. Rutgers U., 1966—69; asst. prof. law, libr. U. Kans., Lawrence, 1969—74; mem. faculty law sch. Washington U., St. Louis, 1974—95, prof. law, 1976—95, prof. tech. mgmt., 1990—95, libr., 1974—76, acting dean univ. libraries, 1987—88; prof. law, assoc. dean, dir. Law Libr. St. John's U. Sch. Law, Jamaica, NY, 1995—97, assoc. dean acad. affairs, 1997—98; prof., dir. law libr. and info. tech. St. Mary's U., San Antonio, 2000—03, prof. law, 2000. Vis. fellow Max-Planck Inst., Hamburg, 1995, 97-98, 2001; vis. prof. law Seton Hall U., 1998-2000, Inst. World Legal Problems, Innsbruck, Austria, 2002, 05-07, co-dir. 2008-09; guest prof. Leopold-Franzens U. Innsbruck, 2008-09. Author: Law For The Businessman, 1974, Reader in Law Librarianship, 1976, Federal Price and Wage Control Programs 1917-1979: Legis. Histories and Laws, 1980, Education of the Handicapped: Laws, Legislative Histories, and Administrative Documents, 1983, Internal Revenue Acts of the United States: The Revenue Act of 1954 with Legislative Histories and Congressional Documents, 1983, Congress and the Courts: A Legislative History 1978-1984, 1984, University-Industry Research Partnerships: The Major Issues in Research and Development Agreements, 1986, Deficit Control and the Gramm-Rudman-Hollings Act, 1986, The Semiconductor Chip and the Law: A Legislative History of the Semiconductor Chip Protection Act of 1984, 1986, American International Law Cases, 2d series, 1986, Technology Transfer Law: The Export Administration Acts of the U.S., 1987, Insider Trading and the Law: A Legislative History of the Insider Trading Sanctions Act, 1989, Insider Trading and Securities Fraud, 1989, The Health Care Quality Improvement Act of 1989: A Legislative History of P.L. No. 99-660, 1990, The National Organ Transplant Act of 1984: A Legislative History of P.L. No. 98-507, 1990, A Legislative History of Individuals with Disabilities Education Act, 1994, Federal Legislative Histories: An Annotated Bibliography and Index to Officially Published Sources, 1994, Electronic Contracting Law, 1996, Health Care Reform, 1994, The American Experience: Clinton and Congress, 1997, The Omnibus Anti-Crime Act, 1997, The Law of E-SIGN: A Legislative History of the Electronic Signature in Global and National Commerce Act, 2001; co-author: Segregation and the Fourteenth Amendment in the States, 1975, Historic Preservation Law: An Annotated Bibliography, 1976, Congress and the Courts: A Legislative History 1787-1977, 1978, Federal Consumer Protection Laws, Rules and Regulations, 1979, A Guide and Analytical Index to the Internal Revenue Acts of the U.S., 1909-1950, 1979, The Numerical Lists and Schedule of Volumes of the U.S. Congressional Serial Set: 73d Congress through the 96th Congress, 1984, Human Experimentation: Federal Laws, Legislative Histories, Regulations and Related Documents, 1985, American Legal Literature: A Guide to Selected Legal Resources, 1985, U.S.A. Patriot Act: A Legislative History, 2002, Supplement, 2005, Intelligence Reform: A Legislative History of the Intelligence Reform and Terrorism Prevention Act, 2006. Trustees Quincy Found. for Med. Rsch. Charitable Trust, San Francisco; bd. dirs. San Antonio Lighthouse for Blind Fellow Am. Bar Found.; recipient Thornton award for excellence Lynchburg Coll., 1986, Disting. Alumni award, 1989, Joseph L. Andrews Bibliog. award, 1995,; named to Hon. Order Ky. Cols., 1992; named Admiral Tex. Navy, 2005. Mem. ABA, ALA, Am. Law Inst., Am. Soc. Law and Medicine, Nat. Health Lawyers Assn., Am. Assn. Higher Edn., Spl. Librs. Assn., Internat. Assn. Law Libr. Coll. and Univ. Attys., Order of Coif, Phi Beta Kappa, Sigma Xi, Beta Phi Mu, Phi Delta Phi, Phi Delta Epsilon, Kappa Delta Pi, Pi Lambda Theta. Office: St Marys U Sch Law One Camino Santa Maria San Antonio TX 78228 Home Phone: 210-479-1316; Office Phone: 210-431-5030. E-mail: breams@stmarytx.edu.

REAMS, LINDA PIGG, elementary school educator; d. Burton Farris Wesley and Ivie Thomas Pigg; m. James Edward Reams, May 31, 1980 (dec. July 2, 2005); 1 child, Mary Catherine Clark. AS, Columbia State Cmty. Coll., Tenn., 1968; BS, Mid. Tenn. State U., Murfreesboro, 1970. Cert. elem. tchr. N-8 Va., 2006, libr. sci. tchr. K-12 Va., 2006. Elem. tchr. Culleoka Elem. Sch., Tenn., 1970—73; libr. Mt. Pleasant Elem. Sch., Tenn., 1974—78, elem. tchr., 1979—80, Chase City Elem. Sch., Va., 1980—99, title 1 tchr., 1980—92, elem. tchr., 1992—98, title 1 tchr., 1999—2008. Art grantee, 1999, 2001, 2003, 2004, 2006. Mem.: NEA, Mecklenburg Edn. Assn., Va. Edn. Assn., Boydton Fire and Rescue Aux. (v.p. 1988—90, pres. 1990—95, Outstanding award 1994), United Daus. Confederacy. Democrat. Baptist. Office: Chase City Elem Sch 5450 Hwy 47 Chase City VA 23924 Business E-Mail: lreams@meck.k12.va.us.

REAMS, MAX WARREN, geology educator, researcher; b. Virgil, Kans., Mar. 10, 1938; s. Chester Lyle and Arline R.; m. Carol Ann Cushard, July 28, 1961; children: Brian Scott, Anne Rachelle, Kayla Diane. BA, BS, U. Kans., 1961, MS with grad. honors in geology, 1963; PhD, Washington U., St. Louis, 1968. Prof. geology, chair dept. physical sci. Olivet Nazarene U., Kankakee, Ill., 1967—. Contbr. articles to profl. jours. Cons. local city bds., Ill. Sgt. USAR, 1956-64. Rsch. grantee various pub. and pvt. orgns., 1966-80. Fellow Geol. Soc. Am., Sigma Xi; mem. Am. Quaternary Assn., others. Mem. Church of Nazarene. Achievements include defining the origin of cave sediments, and defining first spring-related stromatolites. Home: 6 Castle Coombe Bourbonnais IL 60914-1828 Office: Olivet Nazarene U Dept Physical Scis Bourbonnais IL 60914 Office Phone: 815-939-5394. E-mail: mreams@olivet.edu.

REAMS, PATRICIA LYNN, retired elementary school educator; b. Fresno, Calif., Dec. 10, 1938; d. Chris H. and Marjorie Lois (nee Maul) Pedersen; m. William Everett Harvey (dec.); m. George William Reams, Nov. 10, 1972 (dec.); children: Holly, Richard, George, Susan, Kristin. AA, Colo. Women's Coll., 1958; BA with honors, San Jose State U., Calif., 1960. Cert. tchg. life diploma 1966. Tchr. Salinas Sch. Dist., Calif., 1960—61, Cupertino Sch. Dist., Calif., 1961—63, Spreckels Sch. Dist., Salinas, 1963—68, Alisal Sch. Dist., Salinas, 1971—74, Kingsburg Charter Sch., Calif., 1987—2002; cmty. svc. officer Kingsburg Police Dept., 2006—07. BITSA trainer Fresno County Sch., Kingsburg, 1996—98. Pink lady, women's aux. local hosp., Salinas, Calif., 1972—83, Boulder City, Nev., 1984—87; adv. Rainbow Girls, Salinas, 1980—83; sec. PTA, Boulder City, 1984—86; brownie leader, 1985—86; Girl Scout leader, 1986—87; sec. Kingsburg HS Music Boosters, 1992—94; classroom vol. Lincoln Sch., Kingsburg, 2002—07. Recipient Grand Cross of Color award, Rainbow Girls, 1983. Mem.: PEO (pres. 2004—06, guard 2007), Ladies Oriental Shrine. Republican. Avocations: reading, gardening, travel. Home: 13350 SE 26th St Apt 334 Bellevue WA 98005 Personal E-mail: plreams@gmail.com.

REAMS-JOHNSON, ANSA, history professor; d. Jimmie Reams and Patricia Ellis-Reams; m. Derrick Johnson, Dec. 16, 2005. MA, Valdosta State U., Ga. History instr. Edward Waters Coll., Jacksonville, Fla., 2004—. Mem. Nat. Coun. Negro Women, Jacksonville. Mem.: So. Assn. Women Historians, Am. Hist. Assn., Afro-Am. Hist. & Geneal. Soc. Office: Edward Waters Coll 1658 Kings Rd Jacksonville FL 32209

REAMY, MICHAELIN, marriage and family therapist, educator, consultant; b. NYC, Feb. 20, 1938; d. Judson Reamy and Eleanor Stevens McMichael R.; m. James Donald Cowie, Aug. 29, 1959; children: Jennifer D., James J., David K., Laura S.; m. Richard Ward Stephenson, Aug. 31, 1979; m. David H. Watts, Feb. 14, 2003. BS with distinction in Human Ecology, Cornell U., 1960; MSW, U. Ga., 1979; studied with Carolyn Myss and Norm Shealy. Diplomate NASW; cert. primordial sound meditation instr., 1996. Tchr. swimming, Conn., E. Africa, Lebanon, 1968-75; social work intern, grad. asst., Atlanta, 1978-79; dir. social svcs., assoc. dir., coord. family therapy adult treatment program Brawner Psychiat. Inst., Atlanta, 1980-82; dir. extramural tng., marriage and family therapist Atlanta Inst. Family Studies, 1982-87, Perspective Ctr. for Psychotherapy, 1988-98, Natural Color & Design, 1988—. Mem. Atlanta Com. Children, 1983-85; instr. water safety ARC, 1957—. Recipient DAR Citizen award, 1956, YMCA Svc. award, White Plains, NY, 1958. Contbr. articles to profl. jours. Mem. Nat. Assn. Social Workers, Am. Assn. Marriage and Family Therapy (supervision com.), Cornell U. Human Ecology Alumni Assn., Raven and Serpent Mortar Bd., Omicron Nu, Phi Kappa Phi. Home and Office: Natural Color & Design 11 Garzas Trail Carmel CA 93923 Address: PO Box 190 Apalachicola FL 32329-0190 Office Phone: 831-624-4294.

REARDON, FRANK EMOND, lawyer; b. Providence, May 22, 1953; s. J. Clarke and Dorothy (Emond) R.; m. Deborah Walsh, Sept. 30, 1978; children: Kathleen Elizabeth, Brendan Francis, William James, Sean Patrick. BA, Holy Cross Coll., Worcester, Mass., 1975; JD, Suffolk U., 1978; MS, Harvard U., 1981. Bar: Mass. 1978, R.I. 1978, U.S. Dist. Ct. Mass. 1980, U.S. Dist. Ct. R.I. 1980, U.S. Supreme Ct. 1986. Counsel Nat. Assn. Govtl. Employment and Internat. Brotherhood Police Officers, Cranston, R.I., 1978-81; asst. gen. counsel Brigham and Women's Hosp., Boston, 1981-84; litigation counsel Risk Mgmt. Found. Harvard Med. Instns., Cambridge, Mass., 1984-87; ptnr. Hassan and Reardon, Boston, 1987—. Chmn. bd. dirs. St. Monica's Nursing Home, 1984-89, Med. Area Fed. Credit Union, 1984-89; clk., trustee Deaconess Glover Hosp., Needham, Mass.; ethics com. Boston Children's Hosp., 1993-96. Contbr. articles to profl. jours. Chmn. fin. com. Town of Needham, Mass.; mem. pres.'s council Coll. Holy Cross, 1985—. Beuilacqua scholar, 1978. Mem. ABA, Mass. Bar Assn. (chmn. health law sect. 1987—), Assn. Trial Lawyers Am., Am. Soc. Law and Medicine (cmty. rep. children's hosp. ethics com.). Democrat. Roman Catholic. Avocations: tennis, sailing, golf, writing. Home: 44 Sargent St Needham MA 02492-3434 Office: Hassan Reardon Pc 2 International Pl Fl 16 Boston MA 02110-4101

REARDON, GEORGE MARTIN, lawyer; b. Detroit, Aug. 7, 1947; BS in bus., Ind. U., 1972; JD, U. Fla., Gainesville, 1975. Bar: Fla. 1976, US Ct. Appeals 5th Cir. 1976, US Dist. Ct. Mid., No., So. Districts Fla. 1976, Tex. 1992, US Dist. Ct. So. Dist. Tex. 1992, Mich. 1999. V.p., gen. counsel Charles Stedman & Co. Inc., 1976—82; v.p., asst. gen. counsel Snelling & Snelling, Inc., 1983—90; v.p., gen. counsel, corp. sec. The Talent Tree Corp., 1990-94; atty. pvt. practice, Houston, 1994-98; sr. v.p., gen. counsel Kelly Services Inc., Troy, Mich., 1998—2004, Adecco Group N.Am., 2005—. Served Adj. Gen. Corps US Army, 1970—72, Vietnam. Office: Adecco 175 Broadhollow Rd Melville NY 11747

REARDON, JACK EDWARD, economics professor; b. Norwood, Mass., Oct. 12, 1959; m. Laurie Beth Myers, July 18, 1992; children: Elizabeth Michelle, Patrick John. PhD in Economics, U. of Notre Dame, Ind., 1991. Prof. economics U. Wis. Stout, Eau Claire, 1986—2007, Hamline U., St. Paul, 2008—. Avocation: travel. Office: Hamline Univ 1536 Hewitt Ave MS-A1740 Saint Paul MN 55104-1284 Business E-Mail: jreardon02@hamline.edu.

REARDON, JOHN B., III, state banking agency administrator; b. Youngstown, Ohio, Nov. 25, 1957; s. John B. Jr. and Carole Ann (Shutrump) R. BBA in Econs., Kent State U., Ohio, 1979; MA in Econs., Youngstown State U., 1985. Treas. Mahoning County, Ohio, 1998—2007; supt. fin. instns. Ohio Dept. Commerce, 2007—. Prof. econs. Youngstown State U., 1986—95. Democrat. Roman Catholic. Avocations: reading, music, sports, games, travel. Office: Divsn Fin Instns Ohio Dept Commerce 77 S High St 21st Fl Columbus OH 43215-6120 Office Phone: 614-728-8400. Office Fax: 614-752-9029. E-mail: john.reardon@dfi.com.state.oh.us.*

REARDON, JOHN E., broadcast executive; b. Chgo., Jan. 26, 1954; BA in Bus. Adminstrn. and Fin., Loyola U., 1977. Account exec. WGN-TV, Chgo., 1985—86, regional sales mgr., 1986—87, local sales mgr., 1979—89, dir. sales, 1989—92; sta. mgr. KTLA-TV, LA, 1992—96, v.p. & gen. mgr., 1996—2004; group v.p. Tribune Broadcasting Co., 2004—05, pres. & CEO Chgo., 2005—. Bd. dirs. Lincoln Park Zoo, Chgo. Mem.: Nat. Assn. Broadcasters (TV bd. dirs.), TV Bur. Advt. (bd. dirs.). Office: Tribune Co 435 N Michigan Ave Chicago IL 60611 Office Phone: 312-222-9100.

REARDON, MARTINE, department store executive, marketing professional; Numerous positions Macy's Inc., including v.p., prodn. & mktg. divsn. Macy's East NYC, sr. v.p. sales & promotion, 1997, exec. v.p. mktg. Macy's Home Store divsn., then exec. v.p. strategy, events & pub. rels., Macy's Corp. Mktg. divsn., 2007—09, exec. v.p. mktg., 2009—. Named a Woman to Watch, Advt. Age, 2009. Office: Macys Inc Hdqs 7 W 7th St Cincinnati OH 45202 Business E-Mail: martine.reardon@macys.com.*

REARDON, NANCY ANNE, food products executive; b. Little Falls, NY, Sept. 19, 1952; d. Warren Joseph and Elizabeth Owen (Tiel) Reardon; m. Steven Jonathan Sayer, Aug. 28, 1976; children: Scott

Jason, Kathryn Anne. BS in Psychology, Union Coll., 1974; MS in Social Psychology, Syracuse U., 1978. With GE Co., NYC, 1979-85, Avon Products Inc., NYC, 1985-89, Am. Express, NYC, 1989-91; sr. v.p. human resources Duracell Internat., Inc., Bethel, Conn., 1991-97; sr. v.p. corp. affairs & human resources Borden Inc., Columbus, Ohio, 1997—2004; sr. v.p., chief human resources and comm. officer Campbell Soup Co., Camden, NJ, 2004—. Bd. dir. Warnaco Group Inc. 2006-; adv. bd. mem. Catalyst, 1995. Mem. Human Resource Planning Soc. (bd. dirs. 1991-94, treas. 1992-93), N.Y. Human Resource Planners (bd. dirs., pres. 1989-91), Sr. Pers. Execs. Forum, Nat. Fgn. Trade Coun. (bd. dirs. 1995), Soc. Human Resource Mgmt., Phila. Women's Forum. Avocation: skiing. Office: Campbell Soup Co 1 Campbell Pl Camden NJ 08103-1799

REARDON, ROBERT C., retired psychology professor; b. San Antonio, Nov. 20, 1940; s. Thomas A. and Etta Marie Reardon; m. Janet G. Lenz; children: Elizabeth Bevins, Russell Todd. BS, Tex. Luth. Coll., Seguin, 1959; MS, Fla. State U., Tallahassee, 1963, PhD, 1968. Cert. Nat. Bd. Cert. Counselors, 1983. Prof. & program dir. Fla. State U., 1968—2007, prof. emeritus & sr. rsch. assoc. Author: (book) Career Development and Services: A Comprehensive Approach (Eminent Career award, Nat. Career Devel. Assn., 2003). Mem.: ACA, APA, Nat. Career Devel. Assn. Office: Fla State Univ Career Ctr 100 S Woodward Ave Tallahassee FL 32306-4162

REARDON, ROBERT IGNATIUS, JR., lawyer; b. NYC, Nov. 28, 1945; s. Robert I. and Mildred (Lomax) R.; m. Lise Hofffman; children: Colleen Brooke, Kelly Elizabeth. BS in Econs., Boston Coll., 1967; JD, Fordham U., 1970. Bar: Conn. 1970, U.S. Dist. Ct. Conn. 1974, U.S. Ct. Mil. Appeals 1971, U.S. Ct. Appeals (2d cir.) 1974, U.S. Supreme Ct. 1974, U.S. Ct. Claims 1986. Ptnr. Shapiro & Reardon, P.C., New London, Conn., 1973-83; pres. Reardon Law Firm P.C., New London, 1983—. State trial referee Conn. Superior Ct., 1985—. Chmn. Bd. Fin. Town of Waterford, Conn., 1974-79; mem. Bd. Edn. Town of East Lyme, Conn., 1981-84; trustee Eugene O'Neill Meml. Theater, Inc., 1978-84; active Conn. Commn. Pub. Trust, 1998-2000. Served as capt. USMC, 1970-73. Recipient Disting. Alumnus award, Fordham Law Sch., 2004. Mem. ABA (award of achievement young lawyers sect. 1975), ATLA (bd. dirs. 1998—), Conn. Trial Lawyers Assn. (pres. 1997-98), Conn. Bar Assn. (bd. govs. 1979-81, ho. of dels. 1975-79), New London County Bar Assn. (mem. exec. com. 1975-79)Fordham Law Sch. (Dist. Alumnus award, 2004) Office: 160 Hempstead St New London CT 06320-5638 Office Phone: 860-442-0444. Personal E-mail: reardonlaw@aol.com.

REARDON, SIOBHAN A., library director; m. James Reardon; 2 children. BA in Polit. Sci., SUNY, Purchase; MA in Internat. Polit. Economy and Devel., Fordham U., Bronx, NY; MLS, LI U. Palmer Sch. Libr. Sci., NY. Various fin. roles including mgr. of budget and planning NY Pub. Libr.; acting exec. dir., dir. fin., Bklyn. Pub. Libr., dep. exec. dir., COO, 1999—2005; exec. dir. Westchester Libr. Sys., Tarrytown, NY, 2005—08; dir., pres. Free Libr. of Phila., 2008—. Office: Free Libr of Phila 1901 Vine St Philadelphia PA 19103

REASER, DONALD FREDERICK, retired geology educator; b. Wichita Falls, Tex., Sept. 30, 1931; s. Frederick Summers and Lillian Norene (Wales) R.; m. Bette Jane Forrest, Aug. 2, 1975; 1 child, David Forrest Anderson. BS in Geology, So. Meth. U., Dallas, 1953, MS in Geology, 1958; PhD in Geology, U. Tex., Austin, 1974. Cert. profl. geologist. Tchg. asst. dept. geol. sci. U. Tex., Austin, 1958—61, instr., 1960—63; instr. dept. geology Arlington State Coll., Tex., 1961—63; asst. prof. dept. geology West Tex. State U., Canyon, 1964—68; instr. dept. geology U. Tex., Arlington, 1968—70, asst. prof., 1970—74, assoc. prof., 1974—97, prof., 1997—2003, prof. emeritus, 2004—. Petroleum geologist Humble Oil and Refining Co. (Exxon), Midland, Tex., 1965-66; asst. Tex. Bur. Economic Geology, Austin, 1966-67; cons. Core Labs., Inc. (Western Atlas), Dallas, 1974-78, Halliburton (Gearhart Industries, Inc.), Fort Worth, 1982-84. Author: (Essentials of Earth History, 1996, Geology of the Dallas-Fort Worth Metroplex, 2002. Bd. dirs. Oil Info. Libr. Fort Worth, 1987-90; 2nd v.p. U. Tex. Coll. Sci. Adv. Com., 2007-08. 1st lt. USAF, 1954-56. Fellow Tex. Acad. Sci.; mem. Masons, Shriners, Scottish Rite, Lambda Chi Alpha (v.p., pres. 1952-53). Republican. Methodist. Avocation: rock and mineral collecting. Home: 200 Rock Springs Dr Waxahachie TX 75165-5302 Office: U Tex Arlington Dept Earth and Environ Scis PO Box 19049 Arlington TX 76019-0001 Personal E-mail: breaser_2000@yahoo.com.

REASONER, HARRY MAX, lawyer; b. San Marcos, Tex., July 15, 1939; s. Harry Edward and Joyce Marjorie (Barrett) Reasoner; m. Elizabeth Macey Hodges, Apr. 15, 1963; children: Barrett Hodges, Elizabeth Macey Reasoner Stokes. BA summa cum laude in Philosophy, Rice U., 1960; JD with hons., U. Tex., 1962; postgrad., London Sch. Econs., U. London, 1962—63. Bar: Tex., DC, NY. Law clk. US Ct. Appeals (2d cir.), 1963—64; assoc. Vinson & Elkins, Houston, 1964—69, ptnr., 1970—, mng. ptnr., 1992—2001. Vis. prof. U. Tex. Sch. Law, 1971, Rice U., 1976, U. Houston Sch. Law, 1977; mem. adv. com. Supreme Ct. Tex., 1984—90; chair adv. group U.S. Dist. Ct. (so. dist.) Tex., 1990; adj. prof. U. Tex. Sch Law, 2002; at-large rep. Supreme Ct. Tex. Access to Justice Commn., 2006—. Author (with Charles Alan Wright): Procedure: The Handmaid of Justice, 1965; mem. editl. advisory bd.: Nat. Law Jour., 2004—. Trustee U. Tex. Law Sch. Found., Baylor Coll. Medicine; chair Tex. Higher Edn. Coordinating Bd., 1991; bd. dirs. Houston A+ Challenge, Houston, 1997—; trustee emeritus Ctr. for Am. and Internat. Law; bd. dirs. Supreme Ct. of U.S. Bd. Hist. Soc, 2000—. Recipient Professionalism award, US Court Appeals, Fifth Circuit, Am. Inns Court Found., 2004, Lifetime Achievement award, The Am. Lawyer, 2009; named Disting. Alumnus, U. Tex., 1997, U. Tex. Sch. Law, 1998, Rice U., 2003. Fellow: Tex. Bar Found., ABA Found., Internat. Soc. Barristers, Internat. Acad. Trial Lawyers (bd. dirs. 2005—09), Am. Coll. Trial Lawyers; mem.: ABA (chmn. antitrust sect. 1989—90), Litigation Counsel America, Am. Law Inst., DC Bar Assn., Am. Bd. Trial Advocates, Philos. Soc. Tex., Houston Philos. Soc., Assn. Bar City of NY, Houston Bar Assn., Century Assn. NYC, Cosmos Club DC, Phi Delta Phi, Phi Beta Kappa. Office: Vinson & Elkins LLP 1001 Fannin St Ste 2500 Houston TX 77002-6760 Office Phone: 713-758-2358. Business E-Mail: hreasoner@velaw.com.

REASOR, CLAYTON (CRAIG CLAYTON REASOR, C.C. REASOR), oil industry executive; m. Janet Reasor. BS in Fin., U. Richmond, Va.; MBA, Calif. Polytechnic State U. Joined Phillips Petroleum, 1979, comml. services resource area mgr., Norway divsn., dir. investor rels., 2001—02; gen. mgr. investor rels. ConocoPhillips, 2002—05, pres. US mktg., 2005—09, v.p. corporate affairs, 2009—. Office: ConocoPhillips 600 N Dairy Ashford Rd PO Box 2197 Houston TX 77252 E-mail: c.c.reasor@conocophillips.com.*

REATH, GEORGE, JR., lawyer, mediator, arbitrator; b. Phila., Mar. 14, 1939; s. George and Isabel Duer (West) Reath; m. Ann B. Rowland, 1990; children from previous marriage: Eric(dec.), Amanda. BA, Williams Coll., 1961; LLB, Harvard U., 1964. Bar: Pa. 1965, US Dist. Ct. (ea. dist.) Pa. 1966, US Ct. Appeals (3d cir.) 1996. Assoc. Dechert Price & Rhoads, Phila., 1964-70, Brussels, 1971-74; atty. Pennwalt Corp., Phila., 1974-78, mgr. legal dept., asst. sec., 1978-87, sr. v.p. law, sec., 1987-89; sr. v.p., gen. counsel, sec. Elf Atochem N.Am., Inc. (formerly Pennwalt Corp.), Phila., 1990-92; sr. v.p., gen counsel, sec. Legal Triage Svcs., Inc., Phila., 1993-98; sr. v.p., gen. counsel, sec. Triage Mediation Svcs., Inc., Phila., 1999—. Trustee Children's Hosp., Phila., 1974—2003, sec., 1980—81, vice chmn., 1984—97, trustee emeritus, 2003; bd. mgrs. Phila. City Inst. Libr., 1974—, treas., 1981—88, pres., 1989—99; bd. dirs. Phila. Festival Theatre New Plays, 1983—94, Ctrl. Phila. Devel. Corp., 1987—93, Bach Festival Phila., 1990—98, v.p., 1992—93; bd. dirs. Citizens Crim Commn. Delaware Valley, 1st vice chmn., 1992—94, chmn., 1994—96, exec. com., 1996—2007; bd. trustees Episcopal Cmty. Svcs., 1999—2009, treas., 2000—06. Mem.: ABA, Assn. Conflict Resolution, Am. Corp. Counsel Assn., Phila. Bar Assn., Pa. Bar Assn., Winter Harbor Yacht Club, Penllyn Club, Phi Beta Kappa. Office Phone: 215-235-7711. Business E-Mail: gr@triagemediation.com. E-mail: greath@comcast.net.

REAVLEY, THOMAS MORROW, federal judge; b. Quitman, Tex., June 21, 1921; s. Thomas Mark and Mattie (Morrow) Reavley; m. Florence Montgomery Wilson, July 24, 1943 (dec.); children: Thomas Wilson, Marian, Paul Stewart, Margaret; m. Carolyn Dineen King, Aug. 27, 2004. BA, U. Tex., 1942; JD, Harvard U., 1948; LLD, Austin Coll., 1974, Southwestern U., 1977, Tex. Wesleyan, 1982; LLM, U. Va., 1983; LLD, Pepperdine U., 1993. Bar: Tex. 1948. Asst. dist. atty., Dallas, 1948—49; mem. Bell & Reavley, Nacogdoches, Tex., 1949—51; county atty. Nacogdoches, Tex., 1951; with Collins, Garrison, Renfro & Zeleskey, 1951—52; mem. Fisher, Tonahill & Reavley, Jasper, Tex., 1952—55; sec. state Tex., 1955—57; mem. Powell, Rauhut, McGinnis & Reavley, Austin, Tex., 1957—64; dist. judge Austin, Tex., 1964—68; justice Tex. Supreme Ct., Tex., 1968—77; counsel Scott & Douglass, 1977—79; judge US Ct. Appeals (5th cir.), Austin, Tex., 1979—90, sr. judge, 1990—. Lectr. Baylor U. Law Sch., 1976—94; adj. prof. U. Tex. Law Sch., 1958—59, 1978—79, 1988—95, South Tex. Sch. Law, Pepperdine Law Sch., 1990, Tex. Tech. Law Sch., 1998; mem. Am. Bar Assn., Am Bar Found., Tex. Bar Assn, Am. Law Inst., Am. Judicature Soc. Chancellor S.W. Tex. conf. United Meth. Ch., 1972—93. Lt. USNR, 1943—45. Mem.: Masons (33 degree). Office: US Ct Appeals Rm 11009 515 Rusk St Houston TX 77002-2605 Home Phone: 713-960-9512; Office Phone: 713-250-5185.*

REBACK, CHARLES S., economics professor; b. NYC, 1961; m. Melissa Walker. BS in Economics, U. Pa., 1983; MA, Clemson U., SC, 2001, PhD in Applied Economics, 2005; MS in Fin., Boston Coll., Chestnut Hill, 1987. Vis. lectr. U. NC Charlotte, 2004—05; asst. prof. U. SC. Upstate, Spartanburg, 2005—. Office: Univ SC Upstate 800 Univ Way Spartanburg SC 29303 Business E-Mail: creback@uscupstate.edu.

REBACK, JOYCE ELLEN, lawyer; b. Phila., July 11, 1948; d. William and Sue (Goldstein) R.; m. Itzhak Brook, Aug. 2, 1981; children: Jonathan Zev, Sara Jennie. BA magna cum laude, Brown U., 1970; JD with honors, George Washington U., 1976. Bar: D.C. 1976, U.S. Dist. Ct. D.C. 1976, U.S. Ct. Appeals (D.C. cir.) 1976, U.S. Ct. Appeals (3d cir.) 1983, U.S. Ct. Appeals (Fed. cir.) 1985. Assoc. Fulbright & Jaworski, Washington, 1976—84, ptnr., 1984—87; legal svcs. cons. IMF, Washington, 1987—. Contbr. articles to profl. jours. Mem. ABA, D.C. Bar Assn., Phi Beta Kappa. Jewish. Office: Internat Monetary Fund 700 19th St NW Washington DC 20431-0001

REBAY, LUCIANO, language educator, literary critic; b. Milan, Apr. 23, 1928; came to U.S., 1955; s. Angelo and Pierina (Doniselli) R.; m. Martha Virginia Krauss, Aug. 2, 1952; children: Alexandra, Ilaria. Maturita classica Liceo Manzoni, Milan, 1946; Licence es lettres, U. Aix-en-Provence, France, 1951; PhD, Columbia U., 1960. Instr. Italian Columbia U., NYC, 1957-60, asst. prof., 1960-63, assoc. prof., 1963-65, prof., 1965-73, chmn. Italian Dept., 1970-73, Giuseppe Ungaretti prof. Italian lit., 1973—2005, Giuseppe Ungaretti prof. emeritus Italian lit., 2005—; dir. Ctr. Italian Studies, 1976, 1985—88. Cons. to scholarly jours. Author: Le origini della poesia di Giuseppe Ungaretti, 1962, Invitation to Italian Poetry, 1969, Alberto Moravia, 1970, Giuseppe Ungaretti, Gli scritti egiziani, 1909-1912, 1979, Montale, Clizia e l'America, 1982, Montale per amico, 1994, Montale: dal dire e del non dire, 1998; editor: Giuseppe Ungaretti, Saggi e interventi, 1974, Jean Paulhan-Giuseppe Ungaretti, Correspondance, 1921-68, 1989. Guggenheim fellow, 1966-67; Am. Council Learned Socs. fellow, 1970-71; NEH fellow, 1980-81; Am. Philos. Soc. research grantee, 1970, 75 Mem. MLA, Am. Assn. Tchrs. of Italian, Associazione Internazionale per gli Studi di Lingua e Letteratura Italiana Business E-Mail: lr2@columbia.edu.

REBEIZ, CONSTANTIN ANIS, plant biochemist, lab and foundation administrator, educator; b. Beirut, July 11, 1936; arrived in U.S., 1959, naturalized, 1975; s. Anis C. and Valentine A. (Choueyri) Rebeiz; m. Conness Carole Louise, Aug. 18, 1962; children: Paul A., Natalie, Mark J. BS, Am. U., Beirut, 1959; MS, U. Calif., Davis, 1960, PhD, 1965. Dir. dept. biol. scis. Agrl. Rsch. Inst., Beirut, 1965—69; rsch. assoc. biology U. Calif., Davis, 1969—71; assoc. prof. biochem. plant physiology U. Ill., Urbana-Champaign, 1972—76, prof., 1976—2005, dir. Lab. Plant Biochemistry and Photobiology, 1973—2005, prof. emeritus, 2005—; pres. Rebeiz Found. for Basic Rsch., Champaign, 2005—. Adj. prof. U. Limerick, Ireland, 2003. Contbr. articles to profl. jours. Bd. dirs. Rebeiz Found. for Basic Rsch. Recipient Beckman Rsch. award, 1982, 1985, Funk award, 1985, Sr. Rsch. award, U. Ill., 1994, Presdl. Green Chemistry Challenge award, 1999, Outstanding Sci. Achievement award, Faculty of Agrl. and Food Sci., Am. U. Beirut, 2002; named one of 100 Outstanding Innovators, Sci. Digest, 1984—85; grantee John P. Trebellas Rsch. Endowment, 1986, C.A. and C.C. Rebeiz Endowment for basic rsch., 2000. Mem.: AAAS, Lebanese Assn. Advancement Scis. (exec. com. 1967—69). Achievements include research in pathway of chlorophyll biosynthesis; chloroplast development; bioengineering of photosynthetic reactors; first to biosynthesis of chlorophyll in vitro; duplication of greening process of plants in test tube; development of demonstration of operation of multibranched chlorophyll biosynthetic pathway in nature; formulation of a blue-print chloroplast bioengineering in green plants aimed at improving plant productivity; formulation and design of laser herbicides, insecticides and cancer chemotherapeutic agents. Home: 2209 Edgewater Pl Champaign IL 61822 Office: Rebeiz Found Basic Rsch 2209 Edgewater Pl Champaign IL 61822 Home Phone: 217-356-3675; Office Phone: 217-377-8755, 217-377-8756. Business E-Mail: crebeiz@illinois.edu. *Meaningful scientific discoveries are those that help humans achieve a better understanding of themselves, of their environment or of the universe at large, as well as those that contribute to the betterment of the human spiritual, psychological and physical condition.*

REBEK, ERIC, entomologist, educator; b. Fond du Lac, Wis., Oct. 18, 1972; s. Duane and Elaine Rebek; m. Kimberly Toscano, Nov. 14, 1998; children: Harlan, Xavier, Miles. PhD, Purdue U., West Lafayette, Ind., 2004. Rsch. assoc. Mich. State U., East Lansing, 2004—07; asst. prof. Okla. State U., Stillwater, 2007—. Cub scout den, pack leader Boy Scouts America, Stillwater, Okla., 2007. Mem.: Internat. Orgn. Biol. Control, Entomol. Soc. America. Liberal. Roman Catholic. Office: Okla State Univ 127 Noble Research Center Stillwater OK 74078 Business E-Mail: eric.rebek@okstate.edu.

REBEL, AMY LOUISE, elementary school educator; b. Shaker Heights, Ohio, Feb. 26, 1957; d. Paul Vernon Jr. and Louise Alice (Parme) R. BS, No. Ill. U., 1980; postgrad., Nova U., 1992. Cert. tchr., Fla., Ill.; cert. ednl. leadership, Fla.; nat. cert. in water fitness-master level Am. Sport Edn. Program/Nat. Fedn. Interscholastic Coaches Edn. Program instr.; nat. cert. water fitness program coord. Golf coach, mem. support pers. Hinsdale (Ill.) Cen. Twp. High Sch., 1983-85; instructional pers., swimming coach Boca Raton (Fla.) Community Mid. Sch., 1985-86; tchr. phys. edn., swimming coach Boca Raton Community High Sch., 1987; tchr. phys. edn. Whispering Pines Community Elem. Sch., Boca Raton, 1987-88; tchr. phys. and aquatic edn. Sandpiper Shores Cmty. Elem. Sch., Boca Raton, 1989—, ESOL coord., 1991-92; crisis response team Sandpiper Shores Cmty. Elem. Sch., Boca Raton, Fla., 2002—. Personal cons. Water Exercise Programs, Ill. and Fla., 1976—; coach staff swimming Mission Bay Aquatic Tng. Ctr., Boca Raton, 1986-88; co-sponsor Nat. Jr. Beta Honor Soc., 1998-99. Mem. campaign com. Ill. State Rep. 38th dist., 1976; instr. water safety ARC, Fox River Valley, Ill., 1974-90, educator water safety, 1989—. Mem. ASCD, NEA, Fla. Tchrs. Assn., FAPHERD Palm Beach County Tchrs. Assn., U.S. Water Fitness Assn., Nat. Assn. Profl. Women. Avocations: commercial acting, aquatics, modeling. Home: PO Box 738 Boca Raton FL 33429 Office: Sandpiper Shores Cmty Elem Sch 11201 Glades Rd Boca Raton FL 33498-6818 Office Phone: 561-883-4000. Business E-Mail: rebel@palmbeach.k12.fl.us.

REBELL, ARTHUR LESLIE, diversified holding company executive; Prof. mergers & acquisitions NYU Stern Grad. Sch. Bus.; various positions Schroder Wertheim & Co., NYC; mng. dir. High View Capital Corp., Strategic Mgmt. Co., LLC, NYC, 1997—98; sr. v.p., chief investment officer Loews Corp., NYC, 1998—. Office: Loews Corp 667 Madison Ave New York NY 10021-8087 Office Phone: 212-521-2450.

REBELLO, MARLENE MUNSON, speech pathologist, consultant; b. San Jose, Calif., Oct. 15, 1948; d. Alfred Vernon and Rose Zita (Pereira) Nunes; m. Steven Del Munson, Mar. 21, 1970 (div. 1982); m. William Wayne Rebello, Dec. 5, 1992. BA, San Jose State U., 1970, MA, 1971; MS in Counseling, U. LaVerne, 1990. Speech pathologist Newark Unified Sch. Dist., Calif., 1971—2005, Washington Hosp., Fremont, Calif., 1980-89; pvt. practice Fremont and Pleasanton, Calif., 1980—. Cons. in field. Recipient Bank of Am. award, 1966, Cabrillo scholarship, Nat. Merit scholarship, 1966, Maria Leonard award Outstanding Sr. Grade Point Average, 1970; fellow VA, 1970. Mem. Calif. Speech and Hearing Assn., Pleasanton Sister City Assn. (v.p. 1996-2002, pres. 2003, mem. pres. 2005-, fundraising chair 2005-), Newark Tchrs. Assn. (treas. 1971), Save Our Sunol Found., Calif. Tchrs. Assn., Arthur & Elena Court Conservation Soc., Pleasanton North Rotary (Paul Harris fellow). Avocations: antiques, decorating, gourmet cooking. Home and Office: 10579 Foothill Rd Sunol CA 94586-9464 Personal E-mail: marspot@aol.com.

REBER, DAVID JAMES, lawyer; b. Las Vegas, Mar. 1, 1944; s. James Rice and Helen Ruth (Cusick) R.; m. Jacqueline Yee, Aug. 31, 1968; children: Emily, Brad, Cecily BA, Occidental Coll., LA, 1965; JD, Harvard U., 1968. Bar: Calif. 1969, Hawaii 1975, U.S. Dist. Ct. Hawaii, U.S. Ct. Appeals (9th cir.), U.S. Supreme Ct. Asst. prof. law U. Iowa, Iowa City, 1968-70; assoc. Sheppard Mullin Richter & Hampton, LA, 1970-75, Goodsill Anderson Quinn & Stifel, Honolulu, 1975-76, ptnr., 1976—. Bd. dirs. Enterprise Honolulu, Legal Aid Soc. Hawaii, Lawyers Equal Justice. Mem. ABA (bus. and pub. utilities sects.), Hawaii Bar Assn. Avocations: golf, tennis, softball, travel. Office: Goodsill Anderson Et Al 1099 Alakea St Ste 1800 Honolulu HI 96813-4511 Office Phone: 808-547-5611. E-mail: dreber@goodsill.com.

REBER, RAYMOND ANDREW, chemical engineer; b. Bklyn., Apr. 16, 1942; s. Herbert and Dorothy Agnes (Schmidt) R.; m. Anita Jean Roe, June 22, 1963; children: Laura Jean Bucci, Paul Raymond, Jill Anita Atkinson. BChemE, NYU, 1963, MChemE, 1966. Engr. M.W. Kellogg, NYC, 1964-69; devel. engr. Union Carbide, 1970—81, licensing bus. mgr., 1982-84, tech. mgr., 1985-87; dir. tech. UOP, Tarrytown, 1988-93; exec. v.p., COO Balchem Corp., Slate Hill, NY, 1994-96, pres., CEO, 1997. Commr. Montrose Improvement Dist., NY, 1970—; soccer referee, 1977—93; trustee No. Westchester Joint Water Works, 1995, 1998—2001, cons., 2001—, dir., 2003—08. Mem.: NSPE, AIChE, 32 degree Mason. Episcopalian. Achievements include patents in field. Avocations: soccer, table games, philately. Home: 10 Bonnie Hollow Ln Montrose NY 10548-1314

REBERT, JEPHREY LEE, urban planner, musician; b. Carlisle, Pa., June 10, 1959; s. John Alton and Mary Anna (Feeman) Rebert. BS, Pa. State U., 1982. Residential appraiser County of York, Pa., 1984-85; phys. and environ. planner York County Planning Commn., 1985-87, transp. planner, 1987-93, sr. transp. planner, 1993—. Musician, prodr.: audiotape Peace of Mind (Loose Cannons), 1995; musician: (albums) Colonial Pagoda (Namaste), 1997, Smoke Signals (Anderson's Tool Shed), 2004. Alumni mem. Pa. State Blue Band; treas., bd. dirs. Ctr. Ind. Living Opportunities; bd. dirs. Susquehanna Regional Transp. Partnership; ptnr. York Resuce Mission. Mem.: ASCE, Inst. Transp. Engrs., Am. Planning Assn., Phi Mu Alpha Sinphonia (Alpha Zeta chpt., alumnus). Avocations: anthropology, racquet sports, coin collecting/numismatics. Office: York County Planning Commn 28 E Market St Rm 301 York PA 17401-1580 Personal E-mail: zoombangi@netzero.net.

REBHAN, GAIL, art educator; MFA, Calif. Inst. Arts, Valencia. Prof. photography Northen Va. CC, Woodbridge, 2000—. Exhibitions include Room, Aging. Mem.: Soc. Photo Edn. Office: Northern Va CC 15200 Neabsco Mills Rd Woodbridge VA 22191 Business E-Mail: grebhan@nvcc.edu.

REBHOLZ, ANDREW J., hospitality company executive; CPA. Corp. contr. TravelCenters of Am., Westlake, Ohio, 1997—2002, v.p., contr., 2002—07, sr. v.p., contr., exec. v.p., treas., CFO, 2007—; sr. v.p. Reit Mgmt. and Rsch., 2007. Office: TravelCenters of Am 24601 Center Ridge Rd Ste 200 Westlake OH 44145 Office Phone: 440-808-9100. Office Fax: 440-808-3306.

REBHUN, JOSEPH, allergist, immunologist, medical educator; b. Przemysl, Poland, Oct. 7, 1921; came to U.S., 1950; s. Baruch and Serel R.; m. Maria Birkenhejm, Aug. 10, 1945; children: Lillian Friedland, Richard B.R., Donald. MD, U. Innsbruck, Austria, 1950; MS in Medicine, Northwestern U., 1954, PhD in Medicine. Diplomate Am. Bd. Allergy and Immunology. Intern Barnert Meml. Hosp., Patterson, NJ; resident in internal medicine Tompkins County Meml. Hosp. and Cornell U., NY, 1951-52; fellow in allergy Northwestern U. Med. Sch./Chidlren's Meml. Hosp., Chgo., 1952-54; fellow instr. Northwestern U. Med. Sch., 1954; asst. clin. prof. medicine Loma Linda U.,

1957-93; clin. prof. medicine U. So. Calif., LA, 1965-91, ret., 1998. Chief allergy Chgo. Eye, Ear, Nose and Throat Hosp., 1953-55; cons. Pacific State Hosp., Spadra Pomona Valley Cmty. Hosp., Pomona Casa Colina Hosp. Author: SOS, 1946, The Cry of Democracy for Help, God and Man in Two Worlds, 1985, The Embers of Michael, 1993, Crisis of Morality and Reaction to the Holocaust, 1998, Leap to Life: Triumph Over Nazi Evil, 2000, Why Me?, 2004; contbr. numerous articles to med. jours. Pres. Am. Congress Jews from Poland, 1969—70. Capt. U.S. Mil., San Francisco, capt. med. reserve corps., L.A. Recipient honors City and County of L.A., L.A. Office Dist. Atty., Senate of State of Calif., all 1985. Fellow Am. Acad. Allergy (rsch. coun. 1960-65), Am. Coll. Allergy, Assn. Clin. Allergy and Immunology; mem. West Coast Allergy Soc., Calif. Allergy Assn., L.A. Soc. Allergy, L.A. Med. Assn., Calif. Med. Assn, Pomona Valley (head of Med. Reserve Corp). Office Phone: 909-624-1792. Personal E-mail: joerebhun@yahoo.com.

REBICH, LOIS J., elementary school educator; m. Eli Rebich; 3 children. BBA, MBA, Univ. Pitts. Cert. elem. edn. Chatham Coll. Buyer H.J. Heinz; fin. analyst Rockwell Internat.; tchr. Pitts. City Schs., 1989—91; instructional support tchr., head tchr. Ross Elem. Sch., Pitts., 1991—. Named Pa. Tchr. of Yr., 2007. Office: Ross Elem Sch 90 Houston Rd Pittsburgh PA 15237 Business E-Mail: rebichl@nhsd.k12.pa.us.

REBIK, JAMES MICHAEL, otolaryngologist; b. Marshalltown, Iowa, July 10, 1953; s. Hubert James and Donna Jean (Grandgeorge) Rebik; m. Sue Ellyn Primmer, Dec. 22, 1979; children: Christopher James, Kristin Leigh, Robert James, Jonathan Michael. BA summa cum laude, U. No. Iowa, 1981; DO, Kirksville Coll. Osteo. Med., 1985. Diplomate Am. Osteo. Bd. Ophthalmology and Otorhinolaryngology, Nat. Bd. Med. Examiners Osteo. Physicians and Surgeons, lic. physician Mo., Iowa, Minn., Tex., Okla., Ariz., Kans. Intern Kirksville (Mo.) Osteo Med. Ctr., 1985-86, resident otorhinolaryngology/oro-facial plastic surgery, 1986-90; otolaryngologist Landstuhl (Germany) Army Regional Med. Ctr., 1990-92; chief otolaryngology-head and neck surgery svc. Reynolds Army Hosp., Ft. Sill, Okla., 1992—94, Jackson County Meml. Hosp., Altus, Okla., 1998—2006; with Albert Lea Clinic, Mayo Health System, Minn., 1994—95; pvt. practice Kingman, Ariz., 2007—. Cons. VA Med. Ctr., Big Spring, Tex., 1996—98. Maj. M.C. US Army, 1990—94. Recipient 1st degree brown belt, Gup U.S. Tang Soo Do Moo Duk Kwan Fedn., 1979. Fellow: Am. Osteo. Coll. Otolaryngology-Head and Neck Surgery, Soc. Mil. Otolaryngologists; mem.: VFW, AMA, Am. Coll. Legal Medicine, Am. Acad. Sleep Medicine, Okla. Osteo. Assn., Tex. Osteo. Med. Assn., Am. Acad. Otolaryngology-Head and Neck Surgery, Am. Acad. Otolaryngic Allergy, Assn. Mil. Surgeons U.S., Am. Osteo. Assn., Am. Legion, Mensa. Baptist. Avocations: medieval, WWI and WWII history, Baroque and classical music. Home: 845 Vista Grande Dr Kingman AZ 86409 Office: Kingman ENT Ctr 3116 Stockton Hill Rd Kingman AZ 86401 Personal E-mail: jrebik@npgcable.com.

REBOK, DOUGLAS E., insurance company executive, accountant; BA in acctg., Loma Linda U., Calif.; MBA, U. So. Calif., LA. CPA Oreg. Various positions with Adventist Med. Ctr., Portland, Oreg., 1976—83; sr. v.p., CFO Adventist Health, Roseville, Calif., 1983—. Mem.: Healthcare Fin. Mgmt. Assn., Am. Inst. CPA. Office: Adventist Health 2100 Douglas Blvd Roseville CA 95661*

REBOLLO, ANTHONY ERNEST, lawyer; b. Huntsville, Ala., Feb. 25, 1964; s. Antonio Ernesto and Barbara Brown Rebollo; m. Amy Elizabeth Stetson, Aug. 13, 1988; children: Alexandra Jane, Margaux Isabel, Anthony Ernest. BA, Coll. William and Mary, Williamsburg, Va., 1986; JD, U. Calif., Berkeley, 1989. Bar: Tex. 1989, US Tax Ct. 1990, US Dist. Ct. (we. dist.) Tex. 1990, US Dist. Ct. (no. dist.) Tex. 1991, US Dist. Ct. (so. dist.) Tex. 1994, US Ct. Appeals (5th cir.) 1994, SC 2002, US Dist. Ct., SC 2002, Ga. 2003. Shareholder Matthews & Branscomb, P.C., San Antonio, 1989—96, Wells, Pinckney & McHugh, P.C., San Antonio, 1996—98, Strasburger & Price, LLP, San Antonio, 1998—2001, Richardson, Plowden, Carpenter & Robinson P.A., Columbia, SC, 2002—. Mem. Advanced Tax Law Planning Com., Austin, Tex., 1999—2001; chair tax controversy com. Tex. State Bar, Tax Sect., Austin, 1999—2002, mem. tax coun., Tex., 2001—02; mem. pro bono coll. Tex. State Bar, 2004; mem. tax coun., SC, 08; mem. Coll. of State Bar Tex., 2008. Contbr. articles to profl. jour. Mem.: Rotary. Avocations: fishing, canoeing. Office: Richardson Plowden & Robinson PA 1900 Barnwell St Columbia SC 29201 Office Fax: 803-779-0016. Business E-Mail: trebollo@richardsonplowden.com.

REBOLLO LÓPEZ, FRANCISCO, retired Associate Justice, PR Supreme Court; b. San Juan, Aug. 5, 1938; BA, U. PR, 1959, JD, 1963. Asst. dist atty., San Juan, 1966; asst. prosecutor US Dist. Ct., PR; judge PR Superior Ct., 1973—77; pvt. practice atty., 1977—82; justice PR Supreme Ct., San Juan, 1982—2007.

REBOYRAS, ARIEL E., alderman; b. NYC; BEd, U. Ill., Chgo. Tchr. Roberto Clemente HS, Chgo.; truck driver City of Chgo., equipment dispatcher, head, fleet mgmt. tank remediation program, equipment coord., water dept., dep. commr., dept. gen. services; alderman, 30th ward Chgo. City Coun., 2003—. Co-founder Nat. Youth Basketball Assn., Maraton San-Juan; committeeman 30th Ward, Chgo., 2006—; mem. steering com. Healthy Streets Campaign Dr. with Care; mem. Pace Citizen Adv. Bd. Mem.: Nat. Assn. Latino Elected and Apptd. Officials, Chgo. Bicycle Fedn. Office: 3348 N Milwaukee Ave Chicago IL 60641 also: City Hall 121 N LaSalle St Rm 203 Chicago IL 60602 Office Phone: 773-794-3095, 312-744-3304. Office Fax: 773-794-8576. Business E-Mail: ward30@cityofchicago.org.

RECCHI, MARK, professional hockey player; b. Kamloops, BC, Can., Feb. 1, 1968; m. Alexa Recchi; children: Christina, Cameron, Austin. Right wing Pitts. Penguins, 1988—92, 2004—06, 2006—07, Phila. Flyers, 1992—95, 1999—2004, Montreal Canadiens, 1995—99, Carolina Hurricanes, 2006, Atlanta Thrashers, 2007—08, Tampa Bay Lightning, 2008—09, Boston Bruins, 2009—. Named Most Valuable Player, All-Star Game, 1997; named to NHL All-Star Game, 1991, 1993, 1994, 1997—2000. Achievements include being a member of Stanley Cup Champion Pittsburgh Penguins, 1991, Carolina Hurricanes, 2006. Office: Boston Bruins TD Banknorth Garden 100 Legends Way Boston MA 02114*

RECCHIA, DOMENIC M., JR., city councilman; b. Bklyn., 1959; m to Kimberly Recchia; children: Brianna Lyn, Daniella Marie & Juliana Rose. BS, Kent State Univ.; JD, Atlanta Law Sch. City councilman Dist. 47 NY City Coun., 2002—. Chmn. Cultural Affairs, Libraries & Internat. Intergroup Rels. NY City Coun. Mem. NYC Cmty. Sch. Bd. 21. Democrat. Mailing: Dist Off 445 Neptune Ave Brooklyn NY 11224 Office Phone: 718-373-9673, 212-788-7045. Office Fax: 718-373-0195. Business E-Mail: recchia@council.nyc.ny.us.*

RECCHIA, FABIO ANASTASIO, medical educator; b. Putignano, Italy, Apr. 30, 1965; m. Luigia Notaristefano, Oct. 27, 1996. MD, U. Bari, Italy; PhD, U. Torino, 1998. Cert. in anesthesiology Italy. Assoc. prof. Scuola Superiore Sant' Anna, Pisa, Italy, 2002—, NY Med. Coll., Valhalla, 2003—. Contbr. scientific papers to profl. jours. Reviewer NIH. Grant, Am. Heart Assn., 2007—. Achievements include research in biomedical. Office: NY Med Coll 15 Dana Ln Valhalla NY 10595 Business E-Mail: fabio_recchia@nymc.edu.

RECH, LORI DILLARD, museum administrator; BA in Art History, U. Fla.; MA in Mus. Studies, Syracuse U. Edn. coord. Brandywine Battlefield; edn. dir. Ft. Mifflin on the Del.; dir. edn. and pub. programs Nat. Mus. Am. Jewish History; exec. dir. Betsy Ross House, 2000—07; pres. Independence Seaport Mus, Phila., 2007—. Mem.: Liberty Sailing Club (vice commodore 2002—07). Office: Independence Seaport Mus Penns Landing 211 S Columbus Blvd & Walnut St Philadelphia PA 19106 Office Phone: 215-413-8655.

RECHARD, PAUL ALBERT, retired civil engineering company executive, consultant; b. Laramie, Wyo., June 4, 1927; s. Ottis H. and Mary R. (Bird) R.; m. Mary Lou Roper, June 26, 1949; children: Robert Paul, Karen Ann. BS, U. Wyo., 1948, MS, 1949, CE, 1955. Registered land surveyor, Wyo.; registered profl. engr., Wyo.; cert. profl. hydrologist Am. Inst. Hydrology. Hydraulic engr. U.S. Bur. Reclamation, Cody, Wyo. and Billings, Mont., 1949-54; dir. water resources Natural Resource Bd., Cheyenne, Wyo., 1954-58; prin. hydraulic engr. Upper Colorado River Commn., Salt Lake City, 1958-64; dir. Water Resources Rsch. Inst. U. Wyo., Laramie, 1964-81, mem. faculty dept. civil engring., 1964-82, prof., 1964-82; pres. Western Water Cons., Laramie, 1980-2001, Hydrology Assocs., Laramie, 1978-80; ret. Western Water Consults., Inc., 2001. Owner Paul A. Rechard, P.E., Laramie, 1964-1978, 2001-. Editor: Compacts, Treaties and Court Decrees Affecting Wyoming Water, 1956; contbr. articles to tech. publs. Pres., Thayer Sch. PTA, Laramie, 1965; mem. Laramie City Planning Commn., 1974-80. Served with USNR, 1945-46. Recipient Wyo. Eminent Engr. award Tau Beta Pi, 1993; named Disting. Alumnus U. Wyo., 1998; named Outstanding Engr. Wyo. Engring. Soc., 1999. Fellow ASCE (life mem., pres. Wyo. sect. 1968); mem. NSPE (life), Am. Geophys. Union, Wyo. Engring. Soc. (pres. 1976, hon.), U.S. Com. on Irrigation and Drainage, Lions (pres. Laramie 1968), Masons, Sigma Xi (pres. Wyo. chpt. 1973), Phi Kappa Phi (pres. Wyo. chpt. 1969), Gamma Sigma Delta, Sigma Tau (pres. Wyo. chpt. 1948, selected Wyo. Eminent Engr. 1993). Republican. Presbyterian. Home and Office: 316 Stuart St Laramie WY 82070-4866 Office Phone: 307-745-7477. Personal E-mail: prechard@msn.com.

RECHNITZER, HAIM OTTO, religious studies educator; s. Ruben and Devorah Rechnitzer; m. Claire Ester Nesvisky, July 27, 1988; children: Carmel Philip, Adam Leon, Alma Atara. BA, Hebrew U. Jerusalem, 1993, MA, 1995, PhD, 2003; Rabbi, Hebrew Union Coll. JIR, Cin., 2003. Prof. Franklin and Marshal Coll., Lancaster, Pa., 2004—05; asst. prof. jewish thought Hebrew Union Coll. JIR, Cin., 2005—. Recipient Excellence tchg. award, Greater Cin. Consortium Coll. and U., 2007; fellowship, Brandies Inst. Israel Studies Tauber Inst., 2006. Mem.: AJS, CCAR. Office: Hebrew Union Coll JIR 3101 Clifton Ave Cincinnati OH 45220-2488 Office Fax: 513-221-0321. Business E-Mail: hrechnitzer@huc.edu.

RECHT, RAY, set designer; b. NYC, Aug. 9, 1947; s. Morton and Lillian F. (Dembner) R.; m. Claire Des Becker, June 27, 1982. BFA, Carnegie-Mellon U., 1969; MFA, Yale Drama Sch., 1972; studies with Ming Cho Lee, Tony Walton. Asst. prof. design Marymount Coll., NYC, 1993—. Lectr. Goucher Coll., Balt., 1973-76; guest artist Queensborough Community Coll., Bayside, N.Y., 1977-84, Albright Coll., Reading, Pa., 1983-84; adj. faculty C.W. Post Coll., N.Y., 1981. Set designer numerous plays including Medal of Honor Rag, 1975, Slab Boys, 1983, The Babe, 1984, A... My Name Is Alice, 1984, Planet Fires, 1985, Sarafina, 1989, The Flowering Perch, 1994, Mrs. Klein, 1995, Mrs. Klein Tour, 1996, (TV show) Another World, 1984, (ballet) Wien Staatsoper Ballet co. Don Quixote, 1991; asst. designer: (operas) The Italian Straw Hat, One Christmas Long Ago, The Impressario, Aunt Caroline's Will, Werther, Song of Norway, Peter Grimes; asst. art dir.: (film) Just Tell Me What You Want, 1980; asst. prodn. designer (film) The First Deadly Sin, 1980; art dir. (films) Amityville II: The Possession, 1982, Exposed, 1983, Missing Pieces, 1990, The Search for One Eye Jimmy, 1995, (TV shows) French-American Perspective, 1982, The Babe; prodn. designer (film) The Hanging Ground, 1985, (TV) Way Cool (Group W), 1991; mem. film unit Saturday Night Live, 1987—. Mem. United Scenic Artists. Jewish.

RECINIELLO, RICHARD, physicist; b. NYC, Nov. 25, 1950; s. Nicholas and Evelyn Reciniello. BS, Wagner Coll., Staten Island, NY, 1972; MS, NY U., Washington Sq., 1981. Cert. Am. Bd. Health Physics, 1998. Radiochemist USAEC, NYC, 1973—81, Radiation Mgmt. Corp., Phila., 1981—82; health physicist Brookhaven Nat. Lab., Upton, NY, 1987—. Author: (book) A Cynics Dictionary of Modern American Terms; contbr. articles to profl. jours. Bd. mem. Gloria Dei Luth. Ch., New Hyde Pk., NY, 1990—96. Mem.: Am. Mensa, Am. Chem. Soc., Health Physics Soc. Lutheran.

RECK, ANDREW JOSEPH, philosopher; b. New Orleans, Oct. 29, 1927; s. Andrew Gervais and Katie (Mangiaracina) R.; m. Elizabeth Lassiter Torre, June 17, 1987. BA, Tulane U., 1947, MA, 1949; postgrad., U. St. Andrews, Scotland, 1952—53; PhD, Yale U., 1954; student, U. Paris, 1962, student, 1964. Instr. English U. Conn., 1949-50; instr. philosophy Yale U., 1951-52, 55-58; faculty Tulane U., 1958—2003, prof. philosophy, 1964—2003, chmn. dept., 1969-89, dir. Master Liberal Arts program, 1984—2003, emeritus prof. philosophy, 2003—. Thomasfest lectr. Xavier U., Cin., 1970; Suarez Lectr. Spring Hill Coll., 1971; Niebuhr lectr. Elmhurst Coll., Ill., 1976; vis. prof. Fordham U., 1979; vis. scholar Hastings Ctr., NY, 1981; Woodruff lectr. Emory U., 1982; Fairchild lectr. U. So. Miss., 1982, 87; Matchette Found. lectr. Cath. U. Am., 1991, 95; sr. scholar Inst. Humane Studies, Menlo Park, Calif., 1982; vis. scholar Poynter Ctr., Ind. U., Bloomington, 1983; faculty rep. to bd. adminstrs. Tulane Ednl. Fund., 1988-91; bd. dirs. Internat. Soc. for Study of Human Ideas of Ultimate Reality and Meaning, 1989-2005, La. Endowment for Humanities, 1990-96; mem. philosophy screening com. Coun. Internat. Rsch. Scholars, 1974-76; mem. Am. studies adv. com. Am. Coun. Learned Socs., 1972-76. Author: Recent American Philosophy, 1964, Introduction to William James, 1967, New American Philosophers, 1968, Speculative Philosophy, 1972; co-author: Die Philosophie des 18. Jahrhunderts 1, 2004; editor: George Herbert Mead Selected Writings, 1964, 2d edit., 1981, Knowledge and Value, 1972, (with T. Horvath, T. Krittek and S. Grean) American Philosophers' Ideas of Ultimate Reality and Meaning, 1993; co-editor Ultimate Reality and Meaning, Interdisciplinary Studies in the Philosophy of Understanding, 1990-2005; editor History of Philosophy Quar., 1993-98. Soldier US Army, 1953—55. Howard fellow, 1962-63, Liberty Fund grantee, 1982, Newcomb fellow, 1991-93; Fulbright scholar, 1952-53; Am. Coun. Learned Socs. grantee, 1961-62, Am. Philos. Soc. grantee, 1972, Huntington Libr. grantee, 1973, La. Ednl. Quality State Found. grantee, 1994-96, U.S. Info. Agy. grantee, Brazil, 1993. Mem.: Internat. Soc. for Study of Human Ideas of Ultimate Reality and Meaning (treas. 2001—03, sec., treas. 2003—05), Charles S. Peirce Soc. (sec., treas. 1985—86, v.p. 1986—87, pres. 1987—88), Soc. Advancement Am. Philosophy (exec. com. 1980—82, pres.-elect 1997—98, pres. 1998—2000, exec. com. 2001—03, chair nominating com. 2002—04), Metaphys. Soc. Am. (councillor 1971—75, pres. 1977—78, program com. 1989—90, chair program com. 1995—96), So. Soc. Philosophy and Psychology (treas. 1968—71, pres. 1976—77), Southwestern Philos. Soc. (exec. com. 1965—69, v.p. 1971—72, pres. 1972—73), Am. Philos. Assn. (program com. ea. divsn. 1969, nominating com. western divsn. 1975—76, 1981—82, adv. com. to program com. ea. divsn. 1994—97, chair ad hoc com. on history 1996—2004), Tulane U. Emeritus Club (Outstanding Grad. of Class of 1947 award 1997), Omicron Delta Kappa, Alpha Sigma Lambda (hon. Theta chpt. of La.), Phi Beta Kappa (pres. Alpha of La. 1966—67). Home: 6125 Patton St New Orleans LA 70118-5832 Home Phone: 504-895-5629. E-mail: ereck@cox.net.

RECK, ELIZABETH TORRE, social worker, educator; b. Winston-Salem, NC, June 17, 1931; d. Vernon Clark and Mary (Pfohl) Lassiter; m. Mottram Peter Torre, Apr. 13, 1957 (dec.); m. Andrew Joseph Reck, June 17, 1987. Student, Wellesley Coll., Mass., 1948-49; BA, Duke U., 1952; MRE, Union Theol. Sem., 1957; MSW, Tulane U., 1966, PhD, 1972. Cert. social worker, La. Field dir. undergrad. admissions Duke U., Durham, NC, 1952—53; head tchr. primary dept. Riverside Ch., NYC, 1957—60; instr. Sch. Social Work Tulane U., New Orleans, 1966—72, assoc. prof., 1972—2000, coord. Indsl. Social Work Program, 1982—88, mem. faculty senate, 1972—88, prof. emeritus, 2000—. Non-govtl. orgn. rep. UNICEF, World Fedn. Mental Health, 1957—63; cons. to v.p. cmty. affairs WETA, Washington, 1979; cons. Office Spl. Symposia and Seminars, Smithsonian Instn., Washington, 1979-86; treas. N.Y. Jr. League, 1961-62, v.p., 1962-63; bd. dirs. Cmty. Vol. Svcs., New Orleans, 1965-68; mem. profl. adv. com. Project Pre-Kindergarten, Orleans Paris Sch. Bd., New Orleans, 1967-69; mem. adv. bd. DePaul Cmty. Mental Health Ctr., New Orleans, 1971-72; mem. citizens adv. com. Orleans Parish Juvenile Ct., New Orleans, 1970-73; mem. Coun. on Social Work Edn. Task Force on Prevention, 1981-87; mem. New Orleans Women's Coalition Task Force on Employers and Working Parents, 1985-90; mem. med. social svcs. subcom. Mayor's Adv. Com. on Domestic Violence, 1995-96; v.p. Torre Realty Bd., 1996-2006, mem. exec. bd., 2006-. Grantee NIMH, Summer Inst. grantee Nat. Endowment Humanities, 1982; Newcomb Coll. fellow, 1989-2002. Mem. AAUW (Tulane Corp. rep. 1990-2000), NASW (bd. dir. La. chpt. 1987-89), AAUP (treas. Tulane chpt. 1984-86, 88-91, exec. com. 1991-95, v.p. New Orleans chpt. 1996), World Fedn. Mental Health, Coun. Social Work Edn., Am. Orthopsychiat. Assn. (life), Tulane U. Women's Assn. (v.p. 1996-97, pres. 1997-98, bd. mem. 2006-07), Phi Beta Kappa (Tulane chpt. exec. com. 1990-2002, pres. Tulane chpt. 1991, regional sec. 1994—2002), Wachovia Hist. Soc. life).

RECKAMP, KAREN, medical educator; married. MD, U. Chgo., Ill, 1998. Cert. in internal medicine 2001, in med. oncology, in hematology Nat. Bd. Med. Examiners, 2004. Asst. prof. U. Calif., LA, 2005—06, City Hope, Duarte, Calif., 2006—. Office: City Hope 1500 E Duarte Rd Duarte CA 91010

RECKEN, STEPHEN LOUIS, history professor; b. Portland, Oreg., Nov. 12, 1947; married. PhD, Wash. State U., Pullman, 1979. Assoc. prof. U. Ark., Little Rock, 1980—2005. Contbr. articles to profl. jour. Bd. mem. Nat. Orgn. Pub. Historians, Purdue, Ind., 1979—2005. Recipient award, Nat. Orgn. Pub. Historians, 1980—2005. Democrat. Home: 2801 S Univ Little Rock AR 72205 E-mail: slrecken@comcast.net.

RECKERS, PHILIP MERLE, accountant, educator; b. Quincy, Ill., May 1, 1946; s. Merle Joseph and Frances Adelaide (Friye) R.; m. Patricia Anne Polchinski, May 12, 1979; children: Brian, Colleen, Ashley. BS, Quincy Coll., Ill., 1968; MBA, Washington U., St. Louis, 1972; PhD, U. Ill., 1978. Asst. prof. U. Md., College Park, 1976—80; assoc. prof. Ariz. State U., Tempe, 1980—83, prof. acctg., 1983—; dir. Sch. Accountancy, 1993—2002; dir. rsch. Ctr. for Advancing Bus. through Info. Tech., 2002—05. Vis. prof. Notre Dame, 2004—09. Assoc. editor: Advances in Acctg., 1985—93, mem. editl. bd.: Auditing, 1987—2003, Behavioral Rsch. in Acctg., 1992—2002, Internat. Jour. Auditing, 1999—2009; editor: Advanes in Acctg., 1994—; contbr. articles to profl. jours. With US Army, 1970—72, Vietnam. Auditing rsch. grantee, Peat Marwick Found., 1976, 1985, 1989, 1990, 1991, tax rsch. grantee, Ernst and Young Found., 1991. Mem. Am. Acctg. Assn. (v.p. 2006—, Innovations in Acctg. Edn. award 2003, Edn. Rsch. grant 1982), Fedn. Schs. Accountancy (pres. 2002, Joseph Silvoso Lifetime Achievement award 2006), AICPA (pre-cert. edn. exec. com.), Acctg. Programs Leadership Group (v.p. 2005—) Roman Catholic. Home: 7461 S Rita Ln Tempe AZ 85283-4796 Office: Ariz State Univ Sch Accountancy Ba 267B Tempe AZ 85287 Office Phone: 480-965-2283. Business E-Mail: philip.reckers@asu.edu.

RECKFORD, JONATHAN THOMAS MORE, nonprofit organization administrator; b. Chapel Hill, NC, Aug. 31, 1962; s. Kenneth and Mary (Stevens) Reckford; m. Ashley Louise Richards, June 9, 1990; 3 children. BA in polit. sci., U. NC, Chapel Hill, 1984; MBA, Stanford U., 1989. Fin. analyst Goldman, Sachs & Co., 1984—86; mgr. svc. group strategy and bus. devel. Host Marriott Corp.; mgr. bus. planning The Walt Disney Co., 1991—92, mktg. mgr. Disney Vacation Club, 1993, dir. fin. and bus. planning Disney's Am., 1994, dir. bus. planning and devel. Disney Design and Devel., 1994—95; v.p. Circuit City Stores, Inc., 1995—97, sr. v.p. corp. planning and comm., 1997—99; pres. mall stores divsn. The Musicland Group, Inc., 1999—2000, pres. stores, 2000—02; exec. pastor Christ Presbyn. Ch. of Edina, Minn., 2003—05; CEO Habitat for Humanity Internat., Inc., Americus, Ga., 2005—. Henry Luce Found. Scholarship for Young Am. Leaders. Office: Habitat for Humanity Internat Inc 121 Habitat St Americus GA 31709-3498 Office Phone: 229-924-6935.

RECKLINE, SIGMUND JOSEPH, publishing executive, editor; b. Balt., Oct. 29, 1956; s. Sigmund Joseph Reckline and Regina Ann DeBarry; m. Marilyn Louise Windes, May 2000; children: Clarissa Irene, Sigmund Joseph III, William Joseph, Quinten Christopher. BA in Liberal Arts, W.Va. U., 2002; BS in Applied Sci., Siena Heights U., 2002; MBA, U. Notre Dame, 2002; PhD in Bus. Adminstrn., Madison U., 2003; postgrad., Capella U., 2006, U. Md. Ordained Ch. of Spiritual Humanism. I&C technician Va. Electric Power Co., 1981—82; tech. writer, technician Nuc. Support Svcs., 1982, 1986—88; field engr. Johnson Controls, 1983—84; tech. writer Butler Svc. Group, 1984—85; field engr. Westinghouse Instrument Svc. Co., 1985—86; ops. mgr. Chesapeake Internat., 1988—91; sys. engr. Peak Tech. Svcs., 1991—92; tech. editor GTS/Duratek, Rockhill, SC, 1992—97; engring. mgr. Duke Engring and Svcs., Bridgman, 1997—99, Estes Group, Bridgman, Mich., 1999—2000; aux. operator CMS Energy, Covert, Mich., 2000—02; online instr., instr. Siena Heights U., Adrian, Mich., 2002—05; with Global Transitions Pub., Baroda, Mich., 2005—. Founder Environ. Cancer Res. Inst., Baroda, Mich. Co-author: America Rewired. Mem. Berrien County Cancer Ctr., Bridgman, 2002; amb. Am. Cancer Soc., Kalamazoo, 2005; pres. South Potomac Forest Property Owners Assn., Springfield, W.Va., 1986—88; comdr. Antioch Commandery Knights Templar, 2000; hereditary chief Clan Recklein, 1990—. Sgt. USAF, 1981—87. Mem.: Am. Coll. Heraldry, Royal Order Scotland (life), St. Andrews Soc. Balt. (life), Phi Theta Kappa (disting. prof. 2004), Alpha Sigma Lambda. Republican. Presbyterian. Avocations: writing, genealogy, collecting swords, jewelry design. Home: PO Box 249 Baroda MI 49101-0249 Office Phone: 269-369-9897. E-mail: reckline@hotmail.com.

RECKOWSKY, MICHAEL J., academic administrator; s. Allen D. Reckowsky and Shirley J. Jones; m. Constance L. Albrecht, May 4, 1996; children: Ryan M., Robert A. BA in Polit. Sci., Purdue U., West Lafayette, Ind., 1995. Mem. roll of attys. Clk. of Courts, State of Ind., Indpls., 1996—97; devel. assoc. advancement office Purdue U., West Lafayette, 1997—2000, adminstrv. dir. food sci., 2000—. Mem. task force Ind. Dept. of Health, Food Protection Task Force, 2003—. Author: (publ.) Preparing for Bioterrorism Through Simulation; co-creator (copyright for computer data) Food Defense Simulation. Chmn. 7th Dist. Young Reps., Ind., 1997—98, Tippecanoe County Young Reps., Lafayette, 1995—97; campaign mgr. Pool for Congress, Lafayette, 1995—96; mem. Imagination Sta., Lafayette, Ind., 2006—. Recipient Jack McCord award, Tippecanoe Young Reps., 1997, Ill. Ea. Star scholarship, Ea. Star, 1990. Mem.: Inst. of Food Technologists, Antique and Classic Boat Soc. (sec. 2004—06). Evangelical Covenant. Avocations: sailing, boating, woodworking. Office: Purdue U Dept Food Sci 745 Agriculture Mall Dr West Lafayette IN 47907 Office Fax: 765-494-7953. E-mail: mreckowsky@purdue.edu.

RECKTENWALD, MARK E., state supreme court justice; AB magna cum laude, Harvard Univ.; JD with honors, Univ. Chgo. Bar: Hawaii 1986. Reporter United Press Internat., Honolulu; comm. clk. Hawaii State legis.; law. clk. US Dist. Ct. Chief Judge Harold M. Fong., 1986—87; assoc. Goodsill Anderson Quinn & Stifel, 1988—91; asst. US atty. US Dept. Justice Hawaii Dist., 1991—97; ptnr. Marr Hipp Jones & Pepper, 1997—99; asst. US atty. US Dept. Justice Hawaii Dist., 1999—2003; dir. Hawaii Dept. Commerce & Consumer Affairs, 2003—07; chief judge Hawaii Intermediate Ct. Appeals, 2007—09; assoc. justice Hawaii Supreme Ct., 2009—. Office: Hawaii Supreme Ct 417 S King St Honolulu HI 96813 Office Phone: 808-539-4735.*

RECORD, M. THOMAS, JR., biochemist, educator; BA, Yale Univ.; PhD, Univ. Calif., San Diego. Steenbock prof. in Chem. Sci., John D. Ferry prof. of Chemistry, Biochemistry Univ. Wis., Madison. Recipient Biophysical Soc. Founders award, 2001. Fellow: Am. Assn. Advancement Sci., Biophys. Soc., Am. Acad. Arts & Scis. Office: 4419 Biochemistry 433 Babcock Dr Madison WI 53706 Office Phone: 608-262-5332. Business E-Mail: record@chem.wisc.edu.

RECORD, PHILLIP JULIUS, journalist; b. Ft. Worth, Jan. 12, 1929; s. Phillip Cross and Frances Virginia (McElwee) R.; m. Patricia Ann Edwards, Sept. 29, 1954; children: Christopher Phillip, Gregory Edwards, Timothy James. BA in Journalism, U. Notre Dame, Ind., 1950. Gen. reporter Lubbock Avalanche-Jour., Tex., 1950-54; copy editor, reporter Fort Worth Star-Telegram, 1954-67, asst. city editor, 1967-68, city editor evening edit., 1968-76, mng. editor, 1976-80, assoc. exec. editor, 1980-91, spl. asst. to pub., ombudsman, 1991-97, columnist, 1997—2001. Mem. mass comms. com. Tex. Tech. U., 1971—2000, chmn., 1990—92, bd. dirs., 1992—; journalism profl. in residence Tex. Christian U., 1999—. Mem. Friends of Ft. Worth Pub. Libr., 2004—08; bd. visitors Tex. Christian U.; conciliation-arbitration bd. Cath. Diocese Ft. Worth, 1994—2009, chair, 1996—2009, publs. adv. com., 1982—; bd. dirs. Tarrant County Mental Health Assn., 1990—95; dir. Freedom Info. Found., Tex., 1987—93; bd. dirs. Depression Connection Team, 1999—, Cassata H.S., 2006—; founding mem. Ft. Worth Theatre. With US Army, 1950—52. Recipient Ethics award Tex. Christian U., 1991, others for reporting, photography and headline writing; named to Tex. Tech U. Mass Comms. Hall of Fame. Mem. ABA (nat. commn. on pub. understanding about law 1984-90, commn. on partnership programs 1990-93), Investigative Reporters and Editors Inc., Soc. Profl. Journalists (pres. 1983-84, bd. dirs. Found. 1980-2001, v.p. Found., 1991-94, bd. chair 1994-01, Wells Key 1991), Creative Thinking Assn., Orgn. News Ombudsmen (dir. 1994-98, v.p. 1995-96, pres. 1996-97). Avocation: tennis. Home and Office: 6144 Walla Ave Fort Worth TX 76133 Office Phone: 817-292-0826. Business E-Mail: precord@star-telegram.com. *As a journalist, I strive to be a servant of the truth and a servant of the people. As a follower of Jesus, I try to live my life as he would. But, being human, I fail frequently. But I try and I care. I think that makes me OK in God's eyes.*

RECTOR, DONNA LYNN, writer, photographer, poet, artist; b. Warrenton, Va., July 8, 1959; d. Allen Leon and Elizabeth Ann (Godfrey) R. Freelance photographer, journalist, calligrapher, poet, Culpeper, Va., 1985—; corr. Culpeper Star Exponent, Culpeper News, Culpeper, Va., 1987-95. Pub. info. coord. Va. Dept. Transp., Culpeper, 1988-89; advisor CommonHealth, 1989; vocalist Donna Lynn and the Bluesmen, 1996-98; cons. in field. Editor: Va. Dept. Transp. Newsletter, 1989; columnist, photographer: Va.'s Music Line, The Corridor; blues vocalist, 1996—2002; co-author: (with David Leckie Gilmore) Culpeper, Va.; pub.: Stylus newsletter; columnist: Corridor Mag., Rock and Read Mag., SHAKE! Mag., 1995-2005, (with David Leckie Gilmore) Culpeper, Virginia, Va.'s 250th Anniversary celebration Song, 2009. Vol. Svcs. to Abused Families, Culpeper, 1987-92; vol. art instr. Culpeper County Sch. Vis. Artisan Program; canvasser United Way, 1987-88; coord. fundraisers & major charity events, pub. rels. coord. for charity and community orgns.; spl. events/fund raiser coord. Nat. Multiple Sclerosis Soc., Blue Ridge chpt., 1990-91; coord., publicist Culpeper Music Festival, 2004-05, vol. Culpeper Renaissance Downtown Assn., March of Dimes, Va. Campaign, Culpeper Downtown Renaissance, Culpeper County Pub. Schs., Va. Govtl. Employees Assn., bd. dirs., Vocat. Insl. Clubs America, Sr. Nutrition Ctr. Meals Program, Piedmont Tech. Fund, Culpeper Ruritan Club, Voices Blue Ridge, Culpeper Town Police & Culpeper Sheriff's Dept., Helping Hand Culpeper, Culpeper Jaycees, Richardsville Fire and Rescue, Culpeper Musician's Soc., Culpeper Songwriter's Group and numerous others. Recipient First Place awd. for Poetry, Germanna Community Coll., 1988, 92, 98, Bus. and Profl. Women's Assn. Young Career Woman of Yr. award, Spl. Svc. award Va. Dept. Transp., 1989, Cert. Appreciation Blue Ridge chpt. Nat. Multiple Sclerosis Soc., 1991, Piedmont United Way Gold award, 1993, Cert. Appreciation, Vocat. Indsl. Clubs Am., 1993, Cert. Appreciation Culpeper Downtown Renaissance Inc., 1990, Cert. Recognition for exceptional contribution to Va. employee suggestion program Gov. George Allen, Va., 1994, Top Hat award Windmore Found. for Arts, 1999, Mem. Phi Theta Kappa, Alpha Beta Gamma. Avocations: singing, photography, public relations, music, writing. Personal E-mail: drectorrecords@yahoo.com.

RECTOR, JOHN LAWRENCE, history professor; b. Walla Walla, Wash., Aug. 8, 1943; s. Edris William and Ethel Mae Rector; m. Irene Z. Zadorojny, Oct. 26, 1969; children: John Austin, Andrei Lawrence, William Eric, Irina Elizabeth, Peter Alexander. BA, Whitman Coll., Walla Walla, Wash, 1965; MA, Ind. U., Bloomington, PhD, 1976. Assoc. prof. Pontificia U. Catolica PR, 1977—87; fulbright vis. prof. U. Chile and U. Catolica Chile, Santiago, 1983—84; prof. history Western Oreg. U., Monmouth, 1987—, chair social sci. divsn., 2006—. Chair NW Coun. Study Abroad, Oregon, Wash. Alaska, 1998—2000; vol. Peace Corps, Pucon and Caburgua, Chile, 1965—68; lectr. NEH Summer Inst., Puebla, Mexico, 2004. Author: (books) The History of Chile 2003, (book) Merchants, Trade, and Commercial Policy in Chile. Chair Cultural Awareness Commn., Independence, Oreg., 1990—92; recorder St. Timothy's Episcopal Ch., Salem, Oreg., 2002—; pres., bd. directors Centro Sister Isolina Ferre, Ponce, PR, 1981—82; pres. Western Oreg. U. Faculty Senate, 2005—06. Grants Fulbright, U.S. Govt., 1972. Mem.: Latin Am. Studies Assn. St. Timothy'S Episcopal Church. Office: Western Oregon Univ Humanities and Social Sci Bld Monmouth OR 97361

RECTOR, JOHN MICHAEL, pharmaceutical association executive, lawyer; b. Seattle, Aug. 15, 1943; s. Michael Robert and Bernice Jane (Allison) R.; m. Carmen De Ortiz, 1994; children: Christian Phillip, Ciera Rose, Zachary Ryan BA, U. Calif., Berkeley, 1966; JD, U. Calif., Hastings, 1969; PharmD (hon.), Ark. State Bd. Pharmacy, 1991. Bar: Calif. 1970, U.S. Supreme Ct. 1974; registered corp. counsel Va. Bar, 2006. Trial atty. civil rights divsn. Dept. Justice, 1969-71; dep. chief counsel judiciary com. U.S. Senate, 1971-73, counsel to Sen. Birch Bayh, 1971-77, chief counsel, staff dir., 1973-77; confirmed by U.S. Senate as assoc. adminstr. to Law Enforcement Assistance Adminstrn. and adminstr. of Office Juvenile Justice Dept. Justice, 1977-79; spl. counsel to U.S. Atty. Gen., 1979-80; dir. govt. affairs Nat. Assn. Retail Druggists, Washington, 1980-85; sr. v.p. govt. affairs, gen. counsel Nat. Cmty. Pharmacists Assn., Alexandria, Va., 1986—2005, sr. v.p., gen. counsel, 2006—09, sr. v.p., spl. counsel, 2009—. Chmn. adv. bd. Nat. Juvenile Law Ctr., 1973-77; mem. HEW panel Drug Use and Criminal Behavior, 1974-77; cons. panel Nat. Commn. Protection Human Subjects Biomed. and Behavioral Rsch., 1975-76; chmn. US Interdepartmental Coun. Juvenile Justice, 1977-79; mem. bd. com. civil rights and liberties Am. Dem. Action, 1976-80, Pres.'s Com. Mental Health-Justice Group, 1978; mem. Pharm. Industry Adv. Com.; treas. polit. action com. Nat. Pharmacists Assn., 1981-2006; exec. dir. Retail Druggist Legal Legis. Def. Fund, 1985-2005, founder, chmn. Washington Pharmacy Industry Forum; owner Second Genesis. Mem. editl. bd. Managed Care Law; mem. Hastings Law Jour. 1967-9; contbr. articles to profl. jours. Mem. exec. com. small bus. and fin. couns. Dem. Nat. Com., 1988-92; dir. Dem. Leadership Coun.'s Network, 1989-92, bd. advisers, 1992-94, Clinton-Gore Washington Bus. adv. com.; bd. dirs. Small Bus. Legis. Coun., 1987—, sec., 1999, treas., 2000, chmn. elect, 2001, chmn., 2002; bd. dirs. Nat. Bus. Coalition for Fair Competition, 1984—; policy advisor Presdl. campaigns; active Reagan for Pres. Task Force on Criminal Justice. Perry E. Towne scholar, 1966-67; recipient Children's Express Birch Bayh Juvenile Justice award, 1981, John W. Dargavel medal Nat. Assn. Retail Drug Assn. 2003, J. Leon Lascoff Meml. award Am. Coll. Apothecares, 2004. Mem. ABA (mem. com. youth citizenship 1978-84), ATLA, Calif. Bar Assn., Nat. Health Lawyers Assn., Am. Soc. Assn. Execs. (mem. govt. affairs sect.), Washington Coun. Lawyers, Assn. Former Sr. Senate Aides, SOBs, Vinifera Wine Growers Assn. Va. (life), Health R Us, Am. League Lobbyists, Theta Chi, Germanna Found. Libertarian. Avocations: antiques, books and documents. Office: Nat Cmty Pharmacists Assn 100 Daingerfield Rd Alexandria VA 22314-2885 Business E-Mail: john.rector@ncpanet.org.

RECTOR, M. EUGENE, community pharmacist; b. Sequin, Tex., Aug. 16, 1950; m. Marcia A. Rector, May 15, 1982. AA, Blinn Coll., 1970; BS in Pharmacy, U. Tex., Austin, 1972; BA in Philosophy, U. Tex., Dallas, 1982, MS in Mgmt. and Adminstrn. Scis., 1985; PharmD, Broadmore U., Belize City, Belize, 1998. Staff pharmacist Baylor U. Med. Ctr., Dallas, 1973-81, Presbyn. Hosp., Dallas, 1981-86; dir. pharmacy Madison St. Joseph Health Ctr., Madisonville, Tex., 1986—2001; pharmacist Walgreens #4999, 2001—. Fellow Am. Coll. Apothecaries (assoc.); mem. Am. Soc. Health-Sys. Pharmacists, Tex. Soc. Health-Sys. Pharmacists, Lions Club, Masons (Vickery Lodge 1351, Rogers Prairie Lodge 540 past master), Shriners. Republican. Methodist. Avocations: hunting, ranching. Home: 16584 Fm 3 S Normangee TX 77871-3511 Home Phone: 936-855-2898; Office Phone: 936-291-6764. Personal E-mail: rattlinr@windstream.net.

RECTOR, SUSAN DARNELL, lawyer; b. Wilmington, Del., Feb. 14, 1959; d. W. Thomas and Barbara Joan (Shafer) Darnell; m. Neil Kenyon Rector, Aug. 7, 1982. BA in Econs., Wake Forest U., Winston-Salem, NC, 1981; JD, U. N.C., Chapel Hill, 1984. Bar: Ohio 1984. Lawyer Ohio Legislative Svc. Commn., Columbus, Ohio, 1984-87; assoc. Schottenstein, Zox & Dunn, Columbus, Ohio, 1987-93, ptnr., 1993—. Bd. trustees Firstlink, Inc., 1990-95, v.p., 1993, pres., 1994; apt. to Ohio Small Bus. and Entrepreneurship Coun., 1991-95; bd. dirs. The Wilds. Contbr. articles to profl. jours. Mem. allocation com. United Way, Columbus, 1990-96, campaign cabinet, 1991, 2006, co-chair planning, evaluation and allocation com., 1993-94, bd. trustees, 1996-05, chair health vision coun., 1996-99; trustee Columbus Zool. Park Assn., 2001—, v.p., 2003-04, pres. 2005-06, chmn., 2007—08; chmn. devel. com., 2001-03, chmn. zoo fund, 2000; bd. dir., sec., treas. Cmty. Rsch. Ptnrs., 2000-02; bd. dirs. Children's Hunger Alliance, 2007-, Women's Pres. Orgn., 2008-. Harry S. Truman scholar, Truman Scholarship Found., 1979, named one of 10 Outstanding Young Citizens, Columbus Jaycees, 1993, 40 under 40, Bus. (Columbus); grad. Columbus Area Leadership Program; named one of Best Lawyers in Am., 2003, 2004, 2005, 2006, 2007. Fellow Am. Bar Found.; mem. Ohio Bar Assn., Columbus Bar Assn. (Cmty. Svc. award 1997), Columbus Bar Found. (trustee 1995—2004, pres. 2003), Women Lawyers of Franklin County, Women Pres. Orgn., Jr. League of Columbus (bd. trustees, sec. 1989-90, 95-98, pres. 1997-98), Columbus Club, Columbus Met. Club, Columbus Women's Network (Cmty. Leader award), Mortar Bd., Phi Beta Kappa, Omicron Delta Kappa. Home: 67 E Deshler Ave Columbus OH 43206-2655 Office: Schottenstein Zox & Dunn 250 West Street Columbus OH 43215 Office Phone: 614-462-2219. Business E-Mail: srector@szd.com.

REDBERG, RITA FRAN, cardiologist; b. NYC, 1956; BA, Cornell Univ.; MD, Univ. Pa. Sch. Med., 1982; MSc, London Sch. Economics, 1980. Diplomate Am. Bd. Internal Medicine, 1985, Am. Bd. Internal Medicine, Cardiovascular Diseases, 1989. Intern Columbia-Presbyn. Med. Ctr., NYC, 1982-83, resident, 1983-85, fellow in cardiol. internal medicine, 1985-88; fellow in non-invasive cardiology Mt. Sinai Med. Ctr., NYC, 1988—90; staff mem., asst. prof. through prof. of med., and dir. Women's Cardiovascular Services Univ. Calif. San Francisco Med. Ctr., 1990—. Author: You Can Be a Woman Cardiologist, Heart Healthy: The Step-by-Step Guide to Preventing and Healing Heart Disease, Coronary Disease in Women: Evidence-based Diagnosis and Treatment. Thouron Fellowship, Robert Woods Johnson Fellow in health policy. Mem. AMA (founding mem. Women in Cardiology com., 1994), ACP, Am. Coll. Cardiology (mem. advocacy com.), Am. Heart Assn. (chair Sci. Adv. Bd. for Choose to Move program, chair Communications com., mem. sci. publications com.), Am. Soc. Echocardiology. Office: U Calif San Francisco Med Ctr 505 Parnassus Ave # M314D San Francisco CA 94122-2722 Office Phone: 415-476-6874. Office Fax: 415-502-8627. Business E-Mail: redberg@medicine.ucsf.edu.

REDBURN, TOM, editor; BA in Sociology, Pomona Coll., 1972. With OSHA, US Dept. Labor, 1972—73; editor & reporter The Washington Monthly, 1974—75, Environ. Action, 1975—76; reporter & chief econ. correspondent L.A. Times, 1977—90; internat. econ. correspondent Internat. Herald Tribune, 1991—93; reporter NY Times, 1993—94, editor, Bus. Day sect., 1994—97, asst. bus. editor, 1997—2003, tech. editor, 2003—04, dep. bus. editor, 2004—08; dep. mng. editor for bus. Internat. Herald Tribune, Paris, 2008, mng. editor for bus., 2008—. Named to Athletic Hall of Fame, Pomona Coll., 1992. Office: International Herald Tribune 6 bis, rue des Graviers 92521 Neuilly Cedex Paris France*

REDD, J. DIANE, not-for-profit fundraiser; b. Apr. 10, 1945; d. Robert Fountain and Lillian (Fitts) Redd. BS, W.Va. State Coll., 1967. Instr. bus. subjects Paterson (N.J.) Bus. Edn., 1967—89; with U. Medicine and Dentistry, Newark, 1968—69; adminstrv. asst. rsch. and sponsored programs, 1968—73; asst. dir. health edn., 1973—76; sr. devel. officer, 1976—79; asst. dir. devel., 1979—83; chief devel. and alumni affairs, 1983—89; dir. devel. founds., corps. and major gifts Planned Parenthood Fedn. Am., Inc., NYC, 1989—2002; dir. devel. NAACP-LDF, Inc., NYC, 2002—05; nat. dir. corp. and found. rels. Found. Fighting Blindness, 2005—. Mem. priorities com., devel. com. United Way of Essex and West Hudson, Newark, 1983-85; chmn. human resources com. Cmty. Adv. Bd., U. Medicine and Dentistry N.J., Newark, 1978-82; mem. rsch. bd. advisors Am. Biographical Inst., 1992—. Recipient Recognition of Achievement award Young Women of Am., Inc., Montgomery, Ala., 1979, Black Achiever award YMWCA, 1986. Mem. Assn. of Fund Raising Profls. Inc., Ind. (cert., trustee, v.p., parliamentarian, sec.), Exec. Women N.J. (trustee, chmn. scholarship com.), Women in Fin. Devel. Democrat. Office Phone: 212-965-2205.

REDD, L. HUGH, manufacturing executive; B in Acctg., Brigham Young U., Provo, Utah; M of Profl. Accountancy in Tax Acctg., U. Tex. With tax dept. Arthur Andersen, 1983—86; sr. fin. analyst Gen. Dynamics, 1986—89, sr. tax adminstr. Falls Church, Va., 1989—94, dir. treasury planning and analysis, 1994—98, staff v.p., asst. treas., 1998—2000, v.p., contr. Land Systems Sterling Heights, Mich., 2000—06, sr. v.p., CFO, 2006—. Office: Gen Dynamics 2941 Fairview Park Dr Ste 100 Falls Church VA 22042-4513 Office Phone: 703-876-3000. Office Fax: 703-876-3125.*

REDD, MICHAEL, professional basketball player; b. Columbus, Ohio, Aug. 24, 1979; m. Achea Redd. Attended, Ohio State U., Columbus. Guard Milw. Bucks, 2001—. Mem. US Men's Sr. Nat. Basketball Team, 2006, Beijing, 08. Founder Michael Redd Found. Recipient Gold medal, men's basketball, Beijing Olympic Games, 2008; named to Ea. Conf. All-Star Team, NBA, 2004; finalist Sixth Man of Yr. award, 2003. Office: Milwaukee Bucks 1001 N Fourth St Milwaukee WI 53203*

REDD, SCOTT (JOHN SCOTT REDD), former federal official, retired military officer; b. Sidney, Iowa, Sept. 10, 1944; m. Donna Ford; children: Anne, Scott Jr., Adam. BSc in Math. and Physics, U.S. Naval Acad., 1966; postgrad. studies, Uruguay; MS in Ops. Analysis, Naval Post Grad. Sch.; postgrad. studies for Sr. Execs., MIT; grad., Armed Forces Staff Coll. Commd. ensign USN, 1966, advanced through grades to rear admiral, 1994, ret., 1998; staff mem. to sec. US Dept. Def., Washington; naval officer 5 operational commands, destroyers and frigates USN, acting dep. chief naval ops. for plans, policy and ops. Washington; comdr. US Naval Forces, US Ctrl. Command US Dept. Def., 1994—96; commdr. Fifth Fleet USN, 1995; dir. strategic plans and policy The Joint Staff, Washington, 1996—98; chmn., pres., CEO NetSchools Corp., Atlanta, 1999—2002; COO, dep. adminstr. Civilian Provisional Authority, Baghdad, Iraq, 2003—04; dir. Nat. Counterterrorism Ctr., Washington, 2005—07. Pres. Naval Acad. Class, 1966; exec. dir. Commn. on the Intelligence Capabilities of the US Regarding Weapons of Mass Destruction, 2004-05 Decorated Order Bahrain 1st degree, Legion of Merit (2 awards), Disting. Svc. medal (2 awards), Meritorious Svc. medal (2 awards), Navy Commendation medal (2 awards). Mem. U.S. Naval Acad. Alumni Assn. (past bd. dirs.) Avocation: amateur radio.

REDDEL, CARL WALTER, academic administrator; b. Gurley, Nebr., May 31, 1937; s. Walter Julius and Friedora Regina (Sorge) R.; m. Colette Marie Antoinette Mansuy, Oct. 26, 1963; children: Eric, Damien. BSED, Drake U., 1959; MA in Russian Studies, Syracuse U., 1962; PhD in Russian History, Ind. U., 1973, cert. Russian Studies, 1973. Lectr. U. Md., Toul-Rosieres, France, 1963-66; instr. U.S.A.F. Acad., Colorado Springs, Colo., 1967-68, 71-72, from asst. prof. to assoc. prof., 1972—80; from assoc. prof. to prof., head dept. history, fellow U. Edinburgh, 1980—82; prof., head USAF Acad., 1982—99; pres., CEO Eisenhower World Affairs Inst., 1999—2000; pub. svc. fellow Gettysburg (Pa.) Coll., 2000-01; cons. coord. Dwight D. Eisenhower Meml. Commn., Washington, 2001—02, exec. dir., 2002—. Nat. coord., regional World History Assn., Phila., 1990-95; bd. editors, mem. Joun. Slavic Mil., London, 1988-2007; series editor Military Hist. Symposium Series, Colorado Springs, 1993-2001. Editor: Transformation in Russian and Soviet Military History, 1990; contbr. articles to profl. jours. Mem. Rotary Internat., 1994—. Served to brig. gen. U.S. Air Force, 1962-99. Recipient Young Faculty exch. Internat. Rsch. Exchs. Bd., Moscow State U., 1975; Woodrow Wilson fellow, 1959-60, Danforth Found. fellow, 1959-61. Mem.: Am. Assn. Advancement of Slavic Studies, Am. Hist. Assn., Phi Alpha Theta. Lutheran. Home: 420 7th St NW Apt 809 Washington DC 20004-2214 Office: 1629 K St NW Ste 801 Washington DC 20006-3837 Office Phone: 202-296-0005. Personal E-mail: soloviev@msn.com. Business E-Mail: creddel@eisenhowermemorial.org.

REDDEN, GEORGE DEAN, geochemist; b. Inglewood, Calif., Jan. 8, 1953; s. Richard and Arline Redden; m. Yoshiko Fujita; 1 child, Maya. PhD, Stanford U., Calif., 1991. Rsch. scientist Idaho Nat. Lab., Idaho Falls, 1998—. Home: 2219 E Oakmont Dr Idaho Falls ID 83404 Office: Idaho Nat Lab PO Box 1625 MS 2208 Idaho Falls ID 83415 Personal E-mail: gredden@srv.net. Business E-Mail: george.redden@inl.gov.

REDDEN, JAMES ANTHONY, federal judge; b. Springfield, Mass., Mar. 13, 1929; s. James A. and Alma (Cheek) R.; m. Joan Ida Johnson, July 13, 1950; children: James A., William F. Student, Boston U., 1951; LL.B., Boston Coll., 1954. Bar: Mass., 1954, Oreg., 1955. Pvt. practice, Mass., 1954-55; title examiner Title & Trust Ins. Co., Oreg., 1955; claims adjuster Allstate Ins. Co., 1956; mem. firm Collins, Redden, Ferris & Velure, Medford, Oreg., 1957-73; treas. Oreg., 1973-77; atty. gen., 1977-80; U.S. dist. judge, now sr. judge U.S. Dist. Ct. Oreg., Portland, 1980—. Chmn. Oreg. Pub. Employee Relations Bd.; mem. Oreg. Ho. of Reps., 1963-69, minority leader, 1967-69. With AUS, 1946-48. Mem. ABA, Mass. Bar Assn., Oreg. State Bar. Office: US Dist Ct 1527 US Courthouse 1000 SW 3d Ave Portland OR 97204-2902 Office Phone: 503-326-8370.

REDDEN, SHELTON DENNIS, telecommunications industry executive; b. Cleve., Ohio; s. John Redden and Marian E. Jackson; married; 5 children. AA in Info. Svcs., Cmty. Coll. Air Force; BA in Digital Processing, Golden Gate U., 1976. Prin. computer specialist, chief ARTEL/FEMA Ops., ARTEL Telecom., Reston, Va. Served in USAF, Korea, Japan, Philippines, Thailand, England, served in USAF, 1967—68, TET offensive, Vietnam. Decorated Bronze Star for Valor USAF; named to Power 150, Ebony mag., 2008. Mem.: Prince Hall Masons (maston mason, Lodge 103, Lancaster, Calif. 1970, dep. supreme coun, orient, State of Md. 1988, grand min. state 1991, grand jr. warden, Md. 1993, dist. dep. grand master 13th Masonic Dist., UK 1996, grand master, Md. 1998—, 1st lt. grand comdr., worshipful master Donald E. Jones Lodge 121, mem. King Solomon Lodge 7, former comdr.-in-chief James A. Mingo Consistory 334, former potentate MISR Temple 213, Gold Medal Achievement award 1997). Office: ARTEL Inc 1883 Preston White Dr Reston VA 20191 Office Phone: 703-620-1700. Office Fax: 703-620-4262.

REDDEN, TAYLOR TILGHMAN, musician; b. Swarthmore, Pa., Mar. 2, 1946; s. O. Tilghman Redden and Virginia Dare (Martin) Martin-Redden. Artist diploma, Phila. Conservatory of Music, 1965; BA, Phila. Music Acad., 1967, BFA in Music, 1967. Artist, tchr. Phila. Settlement Music Schs., 1968—70; prof. piano Bryn Mawr Conservatory of Music, Bryn Mawr, Pa., 1971—. Mem.: Music Tchrs. N. Am., U. of Arts Alumni Assn.

REDDEN, WADE, professional hockey player; b. Loydminster, Sask., Can., June 12, 1977; m. Danica Topolnisky, Aug. 2008. Defenseman Ottawa Senators, 1996—2008, NY Rangers, 2008—. Player NHL All-Star Game, 2002, 04; mem. Team Can., World Cup of Hockey, 2004. Recipient Bud Light Plus/Minus Award, NHL, 2006. Achievements include being a member of World Cup Champion Team Canada, 2004. Office: NY Rangers 2 Pennsylvania Plaza New York NY 10121

REDDICK, BRYAN DEWITT, academic administrator; b. Austin, Tex., Feb. 4, 1942; s. DeWitt Carter and Marjorie Alice (Bryan) R.; m. Sheila Ann Farrell, Oct. 3, 1970; children: Bridget Louise, George William. BA, U. Iowa, 1964; MA, Syracuse U., 1966; PhD, U. Calif., Davis, 1969. Fulbright teaching fellow U. Lyon, France, 1969-70; Maitre de Confs. U. Grenoble, France, 1970-71; asst. prof. English Am. U., Washington, 1971-75; prof. Olivet (Mich.) Coll., 1980-86, assoc. dean, 1981-82, acad. v.p., 1982-86, Elmira Coll., NY, 1986—. Author: Student Journalist and Effective Writing Style, 1976; editor: Mass Media and the School, 1984. Contbr. articles to profl. jours. Chmn. Olivet Planning Commn., Mich., 1978; mem. Sch./Community Adv. Coun., 1986-89; mem. exec. com. Sullivan Coun. BSA, 1988-92; trustee Chemung Valley History Mus., 1992—. NDEA fellow, 1966-69. Mem. Phi Beta Kappa. Home: 85 Decker Pkwy W Elmira NY 14905-2303 Office: Elmira Coll 1 Park Pl Elmira NY 14901-2085 E-mail: breddick@elmira.edu.

REDDICK, DEIRDRE SHADEIA, physician assistant; b. Bklyn., Sept. 22, 1967; d. Thomas Boykin and Frances Reddick. BS in Chemistry, cum laude, Claflin U., 1989; BS Physician Asst., CUNY, 2002. Social worker, case mgr. King's County Hosp. Ctr., Bklyn., 1993—99; physician asst. Lyndon Baines Johnson Health Complex, Bklyn., 2002—06, Bedford Stuyvesant Family Health Ctr., Bkln., NY, 2007—. Mem. Christian Cultural Ctr. Mem.: N.Y. State Soc. Physician Assts. (pres.'s award 2001), Am. Acad. Physician Assts., Bklyn.-Tech. HS Alumni Assn., Claflin U. Alumni Assn., CUNY Alumni Assn. Avocations: reading, dance. Home: 134-20 87th Ave 4C Kew Gardens NY 11418

REDDICK, EUNICE, United States Ambassador to Gabon and Sao Tome & Principe; BA in History and Lit., NYU, NYC; M in Internat. Affairs, Columbia U. Sch. Internat. Affairs, NYC, 1975; student in Mandarin Chinese, Am. Inst. Taipei Lang Sch., Taiwan, 1989—90. With Africa-America Inst., NYC, Washington; joined US Fgn. Svc., 1980; consular officer US Dept. State, Harare, Zimbabwe, 1981—83, monitor, Bur. Population, Refugee and Migration Affairs, 1983—86, country officer, Bur. African Affairs Tanzania, 1986—88, sr. watch officer, secretary's 24-hour ops. ctr., 1988—89, polit. sect. assignment Beijing, dep. dir. office Burma, Cambodia, Laos, Thailand and Vietnam affairs, Bur. East Asian and Pacific Affairs, dep. dir. office internat. devel. assistance, Bur. Internat. Orgn. Affairs, dep. dir. office Indonesia, Philippines, Malaysia, Brunei and Singapore affairs, 2000—02, dir. office Philippines, Malaysia, Brunei and Singapore affairs, 2002—04, dir. office East African affairs, Bur. African Affairs, 2005—07, US amb. to Gabon and Sao Tome & Principe Libreville, 2007—; assoc. Georgetown U. Inst. the Study of Diplomacy, 1993—94; chief, polit. sect. Am. Inst. in Taiwan, Taipei. Dean and Virginia Rusk fellow, 1993. Office: DOS Amb 2270 Libreville Pl Washington DC 20521-2270*

REDDICK, LOVETT EVAN, biochemist; b. Chattanooga, June 21, 1978; s. Lovett Pratt and Vicki Rose Reddick; m. Amanda Rae Jegier, May 27, 2006. BS, U. Tenn., Knoxville, 2001, PhD, 2009, grad. in Biochemistry, 2009. Cert. in first responder Wilderness Med. Assocs., 1997. Life guard Wilderness Med. Assocs., Black Mountain, NC, 1996—97; head life guard U. Tenn. Aquatic Ctr., 1998—2001; sci. cons. Jupiter Media, History Channel, 2008—; rsch. technician Oak Ridge Nat. Lab., 2001—03. Contbr. articles to biol. chemistry jours. Campaign contbr. Stacey Campfield State Rep., 2004—; reader, organizer Holy Family Cath. Ch., Seymour, 2006—; pres. Idlewood Townhomes Homeowner's Assn., Knoxville, 2008—. Recipient 1st prize, UTK Scis. Exhbn., 2006, Chancellor's award, U. Tenn., 2008. Mem.: Am. Soc. Biochemistry Molecular Biology, Am. Soc. Cell Biology, Am. Chem. Soc., Am. Soc. Plant Biologists, Sigma Xi Sci. Rsch. Soc., Tri Beta (sec. 1999—2001). Roman Catholic. Avocation: travel. Home: 715 Idlewood Ln Knoxville TN 37923 Office: Univ Tenn BCMB Dept 1414 Cumberland Ave Knoxville TN 37996 Personal E-mail: evan.reddick@gmail.com.

REDDING, ROBERT ELLSWORTH, lawyer; b. South Bend, Ind., Mar. 23, 1919; s. Harry Ellsworth and Lorraine (Livengood) R.; m. Blanche Breisch, Apr. 14, 1941 (div.); children: Rosemary, Robert Ellsworth Jr., Douglas; m. A. Virginia Boender Korn, July 22, 1972 (dec. Aug. 2004). AB, Ohio State U., 1940; LLB, JD, Georgetown U., 1946. Bar: DC 1946, Md. 1949, US Supreme Ct. 1951. Legal asst. to judge U.S. Tax Ct., Wash., 1947—48; legal asst. to mem. CAB, Washington, 1949-51; mem. Bradshaw Shearin Redding & Thomas, Silver Spring, Md., 1951-59; v.p., gen. counsel Transp. Assn. Am., Washington, 1960-69; dir. Office Facilitation Dept. Transp., 1970-76; pvt. practice Washington, Md., 1976—2006. Sec. Cert. Claims Profl. Accreditation Council, Washington, 1981-85; chief judge Appeal Tax Ct., Rockville, Md., 1953-55; internat. cons. GE Co., 1977; cons. Ford Motor Co., 1978-79, UN Devel. Program, NYC, 1980-81, Montgomery County, Md. Office Inspector Gen., 1997-2004; dir. fed. affairs Shippers Nat. Freight Claim Coun., Washington, 1979-89; Washington counsel Japan Airlines; chmn. US dels. at various internat. transp. confs. Author: Community Planning for Air Transportation, 1960; Washington editor Handling and Shipping mag., 1976—81, dir. Olney Big Band, 2005—. Pres. Allied Civic Group (50 assns.), Silver Spring, 1956-58; chmn. rsch. com. Md. Rep. Com., 1965-70; chmn. fin. adv. com. to county coun., Rockville, 1965-70; exec. dir. Montgomery County Taxpayers League, 1994-97. 2d lt. US Army, 1943-46. Mem.: Assn. Intelligence Officers, Univ. Club (bd. govs., Washington), 33 Degree Scottish Rite Mason, Phi Beta Kappa, Phi Alpha Delta (supreme justice 1966—68, exec. v.p. Pub. Svc. Ctr. 1984—91, Disting. Svc. chpt.). Home: 9105 Falls Chapel Way Potomac MD 20854-2452 Home Phone: 301-340-1516. Personal E-mail: robredding@comcast.net.

REDDINGTON, MARY JANE, retired secondary school educator; b. New Rochelle, NY, July 21, 1923; d. Gordon William and Katharine Regina (Coleman) Kann; m. John Martin Reddington, Oct. 11, 1947; children: Terence, Martha, Robert. BA cum laude, Coll. New Rochelle, 1945; postgrad., Columbia U., 1947—49; MA, Hunter Coll., 1954; PhD (hon.), Iona Coll., 1996. Tchr. St. Gabriel's H.S., New Rochelle, NY, 1945—51, Albert Leonard Jr. H.S., New Rochelle, NY, 1960—81; dir. devel. The Ursuline Sch., New Rochelle, NY, 1981—88; ret., 1988. Active Bd. Edn., New Rochelle, 1983—, v.p., 1985—87, pres., 1987—89, Colburn Meml. Home; active New Rochelle Pub. Libr. Found. Bd., New Rochelle Cmty. Svcs. Bd.; vol. Sound Shore Med. Ctr.; bd. dirs. United Way New Rochelle, 1972—, pres., 1979—82, campaign chair, 1976—82; trustee Coll. New Rochelle, 1967—73; lector Holy Family Ch.; active Holy Family Ch. Ladies Guild. Recipient Gold Key award, Columbia Scholastic Press Assn., 1976, Ursula Laurus citation, Coll. New Rochelle, 1962, St. Angela Merici medal, 1970, citation, United Way New Rochelle, 1970—82, Spl. Recognition award, 1986, 2001, St. Angela award, The Ursuline Sch., 1977, Nat. Cmty. Svc. award, AARP, 1994, Loyal Svc. and Dedication award, Colburn Home, 1992, Cmty. Salute honoree, New Rochelle Pub. Libr. Found., 1999, Cmty. Svc. award, New Rochelle YMCA, 2001, honoree, Sr. Pers. Placement Bur., 2002, Interreligious Coun. of New Rochelle, 2002, Meals-On-Wheels of New Rochelle, 2003, New Rochelle Fund for Ednl. Excellence, 2004, Marie Vitt award, Sound Share Med. Ctr., 2005; named to Westchester County Hall of Fame, 2005. Mem.: Bus. and Profl. Women's Club New Rochelle (past pres., Woman of Yr. 1979), So. Westchester Ret. Tchrs. Assn. (co-pres.), Coll. New Rochelle Alumnae Assn. (past pres.), Ladies of Charity (past pres.), Cath. Women's Club Westchester (founder, past pres.), Woman's Club New Rochelle (pres.), LWV, Alpha Delta Kappa (past pres.). Roman Catholic. Avocations: travel, reading, antiques, writing, cross country skiing. Home: 56 Wykagyl Terr New Rochelle NY 10804

REDDY, BOOJALA VIJAY, biology professor; s. Gopal and Narayanamma Reddy; m. Pushpalatha M. Reddy, Aug. 11, 1990; children: Shloka B., Shreya M. PhD, CCMB, U. Hyderabad, India, 1988. Prof. CUNY, Flushing, 2005—. Office: Queens Coll City Univ NY 65-30 Kissena Blvd Flushing NY 11367 Business E-Mail: breddy@qc.cuny.edu.

REDDY, CHADA S., toxicologist, researcher; b. Hyderabad, India, Nov. 5, 1949; m. Chaya C. Reddy, May 18, 1972; 1 child, Ramchandra C. BVSc, A.P. Agrl. U., Hyderabad, India, 1971; PhD, U. Miss., 1980. Asst. prof. Ohio State U., Columbus, 1980-84; assoc. prof. toxicology U. Mo., Columbia, 1984—. Assoc. editor Comments on Toxicology, 1993—; contbr. chpts. to books, some 60 abstracts and articles to profl. jours. Mem. Soc. Toxicology (pres. Ctrl. States chpt. 1989-90), Kiwanis Internat. Avocation: golf. Office: U Mo 1600 W Rollins Rd Columbia MO 65203-1756

REDDY, CHAKRADHAR M., gastroenterologist, educator; m. Deepa M. Reddy. MD, Kurnool Med. Coll., NTR U. Health Scis., Andhra Pradesh, India, 1999. Diplomate Am. Bd. Internal Medicine, 2006. Hepatology fellow U. Miami, 2006—07, faculty, 2007—08, gastroenterology fellow, 2008—. Mem.: AMA.

REDDY, CHAKRAVARTHY B., pulmonologist, educator; s. Ramana V. Reddy and Kavitha R. Pappu. MBBS, Mysore Med. Coll., India, 1996. Bd.cert. in internal medicine Am. Bd. Internal Medicine, 2002, bd.cert. in pulmonary medicine 2005, bd.cert. in critical care medicine 2006. Attending physician St. Barnabas Hosp., Bronx, NY, 2002—03; pulmonary and critical care fellow U. Utah, Salt Lake City, 2003—05, clin. instr., 2006—07, asst. prof.; interventional pulmonology fellow Beth Israel Deaconess Med. Ctr., Harvard Med. Sch., Boston, 2007—08. Cons. pulmonologist 4th St. Clinic, Salt Lake City, 2006. Recipient Resident of Yr. award, St. Barnabas Hosp., 2000—01, Young Investigator award, Am. Coll. Chest Physicians, 2005. Mem.: Am. Thoracic Soc., Am. Assn. Bronchology, Am. Coll. Chest Physicians. Avocations: travel, running. Office: Univ Utah 26 N 1900 E Salt Lake City UT 84132-4701 Office Fax: 801-585-3355. Business E-Mail: c.reddy@hsc.utah.edu.

REDDY, J. PATRICK, former energy executive; Grad., UCLA; MBA, Univ. So. Calif. Mgmt. positions through v.p. planning & adv. services Pacific Enterprises, 1980—98; v.p. corp. develop Atmos Energy, Dallas, 1998, v.p., treas., 1998—2000, sr. v.p., CFO, 2000—08; CFO Spectra Energy, Houston, 2009—. Office: Spectra Energy 5400 Westheimer Ct Houston TX 77056-5310*

REDDY, KAMBHAM RAJA, botanist, educator; b. Ambuvari Palli, India, July 1, 1953; s. Kambi Kambham and Ammannamma (Reddy) R.; m. Anasuya Reddy; 1 son, Sasank. BSc in Biology, S.V. U., Tirupati, India, 1975, MSc in Botany, 1977, PhD in Botany, 1984. Curator in botany S.V. U., 1977-88; prof. plant physiology Miss. State U., 1991—. Editor: Climate Change and Global Crop Productivity, 2000; contbg. author: Climate Change and Agriculture: Analysis of Potential International Impacts, 1995; contbr. articles to profl. jour., chpt. to books. Recipient Career Rsch. award, So. Br. Am. Soc. Agronomy and Assn. Agrl. Scientists Indian Origin, 2004. Fellow Am. Soc. Agronomy, Crop Sci. Soc. Am.; mem. Biol. Sys. Simulation Work Group, Gamma Sigma Delta (Rsch. award of merit 1995). Achievements include development of new theories and concepts in plant growth regulation and incorporated into a cotton simulation model GOSSYM, used by cotton producers, consultants and rschr. across the cotton belt; extensive contributions to the field of climate change, environmental plant physiology, ethnobotany, remote sensing and crop simulation modeling. Home: 505 Banyan Rd Starkville MS 39759-4348 Office: Mississippi State U Box 9555 Mississippi State MS 39762-9555 Home Phone: 662-324-5323; Office Phone: 662-325-9463.

REDDY, KRISHNA NARAYANA, artist, educator; b. Chittoor, India, July 15, 1925; s. Narayana B. and Laksmamma Reddy; m. Judith Blum, June 30, 1967; 1 child, Aparna. Diploma in Fine Arts, Internat. U. Santiniketan, India, 1947; cert. in Fine Arts, Slade Sch. Fine Arts, U. London, 1952; student of Zadkine in sculpture, Academie Grande Chaumière, Paris, 1952—55; student of Marino Marini in sculpture, Academia di Belle Arti di Brera, Milan, 1956—57; specialist in Gravure, Internat. Ctr. for Graphics, Atelier 17, Paris, 1953—55; DLitt (hon.), S.V. Univ., India, 1984. Asst. dir. Internat. Ctr. for Graphics, Atelier 17, Paris, 1957—64, prof., co-dir., 1964—76; from prof. art to prof. emeritus NYU, NYC, 1977—2001, prof. emeritus art and art edn., 2003—. Dir. dept. art Coll. Fine Arts, Kalakshetra, Madras, India, 1947—49; lectr. art Arundale Montessori Tchrs. Tng. Ctr., 1948—49; vis. prof. Am. U., 1964; prof. U. Calif., Davis, 1970—71, U. Wis., Madison, 1973; guest prof. Yale U. Summer Sch. Music and Art, 1973; Andrew Mellon vis. prof. Cooper Union Sch. Art and Arch., 1977; vis. prof. Yale U. Summer Sch. Music and Art, 1978, Kala Inst. Graphics, Berkeley, Calif., 1979, U. Calif., Santa Cruz, 1979. Author: Intaglio Simultaneous Color Printmaking: Significance of Materials and Processes, 1989, New Ways of Colour Printmaking, 1997; exhibitions include Bronx Mus. Arts, 1981-82, Indian Coun. for Cultual Relations, Ministry Culture and India Nat. Acad. Fine Arts, 1984-85, Mus. del Palacio de Bellas Artes, Mexico City, 1988-89. Recipient Gagan-Abani Puraskar Nat. award Viswa-Bharati, 1983, Printmaker Emeritus award So. Graphics Coun. Am., 2000, Kala Ratna award Nat. Acad. Fine Arts, Govt. India, 2007, Lifetime Achievement award Soc. Am. Graphic Artists, 2005; named Featured Guest Artist-Printmaker at the Northwest Print Coun. Ann. Meeting, 1985; Title of Padma Shree awarded by Pres. of India, 1972. Home: 80 Wooster St New York NY 10012-4347 Home Phone: 212-925-4227; Office Phone: 212-998-5756. Personal E-mail: jreddy5@nyc.rr.com.

REDDY, MUNAGALA, agricultural studies educator; b. Ardhavidu, Andhra Pradesh, India, June 1, 1954; s. Venkata Reddy and Eswaramma Munagala; m. Bharathi Boyella, Oct. 3, 1979; children: Pallavi, Pavan. PhD, Simon Fraser U., Canada, 1986. Scientist Exxon Chems., Saskatoon, Canada, 1988—94; sr. scientist Cominco Fertilizers, Saskatoon, 1994—95; mgr. Agrium, Saskatoon, 1995—98; prof. Auburn U., Ala., 1998—. CEO U. Chevron, Auburn, 2002—; owner, pres. Tiger Chevron LLC, Auburn, 2004—; pres. Goal Post, Auburn, 2004—; pres., CEO Glendean Shopping Ctr. LLC, Auburn, 2006—, Century Pk. Apt. LLC, Auburn, 2007—. Dir. Siva Temple, Ardhavidu, 2005—09. Recipient Presdl. award, Agrim Inc., 1997; Nat. Overseas Scholarship, Govt of India, 1981—86. Mem.: Am. Phytopathological Soc. Home: 1784 Lauren Ln Auburn AL 36830 Office: Auburn Univ 209 Life Sci Bldg Auburn University AL 36849 Home Fax: 334-826-7532. Business E-Mail: munagrs@auburn.edu.

REDDY, PRATAP CHANDUPATLA, cardiologist, educator, researcher; b. Laxmipur, Andhra Pradesh, India, Apr. 12, 1944; came to U.S., 1969; s. Chandra C. and Butchamma (Kota) R.; m. Shobha Katangur, May 15, 1971; children: Ashutosh, Kirthi. MBBS, Osmania U., Hyderabad, India, 1968. Diplomate Am. Bd. Internal Medicine, Am. Bd. Cardiovascular Diseases. Resident in internal medicine St. Vincent Med. Ctr., SI, N.Y., 1969-73; fellow in cardiology Maimonide Med. Ctr., Bklyn., 1973-74; rsch. assoc. USPHS Hosp., SI, 1974-76; asst. prof. medicine U. Ky., Lexington, 1976-81, dir. cardiac electrophysiology, 1976-84, assoc. prof., 1981-84; prof. medicine La. State U. Med. Ctr., Shreveport, 1984—, assoc. dir. cardiology, 1984—2003, dir. cardiac electrophysiology program, 1984—; chief cardiology divsn. Health Sci. Ctr. La. State U., 2003—; attending cardiologist VA Med. Ctr., Shreveport, La. Editor: Tachycardia, 1984; contbr. articles to profl. jours. Named Kentucky Colonel Gov. Ky., 1983. Fellow ACP, Am. Coll. Cardiology; mem. AMA, Am. Heart Assn. (v.p. La. affiliate 1988-89, pres. 1991-92, mem. coun. clin. cardiology), Cen. Soc. for Clin. Rsch., N.Am. Soc. Pacing and Electrophysiology. Office: La State U Med Sch 1530 Kings Hwy Shreveport LA 71103-4229 Office Phone: 318-675-5941. Business E-Mail: preddy@usuhsc.edu.

REDDY, RAVINDER, medical educator, director; m. Vasantha Reddy; 1 child, Rishika. PhD in Chemistry, Indian Inst. Tech. Kanpur, Kanpur, India, 1989. Cert. German proficiency Indian Inst. Tech. Asst. prof. radiology U. Pa., Phila., 1994—2000, assoc. prof. radiology, 2000—06, prof. radiology, sch. medicine, 2006—. Dir. grad. level courses U. Pa., 1996—, sci. dir., Metabolic Magnetic Resonance Rsch. & Computing Ctr., 1996—, mem. bioengring. grad. grp., 1998—, dir., multinuclear magnetic resonance lab., 2000—, mem. biomed. grad. grp., 2000—. Contbr. articles to profl. jours. Grantee Rsch. grants, NIH, 1995—, Biomedical Rsch. grant, Whitaker Found., 1996—2000, Rsch. grant, Dana Found., 2004—. Mem.: Am. Chem. Soc., Osteoarthritis Rsch. Soc. Internat., NY Acad. Scis., Internat. Soc. Magnetic Resonance Medicine. Achievements include patents for diagnostic MRI technology.

REDDY, VADIYALA MOHAN, cardiothoracic surgeon; m. Anita Reddy. MD, Kakatiya Med. Coll., Warangal, India, 1983. Resident Delhi U., New Delhi, 1986, 1989; sr. resident, pediatric cardiac surgery Children's Hosp., Boston, 1991; fellow Miami Children's Hosp., Fla., 1992, U. Calif., San Francisco, 1992; dir., pediatric cardiac surgery U. Calif, San Francisco, 1992—2001, assoc. prof., 1992—2001; divsn. chief, pediatric cardiothoracic surgery Cardiothoracic Surgery Clinic, Lucile Packard Children's Hosp. at Stanford U. Med. Ctr., Palo Alto, Calif., 2001—; assoc. prof., cardiothoracic surgery Stanford U. Sch. Medicine, Stanford, Calif., 2001—. Contbr. articles to profl. publs. Mem.: Soc. Thoracic Surgeons, Am. Heart Assn., Am. Assn. for Thoracic Surgeons. Office: Cardiothoracic Surgery 300 Pasteur Dr CVRB MC 5407 Stanford CA 94305 Address: Lucile Packard Childrens Hosp 725 Welsh Rd Palo Alto CA 94304 Office Phone: 650-724-2925, 650-497-8000, 415-476-3501. Fax: 650-724-0707, 415-476-9678; Office Fax: 650-725-3846. Business E-Mail: vmreddy@stanford.edu.

REDEKER, JAMES RUSSELL, lawyer; b. Primghar, Iowa, May 28, 1941; s. Russell James and Alice (Englesmann) Redeker; m. Nancy Vargish; children: Rebecca Hope, Eric James, Tricia Marie. BA cum laude, Ctrl. U. Iowa, 1963; MA with honors, U. Ark., 1964; JD, U. Pa. Sch. Law, 1968. Bar: Pa. 1968, US Dist. Ct. (ea. and mid. dists.) Pa., US Ct. Appeals (3rd cir.), Supreme Ct. Pa., US Supreme St. Assoc. to ptnr. Cohen, Shapiro, Polisher, Shiekman & Cohen, Phila., 1971-78; ptnr. Saul, Ewing, Remick & Saul, Phila., 1978-86; ptnr., chmn. labor law dept., mem. exec. com., strategic planning ptnr. Wolf, Block, Schorr & Solis-Cohen, Phila., 1986; now ptnr. Duane Morris LLP, Phila. Former mem. human resources adv. com. Pa. State Chamber Bus. & Industry. Author: Discipline: Policies, Procedures, 1983, Employee Discipline: Policies and Practices, 1989; contbr. numerous articles to profl. jours., chapters to books; contbg. editor: Personnel jour.; mem. editl. bd. Human Resources Profl. Founder, exec. bd. mem. Support Ctr. Child Advocates, Phila., 1975; former mem. Partnership Econ. Devel. Greater Phila.; past chmn. bd. dirs. Prince Music Theater, Phila. Recipient Disting. Vol. award, HHS, 1983; named Human Resource Profl. of Yr., Internat. Assn. Pers. Women, 1989; named a Leader in Law, Phila. Bus. Jour., 2008; named one of Philly's 100 Hottest New Leaders, Bus. Phila. mag., 1994, Top 50 Employment Attorneys, Human Resource Exec. mag., 2008, Top 100 Employment Attorneys in US, 2009. Mem.: ABA, Pa. Bar Assn., Phila. Bar Assn. (Fidelity Bank award 1976). Republican. Presbyterian. Office: Duane Morris LLP 30 S 17th St Philadelphia PA 19103 Office Phone: 215-979-1846. Office Fax: 215-405-3898. Business E-Mail: jredeker@duanemorris.com.*

REDFEARN, PAUL L., III, lawyer; b. Camp Cook, Calif., Oct. 1, 1951; s. Paul Leslie Jr. and Alice Ruby Redfearn; children: Ashley, Lauren; m. Denise Jean Davis, July 24, 1993. BS, S.W. Mo. State U., 1973; JD, Oklahoma City U., 1976. Bar: Mo. 1977, U.S. Dist. Ct. (we.

and ea. dists.) Mo., U.S. Dist. Ct. Kans., U.S. Dist. Ct. N.D., U.S. Dist. Ct. Mont., U.S. Ct. Appeal (8th ant 11th cirs.); bd. cert. civil trial advocate. Assoc. Sheridan, Sanders & Simpson, P.C., 1977-79, William H. Pickett, P.C., 1979-84; pvt. practice Kansas City, Mo., 1984—. Mem. bd. dirs. Lawyers Encouraging Acad. Performance (LEAP), treas.; lectr. and presenter in field. Contbr. chpts. to books. Bd. govs. S.W. Mo. State U., 1998-2003 Named Best of the Bar, Business Jour., 2003, Mo. and Kans. Super Lawyers, 2005—09. Mem. ABA, Am. Assn. Justice, Mo. Bar Assn., Mo. Assn. Trial Attys. (bd. govs. 1986-94, exec. com. 1990—, pres. 1992), Am. Bd. Trial Advs. (charter, pres. chpt. 1996-97, adv.), Pub. Justice Found., Kansas City Met. Bar Assn., Millon Dollar Advs. Forum. Democrat. Avocation: tennis. Office: 1125 Grand Blvd Ste 1805 Kansas City MO 64106-2518 Office Phone: 816-421-5301. Business E-Mail: predfearn@redfearnlawfirm.com.

REDFERN, CHRIS, political organization administrator, former state legislator; b. 1964; m. Kim Redfern; 1 child, Reese. BA in Polit. Sci., Bowling Green State U., MA in State and Local Govt. Commr. Ottawa County, Ohio, 1993—99; mem. Dist. 80 Ohio State House of Reps., 1999—2006, caucus chmn., 2002—03, minority leader, 2003—06; chmn. Ohio Dem. Party, 2005—. Exec. com. mem. Dem. Nat. Com. (DNC); v.p. Midwestern Region Assn. of State Dem. Chairs. Recipient Builders award, Wood County Dem. Party, Pub. Official award, Ottawa County Sr. Fair Bd., Vol. award, Port Clinton Pks. and Recreation Dept., Pres. award, Friends of Camp Perry, Myrl H. Shoemaker Award, 2003; named Citizen of Yr., Port Clinton Area C. of C., 2004. Mem.: Ohio Employee Ownership Assn., Farm Bur., Lake Erie Charter Boat Assn., Port Clinton City Schs. Champions for Children, Farmers Union Nature Conservancy, Put-in-Bay C. of C., Pheasants Forever, Ducks Unlimited, Friends of Edison Woods, Woodmore HS FFA, Ottawa County Dem. Club, Elks, Kiwanis. Democrat. Office: 727 Brentwood Ave Youngstown OH 44511 also: Ohio Dem Party 340 East Fulton St Columbus OH 43215 Office Phone: 614-221-6563.*

REDFIELD, CAROL ANN LUCKHARDT, computer scientist, educator; b. Greencastle, Ind., July 19, 1958; d. Robert Luckhardt and Helen Kinoshta; m. Josiah Beckley Redfield, Mar. 17, 1990; children: Neil, Crystal. BS Edn., U. Mich., 1980, MS Math, 1982, MS Computer & Controls, 1982, PhD Computer Sci. & Engring., 1989. Cert. secondary tchr. Tchg. asst. U. Mich., Ann Arbor, 1979—87; rsch. engr. Southwest Rsch. Inst., San Antonio, 1987—94; sr. scientist Mei Tech. Corp., San Antonio, 1995—98; asst. prof. St. Mary's U., San Antonio, 1998—2003, assoc. prof., 2003—, dir. Grad. Program, 2004—. Chair Internat. Space Devel. Conf., San Antonio, 1991, co-chair, ITS, 1998, AI in Edn., 2001. Author: AI and Game Playing, 1986; editor, author: Intelligent Tutoring Systems, 1991, 98; editor: 1991 ISDC Procs., 1991, AI in Education, 2001 Dir. Internet team Landmark Edn.; founder Radiance Acad. West Charter Sch. Recipient Ultimate Frisbee Nat. champion, 1993; named to San Antonio Women's Hall of Fame, 1993. Mem. AAAI, Nat. Space Soc., San Antonio Space Soc. (pres. 1988—) Mem. Soc. Of Friends. Avocations: science fiction, games, ultimate frisbee. Home: 609 Ridge View Dr San Antonio TX 78253-5348 Office: St Marys U 1 Camino Santa Maria St San Antonio TX 78228-8524 Office Phone: 210-436-3298. Business E-Mail: CRedfield@stmarytx.edu.

REDFIELD, PAMELA A., state legislator; b. Chgo., Aug. 11, 1948; m. Jerry Redfield; 6 children. BS in Edn., U. Nebr., 1969. Mem. Nebr. Legislature 12th dist., Lincoln, 1998—. Mem. Ralston Bd. Edn. 1992-1998. Coun. State Govt.; Nat. Conf. State Legislatures; Am. Legis. Exch. Conf.; Nat. Coun. Ins. Legislators Mem.: Am. Legis. Exch. conf., Nat. Conf. State Legis., Nat. Coun. Ins. State Legis.

REDFIELD, ROBERT HORACE, mathematician, educator; b. Schenectady, NY, Feb. 24, 1945; s. Robert Horace Redfield and Elizabeth (Carlson) Cherrett; m. Rosemary Jeanne Gagne, Dec. 13, 1970 (div. 1979); 1 child, Signe Anne; m. Mary Eleanor Javorski, Aug. 18, 1984; children: Lisbeth Ellen Sarah, Catherine Mairi Sophia. BA, Reed Coll., 1967; MA, U. Oreg., 1969; PhD, Simon Fraser U., Can., 1973. Rsch. fellow Monash U., Clayton, Victoria, Australia, 1974-77, vis. assoc. prof., 1989-90; vis. asst. prof. math. U. Kans., Lawrence, 1977-78; instr. Okanagan Coll., Kelowna, 1978-86; assoc. prof. math. Hamilton Coll., Clinton, N.Y., 1986-93, prof., 1993-96, Samuel F. Pratt prof.math., 1996—. Vis. lectr. McMaster U., Hamilton, Ont., Canada, 1980; vis. assoc. prof. Simon Fraser U., Burnaby, B.C., Canada, 1985, Monash U., Victoria, Australia, 1989—90; assoc. Internat. Jour. Maths. & Math. Scis., 2007—. Reviewer: for math reviews, published: textbook on abstract algebra; contbr. rsch. papers to math. publs. Organizer, tchr., Kelowna Internat. Dancers, 1981-86, Clinton Internat. Folk Dancers, 1992-2003 Grantee, Australian Rsch. Grants Com., 1974-77. Mem. Am. Math. Soc., Can. Math. Soc., Can. Soc. History and Philosophy of Math., Math. Assn. Am., Kelowna Scottish Country Dance Group (treas. 1981-86), Sigma Xi. Office: Hamilton Coll Dept Math Clinton NY 13323

REDFORD, DONALD BRUCE, historian, archaeologist; b. Toronto, Ont., Can., Sept. 2, 1934; s. Cyril Fitzjames and Kathleen Beryl (Coe) R.; m. Susan Pirritano, Jan. 30, 1982; children: Alexander, Aksel; children by previous marriage: Christopher, Philip. BA, U. Toronto, 1957, MA, 1958; PhD, Brown U., 1965. Lectr. Brown U., 1960-61; lectr. U. Toronto, 1961-64, asst. prof. Egyptian history and language, 1965-67, asso. prof., 1967-69, prof., 1969-98; site supr. Brit. Sch. Archaeol. Excavations, Jerusalem, 1964-67; dir. Soc. Study Egyptian Antiquities Expdn. to, Karnak, Egypt, 1970-72, Akhenaten Temple Project, Luxor, Egypt, 1972—; research assoc. Univ. Museum, U. Pa., Royal Ont. Mus.; prof. classics Pa. State U., 1998—. Vis. prof. Ben Gurion U., Beersheva, Israel, 1986, U. Pa., 1995-96; dir. excavations Mendes and Ted Kedwa, Egypt, 1991—. Author: History and Chronology of the Egyptian 18th Dynasty, 1967, A Study of the Biblical Joseph Story, 1970, Papyrus and Tablet, 1973, The Akhenaten Temple Project, vol. I, 1977, Akhenaten, the Heretic King, 1984; Annals, King-Lists and Daybooks, 1986, The Akhenaten Temple Project, vol. II, 1988, Egypt, Canaan and Israel in Ancient Times, 1992, The Wars in Syria and Palestine of Thutmose III, 2003; From Slave to Pharaoh: The Black Experience of Ancient Egypt, 2003. Killam grantee, 1975-79; Smithsonian Fgn. Currency grantee, 1973-76, 1979, Social Scis. Humanities Research Council Can. grantee, 1980—. Fellow Royal Soc. Can. Achievements include discovering Temple of Akhenaten at Luxor, 1976. Office: CAMS Weaver Bldg State College PA 16803 also: Pa State U Dept Classics & Mediterranean Studies 108 Weaver Bldg University Park PA 16802-5500 Business E-Mail: dbr3@psu.edu.

REDFORD, ROBERT (CHARLES ROBERT REDFORD), actor, film director; b. Santa Monica, Calif., Aug. 18, 1937; s. Charles Robert and Martha Redford; m. Lola Van Wegenen, Sept. 12, 1958 (div. 1985); m. Sibylle Szaggars, July 11, 2009; children: Shauna, Jamie, Amy. Student, U. Colo., Pratt Inst. Design, Am. Acad. Dramatic Arts; LHD (hon.), U. Colo., 1987; D (hon.), U. Mass., 1990. Owner ski resort Sundance, Provo, Utah. Stage appearances include: Tall Story, The Highest Tree, Sunday in New York, Barefoot in the Park; actor: (films) War Hunt, 1961, Situation Hopeless But Not Serious, 1965, Inside Daisy Clover, 1965, The Chase, 1966, This Property Is Condemned, 1966, Barefoot in the Park, 1967, Butch Cassidy and the Sundance Kid, 1969, Tell Them Willie Boy is Here, 1969, Little Fauss and Big Halsey, 1970, The Hot Rock, 1972, Jeremiah Johnson, 1972, The Way We Were, 1973, The Sting, 1973, The Great Gatsby, 1974, The Great Waldo Pepper, 1975, Three Days of the Condor, 1975, A Bridge Too Far, 1977, The Electric Horseman, 1979, Brubaker, 1980, The Natural, 1984, Out of Africa, 1985, Legal Eagles, 1986, Havana, 1990, Sneakers, 1992, Indecent Proposal, 1993, Up Close and Personal, 1996, Anthem, 1997, Enredando sombras, 1998, Forever Hollywood, 1999, Spy Game, 2001, The Last Castle, 2001, The Clearing, 2004, An Unfinished Life, 2005, (voice only) Charlotte's Web, 2006; (TV appearances) Maverick, 1960, Rescue 8, 1960, Tall Story, 1960, The Deputy, 1960, Hallmark Hall of Fame, 1960, Playhouse 90, 1960, Moment of Fear, 1960, Tate, 1960, Perry Mason, 1960, Play of the Week (3 episodes), 1960-61, Naked City, 1961, The Americans, 1961, Whispering Smith, 1961, Route 66, 1961, Bus Stop, 1961, The New Breed, 1961, Alfred Hitchcock Presents, 1961, The Twilight Zone, 1962, Dr. Kildare, 1962, Alcoa Premiere, 1962, The Alfred Hitchcock Hour (2 episodes), 1963-63, The Untouchables, 1963, The Dick Powell Show, 1963, Breaking Point, 1963, The Virginian, 1963, The Defenders, 1964; (TV movies) The Iceman Cometh, 1960; actor, dir., prodr.: (films) Lions for Lambs, 2007; actor, exec. prodr.: (films) Downhill Racer, 1969, The Candidate, 1972, All The President's Men, 1976; dir.: (films) Ordinary People, 1980 (Academy award for Best Director, Golden Globe award for Best Director, 1980), Quiz Show, 1994; dir., prodr.: (films) The Milagro Beanfield War, 1988, A River Runs Through It, 1993; prodr. A Civil Action, 1998, The Legend of Bagger Vance, 2000; exec. prodr.: (films) Promised Land, 1988, Some Girls, 1988, She's the One, 1996, The Dark Wind, 1991, Slums of Beverly Hills, 1998, How to Kill Your Neighbor's Dog, 2000; exec. prodr., narrator Yosemite: The Fate of Heaven, 1989, Incident at Oglala, 1992 Founder, pres. The Sundance Inst., 1981—. Recipient Audubon medal, 1989, Dartmouth Film Soc. award, 1990, Cecil B. Demille Golden Globe Award for Lifetime Achievement, 1994, Screen Actors Guild Award for Life Achievement, 1996, Hon. award, Acad. Awards, 2002, Kennedy Ctr. Honor, John F. Kennedy Ctr. for Performing Arts, 2005, Peter J. Owens award, San Francisco Internat. Film Festival, 2009; named Officer of French Ordre des Arts et des Lettres; named one of 100 Sexiest Stars in film history, Esquire mag., 1994. Fellow: Am. Acad. Arts & Scis.; mem.: Land Trust of Napa County (mem. adv. com.). Office: 3101 E Idas Rd Provo UT 84604*

REDGRAVE, MARTYN ROBERT, retail executive; BA in Econs., Princeton U.; MBA in Finance, NYU. CPA Minn. Various fin. and gen. mgmt. positions PepsiCo, 1980—90; exec. v.p. fin., CFO Kentucky Fried Chicken Corp., 1990—94; CFO, exec. v.p Carlson Cos. Inc., Mpls., 1994—2005; exec. v.p., chief admin. officer Limited Brands, Inc., Columbus, Ohio, 2005—; CFO Limited Brands., Inc., Columbus, Ohio, 2006—07. Vol. United Way. Office: Limited Brands Inc 3 Limited Pkwy Columbus OH 43216

REDICK, J.J. (JONATHAN CLAY REDICK), professional basketball player; b. Cookeville, Tenn., June 24, 1984; s. Ken and Jeanie. BA in History, Duke Univ., 2006. Guard Duke Univ. Blue Devils, 2002—06, Orlando Magic, 2006—. Recipient Sullivan award for top amateur athlete, 2005, Naismith Men's Coll. Player of Yr. award, 2006, John Wooden award, 2006, Oscar Robertson Trophy, 2006; named First Team All-Am., AP, USBWA, NABC, ESPN.com, Sporting News, Baketball News, 2005, 2006, Rupp Nat. Player Yr., 2005, 2006, Player of Yr., Atlantic Coast Conf., 2005, 2006, NCAA Player of Yr., AP, 2006. Office: Orlando Magic 8701 Maitland Summit Blvd Orlando FL 32810*

REDING, JOHN ANTHONY, JR., lawyer; b. Orange, Calif., May 26, 1944; AB, U. Calif., Berkeley, 1966, JD, 1969. Bar: Calif. 1970, U.S. Dist. Ct. (no., ctrl., ea. and so. dists.) Calif., U.S. Claims Ct., U.S. Supreme Ct. Formerly mem. Crosby, Heafey, Roach & May P.C., Oakland, Calif.; ptnr. Paul, Hastings, Janofsky & Walker, LLP, San Francisco, global chmn. litig. dept. Mem. ABA (sects. on litigation, intellectual property, and natural resources, energy and eviron. law, coms. on bus. torts, internat. law, trial practice and torts and insurance), Am. Intellectual Property Law Assn., State Bar Calif. (sect. on litigation), Bar Assn. San Francisco, Assn. Bus. Trial Lawyers. Office: Paul Hastings Janofsky & Walker LLP 55 Second St 24th Floor San Francisco CA 94105-3441 Office Phone: 415-856-7004. Office Fax: 415-856-7100. Business E-Mail: jackreding@paulhastings.com.

REDING, ROBERT W., air transportation executive; m. Sherrill Reding. BS in Aero. Engring., Calif. State Poly. U.; MBA, So. Ill. U. Various positions Air Fla.; v.p., flight opers. Midways Airlines, Chgo.; pres., CEO Reno Air, Canadian Regional Airlines; COO Am. Eagle Airlines; sr. v.p., tech. opers. Am. Airlines, 2003—07, exec. v.p. ops., 2007—. Mem. Pres.'s Coun., Calif. State Poly. U. With USAF, 1972—79. Office: AMR Corp 4333 Amon Carter Blvd Fort Worth TX 76155

REDISH, MARTIN HARRIS, law educator; b. Lynbrook, NY, Aug. 16, 1945; m. Caren Beverly Redish; 1 child, Jessica. AB, U. Pa., 1967; JD magna cum laude, Harvard U., 1970. Bar: NY 1971, US Dist. Ct. (so. dist.) NY 1971, US Ct. Appeals (2d cir.) 1971, US Ct. Appeals (7th cir.) 1973. Law clk. Honorable J. Joseph Smith US Ct. Appeals (2d cir.), 1970—71; assoc. Proskauer, Rose, Goetz & Mendelsohn, NYC, 1971—73; asst. prof. Northwestern U. Sch. Law, Chgo., 1973—76, assoc. prof., 1976—78, prof., 1978—90, Louis and Harriet Ancel prof. law and pub. policy, 1990—. Vis. assoc. prof. law Cornell U., 1977, Stanford U., 1977; vis. prof. law U. Mich., 1987—88; mem. 7th Cir. Rules Adv. Com.; cons. U.S. Senate Jud. Com. Author: Federal Jurisdiction: Tensions in the Allocation of Judicial Power, 1980, Federal Courts: Cases, Comments and Questions, 1983, Freedom of Expression: A Critical Analysis, 1984, The Constitution as Political Structure, 1995, Money Talks: Speech, Economic Power and the Values of Democracy, 2001; co-author: Constitutional Law: Principles and Policy, 1987, Civil Procedure: A Modern Approach, 1989, Understanding Federal Court Jurisdiction, 1999; contbr. articles to profl. jours. Mem.: Am. Coll. Trial Lawyers, Am. Law Inst. Office: Northwestern U Sch Law 357 E Chicago Ave Chicago IL 60611-3059 Office Phone: 312-503-8545. E-mail: m-redish@law.northwestern.edu.

REDLES, DAVID, history professor; b. Abington, Pa., Feb. 14, 1961; PhD, Pa. State U., State Coll, 1995. Assoc. prof. history Cuyahoga CC, Parma, Ohio, 2000. Author: (historical non-fiction) Hitler's Millennial Reich: Apocalyptic Belief and the Search for Salvation. Office: Cuyahoga CC 11000 Pleasant Valley Dr Parma OH 44130 Business E-Mail: david.redles@tri-c.edu.

REDLO, MITCHELL, economics professor, consultant; BA in Economics, Buffalo State Coll., 1981; MPA in Pub. Fin., SUNY, Albany, 1983; MA in Economics, SUNY, Buffalo, 1987. Pub. fin. mgr. Marine Midland Bank, NYC, 1983—86; prof. economics Monroe CC, Rochester, NY, 1988—. Cons. Bistro135, Rochester, 2007—; CFO Maui Fresh Fish LLC, Hawaii, 2007—. Author: (textbook) An Introduction to the Principles of Microeconomics, An Introduction to the Market System. K-12 sch. vol. Rush-Henrietta CSD, Rochester, 1999—2008. Recipient Chancellor's award, SUNY, NISOD award.

REDMAN, BARBARA KLUG, nursing educator; b. Mitchell, SD; d. Harlan Lyle and Darlien Grace (Bock) Klug; m. Robert S. Redman, Sept. 14, 1958; 1 child, Melissa Darlien. BS, S.D. State U., 1958; MEd, U. Minn., 1959, PhD, 1964; LHD (hon.), Georgetown U., 1988; DSc (hon.), U. Colo., 1991; M in Bioethics, U. Pa., 2004, MBE, 2004. RN. Asst. prof. U. Wash., Seattle, 1964-69; assoc. dean U. Minn., Mpls., 1969-75; dean Sch. Nursing U. Colo., Denver, 1975-78; VA scholar VA Cen. Office, Washington, 1978-81; postdoctoral fellow Johns Hopkins U., Balt., 1982-83; exec. dir. Am. Assn. Colls. Nursing, Washington, 1983-89, ANA, Washington, 1989-93; prof. nursing Johns Hopkins U., Balt., 1993-95; dean, prof. Sch. Nursing U. Conn., Storrs, 1995-98; dean Coll. Nursing Wayne State U., Detroit. Vis. fellow Kennedy Inst. Ethics, Georgetown U., 1993-94; fellow in med. ethics Harvard Med. Sch., 1994-95. 2004—; vis. scholar U. Pa. Ctr. for Bioethics, 2004—. Author: Practice of Patient Education, 1968—; contbr. articles to profl. jours. Bd. dirs. Friends of Nat. Libr. of Medicine, Washington, 1987—. Recipient Disting. Alumnus award S.D. State U., 1975, Outstanding Achievement award U. Minn., 1989; visiting scholar, U. Pa. Ctr., 2004-. Fellow Am. Acad. Nursing. Home: 12425 Bobbink Ct Potomac MD 20854-3005 Office: Wayne State U 5557 Cass Ave Detroit MI 48202-3615

REDMAN, DON, Councilman; m. Debbie Redman; 5 children. Bus. ptnr. Safe Place; councilman, Dist. 4 Jacksonville City Coun. Chmn. Mayor's Coun. on Fitness & Well-Being; mem. Land Use & Zoning, Transp., Energy & Utilities Coms., Courthouse Architectural Rev. Com.; ex-officio mem. Downtown Devel. Rev. Bd.; mem. Downtown Vision, Inc.; coun. liaison Jacksonville Housing Authority. Chmn. Englewood High Sch. Adv. Com., Greenfield Elem. Sch. Adv. Com., Englewood Resource Ctr. Full Svc. Sch.; mem. Full Svc. Schs. Leadership Coun., Youth Crisis Ctr. Adv. Bd.; usher Bapt. Ch. Jacksonville. Republican. Avocation: race dir. Office: 117 W Duval St Ste 425 Jacksonville FL 32202 Office Phone: 904-630-1386, 904-630-1394. Business E-Mail: redman@coj.net.*

REDMAN, ERIC, lawyer; b. Seattle, June 3, 1948; s. M. Chandler and Marjorie Jane (Sachs) R.; children: Ian Michael, Graham James, Jing, Amanda; m. Heather Bell, 1996. AB, Harvard U., 1970, JD, 1975; BA, Oxford U., 1972, MA, 1980. Bar: Wash. 1975, U.S. Dist. Ct. (we. dist.) Wash. 1975, D.C. 1979, U.S. Ct. Appeals (9th cir.) 1981, U.S. Supreme Ct. 1983. Asst. U.S. senator W.G. Magnuson, Washington and Seattle, 1968-71, 74-75; assoc. Preston, Thorgrimson et al, Seattle, 1975-78, ptnr., 1979-82, Heller, Ehrman, White & McAuliffe, Seattle, 1983—. Author: Dance of Legislation, 1973; also book revs., articles. Home: Heller Ehrman LLP 1077 Maplewood Pl SW Seattle WA 98146-1076 Home Phone: 206-935-5205. E-mail: eric.redman@hellerehrman.com.

REDMAN, TIMOTHY PAUL, language educator, writer; b. Elmhurst, Ill., June 26, 1950; s. William Charles and Eileen Marie (Keenan) Redman. BA, Loyola U., Chgo., 1973; MA, U. Chgo., 1974, PhD, 1987. Instr. Loyola U., Rome, 1977, Ill. Inst. Tech., Chgo., 1980-84; lectr. English dept. Loyola U., Chgo., 1982-84, DePaul U., 1982—84; lectr. U. Wis., Parkside, 1984-85; instr. Ohio State U., Lima, 1985-87, asst. prof., 1987-89, U. Tex., Dallas, 1989-91, assoc. prof., 1991-98, prof., 1998—, assoc. dean, coll. master, 1991-92. Author: Ezra Pound and Italian Fascism, 1991; editor: Official Rules of Chess, 3d edit., 1987. Whiting fellow, 1981—82, NEH fellow, 1992—93. Mem.: MLA, U.S. Chess Trust (v.p.), PEN U.S.A. (pres. Tex. chpt.), Nat. Coun. Tchrs. English, U.S. Chess Fedn. (past pres.,), World Chess Fedn. (Chess schs. com.). Roman Catholic. Office: U Tex Dallas Sch Arts & Humanities JO31 PO Box 830688 Richardson TX 75083-0688: US Chess Fedn PO Box 3967 Crossville TN 38557 Office Phone: 972-883-2775. Business E-Mail: redman@utdallas.edu.

REDMAN, WILLIAM WALTER, JR., retired NC state senator, NC state utilities commissioner; b. Statesville, NC, Oct. 15, 1933; s. William Walter and Mildred (Huie) R.; m. Elizabeth Ann Wilhelm, Dec. 28, 1956; children: Lisa Dawn, Kathryn Marlene, Adrienne Ann. Student, U. So. Calif., 1966; BS, Embry-Riddle Aeronat. U., 1972; postgrad., Jud. Coll., 1987. Enlisted U.S. Army, 1954, advanced trhough grades to lt. col., 1974, ret., 1974; dir. pub. rels. Northwestern Bank, Statesville, 1974—76; pres. Redman Realty, Statesville, 1976-92; mem. N.C. Senate from 26th Dist., 1978-87, minority leader, 1986-87; commr. pub. utilities State of N.C., 1987-95; chmn. N.C. Utilities Commn., 1995—2001; ret., 2004. Exec. dir. N.C. Telecomm. Industry Assn.; exec. v.p. carolina Vas. Telephone Membership Assn.; mem. exec. com., vice chmn. com. on adminstrn., comm. com. Nat. Assn. Regulatory Utility Commrs.; chmn. bd. dirs. Nat. Regylatory Rsch. Inst., Ohio State U., 1993; mem. exec. com. Southeastern Assn. Regulatory Utilities Commrs.; past trustee Gardner-Webb Coll.; mem. bd. advisors Sch. Bus. Pub. Utility Regulatory Bd., N.Mex. State U.; dir. N.C. Solar Ctr.; past mem. N.C. Energy Policy Coun., N.C. Tax Rev. Bd.; bd. dirs. N.C. Child Advocay Inst., 1997, Assn. Excs. N.C. 1997—; adv. bd. ARC Carolina's chpt., 2003-07. Decorated DFC with oak leaf cluster, Bronze Star medal with two oak leaf clusters, Air medal with sixteen oak leaf clusters, Meritorious Svc. medal; recipient Valand award NC Mental Assns.; named to Inf. Officers Sch. Hall of Fame, Ft. Benning Ga., Disting. Mem. Regt., U.S. Transp. Corps, 1990; recipient Long Leaf Pine award State of NC, 1987, 94, Highest Civilian award in NC. Mem. DAV (life), VFW (life), Ret. Officers Assn. (life), Nat. Assn. Adminstrv. Law Judges, Vietnam Helicopter Pilots Assn., Army Otter-Caribou Assn., Army Aviation Am. Assn., 1st Cavalry Divsn. Assn. (life), Am. Legion (life), Raleigh Exec. Club. Republican. Baptist. Home: 1320 Royalty Cir Statesville NC 28625-8230

REDMON, CYNTHIA ANN, poet, songwriter; b. Royal Oak, Mich., Feb. 10, 1951; d. Martin Lewis and Mary Elizabeth (Andrews) Hook; m. Robert Carl Nelson, Sept. 18, 1971 (div. Apr. 1983); children: Jennifer, Christina, David; m. Robert Marx Redmon, Mar. 23, 1985; 1 child, Karl. Grad., h.S., 1969. Contbr. poetry to 10 Best Poets of the 90s, Watermark Press, 10 Best Poets of the 90s, Nat. Library of Poetry, Poetic Voices of Am., 1998, The Best Poets, Nat. Library of Poets, 1991, others; pub. in numerous anthologies. Sgt. USAF, 1970-75. Recipient awards World of Poetry, 1991, 1997; named to Internat. Poetry Hall of Fame, 1997. Mem. Internat. Soc. Poets (life; bd. advisors), Humane Soc. U.S. Avocations: cooking, reading, gardening, spirituality. Home: 4169 Old Brandon Rd Jackson MS 39208-3010 Personal E-mail: cynthiaaredmon@yahoo.com.

REDMOND, DAVID DUDLEY, lawyer; b. Hartford, Conn., May 12, 1944; s. Robert LaVere and Dorothy Iva (Mylchreest) R.; m. Eugenia Blount Scott, Aug. 24, 1968; children: R. Scott, Sarah D. BA, Washington and Lee U., 1966, LLB, 1969. Bar: Va. 1970, U.S. Dist. Ct. (ea. dist.) Va. 1972, U.S. Ct. Appeals (4th cir.) 1972. Ptnr. Christian & Barton LLP, Richmond, Va., 1972—. Mem. editl. bd. Washington and Lee U. Law Rev., 1968—69. Trustee St. Joseph's Villa, 1998—, chmn. bd. trustees, 2004—06. Capt. US Army, 1970—71. Decorated Bronze Star; named to Washington and Lee U. Athletic Hall of Fame. Mem.: George Washington Soc. (bd. dirs. 2002—06), Richmond Bar Assn. (exec. com. 1980), Va. Bar Assn., Va. State Bar, Washington and Lee Law Alumni Assn. (bd. dirs. 1993—2002, pres. 1995—96), Washington and Lee U. Alumni Assn. (pres. Richmond chpt. 1980—82, bd. dirs. 1997—99, 2003—07, exec. com. 2005—07), Matindale-Hubbell AV (peer review), Legal Elite (Va. Bus. exec. 2001—08), Va. Super Lawyers, Omicron Delta Kappa. Office: Mutual Bldg Ste 1200 Richmond VA 23219 Office Phone: 804-697-4102. Business E-Mail: dredmond@cblaw.com.

REDMOND, DONALD EUGENE, JR., neuroscientist, educator; b. San Antonio, June 17, 1939; s. Donald Eugene and Viola (Kellum) R.; m. Patricia Welder (Robinson), Dec. 22, 1972; one child Andy J. BA, So. Meth. U., 1961; MD, Baylor U., 1968; MAH, Yale U., 1987. Diplomate Am. Bd. Psychiatry and Neurology. With Lab. of Clin. Sci., NIMH, Bethesda, Md., 1973-74; asst. prof. psychiatry Yale U., New Haven, 1974-77; assoc. chief clin. neurol. sci. unit Conn. Mental Health Ctr., New Haven, 1974-87; assoc. prof. psychiatry Yale U., New Haven, 1978-87; pres. St. Kitts Bio Med. Rsch. Found., St. Kitts, West Indies, 1983—, Axion Rsch. Found., Hamden, Conn., 1985—; prof. psychiatry, dir. neurol. behavior lab. Yale U., New Haven, 1987—, dir. neurol. transplant program for neurol. diseases, 1987—; prof. neurol. surgery, 1993—; with Yale Univ., New Haven, 1993. Contbr. articles to profl. jour.; patentee in field. With USPHS, 1972-74. Recipient Rsch. Scientist Award NIMH, 1980-2001; Found. Fund Prize, Am. Psychiatric Assoc., 1981; grantee NIMH, 1974-91; Nat. Inst. Neurol. Diseases and Stroke, 1986—; others. Mem.: Internat. Soc. Motor Disturbances, Am. Soc. Neural Transplantation and Repair (coun. mem. 1994—98, pres. 2002), Am. Coll. Neuropsychopharmacology (fellow 2002—03). Office: Yale Sch Medicine 300 George St 9th Fl Ste 32 New Haven CT 06511-6624 Office Phone: 203-785-4432.

REDMOND, ELSA M., anthropologist; BA in Anthropology, Rice Univ., Houston, 1973; MPH, Yale Univ., 1976, PhD, 1981. Anthropology faculty Univ. Conn., Yale Univ., Hunter Coll., Columbia Univ.; rsch. assoc. Am. Mus. Natural History, NYC, 1991—. Fellow: Am. Acad. Arts & Scis. Office: Anthropology Divsn Am Mus Natural History Central Pk W at 79th St New York NY 10024 Office Phone: 212-769-5898. Office Fax: 212-769-5334. Business E-Mail: eredmond@amnh.org.

REDMOND, RHONDA JEAN, psychologist; b. Rome, NY, Aug. 13, 1962; d. Gerald Redmond Jr. and Norma Joyce Redmond. M, SUNY, Oswego, 1997; PhD attending, Walden U., Maryland, 2008—. Cert. sch. neuropsychologist Tex. Woman's U., 2004. Neuropsychologist Morrisville-Eaton Sch. Dist., NY, 1998—, psychologist, 1998—. Blood donor ARC, Oneida, NY, 2006—08. Mem.: Am. Bd. Sch. Neuropsychologist, Alpha Sigma Lambda (Alpha Sigma Lambda 1991). Home: 1028 Upper Lenox Ave Oneida NY 13421 Office: Morrisville-Eaton Sch Dist PO Box 990 55 Eaton St Morrisville NY 13408 Office Fax: 315-684-7252. Personal E-mail: rredmon2@twcny.rr.com. Business E-Mail: rredmond@m-ecs.org.

REDMON-HOLLIDAY, ROSE MARIE, secondary school educator; b. Pasadena, Calif., Sept. 24, 1952; d. Earl Eugene and Rose Ellen (Jackson) R.; m. Dwight Holliday; 1 child, Matthew Eugene. AA, Midway Jr. Coll., 1972; BS, SUNY, Brockport, 1973; MS, Emporia State U., 1981. Cert. secondary edn. tchr., Minn., NY, Ky. Educator Kansas City (Kans.) Pub. Schs., 1974-81; instr. U. Minn., Morris, 1981-82; educator Spl. Sch. Dist. 1, Folwell Jr., Mpls., 1982-83; educator, mid. sch. coord. Webster Open Sch., Mpls., 1983-2000; mid. sch. coord. Jordan Park Sch. Extended Learning, Mpls., 2000—04; title I Math. tchr. Olson Middle Sch., Mpls., 2004—05; tchr. math. Christian County HS, Hopkinsville, Ky., 2005—. Bd. dirs. Grace Meth. Pre-sch., Mpls., 1988-96. Mem. NEA, ASCD, Am. Fedn. Tchrs., Mpls. Fedn. Tchrs., Nat. Coun. Tchrs. Math., Nat. Youth Leadership Coun., Secondary Edn. Task Force Mpls., Minn. Ednl. Effectiveness Project, Mpls. Edn. Assn. Democrat. Mailing: PO Box 678 Murray KY 42071 Office: Christian County HS 220 Glass Ave Hopkinsville KY 42240-2499 Home: 311 oakdale Dr Murray KY 42071 Home Phone: 270-767-1187. E-mail: mamaredmon@yahoo.com.

REDMONT, BERNARD SIDNEY, dean, communications educator; b. NYC, Nov. 8, 1918; s. Morris Abraham and Bessie (Kamerman) R.; m. Joan Rothenberg, Mar. 12, 1940; children: Dennis Foster, Jane Carol. BA, CCNY, 1938; M.J., Columbia U., 1939; D.H.L., Fla. Internat. U., 1980. Reporter, book reviewer Bklyn. Daily Eagle, 1936-38; free lance corr. Europe, 1939, Mexico City, 1939-40; telegraph editor, editorial writer Herkimer (N.Y.) Evening Telegram, 1941-42; newswriter U.S. Office of Inter-Am. Affairs (Washington shortwave radio newscasts to Latin Am.), 1942-43, dir. News div., 1944-46; staff corr., bur. chief U.S. News & World Report, Buenos Aires and Paris, 1946-51; columnist Continental Daily Mail, Paris, 1951-53; chief corr. English Lang. World News Service Agence France-Presse, Paris, 1953-65; European corr. Paris news bur. chief Westinghouse Broadcasting Co., Paris, 1961-76; corr., bur. chief CBS News, Moscow, 1976-79, corr. Paris, 1979-81; prof. journalism, dir. broadcast journalism program, dean Boston U. Coll. Communication, 1982-86, dean emeritus, prof. journalism, 1986—, mem. adv. bd. Latin Am. journalism program, 1989—. Cons. Exec. Svc. Corps. of New Eng., 1991—, Internat. Exec. Svc. Corps, 1992—. Author: Risks Worth Taking: The Odyssey of a Foreign Correspondent, Univ. Press of Am., 1992, Friendly Moderation, 1997. Served with USMCR, 1943-44. Decorated Purple Heart, chevalier Legion of Honor (France); recipient award for advancement of journalism Columbia U., 1986, Townsend Harris medal for life achievement, 1991, Yankee Quill award for disting. contbns. to betterment of journalism, 1995; Pulitzer travel fellow; named to Commns. Hall of Fame CCNY, 2002 Mem. Overseas Press Club (award best radio reporting from abroad 1968, 73), Soc. Profl. Journalists, Nat. Press Club, Anglo-American Press Assn. of Paris (pres. 1961, treas. 1970-73, sec. 1974-76) Unitarian Universalist. *Life has more meaning when it affirms, with grace, the Yang and the Yin, reconciling opposites--independence, yet cooperative effort and community caring; courage and hard work, yet moderation and generosity; hatred of injustice, yet kindness,fairness and compassion.*

REDNAM, KRISHNA RAO VENKATA, ophthalmologist; b. Visakhapatnam, India, Aug. 1, 1949; MD, Andhra Med. Coll., 1971. Diplomate Am. Bd. Ophthamology. Internist King George Hosp., Visakhapatnam, 1971-73, res. ophthamology, 1973-76; resident in surgery Jewish Hosp. and Med. Ctr., Bklyn., 1976-77; fellow in glaucoma Eye and Ear Infirmary, 1977-79; fellowship retina & citreous Ill. Eye and Ear Infirmary, Chgo., 1979-82; active staff St. Josephs Hosp., Kirkwood, Mo., 1983—; courtesy staff St. Lukes Hosp., Chesterfield, Mo., 1983—, Alexian Bros., St. Louis, Mo., 1984—, Lutheran Med. Ctr., St. Louis, Mo., 1985—; Courtesy staff St. Anthony Med. Ctr., St. Louis, 1985—; assoc. Depaul Med. Ctr., Bridgeton, Mo., 1985—; staff Out Patient Surg. Ctr., St. Louis, 1986—; assoc. St. Marys Eye Ctr., St. Louis, Mo., 1987—, 1988—; courtesy staff Christian Hosp., St. Louis, Mo., 1993—; provisional staff Mo. Bapt. Hosp., St. Louis, Mo., 1995—. Fellow ACS, Am. Acad. Ophthalmology, Internat. Coll. Surgeons; mem. AMA, Am. Assn. Opthamology. Office: St Louis Eye Clin 4530 Hampton Ave Saint Louis MO 63109-2238 also: St Louis Eye Clinic 4530 Hampton Ave Saint Louis MO 63109-2238 Office Phone: 314-821-2002.

REDO, PHILIP LAPPANO, broadcast executive; b. NYC, Jan. 14, 1956; s. S. Frank and Maria (Lappano) R.; m. Jenette Sherman Kerr, Sept. 30, 1981. BA, Colby Coll., 1978. On-air program dir. Sta. WLOM-FM, Orleans, Mass., 1978-80; on-air asst. program dir. Sta. KLIF-Am, Dallas, 1980; on-air broadcaster Sta. WROR-FM, Boston, 1980-83; live voice over Sta. WNEV-TV, Boston, 1982-83; program dir. Sta. WLTW-FM, NYC, 1983-86; mgr. ops., program dir. Stas. WMEX/WMJX, Boston, 1986-89; v.p., gen. mgr. Sta. WLIT-FM, Chgo., 1989-97; v.p. programming and prodn. MJI Broadcasting/Divsn. Premier Radio Networks, NYC, 1997—2002; v.p. operations & strategy WNYC AM/FM, NYC, 2002—06; v.p., gen. mgr. Greater Media Boston March, 2006—. V.p. Spinnaker Comm., Boston, 1980-84; adv. coun. Arbitron Radio, 1997—. Producer: (broadcasts) Magic of Ireland, 1987 (Gold medal), Magic of Thanksgiving, 1988 (Radio Festival of N.Y. award), A Letter Home, 1990 (Ill. Broadcasters award), and others. Vol. Mus. of Sci., Boston, 1980-81; commr. Hanover (Mass.) Conservation Commn., 1988-90; reader, bd. dirs. Chgo. Reading Info. Svcs., 1990—; pres. Radio Broadcasters of Chicagoland, 1991; mem., sponsor Jr. Achievement; bd. dirs. Chgo. Sinfonietta. Named Personality of Yr., Billboard Mag., 1978. Mem. Nat. Assn. Broadcasters, Corp. Respnsibility Coop., Radio Advt. Bur., Boston Ad Club (bd. trustees), Mass. Broadcasters Assn. (bd. trustees). Democrat. Avocations: reading, sailing, tennis, golf, painting. Home: 65 Commonwealth Ave Apt 6B Boston MA 02116 Office Phone: 617-822-6250. Business E-Mail: predo@greatermediaboston.com.

REDONDO, ANTONIO, physicist; b. Guatemala City, Guatemala, Dec. 10, 1948; came to U.S., 1968; s. Mariano and Paz (Muiño) R.; m. Shelby Lynn Dinteman, June 18, 1971; children: Tomás P., Michael D., Rebecca M. BS magna cum laude, Utah State U., 1971; MS, Calif. Inst. Tech., 1972, PhD, 1977. Asst. prof. physics U. de Los Andes, Mérida, Venezuela, 1977-78, assoc. prof. physics, 1978-80; rsch. assoc. Calif. Inst. Tech., Pasadena, 1980-83; mem. staff Los Alamos (N.Mex.) Nat. Lab., 1983—94, group leader, 1994—2005, divsn. leader, 2005—. Contbr. sci. articles to profl. jours. Woodrow Wilson fellow Calif. Inst. Tech., 1972, IBM Predoctoral fellow IBM Corp., 1975. Democrat. Avocations: soccer, camping, reading. Office: Los Alamos Nat Lab Mail Stop B210 Los Alamos NM 87545

REDSTONE, SHARI ELLIN, amusement company executive; b. Washington, Apr. 14, 1954; d. Sumner and Phyllis Gloria (Raphael) Redstone; m. Yitzhak Aharon Korff (div.); 3 children. BS, Tufts U., 1975; JD, Boston U., 1978, M in Tax Law, 1980. Pvt. law practice, Boston, 1978-93; v.p. corp. planning & devel. Nat. Amusements, Dedham, 1993—94, exec. v.p., 1994—2000, pres., 2000—; non-exec. vice chmn. Viacom Inc., 2006—, CBS Corp., 2006—; vice chmn. Midway Games Inc., 2004—07, chmn., 2007—08. Bd. dirs. William Wrigley Jr. Co., 1994—2005, Viacom Inc., 1994—, Midway Games Inc., 2004—, Global Hyatt Corp., LaSalle Bank Corp.; bd. dir. The Marmon Group; chmn., CEO Rising Star Media, CineBridge Ventures, Inc.; co-chmn., co-CEO MovieTickets.com; mem. exec. com. Boston U. Sch. Law. Bd. dir. Jewish Philanthropies; bd. overseers Harvard U., 2002—, co-chair com. on Allston; bd. dir., exec. com. Nat. Assn. Theatre Owners; trustee, Dana Farber Cancer Inst. Tufts U.; mem. adv. com. Tufts Hillel. Named one of 50 Women to Watch, Wall St. Jour., 2005, The 100 Most Powerful Women in Entertainment, Hollywood Reporter, 2006, 2007. Office: Nat Amusements Inc 200 Elm St Dedham MA 02026-4536*

REDSTONE, SUMNER MURRAY, broadcast executive, lawyer; b. Boston, May 27, 1923; s. Michael and Belle (Ostrovsky) R.; married; children: Brent Dale, Shari Ellin. BA, Harvard U., 1944, LLB, 1947; LLD (hon.), Boston U., 1994; LHD (hon.), NY Inst. Tech., 1996. Bar: Mass. 1947, US Ct. Appeals (1st cir.) 1948, US Ct. Appeals (8th cir.) 1950, US Ct. Appeals (9th cir.) 1948, DC 1951, US Supreme Ct. 1952. Law sec. US Ct. Appeals (9th cir.), San Francisco, 1947-48; instr. law and labor mgmt. U. San Francisco, 1947; spl. asst. to atty. gen. US Dept. Justice, Washington, 1948-51; ptnr. Ford, Bergson, Adams, Borkland & Redstone, Washington, 1951-54; CEO Nat. Amusements Inc., Dedham, Mass., 1967—, pres., 1967—99, chmn. bd., 1986—, Viacom, Inc., NYC, 1987—2006, CEO, 1996—2006, exec. chmn. bd., 2006—; chmn. bd. CBS Corp., 2006—. Prof. Boston U. Law Sch., 1982, 85-86; bd. dirs., adv. coun. TV Acad. Arts and Scis. Found.; vis. prof. Brandeis U., Waltham, Mass.; lectr. Harvard Law Sch., Cambridge, Mass.; Judge on Kennedy Libr. Found., (sel. comm. John F. Kennedy Profile in Courage award); bd. trustee Mus. TV and Radio; past pres. Theatre Owners Am. Chmn. met. divsn. NE Combined Jewish Philanthropies, Boston, 1963; mem. exec. bd. Combined Jewish Philanthropies of Greater Boston, chmn. met. divsn.; mem. corp. New Eng. Med. Ctr., 1967—, Mass. Gen. Hosp. Corp.; trustee Children's Cancer Rsch. Found.; founding trustee Am. Cancer Soc.; chmn. Am. Cancer Crusade, State of Mass., 1984-86; Art Lending Libr.; sponsor Boston Mus. Sci.; chmn. Jimmy Fund Found., 1960; v.p., mem. exec. com. Will Rogers Meml. Fund; hon. chmn. Will Rodgers Motion Picture Pioneers Found.; bd. dirs. Boston Arts Festival; bd. overseers Dana Farber Cancer Ctr., Boston Mus. Fine Arts; mem. presdl. adv. com. on arts John F. Kennedy Libr. Found., also judge ann. John F. Kennedy Profile in Courage Award com.; chmn. Corp. Commn. on Edn. Tech., 1996—, presdl. apptd. chmn., 1996. 1st lt. AUS, 1943-45. Decorated Army Commendation medal; named 1 of 10 Outstanding Young Men in New Eng., Boston Jr. C. of C., 1958; recipient William J. German Human Rels. award Am. Jewish Com. Entertainment/Comm. Divsn., 1977, Silver Shingle award Boston U. Law Sch., 1985, Variety New Eng. Humanitarian award, 1989, Golden Plate award Am. Acad. Achievement, 1993, 32d Ann. Salute to Excellence Program, 1993, Bus. Excellence award U. So. Calif. Sch. Bus. Adminstrn., 1994, The Stephen S. Wise award The Am. Jewish Congress, 1994, Man of Yr. award MIPCOM, the Internat. Film and Programme Market for TV, Video, Cable and Satellite, 1994, The Legends in Leadership award Emory U., 1995, Allan K. Jonas Lifetime Achievement award Am. Cancer Soc., 1995, Humanitarian award Variety Club Internat., 1995, Expeditioner's award NYC Outward Bound Ctr., 1996, Patron Arts award Songwriter's Hall Fame, 1996, Vision 21 award NY Inst. Tech., 1996, Trustees award NATAS, 1997, Ripple of Hope award Robert F. Kennedy Meml., 1998, Humanitarian award Nat. Conf. Christians and Jews, 1998; named Communicator of Yr., B'nai B'rith Comm./Cinema Lodge, 1980, Man of Yr., Entertainment Industries Divsn. of UJA Fedn., 1988, Pioneer of Yr., Motion Picture Pioneers, 1991, Grad. of Yr., Boston Latin Sch., 1989, Honoree 7th ann. fundraiser Montefiore Med. Ctr., 1995, Hall of Fame award Broadcasting and Cable mag., 1995; named one of World's Richest People, Forbes Mag., 1999-2007. Mem. ABA, Nat. Assn. Theatre Owners (chmn. bd. dirs. 1965-66, exec. comm. 1995—), Theatre Owners Am. (asst. pres. 1960-63, pres. 1964-65), Motion Picture Pioneers (bd. dirs.), Boston Bar Assn., Mass. Bar Assn., Harvard Law Sch. Assn., Am. Judicature Soc., Masons, Univ. Club, Harvard Club. Office: Viacom Inc 1515 Broadway New York NY 10036 also: Nat Amusements Inc PO Box 9126 Dedham MA 02027-9126 also: CBS Corp 51 W 52nd St New York NY 10019-6188*

REDWANSKI, JOHN, medical educator; s. John Louis Redwanski and Peggy Hicks, Steven Hicks (Stepfather); m. Merrie Noble, Mar. 17, 2001. BS, Ball State U., Muncie, Ind., 1992; PharmD, Purdue U., West Lafayette, Ind., 2003. Asst. prof. Hampton U., Va., 2004—. Peer-reviewer Natural Std., Cambridge, Mass., 2004—. Vol. Soc. Prevention Cruelty to Animals, Va. Named Preceptor of Yr., Hampton U. Sch. Pharmacy, 2006—07. Mem.: Drug Info. Assn., Va. Soc. Health Sys. Pharmacists (faculty liasion 2004—), Am. Assn. Coll. Pharmacy, Am. Soc. Health-Sys. Pharmacists (coun. pharmacy practice 2006—07). Liberal. Office: Hampton Univ Kittrell Hall Hampton VA 23668 Home Fax: 757-728-6696. Business E-Mail: john.redwanski2@hamptonu.edu.

REDWINE, JOHN NEWLAND, state legislator, physician; b. Pratt, Kans., Oct. 28, 1950; s. Albert Herold and Joyce Nadean (Durall R.; m. Barbara Ann Bomgaars, Dec. 27, 1975; children: John Newland II, William Merritt, Adam Boone. BA with honors, U. Kans., 1972; cert. med. technology, U. Tex. at Houston, 1974; DO, U. Medicine and Bioscis., Kansas City, Mo., 1978. Diplomate Am. Bd. Family Medicine. Intern U. Hosp., Ctr. for Health Scis., Kansas City, Mo., 1978-79; family practice resident Siouxland Med. Edn. Found., Sioux City, Iowa, 1979-81; med. dir. Morningside Family Practice, Sioux City, 1981-95; v.p. St. Luke's Health Sys., Inc., Sioux City, Iowa, 1995-2001; primary care physician Cmty. Based Outpatient Clinic Dept. Veterans Affairs, 2001—04; mem. Iowa Senate from 2nd dist., Des Moines, 1996—2003; mem. med. staff Sioux Falls VA Med. Ctr., SD, 2002—04, Fayetteville VA Med. Ctr., Ark., 2004—07; chmn. Siouxland Instnl. Rev. Bd., 2002—04. Sr. aviation med. examiner FAA, 1979—95; clin. lectr. Iowa U. Coll. Medicine, Iowa City, 1983—95; pres. Siouxland Med. Edn. Found., 1982—2001; past chmn. family practice St. Luke's Regional Med. Ctr., Sioux City, Iowa, pres.-elect, 1993—95; chmn. Siouxland Instl. Rev. Bd., 2002—. Contbr. articles to profl. jours. Past v.p. Prairie Gold Area coun. Boy Scouts Am., Sioux City, bd. dirs. Mid.Am. coun., 1984-2004; bd. dirs. New Perspectives, Inc., 1996-2002, Sioux City Cmty. Sch. Dist., 1994-97, Crittenton Ctr., 2000-04, Morningside Coll., 2000-04; elected 2d dist. Iowa Senate, 1996-2003, asst. majority leader, 1998-2002. Recipient achievement award Upjohn Pharm. Co., Kansas City, 1978, Silver Beaver award Prairie Gold Area Coun., Boy Scouts Am., 1997, Pub. Ofcl. award Siouxland Dist. Health Dept., 1998, Leadership award Iowans for LIFE, 2000, Guardian of Small Bus. award Nat. Fedn. Ind. Bus., 2001, Iowa Friend of the Family award Christian Coalition Iowa, 2001, 02, Legis. award Iowa Acad. Family Practice, 2002. Fellow Am. Acad. Family Physicians; mem. AMA, Am. Osteo. Assn., Iowa Med. Soc., Woodbury Med. Soc. (past pres.), Flying Physicians Assn. Republican. Avocation: politics. Personal E-mail: john@redwine.org.

REEBERG, PATRICIA ALDORA, minister, entrepreneur; d. Henrietta Monroe. MDiv., Union Theol. Sem., NYC, 1989. Cert. Cmty. Devel. Leadership Harvard Div. Sch., Mass., 1999, Inst. for Not-for-Profit Mgmt. Columbia U., Grad. Sch. of Bus., NY, 1992. Pres./owner SM&G Corp., Bronx, NY, 1994—; pres./chief exec. officer Concord Cmty. Devel. Corp., Bklyn., 1998—; CEO Coun. of Chs. of the City of NY, NY, 1990—94; asst. pastor St. Paul Bapt. Ch., NYC, 1985—; chaplain NY State Dept. of Correctional Svcs., NYC, 1983—89. Cons. Ford Found., NYC, 2000—01, Rockefeller Found., NYC, 1997—97, Fedn. of Protestant Welfare Agencies, NYC, 2002—, NY Work Alliance, NYC, 2003—. Pastor rejoice ministries Ch. Healing Inc.; commr. Civilian Complaint Rev. Bd., NYC, 1993—95; bd. mem. NY State Regents, NYC, 1995—2001, Harlem Congregation for Cmty. Improvement, NYC, 1994—2005. Recipient Good News Maker Award, NY Christian Times, Dedicated Leadership Award, New Voices of Harlem, Outstanding Women Role Model Award, Nat. Assn. of Negro Bus. & Profl. Women's Club, Cert. of Merit, N.Y. Bd. of Rabbis, Elders of Vision Award, Harlem Congregation for Cmty. Devel.; grantee Rsch. Grant, Louisville Inst.; Charles Merrill Fellowship, Harvard Div. Sch. Achievements include first woman elected as of the CEO council of churches of the city of NY in its 183 year history; first woman appointed assistant pastor of St. Paul Baptist Church in its 112 year history; first chaplain appointed to the NYC board of education. Home and Office: SM&G Corp 3403 Cannon Pl Bronx NY 10463-4301 Office Fax: 718-548-4427; Home Fax: 718-548-4386. Business E-Mail: reebergsmg@aol.com.

REECE, ALTON DAVIS, JR., science educator; b. Greensboro, Nc, Apr. 13, 1950; s. Alton Davis and LaVerne Lee Reece; m. Sarah Dawn Mayhew, Oct. 26, 1959; 1 child, Meredith Ashley. BS - Intermediate Sci. Edn., East Carolina U., Greenville, North Carolina, 1968—72. Science Specialist NSTA, 1990. Sci. tchr. Lincoln Jr. High, Greensboro, NC, 1972—85, Lincoln Mid. Sch., Greensboro, NC, 1985—87; sci. specialist Wash. Magnet Sch. of Sci. and Tech., Greensboro, NC, 1987—95; sci. tchr. Lincoln Mid. Sch., Greensboro, NC, 1995—2001, NE Mid. Sch., McLeansville, NC, 2001—. Content consultant (software) Scholastic Science Explorer, coauthor (textbook) Integrated Science Book I - Teacher's Annotated Edition, Integrated Science Book II - Teacher's Annotated Edition, Integrated Science Book II - Teacher Resource Book, Integrated Science - Change within Systems - Grade 8 - Teacher's Annotated Edition, Integrated Science - System and Diversity - Grade 7 - Teacher's Annotated Edition. Recipient Outstanding Jr. H.S. Tchr. of the Yr. Award, Greensboro PTA Coun., 1980, Disting. Svc. to Sci. Edn. Award, NC Sci. Teacher's Assn., 1981, Tchr. of the Yr., Greensboro Pub. Schools, 1981, Cert. of Recognition for Dedication to the Tchg. of Sci., Sigma Xi Sci. Rsch. Soc., 1987, Calvin H. Wiley Excellence in Pub. Edn. Award, Greensboro Area Chamber of Commerce, 1987, Tchg. Excellence Award, Greensboro Pub. Sch. Fund, 1987, Region 5 Outstanding Sci. Tchr. Award, NC Dept. of Pub. Instrn., 1987, NC Outstanding Sci. Tchr. Award, NC Governor's Bus. Com. for Edn., 1987, Mach S. Baker / Mary Kearns Disting. Svc. to Sci. Award, Guilford County Schools Bus. Adv. Bd. for Sci. and Math., 2002. Mem.: Nat. Sci. Teacher's Assn. (life). Office: Guilford County Schools North Eugene Street Greensboro NC 27401 Personal E-mail: science501@earthlink.net.

REECE, BELYNDA M., minister, military officer, consultant; b. San Diego, May 2, 1956; d. Hubert Jackson and Elizabeth Ann (Seifert) Reece. AS in Environ. Health Tech., Merrit Coll., Oakland, Calif., 1977—83; BS in Liberal Arts, SUNY, Albany, 1994; MDiv in Theology, Colgate Rochester Div. Sch., NY, 1995—97; studied, Capella U., Mpls., 2004—. Gen. duty corpsman Naval Support Activity, New Orleans, 1975—76; gen. duty hosp. corpsman Naval Regional Med. Ctr., New Orleans, 1976—77; preventive medicine tech. Navy Environ. and Preventive Medicine Unit No. 7, Naples, Italy, 1977—80, Navy Environ. and Preventive Medicine Unit No. 5, San Diego, 1980—83; instr. staff Preventive Medicine Tech. Sch., Oakland, Calif., 1983—85; leading chief petty officer, med. dept. Cmdr. Fleet Activities, Chinhae, Republic of Korea, 1985—87; supr., joint coord. preventive medicine svc. Naval Hosp., Camp Pendleton, Calif., 1988—89; leading chief petty officer, med. dept. USS Shenandoah, Norfolk, Va., 1990—92; hosp. corps plan officer Navy Bur. Medicine & Surgery, Washington, 1992—95; chap.

Strong Meml. Hosp., Rochester, NY, 1996—97; asst. pastor United Methodist Ch. N. Chili, Rochester, NY, 1996—97, sr. pastor, 2000—04; pastor for spiritual devel. Kenmore United Methodist Ch., NY, 1997—2000; sr. pastor United Meth. Ch., NY, 2002—04; cons. Webb & Assocs. Chap. Cons., Oceanside, Calif., 2004—. Cons. USMC, Camp Pendleton, Calif., 2004—. Decorated Meritorious Svc. Medal, 2 Navy Commendation Medals, Navy Achievement Medal, Good Conduct Medal, Meritorious Unit Commendation, Nat. Def. Medal, S.W. Asia Svc. Medal (with bronze star), Sea Svc. Deployment Medal, 4 Overseas Svc. Ribbons, Kuwait Liberation Medal; recipient Shore Sailor of Yr., Bur. Medicine and Surgery, 1979; finalist Navy Shore Sailor of Yr., 1979, Stephen W. Brown Preventive Medicine Tech. of Yr., HMCM, 1989. Mem.: VFW, Am. Legion, Internat. Critical Incident Stress Found., Am. Assn. Christian Counselors.

REECE, BETH PAULEY, chaplain; b. Warsaw, Ind., June 4, 1945; d. Lester Elden and Genevene (Walter) Pifer; m. Gyle Barry Reece, June 20, 1987. BA, Grace Coll., 1967; degree in interior design, Harrington Inst. Design, Chgo., 1995; attended, Cambridge U., Oxford U., Eng., Trinity Coll., Dublin, 1999, U. Edinburgh, 2001; grad., Inst. Spiritual Companionship, 2000—02; postgrad., North Park Sem., Chgo., 2004, Loyola Inst. Pastoral Studies, 2006—. Cert. hosp. chaplain Assn. Profl. Chaplains, 2007. Grain trader, hedger Ctrl. Soya Inc., Ft. Wayne, Ind., 1973-82; account exec. ACLI Internat. Inc., Chgo., 1982-83; account exec., hedger Ctrl. States Enterprises, Ft. Wayne, 1983-84; account exec. Stotler & Co., Chgo., 1984-89, LaSalle Brokerage Inc., Chgo., 1989—2003; hosp. chaplain Rehab. Inst. Chgo., 2004—. Mem. Spiritual Dirs. Internat., Alpha Sigma Nu. Presbyterian. Avocations: reading, sailing, travel. Home: 227 E Delaware Pl Apt 5C Chicago IL 60611-7758 E-mail: bethreece64@msn.com.

REECE, DAVID BRYSON, information systems administrator; b. Phoenix, Aug. 5, 1953; s. Frank Williams and Margaret Leonora (Bryson) W.; div.; children: Ashley Cambridge, Christopher David. ADN, Phoenix C.C., 1974; Baccalaureate Sci. Wholistic Nursing, Westbrook U., 1991, Master Sci. Wholistic Nursing, 1992, PhD, 1993. Lic. pvt. glide pilot. V.p. Young Nursing Svc., Kingman, Ariz., 1987-89; dean of nursing, co-founder Sch. Wholistic Nursing Westbrook U., Aztec, N.Mex., 1994-2000; co-founder Auditors Unlimited, Inc., Phoenix, 1997, bd. dirs., 1998-2000; CEO Ashfork (Ariz.) Inst., 2004—, Ashfork Rapid Prototyping R&D Ctr., 2006. Author: Minerals, Metals and Gemstones of the Holy Bible, 1998, Wholistic Nursing Theory, 1998, Homeopathy: Introduction to Healthcare Professional, Computer: Computer Based Training for Nursing, Database Administration Fraud & Abuse Analysis, Software Development, 1% Solution-Ergonomic Designs for the Exceptionally Tall and Big, 2000-04, Pre-Nursing, Preparing for Nursing School, 2004, others. Pres. Healingworks Inst. nursing rsch. ctr., Creative Wellness Inst. edn. ctr. Recipient Silver Badge, two gold and one diamond, Internat. Soaring awards. Mem. Ariz. Assn. Healthcare Agys. (bd. dirs. 1988-90), Soaring Soc. Am., Exptl. Aircraft Assn. Avocations: flying, treasure hunting, amateur radio.

REECE, E. ALBERT, dean, obstetrician, gynecologist, perinatologist; b. Spanishtown, Jamaica, Jan. 3, 1950; came to U.S., 1969; s. Wilfred Anderson Reece and Daisy Lucinda (Price) Reece Batten; m. Sharon Andrea Blake, July 28, 1974; children: Kelie, Brynne, Sharon-Andrea II. BS with honors, L.I. U., 1973; MD, NYU, 1978; PhD in Biochemistry, U. West Indies; MBA, Fox Sch. Bus. Mgmt., Temple U.; ob/gyn specialty diploma, Columbia U., 1982; maternal-fetal subspecialty diploma, Yale U., 1984. Diplomate Am. Bd. Ob-Gyn.; bd. cert. maternal-fetal medicine. Intern, resident Columbia U., Presbyn. Med. Ctr., NYC, 1978-82; materal-fetal medicine fellow Yale U. Sch. Medicine, 1982-84, asst. prof. ob-gyn New Haven, 1984-87, assoc. prof. ob-gyn, 1987-90; Abraham Roth prof., chmn. obstetrics, Gynecology and reproductive sciences Temple U. Sch. Medicine, Phila., 1991—2001; vice chancellor, dean, v.p. for med. sciences U. of Arkansas for Med. Sciences, Coll. of Med., Little Rock, 2002—06; John Z. and Akiko K. Bowers disting. prof., dean U. Md. Sch. of Medicine, 2006—; v.p. med. affairs U. Md., 2006—. Elected IOM (chair pediatrics, obstetrics & gynecology, 2003-), NAS, 1998. Co-editor Diabetes Mellitus in Pregnancy: Principles and Practice, 1st edit., 1988, 2nd edit., 1995, Medicine of the Fetus and Mother, 1992, 2nd edit., 1999, A Study Guide for Medicine of the Fetus and Mother, 1992, A Handbook of Medicine of the Fetus and Mother, 1995; co-author: Fundamentals in Obstetric and Gynecologic Ultrasonography, 1993; contbr. articles, abstract to profl. jours. in excess of 400. Mem. sci. adv. com. March of Dimes, 1993—; mem. sci. adv. bd. NIH-DC Infant Mortality Initiative, 1993—; mem. adv. com. Nat. Inst. Child Health and Human Diseases, NIH, 1994—; trustee Reading Rehab. Hosp., 1992—; mem. bioeffects com. AIUM, 1992-95. Grantee March of Dimes, 1985-87, Friedman Found., 1990-92, William Penn Found., 1989-93, Am. Diabetes Assn., 1991-93, NIH, 1992—; named one of Top 100 Black Physicians in Am., Black Enterprise Mag., 2001. Fellow Am. Coll. Ob-Gyn., Coll. Physicians Phila.; mem. Am. Diabetes Assn. (coun. on diabetes in pregnancy), Am. Inst. Ultrasound in Medicine, Hellenic Perinatal Soc. Greece (hon.), Nat. Med. Assn. (exec. com. 1987-88, chmn. ob-gyn. sect. 1991-93), NAS Inst. Medicine ((in conjunction with NRC) mem. adv. com., Human Embryonic Stem Cell Rsch., 2006-), New Haven Obstet. Soc., Soc. for Gynecol. Investigation, Soc. Perinatal Obstetricians (leader diabetes spl. interest 1992-94, bd. mem. 1995—), Phila. Perinatal Soc. (program chair 1993—), Phila. Obstet. Soc. (mem. coun. 1992-94). Seventh-Day Adventist. Office: U Md Sch Medicine 14-029, Bressler Rsch Bldg 655 W Baltimore St Baltimore MD 21201-1559 Office Phone: 410-706-7410. Office Fax: 410-706-0235. E-mail: deanmed@som.umaryland.edu.*

REECE, GWENDOLYN J., academic administrator; d. Robert D. and Donna W. Reece. MA, U. Calif., Santa Barbara, 1995; MS, Simmons Coll., Boston, 1996; PhD, Am. U., Washington, 2007. Reference, instrn., web libr. Am. U., 1998—2004, access services libr., 2004—08, dir. rsch., tchg., and learning, 2008—. Reference libr. Wright State U., Dayton, Ohio, 1996—97. Contbr. articles to profl. jours. Pres. Theosophical Soc. DC, 2007—08. Office: Am Univ 4400 Massachusetts Ave NW Washington DC 20016 Office Fax: 202-885-1317. Business E-Mail: greece@american.edu.

REECE, JULIA RUTH, systems analyst, entrepreneur; b. Detroit, Oct. 25, 1958; d. William James and Julia Henrietta (Thomas) Coleman; m. Darnell Fuller, Nov. 10, 1984 (div. Dec. 1988); m. Terry Allen Reece, July 2, 2001. BA in Computer Sci., Wayne State U., 1980. Programmer, analyst Mich. Bell Telephone Co., Detroit, 1980—82; tech. support analyst Unisys Corp. (formally Burroughs), Detroit, 1982-91; owner JR & Assocs. Computer Svcs., Detroit, 1991—; computer cons. Comprehensive Data Processing, Detroit, 1991-94; sr. programmer, analyst City of Detroit, 1994-00, prin. programmer/analyst, 2000—. Musician Met. Cmty. Tabernacle, Detroit, 1975—84, 1988—2000, Greater Faith New Covenant Assembly, Detroit, 1985—87. Independent. Avocations: reading, travel, music, cooking, computers. Business E-Mail: fullerj@detroitmi.gov. E-mail: ladyjr@ameritech.net.

REECE, KARYN LYNN, business owner, consultant; d. George John and Eleanor Roberta (O'Donnell) R. BS in Bus., SUNY, Buffalo, 1998. Lic. stockbroker, series 7, insurance lic., fin. cons., NY. Lic. stockbroker, insurance Cook Fin. Group, Buffalo, 1990—; ind. fin. cons., 1992—; psychic cons. Author: Caught Between Two Worlds:" A Psychic Detectives Experience in Solving Crimes and Hidden Agendas, The Lighter Side of the Other Side. Mem. Women Everywhere. Independent. Avocations: drawing, aerobics, figure skating. Office Phone: 866-735-3715.

REECE, MARLENE WILLIAMS, elementary school educator; b. Marshalltown, Iowa, Dec. 24, 1950; d. Arthur L. and Donna Joan (Parsons) Williams; m. Dennis E. Reece; children: Matthew, Christopher, Allison Lakshmi. Student, William Penn Coll.; BA in Early Childhood Edn., U. No. Iowa, 1973, BA in Elem. Edn., 1981. Cert. early childhood and elem. edn. Tchr., presch. dir. Union (Iowa) Sch.; mid. sch. reading and math. tchr. Eldora (Iowa)-New Providence Schs., tchr. 4th grade and talented and gifted, 1st and 2d multiage classrm. tchr., Title I reading specialist. Mem. NEA, Iowa State Edn. Assn., Iowa Reading Assn., Iowa Coun. Tchrs. Math., Eldora-New Providence Edn. Assn. (pres., sec. pub. rels.), Hardy Reading Coun. Avocations: music, reading, travel, creative writing. Home: PO Box 73 New Providence IA 50206-0073

REECE, MAYNARD FRED, artist, writer; b. Arnolds Park, Iowa, Apr. 26, 1920; s. Waldo H. and Inez V. (Latson) R.; m. June Carman, Apr. 7, 1946; children: Mark A., Brad D. Privately educated. Artist Meredith Pub. Co., Des Moines, 1938-40; artist, asst., mus. dir. Iowa Dept. History and Archives, Des Moines, 1940-50. Artist: Fish and Fishing, 1963, Waterfowl of Iowa, 1943; watercolor Trout, Saturday Evening Post (award of Distinctive Merit 1962); watercolors 73 Fish, Life mag. (cert. of merit 1955); print of Water's Edge Canada Geese for Am. Artist Collection, Am. Artist Mag., 1985; author, artist: The Waterfowl Art of Maynard Reece, 1985, The Upland Bird Art of Maynard Reece, 1997. Chmn. Gov.'s Com. Conservation of Outdoor Resource, 1963-64; trustee Iowa Natural Heritage Found., Des Moines, 1979—; hon. trustee Ducks Unltd., Inc., 1983—; trustee J.N. "Ding" Darling Conservation Found., Inc., Des Moines, 1962—. Served with AUS, 1943-45. Recipient awards for duck stamps and others Dept. Interior, 1948, 51, 59, 69, 71; recipient award Govt. Bermuda, 1963, award Iowa Conservation Commn., 1972, 77, 80, 81, award Fish and Game Commn., Little Rock, 1982, 88, award Tex. Parks and Wild Life Dept., 1983, award Nat. Fish & Wildlife Found., 1988, award Wash. State Dept. Wildlife, 1989, award Idaho Dept. Fish & Game, 1998, 4 awards Ill. Dept. of Natural Resources, 1997-2000; named Artist of Yr. Ducks Unltd. Inc., 1973; chosen Master Artist 1989, Leigh Yawkey Woodson Art Mus., Wausau, Wis., 1989. Mem. Nat. Audubon Soc., Nat. Wildlife Fedn., Izaak Walton League Am. (hon. pres. 1974-75). Home and Office: 5315 Robertson Dr Des Moines IA 50312-2133 Office Phone: 515-277-3623.

REECE-PORTER, SHARON ANN, international human rights educator; b. Cin., Nov. 28, 1953; d. Edward and Claudia (Ownes) Reece; div., 1981; children: Erika Lynn, Melanie Joyce. BS in Textiles and Clothing, Edgecliff Coll., 1975; cert. clerical computer, So. Ohio Coll., 1984; MEd in Gen. Edn., SUNY, Buffalo, 1994; PhD in Internat. Human Rights Devel., Brentwick U., London, 2000; EdD in Global Edn. (hon.), Australian Inst. Coordinated Rsch., Victoria, 1995; postgrad. in photojournalism/profl. photography, NY Inst. Photography, 2002—. Cert. tchr. Ohio. Dept. supr., asst. buyer Mabley & Carew, Cin., 1975—76; claims adjuster Allstate Ins. Co., Cin., 1976—78; sales merchandiser Ekco Houseware, Cin., 1979—80; sales rep. Met. Life Inc., Cin., 1981—83; info. processing specialist GPA/Robert Half/Word Source, Cin., Dallas, 1985—87; tchr. adult edn. Princeton City Schs., Cin., 1984—90; with Rainbow Internat. Non-Profit Adult Ednl. Rsch. Ctr., Honolulu, 1990—98, Norfolk, Va., 1998—; specialist edn. rsch. found. SUNY, Buffalo, 1993; human rights investigator Citizens Commn. on Human Rights Internat., LA, 2005—. Prof. computer sci. So. Ohio Tech. and Bus. Coll., Cin., 1986-90; computer software tng. cons., 1987-89; part-time tchr. adult GED classes Adult Learning Ctr. Buffalo Bd. Edn., 1994-95; participant Am. Forum for Global Edn., Honolulu; lectr. photography N.Y. Inst. Photography, N.Y.C., N.Y., 2002—. Tutor U.S. divsn. Internat. Laubach Lit., Clermont County, Ohio, 1984; coordinate workshops Dianetics Found., Virginia Beach, Va.; human rights investigator Citizens Commission for Human Rights, Virgina Beach. Fellow Australian Inst. for Coordinated Rsch. (life); mem. NAFE, ASTD, Internat. DOS Users Group, Am. Ednl. Rsch. Assn., Nat. Assn. Women Bus. Owners, UN Assn., World Assn. Women Entrepreneurs, Boston Computer Soc., Cin. Orgn. Data Processing Educators and Trainers, Internat. Platform Assn., Cin. C. of C. (cert. minority supplier devel. coun.), Dianetics Found. (co-coord. workshops). Home: 2941 Chilton Pl Virginia Beach VA 23456 Office: Global Human Rights & Artistic Impressions PO Box 56544 Virginia Beach VA 23456 Personal E-mail: humanrtssharonan@msn.com.

REED, ADAM VICTOR, psychologist, engineer, information scientist; b. Torun, Poland, Jan. 11, 1946; arrived in US, 1959, naturalized, 1965; s. Henry Kenneth and Eva (Tenenbaum) Reed; m. Barbara Irene Birnbaum, 1982 (div. 2000); 1 child, Halina Brooke. BSEE, MIT, 1967, MS in Biology, MSEE, 1970; PhD, U. Oreg., 1974. Rsch. programmer Artificial Intelligence Lab. MIT, Cambridge, 1965; rsch. engr. Hewlett Packard Co., Palo Alto, Calif., 1966-67; mem. rsch. staff Riverside Rsch. Inst., NYC, 1970-71; postdoctoral fellow, adj. asst. prof. Rockefeller U., NYC, 1974-78; asst. prof., vis. lectr. psychology New Sch. Social Rsch., NYC, 1977-82; mem. tech. staff Bell Labs., 1981—99; from assoc. prof. to prof. Calif. State U., LA, 2000—06, prof. Info. Sys., 2006—. Peer rev. referee NSF, others. Contbr. articles to profl. jours. Sci. and tech. adv. LIbertarian v.p. candidate Tonie Nathan, 1972; mem. Marlboro Twp. Bd. Edn., N.J., 1994-97. NDEA Title IV fellow, 1967-70, NSF fellow, 1970-73, NIMH Rsch. Svc. fellow, 1974-77. Mem. Sigma Xi, Tau Beta Pi, Eta Kappa Nu. Achievements include patents in field; first implementation of steepest descent, first statistically adaptive user interface, first switch-based facsimile server, first commercially deployed autonomous expert system; research on experimental psychology-response signals method. Business E-Mail: areed2@calstatela.edu.

REED, ALFRED DOUGLAS, retired academic administrator; b. Bristol, Tenn., July 18, 1928; s. Roy Theodore and Elizabeth Brown (Tuft) R.; m. Emily Joyce Freeman, Mar. 18, 1950 (dec. March 2005); children: Roy Frederick, Robert Douglas, David Clark, Timothy Wayne, Joseph William AB, Erskine Coll., 1949. Reporter Citizen-Times, Asheville, NC, 1949—51, city editor, 1953—60, mng. editor, 1962—63, assoc. editor, 1963—66, capital corr., 1959—66; asst. editor Presbyn. Jour., Weaverville, NC, 1951—52; assoc. editor Shelby Daily Star, NC, 1961—62; dir. pub. info. We. Carolina U., Cullowhee, NC, 1966—96, asst. to chancellor, 1996—2002. Cons. Devel. Office, East Carolina U., Greenville, 1980; bd. dirs. Wachovia Bank, Sylva, N.C., 1969-2003. Author: Prologue, 1968, Decade of Development, 1984; exec. editor: Western, The Mag. of Western Carolina University, 1991-96. Mem. Asheville City Bd. Edn., 1958-61; vice chmn. bd. dirs. Sta. WCQS FM, We. N.C. Pub. Radio Inc., Asheville, 1978-88; bd. dirs., mem. exec. com. Cherokee Hist. Assn., 1985-2004, We. N.C. Assn. Cmtys., 1985-2001, Jackson County Fund of N.C. Cmty. Found., 1991-93; mem. Hunter Libr. Adv. Bd., 1991-98, Pack Pl. Adv. Coun., Asheville, 1991-95. Recipient Paul A. Reid Disting. Svc. award We. Carolina U., 1980, Disting. Svc. award, 1996. Mem. Pub. Rels. Assn. We. N.C. (bd. dirs. 1988-98, treas. 1966-86), Coll. News Assn. Carolinas (bd. dirs. 1968-71, 80-82), Smoky Mountain Host Assn. (bd. dirs., 1st v.p. 1994-96, pres. 1996-98), Great Smoky Mountains Assn. (bd. dirs. 1998-02, 05-06). Democrat. Presbyterian. Avocations: travel, stamps, gardening. Home: 931 University Heights Rd Cullowhee NC 28723-6953 Personal E-mail: douglasreed@earthlink.net.

REED, ANGELICA DENISE, sculptor, writer, illustrator; b. Murfreesboro, Tenn., Dec. 16, 1955; d. Keith Kenyon and Lester Faye (Todd) Reed; m. David Earl Myers, Apr. 19, 1975 (dec. Mar. 1978); m. John Gregory Bettis, May 11, 1979. Student, Mid. Tenn. State U., 1973-75, 77-78, UCLA, 1981-82, Venice Sculpture Studio, 1983-85, Brucchion Sch. of Art, Culver City, Calif., 1987-90. Artist-in-residence Reed Studio and Gallery, Venice, Calif., 1990-95, The Jerry Solomon Gallery, LA, 1997, Belle Art Galleries, Inc. at Bel Age Hotel, West Hollywood, Calif., 2000—. Cons. Sweet Harmony Music, Sunset Beach, Calif., 1978-83, Bettis Paradise Music, Sunset Beach, 1978-85, John Bettis Music, L.A., 1983—, John Bettis Property Mgmt., L.A., 1986—. Fundraiser Children's Hosp./Santa Monica Bay Aux., 1991, Nat. Acad. Songwriters, 1985, SEA Environ. Assn., Bonaventure Hotel, L.A., 1990, 91; mem. L.A. com. P.E.T.A. People for the Ethical Treatment of Animals, 1992; vol. St. John Hosp., 1998. Avocations: gymnastics, scuba diving, travel, ballet.

REED, ANNE F. THOMSON, management consultant; BA, Goucher Coll., 1973; MPA, Harvard U., 1981. Devel. rschr. Office of Alumni Devel. Vanderbilt U., Nashville, 1973—74; jr. cmty. planner Nashville City Planning Commn., 1974—76; staff asst. to asst. dean for adminstrn. Kennedy Sch. Harvard U., Cambridge, Mass., 1976—77, registrar, admissions officer John F. Kennedy Sch. Govt., 1977—80; presdl. mgmt. intern Dept. Navy, Washington, 1981—83, budget analyst for Naval Sea Sys. Command, 1983—86, numerous mgmt. positions Office Comptroller, 1986—93; dep. asst. sec. agr. for adminstrn. USDA, Washington, 1993—96, chief info. officer, 1997—2000; v.p. govt. global industry group EDS, 2000—02, pres. State and Local Govt., 2002—03; pres. & CEO Aquisition Solutions, Inc., 2003—. Office Phone: 703-253-6309.

REED, AUSTIN F., lawyer; b. Waterbury, Conn., Aug. 4, 1951; m. Mary Cincotta, Dec. 22, 1973; children: George, Patricia, Edward, John. AB in Econs. and Polit. Sci., Boston Coll., 1973; JD, U. Fla., 1975. Bar: Fla. 1976, Conn. 1982, Va. 1997. Atty. Fla. Pub. Employee Rels. Commn., 1976-77; sr. atty. Jack Eckerd Corp., 1977-81; assoc. Cummings & Lockwood, Stamford, Conn., 1981-87; asst. gen. counsel Pittston Co., Greenwich, Conn., 1987-89, v.p., gen. counsel Darien, Conn., 1989-93; v.p., gen. counsel, sec. The Brink's Co. (formerly Pittston Co.), Richmond, Va., 1994—.

REED, BERENICE ANNE, cultural organization administrator, artist, educator; b. Memphis; d. Glenn Andrew and Berenice Marie (Kallaher) R. BFA, St. Mary-of-the-Woods Coll., Ind., 1955; MFA in Painting and Art History, Istituto Pio XII, Villa Schifanoia, Florence, Italy, 1964. Cert. art tchr. Tenn. Comml. artist Memphis Pub. Co., 1955—56; arts adminstr., educator pub. and pvt. instns., Washington, Memphis, 1957—70; arts adminstr. Nat. Park Svc., 1970—73; mem. staff U.S. Dept. Energy, Washington, 1973—81, U.S. Dept. Commerce, Washington, 1983—84, Exec. Office of Pres., Office of Mgmt. and Budget, Washington, 1985; with fin. mgmt. svc. U.S. Treasury Dept., Washington, 1985—2004. Ind. art history rschr. Nat. Gallery of Art, Ctr. Advanced Study in Visual Arts, Washington, 1998—; cons. on art and architecture in recreation AIA, 1972-73; artist-in-residence St. Mary-of-the-Woods Coll., Ind., 1965; guest lectr. instr. Nat. Sch. Fine Arts, Tegucigalpa, Honduras, 1968; exec. com. Parks, Arts and Leisure Project, Washington, 1972-73; rschr. art projects, Washington, 1981-83. Developer (video) In Your Interest, 1992; TV interviewer Am. Fin. Skylink satellite programs, 1996-98. Advisor Royal Oak Found.; bd. dirs. Am. Irish Bicentennial Com., 1974—76. Recipient various awards for painting; installed as Dama of Merit, Sacred Mil. Constantinian Order of St. George, Naples, 1997, awarded Star, 2001, installed as Dama, Order of St. Maurice and St. Lazarus, 2000, Companionate Am. Soc. Italian Legions Merit, 2008; named one of 150 Women Who Made A Difference in 150 years of St. Agnes Acad., 2001. Mem. Soc. Woman Geographers, Nat. Soc. Arts and Letters, Ctr. Advanced Study in Visual Arts, Art Barn Assn. (bd. dir. 1973-83), Patrons Arts in the Vatican Mus., Irish Georgian Soc. Roman Catholic. Avocations: photography, performing arts. Home: PO Box 34253 Bethesda MD 20827-0253

REED, BRIAN ALAN, school system administrator; b. Joliet, Ill., Oct. 12, 1973; s. Marvin Alan and Ann Reed; m. Jennifer Larsen, Nov. 23, 2001; children: Madison Nicole, Alexis Jordan. MA in Spl. Edn., Nat. Lois U., 2006. Cert. LBS1 Ill., 2006. Recreation coord. Joliet Pk. Dist., 1996—2004, asst. supt., recreation, 2004—06. Home: 478 Rebecca Ln Bolingbrook IL 60440 Office: Joliet Twp HS Dist 204 201 E Jefferson St Joliet IL 60432 Business E-Mail: breed@jths.org.

REED, CAROLYN E., thoracic surgeon; b. Farmington, Maine, 1950; BA in Chemistry, U. Maine, 1972; MD, U. Rochester, 1977. Cert. Am. Bd. Surgery, 1983, Thoracic Surgery, 1986. Intern surgery NY Hosp. Cornell Medical Ctr., 1977—78, resident surgery, 1978—81, chief resident surgery, 1981—82, asst. surgeon, 1977—81, surgeon, 1981—82, instr. surgery (thoracic), 1983—85; fellowship surgical oncology Meml. Sloan-Kettering Cancer Ctr., 1982—83; asst. prof. surgery Medical U. SC, 1985—89, assoc. prof. surgery, 1989—93, assoc. prof. surgery with tenure, 1993—96, prof. surgery, 1997—, assoc. program dir. Cardiothoracic Surgery Residency Program, 1996—2000, Alice Ruth Reeves Folk Endowed Chair of Clinical Oncology, 1999; chief thoracic surgery Veterans Adminstrn. Hosp., 1985—98; assoc. dir. clinical affairs Hollings Cancer Ctr., 1998—2000, dir., 2000—04, deputy dir. clinical affairs, 2004—; section chief gen. thoracic surgery Medical U. SC, 2004—. Mem.: Women in Thoracic Surgery, Soc. Thoracic Surg., Am. Assoc. Thoracic Surgery, Am. Bd. Thoracic Surgery. Office: MUSC Ashley River Tower Ste 7018 MSC 295 25 Courtenay Dr Charleston SC 29425*

REED, CHARLES RUFUS (CHUCK REED), Mayor, San Jose, California, lawyer; b. Garden City, Kans., Aug. 16, 1948; s. Ambers Reed and Estelle (Robinson) Sinclair; m. Paula Marie Weeg; children: Kim Nicole, Alexander Ryan. BS, USAF Acad., 1970; M in Pub. Affairs, Princeton U., 1972; JD, Stanford U., 1978. Bar: Calif. 1978. Assoc. Campbell, Warburton et al, San Jose, Calif., 1978-80; ptnr. Glaspy, Elliott et al, San Jose, 1981-85; mng. ptnr. Reed, Elliott, Creech & Roth, San Jose, 1985-96; pres. Reed & Roth, San Jose, 1996—99; mem. San Jose City Council, San Jose, 2000—07; mayor City of San Jose, San Jose, 2007—. Mem. Berryessa Citizens Adv. Coun., 1984—, Friends of the Guadalupe River Park, 1986-88, Horizon 2000 Task Force, 1983-84, Sm. Bus. Assn., 1981-83, Enterprise Zone Design Com., 1983, fund raising com. Vinci Park Sch. Site Coun., 1981-82, Bay Area Lawyers for the Arts, 1981-82, Urban Svcs. and Constn. and Conveyance Tax Task Force, 1982, Citizens for Park Improvements, 1982, Mayor's Com. on Ballot Measures, 1982, Berryessa Union Sch. Dist. Human Rels. Task Force, 1980-81, chmn. community rels. subcom., 1981; mem. San Jose Planning Commn., 1982-90, vice chmn., 1985-86, chmn., 1986-87; mem. Mayor's Task Force on Homeless, 1987; mem. site coun. Piedmont Mid. Sch., 1986-88; bd. dirs. San Jose Repertory Co., 1981-83, bd. counsel, 1982-83; mem. adv. bd. San Jose Shelter Found., 1988—; chmn. Destination Downtown steering com., 1988; San Jose Symphony Chmn.'s Coun., 1989; mem. adv. bd. Community Leadership San Jose, 1989—; v.p. Friends of Edn. for Berryessa Students, 1991—; mem. Santa Clara County Planning Commn., 1994—, chair, 1995-96; chair Santa Clara County Charter Rev. Com., 1997—; co-chair San Jose Gen. Plan Task Force GP 2020, 1991-93; mem. Land Trust for Santa Clara County, 1997-98; mem. Walden West Outdoor Sch. Found., 1997—. Served to capt. USAF, 1970-75. Mem. ABA, NAACP, Calif. Bar Assn., Santa Clara County Bar Assn. (mem. exec. com. bus law com., pub. edn. com.), San Jose C. of C. (v.p., bd. dirs. 1985—, chmn. 1990, chmn. high tech. com. 1983-85, participant leadership San Jose program, chmn. cen. bus. dist. com. 1981-83, chmn. downtown roundtable 1987-88) San Jose Downtown Assn. (1987—, pres. 1989, downtown working rev. com 1989-90, urban design rev. bd. 1989-90, mayor's earthquake relief com. 1989-90), USAF Acad. Assn. of Grads. (founder No. Calif. chpt. 1987, pres. 1987-88). Democrat. Avocations: skiing, jogging, boating. Office: Office of Mayor 200 E Santa Clara St San Jose CA 95113 Office Phone: 408-535-4800. Office Fax: 408-292-6422. Business E-Mail: mayoremail@sanjoseca.gov.*

REED, COLIN V., hotel company executive; Joined Harrah's Entertainment Inc., 1977, fin. controller Holiday Inn Internat. Divsn., 1977—81, head fin. and adminstrn. Holiday Inn Internat. European Divsn., 1981—85, CFO Holiday Inn for Europe, Middle East and Africa Divsn., 1985—87, exec. asst. to chmn., 1987—92, sr. v.p. devel., 1992—97, exec. v.p., CFO, 1997—2001, bd. dirs., 1999—2001; pres., CEO Gaylord Entertainment, Nashville, 2001—, chmn. bd. dirs., 2005—. Bd. dirs. Bass Pro Shops, First Horizon Nat. Corp. Office: Gaylord Entertainment One Gaylord Dr Nashville TN 37214 Office Phone: 615-316-6000.

REED, DAN, sports association executive; b. Ann Arbor, Mich. BA in Econs., Am. Studies, Northwestern U., Evanston, Ill.; MBA, Harvard U. Bus. Sch., 2004. Mgmt. cons. A.T. Kearney, Washington, San Francisco; sr. dir. team mktg. and bus. ops. NBA; pres. NBA Devel. League, 2007—. Recipient Dean's award, Harvard Bus. Sch. Office: Nba Development League 645 5th Ave Fl 19 New York NY 10022-5928 Office Phone: 864-248-1100.*

REED, DANIEL A., computer software company executive; BS in Computer Sci. summa cum laude, U. Mo., 1978; MS in Computer Sci., Purdue U., 1980, PhD in Computer Sci., 1983. Postdoctoral rsch. assoc. Purdue U., Ind., 1983; asst. prof. U. NC, Chapel Hill, 1983-84, chancellor's eminent prof., founding dir. Renaissance Computing Inst., chancellor's sr. advisor strategy and innovation; asst. prof. in computer sci. U. Ill., Urbana, 1984-88, assoc. prof. in computer sci., 1988-91, prof. in computer sci., 1991—, head computer sci., 1996—2001; sr. rsch. scientist Nat. Ctr. Supercomputing Applications, Champaign, Ill., 1995—2000, dir., 2000—07, Nat. Computational Sci. Alliance, Urbana, Ill., 2000—07; computing strategist Microsoft Corp., Redmond, Wash., 2007—09, dir. Cloud Computing Futures initiative, 2008—, corp. v.p. eXtreme computing group, 2009—. Vis. scientist IBM T.J. Watson Rsch. Ctr., 1990; vis. scholar Indonesian Second U. Devel. Project, Jakarta, 1990. Author: Multicomputer Networks: Message-Based Parallel Processing, 1987; editor: Sixth SIAM Conference on Parallel Processing for Scientific Computing, 1993, Debugging and Performance Tuning for Parallel Computing Systems, 1996, Scalable Input/Output: Achieving System Balance, 2001. Bd. dirs. Computing Rsch. Assn., 1998—, chair govt. affairs com., 1999-2001; chair Presdl. IT Adv. Commn. High end Software Rev. Subcom., 1998; mem. adv. com. NSF Computer and Info. Sci. and Engring., 1997-2000, chair high performance computing adv. subcom., 1998-2000. Recipient Presdl. Young Investigator award NSF, 1987-92. Mem. IEEE, ACM, AAAS, Internat. Fedn. Info. Processing (mem. working group WG10.3). Avocations: amateur astronomy, golf. Office: Microsoft Corp One Microsoft Way Redmond WA 98052-6399*

REED, DAVID PATRICK, information scientist; b. Portsmouth, Va., Jan. 30, 1952; s. Sherman Clark and Bernice Lois (Maul) R.; m. Lynn Susan Schwartz, June 10, 1973 (div. Mar. 1979); 1 child, Colin Alexander; m. Jessica Amy Kenn, Sept. 4, 1983; children: Katherine Anne, Carly Diana. BS, MIT, 1973, SM, 1975, Degree in Elec. Engring., 1976, PhD, 1978. Asst. prof. computer sci. and engring. MIT, Cambridge, 1978-84, lectr., 1984-86; chief scientist Software Arts, Wellesley, Mass., 1983-84, v.p. R&D, 1984-85; v.p. R&D, chief scientist Lotus Devel., Cambridge, 1985-92; sr. scientist Interval Rsch. Corp., 1992-96; pvt. practice, 1996—; mem. adv. bd. Vanguard, 1991—. Fellow Diamond Tech. Ptnrs. Exch. program, 1997—; vis. scientist MIT Media Lab., 2001-02; adj. prof. MIT Media Lab., 2003—; mem. tech. adv. coun., FCC, 2003-2004. Contbr. articles to profl. jours. Recipient Tchg. award MIT Elec. Engring. Dept., 1975, Tech. award World Tech. Network Comms., 2004, IP3 award Pub. Knowledge, 2005; fellow Hewlett-Packard Labs., 2003—09. Mem. IEEE, Assn. Computing Machinery, Computer Soc., Sigma Xi. Democrat. Achievements include multiple US patents.

REED, DON COLLINS, philosopher, educator; m. Charlotte Collins, 1982; children: Slocomb, Caldwell. BA, Hendrix Coll., Conway, Ark., 1981; PhD, Vanderbilt U., Nashville, Tenn., 1985. Prof. philosophy Wittenberg U., Springfield, Ohio, 1989—. Sch. bd. Springfield City Schs., 2006—09. Author: (nonfiction book) Following Kohlberg: Liberalism and the Practice of Democratic Community. Exec. com. mem. Clark County Dem. Party, Springfield, 2007. NEH Rsch. fellowship, Nat. Endowment for Humanities, 1996—97. Mem.: Assn. Moral Edn. (exec. bd. mem. 1995—2001). Episcopal. Avocations: running, photography. Office: Wittenberg Univ Ward St at N Wittenberg Ave Springfield OH 45501-0720 Business E-Mail: dreed@wittenberg.edu.

REED, DOUG, Internet company executive; BS in Computer Engring., Ohio State U. Rsch. engr. Ohio State U., 1992—94; software engr. Sun Microsystems, 1994—96; sr. engr. Iona Technologies, 1996—97; sr. software engr. Avolent, 1997—99; architect of info. retrieval Digital Insight/1View Network, 2000—02; cons. internet commerce engring. Wells Fargo Bank, 2002—05; prin. Circular Bin Software, 2002—05; engring. mgr. Intuit, 2005—06; founder, chief info. officer Cake Fin. Corp., San Francisco, 2006; chief tech. officer Common Sense Media, San Francisco, 2009—. Office: Common Sense Media 650 Townsend Ste 375 San Francisco CA 94103

REED, DOUGLAS SCOTT, immunologist; s. Richard James and Moyna Kay Reed; m. Deborah Jane Tubbs; 1 child, Allison Christine. PhD, UT Southwestern Med. Ctr., Dallas, 1995. Chief, dept. animal studies U.S. Army Med. Rsch. Inst. Infectious Diseases, Frederick, Md., 1999—2008; aerobiology mgr. U. Pitts., Pa., 2008—. Regional commr. Am. Youth Soccer Orgn., Hagerstown, Md., 2005—07. Decorated Achievement medal Civilan Svc. U.S. Army; recipient Rsch. & Devel. award Tech. Excellence, 2003. Mem.: Am. Soc. Microbiology, Am. Assn. Immunologists. Avocations: soccer, video games. Office: Univ Pittsburgh 3051 5th Ave Pittsburgh PA 15261

REED, ED (EDWARD EARL REED JR.), professional football player; b. St. Rose, La., Sept. 11, 1978; BA, U. Miami, Coral Gables, Fla., 2001. Defensive back Balt. Ravens, 2002—. Weekly correspondent NFL Network, 2003. Recipient Whitney M. Young award, Greater Balt. Urban League, 2007; named 1st Team All-Am., 2000—01, 1st Team All-Conf., Big East Conf., 2000—01, Co-defensive Player of Yr., 2001, Nat. Player of Yr., Football News, 2001, 1st Team All-Pro, AP, 2004, 2006—08, NFL Defensive Player of Yr., 2004; named to Am. Football Conf. Pro Bowl Team, NFL, 2003, 2004, 2006—08. Achievements include member of the NCAA National Championship winning University of Miami Hurricanes, 2001; leading the NFL in: interception return yards, 2004; interceptions, 2004, 2008; non-offensive touchdowns, 2008. Office: Balt Ravens M&T Bank Stadium 1101 Russell St Baltimore MD 21230*

REED, FRANCES BOOGHER, writer, actress; b. Marion, Ky., May 29, 1938; d. Charles Boogher and Evelyn Shelby (Roberts) R.; m. José Joaquín Solís, June 1, 1957 (div. Sept. 1964); children: Julie, Michael Charles; m. Arnold Haslund, Jan. 30, 1965 (div. May 1967); 1 child, Elizabeth Evelyn Marie; 1 adopted child, Leni Ellis. BA in English and Spanish, U. Houston, 1960; MPH, U. P.R., 1970. Tchr. English as 2d lang. Author: A Dream With Storms, 1979, Thoughts, Feelings and Dreams, 1985, Black Mexican Necklace, 1990, TOEIC Test Guide, 1997, Miguel's Aztec Calendar, 1997, (with Koji Shimada) From Chocolate Bars to CEO, A MacArthur's Kid, 2000, (with Francisco Diaz Infante M.) Pockets and Jingles: Something for His Pockets, 2000, Love Blooms in Mazatlan, 2004; co-artist (with Francisco Diaz Infante M.) Art Works Gallery, Hilton Head, SC, Museo de Arte, Mazatlan, Mex.; ghostwriter: Life On the Run; actress (television shows) General Hospital, Rescue-911, others, also movies. Mem. Am. Pub. Health Assn., Screen Actors' Guild, Mensa, Phi Kappa Phi. Democrat. Methodist. Avocations: teaching, dance, reading. Home: 239 Beach City Rd Apt 2113 Hilton Head Island SC 29926-4713 Office Phone: 843-715-0124. Personal E-mail: ml888888@aol.com.

REED, FRANK E., JR., finance educator; b. Ottumwa, Iowa, Feb. 2, 1947; MBA, Aurora U., Ill., 1996. Ops. mgr. DeLa Rue Card Sys., Naperville, Ill., 1994—96; prof. Indian Hills CC, Ottumwa, Iowa, 1996—. Sgt. US Army, 1968—71, Okinawa. Home: 326 Elmdale Ave Ottumwa IA 52501 Office: Indian Hills CC 626 Indian Hills Dr Ottumwa IA 52501

REED, FRANK FREMONT, II, retired lawyer; b. Chgo., June 15, 1928; s. Allen Martin and Frances (Faurot) Reed; m. Jaquelin Silverthorne Cox, Apr. 27, 1963; children: Elizabeth Matthiessen Mason, Laurie Matthiessen Stern, Mark Matthiessen, Jeffrey, Nancy Reed Watson, Sarah Reed Farmer. AB, U. Mich., 1952, JD, 1957. Bar: Ill. 1958. Assoc. Byron, Hume, Groen & Clement, Chgo., 1958-61, Marks & Clerk, Chgo., 1961-63; pvt. practice law Chgo., 1963-78; dir. Western Acadia (Western Felt Works), Chgo., 1960-75, chmn. exec. com., 1969-71; ret., 1978. Author: History of the Silverthorn Family, 4 vols., 1982, Allen Family of Allen's Grove, 1983, Goddard and Ware Ancestors, 1987, Faurot Family, 1988; contbr. articles to profl. jours. Rep. precinct capt., 1972-78; candidate for 43d ward alderman, 1975; bd. dirs., sec. Chgo. Found. Theater Arts, 1959-64; vestryman St. Chrysostom's Ch., 1975-79, mem. ushers guild, 1964-79, chmn., 1976-78; bd. dirs. North State, Astor, Lake Shore Dr. Assn., 1975-78, pres., 1977-78; bd. dirs. Cmty. Arts Music Assn. Santa Barbara, 1984-93, treas., 1988-93; bd. dirs. Santa Barbara Arts Coun., 1987-89. Cpl. AUS, 1952-54. Mem. ABA, Ill. Bar Assn., Racquet Club, Wausaukee Club (sec., dir. 1968-71, 92-94) (Chgo.), Birnam Wood Golf Club (Santa Barbara), Phi Alpha Delta. Episcopalian. Home: 1944 E Valley Rd Santa Barbara CA 93108-1428

REED, FRANK METCALF, bank executive, director; b. Seattle, Dec. 22, 1912; s. Frank Ivan and Pauline B. (Hovey) R.; m. Maxine Vivian McGary, June 11, 1937 (dec. Jan. 25, 2009); children: Pauline Reed, Frank Metcalf (dec.). Student, U. Alaska, 1931-32; BA, U. Wash., 1937. V.p. Anchorage Light and Power Co., 1937-42; pres. Alaska Electric & Equipment Co., Anchorage, 1946-50; sec., mgr. Turnagain, Inc., Anchorage, 1950-56; mgr. Gen. Credit Corp., Anchorage, 1957; br. mgr. Alaska SBA, Anchorage, 1958-60; sr. v.p. First Interstate Bank of Alaska, Anchorage, 1960-87, also dir., corp. sec. Dir. First Interstate Corp. of Alaska, First Nat. Bank of Fairbanks; pres., dir. Anchorage Broadcasters, Inc.; past pres., chmn. Microfast Software Corp.; dir., treas. RM.R., Inc.; dir. Anchorage Light and Power Co., Turnagain, Inc., Alaska Fish and Farm, Inc., Life Ins. Co. Alaska. Pres., Anchorage Federated Charities, Inc., 1953-54; mem. adv. bd. Salvation Army, 1948-58; mem. Alaska adv. bd. Hugh O'Brian Youth Found., 1987-91; trustee Anchor Age Endowment Fund, 1988-96, chmn., 1991; mem. City of Anchorage Planning Commn., 1956; mem. City of Anchorage Coun., 1956-57; police commr. Territory of Alaska, 1957-58; chmn. City Charter Commn., 1958; mem. exec. com. Greater Anchorage, Inc., 1955-65; mem. Sch. Bd., 1961-64; mem. Gov.'s Investment adv. com., 197-72; mem. Alaska State Bd. Edn.; mem. citizens adv. com. Alaska Meth. U.; chmn. Anchorage Charter Commn., 1975; chmn. bldg. fund dr. Cmty. YMCA, 1976 dir., 1976-97, hon. dir. 1998—; sec.-treas. Breakthrough, 1976-78; bd. dirs. Alaska Treatment Ctr., 1980-87, pres. 1985-86; trustee Marston Found., Inc., 1978, exec. dir. 1988. Served as lt. USNR, 1942-46. Elected to Hall of Fame, Alaska Press Club, 1969; named Outstanding Alaskan of Yr. Alaska C. of C., 1976, Alaskan of Yr., 1990, Outstanding Vol. in Philanthropy Alaska chpt. Nat. Soc. Fundraising Execs., 1991; laureate Jr. Achievement's Alaska Bus. Hall of Fame, 2000. Mem.: Alaska Bankers Assns. (pres. 1970—71), Nat. Assn. State Bds. Edn. (sec.-treas. 1969—70), Am. Inst. Banking Am. (exec. coun. 1971—72), Navy League (pres. Anchorage coun. 1961—62), Pioneers of Alaska, Anchorage C. of C. (presl 1966—67, dir.), San Francisco Tennis Club, Tower Club (life), Elks (life), Lions (life; sec. Anchorage 1953—54, pres. 1962—63, dir. 1988, treas. 2002—04, Melvin Jones fellow 2000—05). Home: 1361 W 12th Ave Anchorage AK 99501-4235

REED, GALEN K., music educator; s. Harold Elias and Barbara Keener Reed. BS in music edn., Millersville U., 1976—81. Instructional II Penna. Dept of Edn., 1981. Tchr. Ephrata Area Sch. Dist., Ephrata, Pa., 1983—. Mem.: Hist. Harp Soc., Am. Harp Soc., Am. String Tchrs. Assn. Christian. Avocation: music. Office: Ephrata Area Sch Dist 803 Oak Blvd Ephrata PA 17522 E-mail: g_reed@easdpa.org.

REED, GARY BRIAN, publishing executive; b. Detroit, May 21, 1956; s. Howard Junior and Edith Florence Reed; m. Jennifer Marie Andrews, Dec. 31, 1977; children: Stephanie Rachel, Jessica Nicole, Alison Michelle, Erica Marie. BS, Ea. Mich. U., Ypsilanti, 1982, MS in Biology, 1984. Pres. Reader's Exch. Inc., Westland, 1981—99, Caliber Pub., Westland, 1989—2001; sr. v.p. TMP Toy Co., Livonia, Mich., 1993—96; pub. Transfusion Pub., Canton, 2008—. Author: (novels) A Murder of Scarecrows, Deadworld, Saint Germaine, Spirit of the Samurai, Puffin Graphics: Dracula. Home: 44114 Parkside Canton MI 48187 Personal E-mail: reedgar@gmail.com.

REED, GEORGE ELLIOTT, surgeon, educator, dean; b. NYC, Aug. 4, 1923; m. Anne Miller Moore, 1995; children from previous marriage: Elizabeth E., George E. Jr. DVM, Cornell U., 1944; MD, NYU, 1951. Diplomate Am. Bd. Surgery, Bd. Thoracic Surgery. Successively intern, resident, chief resident NYU Bellevue Med. Ctr., NYC, 1951-56, Berg fellow in cardiovascular surgery, 1956-59; from asst. prof. to assoc. prof. surgery NYU, NYC, 1959-69, prof., 1969-78; prof. surgery, chief cardiothoracic surgery NY Med. Coll., Valhalla, 1978—2004, vice dean, 1996—2004; pres. med. staff Westchester County Med. Ctr., Valhalla, NY, 1989-93, from acting med. dir. to med. dir., 1992—2004, dir. George E. Reed Heart Ctr., 1994—2002; pres. Med. Faculty Health Alliance, Valhalla, 1994—2004. Cons. surgery N.Y. State Dept. Health, Albany, 1963—90, VA, NYC, 1969—78, Lenox Hill Hosp., NYC, 1971—91, Kingston (N.Y.) Hosp., 1971—90; pres. Federated Faculty Practice Plan, 1996—99; adv. bd. Asian Cardiovasc. Thoracic Annals; presenter in field; med. adv. bd. Columbia Meml. Hosp., Hudson, NY, 2002—; pres. Eastview Found., 1992—. Sect. editor: Heart Disease, mem. editl. bd.: Heart and Health Reports; contbr. articles to profl. jours., chapters to books. Fellow: ACS, Am. Coll. Cardiology; mem.: Internat. Soc. Artificial Internal Organs, Am. Soc. Artificial Internal Organs, Heart Rhythm Soc., Internat. Assn. Cardiac Biol. Implants, Am. Trauma Soc., Soc. Thoracic Surgeons, Am. Assn. Thoracic Surgery, Harvey Soc., Am. Trudeau Soc., Alpha Omega Alpha (faculty). Avocations: woodworking, landscape design. Office: Westchester Med Ctr Macy 128 Valhalla NY 10595 Office Phone: 914-493-8665. Personal E-mail: georgereed23@hotmail.com.

REED, GLEN ALFRED, lawyer; b. Memphis, Sept. 24, 1951; s. Thomas Henry and Evelyn Merle (Roddy) Reed; m. Edith Jean Renick, June 17, 1972; children: Adam Christopher, Alec Benjamin. BA, U. Tenn., 1972; JD, Yale U., 1976. Bar: Ga. 1976. Project dir. Tenn. Rsch. Coordinating Unit, Knoxville, 1972-73; assoc. Alston Miller & Gaines, Atlanta, 1976-77, Bordurant Miller Hishon & Stephenson, Atlanta, 1978-81, ptnr., 1981-85, King & Spalding, Atlanta, 1985—. Author: (book) Practical Hospital Law, 1979. Mem. adv. bd. CARE Atlanta, 1992—2007, chmn., 1994—99; v.p. Ga. Network People with Devel. Disabilities, 1991—92; legal advisor Ga. Gov.'s Commn. on Healthcare, 1994; bd. dirs. Ga. Partnership for Caring, 1999—2002, Ga. Comm. Support and Solutions, 2000—, vice chmn., 2005—07, chmn., 2008—09; bd. dirs. Healthcare Ethics Consortium Ga., 2002—04, MedShare Internat., 1999—2007, chmn., 2005—06; bd. dirs. Ctrl. Health Ctr., 1989—95, Vis. Nurse Health Sys., 1992—2006, chmn., 1996—99; mem. dean's coun. Sch. Pub. Health Emory U., Atlanta, 1998—. Mem.: ABA, Metro Atlanta C. of C., Health Svc. Task Force, Ga. Acad. Hosp. Attys. (pres. 1991—92), Am. Health Lawyers Assn. (bd. dirs. 1997—2000, pres. 1998—99, David J. Greenburg Svc. award 2003, Listed Legal Media Group Best of Best USA 2007, 2009), Am. Acad. Hosp. Attys. (bd. dirs. 1991—97, pres.-elect 1997), Ga. Bar Assn., Assn. Retarded Citizens (gen. counsel 1979—, bd. dirs. 1986—2006, pres. 1992—96), Phi Beta Kappa. Methodist. Office: King & Spalding 1180 Peachtree St NE Atlanta GA 30309-1740 Home Phone: 404-266-3461; Office Phone: 404-572-3393. Business E-Mail: gareed@kslaw.com.

REED, GLENN W., lawyer; b. Melrose Park, Ill., Jan. 18, 1953; AB summa cum laude, Dartmouth Coll., 1975; JD cum laude, Harvard U., 1978. Bar: Ill. 1978, U.S. Dist. Ct. Ill. (No. dist.). With Gardner, Carton & Douglas, Chgo., 1978—99, ptnr., 1985—99; exec. v.p., gen. counsel UICI, North Richland Hills, Tex., 1999—, dir., 2001—. Mem. exec. com. bd. dirs. UICI, mem. privacy com., mem. investment com.; dir., v.p. MEGA Life and Health Ins. Co., Mid-West Nat. Life Ins. Co., Tenn., Chesapeake Life Ins. Co., Fidelity First Ins. Co.; dir. Pepper Companies, Inc., Chgo., 1990—, Peoples Bankcorp, Inc., Arlington Heights, Ill., 1999—. Mem.: Ill. State Bar Assn. Office: UICI 9151 Grapevine Hwy North Richland Hills TX 76180 Office Phone: 817-255-5200. Office Fax: 817-255-5394.

REED, H. OWEN, retired music educator; b. Odessa, Mo., 1910; m. Esther M. Reed (dec.); children: Sara Jo Ferrar, Carol Ann Wetters; m. Mary L. Arwood, 1982. Student, U. Mo., 1929—33; MusB in Music Composition, La. State U., 1934, MusM in Music Composition, 1936, BA in French, 1937; PhD in Music Composition, U. Rochester, 1939. Educator Mich. State U., 1939—76, chmn. theory and composition, 1939—67, acting head, Sch. Music, 1957—58, chmn. music composition, Sch. Music, 1967—76, prof. emeritus, 1976—; ret., 1976. Physics educator Army Spec. Tng. Program, 1943—44; guest prof. Mont. State U., 1950, Gettysburg Coll., Pa., 1969, U. Pacific, Stockton, Calif., 1983; founding mem. Geriatric Six Plus One Jazz Ensemble. Asst. conductor, arranger: The La. Kings Brass Ensemble, second trumpet: Lansing Symphony Orchestra, band leader: The Missourians Jazz Ensemble; composer: (orchestral works) Evangeline, 1938, Symphony No. 1, 1939, Overture, 1940, Symphonic Dance, 1942, Concerto for Cello and Orchestra, 1949, Overture for Strings, 1961, La Fiesta Mexicana, 1964, The Turning Mind, 1968, Ut Re Mi, 1979;: Christmas Eve, 2001, Song of Acapulco, 2001, (winds and percussion) Spiritual, 1947, Missouri Shindig, 1951, Theme and Variations, 1954, Renascence, 1958;: Che-Ba-Kun-Ah, 1959, The Touch of the Earth, 1971, For the Unfortunate, 1972, Ut Re Mi, 1980, The Awakening of the Ents, 1985; composer: (for marching band) La Fiesta Mexicana, 1986; composer: Of Loth Lorien, 1987, The Heart of the Morn, 1987, Frolicking Winds, 2006, Overture 1940 (arranged by William Berz), The Song of Acapulco, 2001, (chamber work) Piano Sonata, 1934, String Quartet, 1937, The Passing of John Blackfeather, 1945, Scherzo for Clarinet & Piano, 1947, Three Nationalities, 1947, Dusk, 1947, Wondrous Love, 1948, Mountain Meditation, 1948, Nocturne, 1953, Symphonic Dance, 1954, Christmas Eve, 1954, The Song of Acapulco, 1954, El Muchacho, 1962, El Son De La Negra, 1975, Give the Fiddler a Dram, 1976, Fanfare for Remembrance, 1986, Make a Joyful Noise, 2005, (choral works) Two Tongue Twisters, 1950, Close Beside the Winding Cedar, 1957, Ripley Ferry, 1958, Proud Chieftains, 1958, A Tabernacle for the Sun, 1963, Lord God of Sea, 1963, Rejoice! Rejoice!, 1977, Make a Joyful Noise, 2004, (stage works) The Masque of Red Death, 1936, Michigan Dream, 1955, Earth Trapped, 1960; author: A Workbook in the Fundamentals of Music, 1947, Basic Music, 1954, Basic Music Workbook, 1954, Composition Analysis Chart, 2004; co-author (with Paul Harder): Basic Contrapuntal Technique, 1964; co-author: (with Greg Steinke) rev. edit., 2003; co-author: (with Joel T. Leach) Scoring for Percussion and the Instruments of the Percussion Section, 1969, rev. edit., 1979; co-author: (with Robert G. Sidnell) The Materials of Music Composition, 1978. Recipient Composers Press Symphonic award for Concerto for Cello and Orchestra, 1949, Disting. $1000 award, Mich. State U., 1962, Recognition and Honors for Scholarly Contbns. and Publ. of La Fiesta Mexicana, 1999, award for Psalm of Praise, Basic Contrapuntal Techniques, Belwin Mills Pub., 2004, Libr. Pub. award for sound recording of Awakening of the Ents, La Fiesta Mexicana, For the Unfortunate, and Missouri Shindig, 2005, Citation for Disting. Contbns. in Arts, George Romney and Greater Mich. Found., 1963, Neil A. Kjos Meml. award for For The

Unfortunate, 1975, various ann. awards, ASCAP, 1978—, award of Merit, Youth Arts Festival, 1978, Hon. Mention for Rejoice! Rejoice!, Brown U. Choral Composition Competition, 1978, Nat. Arts Assoc. award, Sigma Alpha Iota, 1983, First Place award for Butterfly Girl and Mirage Boy, Bklyn. Coll. Chamber Opera Competition, 1985, Edwin Franco Goldman Meml. Citation for conspicuous svc. in interest of bands and band music in Am., Am. Bandmasters Assn., 1994; fellow for Creative Work in Musical Composition, Guggenheim, 1948—49; Resident Fellowship, Huntington Hartford Found., Pacific Palisades, Calif., 1960, Helene Wurlitzer Found., Taos, N.Mex, 1967. Mem.: Nat. Assn. Composers (mem. nat. coun.), Am. Music Ctr., ASCAP, Music Tchrs. Nat. Assn. (chmn. theory composition section), Mich. Sch. Band and Orchestra Assn. (hon.), Phi Mu Alpha Sinfonia (Orpheus award, Gamma Epsilon chpt. 1976). Home: 7500 N Calle Sin Envidia Tucson AZ 85718-7374 Office Phone: 520-648-1096. Personal E-mail: hree75@comcast.net.

REED, HOWARD ALEXANDER, retired historian, educator; b. Izmir, Turkey; s. Cass Arthur and Rosalind Christine (MacLachlan) R.; m. Shafiga Daulet, May 25, 1985; children from previous marriage: Seth Olcott (dec.), Heather MacLachlan, Deborah Lamont; stepchildren: Aylin, Sibel. Student, Phillips Acad., Andover, Mass., 1935-37, Wellington Coll., Berkshire, Eng., 1937-38; BA with high honors, Yale U., 1942; MA, Princeton U., 1949, PhD, 1951; PhD (hon.), Hacettepe U., 1997. Instr. history Princeton U., 1949-50, Yale U., also dir. Internat. Student Ctr., 1950-52; co-founder, asst. dir., prof. Grad. Inst. Islamic Studies, McGill U., 1952-55; dir. Inst. Internat. and Intercultural Studies, U. Conn., 1966—71, prof. history, 1966—89, prof. emeritus, cons., 1989—. Del. UNRRA and World Student Svc., Greece, 1946-47; program specialist internat. tng. and rsch. Ford Found., Beirut and N.Y.C., 1955-57; dir. coll. and youth programs Am. Friends Svc. Com., 1958-60; assoc. dir. Danforth Found., St. Louis, 1960-64; dir. Nat. Survey Non-Western Studies in Liberal Arts Colls. Dept. Edn., Assn. Am. Colls., 1963-64; exec. assoc. Edn. World Affairs, NYC, 1964-66; spl. advisor to 4 successive Turkish Mins. of Nat. Edn., 1991-95; participant internat. confs.; cons. Dept. State, USAID, UN, World Bank, India, Oman, Turkey, various corps. and univs.; vis. prof. Alaska Pacific U., Am. U. Beirut, Bilkent U., Bosphorus U., Hoover Inst. on War, Revolution and Peace, Stanford U., UCLA. Author: Non-Western Studies in the Liberal Arts College, 1964, Issues and Opportunities in Turkish Education, 1991; co-editor Islamic Colloquium, 1953; contbg. author: Ency. Islam, 2d edit., 1954—, Foreign Affairs Bibliography, 1942-52, 55, Abdulhak Adnan Adivar, 1956, Islam and the West, 1957, A Guide to Historical Literature, 1961, Ency. Americana, 1964-, General Education, Current Ideas and Concerns, 1964, The University Looks Abroad, 1966, The Emergence of the Modern Middle East, 1970, Expanding Dimensions of World Education, 1976, Internat. Ency. Higher Edn., 1977, Social and Economic History of Turkey (1071-1920), 1980, Islam in the Contemporary World, 1981, 2d edit. 1986, Contributions à l'histoire économique et sociale de l'empire ottoman, 1980, 83, The Oxford Encyclopedia of the Modern Islamic World, 1995, Children in His Heart Youth on His Mind-Tributes to Ihsan Dogramaci, 2003, Internat. Com. Ottoman Studies, Procs. XIV Symposium, 2004, Lucky Lach Becoming an American, 2007, Studies in Atatürk's Turkey-The American Dimension, 2009; adv. editor: Muslim World, 1970-95; mem. edit. bd.: Middle East Jour, 1977-02, Jour. Am. Studies Turkey, 1995—, Bull. of the Internat. Conf. on Higher Edn., 1997—; contbr. articles to profl. jours. Bd. dirs. Assn. Princeton Grad. Alumni, 1961-63, Lisle Fellowship, 1948-52, 58-60, 65-70, Pendle Hill, Wallingford, Pa., 1958-73, 75-86, Campus Christian Found., 1969-73, Univ. Senate, 1969-72, Am. Rsch. Inst. Turkey, 1969-74, 77-79; co-founder Middle East Studies Assn. N.Am., 1966, bd. dirs. 1977-80; co-founder Turkish Studies Assn., 1970; trustee Friends World Coll., 1976-87; bd. overseers Moses Brown Sch., 1975-77; exec. coun. Conf. Peace Rsch. in History, 1972-75; exec. com. Class of 1942, Yale U. Lt. (s.g.) USNR, 1942—46. Decorated Legion of Merit; D.S.C. (Gt. Britain); fellow Internat. Schoolboy, 1937-38, Mid. East Inst., 1948-49, Rockefeller Found., 1949-50, 52, Ford Found., 1954, Fulbright fellow, 1970, 81, fellow Am. Coun. Learned Socs.-Social Sci. Rsch. Coun., 1977. Fellow Mid. East Studies Assn. (charter, Bacharach Svc. award, 2006), Soc. Values in Higher Edn., Turkish Studies Assn. (co-founder 1970, sec.), Inst. Turkish Studies (hon.), AHEPA (hon.); mem. Am. Hist. Assn., Conf. on Peace Rsch. in History, Mid. East Inst. (Year 2000 award), Internat. Soc. Oriental Rsch., Brit.-Am. Alumni, Turkish Hist. Soc. (hon.), Assn. Turkish Am. Scientists (adv. bd.), Am.-Turkish Friendship Coun. (nat. adv. bd., Chmn.'s award in edn. 1991), Atatürk Soc. Am., Phi Beta Kappa, Phi Kappa Phi. Mem. Soc. Of Friends. Achievements include only American guest speaker at 75th anniversary of Turkish Parliament, 1995. Office: U Conn Dept History U-103 241 Glenbrook Rd Unit U-103 Storrs Mansfield CT 06269-2103

REED, IRVING STOY, electrical engineer; BS in Math., Cal. Inst. Tech., 1944, PhD in Math., 1949. With Northrop Aircraft Co., 1949-50, Computer Rsch. Corp., 1950-51; with Lincoln Lab. MIT, 1951-60; with Rand Corp., 1960-63; prof. dept. elec. engring. and computer sci. U. So. Calif., LA, 1963—. Cons. Jet Propulsion Lab., Hughes Aircraft Co., Rand Corp., Mitre Corp.; Shannon lectr. Internat. Symposium Info. Theory, Les Arcs, France, 1982. Co-author: Theory and Design of Digital Machines, 1962, Error—Control Coding for Data Networks, 1994; contbr. articles to profl. jours. Recipient Roy Carlton award for Outstanding Paper 1985, Disting. Alumni award Calif. Inst. Tech., 1992. Fellow IEEE (life, Charles Babbage Outstanding Sci. award 1986, Richard W. Hamming medal 1989, Masaru Ibuka Consumer Electronics award 1995, Warren White Radar medal 2001); mem. NAE. Office: U So Calif Dept Elec Engring Sys Los Angeles CA 90089-2560 Office Phone: 213-740-7335.

REED, JACK (JOHN FRANCIS REED), United States Senator from Rhode Island; b. Providence, Nov. 12, 1949; s. Joseph Anthony and Mary Louise (Monahan) R.; m. Julia Hart. BS in Engring., US Mil. Acad., 1971; MA in Pub. Policy, Harvard U., 1973, JD cum laude, 1982. Bar: DC 1982, RI 1983. Commd. 2d. lt. US Army, 1971, served with 82d Airborne Div., 1973-77; asst. prof. US Mil. Acad., West Point, NY, 1977-79; resigned US Army, 1979; assoc. Sutherland, Asbill & Brennan, Washington, 1982-83, Edwards & Angell, Providence, 1983-89; mem. R.I. State Senate, 1984-90, US Congress from 2nd R.I. Dist., 1991—97; US Senator from RI, 1997—. Mem. com. armed services US Senate, com. banking, housing, and urban affairs, com. health, edn., labor and pensions, com. appropriations, joint econ. com. Author: (with others) American National Security, 1981. Served to Major US Army, 1967—79. Recipient Disting. Legis. award United Way Southeastern New Eng., 1988, Disting. Svc. award AARP, 1989, John Fogarty award, 1990, Crystal Apple award Am. Assn. Sch. Librarians, 1994, Excellence in Public Svc. award Am. Acad. Pediatrics, 1998, Excellence in Immunization award Nat. Partnership for Immunization, 2001, Congl. Leadership award Coalition to Stop Gun Violence and Edn. Fund to Stop Gun Violence, 2002, Nat. Excellence in Public Health award Assn. State and Territorial Health Officials, 2002, Joan Gallagher Legis. award Mass. Sch. Libr. Media Assn., 2003. Mem. ABA, RI Bar Assn., DC Bar Assn., Environ. and Energy Study Inst., Phi Kappa Phi. Democrat. Roman Catholic. Avocations: reading, hiking. Office: US Senate 728 Hart Senate Ofc Bldg Washington DC 20510-0001 also: District Office Ste 200 1000 Chapel View Blvd Ste 290 Cranston RI 02920-3074 Office Phone: 202-224-4642, 401-943-3100. Office Fax: 202-224-4680, 401-464-6837. E-mail: jack@reed.senate.gov.*

REED, JAMES ELDIN, historian, consultant, educator; b. Walla Walla, Wash., Mar. 13, 1945; s. Eldin Wallace and Mary Ellen (White) R.; m. Deborah Jane Addis, Apr. 14, 1983. AB, Ripon Coll., 1967; AM, Harvard U., 1968, MTS, 1971, PhD, 1976. Cert. mgmt. cons., 1984-89. Tchg. fellow Harvard U., Cambridge, Mass., 1972-77; lectr. Boston Coll., 1973—74; dir. summer writing program Harvard U., 1977-78; founder, pres., chmn. Addis & Reed Cons., Inc., Boston, 1977—; pub. ARC Publs., Boston, 1995—99; sr. rsch. fellow Ctr. on Internat. Governance Innovation, 2004—05; pres. Mass. Fulbright Assn., 2008—. Vis. scholar Harvard U., 1992-94, 96-07, fellow, 2007-; rsch. assoc. North Pacific program Fletcher Sch. Law and Diplomacy, Medford, Mass., 1994-96; v.p., pres. Assn. Mgmt. Cons., Boston, 1985-89; founder, bd. dirs. Nat. Coun. Pub. History, Washington, 1980-83; vis. prof., Fulbright Disting. chair U. Waterloo, 2004-05, lectr., U. Tirana, Albenia, 2007; participant internat. confs.; cons. in field. Author: The Missionary Mind and American East Asia Policy, 1983, China On Our Minds, 2006; editor: Select Bibliography of History, 1970, American Canada Watch; e-book, 2008; contbr. numerous articles, papers, and revs. to profl. publs., websites, Christian Sci. Monitor, Boston Globe, Toronto Globe and Mail, others. Cons. House Agr. Com. Washington, 1978, House Judiciary Com., 1999-2000, invited witness Senate Judiciary Com., 1990, Ontario Coun. on Grad. Studies, 1999-2000; legis. dir. Asbestos Victims Campaign, Boston, 1987-90. Woodrow Wilson fellow, 1967-68, Harvard Grad. Prize fellow, 1967-68, fellow Newberry Libr., Chgo., 1965, Am. Coun. Learned Soc., 1987, Ctr. for Internat. Affairs, Harvard U., 1993-94, James Luther Adams Soc., Harvard Div. Sch., 2001—; Fulbright disting. scholar, 2004-05; Fulbright sr. specialist, 2006-. Mem. Am. Hist. Assn., Authors Guild, Am. Acad. Religion, Harvard Faculty Club, Can. Inst. Internat. Affairs (pres. Boston br. 1998—), Fulbright Assn. (bd. dirs. Mass. chpt. 2006—, pres. 2008-), Soc. for Historians of Am. Fgn. Rels., Boston Athenaeum, Phi Beta Delta, Phi Beta Kappa. Home: 25 Holly Ln Brookline MA 02467-2156 Office: Addis & Reed Cons PO Box 85 Chestnut Hill MA 02467 Office Phone: 617-232-3378. Business E-Mail: jimreed@post.harvard.edu.

REED, JAMES WHITFIELD, internist, educator, endocrinologist; b. Pahokee, Fla., Nov. 1, 1935; s. Thomas Reed and Chineater (Grey) Whitfield; married; children: David M., Robert A., Mary I., Katherine E. BS summa cum laude, W.Va. State Coll., Institute, 1954; MD, Howard U., Washington, DC, 1963. Diplomate Am. Bd. Internal Medicine, Am. Bd. Endocrinology and Metabolism; cert. specialist in clin hypertension, Am. Soc. Hypertension. Commd. US Army, 1963, advanced through grades to col., 1981; postdoctoral rsch. fellow U. Calif. Med. Ctr., San Francisco, 1969—71; resident in internal medicine Madigan Army Med. Ctr., Tacoma, 1966—69, chief endocrinology and metabolism, 1971—76, chief dept. clin. rsch., 1976—78; chief dept. medicine Eisenhower Army Med. Ctr., Augusta, Ga., 1978-81; assoc. prof. internal medicine edn. for FP program U. Tex., Dallas, 1981—84; prof. medicine Morehouse Sch. Medicine, Atlanta, 1985—, chmn. dept., 1985—92, chmn. grad. med. edn., 1992—96, activity chmn., 1986—88, dir. internal medicine residency, 1992—98, dir. Clin. Rsch. Ctr., 1998—2000, assoc. chair and prof. medicine, 1992—, chief endocrinology, 1992—, chief of medicine svc. at Grady. Dir. endocrinology, fellowship Madigan Army Med. Ctr., 1976-78; dir., chief medicine and program dir. internal medicine residency program Eisenhower Army Med. Ctr., 1978-81, chmn. directorate of clin. investigation, 1978-81, dir. endocrinology fellowship program; med. cons. Tuskegee VA Hosp., Ala., 1985—; mem. nat. high blood pressure edn. com. NHLBI/NIH, Nat. Diabetes Mellitus Adv. Coun., Nat. Diabetes Adv. Bd., NHLBI working Com. on Hypertension and Diabetes; chmn. Sub Com. Special Population and Situations, chmn. subcom., exec. com. Joint Nat. Commn. Detection Evaluation and Treatment of High Blood Pressure; diabetes epidemic action coun. Am. Diabetes Assn; mem. IOM/NAS Com. Med. Evaluation Vets. Disability Compensation, 2006-08. Author: Black Man's Guide to Good Health, 1994, rev. edit., 2000, High Blood Pressure: The Black Man and Woman's Guide to Living with Hypertension, 2002, Living with Diabetes: A Guide for Patients and Parents, 2005; contbr. articles to profl. jours. Med. advisor, chmn. March of Dimes, Pierce County, Tacoma, 1976-78; pres. Charles Drew Sickle Cell and Health Bd., Tacoma, 1976-78; task force on cardiovascular risk reduction Am. Heart Assn. Decorated Legion of Merit; recipient Disting. Alumni award Nat. Assn. for Equal Opportunity in Higher Edn., 1988, Nat. Alumnus of Yr. award W.Va. State Coll., 1987; named to ROTC Hall of Fame, W.Va. State Coll., 1987. Master ACP; fellow Am. Coll. Clin. Endocrinologists; mem. Assn. Profs. Medicine, Endocrine Soc., Internat. Soc. Hypertension in Blacks (v.p. 1986-92, pres. 1992—2001, Lifetime Achievement award), Assn. Program Dirs. in Internal Medicine, Am. Heart Assn. (task force on cardiovasc. risk), Alpha Phi Alpha. Democrat. Avocations: bowling, skiing. Home: 380 Mcgill Pl NE Atlanta GA 30312-1069 Office: Morehouse Sch Medicine 720 Westview Dr SW Atlanta GA 30310-1495 Office Phone: 404-756-5788. Business E-Mail: jreed@msm.edu. *One cannot control the circumstance of one's birth, but with keen alertness and honest hard work there are no limits to what one can achieve. So hitch your wagon to a star and never lose sight of it.*

REED, JAN STERN, lawyer; Asst. corp. sec., legal counsel Wheelabrator Technologies Inc., 1995—97; asst. corp. sec., asst. gen. counsel Baxter Internat., 1997—98, corp. sec., assoc. gen. counsel, 1998—2004, chief governance officer, 2003—04; sr. v.p., gen. counsel, sec. Solo Cup Co., Highland Park, Ill., 2004—05, exec. v.p., gen. counsel, sec., 2005—. Office: Solo Cup Co 1700 Old Deerfield Rd Highland Park IL 60035

REED, JOAN-MARIE, special education educator; b. St. Paul, Sept. 8, 1960; d. William Martin Reed and Diana-Marie (Miller) Reed Moss. BA, U. Minn., 1982, BS, 1983; MEd, Tex. Woman's U., 1986. Cert. tchr., Tex. Tchr. emotionally disturbed Birdville Ind. Sch. Dist., Ft. Worth, 1984-86, Goose Creek Ind. Sch. Dist., Baytown, Tex., 1986-92, ctr. leader, 1992-93, dept. chairperson, 1987-91; tchr. emotionally disturbed Conroe (Tex.) Ind. Sch. Dist., 1993-94, Willis (Tex.) Ind. Sch. Dist., 1994-95, Jefferson County (Colo.) Pub. Schs., 1995—. Math. instrnl. leader, 2006—. Co-editor: New Teacher Handbook, 1986—87, Behavior Improvement Program Handbook, 1987—88, Student Teacher Supervisor, 1997, Intern Supervisor, 2005—, Middle School Team Leader, 2006—, Jefferson County Pub. Sch. Mem.: NEA. Congregationalist. Avocations: reading, cooking, travel, running. Office: Sobesky Acad Adolescent Day Treatment Program 2001 Hoyt St Lakewood CO 80215 Business E-Mail: jmreed@jeffco.k12.co.us.

REED, JOHN HATHAWAY, former ambassador; b. Ft. Fairfield, Maine, Jan. 5, 1921; s. Walter and Eva Ruth (Seeley) R.; m. Cora Mitchell Davison, Mar. 24, 1944; children— Cheryl, Ruth. BS, U. Maine, 1942, LL.D. (hon.), 1960, Ricker Coll.; grad., Harvard Naval Supply Sch., 1944. Officer Reed Farms, Inc., Fort Fairfield, Maine, 1948-98; pres. Aroostook Raceway, Inc., 1958-59; adv. com. Fort Fairfield br. No. Nat. Bank of Presque Isle; mem. Nat. Transp. Safety Bd., Washington, 1967-75, chmn., 1969-75; ambassador to Sri Lanka Colombo, 1975-77; dir. govt. rels. Assoc. Builders & Contractors, Inc., Washington, 1978-81; ambassador to Sri Lanka and Republic of Maldives, 1982-85; cons. Dept. State, 1985-90; pvt. practice cons. Washington, 1990—. Chmn. Nat. Govs. Conf. Rep., 1966; rep. Fort Fairfield to Maine Legislature, 1954-56; mem. Senate, 1957-59, pres., 1959-60; gov. State of Maine, 1960-67. Pres. bd. Community Gen. Hosp., Fort Fairfield, 1952-54, No. Maine Fair, 1953-59; trustee Ricker Coll., 1953-60, Oak Grove Sch., Vassalboro, Maine; bd. advisors Coll. of Democracy, 1986—, chmn., 1991-2000. Served to lt. (j.g.) USNR, 1942-46. Mem. Am. Fgn. Svc. Assn., Coun. Am. Abassadors, Soc. Sr. Aerospace Execs. Inc. (bd. dirs. 1987-99, pres. 1988-91), Nat. Inst. Former Govs. (bd. dirs. 1992—), Am. Legion, VFW, Grange, Maine Assn. Agrl. Fairs (pres. 1956), Mil. Order of Carabao, Capitol Hill Club, Driving Club (Ft. Fairfield) (pres. 1950-53), Aeroclub of Washington, Internat. Aviation Club, Rotary, Masons, KP, Anah Temple Shrine. Republican. Congregationalist. Office: 410 O St SW Washington DC 20024-2239

REED, JOHN SHEPARD, retired diversified financial services company executive; b. Chgo., Feb. 7, 1939; divorced; 4 children; m. Cindy McCarthy, 1994. BA, Washington and Jefferson Coll., 1961; BS, MIT, 1961; MS, Sloan Sch. MIT, 1965. With Citicorp/Citibank, 1965—2000, chmn., CEO, 1984-98; co-chmn. Citigroup, Inc., NYC, 1998—2000; interim chmn. NY Stock Exch., NYC, 2003—05, interim CEO, 2003—04; Robert S. Hatfield Fellow, Econ. Edn. Cornell Univ., Ithaca, 1998; sr. visiting fellow Princeton Univ., Bendheim Ctr. for Finance, 2002. Bd. dirs. Citicorp/Citibank, 1975-2000, Altria Group (formerly Philip Morris Inc.), 1975-, Monsanto Co.; mem. Bus. Coun.; mem. policy com., Bus. Roundtable; chmn. Coalition of Svc. Inds., svcs. policy adv. com. to the U.S. Trade Rep. Mem. bd. MIT, Meml. Sloan-Kettering Cancer Ctr., Rand Corp., Spencer Found., Am. Mus. Nat. History. Served with C.E. U.S. Army, Korea, 1962-64.

REED, JOHN WESLEY, lawyer, educator; b. Independence, Mo., Dec. 11, 1918; s. Novus H. and Lilian (Houchens) R.; m. Imogene Fay Vonada, Oct. 5, 1946 (div. 1958); m. Dorothy Elaine Floyd, Mar. 5, 1961; children: Alison A., John M. (dec.), Mary V., Randolph F. (dec.), Suzanne M. AB, William Jewell Coll., 1939, LLD, 1995; LLB, Cornell U., 1942; LLM, Columbia U., 1949, JSD, 1957. Bar: Mo. 1942, Mich. 1953. Assoc. Stinson, Mag, Thomson, McEvers & Fizzell, Kansas City, Mo., 1942-46; assoc. prof. law U. Okla., 1946-49; assoc. prof. U. Mich., 1949-53, prof., 1953-64, 68-85, Thomas M. Cooley prof., 1985-87, Thomas M. Cooley prof. emeritus, 1987—; dean, prof. U. Colo., 1964-68, Wayne State U., Detroit, 1987-92, prof. emeritus, 1992—. Vis. prof. NYU, 1949, U. Chgo., 1960, Yale U., 1963-64, Harvard U., 1982, U. San Diego, 1993; dir. Inst. Continuing Legal Edn., 1968-73; reporter Mich. Rules of Evidence Com., 1975-78, 83-84; mem. faculty Salzburg Sem., 1962, chmn., 1964. Author: (with W.W. Blume) Pleading and Joinder, 1952; (with others) Introduction to Law and Equity, 1953, Advocacy Course Handbook series, 1963-81; editor in chief Cornell Law Quar., 1941-42; contbr. articles to profl. jours. Pres. bd. mgrs. of mins. and missionaries benefit bd. Am. Bapt. Chs. U.S.A., 1967-74, 82-85, 88-94; mem. com. visitors JAG Sch., 1971-76; trustee Kalamazoo Coll., 1954-64, 68-70; bd. dirs., Ann Arbor Area Cmty. Found., 2004-. Recipient Harrison Tweed award Assn. Continuing Legal Edn. Adminstrs., 1983, Samuel E. Gates award Am. Coll. Trial Lawyers, 1985, Roberts P. Hudson award State Bar Mich., 1989. Fellow Internat. Soc. Barristers (editor jour. 1980—); mem. ABA (mem. coun. litigation sect.), Assn. Am. Law Schs. (mem. exec. com. 1965-67), Am. Acad. Jud. Edn. (v.p. 1978-80), Colo. Bar Assn. (mem. bd. govs. 1964-68), Mich. Supreme Ct. Hist. Soc. (bd. dirs. 1991—), Sci. Club Mich., Order of Coif. Office: U Mich Sch Law Ann Arbor MI 48109-1215 Office Phone: 734-763-0165. Business E-Mail: reedj@umich.edu.

REED, JOSEPH DUFFIELD, ancient language educator; b. New Haven, May 30, 1965; BA, Yale, 1987; AM, PhD, Stanford U., 1993. Assoc. prof. Greek and Latin U. Mich., Ann Arbor, 2001—. Office: Dept Classical Studies 2160 Angell Hall Ann Arbor MI 48103

REED, JOSEPH WAYNE, American studies educator, artist; b. St. Petersburg, Fla., May 31, 1932; s. Joseph Wayne and Gertrude (Cain) R.; m. Kit Craig, Dec. 10, 1955; children: Joseph McKean, John Craig, Katherine Hyde Maruyama. BA, Yale U., New Haven, Conn., 1954, MA, 1958, PhD, 1961. Rsch. asst. Yale Libr., 1956-57; instr. English Wesleyan U., Middletown, Conn., 1960-61, assoc. prof., 1967-71, prof., 1971—, chmn. dept., 1971-73, 75-76, 85-86, prof. English and Am. studies, 1987—2004; prof. emeritus, 2004—. Vis. lectr. Yale U., New Haven, 1974; lectr. US dept. State and USIS, Can., India, Nepal, 1974; coord. cultural exch., New Delhi, Bombay, 1992, Mo., 2007; coord. music and writing workshop U. Va., Georgetown U; participant exch. program, New Delhi, 2007, Woodstock Writers Jour., Woodstock Jour. Assn.; lectr. in field. Author: English Biography in the Early Nineteenth Century, 1801-38, 1966, Faulkner's Narrative, 1973, Three American Originals: John Ford, William Faulkner, Charles Ives, 1984, American Scenarios, 1989; editor: Barbara Bodichon's American Diary, 1972, (with W.S. Lewis) Horace Walpole's Family Correspondence, 1975, (with F.A. Pottle) Boswell, Laird of Auchinleck, 1977, 2d edit., 1994; one-man shows include Portal Gallery, London, 1971, USIS Libr., New Delhi, 1974, 92, Addison/Ripley Gallery, Washington, 1987, 92, 95, 98, Sterling Meml. Libr., Yale U., 2004; sculptor Johnson Medal of the Johnsonians, 1984, Elizabethan Medal, Yale Elizabethan Club, 1986, Daniel Patrick Moynihan Medal, Citizens Com. NY, 1999, Vincent Scully Medal, Nat. Bldg. Mus., Wash., Freeman Medal, Wesleyan U., 1999, Moynihan plaque, D.P. Moynihan Courthouse, NYC, 2000, Yale Libr. Assocs., 2008. Chmn. Wesleyan Sesquicentennial, 1982; chmn. bd. trustees Yale Libr. Assocs., 1984-2000, hon. trustee, 2000—. Lt. (j.g.) USNR, 1954-56, participant Woodstand Point's Writers Composers, Mussoorie, India. Mem. Elizabethan Club, The Johnsonians (chmn. 1988). Democrat. Episcopalian. Home: 45 Lawn Ave Middletown CT 06457-3135 Office: 51 Lawn Ave Middletown CT 06459 Business E-Mail: jreed@wesleyan.edu.

REED, KATHERINE (KATHY) E., nursing educator; b. Hereford, Tex., Sept. 22, 1948; d. Joseph T. and Pauline F. Marnell; m. Garry A. Reed, Dec. 27, 1970; children: Clint C., Stacie S. Medrano. BSN, Tex. Woman's U., Denton, 1971. RN Tex., 1970. Registered nurse Hillcrest Med. Ctr., Tulsa, Okla., 1971—74, High Plains Hosp., Amarillo, Tex., 1975—90; assoc. prof., nursing Amarillo Coll., 1983—. Mem.: NLN. Home: 5133 McCarty Amarillo TX 79110-3008 Office: Amarillo Coll 4222 W 9th Amarillo TX

REED, KATHLYN LOUISE, occupational therapist, educator; b. Detroit, June 2, 1940; d. Herbert C. and Jessie R. (Krehbiel) R. BS in Occupl. Therapy, U. Kans., 1964; MA, Western Mich. U., 1966; PhD, U. Wash., 1973; MLIS, U. Okla., 1987. Occupl. therapist in psychiatry Kans. U. Med. Ctr., Kansas City, 1964-65; instr. occupl. therapy U. Wash., Seattle, 1967-70; assoc. prof. dept. occupl. therapy U. Okla. Health Scis. Ctr., Oklahoma City, 1973-77, prof., 1978-85, chmn. dept. occupl. therapy, 1973-85; libr. edn. info. svcs. Houston Acad. Medicine

Tex. Med. Ctr. Libr., 1988-97; assoc. prof. Texas Woman's U., Houston, 2006—. Cons. Okla. State Dept. Health, 1976-77, Children's Convalescent Ctr., Oklahoma City, 1977-80, Oklahoma City Pub. Schs., 1980-81; vis. scholars program Tex. Woman's U., 1991-94, adj. prof. Sch. Occupl. Therapy, 1992-97, vis. prof., 1997-2006. Author: (with Sharon Sanderson) Concepts of Occupational Therapy, 1980, 4th edit., 1999, Models of Practice in Occupational Therapy, 1983, Quick Reference to Occupational Therapy, 1991, 2d edit., 2000, (with Julie Pauls) Quick Reference to Physical Therapy, 1996, 2d edit., 2004; (with S. Cunningham) Internet Guide for Rehabilitation Professionals, 1997; (with Sally Pore) Quick Reference to Speech-Language Pathology, 1999. Vol. crisis counselor Open Door Clinic, Seattle, 1968-72; mem. exec. bd. Seattle Mental Health Inst., 1971-72; Mem. Citizen Participation Liaison Coun., Seattle, 1970-72. Recipient Award of Merit, Can. Assn. Occupl. Therapists, 1988. Fellow: Am. Occupl. Therapy Assn. (chmn. ethics commn. 2008—, Merit award 1983, Slagle lectr. award 1985, Svc. award 1985, 2001); mem.: Rehabilitation Engring. Soc. N.Am., Am. Hippotherapy Assn., Soc. for the Study of Occupations, Tex. Occupl. Therapy Found., Am. Occupl. Therapy Found., Med. Libr. Assn. (Rittenhouse award 1987, Acad. Health Info. Professions), Tex. Occupl. Therapy Assn. (Roster of Merit award 2002, Disting. Svc. award 2004), Okla. Occupl. Therapy Assn. (pres. 1974—76), Coun. Exceptional Children, World Fedn. Occupl. Therapists, N.Am. Riding for Handicapped Assn., Sigma Kappa (Colby award 1994), Pi Theta Epsilon. Democrat. Home: 6699 De Moss Dr Houston TX 77074-5003 Office Phone: 713-794-2166. Personal E-mail: klreed3@juno.com.

REED, KEITH ALLEN, lawyer; b. Anamosa, Iowa, Mar. 5, 1939; s. John Ivan and Florence Lorine (Larson) R.; m. Beth Illana Kesterson, June 22, 1963; children: Melissa Beth, Matthew Keith. BBA, U. Iowa, 1960, JD, 1963. Bar: Ill. 1963, Iowa 1963. Ptnr. Seyfarth Shaw, Chgo., 1963—. Co-author: Labor Arbitration in Healthcare, 1981; co-editor: Chicagoland Employment Law Manual, 1994, Employment and Discrimination, 1996, Federal Employment Law and Regulations, 1989-99, 2001-; co-contbr. articles to Am. Hosp. Assn. publs., 1986-89. Trustee Meth. Hosp. Chgo., 1985—; mem. labor sanctioned adv. com. Am. Hosp. Assn., Chgo., 1980—; bd. dirs. Lyric Opera Chgo. Ctr. for Am. Artists, pres., 1983-86. Mem. ABA (dir. health law forum 1979-82), Chgo. Bar Assn. (chair labor and employment law com. 1996-), Union League Club Chgo. (bd. dirs. 1985-88), Sunset Ridge Country Club (Northfield, Ill.). Republican. Methodist. Avocations: music, theater, tennis, golf. Office: 131 S Dearborn St Ste 2400 Chicago IL 60608 Office Phone: 312-460-5838. E-mail: kreed@seyfarth.com.

REED, KIT, writer; b. San Diego; d. John Rich and Lillian (Hyde) Craig; m. Joseph Reed; children: Joseph, John, Katherine. BA English, Coll. Notre Dame, Balt. Reporter St. Petersburg Times, Fla., New Haven Register; freelance novelist; resident writer Wesleyans, 2007—. Adj. prof. English Wesleyan U., 1974-2007, resident writer, 2008-; USIS lectr. India, 1974; lectr. Smithsonian, 1996 Author: Mother Isn't Dead, She's Only Sleeping, 1961, At War as Children, 1964, The Better Part, 1967, Mr. Da V. and Other Stories, 1967, Armed Camps, 1969, Cry of the Daughter, 1971, Tiger Rag, 1973, Captain Grownup, 1976, The Killer Mice, 1976, The Ballad of T. Rantula, 1979, Magic Time, 1980, Other Stories and The Attack of the Giant Baby, 1981, Story First, The Writer as Insider, 1982, Fort Privilege, 1985, The Revenge of the Senior Citizens Plus, 1986, Catholic Girls, 1987, Revision, 1989, Mastering Fiction Writing, 1991, Thief of Lives and Other Stories, 1992, (radio play) The Bathyscaphe, 1979, Little Sisters of the Apocalypse, 1994, Strait, 1995, J. Eden, 1996, Weird Women, Wired Women, 1998; (as Kit Craig) Gone, 1992, Closer, 1997, Some Safe Place, 1998, Seven for the Apocalypse, 1999, Short Fuse, 1999, @expectations, 2000, Thinner Than Thou, 2004, Dogs of Truth, 2005, Bronze, 2005, The Baby Merchant, 2006, The Night Children, 2008, Enclave, 2009. Co-dir. writers exch. for Indo-U.S. subcommn. on edn. and culture, 1990 Named New Eng. Newspaperwoman of Year, New Eng. Women's Press Assn., 1958, 59; grantee Abraham Woursell Found., 1966-71; Guggenheim fellow, 1964, Rockefeller fellow Aspen (Colo.) Inst. for Humanistic Studies, 1976; recipient Alex award ALA, 2005 Mem. ALA, PEN, Writers Guild Am. East, Nat. Book Critics Circle (bd. dir. 1991-95), Century Assn., Authors League Fund (bd. dirs.) Democrat. Roman Catholic. Personal E-mail: storyfirst@wesleyan.edu.

REED, LAWRENCE SAMUEL, plastic surgeon, medical educator; b. Upland, Pa., Mar. 8, 1943; MD, SUNY Downstate, 1969. Diplomate Am. Bd. Plastic Surgery. Intern in surgery Bronx Mcpl. Hosp.-Einstein, 1969—70; resident in plastic surgery Einstein Affiliated Hosps., 1970—72; resident in gen. surgery U. Pa. Grad. Hosp., 1972—75; resident in plastic surgery NY Hosp./Cornell Med. Ctr., 1975—77; fellow Meml. Sloan-Kettering, 1976; consulting med. staff Southampton Hosp., 1986—; asst. attending surgeon plastic surgery NY-Presbyn. Hosp., Weill Divsn., 1993—; clinical asst. prof. plastic surgery Weill Med. Coll., Cornell U., 1993—; asst. attending plastic surgeon Manhattan Eye, Ear and Throat Hosp., 1996—; pvt. practice Reed Ctr. for Plastic Surgery, NYC. Mem. editl. bd. NewBeauty Mag. Fellow: ACS; mem.: Internat. Coll. Surgeons, NY Met. Breast Cancer Soc., NY State Med. Soc., NY Regional Soc. Plastic and Reconstruction Surgeons, Am. Assn. Accreditation Ambulatory Surgery Facilities (mem. strategic planning com., mem. audit com., mem. disciplinary/investigative review com., chmn. accreditation com., chmn. standards com., treas. exec. bd., sec. bd. dirs.), Northeastern Soc. Plastic Surgeons, Med. Soc. County and State of NY, Am. Soc. Aesthetic Plastic Surgery, Inc. (mem. internet steering com., spokesperson non-surg. procedure com., mem. membership com., vice chmn. corp. sponsorship/fin. com., chmn. bylaws com., mem. bd. dirs.), Am. Soc. Plastic Surgeons. Office: Reed Ctr for Plastic Surgery 45 E 85th St New York NY 10028 Office Phone: 212-772-8300. Office Fax: 212-517-6832. Business E-Mail: info@thereedcenter.com.

REED, LEON SAMUEL, secondary school educator, photographer; b. Warren, Ohio, July 6, 1949; s. Walter Charles and Lois Avalene (Botroff) R.; m. Margaret Smith, Dec. 27, 1975 (div.); m. Lois S. Lembo, Aug. 5, 1997; children: Samuel, Stephen, Catherine. BA in Econs. and Journalism, Antioch Coll., Yellow Springs, Ohio, 1971. Project dir. Coun. on Econ. Priorities, NYC and Washington, 1970-75; sr. mem. profl. staff Joint Com. on Def. Prodn., U.S. Congress, Washington, 1975-77; mem. profl. staff Com. on Banking, Housing and Urban Affairs, U.S. Senate, Washington, 1977-81; analyst TASC, 1981-82, mgr. contingency planning, 1982-85, mgr. instl. resources dept., 1985-91, dir. indsl. and mfg. scis. divsn., 1991-97; freelance writer, photographer, 1996—; rsch. staff Inst. Def. Analyses, 1998—2003; rsch. asst. George Mason U., 2004—; tchr. Woodbridge H.S., 2005—. Author: Resource Management: A Historical Perspective, 1988; co-author: Guide to Corporations, 1973, Report of the National Critical Technologies Panel, 1991; contbr. Strategic Survey, 1981-82, The American Defense Mobilization Infrastructure, 1983; author numerous congressional and exec. br. reports, also mag. and jour. articles. Del. White House Conf. on Youth, 1971; pres. Randolph Civic Assn., 1978—80; v.p. North Bethesda Congress of Citizens Assns., 1983—84, pres., 1984—86; v.p. Md. State Youth Soccer Assn., 1998—2005; bd. dirs. Coun. on Econ. Priorities, 1971—73, Montgomery Soccer, Inc., 1994—, pres., 2001—06.

REED, LOWELL A., JR., federal judge; b. Westchester, Pa., 1930; BBA, U. Wis., 1952; JD, Temple U., 1958. Bar: Pa. 1959, U.S. Dist. Ct. (ea. dist.) Pa. 1961, U.S. Ct. Appeals (3d cir.) 1962, U.S. Supreme Ct. 1970. Corp. trial counsel PMA Group, Phila., 1958-63; assoc. Rawle & Henderson, Phila., 1963-65, gen. ptnr., 1966-88; judge U.S. Dist Ct., Phila., 1988-99; sr. judge U.S. Dist. Ct., Phila., 1999—. Lectr. law Temple U., 1965-81, faculty Acad. Advocacy, 1988-2008, Pa. Bar Inst., 1972—. Contbr. articles to profl. jours. Elder Abington (Pa.) Presbyn. Ch.; past. mem. Pa. Senate Select Com. Med. Malpractice; past pres., bd. dirs. Rydal Meadowbrook Civic Assn.; bd. dirs. Abington Sch. Bd., 1971, World Affairs Coun. Phila., 1983-88; trustee Abington Health Care Corp., 1983-88, 90-93. Lt. Comdr. USNR, 1952-57. Recipient Alumni Achievement award Temple U. 1988, Gen. Alumni Assn., Cert. of Honor, 2001, A. Sherman Christensen award Am. Inns. of Ct. Found., 2003. Mem. ABA, Phila. Bar Assn. (chmn. medico legal com. 1975, constl. bicentennial com. 1986-87, commn. on jud. selection and retention 1983-87), Temple Am. Inn of Ct. (pres. 1990-93, master of bench 1990—), Am. Judicature Soc., Temple U. Law Alumni Assn. (exec. com. 1987-90, 99—), Hist. Soc. U.S. Supreme Ct., Hist. Soc. U.S. Dist. Ct. Ea. Dist. Pa. Republican. Office: US Dist Ct US Courthouse Independence Mall W Philadelphia PA 19106

REED, MARC C., telecommunications industry executive, human resources specialist; B in Bus. Adminstrn., State U. NY. Mem. human resources staff GTE World Hqtrs., 1986—87; various human resources exec. positions including dir. human resources GTE Wireless, 1987—97, v.p. human resources, 1997—2004, Verizon Wireless, NYC; exec. v.p. human resources Verizon Comm., NYC, 2004—. Office: Verizon Comm Inc 1095 Avenue of the Americas New York NY 10036 Office Phone: 212-395-2121. Office Fax: 212-869-3265.*

REED, MARK ARTHUR, research scientist, educator; b. Suffern, NY, Jan. 4, 1955; s. Arthur Julius and Rita Margaret Reed; m. Elizabeth J. Schaffer; 1 child, Victor. BS in Physics with honors, Syracuse U., 1977, MS in Physics, 1979, PhD in Solid State Physics, 1983; MA (hon.), Yale U., 1990. Mem. tech. staff Ctrl. Rsch. Labs., Tex. Instruments, Dallas, 1983—88, sr. mem. tech. staff, 1988—90; prof. elec. engring. and applied physics Yale U., New Haven, 1990—, chmn. elec. engring. dept., 1995—2001, Harold Hodgkinson prof. engring. and applied sci., 1999—; chief tech. officer, dir. Molecular Electronics Corp., 1999—2001; assoc. dir. Yale Inst. Nanosci. and Quantum Engring., 2007—. Chmn., organizer numerous confs.; speaker in field. Editor: Nanostructure Physics and Fabrication, 1989, Nanostructures and Mesoscopic Systems, 1992, Nanostructured Systems, 1992, Compound Semiconductors, 1997, Nanostructured Systems, Molecular Electronics, 2001, Molecular Nanolectronics, 2003; contbr. chapters to books, articles 175 pub. to profl. jours. Recipient Kilby Young Innovator award, 1994, Disting. Alumni award Syracuse U., 2000, Fujitsu Internat. Symposium on Compound Semicondrs. Quantum Device award, 2001, Yale Sci. and Engring. Assn. award for advancement of basic and applied sci., 2002; named one of Fortune Mag.'s 12 most promising young Am. Scientists. Fellow: IEEE (Nanotech. Pioneer award 2007), Am. Phys. Soc.; mem.: Sigma Xi. Achievements include pioneered investigation of "Quantum Dots" and Quantum devices; invention of resonant tunneling transistor; 25 patents for novel quantum effect and heterojunction devices; pioneered research on molecular electronic systems. Office: Yale U PO Box 208284 New Haven CT 06520-8284 also: Dept Elec Engring Yale Univ 15 prospect St New Haven CT 06520-8284 Business E-Mail: mark.reed@yale.edu.

REED, MARK LAFAYETTE, III, retired humanities educator; b. Asheville, NC, Sept. 26, 1935; s. Mark Lafayette Jr. and Edith (Murphy) Fisher; m. Martha Balch Sibley, Aug. 30, 1958; children: Victoria Fisher Reed Gless, Christina Pickering Reed Dowdy. BA, Yale Coll., 1957; MA, Harvard U., 1958, PhD, 1962. From asst. prof. to prof. U. NC, Chapel Hill, 1963—71, Lineberger prof. in the humanities, 1986—2000, prof. emeritus, 2000—. Author: Wordsworth: Chronology of Early Years, 1967, Wordsworth: Chronology of Middle Years, 1975; editor: Wordsworth: Thirteen-Book Prelude, 2 vols., 1991; assoc. editor Cornell Wordsworth Series, 1971—; contbr. articles to profl. jours. Bd. advisors Warren Wilson Coll., Swannanoa, N.C., 1976-86; assoc. trustee Wordsworth Trust, Grasmere, Eng., 1975—. Recipient merit award The Asheville Sch., 1985. Mem. MLA, Wordsworth-Coleridge Assn., Elizabethan Club (New Haven, Conn.), Harvard Club (N.Y.C.), Grolier Club (N.Y.C.), Biltmore Forest Country Club. Personal E-mail: mlr@email.unc.edu.

REED, MARY CAROLYN CAMBLIN, retired music educator, county official; b. North Platte, Nebr., June 22, 1938; d. Brick and Evelyn Camblin; m. Paul E. Reed, Dec. 20, 1960. BA, U. No. Colo., 1960; MA, Calif. State U., 1964; PhD in Ednl. Adminstrn., U. So. Calif., 1976. Cert. administr. Calif., 1970. Music educator Rowland Unified Sch. Dist, Rowland Heights, Calif., 1960—67; tchr and writer instrnl. TV LA County Office Edn., asst. to supt. and chief dep. supt., 1976—79; adminstr. Regional Ednl. TV Adv. Coun., LA, 1979—82; ednl. tech. unit adminstr. Calif. State Dept. Edn., Sacramento, 1982—83; dir. media svcs. Sacramento County Office Edn., 1983—94, dir. ednl. media, 1983—94; mng. cons. Northern Calif. Media/Tech. Consortium, 1994—2004, Ctrl. Calif. Ednl. Tech. Consortium, 1994—2004. Cons. music series PBS Sta. WETA, Washington, 1974—76; bd. dirs. LA (Calif.) Music Ctr., AMAN Folk Dance group, LA, 1975—77, PBS Sta. KQED, San Francisco, 1989—95. Musician: Am. Flute Orch., 2001, 2002, Internat. Flute Orch., 2004—09, Sacramento Symphonic Band, 1995, 2003, Camellia City Flute Choir, 2000—. Recipient Outstanding Alumnus, U. of No. Colo., 1983. Mem.: Calif. Music Educators Assn. (pres. 1976—78), Cosumnes Cmty. Orch, West Sacramento Orch. (prin. flutist 1990—).

REED, MAY J., medical educator; b. Taegu, Republic Of Korea, Sept. 29, 1960; MD, Harvard Med. Sch., Boston, 1986. Diplomate internal medicine & geriat. ABIM. Assoc. prof. medicine U. Wash., Seattle, 2001—. Office: Harborview Med Ctr 325 9th Ave SE Box 359625 Mercer Island WA 98040 Office Fax: 206-897-5396. Business E-Mail: mjr@u.washington.edu.

REED, MICHAEL EUGENE, mathematics professor; s. Morgan Eugene and Carol Reed; children: Mason Eugene, Morgan Elizabeth Renee. PhD, U. Ark., Fayetteville, 2004. Asst. prof. Tenn. State U., Nashville, 2004—. Contbr. articles to jours. Mem. Metro Bapt. Ch., Goodlettsville, Tenn., 2008. HBCU-UP grant, NSF, 2007—. Mem.: Math. Assn. America. Office: Tenn State Univ 3500 John A Merritt Blvd Nashville TN 37209

REED, MICHAEL HAYWOOD, lawyer; b. Phila., Jan. 17, 1949; s. Soloman Taylor and Vivian (Haywood) Reed; m. Yalta Gilmore, Aug. 12, 1978; children: Alexandra Haywood, Michael Haywood Jr. BA in Polit. Sci., Temple U., 1969; JD, Yale U., 1972. Bar: Pa. 1972, U.S. Dist. Ct. (ea. dist.) Pa. 1972, U.S. Dist. Ct. (ea. dist.) Mich. 1982, U.S. Supreme Ct. 1982, U.S. Ct. Appeals (3d cir.) 1985. Assoc. Pepper, Hamilton & Scheetz, Phila., 1972-80; ptnr., corp. restructuring, bankruptcy practice Pepper Hamilton LLP (formerly Pepper, Hamilton & Scheetz), Phila., 1980—. Co-adj. prof. law Rutgers U., Camden, NJ, 1983, 85; adj. prof. sch. law Temple U., Phila., 1989; mem. Pa. Judicial Inquiry and Rev. Bd., 1990-93; chair Ea. Dist. Pa. Bankruptcy Conf., 1997-98; mem. Presdl. Adv. Coun. on Diversity in the Profession, 2006-; bd. mem. United Way of Southeastern Pa., 2009-; spkr. in field. Contbr. articles to profl. jours. Advisor Post 913 Law Explorers, Phila., 1974-84; trustee Acad. Natural Scis., Phila., 1988—, vice chair, 2007-, Episcopal Hosp., Phila., 1986-98; mem. bd. advisors Pub. Interest Law Ctr., Phila., 1992—; mem. Com. Seventy, Phila., 1981—; exec. com., bd. mem. Temple U. Alumni Assn., 2008-, United Way Southwestern Penn., 2008-. Recipient cert. of honor Alumnus of Yr. Coll. of Arts and Scis. Temple U., 1995, Award of Excellence, Thurgood Marshall Scholarship Fund, Inc., 2003, J. Austin Norris award, Barristers Assn. Phila., 2005. Fellow Am. Coll. Bankruptcy; mem. ABA (chmn. subcom. labor and employment law, bus bankruptcy com. sect. bus. law 1991-97, chmn. subcom. on labor and employment law 1997-02, subcom. on avoiding powers 2002-05, subcom. bankruptcy coms. 2005-08, ho. of dels. 2002-, bd. govs. 2005-06, mem. presdl. adv. coun. on diversity in the profession 2006-07, mem. pubs. bd. sect. of bus. law, 2006-, mem. standing com. on bar activities and svcs. 2007—, co-chair, subcom. on chpt. Ill., 2008-), Nat. Bar Assn., Am. Law Inst., Am. Bankruptcy Inst., Pa. Bar Assn. (mem. ho. of dels. 1999-01, chmn. minority bar com. 1988-90, mem. bd. govs. 1993-96, co-chair 1994, v.p. 2002-03, pres.-elect 2003, pres. 2004-05, ann. meeting, Spl. Achievement award 1989, Cert. of Honor award 1995), Barristers Assn. Phila. (1st v.p. 1974-76), Phila. Bar Assn. (chair profl. guidance com. 1986), Yale Club (Phila.), Alpha Phi Alpha, Sigma Pi Phi. Democrat. Baptist. Avocations: racquetball, films, theater, biking, piano. Office: Pepper Hamilton LLP 3000 Two Logan Sq 18th and Arch Streets Philadelphia PA 19103-2799 Office Phone: 215-981-4416. Office Fax: 215-981-4750. Business E-Mail: redm@pepperlaw.com.

REED, MICHAEL JOHN, dentist, dean, educator; b. Wednesbury, Eng., Dec. 25, 1940; came to U.S., 1967, naturalized, 1972; s. Harry Ernest and Ida Veva (Heywood) R.; m. Pamela Twycross, July 4, 1965 (div. Feb. 1976); children: Justine Marianne, Helena Clare; m. Ingrid Liepins, Sept. 8, 1978; children: Kathryn Anne, Matthew Harrison. BS with honors, U. Durham, Eng., 1963; B in Dental Surgery, U. Newcastle-Upon-Tyne, Eng., 1967; PhD, SUNY, Buffalo, 1971. Lic. dentist U.K., N.Y., Miss. Instr. oral biology SUNY, Buffalo, 1971-72, asst. prof. oral biology, 1972-77, assoc. prof., 1977-79; asst. dean Sch. Dentistry, U. Miss., Jackson, 1980-85, assoc. dean, 1985; dean, prof. oral biology Sch. Dentistry, U. Mo., Kansas City, 1985—. Cons. Nat. Inst. Dental Rsch., Washington, 1975-85. Contbr. numerous articles to profl. jours. Recipient rsch. career devel. award NIH, 1975-80. Fellow Acad. Dentistry Internat., Internat. Coll. Dentists, Am. Coll. Dentists; mem. ADA (cons. 1982—, joint com. on nat. dental exam., 1988-93, chair 1992-93), Am. Assn. Dental Schs. (sect. chair 1985-86. chmn. schs. coun. of deans, 1992-93, pres. 1997-98), Am. Assn. Dental Rsch. (councillor 1974-76), Fedn. Dentaire Internat., Am. Assn. for Microbiology, Mid-Am. Masters Club, Omicron Kappa Upsilon. Episcopalian. Avocations: running, European current affairs. Office: U Mo-Kansas City Sch Dentistry 650 E 25th St Kansas City MO 64108-2716 Office Phone: 816-235-2010. Office Fax: 816-235-2157. Business E-Mail: reedm@umkc.edu.

REED, MICHAEL ROBERT, agricultural economist; b. Lawrence, Kans., July 11, 1953; s. Robert Stanley and Marian Lucille (Karr) R.; m. Patricia Gail Gurtler, Mar. 16, 1973; children: Laura Gail, Brian Michael. BS, Kans. State U., 1974; MS, Iowa State U., 1976, PhD, 1979. Asst. prof. U. Ky., Lexington, 1978-83, assoc. prof., 1983-89; prof., 1989—; exec. dir. Ctr. for Export Devel., 1988-95; dir. office of internat. affairs U. Ky., Lexington, 1994-98, dir. office of internat. programs for agr., 1998—. Cons. USDA, 1994-97, 02—, US AID, Washington, 1983-86, 99-01, 04-. Author: (textbook) International Trade in Agricultural Products, 2000; mem. editl. bd. So. Jour. of Agrl. Econs., 1983-86; contbr. articles to profl. jours. Grantee Farmer Coop. Svcs., 1982-84, 87-88, TVA, 1982-85, Fed. Crop Ins. Corp., 1985-87, USDA, 1986-2003, 2005—; recipient Outstanding Jour. Article award Soc. Farm Mgrs. and Rural Appraisers, 1986, Jour. Agrl. and Applied Econs., 2002 Mem. Am. Agrl. Econs. Assn., So. Agrl. Econs. Assn., Gamma Sigma Delta. Home: 2216 Bonhaven Rd Lexington KY 40515-1150 Office: U Ky Dept Agrl Econs 308 Barnhart Bldg Lexington KY 40546-0001 Office Phone: 859-257-7259. Business E-Mail: mrreed@uky.edu.

REED, MIRIAM BELL, legislative staff member; b. NYC, May 31, 1930; d. Samuel Dennis and Miriam Wilkes Bell; m. John Grady Reed, May 1, 1954; children: Roberta, Christine, Karen, Laura, Margaret, Abigail, Elisabeth. BA, Mount Holyoke Coll., 1952. Asst. to adminstrv. asst. Rep. Harlan Hagan, Washington, 1953-54; asst. to econ. prof. Littauer Sch. Pub. Adminstrn., Cambridge, Mass., 1954; producer, treas. Video Ed Prodns., Inc., Hyattsville, Md., 1974-90; Singapore testing coord. Malaysian Am. Commn. on Ednl. Exch., Singapore, 1991-92; legis. aide Del. Constance A. Morella, Annapolis, Md., 1978-86; legis. asst. Hon. Constance A. Morella, Washington, 1987-90, 92, 94-97; staff Friends of Connie Morella for Congress, 1999-2000. Cons. Acad. Arrangements Abroad, NYC, 1974-99. Rsch. and writing of ednl. hist. videotapes, 1974-90 (Pratt Libr. award 1986). V.p., pres. bd. LWV, Bronxville, NY, 1957-74; mem. Montgomery County Commn. on the Humanities, 1985-88; mem. Montgomery County Com. to Celebrate Md.'s 350th Birthday. Mem. Montgomery County Hist. Soc. (dir. 1998-2001), C&O Canal Assn. (info. officer 2000, 02, 2004-06). Avocations: swimming, hiking, backpacking. Home: 8221 Burning Tree Rd Bethesda MD 20817-2908 Personal E-mail: mreed8221@aol.com.

REED, PEARLIE SYLVESTER, federal agency administrator; b. Heth, Ark., 1948; married; 2 children. BS in Animal Husbandry, U. Ark., Pine Bluff, 1970; MPA with honors, Am. U., 1980. Fin. mgr., budget analyst, adminstrv. officer Soil Conservation Svc., Washington, 1977-81, adminstv. officer for Nat. Agrl. Lands Study, 1979, state conservationist in Calif., 1989-94; assoc. chief Nat. Resources Conservation Svc. (NRCS), 1994-97, chief, 1998—2002, regional conservationist we. region US, 2002—03; acting asst. sect. for adminstrn. USDA, Washington, 1997—98, asst. sec. for adminstrn., 2009—. Recipient Presdl. Rank award, Disting. Profl. Svc. award, Nat. Assn. Conservation Districts, Silver Plow Honor award, USDA, George Washington Carver Pub. Svc. Svc. Hall of Fame award. Office: USDA 14th & Independence Ave SW Washington DC 20250-0001*

REED, PEGGY ANNE, education educator; b. Kittaning, Pa., Apr. 25, 1954; d. Clarence Wade and Shirley Anne Pence; m. William Raymond Reed, Aug. 9, 1975; children: Meredith Anne Knapp, Kevin William, Christopher Paul. BS, Evangel U., Springfield, Mo., 1976; MEd, Mo. State U., Springfield, 1982; EdD, Nova Southeastern U., Ft. Lauderdale, Fla., 1990. Cert. tchr. Mo. Dept. Elem. and Secondary Edn., 1976. Kindergarten tchr. Fair Play Sch., Mo., 1976—84; substitute tchr. Pleasant Hope Schs., Mo., 1985, Bolivar Schs., Mo., 1985; assoc. prof. Evangel U., Springfield, Mo., 1985—. Dir. Early Childhood Ctr. Evangel U., 1985—97; child care training cons. State of Mo. Child Care Licensing, Jefferson City, 1998. Reader Ozarks Literacy Coun., Springfield, Mo., 2005—07; fifth grade tchr. First Assembly of God Missionettes, Bolivar, Mo., 1990—2005. Mem.: Nat. Assn. for Edn. of Young

Children. Avocations: crafts, reading. Home: 829 W Hughs St Bolivar MO 65613-2817 Office: Evangel Univ 1111 N Glenstone Springfield MO 65802 Business E-Mail: reedp@evangel.edu.

REED, R. DOUGLAS, music educator; b. Cheboygan, Mich., Apr. 17, 1947; s. Robert G. and Marian L. Reed; 1 child, Eric Douglas. MusB in Organ Performance, U. Mich., 1969, MusM in Organ Performance, 1971; cert. in Performance, U. Rochester, 1974, MusD in Performance and Lit., 1975. Prof. music U. Evansville, Ind., 1975—. Organist The Luth. Ch. Our Redeemer, Evansville, 1975—78; organist, dir. music First Presbyn. Ch., Evansville, 1980—88; prin. organist Cathedral Immaculate Conception, Memphis, 2001—02; cons. in field. Musician: Organ Concerts in United States, Europe, and Japan, William Albright: The King of Instruments, (albums) William Albright: Music for Organ and Harpsichord, Eastman American Music Series, Vol. 3, Douglas Reed Plays the C.B. Fisk Organ, Op. 98, Douglas Reed Plays the Taylor & Boody Organ, In Memoriam William Albright Douglas Reed Plays the C.B. Fisk Organ, Op. 110; author: (chapter) North American Organ Music after 1800 for Cambridge Companion to the Organ; contbr. articles to profl. jours. Recipient The Sadelle and Sidney Berger award, U. Evansville, 1998; grantee, The Mesker Trust Fund Evansville, Ind., 1978, U. Evansville, 1985, Ind. Arts Commn. and NEA, 1987, Friends U. Evansville Music, 1991, 2000, 2005; Global scholar, U. Evansville, 2007—08. Mem.: Westfield Ctr. Early Keyboard Studies, Organ Hist. Soc., Am. Guild Organists (dean 1998—2001), Phi Kappa Phi, Pi Kappa Lamda. Avocations: travel, reading, photography. Office: University of Evansville 1800 Lincoln Avenue Evansville IN 47722 Business E-Mail: dr5@evansville.edu.

REED, RALPH EUGENE, JR., political consultant, former political organization administrator; b. Portsmouth, Va., June 24, 1961; s. Ralph Sr. and Marcy R.; m. Jo Anne Young, 1987; children: Brittany, Ralph III, Christopher, Nicole. BA in History, U. Ga., 1985; Ph.D in Am. History, Emory U., 1991. Exec. dir. Christian Coalition, Chesapeake, Va., 1989-97; founder, pres. Century Strategies, Strategies Cons. Co., Duluth, Ga., 1997—; chmn. Ga. Republican Party, 2001—03; southeast regional campaign chmn. George Bush re-election campaign, 2003—04. Founder Students for Am., Raleigh, NC, 1984; lobbyist; spkr. in field. Author: Politically Incorrect: The Emerging Faith Factor in American Politics, 1994, After the Revolution: How the Christian Coalition is Impacting America, 1995, Active Faith: How Christians Are Changing the Face of American Politics, 1996. Named one of 25 Most Influential Republicans, Newsmax Mag., 2008. Office: Century Strategies 3235 Satellite Blvd Ste 575 Duluth GA 30096-9017*

REED, ROBERT PHILLIP, lawyer; b. Springfield, Ill., June 14, 1952; s. Robert Edward and Rita Ann (Kane) R.; m. Janice Leigh Kloppenberg, Oct. 8, 1976; children: Kevin Michael, Matthew Carl, Jennifer Leigh, Rebecca Ann. AB, St. Louis U., 1974; JD, U. Ill., 1977. Bar: Ill. 1977, U.S. Dist. Ct. (ctrl. dist.) Ill. 1979, U.S.Ct. Appeals (7th cir.) 1983, U.S. Dist. Ct. (so. dist.) Ill. 1992, Colo. 1993. Intern Ill. Legislature, Springfield, 1977-78; assoc. Traynor & Hendricks, Springfield, 1979-80; ptnr. Traynor, Hendricks & Reed, Springfield, 1981-88; pvt. practice Springfield, 1988—. Pub. defender Sangamon County, Ill., Springfield, 1979-81; hearing examiner Ill. State Bd. Elections, Springfield, 1981-88; spl. asst. atty. gen. State of Ill., Springfield, 1983—; instr. Lincoln Land Community Coll., Springfield, 1988. Trustee Springfield Pk. Dist., 1985-89. Mem.: NY Stock Exch. (arbitrator 2006—), Bar Assn. Met. St. Louis, Attys Title Guaranty Fund, Inc., Colo. Bar Assn., Ill. State Bar Assn., Nat. Assn. Securities Dealers, Inc. (arbitrator 1996—), Phi Beta Kappa. Roman Catholic. Office: 1129 S 7th St Springfield IL 62703-2418 Office Phone: 217-528-7333. Personal E-mail: reedlaw@sbcglobal.net.

REED, RONDI, actress, theater director; b. Dixon, Ill., Oct. 26, 1952; Mem. Steppenwolf Theatre Co., Chgo., 1979—. Dir.: (plays) Lydie Breeze, 1986, The Common Pursuit, 1988, Stepping Out, 1988, Ring Round the Moon, 1989; actor: Another Time, 1991 (Sarah Siddons award, 1991), The Rise and Fall of Little Voice, 1993, Picasso at the Lapin Agile, 1994, Side Man, 1999, Man From Nebraska, 2003, The Fall to Earth, 2004 (Joseph Jefferson award); (Broadway plays) The Grapes of Wrath, 1990, The Rise and Fall of Little Voice, 1994, August: Osage County, 2007 (Tony award for Best Featured Actress, 2008); (films) One More Saturday Night, 1986, Mo' Money, 1992, Born Yesterday, 1993, Joshua Tree, 1993, Fearless, 1993, Eye for an Eye, 1996, Jungle 2 Jungle, 1997, The Astronaut's Wife, 1999; (TV films) Desperate Choices: To Save My Child, 1992, Murder in the Heartland, 1993, A Streetcar Named Desire, 1995, Normal, 2003, Fargo, 2003; dir.: (plays) Wendall Greene, 2002. Office: Steppenwolf Theatre Co 4th Ave 758 W North Ave Chicago IL 60610

REED, SALLY GARDNER, cultural organization administrator; b. Greeley, Colo., Sept. 13, 1953; m. Harold F. Reed, 1981; children: Gardner F., Charles A. BA in English, Colo. State U., 1979; MLS, No. Ill. U., 1981. Dir. North Hampton (H.H.) Pub. Libr., 1981-85, Ilsley Pub. Libr., Middlebury, Vt., 1985-93, Ames (Iowa) Pub. Libr., 1993-95; dir. librs. Norfolk (Va.) Pub. Libr., 1995—2001; exec. dir. Friends of Librs. USA, Phila., 2001—07, Assn. Libr. Trustees, Advocates, Friends & Founds., 2007—08. Author: Small Libraries: A Handbook for Successful Management, 1991, 2d edit., 2002, Saving Your Library: A Guide to Getting, Using and Keeping the Power You Need, 1992, Library Volunteers: Worth the Effort!, 1994; editor: Creating the Future: Essays on the Future of Librarianship in an Age of Great Change, 1996, Speaking Out: Voices in Celebration of Intellectual Freedom, 1999, Making the Case for Your Library, 2001, 101+ Great Ideas for Libraries and Friends, 2004, Getting Grants in Your Community, 2005, Even More Great Ideas for Libraries and Friends, 2008; contbr. articles to profl. jours. Bd. dirs. Sheldon Art History Mus., Middlebury, 1988-93, United Way Story County, Ames, 1994-95; mem. cabinet United Way Norfolk, 1996-97, chair city campaign, 1997; chair Libr. Advocacy Inst., 2007. Recipient Recognition award Tidewater Area Minority Libr. Network, 1997, Am. Libr. Assoc. Herb & Virginia White award for Promoting Librarianship, 2000. Mem. ALA (chpt. coun. 1989-93, adv. com. office libr. outreach svcs. 1993-94, nat. libr. week com. 1993-95, presdl. com. pub. awareness 1994-96, councilor at large 1995-99, chair membership com. 1996, resolutions com. 1997, exec. bd. 1997-2001, chair pub. awareness com. 2004-06). Democrat. Office: Assn Libr Trustees Advs Friends & Founds 109 S 13th St # 3n Philadelphia PA 19107-4807 Home Phone: 267-210-0882; Office Phone: 312-280-2161. Business E-Mail: sreed@ala.org.

REED, SAM, Secretary of State, Washington; b. Portland, Oreg. m. Margie Reed, 1963; children: David, Kristen. BA, MA, Wash. State U. Cert. profl. elections officer. Exec. dir. Gov. Evans' Urban Affairs Coun.; asst. sec. state State of Wash., Olympia, 1969—75; dir. State Constl. Reform Commn., 1975—77; auditor Thurston County, 1978—2000; sec. state State of Wash., Olympia, 2001—. Exec. dir. Gov.'s Urban Affairs Coun., 1967—69; sec. Nat. Assn. Secretaries State (NASS), 2004; bd. mem. Fed. Election Commn. Voting System; internat. election observer, Uganda; mem. Americorps Adv. Coun., Wash. State Election Admin. & Cert. Bd. Recipient Gov.'s Disting. Vol. award, Thurston County Citizen of the Year Disting. Svc. award. Mem.: Mainstream Reps. of Wash., Wash. State Assn. County Auditors, Olympia Kiwanis. Republican. Avocations: running, piano, arts, tennis. Office: Office Sec of State Legislative Bldg 2nd Floor PO Box 40220 Olympia WA 98504 Office Phone: 360-902-4151. Office Fax: 360-586-5629. E-mail: sreed@secstate.wa.gov.

REED, SCOTT C., musician, educator, writer; s. Vernon C. Reed and Betty M. Ryan. MusB, U. of So. Calif., 1981. Adj. prof. Gov.'s State U., U. Pk., Ill., 1989—95, Prairie State Coll., Chgo. Heights, Ill., 1994—2005. Author: Getting Into Guitar Improvising: A Systematic Approach To Soloing, 2002, Getting Into Guitar Styles, 2005. Fellow, NEA, 1992—93. Mem.: Las Vegas Fedn. Musicians, Chgo. Fedn. Musicians. Office: Prarie State College 202 South Halsted Chicago Heights IL 60411

REED, SCOTT W., lawyer; b. Klamath Falls, Oreg., Apr. 26, 1928; s. Nelson and Margaret (White) Reed; m. Mary Lou Reed; children: Tara, Bruce. BA, Princeton U., NJ, 1954; LLB, Stanford U., Calif., 1955. Bar: Calif. 1955, Idaho 1956, US Dist. Ct. (9th cir.) Idaho 1956, US Supreme Ct. 1965. Pvt. practice, Coeur d'Alene, Idaho, 1956—59, 1961—; asst. US atty. US Dist. Ct., Boise, 1959—61. Dir. Nat. Audubon Soc., NY, 1975—96. Dir. Western Environ. Law Ctr., Eugene, Oreg., 1996—; trustee North Idaho Coll., Coeur d'Alene, Idaho, 1966—72, Coeur d'Alene Libr. Bd., Coeur d'Alene, Idaho, 1999—2004; bd. mem. City Planning Commn., Coeur d'Alene, Idaho, 1962—70; dir. Idaho Nature Conservancy, Ketchum, Idaho, 1993—2004, Idaho Water Resource Bd., Boise, Idaho, 1971—83. Lt. arty. US Army, 1951—53. Named Environmentalist of Yr., Idaho Fish and Game. Mem.: Calif. Bar Assn., Idaho Bar Assn. (dist. pres. 1967—68). Democrat. Avocations: ice skating, walking, history, travel. Home: 853 N Giesa Rd Coeur D' Alene ID 83814 Office: PO Box A Coeur D' Alene ID 83816 Office Fax: 2080-765-5117. Business E-Mail: scottwreed@imbris.com.

REED, SHERMAN KENNEDY, chemicals executive, consultant; b. Chgo., Apr. 11, 1919; s. Frank Hynes and Helen Louise (Kennedy) R.; m. Octavia Bailey, Oct. 11, 1943; children: Martin Bailey, Holly Anne Johnson, Julie Marie Reed. BS with honors, U. Ill., 1940; PhD, Cornell U., 1949. Asst. instr. chemistry Cornell U., 1940-43; asst. rsch. scientist Manhattan Project, NYC, 1942-46; asst. prof. Bucknell U., Lewisburg, Pa., 1946-50; with FMC Corp., 1950—, mgr., asst. dir. rsch., 1950-60, divisional dir. rsch. and devel., ctrl. rsch. dir., 1960-76, v.p., 1976-82, cons. Chgo., 1983—; dir. Avicon, Inc., 1970-82; pres., dir. FMC Gold Corp.; mng. dir. COGAS Devel. Co., 1975—; dir. Indsl. Rsch. Inst., NYC, Franklin Inst., Phila., 1976-83; chmn. bd. Franklin Rsch. Ctr., Phila., 1976-83. Fellow Am. Inst. Chemists; mem. AAAS, Am. Chem. Soc., Assn. Rsch. Dirs. (pres. 1973). Republican. Home and Office: 2300 Indian Creek Blvd W #C211 Vero Beach FL 32966-2400 Home Phone: 772-562-2003; Office Phone: 772-539-2369. Personal E-mail: shermankreed@bellsouth.net.

REED, STUART C., retail executive, former communications executive; b. Feb. 27, 1961; BA in Materials & Logistics Mgmt., Mich. State U.; MS, MIT. V.p. integrated supply chain IBM Corp., 1999—2002, v.p. strategy, process & systems, 2002—03, v.p. systems & storage, worldwide mfg. ops., 2003—04, v.p. systems, storage & software products, 2004—05; sr. v.p., chief supply chain officer Motorola, Inc., Schaumburg, Ill., 2005—06, exec. v.p., integrated supply chain, 2006—08; sr. v.p., pres. home services unit Sears Holding Corp., 2008—. Recipient Eli Broad sch. Bus. Outstanding Alumni award, 2005, IABC EXCEL award, 2007, Mich. State U. Metro Chgo. Disting. Alumnus award, 2007; Sloan Fellow. Office: Sears Holding Corp 3333 Beverly Rd Hoffman Estates IL 60179*

REED, SUSAN J., elementary school educator; d. Eldora L. and James E. Kraby; m. Terry R. Reed, Apr. 15, 1950; children: Jamie R., Daniel C. BS Phys. Edn., N.D. State U., Fargo, 1972; Elem. Edn. Endorsement, Mayville State U., ND, 1982. Cert. Tchr. Reading N.D. Dept. Pub. Instrn., Title I, 2003, Tchr. Math. N.D. Dept. Pub. Instrn., Title I, 2003. Tchr. h.s. phys. edn. Linton Pub. Sch., ND, 1972—73; office asst. Farmers Home Adminstrn. USDA, Hillsboro, ND, 1974—81; tchr. elem. sch. Hillsboro Pub. Sch., 1984—. Dir. and treas. Hillsboro Scholarship Found., 2002—. Recipient Tchr. of Yr., Hillsboro Edn. Assn., 2005; named to Who's Who Among Am. Tchrs., 2006, 2007. Mem.: Hilsboro Edn. Assn., N.D. Edn. Assn. Avocations: reading, golf.

REED, THOMAS JAMES, law educator; b. Joliet, Ill., Jan. 1, 1940; s. Thomas p. and Bernardine M. (Dorsey) R.; m. Emily A. Fabrycki, Dec. 29, 1962; children: Martin, Valerie. BA, Marquette U., 1962; JD, Notre Dame Law Sch., 1969. Bar: Ind. 1969, US Dist. Ct. (so. dist.) Ind. 1969, US Ct. Appeals (7th cir.) 1974, Mass. 1977, US Dist. Ct. Mass. 1979, Pa. 1982, US Ct. Appeals (3rd cir.) 1982. Assoc. Reller, Mendenhall, Kleinknecht & Milligan, Richmond, Ind., 1969-76; asst. prof. law We. New Eng. Coll. Sch. Law, Springfield, Mass., 1976-79, assoc. prof., 1979-81, Widener U. Del. Law Sch., Wilmington, Del., 1981-84, prof., 1984—; assoc. dean Widener U. Law Sch., Wilmington, Del., 1984-93, prof. law, 1993—; dir. Vets. Law Clinic, 2006—, Taishoff prof. law, 2009—. Hist. preservation planner City Planning Assn., Mishawaka, Ind., 1969-71, Hist. Centerville Inc., Ind., 1970-76, Old Richmond, 1975-76. Contbr. articles to profl. jours. Reporter Del. Appellate Handbook, Wilmington, 1984—. Mem. ABA, Fed. Bar Assn., Ind. Bar Assn., Pa. Bar Assn. Roman Catholic. Avocations: civil war history, genealogy, historic preservation. Office: Widener U Law Sch 4601 Concord Pike PO Box 7474 Wilmington DE 19803-0474 Business E-Mail: tjreed@mail.widener.edu.

REED, TIMOTHY PETER, language educator; PhD, Pa. State U., 2002. Grad. tchg. asst. Pa. State U., State Coll., 1997—2002; asst. prof. spanish Ripon Coll., Wis., 2003—. Office: Ripon Coll 300 Seward St Ripon WI 54971

REED, TRAVIS DEAN, public relations executive; b. Trinity, Tex., Sept. 27, 1930; s. Travis and Alma (Rains) R.; m. Caroline M. McDonald, June 15, 1957; children: Anne Reed Adams, Lisa Reed Lettau. Student, Tex. A&M U., 1948-51, U. Houston, 1951-53. Reporter Houston Post, 1951-53; Washington Bur. corr. McGraw-Hill Pub. Co., 1955-61, Boston Herald-Traveler, 1961-62; with Newhouse News Svc., Washington, 1962-79, chief corr., 1964-67, editor, 1967-79; pub. rels. cons. Washington, 1979—. 1st lt. U.S. Army, 1953-55. Mem. Nat. Press Club, Gridiron Club, Army and Navy Club. Home: 37277 Branchriver Rd Purcellville VA 20132-1922 Office: T Dean Reed Co PO Box 65276 Washington DC 20035

REED, W. FRANKLIN, lawyer; b. Louisville, Dec. 30, 1946; s. William Ferguson and Stella Elizabeth (Richardson) R.; m. Sharon Ann Coss, June 16, 1973; children: Jonathan Franklin, William Brian, Carrie Ann. BA, Williams Coll., 1968; JD, Columbia U., 1971. Bar: N.Y. 1972, U.S. Dist. Ct. (so. dist.) N.Y. 1975, U.S. Ct. Appeals (2d cir.) 1975, Pa. 1982, U.S. Dist. Ct. (we. dist.) 1983. Assoc. Milbank, Tweed, Hadley & McCloy, NYC, 1971-82, Reed Smith Shaw & McClay, Pitts., 1982-83; ptnr. Reed, Smith, Shaw & McClay, Pitts., 1984—. Mem. instnl. devel. com. The Pitts. Cultural Trust; chmn., bd. dirs. Steel Industry Heritage Corp. Mem. ABA, Pa. Bar Assn., Allegheny Bar Assn., Carnegie 100, Williams Coll. Alumni Soc. W. Pa. (sec. 1983—), Rivers Club (Pitts.), St. Clair Country Club (Upper St. Clair, Pa.), Duquesne Club (Pitts.), Phi Beta Kappa. Democrat. Presbyterian. Avocations: fishing, golf. Home: 525 Miranda Dr Pittsburgh PA 15241-2039 Office: Reed Smith LLP 435 6th Ave Pittsburgh PA 15219-1886 E-mail: wreed@reedsmith.com.

REED, WALLACE ALLISON, anesthesiologist; b. Covina, Calif., May 19, 1916; s. Wallace Allison and Mary Julia (Birdsall) Reed; m. Maria Eva Wiemers, Jan. 20, 1938; children: Ellen E., Barbara R., Wallace J., Michael E., Kathryn L., Vikki T. AB, UCLA, 1937; postgrad., U. Cologne, 1937-38, U. Freiburg, 1938-39; MD, U. So. Calif., 1944. Diplomate Am. Bd. Anesthesiology. Intern Santa Fe Coast Lines Hosp., Los Angeles, 1943—44; resident Precept Sanders-Valley Forge Hosp., 1944—46, Los Angeles County Gen. Hosp., 1946-47; asst. to head dept. anesthesiology Precept Dillon-Los Angeles County Gen. Hosp., 1946-47; clin. instr. surgery U. So. Calif. Sch. Medicine, 1946-47; practice medicine, specializing in anesthesiology Phoenix, 1948-89; ret., 1989. Hon. staff mem. Good Samaritan Hosp., St. Joseph Hosp., Maricopa County Gen. Hosp.; mem. hon. staff Children's Hosp.; co-founder John L. Ford, M.D., Surgicenter, 1970; vice pres. Maricopa Found. for Med. Care, 1970-74, pres., 1975-76; mem. House Ways and Means Adv. Com.; adv. coun. Nat. Health Inst., 1975-76; mem. accreditation coun. for ambulatory health care Joint Commn. on Accreditation of Hosps., 1975-79; vice-chmn. Accreditation Assn. for Ambulatory Health Care, 1979-81, pres., 1981-83; mem. panel for study Nat. Health Ins., Congl. GAO; chmn. bd. Alterna Care Corp., 1984-87, now chmn. bd. emeritus; mem. adv. bd. Kino Inst., 1994-95. Bd. dirs. South Phoenix Montessori Sch., pres. bd., 1971—75; bd. dirs. Alzheimer's Assn., Greater Phoenix chpt., 1998—2000, co-v.p., 2000; co-chmn. med. and sci. adv. com. Desert S.W. chpt. Alzheimer's Assn., 2004—05; bd. dirs. Ctrl. Ariz. Health Sys. Agy., 1975—78; exec. dir. Surgictr. of Phoenix, 1987—97. Capt. M.C. AUS, 1944—46. Recipient Pinal award Ariz. Psychiat. Soc., 1967-68, Gerard B. Lambert Merit award for innovative ideas that improve patient care; John L. Ford M.D., 1972; recipient spirit of philanthropy award Alzheimer's Assn., 1996, Samba Disting. Svc. award, 2000; Disting. Svc. award Ariz. Soc. Anesthesiology, 2003. Fellow: Am. Coll. Anesthesiologists; mem.: AMA, Alzheimer's Assn. (co-chmn. med. and sci. adv. com. Desert S.W. chpt. 2004—05, co-v.p. Greater Phoenix (Ariz.) chpt. 2000), Soc. for Advancement Geriatric Anesthesia (charter mem.), Guedel Assn. (pres. 1972), Am. Assn. Founds. for Med. Care (dir. 1970—74), Central Ariz. Physicians Svc. Assn. (pres. 1982—83), Maricopa County Med. Soc. (pres. 1964, dir., Salsbury medal 1967, 1971, Thomas Dooley medal 1970), Internat. Assn. Amb. Surgery (hon.), Soc. for Ambulatory Anesthesia (bd. dirs. 1985—87), Federated Amb. Surgery Assn. (pres. 1974—75, dir.), Acad. Anesthesiology (dir. 1966—72, pres. 1969), Ariz., Maricopa County Socs. Anesthesiologists, Am. Soc. Anesthesiologists, WarMer Rsch. Found., Seed Money for Growth Found. (pres. 1984—). Methodist. Home: 4716 N Dromedary Rd Phoenix AZ 85018-2939 Office: 1040 E Mcdowell Rd Phoenix AZ 85006-2622 Home Phone: 602-840-6349; Office Phone: 602-258-1521. Personal E-mail: somnus4@cox.net.

REED, WILLIAM R., JR., bank executive; Chmn. Nat. Bank of Commerce; vice chmn. Nat. Commerce Bancorporation; COO Nat. Commerce Fin. Corp., 2000—03, pres., CEO, 2003—04; vice chmn. SunTrust Banks Inc., Atlanta, 2004—. Mailing: SunTrust Banks Inc PO Box 4418 Atlanta GA 30308-4418 Office Phone: 404-588-7711. Office Fax: 404-827-6173.

REED, WILLIS, professional sports team executive; b. Hico, La., June 25, 1942; s. Willis and Inell R.; m. Geraldine Oliver (div.); children: Carl, Veronica.; m. Gale Reed. Student, Grambling Coll., 1960—64. Center, forward NY Knicks, 1964—74, head coach, 1977—78, spl. basketball adv., 2003—04; head coach Creighton U., Omaha, 1981—85, NJ Nets, 1988—89, sr. v.p. basketball ops., 1989—92, exec. v.p., gen mgr., 1992—96, sr. v.p. basketball ops, 1996—97, sr. v.p., 1997—2003; asst. coach Atlanta Hawks, 1985—87, Sacramento Kings, 1987—88; v.p. basketball ops. New Orleans Hornets (formerly Charlotte Hornets), 2004—. Author: (with Phil Pepe) The View from the Rim, 1971. Named to NBA All-Star Team, 1965-71, Naismith Meml. Hall of Fame, 1982; named NBA Rookie of Yr., 1965, NBA All-Star Game MVP, 1970, NBA MVP, 1970, NBA Playoffs MVP, 1970, 73. Achievements include winning NBA Championships as a member of the Knicks, 1970, 73. Office: New Orleans Hornets 1250 Poydras St # 19 New Orleans LA 70113-1804 Office Phone: 504-301-4000.*

REEDER, JOE ROBERT, lawyer, former federal official; b. Tacoma, Nov. 28, 1947; s. William Thomas and Marilyn Ruth (Parker) R.; m. Katharine Randolph Boyce, Jan 1, 1983; children: Rachael Anne, Aubrilyn, Julia, Kelsey. BS, U.S. Mil. Acad., West Point, NY, 1970; JD, U. Tex., 1975; LLM, Georgetown U., 1981. Bar: Tex. 1975, D.C. 1979, U.S. Dist. Ct. (so. dist.) Tex 1975, U.S. Ct. Appeals (5th cir.) 1989, U.S. Ct. Claims 1979, U.S. Dist. Ct. D.C. 1982, U.S. Ct. Appeals (Fed. cir.) 1984, U.S. Supreme Ct. 1988, U.S. Ct. Appeals (4th cir.) 1988, Md. 1989, U.S. Dist. Ct. (Md. dist) 1989, U.S. Dist. Ct. (no. dist.) Tex. 1991, U.S. Dist. Ct. (so. dist.) Tex. 1991. Commd. 2d lt. U.S. Army, 1970, advanced through grades to maj., 1985; law clk. to presiding justice U.S. Dist. Ct. (so. dist.) Tex., 1976; trial atty. litigation div. U.S. Army, Pentagon, DC, 1976-78, trial atty. contract appeals div., 1978-79; assoc. Patton, Boggs & Blow, Washington, 1979-82, ptnr., 1983-93; under sec. of U.S. Army U.S. Dept. Def., Washington, 1993; chmn. bd. Panama Canal Commn., 1994; now shareholder-in-charge Mid-Atlantic Region, bd. dir. Greenberg Traurig LLP, Washington. Bd. dirs. Perma-Fix Environ. Svcs., Inc., 2003—. Bd. govs. Nat. Def. Industry Assn., Armed Svcs. YMCA, USO. Mem. ABA (assoc. editor pub. contract law jour. 1985-93), ATLA, Am. Law Inst., Fed. Bar Assn., D.C. Bar Assn., Tex. Bar Assn., Bar Assn. 5th Fed. Circuit, Bd. Contract Appeals Bar Assn., Rotary. Episcopalian. Office: Perma-Fix Environmental Services Inc Ste 250 8302 Dunwoody Pl Atlanta GA 30350 Office Phone: 770-587-9898. Office Fax: 770-587-9937. Business E-Mail: reederj@gtlaw.com.*

REEDER, MIKE FREDRICK, materials engineer, consultant; b. Woodriver, Ill., Mar. 10, 1955; s. Charles Fredrick and Bonnie Bell (Knight) R.; m. Julia A. Hodge, Jan. 15, 1977 (div. Sept. 1992); 1 child, Miranda E.; m. Terri Lynn Eckelbarger, Oct. 24, 1992; children: Shannon M. Crawford, Patric T. Crawford, Kristen E. Crawford. BA, Olivet U., 1977; postgrad., Ctrl. Mich. U., 1989-90. Assoc. engr. Carter Carburetor, St. Louis, 1977-80; pvt. practice Carlinville, Ill., 1981-85; mgr., materials and reliability engr. Walbro Engine Mgmt. Corp., Cass City, Mich., 1986—. Prof. math. and mgmt. Detroit Coll. Bus., Flint, Mich., 1994—; lectr. med. sch. Cass City, 1990-94; organizer Native Am. Aid, Pine Ridge, S.D., 1992—. Mem. AAAS, Soc. Automotive Engrs. (tchr. Vision 2000, 1991—), Am. Soc. Materials. Achievements include patent for a flexible composite membrane; discovery of relationship of performance of fuel metering membranes, of cause of corrosive action of ambient atmosphere in automotive fuel tanks on high pressure fuel pumps. Home: 6364 Cass City Rd Cass City MI 48726-9674 Office: Walbro Engine Mgmt Corp 6242 Garfield Ave Cass City MI 48726-1325

REEDER, ROBERT HARRY, retired lawyer; b. Topeka, Dec. 3, 1930; s. William Harry and Florence Mae (Cochran) Reeder. AB, Washburn U., 1952, JD, 1960. Bar: US Dist. Ct. Kans. 1960, Kans. 1960, US Supreme Ct. 1968. Rsch. asst. Kans. Legis. Coun. Rsch. Dept., Topeka, 1955—60; asst. counsel Traffic Inst., Northwestern U., Evanston, Ill., 1960—67, gen. counsel, 1967—92; exec. dir. Nat. Com. Uniform Traffic Laws & Ordinances, Evanston, 1982—90. Co-author: Vehicle Traffic Law, 1974; author: Interpretation of Implied Consent by the Courts, 1972. Served with US Army, 1952—54. Mem.: Com. Alcohol & Other Drugs (chmn. 1973—75). Republican. Methodist.

REEDER, STACY LYNN, geologist; d. Charles Hoffman and Sherry Hyatt Reeder. BS in Physics and Marine Sci., U. Miami, Coral Gables, Fla., 1999; MS in Applied Marine Physics, U. Miami, Va. Key, Fla., 2003, PhD in Marine Geology and Geophysics, 2007. Postdoc. intern Shell Internat. Exploration & Prodn., Houston, 2007; postdoc. scientist Schlumberger-Doll Rsch., Cambridge, Mass., 2007—, rsch. scientist, 2009—. Cons. asst. Rankey Enterprises, LLC, Miami, 2004—07. Contbr. articles to profl. jours., chapters to books. Youth advisor Plymouth Congl. Ch., Coconut Grove, Fla., 2000—07; with Big Bros. Big Sisters, Miami, 1999—2007. Recipient award, U. Miami Grad. Sch., 2006. Mem.: EAGE, SPWLA, SEPM, AAPG.

REED-PENTTINEN, DAPHNE STEVENSON, artist; b. Hartford, Conn. d. Edward McMurtry and Adele (Vaughan) Stevenson; m: Bruce Penttinen, 2001; children: Bonnie, Laurie, Rory. BA, Am. U., Washington, DC; MFA, U. Mass., Amherst, 1969. Rschr., author, editor, publisher, artist, Amherst, Mass., 1965—; instr., theatre dir. Mt. Holyoke Coll., South Hadley, Mass., 1970-72; tchr., adminstr., theatre dir. Hampshire Coll. and Amherst Coll., 1972-77; staff asst. Five Colls., Inc., Amherst, 1977-83; adminstr. U. Mass., Amherst, 1977-85; freelance editor, writer, artist, English lang. cons. Amherst, 1986—; writer, pub. Owl Pub., 1993—2006. Broadcaster Radio Reading Svcs. Western New Eng., Springfield, Mass., 1982-88; cons. in field. One woman show Artwork, 1994; author/dir. (plays) I Woman, 1970, This Thing Called Freedom, 1972; author The Secret World of Angels, 1999; editor Owl Angels Jour., 2000—06. Organizer Pioneer Valley (Mass.) chpt. P-FLAG, 1985, leader, 1994—, editor Owl Angels Jour. newsletter, 2001-06; founding charter mem. Com. on Race Rels., Amherst, 1970-73. Arts Coun. grantee, Amherst, 1987. Mem. Internat. Women's Writing Guild, Ednl. Theatre Assn., Mothers Against War (founder 2002). Democrat. Congregationalist. Avocations: theater, literature, writing, painting, metaphysical and political research. Home: 305 Middle St Amherst MA 01002-3016 Office Phone: 413-253-3354. Personal E-mail: owlangels@aol.com.

REEDY, WALTER JAY, history professor; b. Long Beach, Calif., Dec. 21, 1947; s. Walter E. and Ella M. Reedy; m. Diane K. Lausen. PHD, U. Calif., Santa Barbara, 1976. Assoc. prof. history ND State U., Fargo, 1978—90; prof. history Bryant U., Smithfield, PR, 1990—2008. Rsch. grant, Am. Philos. Soc., 1980. Office: Bryant Univ 1150 Douglas Pike Smithfield RI 02917 Business E-Mail: jreedy@bryant.edu.

REEHER, JAMES IRWIN, minister; b. Sharon, Pa., Dec. 6, 1948; s. James William and Lillian (Irwin) R.; m. Marian Powell, Oct. 25, 1969; children: Elizabeth Margret, James Michael. BA, U. Tampa, 1975; MDiv, Emory U., 1978; DD, Boston U., 1989. Ordained to ministry United Ch. Ch., 1978. Min. Christ United Meth. Ch., Tampa, Fla., 1972-75, Lamar United Meth. Ch., Barnesville, Ga., 1975-78, 1st United Meth. Ch., Seffner, Fla., 1986-90; asst. min. Grace United Meth. Ch., Venice, Fla., 1978-79; founding min. 1st United Meth. Ch., Sarasota, Fla., 1980-86; min. Forest Hills United Meth. Ch., Tampa, 1990—. Del. bd. ordained ministry Tampa Dist., 1987—; del. stewardship com. Fla. United Meth. Ch., Tampa, 1988—; bd. dirs. Jim Russo Prison Ministries, Bradenton, Fla., 1990—; chmn. anti-gambling campaign Fla. United Meth. Conf., 1986; v.p. Shade and Fresh Water, Inc. Founding chmn. East Hillsborough Orgn., Seffner, 1988; bd. dirs. Life Enrichment Sr. Ctr., Tampa, 1990—; founder Family Hall of Fame. Recipient Outstanding Religious Leader award Sarasota Jaycees, 1985. Mem. Assn. for Clin. Pastoral Edn., Alban Inst., North Tampa Ministerial Assn., West Orange Ministerial Assn. Democrat. Home: 3401 Kings Rd Saint Augustine FL 32086 Office: Grace United Meth Ch 8 Carrera St Saint Augustine FL 32084

REEKER, PHILIP THOMAS, United States Ambassador to Macedonia; b. Pa. m. Solveig Johnson. BA, Yale U., New Haven, 1986; MBA, Thunderbird Sch. Internat. Mgmt., 1991. Asst. info. officer US Dept. State, Budapest, Hungary, 1993—96, pub. affairs officer Skopje, Macedonia, 1997—99, dir. press rels. Washington, 1999—2000, dep. spokesman and dep. asst. sec., Bur. Pub. Affairs, 2000—03, spokesman-at-large, 2003—04, dep. chief of mission Budapest, 2004—07, counselor to the amb. for pub. affairs Baghdad, Iraq, 2007—08, US amb. to Macedonia Skopje, 2008—. Office: DOS Amb 7120 Skopje Pl Washington DC 20521-7120 Office Phone: 389-2-310-2000.

REEL, DAVID MARK, curator, museum director; b. Pitts., Nov. 21, 1969; m. Stephanie L. Wolf. BA in Art Hist. and Studio Art, Dickinson Coll., 1992; M in Visual Arts Adminstrn., NYU, 1994. Rsch. specialist Pa. State Capitol Preservation Com., Harrisburg, 1991; cons. Sotheby's Auction Ho., NYC, 1992; asst. curator, adminstr. Forbes Mag. Collection Forbes, Inc., NYC, 1993-98; chief curator, dir. West Point Mus. US Mil. Acad., NY, 1998—. Author: Guide to PA State Capitol, 1991, A Guide to Quarters 100, 1999 (Gold medallion, 1999); contbg. author: West Point/Points West, 2002. Bd. dirs. art alumni adv. coun. NYU, 1994—; trustee Friends Hermitage, Inc., Ho-Ho-Kus, NJ, 1997—2001, Hist. Soc. Newburgh Bay and Highlands, 2007—. Sr. scholar Victorian Soc., 1996; named among People to Watch Times Herald Record, 2001. Mem. Am. Assn. Mus. (mem. curators com.), Nat. Assn. Corp. Art Curators, Army Mus. Assn., Am. Assn. State and Local History, Nat. Trust Historic Preservation, Mus. Assn. NY, Highlands C. of C. Office: West Point Mus US Mil Acad 2110 South Post Rd West Point NY 10996 Office Phone: 845-938-3590. Office Fax: 845-938-7478.

REEP, EDWARD ARNOLD, artist; b. Bklyn., May 10, 1918; s. Joseph and Elsie (Abramson) R.; m. Karen Patricia Stevens, Dec. 9, 1942; children— Susan Kay, Cristine Elyse, Janine J., Mitchell Jules. Student, Art Center Coll. Design, 1936-41. Instr. painting and drawing Art Center Coll. Design, Los Angeles, 1946-50, Chouinard Art Inst., Los Angeles, 1950-69; prof. painting, chmn. dept., artist in residence E. Carolina U., 1970-85, prof. emeritus, 1985—. Cons. editor Van Nostrand Reinhold Pub. Co.; ofcl. war artist-corr. WWII, Africa and Italy. Author: The Content of Watercolor, 1968, A Combat Artist in World War II, 1987; shows include Whitney Mus. Am. Art Ann., N.Y.C., 1946-48, Los Angeles County Mus. Ann., 1946-60, Corcoran Gallery Art Biennial, Washington, 1949, Nat. Gallery Art, Washington, 1945, They Drew Fire, 2000, Mus. Modern Art, N.Y.C.; represented in permanent collections Los Angeles County Mus., U.S. War Dept., Grunwald Graphic Arts Collection, UCLA, Nat. Mus. Am. Art, Washington, Lytton Collection, Los Angeles, State of Calif. Collection, Sacramento. Guggenheim fellow, 1945-46; Nat. Endowment for Arts grantee, 1975 Mem. AAUP, Nat. Watercolor Soc. (past pres., Lifetime Achievement award 2002), Watercolor USA Honor Soc. (lifetime achievement gold medal 1997). Democrat. Home: 9021 Crowningshield Dr Bakersfield CA 93311-1901 Home Phone: 661-664-1028. *I once was consumed by the desire to become an artist. I feel no differently today. There is work ahead. If I had set goals for myself I no longer can recall what they may have been; I go along painting as well or as inventively as I can. Never have I sacrificed living life as I feel I must for my art. My work is a reflection of my life— experiences real and imagined.*

REES, CLIFFORD HARCOURT, JR., (TED REES), consulting company executive, retired trade association administrator, military officer; b. Newport News, Va., Dec. 11, 1936; s. Clifford Harcourt Sr. and Mary Evelyn (Brooks) R.; m. Joan Elizabeth Mittong, July 26, 1958; children— Clifford Harcourt III, Steven M., Daniel B., William B. BS in Fgn. Svc., Georgetown U., 1958; MS in Polit. Sci., Auburn U., 1969; grad., Air War Coll., Montgomery, Ala., 1978; grad. program for sr. exec. in nat. and internat. security, JFK Sch. Govt., Harvard U. Commd. 2d lt. U.S. Air Force, 1958; advanced through grades to lt. gen., 1988; comdr. 421st Tactical Fighter Squadron, Udorn Royal Thai AFB, 1974-75; chief, house liaison office U.S. Ho. Reps., Washington, 1978-80; asst. col. assignments Randolph AFB, 1980-82; vice-comdr. Air Force Manpower and Personnel Ctr., 1982; dep. dir. legis. liaison Office Sec. Air Force, 1982-84, dir. legis. liaison, 1984-86; comdr. USAF Air Defense Weapons Ctr., Tyndall AFB, Fla., 1986-88; vice comdr. in chief USAF in Europe, Ramstein AB, Federal Republic of Germany, 1988-92, ret., 1992; founder, pres. Rees Group Cons., 1992—; pres. Air Conditioning and Refrigeration Inst., Arlington, Va., 1993—2002. U.S. rep. to v.p. Internat. Coun. Mil. Sports, Brussels, 1982-94; dir. bd. dirs. Armed Forces Benefit Assn. Investment Mgmt. Co., 1996—. Decorated D.S.M. with one oak leaf cluster, DFC with one oak leaf cluster, Legion of Merit with one oak leaf cluster, Meritorious Svc. medal with one oak leaf cluster, Air medal with 11 oak leaf clusters, Das Grosse Verdienstkreuz Mit Stern, Fed. Republic Germany; named comdr. Order of Meritorious Svc. Internat. Mil. Sports Coun., 1993, Order of the Sword, US Air Forces in Europe, 1992. Mem. Delta Phi Epsilon (v.p. membership 1957-58, nat. pres. 1984-86) Methodist. Home: 20 Spring Valley Ct Pinehurst NC 28374 E-mail: ted@thereesgroup.com.

REES, DAVID WILLIAM ALAN, engineering educator, researcher, writer; b. London, Ruislip, Middlesex, England, Mar. 12, 1947; s. Arthur Lovell Rees and Mary Jane Jones. MSc, DIC, Imperial Coll., London, 1971; MA (hon.), Trinity Coll., Dublin, Ireland, 1981; PhD, Kingston U., Kingston-upon Thames, Surrey, 1975; DSc, Brunel U., 2003. C. eng. 1972; mem. I.Mech.E., London, 1971. Apprentice Black & Decker, 1963—68, prodn. engr., 1968—69; rsch. asst., lectr. Kingston Polytech., 1970—77; lectr. Trinity Coll., Dublin, 1977—84; sr. lectr. Brunel U., London, Uxbridge, Middlesex, 1985—. Lectr. in engring. sci. Trinity Coll., Dublin, 1977—84; lectr. Surrey U., Guildford, Surrey, 1984—85; sr. lectr. Brunel U., Uxbridge, Middlesex, 1986—; vis. rschr. Joint Rsch. Ctr., Petten, Netherlands, 1982, Nat. Phys. Lab., Teddington, England, 1983—85. Editl. bd. mem. Internat. Jour. Plasticity, 1985—91, Jour. Strain Analysis Engring. Design, 1994—2006; author: (books) Mechanics of Solids and Structures, 1990, 2nd edit., 2000, Basic Solid Mechanics, 1997, Basic Engineering Plasticity, 2006; contbr. scientific papers and articles to profl. jours. (Fylde Prize, 1993, CEGB Prize, 1997); author: (book) Mechanics of Optimum Structures Design, 2009, Optimum Structural Design, 2009. Grantee Tchg. Co. Schemes, D.t.i., England, 1994-1998, Faraday Partnership, Epsrc, England, 1998-2001. Fellow: Royal Soc. Medicine London; mem.: Old Centralians (assoc.; city and guilds assn. 1985—2003). Liberal. Meth. Achievements include research in plasticity, creep fatigue, fracture. Avocations: photography, bicycling. Office: Brunel Univ Kingston Ln Uxbridge Middlesex London UB8 3PH England Office Phone: 0 1895 265837. Office Fax: 44 0 1895 269763. Business E-Mail: david.rees@brunel.ac.uk.

REES, ELLEN, psychoanalyst, psychiatrist; b. NYC; d. Judson and Katherine Rees; m. David Douglas Olds; 1 child, Beverly Bergund. BA Magna cum Laude, Oberlin Coll., Ohio, 1965; MD, Albert Einstein Coll. Medicine, Bronx, NY, 1974. Diplomate Am. Bd. Psychiatry & Neurology, 1979, Am. Psychoanalytic Assn., 1999. Chair curriculum com. Columbia Ctr. Psychoanalytic Tng. and Rsch., NYC, 1997—2003, tchg. faculty, 1991—, tng. and supervising analyst, 1999—; pvt. practice NYC, 1977—; clin. assoc. prof. Weill Cornell Med. Coll., NYC, 2003—; tchg. faculty Berkshire Psychoanalytic Inst., Stockbridge, Mass., 2003—, tng. and supervising analyst, 2005—, founding mem., chair edn. com., 2006—. Mem. editl. bd. Jour. Am. Psychoanalytic Assn., NYC, 2002—05; mem. bd. editl. readers Psychoanalytic Quar., NYC, 2005—. Recipient Janet M. Glasgow award, Am. Med. Women's Assn., 1974, John F. O'Connor award, Columbia U. Ctr. Psychoanalytic Tng. and Rsch., 1994; grantee Howard Klar Tchr. of the Yr. award, 2000. Fellow: Am. Psychiat. Assn. (Nancy C.A. Roeske, M.D. award 1994); mem.: Berkshire Psychoanalytic Inst. (chair of the edn. com. 2006—), Assn. Psychoanalytic Medicine, Am. Psychoanalytic Assn., Alpha Omega Alpha (award 1974), Phi Beta Kappa (award 1995). Avocations: reading, travel. Office: Ellen Rees MD 108 E 96th St 7F New York NY 10128

REES, FRANK WILLIAM, JR., architect; b. Rochester, NY, June 5, 1943; s. Frank William and Elizabeth R. (Miller) R.; m. Joan Mary Keevers, Apr. 1, 1967; children: Michelle, Christopher. BS in Architecture, U. Okla., 1970; postgrad., Harvard U., Boston, 1979-90; OPM, Harvard U., 1990; DArch, U. Hawaii, 2001. Registered architect, 39 states & D.C.; cert. Nat. Coun. Archtl. Registration Bds.; registered interior designer. Sales mgr. Sta. KFOM, Oklahoma City, 1967-70; project architect Benham-Blair & Affiliates, Oklahoma City, 1970-75; pres., CEO, founder Rees Assocs., Inc., Oklahoma City, 1975—. Pres., chmn. bd. Weatherscan Radio Network, Oklahoma City, 1973-78; chmn. bd. Weatherscan Internat., Oklahoma City, 1972-78; pres. Frontier Communications, Oklahoma City, 1980-84; chmn. architecture bd. U. Okla., Norman, 1988-91; bd. dirs. Century, Inc., Oklahoma City. Past pres. Lake Hefner Trails, Oklahoma City, Hosp. Hospitality House, Oklahoma City, Oklahoma City Beautiful; mem. Leadership Oklahoma City. Mem. AIA, Am. Assn. Hosp. Architects, Am. Healthcare Assn., Tex. Hosp. Assn., World Pres. Orgn. (chmn. 1997-98), Assisted Living Fedn. of Am., Am. Assn. Homes and Svcs. for the Agig. Home: 1104 Stone Gate Dr Irving TX 75063-4676 also: 1801 N Lamar St Ste 600 Dallas TX 75202-1711 Office Phone: 214-522-7337.

REES, MARTIN JOHN, astronomy educator; b. York, Eng., June 23, 1942; s. Reginald and Joan (Bett) R. MA, PhD, Cambridge U., Eng., 1967; DSc (hon.), Sussex U., Eng., 1990, Leicester U., 1993, Uppsala U., Sweden, 1995, Keele U., Eng., 1995, Newcastle U., 1995, Copenhagen U., 1995, Toronto U., Can., 1997, Durham U., Eng., 1999, Oxford U., 2000, Exeter U., 2006, Hull U., 2007, Yale U., 2008, Liverpool U., 2008, Open U., 2008, McMastis, 2009; McMastis, East Anglia, 2009. Rsch. fellow Calif. Tech. Inst., 1968; vis. rsch. fellow Inst. for Advanced Study, Princeton, NJ, 1969, 82, 96, 97; vis. scientist Harvard U., Cambridge, Mass., 1972, 87-90; Regents fellow Smithsonian Instn., 1984-87; prof. Sussex U., 1972-73; Plumian prof. astronomy Cambridge U., 1973-91; dir. Inst. Astronomy, Cambridge, 1977-91; rsch. prof. Royal Soc. Cambridge U., England, 1992—2003, prof. cosmology and astrophysics, 2002—; master Trinity Coll., Cambridge, 2004—; astronomer royal, 1995—2005. Fellow King's Coll., Cambridge U., England, 1969—2003; hon. fellow Trinity Coll., 1995—, Jesus Coll., 1996—, Cardiff U., Wales, 1998, Darwin Coll., 2004—, King's Coll., 2007—; vis. prof. Harvard U., Princeton U., Calif. Tech., Imperial Coll., London, Leicester U., hon. prof.; bd. trustees Brit. Mus., 1996—2002, Nat. Endowment for Sci., Tech. and Arts, 1998—2001, Inst. for Advanced Study, Princeton, 1998—, Kennedy Meml. Trust, England, 1999—2004, Inst. for Pub. Policy Rsch., 2001—, Nat. Mus. of Sci. and Tech., 2003—. Author: (with M.C. Begelman) Gravity's Fatal Attraction, 1995, Perspectives in Astrophysical Cosmology, 1995, Before the Beginning, 1997, Just Six Numbers, 1999, Our Cosmic Habitat, 2001, Our Final Century?, 2003. Decorated officer Order of Arts and Letters (France); recipient Heinemann prize, Am. Inst. Physics, 1984, Gold medal, Royal Astron. Soc., 1987, Balzan prize, 1989, Robinson prize, 1990, Bruce medal, 1993, Sci. Writing award, Am. Inst. Physics, 1996, Bower award, Franklin Inst., 1998, Rossi prize, AAS, 2000, Cosmology prize, Gruber Found., 2001, Einstein award, World Sci. Coun., 2003, Crafoord prize, Royal Swedish Acad., 2005, Niels Bohr prize, UNESCO, 2005; created knight bachelor, 1992, created life peer, 2005. Fellow AAAS, Royal Soc. London (pres. 2005-, Henry Norris Russell lectureship, 2004), Royal Netherlands Acad. Arts and Scis., Indian Acad. Scis. (hon.), Russian Acad. Scis. (hon.), Swedish Acad. Scis., Am. Philosophy Soc.; mem. NAS (fgn. assoc.), Pontifical Acad. Scis., Academia Europea, Inst. Physics (Eng.) (Guthrie prize 1990—), Royal Astron. Soc. (pres. 1992-94), Brit. Assn. Advancement Sci. (pres. 1994-95), Royal Sorority (pres. 2005-), Norwegian Acad. Sci., Acad. Lincei (Rome), Finnish Acad. Arts and Sci. Anglican. Office: Inst Astronomy Cambridge England CB3 0HA also: Trinity Coll Cambridge CB2 1TQ England

REES, MICHAEL A., urologist; MD, U. Mich., Ann Arbor; PhD, U. Cambridge. Resident in urology U. Va., Charlottesville; fellow in transplantation U. Cambridge, England; assoc. prof. urology U. Toledo Med. Ctr., med. dir. Paired Kidney Donation Prog., 2004—; founder Alliance for Paired Donation. Office: U Toledo Med Ctr 3000 Arlington Ave Toledo OH 43614 Office Phone: 419-383-7025. Office Fax: 419-383-3153.*

REES, NORMA S., academic administrator; b. NYC, Dec. 27, 1929; d. Benjamin and Lottie (Schwartz) D.; m. Raymond R. Rees, Mar. 19, 1960; children— Evan Lloyd, Raymond Arthur BA, Queens Coll., 1952; Ma, Bklyn. Coll., 1954; PhD, NYU, 1959; D of Arts and Letters honoris causa, John F. Kennedy U., 2001. Cert. speech-language pathology, audiology. Prof. communicative disorders Hunter Coll., NYC, 1967-72; exec. officer, speech and hearing scis. grad. sch. CUNY, NYC, 1972-74, assoc. dean for grad. studies, 1974-76, dean grad. studies, 1976-82; vice chancellor for acad. affairs U. Wis., Milw., 1982-85, from 1986, acting chancellor, 1985-86; vice chancellor for acad. policy and planning Mass. Bd. Regents for Higher Edn., Boston, 1987-90; pres. Calif. State U. East Bay, Hayward, 1990—. Chmn. Commn. Recognition of Postsecondary Accreditation, 1994-96; mem. adv. com. quality and integrity U.S. Dept. Edn., commn. on internat. edn. Coun. on Higher Edn. Accreditation, 2003—. Contbr. articles to profl. jours. Trustee Citizens Govtl. Rsch. Bur., Milw., 1985-87; active Task Force on Wis. World Trade Ctr., 1985-87; bd. dirs. Am. Assn. State Colls. and Univs., 1995-97, Coun. of Postsecondary Accreditation, Washington, 1985-94, Greater Boston YWCA, 1987-90; mem. Calif. Sch. to Career Coun.; bd. dir. Econ. Devel. Alliance for Bus., Alameda County, 1995—; sec. edn. Nat. Adv. Com. Institutional Quality and Integrity, 1998-2002; bd. dirs. Bay Area World Trade Ctr., 2001—, Alameda County Health Care Found., 2002-. Fellow Am. Speech-Lang-Hearing Assn. (honors); mem. Am. Coun. Edn. (com. internat. edn. 1991-93), Am. Assn. Colls. and Univs. (chair task force on quality assessment 1991-92), Nat. Assn. State Univs. and Land Grant Colls. (exec. com. divsn. urban affairs 1985-87, com. accreditation 1987-90), Hayward C. of C. (bd. dirs. 1995-98), Oakland C. of C. (bd. dirs. 1997-2004). Office: Calif State Univ East Bay 25800 Carlos Bee Blvd Hayward CA 94542-3001 Home Phone: 510-889-8069; Office Phone: 510-885-3877. E-mail: norma.rees@csueastbay.edu.

REES, RAYMOND F., military officer; b. Pendleton, Oreg., Sept. 29, 1944; s. Raymond Emmett and Lorna Doone (Gemmell) R.; m. Karen Kristine Young, Nov. 1966 (div. Mar. 1974); children: Raymond Gordon, Christian Frederick; m. Mary Len Middleton, Dec. 30, 1977; 1 child, Carrie Evelyn. BS, U.S. Mil. Acad., 1966; JD, U. Oreg., 1976. Commd. 2d lt. U.S. Army, 1966, 2005—; platoon leader, troop exec. officer, co. comdr. 2d Armored Cavalry Regiment, Bamberg, Fed. Republic Germany; troop comdr. 2-17 Cavalry 101 Airborn divsn., Camp Eagle, Vietnam, 1969; troop exec. officer 1-17 Cavalry 82 Airborn divsn., Ft. Bragg, N.C., 1972; resigned U.S. Army, 1973; with Oreg. Army Nat. Guard, 1973—, advanced through grades to maj. gen., 1990; asst. ops. officer Infantry Brigade; co. comdr. 2d Battalion, 162d Infantry, Corvallis, Oreg.; with 116th Armored Calvary Regiment, 1976-87; comdr. 116th cavalry regiment, adjutant gen. Oreg. Army Nat. Guard, 1987-91; dir. Army N.G., 1991-92; vice chief N.G. Bur., Washington, 1992-94; adjutant gen. Oreg. N.G., 1994-99; vice chief N.G. Bur., Washington, 1999—2002, acting chief, 2002—03; chief of staff Hdqrs. NORAD and U.S. No. Command, 2003—05. Decorated Bronze Star, Legion of Merit, D.S.M., Def. Disting. Svc. medal. Mem. VFW, Adjutant Gen. Assn. U.S., Nat. Guart Assn. U.S., Assn. of U.S. Army, Oreg. Nat. Guard Assn., U.S. Armor Assn., Oreg. Bar Assn., Am. Legion, Mil. Order World Wars, West Point Soc. Oreg., 101st Airborne Div. Assn., 116th Armored Cavalry Assn., 41st Infantry Div. Assn., Elks. Office Phone: 503-584-3991.

REES, RILEY, medical educator; b. Gunnison, Utah, July 22, 1948; s. Gordan S. Rees and Frances Ford; married. BS, U. Utah, Salt Lake City, 1970, D in Medicine, 1973. Assoc. prof. surgery Vanderbilt U., Nashville, 1980—; prof. surgery U. Mich., Ann Arbor, 1988—. Office: Univ Mich 2130 TC 1500 E Med Ctr Dr Ann Arbor MI 48109-0340 Business E-Mail: rreese@umich.edu.

REESE, AUDREY MARIA, music educator; b. Atlanta, July 25, 1957; d. Charles and Zola Allen. BA, Columbus U., 1981. Ga. Educator Cert., 1981. Violinist Columbus Symphony Orch., Ga., 1976—81; violinist/violist African Am. Philharmonic Orch., Atlanta, 1988—; violinist Eclectic String Quartet and Just Friends, Atlanta, 1987—, Orch. Atlanta, 1994—96; violinist/violist Music South Corp., Atlanta, 1988—; condr. Still Waters Youth Sinfo-Nia, 2002—04; tchr. orch. Atlanta Bd. Edn., 1981—. Music curriculum writing com. Atlanta Bd. Edn., music adv. team, music textbook adoption com., 2004—. Ga. incentive Atlanta Bd. Edn., 1989; star tchr. achievement Ga. Dept. Edn., 1991. Recipient Tchr. of Yr., Atlanta Pub. Schools, 2002—03. Mem.: Nat. String Orch. Assn., Music Educators Nat. Conf., Ga. Music Assn. (sec. 1995—97). African Meth. Episc. Avocations: reading, dance, music, gardening. Home: 1335 Gates Dr Atlanta GA 30316

REESE, C. RICHARD, data processing executive; BS, MS in Ceramic Engring., Clemson Univ.; MBA, Harvard Univ. Former cons.; former pres., dir. PRISM Internat. trade assn.; lectr. Harvard Bus. Sch.; pres., CEO Iron Mountain Inc., Boston, 1981—95, chmn., pres., CEO, 1995—2005, chmn., CEO, 2005—08, exec. chmn., 2008—. Bd. dir. Bird Dog Solutions, Continental Fire & Safety LLC; mem. investment com. Schooner Capital LLC. Recipient New England Entrepreneur of Yr., Ernst & Young, 2003. Office: Iron Mountain 745 Atlantic Ave Boston MA 02111 Office Phone: 617-535-4766.

REESE, CHARLES WOODROW, JR., lawyer, real estate developer; b. San Antonio, June 21, 1944; s. Charles Woodrow and Mary Ruth (Gott) R.; m. Jill Fritschi, Aug. 10, 1979; children: Clarissa, Alexandra. BA cum laude, Washington and Lee U., 1966; JD, U. Calif., Berkeley, 1969. Bar: Calif. 1970, US Sup. Ct. 1976. Assoc. McCutchen, Doyle, Brown & Enersen, San Francisco, 1969-75; staff atty. Kaiser Industries Corp., Oakland, Calif., 1975-78; asst. gen. csl. Kaiser Cement Corp., Oakland, 1978-86; mng. dir. Reese Interests, Houston, 1978—; mng. trustee Clotilde deMartini Trusts, San Francisco, 1977-; prin Lempres & Wulfsberg PC, Oakland, 1986-98; exec. v.p. Wulfsberg Reese & Sykes PC, 1998-2002; pres., CFO Wulfsberg Reese Colvig & Firstman PC, 2002—. Hon. trustee Orinda Found., 1976-79; bd. dirs. Planned Parenthood Alameda/San Francisco, 1981-83, Brown and Caldwell, Walnut Creek, 1987-, PLA Holdings, Inc., Port Costa, 1991-2000. Robert E. Lee Rsch. scholar, 1965-66. Mem. State Bar Calif., ABA, Bar Assn. San Francisco, Alameda County Bar Assn. (coms.), Omicron Delta Upsilon, Pacific Union Club (San Francisco), Orinda (Calif.) Country Club. Republican. Episcopalian. Home: 89 La Salle Piedmont CA 94611 Office: 300 Lakeside Dr 24th Fl Oakland CA 94612-3534 E-mail: creese@wulfslaw.com.

REESE, CLARA COOK, educator; b. Burke County, N.C., Nov. 11, 1931; m. Ned Ervin Reese, Aug. 25, 1950; children: Jerry Alan, Susan Clarice. AB, Lenoir Rhyne Coll., 1969; MA, N.C. State U., 1972, EdD, 1980. With finishing dept., supr. irregular dept. Ellis Hosiery Co., Inc., Hickory, N.C., 1952-62, payroll clk., receptionist, 1962-64; sales staff J.C. Penney Co., Hickory, N.C., 1968-69; tchr. Catawba Valley Tech. Inst., 1972-77, Newton-Conover City Schs., Newton, N.C., 1969-77; prof. dept. vocat. and adult tech. edn. Marshall U., Huntington, W.Va., 1980—. Author, co-author 12 occupational curricula, 1982-89. Chmn. bd. dirs. Career Exploration Clubs N.C., 1974-76; state advisor Career Exploration Clubs W.Va., 1982-92; bd. dirs. Huntington Boys and Girls Clubs, 1986—. Mem. Am. Vocat. Assn., W.Va. Vocat. Assn., Phi Delta Kappa, Epsilon Pi Tau. Democrat. Methodist. Office: Marshall U Dept Adult Tech Edn Huntington WV 25701 Business E-Mail: reese@marshall.edu.

REESE, FLOYD, professional sports team executive; Attended, UCLA, 1966—69. Linebacker Montreal Alouettes, Can. Football League, 1969; head football coach Liberty Union HS, Brentwood, Calif., 1970; asst. coach UCLA Bruins, 1971—73, Ga. Inst. Tech. Yellow Jackets, 1974; strength & conditioning coach Detroit Lions, 1975—77, San Francisco 49ers, 1978; linebackers coach, spl. teams coach Minn. Vikings, 1979—83, defensive. coord., 1984, linebackers coach, 1985, Houston Oilers, 1986—90, asst. gen. mgr., 1990—94, exec. v.p., gen. mgr., 1994—96, Tenn. Oilers (formerly Houston Oilers), 1997—98, Tenn. Titans (formerly Tenn. Oilers), 1999—2000, exec. v.p., gen. mgr., dir. football ops., 2001—06; NFL analyst ESPN, 2007—09; sr. football adv. New England Patriots, 2009—. Office: New England Patriots One Patriot Pl Foxboro MA 02035*

REESE, HAYNE WARING, psychologist, educator; b. Comanche, Tex., Jan. 14, 1931; s. Tom F. and Marion (Waring) R.; m. Patsy Atwood, Aug. 24, 1957 (div. Apr. 1967); children: Anne, William, Margaret; m. Nancy Mann, Dec. 16, 1967; 1 child, Bradley. Student, So. Meth. U., 1949-50; BA, U. Tex., 1953, MA, 1955; PhD, U. Iowa, 1958. Asst. prof. U. Buffalo, 1958-62; assoc. prof. SUNY-Buffalo, 1962-66, prof., 1966-67, U. Kans., Lawrence, 1967-70; Centennial prof. psychology W.Va. U., Morgantown, 1970-2000, dir. grad. tng. in life-span devel. psychology, 1973-2000, Centennial prof. emeritus, 2000—. Mem. initial rev. groups div. research grants NIH, Washington, 1969-71, 74-78, 79-84; vis. prof. SUNY, Buffalo, 1970, U. Iowa, 1972, U. Hawaii, 1975, S.W. China Normal U., 1997, 2000. Author: Perception of Stimulus Relations, 1968, Basic Learning Processes in Childhood, 1976; co-author: Experimental Child Psychology, 1970, Life-Span Developmental Psychology, 1977, 1988, Child Development, 1979; editor: Advances in Child Development and Behavior, 26 vols., 1969-2001; co-editor: Life-Span Developmental Psychology, 8 vols., 1973-97; assoc. editor: Jour. Exptl. Child Psychology, 1975-83, editor, 1983-97, mem. editl. bd. 1965-74, 98-2000. Served with U.S. Army, 1954. Fellow AAAS; mem. Soc. for Rsch. in Child Devel., Assn. for Behavior Analysis, Internat. Soc. for Study Behavioral Devel. Home Phone: 817-346-2865. Personal E-mail: haynereese@aol.com.

REESE, JERRY, professional sports team executive; b. Tiptonville, Tenn., July 22, 1963; m. Gwen Moore; children: Jasmyne, Jerry II. BS in Health & Physical Edn., Tenn.-Martin U., 1987, MA in Edn. Adminstrn. & Supervision, 1988. Grad. asst. Tenn.-Martin U., 1986—88, secondary coach, 1988—93, receivers coach, asst. head coach, 1993—94; regional scout NY Giants, 1994—99, asst., pro pers. dept., 1999—2002, dir. player pers., 2002—06, gen. mgr., 2007—. Named to Tenn.-Martin U. Hall of Fame, 1995. Achievements include being third African-American named Gen. Mgr. of Nat. Football League team, 2007. Office: NY Giants Giants Stadium Way East Rutherford NJ 07073*

REESE, JOHN M., lawyer; b. Spokane, Wash., June 16, 1931; s. William Bryan and Carmen Ardis Reese; m. Mary Elaine Reese, Dec. 28, 1954; children: Daniel, Scott, William, Mary Reese-Senter. BS, Wash. State U., Pullman, 1953; JD, U. Idaho, Moscow, 1956. Bar: Wash. 1956, US Ct. Mil. Appeals 1958. Asst. staff Judge Advocate US Air Force, Hamilton AFB, San Rafael, Calif., 1956—58; pvt. practice Reese, Baffnen, Frol and Grossman PS, Walla Walla, Wash., 1958—; city atty. City Walla Walla, 1960—65. Dir. numerous for-profit & non-profit corps., 1962—. Pres., bd. dirs. Walla Walla Area YMCA, 1962—82; pres. Walla Walla C. of C., 1974; pres., bd. mem. Blue Mt. Cmty. Found., Walla Walla, 1984—2004. 1st lt. USAR, 1956—58, Hamilton AFB, Calif. Mem.: ABA, Am. Trust and Estate Counsel, Wash. Bar Assn., Walla Walla County Bar Assn., Exchange Club. Republican. Presbyn. Avocations: skiing, golf, racquetball. Home: 1121 Alvarado Walla Walla WA 99362 Office: Reese Baffnen Frol & Grossman PS 216 S Palouse St Walla Walla WA 99362

REESE, JULIE, museum director, association administrator; BS in Liberal Arts, Ore. State U. Exec. dir. Umatilla County Hist. Soc. & Heritage Station Mus., Pendleton, Oreg., 1987—. Chair Umatilla County Cultural Coalition; mem. Pendleton Conv. Ctr. Commn. Mem.: Oreg. Museums Assn. (pres.). Office: Umatilla County Historical Soc & Heritage State Mus 108 SW Frazer Ave Pendleton OR 97801-2138 also: Oreg Museums Assn PO Box 1718 Portland OR 97207-1718

REESE, MARILYA VETETO, literature and language professor; BA, Austin Coll., Sherman TX, 1982; MA, PhD, U. Tex., Austin, 1990. Asst prof. NAU, Flagstaff, Ariz., 1990—97, assoc prof., 1997—2005; full prof. German Northern Ariz. U., 2005—. Author (book): (novels) Finding A Voice: German; translator: (TV films) Chairs of Science. Grants, NAU, 1990. Mem.: AATG (exec. coun. & chpt. pres. 1994—2006). Liberal. Universal Unitarian. Avocations: yoga, reading, travel, singing, cooking. Office: Northern AZ Univ NAU Box 6004 Flagstaff AZ 86011-6004 Office Fax: 928-523-0963. Business E-Mail: marilya.veteto.reese@nau.edu.

REESE, POKEY, former professional baseball player; b. Columbia, SC, June 10, 1973; Infielder Cin. Reds, 1997—2001, Pitts. Pirates, 2002—03, Boston Red Sox, 2004, Seattle Mariners, 2005, Fla. Marlins, 2006. Recipient Nat. League Golden Glove Award, 1999—2000. Achievements include being a member of World Series Champion Boston Red Sox, 2004.

REESE, STUART HARRY, insurance company executive; b. Richmond, Va., May 3, 1955; s. Allison and Virginia (Saul) R.; m. Elizabeth Garr, Aug. 21, 1976; children: Katharine, Elizabeth, Jillian, Thomas. BA, Gettysburg Coll., Pa., 1977; MBA, Dartmouth Coll., 1979. Securities analyst investment pvt. placements Aetna, Hartford, Conn., 1979-81, sr. securities analyst dept. fin. guaranty, 1981-82, dir. treas. investment planning, 1982-83, sr. investment officer, 1983-84, asst. v.p., 1984-85, mng. dir., 1985-89, v.p., mng. dir. capital markets, 1989—93; various sr. mgmt. positions, including chmn. & CEO Babson Capital Mgmt. subsidiary, Mass. Mutual Fin. Group, Springfield, Mass., 1993—99, exec. v.p. & chief investment officer, 1999—2005, pres. & CEO, 2005—06, chmn., pres., CEO, 2007—08, chmn., CEO, 2008—. Mem. investment com. Vis. Nurses Assn., Simsbury, Conn., 1991—. Mem. Hartford Soc. Fin. Analysts (v.p. bd. 1991—). Office: Mass Mutual Financial Group 1295 State St Springfield MA 01111*

REESE, SUSAN MARIE, elementary school educator; b. Waseca, Minn., Feb. 21, 1966; d. George Andrew and Donna Frances Cobley; 1 child, David Andrew. BA, U. No. Iowa, Cedar Falls, 1988, MA in Edn., 2006. Cert. Nat. Bd. Profl. Tchg. Stds., 2000. Tchr. Allison-Bristow Cmty. Schs, Allison, Iowa, 1993—2004, North Butler Mid. Sch., Allison, 2004—. Office: North Butler Mid Sch 513 Birch St Allison IA 50602 Business E-Mail: sreese@alli-bris.k12.ia.us.

REESE, TRACY, fashion designer; b. Detroit; d. Claude Reese. Degree, Parsons Sch. Design, 1984. Design asst. to Martine Sitbon Arlequin Paris, 1984-87; designer with Marc Jacobs Perry Ellis Portfolio; design dir. Magaschoni, Inc., 1990—95; launched own label Tracy Reese, 1987—89, 1997—, Plenty by Tracy Reese, 1998—, Plenty by Tracy Reese Home. Featured in Ebony mag., 2007. Office: c/o Factory PR 580 Broadway Ste 602 New York NY 10012*

REESE, WILLIAM LEWIS, philosophy educator; b. Jefferson City, Mo., Feb. 15, 1921; s. William Lewis and Lillian Amelia (Fisher) R.; m. Louise Weeks, June 11, 1945; children: Claudia, Patricia, William Lewis III. AB, Drury Coll., 1942; B.D., U. Chgo., 1945, PhD, 1947; postdoctoral, Yale U., 1955-56. Asst. prof. philosophy Drake U., 1947-49, asso. prof. philosophy, 1949-57, head dept., 1954-57; asso. prof. philosophy Grinnell Coll., 1957-60; vis. prof. philosophy Iowa State U., 1958; prof. philosophy, chmn. dept. U. Del., Newark, 1960-67, dir. seminar in philosophy of sci., 1960-66, H. Rodney Sharp prof. philosophy, 1965-67; prof. philosophy SUNY-Albany, 1967-99, chmn. dept., 1968-74, 84, prof. philosophy emeritus, rsch. prof. philosophy, 1999—, dir. emeritus ctr., 2006—, pres. emeritus ctr. bd., 2006—. Tully Cleon Knoles lectr. U. Pacific, 1962; del. U.S. Nat. Commn. for UNESCO, 1963; gen. mem. 4th East-West Philosophers Conf., 1964 Author, contbr.: Studies in C.S. Peirce, 1952, (with Charles Hartshorne) Philosophers Speak of God, 1953, 2d edit., 2000, The Ascent from Below, 1959, 2d edit., 2000, (with Eugene Freeman) Process and Divinity, 1964, Dictionary of Philosophy and Religion: Eastern and Western Thought, 1980, 3d edit., 1999, Freedom, 2000, Values, 2000; gen. editor: Philosophy of Science, The Delaware Seminar, vols. 1, 2, 1963, vol. 3, 1967; editor: Philosophy and World Religions: The Reader's Adviser, vol. 4, 1988, Fundamental Issues in Philosophy Series, 2 vols., 2000; editl. bd.: State of N.Y. Press, 1968-78; contbr. articles to profl. jours Recipient Ford Found. Study award Argentina, 1967; Fulbright lectr. Argentina, summer 1971; Inst. Humanistic Studies fellow, 1977— Mem.: AAUP, Metaphysical Soc. Am. (sec. 1962—65, treas. 1962—65), Am. Philos. Assn. Mem. Christian Ch. (Disciples Of Christ). Home: Font Grove Rd Slingerlands NY 12159 Office: SUNY Emeritus Ctr Univ Adminstrn Bldg 134 Albany NY 12222-0001 Personal E-mail: reesewl@aol.com. *To have before one always the realistic sense that if one has been successful in one way one has failed in others, and that one's failures surely outnumber one's successes.*

REEVE, FRANKLIN D., writer, retired literature professor; b. Phila., Sept. 18, 1928; m. Laura C. Stevenson, 1997; children: Christopher (dec.), Benjamin, Alison, Brock, Mark, Katharine, Margaret. AB, Princeton U., 1950; PhD, Columbia U., 1958; AM (hon.), Wesleyan, 1964; DLitt (hon.), New Eng. Coll., 2004. Instr., asst. prof. Columbia U., NYC, 1952-61; assoc. prof. Wesleyan U., Middletown, Conn., 1962-66, adj. prof., 1967-87, prof., 1988—2002, prof. emeritus, 2002—. Founding editor The Poetry Rev., 1982—84; bd. govs., v.p. Poetry Soc. Am., 1976—84; sec. Poets House, NYC, 1985—99; bd. govs. Transl. Ctr., NYC, 1980—94; vis. prof. Oxford (Eng.) U., 1964, Columbia U., 1988, Marlboro Vt. Coll., 1999; bd. dirs. Marlboro Rev.; vis. scholar, Moscow, 1961; vis. lectr. Yale U., New Haven, 1972—84; assoc. fellow Saybrook Coll., 1972—96; program scholar Vt. Coun. on Humanities; lectr. poetry Ctr., NYC, 1980—84; lectr. USAID, 1999; cons. in field. Author: Aleksandr Blok: Between Image and Idea, 1962, 2d edit., 1981, Robert Frost in Russia, 1964, 2d edit., 2001, The Russian Novel, 1966, The Red Machines, 1968, In the Silent Stones, 1968, Just Over the Border, 1969, The Brother, 1971, The Blue Cat, 1972, White Colors, 1974, The White Monk, 1989; author: (edited with Jay Meek) After the Storm, 1991; author: (poetry) Concrete Music, 1992; editor: Winged Sprits, 1995, A Few Rounds of Old Maid and Other Stories, 1995, The Moon and Other Failures, 1999, (poetry) A World You Haven't Seen, 2001, The Urban Stampede and Other Poems, 2002, (jazz performance with exit 59) The Return of the Blue Cat, 2005—06, North River, 2006; translator: Five Short Novels by Turgenev, 1961, Anthology of Russian Plays, 2 vols., 1961, 1963, 1975, 1991, Contemporary Russian Drama, 1968, The Garden by Bella Akhmadulina, 1990, The Trouble with Reason by Alexander Griboyedov, 1993, The King and the Fool by Alexander Borschagovsky, 2001, Lions and Acrobats by Anatoly Naiman, 2005; editor: The Toy Soldier, 2007, The Blue Cat Walks the Earth, 2007; Jazz Performance, 2007—, Puzzel Master Opera Short Form, 2007—. Trustee Pettee Meml. Libr.; keynote spkr. Internat. Conference Translators Russian Literature, Moscow, 2007. Recipient Lit. award Am. Acad.-Nat. Inst., 1970, Lifetime Golden Rose award New Eng. Poetry Soc., 1994, Binswanger Excellence in Tchg. award Wesleyan U., 2002, May Sarton award, 1999. Mem.: New Eng. Poetry Club (bd. dirs. 1996—). Home: PO Box 14 Wilmington VT 05363-0014

REEVE, THOMAS GILMOUR, physical education educator; b. Memphis, Sept. 23, 1946; s. Paul Goodwin and Dorothy (Bourke) R.; children: Bourke, Spencer. BS in Phys. Edn., Tex. Tech. U., 1969, MEd, 1972; PhD, Tex. A&M U., 1976. Asst. prof. Auburn (Ala.) U., 1977-82, assoc. prof., 1982-87, prof., 1987-91, asst. v.p. for acad. affairs, 1992-93, alumni prof., 1991-95, prof. phys. edn., 1995-98, W.T. Smith Disting. prof., 1998-99; prof., chair Tex. Tech. U., Lubbock, 1999—2004, dir. strategic planning, 2002—08; HS Pliner prof. La. State U., 2008—. Vis. asst. prof. Tex. A&M U., College Station, 1976-77. Co-editor: Stimulus-Response Compatibility, 1990; sect. editor Rsch. Quar. for Exercise and Sport, 1990-92, editor, 1999-2002; assoc. editor Jour. Sport Behavior, 1983—. Fellow AAHPERD, Rsch. Consortium (pres. 2008-09), Am. Acad. Kinesiology and Phys. Edn. (pres. 2004-05); mem. N.Am. Soc. Psychology Sport and Phys. Activity (publ. dir. 1985-87, pres. 1991-92). Avocation: masters swimming. Office: La State Univ 112 H P Long Fieldhouse Baton Rouge LA 70803 Home Phone: 225-752-0633; Office Phone: 225-578-2913. Business E-Mail: tgreeve@lsu.edu.

REEVES, DENISE MOSELEY, dancer, educator; d. Margaret Ann Freeman and Kenneth Stewart Moseley; m. Dennis Dean Reeves, May 15, 1982. BS, U. N.C., Greensboro, 1979; MEd, Frostburg State U., Md., 1984. Cert. tchr. Royal Acad. of Dance, 1988, level 3 master tchr. True Pilates-Romana's Pilates, 2002. Dancer N.C. Sch. of the Arts, Winston-Salem, 1973; tchr. movement edn. sch. King Intermediate Sch., NC, 1978—82; dancer, instr. Hagerstown and W.Va. Youth Ballet Cos., Md., 1982—83; profl. dancer San Jose Dance Theatre, Calif., 1986—88; ballet dir. Pam East Dance, Cupertino, Calif., 1986—92; profl. dancer Santa Clara Ballet, Calif., 1988—92; dance dir., instr. Pebblebrook H.S., Mableton, Ga., 1994—; sch. dir., dancer Ga. Ballet, Marietta, 1992—97; instr., dancer Atlanta Ballet, 1996—98; dance dir. Ga. Gov.'s Honors Program, Atlanta, 1997—97; dir. Pilates Studio of Atlanta, 1999—2002. Coord., instr. Cobb County Schs. Gov.'s Honor Program, Marietta, Ga., 1994—2006. Mem.: Nat. Dance Edn. Orgn., Nat. Dance Assn. (corr.), Ams. for the Arts (corr.), Corps De Ballet Internat. (corr.), Gamma Beta Phi. Achievements include dance ambassador with Santa Clara University to dance in Poland and Soviet Union. Avocations: travel, fitness, musical theatre, dance. Home: 489 Timberlea Lake Dr Marietta GA 30067 Office: Pebblebrook HS 991 Old Alabama Rd Mableton GA 30126 Office Fax: 770-819-2524. Personal E-mail: dansin1@hotmail.com. E-mail: denise.reeves@cobbk12.org.

REEVES, HALLIE LAWSON, retired music educator, chaplain; d. Andrew William and Gracie Elizabeth (Owens) Lawson; m. William A. Reeves, June 21, 1961 (div.); children: Rona Omega, Princess Mickiko. BA, NC Ctrl. U., 1958; MDiv, Duke U., 1978. Cert. supr. ACPE, 1992. Music tchr. Roxboro Pub. Schs., NC, 1958—59, Oxford Pub. Schs., NC, 1959—60, Durham Pub. Schs., NC, 1960—75; chaplain intern St. Elizabeth's Hosp., DC, 1979—80, chaplain resident, 1980—81, staff chaplain, 1985—2003; dir. chaplain svcs. Provident Hosp., Balt., 1981—85. Owner piano studio, 1958—2003. Mem.: NADCD, Phi Delta Kappa.

REEVES, JENNIFER TODD, filmmaker; b. Colombo, Sri Lanka, 1971; MFA, U. Calif., San Diego. Founder Sparky Pictures, Inc., NYC, 2000—. Part-time prof. Bard Coll. Milton Avery Sch. Arts, Cooper Union, Millennium Film Workshop. Filmmaker (prin. works) The Girl's Nervy, 1995, Chronic, 1996, Darling Internat. (with MM Serra), 1999 (Cinematography award, Cinetexas Film Festival, 2000), Fear of Blushing, 2001, The Time We Killed, 2004 (FIPRESCI Critics prize, Berlin Film Festival, Outstanding Artistic Achievement, OUTFEST, Best NY, NY Narrative Feature, Tribeca Film Festival), Shadows Choose Their Horrors, We Are Going Home (Film Co-op award, Ann Arbor Film Festival, 1999, Juror's Citation, Black Maria Film Festival, 1999), (group shows) Toronto Film Festival, Kill Your Timid Notion: Dundee Contemporary Arts Festival, Whitney Biennial: Day for Night, Whitney Mus. Am. Art, 2006. Recipient Princess Grace award, 2000; grantee Jacob K. Javits fellowship, 1997—2001, Andrea Frank Found. grant, 1999. Office: Sparky Pictures Inc PO Box 136 Planetarium Sta New York NY 10024 Personal E-mail: sparkypix@yahoo.com.

REEVES, JOAN HUTCHINS, painter; b. Seattle, June 22, 1932; d. John Marvin and Bess Irene Hutchins; m. George Catherwood Reeves, Sept. 5, 1953; children: David Alan, John Michael. Exhibitions include Whatcom Mus. History and Art, Frye Mus., Bellevue Art Mus. Mem. Art Stall Gallery Coop. (chmn. 1986-89), Nat. Mus. Women in the Arts (charter), N.W. Watercolor Soc. (life mem., exhbn. chmn. 1986, Purchase award 1988), Women Painters of Wash. (membership chmn. 1986-88, Transparent Watecolor award 1985, 86, 90, Best of Show 1989, 2001, Purchase award, 2004), Mont. Watercolor Soc. (signature mem.), Watercolor West (signature mem.), San Diego Watercolor Soc. (signature mem.) Avocation: travel. Home: 3901 Fremont Ave N Seattle WA 98103-7756

REEVES, JOHN DRUMMOND, retired English language professional, writer; b. Troy, NY, Dec. 8, 1914; s. Robert Brockway and Emma Caroline (Mausert) R.; m. Mary Markwick Moore, Sept. 1, 1951. AB, Williams Coll., Williamstown, Mass., 1937; AM, Columbia U., 1941. Instr. in Eng. Irving Sch., Tarrytown, NY, 1937-40, Horace Mann Sch., NYC, 1940-41, 46-47; asst. prof. of classics and Eng. Whitman Coll., Walla Walla, Wash., 1956-62; assoc. prof. English Millikin U., Decatur, Ill., 1962-65; lectr. in Eng. Hofstra U., Hempstead, NY, 1965-73, ret., 1973. Author: Windows on Melville, 2001; contbr. articles to profl. jours. Lt. USNR, 1941-45, PTO. Mem. AAUP, Coll. Eng. Assn., Am. Coun. Learned Soc. (reg. assoc. 1957-59), Walla Walla Archaeol. Assn. (pres. 1959-62), SR (Conn. state chpt.), Masons. Home: 20 Devonwood Dr Apt 161 Farmington CT 06032-1422 Home Phone: 860-677-0318.

REEVES, KEANU, actor; b. Beirut, Sept. 2, 1964; s. Samuel Nowlin Reeves and Patricia Taylor. Stage appearances: Wolf Boy (debut), For Adults Only, Romeo and Juliet; films: Flying, 1986, Youngblood, 1986, River's Edge, 1987, Permanent Record, 1988, The Night Before, 1988, The Prince of Pennsylvania, 1988, Dangerous Liaisons, 1988, Bill and Ted's Excellent Adventure, 1989, Parenthood, 1989, I Love You to Death, 1990, Tune in Tomorrow, 1990, Bill and Ted's Bogus Journey, 1991, Point Break, 1991, My Own Private Idaho, 1991, Bram Stoker's Dracula, 1992, Much Ado About Nothing, 1993, Little Buddha, 1994, Even Cowgirls Get the Blues, 1994, Speed, 1994, Johnny Mnemonic, 1995, A Walk in the Clouds, 1995, Feeling Minnesota, 1996, Chain Reaction, 1996, Devil's Advocate, 1997, The Last Time I Committed Suicide, 1997, The Matrix, 1999, The Replacements, 2000, The Watcher, 2000, The Gift, 2000, Hard Ball, 2001, Sweet November, 2001, The Matrix Reloaded, 2003, The Matrix Revolutions, 2003, Something's Gotta Give, 2003, Thumbsucker, 2005, Constantine, 2005, A Scanner Darkly, 2006, The Lake House, 2006 (with Sandra Bullock Movie-Choice Liplock, Teen Choice Awards, 2006), Street Kings, 2008, The Day the Earth Stood Still, 2008, The Private Lives of Pippa Lee, 2009; TV films: Letting Go, 1985, Act of Vengeance, 1986, Young Again, 1986, Babes in Toyland, 1986, Under the Influence, 1986, Brotherhood of Justice, 1986, Life Under Water, 1989, Children Remember the Holocaust, 1995, (narrator) The Great Warning, 2003. Named one of 50 Most Powerful People in Hollywood, Premiere mag., 2004—06.

REEVES, MARTHA, Councilwoman; b. Eufaula, Ala., July 18, 1941; d. Elijah and Ruby Reeves. Sec., receptionist Motown Recording Artist, Artists and Repertoire, 1962; leader Martha Reeves Vandellas; pres., CEO Martha Reeves Enterprises, Inc.; founder Itch Records, 2001—; councilwoman Detroit City Coun., 2006—. Bd. mem. Am. Fedn. TV and Recording Artists. Author: (biography) Dancing in the Street, 1996. Recipient Pioneer award, Rhythm and Blues Found., Dick Clark Am. Soul award, Spirit of Detroit award; named to Rock and Roll Hall of Fame, 1995, Ala. Music Hall of Fame, 1994. Office: Detroit City Coun Coleman A Young Mcpl Ctr 2 Woodward Ave Ste 1340 Detroit MI 48226 Office Phone: 313-224-4510. Office Fax: 313-224-0230. Business E-Mail: m-reeves_MB@cncl.ci.detroit.mi.us, marthareeves@att.net.

REEVES, RALPH BERNARD, III, publishing executive; b. Raleigh, NC, Apr. 2, 1947; s. Ralph Bernard Reeves Jr. and Frances Rhoda (Campbell) M.; m. Caroline Holton Green, Apr. 24, 1971 (div. 1986); children: Ralph B. IV, Daniel MacQuarrie; m. Katherine Drewry Reid, June 20, 1998. AB in History, U. NC, 1970. Field coord. FMI Mgmt. Group, Raleigh, NC, 1972-76; gen. mgr., v.p. The Leader Newspaper, Rsch. Triangle Pk., NC, 1976-78; pres., pub., founder Spectator Pubs. Inc., Raleigh, 1978-98, Triad Bus., Greensboro, NC, 1986-88, Triangle Bus., Raleigh, 1985-91, Spectator Pub., NC Architect, 1981-84; pres. Reeves Media, 1998—; pub., editor Raleigh Metro Mag., 1999—. Editor: Mr. Spectator, 1978—98; author: (monthly column) My Usual Charming Self in Metro Mag. 1st v.p. Mordecai Square Hist. Soc., Raleigh, 1980—83; pres. Hilltop Home, 1982—84; coun. mem. NC Mus. Art; founder Raleigh Internat. Spy Conf.; chmn. Downtown Adv. Com., 1983—85; bus. adv. com. NC Sec. of State, Raleigh, 1992—; bd. dirs. NC State U. Friends of Libr., Carolina Ballet. Gov's. Bus. award in the Arts and Humanities, Adv. Bd. Raleigh Hall of Fame, 1986, Benjamin Fine award, 1991, AABP award Triangle Bus., 1st place award Feature Writing, 1991. Mem. Assn. of Intelligence Officers (assoc.), Pumpkin Papers Irregulars, Fifty Group, English Speaking Union (past pres. RTP br. 1988—), Carolina Co. Club, Sphinx Club, Nat. Press Club. Episcopalian. Avocations: golf, history, travel. Home: 3066 Granville Dr Raleigh NC 27609 Office Phone: 919-831-0999. E-mail: reevesmedia@ncttbiz.com.

REEVES, ROBERT K., lawyer, oil industry executive; BSBA, JD, La. State U., Baton Rouge. Ptnr. energy sect. Onebane Law Firm, Lafayette, La., 1983—93; sr. v.p., gen. counsel, sec. Flores & Rucks, Inc., 1993—97; exec. v.p., gen. counsel, sec. Ocean Energy, Inc., 1997—2003; sr. v.p. corp. affairs and law Anadarko Petroleum Corp., The Woodlands, Tex., 2004—07, chief governance officer, 2004—07, sr. v.p., gen. counsel, chief adminstrv. officer, 2007—. Trustee Episcopal HS; mem. vestry St. Martin's Episcopal Ch.; bd. dirs. Family Svcs. Greater Houston. Mem.: ABA, Am. Corp. Counsel Assn., La. Bar Assn., Tex. Bar Assn. Office: Anadarko Petroleum Corp 1201 Lake Robbins Dr The Woodlands TX 77380-1046 Office Phone: 832-636-1000.*

REEVES, TATE, state treasurer; b. Rankin County, Miss. m. Elee Williams; 1 child. BS in Econ., Millsaps Coll. CFA. Investment officer Trustmark, 2000; asst. v.p. AmSouth (formerly Deposit Guaranty Nat. Bank); treas. State of Miss., 2003—. Bd. dir. Public Employees' Retirement Sys., Miss.; chmn. bd. College Savings Plans of Miss. Mem.: Miss. Republican Elected Officials Assn., Nat. Assn. State Treas. (pres. so. region, sr. v.p., pres. 2007—), CFA Inst., CFA Soc. of Miss. (Miss. Soc. Fin. Analysts award 1996). Republican. Meth. Office: State Treasurer PO Box 138 Jackson MS 39205 Office Phone: 601-359-3600. Office Fax: 601-359-2001.*

REEVES, W. BOYD, lawyer; b. Easley, SC, Mar. 24, 1932; s. William C. and Lona Elise Reeves; m. Gladys Frances Brown, Nov. 24, 1978; children: Gabrielle Elaine, Stephanie Clair, William Gordon. BA in Bus. Adminstrn., Furman U., 1954; JD, Tulane U., 1959. Bar: La. 1959, Ala. 1960, US Dist. Ct. (so. dist.), Ala. 1961, US Ct. Appeals (5th cir.) 1962, US Ct. Appeals (11th cir.) 1970, US Supreme Ct. 1971, cert.: Nat. Bd. Trial Advocacy (civil trial lawyer). Law clk. U.S. Dist. Ct. Judge Daniel Thomas, Mobile, Ala., 1959—61; practicing atty. Armbrecht, Jackson LLP, Mobile, Ala., 1961—. Atty. Sheriff of Mobile City, Ala., 1980. Past chmn. Southeastern Admiralty Inst.; past pres. Ala. Am. Bd. Trial Advocates; chancellor St. Luke's Episcopal Ch., Mobile, 1970—. Capt. US Army, 1954—56, Alaska. Fellow, Am. Coll. Trial Lawyers. Fellow: Internat. Soc. Barristers; mem.: ABA, Baldwin County Bar Assn., Am. Coll. Legal Medicine, Maritime Law Assn. (exec. com. 1987—90), Internat. Assn. of Defense Counsel, Ala. Def. Lawyers Assn. (past pres.), Mobile Bar Assn. (past pres.). Episcopalian. Home: 3755 Rhonda Dr S Mobile AL 36608 Office: Armbrecht Jackson LLP PO Box 290 Mobile AL 36601 Office Phone: 251-405-1309. Office Fax: 251-432-6843.

REEVES, WILLIAM, language educator; b. Fort Wayne, Ind., June 26, 1944; s. Leslie and Mary Reeves; m. Catherine Zayat, Aug. 28, 1965; children: Elizabeth, Billy. PhD, Notre Dame, South Bend, Ind., 1972. Instr. Notre Dame, 1970—72; prof. Bklyn. Coll., 1972—. Office: Bklyn Coll 2900 Bedford Ave Brooklyn NY 11210 Business E-Mail: wreeves@brooklyn.cuny.edu.

REEVY-MANNING, GRETCHEN MARIA, psychologist, educator; b. Cortland, NY, Oct. 17, 1964; d. William Robert and Carole May Reevy; m. Todd Royal Manning. AB in Psychology, U. N.C., 1986; PhD in Psychology, U. Calif., Berkeley, 1994. Lectr. psychology dept. Dominican Coll., San Rafael, Calif., 1993—98; lectr. U. Calif., Davis, 1994, Profl. Sch. Psychology, San Francisco, 1995; lectr. psychology dept. Calif. State U., East Bay, 1994—. Co-editor: The Praeger Handbook on Stress and Coping, 2007. Grantee, Rand Corp., 1993. Mem.: APA, Soc. for Psychological Study of Social Issues, Assn. Psychol. Sci., Western Psychol. Assn., Phi Beta Kappa, Psi Chi. Avocations: swimming, reading, running. Office: Calif State Univ Psychology Dept Hayward CA 94542 Office Phone: 510-885-3421. Business E-Mail: gretchen.reevy@csueastbay.edu.

REFAAT, MARWAN, lebanon cardiology fellow; b. Pa., Jan. 1979; MD, Am. U. Beirut, NYC, 2003. Lic. Commonwealth Mass., 2006, Commonwealth Pa., 2007, diplomate Am. Bd. Internal Medicine, 2007. Resident internal medicine Mass. Gen. Hosp., Harvard Med. Sch., Boston, 2004—07, med. rsch. fellow, 2000; clin. fellow medicine Harvard Med. Sch., 2004—07; fellow, cardiovasc. diseases U. Pitts. Med. Ctr., 2007—. Contbr. scientific papers. Prevention cardiovasc. diseases, 2004—08. Recipient Carolyn L. Kuckein Rsch. award, Alpha Omega Alpha, 2002, Physicians Recognition award, AMA, 2005, Dept. Medicine award, Mass. Gen. Hosp., 2007, Am. Heart Assn. Rsch. award, 2008, Heart Rhythm Soc., 2008; grantee Med. Rsch., Mass. Gen. Hosp., 2000. Mem.: AMA, ACP (Rsch. award 2004), Mass. Med. Soc. (resident fellow sect. 2005—07, Rsch. award 2007), Am. Coll. Cardiology. Achievements include research in more than 25 citations of my research work.

REFAAT, TAMER F., electrical engineer, researcher; s. Fawzi Ibrahim Refaat and Zeinab Helmi; m. Rehab Hafez; children: Mostafa, Omar. BS, Alexandria U., 1991, MS, 1995; PhD, Old Dominion U., 2000. Tchg. asst. and lectr. dept. elec. engring. Faculty of Engring., Alexandria U., Egypt, 1991—95; rsch. asst. elec. and computer engring. Phys. Electronics Rsch. Lab., Old Dominion U., Norfolk, Va., 1996, Old Dominion U., 1996—99; on-site contr. NASA Langley Rsch. Ctr., Hampton, Va., 1996—99; sr. lidar and instrumentation engr., Sci. and Engring. Svcs. Inc., Burtonsville, Md., 2000—01; rsch. elec. engr. Sci. and Tech. Corp., Hampton, 2001—06; on-site contr. NASA Langley Rsch. Ctr., Hampton, 2001—; sr. rsch. scientist Applied Rsch. Ctr. Old Dominion U., Norfolk, 2006—. Contbr. articles to profl. jours. Mem.: IEEE (corr.), Internat. Soc. Optical Engring. (corr.). Muslim. Achievements include design of advanced atmospheric water vapor and carbon dioxide differential absorption lidar detection systems; research in characterization and modelling of optical detectors. Office: NASA Langley Research Center 5 North Dryden St MS468 Hampton VA 23681 Office Phone: 757-864-1540. Personal E-mail: tamer.refaat@hotmail.com, tamer.f.refaat@gmail.com. Business E-Mail: trefaat@odu.edu.

REFAELI, BAR, model; b. Hod HaSharon, Israel, June 4, 1985; d. Rafael and Tsipi. Home model Renuar; face of Hurley clothing line, 2008, I Am King cologne, 2008. Appearances on (TV series) Pick Up, 2005, (TV films) Ironic Iconic America, 2008, featured in (magazines) Sports Illustrated Swimsuit Issue, 2007, 2008, cover model Maxim, 2006, Telva, 2006, Elle, 2006, 2007, 2008, DT, 2006, GQ, 2006, Tatler, 2007, Woman, 2007, Marie Claire, 2007, 2008, Arena, 2008, Plaza, 2008, Amica, 2008, Sports Illustrated Swimsuit Issue, 2009. Vol. Project Sunshine, Ahava. Achievements include becoming first Israeli model featured in Sports Illustrated magazine; selected as the 2009 covermodel of the Sports Illustred Swimsuit Issue. Office: c/o Ford Models NY 111 5th Ave New York NY 10003*

REFAELI, YOSEF, biology professor; PhD, Harvard U., Cambridge, Mass., 1999. Faculty mem. Nat. Jewish Health, Denver, 2003—. Grantee RO1, R43, NIH, NCI, NIAID, NHLBI, 2005—. Mem.: AAAS. Achievements include research in basic and applied biology for blood and blood cancer. Office: Nat Jewish Health 1400 Jackson St Denver CO 80206 Office Fax: 303-398-1225. Business E-Mail: refaeliy@njc.org.

REFF, STEVEN M., economics educator; b. Elmhurst, Ill., Aug. 26, 1954; s. Martin L. and Shirlee A. Reff; m. Jill Rene Larson, Feb. 24, 1996; 1 child, Gabriel Nelson. M in Edn., U. Ariz., Tucson, 1981. Cert. Ariz. Dept. Edn., 1978. Economics educator TUSD, Tucson, 1978—. Author: (textbook) Economics University. Named Undergraduate Tchr. of Yr., Eller Coll. U. Ariz., 2008. Office: Pueblo Magnet HS 3500 S 12th Ave Tucson AZ 85721

REFINETTI, ROBERTO, biopsychologist; b. Sao Paulo, Brazil, Nov. 19, 1957; came to U.S., 1988; s. Renato and Maria Stella (Barroso) R.; m. Kathleen Diane Zylan, Mar. 5, 1988 (div. Aug. 1991); 1 child, Lauren Lynne; m. Theresa Kaye Tolleson, Aug. 11, 2000. BA in Philosophy, Pontifical Cath. U., Sao Paulo, 1981; BS in Psychology, U. Sao Paulo, 1981, MA in Psychology, 1983; PhD in Psychology, U. Calif., Santa Barbara, 1987. Asst. prof. U. Sao Paulo, 1986-88; fellow U. Calif., Santa Barbara, 1988-89, U. Ill., Champaign, 1989-90, U. Va., Charlottesville, 1990-92; asst. prof. Coll. William and Mary, Williamsburg, Va., 1992-97; mgr. profl. publs. Montage Media Corp., Mahwah, NJ, 1997-98; pvt. practice Birmingham, Ala., 1998-99; asst. prof. U. S.C., Salkehatchie, 1999—2005, prof., 2005—. Author: Circadian Physiology, 1999, 2d edit., 2005; editor-in-chief Jour. Circadian Rhythms, 2003-; contbr. over 150 articles to profl. jours Area grantee NIH, 1996, 2002; recipient Nat. Rsch. Svc. Individual award NIMH, 1991, Career award NSF, 1995, 2004. Mem. Am. Physiol. Soc., Am. Psychol. Soc., Soc. Neuroscience, Soc. Rsch. on Biol. Rhythms. Office: Circadian Rhythm Lab Univ SC 807 Hampton St Walterboro SC 29488 Home Phone: 843-549-9497; Office Phone: 843-549-6314. E-mail: refinetti@sc.edu.

REFO, PATRICIA LEE, lawyer; b. Alexandria, Va., Dec. 31, 1958; m. Don Bivens; 1 child, Andrew stepchildren: Jody, Lisa. BA with high honors and high distinction, U. Mich., 1980, JD cum laude, 1983. Bar: Ill. 1983, US Dist. Ct. (no. dist.) Ill. 1983, US Ct. Appeals (7th cir.) 1988, US Ct. Appeals (11th cir.) 1989, US Ct. Appeals (5th cir.) 1993, Ariz. 1996, US Dist. Ct., Ariz. 1997, US Ct. Appeals (9th cir.) 1998, US Tax Ct. Assoc. Jenner & Block, Chgo., 1983—90, ptnr., 1990—96, Snell & Wilmer LLP, Phoenix, 1996—. Mem. bd. advisors Comml. Lending Liability News, 1989—, Nat. Law Jour., 2005—; mem. faculty Nat. Inst. Trial Advocacy, 1989—; adv. com. on fed. rules of evidence US Jud. Conf., 2000—06; lectr. ALI/ABA and Practicing Law Inst.; William Reese Smith Jr. disting. lectr. litig. ethics Stetson Law Sch., 2006. Chancellor Episcopal Parish St. Barnabas Desert, 1999—2008; bd. dirs. Ariz. Academic Decathlon Assn., 1997—2001, bd. advisors, 2001—; bd. dirs. Ariz. Found. for Women, 1999—2005; dir. Greater Phoenix C. of C., 2005—; sr. warden Episcopal Parish St. Barnabas Desert, 2008—. Recipient Disting. Achievement Medal, Sandra Day O'Connor Coll. Law at Ariz. State U., 2007; named Southwest Super Lawyer, Law & Politics Mag., 2007; named one of The 50 Most Influential Women Lawyers in Am., Nat. Law Jour., 2007. Fellow: Ariz. Found. for Legal Services and Edn., Am. Bar Found.; mem.: ABA (sec. sect. litig. 1994—98, exec. com. sect. litig. 1994—, ho. delegates 1998—2001, standing com. on membership 2000—03, chmn. sect. litig. 2003—04, chair Am. Jury Project 2004—05, ho. delegates 2005—), Women Lawyers Honoring Justice O'Connor, Nat. Assn. Women Lawyers. Office: Snell & Wilmer LLP One Arizona Ctr Phoenix AZ 85004-2202*

REGAL, RANDALL NATHANIEL, policy analyst; s. Arthur N. and Mildred Fins Regal. BA, NYU, NYC, 2003. V.p. comm. ESB-USA, Inc., Hewlett Bay Park, NY, 1985—88; ptnr. Regal Realty Holdings, L.P., Lawrence, NY, 1987—2000, Hahn Assocs., Bayville, NY, 2000—. Trustee The Regal Found., Bellmore, NY, 1987—2005; mem. Cedarhurst Bus. Improvement Dist., NY, 1995—2000. Founding mem. Cedarhurst Comml. Property Owners Assn., 1993—2000. Merit scholar, NY State Bd. Regents, 1983. Mem.: NYU Young Alumni Leadership Cir. (corr.), Am. Mensa (life). Conservative. Personal E-mail: regal8784@comcast.net.

REGALADO, NANCY FREEMAN, language educator; b. Boston, June 8, 1935; d. Norman Easton and Charlotte H. Freeman; m. Nathan Merl Horwitz, June 25, 1983; children: Mariana Hume, Antonio Eduardo. PhD, Yale U., New Haven, Conn., 1966. Prof. French NYU, NYC, 1968—. Author: Poetic Patterns in Rutebeuf: A Study in Non-Courtly Poetic Modes of the Thirteenth Century, 1970; co-editor (with Edward Roesner): Le Roman de Fauvel in the Edition of Mesire Chaillou de Pesstain, 1990; co-editor: (with E. B. Vitz and Marilyn Lawrence) Performing Medieval Narrative, 2005. Bd. mem. New Yorkers Against Gun Violence, NYC, 1993—2009. Recipient Nat. Endowment Humanities, 1979—80, 1992; named Officer of Ordre des Palmes Academiques, French Govt., 1992; fellowship, Am. Coun. Learned Socs., 1988, Guggenheim Found., 1993. Mem.: MLA, Medieval Acad. America. Office: NYU French Dept 13 University Pl Rm 617 New York NY 10012 Business E-Mail: nfr1@nyu.edu.

REGALADO, SAMUEL, history professor; b. Glendale, Calif., Mar. 22, 1953; s. Salvador and Eva Hemandez. With Calif. State U., Stanislaus, 1987; PhD, Wash. State U., 1987. Faculty fellow Smithsonian, 1994; Davies fellow U. San Francisco, 1998. Chmn. publs. bd. Jour. Sport History, 1992—92. Actor: The American Experience: Roberto Clemente, Quiet Pictures, 2008, Viva Baseball!: Latin Major Leaguers and Their Special Hunger, 2005; author: Viva Baseball!: Latin Major Leaguers and Their Special Hunger, 1987, 2nd edit., 1988, 3rd edit, 2007; co-editor (with Jorge lber): Mexican Americans and Sport: A Reader on Athletics and Barrio Life, 2007. Mem.: Japanese Am. Nat. Mus. (scholars adv. com. 1994—), Am. Civil Liberties Union, Am. Hist. Assn., Orgn. Am. Historians, North Am. Soc. Sport History. Office: Calif State Univ Dept History 1 University Ave Stanislaus Turlock CA 95382

REGALMUTO, NANCY MARIE, small business owner, consultant; b. Bay Shore, NY, Aug. 24, 1956; d. Antonio J. Jr. and Agnes C. (Dietz) R. Student, SUNY, Stony Brook. Sales mgr. Fire, Inc., Hempstead, NY, 1976-78; sports handicapper Red Hot Sport, J. Dime Sports, Diamond Sports, Hicksville, NY, 1978—; small bus. owner, pres. Synergy (vitamin/nutritional product mfr. and distributor), Bellport, NY, 1981—. Cons. on medicine, fin., past life, bus. readings, hypnosis, substance abuse, archeology, law enforcement investigations, family, counseling, inter-species comm., animal therapy, psychic surgery, healing, 1989—; lectr. in field, specializing in holistic remedies and therapies, 1989-91. Columnist Daily Racing Form, 1989-91; appeared on numerous TV programs, worldwide radio, mags., newspapers. Lectr., seminar leader, written about in numerous books. Min. Universal Life Ch., 1996, 97, Ch. of Inner Wisdom, 1996, 97. Mem. NAFE, Internat. Platform Assn., Horse Protection Assn., Therapuetic Riding for the Handicapped, World Wildlife Fedn. Office: 18 Woodland Park Rd Bellport NY 11713-2315

REGAN, DAVID, neuroscientist; b. Scarborough, Eng., May 5, 1935; arrived in Can., 1976; m. Marian Pauline Marsh, Aug. 15, 1959; children: Douglas Lawrence, Howard Michael BSc, London U., 1957, MSc, 1958, PhD, 1964, DSc, 1974. Lectr. physics London U., 1960-65; reader neurosci. Keele U., England, 1965-75; prof. psychology Dalhousie U., Canada, 1976-80, prof. physiology, 1980-84, assoc. prof. medicine, 1978-84, prof. medicine, 1984-87, prof. ophthalmology, 1980-87, prof. otolaryngology, 1980-84, Killam rsch. prof., 1978-82; prof. engring. Rutgers U., 1985-86; prof. psychology York U., 1987—2003, prof. biology; prof. ophthalmology U. Toronto, Ont., Canada, 1987—. Retained inventor Wilkinson-Graviner Group, Eng., 1970-75; cons. Westinghouse, Pitts., 1980-86; co-dir. human performance in space lab. Inst. for Space and Terrestrial Sci., York U., 1989-2002, disting. rsch. prof., 1991-93, emeritus, 1993—; indsl. rsch. chair aviation vision Natural Sci. and Engring. Rsch. Coun. Can./Can. Aviation Electronics, 1993-2003; Spinoza profl. U. Amsterdam, The Netherlands, 1999. Author: Human Evoked Potentials, 1972, Human Brain Electrophysiology, 1989, Human Perception of Objects, 2000; editor: Spatial Vision, 1989, Binocular Vision, 1989, Vision Research, 1992; contbr. over 250 articles to profl. jours.; holder 8 patents. Recipient Forman prize for med. rsch., 1983, Prentice medal, 1990, Sir J.W. Dawson Medal, Royal Soc. Can., 1997, award of excellence Nat. Sci. and Engring. Rsch. Coun. Can., 2000, Proctor medal, 2000, Queen Elizabeth II medal, 2002, Hebb medal, 2003; rsch. grantee NIH, NRC, Air Force Office Sci. Rsch., Nat. Scis. and Engring. Rsch. Coun. Can., Med. Rsch. Coun.; mem. Order of Can., 2001; Killam fellow, 1990. Fellow: Optical Soc. Am., Royal Soc. Can.; mem.: Netherlands Royal Acad. (fgn.), Am. Acad. Optometry, Royal Coll. Sci. (London) (assoc.), Assn. Rsch. in Vision and Ophthalmology, Soc. Clin. Electroretinography, Exptl. Psychology Soc. Avocations: cricket, walking, modern european history. Office: York U Dept Psychology 4700 Keele St North York ON Canada M3J 1P3 Business E-Mail: dregan@yorku.ca.

REGAN, DONALD H., law educator; b. 1944; AB, Harvard U., 1963; LLB, U. Va., 1966; BPh, Oxford U., Eng., 1968; PhD, U. Mich., 1980. Asst. prof. U. Mich., Ann Arbor, 1968—71, assoc. prof., 1972—73, prof., 1974—83, prof. law and philosophy, 1983—, William W. Bishop prof. law, 1991—. Author: Utilitarianism and Co-operation, 1980; editor: U. Va. Law Rev., 1966. Recipient Matchette prize, Am. Philos. Assn., 1981; fellow, Nat. Humanities Ctr., 1989; Guggenheim fellow, 1985. Mem.: Am. Acad. Arts and Scis. Office: U Mich Law Sch 343 Hutchins Hall 625 S State St Ann Arbor MI 48109-1215 Office Fax: 734-763-0269, 734-763-9375. E-mail: donregan@umich.edu.

REGAN, ELLEN FRANCES (MRS. WALSTON SHEPARD BROWN), ophthalmologist, educator; b. Boston, Feb. 1, 1919; d. Edward Francis and Margaret (Moynihan) R.; m. Walston Shepard Brown, Aug. 13, 1955. AB, Wellesley Coll., Mass., 1940; MD, Yale U., New Haven, Conn., 1943. Intern Boston City Hosp., 1944; asst. resident, resident Inst. Ophthalmology, Presbyn. Hosp., NYC, 1944-47, asst. ophthalmologist, 1947-56, asst. attending ophthalmologist, 1956-84; instr. ophthalmology Columbia Coll. Physicians and Surgeons, 1947-55, assoc. ophthalmology, 1955-67, asst. clin. prof., 1967-84; ret., 1984. Mem. AMA, Am. Ophthal. Soc., Am. Acad. Ophthalmology, NY Acad. Medicine, NY State Med. Soc., Mass. Med. Soc., River Club, Tuxedo Club. Home: PO Box 632 Tuxedo Park NY 10987-0632

REGAN, JUDITH TERRANCE, former publishing executive; b. Leominster, Mass., Aug. 17, 1953; d. Leo James and Rita Ann (Impresscia) Regan; children: Patrick, Lara. BA, Vassar Coll., 1975. Reporter Nat. Enquirer; sr. editor, v.p. Simon & Schuster, NYC, 1989—94; pres., pub. Regan Books imprint of HarperCollins, NYC, 1994—2006. TV prodr. Entertainment Tonight, NYC, Geraldo, NYC; prodr. 20th Century Fox Films, Fox TV; anchor Full Disclosure, Fox TV; host Judith Regan Tonight, Fox News Channel. Editor, pub. (books) The Way Things Ought to Be (Rush Limbaugh), 1992, Rogue Warrior (Richard Marcinko), 1992, She's Come Undone (Wally Lamb), 1992, Shampoo Planet and Life After God (Douglas Coupland), 1992, Private Parts, Miss America (Howard Stern), 1993, Judge Robert Bork, Slouching Towards Gomorrah, 1993, I Can't Believe I Said That (Kathie Lee Gifford), 1994, Microserfs, 1996, Shabby Chic (Rachel Ashwell), 1996, The Zone (Dr. Barry Sears), 1996, Brain Lock (Dr. Jeffrey Schwartz), 1997, Wicked, 1997, Confessions of an Ugly Stepsister (Gregory Maguire), 1997—2000, Girlfriend in A Coma, 1998, I Know This Much is True, 1998, Marilu Henner's Total health Makeover, 1998, Story (Robert McKee), 1998, Have a Nice Day, Mick Foley (Mankind), 1999, The Rock Says, 2000, The September 11 Photo Project, 2002, How to Make Love Like a Porn Star (Jenna Jameson), 2004, Juiced (Jose Canseco), 2005, Nanny 911, 2005, The Confession (James McGreevey), 2006, The Confession (James E. McGreevey), 2006, A Million Little Lies (James Pinocchio), 2006, The Zero (Jess Walter), 2006, If I Did It (O.J. Simpson), 2006, and others; exec. prodr.: (TV series) Growing Up Gotti, 2004.

REGAN, MICHAEL PATRICK, lawyer; b. Bklyn., Feb. 22, 1941; s. Cornelius Francis and Marguerite (Cann) Regan; m. Susan Ann Light, July 13, 1974; children: Michael Patrick Jr., Brian Christopher, Mark Dennis. BA in English, U. Notre Dame, 1963; LLB, Union U., Albany, 1967, JD, 1968. Bar: NY 1967, Va. 1975, US Dist. Ct. (we. dist.) Va., US Dist. Ct. (so. dist.) NY, US Ct. Appeals (4th cir.), US Bankruptcy Ct.

Assoc. Medwin & McMahon, Albany, NY, 1967—69; asst. dist. atty. Albany County, NY, 1969; corp. atty. Mohasco Corp., Amsterdam, NY, 1969—74; asst. gen. spl. counsel Dan River, Inc., Danville, Va., 1975, assoc. gen. counsel, 1981—88, acting gen. counsel, asst. sec., 1988, gen. counsel, asst. sec., 1989; assoc. gen. counsel, asst. sec. Dan River Svc. Corp. of Va., Danville, 1984—88; gen. counsel Wunda Weve Carpets, Inc., Greenville, SC, 1990—93; pvt. practice Danville, 1990—. Clarinetist, saxophonist Tightsqueeze Philharm. Band, 1981—; active Danville Symphony Orch., 1991—, prin., 1997—2005; leader The DanceNotes, 1986—; active Starmont Swing Band, 1999—; sec. DanPac Polit. Action Com., 1976—89. Fellow Paul Harris fellow, Rotary Internat. Mem.: ABA, ATLA, Va. Trial Lawyers Assn., Danville Bar Assn., Va. Bar Assn., N.Y. State Bar Assn., Danville Golf Club. Republican. Roman Catholic. Home: 236 Cambridge Cir Danville VA 24541-5233 Office: 703 Patton St Danville VA 24541-1905 Office Phone: 434-793-9670.

REGAN, PETER FRANCIS, III, physician, medical educator; b. Bklyn., Nov. 11, 1924; s. Peter Francis Jr. and Veronica (Tierney) R.; m. Laurette Patricia O'Connor, June 18, 1949; children: Peter, Stephen, William, Elizabeth, John, Carol. MD, Cornell U., Ithaca, NY, 1949. Diplomate Am. Bd. Psychiatry and Neurology, Nat. Bd. Med. Examiners. Intern in medicine N.Y. Hosp., 1949-50; asst. resident psychiatry Payne Whitney Psychiat. Clinic, 1950, 53-54, resident, 1954-56; asst. prof. psychiatry Cornell U. Med. Coll., 1956-58; prof., head dept. psychiatry U. Fla. Coll. Medicine, chief psychiat. svc. Univ. Teaching Hosp., 1958-64; prof. psychiatry SUNY, Buffalo, 1964-84, v.p. health affairs, 1964-67, exec. v.p. univ., 1967-69, exec. v.p., acting pres. univ., 1969-70, vice chancellor acad. programs, 1970-71; assoc. chief staff for edn. Buffalo VA Med. Ctr., 1979-84; prof. psychiatry U. Tex. Health Sci. Ctr., San Antonio, 1984-87, assoc. dean Sch. Medicine, 1986-87; assoc. chief staff for edn. San Antonio VA Med. Ctr., 1984-86, chief staff, 1986-87; dep. assoc. chief med. dir. for acad. affairs VA Cen. Office, Washington, 1987-88, assoc. chief med. dir. for acad. affairs, 1988-92; prof. emeritus / sen. cons. dept. psychiatry SUNY, Buffalo, 1992—; interim chair dept. psychiatry Med. U. S.C., 2001—02. Project dir. Ctr. for Ednl. Rsch. and Innovation, OECD, 1972-74. Author: (with F. Flach) Chemotherapy in Emotional Disorders, 1960, (With E. Pattishall) Behavioral Science Contributions to Psychiatry; contbr. articles to profl. jours. Capt. M.C. AUS, 1951-52. Fellow Am. Psychiat. Assn., Am. Coll. Psychiatrists (bd. regents 1986-95, 2d v.p. 1988, 1st v.p. 1989, pres.-elect 1990, pres. 1991); mem. AMA, Alpha Omega Alpha.

REGAN, RICHARD JOSEPH, political science professor, writer; b. Morristown, NJ, Oct. 26, 1930; s. Joseph Michael and May Catherine (Cella R.). A.B., St. Peter's Coll., Jersey City, 1952; PhL, Woodstock Coll., Md., 1957; STL, 1964; PhD in Polit. Sci., U. Chgo., 1967. Assoc. prof. Fordham U., Bronx, 1968—87, prof., 1987—2007, emeritus prof., 2007. Author: American Pluralism and The Catholic Conscience, 1963, Conflict and Consensus, 1967, Private Conscience and Public Law, 1972, Moral Dimensions of Politics, 1986, On Law, Morality and Politics, 1988, God and Creation, 1994, Just War, 1996, A Summary of Philosophy, 2003, The Cardinal Virtues, 2005, Commentry on Aristotle's Politics, 2007; translator: The De Malo of Thomas Aquinas, 2001. Roman Catholic. Avocation: running. Home and Office: Loyola Hall Fordham Univ Bronx NY 10458 Office Phone: 718-817-5432.

REGAN, SUSAN WRIGHT, dance educator, small business owner, choreographer; b. Cambridge, Mass., Dec. 12, 1946; d. Stephen Ellis Wright and Angela Louise Domenichello; m. David Joseph Regan, June 29, 1968 (dec.); children: Michele, David, Derek. BS in Edn., Lesley Coll., Cambridge, 1968. Tchr. Chelmsford schs., Mass.; owner, dance tchr., choreographer Susan Wright Sch. Dance, Watertown, Mass., 1964—. Performer NY World's Fair, appearances on numerous TV programs, dance cos. Recipient 2d and 3d pl. medals, NY World's Fair, 1st pl. regionals, Miss Dance New Eng., 5th pl., Miss Dance Am., Charles Burke award outstanding dedication and svc.; Sch. rated Best of the Best, Watertown, 1999—2005. Mem.: Watertown-Belmont C. of C. (Charles Burke award 2005), Dance Masters Am., Dance Tchrs. Club Boston, Sons of Italy. Avocations: travel, gardening, decorating, ballroom dancing, cooking. Office Phone: 617-924-6255. Personal E-mail: swrdance@comcast.net.

REGAN, TIMOTHY JAMES, grain company executive; b. Atchison, Kans., July 31, 1956; s. Vincent James and Phyllis (Brull) R.; m. Veronica Sue Kasten, June 25, 1977; children: Katrina Sue, Brian James. BS, Kans. State U., 1978. Corp. acct. Lincoln Grain Co., Atchison, 1978-80; acctg. supr. Pillsbury Co., St. Joseph, Mo., 1980, br. account mgr., 1980-82, Omaha, 1982, internal auditor Mpls., 1983, regional account mgr. Huron, Ohio, 1983-84, Scoular Grain Co., Omaha, 1984-87, controller, 1987-91, v.p., mem. exec. com., 1990-99, CFO, 1991—2000; ex-v.p., CFO J.D. Heiskell & Co., Tulare, Calif., 2000—06, sr. v.p., CFO Elkhorn, Nebr., 2006—, exec. v.p., 2007—; bd. mem. Maur Hill Mount Acad., Atchison, Kans., 2008—, treas., 2009—. Fin. adviser Grace Abbott Sch. PTO, Omaha, 1987, treas., 1990-91; bd. dirs. Cath. Charities, 1994-2000, treas., 1997-99; coach Little League Baseball and Soccer. Mem. KC, Elks. Republican. Roman Catholic. Avocations: jogging, basketball, coaching little league baseball and soccer. Office: 20010 Manderson Elkhorn NE 68022 Business E-Mail: tregan@heiskell.com.

REGAN, WILLIAM JOSEPH, JR., energy company executive; b. Bronx, NY, Mar. 7, 1946; s. William Joseph and Eleanor F. (Malone) R.; m. Mary Lee Wynn; children— Katrina Lee, Thomas Wynn, James William BS, U.S. Air Force Acad., 1967; MBA, U. Wis.-Madison, 1969, PhD, 1972. Asst. prof. Wayne State U., Detroit, 1971-75; with Nat. Bank Detroit, 1975-77; sr. bus. planner Am. Natural Resources Co., Detroit, 1977-78, dir. fin. planning, 1978-82, v.p., treas., 1982-85; v.p. corp. fin. United Svcs. Automobile Assn., San Antonio, 1986-88, sr. v.p., treas., 1988-95; v.p., treas. Entergy Corp., New Orleans, 1995-99; CFO Calif. Ind. Sys. Operator Corp., Folsom, Calif., 1999—2008; mem. bd. dirs. Steak N Shake Co., Indpls., 2008—; consumer credit consulting svcs. San Antonio, 2008—. Home: 8624 FAIRWAY GREEN DR Fair Oaks TX 78015-4480 Home Phone: 830-755-4366; Office Phone: 830-755-4368. Personal E-mail: wregan37@earthlink.net.

REGATTE, RAVINDER R., medical educator; b. Yellareddy Guda, Andhra Pradesh, India, Oct. 15, 1966; s. Venkat R. and Susheela R. Regatte; m. Anitha Kancharla, Feb. 11, 1999; 1 child, Abhijeet R. PhD, Osmania U., Hydearabad, India, 1996. Asst. prof. NY U., 2004—. R01 grant, NIH, 2007—. Mem.: ISMRM.

REGAZZI, JOHN JAMES, III, dean, publishing executive; b. Bklyn., June 8, 1948; s. John James Jr. and Theresa Cecil (Fiore) R.; m. Marie Louise Ford, May 30, 1971; children: John James IV, Thomas Paul, Michael Rees. BS, St. John's U., Queens, NY, 1970; MA, U. Iowa, 1972; MS, Columbia U., 1974; PhD, Rutgers U., 1983. Systems mgr. No. Ill. U., De Kalb, Ill., 1974-76; dir. pub. Found. Ctr., NYC, 1976-79; assoc. prof. Rutgers U., New Brunswick, NJ, 1979-81; v.p. The H.W. Wilson Co., NYC, 1981-88; pres., CEO Engring. Info., Inc., NYC, 1988-99; CEO, pres. Elsevier Inc., NYC, 1999—2005; dean LI U. Coll. Info. and Computer Sci., Brookville, 2005—. Chmn. Article Express Internat., 1992-94; bd. dirs. Bristish Stds. Inst. Group, Nat. Tech. Info. Svc., CAB Internat., Engring. Info. Found., Elsevier Found.; adj. prof. SUNY, Albany, Columbia U., Rutgers U. Author: Guide to Periodicals in Religion, 1974. Mem. AAAS, IEEE, ALA, Am. Assn. Pubs. (bd. dirs. NYC chpt. 1987-88), Nat. Info. Standards Orgn. (vice chmn. 1989-90), Nat. Fedn. of Abstracting and Info. Svcs. (bd. dirs. 1980-81, 88, 2004-), Assn. Computing Machinery, NY Acad. Sci. Avocation: cycling. Office: LI U Coll Info & Computer Sci 720 Northern Blvd Greenvale NY 11548 Office Phone: 516-299-4109. Business E-Mail: john.regazzi@liu.edu.

REGELBRUGGE, ROGER RAFAEL, steel company executive; b. Eeklo, Belgium, May 22, 1930; arrived in U.S., 1953, naturalized, 1961; s. Victor and Rachel (Roesbeke) Regelbrugge; m. Dorcas Merchant; children: Anita, Marc, Laurie, Jon, Craig, Kurt, Christiane, Lauren, Lauren, Roger Rafael Jr. BSME, State Tech. Coll., Ghent, 1951; BS in Indsl. Engring, Gen. Motors Inst., Flint, Mich., 1955; MSME, Mich. State U., 1964. Supr. product engring. dept. Gen. Motors Corp., Antwerp, 1955—58; chief devel. engr., then gen. mgr. Airmaster div. Hayes Industries Inc., Jackson, Mich., 1958—66; with Koehring Co., 1966—74, group v.p. internat. ops. Milw., 1969—74; exec. v.p. Korf Industries, Inc., Charlotte, NC, 1974—77, chmn.; chmn., pres., CEO Georgetown Industries, Inc. (formerly Korf Industries, Inc.), 1977—95; chmn., CEO GS Industries Inc. (formerly Georgetown Industries), 1995—97, chmn., 1997—2001. Mem. adv. coun. Coll. Engring. U. Notre Dame; trustee Belmont (N.C.) Abbey Coll. Mem.: Am. Soc. Automotive Engrs., ASME, Georgetown Club, Carmel Country Club. Roman Catholic.

REGENBOGEN, ADAM, judge; b. Steyer, Austria, June 12, 1947; s. William and Pauline (Feuerstein) R.; m. Paula Ruth Rothenberg, June 27, 1970 (div. Oct. 1992); children: Stacy, Candice; m. Helen Busuttil Drwal, Apr. 20, 1996; 1 stepchild, Jason A. Drwal; 1 adopted child Alex. BA, Temple U., 1969; MSW, U. Pa., 1972; JD, Temple U., 1980. Bar: N.Y. 1983. Social worker VA, Coatesville, Pa., 1974—78, supr. Northport, NY, 1978—80, quality assurance dir., 1980—87; dir. quality assurance N.Y. State Office Mental Health, Willard, 1987—91; workers compensation law judge Binghamton, Oneonta, Norwich, Monticello, 1998—; pvt. practice NY, 1983—98; conciliator, acting judge Workers Compensation Bd., NY, 1992—98, judge NY, 1998—; judge assigned to World Trade Ctr. 9/11 cases, 2002. Organizer/incorporator Ithaca (N.Y.) Reform Temple, 1992; organizer Parents Without Partners, Ithaca, 1992. Recipient Pro Bono Svc. award Suffolk County Bar Assn., 1986. Home: 42 Hawkins Rd Nineveh NY 13813 Office: Workers Compensation Bd 44 Hawley St Binghamton NY 13901-4434 Home Phone: 607-639-4265; Office Phone: 607-721-8331. Business E-Mail: adam.regenbogen@wcb.state.ny.us.

REGENSTREIF, HERBERT, lawyer; b. NYC, May 13, 1935; s. Max and Jeannette (Hacker) R.; m. Patricia Friedman, Dec. 20, 1967 (div. July 1968); m. Charlotte Lois Levy, Dec. 11, 1980 (div. Sept. 2002); 1 child, Cara Rachael. BA, Hobart Coll., 1957; JD, NY Law Sch., 1960; MS, Pratt Inst., 1985. Bar: NY 1961, Ky. 1985, US Dist. Ct. (ea. and so. dists.) NY 1962, US Dist. Ct. (ea. dist.) Ky. 1998, US Tax Ct. 1967, US Ct. Appeals (2d cir.) 1962, US Supreme Ct. 1967. Ptnr. Fried & Regenstreif, P.C., Mineola, NY, 1963—; reservist atty. Fed. Emergency Mgmt. Agy., 1998-99. Cons. in field; arbitrator Dist. Ct., Nassau County, NY, 1989—, NYC Civil Ct., 1984-86; sec.-treas. Sta. WAHY-FM, Inc., 1998-2000. Contbr. articles to profl. jours. County committeeman Dem. Com., Queens County, NY, 1978-79. Mem. Bar Assn. Nassau County, Ky. Bar Assn., Am. Judges Assn., Phi Delta Phi, Beta Phi Mu, Hobart Club of NY (gov. 1968-69). Office Phone: 516-294-6442.

REGENSTREIF, S(AMUEL) PETER, political scientist, educator; b. Montreal, Que., Can., Sept. 9, 1936; s. Albert Benjamin and Miriam Lillian (Issenman) R.; children: Anne Erica, Mitchell Chester, Jeffrey Gershon, Gail Aviva. BA, McGill U., 1957; PhD, Cornell U., 1963. Mem. faculty U. Rochester, 1961—, prof. polit. sci., 1971—; coordinator Can. studies program, 1967—. Editl. cons. Toronto Star, 1968-82, Chgo. Sun-Times, 1988-89; polit. cons. Bunting Warburg, Toronto, 1973-90, Coopers & Lybrand, Ltd., 1981-89, Loewen, Ondaatje, McCutcheon, 1991-94; prin. Policy Concepts Inc., Toronto; broadcaster CKO Radio Network, 1983-89; pvt. polit. cons. Author: The Diefenbaker Interlude: Parties and Voting in Canada, 1965; syndicated columnist: Toronto Star, 1963-82; contbr. articles to profl. jours. Served to lt. Canadian Army, 1957. Ford. Found. fellow, 1960; Can. Council fellow, 1960, 65; Canadian Royal Commn. on Bilingualism and Biculturalism grantee, 1964-66; recipient Edward Peck Curtis award U. Rochester, 1979 Mem. AAAS, Am. Polit. Sci. Assn., Can. Polit. Sci. Assn., Assn. Can. Studies in U.S., Phi Beta Kappa. Jewish. Home: 438C Browncroft Blvd Rochester NY 14609 Office: Univ Rochester Dept Polit Sci Rochester NY 14627 Office Phone: 585-275-5466. Business E-Mail: peter.regenstreif@rochester.edu.

REGER, LAWRENCE LEE, trade association administrator; b. Lincoln, Nebr., June 23, 1939; s. Lawrence John and Bertha (Hergenrader) R. Student, U. Nebr., 1961; LL.B., Vanderbilt U., 1964. Bar: Nebr 1964. Asso. firm Crosby, Guenzel & Binning, Lincoln, 1964-70; gen. counsel Nat. Endowment Arts, 1970-72, dir. program devel. and coordination, 1972-78; dir. Am. Assn. Mus., Washington, 1978-86; pres. Heritage Preservation, Washington, 1988—. Mem. visual arts vis. com. U. Del., 1995—; mem. cultural property adv. com. USIA, 1996—2000; mem. bd. trustees St. Petersburg Internat. Preservation Ctr., 1996—2000; bd. dirs. Peck Stacpoole Found. Chmn. Nat. Humanities Alliance, 1982-86, bd. dirs., 2007—; bd. dirs. Nat. Musical Arts, 1990—96. Recipient Forbes medal Am. Inst. Conservation, 2000, Alumni Achievement award Hixon-Leid Coll. Fine and Performing Arts, U. Nebr., 2004. Home: 5010 Garfield St NW Washington DC 20016-3469 Office: Heritage Preservation 1012 14th St NW Ste 1200 Washington DC 20005 Office Phone: 202-233-0800.

REGES, MARIANNA ALICE, marketing executive; b. Budapest, Hungary, Mar. 23, 1947; arrived in U.S., 1956, naturalized, 1963; d. Otto H. and Alice M. Reges; children: Rebecca, Charles III. AAS with honors, Fashion Inst. Tech., NYC, 1967; BBA magna cum laude, Baruch Coll., 1971, MBA in Stats., 1978. Media rsch. analyst Doyle, Dane, Bernbach Advt., NYC, 1967—70; rsch. supr. Sta. WCBS-TV, NYC, 1970—71; rsch. mgr. Woman's Day mag., NYC, 1971—72; asst. media dir. Benton & Bowles Advt., NYC, 1972—75; mgr. rsch. and sales devel. NBC Radio, NYC, 1975—77; sr. rsch. mgr. Ziff-Davis Pub. Co., NYC, 1977—84; media mgr. Bristol-Myers Squibb Co., 1984—2001, Procter & Gamble Co., 2001—. Mem. Spanish Radio Adv. Coun., NYC, 1986—88, Pan-European TV Audience Rsch. Mgmt. Com., 1988—. Mem. advisor Baruch Coll. Advt. Soc., 1975—; active First Presbyn. Ch., NYC. Mem.: Advt. Rsch. Found., Radio and TV Rsch. Coun., Media Rsch. Dirs. Assn., Am. Advt. Fedn., Am. Mktg. Assn., Anthroposophical Soc., Nature Conservancy, Baruch Alumni Assn., Beta Gamma Sigma. Home: 626 E 20th St New York NY 10009-1509 Personal E-mail: marianna10009@hotmail.com.

REGIER, BRYAN L., music educator; b. Topeka, Kans., Sept. 20, 1970; s. Russell L. and Nancy A. Regier; m. Kelly L. Hitt, Dec. 20, 2003. BS, Tabor Coll., 1992; MS, U. Nebr., Kearney, 2000. Grade 5-12 instrumental music tchr. Rushville (Nebr.) H.S., 1994—96; K-12 music, vocal tchr. Arcadia (Nebr.) H.S., 1996—98; grades 5-12 instr. music Bridgeport (Nebr.) H.S., 1998—2000; grades 6-12 instr. music McCook (Nebr.) H.S., 2000—06; instrumental choir Arch Bishop Bergan Cath. Sch., 2006—. Bd. dirs. S.W. Nebr. Cmty. Theatre Assn., McCook, 2000—06, McCook Arts Coun. Mem.: Nebr. State Bandmasters Assn. (chair 2006—09, award), Nebr. Music Educators Assn., Masons. Republican. Mennonite. Avocations: trap shooting, golf, music, gardening. Home: 1424 E 6th St Fremont NE 68025-5349 Office: 545 E 4th Fremont NE 68025 Home Phone: 402-753-5776. E-mail: berger@esuz.org.

REGIER, DARCY JOHN, professional sports team executive; b. Swift Current, Sask., Can., Nov. 27, 1956; came to U.S., 1977; s. John Melvin and Helen (Neufeld) Regier; m. Katherine Opyr, June 30, 1979; children: Jonathan, Justin, Jarrett. Student, U. Lethbridge (Alta., Can.), 1980-85. Head coach Indpls. Checkers, 1984-85; dir. hockey adminstrn. NY Islanders, Uniondale, 1985-89, asst. coach, 1989-91, Hartford Whalers, 1991—92; gen. mgr., v.p. Buffalo Sabres, 1997—. Mem. all-star team Cen. Hockey League, 1983. Mem. Profl. Hockey Players Assn. (chmn. exec. com. 1980-83). Avocations: bicycling, video productions on sports. Office: Buffalo Sabres HSBC Arena One Seymour H Knox III Plz Buffalo NY 14203-3096

REGISTER, ANNETTE ROWAN, literature educator; b. Doctors Inlet, Fla., Apr. 5, 1931; d. Ernest Ambors and Frances Perlena (Monroe) R.; Henry Ira Register, Oct. 31, 1954; 1 child, Andrew Henry. RN, Greenville Gen. Hosp. Sch. of Nursing, Greenville, 1948-51; BS, Tex. Woman's U., Denton, 1954; MEd, U. Fla., Gainesville, 1959; SEd, Fla. State U., 1983; student, U. West Fla., Okaloosa Walton C.C. Instrn. dir. nursing edn. Alachua Gen. Hosp., Gainesville, Fla., 1955-57; pub. sch. tchr. Okaloosa County, Ft. Walton Beach, Fla., 1966-93. V.p., Internat. Tng. in Communication Ft. Walton Beach, Fla.; active Inst. Sr. Profls. Okaloosa Walton C.C. Pres. Okaloosa Reading Coun., 1976—80; mem. Okaloosa Walton C.C. Symphony Guild, 1998—; pres. United Meth. Women, Ft. Walton Beach, Fla., 1985—87; dist. v.p. Mem. Fla. C. of C. (amb. 1996—), Phi Delta Kappa (1st v.p.). Methodist. Avocations: crafts, painting, sketching, travel. Office: Okaloosa County Sch Bd 10 Lowery Pl SE Fort Walton Beach FL 32548 Personal E-mail: registerannette@yahoo.com.

REGISTER, JESSE, school system administrator; BA in English, U. NC, Charlotte, EdM; D in Edn. Adminstrn., Duke U., Durham, NC; grad. supt.'s exec. program, U. NC; attended Change Leadership Program, Harvard U. Cert. advanced sch. adminstr. U. NC, Chapel Hill. Supt. Iredell-Statesville Schs., NC, 1991; prin. Cabarrus County Schs., NC, asst. supt. curriculum and instrn., asst. supt. adminstrn., supt., Hamilton County Schs., 1997—2006; dir. schs. Met. Nashville Pub. Schs., 2009—. Vis. assoc. prof. urban edn. U. Tenn., Chattanooga, 2007; sr. advisor dist. leadership Brown U. Annenberg Inst. Sch. Reform, Providence, mem. dist. redesign team. Mem. Gov.'s Task Force on Salary Equity, Gov.'s Basic Edn. Plan Rev. Com. Named Outstanding Supt. of Yr., Tenn. PTA, 2001, Supt. of Yr., Tenn. Sch. Plant Mgmt. Assn. Office: Met Nashville Pub Schs 2601 Bransford Ave Nashville TN 37204*

REGNERY, ALFRED SCATTERGOOD, publishing executive; b. Chgo., Nov. 21, 1942; s. Henry and Eleanor (Scattergood) R.; m. Christina Sparrow, Nov. 29, 1969 (dec.); children: George M., Louise S., Alfred W., Charles H; m. Audrey Qarrett, sep. 6, 2008. BA, Beloit Coll., 1965; JD, U. Wis., 1971. Bar: Wis. 1971, D.C. 1987. Pvt. practice law, Madison, Wis., 1971-78; minority counsel Senate Judiciary Com., Washington, 1978-81; dep. asst. atty. gen. for land & nat. resources US Dept. Justice, Washington, 1981-82; adminstr. Office of Juvenile Justice and Delinquency Prevention, 1982-86; pres., CEO Regnery Pub. Inc., Washington, 1986—2003; pres. & pub. The Am. Spectator, Arlington, Va., 2003—. Bd. dirs. Eagle Pub., Inc., Washington. Author (Simon S. Schuster): Upstream: The Ascendance of American Conservatism, 2008. Chmn. Intercollegiate Studies Inst., Wilmington, Del.; bd. dirs. Found. for Am. Studies, Washington, Am. Fgn. Policy Coun., Washington, Jamestown Found. Served with USCG, 1966—67. Office: The American Spectator 1611 N Kent St Arlington VA 22209 Office Phone: 703-807-2011.

REGNIER, NANCY MAE, medical educator; b. Lakeview, Oreg., Nov. 6, 1948; d. Cleo and Peggy Viola Price; children: Sereena Michelle, Sonia Marie. MSN, Calif. State U., Chico, 1979. Assoc. prof. nursing Daytona State Coll., Fla., 1995—; weekend hospice coord. Fla. Hosp. Hospice, Ormond Beach, 2008—. Sr. rn emergency,trauma Orlando Regional Med. Ctr., Fla., 1989—2000; sr. nurse emergency dept. Fla. Hosp. Fish Meml., Orange City, 2000—08. Capt. USAF, 1981—89, US,Turkey & Italy. Decorated Achievement medal, Commendation medal USAF. Mem.: ANA. Avocations: reading, travel, gardening. Home: 1885 Bonkirk Dr Deltona FL 32738 Office: Daytona State Coll 1200 International Speedway Blvd Daytona Beach FL 32120-2811 Home Fax: 386-532-5824. Business E-Mail: regnien@daytonastate.edu.

REGO, SIMON ALEXANDER, psychologist; s. Joseph A.V. and Barbara D. Rego; m. Katherine Lynn Muller, May 15, 2003. BSc with honors, Queen's U., Kingston, Ont., Can., 1994; MA, CUNY, NYC, 1995; M of Psychology, Rutgers U., Piscataway, NJ, 1999, PsyD, 2001. Cert. cognitive therapist Acad. Cognitive Therapy, 2004. Open clinic coord. Ctr. for the Treatment and Study of Anxiety, U. Pa., Phila., 2001—03; clin. and rsch. coord. Anxiety and Depression Clinic Montefiore Med. Ctr., Bronx, NY, 2003—04, assoc. dir. psychology tng., 2004—; asst. prof. psychiatry and behavioral scis. Albert Einstein Coll. Medicine, Bronx, 2004—. Mem. instl. rev. bd. for the protection of human subjects Montefiore Med. Ctr., Bronx, 2004—; clin. supr. Ferkauf Grad. Sch. Psychology, Yeshiva U., Bronx, 2004—, Psychol. Clinic, Grad. Sch. Applied and Profl. Psychology, Rutgers U., Piscataway, 2004—; mem. instl. rev. bd. Biomedical Rsch. Alliance NY, Great Neck, NY, 2005—. Sect. editor: the clinical psychologist Internet Update. Recipient GSAPP Scholars award, Grad. Sch. Applied and Profl. Psychology, 1996, Robert S. Morrow prize for Excellence in the Grad. Forensic Psychology Program, John Jay Coll. Criminal Justice, 1996, Dean's award for Contbn. to Student Life, Grad. Sch. Applied and Profl. Psychology, 1998, 1999, 2000, Robert D. Weitz award, 2002. Mem.: APA, Assn. for Behavioral and Cognitive Therapies (chair profl. issues com. 2004—, spl. interest group insomnia and other sleep disorders, spl. interest group anxiety disorders), Can. Psychol. Assn. (sect. on clin. psychology), NY State Psychol. Assn., Obsessive-Compulsive Found., APA Soc. Clin. Psychology, APA Soc. for a Sci. Clin. Psychology, Internat. Assn. for Cognitive Psychotherapy. Office: Montefiore Medical Center 111 E 210th St Klau 1 Bronx NY 10467 Office Fax: 718-920-6538. Business E-Mail: srego@montefiore.org.

REGULA, RALPH STRAUS, former United States Representative from Ohio, lawyer; b. Beach City, Ohio, Dec. 3, 1924; s. O.F. and Orpha (Walter) Regula; m. Mary Rogusky, Aug. 5, 1950; children: Martha, David, Richard. BA, Mt. Union Coll., Alliance, Ohio, 1948, LLD, 1981; LLB, William McKinley Sch. Law, 1952; LLD, Malone Coll., Canton, Ohio, 1976. Bar: Ohio 1952. Sch. adminstr. Stark County Bd. Edn., 1948-55; lawyer Navarre, 1952—; mem. Ohio State Ho. Reps., 1965-66, Ohio State Senate, 1967-72, US Congress from 16th Ohio Dist., 1973—2009, mem. appropriations com.; ptnr. Regula Brothers. Mem. Pres.'s Commn. Fin. Structures and Regulation, 1970—72. Hon. mem. adv. bd. Walsh Coll., Canton; trustee Mt. Union Coll., Stark County Hist. Soc., Stark County Wilderness Soc.; mem. Ohio Bd. Edn., 1960—64. With USNR, 1944—46. Recipient Cmty. Svc. award, Navarre Kiwanis Club, 1963, Meritorious Svc. award for conservation, Canton Audubon Soc., 1965, Conservation award, Ohio Gov. James Rhodes, 1969, J. Sterling Morton award, Nat. Arbor Day Found., 2000, Sheldon Colemon Great Outdoors award, Am. Recreation Coaltion, 2000, Legis. Excellence award, Nat. Assn. Mfrs., 2001, Pick and Gavel award, Assn. Am. State Geologists, 2001, Spirit of Enterprise award, US C.of C., 2001, Vanguard award, North County Trial Assn., 2001, Thomas Jefferson award, Food Distributors Internat., 2002, Disting. Champion award, Nat. Assn. Cmty. Health Ctrs., 2002, Nat. Ednl. Svc. award, Am. Assn. CC's, 2002, Pub. Svc. award, Creutzfeldt-Jacob Disease Found., 2003, Benjamin Franklin Pub.Policy award, Nat. Assn. Mutual Ins. Cos., 2003, Crystal Apple award, Am. Assn. Sch. Librarians Affiliate Assembly, 2003, Disting. Legis. award, Nat. Devel. & Rsch. Insts., Inc., 2003, Congl. Am. Spirit Medallion, Nat. D-Day Mus., 2004; named Outstanding Young Man of Yr., Canton Jr. C. of C., 1957, Legis. Conservationist of Yr., Ohio League Sportsmen, 1969, Legislator of Yr., Assn. Home Appliances Mfrs., 2001, Policy Maker of Yr., Assn. Corp. Travel Execs., 2002. Republican. Episcopalian.*

REH, THOMAS ANDREW, biologist, educator; b. Chgo., Feb. 17, 1955; s. Carl W. Reh and M. Reh Regina; m. Olivia Mary Bermingham-McDonogh, July 4, 1998; children: Rebecca K., Samuel K. PhD, U. Wis., Madison, 1983. Assoc. prof. U. of Calgary, Calgary, Alberta, Canada, 1984—89; prof. U. Wash., Seattle, 1989—, dir., neurobiology and behavior program, 2001—07. Dir., neurobiology and behavior program U. of Wash., Seattle, 2001—07. Author: (non-fiction book) Development of the Nervous System. Sci. adv. bd. mem. Acucela, Seattle, 2003—08. Fellow, A.E. Sloan Found., 1987—89, Rsch. grant, Found. Fighting Blindness, 1987—, RO1 grant, NIH, 1989—, Rsch. grant, NSF, 1991—2000. Mem.: Soc. Neurosci. Office: Univ Wash 1959 NE Pacific St Seattle WA 98195

REHA, ROSE KRIVISKY, retired finance educator; b. NYC, Dec. 17, 1920; d. Boris and Freda (Gerstein) Krivisky; m. Rudolph John Reha, Apr. 11, 1941; children; Irene Gale, Phyllis BS Bus. and Music Edn., Ind. State U., 1965; MA Bus. and Psychology, U. Minn., 1967, PhD Ednl. Psychology and Counseling, 1971. With US and Minn. State Civil Svc., 1941—63; tchr. pub. schs., Minn., 1965—66; tchg. assoc., instr. U. Minn., Mpls., 1966—68, 1968—85; prof. coll. bus. profl. comm. St. Cloud State U., Minn., 1968—85, prof. emeritus, 1985—, chmn. bus. edn. & office adminstrn. dept., 1982—83. Advisor Small Bus. Inst., 1972-85; ct. advocate for women in distress St. Cloud Women's Shelter, 1986-89; adj. prof. profl. and bus. comm. Fla. Atlantic U., Boca Raton, 1989-90; substitute tchr. Broward County, 1990—; tutor (reading) Lauderdale, Fla., 1990-92; moderator, counselor Posnack Jewish Cmty. Ctr., Davie, Fla.; lectr. comm. Soref Jewish Cmty. Ctr. Continuing Edn. for sr. groups, Sunrise, Fla., 1994-2004; cons., lectr. in field; reviewer bus. comm. and consumer edn. textbooks Contbr. articles to profl. jours Camp dir. Girl Scouts US, Moose Lake, Minn., 1960-62; active various cmty. fund drives; sec., mem. relicensure rev. Com. Minn. Bd. Tchg. Continuing Edn., 1984-85 Recipient Achievement award St. Cloud State U., 1985, St. Cloud State U. Rsch. and Faculty Improvement grantee, 1973, 78, 83 Mem. NEA, ACA (cert.), Am. Vocat. Assn. (cert.), Am. Mental Health Counselors Assn. (cert.), Minn. Econ. Assn., Minn. Women of Higher Edn., Minn. Edn. Assn. (pres. women's caucus 1981-83, award 1983), St. Cloud State U. Faculty Assembly (pres. 1975-76), St. Cloud State U. Grad. Coun. (chmn. 1983-85), Pi Omega Pi, Phi Chi Theta, Delta Pi Epsilon, Delta Kappa Gamma Jewish. Avocation: painting. Home: Summit Place 8505 Flying Cloud Dr Apt 239-I Eden Prairie MN 55344 Office Phone: 952-995-1109.

REHAK, JAMES RICHARD, orthodontist; b. Chgo., Jan. 2, 1938; s. James Joseph and Lydia Ann (Thomas) R.; m. Joann Marie Tabbert, Oct. 15, 1969; 1 child, Suzanne Therese. BS, U. Ill., 1960, DDS cum laude, 1962, MS, 1967, cert. in orthodontics, 1965. Pvt. practice dentistry, Chgo., 1962-63; pvt. practice orthodontics Chgo., Arlington Heights, Ill., Cape Coral, Naples, Fla. Asst. prof. U. Ill. Coll. Dentistry, 1966-68. Pres. bd. trustees St. Ann Sch. Foun.; chmn. bd. dirs. St. John Neumann H.S.; organizer, dir. 1st Nat. Bank, Naples; trustee Catholic Cultural Ctr., Washington. Served to capt. U.S. Army Res., 1962-69. Kellogg Found. fellow, 1958; recipient Blessed Edmund Rice medal, Christian Bros., 1996. Fellow Royal Soc. Health; mem. ADA, Ill. Dental Assn., Chgo. Dental Soc., Fla. Dental Assn., West Coast Dental Soc., Collier County Dental Assn., Am. Assn. Orthodontists, Am. Assn. Lingual Orthodontists, Fedn. Dentaire Internationale, Psi Omega, Omicron Kappa Upsilon.

REHAK, PATRICIA, career planning administrator; MA in Psychology, U. Houston Victoria, 1994. Cert. Lifetime elementary tchr. State Tex., 1982. Divsn. chair tech. and bus. Wharton County Jr. Coll., 2004—05, instrnl. assessment coord. Tex., 2005—, chair instrnl. assessment com. Tex., 2005—. Mem.: Tex. CC Tchrs. Assn. Office: Wharton County Jr Coll 911 Boling Hwy Wharton TX 77488

REHBERG, DENNIS R., United States Representative from Montana; b. Billings, Mont., Oct. 5, 1955; m. Janice Rehberg; 3 children. Student, Mont. State U., 1974; BA in Pub. Adminstrn. and Polit. Sci., Wash. State U., Pullman, 1977. Tchr. gymnastics, Billings, Mont., 1973—74; with Green Giant Co., Dayton, Wash., 1975—76, Ramada Inn, Billings, 1977; ditch digger Lockrem Constrn., Billings, 1977; real estate salesman Billings, 1977—79; legis. aide Staffs of State Senator Bill Mathers and State Senator Sonny Lockrem, 1977; legis. asst. Staff of US Rep. Ron Marlenee, Mont., 1979—82; mgr. Rehberg Ranch, Billings, 1982—2000; mem. Mont. State Ho. Reps. from Dist. 88, 1985—89; state dir. Staff of US Senator Conrad Burns, Mont., 1989—91; lt. gov. Mont., 1991—97; mem. US Congress from Mont. at large, 2001—, mem. appropriations com. Recipient Guardian of Senior's Rights award, 60 Plus Assn., 2002, Presdl. award, for leadership, Nat. Farmers Union, 2003; named a Champion of Small Bus., Small Bus. Survival Com., 2001, 2002, Hero of Taxpayer, Americans for Tax Reform, 2002. Republican. Episcopalian. Office: US House Reps 2448 Rayburn House Office Bldg Washington DC 20515-2601 Office Phone: 202-225-3211. Office Fax: 202-225-5687.*

REHBERG, SHIRLEY M., literature and language professor; d. George Dewey and Velma B. Murray; m. Michael G. Rehberg, Sept. 17, 1977; children: James S., Rachel R. Gongre, Catricia L. MS, Nova Southeastern U., Coral Gables, Fla., 2003. Instr. Santa Fe CC, Gainesville, Ga., 2001—06, Lake City CC, Fla., 2001—. Treas. Fla. Devel. Edn. Assn., Lake City, 2009—. Mem. Columbia County Animal Control Bd., Lake City, 1997—2004. Conservative. Episcopalian. Avocation: dog breeding. Office: Lake City CC 149 SE College Pl Jasper FL 32052 Business E-Mail: gavril@alltel.net, rehbergs@lakecitycc.edu.

REHDER, BOB, psychology professor; PhD, U. Colo., Boulder, 1997. Assoc. prof. NY U., 2001—. Office: NY Univ 6 Washington Pl New York NY 10003 Business E-Mail: bob.rehder@nyu.edu.

REHDER, ROBERT RICHARD, business management educator, management consultant; b. Chgo., Aug. 18, 1930; s. Frederick W. and Elsie (Beilfus) R.; m. Lynne G. Wonderlin, Aug. 21, 1954; children: Mark Richard, David Frederick. AB, DePauw U., 1952; postgrad., U. Ill., 1952-53; MBA, Ind. U., 1958; PhD, Stanford, 1961. Asst. prof., adminstrv. asst. to pres.'s office Stanford (Calif.) U., 1963-66; vis. assoc. prof. Duke U., Durham, N.C., 1967; assoc. prof. U. N.C., Chapel Hill, 1966-69; James L. Rutledge prof. mgmt. U. N.Mex., Albuquerque, 1969—, dean Sch. Bus. and Adminstrv. Scis., 1969-79, founder Robert O. Anderson Grad. Sch. Mgmt., 1976—. Vis. rsch. prof. U. Western Australia, Pert, 1977; mem. Stanford faculty team to establish first grad. sch. of bus. in, Latin Am., Lima, Peru, 1963-65; moderator exec. program Aspen Inst. for Humanistic Studies, 1976; vis. lectr. Institut Superieur De Gestion, Paris, 1973-74; bd. dirs. Pub. Svc. Co. N.Mex. Author: Latin American Managemnet: Development and Performance, 1968; Contbr. articles in field to profl. jours. Trustee Nat. Council on Philanthropy, 1976-79. Served with M.C. AUS, 1954-556. NSF Found. fellow for computer and soc. sci. research, 1968; Wilton Park fellow Eng., 1962 Mem. Acad. Mgmt. Home: 1424 Stagecoach Rd SE Albuquerque NM 87123-4433

REHDING, ALEXANDER, musicologist; b. Hamburg, Germany; BA, MA, MPhil, Cambridge U., England, PhD, 1999. Asst. prof., then prof. music Harvard U., 2003—. Co-editor Acta musicologica. Author: Music and Monumentality: Commemoration and Wonderment in Nineteenth-Century Germany, 2009. Fellow John Simon Guggenheim Meml. Found., 2009, Am. Coun. Learned Societies, Newhouse Ctr. Humanities, Wellesley Coll., Alexander von Humboldt Found.; Derek Brewer fellow, Emmanuel Coll., Cambridge. Mailing: 85 Inman St Apt A Cambridge MA 02139-1212 E-mail: arehding@fas.harvard.edu.*

REHM, PATRICE KOCH, radiologist, educator; b. DeSoto, Mo., Nov. 23, 1954; d. James Clarence and Eleanor (Koch) R. BA in Chemistry, U. Mo., 1977; MD, Yale U., 1981. Diplomate Am. Bd. Radiology, Am. Bd. Nuc. Medicine. Intern in medicine Waterbury (Conn.) Hosp., 1981-82; resident in radiology Yale New Haven Hosp., 1982-83, 84-85, fellow in neuroradiology, 1985-86, fellow in nuclear medicine, 1986-87; resident in radiology SUNY Upstate Med. Ctr., Syracuse, 1983-84; clin. assoc. Cleve. Clinic, 1987-88, staff physician, 1988-89, Presbyn. Hosp., Charlotte, N.C., 1989-91, Georgetown U. Med. Ctr., Washington, 1992—2000; assoc. prof. radiology, dir. nuc. medicine U. Va. Health Sys., Charlottesville, Va., 2000—. Fellow Am. Coll. Radiology, Radiologic Soc. N.Am., Soc. Nuc. Medicine. Office: U Va Health Sys PO Box 800170 Charlottesville VA 22908

REHR, JOHN J., physicist, researcher; b. Carlisle, Pa., May 6, 1945; BSE, U. Mich., 1967; PhD, Cornell U., 1972. Prof. physics U. Washington, Seattle, 1975—. Cons. prof. Stanford Synchrotron Radiation Lightsource Starified, Calif., 1993-. Office: Dept Physics Univ Wash PO Box 351560 Seattle WA 98195-1580

REHTH, ANN, counselor; b. Pennyan, NY, May 28, 1942; d. J. Allen and Jean Eleanor (Stanhope) Henderson; children: Nikki, Douglas, Scott. BA, U. South Fla., 1983; MS, Nova U., 1994. Cert. tchr., ESL tchr. Tchr. Venice H.S., Fla., 1984—94; mental health counselor Meridian Behavioral, Gainsville, Fla., 1994—98, YMCA, Sarasota, Fla., 1998—2001; tchr. Gulf Coast Marine Inst., Venice, 2000—01; tchr. ESOL and reading North Port H.S., Fla., 2001—06; ret., 2006; part-time tchr. Sarasota County Tech. Inst., 2005—. Dir. intervention program for children and teens Meridian Behavioral, Gainsville, Fla., 1994—98; cons. to schs. for abuse and crisis intervention YMCA, Venice, Fla., 1999—2001. Mem.: Sarasota Literacy Coun. Avocations: reading, volunteer projects, walking, tricycle riding. Personal E-mail: annrehth@verizon.net.

REIBEL, KURT, physicist, researcher; b. Vienna, May 23, 1926; came to U.S., 1938; s. Michael and Regina (Pak) R.; m. Eleanor Elvira Mannino, June 10, 1954; children— Leah, Michael, David BA, Temple U., 1954; MS, U. Pa., 1956, PhD, 1959. Jr. research assoc. in physics Brookhaven Nat. Lab., 1957-59; research assoc. U. Pa., Phila., 1959-61; asst. prof. Ohio State U., Columbus, 1961-64, assoc. prof., 1964-70, prof. physics, 1970-92, prof. emeritus, 1992—. Vis. scientist CERN, Geneva, Switzerland, 1968-69, 75-76 Author research papers on nuclear and elementary particle physics NSF fellow, 1954-56 Mem. Am. Phys. Soc., AAUP, Fedn. Am. Scientists, Union Concerned Scientists, Sigma Xi Jewish. Office: Ohio State U Dept Physics 191 W Woodruff Ave Columbus OH 43210-1117

REIBER, PAUL L., state supreme court chief justice; b. Pitts., June 20, 1947; BA, Hampden-Sydney Coll., Va., 1970; JD, Suffolk Law Sch., 1974. Prtnr. Reiber, Kenlan, Schwiebert and Facey, 1984—2003; town moderator Chittenden, 1985—; justice Vt. Supreme Ct., 2003—04, chief justice, 2004—. Former mem. Vt. Jud. Nomination Bd. Mem.: ABA, Vt. Bar Assn. Avocations: bicycling, reading. Office: Vt Supreme Ct 109 State St Montpelier VT 05609-0701*

REIBLE, DANNY DAVID, environmental chemical engineer, educator; b. Rantoul, Ill., Dec. 21, 1954; s. George Anthony and Mavis Otilla (Prause) R.; m. Susanne Cecilia Schulte, Mar. 17, 1979; children: Kristin Nicole, Monica Lynn. BS, Lamar U., 1977; MS, Calif. Inst. Tech., 1979, PhD, 1982. Registered profl. engr., La.; diplomate environ. engr., 2004. Asst. prof. La. State U., Baton Rouge, 1981-86, assoc. prof., 1986-92, prof. chem. engring., 1992—2004, Chevron prof. chem. engring., 1998—2004, dir. Hazardous Substance Rsch. Ctr., 1995—; Shell prof. environ. engring. U. Sydney, Australia, 1993-95; Bettie Margaret Smith chair environ. health engring. U. Tex., Austin, 2004—. Vis. rschr. US Army Engr. Waterways Experiment Sta., Vicksburg, Miss., 1990; sr. visitor Cambridge U., Eng., 1992; mem. bd. environ. studies and toxicology Nat. Rsch. Coun.; cons. in field. Author: Fundamentals of Environmental Engineering, 1999, Diffusion Models of Environmental Transport, 2000; contbr. articles to profl. publs. Environ. Sci. and Engring. fellow AAAS, 1987, 2009. Fellow AIChE (exec. bd. 1990-95, LK Cecil award 1992); mem. NAE, Am. Chem. Soc., Am. Geophys. Union, Am. Soc. Engring. Edn. (New Engring. Educator Excellence award 1985), Ak. Soc, Civil Engring., Assn. Environ. Engring. Sci. Profs., Coms. Nat. Rsch. Coun., Sigma Xi. Achievements include identification and evaluation of new mechanisms for contaminant release in the environment; advances in sediment management techniques; development of widely used nethods of managing contaminated sediments. Home: 10300 Indigo Broom Loop Austin TX 78733 Office: U Tex 1 University Station C1786 Austin TX 78712 Office Phone: 512-471-4642. Business E-Mail: reible@mail.utexas.edu.

REIBOLD, DOROTHY ANN, accountant, researcher; b. Leigh, Nebr., Feb. 22, 1922; d. Herman Ludwig Marty and Frances Jane Harvey; m. Wayne Henry Reibold, Mar. 27, 1947; children: Lillie Frances, Marty John. BEd, Wayne State Tchrs., 1945. Tchr., prin. Nenzel Sch., Nebr., 1941-42; tchr. Cozad Sch., Nebr., 1942-43; sec. Burroughs Adding Machine, Omaha, 1943-44; tchr. Lyons Pub. Sch., Nebr., 1945-47; office mgr. Yoelin Bros. Wholesale, Denver, 1947-52; freelance bookkeeper Henderson, Colo., 1960-00; bookkeeper Hazeltine Heights Water, Henderson, 1964—2007; dir. sch. lunch program Zion Luth. Sch., Brighton, Colo., 1969—78; dir. budget Hazeltine Heights Water, 1982—2007. Author: Ecklin Family Story, 1988, Life of Matthias Harvye, 1998. Mem.: DAR. Republican. Lutheran. Avocations: genealogy, travel. Home and Office: 8181 E 104th Ave Henderson CO 80640-9049 Home Phone: 303-288-8635. Personal E-mail: dotareibold@earthlink.net.

REICH, ABRAHAM CHARLES, lawyer; b. Waterbury, Conn., Apr. 17, 1949; s. Samuel and Esther (Gurvitz) Reich; m. Sherri Engelman, Aug. 15, 1971; children: Spencer, Alexander. BA, U. Conn., 1971; JD, Temple U., 1974. Bar: Pa. 1974, U.S. Supreme Ct. 1979. Assoc. Fox Rothschild LLP, Phila., 1974-81, ptnr., 1981—, mng. ptnr., 2001—05, co-chair, 2005—. Chair lawyers adv. com. U.S. Ct. Appeals (3d cir.), 1998. Fellow: Am. Coll. Trial Lawyers; mem.: ABA (house dels. 1997—2002, 2004—), Phila. Bar Assn. (chair profl. responsibility com. 1983—84, chair bench-bar com. 1985, chair profl. guidance com. 1987—88, bd. govs. 1987—89, chair bd. govs. 1989, chancellor 1995, del. ABA 1996—2000). Office: Fox Rothschild LLP 2000 Market St Ste 10 Philadelphia PA 19103-3231 Home: 1520 Spruce St PH06 Philadelphia PA 19102 Office Phone: 215-299-2090. Business E-Mail: areich@foxrothschild.com.

REICH, ALLAN J., lawyer; b. Chgo., July 9, 1948; s. H. Robert and Sonya (Minsky) R.; m. Lynne Susan Roth, May 23, 1971; children: Allison, Marissa, Scott. BA, Cornell U., 1970; JD cum laude, U. Mich., 1973. Bar: Ill. 1973, U.S. Dist. Ct. (no. dist.) Ill. 1973. Ptnr. McDermott, Will & Emery, Chgo., 1973-93; vice chmn. D'Ancona & Pflaum LLC, Chgo., 1993—2003; ptnr., chair nat. corp. practice group Seyfarth Shaw LLP, Chgo., 2003—. Trustee Oakmark Family of Mutual Funds, 1994—. V.p., mem. exec. com. Coun. for Jewish Elderly, 1989—97; mem. men's coun. Mus. Contemporary Art, Chgo., 1988—89; mem. Chgo. exec. bd. Am. Jewish Com., 1989—, nat. bd. govs., pres., 2007; bd. dirs. Young Men's Jewish Coun., Chgo., 1974—84, Coun. for Jewish Elderly, 1986—97. Fellow: Am. Bar Found.; mem.: ABA, Chgo. Bar Assn., Econ. Club Chgo., Northmoor Country Club (Highland Park, Ill.), Standard Club (Chgo.). Home: 936 Skokie Ridge Dr Glencoe IL 60022-1434 Office: Seyfarth Shaw LLP 131 S Dearborn St Ste 2400 Chicago IL 60603 Home Phone: 847-835-3225; Office Phone: 312-460-5650. Business E-Mail: areich@seyfarth.com.

REICH, BERNARD, communications engineer; b. NYC, Jan. 7, 1926; s. Adolph and Rose (Gluck) R.; m. Sylvia Greenberg, June 15, 1947; children: Robin Reich Murphy, Richard. BS in Physics, CCNY, 1948; MSc, Rutgers U., 2002. Electronic engr., supervisory electronic engr. U.S. Army Electronics R & D Command, Ft. Monmouth, N.J., 1948-81; unit mgr. Semcor, Farmingdale, N.J., 1981-88; telecommunications engr. Telos Corp., Shrewsbury, N.J., 1988-99, retired, 1999. Chmn. spl. working group on semicondrs. and microelectronics NATO, Brussels, 1959-80, chmn. group experts on electronic parts, 1972-80; adv. editor Microelectronics and Reliability, 1970—. Contbr. over 100 articles to tech. jours.; patentee in field. Mem. Juvenile Conf. Com., Ocean Twp., N.J., 1964—; pres. Manor at Wayside Condominium Assn., Ocean Twp., 1990-91. Sgt. U.S. Army, 1945-46, ETO. Recipient decoration for meritorious civilian svc. U.S. Army Electronics R & D Command, 1981. Fellow IEEE (chartered,), IEE (Eng.). Avocation: walking. Home: 45 Gimbel Pl Ocean NJ 07712-2565

REICH, CHRISTOPHER, writer; b. Tokyo, Nov. 12, 1961; arrived in US, 1965; Grad., Georgetown U. Sch. Fgn. Svc., Washington DC, U. Tex. Sch. Bus., Austin. Formerly with Union Bank Switzerland, Geneva, Zurich. Author: (novels) Numbered Account, 1998, The Runner, 2000, The First Billion, 2002, The Devil's Banker, 2003, The Patriots' Club, 2004 (Internat. Thriller Writers award, 2006), Rules of Deception, 2008 (Publishers Weekly Bestseller), Rules of Vengeance, 2009 (Publishers Weekly bestseller). Mailing: c/o Todd Doughty Random House Inc 1745 Broadway New York NY 10019 Office Phone: 212-782-9000. Personal E-mail: creich@christopherreich.com. Business E-Mail: tdoughty@randomhouse.com.*

REICH, DAVID LEE, library director; b. Orlando, Fla., Nov. 25, 1930; s. P.F. and Opal Katherine (Wood) Reichelderfer; m. Kathleen Johanna Weichel, Aug. 2, 1954 (div. Sept. 1964); 1 son, Robert Weichel. PhB magna cum laude, U. Detroit, 1961; AM in LS, U. Mich., 1963. Tchr. English Jefferson Davis Jr. Sch., San Antonio, 1961-62; dir. engring. library Radiation Inc., Melbourne, Fla., 1963-64; asst. to dir. libraries Miami-Dade Jr. Coll., Miami, Fla., 1964-65; dir. learning resources Monroe County C.C., Monroe, Mich., 1965-68; dep. dir. Dallas Pub. Library, 1968-73; dep. chief librarian Chgo. Pub. Library, 1973-74, commr., 1975-78; dir. Bd. Libr. Commrs., Commonwealth of Mass., Boston, 1978-80; exec. sec. New Eng. Libr. Bd., Augusta, Maine, 1980-82, vice chmn., 1979-80; dir. Lakeland (Fla.) Pub. Libr., 1983-99, ret., 1999; exec. sec. Soc. Fla. Archivists, 1999—2001, ret., 2001. Libr. cons. Macomb County C.C., Warren, Mich., 1967; chmn. adv. com. to libr. tech. asst. program El Centro Coll., Dallas, 1969-71; mem. inter-task working group Goals for Dallas, 1968-70, mem. Dallas Area Libr. planning coun., 1970-73; mem. adv. coun. dept. libr. sci. No. Ill. U., 1975-78; v.p., pres.-elect Tampa Bay Libr. Consortium, 1985-86, pres., 1986-87. Co-author: The Public Library in Non-traditional Education, 1974; editor The Villas II News, 1999-2007; contbr. articles to libr. jours. Bd. dirs. The Villas II Homeowners Assn., 1994-96, 98-2001; mem. steering com. Friends of Tampa Bay Libr. Consortium, 2000—. Sgt. U.S. Army, 1952-55. Recipient Disting. Alumnus award U. Mich., 1978; William B. Calkins Found. scholar Orlando, 1963; Carnegie L.S. Endowment scholar, 1963. Mem. ALA (coun.-at-large 1968-72, 75-79), S.E. Libr. Assn., Fla. Libr. Assn. (sec.-treas. coll. and spl. librs. divsn. 1965, steering com. mcpl. librs. caucus 1983-84, chmn. 1984-85, exec. bd. 1984-87), Soc. Fla. Archivists (exec. bd. 1994-96, sec. 1996-97, exec. sec. 1999-2001, treas. 2000-01), Fla. Pub. Libr. Assn. (pres. 1987-88, exec. bd. 1988-89, 94-95, pres. emeritus 1996-98, editor newsletter 1992-93, 96-97, chmn. libr. adminstrn. divsn. 1992, friends and trustees divsn. 1993, 95), Soc. Automotive Historians, Alumni Assn. U. Mich. (pres. Libr. Sch. alumni 1973), Nat. Soc. SAR, Polk Sr. Games (bd. dirs., 2004—, sec. 2007—). Home: 4011 Heron Ave Lakeland FL 33813-1123 E-mail: dreich@tampabay.rr.com.

REICH, EDGAR, mathematics professor; b. Vienna, June 7, 1927; arrived in U.S. in 1938, naturalized, 1944. s. Jonas and Luna Sarah (Lunenfeld) Reich; m. Phyllis Masten, June 10, 1949 (dec. 1994); children: Eugene, Frances; m. Julia Henop, Dec. 14, 1998 (dec. Feb.

2006). BEE, Poly. Inst. Bklyn., 1947; MS, MIT, 1949; PhD, UCLA, 1954. Rsch. asst. Servomechanisma Lab. MIT, Cambridge, 1947—49; mathematician Rand Corp., Santa Monica, Calif., 1949—56; mem. Inst. Advanced Study, Princeton, NJ, 1954—55; prof. math. U. Minn., Mpls., 1961—2001, prof. emeritus, 2001—, head Sch. Math., 1969—71; mem. Forschungsinstitut Mathematik Swiss Poly. Inst., Zurich, 1971—72, 1978—79, 1986—87. Vis. prof. Swiss Poly. Inst., 1982-83; Christmas lectr. Bar-Ilan U., Ramat Gan, Israel, 1989, plenary lectr. Nahariya, 2006. Contbr. articles to profl. jours. Fulbright research scholar Denmark, 1960-61; Guggenheim fellow, 1960-61; NSF sr. postdoctoral fellow, 1954-55; recipient Silver plaque Alpine Motoring Contest, 1968, Bronze medal U. Jyväskylä, 1973. Mem. Am. Math. Soc., Finnish Acad. Sci. and Letters (fgn.) Home: 1235 Yale Pl Apt 301 Minneapolis MN 55403-1943

REICH, HERB, editor; b. NYC; s. Herman S. and Hattie (Davis) R.; m. Gerri Toog, Aug. 7, 1960; children: Amanda Suri, Elizabeth Jo. BA, Bklyn. Coll., 1950; MA, Bklyn. Coll. and Kings County Hosp., 1951; postgrad., Columbia U., 1951-54. Author sketches and lyrics Tamiment Revues (Pa.), 1951; staff writer NBC-TV, NYC and Los Angeles, 1955-57; research coordinator Inst. for Motivational Research, Croton-on-Hudson, NY, 1958-59; research dir. Scientist and Engr. Technol. Inst., NYC, 1960-64; mng. editor SETI Pubs. Inc., NYC, 1961-64; sr. editor Odyssey Press, NYC, 1964-65; editorial dir. Profl. and Tech. Programs Inc., NYC, 1966-72; dir. Behavioral Sci. Book Service, NYC, 1966-72; dir. behavioral scis. program Basic Books Inc., NYC, 1973-79; editor intersci. div. John Wiley & Sons. Inc., NYC, 1979-87, sr. editor profl. and trade divsn., 1987-95; pres. H&G Reich, Cons., Hastings Hdsn., NY, 1980—. Publ., rsch., advt. and polit. cons.; rschr., statistician, rsch. cons. Am. Found. for Blind, Pepsi Cola Co., Nowland and Co., Comms. and Media Rsch. Svcs. Mng. editor: Odyssey Science Library Ency. of Engring., Signs and Symbols, 1965, Dictionary of Physics and Mathematics Abbreviations, Signs and Symbols, 1965, Dictionary of Electronics Abbreviations, Signs and Symbols, 1965, Dictionary of Computers and Control Systems Abbreviations, Signs and Symbols, 1965; contbr. Random House Dictionary of the English Language, 1967, rev. edit., 1987, The Greatest Revue Sketches, 1982, Ency. of Psychology, 2d edit., 1994, Corsini Encyclopedia of Psychology and Behavioral Sciences, 2001, Don't You Believe It; TV writer: Broadway Open House, 1951, Olsen and Johnson Show, 1951, Milton Berle Texaco Star Theatre, 1952, All-Star Revue, 1952, Mel Torme Show, 1952, Eddie Cantor Show, 1953, Red Buttons Show, 1954, Summer Colgate Show, 1954, Jerry Lester Show, 1954, Jan Murray Time, 1955, Howdy Doody Show, 1955-56, Tonight Show, 1956, NBC Comedy Hour, 1956, Wayne and Schuster Hour, 1957. Co-founder, vice chmn. Mt. Vernon United for Better Edn., N.Y., 1970-73; mem. Westchester County Democratic Com., 1972-76; exec. com. Mt. Vernon Dem. City Com., 1973-76; mem. supt.'s adv. com. Hastings Schs., Hastings-on-Hudson, N.Y., 1981-82. Recipient Gold award of excellence for radio advt. Advt. Club of Westchester, 1980; recipient Gold and Bronze awards of excellence for radio advt. Advt. Club of Westchester, 1981 Mem. AAAS, APA, Alpha Phi Omega. Office: 127 Mount Hope Blvd Hastings On Hudson NY 10706 Office Phone: 914-478-4042. Personal E-mail: hgreich@yahoo.com.

REICH, JEROME MARK, pulmonologist, consultant; Cert. ABIM Internal Medicine & Pulmonary Disease. Contbr. scientific papers. Achievements include research in identified and characterized lady windermere syndrome. Home: 7400 SW Barnes Rd Apt 622 Portland OR 97225 Home Fax: 001 503 296 4878. Personal E-mail: reichje@dnamail.com.

REICH, JOHN M., former federal agency administrator; b. 1939; BS, So. Ill. U., 1961; MBA, U. South Fla.; grad., Sch. Banking of South, La. State U. Cmty. banker, Ill., Fla.; pres., CEO Nat. Bank Sarasota, Fla.; staff mem. to Senator Connie Mack, US Senate, 1988—2000, chief of staff, 1998—2000; bd. dirs. FDIC, 2001—09, acting chmn., 2001, vice chmn., 2002—05; dir. Office of Thrift Supervision, US Dept. Treasury, Washington, 2005—09. Chmn. bd. dir. Sarasota Family YMCA, Fla. Republican.*

REICH, LARRY SAM, lawyer; b. Bklyn., Sept. 24, 1946; s. Sidney and Regina (Brown) R.; children: Ilysa Jill, Shari Beth; m. Marcia S. Koltun, Mar. 17, 2002. BA, Hofstra U., 1969; JD, Bklyn. Law Sch., 1973. Bar: NY 1974, US Dist. Ct. (so. and ea. dists.) NY 1974, US Ct. Appeals (2d cir.) 1974, US Ct. Appeals (3d cir.) 2002, US Supreme Ct. 1980. Assoc. S. Edward Orenstein PC, NYC, 1973-78; ptnr. Herzfeld & Rubin PC, NYC, 1978-98, Blank Rome LLP, NYC, 1999—. Arbitrator US Dist. Ct. (ea. dist.) NY, Bklyn., 1986—; adj. prof. law, guest Hofstra U. Sch. Law, 1994—. Mem. ABA, N.Y. State Bar Assn. (chmn. com. on supreme cts. 1986-89, chmn. com. on jud. adminstrn. 1989-92, com. jud. adminstrn. 1989-94), N.Y. County Bar Assn., Nassau County Bar Assn., Assn. Trial Lawyers Am., N.Y. State Trial Lawyers Assn. Avocations: running, rowing, biking, reading. Office: Blank Rome LLP The Chrysler Bldg New York NY 10174 Office Phone: 212-885-5514. Business E-Mail: lreich@blankrome.com.

REICH, LAURENCE, lawyer; b. Jersey City, Jan. 22, 1931; s. Victor and Miriam (Gross) R.; m. Doris Rita Diamond, Oct. 21, 1965 (dec. Apr. 15, 2002). BA, U. Chgo., 1951, JD, 1953. Bar: NJ 1954, NY 1982, US Dist. Ct. NJ 1954, US ct. appeals (3rd cir.) 1958, US Supreme ct. 1963, US Tax Ct. 1971, US Dist. Ct. (so. dist.) NY 1982, US Ct. Appeals (2nd cir.) 1987. From mem. firm to sr. counsel McElroy, Deutsch, Mulvaney & Carpenter, LLP (formerly Carpenter, Bennett & Morrissey), Newark, 1957—2003. Mem. Bur. Nat. Affairs Tax Adv. bd., 1972—; lectr. in field. Author: NJ Corporation Law and Practice; contbr. articles to profl. jours. With US Army, 1955-57. Fellow Am. Coll. Tax Counsel, Am. Bar Found.; mem. ABA (com. chmn. sect. taxation 1972-74, 85-86, mem. coun. 1991-94), NJ Bar Assn. (chmn. taxation sect. 1975-76), Assn. Fed. Bar State NJ (v.p. 1982-94, bd. trustees 1994-99), Essex County Bar Assn. Avocations: opera, music, theater, bridge. Office Phone: 973-565-2003. Business E-Mail: lreich@mdmc-law.com.

REICH, NORBERT OTTO, biochemist, educator; b. Bochum, Germany, Mar. 17, 1952; s. Heniz and Charlotte Reich; m. Elisa Landi; children: Tiffany Charlotte, Trudie Katherina. PhD, U. Calif., San Francisco, 1984. Prof. U. Calif., Santa Barbara, 1987—. Recipient fellowship, Am. Cancer Soc., 1992. Mem.: Epigenetic soc. Achievements include discovery of assays for understanding function and modes of inhibition of various biomedically relevant enzymes. Office: Univ Calif Chemistry and Biochemistry Santa Barbara CA 93106 Business E-Mail: reich@chem.ucsb.edu.

REICH, RICHARD ALLEN, bank executive; b. Rhinelander, Wis., Mar. 12, 1962; s. John E. and Alma Louise (Post) R. BBA, U. Wis., Madison, 1984; MBA, NYU, NYC, 1989. CPA, Okla. Staff acct., cons. Deloitte, Haskins and Sells, NYC, 1984-86; fin. analyst Salomon Bros., Inc., NYC, 1986-89; treasury mgr. Citibank-US Card Products Group, NYC, 1989-90; with Bankers Trust Corp., NYC, 1992-93; v.p., dir. risk mgmt. Nikko Securities Internat., Inc., NYC, 1993-95, CDC Capital, Inc., NYC, 1995-99; dir. risk mgmt. and control OGE Energy Corp., Oklahoma City, 1999—2005, treas.; sr. v.p. corp. fin. BancFirst Corp., Oklahoma City, 2005—. Investment mgr. Wis. Eastern Scholarship Fund, 1996-2001. Mem. AICPA, Okla. Soc. CPA, Okla. Soc. Security Analysts, CFA Inst., U. Wis. Alumni Assn. NY (sec. 1989-91, v.p. 1991-92, pres. 1992-95). Avocations: golf, skiing. Office: BancFirst Corp 101 N Broadway Ste 900 Oklahoma City OK 73102-8405 Home: 2219 Windmere Dr Edmond OK 73034-6600 Office Phone: 405-218-4126. Personal E-mail: richard_a_reich@yahoo.com.

REICH, ROBERT BERNARD, political economics educator, former United States Secretary of Labor; b. Scranton, Pa., June 24, 1946; s. Edwin Saul and Mildred Dorf (Freshman) R.; m. Clare Dalton, July 7, 1973. BA, Dartmouth Coll., 1968, MA (hon.), 1988; MA, Oxford U., Eng., 1970; JD, Yale U., 1973. Asst. solicitor gen. US Dept. Justice, Washington, 1974-76; dir. policy planning FTC, Washington, 1976-81; mem. faculty John F. Kennedy Sch. Govt. Harvard U., Cambridge, Mass., 1981-92; sec. US Dept. Labor, Washington, 1993-97; Maurice B. Hexter prof. econ. & social policy Brandeis U., Waltham, 1997—2006; prof. pub. policy Richard & Rhoda Goldman Sch. Pub. Policy, U. Calif, Berkely, 2006—. Chmn. biotech. sect. U.S. Office Tech. Assessment, Washington, 1990-91; vis. prof., Richard & Rhoda Goldman Sch. Pub. Policy, U. Calif, 2004, 2005 Author: The Next American Frontier, 1983, New Deals: The Chrysler Revival and the American System, 1986, Tales of a New America: The Anxious Liberals's Guide to the Future, 1987, The Resurgent Liberal: And Other Unfashionable Prophecies, 1989, The Work of Nations: Preparing Ourselves for 21st Century Capitalism, 1991, Locked in the Cabinet, 1997, The Future of Success: Working and Living in the New Economy, 2001, I'll Be Short: Essentials for a Decent Working Society, 2002, Reason: Why Liberals Will Win the Battle for America, 2004, Supercapitalism: The Transformation of Business, Democracy, and Everyday Life, 2007; editor: The Power of Public Ideas, 1987; contbg. editor The New Republic, Washington, 1982-93; co-founder, nat. editor, chmn. editl. bd. The Am. Prospect, 1990—; playwright Public Exposure, 2005. Mem. governing bd. Common Cause, Washington, 1981-85; bd. dirs. Bus. Enterprise Trust, Palo Alto, Calif., 1989-93; trustee Dartmouth Coll., Hanover, N.H., 1989-93. Rhodes scholar, 1968; recipient Louis Brownlow award ASPA, 1983, Vaclev Havel Found. prize, 2003 Democrat. Office: Richard & Rhoda Goldman School Pub Policy U Calif Berkeley 2607 Hearst Ave Berkeley CA 94720 E-mail: rreich@berkeley.edu.

REICH, STANLEY BENJAMIN, radiologist, medical educator; b. NYC, Feb. 20, 1921; s. Harry Max Reich and Bessie Bangel; m. Adele Axelrod, Dec. 15, 1944; children: Linda, James, Judi. AB, Cornell U., 1941; MD, NYU, 1944. Diplomate Am. Bd. Radiology, Am. Bd. Nuclear Medicine. Intern Bellevue Hosp., NYC, 1944-45, resident in radiology, 1946-49; asst. prof. NYU/Bellevue Hosp., NYC, 1949-50; clin. prof. radiology U. Calif., San Francisco, 1952-72, 77—; prof. radiology U. Colo., Denver, 1972-77, U. Calif. Davis, Sacramento, 1977—2008; ret.; chief radiology No. Calif. VA Clinics, Martinez, 1979-98. Contbr. articles to profl. jours. Pres. Concordia-Argonaut Club, San Francisco, 1963-65; cons. Travis AFB, Fairfield, Calif., 1977—, Exec. Svc. Corps., San Francisco, 1997-2002. Lt. (sr.) USN, 1944-47, 50-52. Fellow Am. Coll. Radiology; mem. Am. Soc. Thoracic Radiology (sec. 1967), Am. Radium Soc. Avocations: travel, photography. Home: 2 Abbott Way Piedmont CA 94618-2610 Personal E-mail: asreia@att.net.

REICH, STEVE, composer; b. NYC, Oct. 3, 1936; m. Beryl Korot; children: Ezra, Michael. Studies in percussion with Roland Kohloff, 1950—53; BA in Philosophy with honors, Cornell U., 1957; studies in composition with Hall Overton, 1957—58; studies with Bergsma and Persichetti, Julliard Sch. Music, 1958—61; MA in Music, Mills Coll., 1963; studies in drumming, Inst. for African Studies, U. Ghana, 1970; student, Am. Soc. for Ea. Arts, Seattle and Berkeley, 1973—74, Cantillation of Hebrew Scriptures, NYC and Jerusalem, 1976—77; D (hon.), Calif. Inst. Arts, 2000. Organized ensemble Steve Reich and Musicians, 1966; performed throughout the world, 1971—; recs. with various cos. including Columbia Records, Deutsche Grammophon, Nonesuch, Disques Shandar, Hungaraton, Angel, ECM, Phillips, Virgin Classics, Argo. Regents lectr. U. Calif., Berkeley, 2000. Composer, performer: (albums) Come Out, 1967, It's Gonna Rain, 1969, Violin Phase, 1969, Four Organs, 1970, Phase Patterns, 1970, Drumming, 1971, Four Organs, 1973, Six Pianos, 1973, Music for Mallet Instruments, Voices, and Organ, 1973, Music for Eighteen Musicians, 1978 (Grammy award 1999), Octet, 1980, Music for a Large Ensemble, 1980,Tehillim, 1982, The Desert Music, 1984, Sextet, 1986, Six Marimbas, 1986, Electric Counterpoint, 1987, Different Trains, 1988 (Grammy award 1989), The Four Sections, 1987, The Cave, 1994, City Life, 1995, Proverb, 1996, Triple Quartet, 1999, Three Tales, 2002, Dance Patterns, 2002, Cello Counterpoint, 2003, You Are, 2004, others; recordings include (10 CD boxed set) Steve Reich Works: 1965-1995; composer: Vermont Counterpoint, Variations for Winds, Strings and Keyboards, Eight Lines for Chamber Orchestra, Piano Phase, Clapping Music, Pendulum Music, Music for Pieces of Wood, Nagoya Marimbas, other works performed by major orchs. and ensembles; commd. to compose for Holland Festival, 1978, Radio Frankfurt, 1979, San Francisco Symphony, 1980, Rothko Chapel, 1981, West German Radio, Cologne, 1984, Fromm Music Found., 1985, Richard Stoltzman, 1985, Bklyn. Acad. Music, 1987, Kronos Quartet, 1988, St. Louis Sympnony, 1987, (with Beryl Korot) The Cave video opera commd. by Vienna Festival, Holland Festival, Festival d'Automne à Paris, Theatre de la Monnaie, Brussels, Hebbel Theatre, Berlin, South Bank Centre/Serious Speakout, London and the Brooklyn Acad. Music, Next Wave Festival, 1993; 4-concert retrospective Lincoln Ctr. Festival, NYC, 1999, video opera (with Beryl Korot) Three Tales, commd. by Vienna Festival, Barbican Ctr., London, SPoleto Festival, Bklyn. Acad. Music, Music Strassbourg, Hebbel Theater, Berlin. Recipient Koussevitzky Found. award, 1981, 2002, Schuman prize Columbia U., 2000, Praemium Imperiale award (Music), Japan Art Assn., 2006, Polar Music prize, 2007; named Composer of Yr., Musical Am., 2000; Rockefeller Found. grantee 1975, 78, 81, 90, Nat. Endowment for the Arts grantee, 1974, 76, 91, NY State Coun. Arts grantee, 1974; Guggenheim fellow, 1978, Montgomery fellow Dartmouth Coll., 2000; elected to Am. Acad. Arts and Letters, 1994, Bayerische Akademie der Schönen Künst, 1995; named Commr. dans l'Ordre des Arts et des Lettres, 1999. Fellow Am. Acad. Arts & Scis. Office: Howard Stokar Mgmt 879 West End Ave New York NY 10025-4918 also: c/o Elizabeth Sobol-Gomez IMG Artists 152 W 57th St 5th Fl New York NY 10019 also: Boosey & Hawkes Inc 35 E 21st St New York NY 10010-6212 also: Nonesuch Records 75 Rockefeller Plaza New York NY 10019

REICH, VICTORIA J., consumer products company executive; b. Southborough, Mass., Sept. 24, 1957; BS in Applied Math. & Econs., Brown U. With GE Co., 1979—96; v.p., contr. Brunswick Corp., Lake Forest, Ill., 1996-2000, sr. v.p., CFO, 2000—03, pres. Brunswick European Group, 2003—06; sr. v.p., CFO United Stationers Inc., Deerfield, Ill., 2007—. Office: United Stationers Inc One Pkwy N Blvd Ste 100 Deerfield IL 60015

REICHARD, ULRICH H., anthropologist, educator; b. Wolfsburg, Lower Saxony, Germany, Jan. 29, 1964; s. Helmut W. and Elfriede Reichard; m. Fraenze Lanick, July 2, 1980; children: Fidelio Luc, Rio Adam. Scientist Max Planck Inst. Evolutionary Anthropology, Leipzig, Germany, 1998—2006; asst. prof. Southern Ill. U., Carbondale, 2006—. Mem.: Internat. Ethological Soc., Evolutionary Anthropology Soc., Internat. Primatological Soc., Am. Assn. of Phys. Anthropologists, Am. Anthrop. Assn., Sigma Xi.

REICHART, KARALEAH S., anthropologist, educator; d. Edgar R. and Reba P. Jones; m. Daniel E. Reichart, July 7, 1996 (div. Dec. 2007); 1 child, Johnathan E. BA in Polit. Sci. and Anthropology with distinction, Pa. State U.; U. Pk., 1996; MA in Anthropology, Northwestern U., Evanston, Ill., 1998, PhD in Anthropology, 2000. Adj. lectr. Northwestern U., 1999; asst. prof. Marshall U., Huntington, W.Va., 1999—2000, Calif. State U., Fullerton, 2000—02; vis. rsch. asst. prof. U. NC, Chapel Hill, 2002—04, adj. asst. prof., 2004—, lectr. Greensboro, 2004—. Mem. com. applied anthropology web page devel., bd. dirs. dept. anthropology Calif. State U., 2000—01; adv. bd. mem. Rockefeller Found. Ctr. Study Study Ethnicity Gender Appalachia, 2000—; invited lectr. in field. Contbr. articles to profl. jours., chapters to books. Participant Arthritis Found. Annual Walk, 2004—07; designer, webmaster Little Canaries, 2005; donations com. mem. Arthritis Found. Walk, Chapel Hill, 2005. Rsch. fellowship, Rockefeller Found., Marshall U., 2001. Mem.: Soc. Applied Anthropology and Econ. Anthropology, Ctr. Study Ethnicity Gender Appalachia, Appalachian Studies Assn., Am. Anthrop. Assn., Golden Key Nat. Honor Soc., Pi Sigma Alpha, Sigma Xi, Phi Alpha Theta, Am. Mensa, Phi Beta Kappa. Achievements include research in women's strategies of nonviolent resistance, alliance-building, coalition development, and strategic political activism in coal communities regarding labor relations and conflict; political lobbying by parents of autistic children to ban mercury from vaccinations. Avocations: photography, birdwatching, motorcycling, hiking, rock collecting. Office: U NC Dept Anthropology Chapel Hill NC 27599

REICHART, STUART RICHARD, lawyer; b. NYC, Nov. 18, 1924; s. Stanley and Rae (Wein) R.; m. Joan Feirtag, Mar. 28, 1981. LLB, Bklyn. Law Sch., 1948; LLM, NYU, 1951. Bar: N.Y. 1949, D.C. 1971, U.S. Supreme Ct. Adminstrv. judge Armed Services Bd. Contract Appeals, Washington, 1966-72; asst. gen. counsel for procurement USAF, Washington, 1972-75, dep. gen. counsel, 1975-78, gen. counsel, 1978-81; of counsel Fried, Frank, Harris, Shriver & Jacobson, Washington, 1982-90; ind. cons., 1991—. Instr. govt. procurement Ohio State U., U. Dayton, U. Md., 1960-70. Contbr. articles to profl. jours. Served with AUS, 1942-45; served to col. USAF, 1951-71. Decorated Legion of Merit, D.F.C., Air medal with silver oak leaf cluster, Purple Heart; recipient Disting. Civilian Service medals Dept. Air Force, 1979, Dept. Def., 1982, Stuart R. Reichart award USAF, 1982. Mem. Masons. Avocations: bridge, tennis, golf. Home and Office: 16873 C Isle of Palms Dr Delray Beach FL 33484-7008

REICHBLUM, AUDREY ROSENTHAL, public relations and publishing executive; b. Pitts., June 28, 1935; d. Emanuel Nathan and Willa (Handmacher) Rosenthal; m. M. Charles Reichblum, Jan. 25, 1956; children: Robert Nathan, William Mark. Student, Bennington Coll., 1952-53; BS, Carnegie Mellon U., 1956. Founder, creator, chmn. Pitts. Children's Mus., 1970-73; mag. writer Pitts. Mag., 1978; dir. pub. rels. Pitts. Pub. Theater, 1978-79; pres. arPR audrey reichblum PUB. RELS. inc., Pitts., 1980—, arpr, inc., 1996—; pub. "Knowledge in a Nutshell" Series, 1996—99, "The Edible Game A Smart Cookie", 1996—, "Sweet Smarts The Candy With A Brain", 2004. Pub. rels. cons., bd. mem. Pitts. Planned Parenthood, 1980-84, United Jewish Fedn., Bus. and Profl. Women, Pitts., 1980-85, Pitts. City Theater, 1985-94, Pa. Coun. on Aging, 1996-99; chmn. Villa de Marillac Nursing, 1999, Vincencian Collaborative Svcs. Bd.; syndicator The Dr. Knowledge Show. Recipient Gold Cindy award Info. Film Producers Am., 1982, award of excellence Internat. Assn. Bus. Communicators, Pitts., 1986, Matrix award for Three Rivers Arts Festival, Lifetime Achievement award NAWBO-YWCA, Y-Tribute to Women in Comms. award, 1998. Mem. Pub. Rels. Soc. Am. (accredited; award of merit 1983, G. Victor Barkman award for excellence 1984, 1st place award Race For The Cure), Women in Comm. (Matrix-sales promotion award 1987), Nat. Assn. Women Bus. Owners (Life Time Achievement award 1995). Office: 1420 Centre Ave Ste 2213 Pittsburgh PA 15219-3536

REICHE, FRANK PERLEY, lawyer, former federal commissioner; b. Hartford, Conn., May 8, 1929; s. Karl Augustus and LaFetra (Perley) R.; m. Janet Taylor, Sept. 26, 1953; children: Cynthia Reiche Schumacker, Dean S. AB, Williams Coll., 1951; LLB, Columbia U., 1959; MA, George Washington U., 1959; LLM in Taxation, NYU, 1966. Bar: N.J. 1960, D.C. 1981. Assoc. Stryker, Tams & Dill, Newark, 1959-61, Smith, Stratton, Wise & Heher, Princeton, NJ, 1962-64, ptnr., 1964-79; commr. Fed. Election Commn., Washington, 1979-85, chmn., 1982; ptnr. Katzenbach, Gildea & Rudner, Lawrenceville, NJ, 1986-93; pvt. practice law Princeton, 1993-97; of counsel Schragger, Lavine & Nagy, West Trenton, NJ, 1997-2000, Archer & Greiner, Princeton, 2001—. Trustee Westminster Choir Coll., Princeton, 1974-86, Ctr. Theol. Inquiry, Princeton, 1991-97, Wells Coll., Aurora, N.Y., 1994-2003; mem. planned giving com. Williams Coll., Williamstown, Mass., 1973-87, nat. chmn. planned giving, 1983-87; dir., Ctr. Responsive Politics, Washington, 2002—. Lt. USN, 1952-56. Mem. ABA, D.C. Bar Assn., N.J. Bar Assn., Am. Coll. Trust and Estate Counsel (N.J. state chair 1995-2000, bd. regents 2001-07). Clubs: Washington Golf and Country, Capitol Hill. Republican. Presbyterian.

REICHEL, WALTER EMIL, advertising executive; b. Irvington, NJ, Dec. 12, 1935; s. Walter Edwin and Flora Maria (Pfister) R.; m. Priscilla Tedesco, Feb. 1, 1969; 1 son, Bradley Joseph. BA, Columbia U., 1959; MA., NYU, 1971, M Philosophy, 1989, postgrad., 1989—. With Benton & Bowles, NYC, 1959-67, v.p., 1965-67, asso. media dir., 1965-67; with Ted Bates & Co., Inc. NYC, 1967-87; sr. v.p. Ted Bates & Co., Inc., NYC, 1973-82, exec. dir. media and programs, 1974-82, exec. v.p., 1982-87, dir.; cons., 1987-91; mng. ptnr. A.S. Link Inc., NYC, 1991-2000; sr. v.p., dir. client svcs. KSL Media, 2000—01; prof. advt. and comm. Fashion Inst. of Tech., 2002—; ptnr. Media Trust, 2007—. Ptnr. Media Trust, 2007—. Home and Office: 449 1/2 Henry St Brooklyn NY 11231-3011 E-mail: aslreichel@aol.com.

REICHELDERFER, BRENDA L., manufacturing executive; b. May 29, 1958; BSEE, Ohio Northern U. Joined ITT Corp. (predecessor to ITT Industries), 1982; various engring., ops. positions ITT Defense & Electronics, 1982—97; v.p., engring., electrical sys. group, automotive divsn. ITT Industries, 1997—98, pres., fluid specialty group, 1998—2001, pres., motion & flow control group, 2001—03, pres., electronic components group, 2003—05, sr. v.p., chief tech. officer White Plains, NY, 2005—. Bd. dirs. Fed. Signal Corp., 2006—. Recipient Ring of Quality award, 1988, Harold S. Geneen award for creative mgmt., 1991. Office: Itt 1133 Westchester Ave Ste N100 West Harrison NY 10604-3543 Office Phone: 914-641-2000. Office Fax: 914-696-2950.

REICHENBACH, LINDA LOUISE, mathematician, language educator; b. Joliet, Ill., Dec. 3, 1946; d. Frank James and Mary Lavonne Kachelhoffer; m. Michael Joseph Reichenbach, July 19, 1969; children: Heidi Marie, Brian Joseph. BS in Math. with honors, Ill. State U., 1968; MS with honors, U. St. Francis, Joliet, Ill., 1997. Tchr. math Joliet Cath. Acad., Ill.; tchr. math. Lockport Twp. HS, Ill.; chair dept. math. Aurora Ctrl. Cath. HS, Ill.; instr. math. tutoring ctr. Joliet Jr. Coll., 2007—. Inclusive tchr. REI Level One Tng., Ill., 1997—98; dir. program for acad. excellence, scholastic bowl and math team coach Aurora Ctrl. Cath. H.S., Ill.; mem. Diocesan-wide math. assessment com. Joliet Diocese, Ill.; Mu Alpha Theta adv. Joliet Cath. Acad.; local, regional and state sci. fair judge, Ill., 1988—2005. Life mem. Cantigny VFW Ladies Aux., 1968. Named Tchr. of Yr., Aurora Ctrl. Cath. HS, 2002—03. Mem.: Math. Assn. Am., Nat. Coun. Tchrs. Math., Girl Scouts Am. (life Nat. Appreciation award Trailways Coun., Ill.). Avocations: writing, antique cars, gardening, art. Personal E-mail: reichenmom@hotmail.com.

REICHER, DAN WILLIAM, information technology executive, former federal agency administrator; b. Syracuse, NY, June 30, 1956; s. Norbert B. Reicher; m. Carole Lisbeth Parker, July 2, 1989. BS in Biology, Dartmouth Coll., 1979; JD, Stanford Law Sch., 1983; student, Harvard U., 1982. Law clk. to Hon. David Sutherland Nelson US Dist. Ct. Mass., Boston, 1983—84; asst. atty. gen. for environmental protection State of Mass., Boston; sr. atty. Natural Resources Def. Coun., 1985-92; spl. asst. to sec. US Dept. Energy, 1993, dep. chief staff & counselor to sec., 1993-95, acting asst. sec. for energy policy, 1995-96, chief staff, 1996-97, sr. policy advisor to sec., 1997, asst. sec. for energy efficiency & renewable energy, 1997—2001; cons. US Senate Environment & Pub. Works Com., 2001; exec. v.p. Northern Power Systems, 2002; co-founder, pres. New Energy Capital Corp.; dir. climate change & energy initiatives Google.org, 2007—. Staff mem. Pres. Commn. on the Accident at Three Mile Island, 1979—80. Co-editor: Controlling the Atom in the 21st Century; contbr. articles to profl. jour.s Office: Google.org 1600 Amphitheatre Mountain View CA 94043*

REICHERT, CHRISTINE EDWARDS, academic administrator; b. St. Joseph, Mich., May 25, 1949; d. Jerome Calvin Patterson and Jane Edna Wohl; children: Jennifer Elizabeth, Rachel Ariana. BA in English Lit., with hon., Baldwin-Wallace Coll., Berea, Ohio, 1985; MA in English Lit., with hon., U. Toledo, Ohio, 1998. Bureau chief The Morning Journal, Lorain, Ohio, 1987—99, regional editor, 1988—89, reporter, 1985—87; instr. U. Toledo, Monroe County, Toledo, 1997—99; dir. acad. svcs. Lourdes Coll., Sylvania, Ohio, 1999—2008, dir. of retention, 2004—05; coord. tutoring & disability svc. U. Toledo, 2008—. Chair Policy and Procedure Ctr., Sylvania, Ohio, 2003—05; mem. Student Success Task Force Lourdes Coll., 2007—08. Editor: The Learning Assistance Review, 2007—; contbr. articles to profl. jours. Recipient Outstanding Tchg. award, U. Toledo, 1998, Staff Excellence award, Lourdes Coll., 2007. Mem.: Nat. Coll. Learning Ctr. Assn., Coll. Reading Learning Assn., Nat. Tutoring Assn., Modern Lang. Assn. Avocations: art, music, theater, reading. Office: Univ Toledo Mail Stop 1046 3025 Library Cir Toledo OH 43614 Office Phone: 419-383-4274. Office Fax: 419-383-3150. Business E-Mail: Christine.Reichert@utoledo.edu.

REICHERT, DAVID, lawyer; b. Cin., Nov. 23, 1929; s. Victor E. and Louise F. Reichert; m. Marilyn Frankel, May 31, 1959; children— James G., Steven F., William M. BA, Bowling Green State U., Ohio, 1951; JD, U. Cin., 1954. Bar: Ohio 1954, US Supreme Ct. 1963. Of counsel Porter, Wright, Morris & Arthur, formerly sr. ptnr. Reichert, Strauss & Reed and predecessors, Cin. Dir. numerous corps. Monthly columnist: Scrap Age mag, 1966-74; bd. editors: U. Cin. Law Rev, 1953-54. Pres. brotherhood Rockdale Temple, Cin., 1960-61, temple treas., 1973-75, v.p., 1975-79, pres., 1979-81; mem. Amberley Village Planning Commn. & Zoning Bd. Appeals, 1972-79, Ohio Solid Waste Adv. Group, 1974; treas. Contemporary Arts Ctr., Cin., 1973-75, pres., 1976-77, trustee, 1982-88, Cin. Opera, 2009; trustee Cin. Art Mus., 1978-93, v.p., 1992-93, chmn. vis. com. for contemporary art, 1990-92; trustee Jewish Publ. Soc., 1980-86, Cin. Sculpture Coun., 1984-87; mem. acquisitions com. Miami U. Art Mus., 1982-85. Mem. Cin. Print and Drawing Cir. (pres. 1974-76), The Literary Club (sec. 1988-91, v.p. 1991-92, pres. 1992-93, hon. mem. 2007), Losantiville Country Club (bd. govs. 1985-92, sec. 1986-90, pres. 1990-92), ISRI 20th Century Club (hon. 1998, trustee Cin. bd. 2009-), Omicron Delta Kappa, Sigma Tau Delta, Phi Delta Phi, Zeta Beta Tau. Office: Porter Wright Morris & Arthur 250 E 5th St Ste 2200 Cincinnati OH 45202-5118

REICHERT, DAVID G. (DAVE REICHERT), United States Representative from Washington; b. Detroit Lakes, Minn., Aug. 29, 1950; m. Julie Reichert; children: Angela, Tabitha, Daniel. AA, Concordia Lutheran Coll., Portland, Oreg., 1970. Police officer Sheriff's Office King County, Wash., 1972—97, sheriff Wash., 1997—2004; mem. US Congress from 8th Wash. dist., 2005—, mem. sci. com., mem. transp. and infrastructure com., vice chmn. Coast Guard and maritime transp. subcommittee, mem. homeland security com., chmn. emergency preparedness, sci. and tech. Author: Chasing the Devil: My Twenty Year Quest to Capture the Green River Killer, 2004. Co-chmn. Wash. State Ptnrs. in Crisis; mem. adv. bd. Criminal Justice Coun., King County, Wash., Domestic Violence Coun., King County, Wash. Served in USAFR, 1971—76, served in USAF, 1976. Recipient Champion of Freedom award, Wash. Policy Ctr., 2 Medal of Valor awards, King County Sheriff's Office; named Sheriff of Yr., Nat. Sheriffs Assn., 2004. Mem.: Wash. Assn. Sheriffs & Police Chiefs (mem. exec. bd.), Wash. State Sheriffs Assn. (past pres.). Republican. Lutheran. Office: US Ho Reps 1223 Longworth Ho Office Bldg Washington DC 20515-4708 Office Phone: 202-225-7761.*

REICHERT, LEO EDMUND, JR., biochemist, department chairman, endocrinologist; b. NYC, Jan. 9, 1932; s. Leo and Anne (Holsten) R.; m. Gerda Sihler, July 20, 1957; children: Leo, Christine, Linda, Andrew. BS, Manhattan Coll., NYC, 1955; PhD, Loyola U., Chgo., 1960. Asst. prof. biochemistry Emory U. Med. Sch., Atlanta, 1960-66, assoc. prof., 1966-72, prof., 1972-79; prof., chmn. dept. biochemistry Albany (N.Y.) Med. Coll., 1979-88, prof. biochemistry and molecular biology, 1988-99; dir. Tucker Endocrine Rsch. Inst., LLC, Atlanta, 2000—08. Dir. human and animal hormone isolation lab. (NIH), Emory U. Med. Sch., 1960-75; mem. med. adv. bd. Nat. Pituitary Agy., 1971-74; com. on glycoprotein hormones Nat. Hormone and Pituitary Program, 1968-86; mem. reproductive biology study sect. NIH, 1971-75; mem. adv. panel on cellular physiology NSF, 1983-86, divsn. of integrative and neuro biology, 1992; mem. WHO Expert Adv. Panel on Biol. Standardization, 1984-2006, Nat. Bd. Med. Examiners, Part I, 1989-91. Mem. editl. bd. Endocrinology, 1967-75, Molecular and Cellular Endocrinology, 1977-83, 90-94, Biology of Reproduction, 1968-70, 86-90, Andrology, 1983-86, Molecular Andrology, 1989-99; contbr. more than 275 articles to profl. jours.; patentee in field. With USMC, 1949—52. Listed among 75 endocrinologists, 1000 scientists most cited, 1965-78. Mem.: Soc. for Study of Reprodn., Andrology Soc. (coun. 1983—87), Endocrine Soc. (ethics adv. com. 2000—01, Ayerst award 1970), Am. Soc. Biol. Chemists. Home: 1974 Mountain Creek Dr Stone Mountain GA 30087-1018 Personal E-mail: lerjr@aol.com.

REICHERT, PHILIP E., health science association administrator; b. Jacksonville, NC, Dec. 28, 1956; s. Elwin Reichert and Norma Jean Overton; m. Rebecca E. Peters, Nov. 24, 1979; children: Brandon P., Benjamin S. E., Adam V. BS, Fla. State U., Tallahassee, 1978; MPH, U. South Fla., Tampa, 1989. HIV prevention program supr. Fla. Dept. Health, Tallahassee, 1996—2005, hepatitis program adminstr., 2005—. Contbr. articles to profl. jours. Mem.: Fla. Pub. Health Assn. Presbyterian. Avocations: writing, guitar, piano, gardening. Office: Fla Dept Health 4052 Bald Cypress Way Bin #A09 Tallahassee FL 32399-1715 Office Fax: 850-245-4297. Personal E-mail: viperbird1228@yahoo.com. Business E-Mail: phil_reichert@doh.state.fl.us.

REICHERT, STEPHEN JOSEPH, bishop; b. Leoville, Kans., May 14, 1943; Ordained priest Order of Friars Minor Capuchin, 1969; missionary priest in Papua New Guinea; ordained bishop, 1995; bishop Diocese of Mendi, Papua New Guinea, 1995—. Roman Catholic. Office: Diocese of Mendi PO Box 69 Mendi So Highlands Papua New Guinea

REICHGOTT, MICHAEL JOEL, medical educator, dean, physician; b. Newark, July 26, 1940; s. Leo and Gertrude (Millman) R.; m. Lynn Gay Haar, Dec. 22, 1962; children: Jay Howard, Seth Alan, Douglas Jordan. AB, Gettysburg Coll., Pa., 1961; MD, Albert Einstein Coll. Medicine, 1965; PhD, U. Calif., San Francisco, 1973. Diplomate Am. Bd. Internal Medicine. Fellow in clin. pharmacology U. Calif., 1969-72; asst. prof. medicine U. Pa., Phila., 1973-81, assoc. prof., 1981-84, Albert Einstein Coll. Medicine, Bronx, NY, 1984—94, prof., 1994—, assoc. dean students and grad. med. edn., 1989—99, assoc. dean clin. affairs and grad. med. edn., 1999—; med. dir. Bronx Mcpl. Hosp. Ctr., 1984-89. Mem. Liaison Com. on Med. Edn., 2002, chmn. 2008-09, NY State Bd. Profl. Med. Conduct, 2009-; presenter in field. Contbr. articles to profl. jours. V.p. Larchmont Temple, NY, 1990-92, pres., 1992-94. Maj. M.C., US Army, 1967-69, Vietnam. Fellow ACP (com.); mem. Assn. Am. Med. Colls. (com. 1990—), NY Acad. Medicine, Phila. Acad. Medicine, Soc. for Gen. Internal Medicine (com.), AMA (sect. med. schs., chair 2003-04, del. 2007-). Avocations: camping, gardening, print collector. Office: Albert Einstein Coll of Medicine 1300 Morris Park Ave Bronx NY 10461-1926 Office Phone: 718-430-4282. Business E-Mail: reichgot@einstein.yu.edu.

REICHGOTT JUNGE, EMBER DARLENE, broadcast commentator, retired state senator, lawyer, writer, radio personality; b. Detroit, Aug. 22, 1953; d. Norbert Arnold and Diane (Pincich) Reichgott; m. Michael Junge. BA summa cum laude, St. Olaf Coll., Minn., 1974; JD, Duke U., 1977; MBA, U. St. Thomas, 1991. Bar: Minn. 1977, D.C. 1978. Assoc. Larkin, Hoffman, Daly & Lindgren, Bloomington, Minn., 1977-84; counsel Control Data Corp., Bloomington, Minn., 1984-86; ptnr. The Gen. Counsel, Ltd., 1987—2007; mem. Minn. State Senate, 1983-2000, chmn. legis. com. on econ. status of women, 1984-86, vice chmn. senate edn. com., 1987-88, senate majority whip, 1990-94, chmn. property tax divsn. senate tax com., 1991-92, chmn. senate judiciary com., 1993-94, senate asst. majority leader, 1995-2000, chmn. spl. subcom. on ethical conduct; pres. Ember Comm., Inc., 2005—; v.p., chief advancement officer Lutheran Social Svc., Minn., 2007—. Dem. endorsed candidate Minn. Atty. Gen., 1998; instr. polit. sci. St. Olaf Coll., Northfield, Minn., 1993; bd. dirs. Citizens Ind. Bank, St. Louis Park, Minn. 1993-. Host cable TV monthly series Legis. Report, 1985-92. Cand. US Congress, 2006; state co-chair Clinton/Gore Presdl. Campaign, Minn. Dem. Farmer-Labor Party, 1992, 1996; del. Nat. Dem. Conv., 1984, 1992, 1996; pres. Minn. Women's Polit. Caucus, 2002—04; trustee, bd. dirs. N.W. YMCA, New Hope, Minn., 1983—88, United Way Greater Twin Cities, Mpls., 1989—2008, Greater Mpls. ARC, 1988—2004, chair, 2001—03. Recipient Woman of Yr. award North Hennepin Bus. and Profl. Women, 1983, award for contbn. to human svcs. Minn. Social Svcs. Assn., 1983, Clean Air award Minn. Lung Assn., 1988, Disting. Svc. award Mpls. Jaycees, 1984, Minn. Dept. Human Rights award, 1989, Myra Bradwell award Minn. Women Lawyers, 1993, Disting. Alumnae award Lake Conf. Schs., 1993, Disting. Alumnae award St. Olaf Coll., 1998, awards for leadership Am. Lung Assn., 1999, Am. Heart Assn., 1997, Everyday Hero award Up with People, 1995, Unsung Hero award United Way of Mpls., 1999, 2000 Innovations in Am. Govt. award Harvard U. and Ford Found., others; 1st recipient of award named in her honor for prevention of sexual assault, 2000; charter inductee Robbinsdale H.S. Hall of Fame, 2000; named One of ten Outstanding Young Minnesotans, Minn. Jaycees, 1984, Policy Adv. of Yr., NAWBO, 1988, Woman of Achievement, Twin West C. of C., 1989, Marvelous Minn. Woman, 1993; named Hall of Fame, Nat. Charter Sch., 2008. Mem. Minn. Bar Assn. (bd. govs. 1992-96, Pro Bono Publico Atty. award 1990), Hennepin County Bar Assn., Corp. Counsel Assn. (v.p. 1989-96). Home: 500 E Grant St #1308 Minneapolis MN 55404 Personal E-mail: ember@visi.com.

REICHL, RUTH MOLLY, editor-in-chief; b. NYC, Jan. 16, 1948; d. Ernst and (Brudno) Reichl; m. Douglas Wilder Hollis, Sept. 5, 1970 (div.); m. Michael Singer, 1985; 1 child. BA in History Art, U. Mich., 1968, MA in History Art, 1970. Chef, co-owner The Swallow Restaurant, Berkeley, Calif., 1974—77; food writer, editor New West mag., San Francisco, 1977—84; editor restaurant column LA Times, 1984-93, food editor, 1990-93; restaurant critic NY Times, 1993—99, New West and Calif. Mags.; editor-in-chief Gourmet Mag., 1999—. Lectr. in field. Author: (books) Mmmm: A Feastiary, 1972, The Contest Book, 1977, Tender at the Bone: Growing Up at the Table, 1998, Comfort Me with Apples: More Adventures at the Table, 2001; editor: (Modern Library Food Series) Perfection Salad: Women and Cooking at the Turn of the Century, 2001, Life a la Henri: Being the Memories of Henri Charpentier, 2001, Cooking with Pomiane, 2001, Clementine in the Kitchen, 2001, Katish: Our Russian Cook, 2001, High Bonnet: A Novel of Epicurean Adventures, 2001, The Passionate Epicure: La Vie et la Passion de Dodin-Bouffant Gourmet, 2002, The Supper of the Lamb: A Culinary Reflection, 2002;: Endless Feasts: Sixty Years of Writing from Gourmet, 2002, Remembrance of Things Paris, 2004, The Gourmet Cookbook, 2004, Garlic and Sapphires, 2005, Tanner Lectures on Human Values, 2005, History in a Glass: Sixty Years of Wine Writing from Gourmet, 2006, Not becoming My Mother and Other Things She Taught Me Along the Way, 2009; one-woman shows include Leonard Lopate; exec. prodr.: Gourmet's Diary of a Foodie, 2006, Gourmet's Adventures with Ruth, 2009; (films) Garlic and Sapphires. Recipient James Beard award, 1994, 1996, 1998, 2009, Honor medal, Mo. Sch. Journalism, 2007, Nat. Mag. award, Am. Soc. Mag. Editors, 2008, Matrix award, NY Women Comm. Inc., 2008, award, Assn. Am. Food Journalists, YWCA's Elizabeth Cutter Morrow; named Adweek's Editor of Yr. Office: 4 Times Sq New York NY 10036-6518 Business E-Mail: ruth.reichl@gourmet.com.

REICHLIN, SEYMOUR, endocrinologist, educator; b. NYC, May 31, 1924; s. Henry and Celia (Rosen) R.; m. Elinor Thurman Dameshek, June 24, 1951; children: Seth David, Douglas James, Ann Elise. Student, CCNY, 1940-41; AB, Antioch Coll., 1945; MD, Washington U., St. Louis, 1948; PhD, U. London, 1954. Intern N.Y. Hosp., 1948-49; asst. resident Barnes Hosp., St. Louis, 1949-50, N.Y. Hosp., 1950-51; chief resident Barnes Hosp., 1951-52; research fellow physiology dept. Maudsley Hosp., London, Eng., 1952-54; instr. psychiatry Washington U., 1954-55, asst. prof. psychiatry and medicine, 1955-60; asso. prof. medicine U. Rochester, 1960-66, prof., 1966-69; prof., head dept. med. and pediatric spltys. Sch. Medicine U. Conn., 1969-71, prof., head dept. physiology, 1971-72; prof. medicine Tufts U., 1972-97, prof. emeritus, 1997—; rsch. prof. U. Ariz., 1994-2000. Sr. physician New Eng. Med. Ctr., 1972-93, sr. endocrinologist, 1993-96; mem. endocrinology study sect. NIH, 1966-70; mem. adv. panel FDA, 1977-79; mem. coun. Nat. Inst. Kidney, Diabetes, Digestive Diseases, 1987-90. Mem. editl. bd. Endocrinology, 1969-74, New Eng. Jour. Medicine, 1976-79, Jour. Psychoneuroendocrinology, 1979-83, Brain, Behavior and Immunity, 1990—; contbr. articles to profl. jours. Bd. dirs. Founds. Fund, New Haven, 1968-70; med. adv. bd. Med. Found., Boston, adv. bd. MacArthur Found., 1988. Served with AUS, 1943-44. Recipient Berthold medal, German Endocrine Soc., 1983, Disting. Alumnus award, Washington U. Sch. Medicine, 1993, Recipient Rebecca Rice award, Antioch Coll., 1995, Horace Mann Alumni award; Commonwealth Fund fellow, Inst. Psychiatry, U. London, 1952—54, Lowell M. Palmer Med. Rsch. fellow, 1954—56. Master ACP-Am. Soc. Internal Medicine (award 2002); fellow AAAS, Am. Acad. Arts and Scis., Acad. Arts and Scis. U. Bologna (fgn.); mem. Ctrl. Soc. Clin. Rsch., Am. Soc. Clin. Investigation, Assn. Am. Physicians, Am. Physiol. Soc., Endocrine Soc. (Eli Lilly award 1972, Disting. Leadership award 1986, pres. 1975-76), Brit. Soc. Endocrinology, Am. Psychosomatic Soc., Am. Thyroid Assn., Internat. Brain Orgn., Assn. for Rsch. in Nervous and Mental Disease (pres. 1976-79), Pituitary Soc. (pres. 1994-95, Disting. Leadership award 1995), Sociedad Mexicana de Nutricion y Endocrinologia (hon.), Sigma Xi, Alpha Omega Alpha. Home: 685 S La Posada Cir GH 3402 Green Valley AZ 85614 Personal E-mail: reichlin@laposadagv.net.

REICHMAN, HENRY FREDERICK, history educator; b. NYC, Feb. 10, 1947; s. Charles and Vera (Stein) R.; m. Susan Alyne Hutcher, June 27, 1976; children: Daniel, Alice. AB, Columbia Coll., 1969; PhD, U. Calif., Berkeley, 1977. Instr. U. Calif., Berkeley, 1975-76, lectr. history San Diego, 1978; asst. prof. history Northwestern U., Evanston, Ill., 1979-80; asst. dir. office for intellectual freedom Am. Libr. Assn., Chgo., 1980-81; asst. prof. history Memphis State U., 1983-89, Calif. State U., Esat Bay, 1989—91, assoc. prof. history, 1991—96, prof. history, 1996—. Vis. asst. prof. history U. Calif., Davis, 1989; chair dept. history Calif. State U., 1994-2003, academic senate, 2002-; assoc. editor newsletter on intellectual freedom Am. Libr. Assn., 1982—2009, editor, 2009-. Author: Railwaymen and Revolution: Russia, 1905, 1987, Censorship and Selection, 1988, rev. edit., 1993, 3rd edit., 2001; contbr. articles to profl. jours. Mem. Am. Hist. Assn., Am. Assn. for Advancement of Slavic Studies, Freedom to Read Found., Phi Beta Kappa. Democrat. Jewish. Avocations: reading, baseball. Office: Calif State U Dept History Hayward CA 94542 Office Phone: 510-885-3207. Business E-Mail: henry.reichman@csueastbay.edu.

REICHMAN, LEE BRODERSOHN, physician; b. NYC, June 25, 1938; s. Theodore and Elinore (Brodersohn) R.; m. Rose Ehrinpreis, Oct. 9, 1965; children: Daniel Mark, Deborah Gar. AB, Oberlin Coll., Ohio, 1960; MD, NYU, 1964; MPH, Johns Hopkins U., Balt., 1971. Intern Bellevue Hosp., I Med. Divsn., NYC, 1964-65, resident, 1967-68, Harlem Hosp. Ctr., NYC, 1968-69, fellow in pulmonary medicine, 1969-70; dir. Bur. Tb, Bur. Chronic Disease, N.Y.C. Health Dept., 1971-73, asst. commr. health, 1973-74; assoc. prof. medicine U. Medicine and Dentistry N.J. Med. Sch., Newark, 1974-78; prof. medicine N.J. Med. Sch., Newark, 1978—, prof. preventive medicine, cmty. health, 1993—; dir. pulmonary div. U. Medicine and Dentistry N.J.-N.J. Med. Sch. Univ. Hosp., 1974-92; founding exec. dir. N.J. Med. Sch. Nat. Tb Ctr., 1993—2006, N.J. Med. Sch. Global Tubercular Inst., 2006—. Cons. CDC, Atlanta, 1970—; prin. investigator pulmonary complications of HIV infection NHLBI, 1987—95; prin. investigator Model Tb Ctr. CDC, 1993—2003, prin. investigator Nat. Tb Trials Consortium, 1994—99, adv. coun. for elimination of Tb, 2002—; prin. investigator Regional Tng. & Med. Conv. Ctr. CDC, 2003—; sr. advisor WHO Stop TB Partnership, Geneva, 2007—. Editor: Tuberculosis-A Comprehensive International Approach, 2d edit., 2000; author: Timebomb-The Global Epidemic of Multi-Drug Resistant Tuberculosis, 2002; contbr. articles to profl. jours. Bd. dirs. Art Ctr. No. N.J., 1979-86; chmn. N.J. Commn. on Smoking of Health, 1986-87; mem. N.J. TB Adv. Coun., 1976—, chmn. 1991—; chair Nat. Coalition for Elimination of Tb, 1992—2004; mem. N.J. Clean Air Coun., 1987. With USPHS, 1965-67. Recipient Nat. Heart Lung and Blood Inst., Pulmonary Acad. career award, 1975-80, Preventive Pulmonary Acad. career award, 1987-92, Tb Acad. career award, 1993—98, 1st prize trade category Am. Med. Writers Assn., 2002, Solomon A. Berson Med. Alumni Achievement award NYU, 2003. Fellow ACP, Am. Coll. Chest Physicians (gov. 1984-90, pres. N.J. chpt. 1982-84, Simon Rodbard Meml. lectr. 2000); mem. Am. Thoracic Soc. (hon. life 1999-), Internat. Union Against Tb and Lung Disease (exec. com. 1982-92, vice chair exec. com. 1989-91, N.Am. Region Disting. Svc. award 2001), Am. Lung Assn. (hon. life 1999-, nat. bd. dirs. 1980-94, pres. elect 1991-92, pres. 1992-93, past pres. 1993-94, Will Ross medalist 1999), N.J. Thoracic Soc. (pres. 1982-84), Am. Lung Assn. N.J. (hon. life 1996-, bd. dirs. 1976—86, pres. 1984-86), Global Alliance for Tb Drug Devel. Stakeholders Assn. (pres., 2004-05, bd. dirs., 2006—), Paul G Rogers Soc. (amb. 2009-). Office: PO Box 1709 225 Warren St Newark NJ 07101-1709 Home Phone: 201-541-4020; Office Phone: 973-972-3270. E-mail: reichmlb@umdnj.edu.

REICHS, KATHY (KATHLEEN JOAN TOELLE REICHS), forensic anthropologist, educator, writer; BA in Anthropology, Am. U., Washington, 1971; MA in Physical Anthropology, Northwestern U., Evanston, Ill., 1972, PhD in Physical Anthropology, 1975. Diplomate Am. Bd. Forensic Anthropology. Asst. prof. Northern Ill. U., 1974—78; instructor Stateville Correctional Facility, Joliet, Ill., 1975—78; asst. prof. Davidson Coll., Davidson, NC, 1981—83; lectr., dept. sociology and anthropology U. NC, Charlotte, 1978—81, 1983—87, asst. prof., dept. sociology and anthropology, 1987—88, assoc. prof., dept. sociology and anthropology, 1988—96, prof., dept. sociology and anthropology, 1996—. Vis. prof., Semester at Sea U. Pitts., 1987; vis. assoc. prof. Concordia U., 1988—89, McGill U., 1988—97; tchr. Symposium for med. and dental students, U. NC Sch. Medicine, Chapel Hill, NC, Symposium for residents in pathology, Laboratoire de Sciences Jucicaires Legales et de medecine legale, Montreal, Canada; instr. Field Course in the Recovery of Human Remains, FBI Acad., Quantico, Va., 1995—; working mem., affiliate Am. Bd. Forensic Anthropology, Inc., Armed Forces Inst. Pathology, Disaster Mortuary Operational Response Team, FBI Lab. Evidence Response, Fed. Emergency Mgmt. Agy., Joint POW/MIA Acctg. Command, RCMP Nat. Police Services Coun.; anthropologue judiciare Govt du Quebec, Ministere de la Securite publique, Laboratoire de Sciences Judiciaries et de Médecine Légale, 1988—; forensic anthropologist cons. Office of the Chief Med. Examiner, State NC, Chapel Hill, NC, 1985—, Mecklenburg County, NC, Medical Examiner's Office, 1985—; cons. osteological analysis Toulouse rsch. project on the skeletal remains of Thomas Acquinas,

1989—90, Remains of Jeam LeBar, Archdiocese Montreal, 1991; cons. Office of Relocation, NC Dept. Transportation, Charlotte, NC; forensic anthropologist Nat. Med. Sys., D-MORT Team, Region 4, 1994—; external cons. in forensic anthropology, casualty, and mortuary affairs ops. ctr. Ctrl. Identification Lab., Hawaii, 1997—99; Commission d'enquete sur les circonstances entourant la disparition et le deces de M. Louis-Georges Dupont (exhumation, analysis), Trois Rivieres/Montreal, 1996; Commission d'enquete Roberge, Govt. du Quebec (exhumation, analysis), Sept Isles/Montreal, 99; frequent expert witness in criminal trials; presenter. lectr. for various profl. associations, conferences, educational institutions, workshops, and literary festivals worldwide. Author: (Temperance Brennan Series) Déjà Dead, 1997 (NY Times bestseller, Ellis award for Best First Novel, 1997), Death du Jour, 1999, Deadly Decisions, 2000, Fatal Voyage, 2001, Grave Secrets, 2002, Bare Bones, 2004, Monday Mourning, 2004, Cross Bones, 2005, Break No Bones, 2006, Bones to Ashes, 2007, Devil Bones, 2008 (#1 Publishers Weekly bestseller); contbr. articles to peer-reviewed publs.; contbr. (TV series) Anatomy of a Murder (CNN), 2005—, guest appearances Leeza, Today Show, Good Morning America, Montell, Investigative Reports, Court TV, Catherine Crier Live, Larry King Live, Discovery Channel, Learning Channel, A&E, WOR-AM-Joan Hamburg, NY Interactive, CBC and BBC (TV and Radio), ABC, TV and Radio programs in South Africa, Australia, New Zealand, Thailand, & Germany. Mem.: Am. Bd. Forensic Anthropology (bd. dir. 1986—93, v.p. 1989—93), Am. Acad. Forensic Scis. (bd. dir. 1996—2002, sec., physical anthropology sect. 1994—95, chair, physical anthropology sect. 1995—96, exec. com., bd. dir. 2000—), Phi Beta Delta. Achievements include traveling to Rwanda to testify at the UN Tribunal on Genocide in 1999; helping to identify individuals from mass graves in Guatemala; helping with forensic work at Ground Zero in NYC in 2001; working with the Central Identification Laboratory in Hawaii to identify bodies lost in WWII.*

REICIN, ERIC DAVID, lawyer; b. Chgo. s. Ronald Ian and Alyta Reicin; m. Jodi Reicin, 1994, 3 children Student, Regent Coll., Eng., 1990; AB in Econs. and Polit. Sci., U. Mich., 1991; JD cum laude, U. Ill., 1994. Bar: Ill. 1994, U.S. Dist. Ct. (no. dist.) Ill. 1994, DC 1995, U.S. Dist. Ct. DC 1995, U.S. Ct. Appeals (DC cir.) 1995, U.S. Ct. Appeals (4th cir.) 1997, U.S. Supreme Ct. 1998, Va. Intern US Senator Robert W. Kasten, Washington, 1989; intern Office of Policy Devel. White House, Washington, 1990; intern U.S. Congressman Carl Pursell, Washington, 1991; law clk. State's Atty.-Champaign County, 1994; assoc. Laner Muchin Dombrow Becker Levin and Tominberg, Chgo., 1994-95, Birch Horton Bittner and Cherot, Washington, 1995-99; asst. gen. counsel Sallie Mae, Inc., Reston, Va., 1999-2000, assoc. gen. counsel, 2001—03, officer, 2003—05, v.p. & assoc. gen. counsel, 2005—07, dep. gen counsel, 2007—08, sr v.p., dep. gen. counsel, 2008—. Chpt. editor: Employment Discrimination Law, 3d edit., 1999, 2000, 4th edit. 2007. Harno scholar, 1993-94, Congrl. scholar, 1986; Pub. Interest Law Found. fellow. Mem. ABA (exec. lt. gov. 1993-94, EEO com. nat. co-chmn. regional liaison program 1997-98, nat. co-chmn. govt. liaison program 1998-2001, nat. co-chmn. ABA/EEOC joint tng. partnership 1997-2001, nat. chmn. EEO com., corp. coun. 2001—), DC Bar Assn. (litig., labor and employment sect.), Met. Washington Employment Lawyers Assn. (sec., bd. dirs. 1997-99), Washington Met. Area Corp. Counsel Assn. (labor and employment com. chair 1999-2004, bd. mem. 2003-, v.p. 2004-05, pres.2006-07, Assn. Corp. Ctrl. Nat. Bd.2008-, Am. Employment Law Coun. (Advisory Bd., 2008-) Mortar Bd., Pi Sigma Alpha, Omicron Delta Epsilon, Sigma Iota Rho, Alpha Epsilon Pi (Arnold B. Hoffman award 1990). Republican. Office: Sallie Mae Inc 12061 Bluemont Way Reston VA 20190 Office Phone: 703-984-3000.

REICIN, RONALD IAN, lawyer; b. Chgo., Dec. 11, 1942; s. Frank Edward and Abranita (Rome) R.; m. Alyta Friedland, May 23, 1965; children: Eric, Kael. BBA, U. Mich., 1964, MBA, 1967, JD cum laude, 1967. Bar: Ill. 1967, U.S. Tax Ct. 1967; CPA, Ill. Mem. staff Price Waterhouse & Co., Chgo., 1966; ptnr. Jenner & Block, Chgo., 1967—. Bd. dirs. Nat. Kidney Found., Ill., 1978-2003, v.p., 1992-95, pres., 1995-98, life trustee, 2004—; bd. dirs. Ruth Page Found., 1985—, v.p., 1990—; bd. dirs. Scoliosis Assn. Chgo., 1981-90, Kohl Children's Mus., 1991-95, River North Chgo. Dance Co., 1999—. Mem.: Ill. State Bar Assn., Chgo. Mortgage Attys. Assn., Chgo. Bar Assn., ABA, Lawyers Club (Chgo.), Exec. Club, Beta Alpha Psi, Beta Gamma Sigma, Phi Kappa Phi. Office: Jenner & Block LLP 353 N Clark St Chicago IL 60654-4701 Home Phone: 847-831-5969; Office Phone: 312-923-2687. Personal E-mail: rreicin@jenner.com.

REID, ANDY (ANDREW WALTER REID), professional football coach; b. LA, Mar. 19, 1958; m. Tammy Reid; children: Garrett, Britt, Crosby, Drew Ann, Spencer. Student, Brigham Young U., 1979—81. Coach Brigham Young U., 1982, San Francisco State, 1983—85; head coach No. Ariz. U., 1986, Tex.-El Paso U., 1987—88; asst. coach U. Mo., Columbia, 1989—91, Green Bay Packers, 1992-99; head coach Phila. Eagles, 2000—, exec. v.p. football ops., 2001—. Named NFL Coach of the Yr., Sporting News, 2000, 2002, Maxwell Football Club, 2000, 2002, Pro Bowl Football Weekly, 2002, AP, 2002. Achievements include being a member of Super Bowl XXXI winning Green Bay Packers, 1997. Office: Philadelphia Eagles Nova Care Complex 1 Nova Care Way Philadelphia PA 19145-5298*

REID, ANTONIO (L.A. REID), music company executive; b. June 7, 1956; m. Perri Reid (div.); 1 child, Aaron. With musical group The Deele; co-founder La Face Records, 1989; chmn. & CEO Hitco Music Pub., Atlanta, 1996—; pres., CEO Arista Records, NYC, 2000—04; chmn. Island Def Jam Music Group, 2004—. Songwriter with Kenny Edmonds, also occasionally with Darryl Simmons. Songs include Girlfriend, 1987, Rock Steady, 1987, Two Occasions, 1987, Don't Be Cruel, 1988, Love Saw It, 1988, Lover In Me, 1988, Every Little Step, 1988 (Grammy award nomination for R&B Song of Yr. 1989), Dial My Heart, 1988, Way You Love Me, 1988, Secret Rendezvous, 1988, Superwoman, 1988, Roses Are Red, 1988, Can't Stop, 1989, My Kinda Girl, 1989, It's No Crime, 1989, On Our Own, 1989, Ready or Not, 1989, Tender Lover, 1989, Giving You the Benefit, 1990, I'm Your Baby Tonight, 1990, Shock Dat Monkey, 1992, End of the Road, 1996. Recipient three Grammy awards, Legend award, World Music Awards, 2008; named one of Most Influential Black Americans Ebony mag., 2006; named to Power 150 Ebony mag., 2008. Office: Island Def Jam Music Group 825 8th Ave, 28th fl New York NY 10019

REID, CHARLES ADAMS, III, lawyer; b. Plainfield, NJ, Apr. 21, 1947; s. Charles Adams Jr. and Gertrude C. (Egan) R.; m. Teresa Keenan, May 11, 1974. BA, Colgate U., 1969; JD, Columbia U., 1974. Bar: N.Y. 1974, N.J. 1976, U.S. Ct. Appeals (3d cir.) 1983, U.S. Ct. Appeals (fed. cir.) 1989, U.S. Ct. Appeals (2d cir.) 1991, U.S. Ct. Appeals (9th cir.) 2002, Calif. 2002. Law clk. to hon. John R. Bartels U.S. Dist. Ct. (ea. dist.) N.Y., Bklyn., 1974-75; assoc. Coudert Bros., NYC, 1975-77, Shanley & Fisher, Newark, 1977-82, ptnr. Newark and Morristown, N.J., 1983-99, Drinker Biddle & Reath LLP, Florham Park, NJ, 1999—. Mem. planning bd. Peapack-Gladstone, N.J., 1984-88, chmn., 1987-88; bd. dirs. Morris Ctr. YMCA, Cedar Knolls, N.J., 1986-93. Served with U.S. Army, 1970-72, Vietnam. Mem. ABA (litigation sect.), N.J. Bar Assn., Morris County Bar Assn., Essex County Bar Assn., Calif. State Bar. Home: PO Box 716 Gladstone NJ 07934 Office: Drinker Biddle & Reath LLP 500 Campus Dr Florham Park NJ 07932-1047 Office Phone: 973-360-1100. Business E-Mail: Charles.Reid@dbr.com.

REID, DAVID G., lawyer; b. NYC, Oct. 28, 1948; s. Donald D. and Charlotte A. (Marois) Reid. BA, McGill U., Montreal, 1970; JD, Boston U., 1973. Bar: Vt. 1973, U.S. Dist. Ct. Vt. 1973, Mass. 1977, U.S. Supreme Ct. 1978, U.S. Ct. Appeals (2d cir.) 1978, U.S. Dist. Ct. Mass. 1991. Pub. defender Orleans, Caledonia, Essex counties, St. Johnsbury, Vt., 1973-75, Bennington (Vt.) County, 1975-79, Windham County, Brattleboro, Vt., 1979-89; ptnr. Reid & Rodgers, Brattleboro, 1989—. Office: Reid & Rodgers 47 Williston St Brattleboro VT 05301-3202 Office Phone: 802-257-7887. E-mail: reidrodg@sover.net.

REID, DOLORES B., retired social services administrator, consultant; b. Pickens, Miss. d. James Edward and Edna (Snow) Scarborough; m. Walter F. Reid; children: Thomas, Amye BS Sociology and Psychology, Loyola U., Chgo., 1954; MSW, Boston U., 1961; postgrad., U. Pa., 1979; PhD Pub. Adminstrn., Union Inst., Cin., 1985. LCSW, Md. Various social work positions, Chgo., St. Paul, N.H., 1954—60; social worker Mass. Soc. for Prevention of Cruelty to Children, Boston, 1961—62; asst. prof. psychiat. social work Hawaii State Hosp./U. Hawaii, Honolulu, 1963—66; psychiat. social worker Mental Health Clinic, Champaign, Ill., 1969—70; dep. dir. regional tng. Ill. Dept. Children and Family Svcs., 1967—71; asst. dir., dir. social svcs. Rock Island Neighborhood Health Ctr., Ill., 1971—73; dep. dir. program support svcs. Ill. Dept. Children and Family Svcs., Springfield, 1973—78; exec. dir. Montgomery County Children Svcs., Dayton, Ohio, 1978—85; various social work positions, 1985—89; chief assessment and monitoring programs Montgomery County, Rockville, Md., 1989—93, chief family preservation svcs., 1993—94; exec. cons. Met. Washington Coun. Govts., 1994—95; chief bur. children svcs. Dept. Human Svcs., Columbus, Ohio, 1995—98, program adminstr. Office Prevention and Protection, 1998—2000, dep. dir. divsn. children and families Phoenix, 2000—05; cons., lectr., trainer social svcs., 2005—. Peer mem., team leader Commn. Coun. Accreditation, 1999—. Contbr. articles to profl. jours.; presenter in field Mem. Acad. Cert. Social Workers, Child Welfare League Am., Black Adminstrs. in Child Welfare (bd. dirs., v.p., chair kinship care com.), Nat. Network for Social Work Mgrs. (cert. social work mgr.) Personal E-mail: dbreid120193@aol.com.

REID, EDWARD SNOVER, III, lawyer; b. Detroit, Mar. 24, 1930; s. Edward S. Jr. and Margaret (Overington) Reid; m. Carroll Grylls, Dec. 30, 1953; children: Carroll Reid Highet, Richard Gerveys, Jenny Reid McTigue, Margaret Reid Boyer. BA, Yale U., 1951; LL.B. magna cum laude (Sheldon fellow), Harvard U., 1956. Bar: Mich. 1957, N.Y. 1958, D.C. 1982, Gaikokuho jimu-bengoshi, Tokyo 1991-96. Assoc. Davis, Polk & Wardwell, NYC, 1957-64, partner, 1964-95, sr. counsel, 1996—; dir. Gen. Mills, Inc., 1974-89. Mem. N.Y.C. Bd. Higher Edn., 1971—73; trustee Bklyn. Inst. Arts and Scis., 1966—93, chmn., 1974—79; trustee Bklyn. Mus. Art, 1973—93, 1994—; bd. dirs. Bklyn. Bot. Garden Corp., 1977—92, 1996—, Bargemusic Ltd., 1990—93. Active duty USMCR, 1951—53. Mem. ABA, N.Y. State Bar Assn., Assn. of Bar of City of N.Y., Am. Law Inst., Heights Casino Club, Rembrandt Club, Century Assn. Club, Yale Club, Quoque Beach Club, Shinnecock Yacht Club, Quoque Field Club. Home: PO Box 39 Quogue NY 11959-0039 Office: Davis Polk & Wardwell 450 Lexington Ave New York NY 10017-3982 E-mail: ereid@dpw.com.

REID, FRANCES EVELYN KROLL, freelance/self-employed cinematographer, film director, communications executive; b. Oakland, Calif., Mar. 25, 1944; d. William Farnham and Marion Storm (Teller) Kroll. BA, U. Oreg., 1966. Tchr. secondary sch., Los Angeles, 1968-69; sound recordist Churchill Films, Los Angeles, 1971; freelance sound recordist Los Angeles, 1972-75; freelance dir., prodr., 1975—; freelance cinematographer Berkeley, Calif., 1978—; dir. Iris Films, Berkeley, 1977—; lectr. U. Calif. Grad. Sch. Journalism, 2005. Vol. Peace Corps, Malawi, Africa, 1969-70. Producer/dir. Long Night's Journey Into Day, 2000 (Grand Jury award Sundance 2000, Acad. award nominee 2001); dir. (film) In The Best Interests of the Children, 1977 (Blue Ribbon Am. Film Festival 1978), The Changer: A Record of the Times, 1991, The Faces of AIDS, 1992, Skin Deep, 1995, Talking About Race, 1994, Straight from the Heart, 1994 (Acad. award nominee 1995); cinematographer: (film) The Times of Harvey Milk, 1984 (Oscar 1985), Living with AIDS, 1986 (Student Acad. award 1987), Common Threads: Stories from the Quilt, 1989 (Oscar award 1990), Complaints of a Dutiful Daughter, 1994 (Acad. award nominee 1995). Mem. Film Arts Found., Assn. Ind. Video and Filmmakers, Acad. Motion Picture Arts and Scis. Office: Iris Films 2600 10th St Ste 607 Berkeley CA 94710-2522 Office Phone: 510-845-5414.

REID, GERALDINE WOLD (GERALDINE REID SKJERVOLD), retired artist; b. Apr. 11, 1944; d. Alden Elroy and Verna (Kocinski) Wold BA in Fine Art, Calif. State U., Sacramento, 1972, MFA, 1975; postgrad., Ind. U. - Purdue U. Instr. dental aux. edn. U. Minn., 1966-70, anthropol. rsch. asst., 1976-78; mng. editor Nat. Arts Guide, Chgo., 1978-80; freelance artist Chgo., 1981-94; pres. Chgo. Art Emerging Inc., 1983-85; graphic artist Reid Design & Illustration, Chgo., 1981-94; dir. show coordination Circle Fine Art, Chgo., 1981. Instr. comm. art and design Alexandria Tech. Coll., Minn., 1994—2009; seminar lectr., 1977, 86; lectr., art and math. Dept. Math. U. Ill., 1987—88; guest lectr. women's art history AAUW, Alexandria, 1997; lectr. on drawing approaches, 2005. One-woman shows include Artists' Coop. Gallery, Santa Fe, 1976, Artlink, Ft. Wayne, Ind., 1979, 84—, D.E.O. Fine Arts, Inc., Chgo., 1982-83, Union League Gallery, Chgo., 1989, Brodsky Gallery, 1993, Second Floor Gallery, Cen. Square, Glenwood, Minn., 1999, Ann Bickle Heritage House, Glenwood, 2000, Pope County Mus., Glenwood, 2004, Pope Art, Ter. Mill, Minn., 2005; group exhbns. include Crocker Art Mus., Sacramento, 1975, Ft. Wayne Mus. Art, 1978, Artists Guild Chgo., 1982, Charles A. Wustum Mus., Racine, Wis., 1983, Limelight, Chgo., 1986, 87, 88, Neville-Sargent Gallery, 1986, 87, Beacon Street Hull House Gallery, 1988, McDonalds Corp., Chgo., 1988, Prairie Ave. Gallery, Chgo., 1990, Peace Mus., Chgo., 1990, Hyde Park Art Ctr., Chgo., 1990, Lettuce Entertain You Enterprises, Inc., 1990, Olive Tree Gallery, Daley Coll., Chgo., 1991, Crown Ctr. Gallery, Loyola U., Chgo., 1992, Agora Syndicate, Inc., 1992, Kieffer-Nolde/TIC, 1992, Flora '92, 1992, Chgo. Bot. Garden, 1992, Open Spectrum, David Adler Cultural Ctr., 1994, August House Studio, Chgo., 1994—, Upper West Gallery, Alexandria Tech. Coll., Minn., 1995, Plains Art Mus., Fargo, ND, 1997, Regional Art Exhibit, New York Mills, Minn., 1997, Runestone Mus., Alexandria, 1997-98, Art on the Plains, 3d Ann. Regional Exhbn., Plains Art Mus., Fargo, 31st Ann. Fergus Falls CC Invitational Art Show, Minn., 2002-03, Pope County Artists Exhibit, Lake Region Arts Coun. Gallery, Fergus Falls, Minn., 2002, 06, Prairie Renaissance Cultural Alliance Gallery, Morris, Minn., 2002-03, 07, Celebration of Lake Region Arts Coun., Fergus Falls, 2002-03, New York Mills (Minn.) Ann. Regional Exhbn., 2003, Minn. State Cmty. and Tech. Coll., Fergus Falls, 2004, Minn. State Colls. and Univs., 2005-08, Three Havens Art Gallery, Alexandria, Minn., 2007-08, Art Perchance, Mpls. Inst. Art., 2006-08; contbr. artwork to 2 ann. 1994 calendars; artwork selected for inclusion in Alex Tech Coll. greeting card suite, 2005. Mem. New York Mills Cultural Ctr., Mpls. Art Inst., Am. Inst. Graphic Arts, Mpls. Inst. Arts, Glacial Ridge Artists. Personal E-mail: gerae@embarqmail.com.

REID, HARRY MASON, United States Senator from Nevada; b. Searchlight, Nev., Dec. 2, 1939; s. Harry and Inez Jaynes Reid; m. Landra Joy Gould; children: Lana, Rory, Leif, Josh, Key AS, Southern Utah State U., 1959; BS in Hist. and Polit. Sci., Utah State U., 1961; JD, George Washington U., 1964; LLD (hon.), U. So. Utah, 1984. Bar: Nev. Bar 1963. Police officer US Capitol, Washington, 1961—64; city atty. City of Henderson, Henderson, Nev., 1964—66; mem. Nev. State Assembly, 1969—70; lt. gov. State of Nev., 1971—75; chmn. Nev. Gaming Commn., 1977—81; mem. US Congress from 1st. Nev. Dist., Washington, 1983—87; US Senator from Nev. Washington, 1987—; asst. minority leader (minority whip), 1999—2001, 2001, 2003—05; asst. majority leader (majority whip), 2001—03; minority leader, 2004—07; majority leader, 2007—; chmn. US Senate Select Com. on Ethics, 2001—03, US Senate Com. on Environment & Pub. Works, 2001. Chmn. US Senate Democratic Conf., 2005—. Author: Searchlight: The Camp that Didn't Fail, 1998. Bd. dirs. Am. Cancer Soc., Legal Aid Soc., Young Men's Christian Assn.; bd. trustees So. Nev. Meml. Hosp., 1967—69. Recipient Humanitarian award, Nat. Asthma Ctr. and Nat. Jewish Hosp., 1984, Public Svc. award, Am. Found. Suicide Prevention, 1999, Friend of Zion award, The Jerusalem Fund, 2000, MLA award disting. public svc., 2002, Award of Merit, The Military Coalition, 2002, Arthur T. Marix award, Military Officers Assn. Am., 2003, Disting. Svc. award, Am. Public Works Assn., 2003, Inspirational Leadership award, Military Order of Purple Heart, 2003, Nat. Landscape Conservation Sys. Champion award, NLCS Coalition, 2004, Pick and Gravel award, Assn. Am. State Geologists, 2004, TechNet Founders Cir. award, 2005; named one of The 50 Most Powerful People in DC, GQ Mag., 2007. Mem.: Nev. Athletic Commn., Nat. Conf. Lt. Governors, Am. Bd. Trial Advocates, Clark County Bar Assn., Nev. Bar Assn., ABA. Democrat. Lds Ch. Office: US Senate 528 Hart Senate Office Bldg Washington DC 20510-0001 also: Lloyd D George Bldg Ste 8016 333 Las Vegas Blvd South Las Vegas NV 89101 Office Phone: 202-224-3542, 702-388-5020. Office Fax: 202-224-7327, 702-388-5030. E-mail: senator_reid@reid.senate.gov.*

REID, HELEN VERONICA, provost; b. Reading, Eng., Sept. 25, 1956; d. Alan A. and Teresa H. (Thatcher) Ware; m. Gary B. Reid, May 29, 1976; children: Robert, Jennifer, Kristen. BA in Biology, U. Tex., 1976; BSN, U. Tex., Arlington, 1978; MSN, Tex. Women's U., 1983; EdD, U. North Tex., 2000. CCRN, 1980, cert. CPR instr. Asst. nurse coord., staff nurse, float pool nurse Parkland Meml. Hosp., Dallas, 1979—83, float pool nurse, 1987—93; instr. Trinity Valley CC, Kaufman, Tex., 1983—86, leader freshman team, 1986—90, dean health occupations, 1990—2006; provost Health Sci. Ctr., 2007—. Mem.: Tex. Assn. Deans and Dirs. for Profl. Nursing Programs (treas. 2005—), Tex. C.C. Tchrs. Assn., Nat. Orgn. ADN (pub. rels. dir. 1998—2002, treas. 2006—), Tex. Orgn. for ADN (sec. 1988—92, nominating com. chair 1995—96, pres.-elect 2002—03, pres. 2003—05, past pres. 2005—06), Tex. Assn. Vocat. Nurse Educators, Phi Kappa Phi, Sigma Theta Tau. Office Phone: 972-932-4309. Business E-Mail: reid@tvcc.edu.

REID, INEZ SMITH, Associate Judge, DC Court of Appeals, lawyer, educator; b. New Orleans, Apr. 7, 1937; d. Sidney Randall Dickerson and Beatrice Virginia (Bundy) Smith. BA, Tufts U., 1959; LLB, Yale U., 1962; MA, UCLA, 1963; PhD, Columbia U., 1968; LLM in Jud. Process, U. Va., 2004. Bar: Calif. 1963, N.Y. 1972, D.C. 1980. Assoc. prof. Barnard Coll. Columbia U., NYC, 1972-76; gen. counsel youth divsn. State of N.Y., 1976-77; dep. gen. counsel HEW, Washington, 1977-79; inspector gen. EPA, Washington, 1979-81; chief legis. and opinions, dep. corp. counsel Office of Corp. Counsel, Washington, 1981-83; corp. counsel D.C., 1983-85; counsel Laxalt, Washington, Perito & Dubuc, Washington, 1986-90, ptnr., 1990-91; counsel Graham & James, 1991-93, Lewis, White & Clay, P.C., 1994-95; assoc. judge D.C. Ct. Appeals, 1995—. William J. Maier, Jr. vis. prof. law W.Va. U. Coll. Law, Morgantown, 1985-86. Contbr. articles to profl. jours. and publs. Trustee emeritus Lancaster Sem., Pa., 2002—; bd. dirs. Homeland Ministries bd. United Ch. of Christ, NYC, 1978—83, vice chmn., 1981—83; chmn. bd. govs. Antioch Law Sch., Washington, 1979—81; chmn. bd. trustees Antioch U., Yellow Springs, Ohio, 1981—82; trustee Tufts U., Medford, Mass., 1988—98, trustee emeritus, 1999—; trustee Lancaster (Pa.) Sem., 1988—2001; bd. govs. D.C. Sch. Law, 1990—96, chmn., 1991—95. Recipient Emily Gregory award Barnard Coll., 1976, Arthur Morgan award Antioch U., 1982, Service award United Ch. of Christ, 1983, Disting. Service (Profl. Life) award Tufts U. Alumni Assn., 1988. Office: DC Ct Appeals 430 E St NW Washington DC 20001-2138*

REID, IRVIN D., former academic administrator; b. Feb. 1941; m. Pamela Trotman, Aug. 27, 1966; children: Nicole, Dexter. BS, Howard U., MS in Exptl. Psychology; MA, PhD, U. Pa.; PhD (hon.), Montclair State U., 2003. Head dept. mktg. & bus. law U. Tenn., Chattanooga, 1979-83, dean Sch. Bus. Adminstrn., John Stagmaier prof. econs. and bus. adminstrn., Alan Lorberbaum prof. mktg.; assoc. prof. mktg. Howard U., Washington, 1978-79; cons. U.S. Consumer Product Safety Commn., 1977-78; sr. staff specialist mktg. & econ. rsch. NASA, 1976-77, 78-79; asst. prof. mktg. coll. bus. Drexel U., 1970-78; pres. Montclair State U., Upper Montclair, NJ, 1989—97, Wayne State U., Detroit, 1997—2008. Bd. mem. Detroit Renaissance, Handleman Co., Fed. Reserve Bank of Chgo., Mack-Cali Real Estate Trust. Bd. dirs. Detroit 300 Com., 1998—; exec. com. Detroit Med. Ctr., 1997—, Karmanos Cancer Inst., 1997—, New Detroit, 1998—, NJ/Israel Trade Commn., 1994-97, NCAA Pres.'s Commn., 1994-99, Nat. Conf. Christians and Jews, 1992-97, Mich. Econ. Devel. Corp., 1999—, Detroit Urban League, 1999—, Mich. Opera Theater, 1998—; steering com. Mich. Life Sci. Initiative, 2000—. Mem. Econ. Club Detroit, Univ. Cultural Ctr. Assn., Upper Montclair (N.J.) Country Club.

REID, IVONNE FIGUEROA, language educator; b. Santiago, Chile, May 25, 1938; d. Hector Francisco Figueroa and Uberlinda Eulojia Cristi; m. Roderic Eugene Reid, June 13, 1963; children: David Alan, Nancy Gail. B in English, U. Chile, 1960; MS in Edn., U. So. Calif., 1963, PhD in Edn., 1972. Rschr. Inst. Statistical Rsch. U. Chile, 1959—63; prof. statistics Family Edn. Inst. Cath. U., Santiago, Chile, 1960—61; rsch. assoc. in evaluation art in elem. edn. rsch. project U. SC, 1975—80; intermediate sch. tchr. Montebello Unified Sch. Dist., Bell Gardens, 1981—89, h.s. Spanish tchr., 1989—99, literacy facilitator, 1999—2002, cons., 2002—05; vol. cons., 2005—06. Presenter Calif. Edn. Rsch. Assn., 1972, 77, 78, Calf. Assn. of Bilingual Edn., 1997—99, 2003. Named High Sch. Tchr. of the Yr., Calif. Bilingual Edn. Assn., Montebello Chapt., 1997; Fulbright scholarship, Dept. State, U. So. Calif., 1961—62. Mem.: Montebello Tchrs. Assn., Calif. Tchrs. Assn., Nat. Edn. Assn., Calif. Assn. Bilingual Edn., Am. Edn. Rsch. Assn. Avocations: travel, music, art, reading. Personal E-mail: ivonnereid@earthlink.net.

REID, JOHN MITCHELL (JACK REID), biomedical engineer, researcher, consultant; b. Mpls., June 8, 1926; s. Robert Sherman and Meryl (Mitchell) R.; m. Virginia Montgomery, Dec. 31, 1949 (div.); children: Donald, Kathryn, Richard; m. Shadi Wang, June 30, 1983; 1 child Xuang-Xuang Hu. BS, U. Minn., 1950, MS, 1957; PhD, U. Pa., 1965. Engring. assoc. U. Minn., Mpls., 1950-54; rsch. engr. St. Barnabas Hosp., Mpls., 1954-57; assoc. U. Pa., Phila., 1957-66; rsch. asst. prof. U. Wash., Seattle, 1966-72; rsch. engr. Providence Hosp., 1972-74; dir. bioengring. Inst. of Applied Physiology & Medicine, 1973-81; Calhoun prof. Drexel U., Phila., 1981-94, prof. emeritus, rsch. prof., 1994—. Adj. prof. radiology Thomas Jefferson Med. Sch., Phila., 1982—; affiliate prof. U. Washington, 1995—; cons. Inst. Applied Physiology and Medicine, Seattle. Contbr. numerous articles to profl. jours.; 5 U.S. patents on devel. of ultrasonic med. imaging. Scoutmaster Boy Scouts Am., Mpls., 1955-57, Phila., 1960-65, cub and scoutmaster, Seattle, 1965-70. With USN, 1944—46. Recipient Pioneer award Soc. Vascular Technologists, 1994; grantee NIH; Professorship in his named established at Drexel U. Sch. Biomed. Engring. and Health Sys., Phila., 2004. Fellow IEEE, Am. Inst. Ultrasound in Medicine (bd. govs., Pioneer award), Acoustical Soc. Am., IEEE Engring. in Medicine and Biology Soc. (Lifetime Achievement award 1993), Am. Inst. Med. and Biol. Engrs.; mem. World Fedn. Ultrasound in Medicine and Biology (hon.). Home: 16711 254th Ave SE Issaquah WA 98027-6973 Business E-Mail: jmreid@u.washington.edu.

REID, JOHN PHILLIP, law educator; b. Weehawken, NJ, May 17, 1930; s. Thomas Francis and Teresa Elizabeth (Murphy) R. BSS., Georgetown U., 1952; LLB, Harvard U., 1955; MA, U. N.H., 1957; LLM, NYU, 1959, JSD, 1962. Bar: N.H. 1955. Law clk. U.S. Dist. Ct. N.H., 1956; instr. NYU, NYC, 1960-62, asst. prof. law, 1962-64, assoc. prof., 1964-65, prof. Sch. Law, 1966—2003, prof. emeritus, 2003—. Author: Chief Justice: The Judicial World of Charles Doe, 1967, A Law of Blood: The Primitive Law of the Cherokee Nation, 1970, In a Defiant Stance, 1977, In a Rebellious Spirit, 1979, Law for the Elephant: Property and Social Behavior on the Overland Trail, 1980, In Defiance of the Law, 1981, Constitutional History of the American Revolution: The Authority of Rights, 1986, Constitutional History of the American Revolution: The Authority to Tax, 1987, The Concept of Liberty in the Age of the American Revolution, 1988, The Concept of Representation in the Age of the American Revolution, 1989, Constitutional History of the American Revolution: The Authority to Legislate, 1991, Constitutional History of the American Revolution: The Authority of Law, 1993, Policing the Elephant: Crime, Punishment, and Social Behavior on the Overland Trail, 1997, Patterns of Vengeance: Crosscultural Homicide in the North American Fur Trade, 1999, Contested Empire: Peter Skene Ogden and the Snake River Expeditions, 2002, Controlling the Law: Legal Politics in Early National New Hampshire, 2004, Rule of Law: The Jurisprudence of Liberty in the Seventeenth and Eighteenth Centuries, 2004, The Ancient Constitution and the Origins of Anglo-American Liberty, 2005. Fellow Guggenheim Found., 1980, Huntington Library-NEH, 1980, 84; hon. fellow Am. Soc. Legal History, 1986. Fellow Am. Acad. Arts and Scis. Republican. Roman Catholic. Office: NYU Law Sch 40 Washington Sq S New York NY 10012-1099 Home Phone: 603-929-6563; Office Phone: 212-998-6230. Business E-Mail: john.reid@nyu.edu.

REID, KAREN DENISE, aerospace transportation executive, writer; b. Memphis, Jan. 17, 1961; d. L.C. and Shirley (Spencer) Reid. BS in Edn., Memphis State U., 1992; postgrad., Webster U., 2007. Journeyman trainee Memphis Pub. Co., 1977—2000; exec. sec., treas., trustee Raleigh Ch., Memphis, 1985—94; acctg. clk. Nat. Hardwood Lumber Assn., Memphis, 1996—98; customer svc. agt. Pinnacle Airlines divsn. Northwest Airlines, Memphis, 1998—; owner K.K.'s Express Boutique, 1998—. Author: From Mistress to Ministry, 2003, The Transformation of a Pastor's Mistress, 2007. Bd. dirs., CEO Twin Ministries, 2000—. Avocations: travel, bowling, writing. Home and Office: Twin Ministries PO Box 752613 Memphis TN 38175 Office Phone: 901-634-2667. Personal E-mail: thetwinministries@yahoo.com.

REID, KATHERINE LOUISE, artist, educator, writer; b. Port Arthur, Tex., Mar. 25, 1941; d. Clifton Commodore and Helen Ross (Moore) Reid. BA, Baylor U., 1963; postgrad. in design and illustration, Kans. City Art Inst., 1964; MEd, U. Houston, 1973; cert. supervision, U. Houston-Clear Lake City, 1980; postgrad., San Jacinto Coll., 1982. Litho reprodn. artist Hallmark Cards, Kansas City, Mo., 1963-64; tchr. art high sch. Pasadena (Tex.) Ind. Sch. Dist., 1964-77, supr. art, gifted and talented and photography, 1977-85, supr. art and photography InterAct, 1985-90, instrnl. specialist, 1990-2000, photography and art, 1990-93, instrnl. specialist in art and spl. programs, 1993-96, rsch. planning, data disaggregation, 1996-2000; internet tchr. recruiter, 2001—02; mural artist Old Car Barn, Edna, Tex., 2000—. 4 MAT learning styles trainer DuPont Leadership Devel. Process Trainer, Selective Rsch., Inst., tchr. perceiver specialist, performance quality sys. trainer, coop. learning trainer, outcome based edn. trainer, integrated unit devel. and authentic assessment trainer Greater Gulf Coast Adminstr. Assessment Project, Assessor, 1990-2000; head crafts, asst. dir., dir. summer, winter discovery program-ski camp Cheley Colo. Camps, Denver, Estes Park, 1967-75; awards com. John Austin Cheley Found., 1990-92; staff artist, media workshop Tex. Edn. Agy., Austin, 1961; art enrichment tchr. Port Arthur Ind. Sch. Dist. (Tex.), 1961; head crafts Camp Waluta, Silsbee, Tex., 1960; mem. Tex. Edn. Agy., Art Leadership Inst., 1989-90, Tracking Rsch. Com., 1991, Core Strategic Planning Team, 1992-2000, Outcome Based Edn. Dist. Planning Com., 1991-92, Quality Sys. Improvement Team, 1991-92, Outcome Based Edn. Com. Exit Outcomes, 1991; Region IV data disk trainer, 1998-2000, target teach coord., 1993-2000, multiple intelligence trainer, 1997-2000, data disaggregation trainer, 1997-2000, supt.'s rsch. com., 1999. Author: Through Their Eyes, 1989. Mem. Friends of Fine Arts-Baylor U., Waco, Tex., 1981—, Scholastic Art awards Regional Bd., Houston, 1978-84; bd. dirs. Houston Coun. Student Art Awards, Inc., 1984-90, Pasadena Ind. Sch. Dist. Edn. Found., 2005-08; mem. Baylor U. Endowed Scholarship Soc., Baylor U. Old Main Scholarship Soc., 2003—. Named Outstanding Secondary Educator of Am., 1975, Tex. Art Educator of Yr., 1985, Outstanding Vol., City of Pasadena, 2004. Mem. ASCD, Tex. ASCD, Tex. Art Edn. Assn. (rep. editor newsletter 1982-85, chmn. supervision divsn. 1982-83, v.p. membership 1978-80, chmn. pub. info. com., regional chmn. youth art month 1980-82; regional chmn. membership com. 1976-78, pres. elect 1986, sec. 1991-93, Disting. Fellows award 2004), Tex. Alliance for Arts Edn. (bd. vice chmn. 1984-86, treas. 1988-90), Nat. Art Edn. Assn. (conv. com. 1977, 85), Tex. Assn. Sch. Adminstrs., Houston Art Edn. Assn. (sec. 1969), Tex. Ret. Tchrs. Assn. (Dist. IV historian 2001-03), Pasadena Area Ret. Sch. Employees (parliamentarian 2002-04, 1st v.p. 2009-), Delta Kappa Gamma (2d v.p. 1984-86, pres. 2002-2004, state leadership devel. chpt. pres. com., 2003-2005, state banner com., 2004, State Leadership Seminar 2005, area III coord. 2005-07, Internat. Golden Gift Leadership Seminar 2006, state rsch. com. 2007-09, state rsch. com. chairperson 2009-). Baptist. Achievements include patents for pet car seat. Home: 106 Ravenhead Dr Houston TX 77034-1520 Personal E-mail: klreid2@comcast.net.

REID, LANGHORNE, III, merchant banker; b. Dallas, Apr. 3, 1950; s. Langhorne Jr. and Mary Anne (Beasley) R.; m. Sally Wolf, Dec. 26, 1972 (div. Aug. 1977); m. Eve Catherine Murphy, Sept. 6, 1986 (div. 1996); 1 child, Claire Hart Reid; m. Vera Anderson Reid, 1999. BA in Psychology, U. Tex., 1972, JD, 1975; MBA, U. Pa., 1977. Bar: Tex. 1975. V.p. Dillon, Read & Co., Inc., NYC, 1977-82; mng. dir. Drexel Burnham Lambert Inc., NYC, 1982-87; co-dir. mergers and acquisitions Paine Webber Group, NYC, 1987-89; ptnr. Gordon Investment Inc., NYC, 1989-93; pres. Beacon Advisors, Inc., Dallas, 1993-99. Bd. dirs. Windmill Holdings; pres. Partnership Svcs., 1992-93; chmn. Cedco Sys., Inc., 1997—, Amtex Holdings, Inc., 1996—, Garland Broadcast Investors, Inc., 1997—2004, Pogesa SA, 2002-; dir. Tex. Security Bank, 2008-. Trustee, treas. Animal Med. Ctr., N.Y.C., 1981—; trustee St. Mark's Sch. of Tex., 2002-. Mem. Tex. Bar Assn. Home: 4109 Windsor Pkwy Dallas TX 75205-1670 Office: Arcady Capital Inc Ste 330 100 Highland Park Village Dallas TX 75205-2726 Office Phone: 214-528-0441.

REID, MARGARET ELIZABETH, elementary and secondary school educator; b. Tampa, Fla., Feb. 8, 1934; d. James Byron and Zella Mae (Thompson) Bruce; m. Arthur M. Reid Jr., Dec. 28, 1955 (div. Dec. 1982); children: Laura Jean, Nancy Ann. BS in Edn., SUNY, Potsdam, 1956; postgrad., SUNY, Stony Brook, 1975—78; MS in Spl. Edn., L.I. U., 1979, postgrad., 1989—. Cert. spl. edn. tchr., N.Y. Tchr. Harborfields Sch. Dist., Greenlawn, NY, 1956—61; tchr. Project Able Three Village Sch. Dist., Stony Brook, 1971—72; substitute tchr. spl. edn. Smithtown Sch. Dist., 1972—75, substitute tchr., 1972—75, Shoreham Sch. Dist., NY, 1974—76, Mt. Sinai Sch. Dist., NY, 1974—79, Middle Island Sch. Dist, NY, 1974—79; tchr. resource rm. Hempstead Sch. Dist., NY, 1979—96. Tchr. rep. spl. edn. com. Hempstead Sch. Dist., 1985—. Mem. N.Y. Pub. Interest Rsch. Group, N.Y.C. 1987—, Citizens Campaign for the Environment, 1988—, Arthur Murray Sch. Dance (V.I.P. Hon. Student award 2002). NSF grantee Stevens Inst. Tech., 1959. Mem. N.Y. Assn. for Learning Disabled, Hempstead Classroom Tchrs. Assn., Coun. for Exceptional Children, N.Y. Branch Orton Dyslexia Soc., Kappa Delta Pi Republican. Methodist. Avocations: music, art, drama. Home: 64 Walter Ave Hauppauge NY 11788-3425

REID, MICHELE M., school librarian, dean; d. Eston O. and Evelyn F. McFadden; m. William H. Reid, June 13, 1981. BA summa cum laude, U. Ctrl. Fla., Orlando, 1979; MA, U. S.Fla., Tampa, 1981, Rutgers U., New Brunswick, NJ, 1987. Circulation and automation libr. NJ Inst. Tech., Newark, 1981—84; dir. pub. svcs. SD State Libr., Pierre, 1990—97; asst. libr. dir. Washburn U., Topeka, 1997—2000; dir. librs. Ripon Coll., Wis., 2000—02; libr. dir. McDaniel Coll., Westminster, Md., 2002—08; dean librs. ND State U., Fargo, 2008—. Mem.: ALA, Libr. Adminstrn. and Mgmt. Assn., Assn. Coll. and Rsch. Librs. Episcopalian. Office: ND State Univ University Ave Fargo ND 58105

REID, PAMELA TROTMAN, college president, psychology professor; b. Bronx, NY, June 1, 1946; d. Louis Hilary and Gloria Legare (Harris) Trotman; m. Irvin Dexter Reid, Aug. 27, 1966; children: Nicole Legare, Irvin Dexter. BS, Howard U., 1967; MA, Temple U., 1970; PhD, U. Pa., 1975. Psychology asst. prof. Trenton State Coll., NJ, 1974-75; asst. prof. Phila. CC, 1975-76, Howard U., Washington, 1976-79; assoc. prof. U. Tenn., Chattanooga, 1979-84, prof., 1984-90; prof. Grad. Sch. CUNY, NYC, 1990, acting assoc. provost, dean acad. affairs Grad. Sch., 1992; dir. Women's Studies Program, prof. edn. and psychology U. Mich., rsch. scientist Inst. Rsch. on Women and Gender; provost, exec. v.p., prof. psychology Roosevelt U., Chgo., 2004—08; pres. St. Joseph Coll., West Hartford, Conn., 2008—. Dir. Office of Social Responsibility APA, Washington, 1986-87. Author: (with others) Demythologizing the Inner City Child, 1979, Women: A Developmental Perspective, 1982, Eliminating Racism, 1988, The Encyclopedia of Adolescence, 1990, Storming the Academic Tower: Women in the Academic World, 1991, Handbook of Psychology of Women, 1993; editor profl. jours.; contbr. articles to profl. jours. Rsch. assoc. Girls, Inc., Indpls., 1985. Recipient Disting. Publ. award Assn. Women in Psychology, 1994. Fellow APA (pres. Div. Psychology Women 1991-92). Democrat. Avocations: reading, travel, walking, motorcycling. Office: St Joseph Coll Office of Pres 1678 Asylum Ave West Hartford CT 06117-2791 Office Phone: 860-231-5221. Office Fax: 860-231-8396.

REID, ROBERT ALFRED, physician; b. Milan, June 8, 1939; BA in English Lit., U. Colo., 1961, MD, 1965. Intern U. Colo. Med. Ctr., 1965-66, resident, 1968-71; dir. med. affairs Santa Barbara Cottage Hosp., Calif., 1992—2009, med. staff cons. Calif., 2009—. Mem. AMA, Am. Coll. Ob-gyn., Calif. Med. Assn. (pres. 1998). Personal E-mail: rreid@gmail.com.

REID, ROBERT HARDEN, III, news correspondent, journalist; b. Asheville, NC, Apr. 22, 1947; s. Robert H. and Edith Elizabeth (Clanton) Reid; m. Jane Allen Mackey, Aug. 2, 1969; children: Amy Elizabeth, Brian Allen. AB in History, Davidson Coll., 1969. Domestic bur. newsman AP, NC, 1969—77, news editor Ctrl. Europe Bonn, Germany, 1977—82, bur. chief Cairo, 1982—85, roving Middle East corr., 1984—86, bur. chief Manila, 1986—95, chief corr. UN NYC, 1995—98, bur. chief Vienna, 1998—2001, European news editor Brussels, 2001, corr. at large Amman, Jordan, 2003—08, acting chief editor Baghdad, Iraq, bur. chief, 2008—. Author: Corazan Aquino and the Brushfire Revolution, 1995, (plays) Manny Manok, 1995. 1st lt. US Army, 1969—73. Recipient Gramling award for journalism excellence, AP, 2005. Office: AP 450 W 33rd St New York NY 10001

REID, ROBERT LELON, engineering educator, dean; b. Detroit, May 20, 1942; s. Lelon Reid and Verna Beulah (Custer) Menkes; m. Judy Elaine Nestell, July 21, 1962; children: Robert James, Bonnie Kay, Matthew Lelon. ASE, Mott C.C., Flint, Mich., 1961; BChemE, U. Mich., 1963; MME, So. Meth. U., 1966, PhDME, 1969. Registered profl. engr., Tenn., Tex., Wis. Asst. rsch. engr. Atlantic Richfield Co., Dallas, 1964-65; assoc. staff engr. Linde Divsn., Union Carbide Corp., Tonawanda, NY, 1966-68; from asst. to assoc. prof. U. Tenn., Knoxville, 1969-75; assoc. prof. Cleve. State U., 1975-77; from assoc. to full prof. U. Tenn., Knoxville, 1977-82; prof., chmn. U. Tex., El Paso, 1982-87; dean Coll. Engring., Marquette U., Milw., 1987-98, prof. mech. engring., 1998-2001; dean emeritus, 2001. Summer prof. NASA Marshall Space Ctr., Huntsville, Ala., 1970, EXXON Prodn. Rsch., Houston, 1972, 73, NASA Lewis Space Ctr., Cleve., 1986; cons. Oak Ridge Nat. Lab., 1974-75, TVA, 1978, 79, State of Calif., Sacramento, 1985, Tex. Higher Edn. Coordinating Bd., Austin, 1987. Contbr. articles 100 articles on heat transfer and solar energy. Grantee NSF, DOE, TVA, NASA, DOI, 1976-87; named Engr. of Yr. Engring. Socs. El Paso, 1986. Fellow ASME (Centennial medallion 1980, chmn. cryogenics com. 1977-81, chmn. solar energy divsn. 1983-84, chmn. Rio Grande sect. 1985-87, John Yellott award, 1997, Dedicated Svc. award 1998); mem. ASHRAE, Engrs. and Scientists Milw. (bd. dirs. 1988-93, v.p. 1989-90, pres. 1991-92), Wis. Assn. Rsch. Mgmt. (pres. 1996-97). Lutheran. Avocations: travel, classic car restoration. Business E-Mail: bobreid@umich.edu.

REID, ROBERT TILDEN, medical association administrator, internist; b. Dallas, Feb. 20, 1931; s. Robert Tilden and Gldays Tressy (King) R.; divorced; children: Robert Tilden, Richard Thomas, Annette Marie, Randolph Young. BS, So. Meth. U., Dallas, 1957; MD, U. Tex.-Southwestern, Dallas, 1959. Diplomate Am. Bd. Internal Medicine, Am. Bd. Rheumatology, Am. Bd. Allergy and Immunology. Intern Parkland Meml. Hosp., Dallas, 1959-60, resident, 1960-63; with Scripps Clinic and Rsch., La Jollla, Calif., 1963-70; pvt. practice La Jollla, Calif., 1970—; chief staff Scripps Meml. Hosp., La Jollla, Calif., 1976-78; scientific dir. Erik and Ese Banck Clinical Rsch. Ctr., San Diego, 1994—. Mem. San Diego County Med. Soc. (pres. 1991), Calif. Med. Assn. (trustee 1992-95). Office: 8716 Production Ave San Diego CA 92121 Home Phone: 858-481-2910; Office Phone: 858-271-0049. Personal E-mail: banckcrc@pacbell.net.

REID, ROSEMARY ANNE, insurance agent; b. Portland, Maine, June 15, 1951; d. Kenneth Bruce and Mary (Hollywood) R.; m. Ronald E. Walls, May 7, 1977 (div. Mar. 1986); children: Rachel A., Tate A. BS in Edn., U. South Maine, Portland, 1973. V.p. ins. Gruntal and Co., Inc., Portland, 1987-91; pvt. practice Portland, 1973—. Mem. Cape Elizabeth Town Coun., 1990, 95-99; mem. Cape Elizabeth Sch. Bd., 1991-94, fin. chair, 1992-93. Recipient 10 Yrs. Nat. Quality, 10 Yrs. Nat. Sale Achievement award, 1979-89, Nat. Assn. of Life Underwriters, 1974—, Am. Hometown Leadership award WalMart, 1998. Mem. Million Dollar Round Table (life and qualifying mem., Top of Table 1984, 86), South Maine Assn. Life Underwriters (bd. dirs. 1985-91, officer 1987-91, pres. 1989-90, regional v.p., pub. svc. chair, others), Life Underwriter Tng. Coun. (chair 1986-87), Maine Assn. Life Underwriters (bd. dirs. 1988-92, v.p. 1991-92, pres. elect 1992). Roman Catholic. Avocations: skiing, swimming, biking. Office: PO Box 927 Portland ME 04104-0927

REID, RUFUS LAMAR, jazz bassist, composer; b. Atlanta, Feb. 10, 1944; s. Alvin and Sylvia (Lindsey) R.; m. Doris Audrey Bangs; 1 child, Michel Matthew. Assoc. in Music, Olympic Coll., 1967-69; MusB, Northwestern U., 1969-71. Instr. No. Ill. U., Dekalb, 1973-76; prof. William Paterson U., Wayne, N.J., 1979-99. Dir. jazz studies and performance William Paterson U., Wayne, NJ, 1980-99; dir. jazz residency Carter G. Woodson Found., Paterson, NJ; panelist Nat. Found. for Advancement in the Arts, Miami, 1982-85; dir. Jazz for Teens program NJ Performing Arts Ctr., 1998—. Author: The Evolving Bassist, 1974 (internat. trilingual edition), Evolving Upward, 1977; rec. and touring artist with Stan Getz, Dexter Gordon, Thad Jones and Mel Lewis Orch., J.J. Johnson, Nancy Wilson, Freddie Hubbard, Jack DeJohnette, Eddie Harris, Kenny Burrell, others; albums include Perpetual Stroll, 1980, Seven Minds, 1984, Corridor to the Limits, 1989, Double Bass Delights, 1996, Intimacy of the Bass, 1999, The Gait Keeper, 2003, Linear Surroundings, 2003, The Rufus Reid Quintet Live at Kennedy Center, 2007, numerous others; co-leader (recs. with performing ensemble Tana Reid and drummer Akira Tana) Yours & Mine, 1991, Blue Motion, 1992, Passing Thoughts, 1994, Rumor, 1995, Looking Forward, 1996, Back to Front, 1998, (video) Michael Moore and Rufus Reid. Served to E-4 USAF, 1961—66. Recipient Disting. Achievement award, Internat. Soc. Bassists, 2001, Mellon Jazz Living Legacy award, MidAtlantic Arts Found., 2005, Sackler Commn. prize, 2006, ASCAP/Internat. Assn. Jazz Edn. Commn. for Established Jazz Composers, 2006; fellow NJ State Coun. Arts, 2006, John Simon Guggenheim Meml. Found., 2008. Mem. Internat. Assn. Jazz Educators (Humanitarian award, 1997, Jazz Educator Achievement award, 1998, NJ ch. Outstanding Educator, 1999). Avocation: model trains. Office: Rufus Reid PO Box 757 Teaneck NJ 07666-0757 also: Suzi Reynolds & Assocs LLC PH-A 2055 Center Ave Fort Lee NJ 07024 Office Phone: 201-947-0961. Office Fax: 201-947-0962.

REID, SUE TITUS, law educator; b. Bryan, Tex., Nov. 13, 1939; d. Andrew Jackson Jr. and Lorraine (Wylie) Titus. BS with honors, Tex. Woman's U., 1960; MA, U. Mo., 1962, PhD, 1965; JD, U. Iowa, 1972. Bar: Iowa 1972, U.S. Ct. Appeals (D.C. Cir.) 1978, U.S. Supreme Ct. 1978. From instr. to assoc. prof. sociology Cornell Coll., Mt. Vernon, Iowa, 1963-72; assoc. prof., chmn. dept. sociology Coe Coll., Cedar Rapids, Iowa, 1972-74; assoc. prof. law. U. Wash., Seattle, 1974-76; exec. assoc. Am. Sociol. Assn., Washington, 1976-77; prof. law U. Tulsa, 1978-88; dean, prof. Sch. Criminology, Fla. State U., Tallahassee, 1988-90; prof. pub. adminstrn. and policy Fla. State U., 1990—. Acting chmn. dept. sociology Cornell Coll., 1965-66; vis. assoc. prof. sociology U. Nebr., Lincoln, 1970; vis. disting. prof. law and sociology U. Tulsa, 1977-78, assoc. dean 1979-81; vis. prof. law U. San Diego, 1981-82; mem. People-to-People Crime Prevention Del. to People's Republic of China, 1982; George Beto Vis. Disting. Prof. criminal justice Sam Houston U., Huntsville, Tex., 1984-85; lecture/study tour of Criminal Justice systems of 10 European countries, 1985; cons. Evaluation Policy Rsch. Assocs., Inc., Milw., 1976-77, Nat. Inst. Corrections, Idaho Dept. Corrections, 1984, Am. Correctional Inst., Price-Waterhouse. Author (with others): Bibliographies on Role Methodology and Propositions Volume D - Studies in the Role of the Public School Teacher, 1962, The Correctional System: An Introduction, 1981, Crime and Criminology, 12th edit., 2009; author: Criminal Justice, 8th edit., 2008, Criminal Law, 7th edit., 2007, Criminal Law: The Essentials, 2009; editor (with David Lyon): Population Crisis: An Interdisciplinary Perspective, 1972; contbr. articles to profl. jours. Recipient Disting. Alumni award Tex. Woman's U., 1979; named One of Okla. Young Leaders of 80's Oklahoma Monthly, 1980. Mem. ABA, Am. Soc. Criminology, Acad. Criminal Justice Scis., Soc. Criminal Jus. Assn. Avocations: walking, reading, cooking, skiing. Office: Fla State Univ Askew Sch Pub Adminstrn & Policy Tallahassee FL 32306

REID, THOMAS F., mathematics professor; s. Aubra Mathew and Kathryn Faye Reid; m. Marcia Nance Reid, Aug. 27, 1994; children: Matthew Franklin, Laura Kathryn, Timothy Alexander. BS in Math., U. Okla., Norman, 1982; PhD, U. NC, Chapel Hill, 1997. Asst. prof. stats. Air Force Inst. Tech., Wright-Patterson AFB, Ohio, 1996—2002; asst. prof. math. U. SC., Aiken, 2002—. Maj. USAF, 1982—2002, Wright-Patterson. Office: Univ SC Aiken 471 Univ Pky Aiken SC 29801

REID, WILLIAM HILL, mathematics professor; b. Oakland, Calif., Sept. 10, 1926; s. William Macdonald and Edna Caroline (Hill) R.; m. Elizabeth Mary Kidner, May 26, 1962; 1 child, Margaret Frances. BS, U. Calif., Berkeley, 1949, MS, 1951; PhD, Cambridge U., Eng., 1955, ScD (hon.), 1968; AM (hon.), Brown U., 1961. Lectr. Johns Hopkins U., Balt., 1955-56; NSF fellow Yerkes Observatory, Williams Bay, Wis., 1957-58; asst. prof. Brown U., Providence, 1958-61, assoc. prof., 1961-63, U. Chgo., 1963-65, prof., 1965-89, prof. emeritus, 1989—; prof. Ind. U.-Purdue U., Indianapolis, 1989—2007. Cons. research labs. Gen. Motors Corp., Warren, Mich., 1960-73. Author (with P.G. Drazin): Hydrodynamic Stability, 1981; author: 2d edit., 2004; contbr. articles to profl. jours. Served with U.S. Mcht. Marine, 1945-47, with AUS, 1954-56. Fulbright Rsch. scholar, Australian Nat. U., 1964—65. Fellow Am. Phys. Soc., Cambridge Philos. Soc.; mem. Am. Math. Soc., Am. Meteorol. Soc., Sigma Xi. Home: 115 Lake of the Woods Ln #407 Jacksonville FL 32259 Business E-Mail: wreid@math.iupui.edu.

REID-CUNNINGHAM, JAMES, conservator; b. Chgo., May 18, 1953; s. Thomas Gavin and Carolyn Mary Reid; m. Maureen Reid-Cunningham, Jan. 4, 1975; children: Allison, Edward. BA, Johns Hopkins U., Balt., 1975; MA, Tufts U., Medford, Mass., 1982. Cert. profl. assoc. Am. Inst. Conservation of Hist. and Artistic Works, 2002. Conservator, Grad. Sch. Design Harvard U., Cambridge, Mass., 1984—2002; chief conservator Boston Athenaeum, 2003—. Pres. Guild of Book Workers, NYC, 2006—. Recipient Disting. Alumni award, North Bennet St. Sch., 2006. Mem.: New Eng. Conservation Assn., Miniature Book Soc. Home: 10 Harrington Rd Cambridge MA 02140 Office: Boston Athenaeum 10 1/2 Beacon St Boston MA 02108 Personal E-mail: james_reidcunningham@yahoo.com. Business E-Mail: reid-cunningham@bostonathenaeum.org.

REIDENBERG, JOEL R., academic administrator, law educator; AB in Govt., Dartmouth, 1983; JD, Columbia U., 1986; DEA, U. Paris-Sorbonne, 1987, Doctorat en droit, 2003. Bar: N.Y. 1986, D.C. 1988. Friedmann fellow PROMETHEE, Paris, 1986-87; assoc. Debevoise & Plimpton, Washington, 1987-90; prof. law Fordham U. Sch. Law, NYC, 1990—, founder Ctr. Law and Info. Policy, dir. grad. program, 1998—2001; assoc. v.p. academic affairs, assoc. chief academic officer Fordham U., 2008—. Cons. FTC, Washington, 1997-99; expert advisor European Commn., Luxembourg, 1993-96, Brussels, 1997-98, 2003-04. Co-author: Data Privacy Law, 1996, Online Services and Data Protection and Privacy: Regulatory Responses, 1998; contbr. articles to profl. jours. Mem. Assn. Am. Law Schs. (chair sect. law and computers 1997, chair sect. defamation and privacy 1998). Office: Ctr Law & Info Policy Fordham U Sch Law New York NY 10023 Office Phone: 212-636-6843. Fax: 212-636-6899. E-mail: jreidenberg@law.fordham.edu.

REIDENBERG, MARCUS MILTON, physician, educator; b. Phila., Jan. 3, 1934; m. June Wilson, July 14, 1957; children: Bruce, Joel, Julie. Student, Cornell U., 1951-54; MD, Temple U., 1958. Diplomate Am. Bd. Internal Medicine. Intern Community Gen. Hosp., Reading, Pa., 1958-59; resident Temple U. Hosp., Phila., 1962-65; from instr. to assoc. prof. Temple U. Med. Sch., Phila., 1962-75; assoc. prof. Cornell U. Med. Coll., NYC, 1975-76, prof. pharmacology, head div. clin. pharmacology, 1976—, prof. medicine, 1980—, prof. pub. health, 2002—, acting assoc. dean, 1981-82, asst. dean, 1988—; attending physician N.Y. Hosp., 1980—2006. Vis. physician Rockefeller U. Hosp., NYC, 1980—99; mem. project adv. group FDA, Rockville, Md., 1977-82; vice chmn. Joint Commn. on Prescription Drug Use, Washington, 1977-80; mem. study sect. NIH, Bethesda, Md., 1980-86; del. US Pharmacopeal Conv., 1975-80. Author: Renal Function and Drug Action, 1971; editor: various books, Clin. Pharmacology and Therapeutics, 1985—2001; contbr. articles to profl. jours. Served to lt. M.C., USNR, 1960-62. Recipient Research Career Devel. award NIH, 1970, Julius Sturmer award Phila. Coll. Pharmacy and Sci., 1982, Oscar B. Hunter award Am. Soc. Clin. Pharmacology and Therapeutics, 2008. Fellow ACP; mem. Am. Soc. Clin. Investigations, Assn. Am. Physicians, Am. Soc. Clin. Pharmacology and Therapeutics (pres. 1984-85, Rawls Palmer award 1981), Am. Soc. Pharmacology and Exptl. Therapeutics (award 1983, Harry Gold award 1999), Internat. Union Pharmacology (vice chmn. sect. clin. pharmacology 1984-87, chmn. 1987-89), World Health Organization Expert Com. on the Selection and Use of Essential Drugs (vice chmn. essential drugs com. 2003, 05, chmn. essential medicine com. 2007, 2009). Office: Cornell U Med Coll Dept Clin Pharmacology 1300 York Ave New York NY 10021-4805 Office Phone: 212-746-6227.

REIDER, VICTORIA A., state banking agency administrator; Grad. cum laude, Mercyhurst Coll.; JD, Dickinson Sch. Law. Bar: Pa. Supreme Ct., US Dist. Ct. (mid. dist. Pa.). With Pa. Commn. Crime and Delinquency; hearing examiner Pa. Dept. Revenue; exec. policy specialist, Gov.'s staff liaison to export-import bank US Gov.'s Office Policy Devel., Pa.; chief counsel, dep. chief counsel Pa. Ins. Dept.; ind. legal cons.; chief counsel Pa. Dept. Banking, 2004—06, acting sec., 2006—07, exec. dep. sec., 2007—. Chmn. Pa. Housing Fin. Agy., 2006—; exec. dep. sec. Banking and Spl. Asst. to Gov. for Fin. Svcs., 2006—. Mem.: ABA, Am. Corp. Counsel Assn., Pa. Bar Assn. Office: Pa Dept Banking 17 N Second St Ste 1300 Harrisburg PA 17101-2290 Office Phone: 717-783-2255. Office Fax: 717-787-8773. Business E-Mail: vareider@state.pa.us.

REIDINGER, MARTIN KARL, federal judge; b. New Haven, Conn., Dec. 18, 1958; BA, U. NC, 1981, JD with honors, 1984. Bar: NC 1984, US Dist. Ct. (wc. dist.) NC 1984, US Ct. Appeals (4th cir.) 1985, US Supreme Ct. 1994. Assoc. Adams Hendon Carson Crow & Saenger, PA, Asheville, NC, 1984—89, shareholder, 1989—2007; judge US Dist. Ct. (we. dist.) NC, 2007—. Mem.: NC Bar Assn., Buncombe County Bar Assn. (sec., treas. 1989—92, pres. 2003—04). Office: 110 US Courthouse Bldg 100 Otis St Asheville NC 28801 Office Phone: 828-771-7260.

REIDMILLER, DAVID R., atmospheric chemist; b. Rochester, NY, Nov. 15, 1979; s. Stephen G Reidmiller and Sylvia A Hagler. BA, Colgate U., Hamilton, NY, 2001; MS, U. Wash., Seattle, 2005. Rsch. technician Mass. Gen. Hosp., Boston, 2001—02; rsch. asst. grad. student U. Wash., Seattle, 2002—. Contbr. articles to profl. sci. jours. Interdisciplinary and Policy Dimensions Earth Sci. fellowship, U. Wash., 2007—08. Mem.: Union Concerned Scientists, Am. Meteorol. Soc., Am. Geophys. Union. Home: 3631 Densmore Ave N Seattle WA 98103 Office: Univ Wash Dept Atmospheric Sci Box 351640 Seattle WA 98195 Personal E-mail: david.reidmiller@gmail.com.

REIDY, CAROLYN KROLL, publishing executive; b. Washington, May 2, 1949; d. Henry August and Mildred Josephine (Mencke) Kroll; m. Stephen Kroll Reidy, Dec. 28, 1974. BA, Middlebury Coll., 1971; MA, Ind. U., 1974, PhD, 1982. Various positions to mgr. subs. rights Random House, Inc., NYC, 1975-83, assoc. pub., 1987-88; dir. subs. rights William Morrow & Co., NYC, 1983-85; v.p., assoc. pub. Vintage Books, NYC, 1985-87, pub., 1987-88, Anchor Books, Doubleday & Co., NYC, 1988; pres., pub. Avon Books, NYC, 1988-92; pres., pub. trade divsn. Simon & Schuster, Inc., NYC, 1992—2001, pres. adult publ. divsn., 2001—07, pres., CEO, 2007—. Bd. dirs. NAMES Project, 1994—98, Literacy Partners, Inc., 2000—, Nat. Book Found., 2001—. Mem.: NY Women in Comm. (recipient Matrix award 2003), Pubs. Lunch Club. Office: Simon & Schuster Inc 1230 Avenue Of The Americas New York NY 10020-1586 Business E-Mail: carolyn.reidy@simonandschuster.com.

REIDY, CHRISTOPHER R., computer company executive; BS in Acctg., St. Francis Coll., Loretto, Pa.; MBA, Harvard Bus. Sch. CPA. Formerly with Price Waterhouse; ptnr. Deloitte & Touche; CFO NBA Properties; pres., CFO bus. svcs. AT&T Corp., 2001—03, v.p., controller, chief acctg. officer, 2003—06; v.p., CFO Automatic Data Processing, Inc., Roseland, NJ, 2006—. Office: Automatic Data Processing Inc 1 ADP Way Roseland NJ 07068*

REIDY, DANIEL EDWARD, lawyer; b. Chgo., Nov. 21, 1949; s. Francis W. and Ann E. (Harrington) R.; m. Elizabeth Gamble, Aug. 21, 1971; children: David, Patrick, Kevin, Jean. BA in Polit. sci., cm laude, Loyola U., 1971; JD magna cum laude, U. Mich., 1974. Bar: Ill. 1974, US Dist. Ct. (no. Ill. dist.) 1974, Supreme Ct., Ill., 1974, US Ct. Appeals (7th cir.) 1975, US Ct. Appeals (11th cir.) 1992, US Ct. Appeals (fed. cir.) 1994, US Dist. Ct. (ctrl. dist.) Ill. 1995, US Dist. Ct. (so. dist.) Ill. 2002, US Ct. Appeals (1st cir.), 2004. Law clk. to Hon. Walter J. Cummings U.S. Ct. Appeals (7th cir.), Chgo., 1974-75; asst. US atty. US Atty.'s Office, Chgo., 1976—85; first asst. US atty. No. Dist. of Ill., Chgo., 1985—87; ptnr. Jones Day, Chgo., 1987—. Mem. commn. adminstrn. justice Ill., Chgo. Office Supreme Ct., Chgo., 1992-93. Fellow Internat. Acad. Trial Lawyers, Am. Coll. Trial Lawyers; mem. ABA, Chgo. Bar Assn.(sec. 2001-2005), Fed. Bar Assn., Chgo. Coun. Lawyers, Chgo. Inn Ct. Office: Jones Day 77 W Wacker Ste 3500 Chicago IL 60601-1692 Office Phone: 312-782-3939. Business E-Mail: dereidy@jonesday.com.

REIDY, THOMAS MICHAEL, financial executive; b. Elmira, NY, Dec. 22, 1951; s. Bernard Thomas and Betty Pauline Reidy; m. Rosemarie Stella, June 12, 1982; 1 child, Carla. AS, Corning C.C., 1971; BA, St. John Fisher Coll., 1973; Cert. in Exec. Leadership, Cornell U. Cert. fin. planner. Exec. br. dir. YMCA, Rochester, N.Y., 1975-84; fin. planner IDS/Am. Express, Rochester, 1984-86; pres., CEO TMR Adv. Group, Rochester, 1986-95; divsn. mgr. Waddall & Reed, Rochester, 1995-98; pres. Morgan & Alexander Ltd., Rochester, 1998—. Pres. CPA/Bus. Forum, Rochester, 1988—90; prin. Sandler Sales Inst., Pittsford, NY, 2002—. Author: (tng. manual) The NOW Client System, 1996, The True Wealth Revolution, 1999, Quality Life Management System, 1999, Winning and Losing It, 2005. Recipient Outstanding Young Man Am. Jaycees, 1979, Businessman of Yr. Nat. Rep. Congrl. Com., 2003. Mem. Rotary Club, C. of C. Profl. Sales Soc. (bd. dirs. 1988-89). Office Phone: 585-249-9189. Business E-Mail: tom@thomasreidy.com.

REIF, (FRANK) DAVID, artist, educator; b. Cin., Dec. 14, 1941; s. Carl A. and Rachel L. (Clifton) R.; m. Ilona Jekabsons, July 30, 1966; 1 child, Megan Elizabeth. BFA, Art Inst. Chgo., 1968; MFA, Yale U., 1970. Asst. prof. art U. Wyo., Laramie, 1970-74, assoc. prof., 1974-81, U. Mich., Ann Arbor, 1980-81; prof. U. Wyo., Laramie, 1981—2004, acting head dept. art, 1986—87, Disting. prof. emeritus, 2004—; prin., owner Reif Artworks & Design Consulting, Laramie, Wyo., 2005—. Selection cons. Ucross Found. Residency Program, Wyo., 1983—; exhibit juror Artwest Nat., Jackson, Wyo., 1986; panelist Colo. State U., Ft. Collins, 1981; lectr. U. Mich., 1980; apptd. Wyo. Arts Coun., 1993-96; vis. artist lectr. Colo. State U., 1996; vis. artist Colo. State U., Ft. Collins, 1996; 3-D juror, art exhbn. Colo. State Fair, Pueblo, 2001. One-man shows include U. Wyo. Art Mus., 1993, Dorsky Galleries, NYC, 1980, No. Ariz. U., 1977, 87, U. Mich., 1980-81, One West Ctr. Contemporary Art, Ft. Collins, 1991, West Wyo. C.C., Rock Springs, 1999, Casper Coll. Goldstein Gallery, 2003; exhibited in group shows at First, Second and Third Wyo. Biennial Tour, 1984-88, U.S. Olympics Art Exhbn., LA, 1984, Miss. Mus. Art and NEA Tour, 1981-83, LA Invitational Sculpture Tour Exhbn., 1991-92, Nicolaysen Art Mus., Casper, Wyo., 1994, Jackson Hole Ctr. Arts, Wyo., 2006, Gene Siskel Film Ctr. Gall, Art Inst. Chgo., 2006. Apptd. chair Wyo. Arts Coun., 1995-96. With USAR, 1963-69. Recipient F.D. Pardee award Yale U., 1970; Best Sculpture award Joslyn Art Mus. Omaha, 1978; grantee Nat. Endowment Arts, 1978-79, Wyo. Basic Rsch., 1983-84, 86-87; Tchg. Excellence grantee U. Wyo., 1996-97. Mem. Coll. Art Assn., Internat. Sculpture Ctr. Democrat. Home: 3340 Aspen Ln Laramie WY 82070-5702 Office: U Wyo Dept Art PO Box 3138 Laramie WY 82071-3138 Office Phone: 307-745-3110. Business E-Mail: dreif@uwyo.edu.

REIF, JOHN F., state supreme court justice; b. June 19, 1951; married. BA, U. Tulsa, Okla., 1973, JD, 1977. Faculty mem. Nat. Tribal Jud. Ctr., Nat. Jud. Coll., Reno; police officer City of Owasso, Okla., 1973—75; planner and grants specialist, law enforcement assistance adminstrn. Indian Nations Coun. Govt., 1974—77; asst. dist. atty. Tulsa County, 1978—81; spl. dist. judge Okla. 14th Jud. Dist., 1981—84; judge Okla. Ct. Civil Appeals, 1984—2002, vice chief judge, 1993, 2001, chief judge, 1994, 2002; justice Okla. Supreme Ct., 2007—. Bus. law adj. prof. Oral Roberts U., Tulsa, 1983—2007. Recipient Pres.'s Disting. Svc. award, Oral Roberts U., 1995. Mem.: Okla. Bar Assn. Office: Okla Supreme Ct State Capitol Bldg 2nd Fl Oklahoma City OK 73105*

REIF, JOHN HENRY, computer science educator; b. Madison, Wis., Aug. 4, 1951; s. Arnold and Jane (Chess) R.; m. Jane Anderson; children: Katie, Emily. BS in Applied Math. and Computer Sci., Tufts U., 1973; MS in Applied Math., Harvard U., 1975, PhD in Applied Math., 1977. Rsch. asst. Harvard U., Cambridge, Mass., 1975-77; rsch. assoc. U. Rochester, N.Y., 1977-78, asst. prof. computer sci. dept. N.Y., 1978-79, Harvard U., Cambridge, 1979-83, assoc. prof., 1983-86; A. Hollis Edens disting. prof. computer sci. Duke U., Durham, NC, 1986—; pres. RSIC, Inc., Durham, NC, 1987—, Eagle Eye, Inc., 1998—. Cons. IBM Watson Rsch. Inst., Yorktown Heights, N.Y., 1983-84, Thinking Machines, Inc., Cambridge, Mass., 1985—, NASA Goddard Space Flight Ctr., Geenbelt, Md., 1985—, Microelectronics Ctr. N.C., Research Triangle, 1986-88. Editor: VLSI Algorithms and Architectures, 1986, Synthesis of Parallel Algorithms, 1993, Algorithm Derivation and Transformation, 1993; patentee in field. Fellow IEEE, AAAS, Inst. of Combinatorics, Assn. for Computing Machinery; mem. Am. Math. Assn., Soc. for Indsl. and Applied Math. Office: Duke U Dept Computer Sci Box 90129 Durham NC 27708-0129

REIF, L. RAFAEL, academic administrator, engineering educator; m. Christine Reif; children: Jessica, Blake. BS, Universidad de Carabobo, Venezuela, 1973; MS, Stanford U., 1975, PhD, 1979. Asst. prof. Universidad Simon Bolivar, Caracas, Venezuela, 1973—74; faculty mem. MIT, Cambridge, 1980—, Maseeh Professor of Emerging Tech., dir. Microsystems Tech. Labs., 1990—99, assoc. head electrical engring., 1999—2004, head Dept. Electrical Engring. and Computer Sci., 2004—05, provost, 2005—. Recipient US Presdl. Young Investigator Award, 1984, Aristotle Award, Semiconductor Rsch. Corp., 2000. Fellow: IEEE; mem.: Am. Physical Soc., Electrochemical Soc., Tau Beta Pi. Office: MIT Rm 38-403 77 Massachusetts Ave Cambridge MA 02139-4307 Office Phone: 617-253-4601. E-mail: reif@mtl.mit.edu.

REIFENHEISER, THOMAS V., banker; b. Bayside, NY, Sept. 9, 1935; s. Thomas V. and Anna Reifenheiser; m. Marianne Bell, Feb. 3, 1968; children: Thomas V. III, Mary Katherine, Dorothy Elizabeth. Student, Notre Dame U., 1953-56; BBA, Hoftra U., 1958; MBA, Wharton U., 1962. Banker Chase Manhattan Bank, NYC, 1963; mng. dir., group exec. Global Media and Telecommunications Divsn. JP Morgan Chase (and predecessors), 1977—2000. Bd. dirs. Citadel Broadcasting Corp., Las Vegas, Nev., 2007—, Lamar Advertising Co., Mediacom Communications Corp., Cablevision Systems Corp. Trustee Mus. Moving Image, N.Y.C., 1986. Mem. Univ. Club (N.Y.C.), Tokeneke Club (Darien, Conn.).*

REIFF, JAMES STANLEY, osteopathic physician, addictions and psychiatric physician, surgeon; b. Mar. 17, 1935; s. Nathan Edgar and Freda Matilda (Imhoff) R.; m. Sharon Ann Kraybill, June 9, 1956 (div. April 1970); children: Gregory James, James Stanley II, Cynthia Diane, Jeffery Cameron. BA in Chemistry, Goshen Coll., 1957; DO, Chgo. Coll. Osteo Medicine, 1961. Biochemist Miles/Ames Pharm. Co., Elkhart, Ind., 1955-57; pvt. practice Mich. City, Ind., 1962-69; addictions physician Oaklawn Psychiat. Ctr., Elkhart, 1974-84; med. dir. Life Recovery Ctr., Elkhart, 1987-90, Substance Abuse Coun., St. Joe County, Mich., 1990-95, Am. Plasma Mgmt., Inc., various, Mich., Ind, 1991-97; mem. staff Cmty. Mental Health Svcs., St. Joe County, 1993-97; vol. svc. with Lakeland Prison, Mich. Dept. Corrections, 2001—. Bd. dirs. Home for Runaway Kids - Victory House, Elkhart, Ind., 1974-76, 12 Step House Meth. Ch.-Halfway House, Elkhart, 1974-77; bd. dirs., treas. Caldwell Home Corp.-Social Rehab. Ctr. for Alcoholism, Elkhart, 1984-87; bd. dirs. Hope House, Jonesville, Mich.; vol. Dept. Corrections, 2001—. Organist First Presbyn. Ch., Sturgis, Mich., 1993-97. Mem. AMA, Am. Osteopathic Assn., Am. Soc. Addiction Medicine (com. on addiction medicine in correctional facilities 1993—), Mich. State Med. Soc., St. Joe County Med. Soc. Avocation: piano. Home and Office: 28275 E Congress St Sturgis MI 49091-9181 Office Phone: 269-659-4706.

REIFF, PATRICIA HOFER, space physicist, educator; b. Oklahoma City, Mar. 14, 1950; d. William Henry and Maxine Ruth (Hoffer) R.; m. Thomas Westfall Hill, July 4, 1976; children: Andrea Hofer Hill, Adam Reiff Hill, Amelia Reiff Hill. Student, Wellesley Coll., 1967-68; BS, Okla. State U., 1971; MS, Rice U., 1974, PhD, 1975. Cert. secondary tchr., Okla., Tex. Resident rsch. assoc. Marshall Space Flight Ctr., Huntsville, Ala., 1975-76; rsch. assoc. space physics and astronomy dept. Rice U., Houston, 1975, asst. prof. space physics and astronomy dept., 1978-81, asst. chmn. space physics and astronomy dept., 1979-85, assoc. rsch. sci., 1981-87, sr. rsch. scientist, 1987-90. Adj. asst. prof. Rice U., 1976-78, disting. faculty fellow, 1990-92, prof. 1992—, chmn. dept. space physics and astronomy, 1996-99, dir. Rice Space Inst., 1999—; mem. sci. team Atmosphere Explorer Mission, Dynamics Explorer Mission; co-investigator Global Geospace Sci. Mission, ESA/Cluster Mission, IMAGE Mission, Men's Mission; prin. investigator The Public Connection NASA, Mus. Tchg. Planet Earth Immersive Earth; cons. Houston Mus. Natural Sci., 1986—; adv. com. on atmospheric scis. NSF, Washington, 1988-92; mem. stategic implementation study panel NASA, Washington, 1989-91; mem. space sci. adv. com. NASA, 1993-98, mem. space sta. utilization subcom., 1995-98; mem. adv. com. Los Alamos Non-Proliferation Divsn., 1998-2001; univ. rep. U. Space Rsch. Assn., Washington, 1993—, chair Coun. of Instns., 2001-04; exec. com. George Observatory, Houston, 1989-92, others. Designer Cockrell Sundial/Solar Telescope, 1989; editor EOS (sci. newspaper), 1986-89; contbr. articles to profl. jours. Trustee, Citizens' Environ. Coalition, Houston, 1978-98, pres. 1980-85, adv. com. 1998-2000; mem. air quality com. Houston/Galveston Area Coun., 1980-83, Green Ribbon Com., City of Houston, 1981-83; active coms. Macedonia United Meth. Ch., 1988—. Named rsch. fellow NAS/NRC., 1975, an Outstanding Young Women Am., 1977, '80, to Houston's Women on the Move, 1990; named Outstanding Aerospace Educator, Women in Aerospace, 1999; NASA grantee 1993-95, 98, 99, 2001-06; recipient NASA Group Achievement award. Fellow Am. Geophys. Union (fin. com. 1980-82, editor search com. 1992, pub. edn. com., Athelstan Spilhaus award, 2009.); mem. Cosmos Club, Wellesley Club, Internat. Union of Geodesy and Geophysics (del. 1975, 81, 83, 89, 91, 93, 95, chair working group 2F, 1991-95). Avocations: organic gardening, beef ranching, scouting. Office: Rice U Dept Physics and Astronomy 6100 S Main St Houston TX 77251 Business E-Mail: reiff@rice.edu.

REIFFEL, LEONARD, physicist, consultant; b. Chgo., Sept. 30, 1927; s. Carl and Sophie (Miller) R.; m. Judith Eve Blumenthal, 1952 (div. 1962); children— Evan Carl, David Lee; m. Nancy L. Jeffers, 1971. B.Sc., Ill. Inst. Tech., 1947, M.Sc., 1948, PhD, 1953. Physicist Perkin-Elmer Corp., Conn., 1948; engring. physicist U. Chgo. Inst. Nuclear Studies, 1948-49; with Ill. Inst. Tech. Research Inst., Chgo., 1949-65, dir. physics research, 1956-63, v.p., 1963-65; cons. to Apollo program NASA Hdqrs., 1965-70; pvt. practice cons., 1970—; tech. dir. manned space flight expts. bd. NASA, 1966-68; chmn. bd. Instructional Dynamics, Inc., 1966-81, Interand Corp., 1969-91, Telestrator Industries, Inc., 1970-73; sci. editor Sta. WBBM-CBS radio, Chgo.; sci. cons./commentator WBBM-TV, 1971-72; host Backyard Safari, 1971-73; sci. feature broadcaster WEEI-CBS radio, Boston, 1965-75; syndicated newspaper columnist World Book Ency. Sci. Service, Inc. (later Universal Sci. News, Inc.), 1966-72, Los Angeles Times Syndicate, 1972-76; sci. cons. CBS Network, 1967-71; chmn., CEO Exelar Corp., Chgo., 1991—; chmn. bd., pres., CEO Ameraine Corp, Chgo., 1992-95; bd. overseers Armour Coll., bd. advisors engring. depts. Ill. Inst. Tech., 1995—; founder, chmn. Luxelar Corp., 2001—; founder Exelar Med. Corp., 2004, chmn., chief tech. officer, 2004—; founder, chmn., chief tech. officer Iron Mount Corp., 2005—08; chief tech. officer CAPTR Corp., 2007—. Cons. Korean Govt. on establishment atomic energy rsch. program; mem. adv. com. isotope and radiation devel. AEC; com. rsch. reactors NAS, 1958-64; cons. U.S. Army, 1976—; chmn. Reiffel Technologies, LLC; mem. advanced tech. adv. com. Children's Meml. Rsch. Ctr. Chgo., 2005-07. Author: (book) The Contaminant, 1979; author numerous sci. papers; patentee in field. Bd. dirs. Student Competitions on Relevant Engring. Named Outstanding Young Man of Year Chgo. Jr. C. of C., 1954, 61; recipient Merit award Chgo. Tech. Socs., 1968, Peabody award, 1968, IR-100 award Telestrator CBS Chalkboard, 1970, award Aviation Writers Assn., 1971, IR-100 award, 1972, 73, 85, Disting. Alumni Achievement award Ill. Inst. Tech., 1974, Third Annual High Tech Entrepreneur award, 1986, Emmy award, 2004; named to Hall of Fame IIT, 1984. Fellow Am. Phys. Soc.; mem. AAAS, Chgo. Literary Club, Sigma Xi, Tau Beta Pi, Eta Kappa Nu. Achievements include being responsible for world's 1st indsl. nuclear reactor, 1956. Home: 602 W Deming Pl Chicago IL 60614-2618 Office Phone: 773-871-0171. Personal E-mail: lreiffel@gmail.com.

REIFLER, DAVID MARTIN, ophthalmologist; b. Columbus, Ohio, Japan, Aug. 30, 1952; s. Albert Herschel and Helen Lillian (Levin) Reifler; m. Karen Elizabeth Kettelhut, Mar. 4, 2001; m. Cathy Hoffman, Sept. 6, 1972 (div. Dec. 18, 1997); children: Aaron Nathaniel, Jonathan Adam, Elizabeth Yael. BS, U. Mich. Sch. Lit. Sci. and the Arts, Ann Arbor, 1974; MD, U. Mich. Med. Sch., Ann Arbor, 1978. Diplomate Nat. Bd. Med. Examiners, 1979, Am. Bd. Ophthalmology, 1983. Clin. prof. ophthalmology Mich. State U. Coll. Human Medicine, Grand Rapids, Mich., 1989—. Pres. Am. Soc. Ophthalmic Plastic and Reconstructive Surgery, Altamonte Springs, Fla., 2004. Contbr. articles to profl. jours., chapters to books. Mem. Thornapple Valley Lions Club, Ada and Cascade Twps., Mich.; pres. Congregation Ahavas Israel, Grand Rapids, 2008—; officer; med. adv. bd. American-Israeli Ophthal. Soc., NYC, 1986—96; mem. Jewish Fedn. Grand Rapids, 1992—2008. Recipient Disting. Svc. award, Am.-Israeli Ophthal. Soc., 1992. Fellow: ACS, Am. Acad. Ophthalmology (Hon. award 1996, Secretariat award 2005, 1996); mem.: Mich. State Med. Soc. (Disting. Leadership award 2004), Cogan Ophthalmic History Soc., AMA, Galens Hon. Med. Soc., U.

Mich. Jewish. Home: 7474 Cascade Rd SE Grand Rapids MI 49546 Office: David M Reifler MD FACS 1000 East Paris Ave SE St 221 Grand Rapids MI 49546 Business E-Mail: david@davidreifler.com.

REIFLER, STEWART, lawyer; b. Poughkeepsie, NY, May 5, 1954; s. Aaron and Sally Reifler; m. Sheryl Louise Perry, Sept. 19, 1982; 1 child, Jonathan Perry. Student, McGill U., 1972—75; BA, Bard Coll., 1979; JD magna cum laude, NY Law Sch., 1992. Bar: N.Y. 1992, Conn. 1992, U.S. Tax Ct. 1992, U.S. Supreme Ct. 2004. Assoc. Law Offices of Joseph E. Bachelder, NYC, 1992—95, Weil, Gotshal & Manges, 1995—98; dir. PricewaterhouseCoopers, 1998—2001; ptnr., shareholder, head N.Y. exec. compensation group Vedder, Price, Kaufman & Kammholz, 2001—. Steering com. mem., exec. compensation AICPA. Co-author: Compensation Committee Handbook, 2d edit., 2004; contbr. articles to profl. jours. Trustee Westport Pub. Libr., Conn. Recipient Outstanding Editl. Contbn., NY Law Sch. Law Rev., 1991, Law Rev., NY Law Sch., Am. Jurisprudence award, 1991. Mem.: ABA, N.Y. State Bar Assn., Conn. State Bar Assn., Assn. of Bar City of N.Y., WorldatWork, Nat. Assn. Stock Plan Profls., Rockefeller Club, Minuteman Yacht Club, Penn Club. Home: 8 Brightfield Ln Westport CT 06880 Office: Vedder Price Kaufman & Kammholz 1633 Broadway New York NY 10019 E-mail: sreifler@vedderprice.com.

REIFSNIDER, KENNETH LEONARD, metallurgist, educator; b. Balt., Feb. 19, 1940; s. David Leonard and Daisy Pearl (Hess) R.; m. Loretta Lieb, June 15, 1963; children: Eric Scott, Jason Miles. BA, Western Md. Coll., 1963; BS in Engring., Johns Hopkins U., 1963, MS in Engring., 1965, PhD, 1968. Jr. instr. Johns Hopkins U., Balt., 1966-67; asst. prof. Va. Poly Inst. and State U., Blacksburg, 1968-72, chmn. materials engring. sci. Ph.D. program, 1974-92, assoc. prof., 1972-75, prof., 1975-83, Reynolds Metals prof. engring. sci. and mechanics, 1983-90, Alexander Giacco prof., 1990—2002; chmn. adminstrn. bd. Ctr. Composite Materials and Structures, 1984, 1994-97; Pratt and Whitney Chair prof. design and reliability U. Conn., 2002—; dir. Conn. Global Fuel Cell Ctr., Storrs. Dir. Va. Inst. for Material Systems, 1988-2001, Conn. Global Fuel Cell Ctr., 2004-, assoc. provost for interdisciplinary programs, 1996-2001; engr. Lawrence Livermore Nat. Lab., 1981; mem. Nat. M aterials Adv. Bd., 1996—; cons. in materials sci. NATO, 1969, 75. Editor in chief Internat. Jour. of Fatigue; assoc editor Internat. Jour. of Fuel Cell Science and Technology, 2003-; editor, co-editor, author books, book chpts, articles for profl. publs. Mem. troop 44 com. Boy Scouts Am., Blacksburg, Va. Recipient Va. Acad. Sci. J. Shelton Horsley award, 1978, Va. Poly Inst. Alumni award, 1982, Disting. Rsch. award Am. Soc. Composites, 1992. Fellow ASTM (founder Jour. of Composites Tech. and Rsch., vice chmn. standing com. on publs., award of merit 1982); mem. ASME, NAE, Coun. on Engring. Office: Conn Global Fuel Cell Ctr 44 Weaver Rd, Unit 5233 Storrs Mansfield CT 06269-5233 also: 262 United Technologies Bldg 191 Auditorium Rd, Unit 3139 Storrs Mansfield CT 06269-3139 Home: 5 Airy Hall Ct Columbia SC 29209-0801 Office Phone: 860-486-5360, 860-486-3139. Office Fax: 860-486-8378, 860-486-5088. E-mail: reifsnid@engr.uconn.edu.

REIG, JUNE WILSON, writer director and producer; b. Schenectady, NY, June 1, 1933; d. Wallace John and Lillian Lucy (Gay) Wilson; m. Robert Maxwell, Nov. 26, 1969. BA summa cum laude, N.Y. State U., 1954; MA in Dramatic Arts, NYU, 1962. Instr. NYU, NYC, 1962—67; prodr., dir. NYU Theater, NYC, 1963—67; dir.-prodr., writer news and pub. affairs NBC TV Network, NYC, 1963—67, dir., writer, prodr. divsn. entertainment, 1967—73; pres. Bunny/Chord Prodns., NYC, 1972—97. Author: (book) Dairy of the Boy King Tut-Ankh-Amen, Charles Scribner's Sons, 1978; writer: (music spl.) The Heart of Christmas with Skitch Henderson, Robert Shaw Chorale and NBC Symphony, 1965; An Afternoon at Tanglewood with Erich Leinsdorf and the Boston Symphony Orch. (Peabody award); writer, dir. (with Johnny Carson) (TV spl.) Stuart Little, 1966 (Peabody award, Prix Jeunesse); writer with Burr Tillstorm, Kukla, Fran & Ollie The Reluctant Dragon, 1968 (Brotherhood award); writer, dir., prodr. (with Burl Ives) Rabbit Hill, 1966 (ALA award); writer, dir., prodr. Bill Cosby As I See It, 1970 (Ohio State award); A Day with Bill Cosby, 1971; Jennifer & Me, 1972; prodr., writer (with Edward Villella and Joanne Woodward) Little Women, the ballet, 1976; creative cons. dir. (with Orson Welles) Tut, the Boy King, 1978 (Peabody award); writer, dir., prodr.: (TV series) Watch Your Child - The Me Too Show, 1973 (Action for Children's TV Achievement award); films in permanent collections Mus. Broadcasting, N.Y.C. With Nat. Conf. Christians & Jews. Recipient Christopher award; nominee Emmy award, 1966, 1976. Mem.: NATAS, Dirs. Guild Am., Writers Guild Am., Audubon Soc., NYU Alumni Assn., Internat. Soc. Animal Rights, Friends of Animals, Alan Devoe Bird Club (Old Chatham, N.Y.). Avocations: photography, music, animals. Office: Resnick Druckman Group LLC 469 Seventh Ave Ste 1300 New York NY 10018 *Whether I am working on a teleplay or book, I write about things I believe children are interested in: feelings, aspirations, caring, animals, loving. As I see it, too much of the fare for young people gives them a distorted view of how much violence there is in the world, and I want to counteract that impression. I want to write about things that create a sense of worth, warm security, and an absence of unnecessary anxiety. When I do write about the darker things that happen in life, it is to help the young person understand himself and the world a little better.*

REIGEL, MARISSA M., research and development company executive; b. Vail, Colo., May 29, 1983; d. Craig and Narda Reigel. Degree in Metall. and Materials Engring., Colo. Sch. Mines, Golden, Colo., 2005, PhD student, 2005—. Cert. in fundamentals engring., Colo., 2005. Mgr. differential thermal analysis lab. Colo. Sch. Mines, 2005—. Mem.: AIST, ACERS, TMS, ASM, Am. Nuc. Soc. Achievements include patents pending for use of auto-ignition combustion synthesis to produce ceramic powders. Personal E-mail: mreigel@gmail.com.

REIGER, JOHN FRANKLIN, history educator, researcher; b. Augusta, Ga., June 10, 1943; s. Anthony Cutte and Sally Elton (Dance) Reiger; m. Andrea Gladys (Becker), Dec. 26, 1970; children— Caren Dance, Christopher John. BA, Duke U., Durham, NC, 1965; MA, U. Fla., Gainesville, 1966; PhD, Northwestern U., Ill., 1970. Prof. history U. Miami, Coral Gables, Fla., 1970-82, asst. prof., 1970-75, assoc. prof., 1975-80, prof., 1980-82; exec. dir. Conn. Audubon Soc., Fairfield, 1983-88; asst. prof. history Ohio U., Chillicothe, 1988-91, assoc. prof., 1991-94, prof., 1994—. Author: American Sportsmen and the Origins of Conservation, 1975, 86, 01 (award from The Wildlife Soc. 1976), Gifford Pinchot with Rod and Reel, Trading Places: From Historian to Environmental Activist: Two Essays in Conservation History, 1994; editor: The Passing of the Great West, Selected Papers of George Bird Grinnell, 1972, 76, 85. Am. Philos. Soc. grantee 1977, 81; Contbr. articles to profl. jours.; chapter to books. mem. Am. Soc. Environ. History Profl. Assn., N.Am. Soc. Sport History Profl. Assn., Fla. Anthrop. Soc. Profl. Assn. Avocations: fishing, hunting, archeology, birding. Office: Ohio Univ Chillicothe 101 University Dr Chillicothe OH 45601-0629

REIJO PERA, RENEE A., reproductive science director, educator; BS in Biology, U. Wis., 1983; PhD in Molecular and Cell Biology, Cornell U., 1993. Damon-Runyan/Walter Winchell postdoctoral fellow Whitehead Inst. for Biomedical Rsch. Lab., 1993—97; instr., human genetics, dept. biology MIT, 1995; asst. prof. in residence, dept. ob-gyn. & reproductive scis., physiology & urology, programs in human & cancer genetics, develop. & stem cell biology U. Calif., San Francisco, 1997—2003, assoc. prof. in residence dept. ob-gyn. & reproductive scis., physiology & urology, programs in human & cancer genetics, develop. & stem cell biology, 2003—, co-dir., program in human stem cell biology, 2004—, assoc. dir., Ctr. for Reproductive Scis., 2004—. Invited participant, chair German Am. Frontiers of Sci., NAS, 2000—03. Contbr. several articles to profl. jours. Scholar Searle Found., 1998—2001; DuPont Tchg. Fellow, 1989, US Army Biotechnology Grad. Fellowship, 1991—93. Office: U Calif Dept Obstetrics Gynecology & Reproductive Sciences 513 Parnassus Ave Rm HSE 1634 Box 0556 San Francisco CA 94143-0556 Office Phone: 415-476-3178. Office Fax: 415-476-3121. Business E-Mail: reijoperar@obgyn.ucsf.edu.*

REILEY, T(HOMAS) PHILLIP, consultant; b. Ft. Lewis, Wash., May 5, 1950; s. Thomas Phillip and Anne Marie (Russick) R. BSc in Biophysics, Pa. State U., 1973; postgrad. in Bus. Adminstrn., Rutgers U.; MBA, NYU, 1991. Cert. prodn. and inventory mgmt., cert. integrated resource mgmt. Inventory supr. Leland Tube Co., South Plainfield, NJ, 1973-76; prodn. inventory control supr. Bomar Crystal Co., Middlesex, NJ, 1976-79; prodn. control mgr. Codi Semiconductor Inc., Linden, NJ, 1979-81; mfg. systems analyst Western Union Info. Systems, Mahwah, NJ, 1981-85; bus. analyst Nabisco Brands Biscuit Divsn., Parsippany, NJ, 1985-91, sr. systems analyst, 1991-94, tech. advisor, 1994-97; applications cons. SAP Am., Newton Square, Pa., 1997—. Mem. Am. Prodn. and Inventory Control Soc. (past chmn. ednl. com. Raritan Valley chpt.), NY Acad. Scis., Coun. Logistics Mgmt., Am. Inst. Mgmt. Accts., Mensa. Republican. Home: 1308 Centennial Ave #111 Piscataway NJ 08854 Office: 3999 West Chester Pike Newtown Square PA 19073 Office Phone: 610-661-7603. Business E-Mail: phillip.reiley@sap.com, preiley@world.std.com, philip.reiley@sap.com.

REILLEY, JAMES CLARK, artist, cartoonist, retired small business owner; b. Detroit, Nov. 4, 1919; s. James Aloyisus and Lillian May (Cole) R.; m. Beatrice C. Clemente, May 10, 1952 (dec.); children: James A. (dec.), Anthony Francis, Beatrice Anita. Grad., Art Inst. of Pitts., 1948. Artist Banner Advt., Phila., 1948-49; layout artist Lit Bros. Dept. Store, Phila., 1949; comic book illustrator John Prentice, LI, 1950; artist DuPont Co., Wilmington, Del., 1950-59; artist/owner Jim Reilley Studio, Wilmington, 1959-94; ret. Link trainer instr.; jazz harmonica soloist various radio programs and shows, Chanutefield, Ill., Walla Walla, Wash.; instrument flying instr., art editor, cartoonist Air Force Publs. "Thunderbird While Stationed At Rapid City S.D. Air Base". Cartoon series, This is the Life, Hornepipe. Sgt. WWIIVET-USAAF, 1942-45. Inducted to Penns Grove H.S. Personal Achievement Hall of Fame, 1996. Roman Catholic. Avocations: fishing, music, sports. Home: 110 N Broad St Penns Grove NJ 08069-1269 Home Phone: 856-299-1640.

REILLY, ANNE HUEDEPOHL, university educator, researcher; b. Chgo., Sept. 16, 1957; d. E. Bradley and Lynne (Swanson) Huedepohl; m. John J. Reilly, Aug. 12, 1978; children: Kristine Anne, Meghan Lynne, Caroline Hannah. BA in Econs. and Bus. Adminstrn. summa cum laude, Knox Coll., 1978; MBA in Finance, U. Iowa, 1980; PhD in Organizational Behavior, Northwestern U., 1989. Banking officer spl. industries Cont. Ill. Nat. Bank, Chgo., 1980-82; asst. v.p. corp. banking Lloyds Bank Internat., Chgo., 1983-84; lectr. bus. adminstrn. U. Iowa, 1979-80; teaching asst. Northwestern U., Evanston, 1987; asst. prof. mgmt. Loyola U., Chgo., 1988-95, assoc. prof. mgmt., 1995—2000, prof. mgmt., 2000—; faculty mentor Loyala U., 2007—; site visit team NSF Advance Program, 2006—. Presented numerous papers in field; contbr. articles to profl. jours. including Jour. Orgnl. Behavior, Acad. Mgmt. Jour., Sloan Mgmt. Rev., Orgn. Sci., Indsl. Crisis Quar., Jour. Mgmt. Studies, Jour. Vocat. Behavior, Jour. Mgmt. Edn., Strategic Mgmt. Jour., Jour. Advance Developing Human Resource, Jour. Family Business Casebook; book and textbook reviewer. Trustee Knox Coll., Galesburg, Ill., 2000—06. Rsch. grantee Northwestern U. Banking Rsch. Ctr., 1987, 88, Nat. Ctr. for Mgmt. R&D, Can., 1989-90, Employee Relocation Coun., 1989-90, Loyola U. Summer Rsch., 1990, Abbott Labs., 1997-99, Loyola U. Family Bus. Ctr., 2006. Mem. Acad. Mgmt., Orgnl. Behavior Teaching Soc., Phi Beta Kappa, Beta Gamma Sigma, Phi Beta Delta. Democrat. Lutheran. Avocations: travel, reading, swimming. Office: Loyola U Chgo 820 N Michigan Ave Chicago IL 60611-2147 Home Phone: 847-835-2946; Office Phone: 312-915-6537. Business E-Mail: areilly@luc.edu.

REILLY, BRENDAN, alderman; s. Brendan and Janice. Grad., Hobart Coll, Geneva, NY, 1994. Former staff mem. Ill. House of Reps., Springfield; former comm. dir. Ill. House Democrats; press sec. & comm. dir. Paul Vallas Gubernatorial Campaign, 2002; v.p. pub. affairs, Midwest AT&T, 2002; alderman, 42d ward Chgo. City Coun., 2007—. Office: 311 W Superior Ste 212 Chicago IL 60654 also: City Hall 121 N Lasalle St Rm 300 Chicago IL 60602 Office Phone: 312-642-4242, 312-744-3062. Office Fax: 312-642-0420. E-mail: office@ward42chicago.com.*

REILLY, CHRISTINE L., finance company executive; d. Philip J. Reilly; 3 children. MBA, NYU Stern Sch. Bus., NYC. CPA. Accountant Arthur Andersen LLP, NYC; joined CIT Group, Inc., 1994, CFO consumer fin., v.p. ops.-inventory, exec. v.p., chief audit officer, exec. v.p. corp. mergers & acquisitions, pres. CIT Small Bus. Lending Corp., 2006—. Co-chair CIT Women's Leadership Coun. Bd. dirs., northern NJ chpt. Am. Red Cross. Named one of Best 50 Women in Bus., NJBiz, 2007, Top 25 Nonbank Women in Fin., US Banker, 2008. Mem.: Fin. Women's Assn., Com. of 200, Nat. Small Bus. Assn., Nat. Assn. Govt. Guaranteed Lenders. Office: CIT Small Bus Lending Corp Nat Ops Ctr 1 CIT Dr Livingston NJ 07039*

REILLY, DANIEL PATRICK, bishop emeritus; b. Providence, May 12, 1928; s. Francis E. and Mary (Burns) Reilly. Attended, Our Lady of Providence Sem., 1943—48, Grand Seminaire, St. Brieuc, France, 1948—53, Harvard U., 1954—55, Boston Coll., 1955—56; D (hon.), Providence Coll., St. Michael's Coll., Holy Apostles Coll. and Sem., Salve Regina Coll., Our Lady of Providence Coll., Sacred Heart U., Assumption Coll., 1995, Anna Maria Coll., 1995, Holy Cross Coll., 1996. Ordained priest Diocese of Providence, 1953, asst. chancellor, 1954—56, sec. to bishop, 1956—64, became monsignor, 1964, chancellor, 1964—72, adminstr., 1971—72, vicar gen., 1972—75; asst. pastor Cathedral Saints Peter and Paul, Providence, 1953—54; ordained bishop, 1975; bishop Norwich, Conn., 1975—94; Conn. state chaplain K.C., 1976—94; Episcopal moderator Nat. Cath. Cemetery Corp., 1977—87; bishop Diocese of Worcester, Mass., 1994—2004, bishop emeritus, 2004—. Ad hoc mem. to aid ch. in Ea. Europe, adminstrv. com. mem. NCCB/US Cath. Conf., 1976—86, 1992—; pro-life com. mem. NCCB, 1989—92, chmn. 10th anniversary peace pastoral com., 1992—93, chmn. internat. policy com., 1993; mem. Priestly Life and Ministry Commn., 1991—94; past pres. New Eng. Consultation Ch. Leaders; drafting com. mem. U.S. Cath. Conf. Pastoral Letter on Peace, 1983, mem. com. on coms.; active Holy See Pontifical Coun.-Cor Unum, 1984—89. Trustee Cath. Mut. Relief Soc., Omaha, 1979—, St. John's Sem., Brighton, Mass., 1987—, Am. Coll., Louvain, Belgium, St. Mary's Sem., Balt.; chmn. bd. Cath. Relief Svcs. Cath. Relief Svcs., 1978—86; mem. fin. and budget com. U.S. Cath. Conf. U.S. Cath. Conf., 1985—87; chancellor Holy Apostles Coll. and Sem., Cromwell, Conn., 1982—94; pres. Conn. Interfaith Housing, 1975—94; cons. Pontifical Coun. Justice and Peace, 1995; bd. dirs. United Way Southeastern Conn., 1976—94, Conn. Drug and Adv. Coun., 1978—80. Mem.: KC (RI state chaplain 1964—75), Rotary. Roman Catholic. Office: St Paul Cathedral Rectory 38 High St Worcester MA 01609 Office Phone: 508-799-4193, 508-799-0999. Personal E-mail: vocdir@aol.com. Business E-Mail: dreilly@worcesterdiocese.org. *If you would make a true success of your life for time and for eternity, never forget that it will be achieved by your willingness to make countless efforts that will be known only to God.*

REILLY, DAVID HENRY, retired university dean; b. Paterson, NJ, Nov. 7, 1936; s. David Henry and Ethel Taylor (Alt) R.; m. Jean Lockwood, July 2, 1960; children— David Scott, Chris Robert, Sandra Jean. BA, U. Vt., 1959; Ed.M., Rutgers U., 1962, Ed.D., 1965. Diplomate: Am. Bd. Profl. Psychology. Remedial reading instr. Drake Sch. of N.J. Neuro-Psychiat. Inst., Princeton, 1959-62, jr. fellow psychol. services at inst., summer 1962-63; research asst. N.J. Bur. Research Neurology and Psychiatry; also sch. psychologist Woodbridge (N.J.) sch. system, 1962-63; clin. psychologist, then research asso. N.J. Bur. Research Neurology and Psychiatry, 1963-64, 65; sch. and research psychologist Woodbridge sch. system, 1964-65; post doctoral fellow clin. child psychology Devereux Found., Devon, Pa., 1965-66; mem. faculty U. N.C., Chapel Hill, 1966-74, prof. psychology, 1974—, chmn. dept. sch. psychology program, 1966-74; dean U. N.C. (Sch. Edn.), Greensboro, 1974-86; dean Coll. of Grad. and Profl. Studies The Citadel, Charleston, 1992—. Mem. N.C. Bd. Examiners Practicing Psychologists, 1973—, treas., 1975, chmn., 1976, Cons. Tbilist State U., Georgia, 2007- Contbr. articles to profl. jours. Research grantee NIMH, 1963; Fulbright Vis. scholar Republic of Cyprus, 1986-87, USSR, 1990. Fellow APA; mem. Am. Acad. Sch. Psychology (pres.-elect 1996-97, pres. 1997-98), Southeastern Psychol. Assn., N.C. Psychol. Assn. (pres. 1980-81), N.C. Assn. Coll. Tchr. Edn. (pres. 1981), N.C. Sch. Psychology Assn. (pres. 1976-77), S.C. Grad. Deans Assn. (pres. 1998-99). Home: 3311-Seven Lakes W Seven Lakes NC 27376 Personal E-mail: skipreilly@aol.com.

REILLY, DAVID N. (NICK REILLY), automotive executive; b. Wales, 1949; Diploma, U. Cambridge, 1971. Gen. ops. mgr. GM Svc. Parts Ops., 1984—86, dir. mfg., 1986—87; v.p. ops. GM, Isuzu, IBC, Luton, England, 1987—90; dir. mfg. Vauxhall Port Plant, Ellesmere, 1990—94; v.p. GM Europe, Zurich, Switzerland, 1994—96; chmn. mng. dir. Vauxhall Motors, 1996—2001; v.p. GM Corp., 1997—, pres. GM Asia Pacific, 2006—; v.p. sales, mktg. GM Europe, 2001—02; pres., CEO GE Daewoo Auto and Tech. Co., Republic of Korea, 2002—06. Mem. Asia Pacific Strategy Bd. GM. Recipient Cmdr. Order British Empire, 2000. Mem.: Soc. Motor Mfgs. and Traders (pres. 2001—02). Office: GM Corp PO Box 33170 Detroit MI 48232-5170*

REILLY, DINAH, physical therapist; b. Stillwater, Okla., Mar. 23, 1949; d. James Everett and Pat Ruth White; m. John Reilly, June 22, 1974; children: Blaine Colin, Timothy Ray. BS, U. Colo., Boulder, 1971; PhD in Human Physiology, U. Oreg., Eugene, 2005. Cert. in phys. therapy Colo., 1971. Phys. therapist Grand Junciton Regional Ctr., Colo., 1982—87, Boise Sch. Dist., Idaho, 1989—. Phys. therapist Sports Medicine and Fitness Ctr., Grand Junction, 1980—82. Contbr. scientific papers, chapters to books. Mem. Idaho Peace Coalition, Boise, Idaho, 2004—04. Mem.: Pediatric Interest Group Boise, Idaho. Personal E-mail: dinahreilly@cableone.net.

REILLY, EDWARD ARTHUR, lawyer; b. NYC, Dec. 17, 1943; s. Edward Arthur and Anna Marguerite (Sautter) R.; children: M. Teresa, Edward A. AB, Princeton U., 1965; JD, Duke U., 1968. Bar: NY 1969, NC 1971, Fla. 1979, Conn. 1983. Asst. dean law sch. Duke U., 1970-72; assoc. Shearman & Sterling, NYC, 1972-80, ptnr., 1980-87, Harlow, Reilly, Derr & Stark, Rsch. Triangle Park, NC, 1988-90; counsel Morris & McVeigh, NYC, 1991-93, ptnr., 1993—2007; pvt. practice, 2007—. Pres. Am. Friends Paris Opera Ballet, Inc.; sec. Camille and Henry Dreyfus Found., Inc.; sec. Owen Cheatham Found. Decorated Knight of Order of Arts and Letters, French Govt.-Ministry of Culture and Comm., 1992. Fellow Am. Coll. Trust & Estate Counsel; mem. NY State Bar Assn., Fla. Bar Assn., Conn. Bar Assn. Episcopalian. Home: 5 Old Field Pl Norwalk CT 06853-1116

REILLY, EDWARD FRANCIS, JR., commissioner, former state senator; b. Leavenworth, Kans., Mar. 24, 1937; s. Edward F. and Marian C. (Sullivan) R. BA, U. Kans., 1961. V.P. Reilly & Sons, Inc., Leavenworth, 1967-92; pres. Yllier Lake Estates, Inc., Easton, Kans., 1965-89; mem. Kans. House Reps., 1963-64, Kans. State Senate, 1964-92, asst. majority leader, 1977-80, vice-chmn. govtl. orgn., chmn. ins. subcom., chmn. fed. and state affairs com.; mem. US Parole Commn., US Dept. Justice, 1992—, chmn., 1992—97, 2001—09. Commr. Nat. Commn. on Accreditation of Law Enforcement Agys., 1982-96; adv. mem. Am. Justice Inst. fed. and state prisons; mem. cmty. liaison com. U.S. Penitentiary Lansing, Kans. Commr. ex officio U.S. Sentencing Commn., Washington; del. to Rep. Nat. Conv., Miami Beach, Fla., 1968; chmn. Leavenworth County Radio Free Europe Fund, 1972; bd. dirs. St. John's Hosp., Leavenworth, 1970-79, sec.; bd. dirs. Leavenworth Assn. for Handicapped, 1968-69, ARC, Leavenworth chpt., Kans. Blue Cross/Blue Shield, 1969-72; apptd. by Pres. Reagan Nat. Hwy. Safety Adv. Com.; active Trinity Nat. Leadership Roundtable, Cath. Campaign Am., Kans. Adv. Bd. Juvenile Offenders, Nat. Com. Cmty. Corrections, bd. trustees, Am. U. Rome, adv. bd. mem. Sch. Philosophy Cath. U. Recipient Cmty. Leaders of Am., 1971, 85, 86, Hallpac Pub. Svc. award, 1988, Am. Police Hall of Fame award, 1990, Good Samaritan award Order of Michael the Arch Angel Police Legion, 1990, Commendation award mayor and city commn. of Leavenworth, Kans., 1990, Carnegie Hero Fund Commn. award and medallion, 1991, Silver Angel award Kans. Cath. Conf., 1992; named Outstanding Young Men Am., 1965-76. Mem. Nat. Criminal Justice Assn., Nat. Inst. Corrections (adv. bd.), Advisory Bd., Dept. of Philosophy, Catholic Univ. of America, Am. Paroling Authorities Internat., Am. Correctional Assn., Am. Probation and Paroling Assn., Leavenworth C. of C. (hon. dir. 1970-73), No. Assn. Chiefs Police, Assn. U.S. Army (Henry Leavenworth award 1960), Kansas City (Kans.) C. of C., Leavenworth Hist. Soc. (dir. 1968-73), John Carroll Soc., Native Sons of Kansas City, Ancient Order of Hibernians, U.S. Supreme Ct. Hist. Soc., Kiwanis (dir. 1969-70, Connelly award 1991, Legion of Honor award 1996), K.C., Elks, Eagles, Order of Malta, Equestrian Order Holy Sepulchre Jerusalem, Sacred Military Constantinian Order of Saint George, Heritage

Found., Am. Soc. Italian Legion Merit Republican. Roman Catholic. Office: US Parole Commission 5550 Friendship Blvd Ste 420 Chevy Chase MD 20815-7201 Home Phone: 301-897-9186; Office Phone: 301-492-5990.*

REILLY, ELIZABETH ANN, law educator, dean; b. South Bend, Ind., Sept. 9, 1951; d. Edward Leo and Barbara (Nolan) Reilly; m. Scott Robert Piepho, Dec. 30, 1994; children: Chloe, Naomi. AB, Princeton U., NJ, 1973; JD, U. Akron, Ohio, 1978. Bar: Ohio State Supreme Ct. 1978, US Supreme Ct., US Ct. of Appeal, Sixth Cir., Third Cir., US Dist. Ct. No. Dist., Ohio, Ea. Divsn. Atty. Whitaker and Reilly, Akron, 1978—84; asst. prof. U. Akron Sch. Law, 1984—88, assoc. prof., 1988—92, prof., 1992—99, C. Blake McDowell Jr. prof. law, 1999—, assoc. dean, 1995—. Fellow constl. ctr. U. Akron Sch. Law, 1998—; chair juvenile rules subcom., adv. com. Ohio Supreme Ct., Columbus, 1999—2002; chair pres. commn. on equity U. Akron, 1999—2002, fellow symposium tchg. assessment and learning, 2002—03. Contbr. articles to profl. jours. Pres. Unitarian Universalist Ch. Akron, Fairlawn, 2007—08. Recipient Outstanding Tchr. Scholar award, U. Akron, 2004, Outstanding Alumna award, Akron Sch. Law, 2006. Fellow: Akron Bar Foun.; mem.: ABA, Ohio State Bar Assn. (mem. section bd. govs. of women in profession 1999—), Akron Bar Assn. (trustee 2000—03). Avocations: photography, hiking, reading. Office: Univ Akron Sch Law Akron OH 44325-2901 Office Phone: 330-972-7331. Business E-Mail: reilly@uakron.edu.

REILLY, FRANK KELLY, business educator; b. Chgo., Dec. 30, 1935; s. Clarence Raymond and Mary Josephine (Ruckrigel) R.; m. Therese Adele Bourke, Aug. 2, 1958; children: Frank Kelly III, Clarence Raymond II, Therese B., Edgar B. BBA, U. Notre Dame, 1957; MBA, Northwestern U., 1961, U. Chgo., 1964, PhD, 1968; LLD (hon.), St. Michael's Coll., 1991. CFA. Trader Goldman Sachs & Co., Chgo., 1958-59; security analyst Tech. Fund, Chgo., 1959-62; asst. prof. U. Kans., Lawrence, 1965-68, assoc. prof., 1968-72; prof. bus., assoc. dir. divsn. bus. and econ. rsch. U. Wyo., Laramie, 1972-75; prof. fin. U. Ill., Champaign-Urbana, 1975-81; Bernard J. Hank prof. U. Notre Dame, Ind., 1981—, dean Mendoza Coll. Bus. Ind., 1981-87. Bd. dirs., chmn. UBS Funds, Assn. Investment Mgmt. and Rsch.; past chmn. Inst. Chartered Fin. Analysts; past chmn. bd. dirs. NIBCO Corp.; bd. dirs. Internat. Bd. CFPs, Discover Bank, chmn. Ft. Dearborn Income Securities, Battery Park High Yield Fund., Morgan Stanley Trust Fed. Savs. Bank (FSB). Author: Investment Analysis and Portfolio Management, 1979, 8th edit., 2006, Investments, 1982, 7th edit., 2006; co-editor: Ethics and the Investment Industry, 1989; editor: Readings and Issues in Investments, 1975, High Yield Bonds: Analysis and Risk Assessment, 1990; assoc. editor Fin. Mgmt., 1977-82, Quar. Rev. Econs. and Bus, 1979-87, Fin. Rev., 1979-87, 92—, Jour. Fin. Edn., 1981—, Jour. Applied Bus. Rsch., 1986—, Fin. Svcs. Rev., 1989-96, Internat. Rev. Econs. and Fin., 1992—, European Jour. Fin., 1994—. Arthur J. Schmidt Found. fellow, 1962-65; U. Chgo. fellow, 1963-65; recipient faculty award U. Notre Dame, 1999. Fellow Fin. Mgmt. Assn. (pres. 1983-84, chmn. 1985-91, bd. dirs.); mem. Midwest Bus. Adminstrn. Assn. (pres. 1974-75), Am. Fin. Assn., Western Fin. Assn. (exec. com. 1973-75), Ea. Fin. Assn. (exec. com. 1979-84, pres. 1982-83), Midwest Fin. Assn. (pres. 1993-94; Lifetime Achievement award 2007), Fin. Analysts Fedn., Acad. Fin. Svcs. (pres. 1990-91), Inst. Chartered Fin. Analysts (coun. of examiners, rsch. and edn. com., edn. steering com.), Internat. Assoc. Fin. Planners (ednl. resource com., bd. dirs.), Assn. of Investment Mgmt. and Rsch. (C. Stewart Sheppard award 1991, Daniel J. Forrestal III Leadership award for profl. ethics 2001), CFA Soc. Chgo. (bd. dirs. 1988-89), Beta Gamma Sigma. Roman Catholic. Office: U Notre Dame Mendoza Coll Bus Notre Dame IN 46556-5646 Business E-Mail: reilly.1@nd.edu. *Any success I have enjoyed is due to the talents God has given me and my belief that I have an obligation to maximize the output from those talents by hard work, while never forgetting that my family comes first because they have always provided me with the love and support necessary for success and happiness.*

REILLY, HUGH JOSEPH, humanities educator, writer; b. Omaha, Nebr., Aug. 30, 1955; s. Robert Thomas and Regina Marie Reilly; m. Deanna Mary Jansen, Aug. 30, 1986; children: Tacheny Kathleen, McKenzie Joseph, Patrick Temple, Charlotte Regina. MA in Comm., U. Nebr., Omaha, 1997. Dir. donor svcs. Father Flanagan's Boys' Home, Boys Town, Nebr., 1990—2001; assoc. prof. U. Nebr., 2001—. Tour dir. Terry Flynn Tours, Carrick On Suir, Ireland, 1992—; cons. The Alliance, Omaha, 2004—. Author: (biography) Father Flanagan: Man of Vision, (history book) Historical Omaha, (book) Letter From the Front. Pres. Nebr. Writer's Guild, 1999—2003; exec. bd. mem. Am. Mktg. Assn., Omaha, 2002—05. Recipient Pinnacle award, Am. Marketign Assn., 1993, 1999. Mem.: Omaha Fedn. Advt. (com. mem. 2002—05), Pub. Rels. Soc. Am. (bd. mem. 2002—04), Nebr. Writer's Guild (v.p. 2004—07). Democrat. Roman Catholic. Avocations: writing, travel. Office: Univ of Nebraska at Omaha 6001 Dodge St ASH 140-C Omaha NE 68152 Office Fax: 402-554-3656. Business E-Mail: hreilly@mail.unomaha.edu.

REILLY, JAMES DALTON, legislative staff member; b. Tex., Dec. 07; s. James and Alice Reilly; m. Jeanine Hoy, June 2007. BSc in Plant Sci., U. Del., Newark; M in Environ. Mgmt., Duke U. Nicholas Sch. the Environment, Durham, NC. Asst. dir. YMCA Camp Tockwogh; fundraiser Gov. Tom Carper Senatorial Campaign, 1999; legis. asst., Senator Thomas Carper US Senate, Washington, 2000—04, chief of staff to Senator Thomas Carper, 2007—; sr. energy and environment advisor British Embassy, Washington, 2005—07. John A. Knauss Marine Policy fellow, US Senate Commerce, Sci. and Transportation Com., 1997. Democrat. Avocation: sailing. Office: 513 Hart Senate Office Bldg Washington DC 20510-2190 Office Phone: 202-224-2441. Business E-Mail: jim_reilly@carper.senate.gov.*

REILLY, JOAN, nursing educator; b. Johnson, Wash., May 2, 1931; d. Jacob and Vernice Althea (Marine) Steiner; m. Robert Joseph Reilly, June 20, 1960; children— Sean Michael, Patrick Joseph, Bridget Colleen. B.S.N., Wash. State U., 1953; M.S.N., St. Louis U., 1970; EdD, Seattle U., 1989. R.N. Staff nurse VA Hosp., Spokane, 1953-55, 1962-63; office nurse pediatrician's office, Spokane, 1955-56; nursing supr. Bakersfield Meml. Hosp. (Calif.), 1956-58; instr. St. Luke's Sch. Nursing, Spokane, 1958-60; staff nurse Ireland Army Hosp., Ft. Knox, Ky., 1961-62; instr. St. Joseph Sch. Nursing, Tacoma, 1964-65, 66-67, nursing svc. staff asst. St. Joseph Hosp., Tacoma, 1970; charge nurse St. Peter Hosp., Olympia, Wash., 1973-74; vis. nurse Tacoma Gen. Hosp., 1974-77; instr. Tacoma Community Coll., 1977—92, ret., 1992; with Wash. State Nursing Commn., 1992-99. Unit service chmn. ACS, Tacoma, 1977; mem. corp. Hospice of Tacoma, 1981—; vol. ARC, Karlsruhe, Germany, 1971; mem. Tacoma Zool. Soc., 1983; mem. Friends of Libr., Steilacoom, Wash., 1983; mem. Steilacoom Hist. Mus. Soc., 1983; key person United Way, Tacoma, 1983-84; parish nurse St. Luke's Episc. Ch., 2004—, group facilitator Good Grief Ctr., 2004—, chmn. Christian edn. com. 2006—, ch. vestry mem.; 2005-08. Named to Phi Delta Kappa, 1997, Sigma Theta Tau Internat., 1998. Mem. Wash. State Nurses' Assn. (chmn. Ways and Means Com. 1982-83, bd. dirs. 1981-84), Nat. Assn. Alcohol and Drug Abuse Counselors, NW Nurses Soc. on Chem. Dependency, Alcoholism Profl. Staff Soc. Wash., Ft. Steilacoom Running, Irish Cultural (pub. com. Tacoma 1982-83), Phi Kappa Phi, Tacoma Musical Playhouse (bd. mem. 1997-2000). Home: 1521 Willow Pl Wenatchee WA 98801-8005

REILLY, JOHN B., lawyer; b. Bangor, Maine, Sept. 12, 1947; s. Louis J. and Evelyn I. (Lindsay) R.; children: Carolyn, Bridget. BA, U. R.I., 1970; JD cum laude, Suffolk U., 1976. Bar: R.I. 1976, Mass. 1985, U.S. Dist. Ct. R.I. 1976, U.S. Dist. Ct. Mass. 1985, U.S. Dist. Ct. Conn. 1995, U.S. Claims Ct. 1980, U.S. Ct. Appeals (1st and 2d cirs.) 1984, U.S. Ct. Appeals (3d cir.) 1985, U.S. Supreme Ct. 1983; cert. fraud examiner. Sole practice, Providence, 1976-81, Warwick, RI, 1981-83; sr. ptnr. John Reilly & Assocs. and predecessor firms, Warwick, RI, 1984—99, 2002—, Reilly & Nikolyszyn, LLP, Warwick, RI, 2000—01. Mem. Gov.'s Automobile Ins. Task Force, 1992-93. Mem. ABA, R.I. Bar Assn., Def. Rsch. Inst., R.I. Assn. Auth Theft and Arson Investigators (sec. 1995-96, pres. 1997—98), Trucking Ind. Def. Assn., Pi Sigma Alpha, Phi Kappa Psi. Office: John Reilly & Assocs 100 N Main St 4th Fl Providence RI 02903 Home: 80 Paterson Ave Warwick RI 02886-9110 Office Phone: 401-272-2800. Business E-Mail: jreilly@lawyers-online.us.

REILLY, JOHN C., actor; b. Chgo., May 24, 1965; m. Alison Dickey, 1992; 2 children. BFA, DePaul U., 1987. Actor: (films) Casualties of War, 1989, We're No Angels, 1989, Days of Thunder, 1990, State of Grace, 1990, Shadows and Fog, 1992, Out on a Limb, 1992, Hoffa, 1992, What's Eating Gilbert Grape, 1993, The River Wild, 1994, Georgia, 1995, Dolores Claiborne, 1995, Hard Eight, 1996, Boys, 1996, Boogie Nights, 1997, The Thin Red Line, 1998, Never Been Kissed, 1999, For Love of the Game, 1999, Magnolia, 1999 (Nat. Bd. Rev. award for Best Ensemble, 1999), The Settlement, 1999, The Perfect Storm, 2000, The Anniversary Party, 2001, Frank's Book, 2001, The Good Girl, 2002, Gangs of New York, 2002 (Las Vegas Film Critics Award for Best Supporting Actor, 2003), Chicago, 2002 (Golden Globe for Best Supporting Actor, Acad. award nomination for Best Actor, Las Vegas Film Critics Award for Best Supporting Actor, 2003), The Hours, 2002 (Las Vegas Film Critics Award for Best Supporting Actor, 2003), Anger Management, 2003, Piggie, 2003, Criminal, 2004, The Aviator, 2004, Are You the Favorite Person of Anybody?, 2005, Dark Water, 2005, A Prairie Home Companion, 2006, Talladega Nights: The Ballad of Ricky Bobby, 2006, Year of the Dog, 2007, Walk Hard: The Dewey Cox Story, 2007, The Promotion, 2008, Step Brothers, 2008; (plays) True West, 2000 (Spl. Outer Critics Cir. Award, 2000), Streetcar Named Desire, 2005. Roman Catholic.

REILLY, KEVIN DENIS, computer scientist, educator; s. Brian Augustine and Dorothy Evelyn Reilly; m. Jo Ann Grace Caniglia, Feb. 4, 1961; children: Martin Louis, Dennis Patrick(dec.), Ann Marie(dec.), Eileen Marie, Shannon Denise Ray. BS summa cum laude, Creighton U., 1959; MS, U. of Nebr., 1962; PhD, U. of Chgo., 1966. Tchr. U.Calif., LA, 1966—70; sr. lectr. U. of So. Calif., LA, 1968—70; prof. U. Ala., Birmingham, Ala., 1970—2007, prof. emeritus, 2008—. Spkr. in field; cons. in field. Contbr. over 300 articles to profl. jours. Judge various sci. fairs, Birmingham; participant in ecumenical dialogs Greek Orthodox-Cath. Discussion Group, Birmingham. Grantee, NSF, 1966—70, U.S. Office of Edn., 1968—70, NIH, 1972—77, 1977—78, US Army, 1987—90, NSF, 1993, NIH, 1998—2000, 2000—; fellow, Woodrow Wilson Found., 1959, NIH, 1962—66, Mobusho fellow, Ministry of Internat. Trade and Industry, Japan, 1989. Mem.: IEEE, Soc. for Modeling and Simulation, European Acad. Sci., Assn. for Computing Machinery. Independent. Roman Catholic. Avocations: travel, philosophy, history, poetry. Home: 304 N Burbank Dr Bluff Park AL 35226-1608 Office: U Ala Birmingham University Station Birmingham AL 35294-1170 E-mail: reilly@cis.uab.edu.

REILLY, NANCY (ANNE CAULFIELD REILLY), painter; b. Bryn Mawr, Pa., Mar. 29, 1927; d. Ralph Caulfield and Claire Helena (Roesch) Goodman; m. Donald Elliott Reilly, May 14, 1949; children: Kevin Caulfield, William Stockbridge, Peter Elliott. Studies with Samuel E. Brown, Westport, Conn., 1955-63; studies with Mimi Jennewein, Larchmont, NY, 1964-65. Lectr., demonstrator portrait painting Bridgeport Art League, Conn., Milford Art League, Conn., Brush and Palette Club, New Haven, Conn. Classic Arts Assn., Allied Artists Am., Kent Art Assn., Conn., SCAN, Newtown, Conn. Exhibited in group shows at Nat. Acad. Design, N.Y.C., 1964, 1965, 1969, 1970, Stamford (Conn.) Mus., 1965, Wadsworth Antheum, Hartford, Conn., 1966, 1972, Nat. Acad. Arts and Letters, N.Y.C., 1971, Mus. Sci. and Industry, Bridgeport, 1972, Salmagundi Club, N.Y.C., Nat. Arts Club, Butler Inst. Am. Art, Youngstown, Ohio, 2001, New Britain (Conn.) Mus. Am. Art, 2001, exhibitions include invitational travelling exhbn. Allied Artists Am., 2003—05, exhibitions include Bennington Ctr. Arts, 2007; included in slide collection Smithsonian Instn., Washington, U. Conn. Health Ctr., Farmington; Documentary Film About Westport Ct. and It's Artistic Legacy, 2008. Vol. artist rehab. unit Norwalk Hosp., 1984—95. Recipient Gold medal for oil painting, Catherine Lorillard Wolfe Art Club, 1965, Silver medal for oil painting, Nat. Arts Club, 1969, George Height award for portrait, 1969, Blanche Farr award, 1991, Anna Liffey award, New Haven Brush and Palette Club for Portraits, 2008, F. Luis Mora award, 2009. Fellow: Am. Artists Profl. League (Claude Parsons Meml. award 2003, Leila Gardin Sawyer Meml. award 2005); mem.: Conn. Pastel Soc. (signature, Honors award 2003, 2004, J.D. Altobello Meml. award), Artists' Fellowship N.Y., Kent Art Assn. (Best in Show 1991, Gordon C. Aymar award for oil 1993, Mabel Rowe Aiken award for oil 1995, Frances B. Townley award for portrait 1998, 1999, James H. Aiken award Best Pastel 2006), Hudson Valley Art Assn. (Bronze medal for oil painting 1981, Thora M. Jensen Portrait award 1989, 2005), Pastel Soc. Am. (CPS award 2005), Nat. Arts Club (Silver medal for oil painting 1969, Bruce Stevenson award for portrait 1971, 1988, 1991, First prize 106th Annual Exhibiting Artist Mems. Exbhn. 2005), Allied Artists Am. (bd. dirs. 1991—99, participant in travelling exhbn. 2003—05), New Haven Paint and Clay Club (Merit award 1992, 1997). Home: 9 Marilane Westport CT 06880-1008

REILLY, PAUL J., electronics executive; b. Jan. 13, 1957; BS, St. John's U., Queens, NY, 1979. CPA. Audit mgr. KPMG Peat Marwick, NYC, 1979-90; dir. reporting, asst. contr. Arrow Electronics, Inc., Melville, NY, 1991—96, corp. v.p., 1996—99, v.p. fin., 1999—2001, v.p., CFO, 2001—05, sr. v.p., CFO, 2005—. Lectr. St. John's U., Pace U. Office: Arrow Electronics Inc 50 Marcus Dr Melville NY 11747-4210 Office Phone: 631-847-2000.*

REILLY, PETER JOHN, chemical engineer, educator; b. Newark, Dec. 26, 1938; s. Edward Thomas and Anita (Galdieri) Reilly; m. Rae Georgine Messer, July 3, 1976; children: Diane Joyce, Karen Elizabeth. AB, Princeton U., 1960; PhD, U. Pa., 1964. Rsch. engr. E.I. Dupont & Co., Deepwater, NJ, 1964—68; asst. prof. U. Nebr., Lincoln, 1968—74; assoc. prof. Iowa State U., Ames, 1974—79, prof., 1979—92, disting. prof., 1992—. Invited prof. Ecole Poly. Federale, Lausanne, Switzerland, 1983—84, 1992—93. Contbr. chapters to books, articles to profl. jours. Fellow: AIChE; mem.: AAUP, Am. Chem. Soc., Sigma Xi. Home: 1807 Wilson Ave Ames IA 50010-4957 Office: Iowa State U 2114 Sweeney Hall Dept Chem Biol Engring Ames IA 50011-2230 Home Phone: 515-232-1396; Office Phone: 515-294-5968. Business E-Mail: reilly@iastate.edu.

REILLY, ROBERT FREDERICK, investment banker; b. NYC, Oct. 3, 1953; s. James J. and Marie (Griebel) Reilly; m. Janet H. Steiner, Apr. 16, 1975; children: Ashley Lauren, Brandon Christopher, Cameron Courtney. BA in Econs., Columbia U., 1975, MBA in Fin., 1976. CPA Ohio, Ill., cert. mgmt. acct., CFF; CFA, cert. real estate appraiser, rev. appraiser, gen. appraiser Ill., Va., Utah, Oreg., NY, bus. appraiser, accredited bus. valuator, valuation cons. Sr. cons. Booz, Allen & Hamilton, Cin., 1975-76; dir. corp. planning Huffy Corp., Dayton, Ohio, 1976-81; v.p. Arthur D. Little Valuation, Inc., Chgo., 1981-85; ptnr., nat. dir. valuation svcs. Deloitte & Touche, Chgo., 1985-91; mng. dir. Willamette Mgmt. Assocs., Chgo., 1991—. Adj. prof. acctg. U. Dayton Grad. Sch. Bus., 1977—81; adj. prof. econs. Elmhurst Coll., Ill., 1982—87; adj. prof. fin. Ill. Inst. Tech. Grad. Sch. Bus., Chgo., 1985—91; adj. prof. taxation U. Chgo. Grad. Sch. Bus., 1985—87. Co-author: (book) Valuing Small Businesses and Professional Practices, 1993, Business Valuation Video Course, 1993, Valuing a Business, 1995;: 4th edit., 2000, Valuing Accounting Practices, 1997, Valuing Professional Practices--A Practitioner's Approach, 1997, Valuing Intangible Assets, 1998, Handbook of Advanced Business Valuation, 1999, Handbook of Business Valuation and Intellectual Property Analysis, 2004, Guide to ESOP Valuation, 2007, Guide to Property Tax Valuation, 2008; editor, columnist: Ohio CPA Jour., 1984—86, 1991—2001, Small Bus. Taxation, 1989—90, Bus. Valuation Rev., 1989—90, Jour. Real Estate Acctg. and Taxation, 1991—93, Jour. Property Taxation Mgmt., 1993—, Jour. Am. Bankruptcy Inst., 1993—, Valuation Strategies, 2003—; co-editor: (book) Financial Valuation-Valuation of Business and Business Interests, 1997; contbr. articles to profl. jours. Mem.: AICPA (mem. ABV exam. com. 2002—06, mem. bus. valuation com. 2006—), Appraisal Inst., Nat. Assn. Bus. Economists, Am. Econ. Assn., Am. Bankruptcy Inst., Inst. CFAs, Chgo. Soc. Investment Analysts, Bus. Valuation Assn., Accreditation Coun. Accountancy (accredited fed. income taxation), Ohio Soc. CPAs (chpt. dir. 1978—81), Ill. Soc. CPAs, Inst. Property Taxation, Inst. Cert. Mgmt. Accts. (chpt. dir. 1976—96), Nat. Assn. Real Estate Appraisers, Am. Soc. Appraisers (mem. bd. examiners 1985—89), Inst. Bus. Appraisers (life). Home: 310 Algonquin Rd Barrington IL 60010-6109 Office: 8600 W Bryn Mawr Ave Chicago IL 60631-3579 Office Phone: 773-399-4300.

REILLY, WILLIAM KANE, private equity firm executive, preservationist, former federal agency administrator; b. Decatur, Ill., Jan. 26, 1940; s. George P. and Margaret (Kane) M.; m. Elizabeth Bennett Buxton; children: Katherine, Megan. BA in History, Yale U., 1962; JD, Harvard U., 1965; MS in Urban Planning, Columbia U., 1971. Bar: Ill., Mass. 1965. Atty. firm Ross & Hardies, Chgo., 1965; assoc. dir. Urban Policy Center, Urban Am., Inc., also Nat. Urban Coalition, Washington, 1969-70; sr. staff mem. Pres.'s Council Environ. Quality, 1970-72; exec. dir. Rockefeller Task Force on Land Use & Urban Growth, 1972-73; pres. Conservation Found., Washington, 1973-89, World Wildlife Fund, Washington, 1985-89; adminstr. EPA, Washington, 1989-93; Payne vis. prof. Stanford U., 1993-94, vis. prof., 1994-97; pres., CEO Aqua Internat. Ptnrs., Tex. Pacific Group, San Francisco, 1997—. Chmn. Natural Resources Coun. Am., 1982-83; head U.S. del. Earth Summit, 1992; head U.S. del. to negotiate Amendments to Montreal Protocol on the Ozone Layer, 1990, 92; bd. dirs. E.I. DuPont de Nemours and Co., 1993-, ConocoPhillips Co., 1997-, Royal Caribbean Internat., 1998-, Evergreen Holdings, Inc., Ionics Inc., 2000-, Enviance, 2006-, AgraQuest, Inc., 2007-; bd. dirs. Nat. Geog. Soc., Am. Acad. in Rome, Presidio Trust; chmn. emeritus World Wildlife Fund; mem. internat. adv. bd., Lafarge; chair adv. bd. Goldman Sch. Pub. Policy U. Calif. at Berkeley. Editor: The Use of Land, 1973, Environment Strategy America, 1994-96; author articles in field, chpts. in books. Served to capt., CIC U.S. Army, 1966-67; bd. dirs. David and Lucile Packard Found. Named to AAAS, 2007. Fellow: Am. Acad. Arts & Scis.; mem.: University (Washington), Univ. (N.Y.C.).*

REILLY, WILLIAM THOMAS, lawyer; b. Passaic, NJ, Feb. 25, 1949; s. Thomas Edwin and Edna May (Dorritie) R.; m. Sheila Mary Brogan, Aug. 1, 1981; children: Kathleen Anne, Brendan Thomas, Timothy John. BS, Boston Coll., 1971; JD, Harvard U., 1974. Bar: N.J. 1974, U.S. Dist. Ct. N.J. 1974, U.S. Supreme Ct. 1979, U.S. Ct. Appeals (3rd cir.) 1984, U.S. Ct. Claims, 1996, U.S. Ct. Appeals (fed. cir.) 1997. Assoc. McCarter & English LLP, Newark, 1974-81, ptnr., 1982—. Trustee United Hosps. Med. Ctr., Newark, 1983-89, One-to-One/NJ, Inc., 1990-97, chmn., 1993-97; trustee, Assn. Fed. Bar NJ, 2006-. Mem. ABA, N.J. State Bar Assn., Harvard Law Sch. Assn., Eastward Ho Country Club. Avocation: golf. Home: 302 Kensington Dr Ridgewood NJ 07450-1822 Office: McCarter & English LLP Four Gateway Ctr 100 Mulberry St Newark NJ 07102-4004 Office Phone: 973-622-4444, 973-639-2058. Business E-Mail: wreilly@mccarter.com.

REILLY-HUDOCK, PATRICIA A. (TRISH REILLY), legislative staff member; Chief of staff to congressman Tom Holden US House of Reps., Washington, 1992—, comm. dir., 1993—98. Democrat. Mailing: US House Reps 2417 Rayburn HOB Washington DC 20515 Office Phone: 202-225-5546. Office Fax: 202-225-0996.*

REIMAN, AMANDA E., social sciences educator; b. Summit, NJ, June 20, 1976; d. Thomas J. and Wendy W. Reiman; life ptnr. Brian A. Canepa. BA in Psychology, U. Ill., Chgo., 2000, MSW, 2002; PhD, U. Calif., Berkeley, 2006. Predoc. fellow Alcohol Rsch. Group, Emeryville, Calif., 2005—06, postdoc. fellow, 2006—08; lectr. U. Calif. Sch. Social Welfare, Berkeley, 2006—, academic coord., 2008—. Cons. Berkeley Patient's Group, 2008. Contbr. articles to profl. jours. Summer fellow Marijuana Policy Project, Bay Area, Calif., 2005. Named NORML Freedom Fighter of Month, 2008. Green Party. Avocations: tennis, hiking, bicycling. Office: Univ Calif Berkeley 120 Haviland Hall Berkeley CA 94720

REIMAN, DONALD HENRY, language educator; b. Erie, Pa., May 17, 1934; s. Henry Ward and Mildred Abbie (Pearce) R.; m. Mary A. Warner, 1958 (div. 1974); one child, Laurel Elizabeth Reiman Henneman; m. Hélène (Liberman) Dworzan, Oct. 3, 1975. BA, Coll. of Wooster, 1956; MA, U. Ill., 1957, PhD, 1960; LittD., Coll. of Wooster, 1981. Instr. English, Duke U., Durham, NC, 1960—62, asst. prof., 1962—64; assoc. prof. U. Wis., Milw., 1964—65; adj. assoc. prof. grad. program in English City Univ. of N.Y., 1967—68; adj. prof. Columbia U., NYC, 1969—70, sr. rsch. assoc. in English, 1970—73; vis. prof. St. John's U., Jamaica, NY, 1974—75; editor Shelley and His Cir., Carl H. Pforzheimer Libr., NYC, 1965—86, N.Y. Pub. Libr., 1986—92; with Carl and Lily Pforzheimer Found., 1992—. Vis. lectr. U. Ill., 1963; vis. prof. U. Wash., Seattle, 1981, NY U., 1992; Lyell reader in bibliography Oxford U., 1988-89; cons. Harvard U. Press, Yale U. Press, Princeton U. Press, Johns Hopkins U. Press, Garland Pub., Inc., W.W. Norton, Oxford U. Press, others; adj. prof. English, U. Del., 1992-. Author: Shelley's The Triumph of Life, A Critical Study, 1965, 2d edit., 1979, Percy Bysshe Shelley, 1969, 2d edit., 1990, (with D.D. Fischer) Byron on the

Continent, 1974, English Romantic Poetry, 1800-1835, 1979, Romantic Texts and Contexts, 1987, Intervals of Inspiration: The Skeptical Tradition and the Psychology of Romanticism, 1988, The Study of Modern Manuscripts, 1993; editor: Shelley and His Circle, Vols. V-VI, 1973, Vols. VII-VIII, 1986, (with D.D. Fischer) IX-X, 2002, The Romantics Reviewed: Contemporary Reviews of English Romantic Writers, 9 vols., 1972, (with S.B. Powers) Shelley's Poetry and Prose: A Norton Critical Edit., 1977, (with Neil Fraistat) 2nd rev. edit., 2002, The Romantic Context: Poetry, 128 vols., 1976-79, (with M.C. Jaye and B.T. Bennett) The Evidence of the Imagination, 1978; gen. editor: Manuscripts of the Younger Romantics, 1985-98; I The Esdaile Notebook: A Facsimile, 1985, II The Mask of Anarchy: Facsimiles, 1985, III Hellas, 1985, V The Harvard Shelley Poetic Manuscripts, 1991; (with M. O'Neill) VIII Fair-Copy Manuscripts of Shelley's Poems, 1997; editor-in-chief: The Bodleian Shelley Manuscripts, 1986-99, I Peter Bell The Third and the Triumph of Life, 1986, VII Shelley's Last Notebook and Other MSS, 1990, (with M.J. Neth) XVI The Hellas Notebook, 1994, (with N. Fraistat) The Complete Poetry of Percy Bysshe Shelley Vol. I, 2000, Vol. II, 2004; mem. editl. com. adv. bd. Keats Shelley Jour., 1968-73, Milton and the Romantics, 1975-80, Studies in Romanticism, 1977—, Romanticism Past and Present, 1980-86, Text, 1981—, Nineteenth Century Literature, 1986—, Nineteenth Century Contexts, 1987-90; co-founder, editor (with others) Romantic Circles Website; mem. editl. bd., U. Delaware Press, 2003-; contbr. articles to encyclopedias, books, and profl. journals. Active in Common Cause. Am. Coun. Learned Soc. Fellow, 1963-64, Wesleyan Ctr. Advanced Studies Fellow, 1963-64, NEH Fellow, 1978; grantee Am. Coun. Learned Soc., 1961, NEH, 1983-2003, 07—. Mem. AAUP, MLA (life), Modern Humanities Rsch. Assn. (life), Wordsworth Coleridge Assn. Am. (founder), Byron Soc. (Am. com. 1973—, treas. 1999-2002, pres. 2003-05), Keats Shelley Assn. Am. (bd. dir., treas. 1973-91, v.p. 1991-2005, Disting. Scholar Award 1987), Soc. Textual Scholarship (exec. com. 1981-93, pres. 2005-06), Charles Lamb Soc., Assn. Documentary Editing, N.Am. Soc. Study of Romanticism. Democrat. Presbyterian. Home Phone: 302-368-7199. Business E-Mail: dhreiman@udel.edu.

REIMAN, RICHARD J., lawyer; b. July 8, 1939; s. John H. and Rose L. (Coleman) R. BA, CUNY, 1961; JD, U. Mich., 1971. Bar: N.Y. 1974, U.S. Dist. Ct. (so. dist.) N.Y. 1975, (ea. dist.) N.Y. 1975, U.S. Ct. Appeals (2d cir.) 1975. Atty. HUD, NYC, 1972-90; spl. asst. U.S. Atty. So. Dist. N.Y., 1990-96; retired, 1996. Address: 382B Heritage Hls Somers NY 10589-1917

REIMANN, ARLINE LYNN, artist; b. St. Louis, Nov. 25, 1937; d. Albert Robbins and Bess (Kagan) Miller; m. Hans Reimann, Feb. 24, 1957; 1 child, Robert. BA, Rutgers U., NJ, 1974; MA, Montclair State U., NJ, 1980. Exhibited in group shows at Hunterdon Art Ctr., Clinton, NJ, 1982, 96, Galeria San Jeronimo, San Juan, P.R., 1987, Nat. Arts Club, NYC, 1988, 90—, Interch. Ctr., NYC, Butler Inst. Am. Art, Youngstown, Ohio, 1989, 395 West Broadway Gallery, NYC, 1994, 420 West Broadway Gallery, Soho, NY, 1995, Lever House Gallery, NYC, 1995, Art Ctr. Municipality of Athens, Greece, 1996, West Beth Gallery, Montclair in Manhattan, NYC, 1996, ISE Art Found. NYC, 1996, Soc. Am. Graphic Artists, New Rochelle, NY, 1997, Gallery Art 54, NYC, 1997, Jane Voorhees Zimmerli Art Mus., New Brunswick, NJ, 1998-99, Old Print Shop, NYC, 2004, 07, Art Students League of NY, NYC, 2005, Worldwide Feminist Expo, Balt., 2000, Nat. Assn. Women Artists, UN, 2002, Audubon Artists Salmagundi Club, NYC, 2005-09, Ringling Mus. Sch. Art, Sarasota, Fla., 2006, Goggleworks Ctr. Arts, Reading, Pa., 2006, Venezuelan Consulate, NYC, 2006, Longview Mus. Fine Arts, Tex., 2007, Monroe Ctr. for Arts, Hoboken, NJ, 2007, NY Hall Sci., 2008, Nat Assoc. Women Artists Gallery, NYC, 2008, Ormond Meml. Art Mus., Ormond Beach, Fla., 2008, Civic Arts, Shadelands, Walnut Creek, Calif., 2009; represented in permanent collections at Jane Voorhees Zimmerli Art Mus., New Brunswick, NJ, Newark Pub. Libr. Fine Print Collection, Newark, NJ, Montclair (NJ) State U., Bailey Matthews Mus., Sanibel, Fla., Black Hills Inst., Hill City, SD. Recipient Best in Show award Salute to Women in Arts, Lincoln Ctr., N.Y.C., 1981, Hon. mention award Nat. Juried Exhbn. Small Works Montclair State U., N.J., 1995. Aida Whedon Meml. award Nat. Assn. Women Artists, 1996. Mem. Nat. Assn. Women Artists (bd. dirs., chair traveling print exhbn. 1984-89, printmaking jury 1987-89, 95-97), Audubon Artists (bd. dirs., rec. sec. 1991-97), Soc. Am. Graphic Artists, Phi Beta Kappa. Home: 546 Hillrise Pl Walnut Creek CA 94598-4064

REIMANN, JOACHIM OSKAR FERDINAND, psychologist, researcher; b. Berlin, Fed. Republic Germany, Jan. 24, 1951; came to U.S., 1960, naturalized, 1967; s. Bernhard Erwin Ferdinand and Beate Eleonore (Hedwig) R.; m. Dolores I. Rodriguez, Sept. 2, 1989. B.A. in Psychology, U. Tex.-El Paso, 1973, M.Ed., 1985; MA Alliant Internat. U., 1992, PhD in Psychology, 1996; nat. cert. counselor; lic. psychologist, Calif. Musician Fox Harbour, Neoga, Ill., 1973-75, Highway, El Paso, 1975-77; caseworker youth Dept. Human Devel., El Paso, 1978-79, counselor, 1979-82; counselor Pvt. Industry Council, Inc., El Paso, 1982—1990; programs coord. growth conf. Tex. Assn. for Counseling and Devel., 1989; v.p. Profl. and Personal Excellence Internat., San Diego, 1996—; rsch. asst. prof. Grad. Sch. Pub. Health, San Diego State U., 1996—; mem. adj. faculty Alliant Internat. U., San Diego, 1999—, Nat. U., San Diego, 2004—. Contbr. articles to profl. jours. Instr. guitar N.E. YMCA, 1978-84. Recipient Outstanding Contribution award TPACD, 1987-88, Recognition award Am. Acad. Family Physicians, 1999, Golden Apple award San Diego State U., 1998. Mem. Trans Pecos Assn. Counseling Devel. (exec. bd. dirs. 1987-90). Democrat. Avocations: martial arts, stamp collecting, writing. Office: Profl and Personal Excellence Internat Ste 103 3530 Carmino del Rio N San Diego CA 92108-1744 Office Phone: 619-991-0592. Business E-Mail: jreimann@excellenceinternational.com.

REIMER, BRYAN, research scientist; PhD, U. RI, Kingston, 2003. Rsch. scientist MIT, Cambridge, 2003—. Contbr. articles to profl. jours. Office: MIT 77 Mass Ave Rm E40-291 Cambridge MA 02139

REIMER, DENNIS J., retired career military officer; b. Medford, Okla., July 12, 1939; m. Mary Jo Powers; 2 children. BS, U.S. Mil. Acad., 1962; MS, Shippensburg State Coll. Gen. U.S. Army, Ft. McPherson, Ga., chief of staff Washington, 1995—99; ret., 1999; dir. Nat. Meml. Inst. for Prevention of Terrorism, Oklahoma City, 2000—. Bd. mem. Plato Learning Inc., Minn. Decorated Def. Disting. Svc. medal, DSM, two Legions of Merit, DFC, six Bronze Star medals, Purple Heart, Combat Infantryman badge, Parachutist badge, Aircraft Crewman badge, Ranger Tab; recipient Nat. Vets. award, 1999. Office: Nat Meml Inst for Prevention of Terrorism Chief of Staff PO Box 889 Oklahoma City OK 73101-0889

REIMER, NONA BRINKMAN, biology professor; b. Quantico, Va., July 13, 1954; children: Jennifer, Jonathan. BA, U. Calif., Santa Barbara, 1976; MRE, Western Conservative Bapt. Theol. Sem., Portland, Oreg., 1978; Multiple Subject Credential, Calif. State U., Hayward, 1987. Elem. sch. tchr. Capistrano Unified Sch. Dist., San Juan Capistrano, Calif., 1987—; instr. biology Calif. State U., Fullerton, 1999—. Office: John S Malcom Eleme Sch 32261 Charles Ave Laguna Niguel CA 92677 Personal E-mail: f12tch@cox.net. Business E-Mail: nbreimer@capousd.org.

REIMER, PAUL E., physicist; married. PhD, U. Ill., Urbana. Physicist Argonne Nat. Lab., Ill., 1999—. Office: Argonne Nat Lab 9700 S Cass Ave Argonne IL 60439

REIN, BERT WALTER, lawyer; b. Bklyn., Feb. 7, 1941; s. Moe and Florence (Fishman) Rein; m. Jennifer Christine Bulson, July 11, 1966 (dec. Mar. 1989); children: Joanna, Benjamin, Samantha; m. Barbara Jean Kahn, Oct. 18, 1992. BA, Amherst Coll., 1961; LLB, Harvard U., 1964. Bar: DC 1965, U.S. Dist. Ct. DC 1965, U.S. Ct. Appeals (DC cir.) 1968, U.S. Ct. Appeals (2d cir.) 1973, U.S. Ct. Appeals (8th cir.) 1974, U.S. Ct. Appeals (4th cir.) 1976, U.S. Ct. Appeals (11th cir.) 1982, U.S. Supreme Ct. 1982. Law ck. to Justice John M. Harlan U.S. Supreme Ct., Washington, 1966-67; assoc. Kirkland & Ellis, Washington, 1967-69, ptnr., 1973-83; spl. asst. U.S. Dept. State, Washington, 1969-70, dep. asst. sec., 1970-73; ptnr. Wiley, Rein & Fielding, Washington, 1983—2006, Wiley Rein, Washington, 2007—. Bd. dirs., chmn. govt. and regulatory affairs com. U.S. C. of C., 1986—90; bd. dirs. Nat. Chamber Litig. Ctr.; advisor Reagan Dept. Justice Transition, Washington, 1980; mem. adv. com. U.S. Sentencing Commn., 1988—89; edn. gen. counsel Cmty. Learning and Info. Network, 1992—. Contbr. articles to profl. jours. Mem. capitol area adv. bd. Salvation Army. Capt. USAR, 1964—68. Mem.: ABA, Internat. Trade Commn. Trial Lawyers Assn. (pres. 1990—91), Am. Law Inst., Aviation Club. Republican. Jewish. Home: 6423 Shadow Rd Chevy Chase MD 20815-6613 Office: Wiley Rein 1776 K St NW Washington DC 20006-2304 Home Phone: 301-215-7655; Office Phone: 202-719-7080. Business E-Mail: brein@wileyrein.com.

REIN, CATHERINE AMELIA, retired insurance company executive, lawyer; b. Lebanon, Pa., Feb. 7, 1943; d. John and Esther (Scott) Shultz. BA summa cum laude, Pa. State U., 1965; JD magna cum laude, NYU, 1968. Bar: NY 1968, US Supreme Ct. 1971. Assoc. Dewey, Ballantine, Bushby, Palmer & Wood, NYC, 1968-74; with Continental Grp., Stamford, Conn., 1974-85, sec., sr. atty., 1976-77, v.p., gen. counsel, 1980-85; sec., asst. gen. counsel Continental Diversified Ops., 1978-80; v.p. human resources Met. Life Ins. Co., NYC, 1985-88, sr. v.p. human resources, 1988-89, exec. v.p. corp. and profl. svcs. dept., 1989—98, sr. exec., v.p. bus. svcs. grp. and corp. svcs., 1998-99; pres., CEO Met. Life Auto and Home, Warwick, RI, 1999—2004; sr. exec. v.p., chief adminstrv. officer Met. Life Inc., 2004—08. Bd. dirs. Bank of NY, Inc., 2001—, First Energy Corp., 2001—. Trustee NYU Sch. Law Found. Mem.: ABA, Assn. Bar City of NY. Episcopalian. Avocations: decorating, restoration, cooking.

REIN, LINDA S., broadcast executive; BA in English, Barnard Coll., NYC, 1966; JD, Bklyn. Law Sch., 1977. Sr. assoc. Grubman Indursky & Schindler, 1988—94; v.p., bus., legal affairs BMG Classics, 1995—98; assoc. gen. coun. Columbia House, 1999—2000; v.p., bus., legal affairs Lifetime Entertainment Svc., NY, 2001—07, sr. v.p., gen. coun. NY, 2007—.

REINA, CARRILLO JOSÉ GABRIEL, physician, surgery educator; b. Caqueza, Cundinamarca, Colombia, May 15, 1937; s. Hernández Santos Reina and Reina Evidalia Carrillo; m. Uriz María Encarnación Rivas, Dec. 12, 1958; 1 child, Rivas María Teresa. MD, Universidad Javeriana, 1965. Attending vascular surgeon Caprecom, Bogotá, 1970—75; instr. gen. surgery Universidad del Rosario, Bogotá, Colombia, 1973—76, prof. gen. surgery, 1977—78; chief gen. surgery Hosp. Ctrl. de la Policia Nacional, Bogotá, 1975—77; chief dept. surgery Clínica Hosp. Juan N. Corpas, Bogotá, 1977—2005. Author: (book) Nociones de Cirugía General, Nutrición Parenteral. Recipient Medalla al Mérito, Policía Nacional, 1996. Fellow: ACS, Sociedad Colombiana de Cirugía Vascular, Sociedad Colombiana de Gastroenterología, Colegio Colombiano de Cirujanos, Real Colegio Español de Médicos, Internat. Soc. Surgeons. Católica. Avocation: magic. Home: Calle 61 No 9 - 38 Apt 902 Cundinamarca Bogota Colombia Office: Fundación Universitaria Juan N Corpas Cra 111 No 157 - 45 Cundinamarca Bogota Colombia Business E-Mail: gabriel.reina@juanncorpas.edu.co.

REINBOLT, PAUL C., oil industry executive; b. Chapel Hill, NC; B in Acctg., Miami U., Oxford, Ohio, MBA. Sr. fin. analyst Marathon Oil Corp., Pitts., 1984—86, short-term investment mgr. New York, 1986—87, mgr. treasury, 1987—91, dir. corp. fin. analysis Pitts., 1991—94, asst. treas., corp. fin., 1994—98, mgr. fin. and adminstrn. prodn., UK London, 1998—2000; comptr. US Steel, Pitts., 2000—01; v.p. fin. and treas. Marathon Oil Corp., Houston, 2001—. Office: Marathon Oil Corp Corp Headquarters 5555 San Felipe Rd Houston TX 77056-2723*

REINECKE, MANFRED G., chemistry professor; b. Milw., May 19, 1935; s. Fritz Wilhelm and Erna (Rittmeyer) R.; m. Marlene Zwisler, June 15, 1957; children: Kurt, Kryn, Claire. BS in Chemistry, U. Wis., 1956; PhD in Organic Chemistry, U. Calif., 1960. Asst. prof. U. Calif., Riverside, 1959-64, Tex. Christian U., Ft. Worth, 1964-68, assoc. prof., 1968-73, prof., 1973—2006, Cecil and Ida Green disting. emeritus tutor, 2006—. Chmn. health professions adv. com. Tex. Christian U., 1974-91; mem. sci. adv. bd. Univera Pharm., Inc., 1996-2002; vis. prof. U. Tubingen, Germany, 1971-72, U. B.C., Vancouver, Can., 1987; cons. in field. Contbr. more than 85 articles on natural product, organic chemistry and chem. edn. to profl. jours. Recipient W.T. Doherty award Ft. Worth, Dallas sect. Am. Chem. Soc., 1984; NSF Tchg.fellow, 1971-72, NAS fellow, 1979, 90. Mem. Am. Chem. Soc. (chmn. Ft. Worth, Dallas sect. 1976), So. Assn. Advisors Health Professions (bd. dirs. 1986-89), Alpha Epsilon Delta (dir. SW region 1985-2002). Office: Tex Christian Univ Dept of Chemistry PO Box 298860 Fort Worth TX 76129-0001 Business E-Mail: m.reinecke@tcu.edu.

REINEMUND, STEVEN S., dean, educator, retired food products executive; b. Queens, NY, Apr. 6, 1948; s. Ott and Dora (Kramer) R.; m. Gail Timbers, Dec. 14, 1974; children: Steven S. Jr., Jonathan Craig. BS in Naval Sci., U.S. Naval Acad., 1970; MBA, U. Va., 1978. Commd. 2d lt. USMC, 1970, advanced through grades to capt., 1974, resigned, 1975; mktg. rep. IBM Corp., 1975-76; v.p., gen. mgr. Marriott-Roy Rogers, 1978-84; sr. v.p., field operator Pizza Hut, Inc., Wichita, Kans., 1984-86, exec. v.p., 1986, pres., CEO, 1986—92, Frito-Lay N.Am., 1992—96; chmn., CEO Frito-Lay, 1996—99; pres., COO PepsiCo, Inc., 1999—2001, chmn., CEO, 2001—07; dean, prof. leadership & strategy Calloway Sch. Bus. & Accountancy & Babcock Grad. Sch. Mgmt., Wake Forest U., Winston-Salem, NC, 2008—. Bd. dirs. Johnson & Johnson, 2003—08, Marriott Internat., 2007—, American Express Co., 2007—, ExxonMobil Corp., 2007—. Chmn. Nat. Minority Supplier Develop. Council; trustee U.S. Naval Acad. Found.; bd. dir. U. Va., Darden Sch. Alumni Assn. Named one of Outstanding Young Men Am. Republican Presbyterian. Avocations: tennis, running. Office: Wake Forest U Calloway Sch of Bus and Accounta 7285 Reynolda Station Winston Salem NC 27109-7285 E-mail: steve@wfu.edu.*

REINER, CARL, director, actor, writer; b. Bronx, NY, Mar. 20, 1922; s. Irving and Bessie (Mathias) R.; m. Estelle Lebost, Dec. 24, 1943 (dec. Oct. 25, 2008); children: Robert, Sylvia A., Lucas. Student, Sch. Fgn. Service, Georgetown U., 1943. Appeared on Broadway and with road co.: Call Me Mister, 1947-48; on Broadway in:Inside U.S.A, 1948-49, Alive and Kicking, 1950; TV actor, 1950—; appeared: Your Show of Shows, 1950-54, Caesar's Hour, 1954-58 (Emmy award 1956, 57); master ceremonies: Keep Talking, 1958-59; writer-actor: Dinah Shore Show, 1960; producer, writer: The Dick Van Dyke Show (Emmy awards as writer 1962, 63, 64, as producer 1965, 66), The New Dick Van Dyke Show, Enter Laughing, written 1958, directed 1967, The Comics, 1968; dir.: (films) Enter Laughing, The Comic, 1967, The Comic, 1969, Where's Poppa, 1970, Oh, God!, 1977, The One and Only, 1978, The Jerk, 1979, Dead Men Don't Wear Plaid, 1982, The Man With Two Brains, 1983, All of Me, 1984, Summer Rental, 1985, Summer School, 1987, Bert Rigby, You're a Fool, 1989, Sibling Rivalry, 1990, Fatal Instinct, 1993, Ocean's Eleven, 2001, The Majestic, 2001, Ocean's Twelve, 2004, Ocean's Thirteen, 2007; appeared in: movie Happy Anniversary, 1959, The Gazebo, 1960, Gidget Goes Hawaiian, 1961, It's a Mad, Mad, Mad, Mad World, 1963, The Russians Are Coming, 1966, The End, 1978, Dead Men Don't Wear Plaid, 1982, (TV movies) Danny Kaye: A Legacy of Laughter, 1996, The Right to Remain Silent, 1996, The Slums of Beverly Hills, 1998, The Adventures of Rocky and Bullwinkle, 2000, Good Boy!, 2003; writer, dir.: Something Different, 1967; writer: Sid Caesar, Imogene Coca, Carl Reiner, Howard Morris Special (Emmy award, 1967); producer: TV series Good Heavens, 1976 (recipient Emmy award 1957, 58, 62, 63); Author: (novels) Enter Laughing, 1958, All Kinds of Love, 1993, Continue Laughing, 1995, NNNNN, 2005; (memoir) My Anecdotal Life, 2003; short stories; (screenplay) The Thrill of It All; (with Mel Brooks) albums The 2000 Year Old Man, The 2001 Year Old Man, The 2013 Year Old Man; exec. producer: film Heaven Help Us, 1976; dir. The Man with Two Brains, 1983. Served with AUS, 1942-46. Recipient Guest Actor in a Comedy Series Emmy award for Mad About You, 1995, Mark Twain Prize for Am. Humor, Kennedy Center, 1999, 2006 Hon. Life Mem. award, Directors Guild America, Valentine Davies award, Writers Guild America, 2009 Achievements include receiving the greatest number of Emmys (12) for any individual. Office: care George Shapiro Shapiro-West 141 S El Camino Dr Ste 205 Beverly Hills CA 90212-2718*

REINER, GARY M., diversified technology and services company executive; BA, Harvard U., 1976, MBA, 1980. Rsch. analyst Boston Consulting Group, 1980—86, ptnr., 1986—91; v.p. corp. bus. devel. GE, Fairfield, Conn., 1991-96, sr. v.p., chief info. officer, 1996—. Office: GE 3135 Easton Tpke Fairfield CT 06431-0002*

REINER, ROB, film director, actor; b. Bronx, NY, Mar. 6, 1947; s. Carl and Estelle (Lebost) R.; m. Penny Marshall, April 10, 1971 (div. 1979), m. Michele Singer, May 19, 1989; 3 children. Student, UCLA. Co-founder Castle Rock Entertainment, Beverly Hills, Calif. Actor: (TV series) All In the Family, 1971-78 (Emmy award 1974, 78), (TV movies) Thursday's Game, 1974 (films) Enter Laughing, 1967, Halls of Anger, 1970, Summertree, 1971, The Jerk, 1979, This is Spinal Tap, 1984, Throw Momma From the Train, 1987, Postcards From the Edge, 1990, The Spirit of '76, 1990, Sleepless in Seattle, 1993, Bullets Over Broadway, 1994, Mixed Nuts, 1994, Bye Bye, Love, 1995, First Wives Club, 1996, Mad Dog Time, 1996, I Am Your Child (TV), 1997, Primary Colors, 1998, EDtv, 1999, The Muse, 1999, The Story of Us, 1999, (voice) The Majestic, 2001, Dickie Roberts: Former Child Star, 2003, (voice) Everyone's Hero, 2006, (theatre) The Roast, 1980; actor, writer: (films) Halls of Anger, 1970, Where's Pappa?, 1970, Summertree, 1971, Fire Sale, 1971; actor, co-writer, prodr. (TV) More Than Friends, 1978, Million Dollar Infield, 1982; actor, co-writer, dir. (film) This Is Spinal Tap, 1984; dir. (films) The Sure Thing, 1985, Stand By Me, 1986, Rumor Has It, 2005, The Bucket List, 2007; dir. prodr. (films) The Princess Bride, 1987, When Harry Met Sally, 1989, Misery, 1990, A Few Good Men, 1992, North, 1994, The American President, 1995, Ghosts of Mississippi, 1996, The Story of Us, 1999, Alex & Emma, 2003, The Bucket List, 2007; co-creator (TV series) The Super, 1972; co-creator, actor (TV series) Free Country, 1977-78, co-author(dir., prodr.) Flipped, 2009. Mem. SAG, AFTRA, Dir. Guild Am., Writers Guild Am. Office: Castle Rock Entertainment 335 N Maple Dr Ste 135 Beverly Hills CA 90210-3867

REINER, THOMAS KARL, manufacturing executive, engineering scientist; b. Budapest, Hungary, Dec. 29, 1931; came to U.S., 1959; s. Pál and Jozefa (Keller) R.; m. Joyce Kramer (div.); children: Paul A., Reneé K. Hedsand; m. Eleanor Ruth Aldridge (div.); m. Bonnie Sherman, 1995. Diploma optics trade sch., Budapest, 1952; MSME, Tech. U., Budapest, 1955; postgrad., London Coll., 1958, U. Pitts., Carnegie Inst. Tech., 1964; PhD, U. Wexford, England, 2001. Shift charge engr. Power Sta., Hungary, 1954-56; test engr. Blaw-Knox Co., London, 1956-57; sr. engr. Eubank & Ptnrs., London, 1957-59; rsch. engr. Pitts. Plate Glass Co., 1959-60, product mgr. Copes-Vulcan divsn., 1960-62; chief engr. J.W. Fecker divsn. Am. Optical Co., 1962-66; product mgr. Carco Electronics, Calif., 1966-68; chief engr. Fairchild Camera Space and Def. Divsn., Calif., 1968-70; dir. engring. Templeton, Kenly & Co., 1970-72; gen. mgr. Foremark Corp., Calif., 1972-74; owner Kinetron, Inc., Calif., 1974-76, GRW, Inc., Calif., 1977-97; pres. Renmark-Pacific Corp., Calif., 1998—2003; chief engring. scientist Integrated Def. Sys., The Boeing Co., Calif., 2004—. Adj. prof. math. Tech. U., Budapest, 1951-54. Pres. Peacock Ridge Homeowners Assn., Calif. Lt. Hungarian Army, 1951-57. Mem.: ASME, Internat. Soc. Weighing and Measurements. Achievements include patents for concrete post tensioning device, air bearing and slave connector for Satellite Attitude Control Space Simulator; synchronization of hydraulic jacking systems to raise the Freemont Street Bridge in one piece; bending of automotive side windows; invention of a tug/barge latching system, membrane type PANCAKE loadcells, ultra low profile industrial scales, air cargo direct loading device. Home: 14110 Valley Vista Blvd Sherman Oaks CA 91423 Office Phone: 310-367-9997. Personal E-mail: t-reiner@pacbell.net.

REINER, VAN R., museum administrator; b. Lakewood, Ohio; m. Shirley C. Reiner; 3 children. BS, Wittenberg U., Springfield, Ohio, 1970; MS, Lehigh U. With Bethlehem Steel Corp., 1974—2004, coke dept. engr. Lackawanna, NY, 1974—84, asst. supt. slab mill/plate mills dept. Burns Harbor, Ind., 1984—90, supt. slab mill/plate mills dept., 1990—95, supt. galvanized products divsn., 1995—97, sr. mgr. ops. Burns Harbor Divsn., 1997—98, pres. Bethlehem Lukens Plate, 1998—2000, pres. Bethlehem Sparrows Point Divsn. Md., 2000—04; acting exec. Md. Sci. Ctr., Balt., 2004—05, pres., CEO, 2005—, also bd. dirs., 2001—05, mem. sci. coun., 2002—05. Founding mem., treas. Partnership for Balt.'s Waterfront. Mem.: Assn. Sci.-Tech. Centers. Office: Md Sci Ctr 601 Light St Baltimore MD 21230

REINERT, JAMES A., entomology educator; b. Enid, Okla., Jan. 26, 1944; s. Andrew J. and Emma Reinert; m. Anita Irwin; children: Travis J., Gina N., Mindy K., Melanie B., Gregory W., Teresa J. BS, Okla. State U., Stillwater, 1966; MS, Clemson U., SC, 1968, PhD, 1970. Asst. state entomologist U. Md., College Park, 1970; asst. prof. entomology to prof. entomology Ft. Lauderdale Rsch. and Edn. Ctr., U. Fla., 1970-84; resident dir., prof. entomology Tex. A&M Univ. Sys., Dallas, 1984-94, prof. entomology, 1994—2003, prof. entomology, Tex. agrilife rsch. faculty fellow, 2004—, regents fellow, 2005—. Contbr. over 460 articles to profl. jours. Grantee, NDEA, 1968. Mem. Inter-Turfgrass Soc., Entomol. Soc. Am. (S.W. br. sec.-treas. 1998, pres. 2000, chair sec. sect. F 2005, award in urban entomology 2002), So. Nurserymen's Assn. (Porter Henegar Meml. award 1982), Fla. Entomol. Soc. (v.p. 1983, pres. 1984, Entomologist of Yr. 1985), Fla. State Hort. Soc. (v.p. 1982), S.C. Entomol. Soc. (J.H. Cochran award 2002, Rsch. Ctr. Adminstrs. Soc. (v.p. 1994, state rep. 1991-92, sec. 1993), Dallas Agr. Club (bd. dirs. 1989, v.p. 1990, pres. 1991). Roman Catholic. Home: 3805 Covinton Ln Plano TX 75023-7731 Office: Tex A&M Agri Life Rsch and Ext Ctr 17360 Coit Rd Dallas TX 75252-6599 Office Phone: 972-231-5362. Business E-Mail: j-reinert@tamu.edu.

REINERT, NORBERT FREDERICK, lawyer, retired chemicals executive; b. Hamilton, Ohio, Apr. 12, 1928; s. Fred F. and Jennie A. R.; m. Ida Elizabeth Barickman, Jan. 26, 1956; children: Matthew W., Paul H. B.Ch.E., Ohio State U., 1951; LL.B., Cleve.-Marshall Law Sch., 1959. Bar: Ohio 1959, D.C. 1961. Patent agt. Standard of Ohio, Cleve., 1957-59, patent lawyer, 1959-60, E.I. duPont de Nemours & Co., Wilmington, Del., 1960-91, dir. investor relations, 1981-84, mng. counsel, 1985-91; v.p., gen. counsel Endo Labs, Inc. subs. DuPont, Garden City, NY, 1971-73, exec. v.p., 1973-77, pres., 1977-81; pvt. practice patent law, 1991—2002. Served with Chem. Corps AUS, 1955-56. Mem. Am. Patent Law Assn., Tau Beta Pi. Republican. Roman Catholic. Home: PO Box 311 Mendenhall PA 19357-0311

REINERTSEN, NORMAN, retired air transportation executive; b. Bklyn., Mar. 27, 1934; s. Berthin and Malene Katherine (Dahl) R.; m. Elizabeth T. O'Shea, Aug. 30, 1958 (dec. 2003); children: Michael, Christopher, Katherine. BEE, CCNY, 1960; postgrad., Harvard U., 1982. Registered profl. engr., Calif. Various positions Grumman Aerospace Corp., 1960-75; gen. mgr. Grumman Aerospace Corp. (Great River ops.), 1975-77; v.p. automotive Grumman Allied Industries, Melville, NY, 1977-83, sr. v.p. vehicle div., 1983-94; sr. v.p. Olson Bodies, Inc., 1977-79; exec. v.p. Grumman Flexible, Delaware, Ohio, 1979-82; pres. Grumman Olson, Mellville, 1983-85; sr. v.p. Vehicle div. Grumman Allied, 1985-87; v.p. quality ops. Grumman Aircraft Sys. div. Northrop Grumman, 1987-94; ret., 1994. With U.S. Army, 1955-57. Mem. Air Force Assn., Northport Yacht Club. Home: 7 Oleander Dr Northport NY 11768-3438

REINFELDT, MIKE (MICHAEL RAY REINFELDT), professional sports team executive, former professional football player; b. Baraboo, Wis., May 6, 1953; m. Susan Reinfeldt; children: Jared Michael, Elise Marie. BA in Mktg., U. Milwaukee-Wis., 1975; MBA in Mgmt. & Fin., Houston Baptist U., 1985. Safety Oakland Raiders, Calif., 1976, Houston Oilers, Tex., 1976—83; CFO LA Raiders, 1985—87; assoc. athletic dir. U. So. Calif., 1988—90; CFO Green Bay Packers, 1991—98, v.p. admin., 1994—98; sr. v.p. Seattle Seahawks, 1999—2004, consul., v.p. football admin., 2005—07; gen. mgr., Tenn. Titans, 2007—. Named NFL Defensive Player Yr., 1979; named to NFL All-Pro Team, 1979, Am. Football Conf. Pro Bowl Team, 1979. Office: Tenn Titans One Titans Way Nashville TN 37213*

REINGLASS, MICHELLE ANNETTE, lawyer, mediator, arbitrator; b. LA, Dec. 9, 1954; d. Darwin and Shirley (Steiner) R. Student, U. Calif., Irvine, 1972-75; BSL, Western State U., 1977; JD, Western State U., Coll. Law, 1978. Bar: Calif. 1979, U.S. Dist. Ct. (ctrl. dist.) Calif. 1979, U.S. Ct. Appeals (9th cir.) 1981, U.S. Dist. Ct. (so. dist.) Calif. 1990. Pvt. practice employee litig., Laguna Hills, Calif., 1979—. Instr. Calif. Continuing Edn. of Bar, 1990—, Western State Coll., 1991, Rutter Group, 1994—; chmn. magistrate selection com. ctrl. dist. US Dist. Ct.,Calif., LA, 1991, 93-95, com. mem., 1994-97, 2003-06, lawyer rep. to 9th cir. jud. conf.; lectr. in field. Contbr. articles to profl. jours. Pres., bd. dirs. Child or Parental Emergency Svcs., Santa Ana, Calif., 1982-92; bd. dirs. Pub. Law Ctr., Santa Ana, Coalition for Justice, Working Wardrobes; mem. exec. com. and cast CHOC Follies. Recipient Jurisprudence award Anti-Defamation League, 1997; named to Western State U. Hall of Fame, 1993; named one of Top 100 Most Influential Lawyers in Calif., LA Daily Jour., 2001; one of Top 30 Female Litigators in Calif., LA Daily Jour., 2002; one of Top 50 Female Litigators, LA Daily Jour., 2003-04; named to Super Lawyers, LA Mag., 2004-07. Fellow Coll. Labor and Employee Lawyers; mem. State Bar Calif., Assn. Bus. Trial Lawyers (bd. dirs.), Orange County Bar Assn. (del. to state conv. 1980-94, bd. dirs. 1983-94, chmn. bus. litigation sect. 1989, sec. 1990, treas. 1991, pres.-elect 1992, pres. 1993), Nat. Employee Lawyers Assn., Calif. Employee Lawyers Assn. (com. mem., chair 2005-07), Orange County Trial Lawyers Assn. (bd. dirs. 1987-89, Bus. Trial Lawyer of Yr. award 1995, Employee Trial Lawyer of Yr. 2004), So. Calif. Mediation Assn., Orange County Women Lawyers (Lawyer of Yr. award 1996), Vols. in Parole (chmn. adv. com. 1990-91), Peter Elliot Inns Ct. (master), Am. Bd. of Trial Advocates. Avocations: distance running, skiing. Office: 23161 Mill Creek Dr Ste 170 Laguna Hills CA 92653-1650 E-mail: michelle@reinglasslaw.com.

REINGOLD, DAVID AMI, sociologist, educator; b. Chgo., Oct. 30, 1968; s. Haim and Badonna Reingold. BA in Sociology and Social Welfare, U. Wis., 1990; MA in Sociology, U. Chgo., 1992, PhD in Sociology, 1996. Asst. prof. Ind. U., Bloomington, 1997—2003, assoc. prof., 2003—08; dir. rsch. and policy devel. Corp. for Nat. and Cmty. Svc., Washington, 2002—04; dir. pub. affairs and doctoral pub. policy programs Ind. U. Sch. Pub. and Environ. Affairs, 2006—08, assoc. dean, 2009—, prodr., 2009—. Rsch. assoc. Ctr. for the Study of Urban Inequality, Chgo., 1990—94; program assoc. Govs. Task Force on Human Svcs. Reform, Chgo., 1993; rsch. assoc. Dept. Children and Family Svcs., Chgo., 1996; field assoc. Rockefeller Inst. Govt., Albany, NY, 1996—98. Contbr. articles to profl. jours. Family self sufficiency com. Bloomington Housing Authority, 1997—2002, chmn. family self-sufficiency com., 1998—2002; housing commr. Bloomington Housing Authority Bd., 1999—2002, vice chmn., 2000—02; task force for disadvantaged youth White House, 2002—03; chmn. Ind. Commn. on Cmty. Svc. and Volunteerism, 2005—; pres. bd. dirs. South Ctrl. Ind. Cmty. Action Program, 2006—09; mem., editl. bd. Jour. Urban Affairs, 2001—, Jour. Policy Analysis & Mgmt., 2009—, mng. editor & co-editor, 2004—09. Grantee rsch. grantee, Ind. Family Social Svcs. Adminstrn., The Joyce Found., Ind. Twp. Assn., 1998—2000, The Joyce Found., 2001—02, Carnegie Corp. NY, 2005—06; fellow fellwship on race, poverty and social policy, NSF/U. Chgo., 1992—96; scholar Century scholar, U. Chgo., 1990—92. Mem.: Assn. for Pub. Policy Analysis and Mgmt. (policy com. 2003—07), Urban Affairs Assn., Am. Sociol. Assn. Office: Ind Univ, Sch Pub & Environ Affairs 1315 E 10th St Bloomington IN 47405 Office Phone: 812-855-5971. Business E-Mail: reingold@indiana.edu.

REINHARD, CHRISTOPHER JOHN, merchant banker, venture capitalist, biotechnologist, director; b. Bridgeport, Conn., Nov. 11, 1953; s. Warren John and Marian Louise (Dutter) R.; m. Maureen Francis, Sept. 24, 1977; 1 child, Griffin John. BS, Babson Coll., 1976, MBA, 1977. Sr. fin. analyst Gen. Motors Corp., Detroit and NYC, 1977-81; asst. sec. Wheelabrator-Frye Inc., NH, 1981-83; asst. sec., asst. treas. The Signal Cos., Inc., La Jolla, Calif., 1983-86; mng. dir., v.p. The Henley Group, Inc., La Jolla, 1986-90; mng. dir. Fisher Sci. Group, Inc., La Jolla, 1986-90; mng. dir., v.p. Wheelabrator Tech. Inc., Henley Mfg. Corp., 1987-90; founder, pres. Colony Group Inc., Rancho Santa Fe, 1990—, Reinhard Assocs., Rancho Santa Fe, 1990-95; founder, v.p., CFO Advanced Access, Inc., San Diego, 1995-97. Pres. Direct Feedback, Inc., 1990, Dairy Queen Ventures, 1990-94, Winsor Sport Fencing, 1993—; CEO, founder, pres. Collateral Therapeutics Inc., 1995-2005; gen. ptnr. Cabrillo Ventures, 1995-96; founder, pres. ihumon, 2000—; exec. chmn. Artes Med., Inc., 2004—; exec. chmn., CEO, founder Cardium Therapeutics Inc., 2003—. Mem. Boston Athenaeum, N.Y. Athletic Club, San Diego Polo Club, Rancho Santa Fe Polo Club. Office: Cardium Therapeutics 12255 El Camino Real Ste 250 San Diego CA 92130-4090

REINHARD, JOAO PEDRO, chemicals company executive; b. Sao Paulo, Brazil, Aug. 4, 1945; BA, MBA, Escola de Administração de Empresas, da Fundação Getulio Vargas, São Paulo, Brazil, 1967; completed postgraduate studies at the U. Cologne, Germany and Stanford U. Fin. planning supr. Squibb do Brazil, Sao Paulo, 1968; credit mgr. Dow Quimica, Sao Paulo, 1970-72; fin. asst. Dow Latin Am., Miami, Fla., 1973; treas. Latin Am. Dow Lepetit Latin Am., Miami, Fla., 1974-76; corp. fin. planning mgr. Dow Chem. Co., Midland, Mich., 1976-77, treas., 1988—96, v.p., 1990—95, fin. v.p., 1995—96, CFO, 1995—2005, exec. v.p., 1996—2005, sr. advisor, 2005; fin. dir. Dow Quimica S.Am., Sao Paulo, Brazil, 1978-80, Dow Europe, Horgen, Switzerland, 1981-85, asst. treas., 1984, v.p., 1985-87; mng. dir. Dow Italy, Milan, 1985—88. Bd. dirs. Royal Bank of Canada, 2000-, Dow Corning Corp., 1995-2007, Sigma-Aldrich Corp., 2001-, Coca-Cola Co., 2003-06, Colgate-Palmolive Co., 2006-, Liana Ltd., Midland, Mich., Dorinco Reinsurance Co., Midland, Dow Chem. Internat. BV, Midland, DCOMCO Inc., Midland, Dow Chm. Inter-Am. Ltd., Midland, Dow Chem. Internat. Inc. (Panama), Midland, Dow Chem. Internat. Ltd., Midland, Midland Pipeline Corp., Dow Chem. Overseas Capital NV, Midland, Bank Mendes Gans NV, Amsterdam, The Netherlands; mem. Environment Health & Safety Com., Dow Chemical Co. Mem. Fin. Execs. Inst., Fin. Mgmt. Assn., Nat. Assn. Corp. Treasurers, Corp. Fin. Inst.

REINHARDT, DANIEL SARGENT, lawyer; b. Orange, NJ, Jan. 27, 1949; s. Warren Irwin and Winifred Ruth (Sargent) R.; m. Elizabeth Ann Johnson, June 11, 1982; 1 child, Meredith Alexandra. BA, Duke U., 1971; JD, Georgetown U., 1974. Bar: Ga. 1975, U.S. Dist. Ct. (no. dist.) Ga. 1975, U.S. Ct. Appeals (5th and 11th cirs.) 1981, U.S. Dist. Ct. (so. dist.) Ga. 1984, U.S. Dist. Ct. (mid. dist.) Ga. 1985, U.S. Ct. Appeals (4th cir.) 1985. Assoc. Troutman Sanders LLP, Atlanta, 1974—79, ptnr., 1980—, mem. exec. com. Dep. asst. atty. gen. State of Ga., 1975-79. Named a Super Lawyer, Atlanta Mag., 2004. Mem. ABA, Ga. Bar Assn., Atlanta Bar Assn., fellow, Am. Coll. Trial Lawyers, Lawyers Club. Avocation: sports. Office: Troutman Sanders LLP 600 Peachtree St Atlanta GA 30308-2265 Office Phone: 404-885-3206. Office Fax: 404-885-3900. Business E-Mail: daniel.reinhardt@troutmansanders.com.

REINHARDT, GEORGE ROBERT, lawyer; b. Tifton, Ga., Mar. 1, 1954; BBA magna cum laude, U. Ga., 1975; JD, U. Va., 1978. Bar: Ga. 1979. Atty. Reinhardt, Whitley, Wilmot, Summerlin & Pittman, PC, Tifton, Ga. Mem.: Tifton Bar Assn., State Bar Ga. (bd. govs. 1992—, state disciplinary bd. review panel 1993—98, chmn. 1996—98, fin. com. 1996—, program com. 1998—, exec. com. 1998—, chair fin. com. 1999—2000, treas. 2000—01, pres.-elect 2003—, pres. 2004), Sphinx Soc. Office: Reinhardt Whitley Wilmot et al PO Drawer 1287 1001 N Central St Tifton GA 31794

REINHARDT, JOHN EDWARD, former international affairs specialist; b. Glade Spring, Va., Mar. 8, 1920; s. Edward Vinton and Alice (Miller) R.; m. Carolyn Lillian Daves, Sept. 2, 1947; children: Sharman W. Reinhardt Lancefield, Alice N., Carolyn C. Reinhardt Fenstermaker. AB, Knoxville Coll., 1939; MS, U. Wis., 1947, PhD, 1950. Prof. English Va. State Coll., Petersburg, 1950-56; cultural affairs officer USIS, Manila, 1956-58; dir. Am. Cultural Ctr., Kyoto, Japan, 1958-63; cultural attache USIS, Tehran, Iran, 1963-66; dep. asst. dir. Office East Asia and Pacific, USIA, Washington, 1966-68, 70-71, asst. dir. Office for Africa, 1968-70; ambassador to Nigeria, 1971-75; asst. sec. state for pub. affairs, 1975-77; dir. USIA, Washington, 1977-78, U.S. Internat. Communication Agy., Washington, 1978-81; acting dir. Smithsonian Mus. African Art, Washington, 1981-83; asst. sec. for history and art Smithsonian Instn., Washington, 1983-84, dir. directorate internat. activities, 1984-87; prof. polit. sci. U. Vt., Burlington, 1987-90, prof. emeritus, 1990—. Served as officer AUS, 1942-46. Mem. MLA, Am. Fgn. Svc. Assn. (v.p. 1969-71). Clubs: Cosmos. Methodist. Home: 3154 Gracefield RD APT 417 Silver Spring MD 20904-0808 E-mail: john.reinhardt3@verizon.net.

REINHARDT, LEROY JACOB, lawyer; b. Fresno, Calif., Aug. 18, 1924; s. Jacob and Marie Huber Reinhardt; m. Janet Velma Reinhardt, Oct. 2, 1953; children: Garth Lynn, Brad Allen, Stacey Regan, Rodney LeRoy, Rhonda Lee. BA, Fresno State U., Calif., 1947; LLD, Stanford U., Palo Alto, Calif., 1950. Legal assoc. Crossland & Crossland, Fresno, 1950—54; sole practice Fresno, 1954—. Dir. Internat. Water Dist., Fresno; sec. Garfield Dist. Water Coun. Lt. USN, 1943—46. Republican. Avocations: woodworking, gardening, farming. Home: 13155 W Shaw Kerman CA 93630 Office: 1500 W Shaw Fresno CA 93711

REINHARDT, NOLA, economics educator; b. N.Y.C., Jan. 17, 1947; d. Bernard Moses and Judith (Kopper) R.; m. Richard Edward Iacovelli, Sept. 1, 1984; children: Amalia Ann, Elena Grace. AB summa cum laude, U. Conn., 1968; MA, U. Calif.-Berkeley, 1979, PhD, 1981. Programmer, analyst Bunker-Ramo Corp., Trumbull, Conn., 1968-71; sr. systems analyst GTE Info. Systems, N.Y.C., 1971-74; asst. prof. econ. Smith Coll., Northampton, Mass., 1981-88; assoc. prof., 1988—2001, prof., 2001-. Author: Our Daily Bread: The Peasant Question and Family Farming in the Colombian Andes, 1988, The Microeconomics of the New Economic in Latin America, 2000. Contbr. articles to profl. jours. Cons. U.N. Econ. Commn. Latin Am. and Caribbean; spkr. Oxfam-Am., 1983; steering com. Northampton Com. on Central Am., 1983. Univ. scholar U. Conn., 1967; fellowship Boren Com., doctoral fellow Inter-Am. Found., 1978; travel grantee U. Calif.-Berkeley Ctr. for Latin Am. Studies, and Tinker Found., 1978; Picker fellow Smith Coll., 1983.; Mem. Latin Am. Studies Assn. (task force on scholarly rels. with Nicaragua 1983-88), New Eng. Coun. Latin Am. Studies (exec. bd. 1987-89, 99-02, 06-09, dissertation prize 1982, hon. mention book award 1988, Best Article prize, 2001), Soc. Econ. Anthropology (exec. bd. 1987-89, prize com. 1992), Econ. History Assn., Phi Beta Kappa, Mortar Bd. Office: Smith Coll Neilson B 13 Northampton MA 01063-0001

REINHARDT, STEPHEN ROY, federal judge; b. NYC, Mar. 27, 1931; s. Gottfried and Silvia (Hanlon) Reinhardt; children: Mark, Justin, Dana. BA cum laude, Pomona Coll., 1951; LLB, Yale, 1954. Bar: Calif. 1958. Law clk. to Hon. Luther W. Youngdahl US Dist. Ct., Washington, 1956—57; atty. O'Melveny & Myers, LA, 1957—59; ptnr. Fogel Julber Reinhardt Rothschild & Feldman LC, LA, 1959—80; judge US Ct. Appeals (9th cir.), LA, 1980—. Adj. prof. Loyola Law Sch., LA, 1988—90. Pres. LA Recreation and Parks Commn., 1974—75; active Coliseum Commn., 1974—75, LA Police Commn., 1974—78, pres., 1978—80; sec., exec. organizing com. LA Olympics, 1980—84; exec. com. Dem. Nat. Com., 1969—72; nat. Dem. committeeman State of Calif., 1976—80; bd. dirs. Amateur Athletic Found. LA, 1984—92. 1st lt. USAF, 1954—56. Mem.: ABA (labor law coun. 1975—77), Calif. Bar Assn., LA County Bar Assn. Office Phone: 213-894-3639.*

REINHARDT, STEVEN K., computer scientist; BS, Case Western Res. U., 1987; MS, Stanford U., 1988; PhD, U. Wis.-Madison, 1996. Prof. U. Mich., Ann Arbor, 1997—2006; mng. engr. Reservoir Labs Inc., Portland, Oreg., 2006—08; fellow Advanced Micro Devices, Bellevue, Wash., 2008—.

REINHARDT, WILLIAM PARKER, chemical physicist, educator; b. San Francisco, May 22, 1942; s. William Oscar and Elizabeth Ellen (Parker) R.; m. Katrina Hawley Currens, Mar. 14, 1979; children: James William, Alexander Hawley. BS in Basic Chemistry, U. Calif., Berkeley, 1964; AM in Chemistry, Harvard U., 1966, PhD in Chem. Physics, 1968; MA (hon.), U. Pa., 1985. Instr. chemistry Harvard U., 1967-69, asst. prof. chemistry, 1969-72, assoc. prof., 1972-74; prof. U. Colo., Boulder, 1974-84, chmn. dept. chemistry, 1977-80; prof. chemistry U. Pa., Phila., 1984-91, chmn. dept., 1985-88, D. Michael Crow prof., 1987-91; prof. chemistry U.Wash., Seattle, 1991—, assoc. chmn. undergrad. program, 1993-96. Adj. prof. physics U. Wash., Seattle, 1998—; vis. fellow Joint Inst. for Lab. Astrophysics of Nat. Bur. Stds. and U. Colo., 1972, 74, fellow, 1974-84; dir. Telluride Summer Rsch. Ctr., 1986-89, treas., 1989-93; com. on atomic, molecular and optical scis. NRC, 1988-90; sub com. Internat. Union Pure and Applied Physics, Atomic Molecular Physics, 2002—05; vis. scientist Nat. Inst. Stds. and Tech., summers 1993—, Harvard-MIT Ctr. Ultra-Cold Atoms, 2005; vis. prof. chemistry U. Paris VI, 1991, U. Melbourne, Australia, 1997, Harvard U., 1998, Davidson lectr. U. Kans., 2000; Kohler lectr. U. Calif., Riverside, 2002; R.S. Berry pub. lectr. Telluride, Colo., 2004, Bertman Meml. lectr. Wesleyan U., Middletown, Conn., 2005. Mem. editl. bd. Phys. Rev. A., 1979-81, 05-, Chem. Physics, 1985-94, Jour. Chem. Physics, 1987-89, Jour. Physics B. (U.K.), 1992-2004, Internat. Adv. Bd., 2004-; Internat. Jour. Quantum Chemistry, 1994-2001, Digital Libr. of Math. Functions, 1999-; rschr. theoretical chem. physics, theoretical atomic and molecular physics for numerous publs Recipient Camille and Henry Dreyfus Tchr. Scholar award, 1972; Alfred P. Sloan fellow, 1972; J.S. Guggenheim Meml. fellow, 1978; Coun. on Rsch. and Creative Work faculty fellow, 1978; Wilsmore fellow U. Melbourne (Australia), 1997; J.W. Fulbright sr. scholar, Australia, 1997. Fellow AAAS, Am. Phys. Soc., Inst. Physics (U.K.), Phi Beta Kappa; mem. Am. Chem. Soc., Sigma Xi (nat. lectr. 1980-82), Phi Lambda Upsilon (Fresenius award 1977), Phi Beta Kappa (vis. scholar 2002-03, disting. fellow lectr., 2004-, Couper lectr. 2006-07, mem. nat. nominating com. 2006-). Office: U Wash Dept Chemistry Box 351700 Seattle WA 98195-1700 Office Phone: 206-543-0578. Business E-Mail: rein@chem.washington.edu.

REINHART, CONNIE S., academic administrator, educator; BS in Elementary Edn., Edinboro U., Pa., 1972, MEd, 1976; postgrad., U. Alaska, 2003. Cert. in pub. sch. adminstrn. U. Alaska, 1984. Tchr. Polk County Sch. Sys., Fla., 1972—73, Greensville Sch. Dist., Pa., 1973—79; demonstration tchr. U. Pitts., Pa., 1979—80; spl. edn. tchr. Anchorage Sch. Dist., Alaska, 1981—89, tchr. in charge Alaska, 1988—91, tchr. Alaska, 1989—91, asst. prin. Alaska, 1991—92, prin. Alaska, 1992—2003; dir. tchr., edn. assoc. prof. Thiel Coll., Greenville, Pa., 2006—, adj. prof., 2003—05, lectr., 2005—. Curriculam study com. mem. Thiel Coll., 2007—08, middle states steering com. mem., 2008—; consumer reviewer Dept. Defense, Va., 2007—. Contbr. articles to profl. jours. Team leader & field coord. Nat. Breast Cancer Coalition, Washington, 2003—. Recipient Superior Tchr. award, U. Pitts., Pa., 1979, Excellence for Children award, Chester Valley Parents/Tchr. Assn., 1996, ASTE Tech. Using Adminstr. of Yr. award, Alaska Soc. Tech. Edn., 1996—97, Tech. Leadership award, Alaska Assn. Elementary Sch. Prin., 1997, Outstand Svc. award, 1997, Gold Pan award, Anchorage Sch. Dist. & Prin. Assn. Mentor Prog., 2000—01, Suzanne H. Kay Advocacy award, Phila., Pa., 2007, Disting. Tchr. of Yr. award, Thiel Coll., 2009; Bilingual Program Devel. grant, US Dept. Edn.'s Office Bilingual Edn. & Minority Lans. Affairs, 2001—03. Mem.: Alaska Breast Cancer Advocacy Ptnr., Anchorage (bd. mem. 2002—), Am. Assn. U. Profs., Nat. Assn. Elementary Sch. Prin.'s, Kappa Delta Pi. Home: 7740 Lake Blvd Jamestown PA 16134 Office: Thiel Coll 75 Coll Ave Greenville PA 16125 Home Phone: 724-927-9532; Office Phone: 724-589-2065. Personal E-mail: creinhart@zoominternet.net. Business E-Mail: creinhart@thiel.edu.

REINHART, KELLEE CONNELY, journalist; b. Kearney, Nebr., Dec. 15, 1951; d. Vaughn Eugene and Mary Jo (Mullen) Connely; m. Stephen Wayne Reinhart, June 15, 1974; children: Keegan Connely, Channing Mullen. BA, U. Ala., 1972, MS, 1974. Advt. copywriter Stas. WTBC-AM, WUOA-FM, 1970-72; asst. mgr. Ala. Press Assn., 1972-74; asst. to the editor Antique Monthly mag., 1974-75, mng. editor, 1975-77; editorial dir. Antique Monthly and Horizons mags., 1977-89; dir. univ. rels. U. Ala. Sys., Tuscaloosa, 1989—2004, vice chancellor for sys. rels., 2004—. Editor: Wild Birds of America: The Art of Basil Ede, 1991, Centennial Memories, Millennial Hopes, 2000, The People's City, 2003. Bd. dirs. Ala. Humanities Found.; bd. dirs. Ala. Writers Forum, pres., 1999—2001. Recipient Druids Arts award, 1995, Betsy Plank Disting. Achievement award U. Ala., 2006. Mem. Soc. Profl. Journalists, Am. Soc. Mag. Editors, Newcomen Soc. U.S., Art Table, XXI/U. Ala. Women's Hon. Soc. Office: 401 Queen City Ave Tuscaloosa AL 35401-1551 Business E-Mail: kreinhar@uasystem.ua.edu.

REINHART, PETER SARGENT, lawyer; b. Mineola, NY, May 17, 1950; s. Charles Woodham and Martha Way (Sargent) R.; m. Susan Stockwell, Aug. 29, 1970 (div. Jan. 1976); 1 child, Amy Lynn; m. Gale McElroy, Oct. 16, 1976 (div. May 1985); 1 child, James Gharrett; m. Carol O. Gaffney, Jan. 4, 1992 (div. Jan. 2001); m. Nancy Jean Byrne, Nov. 4, 2006. BA, Franklin and Marshall Coll., 1971; JD, Rutgers U., 1975. Bar: N.J. 1975. Atty. Pillsbury and Russell, Atlantic Highlands, NJ, 1975-78; corp. counsel K. Hovnanian Enterprises, Inc., Red Bank, NJ, 1978-81, sr. v.p., gen. counsel, 1981—; also bd. dirs. Pres. Inst. Multi-Family Housing, Plainsboro, N.J., 1989-90. Trustee, mem. editorial bd. Housing N.J. mag., 1991—. Trustee Cmty. Assns. Inst., Arlington, Va., pres. NJ chpt., 1988; trustee Assn. for Children of NJ, Newark, 1988-93, Keep Middlesex Moving, New Brunswick, 1990-93,

Bayshore Cmty. Hosp., Holmdel, NJ, 1992-01, v.p., 1995, chmn., 1997, Meridian Hosp. Corp., 2002—, vice chmn., 2007, chmn. 2005-; chmn. Jersey Shore Partnership, 2003-08; pres. Greater Red Bank Jaycees, 1978-79, Atlantic Highlands Rep. Club, 1978; v.p. Monmouth coun. Boy Scouts Am., Oakhurst, NJ, 1987-94, pres., 1994-95; v.p. Garden State Games, Edison, NJ, 1991-94; mem. Coun. Affordable Housing, Trenton, NJ, 1993-04, chmn. Kaboun Fireworks Navesink Inc., 2008. Named to Community Assns. Inst. Hall of Fame, 1988; named Jaycee of Yr. Greater Red Bank Jaycees, 1977. Mem. N.J. State Bar Assn., N.J. Shore Builders Assn. (pres. 1989-90, Builder of Yr. 1987, Hall of Fame 1991), Nat. Assn. Indsl. and Office Parks (bd. dirs. 1990-92), N.J. Builders Assn. (v.p. 1992-94, pres. 1995-96, Builder of Yr. award 1995, Shore Athletic Club (Oakhurst), Ea. Monmouth C. of C. (trustee 1992-98, Vol. of Yr. 1995). Avocations: road racing, marathon running, golf. Office: Hovnanian Enterprises Inc PO Box 500 110 West Front St Red Bank NJ 07701-5902

REINHARZ, JEHUDA, academic administrator, history educator; b. Haifa, Israel, Aug. 1, 1944; came to U.S., 1961; s. Fred and Anita (Weigler) R.; m. Shulamit Rothschild, Nov. 26, 1967; children— Yael, Naomi BS, Columbia U., 1967; BRE, Jewish Theol. Sem., 1967; MA, Harvard U., 1968; PhD, Brandeis U., 1972; LHD (hon.), Hebrew Union Coll., 1995; DHL (hon.), Jewish Theol. Soc. Am., 1996, Fairfield U., 1999. Prof. modern Jewish history U. Mich., Ann Arbor, 1972—82; Richard Koret prof. modern Jewish history Brandeis U., Waltham, Mass., 1982—84, dir. Tauber Inst. Study of European Jewry, 1984—94; provost, sr. v.p. for acad. affairs Brandels U., Waltham, Mass., 1992—94; pres. Brandeis U., Waltham, Mass., 1994—. Mem. internat. acad. bd. Annenberg Rsch. Inst., 1986-90; bd. dirs. Yad Chaim Weizmann, 1990-2000, Internat. Editl. Bd. Pardès, 1996—; pres. Israel Prize, 1990, Akiba award, Am.-Jewish Com., 1996. Author: Fatherland or Promised Land: The Dilemma of the German Jew 1893-1914, 1975, Chaim Weizmann: The Making of a Zionist Leader, 1985 (Present Tense Literary award 1985, Kenneth B. Smilen Literary award 1985, Nat. Jewish Book award 1986, Shazar prize in history Israel, 1988), (in Hebrew) Hashomer Hazair in Germany, 1931-39, 1989, Chaim Weizmann: The Making of a Statesman, 1993 (Nat. Jewish Book award 1994); also numerous articles in French, German, Hebrew and English; co-author: Zionism and the Creation of a New Society, 1998, 2d edit., 2000, The Era of Political Zionism, 2000; gen. editor: Studies in Jewish History, 1984, European Jewish History, 1985; co-editor: The Jew in the Modern World, 1980, 2d edit. 1995, Mystics, Philosophers and Politicians, 1982, Israel in the Middle East 1948-83, 1984, The Jewish Response to German Culture, 1985, The Jews of Poland Between Two World Wars, 1989, The Impact of Western Nationalisms, 1992, Zionism and Religion, Hebrew edit., 1994, Essential Papers on Zionism, 1996; editor: The Letters and Papers of Chaim Weizmann, 1918-20, 1977, Dokumente zur Geschichte des deutschen Zionismus, 1882-1933, 1981, Living with Antisemitism, 1987. Bd. govs. United Israel Appeal/Jewish Agy., 1994, 2000; bd. dirs., mem. exec. com. Am. Joint Distbn. Com., 1994-2002; mem. acad. com. U.S. Holocaust Mus., 1990-2003, mem. com. on conscience nat. adv. forum, 1996—; mem. Presdl. Adv. Commn. on Holocaust Assets in U.S., 1998-2000; mem. Commn. on Israel-Diaspora Rels., 1996-97; trustee Am. Hebrew Acad., Greensboro, N.C., 2000—. Recipient Akiba award, Am. Jewish Com., 1996. Fellow Leo Baeck Inst., Royal Hist. Soc., Am. Acad. Jewish Rsch., Am. Acad. Arts and Scis.; mem. Yad Vashem Soc. (adv. bd. 1983), Nat. Coun. Shazar Ctr., Assn. for Jewish Studies (sec. 1986-88, treas./sec., 1988-94), Coun. on Fgn. Rels. Home: 66 Beaumont Ave Newton MA 02460-2331 Office: Office Of The Pres Irving Enclave 113 415 South St # Ms100 Waltham MA 02453-9110 E-mail: jreinharz@brandeis.edu.*

REINHERZ, HELEN ZARSKY, social worker, researcher; b. Boston, Aug. 4, 1923; d. Zachary and Anna (Cohen) Zarsky; m. Samuel E. Reinherz, Aug. 29, 1943; 1 son, Ellis. AB magna cum laude, Wheaton Coll., 1944; MS, Simmons Coll., 1946; S.M., Harvard U., 1962, Sc.D., 1965. Social worker Newton Family Service, Mass., 1946-49, Mass. Gen. Hosp., Boston, 1949-51; supr. psychiat. social work State Hosp., Waltham, Mass., 1958-61; faculty mem. Simmons Coll., Boston, 1965—, prof. methods rsch., 1972—, dir. research Sch. Social Work, 1968-93, dir. PhD program, 1993-96. Prin. investigator Identifying Children at Risk, 1976—84, Adaption in Adolescence, 1987—93, Adult Rsch. Project, 1998—2001, Early Adulthood Rsch. Project, 1993—97, Simmons Longitudinal Study, 2001—, Study Adolescent Drug Abuse, 1971—73; rsch. cons. Dept. Mental Health, 1970—80; chmn. Gov.'s Adv. Coun. on Mental Health and Retardation, 1972; mem. adv. com. Mental Health Manpower fo Fed. Govt., 1980—82. Author (with H. Wechler, D. Dobbins): Social Work Research in the Human Services, 1976; author: (with M. Heywood, J. Camp) A Community Response to Drug Abuse, 1976; cons., assoc. editor: Jour. Prevention, 1980—91, mem. fed. adv. com.: Rsch. in Prevention Rev., 1984—87, editl. bd.: Jour. Early Adolescence, cons. editor: NASW Jour.; contbr. articles to profl. jours. Recipient Maida H. Solomon award, Simmons Coll. Alumni, 1961, Disting. Career award, Soc. Social Work and Rsch., 2005, Rsch. Achievement award, NASW, 2005; grantee, Grant Found., 1963, Med. Found., 1967—69, NIMH, 1975—84, 1987—2007; NIH tng. fellow, 1961—65. Fellow Am. Orthopsychiat. Assn.; mem. Acad. Cert. Social Workers, Am. Pub. Health Assn., Coun. Social Work Edn., Harvard Sch. Pub. Health Alumni Assn. (sec.-treas. 1965-68), Phi Beta Kappa, Delta Omega. Home: 17 Corey Rd Malden MA 02148-1116 Office: Simmons Sch Social Work 300 The Fenway Boston MA 02115 Business E-Mail: helen.reinherz@simmons.edu, reinherz@simmons.edu. *As a teacher and researcher my efforts have been directed towards encouraging students to formulate the right questions about human problems as a first step to understanding and change.*

REINHOLD, ALLEN KURT, graphic design educator; b. Salt Lake City, Feb. 21, 1936; s. Eric Kurt and Lillian (Hansen) R.; m. Irene Laura Rawlings, May 4, 1962; children: Cindy Anne, David, Alyce, Bryce, Eugene Patrick. BA, Brigham Young U., 1961, MA, 1962. Cert. secondary and post secondary tech. and indsl., Utah, color cons. Freelance artist Allen Reinhold Art & Design Studio, American Fork, Utah, 1962—; tchr. art Emery County High Sch., Castle Dale, Utah, 1962-63; graphic artist Brigham Young U., 1954-56, 63-66; prodn. artist Evans Advt. Agy., Salt Lake City, 1968; dir. ednl. media Olympus High Sch., Salt Lake City, 1966-68; art dir. Telelecture Utah div. Family Svcs., Salt Lake City, 1968-69; art instr. Utah Tech. Coll., Salt Lake City, 1969-85; prof. graphic design Salt Lake Community Coll., 1985-96, prof. emeritus, 1996—. Advisor, coach Vocat. Indsl. Clubs of Am., Salt Lake City, 1978-91. Illustrator: Book of Mormon Stories, 5 vols., 1971-76; exhibited in group shows at Salt Lake Art Festival, 1982, Pageant of the Arts, Am. Fork, 1980-89. Active Boy Scouts Am., American Fork, 1975-90; bd. dir. art Am. Fork City, 1976-80; team mem. Utah State Bd. for Vocat. Edn. Accreditation, Salt Lake City, 1990; mem. Art Rsch. in Europe, summer 1995; van driver Utah County Foster Grandparents, 2001—. Fellow Delta Phi Kappa (historian 1961-62), Salt Lake Community Coll. Faculty Senate. Republican. Mem. Lds Ch. Avocations: travel, photography, documentary video production, painting. Home: 590 N 200 E American Fork UT 84003-1711 Home Phone: 801-756-3615; Office Phone: 801-592-4112. Business E-Mail: reinhold-art@msn.com.

REINI-GRANDELL, LYNETTE EILEEN, literature and language professor, writer; b. Duluth, Minn., Jan. 21, 1960; d. Einar Elmer and Lois Edith Reini; m. Steven Grandell, June 11, 1983. BA, Carleton Coll., Northfield, 1982; MA, U. Minn., Mpls., 1990, PhD, 1992. Co-host, writer KFAI, Mpls., 2000—; English prof. Normandale CC, Bloomington, Minn., 2003—. Past pres. Minn. Coun. Tchrs. English, St. Paul, 2008—. Vestry mem. St. Mark's Episcopal Cathedral, Mpls., 2009—. Office: Normandale CC 9700 France Ave S Minneapolis MN 55431 Personal E-mail: lynette.reini-grandell@normandale.edu.

REINIKE, IRMA, retired civilian military employee, writer, artist, poet, lyricist; b. White Harbor, Long Beach, Miss., Oct. 20, 1927; d. Chester Henry and Edna Claire (Latille) Reinike; children: Harvey Franklin Linn Shows Jr., George David Shows, Thelma Jewell Shows Hoffman. Student, St. Mary's Dominican Coll.; grad., North Light Art Sch., Cin., 1996, 97, 99. Freelance writer, student Famous Writers Sch., Westport, Conn., 1965—69; editor Seabee Courier, writer US Naval Contrn. Battalion Ctr., Gulfport, 1969—71; adminstr. US Army Corps. Engrs.; ret., 1994. Author: Mystery, 1940—41, Long Beach Movie Personality, 1949, My Beach, 1990, Thelma, 1991, (poetry) My Lady of Medjugorje, 1987—88, Irma Reinike Poetry-Book 1, 2002, I Love My Flag, 2000; columnist Round the Town, Long Beach, Miss., 1963—66, The Illustrated Press, Irma Reinike's Personality Parade, New Orleans, 1952; composer: (songs) See You Tomorrow, 1995—96, Days of Love, 1997, The Blue of Your Eyes, 1997, I Am An American, 2006, No Tear Big Enough for Katrina, 2006—07, Christmas on the Beach, 2009, Songs of Irma Reinike, 2009—, (plays) Ethel Chichester, Peg O' My Heart, Kaye Hamilton, Stage Door, 1949, Song, Dance Dixieland Minstrel and Variety Artists, 1950—52, Charity Performer, Le Petit Theatre de Vieux Carre' Sunday Salon, 1996, Destruction by Hurricane Camille, Times Picayune, 1970; Introduction Camille Book-Hurricane, 1969, Art Work, Oil Painting, Ten Acres, 1970—71, Sunrise Lake Ponchartrain, exhibitions include St. Thomas Parish, Long Beach, Miss., Baton Rouge Gallery, Le Petite Theatre, New Orleans, Mandeville, La., City Long Beach, Miss., 2005, Represented in permanent collections Nat. D-Day Museum, New Orleans, prin. works include Enjoying My Beach, The Road to... No. 1, The Road to... No. 2, My Beach Dolphins; ster lyricist, composer: CD, Songs. Mem. La. Libr. Found. New Orleans Friends Pub. Libr., 1994—96; charter mem. World War II Monument Meml., Washington; mem. Nat. Rep. Senatorial Com., 1994—97, Nat. Rep. Congl. Com., 2000, Rep. Presdl. Task Force, 2007. Named Honored Author, La. Libr. Assn., 1994, 1996, La. State Libr., 1995, Friends Fest New Orleans Pub. Libr., 1994—96, Patron, Le Petit Theatre de Vieux Carre, 1996. Mem.: New Orleans Mus. Art, Long Beach, Miss. Historical Soc. Republican. Roman Catholic. Avocations: fine arts, songwriting, poetry, lyricist, philosophy.

REININGHAUS, RUTH, retired artist; b. NYC, Oct. 4, 1922; d. Emil William and Pauline Rosa (Lazarik) R.; m. George H. Morales, Feb. 20, 1944; children: George James, Robert Charles; m. Allan Joseph Smith, May 28, 1960. Student, Hunter Coll., NYU, Nat. Acad. Sch. of Design, 1960-61, Frank Reilly Sch. of Art, 1963, Art Students League, 1964-68; studied oil painting, with Robert Beverly Hale and Robert Philips, with Morton Roberts and Frank Reilly, Robert Maione, with Rudy Colao. Instr. art Banker's Trust, N.Y.C., 1971-77, 79-99, Kittredge Club for Women, N.Y.C., 1971-98. Exhibited in group shows at Berkshire Art Mus., 1970s, Hammer Galleries, Inc., N.Y.C., 1974, Far Gallery, N.Y.C., 1974, Mufalli Gallery, N.Y. and Fla., 1983-90, Pen and Brush Club, 1985—, Petrucci Gallery, Saugerties, N.Y., 1988-94, Pastel Soc. Am., 1988—, John Lane Gallery, Rhinebeck, N.Y., 1992-97, Regianni Gallery, N.Y.C., 1994, Catherine Lorillard Wolfe Club, Salmagundi Club, Allied Artists Am., Heidi Newhoff Gallery, N.Y.C., Hudson Valley Art Assn., Knickerbocker Artists, N.Y.C., Pen & Brush Club Inc., Pastel Soc. Am., Heritage Mus.; represented in permanent collections at US Navy Art, US Coast Guard Art Program, Hon. Murtogh D. Guinness, Salmagundi Club; contbr. to popular mags. Active Navy Art Coop. and Liaison, Coast Guard Art Program. Recipient 3d prize in Oils, Murray Hill Art Show, 1959, 69; Washington Sq. Outdoor Art Exhibit scholar Nat. Acad., 1962, Frank Reilly Sch. Art, 1963, NYU, 1963, Talens award, 1963, Robert Lehman award, 1968, Richtone Artists award, 1968, Baker Brush award, 1969; Salmagund scholar, 1969; subject NBC TV show You Are an Artist, 1950s. Fellow: Hudson Valley Art Assn. (Claude Parson's Meml. award 1974), Am. Artists Profl. League (2d prize oils 1992, 3d prize pastel 1993, Pres. award 1994, Hon. Mention award 2004); mem.: Helen G. Oehler, Knickerbocker Artists (Flora B. Giffuni PSA Pres.' award 1990), Oil Pastel Assn. (Pen and Brush award 1987, Strathmore award 1989, Pen and Brush award 1990, Salmagundi Club award 1991, Oil Pastel Internat. award 2006—07), Allied Artists Am. (assoc.), Washington Sq. Outdoor Art Assn. (bd. dirs. 1983—90), Nat. Arts Club (Reciprocal) Artists Fellowship, Soc. Illustrators (hon. 1983—87), Pastel Soc. Am. (bd. dirs. 1988—90, J. Giffuni purchase award 1988, Pastel Soc. of West Coast award 1997), Salmagundi Club N.Y. (pres. 1983—87, curator 1989—97, 2003—04, Philip Isenberg award 1974, Salmagundi Club prize 1985, Franklin B. Williams Fund prize 1987, Tom Picard award 1987, Mortimer E. Freehof award 1988, John N. Lewis award 1988—89, Medal of Honor 1989, Philip Isenberg award 1989—90, Helen S. Coes award 1990, Flora B. Giffuni Pres. award 1990, Thomas Moran award 1990, Samuel T. Shaw award 1990, Alphaeus Cole Meml. award 1991, Salmagundi award 1991, Alice B. McReynolds Meml. award 1991, Philip Isenberg award 1992, 1995, Harry Ballinger Meml. award 2000—01, Philip Isenberg award 2001, Jane Impastato award 2003, 1st prize John N. Lewis award 2004, Best Show award 2004, Mortimer Freehof award 2005, Art Spirit Found. Silver medal for Excellence in Pastel 2006, 2d prize for Pastel 2006), Pen and Brush Club (Helen Slotman award 1986, OPA Internat. award 1987, Gene Alden Walker award 1988, Samuel T. Shaw award 1990, Merit award 1991—96, Pen and Brush Solo award 1992, Margaret Sussman award 1996, 1998, Merit award 2000), Catharine Lorillard Wolfe Art Club (bd. dirs. 1987—97, Anna Hyatt Huntington award 1978, Coun. Am. Artists award 1985, Merit Award 1991, Pastel award 1992, Still Life award 1993, 1st prize 2001, 2d prize in Pastel 2007), Alpha Delta Pi. Lutheran. Avocations: travel, technical illustration, oil, pastel and watercolor painting, collecting antique music boxes and watches. Home: 222 E 93rd St Apt 26A New York NY 10128-3758 Personal E-mail: reininghaus@netzero.com.

REINISCH, JUNE MACHOVER, psychologist, educator, researcher; d. Mann Barnett and Lillian (Machover) R. BS cum laude, NYU, 1966; MA, Columbia U., 1970, PhD with distinction, 1976. Cert. in childhood edn. NY. Asst. prof. psychology Rutgers U., New Brunswick, N.J., 1975-80, assoc. prof. psychology New Brunswick, N.J., 1980-82, adj. assoc. prof. psychiatry, 1981-82; prof. psychology Ind. U., Bloomington, 1982-93, dir. Kinsey Inst. Rsch. in Sex, Gender, and Reprodn., 1982-93; prof. clin. psychology Sch. Medicine, Indpls., 1983-93; dir. emeritus Kinsey Inst., 1993—. Dir., prin. investigator Prenatal Devel. Projects, Copenhagen, 1976—, sr. rsch. fellow, trustee The Kinsey Inst., 1993—; pres. R2 Sci. Comms., Inc., Ind., NY, 1985—; vis. sr. rschr. Inst. of Preventive Medicine, Copenhagen Health Svcs., Kommunehospitalet, Copenhagen, 1994—; cons. SUNY; sr. cons. Mus. of Sex, NYC, 1998, dir. acquisitions and new exhbns., 2003-, v.p. sci. affairs, 2003; exec. dir. Health and Sci. Adv. Bd., 2004-. Author: The Kinsey Institute New Report on Sex, 1990, 94, pub. 8 fgn. edits.; editor, contbr. books Kinsey Inst. series; syndicated newspaper columnist: The Kinsey Report; contbr. rsch. reports, revs., articles to profl. jours.; appeared on TV shows including PBS, BBC, ABC and NBC sci. spls., Discovery, A&E, ABC & NBC Science Spls., 20/20, Oprah Winfrey, Geraldo Rivera, Charles Grodin, Montel Williams, Sally Jessy Rafael, Good Morning Am., Today Show, CBS This Morning; guest host TV shows including CNBC Real Personal, TalkLive, also fgn. appearances. Founders day scholar NYU, 1966; NIMH trainee, 1971-74; NIMH grantee, 1978-80, Ford Found. grantee, 1973-75, Nat. Inst. Edn. grantee, 1973-74, Erikson Ednl. Found. grantee, 1973-74, grantee Nat. Inst. Child Health and Human Devel., 1981-88, Nat. Inst. on Drug Abuse, 1989-95; recipient Morton Prince award Am. Psychopath. Assn., 1976, medal for 9th Dr. S.T. Huang-Chan Meml. Lectr. in anatomy Hong Kong U., 1988, Dr. Richard J. Cross award Robert Wood Johnson Med. Sch., 1991, Award First Internat. Conf. on Orgasm, New Delhi, 1991, Disting. Alumnae award Tchrs. Coll. Columbia U., 1992, award for su contbn. Profl. al Conocimiento dela Sexualidad Humana, Assn. Mexicana de Sexologia, Mexico City, 1996; named Regents lectr. UCLA, 1999. Fellow AAAS, APA, Am. Psychol. Soc., Soc. for Sci. Study Sex; mem. Internat. Acad. Sex Rsch. (charter), Internat. Women's Forum, NY Women's Forum Inc., Am. Assn. Sex. Educators, Counselors and Therapists, Sigma Xi. Avocations: travel, scuba diving, flying, skydiving. Office: Kinsey Inst Prenatal Devel Project Ind U Bloomington IN 47405 also: Mus Sex 233 Fifth Ave Ste 3B New York NY 10016 Office Phone: 212-689-6337, 718-373-2221. Business E-Mail: jreinisch@museumofsex.com.

REINISH, GLORIA BROOKS, electrical engineer, educator; b. Bklyn., July 23, 1925; d. Julius Benjamin and Celia Glickman Brooks; m. Martin David Reinish, 1948; children: Nancy Reinish Passow, Julie Brook Askins, James Charles. BSEE, Columbia U., NY, 1945, MSEE, 1948, D of Engring Sci. in Bioengineering, 1974. Mem. tech. staff Bell Telephone Lab., NYC, 1945—46; project. engr. Sperry Gyroscope Co., Lake Success, 1946—51; prof. elec. engring. Fairleigh Dickinson U., Teaneck, NJ, 1962—. Chair elec. engring. dept. Fairleigh Dickinson U., 1975—78, chair bioengring. program; cons. Medical Devices Panel FDA, 1976—86; dir. Matrix Instruments, Orangeburgh, NY, 1980—85. Contbr. numerous articles to profl. jours. Grantee Project Kaleidoscope grant, 2001. Fellow: Soc. Women Engrs.; mem.: Inst. Elec. & Electronic Engrs. (life), Tau Beta Pi (Women's Badge 1945), Sigma Xi. Achievements include patents for a new method of precision ranging; research in electrical stimulation of bone growth; being first woman to earn an engineering degree from Columbia University. Avocations: tennis, golf, piano, bridge, crossword puzzles. Office: Fairleigh Dickinson Univ 1000 River Rd Teaneck NJ 07666

REINKE, DORIS MARIE, retired elementary school educator; b. Racine, Wis., Jan. 12, 1922; d. Otto William Reinke and Louise Amelia Goehring. BS, U. Wis., 1943, MS, 1967. Tchr. kindergarten Elkhorn Area Sch. Sys., Wis., 1943—69, prin. bldg., 1968—70, dir. summer sch., 1974—75, tchr. grade 2, 1970—84, chmn. primary dept., 1967—84, administrv. asst., supervising tchr., 1957—83, student tchr., 1984, ret., 1984; tchr. oriented experience Program Area Sch. Sys., Elkhorn, 1966. Pres. Elkhorn Edn. Assn., 1949-50; rep. dist. State Kindergarten Conf., Oshkosh, Wis., 1966; participant early edn. conf. State Early Edn. Conf., Eagle River, Wis., 1968; tchr. Covenant Harbor Elderhostel, 1997, 98; established Doris M. Reinke Resource Ctr., 2002. Author: Bit of History-Walworth County Historical Society Legacy, 1992—; author: (with Charlotte and William Gates) Guide to Beckwith's History of Walworth County, 2000; author: Images of America-Elkhorn, 2004; contbr. weekly newspaper column Webster Notes, 1989, monthly column in The Week, 1991. Chmn. Sch. Centennial, Elkhorn, 1987; mem. Elkhorn Hist. Preservation Com., 1991—; chmn. Sesquicentennial com., 1997—; dir. Webster House Mus., 1991—; mem. Walworth County Sesquicentennial Com., 1997—98; mem. sesquicentennial com. Walworth County Fair, 1998—; archivist Sugar Creek Luth. Ch., 1992—, mem. ch. coun., 2003, sec., 2005; choir mem. Luth. Ch., 1995—2001; del. dist. constn. conv. Evang. Luth. Ch. Am., Beloit, Wis., 1987; com. mem. Luth. Ch., Elkhorn, 1987, sec., 2005; RSVP Vol. Food Pantry, Elkhorn, 1985—2002, bd. dirs., 1985—88, 1995—. Recipient Wis. Edn. Rsch., West Bend, Wis., 1966, Outstanding Elem. Tchrs., Wash., 1973, Wis. Dept. Edn., Madison, 1980, Local History award State Hist. Soc. Wis., 1993, Outstanding Sr. Citizen award Walworth County Fair, 1999, Cmty. Svc. award Masons, 2000, Disting. Svc. award Rotary, 2004; named one of 50 Who Matter, Janesville Gazette, 2006, Vol. of Yr., Walworth County Area Ret. Educators Assn., 2006, DAR medal of Honor, 2007. Mem.: Walworth County Ret. Tchrs. Assn. (v.p. 1988, pres. 1991), Nat. Ret. Tchrs. Assn., Walworth County Geneal. Soc. (bd. dirs. 1991—92), Walworth County Hist. Soc. (treas. 1985—89, v.p. 1990—91, pres. 1991—96, v.p. 1999—2000, pres. 2000—05), Elkhorn Women's Club (sec. 1999—2000, v.p. 2003, pres. 2005—), Alpha Delta Kappa (state pres. 1968—70, 1976—78, chpt. pres. 2002—03, chpt. historian 2008—). Avocations: reading, baseball, bird watching, travel. Home: 516 N Wisconsin St Elkhorn WI 53121-1119 Office Phone: 262-723-4248. Personal E-mail: walcohistory@elknet.net.

REINKE, RALPH LOUIS, retired academic administrator; b. Elmhurst, Ill., June 22, 1927; s. Louis Fred and Malinda Marie (Beckmann) R.; m. Lois Hermine Borneman, Aug. 28, 1948 (dec. Mar. 1984); children: Janice Reinke Eisenloeffel, Stephan, Sharon Reinke Holaway; m. Carole Louise Reidiehs, June 14, 1986 Student, U. Ill., 1945—46; BS, Concordia U., River Forest, Ill., 1949; MA, Northwestern U., 1952; postgrad., U. Chgo., 1956—63; LittD, Concordia Sem., 1972. Prin. St. John Elem. Sch., Houston, 1949-56; assoc. prof. psychology and edn. Concordia U., River Forest, Ill., 1956-68, CEO, 2003—04; pres., chief exec. officer Concordia Pub. House, St. Louis, 1968-86; pres. Concordia U., Seward, Nebr., 1986—90; ret., 1990; CEO Concordia U., Ill., 2002—04. Author: Christian Spelling Series, 2d edit, 1971. Mem. sch. bd. selecting com., Oak Park, Ill., 1965-67, chmn. lit. commn. Mo. Synod Luth. Ch., 1967-69; bd. dirs. Concordia U., 1992-2004, chair, 1999-2002. With USNR, 1944-46. Mem. Protestant Ch. Owned Pubs. Assn. (dir. 1969-84, pres. 1982-84), St. Louis Printing Assn. (bd. dirs. 1975-77), Am. Assn. Indsl. Mgmt. (bd. dirs. 1981-85), Assn. Ind. Colls. and Univs. of Nebr. (pres. 1988-89), Luth. Edn. Assn. (pres. 1967-69), Rotary, Phi Delta Kappa. Lutheran. Personal E-mail: rlreinke@aol.com. *Life is a most precious and finite gift of God to man. Those who would lead must make a commitment to devote their full energies and intellects to the improvement of the quality of life of their fellowmen. In the highest sense, leadership is the integrity to heed the quiet voice of conscience from within in the quest of that quality.*

REINKE, WILLIAM JOHN, lawyer; b. South Bend, Ind., Aug. 7, 1930; s. William August and Eva Marie (Hein) R.; m. Sue Carol Colvin, 1951 (div. 1988); children: Sally Sue Taelman, William A., Andrew J.; m. Elizabeth Beck Lockwood, 1991. AB cum laude, Wabash Coll., 1952; JD, U. Chgo., 1955. Bar: Ind. 1955. Assoc. Barnes & Thornburg and predecessors, South Bend, Ind., 1957-61, ptnr., 1961—96, of counsel, 1996—, former chmn. compensation com. Mem. mgmt. com. Barnes & Thornburg and predecessors. Trustee Stanley Clark Sch., 1969-80, pres., 1977-80; life mem. adv. bd. Salvation Army, 1973—, pres., 1990-92; bd. dirs. NABE Mich. chpt., 1990-94, pres. 1993-94, Isaac Walton League, 1970-81; bd. dirs. United Way, 1979-81; pres. South Bend Round Table, 1963-65; trustee First Meth. Ch., 1976-70, 2005-07; bd. dirs. So. Bend Civic Theatre, 1997-2003. With U.S. Army, 1955-57. Recipient Outstanding Local Pres. award Ind. Jaycees, 1960-61, Boss of Yr. award, 1979, South Bend Outstanding Young Man award, 1961. Mem. ABA, Ind. State Bar Assn., St. Joseph County Bar Assn., Ind. Bar Found. (patron fellow), Am. Judicature Soc., Summit Club (founders com.), Rotary (bd. dirs. 1970-73, 94-97). Home: 51795 Waterton Square Cir Granger IN 46530-8317 Office: Barnes & Thornburg 1st Source Bank Ctr 100 N Michigan St Ste 600 South Bend IN 46601-1632 Office Phone: 574-233-1171.

REINKING, ANN H., dancer, actress; b. Seattle, Nov. 10, 1949; d. Walter Floyd and Francis Holmes (Harrison) R.; m. Larry Small, 1970; m. Herbert A. Allen; Aug. 25, 1982; (stepchildren): Leslie, Christie, Herbert, Charlie. Student public schs. Guest tchr. NYU, Duke U., Durham, N.C., Rutgers, N.J., Harvard, Cambridge, Mass.; choreographer Pal Joey, Goodman Theater, Chgo., 1988. Broadway appearances include Coco, 1970, Wild and Wonderful, 1972, Pippin, 1973, Over Here, 1974, Goodtime Charlie, 1975, Chicago, 1977, A Chorus Line, 1976, Dancin', 1978, Sweet Charity, 1986-87; TV appearances include Ellery Queen, Doug Henning: Magic on Broadway, 1982, Parade of Stars, 1983, American Treasury, 1985, Salute to Jules Styne, Broadway Salutes Washington, An Introduction to the Dance Gala of the Stars; film appearances include Movie, Movie, 1978, All That Jazz, 1979-80, Annie, 1982, Micki and Maude, 1984; play Ann Reinking... Music Moves Me, 1984; actor, choreographer Broadway shows: Chicago, 1996 (Tony award 1997), Annie Get Your Gun, 1999 (Tony award 1999), Fosse, 2001; choreographer Broadway shows: Annie Get Your Gun, 1999, Look of Love, 2003 Recipient Clarence Derwent award, 1974, Outer Critics Circle award, 1974, Theatre World award, 1974, Dance Educators Am. award, 1979, Harkness Dance award, 1979, two Tony award nominations, Tony award for Choregraphy, 1997; Ford Found. scholar, 1964-66, Hero With a Heart award Nat. Marfan Found., 2007; Robert Joffery scholar, 1967; Harkness scholar; Nat. Dance Educators award. Mem. Actors Equity, AFTRA, Stage Actors Guild. Avocations: horseback riding, skiing, swimming, hiking. also: Steps Contemporary & Classical Dance 2121 Broadway Fl 3 New York NY 10023-1786

REINLEITNER, KATHERINE MINDLIN, psychologist, foundation administrator; b. Scarsdale, NY, May 10, 1948; m. Theodore B. Day, Aug. 25, 1968 (div. Sept. 1980); children: Eleanor Day, T. Eugene Day, Jennifer Day, David A.; m. Lee A. Reinleitner, Sept. 15, 1990; children: Mark A., Paul H. BA, Barnard Coll., 1967; MA, Columbia U., 1968; PhD, U. Wash., 1974. Diplomate Am. Bd. Psychopharmacology and Forensic Psychology, Am. Bd. Advanced Practice Psychologists. Intern Astor Home for Children, Reinbeck, NY; psychologist Children's Hosp., Seattle, 1974-83; pvt. practice, Mercer Island and Bellevue, 1976-2000; pvt. practice Bainbridge Island, 1983—2000; adminstr. The Mindlin Found., Bellevue, 1994—. Lectr., asst. prof. U. Wash., 1975-83; gov.'s coun. on abuse and neglect State of Wash., Olympia, 1978-80; bd. dirs. Prescribing Psychologists Register, 1996—, curriculum com., 1996—. Author childrens books; author: What To Do After You've Seen the Zoo, 1983. Tng. fellowship I and IV, VA, 1970-71, 73-74, NIMH, 1969-70. Mem. AAAS, Internat. Coll. of Prescribing Psychologists, Am. Psychol. Assn., Wash. State Psychol. Assn. Achievements include patents for (with Michael Harrington) water sanitizing system. Office Phone: 425-246-8584. Personal E-mail: drkathyday@aol.com.

REINOEHL, RICHARD LOUIS, artist, scholar, martial artist; b. Omaha, Oct. 11, 1944; s. Louis Lawrence and Frances Margaret (Robinson) R.; 1 child, Joy Margaret Iroff-Reinoehl. BS in Sociology, Portland State U., 1970, postgrad., 1972; MSW, U. Minn., Duluth, 1977; postgrad., Cornell U., 1984-88. Acting dir. Vanguard Group Homes, Virginia, Minn., 1976-77; dir. Minn. Chippewa Tribe Group Home, Duluth, 1978, Human Devel. Consortium, Minn., N.Y., Ohio, 1978—; coord. NE Ohio Green Partys' Vote Recount Observation Teams, 2004; dir. Inner Harmony Coun., 2008—. Faculty Social Work Program U. Wis., Superior, 1981-84, Bohecker Coll., 2005—; adv. bd. Computers in Social Svcs. Network, 1982-85; mem. Com. on Internat. Social Welfare Edn., 1982-86, Am. Evaluation Assn., 1986-89; affiliate scholar Oberlin Coll., 1991—; artist-in-residence Ohio Arts Coun., 1996-97. Editor: Computer Literacy in Human Services Education, 1990, Computer Literacy in Human Services, 1990, Men of Achievement, 16th edit., 1993; mem. editl. bd. Computers in Human Svcs., 1983-96, 99, Jour. Technology in Human Svcs., 1999—; assoc. editor book rev., 1996-99; contbr. numerous articles to profl. jours. Mem. Legis. Task Force Regional Alcoholism Bd., 1972-73, Assn. Drug Abuse, Prevention and Treatment, 1973-74, Minn. Pub. Health Assn., 1976-78, Minn. Social Svc. Assn., 1976-83, Wis. Coun. Social Work Edn., 1983-84, N.Y. State Coun. Family Rels., 1986-89, Nat. Coun. Family Rels., 1986-89; exec. bd. Duluth Community Action Program, 1982-83; Dem. precinct chair, Portland, Oreg., 1972-74; precinct vice-chair Dem. Farmer-Labor Party, Duluth, 1979-81, chair, 1981-83, 2d vice-chair exec. bd., 1981-83; mem. Zoning Appeals Bd., New Russia Twp., Ohio, 1996-2001; mem. art edn. com. Fireland Assn. Visual Arts, 1996-99; mem. land use planning com. New Russia Twp., Ohio, 1998-2000; chair Lorain County Comprehensive Plan Growth Mgmt. Com., 1999-2000; mem. Smart Devel. Coalition of Lorain County, 1998-2002, Lorain County Multi-Modal Transp. Planning Steering Com., 2000-01, airport subcom., 2000-01, roadways sub-com., 2000-01, rails subcom., 2000-01, transit subcom., 2000—, info. tech. sub-com., 2000—; field spl. projects field coord., nat. coord. rural issues Kucinich for Pres. campaign, 2003-; chmn. Smart Devel. Coalition Lorain County, 1996-98, Lorain County Growth Mgmt. Com., mem. Environ. Sub.-Com., 1997-98; New Russia Township Zoning Bd. Appeals, 1995-2000, New Russia Township Land Use Planning Com., 1996-98; coord. Ohio Voters Reform, 2005. Mem. NASW (exec. com., chair program com. Arrowhead Region Minn. chpt., 1980-81, co-chair Minn. task force on computers in social work, 1981-82), Acad. Cert. Social Workers, Cornell U. Sailing Club (pres. 1990). Avocations: canoeing, antique volkswagens, wilderness hiking. Personal E-mail: rreinoehl19@gmail.com. *It's noteworthy that the most sought-after items in a society cannot be bought or sold. Included are wisdom, respect, generosity, truthfulness, and the love of family and friends.*

REINOLD, CHRISTY DIANE, school counselor, consultant; b. Neodasha, Kans., July 21, 1942; d. Ernest Sherman and Faye Etta (Herbert) Wild; m. William Owen Reinold, Dec. 20, 1964; children: Elizabeth, Rebecca. BA Edn., Calif. State U., Fresno, 1964, MA in Edn. and Psychology, 1964. Cert. counselor, Family Wellness instr.; lic. mental health counselor, Fla. Tchr. Clovis (Calif.) Unified Sch. Dist., 1965-66, Santa Clara (Calif.) Unified Sch. Dist., 1966-67, Inst. Internat. Chateaubriand, Cannes, France, 1968-69; tchr., vice prin. Internat. Sch., Sliema, Malta, 1969-70; elem. sch. counselor Duval City Schs., Jacksonville, Fla., 1977-82, Lodi (Calif.) Unified Sch. Dist., 1982—2004. Cons. Calif. Dept. Edn.; mem. Calif. Commn. on Tchr. Credentialing, Sacramento, 1986—2004, mem. adv. panel, 1998—2004; mem. stds. rev. com. Nat. Bd. Cert. Sch. Counselors, 2002—. Co-author: The Best for Our Kids; Counseling in the 21st Century; contbr. articles. Chmn. bd. dirs. Oak Crest Child Care Ctr., Jacksonville, 1979-81. Recipient H.B. McDaniel Individual award, 1986, James Saum Legis. award, Calif. Sch. Counselor's Assn., 1991, Donald Hayes Lifetime Achievement award, Assn. Calif. Sch. Counselors, 2002; named Anne Upton Sch. Counselor of Yr. for Calif., Calif. Sch. Counselor's Assn., 1995; named to H.B. McDaniel Hall of Fame, Stanford U., 2003. Mem.: AAUW (3rd v.p. 1974, 1st v.p. 1980, by-laws chmn. 1990, chmn. pub. policy 1991—93, pres. 1993), Lodi Pupil Pers. Assn. (pres. 1986—87), Calif. Alliance Pupil Svcs. Orgns. (bd. dirs. 1988—95), Fla. Sch. Counselors Assn., Calif. Assn. Counseling and Devel., Calif. Sch. Counselor Assn. (legis. chmn. 1985—90, pres. 1991), Am. Sch. Counselor Assn. (govt. rels. specialist 1993—94). Republican. Avocations: history, travel, politics. Home: 1772 Le Bec Ct Lodi CA 95240 Personal E-mail: creinold@earthlink.net.

REINSCH, WILLIAM ALAN, association executive, educator; b. Evanston, Ill., Jan. 15, 1946; s. Bert and Kathleen (Penn) R.; m. Susan Polley Reinsch, Jan. 3, 1970; children: Andrew, Christian. BA, Johns Hopkins U., 1968; MA in Internat. Rels., Johns Hopkins U.-Sch. Advanced Internat. Studies, 1969. Legis. asst. Congressman Gilbert Gude, Washington, 1973-76, Congressman Richard Ottinger, Washington, 1976; chief legis. asst. Senator John Heinz, Washington, 1977-91; legis. asst. Senator John D. Rockefeller IV, Washington, 1991-93; cons., under sec. for export administrn. Dept. Commerce, Washington, 1994-2001; pres. Nat. Fgn. Trade Coun., Washington, 2001—; mem. U.S.-China Econ. and Security Rev. Commn., 2001—. Tchr. Landon Sch., Bethesda, Md., 1968-73; acting staff dir. Environ. Study Conf. U.S. Ho. Reps., 1976; bd. dirs. KHI Svcs. Contbr. articles to profl. jours. Bd. dirs. Middle East Inst. Mem. Phi Beta Kappa, Omicron Delta Kappa, Alpha Delta Phi. Democrat. Presbyterian. Office: Nat Fgn Trade Coun 1625 K St NW Ste 200 Washington DC 20006 E-mail: breinsch@nftc.org.

REINSDORF, JERRY MICHAEL, professional sports team owner, real estate company executive, accountant, lawyer; b. Bklyn., Feb. 25, 1936; s. Max and Marion (Smith) Reinsdorf; m. Martyl F. Rifkin, Dec. 29, 1956; children: David Jason, Susan Janeen, Michael Andrew, Jonathan Milton. BA, George Washington U., 1957; JD, Northwestern U., 1960. CPA Ill., registered mortgage underwriter; bar: DC, Ill. 1960; cert. specialist real estate securities, rev. appraiser. Atty. staff regional coun. IRS, Chgo., 1960—64; assoc. law firm Chapman & Cutler, 1964—68; ptnr. Altman, Kurlander & Weiss, 1968—74; of counsel Katten, Muchin, Gitles, Zavis, Pearl & Galler, 1974—79; gen. ptnr. Carlyle Real Estate Ltd. Partnerships, 1971—72; chmn. bd. Balcor Co., 1973—87; mng. ptnr. TBC Films, 1975—83; chmn. Chgo. White Sox, 1981—, Chgo. Bulls, 1985—; ptnr. Bojer Fin., 1987—. Lectr. John Marshall Law Sch., 1966—68; bd. overseers Inst. Civil Justice, 1996—98; lectr. real estate, sports, taxation. Co-author (with L. Herbert Schneider): Uses of Life Insurance in Qualified Employee Benefit Plans, 1970. Mem. Chgo. region bd. Anti-Defamation League, 1986—2001; mem., trustee Ill. Inst. Tech., 1991—96; mem. Ill. Commn. on African-Am. Males, 1992—, Nat. Baseball Hall of Fame Bd., 2008—; bd. dirs. Chgo. Youth Success Found., 1992—, Corp. Supportive Housing, 1995—; nat. trustee Northwestern U., 1993—2005, bd. govs., 1993—2005, Hugh O'Brian Youth Found.; mem. internat. adv. bd. Barrow Neurol. Found., 1996—97; active Chgo. Baseball Cancer Charities, 1994, 1998; bd. trustees Equity Office Properties, 1997—2004; bd. dirs. Nat. Baseball Hall of Fame, 2008—. Recipient Hallmark award, Chgo. Baseball Cancer Charities, 1986, Corp. Superstar award, Ill. chpt. Cystic Fibrosis Found., 1988, Chicagoan of Yr. award, Chgo. Park Dist., 1990, Kellogg Excellence award, 1991, Cmty. Hero award, Interfaith Organizing Project, 1991, Op. Push Bridgebuilder award, 1992, Alumni Merit award, Northwestern U., 1992, Ellis Island Medal of Honor award, Nat. Ethnic Coalition of Orgns., 1993, Sportsman of Yr. award, 1994, Lifetime Achievement award, March of Dimes, 1994, Hallmark Hall of Fame Civic award, Ind. Sports Charities, 1994, Am. Spirit award, USAF, 1995, Alpha Epsilon Pi Arthur and Simiteich Outstanding Alumnus award, 1995, Order of Lincoln, 1997, Mayor's medal Honor, 1997, Bklyn. Businessman of Yr., 1997, Guardian of Children award, Jewish Coun. for Youth Svc., 1998, Amb. award, Keshet, 2005, Nat. Humanitarian award, Nat. Conf. Cmty. and Justice, 2006, Merit award, Decalogue Soc. Lawyers, 2007, History Maker award, Chgo. Hist. Soc., 2007, Disting. Honoree award, Cook County Sheriff, 2009, Excellence award, Sports Lawyers Assoc., 2009; named Sportsman of Yr., Nat. Italian-Am. Sports Hall of Fame, 2006; named one of Most Influential People in World of Sports, Bus. Week, 2007; named to B'nai B'rith Nat. Jewish Am. Sports Hall of Fame, 1994, Chgo. Sports Hall of Fame, 1997, Inducted G. Washington U. Sports Bus. Hall of Fame, 2008. Mem.: FBA, ABA, Nat. Sports Lawyers Assn. (Award of Excellence 2009), Chgo. Bar Assn., Ill. Bar Assn., Northwestern U. Law Sch. Alumni Assn. (bd. dirs.), Order of Coif, Comml. Club Chgo., Omega Tau Rho. Achievements include owner, MLB World Series Champions, 2005. Office: Chgo White Sox 333 W 35th St Chicago IL 60616-3651 Office Phone: 312-674-5200.*

REINSHAGEN, YOLANDA P., elementary school educator; b. Recife, Brazil, Mar. 18, 1953; came to U.S., 1977; d. Manoel and Irene Ferreira Pessôa; m. Jerald Alfred Reinshagen Sr., Dec. 22, 1977; children: Jerald Jr., Jerlanda, Janice, Joseph, Judith, Jerson. BA in Theology and Edn., Monte Morelos (Mex.) U., 1979; MA in Health Edn., U. West Fla., 1994. Asst. tchr. Educandarion Advents, Belem de Maria, Brazil, 1972-74; chaplain Hosp. La Carlota, Monte Morelos, 1975-77; tchr. Academia Adventista del Oeste, Mayaguez, P.R., 1979, SDA Elem. Sch., Queens, 1980. Office mgr., treas. Family Practice Clinic, Rockport, Ind., 1985-88; ministry dir. Univ. S.D.A.C., Pensacola, Fla., 1992-94 Counselor Pathfinders, 1999; Spanish transl. SDA, 1990. Mem. SMMA (coord. health project 1997, sec. 1997). SDA. Home: 19 North Pt Hattiesburg MS 39402-7708

REINSMOEN, NANCY LOUISE, medical educator, director; d. LeRoy Richard and Hazel Irene Moe; children: Matthew Peter, Rachel Kaia Reinsmoen Cohn. BA, Luther Coll., Decorah, Iowa, 1969; MS, U. Minn., Mpls., 1979, PhD, 1987. Diplomate Am. Bd. Histocompatibility and Immunogenetics. Med. technologist U. Minn., 1971—77, lab. mgr., 1977—87, sr. scientist, 1987—91, asst. prof., 1991—96, assoc. prof., 1996—97; prof. Duke U., Durham, NC, 1997—2006, dir. clin. transplant immunology lab., 1997—; dir. HLA lab. Cedars-Sinai Med. Ctr., LA, 2006—; prof. UCLA, 2006—. Contbr. scientific papers. Recipient Disting. Svc. award, Luther Coll., 1999; Rsch. grant, NIH, 2002—07. Mem.: Internat. Soc. Head and Lung Transplantation, Am. Soc. Transplantation, United Network for Organ Sharing (bd. mem. 1995), Am. Soc. Histocompatibility and Immunogenetics (pres. 1993—94). Luthern. Avocations: reading, swimming, hiking.

REINSTEIN, JOEL, lawyer; b. NYC, July 23, 1946; s. Louis and Ruth Reinstein; children: Lesli, Louis, Mindy. BSE, U. Pa., 1968; JD cum laude, U. Fla., 1971; LLM in Taxation, NYU, 1974. Bar: Fla. 1971, U.S. Tax Ct. 1973, U.S. Dist. Ct. (so. dist.) Fla. 1976. Atty., office of chief counsel IRS, 1971-74; ptnr. Capp, Reinstein, Kopelowitz and Atlas, P.A., Ft. Lauderdale, Fla., 1975-85; dir., ptnr. Greenberg, Traurig, Hoffman, Lipoff, Rosen & Quentel, P.A., Ft. Lauderdale, 1985-92; gen. counsel Internat. Magnetic Imaging, Inc., Boca Raton, Fla., 1992-94; prin. Law Offices of Joel Reinstein P.A., Boca Raton, 1993—. Lectr. Advanced Pension Planning, Am. Soc. C.L.U.s; lectr. in field. Mem. editl. bd. U. Fla. Law Rev. 1970-71; contbr. articles to profl. jours. Mem. Fla. Bar Assn. (tax sect.), ABA (tax sect.), Order of Coif, Phi Kappa Phi, Phi Delta Pi. Office: 925 S Federal Hwy Ste 325 Boca Raton FL 33432 Office Phone: 561-393-6714. E-mail: joel@reinsteinlaw.com.

REINSTEIN, ROBERT J., law educator, former dean; b. Balt., Mar. 17, 1945; m. Mary Taylor Aspinwall; children: Ellen, Thomas. BS in Engring. Physics with distinction, Cornell U., 1965; JD cum laude, Harvard U., 1968; LLD (hon.), Elizabethtown Coll., Pa., 1993. Bar: Md. 1969, Pa. 1982, U.S. Supreme Ct. 1971. Law clk. to Hon. Frank A. Kaufman U.S. Dist. Ct. Md., 1968-69; from asst. prof. to assoc. prof. Temple U. Sch. Law, Phila., 1969-73, prof., 1973—, chief legal officer, 1982-89, v.p., dean, 1989—2008; sr. atty. appellate sect. Civil Rights Divsn., U.S Dept. Justice, 1977-78, chief litigation sect., 1979-80. Vis. prof. law Hastings Coll. Law, San Francisco, 1975, Georgetown U., 1978-79; cons. atty. NAACP Spl. Contbn. Fund, 1970-77. Contbr. articles to profl. jours. Chair civil rights com. B'nai Brith Anti-Defamation League, Phila. Recipient Friendship Award, People's Rep. China, 2002. Mem. ABA, Pa. Bar Assn. Office: Temple U Sch Law Klein Hall Rm 806 1719 N Broad St Philadelphia PA 19122-6002 E-mail: robert.reinstein@temple.edu.*

REINTHALER, RICHARD WALTER, lawyer; b. NY, Feb. 27, 1949; s. Walter F. and Maureen C. (Tully) R.; m. Mary E. Maloney, Aug. 8, 1970; children: Brian, Scott, Amy. BA in Govt. magna cum laude, U. Notre Dame, 1970, JD summa cum laude, 1973. Bar: N.Y. 1974, U.S. Dist. Ct. (so. and ea. dists.) N.Y. 1974, U.S. Ct. Appeals (2d cir.) 1974, U.S. Ct. Appeals (9th cir.) 1976, U.S. Supreme Ct., 1977, U.S. Ct. Appeals (5th cir.) 1978, U.S. Ct. Appeals (11th cir.) 1981, U.S. Ct. Appeals (1st cir.) 2004, U.S. Ct. Appeals (3d cir.) 2005. Assoc. White & Case, NYC, 1973—81, ptnr., 1981—95, Dewey Ballantine LLP, NYC, 1995—2007, co-chmn. litigation dept., 2002—03, Dewey & LeBoeuf LLP, NYC, 2007—. Mem. adv. group U.S. Dist. Ct. (ea. dist.) N.Y., 1992-2004, chairperson subgroup on ethics, 1993-2000. Contbr. articles to profl. jours. Served to 1st lt. US Army, 1974. Fellow Am. Bar Found.; mem. ABA (2d cir. chmn. discovery com. 1982-87, program coord. 1986, ann. meeting litigation sect., vice chmn. com. on fed. procedure 1988-89, co-chmn. com. on profl. responsibility 1989-92, vice chmn. securities litigation com. 1993-94, vice chair Hong Kong meeting 1995, co-chair energy litigation com. 1996-97, co-chair antitrust litigation com. 1997-2000, mem. Ethics 2000 task force 1999-2000), N.Y. State Bar Assn., Assn. of Bar of City of N.Y. (mem. com. to enhance diversity in the profession 1990-95, mem. Orison S. Marden Meml. Lectrs. com. 1994-2000, chair 1997-2000, spl. com. on mergers, acquisitions and corp. control contests 1995-2002), Scarsdale Golf Club (Hartsdale, N.Y., bd. govs. 1994—2003, pres. 2002-2003), Capital Hill Club (Washington). Republican. Roman Catholic. Avocations: golf, tennis. Office: Dewey & LeBoeuf LLP 1301 Avenue Of The Americas New York NY 10019-6022 Office Phone: 212-259-6090. Personal E-mail: rreinthaler@dl.com.

REINUS, WILLIAM R., radiology educator; b. NYC, Oct. 26, 1953; s. Francis Z. Reinus and Helene (Frank) Margulies; m. Elizabeth Katherine Forrestal, June 17, 1977; children: Sarah, Alexander. BS, Amherst Coll., 1975; MD, NYU, 1979. Cert. Am. Bd. Radiology. Intern internal medicine Washington U., Barnes Hosp, 1979-80; resident Mallinckrodt Inst. Radiology, 1980-83; fellow musculoskeletal radiology Mallinckrodt Inst. Radiology, Washington U., 1983-84; asst. prof. Mallinckodt Inst. Radiology, Washington U., St. Louis, 1984-87; attending radiologist Ernst Radiology Clinic, Bridgeton, Mo., 1987-90; asst. prof. Jewish Hosp., Washington U., St. Louis, 1990—. Contbr. articles to profl. jours. Mem. Am. Coll. Radiology, Radiology Soc. North Am., Roentgen Ray Soc., Soc. Cardiovascular & Int. Radiology, Soc. Computers in Radiology, Sigma Xi, Alpha Omega Alpha. Avocations: computer programming, painting.

REIS, DON, publishing executive; b. NYC, Nov. 19, 1927; m. Barbara Weinberg, 1949; children: Robert, Richard. AB, Princeton U., 1947; MA, NYU, 1955. Rsch. editor Bantam Books, 1952-55, edn. editor, 1955-66; editor-in-chief Washington Square Press Divsn. Simon & Schuster, 1966-68; v.p., editorial dir. Ednl. Directions Inc., Westport, Conn., 1968-85; mng. editor Barron's Ednl. Series, 1985-87; gen. and ednl. editor Barron's, 1987-93, sr. cons. editor, 1993-99; editorial dir. Reis Assocs., Forest Hills, NY, 1993—. Author (with A. Butman and D. Sohn) Paperback Books in the Schools, 1962; editor The Collected Essays of Aldous Huxley, 1958. Home and Office: 57 Summer St Forest Hills NY 11375-6035 Personal E-mail: donjreis@yahoo.com.

REIS, RICARDO, economics professor; b. Oporto, Portugal, Sept. 1, 1978; s. Augusto Rocha and Maria Conceicao Reis; m. Mafalda Reis Janela Cardim; 1 child, Antonio Francisco Cardim. BSc, London Sch. Economics, 1999; PhD, Harvard U., Cambridge, Mass., 2004. Asst. prof. Princeton U., NJ, 2004—08; prof. Columbia U., NYC, 2008—. Mem.: Econometric Soc., Am. Econ. Assn.

REISBERG, BARRY, geriatric psychiatrist, neuropsychopharmacologist; b. Bklyn., Dec. 3, 1947; s. Harry and Claire (Cohen) R.; m. Rosalie DePaola, Feb. 23, 1974 (dec. Oct. 1975); m. Nancy A. Minich, May 7, 1988. BA, CUNY, Bklyn., 1968; MD, N.Y. Med. Coll., 1972. Diplomate Am. Bd. Psychiatry and Neurology, Am. Bd. Geriatric Psychiatry. Intern NY Med. Coll./Met. Hosp., NYC, 1972—73, resident in psychiatry, 1972-75; fellow dept. psychiatry Middlesex Hosp. Med. Sch. U. London, 1975; staff psychiatrist Franklin D. Roosevelt VA Hosp., Montrose, NY, 1975-78; staff psychiatrist Neuropsychopharmacology Rsch. Unit NYU Med. Ctr., NYC, 1978-80, asst. attending psychiatrist, 1978—2001, clin. dir. William and Sylvia Silberstein Aging and Dementia Rsch. Ctr., 1978—, attending psychiatrist, 2002—. Adj. prof. Ctr. for Studies in Aging McGill U., Montreal, Que., 1993—; clin. instr. dept. psychiatry N.Y. Med. Coll., Valhalla, 1975—78; asst. prof. NYU Sch. Medicine, NYC, 1978—84, assoc. prof., 1984—90, prof., 1990—; rsch. collaborator, vis. clinician Brookhaven Nat. Labs., Upton, NY, 1979—90; dir. clin. core NIMH Clin. Rsch. Ctr., 1989—93, Nat. Inst. Aging Alzheimer's Disease Ctr., 1990—; dir. Zachary and Elizabeth M. Fisher Alzheimer's Disease Edn. and Resources Program NYU Sch. Medicine, 1995—; med. and sci. adv. bd. Alzheimer's Assn., Chgo., 1993—97; med. and sci. panel Alzheimer's Disease Internat., 1997—; chmn. Prevention Work Group Alzheimer's Disease Internat., 2008—; cons. psychiatrist N.Y. VA Hosp., 1980—89; chmn. work group WHO, Copenhagen, 1984; mem. aging sect. NIH, 1986—90; vis. prof. Palmerston North Postgrad. Med. Soc., New Zealand, 1991; rsch. adv. bd. WHO Project on Alzheimer's Disease, 1995; Bayer vis. prof. St. Louis U. Sch. Medicine, 1999; vis. prof. Georgetown U. Med. Ctr., 2004; vis. prof. in geriatrics Stony Brook U. Health Scis. Ctr., 2005. Author: Brain Failure, 1981; editor: Alzheimer's Disease, 1983; editor: (with others) Diagnosis and Treatment of Senile Dementia, 1989; guest editor Drug Devel. Rsch., Internat. Psychogeriat., mem. editl. bd. Jour. Am. Aging

Assn., 1985—2004, Alzheimer's Disease and Associated Disorders, 1985—2004, Jour. Geriat. Psychiatry and Neurology, 1986—, Am. Jour. Alzheimer's Disease, 1986—, Internat. Psychogeriat., 1989—96, Am. Jour. Geriat. Psychiatry, 1992—2001, Rsch. and Practice in Alzheimer's Disease, 1999—, Middle East Jour. of Age and Aging, 2004—, Polish Jour. Geriatric Psychiatry, 2005—, assoc. editor Psychiat. Quar., 2007—; contbr. over 275 articles to med. and sci. jours. and books. Recipient Home Care award Vis. Nurse Svc. NY, 1985, Disting. Svc. award, Internat. Psychogeriatric Assn., 2001, Ann. Barry Reisberg Lectr. award Hearthstone Alzheimer's Family Found., 2002-, Lifetime Achievement award Alzheimer's Assn. and 9th Internat. Conf. on Alzheimer's Disease and Related Disorders, 2004; fellow NSF, 1963, Coun. on Internat. Ednl. Exch.-Japan Soc., Tokyo, 1968; grantee NIH, 1979-85, 87-2003, 90-95, NIMH, 1983-85, Adminstrn. on Aging, 1998-2007. Fellow: Am. Aging Assn. (bd. dris. 1990—92), Am. Psychiat. Assn. (life); mem.: Am. Coll. Neuropsychopharmacology, Am. Assn. Geriat. Psychiatry (sec. 1991—92, bd. dirs. 1992—96), Alzheimer's and Related Disorders Soc. India (hon.), Internat. Psychogeriat. Assn. (bd. dirs. 1985—93, treas. 1993—95, pres.-elect 1995—97, pres. 1997—99, Disting. Svc. award 2001). Achievements include patents for assessment of dementia; patents in field; Alzheimer's medications. Office: NYU Sch Medicine William and Sylvia Silberstein Aging and Dementia Rsch Ctr 550 1st Ave New York NY 10016-6402 Office Phone: 212-263-8550. Business E-Mail: barry.reisberg@med.nyu.edu.

REISCHAUER, ROBERT D., think-tank executive; AB, Harvard U., 1963; MIA, Columbia U., 1966, PhD, 1971. Spl. asst. to dir., dep. dir., asst. dir. human resources and cmty. devel. Congl. Budget Office, 1975-81, dir., 1989-95; sr. v.p. Urban Inst., 1981-86, pres., 2000—; chmn. bd. trustees MDRC (formerly Manpower Devel. Rsch. Corp.), 1999—2000; vice chair payment adv. commn. Medicare, 2001—08. Author: (with Henry J. Aaron) Countdown to Reform: The Great Social Security Debate, 2001 (revised and updated); editor: Setting National Priorities: Budget Choices for the Next Century, 1997; co-editor: Medicare: Preparing for the Challenges of the 21st Century, 1998, Setting National Priorities: The 2000 Election and Beyond, 1999; contbr. articles to profl. jours., chpts. to books. Sr. Fellow econ. studies Brookings Inst., 1970-75, 86-89, 95-2000. Office: Urban Inst 2100 M St NW Washington DC 20037 Office Phone: 202-261-5400. Business E-Mail: rreischauer@urban.org.

REISENAUER, ERIC MICHAEL, humanities educator; b. Spokane, Wash., Jan. 5, 1968; s. Thomas Martin and Emma Maxine Reisenauer; m. Kimberly Weiss, May 22, 2004; children: Adam Thomas, Jonah Michael. PhD, Loyola U. Chgo., 1997. Assoc. prof. history U. SC. Sumter, 2003—05, williams-brice-edwards prof. humanities, 2005—. Contbr. articles to profl. jours. Mem. Friends Libr., 1999—2005, Sumter Little Theatre, 2001—08. Recipient Governor's Disting. Prof. award, U. SC, 2000, Hugh T. Stoddard Sr. Outstanding Faculty award, 2002, Warren Spencer prize, 2004; named Outstanding Faculty award, 2009.

REISER, RICHARD SCOTT, lawyer; b. Chester, SD, Apr. 8, 1946; s. Kinney S. and Edna E. (Sweet) R.; m. Mary Lynn Durrie, Aug. 24, 1968; children: Todd S., Sally A. BS, U. Nebr., 1968, JD, 1972. Bar: Iowa 1972, Nebr. 1972, U.S. Dist. Ct. Nebr. 1972, U.S. Ct. Appeals (8th cir.) 1989. Assoc. Nelson & Harding, Omaha, 1972-75, ptnr., 1975-84; dir. Gross & Welch, P.C., Omaha, 1984-92; v.p., gen. counsel Werner Enterprises, Inc., Omaha, 1993—96, exec. v.p., gen. counsel, 1996—. Com. mem. Nebr. Transp. Efficiency Task Force, Lincoln, 1995. Bd. dirs., treas. Fontenelle Forest Assn., Omaha, 1988-94; pres. 2d lt. USAR, 1968-74. Mem. Am. Corp. Counsel Assn., Transp. Lawyers Assn., Omaha Bar Assn. (bd. dirs., exec. com.), Nebr. State Bar Assn. (mem. task force on civil justice sys. 1994-95), Iowa State Bar Assn, Nebr. State Hwy. (comm Dist.2, 2001-), Nebr. Trucking Assn. (bd. dir., sec., 2003-), Am. Trucking Assn. (bd. dir., 1999-). Democrat. Presbyterian. Avocations: hunting, skiing, motorcycling. Office: Werner Enterprises Inc PO Box 45308 Omaha NE 68145-0308

REISERT, CHARLES EDWARD, JR., realtor, real estate developer; b. New Albany, Ind., Apr. 5, 1941; s. Charles Edward, Jr. and Jane W. (Wilcox) Reisert; m. Mary Lynn Nunemacher, Nov. 9, 1963; children: Perry G., Heidi L. BS in Edn., Ind. U., 1963, MA, 1968. Tchr. Ind. Pub. Schs., 1963-67; mgr. Ind. Bell Tel. Co., Indpls., 1967-70; trust officer Ind. Nat. Bank, Indpls., 1970-72; ptnr. R.F.R. Prodns. Inc., Zionsville; dir. Wichita (Kans.) Art Assn., 1972-73; mng. ptnr. Century 21 Realty Group-Reisert, Jeffersonville, Ind., 1973—. Chmn. Ind. Real Estate Commn., 1982—90, pres. Ind., 1990; past pres. Clark County Youth Shelter; bd. dirs., past pres. United Way Clark County; bd. dirs. New Hope, Inc., Sagamore of Wabash; mem. Leadership So. Ind., Leadership Louisville; v.p. Clark County Redevel. Commn.; pres. Jeffersonville Housing Authority; trustee, past pres. Clark Meml. Hosp. Found. Recipient Pinnacle award, Sales Mgmt. and Mktg. Assn. Louisville, Servant Leader award, Leadership So. Ind., 2006. Mem.: Realtors Nat. Mktg. Inst., Ind. Assn. Realtor, Nat. Assn. Realtors, So. Ind. Realtors Assn. (past pres., past bd. dirs., Realtor of Yr. 1983, Realtor Hall of Fame 1998), So. Ind. C. of C. (Profl. Person of Yr. 1990), Rotary (past pres., Paul Harris fellow). Roman Catholic. Home: 14 Abby Chase Jeffersonville IN 47130-9762 Office: Century 21 Realty Group-Reisert 1302 E 10th St Jeffersonville IN 47130-4299 Office Phone: 812-285-5000.

REISH, JOSEPH E., psychology professor; m. Dorothy B. Bauler, Oct. 22, 1975; 1 child, Joseph. BS in Psychology, Va. Poly. Inst. and State U., Blacksburg, 1970; MS, Radford U., Va., 1972; ABD, George Mason U., Fairfax, Va., 2006. Assoc. prof. psychology Tidewater CC, Portsmouth, Va., 2008—. Prodr.: (online educator) Introduction to Psychology I On line. Office: Tidewater CC 7000 Coll Dr Portsmouth VA 23703 Business E-Mail: jreish@tcc.edu.

REISLER, EMIL, biochemist, educator, dean; BA, Hebrew U., Jerusalem; PhD, Weizman Inst.Sci., Rehovot, Israel. Postdoctoral scholar, dept. biology Johns Hopkins U.; joined chemistry & biochemistry dept. UCLA, 1976, prof. dept. chemistry & biochemistry, vice chair., chemistry & biochemistry dept., 1989—91, chair chemistry & biochemistry dept., 1997—2000, assoc. dean, life scis. divsn., 2003, acting dean life scis. divsn., 2003—04, dean, life scis. divsn., 2004—. Contbr. articles to profl. jours. Achievements include research in the formation of myosin and actin filaments from their monomeric protein units; the mechanisms of the assembly reactions and the structural changes which govern the polymerization reactions are studied by biophysical, biochemical, and electron microscopy methods. Office: Dept Chemistry & Biochemistry Paul Boyer Hall 401A-UCLA PO Box 951569 Los Angeles CA 90095-1569 Office Phone: 310-825-3958. Office Fax: 310-206-4038. Business E-Mail: reisler@ewald.mbi.ucla.edu.

REISMAN, JUDITH ANN GELERNTER, media communications executive, educator; b. Hillside, NJ, Apr. 11, 1935; MA in Speech Comm., Case Western Res. U., 1976, PhD in Speech Comm., 1980. Faculty dept. anthropology and sociology Haifa U., Israel, 1981—83; rsch. prof. sch. edn. Am. U., Washington, 1983—85; founder, pres. Inst. Media Edn., 1985—. Cons., reviewer grant proposals audio-visual drug programs for youth Dept. Edn., 1987; rsch. design cons. Alcohol and Tobacco Media Analysis in Mainstream Mags., Dept. HHS, 1987—90; cons., field reviewer Drug Free Youth Sch. Candidates Dept. Edn., 1988; lectr., adj. prof. George Mason U., Va., 1990; expert witness Pres.'s Commn. on Assignment of Women in Armed Forces, 1992, U.S. Atty. Gen. Commn. on Pornography, 1985—86, U.S. Atty. Gen. Task Force on Domestic Violence, Washington, 1985, Mapplethorpe Trial, Cin., 1990, Australian Parliament, 1992, Ga. State Senate, 1992; nominated to panel on sex harassment in the Air Force U.S. Inspector Gen., 2003; sci. advisor Protective Parents Assn.; subcom. junk sci. Am. Legis. Exchange Coun. Edn. Task Force, 1999—2004. Author: Images of Children, Crime and Violence in Playboy, Penthouse and Hustler, 1989, Kinsey, Sex and Fraud, 1990, Softport Plays Hardball, 1991, Kinsey, Crimes and Consequences, 1998, 2003; contbr. preme Ct. cases to profl. jours. Recipient Gold Camera award, 1982, Silver Screen award, 1982, Filmstrip of Yr. award, 1981—82, Silver Plaque award, 1982, Family Svc. Assn. Am. 1st pl. award local TV series, 1974, Best of 1965 award, 1965, Scientist of Yr. for Children award, 1993; co-recipient Scholastic Mag. awards, Dukane award, 1982; U.S. Dept. Justice grantee. Mem.: AAAS, World Net Daily .Com (columnist 1998—), Women in Neurosci., Nat. Black Child Devel. Inst., Soc. Sci. Study Sex, N.Y. Acad. Scis., Internat. Comm. Assn., Am. Statis. Assn., Am. Assn. Composers, Authors and Pubs., Nat. Assn. Scholars. Business E-Mail: jareisman@cox.net.

REISMAN, ROBERT E., allergist, educator; b. Buffalo, Nov. 1, 1932; s. Harry S and Jessie (Goldberg) Reisman; m. Rena Estry, Sept. 5, 1954; children: Jeanne, Linda, Nancy, David. MD, SUNY-Buffalo, 1956; Dr.h.c., U. Montpellier, France, 1982. Diplomate Am. Bd. Internal Medicine, Am. Bd. Allergy and Clin. Immunology. Intern Buffalo Gen. Hosp., 1956-57, resident in medicine, 1957-59; practice medicine specializing in allergy and clin. immunology Buffalo, 1961—; co-dir. Allergy Rsch. Lab., Buffalo Gen. Hosp., 1970—90; clin. prof. pediatrics and medicine SUNY, Buffalo, 1978—. Mem. panel allergenic extracts Bur. Biologists FDA; bd. dirs. Am. Bd. Internal Medicine, 1984—86, Am. Bd. Allergy and Clin. Immunology, 1981—86, chmn., 1985. With US Army, 1968—69. Master: ACP; fellow: Am. Acad. Allergy (pres 1980—81). Home: 113 Carriage Cir Buffalo NY 14221-2163 Office: 295 Essjay Rd Williamsville NY 14221-8216 also: 85 High St Buffalo NY 14203-1149 Office Phone: 716-630-1130. Business E-Mail: rreisman@buffalomedicalgroup.com.

REISMAN, ROSEMARY MOODY CANFIELD, writer, humanities educator; b. Des Moines, Nov. 18, 1927; d. V. Alton and Lois Gloria (Slee) Moody; m. Michael Ellison Canfield, Sept. 6, 1952 (div. May 1961); children: Michael, John Charles, Celia Catherine, Christopher James; m. Maurice Reisman, May 10, 1986 (dec. 1990). BA in English, U. Minn., 1949, MA in English, 1952; PhD in English, La. State U., 1971. Reporter Ames Tribune, Iowa, summer 1944; writer, actor Sta. WOI Pub. Radio, Ames, 1944-48; dir., writer children's plays Sta. KASI, Ames, 1949; tchg. asst. U. Minn., 1949-52; writer Sta. WOI-TV, Ames, summer 1952; writer, show host Sta. WDGY, Mpls., 1952-54; instr. La. State U., 1961-69, NDEA fellow, 1969-71; asst. prof. English Troy State U., 1971-80, assoc. prof., 1980-90, chairperson dept. English, 1985-90, prof., 1990-94. Honors coun. Troy State U., 1985-94, honors faculty, 1986-94, acad. coun., 1989-92, faculty adv. coun., 1990-92, Rhodes scholar instnl. rep., 1987-91; adj. prof. Charleston So. U., 1996-99, vis. prof., 1999—; humanities scholar Richland County Libr., S.C., 2002—; coord. sr. honors seminar Coll. of Charleston, 1996-98; prodr., writer Perspectives project films Ala. ETV, 1977-80; chmn. conf. sessions South Ctrl. Soc. for 18th-Century Studies, 1988, Southeastern Am. Soc. for 18th Century Studies, 1991, 93, workshop Ala. Coun. Tchrs. English, 1987; grant writer, project dir. Ala. Humanities Found., 1980, 89, asst. project dir. summer grad. course, 1990; grant writer, project dir. Ala. Pub. Libr. Sys., 1977-80; presenter, lectr., cons. in field. Author: Perspectives: The Alabama Heritage, 1978; co-author: Contemporary Southern Women Fiction Writers, 1994, Southern Men Fiction Writers, 1998; editor, course writer Coastal C.C., Calif., 2002—; chair editl. adv. bd. Ala. Lit. Rev., 1986-94; mem. editl. bd. Biog. Guide to Ala. Lit., 1985-89; guest editor spl. issue Ala. English 7, 1995; contbr. articles to profl. jours. Baldwin County Humanities scholar Ala. Humanities Found., 1983-84. Mem.: AAUW (past br. pres., mem. steering com.), NEA, Thomas Cooper Soc. (bd. dirs. 2001—04), English Spkg. Union (bd. dirs. Charleston 1997—98, pres. 1998—2002, Sourcelist spkr. 1999—2000, pres. 2006—07, bd. dirs. 2007—08), Troy State U. Edn. Assn. (pres. 1990—93), Ala. Edn. Assn., Assn. Coll. English Tchrs. Ala., Assn. Depts. English (state pres. 1986—88), South Atlantic MLA, Soc. of Mary, Confrat. of the Blessed Sacrament, Gamma Beta Phi (nat. pres. 1978—79, cert. of merit 1979), Phi Beta Kappa (del. to nat. triennial coun. 1991, alt. 1994, pres. Low Country Assn. 1996—98, del. 1997, bd. dirs. 1998—2001, alt. del. 2000, bd. dirs. 2003—05, past pres. S.E. Ala. assn.). Anglican. Home and Office: 121 Innisbrook Bend Summerville SC 29483-5084 Personal E-mail: creisman@bellsouth.net.

REISMANN, HERBERT, engineer, educator; b. Vienna, Jan. 26, 1926; s. Henrik and Olga (Pokorny) R.; m. Edith Falber, Aug. 14, 1952; children: Sandra Jean, Barbara Anne BS Aero. Engring., Ill. Inst. Tech., 1947, MS, 1949; PhD Engring., U. Colo., 1962. Project engr. Convair, Ft. Worth, 1951—53; prin. structures engr. Republic Aviation Corp., Hicksville, NY, 1954—56; chief engr. sys. analysis, chief solid mechanics Martin Marietta Corp., 1957—64; prof., dir. aerospace engring. SUNY, Buffalo, 1964—2001, prof. emeritus, 2002—. Cons. NASA, Bell Aero Sys. Corp. Co-author: Elastokinetics, 1974, Elasticity, 1980; author: Elastic Plates, 1988; contbr. articles to profl. jours Assoc. fellow AIAA (Best Tech. Paper award 1962, Oustanding Aerospace Achievement award 1987); mem. ASME, AAUP, Internat. Assn. Bridge and Structural Engring., Sigma Xi, Tau Beta Pi Home: 71 Chaumont Dr Buffalo NY 14221-3511 Office: SUNY-Buffalo 605 Furnas Hall Buffalo NY 14260-4200 Office Phone: 716-634-5862. Personal E-mail: herreis@msn.com.

REISNER, ANDREW DOUGLAS, psychologist; b. Ithaca, NY, Dec. 28, 1955; s. Gerald Seymour and Estelle Ruth (Siegel) R.; m. Deborah Kay Dermen, Aug. 1, 1981; children: David Aaron, Alyssa Danielle. BA, Allegheny Coll., Meadville, Pa., 1977; MA, Edinboro U., Pa., 1978; D of Psychology, Baylor U., Waco, Tex., 1987. Lic. psychologist, Ohio. Psychology asst. Tiffin Devel. Mental Health Ctr., 1979—80, Cmty. Counseling Svcs., Galion, Ohio, 1980—83, chief clin. officer, 1990—99; pvt. practice, 1996—99; intern in clin. psychology Mich. State U., East Lansing, 1986—87; postdoctoral tng. in clin. psychology Harding Hosp., Worthington, Ohio, 1987—88; psychologist Ctr. for Individual Family Svcs., Mansfield, Ohio, 1988—90, Appalachian Behavioral Healthcare, Cambridge, Ohio, 1999—2008, Athens, Ohio, 2008—. Cons. MedCtrl. Crestline Hosp., Ohio, 1989-99, Forensic Diagnostic Ctr., Byesville, Ohio, 1999—; mem. adj. faculty Ashland U., 1993-96. Contbr. chpt. to book, articles to profl. jours. Mem. APA, Ohio Psychol. Assn. Office: Appalachian Behavioral Healthcare 100 Hosp Dr Athens OH 45701 Office Phone: 740-594-5000. Business E-Mail: reisnera@mh.state.oh.us.

REISNER, STEVEN J., psychologist; b. Bklyn., 1954; AB in Psych., Princeton U., NJ, 1976; MS in Clin. Psych., Columbia U., NYC, 1986, MPhil in Clin. Psych., 1987, PhD in Clin. Psych., 1989. Lic. Clin. Psychologist NY. Intern clin. psych. Yale U. Dept. Psychiatry, New Haven, 1986—87; rsch. fellow clin. psych. SUNY Health Sci. Ctr., Bklyn., 1987—89; pvt. practice individual/couple's treatment NYC, 1993—. Adj. asst. prof. Bklyn. Coll., 1980—81; adj. prof. Columbia U., 1989—; faculty, supr. internat. trauma studies prog. NYU, 1999—; faculty NYU Psychoanalytic Inst., 2002—; clin. asst. prof. NYU Med. Sch., 2006—. Editl. assoc. Jour. Am. Psychoanalytic Assn., 2002—04, editl. bd. Studies in Gender and Sexuality, 2003—; contbr. articles to profl. jours. Dir. trauma/arts prog. REFUGE, NY, 1999—2003; cons. psychosocial/trauma response in Kosovo Internat. Orgn. Migrations, Geneva, 2000—02; cons. trauma treatment Heartland Alliance Human Rights & Human Needs, 2005—06; cons. staff-stress response UN. Recipient Obie award, 1981, Freud Meml. award, Columbia U. Tchrs. Coll., 1990. Mem.: Am. Psychol. Assn. (Doctoral Dissertation award 1989). Office: Steven J Reisner PhD 225 W 15th St Ste C New York NY 10011 Office Phone: 212-633-8391. Business E-Mail: sreisner@psychoanalysis.net.*

REISS, CAROL SHOSHKES, immunology educator; b. Boston, Mar. 14, 1950; d. Milton Abraham and Lila (Topal) Shoshkes; m. Paul Petigrow, Aug. 25, 1971 (div. 1976); m. David Simon Reiss, June 5, 1977 (div. 1992); children: Steven M., Joshua S. AB, Bryn Mawr Coll., Pa., 1972; MS, Sarah Lawrence Coll., 1973; PhD, CUNY, 1978. Postdoctoral fellow Harvard U., Boston, 1978-81, instr. pathology dept., 1981-83; assoc. prof. pathology dept. Med. Sch., 1983-88; assoc. prof. pathology dept. Harvard Med. Sch. Harvard U., Boston, 1988-91; assoc. prof. pediatric oncology div. Dana Farber Cancer Inst., Boston, 1983-91; prof. dept. biology NYU, NYC, 1991—, dir. grad. study masters program, 1993—. Lectr. Found. of Microbiology, 1990-91; mem. exptl. biology study sect. NIH, 1987-91; affiliate mem Ctr. Neural Sci., NYU, 1991—; mem. NIH Reviewers Reserve, 1991—, Kaplan Comprehensive Cancer Ctr., 1991—. Assoc. editor: Jour. Immunology, 1989-93; mem. editl. bd. Cellular Immunology, 1992—, Jour. Virology, 1994—, Immunology and Infectious Diseases, 1994—, Viral Immunology 1994—. Recipient Jr. Faculty Rsch. award Am. Cancer Soc., 1984, New Investigation award USPHS, 1981. Mem. Am. Assn. Immunologists, Assn. for Women in Sci., Am. Soc. for Microbiology, Am. Soc. for Virology, Am. Soc. Cellular Biology, Soc. for Mucosal Immunity, Soc. for Neurosci., N.Y. Acad. Sch. Democrat. Jewish. Office: NYU Main Bldg Rm 1009 Washington Sq East New York NY 10003

REISS, DALE ANNE, corporate financial executive; b. Sept. 3, 1947; d. Max and Nan (Hart) R.; m. Jerome L. King, Mar. 5, 1978; children: Matthew Reiss, Mitchell, Stacey. BS, Ill. Inst. Tech., 1967; MBA, U. Chgo., 1970. CPA, Fla., Ill., Mich., Mo. Cost acct. First Nat. Bank, Chgo., 1967; asst. contr. City Colls. of Chgo., 1967-71; dir. fin. Chgo. Dept. Pub. Works, 1971-73; prin. Arthur Young & Co., Chgo., 1973-80; sr. v.p., contr. Urban Investment & Devel. Co., Chgo., 1980-85; mng. ptnr. Ernst & Young LLP, Chgo., 1985-98, Ernst & Young, NYC, 1998-99; global dir. real estate, hospitality and constrn. Ernst & Young LLP, NYC, 1999—. Bd. dirs. Ill. Inst. Tech., Urban Land Inst.; adv. bd. Kellogg Real Estate, Northwestern U., U. Chgo. Grad. Sch. of Bus. Mem. AICPA, Fin. Execs. Inst., Pension Real Estate Assn., Chgo. Network (bd. dirs.), Econ. Chgo. Club, Met. Club, Chgo. Yacht Club, NY Athletic Club. Office: Ernst & Young 5 Times Sq 16th Fl New York NY 10036-6530 E-mail: dale.reiss@ey.com.

REISS, FRANCIS RONALD, bishop; b. Hamtramck, Mich., Nov. 11, 1940; s. Joseph and Emily Reiss. BA in Philosophy, Sacred Heart Sem. Coll.; MA in Religious Studies, U. Detroit, MEd in Adminstrn.; MDiv, St. John's Provincial Sem.; JCL, Pontifical Gregorian U. Ordained priest Archdiocese of Detroit, 1966, dir. dept. edn., aux. bishop, 2003—; min. U. Mich., Dearborn, Henry Ford Cmty. Coll., Dearborn; dean admissions, academic dean Sch. Theology of Sacred Heart Sem., Detroit; defender of bond Met. Tribunal of Archdiocese of Detroit; pastor Holy Ghost Parish, Detroit, St. Mary Parish, Port Huron, SS. Peter and Paul (Westside), Detroit, St. Frances Cabrini Parish, Allen park, Mich., 1998—; ordained bishop, 2003. Roman Catholic. Office: Archdiocese of Detroit 1234 Washington Blvd Detroit MI 48226

REISS, GEORGE RUSSELL, JR., physician; b. Phila., Dec. 25, 1928; s. G. Russell Sr. and Mary Ellen (Brogan) R.; m. Rosemarie Theresa Curcillo, Sept. 19, 1959; children: Mary Elizabeth, Stephanie, G. Russell III, Charlene. BA, LaSalle U., 1953; MD, Temple U., 1957. Diplomate Am. Bd. Pediatrics. Intern Misericordia Hosp., Phila., 1957-58; resident pediatrics St. Christopher Hosp. for Children, Phila., 1958-60; pvt. practice Glenside, Pa., 1960—. With USCG, 1946-49. Mem. Montgomery County Med. Soc., Pa. Med. Soc., Am. Acad. Pediatrics, AMA, Am. Assn. Pro-Life Pediatricians. Roman Catholic. Office: 2220 Mount Carmel Ave Glenside PA 19038-4610 Office Phone: 215-884-7861. Personal E-mail: grcreissjr@aol.com.

REISS, HOWARD, chemistry professor; b. NYC, Apr. 5, 1922; s. Isidor and Jean (Goldstein) R.; m. Phyllis Kohn, July 25, 1945; children: Gloria, Steven. AB in Chemistry, NYU, 1943; PhD in Chemistry, Columbia U., 1949. With Manhattan Project, 1944-46; instr., then asst. prof. chemistry Boston U., 1949-51; with Ctrl. Rsch. Lab., Celanese Corp. Am., 1951-52, Edgar C. Bain Lab. Fundamental Rsch., U.S. Steel Corp., 1957, Bell Telephone Labs., 1952-60; asso. dir., then dir. rsch. div. Atomics Internat., div. N.Am. Aviation, Inc., 1960-62; dir. N.Am. Aviation Sci. Ctr., 1962-67, v.p. co., 1963-67; v.p. rsch. aerospace systems group N.Am. Rockwell Corp., 1967-68; vis. lectr. chemistry U. Calif. at Berkeley, summer 1957; vis. prof. chemistry UCLA, 1961, 62, 64, 67, prof., 1968-91, prof. emeritus, 1991—2003, disting. prof. emeritus, 2003—; vis. prof. U. Louis Pasteur, Strasbourg, France, 1986, U. Pa., 1989; vis. fellow Victoria U., Wellington, New Zealand, 1989. Vis. fellow Princeton (N.J.) Materials Inst., 1996; vis. sci., Hebrew U., Jerusalem, 1998; cons. to chem.-physics program USAF Cambridge Rsch. Labs., 1950-52; chmn. editor Procs. Internat. Conf. Nucleation and Interfacial Phenomena, Boston; mem. USAF Office Sci. Rsch. Physics and Chemistry Rsch. Evaluation Groups, 1966—, Oak Ridge Nat. Lab. Reactor Chemistry Adv. Com., 1966-68; adv. com. math. and phys. scis. NSF, 1970-72, ARPA Materials Rsch. Coun., 1968—; chmn. site rev. com. NRC Associateships Program, Naval Rsch. Lab., 1989. Author: Methods of Thermodynamics, 1965, republished, 1996; author articles; editor in field.; editor: Progress in Solid State Chemistry, 1962-71, Jour. Statis. Physics, 1968-75, Jour. Colloid Interface Sci; mem. editorial adv. bd. Internat. Jour. Physics and Chemistry of Solids, 1955, Progress in Solid State Chemistry, 1962-73, Jour. Solid State Chemistry, 1969, Jour. Phys. Chemistry, 1970-73, Ency. of Solid State, 1970, Jour. Nonmetals, 1971—, Jour. Colloid and Interface Sci., 1976-79, Langmuir, 1985—. Guggenheim Meml. fellow, 1978; Howard Reiss chair in chemistry and biochemistry established named in his honor, UCLA, 1999. Fellow AAAS, Am. Phys. Soc. (exec. com. div. chem. physics 1966-69); mem. NAS, Am. Chem. Soc. (chmn. phys. chemistry sect. N.J. sect. 1957, Richard C. Tolman medal 1973, Kendall award in colloid and surface chemistry 1980, J.H. Hildebrand award in theoretical and exptl. phys. chemistry of liquids 1991, Van Arkel hon.

chair in chemistry U. Leiden, The Netherlands, 1994), Am. Assn. for Aerosol Rsch. (David Sinclair award 1997), Phi Beta Kappa, Sigma Xi, Phi Lambda Upsilon. Office: U Calif Dept Chemistry And Biochemis Los Angeles CA 90095-0001 Office Phone: 310-825-3029. Business E-Mail: reiss@chem.ucla.edu.

REISS, IRA LEONARD, retired sociology educator, writer; b. NYC, Dec. 8, 1925; s. Philip and Dorothy (Jacobs) R.; m. Harriet Marilyn Eisman, Sept. 4, 1955; children: David, Pamela, Joel. BS cum laude, Syracuse U., 1949; MA, Pa. State U., 1951, PhD, 1953. Asst. prof. sociology Bowdoin Coll., Brunswick, Maine, 1953-55, Coll. William and Mary, Williamsburg, Va., 1955-59; asst. prof. Bard Coll., Annandale-0n-Hudson, N.Y., 1959-61; assoc. to full prof. U. Iowa, Iowa City, 1961-69; prof. U. Minn., Mpls., 1969-96, prof. emeritus, 1996—. Rsch. evaluator U.S. Dept. Edn. and Nat. Inst. Child Health and Human Devel., Washington, 1966-78; rsch. dir. Family Study Ctr., U. Minn., 1969-74; ednl. advisor Kimberly-Clark Corp., Neenah, Wis., 1971-75; chair planning com. and bd. dirs. Inst. for Child, Adolescent Sexual Health, 1992-93; vis. prof. Uppsala Univ., Sweden, 1975-76; lectr. in field. Author: Premarital Sexual Standards in America, 1960, The Social Context of Premarital Sexual Permissiveness, 1967, Family Systems in America, 1971, 4th edit., 1988, Journey into Sexuality: An Exploratory Voyage, 1986, An End to Shame: Shaping Our Next Sexual Revolution, 1990, Solving America's Sexual Crises, 1997, At the Dawn of the Sexual Revolution: Reflections on a Dialogue, 2002, An Insider's View of Sexual Science Since Kinsey, 2006; editor: 3 textbooks; contbr. over 150 papers to jours. and textbooks in field. Mem. ACLU, 1948—, Planned Parenthood, 1960—, Nat. Abortion Rights Action League 1975—, Amnesty Internat., 1984—. With U.S. Army, 1944-46, ETO. Mem. Midwest Sociol. Soc. (pres. 1971-72), Am. Sociol. Assn. (chair family sect. 1975-76), Nat. Coun. on Family Rels. (pres. 1979-80, Reuben Hill award 1980, E.W. Burgess award 1984), Polish Acad. Sexual Sci. (hon., Internat. Sexual Sci. award 1989), Soc. for Sci. Study Sex (pres. 1980-81, Disting. Sci. Achievement award 1982, Alfred Kinsey award 1990), Internat. Acad. Sex Rsch. (pres. 1984-85), Am. Assn. Sex Educators, Counselors and Therapists (leadership award 1993). Democrat. Jewish. Home: 5932 Medicine Lake Rd Minneapolis MN 55422-3328 Home Phone: 763-544-8016. E-mail: irareiss@comcast.net.

REISS, JEROME, retired lawyer; b. Bklyn., Dec. 7, 1924; s. William and Eva (Marenstein) Reiss; m. Naomi Betty Plutzik, June 15, 1947; children: Robert Scott, Harlan Morgan, Andrea Ellen, Samantha Glynis. BA, Bklyn. Coll., 1948; JD, Harvard U., Cambridge, Mass., 1951. Bar: NY 1951, US Dist. Ct. (so. dist.) NY 1954, US Ct. Claims 1960, US Dist. Ct. (ea. dist.) NY 1964, DC 1967, US Dist. Ct. (we. dist.) NY 1979, US Supreme Ct. 1989. Staff atty. civil br. Legal Aid Soc., NYC, 1951—54; asst. corp. counsel City of N.Y., 1954—58; assoc. Max E. Greenberg, 1958-67; sr. ptnr. Max E. Greenberg, Trayman, Cantor, Reiss & Blasky, 1967-80, Max E. Greenberg, Cantor & Reiss, NYC, 1980-88, Thelen, Marrin, Johnson & Bridges, NYC, 1989-97, Thelen, Reid & Priest, 1997-2000, ret., 2000; gen. counsel Kiska Constrn. Co.-USA, Inc., 2004—. Arbitrator Small Claims Ct., 1960—88; bd. adv. Fed. Pub., Inc.; chmn. bd. AMT-Pacific, Israel, 2000—02; former mem. Am. Judges Assn.; rep. various Japanese, British, Turkish, Israeli internat. contractors; lectr. in constrn. field PLI, Fla. Atlantic U.; drafter renovation contracts Statue of Liberty; drafter expansion contracts Met. Mus. of Art; drafter construction contracts NYC Conv. Ctr., Rockefeller U., New Pk. Bldg.; competition organizer FDR Lib., Hyde Pk., NY. Contbr. articles to profl. jours., chapters to books. Trustee Brownsville Boys Club Alumni Assn.; gen. counsel Artist Fellowship, Inc. With USAAF, 1943—46. Fellow: Am. Coll. Constrn. Lawyers (founding mem.); mem.: Wash. (DC) Bar Assn., NY Bar Assn., Internat. Bar Assn., Jacob K. Javits Conv. Ctr. Oper. Corp. (bd. dirs.), Mcpl. Assist. Corp. City NY (bd. dirs.), Am. Arbitrators Assn.

REISS, JOHN BARLOW, lawyer; b. London, Aug. 29, 1939; arrived in U.S., 1963; s. James Martin and Margaret Joan (Ping) R.; m. Mary Jean Maudsley, Aug. 6, 1967 (div. 1978); m. Kathleen Strouse, Aug. 2, 1979; 1 child, Juliette Blanche. BA with honors, Exeter U., Devon, Eng., 1961; AM, Washington U., St. Louis, 1966, PhD, 1971; JD, Temple U., 1977. Bar: Pa. 1977, N.J. 1977, U.S. Dist. Ct. N.J. 1977, D.C. 1980, U.S. Supreme Ct. 1981, U.S. Dist. Ct. D.C. 1982. Economist Commonwealth Econ. Com., London, 1962-63; asst. prof. Allegheny Coll., Meadville, Pa., 1967-71; assoc. prof. Stockton State Coll., Pomona, NJ, 1971-75; asst. health commr. State of N.J., Trenton, 1975-79; dir. office of health regulation U.S. Dept. HHS, Washington, 1979-81; assoc. Baker & Hostetler, Washington, 1981-82, Dechert Price & Rhoads, Phila., 1982—93, ptnr., 1986-93, asst. chair health law group, 1984-91, chmn. health law group, 1991-93; ptnr. Saul Ewing LLP, Phila., 1993—, chmn. health law dept., 1995—2002, chmn. health law practice group, 2002—07. Mem. editl. bd. Topics in Hosp. Law, 1985-86, Hosp. Legal Forms Manual, 1985-2002, Jour. Health Care Tech., 1984-86; contbr. Hosp. Contracts Manual, 1983-2002; contbr. articles to profl. jours., chpts. to books. Bd. dirs. Gateway Sch. Little Children, Phila., 1986-99, ECRI, Plymouth Meeting, Pa., 1994—, chmn. bd., 2001—; mem. bd. vestry All Saints Ch., Wynnewood, Pa., 1993, 96-2001; treas. The U. BC 1871 Found., 2006-07. Pub. Health Svc. fellow, 1979-81, English Speaking Union fellow, 1963-66, Econ. Devel. Adminstr. fellow Washington U., 1966-67. Mem. Nat. Health Lawyers Assn., Phila. Bar Assn., Brit. Am. C. of C. of Greater Phila. (bd. dirs. 1991), Health Care Fin. Mgmt. Assn. (bd. dirs. NJ chpt. 2005-08), Union League Phila., U. Barge Club (sec. 2007—), Brit. Officers Club Phila. (1st v.p. 2003—04, pres. 2005-06), Phila. Club. Avocations: gardening, house restoring, reading, sculling. Home: 415 Wister Rd Wynnewood PA 19096-1808 Office: Saul Ewing LLP 3800 Centre Sq W Philadelphia PA 19102 Home Phone: 610-649-4434; Office Phone: 215-972-7124. Business E-Mail: jreiss@saul.com.

REISS, JOHN CHARLES, bishop emeritus; b. Red Bank, NJ, May 13, 1922; s. Alfred and Sophia (Telljohan) R. Student, Immaculate Conception Sem., 1941-46; BA, Seton Hall U., 1947; STL, Catholic U., 1947, JCD, 1953. Ordained priest Diocese of Trenton, 1947, asst. chancellor, 1954, sec., master ceremonies, 1953-62, vice chancellor, 1956-62, officialis, 1962-80, aux. bishop, 1967-80, bishop, 1982-97, bishop emeritus, 1997—; ordained bishop, 1967. Mem. Trenton Mayor's Adv. Commn. on Civil Rights, 1962-68. Roman Catholic.

REISS, LENORE ANN, language educator, retired secondary school educator; b. Bklyn., Apr. 17, 1936; d. Morris and Alice Shestack; m. Edward Lawrence Reiss, Sept. 13, 1959 (dec. June 5, 2000); children: Stephanie Lynne, Jonathan David. BA cum laude, Boston U., 1957; postgrad., Middlebury Coll., 1956, NYU, 1974—76, U. Miami, 1979. Tchr. Spanish and French Martin Van Buren HS, Queens Village, NY, 1957—59; pvt. tutor NYC, 1960—77; pvt. sch. tchr. Studio on Eleventh St., NYC, 1970—77; tchr. The Livingston Sch., NYC, 1977—78, Chiaravalle Montessori Sch., Evanston, Ill., 1986—87; pvt. tutor Evanston, 1990—95; ret., 1995. Author: White-Robed Recluse: A Study of Emily Dickinson, 1993, Genius of Darkness: A Study of Edgar Allan Poe, 1994, The Good Lady of Nohant: A Study of George Sand, 1995, numerous poems; contbr. articles to profl. jours. Avocations: reading, music, dance, antiques, theater. Home: 2025 Sherman Ave Evanston IL 60201 also: 136 E 76th St New York NY 10021

REISS, MICHAEL, medical oncologist, researcher; b. Addis Ababa, Ethiopia, Sept. 22, 1950; came to U.S., 1982; s. Willy and Lies (Gerzon) R.; m. Elisabeth Meta Souget, Mar. 15, 1977; children: Kim, Daniel J. Student, U. Amsterdam Med. Sch., The Netherlands, 1968-73; MD, U. Amsterdam, 1976, Yale U. Sch. Medicine. Cert. Bd. Internal Medicine, The Netherlands; fed. licensing exam.; lic. physician Conn. Clk., subintern U. Amsterdam Hosps. and Affiliated Hosps., 1974-76; rsch. assoc. Cen. Lab. Netherlands Red Cross Blood Trans. Lab. for Immunology, U. Amsterdam, 1976-77; intern in internal medicine Med. Coll. Ohio, Toledo, 1977-78; resident in internal medicine U. Hosp. Binnengasthuis, Amsterdam, 1978-82; rotation in med. oncology Netherlands Cancer Inst., Amsterdam, 1980; postdoctoral fellow in med. oncology Yale U. Sch. Medicine, 1982-85, instr. in med. oncology, 1985-87, asst. prof. dept. internal medicine Yale Comp. Cancer Ctr., 1987-91, assoc. prof. dept. internal medicine Yale Comp. Cancer Ctr., 1991—2001; attending physician Yale New Haven Hosp., 1985—2001; med. oncologist Yale Comprehensive Breast Care Ctr., 1989—2001, co-dir., 1992—2001; dir. breast cancer rsch. program Yale Cancer Ctr., 1995—2001; prof., molecular genetics, microbiology & immunology Cancer Inst. NJ, 2001—, prof., internal medicine, 2001—. Chmn. rsch. com. sect. med. oncology Yale U. Sch. Medicine, 1986—, fellowship com. sect. med. oncology, 1986—, cancer edn. com. Yale Comprehensive Cancer Ctr., 1989—, funds and fellowships com., 1991-95; mem. instnl. grant rev. com. Am. Cancer Soc., 1988-94; invited mem. Sec.'s Spl. Conf. on Breast Cancer, NIH, 1993; reviewer Netherlands Cancer Found. Rsch. Grants. Reviewer: Cancer Rsch., Blood, Jour. Cell Physiology, Cancer Comms., European Jour. Cancer Clin. Oncology; contbr. articles to profl. jours. 2d lt. Dutch Army, 1975-77. Recipient Swebilius Cancer Rsch. award, 1985-86; clin. fellow Queen Wilhelmina Cancer Found., Amsterdam, 1982-84; rsch. grantee numerous orgns. Mem. AAAS, Am. Assn. for Cancer Rsch., Am. Soc. Clin. Oncology, Am. Soc. Cell Biology, Am. Fedn. for Clin. Rsch. Avocations: complexity theory, computers, fishing, bicycling, music. Office: Univ Medicine Dentistry NJ-Robert Wood Johnson Med Sch Cancer Inst NJ 195 Little Albany St New Brunswick NJ 08903-2681 Office Phone: 732-235-6031. Office Fax: 732-235-6267. Business E-Mail: michael.reiss@umdnj.edu.*

REISS, MITCHELL B., academic administrator, law educator, former ambassador; b. Dayton, Ohio, June 12, 1957; s. Martin H. and Rhea E. (Cohen) R.; m. Elisabeth M. Reiss, Oct. 25, 1986; children: Mathew A., Michael E. BA, Williams Coll., 1979; postgrad., Fletcher Sch., 1982; PhD, Oxford U., Eng., 1985; JD, Columbia U., 1988. Bar: D.C. Spl. asst. to nat. security adv. NSC, Washington, 1988-89; assoc. Covington & Burling LLP, Washington, 1989—94; asst. exec. dir. Korean Peninsula Energy Devel. Orgn. (KEDO), 1994—99; dir., Wendy & Emery Reves Ctr. for Internat. Studies Coll. William & Mary, Williamsburg, Va., 1999—2003, dean for internat. affairs, 1999—2003; prof. law & govt. Marshall-Wythe Law Sch., Williamsburg, Va., 1999—, vice provost for internat. affairs Wiliamsburg, Va., 2005—; dir. policy planning staff US Dept. State, Washington, 2003—05, spl. presidential envoy to No. Ireland, 2004—07. Guest scholar Woodrow Wilson Ctr., 1992-95 Author: Without the Bomb: The Politics of Nuclear Non-proliferation, 1988, Bridled Ambition: Why Countries Constrain Their Nuclear Capabilities, 1995; co-editor: Nuclear Proliferation after the Cold War, 1994, The Nuclear Tipping Point: Why States Reconsider Their Nuclear Choices, 2004. Presdl. Commn. on White House fellows, 1988. Avocations: tennis, squash. Office: William & Mary Sch Law PO Box 8795 Williamsburg VA 23187-8795

REISS, PAUL J., academic administrator; b. Lake Placid, NY, Aug. 10, 1930; s. Julian J. and Daisy M. (Smith) R.; m. Rosemary A. Donohue, June 25, 1955; children: Catherine, Paul, Gregory, Mark, Julia, David, Steven, Martha, John. BS, Holy Cross Coll., 1952; MA, Fordham U., 1954; PhD, Harvard U., 1960; LHD (hon.), Showa U., 1994; LLD (hon.), Middlebury Coll., 1996; LHD (hon.), St. Michael's Coll., 2005. Tutor Harvard U., 1954-57; instr., asst. prof. Marquette U., 1957-63, chmn. dept. sociology, 1961-63; asso. prof. sociology Fordham U., Bronx, NY, 1963-75, prof., 1976-85, chmn. dept. sociology and anthropology, 1964-68; dean Fordham U. (Liberal Arts Coll.), 1968-69, v.p. acad. affairs, 1969-75, exec. v.p., 1975-85; pres. St. Michael's Coll., Colchester, Vt., 1985-96, pres. emeritus, 1996—. Editor: Sociological Analysis: A Journal in the Sociology of Religion, 1961-68; contbr. articles to profl. jours. Chmn. bd. dir. Julian Reiss Found., Lake Placid, NY; trustee Wadhams Hall Sem. Coll.; St. Edmund's Retreat, bd. dirs. Lake Placid Sinfonietta (pres.), Mercy Care for Adirondacks (chmn.); mem. Nat. Assn. Ind. Colls., Assn. Cath. Colls. and Univs., Assn. Vt. Ind. Colls. (pres.), Vt. Higher Edn. Coun. (pres.), Vt. Bus. Roundtable, Vt. World Trade Office (chmn.). Fellow Am. Sociol. Assn.; mem. Assn. Sociology Religion (pres.). Democrat. Roman Catholic. Home: 48 Daisy Way Lake Placid NY 12946 Personal E-mail: proreiss@aol.com.

REISS, RICHARD ARNOLD, theater director, actor; b. Cleve., Jan. 10, 1956; s. Joseph Godfrey and LaVerne Francis Reiss; m. Barbara Ann Oleksa-Reiss, Mar. 21, 1953. BA in Speech and Theatre, U. Tenn., Knoxville, 1979; MFA in Acting, Kent State U., Ohio, 2009. Profl. actor, 1979—2007; film carpenter, scenic painter Austin, Tex., 1992—97; tech. dir. Player's Guild Theatre, Canton, Ohio, 1999—2000; dir., designer, tech. dir. North Canton Playhouse, 2001—04; set carpenter, stage hand Stark Campus Kent State U., 2004—06, grad. asst. acting, undergrad. tutor, 2006—09. Co-founder, artistic dir. Ohio Youth Shakespeare Festival; pres. Kent State U. Theatre Grad. Forum, 2007—08; theatre del. Kent State U. Grad Student Senate, 2007—08. Recipient Dir. Excellence award, Ohio Cmty. Theatre Assn., 2004; named Outstanding Grad. Dir., Kent State U., 2007—08. Mem.: Alpha Psi Omega. Liberal. Avocations: reading, carpentry, hiking, cooking, dogs. Home: 827 Harold Dr Kent OH 44240 Office: Kent State U Dept Theatre and Dance Music & Speech Bldg Kent OH 44240 Office Fax: 330-672-2889. Personal E-mail: theatredesigns@aol.com. Business E-Mail: rreiss@kent.edu.

REISS, ROBERT FRANCIS, physician; b. Watertown, NY, Dec. 11, 1938; s. Ernest Paul and Elizabeth Munk (Clark) R.; m. Giovanna Dora Bassi, Mar. 18, 1964; children: Carroll, Christian, Mark, Dylan. AB, Syracuse U., 1959; MD, U. Bologna, Italy, 1965. Diplomate Am. Bd. Pathology (hematology, transfusion medicine). Dir. lab. hematology and blood bank State U. Hosp., Bklyn., 1975-77; asst. prof. pathology SUNY Downstate Med. Ctr., Bklyn., 1975-77; dir. Hudson Valley Blood Svc., Valhalla, NY, 1978-85; assoc. prof. pathology and medicine N.Y. Med. Coll., Valhalla, 1978-88; med. dir. N.Y. Blood Ctr., NYC, 1985-88; dir. lab. hematology and transfusion medicine Columbia-Presbyn. Med. Ctr., NYC, 1988-98; prof. clin. pathology and clin. medicine Columbia U. Coll. Physicians and Surgeons, NYC, 1988—; v.p., chief med. officer N.Y. Blood Ctr., NYC, 1998—2001, 2006—09. Chmn. steering com. Hudson Valley Blood Resources Assn., Valhalla, 1981-85; chief examiner blood banking N.Y.C. Dept. Health, 1980-86, mem. adv. com. on blood banking, 1988-90; mem. instnl. rev. bd. N.Y. Blood Ctr., N.Y.C., 1991-2001. Editor, co-author: Clinical Laboratory Medicine, 1992; contbr. more than 40 articles to med. jours., chpts. to books. Bd. mgrs. camping plus N.Y.C. Mission Soc., 1975-78; scout leader Boy Scouts Am., N.Y.C., 1975-80. Col. U.S. Army, 1966-69, USAR, 1988—2005. Fellow Assn. Clin. Scientists (vice chair sect. on hematology and transfusion medicine, 1999—; mem. Am. Assn. Blood Banks (dist. advisor 1982-88, mem. editl. bd. Ann. Clin. Labs. Sci. 1999—), Coun. Hosp. Blood Bank Dirs. Greater N.Y. (bd. dirs. 1989-98), Am. Soc. Hematology. Avocations: travel, running, stamps. Home Phone: 718-446-2739; Office Phone: 212-570-3407. Business E-Mail: rfr1@columbia.edu.

REISS, STEVEN, psychology professor; b. NYC, Apr. 10, 1947; s. Benjamin A. and Margaret (Schmidt) R.; m. Maggi B. Reiss, Sept. 4, 1971; children: Michael, Ben AB magna cum laude, Dartmouth Coll., 1964; PhD in Psychology, Yale U., 1972. Registered psychologist, Ill. Prof. psychology U. Ill.-Chgo., 1972-91; prof. psychology and psychiatry Ohio State U., Columbus, 1991—2008, dir. Nisonger Ctr., 1991—. Dir. ISDD Mental Health Clinic, Chgo., 1980-91. Author: Who Am I: The 16 Basic Desires, 2000; editor: Psychophropic Medications, 1998; author psychol. tests: Reiss Screen, 1988, Anxiety Sensitivity Index, 1986, The Normal Personality, 2009, Reiss Motivation Profile ARC Rsch. awardee, 1991, NADD Career awardee, 1998. Fellow APA, Am. Assn. Mental Retardation (bd. dirs. 1987, Svc. award 1987). Office: Ohio State Univ 1581 Dodd Dr Columbus OH 43210-1267 Home Phone: 614-885-4114; Office Phone: 614-292-2390. Personal E-mail: sreiss0410@yahoo.com. E-mail: reiss.7@osu.edu.

REISS, STEVEN ALAN, lawyer, educator; b. NYC, Dec. 18, 1951; s. Louis and Ruth (Harrow) R.; m. Mary A. Mattingly; children: Alexandra Mattingly Reiss, Tyler Brennan Reiss. BA, Vassar Coll., 1973; JD, Stanford U., Calif., 1976. Bar: N.Y., D.C., Calif. Law clk. to John Minor Wisdom U.S. Ct. Appeals for 5th Cir., New Orleans, 1976-77; law clk. to justice William J. Brennan U.S Supreme Ct., Washington, 1977-78; assoc. Miller, Cassidy, Larroca & Lewin, Washington, 1978-80; vis. prof. Georgetown U. Law Ctr., Washington, 1981; asst. prof. Law Sch., NYU, 1981-83, assoc. prof., 1984-87, prof., 1987-91; ptnr. Weil, Gotshal & Manges, NYC, 1990—. Editor-in-chief White Collar Crime Reporter, 1987-91, contbg. editor, 1991—. Trustee Vassar Coll. Poughkeepsie, N.Y., 1978-82; bd. trustees Oxfarm America.; gen. counsel Brennan Ctr. for Justice, 1996—; bd. trustees Vols. of Legal Svcs. Mem. N.Y. State Bar Assn., D.C. Bar Assn., Calif. Bar Assn., Assn. of Bar of City of N.Y. (fed. legis. com. 1981-87), 2d Jud. Conf. (reporter 1984—). Home: 25 E 86th St New York NY 10028-0553 Office: Weil Gotshal & Manges 767 5th Ave Fl Concl New York NY 10153-0119 E-mail: steven.riess@weil.com.

REITAN, BERNT, metal products executive; b. Norway, Apr. 11, 1948; married; 2 children. M in Civil Engring., Tech. U. Trondheim, Norway. Various civil engring. project positions, Stavanger and Lillehammer, Norway, 1972—79; plant mgr. Rodsand magnetite mine Elkem, Norway, 1980—83, gen. mgr. Elkem Chems. Ltd. England, 1983—84, plant mgr. Fiskaa silicon plant Norway, 1985—87, bus. unit mgr. ferro alloys divsn., 1987, sr. v.p. materials and tech., mng. dir. Elkem Aluminium ANS, 1988—2000; gen. mgr. World Alumina Chems. Alcoa, Inc., 2000, pres. World Chems., 2000—01, pres. Alcoa World Alumina and Chems., v.p., 2001—03, pres. Primary Metals, 2003, group pres. Global Primary Products, exec. v.p. NYC, 2004—. Bd. mem. Internat. Primary Aluminium Inst., European Aluminium Assn., Norwegian Employers Fedn., Norwegian Process and Mfg. Assn.; chmn. bd. Norwegian Metall. Industry Assn., 1990—92; bd. dirs. Royal Caribbean Cruise Lines. Office: Alcoa Inc 390 Park Ave New York NY 10022 Office Phone: 212-836-2600.

REITAN, DANIEL KINSETH, electric and computer engineering educator; b. Duluth, Minn., Aug. 13, 1921; s. Conrad Ulfred and Joy Elizabeth R.; m. Marian Anne Stemme, July 18, 1946; children: Debra Leah, Danielle Karen. BSEE, ND State U., Fargo, 1946; MSEE, U. Wis., Madison, 1949, PhD, 1952. Registered profl. engr., Wis. Control engr. GE, Schenectady, NY, 1946-48; transmission line engr. Gen. Telephone Co., Madison, Wis., 1949-50; mem. faculty Coll. Engring. U. Wis., Madison, 1952-85, prof. elec. and computer engring., 1962-85; cons. Energy Industries, 1985-95; dir. power sys. simulation lab. Coll. Engring. U. Wis., 1968-84, also dir. wind power rsch. Energy Ctr. Coll. Engring. Cons. Nat. Inst. Sci. and Tech. (formerly U.S. Nat. Bur. Stds.); dir. electric network calculator lab. Wis. Utilities, 1959-68. Author: Interstellar Space Travel at Near Light Speed, 1995, The Visual Appearance of Relativistically Moving Objects, 1999; contbr. articles to profl. jours.; patentee in field. With US Army, World War II. Recipient Outstanding Tchr. award Polygon Engring. Council., Gov.'s citation for service to State of Wis. Fellow IEEE (Centennial medal and cert. for outstanding achievement 1984, Centennial medal and cert. dept. ECE U. Wis., 1991, IEEE power Engring., Computer Control Indsl. Applications and Edn. Soc.), Conf. Internat. des Grand Reseaux Electriques a Haute Tension, Am. Soc. Engring. Edn., Wis. Acad. Scis., Am. Wind Energy Assn., The Planetary Soc., Sigma Xi, Tau Delta Pi, Tau Beta Pi, Eta Kappa Nu, Kappa Eta Kappa. Lutheran. Achievements include research and study of the cosmos. Home: 1200 Harwood Dr Apt 322 Fargo ND 58104-6294 Personal E-mail: dkreitan@cableone.net. *I believe that in one's career professionalism and perseverance are key factors in success. In one's personal life, the family should be the center, but not the circumference, about which all activities revolve.*

REITAN, PAUL HARTMAN, retired geologist, educator; b. Kanawha, Iowa, Aug. 18, 1928; s. John Olsen and Anna (Meldahl) R.; m. Reidun Engebretsen, Sept. 28, 1962; children: Kirsten Berit, Eric Hartmann. AB (Salisbury fellow), U. Chgo., 1953; PhD, U. Oslo, Norway, 1959. Instr. U. Ill., Chgo., 1955; geologist U.S. Geol. Survey, 1953-56; state geologist Geol. Survey of Norway, 1956-60; asst. prof. mineralogy Stanford U., 1960-66; mem. faculty SUNY, Buffalo, 1966-98, dean, 1975-79, prof. emeritus dept. geology, 1998—. Guest scientist Centre for Geol. Sci., Acad. Sci., Warsaw, Poland, Geol. Survey Prague, Czechoslovakia., Geol. Survey, Norway, Nat. Geophys. Rsch. Inst. and Geol. Survey, India Author: (with Davis and Pestrong) Geology, 1976; contbr. articles to profl. jours. Served with U.S. Army, 1946-49. Fulbright fellow, Norway, 1955-56; NATO sr. fellow in sci., 1972; G. Unger Vetlesen fellow, 1973; Fulbright sr. lectr., India, 1986; Norwegian Marshall Fund grantee, 1986, 93. Fellow AAAS, Geol. Soc. Am., Mineral. Soc. Am.; mem. Internat. Assn. Geochemistry and Cosmochemistry, Royal Norwegian Soc. Scis. and Letters (fgn.), Norsk Geologisk Forening (life), Sigma Xi. Home: 120 Walton Dr Buffalo NY 14226-4556 Office: U Buffalo Dept Geology Buffalo NY 14260-3050 Office Phone: 716-645-3489 ext. 3988. E-mail: preitan@buffalo.edu.

REITAN, RALPH MELDAHL, clinical neuropsychologist, former educator; b. Beresford, SD, Aug. 29, 1922; s. John O. and Anna (Meldahl) Reitan; m. Lucille Ann Kirsch, Feb. 14, 1952 (dec. July 1985); children: Ellen, Jon, Ann, Richard, Erik. BA, Ctrl. YMCA Coll., Chgo., 1944; PhD, U. Chgo., 1950. Cert. in clin. psychology and clin. neuropsychology Am. Bd. Profl. Psychology. Instr. U. Chgo., 1948-51; asst. prof. Roosevelt U., Chgo., 1950-51; from asst. prof. to prof. Ind. U.

Med. Sch., Indpls., 1951-70; prof. U. Wash., Seattle, 1970-77, U. Ariz., Tucson, 1977-86; pres. Reitan Neuropsychology Labs., Tucson, 1981—. Cons. NIH, Bethesda, Md., 1960—71, VA, Washington, 1955—84, NASA, Washington, 1964—66. Author: Traumatic Brain Injury, 1985, Neuropsychological Evaluation of Older Children, 1992, The Halstead-Reitan Neuropsychological Test Battery, 1993, Detection of Malingering and Invalid Test Results, 1998, Mild Head Injury: Intellectual, Cognitive and Emotional Consequences, 2000, 15 others; contbr. more than 300 articles to profl. jours. Trustee Easter Seal Rsch. Found., Chgo., 1974—83. With US Army, 1942—43. Fellow: APA, Nat. Acad. Neuropsychology; mem.: Reitan Soc., Coalition Clin. Neuropsychology Practitioners, Am. Acad. Neurology (affiliate), Am. Neurol. Assn. (Lifetime Svc. awards, Father of Field Clin. Neuropsychology). Avocations: walking, birdwatching. Home: 4831 N Via Serenidad Tucson AZ 85718-5715 Office: Reitan Neuropsychology Labs PO Box 66080 Tucson AZ 85728-6080 Home Phone: 520-299-5725. Personal E-mail: reitanlabs@aol.com.

REITER, BRANDT, artist; b. Phila., Nov. 25, 1964; BA in Am. Studies, Temple U., Phila., 1986; MFA in Theatre, Sarah Lawrence Coll., Bronxville, NY, 2005. Cert. in film theory & criticism Sorbonne, Paris, 1985. Jazz critic LA Weekly, 2000—04, NYC, 2008—. Author: End of Play, 2007. Co-vice chair playwriting Kennedy Ctr. Am. Coll. Theatre Festival Region I, 2008—. Mem.: Soc. Stage Dirs. & Choreographers, Am. Fedn. TV & Radio Artists, Actors' Equity Assn., SAG.

REITER, GLENN MITCHELL, lawyer; b. NYC, Feb. 1, 1951; s. Bernard Leon and Helene (Edson) R.; m. Marilyn Beckhorn, Sept. 5, 1976; children: Benjamin, Diana, Julie. BA, Yale U., 1973, JD, 1976. Bar: N.J. 1976, Pa. 1977, D.C. 1978, N.Y. 1979. Law clk. to judge U.S. Ct. Appeals, Phila., 1976-77; assoc. Schnader, Harrison, Segal & Lewis, Phila., 1977-78, Simpson Thacher & Bartlett LLP, NYC, 1978-84, ptnr., 1984—, resident ptnr. London, 1986-90. Mem.: Phi Beta Kappa. Office Phone: 212-455-3358.

REITER, JOSEPH HENRY, lawyer, retired judge; b. Phila., Mar. 21, 1929; s. Nicholas and Barbara (Hellmann) Reiter; m. Beverlee A. Bearman, Nov. 8, 1993. AB, Temple U., 1950, LLB, 1953. Bar: D.C. 1953, Pa. 1954. Atty. advisor U.S. Army, 1955—61; asst. U.S. atty. Ea. Dist. Pa., 1961—63, asst. U.S. atty. in charge of civil div., 1963—69; chief organized crime and racketeering strike force Western N.Y. State U.S. Dept. Justice, 1969—70, sr. trial atty. tax divsn., 1970—72, regional dir. office of drug abuse law enforcement, 1972—73; dep. atty. gen., dir. Drug Law Enforcement Office of Pa., 1973—77; ptnr. Stassen, Kostos and Mason, Phila., 1978—85, Kostos Reiter & Lamer, 1985—89; judge Armed Svcs. Bd. of Contract Appeals, Falls Church, Va., 1989—95; of counsel Kostos & Lamer, Phila., 1995—. Mem. adv. com. Joint State Commn. on Procurement; lectr. in field. Contbr. articles to profl. jours. With US Army, 1953—55. Recipient Meritorious Svc. award, U.S. Atty. Gen. Clark, 1967, Spl. Commendation, Asst. U.S. Atty. Gen. Tax Divsn., 1969, Outstanding Performance award, U.S. Atty. Gen. Richardson, 1973. Mem.: ABA, Phila. Bar Assn., D.C. Bar Assn., Fed. Bar Assn., Pan Am. Assn. Phila., Vesper Club, Am. Legion. Office: Kostos & Lamer 1608 Walnut St Ste 1300 Philadelphia PA 19103-5407 Home Phone: 305-867-0465; Office Phone: 856-795-7927.

REITER, MICHAEL A., lawyer, educator; b. Pitts., Nov. 15, 1941; BS, U. Wis., 1963, MS, 1964, JD, 1967, PhD, 1969. Bar: Wis. 1967, Ill. 1975, US Supreme Ct. 1975, Supreme Ct. Ill. Ptnr. Holleb & Coff, Chgo., 1987-99, Duane Morris LLP, Chgo., 1999—2007, counsel, 2008—. Adj. prof. law Northwestern U., Chgo., 1977—99; mem. faculty Nat. Inst. Trial Advocacy, 1980—; spkr. in field. Contbr. articles to law jours. Mem.: ABA. Office: Duane Morris LLP Ste 3700 190 S LaSalle St Chicago IL 60603-3433 Office Phone: 312-499-6718. Office Fax: 312-277-6904. E-mail: MAReiter@duanemorris.com.*

REITER, ROBERT E., urologist, educator; b. New Haven, Conn., Aug. 11, 1961; s. Stanley and Marcia Reiter; m. Fredrica Smithline; children: Amanda, Jacob, Dean. BS, Yale U., New Haven, 1983; MD, Stanford, 1984—88; MBA, UCLA, 2007. Founder Agensys Corp., Santa Monica, Calif., 1998—2007; founder and chief med. officer ImaginAb LLC, Culver City, Calif., 2007—08; founder and CEO EMTx Therapeutics, LA; prof. UCLA, 1995—. Dir. rsch. UCLA Urology, 2000—08. Lt. comdr. Pub. Health Svc., 1991—93, Bethesda, MD. Recipient Young Investigator award, Soc. Urologic Oncology, 2005; Fulbright scholarship, Inst. Internat. Edn., 1983—84. Fellow: Am. Soc. Clin. Investigation; mem.: Am. Urol. Assn. Achievements include patents for prostate stem cell antigen; invention of PSCA antibody therapy for cancer. Office: UCLA 66-128 Chs Los Angeles CA 90095 Office Phone: 310-794-7224. Office Fax: 310-206-5343. Business E-Mail: rreiter@mednet.ucla.edu.

REITER, ROBERT EDWARD, banker; b. Kansas City, Mo., Dec. 27, 1943; s. Robert Vincent and Helen Margaret (Petrus) R.; m. Mary J. Darby, June 20, 1964; children: Mollie K., Jennifer M., Ellen R., Robert E. Jr. BA, Rockhurst Coll., 1964; JD, St. Louis U., 1967; LLM, U. Mo., Kansas City, 1969. Bar: Mo. 1967. Assoc. atty. Burke, Jackson & Millin, Kansas City, 1967-69; personal trust adminstr. City Nat. Bank and Trust Co., Kansas City, 1969-71; estate planning officer United Mo. Bank of Kansas City, 1971-73, v.p., 1973-80, sr. v.p., 1980-85; exec. v.p. UMB Bank, N.A., 1985—2009. Pres., corp. bd. Seton Ctr., Kansas City, 1992-95. Contbr. articles to profl. jours. Bd. of Counselors St. Joseph Health Ctr., Kansas City, 1977-85; pres. St. Joseph Health Ctr. Adv. Coun., Kansas City, 1985-86; treas., bd. trustees Endowment Trust Fund for Cath. Edn., 1989—; bd. regents Rockhurst U., 1999—, mem. planned giving coun., 1999—. Grantee St. Louis U. Sch. of Law, 1964-67. Mem. Mo. Bar Assn., Kansas City Bar Assn. (chmn. employee benefits com. 1989-90), Employee Benefit Inst. (adv. bd. 1986—, chmn. 1989), Inst. Cert. Bankers (cert. retirement svcs. profl. 1995—), Estate Planning Soc. Kansas City (pres. 1985-86), Serra Club of Kansas City (v.p. 1987-89). Home: 1024 W 70th St Kansas City MO 64113-2004 Office: UMB Bank NA 1010 Grand Blvd PO Box 419692 Kansas City MO 64141-6692

REITH, MAARTEN EDWARD A., neurochemist; b. Utrecht, Netherlands, Dec. 29, 1946; arrived in US, 1978; s. Jan Franciscus and Katherina (Poelmann) Reith; m. Irma Araujo, Apr. 26, 1980; 1 child, Catherina. BS, U. Utrecht, 1968, MS, 1971, PhD, 1975. Rsch. scientist Rudolf Magnus Inst. Pharmacology, Utrecht, 1971—74; sr. rsch. scientist Inst. Molecular Biology, Utrecht, 1974—78; rsch. scientist Ctr. Neurochemistry, NYC, 1978—80; sr. rsch. scientist, 1980—81; assoc. prof. pharmacology Coll. Medicine U. Ill., Peoria, 1991—95, prof., 1995—2003; prof. psychiatry Sch. Medicine NYU, 2003—. Adj. prof. biol. sci. Ill. State U., Normal, 1996—; consulting mem. study sect. Nat. Inst. Drug Abuse, Rockville, Md., 1987—, NIH, Washington, 1998-; invited panelist Winter Conf. Brain Rsch., 1988, 91, 93-95, 97, 2001. Editor: Neurotransmitter Transporters, 1996, 2d edit., 2002, Cerebral Signal Transduction, From First to Fourth Messengers, 2000, Dopamine and Glutamate in Psychiatric Disorders, 2005; mem. editl. bd. Jour. Neurosci. Methods, 2001—, Neurochem. Rsch., 2004—; editl. cons. European Jour. Pharmacology, 2002-. Grantee, NIH, 1983—. Fellow European Brain Behavior Soc., 1971; mem. Am. Soc. Biochemistry and Molecular Biology, Internat. Soc. Neurochemistry, Soc. Neurosci., Am. Soc. Pharmacol. Exptl. Therapy, NY Acad. Sci. Achievements include first characterization of receptors for cocaine, assessment of allosteric modulation of sodium channels by cocaine congeners, first description of regulation of dopamine transport by arachidonic acid, elucidation of factors determining dopamine interaction with its transporter, discovery of precise binding site for tricyclic and SSRI antidepressant in crystal homologue of monoamine transporters. Office: NYU Sch Medicine Dept Psychiatry Rm MHL-HN518 550 1st Ave New York NY 10016 Home Phone: 212-842-0827; Office Phone: 212-263-8267. Business E-Mail: maarten.reith@med.nyu.edu.

REITINGER, PHILIP RAYMOND, federal agency administrator; b. 1962; BS in Electrical Engring. & Computer Sci., Vanderbilt U., 1984; JD, Yale U., 1987. Law clk. to Hon. Patricia C. Fawsett US Dist. Ct. (middle dist.) Fla.; assoc. Trenam, Simmons, Kemker, Scharf, Barkin, Frye, & O'Neill, Tampa, Fla.; trial atty. Fed. Programs Branch, Civil Divsn. US Dept. Justice, trial atty. Criminal Divsn., spl. asst. US atty. (ea. dist.) Va., 1997, dep. chief computer crime and intellectual property divsn. (CCIPS); exec. dir. Cyber Crime Ctr. US Dept. Def., Linthicum, Md.; sr. security strategist Microsoft Corp., chief trustworthy infrastructure strategist; dep. under sec. Nat. Protection & Programs Directorate US Dept. Homeland Security, Washington, 2009—. Mem. steering com. Info. Assurance Tech. Analysis Ctr.; mem. cyber crime adv. bd. Nat. White Collar Crime Ctr.; mem. exec. subcommittee, chair Next Generation Networks Task Force Pres.'s Nat. Security Telecommunications Adv. Com.; v.p. Info. Tech.-Info. Sharing and Analysis Ctr.; mem. nat. adv. coun. Fed. Emergency Mgmt. Agency (FEMA). Office: US Dept Homeland Security 3801 Nebraska Ave NW Washington DC 20528*

REITMAN, IVAN, film director, producer; b. Komarmo, Czechoslovakia, Oct. 27, 1946; came to Can., 1951; s. Leslie and Clara R.; m. Genevieve Robert, Sept. 12, 1976; children: Jason, Catherine, Caroline. MusB, McMaster U., 1969. Judge FOCUS Nissan-Datsun, NYC, 1981-83. Theatrical prodr.: The Magic show, 1974, The National Lampoon Show, 1975, Merlin, 1983 (also dir.); films include: (dir., exec. prodr.) Cannibal Girls, 1973; (prodr.) They Came From Within (aka Shivers), 1975, Death Weekend (aka The House by the Lake), 1977, Blackout, 1978, National Lampoon's Animal House, 1978, Heavy Metal, 1981, Stop! Or My Mom Will Shoot, 1992, Space Jam, 1996, Private Parts, 1996, Father's Day, 1997, Six Days and Seven Nights, 1998, Doomsday Man, 1999, Evolution, 2001; (prodr., dir.) Foxy Lady, 1971, Meatballs, 1979, Stripes, 1981, Ghostbusters, 1984, Legal Eagles, 1986, Twins, 1988, Ghostbusters II, 1989, Kindergarten Cop, 1990, Dave, 1993, Junior, 1994; (exec. prodr.) Rabid, 1976, Spacehunter: Adventures in the Forbidden Zone, 1983, Big Shots, 1987, Casual Sex?, 1988, Feds, 1988, Beethoven, 1992, Beethoven's 2nd, 1993, Commandments, 1996, Road Trip, 2000, Killing Me Softly, 2002, Old School, 2003, Eurotrip, 2004, That Guy, 2006, Trailer Park Boys: The Movie, 2006, Disturbia, 2007; (dir.) My Super Ex-Girlfriend, 2006; TV series: (prodr., dir.) Delta House, 1978; TV films exec. prodr. The Late Shift, 1996, Fathers Day, 1997. Mem. Dirs. Guild Am. also: Bldg 489 100 University City Plz Universal City CA 91608-1002

REITMAN, JERRY IRVING, advertising agency executive; b. Phila., Jan. 9, 1938; s. Benjamin and Ruth (Eisenberg) R.; m. Monica Birgitta Hall, Oct. 27, 1968; children: Jennifer Sharon, Sarah Beth. BS in Fin., Pa. State U., 1961. Exec. v.p., CEO Brit. Pubs., NYC and London, 1965-69; pres., pub. Acad. Media, Sherman Oaks, Calif., 1969-73; v.p. Pubs. Clearing House, Port Washington, NY, 1973-78; exec. v.p. Ogilvy & Mather, NYC, 1978-81; with Scali, McCabe, Sloves, Inc., NYC, 1981-86; pres. Scali, McCabe, Sloves Direct, NYC; chmn. bd. dirs. The Reitman Group, 1986; exec. v.p. The Leo Burnett Co., Chgo., 1986-96; pres., CEO, vice chair Internat. Data Response Corp., Chgo., 1996—. Dir. Scandinavian Airlines Sys. Pub./Distbn. Svcs.; mem. adv. bd. Ill. Dept. Trade and Tourism, 1988—; internat. awards chmn., bd. dirs. John Caples Internat., 1989—; mem. Internat. Direct Mktg. Symposium, Zürich, Switzerland; dir. Catylst Direct, Goliath Solutions, LLC. Author: A Common Sense Approach to Small Business, 1968, Beyond 2000: The Future of Direct Marketing, 1994; contbr. articles to profl. jours. Trustee Locust Valley Libr. Assn., NY, 1982—; exec. com. mem. Pub. Hall of Fame, 1987—; bd. govs. Children's Miracle Network, 1992-, vice chmn., chmn. bd. govs., 1998—, 1999-2001, chmn. 2002-04, dir.; bd. dirs. Children's Meml. Found. Telethon, The Direct Mktg. Ednl. Found., exec. dir., 1996—. Anderson scholar, 1960; recipient Key to City, New Orleans, 1959, Silver Apple award N.Y. Direct Mktg. Club, 1989, Ed Mayer award Ednl. Found., 1996, Charles S. Downs award, 1997, Direct Marketer of Yr. award. Fellow Psychiat. Re-Edn. Assn.; mem. Am. Mktg. Assn. (at-large mem., 2000, bd. dirs.), Direct Mktg. Assn. (bd. mem. ethics com. 1984), Creative Guild (dir. 1984), Internat. Direct Mktg. Assn. (bd. dirs. 1981-82), Publ. Hall of Fame (exec. com. 1988—), Direct Mktg. Club N.Y. (pres. 1983-84), Beta Gamma Sigma. Avocations: tennis, auto restoration, woodworking. Home and Office: The Reitman Group 2204 N Leavitt St Chicago IL 60647-3204 Home (Summer): Ringso 237 Nasbyviken 64061 Stallanholmen Sweden Office Phone: 773-342-1973. Personal E-mail: jireitman@aol.com.

REITMAN, ROBERT STANLEY, management consultant, not-for-profit advisor; b. Fairmont, W.Va., Nov. 18, 1933; s. Isadore and Freda A. (Layman) R.; m. Sylvia K. Golden, Dec. 24, 1955; children: Scott Alan, Alayne Louise. BS in Acctg., W.Va. U., 1955; JD, Case Western Res. U., 1958. Bar: Ohio 1958. Mem. firm Burke, Haber & Berick, Cleve., 1958-60, ptnr., 1960-68; exec. v.p., vice chmn. Tranzonic Cos. (formerly AAV Cos.), Pepper Pike, Ohio, 1968-70, pres., vice-chmn., 1970-73, chief exec. officer, pres., vice chmn., 1973-82, pres., chmn., CEO, 1982-98, chmn. emeritus, bd. dirs., 1998—; prin. Riverbend Advisors, 1998—. Bus. adv. com. Mandel Ctr. for non-profit Orgn. Case We. Res. U., 1995-99, vis. com. Weatherhead Sch. of Bus., 1995-03, vis. com. Sch. of Law, 1998-03, chmn. dean's nat. adv. com., Sch. of Law, 1997-98; dean's adv. com. Sch. Medicine, 2004-06; pvt. banking adv. bd. Key Bank, N.A., 1997-2007. Mem. Rep. fin. com., Cuyahoga County, 1968-78; mem. Com. for Econ. Growth for Israel, Cleve., 1977-80, pres., 1978-80; adv. coun. Cleve. Mus. Nat. History, 1982-85, Cleve. Opera, 1977—; del. Coun. of Jewish Fedns., NYC, 1981-97; gen. co-chmn. Jewish Welfare Fund, Cleve., 1975-78, 81-85, gen. vice chmn., 1985-89, gen. chmn., 1989-91; sect. and divsn. chmn., team capt. United Way Svcs., 1974-97, del. assembly, 1976-85, trustee, 1977-2000, v.p., 1985-88, chmn. nominating. com., 1988-90, campaign chmn., 1993, chair fund raising planning com., 1994-97, chair bd. trustees, 1997-2000, life trustee, 2000—; employment com. Jewish Vocat. Svc., Cleve., 1974-83; bd. dirs. Capital for Israel, Inc., NYC, 1986-87; nat. vice chmn. United Jewish Appeal, 1987-92, nat. allocations chmn., 1987-90, trustee, 1988-94, chair retirement fund com., 1994-97; trustee B'nai B'rith Hillel Found., 1975-81, Cleve. Jewish News, 1976-79, Ideastream, Cleve., 1976-99, vice chmn. 1986-90, chmn. bd., 1990-97, immediate past chair, 1997-99, chair emeritus, 1999—; trustee, pres. Bus. Volunteerism Coun., 1994-96, chmn. 1996-97; trustee Jewish Cmty. Fedn. Cleve., 1983-98, 1999-03, treas., 1991-94, v.p., 1995-97, life trustee, 2003—, Jewish Edn. Ctr. of Cleve., 1993-96, Cleve. Zool. Soc., 1972—, pres., 1979-87, chmn., 1987-92, chmn. emeritus, 1992—, chmn. JDC-Brookdale Inst. of Gerontology and Human Devel., Israel, 1995; trustee Am. Jewish Joint Distbn. Com., 1988—, United Israel Appeal, 1987-94, Mt. Sinai Med. Ctr., Cleve., 1976-96, chmn., 1982-85; trustee Cleve. State U. Devel. Found., 1988-91, Greater Cleve. Roundtable, 1991-04, The Wilds, 1995-99, adv. bd., 1999-02, trustee Mt. Sinai Health Care Found., 1995-04, life trustee, 2004—, vice chair 1998-2001, chair, 2001-04; trustee Univ. Hosps. Health Sys., 1999-04, 05-08, Univ. Hosps. Cleve., 1999-2007; co-chair Coun. of Diplomats, 2007-; trustee, chair Heather Hill, Inc., 2001-08; coun. mem. Village of Gates Mills, Ohio, 1997-00, clk., 2000-07. Mem. The 50 Club Cleve., Case We. Res. Univ. Sch. of Law Soc. Benchers, Am. Kennel Club (regional del. 1960-75), We. Res. Kennel Club (officer, trustee 1959-75), Beechmont Club (fin. com. 1972-80, house com. 1974), Pepper Pike Club, Union Club, Carambola Golf Club, Masons, Zeta Beta Tau, Tau Epsilon Rho. Avocations: golf, swimming. Office: Riverbend Advisors 2087 Chagrin River Rd Gates Mills OH 44040-9740 Home Phone: 440-423-1515. Business E-Mail: rsrform@core.com.

REITMEISTER, NOEL, planner, advisor, insurance agent, mortgage consultant; b. Bklyn., Aug. 12, 1938; s. Morris G. and Anna (Miller) Reitmeister; m. Elaine Schendelman, Sept. 16, 1961; children: Gregg Allen, Stephen Michael. BA in Econs. and Polit. Sci., Queens Coll., CUNY, 1960; MBA in Occupational Psychology and Mgmt., Erikson Sch. Baruch Coll., CUNY, 1969; diploma, NY Inst. Fin., 1969, Coll. Fin. Planning, Denver, 1974. CFP, cert. Fin. Planning Degree Program; lic. in investments, commodities and futures, options, life, accident, disability and health ins., fixed annuities, variable annuities, variable life, long term care, registered rep. N.Y. Stock Exch., Am. Stock Exch., Chgo. Stock Exch., Pacific Stock Exch., Boston Stock Exch., PBW Exch., Chgo. Bd. Trade, Chgo. Merc. Exch., Comex, NASD, Chgo. Options Exch., lic. investment broker NY, NJ, Mass., Fla., Ariz., Calif., Tex., Mich., Wis., Ill., Ind., Kans., Mo., Va., Ala., NC, LA, DC, N.Mex., OH, registered investment advisor representative. Assoc. merchandise mgr. Bloomingdales, NYC, 1962-63; regional mgr Cosmair div. L'Oreal, Paris, 1963-67; project dir. advt. rsch. Toni Div. Gillette Co., 1967-68; ins. and investment cons. John Hancock, 1968—69; acct. exec., br. coord., spl. ptnr. duPont Walston, 1969—74; sr. fin. cons. A.G. Edwards & Sons Inc., Merrillville, Ind., 1974—79, v.p. investments, 1979-99, trust specialist, 1992—, sr. v.p.-investments, 1999—2007; fin. advisor, sr. v.p., investment officer Wachovia Securities, LLC, 2007—09; sr. v.p. investment officer Wells Paigo Advisors LLC. Ptnr. Ind. Investors, 1980-88, Nat. Property Investors, 1980-84, Petro Lewis, 1979-84, Can. Am. Oil, 1980-94, Nora Assocs., 1981-2000, Commerce Point, LLC, 2004—, Rollingbrook Properties, LLC, 1983-, vice chmn. bd. Menorah Credit Union, 1979-81, chmn. 1981-82, chmn., CEO, pres., 1982-83; owner Le Baron Comms., 1980-96, Anglo Am. Prodns., 1987-98; dir., prin. Arctic Exploration, Inc.; co-mng. ptnr. Filthy Rich Enterprises, 1980-90; conducted Roundtable at Advanced Conf. on Retirement Planning, Washington, 1986, attended White House Briefing by Chief of Pres.'s Coun. Econ. Advisors; lectr. investments and fin. planning Inst. Continuing Edn., Purdue U., Calumet, 1976-92, adj. faculty fin., 1994-97; lectr. Purdue North Ctrl., Roosevelt U., Calumet Coll. St. Joseph; adj. prof. fin. Sch. Bus. and Econs., Ind. U.; adj. prof. fin. Exec.MBA and Undergrad. Programs; adj. faculty Coll. for Fin. Planning, Denver, 1974-92; columnist The Southtown Star, 1984-86, Am. Med. News Jour., Post-Tribune, 1996—2008; fin. planning and retirement cons. BP-Amoco, 1974-94, LTV, 1982-92, Inland Steel, 1983-94, Ford Motor Co., 1987-91, C.B. Geigy Pharm., 1991-93; examiner in fin. planning, 1974-78; examination criteria com., 1999, hearings officer, 2000-02, com. to design exam questions, bd. profl. rev., 2000. Author: Portfolios, Inc. Key Objectives in Investments; co-author text Retirement Planning for Coll. Fin. Planning; producer & host (cable TV) Money Doctor, 1985-94, PBS spl. Market Crisis of October 1987; contbr. articles to profl. jours. including Jour. Inst. Cert. Fin. Planning, Fin. Planning and Nursing, Post Tribune, The Times, Vidette Messenger, The Star, The Economist, Daily Southtown, Fin. Svcs. Weekly, NY Times, Registered Rep. Mag., Merrillville Herald, Fin. Planning News. Exec. com., sec. Ill. Theatre Ctr., 1985-88; bd. dirs. South Suburban HELP, 1968-69, N.W. Ind. Pub. Broadcasting, 1986-92; trustee Temple Anshe Sholom, 1975-82, chmn. adult edn., 1977-82, chmn. house and grounds, 1977-78, co-chmn. social action com., 1979-82, Temple's Endowment Com., 1992-95, 96-2001, Rabbinical Selection Com., 1981-82, budget and fin. com., 1978-82; dir. Vis. Nurse Assn. NW Ind., 1992-98, 2000-02, mem. fin. com., exec. com, 1992-98, 1999-2005, devel. com., chmn. by-laws com., exec. com., co-chmn., 1992-98, bd. mem. Ill. Philharm. Orch., 2002—, chmn. mktg. com., exec. com., planning com., 2004—09; dir. drug and alcohol edn. Sheriff's Dept. Cook County, Ill., 1989-91; v.p. Pinnacle Condominium Assn., 2008-; house com., 2006-07; chair Pet Com., 2007-08; v.p., 2008-, sec. South Suburban Acad. Jewish Studies, 1979-82; troop coord. Boy Scouts Am., 1977-78, vol. Richton Crossing Nursing Home; active Anti-Defamation League Cabinet, 1978-82, exec. com. Anti-Defamation League Chgo., 2004—09; v.p. Young Rep. Club of Queens County NY, 1958-60; Jewish War Veterans, 1971-; v.p. Chgo. B'nai B'rith Coun., B'nai B'rith regional v.p. for ADL, Chai Unit, pres. 5 terms, v.p. 40-terms, parliamentarian, 38 terms; co-founder, treas. SESSA; diversity com. Ind. U. N.W. Staff sgt. USAR, 1960-65, 197th US Army Security Agy. Co., Ft. Dix, Ft. Devens, Ft. Hamilton, Ft. Drum. Decorated Order of William Tell (Switzerland); apptd. Col. on staff Gov. of Ky., 1988; named Man of Yr., B'nai B'rith, 1986, Jewish Fedn. Chgo. United Fund, 2005; recipient Excellence award Nat. Assn. Accts., 1985. Mem.: AAUP, Stephen Wolf Soc., Queens Coll. Alumni Assn., Wachovia Securities (mem, Premier advisor level), Pres.'s Coun., Baruch Coll. Alumni Assn., Alfred U. Alumni assn., Goodman Soc., Friends of Chgo. Opera Theatre, Chmn.'s Coun., Ind. TV Prodrs. Assn. Chgo., Chgo. Coun. on Fgn. Rels., Weisenthal Inst., Registry Fin. Planning Practitioners (charter 1983—95), Fin. Planning Assn., Internat. Soc. Registered Reps., Internat. Assn. Fin. Planners (v.p. Chgo. South chpt.), Michiana Assn. Fin. Planners (charter), Chgo. Assn. Fin. Planners (charter 1973—78, pres. 1975), Internat. Assn. Registered Fin. Planners (charter), Inst. Cert. Fin. Planners (pres. Illiana Soc. 1985—93, chmn. 1993—97, amb. 1997—, charter), Stuyvesant Alumni Assn., Stuyvesant HS Alumni Assn., Shedd Aquariam, Jerusalem Soc., Stratford Shakespeare Soc., Volunteered Optometrists Serving Humanity (life), Flossmoor Arts Coun., Yad Vashem Soc., Steppenwolf Theatre Soc., Am. Friends of the Technicon, Jewish War Vets, Friends of Israel Defense Forces, Friends of Hebrew U. Jerusalem, Am. Friends Ben Gurion U., Art Inst. Chgo., Tech. Soc., Nat. Geog. Soc., Chgo. Shakespeare Theatre Soc., Spertus Inst., Lyric Opera League, Friends of the Ill. Philharm., Art Inst. Chgo., Goodman Theater Prodn., Grant Park Symphony Soc., Smithsonian Soc., Crest Club, A. G. Edward's Million Dollar Club, Ancient Arabic Order of the Noble Mystic Shrine, VIP Club, Chgo. U. Club, Tower Club (assoc.), Union League Club (assoc.), Boston Harvard Club (assoc.), Univ. Club (assoc.), Std. Club Chgo. (assoc.), 12 Million Dollar Club, Six Million Dollar Club, Century Club, Convenant Club, Idlewild Country Club, Homewood-Flossmoor Racquet and Fitness, Williams Club (NYC), Mariners Club, Scotish Rite, Masons (32 degree), Neighbor Lodge (life), Shrine-Medinah Temple (Ancient Arabic Order of Noble Mystic Shrine), Tau Delta Phi (social chmn. Queens Coll., pledge master, co-pres.), Delta Omega Kappa (v.p. Alpha chpt. 1953, pres. Beta chpt. 1954—56, nat. pres. 1955—60), Zeta Beta Tau (pres. pledge class 1956—57, soc. chmn. 1956—57), Alpha Epsilon Pi (social chmn., v.p. for pledge, master Queens Coll. chptr.). Home: 21 E Huron St Unit 1706 Chicago IL 60611 Office: 1477 E 83d Ave Merrillville IN 46410-6307 Office Phone: 219-738-6430. Office Fax: 219-738-6476. Business E-Mail: noel.reitmeister@wfadvisors.com. E-mail: nreit@hotmail.com.

REITNAUER, ANDREW RICHARD, forensic specialist; b. Pottstown, Pa., Aug. 1, 1977; s. Richard Gerald and Cheryl Ann Reitnauer; m. Gina Ann Longobardi, Dec. 6, 2003. B in Criminal Justice, York Coll., Pa., 1999; M in Forensic Exam., Touro Coll., Bay Shore, NY, 2004; B in Biology, Stony Brook U., NY, 2005. Coord. security svcs. York Coll., Pa., 2000—03; sr. criminalist Boston Police Dept. Latent Print Unit, 2005—08; criminalist II Crime Lab. Latent Print Devel. Unit, 2008—; cert. crime scene investigator IAI, 2008. Team mem. Am. Cancer Soc., Pottstown, Pa., 2000—03, co-chair, team capt. Port Jefferson Station, NY, 2004—05. Mem.: New England Assn. Identification, Am. Acad. Forensic Scis., Northeastern Assn. Forensic Scientists (assoc.), Internat. Assn. Identification (assoc.). Office: NYPD Crime Lab 150-14 Jamaica Ave Jamaica NY 11432 Home: 603 High St Port Jefferson NY 11777 Office Phone: 718-558-8774. Personal E-mail: areitnau@hotmail.com. E-mail: reitnauera.bpd@ci.boston.ma.us.

REITSEMA, HAROLD JAMES, aerospace engineer; b. Kalamazoo, Jan. 19, 1948; s. Robert Harold and Bernice Jean (Hoogsteen) R.; m. Mary Jo Gunnink, Aug. 6, 1970; children: Ellen Celeste, Laurie Jean. BA, Calvin Coll., 1972; PhD, N.Mex. State U., 1977. Rsch. assoc. U. Ariz., Tucson, 1977-79, sr. rsch. assoc., 1979-82, vis. scientist, 1987—; sr. mem. tech. staff Ball Aerospace, Boulder, Colo., 1982-85, prin. systems engr., 1985-88, program mgr., 1988-89, staff cons., 1989-96, dir., 1996—2008. Cons. Aerospace Tech., 1987—. Contbr. articles to profl. jours. including Astrophys. Jour., Aston. Jour., Nature, Sci., Icarus. Bd. dirs. EE Barnard Obs., Golden, Colo., 1984-91, Space Sci. Inst., 2005-; adv. bds. N.Mex. State U. Arts & Scis., U. Colorado Dept. Astrophysics, Planetary Scis. Fellow AIAA (assoc., tech. com. chair 1991, Engr. of Yr. Colo. region 1990); mem. Am. Astron. Soc. (planetary sci. com. 1991-94), Internat. Astron. Union. Achievements include discovery of Larissa, fifth satellite of Neptune; co-discovery of Telesto, seventeenth satellite of Saturn; patents for Optically-coupled Shaft Angle Encoder. Home: 4795 Hancock Dr Boulder CO 80303-1103 Personal E-mail: hreitsema@aol.com.

REITZ, BRUCE ARNOLD, cardiac surgeon, educator; b. Seattle, Sept. 14, 1944; BS, Stanford U., 1966; MD, Yale U., 1970. Diplomate: Am. Bd. Surgery, Am. Bd. Thoracic Surgery. Intern Johns Hopkins Hosp., Balt., 1970-71, cardiac surgeon-in-charge, 1982-92; resident Stanford U. Hosp., Calif., 1971-72, 74-78; clin. assoc. Nat. Heart Lung Blood Inst., NIH, Bethesda, Md., 1972-74; asst. prof. Stanford U. Sch. Medicine, 1977-81, assoc. prof., 1981-82; prof. surgery Johns Hopkins U. Sch. Medicine, Balt., 1982-92; prof., chmn. Sch Medicine Stanford (Calif.) U., 1992—2005; prof. Stanford U. Sch. Medicine, 2005—. Developer heart-lung transplant technique, 1981. Office: Stanford U Sch Medicine Dept Cardiothoracic Surgery Stanford CA 94305-5407 Office Phone: 650-725-4497. Business E-Mail: breitz@stanford.edu.

REITZ, CURTIS RANDALL, lawyer, educator; b. Reading, Pa. s. Lester S. and Magdalene A. (Crouse) R.; m. Virginia R. Patterson, Dec. 19, 1953 (div.); children— Kevin R., Joanne E., Whitney A.; m. Judith N. Renzulli, Sept. 18, 1983 BA, U. Pa., 1951, LL.B., 1956. Bar: Pa. 1957, U.S. Supreme Ct. 1959. Law clk. to Chief Justice Earl Warren U.S. Supreme Ct., 1956-57; mem. faculty law U. Pa., Phila., 1957—, asst. prof. law, 1957-60, assoc. prof., 1960-63, prof., 1963—, provost, v.p., 1971—73, Algernon Sydney Biddle prof. law, 1985—. Trustee Internat. House Ctr. Phila.; bd. mgrs. Glen Mills Schs., Pa. Served to 1st lt. U.S. Army, 1951-53 Life Mem. Am. Law Inst., Mem., Nat. Conf. Commrs. on Uniform State Laws, Order of Coif Office: U Pa Law Sch 3400 Chestnut St Philadelphia PA 19104-6204 Business E-Mail: creitz@law.upenn.edu.

REITZ, ELIZABETH J., anthropologist, educator; PhD, U. Fla., Gainesville, 1979. Prof. anthropology U. Ga., Athens, 1979—. Dir. Ga. Mus. Natural History, Athens, 1997—2002, Ctr. Archeol. Scis., Athens, 2005—. Author: (book) Zooarchaeology, Case Studies in Environmental Archaeology, Guangala Fishers and Farmers, A Comparative Zooarchaeological Analysis, Reconstructing Historic Subsistence. Mem.: AAAS, Internat. Coun. Archaeozoology (exec. com. 2002—), Southeastern Archaeol. Conf. (sec. 1989—91), Soc. Hist. Archaeology (pres. 1994—94), Soc. Am. Archaeology (com. chair 2005—06), Sigma Xi (com. mem. 2004—07). Office: Ga Mus Natural History Univ Ga Athens GA 30602-7882 Business E-Mail: ereitz@uga.edu.

REITZAS, JOSHUA T., lawyer, venture capitalist; b. Fall River, Mass., July 9, 1974; s. Richard Arthur Reitzas and Donna Lee Haas. BA, Bowdoin Coll., Brunswick, Maine, 1998; JD, Benjamin N. Cardozo Sch. Law, 2001. Bar: NY 2002, NJ 2002, US Dist. Ct. (3d cir.) NJ 2002, US Dist. Ct. (so. dist.) 2005, US Dist. Ct. (ea. dist.) 2005, US Supreme Ct. 2008. Assoc. Rockefeller & Co., Inc., NYC, 1999—2000, Bear Stearns & Co., Inc., NYC, 2001—02, Jaffe & Asher LLP, NYC, 2002—. Adv. bd. Beacon Capital LLC, Martinsville, 2004—; founder ModernFetch, Inc., NYC, 2002—. Fundraiser Metrolacrosse, Boston, 2003—04; alumni interviewer Phillips Exeter Acad., Exeter, NH, 2004. Mem.: ABA (assoc.), NY State Bar Assn. (mem. com. atty. professionalism), Princeton Club NY, Merges and Acquisitions Group, Harvard Club Private Equity and Hedge Fund Group. Achievements include patents pending for in Business and E-commerce. Office: Jaffe & Asher LLP 600 Third Ave New York NY 10016 Office Fax: 212-687-3601. Business E-Mail: jreitzas@jaffeandasher.com.

REITZFELD, ALAN D., lawyer; b. Bklyn., Mar. 13, 1951; s. William and Jeanette (Winzelberg) Reitzfeld; m. Lois Carol Goldfinger, June 24, 1973; children: Jordan Lawrence, Stacey Elyse. BA, Syracuse U., 1973; JD, Hofstra U., 1976. Bar: NY, 1977, DC, 2009, US Dist. Ct. (So. and Ea. Dists. NY), 1977, US Ct. of Internat. Trade, 1978, US Ct. of Military Appeals, 1978, US Dist. Ct. (No. and Western Dists. NY), 1979, US Ct. of Appeals (2nd and 4th Circs.), 1979, US Ct. of Appeals (7th Cir.), 1980, US Supreme Ct., 1980, US Dist. Ct. (Ea. Dist. Wis.), 1988, US Ct. of Appeals (6th Cir.), 1993, US Ct. of Appeals (8th Cir.), 1997, US Ct. of Appeals (9th Cir.), 2001, US Ct. of Appeals, DC Cir., 2004. Dir. First Yr. Legal Rsch. and Advisement Fellows Program, Hofstra U., 1975—76; assoc. Martin, Van de Walle & Sawyer, Great Neck, NY, 1976—77, Haight, Gardner, Poor & Havens, 1978—97; ptnr. Holland & Knight LLP (previously Haight, Gardner, Poor & Havens), NY, 1997—. Mem. firmwide tech. com. Holland & Knight LLP, NYC, 2003—, chmn., 2003—07, firmwide tech. ptnr., 2003—07; lectr. in field; spkr. in field. Mem. Hofstra Law Review, 1974—76, rsch. editor, 1975—76; contbr. articles to profl. jours. Mem.: Internat. Tech. Law Assn., Def. Rsch. Inst., Nassau County Bar Assn., Internat. Assn. Def. Counsel (vice chair newsletters, aviation and space law com. 2007—), Fed. Bar Coun., Assn. of the Bar City of NY (aero. law com. 2002—06), Internat. Bar Assn. (vice-chair tech. and e-Commerce law com. 2004—06), NY State Bar Assn. (mem. bus. law sect. exec. com. 1996—2006, chmn. bus. law sect. computer law com. 1998—2001, del. Ho. of Dels. 2002—06, mem. bus. law sect. exec. com. 2007—), Zeta Beta Tau (pres. Omicron chpt. 1972—73). Office: Holland & Knight LLP 195 Broadway 24th Fl New York NY 10007 Office Phone: 212-513-3400. Business E-Mail: alan.reitzfeld@hklaw.com.

REJAI, MOSTAFA, political science professor; b. Tehran, Iran, Mar. 11, 1931; came to U.S., 1954; s. Taghi and Forough (Lashgari) R. AA, Pasadena City Coll., 1957; BA, Calif. State U., LA, 1959, MS, 1961; PhD, UCLA, 1964. Teaching fellow UCLA, 1963-64; asst. prof. polit. sci. Miami U., Oxford, Ohio, 1964-67, assoc. prof., 1967-70, prof., 1970-83, Disting. prof., 1983—. Vis. scholar Ctr. for Internat. Affairs, Harvard U., 1972, Hoover Instn. on War, Revolution and Peace, Stanford U., 1973, Inst. Internat. Studies, Iran, 1974-75; vis. prof. Western Coll., Oxford, 1971, 72. Author: World Miltary Leaders: A Collective and Comparative Analysis, 1996, The Strategy of Political Revolution, 1973, The Comparative Study of Revolutionary Strategy, 1977, Comparative Political Ideologies, 1984; (with Kay Phillips) Leaders of Revolution, 1979, World Revolutionary Leaders, 1983, Loyalists and Revolutionaries: Political Leaders Compared, 1988, Political Ideologies: A Comparative Approach, 1991, 2d edit., 1995, Demythogizing an Elite: American Presidents in Empirical, Comparative, and Historical Perspectives, 1993, World Military Leaders: A Collective and Comparative Analysis, 1996, Leaders and Leadership: An Appraisal of Theory and Research, 1997, The Young George Washington in Psychobiographical Perspective, 2000, Concepts of Leadership in Western Political Thought, 2002; editor, contbr.: Democracy: The Contemporary Theories, 1967, Decline of Ideology?, 1971; editor: Mao Tse-Tung on Revolution and War, 1969, rev. edit., 1970; assoc. editor Jour. Polit. and Mil. Sociology, 1973—; contbr. articles to profl. jours., book chpts. Recipient Outstanding Teaching award Miami U., 1970. Mem. Am. Polit. Sci. Assn. (polit. psychology sect.), Am. Sociol. Assn. (polit. soc. sect.), Internat. Polit. Sci. Assn., Internat. Soc. Polit. Psychology, Internat. Studies Assn., Inter-Univ. Seminar on Armed Forces and Soc., Conf. for Study Polit. Thought, Midwest Polit. Sci. Assn., So. Polit. Sci. Assn., Wesetern Polit. Sci. Assn., Pi Gamma Mu, Pi Sigma Alpha. Office: Miami U Dept of Political Science Oxford OH 45056

REJENT, MARIAN MAGDALEN, retired pediatrician; b. Toledo, Aug. 12, 1920; d. Casimir Stanley and Magdalen (Szymanowski) R. BS, Mary Manse Coll., 1943; MD, Marquette U., 1946; MPH, U. Mich., 1960. Diplomate Am. Bd. Pediatrics. Intern St. Vincent Med. Ctr., Toledo, 1946-47; resident communicable diseases City Hosp., Cleve., 1947-48; resident pediatrics Childrens Hosp., Akron, Ohio, 1948-50; pvt. practice Toledo, 1950-54; chief div. maternal child health Toledo Bd. Health, 1953-64; dir. pediatrics Maumee Valley Hosp., Toledo, 1964-69; assoc. prof. pediatrics Med. Coll. Ohio, Toledo, 1969-76; med. dir. State Crippled Childrens Program, Columbus, Ohio, 1976-78; attendant pediatrician St. Vincent Med. Ctr., Toledo, 1978-80, 87-99; chief pediatric svcs. Wake County Health Dept., Raleigh, NC, 1980-87; ret. clin. prof. pediatrics Med. Coll. Ohio, 1998; ret., 1999. Exec. com. March of Dimes, 1988-92. Mem. AMA, APHA, Am. Acad. Pediatrics, Am. Med. Women's Assn., Ohio PHA, Ohio State Med. Assn., NW Ohio Pediatric Assn., Acad. Medicine Toledo, Alpha Omega Alpha. Republican. Roman Catholic. Avocations: travel, photography, painting. Home: The Woodlands Apt 416 4030 Indian Rd Toledo OH 43606

REJMAN, DIANE LOUISE, business analyst; b. Hartford, Conn., Jan. 14, 1956; d. Louis P. and Genevieve (Walukevich) R. BS in Aviation Adminstrn., Embry Riddle Aero. U., 1980; MBA in Internat. Mgmt., Thunderbird Am. Grad. Sch. Internat. Mgmt., 1991; cert. in cross cultural negotiation, Western Internat. Univ., 1994. Lic. ins. agt. Calif., Series 7 lic., Series 66 Lic. Indsl. engr./planner Hamilton Aviation, Tucson, 1980-82; indsl. engr. assoc. Gates Learjet, Tucson, 1984; tech. writer, FAA coord. Dee Howard Co., San Antonio, 1984-86; indsl. engr. McDonnell Douglas Helicopter Systems, Mesa, Ariz., 1986-88; systems analyst McDonnell Douglas Helicopter Sys., Mesa, Ariz., 1988-95; sr. aerospace industry market rsch. analyst Frost & Sullivan, Mountain View, Calif., 1995-97; mfg. sys. applications analyst Ross Systems, Redwood City, Calif., 1997-2000; sr. bus. analyst Charitable Way, San Carlos, Calif., 2000; fin. advisor Am. Express Fin. Svcs., 2001—02; video spokesperson Andiron Technologies, Inc., 2001—. Bd. dirs. McDonnell Douglas Helicopter Sys. Employee Community Fund., adminstr. 1992-95, spkr. in field, docent Hiller Aviation Mus., 2002-05, GI Rights Counselor, 2006-09. Author: (reports) World Commercial Avionics Market, 1996, World Airport Ground Equipment Markets, 1996, World Air Traffic Control Equipment Markets, 1997; contbr. counterpunch.org., Jour. of America; prodr., mgr., cover graphics music CD (by Annie and the Vets) A Name on the Wall, 2004-05. Mem. City of Mesa Leadership Tng. Class of 1995. With U.S. Army, 1977-80. Avocations: dance, photography, travel, reading, music, singing. E-mail: yespeaceispossible@yahoo.com.

REKART, JEROME LEO, science educator, researcher; b. Ill., Mar. 24, 1975; married. BS, Ind. U., Bloomington, 1998; MS, Northwestern U., Evanston, IL, 2001; PhD, Northwestern U., 2005. Postdoc. assoc. McGovern Inst. Brain Rsch., M.I.T., Cambridge, Mass., 2005—06; asst. prof. Rivier Coll., Nashua, NH, 2006—09. Dir. behavioral sci. lab. Rivier Coll., 2007—09. Contbr. to numerous profl. jours. Tng. grant, NIMH, 2003—05, Allen Edwards fellowship, Northwestern U., Dept. Psychology, 2001—05. Mem.: APA, Assn. Psychol. Sci. Office: Rivier Coll 420 S Main St Nashua NH 03060

REKATE, ALBERT C., physician; b. Buffalo, June 12, 1916; s. Gustave E. and Fannie (Hummell) R.; m. Elizabeth Foster, June 12 1943 (dec. 1985); 1 child, Suzanne (Mrs. R. Willis Post); m. Linda Ann Holt, Aug. 1, 1992. MD, U. Buffalo, 1940. Diplomate Am. Bd. Internal Medicine. Intern E.J. Meyer Meml. Hosp., Buffalo, 1940-41, med. resident, 1941-44; asst. prof. medicine SUNY-Buffalo, 1954-61, assoc. prof., 1961-65, prof., 1965-86, prof. emeritus, 1986—; dir. rehab. medicine SUNY, Buffalo, 1965-72, acting dean Sch. Health Related Professions, 1965-66, assoc. dean, 1966-74, acting chmn. dept. rehab. medicine, 1972-75; assoc. dir. medicine E.J. Meyer Meml. Hosp., Buffalo, 1957-63, head dept. rehab. medicine, 1964-69, dir. primary rehab. center, 1965-69, acting head cardiology, 1966-69, dir., 1970-72. Bd. dirs. Buffalo Hearing and Speech Ctr., 1973-99; mem. adv. bd. Coastal Empire Mental Health Ctr., S.C., 1980-81, bd. dirs., 1981-93; mem. dean's adv. coun. SUNY-Buffalo Sch. Medicine and Biomed. Scis., 1995—, med. emeritus faculty group steering com., 2000—. Contbr. articles to profl. jours. Served with M.C. AUS, World War II. Mem. Am. Heart Assn., Western N.Y. Heart Assn. (pres. 1954-55), Assn. Am. Med. Colls., N.Y. State Heart Assembly, N.Y. Acad. Scis., Med. Union (pres. 1974-75), Buffalo Acad. Medicine (pres. 1969-70), Erie County Med. Soc., Med. Alumni Assn. U. Buffalo (pres. 1960-61), Beaufort-Jasper Mental Health Assn. (dir. 1980-86). Home and Office: 52 Hampton Hill Dr Williamsville NY 14221-5840 Personal E-mail: lre1832886@aol.com.

REKATE, HAROLD LOUIS, neurosurgeon; b. Annapolis, Md., Nov. 1, 1944; m. Mary Warren, Feb. 3, 1967; children: Jason Warren, Sarah Connell Rekate Cahalane. BS, Duke U., 1966; MD, Med. Coll. Va., Richmond, Va., 1970. Diplomate Am. Bd. Neurol. Surgery, Am. Bd. Pediat. Neurol. Surgery; lic. Ohio, Ariz. Intern U. Hospitals Cleve., Ohio, 1970—71, resident, gen. surgery Ohio, 1971—72, resident, neurol. surgery Ohio, 1972, Ohio, 1974—78, asst. neurosurgeon Ohio, 1978—84, dir., pediat. neurosurgery Ohio, 1978—84; asst. prof. neurosurgery Case Western Res. U. Sch. Medicine, Cleve., 1978-84, asst. prof. surgery, pediatrics, 1979—84; chief pediat. neurosurgery Barrow Neurol. Inst., Phoenix, 1985—, chmn., pediatric neurosciences, 2001—, dir., hypothalamic hamartoma program; chief, pediatric neurosurgery St. Joseph's Hosp. and Med. Ctr., Ariz.; chief, sect. neurosurgery Phoenix Children's Hosp., 1987—91. Mem. academic adv. coun., Case Western Reserve U. Sch. Medicine, 1980-84, chmn. search com. for chief divsn. pediat. neurology, 1981; mem. child protection team, U. Hospitals Cleve., 1978-84, Birth Defects Ctr., 1978-84, dir. Child's Brain Ctr., 1980-84; mem.trauma and critical care task force, Rainbow Babies and Children's Hosp., 1980-82, mem. planning and priorities bd., 1982-84; clin. prof. dept. surgery, sect. neurosurgery U. Ariz. Sch. Medicine, Tucson, 1985-; adj. assoc. prof. sys. engrng. 1985-91; hosp. affiliation Phoenix Children's Hosp., 1985-2001; sec.-treas., Children's Rehabilitative Svcs.-IPA, 1992; mem. pediat. adv. task force, Children's Health Ctr., St. Joseph's Hosp. and Med. Ctr., Phoenix, Ariz., 1992; bd. dirs. Mercy Healthcare Ariz. 1997-2001; invited lectr. in field. Contbr. several articles to profl. jours.; mem. editl. bd. Clin. Neurosurgery, 1984—87, Pediatric Neurosurgery, Child's Nervous System and Jour. Neurosurgery, Pediatrics, guest editor Neurosurgical Focus-Occipital Plagiocephaly, 1997, Neurosurgical Focus-Hydrocephalus, 2007, ad hoc reviewer Neurology, Neurosurgery, & Cancer. Maj., Med. Corps US Army, 1972—74, Fort Benning, Ga. Recipient award for outstanding edn. and treatment of Spina Bifida, Spina Bifida Assn. So. Ariz., 1986—88, Pudenz award for Excellence in Rsch. in Cerebrospinal Fluid Physiology, 1992, Anthony J. Raimondi, MD Medalist, Outstanding Contbn. in Pediat. Neurology-Oncology, 1999. Mem.: Cleve. Acad. Medicine Trauma Com., Acad. Medicine Cleve., Ohio State Neurosurgical Soc., Northeast Ohio Neurosurgical Soc., European Soc. Pediat. Neurosurgery (permanent vis. faculty 1988—), World Fedn. Neurosurgical Societies (mem. scientific program com., World Congress Neurosurgery 1999), Am. Soc. Pediatric Neurosurgeons (treas. 1996—98, sec. 1998—2000, pres.-elect 1999—2000, pres. 2000), Internat. Soc. Pediat. Neurosurgery (mem. by-laws com. 1986, mem. com. edn. 1986—87, mem. liaison com., rep. N.Am. 1987, chmn., scientific program com. 1994—98, pres. 1999—2000), Congress Neurol. Surgeons (chmn., video libr. com. 1982, chmn., sergeant-at-arms com. 1983, chmn., scientific session IV 1984, chmn., spl. courses 1985), Am. Assn. Neurol. Surgeons (chmn. ad hoc com. joint status pediat. sect. 1985—88, chmn., membership com. pediat. sect. 1986—88, chmn. by-laws com. 1988—90, sec., pediat. sect. 1991—94), Pediat. Oncology Group (edn. com. mem. 1997—2001). Office: Barrow Neurol Inst Barrow Neurol Assocs 500 W Thomas Rd Ste 400 Phoenix AZ 85013 Office Phone: 602-406-3632. Office Fax: 602-406-6126. Business E-Mail: Harold.rekate@chw.edu.

REKHI, SANDEEP, geologist, physicist; s. Ram Prakash Walia and Vimal Bayond; m. Neetu Malhotra, Apr. 29, 2005; 1 child, Aryanka Vimal. PhD in Physics, Delhi U.; PhD in Geology, FIU, Miami, 2001. Rsch. fellow MIT, Cambridge, 2003—05; scientist Brookhaven Nat. Lab, Upton, NY, 2005—08. Rsch. fellow Harvard, Cambridge, 2001—03. Contbr. scientific papers to numerous publs. Mem.: Internat. Ctr. Deffraction Data, Sigma Xi. Achievements include research in the origin of black diamonds. Office: Scientist Panalytical 117 Flanders St Westborough MA 01581

REKOWSKI, LOIS THOMPSON, library director; b. Clearfield, Pa., Feb. 16, 1954; d. Grant Thompson and Hilda Mae Bowery; m. Richard George Rekowski, Dec. 25, 1992. BS in Biology, Pa. State U., State Coll., 1976; MLS, U. Pitts., 1977. Cert. in info. sci. U. Pitts., 1999. Head libr. Stey-Nevant Pub. Libr., Farrell, Pa., 1979—81; dir. Upshur County Pub. Libr., Buckhannon, W.Va., 1981—87, Marion County Pub. Libr., Fairmont, W.Va., 1987—93; dir. libr. svcs. Jefferson CC, Steubenville, Ohio, 1993—, adj. instr., 2000—03. Adj. instr. children's lit. A.M. Pfeiffer Libr., W.Va. Wesleyan Coll., Buckhannon, 1985—86; distance edn. facilitator U. SC, Columbia, 1992. Mem. Lit. Vols. America, W.Va. chpt., Charleston, 1986—92; grant writer Camp Fire USA, Upper Appalachian Coun., Weirton, W.Va., 2004—08; mem., grant writing Jefferson County Hist. Assn., 2007—08. Mem.: ALA, Academic Libr. Assn. Ohio, W.Va. Libr. Assn. (2nd v.p. 1989—90), Delta Kappa Gamma, Beta Phi Mu. Liberal. Presbyterian. Office: Jefferson CC 4000 Sunset Blvd Steubenville OH 43952 Office Fax: 740-264-1338.

RELIAS, JOHN ALEXIS, lawyer; b. Chgo., Apr. 2, 1946; s. Alexis John and Marie Helen (Metos) R.; m. Linda Ann Pontious, Nov. 27, 1971; children: Anne, Alexandra. BA, Northwestern U., Evanston, 1968; LLB, Northwestern U., Chgo., 1972. Bar: Ill., 1972, U.S. Dist. Ct. (no. dist.) Ill. 1972, U.S. Ct. Appeals (9th cir.) 1981, U.S. Ct. Appeals (7th cir.) 1983, U.S. Supreme Ct. 1997. Assoc. Vedder, Price, Kaufman & Kammholz, Chgo., 1972-78, ptnr., 1979-94, Franczek, Sullivan, Mann, Crement, Hein & Relias, Chgo., 1994—. Mem. bd. edn. Wilmette (Ill.) Sch. Dist. 39, 1989-97, 2001—09, pres., 1992-93, 1995-96. Mem. Nat. Assn. Sch. Attys., Ill. Assn. Sch. Attys., Order of the Coif, Phi Beta Kappa. Greek Orthodox. Home: 2500 Kenilworth Ave Wilmette IL 60091-1337 Office: Franczek Sulian Mann Crement Hein & Relias 300 S Wacker Dr Chicago IL 60606-6680 Office Phone: 312-786-6160. Business E-Mail: jar@franczek.com.

RELL, JODI (MARY JODI RELL), Governor of Connecticut; b. Norfolk, Va., June 16, 1946; m. Lou Rell; children: Meredith, Michael. Student, Old Dominion U., Western Conn. State U.; LLD (hon.), U. Hartford, 2001. Mem., dep. minority leader Conn. Ho. Reps., 1984-94; lt. gov. State of Conn., 1995—2004, gov., 2004—. Past vice chmn. Brookfield Rep. Town Com., appt. chair of the Hartford Econ. Devel. Adv. Group, (HEDAG), 1998; trustee YMCA Western Conn; played a key role in raising funds for the Conn. Firefighters Meml.; estab. the Lt. Gov.'s Comm. on State Mandate Reform, Lt. Gov.'s Conn. Treasures award. Recipient Leadership award, Nat. Order of Women Legislators (NOWL), Impact award, Conn. Tech. Coun., 2001, First Kids 2001 Policy Leadership award, Conn. Voices for Children, Arnold Markle Public Service award, Nathan Davis award for Outstanding Govt. Svc., AMA, 2008; named Melvin Jones Fellow, Lions Club Internat. Found., 2003. Mem. Nat. Order Women Legislators (past nat. pres., former v.p., treas., corr. sec.), Women Execs. in State Govt., Brookfield Rep. Women's Club (past pres.), Brookfield Bus. and Profl. Women's Club, Prison and Jail Overcrowding comm., Governor's Law Enforcement Coun., Yale Corp., State Finance Advisory Com. Republican. Office: Office Gov Exec Chambers 210 Capitol Ave Hartford CT 06106 E-mail: Governor.Rell@po.state.ct.us.

RELLE, FERENC MATYAS, chemist; b. Gyor, Hungary, June 13, 1922; came to U.S., 1951, naturalized, 1956; s. Ferenc and Elizabeth (Netratics) R.; m. Gertrud B. Tubach, Oct. 9, 1946; children: Ferenc, Ava, Attila. BSChemE, MS, Jozsef Nador Poly. U., Budapest, Hungary, 1944. Lab. mgr. Karl Kohn Ltd. Co., Landshut, Germany, 1947-48; resettlement officer Internat. Refugee Orgn., Munich, 1948-51; chemist Farm Bur. Coop. Assn., Columbus, Ohio, 1951-56; indsl. engr. N.Am. Aviation, Inc., Columbus, 1956-57; rsch. chemist Keever Starch Co.,

Columbus, 1957-65, Ross Labs. divsn. Abbott Labs., Columbus, 1965-70, rsch. scientist, 1970-89; cons. in field. Congl. sci. counselor, 1971—81. Chmn. Columbus and Ctrl. Ohio UNWeek, 1963; pres. Berwick Manor Civic Assn., 1968; trustee Stelios Stelson Found., 1968-69; deacon Brookwood Presbyn. Ch., 1963-65, 92-93, trustee, 1990-91. Decorated knight St. Ladislaus Order. Mem. Am. Chem. Soc. (emeritus; alt. councilor 1973, chmn. long range planning com. Columbus sect. 1972-76, 78-80), Am. Assn. Cereal Chemists (life; chmn. Cin. sect. 1974-75), Ohio Acad. Sci., Arpad Acad. (gold medal mem.), Internat. Tech. Inst. (adv. dir. 1977-82), Nat. Intercollegiate Soccer Ofcls. Assn., Am. Hungarian Assn., Hungrian Cultural Assn. (pres. 1978-81), Ohio Soccer Ofcls. Assn., Columbus Mannerchor, Germania Singing and Sport Soc., Civitan (gov. Ohio dist. 1970-71, dist. treas. 1982-83, pres. Ea. Columbus 1963-64, 72-73, gen. sec. for Hungary 1991-92, Ea. European growth mgr. 1993-94, amb. at large 1994—, established 1st Civitan club in Hungary 1991, Ukraine, 1992, Slovakia 1994, Internat. Gov. of Yr. award 1971, Internat. Honor Key 1992, Internat. Found. fellow 2000, master club builder award 1992, various other awards), World Fedn. Hungarian Engrs. Home and Office: 2983 Melford Rd Upper Arlington OH 43221-2822

RELLER, TAMI, computer software company executive; b. Grand Forks, ND; BS in Math., Minn. State U., Moorhead; MBA, St. Mary's Coll., Moraga, Calif. Receptionist, acct., v.p. fin. Great Plains Software Inc., 1984—99, CFO, 1999—2001; corp. v.p. Microsoft Bus. Solutions Microsoft Corp., 2001—07, corp. v.p. & CFO platforms & services divsn., 2007—09, corp. v.p. & CFO Windows bus. group, 2009—. Named a Baby Bill, Bus. 2.0 mag. Office: Microsoft Corp Platforms & Services Divsn 1 Microsoft Way Redmond WA 98052-6399

RELMAN, ARNOLD SEYMOUR, physician, editor, educator; b. NYC, June 17, 1923; s. Simon and Rose (Mallach) Relman; m. Harriet Morse Vitkin, June 26, 1953; children: David Arnold, John Peter, Margaret Rose. AB, Cornell U., 1943; MD, Columbia U., 1946; LLD (hon.), U. Pa.; ScD (hon.), Med. Coll. Wis., Union U., Med. Coll. Ohio, CUNY; DMSc (hon.), Brown U.; DLH (hon.), SUNY; LittD (hon.), Temple U. Diplomate Am. Bd. Internal Medicine. House officer New Haven Hosp., Yale, 1946—49; NRC fellow Evans Meml., Mass. Meml. hosps., 1949—50; practice medicine, specializing in internal medicine Boston, 1950—68, Phila., 1968—77; asst. prof., prof. medicine Boston U. Sch. Medicine, 1950—68; dir. Boston U. Med. Services, Boston City Hosp., 1967—68; prof. medicine, chmn. dept. medicine U. Pa.; chief med. services Hosp. of U. Pa., 1968—77; editor New Eng. Jour. Medicine, Boston, 1977—91, editor emeritus, 1991—; sr. physician Brigham and Women's Hosp., Boston, 1977—; prof. medicine and social medicine Harvard Med. Sch., 1977—93, prof. medicine and social medicine emeritus, 1993—95, prof. emeritus, 1995—. Cons. NIH, USPHS; mem. bd. registration in medicine Commonwealth of Mass., 1995—2001. Author: A Second Opinion, 2007; editor: Jour. Clin. Investigation, 1962—67; editor: (with F.J. Ingelfinger and M. Finland) Controversy in Internal Medicine, Vol. 1, 1966, Controversy in Internal Medicine, Vol. 2, 1974; contbr. articles to profl. jours. Trustee Columbia U., 1990—96; bd. dirs. Hastings Ctr., 1981—83. Recipient Columbia Alumni Gold medal, 1980, Disting. Svc. award, Am. Coll. Cardiology, 1987, McGovern award, Cosmos Club Washington, 1991, John Peters award, Am. Soc. Nephrology, 1992, George Polk award in journalism, 2003. Master: ACP (John Phillips medal 1985); fellow: Am. Acad. Arts and Scis.; mem.: AMA, Am. Fedn. Clin. Rsch. (past pres.), Am. Soc. Clin. Investigation (past pres.), Inst. of Medicine of NAS (coun. 1979—82), Mass. Med. Soc., Am. Physiol. Soc., Assn. Am. Physicians (coun., pres. 1983—84, Kober medal 1993), Alpha Omega Alpha, Phi Beta Kappa (senator 1991—98). Office: Brigham and Women's Hosp Dept Medicine 181 Longwood Ave Fl 5 Boston MA 02115-5804

RELYEA, HAROLD CLARENCE, political scientist, writer; b. Oneida, NY, Apr. 5, 1944; s. Clyde Frederick and Pauline Elizabeth R.; children: Jennifer L., Stephen F. AB, Drew U., 1966; PhD, American U., 1971. Specialist in Am. nat. govt. Congl. Rsch. Svc. Libr. Congress, Washington, 1971—2009; ret. Author: A Brief History of Emergency Powers in the United States, 1974, The Evolution and Organization of the Federal Intelligence Function: A Brief Overview 1776-1975, 1988, Silencing Silence: National Security Controls and Scientific Communication, 1994; co-author: Presidential Staffing-A Brief Overview, 1978, United States Government Information: Policies and Sources, 2002; editor, contbg. author: The Presidency and Information Policy, 1981, Striking a Balance: National Security and Scientific Freedom, 1985, The Executive Office of the President, 1997; co-editor, contbg. author: Freedom of Information Trends in the Information Age, 1983, United States Government Information Policies: Views and Perspectives, 1989, Comparative Perspectives on E-Government, 2006; bd. editors Presdl. Studies Quar., 1979-99, Govt. Publs. Rev., 1981-83, Transnational Data Report, 1982-89, Jour. Media Law and Practice, 1982-95, Govt. Info. Quar., 1984—, Internat. Jour. E-Govt. Rsch., 2004—08, Jour. E-Govt., 2004-07, Jour. Info. Tech. and Politics, 2007-; contbr. articles to profl. jours. Mem. adv. bd. Coll. Info. Studies, U. Md., 2004—07. Named Expert's Expert on US Freedom Info. Act, The Economist of London, 1981; recipient Exec. Bd. award for superior pub. svc. Am. Soc. Access Profls., 1983, The Best of 1983 award for essay selection Libr. Lit. 14, 1984, Blue Pencil award Nat. Assn. Govt. Communicators, 1984, Congressiional Rsch. Svc. Director's award, 2008; named to Freedom of Info. Act Hall of Fame, Freedom Forum, 1996. Mem. Pi Sigma Alpha. Personal E-mail: relyea_harold@yahoo.com.

REMAKUS, BERNARD LEO, physician, medical educator, writer, medical journalist; b. Wilkes-Barre, Pa., Oct. 28, 1948; s. Leo W. and Adel Bertha (Macho) R.; m. Charlotte M. Amorebello, Aug. 17, 1974; children: Christopher B., Alexandra T., Matthew B. BS, King's Coll., 1970; MEd, E. Stroudsburg State Coll., 1972; MD, Temple U., 1978. Diplomate Nat. Bd. Med. Examiners, Am. Bd. Internal Medicine. Resident Abington Meml. Hosp., 1978-81; pvt. practice Hallstead, Pa., 1981—; instr. SUNY, Binghamton, N.Y., 1981—; clin. asst. prof. Temple U. Sch. Medicine, 2004—. Chief of staff, dir. emergency medicine, chmn. ethics com. Barnes-Kasson County Hosp., Susquehanna, Pa.; med. journalist Internal Medicine World Report, Old Bridge, N.J., 1991—; lectr. Discovery Internat., Deerfield, Ill., 1994—; spkr. in field. Author: The Malpractice Epidemic, 1990, 2d edit. 2004, Cassidy's Solution, 1995, Medicine from the Heart, 2002, Medicine Between the Lines, 2004, (novel) Mia, 2007, (screenplay), 2008; mem. editl. adv. panel Internal Medicine World Report, 1998—; pub. 221 East Pub.; contbr. over 200 articles to profl. jours. Recipient Physicians Recognition award, AMA, 1981, 1984, 1987, 1990, 1993, 1996, 1999, 2002, 2005, 2008, SUNY Health Sci. Ctr. Tchg. award, 1997, Am.'s Top Physicians award, 2003—. Roman Catholic. Office: Rd 2 PO Box 367 Hallstead PA 18822-0367 Office Phone: 570-879-4800.

REMAR, ROBERT BOYLE, lawyer; b. Boston, Nov. 19, 1948; s. Samuel Roy and Elizabeth Mary (Boyle) R.; m. Victoria A. Greenhood, Nov. 11, 1979; children: Daniel A.G., William B.G. BA, U. Mass., 1970; JD, Boston Coll., 1974. Bar: Ga. 1974, Mass. 1975, US Ct. Appeals (5th cir.) 1978, US Ct. Appeals (11th cir.) 1981, US Ct. Appeals (2d cir.) 1995, US Supreme Ct. 1981. Staff atty. Ga. Legal Svcs. Program, Savannah, 1974-76, Western Mass. Legal Svcs., Greenfield, 1976-77; sr. staff atty. Ga. Legal Svcs. Program, Atlanta, 1977-82; ptnr. Remar & Graettinger, Atlanta, 1983-95, Kirwan, Parks, Chesin & Remar PC, Atlanta, 1993-96, Rogers & Hardin, Atlanta, 1996—. V.p., mem. exec. com., bd. dirs. ACLU, NYC, pres. Ga. chpt., 1985-87, gen. counsel, 1980-83; hearing officer Ga. Pub. Svc. Commn., Atlanta, 1985-98; adj. prof. Ga. State U., Atlanta, 1984-98, spl. asst. atty. gen., 1990-2003; bd. experts Lawyers Alert, Boston, 1985-94; pres. bd. dirs. Fed. Defender Program. Mem. Ga. Energy Regulatory Reform Commn., Gov. of Ga., 1980-82, Ga. Consumer Adv. Bd., 1981-82, City Atl. Bd. Ethics, AAA Comml. Panel; pres. Ga. Consumer Ctr. Inc., 1988-91, pres.; bd. dirs., Ga. Resource Ctr.; v.p. Ga Ctr. Law Pub. Inst., 1991-94; bar coun. U.S.D.C. N.D.G., 1996-99. Fellow Am. Coll. Trial Lawyers; mem. ABA (chmn. individual rights access to civil justice com. 1988-99), Ga. Bar Assn. (chmn. individual rights sect. 1981-83, co-chmn. consumer rights and remedies com. 1979-83, chmn. death penalty re. com. 1993—, mem. legis. adv. com. 1994-97, mem. indigent def. com. 2000—), Atlanta Bar Assn., Lawyers Club Atlanta, Lamar Inn of Ct. (master of the bench). Democrat. Avocations: golf, gardening. Home: 1714 Meadowdale Ave NE Atlanta GA 30306-3114 Office: Rogers & Hardin Internat Tower Peachtree Ctr 229 Peachtree St NE Ste 2700 Atlanta GA 30303-1638 Office Phone: 404-420-4031. Business E-Mail: rbr@rh-law.com.

REMATA, SUSEELA REDDY, environmental science educator, researcher; b. Remata, Andhra Pradesh, India, June 28, 1943; arrived in US, 1989, naturalized, 1989; s. Annapurna Reddy and Govindamma Reddy Remata; m. Satyavathi Reddy Mannapuram, May 20, 1946; children: Srinivas, Shalini, Ragalaxmi, Umesh, Hima Bindu, Praveena, Pavan, Vishal, Aditya, Pranav. BSc, Osmania U., India, 1965; MSc, Andhra U., India, 1968; PhD, U. Poona, India, 1983. Vis. fellow Environment Can., Toronto, 1983—87; scientist Indian Inst. Tropical Meteorology Govt. of India, Pune, 1969—91; assoc. prof. Jackson State U., Miss., 1994—. Author: Faith, Patriotism and Love Poems, 2008. Bd. dirs. Inst. Mentally Destituted for Women, Kurnool, India, 2006—07. Recipient Tchg. Performance award, Jackson State U.; grantee, NOAA, 2001—; fellow, NASA, 1996—2000. Mem.: Indian Sci. Congress Assn., Miss. Academic Scis., Am. Geophys. Union, Am. Meteorol. Soc., Indian Aerosol Sci. and Tech. Assn. (life), Morrison Heights Baptist Ch., Am. Telugu Assn., Internat. Soc. Poets. Democrat. Hindu. Achievements include research in tropical meteorology, climatologic, applying diagnostic studies to climate variations, mesos-cale meteorology and modeling, satellite data analysis, and solar-terrestrial relations. Avocations: poetry, singing, music, meditation. Home: 516 McDonald Dr Clinton MS 39056 Office: Jackson State U Dept Physics, Atmospheric Scis & Geoscis 1400 JR Lynch St PO Box 17660 Jackson MS 39217 Office Fax: 601-979-3630. Business E-Mail: rsreddy@jsums.edu.

REMBERT, VIRGINIA PITTS See LILES, VIRGINIA

REMBOLT, JAMES EARL, lawyer; b. Nov. 13, 1943; s. Earl Lester and Dorothy Elouise (Mehring) Rembolt; m. Marilyn Sue Schmadeke, July 16, 1972; children: Tami Anne, Michelle Sue. BBA, U. Nebr., 1965; MA in Bus. Orgn. and Mgmt., 1967, JD with distinction, 1972. Bar: Nebr. 1972, U.S. Dist. Ct. Nebr. 1972, U.S. Tax Ct. 1978, U.S. Ct. Claims 1978. Pres. Nebr. Moot Ct. Bd., 1972; pilot Nebr. Air Nat. Guard, Lincoln, 1969-74; lecr. legal writing U. Nebr. Coll. Law, 1973-74; ptnr. Rembolt, Ludtke LLP, Lincoln, 1976—2008; of counsel Rembolt Ludtke LLP, Lincoln, 2009—. Chmn. bd. trustees YWCA, Lincoln, 1982—83; mem., past pres. Lincoln/Lancaster Sr. Ctrs. Found., Inc., bd. dirs., 1988—90; mem., past chair bd. dirs. Madonna Found., Inc., 1989—91; trustee, past bd. dirs. U.Nebr. Found.; past bd. dirs., pres. Nebr. Continuing Legal Edn., Inc.; bd. elders Eastridge Presbyn. Ch., Lincoln, 1979—82. Fellow: ABA, Nebr. State Bar Found., Am. Coll. Trust and Estate Counsel; mem.: Am. Arbitration Assn. (mem. panel comml. arbitrators 2005—), Lincoln Estate Planning Coun. (past pres.), Lincoln Probate Discussion Group (charter mem.), Nebr. State Bar Assn. (pres. 2002—03), Lincoln Bar Assn., U. Nebr. Lincoln Coll. Bus. Adminstrn. Alumni Assn. (past pres.). Office: Rembolt Ludtke LLP 1201 Lincoln Mall Ste 102 Lincoln NE 68508-2839 Office Phone: 402-475-5100. Business E-Mail: jrembolt@remboltludtke.com.

REMBOS, STEVEN, podiatrist; Cert. Am. Bd. Foot and Ankle Surgery, Endoscopic Techniques Foot and Ankle, Advanced Ankle Arthroscopy Techniques, Holmium LASER Ankle Arthroscopy Technique. Podiatric med. dir. Ambulatory Surg. Ctr.; podiatrist Hosp. Plaza Foot and Ankle Inst., 1988—. Lectr. on foot and ankle pathologies; tchr. of advanced podiatric surg. techniques of foot and ankle pathologies. Mem. Physicians Adv. Bd., Washington. Fellow: Internat. Soc. Podiatric Laser Surgeons, Am. Coll. Foot and Ankle Surgeons; mem.: Ill. Podiatric Med. Assn., Am. Podiatric Med. Assn. Office: Hosp Plz Foot and Ankle Inst Ste 103 3800 Highland Ave Downers Grove IL 60515 E-mail: drrembos@thefootspecialists.com.*

REMER, LILLIAN GLADYS, public health researcher; d. Wayne Claude and Eleanor Ruth Smith; m. Nicholas Wayne Remer, July 19, 1969; children: Norman Paul, Royce Gerard, Patrick James. AB, U. Calif., Berkeley, 1969; MA, Calif. State U., San Francisco, 1972. Cert. GISP GIS Cert. Inst., 2004. Assoc. rsch. scientist Pacific Inst. Rsch. & Evaluation, Berkeley, Calif., 1983—. User's group coord. SF Bay Area GIS User's Group, San Francisco,Oakland,Berkeley, 2007—; rsch. assoc. gastroenterology U. Calif., San Francisco, 1972—74; rsch. assoc. dept. anatomy Stanford U., Palo Alto, Calif., 1974—76. Contbr. articles to profl. jours. Unit leader & com. chair; dist. & coun. trainer & conservation chmn. Boy Scouts America, Pleasant Hill & Walnut Creek, Calif., 1983—2008; lifetime mem. & bd. mem. Friends Pleasant Hill Libr., Pleasant Hill, 1986—2008. Recipient President's Call Svc.award, President's Coun., more than 25 years, Dist. Merit award, Aklan Dist., Mt. Diablo Coun., BSA, 1986, Silver Beaver, Mt. Diablo-Silverado Coun., BSA, 1991, William T. Hornoday award, BSA, 2008. Avocation: reading. Office: Pacific Inst for Rsch & Evaluat 1995 University Ave Ste 450 Berkeley CA 94704 Office Fax: 510-644-0594. Business E-Mail: lilli@prev.org.

REMES, ROBIN EVA, secondary school educator, cartographer; d. Jeremiah and Sarah Remes; m. Fredrick Biddle; 1 child, Patrick Biddle. BA, William Paterson U., 1974; MA, U. South Fla. Cert. tchr. Tex., NJ. World culture studies educator Houston Ind. Sch. Dist., 2004—, reading educator, reading specialist, ESL educator, English educator, chmn. reading dept.; assoc. educator Pinellas County Schools; oil exploration cartographer; computer cartographer Property Appraiser. Elem. sch. tutor, NJ. Author: Cartography Curriculum and H.S. Math Review. Rep. Young Dems., NJ, 1970. State scholar, NJ, 1971—74. Mem.: Houston Fedn. Tchrs. (bldg. steward, Membership Recruiter award 2001). Avocation: travel. Home: 14547 Broadgreen Dr Houston TX 77079-6505 Business E-Mail: rremes@houstonisd.org.

REMICK, SCOT CLIFTON, oncologist, clinical investigator, educator; b. New Rochelle, NY, Oct. 16, 1956; s. Robert Merrick and Marjorie Allis (Stamm) R. BA, SUNY, Oswego, 1978; MD, N.Y. Med. Coll., Valhalla, 1982. Resident Johns Hopkins Hosp., Balt., 1982-85; fellow Clin. Cancer Ctr. U. Wis. Clin. Cancer Ctr., Madison, 1985-88; assoc. prof. Dept. Medicine Albany (N.Y.) Med. Coll., 1988-96; with Case Western Res. U., Cleve., 1996—, assoc. prof. dept. medicine, dir. devel. therapeutics divsn. hematology/oncology, prof. medicine. Prin. investigator numerous oncology and HIV/AIDS clin. trials, Albany, 1988—. Contbr. over 100 papers, textbook chpts. and abstracts. Active Am. Cancer Soc. (Career Devel. award 1991), Albany. Fellow Am. Coll. Physicians; mem. Am. Assn. for Cancer Rsch., Am. Soc. Clin. Oncology, N.Y. Acad. Sci., Alpha Omega Alpha. Office: Univ Hosps of Cleve Divsn Hematol/Oncol 11100 Euclid Ave Cleveland OH 44106-1736 Office Phone: 216-844-5412. Office Fax: 216-844-5234. Business E-Mail: scr@po.cwru.edu.

REMINGTON, BRUCE A., physics researcher; Hydrodynamics group leader Lawrence Livermore Nat. Lab., 1986—. Recipient Excellence in Plasma Physics award Am. Phys. Soc., 1995. Fellow Am. Physical Soc. (pub. rels. coord. divsn. plasma physics). Office: Lawrence Livermore Nat Lab PO Box 808 Livermore CA 94551-0808

REMINGTON, ROYCE ROGER, design educator; b. West Palm Beach, Fla., Mar. 20, 1936; s. Royce Roberts and Julia Snow Remington; m. M. Suzanne Remington, July 21, 2001; m. Beth-Marie Jelsma, Aug. 4, 1984 (div.); m. Donna Currier Remington, May 30, 1958 (dec.); children: Paula Remington Manchester, Royce Roberts, Leigh. MS Art, U. Wis. Madison, 1960. Instr. design Mont. State U., Bozeman, Mont., 1960—63; vignelli disting. prof. design Rochester Inst. Tech., NY, 1963—2008. Recipient Eisenhart award, Rochester Inst. Tech., 1978, Disting. Alumni award, U. Wis. Madison, 1990, Edn. award, Am. Ctr. Design, 1992. Mem.: Am. Inst. Graphic Arts. Democrat. Office: Rochester Inst Tech 73 Lomb Meml Rochester NY 14534 Office Fax: 585-475-7533. E-mail: rrrfad@rit.edu.

REMINI, LEAH, actress; b. Bklyn., June 15, 1970; m. Angelo Pagan, July 19, 2003; 1 child, Sofia Bella. Actress: (TV series) Living Dolls, 1989, Saved By The Bell, 1991, The Man in the Family, 1991, Getting Up and Going Home, 1992, King of Queens, 1999-2007, (voice) Gabriel Knight: Sins of the Fathers, 1994, (voice) Phantom 2040: The Ghost Who Walks, 1994, The First Time Out, 1995, Glory Daze, 1996, Fired Up, 1997, Follow Your Heart, 1998, guest appearances, including Head of the Class, 1988, Who's the Boss?, 1989, Valerie, 1990, Paradise, 1991, Cheers, 1991 & 1993, Blossom, 1992, Evening Shade, 1993, The Commish, 1994, Renegade, 1994, Diagnosis Murder, 1995, Friends, 1995, NYPD Blue, 1996; (TV movies) Legend of the Lost Tribe, 2002 (voice), Hooves of Fire, 1999 (voice); (films) Follow Your Heart, 1998, Old School, 2003. Office: Gold Marchak & Liedtke 3500 W Olive Ave Ste 1400 Burbank CA 91505-5512

REMINI, ROBERT VINCENT, historian; b. NYC, July 17, 1921; s. William Francis and Lauretta (Tierney) R.; m. Ruth Theresa Kuhner, Oct. 9, 1948; children: Elizabeth Mary, Joan Marie, Robert William. BS, Fordham U., 1943; MA, Columbia U., 1947, PhD, 1951; LHD (hon.), Gov.'s State U., 1989; LittD (hon.), Ea. Ky. U., 1992, Fordham U., 1993, Columbia Coll. Chgo., 2000, So. Ill. U., 2004. Prof. history, emeritus prof. U. Ill. Chgo., 1965—, historian, 1997—, US House of Reps., 2005—; life dir. Ill. Humanities Coun., 2007—. Prof. Fordham U., 1947—65, Columbia U., 1959—60, Jilin U. Tech., China, 1986, U. Richmond, 1992, U. Notre Dame, 1995, 96, Wofford Coll., 1998; Walter Lynwood Fleming lectr. La. State U., 1984. Author: Martin Van Buren and the Making of the Democratic Party, 1959, The Election of Andrew Jackson, 1963, Andrew Jackson, 1966, Andrew Jackson and the Bank War, 1968, The Revolutionary Age of Andrew Jackson, 1976 (award of merit Friends of Am. Writers), Andrew Jackson and the Course of American Empire, 1767-1821, 1977, Andrew Jackson and the Course of American Freedom, 1822-1832, vol. II, 1981 (George Washington medal of Honor, Freedoms Found.), Andrew Jackson and the Course of American Democracy, 1833-1845, vol. III, 1984 (Nat. Book award for non-fiction 1984, Chgo. Found. for Lit. award 1985, English Speaking Union U.S. Ambassador of Honor award 1985); The Legacy of Andrew Jackson: Essays on Democracy, Indian Removal and Slavery, 1988, The Life of Andrew Jackson (abridgement of 3-vol. biography), 1988 (Carl Sandburg Lit. award for non-fiction 1989), The Jacksonian Era, 1989, Henry Clay: Statesman for the Union, 1991 (award for biography Soc. Midland Authors 1992), Daniel Webster: The Man and His Time, 1997, The Battle of New Orleans, 1999, Andrew Jackson and His Indian Wars, 2001, (Am. Hist. Assn. award for scholarly dist., 2001, Western Writers of Am. award, 2002, John Hope Franklin Hist. Maker award, Chgo. Hist. Soc., 2003), John Quincy Adams, 2002, Joseph Smith, 2002 (Freedom award Capitol Hist. Soc. 2004), The House: The History of the House of Representatives, 2006 (George Pendleton award Soc. History in Fed. Govt. 2007), A Short History of the United States, 2008, Andrews Jackson (Great Generals Series), 2008; co-author: We the People: A History of the United States, 1975, The Era of Good Feelings and the Age of Jackson, 1816-1841, 1979, The American People: A History, 1981, Andrew Jackson: A Bibliography, 1991, Fellow Citizens: US Presidential Inaugural Addresses, 2009; also articles, chpts. in books.; editor: The Decline of Aristocracy in the Politics of New York, 1965, The Presidency of Andrew Jackson, 1967, The Age of Jackson, 1972; spl. editor Am. history, Crowell-Collier Co., 1960-68, 72-73; mem editl. bd. Jour. Am. History, 1969-72; editl. cons. Papers of Andrew Jackson, 1972—. Lt. USNR, 1943—46. Recipient Encaenia award Fordham U., 1963; Silver Circle award U. Ill., Chgo., 1981, Univ. Scholar award, 1986; grantee Am. Coun. Learned Socs., 1964, Am. Philos. Soc., 1966, 80; Guggenheim fellow, 1978-79. Mem. Am. Hist. Assn. (council 1979-82), So. Hist. Assn., Orgn. Am. Historians. Roman Catholic. Office: Univ Ill at Chgo Office of Historian 815 W Van Buren Chicago IL 60607

REMIS, ROBIN E., lawyer; b. 1969; BA, Union Coll., 1991; JD cum laude, Catholic U., 1996. Bar: Mass. 1996, NY 1998, DC 1998, US Ct. Appeals (1st Cir.), US Ct. Appeals (5th Cir.), US Ct. Appeals (DC Cir.). Atty.-adv. Office of Adminstrv. Law Judges Fed. Energy Regulatory Commn.; assoc. Verner, Liipfert, Bernhard, McPherson and Hand; counsel Energy Group Sullivan & Worcester LLP, Boston. Bd. dirs. Boston Israel Bus. Forum; mem. leadership com. Internat. Conf. Cooperation for Energy Independence of Democracies in 21st Century. Mem.: Energy Bar Assn., Boston Bar Assn., ABA. Office: Sullivan & Worcester LLP One Post Office Square Boston MA 02109 Office Phone: 617-338-2412. E-mail: rremis@sandw.com.

REMKUS, CONNIE ELAINE, nutritional consultant; d. Charles Edward and Phyllis Mary Remkus. BSBA in Acctg., San Francisco State U., 1986. Registered nutritional cons. Sch. Nutritional Sci., San Jose, Calif. Flight attendant United Air Lines, Chgo., 1966—2002; self-employed property and investment mgr. Chgo., 1973—2003; tax preparer David Nitz & Assocs., San Mateo, Calif., 1975; nutritional cons., ind. distbr. Diamite Corp., San Carlos, Calif., 1988—95; field v.p. Symmetry Direct, Chgo., 1995—. Mem. South Loop Neighbors, Chgo., 2001—05; vol. SPCA, San Mateo, 1984—87. Recipient United Airlines award of Merit, 1987. Mem.: Airline Flight Attendants Union (membership chair grievance com. 1967—70), Bus. Networking Internat. (sec. 2001—03, asst. dir., amb. 2002—03). Avocations: travel, real estate, health and wellness. Office Phone: 773-283-9898.

REMLEY, AUDREY WRIGHT, retired academic administrator, psychologist; b. Dec. 26, 1931; d. Leslie Frank and Irene Lesetta (Graue) Wright; m. Alvin Remley, Mar. 25, 1951 (dec. Mar. 1986); children: Steven Leslie, David Mark. AA, Hannibal-LaGrange Coll., 1951; BS in Edn. cum laude, U. Mo., 1963, MA, 1969, PhD, 1974; LHD (hon.), Westminster Coll., 1996. Lic. psychologist, Mo.; cert. health svc. provider, Mo. From asst. prof. psychology to assoc. prof. to prof. Westminster Coll., Fulton, Mo., 1969-95, prof., assoc. dean faculty, 1989-95; emeritus prof., 1996; chmn. dept. psychology Westminster Coll., Fulton, Mo., 1975-78, dir. counseling svcs., 1975-79, dir. student devel., 1979-80, dir. acad. advising and counseling svcs., 1980-88. Owner It's A Crock Antiques; cons. OVID Bell Press, 1988-89. Mem. adv. bd. Callaway Cmty. Hosp., 1988-95, pres., 1992-95; bd. dirs. Serve, Inc., Fulton, 1989-95, pres., 1991-93; mem. adv. bd. social learning program Fulton State Hosp., chair, 1992-94, mng. county govt. task force fin. mgmt. chair; bd. dirs. Cen. Mo. Food Bank, 1995-96, Ft. Worth Symphony League Bd., 1998-2004, pres., 2002-04, v.p. for projects, 2005, exec. advisor, 2005-; bd. dirs. Jubilee Theatre, 2006—,treasurer, 2007-. Recipient Outstanding Young Woman of Am. award Jaycettes, 1965, Athena award, 1991, Remley Center award (1st recipient) Westminster Coll., 2001; NDEA fellow, 1968; bldg. Remley Women's Resource Ctr. Westminster Coll. named in her honor, 2001 Mem. APA, AACD, Am. Coll. Pers. Assn. (exec. coun. 1982-85, co-editor ACPA Developments 1984-87, v.p. state divns. 1987-89, treas.-elect 1990-91, treas. 1991-93, treas. ednl. found. bd. 1994-96, Outstanding State Divsn. Leader 1982, profl. svc. award 1991, Annuit Coeptis award 1994), Mo. Coll. Pers. Assn. (pres. 1981-82, profl. svc. award 1987), Mo. Psychol. Assn. (lic.), Ft. Worth Newcomers Club (pres. 1998-99), Kiwanis (exec. bd. 1989-92, v.p. 1992, pres.-elect 1992-93, pres. 1993-94, disting. 1995). Presbyterian. Avocations: singing, antiques, knitting.

REMLEY, KAREN, state agency administrator, public health service officer; married. MD, U. Mo., Kansas City, 1980; MBA Health Services Mgmt. Cert., Duke U., Durham. Cert. Am. Bd. Med. Examiners, Am Bd. Pediat. and Pediatric Emergency Medicine. Attending physician Children's Hosp. of the King's Daughters, Norfolk, Va.; cmty. faculty, sch. pub. health Eastern Va. Med. Sch., asst. prof. pediat.; assoc. med. dir. Trigon, 1998—2000; chief med. officer Operation Smile, Inc., 2000—01; CEO Physicians for Peace, 2001—03; med. dir. external quality Anthem Blue Cross Blue Shield, Va., 2004—06; v.p. med. affairs Sentara Leigh Hosp., Norfolk, 2006—08; commr. Va. Dept. Health, 2008—. At-large bd. mem. Virginians Improving Patient Care and Safety. Mem.: Am. Acad. Pediat. Office: Va Dept Health 109 Governor St PO Box 2448 Richmond VA 23218-2448*

REMLEY, R. DIRK, English educator, consultant; b. Cleve., July 27, 1964; s. Roland E. and Anna Marie Remley. BA, Bowling Green State U., 1986, MA, 1988. Lectr. Kent (Ohio) State U., 1990—; prin. Strategic Market Consulting Group, Ravenna, Ohio, 1994—. Author: The Red Notebook, 1998, Snapshots of Americana, 1999, In Transit, 1999; contbr. articles to profl. jours. Lector Immaculate Conception Ch., Ravenna, 1997—; vol. Meals on Wheels, Chagrin Falls, Ohio, 1996-97; mem. com. Playhouse Square Ptnrs., Cleve., 1992-96. Mem.: Nat. Coun. Tchrs. English. Office: Kent State U Dept English Kent OH 44242-0001

REMLINGER, ROLF, music educator, composer; b. Detroit, Mar. 9, 1963; s. Florian and Hermina Remlinger; m. Annette C. Tischler, Apr. 1, 1989; children: Eric, Matthew. BA, Hiram Coll., 1985; MEd, Ashland U., 2006. Cert. tchr. Mich., Ohio. Tchr. music St. Fabian Elem. Sch., Farmington Hills, Mich., 1985—86; dir. marching band percussion sect. Midpark H.S., Middleburg Heights, Ohio, 1986—86; tchr. music, dir. choir Lincoln Elem. Sch., Youngstown, 1987—95; asst. orch. dir. Harding H.S., Marion, 1997—98; tchr. music, dir. choir Taft Mid. Sch., 1995—2004; transition team Marion City Schs., 2001—03; tchr. music, choir dir. Grant Mid. Sch., 2004—05; band dir. Lincoln Elem., 2004—05; gen. music tchr. Delaware City Schs., Dempsey Middle Sch., 2005—; percussion instr. marching band Hayes H.S., 2005—. Tchr. drama tchr., dir. Youngstown Playhouse, Ohio, 1988—95; mem. theater tech. staff Interlochen Summer Arts Camp, Interlochen, Mich., 1984; tchr. youth theater drama Jewish Cmty. Ctr., Youngstown, 1991—94; percussionist Ohio Boy Choir, Cleve., 1985—89; vocal instr. Pleasent City Schools Theater Dept., Marion, 1996. Hockey Daze Hockey Comics, 1993; composer: (songs) Slow Day in City Traffic, 1986, Meadow Walk, 1986, Kyrie, 2001, Praise the Lord!, 2002, Salve Regina, 2002, Ave Regina Coelorum, 2002; contbr. articles to mags. Den leader Boy Scouts of Am., Delaware, 1996—2006, tiger cub coach, 2000—05, merit badge counselor, 2002, instr. Pow Wow Columbus, 2003—06; choir mem., composer and dir. St. Mary's Ch., 1997—, vacation bible sch. tchr., 1998—99. Recipient Bissel Meml. Music award, Hiram Coll., 1984, Profl. Svc. award, Youngstown State U., 1991, Tiger Cub Coach award, Boy Scouts of Am., 2002, Cub Scout Den Leader award, 2002; grantee, Ohio Theatre Alliance, 1990; scholar Hubbell scholar, Hiram Coll., 1984, 1985, Martin scholar, 1985. Mem.: PTA, NEA, Del. Edn. Assn., Nat. Mid. Sch. Assn., Ohio Mid. Sch. Assn., Ohio Edn. Assn., Music Educators Nat. Conf., Ohio Music Edn. Assn., Brigade of Am. Revolution, KC. Roman Catholic. Avocations: music, art, hockey, comic book collecting, collecting sports cards.

REMMEL, RORY PATRICK, pharmacy educator; b. Colorado Springs, Colo., Nov. 26, 1954; s. Urban Charles and Regina V. (Bojarski) R.; m. Cheryl L. Zimmerman, June 25, 1983. BS in Biochemistry, U. Wyo., 1976, BS in Pharmacy, 1977; PhD in Medicinal Chemistry, U. Wash., 1982. Lic. pharmacist, Colo., Wash. Pharmacy intern Target Pharmacy # 6, Glendale, Colo., 1977-78; rsch. fellow pharmacology Harvard Med. Sch., Boston, 1982-83; rsch. assoc. U. Minn., Mpls., 1983-84, asst. prof., 1984-91, assoc. prof., 1991—. Vis. scientist U. Dundee, Scotland, 1992; mem. pharmacology com. NIH AIDS clin. trials Group, 1994—; mem. adv. panel natural products U.S. Pharmacopeia, Bethesda, Md., 1995. Fogarty Sr. Internat. fellow, 1992. Mem. Am. Assn. Colls. Pharmacy, Am. Assn. Pharm. Scientists, Internat. Soc. for Study Xenobiotics, Kappa Psi (grand coun. dep.). Avocations: golf, cross country skiing. Office: U Minn Coll Pharmacy 308 Harvard St SE Minneapolis MN 55455-0353 Home: 500 E Grant St Apt 2709 Minneapolis MN 55404-2184 Business E-Mail: remme001@umn.edu.

REMMELE, RICHARD L., JR., research scientist, director; s. Richard L. Remmele, Sr. and Esther Remmele. BS, Oral Roberts U., Tulsa, 1978; MS, Calif. Poly. U., Pomona, 1983; PhD, Ariz. State U., Tempe, 1988. Postdoctoral fellow Colo. State U., Fort Collins, 1988—93, U. Colo. Sch. Pharmacy, Denver, 1993; protein formulations chemist Immunex Corp., Seattle, 1993—2002; biotherapeutics formulations scientific dir. Amgen, Thousand Oaks, Calif., 2002—. Editor: Current Pharmaceutical Biotechnology; contbr. articles in 22 sci. jours., chapters to books. Recipient DAAD scholarship, Karlsruhe Tech. Inst. of Phys. and Electrochemistry. Mem.: AIChE, Am. Chem. Soc., Am. Assn. of Pharm. Sci., Phi Lambda Upsilon (treas. 1985—86), Alpha Chi Sigma. Achievements include patents for increased recovery of active proteins; Polypeptide Formulation; research in liquid formulation development using differential scanning calorimetry, Real-time in situ monitoring lysozyme during lyophilization using infrared spectroscopy; dehydration stress in the presence of sucrose; designing proteins that work using recombinant technologies, Biophysical characterization of a soluble CD40 ligand (CD154) coiled-coil trimer; low-temperature infrared spectroscopy reveals four stages of water loss during lyophilization of hen egg-white lysozyme, examination of chemical and physical stability using a variety of bio physical techniques, analytical characterization of protein live, peptibodies, antibodies; developed Enbral liquid formulation and leol the development of the lyophilized N-plate formulation. Office: Amgen One Amgen Center Dr Thousand Oaks CA 91320-1799 Office Phone: 805-447-5534. Business E-Mail: remmeler@amgen.com.

REMNICK, DAVID JAY, journalist, editor-in-chief; b. Hackensack, NJ, Oct. 29, 1958; s. Edward C. and Barbara (Seigel) Remnick; m. Esther B. Fein; children: Alexander, Noah, Natasha. BA in Comparative Lit., Princeton U., 1981. Reporter The Washington Post, 1982—88, Moscow corr., 1988—92; staff writer The New Yorker Condé Nast Publs., NYC, 1992—98, editor, 1998—. Lectr. Columbia U., Princeton U. Author: Lenin's Tomb: The Last Days of the Soviet Empire, 1993 (Pulitzer Prize for gen. non-fiction, 1994, George Polk award, 1994), Resurrection, 1997, The Devil Problem (and other True Stories), 1997, King of the World: Muhammad Ali and the Rise of an American Hero, 1998, Life Stories: Profiles from The New Yorker, 2000, Reporting: Writings from The New Yorker, 2006. Recipient Livingston award, 1991, Helen Bernstein award, NY Pub. Libr., 1994, George Polk award for excellence in journalism, 1994, Nat. Mag. award for gen. excellence, Am. Soc. Mag. Editors, 2008, Nat. Mag. award for fistion, 2009, Nat. Mag. award for reviews & criticism, 2009, Nat. Mag. award for photo portfolio, 2009; named Editor of Yr., Advt. Age, 1999, 2000, Benjamin C. Bradlee Editor of Yr., Nat. Press Found., 2006. Fellow: Am. Acad. Arts & Sciences. Office: The New Yorker 4 Times Sq New York NY 10036-6561 Office Phone: 212-286-5774.*

REMONDI, JOHN F. (JACK REMONDI), finance company executive; b. 1962; s. John J. Remondi; m. Judith Barbara Dickstein, Mar. 20, 1993. BA in Econ., Conn. Coll. Sr. v.p. corp. fin. & adminstrn., CFO New England Edn. Loan Mktg. Corp.; sr. v.p., treas. Nellie Mae, Inc., Braintree, Mass., 1999—2001; exec. v.p. fin. SLM Corp. (Sallie Mae), Reston, Va., 2001—05, vice chmn., CFO, 2008—; portfolio mgr. PAR Capital Mgmt., Boston, 2005—08. Chmn. Reading is Fundamental, Inc. Office: Sallie Mae 12061 Bluemont Way Reston VA 20190

REMPALA, GRZEGORZ A., mathematician, statistician, educator; b. Warsaw, Mar. 19, 1968; arrived in US, 1992; s. Jan and Ryszarda Rempala; m. Helena A. Hofmokl, 1991; children: Jas, Antos. BS, U. Warsaw, 1990, MA in Math. summa cum laude, 1991; DSc, Warsaw Tech. U., 2007; PhD, Bowling Green State U., Ohio, 1996. Asst. prof. U. Louisville, 1996—2002, assoc. prof., 2002—08; prof. biostatistics Med. Coll. Ga., Augusta, 2008—. Rsch. fellow Inst. Math. and Its Applications, Mpls., 2003—04, Duke U., Durham, NC, 2006—. Author: (articles) Annals of Applied Probability, Proceedings of AMS, Probability Theory and Related Fields. Grantee, NIH, 2005—, NSF, 2006—. Achievements include research in Applied Mathematics and Statistics. Office: Dept Biostats Med Coll Ga 1469 Laney Walker Blvd Augusta GA 30912 Business E-Mail: dbe@mcg.edu.

REMPT, RODNEY P., retired academic administrator, career military officer; b. Burbank, Calif., June 13, 1945; married. BS, U.S. Naval Acad., 1966; MS in Sys. Analysis, Stanford U.; M.Security and Strategic Studies, Naval War Coll. Commd. ensign USN, advanced through grades to vice admiral; comdr. USS Antelope, Naples, Italy; exec. officer USS Dahlgren; initial project officer MK 41 vertical launch sys. Naval Sea Sys. Command; program coord. AEGIS weapons sys. Chief Naval Officer; adminstrv. asst., aide Vice Chief of Naval Ops.; comdr. USS Callaghan, USS Bunker Hill, Yokosuka, Japan; dir. PCO/PXO dept. Surface Warfare Officers Schs. Command, Newport, R.I.; dir. anti-air warfare requirements divs. Staff of Dep. Chief Naval Ops., Naval Warefare; head surface ships and combat sys. Staff of Chief of Naval Ops.; dir. Theater Air Def., 1994-96, program exec. officer, 1996-98; dep. asst. sec. theater combat sys. USN, Washington, 1998—2001; pres. Naval War Coll., Newport, RI, 2001—03; supt. US Naval Acad., Annapolis, Md., 2003—07. Decorated Disting. Svc. medal, Legion of Merit (3 awards), Meritorious Svc. medal (3 awards), Navy Commendation medal with combat V (3 awards).

REMSON, DEBRA S., music educator; b. Buffalo, Sept. 5, 1953; d. Howard and Mildred (Altman) R. Performance cert. in violin, Hochschule für Musik, Graz, Austria, 1973; BA in Music Edn., Fredonia State U., 1975; MA in Urban Edn., U. Buffalo, 1981; MS in Counseling, Canisius Coll., 1995. Tchr. vocal music Buffalo City Sch. Dist., 1977-78; tchr. instrumental music Elmira (N.Y.) City Sch. Dist., 1975-76, Cleveland Hill Sch. Dist., Cheektowaga, N.Y., 1978-79; tchr. vocal music/theater Lockport (N.Y.) City Sch. Dist., 1979-91; tchr. instrumental music Grand Island (N.Y.) Cen. Sch. Dist., 1991—. Guest condr. Niagara County Music Edn. Assn., NCMEA, Niagara County, N.Y., 1985, 90, 1996, 2000, 2004. Campaign asst. Dem. Party, Grand Island, 1997; vol. Ross Perot campaign, 1992. Recipient Grand Island Celebration Inspiration award, 1996, 1997, 1998, 2000, 2001, 2002. Mem. N.Y. State Music Assn. (adjudicator 1992—, guest spkr. 1991—), Erie County Music Edn. Assn. (guest condr. 1995), N.Y. State Outdoor Edn. Assn. (guest spkr.). Democrat. Avocations: music, fitness training, vocalist with local band. Office: Grand Island Cen Sch Dist 1100 Ransom Rd Grand Island NY 14072-1460 Business E-Mail: debraremson@k12.ginet.org.

REMZ, SANFORD F., lawyer; b. Port Jefferson, NY, Aug. 10, 1954; BA, Brandeis U., Waltham, Mass., 1976; JD, Columbia U., NYC, 1979. Bar: NY State Supreme Ct (appellate divsn) 1980, US Dist. Ct. (so. dist. NY) 1980, Supreme Jud. Ct. Mass. 1986, US Dist. Ct. Mass. 1987, US Ct. Appeals (2nd cir.). Assoc. Weil, Gotshal & Manges, NYC, 1979—86; shareholder Widett, Slater & Goldman, Boston, 1986—92, Hutchins, Wheeler & Dittmar, Boston, 1992—2002, Yurko, Salvesen & Remz, Boston, 2003—. Contbr. articles to profl. jours. Dir. Yed Chessed, Bklyn.; v.p. Nat. Ramah Commn., NYC, 2004; dir. Yad Chessed, Bklyn., Mass., 2008; pres. Camp Ramah New Eng., Needham, Mass., 2004—08; dir. Hillel at Brandeis U., Waltham, Mass., 2001—05. Harlan Fiske Stone scholar, Columbia Law Sch., 1976—77. Mem.: ABA, Boston Bar Assn. (co-chair, com. fed. practice and procedure 2005), Phi Beta Kappa. Office: Yurko Salvesen & Remz PC One Washington Mall 11th Fl Boston MA 02108 Office Fax: 617-723-6905. Business E-Mail: sfr@bizlit.com.

REN, CHIANG H., aerospace engineer; b. Taipei, Taiwan, Aug. 3, 1965; arrived in U.S., 1972; m. Kelly Yoon, May 20, 1995; children: Heather Victoria, Gloria Isabel. BSE magna cum laude in Mech. Engrng., U. Pa., 1987; MS in Aeronautics and Astronautics, MIT, 1989. Sr. aerospace engr. ANSER, Arlington, Va., 1989—2001; chief tech. officer Kepler Rsch., Inc., Arlington, 2002—. Contbr. numerous articles to profl. jours.; author: (3 books) Christian Mission Series, 2000. Deacon Presbyn. Ch.; dir. Inst. for Christianity. Recipient Letter of Recognition, Sec. of the Air Force, 2001, Air Force Space Commn. Task Force, 2001. Fellow: AIAA (assoc.); mem.: Pi Tau Sigma, Tau Beta Pi. Office: Kepler Research Inc 1530 Wilson Blvd #600 Arlington VA 22209 Home Phone: 703-818-0221; Office Phone: 703-465-4035. Business E-Mail: chiangren@keplerresearch.com.

REN, HUIZHEN, language educator; b. Hebei Province, China, June 6, 1951; arrived in US, 1982; d. Fengtian Ren and Xiuting Zhao; m. Changbiao Yue, May 1, 1978. MEd, Temple U., Phila., 1984, EdD, 1988. Cert. ESL tchr. NJ Dept. Edn., 1998. English instr. Tianjin Normal U., China, 1975—82, Temple U., Phila., 1988—90, acting dir. spl. recruitment & admissions prog., 1990—94, dir. English lang. enrichment ctr., 1994—95; coord. ESL prog. & svcs. CC Phila., 1995—. Designer & instr. Chinese lang. program CC Phila.; adv. Asian student club Cmty. Phila., 1998—99; Chinese lang. examiner Drexel U., Phila., 1999—; Chinese & English lang. interpreter Inst. Fgn. Langs., Phila., 2000—. Mem.: TESOL. Office: CC Phila 1700 Spring Garden St Philadelphia PA Office Fax: 215-751-8248. Business E-Mail: hren@ccp.edu.

REN, JIANHUA, education educator; d. Shumin (Zhang) and Shanhou Ren; m. Bogdan Bogdanov, Mar. 18, 2006. PhD, Purdue U., West Lafayette, Ind., 1999. Asst. prof. U. Pacific, Stockton, Calif., 2002—08, assoc. prof., 2008—. Recipient Petroleum Rsch. Fund Type-G grant, Am. Chem. Soc., 2006—08; Rsch. grant, Nat. Sci. Found., 2008—. Achievements include research in phys. organic chemistry. Office: Univ of the Pacific Dept of Chemistry 3601 Pacific Ave Stockton CA 95211 Office Fax: 209-946-2607. Business E-Mail: jren@pacific.edu.

REN, KAILIANG, materials scientist, educator; b. Fengxiang, Shaanxi Province, China, Sept. 5, 1974; s. Runmin Ren and Xuezhui Yao; m. Yanan Sha, May 22, 2001; 1 child, Aaron Boyuan. BS, Tianjin U., China, 1997; MS, Pa. State U., State Coll., 2005, PhD, 2007. Software engr. Tianjin Jinke Electronics, Inc., 1997—2001; rsch. asst. Pa. State U., 2003—07, affiliated asst. prof., 2008—. Device engr. Strategic Polymer Scis. Inc., State Coll., 2007—. Contbr. articles to profl. pubs. Mem.: SPIE Smart Structures, NDE, Materials Rsch. Soc. Achievements include patents pending for method to improve the electromechanical response and reliability of electroactive polymer devices; hybrid actuator integrating shape memory polymer with electroactive polymers, and other active polymer. Office: Strategic Polymer Scis Inc 200 Innovation Blvd Ste 237 State College PA 16803 E-mail: kxr233@psu.edu.

REN, SHUNLIN, medical educator; b. Zhejiang, China; married. MD, Va. Commonwealth U., Richmond, PhD, 1992. Assoc. prof. Va. Commonwealth U., 2006—08. Grant, NIH, 2008.

REN, XING JIAN, physician; b. Shanghai, June 27, 1961; s. Yun Feng Ren and Xin Yi Zhang; m. Bei Xie, June 27, 1990; 1 child, Oriana Leigh. MD, Shanghai First Med. Coll., 1984. Diplomate internal medicine and geriatric medicine Am. Bd. Internal Medicine. Resident in surgery Shanghai Ruhui Hosp., China, 1984-85; resident Ft. Wayne (Ind.) Med. Edn. Program, 1993-94; resident, intern in medicine Loyola U. of Chgo., Maywood, Ill., 1994-97; fellow in medicine Harvard Med. Sch., Boston, 1997-99; staff physician Scripps Clinic Found., La Jolla, Calif., 1999—; asst. clin. prof. medicine U. Calif. Sch. Medicine, 2003—. Co-author: Virology, 1986; contbr. articles to profl. jours. Fellow Harvard Med. Sch., 1998; recipient 1st prize Nat. Med. Student Competition for Knowledge of Med. Lit., 1983, grad. student scholarship U. N.C., Chapel Hill, scholarship Carolina Biotechnolgy Ctr., others. Fellow ACP; mem. AMA, Mass. Med. Soc., Am. Geriatrics Soc., Fell. Am. Coll. Physician. Home Phone: 858-794-9284; Office Phone: 858-268-9500, 858-554-8077, 619-245-2830.

REN, ZHAOHUI, engineer; married. PhD, U. Ky., Lexington, 2005. Sr. rsch. engr. Mohawk Innovative Tech. Inc., Albany, NY, 2005—.

RENARD, PAUL STEVEN, music educator; b. NYC, May 5, 1934; s. Joseph Maurice and Elsie (Wolpow) R. Student, Miami (Fla.) Conservatory, 1947-48, Sch. of Am. Music, 1950-51; cert., Ida Elkan Sch. of Music, 1958. Staff concert organist Hammond Organ Co., NYC, 1950-74; staff organist various TV stas., NYC, 1952-61, King Records and Riverside Records, NYC, 1955-64; staff organist, ednl. dir. Lyon-Healy Music Co., Chgo., 1962-72; founder, dir. Paul Renard's Music Dynamics, Chgo., 1972—. Cons. in field. Co-inventor first electric piano, Wurlitzer Mus. Instruments Co., 1953-54; author (software) Paul Renard's Music Dynamics, 1999; author numerous piano and organ texts; contbr. articles tor profl. jours. Home Phone: 706-736-3263.

RENARD, RONALD LEE, allergist; b. Chgo., July 31, 1949; s. Robert James and Dorothy Mae (Fruik) R.; m. Maureen Ann Gilmore, Aug. 5, 1972 (div. Mar. 1992); children: Jeffrey, Stephen, Justin, Leigh Ellen; m. Catherine L. Walker, Apr. 1, 1992; children: Morgan, Michal, Luke. Degrees in Lang., U. de Montepellier, France, 1970; BS in French, U. San Francisco, 1971; MD, Creighton U., 1976. Dir. med. ICU, lt. U.S. Army Hosp., Ft. Leonard Wood, Md., 1980-81; dir. respiratory therapy, asst. chief allergy svc. Walter Reed Med. Ctr., Washington, 1981-84; staff allergist Chico (Calif.) Med. Group, 1984-86; allergist pvt. practice Redding, Calif., 1986—. Dir. ACLS program Enloe Hosp., Chico, 1988-91; bd. dirs. Am. Lung Assn. Calif., 1989-91, med. dir. asthma camp, Chico, Redding, 1986-95; asst. prof. medicine USPHS, Bethesda, Md., 1982-84; asst. prof. family medicine U. Calif. Davis Med. Sch., Redding, 1990-94; Shasta County Planning Commr., 1994-95. Contbr. articles to profl. jours. Fellow Am. Acad. Allergy and Immunology, Am. Coll. Allergists; mem. Assn. Mil. Allergists, Calif. Thoracic Soc., Alpha Omega Alpha. Republican. Roman Catholic. Avocations: hunting, biking. Office: 1505 Victor Ave Redding CA 96003 Office Fax: 530-246-8856. Personal E-mail: rrenard@juno.com.

RENAUD, BERNADETTE MARIE ELISE, author; b. Ascot Corner, Que., Can., Apr. 18, 1945; d. Albert and Aline (Audet) R. Diploma, Présentation de Marie, Granby, Que., 1962-64. Librarian asst. Schs. of Waterloo, Que., 1964-67, tchr. primary schs. Que., 1967-70; adminstrv. sec. Assn. Medi-Tech-Sci., Montreal, Que., 1972-76. Author: Emilie La Baignoire A Pattes, 1976 (Can. Coun. Children's Lit. prize, 1976, Assn. Advancement of Scis. and Technics of Documentation award, 1976), 2d edit., 2002, Le Chat de l'Oratoire, 1978, Emilie la baignoire á pattes album, 1978, La maison tête de pioche, 1979, La révolte de la courte pointe, 1979, La dépression de l'ordinateur, 1981, Une boîte Magique Très Embêtante, 1981, La grande question de Tomatelle, 1982, Comment on fait un livre?, 1983, The Cat in the Cathedral, 1983, The Computer Revolts, 1984, (book and movie) Bach et Bottine, 1986 (awards for movie, 19 awards across the world, transl. ino 8 langs., subtitled into 18 langs.), Bach and Broccoli, 1986, (short movie) Quand l'accent devient grave, 1989, (novels) Un Homme Comme Tant d'Autres, tome 1, 1992, tome, II, 1993, tome, III, 1994, Prix Germaine Guévremont, 1995, Gala des Arts du Bas-Richelieu (QC); dir., coord.: Ecrire pour la jeunesse, 1990; author: short stories, adaptations of 8 children's classics, 1977—79, La quête de Kurweena, 1997; dir., coord.: album and CD Le petit violon muet, 1997, Héritiers de l'éternité, 1998, Les Funambules D'un Temps Nouveau, 2001, Les Chemins d'Eve Tome I, 2002, Les Chemins d'Eve Tome 2, 2002, Grand Prix du Livre de la

Monteregie, 2001, 2002, Émilie, la baignoire à pattes, rééd, 2002, Drôle de nuit pour Miti, 2004, Les gros bisous, 2004, Pas de chouchous, 2004, Les chemins d'Ève Tome 3, 2005, Casimir, le maladroit, 2006, Mon chat zoo, 2006, Les chemins d'Eve, tome 4, 2006, Isis, ma belle Isis, 2008, Juillet a disparu, 2008, Perdu dans la brume, 2009.

RENAUD, CHRISTINE, classicist, educator; d. Raymond and Mary Judith Renaud, Rhoda Renaud (Stepmother). PhD, U. Tex., Austin, 1990. Grad. asst. U. Tex., 1983—86; asst. prof. classics Duquesne U., Pitts., 1989—93; vis. asst. prof. Lewisburg, 1993—94; prof. classics and religion Carthage Coll., Kenosha, 1995—, chair classics, 1995—, chair heritage oversight com., 1996—99, chair writing assessment task force, 1997, dir. heritage studies program, 1999. Course dir. Racine Odyssey Project, Wis., 2004; rschr., translator, field archaeologist Am. Inst. Roman Culture, Rome, 2005—. Contbr. articles to profl. jours. Humanities adv. Kenosha Literacy Coun., Wis., 2008. Recipient Tech. award, Ameritech Wis., 1996; Rsch. grant, Fulbright-Hays, Italy, 1986—87, grant, Wis. Humanities Coun., 2004—05, Mission grant, Racine Dominicans, 2005. Mem.: Am. Inst. Archaeology, Am. Philol Assn., Phi Beta Kappa, Omicron Delta Kappa. Office: Carthage Coll 2001 Alford Pk Dr Kenosha WI 53140 Office Fax: 262-551-6208. Business E-Mail: crenaud@carthage.edu.

RENBAUM, BARRY JEFFREY, lawyer; b. Balt., Feb. 26, 1948; s. David and Leah (Cohen) R.; m. Carol Barbash, June 22, 1980. BS magna cum laude, Rider U., Princeton, NJ, 1970; postgrad., NYU, 1973; JD, Georgetown U., Washington, DC, 1973. Bar: Md. 1973, US Dist. Ct. Md. 1998. Jud. clk. to Hon. John C. Eldridge, Md. Ct. Appeals, 1974-75; asst. pub. defender State of Md., 1975-79; exec. v.p., gen. counsel Custom Savs. Bank, Tmple Fin. Co., Balt., 1980-91; pvt. practice Glyndon, Md., 1991—. Mem. ATLA, Md. Bar Assn., Alpha Epsilon Zeta. Office: Brydonwood Glyndon MD 21071-0326 Business E-Mail: brydonwood@earthlink.net.

REN-CANG, LI, mathematician, educator; s. Hongjin Li and Houcheng Yuan; m. Liting Chen. PhD, U. Calif., Berkeley, 1995. Asst. prof. U. Ky., Lexington, 1995—2001, assoc. prof., 2001—06; prof. U. Tex., Arlington, 2006—. Cons. HP, Palo Alto, Calif., 2003. Contbr. articles to profl. jours. Recipient Friedman Meml. prize, U. Calif. Berkeley, 1996, Career award, NSF, 1999; Householder fellow, Oak Ridge Nat. Lab., 1995. Mem.: Soc. Indsl. and Applied Math., Am. Math. Soc. Achievements include research in numerical analysis and scientific computations. Office: Univ Tex Arlington Dept Math Arlington TX 76019 Office Fax: 817-272-5802. Business E-Mail: rcli@uta.edu.

RENCE, BRADFORD G., biology professor; b. Monroe, Wis., Sept. 26, 1947; s. William G. and Eva Mae Rence; m. Eileen E. Zahlout, Dec. 10, 1976; children: Nadja P., Erika D. PhD, U. Calif., Berkeley, 1976. Postdoc. fellow U. Calif., 1976—79; prof. and chair biology Lawrence U., Appleton, Wis., 1979—. Recipient Tchg. Excellence award, Lawrence U., 2002; named Young Tchr. of Yr., 1984. Mem.: Soc. Behavioral Ecology, Animal Behavior Soc., Xerces Soc. Office: Lawrence Univ 115 S Drew St Appleton WI 54911 Business E-Mail: renceb@lawrence.edu.

RENCH, STEPHEN CHARLES, lawyer; b. Coffeyville, Kans., Oct. 11, 1930; s. Stephen and Gladys Mae (Carpenter) R.; m. Loraine Pennock, Oct. 11, 1966. BA in Econs., U. Kans., 1952; JD, Georgetown U., 1959. Bar: Colo. 1959, U.S. Dist. Ct. Colo. 1959, U.S. Ct. Appeals (10th cir.) 1961, U.S. Supreme Ct. 1979. Law clk to judge U.S. Ct. Appeals (10th cir.), Denver, 1959; law clk. to chief judge U.S. Dist. Ct. Colo., Denver, 1960-61; assoc. Tippit and Haskell, Denver, 1961-63; clk. Probate Ct., Denver, 1964-65; dep. state pub. defender Denver, 1966-74; tng. dir. Colo. State Pub. Defender System, Denver, 1974-77, tng. dir. as ind. contractor tng. seminars, 1980-82; pvt. practice Denver, 1977—. Mem. permanent lecturing faculty for summer sessions and seminars Nat. Coll. Criminal Def., Houston, 1974—, course dir., 1977; instr. trial tactics and strategy, evidence courses U. Denver Law Sch., 1979-91; lectr. in field throughout U.S. Author: Fingertip Law for Colorado Public Defenders, 1975, Strategy for Colorado Public Defenders, 1979, The Rench Book, Trial Tactics and Strategy, 1990, Courtbook, 1982, monthly columnist Trade Secrets of a Trial Lawyer, Washington Memo, 1977-78; contbr. articles to profl. jours. 1st lt. USAF, 1952-56. Mem. ABA, Colo. Trial Lawyers Assn., Colo. Criminal Def. Bar, Nat. Assn. Criminal Def. Lawyers, Nat. Legal Aid and Defenders Assn., Nat. Practice Inst., Assn. Trial Lawyers Am., Denver Bar Assn., Colo. Bar Assn. Office: 580 S Franklin St Denver CO 80209-4502 Office Phone: 303-777-0134. Business E-Mail: scrench@msn.com.

RENDA, JOSEPH L., nephrologist, educator; s. Paul and Mary Renda; m. Rosemary Demennato, Dec. 16, 1972; children: Mathew, Sara, Katherine, Elizabeth. MD, Yale Univ., New Haven, 1974. Diplomate Am. Bd. Medicine, 1972. Assoc. prof., nephrologist Yale Med. Sch., 1974—. Dir. nephrology Waterbury Hosp., Conn., 1974—. Lcdr USNR, 1970—72, Groton, Conn. Named Tchr. of Yr., Yale Sch. Medicine, 1988; named one of Best Dr. in America. Office: Waterbury Hosp Assoc Specialists Nephrology 140 Grandview Ave Waterbury CT 06708 Personal E-mail: jlrneph@aol.com.

RENDA, LARREE M., retail executive; Joined Safeway, Inc., 1974, exec. v.p. retail ops., human resources, pub. affairs, labor and govtl. rels. Pleasanton, Calif., 1999—. Office: Safeway Inc 5918 Stoneridge Mall Rd Pleasanton CA 94588*

RENDA, PATRICK BLAKE, investment company executive; b. Santa Monica, Calif., July 19, 1968; s. Dominic P. and Patricia Renda; d. Alexandra Elsbeth Renda. BA, U. So. Calif., 1991. Prodn. mgr. NBC, Burbank, Calif., 1991-93; sr. paralegal Fragomen, Del Rey, Bernsen & Loewy, Palo Alto, Calif., 1994-96; v.p., investment officer J&W Seligman & Co., Palo Alto, Calif., 1996—2002; v.p., sr. analyst American Express Asset Mgmt., La Jolla, Calif., 2002—05; mng. ptnr. Conquistador Ventures, LLC, La Jolla, 2005—, Fin. Mgmt. Corp.; v.p. Investment Rsch. & Bus. Devel., 2008—09, health makers, 2009—. Nominee Best of Buyside 2000, 04, Instl. Investor Mag. 2004. Mem.: Naples C. of C. Assn., South Fla. hedge Fund Mgrs., Gold Coast Venture Capital Assn., Churchill Club, Balboa Bay Club. Republican. Roman Catholic. Avocations: athletics, art, travel. Office Phone: 239-298-6276.

RENDA-TANALI, IRMAK, program director, consultant; 1 child. BS in Civil Engring., Mid. East Tech. U., Ankara, Turkey, 1991, MBA with honors, 1995, MS in Civil Engring., 1995; DSc, George Washington U., 2002. Program dir., Homeland Security mgmt. studies Grad. Sch. Mgmt. and Tech., U. Md. U. Coll., 1998—; sr. rsch. scientist Inst. for Crisis, Disaster and Risk Mgmt., Washington, 1998—; sr. emergency mgmt. specialist Dewberry, 2005—. Cons. Irmak Renda-Tanali & Assocs., Gaithersburg, Md., 2002—. Editor: Managing Change through Post-Event Evaluations, 2005, Disaster Prevention Preparedness Planning, 2005. Sch. Engring. and Applied Scis. fellow, George Washington U., 2000—02. Mem.: ASCE, Am. Soc. Indsl. Security, Am. Soc. Engring. Mgrs. Avocations: piano, art. Personal E-mail: rendatan@gwu.edu.

RENDELL, EDWARD GENE, Governor of Pennsylvania, retired mayor, lawyer; b. NYC, Jan. 5, 1944; s. Jesse T. and Emma (Sloat) R.; m. Marjorie Osterlund, July 10, 1971; 1 son, Jesse Thompson. BA in Polit. Sci., U. Pa., 1965; JD, Villanova U., 1968. Bar: Pa. 1968, U.S. Supreme Ct. 1981. Asst. dist. atty., chief homicide unit Office Dist. Atty., Phila., 1968-74; dep. spl. prosecutor Phila., 1976; dist. atty., 1978-86; mayor City of Phila., 1992—2000; gov. Commonwealth of Pa., Harrisburg, 2003—. Gen. chmn. Dem. Nat. Com., 1999—2000. 2d lt. USAR, 1968—74. Recipient Man of Yr. award VFW, 1980, Am. Cancer League, 1981, Disting. Pub. Svc. award Pa. County Detectives Assn., 1981. Mem. ABA, Pa. Dist. Attys. Assn. (legis. chmn. 1979—), Phila. Bar Assn., B'nai B'rith, United Jewish Orgns., Jewish War Vets. Democrat. Jewish. Office: Governor's Office Rm 225 Main Capitol Bldg Harrisburg PA 17120 Office Phone: 717-787-2500. Office Fax: 717-772-8284. E-mail: soverner@state.pa.us.

RENDELL, KENNETH WILLIAM, rare and historical documents dealer, consultant; b. Boston, May 12, 1943; s. Harry H. and Pauline (Walsh) R.; m. Diana J. Angelo, June 3, 1967 (div. 1985); children: Jeffrey H., Jason J. (dec.); m. Shirley L. McNerney, July 14, 1985; 1 child, Julia Louise. Student, Boston U., 1961-63. Pres. Kingston Galleries, Inc., Somerville, Mass., 1960-67, Kenneth W. Rendell, Inc., Newton, Mass., 1967—, Kenneth W. Rendell, Ltd., London, 1970—, Kenneth W. Rendell Gallery, Inc., NYC, Tokyo, 1985—, Mus. World War II. Bd. dirs. John Wilson Autographs Ltd., London, 1961-75, Charles Ede Gallery Ltd., London, 1976-92; chmn. New England Antiquarian Booksellers Assn., 1975-77; pres. Internat. League Autograph and Manuscript Dealers, 1975-77; cons. numerous univ. librs., govtl. and media orgns. Author: The Fundamentals of Autograph Collecting, 1976, Tax Appraisals of Manuscript Collections, 1983, Changing Concepts of Value and Rarity, 1985, The Hitler Diaries: Bad Forgeries But a Great Hoax, 1986, The Mormon Conman, Forger and Killer, 1987, Other People's Mail: 30 Years As a Dealer in Historical Documents, 1988, The One Hundred Americans Who Have Made America What it is Today, 1989, The Detection of Forged Historical Letters and Documents, 1990, With Weapons and Wits: Propaganda and Psychological Warfare in World War II, 1991, Forging History: The Detection of Fake Historical Letters and Documents, 1994, History Comes to Life, !995, The Western Pursuit of the American Dream, 2005; co-editor: Autographs and Manuscripts: A Collector's Manual, 1978 (Outstanding Reference Book award ALA); contbr. numerous articles in field to mags. and profl. jours. Trustee D-Day Mus., New Orleans, 1998, Youth Enrichment Svcs., Boston, 1998, William J. Donovan Meml., N.Y., 1998, Churchill Mus., London, 2000, Churchill Ctr., Washington, 2008. Recipient Dept. Justice award, 1991. Fellow Manuscript Soc. (bd. dirs. 1968-74, pres. 1972-74); mem. Assn. Internat. de Bibliophilie Paris, Grolier Club, Morgan Libr. (fellow), Army and Navy Club, Am. Antiquarian Soc., Bohemian Club (San Francisco), Appalachian Mountain Club (trustee 2000), Explorers Club, Saville Club (London), Spl. Forces Club (London). Avocation: ski racing. Office: Kenneth W Rendell Inc 46 Eliot St Natick MA 01760-6042 also: 989 Madison Ave New York NY 10021-1825

RENDELL, MARJORIE O., federal judge; b. 1947; m. Edward G. Rendell, 1971; 1 child, Jesse. BA, U. Pa., 1969; postgrad., Georgetown U., 1970—71; JD, Villanova U., 1973; LLD (hon.), Phila. Coll. Textile and Sci., 1992, Dickinson Coll., 2009. Ptnr. Duane, Morris & Heckscher, Phila., 1972—93; judge US Dist. Ct. (ea. dist.) Pa., 1994—97, US Ct. Appeals (3d cir.), Phila., 1997—. Mem. Am. Jud. Soc., Fed. Judges Assn. Asst. to dir. ann. giving Dept. Devel. U. Pa., 1973—78; mem. adv. bd. Chestnut Hill Nat. Bank/East Falls Adv. Bd.; mem. alternative dispute resolution com. mediation divsn. Ea. Dist. Pa. Bankruptcy Conf.; active Acad. Vocal Arts, Market St. East Improvement Assn., Pa.'s Campaign for Choice, Phila. Friends Outward Bound; vice chair Ave. of Arts, Inc.; vice chair bd. trustees Vis. Nurse Assn. Greater Phila.; bd. mem. Alumni Trust, U. Penn. Mem.: ABA, Phila. Bar Found. (bd. dirs.), Phila. Bar Assn. (bd. dirs. young lawyers sect. 1973—78), Pa. Bar Assn., Am. Bankruptcy Inst., Internat. Women's Forum, Forum Exec. Women, Phi Beta Kappa. Office: US Courthouse 601 Market St Rm 21613 Philadelphia PA 19106-1715*

RENDELL, RUTH BARBARA (BARBARA VINE), writer; b. Feb. 17, 1930; d. Arthur Grasemann and Ebba Kruse; m. Donald Rendell, 1950; 1 son. Student, Loughton County High Sch., Eng. Author: From Doon with Death, 1964, To Fear a Painted Devil, 1965, Vanity Dies Hard, 1965 (pub. in US as In Sickness and in Health, 1966), A New Lease of Death, 1967 (pub. in US as Sins of the Father, 1970), Wolf to the Slaughter, 1967, The Secret House of Death, 1968, The Best Man to Die, 1969, A Guilty Thing Surprised, 1970, One Across, Two Down, 1971, No More Dying Then, 1971, Murder Being Once Done, 1972, Some Lie and Some Die, 1973, The Face of Trespass, 1974, Shake Hands Forever, 1975, A Demon in my View, 1976 (Gold Dagger award Crime Writers Assn. Eng. 1977), A Judgement in Stone, 1977, A Sleeping Life, 1978, Make Death Love Me, 1979, The Lake of Darkness, 1980 (British Nat. Book award 1981), Put on by Cunning, 1981 (pub in US as Death Notes, 1981), Master of the Moor, 1982, The Speaker of Mandarin, 1983, The Killing Doll, 1984, The Tree of Hands, 1984 (Silver Dagger award Crime Writers Assn. Eng. 1984), An Unkindness of Ravens, 1985, Live Flesh, 1986 (Gold Dagger award Crime Writers Assn. Eng. 1986), Heartstones, 1987, Talking to Strange Men, 1987, The Veiled One, 1988, The Bridesmaid, 1989, Ruth Rendell's Suffolk, 1989, (with Colin Ward) Undermining the Central Line, 1989, Going Wrong, 1990, The Crocodile Bird, 1993, Kissing the Gunner's Daughter, 1992, Simisola, 1994, The Reason Why: An Anthology of the Murderous Mind, 1995, The Keys to the Street, 1996, Road Rage, 1997, A Sight for Sore Eyes, 1998, Harm Done, 1999, The Babes in the Wood, 2002, Adam and Eve and Pinch Me, 2001, The Rottweiler, 2003, Thirteen Steps Down, 2004, End in Tears, 2005, The Water's Lovely, 2006, The Thief, 2006, Not in the Flesh, 2007, Portobello, 2008, (short story collections): The Fallen Curtain, 1976 (Edgar Allen Poe award Mystery Writers Assn. America 1976), Means of Evil, 1979, The Fever Tree, 1982, The New Girl Friend, 1985, The New Girlfriend, 1985, The Copper Peacock, 1991, Blood Lines, 2005, Piranha to Scurfy, 2000, Collected Short Stories Vol. 1, 2006, Collected Short Stories Vol. 2, 2008, (as Barbara Vine): A Dark-Adapted Eye, 1985 (Edgar Allen Poe award Mystery Writers Assn. America 1986), A Fatal Inversion, 1987 (Gold Dagger award Crime Writers Assn. Eng. 1987), The House of Stairs, 1989, Gallowglass, 1990, King Solomon's Carpet, 1991, Asta's Book, 1993, No Night is Too Long, 1994, The Brimstone Wedding, 1995, The Chimney-sweeper's Boy, 1998, Grasshopper, 2000, The Blood Doctor, 2002, The Minotaur, 2005, The Birthday Present, 2008; editor: A Warning to the Curious: The Ghost Stories of M.R. James, 1986, (with others) Women of Mystery, 1993. Recipient Sunday Times award for lit. excellence, 1990, Cartier Diamond Dagger for lifetime's achievement in field, 1991, Grand Master award, Mystery Writers America, 1997, Mystery Ink Gumshoe Lifetime Achievement award, 2004. Avocations: reading, walking, opera. Office: c/o Peter Matson Sterling Lord Literistic Inc 65 Bleecker St New York NY 10012

RENDICH, ANA, painter, collage artist; arrived in U.S., 1988; d. Ernesto Pedro Rendich and Maria Elena Romero de Rendich; m. Glenn D. Millis, Dec. 31, 1993; children: Sara C. Millis, Amy C. Millis, Sophie A. Millis. Student, Sch. Art U. Salvador, Buenos Aires, 1979—81, Inst. Superior del Teatro Colon, 1980—81; M Victor Callegary, Buenos Aires, 1981; M in Franco Zeffirelli with master class, NYC, 1996. Exhibitions include Cork Gallery Lincoln Ctr., NYC, 2002—05, Brush Strokes Art Gallery, Fredericksburg, Va. Mem.: Art First Gallery, Nat. Coll. Soc. Roman Catholic. Achievements include being the first South American painter to specialize in miniature painting. Avocations: art, opera. Personal E-mail: anamrendich@comcast.net.

RENDLEN, CHARLES EARNEST, III, (SKETCH RENDLEN), federal judge, lawyer; b. Hannibal, Mo., Aug. 17, 1950; s. Charles Earnest and Shirley Anne (Raible) R.; m. Susan L. David, Aug. 14, 1976; 1 child, Lindsey D. BS magna cum laude, William Jewell Coll., 1972; JD, U. Mo., 1976. Bar: Mo., U.S. Ct. Claims, U.S. Dist. Ct. (ea. and we. dists.) Mo., U.S. Tax Ct., U.S. Ct. Appeals (8th and Fed. cirs.), U.S. Supreme Ct. Assoc. The Rendlen Law Firm, P.C. (formerly Rendlen, Rendlen, Redington & Bastian, P.C.), Hannibal, Mo., 1976—79, ptnr., 1979—91, mng. ptnr, 1991—2003; US trustee, Reg. 13, Exec. Office US Trustees US Dept. Justice, 2003—06; judge US Bankruptcy Ct. (ea. dist.) Mo., St. Louis, 2006—. Mem. com. for jud. redistricting Mo. Supreme Ct., 1991-92, civil rules com., 1990-92; vice-chmn. worker compensation sect. Mo. Bar, 1992—. Co-author: Hedonics, 1992. Coord. Danforth for Senator, Marion County, 1976, 82, 88; chmn. Marion County Rep. Com., 1976-80, state com. 1992—; field worker Re-Elect the Pres., Mo., 1972; bd. dirs. Mennonite Home Assn., Inc., v.p., 1986—; v.p., bd. dirs. Beth Haven Terrace, Inc., 1986—, Beth Haven Group Homes, 1988—, Beth Haven Mgmt. Svcs., 1986—; bd. dirs. Hannibal Regional Hosp., sec., 1987-89. Mem. Rotary (pres. 1985-86). Avocations: golf, sailing. Office: Thomas F Eagleton US Courthouse 111 S Tenth St Rm 4380 Saint Louis MO 63102

RENDL-MARCUS, MILDRED, artist, economist; b. May 30, 1928; d. Julius and Agnes (Hokr) Rendl; m. Edward Marcus, Aug. 10, 1956. BS, NYU, 1948, MBA, 1950; PhD, Radcliffe Coll., 1954. Economist GE, 1953-56, Bigelow-Sanford Carpet Co., Inc., 1956-58; instr. econs. Hunter Coll. CUNY, 1959-60, Columbia U., 1960-61, rschr., 1961-63; sr. economist Nat. Indsl. Conf. Bd., 1963-66; asst. prof. Pace Coll., 1964-66; assoc. prof. Borough of Manhattan C. of C. CUNY, 1966-71, prof., 1972-85. Lectr. econs. CCNY, 1953-58; vis. prof. Fla. Internat. U., 1986; bd. dirs. N.Y.C. Coun. on Econ. Edn.; coun. mem. Harvard Mus. Natural History, 2002-04; assoc. mem. Allied Artists Am., Inc., 2004—; cons. in field. Exhibited group shows at in New Canaan Art Show, 1982-85, Am. Soc. Bus. and Behavioral Scis., 1990-96, New Cannan Soc. for Arts Ann., 1983, 85, New Canaan Arts, 1985, Silvermine Galleries, 1986, Stamford Art Assn., 1987, Phoenix Gallery, 1988, N.Y.C., Parkview Point Gallery, 1982-89, Miami Beach, Fla., 1982-89, Art Complex, New Canaan, Miami Beach, 1985—, Lever House, N.Y.C., 1990, Cork Gallery, Lincoln Ctr., N.Y.C., 1990, Women's Caucus for Art, San Antonio, 1990, Artist's Equity, Broome St. Gallery, N.Y.C., 1991, Greater Hartford Architecture Conservancy, 1991, N.H. Arts Ctr., 1997, Just Originals Art Web, Albuquerque, 1999, Ward-Nasse Gallery, N.Y.C., 2000—, Art Complex Gallery, Las Vegas, 2000-, Liliana Fine Art Gallery, Lenox, Mass., 2003—, Artists Gallery, Chelsea, N.Y.C., 2003, Nat. Assn. Women Artists, 2003—, 115-Yr. Anniversary Show, World Trade Ctr., N.Y.C., 2004, Pen and Brush Non-Mem. Show, 2004, Allied Artists Am., N.Y.C., 2005, Nat. Assn. Women Artists, N.Y.C., 2005, Catherine Lorillard Wolfe Art Club, 2005 (Rendl Drawing award 2006, 07), Audubon Artists, N.Y.C., 2005, Real Art Ways Gallery, Hartford, 2005, 06, 07, 08, Karpeles Mus., N.Y., 2006, Port of Call Gallery, Warwick, N.Y., 2006; artist participant Nat. Mus. Women in the Arts-Art Auction: Women Painters, Washington, 2007, RENDL Art Complex Las Vegas, Nev., 2000-07, Art Complex Gallery LVNY, Las Vegas, 2008-09; author (with E. Marcus) Investment and Development of Tropical Africa, 1959, International Trade and Finance, 1965, Monetary and Banking Theory, 1965, Economics, 1969, Economic Progress and the Developing World, 1970, Economics, 1978, Fine Art with Many Equilibrium Prices, 1995; editor Women in the Arts Found. Newsletter, 1986-92; contbr. articles to profl. jours. Founder Rendl Fund for Slavic Art, Mus. of Modern Art, NYC, 1999—, Harvard U. Art Mus. Fund for Slavic Art, Cambridge, 2000—, Harvard Mus. Natural History, Peabody Mus. Archeology and Ethnology, Rendl Fund for the Conservation of Slavic Artifacts, 2000—, Rendl Fund for the Conservation of the Ware Collection of Blaschka Glass Models of Plants, 2001—; mem. mus. coun. Harvard Mus. Natural History, 2001—; founder Rendl Fund for Czech Art, 2006—, Met. Mus. Art, NYC. Recipient Merit award Manhattan Arts Internat., 1998, Excellence award 1998, Artist Showcase award Manhattan Arts Internat., 1999; Dean Bernice Brown Cronkhite fellow Radcliffe Coll., 1950-51, Anne Radcliffe Econ. Rsch. Sub-Sahara Africa fellow, 1958-59; fellow Gerontol. Assn. Mem. AAUW, Internat. Schumpeter Econs. Soc. (founding), Met. Econ. Assns. (sec. 1954-56), Indsl. Rels. Rsch. Assn., Women's Econ. Roundtable (program planning com.), N.Y.C. Women in Arts, Allied Social Sci. Assn. (artist 1994), Allied Artists Am. Inc. (assoc.), NYU Grad. Sch. Bus. Adminstrn. Alumni (sec. 1956-58), Radcliffe Club, Women's City Club (art and landmarks com.), Met. Mus. Arts.

RENDOCK, MARY KAY, elementary school educator; b. Conn. m. Doug Rendock; 2 children. AA in Early Childhood Edn., Becker Jr. Coll., 1983; BA in Elem. Edn., Ea. Conn. Univ., 1985; MS in Ednl. Tech. and Media, Ctrl. Conn. State Univ., 1996. Tchr. Bloomfield (Conn.) Sch. Sys., 1985—, J. P. Vincent Elem. Sch., Bloomfield Mid. Sch.; now tchr., fifth grade team leader Carmen Arace Intermediate Sch., Bloomfield, Conn. Named Conn. Tchr. of Yr., 2006. Office: Carmen Arace Intermediate Sch 390 Park Ave Bloomfield CT 06002 E-mail: mkrendock@sbcglobal.net.

RENDON, JOSE RUBEN, library director; s. Ruben and Maria Ines Rendon; m. Sylvia Salazar, May 22, 1982; children: Steven Richard, Veronica Elaine, Kathryn Yvette. BS, Tex. A&M U., Coll. Sta., 1975; MLS, U. Tex., Austin, 1977. Dir. libr. Brownsville Pub. Libr., Tex., 1992—94, Harlingen Pub. Libr., Tex., 1994—. Head libr. Harlingen CISD, Tex., 1986—92. Cabinet sec., region chmn., zone chmn., pres., sec., dir. Lions Club Internat., Harlingen, Tex., 1980—. Office: Harlingen Pub Libr 410 76 Dr Harlingen TX 78550 Office Phone: 956-216-5803. Office Fax: 956-430-6654.

RENEAU, MARVIN BRYAN, military officer, business professor; b. Wharton, Tex., Jan. 22, 1939; s. Marvin Cecil Reneau and Bessie Marie (Petrash) Ward; m. Doris Faye Martin, Jan. 2, 1957; children: Terran Bryan, Kevin Troy, Shannon Lyn. BS, U. Tampa, Fla.; MS, Am. Tech. U., U. Cen. Tex.; MA, PhD, Webster Coll., Madison U. Mil. tng.: armor advanced noncommd. officer course The Armor Sch., armor officer basic course, armor officer advanced course, sr. officer preventive maintenance course; co. level motor officer course Fourth US Army Acad.; USATECOM human factors engring. appreciation course US Army Arctic Test Ctr., USATECOM test report preparation course, USATECOM work simplification course; jungle ops. course US Army Sch. of Americas; race rels. awareness course Wannsee Berlin Race Rels. Inst.; facilities engring. mgmt. course The Engr. Sch., engr. officer advanced course; attended Command & Gen. Staff Coll.; RCNS course Nat. Def. U.; res. forces course Air Command and Staff Coll.; def. strategy course US Army War Coll.; bn., brigade pre-command course ARRTC; allied command Europe staff officer course, The NATO Sch. SHAPE; ordnance officer advanced course, The Ordnance Ctr. and Sch.; civil affairs officer advanced course US Army Spl. Warfare Ctr. and Sch.; dynamics of internat. terrorism course USAF Spl. Ops. Sch. Commd. 2d lt. US Army, 1964, advanced through grade to col., co. comdr., armor Vietnam, 1968, engring. ops. mgr. Ft. Sam Houston, Tex., chief, tng. support div., 1989, sr. tng. analyst Ft. Sam Houston. Cons. US Army C.E., Ft. Worth, 1978—, Army Rsch. Inst., Boise, Idaho, 1987—, Army Tng. Bd., Ft. Monroe, Va., 1987—; asst. prof. bus. Incarnate Word Coll., San Antonio. Author: Beneath the Canopy, 1978, And Where the Rockets Can't Reach; contbr. articles to profl. jours. Mem. Army Mut. Aid Fund, Arlington, Va., 1968; acad. advisor Incarnate Word Coll., San Antonio, 1981; vol. counselor DAV, San Antonio, 1980; referral agt. United Way, San Antonio, 1988. Comdr. Regular Army USAR. Decorated Bronze Star, Purple Heart, 3 Meritorious medals, 2 Air medals (1 for valor), 3 Army Commendation medals, Army Achievement medal, Combat Infantryman badge, Rep. of Vietnam Cross of Gallantry with palm, Legion of Merit, Meritorious Civilian Svc. medal, commd. admiral in Tex. Navy, named to Hon. Order Ky. Cols., named to Gunars Abeles Book. Mem. Am. Mktg. Assn., ASTD, Assn. US Army, Mil. Order of Purple Heart, NSW Leagues, Fed. Mgrs. Assn., SW Mktg. Assn., Res. Officer Assn., Orders and Medals Soc. Am., Orders and Medals Rsch. of Great Britain, 34th Armor Regiment (disting. mem.), Berlin US Mil. Vets. Assn., 2d Bn. 34th Armor Assn., 25th Inf. Divsn. Assn., (Mil. Order Purple Heart Alamo Chpt., 1836, trustee), Orders and Medals Soc. Am., Alpha Kappa Psi (sponsor). Methodist. Achievements include conducted and planned check test of Sheridan Weapon System, M551 under winter artic conditions (-25°F thru -62°F) provided secret classified report of results and recommended technical systems improvement; instrumental in the development and implementation of battle projection simulation program for US Army Reserve components. Avocation: researching and collecting historical artifacts. Home: PO Box 39292 San Antonio TX 78218-1292

RENEE, CHERYL, literature and language professor; b. Spartanburg, SC, Mar. 24, 1969; d. Linda D. and Harold D. Felton; children: Ari A., Chrysta A. AA, Brevard CC, Melbourne, Fla., 1991; BA, Rollins Coll., Winter Pk., Fla., 1993; MA, U. Ctrl. Fla., Orlando, 1995. Adj. instr. English Valencia CC, Orlando, 1994—2000; vis. and adj. instr. English U. Ctrl. Fla., 1994—2000; academic advisor Brevard CC, 2001—03, asst. prof. English, 2003—, program coord. English, 2003—. Mem.: FACC. Office: Brevard CC 3865 N Wickham Rd Melbourne FL 32935 Business E-Mail: reneec@brevardcc.edu.

RENEHAN, RICHARD WILLIAM, lawyer; b. Boston, Dec. 30, 1933; s. Francis Xavier and Mary (Sullivan) R.; m. Mary B. Brophy, Feb. 17, 1962; children: Anne M., Joan F., Richard W., Jr., Mark D. BA, Boston Coll., 1955; LLB, Harvard U., 1958. Bar: Mass. 1958, U.S. Dist. Ct. Mass. 1959, U.S. Ct. Appeals (1st cir.) 1964, U.S. Supreme Ct. 1971. Assoc. Peabody, Koufman & Brewer, Boston, 1959-64; ptnr. Hill & Barlow, Boston; dir., profl. liability, securities litig. Goulston & Storrs, Boston. Mem. Gov's Select Com. on Jud. Needs, Boston, 1978-79, Joint Bar Com. on Jud. Appointments, 1979-84, Gov's Jud. Nominating Coun., Boston, 1987-90. Mem. Milton (Mass.) Housing Authority, 1979-86, chmn., 1981-85. Fellow Am. Bar Found, Am. Coll. Trial Lawyers; mem. ABA, Mass. Bar Assn., Boston Bar Assn. (pres. 1985-86). Office: Goulston & Storrs 400 Atlantic Ave Boston MA 02110-3333 Office Phone: 617-574-4024. Office Fax: 617-574-7593. Business E-Mail: rrenehan@goulstonstorrs.com.

RENEKER, MAXINE HOHMAN, librarian; b. Chgo., Dec. 2, 1942; d. Roy Max and Helen Anna Christina (Anacker) Hohman; m. David Lee Reneker, June 20, 1964 (dec. Dec. 1979); children: Sarah Roeder, Amy Johannah, Benjamin Congdon. BA, Carleton Coll., 1964; MA, U. Chgo., 1970; DLS, Columbia U., 1992. Asst. reference libr. U. Chgo. Libraries, 1965-66; classics libr. U. Chgo. Libr., 1967-70, asst. head acquisitions, 1970-71, personnel libr., 1971-73; personnel/bus. libr. U. Colo. Libr., Boulder, 1978-80; asst. dir. sci. and engring. div. Columbia U., NYC, 1981-85; assoc. dean of univ. librs. for pub. svcs. Ariz. State U. Libr., Tempe, 1985-89; dir. instrnl. and rsch. svcs. Stanford (Calif.) Univ. Librs., 1989-90; assoc. provost for libr. and info. resources Naval Postgrad. Sch., Monterey, Calif., 1993—2005, prof. emerita, 2005—. Acad. libr. mgmt. intern Coun. on Libr. Resources, 1980-81; chmn. univ. librs. sect. Assn. Coll. and Rsch. Librs., 1989-90. Contbr. articles to profl. jours. Trustee Monterey Pub. Libr. Rsch. grantee Coun. on Library Resources, Columbia U., 1970-71, fellow, 1990-92. Mem. ALA, Am. Soc. Info. Sci., Sherlockian Scion Soc., Phi Beta Kappa, Beta Phi Mu. Home: 740 Dry Creek Rd Monterey CA 93940-4208

RENFREW, ANDREW COLIN (LORD RENFREW OF KAIMSTHORN), archaeologist, educator, director; b. July 25, 1937; s. Archibald and Helena Douglas (Savage) R.; m. Jane Margaret Ewbank, Apr. 21, 1965; children: Helena Margaret, Alban Robert, Magnus Archibald. BA, St. John's Coll., Cambridge U., 1962, MA, 1964, PhD, 1965, ScD, 1976. Lectr. archaeology U. Sheffield, 1965-72; prof. U. Southampton, 1972-81; Disney prof. archaeology Cambridge U., 1981—2004; dir. McDonald Inst. Archeol. Rsch., 1990—2004. Vis. lectr. UCLA, 1967; fellow St. John's Coll., 1981-86, hon. fellow 2004-; master Jesus Coll., Cambridge, 1986-97, fellow, 1997-04, hon. fellow, 2004—; George Grant McCurdy lectr. Harvard U., 1977; Patten lectr. Ind. U., 1982; field excavations in Saliagos, 1961-64, Sitagroi, 1968-70, Quanterness, Orkney, 1972-74, Phylakopi, Melos, 1974-76, Dhaskalio Kavos Keros, 2006-08. Author (with J. D. Evans): Excavations at Saliagos Near Antiparos, 1968 in Orkney, 1979; author: Problems in European Prehistory, 1979; author: (with J. M. Wagstaff) An Island Polity, 1982; author: Approaches to Social Archaeology, 1984, The Prehistory of Orkney, 1985, The Archaeology of Cult, 1985, Archaeology and Language, 1987; author: (with G. Daniel) The Idea of Prehistory, 1988; author: The Cycladic Spirit, 1991; author: (with P. Bahn) Archaeology, 1991; author: Loot, Legitimacy and Ownership: The Ethical Crisis in Archaeology, 2000, Figuring It Out, 2003, Prehistory, 2007; editor: The Explanation of Culture Change, 1973, British Prehistory, 1974, Transformations: Mathematical Approaches to Culture Change, 1979, Theory and Explanation in Archaeology, 1982; presenter (TV films) The Tree That Put the Clock Back, 1970, Islands Out of Time, 1973, Orkney Underground, 1974, Aphrodite's Other Island, 1977, Bronze Age Blast Off, 1978, Lost Kings of the Desert, 1980, The Emperor's Immortal Army, 1981, City of the Dead, 1982, Who Built Stonehenge, 1986. Trustee Brit. Mus., 1991-01. With RAF, 1956-58. Recipient European Sci. Found. Latsis Prize, 2003, Rivers Meml. medal Royal Anthrop. Inst., 1979, Huxley Meml. medal, 1991, Balzan prize, 2004; named Fgn. Assoc. NAS, 1996; elevated to peerage, 1991. Fellow Brit. Acad., Soc. Antiquaries London, Royal Soc. Edinburgh (hon.), Austrian Acad. Sci., German Archeol. Inst.; mem. Am. Philos. Soc. (fgn.), Athenaeum. Office: Dept Archaeology Downing St Cambridge CB2 3DZ England also: House of Lords London SW1A 0PW England Office Phone: 01223-333521. Business E-Mail: mcdrenf@hermes.cam.ac.uk.

RENFREW, MALCOLM MACKENZIE, chemist, educator; b. Spokane, Wash., Oct. 12, 1910; s. Earl Edgar and Elsie Pauline (MacKenzie) R.; m. Carol Joy Campbell, June 26, 1938. BS, U. Idaho, 1932, MS, 1934, D.Sc., 1976; PhD, U. Minn., 1938. Asst. physics U. Idaho, 1932-33, Asst. chemistry, 1933-35, U. Minn., 1935-37, duPont fellow, 1937-38; research chemist plastics dept. duPont Co., 1938-44, supr. process devel., 1944-46, supr. product devel., 1946-49; head chem. research dept., research labs. Gen. Mills, Inc., 1949-52, dir. chem. research, 1952-53, dir. chem. research and devel., 1953-54; dir. research and devel. Spencer Kellogg & Sons, Inc., 1954-58; phys. sci. div. head, prof. chemistry U. Idaho, 1959-73, prof., 1973-76, emeritus, 1976—; dir. U. Idaho (Coll. Chem. Cons. Service), 1969-76. On leave as sr. staff assoc. Adv. Coun. Coll. Chemistry, Stanford, 1967-68; mem. materials adv. bd. Nat. Rsch. Coun., 1963-67; exec. v.p. Idaho Rsch. Found., 1977-78, patent dir., 1978-88. Editor: Safety in the Chemical Laboratory, Vol. IV, 1981, (with Peter Ashbrook), Safe Laboratories: Principles and Practices for Design and Remodeling, 1991; safety editor: Jour. Chem. Edn, 1977-91; Contbr. to tech. and trade publs. on plastics, coatings, safety, chem. edn. Recipient Excellence in Teaching award Chem. Mfrs. Assn., 1977, Outstanding Achievement award U. Minn., 1977, Disting. Idahoan award U. Idaho Alumni Assn., 2006; named to U. Idaho Hall of Fame, 1977, Idaho Hall of Fame, 1996. Fellow AAAS, Am. Inst. Chemists; mem. Am. Chem. Soc. (councilor 1948, 59, 67-89, chmn. paint varnish and plastics div. 1949, chmn. chem. mktg. and econs. div. 1958-59, chmn. chem. health and safety div. 1982, James Flack Norris award 1976, Chem. Health and Safety award 1985, Mosher award 1986), Am. Inst. Chem. Engrs., Soc. Chem. Industry, Phi Beta Kappa, Sigma Xi, Phi Kappa Phi, Sigma Pi Sigma, Phi Gamma Delta (disting. Fiji 1986). Presbyterian. Office: U Idaho Coll Sci Dept Chemistry PO Box 442343 Moscow ID 83844-2343 Home: 640 N Eisenhower,Good Samaritan Apt 212 Moscow ID 83843 Business E-Mail: renfrew@uidaho.edu.

RENFRO, PATRICIA ELISE, library director, academic administrator; b. Nelson, Lancashire, Eng. d. Henry Lawrence and Maud (Thompson) Candlin; m. Charles Gilliland Renfro, June 21, 1969; children: Rebecca Elise, James Lawrence. BA in English and History with honors, U. York, Eng., 1966; acad. postgrad. diploma, U. London, 1968; MA in History, U. Ky., 1981. Libr. asst. Holborn br. London Borough of Camden Pub. Librs., London, 1966-67, sr. asst. libr., 1968-69; dep. acquisitions libr. Folger Shakespeare Libr., Washington, 1969-70; cataloger Libr. Co. of Phila., 1970-72; reference libr. U. Pa. Librs., 1972-73, U. Ky. Librs., 1975-76, head of reference svcs., 1976-78; exec. sec. U. Ky. Libr. Assocs., U. Ky., 1979-80; reference libr. U. Pa., 1982-83, head circulation svcs. Van Pelt Libr., 1983-85, asst. dir. librs. for pub. svcs., 1985-89, assoc. dir. librs., 1989—2000; dep. univ. libr. Columbia U., NYC, 2000—. Mem. programs adv. com. Rsch. Librs. Group, 1991-92; mem. circulation interchange com. NISO 1999-2002; bd. dirs. N.Y. State Higher Edn. Initiative, 2004-07. Contbr. articles to profl. jours. Mem. ALA, Assn. Coll. and Rsch. Librs. (rsch. com. 1992-94, ULS program com. 2005). Office Phone: 212-854-2226.

RENGER, JOHN JOSEPH, neurobiologist; b. Buffalo Center, Iowa, Dec. 8, 1968; s. Joseph William and Rose Elaine (Steinberg) R. BS in Biology, U. Iowa, 1991, postgrad., 1991—. Rsch. and teaching asst. U. Iowa, Iowa City, 1991—. Mem. grad. student steering com. U. Iowa, 1993-94. Contbr. articles to profl. jours. Cpl. USAR, 1985-91. Mem. Soc. for Neurosci., AAAS. Republican. Roman Catholic. Achievements include demonstration that enzyme calcium/calmodulia dependent kinase II directly affects neuronal plasticity invivo. Office: Merck and Co Inc WP42 770 Sumneytown Pike West Point PA 19486

REN-HEIDENREICH, LIFEN, engineering executive; married. Sr scientist Organon, Cambridge, Mass., 2005—06; sr. dir. Surexam Bio-Tech. Co. Ltd., Guangzhou, China, 2008—. Office: Surexam Bio-Tech Co Ltd 80 Lan Yue Rd Sci City Guangzhou 510663 China Business E-Mail: lifen.ren@surexam.com.

RENK, PAMELA JEAN, counselor, psychotherapist, small business owner; b. Pitts., Feb. 23, 1956; d. James Voris and Nancy Marie (Vessels) McClain; m. Randy Allen Renk, June 20, 1976; 1 child: Chanelle Renk. BA in Social & Behav. Scis. summa cum, Ind. State U., 1982; M in Clin. and Counseling Psychology, Calif. State U., San Bernardino, 1986. Cert. marriage, family and child counselor Bd. Behavioral Sci. Examiners. Intern counselor U. Calif., Riverside, 1984-85, Fontana (Calif.) Med. Group, 1986-87, Harmonium Inc., Mira Mesa, Calif., 1988-89; owner, marriage family child counselor South Bay Counseling, San Clemente, Calif., 1989—. Spkr. in field. Mem. Calif. Assn. Family Therapists. Avocations: skiing, horseback riding, in-line skating, reading, theater. Office: South Bay Counseling 302 N El Camino Real # 210 San Clemente CA 92672-4778 Office Phone: 949-361-7880.

RENKA, ROBERT JOSEPH, computer science educator, consultant; b. Summit, NJ, Dec. 28, 1947; s. John and Elizabeth (Pierce) R. BA in Computer Sci., BS in Math., U. Tex., 1976, MA in Math., 1979, PhD in Computer Sci., 1981. Numerical analyst Oak Ridge (Tenn.) Nat. Lab., 1981-84; asst. prof. computer sci. U. North Tex., Denton, 1984-89, assoc. prof. computer sci., 1989-99, prof. computer sci., 1999—. Cons. in field. Contbr. articles to profl. jours. With USN, 1967-69, Vietnam. Rsch. grantee U. North Tex., 1984-89, NSF, 1990-93, Nat. Security Agy., 1999—. Mem. Assn. for Computing Machinery (algorithms editor 1988-94, editor-in-chief 1989-94), Soc. Indsl. and Applied Math. Avocations: racquetball, rock climbing. Home: 1700 Kendolph Dr Denton TX 76205-6931 Office: U North Tex Dept Computer Sci and Engring PO Box 311366 Denton TX 76203-1366 Home Phone: 940-566-5487; Office Phone: 940-565-2767.

RENKIEWICZ, MARTIN A., federal agency administrator; b. 1954; married; 2 children. Grad., U. RI, 1976. With Immigration & Naturalization Svc. US Dept. Justice; with US Nat. Ctrl. Bur. INTERPOL, US Dept. Justice, 1992—, sr. rep. from US Dept. Justice, asst. dir. Alien Fugitive Divsn., 2002—03, dep. dir., 2003—06, dir., 2006—. Office: INTERPOL US Nat Ctrl Bur 1301 New York Ave NW 4th Fl Washington DC 20530 Office Phone: 202-616-7820. Office Fax: 202-616-1048. E-mail: martin.renkiewicz@usdoj.gov.

RENKIS, ALAN ILMARS, plastics formulating company executive; b. Preili, Latvia, Apr. 16, 1938; arrived in U.S., 1950, naturalized, 1958; s. Joseph and Malvine (Sturitis) R.; m. Inara Balodis, July 15, 1961; children: Martin Alan, Laura Alise. BSChemE, Pa. State U., State College, 1960. Staff product devel. and tech. svc. divsn. Diamond Alkali Co., Painesville, Ohio, 1960-63; tech. dir. G.S. Plastics Co., Cleve., 1963; founder, pres. Thermoclad Co., Erie, Pa., 1963—, Riverside, Calif., 1972-80, Ocala, Fla., 1985—. Developer comml. PVC resins for formulating fluidized bed and electrostatic coating powders; formulations and compounding techniques. Mem. World Pres. Orgn., Am. Latvian Assn., Erie Yacht Club, Kahkwa Club, Sigma Pi, Fraternitas Metropolitana. Home: 214 Crystal Point Dr Erie PA 16505 Office: Thermoclad Co 361 W 11th St Erie PA 16501-1703 Office Phone: 814-456-1243. Business E-Mail: arenkis@thermoclad.com.

RENNER, ANDREW IHOR, surgeon; b. Buenos Aires, Aug. 1, 1951; came to U.S., 1956; s. Vladimir and Emelia R.; m. Cristina Sasyk, Apr. 17, 1982. MD, Albert Einstein Coll. Medicine, 1975. Diplomate Am. Bd. Surgery. Pvt. practice gen. surgery, Burbank, Calif.; chief of staff Providence-St. Joseph Med. Ctr., 2005, 2006; chief of quality assurance Providence St. Joseph Hosp., 2007—08. Chmn. dept. surgery St. Joseph Hosp., Burbank, 1995-97, vice chief of staff Providence St. Joseph Med. Ctr., Burbank, 2003-04, chief of staff, 2005-06. Fellow ACS, Internat. Coll. Surgeons; mem. Am. Soc. Gen. Surgeons, L.A. Surg. Soc. Office: 2701 W Alameda Ave Ste 300 Burbank CA 91505-4408 Office Phone: 818-843-1492. Office Fax: 818-843-5283.

RENNER, BERND, literature and language professor; s. Erich and Ruth Renner. BA, Friedrich-Alexander U., Erlangen, Germany, 1988; MA, PhD, Princeton U., NJ, 2000. Asst. prof. Bklyn. Coll., 2002—06, Bernard H. Stern assoc. prof. humor studies, 2007—; asst. prof. Grad. Ctr., CUNY, NYC, 2003—06, assoc. prof., 2007—. Author: (book) Difficile est saturam non scribere: L'Hermeneutique de la satire rabelaisienne, 2007. Rsch. Abroad grant, PSC-CUNY Found., 2002—08. Fellow: Whiting Found. (Whiting Excellence Tchg. fellowship 2006); mem.: MLA, Sixteenth Century Studies Soc., Renaissance Soc. America (NYC) (outside evaluator 2005—). Avocation: travel. Office: Bklyn Coll 2900 Bedford Ave Brooklyn NY 11210 Office Fax: 718-951-4235. Business E-Mail: brenner@brooklyn.cuny.edu.

RENNER, JACQUELINE MARIE, industrial and wholesale supply company executive; b. NYC, Feb. 15, 1958; d. Ernest John and Patricia Aurora (Romano) R. BA in Chemistry, U. Pa., 1979; MBA, NYU, 1984. Research chemist Olin Corp., New Haven, 1979-81, comml. devel. mgr. Stamford, Conn., 1981-85, product mgr., 1985-87; comml. dir., N.Am. chemicals and catalysts Johnson Matthey, West Deptford, NJ, 1987-89; mktg. mgr. FMC Corp., Phila., 1989-91, strategic planning mgr. chemical products group, 1991-92, bus. dir. process additives divsn. Manchester, 1992-94, acquisition dir. Chgo., 1995—98; comml. dir. Monsanto Co., St. Louis, 1998—2000, v.p. e-business, 2000—02; v.p. and gen. mgr. Fisher Sci., Chgo., 2003—06; pres., Marmon Group Wells Lamont Corp., 2006—. Patentee novel functional fluids, 1981. Robert Bosch fellow, Germany, 1984-85; recipient, Outstanding Bd. Mem., Arts & Bus. Coun. Chgo., 2006. Office: Wells Lamont Corp 6640 W Touhy Ave Niles IL 60714 Office Phone: 312-504-4879.

RENNER, SWEN, zoologist; PhD, U. Goettingen, Germany, 2004. Rsch. assoc. Smithsonian's Nat. Zoo, Front Royal, Va., 2001—; conservation advisor BirdLife Internat., Hanoi, Vietnam, 2008—. Contbr. articles to profl. sci. jours. Mem.: Am. Ornitholgists' Union, Ecol. Soc. Am.

RENNERT, OWEN MURRAY, pediatrician, geneticist, educator; b. NYC, Aug. 8, 1938; s. David Rennert and Frieda (Weinsteiner) Sommer; m. Sandra Serota, Mar. 22, 1964; children: Laura, Rachel, Ian. BS, BA, U. Chgo., 1957, MD, 1961, MS in Biochemistry, 1963. Diplomate Am. Bd. Pediatrics, Am. Bd. Genetics, Am. Bd. Med. Genetics. Assoc. prof. pediatrics U. Fla. Coll. Medicine, Gainesville, 1968—70, assoc. prof. biochemistry, 1970—71, head instl. divsn. genetics, endocrinology and metabolism, 1970—78, prof. pediatrics, biochemistry and neurosci., 1971-78; prof. biochemistry, prof. and head dept. pediatrics U. Okla., Oklahoma City, 1977-88; chief pediatrics svc. and head genetics, sect. endocrinology and metabolism Okla. Children's Mem. Hosp., Oklahoma City, 1977-88; prof., chmn. dept. pediatrics Georgetown U. Sch. Medicine, Washington, 1988-98, prof. dept. biochemistry and molecular biology, 1995—98, prof. emeritus, 1998—2000; spl. asst. to dir. ctr. rsch. mothers and children Nat. Inst. Child Health Human Devel., NIH, Bethesda, Md., 1998—2000, dir. Ctr. Rsch. Mothers and Children, 2000, sci. dir. divsn. intramural rsch., 2000—. Co-author: Metabolism of Trace Metals in Man: Developmental Biology and Genetic Implications (2 vols.), 1984; contbr. articles to profl. jours. Bd. dirs. Children's Med. Rsch., Oklahoma City, 1984-88. Served to sr. surgeon USPHS, 1964-66. Named Clin. Scientist of Yr., Am. Assn. Clin. Scientists, 1978. Mem. Am. Pediatric Soc., Am. Acad. Pediatrics, Soc. Pediatric Research, Am. Coll. Clin. Nutrition, Biochem. Soc., Am. Soc. Molecular Biology and Biochemistry, Am. Coll. Med. Genetics, Am. Soc. Human Genetics. Office: NICHD/NIH Divsn Intramural Rsch 31 Center Dr Bldg 31 Rm 2A46 Bethesda MD 20892-2425 Home Phone: 301-299-6174; Office Phone: 301-594-5984. Business E-Mail: rennerto@mail.nih.gov.

RENNEY, TOM, professional hockey coach; b. Cranbrook, BC, Can., Mar. 1, 1955; m. Glenda Renney; children: Jessica, Jamie. Head coach Kamloops Blazers (WHL), 1991—93, Team Can., 1993—96, Vancouver Canucks, 1996—97; v.p. hockey Can. Nat. Team, 1998—99, head coach, v.p., 1999—2000; dir. player pers. NY Rangers, 2000—02, asst. coach, 2003—04, v.p. player devel., 2003—04, head coach, 2004—09; assoc. head coach Edmonton Oilers, 2009—. Head coach Team Canada, Lillehammer Olympic Games, 1992. Office: Edmonton Oilers Hockey Club 11230 - 110 St Edmonton AB T5G 3H7 Canada*

RENNIE, JOHN, editor-in-chief; b. 1959; BS in Biology, Yale U., 1981. With Harvard Med. Sch.; sci. writer various publs.; mem. bd. editors Sci. Am., 1989—94, editor-in-chief, 1994—, Sci. Am. Presents, 1998—. TV appearances include ABC World News Hour, ABC News Overnight, The Newshour with Jim Lehrer, Fox News Channel, Entertainment Tonight, Science Friday (National Public Radio), CBS Early Show; contbr. articles to profl. publications including The Economist, The New York Times, Longevity. Recipient Sagan award, Coun. Sci. Soc. Presidents, Navigator award, Potomac Inst. Policy Studies. Avocation: Karate. Office: Sci Am 415 Madison Ave New York NY 10017-1111 Office Phone: 212-754-0550. Business E-Mail: editors@sciam.com.

RENNINGER, MARY KAREN, retired librarian; b. Pitts., Apr. 30, 1945; d. Jack Burnell and Jane (Hammerly) Gunderman; m. Norman Christian Renninger, Sept. 3, 1965 (div. 1980); 1 child, David Christian. BA, U. Md., 1969, MA, 1972, M.L.S., 1975. Tchr. English West Carteret High Sch., Morehead City, NC, 1969-70; instr. in English U. Md., College Park, 1970-72; head network services Nat. Libr. Svc., Libr. of Congress, Washington, 1974-78, asst. for network support, 1978-80; mem. fed. women's program com. Libr. of Congress, Washington, 1978-80; chief libr. divsn. Dept. Vets. Affairs, Washington, 1980-90; chief serial and govt. publs. divsn. Libr. of Congress, Washington, 1991—2006, mem. fed. libr. com., 1980-90, mem. exec. adv. bd., 1985-90; ret., 2006. Mem. USBE pers. subcom., 1982-84; bd. regents Nat. Libr. of Medicine, 1986-90, mem. outreach panel, 1988-89; fed. libr. task force for 1990 White House Conf. on Librs., 1986-90; liaison to The White House Conf. Med. Libr. Assn., 1989-90. Recipient

Meritorious Svc. award Libr. of Congress, 1974, Spl. Achievement award, 1976, Performance award VA, ann. 1982-89, Adminstr.'s Commendation, 1985, Spl. Contbn. award, 1986. Mem. ALA (Govt. Documents Roundtable), Libr. Tech. Assn., Med. Libr. Assn. (govt. rels. com. 1985—), DC Libr. Assn., Soc. Applied Learning Tech., Med. Interactive Videodisc Consortium, Govt. Documents Roundtable, Knowledge Utilization Soc., Nat. Multimedia Assn. Am., US Tennis Assn., Phi Beta Kappa, Alpha Lambda Delta, Friends of Acadia Home: 840 College Pky Rockville MD 20850-1931 Personal E-mail: KarenRenninger@comcast.net.

RENNKE, HELMUT G., pathologist, educator; b. Valparaiso, Chile, Jan. 19, 1945; s. Erich and Gertrud Rennke; children: Stephanie, Christianne Phillips. MD, U. Chile, Santiago, 1971. Prof. pathology Harvard U. Med. Sch., Boston, 1974—; pathologist Brigham & Women's Hosp., Boston, 1974—. Author: (book) Renal Pathophysiology; actor: (book) The Essentials. Recipient Career Devel. award, NIH, 1979—84. Mem.: Renal Pathology Soc. (Jacob Churg award 2007). Office: Brigham and Women's Hosp 75 Francis St Boston MA 02115 Office Fax: 617-264-5223. Business E-Mail: hrennke@partners.org.

RENO, BRAD JEFFREY, political science educator; b. Garden City, Mich., Nov. 12, 1969; s. Llewellyn Kenneth and Martha E. (Johnston) R.; m. Amy Lynn Smith, July 27, 1996. BA in Polit. Sci. summa cum laude, U. Mich., Dearborn, 1993; MA in Polit. Sci., Mich. State U., 1996, postgrad., 1996—. Grad. asst. Mich. State U., East Lansing, 1993-95, instr., 1995—; rsch. dir. Hudson Inst., Lansing, Mich., 1997—. Contbr. articles to newspapers. Precinct del. Mich. Rep. Party, Westland, 1990-94. With U.S. Army, 1987-89. Angell fellow/scholar, 1991-93; H.B. Earhart Found. fellow, 1993-96. Mem. Am. Polit. Sci. Assn., Intercollegiate Studies Inst., Nat. Assn. Scholars. Avocations: herb gardening, classical music, wine tasting. Home: 320 Chamberlain Hill Rd Barre MA 01005-8865

RENO, JANET, former United States Attorney General; b. Miami, Fla., July 21, 1938; d. Henry and Jane (Wood) R. AB in Chemistry, Cornell U., 1960; LL.B., Harvard U., 1963. Bar: Fla. 1963. Assoc. Brigham & Brigham, 1963-67; ptnr. Lewis & Reno, 1967-71; staff dir. judiciary com. Fla. Ho. of Reps., Tallahassee, 1971-72; cons. Fla. Senate Criminal Justice Com. for Revision Fla.'s Criminal Code, spring 1973; adminstrv. asst. state atty. 11th Jud. Circuit Fla., Miami, 1973-76, state atty., 1978-93; ptnr. Steel Hector and Davis, Miami, 1976-78; atty. gen. US Dept. Justice, Washington, 1993-2001. Mem. jud. nominating commn. 11th Jud. Circuit Fla., 1976-78; chmn. Fla. Gov.'s Council for Prosecution Organized Crime, 1979-80; bd. dirs. The Innocence Project. Exec. prodr.: (albums) Song of America, 2007. Recipient Women First award YWCA, 1993, Harvard Law Sch. Assn. award, 2001; named to Nat. Women's Hall of Fame, 2000. Mem. ABA (Inst. Jud. Adminstrn. Juvenile Justice Standards Commn. 1973-76), Am. Law Inst., Am. Judicature Soc. (Herbert Harley award 1981), Dade County Bar Assn., Fla. Pros. Atty.'s Assn. (pres. 1984-86). Democrat. Office: Innocence Project 100 Fifth Ave, 3rd Fl New York NY 10011*

RENO, OTTIE WAYNE, former judge; b. Pike County, Ohio, Apr. 7, 1929; s. Eli Enos and Arbannah Belle (Jones) Reno; m. Janet Gay McCann, May 22, 1947; children: Jennifer Lynn, Lorna Victoria, Ottie Wayne II. A in Bus. Adminstrn., Franklin U., 1949; LLB, Franklin Law Sch., 1953; JD, Capital U., 1966; grad. Coll. Juvenile Justice, U. Nev., 1973. Bar: Ohio 1953. Practiced in Pike County; recorder Pike County, 1957-73, common pleas judge probate and juvenile divsn., 1973-79. Author: Story of Horseshoes, 1963, Pitching Championship Horseshoes, 1971; 2d rev. edit., 1975; author: The American Directory of Horseshoe Pitching, 1983, Ohio vs. Smith, Murder, 1990, Reno and Apsaalooka Survive Custer, 1996. Del. Dem. Nat. Conv., 1972, 1996; mem. Camp Creek precinct Dem. Ctrl. Com., 1956—72, 1983—90, 1999—2002; sec. Pike County Dem. Exec. Com., 1971—72, 1983—90, 1983—87, chmn., 1971—72, 1988—90; mem. Ohio Dem. Ctrl. Com., 1969—70; Dem. candidate 6th Ohio dist. U.S. Ho. of Reps., 1966; Dem. candidate 88th Ohio dist. Ohio Ho. of Reps., 1992; pres. Scioto Valley Local Sch. Dist., 1962—66. Recipient 6 Outstanding Jud. Svc. awards, Ohio Supreme Ct., Disting. Svc. award, Ohio Youth Commn., 1974; named 17 Times Horseshoe Pitching Champion, Ala.; named to Hall of Fame, Alabama Horseshoe Pitchers Assn., 1977, Ohio Horseshoe Pitchers Assn., 1978, Nat. Horseshoe Pitchers Assn., 1978, Ohio Sr. Olympics, 2008. Mem.: Pike County Bar Assn., Nat. Coun.Juvenile Ct. Judges, Ohio Bar Assn., Am. Legion. Mem. Ch. Of Christ In Christian Union. Home: 148 Reno Rd Lucasville OH 45648-9580

RENO, ROGER, lawyer; b. Rockford, Ill., May 16, 1924; s. Guy B. and Hazel (Kinnear) R.; m. Janice Marie Odelius, May 17, 1952 (dec. Aug. 2005); children: Susan Marie, Sheri Jan Reno-Rudolph, Michael Guy. Student, Kenyon Coll., 1943-44, Yale U., 1944, U. Wis., 1946; AB, Carleton Coll., 1947; LL.B., Yale U., 1950. Bar: Ill. 1950. Practiced in Rockford, 1950; assoc. firm Reno, Zahm, Folgate, Lindberg & Powell, 1950-56, partner, 1956-84; of counsel Reno & Zahm LLC, 1984—. Chmn. Amcore Fin. Inc., 1982-95; atty. Rockford Bd. Edn., 1955-64. Past pres., bd. dirs. Childrens Home Rockford; trustee Swedish-Am. Hosp. Assn., 1967-77, Keith Country Day Sch. Served to 1st lt. USAAF, 1943-46. Mem. ABA, Ill. Bar Assn., Winnebago County Bar Assn. (pres. 1979-80) Clubs: Forest Hills Country (Rockford). Methodist. Home: 2515 Chickadee Trl Rockford IL 61107 Office: 2902 McFarland Rd #400 Rockford IL 61107 Home Phone: 815-877-0810. Office Fax: 815-961-4092.

RENO, RUSSELL RONALD, JR., lawyer; b. Gary, Ind., Nov. 28, 1933; s. Russell Ronald Sr. and Katherine Narcissus (White) R.; m. Mary Ellen Klock, Jan. 30, 1956 (dec. June 5, 2004); children: Mary Hall, Russell III, William, Elizabeth. AB, Haverford Coll., 1954; JD, U. Pa., 1957. Bar: Md. 1957, D.C. 1983. Assoc. Venable LLP, Balt., 1958-66, ptnr., 1966—; asst. atty. gen. State of Md., Balt., 1962-64. Author: Maryland Real Estate Law-Practice, 1983. Bd. dirs. Balt. Choral Arts Soc., 1966—; trustee Goucher Coll., Balt., 1978-98, trustee emeritus, 1998—; chancellor Episcopal Diocese of Md., Balt., 1986-2009; bd. mgrs. Haverford Coll., 1990-2002. Fellow Am. Bar Found., Md. Bar Found.; mem. ABA, Md. State Bar Assn., Am. Coll. Real Estate Lawyers, Hamilton St. Club, Wednesday Law Club. Home: 224 Grindall St Baltimore MD 21230 Office: Venable LLP 750 E Pratt St Baltimore MD 21202 Office Phone: 410-244-7480. Business E-Mail: rrreno@venable.com.

RENO, STEPHEN JEROME, former academic administrator; b. Oxnard, Calif., Feb. 27, 1944; s. Warren Jerome and Marie Louise (Fischer) Reno; m. Catherine Royce Motley, Sept. 7, 1974; children: Matthew Stephen, Catherine Hamlen. AB in Philosophy, St. John's Coll., 1965; MA, U. Calif., Santa Barbara, 1968, PhD, 1975. Assoc. Dept. Religious Studies U. Calif., Santa Barbara, 1968—70; assoc. prof., assoc dean Faculty of Arts U. Leicester, England, 1970—79; vis. scholar Harvard Ctr. for Study of World Religions, 1979—80; assoc. provost, interim dean Coll. Arts and Scis. U. So. Maine, 1980—88; provost, dean of faculty So. Oreg. U., Ashland, 1988—94, pres., 1994—2000; chancellor U. Sys. of NH, Durham, 2000—09. Bd. dirs. NH Bus. Industry Assn., NH Coll. and Univ. Coun. Author: The Sacred Tree, 1975; contbr. Penguin Dictionary of Religion, 1981, jour. editor Gen. Theol. Ctr. Maine, 1988—89; contbr. articles to religious jours. Bd. dirs. SALT Ctr. for Field Studies, Assembly of Overseers, Mary Hitchcock Hosp., Dartmouth-Hitchcock Med. Ctr., Ethics Com. Cath. Med. Ctr.; vice chair NH Pub. Radio Bd. Trustees. Recipient Rsch. awards, The British Acad., London, 1976—77, 1978—79, Chmn.'s Award, NH High Tech. Coun. (NHHTC), 2009; hon. fellow, U. Winchester, Eng., 2003. Mem.: Am. Acad. Religion, British Assn. for History of Religion. Roman Catholic. Home: 2124 Elm St Manchester NH 03104-2315*

RENOUF, ANNE, corporate financial executive, consultant; Diploma, Emma Willard Sch., 1954; student, Inst. World Affairs, 1957; AB magna cum laude, honors in Anthropology, Columbia U., 1959; MA, Yale U., 1962, PhD, 1966; JD with honors, Am. U., 1978; postgrad., Duke U. Asst. prof. U. N.C., Chapel Hill, 1966-71; sr. profl. cons. U.S. Govt., Washington, 1972-75; pvt. practice internat. devel. and strategic planning, fin. cons. Washington, 1976—; vis. assoc. prof. George Washington U. Sch. Bus. Adminstrn., Washington, 1983-84; gen. ptnr., v.p. Tech. Mgmt. Corp., Montgomeryville, Pa., 1986-88; chmn. Pivot, Inc., 1988—90; founding prin. SaraTech Fin. Inc., 1990-92; pvt. practice fin. cons.; sr. advisor Wall Street Winterset Walls Inc., mng. dir., natural resources, energy and environment. Founding dir., chmn. bd., CFO/bd. treas. Initiatives in Industry, Inc., 1996-02; corp. dir.; dir. fin. devel. Ctr. for Space and Advanced Tech., 1990; cons. The Brookings Instn., Washington, 1966, U.S. Dept. State, Washington, 1967, World Bank, 1992—; mem. Pres.'s Commn. Grad. Edn., 1967-68, Nat. Chamber Found. Task Force on Space Commercialization, Washington, 1983-86; vis. scholar Carnegie Endowment for Internat. Peace, N.Y.C., 1968-69; fellow U.S. Dept. State, EUR/RPE, 1967; northeastern dir. Va. Advanced Tech. Assn., 1984-88; fin. and tech. spkr.; mem. Coun. on Competitiveness, 1998—2003, Tech. Coun. Washington, 1998—; mem. Greater Washington Bd. Trade, The Potomac Conf., 1999-2001; mem. The World Bank, The Global Devel. Network, 1998— Contbr. articles on tech. commercialization and fin. to profl. jours. Co-chair, charter mem. U.S./China Capital Cities Coun., Washington, 1985-95; advisor Greater Washington D.C. Bd. Trade, 1985-86, Internat. Red Cross, 1987-90; mem. Mayor's Adv. Coun. on Trade and Investment, 1987-91; mem. adv. coun. Ctr. for Internat. Bus. Edn. U. Alaska, Fairbanks, 1990-91, co-chmn. World Trade Day, 1989; bd. dirs. Nat. Symphony Orch., 1990-99, Greater Washington Met. Boys and Girls Clubs, 1992-2000; dir. Initiatives in Industry, Inc., 1996-02. Recipient citation, Washington D.C. Mayor's Office, 1986; Woodrow Wilson fellow, 1958, Bushnell fellow, Yale U., 1964, Hon. Officer-Faculty fellow, U.S. Dept. State, 1967. Fellow Washington Acad. Scis.; mem. Am. Soc. Internat. Law, Internat. Forum U.S. C. of C., Internat. Energy Seminar-Johns Hopkins Sch. for Advanced Internat. Study, Corcoran Gallery of Art (nat. coun.), Washington Internat. Trade Assn., Assn. for Corp. Growth, Phi Beta Kappa. Business E-Mail: arenouf@indevone.com.

RENOUF, EDDA, artist; b. Mexico City, June 17, 1943; d. Edward and Catharine Smith; m. Alain Middleton, Sept. 20, 1977; 1 child, Mélisande. BA, Sarah Lawrence Coll., 1965; M.F.A., Columbia U., 1971. One-woman shows include Yvon Lambert Gallery, Paris, 1972, 1974, 1976, 1978, 1980, 1982, 1984, 1993, Konrad Fischer Gallery, Düsseldorf, Germany, 1974, 1979, Blum-Helman Gallery, N.Y.C., 1978, 1980, 1982, 1985, 1987, 1989, U. Mich. Mus. Art, 1995, Elisabeth Kaufmann Gallery, Basel, Switzerland, 1994, 1996, Galerie Sollertis, Toulouse, France, 1994, 1996, 2007, 1998, Staatliche Kunsthalle Karlsruhe, Germany, 1997, Galerie Hubert Winter, Vienna, Austria, 1998, Galerie Liesbeth Lips, Rotterdam, 1998, 2001, Joseph Helman Gallery, N.Y.C., 2001—02, 2002, Nat. Mus. Women in the Arts, Washington, D.C., 2004, Brenau U. Galleries, Gainesville, Ga., 2004, Arnaud Lefebvre Gallery, Paris, 2006, New Arts Gallery, Litchfield, Conn., 2006, Galeria Charpa, Valencia, Spain, 2007, exhibited in group shows at Mus. Modern Art, N.Y.C., 1973, 1990, 1998, Stedelijk Mus., Amsterdam, 1974, 8th Paris Biennale, 1973, Whitney Mus. Am. Art, N.Y.C., 1979, 1985, Centre Georges Pompidou, Paris, 1979, 2002, 2009, Met. Mus. Art, N.Y.C., 1982, Serpentine Gallery, London, 1984, Galerie Denise René, Paris, 1985, Tel Aviv Mus., 1986, 1998, Mus. Fridericianum, Kassel, Germany, 1988, Mus. d'Art Moderne de Lille, France, 1992, Bibliothèque Nationale, Paris, 1992, Nat. Gallery Art, Washington, 1993—94, 1997, Harvard U. Straus Gallery, 1996, Yokohama (Japan) Mus. Art, 1998, Yale U. Art Gallery, 1998, Cabinet des Estampes et des Dessins, Liege, Belgium, 1999, Corcoran Gallery, Washington, 2001, Neue Galerie, Graz, Austria, 2001—02, Riva Yares Gallery, Santa Fe, N.Mex., 2004, Brit. Mus., London, 2000, 2004, 2007, Staatliche Kunsthalle, Karlsruhe, Germany, 2004, New Arts Gallery, Litchfield, Conn., 2005, Addison Gallery Am. Art, Andover, Mass., 2005, Hayward Gallery and Brit. Mus., 2006—07, Del. Art Mus., 2008, Espai d' Art, Grandia, Spain, 2008, Indpls. Mus. Art, 2008—09, Represented in permanent collections Mus. Modern Art, Whitney Mus. Am. Art, Met. Mus. Art, Centre Georges Pompidou, Paris, Chgo. Art Inst., Mus. of Contemporary Art, Chgo., Phila. Art Mus., Yale U. Art Gallery, Neuberger Mus., Australian Nat. Gallery, Cin. Mus. Art, St. Louis Art Mus., Tel Aviv Mus., La. Mus., Denmark, Walker Art Ctr., Mpls. Bibliotheque Nat. Paris, Bklyn. Mus. Am. Art, Dallas Mus. Fine Art, Detroit Mus. Art, Mus. Contemporary Art, L.A., High Mus., Atlanta, Corcoran Gallery, Washington, Staatliche Kunsthalle, Karlsruhe, Nat. Gallery Art, Washington, Kunstmuseum Winterthur, Switzerland, Neue Galerie, Graz, Nat. Mus. of Women in the Arts, Washington. Nat. Endowment Arts grantee, 1976-77, Pollock-Krasner Found. Inc. grantee, 1990-91, Ctr. Nat. Arts Plastiques grantee, 1996. Address: 37 rue Volta 75003 Paris France Home Phone: 331-42-78-36-49; Office Phone: 331-42-78-3649. Personal E-mail: eddarenouf@mac.com.

RENOUX, ANDRÉ, retired physicist researcher; b. Courbevoie, France, Oct. 27, 1937; s. Robert and Jeanne (Noël) R.; divorced; children: Vincent, Nathalie. Lic. Sci., Faculty Scis. Paris, 1958, D 3d cycle, 1961, D, 1965. Asst. Faculty Scis., Paris, 1959—61, master asst., 1961—66; prof. faculty scis. U. Tunis, Tunisia, 1966—69, U. Brest, France, 1969—80; prof. U. Paris, 1980—2003, dir. lab. phys. aérosols et transfert des contaminations, 1980—2008, dir. DESS (3d cycle) sci. des aerosols-génie de l'Aérocontamination, 1981—2003, prof. emeritus, 2003—08. Gen. chmn. European Aerosol Conf., Blois, France, 1994; del. Internat. Coun. for Engring. and Tech., UNESCO, 2000-; adminstr. Maisons Maternelles, 2005-. Author: (with D. Boulaud, Lavoisier, Ed.) Les Aérosols, Physique et Métrologie, 1998; mem. editl. bd. Idojaras, 1979—, Pollution Atmospherique, 1979-2003, Aerosol Sci. & Tech., 1992-2000, Revue Salles Propres, 2000-02; contbr. over 300 articles to profl. jours. Gen. sec. Syndicat d'initiative, Brest, 1973-77; mem. Cons. Com. Univs., France, 1973-77. Recipient Legion Banner award, United Cultural Conv., 2007. Mem. Am Assn. Advancement Rsch., N.Y. Acad. Scis., Com. Regional Anti-Pollution Brest (pres. 1973-80), Soc. France for Nuclear Energy idFNE (pres. 1987-91), Am. Assn. Aerosol Rsch., Gesellschaft Aerosolforschung, Hungarian Meteorol. soc. (hon.), French Aerosol. Rsch. Assn. (pres. 1983-2000, hon. pres. 2000—), European Aerosol Assembly (co-founder, pres. 1998-2000), Office Professionnel de qualification des Entreprises de l'Ultrapropreté (pres. 1995—), Chevalier des Dames du vin et de la Table, Ordre de l'Echarpe. Avocations: tennis, opera, photography. Home: 11 Sq de L'eau Vive 94000 Creteil France Business E-Mail: renoux.andre@numericable.fr.

REN-PATTERSON, RENEE FENG, neuropathologist, neuroscientist; m. James Reid Patterson. MD, Fourth Mil. Med. U. Xian, P.R. China, 1976; MSc, 1989; PhD, U. Hong Kong, Sch. Medicine, 1994. Physician-in-charge clin. pathologist Xijing Hosp., Dept. Pathology, Xian, 1976—89; rsch. assoc. Dept. Anatomy and Cell Biology, Faculty Medicine, U. Hong Kong, 1989—94; vis. fellow Nat. Cancer Inst., Bethesda, Md., 1994—98; sr. postdoc. rschr. Georgetown U., Washington, 1998—2000; sr. rsch. scientist NIMH, Bethesda, 2000—. Mem.: Soc. Neuroscience. Citizens. Achievements include research in a double-mutant mouse model that should prove valuable in studying gene-gene interactions. Avocations: music, ballet, reading, travel.

RENT, CLYDA STOKES, academic administrator; b. Jacksonville, Fla., Mar. 1, 1942; d. Clyde Parker Stokes Sr. and Edna Mae (Edwards) Shuemake; m. George Seymour Rent, Aug. 12, 1966; 1 child, Cason Rent Lynley. BA, Fla. State U., 1964, MA, 1966, PhD, 1968; LHD (hon.), Judson Coll., 1993. Asst. prof. Western Carolina U., Cullowhee, NC, 1968-70, Queens Coll., Charlotte, NC, 1972-74, dept. chair, 1974-78, dean Grad. Sch. and New Coll., 1979-84, v.p. for Grad. Sch. and New Coll., 1984-85, v.p. acad. affairs, 1985-87, v.p. cmty. affairs, 1987-89; pres. Miss. U. for Women, Columbus, 1989—2001; disting. prof. sociology Miss. State U. Mem. adv. bd. Nat. Women's Hall of Fame; cons. Coll. Eb. N.Y.C., 1983-89; sci. cons. N.C. Alcohol Rsch. Authority, Chapel Hill, 1976-89; bd. mem. So. Growth Policies Bd., 1992-94; adv. bd. Nat. Women's Hall of Fame, Trustmark Nat. Bank, 1991-97; rotating chair Miss. Instns. Higher Learning Pres. Coun., 1990-91; commn. govtl. rels. Am. Coun. Edn., 1990-93; mem. adv. bd. Entergy/Miss., 1994-97, Freedom Forum 1st Amendment Ctr., 1996-2001; mem. Miss. adv. bd. Trustmark Nat. Bank, 1991-97; mem. Mary Baker Eddy Adv. Group, 2000—; mem. Rhodes Scholar selection com. of Miss., 1996-98; mem. Free Sprit Awards selection com., 1996—; mem. ACE Commn. on Women in Higher Edn., 1999—. Mem. editl. bd. Planning for Higher Education, 1995; contbr. articles to profl. jours.; speeches pub. in Vital Speeches; mem. editl. bds. acad. jours. Trustee N.C. Performing Arts Ctr., Charlotte, 1988-89, Charlotte County Day Sch., 1987-89; bd. visitors Johnson C. Smith U., Charlotte, 1985-89; exec. com. bd. dirs. United Way Allocations and Rev., Charlotte, 1982-88; bd. advisors Charlotte Mecklenburg Hosp. Authority, 1985-89; bd. dirs. Jr. Achievement, Charlotte, 1983-89, Miss. Humanities Coun., Miss. Inst. Arts and Letters, Miss. Symphony, Miss. Econ. Coun.; chair Leadership Miss. and Collegiate Miss.; chmn. bd. dirs. Charlotte/Mecklenburg Arts and Sci. Coun., 1987-88; Danforth assoc. Danforth Found., St. Louis, 1976-88, Leadership Am., 1989; mem. golden triangle adv. bd. Bapt. Meml. Hosp., 1999—; pres. So. Univs. Conf., 1994-95; mem. commn. govt. rels. Am. Coun. Edn., 1990-93; mem. alumni bd. First United Meth. Ch., 1996—. Recipient Grad. Made Good award Fla. State U., 1990, medal of excellence Miss. U. for Women, 1995, Women Who Make a Difference award IWF, 2000; named Prof. of Yr., Queens Coll., 1979, One of 10 Most Admired Women Mgrs. in Am., Working Women mag., 1993, One of 1000 Women of the 90's, Mirabella mag., 1994; Ford Found. grantee, 1981; Paul Harris fellow, 1992; OWHE fellow, 1999—. Mem. Am. Assn. State Colls. and Univs. (bd. dirs. 1994-96, 99), Sociol. Soc., So. Assn. Colls. and Schs. (mem. commn. on colls. 1996-98), N.C. Assn. Colls. and Univs. (exec. com. 1988-89), N.C. Assn. Acad. Officers (sec.-treas. 1987-88), Soc. Internat. Bus. Fellows, Miss. Assn. Colls. (pres. 1992), Newcomen Soc. U.S., Internat. Women's Forum, Univ. Club, Rotary. Achievements include 1st female pres. of Miss. U. for Women (1st pub. coll. for women in Am.).

RENTAS, ANGELO GEORGE, biology professor, director; b. Chgo., Ill. s. George James and Frances Rentas; m. Kathleen Lopahs, Aug. 17, 1974; children: Michael Angelo, Laura Fletcher, Daniel Charles, Stephanie Marie. MS in Biology, Northern Ill. U., DeKalb, 1980. Cert. microbiologist ASCP, 1980. Sr. rsch. assoc. Abbott Labs., North Chgo., 1983—85; assoc. prof., biology Trinity Internat. U., Deerfield, Ill., 1985—, dir., sch. sci. & tech., 1999—. Achievements include research in effect of potassium acetate on growth and ultrastructure of bracteacoccus cinnabarinus. Office: Trinity Internat Univ 2065 Half Day Rd Deerfield IL 60015 Business E-Mail: arentas@tiu.edu.

RENTCH, JAMES SPENCER, forester, educator; b. Martinsburg, W.Va., Dec. 12, 1947; s. John Kenneth Rentch and Louise Spencer Taylor; m. Maria Jesus Amores-Aguerra, 2003; children: Sarah Louise Turner, James Casey. PhD, W.Va. U., Morgantown, 2001. Elec. engring. technologist Am. Electric Power, Charleston, W.Va., 1980—98; instr. Marshall U., South Charleston, 1994—98; rsch. asst. prof. divsn. forestry WVU, 2001—. Contbr. scientific papers to profl. jours. Mem.: W.Va. Acad. Sci. (sec. 2001—). Office: WVa Univ Divsn Forestry PO Box 6125 Morgantown WV 26501-6125 Business E-Mail: jrentch2@wvu.edu.

RENTERIA, AMANDA A., legislative staff member; b. Lindsay, Calif. m. Patrick Brannelly, May 28, 2006. BA in Polit. Sci. and Econs. with honors, Stanford U., Calif., 1997; MBA, Harvard U. Bus. Sch., Boston, 2003. Sr. fin. analyst Goldman Sachs & Co., LA, 1997—2000; econs. & algebra tchr., athletic coach Woodlake HS, Calif., 2000—01; spl. cons. Acad. Bus. Leadership, LA, 2002; interim devel. officer, Strong Neighborhoods Initiative, and fin. analyst, spl. projects cons. City of San Jose, Calif., 2003—04; econ. policy advisor, legis. asst., Senator Dianne Feinstein US Senate, Washington, 2005—06, legis. asst., legis. dir., Senator Debbie Stabenow, 2006—07, chief of staff to Senator Debbie Stabenow, 2007—. Mem. Harvard U. Global Leadership Conf. Vol. cons., career advisor COMPASS; mem. Hispanic C. of C., Stanford U. Diversity Task Force. Mem.: Stanford U. Alumni Assn., Harvard U. Alumni Assn. Democrat. Office: 133 Hart Senate Office Bldg Washington DC 20510-2204 Office Phone: 202-224-4822.*

RENTERIA, EDGAR ENRIQUE, professional baseball player; b. Barranquila, Colombia, Aug. 7, 1975; Short stop Fla. Marlins, 1996—98, St. Louis Cardinals, 1999—2004, Boston Red Sox, 2005, Atlanta Braves, 2005—07, Detroit Tigers, 2007—08, San Francisco Giants, 2008—. Recipient Silver Slugger award, 2000, 2002, 2003, Gold Glove award, Maj. League Baseball, 2002, 2003; named to Nat. League All-Star Team, 1998, 2000, 2003, 2004, 2006. Achievements include member of the World Series Championship winning Florida Marlins, 1997. Office: San Francisco Giants AT&T Pk 24 Willie Mays Plz San Francisco CA 94107*

RENTON, HOLLINGS C., health products executive; BS Maths., Colo. State U.; MBA, U. Mich. Pres., COO Cetus Corp., 1981—91; pres., Chiron Corp., 1991—92; chmn., pres., CEO Onyx Pharms. Inc., Emeryville, Calif., 1993—. Office: Onyx Pharms Inc 2100 Powell St Emeryville CA 94608

RENTOS, PETER GEORGE, medical educator; b. Reading, Pa., Aug. 21, 1929; s. George John and Stavroula (Blamblas) R.; m. Margaret Perados, Jan. 22, 1956; children: George, Michael. BA, Albright Coll., 1959; MPH, U. Mich., 1964; PhD, U. Iowa, 1970. Indsl. hygienist Pa. Dept. Health, Harrisburg, 1960—66; health svcs. officer USPHS, Salt Lake City, 1966—68, scientist Cin., 1970—71, sr. scientist, 1971—77, scientist dir., 1977—92; assoc. prof. U. South Fla., Tampa, 1992—. Rsch. grant adminstr. Nat. Inst. for Occupl. Safety and Health, Cin., 1971-76. Editor: Evaluation and Control of the Occupational Environment, 1992, Occupational Safety Research/Personal Protection, 1975, Shift Work and Health, 1976. Chmn. Health and Safety Com., Boy Scouts Am., Pitts., 1962; sec. Jr. C. of C., Meadville, Pa., 1965; pres. Met. Area Religious Coalition, Cin., 1988. Col. USPHS, 1966-92. Recipient Spoke award Boy Scouts Am., 1963. Mem. Am. Indsl. Hygiene Assn., Am. Soc. Safety Engrs., Fla. Fedn. for Safety. Greek Orthodox. Avocations: photography, fishing, bicycling, walking. Home: 3951 Brightside Ln Palm Harbor FL 34685-2630 Office: U South Fla Col Pub Health MDC56 13201 Bruce B Downs Blvd Tampa FL 33612-3805 Office Phone: 813-974-6661. Business E-Mail: prentos@health.usf.edu.

RENUART, VICTOR EUGENE, JR., (GENE RENUART), career military officer; b. Nov. 26, 1949; s. Victor Eugene and Ruthann Wigglesworth Renuart; m. Jill Colleen Jenner; children: Ryan Victor, Andrew John. BS in Prodn. and Indsl. Mgmt., Ind. U., 1971; MA in Psychology, Troy State U., 1975; Disting. grad., Squadron Officer Sch., Maxwell AFB, Ala., 1977; Grad., Air Command & Staff Coll., 1979, Army War Coll., 1992, Sr. Officers in Nat. Security Program, 1997. Commd. 2d. lt. USAF, 1973, advanced through grades to gen., 2007; instr., pilot Craig AFB, 1973-76; asst. prof. aerospace studies U. Notre Dame, South Bend, Ind., 1976-79; A-10 instr. pilot, flight comdr. to ops. officer 81st Tactical Fighter Wing, RAF Bentwaters, Eng., 1980-84; ops. inspector Office of the Inspector Gen. Hdqrs. USAF Europe, Ramstein AB, West Germany, 1984-85, exec. officer to inspector gen., 1985-86; chief wing inspections 23rd Tactical Fighter Wing, England AFB, La., 1986-91, ops. officer to comdr., 1986-91, dir. assignments, 1992-93; comdr. support group Allied Air Forces Ctrl. Europe, England AFB, 1993-94, asst. chief of staff, ops., sr. U.S. rep., 1994-95; dir. ops. plans NATO Combined Air Ops. Ctr. 5th Allied Tactical AF, Vicenza, Italy, 1994-95; asst. dir. ops. Hdqrs. USAF Europe, Ramstein, Germany, 1995-96; comdr. 52nd Fighter Wing, Spangdahlem AB, Germany, 1996-98, 347th Wing, Moody AFB, Ga., 1998—2000; comdr. Joint Task Force-Southwest Asia, comdr. 9th Air & Space Expeditionary Task Force-Southwest Asia US Ctrl. Command, Riyadh, Saudi Arabia, 2000—01; dir. ops. (J-3) US Ctrl Command, MacDill AFB, Fla., 2001—03; vice comdr. Pacific Air Forces, Hickam AFB, Hawaii, 2003—05; dir. strategic plans & policy (J-5) Joint Staff, The Pentagon, Washington, 2005—06; sr. mil. asst. to sec. US Dept. Def., Washington, 2006—07; comdr. N.Am. Aerospace Def. Command (NORAD), Peterson AFB, Colo., 2007—, US No. Command (USNORTHCOM), Peterson AFB, 2007—. Decorated Def. Disting. Svc. medal with oak leaf cluster, Disting. Svc. medal, Def Superior Svc. medal with oak leaf cluster, Meritorious Svc. medal with four oak leaf clusters, Aerial Achievement medal with three oak leaf clusters, Air Force Commendation medal with oak leaf cluster, Air Force Achievement medal with oak leaf cluster, Legion of Merit with oak leaf cluster, Air medal with two oak leaf clusters. Office: US Northern Command 250 Vandenberg Ste B016 Colorado Springs CO 80914*

RENWICK, EDWARD S., lawyer; b. LA, May 10, 1934; AB, Stanford U., 1956, LLB, 1958. Bar: Calif. 1959, U.S. Dist. Ct. (cen. dist.) Calif. 1959, U.S. Ct. Appeals (9th cir.) 1963, U.S. Dist. Ct. (so. dist.) Calif. 1973, U.S. Dist. Ct. (no. dist.) Calif. 1977, U.S. Dist. Ct. (ea. dist.) Calif. 1981, U.S. Supreme Ct. 1985. Ptnr. Hanna and Morton LLP, LA. Mem., bd. vis. Stanford Law Sch., 1967-69; mem. environ. and natural resources adv. bd. Stanford Law Sch. Bd. dirs. Calif. Supreme Ct. Hist. Soc. Fellow Am. Coll. Trial Lawyers, Am. Bar Found.; mem. ABA (mem. sect. on litigation, antitrust law, bus. law, chmn. sect. of nat. resources, energy and environ. law 1987-88, mem. at large coord. group energy law 1989-92, sect. rep. coord. group energy law 1995-97, Calif. del. legal com., interstate oil compact com.), Calif. Arboretum Assn. (trustee 1986-92), L.A. County Bar Assn. (chmn. natural resources law sect. 1974-75), The State Bar of Calif., Chancery Club (pres. 1992-93), Phi Delta Phi. Office: Hanna and Morton LLP 444 S Flower St Ste 1500 Los Angeles CA 90071-2922 Office Phone: 213-628-7131. Business E-Mail: erenwick@hanmor.com.

RENWICK, GLENN M., insurance company executive; b. May 22, 1955; B in Math. & Econs., U. Canterbury, Christchurch, New Zealand; MS in Engring., U. Fla., Gainesville, 1978. With Progressive Corp., 1986—, chief info. officer, 1998—2000, CEO ins. ops., 2000, pres., CEO, 2001—; CEO, ins. ops. and bus. tech. process leader Progressive Casualty Ins. Co., 1998—2000, pres., chmn., CEO, 2000—04. Bd. dirs. Fiserv Inc. Office: Progressive Corp 6300 Wilson Mills Rd Cleveland OH 44143-2109 Office Phone: 440-461-5000.

RENWICK, STEPHEN P., engineer; s. Robert and Margaret Renwick; m. Joyce Wilde. BA, Bates Coll., Lewiston, Maine, 1983; MA, SUNY, Stony Brook, 1985; PhD, Wesleyan U., Middletown, Conn., 1991. Rsch. scientist NC State U., Raleigh, 1991—93; physicist L&W Rsch., Wallingford, Conn., 1993—96; prin. engr. SVG Lithography, Ridgefield, Conn., 1996—2000, Nikon Precision, Inc., Belmont, Calif., 2000—. Contbr. articles to numerous jours. Mem.: CAP (Palo Alto, Calif.) (pilot 2001, squadron comdr. 2005—08), Am. Phys. Soc., Internat. Soc. Optical Engring. Achievements include patents for method to diagnose imperfections in illuminator of a lithographic tool. Office: Nikon Precision Inc 1399 Shoreway Rd Belmont CA 94002 Business E-Mail: srenwick@nikon.com.

RENZETTI, PHYLLIS JEAN, retired technical editor, paleontologist; b. Kingman, Ind., Feb. 3, 1925; d. Claude and Helen (Duchene) A.; divorced; 1 child, Jeanne. BA, Wheaton Coll., Ill., 1947; MA, Columbia U., 1950; PhD, Ind. U., 1961. Tchr. Wheaton Coll., 1948-49; tech. editor U.S. Geol. Survey, Reston, Va., Menlo Park, Calif., 1963-94, ret., 1994. Mem. AAAS, Paleontological Soc. Home: 3266 Hanover Dr Lafayette IN 47909-3252

RENZI, RICK (RICHARD GEORGE RENZI), former United States Representative from Arizona; b. Sierra Vista, Ariz., June 11, 1958; s. Eugene Carmen and Faye Marie Renzi; m. Roberta Renzi; 12 children. BS in Criminal Justice, No. Ariz. U., 1980; JD, Cath. U., 2002. Owner Renzi & Co.; staff mem. to Senator Jon Kyl US Senate; mem. US Congress from 1st Ariz. Dist., 2003—09. Indicted on federal charges (conspiracy, money laundering, wire and insurance fraud and extortion) on Feb. 22, 2008. Recipient Friends of Affordable Housing award, Fed. Home Loan Bank San Francisco, 2004, Unsung Hero award, Ariz. Am. Legion, 2004; named to No. Ariz. U. Hall of Fame, 1998. Republican. Roman Catholic.*

REOCK, ERNEST C., JR., retired social studies educator, director; b. Belleville, NJ, Oct. 13, 1924; s. Ernest C. and Helen Rutan (Evans) R.; m. Jeanne Elizabeth Thomason, Jan. 25, 1953; children: Michael, Thomas, Kathleen. BS, Swarthmore Coll., 1945; AB, Rutgers U., 1948, MA, 1950, PhD, 1959. Rsch. assoc. bur. govt. rsch. Rutgers U., New Brunswick, N.J., 1950-59, asst. prof., dir., 1960-63, assoc. prof., dir., 1963-68, prof., dir., 1968-92. Cons. N.J. Constnl. Conv., New Brunswick, 1966, N.J. State and Local Revenue and Expenditure Commns., 1986-88. Author: Handbook for New Jersey Assessors, 1962, School Budget Caps in New Jersey, 1981 (Govtl. Rsch. Assn. award, 1983), Unfinished Business: The New Jersey Constitutional Conv. of 1966, 2003, Redistricting New Jersey After the Census of 2010, 2008; editor: New Jersey Legislative District Data Book, 1972—92; contbr. Chmn. Middlesex County Charter Study Commn., New Brunswick, 1973—74; cons. State Apportionment Commn., 1981, 1991, 2001, various mcpl. charter commns., 1965—; mem. NJ Property Tax Conv. Task Force, 2004. Lt. USN, 1943—46, lt. USN, 1951—53. Recipient Gov.'s award for Pub. Svc., 1997. Mem.: Am. Soc. Pub. Adminstrn. (Pub. Adminstr. Yr. 1982, 2006), Am. Ednl. Fin. Assn. Avocations: sailing, swimming. Home: 7 Kendall Rd Kendall Park NJ 08824-1010 Office: Rutgers U Ctr Govt Svcs 33 Livingston Ave New Brunswick NJ 08901-1900 Office Phone: 732-932-3640 633.

REPHAN, JACK, lawyer; b. Little Rock, Mar. 16, 1932; s. Henry and Mildred (Frank) R.; m. Arlene Clark, June 23, 1957; children: Amy Carol, James Clark. BS in Commerce, 1954; LLB, U. Va., 1959. Bar: Va. 1959, D.C. 1961. Assoc. Kanter & Kanter, Norfolk, Va., 1959-60; law clk. to Judge Sam E. Whitaker, U.S. Ct. Claims, Washington, 1960-62; assoc. Pierson, Ball & Dowd, Washington, 1962-64; ptnr. Danzansky, Dickey, Tydings, Quint & Gordon, Washington, 1964-77; mem. Braude, Margulies, Sacks & Rephan, Washington, 1977-87; ptnr. Porter, Wright, Morris & Arthur, Washington, 1987-88, Sadur, Pelland & Rubinstein, Washington, 1988-93; counsel Hofheimer Nusbaum P.C., Norfolk, Va., 1993-00; principal Rephan Lassiter PLC, Norfolk, 2001—07; shareholder Pender and Coward, P.C., Virginia Beach, 2007—. Mem. Nat. Panel Arbitrators Am. Arbitration Assn., Nat. Panel Mediators Am. Arbitration Assn., NASD Bd. Arbitrators; lectr. joint com. continuing legal edn. State Bar Va. Contbr. articles to legal jours. Pres. Patrick Henry PTA, Alexandria, Va., 1968-69, Linkhorn Bay Condominium Assn., 2000—; treas. John Adams Mid. Sch. PTA, Alexandria, 1970-71; pres. Seminary Ridge Citizens Assn., 1976-77; Dem. candidate for Alexandria City Com., 1969. 1st lt. AUS, 1955-57. Mem. ABA (chmn. subcom. on procurement of jud. remedies pub. contract sect. 1973-74), Va. Bar Assn. (govt. sect. constrn. law 1979-81, 99—, vice chmn. 1980-81, 2006-, chmn. 1981-82, 2007—08), D.C. Bar Assn., Assoc. Gen. Contractors, Hampton Roads Utility and Heavy Contractors Assn. (gen. counsel), Cavalier Golf and Yacht Club, Kiwanis (pres. Landmark Club 1969). Jewish. Home: 1276 Laskin Rd Ste 402 Virginia Beach VA 23451-5272 Office: Pender & Coward PC 222 Central Park Ave Town Ctr Virginia Beach VA 23462 Home Phone: 757-491-5599.

REPINSKI, SARA, library director; d. Stephen Charles and Sharon Ann Gilles; m. Jeffrey Lawrence Repinski, Dec. 10, 1998. BS in History and Art, U. Wis., La Crosse, 1998; MLIS, U. S.C., 2002. Libr. dir. So. Meth. Coll., Orangeburg, SC, 2002—06; catalog libr. Coleman Karesh Law Libr., U. S.C., Columbia, 2006—07; acquisitions libr. U. SC Coleman Karesh Law Libr., Columbia, 2007—. Mem. accreditation team Transnat. Assn. Christian Colls. and Schs., Lynchburg, Va., 2002—; steering com. Coll. Mass Comm. and Info. Studies Alumni Soc. Patron Civil War Preservation Trust. Mem.: Am. Assn. Law Librs. (collection devel. com. 2007—, OBS-SIS local systems com. 2007—), SC Libr. Assn., South Eastern Assn. Law Librs. (strategic planning com. 2007—). Avocations: scrapbooks, music, football.

REPLOGLE, ROBERT LEE, cardiovascular and thoracic surgeon; b. Ottumwa, Iowa, Sept. 30, 1931; s. Ralph Ruby and Edith Dorothy (Swartz) R.; m. Carol A. Heeschen, Aug. 24, 1958; children: Robert E., Jennifer Bremer, Edith Sheffer. MD cum laude, Harvard U., 1960; DSc (hon.), Cornell Coll., 1972. Diplomate Am. Bd. Surgery, Am. Bd. Thoracic Surgery, Am. Bd. Pediat. Surgery. Intern in surgery U. Minn. Hosp., 1960-61; asst. resident in surgery Peter Bent Brigham Hosp., Boston, 1961-63, Mass. Gen. Hosp., Boston, 1965-66; sr. resident in surgery Children's Hosp. Med. Ctr., Boston, 1966; asst. in surgery Children's Hosp. Med. Ctr. and Harvard Med. Sch., Boston, 1966-67; asst. prof. surgery Pritzker Sch. Medicine U. Chgo., 1967-70, assoc. prof. surgery and head, sect. pediat. surgery, 1970-73, prof. surgery and head, sect. pediat. surgery, 1973-74, prof. surgery and head, sect. cardiac surgery, 1973-80, prof. surgery, sect. cardiac surgery, 1973-90; med. dir. cardiac surgery unit Ingalls Meml. Hosp., 1989-98; chief divsn. cardiac surgery Columbus Hosp., Chgo., 1987-97; pres. CTS Net Inc., Chgo., 1998—. Vis. prof. Albany Med. Coll., 1974, Dalhousie Sch. of Medicine, Halifax, 1975, Walter Reed Army Med. Ctr., 1978, U. Miami Med. Sch., 1992, Philippine Heart Ctr. for Asia March, 1995, Health Inst. Japan, Tokyo, 1982, Creighton Med. Sch., 1988, Brooke Army Med. Ctr., 1993, U. Heidelberg, 1995, Kerkoff Clinic/Max Planct Inst., Bad Nanheim, Germany, 1995, German Heart Ctr., Munich, 1995, Peter Bent Brigham Hosp. Harvard Med. Sch., 1996; mem. surgery and bioengring. study sect. HHS, NIH, 1979-83; mem. ad hoc adv. com. bypass angioplasty revascularization investigation, NIH, 1993-94; mem. subcom. on quality N.Y. State Dept. Health, 1989-96, mem. subcom. on resources and facilities, 1993—, mem. cardiac adv. com., 1989—; pres. Ctsnet.org, Inc., 1999—. Author: (with others) Microcirculation, Perfusion, and Transplantation of Organs, 1970, The Critically Ill Child, 1972, Surgical Clinics in North America, 1976, Biprosthetic Cardiac Valves, 1979, Year Book of Nuclear Medicine, 1981, among others; mem. editl. bd. Jour. Cardiac Surgery, 1982-99; contbr. more than 125 articles to profl. jours. With USN, 1951-54. Recipient Merit award Philippine Heart ctr. for Asia, Manila, 1985, Friendship award Shanghai Chest Hosp., 1987; fellowship U. Chgo., MacLean Ctr. Clin. Ethics. Mem. AMA (diagnostic and therapeutic tech. assessment panel 1995—, ho. of dels. 1992—, joint rev. com. on ednl. programs for physicians assts. 1979-84), ACS (com. on allied health pers. 1979-84, chmn. 1983-84, com. on med. motion pictures 1979-85, com. on membership 1988—, residency rev. com. for thoracic surgery of the accreditation com. for grad. med. edn. 1992-95, 96—), Ill. State Med. Soc., Chgo. Med. Soc., Am. Surg. Assn., European Assn. for Cardiothoracic Surgery, Soc. for Acad. Surgery, Am. Heart Assn. (adv. coun. cardiovasc. surgery 1968-71), Soc. Univ. Surgeons, Internat. Cardiovasc. Soc., Societe Internationale de Chirurgie (N.Am. chpt.), Am. Assn. for Thoracic Surgery (del. AMA 1992—, com. on soc. responsibility 1991—), Soc. Thoracic Surgeons (program com. 1978-81, chmn. 1981, com. on medico-legal affairs, chmn. 1985-88, ad hoc fin. adv. com. 1987-89, ad hoc exhibitors adv. com. 1988-89, ad hoc com. on social responsibility 1992-95, ad hoc database liaison com. 1993-94, database liaison com. 1994—, ad hoc com. on physician-specific mortality for cardiac surgery 1993-96, stds. and ethics com. 1984-88, treas. 1986-92, exec. com. 1986—, pres.-elect. 1995-96, pres. 1996-97, rep. to the coun. of med. specialty socs. 1990—, annals of thoracic surgery liaision com. 1992—, com. on grad. edn. in thoracic surgery 1992—, com. on major issues in thoracic surgery 1993, chmn. 1994, 95, pres.-elect coun. med. splty. socs. 1997-98, pres. coun. med. specialty socs. 1998-99), Coun. of Med. Specialty Socs., German Cardiac Surgery Soc. (hon. mem.). Avocations: wine collecting, photography, travel. Address: CTS Net Inc 1160 E 56th St Chicago IL 60637-1541

REPPEN, KYRA E., Internet company executive; BA, Wellesley Coll.; JD, U. Calif. Hastings Coll. Law. Corp. assoc. Dewey Ballantine, Schulte Roth & Zabel; corp. counsel, MTV Networks law & bus. affairs Viacom, 1996—98, sr. counsel, Nickelodeon law & bus. affairs., 1998; v.p. bus. devel. and ops. Nickelodeon Online, 1999; v.p., gen. mgr. NickJr.com, 2000—06; sr. v.p., gen. mgr. NeoPets Inc., Glendale, Calif., 2006—. Office: Neopets Inc 450 N Brand Blvd Glendale CA 91203

REPPUCCI, NICHOLAS DICKON, psychologist, educator; b. Boston, May 1, 1941; s. Nicholas Ralph and Bertha Elizabeth (Williams) R.; m. Christine Marlow Onufrock, Sept. 10, 1967; children: Nicholas Jason, Jonathan Dickon, Anna Jin Marlow Chapman. BA with honors, U. N.C., 1962; MA, Harvard U., 1964, PhD, 1968. Lectr., rsch. assoc. Harvard U., Cambridge, Mass., 1967-68; from asst. prof. to assoc prof. Yale U., New Haven, 1968-76; prof. psychology U. Va., Charlottesville, 1976—, dir. cmty. psychology tng. program, 1976—, dir. grad. studies in psychology, 1984-95, 97-98. Originator biennial conf. on community rsch. and action, 1986. Author: (with J. Haugaard) Sexual Abuse of Children, 1988; (with P. Britner and J. Woolard) Preventing Child Abuse and Neglect Through Parent Education, 1997; editor: (with J. Haugaard) Prevention in Community Mental Health Practice; (with E. Mulvey, L. Weithorn and J. Monahan) Mental Health, Law and Children, 1984; assoc. editor Law and Human Behavior, 1986-96, mem. editl. bd., 1996-2005; mem. editl. bd. Am. Jour. Cmty. Psychology, 1974-83, 88-91; contbr. articles to profl. jours., chpts. in books. Adv. bd. on prevention Va. Dept. Mental Health, Mental Retardation and Substance Abuse Svcs., Richmond, 1986-92. Recipient Disting. Scholar in psychology award Va. Assn. Social Sci., 1991, Outstanding Psychology Tchg. award, U. Va., 2005, Mentoring and Tchg. award Am. Psychology and Law Soc., 2007. Fellow APA (chmn. task force on pub. policy 1980-84), Am. Psychol. Soc., Soc. for Cmty. Rsch. and Action (pres. 1986, Disting. Contbn. award in theory and rsch. 1998, Inaugural award for ednl. mentoring 1999), Phi Beta Kappa. Office: U Va Dept Psychology PO Box 400400 Charlottesville VA 22904-4400 Office Phone: 434-924-0662. E-mail: ndr@virginia.edu.

REPS, THOMAS WILLIAM, science educator, small business owner; b. Ithaca, NY, May 28, 1956; s. John and Constance Reps; m. Susan Horwitz. BA cum laude, Harvard U., Cambridge, 1977; MS, PhD, Cornell U., Ithaca, 1982. Postdoc. assoc. Dept. Computer Sci., Cornell U., 1982—84, rsch. assoc., 1984—85; asst. prof. Computer Scis. Dept. U. Wis., Madison, 1985—88, assoc. prof., 1988—94, assoc. chmn., 1990—93, prof., 1994—; pres. and co-founder GrammaTech, Inc., Ithaca, 1988—. Guest prof. Datalogisk Inst. U. Copenhagen, 1993—94; cons. Def. Advance Rsch. Projects Agy., Arlington, Va., 1996—97; vis. rschr. Consiglio Nat. delle Rsch., Pisa, Italy, 2000—01; mem. F/A-22 Avionics Adv. Team, Office Dep. Under Sec. Def. (Sci. and Tech.), Washington, 2003. Recipient Presdl. Young Investigator award, NSF, 1986, Humboldt Rsch. award, Alexander von Humboldt Found., 2000—03; fellow, Assn. Computing Machinery, 2005; David and Lucile Packard fellowship, 1988—93, Guggenheim fellowship, John Simon Guggenheim Meml. Found., 2000—01. Achievements include patents for interprocedural slicing of computer programs using dependence graphs. Office: Univ Wis Comp Sci Dept 1210 W Dayton St Madison WI 53703

REPSYS, ANDREW J., aquatic biologist, limnologist, water quality specialist, environmental biologist; b. Zagare, Lithuania, July 2, 1940; BS, SD State Univ., 1970, MS, 1972. Data sys. technician USS Saratoga USN, 1965—68; grad. rsch. asst. SD State Univ., Brookings, 1970—72; rsch. assoc. Univ. Wash., Seattle, 1973—74; assoc. biologist NALCO Chem. Co., Northbrook, Ill., 1974—82; fisheries scientific observer Nat. Oceanic and Atmospheric Adminstrn., Seattle, 1983; natural resources scientist SD Dept. Environ. & Natural Resources, Pierre, 1984—. Cons. Public Power Utilities, Kansas, Nebr., 1976—81; aquatic & environ. biologist COE Engring. Firm, SD, 1998; staff South Dakota Dept. environment & Natural Resources, 1987, 96. Author (articles) Proc. SD Acad. Sci., 1973, J. Fish. Res. Board Canada, 1976, (chapters to books) The Middle Missouri River, 1982. PO3 USN, 1965—68. Recipient Environ. Achievement award, EPA, 2002. Achievements include discovery of Impact predications on aquatic biology resulting from modification of hydrological & thermal dynamics; research in feeding strategies & food selectivity of several fish species; discovery of effects of power plant pump/storage facilities on river biology, zoogeography of zooplankton; changes in zooplankton for lake Oahe a Missouri River mainstem reservoir, following the introduction of rainbow smelt - Osmerus mordax, south dakota department of environment natural resources. Avocations: literature, music, history, hiking, fishing. Office: SD Dept Environ & Natural Resources 523 E Capitol Pierre SD 57501-3181 Home: 205 W Pleasant Dr PO Box 1051 Pierre SD 57501-2405 Home Phone: 605-224-0157; Office Phone: 605-773-4046. Business E-Mail: andrewr@denr.sd.us. E-mail: andrew.repsys@state.sd.us.

RESCH, EDWARD J., investment company executive; BS, Lehigh U.; MBA, Rutgers U. Sr. positions Salomon Brothers Inc., Price Waterhouse, Procter & Gamble; CFO, capital markets group Donaldson, Lufkin & Jenrette, Inc., mng. dir., chief acctg. officer; mng. dir., CFO Pershing; exec. v.p., CFO State Street Corp., Boston, 2002—. Office: State Street Corp 225 Franklin St Boston MA 02110

RESCH, RITA MARIE, retired music educator; b. Minot, ND, Dec. 26, 1936; d. Clement Charles and Magdalena Marie (Zeltinger) Resch. BS in Edn., Minot State U., 1957; MM in Music Lit., Eastman Sch. Music, Rochester, NY, 1960; MA in English Lit., U. N.D., 1967; MFA in Voice, U. Iowa, 1973, DMA in Piano Chamber Music/Accompanying, 1974. Music tchr. (vocal) Biwabik Sch. Dist., Minn., 1957—58, S. Redford Twp., Detroit, 1958—59; instr. music Fontbonne Coll., St. Louis, 1960—63; asst. prof. music Wis. State U., Stevens Point, 1965—68, U. Ctrl. Mo. (formerly Ctrl. Mo. State U.), Warrensburg, 1974—79, assoc. prof., 1979—89, prof., 1989—2005, prof. emerita, 2005—. Adjudicator for vocal music Mo. State High Sch. Activities Assn., Columbia, Kans. State High Sch. Activities Assn., Topeka, other orgns., 1976—. Author (with Judith E. Carman, William K. Gaeddert, Gordon Myers): Art Song in the United States: An Annotated Bibliography, 1976, 2001. Assoc. organist Sacred Heart Cath. Ch., Warrensburg, 1980—. Mem.: Mo. Music Tchrs. Assn. (v.p. auditions 1995—98), Music Tchrs. Nat. Assn., Nat. Assn. Tchrs. Singing, Pi Kappa Lambda, Sigma Alpha Iota.

RESCH, TONDA RAE, language educator; d. Vern Charles and Fern Anna Gulick; m. Gregory Dean Resch, Aug. 23, 1969; 1 child, Timothy Vern. AA, Graceland Coll., Lamoni, Iowa, 1966; EdB, Ctrl. Mich., Mt. Pleasant, 1967; MEd, Ctrl. Mo., Warrensburg, 1989. Spanish tchr. Carson City Consolidate, Mich., 1967—69, Smith Cotton, Sedalia, Mo., 1969—71, La Monte Schs., Mo., 1972—81, Knob Noster Schs., Mo., 1981—; adj. Spanish tchr. State Fair CC, Mo., 1988—. Ch. priesthood

Cmty. Christ, Sedalia, organist & pianist, 1957—, music dir., 1969—, youth dir., 1987—90. Mem.: MSTA, FLAM (bd. mem.). Avocations: camping, cooking. Home: 29068 McCormick Rd Sedalia MO 65301 Office: Knob Noster R8 Schs 504 S Wash Knob Noster MO 65336 Office Phone: 660-563-2283.

RESCHER, NICHOLAS, philosopher, author, educator; b. Hagen, Westphalia, Germany, July 15, 1928; arrived in US, 1938, naturalized, 1944; s. Erwin Hans and Meta Anna Rescher; m. Dorothy Henle, Feb. 10, 1968; children: Mark, Owen, Catherine; 1 child from previous marriage, Elizabeth. BS in Math., Queens Coll., 1949; PhD, Princeton U., 1951; LHD (hon.), Loyola U., Chgo., 1970, Lehigh U., 1993; Dr. honoris causa (hon.), U. Córdoba, Argentina, 1992, U. Constance, Germany, 1995; DS (hon.), CUNY, 1999; PhD (hon.), Fern U., Hagen, 2001; Dr.rer.pol.hc, Helsinki, 2006; LHD (hon.), Cleve. State U., 2007. Instr. philosophy Princeton (N.J.) U., 1951-52; mathematician RAND Corp., 1954-56; assoc. prof. philosophy Lehigh U., Bethlehem, Pa., 1957-61; disting. prof. philosophy U. Pitts., 1961—, chmn. Ctr. for Philosophy of Sci., 1988—. Trustee St. Edmunds Acad., Pitts., 1980—85; nonresident mem. Corpus Christi Coll., Oxford; disting. vis. lectr., Oxford, Salamanca, Munich, Konstanz; cons. in field. Author: The Coherence Theory of Truth, 1973, Methodological Pragmatism, 1977, Scientific Progress, 1978, The Limits of Science, 1985, Luck, 1995, Predicting the Future, 1997, Complexity, 1998, Nature and Understanding, 2000, Paradoxes, 2000, Philosophical Reasoning, 2001, Fairness, 2002, Epistomic Logic, 2004, Epistemetrics, 2006, Free Will, 2009; exec. editor: Am. Philos. Quar., 1961—; mem. editl. bd. 15 jours.; contbr. articles to profl. jours. Sec. gen. Internat. Union History and Philosophy Sci. UNESCO, 1969—72. With USMC, 1952—54. Recipient Alexander von Humboldt Humanities prize, 1983, Prix Mercier, 2005; Ford Found. fellow, 1959—60, Guggenheim Found. fellow, 1970—71. Mem.: Acad. Europaea, Academie Internat. de Philosophie des Scis., Inst. Internat. de Philosophie, C. S. Perice Soc. (past pres.), G. W. Leibniz Soc. Am. (past pres.), Royal Soc. Can., Royal Asiatic Soc., Am. Metaphys. Soc. (past pres.), Am. Cath. Philos. Assn. (past pres.), Am. Philos. Assn. (past pres., Aquinas medal 2007). Roman Catholic. Avocation: reading. Home: 1033 Milton Ave Pittsburgh PA 15218 Office: U Pitts Dept Philosophy 1012 Cathedral Pittsburgh PA 15260 Business E-Mail: rescher@pitt.edu.

RESCHLY, DANIEL J., education educator, psychologist; b. Wayland, Iowa, Dec. 30, 1943; married; 3 children. BS, Iowa State U., 1966; MA, U. Iowa, 1968; PhD, U. Oreg., 1971. Lic. sch. psychologist Iowa, Oreg., Ariz.; nat. cert. sch. psychologist, cert. secondary edn. educator Iowa. Sch. psychologist Louisa County Schs., Wapello, Iowa, 1967—69; dir. summer head start program Louisa County, Iowa, 1969; sch. psychology intern Albina Youth Opportunity Ctr. and Portland (Oreg.) Pub. Schs., 1970—71; asst. prof. U. Ariz., Tucson, 1971—75; assoc. prof. Iowa State U., 1975—80, prof., 1980—91, disting. prof. liberal arts and sciences, 1991—98, dir. Sch. Psychology Program, interim assoc. dean Coll. Edn., 1996—98, dir. Rsch. Inst. for Studies in Edn., 1996—98; prof. edn. and psychology Vanderbilt U., Nashville, 1998—, chair dept. spl. edn., 1998—2006. Presenter in field; editor Sch. Psychology Rev., 1979—81, mem. editl. bd., 1974—2000, Jour. Sch. Psychology, 1982—96, Sch. Psychology Quarterly, 1984—90, Jour. of Psychoeducational Assessment, 1983—88, Canadian Jour. Sch. Psychology, 1990—, Jour. of Learning Disabilities, 1998—. Contbr. chapters to books, articles to profl. jours. Recipient Award for outstanding contributions to the develop. of sch. psycholgy, NJ Assn. Sch. Psychologists, 1983, James B. Stroud award, Iowa Sch. Psychologists Assn., 1989, Dorthy H. Hughes Meml. award for disting. svc. in ednl. and sch. psychology, NYU Dept. Applied Psychology, 1994, Outstanding Alumnus awrad, U. Ore. Coll. Edn., 1996, Award for Exemplary Effort in Support of the University's Commitment to Promoting Opportunities for Persons with Disabilities, Vanderbilt U., 2004. Fellow: APA (fellow Sch. Psych. Divsn. 1985, fellow Edn. Psychology Divsn. 1990); mem.: Am. Psychol. Soc. (charter fellow 1989), Learning Disabilities Assn., Tenn. Assn. Sch. Psychologists, Internat. Sch. Psychology Assn., Coun. for Exceptional Children, Am. Assn. on Mental Retardation, Am. Ednl. Rsch. Assn., Iowa Acad. Edn. (charter), Nat. Assn. Sch. Psychologists (pres., editor Sch. Psychology Rev., chair grad. program approval, Disting. Svc. award 1980, 1987, 1990, Lifetime Achievement award 2000, Legends award 2007).

RESCIGNO, RICHARD JOSEPH, editor; b. NYC, Apr. 13, 1946; s. Vincent James and Rose (Sofia) R.; m. Carol Sue Conyne, Apr. 22, 1978; children: Timothy, Daniel. BA in English Lit., Fairleigh Dickinson U., 1967; MS in Journalism, Columbia U., 1968. Reporter The Hudson Dispatch, Union City, NJ, 1967; reporter, copy editor The Bergen Record, Hackensack, NJ, 1971-75; reporter, copy editor, asst. city editor Newsday, Melville, NY, 1975-81; news editor, asst. mng. editor, mng. editor Barron's, The Dow Jones Bus. and Fin. Weekly, NYC, 1981—, mng. editor, 1987—. With U.S. Army, 1968-70. Avocations: foreign languages, travel, sports. Office: Barron's 1211 Ave of the Americas New York NY 10036 Business E-Mail: rich.rescigno@barrons.com.

RESCIGNO, THOMAS NICOLA, theoretical physicist; b. NYC, Sept. 10, 1947; s. Joseph Aiello and Leona Rees (Llewellyn) R.; m. Erie Ann Mills, May 24, 1986. BA, Columbia U., 1969; MA, Harvard U., 1971, PhD, 1973. Rsch. fellow Calif. Inst. Tech., Pasadena, 1973; staff scientist Lawrence Livermore Lab., Livermore, Calif., 1975-79, group leader, 1979-86, sr. scientist, 1986—. Lectr. atomic and molecular physics U. N.Mex., Albuquerque, summers 1993, 94. Editor 2 sci. monographs; mem. editl. staff Phys. Rev. A, 1996-99; contbr. more than 100 articles to profl. jours., chpts. to books. Recipient Am. Inst. Chemists medal, 1969; Nat. Energy fellow NSF, 1975. Fellow Am. Phys. Soc. (local chair 1990). Office: Lawrence Livermore Nat Lab PO Box 808 Livermore CA 94551-0808

RESCORLA, ROBERT ARTHUR, psychology professor; b. Pitts., May 9, 1940; s. Arthur R. and Mildred J. (Jenkins) Rescorla; m. Shirley Steele; children: Eric, Michael. BA, Swarthmore Coll., 1962; PhD, U. Pa., 1966; MA, Yale U., 1974; PhD (hon.), Ghent U., Belgium, 2006. Successively asst. prof., assoc. prof., prof. Yale U., New Haven, 1966—80; prof. psychology U. Pa., Phila., 1981—, James Skinner prof. sci., 1986—2000, Christopher H. Browne disting. prof. psychology, 2000—, dean of coll. Sch. Arts and Scis., 1994—97. Author: Pavlovian Second-Order Conditioning, 1980; editor: Animal Learning and Behavior, 1995—97; contbr. articles to profl. jours. Recipient Ira Abrams Tchg. award, 1999, Horsley Grant award, Pavlovian Soc., 2005. Fellow: Am. Acad. Arts and Sciences; mem.: AAAS (pres. sect. J., psychology 1988—89), APA (pres. divsn. 3 1985, Disting. Sci.Contbn. award 1986), NAS, Psychonomic Soc. (mem. governing bd. 1979—85, chmn. publ. bd. 1985—86), Ea. Psychol. Assn. (bd. dirs. 1983—86, pres. 1986—87, Warren medal 1991), Soc. Exptl. Psychologists, Am. Psychol. Soc. (William James fellow). Office: U Pa Dept Psychology 3720 Walnut St Philadelphia PA 19104-3604

RESEK, ROBERT WILLIAM, economist; b. Berwyn, Ill., July 2, 1935; s. Ephraim Frederick and Ruth Elizabeth (Rummele) R.; m. Lois Doll, July 9, 1960; 1 child, Richard Alden. BA, U. Ill., 1957; AM, Harvard U., 1960, PhD, 1961. Asst. prof. econs. U. Ill., Urbana, 1961-65, assoc. prof., 1965-70, prof., 1970—2005, prof. emeritus, 2005—; vis. scholar MIT, Cambridge, 1967-68; dir. Bur. Econ. and Bus. Rsch., 1977-89, acting v.p. for acad. affairs, 1987-89, v.p. for acad. affairs, 1989—94, v.p. emeritus, 1995—; prof. Inst. Govt. and Pub. Affairs, 1994—2005, prof. emeritus, 2005—. Tchg. fellow Harvard U., 1959-61; vis. prof. U. Colo., 1967, 74-76, 82, Kyoto (Japan) U., 1976; cons. GM, 1964-66, U.S. Congress Joint Econ. Com., 1978-80, ABA, 1980-82; vis. scholar UCLA, 1994-95; co-dir. Midwest Economy: Issues and Policy, Midwest Govs. Conf., 1981; bd. dirs. Midwest U. Consortium Internat. Activities, 1989-94, v.p., 1991-94; mem. Ill. Gov.'s Econ. Policy Coun., 1999-2003. Co-author: Environmental Contamination by Lead and Other Heavy Metals--Synthesis and Modeling, 1978, Special Topics in Mathematics for Economists, 1976, A Comparative Cost Study of Staff Panel and Participating Attorney Panel Prepaid Legal Service Plans, 1981, Illinois Higher Education: Building the Economy, Shaping Society, 2000; editor: Illinois Economic Outlook, 1982-87, Illinois Economic Statistics, 1981, Economic Edge, 1996-2004; co-editor: The Midwest Economy: Issues and Policy, 1982, Frontiers of Business and Economic Research Management, 1983, Illinois Statistical Abstract, 1987, 2002-04. Mem. exec. com. Assn. Univ. Bus. and Econ. Rsch., 1977-89, v.p., 1978-82, pres., 1982-83. Woodrow Wilson fellow, 1957; Social Sci. Rsch. Coun. grantee, 1964; NSF fellow, 1967-69, grantee, 1974-77; U.S. Dept. State scholar, Japan, 1976; grantee Ill. Bd. Higher Edn., 1998-99. Mem. Econometric Soc., Beta Gamma Sigma, Phi Kappa Phi. Home: 201 E Holmes St Urbana IL 61801-6612 Office: Univ Ill 211 IGPA 1007 W Nevada St Urbana IL 61801-3812 Business E-Mail: resek@illinois.edu.

RESER, DON CLAYTON, lawyer, investment banker; b. San Antonio, Dec. 14, 1950; s. Richard Stair and Mary Luella (Clayton) R. A.B. in Econs., Stanford U., 1973; M.B.A., U. Tex., 1976; J.D., U. Houston, 1978. Bar: Tex. 1977, U.S. dist. ct. (we. and so. dists.), U.S. Ct. Appeals (5th and 11th circs.) 1981, U.S. Supreme Ct. 1981, U.S. Tax Ct. 1980. Jr. law clk. to judge U.S. Dist. Ct. Western Dist. Tex., 1977-78, sr. law clk., 1978-79; assoc. Mathis & Bevil, San Antonio, 1979-80, Plunkett, Gibson & Allen, San Antonio, 1980-84, Don C. Reser, P.C., San Antonio, 1984—, D.C. Reser & Co., 1988-90; pres., dir. The Truck Stop Scale, Co., 1988—. Bd. dirs. U. Houston Law Alumni Assn. Mem. ABA, Fed. Bar Assn., Tex. Bar Assn., San Antonio Bar Assn. Republican. Mem. LDS Ch. Contbr. article to law jour. Office: PO Box 791307 San Antonio TX 78279-1307

RESES, JACQUELINE DAWN, private equity firm executive; b. 1970; d. Stephen W. and Ronnie Reses; m. Matthew Benjamin Apfel, Sept. 13, 1992. BS in Economics, cum laude, U. Pa. Wharton Sch. Bus., 1992. Mergers and acquisitions to v.p. Goldman Sachs Group, Inc.; prin. media and tech. investments Doughty Hanson & Co.; bus. devel. 12 Entrepreneuring, Inc.; CEO iBuilding, Inc., 2001; ptnr., co-head US media group Apax Partners, L.P., 2001—. Bd. dirs. N. Am. membership grp. and trend tech. Doughty Hanson & Co.; bd. dirs. iBuilding, Inc. Mem. Baby Buggy, Inc. Named one of The 100 Most Influential Women in NYC Bus., Crain's NY Bus., 2007. Office: Apax Partners LP 153 E 53rd St 53rd Fl New York NY 10022 Office Phone: 212-753-6300. Office Fax: 212-319-6155.*

RESHCHIKOV, MICHAEL A., physics professor, researcher; b. Leningrad, Russia, June 11, 1959; s. Alexander Pavlovich Reshchikov and Oktyabrina Grigorievna Reshchikova; m. Elena Nikolaevna Petrova, Nov. 25, 1983; children: Paul, Alexander. MSEE, St. Petersburg Poly. Inst., St. Petersburg, Russia, 1976—82; PhD in physics, Ioffe Physico-Technical Inst., St. Petersburg, Russia, 1982—89. Rsch. scientist Ioffe Physico-Technical Inst., St. Petersburg, Russia, 1982—97, Northwestern U., Evanstone, Ill., 1997—99, Dept. of Elec. Engring., Va. Commonwealth U., 1999—2004; asst. prof. Dept. of Physics, Va. Commonwealth U., 2004—. Contbr. more than 100 articles to profl. jours. Mem.: Va. Acad. Scis., Am. Phys. Soc., Materials Rsch. Soc. (assoc.). Achievements include research in deep defects in semiconductors, mostly by luminescence methods. Identification of point defects in GaN, GaAs, InSb, Ge. Avocations: swimming, diving, reading. Office: Dept Physics Virginia Commonwealth Univ 1020 West Main St Richmond VA 23284 Office Fax: 804-828-7073. Business E-Mail: mreshchi@vcu.edu.

RESHOTKO, ELI, aerospace engineer, educator; b. NYC, Nov. 18, 1930; s. Max and Sarah (Kalisky) R.; m. Adina Venit, June 7, 1953; children: Deborah, Naomi, Miriam Ruth. BS, Cooper Union, 1950; MS, Cornell U., 1951; PhD, Calif. Inst. Tech., 1960. Aero. research engr. NASA-Lewis Flight Propulsion Lab., Cleve., 1951-56, head fluid mechanics sect., 1956-57; head high temperature plasma sect. NASA-Lewis Research Center, 1960-61, chief plasma physics br., 1961-64; asso. prof. engring. Case Inst. Tech., Cleve., 1964-66, dean, 1986-87; prof. engring. Case Western Res. U., Cleve., 1966-88, chmn. dept. fluid thermal and aerospace scis., 1970-76, chmn. dept. mech. and aerospace engring., 1976-79, Kent H. Smith prof. engring., 1989-98, Kent H. Smith prof. emeritus, 1999—. Susman vis. prof. dept. aero. engring. Technion-Israel Inst. Tech., Haifa, Israel, 1969-70; cons. Inst. Def. Analyses, Dynamics Tech. Inc., Aerion Corp., Rockwell Sci. Ctr.; adv. com. fluid dynamics NASA, 1961-64; aero. adv. com. NASA, 1980-87, chmn. adv. subcom. on aerodynamics, 1983-85; chmn. U.S. Boundary Layer Transition Study Group, NASA/USAF, 1970—2001, steering com., 2001-; US mem. fluid dynamics panel AGARD-NATO, 1981-88; chmn. steering com. Symposium on Engring. Aspects of Magneto-hydro-dynamics, 1966, Case-NASA Inst. for Computational Mechanics in Propulsion, 1985-92, USRA/NASA ICASE Sci. Coun., 1992; Joseph Wunsch lectr. Technion-Israel Inst. Tech., 1990. Contbr. articles to tech. jours. Chmn. bd. govs. Cleve. Coll. Jewish Studies, 1981-84 (life trustee); bd. govs. Technion-Israel Inst. Tech., Haifa, Israel, 1999-2005; mem. NRC Air Force Studies bd., 2000-06, NRC Aeronautics & Space Engring. Bd., 2008-. Guggenheim fellow Calif. Inst. Tech., 1957-59. Fellow ASME, AAAS, AIAA (Fluid and Plasma Dynamics award 1980, Dryden lectr. in rsch. 1994), Am. Phys. Soc. (vice-chmn. divsn. fluid dynamics 1998, chair-elect 1999, chair 2000, Otto Laporte award in fluid dynamics 1999), Am. Acad. Mechanics (pres. 1986-87); mem. NAE, Ohio Sci. and Engring. Roundtable, Sigma Xi, Tau Beta Pi, Pi Tau Sigma. Home: 1200 Humboldt St Apt 601 Denver CO 80218-2454

RESIDANTE, EL (RENÉ PÉREZ), singer, composer; b. Hato Rey, PR, Feb. 23, 1978; Co-founder & lead singer Calle 13; signed to White Lion records. Singer: (albums) Calle 13, 2005 (Latin Grammy award for Best Urban Music Album, 2006), Residante O Visitante, 2007 (Best Urban Music album, Latin Grammy Awards, 2007, Grammy award, Best Latin Urban Album, 2008), Los de Atrás Vienen Conmigo, 2008, (songs) Atrévete Te, Te!, 2005 (Latin Grammy award for Best Short Form Music Video, 2006), (with Nelly Furtado) No Hay Igual, 2006, Pal Norte, 2007 (Best Urban song, Latin Grammy Awards, 2007). Recipient Best New Artist award, Best Urban Album & Best Short Music Video, Latin Grammy Awards, 2006. Office: White Lion Records Inc Urb Ocean Park 2072 Cacique Santurce PR 00911-1514

RESIKA, PAUL, artist; b. NYC, Aug. 15, 1928; Student, Sol Wilson, NYC, 1940—44, Hans Hofmann Sch., 1945—47, Sch. Venice, Italy, 1950—52, Sch. Venice, Rome, 1953. Adj. prof. art Cooper Union, 1966-78; instr. Art Students League, 1968-69; faculty Skowhagen Sch. Painting and Sculpture, 1973, 76; chmn. M.F.A. program Parsons Sch. Design, 1978-89. Dartmouth Coll. 1972 Artist in Residence. One-man shows include George Dix Gallery, NYC, 1948, Peridot Gallery, 1965, 1967, 1968, 1969, 1970, Washburn Gallery, 1971, 1973, Hopkins Ctr. Dartmouth Coll., 1972, Graham Gallery, 1976, 1979, 1981, 1983, 1985, Longpoint Gallery, Provincetown, Mass., 1979, 1981, 1989, 1992, 1995, 25-yr. survey Artists Choice Mus., 1985, Merideth Long Gallery, Houston, 1986, 1997, 2005, 2007, Walker-Kornbluth Gallery, Fair Lawn, N.J., 1986, 1995, 1997, Crane Kalman Gallery, London, 1986, Graham/Modern Gallery, 1987—88, 1990, Salander-O'Reilly Galleries, NYC, 1993, 1994, 1995, 1999, 2001, 2002, 2005, Benucci, Rome, 2005, 2007, Vered Gallery, East Hampton, N.Y., 1995, 2003, 2004, Gerald Peters Gallery, Santa Fe, 1996, Provincetown Art Assn. and Mus., 1997, Graham & Sons, NYC, 2008, Lori Bookstein Gallery, N.Y.C., 1998, 2001, Berta Walker Gallery, Provincetown, 1998, 2001, 2003, Provincetown, Mass., 2004, 2005, 2006, 2007, 2008—09, Lizan Tops Gallery, East Hampton, N.Y., 1998, Hackett Freedman, San Francisco, 1998, Hackett-Freedman, 1999, 2000, 2002, 2006, Metta Galleria, Madrid, 2000, Camino Real Gallery, Boca Raton, Fla., 2003, Benucci Gallery, Rome, 2005, Lori Bookstein Gallery, 2006, Represented in permanent collections Nat. Mus. Am. Art, Washington, Muson-Williams-Proctor Inst. Mus. Art, Utica, N.Y., U. Nebr. Art Gallery, Indpls. Mus. Art, Chase Manhattan Bank, N.Y.C., Neuberger Mus., SUNY, Purchase, U. Wyo., Laramie, Met. Mus. Art, N.Y., Colby Coll., NAD, Owensboro (Ky.) Mus. Art, U. Ariz., William Benton Mus. Art, Hood Mus., Dartmouth Coll., Hanover, N.H., Tucson Mus. Art, Crackow Mus. Art, Poland, Parish Art Mus., Southampton, N.Y., Heckscher Mus., Huntington, N.Y., Mills Coll. Mus., Oakland, Calif., Meml. Art Gallery, Rochester, Whitney Mus., NYC, Mus. Modern Art, also pvt. collections, Lori Bookstein Fine Art, NY. Recipient award Am. Acad. Arts and Letters, 1977; Altman prize NAD, 1982, 91, 97, 2003, Obrig prize, 1996; Louis Comfort Tiffany grantee, 1959, Ingram Merrill grantee, 1969; John Simon Guggenheim Meml. fellow, 1984. Mem. NAD, Am. Acad. Arts and Letters. Home: Apt 6E 175 Riverside Dr New York NY 10024

RESLER, MICHAEL, literature and language professor; s. Richard and Aminda Resler; m. Charles Lutcavage, Jan. 13, 1948. PhD, Harvard U., Cambridge, Mass., 1976. Prof. & chair, German studies Boston Coll., Chestnut Hill, Mass., 1976—. Fellowship, Fulbright Commn., 1969—71. Mem.: Phi Beta Kappa. Democrat. Home: 24 Churchill St Brookline MA 02446 Office: Boston Coll Lyons Hall 201c Chestnut Hill MA 02467 Office Fax: 617-552-4454. Business E-Mail: resler@bc.edu.

RESMAN-TARGOFF, BETH HOLLY, pharmacist, educator; d. Norman M. and Rowena Resman; m. Ira N. Targoff, June 14, 1981; 1 child, Deborah Judith Targoff. BS in Pharmacy, SUNY, Buffalo, 1973, PharmD, 1976. Registered pharmacist NY, 1974, Okla., 1991. Clin. coord., asst. dir. pharmacy The Buffalo Gen. Hosp., 1976—81; clin. instr. SUNY, 1976—81; clin. prof. U. Okla., Oklahoma City, 1981—. Mem. adv. bd. Annals Pharmacotherapy, 1989—. Contbr. chapters to books. Fellow: Am. Coll. Clin. Pharmacy; mem.: Am. Assn. Colls. Pharmacy, Am. Pharmacists Assn., Okla. Soc. Health-Sys. Pharmacists, Am. Soc. Health-Sys. Pharmacists, Phi Kappa Phi, Rho Chi (region VI councilor 2008—, Outstanding Faculty Mem., U. Okla. Chpt. 1992—2006, 2008—09). Avocations: travel, photography. Office: Univ Okla Coll Pharm 1110 N Stonewall Oklahoma City OK 73117

RESNIC, BURTON S., lawyer; s. Samuel and Theresa Babe Resnic; m. Marjoie C. Meyer, July 1, 1961; children: Laura J. Brounstein, Joanne H. Lippman. BA, Washington U., St. Louis, 1950; LLB, Harvard U., Cambridge, Mass., 1953. Bar: Mass. 1954, D.C. 1954. Ptnr. Resnic, Beauregard, Waite & Driscoll, Holyoke, Mass., 1955—. Bd. dirs. Holyoke Hosp., 1983—; spkr. in field, 1975—2005. Contbr. articles to profl. jours. Past pres. Pioneer Valley Coun. Boy Scouts Am., Hampden County, Mass.; past bd. dirs. Jewish Nursing Home, Longmeadow, Mass., Jr. Achievement, Holyoke; vol. Law Day spkr. various Sr. Citizen Couns.; past. bd. dirs. StageWest; del. Rep. Nat. Conv., 1976, 1980; bd. dirs., pro bono legal counsel Congregation Sons of Zion, Holyoke. With US Army, 1953—55. Recipient Recognition for Successful Major Capital Campaign, Holyoke Hosp., 1986—87. Mem.: Crestview Country Club (bd. dirs. 1978—). Avocations: golf, tennis, skiing. Home: 20 Longfellow Rd Holyoke MA 01040 Office: Resnic Beauegard Waite & Driscoll 330 Whitney Ave Ste 400 Holyoke MA 01040 Office Phone: 413-536-0653. Office Fax: 413-536-4074. Business E-Mail: kstdenis@rbwd.com.

RESNICK, ADRIENNE JO, clinical social worker, psychotherapist; b. NYC, July 19, 1954; d. Martin and Molly Starkman; m. Paul Resnick, Sept. 30, 1978; 1 child, Elana. BA, NYU, 1975, MSW, 1981. Psychotherapist Stamford Child Guidance Clinic, Conn., 1981—83; group facilitator YWCA, White Plains, NY; psychotherapist pvt. practice, Sleepy Hollow, 1983—. Author: Sometimes I Feel Blue, 2002, Food Play, 2002. Recipient Founders Day award, NYU, N.Y.C., 1975. Mem.: NASW (diplomate), Am. Soc. Trial Cons., Acad. Cert. Social Workers, Soc. Clin. Social Work. Avocations: writing, travel, yoga. Office: 239 N Broadway Sleepy Hollow NY 10591 Office Phone: 914-633-3389. Personal E-mail: agres719@aol.com.

RESNICK, ALICE ROBIE, retired state supreme court justice; b. Erie, Pa., Aug. 21, 1939; d. Adam Joseph and Alice Suzanne (Spizarny) Robie; m. Melvin L. Resnick, Mar. 20, 1970 PhB, Siena Heights Coll., 1961; JD, U. Detroit, 1964; LLD (hon.), Heidelberg Coll., 1999, U. Akron, 1994. Bar: Ohio 1964, Mich. 1965, U.S. Supreme Ct. 1970. Atty. priv. practice, 1964—75; asst. county prosecutor Lucas County Prosecutor's Office, Toledo, 1964-75, trial atty., 1965-75; judge Toledo Mcpl. Ct., 1976-83, 6th Dist. Ct. Appeals, State of Ohio, Toledo, 1983-88; instr. U. Toledo, 1968-69; justice Ohio Supreme Ct., 1988—2006. Co-chairperson Ohio State Gender Fairness Task Force. Trustee Siena Heights Coll., Adrian, Mich., 1982—; organizer Crime Stopper Inc., Toledo, 1981—; mem. Mayor's Drug Coun.; bd. dirs. Guest House Inc. Recipient Gertrude W. Donahey award, Ohio Democratic Party, 1999, Woman of Toledo award, St. Vincent Mercy Medical Ctr., 1999; named to Ohio Women's Hall of Fame, 1995. Mem. ABA, Toledo Bar Assn., Lucas County Bar Assn., Ohio State Bar Assn. (Nettie Cronise Lutes award 1995), Nat. Assn. Women Judges (Making A Difference award 1996), Am. Judicature Soc., Toledo Women's Bar Assn., Ohio State Women's Bar Assn. (Alice Robie Resnick Outstanding Lawyer award 1998), Toledo Mus. Art, Internat. Inst. Toledo. Roman Catholic. Personal E-mail: icenick@aol.com.

RESNICK, DONALD IRA, lawyer; b. Chgo., July 19, 1950; s. Roland S. and Marilyn B. (Weiss) R.; m. Jill Allison White, July 3, 1977; children: Daniel, Allison. BS with high honors, U. Ill., 1972; JD, Harvard U., 1975. Bar: Ill. 1975, U.S. Dist. Ct. (no. dist.) Ill. 1975. Assoc. Arvey, Hodes, Costello & Burman, Chgo., 1975-80, ptnr., 1981-83; sr. ptnr. Nagelberg & Resnick, Chgo., 1983-89, Levenstein & Resnick, Chgo., 1989-91; chmn. real estate dept. Jenner & Block, Chgo.,

1992—. Mem. mgmt. com. Jenner & Block, Chgo. Mem. ABA, Birchwood (Highland Park, Ill.) Club. Office: Jenner & Block 1 E Ibm Plz Fl 4000 Chicago IL 60611-7603

RESNICK, ELAINE BETTE, psychotherapist, licensed clinical social worker; b. Orlando, Fla., Apr. 2, 1944; d. Julius Milton and Annette (Chusid) Bernstein; m. Peter Schuyten (div. 1973); m. Richard B. Resnick, May 21, 1975; children: Demian, Jesse, Nora; 1 stepchild, Deborah. BA with honors, NYU, 1966; MSW, CUNY, 1971; postgrad., NYU, 1992—. Cert. Inst. for Study Psychotherapy, 1979, comprehensive tng. program with chronically and terminally ill patients, 2002; lic. clin. social worker, N.Y.; cert. in hypnosis tng. and supervision Columbia U., 1978; diplomate in clin. social work. Field work supr. NYU, NYC, 1973-82; rsch. assoc. N.Y. Med. Coll., NYC, 1973—82; clin. dir. div. drug abuse rsch treatment NY Med. Coll., NYC, 1977—83; field work supr. York Coll., NYC, 1976-77, Wurzweiler Sch. of Social Work, Yeshiva U., 1991—; clin. instr. N.Y. Med. Coll., NYC, 1982-83; pvt. practice NYC, 1973—; lectr. Marymount Manhattan Coll., 1974—75; clin. dir. Psychiatry & Family Therapy, NYC, 1986—. Psychiat. social worker, Divsn. Biol. Psychiat. Met. Hosp., 1971-1973 N.Y. State Psychiat. Inst., 1970-71, Columbia U. Sch. Medicine; social worker Intensive Family Counseling Unit N.Y.C. Dept. Social Svcs., 1969-70; psychiat. social worker, St. Vincent's Hosp., 1970; adj. asst. prof. NYU Grad. Sch. Social Work, 1977-82. Contbr. articles to profl. jours.; responsible for numerous presentations in field. Fellow Soc. Clin. Social Work Psychotherapists; mem. NASW, Nat. Registry Health Care Providers in Clin. Social Work. Office Phone: 212-678-6949. Office Fax: 212-678-6949. E-mail: elaine02@mac.com.

RESNICK, IRVEN MICHAEL, philosophy educator; b. Rochester, NY, Nov. 22, 1952; s. William Resnick and Mary Eskenazi; m. Elizabeth Anne Scofield, May 28, 1989; children: Austin Scofield, Matthew Scofield, Ariel Resnick. BA, Tulane U., 1974; MA, Cath. U. Am., 1980; PhD, U. Va., 1983. Asst. prof. La. State U., Baton Rouge, 1987-90; prof. Dept. Philosophy and Religion U. Tenn., Chattanooga, 1990—. Chair of excellence in Judaic studies; sr. assoc. Oxford Ctr. for Hebrew and Jewish Studies, 2003—. Author: Divine Power and Possibility in St. Peter Damian's De Divina Omnipotentia, 1992, Two Theological Treatises of Odo of Tournai, 1994; co-author, translator: Albertus Magnus On Animals, 1999, An Annotated Bibliography of Albert the Great (1900-2000), 2004, The Letters of Peter Damian, 121-150, 2004, The Letters of Peter Damian, 151-180, 2005, Petrus Alfonsi's Dialogue against the Jews, 2006, Albert the Great's Questions Concerning Aristotle's 'On Animals', 2008. Jerusalem Trust fellow Oxford Ctr. for Hebrew Std., Yarnton, Eng., 1995, corr. fellow Ingeborg Rennert Ctr., Bar-Ilan U., Israel, 1996, C.G. Found. Jerusalem Project, Bar-Ilan U., 1996; named disting. vis. fellow Queen Mary, U. London, 2006. Mem.: Medieval Acad. Am., Assn. for Jewish Studies, Soc. for Medieval and Renaissance Philosophy, Oxford Ctr. for Hebrew and Jewish Studies (sr.). Home: 204 Slayton St Signal Mountain TN 37377-2285 Office: U Tenn Chattanooga 615 Mccallie Ave Chattanooga TN 37403-2504 Office Phone: 423-425-4446. Office Fax: 423-425-4153. Business E-Mail: Irven-Resnick@utc.edu.

RESNICK, JEFFREY I., plastic surgeon; b. Jersey City, Mar. 2, 1954; s. Victor and Regina (Bistritz) R.; m. Michele Gail Zinger, July 12, 1981; children: Andrew Gregory, Daniel Zachary. BS, Yale U., 1975; MD, U. Pa., 1980. Diplomate Am. Bd. Surgery, Am. Bd. Plastic Surgery. Resident in surgery Mass. Gen. Hosp., Boston, 1980—85, resident in plastic surgery, 1985—87; asst. clin. prof. plastic surgery UCLA, 1987—, fellow in craniofacial surgery, 1987—88; asst. prof. clin. surgery U. So. Calif, Santa Monica, 1998—. Contbr. articles to profl. jours. Surgeon Interplast, Vietnam, Nepal, Myanmar. Mem. Am. Assn. Plastic Surgeons., Am. Soc. Plastic Surgeons, Am. Soc. Maxillofacial Surgeons, Am. Cleft Palate-Craniofacial Assn., Plastic Surgery Ednl. Found., Sigma Xi, Alpha Omega Alpha. Office: 1301 20th St Ste 470 Santa Monica CA 90404-2082 Home Phone: 310-471-3532; Office Phone: 310-315-0222. Business E-Mail: jresnick@ucla.edu.

RESNICK, KENNETH, photography director; b. NYC, May 11, 1934; s. Reuben and Helen (Edelson) R.; m. Marijke Koch, Aug. 1960 (div. Aug. 1974); children: Sonya, Paul, Karen; m. Karen louise Matthesius, July 23, 1977; children: Margaret Rose, Charles Andrew. Student, Trinity Coll., 1952—56. Dir. photography Ga. Ctr., U. Ga., Athens, 1960-61; cameraman, editor Milner and Fenwick, Inc., Balt., 1961-63; film maker US Info. Agy., Washington, 1963-66; producer Nat. Ednl. TV, NYC, 1965; cameraman, asst. cameraman NBC-TV, Washington, 1967-68; chief photographer Md. Ctr. for Pub. Broadcasting Sta. WMPB-TV, Owings Mills, 1968-69; cameraman, asst. dir. BF&J Prodns., Balt., 1969-72; news film cameraman Sta. WTTG-TV, Metromedia Prodns., Washington, 1972-78; producer, videographer Cable News Network, Atlanta, 1981-82; video producer Wang Labs., Inc., Lowell, Mass., 1986-90. Photography instr. Md. Inst. Coll. Art, Balt., 1985; conf. participant Arts and Soc., Morgan State Coll, Balt., 1966. Co-produced, co-directed, cinematographer Sunday on the River, 1962 (Bronze medal, Silver Gondola award humanitarian idealism in film Venice Internat. Documentary Film Festival 1962, An Outstanding Film of Yr. Brit. Film Inst. and London Film Festival 1962, Golden Eagle award Council Internat. Nontheatrical Events 1962, 63, work inducted in the Mus. Modern Art Film Archives 1991); produced, directed, photgraphed Men, Marble and Machines, 1984 (Bronze medal Internat. Film and TV Festival of NYC 1984, Golden Eagle award, 1984 Chris plaque Columbus Film Festival 1985, Emmy award 1987); photographed Now and in the Future (Silver Plaque INTERCOM 1988); producer, dir., photographer A Celebration of Architecture (Gold Camera award, 3 Silver Screen awards, U.S. Indsl. Film and Video Festival 1989, Gold CINDY award, Rose Layos Green Meml. award 1989, Chris award Columbus Film Festival 1989, Silver Plaque INTERCOM, 1989, 2 Silver Medals Internat. Film & TV Festival N.Y. 1990, Golden Eagle award 1990). Mem. World Wildlife Fund. Recipient First Prize Gen. News Class award, 1973, Spot News Class award, 1976, 78, White House News Photographer's Assn., First Place Spot News award Nat. Press Photographer's Assn., 1978, Emmy news film photography Washington Chpt. Nat. Acad. TV Arts and Scis., Inc., 1978. Mem. Internat. Photographers of Motion Picture and TV Industries (local 600), Sierra Club. Democrat. Unitarian Universalist. Home: 73 Washington St Concord NH 03301-4172

RESNICK, LYNDA, corporate financial executive; Co-owner, vice chmn. Franklin Mint; co-owner Roll Internat. Chmn. Teleflora. Chmn. mktg. com. Conservation Internat.; bd. dirs. Assn. for Cure of Cancer of the Prostate, CaP CURE, Milken Family Found.; mem. exec. com., trustee, chmn. acquisitions com. LA County Mus. Art; mem. com. on sculpture and decorative arts Met. Mus. Art; trustee Phila. Mus. Art. Recipient Gold Effie award, 1983; named one of Top 50 US Women Bus. Owners, Working Women, Top 100 US art collectors Art & Antiques mag., Top 200 Collectors, ARTnews mag., 2008 #1 L.A.-based woman Bus. Owner, LA bus. Jour. Avocation: collecting Old Masters. Office: Roll Internat Corp 11444 W Olympic Blvd Los Angeles CA 90064-1549

RESNICK, MYRON JAY, retired insurance company executive, lawyer; b. Louisville, July 13, 1931; s. Harry C. and Sybil G. (Glick) R.; m. Alicia M. Ward, Dec. 16, 1967; children— Hugh, Clay, David. BS in Econs., U. Pa., 1953; JD, U. Mich., 1956. Various positions Allstate Ins. Co., Northbrook, Ill., 1959-88, sr. v.p., treas. bd. dirs., 1959-95; chmn. bd. Federated Ins. Co. Ltd. (UK), Sale, Cheshire, England, 1979-81; ret., 1995. Dir. Allstate Ins. Co. Ltd. (U.K.), Sale; pres. Allstate Investment Mgmt. Co.; mem. adj. faculty John Marshall Law Sch., Chgo., 1996-98. Chmn. Chgo. exec. com. Anti-Defamation League, 2006—08; bd. dirs. Chgo. Urban League, 1987-2001, St. Scholastica High Sch., Chgo., 1977-79; trustee George Williams Coll., Downers Grove, Ill., 1981-93, chmn. bd. trustees, 1991-93; trustee Aurora U., 1993—; bd. advisors Inst. Law and Econs. U. Pa., 1994—. With U.S. Army, 1956-58. Mem. ABA, Chgo. Bar Assn., Ill. Bar Assn., Assn. Life Ins. Counsel, Chgo. Mortgage Attys. Assn. (bd. dirs. 1965-75)

RESNICK, STEVEN DAVID, pediatric dermatologist, educator; b. NYC, Mar. 18, 1956; AB, Brown U., Providence, 1978; MD, Yale U. Sch. Medicine, New Haven, 1982. Diplomate Am. Bd. Dermatology, lic. Pediat. Dermatology. Intern pediat. U. Wash./Children's Hosp. Med. Ctr., Seattle, 1982-83; resident dermatology U. Calif. San Francisco, 1983-86, fellowship pediat. dermatology, 1986—87; staff NC Meml. Hosp., 1988—95; asst. prof. dermatology and pediatrics U. NC, Chapel Hill, 1994-95; assoc. clin. prof. dermatology and pediatrics Columbia U. Coll. Physicians & Surgeons, Chapel Hill, 1995—; divsn. chief dermatology Mary Imogene Bassett Hosp., Cooperstown, NY, 1995—. Contbr. articles to profl. jours. Named one of Best Dr.'s in America, Best Dr.'s Inc. Fellow: Soc. Pediat. Dermatology, Am. Acad. Dermatology, Am. Acad. Pediat. (exec. com. mem.). Office: Bassett Healthcare Divsn Dermatology 1 Atwell Rd Cooperstown NY 13326-1301 Office Phone: 607-547-3300. Office Fax: 607-547-4648.

RESNICK, STEWART ALLEN, diversified company executive; b. Jersey City, Dec. 24, 1936; s. David and Yetta (Goldmaker) R.; children from previous marriage: Jeffrey Brian, Ilene Sue, William Jay; m. Lynda Rae Harris, Nov. 26, 1972; children: Jonathan Charles Sinay, Jason Daniel Sinay. BS, UCLA, 1959, LLB, 1962. Co-chmn., CEO, pres. Roll Internat. Corp., LA; chmn., CEO The Franklin Mint, Aston, Pa., 1985—; co-chmn., CEO Teleflora, LA; pres. Paramount Farms, Inc., LA; other subsidiaries of Roll Internat. Corp. include Paramount Citrus, Fiji Water, POM Wonderful. Bd. trustees J. Paul Getty Trust, LA, 2005—; mem. bd. Caltech, Bard Coll., Conservation Internat. Named one of Top 200 Collectors, ARTnews, 2008. Avocations: health and fitness related activities, collecting Old Masters. Office: Roll Internat Corp 10th Fl 11444 W Olympic Blvd Los Angeles CA 90064 Office Phone: 310-966-5700. Office Fax: 310-914-4747.

RESNICK CARSWELL, SARAH JACQUELINE, registrar; b. Washington, Dec. 7, 1958; BA, U. Fla., Gainesville, 1980. Student affairs coord, registrar U. Fla. Pharmacy, 2007—. Office: Univ Fla Coll Pharmacy PO Box 100495 Gainesville FL 32610 Office Fax: 352-273-6219. Business E-Mail: carswell@cop.ufl.edu.

RESNIK, HARVEY LEWIS PAUL, psychiatrist; b. Buffalo, Apr. 6, 1930; s. Samuel and Celia (Greenberg) R.; m. Audrey Ruth Frey, Aug. 30, 1964 (dec. 1993); children: Rebecca Gabrielle, Henry Seth Maccabee, Jessica Ruth. BA magna cum laude, U. Buffalo, 1951; MD, Columbia, 1955; grad., Phila. Psychoanalytic Inst., 1967. Diplomate: Am. Bd. Psychiatry and Neurology. Intern Phila. Gen. Hosp., 1955-56, resident in surgery, 1956-57; resident in psychiatry Jackson Meml. Hosp., Miami, Fla., 1959-61; fellow U. Pa. Hosp., 1961-62, mem. staff, 1962-67; instr; Sch. Medicine, U. Pa., 1962-66; instr. med. hypnosis Sch. Medicine, U. Pa. (Grad. Sch. Medicine), 1963-65; clin. dir. psychiatry E. J. Meyer Meml. Hosp., Buffalo, 1967, dir. psychiatry, 1968; from assoc. prof. to prof., dep. chair Sch. Medicine, SUNY at Buffalo, Buffalo, 1968—70; chief Nat. Center for Studies of Suicide Prevention, NIMH, 1969-74, chief mental health emergencies sect., 1974-76; with Reproductive Biology Rsch. Found., St. Louis, 1971; clin. prof. psychiatry and behavioral sci. Sch. Medicine, George Washington U., 1969—2002, prof. emeritus clin. psychiatry and behavioral scis., 2002—08; dir. Human Behavior Found., 1975—; lectr. Sch. Medicine, Johns Hopkins, Balt., 1969-74; adj. lectr. Johns Hopkins U. Sch. Pub. Health, Balt., 1981-82. Prof. cmty. health Fed. City Coll., 1971-75; med. dir. Johns Hopkins U. Compulsive Gambling Ctr., 1981-83; med. dir. alcohol and substance abuse program, College Park, 1986-2000; vis. prof. Katholieke U., Leuven, Belgium, 1986-93; cons. to Sec.-Gen. Ministry of Health, Belgium, 1986-90, NATO fellow, 1986-87; cons. various hosps. and orgns., Medicare, Pa. Blue Shield, 1984-96, Trailblazer Health, 1996-99, Blue Cross/Blue Shield S.C., 1999; sr. attending Suburban Hosp., Bethesda, Md., 1976—, psychiatry chair, 2006-2008, sr. physician emeritus, 2009. Author: Suicidal Behaviors: Diagnosis and Management, 1968, 2d edit., 1994, (with M. E. Wolfgang) Treatment of the Sexual Offender, 1971, Sexual Behaviors: Social, Clinical and Legal Aspects, 1972, (with B. Hathorne) Suicide Prevention in the Seventies, 1973, (with H.L. Ruben) Emergency Psychiatric Care, 1974, (with others) The Prediction of Suicide, 1974, Emergency and Disaster Management, 1976; (with J.T. Mitchell) Emergency Response to Crisis, 1981; editor: Bull. Suicidology, 1969-74; contbr. articles to profl. jours. Mem. Addictions Adv. Bd. Prince Georges County, 1980-85. Capt. MC USAFR, 1957-59, ETO-Mid., East CDR MC USNR, 1972; ret. 1991 Decorated officer Order of Crown (Belgium), 1989. Fellow Am. Coll. Mental Health Adminstrs. (NC) (life), Am. Coll. Psychiatrists (life), Am. Psychiat. Assn. (life); mem. Med-Chi of Md., Prince Georges County Med. Soc. (co-chair joint com. with Bar Assn. 1996-2001), Washington Psychiatry Soc., Am. Acad. Psychiatry and Law (suicidology com. 1998-2000), Phila. Psychoanalytic Soc., NIH Alumni Assn., Columbia U. Med. Alumni Assn. (bd. dirs. 1993-95), Cosmos Club (Washington), Phi Beta Kappa, Beta Sigma Rho (grand vice warden 1963). Jewish. Office: 4209 Bradley Ln Chevy Chase MD 20815-5234

RESNIK, ROBERT, medical educator; b. New Haven, Dec. 7, 1938; s. Nathan Alfred and Elsie (Hershman) R.; m. Lauren Brahms, Oct. 29, 1966; children: Andrew Scott, Jamie Layne. BA, Yale U., 1960; MD, Case Western Res. U., 1965. Intern in internal medicine Mt. Sinai Hosp., Cleve., 1965-66; resident in ob-gyn. Yale U. Sch. Medicine, 1966-70; asst. prof. Sch. Medicine U. Calif., San Diego, 1974-78, assoc. prof., 1978-82, prof. reproductive medicine, 1982—, chmn. dept., 1982-95, dean clin. affairs, 1988-90, dean admissions, 1995—2003. Cons. Nat. Heart, Lung and Blood Inst. NIH, Washington, 1987; mem. exec. com. Coun. Residency Edn. Ob-Gyn, Washington, 1988-94, residency rev. com., 1988-94. Editor: (textbook) Maternal-Fetal Medicine: Principles and Practice, 1984, 5th edit., 2004; contbr. numerous articles to profl. jours. Major U.S. Army, 1970-72. Recipient Lifetime Achievement award, Soc. Maternal Fetal Medicine, 2004, Mentor of Yr., U. Calif. San Diego, 2005; Rsch. grantee, Nat. Found., NIH. Fellow: Royal Coll. Obstet. Gynecologists (ad eundem), N.W. Obstet. Gynecological Soc., Pacific Coast Obstet. and Gynecol. Soc., Am. Coll. Ob-Gyn. (vice chmn. obs. practice com. 1998—2000), New England Obstet. Gynecological Soc.; mem.: San Diego Gynecol. Soc. (pres. 1982), Am. Gynecologic and Obstet. Soc. (pres. 2009—), Perinatal Rsch. Soc. (pres. 1985), Soc. Gynecologic Investigation (coun. 1983—88), Yale Club, Am. Gynecol. Club (pres. 2002—03). Office: UCSD Med Ctr 200 W Arbor Dr 8433 San Diego CA 92103-8433 Business E-Mail: rresnik@ucsd.edu.

RESO, ANTHONY, geologist, educator, earth resources economist; b. London, Eng., Aug. 10, 1931; arrived in US, 1940, naturalized, 1952; AB, Columbia Coll., 1954; MA, Columbia U., 1955; postgrad., U. Cin., 1956—57; PhD, Rice U., 1960; postgrad., Grad. Sch. Bus. U. Houston, 1964—68. Instr. geology Queens Coll., Flushing, NY, 1954; geologist Atlantic Richfield Corp., Midland, Tex., 1955—56; asst. prof. geology and curator invertebrate paleontology Pratt Mus., Amherst Coll., Mass., 1959—62; staff rsch. geologist Tenneco Oil Co., Houston, 1962—86; mgr. geol. Peak Prodn. Co., Houston, 1986—, v.p., 1988—, bd. dirs., 2000—. Cons. in geol. rsch. Tenn. Gas and Oil Co., 1960—61; lectr. U. Houston, 1962—65; vis. prof. Rice U., 1980; mem. bd. advisers Gulf Univs. Rsch. Corp., Galveston, Tex., 1967—75, chmn., 1968—69. Contbr. articles to profl. jours. Recipient Honor award, 2008; named to Hall of Fame, Varsity Basketball Team, Columbia U., 1950—51; Grantee Rsch., Eastman Fund, 1962, NSF fellow, 1958—59. Fellow: AAAS, Geol. Soc. Am. (com. investments 1984—95, chmn. 1985—92, budget com. 1993—95, found. trustee 1999—2004, Rsch. grantee 1958, Disting. Svc. award 1996); mem.: English-Speaking Union US (dir. Houston br. 1978—, v.p. 1982—88, pres. 1997—98), Houston Geol. Soc. (v.p. 1973—75, pres. 1975—76, chmn. constn. revision com. 1981, Disting. Svc. award 1985), Paleontol. Rsch. Instn., Am. Assn. Petroleum Geologists (life; com. convs. 1977—83, gen. chmn. nat. conv. 1979, chmn. 1980—83, com. investments 1982—88, chmn. com. group ins. 1986—88, treas. 1986—88, found. trustee assoc. 1991, Rsch. grantee 1958, 1959, Disting. Svc. award 1985), SEPM Soc. for Sedimentary Geology (com. investments 1990—2004, chmn. 1992—95, treas. SEPM Found. 1997—2003, Disting. Svc. award 2003), Paleontol. Soc., Varsity C Club, Beta Theta Pi, Sigma Gamma Epsilon, Sigma Xi. Episcopalian. Home: 1805 Brun St Houston TX 77019-5712 Office: care Peak Prodn Co PO Box 130785 Houston TX 77219-0785 Personal E-mail: aresogeo@swbell.net.

RESS, CHARLES WILLIAM, management consultant; b. Columbus, Ohio, Aug. 6, 1933; s. George Leonard and Martha (Lake) R.; m. Virginia M. Beck, Aug. 28, 1954; children: Beverly Beck, Suzanne E., Charles W. Jr., Linda Perrins Foxworth, Jennifer Laurel Brulé. BS, Miami U., 1955; MA in Psychology, Rutgers U., 1969. Buyer The Higbee Co., Cleve., 1956-59; asst. to gen. mdse. mgr. The Halle Bros. Co., Cleve., 1959-64; research dir. The Associated Mdse. Corp., NYC, 1964-73; v.p. Mgmt. Horizons, Columbus, 1973-76; founder, chmn. bd. C.W. Ress & Assoc., Inc., Columbus, 1976-90; gen. mgr. Levi Strauss & Co., Columbus, 1990-94, mgmt. cons., 1994—. Lectr. in field. Author: Future Trends in Retailing, 1983, Trans National Retailing, 1988, Retailing 2000, 1991; contbr. articles to profl. jours. Republican. Congregationalist. Avocations: cooking, wine tasting. Office: 3860 Lyon Dr Columbus OH 43220-4907 Office Phone: 614-457-8885. Personal E-mail: ressandress@wowway.com.

RESS, PATRICIA COLLEEN, editor, writer; b. Sioux City, Iowa, Aug. 7, 1945; d. Charles Francis and Alice Joanna (Krofta) Griffin; m. Lawrence Wright Dec. 13, 1969 (dec.); children: Alice Wendy, Cindy Marie; m. Fred Callsen Ress, Sept. 7, 1979; 1 child, Eric Christopher. BS in Edn., U. S.D., 1967; postgrad. studies in Journalism, U. Iowa, 1968-69; cert. in lab. sci., Gradwohl Sch. Med. Lab. Tech., St. Louis, 1970; environ. lab. sci., S.E. Comty. Coll., Lincoln, Nebr., 1979. Feature writer, columnist Clay County News-Sun, Sutton, Nebr., 1977—; feature writer, photographer Sun Newspapers, Lincoln, Nebr., 1977-78; feature writer -strange and unusual column The Nebr. Voice, Lincoln, Omaha, Kearney, Nebr., 1979-81; reporter, photographer The Walton County Tribune, Monroe, Ga., 1986; feature writer Omaha Met. Update and Midland Bus. Jour., 1990, 91; feature writer, free lance Paragon Publ. Ltd., Bournemouth, England, 1992—; editor The Constitutional Liberator, Omaha, 1995—. Regional story cons. Mike Jarmus radio show; staff feature writer/reporter Lagazette of Broussard, La.; story cons. Doomsday Talk Radio, Media, Pa., 2005—09; co-host Night Search Radio Show, Memphis. Author: Stranger Than Fiction: The True Time-Travel Adventures of Steven L. Gibbs, the Rainman of Time-Travel, 2002, Seven Chilling Things You Should Know About Your Soul, 2002, Travel Tips for Tightwads, 2002, Don't Go To College til' You've Read This Book!, 2002, Time-Travel Odyssey, 2002, Dangerouso Information, 2002, Cures and Treatment You're Not Supposed to Know About - They Actually Work, 2004, Carl's Story, 2004, Invisible Hands of Healing: My Journey Into Trans-Dimensional Medicine, 2004, The Frightenuing Final Piece to the UFO Puzzle, 2004, Conversations With Branton, 2004, Mind Machines and How to Use Them, 2005, Sex in the Afterlife, 2006, Machines You Can Build and Travel Through Time With, 2006, Mystery Cars Memphis, 2007—; co-author: Strangers In the Heartland, 1998, Armageddon: The Last Alien Battle, 1998, (plays) Hell Has Windows, 1969; editor: Summary Mag.; pub.:; contbr. articles to mags. and newspapers.; author: Why I Believe The HDR Works And Time Travel Is Possible, (book) Beyond Earthly Knowledge, (novels) The Letters from Inverness Terrace, 2007, Forever in My Heart, 2009; performer (co-host): (radio show) Nightsearch, 2005—. Mem. Lincoln Civic Symphony and Chorus, Nebr., 1981-82. Recipient scholarship Oelwein (Iowa) Daily Register, 1963, Hon. Mention, Sioux City (Iowa) Jour. Ann. photography contest, 1969, Third Pl. medallion Nat. Libr. of Poetry, Owings Mills, Md., 1995, Editors' Choice award Outstanding Achievement in Poetry, Libr. Poetry, 2004-2005., Named Great Women 21st Century award Am. Biog. Inst. Mem. Oakcrest Inst. Elkhorn, Nebr. (bd. mem. in charge of pub. rels.) Avocations: playing music, listening to short wave radio, riding horses, cooking, painting. Home and Office: 5405 S 101st Plz Apt 2 Omaha NE 68127 Office Phone: 402-301-0517. Personal E-mail: nebspook7@cox.net.

RESS, REGINA, story telling and language professor, actor; b. Pitts. d. Sigmund and Evelyn Ress; 1 child, Arieh Down. BS in English, Carnegie Mellon U.; MA in Theatre, Villanova U. Cert. in TESOL New Sch. U. ESL instr. Northern Manhattan Improvement Corp., NYC, 1998—2008; tchg. artist Arts Horizons and Young Audiences NY, 1999—; workshop facilitator Literacy Assistance Ctr., NYC, 2003—; prof. storytelling NY U., Program in Ednl. Theatre, NYC, 2004—. Prodr. profl. storytelling series NYU, NYC; story teller Numerous Nat. & Internat. Festivals; bd. mem. NY Storytelling Ctr. Actor: Broadway production of The Women, (many roles off-broadway, regional, tours) Various Productions (3 times nominated Carbonell award, South Fla. Critics Assn.); contbr. articles to profl. jours., columns in newspapers. Workshop coord., tellabration prodr., newsletter editor NY Storytelling Ctr., NYC, 1998—. Recipient Oracle award Leadership and Svc., Nat. Storytelling Network, 2003; grant, 2005. Mem.: Am. Fedn. TV and Radio Artists, Screen Actor's Guild, Actors Equity Assn., NY Storytelling Ctr. (bd. dir. 1998—), Nat. Storytelling Network. Personal E-mail: reginaress@rnrproductions-nyc.com.

RESSEGUIE, JAMES LYNN, theology educator; b. Buffalo, Jan. 1, 1945; m. Dianne, 1970; children: Timothy, Carin, Jay. BA, U. Calif., Berkeley, 1967; MDiv, Princeton Theol. Sem., 1972; PhD in New Testament, Fuller Theol. Sem., 1978. Ordained minister Presbyn. Ch.,

1976. Vol. Peace Corps, Cameroon, 1967-69; asst. prof. Winebrenner Theol. Sem., Findlay, Ohio, 1976-78, assoc. prof. New Testament, 1979-83, J. Russell Bucher prof. New Testament, 1984—2008, dean acad. and student affairs, registrar, 1990-97, v.p. acad. and student affairs, 1997, disting. prof., New Testament, 2008—; Fulbright prof. U. Iceland, Reykjavik, 1990. Lectr. in field. Author: Revelation Unsealed: A Narrative Critical Approach to John's Apocalypse, 1998, The Strange Gospel: Narrative Design and Point of View in John, 2001, Spiritual Landscape: Images of the Spiritual Life in the Gospel of Luke, 2004, Narrative Criticism of the New Testament: An Introduction, 2005, Narratologia del Nuovo Testamento, 2008, The Revelation of John: A Narrative Commentary, 2009, Lexegese Narative du Nouvean Testament, 2009; contbr.: Eerdmans Dictionary of the Bible, 2000, Dictionary of Biblical Criticism and Interpretation; contbr. articles to profl. publs., chpts. to books. Trustee Marion Twp., 1991; theologian-in-residence Zoar Luth. Ch., Perrysburg, Ohio, 1996; moderator Dola Presbyn. Ch., Dola, Ohio, 1996-98, Enon Valley Presbyn. Ch., 2002-09. Fellow NEH, 1979, 82, 85, 88, 91, Case Method Inst., 1981, Inst. for Ecumenical and Cultural Rsch., 1983, Coolidge rsch. fellow, 1987, Fulbright fellow, 1990; named Outstanding Educator, 1990, 97, 2001; recipient Cert. of Appreciation for Peace Corps svc. Mem. Soc. Biblical Lit., Maumee Valley Presbytery. Office: Winebrenner Theol Sem Dept New Testament 950 North Main St Findlay OH 45840 E-mail: resseguiej@findlay.edu.

RESSEL, TERESA MULLETT, diversified financial services company executive, former federal agency administrator; BS in Engring., MS in Engring., U. Del.; MBA, Rensselaer Poly. Inst., 1990. V.p., chief compliance officer Kaiser Found. Health Plan, Inc., Kaiser Found. Hosps., Inc.; prin. dep. asst. sec. for mgmt. & budget US Dept. Treasury, Washington, 2001—02, asst. sec. for mgmt. & CFO, 2003—04; COO UBS Investment Bank, 2004—; CEO UBS Securities LLC, 2007—. Recipient Presdl. Citation for Outstanding Alumni Achievement, U. Del., 1996, Disting. Svc. award, US Dept. Treasury, 2003. Office: UBS Securities LLC UBS Warburg Ctr 677 Washington Blvd Stamford CT 06901

RESSI, ADEO (ADEO GREGORY RESSI DI CERVIA), Internet company executive; b. Apr. 3, 1972; s. Arturo and Carol Ressi di Cervia; m. Cindy Cica Rajkov, Sept. 25, 2004; 1 child, Kali. Attended, Carnegie Mellon U., 1990—92, U. Pa., 1992—94. Founder, pres. Total New York, NYC, 1994—95; founder, CEO, chmn. methodfive inc., NYC, 1995—2000; exec. v.p., chief strategy officer Worldwide Xceed Group Inc., NYC, 2000; interim CEO EBusiness.com, NYC, 2000; founding ptnr., mem. exec. com. Sophos Partners, NYC, 2000; founder, CEO Game Trust Inc., NYC, 2002—07; founding mem. TheFunded.com, 2007—. Bd. dir. Sudden Industries Inc., Sonata Inc. Trustee X Prize Found., Life to Mars. Home: 960 Waverley St # 2 Palo Alto CA 94301-2741 Office Phone: 212-367-7336 133.

RESSLER, KERRY, psychiatrist, educator; BS in Molecular Biology, MIT; MD, PhD, Harvard Sch. Medicine. Resident Emory U. Sch. Medicine, asst. prof. psychiatry & behavioral sciences; co-dir. Grady Meml. Hosp. Post-traumatic Stress Disorders Clinic; investigator Howard Hughes Med. Inst. Office: Department of Psychiatry and Behavioral Sciences 954 Gatewood Rd Atlanta GA 30329 Office Phone: 404-727-7739. Office Fax: 404-727-8070. E-mail: kressle@emory.edu.*

RESTANI, JANE A., federal judge; b. San Francisco, Feb. 27, 1948; d. Roy J. and Emilia C. Restani. BA, U. Calif., Berkeley, 1969; JD, U. Calif., Davis, 1973. Bar: Calif., 1973. Trial atty. US Dept. Justice, Washington, 1973-76, asst. chief comml. litigation sect., 1976-80, dir. comml. litigation sect., 1980-83; judge US Ct. Internat. Trade, NYC, 1983—2003, chief judge, 2003—. Mem. Order of Coif. Office: US Ct Internat Trade 1 Federal Plz New York NY 10278-0001*

RESTIVO, JAMES JOHN, JR., lawyer; b. Pitts. s. James J. and Dorothy (Ardolino) R.; m. Gail Sharon Hackenburg, July 11, 1970; 4 children. BA in History, U. Pa., 1968; JD, Georgetown U., 1971. Bar: Pa. 1971, U.S. Dist. Ct. (we. and ea. dists.) Pa. 1971, U.S. Ct. Appeals (3d cir.) 1971, U.S. Supreme Ct. 1979. Ptnr. Reed Smith, Pitts., 1979—; head litig. dept. Reed, Smith, Shaw & McClay, Pitts., 1986-97. Mem. editl. bd.: Georgetown Law Rev., 1970—71. Bd. dirs. Rebuilding Together-Greater Pitts., Pitts. Regional Alliance. Fellow Am. Coll. Trial Lawyers; mem. Acad. Trial Lawyers Allegheny County, Allegheny County Bar Assn., Pa. Economy League (We. divsn.), Def. Rsch. Inst. Home: 209 Deer Meadow Dr Pittsburgh PA 15241-2253 Office: Reed Smith 435 6th Ave Ste 2 Pittsburgh PA 15219-1886 Home Phone: 412-835-2283; Office Phone: 412-288-3122. Business E-Mail: jrestivo@reedsmith.com.

RESTLE, PHILLIP J., engineering company executive; BA in Physics, Oberlin Coll., 1979; PhD in Physics, U. Ill., Champaign-Urbana, 1985. Rsch. staff mem. IBM, Yorktown Heights, NY, 1985—. Contbr. articles to profl. jours. Recipient Best Paper award, Pat Goldberg Meml., 2005, ITC Ned Kornfield, 2008. Mem.: IEEE. Home: 31 Whitlockville Rd Katonah NY 10536 Office: IBM T J Watson Rsch Ctr PO Box 218 Yorktown Heights NY 10598 Home Phone: 914-945-2697; Office Phone: 914-945-2697.

RESTREPO, HUMBERTO, gynecologist, obstetrician, educator; b. Cali, Valle del Cauca, Colombia, Jan. 20, 1951; s. Marino Restrepo and Leonor Candelo; m. Gloria Gutierrez, Oct. 26, 1976; children: Adriana, Gisela. MD, Valle U., Cali, Colombia, 1975; MPH, Johns Hopkins U., Balt., 1982. Medical diplomate Colombian Govt., 1976, cert. Ob-Gyn Valle U., 1981. Head, dept. maternal and child health Colombian Inst. Social Security, Cali, 1988—91; med. dir. Diego Lalinde Pub. Health Ctr., Cali, 1983—85; assoc. prof. Valle U., Cali, 1992—2002; dir. rsch. Children's Heart Ctr., Las Vegas, Nev., 2002—; assoc. prof. U. Nev., Sch. Medicine, Las Vegas, 2003—. Clin. rsch. advisor Valle U., Clin. Epidemiology Unit., 1999—2002; assoc. rschr. WHO Collaborating Ctr. Rsch. and Tng. Human Reproduction, Cali, 1982—86. Contbr. to scientific articles. Vol Colombian Assn. Las Vegas, 2004—08. Tng. Grant, WHO, 1981. Mem.: Assn. of Clin. Rsch. Professionals (assoc.).

RESTREPO, RUBEN DARIO, physician, educator; b. Medellin, Antioquia, Colombia, June 6, 1963; s. Jose Ignacio Restrepo and Maria Alma Panesso; m. Lorena Maria Fernandez, Dec. 1, 2002; children: Andrea, Natalia, Simon Usuga. MD, Universidad Pontificia Bolivariana, Medellin, Colombia, 1987; BS, Ga. State U., Atla., 1994. Primary care physician Comedal, Medellin, 1988—90; pediatric outreach program coord. St. Joseph's Hosp., Atla., 1991—92; pediatric ICU therapist Children's Healthcare of Atla., 1994—2005; clin. instr. Ga. State U., Atla., 1997—98, adj. faculty, 1998—99, asst. prof., 1999—2005; assoc. prof. U. Tex. Health Sci. Ctr., San Antonio, 2005—. Contbr. chapters to books, articles to profl. jours. Usher St. Matthew Cath. Ch., San Antonio, 2005—06; bd. mem. and vol. Habitat for Humanity, San Antonio; bd. mem. Office of Family Concerns, Atlanta, 1995—2002. Recipient Respiratory Therapy award, Am. Lung Assn., 1992, Academic Excellence award, Ga. State U., 1994, Berneice Castella Allied Health Aging Rsch. award, U. Tex. Health Sci. Ctr. San Antonio, 2006—; scholar James Ancil Lewis award, Ga. Soc. for Respiratory Care, 1992. Mem.: Am. Assn. for Respiratory Care, Am. Thoracic Soc., Am. Coll. Chest Physicians, Lambda Beta Soc. Catholic. Achievements include development of Educational CD. Avocations: travel, sports, computer technology. Office: Univ TexHealth Scis Ctr 7703 Floyd Curl Dr San Antonio TX 78229 Business E-Mail: restrepor@uthscsa.edu.

RESWICK, JAMES BIGELOW, former government official, biomedical engineer; b. Ellwood City, Pa., Apr. 16, 1922; s. Maurice and Katherine (Parker) R.; children: James Bigelow, David Parker (dec.), Pamela Reswick; m. Irmtraud Orthlies Hoelzerkopf, Dec., 27, 1973. SBME, MIT, 1943, SM, 1948, ScD, 1952; DEng (hon.), Rose Poly. Inst., 1968. Asst. prof., then assoc. prof., head machine design and graphics div. MIT, 1948-59; Leonard Case prof. engring., dir. Engring. Design Ctr., Case Western Res. U., 1959-70; prof. biomed. engring. and orthopaedics U. So. Calif., also dir. of rsch. dept. orthopaedics, 1970-80; assoc. dir. tech. Nat. Inst. Handicapped Rsch., U.S. Dept. Edn.; dir. VA Rehab. R & D Evaluation Unit VA Med. Ctr., Washington, 1984-88; dir. rsch. scis. Nat. Inst. on Disability and Rehab. Rsch. U.S. Dept. Edn., Washington, 1989—94; ret., 1994; acting dir. Nat. Inst. Disability and Rehab. Rsch., Washington, 1989-91. Engring. cons. on automatic control, product devel., automation and bio-med. engring. Mem. com. prosthetics R & D Nat. Acad. Scis., 1962-; chmn. design and devel. com.; mem. bd. rev. Army R & D Office, 1965-; mem. applied physiology and biomed. engring. study sect. NIH, 1972-. Author: (with C.K. Taft) Introduction to Dynamic Systems, 1967; also articles.; Editor: (with F.T. Hambrecht) Functional Electrical Stimulation, 1977; series on engring. design, 1963-; inventor, patentee in field. Chmn. Mayor's Commn. for Urban Transp., Cleve., 1969. Served to lt. (j.g.) USNR, 1943-46, PTO. Decorated officer Yugoslav Flag with golden wreath medal (Yugoslavia), 1990; recipient Product Engring. Master Designer award, 1969, Isabelle and Leonard H. Goldenson award United Cerebral Palsy Assn., 1973; NSR sr. postdoctoral fellow Imperial Coll., London, 1957. Fellow IEEE, Am. Inst. Med. and Biological Engring. (founder); mem. ASME (honor award for best paper 1956, sr. mem.), Am. Soc. Engring. Edn., Instrument Soc. Am., Biomed. Engring. Soc. (sr. mem., pres. 1973, dir.), Am. Acad. Orthopedic Surgeons (assoc.), Inst. Medicine of NAS, NAE, Internat. Soc. Orthotics and Prosthetics, Orthopaedics Rsch. Soc., Rehab. Engring. Soc. N.Am. (founding pres.), Sigma XI. Home: 1834 Calf Mountain Rd PO Box 549 Crozet VA 22932 Home Phone: 434-987-8040. Personal E-mail: jbreswick@yahoo.com.

RETALLACK, GREGORY JOHN, geologist, educator; b. Hobart, Australia, Nov. 8, 1951; arrived in U.S., 1977; s. Kenneth John Retallack and Moira Wynn (Dean) Gollan; m. Diane Alice Retallack, May 31, 1981; children: Nicholas John, Jeremy Douglas. BA, Macquarie U., Sydney, 1973; BSc with honors, U. New Eng., 1974, PhD, 1978. Vis. asst. prof. No. Ill. U., DeKalb, 1977—78; vis. scholar Ind. U., Bloomington, 1978—81; asst. prof. U. Oreg., Eugene, 1981—86, assoc. prof., 1986—92, prof., 1992—. Author: Late Eocene and Oligocene Paleosols from Badlands National Park, South Dakota, 1983, Soils of the Past, 1990, 2d edit., 2001, Miocene Paleosols and Ape Habitats in Pakistan and Kenya, 1991, Colour Guide to Paleosols, 1997; contbr. articles to profl. jours. Grantee, NSF, 1979—, Wenner-Gren Found., 1983. Fellow: AAAS, Geol. Soc. Am.; mem.: Soc. Econ. Paleontologists and Mineralogists, Oreg. Acad. Sci. (pres. 1986), Paleontology Soc. (pres. Pacific sect. 1986), Bot. Soc. Am., Geol. Soc. Australia, Sigma Xi (pres. U. Oreg. chpt. 1983—84). Home: 2715 Elinor St Eugene OR 97403-2513 Office Phone: 541-346-4558. Business E-Mail: gregr@uoregon.edu.

RETHMEL, CAROL ANN, voice educator, director; b. Takoma Park, Md., Apr. 9, 1953; d. Elmer E. and Donna Elizabeth (Wassum) Parsons; 1 child, Joshua Allan Parsons. MusM, Ea. N.Mex U., Portales, 1988—90. Choral dir. Lea County Pub. Schs., Hobbs, N.Mex., 1996—99, Prince William County Pub. Schs., Woodbridge, Va., 1999—. Mem.: Am. Choral Dirs. Assn. (dist. chmn. 2003—05), Music Educators Nat. Con., Sigma Alpha Iota. Home: 2849 Chablis Cir Woodbridge VA 22192 Office: Woodbridge Sr HS 3001 Old Bridge Rd Woodbridge VA 22192 Office Fax: 703-497-8172. Personal E-mail: primadiva1@comcast.net.

RETHORE, BERNARD GABRIEL, manufacturing and mining company executive, consultant; b. May 22, 1941; s. Francis Joseph and Katharine Eunice (MacDwyer) Rethore; m. Marilynn Irene Watt, Dec. 1, 1962 (div. Apr. 2002); m. Shirley Ann Michels, July 7, 2007; children: Bernard Michael, Tara Jean, Kevin Watt, Alexandra Marie, Rebecca Ann, Christopher Philip, Abigail Lyn, Ryan Victor (Michels). BA, Yale U., 1962; MBA, U. Pa., 1967. Assoc. McKinsey & Co., Inc., Washington, 1967—73, sr. assoc., 1973; v.p., gen. mgr. Greer div. Microdot, Inc., Darien, Conn., 1973—77, v.p. ops. connector group, 1977—78, pres. bus. devel. group, 1978—82, pres. fastening sys. and sealing devices groups, 1982—84; pres. Microdot Industries, Darien, Conn., 1984—87, pres., CEO, 1988; pres. Microdot Europe Ltd., Darien, Conn., 1984—88; sr. v.p. Phelps Dodge Corp., Phoenix, 1989—95; group exec. Phelps Dodge Industries, Phoenix, 1989—90, pres., 1990—95; pres., CEO, bd. dirs. BW/IP Internat., Inc., Long Beach, Calif., 1995—97, chmn., 1997; CEO, chmn. bd. dirs. Flowserve Corp., Dallas, 1997—2000, chmn. emeritus, 2000—; chmn. McDyre & Spendley, Ltd., 2000—. Bd. dirs. Belden, Inc., Dover Corp., Walter Industries, Inc., Mueller Water Products, Inc.; cons. U.S. Govt., UN; dean's adv. bd. Wharton Sch. Bus., U. Pa., 1972—80. Elected mem. bd. fin. Town of Westport, Conn., 1986-90; trustee Ballet Ariz., 1989-95, vice chmn., 1991-95; bd. dirs. Boys Hope of Phoenix, 1989-95, Franciscan Renewal Ctr., 2005—, vice chair 2006—; trustee Phoenix Country Day Sch., 1992-2003, adv. trustee, 2003-; mem. global coun. Thunderbird Sch. Global Mgmt., 1990—, chmn., 1991-94, trustee, 1994—, vice chmn., 2004—. Served to capt. inf. US Army, 1962—65. Decorated Bronze Star; named Outstanding Dir., Outstanding Dirs.' Exchange, 2008. Mem. Nat. Assn. Mfrs. (bd. dirs. 1994-95, 96-99), Yale Club (NYC), Union League (Chgo.), Nat. Assn. Corp. Dirs. (blue ribbon com. on bd. role in strategic plan 2000), Gainey Ranch Club (Scottsdale, Ariz.). Home: 7010 East Avenida El Alba Paradise Valley AZ 85253 Office: McDyre & Spendley Ltd 6929 N Hayden Rd Ste 4C-401 Scottsdale AZ 85250 Office Phone: 480-368-8033. Personal E-mail: bgreth@aol.com.

RETMAN, DEBORAH W., biology educator; b. Xenia, Ohio, Nov. 10, 1961; d. Thomas Elmer and Gail (Nichol) Welsh; m. Mick Retman, Mar. 24, 1990. BA, Ohio U., 1984; MA, Wright State U., 1996. Pharmacy tech. rugs, Xenia, 1977—79; waitress Red Barn, Xenia, 1979—82; sales clk. Tiffany Jewelers, Xenia, 1982—84; biology tchr. Piqua City Schs., Ohio, 1984—. Emt City of Clayton, Ohio, 1990—; coach Piqua City Schs., 1989—. Named Tchr. of the Yr., McDonalds. Mem.: Clayton Fire Assn., Piqua Edn. Assn. (pres. 2003—05). Methodist. Office: Piqua High Sch 1 Indiann Trl Piqua OH 45356-9257

RETSCH-BOGART, GEORGE Z., pediatric pulmonologist, surgeon; b. 1952; MD, U. Cin., 1978. Diplomate Am. Bd. Pediat., cert. in Pediat. Pulmonology. Resident pediat. U. Minn., Mpls., 1978—81; fellowship pediat. pulmonary U. NC Sch. Medicine, Chapel Hill, 1986—89, assoc. prof. divsn. pediat. pulmonology, dir. Cystic Fibrosis Ctr.; clin. staff NC Children's Hosp. Contbr. articles to profl. jours. Mem.: Cystic Fibrosis Found., Am. Acad. Pediat. Achievements include research in complex airway disorders in children. Mailing: UNC Dept Pediat 101 Manning Dr Chapel Hill NC 27514 Office Phone: 919-966-4131. Office Fax: 919-966-6049.

RETSINAS, NICOLAS PAUL, public policy educator, former federal official; b. 1946; BA in Economics, NYU; MA in City Planning, Harvard U.; D in Pub. Svc. (hon.), R.I. Coll., 2008. Exec. dir. Housing & Mortgage Corp., 1987-93; dir. policy State of R.I., 1991; asst. sec. for housing US Dept. Housing & Urban Devel., Washington, 1993-98; commr. FHA, Washington, 1993-98; dir. Office Thrift Supervision US Dept. Treasury, Washington, 1996; prof., dir. Joint Ctr. Housing Studies Harvard U., 1998—. Adj. asst. prof. urban studies, Brown U. Co-editor: Low-Income Homeownership: Examining the Unexamined Goal, 2002, Building Assets, Building Credit: Creating Wealth in Low-Income Communities, 2005, Revisiting Rental Housing: Policies, Programs, and Priorities, 2008; co-author: Opportunity and Progress: A Bipartisan Platform for National Housing Policy, 2004, Our Communities, Our Homes: Pathways to Housing and Homeownership in America's Cities and States, 2007. Bd. trustees Nat. Housing Endowment, Enterprise Cmty. Partners. Recipient Meritorious Svc. award, US Dept. Treasury, 1997, Excellence in Pub. Svc. award, Rental Housing Assn., 1998, Housing Leadership award, Nat. Low Income Housing Coalition, 2001; named one of The Most Influential People in Real Estate, Nat. Assn. Realtors; named to The Nat. Housing Hall of Fame. Mem. Nat. Coun. State Housing Authorities (past sec.), Nat. Community Devel. Assn. (past pres.); fellow, Nat. Acad. Pub. adminstrn., Urban Inst. Office: Harvard U Joint Ctr Housing Studies 1033 Massachusetts Ave Fifth Fl Cambridge MA 02138*

RETTIG, DWIGHT W., lawyer; b. July 6, 1960; BA, Ind. U., 1982; JD, U. Houston, 1986, MBA, 1993. Bar: Tex. 1986. Chief legal officer NATCO Group, Inc., 1997—98; gen. counsel Distbn. Svcs. Group Nat. Oilwell Varco, Houston, 1998—99, v.p., gen. counsel, 1999—. Mem.: Houston Bar Assn., ABA, State Bar Tex. (mem. Corp., Internat., Banking and Bus. Law Sect.). Office: Nat Oilwell, Inc 10000 Richmond Ave Houston TX 77042 Office Phone: 713-346-7550. E-mail: dwight.rettig@natoil.com.*

RETTIG, JAMES R., university librarian, library association executive; b. Chgo., Nov. 11, 1950; m. Monica Rettig; children: Chris, Tony, Katie. BA cum laude, Marquette U., 1972, MA, 1974; MLS, U. Wis., Madison, 1975. Asst. reference libr. Murray State U. Libr., Ky., 1976—77, head reference libr. Ky., 1977—78; reference libr. Roesch Libr., U. Dayton, Ohio, 1978—83; head reference libr. U. Ill., Chgo., 1983—87; asst. dean univ. librs. for reference & info. svcs. Earl Gregg Swem Libr., Coll. William & Mary, Williamsburg, Va., 1988—98; univ. libr. Boatwright Meml. Libr., U. Richmond, Va., 1998—. Mem. reference svcs. adv. com. Online Computer Libr. Ctr. (OCLC), 1992—95. Author: (columns) Current Reference Books, for Wilson Libr. Bull., Rettig on Reference; editor: (book) Distinguished Classics of Reference Publishing, 1992. Recipient Info. Authorship award, Info. Access Corp., 1997, Faculty Recognition award, Earl Gregg Swem Libr., 1998, Richard A. Mateer Quality of Life award, U. Richmond Student Govt., 2005, Disting. Alumnus award, U. Wis.-Madison Sch. Libr. & Info. Studies, 2006; sr. fellow, UCLA Dept. Info. Studies, 2001. Mem.: ALA (chair pub. com. 1997—99, chair orgn. com. 2000—03, exec. bd. 2003—06, pres. elect 2007—08, pres. 2008—, G.K. Hall award for Libr. Literature 1993), Assn. Coll. Rsch. Librs. (chair news editl. bd. 1986—88), Reference & User Svcs. Assn. (past pres., Mudge Citation 1988, Louis Shores-Oryx Press award 1995). Office: Univ Libr Boatwright Meml Libr U Richmond Richmond VA 23173 Office Phone: 804-289-8456. Office Fax: 804-289-8757. E-mail: jrettig@richmond.edu.

RETTIG, PAM, literature educator; b. Williston, ND, Mar. 11, 1964; d. Vincent Gregory and Agnes Caroline Rettig. BS, Minot State U., 1986; MS in ednl. psychology, U. of Mary, 1994. Tchr. Burke Ctrl. Sch., Lignite, ND, 1986—89; tchr., prin. Manning Sch., Bismarck, ND, 1989—92; reading specialist Bismarck Pub. Sch., Bismarck, ND, 1992—; adj. prof. U. of Mary, Bismarck, 1998—. Internat. tchr. trainer Internat. Reading Assn., Newark, 2004—; trainer of assessors Nat. Bd. of Tchg. Certification, Clemson, SC, 2004; ednl. cons. U. of Mary, Bismarck, 2000—. Co-author: ND Lang. Arts Standards, 1996—2000. Recipient Milken award, Milken Family Found., 2000, Constance McCullough award, Internat. Reading Assn., 2004; Fulbright scholar, Fulbright Meml. Fund Found., 2001. Mem.: South Ctrl. Reading Assn., ND Reading Assn. Office: Bismarck Public School 1227 N 35th St Bismarck ND 58504 Office Phone: 701-224-1784 x 119. Office Fax: 701-250-1172. Business E-Mail: pam_rettig@bismarckschools.org.

RETZ, WILLIAM ANDREW, naval consultant, retired naval officer; b. Blauvelt, NY, June 3, 1940; s. Andrew Macmillan and Katherine (Deyoe) R.; m. Julia Irene, Sept. 23, 1989; children: Andrew, Gregory, Mark, Alyse Reavis, Mark Rogers. Student, Tex. A&M U., Coll. Sta., 1957; BS in Mech. Engring., U. N.Mex., Albuquerque, 1963; MS, George Wash. U., Washington, DC, 1971; grad., Naval War Coll., Newport, RI, 1972. Commd. ensign USN, 1963, advanced through grades to rear adm., 1991, patrol officer river div. 511 Vietnam, 1968-69, flag sec. to comdr. Amphibious Group Two Norfolk, Va., 1972-74, exec. officer USS Ainsworth, 1974-76, commanding officer USS Stump, 1980-82, commodore Destroyer Squadron 22, 1985-87, dep. for ops. US Ctrl. Command Tampa, Fla., 1987—90; comdr. Naval Base Pearl Harbor, 1992-94, Naval Surface Group Mid. Pacific, 1992-94; commanded and closed Naval Base Phila., 1994-95; ret. USN, 1995; v.p. govt. svcs. Aramark Corp., Phila., 1996-99; ind. cons., 1999; CEO Nofire Techs., Inc., 2000—03; exec. dir. Am. Competitiveness Inst., Phila., 2003—05; ind. cons. Retz & Assoc., 2005—; with Def. Solutions, Washington, 2005—. Active Episcopal Ch.; bd. dirs. Indus, Denison Devel. Found., St. Luke's Sch.; adv. bd. U. Tex., Dallas; chmn. Texoma Tech. Enterprise Coun., Denison, Tex. Decorated Disting. Svc. medal, Legion of Merit, Def. Disting. Svc. medal, Meritorious Svc. medal, Bronze Star, Purple Heart. Mem. Surface Navy Assn., Nat. Def. Indsl. Assn. (bd. dirs.). Avocations: gardening, sailing. Office: Def Solutions 1725 Ist NW Ste 300 Washington DC 20006 Personal E-mail: retzw@comcast.net.

RETZER, MARY ELIZABETH HELM, retired librarian; b. Balt. d. Francis Leslie C. and Edna (Smith) Helm; m. William Raymond Retzer, June 28, 1945; children: Lesley Elizabeth, April Christine. BA, Western Md. Coll., Westminster, 1940; MA, Columbia U., NYC, 1946; postgrad., George Washington U., 1941, Ind. U., 1952, U. Ill., 1958-59, Ill. State U., Normal, 1964-66, Bradley U., Peoria, Ill.; PhD, Western Colo. U., 1972. Faculty Rockville Bd. Edn., Md., 1940-47, elem. supr. Md., 1945-47; staff Peoria Pub. Libr., 1957-63, homebound libr., 1961-63; cons., organizer libr. Bergan High Sch., 1964-67; condr. libr. sci. course in reference Bradley U., 1966-83. Libr. Hines Elem. Sch., 1963-66, Roosevelt Jr. H.S., 1966-69; head media ctr. Manual H.S., Peoria, Ill., 1969-83. Instr. water safety courses ARC, 1938-93; pres. Entre Nous, 1949-51; pres. women's bd. Salvation Army, 1952-54; pres. Peoria Nursery Sch. Assn., 1953-54; mem. legis. action com. Ill. Congress PTA,

1955-56; mem. Crippled Children's Adv. Com., Peoria, 1957-60; active various community drives; women's adv. bd. Peoria Jr. Star, 1970-73; vol. Sarasota Internat. Airport, 1990-98. Mem. AAUW (life), NEA, ALA (life), Ill. Edn. Assn. (life), Peoria Edn. Assn. (life), Ill. Libr. Assn., Ill. Valley Librs. Assn. (pres. 1971-72), Ill. Assn. Media in Edn. (cert. com. 1973-80), Ill. Audiovisual Assn., Internat. Platform Assn., Order Ea. Star (life), Ill. State U. Adminstrs. Club, Willowknolls Country Club, Sarasota Yacht Club, Ladies Oriental Shrine. Republican. Presbyterian. Home: 3240 Lake Pointe Blvd Unit 101 Sarasota FL 34231

REUBEN, ALVIN BERNARD, communications and entertainment executive; b. Harrisburg, Pa., Aug. 11, 1940; s. Maurice and Lillian (Katzef) R.; m. Barbara Ann Harrison, Mar. 18, 1968; 1 dau., Mindee Jill. BS in Commerce, Rider U., 1962. Buyer Pomeroy's div. Allied Stores Corp., Harrisburg, 1962-67; sales rep. Random House, Inc., NYC, 1967-74; dir. mktg. Ballantine Books, Inc. (div. Random House), NYC, 1974-76; v.p. sales Simon & Schuster, NYC, 1976-79, sr. v.p. sales Pocket Books div., 1979-81, sr. v.p. mktg., 1981-82, pres. ref. and promotional pub. group, 1982-83, exec. v.p. electronic pub. div., 1983-85; exec. v.p. Prentice Hall div. Simon & Schuster, 1985-86; sr. v.p. mktg., sales and distbn. Vestron, Inc., 1986-89; sr. v.p. St. Martin's Press, NYC, 1989-91; sr. v.p. sales, mktg. Sony Music Video, NYC, 1991-92; sr. v.p. spl. markets Sony Music, NYC, 1992-95; sr.v.p. video and interactive sales and distbn. BMG Entertainment, 1995-97; pres. BMG Video, 1997-99. Instr. edn. in pub. program, grad. program SUNY, 2004-07; bd. advisors, Coastal Carolina Med. Ctr., Hardeeville, SC, 2005-08. With USAFR, 1963-69. Mem. Tau Kappa Epsilon. Home and Office: 5 Tyler Ln Bluffton SC 29909-5028 Home Phone: 843-705-2531. Personal E-mail: alreubenschh@aol.com.

REUBEN, DON, lawyer; s. Michael B. and Sally (Colucci) R.; m. Evelyn Long, Aug. 27, 1948 (div.); children: Hope Reuben Boland, Michael Barrett, Timothy Don, Jeffrey Long, Howard Ellis; m. Jeannette Hurley Haywood, Dec. 13, 1971; stepchildren: Harris Hurley Haywood, Edward Gregory Haywood. BS, Northwestern U., 1949, JD, 1952. Bar: Ill. 1952, Calif. 1996, U.S. Supreme Ct. 1957. With firm Kirkland & Ellis, Chgo., 1952-78, sr. ptnr., Reuben & Proctor, Chgo., 1978-86, Isham, Lincoln & Beale, Chgo., 1986-88; sr. counsel Winston & Strawn, Chgo., 1988-94; of counsel Altheimer & Gray, Chgo., 1994—2003, Fioretti, Lower & Carbonara, Ltd., Chgo., 2007—08, 2008—. Spl. asst. atty. gen. State of Ill., 1963—64, 1969, 84; gen. counsel Tribune Co., 1965—88, Chgo. Bears Football Club, 1965—88, Cath. Archdiocese of Chgo., 1975—88; counsel spl. session Ill. Ho. of Reps., 1964, for Ill. treas. for congl., state legis. and jud. reapportionment, 1963; spl. fed. ct. master, 1968—70; mem. citizens adv. bd. to sheriff County of Cook, 1962—66, jury instrn. com., 1963—73; past mem. pub. rules com. Ill. Supreme Ct., 1963—73; past mem. pub. rels. com. Nat. Conf. State Trial Judges; com. study caseflow mgmt. in law divsn. Cook County Cir. Ct., 1979—88; adv. implementation com. U.S. Dist. Ct. No. Dist. Ill., 1981—82; mem. Chgo. Better Sch. Com., 1968—69, Chgo. Crime Commn., 1970—80; supervisory panel Fed. Defender Program, 1971—78; sec. gen. counsel, chair audit com. Palm Springs Air Mus., 1998—. Bd. dirs. Lincoln Pk. Zool. Soc., 1972—84; trustee Northwestern U., 1977—; mem. vis. com. U. Chgo. Law Sch., 1976—79; bd. dirs. Blood Bank of the Desert, 1999—2004, vice-chmn., 2003—04; chmn. gen. plan adv. com. City of Rancho Mirage, 1994—; dir., sec. Friends of the Animal Campos, 2004—. Recipient Northwestern U. Law Sch. Alumni Merit award, 2002. Fellow: Am. Bar Found., Internat. Acad. Trial Lawyers; mem.: ABA (standing com. on fed. judiciary 1973—79, standing com. on jud. selection, tenure and compensation 1982—85), ADR Sys. America, Desert Bar Assn., Calif. Bar Assn., Am. Arbitration Assn. (nat. panel arbitrators 1998—2008), Am. Coll. Trial Lawyers (Rule 23 com. 1975—82, judiciary com. 1987—91), Am. Law Inst., Chgo. Bar Assn. (chmn. subcom. propriety and regulation of contingent fees com. devel. 1966—69, subcom. on media liaison 1980—82, com. on profl. info. 1980—82), Ill. Bar Assn., Casino Club, Chgo. Club, Mid-Am. Club, Tamarisk Country Club (hon.), Order of Coif, Beta Gamma Sigma, Beta Alpha Psi, Phi Eta Sigma. Roman Catholic. Office: 74-900 Hwy 111 Ste 222 Indian Wells CA 92210 also: 1100 Glendon Ave 10th fl Los Angeles CA 90024 also: 222 S Riverside Plz Ste 1550 Chicago IL 60606-6000 also: 333 W Wacker Dr Ste 1800 Chicago IL 60604 Business E-Mail: dreuben456@yahoo.com.

REUBEN, GLORIA, actress, singer; b. Toronto, Ont., June 9, 1964; m. Wayne Isaak, 1999. T.V. and movie actress; backup singer and dancer Tina Turner's World Tour, 2000. Actress (films) Immediate Family, 1989, Wild Orchid II: Two Shades of Blue, 1992, The Waiter, 1993, Time Cop, 1994, Nick of Time, 1995, David and Lola, 1999, Macbeth in Manhattan, 1999, Bad Faith, 2000, Pilgrim, 2000, Happy Here and Now, 2002, Kettle of Fish, 2005, The Sentinel, 2006, (TV films) The Day They Came to Arrest the Book, 1987, Shadowhunter, 1993, Percy & Thunder, 1993, Confessions: Two Faces of Evil, 1994, Dead Air, 1994, Johnny's Girl, 1995, Indiscreet, 1998, Sara, 1999, Deep in My Heart, 1999, Sole Survivor, 2000, The Agency, 2001, Feast of All Saints, 2001, Little John, 2002, Salem Witch Trials, 2002, Life Support, 2007, host (TV series) Polka Dot Door, 1985, actress ER, 1995—99, The Agency, 2001—02, actress, composer, prodr. 1-800-Missing, 2003—04, appearances in Alfred Hitchcock Presents, 1987, 21 Jump Street, 1988, The Flash, 1990—91, Silk Stalkings, 1993, Homicide: Life on the Street, 1995, The District, 2002, Law & Order: Special Victims Unit, 2002, Numb3rs, 2005, actress (plays) Stuff Happens, 2005 (Lucille Lortel award outstanding lead actress, 2007), A Nervous Smile, 2006, Conversations in Tusculum, 2008; singer: (albums) Just for You, 2004; back-up singer Twenty Four Seven, Tina Turner's World Tour, 2000. Recipient SAG Awards, 1998, 99, Q Award, 1997, 98; named one of 50 Most Beautiful People in World, People mag., 1996. Mailing: c/o Elise Konialian/ Untitled Mgmt Floor 3 23 East 22nd St New York NY 10010 Office Phone: 212-777-1214.

REUBEN, LAWRENCE MARK, lawyer; b. Akron, Ohio, Apr. 5, 1948; s. Albert G. and Sara I. (Rifkin) R. Student, London Sch. Econs., 1969; BS, Ind. U., 1970; JD, Ind. U., Indpls., 1973. Bar: Ind. 1973, U.S. Dist. Ct. (so. dist.) Ind. 1973, U.S. Dist. Ct. (no. dist.) Ind. 1975, U.S. Ct. Appeals (7th cir.) 1975, U.S. Supreme Ct. 1976, U.S. Ct. Appeals (9th cir.) 1978, U.S. Ct. Appeals (D.C. cir.) 1994, U.S. Ct. Appeals (fed. cir.) 1999. Ptnr. Atlas, Hyatt & Reuben, Indpls., 1976-87, Atlas & Reuben, Indpls., 1987-90; chief counsel Ind. Dept. Ins., 1990-91; gen. counsel Ind. Dept. Transp., 1991-93; chief deputy Ind. Atty. Gen., Indpls., 1993-94; gen. counsel State Lottery Commn. Ind., Indpls., 1994-97; pvt. practice Indpls., 1997—. V.p. Ind. Civil Liberties Union, 1975-84; sec., bd. dirs. Indpls. Humane Soc., 1974-85; fellow Indpls. C. of C.-Lacey Leadership Program, 1982; sec., v.p., bd. dirs. Julian Ctr., Inc., 1983-89; mem. ch.-state commn. Nat. Jewish Community Relations Adv. Council, N.Y.C., 1982-89; bd. dirs. Indpls. Consumer Credit Counseling Bur., 1983-89; pres. Bur. Jewish Edn., 1984-86; parliamentarian Ind. State Dem. Party, 1985-86; mem. Indpls. Police Community Relations Rev. Com., 1983. Recipient Robert Risk award Ind. Civil Liberties Union, 1981, David M. Cook Meml. award Indpls. Jewish Community Rels. Coun., 1982; L.L. Goodman Leadership award, Jewish Fed. Indpls., 1989. Mem. Am. Trial Lawyers Assn., Ind. State Bar Assn., Indpls. Bar Assn., Nat. Employment Lawyers Assn., Am. Collectors Assn. (mem. atty. program), Ind. State Bar Assn. Com. Office: 136 E Market St Ste 200 Indianapolis IN 46204-3671 Office Phone: 317-634-2200. Business E-Mail: lmr@reubenlaw.net.

REUBER, GRANT LOUIS, banking insurance company executive; b. Mildmay, Ont., Can., Nov. 23, 1927; s. Jacob Daniel and Gertrude Catherine (Wahl) R.; m. Margaret Louise Julia Summerhayes, Oct. 21, 1951 (dec. Feb. 1998); children: Rebecca, Barbara, Mary. BA, U. Western Ont., 1950; AM, Harvard U., 1954, PhD, 1957; LLD (hon.), Wilfred Laurier U., 1983, Simon Fraser U., 1985, U. Western Ont., 1985, McMaster U., 1994; postgrad., Cambridge U., 1954-55. Mem. research dept. Bank Can., Ottawa, 1950-52; mem. Can. Dept. Finance, Ottawa, 1955-57; asst. prof. econ. U. Western Ont., London, 1957-59, assoc. prof., 1959-62, prof., head dept., 1963-69, 1963-69; mem. bd. govs. U. Western Ont., London, 1974-78, acad. v.p., provost, 1975-78, chancellor, 1988-92; sr. v.p., chief economist Bank of Montreal, Que., Canada, 1978-79, exec. v.p., 1980-81, dep. chmn., dep. chief exec. officer, 1981-83, dir., mem. exec. com., 1981-89, pres., chief operating officer, 1983-87, dep. chmn., 1987-89; dep. minister fin. Can., 1979-80; chmn. Can. Deposit Ins. Corp., 1993-99; sr. adv., dir. Sussex Circle, 1999—. Staff mem. Royal Commn. Banking and Fin., Toronto, 1962—63; chmn. Ont. Econ. Coun., 1973—78; cons. Can. Internat. Devel. Agy., 1968—69; hon. rsch. assoc. in econs. Harvard U., 1968—69; cons. devel. ctr. OECD, 1969—73; lectr. U. Chgo. Sch. Bus., 1992—93. Author: Private Foreign Investment in Development, 1973, Canada's Political Economy, 1980; contbr. articles. Bd. dirs. Can. Merit Scholarship Found., 1994—2000; bd. govs. Royal Ont. Mus., 2000—02; chmn. Can. Ditchley Found., 1981—. Decorated officer Order of Can. Fellow: Royal Soc. Can. Home Phone: 416-924-4971; Office Phone: 416-867-3614.

REUBISH, GARY RICHARD, English language educator; b. Breckenridge, Minn., Jan. 6, 1946; s. Irving Earl and Genevieve Loretta (Miller) R. AA, N.D. State Coll. Sci., Wahpeton, 1969; BS, Valley City State Coll., 1971. Cert. tchr., N.D. Tchr. English Wolford Pub. Sch., ND, 1971-72, Lake Benton Pub. Sch., Minn., 1972-76, Wahpeton Pub. Sch., ND, 1976—2001. With USAF, 1965-71. Mem. N.D. Edn. Assn. Home: PO Box 181 Wahpeton ND 58074-0181

REUCROFT, PHILIP J., retired materials science professor; s. Leonard and Nellie Reucroft; m. Sheila Anne Powers, May 22, 1961; children: Lisa Marie Gough, Miles Alan, Noel Edward. BS, U. London, 1956, PhD, 1959. Postdoc. fellow NRC Can., Ottawa, Ont., 1959—61; rsch. scientist Franklin Inst. Rsch. Labs., Phila., 1961—69; assoc. prof. materials sci. U. Ky., Lexington, 1969—76, prof. materials sci., 1976—2005, emeritus prof., 2005—. Sci. manuscript reviewer various jours., 1961—; proposal reviewer NSF, Arlington, Va., 1990—. Contbr. over 300 articles to profl. jours. Rsch. grants, NSF, 1961—2005, NASA, 1961—2005. Fellow: ASM Internat. (life; chmn. bluegrass chpt. 1976—77); mem.: Am. Phys. Soc., Royal Soc. Chemistry, Am. Chem. Soc. (life). Achievements include research in surface science, catalysis, electronic materials and film studies. Avocations: swimming, golf, travel.

REUDER, MARY E(ILEEN), retired psychology professor, retired statistician; b. Mpls., Mar. 12, 1923; d. Leo Aloysius and Mary Agnes (McGuire) R.; m. Marvin Alvin Iverson, July 11, 1953 (dec. Dec. 1979); children: Carol Mary, Kent Gery. BA, Coll. St. Catherine, St. Paul, 1944; MA, Brown U., 1945; PhD, U. Pa., 1951. Lic. psychologist, N.Y.; diplomate America Coll. Forescic Examiners Specialties. Asst. instr. psychology U. Pa., Phila., 1946-51; work mgmt. specialist U.S. Naval Ammunition Depot, Ft. Mifflin, Pa., 1951-52; rsch. psychologist pers. br. Adj. Gen.'s Office, Dept. Army, Washington, 1952-54; instr. psychology Queens Coll., CUNY, Flushing, 1957-62, asst. prof., 1962-66, assoc. prof., 1966-71, prof., 1971-86, chmn. dept., 1984-85, chmn. acad. senate, 1982-85, prof. emerita, 1986—. Mem. grad. faculty CUNY, 1977-86; mem. adv. bd. Dushkin Press, Guilford, Conn., 1975-84; cons., manuscript peer reviewer Acad. Psychology Bull., 1980-85, Jour. Profl. Psychology, 1986-88, Am. Psychologist, 1987-88, Psychol. Reports, 1995-96. Contbr. articles to profl. jours. and encys., also monographs, chpt. to book. Cons. com. on rsch. and evaluation Nassau coun. Girl Scouts U.S., 1971-74; bd. dirs. Walker Lake Landowners Assn., 1993-. Recipient William James award for outstanding contbns. to psychology Acad. Divsn. N.Y. State Psychol. Assn., 1998; grantee NSF, 1964, Sigma Xi, 1962. Fellow APA (pres. divs. 1 and 36 1987-88, exec. com. div. 1 1981-87, div. 36 1979—, coun. reps. div. 36 1980-83, 91-97, 99-2001, 2005—, award for exceptional svc. to divsn. gen. psychology, disting. svc. award by divsn. of psychology of religion, 1996, accreditation site visitor 1996—, Virginia Staudt Sexton Mentoring award divsn. 36 psychology of religion 1996), Am. Psychol. Soc., NY Acad. Scis., Am. Assn. Applied and Preventive Psychology (charter); mem. AAAS (life), Am. Coll. Forensic Examiners, Ea. Psychol. Assn. (adminstrv. coord. 1961-67, 70), Psychometric Soc., Biometric Soc., Am. Statis. Assn., Queens Coll. Faculty Club (past bd. dirs., v.p.), U. Pa. Club L.I. (bd. govs. 1980—, Jack White award), N.Am. Lake Mgmt. Soc., Pa. Lake Mgmt. Soc., Penn Club NY (charter mem.), Sigma Xi (grantee 1962, lectr. 1977-1986, nat. bd. dirs. 1972-75, 77), Alpha Sigma Lambda, Pi Gamma Mu, Delta Phi Lambda, Kappa Gamma Pi, Alpha Pi Epsilon, Psi Chi. Democrat. Roman Catholic. Avocations: reading, swimming. Home and Office: PO Box C Shohola PA 18458-0080

REUKAUF, WILLIAM E., lawyer; Degree, Hamilton Coll.; JD, Georgetown U. Asst. US atty. DC, 1970—73; sr. trial atty. US EPA, 1973; pvt. practice Washington; mem. legal staff US Office of Spl. Counsel, Washington, 1983—85, assoc. spl. counsel for prosecution, 1985, head investigation and prosecution divsn., 2001, acting spl. counsel. Office: US Office Spl Counsel 1730 M St NW Ste 218 Washington DC 20036-4505*

REUM, JAMES MICHAEL, lawyer; b. Oak Park, Ill., Nov. 1, 1946; s. Walter John and Lucy (Bellegay) R. BA cum laude, Harvard U., Cambridge, Mass., 1968, JD cum laude, 1972. Bar: NY 1973, DC 1974, US Dist. Ct. (so. dist.) NY 1974, Ill. 1979, US Dist. Ct. (no. dist.) Ill. 1982. Assoc. Davis Polk & Wardwell, NYC, 1973-78; assoc. Minority Counsel Com. on Judiciary US Ho. of Reps., Washington, 1974; ptnr. Hopkins & Sutter, Chgo., 1979-93, Winston & Strawn, Chgo., 1994—. Dir. Great Books Found., 2007—; Midwest advance rep. Nat. Reagan Bush Com., 1980; nominee commr. Securities and Exchange Comm., Pres. Bush, 1992; mem. fin. com. G.W. Bush, 2000; mem. US Coun. for Internat. Bus., 2007—. Served to SP4 USAR, 1969—75. Recipient Harvard U. Honorary Nat. Scholarship, 1964-72. Mem.: Monte Carlo Country Club (Monaco), Univ. Club (NYC), Racquet Club Chgo. Republican. Home: 12 E Scott St Chicago IL 60610-2320 Office: Winston & Strawn 35 W Wacker Dr Ste 4200 Chicago IL 60601-1695 Office Phone: 312-558-5644. Business E-Mail: jreum@winston.com.

REUPKE, WILLIAM ALBERT, engineer; b. Chgo., Jan. 22, 1940; BA, Northwestern U., Chgo., 1961; AM, Ind. U., Bloomington, 1967; MS, Ga. Inst. Tech., Atlanta, 1973, PhD, 1977; MD, 2008. Gen. physicist NASA, Cleve., 1963-64; staff physicist Aerospace Rsch. Applications Ctr., Bloomington, Ind., 1965-67; rsch. engr. Lockheed Missiles and Space Co., Sunnyvale, Calif., 1967-68; engring. physicist Stanford (Calif.) Linear Accelerator Ctr., 1968-71; staff mem. Los Alamos (N.Mex.) Nat. Lab., 1977-82; sr. engr. Computer Scis. Corp., Lanham-Seabrook, Md., 1983-95, Sci. Applications Internat. Corp., Seabrook, Md., 1996—2006, Perot Sys. Govt. Svcs., Fairfax, Va., 2006—08, Aerospace Corp., Chantilly, Va., 2009—. Recipient Group Achievement award NASA, 1987, 91, 93, 2001, Dr. Robert H. Goddard Hist. Essay award Nat. Space Club, 1991. Fellow Brit. Interplanetary Soc.; mem. AIAA (sr.), Am. Phys. Soc. Achievements include development of new method of adjusting neutron cross sections to improve fit of measured and calculated reaction rates in nuclear fusion integral experiments and application of that method to show that a neutron cross section important for fusion energy production is significantly smaller than was previously believed. Office: Goddard Space Flight Ctr Greenbelt MD 20771 Business E-Mail: reupke@mailaps.org.

REUSS, MARK, automotive executive; b. Oct. 19, 1963; BME, Vanderbilt Univ., 1986; MBA, Duke Univ., 1990. Cert. ind. pool test driver Nürburgring Motorsport Track, lic. Grand Am. Road racing. Intern, noise vibration lab. GM Corp., 1983, assoc. engr. & project engr. Flint Automotive div., 1986—90, sr. project engr., total vehicle engr. & vehicle line dir., 1990—2001, exec. dir. arch. engring. & GM Performance div., 2001—05, exec. dir. No. Am. vehicle systems, 2005—06, exec. dir. global vehicle integration, 2006—08, pres. & mng. dir. GM Holden Ltd., 2008—. GM Key Exec. Pa. State Univ. Bd. dir. Horizon Upward Bound Cranbrook Schools; mem. bd. vis. Vanderbilt Univ. Sch. Engring. Office: GM Corp 300 Renaissance Ctr Detroit MI 48265*

REUSZER, DIANE CURTIS, humanities educator; d. Norman Nansen Curtis and Irene Beth Summers; m. John Henry Reuszer. MEd, U. Miami, Coral Gables, Fl., 1976. Prof. Pensacola Jr. Coll., Fla., 1993—2000, Northeastern Jr. Coll., Sterling, Colo., 2000—. Mem.: US Equestrian Fedn.

REUTER, FRANK THEODORE, historian, educator; b. Kankakee, Ill., Mar. 18, 1926; s. Frank Theodore and Evelyn Marie (Scott) R.; m. Kathleen Ann Pester, June 16, 1951; children: Mark, Stephen, Christopher, Ann, Katherine. BS, U. Ill., 1950, MA, 1959, PhD, 1960. Instr. West Liberty (W. Va.) State Coll., 1960-62; asst. prof. Texas Christian U., Fort Worth, 1962-66, assoc. prof., 1966-71; prof. history Tex. Christian U., 1971-92, dean Grad. Sch., 1970-75, chmn. dept. history, 1980-83, prof. emeritus, 1992—. Vis. prof. Pázmány Péter Cath. U., Budapest, Hungary, 1999. Author: West Liberty State College: The First 125 Years, 1963, Catholic Influence on American Colonial Policies, 1898-1904, 1967, Trials and Triumphs: George Washington's Foreign Policy, 1983; co-author: Injured Honor: The Chesapeake-Leopard Affair, 1996. Served with USNR, 1944-46. U. Durham Rsch. fellow, 1991. Mem. Orgn. Am. Historians, Am. Hist. Assn., Soc. Historians Early Republic, Soc. Historians Am. Fgn. Relations, Phi Beta Kappa, Phi Alpha Theta. Roman Catholic. Home: 3617 Winifred Dr Fort Worth TX 76133-2126 Office: Tex Christian U Dept History Fort Worth TX 76129-0001 Office Phone: 817-257-7288. E-mail: rfkreuter@sbcglobal.net.

REUTER, HARALD, pharmacologist; b. Düsseldorf, Germany, Mar. 25, 1934; s. Rudolf and Else (Koerfer) R.; m. Lieselotte Speckmann, Aug. 10, 1960; children: Kirsten, Andreas, Sabine. Diploma, U. Freiburg, Germany, 1959; MD, U. Mainz, Germany, 1960. Asst. dept. pharmacology U. Mainz, 1960-65, privatdozent, 1965-69; prof. pharmacology U. Bern, Switzerland, 1969-99, dean med. faculty, 1983-85, chmn. dept. pharmacology, 1971-99, prof. emeritus, 1999—. Vis. prof. various univs. in Eng., Israel, U.S., Japan and China. Co-author: Calcium Movement in Excitable Cells, 1975; editor: Sodium-Calcium Exchange, 1989; mem. editorial bd. numerous sci. jours.; contbr. over 140 articles to internat. jours. Recipient Outstanding Rsch. award Internat. Soc. Heart Rsch., 1984, Ciba-Geigy-Drew award Drew U., 1984, Marcel-Benoist prize Swiss Govt., 1985, Schmiedeberg-Plakette award German Pharmacology Soc., 1987, K.S. Cole award Biophys. Soc., 1993, Ernst-Jung medal for medicine in gold, 2002. Mem. NAS, Academia Europaea, Deutsche Akademie der Naturforscher Leopoldina, Swiss Acad. Med. Scis., Acad. Royale Médecine Belgique. Avocations: reading, arts, music, hiking, skiing. Home: Hofenstrasse 15 CH 3032 Hinterkappelen Switzerland E-mail: reuter@pki.unibe.ch.

REUTER, MARK F., lawyer; b. South Bend, Ind., Sept. 13, 1971; BA, U. Notre Dame, 1992; JD, U. Notre Dame Law Sch., 1996. Bar: Ohio 1996. Ptnr. Keating Muething & Klekamp PLL, Cin. Mem., Bd. Trustees Summit County Day Sch.; mem., Deal Maker Awards Nomination Com. Greater Cin. Assn. for Corp. Growth. Named one of Ohio's Rising Stars, Super Lawyers, 2005, 2006, 2007. Fellow: Cin. Acad. Leadership for Lawyers; mem.: Ohio State Bar Assn. (mem., Corp. Law Com.), Cin. Bar Assn. Office: Keating Muething & Klekamp PLL One E Fourth St Ste 1400 Cincinnati OH 45202 Office Phone: 513-579-6400. Office Fax: 513-579-6457. Business E-Mail: mreuter@kmklaw.com.

REUTER, STEWART RALSTON, retired radiologist; b. Detroit, Feb. 14, 1934; s. Carl H. and Grace M. R.; m. Marianne (Ahfeldt), June 6, 1966. BA, Ohio Wesleyan U., 1955; MD, Case Western Res. U., 1959; JD, U. San Francisco, 1980. Diplomate: Am. Bd. Radiology, Am. Bd. Legal Medicine. Bar: Tex., 1981. Intern U. Calif., San Francisco, 1959—60, resident in radiology, 1960—63; instr. radiology Stanford U., Calif., 1963—64; asst. prof. U. Mich., Ann Arbor, 1966—69; assoc. prof. U. Calif., San Diego, 1969—72; prof. U. Mich., Ann Arbor, 1972—76, U. Calif., San Francisco and Davis, 1976—80; prof., chmn. dept. radiology Health Sci. Ctr., U. Tex., San Antonio, 1980—2001, prof. emeritus, 2001. Co-author: Gastrointestinal Radiology, 3d edit., 1986; mem. editorial bd. Am. Jour. Roentgenology, 1975-91, Iatrogenics, 1990-93; contbr. articles to profl. journals. Picker Fellow, 1964-66. Fellow: Soc. Interventional Radiologists (pres. 1978, Gold medal 2004), Am. Coll. Legal Medicine (bd. gov. 1985—91, 1992—94, sec. 1994, pres. elect 1995, pres. 1996), Am. Heart Assn., Am. Coll. Radiology (councillor 1996—99, fellow emeritus 2000); mem.: Am. Roentgen Ray Soc., Assn., Soc. Gastrointestinal Radiologists, Tex. Radiol. Assn. (trustee 1989—92, pres. 1994, trustee 1995—98, Gold medal 2000), Assn. Univ. Radiologists, Am. Bd. Legal Medicine, Tex. Bar Assn. Home: 3923 Morgans Creek San Antonio TX 78230-1945 Office: U Tex Health Sci Ctr Dept Radiology 7703 Floyd Curl Dr San Antonio TX 78284-6200 Business E-Mail: reuter@uthscsa.edu.

REUTHER, DAVID LOUIS, retired children's book publisher, writer; b. Detroit, Nov. 2, 1946; s. Roy Louis and Fania (Sonkin) Reuther; m. Margaret Alexander Miller, July 21, 1973; children: Katherine Anna, Jacob Alexander. BA with honors, U. Mich., 1968. Tchr. Lewis-Wadhams Sch., Westport, NY, 1969-71; asst. dir. Children's Book Coun., NYC, 1971-73; editor children's books Macmillan Pub. Co., NYC, 1973-76; sr. editor Four Winds Press-Scholastic Inc., NYC, 1976-82; sr. v.p., pub. Morrow Jr. Books, NYC, 1982-98; co-founder Baseball Ink, Inc., 1986-90; pub. Lothrop Lee & Shepard, NYC, 1996-98, Beech Tree Books, NYC, 1997-98; pres., pub. SeaStar Books, NYC, 1999—2002, North-South Books, NYC, 1999—2002. Co-author (with Roy Doty): Fun to Go, A Take-Along Activity Book, 1982; co-author: (with John Thorn and Pete Palmer) Save-the-Animals Activity Book, 1982, The Hidden Game of Baseball, 1984, Total Baseball, 1989, The Whole Baseball Catalog, 1990, Total Baseball II, 1991; editor (with John Thorn): The Armchair Quarterback, 1982, The Armchair Aviator, 1983, The Armchair Mountaineer, 1984, The Armchair Book of Baseball, 1985, The Armchair Angler, 1986, The Transpose Book of Baseball II, 1987, The Armchair Traveler, 1988. Chmn. Children's Book Coun., 1990, bd. dirs., Smith House Family Health Ctr., 2006—, Champlain Area Trails, 2008—, Essex Cmty. Fund, 2008—. Mem.: NSTA (children's book coun. joint com. 1982—85), ALA (co-chmn. children's book coun. joint com. 2000—02), Champlain Valley Film Soc., Am. Bookseller Assn. (childrens book coun. joint com. 1990—93). Home: Box 337 Willsboro NY 12996

REUTIMAN, ROBERT WILLIAM, JR., lawyer; b. Mpls., June 4, 1944; s. Robert William and Elsbeth Bertha (Doering) R.; m. Virginia Lee Traxler, June 25, 1983; children: Robert James, Joseph Lee. BA magna cum laude, U. Minn., 1966, JD, 1969. Bar: Minn. 1969, U.S. Ct. Mil. Appeals 1969, U.S. Dist. Ct. Minn. 1973, U.S. Ct. Appeals (8th cir.) 1976, U.S. Tax. Ct. 1979. Mem. Armstrong, Phleger, Reutiman & Vinokour, Ltd., Wayzata, Minn., 1973-76; ptnr. Phleger & Reutiman, Wayzata, 1976-81; pvt. practice Wayzata, 1981—. Chmn. Spring Pk. Planning Commn., 1978; city ct. judge, Hopkins and Minnetonka, Minn. Capt. U.S. Army, 1969-73. Decorated Army Commendation medal. Mem. Minn. Bar Assn., Hennepin County Bar Assn., Phi Beta Kappa. Lutheran. Avocations: fishing, gardening. Home: 11610 3rd Ave N Plymouth MN 55441-5919 Office: PO Box 367 Wayzata MN 55391 Office Phone: 952-473-7328. Business E-Mail: billreutiman@lycos.com.

REUTTER, EBERHARD EDMUND, JR., education and law educator; b. Balt., May 28, 1924; s. Eberhard Edmund and Irene Louise (Loewer) R.; m. Bettie Marie Lytle, Aug. 16, 1947; 1 son, Mark Douglas. BA, Johns Hopkins U., 1944; MA, Columbia U., 1948, PhD, 1950. Dir., Tokyo Army Edn. Program Sch., 1945-47; head math. dept. Barnard Sch., NYC, 1947-49; mem. faculty Tchrs. Coll., Columbia U., 1950—, prof., 1957-96, prof. emeritus, 1996—. Vis. prof. U. Alaska, 1960, 66, U. P.R., 1954, U. So. Calif., 1960; speaker, cons. Coordinator spl. edn. projects NAACP Legal Def. Fund, 1965-68 Author: The School Administrator and Subversive Activities, 1951, Schools and the Law, 5th edit., 1981, (with W.S. Elsbree) Staff Personnel in the Public Schools, 1954, (with R.R. Hamilton) Legal Aspects of School Board Operation, 1958, (with W.S. Elsbree) Principles of Staff Personnel Administration in Public Schools, 1959, (with L.O. Garber) The Yearbook of School Law, 1967, 68, 69, 70, Legal Aspects of Control of Student Activities by Public School Authorities, 1970, The Law of Public Education, 4th edit., 1994, The Courts and Student Conduct, 1975, The Supreme Court's Impact on Public Education, 1982; also articles, chpts. in books. Chmn. citizens adv. com. Emerson (N.J.) Bd. Edn., 1954-57. Served from pvt. to 1st lt. inf. AUS, 1943-46. Recipient Marion A. McGhehey award for outstanding service in field edn. law, 1986. Mem. NEA, AAUP, Nat. Orgn. Legal Problems of Edn. (pres. 1967), Am. Assn. Sch. Adminstrs., Am. Assn. Sch. Pers. Adminstrs., Internat. Pers. Mgmt. Assn., Phi Beta Kappa, Kappa Delta Pi, Phi Delta Kappa. Home: 316 Grand Blvd Emerson NJ 07630-1157 Office: Columbia Univ Tchrs Coll New York NY 10027

REUTTER, MICHAEL A., biology professor; PhD, U. Fla., Gainesville, 1997. Instr. Normandale CC, Bloomington, Minn., 2005—. Contbr. scientific papers. Mem.: Human Anatomy & Physiology Soc., Soc. Neurosci., Am. Physiol. Soc. Office: Normandale CC 9700 France Ave S Bloomington MN 55431

REUTTY, MICHELE MARIE, library director; b. Passaic, NJ, Oct. 17, 1949; d. Charles Hugo and Jean Cammarano Reutty; children: David Lavern Walters Jr., Jennifer Walters McCoy, Cristian Michael Maiullo. AA, Bergen County C.C., Paramus, NJ, 1979; B in English, Montclair State Coll., NJ, 1987; MLS, Rutgers U., New Brunswick, NJ, 1989. Cert. ESL tutor Bergen County Coop. Libr. Systems/N.J., 1989. Reference libr. Elmwood Pk. Pub. Libr., 1987—88; asst. dir. Cresskill Pub. Libr., NJ, 1988—89; dir. Free Pub. Libr. Hasbrouck Heights, NJ, 1989—2006, Oakland Pub. Libr., NJ, 2006—; pub. libr. rep. HRLC, 2008—. Editor-in-chief, contbg. author: history book Remembering the Past, Looking Toward the Future, 1996. Recipient Downs Intellectual Freedom award, U. Ill., Campaign-Urbana, 2006, Intellectual Freedom award, NJ Library Assn., 2007; named Citizen of the Yr., Mayor and Coun., Hasbrouck Heights, 1992; fellow Snowbird Leadership Inst., Salt Lake City, Utah, Rutgers U., 1991. Mem.: ALA (assoc.), Rutgers Sch. Communication, Info. and Libr. Studies (pres. alumni assn. 2001—02, 2004, mem. exec. bd. 2006—07), NJ Libr. Assn. (assoc.; second v.p./chair adminstrn. and mgmt. com. 2004—05, v.p., pres.-elect 2006—07, pres. 2007—08), Spokes-Women Motorcycle Club (sec.). Democrat. Roman Catholic. Avocations: creative writing, motorcycling, pysanky writing. Home: 189 Lincoln Ave Elmwood Park NJ 07407 Office: Oakland Pub Libr 2 Municipal Plaza Oakland NJ 07436 E-mail: xlibris@optonline.net.

REUTZEL, EDWARD WILLIAM, mechanical engineer; s. Edward Thomas and Georgia Helena Reutzel; m. Jennifer Ankney Reutzel, June 26, 2004; children: Sophia Lynn, Aubrey Elizabeth. PhD, Penn State U., University Pk., Pa. Test engr. GE Fanuc, Charlottesville, Va., 1997—98; head, laser sys. engr. and integration ARL Penn State, State Coll., Pa., 1998—. Rsch. engr. Lockheed Martin INEL, Idaho Falls, 1993—97. Mem.: ASME. Office: Applied Rsch Lab Penn State PO Box 30 State College PA 16804-0030 Business E-Mail: ewr101@psu.edu.

REVARD, STELLA HILL PURCE, English literature educator; b. NYC, June 9, 1933; d. William Edwin and Mae (Hill) Purce; m. Carter C. Revard, 1956; children: Stephen, Geoffrey, Vanessa, Lawrence. BA magna cum laude, Hunter Coll., 1955; MA, Yale U., 1957, PhD, 1961; MA in Greek, Washington U., St. Louis, 1992. Instr. U. Buffalo, 1958-59; prof. English So. Ill. U., Edwardsville, 1961—98. Author: The War in Heaven, 1980, Milton and the Tangles of Neaera's Hair, 1997, Pindar and the Renaissance Hymn-Ode, 2001, Politics, Poetics and the Pindaric Ode, 2009; editor: Acta Conventus Neo-Latini, 1988, Milton's Complete Shorter Poems, 2009; contbr. articles to profl. jours. Fellow NEH, 1976, 85, 90, 93-94, Huntington Libr., 1991, Folger Libr., 1988, 94; honored scholar Milton Soc. Am., 1997; named to Hunter Coll. Hall of Fame, 1999. Mem. MLA (17th Century com. 1981-84), Milton Soc. of Am. (bd. dirs. 1978-80, v.p. 1983, pres. 1984), Spenser Soc., Internat. Assn. for Neo-Latin Studies (pres. 2000-03), Renaissance Soc. Am. Methodist. Avocations: opera, travel, rare books, gardening. Home: 6638 Pershing Ave Saint Louis MO 63130-4642 Home Phone: 314-727-9358. Business E-Mail: srevard@sive.edu.

REVAY, LINDA ANN, principal, educator; b. Warrensville Heights, Ohio, Apr. 29, 1958; d. Florence Helen Seeman; m. David Christopher Revay, Nov. 7, 1980; 1 child, Diane Marie. BA, Notre Dame Coll. Ohio, South Euclid; MA, John Carroll U., Univ. Heights, Ohio; MEd, PhD, U. Akron, Ohio. Cert. ednl. adminstr. State of Ohio, 2002, elem. tchr. State of Ohio, 1988. Part time faculty U. Akron, Ohio, 2006—; prin. St. Adalbert Cath. Sch., Cleve., 2004—. Mem.: Coun. Exceptional Children, Golden Key Soc., Phi Alpha Theta, Pi Lambda Theta, Delta Kappa Gamma Soc. Internat. Roman Catholic. Avocations: reading, swimming, walking. Home: 157 Forestwood Dr Northfield OH 44067-1920 Office: Univ Akron Akron OH 44325 Personal E-mail: lrevay@yahoo.com. Business E-Mail: lar23@uakron.edu.

REVEAL, ERNEST IRA, III, retired lawyer; b. Chgo., Oct. 19, 1948; s. Ernest Ira Jr. and Hazel (Holt) R.; m. Katherine Trennerry, Nov. 24, 1979; children: Genevieve, Adrienne, Danielle. BA, Cornell U., 1970; JD cum laude, U. Mich., 1973. Bar: Minn. 1973, U.S. Dist. Ct. Minn. 1973, U.S. Ct. Appeals (8th cir.) 1974, U.S. Dist. Ct. S.D. 1976, U.S. Ct. Claims 1976, U.S. Ct. Appeals (7th cir.) 1984, U.S. Dist. Ct. (ctrl. dist.) Calif. 1991, U.S. Ct. Appeals (9th cir.) 1991, U.S. Supreme Ct., 1991, U.S. Cir. Ct. Appeals (fed. cir.)2001. Assoc. Robins, Kaplan, Miller & Ciresi, Mpls., 1973—79, ptnr., 1979—2002, mediator, arbitrator, 2003—; temp. judge Orange County Superior Ct., 2007—. Panel mem. Am. Arbitration Assn., Nat. Arbitration Forum, Internat. Inst. Conflict Preservation & Resolution. Author: Public Sector Labor Law, 1983. Pro tem mem. Civil Svc. Commn., St. Paul, 1976; chmn. regional adv. com. So. Calif. Pub. Radio. Mem. ABA, Minn. Bar Assn. (past chair labor and employment law sect.), Calif. State Bar Assn. (adv., past exec. com., antitrust and unfair competition sect.), Cornell Club of Minn. (past pres.). Democrat. Presbyterian. Avocations: history, travel. Office Phone: 949-589-1276. Personal E-mail: ernest.reveal@cox.net.

REVEL, JEAN-PAUL, biology professor; b. Strasbourg, France, Dec. 7, 1930; arrived in U.S., 1953; s. Gaston Benjamin and Suzanne (Neher) Revel; m. Helen Ruth Bowser, July 27, 1957 (div. 1986); children: David, Daniel Neher, Steven Robert; m. Galina Avdeeva Moller, Dec. 24, 1986 (dec. 2004); 1 stepchild, Karen (dec.). BS, U. Strasbourg, 1949; PhD, Harvard U., 1957. Rsch. fellow Cornell U. Med. Sch., NYC, 1958-59; from instr. to prof. Harvard Med. Sch., Boston, 1959-71; prof. Calif. Inst. Tech., Pasadena, 1971—, emeritus, 2006—, AB Ruddock chair in biology, 1978—2006, dean of students, 1996—2005, emeritus, 2006—. Mem. sch. advisors bd. Nat. Insts. Aging, Balt., 1977-80; mem. ad hoc adv. biology NSF, Washington, 1982-83; mem. Nat. High Voltage Microscopy Adv. Group, Bethesda, Md., 1983, Nat. Rsch. Resources Adv. Coun., 1986-90. Author: (with E.D. Hay) Fine Structure of Developing Avian Cornea, 1969, over 150 publs., 1952-99; editor: Cell Shape and Surface Architecture, 1977, Science of Biological Specimen Preparation, 1986; mem. editl. bd. Jour. Cell Biology, 1969-72, Internat. Rev. Cytology, 1970, Cell and Tissue Rsch., 1979—, Molecular and Cell Biology, 1983-91; editor in chief Jour. Microscopy Soc. Am., 1994-96. Fellow AAAS (leader biol. scis. sect. 1991-92, Gordon conf. cell adhesion); mem. Am. Soc. Cell Biology (pres. 1972-73), Electron Micros. Soc. Am. (pres. 1988, Disting. Scientist award 1993), Soc. Devel. Biology. Avocations: watercolors, photography. Office: Calif Inst Tech # 114-96 Pasadena CA 91125-0001 Home Phone: 626-796-0701; Office Phone: 626-395-4986. Business E-Mail: revelj@caltech.edu.

REVELEY, WALTER TAYLOR, III, academic administrator, former dean, law educator; b. Churchville, Va., Jan. 6, 1943; s. Walter Taylor and Marie (Eason) R.; m. Helen Bond, Dec. 18, 1971; children: Walter Taylor IV, George Everett Bond, Nelson Martin Eason, Helen Lanier. AB, Princeton U., 1965; JD, U. Va., 1968. Bar: Va. 1970, D.C. 1976. Asst. prof. law U. Ala., 1968-69; law clk. to Justice Brennan US Supreme Ct., Washington, 1969-70; fellow Woodrow Wilson Internat. Ctr. for Scholars, 1972-73; internat. affairs fellow Coun. on Fgn. Rels., NYC, 1972-73; assoc. Hunton & Williams, Richmond, Va., 1970-76, ptnr., 1976-98, mng. ptnr., 1982-91, cons., 1998—2008; dean William & Mary Sch. Law, 1998—2008, law prof.; interim pres. Coll. William Mary, 2008, pres., 2008—. Lectr. Coll. William and Mary Law Sch., 1978—80; cons. in field. Author: War Powers of the President and Congress: Who Holds the Arrows and Olive Branch, 1981; mem. editl. bd. Va. Law Rev., 1966-68; contbr. articles to profl. jours. Trustee Princeton U., 1986-90, 91-2001, Presbyn. Ch. (U.S.A.) Found., 1991-97, Va. Hist. Soc., 1991-96, 2003—, Union Theol. Sem., 1992-2000, Andrew W. Mellon Found., 1994—, JSTOR, 1995—2008, Va. Mus. Fine Arts, 1995-2005, pres. 1996-99, St. Christopher's Sch., 1996-01, 2004—, Carnegie Endowment for Internat. Peace, 1999—; bd. dirs. Fan Dist. Assn., Richmond, Inc., 1976-80, pres., 1979-80; bd. dirs. Richmond Symphony, 1980-92, pres., 1988-90, pres. symphony coun., 1994-99; bd. dirs. Presbyn. Outlook Found., 1985-2003, 2004-, pres., 1992-95; bd. dirs. Va. Mus. Found., 1990-99; bd. dirs. New Covenant Trust Co., 1997-99, Va. Found. Humanities, 2001-2007. Mem. ABA, Va. Bar Assn., D.C. Bar Assn., Am. Bar Found., Va. Bar Found., Princeton Assn. Va. (bd. dirs. 1981—, pres. 1983-85), Va. State Bar (Edn. Lawyers sect. bd. govs. 1992—2008, chmn. 1992-95), Raven Soc., Phi Beta Kappa, Omicron Delta Kappa. Home: 2314 Monument Ave Richmond VA 23220-2604 Office: Office Pres PO Box 8795 Williamsburg VA 23187-8795 Office Phone: 757-221-7891. Business E-Mail: taylor@wm.edu.

REVELL, HENRY, JR., social services administrator, retired education educator; b. Selma, NC, Apr. 13, 1932; s. Henry William Sr. and Flora (Vinson) Revell; m. Carolyn Yvonne L. Revell (dec.); children: Gary, Keith, Kevan Croper. BS, NC A&T State U., Greensboro, 1974. Facilitator, pres. Family Strengths, Greensboro, NC, 1980—; pres., CEO Kent-FJHB, Inc., Selma, NC, 1989—; owner, dir. Revell's Enrichment Ctr., Greensboro, 2002—. State 4-H youth coord. NC A&T State U., Greensboro, 1974—87; program dir. Another Chance Recovery Ctr., Greensboro, 2002—; presenter in field. Author: 4-H in Public Housing Communities. Pres., bd. dirs. Triad Sickle Cell Reg., Greensboro, 1987—91, Daniel Godfrey Meml. Fund, Greensboro, 1988—; past pres. RH Family Orgn.; deacon Providence Bapt. Ch., Greensboro, 1981—. With US Army, 1956—58. Grantee, Cmty. Found., Greensboro, 2000. Mem.: NACCP (parlimentarian 1990—), Epsilon Sigma Phi (life). Democrat. Baptist. Avocations: baseball, basketball, football, walking, dance. Home: 3316 S Elm-Eugene St Greensboro NC 27406 Personal E-mail: revellh@bellsouth.net.

REVELLE, DONALD GENE, manufacturing and health care company executive, consultant; b. Cape Girardeau, Mo., July 16, 1930; s. Lewis W. and Dorothy R.; m. Jo M. Revelle, Aug. 1, 1954; children—Douglas, David, Daniel, Dianne BA, U. Mo., 1952; JD, U. Colo., 1957; grad., Harvard U. Bus. Sch., 1971. Dir. employee relations Westinghouse Corp., Pitts., 1957-65; asst. to v.p. Diebold Corp., 1966; v.p. human resources TRW Corp., Cleve., 1967-84; sr. v.p. human resources Black and Decker Co., Towson, Md., 1984-86; exec. v.p. corp. rels. Montefiore Acad. Med. Ctr., Bronx, 1987-98; pres., CEO Syzygy, Inc., 1998—. Univ. lectr.; cons. Duerba Ship, Blue Cross N.Y., Windsor Hosp., Salvation Army Contbr. articles to profl. jours. Mem. sch. bd. State of N.Y. Lt. USNR, 1952-54 Mem.: ABA (labor law com.), Human Resource Planning Soc., Fed. Bar Assn., Colo. Bar Assn., MBA Assn., Rotary. Methodist. Home and Office: Syzygy Inc 29903 Baywood Ln Wesley Chapel FL 33543-9744 Home Phone: 813-994-3403; Office Phone: 813-994-3403.

REVENKOVA, EKATERINA, biologist, researcher; b. Moscow, May 22, 1962; arrived in U.S., 2000; d. Vladimir Preobrazhensky and Natalia Alekhina; 1 child, Anton Revenkov. MS in Genetics, Moscow State U., 1984; PhD in Molecular Biology, V.A.Engelhardt Inst. Molecular Biology, Moscow, 1993. Rsch. scientist Ctr. of Bioengineering, Moscow, 1989—94; postdoctoral rsch. fellow Friedrich Miescher Inst., Basel, Switzerland, 1995—99; scientist Basel Inst. for Immunology, 1999—2000; instr. Mt. Sinai Sch. Medicine, NYC, 2001—04, asst. prof., 2004—. Contbr. articles to profl. jours. Mem.: Am. Soc. for Cell Biology. Office: Mount Sinai School of Medicine 1 Gustave L Levy Pl New York NY 10029

REVER, GEORGE WRIGHT, psychiatrist, health facility administrator; b. Balt., May 18, 1928; s. William Benjamin and Amy Blanche (Wright) R.; m. Bridget Valerie Hanley, 1961 (dec. 1988); children: Kurt, Maeve Rever Raedle; m. Ann Roe, Feb. 4, 1994. BS, U. Md., 1950; MD, U. Md., Balt., 1957. Rotating intern Mercy Hosp., Balt., 1957-58; resident psychiatry and neurology VA Hosp., Boston, 1958-60; fellow Harvard Med. Sch., Cambridge, Mass., 1960-64, clin. instr. psychiatry, 1964—2004; psychiatrist divsn. legal medicine Cambridge Ct., 1960-71; psychiatrist Cambridge Ct. Clinic Divsn. of Legal Medicine, Mass., 1960-71; pvt. practice Cohasset, Mass., 1963-90, Easton, Md., 1990-93; psychiatric cons. Travelers Aid Soc., Boston, 1966-74; psychiatrist Eunice Kennedy Shriver Ctr., Waltham, Mass., 1967-90; fellow child psychiatry Mass. Gen. Hosp., Boston, 1960-61, 62-63, fellow community mental health, 1963-64, staff psychiatrist, 1964-90, dir. child psychiatry tng. program neuropsychiatry devel. disabilities sect., 1967-90, asst. pediatrician, 1969-71, psychiat. cons. social svc. dept., 1970-74, psychiatrist Chelsea Health Ctr., 1974-77, hon. psychiatrist, 1991—2004; med. dir. Brockton Family and Community Rsch., Mass., 1979-90; psychiatric cons. Benedictine Sch., Ridgely, Md., 1990—; child and adolescent psychiatrist Wicomico County Health Dept., Salisbury, Md., 1990-91, Queen Anne County Mental Health, Centreville, Md., 1990-92, Talbot County Mental Health, Easton, 1990-92, med. dir., 1992—2002, Regional Mid-Shore Mental Health Svcs., 1998—2005, Caroline County Mental Health Clinic, 2005—, Bay Hundred Behavioral Health Svcs./Choptank Cmty. Health Svcs., 2005—08, Eastern Shore Psychological Svcs., Easton, Md., 2007—. Part-time fellow child psychiatry Mass. Gen. Hosp., Boston, 1961-62, James Jackson Putnam Children's Ctr., Roxbury, Mass., 1961-62; cons. Am. Heritage Dictionaries, 1992; fleet surgeon Miles River Yacht Club, 2000—04. Editl. cons. The Am. Jour. of Child and Adolescent Psychiatry, 1994—. Sgt. U.S. Army, 1950-52, Korea. Decorated Bronze Star medal; Recipient Talbot County Assn. Retarded Citizens award, 1993. Fellow: Am. Psychiat. Assn. (life Disting.), Am. Coll. Forensic Examiners (life); mem.: AMA, Am. Soc. Clin. Psychopharmacology, Soc. Biol. Psychiatry, Assn. Child Psychology and Psychiatry, Am. Neuropsychiat. Assn., Talbot County Med. Soc., Med. and Chururg. Faculty Md., Md. Psychiat. Soc., Am. Assn. Mental Retardation, Am. Assn. Cmty. Psychiatrists, Am. Acad. Child and Adolscent Psychiatry. Home: 8627 North Bend Cir Easton MD 21601-7327 Business E-Mail: rever@shore.intercom.net.

REVERDIN, BERNARD J., lawyer; b. Baden, Switzerland, June 21, 1919; came to U.S., 1948, naturalized, 1954; s. Jean and Germaine Reverdin; m. Marcelle Coicou Reverdin; children: Caroline Reverdin Flanagan, Brigitte, Nathalie. LLB, U. Geneva, 1942; postgrad., Harvard Law Sch., 1949. Bar: Switzerland 1945, N.Y. 1955. Atty., legal asst. Geneva Govt., 1945-48; assoc. Sullivan & Cromwell, NYC, 1949-51; assoc., ptnr. Lovejoy, Wasson & Ashton, NYC, 1951-84; ptnr., counsel Hunton & Williams, NYC, 1984-88; ptnr. Eaton & Van Winkle, NYC, 1988-97, sr. counsel intern, 1998—2009. Dir. subs. of European corps. Contbr. articles to profl. jours.; lectr. in field Mem. N.Y. State Bar Assn. (chair com. internat. trust and estate 1988-90), Am. Fgn. Law Assn. (past pres.), Consular Law Soc. (past pres.), Internat. Law Assn., Union Internat. des Avocats, Swiss Soc. N.Y., German Am. Law Assn. Personal E-mail: breverdin@aol.com.

REVES, JOSEPH GERALD (JERRY REVES), anesthesiology educator, dean; b. Charleston, SC, Aug. 14, 1943; s. George Everett and Frances (Masterson) R.; m. Virginia Cathcart, Jan. 05, 1945; children: Virginia Masterson, Christine Frances, Elizabeth Cathcart. BA, Vanderbilt U., 1965; MD, Medical Coll. S.C., 1969; MS, U. Ala., Birmingham, 1973. Lic. anesthesiologist S.C., Ala., Md., N.C.; Diplomate Am. Coll. Anesthesiology, Am. Bd. Anesthesiology. Rsch. asst., dept. pharmacology Med. Coll. SC, 1965, 1966; intern U. Ala. Hosp. and Clinics, Birmingham, Ala., 1969-70, resident in anesthesiology, 1970-72; postdoctoral, dept. anesthesia and physiology U. Ala. Med. Sch., 1972; instr., dept anesthesiology U. Ala. Hosp. and Clinics, 1973; dept. tng. staff, anesthesiology Nat. Naval Med. Ctr., Bethesda, Md., 1973-75; clin. instr., dept. anesthesiology George Washington U. Sch. Med., Washington, 1973-75; assoc. prof., dept. anesthesiology U. Ala. Hosp. and Clinics, 1975-78; dir., div. anesthesiology rsch. U. Ala., 1977-84, prof. anesthesiology, 1978-84; clin. anesthesia coord. UAB Cardiac Transplant Program, Birmingham, 1982-84; prof. anesthesiology, dir. cardiothoracic anesthesia Duke U. Med. Ctr., Durham, NC, 1984-1991; dir. Duke Heart Ctr., Duke Med. Ctr., Durham, NC, 1987-97; interim chmn., dept. anesthesiology Duke U. Med. Ctr., 1990-91, prof. and chmn., dept. anesthesiology, 1991—2001; dean, v.p. for med. affairs Med. U. SC Coll. Medicine, Charleston, 2001—. Cons. Hoffman-LaRoche, Somatogen, Abbott/Oximetric. Contbr. to numerous profl. jours., refereed jours., chpts. in books, published scientific reviews, selected abstracts, editorials, films, audio visual presentations, letters, positions and background papers; author: Acute Revascularization of the Infracted Heart, 1987, Common Problems in Cardiac Anesthesia, 1987, Intravenous Anesthesia and Analgesia, 1988, Anesthesiology Clinics of North America, 1988, Anesthesia, 1990, International Anesthesiology Clinics, 1991; Cardiac Anesthesia, Privileges and Practice, 1994; editor: Anesthesia and Analgesia, 1984—, cardiovascular sect. editor 1991—; editorial bd. Society Cardiovascular Anesthesia Monograph Series (chmn. 1986-89), Current Opinion in Anaesthesia 1987—, American Antec Newsletter 1989—; co-editor in chief: Current Opinion in Anaesthesiology 1990—. Dir. Clairmont Ave Hist. Preservation Com. 1976-78; Am. Heart Assn. (Durham chpt. pres. 1988-90, com. mem. anesthesiology, radiology and surgery rsch. study com. 1988-91). Grantee NIH 1991—, Janssen Pharmaceutica 1991-93, Anaquest 1989-92, Diprivan Ednl. grant ICI Pharmaceuticals Group 1991-92. Fellow Am. Coll. Cardiology; mem. AMA, Durham County Medical Soc., Internat. Soc. on Oxygen Transport to Tissue, N.C. Soc. Anesthesiologist (edn. com. 1992—), N.C. State Medical Soc., Birmingham Vanderbilt Club (bd. dirs. 1975-80, 1st v.p. 1979, pres. 1980), Southern Med. Assn. (chmn. elect. anesthesiology sect. 1976-77, chmn. 1977-78, chmn. 1988-89), Southern Soc. Anesthesiologists (v.p. 1978-79, pres. elect 1979-80, pres. 1980-81), Soc. Cardiovascular Anesthesiologists (pres. 1979-80), Assn. Univ. Anesthetists (elected to mem. 1980), Assn. Cardiac Anesthesiologists (elected to mem. 1982, pres. 1990), Soc. for Neuroleptanalgesia (bd. dirs. 1988), U. Ala. Birmingham Nat. Alumni Soc. (dist. dir., bd. dirs. 1991-93), Internat. Anesthesia Rsch. Soc. (bd. Trustees 1992—), Am. Soc. Anesthesiologists (com. sub-specialty representation 1980—, subcommittee on clin. circulation 1992—, com. geriatric anesthesia 1992—), Sigma Xi, Alpha Omega Alpha. Achievements include research on effects of age on neurologic response to cardiopulmonary bypass; cerebral blood flow and metabolism during cardiac surgery; automated delivery system of intravenous anesthetic drugs; pathophysiology of cardiopulmonary bypass; redesign of medical education. Office: Med U SC PO Box 250617 96 Jonathan Lucas St Ste 601 Charleston SC 29425 Office Phone: 843-792-2842. Business E-Mail: revesj@musc.edu.

REVESZ, RICHARD LUIS, dean, law educator; b. Buenos Aires, May 9, 1958; BSE in Civil Engring. summa cum laude, Princeton U., 1979; MS, MIT, 1980; JD, Yale U., 1983. Bar: NY 1986, DC 1986, US Supreme Ct. 1989, US Ct. Appeals DC Cir. 1986, US Dist. Ct. So. Dist. NY 1986. Jud. clerk to Chief Judge Wilfred Feinberg US Ct. Appeals 2nd Cir., NYC, 1983-84; jud. clerk to Justice Thurgood Marshall US Supreme Ct., 1984-85; asst. prof. NYU Sch. Law, 1985-88, assoc. prof., 1988-90, prof., 1990—2001, Lawrence King prof. law, 2001—, dir. Program on Environ. Regulation, 1996—, dean, 2002—. Vis. prof. U. Geneva Sch. Law, 1995, Harvard Law Sch., 1995-96, Yale Law Sch., 2001; Shelby Cullum Davis vis. prof. Grad. Inst. Internat. Studies, Geneva, 1995; vis. prof. pub. & internat. law Princeton U., 2002; pro-bono rep. Natural Resources Def. Coun., 1987; term mem. Coun. Fgn. Rels., 1989-94; cons. Environ. Economics Adv. Com. of Sci. Advisory Bd. EPA, 1998-99, mem., 1999-; cons. dept. tech. coop. for devel. UN, 1980-81, Adminstrv. Conf. of US, 1986-89, 1991-92, Carnegie Commn. Sci., Tech., and Govt., 1989-90; mem. internat. adv. bd. Yearbook European Environ. Law, 1998-. Author: Foundations of Environmental Law and Policy, 1997; editor: Distinctive Practices of the Second Circuit, 1989; co-editor: Analyzing Superfund: Economics, Science, and Law, 1995, Environmental Law, the Economy, and Sustainable Development: The United States, the European Union, and the International Community, 2000. Mem. ABA (vice chmn. com. jud. review sect. adminstrv. law 1988-98, chair, 1998—), Am. Law Inst., Assn. Bar City of NY (chmn. com. adminstrv. law 1988-91, sec. com. second century 1986-88, mem. com. environ. law 1986-88), Am. Law and Economics Assn. (bd. dirs. 1999-), Phi Beta Kappa, Sigma Xi, Tau Beta Pi (prize winner); fellow Am. Acad. Arts & Scis. Office: NYU Sch Law Vanderbilt Hall Ste 406 40 Washington Sq S New York NY 10012-1099 Office Phone: 212-998-6000. Office Fax: 212-995-3150. E-mail: richard.revesz@nyu.edu.*

REVIS-PYKE, ROBIN LYNN, director; b. Orlando, Fla., Feb. 16, 1962; d. Ed Revis and Carol Joan Rogers; m. Scott Douglas Pyke; children: Robert Stevin Revis Pyke, Spencer Douglas Pyke, Barrett Harper Pyke. BS in Comm., Trinity Internat. U., Miami; MS in Higher Edn. Adminstrn., Barry U., Miami, post graduate studies in Edn. Preschool tchr. Miami Shores Baptist Ch., 1996—97, fin. asst., 1997—2000; media comm. coord. Archdiocese of Miami, 2000—01; assoc. dir. admission and fin. aid Miami Country Day Sch., Miami, 2001—06; dean of admission Montverde Acad., Fla., 2006—. Assoc. editor The Admission Review. Chair Miami Shores Village Fine Arts Commn., Fla., 1997—2002; mem. Philanthropic Educators Orgn., 1999—2002; exec. bd. mem. Shores Performing Arts Theater, Miami Shores, 2002—04; mem. pres. bd. advisors St. Thomas U.; chair Miami Shores Village Mayors Task Force, Fla., 1998—2001. Mem.: Assn. Ind. Sch. Admission Profls., Secondary Sch. Admission Test Bd., Nat. Coun. Measurement in Edn., Nat. Assn. Independent Schs., Am. Ednl. Rsch. Assn. (grad. student coun. camps liaison 2005—), Am. Assn. U. Women, Phi Delta Kappa, Kappa Delta Pi. Republican. Baptist. Avocations: yoga, cooking, reading, boating, snorkeling. Office: Montverde Academy 17235 Seventh St Montverde FL 34756 Home: 8725 Spyglass Loop Clermont FL 34711-8574 E-mail: robin@revispyke.net.

REVKIN, ANDREW C., writer, reporter; married; 2 children. B in Biology, Brown Univ.; M in Journalism, Columbia Univ. Staff writer LA Times; sr. writer Science Digest; sr. editor Discover mag.; reporter New York Times, 1995—. Lectr. on writing and environment; appearances on Today Show, Good Morning America, NPR, CNN; adj. prof. Columbia U. Sch. Journalism, NYC; contr. writer The New Yorker, Audubon, Conde Nast Traveler. Author: (books) The Burning Season, 1990 (Sidney Hillman Found. Book prize, Robert F. Kennedy Book award, NY Times Notable Book of Yr.), Global Warming: Understanding the Forecast, 1992. Recipient AAAS Journalism award, 2002, Investigative Reporters & Editors award. Avocations: guitar, songwriting. Office: New York Times 620 8th Ave New York NY 10018

REVOILE, CHARLES PATRICK, lawyer; b. Jan. 15, 1934; s. Charles Patrick and Olga Lydia (Zecca) R.; m. Sally Cole Gates, Nov. 8, 1963. BA, U. Md., 1957, LLB, 1960. Bar: Md. 1962, U.S. Dist. Ct. Md. 1962, U.S. Supreme Ct. 1970, U.S. Ct. Claims 1976, U.S. Ct. Appeals (fed. cir.) 1982. Legis. counsel Nat. Canners Assn., Washington, 1960-64; asst. counsel Deco Electronics Inc., Washington, 1964-67; divsn. counsel Westinghouse Electric, Leesburg, Va., 1967-71; v.p., gen. counsel Stanwick Corp., Arlington, Va., 1971-85; sr. v.p., gen. counsel, sec. CACI Internat. Inc., 1985-92, bd. dirs., 1992—, chmn. compensation com., 1995—, exec. com., 1999—, mem. investor rels. com., 2001—, mem. corp. governance com., 2003—. Mem. regional adv. coun. NASD, 1989-92, mem. nominating com., 2004—, mem. audit com., 2008-; lectr., panelist, advisor. Active in Md. Ednl. Found., College Park, 1974-98; assoc. Nat. Symphony Orch., Washington, 1972-93, Smithsonian Instn., 1980-93, M Club Found., 1985-98; lawyer, lobbyist various non-profit orgns., Washington, 1984-98; mem. exec. com. ann. bus. campaign Gallaudet U., 1989-91; chmn. various coms. Kemper Open Championships, 1980-86; exec. com. 1995 USGA Sr. Open, 1997 USGA Open Championships; gen. counsel, mem. exec. com. 1995, 96, 97 Kemper Open Championship. Mem. Md. Bar Assn., Washington Corp. Counsels Assn., Am. Corp. Counsels Assn., Nat. Assn. Corp. Dirs., USGA, Mid. Atlantic Golf Assn. (exec. com. 1989-99, v.p., pres. 1998), Roger Howell Soc. U. Md. Sch. Law (charter), Congl. Country Club (com. chmn. 1966-92, bd. govs. 1987-93, Bethesda, Md.), Ocean Forest Golf Club (Sea Island, Ga.), Sea Island Club (founder), Sea Island Srs. Golf Assn. (pres. 2003), Sea Island Property Owners Ass. (bd. dirs. 2006—). Home: PO Box 31223 Sea Island GA 31561-1223

REW, LAWRENCE BOYD, lawyer; b. Eugene, Oreg., June 22, 1936; BA, Whitman Coll., 1958; JD, Willamette U., 1961. Bar: Oreg. 1961. Ptnr., of counsel Corey, Byler, Rew, Lorenzen & Hojem, LLP, Pendleton, Oreg., 1965—2005; ret., 2005. Fellow Am. Bar Found.; mem. ABA, Oreg. State Bar Assn. (pres. 2000, Pub. Svc. award 1991, bd. bar examiners 1975-79, bd. govs. 1996-2000).

REWCASTLE, NEILL BARRY, neuropathologist; b. Sunderland, Eng., Dec. 12, 1931; arrived in Can., 1955; s. William Alexander and Eva R.; m. Eleanor Elizabeth Barton Boyd, Sept. 27, 1958 (dec. Jan. 1999); 4 children. MB, BChir cum laude, U. St. Andrews, Scotland, 1955; MA, U. Toronto, 1962. Licentiate Med. Coun. Can., 1957; cert. in gen. pathology, 1962, cert. in neuropathology, 1968. Rotating intern Vancouver Gen. Hosp., 1955-56; resident in pathology Shaughnessy Hosp., Vancouver, 1956-57, U. Toronto, Ont., Canada, 1957-60, demonstrator dept. pathology, 1964-65, lectr., acting head divsn. neuropathology, dept. pathology, 1965—69, assoc. prof., 1969-70, prof., head divsn. neuropathology, 1970—81; fellow Med. Rsch. Coun. Can., 1960-64; prof. & head dept. pathology U. Calgary, 1981-91, prof., 1981-2000, prof. emeritus pathology, lab. medicine, clin. neuroscis., 2000—, mem. neurosci. rsch. group, 1982—2003; sr. pathologist Toronto Gen. Hosp., 1970—81. Dir. dept. histopathology Foothills Hosp., Calgary, 1981-91, pathologist, 1981—2003, cons. neuropathology, 1981-2003; spl. acad. adv. to dean faculty medicine U. Calgary, 1995-97; presenter in field. Contbr. over 146 articles to profl. jour., chpts. to books. Recipient Queen Elizabeth Silver Jubilee medal, 1977. Fellow: Royal Coll. Physicians & Surgeons Can.; mem. Can. Assn. Neuropathologists (ret. mem., sec. 1965-69, pres. 1976-79), Am. Assn. Neuropathologists (sr.), Sunshine Coast Power and Sail Squadron (bd. dirs., comdr. 2007-09), Gibsons Curling Club (bd. dirs.) Sunshine Coast Golf and Country Club. Avocations: gardening, philately, golf, curling, sailing. Personal E-mail: rewcastb@telus.net.

REX, JIM, state official, school system administrator; m. Sue Rex; children: Adam, Jeff, Nathan, Siri. BA in English, U. Toledo, MA in Ednl. Adminstrn., EdD in Curriculum and Instruction. Dean edn. Winthrop U., Coastal Carolina U.; pres. Columbia Coll.; v.p. devel. and alumni rels. U. SC, v.p. univ. advancement; supt. edn. SC Dept. Edn., Columbia, 2007—. Cons. Nat. Inst. Edn., SC Educator Improvement Task Force. Contbr. articles to profl. jours. Chair Clean Water SC; bd. dirs. Palmetto Conservation Found. Office: SC Dept Edn Ste 1006 1429 Senate St Columbia SC 29201 Office Phone: 803-734-8500. Office Fax: 803-734-3389.*

REX, LONNIE ROYCE, religious organization administrator; b. Caddo, Okla., May 11, 1928; s. Robert Lavern and Lennie Cordy (Gilcrease) R.; m. Betty Louise Sorrells, Apr. 8, 1949; children: Royce DeWayne, Patricia Louise, Debra Kaye. MusB, Oklahoma City U., 1950; DD (hon.), Am. Bible Inst., 1970; LLD (hon.), Wesley Synod, NYC, 1999, Meth. Wesley Synod, Toledo, 1999; LittD, Wesley Synod, 2000. Advt. mgr. Oral Roberts Evang. Assn., Tulsa, 1955-57; bus. mgr. T.L. Osborn Found., Tulsa, 1957-69; gen. mgr. Christian Crusade, Tulsa, 1969-80; sec.-treas. David Livingstone Missionary Found., Tulsa, 1970-80, pres., 1980—98. Dep. dir. gen. Internat. Biog. Assn.; bd. dirs. Intra-Ch. Pension Fund, Bethany, Okla.; spkr. internat. confs. Eng., Hungary, Korea, Singapore, Spain, N.Y.C., Congress of Arts and Comms., Oxford U., 1997; invited Pyongyang, North Korea to meet as an NGO with Peace Com. and med. aid, 1996, 97; participant peace conf. Carter Ctr. between North Korea and South Korea, 1997. Author: Never a Child, 1989. Mem. Internat. PHC Loan Fund; bd. dirs. Armand Hammer United World Coll. of Am. West, 1993—; bd. mem. Internat. Humanitarian Centre Russia, Moscow, 2000, bd. mem. Global AID Partnership, 2008, Moms Against Hunger, 2009 Recipient Merit award Korea, 1975, Moran medal Republic of Korea, Humanitarian award Senator Hugh Scott, 1983, Svc. to Mankind award Internat. Biog. Congress, Spain, 1987, Internat. Lions Club award, UN award, medal Gen. Ground Forces USSR, 1990, World Humanitarian Leadership award by M. Susan Savage Mayor of Tulsa, 1998, Roseland Cook Bronze award David Livingstone Found., 1998; knighted in Moscow, 1993; Lonnie Royce Rex Day named in his honor by Gov. Keating of Okla., Jan. 24, 1998. Mem. Knights of Malta (Sword of Svc. 1996), Phi Beta Kappa, Moms Against Hunger (bd. mem. 2009), Global & Partnerships(bd. mem. 2008). Home: 7914 Oxfordshire Dr Spring TX 77379-4668 Home Phone: 281-251-4047. Office Fax: 281-636-3955. Personal E-mail: lonnierrex@sbcglobal.net. *In my work among the starving in Ethiopia, I walked into a tent of over 100 mothers, lying on mats, who had given birth during the last three days. It was silent! Morbid silence! That haunting silence lives with me since that moment. I asked why? I was informed the babies did not have the strength to cry. I have given my life to "cry out" for those in need that did not have the strength to "cry".*

REX, WALTER EDWIN, III, humanities educator; b. Bryn Mawr, Pa., Jan. 31, 1927; s. Walter Edwin Jr. and Barbara (Clayton) R. AB, Harvard U., 1950, AM, 1951, PhD, 1956. Instr. Brown U., Providence, 1956-57, Harvard U., Cambridge, Mass., 1957-60; asst. prof. U. Calif., Berkeley, 1960-65, assoc. prof., 1965-72, prof., 1972-92, prof. emeritus, 1992—. Chair James L. Clifford prize com. Am. Soc. 18th Century Studies, 1997—98. Author: Essays on Pierre Bayle and Religious Controversy, 1965, The Attraction of the Contrary, 1987, Diderot's Counterpoints, 1998; collaborator multi-vol. book (7 vols.) Inventory of Diderot's Encyclopédie, 1971-72, 89; mem. editl. bd. Eighteenth-Century Studies, 1979-82, 89-92; asst. editor The French Rev., 1981-86; contbr. to books in field. Grantee Humanities Rsch. Inst., 1966-67, 73-74; Pres.'s fellow U. Calif., 1990-91. Mem. MLA, Am. Soc. 18th Century Studies (Clifford lectr. ann. meeting 2000), Soc. Francaise d'étude du 18 siècle, Arts Club (Berkeley), Kosmos Club (Berkeley). Democrat. Avocation: chamber music. Home: 287 Alvarado Rd Berkeley CA 94705-1512 E-mail: Tedrex@AOL.com.

REXROAT, LARRY P, environmental scientist; children: Laura Jeannne, Rebecca Anne Rexroat Miller. MST, Tarleton State U., Stephenville, TX, 1974. Environ. scientist US Environ. Protection Agy., Dallas, 1980—88; supervisory phys. scientist US GSA, Ft. Worth, 1988—. SP5 US Army, 1967—70, Republic of Vietnam. Decorated Purple Heart, Army Commendation medal US Army.

REXROTH, LAURA JAYNE, conductor; b. Wahoo, Nebr., July 26, 1961; d. Lynn Charles Rexroth and Sharon Lee Shanahan; m. Reed F. Perkins; children: Anna Elizabeth Perkins, Thomas John Perkins. BA in Music Edn., St. Olaf Coll., Northfield, Minn., 1983; MusM in Wind Conducting, Northwestern U., Evanston, Ill., 1986; conducting student, Aspen Sch. Music, Colo., 1988; MusD in Wind Conducting, Ind. U., Bloomington, 2007. Dir. bands Mazeppa HS, Minn., 1983—85; asst. condr. Northwind Ensemble, Chgo., 1986—89; assoc. dir. bands York HS, Elmhurst, Ill., 1987—88; dir. bands Ctrl. Coll., Pella, Iowa, 1989—90, Coll. William and Mary, Williamsburg, Va., 1990—2000; condr. Internat. Conductors' Workshop, Zlin, Czech Republic, 1995; condr. wind ensembles U. Mass. Amherst, 2003—. Guest condr. tchr. Hampton U. Instrumental Conducting Symposium, Va., 1993, Radford Conducting Symposium, Radford U., Va., 1998, NH Band Dir. Assn. Conducting Symposium, Plaistow, 2008, NW Mo. State HS Summer Music Camp, Maryville, 2005. Contbr. articles to profl. jours.; dir. condr. (music) Sweeney Todd, Evanston, Ill., 1986, Working, Bensonville, Ill., 1987, A Chorus Line, Oak Park, Ill., 1987, I Do, I Do, Winnetka, Ill., 1989, Showboat, Williamsburg, Va., 1996. Recipient Thelma A. Robinson Conducting award, Conductors Guild, Nat. Music Clubs, 1994. Mem.: Conductors Guild, Am. Symphony Orch. League, Coll. Band Dirs. Nat. Assn. (va. state chair 1997—2000, mass. state chair 2005), Nat. Band Assn. (mass. state chair 2006), Pi Kappa Lambda. Office: Univ MA Amherst 151 Presidents Dr Amherst MA 01003 Office Fax: 413-545-2092. Business E-Mail: lrexroth@music.umass.edu.

REY, MARK E., federal agency administrator; b. Canton, Ohio; BS in Wildlife Mgmt., U. Mich., BS in Forestry, MS in Natural Resources Policy and Adminstrn. Staff asst. bur. land mgmt. U.S. Dept. of Interior's, 1974—75; various positions Am. Paper Inst./Nat. Forest Products Assn., 1976—84; v.p. pub. forestry programs Nat. Forest Products Assn., 1984—89; exec. dir. Am. Forest Resource Alliance, 1989—92; v.p. forest resources Am. Forest and Paper Assn., 1992—94; staff mem. U.S. Senate Com. on Energy and Natural Resources, 1995—2001; under sec. for natural resources and environ. USDA, Washington, 2001—. Office: USDA 1400 Independence Ave SW Washington DC 20250*

REY, ROBERT M., plastic surgeon; b. São Paolo, Brazil; arrived in US, 1974; m. Hayley Rey; children: Sydney, Robby. BA in Chemistry, Ariz. State U., 1983; M in Health Policy, Harvard U., 1990; MD, Tufts U. Sch. Medicine, 1990. Diplomate Nat. Bd. Med. Examiners. Resident, gen. surgery Harbor-UCLA Med. Ctr., 1995; resident, plastic surgery U. Tenn. Med. Ctr., 1997; aesthetic and breast reconstruction fellowship Harvard Med. Sch., 1998; private practice Beverly Hills, Calif. Former health policy writer Office of the US Surgeon General. Contbr. articles to med. and plastic surgery jours.; cons. (films) Seven, featured on Dr. 90210, 2004—, featured in CBS, WB, E! Channel, Elle Mag. and fgn. media, featured doctor (DVD series) Rey's Anatomy: The Sensual Body (Vol. I, II, & III). Recipient Am. Assn. Clin. Anatomist Student award for original anatomy and biomechanics rsch., Southeastern Soc. Plastic Surgeons Resident's award. Mem.: AMA, SAG. Avocations: Eagle Scout, martial arts. Office: 436 North Bedford Dr Ste 304 Beverly Hills CA 90210 Office Phone: 310-205-3107. Office Fax: 310-205-8822.

REYES, ARTURO PACHECO, civilian military employee; b. Manila, Philippines, Nov. 30, 1951; s. Anastacio Cenon Reyes and Aurora Cruz Pacheco; m. Zenaida Tarlit Abon, Jan. 2, 1975 (div. July 1998); children: Michelle, Heila Leilani. AA, U. of the City of Manila, 1971; BSc in edn., Wayland Bapt. U., 1983; MSc in adminstrn., Ctr. Mich. U., 1997; student in Medicine, Fatima Coll. Cert. nursing asst., 2002. Perm mem., sr. chief U.S. Naval Res., Washington, 1972—; U.S. civil svc. employee U.S. Civil Svc., 1993—2000; capt., pacific eagle U.S. Coast Guard, 2000; dep. clk. U.S. Dist. Ct., Honolulu, 1998; gen. vessel asst. U.S. Dept. of Commerce, 1997; clk. U.S. Census Bur., Honolulu, 2000; contracting ofcl. U.S. Dept. of Veterans Affairs, 1994. Records mgr. privacy act officer U.S. Dept. of the Army, 1994; chief of the boat U.S.N., 1991; adult correction officer Maui Cmty. Corrections Ctr., Hawaii, 1999. City coun. mem. candidate City and County of Honolulu, 1998; U.S. senate candidate U.S. Senate, Washington, 2000; gov. candidate State of Hawaii, 2002; U.S. congress candidate U.S. Congress, Washington, 2002—03. Mem.: Wayland Bapt. Assn., Sigma Iota Epsilon. Independent. Home: 94-1432 Kahuli St Waipahu HI 96797 Office: Friends of Reyes 94-1432 Kahuli St Waipahu HI 96797 Office Phone: 808-671-7450, 808-671-7450. E-mail: ap_reyes@msn.com.

REYES, CZARINA SUZANNE, mathematics educator; d. Suzanne Paulette Reynolds. BA in Math., So. Meth. U., 1998, MA, 2001; PhD in Higher Edn., U. N. Tex., 2008. Cert. tchr. Tex., 1999. Math. tchr. Creekview HS, Carrollton, Tex., 1999—2000; faculty math. Dallas County C.C. Dist.-Brookhaven Coll., Farmers Branch, Tex., 2000—, IAI, 2009, Harvard Inst. Mind, Brain & Edn., 2009. Mem. Tex. Instruments CC Math. Adv. Panel, 2007—08. Recipient LENs award Focusin Excellence, Brookhaven Coll., 2006. Mem.: AAUW, NADE, UNT, Kappa Delta Pi, Tex. CC Tchrs. Assn., Math. Assn. Am., Phi Kappa Phi, Nat. Scholars, Phi Theta Kappa (Outstanding Student Honor Soc. 2004). Office: Brookhaven Coll 3939 Valley View Ln Farmers Branch TX 75244 Office Fax: 972-860-4151. Business E-Mail: creyes@dcccd.edu.

REYES, DIANE S., bank executive; married; 4 children. MBA, U. Pitts.; grad. exec. program, Carnegie Mellon U. Mid. market product and sales exec. treasury mgmt. services JPMorgan Chase, NYC, global payables solutions bus. exec.; head cash, trade and treasury services, N.Am. region Citigroup, COO transaction services, head industrials franchise for global transaction services, mng. dir., global head cash and trade product sales & global transaction svc. Former co-chair, developing talent com. Citigroup, co-chair, women's coun. Active Girl Scouts Am., Gawad Kalinga, Philippines; treas. NY Race for the Cure. Named one of 25 Women to Watch, US Banker, 2007, 25 Most Powerful Women in Banking, 2008. Office: Citi GTS Global Energy & Chemicals Head 388 Greenwich St 25th Fl New York NY 10013 Office Phone: 212-816-6358. Office Fax: 212-816-6030. Business E-Mail: diane.s.reyes@citi.com.*

REYES, ED P., councilman; b. LA; m to Martha Reyes; children: Natalie, Eddie Jr., Adan & Angel. BA, M, UCLA. Planner, econ. development specialist, legislation dep., & chief of staff to LA City Coun. Mem. Mike Hernandez; councilman, Dist. 1 LA City Coun., 2001—, chmn. planning & land use mgmt. com., vice chmn. transp. com., vice chmn. public safety com., mem. housing and cmty. development com.; vice chmn. Pasadena Blue Line Transit Authority. Office: City Hall 200 N Spring St Rm 410 Los Angeles CA 90012 also: Dist Office Rm 202 163 S Ave 24 Los Angeles CA 90031 Office Phone: 213-473-7001, 213-485-0763. Office Fax: 213-485-8907, 213-485-8908. Business E-Mail: councilmember.reyes@lacity.org.*

REYES, J. CHRISTOPHER, food products distribution executive; BS in Fin., U. Md., 1975. Co-founder, co-chmn. Reyes Holdings, Lake Forest, Ill., 1976—. Bd. dirs. Fortune Brands Inc., Wintrust Financial Corp., 1991—, Allstate Corp., Tribune Co., 2005—. Bd. dirs. Lyric Opera of Chgo., Mus. Sci. and Industry, Northwestern Meml. Found., U. Notre Dame. Mem.: Old Elm, Onwentsia. Office: Reyes Holdings LLC 9500 W Bryn Mawr Ave Ste 700 Rosemont IL 60018 Office Fax: (847) 604-9972.

REYES, JOSE BERNABE, professional baseball player; b. Villa Gonzalez, Dominican Republic, June 11, 1983; s. Jose Manuel and Rosa Reyes. Shortstop NY Mets, 2003—. Mem. Dominican Republic nat. team World Baseball Classic, 2009. Recipient Silver Slugger award, MLB, 2006; named to Nat. League All-Star Team, 2006, 2007. Achievements include leading the National League in: at bats, 2005, 2008; triples, 2005, 2006, 2008; stolen bases, 2005, 2006, 2007; hits, 2008. Office: NY Mets Citi Field 126th St & Roosevelt Ave Flushing NY 11368*

REYES, M. JUDE, food products distribution executive; Bachelor's in economics, Wofford College, NC. Co-founder, co-chmn. Reyes Holdings LLC, Lake Forest, Ill. Bd. mem., officer Premium Distributors, Va., bd. mem., DC, Chicago Beverage Sys., Harbor Distributing, Zema Foods, Martin Brower Co.; bd. dirs. Building One Svcs. Corp., Nat. Rehabilitation Hosp. Mem.: Miller Brewing Company Distributors Adv. Panel, VA Beer Wholesalers Assn., Nat. Beer Wholesalers Assn., Young President's Orgn.

REYES, SILVESTRE, United States Representative from Texas; b. Canutillo, Tex., Nov. 10, 1944; m. Carolina Gaytan; children: Monica, Rebecca, Silvestre Jr. AA, El Paso CC, 1976; student, U. Tex., Austin, U. Tex., El Paso. Agt. US Immigration and Naturalization Svc. Border Patrol, 1969, asst. regional commr. Dallas, sect. chief, 1984-95; mem. US Congress from 16th Tex. Dist., 1997—, US House Armed Services Com.; chmn. US House Permanent Select Com. on Intelligence, 2007—. Chmn. Congressional Hispanic Caucus, 2001—02; founder Missing &

Exploited Children's Caucus. Served in US Army, 1966—68, Vietnam. Recipient Moving Forward award, El Paso Hispanic C. of C., Presdl. Outstanding Svc. award, Mex. Am. Bar Assn., Outstanding Leadership award, Hispanic Assn. Colls. and Univs., Disting. Defender award, Nat. Assn. Cmty. Health Ctr., Chmn.'s award, US Hispanic C. of C., Pres.'s award, League United Latin Am. Citizens, Border Health Hero award, Pan Am. Health Orgn., Susan. G. Hadden Pioneer award, Alliance Pub. Tech., Nat. Congl. award, Nat. Pks. Conservation Assn., L. Medel Rivers award for legis. excellence, Air Force Sgts. Assn., Century Coun. Congl. award; named Govt. Bus. Adv. of Yr., US Hispanic C. of C., Govt. Hispanic Bus. Adv. of Yr., Tex. Assn. Mex. Am. C. of C., Elected Ofcl. of Yr., Rio Grande Coun. Govts. Democrat. Office: US Congress 2433 Rayburn House Office Bldg Washington DC 20515 also: 310 N Mesa St Ste 400 El Paso TX 79901-1301 Office Phone: 202-225-4831.*

REYES, VICTOR H., lawyer; b. Mex., Apr. 28, 1964; BA Polit. Sci., Loyola Univ., 1987; JD, DePaul Univ., 1990. Bar: Ill. 1990. Asst. to Mayor City of Chgo., 1989—95, dir. Mayor's Off. Intergovernmental Affairs, 1995—2002; shareholder, governmental and adminstrv. law dept. Greenberg Traurig LLP, Chgo., 2002—. Bd. dir. Park Fed. Savings. Bd. dir. Rehabilitation Inst. Chgo.; bd. overseers Chgo.-Kent Coll. of Law. Mem.: Ill. Inst. Technology (bd. trustees). Office: Greenberg Traurig LLP Ste 2500 77 W Wacker Dr Chicago IL 60601-1732 Office Phone: 312-456-8400. Office Fax: 312-456-8435. Business E-Mail: reyesv@gtlaw.com.

REYGAERT, WANDA C., medical educator; m. James A. Reygaert, July 23. BS, Ind. U., Northwest, 1993; MS, Purdue U., Calumet, 1997; PhD, U. Ill., Chgo., 2004. Cert. in med. tech. Ind., 1993. Med. technologist & generalist NW Family Hosp., Gary, Ind., 1993—95, Starke County Hosp., Knox, Ind., 1996—98, CliniLab, Valparaiso, Ind., 1997—99; med. technologist, microbiology Alverno Labs., Hammond, Ind., 1999—2004; asst. prof. Oakland U., Rochester, Mich., 2004—. Grantee Fluorimeter grant, Turner Bio-sys., 2006. Mem.: Am. Soc. Clin. Lab. Sci. (vice chair, molecular sci. assembly 2008—09, Keys to Future award 2008), Am. Soc. Microbiology. Achievements include research in antimicrobial resistance of escherichia coli isolated from urinary tract infections. Office: Oakland Univ SHS 2200 N Squirrel Rd Rochester MI 48309

REY-GIRAUD, AGNÈS, health products executive; m. Chris Rey-Giraud; children: Charlotte, Julie. MBA, U. Chgo.; M in Engring., Ecole Nationale d'Ingenieurs de Saint-Etienne, France; M of Ops. Mgmt., ESC, Lyon, France. Various mgmt. positions in mktg., gen. mgmt., ops., sales, fin. and info. systems in US and Europe Xerox; v.p., gen. mgr. eBusiness Express Scripts, Inc., Md. Heights, Mo., 2000—02, sr. v.p. prog. devel., 2002—03, sr. v.p. product mgmt., 2003—06, sr. v.p. strategy and bus. devel., 2006—, sr. v.p. supply chain orgn., 2006—07, exec. v.p. trade rels. & develop. markets, 2007—08, pres. internat. ops., 2008—. Office: Express Scripts Inc 13900 Riverport Dr Maryland Heights MO 63043 Office Phone: 314-770-1666.

REYMAN, JONATHAN ERIC, archaeologist, anthropologist, researcher; b. Greenwich, Conn., July 31, 1943; s. Solon Aaron and Ethel Jeanette (Pearlman) R.; 1 child, Mika Ranjit Mini. BA, Ind. U., 1965; PhD, So. Ill. U., 1971. Instr. anthropology So. Ill. U., Carbondale, 1969—70, postdoctoral rsch. assoc., 1971—72; asst. prof. anthropology Ill. State U., Normal, 1972—77, assoc. prof., 1977—82, prof., 1982—91; rsch. assoc. in anthropology Ill. State Mus., Springfield, 1993—2004, curator Anthropology Sect., 2004—. Rsch. collaborator Nat. Park Svc., Mesa Verde Nat. Park, Colo., 1975-76; founder, operator Feather Distbn. Project, Springfield, 1982—; vis. prof. anthropology U. Ill., Urbna, 1994, 95; mem. peer rev. panel tchg. with tech. NEH, Washington, 1996; editor Teocentli, 2009-. Editor: Rediscovering Our Past: Essays on the History of American Archaeology, 1992, The Gran Chichimeca: Essays on the Archaeology and Ethnohistory of Northern Mesoamerica, 1995; co-editor: Aboriginal Ritual and Economy in the Eastern Woodland: Essays in Memory of Howard Dalton Winters, 2004; contbr. over 150 articles and revs. to profl. jours., also chpts. to books. NDEA Title IV grad. fellow So. Ill. U., 1966-69; sr. rsch. grantee NSF, 1973-78, 87-88, rsch. grantee Wenner-Gren Found. for Anthrop. Rsch., 1980, EPA, 2004. Fellow Am. Anthrop. Assn., Soc. Profl. Archeologists (tchg. cert. panel 1989-93, chmn. com. on pub. land use, 1978-79), Soc. for Applied Anthropology (co-chmn. Am. Indian issues com. 1997-2000), Coun. for Mus. Anthropology, Soc. for Am. Archaeology (history of archaeology com. 1987-89), Sigma Xi, Phi Kappa Phi. Avocations: travel, cooking, reading, music. Home: 1220 Larchmont Dr Springfield IL 62704-2110 Office: Ill State Mus Rsch and Collections Ctr 1011 E Ash St Springfield IL 62703-3500 Home Phone: 217-546-5882; Office Phone: 217-785-0069. E-mail: reyman@museum.state.il.us.

REYNA, CLAUDIO, retired professional soccer player; b. Springfield, NJ, July 20, 1973; m. Danielle Egan, 1997; 2 children. Student, U. Va. Midfielder Bayer Leverkusen, Germany, 1994—97, VfL Wolfsburg, Germany, 1997—99, Glasgow Rangers, Scotland, 1999—2000, Sunderland FC, England, 2001—03, Manchester City FC, England, 2003—07, New York Red Bulls, 2007—08. 112 caps, 8 goals U.S. Nat. Soccer Team, 1994—2006, capt., 1999—2006; mem. U.S. World Cup Team, 1994, 98, 2002, 06, U.S. Olympic Team, 1992—96. Recipient Player of Yr. award, Mo. Athletic Club, 1992, 1993; named Nat. H.S. Player of the Yr., Parade Mag., 1989—90, N.J. H.S. Player of the Yr., 1990, Gatorade H.S. Player of the Yr., 1990, Freshman of Yr., Soccer Am., 1991, 3-time first-team All-Am., Nat. Soccer Coaches Assn. Am., 1991—93; named to World Cup All-Tournament Team, 1992. Office: US Soccer Fedn 1801 S Prairie Ave Chicago IL 60616-1319

REYNA, DIANA, city councilwoman; b. Bklyn., 1973; d. Bienvenido and Maria Reyna; married. BA, Pace Univ., 1966. City councilwoman Dist. 34 NY City Coun., 2001—. Chmn. Rules, Privileges & Elections com. NY City Coun. Democrat. Mailing: Dist Off 444 S Fifth St Brooklyn NY 11211 Office Phone: 718-963-3141, 212-788-7095. Office Fax: 718-963-4527. Business E-Mail: reyna@council.nyc.ny.us.*

REYNA, JIMMIE VALDENEBRO, lawyer; b. Tucumcari, N.Mex., Nov. 11, 1952; s. Julian C. and Consuelo (Valdenebro) R.; m. Dolores Ramirez, Mar. 4, 1972. BA, U. Rochester, 1975; JD, U. N.Mex., 1978. Bar: N.Mex. 1979, U.S. Dist. Ct. N.Mex., U.S. Ct. Appeals (10th cir.) 1983, U.S. Ct. Internat. Trade 1987, U.S. Ct. Appeals (fed. cir.) 1989, U.S. Ct. Appeals (D.C. cir.) 1994. Assoc. Shaffer, Butt, Thornton & Baher, 1979-81; sole practice, 1981-86; assoc. Stewart and Stewart, Washington, 1986; ptnr. internat. trade and customs practice group Williams Mullen, Washington, bd. dirs., 2006—. Contbr. articles to profl. jours. Bd. dirs. Therapeutic Recreational Activities, Albuquerque, 1984-86, Hispanic Culture Found., Albuquerque, 1983-86, Community Svcs. for Autistic Children and Adults, Rockville, Md., 1988—; bd. dirs. Albuquerque Hispano C. of C., 1982-85, v.p., 1983, pres., 1984. Recipient Spirit of Excellence award Albuquerque Hispano C. of C., 1985, Disting. Citizen award USAF, 1985. Mem. ABA (internat. law sect., vice chair Mex. law com., chmn. subcom. on U.S.-Mex. fgn. trade 1989-90, 1994-2000, mem. ABA sect. dispute resolution, internat. com., co-chair subcom. MERCOSUR 1999-2001, co-chair subcom. on WTO, 2001-), Nat. Hispanic Bar Assn. (nat. v.p. regions 2004-05. pres.-elect 2005-06, pres. 2006-07), Soc. for Hispanic Profl. Engrs. (life). Office: Williams Mullen 1666 K St NW Ste 1200 Washington DC 20006

REYNA, MAGDALENA BESSY, writer; b. San Luis, Santiago, Cuba, July 22, 1942; d. Ruben and Maria de Reyna. BA magna cum laude, Mount Holyoke Coll., 1970; MA, U. Conn., 1972, JD, 1982. Asst. reporter jud. decisions Office of the Reporter of Jud. Decisions, State Conn., Hartford, 1986—2002; freelance writer, 2002—. Former faculty mem. child devel. and family rels., U. Conn., Storrs; former staff mem. New Haven Legal Assistance; freelance translator Spanish-English langs.; invited poet Second Sunken Garden Poetry Festival, Farmington, Conn., 1992. Author: Terrarium, 1975, She Remembers, 1997, (poems) Battlefield of Your Body, 2005, poetry and short stories, —; editor: Taller Literario, 1986—87, El Extra Cultural arts' page El Extra News, 1996—2000, Latin Arte News, 2000—; opinion columnist: Hartford Courant. Founder, facilitator The Poetry Exch.; organizer, prodr. Sisters of the Americas, 1986; adv. bd. mem., tv presenter Adelante; former adv. bd. mem. The Pump House Gallery, City of Hartford Pk. and Recreation Dept., 1994-96; bd. mem. Hartford Stage SueÑo Adv. Com., Hartford, 1996, Catalyst Endowment of the Hartford Found. for Pub. Giving, 1998-2003, Conn. Ctr. for the Book, Hartford Pub. Libr., 1998-2003; mentor for poetry winning students Sunken Garden Poetry Festival H.S. Competition, 1995—; mentor for student poets Young Writers' Inst., Hartford, 1995—; master-tchg. artist Conn. Commn. on the Arts, Hartford, 1997—. Recipient 1st prize Joseph E. Brodine Poetry Competition, Conn. Poetry Soc., 1996; named Fgn. fellow, Mt. Holyoke Coll., South Hadley, Mass. and Inst. Internat. Edn., N.Y., 1968—70, UNESCO fellow, U. Conn., 1977, Reginald Smith Cmty.-Lawyer fellow, 1983, Artist fellow in fiction, Conn. Commn. on the Arts, 1990, Latina Citizen of Yr., State of Conn. Commn. Latino and Puerto Rican Affairs, 2001; grantee, Greater Hartford Arts Coun., 1996. Democrat. Avocations: reading, movies, concerts. Office: Latin Arte News PO Box 9341 Bolton CT 06043-9341

REYNA, VALERIE FRANCES, psychologist, educator, researcher; b. Miami Beach, Fla., Apr. 20, 1955; d. Benjamin Villa and Patricia Ruth (Wilson) R.; m. Charles J. Brainerd, Oct. 5, 1985; 1 child, Bertrand Reyna-Brainerd. BA, Clark U., 1976; PhD, Rockefeller U., 1981. Asst. prof. U. Tex., Dallas, 1981-87; adj. prof. U. Ariz., Tucson, 1987-88, asst. prof. dept. ednl. psychology, 1988-92, assoc. prof., 1992-1996, assoc. prof. depts. surgery and medicine, 1996—2003, Cornell U., Ithaca, NY, 2005—. Vis. scientist Stanford (Calif.) U., 1982-83. Guest editor: Developmental Review, 1985, Development of Long-Term Retention, 1992; contbr. articles to profl. jours.; author books. Fellow AAAS, APA, Am. Psychol. Soc.; mem. Soc. for Judgment and Decision Making, Soc. Advancement Chicanos and Native Ams. in Sci., Hispanic Profls. Action Com. Edn., Psychonomic Soc., Soc. for Rsch. in Child Devel., Sigma Xi. Democrat. Home: 3 Whispering Pines Dr Ithaca NY 14850-9789 Office: Cornell U B44 Dept Human Devel Psychology Ithaca NY 14853

REYNARD, MURIEL JOYCE, lawyer; b. Miami Beach, Fla., May 20, 1945; d. Hyman and Faye (Feinstein) Friedkin; m. Brian Patrick Delaney, Nov. 27, 1983; children: Kelly, Charlotte. BA, SUNY, Stony Brook, 1967, MS, 1973; JD cum laude, Yeshiva U., 1983. Bar: N.Y. 1984, U.S. Dist. Ct. (so. and ea. dists.) N.Y. 1984. Health planner Nassau-Suffolk RMP/CHP, Centereach, NY, 1972-74; adminstr. NYC Health and Hosps. Corp., 1974-75; health planner AFSCME Dist. Coun. 37, NYC, 1975-76; adminstr. Inst. Emergency Medicine Albert Einstein Coll. Medicine, NYC, 1977-80; asst. atty. US Atty.'s Office (so. dist.) N.Y., NYC, summer 1982; assoc. Skadden, Arps, Slate, Meagher & Flom, NYC, 1983-85, Paskus, Gordon & Mandel, NYC, 1985-86; v.p., sr. assoc. counsel The Chase Manhattan Bank, N.A., NYC, 1986-96; v.p. assoc. gen. counsel Citicorp Credit Svcs. Inc., NYC, 1997—2002, sr. v.p., assoc. gen. counsel, 2002, sr. v.p., dep. gen. counsel, 2006. Notes and comments editor Cardozo Law Rev.; contbr. numerous articles to law jours. Mem. ABA, N.Y.C. Bar Assn., N.Y. State Bar Assn. Office: Citicorp Credit Services Inc One Court Square New York NY 11120

REYNAUD-ROEPKE, SUZANNE, psychologist; b. Kansas City, Kans., Mar. 26, 1954; d. Raymond Lucien and Donna Jean Reynaud; m. Carl Frank Roepke, Jr., Dec. 22, 1985; children: Peter Hague Roepke II, Lucienne Marie Roepke. BA in Psychology, U. Calif., Santa Barbara, 1976; MEd in Spl. Edn., U. Nev., Reno, 1985; MSEd in Counseling Psychology, U. So. Calif., LA, 1989, PhD in Psychology, 1995. Cert. clear pupil pers. credential sch. psychology Calif., clear pupil pers. credential Calif., clear specialist credential in learning handicapped Calif., clear multiple subjects credential Calif., sch. psychologist endorsement Nev. Student intern Linda Mar Elem. Sch., Pacifica, Calif., 1978—79; pvt. practice ednl. therapy Gardnerville, Nev., 1984—85; grad. intern Douglas County Sch. Dist., 1984—85; grad. asst. ind. ednl. programs educationally handicapped U. Nev., Reno, 1984—85; psychol. intern Julia Ann Singer Children's Psychiatric Ctr., LA, 1986—87; outreach L.A. Jewish Orthodox Cmty., 1986—88, Focus on Youth L.A. Unified Sch. Dist., 1988—89; sch. counselor Multnomah St. Magnet Sch., East Los Angeles, 1988—89; psychol. intern Hollywood Counseling Ctr., 1988—89; predoctoral intern Alvarado Parkway Inst., La Mesa, 1991—92; resource specialist North Ter. Elem. Sch., Oceanside, 1994, The Rhoades Sch., Encinitas, 1995; pvt. practice psychology The Dennison Clinic, Carlsbad, 1995—99; NIMH post doctoral rsch. fellow Geriatric Psychiatry Clin. Rsch. Ctr. U. Calif. San Diego Sch. Medicine, 1996—99; sch. psychologist Inyo and Mono Counties Sch. Dists., Calif., 2000—. Doctoral com. mem. LaVerne Coll., Calif.; field work supr. Calif. State U., San Bernardino; spl. edn. cons. region 10 Calif. Preschool Instrnl. Network Spl. Edn. Divsn. Calif. Dept. Edn., 2000—; contract psychologist Cal-Works Dept. Health and Human Svcs., 2000—; presenter to profl. meetings. Co-author (with J. McQuaid, R. Scinta and P. Cutler): Cognitive Behavioral Therapy for Thought Disorder, 1998; co-author: (with J. McQuaid, E. Granholm and F.S. McClure) Group Therapy Manual for Cognitive Behavioral Skills Training (CBSST) for Older Persons with Schizophrenia, 1999; contbr. scientific papers, articles to profl. jours. Task force mem. southwest dist Luth. Ch. (Mo. Synod), Irvine; bd. mem. Bishop (Calif.) Swim Team, 2002—03. Grantee, Am. Assn. Geriatric Psychiatry; fellow, NIMH, 1996—99; Educare scholarship award, U. So. Calif. Sch. Edn., 1985. Mem.: Nat. Assn. Sch. Psychologists, USA Swimming (nat. cert. swim official 1994—), Am. Paint Horse Assn., Phi Delta Kappa (scholarship award 1988). Republican. Lutheran. Avocations: trail riding, photography, cross country skiing, hiking, yoga. Home: 398 Mt Tom Rd Bishop CA 93514-2122 Office: Bernasconi Edn Ctr Big Pine CA 93513 Office Phone: 760-938-2633.

REYNIK, ROBERT JOHN, retired materials scientist, science educator; b. Bayonne, NJ, Dec. 25, 1932; m. Georgiana M. Walker, Apr. 12, 1959; children: Michael, Christopher, Jonathan, Katherine, Steven, Kevin. BS in Math. and Physics, U. Detroit, 1956; MSEE, U. Cin., 1960, PhD in Phys. Chemistry, 1963. Rsch. assoc. Sch. Metall. Engring. U. Pa., Phila., 1963-64, asst. prof., 1964-67; assoc. prof. Drexel U., Phila., 1967-70; assoc. dir. engring. materials program NSF, Washington, 1970-71, dir. engring. materials program, 1971-74, dir. metallurgy program, 1974-82, head metallurgy, polymers, ceramics and electronic materials, 1983-90, head office spl. programs in materials, 1990-94, sr. staff scientist divsn. materials rsch. Arlington, Va., 1994-96; exec. sec. and cognizant program dir. US-USSR Internat. Agreement in Sci. and Tech., Washington, 1974-79; NSF liaison rep. Nat. Materials Adv. Bd., Washington, 1985-94; math. and phys. sci. directorate coord. Integration of Rsch. and Edn., 1996-97; sr. scientist Office of Sci. and Tech. Infrastructure, 1997-98, sr. staff scientist divsn. materials rsch., 1998-99, grantsmanship cons., 1999—2002. Dir. electrometallurgy and materials, corrosion, program US-USSR internat. agreement sci. and tech., 1974-80; mem. First U.S. Metall. Del. People's Republic China, 1978; vis. prof. materials sci. and engring. U. Pa., 1982-83; tech. coord. Sci. & Tech. Ctrs. in Materials Sci. & Engring., 1990-94; co-chair Fed. Coord. Coun. for Sci., Engring. and Tech. joint com. edn. and tng. Office of Sci. and Tech. Policy, 1992-93; co-chair task group edn. and tng. Aeronautics Materials and mfg. Techs. Working Groups Nat. Sci. and Tech. coun., Office of Vice Pres. of U.S., 1994; tech. mgr. rsch. grants mfg. devel. and mfg. Tech. Reinvestment Project, Fed. Govt., 1994-96. Vol. income tax assistance and tax counseling for the elderly programs IRS, 2001—. Fellow Am. Soc. Materials Internat. (mem.-at-large materials sci. coun. 1990-96, mem.-at-large materials sci. tech. sector coun. 1993-96, fed. affairs com. 1996-99, gold medal selection com.); mem. AAAS, AIME (chmn. govt. pub. affairs com. 1994-96), Am. Chem. Soc., Am. Assn. Engring. Socs. (honors and awards com.), The Metals, Minerals and Materials Soc. (mem. and chmn. tech. coms., mem. bd. dirs., 1980-81, Leadership award 2004), Materials Rsch. Soc., Sigma Xi (past chpt. pres., exec. counselor), Tau Beta Pi. Personal E-mail: rreynik@verizon.net.

REYNOLDS, ANDREW, psychologist; b. Elgin, Ill., Feb. 14, 1964; s. Dorothy Reynolds. MS, Cal State East Bay, Calif., 1999. Sch. psychologist Fresno Unified Sch. Dist., Calif., 2001—05, Balsz Elem. Sch. Dist., Phoenix, 2005—. Office: 4505 E Palm Ln Phoenix AZ 85008

REYNOLDS, BURT, actor, film director; b. Waycross, Ga., Feb. 11, 1936; s. Burt R.; m. Judy Carne (div. 1965); m. Loni Anderson, Apr. 29, 1988 (div. 1994). Ed., Fla. State U., Palm Beach Jr. Coll. Owner ranch, Jupiter, Fla. Actor numerous stage prodns. including The Rainmaker; movie appearances include: Angel Baby, 1961, Armored Command, 1961, Operation CIA, 1965, Navajo Joe, 1967, Impasse, 1969, 100 Rifles, 1969, Sam Whiskey, 1969, Skullduggery, 1970, Shark, 1970, Deliverance, 1972, Fuzz, 1972, Everything You've Always Wanted to Know about Sex But Were Afraid to Ask, 1972, Shamus, 1973, The Man Who Loved Cat Dancing, 1973, White Lightning, 1973, The Longest Yard, 1974, At Long Last Love, 1975, W.W. and the Dixie Dance Kings, 1975, Hustle, 1975, Lucky Lady, 1975, Silent Movie, 1976, Nickelodeon, 1976, Smokey and the Bandit, 1977, Semi-Tough, 1977, Hooper, 1978, Starting Over, 1979, Rough Cut, 1980, Smokey and the Bandit II, 1980, Cannonball Run, 1981, Paternity, 1981, The Best Little Whorehouse in Texas, 1982, Best Friends, 1982, Stroker Ace, 1983, The Man Who Loved Women, 1983, City Heat, 1984, Cannonball Run II, 1984, Stick, 1985, Uphill All The Way, 1986, Rent A Cop, 1987, Heat, 1987, Malone, 1987, Switching Channels, 1988, Physical Evidence, 1989, Breaking In, 1989, Modern Love, 1990, Cop and a Half, 1993, also voice in All Dogs Go To Heaven, 1989, The Maddening, 1996, Striptease, 1996, Ravin, 1996, Mad Dog Time, 1996, Frankenstein and Me, 1996, Citizen Ruth, 1996, Meet Wally Sparks, 1997, Crazy Six, 1997, Boogie Nights, 1997, Raven, 1997, Waterproof, 1998, Mystery Alaska, 1998, The Hunter's Moon, 1998, Without a Paddle, 2004, The Librarians, 2004, Grilled, 2005, Forget About It, 2005, The Longest Yard, 2005, The Dukes of Hazzard, 2005, Broken Bridges, 2006, Deal, 2008, In the Name of the King: A Dungeon Siege Tale, 2008, (voice) Delgo, 2008; dir., actor: Gator, 1976, The End, 1978, Sharkey's Machine, 1981; TV appearances include: M Squad, 1959, Alfred Hitchcock Presents, 1960, Zane Grey Theater, 1961, Route 66, 1962, Perry Mason, 1962, The Twilight Zone, 1963, Branded, 1965, Flipper, 1965, Twelve O'Clock High, 1965, The Carol Burnett Show, 1967, The FBI, 1968, Love American Style, 1970, The Golden Girls, 1986, Dolly, 1987, Beverly Hills, 90210, 1993, The Larry Sanders Show, 1993, Hope & Gloria, 1995, Cybill, 1995, (voice) King of the Hill, 1997, The X Files, 2002, Hollywood Squares, 2002, Ed, 2003, Dinner for Five, 2004, The King of Queens, 2005; regular appearances on Gunsmoke, 1962-65; star series Hawk, 1966, Dan August, 1970-71, B.L. Stryker, 1989, ABC Saturday Mystery Movie, 1988, Evening Shade, 1990-94, (TV movie) The Cherokee Kid, 1996. Recipient Emmy award as Outstanding Lead Actor in a Comedy Series ("Evening Shade") Nat. Acad. TV Arts and Scis., 1991. Mem. Dirs. Guild Am. Office: Jeffrey Lane & Associates 155 N Crescent Dr Apt 416 Beverly Hills CA 90210-5430

REYNOLDS, C. LEWIS, JR., materials scientist, educator; b. Roanoke, Va., Dec. 16, 1948; s. Claude Lewis and Lois Anne Reynolds; m. Judith Ann Grenko, May 11, 2002; children: Karen Marie, Brian Lewis, Kristin Marie. BS, Va. Mil. Inst., Lexington, Va., 1970; MS, PhD, U. Va., Charlottesville, Va., 1974. Sr. scientist U. Va., Charlottesville, 1974—75; rsch. assoc. physics U. Ill., Urbana, Ill., 1975—77; sr. project engr. Union Carbide Corp., Indpls., 1977—80; disting. mem. tech. staff AT&T Bell Labs., Reading, Pa., 1980—92, Agere/Lucent Bell Labs., Breinigsville, Pa., 1992—2002; rsch. prof. NC State U., Raleigh, 2003—, tchg. asst. prof., 2004—. Contbr. more than 120 articles to profl. jours. Mem.: IEEE, Am. Assn. Physics Tchrs., Materials Rsch. Soc., Am. Phys. Soc., Sigma Xi. Independent. Methodist. Achievements include 8 patents in field. Avocations: reading, running, hiking. Office: NC State Univ Dept Materials Sci Engring 911 Partners Way Raleigh NC 27695-7907 Office Fax: 919-515-7724. Business E-Mail: lew_reynolds@ncsu.edu.

REYNOLDS, CELIA ROBINSON, academic librarian, educator; d. Guy Ulysses and Vonna Faye Mills Robinson; m. Samuel John Reynolds, May 11, 1985. BA, Hendrix Coll., Conway, Ark., 1976; MLS, La. State U., Baton Rouge, 1979; EdS in Librarianship, U. Ala., Tuscaloosa, 1988. Head reference libr., online search coord. Henderson State U. - Huie Libr., Arkadelphia, Ark., 1980—88; prof., libr., reference svcs. coord., asst. to v.p. academic affairs U. North Ala., Florence, 1988—. Office: Univ of N Alabama One Harrison Plz Florence AL 35632-0001

REYNOLDS, CHRISTINA, federal official; BA in Journalism, U. NC, Chapel Hill. Comm. dir. for Tom Daschle's 2004 Campaign; rsch. dir. John Edwards' Presdl. Campaign, 2004, rsch. dir., sr. comm. adviser for, 2008; rsch. dir. Dem. Congl. Campaign Com.; dir. rapid response Obama-Biden Campaign, 2008; dir. media affairs The White House, Washington, 2009—. Office: The White House 1600 Pennsylvania Ave NW Washington DC 20500*

REYNOLDS, COLLINS JAMES, III, management consultant; b. NYC, Feb. 28, 1937; s. Collins James and Alta Roberta (Carr) R.; m. Harriet Virginia Blackburn (div. 1965); children: Collins James IV, Quentin Scott; m. Carol Ann Miller, June 24, 1967; children: Justin Blake, Carson Jonathan. Student govt. and econs., Harvard U., George Washington U. Data processing supr. missile and space vehicle div. Gen. Electric, Phila., 1961; contract adminstr. Allison div. Gen. Motors, Indpls., 1962-65; country dir. Peace Corps, Mauritania, 1966-67, Sierra Leone, 1971—74; dir. div. ops. Gen. Learning Corp., Time Inc.,

Washington, 1968-71, trustee, sec., treas., exec. dir. Denver, 1974-79; Carter Presdl. appointee, assoc. dir. Internat. Devel. Coop. Agy., AID, 1980; dir. mktg. Am. TV & Communications Corp., Time Inc., Denver, 1980-81; founder, chmn. bd., pres. Omnicom, Inc., Denver, 1981-87; Bush Presdl. appointee, sr. exec. svc., assoc. dir. mgmt. Peace Corps, 1989-92; dir. comms. divsn. Am. Water Works Assn., 1994-97; trustee The Groundwater Found., 1996—2002; v.p., dir. ops. Internat. Resources Group, Wash., DC, 1999—2002; dir. Mesilla Valley Habitat for Humanity, United Way SW N.Mex. Cons., UN Secretariat, Econ. Devel. Adminstrn., OECD, USAID, USDA, U.S. Dept. Labor, U.S. Dept. Edn., U.S. Dept. Commerce, U.S. Dept. Navy; project dir. Model Cities Edn. Plan, HUD, Gen. Learning, Balt., Dept. Labor/HEW Remedial Edn. and Job Placement Program, Transcentury Corp., Washington; program mgr. Ft. Lincoln New Town Sch. System, Washington; supervising dir. VISTA, Boston, N.Y.C., Atlanta; dir. adminstrn. Job Corps, Kansas City. Founder, editor, pub.: The Bridge; patentee in field. Served as aviator USMCR, 1956-60. Home: 2048 Pine Needle Way Las Cruces NM 88012-6032 Personal E-mail: cojare@gmail.com.

REYNOLDS, CRAIG W., research scientist; PhD. Dir. office sci. ops. Nat. Cancer Inst.; project officer SAIC Frederick, Inc., Data Mgmt. Svcs. Inc., Wilson Info. Svcs. Corp.; assoc. dir. Nat. Cancer Inst. at Frederick, Frederick, Md., 2002—. With NCI-Frederick's ednl. outreach program. Achievements include research in the development and production of vaccines for treatment of patients with leukemia and myeloma. Office: NCI-Frederick Bldg 427 Rm 1 PO Box B Frederick MD 21702-1201 Business E-Mail: reynoldsc@ncifcrf.gov.

REYNOLDS, DAVID BURKMAN, biomedical engineer, department assistant chair; b. Arlington, Va., July 5, 1949; s. Robert Theodore and Rosemary Burkman Reynolds; m. Joyce Ann Barkalow, May 6, 1978; children: Mark David, Allison Jean Rice, Robin Karen. BSME, 1971, MSME, 1972; PhD, U. Va., Charlottesville, 1978. Rsch. fellow Mayo Clinic & Found., Rochester, 1978—80; vis. asst. prof. Wright State U., Dayton, Ohio, 1980—82, asst. prof., 1982—88, assoc. prof., 1988—, asst. chair & biomed. engring. program dir., 2000—. Mem.: Am. Soc. Engr. Edn. (BME Divsn. chair 1992—93), Biomed. Engring. Soc., Edn. & Pub. Affairs Com. (chair 1984—88). Avocations: golf, coin collecting/numismatics. Home: 2271 Cobblestone Ct Dayton OH 45431 Office Phone: 937-775-5068. Office Fax: 937-775-7364; Home Fax: 937-775-7364.

REYNOLDS, DON WILLIAM, geologist; b. Centerburg, Ohio, Apr. 6, 1926; s. Loren William and Charlotte Lones (Hunt) R.; m. Betty Jeannette Spears, Sept. 4, 1953; children: Don William Jr., Richard Allen (dec.), Brenda Gay. BS, Ohio State U., 1952. Registered profl. geologist Calif., 1994, environ. assessor Calif. Mgr. Geochem. Engring., Inc., Midland, Tex., 1950-52; geologist Union Oil Co. Calif., Midland, 1953-66, dist. exploration geologist Anchorage, 1966-68, area geologist Bakersfield, Calif., 1968-76, dis. devel. geologist Ventura, Calif., 1976-86, dis. devel. geologist mid-continent divsn. Oklahoma City, 1986-89, regional mgr. mid-continent devel., 1989-90, advisor geology, 1990-92. Gen. ptnr. Reynolds Farm, 1979—; sec. ASF Inc., IFP Inc., Austin, 1989—; chmn. bd. Future Petroleum Corp., 1992-98, bd. dirs., 2001-2004; ptnr. Alianza Solutions, LP, 2004-09, mng. dir. and chief geologist Olvidado Energy Group, 2009-. Pres. Park Stockdale Civic Assn., Bakersfield, 1970, Clearpoint Homeowner's Assn., Ventura, 1980-86; chmn. Kern County Freeway Com. Bakersfield, 1970-73. Served with USAF, 1944-45. Mem. Am. Assn. Petroleum Geologists, West Tex. Geol. Soc. (sec. 1965-66), Kans.-Okla. Oil and Gas Assn. (nomenclature com. 1987-92), San Joaquin Geol. Soc. (treas. 1974-75), Am. Assn. Petroleum Geologists (sec. Pacific sect. 1975-76). Republican. Methodist. Home: 5009 Reynolds Rd Centerburg OH 43011

REYNOLDS, DORIS ELIZABETH, management consultant, poet; b. Nashville, Apr. 16, 1944; children: James Jr., Tony Antonio. BA, Coby Coll., 1990; cert., U. Tenn., Nashville, 2000. Cert. med. terminologist St. Thomas Hosp. Edn. Mgmt. supr. St. Thomas Hosp., Nashville, 1979—90, patient transfer liaison, 1985—90, supr., 1972, 1976. Spkr. in field of people mgmt. Author (under the pseudonym Dynasty): (poetry) Internat. Soc. Poets, 2003 (Cup, 2003). Recipient Cert. of Achievement, Tenn. Hosp. Assn., 1978, George W. Gore honor for outstanding scholarship and acad. excellence, Tenn. State U., 2002, Outstanding Achievement award in poetry, Internat. Soc. Poets, 2006. Mem.: Internat. Soc. Poets. Home: 2006 15th Ave N Nashville TN 37208

REYNOLDS, DOUGLAS D., mechanical engineer, educator; b. Pekin, Ill., July 12, 1943; s. Deane and Vera Reynolds; m. Linda K. Wood, Oct. 14, 1967; children: John T., Jeff T. BSME, Mich. State U., East Lansing, 1967; MSME, Purdue U., West Lafayette, Ind., 1969, PhD, 1972. Asst. prof. archtl. engr. U. Tex., Austin, 1971—77; assoc. prof. mech. engr. U. Pitts., 1977—80; sr. cons. Pelton-Blum, Dallas, 1980—82; v.p. environ. acoustics Joiner-Pelton-Rose, Dallas, 1982—83; prof. mech. engr. U. Nev., Las Vegas, 1983—, dir. ctr. mech. & environ. sys. tech, 1992—. Chair, working group S2.39, human exposure shock and vibration Am. Nat. Stds. Inst., NYC, 1996—, chair, tech. adv. group, 1998—, head USA del. ISO TC 108/SC 4, human exposure shock & vibration, 1998—. Author: (textbook) Engineering Principles of Acoustics - Noise and Vibration Control, Engineering Principles of Mechanical Vibration, Engineering Principles of Acoustics, (book) Redeemed by God - Our Relationship with God through His Son, Jesus Christ. Chair Southern Nev. Walk Emmaus, Las Vegas, 2000—02, bd. dirs., 2000—02. Mem.: ASME, Am. Soc. Heating, Refrigerating, and Air-Conditioning Engrs., Sigma Xi, Pi Tau Sigma, Tau Beta Pi. Methodist. Avocation: travel. Home: 3939 Briarcrest Ct Las Vegas NV 89120-1305 Office: Univ Nev Las Vegas 4505 Md Pky Las Vegas NV 89154 Office Fax: 702-895-4677. Business E-Mail: reynolds@nscee.edu.

REYNOLDS, DOUGLAS R., history professor; b. Detroit, Oct. 2, 1944; s. Ira Hubert and Harriet Robertson Reynolds; m. Aizhen Sun, June 15, 2006; children: Sara Elizabeth Davis, Emily Kathryn; m. Carol Tyson (div. May 2006). PhD, Columbia U., NYC, 1976. Prof., dept. history Ga. State U., Atlanta, 1980—, dir., Asian Studies Ctr., 2006—. Author: (book) East Meets East: Chinese Discover the Modern World - in Meiji Japan, 1877-95, China, 1898-1912: The Xinzheng Revolution and Japan, 1998, 2nd edit., 2006; translator (editor): China, 1895-1912: State-Sponsored Reforms and China's Late-Qing Revolution; contbr. articles to numerous profl. jours. (Modern Sino-Japanese Rels. prize, 1988, 1991). Co-pres. US China Peoples Friendship Assn., Atlanta chpt., 2006. Recipient Meml. prize, To-A Dobun Shoin Meml. Prize Com., Tokyo, 1996; Rsch. fellowship, Social Sci. Rsch. Coun., 1986—87, Luce Found., History Christianity China project, 1987—88. Mem.: Assn. Asian Studies. Achievements include pioneering scholarship on modern Japan-China cultural interactions, 1850-1912. Home: 613 Clairmont Cir Decatur GA 30033-5316 Office: Ga State Univ Dept History 34 Peachtree St Ste 2050 Atlanta GA 30302-4117

REYNOLDS, ERIC WILLIAM, medical educator; b. Frankfort, Ky., Jan. 20, 1971; s. Gary and JoAnn Reynolds; m. Melanie Avent Reynolds, June 26, 1993; 3 children. BS, U. Louisville, 1993, MD, 1997. Resident N.E. Ohio U. Coll. Medicine Children's Hosp., Youngstown, Ohio, 1997—2000; mem. faculty U. Ky., Lexington, 2003. Chmn. rsch. grant com. Assn. Postgrad. Physician Asst. Programs, 2006—; mem. k-30 scholars programs U. Ky., 2003—05. Contbr. articles to profl. jours. Fellow, U. Md., Balt., 2000—02, U. Ky., 2002—03. Fellow: Am. Acad. Pediatrics; mem.: Ky. Pediatric Soc., So. Soc. Pediatric Rsch. (coun. mem. 2007—), Southeast Assn. Neonatologists, Ky. Perinatal Assn. (bd. dirs. 2007—), Physician Asst. Edn. Assn. Office: U Ky 800 Rose St MS 477 Lexington KY 40536 Business E-Mail: ereyn2@uky.edu.

REYNOLDS, ERNEST WEST, retired internist, educator; b. Bristow, Okla., May 11, 1920; s. Ernest West and Florence (Brown) R. BS, U. Okla., 1942, MD, 1946, MS, 1952. Diplomate: Am. Bd. Internal Medicine. Intern Boston City Hosp., 1946-47; resident Grady Meml. Hosp., Atlanta, 1949-50; practice medicine Tulsa, Okla., 1953-54; prof. medicine U Mich., 1965-72; prof. medicine, dir. cardiology U. Wis., 1972-90, prof. emeritus, 1991—. Dir. Kellogg Found. Comprehensive Coronary Care Project, 1967-72; chmn. NIH Cardiovascular Study Sect. A, 1972-73 Mem. editorial bd.: Am. Heart Jour; Contbr. articles to profl. jours. Served to capt. AUS, 1947-49. Mem. Am. Heart Assn. (fellow coun. clin. cardiology), Ctrl. Soc. Clin. Rsch. Home: 17 Red Maple Trl Madison WI 53717-1515 Personal E-mail: ernest_reynolds@yahoo.com. *In the academic environment, research oriented toward the solution of human problems is more productive in career advancement than the pursuit of applications of new technology. In the private sector applied research which solves real problems rather than copies or improves existing technology is met with surprising sales success and few failures.*

REYNOLDS, FELICIA, technologist educator, consultant; d. Gordon Gurley. AAS, Manhattan CC, NY, 1979; BS in Computer Sci., Barry U., Miami, Fla., 1984, MS in Computer Sci. with honors, 1992. Tech. cons. Ecuadorian Line, Miami, 1999—, Pacific Internat. Svcs., 1999—, Pan Am. Trading, 1999—; prof. Broward CC, Ft. Lauderdale, Fla., 2002—. Tech. cons. Texaco Inc., Westerchester, NY, 1997—99. Mem.: IEEE. Democrat. Roman Catholic. Avocations: tennis, travel. Home: 200 SW 85th Ave 210 Pembroke Pines FL 33025 Office: Broward CC 7200 Pines Boulevard Pembroke Pines FL 33025 Personal E-mail: feliciarey@juno.com. Business E-Mail: freynold@mdc.edu.

REYNOLDS, HAROLD CRAIG, sportscaster, retired professional baseball player; b. Eugene, Oreg., Nov. 26, 1960; Student, San Diego State U., Canada Coll., Redwood City, Calif., Calif. State U., Long Beach. Infielder Seattle Mariners, 1983-92, Balt. Orioles, 1993, Calif. Angels, 1994; broadcaster, analyst ESPN, Bristol, Conn., 1996—2006; CEO Harold Reynolds Enterprises; broadcaster MLB.com, 2007—; studio analyst SportsNet NY, NYC, 2008—, MLB Network, 2008—. Bd. mem. Garth Brooks Teammates for Kids Found. Recipient Roberto Clemente award, 1987, Gold Glove award, MLB, 1988, 1989, 1990, Martin Luther King Humanitarian award, City of Seattle, 1991, Kids Outstanding Athlete award, Sports Illus., 1993, Most Caring Baseball Player award, USA Today, 1993, Man of Yr. award, Jaycees, 1994, Emmy award, 2003; named 195th Point of Light, Pres. George Bush; named one of 10 Outstanding Young Men in America, Jaycees, 1996; named to Am. League All-Star Team, MLB, 1987, 1988, State of Oreg. Hall of Fame, Alumni Hall of Fame, Boys & Girls Clubs America, 2004. Achievements include leading the American League in stolen bases, 1987. Office: SportsNet NY 75 Rockefeller Plz New York NY 10019 Office Phone: 212-485-4800.*

REYNOLDS, HELEN ELIZABETH, management consultant; b. Minerva, NY, Aug. 30, 1925; d. Henry James and Margurite Catherine (Gallagher) McNally; m. Theodore Laurence Reynolds, Feb. 27, 1948; children: Laurence McBride, David Scott, William Herbert. BA, SUNY, Albany, 1967; MA, Union Coll., Schenectady, NY, 1971. Cert. grad. Realtors Inst., N.Y. Owner, mgr. Schafer Studio, Schenectady, 1970—73; co-owner, v.p. Reynolds Chalmers Inc., Schenectady, 1971—97; program coord. Schenectady County, 1980—81; adminstr. Wellspring House Albany, NY, 1981—94; pres. HR Mgmt. Cons., Port Charlotte, Fla., 1994—2002; ret. Cons., examiner N.Y. State Civil Svc., Albany, 1971—81; mem. adv. coun. SBA, Washington, 1978—80. Planning bd. Town of Niskayuna, NY, 1977—81, town councilwoman, 1986—94; co-chair Great N.E. Festival Mohawk River, 1989—90; bd. dirs. HAVEN, Schenectady YWCA; mem. N.Y. State Commn. Capital Region, 1994—98, Acad. Women Achievement, Schenectady, 1994; pres. Photo Arts Group Charlotte County, 1998—2003, Buena Vista Property Owners Assn., Port Charlotte, 1998—2003. Named Woman Vision, 1986—87, Today's Woman, Schenectady YWCA, 1987. Mem.: Purita Grada Elks Lodge #2606, Gulf Coast Chpt.Kentucky Col. (pres. 2009), Charlotte County Art Guild, Union Coll. Alumni Assn., Charlotte Symphony League (pres. 2006), Antique and Classic Boat Soc. (bd. dirs. 1974—89, Disting. Svc. award 1979), Charlotte Harbor Yacht Club, Zonta (pres. 1981—82). Avocations: photography, reading, golf, skiing, canoeing. Home and Office: 104 Leland St SW Port Charlotte FL 33952-9131

REYNOLDS, HERBERT YOUNG, internist; b. Richmond, Va., Aug. 20, 1939; s. George Audney and Pearle Maupin (Young) R.; m. Anne Browning Leavell, July 11, 1964; children: Nancy, George, William Stuart. BA in English, U. Va., 1961, MD, 1965; MA (hon.), Yale U., 1979. Diplomate Am. Bd. Internal Medicine, Am. Bd. Allergy and Immunology. Intern NY Hosp., Cornell Med. Ctr., NYC, 1965—66, asst. physician, fellow in medicine, 1966—67; clin. assoc., lab. clin. investigation Nat. Inst. Allergy, Infectious Diseases, NIH, Bethesda, Md., 1967—70, chief clin. assoc., lab. clin. investigation, 1968—69; chief resident, instr. medicine U. Hosp. U. Wash., Seattle, 1970—71; sr. investigator, lab. clin. investigation Nat. Inst. Allergy, Infectious Diseases, NIH, Bethesda, 1971—76; assoc. prof. internal medicine Yale U. Sch. Medicine, New Haven, 1976—79, prof., 1979—88, head pulmonary divsn.; J. Lloyd Huck prof. medicine, chmn. dept. Pa. State U., Milton S. Hershey Med. Ctr., 1988—2002; assoc. chmn. divsn. medicine Pa. State Geisinger Health Sys., 1997—2000, chief medicine ops. Hershey Med. Ctr. Region, 1997—2000; med. officer Lung Biology and Disease br., divsn. lung diseases NHLBI/NIH, Bethesda, 2002—09; prof. medicine emeritus Pa. State U. Coll. Medicine, 2002—. Adj. prof. medicine Uniformed Svcs. U. Health Scis., Bethesda, 2003—; mem. exec. com. Coll. Medicine Pa. State U.-Hershey Med. Ctr., 1988-2002, exec. bd. U. Hosp., 1988-2002, fin. bd. acad. enrichment fun, 1988-95, dean's adv. com., 1988-97, diversity task force, 1995-2002, physicians faculty practice plan exec. com. 1996-97, human resources team leader, 2000-02; dept. chair rep. Milton S. Hershey Med. Ctr. Bd., 2000-2002; cons. in infectious diseases Nat. Naval Med. Ctr., NIH, Bethesda, 1971-76, clin. rsch. com., 1971-76, chmn., 1974-76, pulmonary disease adv. com. divsn. of lung diseases NHLBI, 1978-82, sci. counselors bd., 1984-88, data and safety monitoring bd. registry of patients with deficiency of Alpha-1 Antitrypsin, 1989-96. Mem. editl. bd. Lung, 1978-2005, Am. Jour. Medicine, 1979-89, Jour. Clin. Investigation, 1980-86, Am. Rev. Respiratory Diseases, 1980-87, Jour. Applied Physiology, 1981-89, Resident Physician, 1981-95; contbr. 318 articles to profl. jours. and med. textbooks. Parent com. Troop 1 Boy Scouts Am., Madison, 1979-82; bd. dirs. Neighborhood Music Sch., Guilford, Conn., 1978-87; Music at Gretna, 1994-2002; bd. dirs. Harrisburg Symphony, 1996-2000; active All Saints Episc. Ch., Hershey; pulmonary infections com. Cystic Fibrosis Found., Bethesda, 1980-86; mem. coun. sci. advisors Parker B. Francis Found., Kansas City, Kans., 1983-87; internat. com. World Orgn. for Sarcoidosis and other Granulomatous Disorders, 1987-95; bd. dirs., mem. coun. Am. Lung Assn., 1989-93, bd. govs. 1990-93, com. mem., 1990-93; coach Guilford Soccer League, 1985-88; vol. Mercy Health Clinic, Gaithersburg, Md., 2003—. Surgeon USPHS, 1967-70. John Edward Nobel fellow, 1961-65; named Outstanding Med. Specialist in USA, Town and Country Mag., 1989, 97, The Best Med. Specialists, Town & Country mag., 1995, One of 400 Best Drs. in U.S. Good Housekeeping Mag., 1991, Best Drs. in Am., 1992-2008; recipient Nat. Inst. Health award of Merit, 2006, Nat. Inst. Health Dir. award, 2007, 09. Fellow ACP (coun. subsplty. socs. 1989-2000, gov. Pa. Ea. Region 1, 2000-02), Am. Coll. Chest Physicians (program com. 1978-84), Infectious Disease Soc. Am., Coll. Physicians Phila.; mem. Am. Thoracic Soc. (sec.-treas. 1987-88, bd. dirs. 1989-93, v.p. 1988-89, pres. 1991-92), Am. Soc. Clin. Investigation, Assn. Am. Physicians, Am. Assn. Immunologists, Am. Fedn. Clin. Rsch., Am. Clin. and Climatol. Assoc. (v.p. 2001-02, pres. 2002-03), Acad. Medicine Wash., Interurban Clin. Club (emeritus 1989), Hershey Country Club, Farmington Country Club, Raven Soc., Phi Beta Kappa, Alpha Omega Alpha, Omicron Delta Kappa. Republican. Avocations: tennis, violin. Home: 226 E Caracas Ave Hershey PA 17033-1309 Office: NHLBI/NIH Divsn Lung Diseases 6701 Rockledge Dr Rm 10180 Bethesda MD 20892-7952 Office Phone: 301-435-0218. Business E-Mail: reynoldh@nhlbi.nih.gov.

REYNOLDS, JACKIE SUSAN, biology professor; b. Chgo., Mar. 15, 1952; m. Gordon Reynolds. MS in Med. Microbiology, U. Hawaii, Honolulu, 1973. Clin. microbiologist Parkland Hosp., Dallas, 1978—81; prof. biology El Centro Coll., Dallas, 1981—85, Richland Coll., Dallas, 1985—. Mem.: Tex. Assoc. Advisors Health Professions (sec. treas.), Am. Soc. Microbiology. Office: Richland Coll 12800 Abrams Rd Dallas TX 75243 Office Fax: 972-238-6389. Business E-Mail: jackiesr@dcccd.edu.

REYNOLDS, JAMES, management consultant; s. Richard James and Esther (Nikander) R.; m. Joanne M.J. BA in Econs., NYU, 1965, postgrad., 1965-66. Cons. to pres. Rothrock, Reynolds & Reynolds Inc., NYC, 1966-70; sr. v.p. health, med. div. Booz, Allen & Hamilton, NYC, 1970-80; pres. Reynolds & Co. (mgmt. cons.), San Francisco, NYC, Washington, 1981—. Developer Combining Pay for Performance with Gain Sharing to align incentives, Leap Frog Group, 2007, developer, HAC Focussed Gain Sharing Program, 2008; bd. dirs. Booz, Allen & Hamilton, 1977-79; chmn. bd. J.X. Reynolds Fine Arts, Ltd., 1979—; lectr. Harvard Sch. Pub. Health; faculty mem. Am. Coll. of Healthcare Execs.; bd. dirs. Health Ctr. Mgmt. Inst., Richmond, Va., 1977; mem. health adv. bd. Hunter Coll., 1980—. Mem. editl. bd. Physicians Fin. News. Recipient NYU Founders award, 1965 Mem. Am. Pub. Health Assn., Am. Mgmt. Assn., Assn. Am. Med. Colls., Am. Hosp. Assn., Hosp. Mgmt. Systems Soc., Hosp. Fin. Mgmt. Assn., Asia Soc., China Inst., Phi Beta Kappa, Guggenheim Mus., Mus. Modern Art, Met. Mus. Art, Met. Opera Guild (NYC) Episcopalian. Home and Office: Reynolds & Co 333 E 51st St New York NY 10022-6702 Home: 333 E 51st St New York NY 10022-6702 Office Phone: 212-826-1818. Business E-Mail: jreynolds@jxreynolds.com.

REYNOLDS, JEAN EDWARDS, publishing executive; b. Saginaw, Mich., Dec. 11, 1941; d. F. Perry and Katharine (Edwards) R.; m. Cary Wellington, Sept. 10, 1975 (div. 1982); children, Bradley, Abigail, Benjamin; m. Jon Haddon, Nov. 8, 1997. BA, Wells Coll., 1963; postgrad., CCNY, 1965-67. Asst. editor, sr. editor trade book div. Prentice-Hall, Englewood Cliffs, NJ, 1963—66, dir. children's books, 1966—69, McCall Pub. Co., NYC, 1969—71; sr. v.p., editorial dir. Franklin Watts Inc., NYC, 1971—75; pres. Pet Projects Inc., Ridgefield, Conn., 1975—81; editor in chief young people's publs. Grolier Inc., Danbury, Conn., 1981—89; founder, pub., exec. v.p. The Millbrook Press, Brookfield, Conn., 1989—2004; assoc. pub. Lerner Publs., Mpls., 2004—06, exec. editor, 2006—. Bd. dirs. Jewish Fedn. Greater Danbury; chair Conn. Ctr. for the Book, 1991-94. Mem. Bd. of Govs. for Higher Edn., State of Conn., 2004—; pres. Jewish Fedn. Greater Danbury, 1991—93, 2003—; bd. dirs. Jewish Home for the Elderly, Fairfield, Conn., 1989—90, 1999, Book Industry Study Group, 1991—98, The Wooster Sch., Danbury, Conn., 1992—2007, chair headmaster search, 2002—; bd. dirs. Temple Shearith Israel, Ridgefield, Conn., 1994—97, chair Kehila campaign, 2002; bd. dirs. The Children's Book Coun., 1996—2000, vice chair, 1997—98, chair, 1998—99; bd. dirs. Ridgefield Symphony, 2006—. Mem. ALA, Children's Book Coun., Mensa. Jewish. Avocations: skiing, sailing, needlecrafts. Home and Office: 33 Corntassle Rd Danbury CT 06811-3208 Personal E-mail: jeanreynolds33@gmail.com.

REYNOLDS, JERRY (GERALD A. REYNOLDS), federal agency administrator; BA, CUNY York Coll.; JD, Boston U. Atty. Schatz & Schatz, Conn., Ribicoff & Kotkin; legal analyst Ctr. Equal Opportunity, 1995—97; pres., legal counsel Ctr. New Black Leadership, 1997—98; sr. regulatory counsel Kansas City Power & Light Co., 1998—2002; asst. sec. civil rights US Dept. Edn., Washington, 2002—04; chmn. US Comm. on Civil Rights, Washington, 2004—. Mem. editl. bd.: Am. Jour. Law and Medicine; editor: Race and the Criminal Justice System: How Race Affects Jury Trials. Republican. Office: KCP&L PO Box 418679 Kansas City MO 64141-6979 also: US Commn on Civil Rights 624 Ninth St NW Ste 700 Washington DC 20425*

REYNOLDS, JERRY OWEN, professional sports team executive; b. French Lick, Ind., Jan. 29, 1944; m. Dodie Reynolds; children: Danielle, Jay. Student, Vincennes U.; grad., Oakland City Coll., Ind., 1966; student, Ind. U.; M in Phys. Edn., Ind. State U., 1970. Coach Rockhurst Coll., Kansas City, Mo., 1975—84, Pittsburg State U., Kans., 1984—85; asst. coach Sacramento Kings, 1985—88, head coach, 1987, 1988—89, dir. player pers., 1990—92, gen. mgr., 1992—93, dir. player pers., TV color analyst, 1994—; gen. mgr, v.p. WNBA Sacramento Monarchs, 1998—2003. Mem. USA Basketball Women's Sr. Nat. Team Com., 2001—04. Office: Sacramento Kings 1 Sports Pkwy Sacramento CA 95834-2300*

REYNOLDS, JOCK, artist, curator, art gallery director; m. Suzanne Hellmuth, 1977; 2 children. BA, Univ. Calif., Santa Cruz, 1969; MFA, Univ. Calif., Davis, 1972. Assoc. prof., dir., grad. program, Center for Experimental and Interdisciplinary Art San Francisco State Univ., 1973—83; co-founder 80 Langton St. (now New Langton Arts), 1975; dir. Washington Project of the Arts, Washington, 1983—89, Addison Gallery of Am. Art, Andover, Mass., 1989—98; Henry J. Heinz II dir. Yale Univ. Art Gallery, New Haven, 1998—; and adj. prof. Yale Univ., New Haven, 1998—. Represented in permanent collections Smithsonian Nat. Mus. of Am. Art., Corcoran Gallery of Art, Walker Art Ctr., Mpls. Inst. of Arts., Univ. Washington Henry Art Gallery. Bd. dir. Williamstown Art Conservation Ctr., Mass. Recipient Fulbright Fellowship. Office: Yale Univ Art Gallery Chapel at High St PO Box 208271 New Haven CT 06520-8271 Office Phone: 203-432-0600.

REYNOLDS, JOHN FRANCIS, insurance company executive; b. Escanaba, Mich., Mar. 29, 1921; s. Edward Peter and Lillian (Harris) R.; m. Dorothy Gustafson, May 1, 1946; children: Lois, Margaret, Michael. BS, Mich. State U., 1942. Claims and assoc. surety mgr. Hartford Ins. Co., Escanaba, Mich. and Chgo., 1946-55; asst. v.p., bond mgr. Wolverine Ins. Co., Battle Creek, Mich., 1955-64, v.p. underwriting, 1964-69; Midwest zone underwriting mgr. Transamerica Ins. Co. (Wolverine Ins. Co.), Battle Creek, Mich., 1969-74; pres., gen. mgr. Can. Surety Co. subs. Transamerica Ins. Co., Toronto, Ont., Canada, 1974-75; v.p. midwestern zone mgr. Transamerica Ins. Group, Battle Creek, Mich., 1975-83, pres., chief operating officer Los Angeles, 1983-84, chmn., chief exec. officer, 1984-85; apptd. spl. dep. ins. commr., dep. conservator Cadillac Inc. Co., 1989. Pres. Underwriting Exec. Council Midwest, 1967; dir. Underwriters Adjustment Bur., Toronto, 1974, Underwriters Labs. of Canada, Montreal, 1974; chmn. Mich. Assn. Ins. Cos., Lansing, 1976, Mich. Basic Property Ins. Assn., Detroit, 1973. Commr. City of Battle Creek, 1967-69; dir. Urban League, Battle Creek, 1969, 70, dir. Mich. Ins. Fedn., Lansing, 1975-83. Served to sgt. U.S. Army, 1942-45; New Guinea Roman Catholic. Avocations: golf, fishing. Home: 14037 N Cameo Dr Sun City AZ 85351-2903 Personal E-mail: reynolds213@yahoo.com.

REYNOLDS, JOHN HUGHES, IV, retired research and development executive; b. Rome, Ga., Sept. 25, 1940; s. John Hughes and Catherine (Neal) R.; m. Lee Boling Smith, Aug. 18, 1963; 1 child, Alison Lee. BA, Shorter Coll., 1962; MS, Clemson U., 1965, PhD, 1968. Chemist III R.J. Reynolds Tobacco Co., Winston-Salem, N.C., 1968-76, group leader, 1976-80, divsn. mgr., 1980-90, prin. scientist, 1990-96. Contbr. articles to profl. jours.; patentee designs for smoking articles and machines for lab. smoking of cigarettes. NDEA fellow Clemson U., 1962-65.

REYNOLDS, JUDITH AMY, nutritionist, animal scientist, consultant, educator; d. Jacob Alen and Mary Emeline Lundgren; m. Rodney Roger Reynolds, Aug. 28, 1971; children: Andrea Mary Rickards, James Christopher. AA summa cum laude, Anoka Ramsey CC, 1988; BS summa cum laude, St. Cloud State U., 1990; MS, Tex. A&M U., 1993, PhD, 1997. Cert. Profl. Animal Scientist Am. Registry Profl. Animal Scientists, 1995. Co-owner, mgr. Reynolds Quarter Horses, Palmyra, Mo., 1978—; grad. asst. rschr. Tex. A&M U., College Station, 1990—91, grad. asst. tchr., 1991—95; long term substitute tchr. biology, anatomy physiology, chemistry Princeton and Elk River Pub. Sch. Sys., Minn., 1997—98; divisional equine tech. specialist Archer Daniels Midland Animal Health Nutrition and MoorMan's Inc., Quincy, Ill., 1998—2001; equine nutritionist Archer Daniels Midland Alliance Nutrition Inc., Quincy, 2001—, equine product and tech. mgr., 2007—. Asst. prof. William Woods U., Fulton, Mo., 1995—97; assoc. faculty John Woods CC, Quincy, Ill., 2004—; spkr. in field; ofcl. reviewer Nat. Rsch. Coun., Nutrient Requirements of Horses, 2007; mem. Equine Sci. Soc. Nutrition Com., 2006—. Author: (online source) Equine Nutrition in the 21st Century (1st Pl. Online Svc. To Reader, 2003); contbr. articles in to profl. jours. Vol. Princeton Pub. Schools, Princeton, Minn., 1983—90; vol. leader; horse sci., horse bowl, horse advancement, vet. sci. Isanti County 4-H, Minn., 1983—90; vol. leader horse judging, market steers, poultry Bryan HS Future Farmers of Am., Tex., 1992—94; vol. horse judge Brazos County, College Station, Tex., 1991—94, Tex. A&M U., College Station, 1991—95; vol. horse bowl team coach Mo. State 4-H, 1996—97; vol. 4-H horse judge Audrain and Calloway Counties, Fulton, Mo., 1996—97. Recipient High Point All Around Horse, Minn. Quarter Horse Assn., 1980, Two Register of Merit Horses, Am. Quarter Horse Assn., 1980, 1982, Four High-Point and Res. Performance Gelding awards, Five State Champions, Five Res. State Champions, Minn. Quarter Horse Assn., 1980-1983, One Performance Horse Qualified, Outstanding Horses of World, World Equine Rsch. Inst., 1983; Mensa scholarship, Am. Mensa, 1987, Alliss scholarships, Alliss, 1987-1990, Academic scholarships, Anoka Ramsey CC, 1987-1988, St. Cloud State U., 1988-1990. Mem.: Am. Registry Profl. Animal Scientists, Equine Sci. Soc. (nutrition com. 2006—), Am. Quarter Horse Assn., Nat. Reining Horse Assn., Phi Kappa Phi, Psi Chi, Kappa Delta Pi, Phi Theta Kappa, Gamma Sigma Delta. Achievements include development of equine feeds and supplements, SENIORGLO, MOORGLO, PRO-VITA-MIN 20 supplement tubs, FORAGE FIRST Horse Rewards, MOORGLO Canadian formula, GROSTRONG QuadBLOCK Canadian formula; stay strong metabolic mineral pellets, juniorglo healthy glo nuggets, healthy glo meal. Avocations: horses, reading, writing, cooking. Office: ADM Alliance Nutrition 1000 N 30th St Quincy IL 62305 Office Fax: 217-222-9060. Business E-Mail: judy.reynolds@adm.com.

REYNOLDS, KAREN ANN, retired elementary school educator; b. Mpls., Jan. 20, 1944; d. Herbert Laverne and Doris Emma (Olson) Hinrichs; m. Kenneth Allen Reynolds, Aug. 2, 1975; stepchildren: Terri Lynn Winberry, Sheri Lee DeMaagd, Robert Scott. BS in Elem. Tchr. Edn. cum laude, So. Oreg. Coll., Ashland, 1966, MS in Elem. Tchr. Edn., 1974. Std. tchg. cert. State of Oreg. Tchr. elem. sch. Riddle Sch. Dist., Oreg., 1966—70, Ashland Sch. Dist. # 5, 1970—80; substitute tchr. Coos Bay and North Bend Sch. Dists., Oreg., 1981, Williston Sch. Dist., ND, 1982—83; tchr. County and City Schs. and pvt. kindergarten, Klamath Falls, Oreg., 1983—90; tchr. elem. sch. Klamath Falls City Schs. Dist. 1, Klamath Falls, 1990—98. Dir. Christmas Program Trenton K-12 Sch., ND, 1984; vol. dist.-sponsored program, mentor Conger Elem. Sch., 1990—91. Sunday sch. and Bible sch. tchr. Grace Luth. Ch., Ashland, 1959—65, tchr. confirmation class, 1972—74; children's message presenter Zion Luth. Ch., Klamath Falls, 2000—05, mem. altar guild, banner artist, 2002—08, asst. to pastor, part time doing e-mail prayer chain, 2005—; active Luth. Women's Missionary League, 2007—; mem./sponsor Good Shepherd Luth. Home, Hillsboro, Oreg., 2007—. Recipient State Bd. Full Tuition scholarship, State of Oreg., 1962—65; named Best Student in a Survey Class in Am. History, Faculty of So. Oreg. Coll., 1964, Best Student in Prins. of Econs. Survey Class, 1965, Best Student in a Survey Course in Geography, Faculty So. Oreg. Coll., 1964, Co-Salutatorian of Graduating Class, Ashland Sr. H.S., 1962. Mem.: Ashland Edn. Assn. (mem. salary negotiation team 1972—73), Klamath Falls Edn. Assn. (treas. 1996—98), Riddle Edn. Assn. (v.p. 1967—68, pres. 1968—69, salary negotiations team 1968—69). Lutheran. Avocations: art, genealogy, travel, back country jeeping.

REYNOLDS, LINDA ANN, elementary school educator; b. Teheran, Iran, Jan. 1, 1959; d. John Kendrick and Fatemah Nikou Reynolds; 1 adopted child, Derek. BS in Elem. Edn., Auburn U., Ala., 1991, MEd, 1995, Edn. Specialist degree, 2000. LCSW. Med. transcriptionist St. Margaret's Hosp., Montgomery, Ala., 1980—84, Drs. Reynolds, Little and Thomas, Montgomery, 1981—87; typing instr. Riley Coll., Montgomery, 1987—88; tchr. 5th grade Davis Elem. Sch., Montgomery, 1991—92; edn. instr. Fews Elem. Sch., Montgomery, 1995, tchr. 5th grade, 2000—01, motivational spkr. and ednl. cons., grade 1-6, 2005—; rschr. Ednl. Found. and Curriculum, 2008—. Ednl. instr. CAP Program, Montgomery, 1995; invited motivational spkr. in field. Vol. city crime prevention unit Montgomery Police Dept.; vol. Montgomery Area Food Bank; active Rainbow Com. Recipient Tchr. of Yr., 1991—92. Mem.: Chi Sigma Iota. Home: PO Box 153 Coosada AL 36020-0153 Personal E-mail: lindaannreynolds@yahoo.com.

REYNOLDS, LLOYD GEORGE, economist, educator; b. Wainwright, Alberta, Can., Dec. 22, 1910; came to U.S., 1934, naturalized, 1940; s. George F. and Dorothy (Carl) R.; m. Mary F. Trackett, June 12, 1937; children: Anne Reynolds Skinner, Priscilla Reynolds Roosevelt, Bruce Lloyd. AB, U. Alberta, 1931, LL.D., 1958; A.M., McGill U., 1933; PhD, Harvard, 1936. Instr. econs. Harvard, 1936-39; asso. polit. economy Johns Hopkins, 1939-41, asso. prof., 1941-45; asso. prof. econs. Yale, 1945-47, prof. econs., 1947-52, Sterling prof. econs., 1952-81, chmn. dept. econs., 1951-59; prof. emeritus, 1981—; dir Econ. Growth Center, 1961-67; vis. fellow All Souls Coll., Oxford, 1967-68. Mem. adv. bd. Pakistan Inst. Devel. Econs., 1965-73; cons. to Social Sci. Research Center, U. P.R., 1951-65; dir. Nat. Bureau Econ. Research, 1958-81; Research dir. labor studies 20th Century Fund, 1940-43; research sec., com. on employment Social Sci. Research Council, 1941-42; co-chmn. appeals com. N.W.L.B., 1943-45; cons. Bur. of Budget, 1945-47; Guggenheim fellow, 1954-55, 1966-67; dir. program in econs. and bus. adminstrn. Ford Found., 1955-57 Author: The British Immigrant in Canada, 1935, Control of Competition in Canada, 1940, Labor and National Defense, 1941, An Index to Trade Union Publications, 1945, Labor Economics and Labor Relations, 1949, The Structure of Labor Markets, 1951, The Evolution of Wage Structure, 1956, Economics: A General Introduction, 1963, Wages, Productivity and Industrialization in Puerto Rico, 1965, The Three Worlds of Economics, 1971, Agriculture in Development Theory, 1975, Image and Reality in Economic Development, 1977, The American Economy in Perspective, 1981, Economic Growth in the Third World, 1850-1980, 1985; contbr. articles to profl. jours. Fellow Am. Acad. Arts and Scis.; mem. Indsl. Rls. Rsch. Assn. (pres. 1955), Am. Econ. Assn. (v.p. 1959, exec. com. 1952-54), Am. Acad. Polit. Sci., Am. Statis. Assn., Phi Beta Kappa. Clubs: Graduates (New Haven) (pres. 1961-64); Harvard (Boston); Century (N.Y.C.); Cosmos (Washington).

REYNOLDS, MARJORIE LAVERS, nutritionist, educator; b. Collingwood, Ont., Can., Jan. 10, 1931; d. Henry James and Laura (Wilson) Lavers; m. John Horace Reynolds, Aug. 17, 1963; children: Steven, Mark. BA, U. Toronto, 1953; MS, U. Minn., 1957; PhD, U. Wis., 1964; AS, State Tech. Inst. Knoxville, 1982. Registered dietitian. Rsch. dietitian Mayo Clinic, Rochester, Minn., 1957-59; rsch. dietitian Cleve. Met. Gen. Hosp., 1959-60; rsch. assoc. U. Tenn., Knoxville, 1963-66; instr. Ft. Sanders Sch. Nursing, Knoxville, 1967-76, State Tech. Inst., Knoxville, 1982-88; substitute secondary sch. tchr. Knox County Schs., Knoxville, 1989-93. Contbr. articles to biochem. and nutrition jours.; newsletter editor Juvenile Diabetes Found., Knoxville, 1985-93. Sec. Midway Rehab. Ctr., Knoxville, 1987—2001. Mem.: LWV, Knoxville Dist. Dietetic Assn. (pres. 1971—72, Outstanding Dietitian 1973—74), Tenn. Dietetic Assn. (pres. 1973—74, Outstanding Dietitian 1973—74), Omicron Nu. Democrat. Presbyterian. Avocations: reading, sports. Home: 7112 Stockton Dr Knoxville TN 37909-2534

REYNOLDS, MICHAEL TIMOTHY, lawyer; b. NYC, June 29, 1968; s. Timothy John and Patricia Mary Reynolds. AB in History magna cum laude, Dartmouth Coll., 1990; MPhil in Medieval History, Cambridge U., Eng., 1991; JD, Yale U., 1995. Bar: N.Y. 1996, U.S. Dist. Ct. (so. and ea. dists.) N.Y. 1996, U.S. Dist. Ct. (D.C.) 2002, U.S. Ct. Appeals (3d and 9th cirs.) 2005, U.S. Ct. Appeals (2d cir.) 2006, U.S. Supreme Ct. 2005. Law clk. to Hon. Diarmuid F. O'Scannlain, U.S. Ct. Appeals for 9th Cir., Portland, Oreg., 1995—96; ptnr., litig. Cravath, Swaine & Moore LLP, NYC, 2003—. Exec. editor Yale Law Jour., 1994-95. Mem. bd. proprietors The Dartmouth, Inc., Hanover, NH, 2001—; trustee Lower East Side Tenement Mus., NYC, 2004—. Keasbey Found. scholar Cambridge U., 1990-92. Mem.: Assn. Bar City NY, Phi Beta Kappa. Office: Cravath Swaine & Moore LLP 825 8th Ave Fl 38 New York NY 10019-7475 Office Phone: 212-474-1552. Office Fax: 212-474-3700. Business E-Mail: mreynolds@cravath.com.

REYNOLDS, NANCY REMICK, writer, researcher, editor; b. San Antonio, July 15, 1938; d. Donald Worthington and Edith (Remick) R.; m. Brian Rushton, June 25, 1983; 1 child: Ehren Reynolds. Student, Sch. Am. Ballet, NYC, 1951, student, 1953—61, Juilliard Sch. Music, 1957, Martha Graham Sch. Contemporary Dance, 1959, U. Sorbonne, Paris, 1962; BA in Art History, Columbia U., NYC, 1965; postgrad., Goethe Inst., Prien, 1972, U. Chgo., 1974—77, Sarah Lawrence Coll., Bronxville, NY, 1974—77. Dancer NYC Ballet, 1956—61; editor Praeger Pubs., NYC, 1965—71; dir. rsch. book Choreography by George Balanchine: A Catalogue of Works, 1979—82; dir. rsch. pub. TV spl. Balanchine, NY, 1983—84; assoc. editor Internat. Ency. of Dance, 1998; dir. rsch. The George Balanchine Found., NYC, 1994—. Co-pub. Twentieth-Century Dance in Slides, 1978-93. Author: Repertory in Review: Forty Years of the New York City Ballet, 1977 (De la Torre Bueno prize 1977), The Dance Catalog: A Complete Guide to Today's World of Dance, 1979, co-author: In Performance, 1980, Dance Classics, 1991 (rec. for teen age NY Pub. Libr.), No Fixed Points: Dance in the Twentieth Century, 2003, Remembering Lincoln, 2007; editor: Movement and Metaphor: Four Centuries of Ballet (Lincoln Kirstein), 1970, Dance as a Theatre Art: Source Readings in Dance History from 1581 to the Present (Selma Jeanne Cohen), 1974, School of Classical Dance (V. Kostrovitskaya and A. Pisarev), 1978; contbr. (book) Ballet: Bias and Belief, "Three Pamphlets Collected" and Other Dance Writings of Lincoln Kirstein, 1983; contbr. articles to profl. jours Ford Found. Travel and Study grantee, 1974; Mary Duke Biddle Found. grantee, 1990. Mem. Dance Critics Assn. (pres. 1986-87), Soc. Dance History Scholars, Soc. for Dance Rsch., Am. Soc. for Theatre Rsch., European Assn. Dance Historians, Internat. Fedn. for Theatre Rsch. in affiliation with Societe Internat. des Bibliotheques et Musees des Arts du Spectacle, Phi Beta Kappa. Home: 9 Prospect Park W Brooklyn NY 11215-1758 Home Phone: 718-783-4265; Office Phone: 718-783-4265.

REYNOLDS, PATRICIA ELLEN, artist; b. Apr. 6, 1934; d. Edwin and Anna (Pacewicz) Steeg; m. Carlyle Reynolds, Oct. 4, 1953 (div. 1991); children: Clifford, Stephanie. Student, SUNY, Plattsburg, 1951-52, Moon Bus. Sch., NYC, 1953; studied with Robert Whitney, studied with Mario Cooper. Watercolor painter, Willsboro, N.Y. Condr. workshops in field, mem. art juries. One-woman shows include Gallerie Camille Renaud, Paris, 1979, Hollsworthy Gallery, London, 1980, Ctr. Modern Design, Riyadh, Saudi Arabia, 1981-83, 25 Yr. Retro Art Mus., SUNY, Plattsburgh, Remington Mus., 1996, North Country Cultural Ctr., Plattsburgh, NY, 2005; exhibited in group shows at Schenectady Mus., SUNY, Plattsburgh, St. Lawrence U., Canton, N.Y., Ctr. Music, Drama and Arts, Lake Placid, N.Y., 1980, Audubon Artists Ann., 1980, 94, Fleming Mus. Burlington, Vt., Am. Watercolor Soc., 1982, 87 (Traveling Shows awards, Lena Newcastle award), Salmagundi Club (Gold Medal award), 1983, 88-89, 91-92 (awards 1983, 88), Nat. Works Paper, 1982 (award), Nat. Exhbn. Am. Watercolors, 1983-84, 87 (award), Allied Trusts Exhbn., 1987, 91, 93, Watercolor West, 1988, Mid-West Watercolor Soc., 1983, 89, 92, Nat. Watercolor Soc., 1991. Recipient Best of Show arad No. Vt. Artists, 1970-71, 76, 78-79, Adirondack Art Exhbn. award, 1973, Oustanding Woman Artist award Am. Pen Women, 1975, Benedictine Nat. award, 1975, Lena Newcastle award Am. Watercolor Soc., 1987, Travel Exhbn. award Am. Watercolor Soc., 1987, William Kowalsky Meml. award, 1991, Adirondack Pk. Centennial award, 1992, Multi-Focus award, 1992, Adirondack Art Assn. award, 2003 Mem. Transparent Watercolor Soc. Am. (Signature Mem. award 1992, North Country award), Allied Artist Am. (assoc.), Nat. Watercolor Soc. (assoc.), Ctrl. N.Y. Watercolor Soc. (signature), Gallery Des Beaucy Artes Des Ameriques Montreal, Adirondack Art Assn., No Cmty. Cultural Ctr Friends of art, SUNY, Pitts. Office Phone: 518-963-8356. Fax: 518-963-8382.

REYNOLDS, PATRICIA JEAN, psychiatric social worker, songwriter; d. Joseph Eustacio D'Angelo and Elizabeth Sophie Jakubczyk; 1 child, Aaron D'Angelo. BA in English, U. Hartford; AS in Mktg., Middlesex Coll., Conn.; MA in Social Work, U. Conn., 1992. Abstract writer Inst. of Living, Hartford; treatment mgr. geriatric and adult units and day program Inst. of Living, Hartford Hosp. Songwriter (CD) New State, New Start, New Man, 2000 (CD of Yr. Conn. Country Music Assn., 2000), Another Country Night, 2005; author: Paradise Park, 2003, various books of poetry. Named Songwriter of Yr., N.Am. Country Music Assn. Internat., 2004. Mem.: Conn. Songwriters Assn. (sec. 2000—, Career Accomplishment award), Nashville Songwriters Assn. Internat., Country Music Assn. Avocations: woodcarving, poetry, novels, sports. Home: PO Box 310762 Newington CT 06131 Home Phone: 860-429-1978; Office Phone: 860-545-7219. Personal E-mail: patsongs@snet.net.

REYNOLDS, PAUL L., lawyer, bank executive; b. Covington, Ky., May 29, 1961; BS cum laude, No. Ky. U., Highland Heights, 1983; JD, U. Ky. Coll. Law, Lexington, KY., 1986. Bar: Ohio 1986, US Dist. Ct. (so. dist. Ohio) 1986, Ky. 1987. Gen. counsel, asst. sec. Fifth Third Bank, 1995, asst. sec., 1995, sr. v.p., 1997; exec. v.p. Fifth Third Bancorp, Cin., 1999—, gen. counsel, sec., 2002—. Recipient Am. Jurisprudence award, Constl. Law, Am. Jurisprudence award, Corp. Fin. Law. Mem.: Ky. Bar Assn., Cin. Bar Assn., Ohio State Bar Assn. Office: Fifth Third Bancorp 38 Fountain Square Plz Cincinnati OH 45263

REYNOLDS, PETER JAMES, physicist; b. NYC, Nov. 19, 1949; s. Rudolph and Lydia Mary (Schanzer) R.; m. Louise Perini, Aug. 7, 1982. AB in Physics, U. Calif., Berkeley, 1971; PhD, MIT, 1979. Rsch. assoc., lectr. Boston U., 1978, asst. rsch. prof., 1979-83; mem. sci. staff Nat. Resource for Computation in Chemistry Lawrence Berkeley Lab., U. Calif., 1980-81, mem. rsch. staff materials and chem. scis. divsn., 1982-88; program mgr. Office Naval Rsch., 1988—2003, Army Rsch. Office, 2003—09, assoc. dir. head physics, 2004—06, divsn. chief, 2006—07, chief scientist phys. scis., 2007—. Vis. scientist NEC Fundamental Rsch. Lab., Kawasaki, Japan, 1986, rsch. prof. Georgetown U., Washington, 1996-2005, Inst. Theoretical Physics, Santa Barbara, 1994, U. Insubria, Como, Italy, 2001-02; vis. rsch. chemist U. Calif., Berkeley, 1988; adj. assoc. prof. dept. chemistry San Francisco State U., 1988-91; adj. prof. physics NC State U., 2008-; lectr. and rschr. in field of statis., chem. and computational physics and Monte Carlo Methods; program mgr. atomic and molecular physics, laser cooling and trapping, Bose-Einstein condensates, quantum degeneracy, optical lattices, quantum coherence and control, atom lasers, quantum computing. Editor: On Clusters and Clustering: From Atoms to Fractals, 1993; co-author: Monte Carlo Methods in Ab Initio Quantum Chemistry, 1994; contbr. articles to profl. jours., also rev. articles, book chpts. NATO lectr., NSF fellow, 1971-74; Lawrence Berkeley Lab. grantee, 1982-83. Fellow IBM, Am. Phys. Soc. (chmn. membership com. 1998, nominating com. Divsn. Computational Physics and Forum on Physics and Soc. 1996-97, 2008-, exec. com. Divsn. Computational Physics 1992-96, 2002-04), Army Rsch. Lab.; mem. Am. Jour. Physics (mem. editl. bd. 2002-04), Materials Rsch. Soc., Optical Soc. Am., N.Y. Acad. Scis., Phi Beta Kappa, Sigma Xi. Office: Army Research Office Physics Divsn PO Box 12211 Research Triangle Park NC 27709

REYNOLDS, ROBERT, artist, educator; b. San Luis Obispo, Calif., Mar. 7, 1936; s. Agee Grady and Viola Elizabeth (Curran) R.; m. Sharon Ardelle Bodley, June 17, 1962 (div. 1979); children: Robert Scott, Richard Lance, Jill Elizabeth; m. Patricia Lee Smith, Oct. 5, 1981. BPA with honors, Art Ctr. Coll. Design, LA, 1963; MA, Calif. Poly. U., 1970. Artist Creative Arts Studio, San Luis Obispo, 1955-56; freelance artist/illustrator L.A., San Luis Obispo, 1957—; staff artist Calif. Poly. U., San Luis Obispo, 1964—, assoc. prof. architecture, 1970-75, prof. art & design, 1980-81, dept. chair art & design, 1984-86, acting head dept. art, 1983-84. Artist Ford Times mag., Dearborn, Mich., 1971-79; instr. Cuesta Coll., San Luis Obispo, 1972-76; artist, tchr., co-founder High Sierra Watercolor Workshop, 1975—, Asilomar Watercolor Workshop, Pacific Grove, Calif., 1980-83; free-lance illustrator for variousi studios, Calif., 1972—; painting instr. Robert Reynolds Workshop, high Sierra, 1973-2007; resident dir. London Study Program Calif. Poly. U., London, 1986, 91; art. acquisitions com. mem. Calif. Poly. State U., 1997—, performing arts adv. com., 1995—, London Study Program Com., 1986—. One-man shows include San Luis Obispo Art Ctr., 1975, 2007-08, Solo Art Exhibition, San Luis Obispo Art Ctr., 2008, Calif. State U. Hdqrs./Gallery, 1979, Allan Hancock Coll., Santa Maria, Calif., 1981, Olive Tree Gallery, Santa Maria, 1983, Johnson Gallery, 1998-2007, Harbinger Gallery, 1998-2006, Elverhoj Mus. Art and History, Solvang, Calif. 2004; group shows include Calif. Survey Drawing and Watercolor, Humboldt, 1982, U. Gallery, Calif. Poly. State U., 1985; exhibitions include Florence Biennale Internat. Art Exhbn., Italy, 2003; represented in permanent collections at City of Stockton, Calif., City of San Luis Obispo, Santa Barbara Mus. Natural history, Calif. State U. and CSU Collection, Long Beach, Mid-State Fair Assn., others; works include design of San Luis Obispo bicentennial symbol and coin, design of ofcl. seal County of San Luis Obispo, ofcl. painting 1984 Mozart Festival, San Luis Obispo; designer U.S. Commemorative Postcard Stamp, 1987, Annual Bear Valley Music Festival Poster, Calif., 2004; cover painting design (book): Splash9: Best of Watercolor, 2006, work is in over 20 Art Books and is on the Cover of Splash 9: Best of Watercolor; author: Painting Nature's Peaceful Places, 1993, The Art of Robert Reynolds: Quiet Journey, 2006; executed mural Mus. Nat. History, Calif., 1983; commd. to do poster for Morro Bay Nat. Estuary Program, 2001. Mem. San Luis Obispo Design and Rev. Bd., 1970-73; chmn. San Luis Obispo Glad Design Competition, 1973. With USNR, 1955-63. Recipient Disting. Teaching award Calif. Poly. State U., 1986, Pres. Art award, 1993, Bronze award Nat. Painting Competition Artist mag., 1996, finalist 1999, 2000, Gold medal Art Inst. Calif., 1994, Alumni award Calif. Poly. State U., 2005; Purchase prize IronStone Vineyards Nat Art Competition, 1999; named Calif. Ctrl. Coast Wine Classic Commemorative Artist, 2002, 05,09; subject of article Ctrl. Coast Mag., 2004. Mem. San Luis Obispo Art Assn. (past pres. 1970-71), Ctrl. Coast Watercolor Soc. (co-founder 1978, pres. 1980-81). Achievements include artwork featured in over 20 art books in the US and England. Personal E-mail: rgreynolds@charter.net.

REYNOLDS, ROBERT A., JR., electric distributor executive; Degree in bus., Stonehill Coll., 1972. Joined Graybar Electric Co., St. Louis, 1972, various mgmt. positions, v.p. commn./data divsn., 1991, pres.,

CEO, 2000—, chmn., 2001—. Mem.: Nat. Assn. Wholesaler-Distributors (sec., vice chmn. 2002—05, chmn. elect 2005—). Office: Graybar Electric 34 N Meramec Ave Saint Louis MO 63105

REYNOLDS, ROBERT HUGH, lawyer; b. St. Louis, Jan. 3, 1937; s. Leslie A. and Rebecca (McWaters) R.; m. Carol Jemison, Apr. 8, 1961; children: Stephen H., Cynthia C., Laura M. BA, Yale U., 1958; JD, Harvard U., 1964. Assoc. Barnes & Thornburg, Indpls., 1964—70, ptnr., 1970—2004, chmn. bus. dept., 1983—91, chmn. internat. practice group, 1992—2004, of counsel, 2005—; vice-chmn. TerraLex, 1996—2003, chmn., 2003—06, chmn. emeritus, 2007—. Co-chmn., editor Comml. Real Estate Financing for Ind. Attys., 1968; vice-chmn., co-editor Advising Ind. Businesses, 1974; chmn., editor Counseling Ind. Businesses, 1981, The Purchase and Sale of a Business, 1987. Bd. dir. Crossroads Am. Coun. Boy Scouts Am., v.p., 1971—75, pres., 1987—89, v.p. Area 4 Ctrl. Region, 1989—92, pres., 1992—93, pres. Ctrl. Region, 1993—96, nat. exec. bd., 1993—; bd. dir. Family Svc. Assn. Indpls., 1974—81, pres., 1978—80; bd. dir. Family Svc. Am., 1979—88, Greater Indpls. Fgn. Trade Zone, 1987—2000, Indpls. Conv. and Visitors Assn., 1989—2000, Indpls. Econ. Devel. Corp., 1983—99, Greater Indpls. Progress Com., 1986—2000, exec. com., vice chmn.; trustee Children's Mus. Indpls., 1988—96, chmn., 1992—94; bd. dirs. Indpls. Downtown Inc., chmn., 1996—99; bd. govs. Legacy Fund, 1992—2007, vice chmn., 2000—03, chmn., 2004—06; bd. dir. Noyes Meml. Found., pres., 2004—; bd. dir. Japan-Am. Soc. Ind., pres., 1994—2005, pres. emeritus, 2005—; bd. dir. Ctrl. Ind. Cmty. Found., 2003—07; bd. dirs. Indpls. Symphony Orch. Found., 2004—. With USN, 1958—61, lt. comdr. USNR, 1961—78. Recipient Silver Buffalo award, Boy Scouts Am., Charles L. Whistler award, Greater Indpls. Progress Com., Sagamore of the Wabash award, Gov. Ind.; named hon. Consul Gen. of Japan, 1999—, hon. trustee, Children's Mus. Indpls., 1997—. Fellow Ind. Bar Found., Indpls. Bar Found.; mem. ABA, Ind. Bar Assn. (chmn. corp., banking and bus. law sect. 1981-82, chmn. internat. sect. 1994-96), Internat. Bar Assn., Indpls. Bar Assn., Greater Indpls. C. of C. (bd. dirs., sec. 2000-05, dir. emeritus 2005—), Econ. Club Indpls. (bd. dirs. 1995-2004), Kiwanis. Republican. Office: Barnes & Thornburg LLP 11 S Meridian St Indianapolis IN 46204-3535 Office Phone: 317-231-7227. Business E-Mail: rreynolds@btlaw.com.

REYNOLDS, ROBERT JOEL, economist, consultant; b. Indpls., May 13, 1944; s. Joel Burr and Betty (Schimpf) R.; m. Lucinda Margaret Lewis, May 27, 1979; children: Joel, Sarah. BSBA in Fin., Northwestern U., Evanston, Ill., 1965, PhD in Econs., 1970. Asst. prof. econs. U. Idaho, Moscow, 1969—73, assoc. prof., 1973—75; asst. dir, sr. economist econ. policy office Dept. Justice, Washington, 1973—81; sr. economist, v.p. ICF Inc., Washington, 1981—87, sr. v.p., 1987—91; exec. v.p., prin. Econsult Corp., Washington, 1991—96; chmn., exec. v.p. Econsult of D.C., Inc., Washington, 1997; chmn. Competition Econs., Inc., Washington, 1997—2007; prin. Brattle Group, 2004—. Vis. assoc. prof. U. Calif., Berkeley, 1976-77, Cornell U., Ithaca, N.Y., 1981. Reviewer: NSF, Rand Jour. of Econs., Internat. Econ. Rev., Internat. Jour. Indsl. Orgn., Jour. Indsl. Econs., Am. Econ. Rev.; mem. editl. bd. Managerial and Decision Econs.; contbr. articles to profl. jours. Recipient Dow Jones award Wall St. Jour., 1965; AT&T grantee, 1971-72, Brookings Instl. grantee, 1968-69; NDEA fellow, 1965-69. Mem. AAAS, IEEE (computer sect.), SIAM, Am. Math. Assn., Am. Econ. Assn., Econometric Soc., Royal Econ. Soc., Am. Statis. Assn., European Assn. for Rsch. in Indsl. Econs., Soc. for the Promotion of Econ. Theory, Math. Assn. Am. Congregationalist. Home: PO Box 59712 Potomac MD 20859-9712 Office: Brattle Group 1850 M St NW Ste 1200 Washington DC 20036 Office Phone: 202-955-5050. Personal E-mail: rjrcei@aol.com.

REYNOLDS, ROBERT L., investment company executive; b. Clarksburg, W.Va., Mar. 10, 1952; married; 4 children. BA in Bus. Adminstrn. & Fin., W.Va. U., 1974. Trust officer Wheeling Dollar Bank; joined NCNB Corp., Charlotte, NC, 1977, sr. v.p.; joined Fidelity Investments, 1984, exec. v.p. Fidelity Mgmt. Trust Co., pres. Institutional Retirement Group, 1996—2000, vice chmn., COO, 2000—07, head mgmt. com.; pres., CEO Putnam Investments, Boston, 2008—; pres. Putnam Funds, 2009—. Bd. dirs. FMR Corp.; bd. mem. Fidelity Investments Can. Ltd.; 41st Acordia/Royal & SunAlliance disting. lectr. W. Va. U. Coll. Bus.; former coll. football referee. Bd. mem. Initiative for a Competitive Inner City; bd. dirs. Make-A-Wish Found., Am. Cancer Soc.; bd. mem. Concord Mus.; bd. dirs. W.Va. U. Found. Recipient Boston Coll. Pres.'s Medal of Excellence; named Jaycee of Yr.; named one of Investment News Power 25 Elite. Avocations: golf, fishing. Office: Putnam Investments 1 Post Office Sq # 500 Boston MA 02109

REYNOLDS, RONALD FOSTER, science educator; b. Taunton, Mass., July 13, 1939; s. Alfred Foster and Lillian Belle Reynolds; m. Roberta Babbitt; children: Douglas Sheldon, Geoffrey Scott. EdB, Bridgewater State Coll., 1961, MEd, 1969. Vis. lectr. Bridgewater State Coll., Mass., 2002—; chemistry & physics tchr. Barrington HS, RI, 1981—2002, Oliver Ames HS, Easton, Mass., 1970—80; sci., IA dept. chair Gilford Mid. & HS, NH, 1980—81; earth sci. & chemistry tchr. Joseph Case HS, Swansea, Mass., 1961—70. Pres. RI Sci. Tchrs. Assn., Warwick, 1984—89; sci. tchr. adv. bd. NSTA, Wash.; nat. faculty Challenger Ctr., Wash., 1986—95; short courses chmn. NSTA Nat. Conv., Boston. Contbr. articles to profl. jours. Sch. com. Berkley Pub. Sch., Mass., 1967—74. Recipient Centennial Tchr. award, NIH, Presdl. Award, Office of U.S. Pres.; finalist Tchr. Space Program State, NASA, 1985. Avocations: photography, woodworking. Home: 120 Birch St Bridgewater MA 02324 Office: Bridgewater State Coll Conant Science Bldg Pk Ave Bridgewater MA 02325 Business E-Mail: rreynolds@bridgew.edu.

REYNOLDS, RUTH CARMEN, school administrator, secondary school educator; b. Dec. 30; d. Jim and Beulah Eliza (Woods) R. BS in Math., Chgo. State U., 1973, BS in Acctg., 1983, MS in Edn., 1986; MA in Math. Edn., DePaul U., 1991. Cert. tchr., high sch. math., gen. adminstrv. Tchr. Chgo. Pub. Schs., 1973—; adminstrv. asst. South Shore Cmty. Acad., Chgo., 1995-96, registrar, 1995-96, dir. scheduling, grade coord., 1995-96; dir. scheduling, registrar Phillips H.S. Acad., Chgo., 1996-97; adminstrv. asst. Harper H.S., Chgo., 1997—2000; program officer, grade coord. and registrar, adminstrv. asst. Collins H.S., Chgo., 2000—. Adj. prof. Columbia Coll., Chgo., 1988-89; program officer Lindblom Tech. H.S., Chgo., 1985-95; mem. symposium com. Chgo. Pub. Schs. Student Sci. Fair, Inc.; mem. Ill. Jr. Sci. Fair, Inc. Contbr. articles to profl. jours. Treas. Chgo. Chpt. NAAF, 1988, nat. phone contact. Frye Found. Math. fellow U. Chgo., 1991. Mem. ASCD, Nat. Coun. Tchrs. Math., Ill. Coun. Tchrs. Math. (del. to Japan 1988), Nat. Coun. Suprs. Math., Notaries Assn. Ill., Benjamin Banneker Assn., Andover-Dartmouth Urban Tchr. Inst., Exeter Math. Inst., Nat. Genealogical Soc., Afro-Am. Geneal. and Hist. Soc. Chgo. (bd. dirs., v.p. 2000-2001, treas. 2001-2002), Met. Math. Club Chgo., Daus. of Union Vets. of the Civil War 1861-1865 (mem. Sarah M.W. Sterling Tent # 3, nat. sec. 2002-), U.S. Colored Troops Inst. for Local History and Family Rsch., Internat. Soc. of Sons and Daus. of Slave Ancestry, Phi Delta Kappa, Chgo. Women's Golf Club, (treas. 2002), NAIC, (regional dir. 1998, treas. 2001-02). Avocations: reading mystery novels, travel, genealogy, golf. Home: 2901 S King Dr Apt 1802 Chicago IL 60616-3315 Office: Collins HS 1313 S Sacramento Blvd Chicago IL 60623

REYNOLDS, RYAN RODNEY, actor; b. Vancouver, BC, Can., Oct. 23, 1976; s. Jim and Tammy Reynolds; m. Scarlett Johansson, Sept. 27, 2008. Actor: (TV series) Hillside, 1990, The Odyssey, 1993—94, The Outer Limits, 1995—98, Two Guys, a Girl and a Pizza Place, 1998—2001; (films) Ordinary Magic, 1993, Life During Wartime, 1997, Coming Soon, 1999, Dick, 1999, Big Monster on Campus, 2000, We All Fall Down, 2000, Finder's Fee, 2001, Van Wilder, 2002, Buying the Cow, 2002, The In-Laws, 2003, Foolproof, 2003, Harold & Kumar Go to White Castle, 2004, Blade: Trinity, 2004, The Amityville Horror, 2005, Waiting, 2005, Smokin' Aces, 2006, The Nines, 2007, Chaos Theory, 2007, Definitely, Maybe, 2008, Fireflies in the Garden, 2008, X-Men Origins: Wolverine, 2009, The Proposal, 2009. Office: c/o United Talent Agy 9560 Wilshire Blvd Ste 500 Beverly Hills CA 90212-6700

REYNOLDS, SCOTT WALTON, academic administrator; b. Summit, NJ, July 15, 1941; s. Clark Leonard and Shirley (Hill) R.; m. Margaret Ann Johnson, July 5, 1969; children: Jane, Amy, David. BA, Trinity Coll., Hartford, Conn., 1963; MBA, Harvard U., 1965. Mng. dir. corp. staff Bankers Trust Co., NYC, 1967-94; asst. to the pres. St. Peter's Coll., Jersey City, 1994-96, Trinity Coll., Hartford, Conn., 1996-98, sec., 1998—, interim v.p. fin., treas., 2004—05, 2007—08. Chmn. fund campaign Montclair (N.J.) ARC, 1974; chmn. bus. and fraternal group Montclair Bicentennial Com., 1976; bd. fellows Trinity Coll., 1982-88, trustee, 1992-96, sec., exec. com., 1993-96. 1st lt. U.S. Army, 1965-67. Recipient 150th Anniversary award Trinity Coll., 1978, Alumni medal for Excellence, 1988, Pres.' Leadership medal, 1993. Mem. Montclair Jaycees (treas. 1973), Trinity Coll. Alumni Assn. N.Y. (pres. 1972-73) Clubs: Harvard (N.Y.C.). Episcopalian. Office: Trinity Coll Office of Pres 300 Summit St Hartford CT 06106-3100 Office Phone: 860-297-2093. Business E-Mail: scott.reynolds@trincoll.edu.

REYNOLDS, SHARON JONES, elementary school educator; b. Piedmont, Ala., Feb. 11, 1965; d. Norman E. and Margaret L. Jones; m. Christopher Alan Reynolds, Mar. 11, 1989; children: Christopher Britton, Jordan Lee. BS in Edn., Jacksonville State U., Ala., 1987, MS in Edn., 1991. Music, strings tchr. Gadsden City Schs., Ala., 1988—; pianist and organist Bellevue Bapt. Ch., Gadsden, Ala., 1998—2000. Music and orch. dir. Theatre Gadsden, Ala., 2008—. Pres. Jacksonville State U. Alumni Chpt., Oneonta, 1994—97. Baptist. Avocation: photography. Home: 1406 Monte Vista Dr Gadsden AL 35904 Office: RA Mitchell Elem 1501 Noccalula Rd Gadsden AL 35904

REYNOLDS, STEPHEN PHILIP, utility company executive; b. Berkeley, Calif., Jan. 5, 1948; s. Philip Elmore and Annette (Medefind) R.; m. Sharon Ann Rudd, Sept. 6, 1969; 1 child, Matthew. BA in Econs., U. Calif., Berkeley, 1970; MBA in Prodn. Mgmt., U. Oreg., 1972. Various mktg./rate positions Pacific Gas and Electric Co., San Francisco, 1967-75, sr. rate engr., 1975-77, supervising rate engr., 1977-80, mgr. rate dept., 1980-84, v.p. rates, 1984-87; pres., CEO Pacific Gas Transmission Co. (subs. Pacific Gas and Electric), 1987—98, Reynolds Energy Internat., 1998—2002; chmn., pres., CEO Puget Energy, Bellevue, Wash., 2002—09; pres., CEO Puget Energy (div. Puget Holdings LLC), 2009—. Bd. dirs. UNOVA Inc., Oregon Steel Mills Inc., InfrastruX Group, Interstate Gas of Am., Interstate Gas of Am. Found., Assn. of Northwest Gas Utilities. Contbr. numerous articles to trade publs. and profl. symposiums on rate issues. Served with Calif. Army N.G., 1970-76. Mem. Pacific Coast Gas Assn., Nat. Planning Assn. (Canadian-American Com.), Calif. Found. on Environment & Economy, San Francisco World Affairs Coun., San Francisco Engrs. Club, Commonwealth Club, World Trade Club. Office: Puget Energy 10885 NE 4th St PO Box 97034 Bellevue WA 98009-9734

REYNOLDS, TERRY RAY, curator, anthropologist, educator; d. Raymond Roberts and Harriet Pearl Reynolds. BA, U. Colo., 1962; MA, Stanford U., 1965; PhD, U. BC, 1979. Instr. Calif. State U., Northridge, 1965—68, 1972—74; sessional lectr. U. BC, Vancouver, Canada, 1968—69; dir. mus. studies U. Denver, 1989—98; curator N.Mex. State U., Las Cruces, 1998—. Cons., rschr., Boulder, Denver and Las Cruces, 1979—89. Editor: A Place as Wild as West Ever Was, 2004. Fellow, Can. Coun., 1969—72. Mem.: Am. Soc. Ethnohistory, Am. Assn. Museums (chair profl. standing com. 1994—98). Avocations: dogs, antiques. Office: NMex State U Mus PO Box 30001 MSC 3564 Las Cruces NM 88003 Office Phone: 505-646-4056. Office Fax: 505-646-1419. Business E-Mail: tereynol@nmsu.edu.

REYNOLDS, THOMAS M., former United States Representative from New York; b. Springville, NY, Sept. 3, 1950; m. Donna Reynolds; 4 children. Student, Kent State U., Ohio, 1968—69. Pres. TM Reynolds Ins. Agy.; mem. to dep. supr. Concord Town Bd., 1974—82; mem. Erie County Legislature, 1982—88, NY State Assembly from Dist. 147, 1988-98, Rep. leader, 1995—98, chmn. minority affordable housing task force, mem. corrections com.; mem. US Congress from 26th NY dist., 1999—2009, US House Ways & Means Com.; chmn. Nat. Rep. Congressional Com. (NRCC), 2003—06; sr. strategic policy adv. Nixon Peabody LLP, Washington, 2009—. Rank up to sgt. NY Air Nat. Guard, 1970—76; exec. asst. Staff NY State Assemblyman Ronald Tillis; clk. Erie County Legislature, legis. asst. to minority Rep. leader, 1987, Rep. chmn., 1990—96. Recipient Golden Apple award, US Apple Assn.; named Legislator of Yr., Am. Legis. Exch. Coun., Shooters Com. Polit. Edn.; named a Friend of Law Enforcement, NY State Sheriff's Assn. Mem.: NRA, Southtown Walleye Assn., Am. Legion, Masons. Republican. Presbyterian. Office: Nixon Peabody LLP 401 Ninth St NW Ste 900 Washington DC 20004 Office Phone: 202-585-8000. Office Fax: 202-585-8080. E-mail: treynolds@nixonpeabody.com.*

REYNOLDS, VIRGINIA EDITH, sociologist, anthropologist, educator, artist; b. Lafayette, Ind., July 3, 1941; d. Ira Hubert and Harriet G. (Robertson) Reynolds; m. Antonio G. Arroyo, 1961 (div. 1974); children: Mary-Jane R. Arroyo Young, Joanne R. Arroyo Shirley. BS with hons. in Sociology, Columbia U., 1965, MA in Sociology, 1967; postgrad., Pa. State U., 1974—84. Rsch. asst. demographic divsn. Population Coun., NYC, 1968; tchr. CUNY Borough Manhattan C.C., NYC, 1969; asst. prof. sociology and anthropology Lycoming Coll., Williamsport, Pa., 1970—75, Indiana U. Pa., 1975—2001; ret., 2001. Mem. exec. com. Assn. for Asian Studies Mid-Atlantic Region, 1997—99; Tai Chi tchr. Solo show, Indiana County Hist. Mus., Indiana, Pa., 2007, exhibited in group shows at Old Courthouse Office Gallery, 2002 (Hon. Mention award, 2002), 2003 (2d Pl. award, 2003), Centennial of the Union Street Sanctuary, 2004, Presbyn. Ch. of Punxsutawney, 2004. Singer Indiana County Singers and Ch. Choir; elected Indiana County Dem. Com., Pa., 2001—. Mem.: AAUW (chair nat. conv. 2005), Touchstone Ctr. for Crafts, Indiana (Pa.) Art Assn., Pitts. Ctr. for the Arts. Episcopalian. Avocations: tai chi, community theater musicals, international folk dancing, Chinese painting, Tibetan Buddhism. Home and Studio: 1699 Church St Indiana PA 15701 Office Phone: 724-349-4952. Personal E-mail: veren77@yahoo.com.

REYNOLDS, WILLIAM BRADFORD, lawyer; b. Bridgeport, Conn., June 21, 1942; s. William Glasgow and Nancy Bradford (DuPont) R.; m. Marguerite Lynn Morgan, June 27, 1964 (div. Feb. 1987); children: William Bradford Jr., Melissa Morgan, Kristina DuPont, Wendy Riker; m. Clare Alice Conroy, Aug. 29, 1987 (div. June 2000); 1 child, Linda Matisan; m. Barbara Lynn Wooster, July 15, 2000; children: Courtney Enright, Brooke Ashley. BA, Yale U., 1964; LLB, Vanderbilt U., 1967. Bar: N.Y. 1968, D.C. 1973, U.S. Supreme Ct. 1971. Assoc. Sullivan and Cromwell, NYC, 1967-70; asst. to Solicitor Gen. U.S. Dept. Justice, Washington, 1970-73; ptnr. Shaw, Pittman, Potts & Trowbridge, Washington, 1973-81; asst. atty. gen. Civil Rights div. U.S. Dept. Justice, Washington, 1981-88, counselor to Atty. Gen., 1987-88; ptnr. Ross & Hardies, 1989-91, Dickstein, Shapiro & Morin, 1991-94, Collier, Shannon, Rill & Scott, 1994-2000, Howrey LLP, Washington, 2000—. Chmn. Archtl. Transp. Barriers Compliance Bd., 1982-84. Editor-in-chief Vanderbilt Law Rev., 1966. Disting. scholar Free Congress Found., 1989-93, Disting. fellow Nat. Legal Ctr. for Pub. Interest, Washington, 1989-90. Mem. ABA, Fed. Bar Assn., D.C. Bar Assn., Order of Coif. Republican. Episcopalian. Home Phone: 703-731-8373; Office Phone: 202-383-6912. Business E-Mail: reynoldsw@howrey.com.

REYNOLDS, WILLIAM FRANCIS, mathematics professor; b. Boston, Jan. 31, 1930; s. William Leo and Grace Regina (Devlin) R.; m. Pauline Jane Fitzgerald, Aug. 5, 1962; children: Nancy Elizabeth, Jane Anele. AB summa cum laude, Holy Cross Coll., 1950; A.M., Harvard, 1951, PhD, 1954. Instr. Holy Cross Coll., Worcester, Mass., 1954-55; instr. Mass. Inst. Tech., Cambridge, 1955-57; asst. prof. math. Tufts U., Medford, Mass., 1957-60, assoc. prof., 1960-67, prof., 1967-98, Walker prof. math., 1970-98, prof. emeritus, 1998—. Contbr. articles to math. jours. Mem. Am. Math. Soc. Achievements include research on modular and projective representations of finite groups. Home: 3 Preble Gardens Rd Belmont MA 02478-3460 E-mail: wfr@post.harvard.edu.

REYNOLDS, WILLIAM LEROY, lawyer, educator; b. Balt., July 26, 1945; s. Austin Leroy and Doris (Hill) R.; m. Theodora Hoe, Sept. 3, 1966; children: William, Megan, Sarah. AB, Dartmouth Coll., Hanover, NH, 1967; JD, Harvard U., Cambridge, Mass., 1970. Bar: Md. 1972, US Supreme Ct. 1975. Clk. to judge U.S. Dist. Ct. Md., 1970-71; asst. prof. law U. Md., 1971-74, assoc. prof., 1974-77, prof., 1977—; of counsel DLA Piper, LLP, Balt., 1992—. Bd. dirs. Md. Jud. Inst. Author: Judicial Process in a Nutshell, 1980, 3d edit., 2002, Understanding the Conflict of Laws, 1984, 3d edit., 2002, Cases and Materials on Conflict of Laws, 1990, 2d edit., 2003, The Full Faith and Credit Clause, 2005. Mem. Am. Law Inst., Md. State Bar Assn., Am. Judicature Soc. Clubs: Serjeants' Inn, Wranglers (Balt.); St. Regis Yacht (Paul Smiths, NY), Hamilton St. Office: U Md Sch Law 500 W Baltimore St Baltimore MD 21201-1701 Business E-Mail: wreynolds@law.umaryland.edu.

REYNOLDS COOCH, NANCY D., sculptor; b. Greenville, Del., Dec. 28, 1919; d. Eugene Eleuthere and Catherine Dulcinea (Moxham) duPont; m. William Glasgow Reynolds, May 18, 1940 (dec. Jan. 1987); children: Katherine Glasgow Reynolds, William Bradford Reynolds, Mary Parminter Reynolds Savage, Cynthia duPont Reynolds Farris.; m. Edward W. Cooch, Jr., Sept. 6, 2003. Student, Goldey-Beacom Coll., Wilmington, Del., 1938. One-woman shows include Caldwell Inc., 1975, Nat. Museum of Women in Arts, 1998; exhibited in group shows at Corcoran Gallery, Washington, 1943, Soc. Fine Arts, Wilmington, 1937-38, 40-41, 48, 50, 62, 65, Rehoboth Art League, Del., 1963, NAD, NYC, 1964, Pa. Mil. Coll., Chester, 1966, Del. Art Ctr., 1967, Del. Art Mus., Wilmington, Wilmington Art Mus., 1976, Met. Mus. Art, NYC, 1977, Lever House, NYC, 1979, Nat. Mus. Women in the Arts, Washington, 1998; represented in permanent collections Wilmington Trust Co., E.I. duPont de Nemours & Co., Children's Home, Inc., Claymont, Del., Children's Bur., Wilmington, Stephenson Sci. Ctr., Vanderbilt U., Nashville, Lutheran Towers Bldg., Travelers Aid and Family Soc. Bldg., Wilmington, bronze fountain head Longwood Gardens, Kennett Square, Pa., bronze statue Brookgreen Gardens, Murrells Inlet, S.C., bronze sculpture "Veiled Lady", Nat. Mus. Women in Arts, Washington, 1998, bronze sculpture U. Del., Newark, 2001, bronze sculpture Biggs Mus., Dover, Del., 2002; contbr. articles to profl. jours. Organizer vol. svc. Del. chpt. ARC, 1938-39; chmn. Com. for Revision Del. Child Adoption Law, 1950-52; pres., bd. dirs. Children Bur. Del.; pres., trustee Children's Home, Inc.; del., past regent Gunston Hall Plantation, Lorton, Va.; mem. adv. com. Longwood Gardens, Kennett Sq., Pa.; garden and grounds com. Winterthur (Del.) Mus.; mem. rsch. staff Henry Francis DuPont Winterthur Mus., 1955-63; mem. archtl. com. U. Del., Newark. Recipient Confrerie des Chevaliers du Tastevin Clos de Vougeot-Bourgogne France, 1960; Hort. award Garden Club Am., 1964, medal of Merit, 1976, Dorothy Platt award Garden Club of Phila., 1980, Alumni medal of merit Westover Sch., Middlebury, Conn., Medal of Distinction, U. Del., 1999. Mem. Pa. Hort. Soc., Wilmington Soc. Fine Arts, Mayflower Descs., Del. Hist. Soc., Colonial Dames, League Am. Pen Women, Nat. Trust Hist. Preservation. Garden Club of Wilmington (past pres.), Garden Club of Am. (past asst. zone 4 chmn.), Vicmead Hunt Club, Greenville Country Club, Chevy Chase Club (Washington), Colony Club (NYC). Episcopalian. Address: PO Box 3919 Greenville DE 19807-0919

REYNOLDS-HUFNER, JO S. (JO S. SCHOLZE), educational administrator; b. Sarasota, Fla., Aug. 15, 1941; d. Joseph Wendling and Frances (Amsden) Scholze; m. James Hooks Reynolds, Dec. 27, 1959 (div. May 1985); children: Jamie Jo, James Burton; m. Frederick G. Hufner, Jan. 16, 1989. AA, Palm Beach Jr. Coll., 1967; BS, Fla. Atlantic U., 1968, MEd, 1973; EdD, Nova U., 1987. Tchr. J.I. Leonard HS, Lake Worth, Fla., 1968-73; dean Conniston Jr. HS, West Palm Beach, Fla., 1973-76, Congress Middle Sch., Boynton Beach, Fla., 1976-79; asst. prin. Forest Hill HS, West Palm Beach, 1979-83; prin. Palm Beach pub. sch., Fla., 1983-87, Wellington Landings Community Middle Sch., Fla., 1987-93; personnel specialist Palm Beach County pub. schs., 1993-94; prin. Adult Edn. Ctr., 1994-98, ret. 1998; ret. 1998 sch. distric Palm Beach County; sch.chmn. county secondary curriculum com., 1985-86. Contbr. poetry to various publs. Former Tchrs. Sarasota scholar, 1959; Selby Found. scholar and grantee, 1967. Mem. Nat. Assn. Secondary Sch. Prins., Palm Beach ret. educators assoc.;POA Riverbridge,"The Island" community; tchr. children's Church Gateway comm. Church; fla. Assn. Secondary Sch. Prins., Am. Assn. Sch. Adminstrs., Palm Beach C. of C. Democrat. Personal E-mail: joreynoldshufner@bellsouth.net.

REZA, FARHAD, engineering educator; married. BSc, U. Iowa, Iowa City, 1995; MS in Engring., Clarkson U., Potsdam, NY, 1996, PhD, 2001. Cert. profl. engr., State Bd. Registration, Ohio, 2002, Structural Engring. Cert. Bd., 2008. Civil engr. Morrison Knudsen Corp., Massena, NY, 2000; assoc. prof. Ohio Northern U., Ada, 2001—. Contbr. articles to profl. jour. Recipient Excellence in Edn., Ohio Mag., 2008, Prof. Henry Horldt Outstanding Tchg. award, Ohio Northern U., 2008. Mem.: ASCE, Am. Soc. Engring. Edn., Am. Concrete Inst. Achievements include research in structural health monitoring of pre-stressed concrete bridge; development of high albedo concrete; pavement quality index. Office: Ohio Northern Univ 525 S Main St Ada OH 45810 Office Fax: 419-772-2404. Business E-Mail: f-reza@onu.edu.

REZA, SHAHED, electrical engineer; Scientist Philips Med. Sys., Gainesville, Fla., 2003—. Achievements include research in nanotechnology. Home: 3111 Windsor Ridge Dr Westborough MA 01581-2364 Personal E-mail: sreza@ieee.org.

REZA, YASMINA, author, playwright; b. France; Author: (plays) Conversations After A Burial, 1987 (Moliere award for best author, SACD New Talent award, Johnson Found. award), Winter Crossing, 1990 (Moliere award for best fringe prodn., 1990), The Unexpected Man, 1995 (Moliere award for best author, Olivier award, Evening Standard award, Tony award), Art, 1995, Life x 3, 2000, A Spanish Play, 2004, God of Carnage, 2006 (Laurence Olivier award for Best New Comedy, 2009, Tony award for best play, 2009), (novels) Hammerklavier, 1997, Une Désolation, 2001, Adam Haberberg, 2003, Nulle part, 2005, Dans la luge d'Arthur Schopenhauer, 2005, L'Aube le Soir ou la Nuit, 2007, (translator) (Kafka) Metamorphosis (Moliere award for best translation); screenwriter (TV films) See You Tomorrow, Kunst, 1997, (films) Le Pique-nique de Lula Kreutz, 2000. Office: c/o Casarotto Ramsay & Associates Ltd Waverly House 7-12 Noel St London W1F 8GQ England*

REZAI, ALI, neurosurgeon, educator; MD, U. Southern Calif. Cert. neurological surgery. Intern NYU Med. Ctr., resident, fellow, dir. ctr. functional & restorative neurosurgery; fellow U. Toronto, Karolinska Inst., Stockholm; dir. ctr. for neurological restoration Cleveland Clinic, prof. neurosurgery. Editorial bd. Neurosurgery Jour. Editor: Textbook of Neuromodulation. Recipient Innovation award, NorTech, 2005, Innovator of Yr., Cleveland Clinic, 2007; named one of the Best Doctors in America, Guide to America's Top Doctors, 2001—08. Fellow: Inst. of Physics, Congress Neurological Surgeons (exec. bd. mem.); mem.: Soc. U. Neurosurgeons, Soc. for Neuroscience, Am. Soc. Stereotactic & Functional Neurosurgery (sec. & treas.), North Am. Neuromodulation Soc., Am. Assn. Neurological Surgeons (Investigator award 1998), Alpha Omega Alpha. Office: Cleveland Clinic Main Campus 9500 Euclid Ave MC-S31 Cleveland OH 44195 Office Phone: 216-444-4720.*

REZAIE, BAHMAN, engineering educator, researcher; PhD in Elec. Engring., Southern Meth. U., Dallas, 1984. Instr. Southern Meth. U., 1981—83; prof. & chair, engring. dept. St. Mary's U., San Antonio, 1983—. Named Piper Prof., Minnie Stevens Piper Found., 2001. Office: St Mary's Univ One Camino Santa Maria San Antonio TX 78228 Business E-Mail: brezaie@stmarytx.edu.

REZK, NASER LABEEB, biochemist, researcher; b. Meet Masoud, Egypt, Feb. 21, 1961; s. Labeeb Hasan and Atyate Hasanan Rezk; m. Nesrin Salah Shrsher, Sept. 1, 1991; children: Salma Abdelnaser, Omar Abdelnaser, Ali Abdelnaser. BSc in Chemistry, Monofia U., Egypt, 1983, MSc in Biochemistry, 1994; PhD, Tanta U., Egypt, 2007. Formulation scientist Trimeris Biopharmaceuticals, Durham, NC; from rsch. tech. to rsch. assoc. prof. U. NC, Chapel Hill, 2000—07, rsch. assoc. prof., 2007—. Recipient Chancellor's award, U. NC, 2006, Excellence Innovation award, NC Gov., 2006, Innovation award, 2006. Mem.: ACS (assoc. Membership award 2005), Egyptian Chem. Soc. (assoc. Membership award 2000), Toastmasters. Home: 6220 Dawn Dr Hurdle Mills NC 27541 Office: Univ NC 2405 Kerr Hall CB 7360 Chapel Hill NC 27599 Office Fax: 919-962-0644; Home Fax: 919-962-0644. Personal E-mail: naser21@gmail.com. Business E-Mail: naser2@unc.edu.

REZNICK, RICHARD HOWARD, pediatrician; b. Chgo., Oct. 31, 1939; s. Louis and Mae Reznick; m. Barbara Ann Glantz, June 20, 1965; children: Steven L., Alicia T., Scott M., Stacey R. BS, U. Ill., 1961; MD, Loyola U., Chgo., 1965. Diplomate Am. Bd. Pediatrics. Resident in pediat. Michael Reese Hosp., Chgo., 1966-68; pediatrician USAF, Homestead AFB, Fla., 1968-70; pediatrician pvt. practice Winnetka, Ill., 1970—71, Scottsdale, Ariz., 1971—. Pres. med. staff Phoenix Children's Hosp., 1990-93, bd. dirs. 1990-94. Capt. USAF, 1968-70. Fellow Am. Acad. Pediatrics (treas. Ariz. chpt. 1982-84); mem. Ariz. Med. Assn., Phoenix Pediatric Soc. (treas. 1976-77), Maricopa County Med. Soc. Avocations: aerobics, bicycling, gardening, classical music, collecting stamps. Office: Papago Buttes Pediatric Ctr 8573 E San Alberto Ste E100 Scottsdale AZ 85258-4318 Office Phone: 480-778-1732.

REZNICK, STEVEN MICHAEL, orthopedic surgeon, educator; b. Washington, 1954; 3 children. BS, U. Md., 1975; MD, George Washington U., 1979; MBA, Columbia U., 2000. Diplomate Am. Bd. Orthopedic Surgery. Resident in gen. surgery George Washington U., 1979-81; resident in orthop. surgery U. Mich., Ann Arbor, 1981-84; clin. instr. orthopedic surgery UCLA Sch. Medicine, 1988-94. Sr. aviation med. examiner FAA, 1985-87; talk show host KGIL-Radio, L.A., 1987-90. Mem. Calif. Rep. Party, Calif. Rep. Assembly, bd. dirs. Palm Springs chpt., 1996-98. Fellow Internat. Coll. Surgeons, Am. Coll. Surgeons, Am. Acad. Orthopedic Surgeons, Beta Gamma Sigma Honor Soc. Avocation: commercial pilot. Home: PO Box 101 Somers NY 10589 E-mail: smr50@columbia.edu.

REZNIKOV, VLADIMIR LVOVICH (VADIM LESNIKOV), historian, playwright; b. Donetzk, Ukraine, May 26, 1937; s. Lev Davidovich Reznikov and Sofia Semyonovna Baskina; m. Natalya Klueva, Nov. 4, 1994; children: Lev, Michael, Sonya. MS in History, Moscow State Pedagogic U., 1962; PhD in History, Russain Acad. Scis., 1972; MS in Screenplay Writing (hon.), State Inst. Cinematography, Moscow, 1973. Sci. editor Oriental Book Publishers, Moscow, 1962—69; dept. editor Asia and Africa Today, Moscow, 1977—81; sr. rsch. fellow Inst. Oriental Studies of Russian Acad. of Scis., Moscow, 1969—97, 1981—97; freelance playwright scholar of art history, 1997—. Author: (screenplays) Encounter, 1971, Forgive me, Vietnam, 1971, Personal Case, 1971, Nature and Society, 1980, Voice of the Centuries, 1975, Use of Isotope Control Devices in Automatization of Production Processes, 1975, (plays) True Story of Buratino or the Song of Triumphant Love, 2006, First Performance, 2006, (books) Policy of Caeser's Germany in Oceania, 1975; editor: India - Country and People, 1967 (Hon. Diploma Geog. Soc. of USSR, 1973). Mem.: Journalist Soc. of Russia, Am. Taekwondo Assn. (2d Degree Black belt). Avocation: Tae Kwon Do. Personal E-mail: nklueva@yahoo.com.

REZNYKOV, ILLYA IGOREVICH, mathematician, application developer; b. Kiev, Ukraine, Nov. 20, 1978; s. Igor Fedorovych Reznykov and Iryna Oleksandrivna (Nekrot) Reznykova; m. Polina V. Deineko; 1 child, Diana. MS in Math. (hon.), Kiev Taras Shevchenko U., Ukraine, 1999, PhD in Math., 2002; MS in Computer Sci. (hon.), Nat. Tech. U., Ukraine, 2000. Cert. master's degree Internat. Sci.-Tng. Ctr. UNESCO PII-IIP, 2000. Programmer IKC5 ltd., Kiev, 1994—98, chief computer tech. dept., 2002—; project leader Old City, Kiev, 1998—99. Contbr. scientific papers. Mem.: Kyïv Math. Soc. Avocations: swimming, photography, ballroom dancing, cooking. Office: IKC5 ltd Bldg 5 Ste 2 Krasnogvardeyskaya Str Kiev 02660 Ukraine Office Fax: 38 044 292 6076. Personal E-mail: illya@reznykov.kiev.ua. Business E-Mail: illya.reznykov@ikc5.com.ua.

RHAMES, VING (IRVING), actor; b. NYC, May 12, 1961; m. Valerie Scott, 1994 (div. 1999); m. Deborah Reed, Dec. 25, 2000; children: Tiffany, Rainbow, Freedom. Grad., Julliard Sch. Drama. Actor (Broadway plays) The Winter Boys, 1984; (films) Native Son, 1986, Patty Hearst, 1988, Casualties of War, 1989, The Long Walk Home, 1990, Jacob's Ladder, 1990, Flight of the Intruder, 1991, Homicide, 1991, Stop! Or My Mom Will Shoot, 1992, The People Under the Stairs, 1992, Dave, 1993, The Saint of Fort Washington, 1993, Bound By Honor Blood In Blood Out, 1993, Pulp Fiction, 1994, Drop Squad, 1994, Kiss of Death, 1995, Ed McBain's 87th Precinct, 1995, Mission: Impossible, 1996, Striptease, 1996, Con Air, 1997, Rosewood, 1997, Dangerous Ground, 1997, The Split, 1998, Out of Sight, 1998, Body Count, 1998, Entrapment, 1999, Bringing Out the Dead, 1999, Mission Impossible II, 2000, (voice) Final Fantasy: The Spirits Within, 2001, Baby Boy, 2001, Lilo & Stitch (voice only), 2002, Dark Blue, 2002, Undisputed, 2002, (voice) Stitch! The Movie, 2003, Back in the Day, 2004, Dawn of the Dead, 2004, Mission: Impossible III, 2006, Idlewild, 2006, Animal 2, 2007, I Now Pronounce You Chuck and Larry, 2007, The Goods: Live Hard, Sell Hard, 2009; (TV films) Go Tell It On the Mountain, 1985, Rising Son, 1990, When You Remember Me, 1990, Amerique en otage L', 1991, Terror on Track 9, 1992, Deadly Whispers, 1995, Don King: Only in America, 1997 (Golden Globe for best performance by an actor in a mini-series or motion picture made for TV 1998), American Tragedy, 2000, Holiday Heart, 2000, Little John, 2002, RFK, 2002, Sins of the Father, 2002; (TV series) Another World, 1986, Men, 1989, UC: Undercover, 2001; TV appearances include Miami Vice, 1985, 87, Crime Story, 1986, Tour of Duty, 1987, Spenser: For Hire, 1988, The Equalizer, 1989, ER, 1994, 95, 96, New York Undercover, 1995, The District, 2002, 03, The Adventures of Jimmy Neutron: Boy Genius, 2003. Office: William Morris Agy 151 S El Camino Dr Beverly Hills CA 90212-2775

RHEAULT, KEITH W., state official, school system administrator; m. Denise Rheault; 4 children. BS, ND State U., 1976, MS in Agrl. Edn., 1980; PhD in Agrl. Edn., Iowa State U., 1985. With Nev. Dept. Edn., 1986—, agriculture edn. cons., state FFA adv., asst. dir. to dir. Office of Occupational and Continuing Edn., dep. supt. for Instructional, Rsch. and Evaluative Svcs., supt. pub. instrn., 2004—. Adj. prof. Agrl. Engring. Dept. Iowa State U. Officer USAR, 1977—85. Office: Nev Dept Edn 700 E Fifth St Carson City NV 89701-5096 Office Phone: 775-687-9217. Office Fax: 775-687-5660, 775-687-9101. E-mail: krheault@doe.nv.gov.*

RHEE, GWANG HOON, mechanical engineer, educator; b. Goseonggun, Gyung Nam, Republic of Korea, Mar. 18, 1968; s. Pan Soo and Young Ja (Kim) Rhee; m. Mi Kyung Rhee, Jan. 11, 1998; children: Gyung Goo, Yena. BA magna cum laude, Korea Advanced Inst. Sci. and Tech., Daejeon, 1993, MA, 1995, PhD, 2000. Rsch. asst. Korea Advanced Inst. Sci. and Tech., Daejeon, Republic of Korea, 1995—2000, rschr., 2000—01; prof. dept. mech. and info. engring. U. Seoul, Republic of Korea, 2001—, chmn. dept. mech. and info. engring., 2003—05, vice dean coll. engring., 2007—. Lectr. Hoseo U., Asan, Chung Nam, 1997—98; invited rsch. fellow Nat. Aerospace Lab., Tokyo, 1996; rschr. Samsung Motor Co., Suwon, Gyung Gi, 1995—98. Trustee Korean Soc. Indoor Environ., 2008—. Cpl. Korean Army, 1988—89. Recipient Citation, Small and Medium Bus. Adminstrn., 2004, Disting. Svc. award, Seoul Coun. Industry-Acad. Coop., 2004. Fellow: Internat. Soc. Ondol (v.p. 2008—); mem.: Korean Soc. Mech. Engring. (dir. 2008—), Soc. Air-Conditioning and Refrigerating Engring. Korea (life), Korean Soc. Mech. Engrs. (life Best Paper award 1999), Korean Soc. Indoor Environ. (dir. 2008—). Achievements include patents in field. Home: Unit 103 301 Youngpoong Madlevill APT 801 Sinnae Dong Joongnang Gu Seoul 131 865 Republic of Korea Office: Univ Seoul 90 Jeonnong Dong Dongdaemun Gu Seoul 130 743 Republic of Korea Office Fax: 82222105575. Personal E-mail: ghrhee@gmail.com. Business E-Mail: ghrhee@uos.ac.kr.

RHEE, MICHELLE A., school system administrator, former educational association administrator; b. Ann Arbor, Mich., Dec. 25, 1969; d. Shang and Inza Rhee; m. Kevin Huffman (div.); children: Starr, Olivia. BA in Govt., Cornell U., 1992; MA in Pub. Policy, John F. Kennedy Sch. Govt., Harvard U. Joined Teach For Am., 1992; tchr. Harlem Park Cmty. Sch., Balt., 1993—96; founder, pres., CEO The New Tchr. Project (TNTP), NYC, 1997—2007; chancellor DC Pub. Schs., 2007—. Adv. bd. Nat. Coun. Tchr. Quality, Nat. Ctr. for Alternative Certification, Project REACH, U. Phoenix Sch. Edn. Ex-officio mem. Kennedy Ctr. Bd. Trustees. Recipient Trinity Washington Woman of Genius award, 2007; named one of 12 People to Watch, Newsweek mag., 2008. Office: DC Pub Schs 825 N Capitol St, NE Washington DC 20002 Office Phone: 202-442-5885. Office Fax: 202-442-5026. E-mail: michelle.rhee@k12.dc.us.*

RHEIN, KEVIN A., bank executive; B in Psychology, U. Ill.; MBA, U. Chgo. Regional dir. Citicorp Mortgage; dir., retail branch ops., dir., retail banking Citibank Ariz., Ariz.; pres., CEO Wells Fargo Card Svcs. Inc., 1999—2004; exec. v.p. Wells Fargo Bank, 2004—09; exec. v.p., Card Svcs. & Consumer Lending Wells Fargo & Co., 2009—. Mem. consumer adv. com. Federal Reserve Bank. Bd. dirs. Ctr. Fin. Svcs. Innovation, First Children's Fin. Office: Wells Fargo & Co 420 Montgomery St San Francisco CA 94163 Office Phone: 866-249-3302. Office Fax: 651-450-4033.*

RHEINECK, WENDY LYNN, science educator; b. Milw., Mar. 8, 1965; d. John Walter and Diane Lee (Goodrum) Hufnagel; m. Patrick Jay Huberty (div.); children: Nicholas Huberty, Joseph Huberty, Jessica Huberty; m. John Richards Rheineck, Aug. 10, 2001. BA, San Diego State Coll., 1993; MA, Cardinal Stritch Coll., Milw., 2001. Substitute tchr. Miller Sch., Escondido, Calif., 1993—98, Merton Sch., Wis., 1998—99, instrnl. asst., 1999—2001; sci. and math. tchr. Merton Intermediate Sch., 2001. Graduation advisor Merton Sch., 2001—, WebGrader liaison, 2003—, mem. staff devel. com., 2003—. Home: N 74 W29117 Winzer Rd Hartland WI 53029 Office: Merton Sch W28320 Sussex Rd Merton WI 53056

RHEINGOLD, TED, Internet company executive; BA in Internat. Rels., U. Penn., 1992. Adminstrv. dir. Calif. Coun. Internat. Trade, San Francisco; web designer, software engr. Preview Travel (now Travelocity.com); sr. web application developer Voquette, Inc. (now Semagix); founder OneMatchFire.com, San Francisco, 2002; founder, CEO Dogster.com, San Francisco, 2004—, Catster.com, 2004—. Fellow Internat. Devel. Exch. Office: Dogster Inc Ste 350 555 De Haro St San Francisco CA 94107 Office Phone: 415-934-0400. Office Fax: 415-864-6261. E-mail: ted@dogster.com.

RHEINHARDT, RICHARD, ecologist, educator; s. Richard M. and Dorothy A. Rheinhardt; m. Martha C. Craig; children: Kathryn R., Lydia. Degree Bus. Mgmt., Coll. William and Mary, Williamsburg, Va., 1976, MS in Biology, 1981; PhD, Va. Inst. Marine Sci., Coll. William and Mary, 1991. Rsch. asst. prof. East Carolina U., Greenville, NC, 1994—99, rsch. assoc. prof., 1999—. Contbr. articles to profl. jours., chapters to books. Numerous grants from state and fed. agys., 1994—. Mem.: Am. Inst. Biol. Sci., Estuarine Rsch. Fedn., Southern Appalachian Bot. Soc., Soc. Wetland Scientist, Torrey Bot. Club. Achievements include research in wetlands and plant ecology; restoration ecology. Avocations: scuba diving, swimming. Office: E Carolina Univ Greenville NC 27858

RHEINS, CARL JEFFREY, historian, educator; b. Cin., Sept. 17, 1945; s. Joseph Melvin and Gertrude (Mandell) R.; m. Brenda Dale Gevertz, July 8, 1979; children: Jason Gabriel, Jaclyn Gail. BS with distinction, U. Wis., 1967; MA, SUNY, Albany, 1970; PhD, SUNY, Stony Brook, 1978. Lectr. Judaic studies SUNY, Stony Brook, 1974-78, asst. to provost, 1978-80, 81-86; dir. acad. affairs Nat. Found. Jewish Culture, NYC, 1980-81; asst. dean Adelphi U., Garden City, NY, 1986-87, assoc. dean, 1987, exec. asst. to pres., 1987-90, dean student life and devel., 1990-92, v.p. student life and devel., 1992-97, v.p. external affairs and comty. rels., 1997—99; exec. dir., CEO Yivo Inst. for Jewish Rsch., NYC, 1999—. Bd. dirs. Coalition on Higher Edn., Jewish Cmty. Rels. Coun., NYC; Delegate (NGO) Vilinius Internat. Forum on Holocaust-Era Looted Cultural Assets, 2000. Contbg. author: Yearbook of the Leo Baeck Inst., 1978, 80, 81; co-editor: Jewish Almanac, 1980 (dual main selection Jewish Book Club Am. 1981). Mem. nat. governing coun. Am. Jewish Congress, NYC, 1986-87, 1st v.p. Suffolk County, NY, 1985-87; bd. govs. LI region Am. Jewish Com., NY, 1984-85; judge Nat. Jewish Book Awards, 1993, 94, 2005-08. Summer fellow NEH, 1987; recipient Frank Cassell Meml. award, 1994. Mem. Garden City C. of C. (bd. dirs. 1997—99), Phi Kappa Phi, Phi Alpha Theta, Alpha Epsilon Pi, Sigma Beta. Office: YIVO Inst for Jewish Rsch 15 W 16th St New York NY 10011-6301 Office Phone: 212-294-6126. Business E-Mail: crheins@yivo.cjh.org.

RHEINSTEIN, PETER HOWARD, healthcare company executive, physician, lawyer; b. Cleve., Sept. 7, 1943; s. Franz Joseph Rheinstein and Hede Henrietta (Neheimer) Rheinstein Lerner; m. Miriam Ruth Weissman, Feb. 22, 1969; 1 child, Jason Edward. BA with high honors, Mich. State U., 1963, MS, 1964; MD, Johns Hopkins U., 1967; JD, U. Md., 1973. Bar: Md. 1973, DC 1980, US Supreme Ct. 2000; diplomate Am. Bd. Family Medicine; cert. added qualifications in geriatric medicine. Intern USPHS Hosp., San Francisco, 1967-68; resident in internal medicine USPHS Hosp. (now Homewood Hosp. Ctr.), Balt., 1968-70, lt., 1967—68, lt. comdr., 1968—70; instr. internal medicine U. Md., Balt., 1970-73; med. dir. extended care facilities CHC Corp., Balt., 1972-74; dir. drug advt. and labeling divsn. FDA, Rockville, Md., 1974-82, acting dep. dir. Office Drugs, 1982-83, acting dir. Office Drugs, 1983-84, dir. Office Drug Stds., 1984-90, dir. medicine staff Office Health Affairs, 1990-99; sr. v.p. for med. and clin. affairs Cell Works, Inc., Balt., 1999—2004; pres. Severn Health Solutions, 2000—. Bd. dirs. Marnac, Inc., Dallas, 2003-09; chmn. FDA Bur. Drugs Com. on Advanced Sci. Edn., 1978-86, Rsch. in Human Subjects Com., 1990-92; adj. prof. forensic medicine George Washington U., 1974-76; WHO cons. on drug regulation Nat. Inst. for Control Pharm. and Biol. Products, China, 1981-90; advisor on essential drugs WHO, 1985-90; FDA del. to US Pharmacopeial Conv., 1985-90, coord. com. for assessment and transfer of tech. NIH, 1990-99, mem. health care fin. adminstrn. tech. adv. com., 1990-98, Nat. Adv. Coun. on Healthcare Policy, Rsch. and Evaluation, 1990-99, Healthy People 2000/2010 Steering Com., 1990-99, US Preventive Svcs. Task Force, 1990-96, CDC Nat. Task Force on Cmty. Preventive Svcs., 1996-99, Nat. Task Force on CME Industry/Provider Collaboration, 1992—, ann. meeting chmn., 2003, mem. com. chmn., 2002-05, US Adopted Names Coun. Rev. Bd., 2004-05, US Adopted Names Coun., 2006—; cons. in legal medicine and regulatory affairs, 1999—; mem. adv. bd. Nat. Commn. for Cert. of CME Profls., 2006-; del. US pharmacopeial convention Md. State Med. Soc., 2008-. Co-author: Human Organ Transplantation, 1987; spl. editl. advisor Good Housekeeping Guide to Medicine and Drugs, 1977-80, Md. State Med. Soc. Del. to US Pharmacy Ofcl. Convention, 2008-; mem. editl. bd. Legal Aspects Med. Practice, 1981-89, Drug Info. Jour., 1982-86, 91-95; pub. Discovery Medicine, 2001-; contbr. articles to profl. jours. V.p. Intercultural Friends Found., 1998—. Recipient Commendable Svc. award, FDA, 1981, Group award of merit, 1983, 1988, Group Commendable Svc. award, 1989, 1992—93, 1995, 1999, Commr.'s Spl. citation, 1993; NIH Nat. Cancer Inst. SBIR grant, 2001. Fellow: Am. Acad. Family Physicians, Am. Coll. Legal Medicine (bd. govs. 1983—93, chmn. fin. com. 1985—88, treas. 1985—88, chmn. publs. com. 1988—93, chmn. fin. com. 1990—91, treas. 1990—91, jud. coun. 1993—95, Pres.'s awards 1985, 1986, 1989—91, 1993, Gold medal 2003); mem.: APHA, AMA (life; ho. of dels. 2002—), ABA, Assn. Clin. Rsch. Profls., Acad. Medicine Wash., Math. Assn. Am., Md. Bar Assn., Johns Hopkins Med. and Surg. Assn., Nat. Assn. Ret. Fed. Employees (life), Soc. Indsl. and Applied Math. (life), Balt. City Med. Soc., Md. State Med. Soc. (del. to US Pharmacopeial Convention 2008—), Fed. Bar Assn. (chmn. food and drug com. 1976—79, Disting. Svc. award 1977), Drug Info. Assn. (bd. dirs. 1982—90, pres. 1984—85, v.p. 1986—87, pres. 1988—89, chmn. ann. meeting 1991, steering com. Ams. 1991—2004, chmn. ann. meeting 1994, Outstanding Svc. award 1990), Am. Bd. Legal Medicine (treas. 2003—), Acad. Pharm. Physicians and Investigators (trustee 1999—2003, pres. Washington-Balt. chpt. 1999—2003, v.p. AMA rels. 1999—, sec./treas. 2008—09, pres. elect 2009—), FDA Alumni Assn., Fed. Exec. Inst. Alumni Assn. (life), Mensa (life), U. Md. Alumni Assn. (life), Johns Hopkins U. Alumni Assn. (life), Mich. State U. Honors Coll. Alumni Assn. (bd. dirs. 1998—2001, pres. 2000—01), Mich. State U. Alumni Assn. (life), John Hopkins Club, Annapolis Yacht Club, Chartwell Golf and Country Club, Delta Theta Phi (life). Achievements include development of precedents for FDA regulation of prescription drug promotion, initiated FDA's first patient medication information program; implemented Drug Price Competition and Patent Term Restoration Act of 1984, authored medication goals for Healthy People 2000 and 2010. Avocations: boating, exercise, real estate. Home and Office: 621 Holly Ridge Rd Severna Park MD 21146-3520 Home Phone: 410-647-9501; Office Phone: 410-647-9500. Office Fax: 410-647-6135. Personal E-mail: phr@jhu.edu.

RHETT, HASKELL EMERY SMITH, educational association administrator; b. Evanston, Ill., Aug. 29, 1936; s. Haskell Smith and Eunice Campbell (Emery) R.; m. Roberta Teel Oliver, Sept. 9, 1961 (div. 1973); children: Kathryn Emery, Cecily Coffin; m. Anita Leone, May 30, 1983 (div. 1993); m. Janet Lee Rollings, Nov. 15, 1997. Diploma, Gov. Dummer Acad., 1954; AB, Hamilton Coll., 1958; MA, Cornell U., 1967, PhD, 1968. Asst. to the pres. Hamilton Coll., Clinton, NY, 1961-64; rsch. asst. Cornell U., Ithaca, NY, 1964-66; rsch. assoc. U. London, 1966-67; dir. program devel. Ednl. Testing Svc., Princeton, NJ, 1967-73; asst. chancellor NJ Dept. Higher Edn., Trenton, 1973—85; v.p. The Coll. Bd., NYC, 1985-90; pres. The Woodrow Wilson Nat. Fellowship Found., Princeton, NJ, 1990—97, pres. emeritus, 1997—. Author: Going to College in New Jersey, 1978; contbg. author: Government's Role in Supporting College Savings, 1990. Commr. NJ Pub. Broadcasting Authority, Trenton, 1983—85; mem. Nat. Task Force on Student Aid Problems, Washington, 1974—75, Gov.'s Adv. Panel on Higher Edn. Restructuring, State of NJ, 1994; trustee Dominican U. of Calif., San Rafael, 1990—99, 2001—07, William Alexander Procter Found., 1998—2002, The Coll. of NJ, 1992—97, vice-chmn., 1995—97, chmn., 1997; trustee The Gov.'s Acad., Mass., 1993—, Heartland Edn. Cmty.,

Ohio, 1992—97, Forums Inst. for Pub. Policy, NJ, 1999—2009, treas., 2000—05, chmn., 2005—09, Woodrow Wilson Presdl. Libr. Found., 2009—; del. Dem. Nat. Conv., Miami, 1972; sr. warden Trinity Episcopal Ch., Princeton, 1988—92, vestryman, 1979—82, 1987—88, 2001—04; dep. Gen. Conv., Detroit, 1988, Phoenix, 1991; mem. standing com. Episcopal Diocese of NJ, 1992—97; bd. dirs. Reach the World, Inc., NYC, 1998—2001, Trenton After Sch. Program, 1989—93, 2001—04. Lt. USNR, 1958—61, Heavy Attack Squadron 5 (VAH-5), USS Forrestal. Nat. Def. fellow US Govt., 1966-67, Eliot-Winant fellow Brit.-Am. Assocs., 1982, fellow Kennedy Sch. Harvard U., 1985, Wilson Coll., Princeton U., 1993-97. Mem. Nat. Assn. State Scholarship and Grant Programs (pres. 1976-78), Princeton Officers Soc., Waynesboro Country Club (Va.). Avocations: travel, tennis, golf, sailing, classic automobiles. Home: 615 Elk Mountain Rd Afton VA 22920

RHEUBAN, KAREN SCHULDER, pediatric cardiologist, educator; b. Jamiaca, NY, 1949; married; 3 children. MD summa cum laude, Ohio State U. Coll. Medicine, 1974. Diplomate Am. Bd. Pediat., Am. Bd. Pediat. Cardiology. Intern pediat. U. Va., Charlottesville, 1974—75, resident pediat. cardiology, 1975—78, fellowship, 1978—80, prof. pediat. cardiology, 1980—, assoc. dean continuing med. edn., 1990—, med. dir. office of telemedicine. Contbr. articles to profl. jours. Recipient Elizabeth Zintl Leadership award, U. Va. Women's Ctr., 2005; named one of Best Dr.'s in America, Best Dr.'s Inc.; named to Nat. Libr. Med. tribute to women physicians, 2003. Fellow: Am. Coll. Cardiology, Am. Acad. Pediat.; mem.: Am. Telemedicine Assn. Achievements include research in congenital heart disease; telemedicine applied to rural health care; tele-echocardiography. Mailing: UVA Main Hosp PO Box 800707 Charlottesville VA 22908 Office Phone: 434-924-2481. Business E-Mail: ksr5g@virginia.edu.

RHEUDE, ELIZABETH ANNE, music educator; b. Canandaigua, NY, May 24, 1955; d. Gregory and Lorraine Rheude. BS in Music Edn., Ind. State U., Terre Haute, 1977; MusM in Clarinet Performance, Mich. State U., East Lansing, 1979. Cert. Music Tchrs. Nat. Assn., 2000. Assoc. prof. clarinet U. ND, Grand Forks, 1986—, co founder, artistic codir., festival women arts, 1998—; clarinet instr. Ind. State U., Terre Haute, 1986. Founder, artistic dir. Nothern Plains Clarinet Symposium, Grand Forks, 1998—. Musician: International Clarinet Association conventions, Idaho Montana Clarinet Symposia, (performer) Michigan Symposium of New Music for the Clarinet, (recital) Great Lakes Clarinet Celebration, 2001, (performer, cd recording) Music from the International Clarinet Association, (cd recording) Kaleidoscope: Music of James Fry. Recipient NC Music Tchr. of Yr., 2000, Tchr. of Yr., Greater Grand Forks Music Tchrs. Assn., 2000. Mem.: Coll. Music Soc., Nat. Assn. Coll. Wind and Percussion Instructors (state chairperson 1992—93), Music Tchrs. Nat. Assn. (nd faculty rep. 1994—95, woodwind repertoire cons. 1995—97, coord., nat. collegiate chamber music competition 1997—99), Internat. Clarinet Assn. (nd state chairperson 1993—2008), Pi Beta Kappa (hon.). Home: 4600 S Washington St 304 Grand Forks ND 58201 Office: Music Dept Univ ND Box 7125 Grand Forks ND 58202 Office Phone: 701-772-8821. Business E-Mail: elizabeth_rheude@und.nodak.edu.

RHEW, PERRY JAMES, federal judge; BS in Psychology/Biology, Southeast Mo. State U., Cape Girardeau, 1980; JD, UMKC Sch. Law, Kansas City, 1983. Lic. Mo., 1983. Pub. defender State of Mo., Kennett, 1983-84; asst. prosecuting atty. Dunklin County, Kennett, Mo., 1985-86; prosecuting atty., 1986-90; adjunct prof. Bus. Law Southeast Mo. State U., Cape Girardeau, 1987-89; assoc. circuit judge 35th Judicial Circuit, Kennett, Mo., 1990; US adminstrv. law judge Social Security Adminstrn., Cleve., 1997—2005; mng. adminstrv. law judge Office of Medicare Hearings and Appeals, US Dept. Health & Human Services, Cleve., 2005, acting chief adminstrv. law judge, 2005—06, chief U.S. adminstrv. law judge, 2006—. Bd. dirs. Family Counseling Ctr., Kennett, Mo., 1986-90, Stapleton Detoxification Ctr., Kennett, Mo., 1986-90, Ctr. for Family Resources, Malden, Mo., 1986-90, Cmty. Caring Counsel, Kennett, Mo., 1993-2005. Author: eight published plays. Elected prosecuting atty., 1986, elected assoc. circuit judge, Dunklin Co. Mo., Kennett, 1990, 94. Recipient Young Alumni Merit award Southeast Mo. State U., Cape Girardeau, Mo., 1993, Denman Dist. Evangelism award United Meth. Ch., 1993. Mem. Mo. Bar Assn., Dunklin County Bar, Lions Club Internat. Mem. United Meth. Ch. Avocations: writing, composer, singing, cooking. Office: Cleveland Regional Office Office of Medicare Hearings & Appeals 200 Public Sq PB Tower Suite 1300 Cleveland OH 44112 Office Phone: 216-615-4000. Office Fax: 216-615-4115.*

RHIEW, FRANCIS CHANGNAM, radiologist, physician; b. Korea, Dec. 3, 1938; came to U.S., 1967, naturalized, 1977; s. Byung Kyun and In Sil (Lee) R.; m. Kay Kyungja Chang, June 11, 1967; children: Richard C., Elizabeth. BS, Seoul Nat. U., 1960, MD, 1964. Cert. Am. Bd. Nuclear Medicine. Intern St. Mary's Hosp., Waterbury, Conn., 1967-68; resident in radiology and nuclear medicine L.I.U.-Queens Hosp. Ctr., NY, 1968-71; instr. radiology W. Va. U. Sch. Medicine, Morgantown, 1971-73; mem. staff Mercy Hosp. and Moses Taylor Hosp. Scranton, Pa., 1973—; also dir. nuclear medicine; clin. instr. Temple U., 1987—. Pres. Radiol. Consultants, Inc., 1984—, F.C.R. Co. Chmn., CEO Francis and Kay Rhiew Charitable Found. With M.C., Korean Army, 1964-67. Recipient Minister of Health and Welfare award, 1963. Mem. AMA, Soc. Nuclear Medicine, Radiol. Soc. N.Am., Am. Coll. Nuclear Medicine, Am. Coll. Radiology, Am. Inst. Ultra Sound, Country Club Scranton, Pres.'s Club U. Scranton, Elks. Home: 14 Lakeside Dr Clarks Summit PA 18411-9419 Office: 746 Jefferson Ave Scranton PA 18510-1624

RHIMES, SHONDA, producer, director, writer; b. Chgo., Jan. 13, 1970; 1 adopted child, Harper. BA in English, Dartmouth Coll., Hanover, NH, 1991; MFA, U. So. Calif., 1994. Dir., writer: (films) Blossoms and Veils, 1998; writer Crossroads, 2002; The Princess Diaries 2: Royal Engagement, 2004; exec. prodr., writer: (TV series) Grey's Anatomy, 2005— (Norman Felton Prodr. of Yr. award in Episodic TV, Prodrs. Guild of America, 2007, NAACP Image award for Outstanding Writing in Drama Series, 2007, 2008, Golden Globe award, Best Drama TV Series, 2007). Named one of The World's Most Influential People, TIME mag., 2007, 40 Under 40, Advt. Age, 2007; named to Power 150, Ebony mag., 2008. Office: c/o ABC TV 500 S Buena Vista St Burbank CA 91521-4551

RHIND, JAMES THOMAS, lawyer; b. Chgo., July 21, 1922; s. John Gray and Eleanor (Bradley) R.; m. Laura Haney Campbell, Apr. 19, 1958; children: Constance Rhind Robey, James Campbell, David Scott. Student, Hamilton Coll., 1940-42; AB cum laude, Ohio State U., 1944; LL.B. cum laude, Harvard U., 1950. Bar: Ill. bar 1950. Japanese translator U.S. War Dept., Tokyo, 1946-47; congl. liaison Fgn. Operations Adminstrn., Washington, 1954; atty. Bell, Boyd & Lloyd, Chgo., 1950-53, 55—, ptnr., 1958-92, chmn. exec. com., 1976—88, of counsel, 1993—. Bd. dirs. Kewaunee Scientific Corp., Statesville, NC. Commr. Gen. Assembly United Presbyn. Ch., 1963; life trustee Ravinia Festival Assn., Hamilton Coll., Clinton, N.Y., U. Chgo.; chmn. Cook County Young Republican Orgn., 1957; Ill. Young Rep. nat. committeeman, 1957-58; v.p., mem. bd. govs. United Rep. Fund Ill., 1965-84; pres. Ill. Childrens Home and Aid Soc., 1971-73, life trustee; bd. dirs. E.J. Dalton Youth Center, 1966- 69; governing mem. Chgo. Symphony Orch., Chgo.; mem. Ill. Arts Council, 1971-75; mem. exec. com. div. Met. Mission and Ch. Extension Bd., Chgo. Presbytery, 1966-68; trustee Presbyn. Homes, W. Clement and Jessie V. Stone Found., Served with M.I. AUS, 1943-46. Mem. ABA, Ill. Bar Assn., Chgo. Bar Assn. (bd. mgrs. 1967-69), Fed. Bar Assn., Chgo. Coun. on Fgn. Rels., Japan Am. Soc. Chgo., Lawyers Club Chgo., Phi Beta Kappa, Sigma Phi. Clubs: Chicago, Glen View (Ill.), U. Club Chgo., Commercial (Chgo.), Economic (Chgo.), U. Club Chgo. Home: 830 Normandy Ln Glenview IL 60025-3210 Office: Bell Boyd & Lloyd 3 First National Plz 70 W Madison St Ste 3200 Chicago IL 60602-4244 Office Phone: 312-372-1121.

RHINEHART, ALYCIA CELESTE, principal; b. NYC, Dec. 8, 1959; d. James Wilfred Osborne and Shirley Ann Peace; 1 child, Tifany Royalyn. BS in Edn., CUNY, 2002, MS in Edn., 2005; MS in Administrn., Coll. St. Rose, Albany, 2007—. Dir. Bklyn Prep. Sch., NYC, 1993—2005; program mgr., curriculum coord. Parkchester Early Learning Ctr., Bronx, 2005; dir. Susan E. Wagner Day Sch., Bronx, 2005—. Acad. coach Kaplan K-12 Learning Svcs., NYC, 2004—05; tutor, reading specialist pvt. practice, NYC, 1994—, tchr. mentor, profl. developer, 1999—; adj. faculty CUNY Grad. Ctr., U. Phoenix Online Campus. Children's ministry Christian Cultural Ctr., Bklyn., 1992—2000. Recipient Excellence Ministry award, Christian Cultural Ctr., 1995. Mem.: ASCD, Nat. Assn. Spl. Edn. Tchrs., Soc. Rsch. Child Devel., Coun. Exceptional Children, Nat. Assn. Edn. Young Children. Avocations: singing, writing. Office: Susan E Wagner Day School 5401 Post Rd Bronx NY 10471 Office Fax: 718-601-0808. Personal E-mail: alyciarhinehart@aol.com.

RHINESMITH, STEPHEN HEADLEY, leadership consultant; b. Mineola, NY, Dec. 13, 1942; s. Homer Kern and Winifred Headley (Long) Rhinesmith; m. Kathleen Alys Law, Aug. 28, 1965; children: Christopher Law, Colin Headley. BA, Wesleyan U., 1965; M in Pub. and Internat. Affairs, U. Pitts., 1966, PhD, 1972. Dir. internat. svcs. McBer and Co., Cambridge, Mass., 1969-71; pres. AFS Intercultural Programs, NYC, 1972-80, 87-89, Holland Am. Cruises, NYC, 1980-82, Moran, Stahl, Boyer, NYC, 1982-84, Rhinesmith & Assocs. Inc., Chatham, Mass., 1984—; ptnr. CDR Internat., 1998—2004; sr. ptnr. Oliver Wyman Leadership Devel., 2004—. Named amb., coord. Pres.'s U.S.-Soviet Exch. Initiative, 1986—87; chmn. dept. orgnl. sociology Moscow State U., 1991—96. Author: Bring Home the World: A Management Guide to Community Leaders of International Programs, 1975, 1985, A Manager's Guide to Globalization: Six Skills for Success in a Changing World, 2d edit., 1996; co-author: Head Heart and Guts: How the World's Best Companies Develop Complete Leaders, 2006, Leading in Times of Crisis: Navigating Through Complexity, Diversity and Uncertainty to Save Your Business, 2009. Baker scholar, Heinz fellow, NDEA fellow. Mem.: ASTD (chair 1994), Quail Creek Country Club, Eastward Ho! Country Club. Home and Office: PO Box 748 Chatham MA 02633-0748 Home Phone: 508-945-5092; Office Phone: 503-223-5678. Personal E-mail: SHRglobal@aol.com.

RHO, MANNQUE, theoretical physicist, researcher; b. Hamyang, Kyung Nam, Korea, Dec. 14, 1936; s. Byung-Serk and Nam-Soon (Baick) R.; m. Helga Rosalinde Heldeis, June 14, 1965; 1 child, Oliver. AB in Chemistry, Clark U., Worcester, Mass., 1960; PhD in Nuclear Physics, U. Calif., Berkeley, 1964. Prof. Commissariat à l'Energie Atomique Saclay, Gif-sur-Yvette, France, 1965—, Korea Inst. Advanced Study, 2001—03. Vis. prof. CERN, 1969-70, SUNY, Stony Brook, 1973-74, 78-79, 82-83, 88-89, U. Nagoya, Japan, 1988, Seoul Nat. U., Korea, 1990; Humboldt award prof. GSI, Darmstadt, Germany, 1995, Korea Inst. for Advanced Study, 1998-2000, Tech. U. Munich, 1996; disting. vis. scholar Pusan Nat. U., Busan, Republic of Korea, 2006, disting. prof. WCU, Hanyang U., Seoul, 2008-. Author: Chiral Nuclear Dynamics, 1996, Chiral Nuclear Dynamics II, 2008; editor: Mesons in Nuclei, 1979; contbr. over 300 articles to profl. jours. Decorated Nat. Order of Merit, Korea, 1996; recipient Paul Langevin prize, 1985, Gay-Lussac Humboldt prize Humboldt Found., 1995, Nat. Acad. Scis. of Korea prize, 1999, Ho-Am Found. prize in Sci., 2002, Korean Broadcasting Svc. Sci. prize, 2004. Mem. French Phys. Soc., NY Acad. Sci., Korean Acad. Scis. and Tech. Avocations: skiing, hiking. Home: 27 Ave Auguste Renoir 78160 Marly-le-Roi France Office: Inst de Physique Theorique CEA Saclay 91191 Gif-sur-Yvette France Office Phone: 33-1-69087469. Business E-Mail: mannque.rho@cea.fr.

RHOADES, EVERETT RONALD, medical educator; b. Lawton, Okla., Oct. 24, 1931; s. Lee Joseph and Dorothy Apasha Rhoades; m. Bernadine Herwona Toyebo, Oct. 22, 1931; children: Lee Charles, Melanie Cheryl Campos, Melinda Sue Yoder, Dorothy Alison, Lisa Patricia. MD, U. Okla., 1956. Diplomate Am. Bd. Internal Medicine, 1963. Chief infectious diseases sect. USAF Hosp., Lackland Air Force Base, Tex., 1961—66; prof. medicine U. Okla. Health Scis. Ctr., Oklahoma City, 1966—92, chief infectious diseases sect., 1966—82; asst. surgeon gen. USPHS, Rockville, Md., 1982—93; dir. Indian Health Svc., 1982—93; assoc. dean cmty. affairs U. Okla. Health Scis. Ctr., 1993—2000; dir. of edn. initiatives Ctr. Am. Indian and Alaska Native Rsch., Balt., 1993—2000; sr. cons. Ctr. Am. Indian Health Rsch., 2000—; dir. Native Am. Prevention Rsch. Ctr., 2000—03; prof. emeritus of medicine U. Okla. Health Scis. Ctr., 2005—. Coun. Nat. Inst. Allergy and Infectious Diseases, Bethesda, Md., 1971—75, Nat. Inst. Deafness and Other Comm. Disorders, 1996—2000, Nat. Ctr. Complementary and Alt. Medicine, 1997—2001; adv. com. Nat. Ctr. Vital and Health Stats., Washington, 1978—82; cons. Nat. Libr. Medicine, Bethesda, 1974, U. Saigon Sch. Medicine, Saigon, Vietnam, 1970—72; adj. prof. internat. health Johns Hopkins Sch. Pub. Health, Balt., 1993—2000. Editor: (text book) American Indian Health - Innovations in Health Care, Promotion and Policy; contbr. scientific papers. Founder, mem., pres. Assn. Am. Indian Physicians, Oklahoma City, 1972—2005. Maj. USAF, 1957—66. Decorated Commendation medal USPHS, Meritorious Svc. medal, DSM, Commendation medal, Surgeon General's Exemplary Svc. award; recipient Recognition Achievement award, Kiowa Tribe Okla., 1988, St. Martin-Beaumont Rsch. award, Indian Health Svc., 1993, Establishment of Everett R. Rhoades prize, U. Okla. Coll. Medicine, 1995, Child Advocacy award, Am. Acad. Pediat., 1995; named Outstanding Am. Indian, Am. Indian Expn., 1996; named to Kiowa Tribal Hall Fame, Kiowa Tribe Okla., 1997; fellow, John Hay Whitney Found., 1952—56; scholar, Zeta Psi Frat., Lafayette Coll., 1949—52, John and Mary Markle Found., 1967—72; Sequoyah fellow, Am. Indian Sci. and Engring. Soc., 1992. Fellow: Infectious Diseases Soc. Am., Am. Coll. Physicians; mem.: Assn. Am. Indian Affairs (bd. dirs.), Am. Fedn. Clin. Rsch., Kiowa Tribal Bus. Com. (vice chmn. 1978—80), Nat. Congress Am. Indians, Assn. Am. Indian Physicians (pres. 2004—05, Excellence award 1980), Commd. Officers Assn., Assn. Mil. Surgeons US, Alpha Omega Alpha, Phi Beta Kappa, Kiowa Gourd Clan (life), Kiowa Blacklegging Soc. (life; sr. counsellor 1970—2005). Methodist. Avocations: hunting, fishing, cave exploring. Home: 1808 Dorchester Dr Oklahoma City OK 73120 Office: U Okla Health Scis Ctr 801 NE 13th St Oklahoma City OK 73104

RHOADES, KEVIN CARL, bishop; b. Mahanoy City, Pa., Nov. 26, 1957; s. Charles and Mary Rhoades. BA in Philosophy, St. Charles Borromeo Sem., Overbrook, Pa., 1979; attended, N.Am. Coll., Rome; STB, Pontifical Gregorian U., Rome, 1982, STL, 1986, JCL, 1988. Ordained priest Diocese of Harrisburg, Pa., 1983; parochial vicar St. Patrick Parish, York, Pa., 1983—85; pastor St. Francis of Assisi Parish, Harrisburg, 1990—95; faculty mem. Mount Saint Mary's Sem., 1995—2004, rector, 1997—2004; ordained bishop, 2004; bishop Diocese of Harrisburg, 2004—. Mem.: Pa. Cath. Conf. (pres.). Roman Catholic. Office: Diocese of Harrisburg Chancery Office PO Box 2153 4800 Union Deposit Rd Harrisburg PA 17105 Office Phone: 717-657-4804. Office Fax: 717-657-2453.

RHOADES, MARK MATTHEW, risk management consultant, educator; s. Forrest Mark and Marie Rhoades; m. Toni Perala Rhoades, June 30, 1990; 1 child, Christian Robert Perala. BS in Aerospace Engring., U. Mich., Ann Arbor, 1983; MS in Aero. Engring., Naval Postgrad. Sch., Monterey, Calif., 1990, MS in Sys. Engring. Mgmt., 2006. Cert. in risk mgmt., IIPER, Calif., 2006. CDR. USN, Monterey, 1983—2005; helicopter aircraft comdr. Helicopter Combat Support Squadron Eleven, San Diego, 1985—88; field svc. dep. program mgr. Naval Aviation Depot, San Diego, 1990—93; Adversary/Topgun class desk officer COMNAVAIRPAC, San Diego, 1993—95; propulsion, power sys. engr. Naval Air Sys. Command, Patuxent River, Md., 1995—98; navy dep. program mgr. GPS Joint Program Office, LA AFB, Calif., 1998—2001; univ. lectr. Naval Postgrad. Sch., Monterey, 2001—. Mem.: DAU Risk Mgmt. Cmty., INCOSE, MOAA. Independent. Office: PO Box 1685 Castroville CA 95012

RHOADES, GERALDINE EMELINE, editor, consultant; b. Phila., Jan. 29, 1914; d. Lawrence Dry and Alice Fegley (Rice) R. AB, Bryn Mawr Coll., 1935. Publicity asst. Bryn Mawr (Pa.) Coll., 1935-37; asst. Internat. Students House, Phila., 1937-39; mng. editor The Woman mag., NYC, 1939-42; editor Life Story mag., 1942-45, Today's Woman mag., NYC, 1945-52, Today's Family Mag., NYC, 1952-53; lectr. Columbia U., 1954-56; assoc. editor Readers Digest, 1954-55; producer NBC, 1955-56; assoc. editor Ladies Home Jour., 1956-62, mng. editor, 1962-63; exec. editor McCall's mag., 1963-66; editor Woman's Day mag., 1966-82, editorial dir., 1982-84, Woman's Day Resource Center, 1984-89; v.p. Woman's Day mag., 1972—84, CBS Consumer Publs., 1977-84; cons. Woman's Day, NYC, 1989-91. Editorial cons., dir. Nat. Mag. Awards, 1991-94. Author: (with others) Woman's Day Help Book, 1988. Mem. journalism awards com. James Beard Found., 1993-2001. Recipient award for profl. achievement Diet Workshop Internat., 1977; Elizabeth Cutter Morrow award YWCA Salute to Women in Bus., 1977; Recipient Econ. Equity award Women's Equity Action League, 1982; March of Dimes Women Editor's citation, 1982 Mem.: Women's Forum (bd. dirs. 1985—87), Advt. Women in N.Y. (bd. govs. 1983—85, 2d v.p. 1985—87, 1st v.p. 1987—89, bd. dirs. 1989—90, Pres.'s award 1987), N.Y. Women in Comm. (Matrix award 1975), Am. Soc. Mag. Editors (chmn. exec. com. 1971—73), Fashion Group (bd. govs. 1977—79, chmn. bd. govs. 1978—80, bd. dirs. Found. 1980—81, treas. bd. govs. 1983—85, bd. govs. 1987—88), Nat. Press Club (dir.), Bryn Mawr Coll. Alumni Assn. (bd. dirs. 1989—94), Turtle Bay Assn. (bd. dirs. 1989—92), Literacy Vols. of N.Y.C. (bd. dirs. 1986—93), YWCA Acad. Women Achievers, Bryn Mawr Club of N.Y.C. (bd. dirs. 1994—2000), Women's City Club of N.Y. (bd. dirs. 1996—, chair comm. 2001—04, Honoree of Yr. 2004). Home: 185 W End Ave Apt 21A New York NY 10023-5548 Personal E-mail: rhoadsge@aol.com.

RHOADS, JAMES BERTON, archivist, consultant, federal official, educator; b. Sioux City, Iowa, Sept. 17, 1928; s. James Harrison and Mary (Keenan) R.; m. S. Angela Handy, Aug. 12, 1947 (dec. Jan. 8, 2007); children: Cynthia Patrice Neven, James Berton, Marcia Marie MacKellar. Student, Southwestern Jr. Coll., 1946-47, Union Coll., Lincoln, Neb., 1947-48; BA, U. Calif.-Berkeley, 1950, MA, 1952; PhD, Am. U., 1965. With GSA-Nat. Archives and Records Service, Washington, 1952-79, asst. archivist for civil archives, 1965, dept. archivist U.S., 1966-68, archivist U.S., 1968-79; chmn. Nat. Archives Trust Fund Bd., 1968-79; chmn. adminstrv. com. Fed. Register, 1968-79; chmn. Nat. Hist. Publs. and Records Commn., 1968-79; mem. Fed. Council on Arts and Humanities, 1970-79; pres. Rhoads Assos. Internat., 1980-84; dir. grad. program in archives and records mgmt. Western Wash. U., Bellingham, 1984-94, prof. history, 1987-94, dir. Ctr. for Pacific N.W. studies, 1994-97; prof. emeritus, 1994—. Trustee Woodrow Wilson Internat. Center for Scholars, 1969-79; v.p. Intergovtl. Coun. UNESCO Info. Program, 1977-79; mem. adv. bd. Wash. State Hist. Records, 1990-97. Recipient Meritorious and Disting. Service awards GSA, 1966, 68, 79 Fellow Soc. Am. Archivists (pres. 1974-75); mem. Internat. Coun. Archives (pres. 1976-79), Am. Antiquarian Soc., Am. Coun. Learned Socs. (com. Soviet-Am. archival coop. 1986-91), Mass. Hist. Soc. (corr.), Wash. State Hist. Soc. (trustee 1986-95), Acad. Cert. Archivists (pres. 1992-94).

RHOADS, JON MARC, pediatric gastroenterologist, educator; b. Nov. 7, 1953; BA, Johns Hopkins U., Balt.; MD, Johns Hopkins Med. Sch., 1980. Diplomate Am. Bd. Pediat., Am. Bd. Pediat. Gastroenterology. Resident UCLA Hosp. & Clinic; fellowship Hosp. for Sick Children, Toronto, Ontario, Canada; prof. pediat. gastroenterology & nutrition U. Tex Med. Sch., Houston, 2006—. Contbr. articles to profl. jours. Mem.: N. Am. Soc. Pediat. Gastroenterology, Hepatology & Nutrition. Mailing: U Tex Med Sch 6431 Fannin St MSB 3137 Houston TX 77030 Office Fax: 713-500-5750. Business E-Mail: j.marc.rhoads@uth.tmc.edu.

RHOADS, MARK B., lawyer; b. Mar. 1, 1959; BA, Coll. William and Mary, 1981; JD, U. Richmond, 1985. Bar: Pa. 1985, Va. 1988, US Dist. Ct. Ea. Dist. Pa. 1985, US Dist. Ct. Ea. Dist. Va. 1988. With Montgomery McCracken Walker & Rhoads, Pa., 1985—88, McCandlish Holton (formerly Mezzullo McCandlish), Richmond, Va., 1988—2003; ptnr., practice group leader bus. immigration group Reed Smith LLP, Richmond, Va., 2003—05; ptnr., Bus. Immigration Group McCandlish Holton, 2005—. Editor: US Immigration Law Handbook, A Guide for Foreign Business. Office: 1111 E Main St Suite 1500 Richmond VA 23219 Office Phone: 804-775-3824.

RHOADS, STEVEN ERIC, political science professor; b. Abington, Pa., May 12, 1939; s. John Reginald and Barbara Ann (Dugan) Rhoads; m. Diana Cabanis Akers, May 17, 1944; children: Christopher, Nicholas, John. BA, Princeton U., 1961; MPA, Cornell U., 1965, PhD, 1972. Mem. staff Office Mgmt. and Budget, Washington, 1965—66; asst. prof. dept. politics U. Va., Charlottesville, 1970—76, assoc. prof., 1977—86, prof., 1986—. Author: Policy Analysis in the Federal Aviation Administration, 1974, Valuing Life: Public Policy Dilemmas, 1980, The Economist's View of the World: Government, Markets and Public Policy, 1985, Incomparable Worth: Pay Equity Meets the Market, 1993, Taking Sex Differences Seriously, 2004; contbr. articles to profl. jours. Lt. (j.g.) USN, 1961—63. Fellow, Sloan NEH, Inst. Ednl. Affairs, Bradley Found., Olin Found. Mem.: Assn. Pub. Policy and Mgmt., Am. Polit. Sci. Assn. Home: 3190 Dundee Rd Earlysville VA 22936-9621 Office: U Va Dept Politics Cabell Hall 232 Charlottesville VA 22903 Office Phone: 434-924-7866.

RHODE, ALFRED SHIMON, retired finance educator; b. Vienna, July 31, 1928; came to U.S., 1940, naturalized, 1949; s. Aron and Olga (Schwarz) Rothkirch; m. Phyllis Mazur, Dec. 28, 1959; children: Yael, Tamar, Yvette, Liane. BCE, CUNY, 1950; MEA, George Washington U., 1959; PhD, Am. U., 1973. Registered profl. engr., Md. Engr. Bur. of Reclamation, Sacramento, 1950—52; various engring. positions U.S. Govt., 1954—63; head logistics rsch. Navy Supply Sys. Command, Washington, 1963—68; head support forces, manpower and logistics br. Navy Program Planning Office, Washington, 1968—75; sr. v.p. nat. security analysis and warfare support group Info. Spectrum, Inc., Arlington, Va., 1976—89, cons., 1989—92; professorial lectr. George Washington U., Washington, 1969—75; adj. faculty Sch. Mgmt. George Mason U., Fairfax, Va., 1990—2002; adj. faculty Sch. Bus. Adminstrn. Georgetown U., Washington, 1998—2009. Exec. dir. Montgomery County Retail Security and Loss Prevention Assn., 1996-2008. Contbr. articles to profl. jours. Capt. USAF, 1952-54. Congl. fellow, 1962. Fellow Mil. Ops. Rsch. Soc. (1st v.p., dir.); mem. Inst. Ops. Rsch. and Mgmt. Scis. (chmn. mil. applications sect.), Washington Inst. for Ops. Rsch. and the Mgmt. Scis. Home: 8305 Fox Run Potomac MD 20854-2576 Home Phone: 301-299-6307. Personal E-mail: arhode@verizon.net.

RHODE, DEBORAH LYNN, law educator; b. Jan. 29, 1952; BA, Yale U., 1974, JD, 1977. Bar: D.C. 1977, Calif. 1981. Law clk. to judge U.S. Ct. Appeals (2d cir.), NYC, 1977-78; law clk. to Hon. Justice Thurgood Marshall U.S. Supreme Ct., Washington, 1978-79; asst. prof. law Stanford U., Calif., 1979-82, assoc. prof. Calif., 1982-85, prof. Calif., 1985—; dir. Inst. for Rsch. on Women and Gender, 1986-90, Keck Ctr. of Legal Ethics and The Legal Profession, 1994—2003; sr. counsel jud. com. Ho. of Reps., Washington, 1998. Trustee Yale U., 1983-89; pres. Assn. Am. Law Schs., 1998; Ernest W. McFarland prof. Stanford Law Sch., 1997—; sr. counsel com. on the jud. U.S. Ho. of Reps., 1998; dir. Stanford Ctr. Legal Profession, 2008-. Author: Justice and Gender, 1989, (with Geoffrey Hazard) the Legal Profession: Responsibility and Regulation, 3d edit., 1993, (with Annette Lawson) The Politics of Pregnancy: Adolescent Sexuality and Public Policy, 1993, (with David Luban) Legal Ethics, 2005, 4th edit., 2004, Speaking of Sex, 1997, Professional Responsibility: Ethics by the Pervasive Method, 1998, In the Interests of Justice, 2000 (with Geoffrey Hazard, Jr.) Professional Responsibility and Regulation, 2002; editor: Theoretical Perspectives on Sexual Difference, 1990, Ethics in Practice, 2000, The Difference Difference Makes: Women and Leadership, 2002, Access to Justice, 2004, Pro Bono in Principle and in Practice, 2005, (with Katherine Bartlett) Gender and Law, 2005, (with Carol Sanger) Gender and Rights, 2005, Moral Leadership: The Theory and Practice of Power, Judgment and Policy, 2006, In Pursuit of Knowledge: Scholars, Status, and Academic Culture, 2006, Women and Leadership: The State of Play and Strategies for Change, 2007; contbr. articles to profl. jours. Mem.: ABA (chmn. commn. on women 2000—02). Office: Stanford U Law Sch Crown Quadrangle Stanford CA 94305

RHODE, EDWARD ALBERT, veterinary medicine educator, veterinary cardiologist; b. Amsterdam, NY, July 25, 1926; s. Edward A. and Katherine (Webb) R.; m. Dolores Bangert, 1955; children: David E., Peter R., Paul W., Robert M., Catherine E. DVM, Cornell U., 1947. Diplomate Am. Coll. Veterinary Internal Medicine. Prof. emeritus vet. medicine U. Calif., Davis, 1964—, chmn. dept. vet. medicine, 1968-71; assoc. dean instrn. U. Calif. Sch. Vet. Medicine, Davis, 1971-81, dean, 1982-91. Mem. AAAS, Nat. Acad. Practices, Am. Coll. Vet. Internal Medicine, Am. Vet. Medicine Assn., Basic Sci. Coun., Am. Heart Assn., Am. Acad. Vet. Cardiology, Am. Physiol. Soc., Calif. Vet Medicine Assn. Office: U Calif Sch Vet Med Davis CA 95616 E-mail: earhode@ucdavis.edu.

RHODE, MARYE FRANCES, paralegal; b. Ft. Defiance, Va., Jan. 29, 1937; d. Silas Caswell Sr. and Mary Ann Frances (James) Rhodes; m. Minter James Rowe, May 1964 (div. 1968); children: Margaret Frances Omar, James Robert Rowe; m. Robert Charles Rhoades Jr., July 25, 1980. Student, Mountain State U., 1956-58, 68, U. Charleston, 1962-63, 74, 89, Antioch U., 1972-73; grad., Mike Tyree Sch. Real Estate, 1984, Evans Coll. Legal Studies, 1990. Educator Nicholas County Sch. Sys., Summersville, W.Va., 1958-61; edit. staff, columnist, staff writer, reporter, photographer Beckley Newspapers Corp., 1962-76; educator Raleigh County Bd. Edn., Beckley, W.Va., 1967-68; exec. editor, columnist Local News Jour., Whitesville, W.Va., 1976-77; libr. bookmobile, asst. ref. libr., outreach coord. Raleigh County Pub. Libr., Beckley, 1977-78; agt. Combined Ins. Co., Chgo., 1978-79; legal sec., paralegal W.Va. Legal Svcs. Inc., Beckley, 1979-82; paralegal Applachian Rsch and Defense Fund Inc., Beckley, 1982-83; exec. dir., owner Rhoades and Rowe, Beckley, 1983—85; paralegal patient advocate Comty. Health Sys. Inc., Beckley, 1986-96; pvt. practice Beckley, 1996—. Contbr. articles to mags. State bd. dirs., pub. resl. LWV, Beckley; pub. rels., various coms. Raleigh County Dem. Women, Beckley; sec., pub. rels. Orchard Valley Women's Club, Crab Orchard, W.Va.; trustee Fraternal Order Eagles; pub. rels., various coms. Loyal Order Moose, Beckley, Beckley Profl. Bus. Women; com. mem. Nat. Coalition to Save the New River; sales rep. So. U.S. Rep. to U.S. Mil. Acad., West Point, N.Y.; active Am. Legion Aux., Mullens, W.Va. Mem. NEA, Classroom Tchrs. Assn., Nat. Paralegal Assn., Nat. Fedn. Paralegals Assn., Nat. Ind. Paralegals Assn., Nat. Com. Save Soc., Sec. Medicare, Nat. Legal Aid and Def. Assn., Nat. Orgn. Social Security Claimants Reps., State Soc. Sec. Task Force, Nat. Vets. Legal Svcs. Project Inc., W.Va. U. Alumni Assn., Community AIDS Edn. Com., W.Va. Edn. Assn., Am. Disability Repr. Specs. Assn. Democrat. Mem. Ch. of God. Avocations: creative arts and music, walking, nascar, doll collecting, writing. Home: PO Box 2173 Beckley WV 25802 Office: Benefit Services PO Box 7265 Beckley WV 25802 Home Phone: 304-252-8431; Office Phone: 304-252-8431. Office Fax: 304-252-1098. Personal E-mail: tv65000@suddenlink.net.

RHODEN, DWIGHT, performing company executive, choreographer, dancer; b. Dayton, Ohio; Dancer Dayton Contemporary Dance Co., Les Ballet Jazz De Montreal; prin. dancer Alvin Ailey Am. Dance Theater; co-founder, artistic dir. Complexions Contemporary Ballet, 1994—. Recipient NY Found. Arts award, 1998, Choo San Goh award for Choreography, 2001, Apex award, Alvin Ailey Sch., 2006. Office: Complexions 7WTC 250 Greenwich St 41st Fl New York NY 10007 Office Phone: 212-777-7771. Office Fax: 212-777-4457. E-mail: info@complexionsdance.org.

RHODES, ALICE GRAHAM, retired lawyer, not-for-profit community development consultant; b. Phila., June 15, 1941; d. Peter Graham III and Fannie Isadora (Bennett) Graham; m. Charles Milton Rhodes, Oct. 14, 1971 (div. Apr. 21, 1997); children: Helen, Carla, Shauna. BS, East Stroudsburg U., Pa., 1962; MS, U. Pa., Phila., 1966, LLB, 1969, JD, 1970, cert. program exec. adminstrn. non-profit, 2004. Bar: NY 1970, US Dist. Ct. (so. and ea. dists.) NY 1971, US Ct. Appeals (2d cir.) 1971, Ky. 1983, US Dist. Ct. (ea. dist.) Ky. 1985. Staff atty. Harlem Assertion Rights, Mobilization for Youth Office Econ. Opportunity, NYC, 1969-70, coord. Cmty. Action Legal Svcs., 1970-72; assoc. dir. in charge of civil representation HUD Model Cities Cmty. Law Offices, NYC, 1972-73; resource assoc. Commn. on Edn. & Employment of Women, NC Dept. Adminstrn., Raleigh, 1975; mgr. policies and procedures Div. for Youth, NC Dept. Human Resources, Raleigh, 1976; in-house counsel, petroleum transactional atty. Ashland, Inc. (formerly Ashland Oil, Inc.), 1980-82; corp. atty. core group Ashland, Inc., 1985-87, 88-91; mem. Ashland City Commn. Human Rights, 1993-99; mem. bd. regents Ea. Ky. U., 1994—2000; asst. county atty. Jefferson County, 1999—2000; atty.-advisor EEOC, 2001. Mem. Property Valuation Appeals Commn., Greenup County, 1994, Pub. Mems. Fgn. Svc.; cons. pub. mem. selection and performance stds. rev. bd. cons. Fgn. Svc., US Dept. State, 1995, Fgn. Agrl. Svc. USDA, 1997; prison program planner, cons. NY City Dept. Corrections, 1971; lectr. NYC Corrections Acad., Riker's, 1971; lectr. juvenile justice NC Law Enforcement Acad., Salemburg, 1976. Vol. Meals on Wheels, 1983—91, Am. Heart Assn., 1982—91; mem. adv. com. task force post secondary edn. Gov. of Ky.; mem. Ky. Gov.'s Conf. on Postsecondary Edn., 1999, Global Interdependence Ctr. U. Pa., 2003—06; bd. dirs. exec. com. Boyd County Dem. Women, 1996—2000; mem. missionary soc., scholarship com. St. Matthew AME Ch., St. Matthew Lay Orgn., SC Club; mem. St. Matthew AME Ch.; bd. dirs. YWCA Ashland, 1983—84, Ashland Heritage Pk. Commn., 1983—85, Negro Baseball Hall of History; bd. dirs., budget com. United Way, Greenup County, Ky., 1988—92; found. bd. dirs. Franciscan Sisters of the Poor, Ky. Health Sys. Found., Inc., 1996—99; mem. presdl. search com. Ea. Ky. U., 1997—98. Recipient Cmty. Svc. award Queens Community Corp., NYC, 1972, Ashland C.C., 1986, Cmty. Svc. award NAACP, Ky.; NSF fellow, 1964, 65; faculty friends of Penn scholar U. Pa. Law Sch., 1966-69, Reginald Heber Smith postgrad. law and cmty. econ. devel. fellow, 1969-71; named to Hon. Order of Ky. Cols., 1989. Fellow Ky. Bar Found., AAUW (bd. dirs. Phila. chpt. 1963-65), NAACP (life), NY Bar, Ky. Bar Assn. (mem. edn. law, corp. house counsel, law sects.), Pilot Club (exec. bd. Ashland 1983), Links, Inc., Penn Club (charter mem.), Phila. Sr. Ctr. (life mem.), Pyramid Club Phila., U. Pa. Edn. Alumni Assn. (bd. dirs. 2006), SC Club (Ann. Day program chair 2006). Democrat. Avocations: interior decorating, sports, dance, gourmet cooking, gardening.

RHODES, ANTHONY H., retired biologist; s. Benjamin Franklin and Wilie Mae Rhodes; m. Shirley Ann Thompson, Mar. 25, 2005; children: Dale, Ray, Angelique, Adia. BS, U. North Ala., Florence, 1979, MS, 1975. Adj. prof. Calhoun CC, Decatur, Ala., 2005—; biology instr. U. North Ala., 2006—. Biol. & agrl. aide TVA, Muscle Shoals, Ala., 1972—78, aquatic biology, toxicologist, 1978—88, safety manger, indsl. hygienist, 1995—2004. Adv. Blacks IN Govtl., Washington, 1976. With USN, 1967—70, San Diego. Mem.: Nat. Orgn. Black Chemists & Chem. Engrs. Office: Univ N Alabama UNA Box 5155 313 Stevens Hall Florence AL 35632-001

RHODES, ARTHUR DELANO, benefits administrator; b. Philadelphia, Miss., Nov. 26, 1960; s. A.D. and Mary (McNair) R.; m. Angela Marie Jolly, May 21, 1988. AA, Miss. Delta Jr. Coll., Moorhead, 1980; BA in Polit. Sci., Millsaps Coll., 1982; JD, U. Miss., 1985. Bar: Miss. 1985, U.S. Dist. Ct. (no. and so. dist.) Miss. 1985. Intern asst. dist. atty. Dist. Atty's Office, Hernando, Miss., 1985; counsel Child Support Unit, Dept. of Human Svcs., Brookhaven, Miss., 1985-87; assoc. Prewitt & Bradley, Jackson, Miss., 1987-88; chief of staff Congressman Mike Parker, Washington, 1988-98; pres., CEO The Benefits Bd., Inc., Cleveland, Tenn., 1999—. Republican. Mem. Ch. Of God. Avocations: travel, reading. Home: 2014 Woodchase Way NE Cleveland TN 37311-1461 Office: The Benefits Bd PO Box 4608 Cleveland TN 37320-4608 Office Phone: 423-478-7131, 423-478-7191. Business E-Mail: artrhodes@benefitsboard.com.

RHODES, DAISY CHUN, writer, researcher, historian; b. Kahuku, Hawaii, Nov. 16, 1933; d. Pyung Chan Chun and Shin Ai Park; children: Joseph, Carmella, Thomas Francese. BA in Creative Writing, Eckerd Coll., 1995. Info. specialist Reconstrn. Devel. Corp., Washington, 1970; specialist indigent funding George Washington U. Hosp., Washington, 1971-74; mgr. hosp. assistance Alexandria (Va.) Hosp., 1975-79; asst. editor Employee Futures Rsch., Luray, Va., 1980-84; editor Inside Negotiations, Rochester, NY, 1985-87, Educators Negotiating Svc., New Port Richey, Fla., 1987-89; novelist, writer New Port Richey, 1989-95; rschr., oral historian Honolulu, 1994; writer Colorado Springs, 1995—; rschr., cons. Donna Ladd, Writer, Colorado Springs, 1996. Rschr., cons. Donna Ladd, Writer, Colorado Springs, 1996; presenter Asian Studies Conf., Honolulu; presenter scholarly and abstract Korean Picture Brides We. Asian Studies Conf., Boulder, Colo., 1997; lectr. Ctr. for Korean Studies U. Hawaii, 1998. Author: Forever Long-Never End, 1990, Wahaiawa Red Dirt, 1991, At Crossroads of Inspiration, 1993, Shirley Temple Feet, 1993, Remembering the Fallen, 1994, Passages to Paradise: Early Korean Immigrant Narratives from Hawaii, 1998; author: (play) I Know About Olympus, 1993; author: (scholarly and abstract) How Oral History of the First Koreans in America Advances Archival Research, 1996; author: Eye of the Dragon, 1994 (finalist Hemingway 1st Novel Competition, 1994), My Father's Voice, Echoes Upon Echoes, 2002, A Place of Noise, 2003, A Literary Lei, 2004. Pres. Colorado Springs Friends of Aquatics, 1997—; bd. dirs. All Souls Unitarian Ch.; mem. adv. bd. City of Colorado Springs Pks. and Recreation, 2004—. Recipient Work Study award for profls., Rotary Internat. Found., South Korea, 1998—99. Mem.: Korean Am. Women's Soc. Greater Washington (pres. 1983—84, bd. dirs., Commendation), Korea Soc., Assn. for Asian Studies, West Pasco Kiwanis (pres. 1990—92).

RHODES, DAVID, academic administrator; s. Silas H. Rhodes. BA in philosophy, Wesleyan Coll.; attended, Columbia U. Pres. Sch. Visual Arts, NYC, 1978—. Mem.: Commn. Higher Edn. Middle States Assn. Coll. & Sch. (appointment 2003—04), Regants Adv. Coun. Instl. Accreditation, Commn. Higher Edn., Assn. Proprietary Coll. (bd. trustees 1989—, chmn. fed. affairs com. 1989—). Office: School of Visual Arts Office of the President 209 East 23 St New York NY 10010

RHODES, DEBORAH JEAN JOHNSON, former prosecutor; b. 1958; BA with high honors, Wheaton Coll.; JD with honors, Rutgers U. Law clk. to Hon. J. William Ditter US Dist Ct. (ea. dist.) Pa; mem. Organized Crime & Racketeering sect., Phila. Strike Force US Dept. Justice, Phila., asst. US atty. San Diego, 1990—2004, counselor to asst. atty. gen., criminal divsn. Washington, 2004—05, US atty. (so. dist.) Ala. Ala., 2005—09. Ex-officio commr. US Sentencing Commn., 2003—. Editor (in chief): Rutgers Law Jour.

RHODES, DONALD ROBERT, musicologist, educator, retired electrical engineer; b. Detroit, Dec. 31, 1923; s. Donald Eber and Edna Mae (Fulmer) R.; children: Joyce R. Holbert, Jane E., Roger C., Diane R. Herran. BEE, Ohio State U., 1945, MEE, 1948, PhD, 1953. Research assoc. Ohio State U., Columbus, 1945-54; research engr. Cornell Aero. Lab., Buffalo, 1954-57; head basic research dept. Radiation, Inc., Orlando, Fla., 1957-61, sr. scientist Melbourne, Fla., 1961-66; Univ. prof. N.C. State U., Raleigh, 1966-94, univ. prof. emeritus, 1994—. Author: Introduction to Monopulse, 1959, 2d edit., 1980, Synthesis of Planar Antenna Sources, 1974, A Reactance Theorem, 1977. Co-founder Central Fla. Community Orch., Winter Park, 1961, pres., 1961-62. Recipient Benjamin G. Lamme medal Ohio State U., 1975; Eminent Engr. award Tau Beta Pi, 1976; named to N.C. State U. Acad. Outstanding Tchrs., 1980. Fellow AAAS, IEEE (John T. Bolljahn award 1963, pres. Antennas and Propagation Soc. 1969); mem. Am. Musicological Soc. Home: 625 Centennial Pkwy Apt 101 Raleigh NC 27606-3255 Office: PO Box 7911 Raleigh NC 27695-7911

RHODES, EDWARD, political science professor; b. Elmhurst, Ill., Oct. 1, 1959; s. C. Harker Rhodes, Jr. and Mae Svoboda Rhodes; m. Kadri Kallikorm; 1 child, Charles Kristian. AB, Harvard U., Cambridge, Mass., 1980; MPA, Princeton U., NJ, 1982, PhD, 1985. Asst. prof. Rutgers U., New Brunswick, NJ, 1986—92, assoc. prof., 1992—2004, dean, social & behavioral scis., 2003—06, prof., 2005—; vis. scholar Harvard U., 1989—90; fellow Office Chief Naval Ops., US Navy, Washington, 1996—97; vis. prof. Princeton U., 2007—09; fellow U. Latvia, Riga, 2000—01. Mem. Adv. Com. Hist. Diplomatic Documentation, US Dept. State, Washington, 2003—09. Author: (book) Power and Madness: The Logic of Nuclear Coercion; co-author: Presence, Prevention, and Persuasion: A Historical Analysis of Military Force and Political Influence; co-editor: The Politics of Strategic Adjustment, Global Politics in a Changing World, International Relations; contbr. articles to profl. jours. Office: Rutgers Univ 89 George St New Brunswick NJ 08901

RHODES, ERIC FOSTER, employee relations consultant, writer; b. Luray, Va., Feb. 5, 1927; s. Wallace Keith and Bertha (Foster) R.; m. Barbara Ellen Henson, Oct. 19, 1946; children: Roxanne Jane, Laurel Lee (dec.); m. Lorraine Endresen, July 29, 1972; m. Daisy Chun, May 31, 1980; m. Barbara Rhodes, Oct. 19, 2004. AA, George Washington U., 1949, AB, 1950, MA, 1952, EdD, 1967. Tchr. high sch., Arlington, Va., 1950-52; counselor Washington Lee High Sch., Arlington, Va., 1952-53, dir. publs., 1953-54, chmn. dept. English, 1954-55; exec. sec. Arlington Edn. Assn., Arlington, Va., 1952-53, Montgomery County Edn. Assn., Rockville, Md., 1955-57; lectr. edn. George Washington U., Washington, 1955—60, adj. prof., 1965—70; salary cons. NEA, Washington, 1957-58, asst. dir. membership div., 1958-60; dir. N.Y. regional office, NYC, 1960-64; ednl. cons. Ednl. Rsch. Svcs., White Plains, N.Y., 1964-65; pres. Ednl. Svc. Bur., Inc., Arlington, Va., 1965-72, chmn. bd., 1972-80; pres. Negotiations Consultation Svcs., Inc., Arlington, 1969-80, Eastern States Advt. Inc., Arlington, 1970-79, EFR Corp., Arlington, 1972-90; exec. dir. Assn. Negotiators and Contract Adminstrs., 1981-89; area coord. U.S. Legal Protection Co., 1989-95; pres. Employee Futures Rsch., New Port Richey, Fla., 1980—, Waterfront Only Real Estate, New Port Richey, Fla., 1988-92, Inst. for Negotiations Tng., New Port Richey, 1989-95, Asset Protection Co., 1991—; asst. supt. for adminstrn. Brighton Schs., Rochester, N.Y., 1983-88; owner Frederick Foster Galleries, Arlington, 1974-80. Cons. Va. Dept. Community Colls., Richmond, 1965-77; vice chancellor Va. Community Coll. System, 1970-71; employee rels. ofcl. City of Orlando, 1980-83; lectr. edn. Frostburg (Md.) State Coll., 1967 Author: Negotiating Salaries, 41 Ways to Cut Budget Costs, Making Good Things Happen Through Negotiation; editor: Inside Negotiations, Wages and Benefits, Employers' Negotiating Service. Mem. Civil Rights Commn., Franklin Twp., N.J., 1962-64; mem. Sr. victim assistance team Colorado Springs Police Dept., 1997-2003; mem. Franklin Twp. Bd. Edn., 1964-65; mem. adv. bd. Keep Am. Beautiful, 1964-75, nat. chmn., 1968; bd. dirs., v.p. Unitarian-Universalist Ch., Tarpon Springs, Fla., 1990-95, pres., 1994-95, bd. dirs., dir. summer programs, 2005—08, v.p. 2007-08; mem. Land Devel. Rev. Bd., New Port Richey, Fla., 2005—. pres. Md., Va. Del. Club, 2009-, With U.S. Army, 1945-47. Mem. Am. Assn. Sch. Adminstrs., Internat. Assn. Sch. Bus. Ofcls., NEA, Edn. Press Assn., Nat. Assn. Ednl. Negotiators (exec. dir. 1971-81), Am. Arbitration Assn. (labor arbitrator), Indsl. Rels. Rsch. Assn., United C. of C. of Pasco County (sec., treas. 1989-90, exec. dir. 1990-91), Am. Legion, Fed. Schoolmen's Club, N.Y. Schoolmen's Club, Lions (v.p. N.Y.C. club 1964-65), Kiwanis (pres. West Pasco club 1991-93, treas. 2004-06), Order of St. John of Jerusalem, Phi Delta Kappa (chpt. pres. 1959-60). Office Phone: 727-849-9484. E-mail: ericrhodes@netzero.com.

RHODES, FRANK HAROLD TREVOR, academic administrator, geologist; b. Warwickshire, Eng., Oct. 29, 1926; came to US, 1968, naturalized, 1976; s. Harold Cecil and Gladys (Ford) R.; m. Rosa Carlson, Aug. 16, 1952; children: Jennifer, Catherine, Penelope, Deborah. BSc, U. Birmingham, 1948, PhD, 1950, DSc, 1963; LLD (hon.), Wooster Coll., Ohio, 1976, Nazareth Coll., Rochester, NY, 1979, Skidmore Coll., Saratoga Springs, NY, 1989, U. Mich., 1990, Clemson U., SC, 1991, Dartmouth Coll., Hanover, NH, 1993, U. Birmingham, Eng., 1999, Fla. Internat. U., Miami, 2000, Trinity Coll., U. Dublin, 2001; LHD (hon.), Colgate U., Hamilton, NY, 1980, Johns Hopkins U., Balt., 1982, Wagner Coll., SI, 1982, Hope Coll., Holland, Mich., 1982, Rensselaer Poly Inst., Troy, NY, 1982, LeMoyne Coll., 1984, Pace U., NYC, 1986, Alaska Pacific U., Anchorage, 1987; LHD, Hamilton Coll., 1987; LHD, DSc, Fla. Atlantic U., Boca Raton, 1996; LHD (hon.), Coll. St. Rose, Albany, NY, 2002; DSc (hon.), U. Wales, Eng., 1981, Bucknell U., Lewisburg, Pa., 1985, U. Ill., 1986, Reed Coll., Portland, 1988, Elmira Coll., NY, 1989, U. Southampton, Eng., 1989, U. Sydney, Australia, 1995, U. Durham, Eng., 1995, Millsaps Coll., 1996; DLitt (hon.), U. Nev., 1982; EdD (hon.), Ohio State U., 1992; D (hon.), U. Stirling, Eng., 1994; LHD (hon.), U. NC, 2003, Ariz. State U., Tempe, 2006. Post-doctoral fellow, Fulbright scholar U. Ill., 1950-51, vis. lectr. geology, summers 1951, 52; lectr. geology U. Durham, 1951-54; asst. prof. U. Ill., 1954-55, assoc. prof., 1955-56; dir. U. Ill. Field Sta., Wyo., 1956; prof. geology, head geology dept. U. Wales, Swansea, 1956-68, dean faculty of sci., 1967-68; prof. geology and mineralogy Coll. Lit., Sci. and Arts, U. Mich., 1968-77, dean, 1971-74, v.p. for acad. affairs, 1974-77; pres., prof. geology Cornell U., Ithaca, NY, 1977-95, pres emeritus, 1995—. Gurley lectr. Cornell U., 1960; Bownocker lectr. Ohio State U., 1966; Case lectr. U. Mich., 1976; Jefferson lectr. U. Calif., Berkeley, 1996-98; dir. NSF, Am. Geol. Inst., summer field inst., 1963; Australian vice-chancellors' visitor to Australian univs., 1964; vis. fellow Clare Hall, Cambridge, 1982; Bye fellow Robinson Coll., Cambridge, 1986-87; Am. Fulbright Disting. fellow, Kuwait, 1987, scholar in residence, Bellagio study and conf. ctr., 1995. Author: The Evolution of Life, 1962, 2d edit., 1976, Fossils, 1963, Geology, 1972, Evolution, 1974, Language of the Earth, 1981, Creation of the Future: The Role of the American University, 2001, Language of the Earth II, 2008; author numerous articles and monographs on sci. and edn.; editor, contbr.: Successful Fund Raising for Higher Edn., 1997. Trustee Carnegie Found. for Advancement Tchg., 1978-86, vice chmn., 1983-85, chmn. 1985-86; trustee The Freedom Forum, 1983-93, Com. for Econ. Devel., 1984-93; prin. Washington Adv. Group, 1997—; bd. dirs. KMI Continental, Inc., 1985-86, Tompkins County Trust Co., 1984-98, Gen. Electric Co., 1984-2002, NBC, 1986-2002, H. John Heinz III Ctr. Sci., Econs. & Environ., 1996-98, Am. Coun. on Edn., 1983-88, vice chair, 1985-86, chair, 1986-88, The Johnson Found., 2000—; mem. Atlantic Philanthropies, 1995-2004, chmn., 2000-04; bd. dirs. Goldman Sachs Found., 2000—; bd. overseers Meml. Sloan-Kettering Cancer Ctr., 1979-91, Koç U., Turkey, 1996—; chmn. adv. bd. Freedom Forum Media Studies Ctr., 1984-93; mem. Nat. Sci. Bd., 1987-98, chair, 1994-96, Internat. Exec. Svc. Corps Coun., 1984-95; v.p. Dyson Charitable Trust, 1996-98; bd. mem. The Johnson Found., 2000—, King Abdullah U. Scis. and Tech. Recipient Clark Kerr medal U. Calif.,

Berkeley, 1995, Reginald Wilson Diversity Leadership award Am. Coun. Edn., 2003; Sr. Vis. Rsch. fellow NSF, 1965-66; scholar U. Calif., Berkeley, 1995. Fellow Am. Acad. Arts and Scis., Geol. Soc. London (coun. 1963-66, Bigsby medal 1967); mem. Am. Philos. Soc. (pres. 1999-2005), Palaeontol. Assn. (v.p. 1963-68), Brit. Assn. Advancement Sci., Geol. Soc. Am., Am. Assn. Petroleum Geologists, Soc. Econ. Paleontologists and Mineralogists, Phi Beta Kappa. Office: Cornell U Office of President Emeritus 3104 Snee Hall Ithaca NY 14853-1504 Office Phone: 607-255-6233.

RHODES, JOHN LEWIS, mathematics professor; b. Columbus, Ohio, July 16, 1937; s. Lewis Rhodes and Ruth McManus; m. Marion Havens (div.); m. Pamela Knutson (div.); m. Irina Anderson (dec.); m. Laura Morland, Jan. 18, 1997; children: Lewis Ambrose, René Rousseau, Christopher Guy. PhD, MIT, 1962. Prof. math. U. Calif., Berkeley, Calif., 1963—99. Founder & editor-in-chief Internat. Jour. Algebra & Computation, 1990—2005. Contbr. scientific papers. Fellow, Inst. Advanced Study, 1968. Liberal. Achievements include discovery of Krohn-Rhodes theorem. Home: 1203 Walnut St Berkeley CA 94709 Business E-Mail: rhodes@math.berkeley.edu.

RHODES, KARIN T., language educator; d. William and Theresia Rhodes. BA in English and Edn., Salem State Coll., Mass., 1978; MA in Am. Lit., Salem State Coll., 1981; Diploma in Anglo-Irish Lit., Trinity Coll., Dublin, 1984. Cert. secondary tchr. Mass. Bd. Edn., 1979. Spl. needs tchr. asst. Salem HS, Mass., 1978; asst. dir., coord. tutorial svcs. Acad. Classics and Scis., Marblehead, Mass., 1978—82; substitute tchr. Marblehead Sch. Sys., Mass., 1978—83; reading and study skills specialist Learning Ctr., Salem State Coll., 1979—80; instr. North Shore CC, Beverly, Mass., 1980—84; instr. English Salem State Coll., 1980—; instr. Marian Ct. Jr. Coll., Swampscott, Mass., 1984—85. Vis. lectr. Endicott Jr. Coll., Beverly, 1985. Mixed media, Powerscourt Waterfall (Judge's Choice award, Coastal Artists Show, Marblehead Arts Assn., Marbelhead Arts Fest, 2005), photographs, Sorosis Farm (1st Prize award, Marblehead Mag., 1979), Forest River (Hon. Mention award, Marblehead Mag., 1979), Grand Canal, Marblehead Arts Fest, 2004, pen and ink, Testing the Waters, Marblehead Arts Assn., 2005; contbr. monographs in field. Recipient Student Appreciation award, Office for Students with Disabilities, Salem State Coll., 1990. Mem.: Nat. Audubon Soc., Mass. Audubon Soc., Trustee of Reservations, Nature Conservancy, Northshore Postcard and Collectors Club, Essex County Ornithol. Club (life). Office: Salem State Coll Dept English Lafayette St Salem MA 01970

RHODES, LAWRENCE, artistic director; b. Mt. Hope, W.Va., Nov. 24, 1939; Studied with Violette Armand. Joined Ballet Russe de Monte Carlo, 1958-60; from dancer to prin. dancer Joffrey Ballet, NYC, 1960-64; prin. dancer Harkness Ballet, 1964-68, dir., prin. dancer, 1968-70; tchr. dance dept. NYU, 1978—, prin. ballet tchr., 1981—, chmn. dance dept., 1981-91; ballet master, choreographer, tchr., artistic dir. Les Grands Ballets Canadiens, Montreal, 1989-99; dir. dance divsn. The Juilliard Sch., 2002—. Guest artist Het Nationale Ballet, Amsterdam, 1970—71, Pa. Ballet, 1971—76, Feld Ballet, NYC, 1973—75; freelance master ballet tchr., coach. Danced with Makarova, Hayden and Fracci, danced for Butler, Joffrey, Ailey, Lubovitch, Harkarvy, Nault, Van Dantzig and Mac Donald, featured dancer (TV films) A Dancer's Vocabulary, PBS's Dance Am. series, CBS's Camera Three. Recipient Lifetime Achievement award, Dance Tchr. Mag., 2009. Office Phone: 212-799-5000 x 255. E-mail: lrhodes@nyc.rr.com.

RHODES, LINDA JANE, psychiatrist; b. San Antonio, May 23, 1950; d. George Vernon and Lucy Agnes (O'Dowd) R. BA, Trinity U., 1972; MD, U. Tex. Med. Br., 1975. Diplomate Am. Bd. Pediat.; bd. certified, Am. Bd. Psychiatry and Neurology. Resident in pediat. U. Tex. Med. Br., Galveston, 1975-78; fellow in ambulatory pediat. U. Tex. Health Sci. Ctr., Houston, 1978-80, resident in psychiatry San Antonio, 1990-92, child and adolescent psychiatrist, fellow in biol. psychiatry, 1992-95, asst. prof. psychiatry, 1995—2004; pediatrician Kelsey Seybold Clinic, P.A., Houston, 1980-95. Pediat. rep. Tex. Lay Midwifery Bd. Tex. Dept. Health, Austin, 1994-95. Active San Antonio Conservation Soc., Nat. Trust for Hist. Preservation, San Antonio Mus. Assn., Trinity U. Assocs., 1992-95; mem. McNay Art Inst.; bd. dirs. Mind. Sci. Found., 1995-2000., Tex. Found. Psychiatric Edn. & Rsch., 1997—, sec., 1998-99, treas., 1999-2004; chair, asst. league Tex. Found. Psychiat. Edn. and Rsch., 2007-09. Fellow Am. Acad. Pediat.; mem. Am. Psychiat. Assn., Am. Acad. Child and Adolescent Psychiatry (past gifts and endowments com., child abuse and neglect com.), Ambulatory Pediat. Assn., Tex. Pediat. Soc., Tex. Soc. Psychiat. Physicians, Tex. Acad. Child and Adolescent Psychiatry, Am. Med. Women's Assn., Am. Soc. Clin. Psychopharmacology, Tex. Med. Assn. (com. on child and adolescent health), AMA, Bexar County Psychait. Soc. (sec. 2000-01, pres. 2002-2003, past pres. 2003-2004), Baxter County Med. Soc.

RHODES, MICHAEL L., federal agency administrator; BS, We. Ky. Univ.; MBA, Chapman Coll.; grad., Army Mgmt. Staff Coll. Fin. analyst for dir. personnel & cmty. activities HQ Staff US Army, Alaska; chief cmty. ops. Fort Richardson, Alaska; cmty. & family activities prog. specialist; gen. mgr. club ops. U.S. Mil. Acad., West Point; bus. cons. cmty. & family activities div. US Army Pacific, Fort Shafter, Hawaii; bus. analyst US Army Cmty. & Family Activities Div., Alexandria, Va.; adv. to comdr. for sustaining base & quality of life affairs US Southern Command, Miami, Fla., 1998—2002; asst. dep. commandant for manpower & reserve affairs US Marine Corps, Washington, 2002—06; dep. dir. adminstrn. & mgmt. & dir. Washington HQ Services US Dept. of Def., Washington, 2006—08, acting dir. adminstrn. & mgmt., 2008—. Served four years US Army. Decorated Meritorious Svc. Medal US Army, Army Achievement medal, Air Assault Badge; recipient Presdl. Rank award for Meritorious Svc., US Dept. of Def., Disting. Civilian Svc. award, US Navy, Meritorious Civilian Svc. award (2), US Army, Joint Meritorious Civilian Svc. award, Commanders awards for Civilian Svc. (2), US Army. Office: Dir Adminstrn & Mgmt 1400 Defense Pentagon Washington DC 20301-1400*

RHODES, PETER EDWARD, label company executive; b. Rochester, NY, Sept. 25, 1942; s. Robert A. and Anne (Ward) R.; m. Cassandra Durkee, May 26, 1962 (div. Sept. 1991); children: Tamara, Amy, Brian; m. Nancy Lewis, Aug. 16, 2002. BS, Rochester Inst. Tech., 1964, MBA, 1970. With Touche Ross & Co., Rochester, 1962-69, sr. auditor, to 1969; with Xerox Co., Rochester, 1969, Fay's Drug Co., Inc., Liverpool, NY, 1970-87, exec. v.p., 1974-87, also dir.; pres. Syracuse Label Co., Inc., Liverpool, 1987—2002, 2002—, also bd. dirs. Bd. dirs. Byrne Dairy Inc. Mem.: AICPA, NY State Soc. CPAs, Bellevue Country Club.

RHODES, RAMONA LAGIERS, medical educator, researcher; d. Jim and Linda Rhodes. BS, Xavier U. La., New Orleans, 1996; MD, U. Ark., Little Rock, 2000; MPH, Brown U., Providence, RI, 2006. Diplomate in geriatrics Am. Bd. Internal Medicine, 2003. Intern/resident Case Western Res. U./MetroHealth Med. Ctr., 2000—03; geriatric medicine fellow Brown U./Rhode Island Hosp., Providence, 2003—06; postdoctoral rsch. fellow Brown U. Ctr. Gerontology and Health Care Rsch., Providence, 2004—06; asst. prof. medicine Brown Med. Sch., Providence, 2006—. Assoc. med. dir. Home and Hospice Care of R.I., Providence, 2006—, mem. diversity task force, 2006—; mem. fellowship exec. com. Brown Med. Sch., divsn. Geriat., Providence. Author: (book chpt.) The Elderly Female Patient; co-author (book chpt.) Pain Management in the Geriatric Patient, (article) Jour. Palliative Medicine, (review) Medicine and Health Rhode Island. Recipient James and Susan Carter Humanitarian award, Dept. Internal Medicine, MetroHealth Med. Ctr., 2003, Haffenreffer award in Fellowship Excellence, R.I. Hosp., Grad. Med. Edn., 2006, Chancellor's List, Nat. Academic Affairs, 2004—06, Tannenbaum Scholarship, U. Ark. for Med. SciS., 1996-2000; grantee, Agy. for Healthcare Rsch. and Quality, 2004—06. Mem.: Am. Acad. Hospice and Palliative Medicine, Am. Geriat. Soc., Nat. Med. Assn., Delta Sigma Theta Sorority, Inc. (mentor 2005). Baptist. Avocations: piano, singing, tennis, travel. Office: Brown Univ Ctr for Gerontology 2 Stimson Ave Box GS-311 Providence RI 02912

RHODES, RANDI, radio personality; b. Bklyn., Jan. 28, 1959; d. Norman and Loretta Bueten; m. Jim Robertson, 1994 (div. 2004); 1 stepchild, Jessica. Jobs at Radio Stations, Seminole, Tex., Mobile, Ala., NY, Dallas, Milw.; former sec., waitress, trucker and US Air Force aircraft mechanic; public relations job then weekend disc jockey WSHE, Coast 97.3 FM, 1987—92; radio talk show host WIOD AM, Miami, Fla., 1992—94, The Randi Rhodes Show, WJNO, West Palm Beach, Fla., 1994—2004, 2008—, The Randi Rhodes Show, Air America Radio, NYC, 2004—08. Served with USAF. Recipient Am. Women in Radio & TV award; named Woman of Yr., Talkers Mag., 2007; named a Most Outstanding Woman in the Air Force, 1979. Mailing: c/o Carmen Shamwell 4th Fl 641 Sixth Ave New York NY 10019*

RHODES, RAYMOND EARL, professional football coach; b. Mexia, Tex., Oct. 20, 1950; Student, Tex. Christian. Asst. def. backs coach San Francisco 49ers, 1981-82, def. backs coach, 1982-91, def. coord., 1994, Green Bay Packers, 1992-93, head coach, 1999-2000, Phila. Eagles, 1995-99; defensive coord. Washington Redskins, 2000, Denver Broncos, 2001—02; def. coord. Seattle Seahawks, 2003—05, spl. projects/def., 2005—07; asst. def. backs coach Houston Texans, 2008—. Named Named NFL Coach of the Yr., The Sporting News, 1995. Office: Houston Texans Two Reliant Pk Houston TX 77054 Office Phone: 832-667-2000.

RHODES, REBECCA LANE, school librarian; b. Boone, NC, Feb. 15, 1948; d. Cecil Elmer Rhodes and Adele Hendricks. BA in Psychology, King Coll., Bristol, Tenn., 1970. Cert. in collegiate profl. Dept. Edn./Va., 2007. Tchr. Franklin County Pub. Schs., Rocky Mount, Va., 1970—82, libr., 1982—. Recipient Tchr. of Yr., Snow Creek Elem. Sch. Mem.: NEA, FCEA, VEA. Independent. Presbyterian. Avocations: reading, games and puzzles. Office: Snow Creek Elementary Sch 5393 Snow Creek Rd Penhook VA 24137 Office Fax: 540-483-5604. Personal E-mail: rebecca.rhodes@gmail.com. Business E-Mail: rebecca.rhodes@frco.k12.va.us.

RHODES, RICHARD LEE, writer; b. Kansas City, Kans., July 4, 1937; s. Arthur and Georgia Saphronia (Collier) R.; children: Timothy James, Katherine Hampton; m. Ginger Kay Untrif, Oct. 3, 1993. BA cum laude, Yale U., 1959; LHD (hon.), Westminster Coll., Fulton, Mo., 1988. Author: The Inland Ground: An Evocation of the American Middle West, 1970, The Ungodly: A Novel of the Donner Party, 1973, The Ozarks, 1974, Holy Secrets, 1978, Looking for America: A writer's Odyssey, 1979, The Last Safari, 1980, Sons of Earth, 1981, The Making of the Atomic Bomb, 1986, Farm, 1989, A Hole in the World: An American Boyhood, 1990, Making Love: An Erotic Odyssey, 1992, Nuclear Renewal: Common Sense about Energy, 1993, How to Write: Advice and Reflections, 1995, Dark Sun: The Making of the Hydrogen Bomb, 1995, Deadly Feasts: Tracking the Secrets of a Terrifying New Plague, 1997, Why They Kill: The Discoveries of a Maverick Criminologist, 1999, Masters of Death: The SS-Einsatzgruppen and the Invention of the Holocaust, 2002, John James Audubon: The Making of an American, 2004, Arsenals of Folly: The Making of the Nuclear Arms Race, 2007; co-author: (with Ginger Rhodes) Trying to Get Some Dignity: Stories of Triumph over Childhood Abuse, 1996; editor: Visions of Technology: A Century of Vital Debate about Machines, Systems, and the Human World, 1999, The Audubon Reader, 2006; Artist: theater play Reykjavik, 2008. Trustee Andrew Drumm Inst., Independence, Mo., 1991-, Atomic Heritage Found., DC, 2004-, Cypress Found., DC, 2005-. Recipient Nat. Book Critics Cir. award for nonfiction, Nat. Book award for nonfiction, 1987, Pulitzer prize, 1988; Guggenheim fellow, 1974-75, fellow Nat. Endowment for Arts, 1978-79, Ford Found., 1981-83, Sloan Found., 1985, 89, 91, 92, 2002-, MacArthur Found., 1990-91. Office: c/o Janklow & Nesbit Assoc 445 Park Ave New York NY 10022-2606 Business E-Mail: richardrhodes1@comcast.net.

RHODES, SAMUEL, violist, educator; b. Long Beach, NY, Feb. 13, 1941; s. Bernard and Martha (Ephraim) R.; m. Hiroko Yajima, Dec. 30, 1968; children— Amy, Harumi. BA, Queen's Coll., CUNY, 1963; M.F.A., Princeton U., 1967; D.F.A. (hon.), Mich. State U., 1984; MusD (hon.), Jacksonville U., 1986, San Francisco Conservatory, 1996. Mem. faculty Juilliard Sch., NYC, 1969—, Mich. State U., East Lansing, 1977-85, SUNY-Purchase, 1982-86; violist Marlboro Festival, 1960-68, 78-81, 91—, Galimir String Quartet, 1961-68, Juilliard String Quartet, 1969—; mem. faculty Tanglewood Music Ctr., 1988—. Office: Juilliard Sch Music Lincoln Ctr New York NY 10023

RHODES, SANDRA LAVERN, retired elementary school educator; b. Susanville, Calif., June 30, 1944; d. Harold Robert and Verdie Lavern Trussell; m. Oran Wayne Rhodes, Apr. 8, 1966; children: Renee, Kevin, Tracey, Mark. BS in Edn., Abilene Christian U., 1966; MS in Edn., Ctrl. Mo. State U., 1992. Cert. tchr. Tex., Mo. Elem. tchr. Moffat County Ind. Sch. Dist., 1966—67; tchr. Killeen (Tex.) Ind. Sch. Dist., 1985—86, Hickman Mills Consol. Sch. Dist., Kansas City, Mo., 1989—2008, curriculum developer, 2002—05, chmn., 2000—08. Tch. advisor Dobbs Elem., Kansas City, 1996—2005, grade level chairperson, 2000—08. Contbr. articles to profl. jours. Prof. women studies Midwestern Sch. Preaching, Sugar Creek, Mo., 1992—2000; workshop presenter, 1979—99. Recipient Appreciation Recognition, Mo. Scholars Acad., 2000; nominee Disney Tchr. of Yr., 2000. Mem.: Mo. State Tchrs. Assn. (local pres. 1995—97). Republican. Mem. Ch. Of Christ. Avocations: genealogy, travel.

RHODES, SHARYN S., education educator, consultant; d. Sigmund Louis Orlowski and May Crystal; m. Thomas Gerald Pokorny, Oct. 14, 2000. PhD, U. Wyo., Laramie, 1975. Tchr. Balt. City Schs., 1971—73; prof. Appalachain State U., Boone, NC, 1975—79; postdoc. fellow Johns Hopkins U., Balt., 1979—80; prof. Loyola Coll., Balt., 1980—. Ednl. cons. Sharyn Rhodes Cons., Balt., 1979—, cons., 1980—. Contbr. articles to profl. jours. Mem.: CHADD (bd. mem.; com. mem. & coord. 2009—). Office: Loyola Coll 4501 N Charles St Baltimore MD 21210

RHODES, SHERRY L., educator; d. Raymond Edward and Audrienne Campbell; m. Arthur Ray Rhodes, June 4, 1966; 1 child, Shelly Raelyn Roop. BA in English, U. North Tex., Denton, 1974, MA in Comm., 1975, postgrad. in Comm. Cert. clin. hypnotherapist Hypnotist Exam. Coun. Calif., 1997. Comm. mgr. C. of C., Dallas, 1977—80; human rels. cons. Sherry Rhodes & Assocs., Richardson, Tex., 1980—98; prof. Collin Coll., Plano, Tex., 1998—. Clin. hypnotherapist CenterPoint Inst., Richardson, Tex., 1993—98. Author: (novel) In Love & Light. Steering com. mem. CCCCD Women's Alliance, Plano, 2003—08; vol. Children's Med. Ctr., Dallas, Spl. Olympics, Dem. Party Collin County. Mem.: Nat. Comm. Assn., Tex. CC Tchrs. Assn. Avocations: travel, reading, swimming, walking, horseback riding. Office: Collin Coll 2800 E Spring Creek Pky Plano TX 75074 Business E-Mail: srhodes@ccccd.edu.

RHODES, THOMAS WILLARD, lawyer; b. Lynchburg, Va., Mar. 9, 1946; s. Howard W. and Ruth R.; m. Ann Bloodworth, May 31, 1975; children: Mildred, Andrew. AB, Davidson Coll., NC, 1968; JD, U. Va., 1971. Bar: Ga. 1971. Assoc. Smith, Gambrell & Russell and predecessor firms, Atlanta, 1971-76, ptnr., 1976—. Dir., pres. Atlanta Vol. Lawyers Found., 1984-89; dir. Fed. Defender Program, Atlanta, 1988-92, 2003—, pres., 1991-92. Contbr. profl. jours. and textbooks; editor: Nonprofit News. Capt. USAR, 1968—72. Recipient Heiner award Atlanta Vol. Lawyers Found., 1989, Anderson Lecture award Am. Acad. Facial Plastic and Reconstructive Surgery, 2004. Fellow Am. Law Inst. (life); mem. Ga. Bar Assn. (past chmn. antitrust law sect.). Office: Smith Gambrell & Russell Promenade II 1230 Peachtree St NE Ste 3100 Atlanta GA 30309-3592

RHODES, WILLIAM C., III, automotive executive; B in Acctg., U. Tenn.; MBA, U. Memphis. CPA. With Ernst & Young, 1988—94, Autozone Inc., Memphis, 1994—, v.p., 1997—99, sr. v.p., 1999—2002, exec. v.p., 2002—05, pres., CEO, 2005—07, chmn., pres., CEO, 2007—. Bd. mem. Memphis Tomorrow; treas. Nat. Civil Rights Mus.; mem. partners bd. FedEx Inst. Tech. Office: Autozone Inc 123 S Front St Memphis TN 38103

RHODES, WILLIAM REGINALD (BILL RHODES), diversified financial services company executive; b. NYC, Aug. 15, 1935; s. Edward R. and Elsie Rhodes; divorced; 1 child, Elizabeth. BA in History, Brown U., 1957, degree (hon.), 2005. Joined Citibank, 1957, served in several sr. positions in Latin Am. and Caribbean, 1957—77; from sr. officer internat. banking group-L.Am. and Caribbean to vice-chmn. Citibank, N.A., NYC, 1977—91, vice-chmn., 1991—2001, sr. vice chmn., 2001—03, 2009—, chmn., 2003—05, chmn., pres., CEO, 2005—09; sr. vice chmn. Citigroup, Inc., 1999—; chmn., CEO Citicorp Holdings, Inc., 2003—05, chmn., pres., CEO, 2005—09. First vice chmn. Inst. Internat. Fin.; mem. Met. Mus. Bus. Com., U.S.-Russia Bus. Coun.; past chmn. adv. com. Export-Import Bank of US; past chmn. U.S. sect. Venezuela-U.S. Bus. Coun.; founding mem. U.S. Nat. Adv. Coun. to the Internat. Mgmt. Ctr., Budapest; active U.S.-Egyptian Pres. Coun.; bd. dirs. ConocoPhillips, Pvt. Export Funding Corp. Chmn. Northfield-Mt. Hermon Sch., Hong Kong-U.S. Bus. Coun.; bd. dirs., gov., trustee NY and Presbyn. Hosp.; bd. overseers Watson Inst. for Internat. Studies, Brown U.; active Lincoln Ctr. Corporate Leadership Com.; vice-chmn. Metropolitan Mus. Art Bus. Com. and chmn. com.; bd. dirs. Africa-Am. Inst.; vice chmn. bd. Nat. Com. on U.S.-China Rels.; hon. chmn., Sister City Program of City of NY. Decorated comdr. and grand officer Nat. Order of the So. Cross (Brazil); officer Legion of Honor (France); Orden de Mayo (Argentina); officer Order Francisco Miranda 1st and 3rd classes, Order Merito en el Trabajo 1st class (Venezuela); Order of Diplomatic Svc., Heung-In medal, Korea; comdr. Order of Distinction (Jamaica); recipient Am.'s award, 1997, African Bus. Devel. award African Am. Inst., 1998, Banker's Lifetime Achievment award Arab Bankers Assn. N.Am., 1999, Stephen P. Duggan award for Internat. Understanding, Inst. for Internat. Edn., 1999, William I. Spencer award NY Blood Ctr., 1999. Mem. Americas Soc. (chmn. bd. dirs.), Coun. of Ams. (chmn. bd. dirs.), Bankers Assn. Fin. and Trade (past pres., Banker of Yr. award 2004), Coun. Fgn. Rels., Venezuelan-Am. C. of C. (past pres.), Fgn. Policy Assn. (bd. dirs.). Avocations: jogging, swimming, archeology, reading. Office: Citigroup Inc 399 Park Ave New York NY 10043-0001*

RHODES, YORKE E(DWARD), organic chemist, educator; b. Elizabeth, NJ, Mar. 25, 1936; s. Yorke Edward and Helen (Pyper) R.; m. Mechthilde Weggenmann, May 24, 1975; children: Yorke Edward III, Christopher A., Matthias Raabe, Timothy A. BS, U. Del., 1957, MS, 1959; PhD, U. Ill., 1963. Chemist Thiokol Chem. Corp., Elkton, Md., 1959; lectr. Yale U., New Haven, 1964-65; asst. prof. chemistry NYU, NYC, 1965-71, assoc. prof., 1971—, asst. dean Coll. Arts and Sci., 1987-89, dir. NYU-Stevens dual degree program in sci. and engring., 1988-2000. Vis. prof. U. Freiburg, Germany, 1972-73, Tech. U. Munich, 1977, Harvard U., 2001; vis. prof. astrophysics U. Grenoble, France, 1987; Humboldt vis. prof. Tech. U. Munich, 1978; Dept. State sci. exch. visitor Zagreb, Yugoslavia, and Prague, Czechoslovakia, 1977. Contbr. articles to sci. jours. Committeeman Englewood Dem. Com., 1968—72; apptd. mem. NYC Mayor's Green Cleaning Adv. Com., 2006—08; chair MARM Exec. Com., 2008—. Recipient Humboldt award, 1978, NYU Great Tchr. award, 2000; NIH fellow, Yale U., 1964—65, fellow, Danforth assoc. Faculty, 1967—72, NASA summer faculty fellow, Jet Propulsion Lab., Pasadena, Calif., 1980, 1981. Mem.: Phi Lambda Upsilon, Planetary Soc., Royal Soc. Chemistry, Am. Chem. Soc. (vice-chmn. N.Y. sect. 1997, chmn. 1998, councilor 1998—, chair nat. local sect. activities com. 2002—04, mem. coun. policy com. 2005—), Sigma Xi. Avocations: opera, photography, travel, gardening, railroads. Office: NYU Dept Chemistry 100 Washington Sq E New York NY 10003-6688 Office Phone: 212-998-8476. Business E-Mail: yorke.rhodes@nyu.edu.

RHODY, RONALD EDWARD, bank, communications executive; b. Frankfort, Ky., Jan. 27, 1932; s. James B. and Mary M. (Clark) R.; m. Patricia Schupp, Apr. 23, 1955; children: Leslie K., Mary M., Virginia K., Ronald C. Student, Georgetown Coll., Ky., 1950-52, U. Ky., 1953-55. Pub. rels. dir. Kaiser Aluminum & Chem. Corp., Ravenswood, W.Va., 1959-62, NYC, 1962-67, corp. v.p. Oakland, Calif., 1967-83; sr. v.p. corp comm. Bank of Am. NT&SA, San Francisco, 1983—, exec. v.p., 1992-94; CEO Rhody, Inc., 1994—. Author: The CEO's Playbook, 1999, Wordsmithing, 2006, Theos Story, 2009; contbr. articles to profl. jours. Founding chmn. adv. bd. San Francisco Acad. Named Pub. Rels. Profl. of Yr., Pub. Rels. News, 1981; recipient Hall of Fame award Page Soc., 1997. Fellow Pub. Rels. Soc. Am.; mem. Pub. Rels. Soc. Am. (accredited, pres.'s adv. coun. Rex Harlow award), Internat. Assn. Bus. Communicators (Gold Quill award 1980), Pub. Rels. Roundtable San Francisco (mem. bd. govs., awards 1980, 85). Home: 187 Juniper Creek Blvd Pinehurst NC 28374-6993 E-mail: ron.rhody@yahoo.com.

RHONE, SYLVIA MARIE MILLER, recording industry executive; b. Phila., Mar. 11, 1952; d. James and Marie (Christmas) Rhone; 1 child, Quinn. BS in Econs., U. Pa. Wharton Sch. Bus. and Commerce, 1974; LHD (hon.), Adelphi U., 1996. Comml. lending trainee Bankers Trust Co., NYC; sec. Buddha Records, 1974, nat. promotion coord., Bareback Records; regional promotions mgr. ABC Records, 1976—78, Ariola

Records, 1978—79; N.E. regional promotions mgr./special markets Elektra Records, 1980—83, dir. mktg./special markets, 1983—85; dir. nat. black music promotion Atlantic Records, NYC, 1985—88, v.p., gen. mgr. black music ops., 1988—88, sr. v.p., gen. mgr. black music ops., 1988—90; CEO, co-pres. EastWest Records America, NYC, 1990—91; chmn., CEO EastWest/Atco Records, NYC, 1991—94; chair/CEO Elektra Entertainment, NYC, 1994—2004; exec. v.p. Universal Records, 2004—06; pres. Motown Records, 2004—06, Universal Motown Records, 2006—. Mem., bd. dirs. Alvin Ailey Am. Dance Theatre, The RIAA, Rock n' Roll Hall of Fame, Jazz at Lincoln Ctr., R&B Found., Studio Mus. of Harlem; bd. dirs. NARAS. Alumni trustee U. Pa., 2001—. Recipient Whitney M. Young Svc. award, Boy Scouts of Am., 1992, Joel Webber Prize for Excellence in Music/Bus. award, New Music Seminar, 1993, Sony Soul of Am. Music Excellence award, 1993, Legacy Life Mem. award, Nat. Coun. of Negro Women, 1995, Urban Network Exec. Yr. award, 1995, Herbert H. Wright award, Nat. Assn. Market Developers, 1995, Studio Mus. Corp. award, 1996, Creative Spirit award, Black Alumni Pratt Inst., Echo & Trumpet awards, Turner Broadcasting, 2004; named one of Most Influential Black Americans, Ebony mag., 2006, The 100 Most Powerful Women in Entertainment, Hollywood Reporter, 2006, 2007, The 100 Most Influential Women in NYC Bus., Crain's NY Bus., 2007; named to Power 150, Ebony mag., 2008. Achievements include becoming 1st African American and first woman chairman and CEO of a major record company. Office: Univeral Motown Records 1755 Broadway # 6 New York NY 10019 Office Phone: 212-275-2805.

RHOTEN, KENNETH DALE, writer; b. Hammond, Ind., Dec. 28, 1950; s. James Edward and Helen Louise (Wasson) R.; m. Virginia Haynie (div.); m. Linda Robin Damron (div.); m. Josephine Meese (dec.); life partner Angela. Draftsman Hahn, Inc., Evansville, Ind., 1973—75; laborer Inland Steel Works, 1975; draftsman N.W. Ind. Regional Planning Com., Highland, 1975—76; draftsman, artist graphic sys. divsn. Rockwell Internat., Cicero, Ill., 1977—78; designer Roper Outdoor Products (in cooperation with Espo Engring.), Bradley, 1978—79; draftsman Fedders Corp., Effingham, 1982—83; freelance writer, inventor, 1983—. Author, editor: Dark Twist of Fate, 1995, 3d edit., 2003, Dark Twist of Fate and Other Works, 1999; author: A Voice From Beyond, 1999, The Complete Works of Kenneth D. Rhoten, 1999, Mathematical Equivalents, 2006; composer pub. songs; patentee automatic brewing apparatus, 1984. Rep. candidate Ill. House of Reps., 1986. Achievements include successful redevelopment of the Edison storage cell and development of new secondary cell; deduced mechanism of Bessler's wheel and constructed model; development of mechanical advantage gravity motors; discovered Ezekiel's wheel; history & physics. Home and Office: PO Box 225 Stoy IL 62464-0225

RHOTON, ALBERT LOREN, JR., neurosurgeon, educator; b. Nov. 18, 1932; s. Albert Loren and Hazel Arnette (Van Cleve) R.; m. Joyce L. Moldenhauer, June 23, 1957; children: Eric L., Albert J., Alice S., Laural A. BS, Ohio State U., 1954; MD cum laude, Washington U., St. Louis, 1959. Diplomate Am. Bd. Neurol. Surgery (bd dirs. 1985-91, vice-chmn. 1991). Intern Columbia Presbyn. Med. Ctr., NYC, 1959; resident in neurol. surgery Barnes Hosp., St. Louis, 1961-65; cons. neurol. surgery Mayo Clinic, Rochester, Minn., 1965-72; chief divsn. neurol. surgery U. Fla., Gainesville, 1972-80, R.D. Keene prof., 1980—, chmn. dept. neurol. surgery, 1980-2000, chmn. emeritus, 2000—. Developer microsurg. tng. ctr.; hon. v.p. World Congress of Neurosurgery, 2005-; hon. prof. Beijing (China) Capital U., 2005—; lectr. in field. Author: The Orbit and Sellar Region: Microsurgical Anatomy and Operative Approaches, 1996, Anatomy and Surgical Approaches to the Temporal Bone, Cranial Anatomy and Surgical Approaches, Chinese and English edits., 2003, Anatomy and Surgery Approaches to the Temporal Bone; mem. editl. bd. Neurosurgery, Jour. Microsurgery, Surg. Neurology, Jour. Fla. Med. Assn., Am. Jour. Otology, Skull Base Surgery; contbr. articles to profl. jours. Hon. pres. World Congress Endoscopic Skull Base Surgery, 2009; bd. dirs. Neurosurgery Edn. and Rsch. Found. Recipient Disting. Faculty award, U. Fla., 1981, Alumni Achievement award, Washington U. Sch. Medicine, 1985, Jones award for outstanding spl. med. exhibit of yr., Am. Assn. med. Illustrators, 1969, Jameison medal, Neurosurg. soc. Australasia, 1997, Outstanding Achievement award, World Congress of Skull Base Surgery, 2000, medal of honor, World Fedn. Neurosurg. Socs., 2001, medal, Neurosurg. Soc. Am., 2001, endowed professorship named in his honor, U. Fla., Lifetime Achievement award, Wall of Fame Honoree, Honorary Alumnus award, 2001, medal of honor, Neurosurg. Soc. of Am., 2001, Bucy award, U. Chgo., 2002; grantee NIH, VA, Am. Heart Assn. Mem. ACS (bd. govs. 1978-84), AMA (Billings Bronze medal 1969), Fla. Brain Tumor Assn. and Moffitt Cancer Ctr. (Lifetime Achievement award, 2008), Congress Neurol. Surgeons (pres. 1978, Exceptional and Disting. Svc. award 2004, honored guest 1993, Founders Laurel award 2006), Nat. Found. Brain Rsch. (bd. dirs. 1990-94), Nat. Coalition for Rsch. in Neurol. Disorders (bd. dirs. 1990-94), Neurol. Soc. Am. (medal 2001), Internat. Congress Meningiomas (hon. pres 2000), Neurosurg. Soc. Brazil (hon., honored guest 2004), Neurosurg. Soc. Japan (hon., Honored guest 2002), Neurosurg. Soc. Mex. (hon.), Neurosurg. Soc. Can. (hon.), Neurosurg. Soc. Uruguay (hon.), Neurosurg. Soc. Venezuela (hon.), Neurosurg. Soc. Turkey (hon.), Korean Neurol. Soc. (hon.), Neurosurg. Soc. Tex. (hon.), Neurosurg. Soc. Okla. (hon.), Neurosurg. Soc. Wis. (hon.), Neurosurg. Soc. Ga. (hon.), Neurosurg. Soc. Rocky Mountain (hon.), Neurosurg. Soc. China (hon.), Neurosurg Soc. Argentina (hon.), Latin Am. Neurosurg. Soc. (hon.), Neurosurg. Soc. Chili (hon.), Fla. Neurosurg. Soc. (pres. 1978), Am. Assn. Neurol. Surgeons (chmn. vascular sect., treas. 1983-86, v.p. 1987-88, pres. 1989-90, exec. com. 1993, Cushing medal 1998), Soc. Neurol. Surgeons (treas. 1975-81, pres. 1993), So. Neurol. Soc. (v.p. 1976), Alachua County Med. Soc. (exec. com. 1978), Fla. Med. Assn., Am. Surg. Assn., Soc. Univ. Neurosurgeons, Am. Heart Assn. (stroke coun., Outstanding Achievement award 1971), N.Am. Skull Base Soc. (pres. 1993-94, honored guest 2001, Lifetime Achievement award 2005), Am. Acad. Neurol. Surgery, Acoustic Neuroma Assn. (med. adv. bd. 1983-2000, chmn. 1992-2001, chmn. emeritus 2001—), Trigeminal Neurol. Assn. (med. advisor bd. 1992—), Hemifacial Spasm Assn. (med. adv. bd. 2002—), Internat. Interdisciplinary Congress on Craniofacial and Skull Base Surgery (pres. 1996-97), Internat. Soc. Neurosurg. Tech. and Instrument Invention (pres. 1997—), Japanese Skull Base Soc. (hon. pres. 2000), Internat. Soc. for Microsurgery Anatomy (hon. pres. 2002, 2004-), World Fedn. Neurosurg. Soc. (hon. v.p. 2005—), World Congress Endoscopic Surgery Brain, Skull Base & Spine (hon. guest), Internat. Levantine Forum, (Turkey) (hon. pres., 2008-), Congress World Fed. SROH Base Socs., Vancouver, BC (honored guest 2008), European Skull Base Soc.(Rotterdam)(hon. mem.), Columbian Neurosurg. Soc., European Skill Base Soc.(hon.) Achievements include design of more than 200 microsurgery instruments; fundraising for 11 endowed chairs at University of Florida. Home: 2505 NW 22d Ave Gainesville FL 32605-3819 Office: U Fla Dept Neurosurgery PO Box 100265 100 S Newell Dr Gainesville FL 32610 Office Phone: 352-273-7788, 352-273-9000. Business E-Mail: rhoton@neurosurgery.ufl.edu.

RHUE, MONIKA RIVERA, archivist; d. Payne Roy and Gloria Williams, Ernest William (Stepfather); m. Stephen Eric Short, July 12, 2003. MLIS, U. NC, Greensboro, 2002. Monika R. Rhue NC Pub. Libr. Bd., 2004, cert. pub. libr. Libr. asst. II Pub. Libr. Charlotte Mecklenburg County, 1995—99; archivist Johnson C. Smith U., Charlotte, 1999—; dir. libr. svc. James B. Duke Meml. Libr. Sci. CEO Preserve Pro, Inc., Charlotte, 2005—; adv. bd. mem. NC Exploring Cultural Heritage Online, Raleigh; exec. bd. mem. Charlotte Black Heritage Grp. Recipient Rsch. grant, Arts & Sci. Emerging Artist, 1993. Mem.: ALA, Afro-Am. Hist. and Geneal. Soc., Soc. NC Archivists (program chair, pres. 2005—07). D-Conservative. Pan African. Avocations: dance, writing. Home: 7419 Balancing Rock Ct Charlotte NC 28262 Office: Johnson C Smith Univ 100 Beatties Ford Rd Charlotte NC 28216 Office Fax: 704-378-3524. Business E-Mail: mrhue@jcsu.edu.

RHYAN, JACK C., pathologist; DVM, Auburn U., Ala., 1975. Vet. pathologist USDA APHIS VS NVSL, Ames, Iowa, 1990—97, wildlife pathologist Ft. Collins, Colo., 1997—. Contbr. scientific papers to profl. jours. Mem.: Wildlife Disease Assn. Achievements include patents pending for wildlife contraceptive product. Office: USDA APHIS 4101 LaPorte Ave Fort Collins CO 80521

RHYS MEYERS, JONATHAN, actor; b. Dublin, July 27, 1977; Actor: (films) A Man of No Importance, 1994, Michael Collins, 1996, La Lengua asesina, 1996, The Disappearance of Finbar, 1996, The Maker, 1997, Telling Lies in Am., 1997, Velvet Goldmine, 1998, The Governess, 1998, The Tribe, 1998, B. Monkey, 1998, The Loss of Sexual Innocence, 1999, Ride with the Devil, 1999, Titus, 1999, Happy Now, 2001, Prozac Nation, 2001, Tangled, 2001, Bend It Like Beckham, 2002, The Tesseract, 2003, Octane, 2003, I'll Sleep When I'm Dead, 2003, The Emperor's Wife, 2003, Vanity Fair, 2004, Alexander, 2004, Match Point, 2005, Mission: Impossible III, 2006, August Rush, 2007; (TV films) Samson and Delilah, 1996, The Magnificent Ambersons, 2002, The Lion in Winter, 2003, Elvis, 2005 (Outstanding Actor in Miniseries or Motion Picture Made for TV, Satellite Awards, 2005, Golden Globe award, 2006); (TV series) The Tudors, 2007—. Recipient Chopard trophy, Cannes Film Festival, 2005. Office: c/o Sharon Sheinwold United Talent Agy 9560 Wilshire Blvd #500 Beverly Hills CA 90212

RIABOV, VLADIMIR VICTOR, aerospace, mechanical, computer engineer, consultant; b. Orel, Russia, 1953; came to U.S., 1992; BS in Aircraft Design, MS in Aircraft Design, Moscow Inst. Physics & Tech., 1976, PhD in Physics and Math., 1979; MS in Computer Info. Sys., So. N.H. U., 1998. Cert. sr. rschr. Vysshaya Attestatsionnaya Kommissiya pri Sovete Ministrov SSSR, Russia. Sr. engr., sr. rschr. Ctrl. Aero-Hydrodynamics Inst., Zhukovsky (Moscow region), Russia, 1979-92, dep. dir., 1989-92; vis. assoc. prof. Worcester (Mass.) Polytech. Inst., 1993-97; software engr. Newbridge Networks, Inc., Andover, Mass., 1998—99; sr. software engr. Nortel Networks, Inc., Billerica, Mass., 2000—01. Cons. Manchester, N.H., 1992—; adj. assoc. prof. U. N.H., 1998—; assoc. prof. Rivier Coll., 2001-08, prof. River Coll., 2008-. Contbr. articles to profl. jours. in Russia and in U.S. including Jour. of Aircraft, Jour. of Thermophysics and Heat Transfer, AIAA Papers, Jour. Engring. Physics, Jour. Applied Mechanics and Tech. Physics, Fluid Dynamics, Fluid Mechanics, Jour. Spacecraft and Rockets, Computers and Structures. Founder Russian br. of Open U. of Great Britain, Zhukovsky, 1990-92. Mem. AIAA (sr.), ACM, IEEE, Math. Assn. America. Business E-Mail: vriabov@rivier.edu.

RIASANOVSKY, NICHOLAS VALENTINE, retired historian, educator; b. Harbin, China, Dec. 21, 1923; arrived in U.S., 1938, naturalized, 1943; m. Arlene Ruth Schlegel, Feb. 15, 1955; children: John, Nicholas, Maria. BA, U. Oreg., 1942; AM, Harvard U., 1947; DPhil, Oxford U., Eng., 1949. Mem. faculty U. Iowa, 1949-57, U. Calif., Berkeley, 1957—, prof. history, 1961—, Sidney Hellman Ehrman prof. European history, 1969—2003, ret., 2003. Vis. rsch. prof. USSR Acad. Scis., Moscow, 1969, Moscow and Leningrad, 1974, 79. Author: Russia and the West in the Teaching of the Slavophiles: A Study of Romantic Ideology, 1952, Nicholas I and Official Nationality in Russia, 1825-1855, 1959, A History of Russia, 1963, 7th edit. (with Prof. Mark Steinberg), 2005, The Teaching of Charles Fourier, 1969, A Parting of Ways: Government and the Educated Public in Russia, 1801-1855, 1976, The Image of Peter the Great in Russian History and Thought, 1985, The Emergence of Romanticism, 1992, Collected Writings 1947-94, 1993, Russian Identities, a Historical Survey, 2005; co-editor: California Slavic Studies, 1960—; editl. bd. Russian rev., Zarubezhnaia Periodicheskaia Pechat' na Russkom Iazyke, Simvol; contbr. articles to profl. jours. Trustee Nat. Coun. Soviet and East European Rsch., 1978—82; mem. Kennan Inst. Acad. Coun., 1986—89. 2d lt. AUS, 1943—46. Decorated Bronze Star; recipient Silver medal Commonwealth Club Calif., 1964; Rhodes scholar, 1947-49; Fulbright grantee, 1954-55, 74, 79; Guggenheim fellow, 1969; sr. fellow NEH, 1975; Fulbright sr. scholar, sr. fellow Ctr. Advanced Studies in Behavioral Scis., 1984-85; sr. fellow Woodrow Wilson Internat. Ctr. for Scholars, 1989-90. Mem. Am. Assn. Advancement Slavic Studies (pres. 1973-76, Disting. Contbr. award 1993), Am. Hist. Assn. (award for Scholarly Distinction 1995), Am. Acad. Arts and Scis.

RIBA, SHIRLEY, artist; d. Arthur Roy and Idell Carolina Riba. BFA, Calif. Coll. Arts and Crafts, Oakland, 1977. Sales/dept. display Gumps Oriental Antique Dept., San Francisco, 1979—; owner ARTRIBA, Laporte, Colo., 1995—. Exhibitions include Corcoran Sch. Art, Washington, D.C., 1977—78, Calif. Coll. of Arts & Crafts, San Francisco, 1977, E.B. Crocker Kingsley, Sacramento, 1979, Gump's Gallery, San Francisco, 1979—90, 1981, 1986, Represented in permanent collections Bohemian Found., Calif., prin. works include Mural After Parrish, 2002, Commissioned Works in Progress, represented in pvt. collections. Home: PO Box 800 Laporte CO 80535

RIBAR, DAVID CHRISTOPHER, economics professor; s. Cynthia Anne Ribar; m. Catherine Avery Moon, Oct. 1, 1988; children: David Tylman, Matthew Karol. PhD, Brown U., Providence, RI, 1990. Asst. prof. Pa. State U., University Park, Pa., 1990—96; asst. assc. prof. George Wash. U., Washington, 1996—2006; prof. U. NC, Greensboro, 2006—. Office: Univ NC Greensboro PO Box 26165 Greensboro NC 27402

RIBARY, URS, neuroscientist, educator; b. Lucerne, Switzerland, Nov. 24, 1955; came to U.S., 1988; m. Evelyne Dahinden, July 11, 1986; 1 child, Samanta R. MS, Swiss Fed. Inst. Tech., Zurich, 1981, DSc, 1985. Rsch. asst. prof. NYU Med. Ctr., NYC, 1988—93, dir. ctr. neuromagnetism, 1989—2005, assoc. prof., 1993—2007; prof. Simon Fraser U., Vancouver, BC, Canada, 2007—. Vis. asst. prof. Simon Fraser U., Can., 1986-88; endowed BC leadership chair Cognitive Neurosci. Childhood Health and Devel., BC, Can., 2007-. Cons. (Time Life series) The Brain, 1990; contbr. articles to profl. jours. Co-founder, chmn. Samanta S. Ribary Found. Inc. Mem. AAAS, Am. Soc. Neurosci., N.Y. Acad. Scis., European Neurosci. Assn., Soc. Cognitive Neuroscience. Achievements include rsch. on using functional brain imaging techniques, to study quantal sequences of dynamic network connectivity in humans during normal cognitive processing, and its alterations in neurological and neuropsychiatric patients. Home: 1068 Sugar Mountain Way Anmore BC V3H 4Y7 Canada

RIBBANS, GEOFFREY WILFRID, language educator; b. London, Apr. 15, 1927; came to U.S. 1978; s. Wilfrid Henry and Rose Matilda (Burton)R.; m. Magdalena Willmann, Apr. 21, 1956; children: Madeleine Elizabeth, Helen Margaret, Peter John. BA with 1st class hons., Kings Coll., U. London, 1948, MA, 1953. Asst. lectr. U. Sheffield, Eng., 1954-56, lectr., 1956-61, sr. lectr. Spanish, 1961-63; Gilmour prof. Spanish U. Liverpool, Eng., 1963-78; vis. Mellon prof. Spanish U. Pitts., 1970-71; Wm. R. Kenan Jr. U. prof. Spanish Brown U., Providence, 1978-99, chmn. dept., 1981-84, prof. emeritus, 1999—. Editor Bull. Hispanic Studies, 1964-78; vis. prof. U. Salamanca, Spain, 1995. Author: Catalunya i Valencia al Segle XVIII, 1955, 2d edit., 1993, Niebla y Soledad: Aspectos de Unamuno y Machado, 1971, Galdós: Fortunata y Jacinta, 1977, Spanish transl., 1988; editor: Antonio Machado, Soledades, Galerias, Otros Poemas, 1984, rev. 17th edit., 2008, Campos de Castilla, 1989, 14th edit., 2003, History and Fiction in Galdós's Narratives, 1993, 2d edit., 1995, Conflicts and Conciliations: The Evolution of Galdós's "Fortunata y Jacinta", 1997. Decorated La Encomienda de la Orden de Isabel la Catolica Spain; recipient prize for excellence in Galdos studies, Las Palmas, 1997, Batista i Roca prize, Barcelona, 2000; Hispanic studies in his honour, Liverpool, 1992, Symposium on Modernism and Modernity in his honor, Brown U., 1998. Mem. MLA, Internat. Assn. Hispanists (v.p. 1974-80), Internat. Assn. Galdós Scholars (pres. 1988-89), N.Am. Catalan Soc. (hon.). Office: Brown U Dept Hispanic Studies PO Box 1961 Providence RI 02912-1961 Business E-Mail: Geoffrey_ribbans@brown.edu.

RIBBLE, JOHN CHARLES, medical educator; b. Paris, Tex., July 26, 1931; s. Elbert Alfred and Dorothy (Pyeatt) R.; m. Anne Blythe Hoerner; 1 stepchild Helen Blythe Strate Kielty. MD, U. Tex., 1955. Diplomate Am. Bd. Internal Medicine. Asst. prof. medicine Cornell U., NYC, 1962-66, assoc. prof. pediatrics, 1966-78, assoc. dean, 1974-78, Med. Sch., U. Tex., Houston, 1978-86, dean, 1986-95; vis. scholar The Health Inst. New Eng. Med. Ctr., Boston, 1995-96; prof. medicine U. Tex., Houston, 1996—. Mem. Nat. Adv. Coun. Gen. Med. Scis. NIH, Bethesda, Md., 1988-91. Episcopalian. Home: 6200 Willers Way Houston TX 77057-2808 Office: U Tex Med Sch 6431 Fannin St Houston TX 77030-1501 Office Phone: 713-500-6709. E-mail: johnribble@comcast.net.

RIBBLE, RONALD GEORGE, psychologist, educator, writer, behavioral consultant; b. West Reading, Pa., May 7, 1937; s. Jeremiah George and Mildred Sarah (Folk) Ribble; m. Catalina Valenzuela Torres, Sept. 30, 1961; children: Christina, Timothy, Kenneth. BSEE cum laude, U. Mo., 1968, MSEE, 1969, MA, 1985, PhD, 1986. Bd. cert. forensic examiner, diplomate in behavioral sci. Am. Bd. Psychol. Spltys., Am. Coll. Forensic Examiners; cert. in homeland security. Enlisted USAF, 1956-60, advance through grades to lt. col., 1976—81; rsch. dir. Coping Resources, Inc., Columbia, Mo., 1986; pres., co-owner Towers and Rushing Ltd. (Pubs. and Psychol. Cons., Troubadour 1997-2001), San Antonio, 1986—; referral devel. Laughlin Pavilion Psychiat. Hosp., Kirksville, Mo., 1987; program dir. Psychiat. Insts. of Am., Iowa Falls, Iowa, 1987-88; lead psychotherapist Gasconade County Counseling Ctr., Hermann, Mo., 1988; sr. lectr. U. Tex., San Antonio, 1989—2002; lectr. Trinity U., San Antonio, 1995-96; assessment clinician Afton Oaks Psychiat. Hosp., San Antonio, 1989-91; ret. from tchg., 2002. Faculty cons. Edn. Testing Svc., 1997; psychologist Olmos Psychol. Svcs., Inc., San Antonio, 1991—93; vol. assessor Holmgreen Children's Shelter, San Antonio, 1992—93; founder Ruth Bohn Weissman Scholarship in Creative Writing U. Tex., San Antonio, 1994—2004; co-sponor Lyric Recovery Festival, Carnegie Hall, 2000; condr. seminars, revs. for maj. publs.; founding mem. U. Mo.-Columbia Bd. Psychology Leaders, 2007. Author: (book) Apples, Weeds, and Doggie Poo, 1995, Dont' Eat the Snake!, 1999; contbr. essays to psychol. refernce books, poetry to anthologies periodicals, lyrics to popular music; interviewer: celebrities in performing and lit. arts, 1995—, columnist: Feelings, 1993—97; pub. access TV appearances, 1991—. Founding cabinet mem. World Peace and Diplomacy Forum; vol. announcer pub. radio sta., Colombia, 1993; vol. Cath. Family and Children's Svc., San Antonio, 1989—91; chpt. advisor Rational Recovery Program for Alcoholics, San Antonio, 1991—92; mem. Pres. Leadership Cir., 1994—2002; contbg. mem. Dem. Nat. Com., 1983—, Presdl. Congl. Task Force, 1994; del. Boone County Dem. Conv., Mo., 1984. Recipient Roberts Meml. prize, Lyric Poetry Jour., 1995, Internat. Peace prize, United Cultural Conv., U.S.A., 2002, DaVinci Diamond award, Internat. Biographical Ctr., 2004, Am. Medal Hon. award, Am. Biographical Inst., 2004; named Legion of Honour, Internat. Biog. Ctr., 2008. Fellow: Am. Coll. Forensic Examiners; mem.: ACLU, USN Inst., Internat. Found. for Protection Officers, Internat. Soc. Genetic Genealogists, MENSA, Assn. Psychol. Sci., London Diplomatic Acad., Academic Coun., Internat. Soc. Polit. Psychology, Acad. Polit. Sci., Soc. for the Psychol. Study of Social Issues, The Jefferson Coun. (founder, dir. 2002), Physicians for Social Responsibility (leadership cir.), So. Poverty Law Ctr. (leadership coun. for tchg. tolerance), Soc. Profl. Journalists, Interfaith Alliance, Mil. Officers Assn., Air Force Assn., Internat. Platform Assn. (Poetry award 1995). Independent. Deist. Avocations: running and fitness, poetry, singing, public speaking. Home: 14023 N Hills Village Dr San Antonio TX 78249-2534 Address: Towers and Rushing Ltd San Antonio TX 78249 Office Phone: 210-558-1393. Business E-Mail: ronribble@usa.net.

RIBEAU, SIDNEY A., academic administrator; b. 1947; m. Paula Whetsel-Ribeau; 3 children. BA, Wayne State U., 1971; M in Interpersonal Comm., U. Ill., 1973, D in Interpersonal Comm., 1979. Prof. comm. studies Calif. State U., LA, 1976—90, chair Pan African studies dept., 1984—87, dean undergraduates studies San Bernadino, 1987—90; dean Coll. Liberal Arts Calif. Polytechnic State U., San Luis Obispo, 1990—92, v.p. acad. affairs Pomona, 1992—95; prof. interpersonal communications Bowling Green U., Ohio, 1995—, pres. Ohio, 1995—2008, Howard U., Washington, 2008—. Bd. dirs. The Andersons Inc., Maumee, Ohio; lectr., spkr. and presenter in field, bd. dirs., Worthington Industries, Inc., 2000- Co-author: African American Communication: Ethnic Identity and Cultural Interpretations, 1994 (Disting. Scholarship award Speech Comm. Assn.); contbr. papers to scholarly jours. Mem. Ohio Bd. Regent's Higher Edn. Funding Commn., Am. Coun. on Edn.'s Leadership and Instnl. Change Commn., Higher Edn. Bus. Coun., Urban League Toledo; bd. dirs. Toledo Symphony Orch. Recipient Disting. Alumnus award, Wayne State U., Calif. Polytechnic State U., U. Ill., President's award, Nat. Assn. Student Pers. Administrators, 2003. Mem. Bowling Green C. of C., Toledo C. of C. Office: Howard University 2400 6th St NW Washington DC 20059 Office Phone: 202-806-6100.*

RIBEIRO, CATHERINE MCKENNA, legislative staff member; d. James and Gloria McKenna; m. Mick Ribeiro. B, Pa. State U.; M, London Sch. Economics. Staff asst., Senator Joe Lieberman US Senate, Hartford, Conn., 2002, constituent services rep., Senator Joe Lieberman, 2002—03, Conn. scheduler and press liaison, Senator Joe Lieberman,

2003, Congl. aide and Conn. press liaison, Senator Joe Lieberman, 2003—04, Congl. aide and press advance, Senator Joe Lieberman, 2004—05, dep. press sec., Senator Joe Lieberman Washington, 2005—07; press. sec., Rep. John F. Tierney US House of Reps., Washington, 2007, Web content mgr. and comm. dir. to Rep. John F. Tierney, 2008—. Democrat. Office: 2238 Rayburn House Office Bldg Washington DC 20515 Office Phone: 202-225-8020. Office Fax: 202-225-5915.*

RIBLEY-BORCK, JOAN GRACE, medical/surgical rehabilitation nurse; b. Schenectady, NY, Jan. 5, 1939; d. Harry Jacob and Lillian Josephine (Cheney) Ribley; m. Walter Carl Borck Jr., Oct. 24, 1964; 1 child, Constance Maria. Diploma, Ellis Hosp. Sch. Nursing, Schenectady, 1960; BSN, Russell Sage Coll., Troy, NY, 1981. RN, NY. Staff nurse operating room Columbia Meml. Hosp., Hudson, NY, 1960-63, staff nurse rusk rehab., 1963-64; staff nurse cardiovascular operating room U. Md. Hosp., Balt., 1965-66; staff nurse, evening charge nurse St. Peters Hosp., Albany, NY, 1968-89; substitute staff nurse Wildwood Program, Schenectady, NY, 1989-96, 2001—02, 2002—03; staff nurse Apria Health Care (formerly Homedco Home Care), 1984—; substitute staff, nurse South Colonie Ctrl. Sch., 1996—; staff nurse Gentiva Health Svcs., Schenectady, 2006—. Ind. provider in nursing Medicaid Mgmt. Info. Sys, NY, 2004—. Mem. ANA, NY State Nurses Assn., Albany Coun. Cath. Nurses. Roman Catholic.

RICAPITO, JOSEPH VIRGIL (GIUSEPPE RICAPITO), literature educator; b. Giovinazzo, Bari, Italy, Oct. 30, 1933; came to U.S., 1935; s. Frank and Filomena (Cervone) R.; m. Carolyn Sue Kitchen, Apr. 7, 1958; children: Frank Peyton, Maria Avadna. BA, CUNY, Bklyn., 1955; MA, U. Iowa, Iowa City, 1956; PhD in Romance Langs., U. Calif., LA, 1966. From instr. to asst. prof. Pomona Coll., Claremont, Calif., 1962-70; from assoc. prof. to prof. Ind. U., Bloomington, Ind., 1970-80; prof. La. State U., Baton Rouge, 1980—, chmn. dept., 1980-85, Joseph Yenni disting. prof. Italian studies, 1999. Author: Bibliografia Razonada y anotada, 1980; editor: La Vida de Laz de Tormes, 1976; translator: Dialogue of Mercury and Charon, 1986, Cervantes's Novelas ejemplares: Between History and Creativity, 1996, Consciousness and Truth in Don Quijote (Juan de la Cuesta Hispanic Series), 2007, Fratelli: A Novel, 2007. Pres. Greater Baton Rouge Am.-Italian Assn., 1984-85. With U.S. Army, 1957-59. Grantee NEH, 1981; named Knight Order of Merit, Republic of Italy, 1988, Knight Order of Queen Isabel, Govt. of Spain, 1990; named Disting. Rsch. Master La. State U., 2001, Cervantes Lectr., Fordham U., 2004. Mem. MLA, Renaissance Soc. Am., Am. Comparative Lit. Assn., Am. Assn. Tchrs. Spanish and Portuguese, Cervantes Soc. Am. Avocations: music, photography, films. Office: La State U 309 Hodges Hall Baton Rouge LA 70803-0001 Home Phone: 225-769-2762; Office Phone: 225-578-6616. Business E-Mail: ricapito@lsu.edu.

RICARD, JOHN HUSTON, bishop, religious studies educator; b. Baton Rouge, Feb. 29, 1940; s. Maceo and Albanie (St. Amant) Ricard. BA, St. Joseph Sem., 1962, MA, 1968; MS, Tulane U., 1970; D, Cath. U. Am., Washington, DC, 1984. Ordained priest St. Joseph's Soc. of the Sacred Heart, 1968; pastor Holy Redeemer Ch., Washington, 1972—75, Holy Comforter Ch., Washington, 1975—84; ordained bishop, 1984; aux. bishop Archdiocese of Balt., 1984—97; assoc. prof. Cath. U. Am., Washington, 1973—; bishop Diocese of Pensacola-Tallahassee, Fla., 1997—. Mem. priest's senate Archdiocese of Washington, 1974—, mem. sch. bd., 1976—. Pres. Cath. Relief Svcs. USCC, 1995—, chair, 1995—2002; mem. Pontifical Coun., COR UNUM, 1996—; Chmn. Com. on Social Devel. and World Peace, Domestic Social Devel., 1992—95. Mem.: Secretariat of Black Caths. Roman Catholic. Office: 11 N B St Pensacola FL 32501

RICARDO-CAMPBELL, RITA, retired economist educator; b. Boston, Mar. 16, 1920; d. David and Elizabeth (Jones) Ricardo; m. Wesley Glenn Campbell, Sept. 15, 1946; children: Barbara Lee, Diane Rita, Nancy Elizabeth. BS, Simmons Coll., 1941; MA, Harvard U., 1945, PhD, 1946. Instr. Harvard U., Cambridge, Mass., 1946—48; asst. prof. Tufts U., Medford, Mass., 1948—51; labor economist U.S. Wage Stabilization Bd., 1951—53; economist Ways and Means Com. U.S. Ho. of Reps., 1954; economist, 1957—60; prof. San Jose (Calif.) State U., 1960—61; sr. fellow Hoover Instn. on War, Revolution, and Peace, Stanford, Calif., 1968—95, sr. fellow emerita, 1995—2008. Lectr. health Stanford U. Med. Sch., 1973—78; bd. dirs. Watkins-Johnson Co., Palo Alto, Calif., Gillette Co., Boston; mgmt. bd. Samaritan Med. Ctr., San Jose. Author: Voluntary Health Insurance in the U.S., 1960, Economics of Health and Public Policy, 1971, Food Safety Regulation: Use and Limitations of Cost-Benefit Analysis, 1974, Drug Lag: Federal Government Decision Making, 1976, Social Security: Promise and Reality, 1977, The Economics and Politics of Health, 1982, 2d edit., 1985, Resisting Hostile Takeovers: The Case of Gillette, 1997, Chinese transl., 2004; co-editor: Below-Replacement Fertility in Industrial Societies, 1987, Issues in Contemporary Retirement, 1988; contbr. articles to profl. jours. Mem. Western Interstate Commn. for Higher Edn. Calif., 1967-75, chmn., 1970-71; mem. Pres. Nixon's Adv. Coun. on Status of Women, 1969-76; mem. Pres. Ford's Adv. Coun. on Status of Women, 1976-79; mem. task force on taxation Pres.'s Coun. on Environ. Quality, 1970-72; mem. Pres.'s Com. Health Svcs. Industry, 1971-73, FDA Nat. Adv. Drug Com., 1972-75; mem. Pres. Reagan's Econ. Policy Adv. Bd., 1981-90, Pres. Reagan's Nat. Coun. on Humanities, 1982-89, Pres. Reagan's Nat. Medal of Sci. com., 1988-91, Pres. Bush's Nat. Medal of Sci. com., 1991-94; bd. dirs. Ind. Colls. No. Calif., 1971-87; mem. com. assessment of safety, benefits, risks Citizens Commn. Sci., Law and Food, Rockefeller U., 1973-75; mem. adv. com. Ctr. Health Policy Rsch., Am. Enterprise Inst. Pub. Policy Rsch., Washington, 1974-80; mem. adv. coun. on social security Quadrennial Health and Human Svcs., 1974-75; bd. dirs. Simmons Coll. Corp., Boston, 1975-80; mem. adv. coun. bd. assocs. Stanford Librs., 1975-78; mem. coun. SRI Internat., Menlo Park, Calif., 1977-90. Mem. Am. Econ. Assn., Mont Pelerin Soc. (bd. dirs. 1988-92, v.p. 1992-94), Harvard Grad. Soc. (coun. 1991-94), Phi Beta Kappa. Home: Classic Residence Hyatt 620 Sand Hill Rd Apt 308D Palo Alto CA 94304 Home Phone: 650-325-7038. Personal E-mail: rricardocampbell@sbcglobal.net.

RICCARDI, VINCENT MICHAEL, pediatrician, educator, entrepreneur; b. Bklyn., Oct. 14, 1940; s. Gabriel John and Frances Mary (Novak) R.; m. Susan Leona Bogda, July 27, 1967; children: Angela M., Ursula M., Mikah F. AB, UCLA, 1962; MD, Georgetown U., 1966; MBA, U. LaVerne, 1993. Intern, resident in medicine U. Pitts., 1966-68; fellow in genetics Harvard Med. Sch., Boston, 1968-70, 72; asst. prof. medicine U. Colo. Med. Ctr., Denver, 1973-75; assoc. prof. medicine, pediatrics Med. Coll. Wis., Milw., 1975-77; prof. medicine, pediatrics Baylor Coll. Medicine, Houston, 1977-90; med. dir. The Genetics Inst., Pasadena, Calif., 1990-92; clin. prof. pediatrics UCLA, 1991—; founder, CEO Am. Med. Consumers, La Crescenta, 1992. Dir. The Neurofibromatosis Inst., La Crescenta, Calif., 1985—. Author: Genetic Approach to Human Disease, 1977, Communication and Counseling in Health Care, 1983, Neurofibromatosis, 1986, rev. edit., 1992, 99. Maj. U.S. Army, 1970-71. Fellow ACP, AAAS, Am. Coll. Med. Genetics; mem. Am. Soc. Human Genetics, Am. Coll. Physician Execs. Avocations: creative writing, acting. Office: Am Med Consumers 5415 Briggs Ave La Crescenta CA 91214-2205 Home Phone: 818-957-4926; Office Phone: 818-957-3508. Business E-Mail: riccardi@medcomsumer.com.

RICCARDS, MICHAEL PATRICK, academic administrator; b. Hillside, NJ, Oct. 2, 1944; s. Patrick and Margaret (Finelli) Riccards; m. Barbara Dunlop, June 6, 1970; children: Patrick, Catherine, Abigail. BA, Rutgers U., 1966, MA, 1967, MPhil, 1969, PhD, 1970. Spl. asst. to chancellor Dept. Higher Edn., Trenton, NJ, 1969-70; from asst. prof. to assoc. prof. SUNY, Buffalo, 1970-77; dean U. Mass., Boston, 1977-82; provost Hunter Coll. CUNY, NY, 1982—83, prof., 1982-86; pres. St. John's Coll., Santa Fe, 1986-89, Shepherd Coll., Shepherdstown, W.Va., 1989-95, Fitchburg State Coll., Mass., 1995—2002; pub. policy scholar-in-residence Coll. Bd., Washington, 2002—05; exec. dir. Hall Inst. Pub. Policy, Trenton, NJ, 2005—. Mem. joint commn. tchr. preparation, 1999—2000. Author: (books) The Making of the American Citizenry, 1973, A Republic, If You Can Keep It, 1987, The Ferocious Engine of Democracy, 2 vols., 1995, 2002, Vicars of Christ, 1998, The Presidency and the Middle Kingdom, 2000, The Odes of DiMaggio, 2001, The Papacy and the End of Christendom, 2003, The Myth of American Miseducation, 2005, The State of the Garden State, 2006, Reaction and Reform in NJ, 2007, State Leason to Abraham Lincoln Bicentennial Commission, 2008. Chmn. N.Mex. Endowment Humanities, 1989; trustee Albuquerque Acad.; mem. Coun. Humanities W.Va., Nat. Skills Stds. Bd., 1993—98; mem. nat. adv. com. Ctr. Study Presidency, 1987—89. Fulbright fellow, 1973, Huntington Libr. fellow, 1974, NEH fellow, Princeton U., 1976—77. Home: 32 Kingston Blvd Hamilton NJ 08690 Office: Hall Inst Pub Policy 130 W State St Trenton NJ 08630 Office Phone: 609-392-2237. Personal E-mail: mriccards@gmail.com.

RICCI, CARLA, psychologist; MA, CAGS, Tufts U., 1995. Elem. classroom tchr. AGBU Sch., Watertown, Mass., 1990—93; psychologist Reading Pub. Schs., Mass., 1995—. Office: Reading Public Schs 365 Summer Ave Reading MA 01867 Business E-Mail: cricci@reading.k12.ma.us.

RICCI, CHRISTINA, actress; b. Santa Monica, Calif., Feb. 12, 1980; Actress: (films) Mermaids, 1990, The Hard Way, 1991, The Addams Family, 1991, The Cemetery Club, 1993, Addams Family Values, 1993, Casper, 1995, Now and Then, 1995, Gold Diggers: The Secret of Bear Mountain, 1995, Bastard Out of Carolina, 1996, The Last of the High Kings, 1996, That Darn Cat, 1996, Ice Storm, 1997, Little Red Riding Hood, 1997, (voice only) Souvenir, 1998, Pecker, 1999, I Woke Up Early When I Died, 1998, Fear and Loathing in Las Vegas, 1998, Desert Blue, 1998, Buffalo 66, 1998, The Opposite of Sex, 1998, Small Soldiers, 1998, (voice only) Souvenir, 1998, 200 Cigarettes, 1999, No Vacancy, 1999, Sleepy Hollow, 1999, Bless the Child, 2000, The Man Who Cried, 2000, All Over the Guy, 2001, Prozac Nation, 2001, The Laramie Project, 2002, The Gathering, 2002, Anything Else, 2003, I Love Your Work, 2003, Monster, 2003, Cursed, 2005, Penelope, 2006, Black Snake Moan, 2006, Home of the Brave, 2006; actress, prodr.(films) Pumpkin, 2002; actress (TV appearances) H.E.L.P., 1990, (voice only) The Simpsons, 1996, Ally McBeal, 2002, Malcolm in the Middle, 2002, Joey, 2005, Grey's Anatomy, 2006. Office: c/o ICM 8942 Wilshire Blvd Beverly Hills CA 90211-1934

RICCIARDI, CYNTHIA BOOTH, writer, researcher, educator; b. Mass., 1959; m. Louis M. Ricciardi. BA, Bridgewater State Coll., Mass.; MA, Boston Coll., Chestnut Hill, Mass.; PhD, Brandeis U., Waltham, Mass. Vis. lectr. Bridgewater State Coll., 1984—2006. Editor: (critic) The Delicate Distress; contbr. chapters to books. Pres. Old Colony Hist. Soc., Taunton, Mass., 2006, Bridgewater State Coll. Alumni Assn., 1997—98. Home: PO Box 228 Taunton MA 02780

RICCIARDI, LAWRENCE ROBERT, lawyer; b. Bronx, NY, Aug. 14, 1940; m. Lucy Ricciardi; children: Andre, Niccol. BA, Fordham U., 1962; JD, Columbia U., 1965; course in executive program, Stamford U., 1978. Bar: N.Y. 1967. Assoc. Gilbert, Segall & Young, 1965-69; counsel Overseas Pvt. Invest Corp./US Dept. State Internat. Devel. Agy., 1969-73; internat. counsel American Express Co., 1973-75; gen. counsel Internat. Banking Corp., 1975-77, Travel Related Services Co., 1977-89; exec. v.p., gen. counsel RJR Nabisco, Inc., NYC, 1989-93, pres., 1993-95; sr. v.p., gen. counsel IBM Corp., Armonk, 1995—2002; sr. adv. Jones Day, Washington, 2003—, Lazard Frères & Co. LLC, 2003—. Bd. dirs. The Reader's Digest Assn., Inc., 1998—, Royal Dutch Shell plc, 2004—, Citigroup Inc., 2008—, Citibank, N.A., 2009—. Trustee Andrew W. Mellon Found., 2003—. Mem. Assn. of Bar of City of N.Y. E-mail: lricciardi@jonesday.com.*

RICCIARDI, LOUIS MICHAEL, brokerage house executive; b. Worcester, Mass., 1959; s. Michael Joseph and Mary Theresa Ricciardi; m. Cynthia Anne Booth. BA, Bridgewater State Coll., 1981. Account exec. Shearson/Am. Express, Brockton, Mass., 1981-83; v.p. Thomson McKinnon, Taunton, Mass., 1983-87; sr. v.p. Morgan Stanley Dean Witter, Taunton, Mass., 1988—2002, UBS Paine Webber, Taunton, 2002—. Bd. corporators Bristol County Savs. Bank, Taunton, Mass., 1985—, bd. trustees, 1992—; trustee Taunton Devel. Corp., 1994—, v.p., treas. 1995—. Weekly investment columnist, 1983-2004. Bd. corporators Morton Hosp., Taunton, 1987—, trustee, 1994—, pres. Heart of Taunton (Mass.) Revitalization Corp., 1988-89, 2004—; trustee Bridgewater (Mass.) State Coll., 1989-99, 2004—, chmn. 1990-94, 2006-, Mass. Bd. Higher Edn., 2009-; trustee Bridgewater Found., 1989—, chmn. 1996-2004; bd. dirs. Taunton Boys & Girls Club, 1999—, pres., 2008-. Named Man of Yr. Com Care SE Mass.; Recipient Rondileau award for Outstanding Profl. Achievement and Cmty. Svc., 1999, Disting. Svc. award Bridgewater State Coll., 2002, Good Scout award Boy Scouts Am., 2003. Mem. Taunton Rotary Club (Paul Harris fellow 2000, pres. 1991-92), Bridgewater Coll. Alumni Assn. (treas. 1992-95). Avocations: guitar, coin collecting/numismatics, baseball, community service, Coca Cola Memorabilia. Home: PO Box 228 Taunton MA 02780-0228 Home Phone: 866-528-6528.

RICCIARDONE, FRANCIS JOSEPH, JR., Deputy Ambassador to Islamic Republic of Afghanistan Kabul; b. Boston, 1951; m. Marie Dunn Ricciardone; 2 children. BS summa cum laude, Dartmouth Coll., 1973. Tchr., Iran, 1976—78; with US Fgn. Svc., 1978—, with Bur. Intelligence and Rsch. Washington, sr. mgmt. positions under dir. gen., chief civilian observer unit Multinational Force and Observers in Egypt Sinai Desert, 1989—91, polit. adv. to U.S. and Turkish commanding gens. Operation Provide Comfort; dep. chief of mission and charge d'affaires US Embassy, Ankara, Turkey, 1995—99; spl. coord. for transition of Iraq US Dept. State, Washington, 1999—2001, US amb. to Philippines and Palau Manilla, 2002—05, US amb. to Egypt Cairo, 2005—08, dep. US amb. to Islamic Republic of Afghanistan Kabul, 2009—. Office: US Embassy 6180 Kabul Pl Dulles VA 20189*

RICCIO, ANGELA, science educator; b. Kankakee, Ill., Dec. 13, 1976; d. Daniel and Patricia Riccio. BS in Elem. Edn., Ill. State U., Normal, 2000; M Sci. Edn., Nat. Louis U., Wheeling, Ill., 2005. Cert. Am. sport edn. program Ill. Sci. tchr. Jefferey C. Still Mid. Sch., Aurora, Ill., 2000—06, Gordan Gregory Mid. Sch., Naperville, Ill., 2006—. Athletic scholar, Ill. State U., 1996—2000. Mem.: NSTA. Home: 522 Majestic Ln Oswego IL 60543-4030

RICCIO, CIRA, art educator; b. Andrews Air Force Base, Md., Oct. 6, 1978; d. Juan and Irma Martinez; m. David Anthony Riccio, May 20, 2000; 1 child, Solomon John. BFA (hon.), Ariz. State U., Tempe, 2003. Cert. tchr. Ariz. State U., 2006. Art tchr. Coronado HS, Scottsdale, Ariz., 2006—. Master: Art Club, Coronado HS. Independent. Avocations: travel, reading, drawing.

RICCIO, FELIX, professional sports team owner; m. Moira Riccio; children: Thomas, Andrew, Catherine, Nicholas. Grad., Princeton U., NJ; law degree, U. Va. Investment banker Morgan Stanley & Co., NYC; atty. Goodwin, Procter & Hoar, LLP, Boston; bd. mgrs. Atlanta Spirit, LLC (parent co. of NBA Atlanta Hawks and NHL Atlanta Thrashers); sr. v.p. corp. devel. Trans Nat. Grp. Mailing: Atlanta Spirit LLC Ste 1900 101 Marietta St NW Atlanta GA 30303

RICCITIELLO, JOHN S., interactive software and gaming executive, venture capitalist; b. Erie, Pa., Aug. 3, 1959; BS cum laude in Mktg., Economics and Finance, U. Calif. Berkeley, 1981. Brand mgr. The Clorox Co., Oakland, Calif., 1981—84; mktg. mgr. Henkel GmbH, Germany, 1984—85; mktg. & sales dir. 17 country Middle East/Greece regions Pepsi-Cola Co., Cyprus, 1985—89, group mktg. dir. then bus. devel. dir.; joined Hagen-Dazs, 1989, London, mng. dir. internat. divisions Paris; pres., CEO Wilson Sporting Goods Co., Chgo., 1993—96; pres., CEO Sara Lee bakery worldwide divsn. Sara Lee Corp., Chgo., 1996—97; pres., COO Electronic Arts, Inc., Redwood City, Calif., 1997—2004; co-founder Elevation Partners, Menlo Park, Calif., 2004; CEO Electronic Arts, Inc., Redwood City, Calif., 2007—. Bd. dirs. Hyperion Solutions, Forbes Media LLC, Electronic Arts Inc., 2007—. Named one of Most Influential People in the World of Sports, Bus. Week, 2008. Office: Electronic Arts Inc 209 Redwood Shores Pkwy Redwood City CA 94065*

RICE, ALAN R., geophysicist; s. Alan H. Rice and Mary Jane Grigware; 1 child, Lorien A. BSc, Columbia U., 1964, MSc, 1968, Doctorate, 1976. Rsch. assoc. dept. earth and planetary scis. Am. Mus. Natural History, NYC, 2003—. Postdoc. appt. U. Newcastle upon Tyne, England, 1977—79, U. Chgo., 1979; asst. prof. U. Colo., Denver, 1983—91; prof. Rhodes U., Grahamstown, South Africa, 1991—92; prof. Inst. Earth Sciences U. Utrecht, Netherlands, 1994—95; prof. dept. geology U. Pretoria, South Africa, 1989—90; prof., dir., mineral formation modeling project U. Natal, Durban, South Africa, Rhodes U., South Africa, Nat. Rsch. Found., South Africa, 1996—2002; rsch. assoc. Los Alamos Nat. Lab., N.Mex. Editor: Volcanism and Fossil Biota, 1990; contbr. numerous articles to profl. jours.; reviewer South African Jour. Sci., Jour. Geophys. Rsch.; reviewer: Jour. of Geology. Dir. Consortium of South African and internat. universities, South Africa, 1996—2002, Nat. Rsch. Found., 1975—2005. Seaman USN, 1956—58. Fellow, U. South Africa, 1997; vis. scholar Fackenthal scholar, Columbia U., 1959—64; AEC fellow, 1972—77, postdoctoral fellow, NSF/NATO, 1977, NSF Postdoctoral fellow, Dept Geophys. Scis. U. Chgo., 1978, Royal Bos Kalis fellow, U. Newcastle upon Tyne, 1978—79, CAMS fellow, Woods Hole Oceanog. Inst., 1982, Hugh Kelly fellow, Rhodes U., 1991—92. Mem.: Am. Meteorol. Soc., Am. Geophys. Union, Sigma K, Explorers Club. Achievements include research in formation of diamonds not restricted to deep, cratonic environments; use of LASERTRACE for continuous geochemical sampling; design of undersea chemical sampler; patents in field. Avocations: wild life management, scuba diving, sailing, outdoors. Personal E-mail: arr80@columbia.edu. E-mail: arice@amnh.org.

RICE, ANDREW, state legislator; b. Okla. City, Apr. 23, 1973; s. Hugh and Cindy Rice; m. Apple Newman Rice; children: Noah David, Parker Harrison. BA in Religious Studies, Colby Coll., 1996; MA in Theol. Studies, Harvard U., 1999. Staff Texas Faith Network, Austin, 2001; freelance doc. prodr. and editor; mem. Dist. 46 Okla. State Senate, 2006—. Founder Hunger Task Force; co-chair Senate Health and Human Resources Com.; mem. Senate Bus. and Labor Com., Senate Criminal Jurisprudence and Pub. Safety Com., Senate Homeland Security Com.; founder Prog. Alliance Found., Red River Democracy Project. Mem. Sept. 11th Families for Peaceful Tomorrows, Fundamentalism Edn. Project; bd. mem. People's Opinion Project; mem. Mayflower Congl. Ch. Democrat. Office: Okla State Senate 2300 North Lincoln Blvd Room 521 Oklahoma City OK 73105 also: PO Box 61333 Oklahoma City OK 73146-1333 Office Phone: 405-521-5610. Business E-Mail: rice@oksenate.gov.*

RICE, ANNE, writer; b. New Orleans, Oct. 14, 1941; d. Howard and Katherine (Allen) O'Brien; m. Stan Rice, Oct. 14, 1961 (dec. Dec. 9, 2002); children: Michele (dec. Aug. 5, 1972), Christopher. Student, Tex. Woman's U., 1959-60; BA, San Francisco State Coll., 1964, MA, 1971. Author: Interview with the Vampire, 1976, The Feast of All Saints, 1980, Cry to Heaven, 1982, The Vampire Lestat, 1985, The Queen of the Damned, 1988, The Mummy or Ramses the Damned, 1989, The Witching Hour, 1990, Tale of the Body Thief, 1992, Lasher, 1993, Taltos, 1994, Memnoch the Devil, 1995, Servant of the Bones, 1996, Violin, 1998, The Vampire Armand, 1998, Pandora: New Tales of the Vampires, 1998, Vittorio the Vampire, 1999, Merrick, 2000, Blood and Gold, 2001, The Master of Rampling Gate, 2002, Blackwood Farm, 2002, Blood Canticle, 2003, Christ the Lord: Out of Egypt, 2005, Christ the Lord: The Road to Cana, 2008, Called Out of Darkness: A Spiritual Confession, 2008; (as A.N. Roquelaure) The Claiming of Sleeping Beauty, 1983, Beauty's Punishment, 1984, Beauty's Release: The Continued Erotic Adventures of Sleeping Beauty, 1985 (as Anne Rampling) Exit to Eden, 1985, Belinda, 1986; screenwriter: (films) Interview with the Vampire: The Vampire Chronicles, 1994.

RICE, BARBARA LYNN, stage manager; b. Hartford, Conn., Nov. 9, 1955; d. Joe Roger and Betty Barbara (Baxter) R. BA in Theatre and French, Ind. U., 1978; MFA in Directing, U. Cin., 1982. Freelance stage mgr., NYC; dir. The Open Eye: New Stagings, NYC, 1989; prodn. stage mgr. Belmont Italian-Am. Playhouse, NYC, 1994, 95; prodn. assn. Silence, Cunning, Exile, NYC, 1995; asst. stage mgr. The Merry Wives of Windsor, NYC, 1995; stage mgr. The Message of Peace, NYC, 2005. Dir. The Open Eye: New Stagings, N.Y.C., 1989; stage mgr. 20 Years Ago Today, Cin., 1989, Fourscore & 7 Years Ago, Paramus, N.J., 1989-90, Hanging the President, N.Y.C., 1990, Message of Peace (Lotus Music and Dance), N.Y.C., 2004; prodn. asst. Kiss of the Spiderwoman, Purchase, N.Y., 1990, (off-Broadway) Beau Jest, N.Y.C., 1992, Belmont Italian-Am. Playhouse, N.Y.C., 1994, 95, Transformations, 1997; listings editor Back Stage, 1998; contbg. writer The Headset, 2005; stage manager The Message of Peace, Lotus Music and Dance, NYC, 2005. Mem. Actors' Equity Assn., Stage Mgrs. Assn. Presbyterian. Avocations: music, history, art, reading, languages. Home: 412 W 56th St Apt 10 New York NY 10019-3647 E-mail: cincydame@aol.com.

RICE, CHARLES LANE, surgeon, educator; b. Atlanta, May 22, 1945; s. Marion Jennings and Molly Black R.; children: Aaron Nicholas, Patrick Marion. AB, U. Ga., 1964; MD, Med. Coll. Ga., 1968. Commd. ensign USN, 1966, advanced through grades to comdr., 1976, ret., 1977; intern Bowman Gray Sch. Medicine, Winston-Salem, NC, 1968-69; resident Nat. Naval Med. Ctr., Bethesda, Md., 1969-73; asst. prof. surgery U. Chgo., 1977-80, assoc. prof. surgery, 1980-84; dir. intensive care unit Michael Reese Hosp., Chgo., 1977-84; prof., vice chmn. dept. surgery U. Wash., Seattle, 1985-92; surgeon-in-chief Harborview Med. Ctr., Seattle, 1985-92; Dr. Lee Hudson- Robert R. Penn prof., chmn., divsn. gen. surgery U. Tex. Southwestern Med. Ctr., Dallas, 1992-93; prof. surgery U. Ill., Chgo., 1993—2005, prof. physiology and biophysics, 1996—2005, vice dean Coll. Medicine, 1994-99, vice chancellor health affairs, 1999—2004; prof. surgery, pres. Uniformed Svcs. U. of Health Scis., Bethesda, Md., 2005—. Robert Wood Johnson Health Policy fellow, 1991-92; legis. asst. to U.S. senator Tom Daschle, 1991-92. Assoc. editor Jour. of Surg. Rsch., 1983-90; contbr. articles to profl. jours. Rep. Accrediting Coun. Grad. Med. Edn., chair elect, 2001—02, chair, 2002—04. Capt. USNR, 1989—2003. Decorated Legion of Merit. Fellow ACS (gov. 1992-98, vice chmn. com. on trauma 1992-93), Am. Surg. Assn., Am. Assn. for Surgery of Trauma (com. chair 1989-91); mem. Soc. Univ. Surgeons, Am. Physiol. Soc., Shock Soc. (pres. 1991-92), Ctrl. Surg. Assn., Pacific Coast Surg. Assn., So. Surg. Assn. Democrat. Episcopalian. Office: Uniformed Svcs U Health Sci Office of Pres 4301 Jones Bridge Rd Bethesda MD 20814-4799 Office Phone: 301-295-3013. Business E-Mail: crice@usuhs.edu.

RICE, CHRIS, telecommunications industry executive; Chief tech. officer AT&T, Inc., San Antonio, exec. v.p. shared svcs., 2008—. Office: AT&T Inc 175 E Houston St San Antonio TX 78205*

RICE, CLARE I., electronics company executive; b. Rice Lake, Wis., Nov. 3, 1918; s. Chris Nilson and Ingeborg (Haugstvedt) R.; m. Virginia M. Bateman; children: Karen Rice, Carol Rice Brannon, David Alan. BSEE, U. Wis., 1943; BS in Law, St. Paul Coll. Law, 1950; DEngring, Rose-Hulman Inst. Tech., 1979. Registered profl. engr., Minn., D.C. Supr. aircraft radio engring. Northwest Airlines, Inc., Mpls., 1946-51; staff engr. Aero. Radio, Inc., Washington, 1951-53; aviation sales mgr., gen. mgr. Bendix Avionics Divsn., Balt., 1953-62; pres. Sunbeam Electronics, Inc., Ft. Lauderdale, Fla., 1962-66; v.p. Nova U., Ft. Lauderdale, 1966-68; asst. v.p., v.p., sr. v.p. Collins Radio Co., pres. Collins Avionics group Rockwell Internat. Corp., Cedar Rapids, Iowa, 1968-83. Dir. Rockwell-Collins Internat., Inc., Dallas. Chmn. United Way, Cedar Rapids, 1973-74; trustee Coe Coll., 1979-83, Hoover Presdl. Libr.; eminent fellow Wisdom Hall of Fame; bd. dirs. St. Luke's Hosp., 1976-82, Mchts. Nat. Bank, 1977-83; chmn. Mcpl. Airport Commn., Cedar Rapids, 1980-84; charter mem. Aviation Hall of Fame; capt. Hon. Dep. Sheriffs Assn., 1987—; pres. Sales and Mktg. Execs. Balt., 1960-61, Cmty. Assn. Bernardo Heights, 1988-91; dir. Rancho Bernardo Cmty. Found. Lt. comdr. USNR, 1943-46. Recipient Disting. Svc. citation U. Wis., 1979, 84; Pioneer award Milw. Sch. Engring., 1981. Sr. mem. IEEE; mem. Iowa Mfrs. Assn. (bd. dirs. 1975-81), Gen. Aviation Mfrs. Assn. (dir. 1970-81, chmn. 1979), U. Wis. Alumni Assn. (chmn. 1981-82, pres. 1980-81, Disting. Svc. award 1984). Clubs: Wings (N.Y.C.); Nat. Aviation (Washington); Rancho Bernardo Heights Country. Lodges: Royal Order of Jesters (dir. 1979). Republican. Presbyterian. Home: The Remington Club 16925 Hierba Dr # 305 San Diego CA 92128

RICE, CLARETHA MAYES, medical/surgical nurse, educator; d. Fred Dossie and Luethisa Mayes; children: William Eugene Mayes, Carisa Denise Brewster. Assoc. in Gen. Studies, C.C. of Phila., 1988. Lic. practical nurse, Pa. Staff nurse Albert Einstein, Phila., 1973—; charge nurse Maplewood Manor, Phila., 1980—84, Stapely Health Care Ctr., Phila., 1984—94; tchr. Sch. Dist. of Phila., 1992—2004. Bereavement counselor Canaan Bapt. Ch., Phila., 1999—. Musician: Canaan Baptist Church Daycare Song (Recommedation from dir. of day care, 1995). Mem. xec. com. Stenton Ave. and Partnership Com., Phila., 1990—2006; tchr. Sunday sch. Disciples of Christ Ch., Phila., 1958—70, Canaan Bapt. Ch., Phila., 1980—2006, deaconess, Bible tchr., 1997—2006, bereavement facilitator and counselor, 1999—2006; coord. women's conf. Canaan Bapt. Ch., Enon Bapt. Ch., Keystone Mercy, 2005. Recipient Cert. of Achievement, Phillippian Bapt. Church-New Hope Ministry, 1999—2006, Cert. of Recognition, Greater Phila. Area Sunday Sch. Assn., Retirement Cert. of Recognition, Am. Fedn. of Tchrs., Cert. of Attendance, Ctr. for Grieving Children, Teens and Families, Cert. of Completion of Mission Study Course, Lott Carey Bapt. Fgn. Mission Conv. of Am.-44Shaw Div. Sch., Name placed on the Wall of Tolerance-So. Poverty Law Ctr., Nat. Campaign for Tolerance, 2005. Democrat. Baptist. Avocations: travel, reading, music, gardening, writing. Personal E-mail: crice63808@aol.com.

RICE, CONDOLEEZZA, political science professor, former United States Secretary of State; b. Birmingham, Ala., Nov. 14, 1954; d. John Wesley and Angelena Ray Rice. BA cum laude in Polit. Sci., U. Denver, 1974; PhD in Polit. Sci., U. Denver Josef Korbel Sch. Internat. Studies, 1981; MA in Polit. Sci., U. Notre Dame, 1975; PhD (hon.), Morehouse Coll., 1991, U. Ala., 1994, U. Notre Dame, 1995, Nat. Def. U., 2002, Miss. Coll. Sch. of Law, 2003, U. Louisville, 2004, Mich. St. U., 2004; degree (hon.), Boston Coll., 2006. Intern, Bur. Ednl. & Cultural Affairs US Dept. State, Washington, 1977; intern The Rand Corp., Santa Monica, Calif., 1978; polit. sci. cons. Stanford U., 1980—81, asst. prof. polit. sci., 1981—87, assoc. prof., 1987—93, prof., 1993—99, 2009—; provost Stanford U., 1993-99; spl. asst. to dir. of the Joint Chiefs of Staff US Dept. Def., Washington, 1986; spl. asst. to the Pres. for nat. security affairs NSC, 1989-91, dir. to sr. dir. Soviet & East European Affairs, 1989—91; sr. fellow The Hoover Instn., Stanford, Calif., 1991—93, 1999—2001, Thomas & Barbara Stephenson sr. fellow on pub. policy, 2009—; nat. security cons. George W. Bush Presdl. Campaign, Washington, 2000; asst. to the Pres. for nat. security affairs NSC, Washington, 2001—05; sec. US Dept. State, Washington, 2005—09. Cons. ABC News, Washington; mem. spl. advisory panel to comdr. and chief strategic air commd.; mem. gov. ind. adv. redistricting state of Calif.; mem. US Delegation to 2+4 talks on German Unification; bd. dirs. Chevron Corp., 1991—2001, Transamerica Corp., 1991—2001, Charles Schwab Corp., 1999—2001; internat. adv. coun. J.P. Morgan & Co., William & Flora Hewlett Found., U. Notre Dame. Author: Uncertain Allegiance: The Soviet Union and the Czechoslovak Army, 1984; co-author (with Alexander Dallin): The Gorbachev Era, 1986; co-author: (with Philip Zelikow) Germany Unified and Europe Transformed, 1995. Ex officio trustee Nat. Gallery Art; trustee John F. Kennedy Ctr. for the Performing Arts. Recipient Dean's award for Disting. Tchg., Stanford U. Sch. Humanities and Scis., 1993, Walter J. Gores award for Excellence in Tchg., Stanford U., 1984, Pres. award, NAACP Image Awards, 2002; named one of The World's Most Influential People, TIME mag., 2005—07, The 100 Most Powerful Women, Forbes mag., 2005—08, The 10 Most Fascinating People of 2005, Barbara Walters Special, The Most Influential Black Americans, Ebony mag., 2006—08, The 50 Most Powerful People in DC, GQ Mag., 2007, Glamour's Women of the Yr., 2008. Fellow: AAAS; mem.: Coun. Fgn. Rels. Republican. Office: Hoover Memorial Stanford University Stanford CA 94305-6010 Office Phone: 650-723-6867, 202-647-4000. Office Fax: 650-723-9376. E-mail: condi@stanford.edu.*

RICE, DANIELLE, museum director; BA, Wellesley Coll., 1973; PhD, Yale U., 1979. With edn. dept. Wadsworth Atheneum, Hartford, Conn., Nat. Gallery, Washington; curator edn. Phila. Mus. Art, 1986—97, sr. curator edn., 1997—2001, assoc. dir. prog., 2001—05; exec. dir. Del. Art Mus., Wilmington, 2005—. Recipient Mus. Educator award, Am. Assn. Museums, 1988, Mus. Educator of Yr. award, Pa. Art. Edn. Assn., 1996. Office: Del Art Mus 2301 Kentmere Pkwy Wilmington DE 19806 Office Phone: 302-571-9590 ext. 537. Office Fax: 302-571-0220. E-mail: drice@delart.org.

RICE, DENIS TIMLIN, lawyer; b. Milw., July 11, 1932; s. Cyrus Francis and Kathleen (Timlin) R.; m. Pamela Stefania Rice, May 8, 2007; children: James Connelly, Tracy Ellen. AB, Princeton U., 1954; JD, U. Mich., 1959. Bar: Calif. 1960. Practiced in, San Francisco, 1959—; assoc. firm Pillsbury, Madison & Sutro, 1959-61, Howard & Prim, 1961-63; prin. firm Howard, Rice, Nemerovski, Canady, Falk & Rabkin, 1964—. Bd. dirs. Anabas, Inc.; chmn., mng. com. San Francisco Inst. Fin. Svcs., 1983—92. Councilman, City of Tiburon, Calif., 1968-72, mayor, 1970-72; dir. Marin County Transit Dist., 1970-72, 77-81, chmn., 1979-81; supr. Marin County, 1977-81, chmn., 1979-80; commr. Marin Housing Authority, 1977-81; mem. San Francisco Bay Conservation and Devel. Commn., 1977-83; bd. dirs. Planning and Conservation League, 1981-2006, Marin Symphony, 1984-92, Marin Theatre Co., 1987-97, Marin Conservation League, 1995-2000, Digital Village Found., 1995—, pres., 1997—; mem. Met. Transp. Commn., 1980-83; mem. bd. visitors U. Mich. Law Sch. 1st lt. AUS, 1955-57. Recipient Freedom Found. medal, 1956 Fellow Am. Bar Found.; mem. ABA (fed. regulation of securities com., chair Asia-Pacific Bus. Law Com., chmn. subcom. on internat. venture law), State Bar Calif. (editor 1978-80, vice-chair sect. bus. law 1978-80, chair com. adminstrn. justice 1997-98, chair com. cyberspace law 1997-2001), San Francisco Bar Assn., Am. Judicature Soc., Internat. Tech. Law Assn. (bd. dirs.), Am. Internat. Property Law Assn., Inter-Pacific Bar Assn. (vice-chmn. securities com.). South End Rowing Club, Tiburon Peninsula Club, Pacific Union Club, Olympic Club, Order of Coif, Phi Beta Kappa, Phi Delta Phi. Office: 3 Embarcadero Ctr Ste 700 San Francisco CA 94111-4003 Office Phone: 415-434-1600. Business E-Mail: brice@howardrice.com.

RICE, DERICA W., pharmaceutical executive; b. Decatur, Ala., 1965; m. Robin Rice; 3 children. BSEE, Kettering U. (formerly GMI Engring. and Mgmt. Inst.), Flint, Mich., 1988; MBA, Ind. U., 1990. Internat. treasury assoc. Eli Lilly and Co., 1990—92, various positions including sales rep., mgr. global fin. planning and analysis for med. devices divsn., global planning mgr. pharms., fin. dir., CFO Can., 1995—97, exec. dir., CFO European ops. London, 1997—2000, gen. mgr. UK and Republic of Ireland, 2000—03, mem. Diversity Leadership Coun., v.p., contr. Indpls., 2003—06, sr. v.p., CFO, 2006—, mem. policy and strategy and ops. coms. Bd. dirs. Clarian Health North. Bd. govs. Indpls. Mus. Art. Office: Eli Lilly and Co Lilly Corp Ctr Indianapolis IN 46285 Office Phone: 317-276-2000.

RICE, DONALD SANDS, lawyer; b. Bronxville, NY, Mar. 25, 1940; s. Anton Henry and Lydia Phipps (Sands) R.; m. Edgenie Higgins, Aug. 27, 1966; children: Alice Rice Perkins, Edgenie Rice Egerton-Warburton. AB magna cum laude, Harvard U., Cambridge, Mass., 1961, LLB/JD cum laude, 1964; LLM in Taxation, NYU, 1965. Bar: NY 1964, US Ct. Claims 1965, US Supreme Ct. 1981. Law clk. judge US Ct. Claims, 1965-67; assoc. Barrett, Smith, Schapiro & Simon, NYC, 1967-71; ptnr. Barrett, Smith, Schapiro, Simon & Armstrong, NYC, 1971-86; vice chmn. bd. Bowery Savs. Bank, NYC, 1986-88; ptnr. Chadbourne & Parke, NYC, 1988-96; mng. dir., prin. Ravitch Rice & Co. LLC, NYC, 1996—; ptnr. Rice & Ravitch LLP, NYC, 1996—; dirs. Flowers Nat. Bank, 2008—. Chmn. Yaddo, 1987—2003; co-chmn. Russian-Am. Banking Law Working Group, 1991—99; v.p., treas., bd. dirs. Soviet Bus. Comml. Law Edn. Found., 1991—96; mem. nat. com. Am. fgn. policy study group dels. to China, Taiwan, 1996, 2000—01; roundtable US China Policy Cross-Strait Rels., 1996—; nat. com. Am. for Pol. Ctrl. Asia Project, 2004—; real estate adv. bd. NY State Comptr., 1987—93; bd. advisors Am.-Russian Investment Forum, 1999—2002; lectr. in field. Contbr. articles to profl. jours. Trustee Nat. Com. Am. Fgn. Policy, 1994—, sr. v.p., 1996—; trustee Chapin Sch., 1980—91, v.p., 1989—91; trustee Marimed Found., 1984—97, Hackley Sch., 1974—81, St. Philip's Episcopal Ch., Mattapoisett, Mass., 1987—, Old Dartmouth Hist. Soc.-New Bedford Whaling Mus., 2006—; pres. Quadequina Co./Mattapoisett Casino, 2001—04; mem. adv. bd. Shorenstein Ctr. on Press, Politics and Pub. Policy, JFK Sch. Govt., Harvard U., 2003—; bd. dirs. African Med. Rsch. Found., 1978—2002. Mem. Coun. Fgn. Rels., Pilgrims of US, NY State Bar Assn., Assn. Bar City NY, Century Assn., Harvard Club NY, NY Yacht Club, Bay Club, Beverly Yacht Club, Mattapoisett Casino. Office: Ravitch Rice & Co LLC 610 5th Ave Rm 420 New York NY 10020-2403 Home: 26-S Ned's Point Rd Mattapoisett MA 02739 Office Phone: 212-218-7880. Personal E-mail: ravricellc@aol.com.

RICE, DOROTHY PECHMAN, medical economist; b. Bklyn., June 11, 1922; d. Gershon and Lena (Schiff) Pechman; m. John Donald Rice, Apr. 3, 1943; children: Kenneth D., Donald B., Thomas H. Student, Bklyn. Coll., 1938—39; BA, U. Wis., 1941; DSc (hon.), Coll. Medicine and Dentistry N.J., 1979. With hosp., and med. facilities USPHS, Washington, 1960—61; med. econs. studies Social Security Adminstrn., 1962—63; health econs. br. Community Health Svc., USPHS, 1964—65; chief health ins. rsch. br. Social Security Adminstrn., 1966—72, dep. asst. commr. for rsch. and statistics, 1972—75; dir. Nat. Ctr. for Health Stats., Rockville, Md., 1976—82; prof. Inst. Health & Aging U. Calif., San Francisco, 1982—94, prof. emeritus, 1994—. Developer, mgr. nationwide health info. svcs.; expert on aging, health care costs, disability, and cost-of-illness. Contbr. articles to profl. jours. Recipient Social Security Adminstrn. citation, 1968, DSM, HEW, 1974, Jack C. Massey Found. award, 1978, UCSF medal, 2002. Fellow: Am. Statis. Assn.; mem.: LWV, APHA (domestic award for excellence 1978, Sedgwick Meml. medal 1988), Assn. Health Svc. Rsch. (President's award 1988), Inst. Medicine. Office: Univ Calif Sch Nursing 3333 California St Ste 340 San Francisco CA 94118 Home Phone: 510-428-9596; Office Phone: 415-476-5685. Personal E-mail: dorothy.rice@comcast.net. Business E-Mail: dorothy.rice@ucsf.edu.

RICE, EDWARD A., JR., military officer; BS in Engring. Scis., USAF Acad., Colorado Springs, 1978; M in Aero. Sci. and Tech., Embry-Riddle U., 1986; M in Nat. Security and Strategic Studies, Naval War Coll., Newport, RI, 1989. 2nd lt. USAF, 1978, 1st lt., 1980; B-52G co-pilot, aircraft comdr., 69th Bombardment Squadron Loring AFB, Maine, 1980—84; capt. USAF, 1982; air staff program tng. asst. dep. chief exec. svcs. divsn., directorate adminstrn. Hdqs. USAF, Washington, 1984—85, programmer air crew mgmt. br., dep. chief staff air and space ops., 1989—90, dep. dir. expeditionary aerospace force implementation, dep. chief staff space ops., 1999—2000; B-52G instr. pilot Mather AFB, Calif., 1985—88, chief standardization and evaluation br., 1985—88, flight comdr. 441st bombardment squadron, 1985—88; maj. USAF, 1986, lt. col., 1990; White House fellow Dept. Health and Human Svcs., Washington, 1990—91; chief standardization and evaluation divsn., 410 ops. group K.I. Sawyer AFB, Mich., 1991—92; comdr. 34th bomb squadron Castle AFB, Calif., 1992—93; nat. security fellow, John F. Kennedy Sch. Govt. Harvard U., 1993—94; col. USAF, 1994; profl. staff mem. comm. on roles and missions of armed forces Office Sec. of Def., Washington, 1994—95, chief of staff for office of rep. and exec. dir. for coalition provisional authority, 2004; dep. comdr. 509th ops. group Whiteman AFB, Mo., 1995—96; comdr. 552 ops. group Tinker AFB, Okla., 1996—97; dep. exec. sec. Nat. Security Coun., Washington, 1997—99; comdr. 28th bomb wing Ellsworth AFB, SD, 2000—02; brig. gen. USAF, 2002; comdr. air force recruiting svc. Hdqs. Air Edn. and Tng. Command, Randolph AFB, Tex., 2002—04; maj. gen. USAF, 2005; comdr. 13th air force Anderson AFB, Guam, 2005; dir. air, space and info. ops., plans and requirements Hdqs. Pacific Air Forces, Hawaii, 2005—06; comdr. 13th air force Hickam AFB, Hawaii, 2005—06, comdr. kenney hdqs., 2006, vice comdr. pacific air forces, 2006—08; comdr. US Forces Japan, 2008—; lt. gen. USAF, 2008; comdr. air force Yokota Air Base, Japan, 2008—. Decorated Legion of Merit with two oak leaf clusters, Disting. Svc. medal, Def. Superior Svc. medal with oak leaf cluster, Meritorious Svc. medal with three oak leaf clusters, Aerial Achievement medal, Air Force Commendation medal; recipient Moller trophy for outstanding wing comdr., Air Combat Command, 2002; named to Power 150, Ebony mag., 2008. Office: US Forces Japan Bldg 714 Yokota Air Base Fussa-shi Tokyo 197-0001 Japan

RICE, EDWARD G., lawyer; b. Pitts., Aug. 13, 1957; s. Richard M. and Theresa A. Rice; m. Ann E. Slyster, July 8, 2000; children: Eric G., Maria C. Murcin, Patrick A., Lindsay P. BS in Indsl. Engring., Pa. State U., State Coll., 1980; JD, Duquesne U., Pitts., 1986. Bar: Supreme Ct., NY 1999, Supreme Ct., Pa. 1986. Mfg. engr. Westinghouse Electric Corp., St. Louis, 1980—83; assoc. atty. Campbell, Sherrard & Burke, P.C., Pitts., 1986—88; sr. atty. Mellon Bank, Pittsburgh, 1988—89; assoc. gen. counsel, vp M&T Bank, Buffalo, 1998—2004; shareholder, dir. Sherrard, German & Kelly, P.C., Pitts., 2004—. Chmn. consumer banking com. Allegheny County Bar Assn., Pitts., 1989—98, treas. corp. banking and bus. law sect., 1996—98; gen. counsel M&T Credit Corp., Buffalo, 2002—04, Highland Lease Corp, Buffalo, 2002—04. Dir. Kingsley Assn., Pitts., 1992—98. Mem.: Millvale Sportsmens Club (assoc.). Roman Catholic. Avocations: fishing, photography. Office: Sherrard German & Kelly PC 620 Liberty Ave Two PNC Plz 28th Fl Pittsburgh PA 15222 Home: 146 Oryx Cir Belgrade MT 59714-7131 Office Fax: 412-261-6221. Business E-Mail: egr@sgkpc.com.

RICE, EDWARD PERRY, secondary school educator; b. Brookline, Mass., Oct. 18, 1947; s. Albert and Ruthe Irene Rice; m. Cheryl Rose Leavitt, June 30, 1974 (div. Apr. 2000); 1 child, Meisha. BA, Northeastern U., 1971; MS Edn., U. So. Maine, 1975. Instr. Journalism dept. U. Maine, Orono, 1987—89; asst. prof. comm. studies Doane Coll., Crete, Nebr., 1989—93; editor Winchester Town Crier, Mass., 1994—96; mng. editor Penobscot Bay Press, Stonington, Maine, 1997—98; tchr. English Katahdin H.S., Sherman Station, Maine, 1998—99; tchr. English, coach cross country Forest Hills H.S., Jackman, Maine, 1999—2001; meeting facilitator Amicus, Bangor, Maine, 2002—04; adj. instr. Ea. Maine C.C., 2004—. Theater critic Portland Press Herald/Maine Sunday Telegram, 1972—77; theater/film critic Maine Pub. Broadcasting-Radio, Orono, 1980—84; theatre critic Maine Times, Topsham, 1984—89; adj. instr. U. Maine, Orono, 2006—. Author: Baseball's First Indian, Louis Sockalexis: Penobscot Legend, Cleveland Indian, 2003, Native Trailblazer Andrew Sockalexis: Penobscot Indian Who Followed The Maine Running Path to Glory and Tragedy, 2008; editor: If They Could Only Hear Me, 2005. With U.S. Army Nat. Guard, Air Nat. Guard, USAR, 1971—93. Decorated Keith L. Ware award, 1st Pl. Dept. Army, Thomas Jefferson award, 2d Pl. Dept. Def.; recipient Cmty. Support award, Cancer Care Maine, 2002; Eugene O'Neill fellow, Nat. Com. for Performing Arts, 1976. Independent. Jewish. Achievements include founded and organized for over 20 years the annual Terry Fox 5-K Run in Bangor, Maine; co-founder Angel Fund, supporting rsch. efforts to find a cure for Lou Gehrig's disease. Home: PO Box 21 Orono ME 04473-0021 Personal E-mail: edrice111@hotmail.com.

RICE, FERILL JEANE, writer; b. Hemingford, Nebr., July 4, 1926; d. Derrick and Helen Agnes (Moffatt) Dalton; m. Otis LaVerne Rice, Mar. 7, 1946; children: LaVeria June McMichael, Larry L. Student, U. Omaha, 1961. Dir. jr. and sr. choir Congl. Ch., Tabor, Iowa, 1952-66; tchr. Fox Valley Tech. Inst., Appleton, Wis., 1970-77; activity dir. Family Heritage Nursing Home, Appleton, Wis., 1972-75; dir. activity Peabody Manor, Appleton, Wis., 1975-76. Editor: Moffatt and Related Families, 1981; asst. editor (mag.) Yester-Year, 1975-76; contbr. articles to profl jours. Chmn. edn. Am. Cancer Soc., Fremont County, 1962-64; founder, 1st pres. Mothers Club Nishna Valley chpt. Demolay for Boys. Mem. DAR, Heisey Collectors Am., Iowa Fedn. Women's Clubs (Fremont county chmn. 1964, 65, 66, 67, 7th dist. chmn. libr. svcs. 1966-67), Tabor Women's Club (pres. 1962, 63, 64), Jr. Legion Aux. (founder, 1st dir. 1951-52), Fenton Art Glass Collectors Am. (co-founder 1977, sec., editor newsletter 1976-86, editor/sec. 1988-93, pres./editor 1993-95, treas. 1995-96, pres. 2000-01), Mayflower Soc., John Howland Soc., Ross County Ohio Geneal. Soc., Dallas County Mo. Geneal. Soc., Clay County (Ind.) Geneal. Soc., Fenton Finders of Wis. (chpt. #1 pres. 1988-90). Republican. Methodist: Lodges: Order Ea. Star (worthy matron 1956, 64), Rainbow for Girls (bd. dirs. 1964), Internat. Order Job's Daus. (honored queen 1945).

RICE, GARY RUSSELL, retired special education educator; b. Franklin, Pa., Oct. 11, 1951; s. Robert Russell and Della Elizabeth Rice. Grad. cum laude, Cleve. State U., 1973. Cert. polit. sci. tchr., learning disabilities, behavioral disorders, Ohio. Substitute tchr. Lakewood, Rocky River, Westlake (Ohio) Schs., 1973—77; instr. West Side Inst. Tech., Cleve., 1977—78; spl. edn. tchr. Parma (Ohio) City Sch. Dist., 1978—2005, ret., 2005. Learning disabilities tutor, Lakewood, 1974-75; guitar cons. Rock and Roll Hall of Fame and Mus., Cleve. Asst. scoutmaster, leader Boy Scouts Am., Cleve.; former Sunday sch. tchr. local chs., Lakewood; columnist, spkr. to various groups on Exceptional Children, the Holocaust and Native Americans; charter mem. U.S. Holocaust Meml. Mus. Recipient Outstanding Spl. Educator award Parma PTA Spl. Edn. com., 1985, Thanks to Tchrs. award Sta. TV-8 WJW, Cleve., 1994, dist. award of merit Boy Scouts Am., 1997, Daniel Carter Beard Masonic Scouter award, 2005. Mem. Cleve. Fedn. Musicians, DeMolay (active Legion of Honor 1996), Masons, Shriners. Avocations: music, photography.

RICE, J. JEFFREY, lawyer; JD, Case Western Res. U., Cleve., 1975. Bar: Fla. (in civil trial law, bus. litigation law and construction law) 1975, cert.: Fla. Supreme Ct. (cir. and county ct. mediator). Ptnr. Goldstein, Buckley, Cechman, Rice, And Purtz, P.A., Ft. Myers, Fla., 1975—. Mem. adv. bd. Hillmyer Tremont Athletic Found., Fr. Myers; chmn. bd. dirs. PFRA Charities; bd. dirs. Dr. 4 Hope. Named Civil Trial

Adv., Nat. Bd. Trial Advocacy, 1984. Master: Calusa Inn Of Ct. (life; pres. 2001—02). Office: Goldstein Buckley Cechman Rice & Pur 1515 Broadway Fort Myers FL 33901 Office Fax: 239-332-6508. Business E-Mail: jrice@gbclaw.com.

RICE, JAMES BRIGGS, JR., lawyer; b. Kansas City, Mo., Dec. 31, 1940; s. James Briggs and Oma J. Rice; m. Carolyn Ryan Rice, Aug. 11, 1962 (div.); children: James Briggs III, Cynthia L.; m. Beverly Sue Rice, Oct. 24, 1980. AB, U. Mo., 1962; JD, 1965. Bar: Mo. 1965, US Dist. Ct. (we. dist.) Mo. 1968. Assoc. Rogers, Field & Gentry, Kansas City, 1967—72; ptnr. Wesner, Wesner & Rice, Sedalia, Mo., 1972—75, Rice & Romines, Sedalia, 1975—80; pvt. practice Sedalia, 1980—; atty. Sedalia Area Devel. Corp., 1976—79. Chmn. Police Pers. Bd., Sedalia, 1976. Capt. US Army, 1965—67, Vietnam. Mem.: VFW, ABA, Vietnam Vets. Pettis County, Mo. Assn. Trial Atty.'s, Am. Judicature Soc., Pettis County Bar Assn. (pres. 1975), Mo. Bar Assn., Shriners, Masons, Noon-day Optimist, Kiwanis (pres. 1975). Republican. Methodist. Office: 701 S Ohio Ave Sedalia MO 65301-4415 Home: 1940 Ashwood Cir Sedalia MO 65301-9296 Office Phone: 660-827-1631.

RICE, JERRY LEE, retired professional football player; b. Starkville, Miss., Oct. 13, 1962; s. Joe Nathan and Eddie Rice; m. Jackie Rice; children: Jaqui, Jerry Jr. Student, Miss. Valley State U., 1981—84. Wide receiver San Francisco 49ers, 1985—2000, Oakland Raiders, 2001—04, Seattle Seahawks, 2004—05, Denver Broncos, 2005. Celebrity dancer Dancing With the Stars, 2006; co-author (with Brian Curtis): Go Long!: My Journey Beyond Fame and the Game, 2007. Recipient Pro Bowl MVP, 1995; named MVP, NFL, 1987, Super Bowl XXIII, 1989, AP/NFL/Sports Illustrated Offensive Player of Yr., 1993; named to Sporting News Coll. All-Am. team, 1984, Pro Bowl team, 1986—96, 1998, 2002. Achievements include holds NFL career records for most touchdowns, receptions, touchdown receptions; having the most consecutive games with one or more touchdowns (13), 1987; holds the NFL single-season record for most touchdown receptions (22), 1987; shares NFL single-game record for most touchdown receptions (5), 1990; holds NFL record of 274 consecutive games with a reception, 1985-2004; led NFL in receptions, 1990, 1996; led NFL in recieving touchdowns, 1986, 1987, 1989-1991, 1993; led NFL in recieving yards, 1986, 1989, 1990, 1993-1995; being a member of SuperBowl XIX, XXIII, XXIV, XXIX Champion San Francisco 49ers.

RICE, JERRY MERCER, biochemist, consultant, pathologist; b. Washington, Oct. 3, 1940; s. John Earle Rice and Leona (Mercer) Greiner; m. Mary Jane Janocha, Jan. 10, 1978; children: Stacey Lynn, Stephen Mark. BA, Wesleyan U., 1962; PhD, Harvard U., 1966. Commd. officer USPHS, 1966, ret., 1996; rsch. scientist Nat Cancer Inst., Bethesda, Md., 1966-81, chief Lab. of Comparative Carcinogenesis Frederick, Md., 1981-94, 96, assoc. dir. Frederick Cancer Rsch. and Devel. Ctr., 1994-95, acting dir. divsn. cancer etiology, 1994-95, ret., 1996; sr. scientist WHO, 1996—2002, ret., 2002; chief unit of carcinogen identification and evaluation Internat. Agy. for Rsch. on Cancer, Lyons, France, 1996—2002, cons. in toxicology, 2003—; Disting. prof. dept. oncology Georgetown U., Washington, 2003—. Editor: Perinatal Carcinogenesis, 1979; co-editor: Organ and Species Specificity in Chemical Carcinogenesis, 1983, Perinatal and Multigeneration Carcinogenesis, 1989, The Use of Short and Medium Term Tests for Carcinogens and Data on Genetic Effects in Carcinogenic Hazard Evaluation, 1999, Species Differences in Thyroid, Kidney and Urinary Bladder Carcinogenesis, 1999, Mech. of Carcinogenesis-contributions of molecular epidemiology, 2004,; contbr. rsch. articles and revs. in mechanisms of chem. carcinogenesis to profl. jours.; dir. emeritus IARC monographs on the evaluation of carcinogenic risks to humans. Mem. James Smithson Soc., Smithsonian Instn. Recipient Outstanding Svc. medal, US Pub. Health Svc., 1990, Meritorious Svc. medal, 1996, George Scott Meml. award, Toxicology Forum, 1997. Mem. Internat. Soc. Differentiation (emeritus), Soc. Toxicology, Am. Assn. Cancer Rsch. (emeritus), Phi Beta Kappa, Sigma Xi. Avocations: viticulture, tropical orchids, wild mushrooms. Home: 3213 Coquelin Ter Bethesda MD 20815-4840 Personal E-mail: jmricewas@aol.com. Business E-Mail: jr332@georgetown.edu.

RICE, JIM (JAMES EDWARD RICE), sportscaster, professional baseball coach, retired professional baseball player; b. Anderson, SC, Mar. 8, 1953; m. Corine Gilliard, 1972; 1 child, Chauncy. Outfielder Boston Red Sox, 1974—89; ret., 1989; roving batting coach Boston Red Sox, 1992—94, hitting instr., 1995—2000, instrnl. batting coach, 2001—; studio analyst New Eng. Sports Network, Mass. Pub. rels. rep. So. Bank & Trust Co., Greenville, SC. Recipient Silver Slugger award, 1983, 84; named Most Valuable Player and Rookie of Yr. Internat. League, 1974, Player of Yr. Sporting News, 1974; co-winner Tucson Pro-Am Golf Tournament, 1977; Am. League Most Valuable Player Baseball Writers' Assn. America, 1978; named to Am. League All-Star Team, 1977-80, 83-86, Nat. Baseball Hall of Fame, 2009. Achievements include leading the American League in: home runs, 1977, 78, 83; slugging percentage, 1977, 78; hits, triples, 1978; runs batted in, 1978, 83. Office: c/o Boston Red Sox Fenway Pk 4 Yawkey Way Boston MA 02215-3409 also: New Eng Sports Network 480 Arsenal St Bldg #1 Watertown MA 02472*

RICE, JIM, state supreme court justice; b. Ramore AFB, Ont., Canada, Nov. 15, 1957; (parents Am. citizens); BA in Polit. Sci., Mont. State U., 1979; JD U. Mont., 1982. Former firefighter Mont. Dept. of Natural Resources & Conservation; former legal intern Missoula City Atty. Office, Lewis and Clark County Atty. Office; former pub. defender Lewis and Clark County; mem. Mont. House Reps., 1989—95, house majority whip, 1993; ptnr. Jackson & Rice, Helena, Mont., 1985—2001; assoc. justice Mont. Supreme Ct., 2001—. Active in Montana Hope Project, Kiwanis; mem. Governor's Council on Food and Nutrition. Recipient Thomas McHugh Disting. Community Service award, Helena Jaycees, 1993. Mem.: Mont. Bar Assn. Office: Justice Bldg Rm 323 PO Box 203003 Helena MT 59620-3003*

RICE, JOHN D., agricultural products executive; BS, Univ. Ill., 1977. Plant mgmt. positions A.E. Stanley Mfg. Co., 1977—85; mgmt. positions Archer Daniels Midland Co., Decatur, Ill., 1985—90, v.p., dir. corp. transp., 1990—93, v.p., pres. ADM-Transp., 1993—96, v.p., pres. food oils divsn., 1996—2000, group v.p., pres. N.Am. oilseed processing divsn., 1999—2000, sr. v.p. corn processing and food specialties, 2000—05, exec. v.p. global mktg. & risk mgmt., 2005—07, exec. v.p. comml. & production, 2008—. Office: Archer Daniels Midland Co 4666 Faries Pkwy Decatur IL 62526*

RICE, JOHN G., diversified technology and services executive; b. 1956; BA in Economics, Hamilton Coll., 1978. Mem. fin. mgmt. program GE, 1978-81, mem. corp. audit staff, 1981-84; mgr. materials GE Appliances, 1984-86, mgr. quality control prodn. engring. and materials ops., 1986-87; pres. GEM Products, Inc., Garden Grove, Calif., 1987-90; gen. mgr. material resources GE Appliances, 1990-92; pres., COO Camco, Inc., Canada, 1992-94; head corp. audit staff GE, 1994-95; pres. GE Plastics Pacific, Singapore, 1995-97; pres., CEO GE Transp. Sys., Erie, Pa., 1997—2000, GE Energy, Fairfield, Conn., 2000—05; vice chmn. GE, 2005—; pres., CEO GE Industrial, 2005—06, GE Infrastructure Inc., 2006—08, GE Technological Infrastructure, 2008—. Chmn. U.S. Energy Assn. Chmn. elect Metro Atlanta C. of C.; trustee Hamilton Coll., Woodruff Arts Ctr., Walker Sch.; mem. adv. bd. Ga. Tech. Univ.; dir. Emory Healthcare. Office: General Electric Co 3135 Easton Tpke Fairfield CT 06828*

RICE, JOSEPH ALBERT, retired bank executive; b. Cranford, NJ, Oct. 11, 1924; s. Louis A. and Elizabeth J. (Michael) R.; m. Katharine Wolfe, Sept. 11, 1948; children: Walter, Carol, Philip, Alan. B in Aero. Engring., Rensselear Poly. Inst., 1948; M in Indsl. Engring., NYU, 1952, MA, 1968. With Grumman Aircraft Engring. Corp., 1948-53, IBM, NYC, 1953-65, mgr. ops., real estate, constrn. divsns., 1963-65; dep. group exec. N.Am. comml. telecom. group, pres. telecom. divsn. ITT, NYC, 1965-67; sr. v.p. Irving Trust Co., NYC, 1967-69, exec. v.p., 1969-72, sr. exec. v.p., 1972-73, vice chmn., 1973-74, pres., 1974-83, chmn., 1984-88, ret., 1988. Exec. v.p. Irving Bank Corp., 1971-74, vice chmn., 1974-75, pres., 1975-83, chmn. bd., CEO, 1984-88. Chmn., trustee John Simon Guggenheim Meml. Found., 1997-2009; Hist. Hudson Valley, 1998-2009, vice chmn., 1998-2008. Mem. Coun. Fgn. Rels., Univ. Club, Links, Union League Club.

RICE, JOSEPH AUBREY, physics professor, researcher; b. Cin., Mar. 31, 1958; s. Joseph Aubrey and Patricia Ann Rice; m. Cathleen Christl Rice, Apr. 9, 1994; children: Katherine Rose, Megan Marie, Kelly Claire. BS in Engring. Sci., U. Cin., BA in Math., 1981; MS in Elec. Engring., Applied Ocean Sci., U. Calif. Scripps Instn. Oceanography, San Diego, 1990. Engr. Space & Naval Warfare Sys. Ctr., San Diego, 1981—2000; SSC San Diego engring. acoustics chair Naval Postgrad. Sch., Monterey, 2001—07, rsch. prof. physics, 2007—. Recipient Meritorious Civilian Svc. award, Dept. Navy, 1998, Bronze medal, Nat. Def. Indsl. Assn., 2004, Lauritsen-Bennett Engring. award, Space & Naval Warfare Sys. Ctr., 2006. Achievements include invention of Seaweb underwater acoustic network. Home: 25009 Valley Pl Carmel CA 93923 Office: Naval Postgrad Sch Dept Physics Monterey CA 93943 Business E-Mail: joe.rice@navy.mil.

RICE, JOSEPH LEE, III, lawyer; b. Bklyn., Feb. 24, 1932; s. Joseph Lee Jr. and Frances (Plunkett) R.; m. Franci Blassberg, Jan. 4, 1992; children: Kimberley, Daniel, Lee Ann. BA, Williams Coll., Williamstown, Mass., 1954; LLB, Harvard U., 1960. Assoc. Sullivan & Cromwell, NYC, 1960-66; v.p. Laird Inc., NYC, 1966-68, McDonnell & Co., NYC, 1968-69; founding ptnr. Gibbons, Green & Rice, NYC, 1969-78; founder, chmn. Clayton, Dubilier & Rice, Inc., NYC, 1978—. Trustee, Williams Coll., 1988-92. Lt. USMC, 1954-57. Mem. Maidstone Club, The Links Club, River Club. Office: Clayton Dubilier & Rice Inc 375 Park Ave New York NY 10152-0002 E-mail: jrice@cdr-inc.com.*

RICE, JOY KATHARINE, psychologist, education educator; d. Joseph Theodore and Margaret Sophia (Bednarik) Straka; m. David Gordon Rice, Sept. 1, 1962; children: Scott Alan, Andrew David. BFA with high honors, U. Ill., 1960; MS, U. Wis., 1962, MS, 1964, PhD, 1967. Lic. clin. psychologist. USPHS predoctoral fellow dept. psychiatry Med. Sch. U. Wis., Madison, 1964-65, asst. dir. Counseling Ctr., 1966-74, dir. Office Continuing Edn. Svcs., 1972-78, prof. ednl. policy studies and women's studies, 1974-95, clin. prof. psychiatry, 1995—; pvt. practice psychology Psychiat. Svcs., S.C., Madison, 1967—. Mem. State Wis. Ednl. Approval Bd., Madison, 1972—73; mem. Adult Edn. Commn. U.S. Office Career Edn., Washington, 1978; co-chmn. Wis. Lt. Gov.'s Task Force on Women and Depression, 2005—. Author: Living Through Divorce, A Developmental Approach to Divorce Therapy, 1985, 2d edit., 1989, Transforming Leaderships Diverse Visions and Women's Voices, 2007; mem. editl. bd. Lifelong Learning, 1979—86; cons. editor: Psychology Women Quar., 1986—88, assoc. editor:, 1989—94, cons. editor: Handbook of Adult and Continuing Education, 1989, Encyclopedia of Women and Gender, 2001, Handbook of Girls' and Women's Psychological Health, 2005; contbr. articles to profl. jours. Pres. Big Bros. Big Sisters Dane County, 2002, bd. dirs.; co-chair Wis. Lt. Gov.'s Task Force on Women and Depression, 2005—06. Recipient Disting. Achievement award, Ednl. Press Assn. Am., 1992, John Fritschler Jr. award for Disting. Achievement, 2004; Knapp fellow, U. Wis., Madison, 1960—62, Tchg. fellow, 1962—63. Fellow: APA (exec. bd. psychology women divsn. 1994—, internat. psychology divsn. 1998—, exec. bd. 1998—, chair internat. com. women 2000—02, chair com. internat. rels. psychology 2005, divsn. pres. 2006, Disting. Leadership award 2000—02, Woman of Yr. award, Sect. for Advancement of Women in Counseling Psychology 2007); mem.: Am. Assn. Continuing and Adult Edn. (Meritorious Svc. award 1978—80, 1982), Internat. Coun. Psychologists (bd. dir. 1998—2001, sec. 2002—04, bd. dir. 2004—), Nat. Assn. Women Edn. (editl. bd. jour. 1984—88, cons. editor Initiatives 1988—91), TEMPO Internat. (bd. dir., sec. 2000—03, 2006—, pres. elect 2009), Rotary, Phi Delta Kappa. Avocations: interior decorating, painting, gardening, travel. Home: 4230 Waban Hl Madison WI 53711-3711 Office: 2727 Marshall Ct Madison WI 53705-2255 Office Phone: 608-238-9354.

RICE, KAROLYN KAYE, elementary school educator; b. Marinette, Wis., Jan. 16, 1949; d. Rudolph C. and Ruby E. Johnson; m. Roger Ruben Rice, June 15, 1974; 1 child, Melanie Kaye. BA cum laude, U. Wis., 1971. Elem. tchr. Garfield Sch., Marinette, Wis., 1971—74, Jenkins Elem. Sch., Mo., 1978—79; English, music tchr. St. Thomas Aquinas Acad., Marinette, 1979—. Pianist, organist Calvary Temple, 1999—2003, Holy Family Parish, Marinette, 2000—. Recipient Tchr. of Yr., Marinette C. of C., 1984. Bapt. Avocations: travel, reading, knitting. Home: 1640 Stanton ST Marinette WI 54143

RICE, KAY DIANE, elementary school educator, consultant; d. Ray H. and Patricia Quibell; 1 child, Brooke Elise; m. F. Scott Rice. AA in Gen. Edn., Shasta Coll., Redding, 1972; BA in Liberal Studies, Calif. State U., Chico, 1975; EdM in Policy and Govt., U. Wash., 1991. Cert. tchr., Calif., Wash., cert. prin., Wash. Tchr. grade 3 Anderson (Calif.) Schs., 1976-79; tchr. grades 1, 2, and 3 Redding (Calif.) Elem. Schs., 1979-81, tchr. grade 1, 1981-83, tchr. grade 5, 1986-87; tchr. grade 2 Bellevue (Wash.) Pub. Schs., 1987-88; tchr. grade 4 Lake Wash. Sch. Dist., Kirkland, Wash., 1988-89; tchr. grades 3-4 Bellevue (Wash.) Pub. Schs., 1989-90; prin. intern Bellevue (Wash.) and Mercer Island (Wash.) Schs., 1990-91; tchr. grades K-1 Bellevue (Wash.) Pub. Schs., 1991-93, tchr. grades 1-2, 1993—. Mem. early childhood assessment project Bellevue Pub. Schs., 1993-99; presenter in field. Vol. ZEST Sch. Dist. Vol. Program, Bellevue, 1991-93. Recipient Pres.'s Merit award Parent Student Tchr. Assn., 1988, U.S. Presdl. EPA award, 1987; grantee Bellevue Schs. Found., 1987, 95-96, 96-97, 98-2006, Danforth Edn. Leadership grantee Bellevue Pub. Schs., 1990-91, Shunju Club, Japanese Bus. People Wash., 1994, Seattle Chinese Sch., 2004. Mem. ASCD, NEA, AAUW (hospitality com. 1982), PTSA, Wash. Orgn. for Reading Devel., PEO. Avocations: cooking, outdoor sports, reading, writing, religious studies. Home: 6818 205th Ave NE Redmond WA 98053-4721 Office: Somerset Elem Sch 14100 Somerset Blvd SE Bellevue WA 98006-2399

RICE, KENNER CRALLE, medicinal chemist; s. Kenner Cralle Jr. and Annie Grace Rice. BS, Va. Mil. Inst., 1961; PhD, Ga. Inst. Tech., 1966. Sr. scientist Ciba-Geigy Corp., Summit, 1969—72; sr. staff fellow NIH, Bethesda, Md., 1972—76, rsch. chemist, 1977—86; chief sect. drug design and synthesis Nat. Inst. Diabetes, Digestive and Kidney Diseases, Bethesda, Md., 1987—88; chief lab. medicinal chemistry NIDDK, NIH, Bethesda, Md., 1989—2006; chief chem. biology rsch. br. Nat. Inst. on Drug Abuse, 2006—. Adj. prof. pharmacology U. Md., Balt., 1985—; mem. Fed. Sr. Exec. Svc., Bethesda, 1989—98, Fed. Sr. Biomed. Rsch. Svc., 1998—; affiliate prof. Va. Commonwealth U., Richmond, 1995—; vis. prof. pharmacology U. Ill., Peoria, 1995—; adj. prof. medicinal chemistry Comprehensive Drug Rsch. Ctr. U. Miami, 1995—. Author (with others): Pharmacological Reviews, 1987; editor: NIDA Research Monograph 96, 1990; contbr. more than 600 rsch. papers to profl. jours. Capt. US Army, 1966—68. Recipient Internat. Sato Meml. award, Japanese Pharm. Soc., 1983, Rsch. Achievement award, Am. Pharm. Assn., 1987, Hillebrand prize, Chem. Soc. Washington, 1986, Divsn. Medicinal Chemistry award, Am. Chem. Soc., 1996, Rsch. Achievement award, Am. Assn. Pharm. Scientists, 1998, Chem. Pioneer award, Am. Inst. Chemists, 2000, Nathan B. Eddy award, Coll. Problems of Drug Dependence, 2001, Bristol-Myers Squibb Smissman award, Am. Chem. Soc. Divsn. Medicinal Chemistry, 2007; named to Medicinal Chemistry Hall of Fame, 2007. Fellow: Coll. on Problems of Drug Dependence (bd. dirs. 1988—92, 1997—2001); mem.: Am. Coll. Neuropsychopharmacology, Cosmos Club. Achievements include 42 patents in organic chemical synthesis and pharmacology of drugs of abuse; development of NIH opiate total synthesis as first practical synthesis of opium alkaloids and derivatives as narcotics and narcotic antagonists. Office: NIH NIDA Chem Biology Rsch Br 5625 Fishers Ln Rm 4N 03 Mail Stop 9415 Rockville MD 20852 Business E-Mail: kr21f@nih.gov.

RICE, LINDA JOHNSON, publishing executive; b. Chgo., Mar. 22, 1958; d. John J. and Eunice Johnson; m. Andre Rice, 1984; 1 child, Alexa Christine; m. Mel Farr Sr. BA Journalism, U. So. Calif., LA, 1980; MBA, Northwestern U., Evanston, Ill., 1987. V.p., asst. to pub. Ebony mag., Jet mag. Johnson Pub. Co., Inc., 1980—87, COO, 1987—2002, pres. Chgo., 1987—, CEO, 2002—. Pres. Fashion Fair Cosmetics, Ill., 1987—. Recipient Women of Power award, Nat. Urban League, Trumpet award, Turner Broadcasting, Alumni Merit award, Univ. So. Calif., Alumni of Yr. award, Northwestern U. Kellogg Grad. Sch. Mgmt.; named one of 100 Most Powerful Women in Chgo., Chgo. Sun Times, Chicago's 40 Under 40, Crain's Chgo. Bus.; named to Power 150, Ebony mag., 2008. Mem.: Exec. Club Chgo., Econ. Club Chgo., Young Presidents Orgn., Nat. Assn. Black Journalists, Fashion Group Internat., Comml. Club Chgo. Office: Johnson Pub Co Inc 820 S Michigan Ave Chicago IL 60605-2191 Business E-Mail: ljr@ebony.com.*

RICE, LOIS DICKSON, retired computer company executive; b. Portland, Maine, Feb. 28, 1933; d. David A. and Mary D. Dickson; m. Alfred B. Fitt, Jan. 7, 1978 (dec. 1992); children: Susan, John Rice. AB magna cum laude, Radcliffe Coll., 1954; postgrad. (Woodrow Wilson fellow), Columbia U., 1954—55; LLD (hon.), Brown U., 1981, Bowdoin Coll., 1984. Dir. counseling services Nat. Scholarship Service and Fund for Negro Students, NYC, 1955-59; with The Coll. Bd., NYC and Washington, 1959-81, v.p. Washington, 1973-81; sr. v.p. govt. affairs Control Data Corp., 1981-91. Guest scholar The Brookings Inst., Washington, 1991—; bd. dirs. McGraw Hill, Inc., 1987—2003, Internat. Multifoods, 1991—2003, UNUM Corp., 1992—2003; overseer Tuck Sch. Mgmt. Dartmouth Coll., 1990—94; mem. Pres.'s Fgn. Intelligence Adv. Bd., 1993—2001; trustee George Washington U., 1992—98, trustee Mgmt. Leadership for Tomorrow, 1994—; trustee CNA Corp. Pub. Agenda Found., Harry Frank Guggenheim Found., 1994—. Contbr. articles on edn. to profl. publs.; editor: Student Loans: Problems and Policy Alternatives, 1977. Mem. adv. bd. to dir. NSF, 1981—89, chair, 1986—89; mem. Gov.'s Commn. on Future of Postssecondary Edn. in N.Y. State, 1976—77, Carnegie Coun. on Higher Edn., 1975—80; trustee Radcliffe Coll., 1969—75, Stephens Coll., Mo., 1976—78, Beauvoir Sch., Washington, 1970—76, Children's TV Workshop, 1970—73; bd. dirs. Potomac Inst., 1977—92, German Marshall Fund, 1984—94, Joint Ctr. Polit. and Econ. Studies, 1991—94, Reading is Fundamental, 1991—2004. Recipient Disting. Service award HEW, 1977 Mem. Cosmos Club, Phi Beta Kappa. Episcopalian. Home: 2332 Massachusetts Ave NW Washington DC 20008 Office: The Brookings Instn 1775 Massachusetts Ave NW Washington DC 20036-2103

RICE, LOUISE ALLEN, fraternal organization administrator, reading educator; b. Augusta, Ga., 1941; m. Wilson L. Rice, Apr. 4, 1965; children: Wilson L. Jr., Robert Christopher. BS, Tuskegee U., 1963; MA, Columbia U. Tchrs. Coll., 1969; PhD, U. Ga., 1979. Instr. English Washington High Sch., Cairo, Ga., 1963-66; instr. reading and English Lucy Laney High Sch., Augusta, Ga., 1966-68, Paine Coll., Augusta, 1968-70, reading specialist, instr., 1972-73, asst. prof. reading, 1973-77, 79-80, assoc. prof. reading, coord. reading dept., 1980-81; instrnl. lead tchr. Joseph Lamar Elem. Sch., Augusta, 1981-84; assoc. dir. admissions Augusta State U., 1984—88, asst prof. edn., reading, 1988—2003; So. regional dir. Delta Sigma Theta Sorority, Inc., 1986—91, nat. sec., 1992—96, nat. first v.p., 2000—02, nat. pres., 2004—. Mem. adv. bd. Richmond County Board Edn.; human rels. com. Edn. Commn. Augusta. Bd. dirs. Ctrl. Savannah River Area Economic Opportunity Authority Inc. Recipient Urban Builders award, Augusta Black Hist. Com., 1985, Educator of Yr., Lincoln League of Augusta, 1988, Distinguished Leadership award, United Negro College Fund, 1990, Citizen of Yr., Augusta Chapter Nat. Social Workers, 1999; named to Power 150, Ebony mag., 2008. Mem.: Internat. Reading Assn., Ga. Assn. Devel. Edn., Nat. Assn. Devel. Edn., Coll. Reading and Learning Assn., Nat. Assn. Univ. Women, Nat. Coun. Negro Women (life). Office: Delta Sigma Theta 1707 NH Ave Washington DC 20009-4562

RICE, LUANNE, writer; b. 1955; B in Humane Letters, Conn. Coll., 1977, degree (hon.), 2002. Author: Angels All Over Town, 1985, Crazy in Love, 1988, Stone Heart, 1990, Secrets of Paris, 1991, Blue Moon, 1994, Home Fires, 1996, Cloud Nine, 2000, Follow The Stars Home, 2001, Firefly Beach, 2001, Dream Country, 2002, Summer Light, 2002, True Blue, 2002, Safe Harbor, 2003, The Secret Hour, 2003, The Perfect Summer, 2003, Dance With Me, 2004, Summer's Child, 2005, Summer of Roses, 2005, Sandcastles, 2006, The Edge of Winter, 2006, What Matter Most, Light of the Moon, 2008, (TV miniseries) Blue Moon, Silver Bells, Beach Girls. Mailing: c/o Andrea Cirillo Jane Rotrosen Agency 318 E 51st St New York NY 10022

RICE, MARY ESTHER, biologist; b. Washington, Aug. 3, 1926; d. Daniel Gibbons and Florence Catharine (Pyles) R. AB, Drew U., 1947; MA, Oberlin Coll., 1949; PhD, U. Wash., 1966. Instr. biology Drew U., Madison, NJ, 1949-50; rsch. assoc. Columbia U., NYC, 1950-53; rsch. asst. NIH, Bethesda, Md., 1953-61; curator invertebrate zoology and dir. Smithsonian Marine Sta., Smithsonian Instn., Washington, 1966—2002, sr. rsch. scientist emeritus, 2002—. Mem. adv. panel on systematic biology NSF, Washington, 1977-78; mem. com. on marine invertebrates Nat. Acad. Sci., 1976-81; mem. overseers com. on biology Harvard U., Cambridge, Mass., 1982-88. Assoc. editor Jour. Morphology, Ann Arbor,

Mich., 1985-91, Invertebrate Biology, 1995—; editor: (with M. Todorovic) Biology of Sipuncula and Echiura, 1975, 2nd vol., 1976, (with F.S. Chia) Settlement and Metamorphosis of Marine Invertebrate Larvae, 1978, (with F.W. Harrison) Microscopic Anatomy of Invertebrates, Vol. 12, 1993; contbr. articles to profl. jours. Recipient Drew U. Alumni Achievement award in sci., 1980. Fellow AAAS; mem. Am. Soc. Zoologists (pres. 1979), Am. Microscopical Soc. (pres. 1999), Phi Beta Kappa. Office: Smithsonian Marine Sta 701 Seaway Dr Fort Pierce FL 34949-3140

RICE, MARY KATHLEEN, literature and language professor; b. Moline, Ill., Jan. 9, 1956; d. Doris Lancaster; m. Donald Rice, Jan. 7, 1978; children: Anna, Sarah. BA, Luther Coll., Decorah, 1978; MA, U. Iowa, PhD, 1988. Instr. Spanish Coe Coll., Cedar Rapids, Iowa, 1985—88; asst. prof. Spanish Concordia Coll., Moorhead, Minn., 1988—94, assoc. prof. Spanish, 1994—2001, chair, dept. Spanish, 2001—06, prof. Spanish, 2001—, chair, divsn. lang., lit. and culture, 2007—. Fundraising Moorhead HS Theatre, Minn., 2007—08. Grant, Concordia Coll., 2000. Dfl. Lutheran. Avocations: music, theater, travel. Business E-Mail: mrice@cord.edu.

RICE, MELISSA ANN, mathematics educator; b. Jerome, Idaho, Dec. 24, 1978; d. Barry Howard and Carolyn Jean Sullivan; m. Todd Douglas Rice, Dec. 31, 2000. BS, BA, Boise State U., Idaho, 2002. H.s. math. tchr. Valley Sch. Dist., Eden, Idaho, 2002—04, Jerome Sch. Dist., 2004—. Tchr., High Schs. That Work site coord. Jerome H.S., 2005—. Mem.: Am. Quarter Horse Assn. Home: 9 Horseshoe Cir Jerome ID 83338 Personal E-mail: ricem@d261.k12.id.us.

RICE, NANCY E., state supreme court justice; b. Denver, June 2, 1950; 1 child. BA cum laude, Tufts U., 1972; JD, U. Utah, 1975. Law clerk U.S. Dist. Ct. of Colo., 1975-76, dep. state pub. defender, appellate divn., 1976-77; asst. U.S. atty. Dist. of Colo., 1977-87; dep. chief civil divn. U.S. Attorney's Office, 1985-88; judge Denver Dist. Ct., 1988-98; justice Colo. Supreme Ct., 1998—. Adjunct prof. law, trial advocacy U. Colo. Sch. of Law, 1987—. Contbr. articles to profl. jours. Mem. Denver Bar Assn. (Judicial Excellence award 1993), Colo. Bar Assn. (bd. govs. 1990-92, exec. coun., 1991-92), Women's Bar Assn., Rhone-Brackett Inn of Ct. (master 1993-97), Women Judges Assn. (co-chair nat. conf. 1990). Office: Colo Supreme Ct Colo State Jud Bldg 2 E 14th Ave Fl 4 Denver CO 80203-2115*

RICE, PATRICIA JANE, journalist; b. St. Louis, Oct. 20, 1942; d. Canice T. and Jane Elizabeth Tobin) R. BA, Maryville Coll., Tenn., 1964; postgrad., St. Louis U., 1965—66. Copywriter Wohl Co., St. Louis, 1964-67; free-lance journalist Paris, 1967; copywriter D'Arcy Advt. Co., St. Louis, 1968; feature writer, columnist St. Louis Post, 1969-94, religion editor, 1994—2004, South reporter, 2004—05; freelance writer, 2005—. Moderator Rutgers U./Eagleton Ctr. Women in Politics Conf., 1980, 82, 84; lectr. in field. Author: City House, 1968, The Eclectic Shopper, 1973, A Catholic Funeral, 2005; co-author: In the Running: The New Political Woman, 1981 V.p. The St. Louis Forum, 1997-2002; bd. dirs. Leadership St. Louis, 1985-90. Recipient Quest award Mo. Press Women's, 1998; Knight Ctr. fellow U. Md., College Park, 1996, 2004. Mem. Journalism Found. Met. St. Louis (pres. 1984-91), St. Louis Newspaper Guild (treas. 1977-87), Soc. Profl. Journalists; St. Louis Regional Arts Commn. (grants com., 2007-); St. Louis Lyon France Sister Cites Beak Club (bd. dirs., 2008-). Avocations: gardening, skiing. Office: Rice Assoc 1221 Locust St Ste 800 Saint Louis MO 63103 Office Phone: 314-241-8000.

RICE, PATRICIA OPPENHEIM LEVIN, retired special education educator, consultant; b. Detroit, Apr. 5, 1932; d. Royal A. and Elsa (Freeman) Oppenheim; m. Charles L. Levin, Feb. 21, 1956 (div. Dec. 1981); children: Arthur David, Amy Ragen, Fredrick Stuart; m. Howard T. Rice, Dec. 16, 1990 (div. Apr. 1994). AB in History, U. Mich., 1954, PhD, 1981; MEd, Marygrove Coll., 1973. Cert. elem. tchr., Mich. Tchr. reading and learning disabled, cons., Detroit Pub. Schs., 1967-76; assoc. prof., coord. spl. edn., Marygrove Coll., 1976-86; adj. prof. Oakland U., 1987-90, U. Miami, 1989-95, ret.; edn. curriculum cons. Lady Elizabeth Sch., Jávea (Alicante) Spain, 1988-91; v.p. Machpelah Non-profit Cemetery Bd., Ferndale, Mich., 1978-87, co-pres., 1987—; adv. bd. Eton Acad., Birmingham, Mich., 1991-93; workshop presenter Dade City Schs., 1992-97; presenter in field. Mem. Mich. regional bd. ORT, 1965-68; mil. affairs and youth svcs. SE Mich. chpt. ARC Bd., 1973-79; v.p. exec. bd. Women's Aux. Children's Hosp. Mich., 1968-73; bd. dirs. women's com. United Cmty. Svcs., 1968-73; judge Dade County Schs. for Tchr. Grants, 1996—2004; bd. dirs. Detroit Grand Opera Assn., 1970-75; com. chair morning of music benefits Detroit Symphony Orch.; torch drive area chmn. United Found., 1967-70; benefactor Fla. Grand Opera, 1990-2001, grand benefactor, 2002—, guild exec. bd., 1992-, v.p., 1998-99, co-pres. 2000-02, chair, found. bd. dirs., 2000-01; guild exec. bd. Miami City Ballet, 1996-2000, Choreographers Cir., 1990-; chair Lincoln Rd. Walk, 1996, co-chair All Star Luncheon, 1996, Ball Com., 1992; active Diabetes Rsch. Inst. & Found. Love & Hope Com., Fla. Concert Assn. Cresendo Soc., 1993-97, Villa Maria Angel, 1996—, v.p. angel bd. 1998—2005, co-pres. Angels of Villa Maria, 2005-, found. bd. dirs. 2000—; v.p. Miami Children's Hosp. Bd., 2004-, aux. bd., 2005—; panel judge Dade County Cultural Affairs Coun., 2002-04; v.p., amb. Mt. Sinai Hosp. Alzheimer's Bd. Mem. NAACP (life), Navy League, Greater Miami Social Register, Citizens Interested in the Arts (charter, grant chair, exec. bd. 1997—), Hadassah (life), Williams Island Club, Miami Shores Country Club, Surf Club, Phi Delta Kappa, Pi Lambda Theta.

RICE, PETER, broadcast executive; Degree, U. Nottingham, England, 1989. Dir. acquisitions Twentieth Century Fox, 1994, dir. prodn., v.p. prodn., sr. v.p. prodn.; pres. prodn. Fox Searchlight Pictures, 2000—09; chmn. Fox Entertainment Group, 2009—. Named one of The 50 Smartest People in Hollywood, Entertainment Weekly, 2007. Office: Fox Entertainment Group 10201 W Pico Blvd Ste 100 Los Angeles CA 90035*

RICE, PHILIP L., bank executive; BBA, U. Akron, Ohio; MBA, Case Western Res. U., Cleve. Mgmt. trainee Nat. City Corp., Cleve., 1980, mng. dir. Nat. City Venture, mgr. regional and nat. comml. real estate businesses, pres. Ohio for Corp. Banking bus. unit, corp. exec. v.p., pres., CEO Nat. City Bank. Bd. dirs., chmn. bd. trustees Cleve. Devel. Advisors. Mem. corp. cabinet Harvest for Hunger; mem. vis. com. Case Western Res. U. Weatherhead Sch. Mgmt.; bd. dirs., vice chairperson, exec. com. mem. Cuyahoga Cmty. Coll. Found. Office: Nat City Corp Nat City Ctr 1900 E Ninth St Cleveland OH 44114-3484 Office Phone: 216-222-2000.

RICE, RAY, professional football player; b. New Rochelle, NY, Jan. 22, 1987; s. Janet Rice. Attended, Rutgers U., New Brunswick, NJ, 2005—08. Running back Balt. Ravens, 2008—. Named Freshman All-Am., The Sporting News, 2005, First Team All-Conf., Big East, 2006, 2007; finalist Maxwell award, 2006, 2007, Doak Walker award, 2007. Office: Balt Ravens M&T Bank Stadium 1101 Russell St Baltimore MD 21230*

RICE, RONALD JAMES, hospital administrator; b. Springfield, Mo., Feb. 5, 1944; s. Glen Elwood and Alice Jeanett (Robinson) R. BSBA, Cen. Mo. State U., 1966, MABA, 1969, Specialist, 1972. Lic. nursing home adminstr.; lic. risk mgr. Unit mgr. Bapt. Med. Ctr., Kansas City, Mo., 1970-71; dir. unit mgmt. Ind. Health Ctr., Independence, Mo., 1971-72; adminstrv. officer Meth. Hosp., Jacksonville, Fla., 1972-73, dir. personnel, 1973-74; assoc. adminstr. Humana Hosp. Orange Park (Fla.), 1974-77; adminstr. Cathedral Rehab. Hosp., Jacksonville, 1977-79, Marion County Gen. Hosp., Hamilton, Ala., 1979-80, Nassau Gen. Hosp., Fernandina Beach, Fla., 1980-85, Reception Med. Ctr., Lake Butler, Fla., 1985-91; regional adminstr. health svcs. Dept. Corrections, Gainesville, Fla., 1991—; sr. health svc. adminstr. Columbia Correctional Instn., 1999—2006. Cons. Clay Meml. Hosp., Green Cove Springs, Fla., 1976-77, Allied Health Care, Jacksonville, 1989. Mem. Polit. Action Com., Fla. Hosp. Assn., 1990, Coun. on Crime and Delinquency, Gainesville, 1990, Human Resources Com., Orlando, 1991; active Orange Park Presbyn. Ch. With U.S. Army, 1967-69. Decorated Army Commendation medal. Fellow Am. Coll. Health Care Execs.; mem. Am. acad. Med. Adminstrs., Am. Coll. Health Care Adminstrs., Am. Soc. Personnel Adminstrs., Fla. Hosp. Assn., Rotary (pres. 1984-86). Democrat. Avocations: boating, collecting model cars, antique juke box collecting, reading. Home: 1744 Horton Dr Orange Park FL 32073-2757 Personal E-mail: ricerjq45@aol.com.

RICE, ROSE ANN M., secondary school educator; b. Washington, Mo., Nov. 9, 1948; d. Martin Henry and Mary Ann Kraft; m. Frank William Rice, July 1, 1995. B in Chemistry and Math, Notre Dame Coll., St. Louis, 1971; MS in Edn., Creighton U., 1981. Cert. tchr. Mo., FAST 1 and FAST 2 sci. tchr. Sci. tchr. St. Gabriel Sch., St. Louis, 1971—75, Hannibal Cath. Sch., Mo., 1975—84, St. Aloysius Sch., St. Louis, 1984—88, Immaculate Conception Sch., Union, Mo., 1991—95, Notre Dame HS, St. Louis, 2001—; sci. and math. tchr. St. Cecilia Sch., St. Louis, 1995—97, St. Dominic Savlo Sch., St. Louis, 1997—2001; prin., sci. and math. tchr. St. Anthony's Sch., Sullivan, Mo., 1988—91. Regional sci. coord. East Ctrl. Coll., Union, 1991—95; tutor Sylvan Learning Ctr., Fenton, Mo., 2002—04, Notre Dame Tutorial Ctr., St. Louis, 2004—05; speech coach, judge in field; moderator sch. sci. fairs. Bd. dirs. Phoenix Homeless Shelter, Washington, Mo., 1992—94; mem. ch. coun. Hannibal (Mo.) Cath. Ch., 1980—84, Mary Mother Ch., St. Louis, 2000—01. Recipient ribbons for needlework and crafts, Washington Town & Country Fair; grantee, Litzinger Ctr., Mo. Bot. Gardens, St. Louis, 1998—2001. Mem.: NSTA, Sci. Tchrs. Mo. Roman Catholic. Avocations: needlecrafts, reading, walking, golf, travel. Office: Notre Dame HS 320 E Ripa Ave Saint Louis MO 63125 Business E-Mail: ricer@ndhs.net.

RICE, STEPHEN GARY, pediatrician, sports medicine physician, educator; b. Bklyn., Dec. 21, 1945; s. Abraham S. Rice and Anne (Shelling) Rice-Brown; m. Hilary Jo Turett, May 10, 1987; children: Adam, Bryan. AB, Columbia Coll., 1967; MD, PhD, NYU, 1974; MPH, U. Wash., 1983. Diplomate in pediat. and sports medicine Am. Bd. Pediat. Intern, resident Children's Hosp. and U. Wash., Seattle, 1974-77; faculty mem. sports medicine U. Wash., Seattle, 1977-96; program dir. primary care sports medicine fellowship Jersey Shore Univ. Med. Ctr., Neptune, NJ, 1996—; clin. assoc. prof. pediat. Robert Wood Johnson Med. Sch. U. Medicine and Dentistry NJ, New Brunswick, 1999—. Team physician U. Wash., 1977-81, Georgian Ct. U., 1997-; developer, dir. Athletic Health Care Sys., 1978—; dir. Jersey Shore Sports Medicine Ctr., 1997-; med. cons., NJ Youth Soccer Olympic Devel. Program, 2002-; cons. in field. Author: Athletic Health Care System, 1988. Mem. Alumni Representative Com., Columbia Coll., 1974-, Concussion in Sports Steering Com., Brain Injury Assn. NJ, 2005-. Recipient Commendation award, Washington State Interscholastic Activities Assn., 1981, 1995, Vol. Faculty Tchg. award, UMDNJ-Robert Wood Johnson Med. Sch., 2000, Silvio O. Conte award, Brain Injury Assn. NJ, 2006; named Top Doctor in Sports Medicine, NJ, NJ Mag., 2001, 2003, 2005, Top Doctor in Greater NY Metro. Area, Castle Connelly, 2002—09. Fellow: Am. Coll. Sports Medicine (sec. Greater NY regional chpt. 1997—2002, chmn. health and sci. policy com. 2000—, mem. bd. trustees 2007—), Am. Acad. Pediat. (chmn. sports medicine com. NJ chpt. 1999—, chmn. govt. affairs com. NJ chpt. 2000—06, sec.-editor NJ chpt. 2002—04, exec. com. of sports medicine and fitness coun. 2003—, treas. NJ chpt. 2004—06, v.p.-elect NJ chpt. 2006—, v.p. 2008—); mem.: AAHPERD, Med. Soc. NJ, Am. Med. Soc. Sports Medicine, Nat. Strength and Conditioning Assn. Avocations: sports, cooking, gardening, gilbert & sullivan, chess. Home: 6 Wildflower Ct Manalapan NJ 07726-2861 Office: Jersey Shore Univ Med Ctr Dept Pediat PO Box 397 Neptune NJ 07754-0397 Office Phone: 732-776-2384. Business E-Mail: srice@meridianhealth.com.

RICE, STUART ALAN, chemist, educator; b. NYC, Jan. 6, 1932; s. Harry L. and Helen (Rayfield) Rice; m. Marian Ruth Coopersmith, June 1, 1952 (dec. June 1994); children: Barbara, Janet; m. Ruth O'Brien, Sept. 27, 1997; 1 child, David Lawrence. BS, Bklyn. Coll., 1952; MA, Harvard, 1954, PhD, 1955. Jr. fellow Harvard, 1955—57; faculty U. Chgo., 1957—60, prof. chemistry, 1960—69, Louis Block prof. phys. scis., 1969—77, chmn. dept. chemistry, 1971—76, Frank P. Hixon disting. service prof., 1977—, dean phys. scis. div., 1981—95, dir. Inst. Study Metals, 1957—59; Newton Abraham prof. Oxford U., 1999—2000. Mem. Nat. Sci. Bd., 1980—86. Author: Polyelectrolyte Solutions, 1961, Statistical Mechanics of Simple Liquids, 1965, Physical Chemistry, 1980, 2d edit., 2000, Optical Control of Molecular Dynamics, 2000; contbr. articles to profl. jours. Recipient Centennial medal, Harvard U., 1997, Nat. Medal of Sci., 1999, Hirschfelder award for Theoretical Chemistry, 2002; named Falk-Plautt lectr., Columbia U., 1964, Riley lectr., Notre Dame U., 1964, U. lectr. chemistry, U. Western Ont., 1970, Seaver lectr., U. Soc. Calif, 1972, Noyes lectr., U. Tex., 1975, Foster lectr., SUNY, 1976, Frank T. Gucker lectr., Ind. U., 1976, Fairchild lectr., Calif. Inst. Tech., 1979, Baker lectr., Cornell U., 1985—86, Centenary lectr., Royal Soc. Chemistry, 1986—87, Nat. lectr., Phi Beta Kappa, 1994—95, Kennedy lectr., Washington U., 2002, Noyes lectr., U. Oreg., 2002; fellow, Guggenheim, 1960—61, Sr. Postdoctoral fellow, NSF, 1965—66, USPHS Spl. Postdoctoral fellow, U. Copenhagen, 1970—71. Fellow: Royal Irish Acad. Scis., Am. Philos. Soc.; mem.: AAAS, Danish Acad. Sci. and Letters, N.Y. Acad. Scis. (A. Cressy Morrison prize 1955), Faraday Soc. (Marlowe medal 1963), Am. Phys. Soc., Am. Acad. Sci. (Hirschfelder award for theoret. chemistry 2002, Willis Lamb medal 2004), Nat. Acad. Sci., Am. Chem. Soc. (Pure Chemistry award 1963, Leo Hendrik Baekland award 1971, Peter Debye award 1985, Hildebrand award 1987). Business E-Mail: s-rice@uchicago.edu.

RICE, SUE ANN, retired dean, psychologist; b. Ponca City, Okla., Sept. 17, 1934; d. Alfred and Helen (Revard) R. BS in Edn., U. Okla., 1956; MA, Cath. U., 1979, PhD, 1988. Ensign USN, 1956, advanced through grades to comdr., 1973; ednl. svcs. officer 9th Naval Dist., Great Lakes, Ill., 1956-58; adminstr., asst. staff, comdr. in-chief Pacific Fleet, Honolulu, 1958-61; head edn. div. Naval Air Sta., Lemoore, Calif., 1961-63; instr., acad. dir. Women Officers' Sch., Newport, R.I., 1963-66; head. tng. div. Naval Command Systems Support Activity, Washington, 1966-70; head, ops. support sec. staff, comdr.-in-chief Lant FLT, Norfolk, Va., 1970-74; sr. U.S. rep. NATO, subgroup 5 orgn. JCS, Washington, 1974-77; ret. USN, 1977; head vocation office Archdiocese of Washington, 1977-78; cons. Notre Dame Inst., Arlington, Va., 1989-97, dean of students, 1990-95; ret., 1995. Lectr. Cath. U. Am., Washington, 1983-84; bd. dirs. Villa Cortona Apostolic Ctr., Bethesda, 1984-94. Tech. reviewer Personnel Administration, 1964; editor (newsletter) Vocation News, 1978. Conoco scholarship Continental Oil Co., 1952-56; recipient Meritorious Svc. medal Pres. of U.S., 1977, rsch. grant Cath. U., Sigma Xi, 1986. Mem.: Lay Women's Assn. (internat. v.p., administrv. commn.), Cath. War Vets. (nat. membership task force com., nat. youth act com., nat. co-chmn. pub. rels. com.), Gamma Phi Beta, Kappa Delta Pi. Roman Catholic. Avocations: travel, music, gardening, woodworking. Home: PO Box 2742 Ponca City OK 74602-2742

RICE, SUSAN ELIZABETH, Permanent United States Representative to the United Nations; b. Washington, Nov. 17, 1964; d. Emmett J.& Lois Dickson (Fitt) R.; m. Ian Cameron, Sept. 12, 1992; 2 children BA in History, Stanford U., Calif., 1986; MPhil in Internat. Rels., Oxford U., England, 1988, PhD, 1990. Mgmt. cons. McKinsey & Co., Toronto, Ont., Canada, 1991-93; dir. internat. organizations & peacekeeping NSC, Washington, 1993-95, spl. asst. to the Pres., sr. dir. African affairs, 1995-97; asst. sec. for African affairs US Dept. State, Washington, 1997—2001; sr. fellow fgn. policy The Brookings Instn., Washington, 2002—09; sr. fgn. policy adv. Barack Obama's Presdl. Campaign, 2008; permanent US rep. to UN US Dept. State, NYC, 2009—. Mem. Coun. on Fgn. Rels.; mem. adv. bd. Obama-Biden Transition Project, 2008; bd. dirs. US Fund for UNICEF, Nat. Democratic Inst., Internews Corp.; mem. adv. coun. U. Tex. Lyndon B. Johnson Sch. Pub. Affairs. Harry S. Truman scholar, 1984, Rhodes scholar, 1986; recipient Walter Frewen Lord prize, Royal Commonwealth Soc., 1990, Assn. prize, Chatham House-British Internat. Studies, 1992, Samuel Nelson Drew Meml. award, NSC, 2000; named to Stanford's Black Alumni Hall of Fame, 2002 Mem. Phi Beta Kappa, Coun. Fgn. Relations, Aspen Strategy Group Office: Permanent Mission of US to UN 140 E 45th St New York NY 10017*

RICE, THOMAS CHARLES, lawyer; b. NYC, Jan. 18, 1956; s. Thomas P. and Laura T. (Hage) R.; m. Cheryl A. Christman, Sept. 15, 1984; children: Thomas Christman, Matthew David. BA in math. magna cum laude, St. John's U., 1978, JD, 1981. Bar: US Dist. Ct. (so. dist.) NY, US Dist. Ct. (ea. dist.), NY, US Dist Ct. (we. dist.) NY, US Dist. Ct. (no. dist.) NY, US Dist. Ct. (no. dist.) Tex., US Dist. Ct. Colo., US Dist Ct. (no. dist.) Okla., US Ct. Appeals (2nd cir.) (U.S. Ct. Apeals), US Ct. Appeals (3rd cir.), US Ct. Appeals (5th cir.), US Supreme Ct, US Dist. Ct. (ea. dist.), Mich. Assoc. Simpson Thacher & Bartlett, NYC, 1981-88, ptnr., 1989—, mem. exec. com. Contbr. articles to profl. jours. Mem. ABA (litigation sect.), N.Y. State Bar Assn., Assn. Bar City of N.Y. (vice chair Judiciary Comm.) Office: Simpson Thacher & Bartlett LLP 425 Lexington Ave Fl 15 New York NY 10017-3954 Office Phone: 212-455-3040. Office Fax: 212-455-2502. Business E-Mail: trice@stblaw.com.

RICE, THOMAS HOWARD, healthcare educator; b. Washington, Apr. 21, 1954; s. John Donald and Dorothy Pechman R.; m. Katherine Anne Desmond, Oct. 21, 1953; children: Clara, Daniel. BA, U. N.C., 1976; MA, U. Calif., Berkeley, 1979, PhD, 1982. Sr. health economist SRI Internat., Menlo Park, Calif., 1979—83; assoc. prof. U.N.C. Sch. Pub. Health, Chapel Hill, 1983—91; prof. UCLA Sch. Pub. Health, 1991—, vice chancellor for academic personnel, 2006—. Chmn. bd. dir. Acad. Health, Washington, 2005—06; editor Med. Care Rsch. and Rev., Thousand Oaks, Calif., 1994—2000; chair Dept. Health Svcs., UCLA Sch. of Pub. Health, 1996—2000. Author: Economics of Health Reconsidered, 2003; editor: Changing the U.S. Health Care System, 2006. Recipient Young Investigator of the Yr. award, Assn. Health Svcs. Rsch., 1988, Thompson prize, Assn. U. Programs in Health Adminstrn., 1992, Article of the Yr. award, Assn. Health Svcs. Rsch., 1998. Mem.: Inst. of Medicine. Office: 2138 Murphy Hall Los Angeles CA 90095-1405 Office Phone: 310-206-9345. Business E-Mail: trice@conet.ucla.edu.

RICE, WAYNE, artist, educator, small business owner; b. Chgo., Ill., Jan. 13, 1950; s. Raymond and Genevieve (Kocol) Rice; 1 child, Conor Raymond. Student, U. Calif. Berkeley, 1968—70, Nothern Ill. U., 1971; BA in art studio, U. N.Mex., 1980; cert. in tchg., U. Colo., 1988. Cert. tchr. cert. K-12 U. Colo., 1988. Graphic artist Webb-Pantaleoni Design, Taos, N.Mex., 1980—81; art dir. Artlines Inc., Taos, 1981—84; graphic designer Westview Press Inc., Boulder, Colo., 1985—87; designer, mus. educator Mus. of N. Mex., Office of Statewide Programs and Edn., Santa Fe, 1989—92; curator of edn. Mus. of N. Mex., Palace of Gov., Santa Fe, 1992; creative dir., owner Design Arts, 1984—; visual info. specialist The Imagination Team, US Dept. of Interior, Bur. Land Mgmt., Dolores, Colo., 1992—2007, Dolores Pub. Lands Ctr., 2007—. Cons. Design Arts, Boulder, Colo., 1986—2007; staff designer, edn. divsn. Mus. of N.Mex., Santa Fe, 1989—91; curator of edn. Mus. of N.Mex., Palace of the Gov. Mus., Santa Fe, 1991—92. Numerous group shows including, exhibited in group shows at Internat. Art Competition, LA, 1984, Palo Alto Cultural Ctr., Calif., 1986, Gallery at the Rep, Santa Fe, N.Mex., 1989, Richmond Art Ctr., Calif., 1997, Ctr. Visual Arts, Chautauqua, NY, 2000, Mus. Contemporary Art, Ft. Collins, Colo., 2004, one-man shows include Sq.: Gallery, Claremont, Calif., 2009—, Harwood Found. U. N.Mex., Taos, N.Mex., 1981, The Bridge Gallery Boulder Pub. Libr., Colo., 1985, Art and Crafts Cooperative, 1986, Tybie Davis Satin Gallery Santa Fe Pub. Libr., N.Mex., 1992, Centennial Savings Bank, Durango, Colo., 1996, Represented in permanent collections City Cortez Pub. Libr., Taos Coutny Assn. Retarded Citizens. Recipient Design award, N. Mex. Route 66 Assn., Shadow Ridge Corp., Town of Taos Adminstrn., Leopold's Records, U. Calif., Artist-in-residence, Nat. Pk. Svc., USDA Forest Svc., Colo., Wy., N. Mex., Silver award, Nat. Assn. Interpretation, 2005; finalist Nat. Forest Sys. Stamp Contest, USDA, 1992; grantee, N.Mex. Arts Divsn., 1982, 1983. Mem.: Colo. Arts Assn., Four Corners Club-Toastmasters Internat. (pres.). Avocations: visual arts, creative writing, hiking, walking, bicycling. Mailing: PO Box 746 Dolores CO 81323 Personal E-mail: desarts@gmail.com.

RICE, WILLIAM EDWARD, journalist; b. Albany, NY, July 26, 1938; s. Harry Edward, Jr. and Elizabeth (Lally) R.; m. Carol Timmon, June 3, 1978 (div.); m. Jill Van Cleave, Aug. 20, 1983. BA in History, U. Va., 1960; MS with honors, Columbia U., 1963. Reporter, editorial writer, critic Washington Post, 1963-69; student LeCordon Bleu, Paris, 1969-70; dir. L'Ecole de Cuisine, Bethesda, Md., 1971-72; freelance writer, restaurant critic Washingtonian Mag., 1971-72; exec. food editor Washington Post, 1972-80; editor-in-chief Food and Wine Mag., NYC, 1980-85; food and wine columnist Chgo. Tribune, 1986—2003. Dining In columnist Gentlemen's Quarterly, 1987-89; chmn. restaurant awards com. James Beard Found., 1993-2003, chmn. who's who food and beverage in Am. com., 2005-08. Author: Feasts of Wine and Food, 1986, Steak Lovers Cookbook, 1997; editor: (with others) Where to Eat in

America, 1978, 2d edit., 1980, 3d edit., 1987. Served with USN, 1960-62. Recipient Vesta award as outstanding newspaper food editor, 1979, Ordre du Merite Agricole (France), 1983 Home: 655 W Buena Ave Chicago IL 60613-2201 Office Phone: 773-975-6685. Personal E-mail: wricechicago@yahoo.com.

RICE, WINSTON EDWARD, lawyer, priest; b. Shreveport, La., Feb. 22, 1946; s. Winston Churchill and Margaret (Coughlin) R.; m. Barbara Reily Gay, Apr. 16, 1977; 1 child, Andrew Hynes; children by previous marriage: Winston Hobson, Christian MacTaggart. Student, Centenary Coll. La., 1967; JD, La. State U., 1971. Bar: La. 1971, Colo. 1990, Tex. 1992; ordained to priesthood Episcopal Ch., 2005. Cons. geologist, Gulfport, Miss., 1968-70; ptnr. Phelps, Dunbar, New Orleans, 1971-88; sr. ptnr. Rice, Fowler, New Orleans, Houston, Miami, Fla., London and Bogota, 1988-2000; gen. mgr. Winston Edw. Rice LLC, Covington, La., 2000—. Instr. law La. State U., Baton Rouge, 1970-71. Assoc. editor La. Law Rev., 1970-71. Asst. rector Christ Ch., Covington, La., 2005—. Mem.: Trucking Industry Def. Assn., Ctr. Transp. Law and Policy, Soc. Ins. Trainers and Educators, Assn. Average Adjusters (U.K.), Assn. Average Adjusters U.S., Maritime Law Assn. U.S. (chmn. subcom. on offshore exploration and devel. 1985—88, vice chmn. com. internat. law of the sea 1988—91, chmn. 1991—95, membership sec. 1998—2002), Com. Maritime Internat. (titulary mem.), Fedn. Ins. and Corp. Counsel, La. Assn. Def. Counsel, New Orleans Assn. Def. Counsel, Can. Transp. Lawyers Assn., New Orleans Bar Assn., Tex. State Bar, Colo. State Bar Assn., La. Bar Assn., Stratford Club, Boston Club, Mariners Club (treas. 1974—75, 1978—79, sec. 1975—76, v.p. 1976—77, pres. 1977—78), Kappa Alpha, Phi Kappa Phi, Phi Delta Phi, Order of Coif. Republican. Episcopalian. Office: 512 E Boston Ave Covington LA 70433-2943 Home Phone: 985-893-8934; Office Phone: 985-893-8949. Business E-Mail: rice@ricellc.com.

RICH, ADRIENNE, poet; b. Balt., May 16, 1929; d. Arnold Rice and Helen Elizabeth (Jones) R.; m. Alfred H. Conrad (dec. 1970); children: David, Paul, Jacob. AB, Radcliffe Coll., Cambridge, Mass., 1951; LittD (hon.), Wheaton Coll., Norton, Mass., 1967, Smith Coll., Northampton, Mass., 1979, Brandeis U., Waltham, Mass., 1987, Coll. Wooster, Ohio, 1988, CCNY, Harvard U., Cambridge, Mass., 1990, Swarthmore Coll., Pa., 1992. Tchr. workshop YM-YWHA Poetry Ctr., NYC, 1966-67; vis. lectr. Swarthmore Coll., 1967-69; adj. prof. writing divsn. Columbia U., 1967-69; lectr. CCNY, 1968-70, instr., 1970-71, asst. prof. English, 1971-72, 74-75; Fannie Hurst vis. prof. creative lit. Brandeis U., 1972-73; prof. English Douglass Coll., Rutgers U., 1976-79; Clark lectr., disting. vis. prof. Scripps Coll., 1983-84; A.D. White prof.-at-large Cornell U., 1981-87; disting. vis. prof. San Jose State U., 1984-85; prof. English and feminist studies Stanford U., 1986-93. Marjorie Kovler vis. lectr. U. Chgo., 1989. Author: Collected Early Poems, 1950-1970, 1993, Diving into the Wreck, 1973, The Dream of a Common Language, 1978, A Wild Patience Has Taken Me This Far, 1981, Your Native Land, Your Life, 1986, Time's Power, 1989, An Atlas of the Difficult World, 1991, Dark Fields of the Republic, 1995, Midnight Salvage, 1999, Fox, 2001, The Fact of a Doorframe: Selected Poems 1950-2001, 2002, The School Among the Ruins, 2004 (Nat. Book Critics Cir. prize poetry, 2005, Telephone Ringing in the Labyrinth, 2006; (prose) Of Woman Born: Motherhood as Experience and Institution, 1976, 10th anniversary edit., 1986, On Lies, Secrets and Silence, 1979, Blood, Bread and Poetry, 1986, What Is Found There: Notebooks on Poetry and Politics, 1993, 2d edit., 2003, Arts of the Possible: Essays and Conversations, 2001, Poetry and Commitment, 2007, A Human Eye: Essays on Poetry in Society, 1996-2008, 2009; editor: Muriel Rukeyser, A Jewish Voice for Peace, Selected Poems, 2004. Mem. nat. adv. bd. Nat. Writers Union, Rosenberg Fund for Children. Recipient Yale Series of Younger Poets award, 1951, Nat. Inst. Arts and Letters award in poetry, 1961, Eunice Tietjens Meml. prize, 1968, Shelley Meml. award, 1971, Nat. Book award, 1974, Fund for Human Dignity award Nat. Gay Task Force, 1981, Ruth Lilly Poetry prize, 1986, Brandeis U. Creative Arts medal for Poetry, 1987, Nat. Poetry Assn. award, 1989, Elmer Holmes Bobst award arts and letters NYU, 1989, MacArthur fellowship, 1994-99, Dorothea Tanning award Acad. Am. Poets, 1996, others; chancellor Acad. Am. Poets, 1999-2001, Lannan Found. Lifetime Achievement award, 1999, Bollingen prize, 2003, Nat. Found. Jewish Culture award, 2003, Nat. Book Found. medal for Disting. Contribution, 2006. Mem. PEN, Nat. Writers Union, A Jewish Voice for Peace. Office: c/o W W Norton Co 500 5th Ave New York NY 10110-0002

RICH, ALAN, music critic, writer; b. Boston, June 17, 1924; (parents Am. citizens); s. Edward and Helen (Hirshberg) R. AB, Harvard, 1945; MA, U. Calif-Berkeley, 1952. Alfred Hertz Meml. Traveling fellow in music, Vienna, 1952-53; Asst. music critic Boston Herald, 1944-45, N.Y. Sun, 1947-48; contbr. Am. Record Guide, 1947-61, Saturday Rev., 1952-53, Mus. Am., 1955-61, Mus. Quar., 1957-58; tchr. music U. Calif. at Berkeley, 1950-58; program and music dir. Pacifica Found., FM radio, 1953-61; asst. music critic N.Y. Times, 1961-63; chief music critic, editor N.Y. Herald Tribune, 1963-66; music critic, editor N.Y. World Jour. Tribune, 1966-67; contbg. editor Time mag., 1967-68; music and drama critic, arts editor N.Y. mag., 1968-81, contbg. editor, 1981-83; music critic, arts editor Calif. (formerly New West mag.), 1979-83, contbg. editor, 1983-85; gen. editor Newsweek mag., NYC, 1983-87; music critic L.A. Herald Examiner, 1987-89, L.A. Daily News, 1989-92, L.A. Weekly, 1992—2008. Tchr. New Sch. Social Rsch., 1972-75, 77-79, U. So. Calif. Sch. Journalism, 1980-82, Calif. Inst. Art, 1982-94, UCLA, 1990-91; artist-in-residence Davis Ctr. Performing Arts CUNY, 1975-76. Author: Careers and Opportunities in Music, 1964, Music: Mirror of the Arts, 1969, Listeners Guides to Classical Music, Opera, Jazz, 3 vols., 1980, The Lincoln Center Story, 1984, Play-by-Play: Bach, Mozart, Beethoven, Tchaikovsky, 4 vols., 1995, American Pioneers, 1995, So I've Heard: Notes of a Migratory Music Critic, 2006; author: (interactive CD-ROM computer programs): Schubert's Trout Quintet, 1991, So I've Heard: Bach and Before, 1992, So I've Heard: The Classical Ideal, 1993, So I've Heard: Beethoven and Beyond, 1993; contbr. articles to entertainment mags. Recipient Deems Taylor award ASCAP, 1970, 73, 74 Mem. Music Critics Circle N.Y. (sec. 1961-63, chmn. 1963-64), N.Y. Drama Critics Circle, Am. Theatre Critics Assn., Music Critics Assn., PEN. Democrat. Avocations: gardening, cooking. Home: 2925 Greenfield Ave Los Angeles CA 90064-4019 Office Phone: 310-475-5102. Office Fax: 310-694-0115. Personal E-mail: alanrich1@mac.com.

RICH, ANDREA LOUISE, former museum administrator; BA, UCLA, 1965, MA, 1966, PhD, 1968. Asst. prof. comms. studies UCLA, LA, 1976, asst. dir. office learning resources, 1976, acting dir. Media Ctr., 1977, dir. office of instructional devel., 1978-80, asst. vice chancellor office of instructional devel., 1980-86, asst. exec. vice chancellor, 1986-87, vice chancellor acad. adminstrn., 1987-91, exec. vice chancellor, 1991-95; pres., CEO L.A. County Mus. of Art, 1995—2006, pres., Wallis Annenberg dir., 2003—06.

RICH, BENJAMIN JACOBS, legislative staff member; s. Robert and Judith Rich; m. Karen Marie Ancharski, Nov. 2005. Grad., U. Mich. Legis. asst., Rep. Bill Pascrell US House of Reps., Washington, sr. legis. asst., Rep. Bill Pascrell, 2002—03, legis. dir., Rep. Bill Pascrell, 2003—05, chief of staff to Rep. Bill Pascrell, 2005—. Democrat. Office: 2464 Rayburn House Office Bldg Washington DC 20515 Office Phone: 202-225-5751. Office Fax: 202-225-5782.*

RICH, CHARLES ANTHONY, hydrogeologist, consultant; b. London, Nov. 5, 1951; came to U.S., 1955; s. Eric Hebert and Ilse (Renard) R.; m. Linda Christine Johnson, June 23, 1984; 1 child, Oliver Sandor. BS in Geology, Syracuse U., 1973; MA in Geology, CUNY, 1975. Cert. in dispute resolution; cert. profl. geologist. Hydrologic technician U.S. Geol. Survey, Mineola, NY, 1973—75; hydrogeologist H2M Corp., PC, Melville, NY, 1975—76, Geraghty & Miller, Inc., Port Washington, NY, 1976—79; prin.-in-charge Dames and Moore, Cranford, NJ, 1979—82; pres. C.A. Rich Cons., Inc., Plainview, NY, 1982—. Expert witness Nat. Forensic Ctr., 1989; environ. cons., spkr. in field. Bd. dirs. L.I. Real Estate Practitioners Inst., 2001—, vice chmn. white paper com., chmn., 2003—. Mem. ASTM (stds. com., environ. audits for real property transfer com., environ. monitoring com. water supply exploration and devel.), Am. Inst. Profl. Geologists (pres. N.E. sect. 1981-92, nat. govt. affairs com. 1983—, chair N.E. U.S. membership screening bd. 2000—), Am. Water Resources Assn., Am. Water Works Assn., Nat. Ground Water Assn. (cons. com.), N.Y. Water Pollution Control Assn., Am. Geol. Inst./Geol. Soc. Am., Nat. Forensic Ctr. (expert writer) Cons. Bus. and Industry Assn., Conn. Ground Water Assn., N.Y. State Coun. Profl. Geologists (v.p.), L.I. Assn., L.I. Geologists (govt. affairs liaison 2003—). Home: 168 Baldwin Ave Locust Valley NY 11560-1920 Office: CA Rich Cons 17 Dupont St Plainview NY 11803-1602 Office Phone: 516-576-8844. Business E-Mail: crich@carichinc.com.

RICH, FRANK, journalist, writer; b. Washington, June 2, 1949; s. Frank Hart Rich and Helene Bernice (Aaronson) Fisher; m. Alexandra Rachelle Witchel, 1991; children from previous marriage: Nathaniel Howard, Simon Hart. BA in Am. Hist. and Lit., with honors, Harvard U., 1971. Co-editor Richmond Mercury, Va., 1972-73; sr. editor, film critic New Times mag., NYC, 1973-75; film critic NY Post, NYC, 1975-77; film and TV critic TIME mag., NYC, 1977-80; chief drama critic NY Times, NYC, 1980-93; columnist NY Times Sunday Mag., NYC, 1993; Op-Ed columnist NY Times, NYC, 1994—2003, 2005—, assoc. editor, columnist, 2003—05; creative cons. Home Box Office (HBO), 2008—. Author: The Theatre Art of Boris Aronson, 1987, Hot Seat: Theater Criticism for the New York Times 1980-93, 1998, Ghost Light: A Memoir, 2000, The Greatest Story Ever Sold: The Decline and Fall of Truth from 9/11 to Katrina, 2006. Recipient George Polk award for contbn. to journalistic integrity and investigative reporting, LI U., 2005. Office: The NY Times 620 Eighth Ave New York NY 10018-1405 Business E-Mail: frrich@nytimes.com.

RICH, HAROLD W., history professor; s. Hugh W. and Edith M. Rich; 1 child, James Scott. PhD, Tex. Christian, Ft. Worth, 2006. Instr. Tarrant County Coll., Ft. Worth, 2003—. Contbr. articles to hist. jour. Achievements include research in Ft. Worth history. Home: 4760 Melita Ave Fort Worth TX 76133 Office: Tarrant County Coll 4801 Marine Creek Fort Worth TX 76179 Personal E-mail: hwrich@hwrich.com.

RICH, JEFFREY A., former information technology company executive; b. 1960; BA, U. Mich., 1982. Asst. v.p. Interfirst Bank Dallas, 1982-86; v.p. Citibank, 1986-89; sr. v.p., CFO Affiliated Computer Svcs., Inc., Dallas, 1989-95, COO, 1995—2001, pres., 1995—2002, CEO, 1999—2005. Dir. Pegasus Solutions Inc. Dir. US C. of C., Edn. is Freedom Found.; mem. Young President's Orgn., Dallas Citizen's Coun.; bd. gov. Dallas Symphony Orchestra.

RICH, JOHN HUBBARD, JR., retired news correspondent; b. Cape Elizabeth, Maine, Aug. 5, 1917; s. John Hubbard Rich and Alma Estella Glidden Rich; m. Doris Lee Halstead, Sept. 2, 1954; children: Barbarine, John III, Whitney, Nathaniel. AB, Bowdoin Coll., 1939, LittD (hon.), 1974. News reporter Daily Kennebec Jour., Augusta, Maine, 1939—40, Portland (Maine) Press Herald, 1941—42; reporter, fgn. corr. Internat. News Svc., Tokyo, 1945—50; fgn. corr. NBC News, Tokyo, 1950—54; fellowship Coun. on Fgn. Rels., NYC, 1954—55. With US Corps. Maj. USMCR, 1943—45, PTO. Decorated Bronze star; recipient Peabody award, 1974. Mem.: Tokyo Fgn. Corrs. Club, Overseas Press Club (award 1974), Sigma Delta Chi. Avocations: tennis, sailing. Home: 13 Rocky Point Ln Cape Elizabeth ME 04107 Home Phone: 207-799-5978; Office Phone: 207-831-2103.

RICH, JOHN MARTIN, humanities educator, researcher; b. Tuscaloosa, Ala., Dec. 14, 1931; s. Emanuel Morris and Bertha (Rose) R.; m. Martha Elaine Schur, June 6, 1955 (div. June 1966); children— Jeffrey Brian, Suzanne Elon; m. Joyce Ann Stegemoller, Aug. 28, 1967 (div. Mar. 1985); m. Audrey Faye Arnold, Aug. 1, 1987. BA, U. Ala., 1954, MA, 1955; PhD, Ohio State U., 1958. Grad. asst. Ohio State U., Columbus, 1955, asst. instr. edn., 1956-58; asst. prof. edn. U. Tenn.-Martin, 1958-60; assoc. prof. edn. Coll. SUNY-Oneonta, 1960-61; from asst. prof. to assoc. prof. Iowa State U., Ames, 1961-66; assoc. prof. social and philos. studies U. Ky., Lexington, 1966-69; prof. cultural founds. edn. U. Tex., Austin, 1969-96, prof. emeritus, 1996—, chmn. dept. cultural founds. edn., 1969-75. Vis. lectr. Nat. Kaohsiung (Taiwan) Normal U., 1993. Author: (books) Education and Human Values, 1968, Humanistic Foundations of Education, 1971, Portuguese translation, 1975, Korean translation, 1985, Challenge and Response, 1974, New Directions in Educational Policy, 1974, Discipline and Authority in School and Family, 1982, Professional Ethics in Education, 1984, Innovative School Discipline, 1985, Foundations of Education, 1992; co-author: Theories of Moral Development, 1985 (named an Outstanding Book of 1985-86 Choice mag.), 2d edit., 1994, Korean translation, 1999, Helping and Intervention, 1988, Competition in Education, 1992, The Success Ethic, Education, and the American Dream, 1996, Korean translation, 1998; editor: Readings in the Philosophy of Education, 1966, 2d edit., 1972, Conflict and Decision, 1972, Innovations in Education, 6th edit., 1992; co-editor, editl. adv. bd. Ednl. Studies, 1970-74, 77-80, 89-91; bd. contbg. editors Rev. Edn., 1977-85; editl. bd. Focus on Learning, 1980-84, Educational Foundations, 1985-91; bd. cons. Jour. Rsch. and Devel. in Edn., 1982-96, Ednl. Theory, 1991-95; contbr. articles to profl. jours., U.S., Can., Eng., Australia. Recipient Faculty Research Assignment award Univ. Research Inst., Austin, Tex., 1983-84; vis. scholar U. London, 1977; Univ. Research Inst. grantee, 1981-82, 84-85 Mem. North Central Philosophy of Edn. Soc. (pres. 1966-67), Ohio Valley Philosophy of Edn. Soc. (pres. 1967-68), Philosophy of Edn. Soc. (exec. bd. 1967-68, 80-82, Cert. Significant Svc.), Am. Ednl. Studies Assn. (exec. council 1972-74, pres. 1975-76) Home: 1801 Lavaca St Apt 8M Austin TX 78701-1312 Office: U Tex Edn Bldg 406 Austin TX 78712 E-mail: john1931@webtv.net.

RICH, KAREN, nursing educator; BSN, La. State U. Health Sci. Ctr., New Orleans, 1983; MN, La. State U. Health Sci. Ctr., 1988; PhD, U. Southern Miss, Hattiesburg, 2005. Cert. nurse, Miss. Author: (book) Nursing Ethics Across the Curriculum and Into Practice; contbr. articles to jours. Recipient Gt. Nurse award, La. Nurses Assn., 1989; grant, Gamma Lambda Chpt. Sigma Theta Tau Internat., 2005, HRSA, 2007—08, U. Southern Miss., 2009—. Mem.: ANA, Assn. Cmty. Health Nurse Educators, Sigma Theta Tau Internat., Phi Kappa Phi.

RICH, KAREN VERNA STONEBRIDGE, nursing educator; b. Montreal, Can., Feb. 3, 1948; d. Alfred Basford and Alice (Thornly) Stonebridge; children: Kimberly Allison, Jason John Gordon. AAS, Alfred Agrl. and Tech. Coll., 1976; BSN, Alfred U., 1984; MS, U. Rochester, NYC, 1986; postgrad., Plymouth State Coll., U. Maine, Orono; doctoral student, Calif. Inst. Integral Studies, 1995—. Staff nurse Cuba (N.Y.) Meml. Hosp.; staff nurse ICU VA, Bath, N.Y., gerontol. nurse practitioner Manchester, N.H.; Concord Regional Vis. Nurses Assn.; assoc. prof. nursing N.H. Tech. Inst., Concord, to 1992; asst. prof. Husson Coll., Bangor, 1992—; community health nurse Community Health and Counseling, Bangor, 1993—. Teagle scholar. Mem. ANA (cert. gerontol. nurse practitioner), Am. Holistic Nurses Assn., Maine Gerontol. Assn. (bd. dirs.), Sigma Theta Tau. Home: 271 Fern St Bangor ME 04401-4041 Office: Husson Coll Bangor ME 04401

RICH, MICHAEL DAVID, think-tank executive, lawyer; b. LA, Jan. 23, 1953; s. Ben Robert and Faye (Mayer) Rich; m. Debra Paige Granfield, Jan. 12, 1980; children: Matthew, William. AB, U. Calif., Berkeley, 1973; JD, UCLA, 1976. Bar: Calif. 1976. Extern law clk. to judge U.S. Dist. Ct., Boston, 1975; staff mem. RAND, Santa Monica, Calif., 1976—85, dir. resource mgmt. program, 1980—85, dep. v.p., 1986, v.p. nat. security rsch. and dir. Nat. Def. Rsch. Inst., 1986—93, sr. v.p., 1993—95, exec. v.p., 1995—. Co-chmn. bd. overseers Rand-Qatar Policy Inst., 2003—. Author: numerous classified and unclassified reports and articles. Bd. dirs. WISE & Healthy Aging, Coun. Aid to Edn., chmn., 1996—2005; mem. bd. councillors UCLA Found., 2000—; mem. fin. oversight com. Santa Monica-Malibu Unified Sch. Dist., 2000—04; bd. advisers Santa Monica-UCLA Med. Ctr.; mem. adv. coun. Everychild Found.; chmn. bd. trustees The Comm. Inst., 2003—09. Mem.: Internat. Inst. Strategic Studies (mem. governing coun. 2001—07, chmn. bd. trustees IISS-US 2004—), Coun. Fgn. Rels. Office: RAND PO Box 2138 1776 Main St Santa Monica CA 90407-2138 Office Phone: 310-451-6934. E-mail: mrich@rand.org.

RICH, MICHAEL JOSEPH, lawyer; b. NYC, June 19, 1945; s. Jesse and Phyllis (Sternfeld) R.; m. Linda Christine Kubis, July 19, 1969; children: David Lawrence, Lisa Diane. BA, Gettysburg Coll., 1967; JD, Am. U., 1972. Bar: Del. 1973, U.S. Dist. Ct. Del. 1973, U.S. Supreme Ct., 1976, Pa., 1981. Law clk. Del. Supreme Ct., Georgetown, 1972-73; assoc. Tunnell & Raysor, Georgetown, 1973-76; ptnr. Dunlap, Holland & Rich, P.A., Georgetown, 1976-80; gen. counsel Pearlette Fashions, Inc., Lebanon, Pa., 1981-83; assoc. Morris, Nichols, Arsht & Tunnell, Georgetown, 1983-86; ptnr., 1987-91, Twilley, Street, Rich Braverman & Hindman, P.A., Dover, Del., 1991-95; state solicitor, 1995-2001; dep. atty. gen., 2001—07; v.p., regulatory counsel Fidelity Nat. Fin. Inc., 2007—. Mem. Bd. Bar Examiners, Del., 1986-97, chmn., 1996-97;minority counsel Del. Ho. of Reps., Dover, 1977-79; mem. Del. Gov's Magistrate Commn., 1980, 83-86; sec. Del. Gov's. Jud. Nominating Commn., 1986-89. Bd. dirs. People's Place II, Inc., Milford, Del., 1973-77; pres. Bi-County United Way, Inc., Milford, 1977-78; mem. Partnership Greater Milford Commn., 1987-89, Friends Milford Library. Served to 1st lt. U.S. Army, 1967-69, Vietnam. Dean's fellow Am. U., 1971-72. Mem. Del. Bar Assn. (pres. 1990-91), Sussex County Bar Assn. (pres. 1987-89). Office Phone: 904-854-3558. Business E-Mail: michael.rich@fnf.com.

RICH, PATRICIA R., lawyer; b. Bridgeport, Conn., Apr. 8, 1970; BA cum laude, U. Conn., 1991; MSW, U. Hawaii, Manoa, 1995; JD, Northeastern U., 1998. Bar: Conn., Mass., US Dist. Ct. (Dist. Mass.), US Dist. Ct. (Dist. Conn.). Assoc. Testa, Hurwitz & Thibeault, LLP, Boston, 1998—2002, Duane Morris LLP, Boston, 2002—06, ptnr., 2007—. Spkr. in field. Contbr. articles to law jours. Mem.: ABA, Women's Bar Assn., Fed. Bar Assn., Boston Bar Assn., Mass. Bar Assn. Office: Duane Morris LLP Ste 500 470 Atlantic Ave Boston MA 02109 Office Phone: 857-488-4290. Office Fax: 857-401-3049. E-mail: PRich@duanemorris.com.*

RICH, PAUL JOHN, policy educator, consultant; b. Buffalo, Dec. 10, 1938; BA with honors, Harvard U., 1959, EDM, 1963; PhD, U. Western Australia, Perth, 1989. Cons. Ministry Higher Edn., Saudi Arabia, 1979-81; faculty King Saud U., Saudi Arabia, 1979-81; adviser Govt. Qatar, 1981-90; rsch. fellow U. Western Australia, Perth, 1990-93, mem. univ. coun., 1991-93; prof. Univ. de las Americas, Puebla, Mexico, 1993—2007; adj. prof. George Mason U., 2006—. Bd. dirs. Nat. Intelligence study Ctr., Digest of Mid. East Studies, Acad. Coun. UN Sys., Coun. European Studies, U.S. Commn. Mil. History; gov. Harris Manchester Coll. Oxford U.; rsch. assoc. Fed. Res. Bank, Dallas, 1995—; Huntington lectr. Libr. Congress, 2000. Author: Elixir of Empire, 1989, Invasions of the Gulf, 1991, Chains of Empire, 1991, Tenure and the Demise of Academic Accountability, 1995; editor: (8 books) Middle East Series, 1992; co-author: Benefits Bestowed?, 1988, Secret Texts, 1995, Promise Keepers, 2000, Freemasonry in Context, 2004; editor: (series) Allborough Middle East Classics; prodr.: (films) The Night of Death, 1995; co-author: Creating the Arabian Gulf, 2009. Mem. Govt. House Found.; bd. dirs. Roosevelt Inst., 2005—. Vis. fellow Hoover Instn., Stanford U., 1992—; recipient Cameron medal for Rsch., James award for Rsch., Grand Lodge of Tex. Fellow: Royal Soc. West Australia, Royal Soc. Arts, Royal Microscopical Soc. (hist. sect.), Royal Numis. Soc., Royal Soc. Antiquaries, Royal Anthrop. Inst., Royal Asiatic Soc. (Hong Kong br.), Royal Geog. Soc., Royal Meteorol. Soc.; mem.: KP, ALA, AAAS, U. Club (DC), Diplomatic Club(Club), Am. Polit. Sci. Assn. (mem. awards com. 2003—, chair libr. com. 2003—, Lane award for Pub. Svc. 2002), Am. Hist. Assn. (life), Archeol. Inst. Am. (life), Assn. Geographers (life), Col. Mil. Historians (life), Nat. Coun. Geographic Edn. (life), Inst. Advanced Philos. Rsch. (life), Philos. Soc. Washington (life), Policy Studies Orgn. (pres. 2002—), Calif. Inst. Internat. Studies (v.p. 1994—2000), Am. Culture Assn. (chmn. endowment com. 1999—2003), Popular Culture Assn., Brit. Soc. Middle East Studies, Geog. Soc. India, Coll. Preceptors, U. Arts, Wash., Congress of Ams. (pres. 1995—), Tangier Am. Legation Soc., Sutton Ho Soc. (life), Royal Soc. Lit., Washington Club, Bostonian Soc. (life), Pilgrim Soc. (life), Women's Nat. Dem. Club DC, Stanford Faculty Club, Explorers Club Lima, Authors Club London, Challoner Club, Scottish Rite Rsch. Soc., Grange, Knight of Malta, Knight Templar, Masons, Shriners, Phi Sigma Omega (chancellor 2004—), Pi Lambda Theta, Phi Beta Delta (internat. pres. 2003—04, v.p. southeast and Europe, historian), Delta Phi Epsilon. Democrat. Unitarian Universalist. Avocations: water lily propagation, speleology, croquet, collaging. Office: 1527 New Hampshire Ave NW Washington DC 20036 Office Phone: 202-483-2512. Personal E-mail: rich@hoover.stanford.edu.

RICH, PHILIP DEWEY, publishing executive; b. Nashua, NH, Feb. 1, 1940; s. John Parker and Olive Frances (Hussey) R.; m. Leslie Ann Burke, June 14, 1974 (div. 1982). AB magna cum laude, Harvard U., 1961; MA, NYU, 1962; postgrad., Princeton U., 1962. Editor Houghton Mifflin Co., Boston, 1964-73; asst. mng. editor UpCountry Mag. Berkshire Eagle, Pittsfield, Mass., 1976-77; editor Book Creations Inc., Canaan, NY, 1977-80, editor-in-chief, 1980-91, v.p., exec. editor, 1991-92; cons. editor Berkshire Ho. Publs., Lee, Mass., 1992-93, mng. editor,

1993-96, mng. editor and prodn. editor, 1996-99, editl. dir., prodn. dir., 1999—2003; editl. cons. Pittsfield, Mass., 2003—. Office: 18 Boylston St Pittsfield MA 01201-6748 Office Phone: 413-443-1737. Personal E-mail: prich@bcn.net.

RICH, ROBERT E., JR., frozen foods company executive; b. 1941; s. Robert E. Rich Sr. and Janet Rich; m. Mindy Rich. BA, Williams Coll., 1963; MBA, U. Rochester, 1969; Ph.D (hon.), St. Bonaventure U., Niagra U., Johnson & Wales U. Pres. Rich Products Corp., Buffalo, 1978—, chmn., 2006—. Co-founder Western NY United Against Drug & Alcohol Abuse, Inc., 1986; chmn. Nat. Grocery Mfrs. Assn., 1999—, Students in Free Enterprise, 2003—06, Nat. Frozen & Refrigerated Foods Assn., 2006—. Author: Fish Fights: A Hall of Fame Quest, 2001, The Fishing Club, 2006. Recipient Peter Medaille medal, Outstanding alumni award, U. Rochester; named Citizen of the Yr., Buffalo News, 1983, Buffalo/Niagra Frontier Sales & Mktg. Exec. of the Yr., 1984, Exec. of the Yr., Am. Assn., 1986, Triple-A Exec. of the Yr., The Sporting News, 1988, Exec. of the Yr., Refrigerated & Frozen Foods mag., 1996; named a Diplomat, Nat. Restaurant Assn., 2000; named to, Nat. Frozen Food Ind. Hall of Fame, 1996, Buffalo Baseball Hall of Fame, S. Fla. Fishing Hall of Fame, 1999, Greater Buffalo Sports Hall of Fame, Nat. Restaurant Assn. Ednl. Found. Coll. Diplomats, 2000. Office: Rich Products Corp One Robert Rich Way Buffalo NY 14213

RICH, ROBERT EDWARD, lawyer; b. Corbin, Ky., Feb. 4, 1944; s. Edward Bluch and Marjorie Brooks (Wentworth) R.; m. Janet Sue Shearer, May 14, 1966; children: Susan M., Christopher R., David E., Sarah M. AB, U. Ky., 1966; JD, Harvard U., 1969. Bar: Ohio 1970. Jud. clk. U.S. Ct. Appeals for 6th Cir., Louisville, 1969-70; assoc. Taft, Stettinius & Hollister, Cin., 1970, ptnr., 1978—. Pres. Lighthouse Youth Svcs., Inc., Cin., 1985, Ky. YMCA Youth Assn., Frankfort, 2001; mem. exec. bd. Ky. Hist. Soc.; pres. Cin. Bar Found., 1991. Mem. ABA, Cin. Bar Assn. Republican. Presbyterian. Home: 215 Hilltop Ln Wyoming OH 45215-4121 Office: 1800 US Bank Tower 425 Walnut St Cincinnati OH 45202-3923 Office Phone: 513-357-9355. E-mail: rich@taftlaw.com.

RICH, ROBERT F., law and political science professor; married; 3 children. BA in Govt. with honors, Oberlin Coll., 1971; student, Free U. of Berlin, 1971-72; MA in Polit. Scis., U. Chgo., 1973, PhD in Polit. Scis., 1975. Project dir., asst. rsch. scientist Ctr. for Rsch. on Utilization Sci. Knowledge, Inst. Social Rsch., U. Mich., lectr. dept. polit. sci., 1975-76; asst. prof. politics and pub. affairs Princeton U., 1976-82, coord. domestic and urban policy field Woodrow Wilson Sch., 1976-82; assoc. prof. polit. sci., pub. policy and mgmt. Sch. Urban and Pub. Affairs, Carnegie-Mellon U., 1982-86; prof. U. Ill., Urbana, 1986—, dir. Inst. Govt. and Publ. Affairs, 1986-97, 2005—, acting head med. humanities and social scis. program Urbana-Champaign, 1988—97; fellow Johns Hopkins U. Ctr. for Study of Am. Govt., Washington, 1993-95; Mercator prof. Humboldt U., Berlin, 2002—03; vis. fellow Max Planck Inst. Fgn. Internat. Social Awareness, 2004. Cons. U.S. Dept. Health and Human Svcs., Carnegie-Mellon U., 1986—, MacArthur Found., NIMH, 1988-89, Food, Drug and Law Inst., HHS, 1989, Am. Career Soc., 1996-97; disting. lectr. German Marshall Fund, Hamburg, Germany, 1997. Author: Social Science Information and Public Policy Making: The Interaction Between Bureaucratic Politics and the Use of Survey Data, 1981; co-author: Government Information Management: A Counter-Report of the Commission on Federal Paperwork, 1980; editor: Translating Evaluation into Policy, 1979, The Knowledge Cycle, 1981, Knowledge, Creation, Diffusion, Utilization, 1979-88, 88-91; co-editor: Competitive Approaches to Health Policy Reform, 1993, Health Policy, Federalism and the Role of the American States, 1996; assoc. editor Society, 1984-88, Evaluation Rev., 1985-89; mem. editl. bd. Policy Studies Rev. Series, 1980-83, Evaluation and Change, 1979-82, Law and Human Behavior, 1983-87; contbr. articles to profl. jours., book chpts. Recipient Emil Limbach Teaching award Carnegie-Mellon U., Sch. Urban and Pub. Affairs, 1985; fellow German Acad. Exch. Program, Fed. Republic Germany, 1971-72, Nat. Opinion Rsch. Ctr. fellow, 1972-73, German Govt. fellow, 1974, Russel Sage Found. Rsch. fellow, 1974-75; vis. scholar Hastings Ctr. for Society, Ethics and Life Scis., 1982. Mem. APA (task force on victims of crime and violence 1982-84), Soc. for Traumatic Stress Studies (bd. dirs. 1980—), World Fedn. for Mental Health (chmn. com. on mental health needs of victims 1985—, vice chmn. 1981-83, Robert F. Rich rsch. ann. award established in his honor, sci. com. on mental health needs of victims 1983), Howard R. Davis Soc. for Knowledge Utilization and Planned Change (pres. 1986-89), Polit. Sci. 400, Policy Studies Assn. (Aaron Wildausky award 1994), Phi Beta Kappa, Sigma Xi, Phi Kappa Phi. Office: U Ill Inst Govt & Pub Affairs 1007 W Nevada St # 204 Urbana IL 61801-3812 also: 815 W Van Buren St Chicago IL 60607-3506 Office Phone: 217-244-8550. Business E-Mail: rfrich@uillinois.edu.

RICH, ROBERT REGIER, academic administrator, immunologist, medical educator; b. Newton, Kans., Mar. 7, 1941; s. Eldon Stahly and Margaret Joy (Regier) R.; m. Susan Jepsen Solliday, Mar. 22, 1974; children from previous marriage: Kenneth Eldon, Cathryn Louise; 1 stepchild, Lynn Solliday Todorov. AB, Oberlin Coll., 1962; MD, U. Kans., 1966. Diplomate Am. Bd. Internal Medicine (bd. dirs. 1990-93), Am. Bd. Allergy and Immunology (bd. dirs. 1987-93, chmn. 1991); cert. spl. qualification Diagnostic Lab. Immunology. Intern, resident in internal medicine U. Wash., Seattle, 1966-68; clin. asso., chief clin. asso., sr. staff fellow NIH, Bethesda, Md., 1968-71; research asso. Harvard Med. Sch., Boston, 1971-73; asst. in medicine Peter Bent Brigham Hosp., 1972-73; asst. prof., assoc. prof. microbiology, immunology and internal medicine Baylor Coll. Medicine, Houston, 1973-78, prof., 1978-95, Disting. Svc. prof., 1995—2002, head immunology sect., 1978-98, chief clin. immunology, 1979-91, v.p., dean rsch., 1990-98; exec. assoc. dean, prof. medicine & microbiology/immunology Emory U. Sch. Medicine, 1998—2004; sr. v.p. for medicine, dean Sch. Medicine U. Ala., Birmingham, 2004—, prof. medicine and microbiology, 2004—. Investigator Howard Hughes Med. Inst., Bethesda, Md., 1977-91; mem. immunobiology study sect. NIH, 1977-81; mem. transplantation biology and immunology com. Nat. Inst. Allergy and Infectious Disease, 1982-86, chmn., 1984-86; mem. nat. ctr. grants com. Arthritis Found., 1983-86, chmn., 1984-86, nat. rsch. com., 1984-89, chmn., 1986-89, ho. of dels., 1985-91, Blue Ribbon com. on rsch. 2000-01; mem. rsch. adv. com. Nat. Multiple Sclerosis Soc., 1989-94, chmn., 1993-94; adv. panel on rsch. Assn. Am. Med. Coll., 1990—, shared responsibility advocacy com., 1997-98; chmn. ctrs. working group Nat. Inst. Arthritis Musculoskeletal Skin Diseases, 1996-97; mem. nat. human rsch. protections adv. com., dept. health and human svcs., 2000-02; vice chmn. UAB Health Sys., 2004—, bd. dirs.; vice chmn. bd. dirs. Ctr. Infectious Diseases Rsch., Zambia, 2006—08, chmn. bd. dirs., 2008-. Assoc. editor: Jour. Immunology, 1978-82, sect. editor, 1991-96, deputy editor, 1997-2002, editor-in-chief, 2003—08; assoc. editor: Jour. Infectious Diseases, 1984-88; adv. editor: Jour. Exptl. Medicine, 1980-84; mem. editl. bd. Jour. Clin. Immunology, 1989-96, Clin. and Exptl. Immunology, 1995-2000; editor-in-chief Clin. Immunology: Principles and Practice, 1996, 2d edit., 2001, 3rd edit., 2008; contbr. articles to profl. jours. With USPHS, 1968—70. Recipient Rsch. Career Devel. award, NIH, 1975—77, Merit award, 1987. Fellow ACP, Am. Acad. Allergy, Asthma, and Immunology (chmn. basic and clin. immunology interest sect. 1992-93, chmn. profl. edn. coun. 1996-98, v.p. 2001-2002), Infectious Diseases Soc. Am.; mem. AMA, AAAS, Am. Bd. Internal Medicine (diplomate, bd. dirs. 1990-93), Am. Bd. Allergy and Immunology (diplomate, bd. dirs. 1987-93, chmn. bd. 1992), Assn. Am. Physicians, Am. Soc. Clin. Investigation, Am. Assn. Immunologists (chmn. pub. affairs com. 1994-2000, Disting. Svc. award 1999, Lifetime achievement award 2008), Am. Soc. Microbiologists, Am. Clin. Climatological Assn. (councillor 2001-05), Fedn. Am. Socs. for Exptl. Biology (bd. dirs. 1998-2003, pres. and chmn. bd. dirs. 2001-02), Clin. Immunology Soc. (coun. 1990-96, pres. 1995), Nat. Assn. Biomed. Rsch. (bd. dirs. 2002-05), Assn. for Assessment and Accreditation of Lab. Animal Care Internat. (trustee 2003-05), Alpha Omega Alpha, Sigma Xi. Office: Univ Ala Birmingham Sch Medicine 1530 3d Ave S Birmingham AL 35294-3412 Office Phone: 205-934-1997. Business E-Mail: rrich@uab.edu.

RICH, ROBERT STEPHEN, lawyer; b. NYC, Apr. 30, 1938; s. Maurice H. and Natalie (Priess) R.; m. Myra N. Lakoff, May 31, 1964; children: David, Rebecca, Sarah. AB, Cornell U., 1959; JD, Yale U., 1963. Bar: N.Y. 1964, Colo. 1973, U.S. Tax Ct. 1966, U.S. Supreme Ct. 1967, U.S. Ct. Claims 1968, U.S. Dist. Ct. (so. dist.) N.Y. 1965, U.S. Dist. Ct. (ea. dist.) N.Y. 1965, U.S. Dist. Ct. Colo. 1980, U.S. Ct. Appeals (10th cir.) 1978; conseil juridique, Paris, 1968. Assoc. Shearman & Sterling, NYC, Paris, London, 1963-72; ptnr. Davis, Graham & Stubbs, Denver, 1973—. Adj. faculty U. Denver Law Sch., 1977—; mem. adv. bd. U. Denver Ann. Tax Inst., 1985—, global bus. and culture divsn., U. Denver, 1992—, Denver World Affairs Coun., 1993—; mem. Colo. Internat. Trade Coun., 1985—; mem. Rocky Mt. Dist. Export Coun., US Dept. Commerce, 1993—; tax adv. com. US Senator Hank Brown; bd. dirs. Clos du Val Wine Co. Ltd., Danskin Cattle Co., Ouray Ranch, Areti Wines, Ltd., Taltarni Vineyards, Christy Sports, others. Contbr. articles to profl. jours. Actor, musician N.Y. Shakespeare Festival, 1960; sponsor Am. Tax Policy Inst., 1991—; adv. bd. Middle Park Land Trust, Granby, Colo., 2003—; pres. So. Boulder Park Ecol. Assn., 1999—; sec. Bhutan Found.; sec., treas. Citizens for Arts to Zoo; bd. dirs. Alliance Francaise, 1977—, Copper Valley Assn., Denver Internat. Film Festival, 1978—79, Anschutz Family Found.; trustee, sec. Denver Art Mus., 1982—; pres., bd. dirs. Ouray Ranch, Granby, Colo., 2001—; pres. Ouray Anglers Club, 2009—; bd. dirs. Aspen Music Festival and Sch., 2004—. Capt. US Army, 1959—60. Fellow Am. Coll. Tax. Coun. (bd. regents 10th cir. 1992—), Soc. Fellows Aspen Inst.; mem. ABA, Internat. Bar Assn., Colo. Bar Assn.(James Bye Lifetime Achievement award 2009), NY State Bar Assn., Assn. Bar City of NY, Asia-Pacific Lawyers Assn., Union Internat. des Avocats, Internat. Fiscal Assn. (pres. Rocky Mt. br. 1992—, US regional v.p. 1988—), Japan-Am. Soc. Colo. (bd. dirs. 1989—, pres. 1991-93), Confrerie des Chavaliers du Tastevin, Rocky Mt. Wine and Food Soc., Meadowood Club, Denver Club, City Club Denver, Mile High Club, Cactus Club Denver, Yale Club, Denver Tennis Club. Home Phone: 303-321-4965; Office Phone: 303-299-1230. Personal E-mail: robertrich@aya.yale.edu. Business E-Mail: robertrich@tac-denver.com.

RICH, RONALD LEE, chemistry professor; b. Washington, Ill., Mar. 29, 1927; s. Rufus Joseph and Lillian May (Lantz) Rich; m. Elaine Horner Sommers, June 14, 1953; children: Jonathan Joseph, Andrew Forrester, Miriam Sommers, Mark Monroe. BS in Math. and Chemistry, Bluffton Coll., 1948; PhD in Chemistry, U. Chgo., 1953. Rsch. fellow Harvard U., Cambridge, Mass., 1963-64; prof. chemistry Bethel Coll., North Newton, Kans., 1964-66, Internat. Christian U., Tokyo, 1966-79; dean acad. affairs Bluffton (Ohio) Coll., 1979-80, scholar in residence, 1981—. Vis. prof. Stanford (Calif.) U., 1974, U. Ill., Urbana, 1975, U. Oreg., Eugene, 1984; electrochemical engr. N.C. State U., Raleigh, 1989—90. Author: Periodic Correlations, 1965, Inorganic Reactions in Water, 2008; co-author: Chemical English (for Japanese), 1969, 2 vols., 1976; contbr. articles to profl. jours. Achievements include a general way to predict boiling points; a qualitative-analysis scheme whose groups fit in the periodic chart. Home and Office: 327 S Jackson St Bluffton OH 45817-1011 Business E-Mail: richr@bluffton.edu.

RICH, S. JUDITH, public relations executive; b. Chgo., Apr. 14; d. Irwin M. and Sarah I. (Sandock) R. BA, U. Ill., 1960. Staff writer, reporter Economist Newspapers, Chgo., 1960—61; asst. dir. pub. rels. and communications Coun. Profit Sharing Industries, Chgo., 1961—62; dir. advt. and pub. rels. Chgo. Indsl. Dist., 1962—63; account exec., account supr., v.p., sr. v.p., exec. v.p and nat. creative dir. Edelman Pub. Rels. Worldwide, Chgo., 1963—85; exec. v.p., dir. Ketchum Pub. Rels. Worldwide, Chgo., 1985—89, exec. v.p., exec. creative dir. USA, 1990—97, exec. v.p., chief creative officer worldwide, 1998—2001; pres. Rich Rels. A Creativity Consultancy, Chgo., 2002—. Frequent spkr. on creativity and brainstorming; workshop facilitator. Contbr. articles to popular mags. Mem. pub. rels. adv. bd. U. Chgo. Grad Sch. Bus., Roosevelt U., Chgo., DePaul U., Chgo., Gov.'s State U. Recipient Pub. Rels. All-Star award for Creativity, Inside PR mag., 1999. Mem. Pub. Rels. Soc. Am. (Silver Anvil award, judge Silver Anvil awards), Counselors Acad. of Pub. Rels. Soc. Am. (exec. bd.), Chgo. Publicity Club (8 Golden Trumpet awards). Avocations: theater, swimming, bicycling, racquetball. Office: Rich Rels A Creative Consultancy Ste 2603 2500 N Lakeview Ave Chicago IL 60614

RICH, TRACY LEON, lawyer, insurance company executive; b. Nesmith, SC, Jan. 31, 1952; BA in Political sci., Union Coll., 1974; JD, NYU Sch. of Law, 1977; LLM in Taxation, Boston U. Sch. of Law, 1985. Bar: NY 1978, Conn. 1981, Mass. 1997. Trial atty. office of chief counsel IRS, NYC, 1977—81; atty. Robinson and Cole, Hartford, Conn., 1981—82; v.p., gen. counsel Conn. Mutual, Hartford, Conn., 1982—96; sr. v.p., dep. gen. counsel Mass. Mutual Life Insurance Co., Springfield, Mass., 1996—2000; sr. v.p., gen. counsel Phoenix Life (div. of The Phoenix Co., Inc.), Hartford, Conn., 2000—02; exec. v.p., gen. counsel, sec. The Phoenix Co., Inc., Hartford, Conn., 2002—09; exec. v.p., sec., gen. counsel Guardian Life Ins. Co., NYC, 2009—. Lecturer U. Conn. Law Sch., 1998—2000. Mem.: ABA, Tax Club of Hartford. Office: Guardian Life 7 Hanover Sq New York NY 10004*

RICH, WILLIS FRANK, JR., banker; b. Ft. Dodge, Iowa, July 26, 1919; s. Willis Frank and Agnes Reed (Paterson) R.; m. Jo Ann Rockwell, Apr. 12, 1947; children: Ronald Rockwell, Roxanne, Andrew Paterson. BA, Princeton U., 1941. Credit analyst Northwestern Nat. Bank, Mpls., 1947-52, asst. cashier, 1952-55, asst. v.p., 1955, v.p., 1955-57; pres. N.W. Nat. Bank, Bloomington-Richfield, Minn., 1952-58, v.p., cashier, 1957-60, v.p. div. A, 1960-68, sr. v.p. nat. and internat. divs., 1968-73, exec. v.p. Mpls., 1973-81, vice chmn. bd. dirs., chief credit officer, 1981-84; fin. cons., 1984—. Dir. Advance Acceptance Corp., 1985-2000. Pres. Viking coun. Boy Scouts Am., 1970-71, trustee found., 1971-86; mem. exec. bd. Minn. Cmty. Rsch. Coun., 1969-77; dir. Minn. Zoo, 1987-95; trustee St. Martin's Found., 1986-90; vestry mem. St. Martin's-By-The-Lake Ch. With AUS, 1941-46. Decorated Bronze Star. Mem. Robert Morris Assocs. (nat. pres. 1977-78), Mpls. Suburban Gyro Club. Club: Swan Lake Country. Episcopalian. Home: 378 Waycliffe N Wayzata MN 55391-1390 Personal E-mail: WFRJR@msn.com.

RICHARD, A. KERBER, medical educator; b. Ft. Washington, Pa., Feb. 19, 1959; s. Richard Ade Kerber and Elizabeth Ann Bogar; m. Elizabeth O'Brien, July 6, 1986; children: Rose Ellen Kerber, William James Kerber. BA, Kenyon Coll., Gambier, Ohio, 1980; MA, Northwestern U., Evanston, Ill., 1982, PhD, 1986. Asst. to assoc. prof. U. Utah, Salt Lake City, 1991—2008; assoc. prof. U. Louisville, 2008—. Acting dir. Utah Cancer Registry, Salt Lake City, 1995—96. Contbr. articles to profl. jours. Rsch. grant, Nat. Cancer Inst., 1995—2001, Susan B. Komen Found., 2008—. Mem.: Internat. Genetic Epidemiology Soc., Soc. Epidemiologic Rsch. Achievements include research in nuclear weapons testing on health of downwind populations; discovery of relationship between human telomere length and mortality; gene expression linked to aging and mortality. Business E-Mail: rich.kerber@louisville.edu.

RICHARD, BILL, legislative staff member; b. St. Paul, Dec. 18, 1946; m. Carlotta Bang, 1972; 4 children. Diploma, St. John's U., Collegeville, Minn., 1965, U. Minn., 1966, Def. Lang. Inst., Monterey, Calif., 1968. Clk. Finlayson Twp., Minn., 1978—80; candidate Minn. House of Reps., 1980; dist. staff dir. for Rep. James Oberstar US House of Reps., 1981—90, chief of staff Washington, 1990—. Russian linguist Soviet spage program Army Security Agy., Asmara, Ethiopia, with US Army, 1966, staff sgt., 1970. Mem.: Pine County (Minn.) (chair 1978—80). Democrat. Office: Office of Congressman James L Oberstar 2365 Rayburn House Office Bldg Washington DC 20515 Office Phone: 202-225-6211. Business E-Mail: bill.richard@mail.house.gov.*

RICHARD, CANDACE L., music educator; d. James S. and Nelda M. (Northrup) Terrill; m. Loren D. Richard, July 20, 1974; children: Christopher L., Colby A. MusB in Edn., Emporia State U., 1970; MusM, Kans. State U., 1993. Cert. tchr. Kans. Vocal music tchr. Unified Sch. Dist. 322, Onaga, Kans., 1970—73, Unified Sch. Dist. 457, Garden City, Kans., 1973—76; vocal and instrumental music tchr. Trinity Cath. HS, Hutchinson, Kans., 1982—84; applied vocal music instr. Cloud County CC, Concordia, Kans., 1985—2000; vocal music tchr. Unified Sch. Dist. 333, Concordia, 1990—2000, Unified Sch. Dist. 480, Liberal, Kans., 2000—. Choral clinician, adjudicator, Kans. Bd. dirs. Cmty. Concert Assn., Concordia, 1987—2000, Liberal, 2000—04, Live on Stage II, 2004—. Mem.: NEA, Music Edn. Nat. Conf., Seward County Hist. Soc., DAR, PEO, Delta Kappa Gamma. Lutheran. Avocation: genealogy.

RICHARD, EDWARD H., manufacturing executive, retired municipal official; b. Mar. 15, 1937; s. Henry and Ida Richard. BA, Antioch Coll., 1959. Pres., chmn., bd. dirs. Magnetics Internat. Inc., Maple Heights, Ohio, 1967-86; exec. v.p. Stearns Magnetics S.A., Brussels, Belgium, 1974-77; prin. Edward H. Richard & Assocs., Cleve., 1967-96; pres., treas. David Round & Son, Inc., Cleve. Chmn. Cleve. dist. adv. council Small Bus. Adminstrn., 1975-79; past nat. adv. council Dept. Treasury; cons. and advisor in field; del. world trade fairs. Former trustee Regional Econ. Devel. Coun., Met. Cleve. Jobs. Coun., Cleve. Devel. Found., Cleve. BBB; former trustee Hiram House, Antioch U., former treas., 1972-77; N.E. Ohio Regional Sewer Dist., Greater Cleve. Domed Stadium Corp., Greater Cleve. Conv. and Visitor Bur.; former trustee, vice-chmn. Cleve. Ctr. Econ. Edn.; former pres. Bratenahl Condominium Assn.; chmn. fin. com. Bratenahl Bd. Edn., 1971-75; former trustee, chmn. nominating com., exec. com. La Jolla Playhouse; CFO Mainly Mozart Festival, 1998—; CFO, chmn. bd. orch. rels. com., exec. com., fin. com., trustee San Diego Symphony Orch. Mailing: 1811 Englewood Rd Ste 217 Englewood FL 34223

RICHARD, ELLEN, theater executive; b. Bridgeport, Conn., Dec. 12, 1957; d. Laurent and Anne (Markham) R. Bus. mgr. Atlas Scenic Studio, Bridgeport, 1977-82; theater mgr. Stamford (Conn.) Ctr. for Arts, 1980-83; bus. mgr. Westport (Conn.) Country Playhouse, 1982-84; gen. mgr. Roundabout Theatre Co. Inc., NYC, 1983—; dir. design and constrn. Am. Airlines Theatre, Studio 54, Harold and Mirium Steinberg Ctr. Theatre, Laurel Pels Theatre, various Broadway Theatres. Dir. design and constrn. Am. Airlines Theatre, Studio 54, Harold and Miriam Steinberg Ctr. for Theatre, Laura Pels Theatre, Broadway theatres. Mng. dir.: (Broadway plays) A View From the Bridge, 1997-98 (Tony award Revival of a Play 1998), Cabaret, 1998-2004 (Tony award Revival of a Musical 1998), The Deep Blue Sea, 1998, Side Man, 1998-99 (Tony award Best Play 1999), Little Me, 1998-1999, Death of a Salesman, 1999, The Lion in Winter, 1999, The Rainmaker, 1999-2000, Uncle Vanya, 2000, The Man Who Came to Dinner, 2000, Betrayal, 2000-01, Design for Living, 2001, Major Barbara, 2001, The Women, 2001-02, An Almost Holy Picture, 2002, The Crucible, 2002, The Man Who Had All the Luck, 2002, An Evening with Mario Cantone, 2002, The Boys from Syracuse, 2002, Tartuffe, 2003, A Day in the Death of Joe Egg, 2003, As Long As We Both Shall Laugh, 2003, Nine, 2003 (Tony award Best Revival of a Musical, 2003), The Look of Love, 2003, "MASTER HAROLD"...and the boys, 2003, Big River, 2003, The Caretaker, 2003-04, Twentieth Century, 2004, Assassins, 2004 (Tony award Best Revival of a Musical, 2004); prodr.: Sideman, 1999 (Tony award New Play). Mem. NY Cycling Club. Avocations: bicycling, antiques, art, sailing. Office: 203 Brewster St Bridgeport CT 06605-3112 Personal E-mail: ellrch2@aol.com.

RICHARD, HOLLINGER VERNON, archivist, historian; s. Vernon Kenneth and Dolly Jean Hollinger; m. Sandra Lynn Hutchison, May 14, 1995; 1 child, Shira Hollinger. BA, Calif. State U., San Bernardino, 1981; MA, UCLA, 1984, Calif. State U., Dominguez Hill, 1993. Archivist NY Pub. Libr., NYC, 1990—94; head archives and spl. collections Columbia U., Health Scis. Libr., NYC, 1994—96, U. Sci. and Tech., Hong Kong, 1996—99. Instr., archival principles and practices Chinese U. Hong Kong, 1998—99; curator manuscripts NJ Hist. Soc., Newark, 1999—2000; head spl. collections U. Maine, Orono, 2000—. Editor: (books) Community Histories:(Studies in Babi and Bahá'í History, vol. 6); author: An Iranian Enclave in Lebanon in Distant Relations: Iran and Lebanon in the last 500 years. Rsch. felllowship, NHPRC. Achievements include research in history of record keeping, history of Baha'i religion. Office: 5729 Fogler Libr Univ Maine Orono ME 04473 Business E-Mail: richard.hollinger@umit.maine.edu.

RICHARD, HOWARD M., lawyer; b. Oak Park, Ill., Sept. 20, 1944; BA, Cornell U., 1965; LLB, Harvard U., 1968. Bar: Ill. 1968. Ptnr. Katten Muchin Rosenman, Chgo. Bd. editors Harvard Law Rev., 1967-68. Mem. ABA (sect. real property, probate and trust law), Chgo. Bar Assn. Office: Katten Muchin Rosenman 525 W Monroe St Ste 1900 Chicago IL 60661-3693 Home Phone: 847-432-7924; Office Phone: 312-902-5219. Office Fax: 312-577-8670. E-mail: howard.richard@kattenlaw.com.

RICHARD, LOREN DRU, bank executive; b. Ellsworth, Kans., Feb. 12, 1947; s. Loren Clarence and Drucilla Ruth Richard; m. Candace Leigh Terrill, July 20, 1974; children: Christopher Loren, Colby Alexander. BS, Kans. State U., Manhattan, 1970. HS agr. instr., Garden City, Kans., 1972—75; field rep. Evans Grain Co., Garden City, 1975—76; asst. v.p. Fidelity State Bank, Garden City, 1977—80; agr. loan officer Hutchinson Nat. Bank, Kans., 1980—84; sr. v.p. UMB Bank, Concordia, Kans., 1984—2000, Cmty. Bank, Liberal, Kans., 2000—. Pres. Kans. Assn. Bank Agr. Reps., 1984—85; chmn. agr. com. Kans. Bankers Assn., 1984—85; mem. adv. bd. UMB, Concordia, 1998—2000. Chmn. agr. com. C. of C., Liberal, 2003—04; v.p. Crossroads Ctr., Liberal, 2005—06; chmn. Luth. Ch. Coun., Liberal, 2005—06. 1st lt. US Army, 1970—72. Mem.: Kans. Agr. Bankers, Panhandle Team Penning Assn., Fellowship Christian Cowboys (sr.), Am. Quarter Horse Assn., Lions (Liberal club 2006, pres. Concord Club 1988). Office: The Cmty Bank Liberal KS 67905 Office Phone: 620-624-6898. Office Fax: 620-624-2381. E-mail: dru@communitybankliberal.com.

RICHARD, N. LANDERS, psychology professor; m. Amy Landers. PhD in Psychology, U. Minn., Twin Cities, 2009. Grad. student, instr. U. Minn., 2004—09; asst. prof. Old Dominion U., Norfolk, Va., 2009—. Mem.: APA, ASTD, Soc. Indsl. and Orgnl. Psychology. Personal E-mail: richdiesal@hotmail.com.

RICHARD, ORR KENNETH, oncologist, educator; b. Ft. Wayne, Ind., Aug. 1, 1952; s. Kenneth and Marilyn Meyer Orr; m. Elizabeth Orr, June 25, 2005; children: Jenna Orr, Rebecca Porter Orr. BA, Vanderbilt U., Nashville, Tenn., 1974; MD, U. South Fla., Tampa, 1977; MPH, U. Mass., Amherst. Diplomate Am. Bd. Surgery, 1985. Asst. prof. urgery U. Miami, Fla., 1984—86; surg. oncologist Fallon Clinic, Worcester, Mass., 1986—97, Marshfield Clinic, Wis., 1997—99; dir. surg. oncology & endocrine surgery Spartanburg Regional Med. Ctr., SC, 1999—, dir., surg. residency program, 2001—. Assoc. prof. surgery Med. U. SC., Charleston, 2004—. Contbr. scientific papers to profl. publs. Mem.: ACS, Soc. Med. Decision Making, Southeastern Surg. Congress, Soc. Surg. Oncology, New Eng. Surg. Soc., Am. Hepatopancreatobiliary Assn., Am. Assn. Endocrine Surgeons. Office: Spartanburg Regional Med Ctr 101 E Wood St Spartanburg SC 29303

RICHARD, ROBERT CARTER, psychological consultant; b. Waterloo, Iowa, Apr. 4, 1938; s. Quentin Leroy and Adeline Pauline (Halverson) R.; m. Shirley Ruth Jones, Aug. 25, 1962 (div. Mar. 1999); children: David, John; m. Jacqueline J. Mendes, Feb. 19, 2000; stepchildren: Julianne Mendes, Katherine Mendes. BA Wheaton (Ill.) Coll., 1960; BD, Fuller Theol. Sem., 1963, PhD, 1973; STM, Andover Newton Theol. Sch., 1964. Ordained to ministry Am. Bapt. Conv., 1963; lic. psychologist, Calif. Pastor Peninsula Bapt. Ch., Gig Harbor, Wash., 1965-68; marriage, family counselor Glendale Family Svc., Calif., 1970-71; psychol. asst. Oakland and Pleasant Hill, Calif., 1972—73; psychologist Rafa Counseling Ctr., Pleasant HIll, 1974—2006; ret., 2006. Mem. faculty John F. Kennedy U., Orinda, Calif., 1975-78; adj. faculty mem. New Coll., Berkeley, Calif, 1986; mem. dean's nat. adv. coun. Sch. Psychology, Fuller Theol. Sem., 2005—; co-founder, bd. dirs. New Directions Counseling Ctr., 1974-81; rschr. assertiveness tng., lay counselor tng., psychotherapy and religious experience, treatment of adults abused as children; bd. dirs. Fuller Psychological and Family Svc., 2008-. Author: (with Deacon Anderson) The Way Back: A Christian's Journey to Mental Wholeness, 1989; contbr. articles to profl. publs. Recipient Integration of Psychology and Theology award, 1973. Mem.: APA, Calif. Psychol. Assn. Republican. Avocations: boating, astronomy, photography, art, tennis.

RICHARD, STEPHEN O., sports association executive; BS in Acctg., Northeastern U., Boston; MBA in Fin., Columbia Bus. Sch., NYC. Sr. audit mgr. Deloitte & Touche, LLP; dist. mgr. fin. planning & analysis AT&T; v.p., region dir. corp. audit grp. Citibank N.A.; sr. v.p. fin. NBA, NYC, 1998—. Mem.: Nat. Assn. Black Accts. (pres. no. NJ chpt.), NJ Soc. CPA, AICPA. Office: NBA Olympic Tower 645 5th ave Fl 10 New York NY 10022-5986*

RICHARD, THELMA SHINN, literature and language professor; b. Flint, Mich., Sept. 10, 1942; d. Louis George Wardrop and Erma Helen Sullivan; m. Jon Richard, Oct. 21, 1995; m. Raymond James Shinn, Sept. 19, 1961 (div. Sept. 1966); children: Ramona Sue Ferrara, Rebecca Sharon John, Joseph Raymond Shinn, James Malcolm Shinn, Rachel Sarah Shinn. BA, Ctrl. Conn. State, New Britain, 1965; MA, Purdue U., West Lafayette, Ind., 1967, PhD, 1972. Instr. Coll. Our Lady Of Elms, Chicopee, Mass., 1971—73; asst. prof. Westfield State Coll., Mass., 1973—75; prof. Ariz. State U., 1975—2004, founding dir., womens studies, 1977—80, prof. emeritus, 2004—. Vis. faculty AIFS, London, 1987—88; sr. lectr. CIES Fulbright, Granada, Spain, 1994, Stellenbosch, South Africa, 2000; sr. editor JRLA, Riverside, Calif., 2001—08. Author: (books) Radiant Daughters, Worlds Within Women, Women Shapeshifters, (plays) Don't Worry, Mary's Pregnant Again, Time For Love; contbr. articles to profl. jours. Theater edn. del. People To People Internat., South Africa, 1998. Recipient Outstanding Achievement and Contbs. award, Commn. Status Of Women, 2001, Above and Beyond award, ASU Womens Studies Program, 2002; named Notable Ariz. Women, Assn. Women In Psychology, 1990, Disting. Mentor Women, ASU Faculty Womens Assn., 1999; Womens Studies grant, Ariz. Humanities Coun., 1978—79, Fulbright Sr. scholar, 2006. Mem.: RMMLA. Avocations: travel, reading, writing. Home: 11542 Cornell Ave Riverside CA 92507 Office: Ariz State Univ PO Box 870302 Tempe AZ 85287 Office Fax: 480-965-3241. Personal E-mail: jonandthelma@gmail.com. Business E-Mail: tjrichard@asu.edu.

RICHARD, THOMAS LEHMAN, agricultural engineer, educator; BS in Polit. Economy of Natural Resources, U. Calif., Berkeley, 1978; MS in Agrl. Engring., Cornell U., Ithaca, NY, 1987; PhD in Biol. Engring., Cornell U., 1997. Rsch. support specialist dept. agrl. and biol. engring. Cornell U., 1987—97; asst. prof. dept. agrl. and biosystems engring. Iowa State U., Ames, 1997—2003, assoc. prof., 2003—04; assoc. prof. dept. agrl. and biol. engring. Pa. State U., State College, 2004—. Vis. prof. dept. environ. tech. Wageningen U. Rsch. Ctr., Netherlands, 2000. Contbr. articles to sci. jours., chapters to books. Mem.: Water Environment Fedn., Soil and Water Conservation Soc., Internat. Soc. Indsl. Ecology, Am. Soc. Engring. Edn., Am. Soc. Agrl. and Biol. Engrs. (Iowa Sect. Newcomer Engr. of Yr. 2001, Blue Ribbon award 1991, 1993, 2001, 2003), Inst. Biol. Engring. (pres., treas. 1998—2001, 2004—06), Sigma Xi, Phi Beta Kappa. Office: Dept Agrl and Biol Engring Pa State U 225 Agricultural Engring Bldg University Park PA 16802 Office Phone: 814-865-3722. Office Fax: 814-863-1031. E-mail: trichard@psu.edu.

RICHARDS, ANN ADAIR, psychologist; b. Tulsa, Jan. 28, 1949; d. William Jenkins and Virginia Ann (Daniels) Richards; 1 child, Desiree Ann Perkins. BS in bus. edn., U. Okla., 1970; BA in theatre arts, U. No. Colo., 1983, MA in agy. counseling, 1985, EdS, 2002. Nationally Certified School Psychologist, lic. Professional Counselor Colo. Regulatory Bd. Workshop coord. Rocky Mtn. Planned Parenthood, Denver, 1977—79; para profl., remedial reading Denver Pub. Schools, 1979—80; generalist clinician Centennial Mental Health Ctr., 1986—95; children and family therapist No. Range Behavior Health, Greely, Colo., 1995—99; pvt. practice Greely, 1999—2000; sch. psychologist intern Northeast Bd. Cooperative Ednl. Svcs., Haxton, Colo., 2000—01; sch. psychologist East Ctrl. Bd. Cooperative Ednl. Svcs., Limon, Colo., 2001—. Chair and vice chair Logan County Sexual Assault Team, Sterling, Colo., 1989—95; co-dir. drama club play Woodlin Sch., 2000, participant reading challenge, 06, 07; crisis response coord. East Ctrl. Bd. Cooperative Ednl. Svcs., 2001—, autism coord., 2005, rti coord., 2005—07, supr. sch. psychologists, interns, practicum students, 2006, supr. sch. psychologists, interns, practicum students neuropsych.spec, 08; mem. crisis response team Colo. Soc. Sch. Psychologists, 2004—09. Spl. olympics vol. Sterling H.S., 1992—94; bd. mem. Yuma Cmty. Resource Ctr., Yuma, Colo., 1986—88, Help for Abused Ptnrs., Sterling, Colo., 1989—95, sec., 1989—95; com. mem. Arts Picnic, Greeley, Colo., 1983. Recipient Women of the Yr., Beta Sigma Phi Social Svc. Sorority, 2000, Scholarship, Am. Assn. of U. Women; Circle Key Alumni grant, Kappa Kappa Gamma Found., 1994, 1995, Mildred Guch Scholarship, U. No. Colo., 1984—85. Mem.: Colo. Soc. Sch. Psychologists, Nat. Assn. Sch. Psychologist. Democrat. Lutheran. Avocations: weightlifting, aerobics, movies, reading, interior decorating. Home: 15400 CR L Box 180 Woodrow CO 80757 Office: East Ctrl Bd Ednl Svcs 820 2d St Limon CO 80828

RICHARDS, BERNARD, investment company executive; b. NYC, July 12, 1927; s. Charles and Sadie (Rubin) R.; m. Arlene Kaye, Dec. 23, 1948; children: Carol Leslie, Patricia Ellen, Lori Gale. BBA, Baruch Coll., 1949. CPA, NY. Acct. Eisner & Lubin, NYC, 1949-53, S.D. Leidesdorf, NYC, 1953-56; from contr. to treas. to v.p. fin. to pres. Slattery Group Inc., NYC, 1956-87; pres. Slattery Investors Corp., NYC, 1988—; chmn. bd. dirs. Slattery Assocs., Inc., NYC, 1968-87. Trustee Temple Sinai, Roslyn, NY, 1969-89; bd. dirs. Variety Boys Club, Queens, NY, 1972-96; bd. dirs. NYC Indsl. Devel. Bd., 1973-76; bd. dirs. Baruch Coll. Fund, NYC, 1975—, pres., 1996-98. Recipient Heavy Constrn. award United Jewish Appeal, 1980, Pres.'s medal Baruch Coll., 1989; named Oustanding Alumnus of Yr. Baruch Coll., 1979, Man of Yr. United Jewish Appeal, 1980, March of Dimes, 1983, Man of Yr. Baruch Coll. Fund, 1972; Wood fellow Baruch Coll., 1979. Mem. AICPA, N.Y. State Soc. CPAs, Moles, Beavers (bd. dirs. 1982-96), Shelter Rock Tennis Club. Republican. Jewish. Avocations: tennis, travel, bicycling, swimming, hiking. Home: 18 Applegreen Dr Old Westbury NY 11568-1203 Office: Slattery Investors Corp 1 Hollow Ln Ste 311 New Hyde Park NY 11042-1215

RICHARDS, BRAD, professional hockey player; b. Murray Harbour, Prince Edward Island, May 2, 1980; Center Rimouski Oceanic (QMJHL), 1998—2000, Tampa Bay Lightning, 2000—08, Dallas Stars, 2008—. Mem. Team Can., World Championships, 2001, Team Can., World Cup of Hockey, 2004. Recipient Conn Smythe Trophy, 2004, Lady Byng Trophy, 2004; named to, NHL All-Rookie Team, 2000, NHL YoungStars Game, 2002. Achievements include being a member of Stanley Cup Champion Tampa Bay Lightning, 2004; being a member of World Cup Champion Team Canada, 2004. Office: c/o Dallas Stars 2601 Avenue of the Stars Frisco TX 75034

RICHARDS, CAROL ANN RUBRIGHT, lecturer, retired editor, journalist; b. Buffalo, Sept. 24, 1944; d. Jesse Bailey and Emma Amanda (Fisher) Rubright; m. Clay F. Richards, Aug. 12, 1967; children: Elizabeth Amanda, Rebecca Diana. BA, Syracuse U., 1966. Reporter Rochester (N.Y.) Times-Union, 1966; legis. corr. Gannett News Svc., Albany, NY, 1967-73, White House corr. Washington, 1974-76, regional/nat. editor, 1979-84; founding editor USA Today, Arlington, Va., 1982, mem. editl. bd., 1985-87; dep. editor editl. page Newsday, Melville, NY, 1987—2006; ret., 2006. Adj. prof. journalism U. Maryland, Coll. Pk., Md., 2008—; freelance editor. Pres. Washington Press Club, 1981-82, editor-at-large The Brook, Stony Brook U. Mag. Mem.: Women's Press Club N.Y. (named to Hall of Honor 2003), Nat. Press Club. Episcopalian. Home and Office: 101 Edge Hill Rd Sherwood Forest MD 21405 Office Phone: 631-896-4571. Business E-Mail: carol.richards@yahoo.com.

RICHARDS, CECILE, healthcare network executive; b. 1957; d. David and Ann Richards; 3 children. BA in History, Brown U., 1980. Labor organizer, La., Calif., Tex., 1980—95; founder Texas Freedom Network, 1995—2002; dep. chief of staff to Rep. Nancy Pelosi US Congress, Washington, 2002—03; founder, pres. America Votes, Washington, 2003—06; pres. Planned Parenthood Fedn. America, Inc., NYC, 2006—. Bd. dirs. NARAL Pro-Choice Am., Planned Parenthood Action Fund; founder, bd. dirs. Tex. Freedom Network, 1995. Democrat. Office: Planned Parenthood Fedn Am Inc 434 W 33rd St New York NY 10001-2601 Office Phone: 212-541-7800. Office Fax: 212-245-1845.

RICHARDS, CHRISTINE P., delivery service executive, lawyer; b. Amityville, NY, Jan. 8, 1955; BA magna cum laude, Bucknell U., 1976; JD, Duke U., 1979. Bar: Tenn. 1987, NC 1980. Joined FedEx Corp., 1984, corp. v.p. customer and bus. transactions & gen. counsel FedEx Corp. Services, exec. v.p., gen. counsel, sec., 2005—. Office: FedEx Corp 942 S Shady Grove Rd Memphis TN 38120 Office Phone: 901-818-7500. Office Fax: 901-395-2000.*

RICHARDS, CRAIG EDWARD, academic administrator, educator; b. Menominee, Mich. s. Edward Richards; m. Elizabeth Clegg-Richards; 1 child, Michael. PhD, Stanford U., Calif., 1983. Dept. chair, dept. orgn. & leadership Tchrs. Coll., Columbia U., NYC, 2004—06, founding dir., Summer Prins. Acad., 2004—. Author: (book) Financing Education Systems. Independent. Buddhist. Avocations: meditation, poetry, jazz, guitar. Office: Tchrs Coll Columbia Univ 525 W 120th St New York NY 10027

RICHARDS, DAVID ALAN, lawyer; b. Dayton, Ohio, Sept. 21, 1945; s. Charles Vernon and Betty Ann (Macher) R.; m. Marianne Catherine Del Monaco, June 26, 1971; children: Christopher, Courtney. BA summa cum laude, Yale U., 1967, JD, 1972; MA, Cambridge U., Eng., 1969. Bar: N.Y. 1973. Assoc. Paul, Weiss, Rifkind, Wharton & Garrison, NYC, 1972-77, Coudert Bros., NYC, 1977-80, ptnr., 1981-82; ptnr., head real estate group Sidley & Austin, NYC, 1983-2000; ptnr. McCarter & English, NYC, 2001—, mng. ptnr. N.Y. office, 2002—06. Gov. Anglo-Am. Real Property Inst. U.S./U.K., 1983-88, chair, 1993; mem. Chgo. Title N.Y. Realty Adv. Bd., 1992—. Author: Rudyard Kipling: The Books I Leave Behind, 2007, Rudyard Kipling:A Bibliography, 2009; co-editor: Kipling and His First Publisher, 2001; co-author: The Commercial Office Lease Handbook, 2003; contbr. articles to profl. jours. Trustee Scarsdale Pub. Libr., 1984-89, pres., 1988-89; co-chair N.Y. Lawyers for Clinton/Gore, 1996. Fellow Am. Bar Found.; mem. ABA (real property, probate and trust sect., coun. 1982-88, chair 1991-92), Am. Coll. Real Estate Lawyers (gov. 1987-93), Assn. of Bar of City of N.Y. (real property com. 1978-80, 84-87), Century Assn., Kipling Soc. (N.Am. rep., v.p. 2005—), Assn. Fellows of Morgan Libr., Shenorock Shore Club (Rye, N.Y.), The Grolier Club (N.Y.C., coun. 2003—, sec. 2006-2009), Yale Club (N.Y.C.), Yale Libr. Assn. (trustee 2003—, vice chair 2009-). Democrat. Home: 18 Forest Ln Scarsdale NY 10583-6464 Office: McCarter & English 245 Park Ave Fl 27 New York NY 10167 Office Phone: 212-609-6817. Personal E-mail: darichards21@aol.com. Business E-Mail: drichards@mccarter.com.

RICHARDS, DAVID GLEYRE, German language educator; b. July 27, 1935; s. Oliver L. and Lilian Marie (Powell) R.; m. Annegret Horn, Sept. 3, 1959 (div. 1992); 1 child, Stephanie Suzanne; m. Friederike Hensler, Oct. 11, 1997. BA, U. Utah, 1960, MA, 1961; PhD, U. Calif., Berkeley, 1968. Asst. prof. German SUNY, Buffalo, 1968, assoc. prof., 1974—84, prof., 1984—99, chair dept., 1986—92, prof. emeritus, 1999—. Author: Georg Buchners Woyzeck, 1975, George Buchner and the Birth of the Modern Drama, 1976, The Hero's Quest for the Self: An Archetypal Approach to Hesse's Demian and other Novels, 1987; editor: (with H. Schulte) Crisis and Culture in Post-Enlightenment Germany: Essays in Honor of Peter Heller, 1993, Exploring the Divided Self: Hermann Hesse's Steppenwolf and its Critics, 1996, Georg Buchner's Woyzeck: A History of Its Criticism, 2001. SUNY grantee, 1973; NEH grantee, 1977-78, Fulbright Commn. grantee, 1980. Rsch. Found. of SUNY fellow, 1982. Democrat. Avocation: photography. Personal E-mail: dgrich@nc.rr.com.

RICHARDS, DENISE, actress; b. Downers Grove, Ill., Feb. 17, 1971; m. Charlie Sheen, June 15, 2002 (div. Nov. 17, 2006); children: Sam, Lola Rose. Former model. Actor: (films) Loaded Weapon 1, 1993, Nowhere, 1997, Starship Troopers, 1997, Wild Things, 1998, Lookin' Italian, 1998, Drop Dead Gorgeous, 1999, The World is Not Enough, 1999, Tail Lights Fade Away, 1999, Valentine, 2001, Good Advice, 2001, Empire, 2002, Undercover Brother, 2002, The Third Wheel, 2002, You Stupid Man, 2002, Love Actually, 2003, Scary Movie 3, 2003, Elvis Has Left the Building, 2004, Edmond, 2005, Blonde and Blonder, 2007, Jolene, 2008; (TV films) 919 5th Avenue, 1995, In the Blink of an Eye, 1996, Pier 66, 1996, I Do (But I Don't), 2004; (TV series) Sex, Love, & Secrets, 2005; actor, exec. prodr. (TV reality series) Denise Richards: It's Complicated, 2008—, guest appearances (TV series) Life Goes On, 1990, Saved By the Bell, 1991, Married With Children, 1991, Doogie Howser, MD, 1991, Beverly Hills 90210, 1992, Seinfeld, 1993, Lois and Clark: The New Adventures of Superman, 1994, Melrose Place, 1996, Spin City, 2001, Friends, 2001, Two and Half Men, 2003, 2004, Secrets in a Small Town, 2006. Office: 722 Elvira Ave #A Redondo Beach CA 90277

RICHARDS, EARL FREDERICK, electrical engineer, educator; b. Detroit, Mar. 11, 1923; s. Earl Frederick Richards and Esther Branning; m. Marjorie Phyllis Holt, Jan. 12, 1946; 2 children. BSEE, Wayne State U., 1951; MSEE, Mo. Sch. of Mines and Metallurgy, Rolla, 1961; PhD, U. Mo., 1971. Registered engr., Mo., Mich. Elec. engr. Electronic Control Corp., Detroit, 1951—52, Pa. Salt Mfg. Co., Wyandotte, Mich., 1952—53; chief elec. engr. Revere Copper and Brass, Detroit, 1954—58; prof. elec. engring. U. Mo.-Rolla, 1958—92, prof. emeritus, 1992—. Cons. in field. Author: (book) Handbook of Small Electric Motors, 2000; contbr. articles to profl. jours. and publs. With Office Strategic Svcs. US Army, 1942—46. Named to Hall of Fame, Sml. Motors Mfrs. Assn., 1995. Mem.: Eta Kappa nu, Sigma Xi. Avocations: antiques, woodworking, reading. Home Phone: 573-364-3178; Office Phone: 573-341-4516. Personal E-mail: richards@mst.edu.

RICHARDS, FREDERICK FRANCIS, JR., manufacturing executive, consultant; b. Payette, Idaho, Jan. 28, 1936; s. Frederick Francis and Dorothy Lucille (Taylor) R.; m. DeAnne Aden, Aug. 10, 1958; children: Frederick Francis III, Craig, Jeffrey. BS in Indsl. Engring., So. Meth. U., 1959; MBA, Harvard U., 1961. Indsl. engr. Collins Radio Inc., 1955—59; rsch. asst. Harvard U., 1961—62; fin. analyst H.F. Linder & William T. Golden, NYC, 1962—65; pres., CEO Adrich Corp. and subs., Dallas, 1965—; pres. Resource Locators Inc., Dallas, 1992—95. Exec. v.p. FSE Corp., Plano, Tex., 1990-92; v.p. and prin. Capital Alliance Corp., Dallas, 1985-91; v.p. GTex., Inc., Dallas, 1986-87; pres. Work Lite Dist., Dallas, 1990-95, AR Assocs., internat. mgmt. cons., Dallas, 1972—2002; dir. Dallas Pub. Inc., 1982-84, Aden-Richards Inc., 1979—. Author papers in field; bus. and fin. columnist. Mem. ASTM, Am. Inst. Indsl. Engrs. (sr.), Assn. for Tech. Analysis, Airplane Owners and Pilots Assn., Am. Soc. Indsl. Security, Internat. Assn. Chiefs Police, Nat. Pilots Assn., Exptl. Aircraft Assn., Harvard Club (N.Y.C.), The Tech. Club of Dallas. Home and Office: 3 Cumberland Pl Richardson TX 75080-4926 Office Phone: 972-783-8625. E-mail: ffr@adrich.com.

RICHARDS, GERALD THOMAS, lawyer, educator, writer; b. Monrovia, Calif., Mar. 17, 1933; s. Louis Jacquelyn Richards and Inez Vivian (Richardson) Hall; children: Patricia M. Richards Grauf, Laura J., Dag Hammarskjold; m. Mary Lou Richards, Dec. 27, 1986. BS magna cum laude, Lafayette Coll., Easton, Pa., 1957; MS, Purdue U., 1963; JD, Golden Gate U., San Francisco, 1976. Bar: Calif. 1976, US Dist. Ct. (no. dist.) Calif. 1977, US Patent Office 1981, US Ct. Appeals (9th cir.) 1984, US Supreme Ct. 1984. From computational physicist to asst. lab. counsel Lawrence Livermore Nat. Lab., Calif., 1967—84, asst. lab. counsel, 1984—93; sole practice Livermore, Calif., 1976-78, Oceanside, Calif., 1994-97; emeritus atty. pro bono participant Calif. State Bar, 1998—; staff atty. Contra Costa Sr. Legal Svcs., Concord, 1998—, mem. bd. dirs., 2009—. Constrn. law instr. Contrs. State License Schs., Van Nuys, Calif., 1998; mem. exec. com., policy advisor Fed. Lab. Consortium for Tech. Transfer, 1980-88; panelist, del. White House Conf. on Productivity, Washington, 1983; del. Nat. Conf. on Tech. and Aging, Wingspread, Wis., 1981. Author: (novel) Jimmy, 2003. Commr. Housing Authority, City of Livermore, 1977, vice chmn., 1978, chmn., 1979; mem. Bd. Administrn. Appeals, City of Antioch, Calif., 2003-2005, Contra Costa Count Adv. Coun. on Aging, 2005—, sec., 2007, pres., 2008-; with Contra Costa for Every Generation, 2006-; pres. Housing Choices, Inc., Livermore, 1980-84; bd. dirs. Valley Vol. Ctr., Pleasanton, Calif., 1983, pres., 1984-86; staff Calif. Boys' State Am. Legion, 1996—. Maj. U.S. Army, 1948-67 Recipient Engring. award GE, 1956, Wesley S. Mittman Bible prize, 1957; decorated Army Commendation medal, 1967. Mem. ABA, Calif. State Bar (conv. alt. del. 1990-92, del. 2000, 04-, mem. com. sr. lawyers 2002-05), Alameda County Bar Assn., Contra Costa County Bar Assn., Ea. Alameda County Bar Assn. (sec. 1978, bd. dirs. 1991-92, chair lawyers referral com. 1992-93), LA County Bar Assn., Santa Barbara County Bar Assn., San Diego County Bar Assn., Bar Assn. No. San Diego County, San Francisco Bar Assn., Phi Beta Kappa (No. Calif. chpt. bd. dirs., newsletter chair 2001-07), Tau Beta Pi, Sigma Pi Sigma. Democrat. Home: 1099 Baywood Ln Hercules CA 94547-2739 Personal E-mail: hesiod@calbears.com.

RICHARDS, GLENORA, artist; b. Feb. 18, 1909; d. Tracy Henry and Bertha (Huber) Case; m. Walter DuBois Richards, June 20, 1931 (dec. May 2006); children: Timothy, Henry Tracy(dec.). Student, Cleve. Sch. Art, 1927-30. Exhibited in group shows at Nat. Collection Fine Arts (Smithsonian Inst.), NAD, Portraits, Inc., N.Y.C., Phila., Pa. Soc. Miniature Painters, L.A., Royal Soc. Miniature Painters, Sculptors and Gravers, R.W.S. Galleries, London, 1958, 95, IBM Gallery Arts and Scis., N.Y.C., 1966; represented in permanent collection Phila. Mus. Arts, Smithsonian Inst., Worcester (Mass.) Art Mus., Yale Mus. Fine Arts; contbr. articles to profl. jours.; designer commemorative stamp of Edna St. Vincent Millay, 1981, of Dr. Mary Walker, 1982. Recipient Pa.

Soc. prize Pa. Soc. Miniature Painters, 1947. Mem. Am. Soc. Miniature Painters (Levantia White Boardman Meml. medal 1947), Nat. Assn. Women Artists (medal of honor 1953, 74, Aileen O. Webb prize 1971), Miniature Painters, Sculptors and Gravers Soc. Washington (Elizabeth Muhlhoffer award 1956, 57, 61, hon. award for miniature portrait 1969, Levantia White Boardman Meml. prize 1979, 81), Miniature Art Soc. N.J. (Best on Ivory 1974, 77), Miniature Soc. Fla. (Richard B. Baumgardner award 1989). Home: 100 Duval Rd Lancaster MA 01523-3234

RICHARDS, KEITH, musician; b. Dartford, Kent, Eng., Dec. 18, 1943; s. Bert and Doris (Dupree) R.; children with Anita Pallenberg: Marlon, Angela (Dandelion), Tara (dec. June 4, 1976); m. Patti Hanson, Dec. 18, 1983, children: Hansen, Theodora, Alexandra Student, Sidcup Art Sch. Guitarist The Rolling Stones, 1962—. Guitarist (albums with The Rolling Stones) England's Newest Hitmakers: The Rolling Stones, 1964, 12 X 5, 1964, The Rolling Stones, Now!, 1964, Out of Our Heads, 1965, December's Children (And Everybody's), 1965, Big Hits, High Tide, & Green Grass, 1966, Aftermath, 1966, Got Live if You Want It!, 1966, Between the Buttons, 1967, Flowers, 1967, Their Satanic Majesties Request, 1967, Beggars Banquet, 1968, Through the Past, Darkly (Big Hits Vol. II), 1969, Let It Bleed, 1969, Get Yer Ya-Yas Out !: The Rolling Stones in Concert, 1970, Hot Rocks, 1964-1971, 1971, Sticky Fingers, 1971, More Hot Rocks: Big Hits and Fazed Cookies, 1972, Exile on Main Street, 1972, Goats Head Soup, 1973, It's Only Rock and Roll, 1974, Metamorphosis, 1975, Made in the Shade, 1975, Rolled Gold+: The Very Best of the Rolling Stones, 1975, Black and Blue, 1976, Love You Live, 1977, Some Girls, 1978, Emotional Rescue, 1980, Sucking in the Seventies, 1981, Tattoo You, 1981, "Still Life" (American Concert, 1981), 1982, Undercover, 1983, Rewind (1971-1984), 1984, Dirty Work, 1986, Singles Collection: The London Years, 1989, Steel Wheels, 1989, Flashpoint, 1991, Jump Back: The Best of The Rolling Stones, 1993, Voodoo Lounge, 1994 (Grammy award for Best Rock Album, 1994), Stripped, 1995, Bridges to Babylon, 1997, No Security, 1999, Forty Licks, 2002, Singles: 1965-1967, 2004, Live Licks, 2004, A Bigger Bang, 2005, Rarities 1971-2003, 2005, (soundtrack) Shine a Light, 2008, (albums with The Rolling Stones & other artists) The Rolling Stones Rock 'N' Roll Circus, 1996, singer, guitarist (solo albums) Talk Is Cheap, 1988, Keith Richards & The X-Pensive Winos Live At The Hollywood Palladium, 1991, Main Offender, 1992; performer: (films) Gimme Shelter, 1970, Sympathy for the Devil, 1970, Ladies and Gentlemen: The Rolling Stones, 1974, Let's Spend the Night Together, 1983, 25 X 5: The Continuing Adventures of the Rolling Stones, 1989, Rolling Stones: Live At the Max, 1991, Voodoo Lounge, 1994, The Rolling Stones Rock 'N' Roll Circus, 1996, The Rolling Stones Bridges to Babylon Tour '97-98, 1997, Four Flicks, 2003, The Biggest Bang, 2007, Shine a Light, 2008; performer, musical dir. (films) Hail! Hail! Rock & Roll, 1987, appeared in (documentaries) Being Mick, 2001; actor: (films) Pirates of the Caribbean: At World's End, 2007 (Spike TV's Best Cameo award, 2008). Recipient Living Legend award Internat. Rock, Nordoff Robbins Silver Clef award, 1982, Grammy award for Lifetime Achievement, 1986, Ivor Novello award for Outstanding Contribution to British Music, 1991, Greatest Touring Band of All Time, World Music Awards, 2006; named to The Rock and Roll Hall of Fame (as mem. of The Rolling Stones), 1989. Office: Universal Music Group 1755 Broadway New York NY 10019

RICHARDS, LEONARD MARTIN, investment executive, consultant; b. Phila., June 4, 1935; s. Leonard Martin and Marion Clara (Lang) R.; m. Phyllis Janelle Mowrey, Aug. 26, 1961 (div. Aug. 1978); children: Lisa, David Reed. BS, Pa. State U., 1957; MBA, U. Pa., 1963; MTh, Universal Sem., 1996, ThD, 2000. Asst. to sr. ptnr. Van Cleef, Jordan & Wood, NYC, 1963-68; v.p., portfolio mgr. Bernstein-Macaulay, Inc., NYC, 1968-72; ptnr. G. H. Walker, Laird Co., NYC, 1972-74; v.p., trust officer, mgr. instnl. funds group Republic Bank N.A., Dallas, 1974-77; v.p., sr. investment officer, mem. exec. com. Variable Annuity Life Ins. Co., Houston, 1977-88; v.p., sr. investment officer Am. Gen. Series Portfolio Co., 1985-88; pres. L.M. Richards & Co., Houston, 1982—, also bd. dirs.; mem. adv. bd. Trinity Life Ctr., Houston, 1996-2000; mng. dir. The Enhancement Inst., Houston, 2003—; pres. Lenan Holdings, Inc., Houston, 2005—. Pres., bd. dirs. Sand Dollar, Inc., Houston, 1985—96; trustee Post Oak Sch., Houston, 1997—99, Universal Sem., 1997—2000, pres., 2001—; mem., bd. dir. Capital Institutional Services, Dallas, 1991—99; trustee PAIRS Found., Weston, Fla., 2004—06; bd. dirs. Houston Chorale, 1988—90. Capt. US Army, 1957—65. Mem. ACFA Inst., Houston Soc. Fin. Analysts, Wharton Club (Houston), Houstonian Club Independent. Avocations: skiing, travel, scuba. Home: 9023 Briar Forest Dr Houston TX 77024-7220 Office: LM Richards & Co 1900 St James Pl Ste 800 Houston TX 77056 Office Phone: 713-961-0400. Business E-Mail: lrichards@enhancementinstitute.com.

RICHARDS, LORIE GAGE, occupational therapist, educator; b. Ilion, NY, May 22, 1961; d. Gerald LaMont and Doris Jean (Wilcox) Gage; m. Thomas Edward Richards, May 20, 1989; children: Alia Irene, Ian Andrew. BS in Occupational Therapy, Elizabethtown Coll., 1983; MS in Exptl. Psychology, Syracuse U., 1989, PhD, 1992. Cert. occupational therapist. Staff occupational therapist Plaza Health & Rehab. Ctr., Syracuse, N.Y., 1983-85, The Neurologic Ctr. at Cortland, N.Y., 1985-86; teaching and rsch. asst. dept. psychology Syracuse U., 1986-92; asst. prof. U. Kans. Med. Ctr., Kansas City, 1992—, assoc. scientist ctr. on aging, 1993—; courtesy asst. prof. dept. psychology U. Kans., Kansas City, 1993—. Contbr. articles and revs. to profl. jours. Recipient Dissertation award Am. Psychol. Assn., 1991-92. Mem. Am. Occupational Therapy Assn., Psychonomics Soc. (assoc.), Midwestern Psychol. Assn., Kans. Occupational Therapy Assn. (co-chair conf. program 1995-96), Am. Psychol. Soc. Methodist. Avocation: craftwork. Office: U Kans Med Ctr Dept Occupational Therapy 3033 Robinson 3901 Rainbow Kansas City KS 66160-0001 Home: 4426 NW 60th Ter Gainesville FL 32606-4297

RICHARDS, MADGE MARIE, business owner, professor, consultant, recruiter, professional fundraiser; b. Washington, Oct. 4, 1952; d. Benjamin Ellsworth and Virginia (Oliver) Richards; children: Jared Benjamin, Jessica Lauren. B.S. in Bus. Mgmt., Strayer Coll., 1973; MBA Columbia Union Coll. 2004, Nat. govt. sales rep. G.F.C. Mfg. Co., Bklyn., 1972-75; ter. sales rep. John H. Breck, Am. Cyanamid, Wayne, NJ, 1975-1977; ter. sales mgr. Drackett Products Co., Cin., 1977-81, E.J. Brach & Sons., Chgo., Annapolis, Md., 1981-87, owner, pres. Madge Johnson Ltd., 1987—2009; sec.-treas. Recreation Environments Co., Annapolis, Md., 1988-90, recruiter, asst. dir. Columbia Union Coll. Takoma Park, Md., 1999—2008; prof. Prince Georges Cmty. Coll., 2008-; treas. Martin Barr Sch., 1989-90 Mem. NAFE, Grocery Mfrs. Reps., Women in Consumer Product Sales. Home and Office: 17205 Magruders Ferry Rd Brandywine MD 20613-8358 Home Phone: 301-888-9392. Personal E-mail: mjatcuc@aol.com.

RICHARDS, MARK A., dean, earth and planetary science professor; BS in Engring. Sci., U. Tex., Austin, 1977; MS in Applied Physics, Calif. Inst. Tech., Pasadena, 1978, PhD in Geophysics, 1986. Faculty mem. U. Oreg., Eugene, 1987—89, U. Calif., Berkeley, 1989—, chair dept. geology & geophysics (now earth and planetary sci.), 1997—99, prof. earth and planetary sci., dean divsn. math. and phys. scis., 2002—, exec. dean Coll. Letters and Sci., 2006—. Vis. scholar Los Alamos Nat. Lab., N.Mex., 1997—98. Contbr. articles to profl. publs. Fellow: Am. Geophys. Union. Achievements include patents in field. Office: Coll Letters and Sci U Calif Berkeley 201 Campbell Hall Berkeley CA 94720-2920 Office Phone: 510-642-5872. Office Fax: 510-642-7578. E-mail: Mark_Richards@berkeley.edu.

RICHARDS, MICHAEL, actor, comedian; b. Culver City, Calif., July 24, 1949; 1 child. Stand-up comedian, 1999—. TV appearances include Fridays, 1980-82, Marblehead Manor, 1987, Seinfeld, 1990-1999 (Emmy award, Outstanding Supporting Actor in a Comedy Series, 1993, 94), The Michael Richards Show, 2000, David Copperfield, 2000; films include Young Doctors in Love, 1982, Transylvania 6-5000, 1985, Whoops Apocalypse, 1986, UHF, 1989, Problem Child, 1990, Coneheads, 1993, So I Married and Axe Murderer, 1994, Airheads, 1994, Unstrung Heroes, 1995, Trial ad Error, 1997, Bee Movie (voice), 2007; TV movie London Suite. Office: Untitled Entertainment 322 8th Ave Ste 601 New York NY 10001-6715

RICHARDS, MIKE, professional hockey player; b. Kenora, Ont., Can., Feb. 11, 1985; Center Kitchener Rangers (Ontario Hockey League), 2001—05, Phila. Flyers, 2005—, capt., 2008—. Mem. Team Can., World Jr. Championships, Helsinki, Finland, 2004, Grand Forks, ND, 05. Named to NHL All-Star Game, 2008. Achievements include being a member of Gold Medal Team Canada, World Junior Championships, 2005; being a member of Calder Cup champion Philadelphia Phantoms, 2005. Office: Philadelphia Flyers Wachovia Ctr 3601 S Broad St Philadelphia PA 19148

RICHARDS, NORMAN BLANCHARD, lawyer; b. Melrose, Mass., May 27, 1924; s. Henry Edward and Annie Jane (Blanchard) R.; m. Diane Maionchi, July 9, 1977; children— Terri, Jeffrey. BS, Bowdoin Coll., 1945; JD, Stanford U., 1951. Bar: Calif. bar 1951. Mem. firm McCutchen Doyle Brown & Enersen, San Francisco, 1951—, partner, 1960—. Mem. faculty Tulane Admiralty Law Inst., Hastings Coll. Advocacy. Bd. visitors Stanford Law Sch. With USN, 1943-46. Fellow Am. Coll. Trial Lawyers; mem. ABA, Calif. State Bar, San Francisco Bar Assn., Maritime Law Assn. U.S. Home: 85 Platt Ave Sausalito CA 94965-1897 Office: Bingham McCutchen 3 Embarcadero Ctr San Francisco CA 94111-4003 Home Phone: 415-332-0894.

RICHARDS, PATRICIA JONES, artist, poet, musician, composer; b. Pomona, Calif., Nov. 20; d. Earle Feurte Jones and Florence Frable Slawson; m. Addison Whitaker Richards, May 1, 1950 (dec. Mar. 1964). BA, Pomona Coll., 1944; cert. nursery sch. tchr., Scripps Coll., 1944. Acquistions libr. Calif. State Polytechnic U., Pomona, 1979-85. Author: Self-Expression-Poems and Watercolors, 1996, "Old Friends" Through Sun and Showers, 1997, Pensativo-Poems and Watercolors (Golden Leaves award 1996-97, 99-2000), 2000, Afterthoughts - Poems and Watercolors, 2004; pianist Jazz CD, To a Woven Fitness, 2001; co-author, composer A Twist of Hate, a musical, 2004; composer (CD) A Twist of Hate, 2007, Iwant you back, 2009. Personal E-mail: patpj3@yahoo.com.

RICHARDS, PAUL GRANSTON, seismologist, geophysics educator; b. Cirencester, Eng., Mar. 31, 1943; arrived in US, 1965; naturalized, 1980; s. Albert George and Kathleen Margaret (Harding) R.; m. Jody Margaret Porterfield, June 1, 1968; children: Mark, Jessica, Gillian. BA, Cambridge U., Eng., 1965; MS, Calif. Inst. Tech., Pasadena, 1966, PhD, 1970. Asst. prof. geology Columbia U., NYC, 1971—76, chmn. geol. scis., 1980-83, assoc. prof. geol. scis., 1976—79, prof. geol. scis., 1979—96; Mellon prof. natural scis. Columbia. U., NYC, 1987—; prof. earth and environ. scis. Columbia U., NYC, 1996—; assoc. dir. Lamont-Doherty Geol. Obs., Columbia U., Palisades, 1980—83, mem. adminstrv. com., 1987—90, 1994—98. Seismic rev. panel USAF Tactical Applications Ctr., 1985—; mem. Coun. Fgn. Rels., 1992—. Co-author: Quantitative Seismology, 2 vols., 1980, 2nd edit., 2002; bd. editors Wave Motion, 1985-92, Jour. Computational Acoustics, 1991-97. Recipient Leo Szilard lectureship award, Am. Phys. Soc., 2006; Sloan Found. rsch. fellow, 1973-77, Guggenheim Found. fellow, 1977-78, MacArthur Found. fellow, 1981-86, fellow Royal Norwegian Coun. Scientific and Indsl. Rsch., 1989; William C. Foster fellow and vis. scholar, US Arms Control and Disarmament Agy., 1984-85, 1993-94; vis. scholar Los Alamos Nat. Lab., 1997, Phi Beta Kappa vis. scholar, 2000-01. Fellow AAAS, Royal Astron. Soc., Am. Acad. Arts and Scis., Am. Geophys. Union (mem. coun. 1990-94, pres. seismology sect., 1992-96; Macelwane award 1976); mem. Inc. Rsch. Institutions for Seismology (chmn. presdl. search com., 1985, 1990, exec. com., 1987-90, vice-chmn. bd. dirs., 1988-90, standing com. data mgmt. ctr., 1996-99, nominating com., 2003-04), Seismological Soc. America (bd. dirs. 2002-09, Reid medalist 2009), Soc. Exploration Geophysicists, Arms Control Assn. Episcopalian. Office: Lamont-Doherty Earth Obs 61 Rte 9W Palisades NY 10964 E-mail: richards@ldeo.columbia.edu.

RICHARDS, PRISCILLA ANN, medical/surgical nurse; b. Providence, Nov. 10, 1949; d. Frank L. Thornton and Dorothy A. Maker; children: Tanya Rene, Jason Edward. Assoc. Degree Nursing, Lincoln Land C.C., Springfield, Ill., 1980. RN Ill., 1980, R.I., 1997. Cert. nursing asst. Meml. Med. Ctr., Springfield, 1971—73, lic. practical nurse, 1973—80, RN, 1980—97, South County Nursing and Subacute Ctr., North Kingstown, RI, 1997—2000, Elmhurst Extended Care, Providence, 2000—05, Maxim Health Care, Providence, 2005—. Sgt. USAF, 1968—71. Baptist. Avocations: reading, swimming, yard work. Home: 71 Wells Ave Warwick RI 02889 Personal E-mail: prissy200959@yahoo.com.

RICHARDS, SIR REX EDWARD, research scientist, academic administrator; b. Colyton, Devon, Oct. 28, 1922; s. H.W. and E.N. Richards; m. Eva Edith Vago, 1948; 2 children. BA, Oxford U., 1945. Prof. chemistry Oxford U., 1964-69. Warden Merton Coll. Oxford U., 1969-84, vice chancellor, 1977-81; chmn. Oxford Enzyme Group, 1969-83; chmn. Br. Postgrad. Med. Fedn., 1986-93; pres. Royal Soc. Chemistry, 1990-92; commr. Royal Commn. Exhbn. 1851, 1984-97; chancellor U. Exeter, 1982-98; dir. The Leverhulme Trust, 1984-94. Trustee Ciba Found., 1978-97, Nat. Heritage Meml. Fund, 1980-84, Tate Gallery, 1982-88, 91-93, Nat. Gallery, 1982-88, 89-93, Nat. Gallery Trust, 1997-2006, Henry Moore Found., 1989-2003 Fellow Royal Soc. Address: Unit 4 West Heanton Buckland Filleigh Beaworthy Devon EX21 5PJ England E-mail: rex.richards@merton.ox.ac.uk.

RICHARDS, STEPHEN HAROLD, engineering educator; b. Austin, Tex., July 19, 1952; s. Harold Richards Jr. and Janice Valerie (Mahone) Jackson; m. Mary Kathryn King Coleman, Aug. 15, 1974 (div. July 1981); 1 child, Adam King; m. Elizabeth "Jeannie" Stevens, Apr. 5, 2006. BSCE, U. Tex., 1976; MCE, Tex. A&M U., 1977; PhDCE, U. Tenn., 1989. Registered profl. engr., Tenn., Tex. Rsch. asst. Tex. Transp. Inst., Tex. A&M U., 1976-77, engring. rsch. assoc., 1977-81, asst. rsch. engr., 1982-84; asst. dir. transp. ctr. U. Tenn., Knoxville, 1984-87, acting dir. transp. ctr., 1987-89, dir. transp., 1989—, assoc. prof. civil engring., 1989—; traffic engring. cons. Ctr. Transp. Rsch., 1976—. Engr., mgr. Walton & Assocs./Cons. Engrs., Inc., Houston, 1981-82; lectr. in civl engring. U. Houston, 1982, Tex. A&M U., 1978-81, 83-84; instr. Tex. Engring. Extension Svc., Tex. A&M U., 1978-84; Dwight D. Eisenhower Fellowship Rev. Com., Tenn. State U., 1993, N.C. A&T Univ., 1992; Bicentennial planning Com. U. Tenn., 1993, dir. program for minority student recruitment into transp. careers, 1992—, coll. engring. awards com., 1991—, chmn. spl. events traffic planning com., 1985—. Contbr. numerous articles to profl. jours. Mem. Cumberland Gatewaa Com., 1993—; edn. com. Southeastern Transp. Ctr., 1992—; exec. dir. Southeastern Consortium of U. Transp. Ctrs., 1992—; chmn. Knoxville Transp. Authority, 1992-94, vice-chmn., 1990-92, commr., 1989-93; rep. Coun. of Univ. Transp. Ctrs. U. Tenn., 1987—, bd. dirs. 1992—, sec., 1994-95, v.p., 1995-96, pres., 1996—; adv. com. Ga. State U. Transp. Ctr., 1989—; traffic control device subcom. Transp. Rsch. Bd., 1989-91, traffic control devices, 1991—, many other coms. Hwy. Safety fellowship Fed. Hwy. Adminstrn., U.S. Dept. Transp., 1976-77. Mem. ASCE, Inst. of Transp. Engrs. (chmn. tech. com. Tenn. sect. 1988—, area coord. Tex. sect. 1982-84, guidelines for driveway design and location), Transp. Rsch. Bd., Soc. Profl. Engrs., Am. Road and Transp. Builders Assn. (edn. com. 1988—), Phi Kappa Phi, Chi Epsilon. Office: Ctr Transp 600 Henley St Ste 309 Knoxville TN 37996-4133 Home Phone: 865-382-0123; Office Phone: 865-974-5255. Personal E-mail: shrichards@tds.net.

RICHARDS, SUZANNE V., lawyer; b. Columbia, SC, Sept. 7, 1927; d. Raymond E. and Elise C. (Gray) R. AB, George Washington U., 1948, JD with distinction, 1957, LLM, 1959. Bar: D.C. 1958. Sole practice, Washington, 1974—. Mem. D.C. Jud. Conf., 1975—2007; lectr. in family and probate law. Bd. dirs. Coun. for Ct. Excellence. Recipient John Bell Larner award George Washington U., 1958; named Woman Lawyer of Yr., Women's Bar Assn. D.C., 1977. Mem. ABA (ho. of dels. 1988-90), Bar Assn. D.C. (pres. 1989-90, named Lawyer of Yr. 2002), Women's Bar Assn. (pres. 1977-78), Trial Lawyers Assn. of D.C. (bd. govs. 1978-82, 85-2001, treas. 1982-85), D.C. Bar. Home: 530 N St SW Washington DC 20024-4546 Office: PO Box 65466 Washington DC 20035-5466

RICHARDS, THOMAS EDWARD, information technology executive, former telecommunications industry executive; b. 1954; m. Mary Beth Richards; 2 children. BA in Economics, U. Pitts.; MS in Mgmt., MIT, Cambridge. Various mgmt. positions Bell of Pa., 1976—83, Bell Atlantic, 1983—95; exec. v.p. comm. & info. products Ameritech, 1995—99; chmn., pres., CEO Clear Comm., 1999—2003; exec. v.p. bus. markets group Qwest Comm. Internat., Inc., Denver, 2005—08, COO, 2008—09; pres., COO CDW Corp., Vernon Hills, Ill., 2009—. Bd. dirs. Nat. Alliance Bus., Tele Danmark (TDK). Mem. Pitts. coun. Boy Scouts America; bd. dirs. Pa. Econ. League, Pa. SW Econ. Devel. Assn., Pitts. C. of C. Alfred P. Sloan Fellow. Office: CDW Corp 200 N Milwaukee Ave Vernon Hills IL 60061*

RICHARDS, TODD, professional hockey coach; b. Crystal, Minn., Oct. 20, 1966; m. Maryann Richards; children: Zachary, Justin. Grad., U. Minn., 1989. Defenseman Sherbrooke Canadiens, 1989—90, Fredericton Canadiens, 1990, Springfield Indians, 1990—93, Hartford Whalers, 1990—92, Las Vegas Thunder, 1993—95, Orlando Solar Bears, 1996—2001; asst. coach Milw. Admirals, 2002—06; head coach Wilkes-Barre/Scranton Penguins, 2006—08; asst. coach San Jose Sharks, 2008—09; head coach Minn. Wild, 2009—. Office: Minn Wild 317 Washington St Saint Paul MN 55102*

RICHARDS, VINCENT PHILIP HASLEWOOD, librarian; b. Sutton Bonington, Nottinghamshire, Eng., Aug. 1, 1933; arrived in Can., 1956, naturalized, 1961; s. Philip Haslewood and Alice Hilda (Moore) R.; m. Ann Beardshall, Apr. 3, 1961; children: Mark, Christopher, Erika. ALA, Ealing Coll., London, 1954; BLS with distinction, U. Okla., 1966. Cert. profl. libr., B.C. Joined Third Order Mt. Carmel, Roman Cath. Ch., 1976; with Brentford and Chiswick Pub. Librs., London, 1949-56; asst. librarian B.C. (Can.) Pub. Libr. Commn., Dawson Creek, 1956-57; asst. dir. Fraser Valley Regional Libr., Abbotsford, B.C., 1957-67; chief librarian Red Deer Coll., Alta., Canada, 1967-77; dir. librs. Edmonton (Alta.) Pub. Libr., Edmonton, 1977-89; libr. and book industry cons. Victoria, Canada, 1990—. Pres. Faculty Assn. Red Deer Coll., 1971-72, bd. govs., 1972-73; pres. Libr. Assn. Alta., 1984-85. Contbr. articles to profl. jours. V.p. Jeunesses Musicales, Red Deer, 1969-70; bd. dirs. Red Deer TV Authority, 1975-76; dir. Alta. Found. Lit. Arts, 1984-86. Served with Royal Army Ednl. Corps, 1951-53. Home and Office: 105 1049 Costin Ave Victoria BC Canada V9B 2T4 Home Phone: 250-391-9892; Office Phone: 250-391-9892. Personal E-mail: v.p.h.richards@gmail.com. *Dedication to public service, in spite of its frustrating aspects, diversity of experience, people and places, and the avoidance of overspecialization are great contributors to an enjoyable working life.*

RICHARDSON, ALBERT EDWARD, chemistry professor, researcher; b. Lovelock, Nev., Feb. 4, 1929; s. James Harold and Mary Lorraine Richardson; m. Shirley Arlene Richardson, June 10, 1959 (dec. Apr. 1997); children: Anne Ikard, John (dec.), Stephen; stepchildren: Corinne Jameson, Elisabeth Anderson, David Beckman, Margaret Chambers. BS in Chemistry, U. Nev., 1950; PhD, Iowa State U., 1956. Accredited profl. chemist Am. Inst. Chemists. Rsch. chemist Ames (Iowa) Lab. of the Atomic Energy Commn., 1950—55; asst. prof. chemistry N.Mex. State U., Las Cruces, 1955—60, radiation safety officer, 1957—75, assoc. prof. chemistry, 1960—91, assoc. prof. emeritus, 1991—. Vis. scientist N.Mex. secondary schs., 1960—91; vis. prof. chemistry Adams State Coll., Alamosa, Colo., 1963; summer rschr. Ames Lab. Atomic Energy Commn., 1964, Lawrence Livermore (Calif.) Nat. Lab., 1979; cons. White Sands (N.Mex.) Missile Range, 1965—71, contractor, 1973—74, chemist, 1981—82, 1984—92; vis. staff mem. Los Alamos (N.Mex.) Nat. Labs., 1975—80; summer faculty Sandia Nat. Lab., Albuquerque, 1983; owner, mgr. Timberline Bed and Breakfast, Cedaredge, Colo., 1992—98. Contbr. over 20 articles to profl. jours. Mem. founding cabinet The World Peace and Diplomacy Forum, 2003—; bus. mgr. Coll. Cmty. Chorus, Las Cruces, 1956—57; pres. U. Park Toastmaster's Club, Las Cruces, 1961; dir. Southwestern N.Mex. Regional Sci. Fair, Las Cruces, 1967—68; vol. reading aide to elem. schs. Las Cruces, 2000—03. Rsch. grantee NASA, 1966, Equipment grantee Atomic Energy Commn., 1968; postdoctoral rsch. fellow Atomic Energy Commn., 1968-69. Mem. Am. Chem. Soc. (chmn. so. N.Mex. sect. 1962, chmn. Rio Grande Valley sect. 1977), World Peace and Diplomacy Forum (charter), Sigma Xi, Phi Kappa Phi (pres. N.Mex. State U. chpt. 1972-73), Phi Lambda Upsilon, Sigma Pi Sigma. Democrat. Avocations: photography, collecting coins and CD's, travel, gardening, cultural activities. Home: 3045 Buena Vida Cir Apt 202 Las Cruces NM 88011-9122 Personal E-mail: aerinlc@earthlink.net.

RICHARDSON, ALFONSO AUSTIN, accountant, financial services executive; b. St. Nicholas, Aruba, W.I., Feb. 29, 1932; came to U.S., 1951; s. Ashley A. and Elvia H. Richardson; m. Florence C. St. Hilaire, Sept. 7, 1957 (dec. Nov. 17, 1998); children: Paula, Kathy, Peter, Steven, Edward, Vernon; m. Jennifer Harrypersad Dec., 24, 2002; stepchildren:

Nicholas Binda, Devon Binda. BS, L.I. U., 1959. Cert. internat. financier. V.p., treas. Node 4 Assocs., Inc., Bklyn., 1970-71; asst. contr. Kings County Hosp. Ctr., Bklyn., 1971-74; owner Richardson Mgmt. Assoc., 1971—; contr. Kings County Hosp. Ctr., Bklyn., 1974-79; contr., CFO Harlem Hosp. Ctr., NYC, 1979-95; CFO L.B.J. Health Complex, Inc., Bklyn., 1996-98; pres., CEO Accudata Sys. Svcs., Inc., NYC, 1997—; CFO, cons. Concord Nursing Home, Inc., 2002—07. Owner Empire Trading Co. Internet Mktg., 2002, Richardson Bus. Svcs. ISP. Contbr. articles to profl. publs. Dir., treas. Bklyn. Local Econ. Devel. Corp., 1965-70, L.B.J. Health Complex, Inc., Bklyn., 1991-96; mem. Pub. Citizens; ordained minister, 1992. Sgt. US Army, 1952—55, Korea. Recipient Bus. Visionary award, Cacci, 2007. Mem. Healthcare Fin. Mgmt. Assn. (Follmer Bronze Merit award 1996), Nat. Soc. Accts., Ind. Assn. Accts. Bklyn., Caribbean Am. C. of C., Oxford Club, VFW, Disabled Am. Vets., Contrs. Orgn. (past pres.), Internat. Assn. Fin. Planning, Internat. Soc. Financiers; Am. Legion. Avocations: bowling, Scrabble, stamp collecting, coin collecting, bicycling. Home: 704 Empire Blvd Brooklyn NY 11213-5309

RICHARDSON, ANN BISHOP, foundation executive, lawyer; b. New Rochelle, NY, Dec. 15, 1940; d. Erwin Julius and Mary Frances (Stuart) Heilemann; children: Timothy William, Lynn Patricia, Melanie Elizabeth. BA summa cum laude, Georgetown U., 1977; JD, George Washington U., 1984; cert., Oxford U., Eng., 1986. Bar: Md. 1988, DC 1989. Student counselor Amideast, Beirut, 1967-68, program specialist, 1970-73; adminstrv. asst. UN Devel. Program, Yaounde, Cameroon, 1968-70; adminstrv. mgr. Antioch Sch. Law, Washington, 1977-79; chief adminstrv. officer for internat. ops. Peace Corps, Washington, 1980-84; dir. adminstrn. and fin. African Devel. Found., Washington, 1984-87; atty. Karr and McLain, Washington, 1987-92; v.p., gen. counsel Time Dollar, Inc., Washington, 1992-98; adj. prof. law DC Sch. Law, Washington, 1994-98; prof., acad. dean U. DC David A. Clarke Sch. Law, Washington, 1998—. Bd. dirs. Bur. Rehab., Inc. Active Neighbors, Inc., Washington, 1976—, Time Dollar, Inc. Recipient Spl. Achievement award Peace Corps, 1981, 82, African Devel. Found., 1986. Mem. ABA, ACLU, DC Bar Assn., Am. Women Univ. Grads., Soc. for Internat. Devel., Phi Beta Kappa. Office: David A Clarke Sch Law 4200 Connecticut Ave NW Washington DC 20008-1122

RICHARDSON, ANNE WORSHAM, art gallery owner, artist; b. Turbeville, SC, Oct. 22, 1922; d. George Talbert and Jessie Phillips Worsham; m. Marvin D. Richardson, 1946 (dec.); 1 child, Marvin D. Jr. (dec.); m. John Peter Paszek, 1972 (dec. 2005). Student, Rice Bus. Coll., Charleston, SC, 1938. Artist, gallery owner Birds I View Gallery, Charleston, 1972—. Lectr. in field. Exhibitions include Ga. Ornithological Soc., 1949, Carolina Bird Club, Lake Mattamuskeet, NC, 1950, Kennedy Gallery, NYC, 1958, East Clarendon HS, Turbeville, 1958, Dock St. Theatre Green Rm., Charleston, 1962, Wilson Ornithological Soc., Charleston Mus., 1963, The Gibbes Mus. Art, Charleston, 1965, Bob Jones U., Greenville, SC, 1966, The Berkshire Mus., Pittsfield, Mass., 1966, Columbia Mus. Art, 1967, Calif. State Mus., LA, 1970, 1972, 1977, Harbour Town Mus., Hilton Head Island, SC, 1971, St. Louis Art and Sci. Mus., 1974, The Sumter Art Gallery, SC, 1974, Nat. Wildlife Fedn., Washington, 1975, Nat. History Mus., Anniston, Ala., 1976, Vt. Art Ctr., Manchester, Vt., 1977, The Arts Club of Washington, 1978, Schloss Gluecksburg, Germany, 1978, Morton Arboretum Mus., Chgo., 1991, York County Natural History Mus., Rockhill, SC, 1991, Darlington Garden Club, SC, 2003, Delta Kappa Gamma, Florence, SC, 2004, Florence Mus., Represented in permanent collections SC State Ho., Columbia. Recipient award, Summerville Art Guild, 1959, Medway Art Festival 1st award purchase prize, Gibbes Mus. Art, 1959, Commendation award, Calif. State Mus., LA, 1972, commendation for conservation, Dept. of Interior, Washington, 1985, Lifetime Svc. award, Horry County Literacy Coun., 2002; named to SC Fedn. Women's Clubs Hall of Fame, 1978, SC Hall of Fame, Myrtle Beach, 1991; grantee, Charleston Cultural and Sci. Found., 1962. Mem.: Charleston Artists Guild, Nat. Wildlife Fedn. (Art Print of Yr. award 1970), Nat. Audubon Soc., Cornell Ornithological Soc., USN League (life), Alpha Kappa Gamma (hon.), Delta Kappa Gamma (hon.). Office: Birds I View Gallery 119-A Church St Charleston SC 29401 Office Phone: 843-723-1276. Personal E-mail: 4awr@bellsouth.net.

RICHARDSON, ARTEMAS P(ARTRIDGE), retired landscape architect; b. Phila., May 24, 1918; s. Eugene Stanley and Jessica (Ripple) R.; m. Frederica McAfee, Sept. 2, 1945; children: Steven, David, Ann, Vida, Stanley. BA in Fine Arts, Williams Coll., 1940; student, Pa. State U., 1940-42; BS in Landscape Architecture, Iowa State U., 1947. Registered landscape architect, Conn., Fla., Md., Mass., Miss., N.Y., Ohio, R.I., Tenn. Asst. landscape architect McCloud & Scatchard, Lilitz, Pa., 1947-48, Olmsted Bros., Brookline, Mass., 1949-50, ptnr., 1950-61, Olmsted Assocs., Brookline, 1961-64, pres, treas., 1964-80; owner The Olmsted Office, Fremont, NH, 1980-2000; ret. Lectr. Harvard U., Cambridge, 1961; mem., chair Bd. Registration Landscape Architects, Mass., 1968-77. Illustrator: Trees for Every Purpose, 1980. Mem., chair Planning Bd., Needham, Mass., 1956-62, Conservation Commn., Fremont, 1982-2000, chair, 1984-2000; mem. N.H. Gov.'s Task Force on Community Trees, Concord, 1989-91; mem., chair Exeter River Local Adv. Com., 1995-2001. Lt. USNR, 1942-46, ETO. Named Outstanding Mcpl. Vol., N.H. Mcpl. Assn., 1993. Fellow Am. Soc. Landscape Architects, Boston Soc. Landscape Architects (pres. 1952-56); mem. N.H. Landscape Assn. (bd. dirs. 1984-87), Granite State Landscape Architects (vice chair 1990-91), Herb Soc. Am. (life), Scarab, Rotary (pres. local club 1965-66, dist. trustee 1968-69, dist. gov. 1970-71, bd. dirs. R.I. 1978-80), Delta Phi, Tau Sigma Delta, Pi Gamma Alpha. Avocations: photography, woodworking, gardening. Home: Langdon Pl 17 Hampton Rd Apt 108 Exeter NH 03833-4822 Personal E-mail: aprich@verizon.net.

RICHARDSON, BILL (WILLIAM BLAINE RICHARDSON III), Governor of New Mexico, former United States Secretary of Energy; b. Pasadena, Calif., Nov. 15, 1947; s. William Blaine & María Luisa López-Collada Márquez Richardson; m. Barbara Flavin, 1972. BA, Tufts U., Medford, Mass., 1970; MA, Fletcher Sch. Law and Diplomacy, 1971. Mem. staff US Congress, 1971-72, US Dept. State, 1973-75; mem. staff fgn. relations com. US Senate, 1975-78; exec. dir. N. Mex. State Democratic Com., 1978, Bernalillo County Democratic Com., 1978; businessman Santa Fe, 1978-82; mem. US Congress from 3rd N.Mex. Dist., Washington, 1982-96; permanent US rep. to UN US Dept. State, NYC, 1997-98; sec. US Dept. Energy, Washington, 1998-2001; sr. mng. dir. Kissinger McLarty, Washington, 2001—02; gov. State of N. Mex., Santa Fe, 2003—. Ranking minority mem. Resources Com. on Nat. Pks., Forests and Lands; mem. Select Com. on intelligence, Helsinki Commn.; adj. prof. pub. policy Harvard U., 2001; cons. Salomon Smith Barney; chair Democratic Governor's Assoc.; Western Governors Assoc. Author (with Michael Ruby): Between Worlds: The Making of an American Life, 2005; author: Leading By Example: How We Can Inspire an Energy and Security Revolution, 2007. Vice chair Dem. Nat. Com.; active Big Bros.-Big Sisters, Santa Fe; US amb. to UN, 1997-98; mem. Presdl. Consolidate-Dew Party, 2008. Named one of 25 Most Influential Hispanics, Time Mag., 2005. Mem. Santa Fe Hispanic C. of C., Santa Fe C. of C., Council Fgn. Relations, NATO 2000 Bd., Congl. Hispanic Caucus, Am. G.I. Forum Democrat. Catholic. Office: Office of the Gov State Capitol Rm 400 Santa Fe NM 87501 Office Phone: 505-476-2200. Office Fax: 505-476-2226. Business E-Mail: bill.richardson@state.nm.us.

RICHARDSON, BRENT EARL, otolaryngologist; BA in Biology and Anthropology, Washington U., St. Louis, 1986; MD with honors, U. Wash., Seattle, 1990; MS in Otolaryngology, U. Minn., Mpls., 1996. Cert. Am. Bd. Otolaryngology, 1997. Fellow, laryngology and voice Loyola U. Med. Ctr., Maywood, Ill., 1996—97; intern, dept. surgery Hennepin County Med. Ctr., Minneapolis, Minn., 1990—91, resident, dept. surgery, 1991—92; resident, dept. otolaryngology U. Minn., Minneapolis, 1992—96; attending physician, surgical svc., divsn. otolaryngology Hines VA Med. Ctr., Ill., 1997—2002; attending physician Foster McGaw Hosp., Loyola U. Med. Ctr., Maywood, Ill., 1997—2003; asst. prof., otolaryngology Stritch Sch. Medicine, Loyola U. Chgo., Maywood, Ill., 1997—2003; attending physician Advocate Good Samaritan Hosp., Downers Grove, Ill., 2003—; laryngologist Bastian Voice Inst., Downers Grove, Ill., 2003—. Cons., surgical svc., divsn. otolaryngology Hines VA Med. Ctr., Ill., 2002—03; invited presenter in the field. Contbr. articles to profl. jours. Named to Guide to America's Top Physicians, Consumers' Research Coun. Am., 2003. Mem.: Nat. Assn. Teachers of Singing, Am. Speech-Language-Hearing Assn., Dysphagia Rsch. Soc., Christian Soc. Otolaryngology/Head and Neck Surgery, Christian Med. Assn., Chgo. Laryngological and Otological Soc., Am. Acad. Otolaryngology/Head and Neck Surgery, Am. Acad. Med. Ethics, Phi Kappa Phi, Alpha Omega Alpha. Office: Bastian Voice Inst 3010 Highland Pkwy Ste 550 Downers Grove IL 60515 Office Phone: 630-724-1100. Office Fax: 630-724-0084.

RICHARDSON, CAMPBELL, retired lawyer; b. Woodland, Calif., June 18, 1930; s. George Arthur and Mary (Hall) R.; m. Patricia Packwood, Sept. 3, 1957 (dec. Oct. 1971); children: Catherine, Sarah, Thomas; m. Carol Tamblyn, June 1975 (div. Dec. 1977); m. Susan J. Lienhart, May 3, 1980; 1 child, Laura. AB, Dartmouth Coll., 1952; JD, NYU, 1955. Bar: Oreg. 1955, U.S. Dist. Ct. Oreg. 1957. Ptnr. Stoel Rives LLP, Portland, 1964-2000; ret., 2000—. Co-author: Contemporary Trust and Will Forms for Oregon Attorneys, 2003, and for Idaho Attorneys, 2001; contbr. articles to profl. jours. Mem. Portland/Metro Govt. Boundary Commn., 1976; mem. Oreg. Adv. Com. to U.S. Commn. on Civil Rights, 1976-84; bd. dirs. Ctr. for Urban Edn., Portland, 1980-84, Dorchester Conf., Inc., 1982, Oreg. Zoo Found., 1993-2003; chmn. planned giving com. St. Vincent Med. Found., 1988-98; mem. planned giving coun. Oreg. Health Scis. Found., 1994-2003; trustee Met. Family Svc. Found., 1990-98; bd. dirs. Elders in Action, Portland, 2000-06. Served with U.S. Army, 1955-57. Mem. ABA, Oreg. Bar Assn., Multnomah County Bar Assn., Estate Planning Coun. Portland (pres. 1978), Am. Coll. Trust and Estate Counsel, City Club, Multnomah Athletic Club (Portland). Republican. Home: 1500 SW 5th Ave Unit 1701 Portland OR 97201-5430 Office: Stoel Rives LLP 900 SW 5th Ave Ste 2300 Portland OR 97204-1229 Office Phone: 503-294-9337. E-mail: crichardson@stoel.com.

RICHARDSON, CHARLES CLIFTON, biochemist, educator; b. Wilson, NC, May 7, 1935; s. Barney Clifton and Florence Elizabeth (Barefoot) R.; m. Ute Ingrid Hanssum, July 29, 1961; children: Thomas Clifton, Matthew Wilfrid BSM., Duke U., 1959, MD, 1960; A.M. (hon.), Harvard U., 1967. Intern dept. medicine Duke U., Durham, NC, 1960-61; postdoctoral fellow dept. biochemistry Stanford U. Med. Sch., Calif., 1961-63; asst. prof. biol. chemistry Harvard Med. Sch., Boston, 1964-67, assoc. prof., 1967-69, prof. biol. chemistry, 1969—, chmn. dept. biol. chemistry, 1978-87, Edward S. Wood prof., 1979—. Physiol. chemistry study sect. NIH, 1970-74; mem. Fachbeirat of Max-Planck Inst. für Moleculare Genetik, Berlin, Fed. Republic Germany, 1980-89; sci. adv. com. U.S. Biochem. Corp., Cleve., 1983-93, Genetics Inst., Cambridge, Mass., 1986-99, NYCOMED-Amersham, U.K., 1998-2000; mem. Nat. Bd. Med. Examiners, 1973-76; nucleic acids and protein adv. com., Am. Cancer Soc. Inst., 1975-78; vis. com. Boston Biomed. Rsch. Found., 1985—; assoc. Helicon Found., San Diego, 1983-2000; sci. adv. bd. Amersham Life Sci. Inc., 1994-98. Assoc. editor: Ann. Rev. Biochemistry, 1973-82, editor, 1983-2003; mem. editl. bd. Jour. Biol. Chemistry, 1968-73, 84-88, Jour. Molecular Biology, 1976-79. Recipient Career Devel. award, NIH, 1967—76, Merit award, 1986, Herbert Tabor lectureship award, Jour. Biol. Chemistry, 2006. Fellow Am. Acad. Arts and Scis., Inst. of Medicine; mem. Nat. Acad. Scis., Am. Chem. Soc. (Eli Lilly Co. biol. chem. award 1968), Am. Soc. Biol. Chemists (mem. nominating com. 1974-75, 1983-84), Am. Cancer Soc. (coun. for rsch. and clin. investigation 1989-92), Am. Soc. Biochemistry and Molecular Biology (Merck award in biochemistry and molecular biology 1996, Herbert Tabor/Jour. Biol. Chemistry Lectureship award 2006). Business E-Mail: ccr@hms.harvard.edu.

RICHARDSON, CURTIS JOHN, ecology educator; b. Gouverneur, NY, July 27, 1944; s. Nilie John and Rose Marie (LaPierre) R.; m. Carol Bartlett, Aug. 22, 1972; children: John, Suzanne. BS in Biology, SUNY, Cortland, 1966; PhD in Ecology, U. Tenn., 1972. Asst. prof. resource ecology Sch. Natural Resources U. Mich., Ann Arbor, 1972-77, asst. prof. plant ecology Biologican Station, Mich., summer 1973; assoc. prof. resource ecology Sch. Forestry and Environ. Studies Duke U., Durham, N.C., 1977-87, prof. resource ecology, 1988—, dir. Wetland Ctr., 1990—; sr. rsch. fellow in applied ecology and forestry U. Edinburgh, Scotland, 1982. Mem. sci. adv. bd. Nat. Wetland Rsch. Plan, U.S. EPA, Washington, 1991, chmn. Nat. Wetland EMAP rev. panel, 1992; panel mgr. competitive grants program water quality USDA, Washington, 1990-91. Fellow Soil Sci. Soc. Am., AAAS; mem. Am. Inst. Biol. Scis., Am. Soc. Agronomy, Ecol. Soc. Am., Soc. Wetland Scientists (v.p. 1986-87, prs. 1987-88, assoc. editor 1987-93). Avocations: jogging, hiking, fishing. Office: Duke U Wetland Ctr Nichols Sch Environ LSRC Research Dr Durham NC 27708-0333 Home: 717 Anderson St Durham NC 27705-1013

RICHARDSON, CYNTHIA TERESA, music educator; d. Louis Bernard and Margaret Hyrne Richardson. BA, Montclair State Coll., NJ, 1981; ThM, Christian Bible Inst., Bloomfield, NJ, 1991. Tchr., music Paterson Pub. Schs., NJ, 1982—. Pvt. piano & voice tchr., 2008—. Tither, giver, servant, psalmist Shekinah Glory Christian Ch., Irvington, NJ, 2005. Democrat. Office: Paterson Public Schs 33 Church St Paterson NJ 07513 Business E-Mail: crichardson@paterson.k12.nj.us.

RICHARDSON, DANA ROLAND, technology consultant; b. Mason City, Iowa, Jan. 11, 1945; s. Dana Roland Richardson and Louise Marion (Duke) Sarles; m. Sandra Anderson, June 12, 1966; children: Patricia Nan, Dana Roland, Jr. BS, UCLA, 1966, MBA, 1967. CPA, Calif., N.Y. Staff acct. Arthur Young, LA, 1967—72, mgr., 1972—76, prin. NYC, 1976—78; ptnr. Ernst & Young, NYC, 1978—94; founder, ptnr. Dream Street Prodns., New Canaan, Conn., 1994—2002; pres. Richardson Media & Tech. LLC, 2003—. Author: A Manager's Guide to Computer Timesharing, 1975, Audit and Control of Information Systems, 1987. Staff sgt. Reserves USANG, 1967-73. Recipient Nat. Videographer award, Nat. Videography Assn., 1998, 1999, Telly award, 1999; named one of Techology 100 Top 100 Achievers in Techn. in Am., Tech. Mag., 1982, Top 100 Influential People in Acctg., Acctg. Today mag., 2005. Mem. AICPA (Lifetime Achievement award 2003), Calif. Soc. CPA's, Conn. Soc. CPA's. Republican. Episcopalian. Avocations: boating, fishing, music, videography, multimedia. Office: Richardson Media & Tech LLC 24 Blueberry Ln Canton CT 06019 Home: 24 Blueberry Ln Canton CT 06019-4503 Business E-Mail: rick@richardson-media-tech.com.

RICHARDSON, DAVID WALTHALL, cardiologist, educator, consultant; b. Nanking, China, Mar. 22, 1925; s. Donald William and Virginia (McIlwaine) R.; m. Frances Lee Wingfield, June 12, 1948; children: Donald, Sarah, David. BS, Davidson Coll., 1947; MD, Harvard U., 1951. Diplomate Am. Bd. Internal Medicine, Am. Bd. Cardiology. Intern, resident Yale New Haven Hosp., 1951-53; resident, fellow Med. Coll. Va., Richmond, 1953-56, assoc. prof. to prof. medicine, 1962-95, prof. emeritus, 1995—2007, prof. medicine, 2007—. Chmn. divsn. cardiology, 1972-87; interim chmn. dept. medicine, 1973-74; chief cardiology, assoc. chief staff for rsch. VA Hosp., Richmond, 1956-61, dir. cardiology tng. program, 1990-95, prof. medicine Health Sci. Disease Va. Commonwealth U., 1995-; vis. scientist Oxford U., Eng., 1961-62; vis. prof. U. Milan, Italy, 1972-73. Contbr. articles to profl. jours. Moderator Hanover Presybery, Presbyn. Ch. U.S., Richmond, 1970; chmn. events com., NHLBI Cardiac Arrhythmia Suppression Trial, 1983-92, NHLBI Anti-Arrhythmics versus Implantable Defibrillators Trial, 1993-97. Served with USN, 1944-46. Fellow Am. Coll. Cardiology (gov. VA 1970-72), Am. Heart Assn. (coun. clin. cardiology and high blood pressure rsch.); mem. Am. Soc. Clin. Investigation, Am. Clin. and Climatol. Assn. Democrat. Presbyterian. Home: 1500 Westbrook Ct CYA 1105 Richmond VA 23227-3366 Office Phone: 804-200-1256. Personal E-mail: dwr1@wcrichmond.org.

RICHARDSON, DEAN WHEELER, equine surgeon, veterinary educator; b. Aug. 30, 1953; married; 1 child. BS, Dartmouth Coll., Hanover, NH, 1974; DVM, Ohio State U., Coll. Vet. Medicine, 1975—79. Internship surgical residency training prog., U. Pa., 1979; with New Bolton Ctr., U. Pa. Sch. Vet. Medicine, Kennett Sq., Pa., 1979—, Charles W. Raker prof. equine surgery, chief of Large Animal Surgery. Mem. editl. bd. Specialty Mag. in the Sci. Biol. Chemicals, mem. adv. editl. bd. Zeitschrift für Metallkunde. Recipient Norden Disting. Teaching award, Disting. Alumni award, Coll. Vet. Medicine, Ohio State U., 2005. Mem.: Osteosynthesis Soc., Grayson-Jockey Club (mem. scientific adv. bd.). Achievements include recognized for teaching AO Veterinary in North America and Switzerland; leading authority in orthopedic surgery and long bone fractures in horses; renown for performing life saving surgery on Kentucky Derby winner Barbaro, 2006. Avocations: horseback riding, basketball, golf, birdwatching. Office: U Pa New Bolton Ctr 382 W St Rd Kennett Square PA 19348 Office Phone: 610-925-6264. Office Fax: 610-925-8120. E-mail: dwr@vet.upenn.edu.*

RICHARDSON, DENNIS MICHAEL, lawyer, educator; b. LA, July 30, 1949; s. Ralph Lee and Eva Catherine (McGuire) R.; 1 child from previous marriage, Scott Randol; m. Catherine Jean Coyl, July 27, 1973; children: Jennifer Eve, Valerie Jean, Rachel Catherine, Nicole Marie, Mary Rose, Marie Christina, Laura Michelle, Alyssa Rose. BA, Brigham Young U., 1976, JD, 1979. Bar: Oreg. 1979. Owner Law Firm of Dennis Richardson, P.C., Central Point, Oreg., 1979—; pvt. practice law Central Point, Oreg., 1979—; mem. Oreg. House of Reps., 2003—, spkr. pro tem, 2005—07. Guest lectr. in field. Contbr. articles to profl. jours. Bd. dirs. Oreg. Lung Assn., 1980, Shakespearean Festival, Ashland, 1981, Jackson County Legal Services, 1982; chmn. GOP Oreg. 2d. Congl. Dist., 1996-2000, treas. GOP Oreg. Exec. Com., 1996-2002; councilman Ctrl. Point City, 2001-2002. Served as helicopter pilot U.S. Army, 1969-71, Vietnam. Decorated Vietnamese Cross Gallantry. Republican. Office: Law Firm of Dennis Richardson PC 55 S 5th St Central Point OR 97502-2474 Office Phone: 541-664-6622. Business E-Mail: dennis@justiceonline.com.

RICHARDSON, DESMOND, dancer; b. Sumter, NC; Ed., Alvin Ailey Am. Dance Ctr., 1983—86, Internat. Sommer Acad. Tanz, Koln, Germany, 1984—85. Dancer Alvin Ailey Repertory Ensemble, Alvin Ailey Am. Dance Theater, 1987-93; soloist Frankfurt Ballet, Germany, 1994-96; prin. dancer Am. Ballet Theatre, NYC, 1997—; co-artistic dir. (with Dwight Rhoden) Complexions Contemporary Ballet, 1994—. Dancer (Broadway plays) Fosse, 1999, Moving Out, 2002, The Look of Love, 2003, (ballets) Soul Possessed, 1999, Othello, 2003, (solo show choreographed by Taye Diggs) Loose Change, 2007; actor: (films) One Last Dance, 2003, Chicago, 2002, Light and the Sufferer, 2004; dancer (films) Across the Universe, 2007, (TV films) Mosè e Faraone, o Il passaggio del Mar Rosso, 2003. Recipient Presdl. Scholar Arts award, 1986, Bessie award, 1991, Monarch award, Apex award, Alvin Ailey Sch., 2006, Dance Mag. award, 2007. Office: Complexions Contemporary Ballet 7 World Trade Ctr 250 Greenwich St New York NY 10007 Office Phone: 212-777-7771. Office Fax: 212-777-4457.

RICHARDSON, DONALD EDWARD, neurosurgery educator; b. Vicksburg, Miss., Oct. 5, 1931; s. Edward K. and Ina Mae (Cooper) R.; children: Donna Richardson Boas, Scott, David, W. Jeffrey, Cooper E.H. BS in Chemistry, Millsaps Coll., Jackson, Miss., 1953; MD, Tulane U., New Orleans, 1957. Diplomate Am. Bd. Neurol. Surgery. Intern in surgery Charity Hosp., New Orleans, 1957-58, resident in neurosurgery, 1961-62, Ochsner Found. Hosp., New Orleans, 1958-60, VA Hosp., New Orleans, 1960-61; instr. Dept. Neurosurgery, Tulane U., 1962-64, asst. prof., 1964-67, assoc. prof., 1967-74, prof., chmn., 1980—, program dir. residence-tng. program, 1980, adj. prof. dept. biomed. engring., 1984—; clin. assoc. prof. dept. neurosurgery La. State U., New Orleans, 1974-80. Dir. Pain Treatment Ctr. Hotel Dieu Hosp., New Orleans, 1978-93, mem.-at-large exec. com., 1978-84, chmn. spl. procedures com., 1984-93; chief neurosurgery sect. Charity Hosp. La. New Orleans, 1980—, VA Hosp. New Orleans, 1980—; mem. neurosurgery staff, Toure Infirmary, So. Bapt. Hosp., Pendelton Meml. Meth. Hosp., St. Jude Med. Ctr.; chmn. Neurosurgery dept. Tulane U. Med. Ctr. Hosp., 1980—, oper. rm. and exec. coms., 1980—; invited presenter in field; lectr. and expert in field. Contbr. articles to profl. jours.; featured on Miracle Workers, ABC, 2006. Fellow ACS; mem. AAAS, AMA, Am. Assn. Neurol. Surgeons, Am. Pain Soc., Am. Soc. for Stereotactic and Functional Neurosurgery, Assn. for Acad. Surgery, Congress Neurol. Surgeons, Internat. Assn. for Study Pain, Internat. Neurosurg. Soc., La. Neurol. Soc. (pres. 1979), La. State Med. Soc., Neuroelectric Soc., N.Y. Acad. Sci., Orleans Parish Med. Soc., Research Soc. Neurol. Surgeons, Royal Soc. Medicine, Soc. for Neurosci., So. Med. Assn., So. Neurosurg. Assn., Oscar Creek Surg. Soc., Midwest Pain Soc., Can. Neurosurg. Soc., Am. Acad. Pain Medicine, Alton Ochsner Med. Found. Soc., Soc. Neurol. Surgeons, La. Med. Rev. Found., Am. Acad. Clin. Neurophysiology, Alpha Omega Alpha. Lodges: Rotary. Achievements include first to pioneer in the field of brain stimulation for the treatment of chronic pain; performed the first deep brain stimulation for Parkinson's disease in the state of Louisiana; performed the first deep brain stimulation for Tourette's Syndrome in Louisiana, which was the second one performed in the US. Avocations: boating, travel, collecting art. Office: Tulane U Sch of Medicine Dept of Neurosurgery 1430 Tulane Ave New Orleans

LA 70112-2699 also: Tulane U Hosp and Clinic 1415 Tulane Ave New Orleans LA 70112 Address: Lakeview Regional Med Ctr 95 E Fairway Dr Covington LA 70433 Office Phone: 504-988-5565. Business E-Mail: der@tulane.edu.*

RICHARDSON, DUNCAN W., investment company executive; b. 1958; Grad., US Navel Acad., 1979; MBA, Harvard U., 1987. With Booz-Allen & Hamilton; joined Eaton Vance Corp., 1987, v.p., 1990—2000, sr. v.p., 2000—06, chief equity officer, 2001—, exec. v.p., 2006—. Spkr. in field; bd. dirs. Eaton Vance Corp., 2008—. Office: Eaton Vance Corp 255 State St Boston MA 02109*

RICHARDSON, EDWARD R., former academic administrator; b. Pensacola, Fla., Jan. 24, 1939; s. Edward H. and Doria (Parker) R.; m. Nell C.; children: Merit Lynn Richardson Smith, Laura Leigh. BS, Auburn U., 1962, MEd, 1967, EdD, 1972. Sci. tchr. Montgomery Pub. Schs., Montgomery, Ala., 1962-64, prin., 1967-70, Andalusia High Sch., Andalusia, Ala., 1972-80; asst. prof. Auburn U., Montgomery, Ala., 1980-82, interim pres., 2004—06, pres., 2006—07; supt. Auburn City Schs., Auburn, Ala., 1982-95; supt. edn. State of Ala., Montgomery, Ala., 1995—2004. Bd. mem. So. Regional Edn. Bd., Atlanta, 1989—; co-dir. Ala. Mgmt. Inst. Sch. Leaders, Montgomery, 1980-82. Ednl. advisor Gov. Guy Hunt, Montgomery, 1987—; active Landmarks Found., Montgomery, 1968-69. Named Supt. of Yr., State PTA, Montgomery, 1986-87, Educator of Yr., Andalusia Jaycees, 1973-74. Mem. Ala. Assn. Secondary Sch. Adminstrs. (pres. 1978-79), Ala. Assn. Sch. Adminstrs. (pres. 1986-87), Rotary (Auburn chpt. pres. 1987-88), Capitol Lions Club (pres. 1968-69), Phi Delta Kappa (Auburn U. chpt. pres. 1971-72). Republican. Methodist. Avocations: tennis, reading, gardening. Office Phone: 334-844-4650. E-mail: president@auburn.edu.

RICHARDSON, ERIC W., lawyer; b. Ft. Thomas, Ky., 1973; BA, Thomas More Coll., 1993; JD, U. Cin., 1996. Bar: Ohio 1996, Ky. 1997, US Supreme Ct., US Ct. of Appeals Sixth Cir., US Ct. of Appeals Fed. Cir., US Dist. Ct. Southern Dist. Ohio, US Dist. Ct. Eastern Dist. Ky., US Dist. Ct. Western Dist. Ky. Law clerk Hon. R. Guy Cole, Jr., US Ct. of Appeals Sixth Cir., 1996—97; ptnr. Vorys, Sater, Seymour and Pease LLp, Cin. Named one of Ohio's Rising Stars, Super Lawyers, 2006. Mem.: Ky. Bar Assn., Cin. Bar Assn., Order of Coif, Delta Epsilon Sigma. Office: Vorys Sater Seymur and Pease LLP Atrium Two Ste 2000 221 E Fourth St PO Box 0236 Cincinnati OH 45202-0236 Office Phone: 513-723-4019. Office Fax: 513-852-7885. E-mail: ewrichardson@ussp.com.

RICHARDSON, EVERETT VERN, hydraulic engineer, educator, administrator, consultant; b. Scottsbluff, Nebr., Jan. 5, 1924; s. Thomas Otis and Jean Marie (Everett) R.; m. Billie Ann Kleckner, June 23, 1948; children: Gail Lee, Thomas Everett, Jerry Ray. BS, Colo. State U., 1949, MS, 1960, PhD, 1965. Registered profl. engr., Colo. From hydraulic engr. to project chief US Geol. Survey, Wyo., 1949—52, Iowa, 1952—56, rsch. hydraulic engr., 1956—63, project chief Ft. Collins, Colo., 1963—68; adminstr. Engring. Rsch. Ctr. Colo. State U., Ft. Collins, 1968—88, dir. Egypt water use project, 1977-84, prof. in charge of hydraulic program, 1982-88, dir. hydraulic lab. Engring. Rsch. Ctr., 1982-88, prof. emeritus, 1988—, dir. Egypt irrigation improvement project, 1985-90; dir. Egypt Water Rsch. Ctr. Project, Ft. Collins, 1988-89; sr. assoc. Ayers Assocs. Inc. (formerly Resource Cons./Engr., Inc.), Ft. Collins, 1989—. Dir. Consortium for Internat. Devel., Tucson, 1972-87; developer stream stability and scour at hwy. bridges course for State Dept. Transps. for NHI, FHWA; investigator for NTSB 1987 I-90 bridge failure, NY, 1997, railroad bridge failure, Ariz., CALTRAN 1995 I-5 bridge failure; chmn. peer rev. panel Turnefairbanks Rsch. Ctr. Hydraulics Lab., 2004; cons. in field; lectr. in field. Sr. author Highways in the River Environment: Hydraulic and Environmental Considerations, FHWA, 1975, 1990, Evaluating Scour at Bridge, FHWA, 1991, 1993, 1995, 2001, FHWA Hydr. Design Series No. 6: River Engineering for Highway Encroachments, 2001, Civil Engring. Handbook, 1995; co-author: Engring. Handbook, 1995, 2003; contbr. Handbook of Fluid Dynamics and Fluid Machinery, 1996, Water Resources-Environmental Planning, Management and Development, 1996, more than 200 articles to profl. jours. Mem. Ft. Collins Water Bd., 1969-84; mem. NY State Bridge Safety Assurance Task Force, 1988-91. Decorated Bronze Star, Purple Heart, Combat Infantry Badge; named hon. diplomate Am. Acad. Water Resources Engring. 2005; U.S. Govt. fellow MIT, 1962-63. Fellow: ASCE (chair task com., bridge scour rsch. 1990—96, editor Compendium of Stream Stability and Scour Papers 1991—98, vice chair 1997—2002, J.S. Stevens award 1961, hydraulics divsn. task com. excellence award 1993, Hans Albert Einstein award 1996); mem.: Am. Acad. Water Resource Engrs. (hon. diplomate 2005), Internat. Congress for Irrigation and Drainage, Sigma Xi, Sigma Tau, Chi Epsilon. Home: 824 Gregory Rd Fort Collins CO 80524-1504 Office: Ayres Assocs PO Box 270460 Fort Collins CO 80527-0460 Office Phone: 970-223-5556. Personal E-mail: mudih2o@aol.com. Business E-Mail: richardsone@ayresassociates.com.

RICHARDSON, HERBERT HEATH, retired mechanical engineer, educator, dean, academic administrator; b. Lynn, Mass., Sept. 24, 1930; s. Walter Blake and Isabel Emily (Heath) R.; m. Barbara Ellsworth, Oct. 6, 1973. SB, SM with honors, MIT, 1955, ScD, 1958. Registered profl. engr., Mass., Tex. Rsch. asst., rsch. engr. Dynamic Analysis and Control Lab. MIT, 1953-57, instr. dept. mech. engring., 1957-58, mem. faculty, 1958-84, prof. mech. engring., 1968-85, head dept., 1974-82, assoc. dean engring., 1982-84; disting. prof. engring. Tex. A&M U. Sys., Coll. Sta., 1984—2006, regents prof., 1993—2006, dean, vice chancellor engring., 1984-85, dep. chancellor, dean, dir. Tex. Engring. Expt. Sta., 1985-91, chancellor, 1991-93, assoc. vice chancellor engring., assoc. dean engring., dir. Tex. Transit Inst., 1993—2006, dir. emeritus Tex. Transp. Inst., 2006—, disting. prof. engring. emeritus, chancellor emeritus, 2006—. With Ballistics Rsch. Lab. Abderdeen Proving Ground, Md., 1958; chief scientist U.S. Dept. Transp., 1970-72; chmn. adv. com. for engring. NSF, 1987-89, adv. com. basic energy scis. U.S. Dept. Energy, 1987-91. Author: Introduction to System Dynamics, 1971; contbr. articles to profl. publs. Trustee S.W. Rsch. Inst. Officer U.S. Army, 1968. Recipient medal Am. Ordnance Assn., 1953, Gold medal Pi Tau Sigma, 1963, Meritorious Svc. award and medal Dept. Transp., 1972, Disting. Svc. award Coun. U. Transp. Ctrs., 2006. Fellow AAAS, ASME (Moody award fluid engring. divsn. 1970, Centennial medallion 1983, Rufus Oldenberger medal 1984, Meritorious Svc. medal 1986, Disting. Svc. award 1986, hon. mem. 1987), Transp. Rsch. Bd. (Roy Crumm award 2007); mem. NAE (coun. 1986-92, com. on engring. edn.), Am. Soc. Engring. Edn. (Disting. Svc. medal 1993, Lamme award 1997), Nat. Rsch. Coun. (gov. bd. 1986-92, chmn. transp. rsch. bd. 1988-89), Nat. Acads. (nat. assoc., life), Sigma Xi, Tau Beta Pi. Office: Tex A&M U Sys MS 3135 College Station TX 77843-3135 Home Phone: 979-774-9616. E-mail: herbert-richardson@tamu.edu.

RICHARDSON, JAMES DAVID, surgeon; b. Morehead, Ky., 1945; MD, U. Ky., 1970. Diplomate Am. Bd. Surgeons, Am. Bd. Vascular Surgery, Am. Bd. Thoracic Surgery, Am. Bd. SCC. Intern U. Ky. Med. Ctr., Lexington, 1970, resident, 1971-72, U. Tex., San Antonio, 1972-76; surgeon Norton Hosp., Louisville, 1977—; prof. surgery U. Louisville, 1979—; pres. Am. Bd. Surgery, 1998-99. Past pres. So. Surg. Assn., Western Surg. Assn. Editor: (jour.) Am. Surgeon, 2005—. Fellow ACS (bd. regents); mem. AMA, Am. Assn. Surgery of Trauma, Soc. Surgergy Alimentary Tract, Alpha Omega Alpha. Office: U Louisville Dept Surgery 550 S Jackson St Louisville KY 40202-1622 Office Phone: 502-583-8303, 502-852-5452.

RICHARDSON, JAMES MICHAEL, lawyer; b. Hanford, Calif., Dec. 6, 1953; s. Louis Lee and June Richardson. BA, UCLA, 1977; JD, U. Tulsa, 1981. Bar: Tex. 1981, cert.: Tex. Bd. Legal Specialization (civil trial specialist) 2002, Nat. Bd. Trial Advocacy 2002. Atty. Fulbright & Jaworski, LLP, Houston, 1981—85; ptnr. Bankston, Wright & Greenhill, P.C., Austin, 1985—91, Maroney, Crowley, Bankston, Richardson & Hull, LLP, Austin, Tex., 1992—98, Bankston & Richardson, LLP, Austin, 1999—. Editor-in-chief Tulsa Law Rev., 1980—81. Recipient Outstanding Law Grad. award, 1980; named to Tex. Super Lawyer, Tex. Monthly, 2006, 2007—08. Fellow: Okla. Bar Assn., Austin Bar Assn. (bd. dirs. 1994—96), Tex. Bar Found. (life). Office: Bankston & Richardson LLP 400 West 15th St Ste 710 Austin TX 78701 Office Fax: 512-499-8886. Business E-Mail: jrichardson@bankrichlaw.com.

RICHARDSON, JASON ANTHONY, professional basketball player; b. Saginaw, Mich., Jan. 20, 1981; Attended, Mich. State U., East Lansing, 1999—2001. Guard Golden State Warriors, Oakland, Calif., 2001—07, Charlotte Bobcats, 2007—08, Phoenix Suns, 2008—. Named to NBA All-Rookie First Team, 2002. Achievements include member of the NCAA National Championship winning Michigan State University Spartans, 2000; winner of the NBA All-Star Slam Dunk Competition, 2002, 2003; leading the NBA in: 3-point field goals (243), 3-point field goal attempts (599), 2007. Office: Phoenix Suns 201 E Jefferson St Phoenix AZ 85034*

RICHARDSON, JOHN, retired international relations executive; b. Boston, Feb. 4, 1921; s. John and Hope (Hemenway) R.; m. Thelma Ingram, Jan. 19, 1945; children: Teren de Cossy, Hope Gravelly, Catherine Munch, Hetty L AB, Harvard U., 1943, JD, 1949. Bar: NY 1949. Assoc. Sullivan & Cromwell, NYC, 1949-55; with Paine, Webber, Jackson & Curtis, NYC, 1955-69, gen. ptnr., 1958-61, ltd. ptnr., 1961-69; pres., chief exec. officer Free Europe, Inc. (Radio Free Europe), 1961-68; asst. sec. for ednl. and cultural affairs Dept. State, 1969-77, also acting asst. sec. state for pub. affairs, 1971-73; exec. dir. for social policy Ctr. for Strategic and Internat. Studies; rsch. prof. internat. comm. Sch. Fgn. Svc., Georgetown U., Washington, 1977-78; pres., chief exec. officer Youth for Understanding, Inc., 1978-86, bd. dirs., 1986-98; counselor US Inst. of Peace, 1987-90. Spl. advisor Aspen Inst. Humanistic Studies, 1977—80. Founder Polish Med. Aid Project, 1957—61; co-founder, chmn. bd. Am. Com. to Aid Poland, 1989—95; pres. Internat. Rescue Com., 1960—61, bd. dirs., 1958—61, 1978—2004, bd. overseers, 2004—; chmn. Am. Coun. for UN U., 1977—87, Consortium for Internat. Citizens Exch., 1980—84, Delphi Internat., 1995—99, bd. dirs., 1999—2001; chmn., bd. dirs. Nat. Endowment for Democracy, 1984—88, 1991—92, chmn. emeritus, 1992—; bd. dirs. Freedom House, 1963—69, pres., 1977—84; mem. Coun. Fgn. Rels., 1957—; Citizens Commn. on S.E. Asian Refugees, 1978—85; bd. dirs. Fgn. Policy Assn., 1958—68, 1977—86, Japan-US Friendship Commn., 1976—77; chmn. NYC Met. Mission United Ch. of Christ, 1966—69; bd. dirs. Kennedy Ctr. for the Performing Arts, 1970—77, Inter-Am. Found., 1970—77, East-West Ctr., 1975—77, Am. Forum for Global Edn., 1977—, Social Sci. Found., U. Denver, 1992—2004, World Learning, 2001—05, Meridian House Internat., 1978—83, Atlantic Coun. U.S., 1982—84, Fgn. Student Svc. Coun., 1978—82, Coun. for Advancement of Citizenship, 1991—96, Coun. Cmty. of Democracies, 1996—, chmn., 1999—2001, chmn. emeritus, 2001—. With paratroops USAR, WWII. Decorated Bronze Star with v device, Japan Order of the Sacred Treasure, Gold and Silver Star; Germany Order of Merit, Commdr.'s Cross, Poland Order of Merit, Knight Cross. Home: 9707 Old Georgetown Rd Apt 1104 Bethesda MD 20814-1746 Home Phone: 301-896-0341.

RICHARDSON, JOHN CARROLL, lawyer, financial consultant; b. Mobile, Ala., May 3, 1932; s. Robert Felder and Louise (Simmons) R.; m. Cicely Tomlinson, July 27, 1961; children: Nancy Louise, Robert Felder III, Leslie. BA, Tulane U., 1954; LLB cum laude, Harvard U., 1960. Bar: Colo. 1960, N.Y. 1965, D.C. 1972. Assoc. Holland & Hart, Denver, 1960-64; legal v.p. Hoover Worldwide Corp., NYC, 1964-69; v.p., gen. counsel Continental Investment Corp., Boston, 1969; dep. tax legis. counsel U.S. Dept. Treasury, Washington, 1970-71, tax legis. counsel, 1972-73; ptnr. Brown, Wood, Ivey, Mitchell & Petty, NYC, 1973-79, LeBoeuf, Lamb, Leiby & MacRae, NYC, 1979-88, Morgan, Lewis & Bockius, NYC, 1988-93; ret., 1993. Tax legis. cons., Orford, N.H., 1993—; adj. prof. Law Sch. Fordham U., 1990-94. Served to lt. comdr. USN, 1954-58. Mem. ABA (chmn. com. adminstrv. practice tax sect. 1984-86), N.Y. State Bar Assn. (exec. com. tax sect. 1975-84), D.C. Bar Assn., Am. Coll. Tax Counsel, N.Y. Athletic Club. Office Phone: 603-353-4608. Personal E-mail: jctr@together.net.

RICHARDSON, JOHN VINSON, JR., library and information science professor; b. Columbus, Ohio, Dec. 27, 1949; s. John Vinson Sr. and Hope Irene (Smith) R.; m. Nancy Lee Brown, Aug. 22, 1971. BA, Ohio State U., 1971; MLS, Peabody Coll., 1972; PhD, Ind. U., 1978. Asst. prof. UCLA, 1978-83, assoc. prof., 1983-98, editor The Libr. Quar., 1994—2003, editor emeritus, 2003—, prof., 1998—, assoc. dean grad. divsn., 2002—07, mem. editl. bd., The Libr. Quar., 2004—08. Faculty coord. UCLA-St. Petersburg State Acad. of Culture Exch. Program, 1996—; fellow advanced rsch. Inst. U. Ill., 1991; pres. Info. Transfer, Inglewood, Calif., 1988—; vis. fellow Charles Sturt U. NSW Australia, 1990; vis. scholar ALISE Russia Project, St. Petersburg and Moscow, 1996; vis. disting. scholar OCLC Inc., Dublin, Ohio, 1996-97; presidential scholar, Libr. Sys. & Svcs., LLC, 2002—03; chmn. Calif. Pacific Ann. Conf. Com. on Archives and History, 1992-96; Henderson lectr. U. N.C., Chapel Hill, 1997; mem. UCLA Privilege and Tenure, 1999-2000, chair, 2000-02; Fulbright sr. specialist Vladivostok State U. Econ. and Svc., Russia, 2005.; cons. to U.S. Dept of State, Vladivostok, 2000, Uganda and Zambia, 2001, Eritrea, 2003, Turkmenistan, 2005. Author: Spirit of Inquiry, 1982, Government Information, 1987, Gospel of Scholarship, 1992, Knowledge-based Systems for General Reference Work, 1995, Understanding Reference Transactions, 2002; mem. editl. bd. Ref. Svcs. Rev., Ann Arbor, Mich., 1991—, Jour. Govt. Info., Oxford, Eng., 1975-2005, Index to Current Urban Documents, Westport, Conn., 1987—, U. Calif. Press Catalogues and Bibliographies series, 1994-97, Jour. Edn. for Libr. and Info. Sci., 2005-07. Mem. UCLA Grad. Coun., 1992-96, chair, 1995-96; mem. U. Calif. systemwide coord. com. on grad. affairs, 1993-96; pres. Wesley Found., L.A., 1981-87; lay del. Cal-Pac Conf. United Meth. Ch., 1985, 86, 92-96, chair conf. commn. on archives and history, 1992—96. Rsch. grantee Coun. on Libr. Resources, 1985, 90, Assn. Libr. and Info. Sci. Educators rsch. grantee, 1984, 87, 98, Online Computer Libr. Ctr. Libr. and Info. Sci. rsch. grantee, 1999; Harold Lancour scholar Beta Phi Mu, 1986, 99, Kaliper Sr. scholar U. Mich., 1998-99, Presdl. scholar Libr. Systems and Svcs. LLC, 2002—03; recipient Louise Maxwell award Ind. U. Alumni Assn., 1995. Mem. ALA (Justin Winsor prize 1990, Ref. and Adult Svcs. divsn. Outstanding Paper award 1992), AAAS, Assn. Libr. and Info. Sci. Educators (rsch. paper prize 1986, 91, rsch. grants 1984, 87, 98), Am. Soc. for Info. Sci. (Best Info. Sci. book 1995), Am. Assn. Adv. Slavic Studies, Sigma Xi. Democrat. Avocations: wine tasting, bread baking, reading, foreign travel. Office: UCLA GSE&IS DIS Campus Box 951520 Los Angeles CA 90095-1520 Office Phone: 310-206-9369. Business E-Mail: jrichard@ucla.edu. *By our common action, we can bend the flow of history.*

RICHARDSON, JOSEPH HILL, physician, medical educator; b. Rensselaer, Ind., June 16, 1928; s. William Clark and Vera (Hill) R.; m. Joan Grace Meininger, July 8, 1950; children: Lois N., Ellen M., James K. MS in Medicine, Northwestern U., 1950, MD, 1953. Diplomate Am. Bd. Internal Medicine. Intern U.S. Naval Hosp., Great Lakes, Ill., 1953-54; physician internal medicine, hematology pvt. practice, Marion, Ind., 1959-67, Ft. Wayne, Ind., 1967—. Assoc. clin. prof. medicine Ind. U. Sch. Medicine, 1993—; founding mem. The Reviewing Physician Group, 2001—08. Contbr. articles to profl. jours. Fellow in medicine Cleve. Clinic, 1956-59. Fellow: AAAS, ACP; mem.: AMA, Masons. Home and Office: 8726 Fortuna Way Fort Wayne IN 46815-5725 Office Phone: 260-485-1391.

RICHARDSON, JOSEPH J., JR., insurance company executive; b. Pa. BA, Temple U., Phila. Joined Allstate Ins. Co., 1977, various positions in distbn., claims and underwriting, chmn. Allstate NJ, CEO Allstate Floridian, v.p. Eastern Market Operating Com., sr. v.p. protection distbn., 2008—. Bd. mem. Allstate Bank, ALLPAC. Bd. mem., treas. Nat. Adoption Ctr., Phila. Office: Allstate Ins Co Corp Hdqs 2775 Sanders Rd Northbrook IL 60062 Office Phone: 847-402-5000.*

RICHARDSON, JUDY MCEWEN, investment banker, consultant; b. Appleton, Wis., June 3, 1947; d. John Mitchell and Isabel Annette (Ruble) McEwen; m. Larry Leroy Richardson, Mar. 19, 1972 (div. Oct. 1983). BA in English, Stanford U., 1968, MA in Edn., 1969; PhD in Higher Edn., U. Wash., 1975. Dir. ednl. rsch. St. Olaf Coll., Northfield, Minn., 1975-79; evaluation specialist Northwest Regional Ednl. Laboratory, Portland, 1980-82; legis. rsch. analyst Ariz. State Sen., Phoenix, 1982-87; dir. sch. fin. Ariz. Dept. Edn., Phoenix, 1987-92, assoc. supt., 1992-94; ednl. cons. Scottsdale, Ariz., 1994-96; exec. dir. Ariz. State Bd. for Sch. Capital Facilities, Phoenix, 1996-98; sch. fin. cons. Peacock, Hislop, Staley & Given, Phoenix, 1998—2002; v.p. Stone & Youngberg, Phoenix, 2002—. Cartoonist for the Ariz. Capitol Times, 1995-96. Office: Stone & Youngberg LLC 2555 E Camelback Rd Ste 280 Phoenix AZ 85016 Office Phone: 602-794-4012. Business E-Mail: jrichardson@syllc.com.

RICHARDSON, JULIE G., private equity firm executive; b. Mpls., 1963; married. BA, U. Wis., Madison, 1985; PhD in Fin., Stanford U. Grad. Sch. Bus. Mng. dir. Merrill Lynch & Co., Inc., 1986—98; vice chmn., co-chair JP Morgan Chase & Co., NYSE, 1998—2003; mng. dir. Providence Equity Partners Co., Providence, 2003—. Named one of 40 Under 40, Crain's NY Bus., 1999, The 100 Most Influential Women in NYC Bus., 2007. Office: Providence Equity Partners Co 50 Kennedy Plaza, 18th Flr Providence RI 02903*

RICHARDSON, LAURA A., United States Representative from California; b. LA, Apr. 14, 1962; m. Anthony W. Batts (div.). BA in Polit. Sci., UCLA, 1984; MBA, U. So. Calif., 1996. With Xerox Corp., 1987—2001; So. Calif. dir. office Lt. Gov. Cruz Bustamante State of Calif., 2001—06; mem. Calif. State Assembly from Dist. 55, 2006—07, asst. spkr. Pro Tempore Leadership Team, 2006—, mem. budget, human svcs., utilities & commerce, govt. orgn., and joint legis. budget coms.; mem. US Congress from 37th Calif. Dist., 2007—, mem. sci. & tech. com., transp. & infrastructure com. Field dep. to congresswoman Juanita Millender-McDonald US Congress, 1997; mem. Long Beach City Coun., 2000—06. Named to Power 150, Ebony mag., 2008. Mem.: Calif. Mfg. & Tech. Assn. (bd. mem.). Democrat. Methodist. Office: US Congress 2233 Rayburn House Office Bldg Washington DC 20515 also: PO Box 50080 Long Beach CA 90815*

RICHARDSON, LAUREL WALUM, sociology educator; b. Chgo., July 15, 1938; d. Tyrrell Alexander and Rose (Foreman) R.; m. Herb Walum, Dec. 27, 1959 (div. 1972); children: Benjamin, Joshua; m. Ernest Lockridge, Dec. 12, 1981. AB, U. Chgo., 1955, BA, 1956; PhD, U. Colo., 1963. Asst. prof. Calif. State U., Los Angeles, 1962-64; postdoctoral fellow Sch. Medicine Ohio State U., Columbus, 1964-65, asst. prof. sociology, 1970-75, assoc. prof., 1975-79; prof. sociology Sch. Medicine Ohio State U., Columbus, 1979—, prof. cultural studies, edn. policy and leadership; asst. prof. sociology Denison U., Granville, Ohio, 1965-69. Mem. editl. bd. Jour. Contemporary Ethnography, Symbolic Interaction, Gender and Soc., Qualitative Sociology, The Sociol. Quar.; disting. lectr. Acad. Creative Writing, U. Iceland, 2005; Miegunyah disting. fellow U. Melbourne, 2006. Author: Dynamics of Sex and Gender, 1977, 3d edit. 1988, The New Other Woman, 1985, Die Neve Andere, 1987, A Nova Outra Mulher, 1987, Writing Strategies: Reaching Diverse Audiences, 1990, Gender and University Teaching: A Negotiated Difference, 1995; editor: Feminist Frontiers, 1983, 5th edit., 2000, Fields of Play Constructing an Academic Life, 1997 (Charles H. Cooley award for best sociology book 1998), (with Ernest Lockridge) Travels with Ernest: Crossing the Literary/Sociological Divide, 2004, Last Writes: A Daybook for a Dying Friend, 2007; assoc. editor Symbolic Interaction; author more than 120 rsch. articles and papers. Ford Found. fellow, 1954-56; NSF dissertation fellow, 1960-62; post doctoral fellow Vocat. Rehab., Columbus, 1964; grantee Ohio Dept. Health, 1986-87, Nat. Inst. Edn., 1981-82, NIMH, 1972-74, NSF, 1963-64, NEH, 1992; internat. fellow Copenhagen, 2000, Iceland, 2005, Miengalow Fellow, Melbourne, 2006; recipient Disting. Affirmative Action award Ohio State U., 1983, Feminist Mentor award, 1998. Mem. Am. Sociol. Assn. (com. on coms. 1980-81, com. on pub. info. 1987—), North Ctrl. Sociol. Assn. (pres. 1986-87), Sociologists for Women in Soc. (coun. mem. 1978-80), Ctrl. Ohio Sociologists for Women in Soc. (past pres.), Women's Poetry Workshop, Soc. for Study of Symbolic Interaction (publs. com.). Avocations: hiking, poetry, book arts. E-mail: richardson.9@osu.edu.

RICHARDSON, LEATRICE JOY, artist; b. NYC, Dec. 26, 1940; d. Sidney and Ottila (Moldovan) Mayer; m. Robert John Richardson, Aug. 7, 1965; children: Todd Harper, Tiffany Jill. Student, Chouinard Art Inst., LA, 1960—65. Tchr. art Calif. Inst. Art, Thousand Oaks. Tchr. Figure in Watercolor Calif. Art Inst., 2006. Group shows and exhbns. include: Akron Soc. Artists, 1998, Houston Watercolor Soc., 1994, 97, 98, 99, 2002, La. Watercolor Soc., 1996, Midwest Watercolor Soc., 1993, 95, 97, 98, 99, Miss. Watercolor Soc., 1994, Nat. Assn. Women Artists, N.Y.C., Northwest Watercolor Soc., 1994, 95, San Diego Watercolor Soc., 1995, Taos Nat. Exhbn. of Watercolor II, 1996, Watercolor USA, 1996, We. Colo. Watercolor Soc., 1995, We. Fedn. of Watercolor Socs., 1996, 99, 2001, Nat. Watercolor Soc. Viva Gallery, 2006, Watercolor West Exhbn., 2009, others; publs. include People in Watercolor, 1996, Best of Watercolor: Painting Color, 1997, Internat. Artists Mag., Apr./May, 2002; One Woman Show "Stodioc" Thousand, Oaks, CA. Recipient 2d award Houston Watercolor Soc., 1997, Art Study Club award Miss. Watercolor Soc., 1994, Northwest Watercolor Soc., Margaret Malloy Merit award, 1994, Svoir Faire, Lana Paper Merchandise award 1992, Winsor Newton Merchandise award 1994, 2000-01 Mem.: Nat. Assn. Women Artists (Miriam Russo Enders award 2004), Women Painters West, Midwest Watercolor Soc. (Jack Richeson & Co. Merit award 1995), Watercolor West (Founders award 2001—02, San Diego Watercolor award 1991). Avocations: films, animation. Home and Office: 3540 Ridgeford Dr Westlake Village CA 91361-4820 Office Phone: 818-889-8835. Personal E-mail: cartoonbiz@roadrunner.com.

RICHARDSON, M. CATHERINE, lawyer; b. Syracuse, NY, July 14, 1941; d. George Lynch and Margaret (Mansfield) R. BS, SUNY, 1963; MA, U. No. Colo., 1969; JD magna cum laude, Syracuse U., 1977; LLD (hon.), SUNY, 2005. Bar: NY 1978, SUNY Oswego, 1963, US Dist. Ct. (ND dist.) NY 1978, NY Ct. Appeals (2d cir.) 1982. Math. tchr. Westhill HS, NY, 1963-67, Jamesville-Dewitt (NY) HS, 1969-74; lawyer Bond, Schoeneck & King, PLLC, Syracuse, 1977—2003; ret., 2003. Mem. com. on profession and the cts. and profl. edn. project Chief Judge State NY With St. Camillus Health and Rehab. Ctr.; Frank H. Hiscock Legal Aid Soc. (pres. 1994-96, bd.dir.); mem. Syracuse Rsch. Corp. Recipient Take the Lead award Ctrl. NY Girl Scout Coun., 1988, Athena award Greater Syracuse C. of C. Small Bus. Bur., 1989, Spirit of Am. Women award Girls Inc. of Ctrl. NY, 1994, Syracuse Law Rev.'s Alumni Achievement award, 1995; named Outstanding Alumni SUNY Oswego, 1995; Kate Stoneman award, Albany Law Sch., 1996. Fellow ABA (bd. govs.; 2003-06), Am. Bar Found., NY State Bar Found. (bd. dirs. 1992—, Ruth G. Shapiro award 2002); mem. NY State Bar Assn. (pres. 1996-97), NY State Jud. Inst., Hist. Soc. Cts. State NY, Onondaga County Bar Assn. (pres. 1987, Pro Bono award), Onondaga County Bar Found. (bd. dirs.), Lambda Sigma Tau, Kappa Delta Pi, Delta Kappa Gamma, Phi Kappa Phi, Justinian Hon. Law Soc., Ordr of Coif. Office: Bond Schoeneck & King LLP One Lincoln Ctr Syracuse NY 13202 Home Phone: 315-428-0521; Office Phone: 315-218-8230. Business E-Mail: crichardson@bsk.com.

RICHARDSON, MARGARET MILNER, lawyer; b. Waco, Tex., May 14, 1943; d. James W. and Margaret Wiebusch Milner; m. John L. Richardson, July 22, 1967; 1 child, Margaret Lawrence. AB in Polit. Sci., Vassar Coll., 1965; JD with honors, George Washington U., 1968. Bar: Va. 1968, D.C. 1968, U.S. Dist. Ct. D.C. 1968, U.S. Ct. Appeals (4th, 5th, D.C. and Fed. cirs.) 1968, U.S. Claims Ct. 1969, U.S. Tax Ct. 1970, U.S. Supreme Ct. 1971. Clk. U.S. Ct. Claims, Washington; with Office Chief Counsel IRS, Washington, 1969-77; with Sutherland, Asbill and Brennan, Washington, 1977-80, ptnr., 1980-93; commr. IRS, Washington, 1993-97; ptnr. Ernst & Young, Washington, 1997—2003. Mem. commr.'s adv. group IRS, 1988-90, chair, 1990; bd. advisors George Washington Law Sch.; mem. D.C. Bar Commn. on Multidisciplinary Practice, Presdl. Commn. on Holocaust Assets; bd. dirs. Legg Mason, Inc., JacksonHewitt, Eurasia Found., former chair, USA4UNHC. Contbr. articles to profl. jours. Assisted Clinton 1992 primary and gen. election campaign; served as team leader Justice Dept./Civil Rights Cluster during Presdl. Transition; mem. bd. Mayor's Transition Team, 1998, Women's Campaign Fund, Nat. Cathedral Sch., Hosp. for Sick Children; trustee Eurasia Found., USA for UNHCR, U.S.-Russia Bus. Coun., 1999-03; mem. bd. dirs. Nat. Mus. Women in the Arts, Protestant Episcopal Cathedral Found. Piedmont Environ. Coun. Mem. ABA, D.C. Bar Assn. (tax sect.), Va. State Bar, Fed. Bar Assn. (com. taxation), Fin. Women's Assn. N.Y., Washington Women's Forum. Avocations: travel, antiques, needlepoint, gardening. Home Phone: 540-364-0241. Personal E-mail: margaretrichardson@yahoo.com.

RICHARDSON, MARK P., protective services official, educator; b. St. Paul, June 27, 1962; m. Mary K Sanford, Oct. 8, 1988; children: Lara S., Sonja S. BS, St. Cloud State U., Minn., 1992; Med, St. Mary's U., Minn., 1998; JD, William Mitchell Coll. of Law, Minn., 2004. Tchr. Ind. Sch. Dist. #728, Elk River, Minn., 1993—; firefighter Elk River Fire Dept., Minn., 1997—. E-5 staff sargeant USAF, 1982—86, Ramstein Airbase, Germany. Avocations: Karate, scuba diving, horseback riding, travel. Office: Ind Sch Dist #728 900 School St Elk River MN 55330 E-mail: mrichardson@elkriver.k12.mn.us.

RICHARDSON, MARTHA (MARCIE) KIRK, obstetrician, gynecologist; b. Peterborough, NH, Sept. 12, 1949; Grad., Radcliffe Coll.; MD, U. Calif. San Diego Sch. Medicine, 1974. Intern, ob-gyn. Cambridge Hosp., 1974—75; resident & dept. gen. obstetrics & gynecology Beth Israel Deaconess Hosp., Mass., 1975—79; dir. menopause consultation svc. Harvard Vanguard Med. Assocs., asst. med. dir. dept. obstetrics & gynecology; clinical instr. obstetrics & gynecology Harvard Med. Sch., 1980—. Adv. bd. Harvard Women's Health Watch. Editorial adv. Our Bodies, Ourselves: Menopause, 2006. Mem.: North Am. Menopause Soc. (bd. trustees, former chmn. edn. com.). Office: 165 Dartmouth St Boston MA 02116-3502 Office Phone: 617-859-5250. Office Fax: 617-859-5051.*

RICHARDSON, MARY L., psychotherapist; b. Topeka, Oct. 4, 1953; d. Darrell and Beverly Nutter; m. Kenneth T. Richardson Jr. children: Shad Martin, Cheralyn Pasbrig, Kenneth T. Richardson III, Russ Richardson. BS in Addictions Counseling, Westbrook U., W.Va., 2001, MPhil in Transpersonal Psychology. Lic. ind. substance abuse counselor, Ariz. State Behavioral Health; cert. Ariz. Bd. Cert. Addictions Counselors, IROC, cert. Internat. Addictions Counselor, cert. addictions counselor, Hawaii. Counselor The Meadows Treatment Ctr., Phoenix, 1986-88; co-founder Co-Dependents Anonymous, 1986—; co-founder, adminstr. The Orion Found., 1988—90; co-owner Phoenix Cons. & Counseling Assocs., Ariz., 1989—; lectr. workshop presenter Las Vegas Recovery Ctr., Nev. Founder, adminstr. The Orion Found., Ariz.; project mem. The Hutoomkhum Com. and Support Program, Hopi Reservation, Ariz.; cons. Baywood Hosp., 1988-89; faculty instr. The Recovery Source, 1989-90; chair Nat. Conv. Women, 1992; facilitator Your Healing Journey Workshop, 2002-. Author: Women's Acts of Power, 1991-93, Relationship Recover, 1992—, Women's Empowerment, 1992—, Body, Mind & Spirit, 1994—. Mem. Nat. Assn. Alcoholism & Drug Abuse Counselors, Nat. Reciprocity Consortium. Avocations: writing, sculpting, dance, herbology. Office: 1121 E Missouri Ave #125 Phoenix AZ 85014 Office Phone: 602-230-8994.

RICHARDSON, MICHAEL, physics professor, department chairman; b. Glendale, Calif., Apr. 23, 1945; s. Bruce and Zelta Richardson; m. Jane Sherriff, Aug. 1, 1986; children: Christine, Russell. MA in Math., Calif. State U., Sacramento, 1971; MA in Physics, U. Calif., Davis, 1974. Physics prof. Sacramento City Coll., 1986—, physics dept. chmn., 1990—. Mem.: Planetary Soc., Union Concerned Scientists. Office: Sacramento City Coll 3835 Freeport Blvd Sacramento CA 95822 Business E-Mail: richarm@scc.losrios.edu.

RICHARDSON, MIRANDA, actress; b. Lancashire, Eng., Mar. 3, 1958; Studied, Drama Program Bristol. Stage performances include Moving, All My Sons, Who's Afraid of Virginia Woolf, The Life of Einstein, A Lie of the Mind, Edmond, Insignificance, Aunt Dan & Lemon, The Changeling, Mountain Language, Educating Rita, The Maids, The Designated Mourner, Etta Jenks, Erasser of A Thousand Colors; actor(TV appearances): The Hard Word, Sorrel and Son, A Woman of Substance, Underworld, Death of the Heart, The Scold's Bridle, 1998, Merlin, 1998, Alice, 1999,: (TV series) Black Adder II & III, Sweet as You Are, The Life and Times of Vivian Vyle, 2007; (TV miniseries) Die Kinder, The James Bond Story, 1999, (voice): The Miracle Maker, 2000,: (films) Dance with a Stranger, 1985, The Innocent, 1986, Empire of the Sun, 1987, Eat the Rich, 1987, Twisted Obsession, 1990, The Bachelor, 1991, Enchanted April, 1992 (Golden Globe award), Damage, 1992 (B.A.F.T.A. award for Best Supporting Actress, Acad. award nominee for Best Supporting Actress), The Crying Game, 1992, Fatherland, HBO, 1994 (Golden Globe award), Tom & Viv, 1994 (Acad. award nominee for best actress, 1995), La Nuit et Le Moment, 1994, Kansas City, 1996, The Evening Star, 1996, Swann, 1996, Saint-Ex, 1997, The Apostle, 1997, The Designated Mourner, 1997, All for Love, 1998, Jacob Two Two and the Hooded Fang, 1998, Sleepy Hollow, 1999, Blackadder Back and Forth, 1999, Get Carter, 2000, Spider, 2001, The Hours, 2001, Rage on Placid Lake, 2002, Young Victoria, 2007, The Lost Prince, 2002, Chicken Run, 2000, Snow White, 2000, The Actors, 2002, Falling Angels, 2003, The Prince and Me, 2003, Phantom of the Opera, 2003, Churchill The Hollywood Years, 2003, Wah-Wah, 2004, Harry Potter and the Goblet of Fire, 2005, Gideon's Daughter, 2005, Provoked, 2005, Merlin's Apprentice, 2005, Final Chance To Save, 2005, Southland Tales, 2005, Spinning Into Butter, 2006, Puffball, 2006, Fred Claus, 2007, Young Victoria, 2008, Dagenham Girls, 2009. Address: c/o Paul Lyon Maris 76 Oxford St London W1D 1BS England Office Phone: 0207 636 6565.

RICHARDSON, RICHARD COLBY, JR., leadership and policy studies educator, researcher; b. Burlington, Vt., Sept. 10, 1933; s. Richard Colby and Florence May (Barlow) R.; m. Patricia Ann Barnhart, Dec. 21, 1954; children: Richard Colby III, Michael Donald, Christopher Robin. BS, Castleton State Coll., 1954; MA, Mich. State U., 1958; PhD, U. Tex., 1963; LittD (hon.), Lafayette Coll., 1973. Instr., counselor Vt. Coll., Montpelier, 1958-61; dean instrn. Forest Park C.C., St. Louis, 1963-67; pres. Northampton County Area C.C., Bethlehem, Pa., 1967-77; chmn. dept. higher edn. and adult edn. Ariz. State U., Tempe, 1977-84, prof. edn. leadership and policy studies, 1984-99, prof. emeritus, 1999—; prof. higher edn. NYU, 1999—, chair Dept. of Adminstrn., Leadership and Tech., 2003—08. Jr. author: The Two Year College: A Social Synthesis, 1965; sr. author: Governance for the Two-Year College, 1972, Functional Literacy in the College Setting, 1981, Literacy in the Open Access College, 1983, Fostering Minority Access and Achievement in Higher Education, 1987, Achieving Quality and Diversity, 1991, Designing State Higher Education Systems for a New Century, 1999, Policy and Performance in America Higher Education: An Examination of Cases Across State Systems, 2009. Bd. dirs. Easton Hosp., 1973-77, v.p., 1975-77; exec. coun. Minsi Trails coun. Boy Scouts Am., Bethlehem, 1973-77; bd. trustees First Presbyn. Ch. N.Y.C., 2004-06. Named Disting. Grad., Coll. Edn., U. Tex., Austin, 1982; recipient Outstanding Rsch. Publ. award Coun. Univ. and Colls.-Am. Assn. Cmty. and Jr. Colls., 1983, Disting. Svc. award, 1984. Mem. Am. Assn. Higher Edn. (charter life, dir. 1970-73), AAUP, Assn. for Study of Higher Edn. (bd. dirs. 1984), Am. Assn. Cmty. and Jr. Colls. (dir. 1980-83). Democrat. Office: New York Univ Dept Adminstrn Leadership & Technology New York NY 10003-6674 Home Phone: 212-533-0393; Office Phone: 212-998-5640. Business E-Mail: richard.richardson@nyu.edu.

RICHARDSON, RICHARD JUDSON, retired political science professor; b. Poplar Bluff, Mo., Feb. 16, 1935; s. Jewell Judson and Naomi Fern (Watson) R.; m. Sammie Sue Cullum, Dec. 29, 1961; children: Jon Mark, Anna Cecile, Ellen Elizabeth, Megan Leigh. BS, Harding Coll., Searcy, Ark., 1957; cert., U. Dublin, Trinity Coll., Ireland, 1958; MA, Tulane U., New Orleans, 1961, PhD, 1967. Instr. Tulane U., 1962—65; asst. prof. polit. sci. Western Mich. U., Kalamazoo, 1965, assoc. prof., 1967—69; vis. assoc. prof. U. Hawaii, 1967—68; Burton Craige prof. UNC, Chapel Hill, 1985—90, assoc. v.p. acad. affairs univ. gen. adminstrn., 1991—92, chmn. dept. Adj. prof. Duke U., Durham, 1972-74; provost, vice chancellor acad. affairs U. N.C., 1995-2000; cons. in field. Author: (with Kenneth Vines) The Politics of Federal Courts, 1971, (with Darlene Walker) People and the Police, 1973, (with Marian Irish, James Prothro) The Politics of American Democracy, 1981. Del. County Dem. Conv., 1972, 83; vice chmn. Dem. Party Precinct, 1983-85; chmn. bldg. fund YMCA, 1976; chmn. Carolina Challenge for endowment U. N.C., Chapel Hill, 1979-80; chmn. U. N.C. Bicentennial Observance, 1991-94; chmn. United Way, 1983, pres., 1985; pres. PTA County Coun., 1984. Recipient Edward S. Corwin award Am. Polit. Sci. Assn., 1967, Tanner Disting. Teaching award U. N.C., 1972, Univ. award for Outstanding Teaching, 1981, Thomas Jefferson award, 1987, James Johnston Disting. Tchg. award, 1993, Alumni Faculty Disting. Svc. award, 1994, Disting. Eagle Scout award Boy Scouts Am., 1998, Laura Thomas award, 1999, C. Knox Massey award, 2000, Disting. Svc. medal U. N.C. Alumni Assn., 2001, William Richardson Davie award, 2005; named life regent Boy Scouts Am., 1998; Edgar Stern fellow, 1959-61; Paul Harris fellow, Rotary Internat. Found. 2008, Humanity award Rotary Internat. Global Svc., 2009; NEH grantee, 1970 Mem. N.C. Polit. Sci. Assn. (pres. 1978-79), Am. Polit. Sci. Assn., So. Polit. Sci. Assn., ACLU (bd. dirs. local chpt. 1985-88, state bd. dirs. 1988-89), Order of Janus, Order of the Long Leaf Pine, Order of Golden Fleece, Order of the Grail. Home: 234 Terrells Creek Ln Pittsboro NC 27312-5145

RICHARDSON, ROBERT, cinematographer; b. Hyannis, Mass., Aug. 27, 1955; m. Monica Wali (div.); 3 children. BFA, RI Sch. Design; MFA, Am. Film Inst. Cinematographer: (films) An Outpost of Progress, 1982, Salvador, 1986, Platoon, 1986 (Academy Award Nomination for Best Cinematography 1986), Wall Street, 1987, Dudes, 1987, Eight Men Out, 1988, Talk Radio, 1988, Born on the Fourth of July, 1989 (Academy Award Nomination for Best Cinematography 1989), City of Hope, 1991, The Doors, 1991, JFK, 1991 (Academy Award for Best Cinematography 1991), A Few Good Men, 1992, Heaven and Earth, 1993, Natural Born Killers, 1994, Casino, 1995, Nixon, 1995, U-Turn, 1997, Fast, Cheap & Out of Control, 1997, Wag the Dog, 1997, The Horse Whisperer, 1998, Snow Falling on Cedars, 1999, Bringing Out the Dead, 1999, The Hire: Power Keg, 2001, The Four Feathers, 2002, Kill Bill: Vol. 1, 2003, Kill Bill:Vol. 2, 2004, The Aviator, 2004 (Academy Award for Best Cinematography, 2005), The Good Shepherd, 2006, Shine A Light, 2008; (documentaries) Standard Operating Procedure, 2008; exec. prodr.: (films) The Wind Effect, 2003 Mem.: Am. Soc. Cinematographers.

RICHARDSON, ROBERT COLEMAN, physics professor, researcher; b. Washington, June 26, 1937; s. Robert Franklin and Lois (Price) R.; m. Betty Marilyn McCarthy, Sept. 2, 1962; children: Jennifer, Pamela. BS in Physics, Va. Poly. Inst. and State U., 1958, MS, 1960; PhD in Physics, Duke U., 1966; PhD (hon.), Ohio State U., 2000. Research assoc. Cornell U., Ithaca, NY, 1966-67, asst. prof., 1968-71, assoc. prof., 1972-74, prof., Low Temp. Physics, 1975—86, Floyd R. Newman prof. physics, 1987—, dir., Lab. of Atomic and Solid State Physics, 1990—97, vice provost for rsch. Ithaca, NY, 1998—. Chmn. Internat. Union Pure and Applied Physics Commn. (C-5), 1981-84; mem. bd. assessment Nat. Bur. Standards, 1983—; vis. scientist Bell Labs., Murray Hill, N.J., 1984; mem. adv. panel for MIT v.p. rsch., 1998-; mem. NASA Life and Microgravity Sci. and Applications Adv. Panel, 1999-; mem. Internat. Space Station Mgmt. and Cost Evaluation Task Force, NASA, 2001-02; trustee Duke U., 1997—, exec. com. bd. trustees, 2001—; bd. dirs. Brookhaven Sci. Assocs.; mem. ecec. com. of sr. rsch. officers, Am. Assn. Univs., 2002-. Author: Experimental Techniques in Condensed Matter Physics at Low Temperatures, 1988, (videotape lectr.); College Physics, 2003; mem. editorial bd. Jour. of Low Temperature Physics, 1984—. Served to 2d lt. U.S. Army, 1959-60. Guggenheim fellow 1975-76, 82-83; recipient Simon Meml. prize Brit. Phys. Soc., 1976, Dinting. Grad. Sch. Alumnus Award, Va. Polytechnic Inst. and State U.; co-recipient Nobel prize in physics, 1996; commendation, Va. Gen. Assembly, 1988. Fellow AAAS (bd. dirs. 2000—), Am. Phys. Soc. (Oliver E. Buckley prize 1981), Am. Philos. Soc, Am. Acad. Arts & Scis.; mem. NAS, Nat. Sci. Bd. (exec. com. 2000—); Finnish Acad. Sci. & Letters. Achievements include research in experimental low temperature physics, especially the properties of liquids and solids at sub-millikelvin temperatures. Avocations: photography, gardening. Office: Cornell U Lab of Atomic and Solid Physics 529A Clark Hall Ithaca NY 14853-2501*

RICHARDSON, ROBERT DALE, JR., language educator; b. Milw., June 14, 1934; s. Robert Dale and Lucy Baldwin (Marsh) R.; m. Elizabeth Hall, Nov. 7, 1959 (div. 1987); m. Annie Dillard, Dec. 10, 1988; children: Elisabeth, Anne, Rose. AB magna cum laude in English, Harvard U., 1956, PhD in English Lit., 1961; DHL (hon.), Meadville-Lombard Theol. Sch., 2003, U. Denver, 2008. Instr. English Harvard U., Cambridge, Mass., 1961-63; asst. prof. English U. Denver, 1963-68, assoc. prof., 1968-72, prof., 1972-87, Lawrence C. Phipps prof. humanities, 1979-82, chmn. dept., 1968-73, pres. Univ. senate, 1972-73, assoc. dean grad. studies, 1975-76; prof. English, U. Colo., Boulder, 1987; vis. prof. letters Wesleyan U., Middletown, Conn., 1989-94. Vis. prof. Harvard U., summer 1976, CUNY, 1978, Sichuan U., 1983, U. N.C., Chapel Hill, 2002, 05; vis. fellow Huntington Libr., 1973-74; vis. instr. Yale U., 1988; bd. dirs. David R. Godine Pub., R. W. Emerson Inst. Author: Literature and Film, 1969, Henry Thoreau: A Life of the Mind, 1986 (Melcher award, 1986), Emerson: The Mind on Fire, 1995 (Parkman prize, 1995, Melcher award, 1995, Washington Irving award, 1995), Myth and Literature in the American Renaissance, 1978; author: (with Burton Feldman) The Rise of Modern Mythology 1680-1860, 1972; author: (with Allen Mandelbaum) Three Centuries of American Poetry, 1999; author: William James: In the Maelstrom of American Modernism, 2006 (Bancroft prize, 2006), First We Read, Then We Write: Emerson on the Creative Process, 2009. Trustee Meadville-Lombard Theol. Sch., 1981-87. Fellow Guggenheim Found., 1990, Nat. Humanities Ctr., 1999-00; recipient Acad. award in lit. Am. Acad. Arts and Letters, 1998. Mem. Soc. Am. Hist., Author's Guild, Thoreau Soc., Emerson Soc., Assn. Lit. Scholars and Critics, William James Soc. Democrat. Unitarian Universalist. Personal E-mail: rrchardson@gmail.com.

RICHARDSON, R(OSS) FRED(ERICK), insurance company executive, consultant; b. Renfrew, Ont., Can., Feb. 4, 1928; came to U.S., 1980; s. Garfield Newton and Grace Mary (MacLean) R.; m. Betty Blanche Betts, Feb. 4, 1972; children by previous marriage: Sheri Joan, Robert John, Paul Frederick. BA in Math. and Physics with honors, Queens U., 1950. Actuarial asst. Empire Life Ins. Co., Kingston, Ont., Canada, 1950-55; sec. Maritime Life Ins. Co., Halifax, N.S., Canada, 1955-59, dir. sales, 1959-65, chief exec. officer, 1967-72; mng. dir., chief exec. officer Abbey Life Ins. Co., England, 1972-80; group gen. mgr. Hartford Europe Group, 1975-80; sr. v.p., dir. worldwide life ins. ops. Hartford Ins. Group, Conn., 1980-83, dir. worldwide life ins. ops. Conn., 1983-88; pres., COO, Hartford Life Cos., 1983-88; pvt. ins. cons., Boca Raton, Fla., 1988; pres., CEO, Crown Life Ins. Co., 1988-93; cons. INSCE, Boca Raton, 1993—. Fellow Soc. Actuaries, Can. Inst. Actuaries. Home: 401 E Linton Blvd Apt 263 Delray Beach FL 33483-5083 Personal E-mail: rfredr@gmail.com.

RICHARDSON, RUDY JAMES, toxicology and neurosciences educator; b. May 13, 1945; BS magna cum laude, Wichita State U., 1967; Sc.M., Harvard U., 1973, Sc.D., 1974. Diplomate Am. Bd. Toxicology. Rsch. geochemist Columbia U., NYC, summer 1966; NASA trainee SUNY, Stony Brook, 1967-70; rsch. biochemist Med. Research Council, Carshalton, England, 1974-75; asst. prof. U. Mich., Ann Arbor, 1975-79, assoc. prof., 1979-84, prof. toxicology, 1984—, assoc. prof. neurotoxicology neurology dept., 1987—, Dow prof. toxicology, 1998—, acting dir. toxicology program, 1993, dir., 1994-99, dir. toxicology tng. program, 2003—. Vis. scientist Warner-Lambert Co., Ann Arbor, 1982-83; vis. prof. U. Padua, Italy, 1991; cons. NAS, Washington, 1978-79, 84, Office Tech. Assessment U.S. Congress, 1988-90, Nat. Toxic Substance Disease Registry, 1990—; mem. sci. adv. panel on neurotoxicology EPA, 1987-89; chmn. work group on neurotoxicity guidelines Orgn. for Econ. Coop. and Devel., 1990, Nat. Inst. Orgnl. Safety and Health, 1990, 94; mem. acute cholinesterase risk assessement expert panel Internat. Life Scis. Inst., 1996; mem. steering com., working group Risk Sci. Inst., 1997; presenter sci. adv. panel U.S. EPA, 1998-99, WHO, Geneva, 1998; chair expert panel on dichlorvos neurotoxicity and cholinesterase inhibition SRA Internat., Washington, 1998-99, guest panel mem. Mich. Environ. Sci. Bd., 2003—; invited spkr. in field. Mem. editorial bd. Neurotoxicology, 1980—, Toxicology and Indsl. Health, 1986—, Toxicology and Applied Pharmacology, 1989-97, Jour. Toxicology and Environ. Health, 1997—; contbr. articles to profl. jours., chpts. to books. Mem. Mich. Lupus Found., Ann Arbor, 1979—. Grantee NIH, 1977-86, 95—, EPA, 1977-86, U.S. Civilian R & D Found., 1996—, U.S. Army Rsch. Office, 2002—. Mem. AAAS, Am. Coll. Toxicology, Soc. Toxicology (pres. neurotoxicology sect. 1987-88, councillor 1988-89, co-recipient Best Paper award 2003), Soc. for Neurosci., Am. Diabetes Assn., Am. Chem. Soc., Internat. Soc. Neurochemistry, Internat. Brain Rsch. Orgn. Achievements include codiscoverer (with B.R. Dudek) of lymphocyte neuropathy target esterase (NTE); development of lymphocyte NTE as biomarker of exposure to neuropathic organophosphates; refinement of NTE assay for use in neurotoxicity testing; use of protein mass spectrometry in mechanistic toxicology and sensor development. Office: U Mich 1420 Washington Heights Ann Arbor MI 48109-2029 Office Fax: 734-763-8095. Business E-Mail: rjrich@umich.edu.

RICHARDSON, SALLY KEADLE, academic administrator; b. Mar. 2, 1933; d. Okey P. and Viola Miriam (Graybeal) Keadle; m. Don Rule Richardson, Dec. 15, 1961; children: Miriam Paige, Ruth Evan. AB, Vassar Coll., 1954. Regional pub. info. rep. Columbia Gas Sys., Charleston, W.Va., 1958-62; dir. Children's Mus., Charleston, 1963; coord. space-related sci. project Kanawha County Schs., Charleston, 1967-68; vol. dir. Rockefeller for Gov. Campaign, Charleston, 1972, program dir., 1976, 80; dir. admissions W.Va. Wesleyan Coll., Buckhannon, 1974-75; spl. asst. Office of Gov. State of W.Va., 1977, dep. commr. dept. welfare, 1978-79, dep. dir. dept. health, 1979-83; chmn. W.Va. Health Care Cost Rev. Authority, Charleston, 1983-85. Health care cons., Charleston, 1985-89; dir. W.Va. Pub. Employees Ins. Agy., Charleston, 1989-93; vice-chmn. W.Va. Health Care Planning Task Force, 1992-93; mem. White House Health Care Reform Task Force,

Washington, 1993; dir. Medicaid Bur., Health Care Financing Adminstrn., U.S. DHHS, Balt., 1993-96; acting dep. adminstr. HCFA, U.S. DHHS, Washington, 1996-97; dir. HCFA Ctr. for Medicaid and State Ops., 1997-99; mem. U.S. DHHS Governing Coun. on Children and Youth, 1993-97, co-chmn. U.S. DHHS Children's Health Initiative, 1997-99; co-chmn. U.S. DHHS Home and Cmty. Based Svcs. Task Force, 1996-99; mem. U.S. DHHS Pub. Health Coun.'s D.C. Task Force, 1994-99; mem. Nat. Adv. Com. on Rural Health, DHHS, 2000-04; bd. dirs. Molina Healthcare, Inc. W.Va. rep. Task Force on So. Children, So. Growth Policies Bd., 1978-79; co-chmn. exec. com. W.Va. Internat. Yr. of Child, 1979; staff mem. Com. on Human Resources Nat. Gov. Assn., 1983-85; trustee U. Charleston, 1994-; bd. dirs. Children's Home Soc., Charleston, 1999—. Mem. Acad. Health, Nat. Rural Health Assn. Democrat. Office: WVa U Inst Health Policy Rsch 3110 Maccorkle Ave SE Rm 3015 Charleston WV 25304-1210

RICHARDSON, SCOTT, federal official, researcher, writer; s. Stewart and Jeanne Richardson; m. Leighann Lowley, Nov. 12, 1994; 1 child, Evan Stewart. BA, Thomas Edison Coll., Trenton, NJ, 1981. Cert. in public health Bloomberg Sch. Public Health, Johns Hopkins U., Balt., 2001. Project mgr., coord. Nat. Evaluation Sys., Amherst, Mass., 1981—88; project dir. Nat. Evaluation Systems, Inc., Austin, Tex., 1988—90; mgr. bur. of labor stats. programs Tex. Workers' Compensation Commn., 1991—94, chief safety info. sys, 1994—99; dir. office of stats. Occupl. Safety and Health Adminstrn., Washington, 1999—2000; program mgr. census of fatal occupl. injuries Bur. Labor Stats., Washington, 2000—. Contbr. articles to profl. jours., chapters to books. Sr. warden, vestry Christ Our Lord Ch., Woodbridge, Va., 2004—06. Mem.: APHA. Anglican. Office: Bureau of Labor Statistics 2 Massachusetts Ave Washington DC 20212 Business E-Mail: richardson.scott@bls.gov.

RICHARDSON, SELMA KATHERINE, retired library and information scientist; b. McCandless, Pa., Oct. 23, 1931; d. John J. and Laura Ingrid Richardson. BM, St. Olaf Coll., Northfield, Minn., 1953; MA, U. Mich., Ann Arbor, 1959, MALS, 1962, PhD, 1969. Tchr. Berkley Sch. Dist., Mich., 1953—60; libr. Oak Park Sch. Dist., Mich., 1960—69; prof. Ball State U., Muncie, Ind., 1969—70; libr. Oak Park-River Forest Sch. Dist., 1970—74; prof. libr. sci. U. Ill., Urbana, 1974—95, prof. emeritus, 1995—. Author: Periodicals for School Media Programs, 1978, Magazines for Children, 1983, 2d edit., 1991, Magazines for Young Adults, 1984; editor: Children's Services of Public Libraries, 1978, Study and Collecting of Historical Children's Book, 1979, Research About Nineteenth-Century Children and Books, 1980; contbr. articles to profl. jours. and mags., chapters to books. Named Disting. Alumnus, Sch. Libr. Sci. U. Mich., 1978. Mem.: ALA (mem. coun. 1972—76), Beta Phi Mu, Pi Lambda Theta, Phi Kappa Phi. Avocation: travel. Home: 814 Phoenix Dr Champaign IL 61820 Office: U Ill Sch Libr and Info Sci 501 E Daniel St Champaign IL 61820

RICHARDSON, STEPHEN GILES, biotechnologist, research and development company executive, writer; b. Mpls., Sept. 17, 1951; s. Richard Giles and Constance Bernice (Krieg) R. BA in English and Chemistry, cum laude, Wartburg Coll., 1972; MS in Chemistry, U. Iowa, Iowa City, 1974, PhD in Organic Chemistry, 1981; postdoctoral, Duke U., Durham, NC, 1982—84. Cert. project mgmt. profl. Project Mgmt. Inst. Ter. mgr. Wyeth Labs., Phila., 1974-76; rsch. asst. U. Iowa, Iowa City, 1976-82; rsch. assoc. Duke, Durham, NC, 1982-84; scientist Becton Dickinson Rsch. Ctr., Research Triangle Park, NC, 1984-86; devel. group leader Dade Diagnostics divsn. Baxter Healthcare, Miami, Fla., 1986; rsch. group leader Organon Teknika Corp divsn., Akzo Nobel N.V, Durham, NC, 1987-89, R & D sect. head, internat. R & D area mgr., 1989-90, program mgr., 1990-94, assoc. dir., head product devel., 1994-96, project mgmt. dir., microbiology bus. area R & D, 1997—2001; program dir. global mktg. and strategic devel. bioMerieux, Inc., Durham, NC, 2001—04; pres. Adamantane Corp., 2004—. Contbr. articles to profl. jours.; patentee in field; bd. readers IVD Technology Mag. Co-founder Libertarian Party Minn., Mpls., 1972, del. nat. conv., 1998; exec. sec. Iowa Coun. to Repeal Conscription, Waterloo, 1971. Mem. Am. Soc. for Microbiology, Am. Chem. Soc., Royal Soc. Chemistry UK, NY Acad. Scis., Electronic Frontier Found., Traingle Stamp Club (pres. Chapel Hill, 1997-98, 2008), Sigma Xi. Libertarian. Achievements include discovery of transient neutral heteroaryl radicals as viable organic synthetic intermediates, such as, to halopurine nucleosides; MDA-180 hemostasis analyzer system, BacT/ALERT 3D blood culture system family. Office Phone: 919-643-3021. Office Fax: 919-640-1344. Business E-Mail: adamantane@embarqmail.com.

RICHARDSON, TIMOTHY WAYNE, language educator; b. Mesa, Ariz., Feb. 18, 1951; s. Joseph Wayne and Doralynn Millett Richardson; m. Helen Carpenter, Dec. 20, 1986; children: Sarah Jacquier, Nathan Joseph, Timothy Seth, Jacob Enoch, Abigail, Susanna, Isaac Nathanael, Samuel James. BA in Spanish Lang., 1975, MPA, 1977, MA in Spanish Lang., 1987, PhD in Fgn. Lang. Edn., 1998. Instr. Spanish Brigham Young U., 1983—87, 1988—89; fgn. expert Xian Fgn. Langs. U., Shaanxi, China, 1987—88, 1989—90; instr. Internat. Ctr. & Dept. Fgn. Langs. Snow Coll., 1990—92, 1995—98, asst. prof. chair, fgn. langs., 1998—2001; asst. instr. Portuguese, Spanish U. Tex., Austin, 1992—95; asst. prof. Spanish, Chinese Brigham Young U. Hawaii, 2001—, coord. world lang., 2002—, assoc. prof., 2009; vis. rsch. fellow Nanzan Inst. Religion & Culture Nanzan U., Nagoya, Japan, 2006—09. Spanish tchr. Lang. Training Mission, Provo, Utah, 1972—74; intern US Agy. Internat. Development, Washington, 1978; ops. mgr. Swepco do Brasil, Southwestern Petroleum Corp., Tex., 1979—80; coord. Internat. Personnel & Adminstrn., Presiding Bishopric Internat. Offices, Ch. Jesus Christ Latter-day St., Utah, 1981—83; cons. trainer Durham & Co., Ariz., 1997. Contbr. scientific papers to profl. pubs.; co-author: Chinese Character Learning. Recipient Tchg. award, Snow Coll., 1999—2000, Faculty Appreciation award, 2009; named Tchr. of Yr., Brigham Young U. Hawaii, 2001—02, Favorite Lang. Tchr., 2005; nominee Model Tchr. award, Xian Fgn. Lang. U., 1990. Mem.: Rsch. Network Learner Autonomy Lang. Learning, Chinese Lang. Tchrs. Assn., Am. Assn. Tchrs. Spanish & Portuguese, Sigma Delta Pi, Phi Kappa Phi. Independent. Avocations: reading, music, basketball. Office: Brigham Young Univ Hawaii 55-220 Kulanui St Laie HI 96762-1294 Business E-Mail: timothyr@byuh.edu.

RICHARDSON, TODD H., literature and language professor; b. Wilmington, Del., May 3, 1968; s. William Smith Richardson and Margaret Anne Pepper. BA, Coll. Wooster, Ohio, 1990; MA, U. Del., Newark, 1997; PhD, U. SC, Columbia, 2002. Vis. asst. prof. U. SC., 2002—03; asst. prof. U. Tex. Permian Basin, Odessa, 2003—09, assoc. prof., 2009—. Contbr. articles to profl. jours. Mentor Big Bros., Big Sisters, Midland, Tex., 2003—; founding mem. Sierra Club: Permain Basin Conservation Com., Odessa, Tex. Recipient Golden Windmill award, La Mancha Soc., 2007; named Big Bro. of Yr., Big Bros., Big Sisters Midland, 2007; fellowship, Nat. Endowment Humanities, 2005. Mem.: Thoreau Soc., Modern Lang. Assn., Ralph Waldo Emerson Soc. (bd. mem., program chair 2004—09, sec., treas. 2009—), Phi Beta Kappa. Office: Univ Tex Permian Basin 4901 E University Odessa TX 79762 Office Fax: 432-552-3280. Business E-Mail: richardson_t@utpb.edu.

RICHARDSON, VERNAL EDWARD, retired music educator; b. Bloomington, Ind., May 20, 1932; s. Edgar Lee and Olive Mae Richardson; m. Elpha Ernestine Patton, Aug. 10, 1958; children: Ernest Todd, Patricia Beth Niemann, Edward Scott. MusB, Ind. U., Bloomington, 1950—55, MusM, 1959—63; PhD in Musical Arts, Cath. U. Am., DC, 1970—77. Cert. orch. tchr. Ga., 1989. Orch. dir. Manatee Pub. Schs., Bradenton, Fla., 1985—89, Atlanta Pub. Schs., 1989—2004. First violin sect. Atlanta Symphony Orch., 1955—56; pilot USAF, Lincoln AFB, Nebr., 1956—59; asst. prof., music David Lipscomb Coll., Nashville, 1959—63, Southeastern La. U., Hammond, 1963—65, Harding Coll., Searcy, Ark., 1965—68, Towson State U., Md., 1968—79; assoc. prof., music Lebanon Valley Coll., Annville, Pa., 1979—82, Moorhead State U., Minn., 1982—85. 1st lt. USAF, 1956—59, Lincoln, Nebr. Mem.: Am. Fedn. Musicians. Democrat. Methodist. Avocations: aviation, photography, music. Home: 5968 Brasstown Creek Estates Young Harris GA 30582 Office: Richardson String Studios 5968 Brasstown Creek Estates Young Harris GA 30582 Business E-Mail: verned@windstream.net.

RICHARDSON, W. C., painter; Exhibitions include W.C. Richardson: New Paintings, Kiang Gallery, Atlanta, 2004, one-man shows include, Loyola U., Baltimore, 2004, Fusebox Gallery, Washington DC, 2002, 2003, Baumgartner Gallery, NYC, 2000, displayed in, Hirshhorn Twenty-five: Celebrating Modern & Contemporary Art, Hirshhorn Mus. & Scuplture Garden, 1999, two painted triptychs, reproduced in porcelanized steel, North Terminal, Ronald Reagan Nat. Airport; co-curator with Paula Crawford (exhibitions) Recent Paintings, Projectspace, Washington DC, 1998. Grantee Individual Artist Award, Md. State Arts Coun., 2002, Visual Arts Fellowship, 2002, 1998, 1987, 1981Md. State Arts Coun. Office: U Maryland 1211 Art/Sociology Bldg College Park MD 20742-1311 Office Phone: 301-405-1460. Office Fax: 301-314-9740. E-mail: wr8@umail.umd.edu.

RICHARDSON, WILLIAM CHASE, retired university and foundation executive; b. Passaic, NJ, May 11, 1940; s. Henry Burtt and Frances (Chase) R.; m. Nancy Freeland, June 18, 1966; children: Elizabeth, Jennifer. BA, Trinity Coll., 1962; MBA, U. Chgo., 1964, PhD, 1971; PhD (hon.), from 11 Univs. including, U. Mich., 2006. Rsch. assoc., instr. U. Chgo., 1967-70; asst. prof. health services U. Wash., 1971-73, assoc. prof., 1973-76, prof., 1976-84, chmn. dept. health services, 1973-76, assoc. dean Sch. Pub. Health, 1976-81, acting dean, 1977, 78, dean Grad. Sch., vice provost, 1981-84; exec. v.p., provost, prof. dept. family and community medicine Pa. State U., 1984-90; pres. Johns Hopkins U., Balt., 1990-95, pres., prof. emeritus, 1995, prof. dept. health policy, mgmt., 1990-95, prof. emeritus, 1995—; pres., CEO W.K. Kellogg Found, Battle Creek, Mich., 1995—2005; prof. policy Kalamazoo Coll., 2005—. Cons. in field; chmn., bd. dir. Coun. on Founds.; chmn. Kellogg Trust, 1996-2006, Kaiser Family Found., 1985-1998. Author: books, including Ambulatory Use of Physicians Services, 1971, Health Program Evaluation, 1978; contbr. articles to profl. jours. Mem. adv. com. Rand Corp. Kellogg Coll. fellow, Oxford U., 1995—. Mem.: Am. Acad. Arts and Scis., Inst. Medicine, Am. Public Health Assn.

RICHARDSON, WILLIE FORREST, JR., physician, consultant; s. Willie Forrest Richardson and Linda Lou Cummings. BS in Biology (hon.), Pembroke State U., 1996; MD, East Carolina U., 2000. Diplomate Am. Bd. Dermatology, lic. dermatologist N.Mex., Fla. Intern in internal medicine Med. U. S.C., Charleston, 2000—01; resident indermatology U. N.Mex. Health Scis. Ctr., Albuquerque, 2001—04; staff dermatologist Gallup Indian Med. Ctr., N.Mex., 2003—; dermatologist Presbyn. Med. Group-Kaseman Dermatology, Albuquerque, 2004—05; staff dermatologist Broward Gen. Med. Ctr., Ft. Lauderdale, Fla., 2005—; dermatologist Las Olas Dermatology, Ft. Lauderdale, Fla., 2005—. Author: (textbook) Native American Skin Disease, 2005; contbr. articles to profl. jours. Recipient Indian Health Svc. scholarship, U.S. Dept. HHS, 1994—96, Premedical scholarship, Indian Health Svc., 1993-1996, Outstanding Clin. Excellence award, Gallup Indian Svc. Divsn., 2003. Fellow: Am. Soc. Mohs Surgery; mem.: AMA, Broward County Dermatology Soc., Broward County Med. Assn., Am. Acad. Dermatology, Alpha Chi. Achievements include research in Native American skin disease. Personal E-mail: nativehealer@aol.com.

RICHARDSON-WENINEGAR, LORETTA LYNNE, biologist, educator; b. Ft. Riley, Kans., Sept. 19, 1954; d. Woodrow and Florence Myrtle Denton; children: Jennifer Lynne Weninegar-Canady, Jessica Leigh Weninegar, James Christopher Weninegar. BS in Biology and Secondary Edn./Minor Psychology, U. Mobile, 1976, MSEd in secondary edn./biology, 1993; MS in biology, Jacksonville State U., 2002. Cert. Tchr. #252735, Type B Ala., 1976, Tchr. #252735, Type A Ala., 1993. Sci. tchr. Arnold Sch. of Ala., Mobile, 1976, Berney Points Sch., Birmingham, Ala., 1977—79, Hueytown H.S., Ala., 1995—98, Jacksonville H.S., Ala., 1990—91; grad. tchg. asst., biology Jacksonville State U., Ala., 1993, adj. instr. biology, 1993—98; asst. project dir. Ala. Sci. in Motion Ala. A&M U., Huntsville, 1998—; tchr. of sci. Columbia H.S., 2006—. Field technician, botanist Natural Resource Conservation Svc., Ala., 1996; chmn., pers. com. Berney Points Sch., Birmingham, 1979—81; asst. dir. Chattooga river environ. edn. and water quality project Jacksonville State U., Ala., 1994—95, facilitator environ. edn. From Awareness to Action, 1993, staff, Little River Field Sch., 1993—97; trainer Ala. Water Watch Ala. A&M U., Huntsville, 1998—; adj. instr. Biology Calhoun C.C., Decatur/Huntsville, Ala., 2004—; mem. Ala. Invasive Plant Coun., 2007. Spkr. bur., hike leader The Land Trust of Huntsville and North Ala.; strategic planning com. Columbia HS, Huntsville, 2005—; outdoor amb. Ala. Bur. Tourism and Travel, 2006; spkr. Ala. Wildflower Soc., Huntsville. Grantee Toyota Tapestry 10K grant, 2007. Mem.: NEA, Ala. Invasive Plant Coun., Nat. Sci. Tchr. Assn., Nat. Assn. Biology Tchrs., Ala. Edn. Assn., The LandTrust of Huntsville and North Ala. (speaker's bur., hike leader), Beta Beta Beta, Delta Kappa Gamma (membership chmn. 2002—04). Achievements include research in water quality analysis of Cane Creek in Calhoun County, Ala; STS-106 Atlantis; Vascular Flora of Choccolocco Creek, Calhoun, Cleburne, and Talladega Counties, Ala. Avocations: hiking, camping, gardening, birdwatching, dance. Home: 9507 Hemlock Dr SE Huntsville AL 35803-1161 Personal E-mail: bcdh@aol.com.

RICHARDS-VITAL, CLAUDIA, small business owner, recreational facility executive; b. Banes, Oriente, Cuba, May 18, 1935; arrived in U.S., 1951; d. Vasper Zacharia Richards and Ana Louisa Coombs - Vital; m. Eugene Blackman, July 22, 1956 (div. Apr. 20, 1965); children: Emery, John, Veronica. AA in Bus. Adminstrn./English, Havana Bus. Acad., 1951; diploma in Early Childhood Devel., Miami Dade C.C., 1972. Pvt. practice nanny, Miami Beach, Fla., 1951—56; seamstress Playboy Club, Miami, Fla., 1961—65; prodn. supr. So. Bakery, 1965—69; care mother James E. Scott Cmty. Agy., 1970—75; nurse asst. North Shore Hosp., 1970—75; home health aide Total Care Home Health Agy., 1975—85; site dir. YMCA, 1985—95; sole propr. Veronica's Boutique, 1982—89, Claudia's Formal Wear, 1989—. Pres. Local #249 Am. Bakery and Confectionery Workers Internat. AFL-CIO, Fla., 1966—69. Recipient Diamond Pendant, Queen Elizabeth II, 1965, cert. of Appreciation, YMCA of Miami, Fla., 1990; named Parent of Yr., Metro Dade County, 1993. Mem.: NAFE, NAACP. Democrat. Roman Catholic. Avocations: sewing, decorating, gardening, babysitting, animals.

RICHARZ, CHARISSE ELAINE, language educator; d. Wilbert Harold and Ann Sherrill Richarz; 1 child, Sherrill Simone Xia. BA, Trinity U., San Antonio, 1971; MA, U. Tex., Austin, 1976. Tchg. asst. U. Tex., 1974—76, Tex. Tech U., Lubbock, 1992; instr. Blinn Coll., Brenham, Tex., 1976—. Office: Blinn Coll 901 College Ave Brenham TX 77833 Business E-Mail: cricharz@blinn.edu.

RICHE, DENNIS M., retired history professor; s. Earle A. and Virginia A. Riche; m. Vivian L. Ross; children: Stephanie R. Ray, Brad David Robinson, Sherri K. Taylor, Bryan Ross Robinson, Michael A. MA in Am. History, NorthWest Mo. State U., Maryville, 1970. Cert. in secondary edn. tchg. Mo., 1967. Tchr. Sch. Dist., St. Joseph, 1967—99, Mo. Dept. Mental Health, St. Joseph, 1971—80; trainer Mo. Dept. Correction, St. Joseph, 1999—2003; adj. instr. methods tchg. Mo. Western U., St. Joseph, 1994—99; adj. instr. Mineral Area Coll., Pk. Hills, Mo., 2004—. Meal delivery Sr. Ctr., Farmington, Mo., 2004—08; vol. AARP, Farmington, Mo., 2004—08. Mem.: Red Coat Club, Lions Club, Ea. Star Lodges, Elks Lodges, Masonic. Conservative. Baptist.

RICHELS, JOHN, energy executive, lawyer; BA, York Univ.; LLB, Univ. Windsor, 1978. Mng. ptnr., COO, mem. exec. com. Bennett Jones; bd. dir. Northstar Energy Corp., 1993—96, exec. v.p., CFO, 1996—98; pres., CEO Devon Canada, 1998—2001; sr. v.p. Canadian div. Devon Energy Corp., Oklahoma City, 2001—04, pres., 2004—. Gen. counsel XV Olympic Winter Games, Calgary, 1986—88. Office: Devon Energy Corp 20 N Broadway Oklahoma City OK 73102-8260

RICHELSON, PAUL WILLIAM, curator; b. Montpelier, Idaho, Sept. 27, 1939; s. Paul Newton and June (Quayle) R. BA, Yale U., 1961; MFA, Princeton U., 1967, PhD, 1974. Asst. prof. Lawrence U., Appleton, Wis., 1970-77, U. Denver, 1977-84; asst. dir., curator Trisolini Gallery of Ohio U., Athens, 1984-87; chief curator Grand Rapids (Mich.) Mus., 1987-91; curator of Am. art Mobile Mus. Art, Mobile, Ala., 1991-97, asst. dir., chief curator, 1997—. Author: (book) Studies in the Personal Imagery Collection of 20th Prints Ohio University, 1985, (catalogue) The Golden Age 19th Century Prints by David Roberts, 1988, Lee Loring: A Southern Sophisticate, 1992, Modernism and American Painting of the 1930s, 1993, ThirtySomething, 1994, Alabama Impact: Contemporary Artists with Alabama Ties, 1995, Louise Lyons Heustis (1965-1951): A Retrospective, 1995, The French Connection: Jean Simon Chaudron Returns To Mobile, 1996, John Roderick Dempster MacKenzie (1865-1941): A Retrospective, 1997, Celebrating the Creative Spirit, 1998, Contemporary Southeastern Furniture, 1998, Coming Home: American Paintings, 1930-1950, from the Schoen Collection, 2003, Craig Nutt: Certified Organic, 2008; A Perfect Marriage: Wood and Color, 2008; Alabama Masters: Artists and Their Work, 2008. Lt. (j.g.) USN, 1961-63. Recipient Elizabeth B. Gould Rsch. award Mobile Hist. Devel. Commn., 1997; Fulbright-Hays fellow to Italy, 1967-69; Mus. Purchase Plan grantee Nat. Endowment for the Arts, 1991; grantee Mus. Loan Network, 2002. Mem. Southeastern Museums Conf. Home: 6427 Grelot Rd Apt 405 Mobile AL 36695-2630 Office: Mobile Museum of Art 4850 Museum Dr Mobile AL 36608-1917 Home Phone: 251-633-8596; Office Phone: 251-208-5215. Fax: 251-208-5201. E-mail: prichelson@mobilemuseumofart.com.

RICHENHAGEN, MARTIN H., manufacturing executive; b. July 1, 1952; married; 3 children. Grad., Univ. Bonn, Germany, 1975. Vice-pres. field ops. Schindler Aufzugefabrik GmbH, Germany, 1995—98; group pres. GLAAS KgaA mbH, Germany, 1995—2003; group exec. vice-pres. Forbo Internat. SA, 2003—04; pres., CEO AGCO Corp., Duluth, Ga., 2004—, chmn., 2006—. Bd. dir. PPG Industries, 2007—. Office: AGCO Corp 4205 River Green Pkwy Duluth GA 30096 Office Phone: 770-813-9200.

RICHERSON, JAMES J., museum administrator, consultant; b. Chgo., Mar. 26, 1956; s. John Richerson and Ann Kanarski; m. Judith E. Lee, June 29, 1985; children: Austin Lee-Richerson, Zachary Lee-Richerson. BA, Coe Coll., 1979; MFA, U. Chgo., 1984; attended, Bouguiba Inst., 1991—92. Cert. in Mus. Mgmt. U. Colo.-Boulder, 1999. Exhibit designer Oriental Inst. Mus., U. Chgo., 1981—91; Fulbright lectr. Nat. Mus. Carthage, Tunisia, 1991—94; planning, design cons. Nat. Mus. Archaeology, Valetta, Malta, 1994—96, academic specialist US info. svc., 1989—91, 1994; exec. dir. Cayuga Mus. History and Art, Auburn, NY, 1997—2000; CEO, pres. Lakeview Mus. Arts and Scis., Peoria, Ill., 2000—. Contemporary art exhibit coord. Chgo. Merc. Exch., 1979—90; earthwatch prin. investigator, grantee, Carthage, 1990—93; grant reviewer Inst. Mus. and Libr. Svcs., 1998—; panelist in field, 1999; guest lectr. in field, 2002—04. Contbr. articles to profl. jours. and mags. in field. Scoutmaster Boy Scouts Am. Grants, Am. Tunisian Assn., 1990—92. Office: Lakeview Mus 1125 W Lake St Peoria IL 61614

RICHERT, JOHN ROLIN, neuroimmunologist, educator; b. Boston, June 9, 1945; s. Daniel Arnold and Esther (Beamer) Richert; m. Nancy Dembeck, July 5, 1969. BA, Cornell U., 1966; MD, U. Rochester, 1970. Diplomate Am. Bd. Med. Examiners, Am. Bd. Psychiatry and Neurology. Intern, resident in medicine Strong Meml. Hosp. U. Rochester, NY, 1970-72; resident in neurology Mayo Clinic, Rochester, Minn., 1974-77; fellow Nat. Multiple Sclerosis Soc. NIH, Bethesda, Md., 1977-80; rsch. asst. prof. neurology Georgetown U. Med. Ctr., Washington, 1980-83, asst. prof. neurology, 1983-89, assoc. prof. neurology, 1989-93, prof. neurology, 1993—2005, prof., chair dept. microbiology and immunology, 1997—2005; v.p. rsch. and clin. programs Nat. Multiple Sclerosis Soc., NYC, 2005—07, exec. v.p. rsch. and clin. programs, 2007—; mem. data and safety monitoring bd. Acorda Therapeutics, Hawthorne, NY, 2005—07, Novartis, Basel, Switzerland, 2005—06; mem. data and safety monitoring com. Biogen Idec, Cambridge, 2007—. Mem. physician adv. bd. Biogen Inc., Cambridge, Mass., 1994-2000; cons. Immunex, Inc., Seattle, 1998-2000; external adv. com. VA Multiple Sclerosis Ctr. of Excellence, U. Md. Multiple Sclerosis Ctr., Balt., 2003-2005; sci. adv. bd. TolerGenics, Inc., Rockville, Md., 2001-2005; cons. Health Sci. Ctr. for Continuing med. Edn., NY, 2003; mem. med. adv. com. Multiple Sclerosis Soc. Can., 2006—, sci. review com. mem. World Congress On Treatment and Rsch. Multiple Sclerosis, 2007-08, rsch. ref. group mem. MS Internat. Fedn., 2007-, sci. adv. bd. BIOMS European Biomaker Gr., 2008- Mem. editl. bd.: Neurotherapeutics. Mem. immunol. scis. study sect. NIH, 1989, mem. mental health AIDS and immunology rsch. study sect., 1992, mem. neurol. disorders program project com., 2003, Brain Disorders and Clin. Neuroscience spl. emphasis panel, 2003-2004. Maj. USAF, 1972-74. Fellow Am. Acad. Neurology; mem. Internat. Soc. Neuroimmunology, Nat. Multiple Sclerosis Soc. (med. adv. bd. 1988-91, 93-96, profl. adv. com. 1988-2005, sci. peer rev. com. 1993-98), Am. Neurol. Assn., Am. Assn. Immunologists, Am. Soc. for Biochemistry and Molecular Biology, Am. Soc. for Exptl. Neurotherapeutics (pub. com. 2006—), Assn. Med. Sch. Microbiology and Immunology Chairs(pub policy com. chair 2004-05, chair 1997-2005), Alpha Omega Alpha, MS Internat. Fedn. (rsch. reference group 2007-), Bioms European Biomarker Group Proteomic Based Biomarker Study (sci. adv. bd. 2008-). Avocations: tennis, golf, skiing. Office: Nat Multiple Sclerosis Soc 733 3d Ave New York NY 10017 Home Phone: 301-654-6293; Office Phone: 212-476-0423. Business E-Mail: john.richertj@nmss.org.

RICHERT, PAUL, law educator; b. Elwood, Ind., Aug. 31, 1948; m. Catherine George Stanton, June 24, 1972; children: John, William. AB, U. Ill., Urbana, 1970, MS, 1971; JD, Tulane U., New Orleans, 1977. Bar: Ohio 1977. Asst. law libr. U. Akron, 1977-78, law libr., asst. prof. law, 1978-83, assoc. prof., 1983-87, prof. law, 1987—. Local bd. dirs. Selective Svc. sys. Co-author: Searching the Law, 3d edit., 2005. Mem. United Chs. of Christ. With U.S. Army, 1971-74. Mem. Am. Assn. Law Libr., Akron Bar Assn., ABA. Home: 2030 Ganyard Rd Akron OH 44313-6050 Office: Univ Akron Sch Law Library 302 Buchtel Common Akron OH 44325-2902 Home Phone: 330-867-8272; Office Phone: 330-972-6350. Business E-Mail: richert@uakron.edu.

RICHESON, HUGH ANTHONY, JR., lawyer; b. Aberdeen, Md., Apr. 22, 1947; s. Hugh Anthony Sr. and Mary Evelyn (Burford) R.; m. Melissa Anne Baum, Apr. 4, 1970; children: Hugh Anthony III, Heidi E., Holly K., Hagin G., Herald Joshua. BS in Bus. Adminstrn., U. Richmond, 1969; JD, U. Fla., 1973; student, St. Catherine's Coll., Oxford U., Eng., summer 1973. Bar: Fla. 1974, US Dist. Ct. (mid. dist.) Fla. 1975, U.S. Supreme Ct. 1992. Assoc. Bryant, Dickens, Rumph, Franson & Miller, Jacksonville, Fla., 1974—76, ptnr., 1977, Smith, Hallowes & Richeson, Orange Park, 1982—83; sole practice Orange Park, Fla., 1977—82, Palm Harbor, Fla., 1984—98; of counsel Carey & Hilbert, Clearwater, Fla., 1998—2005, Florin Roebig P.A., Palm Harbor, Fla., 2005—. Author: Legally Yours, 2002. Pres. Full Gospel Bus. Men's Fellowship Internat., Orange Park, 1983-84, Palm Harbor, 1985-92, field rep., 1987—; bd. dirs. Religious Freedom Coalition, Washington. Mem. Fla. Coun. Bar Assn. Pres. (life), Gideons Internat., Phi Delta Phi, Sigma Phi Epsilon. Republican. Methodist. Office: Florin Roebig PA 777 Alderman Rd Palm Harbor FL 34683 Office Phone: 727-785-5858. Personal E-mail: hariia@aol.com.

RICHESON, JAMES GRADY, JR., dentist; m. Nancy Richeson; 1 child, Suzanne. DDS, Georgetown U. Dentist, Washington. Recipient Disting. Svc. award, Georgetown Dental Alumni, 2003. Fellow: Pierre Fauchard Acad., Am. Coll. Dentists, Acad. Gen. Dentistry (pres.-elect 2001—02, pres. 2002—03, v.p., treas., bd. trustee, budget and fin. com., regional dir., Found. bd. dirs.); mem.: ADA (alt. del. 2001—, del. 2004), DC Dental Soc. (The Sterling V. Meade Disting. Svc. award 2004), DC Acad. Gen. Dentistry (past pres.), Georgetown U. Alumni Club of Met. Washington (past pres.). Office: 4400 Jenifer St NW Ste 340 Washington DC 20015-2113 Office Phone: 202-364-5246. Business E-Mail: jim@yourdentaldr.com.

RICHEY, JAMES D., JR., literature and language professor; married. BA, AA, MA, EdD, Tex. A&M. Academic coord. Chapel Hill ISD, Mt. Pleasant, Tex., 1999—2004; prof. English & faculty senate pres. Tyler Jr. Coll., Tex., 2004—. Musician: Identifying Lucy. Recipient Endowed Excellence Tchg. award, Tyler Jr. Coll., 2009—.

RICHEY, P. JEROME, lawyer, energy executive; b. Pitts., Feb. 23, 1949; BA, U. Pa., 1971, JD cum laude, 1974. Bar: Pa. 1974. Shareholder Buchanan Ingersoll, PC, Pitts.; v.p., gen. counsel CONSOL Energy Inc., Pitts., 2005—07, sr. v.p., gen. counsel, 2007—09, exec. v.p. corp. affairs, chief legal officer, 2009—. Mem. ABA (individual rights and responsibilities in the workplace com. 1984-05), Allegheny County Bar Assn. Office: Consol Energy 1000 Consol Energy Dr Canonsburg PA 15317-6506 Office Phone: 412-831-4021.

RICHIE, BOYD LYNN, lawyer, political organization administrator; b. Breckenridge, Tex., July 11, 1945; s. Bradie Eugene adn Billie June (Robinson) R.; m. Betty Zoe Furr, May 28, 1966; children: Christophber Robin, Tracy Lynn. BA in Polit. Sci. and History, Midwestern State U., 1967; JD, Tex. Tech. U., 1970. Bar: Tex. 1970, U.S. Dist. Ct. (no. dist.) Tex. 1975. Trial atty. Fed. Power Commn., Washington, 1970-71; assoc. John Bradshaw, Graham, Tex., 1971-72; sole practice Graham, 1972-77; dist. atty. 90th Jud. Dist., Graham, 1977-80; asst. dist. atty. Wichita County, Wichita Falls, Tex., 1980-81; ptnr. Neal, Neal, Richie & Hill, Graham, 1981—; atty. Young County, Tex., 1996—. Co-op, Inc, Bluegrove, Tex., 1979-83, Ft. Belknap Electric Coop., Inc., Olney, Tex., 1984—. Chair Audit Subcommittee of Fin. Com. Tex. Dem. Party, chmn., 2006—. Fellow: Texas Bar Assn. (life); mem.: Young County Bar Assn. (pres. 1972—73). Democrat. Episcopalian. Office: Young County Courthouse Rm 102 PO Box 2256 Graham TX 76450-8256 also: Tex Dem Party Ste 200 505 W 12th St Austin TX 78701 Office Phone: 512-478-9800. Office Fax: 512-480-2500. Business E-Mail: yellowdog@txdemocrats.org.*

RICHIE, RODNEY CHARLES, critical care and pulmonary medicine physician; b. Big Springs, Tex., Aug. 17, 1946; s. Howard Mouzon and Gloria (Hollingshead) R.; m. Sara Lee Dilley, July 13, 1968; children: Megan Kathryn, Paul Nathan. BA in Chemistry, So. Meth. U., 1968; MD cum laude, Baylor Coll., 1972. Diplomate in Internal Medicine, Pulmonary, Ins. Medicine. Resident in medicine Baylor Affiliated Hosps., Houston, 1973-75, chief med. resident, 1975, fellow in pulmonary medicine, 1976-77; pres. Waco Lung Assocs., Tex., 1977—2007; assoc. clin. prof. cmty. medicine Heart of Tex. Cmty. Health Ctr./U. Tex. SW Med. Sch., 2004—. Med. dir. Tex. Life Ins., Waco, 1985—, Cmty. Hospice of Waco, 1996—, EMSI, Waco, Tex., 1997—. Chmn. med. staff Hillcrest Bapt. Med. Ctr., Waco, 1993; chmn. bd. dirs. GH Pape Found., Waco, 1993. Fellow: ACP, Am. Coll. Chest Physicians; mem.: AMA, Am. Thoracic Soc., Am. Acad. Internal Medicine (del. to AMA), Tex. Club Internists. Episcopalian. Avocations: skiing, writing, reading. Home: 3509 Lake Heights Dr Waco TX 76708-1005 Office: Waco Med Group 7125 New Sanger Rd Ste B Waco TX 76712 Office Phone: 254-741-1688. Personal E-mail: rcrichie@earthlink.net.

RICHIERI, KENNETH A., lawyer, publishing executive; b. Jersey City, June 5, 1951; m. Kathryn Obler; children: Julia, Camille, Peter. AB, Brown U., 1973; JD cum laude, Harvard U., 1976. Bar: 1977. Assoc. Cahill Gordon & Reindel, 1976—82; legal counsel The NY Times Co., NYC, 1983—89, sr. counsel, 1989—93, asst. gen. counsel, 1993—2001, dep. gen. counsel, 2001—05, v.p., dep. gen. counsel, 2005, v.p., gen. counsel, 2006—07, sr. v.p., gen. counsel, 2007—; gen. counsel NY Times Digital, 1999—2004. Office: The NY Times Co 229 W 43rd St New York NY 10036

RICHLAND, KENT LEWIS, lawyer; b. Nov. 1946; m. Barbara Sue Circle, 1969; children: Justin Blake, Sara Circle. AB, U. Calif., Berkeley, 1968; JD, UCLA, 1971. Bar: Calif. 1972, US Supreme Ct. 1975, US Ct. Appeals (9th cir.) 1972, US Dist. Ct. (ctrl. dist.) Calif. 1972. Supervising dep. atty. gen. Calif. State, 1972—76; supervising atty. for Calif. State Pub. Defender, 1976—78; sr. rsch. atty. to Presiding Justice Otto M. Kaus Calif. Ct. Appeals, 1978—79; atty. Horvitz & Greines, 1980—83; founding mem. Greines, Martin, Stein & Richland LLP, LA, 1983—. Trustee state appellate jud. evaluation com., 1998—2000; chair appellate cts. com., 1985—88, Calif. jud. sys. com., 1988—90, jud. appts. com., 2001—03; adj. prof. law Southwestern Sch. Law, 1986—87; guest lectr. U. So. Calif. Law Ctr., UCLA Sch. Law, U. West LA Sch. Law. Bd. editors LA Bar Jour. and LA Lawyer, 1973—78, articles editor and mng. editor, 1977—78, bd. advisors Hastings Constl. Law Quarterly, 1978—88; contbr. articles to law jours. Fellow: Am. Acad. Appellate Lawyers; mem.: ABA (co-chair Nat. Inst. on Med. Malpractice 1989—90, mem. appellate adv. com. 2001—, mem. torts and ins. practice sect. appellate advocacy com.), Calif. Judicial Coun., LA County Bar Assn. (trustee 1998—2000), Calif. Acad. Appellate Lawyers (pres. 1995—96), Calif. Supreme Ct. Hist. Soc. (bd. dirs. 1998—, pres. 1999—2005). Achievements include successful arguing Marshall versus Marshall (Anna Nicole Smith case) in the United States Supreme Court, 2006. Office: Greines Martin Stein Richland Llp 5900 Wilshire Blvd Ste 1200 Los Angeles CA 90036-5009 Office Phone: 310-859-7811. Office Fax: 310-276-5261. Business E-Mail: krichland@gmsr.com.

RICHLER, ZENIA H., naturopath educator, health facility administrator; B in Bio-Energetics, Acad. Bio-Energetics, 1997, M in Bio-Energetics, 1999, D in Bio-Energetics, 2001; D of Naturopathic Medicine, So. Coll. Naturopathic Medicine, 2001. Dir. Health Alternatives, Atlanta, 1986—98, dir., nmd Humansville, 1998—; pres., CEO, chief instr. Acad. BioEnergetics, Humansville, Mo., 1999—. Assoc. dir. new bus. devel. Transformation Group, Inc., Houston, 2006—; acad. cons. EMR Techs., Inc., Las Vegas, Nev., 2006—; instr. Neurotherapy BioFeedback Certification Bd., 2006—; cert. instr. SounderSleep, 2006—. Fellow: AAIM, Am. Assn. Integrated Medicine; mem.: Am. Assn. Drugless Practitioners, Noetic Scis., Natural Resources Def. Coun., Coalation for Natural Health, Nat. Health Fedn., Am. Holistic Health Assn., Am. Alternative Med. Assn. Avocations: swimming, reading, yoga. Office: Acad BioEnergetics 18820 E Hwy N Humansville MO 65674 Business E-Mail: academybe@tri-lakes.net.

RICHLOVSKY, THOMAS ANDREW, bank executive; b. Cleve., July 26, 1951; s. Simon Andrew and Arline Miriam (Uresh) R.; m. Rhonda Marie Dolens, June 30, 1973; children: Paul, Abbey, Jill. BBA in Acctg., Cleve. State U.; grad., Stonier Grad. Sch. Banking. CPA. Audit supr. Ernst & Whinney, Cleve., 1973-78; v.p., treas. Nat. City Corp., Cleve., 1978, sr. v.p., treas. Bd. dirs. Banic Adminstrn. Inst., Cleve., 1982-84. Treas. Urban Cmty. Sch., Cleve., 1974, bd. trustees; mem. vis. com. Cleve. State U., Coll. Bus., 1985-86.; mem. fin. com. Magnificat HS; bd. dirs., treas. Jesuit Retreat House. Mem. AICPA, Fin. Execs. Inst., Nat. Investor Rels. Inst. (bd. dirs. Cleve. chpt.), Bank Adminstrn. Inst., Ohio Soc. CPAs, Greater Cleve. Growth Assn. Roman Catholic. Avocation: running. Office: Nat City Corp Nat City Ctr 1900 E 9th St Cleveland OH 44114-3484 Office Phone: 216-222-2000.

RICHMAN, ALAN, magazine editor, educator; b. Bronx, NY, Nov. 12, 1939; s. Louis and Sonia (Carity) R.; m. Kelli Shor, June 21, 1964; children: Lincoln Seth Shor, Matthew Mackenzie Shor. BA, Hunter Coll., 1960. Reporter Leader-Observer, NYC, 1960-61; asst. editor Modern Tire Dealer, NYC, 1962-64; assoc. editor ASTA Travel News, NYC, 1964-65; pub. rels. rep. M.J. Jacobs, Inc., NYC, 1965-66; mng. editor Modern Floor Coverings, NYC, 1966-68; editor Bank Systems & Equipment, NYC, 1968-79, Health Care Product News, NYC, 1976; from assoc. pub. to pub. Bank Systems & Equipment, NYC, 1969-79; editorial dir. Nat. Jeweler, NYC, 1979-81; editor Health Foods Bus.; editorial dir. Army/Navy Store and Outdoor Merchandiser, 1981-88, The Pet Dealer, 1983-88; editor Cabinet Mfg. and Fabricating KBC Publs., 1988-94. Program dir. Cabinet Mfg. Fair, 1989-94; adj. faculty NYU, 1989—, Brookdale CC, 1992—, Bergen County CC, 1994-. Exec. editor: Kitchen and Bath Design News, 1992-93; editor-in-chief Wood Digest, PTN Pub. Co., 1992-94; editor: Whole Foods, 1994-2007; proprieter, freelance writer and cons. Alan Richman Comm. Svcs., 2007-; author: Czechoslovakia in Pictures, 1969, A Book on the Chair, 1968. With AUS, 1961-62. Recipient Jesse H. Neal certificate merit Am. Bus. Press, 1973. Achievements include invention of patent pending method of teaching writing to non-writers.

RICHMAN, DANIEL CHARLES, law educator; b. NYC, Oct. 21, 1958; s. Harold Lloyd and Sylvia (Batlan) R.; m. Alexandra S. Bowie, Dec. 4, 1988; children: Matthew, Rebecca. AB summa cum laude in Hist., Harvard Coll., 1980; Grad. English, Hist., Oxford U., Eng., 1980—81; JD, Yale Law Sch., 1984. Bar: N.Y. 1986, U.S. Dist. Ct. (so. dist.) N.Y. 1992, U.S. Dist. Ct. (ea. dist.) N.Y. 1992, U.S. Ct. Appeals (2d cir.) 1987, U.S. Supreme Ct. 1991. Law clk. to Hon. Wilfred Feinberg US Ct. of Appeals, NYC, 1984-85; law clk. to Justice Thurgood Marshall US Supreme Ct., Wash., 1985-86; assoc. Patterson, Belknap, Webb & Tyler, 1986—87; asst. US atty. (so. dist.) NY US Dept. Justice, 1987-92, spl. asst. US atty. (so. dist.) NY NYC, 1992—94; prof. law Fordham Law Sch., NYC, 1992—2007, Columbia U. Law Sch., NYC, 2007—. Vis. assoc. prof. of Law U. Va. Sch. Law, 1996—97; vis. prof. Columbia U. Sch. Law, 2002. Cons. (treasury dept.) Waco Administrv. Rev., 1993—94. Mem. Assn. Bar of NYC, Phi Beta Kappa, Fed. Bar Coun. Office: Columbia Law Sch 435 West 116th St New York NY 10027 Office Phone: 212-854-9370. Business E-Mail: drichm@law.columbia.edu.

RICHMAN, DAVID PAUL, neurologist, educator, researcher; b. Boston, June 9, 1943; s. Harry S. and Anne (Goodkin) R.; m. Carol Mae von Bastian, Aug. 31, 1969; children: Sarah Ann, Jacob Charles. AB, Princeton U., 1965; MD, Johns Hopkins U., 1969. Diplomate Am. Bd. Psychiatry and Neurology. Intern, then asst. resident in medicine Albert Einstein Coll. Medicine, NYC, 1969-71; resident in neurology Mass. Gen. Hosp., Boston, 1971-73, chief resident, 1973-74; instr. neurology Harvard U. Med. Sch., Boston, 1975-76; asst. prof. neurology U. Chgo., 1976-80, assoc. prof., 1981-85, prof., 1985-91, Straus prof. neurol. Scis., 1988-91; prof. neurology U. Calif., Davis, 1991—, chmn. dept., 1991-97. Mem. com. Nat. Inst. Aging, NIH, 1984-85, mem. immunogical scis. study sect., 1986-90. Mem. AAAS, Am. Assn. Immunologists, Am. Acad. Neurology, Am. Neurol. Assn., Phi Beta Kappa, Sigma Xi. Office: U Calif Davis Dept Neurology 1515 Newton Ct Davis CA 95616-4859 Office Phone: 530-752-5013. Business E-Mail: dprichman@ucdavis.edu.

RICHMAN, DOUGLAS DANIEL, medical virologist, educator, internist; b. NYC, Feb. 15, 1943; s. Daniel Powell and Louise Kohnstamm (Woolf) R.; m. Eva Acquino, June 21, 1965; children: Sara, Matthew. AB cum laude, Dartmouth Coll., 1965; MD, Stanford U., 1970. Diplomate Am. Bd. Internal Medicine, Am. Bd. Infectious Diseases, Am. Bd. Med. Examiners. Intern Stanford Med. Sch., Calif., 1970—71, resident, 1971—72; rsch. assoc. LID/NIAID NIH, Bethesda, Md., 1972—75; fellow Beth Israel and Children's Hosps., Harvard Med. Ctr., Boston, 1975—76; asst. prof. depts. pathology and medicine U. Calif., San Diego, 1976—82, assoc. prof., 1982—88, prof., 1988—, Florence Seeley Riford chair in AIDS rsch., 2004—. Vis. prof. Hubei Med. Coll., Wuhan, People's Republic of China, 1987, Tokyo Med. and Dental U., Kumamoto U. Sch. Medicine, Inst. for Virus Rsch. at Kyoto U., St. Marianna U., Tokyo, Inst. Med. Rsch., Tokyo, Fukishima Prefecture Med. Sch., Japan, 1990; vis. fellow Clare Hall, U. Cambridge, 1984-85; mem. U. Calif. Pres.'s Cancer Rsch. Coord. Com., 1984-89, NIH AIDS Rsch. Rev. Com., 1987-90; cons. FDA Ctr. for Drugs and Biologics, 1986-89; dir. U. Calif.-San Diego Ctr. for AIDS Rsch., AIDS Rsch. Inst. Co-editor: Clin. Virology, —; mem. editl. bd.: Antimicrobial Agts. and Chemotherapy, 1987—, Jour. of AIDS, 1988—, Antiviral Agts., 1988—, AIDS, 1990—, AIDS Alert, 1990—, Antiviral Drug Resistance, 1996—, Virology, 1997—, others; contbr. more than 550 articles to profl. jours. Recipient Lowell Rantz award in infectious diseases, 1970, AMA Physicians Recgonition award, 1976, 79, 82, 85, 88, William S. Middleton award Dept. Vet. Affairs, 2002; John Simon Guggenheim fellow, 1984. Fellow: ACP, AAAS, We. Assn. Physicians, Am. Assn. Physicians, Infectious Diseases Soc. Am.; mem.: Am. Clin. and Climatologic Assn., VA Soc. for Physicians in Infectious Diseases, Internat. AIDS Soc., Internat. Soc. Antiviral Rsch., Am. Soc. for Virology, Am. Fedn. for Clin. Rsch., Am. Soc. for Microbiology. Office: U Calif San Diego Dept Pathology & Medicine 9500 Gilman Dr La Jolla CA 92093-0679

RICHMAN, JACK M., social sciences educator; b. NYC, July 25, 1950; m. Carol R. Kramer, July 14, 1974; children: Alice R., Erica L. MSW, U. Albany, NY, 1974; PhD, Fla. State U., Tallahassee, 1977. Asst. prof. Nebr. Wesleyan U., Lincoln, 1977—82, assoc. prof. & program chair, 1982—83; prof. and dean U. NC, Chapel Hill, 1983—. Home: 111 Birchcrest Pl Chapel Hill NC 27516 Office: Univ NC Chapel Hill 325 Pitsboro St Chapel Hill NC 27599

RICHMAN, JESSE, ophthalmologist, researcher; s. Jeffrey and Wendy Richman; m. Jamie Jacobs, May 25, 2008. MD, Jefferson Med. Coll., Phila., 2007. Clin. rsch. coord. Glaucoma Rsch. Ctr. Wills Eye Inst., Phila., 2002—03; intern Frankford Hosp., Phila., 2007—08; ophthalmology resident RI Hosp., Providence, 2008—. Contbr. conf. presentation (NEI Award, 2008). Recipient Award, Am. Acad. Orthop. Surgeons, 2007. Mem.: Am. Acad. Ophthalmology. Office: Brown Med Sch 593 Eddy St APC 7th Fl Providence RI 02903 Business E-Mail: jesse.richman@hotmail.com.

RICHMAN, JOHN MARSHALL, lawyer, food products executive; b. NYC, Nov. 9, 1927; s. Arthur and Madeleine (Marshall) R.; m. Priscilla Frary, Sept. 3, 1951; children: Catherine Richman Wallace, Diana H. BA, Yale U., 1949; LLB, Harvard U., 1952. Bar: N.Y. 1953, Ill. 1973. Assoc. Leve, Hecht, Hadfield & McAlpin, NYC, 1952-54; mem. law dept. Kraft, Inc., Glenview, Ill., 1954-63, gen. counsel Sealtest Foods div., 1963-67, asst. gen. counsel, 1967-70, v.p., gen. counsel, 1970-73, sr. v.p., gen. counsel, 1973-75, sr. v.p. adminstrn., gen. counsel, 1975-79, chmn. bd., chief exec. officer, 1979, Dart & Kraft, Inc. (name changed to Kraft, Inc. 1986), Glenview, 1980; chmn. Kraft Gen. Foods, Glenview, Ill., 1988-89; counsel Wachtell, Lipton, Rosen & Katz, Chgo., 1990-98. Life trustee Chgo. Symphony Orch., Northwestern U.; bd. dirs. Chgo. Coun. Global Affairs, Lyric Opera Chgo., Norton Mus. Art, West Palm Beach. Fla. Mem. Coun. Ret. Chief Exec., Comml. Club, Chgo. Club, Casino Club (Chgo.), Westmoreland Country Club (Wilmette, Ill.), Old Elm Club (Highland Park, Ill.), Lost Tree Club (N. Palm Beach, Fla.), Racquet Club of Chgo. Congregationalist. Office: 179 E Lake Shore Dr Chicago IL 60611-1306 E-mail: johnrichman@att.net.

RICHMAN, JOSEPH HERBERT, retired public health service officer; b. Balt., Aug. 13, 1941; s. Samuel and Beatrice Richman. BS, Howard U., 1962, MD, 1966; MPH, Johns Hopkins U., 1974. Intern Maimonides Med. Ctr., Bklyn., 1966-67; resident in pediat. Sinai Hosp. of Balt., 1967-69; chief sch. health P.G. Health Dept. of Md., Cheverly, Md., 1972-75; dir. area health svcs. Montgomery County Health Dept., Bethesda, Md., 1975-82; county chief pub. health physician State of Del., Dover, 1982-99; ret., 2000; med. cons. Ariz. Med. Bd., 2009—. Capt. USAF, 1969—71. Recipient Outstanding Svc. award, Delaware Health and Soc. Svc., 1999. Fellow Am. Acad. Pediatrics (emeritus), Am. Coll. Preventive Medicine, Am. Coll. Physician Exec., Am. P.H. Assn.; mem. AMA, Masons, Phi Beta Kappa. Democrat. Jewish. Avocations: golf, photography. Home: PO Box 880852 Boca Raton FL 33488-0852 Home Phone: 561-482-3154. Personal E-mail: joefortsedgwick@aol.com.

RICHMAN, LAWRENCE I., lawyer; b. Chgo., Aug. 8, 1954; s. Jack and Reggie (Heller) R. BA magna cum laude, Columbia U., 1974; JD, U. Chgo., 1977. Bar: Ill. 1977. Atty. McDermott Will & Emery, Chgo., 1977-80, Neal Gerber & Eisenberg, Chgo., 1980—. Elected fellow Am. Trusts and Estates Coun., 2008—. Named one of Top 100 Attys., Worth mag., 2006—08. Mem. ABA (generation shipping transfer tax com. 1990, recipient cert. of appreciation 1989), Chgo. Bar Assn. (chmn. trust law com. 1988-89), Am. Technion Soc. (bd. dirs. 1987), Phi Beta Kappa. Avocation: skiing. Office: Neal Gerber & Eisenberg LLP 2 N LaSalle St Ste 2200 Chicago IL 60602-3801 Office Phone: 312-269-8070. Office Fax: 312-750-6460. E-mail: lrichman@ngelaw.com.

RICHMAN, MARC HERBERT, engineer, forensic specialist, educator; b. Boston, Oct. 14, 1936; s. Samuel and Janet (Gordon) R.; m. Ann Raeshel Yoffa, Aug. 31, 1963. BS, MIT, 1957, ScD, 1963; MA, Brown U., 1967. Registered profl. engr., Conn., Mass., R.I.; cert. forensic examiner. Cons. engr., 1957—; engr. shipbldg. div. Bethlehem Steel Corp., Quincy, Mass., 1957; instr. metallurgy MIT, Cambridge, 1957-60, research asst. dept. metallurgy, 1960-63; instr. metallurgy div. univ. extension Commonwealth of Mass., 1958-62; asst. prof. engring. Brown U., Providence, 1963-67, assoc. prof., 1967-70, prof., 1970-98, dir. central electron microscopy facility Materials Research program, 1971-86, dir. undergrad. program in engring., 1991-98; prof. emeritus, 1998—; pres. Ednl. Aids of Newton Inc., Providence, 1968-71, Marc H. Richman Inc., Providence, 1981—. Guest scientist Franklin Inst., Phila., 1959; vis. prof. U. R.I., Kingston, 1970-71; biophysicist dept. medicine Miriam Hosp., Providence, 1974-87; biogengr. dept. orthopaedics R.I. Hosp., 1979-93; prof. emeritus Brown U., Providence, 1998—. Author: Introduction to Science of Metals, 1967; also articles; editor Soviet Physics: Crystallography, 1970-94; mem. editl. adv. bd. Materials Characterization, 1970—98, Jour. Forensic Engring., 1985-88. Served to maj. Ordnance Corps, U.S. Army, 1963. Recipient Engr. of Yr. award R.I. Soc. Profl. Engrs., 1993. Fellow Nat. Acad. Forensic Engrs. (cert.), Am. Coll. Forensic Examiners (cert.), Am. Inst. Chemists, Inst. Materials (U.K.); mem. ASCE, AIME, NSPE, ASEE (Outstanding Young Faculty award 1969), NAFE (bd. cert. diplomate in forensic engring.), Am. Soc. Metals (sec.-treas. 1965-68, chmn. R.I. chpt. 1968-69, Albert Sauveur Meml. award 1968, 69), Providence Engring. Soc. (pres. 1991-92, Freeman award for engring. achievement 1989), B'nai B'rith, Sigma Xi, Tau Beta Pi. Home: 291 Cole Ave Providence RI 02906-3452 Office: One Richmond Sq Providence RI 02906 Office Phone: 401-751-9656. Personal E-mail: mhrichman@aol.com.

RICHMAN, MARTIN FRANKLIN, lawyer; b. Newark, Feb. 23, 1930; s. Samuel L. and Betty E. (Goldstein) R.; stepson Doris (Bloom) R.; m. Florence E. Reif, May 6, 1962; children— Judith, Andrew. BA magna cum laude, St. Lawrence U., 1950; LL.B. magna cum laude, Harvard U., 1953. Bar: N.Y. 1953. Law clk. to Judge Calvert Magruder and Chief Justice Earl Warren, 1955-57; assoc., mem. firm Lord Day & Lord, Barrett Smith (and predecessors), NYC, 1957-66, 69-94; of counsel K & L Gates LLP, NYC, 1994—; dep. asst. atty. gen. Office

Legal Counsel, Dept. Justice, Washington, 1966-69. Public mem. Adminstrv. Conf. U.S., 1970-76; bd. dirs. Community Action for Legal Services, 1977-80 Trustee St. Lawrence U., 1979-95, trustee emeritus, 1995—, vice chmn. bd., 1988-95; bd. dirs. Friends of Law Libr. of Congress, 1992-99. Recipient Alumni citation St. Lawrence U., 1972 Fellow Am. Bar Found., N.Y. Bar Found.; mem. ABA (chmn. sect. adminstrv. law 1983-84), N.Y. State Bar Assn. (ho. of dels. 1981-84), Assn. of Bar of City of N.Y. (sec. and mem. exec. com. 1976-79, chmn. com. fed. legislation 1972-75, com. lawyer's pro bono obligations 1977-81), Am. Law Inst. Office: K & L Gates LLP 599 Lexington Ave New York NY 10022-6030 Office Phone: 212-536-3945. E-mail: martin.richman@klgates.com.

RICHMAN, MICHAEL F., thoracic surgeon, consultant; b. Chgo., Ill., June 1, 1965; MD, Georgetown U., 1991. Diplomate Am. Bd. Surgery, Am. Bd. Thoracic Surgery. Intern, surgery U. Southern Calif. Med. Ctr., LA, 1991—92, resident, suregery, 1992—96; fellow in cardiothoracic & vascular surgery U. Miami Jackson Meml. Hosp., 1997; clin. instr. surgery U. Southern Calif. Sch. Medicine, LA, 1996; founder Ctr. for Cholesterol Mgmt., 2005—, Elite Laser Vein Ctr., 2006—. Cholesterol expert WebMD; editorial bd. Clinical Jour. Lipidology. Fellow: Nat. Lipid Assn., Am. Coll. Chest Physicians, ACS. Office: Ctr for Cholesterol Management 1950 Sawtelle Blvd Los Angeles CA 90025 Office Phone: 310-481-3939. Office Fax: 310-481-3949.*

RICHMAN, MURRAY W., lawyer; b. Bronx, NY, Oct. 3, 1937; m. Andrea Richman, 1963 (dec. 2001); children: Stacey Gayle, Nicole; m. Rene Arias, Sept. 22, 2002. BA, CCNY, 1959; JD, NY Law Sch., 1964. Bar: US Dist. Ct. (so. dist.) NY 1969, US Dist. Ct. (ea. dist.) NY 1969, US Ct. Internat. Trade 1982, US Tax Ct. 1979, US Ct. Appeals (2nd cir.) 1975, US Supreme Ct. Sole practice Law Offices of Murray Richman, Bronx, NY, 1964—. Numerous TV appearances. Subject of profile New Yorker mag., 2001, subject of book A Cold Case by Philip Gurevich. Recipient Humanitarian award, Black Econ. Survival Assn., 1976, Honor award, Borough Pres. Bronx County, 1972, Lawyer of Yr. award, United Jewish Appeal, 1985, Man of Yr. award, Black Bar Assn., 2005, Thurgood Marshall award, 2005; named Man of Yr., Am. Jewish Congress, 1972. Master: Bronx Bar Assn. (bd. dirs.); mem.: NY Assn. Criminal Def. Lawyers, Bronx Criminal Bar Assn. (v.p., Humanitarian award 1981), B'nai B'rith. Office: Law Offices of Murray Richman 2027 Williamsbridge Rd 3rd Fl Bronx NY 10461-1605 Office Phone: 718-892-8588. Personal E-mail: mrichman_mr@msn.com.*

RICHMAN, PAUL, semiconductor industry executive, educator; b. NYC, Nov. 17, 1942; s. Harry and Molly (Armel) Richman; m. Ellen Margaret Kleiman, July 3, 1966; children: Lee Stuart, Alyson Michelle, Daniel Noah. BSEE, MIT, 1963; MSEE, Columbia U., 1964. V.p. R & D Standard Microsystems Corp., Hauppauge, NY, 1971-76, pres., 1976-81, pres., chief exec. officer, 1981-83, pres., chmn. bd., chief exec. officer, 1983-2000; co-founder Toyo Microsystems Corp., Tokyo, 1987—. Pres Consortium Technology Licensing Ltd, Nissequogue, NY, 1994—99, chmn bd dirs, CEO, 1999—; vis prof elec eng SUNY, Stony Brook, 1976—85; mem vis comt elec eng and computer sci dept MIT, 1996—; adj. prof. elec. engring. CUNY, 1973—75; bd. dirs. Wi-LAN, Inc., Ottawa, Canada, 2007—. Author: (book) Characteristics and Operation of MOS Field Effect Devices, 1967, MOS Field Effect Transistors and Integrated Circuits, 1974. Recipient Ann Award Achievement in Electronics, Electronics Mag, 1978; named one of 30 Most Important Contributors in the World to Devel Integrated Circuit Technology, Elec Eng Times/Elec Buyer's News/VLSI Sys Design, 1988. Fellow: IEEE (Award for Outstanding Technical Achievement 1980, Third Millennium Medal 2000). Achievements include invention of COPLAMOS technology. Personal E-mail: richman.paul@gmail.com. E-mail: paul_consortium@verizon.net.

RICHMAN, PETER, electronics executive; b. NYC, Nov. 7, 1927; s. Emil H. and Janet (Seidler) R.; m. Vivian Hoffman, July 29, 1951; children: Meredith, Jeremy. BS, MIT, 1946; MS, NYU, 1953. Asst. chief engr. Reeves Instrument Corp., Garden City, NY, 1948-58; chief engr. Epsco, Inc., Cambridge, Mass., 1959-60; v.p., co-founder Rotek Instrument Corp., Watertown, Mass., 1960-64; v.p. Weston-Rotek, Lexington, Mass., 1964-67; cons. electronics engr. Lexington, 1967—. Bd. dirs. Thermo Voltek Corp, Thermo Sentron Corp.; founder, pres. KeyTek Instrument Corp., 1975-93; mem. NRC/NAS/Nat. Acad. Engring. Evaluation Panel for electricity divsn. Nat. Bur. Standards; mem. sci. adv. groups for several indsl. and sci. orgns. Patentee in precision electronic instrumentation; pioneer in precision dc and audio-frequency measurements, surge electrostatic discharge generation and electrostatic discharge measurements; author: The Insider's Guide to Growing a Small Business, 1996; contbr. articles to profl. jours. Mem. bd. overseers Boston Mus. Sci. Fellow IEEE; mem. Electromagnetics Acad., Instrument Soc. Am. (sr.), Sigma Xi, Tau Beta Pi.

RICHMAN, PETER MARK, actor, painter, writer, film producer; b. Phila., Apr. 16, 1927; s. Benjamin and Yetta Dora (Peck) Richman; m. Theodora Helen Landess, May 10, 1953; children: Howard Bennett, Kelly Allyn, Lucas Dion, Orien, Roger Lloyd. BS in Pharmacy, U. of the Scis., 1951; student of Lee Strasberg, NYC, 1952-54; mem., Actors' Studio, NYC, 1954—. Registered pharmacist Pa., NY. Actor: (plays), 1946—51, Have I Got a Girl for You, 1963, Ctr. Theater Group, 1965, Grove Theater, 1952, Westchester Playhouse, 1953, Drury Ln., 1957, Strand, 1957, Capri, 1959, Ongonquit Playhouse, 1955—62, 1955, 1953—55, 1955, 1962, 1955—62, Phila. Playhouse in Pk., 1962—63; (Broadway plays) End as a Man, 1953, Hatful of Rain, 1956—57, Masquerade, 1959; (plays) End as a Man, 1953, The Dybbuk, 1954, The Zoo Story, 1960—61, Rainmaker, Private Lives, Angel Street, Arms and the Man, Rose Tattoo, Liliorn, Funny Girl, Owl and the Pussycat, Hold Me, Equus, Night of the Iguana, Blithe Spirit, Twelve Angry Men, 1985, Babes in Toyland, 1988, Ray Bradbury's Next in Line, 1992, numerous others, stage, radio, TV, 1948—65; writer, performer: 4 Faces, 1995 (Drama-Logue Critics Performance award, 1996), 1996; The Actors Studio, 1996; others; narrator 7 Circles of Life: A Subud Cantata, 1997, Inssbruck, Austria, 2005, A Lincoln Portrait, 2004, 2007; actor: (films) Friendly Persuasion, 1956, The Strange One, 1956, Black Orchid, 1958, The Dark Intruder, 1965, Agent for HARM, 1965, For Singles Only, 1967, Judgement Day (formerly The Third Hand), 1988, Friday the 13th, Part 8: Jason Takes Manhattan, 1989, Naked Gun 2 1/2: The Smell of Fear, 1991, Pool Hall Junkies, 2003; prodr., writer, actor: 4 Faces, 2000; actor: (TV series) Cain's Hundred, 1961—62, David Chapter III, 1966, Longstreet, 1971—72, Three's Company, 1978—79, Heroes of the Bible, 1979, Dynasty, 1981—84, Santa Barbara, 1984, Defenders of the Earth, 1986, My Secret Summer (formerly Mystery of the Keys), 1991; guest actor: Hotel; Dallas; Hart to Hart; Fantasy Island; Murder She Wrote; Nothing Sacred; Three's Company; Knight Rider; Star Trek: The Next Generation; Matlock; Beverly Hills 90210; Over 500 Shows; actor: (TV films) House on Greenapple Road, 1968, McCloud, 1969, Yuma, 1970, Nightmare at 43 Hillcrest, 1974, Mallory, 1975, The Islander, 1978, Greatest Heroes of the Bible, 1979, Blind Ambition, 1979, The PSI Factor, 1981, Dynasty, 1981, Dempsey, 1983, City Killer, 1984, Bonanza: The Next Generation, 1988; one-man shows include Am. Masters Gallery, LA, 1967, Orlando Gallery, 1966, McKenzie Gallery, 1969, 1973, Hopkins Gallery, 1971, Goldfield Gallery, 1979, Galerie des Stars, 1968, Crocker Mus., Sacramento, 1967, Parkhurst Gallery, Seal Beach, Calif., 1991, Henley Gallery, Chapman U., Orange, Calif, 1996, exhibited in group shows at Bednarz Gallery, LA, 1968, Dohan Gallery, 1966, Celebrity Art Exhibits, 1964—65; author: (plays) Heavy, Heavy What Hangs Over?, 1971, A Medal for Murray, 1991, 2008, 4 Faces, 1995 (Commendation award Prism Film Festival, 2002); dir.: (plays) Apple of His Eyes, 1954, Glass Menagerie, 1954; author: Hollander's Deal, 2000, The Rebirth of Ira Masters, 2001; performer: (albums) Twilight Zone, 2005. Trustee Motion Picture and TV Fund. With USN, 1945—46. Recipient Silver medallion, Motion Picture TV Fund, 1990, Sybil Brand Humanitarian award, Jeffrey Found., 1990, Spl. award, 1997, Golden Halo Eagle award, So. Calif. Motion Picture Coun., 1997, Lifetime Achievement award, 2004. Mem.: AFTRA, SAG, Dramatists Guild America, Acad. TV Arts and Scis., Acad. Motion Picture Arts and Scis., Assn. Can. TV and Radio Artists, Actors Equity Assn. Office: 4 Faces Prodns 19528 Ventura Blvd Ste 385 Tarzana CA 91356 Office Phone: 818-623-6476. *I have always been grateful to be able to work in more than one medium. In a way they are all related, each solidifying and nurturing the other. I have a strong belief in God...and spiritual values. This, along with my marriage, children, and family life, has helped me enormously to express my own individuality as an artist.*

RICHMAN, STACEY GAYLE, lawyer; b. 1966; d. Murray W. and Andrea Richman. BA, Brandeis U., 1988; JD, Yeshiva U., 1991. Bar: Calif. 1993, NJ, NY. With Law Offices Murray Richman. Office: 2027 Williamsbridge Rd. 3rd Fl Bronx NY 10461 Office Phone: 718-892-8588. Office Fax: 718-518-0674. E-mail: srichman@murrayrichman.net.*

RICHMAN, STEPHEN ERIK, retired lawyer, consultant; b. Austin, Tex., Mar. 10, 1945; s. Allen A. and Erika (Zimmerman) Richman; m. Frances Ellen Sharpe, Aug. 29, 1971; children: Joshua Eric, Wendy Michelle. BA magna cum laude, Amherst Coll., Mass., 1967; JD cum laude, Harvard U., Cambridge, Mass., 1970. Bar: Wis. 1972. Assoc. Webster Sheffield, NYC, 1970-72, Quarles & Brady, Milw., 1972-78, ptnr., 1978—2006; ret., 2006. With Richman Nonprofit Strategies, LLC, 2005—. Pres. Milw. Youth Symphony Orch., 1985—87; bd. dirs. Milw. Symphony Orch., 1995—2004, chmn., 2000—02; chmn. steering com. Milw. Youth Arts Ctr., 2003—05; pres. Milw. Jewish Fedn., 1996—98; bd. dirs. United Performing Arts Fund, Milw., 2007—. Mem.: Phi Beta Kappa. Home and Office: 1611 W Eastbrook Ct Mequon WI 53092

RICHMOND, ALICE ELENOR, lawyer; b. NYC; d. Louis A. and Estelle (Muraskin) R.; m. David L. Rosenbloom, July 26, 1981; 1 child, Elizabeth Lara. BA magna cum laude, Cornell U., Ithaca, NY, 1968; JD, Harvard U., 1972, grad. Owners and Pres.'s Mgmt. Program, 2001; DLH (hon.), North Adams State U., 1987. Bar: Mass. 1973, US Dist. Ct. Mass. 1975, US Ct. Appeals (1st cir.) 1982, US Supreme Ct. 1985. Law clk. to justices Superior Ct., Boston, 1972-73; asst. dist. atty. Office of Dist. Atty., Boston, 1973-76; spl. asst. atty. gen. Office of Atty. Gen., Boston, 1975-77; asst. prof. New Eng. Sch. of Law, Boston, 1976-78; assoc. Lappin, Rosen, Boston, 1978-81; ptnr. Hemenway & Barnes, Boston, 1982-92, Deutsch, Williams, Boston, 1993-95, Richmond, Pauly & Ault, Boston, 1996—2003; prin. Richmond & Assocs., Boston, 2003—. Asst. team leader, faculty Trial Advocacy Course, 1978—82; examiner Mass. Bd. Bar Examiners, Boston, 1983—2008; trustee Mass. Continuing Legal Edn., Inc., Boston, 1985—96, Boston, 1998—2004; treas. Nat. Conf. Bar Examiners, 1995—2005, chmn., 2003—04; analyst CBS TV WBZ, 1991—; v.p., bd. dirs. Am. Bar Ins., Inc., 1995—; bd. dirs. Valora Tech., Inc. Conbr. chpts. to book; contbr. articles to profl. jours. Mem. Pres. Adv. Com on the Arts, 1995—99; bd. overseers Handel & Haydn Soc., 1985—2006, bd. govs., 1994—2007, v.p., 1996—2002; mem. Boston 2000 Millennium Commn., 1997—98; sec., dir. Boston 2000, Inc., 1998—2001; mem., pres. Coun. of Cornell Women, Cornell U. Coun.; trustee Red Auerbach Youth Found., Fund for Justice and Edn., 1997—2002; mem. adv. bd. Ctrl. and Ea. European Law Initiative, 1998—2002; mem. Angell Meml. Hosp. Coun. of Fellows, 2001—; trustee Nature Conservancy, Mass Chapter, 2007—. Named one of Outstanding Young Leaders, Boston Jaycees, 1982; Sloan Found. Urban fellow, NYC, 1969. Fellow: Am. Coll. Trial Lawyers; mem.: NOW, Legal Def. and Edn. Fund (trustee 1995—2002, sec. 1998—2002), ABA (house dels. 1980—, vice chmn. com. on rules and calendar 1986—88, bd. govs. 2002—05, task force on GATS 2003—, standing com. on audit 2005—, treas. 2008—), Latin Am. Legal Initiatives Coun., Mass. Bar Found. (pres. 1988—91), Mass. Bar Assn. (pres. 1986—87), Am. Law Inst., Bostonian Soc. (dir.), Corp. Dirs. Club, Boston Club. Office: Richmond & Assocs 39 Brimmer St Boston MA 02108 Home Phone: 617-523-0331; Office Phone: 617-523-8187.

RICHMOND, ANGELA, music educator; b. Vancouver, Wash., Oct. 2, 1978; d. Robert and Susan Porter; m. Adam Richmond, Apr. 2, 2005. MusB in Music Edn., Ctrl. Wash. U., Ellensburg, 2002. Cert. tchr. Wash., 2002. Music & strings specialist Wenatchee Sch. Dist., Wash., 2002—; funeral asst. Jones & Jones Funeral Home, Wenatchee, Wash., 2005—07. Tech. resource tchr. Wenatchee Sch. Dist., 2004—. Worship team leader Valley Cmty. Ch., Wenatchee, 2004—. Mem.: NEA, Wenatchee Edn. Assn., Wash. Edn. Assn., Wash. Music Educators Assn., Nat. Assn. Music Edn. Avocations: computers, drawing, dance.

RICHMOND, GAIL LEVIN, law educator; b. Gary, Ind., Jan. 9, 1946; d. Herbert Irving and Sylvia Esther (Given) Levin; children: Henry, Amy. AB, U. Mich., 1966, MBA, 1967; JD, Duke U., 1971. Bar: Ohio 1971, U.S. Claims Ct. 1986, U.S. Ct. Mil. Appeals, 1994; CPA, Ill. Acct. Arthur Andersen & Co., Chgo., 1967-68; assoc. Jones, Day, Cleve., 1971-72; asst. prof. Capital U. Law Sch., Columbus, Ohio, 1972-73, U. N.C. Law Sch., Chapel Hill, 1973-78; vis. asst. prof. U. Tex. Law Sch., Austin, 1977-78, Nova U. Law Ctr., Ft. Lauderdale, Fla., 1979-80, assoc. prof., 1980-81, assoc. prof., assoc. dean, 1981-85, prof., assoc. dean., 1985—93, 1995—2009, prof., acting dean, 1993-95, prof., 2009—. Author: Federal Tax Research, 7th edit., 2007, Mastering Corporate Tax, 2009; co-author: Tax Planning for Lifetime and Testamentary Dispositions, 1997, A Complete Introduction to Corporate Taxation, 2006, Florida Wills, Trusts and Estates: Cases and Materials, 2007; contbr. articles to profl. jours. Pres. Greater Ft. Lauderdale Tax Coun., 1987-88; trustee Law Sch. Admission Coun., 1994-99, chair audit com., 1991-93, chair svcs. and programs com., 1997-99. Mem. ABA (chair commn. on individual income, tax sect. 2001-03, supervising editor News Quar. 2006—, chair AMT task force 2003-2004, chair adj. com., legal edn. sect. 2002-05), Am. Assn. Atty.-CPAs (dir. Fla. chpt. 1992-98), Assn. Am. Law Schs. (chmn. audit com. 1992, chair sect. adminstrn. of law schs. 1996, pres. S.E. chpt. 1993-94, sec. S.E. chpt. 1995-2002), S.E. Assn. Law Schs. (pres. 2002-03, sec. 2004—). Office: Nova Southeastern Univ Shepard Bd Law Ctr 3305 College Ave Davie FL 33314-7721

RICHMOND, HAROLD NICHOLAS, lawyer; b. Elizabeth, NJ, Apr. 5, 1935; s. Benjamin I. and Eleanor (Turbowitz) R.; m. Elaine Zemel, June 16, 1957 (div. Nov. 1972); children: Bonnie J. Ross, Michele Weinfeld; m. Marilyn A. Wenrich, Aug. 26, 1973; children: Eric L., Kacy L. BA, Tulane U., 1957; LLB, NYU, 1961, LLM in Taxation, 1965. Estate tax examiner IRS, Newark, 1963-65; tax mgr. Puder & Puder/Touche Ross & Co., CPAs, Newark, 1965-73; ptnr. Sodowick Richmond & Crecca, Newark, 1973-84; prin. Harold N. Richmond, West Orange, N.J., 1984-86; ptnr. Wallerstein Hauptman & Richmond, West Orange, 1986-91, Hauptman & Richmond, West Orange, 1992—. With US Army, 1959—60. Mem. ABA (tax sect. closely held bus. com., real property and probate sect.), N.J. Bar Assn. (tax, real property and probate sects.), Essex County Bar Assn. (chmn. tax com. 1989, real property and probate sect.). Avocations: running, tennis. Office: Hauptman & Richmond 100 Executive Dr Ste 330 West Orange NJ 07052-3309 Office Phone: 973-731-1100. Business E-Mail: hnr@hrlawfirm.com.

RICHMOND, HUGH MACRAE, English language educator; b. Burton-upon-Trent, Eng., Mar. 20, 1932; came to U.S., 1957; s. Ronald Jackson and Isabella (MacRae) R.; m. Velma Elizabeth Bourgeois, Aug. 9, 1958; children: Elizabeth Merle, Claire Isabel. Diploma, U. Florence, Italy, 1952, U. Munich, 1956; BA in English with honors, Cambridge U., Eng., 1954; DPhil in English, Oxford U., Eng., 1957. Asst. d'Anglais Lycée Jean Perrin, Lyon, France, 1954-55; prof. English U. Calif., Berkeley, 1957—, dir. Shakespeare Program, 1974—, dir. Shakespeare Forum, 1981-95. Edn. dir. Shakespeare Globe Ctr. US, 1995-98; dir. scholarly website U. Calif. Shakespeare, Berkeley. Author: The School of Love, 1964, Shakespeare's Political Plays, 1967, Renaissance Landscapes, 1973, Shakespeare's Sexual Comedy, 1971, The Christian Revolutionary: John Milton, 1974, Puritans and Libertines, 1981, Shakespeare in Performance: King Richard III, 1990, Shakespearean Performance King Henry VIII, 1994, Shakespeare's Theatre, 2000; prodr. videos Shakespeare and the Globe, 1985, Shakespeare's Globe Restored, 1997, Shakespeare and the Spanish Connection, 2005; dir., prodr. stage and videos for NEH, 1984—. Bd. dirs. Calif. Shakespeare Festival, Berkeley, 1980-90; chair adv. coun. Shakespeare Globe Ctr., 1988-98, dir. edn., 1995-98. 2d lt. Royal Arty., U.K., 1950-51. Fellow Am. Coun. Learned Socs., 1964-65, NEH, 1977, 88; grantee, 1984-86. Mem. MLA, Shakespeare Assn. Am. Roman Catholic. Avocation: maritime history. Office: U Calif English Dept Berkeley CA 94720-1036 Business E-Mail: hmr@berkeley.edu.

RICHMOND, JAMES ELLIS, retired restaurant company executive; b. Chgo., Feb. 16, 1938; s. Kenneth E. and Irene M. (Anderson) R.; m. Karen Ann Ryder, Oct. 6, 1956; children: Scott, Brian, Ann, Susan. BBA, Case Western Res. U., 1960. CPA, Ohio. Sr. auditor Ernst & Ernst, Cleve., 1960-64; treas. Cook United, Inc., Cleve., 1964-75, Fairmont Foods Co., Houston, 1975-80, v.p. ops., 1980-82; v.p., treas. U-tote-M, Inc., 1982-84; mktg. exec. Circle K Convenience Stores, 1984-86; v.p. Consol. Products, Inc., Indpls., 1986-2000; ret. Lutheran. Home: 331 Wild Turkey Blvd Boerne TX 78006- E-mail: jkrich@gvtc.com.

RICHMOND, LYLE L., Associate Justice, American Samoa High Court; BA, Wesleyan U., 1952; LLB, Yale U., 1955. Dep. dist. atty., San Diego, 1959—64; pvt. practice Calif., 1964—70; dist. atty. Truk/Ponape dists., 1970—73; head legal divsn. atty.'s gen. office Trust Territory of the Pacific Islands, Saipan, 1973—75; atty. gen. American Samoa, 1975—77; legal counselor to American Samoa govs. Peter T. Coleman and A. P. Lutali, 1978—89; adminstr., legal mgr. Samoa Packing Co., Pago Pago, American Samoa, 1989—91; assoc. justice High Ct., Pago Pago, American Samoa, 1991—. With USN, 1955—58, capt. JAGC USNR, ret., 1984. Office: Courthouse PO Box 309 Pago Pago AS 96799 Office Phone: 684-633-1261. Business E-Mail: lylerichmond72@hotmail.com.*

RICHMOND, MARISA JEANNE, columnist; b. Nashville, Oct. 3, 1958; AB, Harvard U., 1980; MA, U. Calif., Berkeley, 1985; PhD, George Washington U., 1992. Columnist Tenn. Vals, Nashville, 1994—; also bd. dirs.; columnist Transgender Cmty. News, 1999—. Contbr. articles to Transgender Tapestry, Chrysalis. Bd. dirs. Gender Polit. Action Com., Washington, 1996-99; com. mem. Ctr. for Gay, Lesbian, Bi and Transgendered Life, Nashville; co-founder Magnolia Transgender Alliance, Ashville, N.C., 1994—. Mem. Am. Hist. Assn., Soc. History of Tech., Orgn. Am. Historians, Tenn. Hist. Soc., Phi Kappa Phi. Office: Tenn Vals PO Box 92335 Nashville TN 37209-8335 E-mail: marisaval@aol.com.

RICHMOND, MITCHELL JAMES, professional sports team executive, retired professional basketball player; b. Ft. Lauderdale, Fla., June 30, 1965; m. Juli Richmond; children: Phillip Mitchell, Jerin Mikell, Shane, Tearra. Attended, Moberly Area Jr. Coll., Mo.; B in Social Sci., Kans. State U., Manhattan, 1988. Guard Golden State Warriors, 1988—91, spl. asst., 2004—07, dir. player pers., 2007—; guard Sacramento Kings, 1991—98, Washington Wizards, 1998—2001, LA Lakers, El Segundo, Calif., 2001—02. Mem. US nat. team Summer Olympic Games, Seoul, 1988, Atlanta, 96. Established Solid As A Rock Scholarship Found., Ft. Lauderdale, Fla., 1992; hon. bd. dir. NCPCA. Recipient Spl. Friend award, NCPCA, Bronze medal, Summer Olympic Games, 1988, Gold medal, 1996; named Rookie of the Yr., NBA, 1989, All-Star Game MVP, 1995; named to Western Conf. All-Star Team, 1993—98. Achievements include member of NBA Finals championship winning Los Angeles Lakers, 2002. Avocations: bowling, video games. Office: Golden State Warriors 1011 Broadway Oakland CA 94607*

RICHMOND, NANCY MASON, retired state agency administrator; b. Buxton, Maine, Mar. 14, 1933; d. Ansel Robert and Kate Douglas (Libby) M. Grad., Bryant Coll., Providence, RI, 1952; BA, U. Mass., Boston, 1977; postgrad., Inst. Governmental Services, Boston, 1985, The Auditor's Inst., 1988. Asst. to chief justice Mass. Superior Ct., Boston, 1964-68; cmty. liaison Action for Boston Cmty. Devel., Boston, 1968-73; mgmt. cons. East Boston Cmty. Devel. Assn., Boston, 1973-78; asst. dir. Mass. Office of Deafness, Boston, 1978-86; dir. of contracts Mass. Rehab. Commn., Boston, 1986-98; ret., 1998. Cons. Jos. A Ryan Assocs., Boston and Orleans, Mass., 1981-86, Radio Sta. WFCC, Chatham, Mass., 1987-91, Networks, Inc., 2003-05. Author: Bromley-Heath Security Patrols, 1974, Reorganization of East Boston Community Development Corporation, 1976, How to Start Your Own Small Business, 1981. Bd. dirs. Deaf-Blind Contact Ctr., Boston, 1988-91; vol. Am. Cancer Soc., Winchester, Mass., 1986-93, Tax Equity Alliance Mass., 1994; treas. Sunset Bay Condo Assn., 1998-99, bd. dirs. 1998-2001, Highland Cemetery Assn., 2002-; mem. vestry Trinity Episc. Ch., Saco, Maine, 2005-07. Recipient Good Citizen award DAR, 1950, Community Svc. award Northeastern U., 1986, Gov.'s citation for outstanding performance, 1993; named to Outstanding Young Women of Am., 1965. Mem. NOW, Mass. State Assn. Deaf, Mass. Rehab. Commn. Statewide Cen. Office Dirs. (chair 1995-98, MRC procurement mgmt. team 1997-98, co-chair Take Your Daughters to Work Day 1998-99), Red Hat Soc. Democrat. Episcopalian. Avocations: reading, music, swimming, sign language. Home: 12315 SR 674 #34 Lithia FL 33547-1417

RICHMOND, ROCSAN, television executive producer, investigative reporter, small business owner; b. Chgo., Jan. 30; d. Alphonso and Annie Lou (Combest) Richmond; 1 child from previous marriage, Tina S. Student, Wilson Jr. Coll., 1963, 2d City Theatre, Chgo., 1969, Alice Liddel Theatre, 1970; cert. fingerprint classifier, LA City Coll., 1996.

Lic. 3d class radio/tel. operator FCC. Vegetarian editor Aware mag., Chgo., 1977—78; investigative reporter, film critic Chgo. Metro News, 1975—81; prodr., talk show host Sta. WSSD, Chgo., 1980—81; dir. pub. rels. IRMCO Corp., Chgo., 1981—82; dir. pub. rels., newsletter editor Hollywood (Calif.) Reporter, 1985—86; exec. prodr. Donald Descendent's Prodns., Hollywood, 1983—, Future News, TV show, 1983—86; pres. Richmond Estates; tchr. TV prodn. Profl. Bus. Acad., Hollywood, 1998—2000; founder, pres. Richmond Acad. Fine Manners, 2000—; v.p. adminstrv. svcs. S.G. Mgmt. Co., Manhattan Beach, Calif., 2000—06; pres. Integrity Mgmt. Co. Invention invisible drapery tieback. Jehovah's Witness. Achievements include invention of invisible drapery tieback. Personal E-mail: estateofrichmond@aol.com.

RICHT, MARK, college football coach; b. Omaha, Nebr., Feb. 18, 1960; m. Katharyn Francis; children: Jonathan, David, Zach, Anya. B, U. Miami, Coral Gables, Fla., 1982. Grad. asst. Fla. State U. Seminoles, 1985—86, vol. asst., 1987—88, quarterbacks coach, 1990—2000, offensive coord., 1994—2000, East Carolina U. Pirates, 1989; head football coach U. Ga. Bulldogs, 2000—. Named Coach of Yr., SEC Conf., 2002, 2005; finalist Bear Bryant Nat. Coach of Yr. award, 2002. Office: Univ Ga Athletic Dept PO Box 1472 Athens GA 30603 Office Phone: 706-542-1515.*

RICHTEL, MATT (THERON HEIR), reporter, cartoonist; m. Meredith Jewel, 2006. BA, Univ. Calif., Berkeley; MS in Journalism, Columbia Univ. Reporter & editor Peninsula Times Herald; reporter Oakland Tribune; freelance reporter NY Times, 1996—2000, telecommunications reporter, 2000—. Co-author (with Darrin Bell, under pen name Theron Heir): (syndicated comic strip) Rudy Park, 2001—; author: Hooked, 2007. Finalist Gerald Loeb award, 2007. Office: New York Times 201 Spear St San Francisco CA 94105 Office Phone: 415-836-6700. Business E-Mail: mattr@nytimes.com.

RICHTER, ANDY, actor; b. Grand Rapids, Mich., Oct. 28, 1966; m. Sarah Thyre, Mar. 18, 1994; children: William, Mercy. Attended, U. Ill. Urbana/Champaign, Columbia Coll. Actor: (TV films) The Positively True Adventures of the Alleged Texas Cheerleader-Murdering Mom, 1993, The True Meaning of Christmas Specials, 2002, The Lunchbox Chronicles, 2003, Harry's Girl, 2003, A.S.S.S.S.C.A.T.: Improv, 2005; (films) Cabin Boy, 1994, Good Money, 1996, The Thin Pink Line, 1998, Dr. T and the Women, 2000, Dr. Dolittle 2, 2001, Pootie Tang, 2001, Scary Movie 2, 2001, Run Ronnie Run, 2002, Martin & Orloff, 2002, Big Trouble, 2002, The Cat Returns, 2002, My Boss's Daughter, 2003, Elf, 2003, (voice) Lenny the Wonder Dog, 2004, Death and Texas, 2004, New York Minute, 2004, Seeing Other People, 2004, (voice) Madagascar, 2005, Talladega nights: The Ballad of Ricky Bobby, 2006, If I Had Known I Was a Genius, 2007, Blades of Glory, 2007, Semi-Pro, 2008, (voice) Madagascar: Escape 2 Africa, 2008, Aliens in the Attic, 2009; (TV series) Quintuplets, 2004—05, The New Adventures of Old Christine, 2006—08; actor, prodr. (TV series) Andy Richter Controls the Universe, 2002—04, Andy Barker, P.I., 2007, writer Late Night with Conan O'Brien, 1993—2000 (Writers Guild Am. award, 1997, 2000). Office: c/o United Talent Agy Ste 350 9150 Wilshire Blvd Beverly Hills CA 90212

RICHTER, BURTON, physicist, educator; b. NYC, Mar. 22, 1931; s. Abraham and Fanny (Pollack) Richter; m. Laurose Becker, July 1, 1960; children: Elizabeth, Matthew. BS, MIT, 1952, PhD, 1956; degree in physics (hon.), U. Pisa, 2001. Research assoc. Stanford U., 1956—60, asst. prof. physics, 1960—63, assoc. prof., 1963—67, prof., 1967—2006, Paul Pigott prof. phys. sci., 1980—2005, tech. dir. Linear Accelerator Ctr., 1982—84, dir. Linear Accelerator Ctr., 1984—99; dir. emeritus, 1999—2006. Loeb lectr. Harvard U., 1974; DeShalit lectr. Weizmann Inst., 1975; pres. Internat. Union of Pure and Applied Physics, 1997; Astor vis. lectr. Oxford U., 2000; cons. NSF, 1999—2002, advisor, chair NERAC subcom. adv. nuc. transmutation tech., 2002—; sec., bd. dirs. AREVA Enterprises, Inc., Litel Instruments. Contbr. over 300 articles to profl. publs. Recipient E.O. Lawrence medal, Dept. Energy, 1976, Nobel prize in Physics, 1976. Fellow: AAAS, Am. Acad. Arts and Scis., Am. Phys. Soc. (pres. 1994, chmn. energy efficiency study group); mem.: NAS, Nat. Rsch. Coun. (mem. bd. physics and astronomy, chair 2003—), Internat. Coun. Sci. (mem. exec. bd. 2002—05), Regents Mercersbury Acad. (hon.), Nat. Climate Change Assessment (PCAST rev. panel), Am. Phil. Soc. (bd. dirs.). Achievements include research in elementary particle physics. Office: SLAC 2575 Sand Hill Rd Menlo Park CA 94025*

RICHTER, DONALD PAUL, lawyer; b. New Britain, Conn., Feb. 15, 1924; s. Paul John and Helen (Racoske) R.; m. Jane Frances Gumpright, Aug. 10, 1946; children: Christopher Dean, Cynthia Louise. AB, Bates Coll., 1947; LL.B., Yale U., 1950. Bar: NY 1951, Conn. 1953. Assoc. Winthrop, Stimson, Putnam & Roberts, NYC, 1950-52; ptnr. Murtha, Cullina, Richter and Pinney, Hartford, Conn., 1954-94; counsel Murtha Cullina LLP, Hartford, Conn., 1994—. Trustee Bates Coll., 1962-94, Manchester (Conn.) Meml. Hosp., 1963-94, Hartford Sem., 1973-85; trustee Suffield Acad., 1974—, pres., 1982-89; bd. dirs. Met. YMCA Greater Hartford, 1970-94, pres., 1976-81, trustee, 1994—; mem. nat. coun. YMCA, 1978-82; bd. dirs. Church Homes, 1967-81; trustee, v.p., Silver Bay Assn., 1971-96. With USNR, 1943-46. Fellow Am. Coll. Trust and Estate Counsel; mem. ABA, Conn. Bar Assn., Univ. Club, Hartford Club, 20th Century Club, Rotary (Paul Harris fellow 1996), Phi Beta Kappa, Delta Sigma Rho. Congregationalist. Home: 140 Boulder Rd Manchester CT 06040-4508 Office: Murtha Cullina LLP City Place I 185 Asylum St Hartford CT 06103-3469 Office Phone: 860-240-6003.

RICHTER, ELIZABETH MARGOT, music educator; d. Goetz Wilfried and Lucretia Henry Richter; m. Steven Charles Turpin, Nov. 30, 1991. MusM, Boston U. Sch. Arts, 1979. Prin. harp Kans. City Philharm., Mo., 1979—81; adj. asst. prof. U. Mo. Kans. City, 1979—82; prof. harp Ball State U. Sch. Music, Muncie, Ind., 1982—. Musician: (recording) Looking Glass River: Music for Solo Harp, Montage: Four Centuries of Music for Flute and Harp. Recipient Dean's Tchg. award, Ball State U. Coll. Fine Arts, 2001; Individual Artist fellowship, Ind. Arts Commn., 1986, Creative Arts grant, Ball State U., 2004. Mem.: Am. Harp Soc. (1st v.p. 2000—02, bd. dirs. 2000—, Outstanding Svc. award 2003), Pi Kappa Lambda. Office: Ball State Univ Sch Music Muncie IN 47306 Office Phone: 765-285-5416. Business E-Mail: erichter@bsu.edu.

RICHTER, GERHARD, artist; b. Dresden, Germany, Feb. 9, 1932; m. Isa Genzken, 1982; 1 child, Betty. Student, Hochschule fur Bildende Kunste, Dresden, 1952-57; studied with, Karl-Otto Gotz Staatliche Kunstakademie, Dusseldorf, 1961-64. Scenery painter Stadttheatre Zittau, East Germany, 1949-50; commercial artist numerous firms Zittau, 1950-51; photolab. technician Dresden, 1957-60; painter Dusseldorf, 1963—; visual artist Staatliche Kunstakademie, Germany. Prof. Staaliche Kunstakademie, Dusseldorf, 1971; lectr. in field. One man shows include Mobelhaus Berges, Dusseldorf, 1963, Galerie Heiner Friedrich, Munich, 1964, 67, 70, 72, Galerie Rene Block, 1965, 69, 74, White Wide Space Gallery, Antwerp, 1967, Galerie Ricke, Kassel, 1968, Galleria del Naviglio, 1969, Palais des Beaux-Arts, Brussels, 1970, Galerie Konrad Fischer, Dusseldorf, 1970, 72, 75, 83, Mus. Folkwang, Essen, 1970, 80, Kunstverein, Dusseldorf, 1971, Galerie Thomas Borgmann, Cologne, 1971, 84, Galerie Rudolph Zwirner, Cologne, 1972, Galerie Seriaal, Amsterdam, 1973, Onnasch Gallery, NY, 1973, Galleria La Bertesca, Milan, 1973, Galerie Rolf Preisig, Basle, 1975, Nova Scotia Coll. Art, Halifax, 1978, Whitechapel Art Gallery, London, 1979, Sperone-Westwater-Fischer, NY, 1980, 83, Kunsthalle, Dusseldorf, 1981, Galerie Hetzler, 1982, Padiglione d'Arte Contemporanea, Milan, 1982, Galleria Lucio Amelio, Naples, 1983, Galleria Maria Pieroni, Rome, 1983, Musée d'Art et d'Industrie, St. Etienne, France, 1984, Marian Goodman Gallery, NY, 1985, Sperone-Westwater, NY, 1985, Anthony d'Offay Gallery, London, 1988, Art Gallery Ont., 1988, others; exhibited in group shows at Whitechapel Art Gallery, London, Stedelijk Mus., Amsterdam, Kunsthalle, Royal Acad. London, LA County Mus. Art; represented in permanent collections Kunstmuseum, Dusseldorf, Neue Gallery, Mus. Folkwang, Nationalgalerie, Berlin, Kunstmuseum, Basle, Guggenheim Mus., NY; author: Bericht uber eine Demonstr., 1963, Gerhard Richter: Atlas von de fot., 1972, Gerhard Richter: Atlas der Fotos, Collgen und Skizzen, 1976. Recipient Kunstpreis Junger Westen, Recklinghausen, 1967, Arnold Bode prize, Kassel, 1982, Wolf prize in arts (painting) Wolf Found., 1994/5 Mem.: Am. Acad. Arts and Sciences (hon. fgn.). Mailing: Staatliche Kunstakademie Eiskellerstraße 1 Alstadt Germany

RICHTER, HARVENA, retired literature educator, poet; b. Reading, Pa., Mar. 13, 1919; d. Conrad Michael and Harvena Maria (Achenbach) R. BA, U. N.Mex., 1938; MA, NYU, 1955, PhD, 1967. Advt. copywriter Saks 5th Ave., NYC, 1942-43, R.H. Macy, NYC, 1944-46; copy chief Elizabeth Arden, NYC, 1946-47; advt. dir. I. Miller, NYC, 1947-48; European corr. various newspapers, 1948-49; lectr. NYU, NYC, 1952-66, U. N.Mex., 1969-89. Author: The Human Shore, 1959, Virginia Woolf: The Inward Voyage, 1970, Writing to Survive: The Private Notebooks of Conrad Richter, 1988, The Yaddo Elegies and Other Poems, 1995, Green Girls, Poems Early and Late, 1996, The Innocent Island, 1999, Frozen Light, the Crystal Poems, 2002, The Golden Fountains, Sources of Energy and Life, 2002, Passage to Teheran, 2004; author numerous poems; short stories to Sat. Eve. Post, New Am., Blue Mesa Rev.; essays to Atlantic, Modern Fiction Studies, C.S. Monitor, others. AAUW fellow, 1964-65; grantee Yaddo, 1963-64, MacDowell Colony, 1965-66, Wurlitzer Found., Taos, N.Mex., 1968, 73-75, Va. Ctr. for Creative Arts, 1983, 85, Ragdale Found., 1990. Mem. Author's Guild, Virginia Woolf Soc., Kappa Kappa Gamma. Avocation: gardening. Home and Office: 1932 Candelaria Rd NW Albuquerque NM 87107

RICHTER, JOHN CHARLES, prosecutor; Grad., Emory U.; JD, U. Va. Law clk. to Hon. J. Owen Forrester US Dist. Ct. (no. dist.) Ga.; asst. dist. atty. Cobb County, Ga., 1998; chief of staff, criminal divsn. US Dept. Justice, 1998, acting asst. atty. gen. criminal divsn., acting US atty. (we. dist.) Okla., 2005—06, US atty. (we. dist.) Okla., 2006—. Office: US Attys Office 210 W Park Ave Ste 400 Oklahoma City OK 73102*

RICHTER, PETER CHRISTIAN, lawyer; b. Opava, Czechoslovakia, June 13, 1944; came to U.S., 1951; s. Hanus and Alzbeta (Kindlarova) R.; m. Leslie Diane Rousseau, Nov. 25, 1967; children: Timothy Jason, Lindsey Berta. BS, U. Oreg., 1967, JD, 1971. Bar: Oreg. 1971, U.S. Dist. Ct. 1972, U.S. Ct. Appeals (9th cir.) 1972, U.S. Supreme Ct. 1983. Assoc. Veatch, Lovett & Stiner, Portland, Oreg., 1971-73; ptnr. Miller Nash LLP, Portland, 1978—. Adj. prof. law trial advocacy Northwestern Sch. of Law, Lewis and Clark Coll., Portland, 1986—; pro tempore judge Multnomah County Cir. Ct., Portland, 1985—1998, Oreg. State Bar Trial Advocacy Seminars, 1988—; trial advocacy coll. planner, instr. Oreg. State Bar, 1998—. Author: (handbook) Oregon State Bar, 1987, 88, 89; co-author: (chpt. in book) Oregon State Bar Damage Manual, 1985, 90, editor, program planner Sales: The Oregon Experience, 1989. Trustee, bd. dirs. Parry Ctr. for Children, Portland, 1990; former bd. dir. Boy Scouts of Am., Columbia Pacific Coun., Portland, Nat. Conf. Christians and Jews, Portland, 1983; bd. advisers Pacific Crest Outward Bound, 2000. With Oreg. Army N.G., 1967-75. Recipient Cert. of Appreciation Northwestern Sch. of Law, 1990; named one of ten Best Litigators in Oreg, Nat. Bar Jour. Fellow Am. Bar Found.; mem. ABA (trial techniques com.), Fed. Bar Assn. (Oreg. chpt.), Am. Bd. Trial Advocates (advocate), Internat. Assn. of Def. Counsel, Oreg. Bar Assn. (lectr. trial advocacy seminars 1988—, mem. jud. adminstn. com, bus. lit. sec. exec. comm.), Multnomah Bar Assn. (former bd dirs.), Oreg. Assn. Def. Counsel (cert. of appreciation 1987, 89) Inns of Ct., Multnomah Athletic Club (trustee, pres.), Arlington Club. Avocations: squash, tennis, skiing, golf, reading, motorcycling riding. Office: Miller Nash LLP 111 SW 5th Ave Ste 3500 Portland OR 97204-3699 Office Phone: 503-224-5858. Business E-Mail: peter.richter@millernash.com.

RICHTER, W.D., screenwriter, director, producer; b. New Britain, Conn., Dec. 7, 1945; s. Walter Oswald and Hedwig (Duch) R.; m. Susan Booth, June 22, 1968. BA, Dartmouth Coll., 1968; postgrad., U. So. Calif., 1968-70. Freelance writer, producer, director, 1973—. Screenwriter: Slither, 1973, Peeper, 1975, Nickelodeon, 1976, Invasion of the Body Snatchers, 1978, Dracula, 1979, Brubaker, 1980 (Academy award nomination best original screenplay 1980), All Night Long, 1981, Hard Feelings, 1982, Big Trouble in Little China, 1986, Needful Things, 1993, Home for The Holidays, 1995, Stealth, 2005; prodr., dir.: (films) Buckaroo Banzai, 1984, Late for Dinner, 1991. Mem. Writers Guild Am., Dirs. Guild Am.

RICHTER, WILLIAM LOUIS, social sciences educator; b. Covina, Calif., Apr. 9, 1939; s. Louis Ernest and Gwendolyn Marguerite (Hughes) R.; m. Linda Kay Clark, Aug. 29, 1964; children: Mark William, Robert Clark. BA, Willamette U., 1961; MA, U. Chgo., 1963, PhD, 1968. Instr. Ill. Inst. Tech., Chgo., 1964, U. Hawaii, Honolulu, 1964-66; asst. prof. Kans. State U., Manhattan, 1966-73, assoc. prof., 1973-81, prof., 1981—2008, prof. emeritus, 2008—, dept. head, 1984-93, asst. provost, 1991-96, assoc. provost for internat. programs, 1996—2002. Vis. Fulbright lectr. Panjab U., Chandigarh, India, 1969-70; faculty rsch. fellow Am. Inst. Indian Studies, New Delhi, India, 1972-73, 1985; faculty rsch. fellow Am. Inst. Pakistan Studies, Lahore, Pakistan, 1976-77; cons. USAID, NDI, 1990—. Co-editor: (books) The Landon Lectures, 1987, Combating Corruption, Encouraging Ethics, 1990, 2d edit., 2007, (Lanham, MD:Rowman & Littlefield) Approaches to Political Thought, 2009. Mem. Rotary (Rotarian of Yr., 1993). Home: 2383 Grandview Ter Manhattan KS 66502-3729 Office: Kans State U Dept Polit Sci 226 Waters Hall Manhattan KS 66506-4030 E-mail: wrichter@ksu.edu.

RICHTON, SAMUEL M., pediatric endocrinologist; b. Pittsfield, Mass., Aug. 17, 1948; m. Marsha Lee Richton, May 25, 1975; children: Jonathan, Joshua, Jeanette, Simcha, Jesse. BS, U. Mass., 1970; MS, Yale U., New Haven, 1972; MD, Albert Einstein Coll. Medicine, Bronx, NY, 1975. Diplomate Am. Bd. Pediat., Am. Bd. Pediat. Endocrinology. Resident pediat. Rainbow Babies & Children's Hosp., Cleve., 1975-77; fellow pediat. endocrinology and metabolism U. Md., Balt., 1977-78; fellow pediat. Harvard Med. Sch., Boston; rsch. fellow Juvenile Diabetes Found. Children's Hosp., Boston, 1978-80; physician Diabetes Med. Group, LA, 1980-81; asst. prof. U. Ill. Coll. Medicine, Chgo., 1981-84, Chgo. Med. Sch., 1984-87; dir. endocrinology Cook County Children's Hosp., Chgo., 1984-87; dir. divsn. pediat. endocrinology Miami Children's Hosp., 1987—. Med. dir. South Fla. Diabetes Camp, Miami, 1987—. Contbr. articles to profl jours. Fellow: Am. Acad. Pediat.; mem.: Lawson Wilkens Pediat. Endocrine Soc., Internat. Diabetes Found., Am. Diabetes Assn. Office: Miami Childrens Hosp 3100 SW 62nd Ave # 122 Miami FL 33155-3009 Office Phone: 305-662-8398. Office Fax: 305-663-8581.

RICK, ROSELEEN P., lawyer; b. NYC, 1941; BA, Va. Commonwealth Univ., 1976; JD, Univ. Richmond, 1980. Bar: Va. 1980. Ptnr., practice group leader, multi-family housing Troutman Sanders LLP, Richmond, Va. Mem.: ABA, Nat. Assn. Women Bus. Owners, Va. Bar Assn., Richmond Bar Assn. Office Phone: 804-697-1462. Office Fax: 804-698-6007. Business E-Mail: roseleen.rick@troutmansanders.com.

RICKABAUGH, RENÉ LANE, principal; b. Newcastle, Wyo., Sept. 1, 1957; d. James Austin and Patricia Lee (Baumgartner) Lane; m. Ronald J. Rickabaugh, Aug. 1, 1981. BA in Elem. and Spl. Edn. cum laude, U. Wyo., Laramie, 1979, MA in Spl. Edn., 1989. Spl. summer program dir. Assn. for Retarded Citizens Weston County, Newcastle, 1979; spl. edn. tchr. Natrona County Sch. Dist. 1, Casper, Wyo., 1979—84, ednl. resource specialist, cons. for instrn., curriculum and materials for handicapped students, 1984—92, prin. spl. edn., 1992—94; elem. prin., Title I dir. Bar Nunn Sch., 1994—. Mem. Wyo. state com. North Ctrl. Assn. Edn. chmn. First United Meth. Ch., chair staff/parish rels. com. Recipient Medallion Excellence award, NCSD, 2005. Mem. NEA, AAUW, Wyo. Assn. Elem. Prins. (past treas., pres.-elect 2005, pres. 2006), Nat. Assn. Elem. Prins., Coun. Exceptional Children (past membership chmn.), Assn. Direct Instrn., Assn. Retarded Citizens (past sec. N.C. chpt.), U. Wyo. Alumni Assn., PEO (past pres. chpt.), Omicron Delta Kappa, Kappa Delta Pi (past v.p.), Phi Delta Kappa (past chpt. pres.), Phi Kappa Phi. Home: 80 Magnolia St Casper WY 82604-4063 Home Phone: 307-266-5526; Office Phone: 307-577-4507. Personal E-mail: rener_9@msn.com.

RICKARD, DAVID B., retail executive; b. Oneida, NY, 1946; BS, Cornell U., 1969; MBA, Harvard U., 1971. From internat. acct. to fin. control mgr. U.S. mktg. S.C. Johnson Wax, Inc., 1971-74; with Gen. Foods Corp., fin. dir. internat.; dir. investor rels. Kraft Gen. Foods; v.p. fin. and strategy Kraft USA; sr. v.p., CFO Grand Metropolitan, 1991-94, group contr. London, 1994-95; fin. dir. Internat. Distillers and Vintners, Ltd., 1995-96; exec. v.p. Internat. Distillers and Vintners-Americas, 1996-97; sr. v.p., CFO RJR Nabisco, NYC, 1997-99; exec. v.p., CFO, chief adminstrv. officer CVS Corp., Woonsocket, RI, 1999—2007, CVS/Caremark Corp., Woonsocket, RI, 2007—. Bd. dirs. Harris Corp., 2001—, May Dept. Stores, 2005—. Mem.: Worldwide Retail Exchange, Financial Acctg. Standards Advisory Coun. (mem. steering comt.). Office: CVS Caremark Corp 1 CVS Dr Woonsocket RI 02895*

RICKARD, LISA ANN, lawyer; b. Englewood, NJ, Oct. 22, 1955; d. Joseph Mitchell and Ann Marie (Samen) Moore; m. J. Scott Rickard, June 18, 1977; children: Jack Taylor, Justin Moore. BA in Govt. and French, Lafayette Coll., 1977; JD, Am. U., 1982. Legis. asst. Bank of Am., Washington, 1977-78; spl. asst. and press asst. to Sen. Richard Stone, Washington, 1978-80; legis. asst. to Sen. Frank Murkowski, Washington, 1981; assoc. and ptnr. Akin, Gump, Strauss, Hauer & Feld, Washington, 1982-93; v.p. federal affairs Ryder System, Inc., Washington, 1993-97, sr. v.p. govt. affairs, 1997; v.p. fed. & state govt. affairs Dow Chemical Co.; pres. U.S. C. of C. Inst. for Legal Reform, Washington. Bd. dirs., mem. corp. adv. coun. Women's Rsch. and Edn. Inst., Washington, 1991—. Diplome D'Etudes Francaises Cours Moyen, Deuxieme Degres, U. Strasbourg, France, 1976. Mem. ABA, D.C. Bar Assn. Episcopalian. Avocation: travel. Office: Institute for Legal Reform 1615 H St NW Washington DC 20062-2000 Office Phone: 202-463-3107. E-mail: lrickard@uschamber.com.

RICKARD, MARGARET LYNN, library director, consultant; b. Detroit, July 31, 1944; d. Frank Mathias and Betty Louise (Lee) Sieger; m. Cyriac Thannikary, Nov. 13, 1965 (div. Feb. 1973); 1 child, Luke Anthony Thannikary; m. Marcos T. Perez, Mar. 1973 (dec. Oct. 1973); m. Lui Gotti, Dec. 23, 1984 (dec. Aug. 1997); m. William A. Rickard, Aug. 22, 1998 (dec. Aug. 21, 2005). AB, U. Detroit, Mich., 1968; MLS, Pratt Inst., Bklyn., 1969; postgrad., NYU, 1976—77. Cert. libr. N.Y. Sr. libr. Queens Pub. Libr., Jamaica, NY, 1969-77; libr. dir. El Centro (Calif.) Pub. Libr., 1977-99; ret., 1999. Vice chmn., chmn. Serra Coop. Libr. Sys., San Diego, 1980—82, libr. cons., 1998—; county libr./cons. Imperial County Free Libr., 1993—99. Pres. Hist. Site Found., El Centro, 1988—99, 1992, sec., 1989, trustee, 1989—99, v.p., 1991—92; mem. Downton El Centro Assn., mem. arches bus. improvement dist.; mem. comm. and arts task force Imperial County Arts Coun.; coord. arts and culture com. City of El Centro Strategic Plan; fin. sec. St. Elizabeth Luth. Ch., El Centro, 1988. Recipient Disting. Svc. award, El Dorado County ACSA, 2004, El Dorado County Disting. Employee Svc. award, ACSA, 2004; Title IIB fellow, Pratt Inst., 1968—69. Mem.: AAUW (v.p. El Centro 1988), ALA, Calif. County Librs. Assn., Calif. Libr. Assn., Toastmasters, El Centro C. of C., Women of Moose (sr. regent El Centro 1988—89, ednl. advancment chmn. 1999—2000), Soroptomists (life; v.p. El Centro 1978, corr. sec. 1990—91, 1st v.p. 1991—92, pres. 1992—93, 2d v.p. 1995—96, 1998—99, rec. sec. 1997—98). Democrat. Lutheran. E-mail: rickmeg@worldnet.att.net.

RICKARDS, JOHN PATRICK, psychology professor; b. Albany, Oct. 22, 1941; s. Robert P. and Kathryn A. Rickards; m. Karin Sheehan; children: Kristine Alexis Rickards-Schlichting, Claire Alison. PhD, Penn State U., Univ. Pk., 1971. Assoc. prof. edn. and psychology Purdue U., West Lafayette, Ind., 1971—81; prof. psychology U. Conn., Storrs, 1981—. Contbr. articles to profl. jours. Fellow: APA. Avocations: travel, hiking, bicycling. Home: 51 Storrs Heights Rd Storrs Mansfield CT 06268 Office: Univ Cin Bousfield Bldg Storrs Mansfield CT 06269 Business E-Mail: john.rickards@uconn.edu.

RICKEL, ANNETTE URSO, psychology and psychiatry researcher, educator; b. Phila. d. Ralph Francis and Marguerite (Calcaterra) Urso; 1 child, John Ralph Rickel. BA, Mich. State U., 1969; PhD, MD, U. Mich., 1972. Lic. psychologist, Mich. Faculty early childhood edn. Merrill-Palmer Inst., Detroit, 1967-69; adj. faculty U. Mich., Ann Arbor, 1969-75; asst. dir. N.E. Guidance Ctr., Detroit, 1972-75; asst. prof. psychology Wayne State U., Detroit, 1975-81; vis. assoc. prof. Columbia U., NYC, 1982-83; assoc. prof. psychology Wayne State U., 1981-87, asst. provost, 1989-91, prof. psychology, 1987-95; Am. Coun. on Edn. fellow Princeton and Rutgers Univs., 1990-91; clin. prof. dept. psychiatry Georgetown U., Washington, 1995—2000; program officer Rockefeller Found., 2000—03; pres. Annette Urso Rickel Found., 2003—; prof. Weill Cornell Med. Sch., 2005—. AAAS and APA Congl. Sci. fellow on Senate Fin. Subcom. on Health for Senate's Nat. Health Care Reform Task Force, 1992—93. Cons. editor Jour. of Cmty. Psychology, Jour. Primary Prevention; co-author: Social and Psychological Problems of Women, 1984, Preventing Maladjustment..., 1987; author: Teenage Pregnancy and Parenting, 1989, Keeping Children From Harm's Way, 1997, High Risk Sexual Behavior, 1998, Understanding Managed Care,

2000, Attention Deficit Hyperactivity Disorder in Children and Adults, 2006, Chronic Illness in Children and Adolescents, 2007; contbr. articles to profl. jours. Mem. Pres.'s Task Force on Nat. Health Care Reform, 1993; bd. dirs. Children's Ctr. of Wayne County, Mich., 1989—, The Epilepsy Ctr. of Mich., 1984-92, Nat. Symphony Orch., 1997—, Reading is Fundamental, 2000—, Chamber Music Soc. of Lincoln Ctr., 2002—, Soc. Meml. Sloan Kettering Cancer Ctr., 2002—, The Kellogg Found., 1996-97, The John D. and Catherine T. MacArthur Found., 1998-99. Grantee NIMH, 1976-86, Eloise and Richard Webber Found., 1977-80, McGregor Fund, 1977-78, 82, David M. Whitney Fund, 1982, Katherine Tuck Fund, 1985-90, NIH, 2000; recipient Career Devel. Chair award, 1985-86. Fellow APA (div. pres. 1984-85); mem. Internat. Women's Forum, Soc. for Rsch. in Child Devel., Soc. for Rsch. in Child and Adolescent Psychopathology, Internat. Assn. of Applied Psychologists, Sigma Xi, Psi Chi. Roman Catholic. Office Phone: 212-710-1040. Personal E-mail: rickelau@aol.com.

RICKEL, JOHN C., automotive executive; b. 1961; B in Finance, Ohio State U., MBA. Various exec. and managerial positions including contr. Ford Americas and CFO Ford Europe Ford Motor Co., 1984—2005, mem. audit com., bd. dirs. Ford Otosan Turkey, chmn. bd. dirs. Ford Russia, 2002—04; sr. v.p., CFO Group 1 Automotive, Inc., Houston, 2005—. Office: Group 1 Automotive Inc 800 Gessner Ste 500 Houston TX 77024 Office Phone: 713-647-5700.*

RICKELS, KARL, psychiatrist, educator; b. Wilhelmshaven, Germany, Aug. 17, 1924; came to U.S., 1954, naturalized, 1960; s. Karl E. and Stephanie (Roehrhoff) R.; m. Rosalind Wilson, June 27, 1964; children: Laurence Arthur, PhD, Stephen W., Michael R. MD, U. Muenster, 1951. Intern Dortmund (Germany) City Hosp., 1951-52; postgrad. tng. U. Erlangen, U. Frankfurt, City Hosp. Kassel, 1952-54; resident in psychiatry Mental Health Inst., Cherokee, Iowa, 1954-55, Hosp. U. Pa., Phila., 1955-57; from instr. to assoc. prof. U. Pa., Phila., 1957-69, prof. psychiatry, 1969—, prof. pharmacology, 1976-98, Stuart and Emily B.H. Mudd prof. human behavior, 1977—, chief mood and anxiety disorders program, 1964—, chmn. com. on studies involving human beings Phila., 1985-98. Chief psychiatry Phila. Gen. Hosp., 1975-77. Editor, author 9 books; contbr. over 570 articles to profl. publs. Fellow Am. Coll. Neuropsychopharmacology (life; charter), Am. Psychiat. Assn. (life), Coll. Physicians Phila., Collegium Internat. Neuro-Psychopharmacologicum, Psychiat. Rsch. Soc., European Coll. Neuropsychopharmacology (corr.). Home: 1324 Youngsford Rd Gladwyne PA 19035 Office: U Pa Dept Psychiatry Ste 670 3535 Market St Philadelphia PA 19104-3515 Home Phone: 610-649-4838; Office Phone: 215-746-6417. Business E-Mail: krickels@mail.med.upenn.edu.

RICKELS, LAURENCE ARTHUR, foreign language educator; b. Cherokee, Iowa, Dec. 2, 1954; s. Karl and Crista (Loessin) R. BA in English Lit., U. Pa., Phila., 1975; Hauptseminaraufnahmeprufung, Freie U. Berlin, Germany, 1975; MA, PhD in German Lit., Princeton U., NJ, 1978-80; MA in Clin. Psychology, Antioch U., Santa Barbara, Calif., 1994. Lectr. U. Dusseldorf, Germany, 1980-81; asst. prof. U. Calif., Santa Barbara, 1981-86, assoc. prof., 1986-90, prof., 1990—, chair dept. Germanic, Slavic and Semitic studies, 1989-95, Sigmund Freud prof. European grad. sch., 2006—. Cons. Psychiat. Rsch. Group, 1982—; mem. Film Studies Adv. Bd., U. Calif. Santa Barbara, 1987-96. Author: Aberrations of Mourning, 1988, Der Unbetrauerbare Tod, 1989, The Case of California, 1991, The Vampire Lectures, 1999, Nazi Pscyhoanalysis, 2002; editor: Looking After Nietzsche, 1990, Acting Out In Groups, 1999; founding editor Art US, 2003—; contrb. articles to profl. jours. Recipient Rsch. Assistance awards Ctr. for German and European Studies, Berkeley, 1991, 93, 94; rsch. fellow Alexander Von Humboldt-Stiftung, Berlin, 1985-86, 88, 89; rsch. fellow Zentrum Literatur Forschung, Berlin, 2006. Mem. MLA (del. assembly mem. 1988-90), Internat. Initiative on Tech. and the Unconscious-U. Calif. Humanities Rsch. Inst. (founding). Office: Univ Calif Dept Germanic Slavic & Semitic Studies Santa Barbara CA 93106 Home: 8400 De Longpre Ave Apt 209 West Hollywood CA 90069-2625 Business E-Mail: rickels@gss.uscb.edu.

RICKEN, DAVID LAURIN, bishop; b. Dodge City, Kans., Nov. 9, 1952; s. George William and Bertha H. (Davis) Ricken. Attended, Pontifical Coll. Josephinum, Worthington, Ohio, 1970—72; BA in Philosophy, Conception Sem., Mo., 1974; MA, STB, Cath. U. Louvain, Belgium, 1980; JCL, Pontifical Gregorian U., Rome, 1989. Ordained priest Diocese of Pueblo, Colo., 1980; assoc. pastor Cathedral of Sacred Heart, Pueblo, 1980—85; vice-chancellor Diocese of Pueblo, Pueblo, 1985—87; adminstr. Holy Rosary Parish, Pueblo, 1985—87; vocation dir., vicar, ministry formation Diocese of Pueblo, 1992—99, chancellor, 1992—99, with, Diocesan Tribunal, 1992—99; ordained bishop, 2000; coadjutor bishop Diocese of Cheyenne, Wyo., 2000—01, bishop, 2001—08, Diocese of Green Bay, Wis., 2008—. Com. chmn. Am. Coll. Louvain; com. mem. Protection of Children and Young People; bd. trustees Our Lady of New Advent Theol. Inst., Denver. Mem.: US Conf. Cath. Bishops. Office: Diocese of Green Bay 1910 S Webster Ave PO Box 23825 Green Bay WI 54305-3825 Office Phone: 920-437-7531. Office Fax: 920-435-1330.

RICKERT, JONATHAN BRADLEY, retired foreign service officer; b. Washington, July 23, 1937; s. Van Dusen and Margaret Eleanor (Bradley) R.; m. Ulla Gerd Margareta Granstrand, June 20, 1969; children: Ulla Margaret, Jonathan Bernt. AB cum laude, Princeton U, 1959; diploma Russian lang., U.S. Army Lang. Sch., 1962; student, Harvard U., 1976-77; MA, George Washington U., 1982. Rotational jr. officer Exec. Sec. State Dept., 1963-65; consular officer Embassy, London, 1965—66, staff aide to amb., polit. officer Moscow, 1966-68; exchanges officer Office Soviet and Eastern European Exchanges State Dept., 1969-70, with Romanian Lang. Tng. FSI, 1971; consular officer Embassy Bucharest, 1971-73, polit. officer, 1973-74; spl. asst. to U.S. Rep. U.S. Delegation MBFR, Vienna, 1974-76; polit./labor officer Embassy Port of Spain, 1977-80; desk officer Trinidad, Guyana, Suriname, acting dep. dir. Office Caribbean Affairs State Dept., 1980-82, desk officer Romania, Office Eastern European and Yugoslav Affairs, 1982-84, with Bulgarian Lang. Tng., 1984-85; dep. chief mission Embassy Sofia, 1985-88; chief European Assignments divsn. State Dept., 1988-90; legis. asst. to Sen Bob Packwood, 1990-91; dep. chief mission Embassy Bucharest, 1991-95; dir. Office of N. Cen. European Affairs State Dept., 1995-98, program officer Office of the Coord. for U.S. Assistance to Europe and Eurasia, 1998—2005, pub. diplomacy officer Bur. European and Eurasian Affairs, 2006—07; bd. dirs. Project on Ethnic Rels., Princeton, N.J., 1999. With U.S. Army, 1961-62. Mem. Am. Fgn. Svc. Assn. Episcopalian. Personal E-mail: therickets@hotmail.com.

RICKETSON, GEORGE MANNING, III, retired surgeon; b. Atlanta, Ga., 1937; MD, U. Fla., 1966. Diplomate Am. Bd. Surgery. Intern Bethesda Naval Hosp, Md., 1966-67; resident in surgery USN Hosp., Portsmouth, Va., 1967-71; pvt. practice Sacred Heart Hosp., Pensacola, Fla.; pvt. practice, group partnership McMahon Ricketson Stockamp, Pensacola, Fla.; ret., 2002. Fellow: ACS; mem.: Southeastern Surg. Congress. Office: McMahon Ricketson Stockamp 5014 Barranca Lora Pensacola FL 32514 Home Phone: 850-477-5146. Personal E-mail: pricketson@cox.net.

RICKETSON, MARY E., former dean, lawyer; m. Nathan Ben Coats. JD, U. Denver, 1978. Asst. atty gen., Colo.; dep. dist. atty. Colo.; pvt. practice specializing in employment dispute mediation, arbitration; exec. dir. Colo. Lawyer's Com.; dean, univ. prof. U. Denver Sturm Coll. Law, 2000—06. Affiliated Jud. Arbitrators and Mediators. Trustee Dian Fossey Found. Internat.; co-chair Mayor Wellington Webb's 2025 Commn., 2002. Recipient Women of Distinction award, Mill High Girl Scouts, 2004, Edwin Wolf award, Lawyers Com. Civil Rights Under Law, 2004, Mile High Coun. Girl Scouts award, 2004. Mem.: Am. Bar Found., Am. Law Inst., Colo. Hispanic Bar Assn. (Cmty. Svc. award 2003), Colo. Profl. Soc. on Abuse of Children (former pres.), Colo. Women's Bar Found. (former pres.), Colo. Women's Bar Assn. (former pres., Mary Lathrop award 2003).

RICKETTS, THOMAS, investment company executive; s. J. Joe Ricketts; married. AB, U. Chgo., 1987; MBA, U. Chgo. Grad. Sch. Bus., 1993. CFA. Summer intern TD Ameritrade Holding Corp.; pit trader Chgo. Bd. Options Exch.; fin. exec. Chgo. Corp.; founder, pres., CEO Incapital Holdings LLC, Chgo., 2001—. Recipient Young Alumni award, U. Chgo., 2005. Office: Incapital LLC 200 S Wacker Dr Ste 3700 Chicago IL 60606 Office Phone: 312-379-3700. Office Fax: 312-379-3701.*

RICKETTS, VIRGINIA LEE, historian, researcher; b. Jamestown, Kans., Jan. 12, 1925; d. Roy Earl Eastman and Alma Anna Hunter; m. Clair Keith Ricketts, June 3, 1944; children: Keith Alan, Dennis Lee, Donald Gene. Grad. H.S., Filer, Idaho. Clk. dist. ct., auditor, recorder Jerome County, Idaho, 1972—79; pvt. practice historian, rschr. Jerome, 1979—. Mem. Idaho State Hist. Records Adv. Bd., Boise, 1976-2002; pres. Idaho Assn. Recorders and Clks., 1977-78; cons. Idaho State Supreme Ct., Boise, 1979-81; tour dir., instr. Coll. So. Idaho, Twin Falls, 1984-97; mem. Bur. Land Mgmt. Adv. Bd., Shoshone, Idaho, 1989-95, Upper Snake River Ecosystem Adv. Bd., Idaho, 1995-98; Internat. Toastmistress communicator, 1988; lectr. in field Author: The History of the North Side-The First 75 Years, 1982, Greater Twin Falls Historical Guide, 1988, A History of the Middle Snake River, 1996, Then and Now in Southern Idaho, 1998, Shoshone Falls the Magnificent Spectacle, 2005 Organizer Friends St. Stricker Ranch, Inc., Twin Falls, 1984 Recipient Cert. of Commendation, Am. Assn. for State and Local History, 1984, Cert. of Resolution of Appreciation, Idaho State Bd. Edn., 1998, Esto Perpetua award Idaho State Hist. Soc., 2004; named Idaho Disting. Citizen, Idaho Statesmen, 1988, Centennial Citizen, Citizens of Jerome County Idaho, 1990 Mem. Idaho State Hist. Soc. (trustee 1987-99, chair bd. trustees 1991-98), Oreg. Calif. Trails Assn. (organizer Idaho chpt. 1984, treas. 1985-99), Jerome County Hist. Soc., Inc. (co-organizer 1984, former pres., curator 1985-2004), Idaho Assn. Mus. (Outstanding Svc. award 1998), Soroptomist Internat. Am. (Woman of Distinction 1999, Cmty. Svc. award Jerome Masonic Lodge, 2007-.), PEO (historian Ea. Idaho chpt. 1987-98). Republican. Presbyterian. Avocations: needlecrafts, gardening, sports. Home: Chaparelle House #117 1880 N Harrison St Twin Falls ID 83301

RICKLEFS, DALE LYNNE, library director; b. Chgo., July 29, 1953; d. Glenn Harley and Eleanor Clara Rogers; 1 child, Reyhan. BA, Ill. Wesleyan U., 1974; MLS, U. Tex., 1977. Libr. Radian Corp., Austin, Tex., 1975—80; libr. dir. City of Round Rock, Tex., 1980—. Mem. ex officio Friends Round Rock Pub. Libr., 1983—, Round Rock Pub. Libr. Found., 1991—; bd. dirs. Round Rock Cmty. Choir, 1998—2003; pres. United Way Greater Williamson Co., Round Rock, 2003—05; treas. Williamson County Hist. Mus., 2007—; boy scout dist. cub trainer Boy Scouts Am. Tomahawk Dist., Austin-Georgetown, Tex., 1991—92; pres. Main St. Quilt Guild, 2002—03. Recipient Dist. Cubscouter of Yr., Boy Scouts Am. Tomahawk Dist., Texas, 1992. Mem.: ALA, Texas Mcpl. League Libr. Dir.'s Divsn. (pres. 1988—89), Tex. Libr. Assn. (chmn. dist. 3 1984—85). Avocations: machine embroidery, quilting. Office: City Round Rock Pub Libr 216 E Main St Round Rock TX 78664 Office Phone: 512-218-7010. Business E-Mail: dale@round-rock.tx.us.

RICKLES, DONALD JAY, comedian, actor; b. LI, NY, May 8, 1926; s. Max S. and Etta (Feldman) R.; m. Barbara Sklar, Mar. 14, 1965; children: Mindy Beth, Lawrence Corey. Grad., Am. Acad. Dramatic Arts, NYC. Appeared in TV shows The Don Rickles Show, 1971-72, C.P.O. Sharkey, 1976-77, Foul-Ups, Bleeps and Blunders, 1984, Daddy Dearest, 1993; appeared in movies Run Silent, Run Deep, 1958, The Rat Race, 1960, Kelly's Heroes, 1992, Casino, 1995, Toy Story, 1995, Quest for Camelot, 1998, Toy Story 2, 1999, The Wool Cap, 2004, others; Reno and Lake Tahoe, Nev., Orleans, Las Vegas, Borgata, Atlantic City, numerous other nightclubs; numerous appearances TV variety shows, (HBO documentary) Mr. Warmth: The Don Rickles Project, 2007 (Primetime Emmy for Outstanding Individual Performance in a Variety or Music Program, Acad. TV Arts and Scis., 2008), DVD, 2008; rec. albums include Don Rickles Speaks, Hello Dummy; author: Rickles Book, 2007 (NY Times Bestseller), Rickles' Letters, 2008. With USN, 1943—45. Named Entertainer of Yr. Friars Club, 1974, Entertainer of Yr., Am. Gaming Assn., 2004, Las Vegas Comedian of Yr., Las Vegas Conv. and Visitor's Authority, 2004; awarded star on Hollywood Walk of Fame, 2000; recipient Pinnacle award US Comedy and Arts Festival, 2007, TV Land Legend award, 2009. Office: care Shefrin Co 808 S Ridgeley Dr Los Angeles CA 90036-4727 Office Phone: 323-931-8200.

RICKMAN, ALAN, actor; b. London, Feb. 21, 1946; Student, Royal Acad. of Dramatic Art. Stage appearances: The Seagull, Mephisto, Les Liaisons Dangereuses, 1985, 87 (Tony nominee Best Actor 1987), Tango at the End of Winter, 1991, Hamlet, 1992, Anthony and Cleopatra, 1998, Private Lives (Tony nominee, Best Stage Actor award Variety Club Show Bus. Awards 2002); dir.: My Name is Rachel Corrie, London & NY, 2005-06; (TV movies) Romeo and Juliet, Masterpiece Theater, 1978, Therese Raquin, 1980, Barchester Chronicles, 1984, Spirit of Man, 1989, Revolutionary Witness, 1989, Victoria Wood's All Day Breakfast, 1992, Fallen Angels, 1993, Rasputin, 1996 (Golden Globe, Emmy and SAG awards for Best Actor), Victoria Wood with All the Trimmings, 2000, We Know Where You Live, 2001 (Emmy Nomination Best Actor, 2004); (films) Die Hard, 1988, The January Man, 1989, Robin Hood: Prince of Thieves, 1991, Quigley Down Under, 1990, Truly, Madly, Deeply, 1991, Closet Land, 1991, Close My Eyes, 1991, Bob Roberts, 1992, Mesmer, 1993, An Awfully Big Adventure, 1994, Sense and Sensibility, 1995, Michael Collins, 1996, Judas Kiss, 1998, Dogma, 1998, Dark Harbor, 1998, Galaxy Quest, 1999, Play, 2000, Blow Dry, 2001, Harry Potter and the Sorcerer's Stone, 2001, Search for John Gissing, 2001, Harry Potter and the Chamber of Secrets, 2002, Love Actually, 2003, Harry Potter and the Prisoner of Azkaban, 2004, (voice) The Hitchhiker's Guide to the Galaxy, 2005, Harry Potter and the Goblet of Fire, 2005, Snowcake, 2006, Perfume: The Story of a Murderer, 2006, Nobel Son, 2007, Harry Potter and the Order of the Phoenix, 2007, Sweeney Todd: The Demon Barber of Fleet Street, 2007, Bottle Shock, 2008, Harry Potter and the Half-Blood Prince, 2009; writer, dir.: The Winter Guest, 1997 (Best Film award Chgo. Film Festival). Office: Oxford House 76 Oxford St London W1N 0AX England

RICKMAN, CONNIE GARZA, retired principal; d. Manuel and Guadalupe Costello Garza; m. Raymond Douglas Rickman, Jan. 20, 1961; children: John Joseph, Rise, Ric. BS in Edn., Tex. Woman's U., Denton, 1957; MEd, Ctrl. State U., Wilberforce, Ohio, 1968. Cert. in secondary adminstrn. Seattle, 1974, in tng. Heidelburg, Germany, 1964. Tchr. Gregory Pub. Sch. Dist., Tex., 1958—59; fifth and sixth grade tchr. Elmira Heights Sch. Dist., NY, 1959—60; tchr. DuPont-Ft. Lewis Sch. Dist., Wash., 1960—63, Dept. Def., European Theater, Frankfurt, Kaiserslautern, Germany, 1963—66, Xenia Sch. Dist., Ohio, 1966—69; vocat. counselor, student suspensions hearing officer, jr. high/HS vice-prin. to prin. Tacoma Sch. Dist. #10, 1969—97. Staff devel. trainer USDEA, Dept. Army, Kaiserslautern, 1965—66; staff developpment leader Xenia Sch. Dist., Xenia, Ohio, 1966—69; edn. advisor Local Am. Cancer Soc., Xenia, 1967—69; lectr. Wright State U., Fairborn, Ohio, 1968—69; congl. area rep. Assn. of Wash. State Secondary Principals, Olympia, Wash., 1974—97; edn. com. chair Educators Against I-601-602, Wash.; edn. com. Senator Slade Gorton, Seattle; advisor, chaperone US ho. reps. conf. Voices Against Violence. Contbr. letter books. State chair, nat. liaison Wa. State Sch. Retirees Assn., Lacey; organizer help a student fund Tacoma Edn. Assn., 1973—2008; com. mem. St. Leo's, Tacoma, 1982—83; youth leader Tobacco and Substance Abuse Prevention; abuse prevention mem. Wash. State Prevention Summit; svc. chair State Liaison to Nat. Sch. Retirees; adult leader Area Schs. Students' Com.; organizer Tacoma Principals Assn., 1974—97; chaperone U.S. Ho. of Representatives, Washington DC, DC, 1999—2000; mem. congl. dist. #6 Fed. Rels. Network, Tacoma, Olympia, 2003—08; dir., pres. Tacoma Sch. Bd., 2003—; com. chair St. Leo's Bldg. Project, Tacoma, 1986—87; bd. mem. County Sheriff's Advisory Bd.; bd. dirs. TPS. Recipient Sustained Superior award, 1966;, 1966, Wash. State award, Tobacco and Substance Abuse Prevention Program, 2000, Dept. Plaque of Distinction award, County Sheriff, 2005, Letters of Commendation award, US House Reps., Pres. Plaque, Tacoma Pub. Schs.; nominee Wa. State Prin. of Yr., Stadium HS, 1994. Mem.: Safe Streets (fin. com. 2006—08, Cert. Appreciation award 2006—07), Wa. State Retired Tchrs. Assn. (pres., Unit Pres. Recognition award), Tacoma Principals Assn. (leadership bd. mem. 1975—96), Ft. Lewis Edn. Assn. (pres.-elect 1960—63). Independent. Roman Catholic. Home: 7023 N 10th St Tacoma WA 98406 Office: Tacoma Sch Dist # 10 PO Box 1357 Tacoma WA 98401-1357 Office Fax: 253-571-7438; Home Fax: 253-759-7607. Personal E-mail: connie.rickman@nventure.com. Business E-Mail: crickma@tacoma.k12.wa.us.

RICKMAN, ELLEN ERWIN, museum administrator; BA in Lit., U. NC, Asheville. Cert. in mgmt. U. SC. Various positions including curator, collections mgr. and registrar Biltmore Estate, Asheville, NC, 1977—2000, dir., mus. svcs., 2000—. Mem. pub. art bd. City of Asheville. Mem.: NC Mus. Conf., Southeastern Mus. Conf., Am. Assn. Mus. Office: Biltmore Estate 1 Approach Rd Asheville NC 28803 Office Phone: 828-225-1333.

RICKMAN, GREGG, United States Special Envoy to Monitor and Combat Anti-Semitism; B, M, John Carroll U., University Heights, Ohio; PhD in Internat. Rels., U. Miami, Coral Gables, Fla. Dir. Congl. affairs Rep. Jewish Coalition; dir. banking com. investigation into the disposition of assets of Holocaust victims held by Swiss banks since World War II US Senate, 1995—98; staff mem., staff dir. US House Internat. Rels. Com.; spl. envoy to monitor and combat anti-semitism US Dept. State, 2006—. Author: Swiss Banks and Jewish Souls, 1999, Conquest and Redemption, A History of Jewish Assets from the Holocaust, 2006. Office: US Dept State Bur Democracy Human Rights and Labor 2201 C St NW Washington DC 20520*

RICKS, JOYCIA CAMILLA, retired lawyer; b. Atlanta, Feb. 17, 1949; d. George Palmer and Johnnie Mae (Ricks) Redd. BBA, Albany State Coll., 1971; MS, Ga. State U., 1977; JD, Woodrow Wilson Coll. Law, Atlanta, 1979, LLM, 1987. Bar: Ga. 1979, US Dist. Ct. (no. dist.) Ga. 1979, US Ct. Appeals (5th cir.) 1979. Acctg. clk. Gulf Oil Corp., Atlanta, 1971; clk. EEOC, Atlanta, 1971-73, paralegal specialist, 1973-79, investigator, 1979-91, supervisory investigator, 1992-2000; complaints mgr. CDC, Atlanta, 2000—03; gen. counsel Albany State U. Alumni Assn., 1986—90, 2005—08. Recipient Presdl. citation award Equal Opportunity in Higher Edn., Washington, 1981. Mem. AAJ, Atlanta Bar Assn., Albany State Coll. Alumni Assn. (pres. Atlanta chpt. 1983-85), Ga. State U. Alumni Assn., State Bar Ga., Women of the Ch. Presbyn. (hon. life), Am. Bus. Women's Assn. (Woman of Yr., Tara chpt. 1985, 91, Peach chpt. 2003), Spreading Oak Cmty. Club. Democrat. Baptist. Business E-Mail: jycric5@bellsouth.com.

RICKS, MARK G., former lieutenant governor, state senator; b. Rexburg, Idaho, July 4, 1924; s. Peter J. and Emily E. (Arnold) Ricks; m. Evelyn Tonks, Aug. 9, 1944; children: Michael T., Gary M., Alan D., Adele Ricks Nielson, Glen L., Kathie Ricks Tensmeyer, Grant H., Merle K., Douglas T. AS in Agrl., Ricks Coll. Mem. Idaho State Senate, 1979—94, chmn. senate commerce and labor commn., 1981—82, chmn. reapportionment com., 1982, 1990—94, majority leader, 1983—88, vice chmn. senate fin. com., 1989—94, mem. state affairs com., chmn., 1989—94, chmn. revenue and projection com., 1989—94; lt. gov. State of Idaho, 2006—07. Mem. exec. and adv. bd. coun. Boy Scouts Am. Recipient Cmty. Svc. Prodn. and Example award, Rexburg C. of C., 1976, Outstanding Svc. award, Madison Sch. Dist., 1987, Disting. Alumni award, Ricks Coll., 1988; named one of Ten Outstanding Legislators, Nat. Rep. Legislators Assn., 1987; named to, Eastern Idaho Agrl. Hall of Fame, 1989, Idaho Blue Ribbon Task Force, 2002. Mem.: Rexburg C. of C. (maj. gifts com. Ricks Coll.), Nat. Fedn. Ind. Bus., Idaho Wheat Growers, Counc. State Govts. (chmn. western legis. conf. 1988—89, chmn. ann. meeting com. 1988—90, mem. budget com. 1989—90, mem. exec. com.), Nat. Conf. State Legis. (mem. exec. com. 1985—87, chmn. nom. com. 1988, mem. rsch. and grants com., vice chmn. fed. taxation com., vice chmn. trade and econ. devel. com., mem. budget and rules com., co-chmn. reapportionment com. 1989, vice chmn. state fed. assembly 1988). Republican. Mem. Lds Ch.

RICKS, RON, air transportation executive; b. Del Rio, Tex., Sept. 25, 1949; s. Philip A. and Leota B. (Petty) R.; m. Eileen Susan Townley, Jan. 8, 1972; 1 child: Alan A. BA in history, U. Tex., 1972; JD, George Washington U., 1977. Bar: N.M. 1977, Tex. 1981. Legis. aide to Congressman O.C. Fisher US Congress, Washington, 1972-74; ptnr. Zinn & Donnell, Santa Fe, 1977-81, Oppenheimer, Rosenberg, Kelleher & Wheatley Inc., San Antonio, 1981-86; v.p. govt. affairs Southwest Airlines Co., Dallas, sr. v.p. for law airports & pub. affairs, 2004—06, exec. v.p. for law, airports & pub. affairs, 2006—08, exec. v.p. for corp. services, corp. sec., 2008—; adv. bd. mem. Mitre Corp. Aviation. Recipient Graduate award, Leadership Dallas, 1987. Mem. N.Mex. Bar Assn., Tex. Bar Assn., Air Transport Assn., North Dallas C. of C. (bd.

dirs.), North Dallas Chamber Aviation Com. (co-chmn.), Dallas C. of C. Aviation Com. (exec. com.). Clubs: Dallas Friday Group. Democrat. Office: Southwest Airlines Co PO Box 36611- 4GA Dallas TX 75235

RICKS, THOMAS EDWIN, journalist, writer; b. Beverly, Mass., Sept. 25, 1955; s. David Frank and Anne (Russell) Ricks; m. Mary Catherine Giblin, Oct. 10, 1981; 2 children. BA, Yale U., 1977. Instr. Lingnan Coll., Hong Kong, 1977-79; asst. editor Wilson Quar., Washington, 1979-81; reporter Wall St. Jour., Atlanta, Miami, 1982-86, dep. bur. chief Miami, 1986, reporter Washington, 1987-89, feature editor, 1989-92, Pentagon corr., 1992—99; mil. corr. Washington Post, 2000—. Author: Making the Corps, 1997, A Soldier's Duty, 2001, FIASCO: The American Military Adventure in Iraq, 2006, The Gamble: General David Petraeus and the American Military Adventure in Iraq, 2006-2008, 2009 (Publishers Weekly bestseller). Co-recipient Pulitzer prize for Nat. Reporting, 2000, 2002. Office: The Washington Post 1150 15th St NW Washington DC 20071*

RICKS, THOMAS MILLER, retired historian, faculty researcher, academic administrator, independent scholar; b. Lafayette, Ind., Oct. 15, 1938; s. Michael T. and Veronica K. (Jordan) R.; m. Janice D. Grasso, Aug. 26, 1967; children: Cynthia C., Laila M. BA, U. Notre Dame, 1961; MA, Ind. U., 1968, PhD, 1975. Tchr. history Tehran Internat. Sch., 1972-73; instr. history Macalester Coll., St. Paul, 1974-75; asst. prof. history Georgetown U., Washington, 1975-83; asst. dir. Ctr. for Arab and Islamic Studies Villanova U., Pa., 1985-91, dir. internat. studies Pa., 1985—2002; lectr. history U. Pa., 2002—05. Adj. assoc. prof. history Ctr. for Arab and Islamic Studies, Villanova U., 1985-2002; vis. asst. prof. history Birzeit U., Palestine, 1983-85; mem. Am. Friends Svc. Com., Mid. East Panel, 1996-2006 Author: Turbulent Times: The Diaries of Khalil Totah, 1886-1955, 2009; editor, compiler, author: (bibliography) Persian Studies: A Bibliography, 1970, editor and compiler, Iran: Contemporary Persian Literature, 1974, editor and compiler, Critical Perspectives on Persian Literature, 1976; co-author: (textbook) Middle East: Past and Present, 1986; co-founder, co-editor: (jour.) Rev. of Iranian Polit. Economy and History, 1976-80, Internat. Jour. Mid. East Studies, 1980-82, (co-founder)Birzeit Rsch. Rev., 1985-86; assoc. editor, co-founder: Frontiers: An Interdisciplinary Jour. of Study Abroad, 1994—. Vol. Iran III program Peace Corps, Mashhad and Mahabad, Iran, 1964-66. Asian Scholar, Ind. U., 1966-67, Birzeit U., 1983-85, Fulbright Found., 1993-95, Gest scholar Haverford Coll., 2003, Spencer Found., 2005-07; Nat. Def. Edn. Act grant US Dept. Edn., 1967-70, grantee Fulbright-Hays Scholar, 1971-72, NEH, 1976, 91-92, Social Sci. Rsch. Coun., 1977, US Dept. Edn., 1988-90, Pa. Dept. Edn., 1990-94, US Dept. State Overseas U. Partnership Program, Palestinian Am. Rsch. Ctr., 2003, Bethlem U., 1995-98 & Lebanese Am. U., 1998-2002, Spencer Found. fellow, 2005-07. Mem. Coun. for Internat. Ednl. Exch. (bd. dirs. 1997-2000), Coun. for Internat. Exch. of Scholars (bd. dirs. 1996-04), Pa. Coun. for Internat. Edn. (bd. dirs. 1994-03, pres. 1994-99), Mid. East Studies Assn., Ctr. Iranian Rsch. and Analysis (bd. dirs. 1997-2000), Internat.Soc. for Iranian Studies (treas. 1974-76), Mid. East Inst., Am. Hist. Assn., Oral History Assn., Hist. Soc. Pa., Presbyn. Hist. Soc., Sons of the Union Vets. the Civil War, 28th PVI Hist. Assn., Palestinian Am. Rsch. Ctr., Assn. Study Persianate Soc. Democrat. Roman Catholic. Avocations: civil war living history/reenactment, musician, history. Home Phone: 610-449-3015. Business E-Mail: tmricks@sas.upenn.edu.

RICO, CHRISTOPHER, artist; b. Tucson, Ariz., Nov. 4, 1966; s. Beverly Rico; m. Miriam Ragland, Dec. 17, 2005; children: Clementine Rico-Ragland, Magdalene Rico-Ragland. BA, U. Memphis, 1995. Exhibitions include Paintings, 2008, Contemporaries' Artist of the Year exhibition, Festival of Flowers, New Paintings, Depot invitational, Small Works Series, Road Sketchbook. Recipient award, Memphis Theatre Assn., 1998. Office: Christopher Rico Studios 215 W Main St Clinton SC 29325 Business E-Mail: details@christopherrico.com.

RICOL, RENE JEAN, accountant; b. Lyon, France, Dec. 26, 1950; s. Benoit and Marie Antoinette (Mercier) R.; children: Raphaelle, Stephane, Matthieu, Antoine, Arthur, Victor. MBA in Econs., Lyon U., France, 1973. Ptnr. Calan Ramolino Ricol, Paris, 1978—80, mng. ptnr., 1980—86; pres. Ricol-Lasteyrie & Assocs., Paris, 1986—; hon. pres. France Defi, Paris, 1989-97, Euro Defi, 1991-94. Pres. Compagnie Regionale Des Commissaires Aux Comptes, 1982-84, Compagnie Nationale des Commissaires Aux Comptes, 1985-89, Conseil Superieur de l'Ordre des Experts-Comptables, 1994-98, Internat. Fedn. Accts., NY, 2002-04, Tous pour l'Emploi, 2004, France Investments, 2006-. Decorated comdr. Legion of Honor, Grand Officer Order of Merit (France). Office: Ricol Lasteyrie 2 Ave Hoche 75008 Paris France Business E-Mail: rr@ricol-lasteyrie.fr.

RICORDI, CAMILLO, surgeon, researcher; b. NYC, Apr. 1, 1957; m. Valerie A. Grace, Aug. 8, 1986; children: M. Caterina, Eliana G., Carlo A. MD, Milan U., Italy, 1982. Trainee in gen. surgery San Raffaele Inst., Milan, 1982-85; NIH trainee Washington U. Sch. Medicine, St. Louis, 1985-88; attending surgeon San Raffaele Inst., Milan, 1988-89; asst. prof. to assoc. prof. surgery U. Pitts., Pa., 1989-93; disting. prof. medicine, prof. biomed. engring., microbiology and immunology, chief divsn. cellular transpl., dir. cell transplantation ctr. Diabetes Rsch. Inst., U. Miami, Fla., 1993—, sci. dir., chief acad. officer Fla., 1996—, Stacy Joy Goodman chair in Diabetes Rsch., 1998—. Reviewer of applications for grants Can. and Am. Diabetes Assns., Juvenile Diabetes Found., NIH; chmn. First and Third Internat. Congresses of Cell Transplant Soc., Pitts., 1992, Miami, 1996, 5th Internat. Congress on Pancreas and Islet Transplantation, Miami, 1995, others; mem. editl. bd. Transplantation, Cell Transplantation, Transplantation Procs., Jour. Tissue Engring. Editor: Pancreatic Islet Cell Transplantation, 1992, Methods in Cell Transplantaion, 1995; co-editor-in-chief Cell Transplantation, Graft; assoc. editor Am. Jour. Transplantation, 2003—; contbr. numerous chpts. to books and articles to jours. including Immunology Today, Jour. Clin. Investigation, New Eng. Jour. Medicine, Hepatology, Diabetes, Transplantation, Endocrinology, Procs. NAS, USA, Am. Jour. Physiology, Surgery, Nature, Nature Genetics, Lancet, Nature Immunology Rev. Grantee Juvenile Diabetes Found. Internat., 1988—, NIH, 1993—, Galileo Lectr., EASD, Rome, 2008; recipient Nessim Habif World prize of surgery, 2001. Mem. AAAS, Cell Transplant Soc. (founder, pres. 1992-94), Am. Soc. Transplant Surgeons, Internat. Pancreas and Islet Transplant Assn. (v.p. 1979-99, pres. 1999-2001), The Transplantation Soc., Am. Diabetes Assn. (councillor, 2003-, Outstanding Sci. Achievement award 2002). Achievements include patents in cellular biotechnologies. Office: U Miami Diabetes Rsch Inst PO Box 016960 Miami FL 33101 Business E-Mail: ricordi@miami.edu.

RIDD, BRIAN V., chemicals executive; With Huntsman Corp., Salt Lake City, 1984—, v.p. purchasing Huntsman Chem. Corp. subs., v.p. purchasing Huntsman Petrochemical Corp. subs., v.p. Olympus Oil subs., v.p. purchasing, 1995—2000, sr. v.p. purchasing, 2000—. Office: Huntsman Corp 500 Huntsman Way Salt Lake City UT 84108 Office Phone: 801-584-5700.

RIDDELL, MALCOLM, investment banker; b. Zanesville, Ohio, Nov. 11, 1952; s. William Roy Riddell and Martha Cottingham. BA, U. S. Fla., 1973; JD, Stetson U., 1976; M in Internat. Affairs, Columbia U., 1985; MBA, Harvard U., 1986. Bar: Fla. Assoc. Icard, Merrill, Cullis & Timm, Sarasota, Fla., 1976-77; city prosecutor City of Sarasota, 1977-78; fgn. svc. officer U.S. Dept. State, Washington, 1978-84; investment banker Salomon Bros., NYC, 1986-88; pres. Riddell & Tseng, Taipei, Taiwan, 1988—. Bd. dirs. Fla. Export Fin. Corp. Undersecretary internat. affairs Fla. Dept. State, Tallahassee, 1999-2000; bd. dirs. Ctr. Internat. Bus. Edn. U. S. Fla., Tampa, 1999—. Mem. Coun. Fgn. Rels. Avocations: sculpting, classical guitar, collecting ming dynasty furniture.

RIDDER, PAR, former publishing executive; b. 1969; s. Tony Ridder; m. Sara Ridder; 2 children. BA, U. Wash., 1990; MBA, U. Mich., 1996. Retail sales rep. Washington Post, 1990—94; circulation zone mgr. Akron Beacon Jour., 1996—97; recruitment mgr. Contra Costa Times, 1996—97; pub. San Luis Obispo Tribune, Calif., 2001—04, v.p. & advt. dir. Calif., 1997—99; pub. & pres. St. Paul Pioneer Press, St. Paul, 2004—07; pub. & CEO Star Tribune, Mpls., 2007. Recipient Alvah H. Chapman award, San Luis Obispo Tribune, 2003. Home: 2419 E Lake Of the Isles Pkwy Minneapolis MN 55405-2479 Office Phone: 612-673-1708. E-mail: publisher@startribune.com.

RIDDICK, DANIEL HOWISON, obstetrician, gynecologist, priest; b. Lynchburg, Va., Dec. 12, 1941; s. Joseph Henry and Nancy Eloise (Gordon) R.; m. Louisa McIntosh Spruill, June 9, 1963; children: Ellen, Daniel. BA, Duke U., 1963, MD, 1967, PhD in Physiology, 1969. Diplomate Am. Bd. Ob-Gyn, Am. Bd. Reproductive Endocrinology; ordained priest Episc. Ch., 1969. Asst. prof. physiology Duke U., Durham, NC, 1973-74; asst. prof. ob-gyn U. Conn. Sch. Medicine, Farmington, 1974-76, dir. reproductive endocrinology and infertility, 1974-85, assoc. prof. ob-gyn, 1976-81, prof. ob-gyn, 1981-85; prof., chmn. ob-gyn dept. U. Vt., Burlington, 1985-97, assoc. dean grad. med. edn., 1987-88. Editor: Reproductive Endocrinology in Clinical Practice, 1987; editor: (with others) Pathology of Infertility, 1987. Mem. ACOG, Am. Fertility Soc. (pres. 1992-93), Am. Gynecol. and Obstet. Soc. Avocation: sheep-raising. Home: 680 Mayo Rd Huntington VT 05462-9410 Office: Fletcher Allen Health Care Dept of Obstetrics & Gynecology 111 Colchester Ave Burlington VT 05401-1416 Office Phone: 802-847-1400. E-mail: dan.riddick@vtmednet.org.

RIDDICK, FRANK ADAMS, JR., physician, healthcare administrator; b. Memphis, June 14, 1929; s. Frank Adams and Falba (Crawford) Riddick; m. Mary Belle Alston, June 15, 1952; children: Laura Elizabeth Dufresne, Frank Adams III, John Alston. BA cum laude, Vanderbilt U., 1951, MD, 1954. Diplomate Am. Bd. Internal Medicine. Intern Barnes Hosp., St. Louis, 1954—55, resident in medicine, 1957—60; fellow in metabolic diseases Washington U., St. Louis, 1960—61; staff Ochsner Clinic (Ochsner Found. Hosp.), New Orleans, 1961—, head sect. endocrinology and metabolic disease, 1976—83, asst. med. dir., 1968—72, assoc. med. dir., 1972—75, med. dir., 1975—92; CEO Alton Ochsner Med. Found., New Orleans, 1992—2001; CEO emeritus Ochsner Clinic Found., 2001—. Bd. govs. Am. Bd. Internal Medicine, 1973—80; clin. prof. Tulane U., New Orleans, 1977—; trustee Alton Ochsner Med. Found., 1973—, CEO, 1991—; chmn. bd. Ochsner Health Plan, 1983—92; pres. Orleans Svc. Corp., 1976—80, South La. Med. Assocs., New Orleans, 1978—; dir. Brent House Corp., New Orleans, 1980—; chmn. Accreditation Coun. on Grad. Med. Edn., 1986—87, v.p. nat. resident matching program, 1986—90, mem. accreditation coun. on med. edn., 1988—90. Bd. govs. Isidore Newman Sch., New Orleans, 1987—93; trustee St. Martin's Protestant Episc. Sch., Metairie, La., 1970—84. Recipient Tchg. award, Alton Ochsner Med. Found., 1969, Disting. Alumnus award, Castle Heights Mil. Acad., 1979, Physician Exec. award, Am. Coll. Med. Group Adminstrs., 1984, Disting. Alumnus award, Vanderbilt U. Sch. Medicine, 1988. Master: ACP; fellow: Am. Coll. Physician Execs. (pres. 1987—88); mem.: NAS Inst. Medicine, AMA (ho. dels. 1971—92, chmn. coun. on med. edn. 1983—85, coun. on jud. and ethical affairs 1995—2002, chair 2001—02, Disting. Service award 2003), Am. Group Practice Assn. (pres. 1992—94), Soc. Med. Adminstrs. (pres. 1995—), Am. Diabetes Assn., Endocrine Soc., Am. Soc. Internal Medicine (trustee 1970—76, Disting. Internist award), Cosmos Club, New Orleans Country Club, Boston Club. Office: Ochsner Clinic 1516 Jefferson Hwy New Orleans LA 70121-2429 Home: 150 Broadway 709 New Orleans LA 70118-7610 Office Phone: 504-842-4019. Business E-Mail: friddick@ochsner.org.

RIDDIFORD, LYNN MOORHEAD, biologist, educator; b. Knoxville, Tenn., Oct. 18, 1936; d. James Eli and Virginia Amalia (Berry) Moorhead; m. Alan W. Riddiford, June 20, 1959 (div. Jan. 1966); m. James William Truman, July 28, 1970. AB magna cum laude, Radcliffe Coll., 1958; PhD, Cornell U., 1961. Rsch. fellow in biology Harvard U., Cambridge, Mass., 1961-63, 65-66, asst. prof. biology, 1966—71, assoc. prof., 1971—73; instr. biology Wellesley Coll., Mass., 1963—65; from assoc. prof. to prof. zoology U. Wash., Seattle, 1973—2003, prof. biology, 2003—07, prof. biology emeritus, 2007—, Virginia and Prentice Bloedel prof., 2000—05, assoc. chmn., 2003—04; sr. fellow Janelia Farm Howard Hughes Med. Inst., Ashburn, Va., 2007—. Mem. study sect. tropical medicine and parasitology NIH, Bethesda, Md., 1974—78, 1997; mem. Competitive Grants panel USDA, 1979, 89, 95; mem. regulatory biology panel NSF, 1984—88, 2001, 05, 07, mem. biol. adv. com., 1992—95; mem. governing coun. Internat. Ctr. for Insect Physiology and Ecology, 1985—91, chmn. program com., 1989—91; chmn. adv. com. SeriBiotech, Bangalore, India, 1989; mem. coun. Internat. Cong. Entomology, 1988—2008, pres., 2000—04; mem. coun. Internat. Fedn. Comparative Endocrine Socs., 1996—, pres., 2001—05. Mem. editl. bd. profl. jours.; contbr. articles to profl. jours. Bd. dirs. Entomol. Found., 1998—2001, chmn., 2001; bd. dirs. Whitney Lab., 2000—04, chmn., 2004. Recipient Gregor J. Mendel award, Czech Republic Acad. Scis., 1998, Ann. Dinner honors, Entomol. Found., 2006; grantee, NSF, 1964—65, 1967—, Rockefeller Found., 1970—79, USDA, 1978—82, 1989—2006, NIH, 1975—; fellow, NSF, 1958—60, 1961—63, NIH, 1960—61, John S. Guggenheim Found., 1979—80, NIH, 1986—87. Fellow: AAAS, Entomol. Soc. Am. (Recognition award in insect physiology, biochemistry and toxicology), Royal Entomol. Soc., Am. Acad. Arts and Sci.; mem.: Soc. Exptl. Biology, Soc. Devel. Biology, Am. Soc. Biochem. and Molecular Biology, Soc. Integrative and Comparative Biology. Methodist. Office: Janelia Farm Howard Hughes Med Inst 19700 Helix Dr Ashburn VA 20147 Home: 40733 Manor House Rd Leesburg VA 20175 Business E-Mail: riddifordl@janelia.hhmi.org.

RIDDLE, CHARLES ADDISON, III, district attorney, former state legislator; b. Marksville, La., June 8, 1955; s. Charles Addison Jr. and Alma Rita (Gremillion) R.; m. Margaret Susan Noone, Mar. 24, 1978; children: Charles Addison IV, John H., Michael J. BA, La. State U., 1976, JD, 1980. Bar: La. 1980, U.S. Dist. Ct. (mid. and we. dists.) La. 1983, U.S. Ct. Appeals (5th cir.) 1988, U.S. Supreme Ct. 1991, U.S. Ct. Vets. Appeals 1994. Ptnr. Riddle & Bennett LLC, Marksville, 1980; pvt. practice Marksville, 1981—2004; mem. La. Ho. of Reps., Baton Rouge, 1992—2003; reelected La. House of Reps., Baton Rouge, 1995—99, 1999—2003; dist. atty. Avoyelles Parish 12th Jud. Dist., 2003—. Elected La. State Dem. Cen. com., Avoyelles Parish, 1983-87, Parish Exec. Demo. Com. 1987-91. Mem. Avoyelles Bar Assn. (pres. 1987-88), Bunkie Rotary (bd. dirs.), Marksville Lions, Marksville C. of C. (pres. 1988-92). Office: PO Box 608 208 E Mark St Marksville LA 71351-2416 Office Phone: 318-253-4551. Personal E-mail: criddle777@aol.com.

RIDDLE, JOHN MARION, retired humanities educator; s. Jack Parson and Betty Magill Riddle; m. Margaret Crenshaw Riddle, June 8, 1963; 1 child, Erika Mangrum. AB, MA, PhD, U. NC, Hickory, Chapel Hill, 1963. Alumni disting. prof. emeritus NC State U., Raleigh, NC, 1965—2008, head, divsn. U. studies, 1982—88. Author: (book) History of the Middle Ages, 300-1500. Bd. Wake County Dem. Men's Club, Raleigh, 2008—. Liberal. Episcopal. Avocation: tennis. Office: NC State Univ Withers Hall Raleigh NC 37695 Office Fax: 919-515-3886; Home Fax: 91951533886. Business E-Mail: john_riddle@ncsu.edu.

RIDDLE, MICHAEL LEE, lawyer; b. Oct. 7, 1946; s. Joy Lee and Francis Irene (Brandes) R.; m. Suzan Ellen Shaw, May 25, 1969 (div.); m. Carol Jackson, Aug. 13, 1977; 1 child, Robert Andrew. BA, Tex. Tech U., 1969, JD with honors, 1972. Bar: Tex. 1972, U.S. Dist. Ct. (no. dist.) Tex. 1972, U.S. Ct. Appeals (5th cir.) Tex. 1972, U.S. Supreme Ct. 2007. Assoc. Geary Brice Barron & Stahl, Dallas, 1972-75; ptnr. Baker Glast Riddle Tuttle & Elliott, Dallas, 1975-80; ptnr., mng. ptnr. Middleburg, Riddle & Gianna, 1980—; chmn., CEO MRG Document Techs., 2000—. Bd. dirs. Dallas Opera. Bd. dirs. U.S.A. Film Festival, pres., 1984-86, North Tex. Pub. Broadcasting, 1992-97; chmn., bd. dirs. Provident Bancorp Tex., 1987-90. Mem. ABA, Tex. Bar Assn., Dallas Bar Assn., Coll. of State Bar of Tex., Lakewood Country Club, Crescent Club. Democrat. Lutheran. Office: 717 N Harwood Ste 2400 Dallas TX 75201 Office Phone: 214-220-6300. Personal E-mail: mriddle@midrid.com.

RIDDLE, VERYL LEE, lawyer; b. Campbell, Mo., Dec. 6, 1921; s. Elvis Lloyd and Etter Whitehead (Wood) R.; m. Mary J. Riggs, Jan. 15, 1941 (div. 1967); children: Kay, Jo, Janet, Veryl Lee, Jr.; m. Janet Lewis, Nov. 24, 1985. Student, Southeast Mo. U., 1939-41; student, U. Buffalo, 1942, 45-46; JD, Washington U., St. Louis, 1948. Bar: Mo. 1948, US Dist. Ct. (ea. and we. dists.) Mo. 1949, US Ct. Appeals (8th cir.) 1949, US Supreme Ct. 1969, US Ct. Appeals (7th cir.) 1970, US Ct. Appeals (5th cir.) 1974, US Ct. Appeals (3d cir.) 1975. Agt. US Dept. Justice, NY, Ohio, Tex., Mex., 1942-43; US atty. Eastern Dist. Mo. Dept. Justice, St. Louis, 1967-69; ptnr. Riddle, Baker & O'Herin, Malden, Mo., 1948-67; sr. ptnr. Bryan Cave, St. Louis, 1969—. Pros. atty. Dunklin County, Mo., 1950-53; chmn. merit selection panel for US Magistrate, St. Louis, 1983-84 Del., Nat. Democratic Conv., Chgo., 1956, Los Angeles, 1960. With US Army, 1943-45, European Theatre, Military Intelligence. Recipient Disting. Alumni award Washington U. Sch. Law, 1993. Fellow Am. Coll. Trial Lawyers, Internat. Acad. Trial Lawyers; mem. Acad. Mo. Squires. Clubs: Bellerive Country, Noonday, Round Table (St. Louis). Baptist. Office: Bryan Cave 211 N Broadway Saint Louis MO 63102-2733 Office Phone: 314-259-2235. Business E-Mail: vlriddle@bryancave.com.

RIDE, SALLY KRISTEN, physics professor, research scientist, retired astronaut; b. L.A., May 26, 1951; d. Dale Burdell and Carol Joyce (Anderson) R.; m. Steven Alan Hawley, July 26, 1982 (div.). BA in English, Stanford U., 1973, BS in Physics, 1973, PhD in Physics, 1978. Tchg. asst. Stanford U., Palo Alto, Calif., rschr. dept. physics, sci. fellow, 1987-89; astronaut candidate, trainee NASA, 1978-79, astronaut, 1979-87, on-orbit capsule communicator STS-2 mission Johnson Space Ctr. Houston, on-orbit capsule communicator STS-3 mission, mission specialist STS-7, 1983, mission specialist STS-41G, 1984; dir. Calif. Space Inst. U. Calif. San Diego, La Jolla, 1989—96, pres. space com., 1999-2000; prof. dept. physics U. Calif. San Diego, 1989—. Pres., CEO Space web site, 1999—2000, Imaginary Lines, Inc., 2001—; mem. Presdl. Commn. on Space Shuttle Challenger Accident, 1986, World Resources Inst. Global Coun., 1993—, Presdl. Com. Advisors on Sci. and Tech., 1994—, U. Calif. Oversight Com. for Nat. Labs, Pacific Coun. on Internat. Policy; intiated NASA EarthKAM project; bd. dir. Nat. Rsch. Coun. Space Studies, Congressional Office of Tech. Assessment, Carnegie Instn. Washington; past bd. dir. NCAA Found.; bd. trustee Caltech; lectr. in field. Author: (with Susan Okie) To Space and Back, 1986, (with T.O'Shaughnessy) Voyager: An Adventure to the Edge of the Solar System, 1992, The Third Planet: Exploring the Earth From Space, 1994, (revised 2004), The Mystery of Mars, 1999, Exploring Our Solar System, 2003. Recipient Jefferson award for Pub. Svc., Nat. Spaceflight medal (twice), Von Braun award, Lindbergh Eagle award, Silver Anniversary award, NCAA, 1998, Golden Plate award, Acad. Achievement, 2004, Theodore Roosevelt award, NCAA, 2005; named to The Nat. Women Hall of Fame, 1988, Astronaut Hall of Fame, Kennedy Space Center, 2003, Nat. Aviation Hall of Fame, 2007. Fellow: Am. Physical Soc. Achievements include becoming the first American woman to orbit Earth when she flew aboard Space Shuttle Challenger, June, 18 1983. Avocations: tennis, running, volleyball, softball, stamp collecting. Office: U Calif San Diego Dept Physics 0426 La Jolla CA 92093-0426 Address: Sally Ride Science 9191 Towne Centre Dr San Diego CA 92122*

RIDENOUR, JIM, Mayor, Modesto, California; b. Modesto, CA; m. Renee Ridenour; 3 children. Paramedic Santa Barbara County, 1974; dep. sheriff Stanislaus & Santa Barbara County; ops. exec. Central Valley Ops. Am. Med. Response; mayor City of Modesto, 2003. Chmn. Calif. Ambulance Assoc. With Nat. Guard US Army. Office: 1010 10th St Modesto CA 95354 Mailing: PO Box 642 Modesto CA 95353 Office Phone: 209-571-5597. Office Fax: 209-571-5586. Business E-Mail: mayor@modestogov.com. E-mail: jridenour@modestogov.com.*

RIDER, LISA G, pediatric rheumatologist, researcher; b. Newark; MD, Duke U. Sch. of Medicine, 1983—87. Pediatric Rheumatologist Am. Bd. Pediat. Med. officer and staff scientist Ctr. for Biologics Evaluation and Rsch., FDA, Bethesa, Md., 1993—2001; dep. chief Environ. Autoimmunity Group, Nat. Inst. Environ. Health Scis. NIH, Bethesda, Md., 2001—. Med. adv. bd. mem., chri rsch. com. The Myositis Assn., Washington, 1996—2009; spl. govt. employee FDA, Rockville, Md., 2001—03; adv. coun. Pediatric Rheumatology Collaborative Study Group, Cincinnati, Ohio, 1998—. Editor: Myositis and You; contbr. articles to profl. jours., chapters to books. Vol. Garrett Pk. Elem. Sch., Md., 2002—06. Capt. US Pub. Health Svc., 1991—, Bethesda, MD. Fellow, PhRMA, 1985—86; Eugene Stead Rsch. fellow, Duke U., 1985—86. Fellow: Am. Acad. Pediat., Am. Coll. Rheumatology (exec. coun. pediatric rheumatology sect. 2003—08); mem.: Phi Beta Kappa. Achievements include research in juvenile myositis, rheumatic disease, environmental risk factors, autoantibodies, immunogenetics, outcome measures. Office: NIEHS NIH CRC 4-2352 MSC 1301 10 Center Dr Bethesda MD 20892-1301 Business E-Mail: riderl@mail.nih.gov.

RIDER, ROGER ALAN, lawyer; b. Sweickley, Pa., May 28, 1945; s. Joseph W. and Evelyn M. (Kuntzman) R.; m. Nancy Lucille Huston, May 8, 1982; children: Matthew Huston, Zachary Alan Huston. BS in

Psychology, U. Houston, 1971, JD magna cum laude, 1974. Bar: Tex. 1974; cert. in civil trial, Tex. Bd. Legal Specialization, Nat. Bd. Trial Advs. Assoc. Butler, Binion, Rice, Cook & Knapp, Houston, 1974-80, ptnr., 1980-82; founding ptnr. Mayor Day & Caldwell, Houston, 1982-90; founder Rider & Assocs., Houston, 1990-96; ptnr. Doyle, Rider, Restrepo, Harvin & Robbins, 1996—2000; pvt. practice, 2000—. Sec., treas., v.p., pres.-elect, pres. Houston Young Lawyers Assn., 1976-81; faculty Tex. Legal Svcs. Ctr., 1993; speaker, instr. U. Houston Law Ctr., 1991-92, adj. prof., 2008-09. Editor Houston Law Review, 1974. Mem. steering com. numerous judicial election campaigns, Houston, 1991—; mgr., coach youth sports YMCA, Houston, 1987-93; mgr. youth sports United Ch. Athletic League, Houston, 1993—; mgr., coach youth baseball West Univ. Little League, Houston, 1990—. Cpl. USMC, 1966-68, Vietnam. Named a Tex. Super Lawyer, 2003, 2004, 2006—08; named one of Houston's Top Lawyers, H Tex. Mag., 2004, 2006. Fellow Houston Bar Found. (life), Tex. Bar Found. (life); mem. ABA (torts and ins. practice sect. 1985-94), Tex. Bar Assn. (Cert. of Merit 1986), Houston Bar Assn. (sec. 1987-89, dir. 1981-85, 90, Pres.'s award 1980, 90, 91), Inns of Ct. (chmn. bd. dirs. 1990-92), Order of Barons (pres. 1974). Avocations: coaching youth sports, physical fitness, skiing. Home: 2064 Timber Ln Houston TX 77027-4118 Office: Comerica Bank Bldg 1 Sugar Greek Ctr Ste 980 Sugar Land TX 77478 Home Phone: 713-805-5001; Office Phone: 281-980-4529. Business E-Mail: rrider@rogerrider.com.

RIDER STEVENSON, JANE, artist, educator; b. Brownfield, Tex., Sept. 11, 1919; d. Oscar Thomas and Florence Myrtle (Bliss) Halley; m. Rolla Wilson Rider Jr., Mar. 26, 1944 (dec. July 1992); 1 child, Dorothy Jo Neil. BA, UCLA, Westwood, 1943, tchg. diploma in secondary art; postgrad., Chgo. Art Inst., 1945, Chouniards, LA, U. Oreg., Scripps, Claremont, Calif. Art supr., elem. and jr. high art tchr. Tulare (Calif.) City Schs. Dist., 1943-44, 44-45; art tchr. Beverly Hills (Calif.) High Sch., 1946-47; art tchr. jr. high gen. art and ceramics Santa Barbara City Schs., Goleta, Calif., 1964-66; head art dept., tchr. Morro Bay (Calif.) Jr.-Sr. High Sch. Dist., 1967-70; pvt. practice studio potter Cambria, Calif., 1961-85; artist, Santa Rosa, Calif., 1985—. Founder, dir., tech. La Canada (Calif.) Youth House Art Program, 1953-60; dir. Pinedorado Art Show, Allied Arts Assn., Cambria, 1970-85. Exhibited in group shows Santa Rosa Art Guild, 1986-95, Nat. League Am. Pen Women, 1994-98, Wine Country Artist's Spring Show, 1991, 92, 93, 94, 95, 97, Gualala Art in Redwoods, 1986-88, 96-2000, (merit award for watercolor), Rodney Strong Vineyards Art Guild, 1994, Oakmont Art Assn., 1985-2000, revolving exhibits Berger Ctr., Chalais, Oakmont, Santa Rosa, Santa Rosa Art Guild, 1986—; statewide art shows Spring Palettes Mumm Cuvee Winery, Napa, Calif., 1994, Luther Burbank Ctr., 1995, Summer House Gallery, Healdsberg, 1995, Armida Winery Show, 1995, Watercolor Artists of Sonoma Co., Aqua Area Shows, 1995-2000, Coddingtown Mall, Audubon-Bouverie Preserve, Glen Ellen, Calif., 1996, Pedroncelli Winery, 1996, Watercolor Artists of Sonoma County, 1995-2000, Marin Art Assn. Gallery, 1996, Kendall Jackson Winery, Santa Rosa, 1997—, others. Mem. Santa Rosa Art Guild (rec. sec. 1989), Ctrl. Coast Watercolor Soc. (charter 1977). Republican. Avocations: photography, gardening, listening to music, travel, tennis. Home: 32 Cliffwood Pl Santa Rosa CA 95709-6352

RIDGE, ROBERT A., oil industry executive; b. Walsenburg, Ohio, 1948; BS in Chem. and Petroleum Refining Engring., Colo. Sch. Mines, 1971. Process sect. supr. Sweeney refiney Phillips 66 Co., Tex., 1978, mgr. planning/budgeting, 1992—94, gen. mgr. refining assets Sweeny bus. unit, 1994—2001; v.p. health, safety & environ. Phillips Petroleum Co., 2001—02, ConocoPhillips, Houston, 2002—. Past bd. dirs. Tex. Inst. Advancement of Chem. Tech. Liaison Colo. Sch. Mines. Mem.: Am. Petroleum Inst. (mem. op. practices com.). Office: ConocoPhllips PO Box 2197 Houston TX 77252-2197*

RIDGE, TOM (THOMAS JOSEPH RIDGE), consulting company executive, former United States Secretary of Homeland Security; b. Munhall, Pa., Aug. 26, 1945; s. Thomas Regis Ridge and Laura A. Sudimack; m. Michele Moore, 1979, children, Lesley, Tommy. BA in govt. studies, Harvard U., 1967; JD, Dickinson Sch. Law, Carlisle, Pa., 1972. Bar: Pa. 1972. Pvt. law practice, Erie, Pa., 1972-82; asst. dist. atty. Erie County, Pa., 1979-82; mem. US Congress from 21st Pa. dist., Washington, 1983—95; mem. Banking, Fin., Urban Affairs com., Veteran's Affairs com.; gov. State of Pa., Harrisburg, 1995—2001; asst. to pres. for homeland security The White House, Washington, 2001—03; sec. US Dept. Homeland Security, 2003—05; founder, pres., CEO Thomas Ridge LLC, Washington, 2005—06, Ridge Global LLC, Washington, 2006—. Bd. dirs. Vonage Holdings Corp., Holmdel, NJ, 2005—, Exelon Corp., Chgo., 2005—, The Hershey Co., Hershey, Pa., 2007—. Co-author (with Larry Bloom): The Test of Our Times: America Under Seige...And How We Can Be Safe Again, 2009. Staff Sergeant, U.S. Army, 1968-70, Vietnam; Awarded a Bronze Star for Bravery. Republican. Office: Ridge Global LLC 110 116th St Suite 308 Washington DC 20036 Office Phone: 202-833-2008. E-mail: tridge@ridgeglobal.com.

RIDGELY, HENRY DUPONT, state supreme court justice; b. Dover, Del., May 31, 1949; s. Henry Johnson and Mary Lil (Berry) R.; m. Barbara Shepard, Mar. 17, 1973; children: Daniel, Michael. BS in Business Administration, Syracuse U., 1971; JD, Cath. U. Am. Columbus Sch. Law, 1973; LLM in Corp Law, George Washington U. Nat. Law Ctr., 1974. Atty. Ridgely and Ridgely, Dover, 1974—84, Del. State Senate, Dover, 1981—84; judge Superior Ct. Del., Dover, 1984—2004; justice Del. Supreme Ct., Dover, 2004—. Recipient Chief Justice's Annual award for Outstanding Judicial Service, 1997, Judicial Professionalism and Civility award, Am. Bd. Trial Advocates- Del. Chapter, 2000. Fellow: Am. Bar Found.; mem.: ABA (co-chair Ct. Technology Com. 2003—), Terry-Carey Am. Inn of Ct. (pres. 1996—98, bd. dirs. 2007—), Nat. Assn. for Ct. Mgmt., Am. Judicature Soc. (bd. dirs. 2003—05). Republican. Episcopalian. Office: Del Supreme Ct 502 S State St Dover DE 19901*

RIDGEWAY, JAMES FOWLER, journalist; b. Auburn, NY, Nov. 1, 1936; s. George L. and Florence (Fowler) Ridgeway; m. Patricia Carol Dodge, Nov. 1966; 1 child, David Andrew. AB, Princeton U., 1959. Assoc. editor New Republic, Washington, 1962-68, contbg. editor, 1968-70; editor Hard Times, 1968-70, Elements, 1974-78; assoc. editor Ramparts, 1970-75; assoc. fellow Inst. for Policy Studies, 1973-77; mem. Pub. Resource Center, 1977—; staff writer Village Voice, 1973—2006; corr. Washington Mother Jones, 2006—. Author: (book) The Closed Corporation, 1969, Politics of Ecology, 1970, The Last Play, 1973, New Energy, 1975; author: (with Alexander Cockburn) Smoke, 1978; author: Political Ecology, 1979, Energy-Efficient Community Planning, 1979, Who Owns the Earth, 1980, Powering Civilization, 1983, Blood in the Face, 1991, The March to War, 1991; author: (with Jean Casella) To Cast a Cold Eye, 1991; author: The Haiti Files, 1994; author: (with Jasmika Udovicki) Yugoslavia's Ethnic Nightmare, 1995; author: (with Sylvia Plachy) Red Light, 1996; author: (with Jeffrey St. Clair) Environmental Bad Guys, 1999; author: (with Kevin Rafferty, Fran K. Kerandren) Who Wants to Be President; prodr., dir. (with Anne Bohlen, Kevin Rafferty): (films) Blood in the Face, 1990; prodr., dir. (with Kevin Rafferty) Feed, 1992; cons. prodr. Awful Truth, 1999; author: It's All For Sale, 2004, The 5 Unanswered Questions about 9/11, 2005, Baghdad Burning, 2005. With N.G. US Army, 1959. Home: 3103 Macomb St NW Washington DC 20008-3325 Personal E-mail: jridgew@yahoo.com.

RIDGLEY, THOMAS BRENNAN, lawyer; b. Columbus, Ohio, Apr. 29, 1940; s. Arthur G. and Elizabeth (Tracy) R.;); children: Elizabeth, Jennifer, Kathryn; m. Lisa Lester, Nov. 27, 1999. BA, Princeton U., NJ, 1962; JD with honors, U. Mich., 1965. Bar: Pa. 1965, Ohio 1968, U.S. Dist. Ct. (so. and no. dists.) Ohio, U.S. Dist. Ct. (ea. dist.) Pa., U.S. Ct. Appeals (6th, 3d and 10th cirs.), U.S. Supreme Ct. Assoc. Dechert, Price and Rhoades, Phila., 1965-67; ptnr. Vorys, Sater, Seymour and Pease LLP, Columbus, 1967—. Author: Interstate Conflicts and Cooperation, 1986, (with others) Fending Off Corporate Raiders, 1987. Bd. dirs., mem. exec. com. United Way of Franklin County, Columbus, 1986-98; bd. dirs. Cmty. Shelter Bd., 1992-98, pres. 1997-98; bd. dirs. Columbus Bar Found., 1992-99, pres., 1998. Fellow Am. Coll. Trial Lawyers. Office: Vorys Sater Seymour and Pease LLP 52 E Gay St Columbus OH 43215-3161 Office Phone: 614-464-6229. Business E-Mail: tbridgley@vssp.com.

RIDGWAY, DELISSA ANNE, federal judge; b. Kirksville, Mo., June 28, 1955; d. Kenneth Driggs and Margaret Anne (Warner) R. BA with honors, U. Mo., 1975, postgrad., 1976; JD, Northeastern U., 1979. Bar: DC Ct. Appeals 1979, US Dist. Ct. DC 1980, US Ct. Appeals (DC cir.) 1980, US Supreme Ct. 1983, US Ct. Appeals (1st circuit) 1988. Law clk. to presiding justice US Dist. Ct. DC, Washington, 1979; assoc. Shaw, Pittman, Potts & Trowbridge, Washington, 1979-88, counsel, internat. practice group, 1988—94; chair, US Fgn. Claims Settlement Commn. US Dept. Justice, Washington, 1994—98; judge US Ct. Internat. Trade, NYC, 1998—. Lectr. nuclear and environ. law to various orgns. Mem. Women's Legal Def. Fund. Recipient: Hardin-Craig fellow U. Mo., Columbia, 1974, Frederick B. Abramson award, DC Bar Assn., 1996, Earl W. Kintner award, Fed. Bar Assn., 2000, Woman Lawyer of The Year, Washington, 2001. Mem. ABA, Women's Bar Assn. (sec. 1989-90), Fed. Bar Assn. (chair adminstrv. law sect. com. agy. adjudication 1985-89, chair adminstrv. law sect. com. regulatory reform 1984-85), American Law Inst., Fellow, Amerocam Bar Found. Roman Catholic. Office: US Ct Internat Trade One Federal Plz New York NY 10278-0001*

RIDGWAY, ELI CHESTER, medical educator; s. Eli Chester and Emily Shafer Ridgway; children: Emily Boye, Eli Chester, Abigail Barkley. BA, Dartmouth Coll., 1964; MD, U. Colo., Denver, 1968. Assoc. prof. medicine Harvard Med. Sch., Boston, 1972—85; prof. medicine U. Colo., Aurora, 1985—, sr. assoc. dean, academic affairs, 1994—. Pres. Elk Creek Ranch, Cody, Wyo., 1983—, Endocrine Soc., Washington, 2003—04. Author: (book) Your Thyroid; contbr. articles to numerous med. publs. Lt comdr. USN, 1973—75, San Diego. Recipient Joseph Addison Sewall award, U. Colo., 1999, Mentor award, Women in Endocrinology, 2005. Master: ACP; mem.: Endocrine Soc. (pres. 2003—04), Am. Thyroid Assn. (pres. 1996—97, Disting. Svc. award 1999, Paul Starr award 2003, Stanbury medal 2008, Williams Disting. Leadership award 2009). Office: Univ Colo Denver Sch Medicine 13001 E 17th St C-290 Aurora CO 80045 Business E-Mail: e.chester.ridgway@ucdenver.edu.

RIDGWAY, R. HUNTER, legislative staff member; BA, U. Va., Charlottesville, 1986; JD, Southern Meth. U., Dallas, 1990. Bar: Tex. 1990, DC 1992. Legis. asst. for Sen. Wyche Fowler, Jr. US Senate, Washington, 1990—91; legis. asst. & budget com. assoc. for Rep. Louise M. Slaughter US House of Reps., 1991—94, legis. dir. for Rep. Jane Herman, 1995, legis. dir. for Rep. John W. Olver, 1995—97, chief of staff, 1997—99, 2000—. Office: Office of Congressman John W Olver 1111 Longworth House Office Bldg Washington DC 20515 Office Phone: 202-225-5335. Business E-Mail: hunter.ridgway@mail.house.gov.*

RIDGWAY, ROZANNE LEJEANNE, corporate director, retired ambassador; b. St. Paul, Aug. 22, 1935; d. H. Clay and Ethel Rozanne (Cote) R.; m. Theodore E. Deming. BA, Hamline U., 1957, LLD (hon.), 1978, George Washington U., 1986, Elizabethtown Coll., 1990, U. Helsinki, 1992; LLD in Pub. Svc. (hon.), Coll. of William and Mary, 1994; DHL (hon.), Hood Coll., 1994; LLD (hon.), Albright Coll.; DHL in Pub. Adminstrn. (hon.), The Citadel, 2003; DHL (hon.), Ill. Coll., 2003. Career diplomat U.S. Fgn. Svc., 1957-89, amb. at large for oceans and fisheries, 1975-77, US amb. to Finland Helsinki, 1977—80; counselor State Dept., 1980—81, spl. asst. to sec., 1981, amb. to German Dem. Republic, 1982-85, asst. sec. Europe and Can., 1985-89; pres. Atlantic Coun. US, 1989-92, co-chmn., 1993-96; chmn. Baltic-Am. Enterprise Fund, Washington, 1994—, Ctr. Naval Analyses, 2009—. Bd. dirs., Emerson Electric Co., Sara Lee Corp., New Perspective Fund, Europacific Fund, New World Fund. Life trustee Hamline U.; trustee Nat. Geog. Soc. Decorated Grand Cross Order of the Lion (Finland); recipient Profl. awards Dept. State, Presdl. Disting. Performance awards, Joseph C. Wilson Internat. Rels. Achievement award, 1982, Sharansky award Union Couns. Soviet Jewry, 1989, U.S. Presdl. Citizens medal, 1989; named Person of Yr. Nat. Fisheries Inst., 1977, Knight Comdr., Order of Merit, Germany; inducted into Nat. Women's Hall of Fame, 1998. Fellow Nat. Acad. Pub. Adminstrn.; mem. Am. Acad. Diplomacy, Army-Navy Country Club.

RIDINGS, DOROTHY SATTES, former association executive; b. Charleston, W.Va., Sept. 26, 1939; d. Frederick L. and Katharine E. (Backus) Sattes; m. Donald Jerome Ridings, Sept. 8, 1962 (dec. June 1997); children: Donald Jerome Jr., Matthew Lyle. Student, Randolph-Macon Woman's Coll., 1957-59; BSJ, Northwestern U., 1961; MA, U. NC, 1968; D.Pub. Svc. (hon.), U. Louisville, 1985; LHD (hon.), Spalding U., 1986; LLD (hon.), U. Charleston, 1999. Reporter Charlotte Observer, NC, 1961-66; instr. U. NC Sch. Journalism, 1966-68; freelance writer Louisville, 1968-77; news editor Ky. Bus. Ledger, Louisville, 1977-80, editor, 1980-83; comm. cons., editor, 1983-86; mgmt. assoc. Knight-Ridder Inc., Charlotte, NC, 1986-88; pres., pub. Bradenton Herald, Fla., 1988-96; pres., CEO Coun. on Founds., Washington, 1996—2005. Adj. prof. U. Louisville, 1982-83; v.p. Nat. Mcpl. League, 1985-86; bd. dirs. com. on Constl. Sys., Nat. Com. Against Discrimination in Housing, 1982-87, Com. Study of Am. Electorate, 1982—; bd. dirs. Ind. Sector, 1983-88, 92-97; mem. exec. com. Leadership Conf. Civil Rights, 1982-86; mem. Accrediting Coun. on Edn. in Journalism and Mass Comm., 2000-06. Pres. LWV U.S., 1982-86, 1st v.p., 1980-82, human resources dir., 1976-80, chair edn. fund, 1982-86, 1st vice chair, 1980-82, trustee, 1976-80, pres. Louisville/Jefferson County, 1974-76, bd. dirs., 1969-76; chmn., bd. dirs. Nat. Civic League, 2000-04; trustee Louisville Presbyn. Theol. Sem., 1992-2008,2009-, chmn., 2000-2008; dir. Assn. Theol. Schs., 2008-; trustee Ford Found., 1989-96, Manatee C.C., 1992-96; bd. dirs. Benton Found., 1989-96, Fla. Press Assn., 1994-96, Leadership Ky., 1984-87, Leadership Louisville, 1983-86, Louisville YWCA, 1978-80, Jr. League Louisville, 1972-74; mem. ABA Accreditation Com., 1987-93, ABA coun. legal edn. and admissions to bar, 1997-03, Gov.'s Coun. Ednl. Reform, 1984-85; chair Prichard Com. Acad. Excellence, 1985-86; mem. Gov.'s Commn. Full Equality, 1982-83; mem. state adv. coun. US Commn. Civil Rights, 1975-79; mem. steering com. Task Force for Peaceful Desegregation, 1974-75; elder 2nd Presbyn. Ch., 1972-75, 78-81, 2008-; mem. adv. coun. on ch. and soc. United Presbyn. Ch. in USA, 1978-84; mem. bd. visitors U. NC, 1993-96; mem. Nat. Commn. on Presdl. Debates, 1997—; mem. Urban Librs. Coun. Exec. Bd., 2005—, sec. 2008-, treas. 2008-; bd. dirs. Editl. Projects in Edn., 2004—; trustee U. Charleston, 2008-. Recipient Northwestern U. award of merit, 1994, Disting. Alumna award U. NC., 1995, Leadership award Nat. Assn. Cmty. Leadership Orgns., 1986, Alumnae Achievement award Randolph-Macon Woman's Coll., 1985, Disting. Citizen award Nat. Mcpl. League, 1983; inducted into Northwestern U. Medill Sch. Journalism Hall of Fame, 1996, U. NC Journalism Hall of Fame, 1997.

RIDKER, PAUL M., cardiologist, medical educator; b. St. Louis, Oct. 2, 1959; BS, Brown U., Providence, 1981; MD, Harvard Med. Sch., 1986; MPH, Harvard Sch. Pub. Health, 1992. Diplomate Am. Bd. Internal Medicine, cert. in Cardiovasc. Disease. Intern Brigham & Women's Hosp./Harvard Med. Sch., Boston, 1986—87, resident internal medicine/cardiology, 1987—89, fellow cardiology, 1989—91, assoc. physician, dir. Ctr. Cardiovasc. Disease Prevention, 1991—; also co-dir. Leducq Ctr. Cardiovasc. Rsch. Brigham & Women's Hosp.; co-dir. Reynolds Ctr. Cardiovasc. Rsch. Harvard Med. Sch., 2003—, Eugene Braunwald prof. medicine. Chief med. resident Vets. Adminstrn. Boston Health Care, 1989; Simon Dack vis. prof. Mt. Sinai Med. Ctr., 2000; cons. cardiologist So. Jamaica Plain Health Ctr., Boston. Consulting editor: Circulation jour.; contbr. articles to profl. jours., chapters to books. Recipient Clinician Scientist award, Am. Heart Assn., 1992—97, Established Investigator award, 1997—2002, SmithKline Beecham Faculty Devel. award, 1997—99, Disting. Clin. Scientist award, Doris Duke Charitable Found., 2000, Linus Pauling Lecture & Prevention award, Am. Coll. Advancement Medicine, 2000; named one of America's Ten Best Rschrs. in Sci. & Medicine, TIME mag., 2001, 100 Most Influential People, 2004. Fellow: Am. Coll. Cardiology; mem.: Am. Assn. Physicians, Am. Soc. Clin. Investigation, Am. Epidemiol. Soc. Achievements include research in arterial inflammation, an immune-system reaction that is the most powerful contributor after cholesterol to heart attacks; design of federal guidelines advocating CRP evaluation as a new method for cardiovascular disease detection; patents in field. Office: Brigham & Womens Hosp Divsn Preventive Medicine 900 Commonwealth Ave E 3rd Fl Boston MA 02215 Office Phone: 617-278-0869. E-mail: pridker@partners.org.*

RIDLEY, BETTY ANN, theology studies educator; b. St. Louis, Oct. 19, 1926; d. Rupert Alexis and Virginia Regina (Weikel) Steber; m. Fred A. Ridley, Jr., Sept. 8, 1948; children: Drue Alexis, Clay Kent. BA, Scripps Coll., Claremont, Calif., 1948. Christian Sci. practitioner, Oklahoma City, 1973—. Tchr. Christian Sci., 1983—; mem. Christian Sci. Bd. Lectureship, 1980-85. Trustee Daystar Found., 1990-; mem. First Ch. of Christ Scientist, Boston, 1956-2005, Fifth Ch. of Christ Scientist, Oklahoma City. Mem. Jr. League Am. Home: 2933 Lansdowne Ln Oklahoma City OK 73120-4343 Office: Suite 100-G 3000 United Founders Blvd Oklahoma City OK 73112 Office Phone: 405-848-7565. Personal E-mail: baridley@aol.com.

RIDLEY, CLARENCE HAVERTY, retail executive; b. Atlanta, June 3, 1942; s. Frank Morris Jr. and Clare (Haverty) R.; m. Eleanor Horsey, Aug. 22, 1969; children: Augusta Morgan, Clare Haverty. BA, Yale U., 1964; MBA, Harvard U., 1966; JD, U. Va., 1971. Bar: Ga. 1971. Ptnr. King & Spalding, Atlanta, 1977—2000, chmn., policy com., 1995—97; chmn. bd. Haverty Furniture Cos., Inc., 2001—. Bd. dirs. Crawford & Co., Inc.; bd. trustees STI Classic Funds and Variable Trusts, 2001—. Co-author: Computer Software Agreements, 1987, 3d edit., 2003; exec. editor Va. Law Rev., 1970-71. Chmn., bd. trustees St. Joseph's Health Sys., 2003-04; founding trustee Atlanta Girls Sch., 2000-2003; chmn., bd. visitors Emory U., 1999-2000; bd. councilors Carter Ctr., 2000-. Lt. US Army, 1967—68, Korea. Mem.: Atlanta Rotary Club. Roman Catholic. Home: 2982 Habersham Rd NW Atlanta GA 30305-2854 Office: Haverty Furniture Companies Inc 780 Johnson Ferry Rd Atlanta GA 30342

RIDLEY, JOHN A., lawyer; b. Jersey City, Oct. 27, 1943; AB, St. Peter's Coll., 1965; LLB, U. Va., 1968. Bar: Va. 1968, N.J. 1968, U.S. Supreme Ct. 1979. Law sec. to Hon. Lawrence A. Whipple U.S. Dist. Ct. N.J., 1968-70; mem. Gibbons, Del Deo, Dolan, Griffinger & Vecchione, Newark, 1970—2002; ptnr. labor & employment law practice group Drinker Biddle & Reath LLP, Florham Park, 2002—. Mem. ABA (labor and employment law, litigation, tort and ins. practice sects.), N.J. State Bar Assn., Essex County Bar Assn. Office: Drinker Biddle & Reath LLP 500 Campus Dr Florham Park NJ 07932-1047 Office Phone: 973-549-7030. Office Fax: 973-360-9831. Business E-Mail: john.ridley@dbr.com.

RIDOLFI, PATRICK MURPHY, music educator, tenor; b. San Francisco, Calif., July 29, 1954; s. Joseph Oreste Ridolfi and Lillian Ruth Scott; m. Margie Gayatin, May 22, 1993; 1 child, Justin Robert; m. Barbara Ridolfi, Sept. 20, 1980 (dec. Nov. 6, 1989); 1 child, Joseph Patrick. BA, U. of Calif. at Santa Barbara, Santa Barbara, CA, 1977; BM, Calif. State U. at Northridge, Northridge, CA, 1987. Free-lance operatic tenor LA Opera, LA Master Chorale, Long Beach Opera, Carnegie Hall, Roger Wagner Chorale, 1981—; elem. tchr. LA Unified Sch. Dist., 1991—2007, elem. music tchr., 1995—. Grantee ELSA Grant, Fed. Arts Grant, 1999, 2000. Mem.: UTLA, MENC. Avocations: swimming, snorkeling, travel.

RIDYARD, SUSAN J., history professor; b. Clitheroe, Lancashire, Eng., Jan. 14, 1957; d. George S. and Edna Ridyard. BA, Cambridge U., 1978, PhD, 1983. Fellow Lucy Cavendish Coll., Cambridge, 1982—89; asst. to prof. U. South, Sewanee, Tenn., 1989—2009. Dir. Sewanee Medieval Colloquium. Contbr. conf. papers. Bd. mem. Franklin County Humane Soc., Winchester, Tenn., 2008—. Harkness fellowship, Commonwealth Fund, NY, 1986—87, fellowship, Nat. Endowment Humanities, 2003. Mem.: Medieval Acad. Am., Am. Hist. Assn. Episcopalian. Avocation: travel. Office: Univ South 735 Univ Ave Sewanee TN 37383 Office Fax: 931-598-9260. Business E-Mail: sridyard@sewanee.edu.

RIECKEN, CLAUDIA, researcher, director; b. São Paulo, Brazil, Nov. 8, 1966; d. Gottfried Kurd Riecken and Maria Auxiliadora (Zuquim) Lia De Paoli; children: Liliane Riecken (Caldeira), Isabella Riecken (Calvo), Luanna Riecken (Calvo) 3 stepchildren. Degree in Neurol. Behavioral Studies, Inst. Systematic Psychology of Ocident & Quantum Leap, Guadalajara, Mex., 1998. Cert. Fed. Therapy Counsel, 1995. Chair woman Quantum Assessment, São Paulo, 1987—. Customer rels. dir. Editora Três, 1989—93; lectr. Free State U., 3Peom Found., South Africa. Author: (book) Empowerment to Win, 1999, Alive Winner's Story, 2006, Melissa Raywoods & Erotical Patterns of Human Interest, 2009. Sponsor searcher Brazilian Assn. Multiple Sclerosis, São Paulo, 2003—07. Mem.: UN East Timor (cons.), Endeavor (assoc.). Avocations: ice skating, dance, horseback riding, motorcycling, travel. Office: Quantum Assessment Av Brig Faria Lima 2894 conj 73 & 81 São Paulo

01451902 Brazil Home: Rua Joaquim Nabuco 1005 Casa 44 Brooklin CEPI 04617003 Sao Paulo Brazil Home Phone: 551155330009. Home Fax: 5511 37093398. Personal E-mail: elaclau@hotmail.com. Business E-Mail: claudia@metodoquantum.com.br.

RIEDEL, ALAN ELLIS, manufacturing executive, lawyer; b. Bellaire, Ohio, June 28, 1930; s. Emil George and Alberta (Shafer) R.; m. Ruby P. Tignor, June 21, 1953; children: Ralph A., Amy L., John T. AB magna cum laude, Ohio U., 1952, LLD (hon.), 1994; JD, Case Western Res. U., 1955; grad., Advanced Mgmt. Program, Harvard, 1971. Bar: Ohio 1955, Tex. 1968. Assoc. Squire, Sanders & Dempsey, Cleve., 1955-60; from gen. counsel to sec. Cooper Industries Inc. (formerly Cooper Bessemer Co.), Mt. Vernon, Ohio, 1960-68; from sec. to v.p. indsl. rels. Cooper Industries Inc., Mt. Vernon, Ohio, 1963-73; from sr. v.p. adminstrn. to vice chmn. Cooper Industries, Inc., Houston, 1973-94. Dir. Factory Mut. Ins., 1999-2000; bd. dirs. Belden Inc., St. Louis, 1993-2000, Gardner Denver Inc., Quincy, Ill., 1994-2000, chmn. bd. dirs., 1994-98; of counsel Squire, Sanders & Dempsey, Houston, 1994-2000. Past chmn. bd. dirs. Jr. Achievement of S.E. Tex.; trustee, past chmn. bd. trustees Ohio U. Endowment Found. Mem. Order of Coif, Phi Beta Kappa, Omicron Delta Kappa, Delta Tau Delta. Home: Bunker Hill Village 4 Heritage Ct Houston TX 77024 Personal E-mail: aeriedel@swbell.net.

RIEDER, NAOMI, artist; b. Bklyn., Mar. 12, 1937; d. Jacob and Pearl Rieder; children: Mara Yolken, Thea Clark. BA, Bklyn Coll., 1958; MA, Columbia U., NYC, 1967. Instr. fine arts Bd. Edn., NYC, 1966—75; substitute instr. sculpture and drawing Ft. Mason Art Ctr., San Francisco, 1977—80; instr. life sculpture Conn. Coll., New London, 1985, Ft. Mason Art Ctr., 1980—81. Exhibited in group shows at Marina View Gallery, San Francisco, 1977, No. Calif. Women's Art Festival, Santa Rosa, Calif., 1979, Fort Mason Art Ctr., San Francisco, 1977—80, Conard Gallery, 1980, Mystic Art Assn., Conn., 1983, Stonington Art Gallery, 1984, Vanguard Gallery, New London, Conn., 1986, Feats of Clay XIII, Lincoln, Calif., 2000 (2 Merit awards, Purchase award), Blink Gallery, Andes, NY, 2006, WAAM, Woodstock, NY, 2007; contbr. works to ceramic publs. Avocations: gardening, crossword puzzles. Home: PO Box 134 Glenford NY 12433-0134 Personal E-mail: naomirdr@aol.com.

RIEDESEL, CLARK ALAN, retired education educator; b. Davenport, Iowa, July 21, 1930; s. F. Clark and Dorothy H. (Franco) R.; m. Ardeth Scott, 1951; children: Christine, Mark, Claudia, Matthew, Craig. BA, Cornell Coll., 1951; MA, U. Iowa, 1956, PhD, 1962. Tchr. Lisbon (Iowa) Schs.; tchr., elem. prin. Albany (Ill.) Schs., 1953-56; prof. edn. SUNY, Plattsburgh, 1956-61, Kansas State U., Manhattan, 1962-63, Pa. State U., University Park, 1963-69, Ga. State U., Atlanta, 1970-72; prof., edn. dept. dir., software lab. dir. SUNY, Buffalo, 1972—95, prof. emeritus, 1995—. Author: Teaching Elementary School Math, 1967, 75, 80, 85, 90, 98, Handbook: Elementary School Math, 1975, Mathematics for Elementary Teachers, 1975; developer: (series) Essentials in Teaching, 1994, 2000; software author: Sunburst, 1989, 90; contbr. articles to profl. jours. Recipient Disting. Prof. award, 1995; NSF grantee, 1962, 66, 68, 74. Mem. ASCD, Nat. Coun. Tchrs. Math (editor The Arithemtic Teacher, 1967-72), Nat. Coun. Social Studies Tchrs. Anglican. Assembly Of God. Avocations: nature, bird carving, woodworking. Home Phone: 716-753-7895; Office Phone: 716-753-7895. Personal E-mail: anaried@fairpoint.net.

RIEDL, GEORGE J., retail executive; b. 1960; BS, U. Ill., 1983. Pharmacist, dist. supr. Walgreen Co., Deerfield, Ill., 1982—91, gen. mdse. mgr., 2000—01, divisional v.p., 2001—03, sr. v.p. mktg., 2003—06, exec. v.p. mktg., 2006—08, exec. v.p. merchandising, 2008—09, sr. v.p. pharmacy innovation & purchasing, 2009—. Bd. mem. Nat. Assn. Chain Drug Stores Inc. Office: Walgreen Co 200 Wilmot Rd Deerfield IL 60015*

RIEDL, JOHN ORTH, retired university dean; b. Milw., Dec. 9, 1937; s. John O. and Clare C. (Quirk) R.; m. Mary Lucille Priestap, Feb. 4, 1961; children: John T., Ann E., James W., Steven E., Daniel J. BS in Math. magna cum laude, Marquette U., Milw., 1958; MS in Math., U. Notre Dame, 1960, PhD in Math., 1963; postgrad., Northwestern U., 1963; degree (hon.), MedCentral Coll. Nursing, 2003. Asst. prof. math. Ohio State U., Columbus, 1966-70, assoc. prof., 1970—2003, asst. dean Coll. Math. and Phys. Sci., 1969-74, assoc. dean, 1974-87, acting dean, 1984-86, spl. asst. to provost, 1987—2003, dean, dir. Mansfield (Ohio) Campus, 1988—2003, exec. dean regional campus, 1988—2003, assoc. prof. emeritus, 2003—; ret., 2003; interim pres. MedCentral Coll. Nursing, 2007—08. Panelist sci. edn. NSF, 1980-91; cons. Ohio Dept. Edn., 1989, Ohio bd. regents subsidy cons., 1991, 95, 97, 99, 2001, 03; bd. dirs. Richland County Univ. and Coll. Access Network, 2001—, pres. treas. Richland County bus. adv. coun., 2004-06; trustee Mansfield Meml. Homes, 2007—. Pres., Ohio State U. Alumni Club Richland County, 1989-; treas. Univ. Cmty. Assn., Columbus, 1970-78; mem. edn. commn. St. Peter's Schs., Mansfield, 1989-95; trustee Rehab. Svc. N. Ctrl. Ohio, Mansfield, 1990-99, v.p., 1993-94, pres., 1995-97; pres. Ohio Assn. Regional Campuses, 1993-94; co-chair capital campaign St. Peter's Schs., 1998. Recipient Faculty Svc. award, Nat. U. Continuing Edn. Assn., 1988, Creative Programming award, 1988; NSF grad. fellow, 1960—62. Mem. Math. Assn. Am. (chair com. on minicourse 1981-87), Downs Am. Chestnut Found. of Ohio (bd. dirs. 2001-04), Rotary Internat. (bd. dirs., pres.-elect, pres.) C. of C. (bd. dirs.). Democrat. Roman Catholic. Avocations: fishing, woodworking, gardening, tennis. Home: 789 Clifton Blvd Mansfield OH 44907-2284 Office: Ohio State U 1680 University Dr Mansfield OH 44906-1547 Business E-Mail: riedl.1@osu.edu.

RIEDLINGER, STEPHEN C., federal judge; b. 1950; BA, La. State U., 1971, JD, 1977. Bar: La. 1977, U.S. Dist. Ct. (ea. dist.) La. 1979, U.S. Dist. Ct. (mid. dist.) 1978, U.S. Ct. Appeals (5th cir.) 1983. Law clk. U.S. Dist. Ct. La., 1977-78; pvt. practice Baton Rouge, 1978-86; magistrate judge U.S. Dist. Ct. (mid. dist.) La., Baton Rouge, 1986—. With USNR, 1971-77. Office: Russell B Long Fed Bldg & Courthouse 777 Florida St Ste 260 Baton Rouge LA 70801-1717 Office Phone: 225-389-3584. Office Fax: 225-389-3585.

RIEDMAN, MARY SUZANNE, lawyer; b. June 1951; JD, Yale U. Bar: Wash. 1980, DC 1983, Calif. 1988. Various positions Beverly Enterprises Inc., Forth Smith, Ark.; counsel Vencor Inc., Louisville, 1995—96, assoc. gen. counsel, 1996—97, v.p., assoc. gen. counsel, 1997—98, Vencor Inc. (renamed Kindred Healthcare Inc. in 2001), Louisville, 1998—99, sr. v.p., gen. counsel, 1999—. Office: Kindred Healthcare Inc 680 S 4th St Louisville KY 40202-2412

RIEDY, MARK JOSEPH, finance educator; b. Aurora, Ill., July 9, 1942; s. Paul Bernard and Kathryn Veronica R.; m. Erin Jeanne Lynch, Aug. 29, 1964; children: Jennifer Erin, John Mark. BA in Econs. maxima cum laude, Loras Coll., 1964; MBA, Washington U., St. Louis, 1966; PhD, U. Mich., 1971. Asst. prof. bus. adminstrn. U. Colo., Boulder, 1969-71; sr. staff economist Council of Econ. Advisers, Washington, 1971-72; spl. asst. to chmn. Fed. Home Loan Bank Bd., Washington, 1972; v.p., dir. research PMI Investment Corp., San Francisco, 1973; v.p., chief economist Fed. Home Loan Bank of San Francisco, 1973-77; exec. v.p., chief operating officer Mortgage Bankers Assn. of Am., Washington, 1978-84; pres., chief operating officer Fed. Nat. Mortgage Assn., Washington, 1985-86, cons., 1986-87; pres., chief operating officer J.E. Robert Cos., Alexandria, Va., 1987-88; pres., chief exec. officer Nat. Coun. Community Bankers, Washington, 1988-92, also bd. dirs.; prof. real estate fin. U. San Diego, 1993—, exec. dir. Burnham-Moores Ctr. Real Estate, 1993—. Mem. adv. coun. Credit Rsch. Ctr., Purdue U., 1981-82; bd. dirs. Fed. Nat. Mortgage Assn., Continental Savs. Bank, AccuBanc Mortgage Corp., Pan Pacific Retail Properties, Inc., Am. Mortgage Network, Inc., Bio-Med. Realty Trust, Noble Broadcast Group, Drayton Ins. Cos., Perpetual Savs. Bank, Ctr. for Fin. Studies; chmn., bd. dirs., Neighborhood Bancorp; mem. San Diego Mayor's Renaissance Commn. Bd. dirs. Lambda Alpha Internat. Woodrow Wilson scholar, 1964; Nat. Def. scholar, 1964-66; U.S. Steel Found. fellow, 1966-68; Robert G. Rodkey Found. fellow, 1966-69; Earhart Found. fellow, 1968-69 Mem. Am. Econ. Assn., Am. Fin. Assn., Nat. Assn. Bus. Economists, Am. Soc. Assn. Execs., NAIOP, Urban Land Inst. Office: U San Diego Sch Bus Adminstrn 5998 Alcala Park San Diego CA 92110-2492 Business E-Mail: mriedy@sandiego.edu.

RIEFF, DAVID SONTAG, editor, writer, critic; b. Boston, Sept. 28, 1952; s. Philip and Susan (Sontag) R. Student, Lycee Francais de NY, New Lincoln Sch., BA, Princeton U., 1978. Dir. publs. NY Inst. Humanities, 1980-85, program dir., 1984—85, now fellow; sr. editor Farrar, Straus & Giroux Inc., NYC, 1979—89. vis. prof., creative writing, City U. NY, 1985-86; writing faculty, Empire State Summer Writing Program, Skidmore Coll., 1990-95; freelance writer, 1989-, dep. editor, World Policy Jour., 1998-; contbg. editor, The New Republic, 1990-, Author: Texas Boots, 1979, Going to Miami: Exiles, Tourists, and Refugees in the New America, 1987, Los Angeles: Capital of the Third World, 1991, The Exile: Cuba in the Heart of Miami, 1993, Slaughterhouse: Bosnia and the Failure of the West, 1995, A Bed for the Night: Humanitarianism in Crisis, 2002, At the Point of a Gun: Democratic Dreams and Armed Intervention, 2005, Swimming in a Sea of Death A Son's Memoir, 2008; contbr. numerous articles, short stories to various publs. Club: Princeton (NYC). Office: Pentagram Design 204 5th Ave New York NY 10010-2103 Address: c/o Wylie Agy Ste 2114 250 W 57th St New York NY 10107 E-mail: davidrieff@compuserve.com.

RIEFLER, DONALD BROWN, financial consultant; b. Washington, Nov. 10, 1927; s. Winfield W. and Dorothy (Brown) R.; m. Patricia Hawley, Oct. 12, 1957; children: Duncan, Linda, Barbara. BA, Amherst Coll., 1949. With J.P. Morgan & Co. Inc., NYC, 1952-91; v.p. Morgan Guaranty Trust Co. of N.Y., 1962-68, sr. v.p., 1968-77, chmn. sources and uses of funds com., 1977—88, chmn. market risk com., 1989—91; fin. mkts. cons., 1991—. With U.S. Army, 1950-52. Mem. John's Island Club, Riomar Country Club, Quail Valley River Club, Birchwood Farms Club, Harbor Point Club, Creek Club. Home: 512 Bay Dr Vero Beach FL 32963-2107

RIEGEL, BYRON WILLIAM, ophthalmologist; b. Evanston, Ill., Jan. 19, 1938; s. Byron and Belle Mae (Huot) Riegel; m. Marilyn Hills, May 18, 1968; children: Marc William, Ryan Marie, Andrea Elizabeth. BS, Stanford U., 1960; MD, Cornell U., 1964. Diplomate Nat Bd Med Examiners, Am Bd Ophthalmology 2007. Intern King County Hosp., Seattle, 1964-65; asst. resident in surgery U. Wash., Seattle, 1965; resident in ophthalmology U. Fla., Fla., 1968-71; pvt. practice medicine specializing in ophthalmology Sierra Eye Med. Group, Inc., Visalia, Calif., 1972—2007, cons., 2008—. Mem staff Kaweah Delta Dist Hosp, chief staff, 1978—79, bd dirs, asst secy, 1983—90; asst. med. dir. Sierra Ambulatory Surg Ctr, Visalia, Calif., 2000—07. Flight surgeon USN, 1966—68. Co-recipient Fight-for-Sight Citation for rsch. in retinal dystrophy, 1970. Fellow: ACS, Am. Acad. Ophthalmology; mem.: Am. Soc. Cataract and Refractive Surgery, Calif. Acad. Ophthalmology (v.p. 3d party liaison 1994—96, dir. 1996—98), Tulare County Med Asn, Calif. Med. Assn. (del. 1978—79), Rotary. Roman Catholic. Home: 3027 Keogh Ct Visalia CA 93291-4228 Personal E-mail: briegel@pacbell.net.

RIEGER, MICHAEL IRA, lawyer; b. NYC, Oct. 19, 1952; s. Joseph and Adrienne R. BA in Sociology, SUNY, Buffalo, 1973; JD, George Mason U., 1977. Bar: Va. 1977. Pvt. practice, Fairfax, Va., 1977—. Lectr. in field. Mem. Va. State Bar Assn., Fairfax Bar Assn. co-chmn. com. law related edn. 1996-97, co-chmn. com. continuing legal edn. 1995-96, chmn. subcom. gen. dist. ct. criminal law 1993-95, com. mem.) Office: Ste 301-B 10623 Jones St Fairfax VA 22030 Office Phone: 703-352-1400. Business E-Mail: riegerlaw@aol.com.

RIEGLER, ROXANE, language educator, researcher; b. Vienna, Austria, Feb. 26, 1959; d. Lydia and Otto Ignaz Riegler; m. Joshua Simon Easterling, July 7, 2005. MA, Salzburg U., 1992; PhD, U. Md., Coll. Pk., 2003. Cert. tchr. Salzburg U., 1992. Asst. prof. Emporia State U., Kans., 2005—, German program dir., 2005—. Contbr. articles to profl. jours. Recipient Audrey award, Emporia State U., 2006; Prahl fellowship, U. Md., 2007, Curriculum Change Program grant. Mem.: MLA, German Studies Assn. Office: Emporia State Univ 1200 Commercial St Emporia KS 66801

RIEHECKY, JANET ELLEN, writer; b. Waukegan, Ill., Mar. 5, 1953; d. Roland Wayne and Patricia Helen (Anderson) Polsgrove; m. John Jay Riehecky, Aug. 2, 1975; 1 child, Patrick William. BA summa cum laude, Ill. Wesleyan U., 1975; MA in Comm., Ill. State U., 1978; MA in English, Northwestern U., 1983. Tchr. English Blue Mound (Ill.) H.S., 1977-80, West Chicago (Ill.) H.S., 1984-86; editor Child's World Pub. Co., Elgin, Ill., 1987-90; freelance writer Elgin, 1990—. Author: Dinosaur series, 24 vols., 1988, UFOs, 1989, Saving the Forests, 1990, Irish Americans, 1995, The Mystery of the Missing Money, 1996, The Mystery of the UFO, 1996, Stegosaurus, 1998, Triceratops, 1998, Tyrannosaurus, 1998, Velociroptor, 1998, A Ticket to China, 1999, Greece, Sweden, 2000, George Lucas, 2001, The Emancipation Proclamation, 2002, The Osage Nation, 2002, The Cree Nation, 2002, Indonesia, 2002, The Plymouth Colony, 2002, The Settling of Jamestown, 2002, The Settling of St. Augustine, 2002, The Siege of the Alamo, 2002, Benjamin Franklin, 2003, Daniel Boone, 2003, The Wampanoag, 2003, Ulysses S. Grant, 2004, William McKinley, 2005, Respect, 2005, Citizenship, 2005, Cooperation, 2005, Iguanodon, 2006, Diplodocus, 2006, Pteranodon, 2006, Megalodon, 2006, Cave Bear, 2007, Sabertooth Cat, 2007, Tasmanian Tiger, 2007, Great White Shark, 2009, Komodo Dragon, 2009, Cobras, 2009, Megalosaurus, 2009, Giant Ground Sloth, 2009, Giganotosaurus, 2009, Giant Rhinoceros, 2009. Nat. dir. Kids Love a Mystery, 1999-2004. Recipient Summit award for best children's nonfiction Soc. Midland Authors, 1988. Mem. Soc. Am. Magicians, Soc. Children's Book Writers and Illustrators (network rep. 2006), Mystery Writers Am. (midwest bd. dirs. 2000-04), Sisters in Crime, Phi Kappa Phi. Democrat. Baptist. Avocations: reading, hiking, dinosaur hunting. Office Phone: 847-695-9781. Personal E-mail: jr@janetriehecky.com.

RIEHL, JANE ELLEN, education educator; b. New Albany, Ind., Oct. 17, 1942; d. Henry Gabbart Jr. and Mary Elizabeth Willham; m. Richard Emil Riehl, June 15, 1968; 1 child, Mary Ellen. BA in Elem. Edn., U. Evansville, 1964; MS, Ind. U., Bloomington, 1966; postgrad., Spalding U., 1979, Ind. U. S.E., New Albany, 1991—2002. Cert. 1-8 and kindergarten tchr., Ind.; lic. profl. elem adminstrn., reading minor kindergarten tchr., Ind. Elem. tchr. Clarksville (Ind.) Cmty. Sch., 1964-68, 70-75, 81-82, tchr. kindergarten, 1975-81; elem. tchr. Chapelwood Sch. Wayne Twp., Indpls., 1968-70; lectr. edn. Ind. U. S.E., 1988-97, dir. tchg. and rsch. project, 1990-91, 92-93, dir. field and career placement, cert./lic. grad advisor New Albany, 1998, coord. elem./spl. edn. field and career placement, license and grad. advisor, 1998—. Cons. Riehl Assocs., Jeffersonville, Ind., 1995—. Co-author: An Integrated Language Arts Teacher Education Program, 1990, The Reading Professor, 1992, Multimedia: HyperStudio and Language Education, 1996, Technology: Hypermedia and Communications, 1997, others; author procs. Parent vol. Girl Scouts U.S.A., Jeffersonville, 1988-95; mem. adminstrtv. bd. Wall Street United Meth. Ch., Jeffersonville, 1993-95; mem. women's health adv. coun. Clark Meml. Hosp., Jeffersonville, 1995—; bd. dirs. Clark Meml. Hosp. Found., vice chair, 1999, chair 2000, sec. 2002-03; team mem. People to People Citizen Amb. Program, 1993, 95, 96; chair internat. bylaws Altrusa Internat., Inc., 2001—. Named Young Career Woman of Yr. Bus. and Profl. Women New Albany and Dist. 13 Ind., 1966; tchg. and rsch. grantee Ind. U. S.E., 1990, 94, 95, 96, 97, 2000; recipient Disting. Tchg. award Ind. U. S.E., 1997, Tchg. Excellence Recognition award, 1997. Mem. Nat. Coun. Tchrs. English, Profs. Reading Tchr. Edn., Ind. State Med. Assn. Alliance (v.p. so. area 1999-2000), Clark County Med. Soc. Alliance (pres.-elect 1997-98, pres. 1998-99), Altrusa Internat. Inc. (internat. bd. 1993-95, dist. gov. 1993-95, svc. award 1995), Phi Delta Kappa (v.p. 1991-92, pres. 1997—, svc. award 1991), Kappa Kappa Kappa (pres. Jeffersonville 1975-76, 90-91, Outstanding Mem. award 1987). Avocations: travel, reading, crafts, decorating. Home: 1610 Fox Run Trl Jeffersonville IN 47130-8204 Office: Ind U SE 4201 Grant Line Rd New Albany IN 47150-2158

RIEHLE, B. HUDSON, trade association executive; b. Cin., Sept. 10, 1953; s. Robert Arthur Riehle and Lois W. Hudson; m. Eileen Patricia Betit, Aug. 2, 1986; children: B. Hudson Jr., Bradley Patrick. BA, Skidmore Coll., 1975; MBA, U. Pa., 1986. Rsch. cons. Avmark, Inc., Washington, 1976-78; rsch. analyst Airline Pilots Assn., Washington, 1978-81, supr. econ. analysis, 1981-84; rsch. mgr. Nat. Restaurant Assn., Washington, 1986-91, sr. rsch. mgr., 1991-95, dir. rsch., 1995-97, sr. dir. rsch., 1997-99, v.p. rsch. & info. svcs., 1999-2000, sr. v.p. rsch. and info. svcs., 2000—; bd. dirs. Alexandria Econ. Devel. Partnership, 2002—04. Bus. rsch. adv. coun. Bureau of Labor Stats., 2003—07. Editor: Comml. Airline Fleets, 1976—78, Restaurant Industry Ops. Report, 1986—; contbr. Airline Pilot, 1978—84, Restaurants USA, 1986-2002; reviewer: Cornell Hotel and Restaurant Adminstrn. Qrly., 2007—. Mem., bd. dirs., 1st v.p. Fairlington Meadows, Arlington, 1990—92. Mem.: Alexandria Conv. and Visitors Assn. (vice chmn. bd. govs. 2001—02, chmn. bd. govs. 2002—04, treas. 2004—05). Avocations: geology, cross country skiing, photography. Home: 2431 Davis Ave Alexandria VA 22302-3209 Office: Nat Restaurant Assn 1200 17th St NW Ste 700 Washington DC 20036-3006 Office Phone: 202-331-5962. E-mail: hriehle@restaurant.org.

RIEKE, MARCIA J., astronomer, educator; BS in Physics, MIT, 1972, PhD, 1976. Prof. astronomy Univ. Ariz., Tucson. Fellow: Am. Acad. Arts & Scis.; mem.: NSF (math, phys. sci. adv. com. 2006—07), NAS, Am. Astronomical Soc. Office: Steward Observatory 262 Univ Ariz PO Box 210065 Tucson AZ 85721 Office Phone: 520-621-2731. Office Fax: 520-621-1532. Business E-Mail: mrieke@as.arizona.edu.

RIELLY, JOHN EDWARD, educational association administrator; b. Rapid City, SD, Dec. 28, 1932; s. Thomas J. and Mary A. (Dowd) R.; m. Elizabeth Downs, Dec. 28, 1957 (marriage annulled 1976); children: Mary Ellen, Catherine Ann, Thomas Patrick, John Downs; m. Irene Diedrich, Aug. 1, 1987. BA, St. John's U., Collegeville, Minn., 1954; postgrad. (Fulbright scholar), London Sch. Econs. and Polit. Sci., 1955-56; PhD, Harvard U., 1961. Faculty dept. govt. Harvard U., 1958-61; with Alliance for Progress programs Dept. State, Washington, 1961-62; fgn. policy asst. to Sen. then Vice Pres. Hubert Humphrey, Washington, 1963-69; cons. office European and internat. affairs Ford Found., NYC, 1969-70; sr. fellow Overseas Devel. Council, Washington, 1970-71; exec. dir. Chgo. Council on Fgn. Relations, 1971-74, pres., 1974—2001. Adj. prof. Northwestern U., 2001—; vis. prof. Grad. Sch. Internat. Rels. U. Calif., San Diego, 2003-; cons. NSC; adv. bd. Grad. Sch. Arts and Scis., Harvard U. Alumni Assn.; bd. dirs. Am. Coun. on Germany, Nat. Com. on U.S.-China Rels., China Coun. of Asia Soc., Am. Ditchley Found., Trilateral Commn., commn. on U.S.-Brazilian Rels.; past pres. Nat. Coun. Comty. World Affairs Orgns. Contbr. articles to profl. jours.; editor: American Public Opinion and U.S. Foreign Policy, 1975, 2d edit., 1979, 83, 87, 91, 95, 99; editl. bd. Fgn. Policy Quar., 1974—. Former trustee St. John's U. Recipient Legion d'Honneur, France, Distinguished Service Cross, Germany, Commendatore of the Italian Republic, Bernardo O'Higgins Award, Chile, The Golden Decoration, Austria, European Friendship Award, European Union, Order of Leopold (Belgium), Nat. Hon. Southern Cross, Brazil. Mem.: Council on Fgn. Relations, N.Y.C. Home: 2021 Kenilworth Ave Wilmette IL 60091-1519 Office: Ctr for Internat & Comparative Studies 1902 Sheridan Rd Evanston IL 60208 Office Phone: 847-467-4409.

RIELLY, J(OHN) P., oil industry executive; Ptnr. Ernst & Young; v.p., controller, chief acctg. officer Amerada Hess Corp., NYC, 2001—04, sr. v.p., CFO. Office: Amerada Hess Corp 1185 Avenue of the Americas New York NY 10036 Office Phone: 212-997-8500. Office Fax: 212-536-8390.*

RIEMANN, STANLEY A., oil industry executive; BS, Univ. Nebr., 1973; MBA, Rockhurst Univ., 1992. Various mgmt. positions Farmland Industries Inc., 1974—99, exec. v.p., pres. energy & crop nutrient divsn., 1999—2004; COO Coffeyville Resources LLC, 2004—06, CVR Energy Inc., Sugar Land, Tex., 2006—. Bd. mem. The Fertilizer Inst.; past bd. mem. Phosphate Potash Inst., Fla. Phosphate Coun., Internat. Fertilizer Assn. Office: CVR Energy Inc Ste 500 2277 Plaza Dr Sugar Land TX 77479*

RIEMKE, RICHARD ALLAN, nuclear engineer; b. Vallejo, Calif., Oct. 11, 1944; s. Allan Frederick and Frances Jewell (O'Brien) R. BA in Physiology, U. Calif., Berkeley, 1967, MA in Physiology, 1971, PhD in Engring. Sci., 1977. Postdoctoral fellow U. So. Calif., LA, 1977-78; rsch. engr. Del Mar Avionics, Irvine, Calif., 1979; staff fellow NIH, Bethesda, Md., 1980; nuc. engr. Battelle Energy Alliance, Idaho Nat. Lab., Idaho Falls, 1980—. With USAR, 1969—75. Mem. AAAS, ANS, ASME, Biomed. Engring. Soc., Soc. Computer Simulation, Soc. Math. Biology, Soc. Engring. Sci., Order of Golden Bear, Alpha Sigma Phi. Republican. Roman Catholic. Avocations: swimming, surfing. Home: 1727 Grandview Dr # 4 Idaho Falls ID 83402-5016 Office: Battelle Energy Alliance Idaho Nat Lab Idaho Falls ID 83415-3870

RIENDL, ROBIN W., wealth advisor LPL branch manager; b. Madison, Wis., Feb. 8, 1966; d. Jim McCaslin and Dean Naomi Brown; m. Paul Alex Riendl, Feb. 4, 1994. B in Natural Resources Mgmt., U. Alaska, Fairbanks, 1988; MBA, U. Alaska, 1991. Field investigator Harding Lawson Assocs., Anchorage, 1988—89; rsch. asst. U. Alaska, Fairbanks, 1989; planner Fairbanks N. Star Borough, 1989—90; forestry tech. Environ. Rsch. Inst., 1989—90; environ. analyst State of Alaska Dept. Transportation, Anchorage, 1992—96; fin. advisor Morgan Stanley, 1996—2002, Citi Smith Barney, 2002—09, provisio, 2009—. Recipient Outstanding Young Woman of Am., 1997. Mem.: Fin. Planning Assn., U. Alaska Fairbanks Alumni Assn. Avocations: martial arts, skiing, scuba diving. Office: Provisio 1000 O'Malley Rd Ste 201 Anchorage AK 99515 Business E-Mail: robin@provisioalaska.com.

RIENHOFF, HUGH, venture capitalist, physician, geneticist; m. Lisa Hane, 1998; 3 children. BA in Biology and English Lit., Williams Coll.; MD, Johns Hopkins U. Genetics researcher Fred Hutchinson Cancer Rsch. Ctr., Seattle; ptnr. biotechnology investing New Enterprise Associates, Menlo Park, Calif.; dir. Abingworth Mgmt. Ltd., London; founder, chmn., CEO DNA Sciences (formerly Kiva Genetics), 1998—2001; gen ptnr. Vanguard Ventures, 2002; joined bd. dirs. GeneEd, 2004—, chmn. Faculty mem., dept. molecular biology and genetics John Hopkins U. Sch. Medicine; founder MyDaughtersDna.org, 2007—. Office: GeneEd 100 Pine St 10th Fl San Francisco CA 94111 Office Phone: 415-856-0097. Fax: 415-856-0096.*

RIEPE, CHARLEINE WILLIAMS, secondary school educator; b. Lackawanna, NY, Oct. 28, 1924; d. Edward and Dorothy Hayd (VanAllen) Williams; m. Dale Maurice Riepe, May 24, 1948; children: Kathrine Leigh Herschlag, Dorothy Lorraine. BA cum laude, D'Youville Coll., 1945; MA, U. Mich., 1947; postgrad., U. Hawaii, 1949, SUNY, Buffalo, 1966-70. Tchr. Holy Angels Acad., 1945-47, Carleton Coll., 1950-52; instr. U. S.D., 1952-54, Kokusai Bunka Shinkokai, Internat. House of Japan, 1957—, Tsuda Women's Coll., Tokyo, 1958, U. N.D., 1959-61, Tappan Middle Sch., 1960-61; tchr. Oyster Bay (N.Y.) Middle Sch., 1963; instr. SUNY, Buffalo, 1963-69; tchr. Latin Amherst (N.Y.) Ctrl. Sr. H.S., 1971-85, chmn. dept. fgn. langs., 1975-81. Cons. N.Y. State Regents Exams, 1978-80. Editor: Reading Selections for Latin Level III, 1973, Classical Currents, 1976-79; sec., treas., mng. editor Arethusa, 1968-71. Bd. dirs. Evergreen Coll. Cmty. Orgn., treas., 1990-93; bd. dirs. Wash. State Capital Mus., Friends of Evergreen State Coll. Libr., 1993-99; assoc. State Capitol Mus. Recipient Tchg. Excellence award PTA Amherst, 1978; N.Y. Regents scholar, 1942-46. Mem. Archeol. Inst. Am. (treas. Western N.Y. 1977-79), Classical Assn. Western N.Y. (v.p. 1972-74, pres. 1974-76, exec. coun. 1976-85), Classical Assn. Atlantic States (regional rep. 1980-82), Am. Classical League, Classical Assn. New Eng. States, Nat. Jr. Classical League, N.Y. Assn. Fgn. Lang. Tchrs., N.Y. State Jr. Classical League, Pompeliana, Western N.Y. Fgn. Lang. Educators Coun. (life), Western N.Y. Archeol. Soc. (treas. 1977-79), Wash. Ctr. Performing Arts, Palm Springs Desert Mus., Frye Art Gallery, Henry Gallery U. Wash., Delta Kappa Gamma. Home: 14325 Eagle Run Dr #406 Omaha NE 68164

RIES, ANDREW, dean, educator; MD, Yale U., New Haven, 1974; MPH, San Diego State U., 1991. Prof. medicine U. Calif., La Jolla, 1981—, assoc. dean, acad. affairs, Sch. Medicine, 2004—. Office: Univ Calif San Diego 9500 Gilman Dr La Jolla CA 92093-0602

RIES, EDWARD RICHARD, petroleum geologist, consultant; b. Freeman, SD, Sept. 18, 1918; s. August and Mary F. (Graber) R.; m. Amelia D. Capshaw, Jan. 24, 1949 (div. Oct. 1956); children: Rosemary Melinda, Victoria Elise; m. Maria Wipfler, June 12m 1964. AB magna cum laude, U. S.D., 1941; MS, U. Okla., 1943, PhD, 1951; postgrad., Harvard U., 1946-47, Harvard, 1946-47. Asst. geologist Geol. Survey S.D., White River area, 1941; geophys. interpreter Robert Ray Inc., Western Okla., Okla., 1942; jr. geologist Carter Oil Co., Mont., Wyo., 1943-44; geologist Standard Vacuum Oil Co., Mont., Wyo., Colo., India, 1944-49, sr. geologist Asam, Tripura, Bangladesh, India, 1951-53; sr. regional geologist NY Standard Vacuum Petroleum, Maatschappij, NY, Indonesia, 1953-59, geol. advisor Far East and Africa White Plains, NY, 1959-62, Oceania, Mobile Petroleum Co., NYC, 1962-65; geol. advisor Europe, Far East Mobil Oil Corp., NYC, 1965-71, sr. regional explorationist Far East, Australia, New Zealand, 1971-73, sr. regional explorationist Asia-Pacific, Dallas, 1973-76, sr. geol. advisor Rsch. Geology, 1976-79; assoc. geol. advisor Geology-Geophysics, Dallas, 1979-82; sr. geol. cons., 1982-83. Ind. internat. petroleum geol. cons. Europe, Africa, Sino-Soviet and S.E. Asia, 1986—; grad. asst., teaching fellow U. Okla., 1941-43, Harvard, 1946-47. Contbr. numerous domestic and internat. proprietary and pub. hydrocarbon generation and reserve evaluations, reports and profl. papers. With AUS, 1944-46. Warden-Humble fellow, U. Okla., 1951. Mem. AAAS, Am. Inst. Econ. Rsch., Am. Assn. Petroleum Geologists (assoc. editor 1978-83, 50 Yr. Mem. Svc. award 1993, 60 Yr. Mem. Svc. award 2003), Geol. Soc. Am., Am. Geol. Inst., Nat. Wildlife Fedn., Nat. Audubon Soc., NY Acad. Sci., Soc. Exploration Geophysicists, Wilderness Soc., Am. Legion, Harvard Club (Dallas), Phi Beta Kappa, Sigma Xi, Sigma Gamma Epsilon. Republican. Mennonite. Home and Office: 810 E 6th St Freeman SD 57029

RIES, MARCIE BERMAN, former ambassador; b. Boston, 1950; m. Charles Parker Ries; 2 children. BA, Oberlin Coll., Ohio, 1972; MA, Johns Hopkins U. Sch. Advanced Internat. Studies, 1974. Mgr., internat. investment policy Motor Vehicle Manufacturers Assn., 1975—78; consular/polit. officer US Embassy Santo Domingo US Dept. State, 1978—80, internat. rels. officer, Office Strategic Nuclear Policy, 1981—83, polit. officer US Embassy Ankara, Turkey, 1984—86, desk officer Malta and the Vatican, Office We. European Affairs, 1986—88, dep. head polit. sect., Office European Regional Polit. Military Affairs, 1988—90, officer in charge French desk, Office We. European Affairs, 1990—91, Pearson fellow, House Internat. Relations Com., 1991—92, dep. polit. counselor, US Mission to European Union Brussels, 1992—96, polit. counselor US Embassy London, 1996—2000, dir. Office UN Polit. Affairs, 2001—03, chief of mission Pristina, Kosovo, 2003—04, US amb. to Albania, 2004—07. Recipient Superior Honor awards, US Dept. State.*

RIESEL, SHEILA GINSBERG, lawyer; b. Bklyn., Oct. 5, 1944; BA, Vassar Coll., 1966; JD, Fordham U., 1969. Bar: NY 1969, US Supreme Ct., US Ct. Appeals (2nd cir.), US Dist. Ct. (ea. dist. NY), US Dist. Ct. (so. dist. NY). With Legal Aid Soc.; ptnr. Blank Rome, LLP, NYC. Adj. prof. law, appellate advocacy and legal writing Fordham Law Sch., 1976—82. Mem. Matrimonial Commn., 2005. Named one of Top 100 Attys., Worth mag., 2006, 2007. Mem.: Women's Bar Assn., NY State Bar Assn., NYC Bar Assn., Fed. Bar Coun. Office: Blank Rome LLP Chrysler Bldg 405 Lexington Ave New York NY 10174-0208 Office Phone: 212-885-5535. Office Fax: 212-885-5002. E-mail: SRiesel@BlankRome.com.

RIESELMAN, DEBORAH SUE, editor; b. Cin., Jan. 15, 1953; d. Robert Henry and Gail Dixon (Cato) R.; div. Apr. 1995; 1 child, Charles R. Hamilton. Student, U. Ky., U. Aberdeen, Scotland, U. Cin. News editor Dixie News, Florence, Ky., 1974-79; mng. editor Recorder Newspapers, Burlington, Ky., 1979-84, Christian Music Place, Close to Home Website, 1996-97; digital exec. editor, asst. dir. U. Cin., 1984—. Writing instr. U. Cin., 1999-; editl. judge Internat. Assn. Bus. Communicators, 1992-99, 2007, Cath. Press Assn., 2001, 05, Cin. Overature Awards, 2005; accredited bus. communicator, 2008; presenter in field. Editor, author: UC Mag., 1988— (49 awards Cin. Editors Assn. 1988-2000, 36 awards Internat. Assn. Bus. Communicators 1992-2008, IABC Quill Gold medal Coun. Advancement and Support of Edn. 1998, 4 Regional Coun. Advancement and Support Edn. awards 2004-2006, Soc. Profl. Journalists Two awards, 2008); contbg. author: Mentors, Models and Mothers, 1997. Pub. chmn. 2 state senatorial races, Ky., 1980s; site coord., pub. rels. dir. NAMES Project AIDS Meml. Quilt, Cin., Covington, Ky., Lexington, Ky., Washington, 1989-98; interpreter and storyteller Cin. Hist. Soc., 1996-2001; bd. dirs. Women of Evang. Luth. Ch., Ind.-Ky. Synod, 1999-2002; Nat. WELCA Delegate, 2008. Named Outstanding Citizen of Erlanger, Erlanger (Ky.) City Coun., 1982, one of Outstanding Young Women of Am., 1985. Pres. Internat. Assn. Bus. Communicators (Bronze Quill judge 1995—); mem. Cin. Editors Assn. (various membership coms. 1988-00), U. Cin. Assn. Women Adminstrs. (former bd. dirs.), Kappa Kappa Kappa. Lutheran. Avocations: teaching clogging, mountain dulcimer performer. Office Phone: 513-556-5225. Fax: 513-556-3237. E-mail: Deb.Rieselman@UC.edu.

RIESER, JOSEPH A., JR., tax specialist; b. Pitts., Aug. 28, 1947; s. Joseph Alexander and Ruth Margaret (Piper) R.; m. Susan Jean Irving, Feb. 28, 1976; 1 child, Alexander H.I. AB, Princeton U., 1969; JD, MPP, Harvard U., 1974. Bar: Pa. 1974, D.C. 1976, U.S. Supreme Ct. 1979. Assoc. Reed Smith LLP, Pitts. and Washington, 1974-82, ptnr. Washington, 1983—2003, Arent Fox LLP, Washington, 2003—. Mem. D.C. Office of Tax and Revenue Adv. Group, 1997-2001. Chmn. nat. alumni assn. Kennedy Sch. Govt., Cambridge, Mass., 1979-82; bd. dirs. Harvard U. Alumni Assn., 1982-84; gen. counsel 1984 Dem. Nat. Conv., Washington, 1983-84; gen. counsel Nat. Dem. Party, Washington, 1985-89; spl. counsel Clinton/Gore '92, Inc.; mem. Clinton-Gore 1992 Presdl. Transition Team. Mem. D.C. Bar (chmn. bus. related taxes com. 1989-92, tax policy steering com., chmn. D.C. Bar Nat. Fed. Tax Inst. 1991, 92, 2000, chmn. state and local taxes com. 1994-97, tax sect. steering com. 1997-2003, co-chair tax sect. 1998-2001), Ctr. for Nat. Policy Bd. Advisors, Cosmos Club. Presbyterian. Home: 3517 Davis St NW Washington DC 20007-1426 Office: Arent Fox LLP 1050 Connecticut Ave NW Washington DC 20036 Office Phone: 202-857-8964.

RIESER, RICHARD M., JR., banker; b. Buffalo, Apr. 7, 1943; s. Richard M. and Eleanor (Berger) Rieser; m. Susan Ellen Gecht; children: Abigail L., Jon A., Nicholas A. AB in Am. Civilization, Brown U., Providence, 1965; JD, U. Chgo., 1968. Bar: Ill. 1968, US Dist. Ct. (no. dist.) Ill., US Ct. Appeals (7th cir.). Lawyer VISTA, U.S. OEO, New Orleans and Altus, Okla., 1968-69; assoc. D'Ancona, Pflaum, Wyatt & Riskind, Chgo., 1969-70; sr. v.p. Amalgamated Trust & Savs. Bank, Chgo.; chmn., pres., chief exec. officer 1st Oak Brook Bank, Glenview, Ill., 1974—2006; pres. 1st Oak Brook Bancshares, Inc. (merged with MB Financial 2006); exec. v.p., chief mktg. officer, legal strategist MB Financial, Inc., 2006—. Pres. bd. Village of Northfield, Ill.; former chmn. Northfield Traffic Commn.; former mem. bd. caucus Northfield Sch.; adv. dir. Northwestern U. Kellogg Grad. Sch. Mgmt. Banking Rsch. Ctr.; mem. nat. alumni schs. prog. Brown U. Mem.: Brown U. Alumni Assoc. (past bd. dirs.), Conf. State Bank Suprs., Chgo. Bar Assn., Ill. Bar Assn., Brown Club Chgo. (past pres.). Office: MB Fianacial Inc Hdqs 800 W Madison St Chicago IL 60607 Office Phone: 888-422-6562.

RIESS, ADAM GUY, astronomer, educator; b. Dec. 16, 1969; BS in Physics, MIT, 1992; AM in Astrophysics, Harvard U., 1994, PhD in Astrophysics, 1996. Undergraduate rsch. asst. MIT, 1990—92, sr. thesis student, 1991—92; rsch. assoc. Lawrence Livermore Nat. Lab., 1992; doctoral student Harvard U., 1992—96; Miller Fellow U. Calif., Berkeley, 1996—99; asst. astronomer Space Telescope Sci. Inst., Balt., 1999—2001, assoc. astronomer, 2001—; assoc. adj. prof. John Hopkins U., 2002—06, prof., physics and astronomy, 2006—. Tchg. fellow, physics dept., The Physics of Sports MIT, 1992; tchg. fellow, astronomy Harvard U., 1993, 94; co-taught, Hot Topics in Astrophysics, astronomy and physics dept. John Hopkins U., 2003; invited spkr. in field. Contbr. articles to profl. jours.; guest appearance Quirks and Quarks, CPR, 1998, News, BBC, 1998, Science Friday, NPR, 1998, 2001, Headline News, CNN, 1998, Jim Lehrer News Hour, PBS, 1998, Sound Prints, NPR, 2000, NOVA, PBS, 2000, 60 Minutes, CBS, 2003, Scientific American Frontiers, PBS, 2004. Recipient Nat. Merit Scholar, 1988, Trumpler award, Astronomical Soc. Pacific, 1999, AURA Sci. award, 2000, Innovator award, Time Mag., 2000, Bok prize, Harvard U., 2001, Helen B. Warner prize, Am. Astronomical Soc., 2003, Best and Brightest award, Esquire Mag., 2003, Raymond and Beverly Sackler prize, Tel-Aviv U., 2004, Gruber prize in Cosmology, 2007; co-recipient Shaw prize in Astronomy, Shaw Found., Hong Kong, 2006; named a MacArthur Fellow, The John D. and Catherine T. MacArthur Found., 2008; finalist Innovator award, Discover Mag., 2003; Margaret Weyerhaeuser Jewett Meml. fellowship, 1993, Harvard GSAS Merit fellow, 1995, Kavli Frontier of Sci. fellow, 2007. Fellow: Am. Acad. Arts and Sciences; mem.: Phi Beta Kappa. Achievements include design of Space Shuttle, Leap Frog Toys, children's educational astronomy toy, 1997-98; published the first evidence that the expansion of the Universe was accelerating % filled with Dark Energy, as a result, Science Magazine called this the Breakthrough Discovery of the Year in 1998. Avocations: bicycling, coin collecting/numismatics, home improvement. Office: Space Telescope Sci Inst 3700 San Martin Dr Baltimore MD 21218 Office Phone: 410-338-4509. Office Fax: 410-338-5090. Business E-Mail: ariess@stsci.edu.

RIESS, WERNER, ancient history and classics professor; b. Altoetting, Bavaria, Germany, Aug. 8, 1970; s. Heinrich and Maria Riess; m. Claudia Zech; 1 child, Philipp Benjamin. Habilitation, U. Augsburg, Germany, 2008; PhD, U. Heidelberg, Germany, 2000. Wissenschaftlicher Mitarbeiter U. Heidelberg, 1999—2003; asst. prof. classics UNC, Chapel Hill, 2004—07, assoc. prof. classics, 2007—. Recipient Jr. Faculty Devel. award, UNC, Chapel Hill, 2004, Ruprecht-Karls-prize, U. Heidelberg, 2001—02; Advanced Study grant, German Rsch. Found., 1997—99, Feodor-Lynen fellowship, Alexander-von-Humboldt Found., 2002—03, Jr. fellowship, Harvard Ctr. Hellenic Studies, 2007—08, Spray-Randleigh fellowship, UNC, Chapel Hill, 2006—07. Office: UNC-Chapel Hill Dept Classics 212 Murphey Hall CB #3145 Chapel Hill NC 27599-3145 Business E-Mail: wriess@email.unc.edu.

RIESZ, PETER CHARLES, marketing educator, consultant; b. Orange, NJ, Apr. 30, 1937; s. Kolman and Ellen (Wachs) R.; m. Elizabeth Strider Dunkman, Dec. 28, 1968; children: Sarah Kathleen BS, Rutgers U., 1958; MBA, Columbia U., 1963, PhD, 1971. From asst. prof. to assoc. prof. U. Iowa, Iowa City, 1968-80, prof. mktg., 1980—2007, chmn. dept. mktg., 1981-87, Williams prof. tchg., 1994-97, prof emeritus, 2007—. Vis. prof. Boston U., 1974-75, Duke U., Durham, N.C., 1984-85; guest prof. Meiji U., Japan, summer 2004; cons. in field. Contbr. articles to profl. jours. Recipient Teaching Excellence award HON Industries, 1989; named MBA Prof. of Yr., 1990; Old Gold fellow U. Iowa, 1972. Mem. Am. Chem. Soc. Democrat. Presbyterian. Avocation: photography. Home: 2411 Tudor Dr Iowa City IA 52245-3638 Office: U Iowa Dept Mktg Tippie Coll Bus Adminstrn Iowa City IA 52242 Business E-Mail: peter-riesz@uiowa.edu.

RIEW, K. DANIEL, cervical spine surgeon; b. Seoul, Republic of Korea, July 28, 1958; arrived in U.S., 1966; s. C. Keith and H. Kim Riew; m. Mary Kahng, Sept. 12, 1992. MD, Case Western Res. U., 1984. Diplomate Am. Bd. of Orthopaedic Surgery. Asst. attending physician, instr. medicine Cornell U. Med. Ctr., NYC, 1987—89; resident gen. surgery Beth Israel Med. Ctr., NYC, 1989—90; resident orthop. surgery George Washington U. Hosp., Washington, 1990—94; fellow spine surgery U. Hosps. Cleve./Case We. Res. U.; from asst. prof. to prof. Washington U. Sch. Medicine, St. Louis, 1995—2005, Mildred B. Simon disting. prof. orthop. surgery, prof. neurol. surgery, 2006—, chief cervical spine surgery, dir. Orthopedic-Rehab. Inst. for Cervical Spine Surgery. Contbr. articles to profl. jours. (Cervical Spine Rsch. Soc. Outanding Basic Sci. Rsch. award, 2000, Mayfield award for basic sci. Am. Assn. of Neurol. Surgeons, 2000, North Am. Spine Soc. Outstanding Paper award, 2000, Russell S. Hibbs Basic Sci. award Scoliosis Rsch. Soc., 2000). Recipient C. Richard Bowman award, N.Y. Hosp., Cornell Med. Ctr., 1987, Caring Spirit award, Barnes-Jewish Hosp., 2001, Best Paper award, Am. Soc. Spine Radiology, 2005, Mentor award, 2006, Excellence in Tchg. award, 2007; grantee, Orthopaedic Rsch. and Edn. Found., 2002—05. Fellow: Am. Acad. Orthop. Surgeons; mem.: Mo. State Orthop. Assn., Mid. Am. Orthop. Assn., Am. Orthop. Assn., Scoliosis Rsch. Soc., Orthop. Rsch. Soc., N.Am. Spine Soc. (CME com. and surg. care com. 2000, Outstanding Paper award 2003), Cervical Spine Rsch. Soc. (clin. outcomes com. 2001, Outstanding Clin. Rsch. award 2004, Clin. Poster award 2005, Outstanding Clin. Rsch. award 2006, Outstanding Clin. Poster award 2006). Avocations: skiing, golf. Office: Washington U Sch of Medicine ste 11300 One Barnes-Jewish Hosp Plz Saint Louis MO 63110

RIEZMAN, RAYMOND, economics professor; m. Patricia Beasley, May 12, 2000; children: Rachel, Matthew. PhD, U. Minn., Mpls., 1977. Henry B. Tippie rsch. prof. economics U. Iowa, 1976—. With Army Res., 1969—75, Mpls. Office: Dept Economics Univ Iowa Clinton & Jefferson Iowa City IA 52242

RIFBJERG, KLAUS THORVALD, writer; b. Copenhagen, Dec. 15, 1931; s. Thorvald Frants and Lilly (Nielsen) R.; m. Inge M.G. Andersen, May 28, 1955; children— Lise Beate, Synne Marie, Frands Carl. Student, U. Copenhagen, Princeton U.; PhD (hon.), Lund U., 1992. Freelance writer, poet and dramatist; lit. critic Info., 1955-57, Politiken, from 1959; lit. dir. Gyldendal Pubs., 1984-92. Hon. prof. Danish Tchrs. Coll., 1987, Copenhagen Bus. Sch., 2003. Author (novels) Den Kroniske Uskyld, 1958, Til Spanien, 1971, Brevet til Gerda, 1972, Det sorte hul, 1980, numerous others, (short stories) Og Andre Historier, 1964, Sommer, 1974, (plays) Gris Pa Gaflen, 1962, Udviklinger, 1965, numerous other books of short stories, plays, also criticism. Recipient award Danish Acad., 1967, Nordic Council prize, 1970, Holberg medal, 1979, Nordic prize The Swedish Acad., 1999, others. Mem. Danish Acad. Arts and Letters, Princeton Colonial Club (hon.). Office: care Gyldendal Pubs 3 Klareboderne 1001 Copenhagen Denmark Personal E-mail: thorvaldrif@mail.dk.

RIFENBURGH, RICHARD PHILIP, investment company executive; b. Syracuse, NY, Mar. 3, 1932; s. Russell D. and Edna (MacKenzie) R.; m. Doris Anita Hohn, June 24, 1950; children: David, Susan, Robert. Student, Wayne State U. With Mohawk Data Scis. Corp., Herkimer, NY, 1964-74, pres., 1970-74, chmn., 1974, Moval Mgmt. Corp., Herkimer, 1968—; CEO, GCA Corp., Andover, Mass., 1986-87; gen. ptnr. Hambrecht and Quist Venture Ptnrs., 1987-90; chmn. Miniscribe Corp., Longmont, Colo., 1988-91, Ironstone Group Inc., 1988-91, St. G Crystal Ltd., Jeannette, Pa., 1985—2008, Paradise Music and Entertainment Inc., 2000—. Chmn. Tristar Corp., 1992—2002. With USAF, 1951-55. Address: Moval Mgmt Corp PMB 133 2637 E Atlantic Blvd Pompano Beach FL 33062-4939 Home Phone: 954-941-9182; Office Phone: 954-494-0811. Personal E-mail: dickrif@gmail.com.

RIFF, LAWRENCE P., lawyer; BA in History with highest honors and high distinction, U. Mich., 1978; JD, U. Oreg., 1982. Bar: Calif. 1982, Oreg. 1985, Washington 1987. Lawyer So. Pacific Transp. Co., San Francisco, 1982—86; mng. ptnr., toxic tort, transp. & litig. depts. Steptoe & Johnson LLP, LA, 1997—. John Williams Fellowship. Mem.: Am. Bd. Trial Advocacy, LA County Bar Assn. (Litig. Sect.), Internat. Moot Ct. Team, Jessup Competition. Office: Steptoe & Johnson LLP 633 W 5th St Ste700 Los Angeles CA 90071 Office Phone: 213-439-9494. Office Fax: 213-439-9599. Business E-Mail: lriff@steptoe.com.

RIFFEE, WILLIAM H., dean, pharmacy educator; BS in Pharmacy, W.Va. U., 1967; PhD in Pharmacology, Ohio State U., 1975. Clin. pharmacy officer divsn. hosps. USPHS Commd. Corps, 1967—70; prof. divsn. pharmacology/toxicology U. Tex. Coll. Pharmacy, Austin, 1975—96; prof. dept. pharmacodynamics, dean U. Fla. Coll. Pharmacy, Gainesville, 1996—. Achievements include research in the area of educational technology and its utility in the classroom; innovation in the area of teaching and the use of television and computer-based presentation technology as well as the use of the computer as a learning tool; design of electronic classrooms that incorporate video with computer workstations for student's use. Office: U Fla Coll Pharmacy PO Box 100484 Gainesville FL 32610 Office Phone: 352-392-9714. Office Fax: 352-392-3480. Business E-Mail: riffee@cop.ufl.edu.*

RIFFEL, LAURA ANN, director, special education educator; d. Melvin Ell and Deloris Ann Warford; m. Thomas Edward Riffel, Dec. 23, 1978; children: Jessica Regan, Brandon Daniel. BS in elem. edn., Kans. State U., Manhattan, 1979, MS in Spl. Edn., 1986; PhD in Spl. Edn, U. Kans., Lawrence, 2002. Tchr. LD grades 1 and 3 Geary County Schs., Junction City, Kans., 1979—87; tchr. EMH grade 4 Cabarrus County Schs., Concord, NC, 1987—89; tchr. LD kindergarten, grade 6 and SMH grades 3 and 4 Olathe (Kans.) Dist. Schs., 1989—2000; tchr. asst. U. Kans., Lawrence, 2000—02; dir. Behavioral Intervention Program, Forest Park, Ga., 2002—; webmaster Office of Spl. Edn. Programs Tech. Assistance Ctr. Positive Behavior Support, Eugene, Oreg., 2000—; rschr. Abt Corp., Balt., 2001—02. Adj. prof. applied behavior analysis Ga. State U.; presenter parent mentor programs State of Ga., 2000—; mem. steering com. Effective Behavioral and Instl. Supports, Ga., 2001—; agy. trainer functional behavior assessment and mgmt. Contbr. articles to profl. jours. Finalist Kans. Tchr. of Yr., 1997. Mem.: TASH, Assn. Behavior Analysis, Assn. Positive Behavior Support (web cons. 2002—), Coun. Exceptional Children, Phi Kappa Phi, Delta Kappa Gamma, Pi Lamda Theta. Methodist. Avocations: decorating, knitting, children's drama. Home: 1617 Alabama St Lawrence KS 66044-4033 Office Phone: 404-362-2025.

RIFFENBURGH, GERRYE H., artist, educator; d. Herman Harvey and Mary (Beryl) Harlow; m. Robert Harry Riffenburgh, Nov. 22, 1952; children: Robin, Scott, Marc, Karen, Douglas. BS, Coll. William and Mary, 1951, MS, 1955; BA summa cum laude, San Diego State U., 1979. Exhibiting artist and instr. San Diego Adult Coll., 1978—81; exhibiting artist The Hague, Netherlands, 1982—86, La Spezia, Italy, 1986—89, San Diego, 1990—. Rep. exhibitor Cosmopolitan Fine Arts Gallery, La Jolla, Calif., 2001—, Timmons Courtyard Gallery, Encinitas, Calif., 2001—. Author: (article on color choice) Jour. of Gen. Psychol.; over 45 juried exhibitions, Europe, U.S. Vol. Coastal Planning Coun., San Diego, 1971—73; leader Girl Scouts, San Diego, 1968—74, Girl Guides, Pembrokeshire, Wales, 1974—77; vol. polit. groups, San Diego, 1978—81; fund raiser vol. COTA, San Diego, 1978—82. Recipient 1st pl., Pembrokeshire Artists Assn., UK, 1974, hon. mention, Nat. Annual Galleon Exhibit, London, 1975, 3d pl., Congressgebouw, Netherlands, 1984, Cenacolo Buttini, Italy, 1988, 1st pl., Maurice Braun Meml. Plein Air Exhbn., Calif., 2000, cert. merit, LaJolla Art Assn., 2001, 3d pl., Offtrack Gallery, Leucadia, Calif., 2002, William Schultz award, Am. Impressionist Soc., Fla., 2002, 2d pl., Mcpl. Art Gallery, Escondido, Calif., 2003, spl. merit, Coos Mus. Art, Oreg., 2003, Nat. Arts Club, N.Y.C., 2003—05, Spl. Merit award, Internat. Mus. Contemporary Masters Fine Art, San Antonio, 2004—05, Arts for the Pks. award for excellence, 2005, cert. merit, LaJolla Art Assn., 2006; named hon. mention, Associazione Artisti Versiliese, Italy, 1989; named to Gold Medal Exhbn., Salon d'Automne/Pasadena, Calif., 2002. Mem.: Internat. Plein Air Painters (signature mem.), Am. Soc. Marine Artists (juried artist mem.), Artists' Guild San Diego Mus. Art, Oil Painters Am., Plein Air Painters Assn. San Diego (founder), Am. Impressionists Soc. (signature mem.), La Jolla Art Assn. (life; treas., bd. dir. 1996—2001), Calif. Art Club (juried artist mem.). Avocations: photography, piano, walking, tennis, yoga. E-mail: gerryeriff@yahoo.com.

RIFFENBURGH, ROBERT HARRY, biostatistician, researcher; b. Christiansburg, Va., June 19, 1931; s. Harry Buchholz and Ada Swallow Riffenburgh; m. Gerrye Harlow, Nov. 22, 1952; children: Robin, Scott, Marc, Karen, Douglas. BS, Coll. William and Mary, Richmond, Va., 1951, MS, 1953; PhD, Va. Poly. Inst., Blacksburg, 1957. Asst. prof. math. Va. Poly. Inst., Blacksburg, 1955—57, U. Hawaii, Honolulu, 1957—61; prof., head dept. stats. U. Conn., Storrs, 1962—70; prof. stats. San Diego State U., 1968—74, 1979—82, 1990—93, 2006—; head, biomedical program Naval Undersea Ctr., San Diego, 1970—73; scientist Naval Facility, Brawdy, Wales, 1974—77; math. statistician Naval Ocean Systems Ctr., San Diego, 1977—82; leader, naval ops. rsch. NATO SHAPE Tech. Centre, The Hague, Netherlands, 1982—86; head, ops. rsch. NATO SACLANT Undersea Rsch. Centre, La Spezia, Italy, 1986—90; chief biostats. Naval Med. Ctr. San Diego, San Diego, 1991—. Pres. and ceo Gen. Systems Analysis Co., Storrs, Conn., 1963—70. Author: Statistics in Medicine; contbr. articles to profl. jours. Capt. NATO, 1982—89. Decorated Navy Commendation Medal; Predoctoral fellow, NIH, 1954-1956. Fellow: Am. Statis. Assoc., Royal Statis. Soc. (life); mem.: Internat. Biometrics Soc., Phi Kappa Phi, Sigma Xi.

RIFKIN, ARNOLD, film company executive; b. Bklyn. m. Nikki MacGregor five children. BA, U. Cin. Founder Rifkin-David, 1974-80; merged to form Rifkin/David/Kimble/Parseghian, 1980-81, DHKPR, 1981-84; head motion picture dept. Triad Artists, Inc., 1984-92, founding ptnr.; exec. v.p., worldwide head motion picture divsn. William Morris Agy., Beverly Hills, Calif., 1992-96; pres. William Morris Talent and Lit. Agy., Beverly Hills, Calif., 1996-2000; CEO Cheyenne Enterprises, LLC, Santa Monica, Calif., 2000—06; co-CEO Rifkin/Eberts LLC, 2007—08; CEO Cheyenne Enterprises LLC, 2008—. Bd. dirs. Am. Cinematheque; faculty, co-chair UCLA Sch. Theatre, Film & TV; lecturer Yale Law Sch., Harvard Sch. Bus., 2002-. Bd. councillors U. So. Calif. Office: Cheyenne Enterprises LLC 406 Wilshire Blvd Santa Monica CA 90401-1410

RIFKIN, BARRY R., dean, dental educator, researcher; b. Trenton, NJ, Mar. 30, 1940; s. Samuel H. and Ida M. Rifkin; m. Harriet Smith, Mar. 1960 (div. Sept. 1981); children: Avery, Carl; m. Linda Ruth Rosenberg, Nov. 1993; 1 child, Hannah. BS, Ohio State U., 1961; MS, U. Ill., 1964; DDS, Temple U., 1968; PhD, U. Rochester, 1974. Andrew Mellon fellow U. Rochester Med. Ctr., 1974; assoc. pathologist Strong Meml. Hosp., 1974—80; assoc. prof. NYU, NYC, 1980—84, chmn. dept. oral medicine, 1980—87, prof., 1984—91, chmn. dept. oral medicine and pathology, 1987—91, head divsn. basic scis., 1991—98, prof. emeritus, 1998—; prof. oral biology and pathology, dean SUNY Stony Brook Health Sciences Ctr. Sch. Dental Medicine, 1998—. Rschr. in field; bd. mem. Friends of the Nat. Inst. of Dental and Craniofacial Rsch., 2005—. Sr. editor Biology and Physiology of the Osteoclast, 1992; mem. editl. bd.: Jour. Dental Rsch.; contbr. articles and abstracts to profl. jours. Fellow: Am. Coll. Dentists; mem.: AAAS, Am. Soc. Bone and Mineral Rsch., Internat. Assn. Dental Rsch., Am. Soc. Cell Biology, N.Y. Acad. Scis., Am. Assn. Oral Biologists (pres. 1992—93), Sigma Xi, Omicron Kappa Upsilon. Office: Stony Brook Univ Sch Dental Medicine 160 Rockland Hall Stony Brook NY 11794-8700 Office Phone: 631-632-8950. Office Fax: 631-632-9105. E-mail: barry.rifkin@stonybrook.edu.

RIFKIN, DEBORAH, music educator; b. NY; MusM, U. Mich., Ann Arbor, 1993; PhD in Music Theory, Eastman Sch. Music, Rochester, NY, 2000. Asst. prof. music theory Oberlin Coll., Ohio, 2000—06, Ithaca Coll., NY, 2006—. Office: Ithaca Coll 953 Danby Rd Ithaca NY 14850

RIFKIN, MATTHEW D., radiologist; b. NYC, Mar. 26, 1949; m. Susan Greenberg, 1971; children: Adam, Jason. BA, Brandeis U., 1971; MD, Albert Einstein Coll., 1974. Intern in medicine Montefiore Hosp. and Med. Ctr., Bronx, NY, 1974—75, resident in diagnostic radiology, 1975—78; fellow in ultrasound/CT Johns Hopkins Hops. and Med. Ctr., Balt., 1978—79; instr. radiology Johns Hopkins Hosp. and Med. Sch., Balt., 1978—79; clin. asst. prof. radiology U. Miami Sch. Medicine, Fla., 1979—81, Jefferson Med. Coll., Thomas Jefferson U., Phila., 1981—83, asst. prof. radiology, 1983—85, assoc. prof. radiology, 1983—86, prof. urology, 1985—91, prof., assoc. chair dept. radiology, 1986—91; clin. prof. Coll. Allied Health Sci., Thomas Jefferson U., Phila., 1984—91, 1991; chair dept. radiology Albany Med. Coll., 1991—98, prof. radiology, 1991—98, prof. surgery, 1995—99; prof., vice chmn., chief diagnostic radiology SUNY Sch. Medicine, Stony Brook, 1999—2003, prof. urology, 1999—2003, prof. radiology, 2009—; chmn. radiology Good Samaritan Hosp., West Islip, NY, 2002—; dir. radiology St. Catherine of Siena Hosp., Smithtown, NY, 2004—, St. Charles Hosp., Port Jefferson, NY, 2005—, Mather Hosp., Port Jefferson, 2007—; dir. Mother Hosp., Port Jefferson, NY, 2007—; adj. prof. radiology SUNY Sch Medicine, Stony Brook, 2009—; prof. radiology NY Coll. Osteo. Medicine, 2004—. Cons. radiology VA, Perry Point, Md., 1978—79; staff radiologist Johns Hopkins Hosp., Balt., 1978—79, Plantation Gen. Hosp., Fla., 1979—80, St. Mary's Hosp., West Palm Beach, Fla., 1980—81; med. and ednl. dir. med. sonography St. Mary's Hosp. Sch. Diagnostic, West Palm Beach, 1980—81; staff radiology Thomas Jefferson Univ. Hosp., Phila., 1981—91; dir. radiology rsch. Jefferson Med. Coll., Thomas Jefferson U. Hosp., 1986—91, dir. divsn. magnetic resonance imaging, 1986—91; med. svc. dir. dept. radiology Albany Med. Ctr. Hosp., 1996—98, chief radiologist, 1991—98; vice chair, chief diagnostic radiology, chief clin. ops., chief abdominal radiology SUNY Health Sci. Ctr., Stony Brook, 1999—2003; dir. Mather Meml. Hosp., 2007—; presenter in field. Contbr. scientific papers and articles to profl. jours.; author: Diagnostic Imaging of the Lower Genitourinary Tract, 1985, Handbook of Normal Ultrasound Anatomy, 1985; author: (editor) Intraoperative and Endoscopic Ultrasound, 1987; author: Ultrasound of the Prostate, 1988, 1997, Ultrasound, 1991; editor: Ultrasound of the Urinary Tract, 1991; co-editor: Interventional Radiology of the Genitourinary Tract, 1993; co-author: Pocket Atlas of Normal Ultrasound Anatomy, 2001, Diagnostic Imaging of the Scrotum and External Male Genitalia, 2002. Fellow: Phila. Coll. Physicians, Am. Coll. Radiology, Am. Inst. Ultrasound Medicine; mem.: Soc. Uroradiology. Home: 198 Field Rd East Setauket NY 11733 Office: Good Samaritan Hosp and Med Ctr Dept Radiology 1000 Montauk Hwy West Islip NY 11795 Office Phone: 631-376-4030. Personal E-mail: matthew.rifkin@chsli.org.

RIFKIN, NED, former museum director; b. Florence, Ala., Nov. 10, 1949; s. Arthur Robert and Ina Blanche (Steinberg) R.; children: Moses Kleinman, Amos Kleinman. BA, Syracuse U., 1972; MA in Art History, U. Mich., 1973, PhD in Art History, 1976. Asst. prof. dept. art U. Tex., Arlington, 1977-80; curator, asst. dir. New Mus. Contemporary Art, NYC, 1980-84; curator contemporary art Corcoran Gallery Art, Washington, 1984-86; chief curator exhbns. Hirshhorn Mus. and Sculpture Garden, Washington, DC, 1986-90, chief curator, 1990-91, dir., 2002—05; Nancy and Holcombe T. Green Jr. dir. High Mus. Art, Atlanta, 1991—99; dir. Menil Collection and Found., Houston, 2000—01; under sec. for art Smithsonian Inst., Washington, 2004—08.

RIFKIN, STEPHEN, nephrologist; s. Morris and May Rifkin; children: Steven, Laura. AB, U. Rochester, 1963, MD, 1967. Diplomate in internal medicine and in nephrology Am. Bd. Internal Medicine. Pvt. practice nephrology, Tampa, Fla., 1980—; assoc. prof. medicine U. South Fla. Coll. Medicine, Tampa, 1999—. Chief of staff Tampa Gen. Hosp., 1988—90, chief nephrology sect., 2002—; pres. Fla. End Stage Renal Disease Network #7, Tampa, 1990—92, bd. dirs., 1999—2004. Capt. U. S. Army, 1969—71. Recipient Exemplary Practice award for nephrology, Nat. Kidney Found. of Fla., 1996. Fellow: ACP; mem.: Internat. Soc. Nephrology, Am. Soc. Nephrology. Avocations: tennis, travel.

RIFKIND, ARLEEN B., pharmacologist, researcher, educator; b. NYC, June 29, 1938; d. Michael C. and Regina (Gottlieb) Brenner; m. Robert S. Rifkind, Dec. 24, 1961; children: Amy, Nina. BA, Bryn Mawr Coll., 1960; MD, NYU, 1964. Resident Bellevue Hosp., NYC, 1965; clin. assoc. Endocrine br. Nat. Cancer Inst., 1965—68; rsch. assoc., asst. resident physician Rockefeller U., 1968—71; from asst. prof. to assoc. prof. Weill Med. Coll. Cornell U., NYC, 1971—83, prof. pharmacology Weill Med. Coll., 1983—, chmn. Gen. Faculty Coun. Weill Med. Coll., 1984—86. Mem. Nat. Inst. Environ. Health Scis. Rev. Com., 1981-85, chmn., 1985-86; mem. toxicology study sect. NIH, 1989-91, chmn., 1991-93; bd. sci. counselors USPHS Agy. for Toxic Substances and Disease Registry, 1991-95; adv. com. FDA, Spl. Studies Relating to the Possible Long-Term Health Effects of Phenoxy Herbicides and Contaminents, 1995-99; external adv. bd. Environ. Health Scis. Ctr., Wayne State U., 1999—. Assoc. editor Drug Metabolism and Disposition, 1997-2005; mem. editl. bd. Toxicology and Applied Pharmacology, 1996-2002, Biochem. Pharmacology, 1996—2003; contbr. articles to profl. jours. Chair Friends of Libr., Jewish Theol. Sem. Am., 1984-86; trustee Dalton Sch., 1986-92; bd. govs. Am. Jewish Com., 1999—; bd. dirs. N.Y. chpt. Am. Jewish Com. Recipient Andrew W. Mellon Tchr.-Scientist award, 1976-78, Excellence in Tchg. award Weill Med. Coll. Cornell U., 2004 Mem. AAAS, Internat. Soc. Study Xenobiotics, Am. Soc. Clin. Investigation, Am. Soc. Pharmacology and Exptl. Therapeutics, Endocrine Soc., Soc. Toxicology. Office: Cornell U Med Coll Dept Pharmacology 1300 York Ave New York NY 10021-4805 Business E-Mail: arifkind@med.cornell.edu.

RIFKIND, ROBERT S., lawyer; b. NYC, Aug. 31, 1936; s. Simon H. and Adele (Singer) R.; m. Arleen Brenner, Dec. 24, 1961; children: Amy, Nina. BA, Yale U., 1958; JD, Harvard U., 1961; LHD (hon.), Jewish Theol. Sem. Am., 1998. Bar: N.Y. 1961, U.S. Supreme Ct. 1965. Asst. to solicitor gen. Dept. Justice, 1965-68; assoc. firm Cravath, Swaine & Moore LLP, NYC, 1962-65, 68-70, ptnr., 1971—2001, sr. counsel, 2002—. Trustee Dalton Sch., N.Y.C., 1975-83, hon. trustee, 1983—, pres., 1977-79; trustee Brandeis U., 1998—, The Loomis Inst., 1987-95; bd. dirs. Charles H. Revson Found., 1991-2005, chmn., 1997-2003; bd. dirs. Jewish Theol. Sem. Am., 1983—, Jerusalem Found., 1998-2006, Leo Baeck Inst., 1999—, Benjamin N. Cardozo Sch. Law, 1984-89, UN Assn., 2006—; pres. Am. Jewish Com., 1994-98; chmn., adminstr. coun., Jacob Blaustein Inst. Advancement of Human Rights, 1999-2007. Fellow Am. Coll. Trial Lawyers, Am. Bar Found.; mem. ABA, Coun. Fgn. Rels., Am. Law Inst., Assn. of Bar of City of N.Y., The Century Assn., Phi Beta Kappa. Democrat. Office: Cravath Swaine & Moore LLP Worldwide Pla 825 8th Ave Fl 40 New York NY 10019-7475 Office Phone: 212-474-1450. Business E-Mail: rrifkind@cravath.com.

RIGALI, JUSTIN FRANCIS CARDINAL, cardinal, archbishop; b. LA, Apr. 19, 1935; s. Henry Alphonsus and Frances Irene (White) Rigali. B in Sacred Theology, Cath. U. Am., 1961; Lic. in Canon Law, Gregorian U., Rome, 1963, D in Canon Law, 1964; LHD (hon.), St. Louis U., 1995. Ordained priest Archdiocese of LA, 1961; served at Apostolic Nunciature Madagascar, 1966—70; named Papal Chamberlain to Pope Paul VI, 1967; ordained bishop, 1985; titular archbishop Volsinium, 1985—94; pres. Pontifical Ecclesiastical Acad., Rome, 1985—89; sec. Congregation of Bishops, Rome, 1989—94, Coll. of Cardinals, Rome, 1990—94; archbishop Archdiocese of St. Louis, 1994—2003, Archdiocese of Philadelphia, Pa., 2003—; elevated to cardinal, 2003; cardinal-priest S. Prisca, 2003—. Pres. Pontifical Ecclesiastical Acad., 1985—89. Roman Catholic. Office: Archdiocese of Philadelphia 222 N 17th St Philadelphia PA 19103

RIGAS, JOHN NICHOLAS, lawyer; b. Muncie, Ind., Feb. 24, 1949; s. Nicholas Peter and Edna (Krestakos) Rigas; m. Rosemary Ann Dzienis, May 19, 1979; children: Margaret Rosemary, Nicholas John. BA, Mich. State U., 1971; MA in history and polit. sci., U. Mich., 1972; JD, U. Conn., 1979. Bar: Mich. 1979, US Dist. Ct. Mich. 1979. Joined Dow Corning Corp., 1982; sr. internat. atty. Dow Corning Europe, Brussels, 1988-91; mng. counsel for bus. and comml. law Dow Corning Corp., Midland, Mich., 1992-94, sr. mng. counsel for litigation and claimant law, 1994—99; dep. gen. counsel litig. Armstrong World Industries Inc., 1999—2000, sr. v.p., gen. counsel, sec., 2001—, Armstrong Holdings Inc., Lancaster, Pa., 2000—. Dir. Armstrong Found. Bd. dirs. Lancaster C. of C. and Industry, 2000—03. Mem. ABA, State Bar Mich., Am. Corp. Counsel Assn., Internat. Bar Assn., Midland Country Club (bd. dirs.). Office: Armstrong Holdings Inc PO Box 3001 Lancaster PA 17604-3001

RIGBY, JOSEPH M., utilities executive; B in acctg., Rutgers Univ.; MBA, Monmouth Univ. CPA NJ. Mgmt. positions Pepco Holdings Inc. & subsidiaries, 1979—; v.p., gen. mgr. gas delivery Atlantic City Elec., v.p., gen. mgr. elec. delivery, pres., 2002—04; sr. v.p., pres. Connectiv power delivery Pepco Holdings Inc., Washington, 2002—04, sr. v.p., CFO, 2004—07, exec. v.p., CFO, 2007—08, pres., COO, 2008—09, chmn., pres., CEO, 2009—. Mem. exec. adv. bd. Rutgers-Camden Sch. Bus.; mem. cabinet United Way Del.; mem. adv. bd. Girl Scouts Chesapeake bay. Mem.: Am. Inst. CPAs, NJ Soc. CPAs. Office: Pepco Holdings Inc 701 9th St NW Washington DC 20068*

RIGBY, RANDY, professional sports team executive; m. Sandra Rigby; 5 children. Grad. in bus. mgmt., Brigham Young U., 1979. Sr. v.p. CFS Financial Corp.; sr. v.p. sales, CMO Larry H. Miller Sports & Entertainment Group, gen. mgr., Sta. KJZZ-TV, sr. v.p. broadcasting, pres., COO, 2007—. Alt. NBA Bd. Govs. Mem. NBA Broadcasting Adv. Bd.; past pres., bd. mem. Utah Broadcasters Assn. Avocations: golf, scuba diving, fly fishing. Office: Larry H Miller Group 9350 S 150 E Rte 1000 Sandy UT 84070 also: Utah Jazz 301 W South Temple Salt Lake City UT 84101 Office Phone: 801-563-4100. Office Fax: 801-563-4191.*

RIGBY, WELDON, realtor; Cert. Residential Specialist, Accredited Buyer Rep. Owner, realtor Weldon Rigby Inc. Realtors, Houston; realtor Keller Williams Realty, Houston. Named #1 GCI, Keller Williams Realty Houston Region, 2007, #4 GCI, Keller Williams North America and Can., 2007. Office: Keller Williams Realty 550 Post Oak Blvd Ste 350 Houston TX 77027 Office Phone: 713-621-2555. Office Fax: 713-621-2550.*

RIGDEN, JOHN SAXBY, physicist; b. Painesville, Ohio, Jan. 10, 1934; s. William Percy and Eltheda Xelpha (Weaver) R.; m. Dorothy Lois Takala (div.); children: Jeffrey William, Gregory John, Jonathan Robert, Keith David, Karen Ruth Montes-De-Oca, Lawrence Brick; m. Diana Elizabeth Wyllie, May 15, 1985. BS, Ea. Nazarene Coll., 1956; PhD, Johns Hopkins U., 1960. Prof. physics Ea. Nazarene Coll., Quincy, Mass., 1961-67, Middlebury (Vt.) Coll., 1967-68, U. Mo., St. Louis, 1968-90; dir. physics programs Am. Inst. Physics, NYC, 1987—97. Editor Am. Jour. Physics, 1978-88; Co-Editor Physics in Perspective, 1998-; author: (biography) Rabi: Scientist and Citizen, 1987, (text) Physics and the Sound of Music, 1977, 85, Hydrogen: The Essential Element, 2002, Einstein 1905: The Standard of Greatness, 2005; contbr. 20 papers to refereed jours., 37 articles and revs. to jours., mags., newspapers, 100 editorials to Am. Jour. Physics. Grantee NSF, 1961-67, 68, 69-71, 79-80, 87-89, Sloan Found., 1981-85, 86-88, NEH, 1970; Fulbright fellow, 1971, 75, Robert A. Millikan medal, 2005; Andrew Gemant award, 2008 Fellow AAAS; Am. Phys. Soc., mem. Am. Assn. Physics Tchrs., History of Sci. Soc., N.Y. Acad. Scis., St. Louis Acad. Scis. Office: 822 Havenwood Count Saint Louis MO 63122 also: Dept Physics Wash Univ Saint Louis MO 63130

RIGDON, KEVIN LEIGH, theater educator, lighting designer, set designer; b. Pontiac, Mich., Feb. 17, 1956; s. Donald Lee and Arlene Mae Rigdon; m. Patricia Patrick, June 21, 1998. Student, Drake U., Des Moines, Iowa, 1974—75. Resident designer Steppenwolf Theatre Co., Chgo., 1976—97; from vis. prof. to prof. U. Houston, 1997—2001, prof., 2001—. Adj. faculty The Theater Sch. De Paul U., 1991—96; assoc. dir. design The Alley Theater, Houston, 1998—. Lighting designer (plays) Steppenwolf Theatre, 1980 (The Joseph Jefferson award, 1980), Remains Theatre, 1982 (The Joseph Jefferson award, 1981, 1982), Glengarry Glen Ross, 1984, Speed the Plow, 1988, Ghetto, 1989, Our Town, 1989 (nominated Drama Desk award, 1989), The Grapes of Wrath, Broadway, 1990 (nominated Drama Desk award, 1990, Am. Theatre Wing Design award, 1990, nominated Tony award, 1990), A Streetcar Named Desire, 1992, Steppenwolf Theatre, 1994 (The Joseph Jefferson award, 1994), The Rise and Fall of Little Voice, 1994, Buried Child, 1996, Mark Taper Forum, 1997 (Drama-Logue Critic's award, 1997), One Flew Over the Cuckoo's Nest, 2001, Lincoln Ctr. Theater (Am. Theatre Wing Design award, 1985, nominated Drama Desk award, 1985, 1985, Am. Theatre Wing Design award, 1985), A Clockwork Orange (The Joseph Jefferson award, 1997), Goodman Theatre (The Joseph Jefferson award, 1988), Remains Theatre, scenic designer, lighting designer The Caretaker, 1986, The Song of Jacob Zulu, 1993, Coast Playhouse, 1994 (The L.A. Weekly award, 1994, LA Weekly award, 1994), The Old Neighborhood, 1997, designer (over 300 other plays off-Broadway plays). Recipient Outstanding Faculty award, The Houston Alumni Orgn., 2003. Mem.: United Scenic Artists. Home: 2115 Runnels St Apt 5308 Houston TX 77003 Office: Univ Houston 133 Cynthia Woods Mitchell Houston TX 77204-4016 Home Fax: 713-236-0986. Personal E-mail: rigdondesign@sbcglobal.net. Business E-Mail: krigdon@uh.edu.

RIGEL, DARRELL SPENCER, dermatologist, educator, skin cancer researcher; b. Montclair, NJ, June 20, 1950; s. Geldon and Gertrude (Kochansky) R.; m. Beth Carol Hollander, Aug. 4, 1974; children: Ethan, Adam, Ashlee. SB, MIT, 1972, SM, 1974; MD, George Washington U., 1978. Diplomate Am. Bd. Dermatology. Intern N.Y. Hosp.-Cornell Med. Ctr., NYC, 1978-79; resident in dermatology NYU Med. Ctr., 1979-82, dermatologic surgery and oncology fellow, 1982; chief resident NYU Hosp., Bellevue Hosp., Manhattan VA Hosp., 1981-82; pvt. practice NYC, 1982—; dir. dermatology PMI Strang Clinic, NYC, 1982-90. Attending physician NYU Hosp., NYC, 1983—, Bellevue Hosp. Ctr., NYC, 1983—; clin. instr. dermatology NYU Med. Ctr., 1983-86, clin. asst. prof., 1986-90, clin. assoc. prof., 1991-97, clin. prof., 1997—; sci. cons. to numerous cos. and orgns.; pres., chief exec. officer Iris, Inc., NYC, 1987—. Author, editor: Pigmentated Lesions, 1985, Cancer of the Skin, 2005; contbr. numerous articles to profl. jours. Bd. dirs. Am. Cancer Soc., NYC, 1985—. Recipient nat. citation Am. Cancer Soc., 1987. Fellow Am. Acad. Dermatology (nat. sec.-treas., 1997-99, bd. dirs., chmn. pres. 1999-2000, presdl. comm. on melanoma and skin cancer, chmn. on computer tech. 1985-89, Presdl. citation 1985, pres., 1999-2000); mem. AMA, Am. Dermatologic Assn. (sec., treas. 2001-07, pres. 2007-08), Dermatologic Soc. Greater N.Y. (v.p. 1988, pres. 1989), Iris Golf Club (pres. 1987-89). Avocations: golf, fishing, chess, sailing. Office: 35 E 35th St Ste 208 New York NY 10016-3814

RIGG, CHARLES ANDREW, pediatrician; b. Hamilton, Victoria, Australia, Oct. 18, 1926; arrived in U.S., 1963; s. Arthur Oscar and Mary Eileen (Wingrove) Rigg. B Medicine, Surgery with honors, Sydney U., 1951. Registrar pediat. unit St. Mary's Hosp., London, 1956, 1958; registrar professorial unit Children's Hosp., Sydney, 1954—56; fellow adolescent medicine Boston Children's Hosp., 1963—64, staff adolescent medicine, 1964—65; asst. prof. pediat. Georgetown U. Med. Sch., 1965—67; chief dept. adolescent medicine Children's Nat. Med. Ctr., Washington, 1967—80, Boston City Hosp., 1981—83; med. dir. Outer Cape Health, Provincetown, Mass., 1983—88; pediatrician, med. dir. Medicenter Five, Harwich, Mass., 1988—95, pediatrician, 1995—97; cons. pediatrician May Ctr. Child Devel., Chatham, Mass., 1990—; pediatrician Harwich Town Pub. Sch. Sys., 1997—. Cons. Nat. Naval Med. Ctr., Bethesda, Md., 1973—80, Walter Reed Army Med. Ctr., Washington, 1973—80; courtesy staff medicine Children's Hosp., Boston, 1983—2005, emeritus mem. courtesy staff, 2005—; vis. prof. Philippine Pediat. Soc., 1978, 9th Congress Brazilian Med. Assn., 1979, 16th Internat. Congress Pediat., Barcelona, 1980; from asst. prof. to assoc. prof. child health George Washington U. Med. Sch., 1967—80;

assoc. prof. pediat. Boston U., 1981—83. Editor: Adolescent Medicine Present and Future Concepts, 1980; contbr. articles to profl. jours. Mem. Shakespeare Libr., Washington, Nat. Trust Hist. Preservation, Nat. Trust Australia, Tasmania, Royal Oak Soc. Maj. M.C. Royal Australian Army, 1951—60, lt. col. USAR, 1985—91. Model Tng. Program Adolescent Medicine grantee, Maternal and Child Health Svcs.-U.S. Govt., 1967—80, Comprehensive health Svcs. Adolescent Ctr. grantee, Mass. Dept. Pub. Health, 1981—83. Fellow: Royal Australasian Coll. Physicians, Am. Acad. Pediatrics (life); mem.: Soc. Adolescent Medicine (Washington, DC chpt. pres. 1974—76, New Eng. chpt. pres. 1982—84, charter, treas., chmn., legis. com.), Folger Shakespeare Libr., Royal Sydney Golf Club. Episcopalian. Avocations: historic preservation, gardening, theater, music, walking. Office Phone: 508-945-1147.

RIGGEN, PATRICIA, film director, film producer; b. Guadalajara, Mexico; MFA in Film Studies, Columbia U., NYC. Prodn. vice chmn. shorts Mex. Film Inst., 1997—98. Prodr.: (films) Adiós mama, 1997, No Support, 1998; exec. prodr.: In the Mirror of the Sky, 1998; writer, prodr., dir. (films) The Cornfield, 2002 (Gold medal Student Acad. Awards, 2002, OCIC award - Spl. Mention Havana Film Festival, 2002, Silver Goddess award for Best Short Film Mex. Cinema Journalists, 2003, Best Short Fiction Film Ariel Awards, 2003, DGA East Coast Student Filmmaker award, 2003, first place ATAS Found. Coll. TV Awards, 2004), Family Portrait, 2004 (Short Filmmaking award Sundance Film Festival, 2005), prodr., dir. Under the Same Moon, 2007 (Best Dir. Imagen Found., 2008). Office: Fox Searchlight 10201 W Pico Blvd Bldg 38 Los Angeles CA 90035

RIGGENBACH, JEFF, journalist, broadcaster; b. Highland Park, Mich., Jan. 12, 1947; s. Frank Riggenbach and Dorothy Jane Miller; m. Suzanne Hoy Riggenbach, Mar. 10, 1996; m. Leslee J. Newman, Sept. 5, 1976 (div. 1989); m. Patricia Streeter, Mar. 29, 1967 (div. 1973); children: Max Rigman, Blaine Streeter. BS in Liberal Studies, Excelsior Coll. (formerly Regents Coll.); MA in Humanities, Calif. State U., 2004. Anchor/newswriter KNUZ, KQUE Radio, Houston, 1967—72; anchor/book critic/cultural affairs reporter KFWB All News Radio, LA, 1972—78; editor The Castalian (mag.), LA, 1972—74; instr. (journalism) Pierce Coll., LA, 1977—78; freelance writer L.A. Times, 1977—86; reporter, prod. Pub. Affairs Broadcast Group, Los Angeles, 1977—79; exec. editor The Libertarian Rev., San Francisco, 1978—82; exec. prodr., Byline Cato Inst., Washington, 1979—90; contbg. editor Inquiry mag., Washington, 1982—85; freelance writer San Jose (Calif.) Mercury News, 1983—88, U.S.A. Today, 1983—95; editl. writer Oakland Tribune, Calif., 1984—85; contbg editor Reason mag., LA, 1984—90; editl. writer/columnist Orange County Register, Santa Ana, Calif., 1985—87; daily economics commentator CNN Radio, Atlanta, 1985—87; prodr./program host KFAC Classical Radio, LA, 1987—89; mng. editor Pacific Bus. Rev., San Francisco, 1992—93; prodr./program host KKHI Classical Radio, San Francisco, 1993—94; instr. (liberal arts) Acad. of Art Coll., San Francisco, 1996—2000; contbg. editor Liberty mag., Port Townsend, Wash., 2001—08. Co-founder, vice chair Free Press Assn., Columbus, Ohio, 1983—87; sr. fellow Randolph Bourne Inst., Redwood City, Calif., 2005—. Author: (books) In Praise of Decadence, 1998, Why American History Is Not What They Say, 2009; books columnist: Rational Review.com, 2005—. Mem.: Orgn. of Am. Historians. Home: 5622 Allendale Rd Houston TX 77017 Personal E-mail: jriggenbach@bigfoot.com.

RIGGINS, TRACY, neurologist, educator; d. Donald and Wendy DeBoer; m. Brock Riggins. PhD, U. Minn., 2005. Postdoc. fellow U. Calif., Davis, Sacramento, 2005—07, U. Md., Sch. Medicine, Balt., 2007—08; asst. prof. U. Md., Coll. Pk., 2008—. Contbr. articles to profl. jours. Democrat.

RIGGINS, WILLIAM G., electric power industry executive; b. 1958; BS, JD, U. Kans.; MS, U. Mo., Kansas City. Bar: Mo. 1984. Atty. Great Plains Energy, Inc., Kansas City, Mo., 1991—92, staff atty., 1992—94, sr. atty., 1994—96, mng. atty., 1996, asst. gen. counsel, 1996—98, asst. chief legal officer, 1998—2000, gen. counsel, corp. sec., 2000—. Bd. mem. vice chmn. Swope Health Found. Office: Great Plains Energy Inc PO Box 418679 1201 Walnut St Kansas City MO 64141

RIGGINS-EZZELL, LOIS, museum administrator; b. Nashville, Nov. 18, 1939; d. Percy Leon and Lula Belle Prather (Traughber) Von Schmittou; 1 son, Nicholas. B.S., Belmont Coll., 1968; postgrad., U. Western Ky., 1969-72, George Washington U., 1978. Cert. tchr., Ky., Tenn. Tchr. Ky. Pub. Schs., Adairville, 1962-71; tour supr. Tenn. State Capitol, Nashville, 1972-74; curator of extension services Tenn. State Mus., Nashville, 1975-77, curator edn., 1977-81, exec. dir., 1981—. Chmn. Nashville Flight of Tenn. Friendship Force, Caracas, Venezuela, 1977, Tenn. Am. Revolution Bicentennial Arts Competition, 1976, Gov.'s Quicentennial Com., 1991-92; bd. dirs. Tenn. State Mus. Found., Inc., 1981—, Zool. Soc. Mid. Tenn., 1986-88, So. Folk Cultural Revival Project, 1986-93, Tenn. Pres. Trust, 1989—, Hist. Coun., Girl Scouts U.S.; mem. commning. com. USS Tenn., 1990; keynote speaker nat. forums Corp. Philanthropy Report, Chgo., Atlanta, 1991. Named Woman for Lears, Lears Mag., 1990, Tenn. Woman of Distinction, 1993. Mem. Southeastern Mus. Conf. (edn. com., rep. to Am. Assn. Mus. council, publs. advt. com. 1983), Inter Mus. Council of Nashville (chmn. edn. 1980-81), Am. Assn. Mus., Am. Assn. State and Local History (edn com. 1988-90), Am. Fedn. Art., Art Dirs. Forum. Office: Tenn State Mus 505 Deaderick St Nashville TN 37243-1402

RIGGIO, KERRY KERSTIN, elementary school worker, researcher; d. Patrick Peter and Giedre Grazina (Lisauskas) Riggio. BA in Econs., Pa. State U., University Park, 1993. Cert. United Animal Nations Emergency Rescue Svc., EMT NJ. Patient care rep. Hunterdon Med. Ctr., Flemington, NJ, 1998—2000; statis. analyst A.M. Best, Oldwick, NJ, 2000; aftercare asst. Immaculate Conception Sch., Annandale, NJ, 2003—. Author: Calls of the Tame: Dog Sounds Explained, 1999. Pet therapy vol. St. Hubert's Geralda, Madison, NJ, 1994; CCD aide Immaculate Conception Ch., 2004. Recipient award for slogan, Mellon Bank, 1992; scholar, Garden State, Lithuanian Am. Club No. NJ. Mem.: Am. Mensa Ltd. Roman Catholic. Avocations: collecting Sleeping Beauty memorabilia, ceramics. E-mail: savekoala@aol.com.

RIGGIO, LEONARD, book store company executive; b. 1941; married; 3 children. Student, NYU; D (hon.), CUNY Baruch Coll., Bentley Coll. Mdse. mgr. NYU Bookstore, NYC, 1962—65; pres., CEO, bd. dirs. Barnes & Noble Bookstores, Inc., 1965—86; founder, CEO, pres., treas. Barnes & Noble Inc., NYC, 1986—2002, chmn. bd., 1986—; chmn. bd., prin. beneficial owner Software Etc. Stores, Inc., Mpls., MBS Textbook Exch. Inc., Columbia, Mo. Chmn. bd. Dia Art Found., 1998—2006, bd. mem., 2006—; bd. dirs. Children's Def. Fund, Black Children's Cmty. Crusade, Bklyn. Tech Found., Italian Am. Found. Recipient Ellis Island Medal of Honor, Frederick Douglas Medallion, Americanism award, Anti-Defamation League, 2002; named one of Top 200 Collectors, ARTnews mag., 2003—08; named to Acad. of Disting. Entrepreneurs, Babson Coll., Retailing Hall of Fame, Tex. A&M U., 2005. Avocation: collecting contemporary art. Office: Barnes & Noble Inc 4th Fl 122 5th Ave Fl 4 New York NY 10011-5605

RIGGIO, MILLA C., language educator, researcher; d. Morgan William Cozort and Mildred Ella Robison; m. Thomas P. Riggio, June 21, 1969; children: Anna Riggio-Rosen, Thomas P. II 1 stepchild, Robert Brink. BA, So. Meth. U., Dallas; AM, Harvard U., Cambridge, Mass., 1968, PhD, 1973. Lectr. U. Sydney, 1968, Harvard U., Cambridge, 1971; from asst. prof. to prof. Trinity Coll., Hartford, Conn., 1973—96, James J. Goodwin prof. English, 1996—. Dramaturg, panelist, cons. Hartford Stage Co., 1995—; cons. West Indian Found., Hartford, 1998—; vis. prof. in residence U. W. Indies, St. Augustine, Trinidad and Tobago, 2000. Author, editor: Teaching Shakespeare thru Performance, 1989, Carnival: Culture in Action - The Trinidad Experience, 2004, In Trinidad, 2008; editor: Trinidad & Tobago Carnival, 1998. Exec. bd. Hemispheric Inst. of Performance and Politics, NYC; trustee E. Coast Artist, NYC; bd. dirs. Charter Oak Cultural Ctr., Hartford, 2001—02; mem. adv. bd. Cinestudio, Trinity Coll., 2008. Recipient award for Contbn. to West Indian Hartford Cmty., T.C. Brownell Disting. Tchg. award, Trinity Coll. Trustee Faculty Excellence award; fellow, NEH, 1998—99; vis. scholar, NYU, 2005—06; Nat. Merit scholar, Fulbright fellow, Australia, 1964. Mem.: MLA, Medieval/Renaissance Drama Soc. (sec., v.p., pres. 1988—2001), Shakespeare Assn. Am. Avocations: music, tennis, films. Home: 20 Dearborn Dr Manchester CT 06040 Office: Trinity Coll English Dept Hartford CT 06106

RIGGIO, STEPHEN, book store company executive; married; 3 children. BA in Anthropology, Bklyn. Coll., 1974. Buying, mktg. areas Barnes & Noble Bookstores, Inc., NYC, 1974-78, gen. mdse. mgr., 1978-81, head direct mail bus., 1981-86, exec. v.p. merchandising, 1986-90, exec. v.p., chief oper. officer, 1990—97; vice-chmn. & acting CEO barnesandnoble.com, 2000—02; vice-chmn. Barnes & Noble, Inc., 1997—, CEO, 2002—. Originator Children With Special Needs collection books about and for children with learning disabilities. Bd. dirs. N.Y. chpt. Assn. Help Retarded Children. Office: Barnes & Noble, Inc 122 5th Ave New York NY 10011-5605

RIGGLEMAN, JIM (JAMES DAVID RIGGLEMAN), professional baseball coach; b. Fort Dix, NJ, Nov. 9, 1952; 1 child. B in Phys. Edn., Frostburg State U., Md., 1974. Minor league player Waterbury, Ark., New Orleans, Springfield, 1974—81; minor league mgr. St. Louis Cardinals, 1982—88, dir. player devel., 1988—89, first base coach, 1989—91, minor league field coord., 2005—07; minor league mgr. AAA Las Vegas, 1991—92; mgr. San Diego Padres, 1992—94, Chgo. Cubs, 1995—99; bench coach LA Dodgers, 2001—04, Seattle Mariners, 2008, mgr., 2008; bench coach Washington Nationals, 2008—09, interim mgr., 2009—. Office: Washington Nationals Nationals Pk 1500 S Capitol St SE Washington DC 20003-1507*

RIGGS, ARTHUR D., health facility administrator, research scientist; b. Modesto, Calif., Aug. 8, 1939; s. John Arlis and Nelly Laura Riggs; m. Jane Merill, June 12, 1960; children: Karen, Lynelle, Derrick. AB in Chemistry, U. Calif., Riverside, 1961; PhD in Biochemistry, Calif. Inst. Tech., Pasadena, 1966. Predoctoral fellow biology dept. Calif. Inst. Tech., 1961—66; postdoctoral fellow Salk Inst. for Biol. Studies, La Jolla, Calif., 1966—69; assoc. rsch. scientist dept. molecular biology City of Hope Nat. Med. Ctr., Duarte, Calif., 1969—74, sr. rsch. scientist, 1974—83, assoc. chmn. divsn. biology, 1979—81, chmn. divsn. biology, 1981—83, assoc. dir. rsch., 1998—99; adj. prof. U. So. Calif., Los Angeles, 1978—; assoc. dir. for lab. rsch. City of Hope Cancer Ctr., 1981—87, dir. shared resources, 1993—95; chmn. divsn. biology Beckman Rsch. Inst. City of Hope, 1983—87, 1994—2000, dir., 1999—, 2000—; founding dean City of Hope Grad. Sch., Duarte, 1994—98. Contbr. articles to profl. jours. Recipient Rsch. award, Juvenile Diabetes Found., 1979, Disting. Alumnus award, U. Calif., Riverside, 1988, Tech. Leadership award, 2004. Mem.: NAS. Achievements include first human protein produced in bacteria; first man-designed and man-made gene; discovery of new type of genetics. Avocations: hiking, kayaking, mountain biking. Office: Beckman Rsch Inst City of Hope 1450 E Duarte Rd Duarte CA 91010

RIGGS, ARTHUR JORDY, retired lawyer; b. Nyack, NY, Apr. 3, 1916; s. Oscar H. and Adele (Jordy) R.; m. Virginia Holloway, Oct. 15, 1942 (dec.); children: Arthur James (dec.), Emily Adele Riggs Freeman, Keith Holloway, George Bennett; m. Priscilla McCormack, Jan. 16, 1993. AB, Princeton U., 1937; LLB, Harvard U., 1940. Bar: Mass. 1940, Tex. 1943; cert. specialist in labor law. Assoc. Warner, Stackpole, Stetson & Bradlee, Boston, 1940-41; staff mem. Solicitors Office U.S. Dept. Labor, Washington, Dallas, 1941-42; mem. Johnson, Bromberg, Leeds & Riggs, Dallas, 1949-81; of counsel Geary & Spencer, Dallas, 1981-91. Mem. ABA, State Bar Tex., Phi Beta Kappa. Avocations: maya archeology, history, photography. Home and Office: 2110 Antibes Dr Carrollton TX 75006-4326

RIGGS, AUDREY, psychologist; b. Wichita, Kans. d. Gary Rex and Phyllis Maurine Armstrong; m. Thomas Walker Riggs; children: Grace Anne, Mary Elizabeth. BS in Psychology, Mo. Western State U., St. Joseph, Mo., 1991; MA, Stephen F. Austin State U., Nacogdoches, Tex., 1996. Cert. psychology Tex., 1997. Lic. specialist sch. psychology Pine Tree ISD, Longview, Tex., 1996—2001, Pearland ISD, Pearland, Tex., 2002—04, Grapevine-Colleyville ISD, Tex., 2005—08. Active Christian Edn., Youth Ministry, Music Ministry, 1985—2008. Recipient Magna Cum Laude, Mo. Western State U., 1991, Outstanding Sr. Psychology, 1991; grantee, State Kans., 1984. Mem.: Tex. Assn. Sch. Psychologists, Assn. Tex. Profl. Educators, Alpha Chi, Psi Chi. Home: 937 Brown Trail Bedford TX 76022

RIGGS, BYRON LAWRENCE, JR., physician, educator; b. Hot Springs, Ark., Mar. 24, 1931; s. Byron Lawrence and Elizabeth Ann (Patching) R.; m. Janet Templeton Brewer, June 24, 1955; children: Byron Kent, Ann Templeton. BS, U. Ark., 1953, BS in Medicine, 1955, MD, 1955; MS in Medicine, U. Minn., 1962. Diplomate Am. Bd. Internal Medicine, Am. Bd. Endocrinology. Intern Letterman Army Hosp., San Francisco, 1955-56; resident in internal medicine Mayo Grad. Sch. Medicine Hosp., Rochester, Minn., 1958-61; asst. to staff Mayo Clinic and Found., Rochester, 1961, mem. staff internal medicine and metabolism, 1962—; faculty U. Minn. Med. Sch., Rochester, 1962—74, assoc. prof., 1970-72, prof., 1972—; Purvis and Roberta Tabor prof. med. rsch. Mayo Clinic Coll. Medicine Sch., Rochester, 1974—2003, chmn. divsn. endocrinology and metabolism, 1974—84, prof. emeritus, 2003—; mem. gen. medicine B study sect. NIH, 1979-82. Nat. adv. bd. NIAMS/NIH, 1987-91, disting. investigator Mayo Found., 1991-2003 Contbr. articles to profl. jours. Dist. investigator Mayo Found., 1991—. Served with M.C. AUS, 1956-58. Recipient Postgrad. Travel award Mayo Found., 1961, Kappa Delta award Am. Acad. Orthopedic Surgery, 1972, Disting. Alumni award U. Ark., 1998, Mayo Found., 2000, Cable Disting. Svc. award AACE, 2002; Traveling fellow Royal Soc. Medicine, 1973 Master ACP; mem. AMA, AAAS, Am. Coll. Endocrinology, Assn. Am. Physicians, Am. Soc. Clin. Investigation, Endocrine Soc. (Rorer Clin. Investigator award 1989), Am. Fedn. Clin. Rsch. (councillor Midwest sect. 1969-71), Am. Soc. for Bone and Mineral Rsch. (pres. 1985-86, Bartter Clin. Investigation award 1990, Career Recognition award, Newman Disting. Svc. award 2002, Outstanding Mentorship Rodam award 2005), Ctrl. Soc. Clin. Rsch. (councillor, Nat. Osteoperoisis Found. (Legands In Osteoperoisis award 2009). Office: Mayo Clinic 200 1st St SW Rochester MN 55905-0002 Home: 801 Pleasant Valley Dr Unit 22 Little Rock AR 72227-2163

RIGGS, FLETCHER EUGENE, economist, consultant; b. Kansas City, Mo., Dec. 21, 1923; s. Fletcher and Martha Mae (Pitcher) Riggs; m. Frances Maude Cooley, Feb. 5, 1944 (dec.); children: Fletcher Vincent, Roger Eugene, Keturah Ann, Russell Craig. BS in Agrl. Econs., Kans. State U., Manhattan, 1948, MS in Agrl. Econs., 1949; PhD in Econs., Vanderbilt U., Nashville, 1956. Asst. prof. agrl. econs. Kans. State U., 1951—56; agrl. economist, regional econ. analyst Tenn. Valley Authority, 1956—64; agrl. economist, regional econ. analyst, dep. chief rural devel. divsn. AID, Republic of Korea, 1964—70, asst. dir. agr. and rural devel. Thailand, 1970—75, chief. agr. and rural devel. bur. Asia Washington, 1975—77, dep. assoc. asst. adminstr. bur. devel. support, 1977—78, chief agr. and rural devel. New Delhi, 1978—81; cons., 1981—91; housing constrn. and land developer Costa Rica, 1991—2000; exotic hardwood mfr., Peru, 2000—07. Co-author: Economics of Watershed Planning, 1961. With US Army, 1942—46, ETO. Decorated Most Noble Order of Crown of Thailand Royal Thai Govt.; recipient Disting. Career Svc. award, Agy. Internat. Devel., 1975, 1979. Avocations: sculpting, painting. Office: Mar de Sueños LLC 852 1st Ave S Naples FL 34102 Home: 1100 13th Sr N Naples FL 34102

RIGGS, GREGORY LYNN, lawyer; b. Columbus, Ohio, Apr. 21, 1948; s. Roy Albert and Edith Myrtle (Riggins) R.; m. Janet Kaye Adams, June 26, 1982; children: Caroline Ashley, Kristen Nicole. BA, U. NC, 1971; BA in jurisprudence, Oxford U., 1976; JD, Emory U., 1979. Bar: Ga. 1979, US Dist. Ct. No. Dist. Ga. 1979, US Ct. Appeals 7th cir. 1982, US Ct. Appeals 11th cir. 1985, US Ct. Appeals 5th cir. 1986. Atty. Delta Air Lines, Atlanta, 1979-84, sr. atty., 1984-92, asst. gen. counsel, 1992-94, assoc. gen. counsel, 1994-98, v.p., dep. gen. counsel, asst. sec., 1998—2003, sr. v.p., gen. counsel, 2003—04, sr. v.p., gen. counsel, chief corp. affairs, 2004—05; chmn. exec. com., corp. counsel sect. State Bar Ga., 2005—. Mem.: Atlanta Vol. Lawyers Found. (bd. dirs. 2000—04), Am. Corp. Counsel Assn. (chair law dept. mgmt. com. 1995—96, bd. dirs. Ga. chpt. 1998), State Bar of Ga. (access to justice com. 1999, chair exec. com. corp. counsel sect. 2005—). Office: Delta Air Lines Inc Dept Law Hartsfield Internat Airport Atlanta GA 30320 E-mail: greg.riggs@comcast.net.

RIGGS, HENRY EARLE, academic administrator, engineering educator; b. Chgo., Feb. 25, 1935; s. Joseph Agnew and Gretchen (Walser) Riggs; m. Gayle Carson, May 17, 1958; children: Elizabeth, Peter, Catharine. BS, Stanford U., 1957; MBA, Harvard U., 1960; Doctorate (hon.), Harvey Mudd Coll., 2006, Kech Grad. Inst., 2007. Indsl. economist SRI Internat., Menlo Park, Calif., 1960—63; v.p. Icore Industries, Sunnyvale, Calif., 1963—67, pres., 1967—70; v.p. fin. Measurex Corp., Cupertino, Calif., 1970—74; prof. engring. mgmt. Stanford U., Calif., 1974—88, Ford prof. Calif., 1986—88, Ford prof. emeritus Calif., 1990, v.p. for devel. Calif., 1983—88; pres. Harvey Mudd Coll., Claremont, Calif., 1988—97, pres. emeritus, 1997; pres. Keck Grad. Inst., Claremont, 1997—2003, pres., trustee emeritus, 2003—. Bd. dirs. Capital Rsch. Group, 1989—; dir. Inst. for Sys. Biology, 2006—. Author: Accounting: A Survey, 1981, Managing High-Tech Companies, 1983, Financial and Economic Analysis, 1994, 2d edit., 2004, Understanding the Financial Score, 2007; contbr. articles to profl. jours. Recipient Gores Tchg. award, Stanford U., 1980; Baker scholar, Harvard Bus. Sch., 1959. Mem.: Stanford U. Alumni Assn. (bd. dirs. 1990—94, chmn. 1993), Palo Alto Club, Sunset Club, Calif. Club, Tau Beta Pi, Phi Beta Kappa. Home: 24 Peter Coutts Circle Stanford CA 94305 Personal E-mail: henryriggs@comcast.net.

RIGGS, JANET MORGAN, academic administrator, psychology professor; married; 3 children. BA summa cum laude, Gettysburg Coll., 1977; MA in Social Psychology, Princeton U., 1979, PhD in Social Psychology, 1982. Instr. to prof. psychology Gettysburg Coll., Pa., 1981—, exec. asst. to pres., 1991—94, interim provost, 1995—96, 2006—07, provost, 2007—08, interim pres., 2008—09, pres., 2009—. Cons. editor The Psychology of Women Quarterly; contbr. articles to profl. jours. Recipient Thompson Award for Disting. Tchg. Office: Gettysburg Coll Campus Box 0418 300 N Washington St Gettysburg PA 17325 Office Phone: 717-337-6820. E-mail: riggs@gettysburg.edu.*

RIGGS, KRISTA DYONIS, music educator, librarian; b. Aurora, Colo., June 17, 1977; d. Donald Eugene and Jane (Vasbinder) Riggs. MusB summa cum laude, Ariz. State U., 1999; MusM, Ind. U., 2000, MLS, 2004, MusD with high distinction, 2004. Libr. Woodward Park Regional Libr., Fresno, Calif., 2004—; tchr. oboe and music theory Calif. State U., Fresno, 2006—. Invited spkr. World Conf. Internat. Soc. Music Edn., Internat. Symposium on Philosophy of Music Edn., Nat. Conf. Coll. Music Soc.; invited peformer recital Internat. Double Reed Soc. Author: (articles) Double Reed Jour., Philosophy of Music Edn. Rev. Recipient Nina Neal merit scholarship, Ind. U., 2000—04. Mem.: Internat. Double Reed Soc., Coll. Music Soc., Internat. Soc. Philosophy of Music Edn. Office: Calif State Univ Music Dept 2380 Keats Ave M/S 77 Fresno CA 93740 Business E-Mail: kdriggs@csufresno.edu.

RIGGS, LEW, foundation executive; b. Indpls., Apr. 1, 1937; s. Frank Lloyd Riggs and Marie Loretta (Shaner) Ellis; m. Christine Marie Stiemke, Dec. 2, 2000. BS in Bus. Adminstrn., U. Ariz., 1961, EdD, 1976; MBA, George Washington U., 1964. Mktg. adminstr. TRW Systems, LA, 1964-67; assn. exec. Electric League Ariz., Phoenix, 1967-68; pub. affairs adminstr. Ariz. Regional Med. program Coll. of Medicine, U. Ariz., Tucson, 1968-73; dir. community affairs Tucson Med. Ctr., 1973-82; dir. pub. rels. Good Samaritan Med. Ctr., Phoenix, 1982-85; pres. The Lew Riggs Co., Phoenix, 1985-88; chief exec. officer Tucson Osteo. Med. Found., Tucson, 1988—. Adj. prof. U. Ariz. Coll. Edn., Tucson, mem. internat. adv. bd., 1996-99, pres., 2000; cons. to hosps. and physicians in group practice nationally; presenter in field. Editor: Public Relations Handbook, 1982; co-author booklets; contbr. articles to profl. jours. Chmn. pub. rels. Nat. Arthritis Found., Atlanta, 1985-87; participant Ariz. Strategic Planning and Econ. Devel., 1991-92. Lt. col. USAFR, 1987. Recipient IABC gold quill award, Silver Anvil award Pub. Rels. Soc. Am., Golden Mike award Am. Legion Aux., MacEachern citation Acad. Hosp. Pub. Rels., Pres.'s citation Pub. Rels. Soc. Mem. Pub. Rels. Soc. Am. (trustee 1999—), Nat. Assn. Osteo. Founds. (pres. 1991-93), Student Osteo. Med. Assn. (found. bd. dirs. 1990—), Soc. Assn. Execs. (bd. dirs. 1995—), Rotary. Republican. Presbyterian. Home: 4566 E Camino De Oro Tucson AZ 85718-4475 Office Phone: 520-299-4545. Business E-Mail: lriggs@tomf.org.

RIGGS, MICHAEL DAVID, editor, writer; b. Frankfort, Ky., Apr. 30, 1951; s. Homer David and Helen Marion (Webber) R.; m. Elizabeth Susan Borman, Apr. 24, 1983; children: David B., William B. AB, Washington U., 1973. Chief trader Thomte & Co., Boston, 1975-77; tech. writer Saddlebrook Corp., Cambridge, Mass., 1977-79; assoc. editor Mini-Micro Systems Mag., Boston, 1979-80; editor High Fidelity Mag., NYC, 1980-89; exec. editor Stereo Review Mag., NYC, 1989-95; editor-in-chief Audio Mag., NYC, 1995-2000; ind. technology writer, editor, cons. Westfield, NJ, 2000—. Author: Understanding Audio and

Video, 1989; sr. contbg. editor: Sound and Vision Mag., 2001—04, sr. editor:, 2004—05, online editor:, 2006—07. Mem. Audio Engring. Soc., Boston Audio Soc. Personal E-mail: michael@riggsnet.com.

RIGGS, PENNY KAYE, molecular geneticist; b. Laredo, Tex., Aug. 24, 1965; d. Michael Gene and Karen Ann (Redic) R. BS in Biology, Purdue U., 1987, MS in Animal Cytogenetics, 1991; PhD in Molecular Genetics, Tex. A&M U., 1996. Rsch. assoc. Purdue U. Cytogenetics Lab., West Lafayette, Ind., 1987-91; Regents' fellow Tex. A&M U., College Station, 1991-92, grad. rsch. asst., 1992—. Author: (with others) Advances in Veterinary Science, 1990, Methods in Molecular Medicine, 1997. Pres. Vet. Med. Student Coun. Recipient Grad. Travel award Purdue U. Dept. Animal Sci., 1990, Grad. Rsch. grant and Travel award Tex. A&M U. Coll. of Vet. Medicine, 1995; Aerospace Postdoctoral fellow U. Houston/Johnson Space Ctr., 1996—. Mem. Am. Genetic Assn., Radiation Rsch. Soc., Tissue Culture Assn., Gamma Sigma Delta. Achievements include first to describe chromosomal fragile sites in the domestic pig, first to develope a bovine interspecific hybrid backcross panel for use in gene mapping.

RIGGS, ROBERT MELDRUM, French educator; b. Washington, Aug. 1, 1932; s. Theodore Scott and Phillis Wey (Symmonds) R.; B.A. with distinction, George Washington U., 1955; Fulbright scholar, U. Toulouse (France), 1955-56; M.A. (Miller fellow), U. Ill., 1957, postgrad., 1957-62. Grad. asst. U. Ill., 1957-62; instr. French, then asst. prof. George Washington U., 1964-70, asst. to chmn. dept. Romance langs., 1963-70; assoc. prof. French, Frostburg (Md.) State Coll., 1970—94, prof. emeritus, 1994, chmn. dept. fgn. langs., 1984-88. Bd. dirs. Allegany County Mental Health Assn., 1975-81; trustee Cumberland Theatre, 2000-05; bd. mem. Cumberland Cultural Found., 2007; bd. mem. Cumberland Bicentennial Com.; layreader, chmn. Christian edn. com. Emmanuel Episcopal Ch., Cumberland, 1979—, vestryman, 1981-85, 2004-07. May Flower Soc. Denison Soc., Gallup Family Assn., Allegany County Hist. Soc. (curator 1976-78, 1st v.p. 1978-80, trustee 1980-82), Phi Beta Kappa, Phi Kappa Phi, Omicron Delta Kappa, Pi Delta Epsilon, Pi Delta Phi, Sigma Delta Pi, Acacia. Democrat. Home: 101 Washington St Cumberland MD 21502-2966 E-mail: rmriggs264@hotmail.com.

RIGGS, TIMOTHY ALLAN, museum curator; b. New Haven, Feb. 15, 1942; s. Douglas Shepard and Robin (Palmer) R.; divorced; 1 child, Emma; m. Carolyn P. Coolidge, June 25, 1995. BA, Swarthmore Coll., 1964; MA, Yale U., 1966, PhD, 1971. Rschr. Print Coun. Am., 1970-73; asst. curator Worcester (Mass.) Art Mus., 1973-76, curator prints and drawings, 1976-84; asst. dir. Ackland Art Mus., Chapel Hill, NC, 1984—, acting dir., 1986, 1994, curator collection, 2003—; adj. prof. U. NC, Chapel Hill, 1984—. Adj. prof. U. N.C., Chapel Hill, 1984-2003, curator of collections, 2003—. Contbr. catalogs. Mem. Print Coun. Am. (bd. dirs. 1981-84), Historians Netherlandish Art. Office: Ackland Art Mus CB #3400 UNC-CH Chapel Hill NC 27599-3400

RIGGSBY, DUTCHIE SELLERS, education educator; b. Montgomery, Ala., Oct. 26, 1940; d. Malcolm Sellers and Marcelia Sellers Dickman; m. Ernest Duward Riggsby, Aug. 25, 1962; 1 child, Lyn. BS, Troy State Coll., 1962, MS, 1965; postgrad., George Peabody Coll., 1963; EdD, Auburn U., 1972. Cert. tchr., Ala., Ga.; cert. libr., Ga. Tchr. Montgomery Pub. Schs., 1962—63, Troy City Schs., 1963—67; instr. Auburn U., Ala., 1968—69, dir. media svcs., 1972—77; asst. prof. Columbus Coll., Ga., 1972—77, assoc. prof., 1978—83, prof., 1983—2009, parttime prof., 2009—. Vis. prof. U. P.R., Rio Piedras, 1972—73; leader various workshops, 1989, 1993—; sorfware reviewer NSTA, 2000—; chmn. publicity Ga. Ednl. Tech. Conf., 1997—, bd. dirs.; bridal cons. Hist. Moments, Inc., v.p., 1998—2001; coord. instrnl. Tech. Sch. Edn., 1996—97; coord. program Ednl. Founds., 2001—04; bd. dirs. Ga. Ednl. Tech. Consortium, 2002—. Contbr. more than 90 articles on state, regional, nat., and internat. programs to profl. jours., 1968—. Active Internal Aerospace Edn. CAP, Maxwell AFB, 1980-90; dir. Air and Space Camp for Kids, 1990-98; apptd. selection com. Coll. Edn. Columbus State U. Hall of Fame, 2005—09 Recipient STAR Tchr. award NSTA, 1968; named to Lee H.S. Hall of Fame, Montgomery, 1997. Mem.: Ga. Assn. Instrnl. Tech. (bd. dirs. 1982—84), World Aerospace Edn. Orgn. (v.p. for Ams. 1996—98, pres. for Ams. 1998—2008), Nat. Congress on Aviation and Space Edn. (dir. spl. promotions 1986—90), Assn. for Ednl. Commn. and Tech. (awards com. 1994—96, non-periodical publs. com. 1994—99, chair meml. awards com. 1996—99), Phi Delta Kappa (pres. Chattahoochee Valley chpt. 1986—87, v.p. 2008—09, membership v.p. 2005—06, pres. Chattahoochee Valley chpt. 2006—07, membership v.p. 2008—, Svc. award 1989, Svc. Key award 1993). Baptist. Avocations: photography, mining for gemstones. Office: Columbus State U Coll Edn 4225 University Ave Columbus GA 31907-5679 Office Phone: 706-565-7802.

RIGHETTI, DAVID ALLEN (DAVE RIGHETTI), professional baseball coach, retired professional baseball player; b. San Jose, Calif., Nov. 28, 1958; s. Leo Righetti; m. Kandice Righetti, Feb. 11, 1989; children: Nicolette, Natalee, Wesley. Pitcher NY Yankees, 1981-90, San Francisco Giants, 1990—93, minor league pitching instr., 1999, pitching coach, 2000—; pitcher Oakland Athletics, 1994, Toronto Blue Jays, 1994, Chgo. White Sox, 1995. Active Boys and Girls Clubs America, Leukemia Soc.; bd. dirs. Jean Weingarten Peninsula Oral Sch. for the Deaf. Named Am. League Rookie of Yr., Maj. League Baseball, 1981, Am. League Rolaids Relief Man of Yr., 1986, 1987; named to Am. League All-Star Team, Maj. League Baseball, 1986, 1987. Achievements include leading the American League in: ERA (2.05), 1981; saves (46), 1986; throwing a no-hitter, July 4, 1983. Office: San Francisco Giants AT&T Pk 24 Willie Mays Plz San Francisco CA 94107*

RIGHINI, MARILOU MAUSTELLER, editor, consultant; b. Savannah, Ga., June 17, 1937; d. John Ellis and Ethel Mae Mausteller; m. Massimo A. Righini, May 5, 1962; children: Giovanna, John Paolo. BA in Polit. Sci. magna cum laude, Mich. State U., East Lansing, 1958; attended, Johns Hopkins U., Bologna, Italy, 1958—60; MA in Internat. Rels., Johns Hopkins U., Washington, DC, 1963. Editor Internat. Legal Materials Am. Soc. Internat. Law, Washington, 1968—97, dir. pubs., 1992—97; editor, mem. editl. bd. Transnational Pubs., Inc., Ardsley, NY, 1998—, aquisitions editor, cons., 1998—2001. Translator IBM, Milan, 1960—61; tchr. polit. sci., internat. law, am. lit. Istituto Ugo Foscolo, Bologna, Italy, 1961—62; rschr., editl. asst. Washington Ctr. Fgn. Policy Rsch., 1963—68; program chmn. Internat. Devel. Conf., Washington, 1977; program coord. Washington Fgn. Law Soc., 1980—81, bd. govs., 1980—82; chmn. Coun. Washington Reps. UN, 1983—85; tchr. internat. law and orgn. Trinity Coll., Washington, 1985; elected com. rep. DC Dem. State Com., Ward 1, 1988—92; chmn., nominating com. Worldwise 2000, 1989, bd. dirs., 1989—91; ann. mtg. roundtable chair Am. Soc. Internat. Law, 1991, ann. mtg. panel chair, 92; program developer Am. Assn. Law Librs., 1999, 2000. Mem.: Mich. State U. DC Study Devel. Coun., Am. Soc. Internat. Law, UN Assn. U.S.A., Meridian Internat. Ctr., Delta Gamma.

RIGHTER, WALTER CAMERON, retired bishop; b. Phila., Oct. 23, 1923; s. Richard and Dorothy Mae (Bottomley) R.; m. Nancy Ruth DeGroot, Aug. 22, 1992; children: Richard, Rebecca. BA, U. Pitts., 1948; MDiv, Berkeley Div. Sch., New Haven, 1951, DD, 1972; DCL, Iowa Wesleyan U., 1982; DD, Seabury Western Sem., 1984. Ordained priest Episcopal Ch., 1951, consecrated bishop, 1972; lay missioner St. Michael's Ch., Rector, Pa., 1947-48; priest-in-charge All Saints Ch., Aliquippa, Pa., 1951-54, St. Luke's, Georgetown, Pa., 1952-54; rector Ch. of Good Shepherd, Nashua, NH, 1954-71; bishop Diocese of Iowa, Des Moines, 1972-89; asst. bishop Dio. of Newark, 1989-91; interim rector St. Elizabeth's, Ridgewood, NJ, 1991; assisting bishop Diocese of Mass., 2000—03; ret. Mem. exec. coun. Protestant Episcopal Ch. U.S.A., 1979-85; spl. adv. NH Cursillo, 1994-96; interim rector Emmanuel, Rockford, Ill., 1989. Author: A Pilgrim's Way, 1998. Mem. N.H. com. White House Conf. on Youth, 1962, Regional Crime Commn., Hillsboro County, N.H., 1969-71; trustee Nashua Libr., 1968-71, Seabury Western Sem., 1986-89; founding trustee The Morris Fund, Des Moines; planning com. Town of Alstead, N.H., 1993-96. Fellow Coll. Preachers, Washington Cathedral. Episcopalian. Personal E-mail: wcrighter@alltel.com.

RIGHTMIRE, GEORGE PHILIP, anthropology educator; b. Boston, Sept. 15, 1942; s. Brandon Garner and Marcia (Ham) R.; m. Berit Johansson, Aug. 20, 1966; children: Anna Marcia, Eric Philip. AB, Harvard U., 1964; MS, U. Wis., 1966, PhD, 1969. Asst. prof. SUNY, Binghamton, 1969-73, assoc. prof., 1973-82, prof., 1982—2002, chmn., 1976-78, disting. prof., 2002—; rsch. assoc. Harvard U., 2006—. Vis. in archaeology U. Cape Town, South Africa, 1975-76; rsch. fellow in osteology U. Stockholm, Sweden, 1973. Author: The Evolution of Homo erectus, 1990; contbr. articles to profl. jours., chpts. to books and encyclopedias. Fellow Nat. Inst. Gen. Med. Scis., 1973; rsch. grantee NSF, 1975—, Nat. Geographic Soc., 1978-79, L.S.B. Leakey Found., 1990-91, 1992-93, 1995-96, 98-99. 2001-2003, 2006—09, Am. Philos. Soc., 2003-04. Fellow AAAS; mem. Am. Assn. Phys. Anthropologists, Human Biology Assn., Paleoanthropology Soc., Sigma Xi Achievements contributions to systematics of genus Homo, research and field work in paleoanthropology, fossil evidence for hominid evolution examined in East Africa, South Africa, Europe, the Near East, the Caucasus, China and Southeast Asia. Office: Harvard Univ Dept Human Evolutionary Biology Peabody Mus Cambridge MA 02138 Home: 24 Whittier Dr Scituate MA 02066-2436 Office Phone: 617-495-5703. Business E-Mail: gprightm@fas.harvard.edu.

RIGHTS, GRAHAM HENRY, retired minister; b. Winston-Salem, NC, Jan. 14, 1935; s. Douglas LeTell and Cecil Leona (Burton) R.; m. Sybil Critz Strupe, Sept. 7, 1963; children: Susan Elizabeth, John Graham. BA, U. N.C., 1956; BD, Yale U., 1959; postgrad., Moravian Theol. Sem., 1959-60, DHL (hon.), 1997; postgrad., U. Edinburgh, Scotland, 1965-66; DD (hon.), Wofford Coll., 1989. Ordained to ministry Moravian Ch., 1960. Pastor Union Ch., Managua, Nicaragua, 1960-63, Managua Moravian Ch., 1960-65, Mayodan (N.C.) Moravian Ch., 1966-72, Messiah Moravian Ch., Winston-Salem, 1972-81; exec. dir. Bd. World Mission Moravian Ch., Bethlehem, Pa., 1981-83, pres. exec. bd. so. province Winston-Salem, 1983-95, pres. exec. bd. worldwide, 1991-94; pastor First Moravian Ch., Greensboro, NC, 1995-2000; ret. Bd. dirs. Crisis Control Ministry, Forsyth County, 1976-, Wachovia Hist. Soc., 2004-, Cherokee-Moravian Hist. Assn., 2004-. Mem. N.C. Soc. Mayflower Descendants (elder 2000—). Mem. Moravian Ch. Home: 553 Steeple View Ct Winston Salem NC 27101-5850

RIGOLE, ROSE HICKMAN, lawyer; BA in Philosophy, Coll. William and Mary, Williamsburg, Va., 1997, BS in Physics, 1997; JD, U. So. Calif., LA, 2001. Atmospheric sci. rschr. NASA Langley, Norfolk, Va., 1996—97, Ga. Inst. Tech., Atlanta, 1997—97; programmer/analyst BellSouth Intelliventures, Atlanta, 1997—98; judicial extern, Hon. Mitchell R. Goldberg Riverside, Calif., 1998; law clk. Blakely, Sokoloff, Taylor & Zafman, LA, 1999—2000; summer assoc. Pretty, Schroeder, & Poplawski, LA, 2000; atty. Christie, Parker & Hale, LLP, Pasadena, Calif., 2001—06, Hogan & Hartson, LA, 2006—. Contbr. INTA Bulletin newsletter. Named Rising Star Super Lawyer, Law & Politics Mag., 2004—08, L.A. Mag., 2004—08. Mem.: LA County Bar Assn. IP and Entertainment Law Sect. (exec. com. mem. 2007—), Internat. Trademark Assn. (bull. com. mem. 2006—), LA County Bar Assn. Barristers (exec. com. mem. 2003—, networking com. chair 2003—, v.p. 2006—07), US Patent Bar, Calif. Bar, LA Intellectual Property Law Assn. Achievements include prosecuting patents for the design of the Mars Exploration Rover Athena; worked on the successful Markman brief and summary judgment motion dealing with inoperable claim limitations, affirmed by the Federal Circuit in Chef America, Inc. v. Lamb-Weston. Office: Hogan and Hartson LLP Ste 1400 1999 Ave of the Stars Los Angeles CA 90067 Personal E-mail: roserigole@yahoo.com. Business E-Mail: rigole@hhlaw.com.

RIGOLOSI, ELAINE LA MONICA, lawyer, educator; b. Astoria, NY, Oct. 12, 1944; d. Richard Anthony La Monica and Caroline La Monica; m. Robert Salvatore Rigolosi, June 15, 1997. BS, Columbia Union Coll., Takoma Park, Md., 1964; MN, U. Fla., 1967; EdD, U. Mass., 1975; JD, Benjamin N. Cardozo Sch. Law, NYC, 1993. Bar: N.J. 1994, N.Y. 1994, D.C. 1995; RN, N.Y. Chair dept. nursing edn. Tchrs. Coll., Columbia U., NYC, 1988-91, prof. nursing edn., 1982-96, acting chair dept. nursing edn., 1994-96, prof. dept. orgn. and leadership, 1996—; health care mgmt. cons. in pvt. practice, NYC, 1974—. Bd. dirs. Hooper Holmes, Inc., Basking Ridge, N.J., 1989—; cons. Delaware Valley Transplant Program, Phila., 1998, U. Tenn. Coll. Pharmacy, Memphis, 1995-98. Author: The Nursing Process: A Humanistic Approach, 1979 (Am. Jour. Nursing Book of Yr. 1979), Management in Health Care, 1994, Management and Leadership in Nursing and Health Care, 2005. Dept. HHS grantee, 1977-80, 80-83. Fellow Am. Acad. Nursing; mem. ABA, Assn. Bar City NY, Am. Health Lawyers Assn., Am. Assn. Nurse Attys., Am. Coll. Legal Medicine, Sigma Theta Tau. Avocations: tennis, needlepoint, interior design. Home: 158 Summit Dr Paramus NJ 07652-1312 Office: Tchrs Coll Columbia U 525 W 120th St New York NY 10027-6625

RIGOPULOS, ALEXANDER PETER, video game development company executive; BS in Music Composition, MIT, 1992, MS in Media Arts and Scis., 1994. Design cons. Yamaha Musical Instruments, Japan; co-founder, pres., CEO Harmonix Music Sys., Inc., Cambridge, Mass., 1995—, exec. prodr., game design contbr. Co-recipient Maverick Award, 2006; named one of The 100 Most Influential People in the World, TIME mag., 2008. Office: Harmonix Music Sys, Inc 625 Massachusetts Ave, 2nd Fl Cambridge MA 02139

RIGOTTI, NANCY, medical educator; d. Victor and Lucille Rigotti; life ptnr. Stanley Rowin. MD, Harvard Med. Sch., Boston, 1978. Cert. physician Mass., 1978, diplomate specialist Am. Bd. Internal Medicine, 1981. Prof. medicine Harvard Med. Sch., 2006—. Dir. Tobacco Rsch. & Treatment Ctr., Boston, 1992—. Office: Mass Gen Hosp 50 Staniford St 9th fl Boston MA 02114

RIGSBY, LINDA FLORY, lawyer, director; b. Topeka, Dec. 16, 1946; d. Alden E. and Lolita M. Flory; m. Michael L. Rigsby, Aug. 14, 1963; children: Michael L. Jr., Elisabeth A. MusB, Va. Commonwealth U., 1969; JD, U. Richmond, 1981. Bar: Va. 1981, D.C. 1988. Assoc. McGuire, Woods, Battle & Boothe, Richmond, Va., 1981-85; dep. gen. counsel and corp. sec. Crestar Fin. Corp., Richmond, 1985-99, gen. counsel, 1999-2000; mng. atty. Sun Trust Banks Inc., 2000—05, deputy gen. coun., 2006; ret., 2007; of counsel Williams Mullen law, 2007—. Mem. audit com. Bon Secours Health Systems, Richmond, 1999—. Bd. dirs. Commonwealth Cath. Charities, 2004-, vice chmn., 2008; mem. Bar Secours Foundation Bd, 2008- Recipient Disting. Svc. award U. Richmond, 1987; named Vol. of Yr. U. Richmond, 1986, Woman of Achievement, Met. Richmond Women's Bar, 1995. Mem. Va. Bar Assn. (exec. com. 1993-96), Richmond Bar Assn. (bd. dirs. 1992-95), Va. Bankers Assn. (chair legal affairs 1992-95), U. Richmond Estate Planning Coun. (chmn. 1990-92), Va. Bar Assn. (elected fellow 2008). Roman Catholic. Avocations: music, gardening. Home: 163 W Square Pl Richmond VA 23238-6157 Office: Williams Mullen Law Firm PO Box 1320 Richmond VA 23218-1320 Home Phone: 804-784-7479; Office Phone: 804-783-6404. Personal E-mail: mlrigsby163@comcast.net.

RIGSBY, MARY SUE, retired elementary school and adult education educator; b. Big Stone Gap, Va., June 22, 1936; d. Sherman Coomer and Jenelle Kilbourne; m. Hobert Herchel McElyea (div. 1978); children: Gary A. McElyea, Tammy Sue McElyea, Jeffrey Earl McElyea; m. Elmer Virgil Rigsby Jr., June 1, 1985 (dec. July 12, 2001). BS, East Tenn. State U., Johnson City, 1979, MEd, 1989. Cert. postgrad. profl. Va., early edn., mid. edn., learning disabilities tchr., reading specialist Va. Tchr. aide Lee County Schs., Pennington Gap, Va., 1971—74; tchr. Tazewell County Pub. Schs., Tazewell, Va., 1979—86, Rogersville City Schs., Tenn., 1988—89, Scott County Pub. Schs., Gate City, Va., 1989—2004; ret., 2004; part-time tchr. adult edn. Scott County Pub. Schs., Weber City, Va., 2004—06, substitute tchr., 2006—. Home: 101 Milton Ct Kingsport TN 37664-3570 Personal E-mail: suerigsby@hotmail.com.

RIHANNA, (ROBYN RIHANNA FENTY), singer, actress; b. St. Michael, Barbados, Feb. 20, 1988; d. Ronald and Monica Fenty. Model, spokesperson Covergirl. Singer: (albums) Music of the Sun, 2005 (Album of Yr., Barbados Music Awards, 2006), A Girl Like Me, 2006 (Album of Yr., Barbados Music Awards, 2007), Good Girl Gone Bad, 2007, (songs) Pon de Replay, 2005 (Best Dance Single Song of Yr., Barbados Music Awards, 2006), SOS, 2006 (Best New Video Artist, MTV Video Music Awards Japan, 2006), Unfaithful, 2006 (Best R&B Single, Song of Yr., Barbados Music Awards, 2007), Umbrella, 2007 (Monster Single of Yr. and Video of Yr., MTV Video Music Awards, 2007, Grammy award, Best Rap/Sung Collaboration, 2008); actor: (films) Bring It On: All or Nothing, 2006. Recipient Best Internat. Artist award, MuchMusic Video Awards, 2006, Female Breakout Artist award, Teen Choice Awards, 2006, Choice R&B Artist award, 2006, Best R&B award, MTV Europe Music Awards, 2006, Female Artist of Yr. award, Billboard Music Awards, 2006, Female Hot 100 Artist of Yr., 2006, Pop 100 Artist of Yr., 2006, 7 awards, including Best New Artiste, Female Artiste of Yr., Best-Selling Female Artiste of Yr., and Entertainer of Yr., Barbados Music Awards, 2006, 7 awards, including Worldwide Best-Selling Recording Artiste, Female Entertainer of Yr., and Entertainer of Yr., 2007, Barbados Music Awards ring, 2007, Favorite Female R&B Artist award, Am. Music Awards, 2007, 2008, Favorite Female Pop Artist award, 2008, Entertainer of Yr., Best Female R&B Artist, and Best Pop Female Artist, World Music Awards, 2007, Favorite R&B Song, People's Choice Awards, 2008; named one of Top 25 Entertainers of Yr., Entertainment Weekly, 2007. Office: c/o Island Def Jam Music Group 28th Fl 825 8th Ave New York NY 10019

RIKLEEN, LAUREN STILLER, lawyer; b. Winthrop, Mass., Apr. 29, 1953; d. Joseph and Elaine Lillian (Brodie) Stiller; m. Sander A. Rikleen, May 25, 1975. Student, Clark U., 1971—73; BA magna cum laude, Brandeis U., 1975; JD, Boston Coll., 1979. Bar: Mass. 1979, US Dist. Ct. Mass. 1980, US Ct. Appeals (1st cir.) 1980, US Supreme Ct. 1985. Asst. dir. Flaschner Jud. Inst., Boston, 1979—81; atty. region one EPA, Boston, 1981—84; asst. v.p. negotiations Clean Sites Inc., Alexandria, Va., 1984—87; asst. atty. gen. Mass. Dept. Atty. Gen., 1987—88; chair environ. practice group Bowditch & Dewey, Mass., 1988—, sr. ptnr. real estate and environ. law practice group. Mem. bd. trustees Clark U., 1998—; pres. Metrowest Harvest; bd. dirs. Environ. League Mass. Named Woman of Yr., Middlesex News, 1991. Fellow: Am. Bar Found.; mem.: ABA (bd. govs. 2008—, mem. natural resources com.), Metrowest C. of C. (chair 1994—95), Boston Bar Assn. (mem. environ. sect., chair 1993—95, sec. 1995, pres. 1998—99, co-chair work family balance com. 2001, v.p. 1996—97). Office: Bowditch Dewey Llp 175 Crossing Blvd Ste 500 Framingham MA 01702-4490 Office Phone: 508-416-2411. Office Fax: 508-929-3043. E-mail: lrikleen@bowditch.com.*

RIKLI, DONALD CARL, lawyer; b. Highland, Ill., June 16, 1927; s. Carl and Gertrude Louise (Stoecklin) R.; m. Joan Tate, Oct. 10, 1953; children: Kristine, David. AB, Ill. Coll., 1951; JD, U. Ill., 1953. Bar: Ill. 1953, U.S. Dist. Ct. (so. dist.) Ill. 1961, U.S. Ct. Appeals (7th cir.) 1968, U.S. Supreme Ct. 1974. Pvt. practice law, Highland, 1953-97. Atty. City of Highland, 1956-59; lectr. in field. Author: The Illinois Probate System, 1974, 75, 77, 78; bd. editors Illinois Real Property I, 1966, 71, Lawyers World, 1970-72, Law Notes, 1981-83, The Compleat Lawyer, 1985-87; contbr. over 60 articles to profl. jours. Mem. consistory United Ch. of Christ, 1960-62, 93-95. With U.S. Army, 1945-47. Fellow Am. Coll. Trust and Estate Counsel, Ill. Bar Found., Am. Bar Found.; mem. ABA (sec. chairperson gen. practice sect. 1990-91, Ho. of Dels. 1991-93, mem. coun. gen. practice sect. 1981-93, Sole Practitioner of Yr. 1990, posthumous Donald C. Rikli Solo Lifetime Achievement award gen. practice, solo practice and small firms sect.), Ill. Bar Assn. (chmn. Bill of Rights com. 1967-68, coun. estate planning probate and trust sect. 1976-81, sec. 1980-81), Madison County Bar Assn. (pres. 1966-67), Am. Acad. Estate Planning Attys. (bd. govs. 1994-95). Address: PO Box 366 Edwardsville IL 62025-0366

RIKON, MICHAEL, lawyer; b. Bklyn., Feb. 2, 1945; s. Charles and Ruth (Shapiro) R.; m. Leslie Sharon Rein, Feb. 11, 1968; children: Carrie Rachel, Joshua Howard. BS, NY Inst. Tech., 1966; JD, Bklyn. Law Sch., 1969; LLM, NYU, 1974. Bar: NY 1970, U.S. Dist. Ct. (so. and ea. dists.) NY 1971, U.S. Ct. Appeals (2d cir.) 1972, U.S. Supreme Ct. 1973, U.S. Ct. Appeals (5th and 11th cirs.) 1981. Asst. corp. counsel City of NY, 1969-73; law clk. NY State Ct. Claims, 1973-80; ptnr. Rudick and rikon, P.C., NYC, 1980-88; pvt. practice NYC, 1988-94; ptnr. Goldstein, Goldstein Rikon & Gottlieb PC, NYC, 1994—. Contbr. articles to profl. jours. Pres. Village Greens Residents Assn., 1978-79; chmn. bd. Arden Heights Jewish Ctr., S.I., NY, 1976-77; pres. North Shore Rep. Club., 1977; mem. cmty. bd. S.I. Borough Pres., 1977. With SSGT 99th Signal Batallion USAR. Recipient Bus. Leadership award, NYIT Alumni Fed., 2006; named Best Lawyers in Eminent Domain and Condemnation Law, NY, 2006—09. Fellow Am. Bar Found.; mem. ABA (chair com. Condemnation) NY State Bar Assn. (spl. com. of condemnation law), Suffolk County Bar Assn., Nassau County Bar Assn., NY

County lawyers Assn. (chair condemnation com.), Assn. Bar City of NY (condemnation com.), Owners Counsel Am. (dir.). Republican. Jewish. Avocations: collecting stamps, photography, collecting miniature soldiers. Office: 80 Pine St New York NY 10005-1702 Home: 105 East 29th St New York NY 10016-8014 Office Phone: 212-422-4000 23. Business E-Mail: mrikon@ggrgpc.com.

RIKOON, JONATHAN J., lawyer; b. 1955; AB cum laude, U. Pa., 1976; JD cum laude, NYU, 1979. Bar: NY 1980. Assoc., prin. atty. Paul, Weiss, Rifkind, Wharton & Garrison; of counsel Mudge, Rose, Guthrie, Alexander & Ferdon; counsel to ptnr. Debevoise & Plimpton, LLP, NYC, 1995—. Prin. author: Essential Facts: Estate Planning and Family Wealth Transfers, 1995, Stocker and Rikoon on Drawing Wills and Trusts, 2000, 2001—08; contbr. articles to profl. publs. Named one of Top 100 Attys., Worth mag., 2005, 2007—08. Fellow: Am. Coll. Trust and Estate Counsel; mem.: NY EPTL and SCPA (liason, mem. legislative adv. com. 2009—), US Commn. Preservation America's Heritage Abroad, NY State Bar Assn. (privilege subcommittee 1992—95, mem. estate litig. com. 1992—, fees subcommittee 1995—, tax aspects of settling probate litig. subcommittee 1998—99, chair estate liitg. com. 2003—06, exec. com. 2003—, first dist. rep. 2007—, trusts and estates sect.), Assn. of Bar of the City of NY (estate and gift taxation com. 1993—96, chair allocation of estate taxes subcommittee 1993—96, chair dead man statute subcommittee 1996, estates, trusts & surrogate's ct. com. 1996—99, chair working grp. on prin. and income 1998—99, estates, trusts & surrogate's ct. com. 2007—, chair subcom. on trust formalities 2008—09). Office: Debevoise & Plimpton LLP 919 Third Ave New York NY 10022-3904 Office Phone: 212-909-7217. Office Fax: 212-909-6836. E-mail: jjrikoon@debevoise.com.

RIKOSKI, RICHARD ANTHONY, electrical engineering executive; b. Kingston, Pa., Aug. 13, 1941; s. Stanley George and Nellie (Gober) R.; m. Giannina Batchelor Petrullo, Dec. 18, 1971 (div. 1979); children: Richard James, Jennifer Anne; m. Carol Westbrook. BEE, U. Detroit, 1964; MSEE, Carnegie Inst. Tech., 1965; PhD, Carnegie-Mellon U., 1968; postdoctoral fellow, Case-Western Res. U./NASA, 1971. Registered profl. engr., Ill., Mass., Pa. Engr. 1st communication satellite systems Internat. Tel. & Tel., Nutley, NJ, 1961-64; engr. Titan II ICBM program Gen. Motors, Milw., 1964; trainee NASA, 1964-67; instr. Carnegie-Mellon U., Pitts., 1966-68; asst. prof. U. Pa., Phila., 1968-74; assoc. prof., dir. hybrid microelectronics lab., chmn. ednl. TV com. IIT, Chgo., 1974-80, chmn. ednl. TV com., 1974-80; rsch. engr. nuclear effects ITT Rsch. Inst., Chgo., 1974-75; pres. Tech. Analysis Corp., Chgo., 1980—. Engr. color TV colorimetry Hazeltine Rsch., Chgo., 1969; engr. Metroliner rail car/roadbed ride quality dynamics analysis US Dept. Transp., ENSCO, Inc., Springfield, Va., 1970; pres. Tech. Analysis Corp., Chgo., 1978-91; contractor analysis of color TV receiver safety hazards US Consumer Product Safety Commn., 1977, analysis heating effect in aluminum wire Beverly Hills Supper Club Fire, Covington, Ky., 1978; engr. GFCI patent infringement study 3M Corp., St. Paul, 1979-81; elec. systems analyst Coca-Cola Corp., Atlanta, 1983-91; fire investigator McDonald's Corp., Oak Brook, Ill., 1987-90; engring. analyst telephone switching ctrs. ATT, Chgo., 1990-91; expert witness numerous other govtl. and corp. procs.; evaluator Accreditation bd. Engring. and Tech., 2000—. Author: Hybrid Microelectronic Circuits, 1973; editor: Hybrid Microelectronic Technology, 1973; contbr. articles to profl. jours. Officer Planning Commn., Beverly Shores, Ind., 1987-93, trustee town coun., 1992—, police liason 1993-96, dir. emergency mgmt., 1998, coun. pres., 1999-2000; mem. Chgo. Coun. Fgn. Rels., USAF SAC Comdrs. Disting.is. Program; adv. coun. Nat. Park Svc. Ind. Dunes Nat. Lake Shore, 1993—. NASA fellow, 1964-67, 70. Mem. IEEE (sr. ednl. activities bd. NYC 1970-74, USAB career devel. com. 1972-74, editor Soundings 1973-75, Cassette Colloquia 1973-74, del. Popov Soc. Tech. Exch. USSR, mgr. Dial Access Tech. Edn. program 1972), Assn. for Media Based Continuing Engring. Edn. (bd. dirs.), Nat. Fire Protection Assn., Sigma Xi, Tau Beta Pi, Eta Kappa Nu. Republican. Avocations: sailing, travel. Home: One E Lakefront Dr Beverly Shores IN 46301-0444 Office: 211 E Ontario St Chicago IL 60611 Office Phone: 773-883-1333. Personal E-mail: rikoski@earthlink.net.

RIKVOLD, PER ARNE, physicist, educator; b. Hadsel, Norway, Oct. 4, 1948; arrived in U.S., 1980; s. Per and Inger-Johanne (Corneliussen) Rikvold. BS, U. Oslo, 1971, MS in Physics, 1976; cert. Japanese lang., Osaka U., Japan, 1977; PhD in Physics, Temple U., 1983. Rsch. assoc. dept. physics U. Oslo, 1978-81; rsch. assoc. dept. mech. engring. SUNY, Stony Brook, N.Y., 1983-85; sr. rsch. chemist ARCO Chem. Co., Newtown Square, Pa., 1985-87; assoc. prof. physics Fla. State U., Tallahassee, 1987-92, prof. physics, 1992—2004, James G. Skofronick prof. physics, 2004—, prof. Sch. Computational Sci., 2005—08. Vis. scientist Kyushu U., Fukuoka, Japan, 1979, U. Geneva, 1981—82, Inst. Solid State Physics, Jülich, Germany, 1982; vis. scholar Temple U., Phila., 1986—87; vis. rschr. IBM, Bergen, Norway, 1987, 88; vis. scholar Tohwa Inst. Sci., Japan, 1991, Kyushu (Japan) U., 1991, Kyoto (Japan) U., 1993, 96, 98, 2001, 05, McGill U., Monteral, Que., Canada, 1995; vis. rschr. U. Colo., Boulder, 1997, U. Tex., Austin, 1999, Va. Poly. Inst. and State U., 2002—03, U. Tokyo, 2007, 08, 09; vis. rsch. prof. Miss. State U., 2003. Contbr. numerous articles to profl. jours. and books. Grantee, Petroleum Rsch. Fund, 1988—91, NSF, 1991—; fellow, Japanese Ministry Edn., 1976—78, Norwegian Rsch. Coun., 1981—83, Japan Found. Ctr. Global Partnership, 1996. Fellow: Am. Phys. Soc.; mem.: AAAS, European Phys. Soc., Norwegian Acad. Sci. and Letters, Norwegian Phys. Soc., Electrochem. Soc., Materials Rsch. Soc., Sigma Xi. Democrat. Achievements include research in statistical and condensed-matter physics and complex systems theory with applications to materials science, electrochemistry, engineering, computer science and ecology and evolutionary biology. Office: Fla State U Physics Dept Tallahassee FL 32306 Business E-Mail: prikvold@fsu.edu.

RILEY, BENJAMIN ROBERTSON, engineering educator; married. Asst. prof. Ill. Inst. Tech., Chgo., 1999—. Office: Ill Inst Tech 3360 S State St Chicago IL 60616 Business E-Mail: rileyb@iit.edu.

RILEY, BOB (ROBERT RENFROE RILEY), Governor of Alabama; b. Ashland, Ala., Oct. 3, 1944; m. Patsy (Adams) Riley; children: Rob, Jenice, Minda, Krisalyn. Degree in bus. administrn., U. Ala. Past poultry and egg bus. co-owner, Ala.; past owner automobile dealership, Ala.; owner trucking co., Ala.; past owner grocery store and local pharmacy, Ala.; mem. Ho. of Reps. from 3d Ala. dist., 1996—2002, asst. whip, mem. house armed svcs. com., mem. house banking and fin. svcs. com., mem. house agr. com., house-senate conferee on FY 1998 Def. Authorization bill, 1997, mem. ho. agrl. com.; gov. State of Ala., 2003—. Past chmn. fin. com. Clay County Hosp.; mem. First Baptist Ch., men's Sunday sch. tchr., past chmn. bd. trustees; pres., Ala. State Bd. Edn, 2003-. Named Pub. Official of Yr., Governing mag., 2003. Mem. Masons, Shriners, Jaycees (past pres. Ashland chpt.). Republican. Baptist. Office: Office of the Gov State Capitol 600 Dexter Ave Montgomery AL 36130 Office Phone: 334-242-7100. Office Fax: 334-242-0937.

RILEY, DAN, entertainer; s. James Harry and Iris Riley. Degree, U. Wis., Milw., 1970. Entertainer Dan Riley Entertainment Group, Brussels, Wis., 1977—. Actor(with Frank Sinatra, Sammy Davis and many others):,: Klutz Around the House. Entertainer Multiple local, nat. and internat. charities, 1977—; telethon host Cerebral Palsy Inc., Green Bay, Wis., 1977—; with Dan Riley Scholarship Performing Arts, Brussels, 1993—. Office: Dan Riley Entertainment Group PO Box 102 Luxemburg WI 54217

RILEY, DYANNE SCHROCK, music professor; b. San Diego, Feb. 16, 1944; d. Ralph Ellis Schrock and Coral Jean Clark; m. Michael Arthur Riley; children: Michael Timothy, AnnaMarie, David Patrick, Keri Jo, Suzanne. BA in Music with distinction, San Diego State U.; MusM, Brigham Young U. Tchr. Mt. Miguel High Sch.; grad. asst. Brigham Young U., Provo; assoc. prof., dir. choral activities Utah Valley U. Vocal specialist Tng. Sch. of Mormon Tabernacle Choir, 2003—07; condr. Utah Valley Choral Soc.-Wasatch Chorale, 2005—. Singer: Mormon Tabernacle Choir, 1995—2004. Named Adj. Faculty of Yr., Utah Valley State Coll., 1998—99, 2002—03. Mem.: Soc. Music Theory, Am. Choral Dirs. Assn., Nat. Assn. Tchrs. Singing. Avocations: harp, quilting. Home: 4323 N Imperial Way Provo UT 84604 Office: Utah Valley Univ 800 W Univ Pky Orem UT 84058 Office Phone: 801-863-7432. Business E-Mail: dyanne.riley@uvu.edu.

RILEY, ENRICO, painter; b. Waterbury, Conn., 1973; BA in visual studies, Dartmouth Coll., 1995; MFA, Yale U., 1998. Sr. lectr. studio art, area head of painting and drawing Dartmouth Coll., Hanover, NH. Resident Vt. Studio Ctr., 2000, 01. One-man shows include Sounding Silence, Karl Drerup Gallery, Plymouth, NH, 2004, Polar/Solar, Pageant Gallery, Phila., 2005, exhibited in group shows at Invitational Exhbn. Visual Arts, AAAL, 2004 (Purchase award, AAAL, 2004), Rhythmic Brushwork, Mus. Nat. Ctr. Afro-Am. Artists, Roxbury, Mass., 2005, The Grid, Reeves Contemporary, NYC, 2006, Color as Structure: Structure as Color, Lori Bookstein Fine Art, NYC, 2007. Fellow John Simon Guggenheim Meml. Found., 2008. Office: Studio Art Dept Hinman Box 6081 Dartmough Coll Hanover NH 03755 also: Reeves Contemporary 2nd Fl 535 W 24th St New York NY 10011*

RILEY, FRANCENA, nurse, retired non-commissioned officer; b. New Smyrna Beach, Fla., May 5, 1957; d. Willard Harrell and Jacqueline Delores (Griffen) R. 1 child, Daniel Albert Cross (dec.). AA, U. Md., Heidelberg, Fed. Republic Germany, 1987; BS, Upper Iowa U., 1994; MA in Edn., Ctrl. Mich. U., 2001. Enlisted U.S. Army, 1980, advanced through grades to sgt. 1st class, 1991, expert field med. badge, parachutist; practical nurse emergency room Keller Army Hosp., West Point, N.Y., 1981; bn. tng. noncommd. officer 34th Med. Bn., Ft. Benning, Ga., 1988-89, practical nurse 2d Mobile Army Surg. Hosp., 1989-91; wardmaster intensive care unit #1 2d MASH, 1990-91; practical nurse pediatric ward Walter Reed Army Med. Ctr., Washington, 1982-84; practical nurse, then nursing supr. 913th Med. Detachment, Kaiserslautern, Fed. Republic Germany, 1984-86; wardmaster surgery clinic Army Regional Med. Ctr., Landstuhl, Fed. Republic Germany, 1987; with 2D MASH 44th med. brigade operation desert shield U.S. Army, Saudi Arabia, 1990-91; ops. non-commd. officer 2d MASH, 1991-92; wardmaster newborn nursery USA MEDDAC, Ft. Polk, La., 1992-94; wardmaster med. surg. unit USAMEDDAC, Ft. Polk, 1994-95; ret., 1995; distbn. clk. USPS, Atlanta, 1995-2000; anesthesia nurse Northside Hosp., Atlanta, 2002—04; jr. planner Eagle Group Internat. Inc., Atlanta, 2004—. Maintenance support clk. USPS, Atlanta; adj. instr. Ga. Perimeter Coll., Clarkston, Ga., 2001—. Mem. handbell choir, sr. usher bd. hist. com. Ebenezer Bapt. Ch., Atlanta. Recipient med. badge U.S. Army, 1991. Baptist. Avocations: bicycling, plate collecting, visiting zoos and nature parks. Home: 8773 Valley Lakes Ct Union City GA 30291-6011 Personal E-mail: alberta959@aol.com.

RILEY, HENRY CHARLES, banker; b. Newton, Massachusetts, Mar. 23, 1932; s. Charles Matthew and Marion Anna (Armstrong) R.; m. Patricia Ann (Buchanan), Mar. 3, 1962; children: Lauren Elizabeth, Carolyn Ann, Julie Louise. BA, Yale U., 1954; MBA, Boston Coll., 1965. With BayBank Harvard Trust Co., Cambridge, Mass., 1958—89, treas., sec., 1967—70, sr. v.p., sec., 1972—82, exec. v.p., 1982—87; mng. dir. cmty. banking BayBank Systems Inc., Waltham, Mass., 1987—90; exec. v.p., dir. cmty. banking BayBank Boston, 1990—92; exec. v.p. BayBank Systems, Inc., Waltham, Mass., 1992—97; bd. dir. BayBank F.S.B., BayBank N.A., NH, 1995—96. Mem. pvt. banking adv. com. Fleet Boston, Sarasota, Fla., 2000-04. Trustee, treas. Longy Sch. Music, 1970-92; bd. dir. Richard Warren Surg. Rsch. and Ednl. Fund Inc., 1984-2009; bd. dir., pres. Cambridge Econ. Devel. Corp., 1982-87; corporator, past asst. treas. Mt. Auburn Hosp.; mem. exec. bd. Gettysburg Coll. Parents Assn.; treas. St. John's Episcopal Ch., sr. warden, Westwood, Mass., 1982-85; mem. St. Paul's Cathedral chpt., Boston, 1990-93. Served in USNR, 1956-57. Mem. Am. Bankers Assn. (chmn. 1991-92, exec. com. br. adminstrv. divsn. 1992, chmn. nat. retail banking conf. 1990), Nat. Br. Adminstr. Roundtable, Boston Coll. Sch. Mgmt. Alumni Assn. (past dir., pres.), Harvard Sq. Bus. Assn. (past dir.), Cambridge C. of C. 1975-87 (past dir., past treas., v.p.) Rotary (club dir. 1976-80, pres. 1979-80), Yale Club, Boston, Yale Club of the Suncoast (bd. dir. 2001—, v.p., 2004), Harvard Club, Dennis Yacht Club (mem. bd. govs., treas. 1993-94), The Meadows Country Club, Ivy League Club, The Club at Yarmouthport. Episcopalian. Home: 33 York Way Westwood MA 02090-2633 also: PO Box 1192 240 New Boston Rd Dennis MA 02638-2121 also: 5284 Huntingwood Ct Sarasota FL 34235-5600 Personal E-mail: Marshwind@aol.com.

RILEY, JAMES B., JR., lawyer; b. Evanston, Ill., 1954; BA magna cum laude, U. Ill., 1976; JD cum laude, George Wash. U., 1979. CPA; bar: Ill. 1979, US Dist. Ct. No. Dist. Ill. 1979, US. Ct. Fed. Claims. Ptnr. Ross & Hardies (merged with McGuireWoods LLP in 2003), Chgo., 1985—2003, McGuireWoods LLP, Chgo., 2003—, co-chair firm health care dept., 2003—. Bd. dirs., past pres. Rebuilding Together North Suburban Chgo. Mem.: ABA (health law sect.), Ill. Assn. Hosp. Attorneys, Am. Health Lawyers Assn. Office: McGuireWoods LLP Ste 4100 77 W Wacker Dr Chicago IL 60601-1815 Office Phone: 312-750-8665. Office Fax: 312-920-6133. Business E-Mail: jriley@mcguirewoods.com.

RILEY, JAMES KEVIN, lawyer; b. Nyack, NY, July 21, 1945; s. Charles A. and Mary Lenihan R.; m. Joan Leavy Riley, Oct. 4, 1969; children: Carolyn, Tara, Sean. AB, Fordham Coll., 1967; JD, Rutgers U., 1970. Bar: N.Y. 1971, N.J. 1983, U.S. Supreme Ct. 1984; cert. fin. planner; accreditated real estate planner. Asst. dist. atty. Rockland County, New City, NY, 1973-74; ptnr. Amend & Amend, NYC, 1974-78, O'Connell & Riley, Pearl River, NY, 1978—. Pub., pres. 1099 Express Software, 1099 Express Ltd., Pearl River, 1987-97; adj. prof. estate planning Pace Univ., White Plains, N.Y.; town atty. Town of Orangetown; adj. prof. pub. edn. law LI U., Sparkill, NY. Bd. dirs. United Way of Rockland County, N.Y., 1974-80, Rockland Family Shelter for Victims of Domestic Violence, 1981-85, Literacy Vols. Rockland County, 1989-99; chmn. bd. dirs. New Hope Manor, Barryville, N.Y., 1985-88. Mem. ABA, Am. Soc. Hosp. Attys., Nat. Coun. Sch. Dist. Attys., N.Y. State Bar Assn. (ho. of dels. 1988-92, 2000-04), Rockland County Bar Assn. (bd. dirs. 1986—, pres. 1997-98), Nat. Acad. Elder Law Attys., Rotary Club of Pearl River (pres. 1999-2000). Democrat. Roman Catholic. Home: 145 Franklin Ave Pearl River NY 10965-2510 Office: O'Connell & Riley 144 E Central Ave Pearl River NY 10965 also: 210 Summit Ave PO Box 532 Montvale NJ 07645

RILEY, JOCELYN CAROL, writer, television producer; b. Mpls., Mar. 6, 1949; d. G.D. Riley and D.J. (Berg) Riley-Jacobson; m. Jeffrey Allen Steele, Sept. 4, 1971; children: Doran Riley, Brendan Riley. BA in English, Carleton Coll., Northfield, Minn., 1971. Mng. editor Carleton Miscellany, Northfield, Minn., 1971; mkgt. asst. Beacon Press, Boston, 1971-73; freelance writer, editor, prodr., 1973—. Author: (books) Only My Mouth is Smiling, 1982, Crazy Quilt, 1984; prodr.: (TV series) Her Own Words, 1986, Belle: The Life and Writings of Belle Case La Follette, 1987, Gold Medal Internat. Film and TV Festival, 1988, Zona Gale, 1874-1938, 1988, Patchwork, 1989, Prairie Cabin, 1991, Winnebago Women Songs & Stories, 1992, Ethel Kvalheim, Rosemaler, 1992, Her Mother Before Her, 1992, Women in Construction, 1993, America Fever, 1994, Women in Policing, 1994, Sisters & Friends, 1994, Big Sister, Little Sister, 1995, Audrey Handler, Glass Artist, 1995, Women in Dentistry, 1996, Sewing Together, 1996, Women in Nontraditional Careers, 1996, Women in Firefighting, 1996, Women in Machining, 1997, Women in Welding, 1997, Prairie Child, 1997, Math at Work, 1998, Writing on the Lakes, 1998, Women in Engineering, 2000, Work Talk, 2000, Women in Highway Construction, 2001, Women in Building Construction, 2002, The Art of Ethel Kvalheim, 2002, Writing at Work, 2003, Shifting Gears: Changing Careers, 2004, Women Entrepreneurs, 2005, Women in the Automotive Industry, 2005, Women in Electronics, 2006, Broken Dishes, 2009; columnist: Wis. State Jour., 1986—91; contbr. articles to profl. jours. Active United Way of Dane County, 1984-90, On-Site Rev. Com., Madison Area Tech. Coll., 1993, Boy Scouts Am., 1996-2008, Nat. Alliance Partnerships Equity Ednl. Found. Bd., 2007-, v.p., 2008-. Hon. fellow Women's Studies Rsch. Ctr., U. Wis., Madison, 1986-91; Film in the Cities Regional Film/Video grantee; Dane County Cultural Affairs Comm. grantee, 1986-94, 96-97, 2002, 04; Wis. Arts Bd. grantee, 1986, 88-93; Wis. Humanities Coun. grantee, 1997; Wis. Sesquicentennial grantee, 1997, Madison CitiArts grantee, 1986-87, 89-90, 92-93, 96-97, 2002; Bronze Apple award Nat. Ednl. Film & Video Festival, 1988; cert. of commendation Am. Assn. State and Local History, 1988, Gold medal Internat. Film & TV Festival, 1988, cert. of recognition Wis. Dept. Pub. Instrn. Am. Indian History & Culture Program, 1991, Write Women Back into History award Nat. Women's History Project, 1995, ALA award, 1996, Barb Landers Meml. award Assn. for Gender Equity Leadership in Edn., 2004, Rotary Paul Harris fellow, 2009. Mem. Women in Comm. (pres. Madison chpt. 1984-85, nat. del. 1983, Writer's Cup 1985), Coun. for Wis. Writers (1st pl. for nonfiction article 1986), Authors Guild, Madison Assn. for Multi-Image (pres. 1986-87, nat. del. 1986), Downtown Madison Rotary Club (Paul Harris fellowship, 2009), Nat. Alliance Patnerships Equity Edn. Found. (bd. mem. 2007, v.p. 2008). Address: PO Box 5264 Madison WI 53705-0264

RILEY, LAURA E., obstetrician, gynecologist; MD, U. Pitts. Sch. Medicine. Cert. maternal & fetal medicine Am. Bd. Obstetrics & Gynecology. Resident U. Pitts. Med. Ctr.; dir. labor, delivery & infectious disease Mass. Gen. Hosp. Spokeswoman Soc. for Maternal Fetal Medicine. Office: Mass General Hospital Vincent OB/GYN Service 55 Fruit St YAW 4 Boston MA 02114 Office Phone: 617-724-2229. Office Fax: 617-724-3498.*

RILEY, MARK RICHARD, biochemical engineer, educator; b. Dearborn, Mich., Mar. 16, 1969; s. Richard A. and Mary Alice Stella (Malaski) R.; m. Jill Susan Bonita Riley, Oct. 7, 1995. BSE in Chem. Engring. cum laude, U. Mich., 1990; MS in Chem. and Biochemical Engring., Rutgers U., 1994, PhD in Chem. and Biochemical Engring., 1995; Post Doctoral in Biochemical Engring. and Analytical Chemistry, U. Iowa, 1997. Undergraduate rsch., cellular bioengineering lab., dept. chemical engring. U. Mich., 1989—90; grad. dissertation rsch., dept. chemical and biochemical engring. Rutgers U., NJ, 1992—95; postdoctoral rschr., dept. chemical and biochemical engring. and dept. chemistry U. Iowa, Iowa City, 1995-97; faculty mem. of grad. interdisciplinary program in biomedical engring. U. Ariz., Tucson, 1997, chair, activities subcommittee, 1999—, asst. prof. dept. agrl. and biosystems engring. and program in biomedical engring., 1997—2003, assoc. prof., dept. agrl. and biosystems engring., biomedical engring., 2003—, assoc. prof., chemical and environ. engring., 2004—, assoc. prof., materials sci. and engring., 2005—, assoc. prof., Bio5 Inst., 2005—. Undergraduate tchg. asst. for self-paced biochemistry class, dept. biochemistry U. Mich., 1990; tchg. asst. for grad. and undergraduate classes in transport phenomena, dept. chemical and biochemical engring. Rutgers U., 1993—94, Merck Excellence fellow, NJ, 1993—95, instructor of undergraduate class in momentum transport phenomena, dept. chemical and biochemical engring., NJ, 1994; tchg. of several workshops/seminars for small groups of students U. Ariz., 1997—2001; indsl. intern Ortho Pharma., Raritan, NJ, 1991, Exxon Rsch. and Engring., Annandale, NJ, 1993, Annandale, 94. Refereed articles for peer-reviewed jours.; contbr. chapters to books; editor for patents and lit. reviews Applied Biochemistry and Biotechnology, 1998—, biol. engring. representative to resource mag. editl. bd., 2004—06. Recipient Nat. Assn. Coll. anf Teachers of Agr., Tchg. award of merit, U. Ariz, Coll. Agr. and Life Sciences, 2002; U. Ariz. Dean of Students Faculty Fellow, 2001—. Mem. Am. Chem. Soc. (membership chair for biochemical tech. divsn. 1998-2002), Biomed. Engring. Soc., AIChE, Am. Soc.Agrl. Engring. (chair, biol. engring. divsn., 1999-2000, assoc. editor, Transactions, 2005-), Am. Soc. of Engring. Soc., Inst. Biol. Engring. (councilor, 2000-02, 2003-04), Alpha Epsilon. Achievements include development of methods to predict the rates of nutrient transport and reaction in immobilized cell systems; developed near infrared spectroscopic techniques for bioreactor monitoring; invented a sticker that can tell consumers if a fruit or vegetable is ripe. Office: Dept Agrl and Biosystems Engring U Ariz Shantz Bldg Rm 403 Tucson AZ 85721-0038 Office Phone: 520-626-9120. Office Fax: 520-621-3963. Business E-Mail: riley@ag.arizona.edu.

RILEY, MARY JANE STEWART, secondary school educator; d. Norman Stewart and Martha Veronica Venzuch; m. Richard Michael Riley, Jan. 11, 1980 (div. Mar. 23, 1987); children: Megan Stewart, Erin Courtney Stewart. BS, We. Mich. U., Kalamazoo, 1967—71; MA in Tchg., Oakland U., Rochester, Mich., 1971—77. Profl. edn. cert. Mich. Guest tchr. Birmingham Pub. Schs., Mich., 1993—95; HS tchr. Ferndale Pub. Schs., Ferndale, Mich., 1995—96; HS tchr. in adult edn. Royal Oak Pub. Schs., Mich., 1995—97; mid. sch. tchr. Sch. Dist. Pontiac, Mich., 1996—2005. Exec. bd. mem. Mich. Coun. Social Studies (MCSS), Ann Arbor, Mich., 1999—, state conf. chmn., 1999—2005; state contest judge Mich. Social Studies Olympiad (MSSO), Shelby Twp., Mich., 1996—; tech. writer for curriculum Pontiac Public Schs., 1996—; mem. social studies steering com. Mich. Dept. Edn., 2001—; mem. tchr. del. to Kusatsu, Japan. Chmn. Marine Safety Edn. Commn., Lansing, Mich., 1989—90; mem. house dels. Nat. Coun. Social Studies, 2002. Recipient Top Fellow award, Goethe Inst., 2002. Mem.: Pontiac Edn. Assn. (dir. 2006—, contract labor negotiator, Pontiac Public Schs. 2006—07).

Independent Thinkers. Achievements include writing a senate bill in 1989 for boating safety that passed the Michigan state legislature, and signed into law by former Governor James Blanchard, causing boating regulations in other states. Avocations: golf, travel, reading, photography, karaoke. Office: Madison Mid Sch 1275 N Perry St Pontiac MI 48340

RILEY, MICHAEL, college football coach; b. Wallace, Idaho, July 6, 1953; m. Dee Riley; children: Matthew, Kate. BS in Soc. Sci., U. Ala., 1975; MS, Whitworth Coll., 1976. Defensive back Crimson Tide U. Ala., 1971-74; grad. asst. coach U. Calif. Golden Bears, 1975; def. coord., secondary coach, asst. athletic dir. Linfield Coll. Wildcats, McMinnville, Oreg., 1977-82; secondary coach Winnipeg Blue Bombers, CFL, 1983-84, head coach, 1987-90; defensive coord., sec. coach U. No. Colo. Bears, 1986; head coach San Antonio Riders, World League Am. Football, 1991-92; asst. head coach, offensive coord./quarterbacks coach U. So. Calif. Trojans, 1993-96; head coach Oreg. State U. Beavers, 1997-98, 2003—, San Diego Chargers, 1998—2001; asst. coach New Orleans Saints, 2002. Named Coach of Yr., Canadian Football League, 1988, 1990; named to Winnipeg Blue Bombers Hall of Fame, 2007. Achievements include being a member of the Grey Cup Championship winning Winnepeg Blue Bombers, 1988, 1990. Office: c/o Oreg State U Athletics Comm 104 Gill Coliseum Corvallis OR 97331 Office Phone: 541-737-2614. Business E-Mail: kelly.harness@oregonstate.edu.

RILEY, MICHAEL ROBERT, marketing and business development executive; b. Wisconsin Rapids, Wis., Apr. 17, 1938; s. Robert William and Anne Bates (Clark) R.; m. Judith Wood, Aug. 12, 1961; children: David T., Christopher W. BS, Hampton U., 1974; MS, Indsl. Coll. of Armed Forces, Washington, 1975; MPA, Golden Gate U., 1976, MBA, 1977. Commd. 2d lt. USAF, 1958, advanced through grades to lt. col., 1977, ret., 1979; mktg. exec. McDonnell Douglas Corp., St. Louis, 1979-90; pres. MRR Assocs., St. Louis, 1990—. Cons. Regional Commerce and Growth Assn., St. Louis, 1980-85, 90—. Pres. trustees Lake of the Woods Subdiv., St. Louis, 1980-85; pres. bd. dirs. St. Louis Chamber Chorus, 1986-88; mem. St. Louis Ambassadors, 1990—. Decorated D.F.C. with 2 oakleaf cluster, Bronze Star, Air medal with 23 oakleaf clusters; named Swimmer of the Yr., U.S. Amateur Athletic Union/NCAA, Portland, Oreg., 1956; recipient USAF Navigator Wings, Harlingen, Tex., 1959, USAF Pilot Wings, Chandler, Ariz., 1964, USN Wings, Beeville, Tex., 1971. Mem. Air Force Assn., Assn. Naval Aviation, Am. Mgmt. Assn., Internat. City Mgrs. Assn., Army Aviation Assn. Am., Am. Helicopter Soc., Navy League, River Rats. Avocations: sailing, golf, flying. Office: MRR Assocs 5846 Mango Dr Saint Louis MO 63129-2243

RILEY, MIKE, college football coach; b. Wallace, Idaho; s. Bud Riley; m. Dee Riley; children: Matthew, Kate. B in Social Sci., U. Ala., 1975; M in Phys. Edn., Whitworth Coll., Spokane, Wash., 1977. Grad. asst. coach U. Calif. Golden Bears, Berkeley, 1975, Whitworth Coll. Pirates, 1976; defensive coord., secondary coach, asst. athletic dir. Linfield Coll. Wildcats, 1977—82; secondary coach Winnipeg Blue Bombers, Can. Football League, 1983—85, head coach, 1987—90; defensive coord. U. No. Colo. Bears, 1986; head coach San Antonio Riders, World Football League, 1991—92; offensive coord., quarterbacks coach, asst. head coach U. So. Calif. Trojans, 1993—96; head coach Oreg. State U. Beavers, 1997—98, 2003—, San Diego Chargers, 1999—2001; secondary coach, asst. head coach New Orleans Saints, 2002. Named Coach of Yr., Can. Football League, 1988, 1990; named to Winnipeg Blue Bombers Hall of Fame, 2007. Achievements include being head coach of the Grey Cup Championship winning Winnipeg Blue Bombers, 1988, 1990. Office: Oreg State Univ Dept Athletics Corvallis OR 97331-4501*

RILEY, MONICA, microbiologist, educator; b. New Orleans, Oct. 4, 1926; d. Chauncey Wesley and Maude (Kemper) R.; children: Adam, Christine (dec.), Katherine. BA, Smith Coll., 1947; PhD, U. Calif.-Berkeley, 1960. Asst. prof. U. Calif., Davis, 1960-66; assoc. prof. SUNY-Stony Brook, 1966-75, prof. and provost biol. scis., 1975-78, prof. biochemistry, 1975-89, acting chmn., 1984-85, emeritus prof., 1989—; sr. scientist Marine Biol. Lab., Mass., 1989-06; vis. prof. U. Paris-Sud-Orsay, 1991, 94; mem. program com. for meeting Engineered Organisms in the Environment, 1985; mem. rev. panel NSF; organizer Conf. on Orgn. Bacterial Chromosome, 1988; chair Gordon Rsch. Conf. on Population Biology of Microorganisms, 1989; mem. Recombinant DNA Adv. Com. NIH, 1988-91; lectr. Found. for Microbiology, 1987-88; co-organizer 1st Internat. Conf. on E coli Genome, 1992, organizer 3d conf., 1993-94; organizer Internat. Workshops Annotation Ecoli genome, 2003, 05. Editor: The Bacterial Chromosome, 1990; co-editor: Escherichia coli and Salmonella typhimurium, 1st edit.; contbr. articles to profl. jours., chpts. to books. Bd. dirs. Brookhaven chpt. LWV, N.Y., 1982-87, Falmouth chpt., Mass., 1990-00. Grantee NIH, 1960-00, 05, NSF, 1960-90, DOE, 1999-06. Fellow Am. Acad. Microbiologists; mem. Am. Soc. Microbiology (chmn. com. genetic and molecular microbiology of pub. and sci. affairs bd. 1984-88), Phi Beta Kappa, Sigma Xi. As a graduate student at the University of California at Berkeley in the 1950s, Ms. Riley's work on how genes make protein helped forge the field of Molecular Biology. When the complete DNA sequence of the bacterium Escherichia coli was determined in the mid 1990s, she played an important role by interpreting gene functions from their sequences. As a leader in the field, she organized international workshops in 2003 and 2005 to update the annotation of this model organism, which was a major step toward learning how all the genes of a cell work. Business E-Mail: mriley@mbl.edu.

RILEY, NANCY MAE, retired secondary school educator; b. Grand Forks, ND, May 1, 1939; d. Kenneth Wesley and Jeanne Margaret Olive (Hill) R. BS in Edn., Miami U., 1961; postgrad., Ohio U., 1964—69; MA, Marietta Coll., 1989. Cert. high sch. tchr. Tchr. home econs. Malta-McConnelsville (Ohio) High Sch., 1961-67; tchr. home econs. Waterford (Ohio) High Sch., 1968-92. Advisor Malta-McConnelsville Future Homemakers, 1961-66, Waterford Future Homemakers Am., 1968-92; advisor to state officer Ohio Future Homemakers Am., McConnelsville, 1963, Waterford, 1976. Leader Girl Scouts Am., McConnelsville, 1962-66, camp counselor, 1962-76; fair judge Waterford Cmty. Fair, Waterford, 1970-85. Mem.: DAR (Marietta chpt.) (pres. 2007—), NEA, Ohio Vocat. Assn. (life), Ohio Edn. Assn. (life; del. 1979), Am. Vocat. Assn. (life), Ohio Geneal. Soc., Daus. War of 1812 (pres. 1991—2004, state sec. 1995—97, state 2d v.p. 2001—05, v.p., registrar), Daus. Union Vets. (del. 1992—, tent pres. 1993—98, dist. pres. 1996, Ohio Dept. pres. 1999, nat. historian 2002, tent pres. 2009), White Shrine of Jerusalem (worthy high priestess 1979—81, 1983), Order Eastern Star (worthy matron 1968, dep. grand matron 1978, worthy matron 2003). Republican. Baptist. Avocations: ceramics, genealogy, camping, reading, handcrafts. Office Phone: 740-373-6684. E-mail: rileyn@localnet.com.

RILEY, PATRICK JAMES, professional sports team executive; b. Rome, NY, Mar. 20, 1945; s. Leon R.; m. Chris Riley; children: James Patrick, Elisabeth Marie. Grad., U. Ky., 1967. Guard San Diego Rockets, 1967-70, Phoenix Suns, 1975-76, LA Lakers, 1970-75, asst. coach, 1979-81, head coach, 1981-90, NY Knicks, 1991-95, Miami Heat, 1995—2003, 2005—08, pres. basketball ops., 2003—. Broadcaster LA Lakers games Sta. KLAC and Sta. KHJ-TV, 1977—79; broadcaster NBC Sports, 1990—91. Author: Show Time: Inside the Laker's Breakthrough Season, 1988, The Winner Within: A Life Plan for Team Players, 1993. Named NBA Coach of Yr., 1990, 93, 97; named to Naismith Meml. Basketball Hall of Fame, 2008. Head coach, NBA Champions, LA Lakers, 1982, 85, 87, 88, NBA Champions, Miami Heat, 2006. Achievements include setting the NBA record for most playoff wins (137). Office: Miami Heat Am Airlines Arena 601 Biscayne Blvd Miami FL 33132*

RILEY, REBECCA MICHELLE, music educator; b. Carthage, Mo., June 23, 1974; d. Russell and Ruby Richmond; m. Ben Lee Riley; children: Raecancia Ann, Matthew Lee. BS in Edn. and Music, Mo. So. State U., 1997; M, William Woods U., Fulton, Mo., 2003. Cert. tchr. Mo. Elem. music tchr. Diamond Elem. Sch., Mo., 1997—2000; music tchr. Jasper HS, Mo., 2000—02, Noel Sch., Mo., 2002—06; music and HS choral tchr. Seneca, Mo., 2006—. Mem.: Mo. State Tchrs. Assn. (assoc.), Music Educators Nat. Conf. (assoc.), Mo. Music Educators Assn. (assoc.). Business E-Mail: rriley@seneca.k12.mo.us.

RILEY, RICHARD WILSON, lawyer, former United States Secretary of Education; b. Greenville, SC, Jan. 2, 1933; s. Edward Patterson and Martha Elizabeth (Dixon) Riley; m. Ann Osteen Yarborough, Aug. 23, 1957; children: Richard Wilson, Anne Y., Hubert D., Theodore D. BA, Furman U., 1954; JD, U.S.C., 1959. Bar: S.C. 1960. Ptnr. Riley & Riley, Greenville, 1959—78, Nelson, Mullins, Riley & Scarborough, Greenville and Columbia, 1987—93, Greenville, 2001—; gov. State of S.C., 1979—87; sec. US Dept. Edn., Washington, 1993—2001; disting. univ. prof. U. S.C., Columbia, 2001—; disting. prof. govt., politics, and pub. policy Furman U., 2001—. Spl. asst. to subcom. U.S. Senate Jud. Com., 1960; mem. S.C. Ho. of Reps., 1963—66, S.C. Senate from Greenville-Laurens Dist., 1966—76; sr. adv. and chair Richard W. Riley Inst. Govt., Politics and Pub. Leadership, Furman U., 2001—; bd. dirs. ACT (Am. Coll. Testing Program); bd. trustees Knowledge Works Found., 2001—; trustee Carnegie Corp. N.Y., 2004—, Furman U., 2001—; former bd. dirs. Pub. Broadcasting Svc. (PBS). Lt. (j.g.) USNR, 1954—56. Recipient Dist. Svc. award, Coun. Chief State Sch. Officers, 1994, James Bryant Conant award, Edn. Comm. of the States, 1995, T.H. Bell award for outstanding edn. advocacy, Com. for Edn. Funding, 1996, Dist. Svc. award, Am. Coun. on Edn., 1998; disting. sr. fellow, NAFSA: Assn. Internat. Educators, Wash., D.C. Mem.: Greenville Bar Assn., S.C. Bar Assn., Rotary, Phi Beta Kappa. Office: Nelson Mullins Riley & Scarborough Poinsett Plaza Ste 900 104 S Main St Greenville SC 29601 Office Phone: 864-250-2300. Business E-Mail: dick.riley@nelsonmullins.com.

RILEY, ROBERT BARTLETT, landscape architect; b. Chgo., Jan. 28, 1931; s. Robert James and Ruth (Collins) R.; m. Nancy Rebecca Mills, Oct. 5, 1956; children: Rebecca Hill, Kimber Bartlett. PhB, U. Chgo., 1949; BArch, MIT, 1954. Chief designer Kea, Shaw, Grimm & Crichton, Hyattsville, Md., 1959-64; prin. partner Robert B. Riley (A.I.A.), Albuquerque, 1964-70; campus planner, asso. prof. architecture, dir. Center Environ. Research and Devel., U. N.Mex., 1966-70; prof. landscape architecture and architecture U. Ill., Urbana-Champaign, 1970—, head dept. landscape architecture, 1970-85, dir. PhD program, 1999—; vis. prof. Harvard U., 1996-97; prof. emeritus, dir. joint PhD program U. Ill., 1997—. Sr. fellow landscape architecture studies Dumbarton Oaks/Harvard U., 1992—, chmn. fellows, 1996—; mem. rev. panel landscape architects Fed. Civil Service-Nat. Endowment Arts. Assoc. editor Landscape mag., 1967-70; editor Landscape Jour., 1987—. Served with USAF, 1954-58. Nell Norris fellow U. Melbourne, Australia, 1977; project fellow Nat. Endowment Arts, 1985 Fellow Am. Soc. Landscape Architects (Nat. Honor award 1979); mem. Coun. of Educators in Landscape Architecture, pres. 1984-85, chmn. bd. dirs. 1985-86, Outstanding Educator award 1992, Pres.'s award 1994, chmn. editl. adv. bd. Landscape Architecture 1996-99), AIA (Design award Md. 1962, N.Mex. 1968, Environ. Svc. award N.Mex. 1970), Environ. Design Rsch. Assn. (chmn. bd. 1990-91, Career award 2003), Phi Beta Epsilon. Unitarian Universalist. Office: Univ Ill 101 Temple Buell Hall 611 E Lorado Taft Dr Champaign IL 61820-6921 Home: 407 E George Huff Dr Urbana IL 61801-6703 Business E-Mail: rbriley@uiuc.edu.

RILEY, ROBERT EDWARD, financial services company executive; b. Boston, Feb. 19, 1930; s. Edward Gerard and Nina Loretta (Wolfe) R.; m. Ann Elizabeth McCourt, Nov. 10, 1956 (div. 1972); children: Robert Edward, David, Thomas; m. Carol Lee Anthony, June 22, 1974; children: Michael, Brian. AB, Holy Cross Coll., 1951; MBA, Harvard U., 1953. Pres., chief exec. officer Putnam Mgmt. Co., Boston, 1970-80, Marsh & McLennan Asset Mgmt. Co., Boston, 1974-81; sr. v.p. Am. Express Co., NYC, 1981-84; sr. v.p. group pensions Prudential Ins. Co. Am., Newark, 1984-85; pres. Prudential Asset Mgmt. Co., Newark, 1985-86; exec. v.p. Prudential Investment Corp., Newark, 1986-94; chmn. Prudential Realty Group, Newark, 1986-90; chmn., CEO Prudential Residential Svcs. Co., Boston, 1990-93, Prudential Reins. Co., 1993-94; pres., COO Dreyfus Corp., 1995; pres., CEO Leggat McCall Properties, 1995—98, Joseph P. Kennedy Enterprises, 1998—2005; mng. dir. J.W. Childs Assocs., 2005—09. Assoc. trustee Holy Cross Coll.; bd. dirs. John F. Kennedy Libr.; overseer New Eng. Deaconess Hosp.; trustee assoc. Boston Coll. HS. Lt. comdr. USNR, 1953-56, Korea. Named Chief Exec. Officer of Yr. Fin. World Mag., 1975, 79. Mem.: Union (Boston); Univ. (N.Y.C.). Republican. Roman Catholic. Avocations: boating, skiing, ice hockey. Office: 50 Derby St Hingham MA 02043 Personal E-mail: rereiley19@yahoo.com.

RILEY, SALLY JEAN, retired science educator; b. Pasadena, Calif., Feb. 24, 1941; d. Richard Dunlap Hopping and Nelle Bernice Webb-Hopping; m. Robert William Riley, Sept. 27, 1977; children: Stacie Lynn Scripter, Derrick Wayne, Stefanie Lyn Campbell. BA, Calif. State U., LA, 1963; Tchg. Credential, U. Calif., Irvine, Calif., 1982. Social worker County of LA, Covina, Calif., 1967—71, County of Orange, Santa Ana, Calif., 1974—76; sci. tchr. Irvine Unified Sch. Dist., Irvine, Calif., 1982—2008. Mem. Sch. Site Coun., Irvine, Calif., 1995—. Vol. Pacific Wildlife Orgn., Laguna Niguel, Calif., 2000—04. Mem.: NEA, Calif. Tchrs. Assn., Irvine Tchrs. Assn. R-Liberal. Christian Scientist. Achievements include Dean's List - Univ. Calif., Irvine. Avocations: genealogy, gardening, reading, travel.

RILEY, TERENCE, curator, architect; Architect, ptnr. (with John Keenen) architectural practice; dir. Arthur Ross Architectural Galleries, Columbia U.; curator dept. arch. and design MoMA, NYC, 1991, chief curator, 1992—2002, Philip Johnson chief curator arch. and design, 2002—06; dir. Miami Art Mus., Fla., 2006—. Prof. Harvard U., Columbia U. Curator (exhibitions) Paul Nelson: Filter of Reason, Arthur Ross Architectural Galleries, Columbia U., 1989, Light Construction, The Un-Private House, Mies in America, 2001, On-Site: New Architecture in Spain, 2006; contbr. articles to profl. jours. Trustee Fundació Mies van der Rohe, Barcelona; adv. bd. Parsons Grad. Sch. Design. Office: Miami Art Museum 101 West Flager St Miami FL 33130

RILEY, THOMAS, United States Ambassador to Morocco; BS in Indsl. Engring., Stanford U., Calif., 1972; MBA, Harvard U., Mass., 1975. Assoc. engr. Boeing Co., Seattle; various positions including mgr. European ops. TRW, No. Ireland, England, France; co-founder Gen. Resources Corp., Calif.; pres., CEO Unity Systems, Web State, Active-Photo; US amb. to Moroco US Dept. State, 2003—. Vol. Bizworld, Hope Rehab. Services. Achievements include patents for an energy management system. Office: DOS Amb 9400 Rabat Pl Washington DC 20521-9400*

RILEY, THOMAS EDWARD, lawyer; BA, SUNY, Binghamton, 1976; JD, NYU, 1979. Bar: NY 1980, US Dist. Ct. (so. dist.) NY 1983, US Dist. Ct. (ea. dist.) NY 1983, US Dist. Ct. Ariz. 1992, US Ct. Appeals (4th cir.) 1995, US Ct. Appeals (6th cir.) 1998, US Dist. Ct. (no. dist.) NY 2002, US Ct. Appeals (3rd cir.) 2004, US Ct. Appeals (2nd cir.) 2004. Staff atty. Mfrs. Hanover Trust Co., NYC, 1979-80; law clk. to presiding justice US Dist. Ct. (We. Dist.) NY, Buffalo, 1980-82; with Chadbourne & Parke LLP, NYC, 1982—, ptnr., head litig. dept. Staff mem. NYU Jour. Internat. Law & Politics, 1977—78, rsch. editor, 1978—79; contbr. articles to profl. jours. Bd. dirs. U. Settlement Soc. of NY, 1992—2004. Mem.: ABA, Internat. Assn. Def. Counsel (mem. Amicus Curiae com.), NY State Bar Assn. Office: Chadbourne & Parke LLP 30 Rockefeller Plz Fl 31 New York NY 10112-0129 Office Phone: 212-408-5408. Office Fax: 212-541-5369. Business E-Mail: triley@chadbourne.com.

RILEY, THOMAS JOSEPH, anthropologist, academic administrator; b. Portland, Maine, Nov. 2, 1943; s. Joseph Gerard and Virginia C. (Cunningham) R.; m. Karma Jean Ibsen, July 10, 1967 (div. 1985); children: Kirsten, Katharine, Erin; m. Carol Ann, Nov. 21, 1989; 1 child, Julia Wade. BA, Boston Coll., 1965; MA, U. Hawaii, 1970, PhD, 1973. Asst. prof. NYU, 1972—74; from asst. prof. to prof. anthropology U. Ill., Urbana, 1974—96; dean Coll. Arts, Humanities/Social Scis., prof. anthropology N.D. State U., Fargo, 1996—. Acad. adv. bd. SALT Ctr., Portland, 1980-96; assoc. dean Grad. Coll. U. Ill., 1983-86, head dept. anthropology, 1986-93, chmn. senate coun., 1995-96; dir. N.D. Inst. Regional Studies, 1996— Co-author: Prehistoric Agriculture, 1972; mem. editl. bd. Ency. World Cultures, 1993-96, Ency. Cultural Anthropology, 1994-95, Ency. World Pre-history, 1996-2001; contbr. over 100 articles to profl. jours Chmn. bd. Devel. Svcs. Ctr., Champaign, 1986—89, Human Rels. Area Files at Yale U., 1985—96, v.p., 1995, pres., 1996; sec. bd. C-U Independence, Champaign, 1987—96; bd. dirs. Disabled Citizens Found., Champaign, 1988—96, Ill. Assn. Retarded Citizens, Chgo., 1988—94, Champaign County Mental Health Bd., 1993—96, Prairie Pub. Broadcasting, 1999—2005, Plains Art Mus., Fargo, 2001—07, vice-chair, 2003—05, chair, 2005—06; bd. dirs. ND State Hist. Soc. Found., 2001—, Ill. State Hist. Sites Adv. Coun., 1986—89, United Way Cass-Clay, 2001—. Grantee, NSF, 1978—79. Mem. Am. Assn. State and Local History, Am. Anthropology Assn., AHRS, Soc. Am. Archaeology, Soc. Archeol. Scis. (treas. 1982-83), Sigma Xi (chpt. v.p. 1987-88, chpt. pres. 1988-91), Rotary Internat. (gov. nominee, Dist 5580 2009-), FM Am Rotary (pres. 2001-02) Roman Catholic. Office: ND State U 221 Minard Hall Fargo ND 58105 Office Phone: 701-231-8338. Business E-Mail: thomas.riley@ndsu.edu.

RILEY, TOM JOSEPH, lawyer; b. Cedar Rapids, Iowa, Jan. 9, 1929; s. Joseph Wendell and Edna (Kyle) R.; m. Nancy Evans, Jan. 21, 1952; children: Pamela Chang, Peter, Lisa Thirnbeck, Martha Brown, Sara Riley, Heather Mescher. BA, U. Iowa, 1950, JD, 1952. Bar: Iowa 1952, U.S. Dist. Ct. (no. dist.) Iowa 1952, U.S. Ct. Appeals (8th cir.) 1960, U.S. Ct. Appeals (7th cir.) 1977, U.S. Ct. Appeals (9th cir.) 1996, U.S. Supreme Ct. 1966. Assoc. Simmons, Perrine, Allbright & Ellwood, Cedar Rapids, 1952-60, ptnr., 1960-80; pres. Tom Riley Law Firm, P.C., Cedar Rapids, 1980—. Adj. prof. trial advocacy Coll. Law, U. Iowa, Iowa City, 1979. Author: Proving Punitive Damages, 1981, The Price of a Life, 1986, Trial Handbook for Iowa Lawyers (Civil), 1997, Iowa Practice: Civil Litigation Handbook, 2003, 5th rev. edit., 2007. Active Iowa Ho. of Reps., 1960-64, Iowa Senate, 1965-74. First lt. USAF, 1952-54. Named Outstanding Freshman Legislator, Des Moines Press and Radio Club, 1961. Fellow Iowa Acad. Trial Lawyers (bd. govs. 1982-91); mem. Iowa Trial Lawyers Assn. (bd. govs. 2000-2002), Cedar Rapids Country Club. Democrat. Presbyterian. Avocations: tennis, sailing. Home: 5300 Lakeside Rd Rural Route Marion IA 52302 Office: 4040 1st Ave NE Cedar Rapids IA 52402-3143 Office Phone: 319-363-4040. Business E-Mail: rtom@trlf.com, ellena@trlf.com, tnrlakeside@cs.com.

RILEY, WAYNE JOSEPH, academic administrator, medical educator; b. New Orleans, May 3, 1959; s. Emile E. Jr. and Jacqueline Jean (Cerf) R.; m. Charlene Maria Dewey, May 1, 1959; children: Erin Elizabeth, Alexis Camille. BA in Med. Anthropology, Yale U., New Haven, 1981; MPH in Health Systems Mgmt., Tulane U., 1988; MD, Morehouse Sch. Medicine, Atlanta, 1993; MBA, Rice U., 2002. Adminstrv. asst. to mayor City New Orleans, 1981—86, exec. asst., 1986; instr. sect. gen. internal medicine to v.p., vice dean health affairs and govtl. rels. and assoc. prof. medicine Baylor Coll. Medicine, Houston, 1996—2006, asst. dean edn., 2000—04; asst. chief medicine, practicing gen. internist Ben Taub Gen. Hosp., Houston; mem. med. staff, attending physician Michael E. DeBakey Vet. Affairs Med. Ctr., Meth. Hosp., St. Luke's Episcopal Hosp.; pres. & CEO Meharry Med. Coll., Nashville, 2007—. Adv. bd. La. State U., 1993; adj. prof. mgmt. Rice U. Jesse H. Jones Grad. Sch. Mgmt.; chmn. Harris County Hosp. Dist. Med. Bd., 2003. Mem. Am. Coll. Physicians (assoc., vice chair coun. assocs. 1995-96, health & pub. policy com. 1996), Yale Club Houston, Morehouse Sch. Medicine Nat. Alumni Assn., Alpha Phi Alpha, Alpha Omega Alpha. Roman Catholic. Avocations: jazz, golf, reading. Office: Meharry Med Coll 1005 Dr DB Todd Jr Blvd Nashville TN 37208-3599 Office Fax: 615-327-6540. Business E-Mail: wjriley@mmc.edu.

RILEY, WILLIAM, wholesale distribution executive, writer, conservationist; b. Indpls., June 30, 1931; s. Leo Michael and Edna (Wilhelm) R.; m. Laura Etz, Apr. 20, 1957. AB, U. Notre Dame, 1952; LLB, Yale U., 1955. V.p., dir., chmn. Ivy Corp., Atlanta, 1960-80; CEO, chmn. Moore-Handley, Inc., Birmingham, Ala., 1981—. Bd. dirs. Fabco-Air, Inc., Gainesville, Fla. Author: (with Laura Riley) Guide to the National Wildlife Refuges, 1979 (Pulitzer prize nominee), 2d edit., 1993, Lifetime Conservation award Nat. Audubon Soc., 2000. Trustee The Raptor Trust, Basking Ridge, N.J., 1980-2000; bd. dirs. Nat. Wildlife Refuge Assn., Potomac, Md., 1985-94, Hawk Mountain Sanctuary Assn., Kempton, Pa., 1989-98, Nat. Audubon Soc., N.Y.C., 1990-94; chmn. exec. com. Everglades Fdn., 1997-2003, chmn. program com. 2003-. With U.S. Army, 1957-58. Recipient Conservationist of Yr. award Everglades Coalition, 2001. Mem.: Explorers Club of N.Y.C., Met. Club of N.Y.C. Office: 444 Madison Ave 33 Fl New York NY 10022

RILEY, WILLIAM JAY, federal judge; b. Lincoln, Nebr., Mar. 11, 1947; s. Don Paul and Marian Frances (Munn) R.; m. Norma Jean Mason, Dec. 27, 1965; children: Brian, Kevin, Erin. BA, U. Nebr., 1969, JD with distinction, 1972. Bar: Nebr. 1972, US Dist. Ct. Nebr. 1972, US Ct. Appeals (8th cir.) 1974; cert. civil trial specialist Nat. Bd. Trial Advocacy, 1994-2004. Law clk. US Ct. Appeals (8th cir.), Omaha,

1972-73; assoc. Fitzgerald, Schorr Law Firm, P.C., LLO, Omaha, 1973-79; shareholder Fitzgerald, Schorr Law Firm, Omaha, 1979—2001; judge US Ct. Appeals (8th cir.), 2001—. Adj. prof. trial practice Creighton U. Coll. Law, Omaha, 1991—, Nebr. Law Sch., Lincoln, 2006-; chmn. fed. practice com. Fed. Ct., 1992-94; mme. criminal law com. Jud. Conf. US, 2005—. Scoutmaster Boy Scouts Am., Omaha, 1979—89, scout membership chair Mid. Am. coun., 1995—98, trustee, 2001—. Recipient Silver Beaver award Boy Scouts Am., 1991. Fellow Am. Coll. Trial Lawyers (chair state com. 1997-99), Nebr. State Bar Found.; mem. Am. Bd. Trial Advs. (Nebr. chpt. pres. 2000), Nebr. State Bar Assn. (chmn. ethics com. 1996-98, ho. of dels. 1998—, profl. com. 2002—), Omaha Bar Assn. (treas. 1997-98, pres. 2000-01), Robert M. Spire Inns of Ct. (master 1994—2001, counselor 1997-98, 2007-, jud. mem. 2001-07), Order of Coif, Phi Beta Kappa. Republican. Methodist. Avocations: reading, hiking, bicycling. Office: Roman L Hruska US Courthouse 111 S 18th Plaza Ste 4303 Omaha NE 68102-1325 Office Phone: 402-661-7575.*

RILEY, WILLIAM JOHN, neurologist; b. Seattle, Oct. 24, 1930; s. William John and Virginia (McCarthy) R.; m. Joan Marie Weismann, 1956 (div. 1976); children: Sean, Kevan, Megan, Janeen, Michael; m. Margit Mary Winstrom, 1976; children: Britta, Shane, Timothy. MS in Anatomy, U. Chgo., 1958, MD, 1960; PhD, U. Minn., 1965. Intern Mpls. Gen. Hosp., 1961-62; resident U. Minn. Hosps., 1962-65; asst. chief neurology Mpls. Gen. Hosp., 1965-69; chief neurology St. Luke's Episcopal Hosp., Houston, 1970-85; pres., CEO Tex. Neurol. Clinic Assn., Houston, 1969—. Staff sgt. USAF, 1951-55. Recipient Disting. Tchg. award Minn. Med. Found., Mpls., 1969. Fellow: ACP, Tex. Neurol. Soc. (pres. 2002—, Lifetime Achievement award 2005), Am. Acad. Neurology; mem.: Alpha Omega Alpha, AMA, Tex. Med. Assn. (pres. 9th dist. 1991), Sigma Xi. Roman Catholic. Avocation: ranching. Office: Tex Neurol Clinic Assn 4126 SW Freeway # 1210 Houston TX 77027-7306 Office Phone: 713-621-9291. Personal E-mail: wjrileymd@aol.com.

RILLING, JOHN ROBERT, history professor; b. Wausau, Wis., Apr. 28, 1932; s. John Peter and Esther Laura (Wittig) R.; m. Joanne Marilyn McCrory, Dec. 21, 1953; children: Geoffrey Alan, Andrew Peter. BA summa cum laude, U. Minn., 1953; AM, Harvard U., 1957, PhD, 1959. Asst. prof. history U. Richmond, Va., 1959-62, assoc. prof. history, 1962-68, prof. history, 1968-99, prof. English history emeritus, 1999—, chmn. dept. history, 1977-83, Westhampton Coll., 1965-71. Pres. Faculty Senate of Va., 1975—77, Shepherd's Ctr., Richmond, Va., 2008—. Contbr. articles to profl. jours. Elder, Ginter Park Presbyn. Ch., 1973-83. Served with U.S. Army, 1953-55. Recipient U. Richmond Disting. Educator award, 1975, 76, 77, 80, 87, Prof. of Yr. finalist Coun. for Advancement and Support of Edn., 1981. Woodrow Wilson fellow, 1955-59; Harvard U. travelling fellow, 1958; Coolidge fellow, 1955-56; Folger Libr. fellow, 1960. Mem.: Agecroft Assn. (bd. dir.), Am. Hist. Assn., Omicron Delta Kappa (Prof. of Yr. 1995), Phi Beta Kappa. Avocations: hiking, bicycling, enology. Home: 1507 Wilmington Ave Richmond VA 23227-4429 Office: U Richmond Dept History Richmond VA 23173 Business E-Mail: jrilling@richmond.edu.

RILLING, WILLIAM S., radiologist; m. Kathryn A. Perelli, Sept. 7, 1991. MD, U. Wis., Madison, 1990. Cert. in interventional radiology Am. Bd. Radiology, 2007. Dir., interventional radiology Med. Coll. Wis., 2002—. Office: Med Coll WI Dept Radiology 9200 W WI Ave Rm 2803 Milwaukee WI 53226

RIMA, INGRID HAHNE, economics professor; b. Germany; d. Max F. and Hertha G. (Grunsfeld) Hahne; m. Philip W. Rima; children: David, Eric. BA with honors, CUNY, 1945; MA, U. Pa., 1946, PhD, 1951. Prof. econs. Temple U., Phila., 1967—. Author: Development of Economic Analysis, 1967, 6th edit., 2000, 7th edit., 2009, Labor Markets Wages and Employment, 1981, The Joan Robinson Legacy, 1991, The Political Economy of Global Restructuring, Vol. I, Production and Organization, Vol. II, Trade and Finance, 1993, Measurement, Quantification and Economic Analysis, 1994, Labor Markets in a Global Economy, 1996. Fulbright Disting. Lectr., Lingnan U., China, 2000. Fellow Ea. Econ. Assn.; mem. Am. Econ. Assn., History of Econs. Soc. (pres. 1993-4), Phi Beta Kappa (pres. chpt. 2006). Office: Temple U Broad & Montgomery Ave Philadelphia PA 19122 Personal E-mail: irima@aol.com.

ŘÍMAN, JOSEF, biology professor; b. Horní Suchá, Karviná, Czechoslovakia, Jan. 30, 1925; s. Alois and Hilda (Glaserová) Říman; m. Věra Tomková, July 16, 1950. MD, Charles U., Prague, Czechoslovakia, 1950; PhD, Czechoslovak Acad Sci., Prague, 1955, DSc in Chemistry, 1966; DSc in Biology (hon.), J.E. Purkyně U., Brno, Czechoslovakia, 1987. Rsch. physician 1st Clinic Pediatrics Charles U., Prague, 1950-51, prof. med. faculty, 1967-72; sr. scientist Inst. Organic Chemistry Czechoslovak Acad. Sci., Prague, 1951-74, founder, dir. Inst. Molecular Genetics, 1976—91, sci. sec., 1978-81, v.p., 1981-86, pres., 1986-90; vis. prof. Duke U., Durham, NC, 1968; acad. rep. UNESCO, 1980-86; Czechoslovak nat. rep. Internat. Coun. Sci. Unions, 1982-84. Dep. Ho. Nations Fed. Assembly, Prague, 1986—89; chmn. commn. INTERKOSMOS, 1986—90; founder Czechoslovak Biochemistry Retroviruses Inst. Molecular Genetics, Prague; participant UNESCO Symposium Sci. and Culture 21st Century, Vancouver, Canada, 1989. Mem. editl. bd. Neoplasma Slovak Acad. Scis., 1967, Acta Virologica, 1970, Biologica, 1982, Cancer Biochemistry and Biophysics, 1985; chmn., chief editor: Czechoslovak Encyclopaedia, 1986—90; contbr. articles to profl. jours. Recipient State prize, Govt. of Czechoslovakia, 1969, 1977, J. E. Purkeyne medal, 1979, Order of Labor, 1983, J. E. Purkyne Silver medal, Czechoslovak Med. Soc., 1986, Gold medal, Slovak Acad. Sci., 1989, State prize, USSR, 1978, Gold G. Dimitrov medal, Govt. of Bulgaria, 1986, Gold Einstein-Russel Pugwash medal, Pugwash Conf., 1987, Hippocrates medal, Kyoto U. Med. Sch., 1988, J. E. Fogarty medal, NIH, 1988, Gold medal, Nagoya U. Med. Sch., 1990, Kunio Yagi Gold Meml. medal, 1990. Fellow: Indian Nat. Sci. Acad. (fgn.); mem.: Academician, Ctrl. European Acad. Sci. and Art, G. W. Liebniz Soc., German Soc. Biol. Chemistry (fgn.), Czechoslovak Soc. Immunology (hon.), Hungarian Acad. Sci. (hon.), Slovak Soc. Biochemistry (hon.), Bulgarian Acad. Sci. (fgn.), German Acad. Scis. (fgn.), Czechoslovak Acad. Sci. (chief editor Folia Biologica 1975, G. J. Mendel Gold plaque 1975, Gold pin G. W. Leibniz 2005, medal of Honor, numerous others), Russian Acad. Sci. (fgn., M. L. Lomonosov Gold medal 1987). Avocation: history of science. Office: Acad Sci Inst Molecular Genetics Fleming Square 2 166 37 Prague Czech Republic Office Phone: 420 2 3333 09 71. E-mail: riman@img.cas.cz.

RIMBACH, EVANGELINE LOIS, retired music educator; b. Portland, Oreg., June 28, 1932; d. Raymond Walter and Viola Clara (Gaebler) Rimbach. BA, Valparaiso U., Ind., 1954; MMus, Eastman Sch. Music, Rochester, NY, 1956; PhD, Eastman Sch. Music, 1967; student, Pacific Luth. U., Parkland, Wash., 1950—52. Vocal music instr. Goodwin Jr. High Sch., Redwood City, Calif., 1956-57; music instr. Calif. Concordia Coll., Oakland, Calif., 1957-62; prof. music Concordia U., River Forest, Ill., 1964-97, chmn. dept., 1989-97; ret., 1997. Contbg. editor: Church Music, 1965—80; editor: (book) Johann Kuhnau: Magnificat, 1980, (cantata) Johann Kuhnau: Lobe den Herrn, meine Seele, 1994, 2008; contbr. (essays) Hymnal Supplement '98 Handbook, Keywords in Church Music, 2004, Thine the Amen, 2005; editor: (book) Johann Kuhnau:Missa in F, 2008; contbr. articles to profl. jours. Bd. dirs. Civic Symphony of Oak Park-River Forest, 1974-80, concert com. chmn., 1976-78, prog. annotator, 1976-80; mem. choir Grace Luth. Ch., River Forest, 1964-97. AAUW postdoctoral fellow, 1969-70; DAAD grantee, Munich, 1980; recipient Rose of Honor award, Sigma Alpha Iota, 1987. Mem. Am. Musicol. Soc., Assn. Luth. Ch. Musicians (editor newsletter 1998—), Sigma Alpha Iota (Rose of Dedication award 1997). Republican. Lutheran. Avocations: travel, cooking, needlecrafts. Home: Unit B 4320 S Pine St Tacoma WA 98409 Home Fax: 253-292-1165. Personal E-mail: evangelinerimbach@comcast.net.

RIMEL, IRA WESLEY, writer, US Navy supply officer, real estate specialist, real estate appraiser, real estate broker; b. Wibaux, Mont., Jan. 10, 1921; s. Ira Dice and Hazel Barbara (Webber) Rimel; m. Mary Mackinlay Weir, Dec. 13, 1943 (div.); children: Patricia, Valerie, Linda, David, Glenn. Basic sci./engring, Mont. Sch. Mines, 1943—44; BA in mgmt./acctg., U. Wash., 1943—47; Navy supply, acctg. grad., Harvard Grad. Sch. Bus., 1945—46; nat. security, econ., Indust. Coll. Armed Forces, 1965. Tech. writer Military Manuals Co., Renton, Wash., 1952—55; indsl. agent No. Pacific Railway, Seattle, 1955—58; right of way agent/supr. Mont. Hwy. Dept., Helena, 1958—65; right of way agent Lane County, Eugene, Oreg., 1965—86; columnist Fishing & Hunting News, Seattle, 1992—95; freelance writer, 1956—. Ensign, reserve, supply, disbursing, acctg. officer U.S. Navy Naval Prison, Norfolk, Va., 1946; LTJG supply officer liaison U.S. Navy, Republic of Korea, 1950—51. Author: (short stories) Dynamic Tension, 1990 (First Prize, 1990), Lucky Man, 2002 (Best of Show/Class, 2002), Winter Travel, 2002 (First Prize, 2002). Adj., publicity officer/comdr. Disabled Am. Vet., Renton, Wash., 1952—58, Wash. publicity officer Seattle, 1953—58; lifetime mem. VFW, Marcola, Oreg., 1960—2003. Lt. jr. grade USN, 1942—46, WWII, Korea, lt. jr. grade USN, 1950—51, WWII, Japan, selected for V-12 Coll. Prog. USN. Recipient corr., Mont. Sports Outdoors, Missoula, 1959, Author "Lady Gets Her Buck", 1959; named rep. to Rep. Korea, Yokosuka, Japan, Celebration of Commissioning Frigates to Korea, U.S. Navy, 1950. Mem.: Am. Legion, DAV. Avocations: hunting, fishing, boating, horseback riding, gardening.

RIMEL, REBECCA WEBSTER, foundation administrator; b. 1951; BS, U. Va., 1973; MBA, James Madison U., 1983. Head nurse, emergency dept. U. Va. Hosp., Charlottesville, 1973-74, coord. med. out-patient dept., 1974-75, nurse practitioner dept. neurosurgery, 1975-77, instr. in neurosurgery, 1975-80, asst. prof., 1981-83; program mgr. health Pew Charitable Trusts, Phila., 1983-84; asst. v.p. Glenmede Trust Co., Pew Charitable Trusts, Phila., 1984-85; v.p. for programs Pew Charitable Trusts, Phila., 1985-88, exec. dir., 1988-94, pres., CEO, 1994—. Mem. Coun. on Founds., Washington; prin. investigator dept. neurosurgery U. Va., 1981—83; adv. com. Boxing U.S. Olympics, 1983—86; adv. coun. Nat. Inst. of Neurol. Disorders and Strokes, 1988—91, bd. dirs., Thomas Jefferson Meml. Found., Deutsche Banc Flag Investors Fund, VIASYS Healthcare Inc., 2007—, CardioNet, Inc., 2009—. Contbr. chpts. in books, articles and abstracts to profl. jours. Recipient Disting. Nursing Alumni award, U. Va., 1988; fellow Kellogg Nat. fellow, 1992. Mem.: APHA, ANA, Va. State Nurses Assn. (membership and credentials com. 1982—86), Emergency Dept. Nurses Assn., Am. Assn. Neurosurg. Nurses, Am. Acad. Nursing. Address: The Pew Charitable Trusts 2005 Market St Ste 1700 Philadelphia PA 19103-7017*

RIMER, BARBARA K., dean, healthcare educator; b. Wilkes Barre, Pa., Jan. 14, 1949; married. BA in English, U. Mich., 1970, MPH in Med. Care Adminstrn. and Health Edn., 1973; PhD in Health Edn., Johns Hopkins Sch. of Hygiene and Public Health, 1981. Instr. Wayne State U. Sch. Medicine, Detroit, 1973-75; program dir. Nat. Cancer Inst., Bethesda, Md., 1975-77; intervention coord. Johns Hopkins Oncology Ctr., Balt., 1977-79; rsch. assoc. Johns Hopkins Sch. Hygiene and Public Health, Balt., 1977-79; sr. health educator Fox Chase Cancer Ctr., Phila., 1981-87, dir. health comms. rsch., 1981-87, dir. behavioral rsch., 1987-91, dir. population sci. for behavioral rsch., 1990-91; dir. cancer prevention, detection and ctrl. rsch. Duke Comprehensive Cancer Ctr., Durham, NC, 1991-97; sr. fellow Aging Ctr. Duke U. Med. Ctr., Durham, NC, 1991-97, assoc. prof. in cmty. and family medicine, 1991-93, prof. cmty. and family medicine, 1993-97; acting dep. dir. Duke Comprehensive Cancer Ctr., Durham, NC, 1995-96; dir. cancer ctrl. and population scis. Nat. Cancer Inst., Rockville, Md., 1997—2002; dep. dir. population scis. Lineberger Cancer Ctr. U. NC, Chapel Hill, 2003—05, alumni disting. prof. Dept. Health Behavior & Health Edn., 2003—, dean Sch. Pub. Health, 2005—. Adj. assoc. prof. dept. health behavior and health edn. U. N.C. Sch. of Public Health, Chapel Hill, NC, 1992-97; adj. mem. Fox Chase Cancer Ctr., Phila., 1992-97; preceptor, lectr. Temple U., 1983-91; guest lectr. Duke U. Med. Ctr., 1991-97, U. N.C. Sch. Public Health, 1991-93; Judith P. Schlager vis. prof. Dana-Farber Cancer Inst., 1995; disting. vis. lectr. Harvard U., 1998; mem. institutional review bd. Fox Chase Cancer Ctr., 1983-88, vice chair, 1988-91; proposal review, site visitor Nat. Cancer Inst., 1985-95; chairperson tech. advisory com. Am. Lung Assn., 1987; external advisory com. Vermont Regional Cancer Ctr., 1988-89; advisory com. Brown U., U. R.I. Cancer Prevention Rsch. unit, 1988-95; mem. Am. Assn. Retired Persons task force on smoking, 1989-91, Health Promotion adv. bd. Wesley Found., 1990-91, program com. annual mtg. Am. Soc. Preventive Oncology, 1990-93, chair, 1993 mtg., expert adv. com. AMC Cancer Rsch. Ctr./Ctrs. for Disease Ctrl. Coop. Agreement, 1991, adult edn. subcom. and tobacco materials review group Am. Cancer Soc., 1991; mem. Nat. Task Force on Breast Cancer Ctrl. Am. Cancer Soc., 1992, chair Nat. and State (NC) Task Force on Breast Cancer Ctrl., 1992; mem. Pub. Edn. subcom. on Adult Edn. Am. Cancer Soc., 1992; mem. adv. bd. Office of Cancer Comms., NCI, 1992; mem. Clin. Cancer com. Duke U. Med. Ctr., 1992-95; mem. Cancer Ctrs.' Support com. NCI, 1993-94, Recruitment and Adherence com. Office of Women's Health NIH, 1993, Report com. Internat. Workshop on Screening for breast cancer NCI, 1993, Detection and Treatment subcom. on Breast Cancer Am. Cancer Soc., 1993, 94, Nominating com. Soc. Behavioral Medicine, 1993-96, adv. com. on cancer coordination and ctrl. State of NC, 1993-97; invited participant and com. chair Frontiers of Behavioral Medicine mtg., Chantilly, Va., 1993; invited co-chair Sec. Shalala's Mtg. to develop nat. strategic plan for breast cancer, Bethesda, Md., 1993; chair, mem. Nat. Cancer Adv. Bd. (presdl. appointment), 1994-97; bd. dirs. Am. Family Life Assurance Corp., 1995—; fellowship selection com. Am. Assn. Cancer Rsch., 1996; mem. exec. com. Acad. Behavioral Medicine Rsch., 1998, Charles S. Mott Selection com. of Gen. Motors Cancer Rsch. Found., 1999, Inst. Medicine com. effective health comm. and behavior change strategies for diverse populations, 2000. Editor: special cancer issue Health Education Research, 1998-89; editl. bd. Health Education Quarterly, 1985-87, guest editl. bd. 1983; editl. bd. Jour. of Compliance in Health Care, 1989-90, Health Edn. Rsch., 1990-98, Cancer Prevention, Epidemiology and Biomarkers, 1990—, Patient Edn. and Counseling, 1994—, Breast Diseases, 1998—, Cancer Causes and Control, 1998—, Effective Clin. Practice, 2000—; assoc. editor: Preventive Medicine, 1990—; reviewer Am. Jour. Preventive Medicine, Am. Jour. Public Health, Annals of Internal Medicine, Health Edn. Quarterly, Health Services Research, Jour. of Am. Med. Assn., Jour. Nat. Cancer Inst., Milbank Quarterly, Women's Health, 1986—; contbr. numerous articles, papers to profl. pubs. Fellow Johns Hopkins Sch. of Hygiene and Public Health, 1979-81, Soc. of Behavioral Medicine, 1997; recipient Mayhew Derryberry award Am. Public Health Assn., 1992, Best Visual Presentation of Session award Soc. of Behavioral Medicine, San Diego, 1995, Citation award Soc. Behavioral Medicine, 1996, Disting. Achievement award Am. Soc. Preventive Oncology, 1997, Herbert J. Block Leadership award Ohio State U., 1997, John P. McGovern award in Health Promotion U. Tex. Sch. Public Health, 1999. Mem.: Inst. Medicine. Office: Sch Public Health Univ North Carolina 170 Rosenau Hall Campus Box 7400 Chapel Hill NC 27599-7400 Office Phone: 919-966-3215. Office Fax: 919-966-7678. E-mail: brimer@unc.edu.*

RIMER, JOHN THOMAS, language educator, academic administrator, writer; b. Pitts., Mar. 2, 1933; s. John T. and Naomi (Bowser) R.; m. Laurence E. Mus., Apr. 18, 1964; children: John, Mark. BA, Princeton U., 1954; MA, Columbia U., 1969, PhD, 1971. Asst. cultural officer USIA, Laos, Japan; then dir. Am. Cultural Ctr. Kobe, Japan, 1958-67; assoc. prof., then prof. Japanese lang. and lit. Washington U., St. Louis, 1973-83, chmn. dept. Chinese and Japanese, 1973-83; chief Asian div. Library of Congress, Washington, 1983-86; chmn. Hebrew and East Asian langs. and lits. U. Maryland, College Park, 1986-91; chmn. East Asian langs. and lits. U. Pitts., 1991—2005; ret., 2005. Author: Toward a Modern Japanese Theatre, 1974, Traditions in Modern Japanese Fiction, 1978; translator: stories Mori Ogai, 2 vols., 1977, Mask and Sword: Two Plays for the Contemporary Japanese Theatre, 1980, On the No Drama, 1983, Pilgrimages, 1988, A Reader's Guide to Japanese Literature, 1988; editor: Multiple Meanings, 1987; editor, contbr.: Culture and Identity, Japanese Intellectuals during the Interwar Years, 1990, Shisendo, 1991, Youth and Other Stories by Mori Ogai, 1994, Kyoto Encounters, 1995, A Hidden Fire: Russian and Japanese Cultural Encounters, 1868-1929, 1995, The Blue-eyed Tarōkaja: Essays by Donald Keene, 1996, Nara Encounters, 1997, The Voyage of Japanese Theatre: Theatre Criticism of Senda Akihiko, 1997, Poems to Sing: The Wakan Roeisu, 1997; (with Marlene J. Mayo) War, Occupation, and Creativity: Japan and East Asia 1920-1960, 2001, Collected Writings of J. Thomas Rimer, 2004; (with Van Gessel) The Columbia Anthology of Modern Japanese Literature, vol. 1, 2005, vol. 2, 2007; (with Stephen Addiss and Gerald Groemer) Traditional Japanese Arts and Cultures: An Illustrated Sourcebook, 2006. Served with U.S. Army, 1955-58. NEH fellow France, 1976-77; NEH grantee, 1979-81; recipient Order of the Sacred Treasure award Japanese Govt., 1997. Episcopalian. Achievements include research in Japanese literature, theatre, and cultural history. Avocation: classical music. Home: 4319 Redwood #1 Marina Del Rey CA 90292-7643

RIMER, MENDELL DE JESUS, healthcare educator; s. Jorge Rimer and Beatriz Elena Gaviria; m. Haydee Coromoto D'Alessandro; children: Daniela Beatriz, Austin Daniel. Degree Summa Cum Laude, U. Los Andes, Merida, Venezuela, 1986; PhD, U. Md., Balt., 1993. Postdoc. fellow NY U. Med. Sch., NYC, 1999—2000, Stanford U., Palo Alto, Calif., N.Mex State U., Las Cruces, instr., 1998; asst. prof. Austin, Tex., 2000—07, Tex. A&M Health Sci. Ctr., Coll. Sta., 2007—. Contbr. articles to profl. jours. Recipient Tchg. Excellence award, U. Tex. Austin, 2006; Postdoc. fellowship, Myasthenia Gravis Found. America, 1995—96. Mem.: AAAS, Internat. Soc. Devel. Neurosci., Internat. Brain Rsch. Orgn., Soc. Neurosci. Office: Tex A&M Univ Health Sci Ctr 228 Joe H Reynolds Med Bldg College Station TX 77843-1114 Office Fax: 979-845-0790. Business E-Mail: mjrimer@medicine.tamhsc.edu.

RIMES, LEANN, country music singer; b. Jackson, Miss., Aug. 28, 1982; d. Wilbur and Belinda Rimes; m. Dean Sheremet, Feb. 23, 2002 (div. 2009). Singer: (albums) Blue, 1996, Unchained Melody: The Early Years, 1997, You Light Up My Life: Inspirational Songs, 1997 (Contemporary Christian Album of Yr., 1998), Sittin' on Top of the World, 1998, LeAnn Rimes, 1999, I Need You, 2001, God Bless America, 2001, Twisted Angel, 2002, Greatest Hits, 2003, What a Wonderful World, 2004, This Woman, 2005, Whatever We Wanna, 2006, Family, 2007; co-writer: (TV films) Holiday in Your Heart, 1997; guest appearance (TV films) Holiday in Your Heart, 1997, (TV series) American Dreams, 2003, (TV) Days of Our Lives, 1998, Moesha, 1999, MadTV, 2000, Tinseltown TV, 2003, and several others, (films) Coyote Ugly, 2000, host (TV series) Nashville Star, 2003—; performer: (TV) LeAnn Rimes Live, 2003, LeAnn Rimes: Custom Concert, 2004; author: (children's books) Jag, 2003, Jag's New Friend, 2004; singer: (soundtrack) Can't Fight The Moonlight for Coyote Ugly (Favorite Song, Blockbuster award, 2001), Looking Through Your Eyes for Quest for Camelot, (soundtrack-TV miniseries) I Need You for Jesus, 2000. Internat. spokesperson Children's Miracle Network; established LeAnn Rimes Adventure Gym (Vanderbilt Children's Hosp.), Nashville. Nominated Best Country Singer award, Country Music Assn., 1996; recipient Best New Artist,(youngest person to win a top award) & Best Female Country Vocal Performance, Grammy award, 1997, Song of Yr. & Single Record of Yr., Blue, Top New Female Vocalist, Acad. Country Music, 1997, Home Depot Humanitarian award, 2009, Horizon award, Country Music Assn., 1997, Favorite Female Artist, Blockbuster award, 1998; named Female Rising Video Star of Yr., Country Music TV, 1997, New Country Act of Yr., Internat. Touring Talent Pub., Internat. Rising Star, British Country Music Awards, Artist of Yr., North Tex. Music Festival, Country Single Sale Artist of Yr., Female Country Artist of Yr., Contemporary Christian Artist of Yr., Billboard, 1998, and others. Office: c/o Alix Gucovsky Special Artists Agy 9465 Wilshire Blvd Ste 890 Beverly Hills CA 90212 also: c/o Curb Records 2d Fl 3907 W Alameda Ave Burbank CA 91505-4332*

RIMLAND, LISA PHILLIP, writer, composer, lyricist; b. Stamford, Conn., Mar. 27, 1954; d. Maurice Louis and Eva (Kreiz) R. BA, U. Conn., 1978. Owner Ph Rimland Press, Storrs, Conn., 1991—. Composer numerous songs, including Your Heart or Mine, 1990, Drive Me Crazy, 1991, Send Me an Angel, 1992, Geography of Heaven, 1990, 2002, The Winds of Time (The Cloning Song), 2003, I Bleed, 2009; author: The Candida Manual: Candida Overgrowth and the Quest for Human Wellness, 1999, Voices From the Farm, 1999, Machronomarker Observations Conducted During the First Three Months of the Life of a Cloned Heifer Dairy Calf, 2000, An Evaluation of Machronomarker Observations, 2001, Amy and Aspen: Behavioral Observations of a Cloned Holstein Cow and Her Genetic Donor Living Together In Pasture, 2003, Betty and Cathy With Aspen In Summer, 2004, Behavioral Observations of Two Cloned Holstein Cows and Their Genetic Donor Living Together in Pasture, 2006; contbr. articles, poems, essays to profl. jours. Vol. dairy barn U. Conn., 1992—, vol. photographer Morgan horse facility, 1982-91. Recipient DAR award, 1969, Soc. Women Engrs. award, 1971, Editor's Choice award Nat. Libr. Poetry, 1995, 96; Nat. Merit scholar, 1972. Mem. ASCAP. Avocations: film and drama, art, poetry, athletics, morgan horses. Home: 51 Cheney Dr Storrs Mansfield CT 06268-2008

RIMOIN, DAVID LAWRENCE, medical geneticist; b. Montreal, Nov. 9, 1936; s. Michael and Fay (Lecker) Rimoin; m. Mary Ann Singleton, 1962 (div. 1979); 1 child, Anne; m. Ann Piilani Garber, July 27, 1980; children: Michael, Lauren. BSc, McGill U., Montreal, 1957, MSc, MD, CM, 1961; PhD, Johns Hopkins U., 1967; LHD (hon.), Finch U., 1997. Asst. prof. medicine, pediat. Washington U., St. Louis, 1967—70; assoc. prof. UCLA, 1970—73, prof., 1973—, chief med. genetics, Harbor-UCLA Med. Ctr., 1970—86; chair dept. pediat., dir. Med. Genetics and Birth Defects Ctr. Cedars-Sinai Med. Ctr., LA, 1986—2004, Steven Spielberg chair, 1989—, dir. Med. Genetics Inst., 2004—. Chmn. coun. Med. Genetics Orgn., 1993. Co-editor: Emory and Rimoin's Principles and Practice of Medical Genetics, 1983, 5th edit., 2007; contbr. chapters to books, articles to profl. jours. Recipient E. Mead Johnson award, Am. Acad. Pediat., 1976, Col. Harland Saunders award, March of Dimes, 1997, Pioneer in Medicine award, Cedars Sinai Med. Ctr., 2001, Extraordinary Merit award, UCLA Med. Alumni Assn., 2005, Legends Harbor award, LA Biomed. Found., 2006, Leadership award, Am. Soc. Human Genetics, 2006. Fellow: Am. Coll. Med. Genetics (pres. 1991—96, bd. dirs. 1996—2000), AAAS, ACP; mem.: Inst. of Medicine, Assn. Am. Physicians, Am. Pediat. Soc., Am. Soc. Human Genetics (pres. 1984, Leadership award 2006), Am. Bd. Med. Genetics (pres. 1979—83), Western Soc. Pediat. Rsch. (pres. 1995, Ross Outstanding Young Investigator award 1976), Western Soc. Clin. Rsch. (pres. 1978), Am. Fedn. Clin. Rsch. (sec.-treas. 1972—75), Am. Coll. Med. Genetics Found. (pres. 1999—2002, bd. dirs. 2002—), Johns Hopkins Soc. Scholars. Office: Cedars Sinai Med Ctr 8700 Beverly Blvd Los Angeles CA 90048-1865 Office Phone: 310-423-4461. Business E-Mail: david.rimoin@cshs.org.

RINAKER, SAMUEL MAYO, JR., retired utilities executive; b. Chgo., Sept. 29, 1922; s. Samuel Mayo and Marjorie (Horton) R.; m. Alice Benthey, Dec. 17, 1949 (div. 1974); children: Elizabeth Cherry, Samuel M. III, Laura Frazier, Mary Clark. Student, UCLA, 1941-42. Farmer, Nebr. and Ill., 1946-49; exec. sec. to atty. gen. Olympia, Wash., 1949-52; news dir. Sta. KTNT-TV, Tacoma, Wash., 1952-57, Sta. KIRO-TV, Seattle, 1957-60; assoc. news dir., news anchor Sta. KGTV, San Diego, 1960-75; dir. pub. policy San Diego Gas & Electric Co., 1976-84. Bd. dirs. 1st Nat. Bank, Beatrice, Neb., 1976-93. Maj. U.S. Army Air Corps, 1942-46, ETO. Mem. Rotary (bd. dirs. 1965-67), La Jolla Beach Tennis Club. Republican. Presbyterian. Avocation: golf. Home: 5935 Rutgers Rd La Jolla CA 92037-7834 E-mail: smr11@san.rr.com.

RINALDI, EMILIA, finance educator; b. Rome, Sept. 10, 1977; d. Massimo Rinaldi and Rosalba Leone. BA in Bus. Adminstrn., John Cabot U., Rome, 2005; MA in Economics, U. Iowa, 2008. Rsch. asst. FAO UN, Rome, 2005—06; tchg. asst. U. Iowa, 2006—. Campain vol. A.N. Giovani, Rome, 2003—04; troop leader A.G.E.S.C.I., Rome, 1998—2006. Recipient Academic Excellence award, John Cabot U., 2005. Personal E-mail: rinaldi.emilia@gmail.com. Business E-Mail: emilia-rinaldi@uiowa.edu.

RINAMAN, JAMES CURTIS, JR., lawyer; b. Miami, Fla., Feb. 8, 1935; s. James Curtis and Ruth Marie (Rader) R.; m. Gloria Margaret Kaspar; children: James, Mark, Christine, Karen BA, U. Fla., 1955, JD, 1960. Bar: Fla. 1960, U.S. Dist. Ct. (so. dist.) Fla. 1960, U.S. Ct. Appeals (5th cir.) 1960, U.S. Supreme Ct. 1963, U.S. Dist. Ct. (mid. dist.) Fla. 1967, U.S. Dist. Ct. (no. dist.) Fla. 1981, U.S. Ct. Appeals (11th cir.) 1981, U.S. Ct. Claims 1991, U.S. Ct. Mil. Appeals 1994; cert. civil trial lawyer Fla. Bar. With Marks, Gray, Conroy & Gibbs, P.A., Jacksonville, Fla., 1960—. Gen. counsel Fla. Bd. Architecture, 1965-79, City of Jacksonville, 1970-71, Jacksonville C. of C., 1973-76, 90; adj. prof. Coll. Architecture, U. Fla., 1975-90; dir. gen. The Southern Acad. Letters, Arts and Scis., 1997—. Pres. Jacksonville Cmty. Coun. Inc., 1985. Leadership Jacksonville, Inc., 1987; mem. Jacksonville Transp. Authority, 1971-80, Jacksonville Base Realignment and Closure Commn., 1993-95. Jacksonville Cecil Field Devel. Commn., 1994-96; chmn. N.E. Fla. chpt. ARC, 1996; chmn. ICCI Elections, 2001; trustee US 11th Cir. Ct. Appeals Nat. Soc., 2007-. With U.S. Army, 1955-57, Fla. NG, 1957-92. ret. brig. gen., 1992. Named to U. Fla. Hall of Fame. Fellow Am. Coll. Trial Lawyers, Am. Bar Found., Fla. Bar Found. (bd. dirs. 1982-87, 88, Disting. Svc. award 1983, 86, Medal of Honor 1988); mem. ABA (ho. of dels. 1982-86), Jacksonville Bar Assn. (pres. 1972-73, Lawyer of Yr. 1994), The Fla. Bar (pres. 1982-83), Def. Rsch. Inst. (so. regional v.p. 1980-83, bd. dirs. 1976-78, 83-87), Am. Judicature Soc. (Herbert Harley award 1987), Fla. Coun. Bar Pres. (Outstanding Past Pres. award 1989), Lawyers for Civil Justice (pres. 1989-91, chmn. bd. dirs. 1991-94), Vol. Lawyers Resource Ctr. of Fla., (pres. 1984-89, chmn. bd. dirs. 1989-93), So. Conf. of Bar, Nat. Conf. of Bar, Assn. Def. Trial Attys. (internat. pres. 1976-77), Internat. Assn. Def. Counsel, Jacksonville Assn. Def. Counsel, Fla. Defense Lawyers Assn. (pres. 1973), Fla. C. of C., Jacksonville C. of C. (chmn. 1994), Meninak Civic Club (pres. 1986), Jacksonville Commodores League (Flag Commodores 2008-09), The Army War Coll. Alumni Assn. (life), Fla. Blue Key, San. Jose Country Club, River Club, Phi Gamma Delta (bd. trustees ednl. found. 1995—), Phi Alpha Delta. Republican. Methodist. Office: Marks Gray Conroy & Gibbs 1200 Riverplace Blvd Ste 800 Jacksonville FL 32207-1805 also: PO Box 447 Jacksonville FL 32201-0447 Office Phone: 904-398-0900. E-mail: jrinaman@marksgray.com.

RINCKEY, GREG T., state attorney general; s. Tom and Marie Rinckey; m. Tara L. Rinckey; 1 child, Grant K. BBA, Hofstra U., Hempstead, NY, 1951; JD, Touro Law Sch., Ctrl. Islip, NY, 1998. Bar: NJ (attorney) 1998, NY State Bar Assn. 2003, Washington 2004. Columnist Fed. Times, 1997—; mng. ptnr. Tully Rinckey PLLC, Albany, NY, 2003—; dep. chief, law enforcement Schenectady County SPCA, Niskayuna, NY, 2007—; firefighter EMT East Meadow, NY Fire Dept., East Meadow, NY; co-host Tully Rinckey Legal Power Hour, Albany, NY, 2008; com. mem. Character and Fitness, 3rd Judicial Dist., Appellate Divsn., NY. Jag officer, capt. US Army, 1999—2004. Decorated Meritorious Svc. medal US Army. Office: Tully Rinckey PLLC 441 New Karner Rd Albany NY 12205 Office Fax: 518-218-0496. Business E-Mail: grinckey@tullylegal.com.

RINCON, FRED, neurologist, researcher; b. Barrancabermeja, Santander, Colombia, May 5, 1973; s. Saul Rincon and Rosalba Rodriquez; m. Erine A. Kupetsky, June 4, 2005. MD, U. Mil. Nueva Granada, Bogota, Colombia, 1996; MSc in Epidemiology, Colombia U., NYC, 2008. Cert. Ednl. Commn. Fgn. Med. Grads., 1996; United Coun. Neurol. Specialties, Neurocritical Care, 2008, lic. Colombian Nat. Inst. Health, 1996, State Bd. Med. Examiners NJ, 2004, Commonwealth Pa., 2005, U. State NY, 2005, diplomate Am. Bd. Psychiatry and Neurology, 2008. Lt., rev. Colombian Army Med. Corps., 1996—; rsch. scholar, vascular biology, dept. surgery U. Medicine and Dentistry NJ, Newark, 1998—2000, advanced trauma and cardiac life support instr., 1998—; advanced trauma life support instr. Harlem & Lincoln Med. Ctr., Bronx, NY, 2000—; resident internal medicine Cornell U., NYC, 2000—02, Lincoln Hosp., 2000—02; house staff rep. Lincoln Med. Ctr., 2000—02, mem, GME residency rev. com., 2001—02; resident neurology Neurol. Inst. NY, NYC, 2002—05, Columbia U. Med. Ctr., NYC, 2002—05, postdoc. fellow, neurocritical care and stroke, dept neurology, 2005—08; clin. asst. neurology NY Presbyn. Hosp., NYC, 2005—, cons. neurology, 2005—. Mem. editl. bd. U. Mil. Nueva Granada, 1993—94. Contbr. articles to profl. med. jours., scientific papers to numerous clin. publs. Physician social sci. Colombian Red Cross, Bogota, 1996—97, gen. practitioner, 1997—98. Spotrias, Tng. grant, NIH, Nat. Inst. Neurol. Disorders and Stroke, NY, 2006—08, Neuro-Epidemiology Tng. grant, 2007—08, fellowship, neurocritical care, Cooper U. Hosp., Robert Wood Med. Sch., Camden, NJ, 2008—. Mem.: AMA (Physician's Recognition award 2002, 2007), ACP, Am. Acad. Neurology, Neurol. Care Soc., Soc. Critical Care Medicine. Achievements include research in Cerebrovascular disease: acute brain resuscitation after ischemic stroke, management of the moribund patient with ischemic stroke and ICH, physiopathology of SAH and management of its complications; Neurocardiology: effects of cerebrovascular disease in cardiac rhythm, arrhythmogenesis, and outcomes; Interventions: multi-modality monitoring, therapeutic hypothermia, cardiac arrest, and resuscitation medicine. Avocations: sailing, carpentry, history of medicine. Office Phone: 212-305-7236. Office Fax: 212-305-2792. Personal E-mail: fr2034@gmail.com. Business E-Mail: doc@fredrincon.com.

RINE, JASPER, geneticist, educator; BS, SUNY Albany, 1975; PhD in molecular genetics, U. Oreg., 1979. Prof. genetics, genomics and devel. U. Calif., Berkeley, dir. Ctr. Computational Biology; prof. Howard Hughes Med. Inst., 2006—. Recipient Disting. Tchg. award, U. Calif. Berkeley, 1997. Fellow: Am. Acad. Arts and Sciences, Am. Soc. Miocrobiology; mem.: NAS, AAAS. Office: Rine Lab 176 Stanley Hall #3220 U Calif Berkeley Berkeley CA 94720-3220 Office Phone: 510-642-7047. Office Fax: 510-642-6420. E-mail: jrine@berkeley.edu.

RINE, ROSE MARIE, physical therapist, educator; b. Worcester, Mass., Jan. 17, 1951; d. Nicholas and Bienvenida DiPilato; m. Stephen Scott DiPilato, Feb. 3, 1974; children: Kristen, Anthony, Jonathan. BS, U. Conn., Storrs, 1973, MS, 1983; PhD, Northeastern U., Boston, 1990. Cert. Am. Phys. Therapy Assn., 1973. Lectr. Northeastern U., 1984—89; assoc. prof. U. Miami Sch. Medicine, Coral Gables, Fla.; rsch. prof. U. North Fla., Jacksonville, 2006—. Recipient Rsch. award, Sect. Pediat. APTA, 2002, Alumni Rsch. award, U. Conn. Coll. Allied Health, 2004. Office: Univ N Fla 1 UNF Dr Jacksonville FL 32224 Business E-Mail: r.m.rine@unf.edu.

RINEBOLD, ALICE JUNE, environmental scientist; b. Fostoria, Ohio, June 24, 1953; d. Rex Gene and Hilma Alice (Huff) Rinebold; 1 child, Nicholas Jeremy. AA, USAF C.C., 1982; BA in Psychology and Biol. Sci., U. No. Colo., 1983. Cert. Nat. Environ. Health Trainer NEHA, 2003, Administr. Profl. Excellence APEX, 2005. Vet. food insp. WAC, Ft. Carson, Colo., 1972—75; environ. health specialist Weld County Health Dept., Greeley, Colo., 1986—91; environ. specialist Environ. Health, City and County Denver, 1991—. Trainer Nat. Environ. Health Assn., Denver; environ. medicine tech. Master sgt. USAF Reserves, Colorado, ret., 1998. Recipient Outstanding Achievement Humanitarian award, USAF Caledonia, San Blas Islan. Mem.: Colo. Environ. Health Assn. (Honary award 1993), Nat. Environ. Health Assn. Achievements include being one of the first 5 women food inspectors in the US Army in 1972.

RINEER, CARLA MARY, literature and language professor; b. Lancaster, Pa., Aug. 22, 1950; d. Charles Elvin and Dorothy Mae Rineer; 1 child, Tara Rineer Ritter Poag. PhD, Temple U., Phila. Pa., 1998. Asst. prof. English Millersville U., 1990—. Recipient Dissertation Completion award, Temple U., 1997—98. Mem.: MLA. Home: 1437 Glen Moore Cir Lancaster PA 17601 Office: Millersville Univ George St Millersville PA 17551 Personal E-mail: carlarineer@yahoo.com. Business E-Mail: crineer@millersville.edu.

RINEHART, CHARLES R., savings and loan association executive; b. San Francisco, Jan. 31, 1947; s. Robert Eugene and Rita Mary Rinehart; married; children: Joseph B., Kimberly D., Michael P., Scott. BS, U. San Francisco, 1968. Exec. v.p. Fireman's Fund Ins. Cos., Novato, Calif., 1969-83; pres., CEO Avco Fin. Services, Irvine, Calif., 1983-89, H.F. Ahmanson & Co., Irwindale, Calif., 1989-93; chmn., CEO Home Savs. of Am., H.F.Ahmanson & Co., Irwindale, 1993—98; CEO Downey Savings and Loan Assn. F.A., Newport Beach, Calif., 2008—. Mem. Fannie Mae Nat. Adv. Coun., Thrift Instn. Adv. Coun., 1998-99; bd. dirs. Fed. Home Loan Bank San Francisco, 1995-2001, L.A. Bus. Advisors, Kaufman and Broad Home Corp., 1996-99, H.F. Abramson, 1993-98, Union Bank Calif., 2002-05, Pacificare, 2002-05, Ins. Co. America, 2007-, Verifone, 2007-, Mem. adv. com. Drug Use is Life Abuse; mem. Tustin Pub. Sch. Found. Camp com. Served to 2d lt. U.S. Army, 1968-69. Fellow Casualty Actuarial Soc.; mem. Am. Mgmt. Assn., Am. Acad. Actuaries. Republican. Roman Catholic. Avocations: athletics, gourmet cooking, model trains. Office: Downey Savings and Loan Assn FA 3501 Jamboree Rd Newport Beach CA 92660*

RINEHART, JAMES FORREST, political science professor, department chairman; b. Kansas City, Mo., Dec. 1, 1950; s. Kenneth Perry and Eleanor Louise (Lane) R.; m. Betty Keller, Feb. 3, 1973; children: Erica Christine, Andrew James. BA, U. Fla., Gainesville, 1972; M of Social Sci., Syracuse U., NY, 1991, PhD, 1993. Vis. prof. internat. rels. U. Tenn., Chattanooga, 1993-95; dir., prof. grad. program in internat. rels. U.S. Army John F. Kennedy Spl. Warfare Sch. Troy U., 1995—2001, lectr. regional studies program, 1996—2001; prof., chair dept. polit. sci. Troy U., Ala., 2001—, dir. grad. program in internat. rels., 2001—. Author: Revolution and the Millennium: China, Mexico and Iran, 1997, Apocalyptic Faith and Political Violence: Prophets of Terror, 2006; contbr. articles to profl. jours. Mem. Coun. on Peace Rsch. in History, 1992-94; active Program on Analysis and Resolution of Conflict, Syracuse U., 1991-93; bd. dirs. Ulster Project Chattanooga, 1993-94. Capt. USAR, 1972-80. Recipient Cert. of Achievement U.S. Army JFK Spl. Warfare Ctr. and Sch., 1996. Mem. Am. Polit. Sci. Assn., Internat. Studies Assn. (exec. cou. South 2002-05, treas. 2005—), Internat. Soc. Polit. Psychology, Am. Radio Relay League, Fla. Blue Key Soc., Phi Gamma Delta. Democrat. Presbyterian. Home: 201 Hampton Ave Troy AL 36081-4045

RINER, DEBORAH LILLIAN, mental health services professional; b. Brunswick, Ga., Mar. 20, 1960; d. Lee Calvin and Lillian Rosebell Jacobs. A in Allied Health, Calif. Coll. Health Sci., 2005. Cert. medical hypnotherapist, difficult & complex issues Omni Hypnosis Tng. Ctr., 2002, notary pub. Ga. Exec. sec. Greater Jax Christian Sch., Jacksonville, 1984—87; med. transcription coord. St. Vincent's Med. Ctr., Jacksonville, 1987—89; claims processor Allen Med. Claims Adminstrs., Ft. Valley, Ga., 1990—91; registration technician Houston Health Care Complex, Perry, Ga., 1991—92; med. asst. Peace Sun Med. Clinic, Khamis Mushayt, Saudi Arabia, 1993—95; owner and hypnotherapist Coastal Hypnosis Ctr., Brunswick, 2002—. Mem. Immediate Past Pres. Healthy Glynn.com, Brunswick; amb.,Ga. State lead ambassador CDI ACT Am. Cancer Soc., 2006—; bd. dir. YWCA, Golden Isles Children Advocacy, Rape Crisis Ctr. Mem.: Nat. Guild Hypnotists, Nat. Guild Hypnotists, Brunswick Golden Isles C. of C., Order Ea. Star. Mem. Ch. Of Christ. Avocations: genealogy, travel, antiques, Reiki. Office: Coastal Hypnosis Ctr 40 Carteret Ct Brunswick GA 31525 Home Phone: 912-267-6451; Office Phone: 912-261-8906. Business E-Mail: coastalhypnosis@aol.com.

RING, ALICE RUTH BISHOP, retired preventive medicine physician; b. Ft. Collins, Colo., Oct. 11, 1931; d. Ernest Otto and Mary Frances Bishop; m. Wallace Harold Ring, 1956 (div. 1969); children: Rebecca, Eric, Mark; m. Robert Charles Diefenbach, Sept. 10, 1977. BS, Colo. State U., 1953; MD, U. Colo., 1956; MPH, U. Calif., Berkeley, 1971. Diplomate Am. Bd. Preventive Medicine. Physician cons. Utah State Divsn. Health, Salt Lake City, 1960—65; med. dir., project head start Salt Lake City Cmty. Action Program, 1965—70; resident Utah State Divsn. Health, 1969—71; asst. assoc. regional health dir. USPHS, San Francisco, 1971—75, med. cons. Atlanta, 1975—77, dir. primary care, 1977—84; dir. divsn. diabetes control Ctrs. Disease Control, Atlanta, 1984—88; dir. WHO Collabor Ctr., Atlanta, 1986—91; dir. preventive medicine residency Ctrs. Disease Control, Atlanta, 1988—93; exec. dir. Am. Bd. Preventive Medicine, 1993—98. Trustee Am. Bd. Preventive Medicine, 1990—92; lectr. Emory U. Sch. Pub. Health, 1988—94; bd. dirs. Redwood Coast Med. Svcs., v.p., 1994—2004; mem. adv. com. Shamli Hospice, Gualala, Calif.; mem. adv. coun. Sonoma County Area Agy. on Aging, Santa Rosa, Calif., 2001—07, sec., 2004—06, v.p., 2006—07; bd. dirs. Alliance Rural Cmty. Health, Calif., 2002—04. Co-author: Clinical Diabetes, 1991; author: History of the American Board of Preventive Medicine, 2002. Bd. dirs. Diabetes Assn. Atlanta, 1985—90. Recipient Disting. Svc. award, Am. Bd. Med. Splties, 2004. Fellow: Am. Coll. Preventive Medicine (bd. dirs. 1990—94, Spl. Recognition award 1998); mem.: AMA (grad. med. edn. adv. com. 1993—97), Steering Com. Environ. Commons, Am. Bd. Med. Specialists (Disting. Svc. award 2004), Am. Acad. Pediat., Assn. Tchrs. Preventive Medicine. Office: PO Box 364 Gualala CA 95445-0364 Business E-Mail: ard@mcn.org.

RING, ALVIN MANUEL, pathologist, educator; s. Julius and Helen (Krolik) R.; m. Cynthia Joan Jacobson, Sept. 29, 1963; children—Jeffrey, Melinda, Heather. BS, Wayne State U., 1954; MD, U. Mich., 1958. Intern Mt. Carmel Hosp., Detroit, 1958-59; resident in pathology Michael Reese Hosp., Chgo., 1960-62; asst. pathologist Kings County Hosp., Bklyn., 1962-63; assoc. pathologist El Camino Hosp., Mountain View, Calif., 1963-65; chief pathologist, dir. labs. St. Elizabeth's Hosp., Chgo., 1965-72, Holy Cross Hosp., Chgo., 1972-87, Silver Cross Hosp., Joliet, Ill., 1990—. Instr. SUNY, 1962-63, Stanford U., 1963-65; asst. prof. pathology U. Ill., Chgo., 1966-69, assoc. prof., 1969-78, prof., 1978—; adj. clin. prof. No. Ill. U., 1981-87; adj. prof. med. edn. U. Ill. Coll. Medicine, 1988—; chmn. histotech. Nat. Accrediting Agy. for Clin. Lab Scis., 1977-81; mem. spl. adv. com. Health Manpower, 1966-71; pres. Spear Computer Users Group, 1981-82; mem. adv. com. Mid-Am. chpt. ARC, 1979-85; pres. Pathology and Lab Cons., Inc., 1985—; adj. prof., med. dir. Med. Tech., Moraine Valley C.C., 1994—; originator, coord. pathology, med. decision-making courses Nat. Ctr. for Advanced Med. Edn., 1981—, others; co-coord. computer courses Midwest Clin. Conf., 2000—. Author: Laboratory Correlation Manual, 1968, 82, 86, Laboratory Assistant Examination Review Book, 1971, Review Book in Pathology, Anatomic, 1986, Review Book in Pathology, Clinical, 1986; mem. editorial bd. Lab. Medicine, 1975-87; contbr. articles to med. jours. Fellow: Am. Soc. Clin. Pathology, Coll. Am. Pathology (insp. 1973—, ins. com. 2002—06, membership com. 2005—06, PathPac bd. dirs. 2007—, adv. com. on health care delivery, mem. House of Delegates 2007—); mem.: AMA, Assn. Brain Tumor Rsch. (cons.), Am. Assn. Blood Banks, Chgo. Pathol. Soc. (censor 1980—88, exec. com. 1985—89, program com. 1987—), Ill. Pathol. Soc. (trustee 1997—), Chgo. Med. Soc. (alt. councilor 1980—85), Ill. Med. Soc., Exec. Svc. Corps (exec. cons. 1988—), Phi Lambda Kappa (chpt. pres.). Home: 100 Graymoor Ln Olympia Fields IL 60461-1213 Office: Silver Cross Hosp 1200 Maple Rd Joliet IL 60432-1497

RING, BONNIE, psychologist, consultant, priest; b. NYC, Apr. 22, 1940; Attended, Vassar Coll., 1957—59; BA, NYU, 1962; EdM, Boston U., 1964, EdD, 1972. Lic. psychologist Calif., 1974. Tchg. fellow Boston U. Sch. Mgmt.; fellow Ctr. Applied Behavioral Scis., Boston U., 1963—65; tng. specialist Econ. & Youth Opportunities Program, LA, 1966; rsch. asst. UCLA, 1966—67; tng. assoc., coord. intern program U. Calif., Statewise Ext., 1967—68; counseling psychologist U. Calif., Santa Cruz, 1969—73, assoc. dir. clin. svcs. Irvine, 1973—75; assoc. dean Calif. Coll. Podiatr. Medicine, San Francisco, 1975—77; pres. Bonnie Ring, EdD, A Psychol. Corp., San Francisco, 1977—86, Coastside Resources, 2000—; mem. tng. staff Exec. Effectiveness Seminar Am. Mgmt. Assn., 1978—82; host daily psychol. call-in talk show Sta. KSFO, San Francisco, 1980—81; cons. AT & T, San Francisco, Pleasanton, Calif., 1982—86; psychologist pvt. practice, 1986—. Ordained Episcopal priest, 1992; dir. elder ministry St. Johns Episcopal Ch., Oakland, 2004—05. Mem.: Spiritual Dirs. Internat., Eye Movement Desensitization & Regroceesing Internat. Assn., Nat. Register Health Svc. Providers, Calif. Psychol. Assn., Am. Psychol. Assn., Pi Lambda Theta. Democrat. Office: 2305 Asbby Ave Berkeley CA 94705 Office Phone: 650-728-0555.

RING, CAMERON, Internet company executive; BS, MS, Stanford Univ. Co-founder, chief server engr. netElement, 1999—2001; co-founder, chief architect Plaxo Inc., Mountain View, Calif., 2001—. Named a President's Scholar, Stanford Univ. Office: Plaxo Inc 203 Ravendale Dr Mountain View CA 94043 Office Phone: 650-254-5400.

RING, GERALD J., real estate developer, insurance company executive; b. Madison, Wis., Oct. 6, 1928; s. John George and Mabel Sarah (Rau) R.; m. Armella Marie Dohm, Aug. 20, 1949; children: Michael J., James J., Joseph W. Student public schs., Madison. With Sub-Zero Freezer Co., Madison, 1948-70, mfr.'s rep., 1954-70; founder, chmn. bd. Parkwood Hills Corp., Madison, from 1965; founder, pres. Park Towne Devel. Corp., Madison, from 1969, Ring Devel. Co., 1992—. Bd. dirs. CUNA Mut. Ins. Soc., CUNA Mut. Ins. Group, CUNA Mut. Investment Corp., CUDIS Ins. Soc., all Madison, 1968-98, exec. com., 1973-83, chmn. bd., 1979-81; bd. dirs. CUMIS Ins. Soc., mem. exec. com., 1973-83, chmn. bd., 1977-79; bd. dirs. CMCI Corp., mem. exec. com., 1974-83, chmn. bd., 1981-83; treas. CUNADATA Corp., 1974-81; bd. dirs. Wis. Credit Union League, 1958-79, pres., 1965-67; mem. Wis. Credit Union Rev. Bd., 1967-83, chmn., 1973-76, 82-83; bd. dirs. CUNA Credit Union Nat. Assn., Inc., 1964-81, League Life Ins. Co., League Gen. Ins. Co., Southfield, Mich., CUNA Mut. Fin. Svcs. Corp., Century Ins. Co. Am., Waverly., Iowa. Chmn. Greater Madison C. of C., 1980, bd. dirs., 1976-89, v.p. econ. devel., 1983-85, v.p. govtl. affairs, 1985-89, mem. capital fund raising com., 1983—, chmn. 1983-86; mem. Mayor's Emergency Housing Com., 1984-85; chmn. fin. com. St. Patrick's Congregation, 1983-89; bd. dirs. Cath. Charities of Madison, 1995-2004, pres., 1996-99; bd. dirs. Future Madison Housing Fund, 1997—, pres, 2005—. Served with USMC, 1951-53, bd. dir., All Saints Retirement Ctr., 2004-. Mem. Aircraft Owners and Pilots Assn. Lodges: Rotary. (bd. dirs. 1981-83). Roman Catholic. Home: 607 Farwell Dr Madison WI 53704-6029 Office: 402 S Gammon Rd Madison WI 53719-1002

RING, JACK, systems engineer, educator; BSEE, Iowa State U., 1964, MSEE, 1966; PhD in Elec. Engring., Ariz. State U., 1971. Sys. engr. Gen. Electric, 1966—74, Fleet Analysis Ctr., 1971—84; prof. elec. engring. Calif. State U., Fullerton, 1977—; sys. engr. cons. Raytheon Naval and Marine Sys. Divsn., Fullerton, Naval Warfare Analysis Divsn., Corona, Calif., Naval Warfare Ctr., Dahlgren, Va., Rockwell Mission Analysis Unit, Anaheim, Calif., Rockwell STSD Simulation Lab., Downey, Calif., FORELL Enterprises, Buena Pk., 1984—. Contbr. scientific papers to numerous rsch. jours.; author: (textbook) The Engineering Design of Systems: Models and Methods, Computer Simulation of Continuous System, 2000, Simulation-Based Engineering of Complex Systems, 2001. Recipient Hughes Faculty Rsch. award, 1989—90. Fellow: IEEE (Orange County, Calif.) (sect. chair), Orange County Calif. Engring. Coun., Internat. Coun. Sys. Engring.; mem.: Mil. Ops. Rsch. Soc., Sys., Man, Cybernetics Soc. Office: Internat Coun Sys Engring 442 N Sage Ln Gilbert AZ 85234

RING, JAMES WALTER, physics professor; b. Worcester, NY, Feb. 24, 1929; s. Carlyle Conwell and Lois (Tooley) R.; m. Agnes Elizabeth Muir, July 18, 1959; 1 son, Andrew James. AB, Hamilton Coll., 1951; PhD (Root fellow), U. Rochester, 1958. Asst. prof. physics Hamilton Coll., Clinton, NY, 1957—62, assoc. prof., 1962—69, prof., 1969—75, Winslow prof., 1975—2003, chmn. dept. physics, 1968—80, 1987—88, 1991—92, radiation safety officer, 1964—84, engring. liaison officer, 1969—2002, prof. emeritus, 2003—. Attached physicist Atomic Energy Rsch. Establishment, Harwell, Eng., 1965-66; vis. physicist Phys. Chemistry Lab., Oxford (Eng.) U., 1973; vis. fellow Ctr. for Energy and Environ. Studies, Princeton U., 1981; vis. scientist Lab. for Heating and Air Conditioning, Danish Tech. U., Copenhagen, 1987. Contbr. articles to profl. jour. and books in physics, chemistry, solar energy, environ. sci., health physics, archaeology, and engring. Recipient prize Acad. Edn./Devel., 1980, medal for outstanding achievements in physics Hamilton Coll., 2005; NSF grantee, 1959-66; NSF sci. faculty fellow, 1965-66. Mem. AAUP (chpt. pres. 1987-92), Am. Phys. Soc., Am. Assn. Physics Tchrs., Phi Beta Kappa, Sigma Xi. Achievements include solar house design and testing; indoor air studies in radon dangers and thermal comfort; study of the use of solar energy by the Romans during the Roman Empire; analysis of experimental evidence for the validity of continuous spontaneous localization theory as an alternative to standard quantum mechanics; detection of Pb210 gamma radiation to establish geochronology for sediment core samples taken in antarctic peninsula bay and straits; to study global warming; planning to decrease Hamilton college's carbon footprint 40% by 2025 as a member of the sustainability committee. Avocations: reading, cross country skiing, landscape painting, visiting wine country, studying architecture. Office: 3926 Griffin Rd Clinton NY 13323 Home Phone: 315-853-8307; Office Phone: 315-859-4366, 315-859-4367. Business E-Mail: jring@hamilton.edu.

RING, JUDITH A., state librarian; BS in Elem. Edn., Edinboro Coll., Pa., BLS; MLS, Clarion U., Pa. Exec. dir. Erie County Libr. System, Pa.; dep. divsn. dir. Lee County Libr. System, interim libr. dir.; asst. divsn. dir. Divsn. Libr. and Info. Services, Tallahassee, 2001—03, state libr., 2003—. Mem. adv. com. Fla. Book Awards, 2007. Mem.: Chief Officers of State Libr. Agys., Fla. Libr. Assn. (mem. exec. bd. 2007—08). Office: Fla State Libr RA Gray Bldg 500 South Bronough St Tallahassee FL 32399-0250 Office Phone: 850-245-6600. Office Fax: 850-245-6735. Business E-Mail: jring@dos.state.fl.us.

RING, LEONARD M., lawyer, writer; b. Taurage, Lithuania, May 11, 1923; came to U.S., 1930, naturalized, 1930; s. Abe and Rose (Kahn) R.; m. Donna R. Cecrle, June 29, 1959; children: Robert Steven, Susan Ruth Student, N.Mex. Sch. Mines, 1943-44; LLB, DePaul U., 1949, JD; LLD (hon.), Suffolk U., 1990. Bar Ill. 1949. Spl. asst. atty. gen. State Ill., Chgo., 1967-72; spl. atty. Ill. Dept. Ins., Chgo., 1967-73; spl. trial atty. Met. San. Dist. Greater Chgo., 1967-77; lectr. civil trial, appellate practice, tort law Nat. Coll. Advocacy, San Francisco, 1971, 72; chmn. and spl. atty. com. jury instrns. Ill. Supreme Ct., 1967—. Nat. chmn. Attys. Congl. Campaign Trust, Washington, 1975-79. Author: (with Harold A. Baker) Jury Instructions and Forms of Verdict, 1972. Editorial bd. Belli Law Jour., 1983—; adv. bd. So. Ill. U. Law Jour., 1983—. Contbr. chpts. to books including Callaghan's Illinois Practice Guide, Personal Injury, 1988 and chpt. 6 (Jury Selection and Persuasion) for Masters of Trial Practice, also numerous articles to profl. jours. Trustee, Roscoe Pound-Am. Trial Lawyers Found., Washington, 1978-80; chmn. bd. trustees Avery Coonley Sch., Downers Grove, Ill., 1974-75. Served with U.S. Army, 1943-46 Decorated Purple Heart. Fellow Am. Coll. Trial Lawyers, Internat. Acad. Trial Lawyers, Internat. Soc. Barristers, Inner Circle Advs.; mem. Soc. Trial Lawyers, Am. Judicature Soc., Appellate Lawyers Assn. (pres. 1974-75), Assn. Trial Lawyers Assn. (nat. pres. 1973-74), Ill. Trial Lawyers Assn. (pres. 1966-68), Trial Lawyers for Pub. Justice (founder, pres. 1990-91), Chgo. Bar Assn. (bd. mgrs. 1971-73, 2d v.p. 1993), ABA (coun. 1983—, chair tort and ins. sect. 1989—, fed. jud. standing com. 7th cir. 1991—), Ill. Bar Assn., Kans. Bar Assn. (hon., life), Lex Legion Bar Assn. (pres. 1976-78), Met. Club, Plaza Club, Meadow Club, River Club, Monroe Club. Home: Ginger Creek 6 Royal Vale Dr Oak Brook IL 60523-1648 Office: Ill Supreme Ct PO Box 4987 Oak Brook IL 60522-4987

RING, LUCILE WILEY, lawyer; b. Kearney, Nebr., Jan. 2, 1920; d. Myrtie Mercer and Alice (Cowell) W.; m. John Robert Ring, Mar. 28, 1948; children: John Raymond, James Wiley, Thomas Eric. AB, U. Nebr., Kearney, 1944; JD, Washington U., 1946. Bar: Mo. 1946, U.S. Dist. Ct. (ea. dist.) Mo. 1947, U.S. Ct. Appeals (8th cir.) 1972. Atty.-adviser, chief legal group adjudications br. Army Fin. Ctr., St. Louis, 1946-52; exec. dir. lawyer referral svcs. St. Louis Bar, 1960-70; pvt. practice St. Louis, 1960-2000; staff law clk. U.S. Ct. Appeals (8th cir.), St. Louis, 1970-72; exec. dir. St. Louis Com. on Cts., 1972-85. Legal advisor Mo. State Anat. Bd., 1965-95; adj. prof. adminstrv. law Webster Coll., Webster Groves, Mo., 1977-78; mem. Mo. Profl. Liability Rev. Bd., State of Mo., 1977-79. Author, editor: Guide to Community Services - Who Do I Talk To, 1974, 75, 76-79, St. Louis Court Directories, 1972, 73, 74, 75, Felony Procedures in St. Louis Courts, 1975; author: Breaking Barriers: The St. Louis Legacy of Women in Law 1869-1969, 1996; author (series): Women Lawyers in St. Louis History, 1996, Women Breaking Barriers, 1998; contbr. articles to profl. jours. Mem. Mo. Mental Health Authority, 1964-65; bd. dirs., v.p. Drug and Substance Abuse Coun., met. St. Louis, 1976-83; adv. coun. St. Louis Agy. on Tng. and Employment, 1976-83; mem. Mayor's Jud. Reform Subcom., St. Louis, 1974-76. Recipient letter of commendation Office of Chief of Fin., US Army, 1952, Outstanding Alumni award, U. Nebr., Kearney, 1994, Disting. Alumni award, 2005; scholarship, Washington U. Sch. Law, 1944—46, 1st Mo. woman nominated for Mo. Ct. Appeals, St. Louis Dist., Mo. Appellate Commn., 1972, 1st woman nominated judgeship Mo. Non-Partisan Ct. Plan, 1972. Mem. Bar Assn. Met. St. Louis (v.p. 1975-76), Legal Svcs. Ea. Mo., Inc. (v.p. 1978-79, dir.), Legal Aid Soc. St. Louis City and County (bd. dirs. 1977-78), HUD Women and Housing Commn. (commr. 1975), Women's Bar Assn. (treas. St. Louis chpt. 1949-50), Mo. Assn. Women Lawyers (treas. 1959-60, pres. 1960-61), Washington U. Dental Faculty Wives (pres. 1972-74), Mortar Board, Pi Kappa Delta, Sigma Tau Delta. Methodist. Home and Office: 2041 Reservoir Loop Rd Selah WA 98942-9616 Home Phone: 509-697-7740.

RING, NANCY GAIL, artist, educator, writer; b. Irvington, NJ, Dec. 24, 1956; d. Frank and Dorothy (Kasoff) R. Student, Sch. of Mus. of Fine Arts, Boston, 1975-76; BFA, Syracuse U., 1978. Food history columnist, feature food article contbr. N.J. Star Ledger, Newark, 1998—2004; art educator Far Brook Sch., NJ, 2004—. Muralist pvt. commns., 2000—. Author (and illustrator): Walking on Walnuts, 1996; exhibitions include Iandor Fine Art Gallery, Newark, 2005, New Door Creative Gallery, Balt., 2005. Recipient Drawing award Barbara Chase Burke, 1978; fellow Mid-Atlantic Arts Found., 1988, N.Y. Found. for Arts, 1987, Montalvo Ctr. for Arts, 1987. Avocations: baking, cooking, exercise, travel, reading.

RING, RENEE ETHELINE, lawyer; b. Frankfurt, Germany, May 29, 1950; arrived in U.S., 1950; d. Vincent Martin and Etheline Bergetta (Schoolmeesters) Ring; m. Paul J. Zofnass, June 24, 1982; children: Jessica Renee, Rebecca Anne. BA magna cum laude, Catholic U. Am., 1972; JD, U. Va., 1976. Bar: NY 1977. Assoc. Whitman & Ransom, NYC, 1976-83, Carro, Spanbock, Fass, Geller, Kaster & Cuiffo, NYC, 1983-86, ptnr., 1986, Finley Kumble Wagner et. al., NYC, 1987; of counsel Kaye, Scholer, Fierman, Hays & Handler, NYC, 1988; ptnr. Kaye, Scholer, Fierman, Hays & Handler, LLP, NYC, 1989-97, Hunton & Williams, NYC, 1997—2002, McKee Nelson LLP, NYC, 2006—. Trustee The Spence Sch., 2001—02; advisor WestWind Found., 2001—; mem. exec. com. Lawyers for Clinton, Washington, 1991—92; team capt. Clinton Transition Team, Washington, 1992—93; mem. Nat. Lawyers Coun. Dem. Nat. Com., 1993—98; trustee The Clinton Legal Expense Trust, 1998—2002, Pound Ridge Land Conservancy, 2003—, v.p., 2006—; mem. alumni coun. U. Va. Sch. of Law, 1997—2005, 2d v.p., 2000—01, 1st v.p., 2001—03, pres., 2003—05. Mem.: ABA, Women's Campaign Forum (mem. bd. dirs. 2009—), Queens Bot. Garden Soc. (trustee 2003—08, mem. exec. coun. 2004—08, vice chmn. 2007—). Democrat. Roman Catholic. Office Phone: 917-777-4527.

RING, TIMOTHY MICHAEL, pharmaceutical executive; b. Buffalo, Sept. 30, 1957; s. Roger Michael and Leone Ann (Reitmeier) R.; m. Kathryn L. Gleason; 4 Children. BS in Indsl. Labor Relations, Cornell Univ., 1979. Coll. grad. in tng. GM, Detroit, 1979-80, labor relations rep., 1980, salaried personnel rep., 1980-81, sr. salaried personnel rep., 1981-82, sr. labor relations rep., 1982-83; div. personnel mgr. Abbott Labs., North Chicago, Ill., 1983-84, regional personnel mgr., 1984-86, dir. personnel Pacific, Asian and African ters., 1986-87, dir. personnel Pacific, Asian, African and European ters., 1987—92; corp. v.p., human resources CR Bard Inc., NJ, 1992—93, group v.p.-internat., 1993—97, group pres.-coronary vascular products, 1997—99, group pres.-electrophysiology, peripheral vascular products, 1999—2003, chmn, CEO, 2003—. Mem. Delta Upsilon. Republican. Roman Catholic. Avocations: real estate investments, tennis, golf, sailing. Office: CR Bard 730 Central Ave Murray Hill NJ 07974 Office Phone: 908-277-8000.*

RING, W(ILLIAM) STEVES, thoracic and cardiovascular surgeon; b. Patterson, NJ, Aug. 12, 1945; s. William Steves and Nancy J. (Gettings) R.; m. Denise B. Passmore, 1969; children: William Steves III, Ashley Brinton. BA, Brown U., 1967, MMS, 1969; MD, Harvard U., 1971. Diplomate Am. Bd. Surgery, 2001, Am. Bd. Thoracic Surgery, 2004; cert. Nat. Bd. Med. Examiners, 1972, Tex. State Bd. Med. Examiners. Intern, then resident in surgery, fellow Duke U., Durham, NC, 1971-73, 75-77, resident in surgery, fellow, 1977-82; instr. surgery U. Minn., Mpls., 1983-85, asst. prof., 1985-87, dir. cardiac transplantation, 1984-87; prof., chmn. divsn. thoracic surgery U. Tex. Southwestern Med. Ctr., Dallas, 1988—2000, Frank M. Ryburn, Jr. disting. chair cardiothoracic surgery, 1989—, chmn. dept. cardiovascular thoracic surgery, 2000—; chief thoracic and cardiovascular surgery Parkland Meml. Hosp., Dallas, 1988—, Zale Lipshy Univ. Hosp., Dallas, 1988—; dir. cardiac transplantation St. Paul Med. Ctr., Dallas, 1988—. William D. Seybold lectr. in surgery U. Tex. Southwestern Med. Ctr., 1988, presenter, president's lecture series, 2007. Mem. editl. bd. Clin. Transplantation; contbr. articles to profl. jours. Mem. exec. com. Dallas affiliate Am. Heart Assn., 1988—, pres., 1992-93; mem. exec. com. S.W. Organ Bank, 1988—. Maj. USAF, 1973-75. Recipient Nat. Rsch. Svc. award NIH, 1978 79, Gladys Faschena award Dallas affiliate Am. Heart Assn., 1990. Fellow ACS, Am. Coll. Cardiology, Am. Coll. Chest Physicians; mem. Am. Soc. Transplant Surgeons (mem. membership com. 1991—), Internat. Soc. Heart and Lung Transplantation, Am. Assn. Thoracic Surgery, Transplant Soc, World Soc. Pediatric and Congenital Heart Surgery, Southern Thoracic Surg. Assn. (councilor 2004, Kent Trinkle edn. lectr. 2002) Home: 3501 Euclid Ave Dallas TX 75205-3213 Office: U Tex Southwestern Med Ctr 5323 Harry Hines Blvd Dallas TX 75390-7208

RINGEL, DEAN, lawyer; b. NYC, Dec. 12, 1947; m. Ronnie Sussman, Aug. 24, 1969; children: Marion, Alicia. BA, Columbia Coll., 1967; JD, Yale U., 1971. Bar: NY 1972, US Ct. Appeals (6th cir.) 1972, US Ct. Appeals (2d and DC cirs.) 1974, US Supreme Ct. 1976, US Ct. Appeals (10th cir.) 1982, US Ct. Appeals (11th cir.) 1997, US Ct. Appeals (9th cir.) 2000. Law clk. to Judge Anthony J. Celebrezze U.S. Ct. Appeals (6th cir.), 1971—72; assoc. Cahill Gordon & Reindel, NYC, 1972—79; ptnr. Cahill, Gordon & Reindel LLP, NYC, 1979—. Pres. def. coun. sect. Media Law Resource Ctr., 2008, pres. emeritus, 2009—. Mem.: ABA (vice chmn. com. on freedom of speech and press 1978—79), Pub. Edn. Assn. (trustee, sec. 1997—2000, trustee CEI-PEA 2000—), Assn. Bar City NY (commn. comm., fed. litigation, antitrust and trade regulation), NY State Bar (chmn. antitrust litigation com., sect. comml. and fed. litigation 1994—96, co-chmn. fed. judiciary com. 1997—2001, co-chair newsgathering com. Media Law Resource Ctr. 2001—05). Office: Cahill Gordon & Reindel LLP 80 Pine St 17th Fl New York NY 10005-1790 Office Phone: 212-701-3521.

RINGEL, FAYE JOYCE, retired literature educator; b. Norwich, Conn., Aug. 17, 1951; d. Harold L. and Toube Marilyn (Barsky) Ringel; m. E. Paul Hazel, 1990 (div. 1993). AB in Comparative Lit. summa cum laude, Brandeis U., Waltham, Mass., 1972; PhD in Comparative Lit., Brown U., Providence, 1979. Instr. English Ea. Conn. State U., Willimantic, Conn., 1981—84, Three Rivers C.C., Norwich, Conn., 1981—85; prof. English dept. humanities USCG Acad., New London, Conn., 1985—2009; cons. USCGA Alumni Assn., 2009—. Author: New England's Gothic Literature, 1995; singer, pianist: CD recording Hot Chestnuts, 2002. Founding pres. Norwich Arts Coun., 1987; bd. mem. Norwich chpt. Hadassah, 1998—, Beth Jacob Synagogue, Norwich, 1999—2008, pres., 2004—06. Recipient Hand of Healing award, Conn. Region Hadassah, 2006, Disting. Faculty award, Coast Guard Acad. Alumni Assn., 2006, Disting. Career Svc. award, Dept. Homeland Security, 2009. Mem.: Nat. Coun. Tchrs. English, Internat. Assn. for the Fantastic in the Arts, NE Popular Culture Assn. (area chair 1999—2009), Internat. Gothic Assn. (editl. bd. mem. 1996—), New Eng. Assn. Tchrs. English (exec. bd., sec. 1994—, Charles Swain Thomas award 2005), Phi Beta Kappa. Jewish. Avocations: vocal and instrumental music, theater. Home: 6 Taylor Dr Norwich CT 06360

RINGEL, JUDY G., writer; b. Cleve., Aug. 31, 1940; d. Leo and Ernestine F. Greenberger; m. Neil E. Ringel, June 30, 1960; children: Elizabeth Ringel Saslawsky, James M., Jonathan L. Student, Goucher Coll., 1958—60; BA magna cum laude, Cast Western Res. U., 1962. Assoc. editor Memphis Mag., 1982—86, sr. editor, 1986—91, assoc. pub., 1991—92; freelance writer Memphis, 1992—. Author: Children of Israel, 2004 (cert. of commendation Am. Assn. State and Local History, 2005); contbr. numerous articles to mags. Chmn. bd. dirs. Memphis Planned Parenthood, Memphis, 1995—97; pres. Jewish Fedn. Women's Divsn., Memphis, 1976—77. Mem.: Memphis Jewish Hist. Soc., West Tenn. Hist. Soc., Am. Assn. for State and Local History, Phi Beta Kappa. Avocations: golf, gardening, jogging, reading.

RINGEL, STEVEN PETER, neurology educator; b. Hamilton, Ohio, Feb. 17, 1943; s. Edward and Hedy (Fried) R.; m. Joan Deutsch, May 29, 1969; children: Andrew, Timothy. MD, U. Mich., 1968. Diplomate Am. Bd. Neurology and Psychiatry. Intern in medicine Rush Presbyn. St. Luke's Hosp., Chgo., 1968-69, resident in neurology, 1969-72; rsch. fellow NIH, NINDS, Bethesda, Md., 1974-76; from asst. to prof. U. Colo., Denver, 1976—. Vis. prof. U. Padua, Italy, 1983; dir. Office of Clin. Practice, U. Hosp., Denver, 1994—2005, v.p., Qualdy U. Colo. Hosp. Author 4 books; contbr. over 300 articles to profl. jours. Maj. U.S. Army Med. Corps, 1972-74. Robert Wood Johnson Health Policy fellow U.S. Senate, 1991-92; resident scholar Inst. Medicine, 1991-92; recipient Postdoctoral Rsch. fellowship NIH, 1974-76, Rsch. fellowship NATO, 1982-84. Mem. Am. Acad. Neurology (treas. 1989-91, pres. 1997—). Office: Univ Colo 12631 E 17th Ave B-185 Aurora CO 80045

RINGENBERG, WILLIAM CAREY, historian, minister; b. Ft. Wayne, Ind., Aug. 18, 1939; s. Loyal Robert and Rhoda (Roth) R.; m. Rebecca Helen Lehman, Aug. 18, 1962; children: Matthew, Mark, Peter, Melodie. BS, Taylor U., 1961; MA, Ind. U., 1964; PhD, Mich. State U., 1970. Ordained to ministry Evang. Mennonite Ch., 1979. From asst. prof. to prof. history Taylor U., Upland, Ind., 1968—, assoc. dean acad. affairs, 1974-79, chmn. dept. history, 1982—2008, dir. honors program, 1983—98; min. Bailey Chapel United Meth. Ch., Anderson, Ind., 1979-80, Mt. Carmel United Meth. Ch., Hartford City, Ind., 1980-85, Cammack United Meth. Ch., Hartford City, Ind., 1985-89. V.p. Conf. on Faith and History, 1987-88, pres., 1989-90. Author: Taylor University: The First 125 Years, 1973, Taylor University: The First 150 Years, 1996, The Christian College: A History of Protestant Higher Education in America, 1984, 2006, The Business of Mutual Aid: Seventy-five Years of the Brotherhood Mutual Insurance Company, 1993, Letters to Young Scholars: An Introduction to Christian Thought, 2003; mem. editorial bd. Christian Scholar's Rev., 1970-74; contbr. articles and revs. to hist. & religious publs. Lilly fellow Ind. U., 1962-63; scholar Inst. for Advanced Christian Studies, 1981; Lilly Endowment Rsch grant, 2005-06; Rsch fellow Ctr. Study Religion & Am. Culture. Mem. Am. Soc. Ch. History, Conf. Faith & History, Chi Alpha Omega. Mennonite/Methodist. Office: Taylor U Dept History Reade Ave Upland IN 46989 *What you are is more important than what you do. Wisdom is of greater value than knowledge, character than craft, love and kindness than control.*

RINGER, DARRELL WAYNE (DAN), lawyer; b. Elizabeth, NJ, Apr. 14, 1948; s. Darrell Wayne and Elva (Brown) R.; m. Rebecca Ruth Bonner, Feb. 23, 1979; children: Daniel Benjamin, Darren Wayne. BS in Physics, W.Va. U., 1971; MBA, U. N.D., 1975; JD, W.Va. U., 1978. Bar: W.Va. 1978, U.S. Dist. Ct. (no. and so. dists.) W.Va. 1978. Assoc. Jones, Williams, West & Jones, Clarksburg, W.Va., 1978-80, Moreland & Ringer, Morgantown, W.Va., 1980-83, Reeder, Shuman, Ringer & Wiley, Morgantown, 1983-91, Ringer Law Offices, Morgantown, 1991—. 1st asst. prosecutor Monongalia County, W.Va., 1985-87; host W.Va. Pub. TV, PBS Pub. Affairs Programming, 1991—. Bd. dirs. Monongalia County (W.Va.) Mental Health Assn., Morgantown, 1981-83; mem. W.Va. U. Animal Care and Use Com., 1985-2003. Capt. USAF, 1971-75. Named W.Va. Bar Found. Lawyer Citizen of Yr., 1996. Fellow W.Va. Bar Found.; mem. ABA (named Sole Practitioner of Yr., 2000), ATLA, W.Va. State Bar (pres. 1999-2000), Monongalia County Bar Assn. (sec. 1980-92, pres. 2001), W.Va. Trial Lawyers Assn. (bd. govs. 1982-91, Pres.'s award 2001). Democrat. Avocation: amateur radio. Office: 823 Fairmont Rd Morgantown WV 26501-3812 Home Phone: 304-296-1718; Office Phone: 304-292-1999. Business E-Mail: dringer@ringerlaw.com.

RINGER, JOHN WILLIAM, lawyer; b. Dexter, Mo., July 18, 1936; s. John Lee and Helen (Boyd) R.; m. Carolyn Irvin, July 18, 1954 (div. 1967); 1 child, Lisa Denise; m. Debra Lou Calhoun, Dec. 4, 1976 (div. 2001); 1 stepchild, Lora Brooke Cecil; 1 child, James M. BA, William Jewell Coll., 1958; JD, U. Mo., 1960. Bar: Mo. 1960, U.S. Dist. Ct. (ea. dist.) Mo. 1964, U.S. Tax Ct. 1974. Assoc. Powell, Ringer & Bischof, and predecessors, Dexter, 1960-63, ptnr., 1963-79, sr. ptnr., 1979-86; assoc. judge juvenile and criminal divsn. Mo. 35th Jud. Cir., Mo., 1986-87; ptnr. Powell, Ringer, Bischof & Rogers, Dexter, 1987-97; pvt. practice, Dexter, 1998—; sr. judge Mo., 1999—; state and fed. mediator Mo., 2004—. Bd. dirs. Regional Healthcare Found., gen. counsel, 1999—. Contbr. to and revising editor Mo. Law Rev. Pres. Dexter Meml. Hosp., 1964-89; campaign dir. Stoddard County March of Dimes, 1960-64, campaign treas., 1964-67; co-chmn. Cmty. Betterment Com., 1971-73; pres., bd. dirs. Bapt. Ch., 1968-77, music dir., 1960-80, gen. counsel, 1960—, by laws com., 2006—; chmn. John Wesley White Areawide Evang. Crusade, 1986; tchr. Sunda Sch., 1981—. Mem. ABA, Nat. Health Lawyers Assn., Mo. State Bar (health and hosp. law com. 1992—), Mo. Bar Assn., Stoddard County Bar Assn., Mo. Soc. Hosp. Attys. (bd. dirs. 1992-97), Mo. Hosp. Assn. (Excellence in Govt. award 1995), Dexter C. of C. (past bd. dirs., Cmty. Leadership award 1964), Kiwanis (past pres.), Mo. Bar Fee Dispute Resolution Mediator, Mo. Bar Lawyer-to-Lawyer Dispute Resolution (mediator 2008-), Mo. Bar Approved Mediator Democrat. Baptist. Avocations: yard work, model airplanes and trains, boating, computing. Home: 405 N Walnut PO Box 337 Dexter MO 63841-0337 Office: 21 Vine St PO Box 337 Dexter MO 63841-0337 Office Phone: 573-624-4567. E-mail: jwringerlaw@yahoo.com.

RINGGOLD, FAITH, artist; b. NYC, Oct. 8, 1930; BS, CCNY, 1955, MA, 1959; DFA (hon.), Moore Coll. Art, Phila., 1986, Coll. Wooster, Ohio, 1987, Mass. Coll. Art, Boston, 1991, CCNY of CUNY, 1991, RI Sch. Design, 1994, Russell Sage Coll., NY, 1996, Parsons Sch. Design, 1996, Marymount Coll., 1999, Mary Grove Coll., 2000, William Patterson U., 2001, Chgo. Art Inst., 2001, Bloomfield Coll., 2005; DSc (hon.), Brockport State U., NY, 1992, Calif. Coll. Arts and Crafts, Oakland, 1993; DHL (hon.), Malloy Coll., 1997, Bank St. Coll., 1999, William Patterson U., 2001, St. Joseph Coll., 2004; DEd (hon.), Wheelock Coll., 1997. Art tchr. NY Pub. Schs., 1955-73; lectr. Bank St. Coll. Grad. Sch., NYC, 1970-80; prof. art U. Calif., San Diego, 1984—2002, prof. emeritus, 2002—, ret., 2002. Solo exhbns. include Bernice Steinbaum Gallery, 1991, ACA, 2000, Spectrum Gallery, NYC, 1967, 70 10 year retrospective, Studio Mus. in Harlem, NYC, 1984, Bernice Steinbaum Gallerym NYC, 1987-88, Balt. Mus., Deland Mus., Fla., Faith Ringgold 25 Yr. Survey Fine Arts Mus. LI, Hempstead, 1990-93, Textile Mus., Washington, 1993, Children's Mus. of Manhattan, NYC, 1993-95, Hewlett-Woodmere Pub. Libr., Hewlett, NY, 1993-94, St. Louis Art Mus., 1994, Athenaeum, La Jolla, Calif., 1995, A.C.A. Gallery, NYC, 1995, 98, Ind. U. of Pa., 1995, Bowling Green State U., Ind., 1996, New Mus. Contemporary Art, NYC, 1998; exhibited in group shows at Harlem Cultural Coun., NYC, 1966, Meml. Exhibit for MLK, Mus. Modern Art NYC, 1968, Chase Manhattan Bank Collection, Martha Jackson Gallery, NYC, 1970, Am. Women Artists, Gedok, Kunstalle, Hamburg, Ger., 1972, Jubliee, Boston Mus. Fine Arts, 1975, Major Contemporary Women Artists, Suzanne Gross Gallery, Phila., 1984, Committed to Print Mus. Modern Art, NYC, 1988, The Art of Black Am. in Japan, Terada Warehouse, Tokyo, Made in the USA, Art in the 50s and 60s U. Calif. Berkeley Art Mus., Craft Today Poetry of the Physical, Am. Craft Mus., NYC, Portraits and Homage to Mothers Hecksher Mus. Huntington, 1987, NJ State Mus., Trenton, 1992-94, Fukui Fine Art Mus., Fuki, Japan, 1992, Takushima Modern Art Mus., Japan, 1993, Otani Meml. Art Mus., Japan, 1993, Salina Art Atr., Kans., 1993, Bruce Watkins Ctr. Kansas City, Mo., 1993, Barton County CC, Great Bend, Kans., 1993, Del. State Coll. Arts Ctr. Gallery, Dover, 1993-94, Roswell Mus. and Art Ctr., N.Mex., 1994, Aknaton Gallery, Cairo, Alexandria, Egypt, Exit Art, NYC, 1994, New Mus. Contemporary Art, NYC, 1996, Spellman Coll. Mus., Atlanta, 1996, Whitney Mus., NYC, 1996, Centre Georges Pompidou, Paris, 1997, Mus. Art, Ft. Lauderdale, Fla., 1997, NJ Ctr. Arts, Summit, NJ, 1997, Trout Gallery Dickenson Coll., Carlisle, Pa., numerous others; represented in collections at Chase Manhattan Bank, NYC, Philip Morris Collection, NYC, Children's Mus., Bklyn., Newark Mus., The Women's House of Detention, Rikers Island, NY, The Studio Mus., NYC, High Mus., Atlanta, Guggenheim Mus., Met. Mus. Art, Boston Mus. Fine Arts, MOMA, AARP, Washington, Am. Craft Mus., NYC, Clark Mus., Williamstown, Mass., ARCO Chem., Phila., Coca-Cola, Atlanta, Ft. Wayne Mus. Fine Art, Ind., Harold Washington Libr. Ctr., Chgo., Lang Comm. Corp., Coll., Phila. Mus. Art, Pub. Art Pub. Schs., P.S. 22, Bklyn., Spenser Mus. Lawr., Kans., St. Louis Mus. Art, Balt. Mus., Nat. Mus., Washington, Woman's Mus., Washington, Eugenio Maria de Hostos CC, NYC, MTA 125th St. IRT subway sta. installation, NYC, numerous others; author: Tar Beach, 1991, Aunt Harriet's Underground Railroad in the Sky, 1992 (Picture Book award 1993, Best Children's Book of Yr. 1993), Dinner at Aunt Connie's House, 1993 (Reading Magic award 1993), We Flew Over the Bridge: Memoirs of Faith Ringgold, 1995, Talking to Faith Ringgold, 1995, Bonjour Lonnie, 1996, My Dream of Martin Luther King, Jr., 1996, The Invisible Princess, 1999, If a Bus Could Talk: The Story of Rosa Parks, 1999, Counting to Tar Beach, 1999, Cassie's Colorful Day with Daddy, 1999, Cassie's Word Quilt, 2000, O Holy Night, 2004, Three Witches, 2006; author: (video prodn.) Goodnight Moon: and Other Sleepy Time Tales, Tar Beach, 2000; contbr. articles to profl. jours. Recipient AAUW travel award to Africa, 1976; John Simon Guggenheim Meml. Found. Fellowship (painting), 1987, NY Found. for Arts award (painting), 1988, Nat. Endowment Arts award (sculpture), 1978, (painting) 1989, La Napoule Found. award (painting in So. of France), 1990, Video and Software award Calif. children's book, 1991, Parent's Choice Gold award, 1991, Artist award Studio Mus., Harlem, 1991, Artist of Yr. award Sch. Art League NY, 1991, Coretta Scott King award for illustration, 1992, Dist. Artist award Nat. Coun. Art Adminstrs., 1992, award, 1993, Arts Internat. award (travel to Morocco), 1992, Honors award for outstanding achievement in the visual arts Woman's Caucus Arts, NY, 1994, Towsend Harris medal City Coll. Alumni Assn., 1995, NJ Artist of Yr. award NJ Ctr. Visual Arts, 1997, 31st NAACP Image award, 1999, Visionary Woman award, Moore Coll. Art & Design, 2005. Home: PO Box 429 Englewood NJ 07631-0429 Office: ACA Galleries 529 W 20th St Fl 5 New York NY 10011-2800 Office Phone: 858-576-0397. Business E-Mail: ringgoldfaith@aol.com.

RINGKAMP, STEPHEN H., lawyer, educator; b. St. Louis, Nov. 14, 1949; s. Aloysius G. and Melba Ann (Finke) Ringkamp; m. Patricia Sue Fuse, July 5, 1971; children: Christa, Angela, Laura, Stephen M., Kara. BSEE, St. Louis U., 1971, JD cum laude, 1974. Bar: Mo. 1974, U.S. Dist. Ct. (ea. dist.) Mo. 1974, U.S. Ct. Appeals (8th cir.) 1974, U.S. Supreme Ct. 1990. Law clk. 22d Jud. Cir. Mo., St. Louis, 1974-75; mng. prin. The Hullverson Law Firm, St. Louis, 1976—. Chmn., mem. com. on civil instrns. Mo. Supreme Ct., 1981—; adj. prof. law St. Louis U., 1983—1997; mem. faculty Mo. Jud. Coll., 1993-2008; lectr. legal seminars. Contbr. articles to legal jours. Recipient Trial Lawyer award Mo. Bar Found. 1983, Smithson award for Excellence, 1996. Mem. ABA, ATLA, Mo. Bar Assn. (vice chmn. civil practice com. 1983-84), Mo. Assn. Trial Attys. (pres. 1991), Bar Assn. Met. St. Louis, Lawyers Assn. St. Louis. Office: The Hullverson Law Firm 1010 Market St Ste 1480 Saint Louis MO 63101-2026 Home Phone: 314-849-3403; Office Phone: 314-421-2313. E-mail: sringkamp@hullverson.com.

RINGLE, BRETT ADELBERT, lawyer, oil and gas industry executive, trustee; b. Berkeley, Calif., Mar. 17, 1951; s. Forrest A. and Elizabeth V. (Darnall) R.; m. Sue Kinslow, May 26, 1973. BA, U. Tex., 1973, JD, 1976. Bar: Tex. 1976, US Dist. Ct. (no. dist.) Tex. 1976, US Supreme Ct. 1980, US Ct. Appeals (5th cir.) 1984. Ptnr. Shank, Irwin & Conant, Dallas, 1976-86, Jones, Day, Reavis & Pogue, Dallas, 1986-96; v.p. Hunt Petroleum Corp., Dallas, 1996—2008; trustee Margaret Hunt Trust Estate, 2008—. Adj. prof. law So. Meth. U., Dallas, 1983. Author: (with J.W. Moore and H.I. Bendix) Moore's Federal Practice, 2d edit., Vol. 12, 1980, Vol. 13, 1981, (with J.W. Moore) Vol. 1A, 1982, Vol. 1A Part 2, 1989. Mem. Dallas Bar Assn. Home: 3514 Gillon Ave Dallas TX 75205-3220 Office: Margaret Hunt Trust Estate Ste 4900 1601 Elm St Dallas TX 75201 Office Phone: 214-922-1004. Business E-Mail: bringle@hh-services.com.

RINGLE, PHILIP HAMILTON, JR., retired lawyer; b. Portland, Oreg., Mar. 23, 1931; s. Philip Hamilton and Audrey Louise (Smallhouse) R.; children: James B., Sara Louise; m Marva Fabien, June 8, 2000. BA, Willamette U., 1953, JD, 1956. Bar: Oreg. 1957, US Dist Ct. (9th cir.), 1958 Oreg. Assoc. Green, Richardson, Green & Griswold, Portland, Oreg., 1958-63, Hibbard, Jacobs, Caldwell & Kincart, Oregon City, Oreg., 1963-65, Misko, Njust & Ringle, Oregon City, 1965-67; ptnr. Ringle & Herndon, Gladstone, Oreg., 1968-76; pres. Ringle, Herndon & Beck, P.C., Gladstone, Oreg., 1976-85, Ringle & Herndon, P.C., 1985-86; sole practice, Gladstone, 1986-98, Oregon City, 1999—2008,; Mcpl. ct. judge City of Gladstone, 1965—; ptnr. Ringle & Son Tree Farms, 1986-. Chmn. Nat. Caterpillar Show, Brooks, Oreg., 2006. Contbr. articles to profl. jours. Named Caterpillar 2006 Man of Yr. Mem. ABA, Oreg. Trial Lawyers Assn., Oreg. State Bar Assn., Clackamas County Bar Assn., Multnomah Bar Assn., Oreg. Mcpl. Judges Assn. (pres. 1975-77), Schnee Vögeli Ski (Portland) (pres. 1960-61), Elks, Rotary, Oregon City Club (pres. 1970-71), Oreg. Old Time Fiddlers Assn., Pacific N.W. Christmas Tree Assn. Co-editor: Oregon Special Court Bench Book, 1978. Democrat. Presbyterian (elder). Office: PO Box 307 Aurora OR 97002

RINGLEE, ROBERT JAMES, retired consulting engineering executive; b. Sacramento, Apr. 23, 1926; s. Francis and Marie N. R.; m. Helen Laura Carleton, Aug. 27, 1949; children— Sarah N., Jane C., Robert K. BSEE, U. Wash., Seattle, 1946, MSEE, 1948; PhD in Mechanics, Rensselaer Poly. Inst., Troy, NY, 1964. With advanced engring. program Gen. Electric Co., 1948-51, advanced devel. engr., power transformer dept., 1951-55, supr. power transformer design, 1955-60, sr. analytical engr., 1960-65, mgr. system and equipment reliability, 1965-69; prin. engr. dir. Power Technologies, Inc., Schenectady, 1969-86, prin cons., 1986-93; TAG assoc. Power Techs., Inc., 1993-94, assoc. cons., 1994-98. Contbr. articles to profl. publs.; patentee in field. Active Schalmont Bd. Edn., 1966—70, pres., 1968—69; environ. adv. coun. NYISO, 2004—; sec. Friends of the Pine Bush Cmty. Inc., 2005—. With USNR, 1944—46. Recipient Managerial award Gen. Electric Co., 1953 Fellow IEEE (3 prize paper awards), AAAS; mem. Internat. Conf. on High Voltage Power Systems (expert advisor, Attwood Assoc.), Adirondack Mountain Club (pres. 1990-93, acting exec. dir. 1994). Democrat. Unitarian Universalist. Home and Office: 315 Juniper Dr Schenectady NY 12306-1705

RINGLER, JAMES M., computer services company executive; b. 1945; BS, U. Buffalo, 1967, MBA, 1968. Mgr., cons. Arthur Andersen & Co., 1968-76; v.p. appliance group Tappan Co., Mansfield, Ohio, 1976-78, gen. v.p., mgr. appliance div., 1978-87, pres., COO, 1987-90, also bd. dirs., 1987-90; exec. v.p. Premark Internat., Inc., Deerfield, Ill., 1990-92, pres., COO, 1992-96, pres., CEO, 1996—99, chmn., 1997—99; vice chmn. Ill. Tool Works, Inc., Glenview, 1999—2004; interim CEO NCR Corp., Dayton, Ohio, 2005, chmn., 2005—07, Teradata Corp., Miamisburg, Ohio, 2007—. Bd. dir. Union Carbide Corp., 1996—2001, Dow Chemical Co., 2001—, Corn Products Internat., 2001—, FMC Tech., 2001—, Autoliv Lic., 2002—, NCR Corp., 2003—07, JBT, 2008—. Bd. mem. Lyric Opera Chgo.; trustee Boys & Girls Club of No. Am., Midwest region. Office: Teradata Corp 2835 Miami Village Dr Miamisburg OH 45342

RINGLESBACH, DOROTHY LOUISE, retired nurse, writer; b. Ft. Wayne, Ind., Aug. 14, 1925; d. Paul Frederich and Elizabeth Barbara Preusser; m. Robert J. Salisbury, 1946 (div.); children: David, Claudia Ann, Evelyn, Claude, Jane; m. John C. Ringlesbach, July 5, 1980 (dec. Sept. 27, 2008). RN, Wishard Meml. Hosp., 1947. RN Ind., Ky., Va. RN staff Mary Chiles Hosp., Mt. Sterling, Ky., 1958—60; interperter Colonial Williamsburg, Williamsburg, Va., 1968—73; house supr. Williamsburg Cmty. Hosp., Williamsburg, Va., 1973—80, 1985—93; ret. Author: OSS Stories that can Now Be Told, 2005; contbr. articles pub. to profl. jour. Mem. US Cadet Nurse Corps., 1944—47; state pres. Aux. to Kymedical Assn., Louisville, 1965—66, rec. sec., 1962—65. Cadet nurse corps, 1944—47. Mem.: Women in Military Service for America, OSS Carpet Bagger, OSS Com. Vets, OSS Soc. Luth. Avocations: reading, raise orchids, travel, writing. Home: 303 Farmville Ln Williamsburg VA 23188-1006 Office Phone: 757-564-8299. Personal E-mail: esp22693@widomaker.com.

RINGWALD, MOLLY, actress; b. Sacramento, Feb. 18, 1968; d. Bob and Adele Ringwald; m. Valery Lameignère, July 28, 1999 (div. Nov. 2002); m. Panio Gianopoulos; children: Mathilda Ereni, Adele Georgiana, Roman Stylianos. Grad. high sch., Los Angeles. Actress: (stage prodns.) The Glass Harp, 1973, Annie, 1977, Cabaret, 2001, Enchanted April, 2004, When Harry Met Sally, 2004, Sweet Charity, 2006;(feature films) Tempest, 1982, Spacehunter: Adventures in the Forbidden Zone, 1983, Sixteen Candles, 1984, The Breakfast Club, 1985, Pretty in Pink, 1986, The Pick-Up Artist, 1987, For Keeps, 1988, Betsy's Wedding, 1990, Seven Sunday, 1994, Office Killer, 1996, Kimberly, 1999, Requiem For Murder, 1999, Teaching Mrs. Tingle, 1999, Cut, 2000, In the Weeds, 2000, Ring of Fire, 2000, Not Another Teen Movie, 2001, The Tulse Luper Suitcases: The Moab Story, 2003; (TV movies) Packin' It In, 1983, P.K. and the Kid, Something to Live For: The Alison Gertz Story, 1992, Twice Upon a Time, 1998, Since You've Been Gone, 1998, The Big Time, 2002, The Wives He Forgot, 2006, Molly: An American Girl on the Home Front, 2006; (TV mini-series) The Stand, 1994; regular (TV series) The Facts of Life, 1979-80, Townies, 1996, The Secret Life of the American Teenager, 2008-; guest-star: (TV shows) Diff'rent Strokes, The Merv Griffin Show; (Album) Molly Sings, 1974. Office: ABC Family 500 S Buena Vista St Burbank CA 91521-6078*

RINI, JOEL, language educator, linguist; b. Cleve., Dec. 4, 1957; s. Joseph Charles and Virginia Ann Rini; m. Pamela Jean De Vries; children: Christopher Michael, Marcus Joel. BS in Edn., Kent State U., 1981; PhD, U. Mich., 1987. Asst. prof. Spanish linguistics U. Va., Charlottesville, 1987—93, assoc. prof. Spanish linguistics, 1993—2000, prof. Spanish linguistics, 2000—, chmn. Spanish, Italian and Portuguese, 1998—2004. Author: (books) Motives for Linguistic Change in the Formation of the Spanish Object Pronouns, 1992, Exploring the Role of Morphology in the Evolution of Spanish, 1999; contbr. articles to profl. jours. Home: 1039 Hayrake Ln Charlottesville VA 22903 Office: Univ Virginia 115 Wilson Hall Charlottesville VA 22904 Personal E-mail: jrini@adelphia.net. E-mail: jr6b@virginia.edu.

RINK, THOMAS, nuclear medicine physician; b. Hanau, Hessen, Germany, May 20, 1963; s. Karl-Heinz and Gisela (Goebel) R. MD, U. Frankfurt, 1989. Physician in-tng. Nuc. Medicine Mcpl. Hosp., Hanau, affiliated to Johann-Wolfgang-Goethe-U., Frankfurt/Main, 1989—90; asst. physician Nuc. Medicine Mcpl. Hosp., Wiesbaden affiliated to Johannes-Gutenberg-U., Mainz, 1991—93; asst. physician surgery St. Vinzenz Hosp., Hanau, 1993—94; asst. physician nuc. medicine U. Frankfurt, 1995—96; chief dept. nuc. medicine Mcpl. Hosp., Hanau affiliated to Johann-Wolfgang-Goethe-U., Frankfurt/Main, 1996—. Contbr. articles to profl. jours. Mem. Soc. of Nuc. Medicine, European Assn. of Nuc. Medicine, Rotary Internat. Home: Röntgenstr 36 63454 Hanau Germany Office: Mcpl Hosp Dept Nuclear Med Leimenstr 20 D-63450 Hanau Germany Office Fax: 01149-6181-23368. Business E-Mail: rink@em.uni-frankfurt.de.

RINKER, CHARLES F., II, surgeon; b. Washington, Aug. 29, 1945; s. Royden Carrington and Elsie Margaret (Kilroy) R.; m. Katherine Ann Bogenreif, Oct. 10, 1982; children: Neil, Brian, Lindsay, Charles. AB, Hamilton Coll., Clinton, NY, 1967; MD, Case Western Res. U. Sch. Medicine, Cleveland, 1971. Diplomate Am. Bd. Surgery. Gen. surgeon Bozeman Deaconess Hosp., Bozeman, Mont., 1976—2008. Vice-chairman ACS Com. Trauma, Chgo., 1994—98; mem. Govs. Trauma Care Com., Helena, Mont., 1996—2001; adv. coun. gen. surgery ACS, 2000—05, chair, rural subcom., adv. coun. gen. surgery, 2003—05. Co-prodr. (documentary film) Trauma Care in Montana, 1994. Trustee Intermountain Opera, Bozeman, 1985-89, Mus. of the Rockies, Bozeman, 1987-93, Polit. Economy Rsch. Ctr., Bozeman, 1988-94. Recipient Meritorious Svc. award, ACS Com. Trauma, 1993; fellowship, Southwestern Surg. Congress, Am. Assn. Surgery Trauma, 1997. Fellow: ACS (pres. Mont-Wyo. chpt. 1987—88, gov. at large Mont. 1992—, vice-chair com. on trauma 1994—98, chair regional com. on trauma 1994—98, advisory coun. gen. surgery 1999—, Trauma Achievement award 1993), Southwestern Surg. Congress. Avocations: golf, running, fishing, skiing, hunting.

RINKER, CRAIG WAYNE, minister, educator; b. Phila., Aug. 9, 1945; s. Berl Leroy and Maxene Betsy (Abshier) R.; m. Kathlyn Louise Waugh, Dec. 19, 1970 (div.); children: Sheri Lou, Amy Kathlyn, Craig Wayne II; m. Bonita Lee Dupre, Feb. 16, 1991 (div.); m. T. Gaynell Pierce, May 20, 2005 AA, St. Johns Coll., Winfield, Kans., 1965; BA in Philosophy, Concordia Sr. Coll., 1967; M of Divinity, Concordia Sem., 1971; MST, Luth. Sch. of Theology, 1975; PhD, U. Okla., Norman, 1979. Ordained pastor Luth. Ch., 1972. Pastoral asst. Luth. Ch. of Our Savior, Bethany, 1972-75; assoc. pastor Good Shepherd Luth. Ch., Hayward, Calif., 1975-78; pastor Grace Luth. Ch., Houma, La., 1978—92, Zion Luth. Ch., New Orleans, 2007—; asst. pastor First English Luth. Ch., New Orleans, 1993—95, interim sr. pastor, 1997—2002; spl. edn. tchr. Jefferson Parish Sch. Bd., 1992—94; assoc. prof. Concordia U. Wis.- New Orleans Ctr., 1993—2006. Vicar supr. Concordia Theol. Sem., Fort Wayne, Ind., 1981—82, Fort Wayne, 2001—02; distance educator leading to ordination mentor Concordia Sem., St. Louis, 1998—. Contbr. articles to profl. jours. Mem. bd. commrs. Terrebonne Gen. Hosp., Houma, La., 1986—92. Mem. So. States Speech Communication Assn. (sect. chmn. conv. Baton Rouge, 1984, Birmingham 1990, panelist New Orleans 1988), Speech Communication Assn., Terrebonne Assn. Mins. (officer 1978-92), Rotary (bd. dirs. 1980-06). Republican. Lutheran. Avocations: bowling, reading. Office: Zion Luth Ch 1924 St Charles New Orleans LA 70130 Office Phone: 504-524-1025. Personal E-mail: rinkercw@aol.com.

RINO, BARBARA ELIZABETH, musician, educator; b. Lincoln, Nebr., Jan. 14, 1945; d. Howard Gillette and Elizabeth Lucille Cook; m. Louis Stanislaus Rino, Dec. 22, 1974 (dec. Aug. 31, 2004); 1 child, John Gaspare. MusB (with distinction), Nebr. Wesleyan U., Lincoln, 1966; violin study, Harold Wippler, Denver, Colo., 1974—77. Lic. tchr. Colo., 1967. Violinist Lincoln Symphony Orch., Lincoln, Nebr., 1962—66; music educator Denver Pub. Sch., Denver, 1966—68; orch. dir. Adams County Sch. Dist. 50, Westminster, Colo., 1969—78, Adams County Sch. Dist. 12 Five Star Schs., Thornton, Colo., 1988—2001; pvt. studio tchr. self employed, Westminster, Colo., 1971—; concertmaster Brico Symphony Orch., Denver, 1972—74; dir. orch. Denver Youth Musicians Inc., 1973—77, 1984—89; free lance violinist Denver Musicians Assn., Denver, 1973—95; orch. clinician, adj. Solo and Group Competitions Youth Orch. Chair Auditions, Colo., 1973—; concertmaster Rocky Mountain Chamber Orch., 1985—87. Conductor: Colo. Music Educators State Conf., 1972, 1975; musician: Disneyland and Universal Studios, Kennedy Arts Ctr., 1976, Expo '86; author (curriculum): Dist. Orch. grades 6-12, 1990. Music activities Westminister United Meth. Ch., Colo., 1980—2005. Recipient Outstanding Alumni award, Nebr. Wesleyan U. Dept. Music, 2006. Mem.: Music Tchrs. Nat. Assn., Am. String Tchrs. Assn. (Colo. Outstanding Tchr. of the Yr. 2003), Music Educators Nat. Conf., Phi Kappa Phi, Kappa Delta Pi. Meth.

RINSCH, MARYANN ELIZABETH, occupational therapist; b. LA, Aug. 8, 1939; d. Harry William and Thora Analine (Langlie) Hitchcock; m. Charles Emil Rinsch, June 18, 1964; children: Christopher, Daniel, Carl. BS, U. Minn., 1961. Registered occupational therapist Calif., lic. Calif., 2003. Staff occupl. therapist Hastings State Hosp., Minn., 1961-62, Neuropsychiat. Inst., LA, 1962-64; staff and sr. occupl. therapist Calif. Children's Svcs., LA, 1964-66, head occupl. therapist, 1966-68; rschr. A. Jean Ayres, U. So. Calif., LA, 1968-69; pvt. practice neurodevel. and sensory integraton Tarzana, Calif., 1969-74; pediat. occupl. therapist neurodevel. & sensory integration St. Johns Hosp., Santa Monica, Calif., 1991-95; pvt. practice, cons. Santa Monica-Malibu Unified Sch. Dist., 1994-2001; pvt. practice, 2001—. Mem. alliance bd. Natural History Mus., LA County, 1983-2009; cub scouts den mother Boy Souts Am., Sherman Oaks, Calif., 1986-88, advancement chair Boy Scout Troop 474, 1989-92; mem. Vol. League San Fernando Valley, Van Nuys, Calif., 1985-93; trustee Viewpoint Sch., Calabasas, Calif., 1987-90; bd. dirs. Valley Women's Ctr., 1990-91. Mem. Am. Occupl. Therapy Assn., Calif. Occupl. Therapy Assn. Home: 430 S Oakhurst Dr Beverly Hills CA 90212 Personal E-mail: merinsch@yahoo.com.

RINSKY, JUDITH SUE LYNN, foundation administrator, consultant, educator; b. Sept. 12, 1941; d. Allan A. and Sophie (Schwartz) Lynn; m. Joel C. Rinsky, Jan. 29, 1963; children: Heidi Mae Schnapp, Heather Star Maxon, Jason Wayne. BA in Home Econs., Montclair State U., 1963. Tchr. home econs. Florence Ave. Sch., Irvington, NJ, 1963—66; substitute tchr. Millburn-Short Hills Sch. Sys., Millburn Twp., NJ, 1978—82, Milburn-Short Hills Sch. Sys., Milburn Twp., 1990—98; sr. citizen coord. Millburn-Short Hills Sch. Sys., Millburn Twp., 1982—87; coord. respite care Essex County Divsn. on Aging, East Orange, NJ, 1988—90; pvt. practice educator Short Hills, NJ, 1990—98; tchr. basic skills Millburn H.S., 1998—. Bd. mem. adv. com. gerontology Seton Hall U., 1984—90; coord. Mayor's Adv. Bd. Sr. Citizens, Millburn-Short Hills, 1982—87; home instrn. Millburn-Short Hills Sch. Sys., 1997—98; tchr. adv. Millburn H.S. Interart Club, 2000—; cons. Gerontology Life Mgmt. Resources, LLC, 2008—; caregiver family adv. Elder Care Cons. Pres. Deerfield Sch. PTA, 1979-80, Millburn H.S. PTA, 1983-85; co-chmn. dinner dance Charles T. King Student Loan Fund, 1981; active Handicapped Access Study Com., 1983-85; bd. dirs. Coun. on Health and Human Svcs., 1985-90, 94-97; acting dir. B'nai Israel Nursery Sch., 1994. Mem. Lake Naomi Assn. (chmn. sailing com. 1981), N.J. Home Econs. Assn., Am. Home Econs. Assn., Rotary (hon., pres. Millburn-Short Hills club 1992-93, bd. dirs. 1992-2000, advisor Millburn interact club 1987-98, 2000-04, chmn. internat. interact dist. 7470 1993-95, advisor 1995-98). Home and Office: 87 Sullivan Dr West Orange NJ 07052-2262 Home Phone: 973-669-8687; Office Phone: 973-376-3600. Personal E-mail: jsr_07041@yahoo.com. Business E-Mail: rinsky@millburn.org.

RIOFRIO, JOSÉ ANTONIO, electronics engineer; b. Lima, Peru, June 19, 1981; s. Javier Arturo and Margot Riofrio. BS, Elizabethtown Coll., Pa., 2003; MS, Vanderbilt U., Nashville, 2005, PhD, 2008. Rsch. asst. Vanderbilt U., 2003—08; mechatronics engr. Enfield Techs., Trumbull, Conn., 2008—. Contbr. articles to profl. publs.

RIOJAS, JOSE DAVID, federal agency administrator, career military officer; b. 1954; BA, US Mil. Acad., West Point, 1976; grad., US Army War Coll., 1997. Second lt. Field Artillery US Army, 1976, advanced through grades to brig. gen.; polit. and mil. affairs officer Arms Control and Disarmament Agency US Dept. State; chief Army requirements US Dept. Defense, rep. Joint Requirements Oversight Panel, Joint Requirements Oversight Coun., exec. officer to chief of staff of US Army; asst. divsn. comdr. 3rd Infantry Divsn. US Army, Fort Stewart, Ga., condr. Joint Task Force North (JTF-N) Fort Bliss, Tex., 2004—06; v.p. strategic initiatives U. Tex., El Paso, 2006—09, exec. dir. Ctr. for Defense Sys. Rsch., dir. Ctr. of Excellence for Border Security and Immigration, US Dept. Homeland Security, 2008—09; asst. sec. ops., security & preparedness US Dept. Veterans Affairs, Washington, 2009—. Sr. asst. prof. mil. sci. Bowling Green State U., Ohio; project mgr. Extending the Littoral Battlespace, Advanced Concepts Tech. Demonstration; mem. adv. com. Border Biomedical Rsch. Ctr.; bd. dirs. El Paso Regional Econ. Devel. Corp.; mem. Tex. Gov.'s Emerging Tech. Fund Adv. Com. Office: US Dept Veterans Affairs 810 Vermont Ave NW Washington DC 20420*

RIOLA, PATRICIA ANNE, computer engineer, educator; BA, Bloomsburg U., Pa., 1982; MS in Info. Sys., DeSales U., Ctr. Valley, Pa., 1995; PhD in Bus. Admnstrn. And Applied Computer Sci., Northcentral U., Prescott, Ariz., 2003. Cert. CCNA CISCO, Pa., 2000, CCAI CISCO,

Pa., 2002, MCSE Microsoft, Pa., 2000. Sr. sys. analyst Ingersoll-Rand Corp., Bethlehem, Pa., 1990—97; prof. Lehigh Carbon C.C., Schnecksville, Pa., 1997—. Info. tech. Mack Trucks, Inc., Allentown, Pa., 1987—90. Contbr. scientific papers. Mem.: ACM, IEEE, Phi Theta Kappa. Office: Lehigh Carbon Cmty Coll 4525 Education Park Dr Schnecksville PA 18078

RIORDAN, CORNELIUS, sociology educator, writer, consultant; b. Worcester, Mass., May 29, 1940; s. Cornelius H. and Mary J. Riordan; m. Arline K. Riordan; children: Julie, Kate. BS in Edn., Fitchburg U., Mass., 1962; MA in Sociology, Clark U., 1970; PhD in Sociology, Syracuse U., NY, 1975. Prof. sociology Providence Coll., 1972—; postdoctoral fellow The Johns Hopkins U., Balt., 1979-81. Cons. Childreach, USA, Warwick, R.I., 1993-2002, Regional Lab. at Brown U., Providence, 1997-98, NSF, 2000-02; expert witness cases involving single-sex schooling, 1989-2000; project dir. U.S. Dept. Edn. funded study on single-sex Pub. Schs: Perceptions and characteristics,2004—08, internat. spkr. Single Sex Schs. Author: Girls and Boys in School: Together or Separate, 1990, Equality and Achievement, 2d edit., 2004; contbr. articles to profl. jours. Vol. U.S. Peace Corps, Kerman, Iran, 1963-65; dir. Encampment for Citizenship, N.Y.C., 1965-69. Mem. Am. Sociol. Assn. (coun. 1990-92), Am. Ednl. Rsch. Assn. (grantee 1992-93, 2000-2002). Office: Dept Sociology Providence Coll River & Eaton Sts Providence RI 02918 Business E-Mail: criordan@providence.edu.

RIORDAN, MICHAEL C., hospital administrator; b. NJ, 1959; BA in Liberal Arts and English, Columbia U., 1980, MA in Edn. and Psychology, 1981; M in Health Sys., Ga. Inst. Tech., 1986. Various positions Crawford Long Hosp., Atlanta; COO, sr. assoc. adminstr. Emory U. Hosp. Sys., Atlanta, 1995—2000; exec. v.p. and COO U. Chgo. Hospitals, 2000—01, pres. and CEO, 2001—06; pres., CEO Greenville Hosp. Sys., 2006—. With USMC, 1981—85. Office: Greenville Hosp Sys 701 Grove Rd Greenville SC 29605*

RIORDAN, SEAN PATRICK JOSEP, lawyer, educator; b. Amityville, NY, Jan. 17, 1978; s. John Michael and Anne Veronica (Saunders) Riordan; m. Elizabeth Abrahams, Jan. 25, 1980; children: Jackson Patrick, Isabella Sydney. BA summa cum laude, Molloy Coll., 2000; JD, St. John's U., Jamaica, NY, 2004. Bar: NY 2005. Law clk. Brecher Fishman Pasternack Popish Heller Rubin & Reif, Bklyn., 2003—04; atty. Brecher Fishman Pasternack Popish Heller Reif & Walsh, Garden City, 2004—06. Intern Hillary Clinton for US Senate, NYC, 1999—2000. With USAR, 1999—2000. Mem.: ABA, ATLA, Brehon Law Soc., NY Count Lawyers Assn., NY State Bar Assn., Friendly Sons of St. Patrick. Liberal. Roman Catholic. Avocations: running, baseball, basketball, kayaking, football. Office: Brecher Fishman Pasternack Popish Heller 1325 Franklin Ave Ste 250 Garden City NY 11530 Office Fax: 516-742-3994. Personal E-mail: spjriordan@aol.com. Business E-Mail: seanr@brecherfishman.com.

RIORDAN, THOMAS J., manufacturing executive; BS, Northwestern Univ.; MS, Purdue Univ. Mgmt. positions Borg-Warner Automotive, J.I. Case; pres. Consolidated Sawmill Machinery Internat.; mgmt. positions through exec. v.p., COO SPX Corp., 1997—2006; pres., COO TEREX Corp., Westport, Conn., 2007—. Office: TEREX Corp 500 Post Rd E Westport CT 06880

RIOS, ALEXIS ISRAEL, professional baseball player; b. Coffee, Ala., Feb. 18, 1981; Outfielder Toronto Blue Jays, Canada, 2004—09, Chgo. White Sox, 2009—. Mem. Puerto Rican nat. team World Baseball Classic, 2006, 09. Named to Am. League All-Star Team, Maj. League Baseball, 2006, 2007. Office: Chgo White Sox 333 W 35th St Chicago IL 60616*

RIOS, EVELYN DEERWESTER, columnist, musician, artist, writer; b. Payne, Ohio, June 25, 1916; d. Jay Russell and Flossie Edith (Fell) Deerwester; m. Edwin Tietjen Rios, Sept. 19, 1942 (dec. Feb. 1987); children: Jane Evelyn, Linda Sue Rios Stahlman. BA with honors, San Jose State U., 1964, MA, 1968. Cert. elem., secondary tchr. Calif. Lectr. in music San Jose (Calif.) State U., 1969-75; from bilingual cons. to assoc. editor Ednl. Factors, Inc., San Jose, 1969-76, mgr. field rsch., 1977-78; writer, editor Calif. MediCorps Program, 1978-85; contbg. editor, illustrator Cmty. Family Mag., Wimberly, Tex., 1983-85; columnist The Springer, Dripping Springs, Tex., 1985-90. Author, illustrator, health instr. textbooks elem. schs., 1980—82. Author: The Best of It Seems To Me, 2002. Chmn. Dripping Springs Planning and Zoning Commn., 1991—93; music dir. Cambrian Park (Calif.) Meth. Ch., 1961—64; choir dir. Bethel Luth. Ch., Cupertino, Calif., 1965—66, 1968—83; dir. music St. Aban's Ch., Bogota, Colombia; organist Holy Spirit Episcopal Ch., Dripping Springs, 1987—94. Mem.: Am. Guild Organists (dean 1963—64), Phi Kappa Phi (pres. San Jose chpt. 1973—74). Avocations: weaving, stitching, painting. Home: PO Box 3175 Atascadero CA 93423-3175

RIOS, MARJORIE EVANS, language educator; b. Ft. Bragg, NC, Feb. 21, 1941; d. Giles Lincoln Evans and Claudine Margaret Smelser; m. Eliseo Rios, Sept. 17, 1965; children: Rocio Rebecca, Malcolm Alexander. AB, Gettysburg Coll., Pa., 1963; EdS, Tenn. Technol. U., Cookeville; MEd, U. Fla., Gainesville. Cert. tchr. Tenn. HS Spanish tchr. Livingston Acad., Tenn., 1985—2006; adj. Spanish prof. Tenn. Tech. U., Cookeville, 2006—. With Tenn. Ed. Assn., Nashville, 1974—. Deacon, choir mem. First Presbyn. Ch., Cookeville, 1972—. Mem.: Phi Delta Kappa (past pres.). Office: Tenn Technol Univ Cookeville TN 38505

RIOS, ROSA GUMATAOTAO, federal agency administrator; b. 1966; d. Guadalupe Rios; m. Joe Gumataotao; children: Joey, Brooke. BA in Sociology and Romance Languages & Lit., Harvard U., 1987. Comml. property underwriter Gen. Reinsurance Corp., San Francisco; mgr. Union City Redevelopment Agy., Calif.; devel. specialist City of San Leandro, Calif.; dir. econ. devel. City of Fremont, Calif., 1997—2001; dir. redevelopment and econ. devel. City of Oakland, Calif., 2001—03; prin. Red River Assocs., 2003—06; mng. dir. investments MacFarlane Ptnrs., 2006—09; US treas. US Dept. Treasury, Washington, 2009—. Mem. Treasury/Fed. Res. Transition Team for Obama Adminstrn., 2008; trustee Alameda County Employees' Retirement Assn.; bd. mem. Calif. Assn. Local Econ. Devel., Fruitvale Spanish-Speaking Unity Coun., Toigo Found. Fellow: Royal Soc. Arts. Office: US Dept Treasury 1500 Pennsylvania Ave NW Washington DC 20220 Office Phone: 202-622-2000.*

RIOTTO, JOSEPH, finance educator; m. Jeannine Riotto; children: Raffaella, Giancarlo, Lucia. DBA, Nova Southeastern U., Fla. CPA NJ. Assoc. prof. NJ City U., Jersey City, 2002—. Office: NJ City Univ 2039 John F Kennedy Blvd Jersey City NJ 07305 Business E-Mail: jriotto@njcu.edu.

RIOUX, PIERRE AUGUST, psychiatrist; b. Hartford, Conn., Sept. 2, 1953; s. Berchmans and Mary (Sauter) R. BA, Concordia Coll., 1975; MD, U. N.D., 1981. Diplomate Am. Bd. Psychiatry and Neurology. Intern U. Mich., 1981-82, resident, 1982-85; asst. prof. dept. psychiatry Emory U., Atlanta, 1985-86; attending physician VA Med. Ctr., Atlanta, 1985-86; staff physician UniMed Med. Ctr., Minot, ND, 1986-87, med. dir. adult partial hospitalization program, 1988-98, dir. behavioral health svcs., 1990—2001; med. dir. North Ctrl. Human Svc. Ctr., Minot, 1987-98; med. dir. stress unit Austin Med. Ctr., 2001—; med. dir. behavioral health Mayo Health Sys., Austin, 2003—06, med. dir. dept. psychiatry and psychology, 2006—; instr. Mayo Med. Sch., 2003—. Cons. North Ctrl. Human Svc. Ctr., 1986—2001; mem. chem. dependency unit UniMed Med. Ctr, 1986—; mem. adv. bd. UniMed Med. Ctr., 1998—2001; clin. prof. neurosci. U. N.D. Sch. Medicine, 1986—96; mem. family practice residence adv. bd. com. U. N.D., 1987—95; physician advisor N.D. Health Care Rev., Inc., 1987—2001; dir. psychiat. svcs. Dakota Boys Ranch, Minot, 1990—94; med. dir. Rural Mental Health Consortium, 1999—2001; instr. Mayo Med. Sch., 2003—. Bd. Am. Coll. of Heraldry, 2003; comsumer rsch. coun. America's Top Psychiatrists, 2002—. Recipient Nat. Alliance for the Mentally Ill Exemplary Psychiatrist award, 1993, Top Psychiatrists in Am. award Consumers Rsch. Coun. Am., 2003. Fellow Am. Coll. Forensic Examiners (life); mem. AMA, Am. Psychiat. Assn. (pres. N.D. dist. br. 1993-96, dep. rep. area IV coun. 1993-98, mem. psychiat. svcs. achievement awards bd. 1996-97, chmn. 1998, fellowship award 1996, disting. fellowship award 2003), Assn. Am. Physicians and Surgeons, Am. Soc. Clin. Psychopharmacology, N.D. Psychiat. Assn. (dist. br. exec. coun. 1997-2001), N.D. Med. Assn. (mem. commn. on socio-econ. affairs 1997-2001), Internat. Soc. for Philos. Enquiry (pres.2002-05) Avocation: art. Office: PO Box 188 Austin MN 55912-0188

RIPA, KELLY MARIA, television personality, actress; b. Stratford, NJ, Oct. 2, 1970; d. Joseph and Esther Ripa; m. Mark Consuelos, 1996; children: Michael Joseph, Lola Grace, Joaquin Antonio. Student, Camden CC, NJ. Co-host Live with Regis and Kelly, NY, 2001—. Spokesperson Electrolux kitchen appliances, 2008. Dancer (TV series) Dance Party USA, 1986; actor: (TV series) All My Children, 1990—2002 (Soap Opera Digest award, 1996, 1998, 2000, 3 Daytime Emmy nominations); (films) Marvin's Room, 1996, The Stand-In, 1999 (Best Actress award N.Y. Internat. Ind. Film and Video Festival, 1999), It's a Very Merry Muppet Christmas Movie, 2002; voice: Kim Possible: A Stitch in Time, 2003; actor: Cheaper by the Dozen, 2003, (voice) Fly Me to the Moon, 2008, Delgo, 2008,: (TV films) Someone to Love, 2001; voice: (films) Batman: Mystery of the Batwoman, 2003; actor: (TV series) Hope & Faith, 2003—. Named one of 25 Most Intriguing People, People Mag., 2001, Top 20 Entertainers of Yr., E! Entertainment, The 50 Most Powerful Women in NYC, NY Post, 2008; nominee Outstanding Talkshow Host award, Daytime Emmy. Office: Live with Regis and Kelly 7 Lincoln Sq New York NY 10023

RIPERT, ERIC FRANK, chef; b. Antibes, France, Mar. 2, 1965; arrived in US, 1989; m. Sandra Ripert. Grad., Culinary Sch., Perpignan, France, 1982. Apprentice La Tour D'Argent, Paris; with Jamin; sous chef Watergate Hotel, Washington, 1989—91, Bouley, NYC; exec. chef Le Bernardin, NYC, 1991—94, chef., 1994—, co-owner; culinary dir. West End, Washington, 2007—, 10 Aets, Phila., 2008—. Chair City Harvest's Food Coun. Co-author (with Maguy Le Coze): Le Bernardin Cookbook: A Return to Simplicity, 1998; author: A Return to Cooking, 2002, On The Line, 2008. Recipient Top Chef in NYC award James Beard Found., 2003, 2008 Am.'s Top Restaurants award for Le Bernardin, Zagat Survey. Achievements include awarded 3 stars by Michelin Guide. Avocations: travel, skiing. Office: Le Bernardin 787 7th Ave New York NY 10019 Office Phone: 212-554-1515.*

RIPERT, JEAN-MAURICE, ambassador; b. June 22, 1953; married; 1 child. Grad., Inst. Polit. Studies, Paris, 1973, Nat. Sch. Adminstrn., 1980. With legal affairs divsn. French Ministry Fgn. Affairs, 1980—82, with econ. and fin. affairs divsn., 1982—83, tech. advisor, mem. staff of the min. for cooperation and devel., 1983—84, tech. advisor, mem. staff of the min. for European affairs, 1984, tech. advisor, mem. staff of the min., 1984, 2nd counselor Washington, 1986—88, tech. advisor, mem. staff of the prime min., 1988—90, diplomatic advisor to prime min., 1991, chief of staff to sec. state for humanitarian action, 1991—92, advisor to min. health and humanitarian action, 1992—93, consul gen. LA, 1993—96, dep. dir. UN and Internat. Orgns. desk, 1996—97, diplomatic advisor to prime min., 1997—2000, amb. to Greece, 2000—03, dir. UN and Internat. Orgns. desk, 2003—05, amb., permanent rep. to UN Geneva, 2005—07, NYC, 2007—. Office: French Mission to UN 245 E 47th St New York NY 10017 Office Phone: 212-308-5700. Office Fax: 212-355-2763.

RIPKA, JUDITH, jewelry designer; b. NY; m. Ronald J. Berk. Studied design, Parson's Sch. Design. Owner, designer The Judith Ripka Companies, Inc., 1977—. Launched first 18K Gold Collection, 1977; hdqs. and mfg. facilities open, NYC, 77; first leased dept. in Boutique Tango, Roslyn, NY, 82; first free-standing store opens, Manhasset, NY, 93; designs PN 1 Pearl Necklace, 86; opens store on Madison Ave., NYC, 95; opens Aspen store, 95; opens Chgo. store, 97; opens Atlanta stores, 98; opens Boca Raton store, 99; Beverly Hill store opens on Rodeo Drive, 2000; San Francisco store opens on Geary St., 00; styled 9th annual Victoria Secret's Runway Show, 03; launched sterling silver & 18K Gold collection, 01; flagship store opens at 777 Madison Ave, NYC, 05; Bal Harbour Store opens at the Bal Harbour Shops, 05; Atlantic City store opens at The Piers, 06; Las Vegas store opens at The Forum Shops at Caesars, 07; NY store opens at Woodbury Common, 07; Fla. store opens at the Colomade at Seagrass, 07; Dallas store open, Highland park, 08; Fla. store opens at Prime 1 in Orlando, 08. Serves on several boards and steering committees, including Rita Hayworth Gala in support of Alzheimer's Assn. Recipient Albert Einstein Spirit of Achievement award, 2005; named Official Jewelry Designer for Mercedes-Benz Fashion Week in NY and LA, 2004; named one of The Leading Entrepreneur of the World, 2000. Mem.: Coun. Fashion Designers of Am. Achievements include being honored by many prestigious organizations, including Albert Einstein College Medicine and Crohn's & Colitis Foundation; has created commemorative pieces of jewelry for Austism Speaks, US Holocaust Museum, Mother's Voices AIDS Organization and Long Island Philharmonic; created First Lady Hillary Clinton's Inauguration Pin in 1996; chosen as one of Oprah's Favorite Things for Holiday Gifts in 2003. Office: Judith Ripka Companies Inc 777 Madison Ave New York NY 10065*

RIPKEN, CAL (CALVIN EDWIN RIPKEN JR.), retired professional baseball player, sportscaster; b. Havre de Grace, Md., Aug. 24, 1960; s. Calvin and Viola Ripken; m. Kelly Geer, Nov. 13, 1987; children: Rachel, Ryan. Played for minor league teams, Bluefield, Miami, Charlotte, Rochester, 1978—81; shortstop Balt. Orioles, 1981—2001; pres., CEO Ripken Baseball Group, 1999—; studio analyst, Maj. League Baseball Turner Sports, 2007—. Author: The Longest Season: The Story of the Orioles 1988 Losing Streak, 2007; co-author (with Mike Bryan): The Only Way I Know, 1997, Cal Ripken, Jr.: Play Ball!, 1999; co-author: (with Bill Ripken & Larry Burke) Play Baseball The Ripken Way: The Complete Illustrated Guide to the Fundamentals, 2004; co-author: (with Rick Wolff) Parenting Young Athletes the Ripken Way: Ensuring the Best Experience for Your Kids in Any Sport, 2006; co-author: (with Bill Ripken & Scott Lowe) Coaching Youth Baseball the Ripken Way, 2007; co-author: (with Donald T. Phillips) Get in the Game: Eight Elements of Perseverance That Make the Difference, 2007. Co-founder The Cal Ripken Sr. Found., 2001—; spl. sports envoy US Dept. State, Washington, 2007—. Recipient Am. League Rookie of Yr. award, 1982, Am. League Silver Slugger award, 1983—86, 1989, 1991, 1993—94, Am League Golden Glove award, 1991—92, Lou Gehrig Meml. award, 1992; named Am. League MVP, 1983, 1991, MLB All-Star Game MVP, 1983, 2001, Sportsman of Yr., SI mag., 1995, Male Athlete of Yr., AP, 1995; named to Am. League All-Star Team, 1983—2001, MLB All-Century Team, 1999, Nat. Baseball Hall of Fame, 2007. Achievements include being a holder of the major league record for consecutive games played; breaking Lou Gehrig's record of 2131 consecutive games played, 1995; maj. league record home runs by shortstop; highest single season fielding percentage (.996), 1990; most consecutive errorless games at shortstop (95); led Am. League in Runs (121), Hits (211), 1983. Office: Ripken Baseball 1427 Clarkview Rd Ste 100 Baltimore MD 21209*

RIPLEY, AFA, JR., (FEPULEA'I A. RIPLEY JR.), attorney general; b. 1949; BBA, MBA, Kans. State Teachers Coll., Emporia, Kans.; JD, Calif. Western Sch. Law, San Diego, 1978. Dep. atty. gen. Atty. Gen. Office, Hawaii, 1978; dep. pros. atty. City and County of Honolulu, 1979—80, dep. corp. counsel, trial divsn., 1980—82; atty. Minn & Ripley, Hawaii, 1982—89; chmn., bd. mem. Am. Samoa Power Authority; lawyer pvt. practice; atty. gen. Am. Samoa, 2007—. Office: American Samoa Govt Exec Office Bldg Utulei Territory of American Samoa Pago Pago AS 96799 Office Phone: 684-633-4163.*

RIPLEY, ALICE H., actress; b. San Leandro, Calif., Dec. 14, 1963; m. Shannon Ford. BFA, Kent State U. Performer: (Broadway plays) The Who's Tommy, 1993, Sunset Boulevard, 1994, King David, 1997, Side Show, 1997, Les Misérables, 1998—99, James Joyce's The Dead, 2000, The Rocky Horror Show, 2000, Next to Normal, 2009 (Tony award for Best Performance by a Leading Actress in a Musical, 2009), (plays) The Vagina Monologues, 1999, Company, 2002, The Baker's Wife, 2005, Next to Normal, 2008; actor: (films) The Adulterer, 2000, Temptation, 2004.*

RIPLEY, CHARLENE A., lawyer; BA, U. Alta.; JD, Dalhousie U., Nova Scotia. Counsel Amoco Can. Petroleum Co. Ltd., 1990—97; sr. counsel Norcen Energy Resources Ltd. (predecessor to Anadarko Can. Corp.), 1997—98, v.p., gen. counsel, corp. sec., 1998—2003; v.p., gen. counsel Anadarko Petroleum Corp., 2003—, corp. sec., 2004—, chief legal officer, 2003; sr. v.p., gen. counsel, corp. sec. LINN Energy, LLC, 2007—. Bd. adv. Houston Mayor's Internat. Affairs and Devel. Coun., past chmn.; mem. Women's Energy Network, The United Way of Greater Houston Women's Initiative; mem., Exec. Women's Partnership Greater Houston Partnership. Mem.: The Woodlands Bar Assn., Can. Bar Assn., Law Soc. Alta., Assn. Corp. Counsel, Tex. Gen. Counsel Grp., API Gen. Com. on Law, Alta. Arbitration & Mediation Soc., Tex. State Bar. Office: Linn Energy LLC Ste 7000 600 Travis St Houston TX 77002 Office Phone: 281-605-4100.*

RIPLEY, JUDITH G., state banking agency administrator; Student, U. Cin.; LLB, Ind. U., Indpls., 1981. Mem. Ind. Utility Regulatory Commn., 1998—2005; dir. Ind. Dept. Fin. Instns., 2005—. Mem. fed.-state joint bd. jurisdictional separations FCC, 2003. Adv. coun. N.Mex. State U. Ctr. Pub. Utilities. Mem.: Conf. State Bank Suprs. (vice chmn. dist II, vice chmn. legis. com.). Office: Dept Fin Instns Ste 300 30 S Meridian St Indianapolis IN 46204 Office Phone: 317-232-3955.*

RIPLEY, RANDALL BUTLER, political scientist, educator; b. Des Moines, Jan. 24, 1938; s. Henry Dayton and Aletha (Butler) R.; m. Grace A. Franklin, Oct. 15, 1974; children: Frederick Joseph, Vanessa Gail. BA, DePauw U., 1959; MA, Harvard U., 1961, PhD, 1963. Tchg. fellow Harvard, 1960-62; mem. staff Brookings Inst., Washington, 1963-67, rsch. asst., 1963-64, rsch. assoc., 1964-67; intern Office Dem. Whip, US Ho. of Reps., Washington, 1963; assoc. prof. dept. polit. sci. Ohio State U., Columbus, 1967-69, prof., 1969—2005, prof. emeritus, 2005, chmn., 1969-91, dean Coll. Social and Behavioral Scis., 1992—2004. Lectr. Cath. U., Washington, 1963-64; professorial lectr. Am. U., Washington, 1964-67; vis. prof. U. Okla., 1969-91. Author: Public Policies and Their Politics, 1966, Party Leaders in the House of Representatives, 1967, Majority Party Leadership in Congress, 1969, Power in the Senate, 1969, The Politics of Economic and Human Resource Development, 1972, Legislative Politics U.S.A, 1973, American National Government and Public Policy, 1974, Congress: Process and Policy, 1975, 4th edit., 1988, Policy-making in the Federal Executive Branch, 1975, Congress, the Bureaucracy, and Public Policy, 1976, 5th edit., 1991, National Government and Policy in the United States, 1977, A More Perfect Union, 1979, 4th edit., 1989, Policy Implementation and Bureaucracy, 1982, 2d edit., 1986, CETA: Politics and Policy, 1973-82, 1984, Policy Analysis in Political Science, 1985, Readings in American Government and Politics, 1989, 2d edit. 1993, 3d edit., 1999, Congress Resurgent, 1993, U.S. Foreign Policy After the Cold War, 1997, American Labor Unions in the Electoral Arena, 2001; contbr. articles to profl. jours. Bd. govs. Stratford Festival, Ont., Can., 1994-98. Woodrow Wilson fellow, 1959-60; Danforth fellow, 1959-63; recipient Sumner prize Harvard, 1963 Mem. Am. Polit. Sci. Assn. (sec. 1978), Phi Beta Kappa. Democrat. Home: 11465 Cable Rd SW Pataskala OH 43062-8809 Home Phone: 740-964-6977; Office Phone: 614-292-4392. Personal E-mail: ripley.1@osu.edu.

RIPP, JOSEPH ALLEN, information technology executive; b. NYC, Nov. 29, 1951; m. Virginia Nolan. BA, Manhattan Coll.; MBA, Bernard M. Baruch Coll. CUNY, 1980. Mgr. Ernst & Whinney, NYC, 1973-82; asst. contr. Time Inc., NYC, 1982-85, v.p. fin., 1985-90, v.p., CFO, 1990-92, sr. v.p., CFO, 1992-94, exec. v.p., CFO, 1994-99, Time Warner Inc., NYC, 1999-01; CFO America On-Line, Inc., 2001—03, vice chmn., 2002—04; sr. v.p. media & comm. group Time Warner Inc., 2004—05; pres., COO Dendrite Internat. Inc., Bedminster, NJ, 2005—. Bd. dirs. Greenfield Online Inc. Trustee Manhattan Coll.; bd. dir. Advt. Edn. Found; bd. dir., mem. exec. com., chmn. fin. com. Ad Council Office: Dendrite Internat Inc 1405-1425 Rt 206 S Bedminster NJ 07921

RIPPE, LYNN E., portfolio manager; b. Superior, Nebr., Dec. 27, 1947; children: Douglas E., Christopher C. BA in Econs., Kansas State U., 1969; MBA, So. Ill. U., Edwardsville, 1977. Contract specialist, contracting officer Naval Constrn. Bn. Ctr., Port Hueneme, Calif., 1989-93; sr. contract adminstr. U. Calif. Lawrence Livermore (Calif.) Nat. Lab., 1993-98; computing scis. subcontracts mgr. U. Calif. Lawrence Berkeley Nat. Lab., 1998—. Mem. Nat. Contract Mgmt. Assn. (v.p. Tri Valley chpt. 1995-96, pres. 1996-97, nat. dir. 1997-98, 2000-01, nat. v.p. 2001-03). Republican. Roman Catholic. Home: 3478 FM 1670 Belton TX 76513 Office: U Calif Lawrence Berkeley Nat Lab M-50B One Cyclotron Rd Berkeley CA 94720 Office Phone: 254-939-5514. E-mail: lerippe@nersc.gov.

RIPPERT, ERIC THEODORE, oral and maxillofacial surgeon, healthcare consultant, author, writer; b. Ft. Devens, Mass., Feb. 22, 1942; s. Jacob Kopf and Kathleen (Faughnan) R.; m. Mary Ellen Dormer, Nov. 25, 1965; children: Thomas, Kathleen. AB, Holy Cross Coll., 1964; DMD, U. Pa., 1968. Diplomate Am. Bd. Oral and Maxillofacial Surgery. Intern Phila. Gen. Hosp., 1968-69, resident, 1973-76; dental officer U.S. Navy, 1965-95; asst. prof. oral and maxillofacial surgery U. Nebr., Lincoln, 1996-99; asst. prof. U. Pitts., 1999-2000; assoc. prof. Med. Coll. Va., Richmond, 2000—02; assoc. prof., dir. residency tng., oral and maxillofacial surgery Med. Coll. Ga., Augusta, Ga., 2002—05; cons. in health care, 2005—. Clin. asst. prof. Med. Coll. Va., Richmond, 1979-81; adj. assoc. prof. Temple U., Phila., 1984-87; asst. prof. U. Calif., San Francisco, 1991-93. Author: (book) Defense of the Hudson Highlands, 1775-1783, 2008, The Executive Handbook, 2008. Fellow Am. Assn. Oral and Maxillofacial Surgeons, Am. Coll. Dentists, Internat. Coll. Dentists; mem. Varsity Club Coll. Holy Cross, Delta Sigma Delta. Republican. Roman Catholic. Avocations: tennis, skiing, speech and dialogue, writing. Office Phone: 706-836-0304.

RIPPETEAU, DARREL DOWNING, retired architect; b. Clay Center, Nebr., Jan. 14, 1917; s. Claude LaVerne and Eva (Downing) R.; m. Donna Doris Hiatt, Jan. 8, 1939 (dec. 1988); children: Bruce Estes, Darrel Downing, Jane Upson Heffron; m. Joyce Spencer, May 18, 1991. BA in Architecture, U. Nebr., 1941. Staff architect FHA, Omaha, 1941-42; project mgr., mng. ptnr. Sargent-Webster-Crenshaw & Folley, Archs. and Engrs., Watertown, Buffalo, Syracuse, NY, Burlington, Vt, Bangor, Maine, 1946-81; treas., dir. Empire Forest System, Albany, N.Y., 1984-89; ret., 1990. Bd. dirs. Archtl. Corp. Atlanta, Key Bank No. N.Y., Watertown, Assn. Island Recreational Corp.; commr. N.Y. State Coun. Architecture, 1975-85; mem. N.Y. State Forest Practice Bd., 1980-2000, chmn., 1994-98; nat. adv. bd. mem. Remington Art Mus., Ogdensburg, N.Y., 1983-95. Prin. works include Justice Bldg, Albany, N.Y. State Office Bldg Watertown, Toomey Abbott Towers Syracuse, State U. N.Y. Cortland, U.S. P.O. Facility Syracuse. Mem. nat. fin. com. Rep. Party, 1971-73; bd. trustees The Antique Boat Mus., Clayton, N.Y., 1973-99, Glenn Curtiss Mus., Hammondsport, N.Y. Maj. U.S. Army, 1942-46; lt. col. Corps of Engrs. retired, 1977. Recipient North Country citation St. Lawrence U., Canton, N.Y., 1971; Sears-Roebuck scholar, 1936-37; U. Nebr. Dept. Architecture grantee, 1940-41; Nebr. master U. Nebr., 1971; Disting. Alumni award Coll. of Architecture Alumni Assn., U. Nebr., 1996. Fellow AIA (nat. dir. 1969-73, trustee AIA Found. 1970-73); mem. Greater Watertown C. of C. (past pres.), NY State Assn. Indsl. Devel. Agys. (past v.p.), N.Y. State Assn. Architects (pres. 1968-69, polit. action com. 1980-98, James Kideney award 1987), Bldg. Rsch. Inst., Res. Officers Assn. (past pres.), Am. Tree Farm Assn., Jefferson County Hist. Soc. (dir. 1974-78), OX-5 Aviation Pioneers (chpt. pres.), Assn. US Army (Ft. Drum NNY chpt. pres. 1985-86). Republican. Presbyterian. Home: 1011 NW 3rd Ave Delray Beach FL 33444-2938 Home Phone: 561-272-2836.

RIPPLE, KENNETH FRANCIS, federal judge; b. Pitts., May 19, 1943; s. Raymond John and Rita (Holden) Ripple; m. Mary Andrea DeWeese, July 27, 1968; children: Gregory, Raymond, Christopher. AB, Fordham U., 1965; JD, U. Va., 1968; LLM, George Washington U., 1972, LLD (hon.), 1992. Bar: Va. 1968, NY 1969, US Supreme Ct. 1972, US Supreme Ct. 1972, DC 1976, Ind. 1984, US Ct. Appeals (7th cir.), US Ct. Mil. Appeals, US Dist. Ct. (no. dist.) Ind. Atty. IBM Corp., Armonk, NY, 1968; legal officer US Supreme Ct., Washington, 1972—73, spl. asst. to chief justice Warren E. Burger, 1973—77; prof. law U. Notre Dame, 1977—; judge US Ct. Appeals (7th cir.), South Bend, 1985—. Reporter Appellate Rules Com., Washington, 1978—85; commn. on mil. justice US Dept. Def., Washington, 1984—85; cons. Supreme Ct. Ala., 1983, Calif. Bd. Bar Examiners, 1981, Anglo-Am. Jud. Exch., 1977; adv. com. Bill of Rights to Bicentennial Constn. Commn., 1989; adv. com. on appellate rules Jud. Conf. US, 1985—90, chmn., 1990—93; chmn. adv. com. on appellate judge edn. Fed. Jud. Ctr., 1996—2003; mem. jud. conf. adminstrv. office US Cts. Com., 2003—06; mem. faculty Law Clerkship Inst., Pepperdine U., 2001—04; mem. vis. com. U. Chgo. Sch. Divinity, 2005—, U. Chgo. Sch. Law, 2005—08; mem. com. on jud. resources Jud. Conf. U.S., 2006—09. Author: Constitutional Litigation, 1984. With JAGC USN, 1968—72. Mem.: ABA, Am. Law Inst., Phi Beta Kappa. Office: US Ct of Appeals 208 US Courthouse 204 S Main St South Bend IN 46601-2122 also: Fed Bldg 219 S Dearborn St Ste 2660 Chicago IL 60604-1803*

RIPPLINGER, GEORGE RAYMOND, JR., lawyer; b. East St. Louis, Apr. 19, 1945; s. George Raymond and Virginia Lee (Toupnot) R. AB, U. Ill., 1967, JD, 1970. Bar: Ill. 1970, U.S. Dist. Ct. (so. dist.) Ill. 1970, U.S. Ct. Appeals (7th cir.) 1970, U.S. Dist. Ct. (ctrl. dist.) Ill. 1972, U.S. Tax Ct. 1971, U.S. Claims Ct. 1973, U.S. Ct. Mil. Appeals 1985, U.S. Supreme Ct. 1973, U.S. Ct. Internat. Trade 1973, U.S. Dist. Ct. (ea. dist.) Mo. 1977, U.S. Ct. Appeals (8th cir.) 1977. Assoc. Meyer & Meyer, Belleville and Greenville, Ill., 1970-72; assoc. Meyer & Kaucher, 1972—73; sole practice Belleville, 1974; ptnr. Ripplinger & Walsh, Clayton, Mo., 1974-76, Ripplinger, Dixon & Johnston, Belleville, Ill., St. Louis, Scott AFB, and Bellvue, Neb., 1976-94; prin. George Ripplinger & Assocs., Belleville, 1994—2005; mng. mem. Ripplinger & Zimmer LLC, Belleville, 2006—. Mem. com. minimum continuing legal edn. Ill. Supreme Ct., 2005—. Bd. visitors Coll. Law U. Ill., 1979-86, pres., 1983-84; pres., bd. dirs. Ill. Legal Aid on Line, 2006-2008, bd. dirs. 2005-2008. Col. USAR, 1970-2001. Recipient Disting. Alumnus award, U. Ill., Coll. Law, 2006, BF Fellows award. Fellow Am. Bar Found., Ill. Bar Found. (bd. dirs. 1988-2004, treas. 1998-2004); mem. ABA (ho. of dels. 1989-93, 95-99, chmn. workers compensation com. 1985-88, divsn. dir. 1988-89, 95-99, mem. coun. 1989-93, 99-2003, sec. 1999-2000, vice-chmn. 2000-2001, chmn. 2001-02, gen. practice/solo and small firm divsn.), ATLA, Lawyers Trust Fund Ill. (bd. dirs. 1988-94), Ill. Bar Assn. (bd. govs. 1981-83, 87-93, sec. 1991-92), St. Clair County Bar Assn., Bar Assn. Met. St. Louis, Mo. Bar Assn., Ill. Trial Lawyers Assn. (bd. advs. 1993—), Land of Lincoln Legal Assistance Found. (bd. dirs. 1982-88, vice-chmn. 1987-88), Res. Officers Assn. Democrat. Office: Ripplinger and Zimmer LLC 2215 W Main St Belleville IL 62226-6668 Home Phone: 618-398-6112; Office Phone: 800-733-8333. Business E-Mail: george@ripplingerlaw.com.

RIPPS, HARRIS, ophthalmologist, educator; b. NYC, Mar. 9, 1927; s. Abraham and Molly Ripps; m. Jeanne Meisler; children: Bradford Reed, Glenn Jay. BS, MS, MA, PhD, Columbia U., NYC, DSc, 1959. Cert. in accreditation Ill., 2006. Prof. ophthalmology & visual scis., anatomy & cell biology, physiology & biophysics UIC Coll. Medicine, Chgo., 1985—2008, prof. emeritus ophthalmology, anatomy & cell biology, physiology & biophysics, 2007—. Pres. Assoc. Rsch. Vision & Ophthalmology, 1986—87; vis. prof. Inst. Pasteur, Paris, 1998—99; sr. rsch. scientist Marine Biol. Lab., Woods Hole, 2006—. Contbr. scientific papers to profl. jours. (Rsch. award, 1987). With USN, 1944—46, San Diego. Recipient Rsch. Career Devel. award, US Pub. Health Svc., NIH, 1964—73, Vis. Prof., Inst. Ophthalmology, U. London, 1979, Sr. Sci. Investigator, Rsch. Prevent Blindness, 1991—2005, Rsch. award, U. Ill. Coll. Medicine, 1992—2008, Presdl. award, 1994, Disting. Faculty award, 1995, Disting. Lectr. & Vis. Prof. award, Cole Eye Inst., Cleve. Clinic, 2001, Excellence award, Alcon Rsch. Inst., 2002; Spl. Fellowship, Nat. Inst. Neurol. Diseases & Blindness, 1962—63. Mem.: RCS (Edridge-Green award 1975), Internat. Soc. Eye Rsch., Assn. Rsch. Vision & Ophthalmology (pres. 1986—87, Proctor medal 1982), Soc. Neurosci. Achievements include first to obtain photochemical recordings in the living human retina. Home: 7235 Promenade Dr Boca Raton FL 33433 Business E-Mail: harripp@uic.edu.

RIPS, LANCE JEFFREY, psychology professor; b. Omaha, Dec. 19, 1947; s. Norman Julian and Barbara (Taxman) R.; m. Julie West Johnson; 1 child, Eve Clare Johnson. BA, Swathmore Coll., Pa., 1970; PhD, Stanford U., 1974. Asst. prof. U. Chgo., 1974-80, assoc. prof., 1980-91, prof., 1991-93, Northwestern U., Evanston, Ill., 1993—. Author: Psychology of Proof, 1994, Psychology of Survey Response, 2000; mem. editl. bd. Cognition; contbr. articles to profl. jours. James McKeen Cattell fellow, 1989-90, Fulbright fellow, 2004-2005, Guggenheim Fellow, 2008-. Fellow APA, Am. Psychol. Soc.; mem. Psychonomic Soc., Soc. Exptl. Psychologists, Cognitive Sci. Soc., Phi Beta Kappa. E-mail: lrips@attglobal.net.

RISCASSI, ROBERT W., communications systems company executive, retired military officer; Comdr. Combined Arms Ctr. US Army, dep. chief of staff Ops. and Plans, dir. joint staff Joint Chief of Staff, vice chief of staff, comdr. in chief UN Command/Korea; positions up to v.p. land systems Washington ops. Loral Corp., 1993—96; v.p. land systems C3I and Systems Integration Sector Lockheed Martin; sr. v.p. Washington ops. L-3 Comm. Holdings, Inc. Office: L-3 Comm Holdings Inc 1215 S Clark St Ste 1205 Arlington VA 22202 Office Phone: 703-412-7190.

RISCH, HARVEY A., epidemiologist, educator; BSc, Calif. Inst. Tech., 1972; MD, U. Calif., San Diego, 1976; PhD, U. Chgo., 1980. Prof. epidemiology Yale U. Sch. Medicine, New Haven, 1991—. Office: Dept Epidemiology Public Health Yale U Sch Medicine PO Box 208034 New Haven CT 06520-8034

RISCH, JIM (JAMES ELROY RISCH), United States Senator from Idaho, former Governor of Idaho; b. Milw., May 3, 1943; s. Elroy A. and Helen B. (Levi) R.; m. Vicki L. Choborda, June 8, 1968; children: James E., Jason S., Jordan D. BS in Forestry, U. Idaho, 1965, JD, 1968. Dep. pros. atty. Ada County, Idaho, 1968-69, chief dep. pros. atty. Idaho, 1969-70, pros. atty. Idaho, 1971-75; mem. Idaho Senate from Dist. 18, Boise, 1974—88, 1995—2002, majority leader, 1977—82, 1997—2002, pres. pro tem, 1983-88; ind. counsel to Gov. State of Idaho, Boise, 1996; ptnr. Risch Goss & Insinger, Boise, 1975—; lt. gov. State of Idaho, Boise, 2003—06, 2007—09, gov., 2006—07; US Senator from Idaho, 2009—; mem. US Senate Fgn. Rels. Com., 2009—, US Senate Energy & Nat. Resources Com., 2009—, US Senate Select Com. on Ethics, 2009—, US Senate Select Com. on Intelligence, 2009—, US Senate Joint Econ. Com., 2009—. Prof. law Boise State U., 1972-75. Bd. dirs. Nat. Dist. Attys. Assn., 1973, Idaho Co., 1992-94, State Legis. Leaders Found., 2002; chmn. bd. dirs. Am. Trailer Mfg. Co., 1995—; pres. Idaho Pros. Attys., 1970-74; chmn. George Bush Presdl. Campaign, Idaho, 1988; gen. counsel Idaho Rep. Party, 1991-2002. Mem. ABA, Idaho Bar Assn., Boise Bar Assn., Ducks Unlimited, Nat. Rifle Assn., Nat. Cattlemans Assn., Idaho Cattlemans Assn., Am. Angus Assn., Idaho Angus Assn., Am. Legis. Exch. Coun., Boise Valley Angus Assn., Phi Delta Theta, Xi Sigma Pi Republican. Roman Catholic. Avocations: hunting, fishing, skiing. Office: US Congress 2 Russell Courtyard Washington DC 20510 also: 350 N 9th St Ste 302 Boise ID 83702 Office Phone: 202-224-2752, 208-342-7985. Office Fax: 208-343-2458, 202-224-2573.

RISCH, TROY H., retail executive; Group dir. stores Target Corp., Mpls., 2002—05, group v.p., 2005—06, exec. v.p. stores, 2006—. Bd. mem. Sci. Mus. of Minn. Office: Target Corp 1000 Nicollet Mall Minneapolis MN 55403-2467 Office Phone: 612-304-6073. Office Fax: 612-370-5502.*

RISCHBIETER, MICHAEL O., biology professor; m. Diane Flynn, June 22, 1984. PhD, U. SC., Columbia, 1992. Tchg. fellow UNC Chapel Hill, 1986—87; prof., biology Presbyn. Coll., Clinton, SC, 1987—. Sci. olympiad coach Clinton HS, 2000—.

RISDEN, EDWARD L., literature and language professor; b. Warren, Ohio, Oct. 10, 1957; s. Gary E. Risden and Patricia A. Irwin; m. Kristy J. Deetz, Dec. 22, 1990. BS, Baldwin-Wallace Coll., Berea, Ohio, 1979; MA, John Carroll U., Univ. Heights, Ohio, 1985; PhD, Purdue U., West Lafayette, Ind., 1990. Prof. English St. Norbert Coll., De Pere, Wis., 1990—. Author: (novel) Odysseus on the Rhine, (textbook) How English Works, (novel) A Living Light, Sir Severus le Brewse, (poems) A Second City Street Prophet Sings the Blues, Through a Glass Darkly, (book) Beowulf for Business, Herros, Gods and the Role of Epiphery in English Epic Poetry. Mem.: Medieval Assn. Midwest (pres., v.p., councillor 1994—2009). Avocations: golf, tai chi. Office: St Norbert Coll 100 Grant St De Pere WI 54115 Office Fax: 920-403-4086.

RISDON, MICHAEL PAUL, manufacturing executive; BS, Iowa State U., Ames, 1967, U. Ky., Lexington, 1968; MBA, U. Pitts., 1971. Sr. acct. Ernst & Young, Indpls., 1971-75; audit supr. Ashland Oil, Inc., Ky., 1975—77; v.p. fin. and sys. Diesel ReCon Co., Memphis, 1982-86; budget analyst Cummins Engine Co., Columbus, Ind., 1969-70, mgr. corp. audit, 1977-78, dir. corp. and EDP audit, 1978-82, dir. fin. and planning power sys. group, 1987-88; v.p. Cummins Power Generation, Columbus, 1989; v.p. fin., CFO Metal Powder Products Co., Inc., Indpls., 1989-99; pres. MPM LLC, Carmel, Ind., 1998-99; pres., CEO The Cumbernauld Group, 1999—; exec. v.p., chief adminstrv. officer PiezoTech, LLC, Indpls., 1999—2003; v.p. Alpha Natural Resources, 2007—. Vol. Big Sisters Ctrl. Ind., 1994-98; trustee exec. com. Barter Theatre. Mem. AICPA, Ind. CPA Soc., Metal Powder Industry Fedn. (fin. com. 1991-98, chmn. 1994-98), Fin. Execs. Internat. (sec. 1997-98, v.p. 1998, pres. 1999), Inst. Mgmt. Accts. (nat. bd. dirs. 1981-87, v.p. 1985), Kiwanis (v.p. Columbus 1981). Roman Catholic. Avocations: bicycling, hiking, sports.

RISEBROUGH, DOUG, former professional sports team executive; b. Guelph, Ont., Can., Jan. 29, 1954; m. Marilyn Risenbrough; children: Allison, Lindsay. Former player Montreal Canadiens, for 8 years, Calgary Flames, for 5 years, former asst. coach, 1987-89, asst. gen. mgr., 1989-90, head coach, 1990-92, gen. mgr., 1992—95; v.p. hockey ops. Edmonton Oilers, 1996—99; gen. mgr. Minn. Wild, 1999—2009; pres. Minn. Sports & Entertainment (MSE), 2003—09. Named NHL Exec. of Yr., Sporting News, 2003.

RISEN, JAMES E., journalist; b. Cin., Apr. 27, 1955; married; 3 children. BA in history, Brown U., 1977; MS in journalism, Northwestern U., 1978. Reporter Detroit Free Press, 1981—84; bur. chief LA Times, Detroit, 1984—90, chief econ. corr. Washington, 1990—95, nat. sec. & intelligence corr., 1995—98; investigative corr. NY Times, Washington, 1998—. Recipient Pulitzer Prize for nat. reporting, 2006. Fellow: Am. Acad. Arts & Scis. Office: NY Times Washington Bur 7th Fl 1627 I St NW Washington DC 20006 Office Phone: 202-862-0355. Office Fax: 202-862-0340. Business E-Mail: risenj@nytimes.com.

RISEN, WILLIAM MAURICE, JR., chemistry educator; b. St. Louis, July 22, 1940; ScB, Georgetown U., 1962; PhD, Purdue U., 1967. Asst. prof. chemistry Brown U., Providence, 1967-72, assoc. prof. chemistry, 1972-75, prof. chemistry, 1975—2008, chmn. chemistry dept., 1972-80, chmn. of faculty, 1993-94, prof. emeritus & adj. prof., 2009—. Cons. in field. Contbr. over 100 articles to profl. jours. Grantee in field. Mem. Am. Chem. Soc., Materials Rsch. Soc. Office: Brown U Dept of Chemistry 324 Brook St Providence RI 02912-9019 Business E-Mail: wrisen@brown.edu.

RISHEL, KENN CHARLES, school superintendent; b. Utica, NY, Nov. 19, 1946; s. Lester and Lois (Keehle) R.; m. Leslie Ann Syposs, Dec. 30, 1967; children: Samantha D., Andrea L. BS, SUNY, Oneonta, 1968; MS in Edn., SUNY, Cortland, 1973, Cert. Advanced Study/Adminstrn., 1985. Cert. notary pub. N.Y. Elem. tchr. Holland Patent (N.Y.) Ctrl. Sch., 1968-81, math coord., 1977-81; cons. CIMS program Oneida/Madison BOCES, New Hartford, N.Y., 1977-81; asst. supt. for bus. Carthage (N.Y.) Ctrl. Sch., 1981-87, supt., 1987-96; supervising adminstrn., CEO Carthage Area Hosp., 1994-98; cons. Sch. Constrn. & Collective Bargaining Radio Broadcaster, Lowille, N.Y., 1998-99; supt. S.A.U: #30, Laconia, NH, 1999—2001. Excelsior examiner N.Y. State Award for Quality, Albany, 1992—94; adj. prof. SUNY-Oswego, Watertown, 1994, SUNY, Oneonta, 2001—, Mohawk Valley C.C., 2005—. Author: The Disappearing Man, 2006. Recipient Pathfinder award NYSAWA, 1995. Mem. N.Y. Coun. Sch. Supts. (mem. ethics com. 1991-95, Black River Coun. Sch. Supts., Am. Assn. Sch. Adminstrs., Assn. U.S. Army, Rotary (v.p., pres. 1981-86), Lions, Elks. Home: 1006 Trackside Dr Marcy NY 13403 Personal E-mail: mgtcon1@netzero.net. Business E-Mail: rishelkc@oneonta.edu.

RISHEL, TRACY D., finance educator, director; d. Richard and Connie Rishel. BS, MS, PhD, Pa. State U., State Coll. Cert. in prodn. and inventory mgmt. APICS. Prodn. line supr. Corning Glass Works, State Coll., asst. bus. planner Corning, NY; asst.-assoc. prof. Susquehanna U., Selinsgrove, Pa.; sr. cons. McGladrey and Pullen, Charlotte, NC; assoc. prof. U. NC, Wilmington, NC A&T State U., Greensboro; dir. motorsports mgmt., assoc. prof. Belmont Abbey Coll., NC. Contbr. articles to profl. jours. Mem. Office: Belmont Abbey Coll 100 Belmont-Mt Holly Rd Belmont NC 28112 Business E-Mail: tracyrishel@bac.edu.

RISHER, WILLIAM HENRY, cardiothoracic surgeon, educator; b. New Orleans, Oct. 3, 1958; m. Michele Helene Van Kuren, July 11, 1981; children: Amelia Alexandra, Jordan Prescott, Olivia Leigh. Student, U. New Orleans, 1981; BS in Biomed. Engring., Tulane U., 1981; MD, La. State U., 1985. Diplomate Am. Bd. Surgery, Am. Bd. Thoracic Surgery; lic. surgeon, N.Y.; cert. ACLS, advanced trauma life support, pediatric advanced life support provider, basic life support provider. Resident in gen. surgery Alton Ochsner Med. Found., New Orleans, 1985-90, chief resident, 1989-90, resident and fellow in cardiovascular surgery, 1990-92, chief resident, 1991-92; flight care physician Ochsner Flight Care, 1986-92; assoc. prof. cardiothoracic surgery Med. Ctr. U. Rochester, NY, 1992—2002; chief St. Luke's Regional Heart Program, Bethlehem, Pa., 2002—. Presenter in field. Contbr. over 20 articles to med. and sci. jours. T.H. Harris scholar Tulane U, 1977-79, full scholar, 1979-81. Fellow ACS, Am. Coll. Cardiology (assoc.); mem. AMA, Am. Coll. Chest Physicians, Soc. Thoracic Surgeons, Internat. Soc. Heart and Lung Transplantation, S.E. Surg. Congress, So. Med. Assn., Med. Soc. County Monroe, Rochester Acad. Medicine, Rochester Cardiovascular Soc., Upstate Soc. Thoracic Surgeons, Rochester Surg. Soc., Assn. for Advancement of Med. Instrumentation, Alton Ochsner Med. Soc., Tau Beta Pi, Alpha Omega Alpha. Home: 1875 Augusta Dr Center Valley PA 18034-8924 Office Phone: 610-954-3990. Personal E-mail: mbaj05@aol.com.

RISHI, ARUN K., molecular biologist, educator; married. PhD, U. London, 1987. Asst. prof. U. Md., Balt., 1994—98; assoc. prof. Wayne State U., Detroit, 1998—. Asst. prof. Boston U., 1991—94. Grantee Rsch. grant, Susan G Komen Found. Breast Cancer Rsch., 2004—. Office: Wayne State Univ 4646 John R Detroit MI 48201 Office Fax: 313-576-1112. Business E-Mail: rishia@karmanos.org.

RISHWAIN, JAMES MICHAEL, JR., lawyer; b. Stockton, Calif., Apr. 28, 1959; BA with honors, UCLA, 1981; JD cum laude, Pepperdine U., 1984. Bar: Calif. Firm chair and CEO Pillsbury Winthrop Shaw Pittman LLP, LA, 2006—, leader real estate group, 1995—2006. Editor (Note & Comment): Pepperdine Law Rev. Mem. adv. bd. LA City Coun. for Holmby Pk., Calif. Coalition for Adequate Sch. Housing, Jonathan Club; bd. mem. Bldg. Owners and Mgrs. Assn.; bd. experts Internat. Real Estate Trade Orgn., mem. pres.'s cir. Recipient Calif. Lawyer of Yr. award, 2004, 2005; named Best Lawyer Am., 2005—06; named one of Calif. Super Lawyers, 2004, 2005, 2006—08. Mem.: ABA, State Calif. Bar Assn., LA County Bar Assn., Urban Land Inst. Office: Pillsbury Winthrop Shaw Pittman LLP Ste 2800 725 S Figueroa St Los Angeles CA 90017-5406 Office Phone: 213-488-7111. Office Fax: 213-488-7400. E-mail: jrishwain@pillsburylaw.com.

RISI, LOUIS JAMES, JR., manufacturing executive; b. Highland Park, Ill., July 2, 1937; s. Louis J. and Ann E. Risi; m. Mary Jean Anson, Jan. 15, 1958; children: Steven, Janet, Andrew. BS, Bradley U.; MBA, U. Chgo. Pres. and CEO, bd. dirs., mem. exec. com. Norin Corp., Miami, Fla., 1969-81; exec. com. dir. Maple Leaf Mills Ltd., Toronto, Can., 1970-81, Corp. Foods, Inc., 1970-81; chmn. bd. dirs. Louis Sherry, Inc., 1976-81; chmn. bd., CEO Nat. Investors Fire & Casualty Co., 1975-77; exec. com. dir. Investors Equity Life Ins. Co. of Hawaii, 1970-75; pres., dir. The Abbey, Lake Geneva, 1970-75; exec. com., dir. Upper Lakes Shipping, Ltd., Toronto, Can., 1970-76; pres., dir. The Pioneer, Lake Oshkosh, 1971-76; exec. com., dir. Port Weller and St. Lawrence Dry Dock, Ltd., St. Catharines, Can., 1971-76; pres., dir. Homosassa Springs, Fla., 1971-78, Ivan Tors Films Inc., Culver City, Calif., 1971-78, Ivan Tors Studios Inc., Miami, Fla., 1976-80; exec. com. dir. Midland Nat. Bank, 1976-80; pres., dir. Norris Grain Co., 1980-82; chmn. bd., CEO CTC Corp., 1981-83. Exec. com. Nat. Investors Life Ins. Co., 1970-77; chmn. bd., pres. Victory Industries, Inc.; chmn. bd. dirs. Red Wing Co., Oklawaha Farms, Inc., Assured Security Co.; dir. Breckinridge Group; exec. v.p. Ft. Worth Red Wings Hockey Club, Inc., 1975-78, Detroit Red Wings Hockey Club, Inc., 1976-82, Adirondack Red Wings Hockey Club, Inc., 1976-82; bd. govs. Nat. Hockey League, 1976-82; bd. dirs. Chgo. Rock Island and Pacific R.R.; exec. com. AfriAir Corp., 1972-79, Southeastern Airlines, Inc., 1972-78; exec. com., bd. dirs. Peter Bowden Drilling Ltd., Bankmgrs. Corp.; U.S. rep. Grain negotiations with USSR; U.S. rep. Feedstuffs negotiations with China; adv. coun. Am. Stock Exch.; mem. Agrl. Processors Liaison com. FTC; adv. bd. Nat. Millers Assn.; bd. govs. Internat. Hockey League, 1978-82, Am. Hockey League, 1975-79; pres., chmn. bd. dirs. Kinnard Body Works, Inc., 1970-73. Trustee Fairchild Tropical Garden, Miami, Fla. Lt. comdr. USNR, 1959—67. Mem. Ocean Reef Yacht Club (Key

Largo, Fla.), Santa Rosa (Calif.) Country Club, Riviera Country Club (Coral Gables, Fla.), Lake Toxaway Country Club (Lake Toxaway, NC), Coral Reef Yacht Club (Miami, Fla.), Anabelle's Club (London), St. James Club (London).

RISICA, PATRICIA, medical researcher, educator; d. James D. and Anne H. Markham; m. Robert Risica. BS, Ohio State U., Columbus, 1987; MPH, Johns Hopkins U., Balt., 1993, DPH, 1998. Rsch. assoc. U. of Alaska Anchorage, Anchorage, Alaska, 1993—98; asst. prof. Brown U., Providence, 1998—2008. Advocacy chair, pres. RI Pub. Health Assn., Providence, 1998—2008. Office: Brown Univ Providence RI 02901

RISIN, DIANA, biomedical researcher; d. Jacob and Khinya Ratner; m. Semyon Aaron Risin, July 4, 1970; 1 child, Misha. MD, Minsk State Med. Inst., Minsk, 1971; PhD, Belorussian Inst. Continuing Edn. Physicians, Minsk, 1982. Investigator Clin. and Rsch. Inst. Oncology and Med. Radiology, Minsk, 1973—84, sr. investigator, 1984—88, chief, lab. immunology, 1988—89; rsch. assoc. UT M.D. Anderson Cancer Ctr., Houston, 1990—93, instr. surgery basic rsch. and asst. immunologist, 1993—94; cell scientist KRUG Life Scis. Inc., Houston, 1994—96, sr. cell scientist, 1996—97, WYLE Labs. Inc., Houston, 1997—2000, sect. supr., advanced programs, 2000; mgr. sci. coordination NASA Johnson Space Ctr., 2000—05, element scientist exploration medicine, 2006—08, project mgr. biomed. results space shuttle missions program, 2008—. Supervisory com. mem., PhD program Ga. Inst. Tech. and Emory U., Atlanta, 2005—08. Recipient numerous awards, Inst. Oncology and Med. Radiology, NASA/JSC, 1998, 2001—07, R&D 100 award, 2007; fellowship, Inst. Oncology and Med. Radiology, 1974, UT M.D. Anderson Cancer Ctr., 1992. Achievements include patents for treatment of patients with secondary skin melanoma, method of B lymphocytes detection. Avocation: travel.

RISIN, SEMYON AARON, pathologist, educator; b. Belarus; m. Diana Risin; 1 child, Michael. MD, PhD, Minsk State Med. Inst., Belarus, 1964. Diplomate Am. Bd. of Pathology, 2003. Physician, physician-in-chief Village Hosp., Khominka, Belarus, 1964—66; rschr. Minsk State Med. Inst., 1971—79, prof., 1979—89; rsch. prof. U. Tex. M. D. Anderson Cancer Ctr., Houston, 1990—97; resident physician dept. pathology & lab. medicine U. Tex.-Houston Med. Sch., 1997—2001, prof. dept. pathology & lab. medicine, 2001—. Med. cons. Am. Biomed, Houston, 1990—91; med. interpretor and cons. Johnson Space Ctr., NASA, Houston, 1996—97. Avocation: travel. Office: UT-Houston Medical School 6431 Fannin Street MSB 2290 Houston TX 77030 Office Fax: 713-500-0730.

RISING, CATHARINE CLARKE, author; b. Berkeley, Calif., Jan. 7, 1929; d. Philip Seymour and Helen Katharine (Davis) Clarke; m. Boardman Rising, Sept. 16, 1950. BS, U. Calif., Berkeley, 1950, PhD, 1987; MA, San Francisco State U., 1979. Cert. cmty. coll. instr., Calif. Author: Darkness at Heart: Fathers and Sons in Conrad, 1990, Outside the Arch: Kohut and Five Modern Writers, 1999; contbr. articles to profl. jours. Mem. MLA, Phi Beta Kappa.

RISINGER, BETH N., elementary school educator; b. New Orleans, June 24, 1959; d. Merrill J. and Betty Nunez; m. Kurt Risinger, May 21, 1983; children: Kristofer, Kevin. BA in Elem. Edn., Nicholls State U., 1982. Life cert. in elem. edn., grades 1-8. Sci. tchr. St. Bernard Parish Schs., Chalmette, La., 1982—83; 4th and 5th grade tchr. West Ascension Elem., Donaldsonville, La., 1986—92; 3rd and 4th grade tchr. G.W. Carver Primary, Gonzales, La., 1992—2008; 4th grade tchr. Riveroaks Elem., Baton Rouge, 2008—. Vol. Children's Miracle Network. Named Tchr. of Yr., Carver Primary, 1996—97, Riveroaks Elem. Sch., 2009—. Mem.: La. Fedn. Tchrs., Nat. Coun. Math. Tchrs., Internat. Reading Assn. Home: 13668 Parwood Ave Baton Rouge LA 70816-1473

RISINGER, C. FREDERICK, social studies educator; b. Paducah, Ky., July 15, 1939; s. Charles Morris and Mary Neal (Barfield) R.; m. Margaret M. Marker, July 4, 1994; children: Donna Lyne, Alyson, Laura, John. BS in Edn., So. Ill. U., 1961; MA in History, No. Ill. U., 1968. Newscaster, disc jockey WMOK Radio, Metropolis, Ill., 1955-61; tchr., adminstr., coach Lake Park H.S., Roselle, Ill., 1962-73; coord. sch. social studies Ind. U., Bloomington, 1973-86, assoc. dir. social studies devel. ctr., 1986-90, dir. nat. clearinghouse for U.S.-Japan studies, 1990—2004, assoc. dir. tchr. edn., 1995—2004, dir. profl. devel., sch. svcs. and summer sessions, 1997—2004. Mem. adv. bd. Learning Mag., Boston, 1988-. Co-author: America! America!, 1974, America's Past and Promise, 1997, Surfing Social Studies: The Internet Book, 1999, Creating America, 2000, Scott Foresman Social Studies K-6 Series, 2004, American History, 2008; editor jour. News and Notes on the Social Sciences, 1973-86. Pres. Social Studies Suprs. Assn., Washington, 1985-86; exec. dir. Ind. Coun. for Social Studies, Bloomington, 1975-87. Recipient numerous pub. and pvt. edtl. grants; named Tchr. of Yr. DuPage County Edn. Assn., 1973. Mem. ASCD, Nat. Coun. for Social Studies (pres. 1990-91), Nat. Coun. History Edn., Ind. Assn. Historians, Social Sci. Edn. Consortium (pres. 2006-08), Phi Delta Kappa. Democrat. Home: 7039 E State Rd 45 Bloomington IN 47408-9580

RISINGER, D. MICHAEL, lawyer, educator; b. Kansas City, Mo., Mar. 31, 1945; s. Homer D. and Madeline F. Risinger; m. Celia A. Defensor, Oct. 17, 1977 (div. Jan. 1990); children: Ariel Michelle, Michael R. Defensor, Jonathan Marshall; m. Barbara B. Comerford, Jan. 1991; 1 child, Caroline Violet Comerford. BA magna cum laude in Polit. Sci, Yale U., 1966; JD cum laude, Harvard U., 1969. Bar: Pa. 1973, N.J. 1978, N.Y. 1983. Asst. counsel Mass. Joint Legis. Com. on Drugs and Drug Abuse, 1969; tchr. N.Y.C. Public Schs., 1969-71; law clk. to hon. Clarence C. Newcomer US Dist. Ct. (ea. dist.) Pa., 1972-73; asst. prof. law Seton Hall U., Newark, 1973-76, assoc. prof., 1976-79, prof., 1979—. Vis. sr. fellow Nat. U. Singapore, 1985-86; mem. faculty Nat. Jud. Coll., 1988; lectr. on evidence N.J. Inst. Continuing Legal Edn., N.J. Jud. Coll., N.J. Adminstrv. Law Inst., N.Y. Practising Law Inst., N.Y.C.; trial adv. trainer Nat. Legal Services Corp.; mem. N.J. Supreme Ct. Com. on Evidence. Author: (with Mark P. Denbeaux) Trial Evidence, 1978; co-author of Trial Evidence, Continuing Legal Education Casebook, contbr. articles to profl. jours. Grantee Dean's Rsch. Fellows, Seton Hall's, 2002—04. Mem. ABA, Am. Law Inst., past chair Assn. Am. Law Sch., chair-elect AALS Sect., mem. NJ Supreme Ct. Com. Office: Seton Hall U School of Law 1 Newark Center Newark NJ 07102-5206 Office Phone: 973-642-8834. Office Fax: 973-642-8876. Business E-Mail: risingmi@shu.edu.

RISINGER, PETRA EVEREST, school librarian; b. Seattle, Oct. 31, 1951; d. David M. and Mildred Fay Everest; m. Johnny Bryan Risinger; children: Tate A. Brock, David L. Brock, Darrin M. Minderman. A, Panola Jr. Coll., Carthage, Tex., 1999. Cert. in para profl. Tex., 2006. Libr. sec. Westminster Presbyn. Ch., Nacogdoches, Tex., 1978—80; traffic dir. KSFA-KTBC Radio, Nacadoches, 1980—81; asst. libr. Timpson I. S. D., Tex., 1985—2000. Attendance com. Presbyterian Womens Nat. Meeting, Houston, 1978. Mem.: Waskom Women (historian 2000—08). Conservative. Presbyterian. Avocations: travel, gardening. Business E-Mail: prisinger@chireno.esc7.net.

RISKAS, MIKE, retired physical education educator, coach, actor; b. Ely, Nev., June 22, 1934; s. Nicholas Vasiliou and Helen (Massouris) Riskas; m. Barbara Lou Watson, July 16, 1960; children: Michelle Dee Johnston, Steven Dean. BS, U. Calif., LA, 1958, MS, 1967. Player, football and baseball U. Calif., LA, 1953—55, 1958—59; freelance actor Hollywood, Calif., 1959—; coach football and baseball Alhambra (Calif.) HS, 1960; prof. Pomona Coll., Claremont, Calif., 1961—2003, coach football, 1961-85, coach baseball, 1963-86, ret., 2003. Course advisor, editor Azusa Pacific U., Calif., 1972-73; curriculum advisor, editor U. LaVerne, Calif., 1974-79; coach baseball U. Calif., LA, 1980; baseball clinician Am. Baseball Assn./European Dept. of State, 1970, Am. Baseball Assn./US Olympic Com., Colombia, S.A., 1984, US Baseball Fedn., Eng., 1987; head baseball Coach French Nat. Team, France, 1988, 1995; instr. major league baseball envoy, France, 1993; coach Greek Baseball Nat. Team, 2000-07, Greek Baseball Olympic Team, Athens, 2004. Named to Baseball Hall Fame, U. Calif., LA, 1996, Athletic Hall Fame, Pomona-Pitzer Coll., 1997. Mem. Am. Football Coaches Assn. (life), Am. Baseball Coaches Assn., Nat. Athletic Intercollegiate Assn. (life) (chmn. div. III 1967, chmn. western region 1985-86), U.S. Baseball Fedn., Internat. Baseball Assn., UCLA 10th Player. Democrat. Greek Orthodox.

RISKOWSKI, GERALD LEE, engineering educator; b. Loup City, Nebr., Feb. 26, 1952; s. Stanley George and Rose Marie (Eurek) R.; 1 child, Ryan Lee. BS in Agrl. Engring., U. Nebr., 1974, MS in Agrl. Engring., 1976; PhD in Agrl. Engring., Iowa State U., 1986. Registered profl. engr., Ill., Iowa, Wis. Design engr. Lesters Bldgs., Lester Prairie, Minn., 1976-77; product engr. Wick Bldg. Systems, Mazomanie, Wis., 1977-80; instr. Iowa State U., Ames, 1980-86; prof. dept. agrl. engring. U. Ill., Urbana, 1986—2001; prof., head biol. and agrl. engring. dept. Tex. A&M U., College Station, 2002—. Swine facilities cons. Am. Tech. Products, Savoy, Ill., 1997-2002; pres. Internat. Air Technologies, Savoy, 1994-2003. Author: Designing Facilities for Pesticide and Fertilizer Containment, 1991 (Am. Soc. Agrl. Engrs. Blue Ribbon 1992); editor: Swine Housing and Equipment Handbook, 1983 (Am. Soc. Agrl. Engrs. Blue Ribbon 1984), Livestock Waste Facilities, 1985, Farm Buildings Wiring Handbook, 1986 (Am. Soc. Biological and Agrl. Engrs. Blue Ribbon 1987). Named to Rural Builders Hall of Fame, 1998. Mem. ASHRAE (TC.2 Handbook chair 1993-2000), Am. Soc. Biological and Agrl. Engrs. (fellow 2007, S&E program chair, stds. chair, Henry Giese award 2001). Office: Tex A&M U 2117 TAMU College Station TX 77843-2117 E-mail: riskowski@tamu.edu.

RISLEY, ROD ALAN, educational association administrator; b. Hutchinson, Kans., Oct. 17, 1954; s. Ralph Edward and Patricia Ann (Gaulding) R. AA, San Jacinto Coll., Tex., 1975; BBA, Sam Houston State U., Huntsville, Tex., 1982; AA (hon.), Austin Community Coll., Tex., 1991; MBA, Millsap Coll., 1995; PhD (hon.), Highpoint U., 1996, Mt. Ida Coll., Newton Centre, Mass., 1996, Landmark Coll., Putney, Vt., 2003; ABD, Miss. State U., 2003. Dir. alumni affairs Phi Theta Kappa, 1976-82; assoc. dir. Phi Theta Kappa Internat. Hdqrs., Jackson, Miss., 1982-85, exec. dir., 1985—. Chmn. bd. dirs. Miss. Humanities Coun.; bd. dirs. Jack Kent Cooke Found., CC Transfer Initiative; chmn. bd. devel. com. Miss. Ctr. Non-Profit Orgns., Am. Soc. Assn. Execs.; grant reviewer NSF, CC Humanities Assn., NEH; mem. adv. bd. Horne CPA Group. Judge Truman Scholarship Found., 1993, 94, Coca-Cola Scholars Found., 2001-04, USA Today's All-USA Acad. Team HS, 2003-04, Jack Kent Cooke Found., 2004-06, Nat. Assn. C.C. Tchr. Edn. Program, 2004-07. Named one of Outstanding Young Men Am., 1982, 83, 84, 85, 86, 87, 88, 89, Top Bus. Leaders Miss., 1994, Disting. Alumnus, San Jacinto Coll., 1997; Mid South Found. C.C. fellow, 2001, Am. Assoc. Comm. Coll. Leadership award, 2008. Mem. Am. Assn. of Cmty. Colls. (commr. coun. for acad., student and cmty. devel., grant reviewer, Disting. Alumnus award 1996), Am. Soc. Assn. Execs., Phi Theta Kappa (sec., pub. jour.), Phi Kappa Phi. Episcopalian. Office: Phi Theta Kappa Soc PO Box 13729 Jackson MS 39236-3729 Office Phone: 601-984-3518. Business E-Mail: rod.risley@ptk.org.

RISMAN, MICHAEL, lawyer, real estate developer, broker; b. Everett, Mass., Apr. 2, 1938; s. Morris Charles and Doris (Rosenbaum) R.; m. Rebecca R. Fuchs, Mar. 23, 1974; 1 stepchild, Ian Carlton Murray; children: Matthew Craig, Deborah Risman Kyle, Jared Evan. BA, U. Mich., 1960; LLB, Georgetown U., 1964. Bar: D.C. 1964. Staff mem. Democratic Nat. Com., Washington, 1964; atty. U.S. Fgn. Claims Settlement Commn., Washington, 1964-66, SEC, Washington, 1966-67; counsel Seaboard Planning Corp., Beverly Hills, Calif., 1967-72, pres., 1970-72; v.p. Seaboard Corp., Beverly Hills, 1970-72; sec. B.C. Morton Realty Trust, 1967-71; with Arlington Investments Corp., Santa Monica, Calif., 1979-86; founder The Quincey Group, 1986; owner, pres. Armstrong Kitchens, San Francisco, 1988-90; sr. v.p. AFC Am. Housing Corp., LA, Calif., 1991-97; mng. dir. Hollingsworth & Lord, LA, 1997—; ptnr. Dorama, L.L.C., 2002—. Bd. dirs. Competitive Capital Fund, Income Fund Boston, Inc., Admiralty Fund. Named Businessperson of Yr., Desert Hot Springs C. of C., 2007. Home: 1133 Centinela Ave Santa Monica CA 90403-2316 Office Phone: 310-890-6011. Personal E-mail: mrisman02@aol.com.

RISOM, JENS, furniture designer, consultant, manufacturing executive; b. Copenhagen, May 8, 1916; came to U.S., 1939; naturalized, 1944; s. Sven J. and Inger Risom; m. Iben Haderup, Dec. 12, 1939 (dec. Jan. 1977); children: Helen Ann, Peggy Ann, Thomas Christian, Sven Christian; m. Henny Panduro, May 12, 1979. Student, Krebs, Denmark, 1922-27, St. Annae, 1927-32, Niels Brock Bus. Coll., 1932-34, Sch. for Arts and Indust., Denmark, 1935—37; DFA (hon.), R.I. Sch. Design, 2003. With design and decorating divsn. Nordiska Kompanet, Stockholm, Inge Westin, Stockholm, 1934-35, Ernst Kühn, Arch., Copenhagen and NYC, 1937-38; with Dan Cooper, Inc., N.Y., 1939-41; freelance furniture designer, 1941-46; founder, pres. Jens Risom Design Inc., 1946-71; pres. Jens Risom Design, Inc. (became subs. Dictaphone Corp. 1971); v.p. Dictaphone Corp., 1971-73; pres. Design Control, New Canaan, Conn., 1973—. Cons. design, mktg., space planning. Trustee RISD, New Canaan Libr., Indsl. Design Soc. Am. With U.S. Army, 1943-45, ETO. Decorated Danish Knight's Cross (Denmark); recipient awards Archtl. League, Am. Inst. Internat. Design, Lifetime Achievement award Bklyn. Mus. Art, 1994, Russell Wright Manitoga Design award RI Sch. Design, 2004, numerous Danish and Am. design awards. Home and Office: 24 Parade Hill Ln New Canaan CT 06840-4119 also: PO Box 596 Block Island RI 02807-0596 Office Phone: 203-966-5009.

RISS, ERIC, psychologist; m. Miriam Barbara Schoen; children: Arthur, Suzanne, Wendy. BA, Bklyn. Coll., 1950; PhD, NYU, 1958. Diplomate Am. Bd. Psychotherapy. Pvt. practice psychotherapy, family therapy and marriage counseling, NYC, 1952; sr. psychologist N.Y.C. Diagnostic Ctr., 1954-57; with Marriage and Family Life Inst., NYC, 1956-92, cons., 1956-58, dir. pub. edn., 1960-73, chmn. bd. dirs., 1961-73, dir., 1973-92; mem. attending staff, supr. psychotherapy and family therapy Payne Whitney Psychiat. Clinic, N.Y. Hosp., NYC, 1971-78; clin. instr. psychology and psychiatry Cornell U. Med. Coll., 1971-72, clin. asst. prof., 1973-78; dir. Inst. for Exploration of Marriage, 1976-84; chief psychologist Artists, Writers and Performers Psychotherapy Ctr., 1978-92. Sr. psychologist N.Y.C. Diagnostic Center, 1954-57; with Marriage and Family Life Inst., N.Y.C., 1956-92; cons., 1956-58, dir. pub. edn., 1960-73, chmn. bd. dirs., 1961-73, dir., 1973-92; mem. attending staff, supr. psychotherapy and family therapy Payne Whitney Psychiat. Clinic, N.Y. Hosp., N.Y.C., 1971-78; clin. instr. psychology and psychiatry Cornell U. Med. Coll., 1971-72, clin. asst. prof., 1973-78; dir. Inst. for Exploration of Marriage, 1976-84; chief psychologist Artists, Writers and Performers Psychotherapy Center, 1978-92; lectr. Bklyn. Coll., 1955-62; cons. Fordham Hosp., 1956-68; psychotherapist N.Y. Neuropsychiat. Center, 1958-60; psychotherapist Community Guidance Service, N.Y.C., 1958-61; founder, head Natural Psychotherapy Internat., 1999—; webmaster www.naturalpsychotherapy.com. Contbr. numerous articles to profl. jours. Mem. APA, N.Y. State Psychol. Assn., Am. Acad. Psychotherapy, N.Y. State Marriage, Family and Child Counseling Assn. (pres. 1971-72), Acad. Family Psychology. Office: 174 E 73rd St New York NY 10021-4352 Office Phone: 212-988-4700. E-mail: eriss@naturalpsychotherapy.com, eriss@npsy.com.

RISSE, GUENTER BERNHARD, physician, historian, educator; b. Buenos Aires, Apr. 28, 1932; s. Francisco B. and Kaete A. R.; m. Alexandra G. Paradzinski, Oct. 14, 1961; children— Heidi, Monica, Alisa. MD, U. Buenos Aires, 1958; PhD, U. Chgo., 1971. Intern Mercy Hosp., Buffalo, 1958-59; resident in medicine Henry Ford Hosp., Detroit, 1960-61, Mt. Carmel Hosp., Columbus, Ohio, 1962-63; asst. dept. medicine U. Chgo., 1963-67; asst. prof. dept. history of medicine U. Minn., 1969-71; asso. prof. dept. history of medicine and dept. history of sci. U. Wis., Madison, 1971-76, prof., 1976-85, chmn. dept. history of medicine, 1971-77; prof. dept. history health scis. U. Calif., San Francisco, 1985-99, prof. dept. anthropology, history and social medicine, 1999-2001, prof. emeritus, 2001—, dept. chair, 1985—99; affiliate prof. dept. bioethics and humanities U. Wash. Sch. Medicine, Seattle, 2002—. Author: Paleopathology of Ancient Egypt, 1964, Hospital Life in Enlightenment Scotland, 1986, Mending Bodies-Saving Souls: A History of Hospitals, 1999, New Medical Challenges During the Scottish Enlightenment, 2005; editor: Modern China and Traditional Chinese Medicine, 1973, History of Physiology, 1973, Medicine Without Doctors, 1977, AIDS and the Historian, 1991, Culture, Knowledge and Healing, Historical Perspectives of Homeopathic Medicine in Europe and North America, 1998; mem. editl. bd. Jour. History of Medicine, 1971-74, 90-93, Clio Medica, 1973-88, Bull. History of Medicine, 1980-94, Medizinhistorisches Jour., 1981—, Med. History, 1989-95, NTM Internat. Jour. of History, Ethics, Medicine, 1992—, History of Philos. Life Scis., 1993—, Asclepio, 1995—, Health and History, 1998—. With Argentine Armed Forces, 1955. Recipient NIH grants, 1971-73, 82-84, WHO grant, NIH grant San Francisco's Plague: The View from Chinatown, 2007-09, fellowship History & L.Am. Med. Sys., 1979; named Logan Campbell Disting. Lectr., New Zealand, 1994, Karl Sudhoff Meml. Lectr., Germany, 2000. Mem. Am. Assn. History of Medicine (pres. 1988-90, William H. Welch medal 1988, Lifetime Achievement award 2005), History Sci. Soc., Deutsche Gesellschaft fur Geschichte der Medizin, European Assn. History of Medicine and Health, Internat. Network for History of Pub. Health, Mex. Soc. History and Philosophy of Medicine, Peruvian Assn. Med. Ethnology and History, Brit. Soc. for Social History of Medicine, Argentine Ateneo de Historia de la Medicina, AIDS History Group (co-chair 1988-94), Internat. Network for History of Hosps. (convenor 1995—), Bay Area Med. Hist. Club (pres. 1994-96). Home: 2612 SW 167th St Burien WA 98166-3228 Business E-Mail: risseg@u.washington.edu.

RISSECH, CARME, research scientist; d. Pere Rissech and Rosa Badalló; m. Lluís Lloveras, Dec. 7, 1990; 1 child, Zoé Lloveras. Master in Human Biology, U. Autónoma Barcelona, Spain, 1989; PhD in Biology, 2001. Lab. worker Hosp. Sant Jaume, Calella de la Costa, Barcelona, 1988—88; prof. hs Col.legi Immacolada Concepcció, Lloret de Mar, Girona, Spain, 1989—91; Postdoc rschr. Coimbra U., Portugal, 2002—06; colaborator rschr. U. de Barcelona, 2008—. Assoc. prof. U. Autónoma de Barcelona, 2006—07. Contbr. scientific papers to profl. jours. Office: Faculty Biology Univ de Barcelona Avd Doagonal 645 Barcelona 08028 Spain Office Fax: (34)934035740. Personal E-mail: carme.rissech@gmail.com. Business E-mail: carme.rissech@ub.edu.

RISSEL, HILDEGARD, language educator; b. Westerholt, Germany, May 21, 1956; d. Herbert Joseph Rissel and Hannelore Halsband. PhD, Georgetown U., Washington, 1990. Asst. prof. U. Wis. Wash. County, West Bend, 1991—96; assoc. prof. Va. State U., Petersburg, 1996—. Contbr. articles to profl. jours. Regent Cath. Daus.-Ct. Regina Coeli, Colonial Heiths, Va., 2001—04. Mem.: Phi Beta Kappa. Roman Catholic. Avocations: travel, reading. Office: Va State Univ 1 Hadyen Dr Petersburg VA 23806 Office Fax: 804-524-5184. Business E-Mail: hrissel@vsu.edu.

RISSER, JAMES VAULX, JR., journalist, educator; b. Lincoln, Nebr., May 8, 1938; s. James Vaulx and Ella Caroline (Schacht) R.; m. Sandra Elizabeth Laaker, June 10, 1961; children: David James, John Daniel. BA, U. Nebr., 1959, cert. in journalism, 1964; JD, U. San Francisco, 1962. Bar: Nebr. 1962. Pvt. practice law, Lincoln, 1962-64; reporter Des Moines Register and Tribune, 1964-85, Washington corr., 1969-85, bur. chief, 1976-85; dir. John S. Knight fellowships for profl. journalists, prof. communication Stanford U., 1985-2000. Lectr. Wells Coll., 1981; mem. com. on agrl. edn. in secondary schs. Nat. Acad. Scis., 1985-88. Trustee Reuter Found., 1989-00, Am. Conservatory Theater, 2000-03, Oreg. Shakespear Fest., 2003—, Jefferson Pub. Radio, 2003-; mem. Pulitzer Prize Bd., 1990-99; mem. journalism adv. com. Knight Found., 2000-06. Profl. Journalism fellow Stanford U., 1973-74; recipient award for disting. reporting public affairs Am. Polit. Sci. Assn., 1969; Thomas L. Stokes award for environ. reporting Washington Journalism Center, 1971, 79; Pulitzer prize for nat. reporting, 1976, 79; Worth Bingham Found. prize for investigative reporting, 1976; Raymond Clapper Meml. Assn. award for Washington reporting, 1976, 78; Edward J. Meeman award for Conservation Reporting, 1985. Mem.: Com. Concerned Journalists, Soc. Profl. Journalists (Disting. Svc. award 1976), Soc. Environ. Journalists, Gridiron Club. Home: 71 Water St 206 Ashland OR 97520 Personal E-mail: risserjv@gmail.com.

RISSER, PAUL GILLAN, academic administrator, botanist; b. Blackwell, Okla., Sept. 14, 1939; s. Paul Crane and Jean (McCluskey) R.; children: David, Mark, Stephen, Scott. BA, Grinnell Coll., 1961; MS in Botany, U. Wis., 1965, PhD in Botany and Soils, 1967. From asst. prof. to prof. botany U. Okla., 1967-81, also asst. dir. biol. sta., chmn. dept. botany and microbiology, 1977-81, prof., chmn. rsch. cabinet, 2006—, exec. dir. Econ. Devel. Generating Excellence, 2008—; dir. Okla. Biol. Survey, 1971-77; chief Ill. Natural History Survey, 1981-86; program dir., ecosystem studies NSF; provost and v.p. acad. affairs U. N.Mex., 1989-92; former pres. Miami U., Oxford, Ohio; pres. Oreg. State U., 1996—2002; chancellor Okla. Sys. Higher Edn., 2003—06; acting dir. Nat. Mus. Nat. History, Washington, 2007—08; exec. dir. Econ. Devel. Generating Excellence (EDGE), Okla. Author: (with Kathy Cornelison)

Man and the Biosphere, 1979, (with others) The True Prairie Ecosystem, 1981; research, numerous publs. in field. Trustee Pioneer Multi-County Library Bd. Mem. Am. Acad. Arts and Scis., Ecol. Soc. Am. (pres.), Brit. Ecol. Soc., Soc. Range Mgmt., Southwestern Assn. Naturalists (pres.), Am. Inst. Biol. Sci. (pres.), Torrey Bot. Club. Presbyterian. Office: U Okla Rsch Cabinet 1 Partners Pl 350 David L Boren Ave Norman OK 73072 E-mail: risserp@ou.edu.

RISSETTO, HARRY A., lawyer; b. Dec. 1, 1943; AB, Fairfield U., 1965; JD, Georgetown U., 1968. Bar: N.Y. 1969, D.C. 1970, U. S. Supreme Ct. Law clk. to Hon. John J. Sirica US Dist. Ct. D.C., 1968-69; law clk. to Chief Justice Warren E. Burger US Supreme Ct., 1969-70; sr. counsel Morgan, Lewis & Bockius, Washington. Adj. prof. Law Ctr., Georgetown U., 1986-89. Mem. ABA (co-chmn. railway labor act com. sect. of labor and employment law 1987-89), Coll. Labor & Employment Lawyers. Office: Morgan Lewis & Bockius 1111 Pennsylvania Ave NW Washington DC 20004 Home Phone: 703-241-0442; Office Phone: 202-739-5130. Business E-Mail: hrissetto@morganlewis.com.

RISSMAN, BURTON RICHARD, lawyer; b. Chgo., Nov. 13, 1927; s. Louis and Eva (Lyons) R.; m. Francine Greenberg, June 15, 1952; children: Lawrence E., Thomas W., Michael P. BS, U. Ill., 1947, JD, 1951; LLM, NYU, 1952. Bar: Ill. 1951, U.S. Dist. Ct. (north dist.) Ill. 1954, U.S. Ct. Appeals (7th cir.) 1978, U.S. Supreme Ct. 1982. Assoc. Schiff, Hardin & Waite, Chgo., 1953-59, ptnr., 1959—2003, mem. mgmt. com., 1984-92, chmn. mgmt. com., 1986-90; ret., 2003. Mem. faculty Practicing Law Inst. Bd. editor U. Ill. Law Forum, 1949-51; contbr. articles to profl. jours. 1st lt. JAGC USAF, 1952—53. Food Law fellow, 1951. Mem. ABA, Ill. Bar Assn., Chgo. Bar Assn., Chgo. Coun. Lawyers, Carlton Club.

RISTER, GENE ARNOLD, humanities educator; b. Merkel, Tex., Apr. 18, 1943; s. Jettie William and Mary Evelyn (Scott) R.; m. Janet Kathleen Ledermann, Jan. 21, 1967. BA summa cum laude, McMurry U., 1965; MA, Tex. Christian U., 1966; PhD, U. Wis., 1972; postgrad., U. Ariz., 1990, No. Ariz. U., 1990. Prof., divsn. chmn. McMurry U., Abilene, Tex., 1970-81, East Ctrl. U., Ada, Okla., 1981-83, Paradise Valley Coll., Maricopa C.C., Phoenix, 1983—. Adj. prof. No. Ariz. U., Phoenix, 1994—; del. Nat. Inst. Higher Edn. for Mex.-Ams., Albuquerque, 1975. Author: (poems) Canticles I, 2002, Canticles II, 2003, Canticles III, 2004, Rumors of Unruh, 2006, Asia Ste, 2008; book reviewer Tex. Rev., 1985; illustrator Tex. Rev. and Tex. Anthology, 1979-82; contbr. articles to profl. jours.; contbr. numerous poems to jours., anthologies. Regional cons. Human Rels. Coun., Midland; moderator, dir. West Tex. Coun. Govts.; mem. Tex. Com. for Humanities and Pub. Policy, 1975-81; ECU rep. Intertribal Coun., Five Nations, Sulphur, Okla., 1981; co-sponsor Tex. Reading Cir. Consortium of Univs., 1977-79. Recipient Faculty Recognition award Consortium for C.C. Devel., 1996; named Innovator of the Yr. Maricopa CCD/League for Innovation, 1988, Outstanding Faculty Employee award Maricopa C.C. Dist., 1985, 89, 92; NDEA Title VI fellow, 1965-67, Am. Grad. Sch. Internat. Mgmt. fellow, 1995, East-West Ctr. fellow, 1994, Japan Found. fellow, 1995; U.S. Dept. Edn. Title VIA grantee, 1996-98. Mem. C.C. Humanities Assn. (Ariz. state rep. to nat. bd. 1992). Democrat. Baptist. Avocations: archaeology, art, movies, music, travel. Home: 14407 N 60th St Scottsdale AZ 85254-5540 Office: Paradise Valley Cmty Coll 18401 N 32nd St Phoenix AZ 85032-1210 Home Phone: 480-991-6501; Office Phone: 602-787-6575. E-mail: gene.rister@pvmail.maricopa.edu.

RISTOW, BRUNNO, plastic surgeon; b. Brusque, Brazil, Oct. 18, 1940; s. Arno and Ally Odette (von Bruettner) Ristow; m. Urannia Carrasquilla Gutierrez, Nov. 10, 1979; children from previous marriage: Christian Kilian, Trevor Roland. Student, Coll. Sinodal, Brazil, 1956—57; MD magna cum laude, U. Brazil, 1966. Diplomate Am. Bd. Plastic and Reconstructive Surgery. Intern in surgery Hosp. dos Estrangeiros, Rio de Janeiro, 1965, Hosp. Estuadual Miguel Couto, Brazil, 1965—66, Instituto Aposentadoria Pensao Comerciarios Hosp. for Gen. Surgery, 1966; resident in plastic and reconstructive surgery Dr. Ivo PItanguy Hosp. Santa Casa de Misericordia, Rio de Janeiro, 1967; fellow Inst. Reconstructive Plastic Surgery NYU Med. Ctr., NYC, 1967—68, jr. resident, 1971—72, sr. and chief resident, 1972—73; practice medicine specializing in plastic surgery Rio de Janeiro, 1967, NYC, 1968—73, San Francisco, 1973—; asst. surgeon NY Hosp., Cornell Med. Ctr., NYC, 1968—71. Clin. instr. surgery NYU Sch. Medicine, 1972—73; chmn. plastic and reconstructive surgery divsn. Presbyn. Hosp., Pacific Med. Ctr., San Francisco, 1974—92, chmn. emeritus, 1992—. Contbg. author: Cancer of the Hand, 1975, Current Therapy in Plastic and Reconstructive Surgery, 1988, Male Aesthetic Surgery, 1989, How They Do It: Procedures in Plastic and Reconstructive Surgery, 1990, Middle Crus: The Missing Link in Alar Cratilage Anatomy, 1991, Surgical Technology International, 1992, Aesthetic Plastic Surgery, 1993, Mastery of Surgery: Plastic and Reconstructive Surgery, 1993, Reoperative Aesthetic Plastic Surgery of the Face and Breast, 1994; contbr. articles to profl. jours. With M.C. Brazilian Army Res., 1959—70. Decorated knight Venerable Order of St. Hubertus, Knight Order St. John of Jerusalem; fellow in surgery, Cornell Med. Sch., 1968—71. Fellow: ACS, Internat.Coll. Surgeons; mem.: AMA (Physician's Recognition award 1971—83), San Francisco Med. Assn., Calif. Med. Assn., Calif. Soc. Plastic Surgeons, Internat. Soc. Aesthetic Plastic Surgeons, Am. Soc. Plastic and Reconstructive Surgeons, Am. Soc. Aesthetic Plastic Surgery (chmn. edn.), San Francisco Olympic Club. Republican. Evangelical. Office: Calif Pacific Med Ctr 2100 Webster St Ste 501 San Francisco CA 94115-2373 Home Phone: 415-346-0465; Office Phone: 415-202-1507. Office Fax: 415-202-0131. Personal E-mail: info@brunnoristow.com.

RISTOW, GEORGE EDWARD, neurologist, educator; b. Albion, Mich., Dec. 15, 1943; s. George Julius and Margaret (Beattie) R.; 1 child, George Andrew Martin. BA, Albion Coll., 1965; DO, Coll. Osteo. Medicine/Surgery, Des Moines, 1969. Diplomate Am. Bd. Psychiatry and Neurology. Intern Garden City Hosp., 1969-70; resident Wayne State U., 1970-74; fellow U. Newcastle Upon Tyne, 1974-75; asst. prof. dept. neurology Wayne State U., Detroit, 1975-77; assoc. prof. Mich. State U., East Lansing, 1977-83, prof., 1983-84, 95—, prof., chmn., 1984-95, prof. emeritus, 2001—. Fellow Am. Acad. Neurology, Royal Soc. Medicine; mem. AMA, Am. Osteo. Assn., Pan Am. Med. Assn., World Fedn. Neurology, Am. Coll. Neuropsychiatrists (sr.). Home: 10216 Regal Dr Apt 501 Largo FL 33774-4948 also: 19534 Gulf Blvd Apt 102 Indian Shores FL 33785 Office Phone: 517-374-7600. Personal E-mail: gristow@cimamed.com, ristowge@aol.com.

RISTOW, THELMA FRANCES, retired elementary school educator; b. Plymouth, Wis., Sept. 9, 1938; d. Ambrose J. and Marie A. (Lauby) Enders; m. William A. Ristow, Nov. 7, 1964; children: James, Lora, Kim, Robert, Donald. BS, U. Wis., Oshkosh, 1960, MS in Elem. Edn., 1995. Cert. elem. tchr. Peer coach Oshkosh Area Sch. Dist., 2000—. Contbr. chapters to books; co-author (with Dr. Ava McCall): Teaching State History: A Guide to Developing a Multicultural Curriculum. Mem. Internat. Reading Assn. (state coord.), Wis. State Reading Assn., Ctrl. Wis. Reading Coun., Mid-East Reading Coun., Wolf River Reading Coun., Fox Valley Reading Coun., Headwaters Reading Coun., Menominee Indian Reading Coun., ABC Literacy Coun. Home: 1600 Northpoint St Oshkosh WI 54901-3119 Personal E-mail: tfristow@new.rr.com.

RITCH, KATHLEEN, diversified financial services company executive; b. Harbor Beach, Mich., Jan. 23, 1943; d. Eunice (Spry) R. BA, Mich. State U., 1965; student, Katharine Gibbs Sch., 1965—66. Exec. sec., adminstrv. asst. to pres. Katy Industries, Inc., NYC, 1969-70; exec. sec., adminstrv. asst. to chmn. Kobrand Corp., NYC, 1970-72; adminstrv. asst. to chmn. and pres. Ogden Corp., NYC, 1972-74, asst. sec., adminstr. office svcs., asst. to chmn., 1974-81, corp. sec., adminsr. office svcs., 1981-84, v.p., corp. sec., adminstr. office svcs., 1984-92, v.p. corp. sec., 1992-2000; freelance executive NYC, 2000—. Co-owner Unell Mfg. Co., Port Hope, Mich., 1966-87. Bd. dir. Young Concert Artists, Inc. Home: 500 E 77th St New York NY 10162-0025

RITCH, ROBERT HARRY, ophthalmologist, educator; b. New Haven, May 14, 1942; s. Edward Lewis and Minerva (Grosberg) R. BA cum laude, Harvard U., 1965, MA, 1967; postgrad., Rice U., 1967—68; MD, Albert Einstein Coll. Medicine, 1972. Diplomate Am. Bd. Ophthalmology, Am. Bd. Laser Surgery. Intern St. Vincent's Med. Ctr., NYC, 1972-73; resident in ophthalmology Mt. Sinai Sch. Medicine, NYC, 1973-75, chief resident, 1975-76, Heed Ophthalmic Found. fellow, 1976-77, NIH-Nat. Rsch. Svc. fellow, 1976-78, asst. clin. ophthalmologist, 1976-77, instr., 1977-78, asst. prof., 1978-80, assoc. prof., 1980-82; attending ophthalmologist Beth Israel Med. Ctr., NYC, 1978—; chief Glaucoma Svc. NY Eye and Ear Infirmary, NYC, 1983—, surgeon dir., 1991—; Shelley and Steven Einhorn Disting. chair in ophthalmology, 2007—. Cons. ophthalmologist VA Hosp., Bronx, 1978—82, Manhattan Eye, Ear & Throat Hosp., 1989—; dir. glaucoma svc. Elmhurst Hosp., 1978—82, acting dir. dept. ophthalmology, 1979—82; chief glaucoma svc. NY Eye and Ear Infirmary, NYC, 1983—, surgeon dir., 1991—; adj. sr. scientist Singapore Eye Rsch. Inst., 1997; adj. prof. Mt. Sinai Sch. Medicine, 2005—; prof. clin. ophthalmology NY Med. Coll., Valhalla, 1983—2008, prof. ophthalmology, 2008—; Arthur Bedell Meml. lectr. Wills Eye Hosp., Phila., 1995; John Edwin Brown Meml. lectr. Ohio State U., Columbus, 1996; Schoenburg Meml. lectr. Ill. Eye and Ear Infirmary, Chgo., 1996; Schlaegel lectr. U. Ind., Indpls., 1996; Gerasimos Frenimopoulos Meml. lectr. Duke U., 1997, Joseph M. Bryan Meml. lectr., 97; Roger P. Mason Meml. lectr. Howard U., 1997; Abraham S. Ticho lectr., Jerusalem, 98; Anagnostakis-Trantus lectr., Athens, 98; Sanford Gifford Meml. lectr., Chgo., 98; Annie Wong lectr. Chinese U., Hong Kong, 1999; Arthur Lim lectr., Hong Kong, 2001; Am. Glaucoma Soc. Subspecialty Day lectr. Am. Acad. Opthalmology, New Orleans, 2001; King Khaled Meml. lectr., Riyadh, 03; Chew Sek-Jin Meml. lectr., Hong Kong, 03; Irving Leopold Meml. lectr., Irvine, Calif., 04; Francis Proctor Meml. lectr., San Francisco, 05; Julius Silver Meml. lectr., NY, 06; Irving Leopold Meml. lectr., NY, 06; Robert Shaffer lectr. Am. Acad. Opthalmology, 2007; program chmn. East Coast Glaucoma Symposium, NY, 2000; cons. Sukhumvit Hosp., Bangkok, 1994; pres. Internat. Eye Cons., Ltd., 1995—, NY Glaucoma Rsch. Inst., 1996; mem. adv. bd. Dr. to Dr., Berkeley, Calif., 1995—; sec., treas., chmn. sci. adv. bd. Glaucoma Found., 1984—; med. dir., chmn., grant rev. com.; med. dir. Children's Right to Sight, prin. investigator Collaborative Initial Glaucoma Treatment Study, 1993—2003; mem. adv. bd. Sturge-Weber Found., 1996; mem. glaucoma adv. com. Nat. Soc. to Prevent Blindness, 1986—; organizing chmn. Bangkok Ophthal. Congress, 1985—93, Optic Nerve Rescue & Restoration Think Tank, NY, 1994—2003, First Internat. Think Tank on Exfoliation Syndrome, NY, 1999, Myanmar Internat. Ophthal. Congress, 1997, 99, 2003; internat. sci. com. Internat. Congress of Ophthalmology, Sydney, 2002; sci. organizing com. mem. 4th Internat. Glaucoma Congress, Barcelona, 2003; external assessor U. Malaya, 1988—96; cons. Tun Hussein Onn Nat. Eye Hosp., Kuala Lumpur, Malaysia, 1996—; internat. adv. bd. 4th Internat. Symposium of Ophthalmology, Shantou, China, 2002; mem. steering com. Assn. Internat. Glaucoma Soc., 2002—; internat. advisor Tianjin Med. Ctr., China, 2002—; hon. pres. Chinese Internat. Glaucoma Congress, Beijing, 2004; mem. sci. organizing com. 5th Internat. Glaucoma Congress, Capetown, South Africa, 2005; chmn. sci. organizing com. glaucoma sect. World Congress Ophthalmology, Sao Paulo, Brazil, 2006; organizing chmn. Kazakhstan Ophthalmological Congress, Almaty, 2006, ARVO/AAO Symposium on Nanotech., Am. Acad. Ophthalmology, 2007; organizing com. World Glaucoma Congress, Singapore, 2007; bd. dirs. Helen Keller Internat.; hon. prof., dept. anatomy Hong Kong U., 2008—; lectr. in field; Robert Herbst lectr., 2008; Tkc Liv meml. lectr., 08; Huang-Uhan meml. lectr., 08; hon. lectr. Optometric Glaucoma Soc., 2008; lectr. 17th Am. Glaucoma Soc., 2008; spl. lectr. APAO, 2009; organizing chmn. Glaucoma Sect. World Ophthlmology Congress, Hong Kong, 2008; co-chmn. & organizer First Annual World Glaucoma Day, 2008; program chmn. Glaucoma Asia-Pacific Acad. Ophthalmology, Bali, 2009; organizing chmn. Hong Kong Nenotech. Symposium, 2009, Internat. Update Eye Disease, Lima, Peru, 2009. Author (with M.B. Shields): The Secondary Glaucomas, 1982, The Glaucomas, 1988, 1996; author: (with R. Caronia) Classic Papers in Glaucoma, 2000; spl. sect. editor: Jour. Glaucoma, 1991—98, mem. editl. bd.: Sightsaving, 1981—86, Opthalmic Laser Therapy, 1984—88, Ophthalmic Resident, 1992—95, Ophthalmic Surgery and Lasers, 1995—, Microsurgery, 1994—2004, Ophthalmology Times, 1996—2001, Jour. Glaucoma, 1998—, Internat. Glaucoma Rev., 1999—, Archives Ophthalmology, 2004—08, BMC Ophthalmology, 2005—, Expert Rev. Ophthalmology, 2005—, Asian Jour. Ophthalmology, 2006—, contbg. editor: Ophthalmic Practice, 1993—2005; contbg. editor Jour. Ocular Biology, Diseases, and Informatics, 2007—, advisory panel US Ophthalmic Review, 2007—; contbr. to films on laser therapy, over 1400 articles and abstracts in field. Bd. dirs. Dooley Found./Intermed. USA, 1991—, UN, Southeastern Nigeria Eye Care Outreach Coll. Med. Scis. U. Calabar, Nigeria, 1996—; vol. Devel. Coun., 1991-93; chmn. bd. dirs. I-Med. Devel Corp., 1991-94; sci. adv. bd. Singapore Eye Rsch. Inst.; bd. govs. Internat. Soc. for Imaging of the Eye, 2002—; adv. com. Internat. Coun. Ophthalmology, 2002—, chmn., adv. com. to bd. dirs., 2009-. Hon. scholar, Harvard U., 1965, NSF fellow, 1966—67, Harvard Traveling fellow, Rice U., 1967—68; recipient Acad. Investigator award, NIH, 1978—81, Disting. Svc. award, Internat. Ctr. NY, 1981, Exec. Dirs. award, 1985, Founders award, Nat. Exhibits by Blind Artists, 1985, Gold medal of Merit and Honor, Greek Glaucoma Soc., 1998, Ophthalmology Times Achievement in Ophthalmology award, 1998, Louis Rudin award for rsch. in glaucoma, 1999, Dean's Disting. Rsch. award NY Med. Coll., 2008, Decorated comdr. Grace Sovereign Order of Orthodox Knights Hospitalier of St. John of Jerusalem; named spl. honoree, Helen Keller Found., 2000, Glaucoma Found., 2000; Jesse H. Neal award for editl. achievement, 2000, John Kearny Rodgers Physician of Yr. award, NY Eye and Ear Infirmary, 2005; Albion O. Bernstein award, Med. Soc. State of NY, Dean's Disting. Rsch award, NY Med. Coll., 2007, TKC Liu Meml. award for Leadership in Ophthalmology, Hong Kong 2008, Glaucoma Found. award for Innovation and Excellence in Glaucoma 2008, Ronald F. Lowe Medal of the Australia-New Zealand Ophthalmol Soc., 2008, Dominick Purpura Disting. Alumnus Annual award, Albert Einstein Coll. of Medicine 2009. Fellow Am. Acad. Ophthalmology (edn. distbn. subcom. 1994-97, book/jour. link subcom. 1994-97, distbn. adv. subcom. 1997-2000, chmn. subcom., 2001—, Honor award, 1985, sr. honor award 1995, Lifetime Achievement Honor award 2007, Leaders in Edn. Ophthalmology award 2007), Heed Ophthalmic Found. (ophthalmologist of Yr. 1996), Am. Ophthalmol. Soc. (program com. 2002-2004), NY Acad. Medicine, Royal Coll. Ophthalmologists (UK), ACS, Internat. Coll. Surgeons, Am. Soc. Laser Surgery Medicine (chmn. ophthalmology sect. 1991-92, moderator and program chmn. joint sci. symposium on glaucoma 1991), NY Acad. Medicine (sec. sect. on ophthalmology 1991-92, chmn. 1993-94, Charles May Meml. Lectr. 1991, bd. trustees 2003—); mem. AMA, AAAS, NY State Med. Soc., NY County Med. Soc., Assn. Rsch. in Vision and Ophthalmology (program com., glaucoma sect. 1991-93, program chmn. 1993-94, internat. com. 2003—, bd. trustees 2003—08, v.p. 2007-08, Disting. Svc. award 2009, Gold fellow 2009), Am. Assn. Ophthalmology, Ophthal. Soc. UK, Internat. Assn. Ocular surgeons, Internat. Congress Ophthalmology (glaucoma com. 1994—), NY Intra-Ocular Lens Implant Soc., Manhattan Ophthal. Soc., Assn. Internat. Glaucoma Soc., Internat. Soc. Eye Rsch., Soc. Clin. Trials, Pan-Pacific Anterior Segment Soc. (v.p. 1985-88), Internat. Coun. Ophthalmology (adv. com.), NY Acad. Sci., Ophthalmic Laser Surgery Soc. (sec.-treas. 1982-98, 2000-, pres. 1998-2000), NY Soc. Clin. Ophthalmology (rec. sec. 1988-90, program chmn. 1990-91, pres. 1991-92), NY Glaucoma Rsch. Inst. (pres. 1996—), Am. Soc. Cell Biology, Am. Telemed Assn., Internat. Soc. On-Line Ophthalmologists (mem. orgn. com., chmn. glaucoma sect. 1995—), Internat. Fedn. Cell Biologists, Philippine Soc. Ophthalmology (hon.), Thailand Ophthal. Soc. (hon.), Italian Assn. for Study of Glaucoma (hon.), La.-Miss. Ophthal. and Otolarygol. Soc. (hon.), Can. Implant Soc. (hon). Home: 455 E 57th St # 14D New York NY 10022-3065 Office: NY Eye and Ear Infirmary 310 E 14th St New York NY 10003-4201 Home Phone: 212-980-7187; Office Phone: 212-477-7540. Personal E-mail: ritchmd@earthlink.net.

RITCHEY, KATHY J., history professor; b. Dallas, June 21, 1961; d. Aeron and Gladys Oden; children: Jennifer, Josh, Kristen Ritchey-Vian. BS, Hardin-Simmons U., Abilene, Tex., 1994; MA, Sul Ross State U., Alpine, Tex., 1996. Cert. tchr. Tex., 1994. Adj. prof. history Brookhaven Coll., Dallas, 2003—; prof. polit. sci. Cisco Jr. Coll., Abilene, 2005—. Vol. coord. Cisco Coll., 2003—08. Office: Brookhaven Coll 3939 Valley View Ln Dallas TX 75244 Business E-Mail: kritchey@dcccd.edu.

RITCHEY, KENNETH WILLIAM, human services administrator; b. Washington, June 7, 1947; s. Conrad Monroe and Katherine Costance (Sheris) (dec. 2004) R.; m. Nancy Jayne Kirk, Aug. 22, 1970; children: Kirk Damon, Erin Kathryn (dec. Apr. 1988). BS in Edn., Shippensburg U., 1969; MEd in Spl. Edn., U. Va., 1972; MS in Edn1. Adminstrn., U. Dayton, 1980, D in Leadership, 1991; grad. sr. execs. in state & local govt. program, Harvard U., 1992. Spl. edn. tchr. Shippensburg Area Sch. Dist., Pa., 1969-71; head cross country and track coach Shippensburg U., 1970-74; master tchr., coord. work experience program Lincoln Intermediate Unit, New Oxford, Pa., 1971-76; adult edn. tchr. Franklin County Prison, Chambersburg, Pa., 1972-76; asst. supt. mgmt. svcs. Montgomery County Bd. Mental Retardation & Devel. Disabilities, Dayton, Ohio, 1977-83, supt. bd., 1983-99; dir. Ohio Dept. Mental Retardation and Devel. Disabilities, Columbus, 1999—2007; asst. commr. divsn. devel. disabilities NJ Dept. Human Svcs., 2007—. Mem. part-time faculty edn. dept. U. Dayton, 1983-97; mem., vice-chair cmty. and mil. adv. com. ARC, 1986-95, needs and priorities com. Human Svcs. Levy Coun., 1982-84, 87-99; trustee Ohio Polit. Action Com., Brighter Tomorrow Found., 1990-2000, County Corp., 1992-98. Former editor statewide newsletter for tchrs. and profls. in Work Experience. Vol. mem. cmty. and agys. resources coun. United Way, 1986—98; v.p. HelpLink Bd., pres.; mem. Gov.'s Vision Com., Ill., 1997—2000, Gov.'s Cabinet; bd. dirs. Ohio Pub. Images, Inc., past pres. Recipient Harold Hilty Humanitarian award, United Cerebral Palsy Rehab. Svcs., 1994, Robert Weaver Disting. Svc. award, Montgomery County Bd. Mental Retardation and Devel. Disabilities, 1999, Svc. award, Profl. Assn. on Retardation, 2002, Chair's Recognition award, Wright State U. Dept. Psychiatry, 2005, Cmty. Star award, Franklin County, 2006, Ray Ferguson Advocacy award, ARC, Ohio, 2007; honored by, Ohio Assn. County Bds., 2005. Mem.: Ohio Self Determination Assn. (Catalyst award 2003), Nat. Assn. State Dirs. Devel. Disabilities Svcs. (chair nat. policy work group 2002, bd. trustees 2004, sec.-treas. 2005—, v.p./pres. elect 2007), Supts. Assn. (exec. com.), Ohio Supts. County Bds. Mental Retardation (v.p., pres.), Phi Beta Kappa. Democrat. Methodist. Home: 86 Lochatong Rd Ewing NJ 08628 Office: Division Devel Disabilities PO Box 726 Trenton NJ 08025 Home Phone: 609-882-4648; Office Phone: 609-631-6500. Personal E-mail: k1ritchey@aol.com.

RITCHEY, SAMUEL DONLEY, JR., retired retail executive; b. Derry Twp., Pa., July 16, 1933; s. Samuel Donley and Florence Catherine (Litsch) R.; m. Sharon Marie Anderson, Apr. 6, 1956; children: Michael Donley, Tamara Louise, Shawn Christopher. BS, San Diego State U., 1955, MS, 1963; postgrad., Stanford U., 1964. With Lucky Stores Inc., 1951-61, 64-86, pres., chief operating officer, 1978-80, pres., chief exec. officer, 1980-81, chmn., chief exec. officer, 1981-85, chmn. bd., 1981-86. Bd. dirs. The McClatchy Co., De La Salle Inst., John Muir Health; chair Coll. Bus., San Diego State U.; grad. mgr. San Diego State U., 1961-63; lectr. in field; past chmn. Calif. Power Exch., mem. AT&T bd. audit com. chair, adv. coun. Grad. Sch. Bus., Stanford U. Sloan Found. fellow Mem. Mex. Am. Legal Def. and Edn. Fund, Western Assn. Food Chains (bd. dirs., pres.), Food Mktg. Inst. (bd. dirs., vice chmn.), Sloan Alumni Assn. (adv. bd., pres.).

RITCHIE, ALBERT, lawyer; b. Charlottesville, Va., Sept. 29, 1939; s. John and Sarah Dunlop (Wallace) R.; m. Jennie Wayland, Apr. 29, 1967; children: John, Mary. BA, Yale U., 1961; LLB, U. Va., 1964. Bar: Ill. 1964, Tenn. 2000. Assoc. Sidley & Austin, Chgo., 1964-71, ptnr., 1972-99, ret., 1999. Bd. dirs. Erie Neighborhood House, Chgo., 1978-88; bd. dirs. United Charities of Chgo., 1979-90; trustee U. Va. Law Sch. Found., 1997-99. Capt. U.S. Army, 1965-67. Mem. ABA, Am. Coll. Real Estate Lawyers, Chgo. Legal Aid Soc., Legal Club Chgo. (pres. 1986-87), U. Va. Law Sch. Alumni Assn. (v.p. 1989-93, pres. 1993-95), Cherokee Country Club, Hillsboro Club. Methodist. Home: 436 Boxwood Sq Knoxville TN 37919-6627 Personal E-mail: ritchiea@bellsouth.net.

RITCHIE, ALEXANDER BUCHAN, lawyer; b. Detroit, Apr. 19, 1923; s. Alexander Stevenson and Margaret (May) R.; m. Sheila Spellacy, June 1998; 1 child, Barbara Ritchie Drolshagen. BA, Wayne State U., 1947, JD, 1949. Bar: Mich. 1949. Pvt. practice, Detroit, 1949-52, 84—; asst. gen. counsel, asst. v.p. Maccabees Mutual Life Ins. Co., Detroit, 1952-65, v.p., sec., gen. counsel Southfield, Mich., 1977-84; sec., house counsel Wayne Nat. Life Ins. Co., Detroit, 1966-67; ptnr. Fenton, Nederlander, Dodge & Ritchie, Detroit, 1967-77. Spl. asst. atty. gen. State Mich., 1974-77. Bd. mem. Detroit Bd. Edn., 1971-77, Detroit Ctrl. Bd. Edn., 1971-73; bd. Police Commrs., Detroit, 1974-77; bd. dirs. Doctor's Hosp., Detroit, 1974-89. With U.S. Army, 1943-46. Recipient Key to the City of Detroit, Mayor Coleman Young, 1977. Mem. Mich. State Bar Assn. Avocations: reading, golf, theater, gourmet. Home: 29255 Laurel Woods Dr Apt 201 Southfield MI 48034-4647

RITCHIE, COY DOYLE, management consultant; b. Blythe, Calif., Dec. 30, 1937; s. Coy Doyl Ritchie and Carolyn Helen Schwacofer; m. Juanita Pacita Domingo, June 13, 1959; children: Coy C., Harold M. BSBA, Roosevelt U., Chgo., 1965; MBA, City U., Bellevue, Wash., 1984; D of Mgmt., Colo. Tech. U., Colorado Springs, 1996. Dir., officer-in-charge Navy Elec. Tng. Sch., Norfolk, Va., 1975—78; dir., area mgr. ITT Tech. Inst., Portland, Oreg., 1978—86; v.p. acad., dean Colo. Tech. Coll., 1986—88; dir. ITT Tech. Inst., Sacramento, 1988—91, Aurora, Colo., 1991—96; v.p., chancellor Colo. Tech. U., 1997—2002; pres. Ritchie Mgmt. Svcs., Aurora, 2003—. Author: Digital Computers, 1965. Treas. Spring Creek Homeowners Assn., Aurora, 2003—07; sec. Colo. Pvt. Sch. Assn., Denver, 1994—95; chmn. edn. com. Aurora C. of C., 1995—96. Mem.: Mil. Order of the World Wars (chpt. comdr.), Navy League US (Denver coun. bd. dirs. 2006—09), Mile High Mil. Officers Assn. (pres.), Beta Gamma Sigma. Republican. Roman Catholic. Avocations: genealogy, gardening, classic automobiles. Home: 4198 S Kirk Ct Aurora CO 80013-6022 Office Phone: 303-981-5519. Personal E-mail: coyritchie@aol.com.

RITCHIE, DAVID, communications educator, researcher; b. Kellogg, Idaho, Aug. 5, 1943; s. Lloyd Ritchie and Lois Brannan; m. LaJean Humphries. PhD, Stanford, Calif., 1987. Asst. prof. U. Puget Sound, Tacoma, U. Wis., Madison; prof. Portland State U., Oreg., 1990—. Contbr. articles to profl. publs. Lt. USN, 1966—69, USS Chikaskia. Mem.: Internat. Comm. Assn. Liberal. Avocations: hiking, skiing, travel. Office: Portland State Univ 724 SW Harrison Portland OR 97207 Business E-Mail: cgrd@pdx.edu.

RITCHIE, DORIS LEE, executive secretary; b. Oak Park, Ill., May 18, 1926; d. Joseph Bulicek and Janette Louise Whitmire; m. H. R. Ritchie, Nov. 7, 1947 (dec.); children: H. Russell III, Jane Lee, Dara Kim. AA, Harper Coll., Palatine, Ill., 1972; BA, Elmhurst Coll., Ill., 1975; MS, Northern Ill. U., 1979; EdD, No. Ill. U., 1987. Exec. sec. Motorola, Chgo., 1943—45, Englander Bedding, Chgo., 1945—48, Pioneer Press, Oak Park, Ill., 1949—50, ABC, Chgo., 1948—49; tchr. Rolling Meadows Ill. Sch. Dist., 1979—81; vol. cons. Palatine, Ill., 1980—83. Spkr. in field. Sr. commr. City of Carlsbad, 1986—91, housing commr., 2000—09. Recipient Woman of Distinction, Soroptimist Club, 1990, DAR, 2000, Rookie of Yr., Hi Noon Rotary Club, 1989. Mem.: Hospice North Coast (life), Belleek Collector's Soc., Country Friends (life), Widows and Widowers Club. Avocations: antiques, reading, bridge. Home: 3379 Garibaldi Pl Carlsbad CA 92010 Personal E-mail: dl-ritchie@sbcglobal.net.

RITCHIE, J., computer software company executive; b. Little Rock; B, U. Ark.; MBA, Okla. State U. Fin. profl. Wash. Mutual, Aetna; head compensation and benefits Frito-Lay Internat.; global dir. exec. compensation and variable rewards Nokia, Helsinki, Finland; gen. mgr. global compensation, benefits and performance mgmt. Microsoft Corp., Redmond, Wash., 2004—08, corp. v.p. worldwide compensation and benefits, 2008—. Mem.: Global High Tech Compensation and Benefits Roundtable, Conf. Bd. (mem. compensation coun.), World at Work. Office: Microsoft Corp One Microsoft Way Redmond WA 98052-6399*

RITCHIE, KEVIN, electronics executive; BSEE, U. Dayton, Ohio, 1978. Product engr. def. bus. Tex. Instruments Inc., 1978—80, with semiconductor group, 1980—90, wafer fab mgr., 1990—96, mgr. worldwide application-specific products mfg. ops., 1996—2000, sr. v.p. worldwide mfg. ops., tech. and mfg. group Dallas, 2000—. Office: Tex Instruments Inc PO Box 660199 Dallas TX 75266-0199 Office Phone: 972-995-2011. Office Fax: 972-995-4360.

RITCHIE, MARK, Secretary of State, Minnesota; b. 1951; m. Nancy Gaschott; 1 child, Rachel (dec.). Grad., Iowa State U., 1971. Founder League of Rural Voters, 1986—2005; founder, pres. Inst. Agr. and Trade Policy, Mpls., 1986—2005; founder, nat. coord. Nat. Voice NOVEMBER 2 Campaign, 2003—04; founder, coord. Internet Resources on Election Protection, 2003—; founder, vol. leader Ctr. Civic Participation, 2004—05; sec. state State of Minn., St. Paul, 2007—. Recipient Activist of Yr. award, Minn. Alliance for Progressive Action, 2004, Progressive Campaign award to Voting Rights Coalition, 2005, Nat. Progressive Leadership award, US Action, 2005, Carl King Disting. Svc. award, Am. Corn Growers Assn., Civic Engagement award, Minn. Commn. Serving Deaf and Hard of Hearing People; named a Patriotic Employer, Employers Support the Guard and Res., 2007. Democrat. Office: Office Sec State 180 State Office Bldg 100 Rev Dr Martin Luther King Jr Blvd Saint Paul MN 55155-1299 Office Phone: 651-201-1328.

RITCHIE, ROBERT JAMES See KID ROCK

RITCHIE, ROBERT OLIVER, materials science educator, department chairman; b. Plymouth, Devon, Eng., Jan. 2, 1948; arrived in US, 1974, naturalized, 1990; s. Kenneth Ian and Kathleen Joyce (Sims) Ritchie; m. Connie Olesen (div. 1978); 1 child, James Oliver; m. HaiYing Soong, 1991; 1 child, Duncan Soong. BA with honors, U. Cambridge, Eng., 1969, MA, PhD, 1973, ScD, 1990. Cert. engr., UK. Goldsmith's rsch. fellow Churchill Coll. U. Cambridge, 1972-74; Miller fellow in basic rsch. sci. U. Calif., Berkeley, 1974-76, prof., 1981—, chair Materials Sci. and Engring. Dept., 2005—; assoc. prof. mech. engring. MIT, Cambridge, 1977-81; dep. dir. Materials Scis. Divsn. Lawrence Berkeley Nat. Lab., Cambridge, 1990-94, dir. Ctr. for Advanced Materials, 1987-95, head structural Materials Dept., Materials Scis. Divsn., 1995—. Cons. Alcan, Allison, Applied Materials, Boeing, Chevron, Cordis, Exxon, GE, GM, Grumman, Guidant, Instron, Northrop, Rockwell, Westinghouse, Baxter, Carbomedics, Med. Inc., Shiley, St. Jude Med.; Van Horn Disting. lectr. Case Western U., 1997. Editor: 19 books; contbr. more than 600 articles to profl. jours. Recipient G. R. Irwin medal, ASTM, 1985, Mathewson gold medal, TMS-AME, 1985, Curtis W. McGraw Rsch. award, Am. Soc. Engring. Educators, 1987, Rosenhain medal, Inst. Materials London, 1992, Wohler medal, European Structural Integrity Soc., 2006, Van Horn Disting. Lectr. award, Case Western U., 1997; named one of Top 100 Scientists, Sci. Digest mag., 1984. Fellow: Royal Acad. Engring. (London), Minerals, Materials and Metals Soc. (Mathewson Gold medal 1985, Disting. Structural Materials Scientist/Engr. award 1996), Am. Soc. Metals Internat. (Marcus A. Grossman award 1980), Internat. Congress on Fracture (pres. 1997—2001, Cottrell Gold Medal 2009), Inst. Materials (London, AA Griffith medal 2007); mem.: NAE, ASME (NADAI medal 2004), Am. Acad. Arts and Scis., Am. Ceramic Soc., Materials Rsch. Soc. Avocations: skiing, hiking, antiques, orchids. Home: 590 Grizzly Peak Blvd Berkeley CA 94708-1238 Office: U Calif Dept Materials Sci and Engring Berkeley CA 94720-1760 Office Phone: 510-486-5798. Business E-Mail: roritchie@lbl.gov.

RITCHIE, WALLACE PARKS, JR., retired surgeon, educator; b. St. Paul, Nov. 4, 1935; s. Wallace Parks and Alice Ransome (Otis) R.; m. Barbara Carey Jewell, Aug. 10, 1960; children: Stephanie, David, Jessica. BA, Yale U., 1957; MD, Johns Hopkins U., 1961; PhD, U. Minn., 1971. Diplomate Am. Bd. Surgery. Intern, resident in surgery Yale U., New Haven, 1961-63; resident in surgery U. Minn. Hosps., Mpls., 1963-69, instr. in surgery, 1969-70; from asst. prof. to prof. surgery U. Va. Sch. Medicine, Charlottesville, 1973-83; prof., chmn. dept. surgery Temple U. Sch. Medicine, Phila., 1983-93; exec. dir. Am. Bd. Surgery, Phila., 1994—2002; ret. Editor textbook: Essentials of Surgery, 1994; contbr. over 160 sci. articles to profl. jours. Lt. col. M.C., U.S. Army, 1970-73. USPHS grantee, 1974-85. Office: Am Bd Surgery Inc 1617 John F Kennedy Blvd Philadelphia PA 19103-1821 Office Phone: 215-525-3809. Personal E-mail: wallace.ritchie@verizon.net.

RITCHIE, WILLIAM PAUL, lawyer; b. Columbus, Ohio, June 3, 1946; s. Austin Everett and Helen (Drake) Ritchie; m. Diane Smith, Aug. 2, 1969; 1 child, Elizabeth Drake. BS in Bus. Adminstrn., Ohio State U., 1968; JD, U. Va., 1971. Bar: Ohio 1971, Calif. 1973, Ill. 1987. Assoc. Jones, Day, Reavis & Pogue, Cleve., 1971—77, ptnr., 1977—, ptnr.-in-charge Chgo., 1987—. Served to lt. USAR, 1972. Mem.: ABA, Chgo. Bar Assn., Calif. Bar Assn., Ohio Bar Assn., Chgo. Club, Mayfield Country Club Cleve. Republican. Office: Jones Day 77 W Wacker Dr Fl 35 Chicago IL 60601-1662 Office Phone: 312-782-3939. Office Fax: 312-782-8585. Business E-Mail: wpritchie@jonesday.com.

RITCHLIN, CHRISTOPHER TREVOR, rheumatologist; s. Raymond F. and Muriel C. Ritchlin; m. Doria A. Scortichini, May 29, 1982; children: Emily Y., Christina L. MD, Albany Med. Coll., NY, 1982; MPH, U. Rochester Sch. Medicine & Dentistry, NY, 2008. Cert. in internal medicine NY, 1983, Am. Bd. Internal Medicine, 1986, rheumatology 1988. Head Rheumatology Unit, Rochester Gen. Hosp., 1991—98; dir. clin. immunology rsch. unit U. Rochester Med. Ctr., 1998—. Mem. med. bd. CORRONA, Albany, 2003—08, Nat. Psoriasis Found., Portland, Oreg., 2004—08. Fellow: ACP (life). Achievements include research in psoriatic arthritis. Office: Univ Rochester Med Ctr 602 Elmwood Ave Box 695 Rochester NY 14642 Business E-Mail: christopher_ritchlin@urmc.rochester.edu.

RITER, ROBERT C., JR., lawyer; b. Pierre, SD, July 8, 1948; BS, U. SD, 1970, JD, 1973. Bar: SD 1973. Asst. city atty., 1973—; with Riter, Rogers, Wattier & Brown, LLP, Pierre, SD, 1973—, ptnr. Lectr. in field. Contbr. articles to profl. jours. Fellow: Am. Bar Found., Am. Bd. Trial Advocates, Am. Coll. Trial Lawyers; mem.: ABA, Def. Rsch. Inst. (state rep. 1994—99, bd. dirs. 1999—2003), Am. Counsel Assn., SD Def. Lawyers Assn. (pres. 1994—95), State Bar SD (chmn. adminstrv. law com. 1979—81, continuing legal edn. com. 1981—84, ethics com. 1986—89, commr. 1992—95, pres. 2005—06), Phi Delta Phi. Office: Riter Rogers Wattier & Brown LLP Profl and Exec Bldg 319 S Coteau St PO Box 280 Pierre SD 57501 Office Phone: 605-224-5825. Office Fax: 605-224-7102. E-mail: r.riter@riterlaw.com.

RITMAN, BARBARA ELLEN, counselor; b. LA, Oct. 19, 1946; d. Jack and June Harriett (Marcus) R. AA, Long Beach City Coll., 1969; BA (magna cum laude), Calif. State U., Long Beach, 1974; MA, Chapman Coll., 1976. Lic. marriage, family and child counselor. Instr. Mt. San Antonio Coll., Walnut, Calif., 1976-78; mental health worker Orange County (Calif.) Mental Health, 1978-80; therapist Family Svc., Long Beach, Calif., 1980-82; clin. dir. Neighborhood Youth Assn., Wilmington, Calif., 1981-88; head psychology svcs. Bellflower (Calif.) Med. Group, 1988-89; chem. dependency counselor Kaiser Permanent, Orange, Calif., 1990—. Cons. Child Abuse Info. Ctr., L.A., 1976-78, Action Seminars for Progress, Santa Monica, Calif., 1976-82. Vista vol., Salt Lake City, Houston, 1967—68. Fellow mem. Calif. Assn. Marriage & Family Therapists. Avocations: film, music, theater, photography.

RITSCH, FREDERICK FIELD, academic administrator, historian; b. Covington, Va., Nov. 25, 1935; s. Frederick Field and Harriet Curtis (Miller) R.; m. Jeannette McClung, June 14, 1957 (dec.); children: Frederick Field III, Lise Catherina; m. Debra Ronning, Dec. 21, 1991; 1 child, Anne Ronning. BA, U. Va., 1956, MA, 1959, PhD, 1962; student, Univ. de Strasbourg, France, 1957-58. Instr. Randolph-Macon Women's Coll., Lynchburg, Va., 1959; vis. lectr. Sweet Briar (Va.) Coll., 1959-60; from asst. prof. to prof. Dana history and humanities Converse Coll., Spartanburg, SC, 1960-83, dir. ctr. for humanities, head div. humanities; dean of faculty Elizabethtown (Pa.) Coll., 1984-85, provost, 1986-96, prof., 1997—2003, prof. and provost emeritus, 2004—. Cons. Ednl. Svcs., Inc., Washington, 1975-77; vice chmn. Comm. Svcs., Inc., Spartanburg, 1978-82; dir. Ctr. for Study Contemporary Humanities, Spartanburg, 1972-81. Author: French Left and European Idea, 1967; author, editor: Issues and Commitment, 1976; editor: (with M. Goldberg) Probes and Projections, 1974; contbr. articles to profl. jours. and collections. Elder Donegal Presbyn. Ch., Mt. Joy, Pa.; sch. bd. Elizabethtown Area Sch. Dist., 2005—. Fulbright fellow, 1957-58; NEH grantee, 1969; recipient Cert. Merit, Inst. Internat. Edn., 1978. Mem. Am. Hist. Assn., Pa. Acad. Deans Conf. (program chmn. 1984), So. Humanities Conf. (editor jour. Humanities in the South 1971-83, chmn. 1984), Phi Beta Kappa. Home: 102 Meadowbrook Ln Elizabethtown PA 17022-2239 Home Phone: 717-367-7871.

RITSCHEL, WOLFGANG ADOLF, medical educator, sculptor, artist; b. Trautenau, Bohemia, Jan. 10, 1933; came to U.S., 1968; s. Karl and Eleonore (Olbert) R.; m. Ingrid M. Wallner, Aug. 5, 1991; children from previous marriage: Alexander, Barbara. Mr.Pharm., U. Innsbruck, Austria, 1955; Dr.Univ., U. Strasbourg, France, 1960; PhD, U. Vienna, Austria, 1965; MD, U. Villarreal, Peru, 1989. Chief pharmacist Girol AG, Zurich, Switzerland, 1958-59; head pharmacy rsch. Biochemie AG, Kundl, Austria, 1959-61; seminar docent Teaching Hosp., Kufstein, Austria, 1959-61; head rsch. Albert David Rsch. Inst., Dacca, Pakistan, 1961-64; prof. Dacca U., 1961-64, U. Basel, Switzerland, 1965-68, U. Cin., 1969-97, prof. emeritus, 1997—. Divsn. head U. Cin., 1985-94; vis. prof. Med. Acad. Krakow, Univ. Clermont-Ferrand, S. Marcos, Lima. Author: The Tablet, 1966, Applied Biopharmaceutics, 1973, Laboratory Manual of Biopharmaceutics and Pharmacokinetics, 1974, Handbook of Basic Pharmacokinetics, 6th revised edit., 2004, Graphic Approach to Clinical Pharmacokinetics, 1993, 2d edit., 1994, Japenese edit., 1998, Antacids and Other Drugs in GI Diseases, 1984, Gerontokinetics, 1988, Japanese edit., 1994, (with Betzien, Kaufmann and Schneider) KINPAK: A Comprehensive Approach to Evaluating Blood Level Curves, 1985, (with Koch) Synopsis der Biopharmazie und Pharmkokinetik, 1986; editor: Clinical Pharmacokinetics: Proceedings of An International Symposium at Salzgitter-Ringelheim, 1977, (with Bauer-Brandl) Die Tablette, 2003, Wolfgang A. Ritschel - The Other Life, 1999; contbr. more than 450 articles to profl. jours., 28 chpts. to books; 23 patents in field; numerous solo and group exhbns. of paintings and sculptures in U.S. and Europe, including Internat. Biennale, Florence, Italy 2005; (travel exhbn.) Learned in Science, Explored in Art, 2009-. Recipient Theodor-Koerner prize Austria Ministry of Edn., 1962, Cross of Honor, Pres. Fedn. Republic Austria, 1975, numerous art awards; named Hon. Prof. U. San Marcos, 1973, U. Cayetano Heredia, 1979; Hon. Senator U. Pisa, 1978; Fulbright sr. scholar, 1993, 1996; named to Internat. Order of Merit, Cambridge, 1993. Fellow Am. Coll. Clin. Pharmacology, Am. Assn. Pharm. Scientists; mem. Acad. Am. Pharm. Assn., Fedn. Internat. Pharm., Royal Acad. Sci. (Spain), Acad. of Sci. (hon.). Roman Catholic. Home: 3436 Cornell Pl Cincinnati OH 45220-1502 Office: Univ Cin Med Ctr 3223 Eden Cincinnati OH 45267-0004

RITTENBERRY, HAROLD W., JR., sculptor; b. Athens, Ga., Dec. 25, 1938; Metal sculptor, Athens. Sculpture, drawings, Gate for Atlanta City Ct., sculpture, Wisdom sculpture for East Point. library, Fulton Co Pub Art Program, Steel Screens for Coll. Pk. Libr., Fulton Co. Pub. Art Prog., sculptured steel bench, Mobile Museum Art, exhibitions include one man sculpt, Ga. mus. art Spirit Yard sponsored by Florsheim Found. Soldier US Army, 1956—59. Grantee, Florsheim found., 2003. Home: 268 Colima Ave Athens GA 30606 Business E-Mail: rclements1@charter.net.

RITTENHOUSE, MICHELE RAPER, playwright, theater educator; b. Tupelo, Miss., Jan. 8, 1952; d. Finas Baynard Raper and Suzanne Madeleine Drouard; m. Michele Raper. BA in Theater, U. Miss., Oxford, 1974; MFA in Playwriting, Rutgers U., New Brunswick, NJ, 1995. Asst. theatre dir. NJ Inst. Tech., Newark, 1974—, adj. prof., 1984—, mng. dir. Rutgers-NJIT Theatre Arts Program, 1995—; adj. prof. Rutgers U., Newark, 1989—. Resident playwright Nat. Playwrights Conf. O'Neill Theatre Ctr., Waterford, Conn., 1997—97; coord. profl. playwright seminar Playwrights Horizon Sch., NYC, 2003—05; playwright resident Abingdon Theatre Co., NYC, 2004—05. Author: (drama) The Scenario, Angel On My Shoulder, The Scenario, Heartland, In The Arms of Baby Jesus, Weep No More Today, Out of the South, Angel On My Shoulder, Weep No More Today, (comedy) Lost Armadillo Cafe, (dramatized folk tales) Xotika, Stories From Home, Sonnet One, Sonnet Two. Recipient One Act Play Competition finalist, Louisville Theatre Ctr., Avy award, NJ Arts Group, 1991—94, award, Nat Horne New Playwrights Festival, 1993, Nat. New Play Contest finalist, SW Theatre Assn., 2000, New Century Writers award, Moxie Films, 2002—03, Christopher Wolk Playwriting finalist, Abingdon Theatre Co., 2003; finalist Julie Harris Playwright award, Chesterfield Film Project, 1998—99; fellow Witter Bynner fellowship, Abingdon Theatre Co., 2004—05. Mem.: AAUP, Alpha Pi Omega, Actor's Frat., Pi Kappa Delta, Forensic Frat., Austin Playwright & Screenwriters Guild, Theatre Devel. Fund, Theatre Comm. Group, Drama Leaque, Authors Leaque America Inc., PSA Profl. Staff Assn., AAUP Profl. Staff Assn., Dramatists Guild America. Office: NJ Inst Tech 323 M L King Jr Blvd Newark NJ 07102 Office Fax: 973-596-5820. Business E-Mail: rittenhouse@njit.edu.

RITTENHOUSE, NANCY CAROL, elementary school educator; b. Humeston, Iowa, May 26, 1941; d. Myrl Matthews and Opal L. (McCartney) Hixson; m. J. Kent Rittenhouse, Dec. 18, 1960 (div. Mar. 1984); children: Brenda L. Carroll, J. Aaron, Timothy K. Grad., Kirksville State Tchrs. Coll., 1960; student, St. Mary of the Plains Coll., 1984-87; degree in elem. edn., Ft. Hays State Coll., 1989. Cert. tchr., Kans. Reading instr. Sacred Heart Sch., Dodge City, Kans., 1984; elem. tchr. Miller Sch., Dodge City, Kans., 1985-86, Washington Sch., Hays, 1987; city-county recreation dir. Sherman County, Goodland, 1988; elem. tchr. Northside Sch., Larned, 1989-90; with Great Bend (Kans.) Tribune. Artist numerous paintings; author poetry. Mem. Menninger Found., Topeka, 1984—; hon. mem. Boy Scouts Am., 1978; camp instr. Spl. Olympics Blind Found., Junction City, Kans., 1985-90, Dodge City, 1984; leader Girl Scouts USA, 1975-77. Recipient Hon. award Spl. Olympics, 1984, 1st pl. poetry award, 1990, watercolor award, 1990, oils award, 1988, pen and ink award, 1984. Mem. AAAS, Nat. Trust for Hist. Preservation, Nat. Geog. Soc., Planetary Soc., Smithsonian Assn., MIT. Republican. Avocations: painting, drawing, walking, swimming, writing prose. Home: PO Box 1872 Great Bend KS 67530-1872 Office: Great Bend Tribune 2012 Forest Ave Great Bend KS 67530-4014

RITTENMEYER, RONALD ALLEN, information technology executive; b. Wilkes-Barre, Pa., May 22, 1947; s. Harold E. and Shirley A. (Hitchner) R.; m. Hedy A. Wrightson; children: Christopher, Ashley. BS in Commerce & Fin., Wilkes U., 1972; MBA, Rockhurst U., 1984. Fin. officer US Dept. Housing & Urban Devel., Washington, 1972-74; shipping mgr. Frito-Lay, Inc., Kirkwood, NY, 1974-76, distbn. mgr. Fall River, Mass., 1976-77, Louisville, 1977-78, Charlotte, NC, 1978-80, prodn. mgr., 1980-82, ops. analyst Dallas, 1982, plant mgr. Topeka, 1982-85, v.p. zone ops. Dallas, 1985-86, v.p. sales and strategic planning, v.p. ops.; v.p. Mid. Ea. & worldwide ops. PepsiCo Food Internat.; pres., COO Merisel; COO Ryder TRS, 1997-98; pres., CEO RailTex, Inc., San Antonio, 1998—2000; chmn., pres., CEO Safety-Kleen Inc., 2001—04; mng. dir. The Cypress Group LLC, 2004—05; exec. v.p. global svc. delivery Electronic Data Systems Corp., Plano, Tex., 2005—06, co-COO, 2005—06, pres., COO, 2006—07, pres., CEO, 2007—, chmn., 2007—. Bd. mem. U.S. C. of C., Am. Heart Assn., No. Tex. Kidney Assn.; mem. exec. bd. Cox Sch. Bus. So. Methodist Univ. Recipient Outstanding Achievement award U.S. HUD, 1974. Avocations: diving, aviation. Office: Electronic Data Systems Corp 5400 Legacy Dr Plano TX 75024 E-mail: ron.rittenmeyer@eds.com.

RITTER, ANN L., lawyer; b. NYC, May 20, 1933; d. Joseph and Grace (Goodman) R. BA, Hunter Coll., 1954; JD, N.Y. Law Sch., 1970; postgrad. Law Sch., NYU, 1971-72. Bar: N.Y. 1971, U.S. Ct. Appeals (2d cir.) 1975, U.S. Supreme Ct. 1975. Writer, 1954-70; editor, 1955-66; tchr., 1966-70; atty. Am. Soc. Composers, Authors and Pubs., NYC, 1971-72, Greater N.Y. Ins. Co., NYC, 1973-74; sr. ptnr. Brenhouse & Ritter, NYC, 1974-78; sole practice NYC, 1978—. Editor N.Y. Immigration News, 1975-76. Mem. ABA, Am. Immigration Lawyers Assn. (treas. 1983-84, sec. 1984-85, vice-chair 1985-86, chair 1986-87, chair program com. 1989-90, chair spkrs. bur. 1989-90, chair media liaison 1989-90), N.Y. State Bar Assn., N.Y. County Lawyers Assn., Assn. Trial Lawyers Am., N.Y. State Trial Lawyers Assn., N.Y.C. Bar Assn., Watergate East Assn. (v.p., asst. treas. 1990—). Democrat. Jewish. Home: 47 E 87th St New York NY 10128-1005 Office: 420 Madison Ave Rm 1200 New York NY 10017-1171 Home Phone: 212-534-0980. Personal E-mail: annlritter@aol.com.

RITTER, ANN MARIE, pediatric neurosurgeon; b. Bryn Mawr, Pa., May 27, 1964; d. Thomas F. Ritter and Mae Groover; m. Albert S Diradour, May 23, 1998; children: Cannon A Diradour, Madelyn O Diradour. BS in Nutrition with honors, U. Tex., Austin, 1986; MD, Baylor Coll. Medicine, Houston, 1991. Diplomate neurological surgeons Am. Bd. Neurol. Surgeons, 2004, pediatric neurosurgeons Am. Bd. Pediatric Neurosurgeons, 2007. Intern Baylor Coll. Medicine, 1991—93; resident Med. Coll. Va., 1993—99; fellow U. Tex., Dallas, 1999—2000; pediatric neurosurgeon, chief pediatric neurosurgery U. NC, Chapel Hill, 2000—05; pediatric neurosurgeon A. I. duPont Hosp. for Children, Wilmington, 2005—. Lectr. Houston C.C., 1989—94, Baylor Coll. Medicine-Neuroanatomy, Houston, 1994, U. NC, 2000—05. Contbr. articles various profl. jours., chapters to books, numerous medical presentations. Chmn. Pedal for Pediat., Chapel Hill, 2003—05. Mem.: AMA, Richmond Acad. Medicine, Women in Neurosurgery, Am. Acad. Pediat., Va. Med. Soc., Am. Soc. Pediatric Neurosurgeons, Am. Assn. Neurol. Surgeons, Congress Neurol. Surgeon. Avocations: scuba diving, gardening. Business E-Mail: amritter@nemours.org.

RITTER, BILL (AUGUST WILLIAM RITTER JR.), Governor of Colorado, former prosecutor; b. Aurora, Colo., Sept. 6, 1956; s. August William and Ethel Ritter; m. Jeannie L. Ritter; children: August, Abe, Sam, Tally. BA, Colo. State U., 1978; JD, U. Colo. Sch. Law, 1981. Dep.

dist. atty. City of Denver, 1981—84, chief dep. dist. atty., 1984—87, 1992—93, dist. atty. Denver, 1993—2005; asst. US atty. criminal divsn. Dist. Colo. US Dept. Justice, Denver, 1990—91; coord. Mongu Nutrition Grp., Zambia, 1987—90; gov. State of Colo., Denver, 2006—. Bd. mem. Nat. Assn. Drug Ct. Profls., 1995—2002; v.p. Nat. Dist. Attys. Assn., 1995—2004; chmn. Am. Prosecutors Rsch. Inst., 1998—2004; pres. Colo. Dist. Attys. Coun., 1999—2000, 2003—04. Bd. chair Project PAVE (Promoting Alternatives to Violence through Edn.), 1992—2003; bd. mem. Mile High United Way, 1999—2004. Democrat. Roman Catholic. Office: Office Gov 136 State Capitol Denver CO 80203-1792

RITTER, C. DOWD, diversified financial services company executive; b. Birmingham; m. Susan; 2 children. BA, Birmingham-Southern Coll., 1969; grad., Sch. Banking of South, L.S.U. With AmSouth Bancorporation and AmSouth Bank, Birmingham, Ala., 1969—2006, exec. v.p., 1980-88, sr. exec. v.p., 1988-93, vice chmn. bd., 1993-94, pres., COO, 1994-96, chmn., pres., CEO, 1996—2006; pres., CEO Regions Fin. Corp., Birmingham, Ala., 2006—07, chmn., pres., CEO, 2008—. Bd. dirs. Ala. Power Co., Protective Life Corp. Bd. trustees Tuskegee Inst., Bus. Council Ala., Ala. Econ. Develop. Partnership, Region 2020 Inc., Birmingham Mus. Art, Birmingham-Southern Coll., Leadership Birmingham, adv. bd. Birmingham Crime Commn., Juvenile Diabetes Found., bd. visitors U. ala. Coll. Commerce and Bus. Adminstrn., campaign co-chmn. Am. Cancer Soc. Five Points South Ctr. and Hope Lodge, campaign steering com. YWCA Birmingham, pres's. coun. U. Ala., campaign chmn. United Way Central Ala., 1993. Named Ala. Outstanding Young Banker 1984. Mem. Ala. Young Bankers (past pres.), Birmingham Festival Arts (past pres.). Office: Regions Fin Corp 417 20th St N Birmingham AL 35203

RITTER, DALE WILLIAM, obstetrician, gynecologist; b. Jersey Shore, Pa., June 17, 1919; s. Lyman W. and Weltha B. (Packard) Ritter; m. Winnie Mae Bryant, Nov. 13, 1976; children: Eric, Lyman, Michael, Gwendolyn, Daniel. AB, UCLA, 1942; MD, U. So. Calif., 1946. Diplomate Am. Bd. Ob-Gyn. Intern LA County Hosp., 1945—46, resident, 1948—52, admitting room resident, 1948—52; pvt. practice Chico, Calif., 1952—98; founder, mem. staff, past chmn. bd. dirs. Chico Cmty. Meml. Hosp. Guest lectr. Chico State Coll., 1956—; staff Enole Hosp., Chico, 1952—, Glenn Gen. Hosp., Willows, Calif., 1953-98, Gridley Meml. Hosp., Calif., 1953-80; spl. cons. obs. Calif. Dept. Pub. Health, No. Calif., 1958-70. Contbr. articles to profl. jours. Bd. dirs. No. dist. Children's Home Soc., Chico, 1954-70. With AUS, 1943-45, M.C., AUS, 1946-48. Recipient Pro-Life award, Calif. KC, Citizenship award, SAR. Fellow ACS, Am. Coll. Ob-Gyn; mem. AMA, AAAS, DAV, Calif. Med. Assn., Internat. Soc. Hypnosis, Am. Soc. Clin. Hypnosis, Am. Fertility Soc., Pacific Coast Fertility Soc., Assn. Am. Physicians and Surgeons, Pvt. Drs. Am., Butte-Glenn County Med. Soc. (past pres.), Am. Cancer Soc. (past bd. dirs. Butte County), Christian Med. Soc., Am. Assn. Pro-life Obstetricians and Gynecologists, Butte-Glenn County Tumor Bd., Anthrop. Assn. Am., Archaeol. Inst. Am., Soc. Calif. Archaeology, Oreg. Archaeology Soc., Archeol. Survey Assn., Southwestern Anthrop. Soc., Am. Rock Art Rsch. Assn. (Pioneer award), Calif. Hist. Soc., Calif. Oreg. Trails Assn., Australian Rock Art Rsch. Assn., Internat. Assn. for Study of Prehistoric and Ethnologic Religions, Fretted Instrument Guild Am. (dir. Banjo Kats 'n Jammers), North Valley Banjo Band, Am. Philatelic Soc., Am. Horse Coun., Peruvian Paso Horse Registry of N.Am., Assn. Owners Breeders Peruvian Paso Horses, Sons of Am. Revolution, Am. Legion, named Sons Am. Revolution, Citizenship award, WWII, Rotary (Paul Harris fellow), Gideons Internat., Phi Chi, Lambda Sigma, Zeta Beta Sigma. Republican. Home: PO Box 156 975 East Ave Chico CA 95926-1308

RITTER, DANIEL BENJAMIN, lawyer; b. Wilmington, Del., Apr. 6, 1937; s. David Moore and Bernice Elizabeth (Carlson) R.; m. Shirley F. Sether, Jan. 29, 1971 (dec. Jan. 1998); 1 child, Roxane Elise. AB with honors, U. Chgo., 1957; LLB, U. Wash., 1963. Bar: Wash. 1963, U.S. Dist. Ct. (we. dist.) Wash. 1963, U.S. Tax Ct. 1965, U.S. Ct. Appeals (9th cir.) 1963. Assoc. Davis, Wright Tremaine LLP (formerly Davis, Wright and Jones), 1963-69, ptnr., 1969—2006; ret., 2006. Lectr. Bar Rev. Assocs. Wash., Seattle, 1964—86; chmn. internat. dept. Davis, Wright and Jones, Seattle, 1984—85, chmn. banking dept., 1986—89. Casenote editor U. Wash. Law Rev., 1962-63; editor-in-chief, contbg. author Washington Revised Article 9 Deskbook, 2003; contbg. author: Washington Commercial Law Desk Book, 1982, rev. edit., 1987, Washington Community Property Desk Book, 1977. Trustee Cathedral Assoc., Seattle, 1980-86; legal counsel Wash. State Reps., Bellevue, 1983-92; bd. dirs. U. Chgo. Club Puget Sound, Seattle, 1982-95, pres., 1984-86; bd. dirs. Am. Lung Assn. Wash., Seattle, 1983-92; mem. vis. com. U. Wash. Law Sch., 1984-88; trustee U. Wash. Law Sch. Found., 1989-92; chmn. alumni rels. coun. U. Chgo., 1986-88; mem. statute law com. State of Wash., 1978-87; bd. dirs. Seattle Camerata, 1991-93; bd. dirs. Early Music Guild, Seattle, 1993-96. Mem. ABA (bus. law sect.), Wash. State Bar Assn. (chmn. bus. law sect. 1988-89, uniform comml. code com. 1980—, chmn. 1980-86, chmn. internat. law com. 1979-81, jud. recommendations com. 1991-93), Seattle-King County Bar Assn. (chmn. internat. and comparative law sect. 1980-82), Rainier Club, Order of Coif. Republican. Lutheran. Avocations: reading, theater, early music. Home: 907 Warren Ave N Apt 202 Seattle WA 98109-5635 Personal E-mail: dan.b.ritter@gmail.com.

RITTER, DEBORAH ELIZABETH, anesthesiologist, educator; b. Phila., May 16, 1947; d. Charles William and Elizabeth Angeline (Coffman) R. BA, Susquehanna U., 1968; MS, U. Pa., 1969; MD, Med. Coll. Pa., 1973. Diplomate Am. Bd. Anesthesiology (assoc. examiner oral bds. 1990, 92). Intern Thomas Jefferson Univ. Hosp., Phila., 1973-74, resident in anesthesia, 1974-76, clin. fellow in anesthesiology, 1976-77; affiliate resident in anesthesia Children's Hosp. Pa., Phila., 1975; assoc. in anesthesiology Frankford Hosp., Phila., 1977-78; clin. instr. anesthesiology Med. Coll. Pa., Phila., 1977-78, Thomas Jefferson U., 1978-80, clin. asst. prof., 1980-86, clin. assoc. prof., 1986—, vice chmn. dept. anesthesiology, 1985—. Contbr. articles to profl. jours. Named Top Doc, Phila. Mag., 1994, 96. Mem. AMA, Am. Women's Med. Assn., Am. Soc. Anesthesiologists, Internat. Anesthesia Rsch. Soc., Soc. Edn. Anesthesia, Assn. Anesthesia Clin. Dirs. Lutheran. Avocations: gardening, music, history, wilderness preservation, american indian culture. Office: Thomas Jefferson U Dept Anesthesiology 111 S 11th St Ste 8490G Philadelphia PA 19107-5084

RITTER, JASON, actor; b. LA, Calif., Feb. 17, 1980; s. John Ritter and Nancy Morgan. Attended, NYU. Actor: (TV series) Joan of Arcadia, 2003—05, The Class, 2006—; (TV films) The Dreamer of Oz, 1990, Who's Your Momma?, 2004; (films) Mumford, 1999, PG, 2002, Swimfan, 2002, Smash the Kitty, 2003, Freddy vs. Jason, 2003, Raise Your Voice, 2004, Perceptions, 2005, Happy Endings, 2005, Our Very Own, 2005, Placebo, 2005, The Wicker Man, 2006, The Education of Charlie Banks, 2007, Good Dick, 2008, The Deal, 2008, W., 2008, Peter and Vandy, 2009, (off-Broadway) The Beginning of August; (plays) The Distance from Here, Third, 2005 (Clarence Derwent award, Actors' Equity Found., 2006). Mailing: c/o The Burstein Co Ste 208 15304 Sunset Blvd Pacific Palisades CA 90272*

RITTER, JOSEPH MICHAEL, chemistry professor, dean; s. Edward Joseph and Margaret Mary Ritter; m. Janice Lee Hughart, Dec. 28, 1984; children: Brian Joseph, David Michael, Jennifer Lee, Susan Michelle, Rebecca Jo. BS in Chem. Engring., U. Ill., Urbana, 1984; MS in CIS, U. Del., Newark, 1991, PhD in Chem. Engring., 1989. Rsch. engr. Amoco Oil Co., Naperville, Ill., 1989—92, sr. process control engr. Whiting, Ind., 1992—94, ops. engr., 1994—95; asst. prof. chemistry Principia Coll., Elsah, Ill., 1995—2000, solar car project faculty advisor, 1996—, assoc. prof. chemistry, 2000—05, dir. engring. sci., 2000—08, chair chemistry dept., 2004—08, prof. chemistry, 2005—, asst. dean academics, 2008—. Asst. scoutmaster Boy Scouts America, Town & Country, Mo., 2004—06; sunday sch. tchr. First Ch. Christ Scientist, Elsah, 1995—, chair, 2001—02; soccer coach Alton Parks and Recreation, Ill., 1997—2005. Recipient Order of Engr. award, 1989; named Outstanding Young Man of America, 1998; Grad. fellowship, Merck Corp., 1986—88, Dorothy Moller Rsch. fellowship, Principia Coll., 2005. Mem.: AIChE, Am. Chem. Soc., Phi Lambda Upsilon, Tau Beta Pi. Office: Principia Coll 1 Maybeck Pl Elsah IL 62028

RITTER, PHILIP WAYNE, library administrator; b. Ft. Myers, Fla., May 29, 1945; s. Ozzie Clarence and Connie (Copeland) R.; m. Barbara Ann Barnes, June 3, 1967; children— Andrew Philip, Cynthia Leigh. B.A., Atlantic Christian Coll., Wilson, N.C., 1967; M.Div., Vanderbilt U., 1970; M.S. in L.S., U. N.C., Chapel Hill, 1971. Cert. librarian, N.C., Va., NY. Librarian, Southside Va. Community Coll., Alberta, Va., 1971-72; extension librarian Wake County Pub. Libraries, Raleigh, N.C., 1972-75; dir. Central N.C. Regional Library, Burlington, 1976-80; dir. Gaston-Lincoln Regional Library, Gastonia, N.C., 1980—95, Gaston County Pub. Library; dir. Greenville County Libr., SC, 1995-2000; exe. dir. Upper Hudson Libr. Sys., Albany, NY, 2000-. Gaston Literacy Council, 1986-95, past chmn.; pres. Sherwood Elem. Sch. Parent Tchr. Orgn., 1984-85. Mem. United Way Community Resources Div. Bd., Gastonia, 1983-86. Recipient Gaston County Vol. award, 1995, Gov's award, NC, 1995, Intellectual Freedom award, SC Libr. Assn., 1998. Mem. ALA, Southeastern Library Assn., N.C. Library Assn. (past v.p.), N.C. Pub. Library Dirs. Assn. (exec. bd. 1986-95, past pres.), Metrolina Library Assn. (past pres., 1995), Alpha Chi, Sigma Pi Alpha, Beta Phi Mu. Lodge: Rotary (bd. dirs. 1985-95, past pres.) NY Libr. Assn., United Way Gaston County (past chmn.). Contbr. in field. Office: 28 Essex St Albany NY 12206

RITTMAN, BENITA GRIFFIN, psychologist; b. Fla., Sept. 19, 1968; d. Locester Young Presha; m. Jarvis Rittman, July 18, 1992; children: Maiya Patrice, Jarvis Dejuan. MS, Fla. A&M U., Tallahassee, 1994. Cert. in sch. psychology Dept. Edn., Fla. Sch. psychologist Gadsden County Sch. Bd., Quincy, Fla., 1996—. Pres., life mem. Gadsden County Chpt. FAMU-NAA, Quincy, 2001—08. Mem.: Alpha Kappa Alpha Sorority Inc. (sec. 2006—08). Dfl. Office: Gadsden County Sch Bd 35 Martin Luther King Jr Blvd Quincy FL 32351 Office Fax: 850-875-1175. Business E-Mail: rittmanb@mail.gcps.k12.fl.us.

RITTNER, LINDA, educational consultant, director; d. Leland W. Porter and Bernice H. Greene; m. Clark Rittner; children: Christian, Michael, William David, Matthew, Katilyn. BS, Colo. State U., Fort Collins; BA, U. Northern Colo., Greeley, 2004, MA, 2005, PhD, 2009. Dir. Pleasant Hill Acad., Longmont, Afghanistan, 1988—. Ednl. cons., Longmont. Office: Univ Northern Colo 505 20th St Greeley CO 80639

RITTS, LESLIE SUE, lawyer; b. Boston, Mar. 20, 1955; d. Roy Ellot Ritts, Jr. and Hilda Jo Ritts; m. George Y. Sugiyama, Oct. 7, 1989; 1 child, James Ellot Sugiyama. AB cum laude, Princeton U., NJ, 1977; JD, William & Mary Law Sch., Williamsburg, Va., 1980. Bar: Va. 1980, DC 1984, US Ct. Appeals (DC cir.) 1992, US Supreme Ct. 2006. Sr. atty. Environ. Law Inst., Washington, 1984—90; assoc. Morgan, Lewis & Bockus, Washington, 1990—95; counsel Chadbourne & Parke, Washington, 1995—2006; ptnr. Hogan & Hartson, LLP, Washington, 1990—2009. Gen. counsel clean air project Nat. Environ. Devel. Assn., Washington, 1984—2006; mem. new source rev. adv. coun. clean air act US EPA, Washington, 1993—94, mem. clean air operating stateholder group, 1994—98. Contbr. articles to profl. jours. Mem.: ABA, Va. State Bar. Home: 620 Ft Williams Pkwy Alexandria VA 22304 Office: Ritts Law Group PLLC The Carriage House 620 Ft Williams Pkwy Alexandria VA 22304 Personal E-mail: lsritts@gmail.com.

RITVO, HARRIET, historian; b. Cambridge, Mass., Sept. 19, 1946; d. Martin and Zelma R. AB, Harvard U., 1968, PhD, 1975; student, U. Cambridge, Eng., 1968-69. Staff assoc. AAAS, Boston, 1976-79; from asst. prof. to prof. MIT, Cambridge, 1979—, assoc. dean humanities and social scis., 1992-95, Arthur J. Conner prof. of history, 1995—, head history faculty, 1999—2006; v.p. Am. Soc. Environ. History, 2007—09, pres., 2009—. Author: The Animal Estate, 1987, The Platypus and the Mermaid, 1997, The Dawn of Green, 2009; co-editor: Macropolitics of 19th Century Literature, 1991. Rsch. fellow Stanford Humanities Ctr., 1985-86, fellow NEH, 1989, Guggenheim fellow, 1990, sr. fellow Nat. Humanities Ctr., 1990, 2002-03; recipient Whiting Writer's award Whiting Found., 1990. Fellow: Am. Acad. Arts and Scis. Office: MIT E51-285 Cambridge MA 02139 Office Phone: 617-253-6960. Business E-Mail: ritvo@mit.edu.

RITVO, JACOB, legislative staff member; B, Cornell U., Ithaca, NY, 2005. Legis. asst., systems adminstr., Rep. Grace Napolitano US House of Reps., Washington, 2007—08, comm. dir. to Rep. Peter Visclosky, 2008—. Democrat. Office: 2256 Rayburn House Office Bldg Washington DC 20515 Office Phone: 202-225-2461. Office Fax: 202-225-2493. Business E-Mail: jacob.ritvo@mail.house.gov.*

RITVO, ROGER ALAN, research management professor, health management-policy educator; b. Cambridge, Mass., Aug. 12, 1944; s. Meyer and Miriam R.S. (Meyers) R.; m. Lynn Lieberman; children: Roberta, Eric. BA, Western Res. U., 1967; MBA, George Washington U., 1970; PhD, Case Western Res. U., 1976. Asst. adminstr. N.Y. Mental Health System, 1968-70; asst. prof., asst. dean Sch. Applied Social Scis. Case Western Res. U., Cleve., 1976-79, assoc. prof., 1981-83; assoc. prof., founding dir. Grad. Program in Health Adminstrn. Cleve. State U., 1983-87; prof. health mgmt. and policy, dean Sch. Health and Human Svcs. U. N.H., Durham, 1987-97; sr. health policy analyst to sec. DHHS, Washington, 1980-81; vice chancellor acad. and student affairs Auburn U. Montgomery, Ala., 1997—2005. Vis. rsch. scholar WHO, Copenhagen, 1978; vis. prof. Am. U., Washington, 1980-81, U. W.I., 1993; chair Ala. Coun. Chief Acad. Officers, 1998-2000; vis. scholar U. Sheffield, Eng., 1985; cons. to numerous orgns. on profit and non-profit strategic planning. Editor, author 8 books, including Managing in the Age of Change, 1994, Improving Governing Board Effectiveness, 1996, Sisters in Sorrow Voices of Care in the Holocaust, 1998, Ethical Governance in Health Care, 2004, Nonprofit Organizations: Principles and Practices, 2008; mem. cmty. editl. bd. Montgomery Advertiser newspaper, 1999; contbr. articles to profl. jours. Trustee Hosp. Sisters of Charity, Cleve., 1980-85, Greater Seacoast United Way, 1991-93; chmn. health care adv. com. Ohio Senate, 1983-85; bd. mem. Fairmount Temple, Beachwood, Ohio, 1980-85; trustee Leadership Seacoast, 1991-93, bd. dirs., 1992-95; bd. dirs. N.H. chpt. United Way, 1992-95, Higher Edn. Leadership Partnership, 1998-2000; chair higher edn. divsn. United Way, Montgomery, Ala., 2004. Recipient Outstanding Adminstr. award, 1992, Cert. of Merit U. N.H. Pres.'s Commn. on Women, 1994; Govt. fellow Am. Coun. Edn., 1980-81; Fulbright scholar Azerbaijan, 2006. Mem. Nat. Tng. Labs. Inst. (bd. dirs. 1981-85, 92-96), Cert. Cons. Internat., Jewish Philatelic, Hist. Soc. N.Y.C. Avocations: collecting flat irons and masks, philatelist, white water rafting. Office Phone: 334-244-3603.

RITZENTHALER, BEATRIZ AUGUSTA, musician, educator; arrived in U.S., 2001; d. Adilson Ferreira and Beatriz Pereira Da Silva; m. Robert Joseph Ritzenthaler, Aug. 10, 2003. BA in Piano Performance with honors, Brazilian Conservatory Music, 1998; MusM with honors, Andrews. U., 2004. Piano instr. Villa Lobos Conservatory Music, Aracatuba, Brazil, 1991—2000; piano instr., adj. prof. Andrews U., Berrien Springs, Mich., 2001—06. Concert pianist Brazil, Europe and US, Brazil. Performer: (recordings) Sacred Concerts for Piano, 1998. Pianist Seventh Day Adventist Ch., Berrien Springs, Mich., 2001—04. Recipient 1st pl., Internat. Piano Competition, France, 1992, 2d pl. nat. piano competition, Heitor Villa Lobos, 1986; named winner young artists competition, Andrews U., 2004; grantee, Fundação Manoel de Barros, Brazil, 2001—04; scholar, Music Dept. Andrews U., 2001—04. Mem.: Phi Kappa Phi. Home: 2472 Honeysuckle Ln Berrien Springs MI 49103 Office Phone: 269-408-1479. Business E-Mail: beapianist@hotmail.com.

RITZI-MAROUF, VIVIANE COSETTE, language educator, department chairman; b. Geneva, Nov. 10, 1956; d. William Ritzi and Therese Carreras; m. Said Marouf, Sept. 25, 1998. BA, Brigham Young U., Provo, Utah, 1982; MA in French, U. Calif., Davis, 1985, MA in Spanish, 1987. French and Spanish lectr. U. Calif., 1989—99; Spanish prof. Cosumnes River Coll., Sacramento, 1989—99; French and Spanish prof. Solano CC, Fairfield, Calif., 1989—99, Folsom Lake Coll., Calif., head French dept., 1999—. Author: (textbook) Dimelo tu. Office: Folsom Lake Coll 100 Scholar Way Folsom CA 95630 Business E-Mail: ritzimv@flc.losrios.edu.

RIVA, CARLOS, pharmaceutical executive; BS in Civil Engring., MIT; MS in Civil Engring., Stanford U.; MBA, Harvard U. Pres., COO J. Makowski Co., 1992—94; COO InterGen, 1995—2003; exec. dir. Amec plc, 2003—05; chmn., CEO Celunol, 2005—07; pres., CEO, dir. Verenium Corp., Cambridge, Mass., 2007—. Office: Verenium Corp 55 Cambridge Pkwy 8th Fl Cambridge MA 02142*

RIVADENEIRA, DAVID EDWARD, colon and rectal surgeon, researcher; b. NYC, Dec. 27, 1969; s. Eduardo and Manuela Rivadeneira; m. Anabela Alves, June 3, 1995; children: Sophia Bella, Gabriella. MD, Howard U., Washington, 1995. Diplomate in laparoscopic, minimally invasive colon & rectal surgery Am. Bd. Surgery, Am. Bd. Colon & Rectal Surgery. Intern NY Hosp. - Cornell Med. Ctr., 1995—96; NIH rsch. fellow Cornell Med. Sch., NYC, 1997—99; surgery resident Meml. Sloan-Kettering Cancer Ctr., NYC, 1995—2002, NY Presbyn. Hosp.-Cornell Med. Ctr., NYC, 1995—2001, surgery chief resident, 2001—02; fellow Lahey Clinic, Burlington, Mass., 2002—03. Contbr. articles to profl. jours. Recipient Scholar award, Am. Assn. Cancer Rsch., 1995, Outstanding Academic Achievement award, Lahey Clinic Med. Ctr., 2003. Fellow: ACS (licentiate; diplomate), Am. Soc. Colon and Rectal Surgeons (diplomate); mem.: Assn. for Academic Surgery, NY Surg. Soc. (licentiate), Soc. Am. Gastrointestinal Endoscopic Surgeons (licentiate), Soc. for Surgery of the Alimentary Tract (licentiate). Office Phone: 631-862-3000. Office Fax: 631-862-3660. Personal E-mail: drivad@aol.com. Business E-Mail: david.rivadeneira@chsli.org.

RIVARA, FREDERICK PETER, pediatrician, educator; b. Far Rockaway, NY, May 17, 1949; s. Frederick P. and Mary Lillian (Caparelli) R.; m. J'May Bertrand, May 17, 1975; children: Matthew, Maggie. BA, Holy Cross Coll., 1970; MD, U. Pa., 1974; MPH, U. Wash., 1980. Diplomate Am. Bd. Pediatrics. Intern Children's Hosp. and Med. Ctr., Boston, 1974-75, resident, 1975-76, Seattle, 1978-80; RWJ clin. scholar U. Wash., Seattle, 1978-80, assoc. prof. pediatrics, 1984-89, prof. pediatrics, head divsn. gen. pediatrics, 1994—; mem. staff Nat. Health Svc. Corps, Hazard, Ky., 1976-78; asst. prof. pediatrics U. Tenn., Memphis, 1981-84. Editor Archives of Pedatrics and Adolescent Medicine. Fellow Am. Acad. Pediatrics; mem. Ambulatory Pediatrics Assn., SPR, Am. Pediat. Soc., Internat. Assn. Child, Adolescent and Injury Prevention (pres. 1993-2000), Inst. Medicine (Washington), Acad. Sci. Office: Harborview Med Ctr 325 9th Ave PO Box 359960 Seattle WA 98195-9960 Business E-Mail: fpr@uwashington.edu.

RIVARA, SARA, language educator; BA, Kalamazoo Coll., Mich., 1999; MFA in Creative Writing, Warren Wilson Coll., Asheville, NC, 2002. Instr. English Kalamazoo Valley CC, 2004—. Singer: Aspire Ensemble Vocal Quartet. Chairperson, bd. music and arts First Congl. UCC Kalamazoo, 2007—; mem. Bach Festival Soc. Kalamazoo, 1999—2006, sec., 1999—2006. Mem.: AWP Club. Office: Kalamazoo Valley CC 6767 W O Ave Kalamazoo MI 49009

RIVARD, ROBERT, editor, publishing executive; b. Nov. 17, 1952; m. Monika Maeckle, Sept. 19, 1981; children: Nicolas, Alex. BA in Polit. Sci., U. Tex., San Antonio, 1996; postgrad., Northwestern U., 1996. Sportswriter Brownsville Herald, 1977-78; news reporter Corpus Christi Caller, Tex., 1978-79; reporter Dallas Times Herald, 1979-81, Ctrl. Am. bur. chief, 1981-83, Newsweek, 1983-85, sr. editor, chief corrs. NYC, 1985-90; dep. mng. editor San Antonio Light, 1990-93; mng. editor San Antonio Express-News, San Antonio, 1993-97, editor, exec. v.p., 1997—. Bd. dirs. InterAm. Press Assn. Author: (non-fiction) Trail of Feathers: Searching for Philip True, 2005. Recipient Maria Moor Cabot award, Columbia U., 2002; named Editor of Yr., Editor & Pub. mag., 2000. Mem.: Soc. Profl. Journalists (Disting. Svc. award 1982). Office: San Antonio Express-News 301 Ave E San Antonio TX 78205 Office Phone: 210-250-3111. E-mail: rrivard@express-news.net.*

RIVAS, ANDRES ELOY, economics professor; b. Puerto La Cruz, Anzoategui, Venezuela, Nov. 16, 1966; s. Antonio Clemante and Luz Isabel Rivas; m. Daglys Angela Martinez, Oct. 16, 1993; children: Daglys Andrea Rivas-Martinez, Dylan Andres Rivas-Martinez, Andres Juan Antonio Rivas-Martinez. PhD, U. Tex.-Pan America, Edinburg, 2003. Cert. faculty development internat. bus.-finance U. SC, 2007. Lectr. U. Tex., Bronwsville, 2002—04; asst. prof. economics & fin. Tex. A&M Internat. U., Laredo, 2004—. Dir. internat. bus. & fin. Internat. Machinery Exch., Deerfield, Wis., 1997—98. Contbr. articles to profl. jours. Lector Santo Nino Ch., Laredo, Tex., 2007—08. Mem.: Fin. Mgmt. Assn. Office: Tex A&M Internat Univ 5201 University Blvd Laredo TX 78041 Business E-Mail: arivas@tamiu.edu.

RIVAUX, LOIS ELAINE, music educator; b. Galveston, Tex., Aug. 4, 1947; d. Jake Richard and Lois Catherine Dodson; children: Tania R., Rich, Benjamin R., Jorge Ariel Nevarez-Rivaux. BS in Elem. Edn., Southwestern Adventist U., Keene, Tex., 2003. Cert. tchr. Tex. Exec. dir. YMCA, Galveston, 1988—94; paraprofl. Groesbeck (Tex.) Ind. Sch.

Dist., 1995—2002; tchr. elem. music Galveston Ind. Sch. Dist., Galveston, 2002—. Children's min. First United Meth. Ch., Groesbeck, Tex., 1999—2002. Recipient Disting. Honor award, 1988; named Citizen of Yr., Groesbeck C. of C., 2000. Democrat. Lutheran. Office: L A Morgan Elem 1410 37th Galveston TX 77550 Home: 1807 Avenue L Galveston TX 77550-6025 Personal E-mail: 1er4@hotmail.com.

RIVELLI, SUSAN VERONICA, nurse; b. Des Moines, Aug. 28, 1954; d. Thomas James Dobberthein and Naomi M. (Edwards) Dutch; 1 child, Carly Vanessa; m. Prospero Rivelli, Jr., Aug. 20, 1989. Diploma in practical nursing, Des Moines Area CC, 1976; ASN, St. Petersburg Jr. Coll., 1983, AA, 2001. RN, Fla.; cert. risk mgr., Fla., quality assurance profl.; cert. hospice and palliative nurse; Registered Health Info. Technician. Dir. quality assurance and med. records Horizon Hosp., Clearwater, Fla., 1980-89; DON Palm Gardens of Clearwater, 1989-90; quality assurance/risk mgr. liaison, cons. The Manors, Tarpon Springs, Fla., 1990-94; instr. Ultimate Learning Ctr., Clearwater, Fla., 1994—; shift adminstr. The Manors, Tarpon Springs, Fla., 1994-97; staff nurse Hospice of Fla. Suncoast, Largo, Fla., 1997—2001; sr. staff nurse Hospice of the Fla. Suncast, Largo, 2002—03; admissions nurse Hospice of the Fla. Suncoast, Largo, 2003—04, admissions clin. coord., 2005—07, health info. mgr., 2007—. Cons. in field. Pres. Knollwood Civic Assn., Largo, Fla., 1985, editor, pub. newsletter, 1984. Scholar Tampa Bay Orgn. Nurse Exec., 2001. Mem. Am. Health Info. Mgmt. Assn., Nat. Assn. of Quality Assurance Profls., Bay Area Healthcare Risk Mgrs, Nat. Hospice/Palliative Care Orgn., West Coast Fla. Hospice and Palliative Nurse Assn. (sec.), Phi Theta Kappa. Roman Catholic. Avocations: writing, reading, alpine skiing. Home: 3149 Harvest Moon Dr Palm Harbor FL 34683-2124 Office Phone: 727-523-3252. Business E-Mail: svr828@verizon.net.

RIVENBARK, CHRISTINE KLEMENZ, science educator, researcher; b. Estavayer-le-Lac, Switzerland; arrived in US, 2001, naturalized; d. Heinz H. Klemenz and Irene D. Felchlin; m. Stephen D. Rivenbark, Oct. 11, 2003. Biomed. scientist, Coll. for Med. Professions, Lausanne, Switzerland, 1980; chem. engr., Coll. Engring. and Archtecture, Fribourg, Switzerland, 1990; PhD, U. of Tokyo, 2000. Rsch. engr. Swiss Fed. Inst. of Tech., Lausanne, 1990—2001; rsch. scholar U. Ctrl. Fla., Orlando, 2001—02, faculty, 2002—09; gen. mgr., tech. dir. Krystal Engring. LLC, Titusville, Fla., 2009—. Co-organizer 34th Course of Assn. Vaudoise Chercheurs Physique, Grimentz, Switzerland, 1992, First Internat. Sch. on Crystal Growth Tech., Beatenberg, Switzerland, 1998; lectr. Internat. Sch. on Advanced Materials, Madras, India, 1994, 10th Internat. Summer Sch. on Crystal Growth-10, Rimini, Italy, 1998. Recipient Young Scientist award, Internat. Union of Crystallography, 1994, Best Thesis award, Fribourg Industries Group, 1990, Outstanding Achievement award, Swiss Fed. Inst. of Tech., 1999, 2000. Mem.: IEEE (program com. mem. internat. frequency control sys.), Crystal Growth Commn. of Internat. Union Crystallography, Am. Assn. for Crystal Growth, Am. Ceramics Soc., Materials Rsch. Soc., Air Force Assn. Achievements include research in First single-crystalline high-temperature superconducting NdBCO and YBCO films by LPE; First colorless transparent anatase single-crystals by CTR - enabled for first time photoelectrochemical investigations (for Graetzel solar cells development); Nitride films by LPE; LGS, LGT, LGN (langasite-type) films by LPE bulk ternary and quaternary langasites by Czochralski technique; laser and NLO single-crystals. Avocations: horses, travel, history, music. Office: Krystal Engring LLC 1429 Chaffee Dr Titusville FL 32780

RIVENES, SHANNON MARIE, pediatric cardiologist; b. Calgary, Alberta, Canada, Dec. 3, 1966; d. Steven Bryce Holmgren and Gayle Marie Cooper; m. Scott Richardson Rivenes, Oct. 7, 1995; children: Bradley S., Bailey M. BA, BS, So. Meth. U., Dallas, 1989; MD, U. Ariz., Tucson, 1993. Diplomate in pediat. Am. Acad. Pediat., 1996, in pediat. cardiology 2000. Pediatric cardiologist Tex. Children's Hosp., Houston, 1999—; asst. prof. pediat. Baylor Coll. Medicine, Houston, 1999—. Dir. Tex. Children's Health Ctrs. Cardiology Clinics, Houston, 2006—. Contbr. articles to profl. jours. Com. mem. Am. Heart Assn. Operation Heartbeat, Houston, 2002—04; bd. mem. Am. Heart Assn., Sugar Land, Tex., 2001—06, Health Edn. Adv. Coun., Ft. Bend ISD, Sugar Land, 2003—07. Recipient Merck Manual award, U. Ariz., 1993; grantee We. Fedn. Clin. Rsch., 1991. Fellow: Am. Acad. Pediat.; mem.: Soc. Pediat. Echocardiography, Am. Soc. Echocardiography, Am. Coll. Cardiology, Am. Heart Assn., Alpha Omega Alpha. Office: Texas Children's Hosp Cardiology 6621 Fannin MC 19345-C Houston TX 77030 Office Fax: 832-825-5630. Business E-Mail: smrivene@texaschildrenshospital.org.

RIVERA, GERALDO, television personality, journalist; b. NYC, July 4, 1943; s. Cruz Allen and Lillian (Friedman) R.; m. Sheri Rivera (div. 1984); m. C.C. Dyer, 1987 (div. 2002); children: Gabriel, Cruz, Isabella, Simone, m. Erica Levy, 1 child, Solita Liliana. BS, U. Ariz., 1965; JD, Bklyn. Law Sch., 1969; postgrad., U. Pa., 1969, Sch. Journalism, Columbia U., 1970. Bar: NY 1970. Mem. anti-poverty neighborhood law firms Harlem Assertion of Rights and Community Action for Legal Svcs., NYC, 1968-70; with Eyewitness News, WABC-TV, NYC, 1970-75; reporter Good Morning America program ABC-TV, 1973-76, corr., host Good Night America program, 1975-77, corr., sr. producer 20/20 Newsmag., 1978-85; host syndicated talk show The Geraldo Rivera show, NYC, 1987-98; host investigative show on cable CNBC Rivera Live, NYC, 1994—2001; host nightly news show on cable CNBC Upfront Tonight, NJ, 1998—2000; spl. corr. Fox News Channel, 2001—; host weekend show on cable At Large with Geraldo Rivera; contbr. Fox newsmag. The Pulse; host Fox News Channel, NYC, 2001—. Author: Willowbrook, 1972, Island of Contrasts, 1974, Miguel, 1972, A Special Kind of Courage, 1976, Exposing Myself, 1991, His Panic: Why Americans Fear Hispanics in the U.S., 2008, The Great Progression: How Hispanics Will Lead America to a New Era of Prosperity, 2009; co-author: (with Daniel Paisner) Exposing Myself, 1991; film appearances: The Bonfire of the Vanities, 1990; (TV movies): Perry Mason: The Case of the Reckless Romeo. Recipient 7 Emmy awards, Peabody award, Kennedy Journalism award, 1973, 75, numerous others; named Broadcaster of Yr. N.Y. State AP, 1971, 72, 74; Smith fellow U. Pa., 1969, 2000 Robert F. Kennedy journalism award, Scripps Howard Found. nat. journalism award, George Foster Peabody award. Jewish. Office: Fox News Channel 2nd fl 1211 Ave of Ams New York NY 10036 Office Phone: 212-301-3000. Office Fax: 212-301-8588. Business E-Mail: foxnewsonline@foxnews.com.*

RIVERA, JOEL, city councilman; son of Jose Rivera. Attended, Iona Coll., Fordham Univ. City councilman Dist. 15 NY City Coun., 2001—. Majority leader NY City Coun., 2002—, chmn. Charter Revision com., Fed. & State Legis. com. Bronx Young Dems; Not in My Neighborhood You Don't; Friends of Crotona Park; Tremont Crotona Day Care; Tanima Productions. Democrat. Mailing: Dist Off 1901 Southern Blvd Bronx NY 10460 Office Phone: 718-842-8100. Office Fax: 718-842-6280. Business E-Mail: rivera@council.nyc.ny.us.*

RIVERA, JOHN ZARATE, director; s. Albino and Pura Zarate Rivera; m. Maria Lourdes Valdivia, Jan. 25, 1997; 1 child, John Avery-Miles. BA in Comm., U. Calif., Santa Barbara, 1993; MA in Ednl. Adminstrn., Calif. State U., Northridge, 2006. Tchg. credential Calif. Commn. Tchr. Credentialing, 1998, adminstrv. credential Calif. Commn. Tchr. Credentialing, 2007. Tchr. Annandale Elem. Sch., LA, 1996—2003; instrnl. tech. applications facilitator LA Unified Sch. Dist., 2003—. Tech. lead instr. Teach the Tchrs. Collaborative, Ojai, Calif., 1998—2006; nat. tchr. advisor Cable in the Classroom, Washington, 2002—04; lead tchr. Instrnl. Tech. Inst., Long Beach, Calif., 2002. Mem. Ch. of the Open Door, Glendora, Calif., 1998—2007. NEA Found. Innovation in Edn. grantee, NEA, 2002, Help Us Help You grantee, Oracle, 2002, Tech. grantee, Computer-Using Educators LA, 2002. Mem.: Computer-Using Educators (bd. mem. 2004—07), Phi Kappa Phi, Phi Lambda Theta. Office: Los Angeles Unified School District 2151 N Soto St Los Angeles CA 90032

RIVERA, JOSE DE JESUS, lawyer; b. Zacatecas, Mex., 1950; m. Nina Rivera; 5 children. BA, No. Ariz. U.; JD, Ariz. State U. Atty. civil rights divsn. Dept. of Justice, 1976—77; asst. U.S. atty. Dist. Ariz., 1977—81; with Langerman, Begam, Lewis and Marks, 1981—84; ptnr. Rivera, Scales and Kizer, 1984—98; atty. City of El Mirage, U.S. Atty., Dist. of Ariz., 1998—2001; with Haralson, Miller, Pitt & McAnally PLC, Phoenix, 2001—. Vice-chair adv. com. civil rights Atty. Gen. Ariz. dist., 1998-2001, adv. com. Native Am. issues, domestic terrorism subcom., 1998-2001, chair subcom. no Mem. com. Los Abogados; bd. dirs. Inst. for County Initiatives, 1996-98; with N.G. Mem. Ariz. State Bar. (bd. govs. 1995-98, bd. officer, sec. treas. 1996, 2d v.p. 1997-98, exec. dir. search com. 1996-97, chair appointments com. 1997-98), Hispanic Bar Assn., Los Abogados Bar Assn. (bd. dirs. 1981-83). Democrat. Avocation: reading. Office: Haralson Miller Pitt Feldman & McAnally PLC 2800 N Ctrl Ste 840 Phoenix AZ 85004 Home Phone: 602-279-5687; Office Phone: 602-266-5557. Business E-Mail: jrivera@hmpmlaw.com.

RIVERA, JOSIE, elementary school educator; b. Victoria, Tex., Apr. 29, 1947; d. Jose Jr. and Emilia (Ramirez) Lopez; m. Mike Rivera, Jan. 10, 1964; children: Diana Lynn, Mike Jr., Michele Yvonne. AA, Victoria Coll., 1983; BS in Edn., U. Houston, 1984, MEd, 1985, 1995, EdD, 1997. Tchr., aide Bloomington Ind. Sch. Dist., Tex.; vis. prin. Bloomington ISD Supt.; tchr. Victoria Ind. Sch. Dist., asst. prin.; adj. prof. Victoria Coll.; spl. projects U. Houston-Victoria. Mem. spl. projects com. U. Houston-Victoria, 2004—09, pres.'s adv. cun. Mem. Vision Victoria, U. Houston PAC; bd. trustees Victoria Coll., 2006—; Supt. Outreach Word Acad., 2005; bd. mem. Victoria Coll. Found., 2007; disting. Victoria Coll., 2001; Treas. Affectionate Arms, 2008, pres., bd. dirs.; v.p. bd. dirs. Hope Chest; v.p. Latina Forum; bd. dirs. DeTar Healthcare Sys.; co-chair FOU Fundraising for U. Houston-Victoria, lead sr. program devel. coord. Named one of South Tex. Women, 2000. Mem. Tex. Elem. Prins. and Suprs. Assn. (Nat. Disting. Prin. 1999, Hometown Hero award), Tex. Assn. Biligual Educators(TEA Textbook Review Panel mem.), Alpha Delta Kappa, Phi Delta Kappa. Home: PO Box 129 Placedo TX 77977-0129 Office Phone: 361-570-4109. Personal E-mail: jo1947@hotmail.com.

RIVERA, LIONEL, Mayor, Colorado Springs, Colorado; b. El Paso, Tex. B in Microbiology, Tex. Tech. U.; MBA, Jacksonville State U., 1986. V.p. investments UBS Fin. Svc.; mem. Colorado Springs City Coun., Colo., 1997—2001; vice mayor City of Colorado Springs, Colo., 2001—03, mayor Colo., 2003—; ret., 2009. Founder, past pres. Colorado Springs Hispanic C. of C.; trustee United Way; mem. exec. com., co-chair The Springs Cmty. Action Plan; mentor Big Bros.-Big Sisters. Capt. US Army, 1979—87. Office: PO Box 1575 Colorado Springs CO 80901 Office Phone: 719-385-5986. Office Fax: 719-385-5495. E-mail: lrivera@springsgov.com.*

RIVERA, MARIANO, professional baseball player; b. Panama City, Panama, Nov. 29, 1969; m. Clara Rivera, Nov. 9, 1991; children: Mariano Jr., Jafet, Jaziel. Pitcher NY Yankees, 1995—. Recipient Reliever of Yr. award, The Sporting News, 1997, 1999, 2001, 2004—05, Babe Ruth award, 1999, Am. League Rolaids Relief award, 1999, 2001, 2004—05, MLB.com's Closer of Yr. award, 2004—06, DHL Delivery Man of Yr. award, 2005—06; named World Series MVP, 1999, Am. League Championship Series MVP, 2003, NY Yankees Player of Yr., 2005; named to Am. League All-Star Team, Maj. League Baseball, 1997, 1999—2002, 2004—06, 2008, 2009. Achievements include being a member of the World Series Champion New York Yankees, 1996, 1998, 1999, 2000; holding the Major League Baseball record for most appearances in postseason history; being the only pitcher in Major League history to close out three World Series; setting the Major League record for: most All-Star Game saves (4), postseason saves (34) and World Series saves (9); setting the American League record for most regular season saves (443), 2007; becoming the second player in Major League Baseball history to save 500 games, 2009. Office: NY Yankees Yankee Stadium One E 161st St Bronx NY 10451*

RIVERA, MAXIMIANO MARQUEZ, academic administrator, educator, researcher, writer; b. Mindoro, Philippines, Aug. 24, 1946; arrived in U.S., 1991; s. Maximiano Corea Rivera, Sr. and Rosita Marquez Rivera; m. Roela Victoria Rivera, Oct. 5, 1974; children: Paul Christian, Paul John, Norman Vincent Paul. BS, U. East, Manila, 1967, BS Biosci., 1969, BS Edn., 1970, MEd, 1974; diploma aquaculture, U. Philippines, 1985, M Aquaculture, 1985; profl. diploma, Centro Escolar U., Manila, 1979, DEd, 1980. Cert. sci./technol. specialist. Supervising tchr. Secondary Sch. U. East, Manila, 1969—70, prof., 1971—81; rschr., sta. head S.E. Asian Fisheries, Iloilo, Philippines, 1982—85; gen. mgr., rschr. Seahorse Aquaculture, Mindoro, 1986—87; exec. asst. Dept. Edn., Pasig, Philippines, 1988—92; v.p., prof. Makati U., Philippines, 1993—96; coord. NSE program Tenn. State U., Nashville, 1997—, asst. dir. honors program, 2004—. Cons. Seoul Art Theol. Sch., Korea and the Philippines, 1994—95; adj. faculty Vol. State C.C., Gallatin, Tenn., 1997—98; faculty honors program Tenn. State U., Nashville, 1998—2004; pres. Tenn. Collegiate Honors Coun., 2005—06, PKP Tsu Chpt., 2007—08; asst. dir. TSK Honors Program, 2004—08; rep. Primerica Fin. Svc., 2009—. Author: (book) Thesis/Dissertation Writing, 1999; co-author: Practical Guide to Thesis and Dissertation, 1996, 2007; contbr. articles to profl. jours. Election coord., supr. Election Commn. Makati U., 1993—95. Recipient Man of Yr. award, New Life Family Devel. Coun., 1994, Golden medal of honor, Philippine Exptl. Ednl. Rsch. Soc. Inc., 1995, Profl. Achievement award, Media for Devel. and Progress Inc., 1995, Golden Record Achievement award in field of edn., Asian Inst. Humanitarian Devel., 1995, Dr. Jose Rizal Immortal award, Philippine Exptl. Ednl. Rsch. Soc. Inc., 1994, Golden Leadership award for outstanding educator, Social Action and Civic Movement Inc., 1994, Golden Scroll of Honor award, New Life on Family Devel. and Youth Coun. Inc., 1997, Recognition Outstanding Svc. and Leadership cert., City of Nashville, 2004, Noble Svc. Disting. Univ. Svc. cert., Tenn. State U., 2004, Recognition Outstanding Svc. to Nat. Student Exch. Program cert., Tenn. State U. Honors Program, 2005, Advisor of Yr. award, Golden Key, 2007; named Outstanding Father, Devel. of Filipino Youth Inc., 1998; grantee, Tenn. State U.; fellow, Exxon Mobil; scholar, Japan Internat. Coop. Agy., SEAFDEC, AQD, State of Israel, Fund for Assistance to Pvt. Edn., U. East, Coun. Internat. Ednl. Exch. Mem.: So. Regional Honors Coun., Am. Soc. Pub. Adminstrn., Philippine Geog. Soc. (life), Philippine Soc. Microbiology (life; bus. mgr. 1980—), Philippine Assn. for Advancement of Sci. (life), Biology Tchrs. Assn., Inc. (life; bd. dirs., Outstanding Svc. award 1991), Phi Kappa Phi (scholarship chair 1999—, chpt. pres.-elect 2006—07, Meritorius Svc. award 2009, Honors Program Outstanding Svc. award 2009, Dedicated Svc. award 2009, Lifetime Membership award 2009). Achievements include patents for anti-pimples formula; massaging device. Avocations: reading, sitar, gardening. Office: Tenn State U Honors Program 3500 John A Merritt Blvd Nashville TN 37209 Office Phone: 615-963-5612, 713-722-9666. Business E-Mail: mrivera@tnstate.edu.

RIVERA, MILUKA, actress, journalist, poet; b. San Juan, Mar. 24, 1953; d. Francisco and Fidelina (Rabell) R.; m. Paul Navarre Matlovsky, Sept. 28, 1981; children: Élan Lixander, Miluette Nalin Matlovsky. Student, Inter-Am. U., Hato Rey, PR, 1971-74; diploma in pub. rels., U. P.R., Rio Piedras, 1974; student in writing and journalism, UCLA, 1986. Lic. in real estate, Calif. Model Polianna/Barbizon, San Juan, 1968-74; instr. modeling, advisor, co-founder Barbizon Sch. of Modeling, San Juan, 1971-74; freelance dir., 1994—; hostess Buena Vista Cable TV, LA, 1997—; instr. acting, modeling and etiquette Creative Arts Ctr., Burbank, Calif., 1998—2004; co-founder, artistic dir., instr. Kumaras Ctr. Arts and Etiquette, 2004—. Appeared in T.V. shows including Kojak, Nurse and General Hospital; films include Taxi Driver, All That Jazz, Fort Apache: The Bronx, Alma Boricua Alma Boreal, Legado Puertorvauen En Hollywood; prodr. documentaries; author (poems), "Unequaled Raul Julia", Hollywood Latinos Offspring, 1998; contbr. articles to profl. publs. Founder, pres. Alliance of Latin Artists, N.Y.C., 1982-84. Recipient Governor Mario Cuomo's Citation award for service, N.Y.C., 1984, Excellent Svc. award Assn. Cronistas Espectaculo, N.Y.C., 1996, Best of Burbank award Kumaras Ctr. for Arts Etiquette, 2005, 06, 08. Mem. AFTRA, SAG (nat. bd. dirs. 1992-93, chair com., 1998—), Actors Equity Assn. Avocations: poetry, drawing, ballroom dancing, horseback riding, skiing. Office: Kumaras Ctr for Arts & Etiquette 1616 W Magnolia Blvd Burbank CA 91506 Home Phone: 818-606-5536; Office Phone: 818-848-9333. Business E-Mail: kumarascenter@aol.com.

RIVERA, SUSAN FRANCES, elementary school educator; b. San Bernardino, Calif., Dec. 11, 1963; d. Oscar C. and Shirley Boyd Gonzalez; children: Jacob Tomas, Aaron Seth. BA in Human Comm., U. Northern Colo., Greeley, 1999; MEd, Grand Canyon U., Phoenix, 2004. Lic. elem. edn. CDE, 2000. Tchr. Aurora Pub. Schs., Colo., 2000—05, math tchr., 2006—. Named Outstanding first yr. tchr., Aurora Pub. Schs., 2001. Home: 17182 E Mercer Dr Aurora CO 80013

RIVERA, VICTOR M., medical educator, director; b. Guadalajara, Jalisco, Mexico, July 21, 1941; s. Manuel and Dolores Olmos de Rivera; m. Cristina Maria Montero, Oct. 12, 1994; children: Maria-Celina, Victor M. MD, Nat. Autonomous U. Mex., Mexico City, 1965. Diplomate Am. Bd. Neurology and Psychiatry, 1978. Prof. Baylor Coll. Medicine, Houston, 1993—. Med. dir. Maxine Mesinger Multiple Sclerosis Clinic, Houston, 2003—; disting. neurologist Nat. MS Soc., 2005. Bd. mem. Nat. Multiple Sclerosis Soc. Named to Hall of Fame, Mexican Acad. Neurology, 2003. Fellow: Am. Acad. Neurology; mem.: Venezuelan Soc. Neurology. Independent. Roman Catholic. Achievements include research in new tretaments for MS. Office: Baylor Coll Medicine 6501 Fannin St NB 100 Houston TX 77030 Office Phone: 713-798-7707. Office Fax: 713-798-0115.

RIVERA-AMILL, VANESSA, medical educator; married. PhD, Wash. State U., Pullman, 2001. Asst. prof. San Juan Bautista Sch. Medicine, Caguas, PR, 2002—05, Ponce Sch. Medicine, PR, 2005—. Mem.: Soc. Neuroimmune Pharmacology. Office: Ponce Sch Medicine Rsch Bldg 395 Indsl Rep 2 Ponce PR 00716 Business E-Mail: vrivera@psm.edu.

RIVERA-DOMINGUEZ, ALBERTO, mathematician, educator, mechanical engineer; b. Vega Baja, PR, June 17, 1958; s. Angel Rivera-Delgado and Concepcion Dominguez-Suarez; m. Elli Reyes-Grote, Jan. 6, 1985; 1 child, Albert Vincent Rivera-Reyes. BSME magna cum laude, U. P.R., 1981; MSME, La. Tech. U., 1990. Engr. Boeing Comml. A/P Co., Seattle, 1981-82; lectr. U. P.R., Mayaguez, P.R., 1983-84, asst. to the assoc. dean of engring., 1984; tchg. asst. La. Tech. U., Ruston, 1985-86; mech. engr. U.S. Army, Fort Buchannan/San Juan, P.R., 1987-90, USN/AFWTF, Ceiba, P.R., 1990-91; gen. engr. USN - NUWC, Newport, R.I., 1991-95; engr. Breeze-Eastern, Union, NJ, 1995—2001; tchr. h.s. math NJ, 2001—. Lectr. U. P.R., 1983-84. Contbr. articles to profl. jours. Recipient tuition award MIT, Cambridge, Mass., 1982, 84, Panam. Surety Assn. scholarship La. Tech. U., Ruston, 1986; inductee Nat. Honor Roll's Outstanding Am. Tchr., 2005-06. Mem. ASME, NSPE, Am. Soc. for Composites, Colegio de Ingenieros Y Agrimensores de P.R. Achievements include research on viscoelastic characterization of composite materials; theoretical rsch. findings include: co-established the prin. of virtual equillibrium state of viscoelasticity; devel. a generalized predictive creep response formulation suitable for composite materials; developed algorithm and techniques for performance and reliability prediction of assembled products. Home: PO Box 868 Matawan NJ 07747-1370

RIVERA-DUEÑO, JAMIE, state agency administrator, public health service officer; MD, U. PR Sch. Medicine, 1960. Specialty in pediat. Univ. Hosp. U. PR, 1966. Prof. pediat. Universidad Ctrl. del Caribe; pres., dean Ponce Sch. Medicine, PR; sec. health PR Dept. Health, San Juan, 1977—84, 2009—; exec. dir. San Juan AIDS Inst., Santurce, PR; sr. v.p. med. affairs HIMA San Pablo Hosp. Group; pres. PR Hosp. Assn. Office: PR Dept Health PO Box 70184 San Juan PR 00936*

RIVERA PÉREZ, EFRAÍN E., territorial supreme court justice; b. Mayaguez, PR, July 15, 1951; s. Efrain Rivera Padilla and Irene Perez Camacho; 1 child, Mariela. BBA, U. PR, 1971; JD, Pontifica Cath. U., PR, 1975. Pvt. practice, 1976—82, 1985—92; dist. judge, 1983—84; superior ct. judge Judicial Region Mayaguez, 1984—85; prof. U. PR, 1986—92; atty. general PR, 1993; dir. Comml. Jud. Reform, 1993—95, Jud. Nominations, 1993—95; judge Cir. Ct. Appeals Judge, 1995—2000; assoc. justice PR Supreme Ct., 2000—. Office: PO Box 902 2392 San Juan PR 00902-2392 Personal E-mail: efrain.erp@hotmail.com. E-mail: efrain.rivera@ramajudicial.pr.*

RIVERA-SOTO, ROBERTO A., state supreme court justice; b. NYC, 1954; m. Mary Catherine Mullaney; 3 children. Grad., Colegio Nuesra Senora Del Pilar, Rio Piedras, PR, 1970, Haverford Coll., 1974; JD, Cornell U. Sch. of Law, 1977. Asst. US atty. criminal divsn. US Atty. Office, Pa., 1978—80; litigation assoc. Fox Rothschild, O'Brien & Frankel, 1980—83; v.p., gen. counsel, corp. sec. Sands Hotel Casino, Atlantic City, 1984—94, Caesars World, Las Vegas, 1994—99; prtnr. Fox Rothschild, Princeton, NJ, 1999—2004; justice NJ Supreme Ct., 2004—. Former instructor trial advocacy Rutgers Sch. of Law; certified mediator U.S. Dist. Ct. for Dist. of N.J.; mem., chair N.J. Supreme Ct. Dist. VII Ethics Com. Former mem. bd. dirs. Please Touch Museum,

N.J. Devel. Authority for Small Bus., Minorities and Women's Enterprises. Recipient Director's award for superior performance as asst. U.S. atty., U.S. Dept. Justice, 1980. Office: NJ Supreme Ct PO Box 970 Trenton NJ 08625*

RIVERO, ANDRIA, psychology educator; b. Alacranes, Matanzas, Cuba, Feb. 04; came to the U.S. d. Javier and Juana Maria Rivero; children: Hermann J., Karina J. BS, Fla. Internat. U., 1974; MS, Nova U., 1981. Elem. tchr. St. Patrick Cath. Sch., Miami Beach, Fla., 1979-81; instr., dean instrn. Ft. Lauderdale Coll., Miami, Fla., 1981-84; prof., disability svcs. advisor St. Thomas U., Miami, 1984-99. Ed. specialist Accrediting Comm. for Colls. and Tech. Career Schs., 1993—; adv. bd. Tech. Career Inst., Miami, 1997-2000; adj. prof. MDC, 2000—, Fla. Internat. U., 2000—; lic. cmty. assn. mgr., Dade County, Fla., 2000. Mem. safety com. City of Miami Beach, 1995-97, lic. property mgr., 2002. Roman Catholic. E-mail: arivero@bellsouth.net.

RIVERO, DENNIS P., orthopedist; b. Albuquerque, Mar. 11, 1952; MD, Ctrl. U. Venezuela, Caracas, 1981. Chief sect. adult reconstrn. U. N.Mex., Albuquerque, 1992—. Author: (with others) Surgical Infections, 1995. Mem. Am. Acad. Orthopaedic Surgeons, Am. Assn. Hip and Knee Surgeons. Office: U NMex Sch Med Dept Orthopaedics MSC 105600 Albuquerque NM 87131-0001 Office Phone: 505-272-4107. Business E-Mail: drivero@salud.unm.edu.

RIVERO, LUIS RAUL, aerospace physician, military officer; b. San Juan, July 7, 1968; s. Luis Raul Rivero and Ana Luisa Marin de Rivero; m. Maria Judith Stillwell, Dec. 19, 1993. BS in Biology, Georgetown U., Washington, 1990; MD cum laude, U. Ctrl. Caribbean Sch. Medicine, Bayamon, PR, 1994; MPH, U. Tex. Med. Br., Galveston, 2005. Lic. PR, 1995, cert. preventive and aerospace medicine Am. Bd. Preventive Medicine, 2007. Intern surgery U. Dist. Hosp. U. PR, San Juan, 1994—95; gen. med. officer US Army Health Clinic Darmstadt, Germany, 1995—97; emergency med. treatment physician 212th Mobile Army Surg. Hosp. Operation Joint Endeavor, Bosnia-Herzegovina, 1996—97; gen. med. officer Rodriguez Army Health Clinic, Fort Buchanan, PR, 1997—2000; bn. field surgeon 296th Brigade Support Bn., 3rd BDE, 2nd ID, Fort Lewis, Wash., 2000—02; flight surgeon Raymond W. Bliss Army Health Clinic, Fort Huachuca, Ariz., 2002—03; bn. flight surgeon 5th Bn., 158th Rgt., 12th Aviation BDE Operation Iraqi Freedom, 2003—04; resident aerospace medicine Naval Aerospace Med. Inst., Pensacola, Fla., 2004—06, asst. chief resident, 2006—07; stationed at Schofield Barraks, Hawaii, 2007—. Dep. comdr. Rodriguez Army Health Clinic, Fort Buchanan, 1997—99; chief dept. mil. medicine Raymond W. Bliss Army Health Ctr., Fort Huachuca, 2003. Author: (research) A Study of the 1993 Healthcare Reform in Puerto Rico; contbr. scientific papers, articles to profl. jours. Lt. col. US Army, 1994—. Decorated Bronze Star US Army, Nat. Def. Svc. medal with Bronze Star, Global War on Terrorism Svc. medal, Global War on Terrorism Expeditionary medal, Meritorious Svc. medal with Oak Leaf Cluster, Army Commendation medal with 2 Oak Leaf Clusters, Armed Forces Svc. medal, Armed Forces Expeditionary medal, Humanitarian Svc. medal, NATO medal, Army Superior Unit award, Army Presdl. Unit citation. Mem.: Am. Coll. Preventive Medicine, Aerospace Medicine Student and Resident Orgn. (mil. liaison 2006—07), Aerospace Med. Assn., Coll. Physicians and Surgeons of PR, Soc. US Army Flight Surgeons (life). Roman Catholic. Avocation: travel. Home: 26445 Misty Ridge Pl Canyon Country CA 91387 Personal E-mail: luis.r.rivero@us.army.mil.

RIVERS, BEVERLY D., former district secretary; b. 1965; JD U. Ala. Sch. Law; BS in bus. mgmt., Oakwood Coll., Huntsville, Ala. Sec. D.C.; spl. asst. CFO; chief legis. asst. State Senator Henry L. Marsh, Richmond, Va.; atty. Hill Tucker Firm, Marsh Firm; acting sec. of dist. D.C. Govt., 1999, sec. of dist., 1999—2003. Mem.: Nat. Forum Black Pub. Adminstr., Wash. Bar Assn., Ala. Bar Assn., D.C. Bar Assn.

RIVERS, DOC (GLENN ANTON RIVERS), professional basketball coach; b. Maywood, Ill., Oct. 13, 1961; s. Grady Alexander and Betty Rivers; m. Kris Rivers, 1987; children: Jeremiah, Callie, Austin, Spencer. Student, Marquette U., 1980-83, BA in Pre-Law & Polit. Sci., 1985. Player Atlanta Hawks, 1983-91, LA Clippers, 1991-92, NY Knicks, 1992-94, San Antonio Spurs, 1994-96; sports analyst Turner Sports, 1996—99, ABC Sports, 2003—04; head coach Orlando Magic, 1999—2003, Boston Celtics, 2004—. Asst. coach U.S.A. Men's Basketball Team Goodwill Games, Brisbane, Australia, 2001. Recipient J. Walter Kennedy Basketball Citizenship award, Pro Basketball Writers, 1990; named Coach of Yr., NBA, 2000, Head Coach Eastern Conf. All-Star Team, 2008, Male Coach of Yr., Rainbow Sports Awards, 2000; named to NBA All-Star Team, 1988. Achievements include coaching the NBA Champion Boston Celtics, 2008. Office: Boston Celtics 226 Causeway St 4th Fl Boston MA 02114-4720*

RIVERS, JOAN (JOAN ALEXANDRA MOLINSKY), entertainer; b. NYC, June 8, 1937; d. Meyer C. Molinsky and Beatrice (Grushman); m. Edgar Rosenberg, July 15, 1965 (dec.); 1 child, Melissa. BA, Barnard Coll., 1958. Formerly fashion coordinator Bond Clothing Store; founder Joan Rivers Classics Collection, 1990, Joan Rivers Worldwide Enterprises, 1996—. Debut entertaining, 1960; mem. From Second City, 1961-62; TV debut Tonight Show, 1965; Las Vegas debut, 1969; nat. syndicated columnist Chgo. Tribune, 1973-76; creator: CBS TV series Husbands and Wives, 1976-77; host: Emmy Awards, 1983; guest hostess: Tonight Show, 1983-86; hostess The Late Show Starring Joan Rivers, 1986-87, Hollywood Squares, 1987, (morning talk show) Joan Rivers (Daytime Emmy award 1990), 1989-93, Can We Shop? Home Shopping Network, 1994, (radio) The Joan Rivers Show, 1997-2002, (TV series) E! Pre-awards Show, 1995-2004, red carpet events, TV Guide Channel, 2005-07; originator, screenwriter TV movie The Girl Most Likely To, ABC, 1973; other TV movies include: How to Murder A Millionaire, 1990, Jackie Collins' Lady Boss, 1992, Tears and Laughter: The Joan and Melissa Rivers Story, 1994; cable TV spl. Joan Rivers and Friends Salute Heidi Abromowitz, 1985; film appearances include The Swimmer, 1968, Uncle Sam, The Muppets Take Manhattan, 1984; co-author, dir.: (films) Rabbit Test, 1978 (also acted), Spaceballs, 1987, Serial Mom, 1994 Goosed, 1998, L'Intern, 2000, Shrek 2, 2004; actress: theatre prodn. Broadway Bound, 1988, Sally Marr...and her escorts, 1994; recs. include: comedy album What Becomes a Semi-Legend Most, 1983; author: Having a Baby Can be a Scream, 1974, The Life and Hard Times of Heidi Abromowitz, 1984, (autobiography with Richard Meryman) Enter Talking, 1986, (with Richard Meryman), Still Talking, 1991, Jewelry, 1995, Bouncing Back: I've Survived Everything... and I Mean Everything... and You Can Too!, 1997, From Mother to Daughter: Thoughts and Advice on Life, Love and Marriage, 1998, Don't Count the Candle, Just Keep the Fire Lit, 1999, Men Are Stupid... And They Like Big Boobs: A Woman's Guide to Beauty Through Plastic Surgery, 2008, Murder at the Academy Awards: A Red Carpet Murder Mystery, 2009; debuted on Broadway (play) Broadway Bound, 1988, creator Seminar You Deserve To Be happy, 1995; columnist (magazines) She Says/She Says, McCall's mag. (with daughter Melissa), 1999-2000, Star Mag. Fashion column (with daughter Melissa), 2002-03; actress (guest appearances), Suddenly Susan, 1998-99, Spaceballs: The Animated Series, 2008. Nat. chmn. Cystic Fibrosis, 1982—; benefit performer for AIDS, 1984; hon. chair Night of A Thousand Gowns, Imperial Court of NY, 2009. Recipient CLIO awards for commls., 1976, 1982, Jimmy award for best comedian, 1987, 1991, Accessories Coun. award of Excellence, 1997, Rebekah Kohut award for Svc. in Cmty., 2004, winner Celebrity Apprentice, 2009; named Hadassah Woman of Yr., 1983, Harvard Hasty Pudding Soc. Woman of Yr., 1984. Mem. Phi Beta Kappa. Office: William Morris Agy 151 S El Camino Dr Beverly Hills CA 90212-2775 also: Joan Rivers Worldwide 150 E 58th St, Ste 2400 New York NY 10155-2402*

RIVERS, PATRICK A., education educator, researcher; b. Oct. 18, 1958; s. Cosmas and Amma Rivers; m. Mary Alice Patton, May 3, 1983; 1 child, Patrick Cosmas. MBA in Fin., Investment and Banking, U. Wis., Madison, 1988; PhD, U. Ala., 1997; cert., Maguire Energy Inst., 2000. Faculty devel. fellow U. Ala., Birmingham, 1993—97; rsch. fellow Rand Corp., Santa Monica, Calif., 1997—98; clin. prof. U. Ariz., Tucson, 1998—; prof. Ariz. State U., Tempe, 1998—; prof., dir. So. Ill. U., 2004—. Recipient Nat. Rsch. Svc. award, Agy. for Health Rch. and Quality, 1997—98; scholar Most Published scholar, U. Ala., 1996—97. Fellow: Am. Coll. Health Care Execs.; mem.: Strategic Mgmt. Soc., Acad. Mgmt. Office: Ariz State Univ PO Box 874506 Tempe AZ 85287-4506 Home: 1175 S Morningside Dr Carbondale IL 62901 Office Phone: 618-453-8842. Business E-Mail: privers@siu.edu.

RIVERS, PHILIP, professional football player; b. Decatur, Ala., Dec. 8, 1981; s. Steve Rivers. B in Bus., NC State U., Raleigh. Quarterback San Diego Chargers, 2004—. Named to Am. Football Conf. Pro Bowl Team, NFL, 2006. Achievements include leading the NFL in: quarterback rating, passing touchdowns, 2008. Office: San Diego Chargers PO Box 609609 San Diego CA 92160-9609*

RIVERS, ROBERT ALFRED, microwave company executive; b. Phillipston, Mass., Sept. 5, 1923; s. Frank Allen and Marie Ange (Pelchat) R.; m. Priscilla Bradford, Oct. 8, 1944; children: Lucy Marie, Rosalind Dolley, Robert Bradford. BSEE, MIT, 1953. Registered profl. engr., NH. Flight radio officer Pan Am. Airways, various locations, 1942-50; design engr. Gen. Electronic Labs., Boston, 1953-54; pres. Aircom, Inc., various cities, 1954—. Editor Tech. Employment and Engring. Manpower Newsletter, 1989-2002; contbr. articles to profl. jours. Inventor wideband cavity resonator; designer over 1300 microwave components, portable and desktop microcomputer systems. Fellow IEEE (life, bd. dirs. 1975-76, mem. numerous coms. and bds., ethics rev. panel 1982-88, Centennial medal 1984, US Activities Bd. citation of hon., Profl. Achievement award 1992, Haradan Pratt award 1997); mem. IEEE Microwave Theory and Techs. Soc. (pres. 1974, mem. numerous coms., chmn. Boston chpt. 1958-59, digest editor 1967, MTT Disting. Svc. award 1978), Eta Kappa Nu, Tau Beta Pi. Republican. Avocations: gardening, travel, reading. Office: Aircom Inc PO Box 98 Orange MA 01364-0098

RIVES, JACK L., judge, career military officer; b. Carrollton, Ga., Apr. 8, 1952; BA in Polit. Sci., U. Ga., Athens, 1974, JD, 1976; postgraduate student, Squadron Officer Sch., 1982, Air Command and Staff Coll., 1983, Nat. Security Mgmt., 1985, Air War Coll., 1990; disting. grad., Naval War Coll., Fort Lesley J. McNair, Washington, 1993. Advanced through ranks to lt., vice maj. lt. gen. USAF, 2008, 2nd lt., 1974—77; asst. staff judge adv. Griffiss AFB, NY, 1977, area def. counsel NY, 1977—78; dep. staff judge adv. Kunsan Air Base, Republic of Korea, 1978—79; asst. staff judge adv. Hellenikon Air Base, Greece, 1979—81; cir. def. counsel (Pacific cir.) Clark Air Base, Philippines, 1981—83; judge adv. air staff tng. officer The Pentagon, Washington, 1983—84, dep. legal counsel to Chmn. Joint Chiefs of Staff, 1993—95; staff judge adv. Plattsburgh AFB, NY, 1984—86; chief officer br., judge adv. profl. devel. divsn. Office of JAG, Washington, 1986—90; appellate judge USAF Ct. Mil. Rev., Bolling AFB, DC, 1990—92; comdt. Air Force JAG Sch., Maxwell AFB, Ala., 1995—98; chief Air Force Exec. Issues Team Office of Sec. of Air Force, Washington, 1998—2000; staff judge adv. Hdqrs. Air Combat Command, Langley AFB, Va., 2000—02; dep. JAG USAF, Washington, 2002—06, JAG, 2006—. Decorated Legion of Merit with oak leaf cluster, Def. Superior Svc. Medal, Meritorious Svc. Medal with silver and bronze oak leaf clusters, Air Force Commendation Medal, DSM. Office: HQ USAF JA 1420 Air Force Pentagon Washington DC 20330

RIVES, STANLEY GENE, retired academic administrator; b. Decatur, Ill., Sept. 27, 1930; s. James A. and Frances (Bunker) R.; m. Sandra Lou Belt, Dec. 28, 1957; children: Jacqueline Ann, Joseph Alan. BS, Ill. State U., 1952, MS, 1955; PhD, Northwestern U., 1963; EdD (hon.), Lincoln Coll., 1998. Instr. W.Va. U., 1955-56, Northwestern U., 1956-58; prof. Ill. State U., Normal, 1958-80, Am. Coun. on Edn. Fellows Program, 1969-70, assoc. dean faculties, 1970-72, dean undergrad. instrn., 1972-80, assoc. provost, 1976-80, acting provost, 1979-80; provost, v.p. acad. affairs, prof. Eastern Ill. U., Charleston, 1981-83, pres., 1983-92, pres. emeritus, 1992—. Vis. prof. U. Hawaii, 1963—64. Author: (with Donald Klopf) Individual Speaking Contests: Preparation for Participation, 1967, (with Gene Budig) Academic Quicksand: Trends and Issues in Higher Education, 1973, (with others) Academic Innovation: Faculty and Instructional Development at Illinois State University, 1979, The Fundamentals of Oral Interpretation, 1981; contbr. articles to profl. jours. Bd. dirs. Ill. State Univs. Ret. Sys., 1992-2005, treas., 1995-2001, pres., 2001-05; bd. dirs. Ea. Ill. Univ. Found., 1993-98, also pres., 1996-98, East Ctrl. Ill. Devel. Corp., 1983-92, Charleston Area Econ. Devel. Found., 1986-92, Coles Together, 1988-92; mem. pres. commn. NCAA, 1986-91; trustee Nat. Debate Tournament, 1967-75. With U.S. Army, 1952-54. Recipient Alumni Achievement award, Ill. State U., 1998; named to Co. of Edn. Hall of Fame. Mem. Am. Assn. State Colls. and Univs., Ill. State C. of C. (bd. dirs. 1990-92), Charleston C. of C. (bd. dirs. 1985-88), Theta Alpha Phi, Phi Kappa Delta, Pi Gamma Mu, Alpha Phi Omega, Alpha Zeta, Sigma Phi Epsilon (hon.). Home: 2231 Andover Pl Charleston IL 61920-3807 Personal E-mail: srives@consolidated.net.

RIVEST, JEAN-FRANÇOIS, conductor; Student, Conservatoire de Montréal, Juilliard Sch., NYC. Artistic dir., prin. condr. Orchestre de l'Université de Montréal, Thirteen Strings Chamber Orch., Ottawa, Orchestre symphonique de Laval; condr. in residence Montréal Symphony Orch., 2006—. Music tchr. McGill U., Conservatoire de musique du Québec; head string dept. Université de Montréal, prof. titulaire conducting. Office: Montreal Symphony Orch 260 de Maisonneuve Blvd W, 2nd Fl Montreal PQ H2X 1Y9 Canada*

RIVET, DIANA WITTMER, lawyer, farmer; b. Auburn, NY, Apr. 28, 1931; d. George Wittmer and Anne (Jenkins) Wittmer Hauswirth; m. Paul Henry Rivet, Oct. 24, 1952; children: Gail, Robin, Leslie, Heather, Clayton, Eric. BA, Keuka Coll., 1951; JD, Bklyn. Law Sch., 1956. Bar: N.Y. 1956, U.S. Dist. Ct. (ea. and so. dists.) N.Y. 1975; cert. organic NOFA, 2001. Sole practice, Orangeburg, NY, 1957—2000; farmer Danny's Backyard Organic Farm, Orangeburg, 2000—. County atty. Rockland County (N.Y.), 1974-77; asst. to legis. chmn. Rockland County, 1978-79; counsel, adminstr. Indsl. Devel. Agy., Rockland County, 1980-91, Rockland Econ. Devel. Corp., 1981-90; counsel, exec. dir. Pvt. IndustryCoun. Rockland county, 1980-90; pres., CEO Environ. Mgmt. Ltd., Orangeburg, 1980-98; mem. air mgmt. adv. com. N.Y. State Dept. Environ. Conservation 1984-92, Orangetown Planning Bd., 1993-2000, master plan com., 2000-03. Pres. Rockland County coun. Girl Scouts U.S., 1981-84; chmn. Rockland County United Way, 1996-97, mem. campaign com., 1983-84, 88-89, 93, sec., 1997-99, bd. dirs., 1988-94, 95-2004, adv., nominating com., 2004-06, cmty. investment com. 2007—; mem. Leadership Rockland, 1991-94. Recipient Cmty. Svc. award Keuka Coll., 1965, Disting. Svc. award Town of Orangetown, 1970, Disting. Svc. award Rockland County, 1989, Econ. Devel. award Rockland Econ. Devel. Corp., 1990, Retirement award Keuka Coll., 2006; named Businessperson of Yr. Jour. News, Rockland County, 1982.E Mem. ABA, NY State Bar Assn. (mcpl. law sect. exec. com. 1976-83, environ. law sect. exec. com. 1974-86), Rockland County Bar Assn. (chair environ. law com. 1994-96), Rockland Bus. Assn. (bd. dirs. 1981-97, small bus. adv. com. 1998, gov. affairs com. 1998-2004), Rockland Computer Users' Group (bd. dirs. 1998-99), Rockland Farm Alliance. Democrat. Mem. Religious Soc. of Friends. Home: 1 Lester Dr Orangeburg NY 10962-2316 Office Phone: 845-359-1515. Personal E-mail: ydannyy@verizon.net.

RIVET, JEANNINE M., health insurance company executive; BS in Nursing, Boston Coll.; MPH, Boston U. Sch. Public Health. V.p. grp. ops. Prudential Ins. Co. Am.; v.p. health svc. ops. to CEO United HealthCare, Minnetonka, Minn., 1990-98, CEO, 1998—2000, Ingenix; exec. v.p. UnitedHealth Grp., 2000—. Office: UnitedHealth Group 9900 Bren Rd E Minnetonka MN 55343-9664*

RIVET, ROBERT J., semiconductor company executive; b. Chgo., Mar. 23, 1954; s. Robert F. and Lucille E. (Fazy) R.; m. Cynthia J. Moderhack, June 11, 1977; children: Scott M., Lauren N. BS, No. Ill. U., 1976; MBA, U. Tex., 1985. CPA, Ill. Sr. acct. Motorola Corp. Hdqs., Schaumburg, Ill., 1976-79, fin. analyst, 1979-81; group contr. Motorola Microprocessor Group, Austin, Tex., 1981-90, v.p., contr., 1990-92, Motorola Semicondr. Europe, Geneva, 1992; CFO Advanced Micro Devices, Sunnyvale, Calif., 2000—01, exec. v.p., CFO, 2001—08, chief ops. & adminstrv. officer, 2008—. Mem. Nat. Assn. Accts. Avocations: tennis, golf, travel. Office: AMD 1 AMD Pl Sunnyvale CA 94088*

RIVIERE, JIM EDMOND, pharmacologist, toxicologist, educator; b. New Bedford, Mass., Mar. 3, 1953; s. Raymond R. Riviere and Gertrude E. Pelletier-Riviere; m. Nancy Ann Monteiro-Riviere, May 31, 1976; children: Christopher, Brian, Jessica. BS, MS, Boston Coll., 1976; DVM, PhD, Purdue U., 1980, DSc (hon.), 2007. Lic. vet. medicine; diplomate Am. Bd. Forensic Medicine, Acad. Toxicological Sci. From asst. prof. to assoc. prof. NC State U., Raleigh, 1981-88, prof., 1988-92, Burroughs-Wellcome disting. prof. pharmacology, 1992—, dir. Ctr. Chem. Toxicology Rsch. and Pharmacokinetics, 1989—, dir. Biomath. Prog., 2005—07. Cons. for govt. and pharm. cos.; mem. com. on revision US Pharmacopeia; mem. sci. bd. FDA. Author, editor 10 books, author over 440 rsch. manuscripts. Recipient Ebert prize Am. Pharm. Assn., 1991, Disting. Alumni award Purdue U., 1991, Outstanding Rsch. award NC State U. Alumni Assn., 1993, Harvey Wiley medal, 1997, FDA Commrs. Spl. citation, 1997, O. Max Gardner award U. NC Sys., 1999; numerous rsch. grants. Fellow Am. Acad. Vet. Pharmacology and Therapeutics (editor 1989-92, 99—, First Rsch. award 1998), Inst. Medicine Nat. Academies (elected); mem. Am. Assn. Pharm. Scientist, Soc. Toxicology, Am. Vet. Med. Assn., Am. Coll. Forensic Examiners, Bd. of Sci. Coun. Nat. Toxicology Prog. Achievements include 5 patents in field. Avocations: baseball, boating, beachcombing. Office: NC State U 4700 Hillsborough St Raleigh NC 27606-1428 Home Phone: 919-881-9219. Business E-Mail: Jim_Riviere@ncsu.edu.

RIVIN, EVGENY (EUGENE) I., engineering educator, researcher, inventor, consultant; b. Moscow, June 11, 1932; came to U.S., 1979; s. Izrail Borisovich and Frida Mikhailovna Rivin; m. Irina Rivin, Dec. 30, 1958; children: Igor, Natasha. MS in Mech. Engring., Moscow Machine Tool Inst., 1954; PhD, Moscow Machine Tool. Inst., 1962; DSc, USSR Supreme Attestation Bd., 1972. Registered profl. engr., Ont., Can. Sr. engr. Moscow Profl. Motion Cameras Plant, 1954—57; sr. rschr. Rsch. Inst. Machine Tools, Moscow, 1957—68; head. lab. Rsch. Inst. Standardization, Moscow, 1968—75; prin. staff engr. Ford Motor Co., Dearborn, Mich., 1976—81; prof. Wayne State U., Detroit, 1981—. Co-prin. The TRIZ Group, West Bloomfield, Mich. Author: Dynamics of Machine Drives, 1966, Mechanical Design of Robots, 1988, The Science of Innovation, 1997, Stiffness and Damping in Mechanical Design, 1999, Passive Vibration Isolation, 2003, Innovation on Demand, 2005; author 13 books/monographs; editor 10 books; contbr. some 150 articles to profl. jours.; holder more than 60 patents. Bd. mem. Inst. Individual and Group Therapy, Farmington Hills, Mich., 2002—. Recipient Shingo prize for excellence in mfg. rsch. Shingo Found., 1992, DeVlieg Rsch. awards Wayne State U., 1987-89; Eminent Scholar Invitation, Loughborough Univ. Tech., 1995. Fellow ASME, Soc. Mfg. Engrs., Internat. Acad. for Prodn. Engring. (CIRP) (membership com. 1990). Achievements include over 60 patents in field. Office: Wayne State Univ 5050 Anthony Wayne Dr Detroit MI 48202 Office Phone: 313-577-3898.

RIVKIN, CHARLES HAMMERMAN, United States Ambassador to France and Monaco; b. 1962; s. William R. Rivkin; m. Susan Melissa Tolson, Aug. 1990. BA in Internat. Rels., Yale U., New Haven; MBA, Harvard U., Mass., 1988. Intern Renault, France; corp. fin. analyst Salomon Brothers, Inc.; from strategic planner to pres. & COO Jim Henson Co., LA, 1988—2000, pres., CEO, 2000—04, W!LDBRAIN, Inc., San Francisco, 2005—09; US amb. to France and Monaco US Dept. State, Paris, 2009—. Bd. dirs. W!LDBRAIN, Inc., 2005—09, EMAK Worldwide, Inc., 2006—09; chmn. bd. Kidrobot, Inc. Exec. prodr.: (TV series) Yo Gabba Gabba!. At-large Calif. del. Dem. Nat. Convention, 2004, 2008. Named one of 100 Most Creative People in Bus., Fast Co. Mem.: Pacific Coun. on Internat. Policy. Democrat. Office: DOS Amb 9200 Paris Pl Washington DC 20521*

RIVKIN, ROBERT SAMUEL, federal agency administrator; b. 1960; s. William R. Rivkin; m. Cindy S. Rivkin, May 7, 1988; 3 children. BA magna cum laude, Harvard Coll., Cambridge, Mass., 1982; JD, Stanford U. Law Sch., Calif., 1987. Law clk. to Hon. Joel M. Flaum US Ct. Appeals (7th cir.), 1987—88; asst. US atty. (no. dist.) Ill. US Dept. Justice, 1988—94; dir. programs & policy legal dept. City of Chgo., 1994—97; litig. ptnr. Schiff, Hardin & Waite, Chgo., 1998—2001; gen. counsel Chgo. Transit Authority, 2001—04; v.p., dep. gen. counsel the Americas Aon Corp., 2004—09; gen. counsel US Dept. Transp., Washington, 2009—. Office: US Dept Transp 1200 New Jersey Ave SE Washington DC 20590 Office Phone: 202-366-4702.*

RIVKIN, WILLIAM B., physicist; b. Latvia, Jan. 6, 1921; arrived in US, 1931; s. Oscar W. and Fannie Mary Rivkin; m. Dolores Cohan Rivkin; children: Francine, Debra Rivkin Haggarty. BSEE, Ill. Inst. Tech., 1945; postgrad., Northwestern U., Evanston, Ill., 1960—61. V.p., gen. mgr. Health Physics Assoc., Northbrook, Ill., 1959—86, Isotope Measurements Labs., 1969—87, Mobile Imaging, Inc., 1970—93; physicist Vets. Adminstrn. Hosp., Hines, 1961—75; health physicist U.

Ill., Chgo., 1970—76; CEO Medx, Inc., Wooddale, 1993—98, Arlington Heights, 2003—. Field engr. Tracerlab, Inc., Boston, 1953—57; criticality engr. Westinghouse Electric Co., Cheswick, Pa., 1957—58; cons. Imaging Concepts, Inc., Highland Park, Ill., 1980—2003. Contbr. chapters to books. Bd. dirs. Northbrook Symphony Orch., 1980—2003, Am. Nuc. Soc., Washington, 1980—85. With Signal Corps. US Army, 1940—42. Mem.: Am. Assn. Physics in Medicine (com. mem. 1965—), Soc. Nuc. Medicine (com. mem. 1970—), Health Physics Soc. (pres. 1970—74), Rotary. Democrat. Jewish. Avocations: sailing, travel. Home: 1190 Ridge Rd Highland Park IL 60035 Office Phone: 947-831-3293. Personal E-mail: wbrivkin@comcast.net.

RIVKIND, PERRY ABBOT, federal railroad agency administrator; b. Boston, Jan. 22, 1930; s. Samuel Alexander and Mae Edna (Polisnor) R.; m. Dolores Russo; children: Robert Douglas, Valerie Jean, Jeff Pettit; m. Kathleen Marie Lysher, Aug. 14, 1989. AA, Columbia U., 1948, Miami CC, Fla., 1963; BA, Fla. State U., 1965; MA, Fla. Atlantic U., 1966; postgrad., Nat. War Coll., Washington, 1981. Comml. charter pilot, 1956-58; police officer Met. Police Dept., Miami, 1958-61; chief investigator Dade County State Atty. Office, Miami, 1961-67; prof., dir. dept. Cen. Piedmont Coll., Charlotte, NC, 1967-68; asst. dir. Fed. Bur. Narcotics, Washington, 1968-74; asst. adminstr. Law Enforcement Assistance Adminstrn., Washington, 1974-81; assoc. commr. U.S. Immigration and Naturalization Svc., Washington, 1981-84, dist. dir. Miami, 1984-88; safety mgr. Miami Herald Pub. Co., 1988-89; dep. adminstr. Fed. R.R. Adminstrn., Washington, 1989—. Chmn. com. on tng. Pres.'s Coun. on Drug Abuse, Washington, 1971-74, chmn. com. on rsch. Working Group on Terrorism Nat. Security Coun., Washington, 1978-81. Capt. Cadet Program USAF, 1943-45, With U.S. Army, 1951-53. Perry A. Rivkind Day established in his honor City of Miami/Dade County/City of Miami Beach, 1985-89. Republican. Avocations: boating, hunting, fishing, motorcycling, camping. Home Phone: 704-992-5675.

RIVLIN, ALICE MITCHELL, economics professor, former federal official; b. Phila., Mar. 4, 1931; d. Allan C. G. and Georgianna (Fales) Mitchell; m. Lewis Allen Rivlin, 1955 (div. 1977); children: Catherine Amy, Allan Mitchell, Douglas Gray; m. Sidney Graham Winter, 1989. AB, Bryn Mawr Coll., 1952; MA, Radcliffe Coll., 1955, PhD, 1958; LLD (hon.), U. Mich., 1975, U. Md., 1975; DSc (hon.), U. Ind., 1976; LLD (hon.), Yale U., 1984; DSc (hon.), N.J. Inst. Tech., 1998; LLD (hon.), U. Dist. of Columbia, 1999, Harvard U., 2001. Mem. staff Brookings Instn., 1957-66, 69-75, 83-93, dir. econ. studies, 1983-87; dep. asst. sec. for program coordination US Dept. Health Edn. & Welfare, Washington, 1966—68, asst. sec. for planning & evaluation, 1968—69; dir. Congl. Budget Office, 1975-83; prof. pub. policy George Mason U., 1992—93; dep. dir. Office Mgmt. & Budget, Exec. Office of the Pres., Washington, 1993-94, dir., 1994-96; mem. bd. governors Fed. Res. Sys., 1996—99, vice chmn. Washington, 1996-99; chair Fin. Assistance and Mgmt. Authority, 1998—2001; sr. fellow, econ. studies program Brookings Instn., Washington, 1999—, dir. Greater Wash. Rsch. Program, 2001—; Henry J. Cohen prof. New Sch. U., 2001—03. Mem. Staff Adv. Commn. on Intergovtl. Rels., 1961-62; bd. dirs. NY Stock Exch., 2005-06, NYSE Group, Inc., 2006-, BearingPoint, Inc., 2001-06, The Washington Post Co., 2002-06 Author: The Role of the Federal Governemnt in Financing Higher Education, 1961, Microanalysis of Socioeconomic Systems, 1961, Systematic Thinking for Social Action, 1971, Caring for the Disabled Elderly: Who Will Pay?, 1988, Reviving the American Dream, 1992; co-author: (with Robert E. Litan), Beyond the Dot.Coms: The Economic Promise of the Internet, 2001; co-editor: (with Robert E. Litan) The Economic Payoff from the Internet Revolution, 2001, (with Isabel Saawhill) Restoring Fiscal Sanity: How to Balance the Budget, 2004, Restoring Fiscal Sanity 2005: Meeting the Long-Run Challenges, 2005, (with Joseph Antos) Restoring Fiscal Sanity 2007: The Health Spending Challenge, 2007 Named a MacArthur Fellow, John D. & Catherine T. MacArthur Found., 1983, Elliot J. Richardson Prize for Excellence in Pub. Svc., 2002, Barnard Medal of Distinction, Barnard Coll., 2002, Lifetime Achievement award, DC Chamber of Commerce, 2004, Daniel Patrick Moynihan prize, Am. Acad. Social & Polit. Sci., 2008 Mem. Am. Econ. Assn. (nat. pres. 1986), Nat. Acad. Pub. Administrn., Nat. Acad. of Social Insurance, Coun. on Fgn. Rels., Women's Econ. Roundtable Democrat. Office: Brookings Instn 1755 Massachusetts Ave Washington DC 20036*

RIVLIN, GARY, writer, reporter; b. NYC, June 20, 1958; s. Kenneth and Naomi Rivlin. BS, Northwestern U., 1980. Staff writer Chgo. Reader, 1985—89; reporter Conta Costa Times, 1990—91; staff writer East Bay Express, 1991—96, editor, 1999; sr. writer & editor Industry Standard, 2000—01; contbg. editor Wired mag., 2001—04; tech. reporter NYTimes, 2004—. Author: Fire on the Prairie, 1992 (Nonfiction Book of the Yr., Chgo. Tribune, 1992, Carl Sandburg award, 1992), Drive-By, 1995 (one of NY Times' notable books of the yr., 1995, non-fiction book of yr. finalist, San Francisco Bay Area Book Reviewers Assn., 1995, non-fiction finalist for Pen-WEST Best of West, 1995), The Plot to Get Bill Gates, 1999, The Godfather of Silicon Valley, 2001; contbr. to magazines such as NY Times Magazine Newsweek, Fortune, The New Republic, Parada and GQ. Recipient print journalism prize, San Francisco Bay Area Media Alliance, 1993, Best Enterprise reporting award, Soc. Profl. Journalists, 1993, Gold Medallion award, Calif. Bar Assn., 1996, Gerald Loeb award for disting. bus. & fin. journalism in the mag. category, 2001, Gerald Loeb award, 2005; named best writer non-daily newspaper, Calif. Newspaper Pub. Assn., 1993. Office: New York Times 201 Spear St San Francisco CA 94105 Office Phone: 415-836-6700. Business E-Mail: rivlin@nytimes.com.

RIVLIN, RACHEL, lawyer; b. Bangor, Maine, Sept. 1, 1945; d. Lawrence and A. Sara (Rich) Lait. BA, U. Maine, 1965; MA, U. Louisville, 1968; JD, Boston Coll., 1977. Bar: Mass. 1977, U.S. Dist. Ct. Mass. 1978, U.S. Ct. Appeals (1st cir.) 1983, U.S. Supreme Ct. 1985. Audiologist Boston City Hosp., 1969-72; dir. audiology Beth Israel Hosp., Boston, 1972-74; atty. Legal Sys. Devel., Boston, 1977-78, Liberty Mut. Ins., Boston, 1978-82; counsel, sec. Lexington Ins. Co., Boston, 1982-85, v.p., assoc. gen. counsel, sec., 1985—. Mem. task force fin. literacy students U.S. Bankruptcy Ct. and Boston Bar Assn., 2004—05. Mem. civil rights com. Anti-Defamation League, Boston, 1982—2005; bd. dirs. Dance Art, Inc., Boston, 1985—92. Mem.: ABA (mem. ins. regulation com. 1980—, vice chair internat. ins. law com. 1983—84, internat. ins. law com. 1985—86, sr. vice chair nat. inst. insurer insolvency 1987—88, sr. vice chair pub. regulation of ins. 1987—90, nat. inst. reins. collections and insolvency 1988, chair excess surplus lines and resins. com. 1988—89, nat. inst. insurer insolvency 1989, internat. ins. law com. 1997—2005, task force ins. and corp. counsel interests and involvement 1999—2003, vice chair corp. counsel com. 2003—08), Boston Bar Assn. (mem. coun. 1983—86, chmn. corp. counsel 1987, steering com. corp. bus. law and fin. sect. 1987—89, chmn. ins. law. com. 1987—2005, nominating com. 1988, edn. com. 1989, 1990—91, chmn. ins. com. 1990—93, ethics com. 1993—2005, edn. com. 1994, multi-disciplinary practice task force 2000—02, comprehensive revision Mass. corp. law 2000—02, mem. coun. 2002—05, edn. com. 2003, mem. task force fin. literacy students 2004—05), Boston Coll. Law Sch. Alumni Assn. (ann. fund com. 1981—89, chmn. telethon com. 1989—94, nominating com. 1990, search com. for dean 1993, search com. for law sch. fund dir. 1993, leadership gifts exec. com. 1994—98, search com. for dir. instl. advancement 1995, reunion com. 2002, Father James Malley award 1996). Office Phone: 941-870-3326. Business E-Mail: rachelrivlin@aol.com.

RIZK, MAGED, cardiologist, researcher; b. Cairo, Apr. 12, 1961; s. Mostafa Rizk; m. Magda Rashad, May 25, 1992; children: Ahmed, Rahma. MD, Ain Shams U., 1985; PhD in Pharmacology and Toxicology, U. Medicine and Dentistry NJ, 1992. Cert. Am. Bd. Internal Medicine, 1996, ABIM Bd. Cert. in Cardiology 2000, Bd. Cert. in Echocardiography 2001. Instr., dept. medicine NY Med. Coll., Valhalla, NY, 1995—97, cardiology fellow, 1997—2000; asst. prof. cardiology St. Louis U., 2000—01; cardiology cons. Cardiovascular Cons., PC, Sterling Heights, Mich., 2001; dir. noninvasive cardiology St. John Macomb Hosp., 2006. Pres. Grad. Student Assn. UMDNJ, Newark, 1990—91; instr. of medicine NY Med. Coll., Valhalla, 1995—96; pres., CEO Medcom Am. Inc., Elmsford, NY, 1995—97; dir. Cardiology So. Ill., Herrin, 2000—01. Doctorate fellowship, UMDNJ, 1987. Mem.: ACP, Am. Soc. Nuc. Cardiology, Am. Soc. Echocardiography, Am. Heart Assn., Am. Assn. Univ. Profs., Am. Coll. Cardiology. Achievements include patents for Anticoagulant effect of aspirin and salicylamide, 1992. Avocation: tennis. Office: Cardiovascular Cons PC 37771 Schoenherr Ste 101 Sterling Heights MI 48312 Office Phone: 586-274-2450. Personal E-mail: maged@sbcglobal.net.

RIZKALLA, SAMI, engineering educator; m. Mary Rizkalla; children: Carolyn, Natalie. BS in Civil Engring., Alexandria U., Alexandria, Egypt, 1965; MS in Civil Engring., NC State U., Raleigh, NC, 1974, PhD in Civil Engring., 1976. Dir., structural engring. and constrn. U. Man., Canada, 1990—95, assoc. dean, faculty engring., 1992—94, pres. and sci. dir., ISIS, 1995—2000, prof., civil engring., adj. prof., 2000—06; prof. civil engring. NC State U., 2000—, dir. constructed facilities lab., dir., NSFI/UCRC repair of buildings; adj. prof. Concordia U., Canada, 1995—98, Ain Shams U., Egypt, 2007—. Mem. Raleigh Rotary Club, Raleigh, NC, 2000; exec. com., St. Mary's Coptic Orthodox Ch., 2005; mem. bd. Raleigh Rotary Club, Raleigh, NC, 2006—07. Recipient Lifetime Achievement award, IIFC, 2006, Martin P. Korn award, 2007, Mirko Ros Gold Medal award, EMPA Switzerland, 2008, Joe W. Kelly award, Am., Concrete Inst., 2008, PCI Jour. Award. Fellow: Can. Soc. Civil Engring., Engring. Inst. Can., Internat. Inst. FRP in Constrn. (Fellow and Coun. Mem.); mem.: Internationsl Concrete Repair Inst., Post-Tension Inst. Office: NC State Univ 2414 Campust Shore Dr CB 7533 Raleigh NC 27695-7533

RIZKIN, IOSIF, retired systems, circuits, and computer scientist, writer; b. Leningrad, Russia, Apr. 10, 1931; came to U.S., 1988; s. Chaim Aronovitch Rizkin and Sosja Eljevna Itsikson; m. Lyudmila Chudnovskaya, Oct. 28, 1930; 1 child, Yelena. PhD, Moscow Telecomm. Inst., 1962, DSc in Engring., 1972. Assoc. prof. Moscow Telecomm. Inst., 1969-88; programmer-analyst Chem. Bank, NYC, 1989-94; programmer Amarex Tech., Inc., NYC, 1994-95, Metropolitan Transp. Authority (MTA), NYC, 1997—2001; freelance cons. NYC, 2001—07. Author: Frequency Multipliers and Dividers, 1966, 2d edit., 1976, Computer Aided Analysis and Design in Engineering, 1985, Night Skies, 1999, Scenes from the Previous Life, Pseudo-Poetry, 2002 (in Russian, in English); contbr. articles to profl. jours. in Russia, Europe and U.S. Mem. sci. adv. bd. N.Y. Assn. for New Americans, 1990-94. Mem. IEEE (sr., former section chmn. Popov Soc.). Jewish. Avocations: poetry, stories and plays. Home and Office: 186 Pinehurst Ave Apt 2B New York NY 10033-1731 Office Phone: 212-795-0478. Personal E-mail: irizonlin@gmail.com.

RIZOWY, CARLOS GUILLERMO, lawyer, educator, political analyst; b. Sarandi Grande, Uruguay, Mar. 5, 1949; arrived in U.S., 1973, naturalized, 1981; s. Gerszon and Eva (Visnia) R.; m. Charlotte Gordon, Mar. 14, 1976; children: Brian Isaac, Yael Deborah, Michal Evie. BA, Hebrew U., Jerusalem, 1971; MA, U. Chgo., 1975, PhD, 1981; JD, Chgo. Kent Coll. Law, Ill. Inst. Tech., 1983. Bar: Ill. 1983, U.S. Dist. Ct. (no. dist.) Ill. 1983, U.S. Ct. Appeals (7th cir.) 1983. Asst. prof. polit. sci. Roosevelt U., Chgo., 1982-89, chmn. dept. polit. sci., 1983-86, dir. internat. studies program, 1986-89; mng. ptnr. Ray, Rizowy & Fleischer, Chgo., 1983-90; ptnr. corp. law dept. Gottlieb and Schwartz, 1990-92; ptnr. Levenfeld, Eisenberg, Janger, Glassberg, Samotny & Halper, 1993-94; of counsel Sonnenschein, Nath & Rosenthal, 1994—2004; internat. bus. cons., 2004—. Hon. consul of Uruguay, Chgo., 1994—; adj. assoc. prof. Spertus Coll. Judaica, Chgo., 1984—; weekly polit. analyst on Mid. East, internat. law and fgn. policy, resource specialist Sta. WBEZ Pub. Radio and BBC L.Am.; mem. panel of arbitrators of Mediation and Arbitration Ctr., Internat. Arbitration Ct. for Mercosur Bolsa de Comercio, Uruguay, 1999—; gen. counsel Assn. Iberoamerican Consuls, 2003-; internat. bus. cons., 2004-; spkr. and presenter to CEOs on Am. fgn. policy. Author: May 17, Elections in Isreal, National Stragey Forum, 1999, Guidelines for US Mideast Policy, National Strategy Forum, 2001; co-editor: Avoiding Premises Liability Suits by Improving Security and Premises Liability Increases as Violence becomes more Forseeble, 1991, Middle East Security: Five Areas to Watch, National Strategy Forum, 1997, Latin American Business Cultures-Crossing Cultural Barriers, Prentice Hall, 2005; contbr. articles to profl. jours. V.p., resource specialist to exec. com. Orgn. Children of Holocaust Survivors, Chgo., 1982; pres. Assn. Children Holocaust Survivors, 1986-91; pres. bd. dirs. Soviet Jewry Legal Advocacy Ctr., 1986-88; rsch. com. Nat. Strategy Forum, bd. dirs. UN Assn. U.S., 1985-89; cmty. rels. com. Jewish Fedn. Met. Chgo., 1983-84; adv. bd., chmn. internat. affairs commn. Am. Jewish Congress, Chgo., 1983-85, chmn. subcom. for Israel, 1986-88; mem. Nat. Spkrs. Bur. United Jewish Appeal, Nat. Spkrs. Bur. Devel. Corp. for Israel; spkr. to CEOs The Exec. Com., 1980-; adv. bd. Chgo. Action for Soviet Jewry, 1983-85; bd. dirs. Am. Friends of Hebrew U., Chgo., 1984-86, Florence Heller Jewish Cmty. Ctr., 1986-88; human rights com. Anti-Defamation League, 1986, bd. dirs. 1989—; bd. dirs. Bd. Jewish Edn., 1989-91, Hispanic Coalition for Jobs, 1991-94; chmn. univ. educators divsn. Jewish United Fund, 1988-90; consular corp. adv. bd. Internat. Vis. Ctr. Chgo., 1995—, com. fgn. affairs Chgo. Coun. Fgn. Rels., 1994—. Scholar Hebrew U., 1967-72, U. Chgo., 1972-78, Hillman Found., 1978, Peter Volid Found., 1980; recipient Globalist award Heritage Internat. Trade Assn., 1997. Mem. ATLA, ABA (chmn. bus. com. 1993-95), Assn. Ibero-Am. Consuls of Chgo., Ill. State Bar Assn., Chgo. Bar Assn. (internat. trade com.), Latin Am. Bar Assn., Nat. Hispanic Bar Assn., Am. Immigration Lawyers Assn., Am. Polit. Sci. Assn., Am. Judicature Soc., Exec. Club Chgo., Internat. Platform Assn., Wexner Heritage Found., Am. Forum, Latin Am. C. of C. (bd. dirs. 1991—, gen. counsel 1992—), Anshe Emet Congregation, Masons. Office Phone: 312-371-5531. Personal E-mail: crizowy49@hotmail.com.

RIZVI, SYED, engineering educator; married. PhD, SUNY, Buffalo, 1996. Prof. and chairperson dept. Engring. Sci. and Physics Coll. Staten Island-CUNY, 2002—. Grant, ARO, 2000—05. Mem.: IEEE. Office: Coll of Staten Island-CUNY Rm 1N-226 2800 Victory Blvd Staten Island NY 10314 Office Fax: 718-982-2830. Business E-Mail: rizvi@mail.csi.cuny.edu.

RIZZA, FRANK ALFONSO, retired surgeon, educator; b. Savannah, Ga., Sept. 28, 1928; s. Alfonso Joseph and Georgia Hall Rizza. BS, Med. Coll. Ga., 1950, MD, 1954. Gen. surgeon, New Orleans, 1960—96; chief surgery West Jefferson Gen. Hosp., Marrero, La., 1980—84. Assoc. prof. La. State Med. Sch., New Orleans. Archives rschr. Savannah (Ga.) Cath. Diocese, 2001—06. Capt. Med. Corps US Army, 1956—58. Fellow: AMA, ACS, Royal Soc. Medicine; mem.: Parish Med. Soc., La. State Med. Soc., AMA of Vienna.

RIZZA, ROBERT ALLAN, physician; b. Balt., Aug. 1, 1945; s. Joseph Charles and Elizabeth Allan Rizza; m. Emily Bonn; children: Stacey Vlalakis, Elizabeth Allan. BA in biophysics, Johns Hopkins U., 1967; MD, U. Fla. Med. Sch., 1971. Diplomate Am. Bd. Internal Medicine, Am. Bd. Endocrinology and Metabolism. Intern, medicine Johns Hopkins U., 1971-72, resident, endocrinology, 1972-73, 75-76; fellow Mayo Clinic, 1976-79; from asst. to Earl and Annette R. McDonough prof. medicine, cons. divsn. endocrinology and dir. rsch. Mayo Found., Rochester, Minn., 1980—, dir., endocrine rsch., vice-chair, dept. medicine; chair, divsn. endocrinology, diabetes, metabolism and nutrition. Assoc. editor Diabetes Care, Diabetes, Am. Jour. Physiology; contbr. articles to peer-reviewed publications. Lt. col. USN, 1973-75. Recipient Yank D. Coble, Jr., MD Disting. Svc. to Endocrinology, Am. Coll. Endocrinology, Bruce Zimmerman award, Minn. Dept. Health and Minn. Diabetes Steering Com., 2006. Mem. Am. Diabetes Assn. (bd. dirs., pres. exec. com., 2005, mem. expert com. on diagnosis and classification of diabetes, profl. practice com., provider recognition com., meeting oversight com., rsch. policy com., Outstanding Physician Clinician in Diabetes award), Am. Assn. Subsplty. Profs. (coun.), Assn. Program Directors Endocrinology, Diabetes and Metabolism (pres.-elect), Am. Soc. Clin. Investigation. Office: Mayo Found 200 1st St SW Rm 5-194 Joseph Rochester MN 55905-0001 Office Phone: 507-255-6515. Office Fax: 507-255-4828.

RIZZELLO, JOSEPH SAMUEL, stock exchange executive; b. Phila., Mar. 5, 1947; s. Samuel Joseph and Helen (Calabree) R.; m. Daria Catherine Sawicky; children: Damien Joseph, Justin Michael, Marcus Samuel. Ops. mgr. Drexel Burnham, Phila., 1970-74; asst. v.p. ops. and sales Thomson McKinnon Securities, Phila., 1974-80, v.p., br. mgr., 1980-85; sr. v.p. mktg. Phila. Stock Exchange, 1985-89, exec. v.p. bus. devel. mktg., new product devel., 1994—98; pres. Phila Bd. Trade subs. Phila. Stock Exchange, 1989; principal Vanguard Brokerage Services, Malvern, Pa., 1998—2000; mng. dir., mem. exec. com. Pershing LLC, 2001; pres. Pershing Trading Co.; bd. dirs. NSX Holdings, Inc., Chgo., 2002—04, special advisor to CEO and bd. dirs., 2004—06, chmn., 2006—; CEO Nat. Stock Exchange, 2006—. Bd. dirs. Internat. Cons. and Investment Techs., Inc., Calif., Found. for Rsch. Internat. Banking and Fin., Calif. With U. S. Army, 1966-67. Mem. Nat. Futures Assn. (bd. dirs. 1989—), Investment Traders Assn. Phila. (bd. dirs. 1987—). Roman Catholic. Office: NSX Holdings 440 S LaSalle St Ste 2600 Chicago IL 60605*

RIZZI, GIANFRANCO, artist; b. Foggia, Italy, June 3, 1946; s. Faldino Rizzi and Jolanda Italia Cusenza. Degree in Scenography, Acad. Albertina of Fine Arts, Torino, 1968. Headmaster, dir. Pinacoteca Albertina Mus. of Turin, Sch. of Painting, 2005—. Head dept. painting Albertina Acad. Fine Arts, Turin, Italy, 1995—, mem. adminstrn. coun., 2005—; v.p. Soc. Promotrice Belle Arti, Turin, Italy, 2000—04; intern painting symposium for Olympic Games, Patra, Greece, 2004; condr. workshops in field; lectr. in field. One-man shows include Baglioni Palace, Florence, 1965, Pianetti Palace Mcpl. Art Gallery, Jesi, 1972, Mcpl. Mus. Pictures Gallery, Foggia, 1972, Guillaume Campo Gallery, Antwerp, Belgium, 1972, Stadthalle, Göppingen, Germany, 1976, Frederic Gallery, Würzburg, Germany, 1988, Galerie Adriana, Stuttgart, Germany, 1987, exhibited in group shows at Royal Palace, Naples, 1969, Turin, 1971, exhibited in group shows at Mcpl. Art Gallery Tessaloniky, Greece, 2006, 2007, Olympische Kunst Onu, Francfurt am Main, Germany, 2006, Intern, Painting in Exposition by Unesco: Let's Talk About Migration, Patras, Greece, 2006; author: Art in the Beginning of the 3rd Millennium, 2000, (F)Atti d'Arte, 2001, Hortus Botanicus Taurinensis, 2002, Thoughts About Art of Painting-Conversation with Historical Artist, 2007, Art and Urban Spaces in a Society Educated by Advertisement, Internat. Sci. Conf. Conjectural Interference in Constrn., Patras, Greece, 2007; Represented in permanent collections Nat. Gallery, Berlin, Biblioteca Aposiolica vaticans Citta Del Vaticano, Modern Art Civic Gallery, Turin, Staat Gallery, Stuttgart, Stadt Gallery, Nurnberg, Ministere Affaires Culteureles, Paris, Civic Mus., Foggia, The Fly, Monument, Gino Lisa Civil Airport, Italy, Gradara Castle, 1971. Recipient Gold medal, Foggia Town, 1969, 1st prize painting, City of Turin, 1969, Prize for drawing, City of Milan, 1969, 1st place nat. competition painting, Acad Fine Art, Milan, Italy, 1985. Home: Largo Orbassano 81 10124 Turin Italy Office: Accademia Albertina di Belle Arti Via Accademia Albertina 6 10123 Turin Italy Office Phone: 011-889020. Personal E-mail: gfrpit@libero.it. E-mail: gianfranco.rizzi@accademiaalbertina.torino.it.

RIZZI, JOSEPH VITO, banker; b. Berwyn, Ill., Dec. 5, 1949; s. Joseph and Mary Catherine (Mancini) R.; m. Candace Kunz, June 24, 1972; children: Jennifer, Joseph, Sammantha. BS in Commerce summa cum laude, DePaul U., 1971; MBA, U. Chgo., 1973; JD magna cum laude, U. Notre Dame, 1976. Bar: Ill. 1976. Law clk. to judge US Dist. Ct. (no. dist.) Ill., 1976—77; exec. v.p. T.B.R. Enterprises, Inc., Downers Grove, Ill., 1977—83; mng. dir. ABN AMRO, NYC, 1983—. Mem. Delta Epsilon Sigma. Roman Catholic. Office: Capital Gen Capital Suite 401 280 Pk Ave 40th Fl New York NY 10017 Home: 389 E 89th St Apt 19E New York NY 10128 Office Phone: 212-542-6874. Business E-Mail: jrizzi@capgen.com.

RIZZO, JEFFREY F., corporate and non-profit financial executive; BA in Econ., Fairfield U., Conn.; post grad. studies, NYU, NYC. Mng. dir. pub. fin. dept. Moody's Investors Svc., NYC, 1976—95; dir. fin. Met. Transportation Authority, NYC, 1995—97; mgmt. cons. NYC, 1997—2000; controller Marble Collegiate Ch., NYC, 2001—04, NY Ch., 2001—04. Mem. Calif. Debt & Investment Adv. Com., US Conf. Mayors, All Am. Mcpl. Analysts Team. Bd. treas. United Charities, Friends of R.S.V.P.; mem. Mayors Leadership Inst. Mem.: Heart Media Found. (bd. treas.), Blue Ocean Inst. (bd. treas.).

RIZZO, RONALD STEPHEN, lawyer; b. Kenosha, Wis., July 15, 1941; s. Frank Emmanuel and Rosalie (Lo Cicero); m. Mary Rizzo; children: Ronald Stephen Jr., Michael Robert. BA, St. Norbert Coll., 1963; JD, Georgetown U., 1965, LLM in Taxation, 1966. Bar: Wis. 1965, Calif. 1967, Ill. 1999. Assoc. Kindel & Anderson, LA, 1966-71, ptnr., 1971-86, Jones & Day, LA, 1986—93, Chgo., 1993—2004, of counsel, 2005—. Bd. dirs. Guy LoCicero & Son Inc., Kenosha, Bristol Oaks Country Club Enterprises, Bristol, Wis. Contbg. editor ERISA Litigation Reporter, 1994-99; mem. internat. adv. editl. bd. Jour. Pensions Mgmt. and Mktg. Schulte zur Hausen fellow Inst. Internat. and Fgn. Trade Law, Georgetown U., 1966. Fellow Am. Coll. Tax Counsel, Am. Coll. Employee Benefits Counsel (charter); mem. ABA (chmn. com. on employee benefits sect. on taxation 1988-89, vice chair com. on govt. submissions 1995-99), Los Angeles County Bar Assn. (chmn. com.

on employee benefits sect. on taxation 1977-79, exec. com. 1977-78, 90-92), State Bar Calif. (co-chmn. com. on employee benefits sect. on taxation 1980), West Pension Conf. (steering com. L.A. chpt. 1980-83). Avocations: reading, golf, travel. Office: Jones Day 77 W Wacker Ste 3500 Chicago IL 60601-1692 Home: PO Box 11 Russell IL 60075-0011 Home Phone: 312-415-1941; Office Phone: 312-269-1568. Business E-Mail: rsrizzo@jonesday.com.

RIZZO, WILLIAM BRADLEY, pediatrician, educator; MD, U. Ill., Chgo., 1977. Cert. Am. Bd. Pediat., 1985, Am. Bd. Med. Genetics, 1987. Prof. pediat., human genetics and biochemistry Med. Coll. Va., Richmond, 1983—2002; prof. pediat. U. Nebr. Med. Ctr., Omaha, 2002—. Lt. comdr. Pub. Health Svc. US Army, 1979—82, Bethesda, Md. Rsch. grant, NIH, 1984—. Mem.: Soc. Inherited Metabolic Disorders, Am. Soc. Human Genetics. Office: Univ Nebr Med Ctr 985456 Nebr Med Ctr Omaha NE 68198-5456 Office Fax: 402-559-2540. Business E-Mail: wrizzo@unmc.edu.

RIZZOTTO, VINCENT MICHAEL, bishop emeritus; b. Houston, Tex., Sept. 9, 1931; Attended, St. Mary's Sem.; degree in Canon Law, Cath. U. Am., 1963. Ordained priest Archdiocese Galveston-Houston, 1956, officialis Marriage Tribunal, 1967—72, consultor to bishop, pres. senate of priests, coord. liturgical commn., dir. secretariat chaplaincy svcs. clergy formation, vicar ethnic ministries, vicar African Am. catholics, aux. bishop, 2001—06, aux. bishop emeritus, 2006—; pastor All Saints Parish, Houston, 1969—72, St. Francis de Sales, Houston, 1972—82, St. Cecilia Cath. Cmty., Houston, 1982—2002; ordained bishop, 2001. Recipient Monsignor John J. Roach Recognition award, Associated Catholic Charities. Roman Catholic. Office: Archdiocese 1700 San Jacinto PO Box 907 Houston TX 77002

RIZZUTO, KATHERINE, publishing executive; married; 3 children. BA in Hist., Rutgers Coll., New Brunswick, NJ. Media planner SSC&B Advt.; acct. exec. YM mag. Gruner & Jahr USA, various positions from advt. dir., assoc. pub. to v.p. Fitness mag.; assoc. pub. Brides mag. Condé Nast Publs., 1997—2000; v.p., pub. Marie Claire Hearst Corp., 2000—04; v.p., pub. Radar/Radaronline.com, 2004—06; pub. Fitness mag., 2005, Condé Nast Bridal Grp., 2006—08; v.p., assoc. pub. advt. In Style mag. Tome Inc., 2008—. Office: In Style 1271 Ave of Americas New York NY 10020 Office Phone: 212-522-1212.

RO, BYUNG TAK, accounting educator; b. Ham Yang, Kyungnam, Korea, Nov. 15, 1939; came to U.S. 1969; s. Wee Sang and Mal Soon (Chung) Ro; m. Eun J. Park, Feb. 1, 1969; children: Young K., Tad K., Jay K. BA, Yeungnam U., Taegu, Korea, 1963; MA, Seoul Nat. U., 1965; MBA, U. Calif., Berkeley, 1971; PhD, Mich. State U., 1976. Controller Carlson's Bakeries & Supplies Inc., Oakland, Calif., 1971-72; prof. Seoul Nat. U., 1967-72; grad. asst. Mich. State U., E. Lansing, 1972-76; prof. accounting Purdue U., West Lafayette, Ind., 1976—, dir. acctg. PhD prog., 1983—. Author: Information Economics and Accounting, 1984; contbr. articles to profl. jours. XL Faculty Rsch. grantee, Purdue U., 1978-79. Mem. Korean Am. Acctg. Profs. Assn. (pres. 1990—), Am. Acctg. Assn. Avocations: reading, travel, walking, swimming. Home: 1831 Sandpiper Dr West Lafayette IN 47906-6517 Office: Purdue University 1831 Sandpiper Dr West Lafayette IN 47906-6517

ROACH, CAROLE HYDE, music educator; d. Clyde Eugene Hyde and Mary Evelyn Springer; m. Samuel Frederick Roach, Nov. 14, 1970. BMus, Ga. State U., 1962; MusM, Fla. State U., 1963; postgrad., U. Ga., 1974. Nat. cert. voice and piano Tchrs. Nat. Assn., 1974, cert. piano & voice Music Tchrs. Nat. Assn., 1985. Voice & piano tchr. Mary Hardin-Baylor Coll., Belton, Tex., 1964—65, Kennesaw State U., Ga., 1967—70, Perimeter Coll., Decatur, Ga., 1970—71; choral dir. Jerusalem Ave. Jr. HS, North Bellmore, NY, 1965—67; choir dir. Ch. of Ascension, Cartersville, Ga., 1993—96, St. Teresa's Episcopal Ch., Acworth, Ga., 2000—; mezzo-soprano soloist Peachtree Presbyterian, Atlanta, 1967—84, Peachtree Meth., Atlanta, 1984—86. Soloist Fletcher Wolfe Chorale, Atlanta, 1968—71, state vocal auditions chmn., 2003, Atlanta, 04; soloist Atlanta Chamber Opera, 1968—71; musical dir. Canton Theatre, Canton, Ga., 2004. Actress: Gooch (Best Supporting Actress, 1991); Bloody Mary (Best Supporting Actress, 1995); dir.: Fantasticks (Best Dir., 1998), Lend Me a Tenor (Best Dir., 1999), I Hate Hamlet (Best Dir., 2000). Pres., treas. Pumphouse Players, Cartersville, Ga., 1990—2003. Mem.: Music Tchrs. Nat. Assn., Ga. Music Tchrs. Assn., Greater Marietta Music Tchrs. Assn. (pres. 2003—), Cobb County Music Tchrs. Assn. (pres. 1975—76, state chair for vocal auditions). Democrat. Episcopalian. Avocations: theater, travel, dog breeding, dog showing, dog rescue. Office: Music Acad So Keyboards 1898-B Leland Dr Marietta GA 30067

ROACH, JAMES CLARK, retired federal agency administrator; b. Charleston, W. Va., Sept. 29, 1943; m. Susan Roelke Roach, June 27, 1970; children: Edward J., Andrew A. BA in Social Studies and History, W. Va. Wesleyan Coll., 1965; MA in Am. History, W. Va. U. Historian Harpers Ferry (W. Va.) Nat. Hist. Pk., 1967-68, 70-72; chief interpretation resource mgmt. Ft. Frederica Nat. Monument, St. Simons Island, Ga., 1972-74; asst. chief interpretation visitor svcs. Colonial Nat. Hist. Pk., Yorktown, Va., asst. chief interpretation, visitor svc. Jamestown, Va.; chief interpretation visitor svcs. Gettysburg (Pa.) Nat. Mil. Pk., Eisenhower Nat. Hist. Site, 1981-94; site mgr. Eisenhower Nat. Hist. Site, 1995—2001; sch.-to-work coord. Adams County Bus. Edn. Partnership, Gettysburg, Pa., 2001—09. Sec., past bd. dirs. Gettysburg Peace Celebration Commn. Inc.; sec. Adams County Econ. Edn. Found.; vice chair Blue and Grey dist. cons. York Adams coun. Boy Scouts Am.; bd. dirs. Adams County Hist. Soc. With US Army, 1968—70, Vietnam. Recipient Freeman Tilden award Mid-Atlantic Region Interpreter of Yr., 1984, Ea. Superior Performance award Nat. Park and Monument Assn., 1985, Spl. Events award GETT Travel Coun. award, 1986, 87. Mem. Assn. Nat. Pk. Rangers, Lincoln Fellowship Pa. (sec., past pres.), Adams County Torch Club (past pres.), Rotary (bd. dirs. Gettysburg club). Lutheran. Avocations: gardening, reading, fishing, stamp collecting/philately, travel. Home: 84 Knoxlyn Orrtanna Rd Gettysburg PA 17325-7215

ROACH, JAMES ROBERT, retired political science professor; b. Rock Rapids, Iowa, Aug. 25, 1922; s. Paul Ramsey and Doris (Kline) R. BA, U. Iowa, 1943; AM, Harvard U., 1948, PhD, 1950. Mem. faculty, adminstrn. U. Tex., Austin, 1949—, prof. govt., 1965-95, prof. emeritus, 1995—, dir. spl. programs, 1965-69, vice provost, dean interdisciplinary programs, 1971-72, dean divsn. gen. and comparative studies, 1972-74; counselor for cultural affairs Am. embassy, New Delhi, 1974-78. Fulbright vis. lectr. polit. sci. Rajasthan U., India, 1961-62; mem. Bd. Fgn. Scholarships, 1965-74, chmn., 1969-71; mem. U.S. Commn. for UNESCO, 1966-69. With USNR, 1943-46. Fulbright rsch. grantee, Australia, 1951-52, Ford Found. fgn. fellow, India, 1956-57. Mem. Phi Beta Kappa, Kappa Tau Alpha, Phi Kappa Psi. Democrat. Congregationalist. Home: 8604 Dorotha Ct Austin TX 78759-8113

ROACH, JOHN D., building products company executive; b. West Palm Beach, Fla., Dec. 3, 1943; s. Benjamin Browning and Margaret (York) Roach; divorced; children: Vanessa, Alexandra; m. Betty Lou Phillips, Aug. 28, 1982; children: Bruce, Bryce, Brian. BS in Indsl. Mgmt., MIT, 1965; MBA, Stanford U., 1967. Dir. mgmt. acctg. and info. sys. Ventura divsn. Northrop Corp., Thousand Oaks, Calif., 1967—70; co-founder, mgr. Northrop Venture Capital, Century City, Calif., 1970—71; v.p., dir. Boston Consulting Group, Boston and Menlo Park, Calif., 1971—80; v.p., world-wide strategic mgmt. practice mng. officer Booz, Allen, Hamilton, San Francisco, 1980—82, Houston, 1982—83; vice chmn., mng. dir. Braxton Assocs., Houston, 1983—87; sr. v.p., CFO Manville Corp., Denver, 1987—88, exec. v.p. ops., 1988-91; pres. Manville Bldg. Products Group, Denver, 1988-90, Manville Mining and Minerals Group, Denver, 1990-91, Celite Corp., Denver, 1990-91; chmn., pres., CEO Fibreboard Corp., Walnut Creek, Calif., 1991—97, Stonegate Resources, Dallas, 1997—2001; founder, chmn., pres., CEO Builders FirstSource, Inc., Dallas, 1998—2001; chmn., CEO, pres. Stonegate Internat., Dallas, 2001—; chmn. Unidare U.S., Muskogee, Okla., 2002—06. Bd. dirs. PMI Group, URS Corp., VeriSign, Mat. Scis., NCI Bldg. Systems, Wash. Group Internat., Am. Stock Exch., Thompson PBE, Magma Power, Fibreboard Corp., Builders First Source, Ply Gem Industries Build Direct. Author: Strategic Management Handbook, 1983. Bd. dirs. Opera Colo., Denver, 1987—91, Bay Area Coun., San Francisco, 1991—96; bd. dirs., mem. exec. com. Dallas Symphony, 1996—2003; mem. exec. com. San Francisco Opera Assn.; trustee Alta Bates Med. Ctr. Mem.: MIT Alumni Club, Stanford Grad. Sch. Bus. Club, Dallas Country Club, Cordillera Country Club (Colo.), Beaver Creek (Colo.) Country Club, Red Sky Golf Club (Wolcott, Colo.), Preston Trail Golf Club (Dallas), Cherry Hills Country Club (Englewood, Colo.). Avocations: golf, skiing, hunting. Office: Stonegate Internat 100 Crescent Ct 7th Fl Dallas TX 75201 Home: 4200 St Johns Ave Dallas TX 75205-3718 Office Phone: 214-459-3460. Personal E-mail: johndcroach@aol.com.

ROACH, MARGARET, former publishing executive; b. 1954; Copy editor., contbr. articles NY Times 1973-1978, 1981-1985; fashion editor Newsday/NY Newsday, 1985—90, garden editor, 1990—95; contbg. editor Martha Stewart Living Omnimedia, 1994—95, sr. v.p., garden editor Martha Stewart Living mag., mgr. devel. and execution marthastewart.com, editor-in-chief Martha Stewart Living mag. NYC, 2001—05, editl. dir., 2005—08; founder online garden blog A Way to Garden, 2008—. Author: A Way to Garden, 1998 (Garden Writers Assn. Am. Best Book, 1998); co-author (with Ken Druse): The Natural Habitat Garden, 2004.

ROACH, MARGOT RUTH, retired biophysicist, educator; d. Robert Dickson and Katherine Roach; m. Franklyn St. Aubyn House, Dec. 20, 1994 (wid. Feb. 2000). B.Sc. in Math. and Physics with honors, U. N.B., Fredericton, Can., 1955; MD, C.M. cum laude, McGill U., Montreal, Can., 1959; PhD in Biophysics, U. Western Ont., Can., 1963; D.Sc. (hon.), U. N.B., St. John, Can., 1981. Lic. lay worship leader Truro Presbytery the United Ch. Can., 2008, grad. cert. in Theol. studies Atlantic Sch. Theology, Can., 2008. Jr. intern Victoria Hosp., London, Ont., Can., 1959-60, fellow in cardiology, 1962-63, asst. resident in medicine, 1963-64, Toronto Gen. Hosp., 1964-65; mem. faculty, dept. biophysics U. Western Ont., London, 1965—98, head dept. biophysics, 1970-78, prof., 1971-98, asst. prof. medicine, 1965-72, assoc. prof., 1972-78, prof., 1978-98, prof. emeritus Biophysics & Med., 1998; chair, worship com. Tatamagouche Pastoral Charge, 2009—. Mem. staff dept. medicine Victoria Hosp., 1967-72, U. Hosp., London, 1972-98; Commonwealth vis. sci., dept. applied math. theoretical physics Cambridge U., 1975; vis. sci. Bioengring. Inst., Chonqing U., People's Republic of China, 1991; mem. bioengring. grants com. Med. Rsch. Coun. Can., 1993-96; cons. and lectr. in field. Mem. editl. bd.: Imprints, 2003—06, Can. Jour. General Internal Medicine, 2007—. Active civic orgns. and coms. including Univ. Rsch. Coun., 1976-79; mem. interview bd. London Conf. of United Ch., 1967-90; steward United Ch. of Can., 1967-73, elder, 1973-82, mem. com. on ministry vocations, 2004-06, chair unified bd. Tatamagouche Pastoral Charge, 2001-07; chmn. stewardship devel. com. Colborne St. United Ch., 1990-93. Recipient A. Wilmer Duff prize in physics U. N.B., 1955, Cushing prize in pediatrics, 1959, Ciba Found. award for research in aging, 1959, Teaching award Faculty of Medicine U. Western Ont., 1990, Dean's award, 1997, Women of Distinction award YWCA, 1997; Med. Research Council fellow U. Western Ont., 1960-62, Arthur Guyton award Internat. Soc. Cardiovascular Medicine and Sci., 1997; numerous other fellowships and grants in medicine. Fellow Royal Coll. Physicians (Can.), Am. Coll. Cardiology (Young Investigator's award 1963); mem. Can. Physiol. Soc., Can. Cardiovascular Soc. (of council), Can. Clin. Investigation Soc. (council 1980-84), Can. Soc. Internal Medicine. Address: RR #1 104 Sea Shore Dr Tatamagouche NS Canada B0K 1V0 Personal E-mail: mrroach@ns.sympatico.ca.

ROACH, MAUREEN S., primary school educator; B, Boston U.; M, U. Mass. Primary sch. educator Lyndon Pilot Sch., West Roxbury, Mass. Presenter Nat. Bd. Insts.; mem. bd. dir. Nat. Bd. Profl. Tchg. Standards, 2005. Mem.: Nat. Bd. for Profl. Tchg. Stds. (bd. mem.). Avocations: cross country skiing, reading. Office: Patrick Lydon School 20 Mount Vernon St West Roxbury MA 02132-2809

ROACH, ROBERT MICHAEL, JR., (RANDY ROACH), lawyer; b. Bronxville, NY, May 27, 1955; s. Robert M. and Mary Dee R. BA, Georgetown U., 1977; JD, U. Tex., 1981. Bar: Tex. 1981, U.S. Dist. Ct. (so. dist.) Tex. 1982, U.S. Ct. Appeals (5th cir.) 1982, U.S. Dist. Ct. (we. dist.) Tex. 1984, U.S. Supreme Ct. 1986, U.S. Dist. Ct. (ea. dist.) 1986, U.S. Dist. Ct. (no. dist.) Tex. 1988. Assoc. Vinson & Elkins, Houston, 1981-83, Ryan & Marshall, Houston, 1983, Mayor, Day & Caldwell, Houston, 1983-88; ptnr. Mayor, Day, Caldwell & Keeton, Houston, 1989-93; founding ptnr. Cook & Roach LLP, Houston, 1993—; dir. appellate advocacy U. Houston Law Ctr., 1994—; adj. prof. U. Tex., 2000—; ptnr. RBS Napa Winery, 2000—. Adj. prof. law U. Houston, 1990-; lectr. continuing legal edn. U. Houston Law Ctr., 1989—; lectr. continuing legal edn. State Bar Tex., U. Tex., U. Houston, South Tex. Coll. Law, So. Meth. U., ABA; rschr., editor U.S. Senate Com. on Nutrition, 1975, 76, 77; rschr. U.S Supreme Ct., Washington, 1977; mem. Tex. Law Rev., 1979-81. Editor Def. Counsel Jour., 1990-93. Mem. Product Liability Adv. Coun., Internat. Assn. Def. Counsel, Fedn. Defense and Corp. Counsel, Def. Rsch. Inst., Tex. Assn. Def. Counsel, State Bar Tex. (appellate sect. chmn. 2006-07, chair of coun. chairs, grievance com., insurance section judicial liaison), Houston Bar Assn. (former chmn., appellate sect.), Meadowood of NAPA Valley, Coronado Club, Houston Racquet Club. Avocations: oenology, music, travel, tennis. Office: Cook & Roach LLP Heritage Plaza Ste 2650 1111 Bagby St Houston TX 77002-2543 Home Phone: 713-459-5550; Office Phone: 713-652-2032. Business E-Mail: rroach@cookroach.com.

ROACH, STEPHEN S., diversified financial services company executive; BS in Economics, U. Wis.; MA, NYU, 1970, PhD, 1973. Rsch. fellow Brookings Instn., Washington; with rsch. staff Fed. Reserve Bd., 1972—79; v.p. econ. analysis Morgan Guaranty Trust Co., NYC; with Morgan Stanley, NYC, 1982—, sr. economist, mng. dir., chief economist, dir. gloal econ. analysis NYC; chmn. Morgan Stanley Asia, Hong Kong, 2007—, acting CEO, 2008. Contbr. articles to profl. jours. Recipient Grad. Sch. Arts and Sciences Alumni Achievement award, NYU, 2006. Mem.: NAS (com. study impact info. tech. on performance of service activities 1994). Office: Morgan Stanley 3 Exchange Sq 30th Fl Central Hong Kong Office Phone: (852) 2848-5200.*

ROACH, WESLEY LINVILLE, lawyer, insurance executive; b. Norlina, NC, Oct. 8, 1931; s. Joseph Franklin and Florence G. (Sink) R.; m. Mary Jon Gerald, Aug. 13, 1955; children: Gerald, Mary Virginia. BS, Wake Forest U., 1953, JD, 1955. Bar: N.C. 1955. With Pilot Life Ins. Co., Greensboro, NC, 1958-86, also bd. dirs.; sr. v.p., gen. counsel Jefferson-Pilot Life Ins. Co., Greensboro, 1986-88; sec. Great Ea. Lif. Ins. Co., 1975-85; of counsel Smith, Anderson, Blount, Dorsett, Mitchell & Jernigan, Attys. at Law, Raleigh, NC, 1988—. Former chmn. bd. dirs. N.C. Life and Accident and Health Ins. Guaranty Assn., Va. Life, Accident and Health Guaranty Assn., S.C. Life, Accident and Health Guaranty Assn.; sec. JP Investment Mgmt. Co., Jefferson-Pilot Equity Sales, Inc., Spl. Services Agy., Inc., 1974-84; mem. exec. com., bd. dirs. N.C. Ins. Edn. Found., 1978—; trustee In-Home Care, Inc., 1999—, chmn., 2001. Mem. fin. com. Greensboro United Fund, 1964-65; mem. fin. com. Greensboro 1st Bapt. Ch., 1963-66, 83-86, chmn., 1983-85, chmn. bd. deacons, 1974-76, 80-81; nat. chmn. alumni coun. coll. fund Wake Forest U., 1971-76, pres. nat. alumni coun., 1975-76, trustee univ., 1978-82, emeritus trustee, 1999—; trustee So. Bapt. Theol. Sem., Louisville, 1973-84; trustee Bapt. Retirement Homes N.C., Inc., 1992-2000, chmn., 1993-94, emeritus trustee, 2001-; trustee In Home Care, Inc., 1997—, chmn., 2001; trustee Bapt. Retirement Homes Found. 2001-. With USNR, 1955-58. Mem. ABA, N.C. Bar Assn., Raleigh Bar Assn., Assn. Life Ins. Counsel (bd. govs. 1984-88), Greensboro C. of C. (chmn. nat. legis. com. 1973—), Nat. Orgn. Life Guaranty Assn. (bd. dirs. 1982-87). Democrat. Home: PO Box 1690 601 Selma Rd Wendell NC 27591-8648 Office: 2500 First Union Capitol Ctr PO Box 2611 Raleigh NC 27602-2611 Office Phone: 919-821-6630.

ROACHE, PATRICK MICHAEL, JR., management consultant; b. Elizabeth, NJ, Oct. 8, 1946; s. Patrick Michael and Rose Marie (Remite) R. BS, St. Peter's Coll., 1969. Adminstrv. aide to a state assemblyman N.J. Assembly, NJ, 1969-71; supr. acctg. Dept. Pub. Works Newark, Newark, 1971-78, asst. to dir. pub. works, 1978-79, mgr. div. motors, 1979-84; mgmt. specialist Dept. Gen. Svcs., Newark, 1985-86, 2002; pvt. practice as mgmt. and fin. cons. Brick, NJ, 1986—. Mem. Lions (treas. 1983-86, pres. 1988-89). Republican. Roman Catholic. Home and Office: 170 Binnacle Rd Brick NJ 08723-6704 Home Phone: 732-477-7036; Office Phone: 732-477-9162. E-mail: proache@haywardnet.com.

ROAN, FORREST CALVIN, JR., lawyer; b. Waco, Tex., Dec. 18, 1944; s. Forrest Calvin and Lucille Elizabeth (McKinney) Roan; m. Vickie Joan Howard, Feb. 15, 1969 (div. Dec. 1983); children: Amy Katherine, Jennifer Louise; m. Leslie D. Hampton, Jan. 2, 1999. BBA, U. Tex., Austin, 1973, JD, 1976. Bar: Tex. 1976, US Dist. Ct. (we. dist.) Tex. 1977, US Dist. Ct. (so. dist.) Tex. 1998, US Ct. Appeals (5th cir.) 1977, US Supreme Ct. 1979, US Ct. Appeals (11th cir.) 1981, US Ct. Appeals (fed. cir.) 1998, US Ct. Internat. Trade 1998. Prin. Roan & Assocs., Austin, 1969-71; counsel, com. dir. Tex. Ho. of Reps., 1972-75; assoc. Heath, Davis & McCalla, Austin, 1975-78; prin. Roan & Gullahorn, P.C., Austin, 1978-85, Roan & Autrey (formerly Roan & Simpson), P.C., 1986-99; sr. ptnr. Cantey, Hanger, Roan & Autrey, 1999—2003; shareholder & chair pub. regulatory law practice group Winstead, P.C. (formerly Winstead, Sechrest & Minick, P.C.), Austin, 2003—. Chair leadership coun. Am. Lung Assn.; bd. dirs. Lawyers Credit Union, chmn., 1982—83; bd. dirs. pub. law sect. State Bar Tex., 1980—84; mem. Littlefield Soc. and Chancellor's Coun. U. Tex.; chmn. Tex. Meml. Life Insurance Gr., 2006—09. With Tex. N.G. US Army, 1966—74. Fellow: Am. Bar Found. (life), Austin Bar Found. (life; founding fellow), Tex. Bar Found. (life); mem.: ABA, Fed. Regulatory Counsel, Assn. Life Ins. Counsel, Austin Bar Assn., Def. Rsch. Inst., Tex. Assn. Bank Counsel, Tex. Assn. Def. Counsel, Austin C. of C., Mensa (life), Tex. Lyceum Assn. (v.p., bd. dirs. 1980—87), Headliners Club, Austin Club, Shriners Masons (Parsons Masonic master 1976—77), Knights of the Symphony (Lord Chancellor 2003—04). Methodist. Office: Winstead PC 401 Congress Ste 2100 Austin TX 78701 Office Phone: 512-370-2999. E-mail: froan@winstead.com.

ROA-PRADA, SEBASTIAN, engineering educator; s. German Roa-Suarez and Esther Prada-Castillo. BSc in Mech. Engring. with cum laude, U. Indsl. Santander, Bucaramanga, Colombia, 2002; attending, Rensselaer Poly. Inst., Troy, NY, 2006—. Prof. U. Autonoma Bucaramanga, Santander, Colombia, 2002—04; rsch. asst. Rensselaer Poly. Inst., 2006—08, tchg. asst., 2008—. Mentor undergrad. engring. student NASA, Cleveland, 2009. Fulbright scholarship, US Dept. of State, 2004. Mem.: ASME. Achievements include research in ultrasonic communication. Personal E-mail: sebastianroa27@hotmail.com.

ROARK, BARBARA ANN, librarian; b. Evanston, Ill., July 24, 1958; d. Edward B. and Ann H. Rowe; m. Paul E. Roark, Sept. 18, 1982; children: Sarah, John. BA in History, U. Ky., 1981, MLS, 1982. Dir. Hopkins County Madisonville (Ky.) Pub. Libr., 1983-85; ops. mgr. Wurzburg Inc., Nashville, 1985-91; dir. Spies Pub. Libr., Menominee, Mich., 1991-98, Franklin (Wis.) Pub. Libr., 1998—. V.p. adv. coun. Mid-Peninsula Libr. Coop., Mich., 1993-95, sec. adv. coun., 1991-93; chair tech. adv. com. Milwaukee County Federated Libr. Sys., 2001—; dir. Libr. Coun. Southeastern Wis., 2007-; chair Libr. Dirs. Adv. Coun., 2007—. Grant writer Title II, 1994, Title I, 1995. Treas. Franklin Area Jr. Woman's Club. Recipient Cert. of Excellence Libr. of Mich., 1995, Cert. of Appreciation Menominee Area C. of C., 1998. Mem. ALA, Wis. Libr. Assn. (pers. and profl. concerns com. 1999—, Muriel Fuller award 2002), Spies Pub. Libr. Found., PEO, Order Ea. Star, U. Ky. Alumni Assn., Franklin Area Jr. Women's Club (treas. 1999—), Kiwanis (pres. Milw. suburban S.W. chpt. 2002—), Zeta Tau Alpha. Methodist. Avocations: golf, reading, cross stitching, travel. Home Phone: 414-427-8397; Office Phone: 414-425-8214. E-mail: barbara.roark@mcfls.org.

ROARK, IAN R., school system administrator; b. Laramie, Wyo., Nov. 11, 1977; s. Ben T. and Eileen R. Roark; m. Landi D. Orr, July 4, 1998; 1 child, Ireland Malone. MusB in Edn. magna cum laude, Angelo State U., San Angelo, Tex., 1999; MA in Edn. and Edni. Leadership, U. of Tex. of the Permian Basin, Odessa, 2004. Cert. prin. Tex., tchr.- all level music Tex., tchr.- social studies composite Tex., tchr.- English as second lang. Tex. Music tchr. choir San Angelo Ind. Sch. Dist., 2000—01; asst. prin. Midland (Tex.) Ind. Sch. Dist., 2004—05; social studies tchr., dept. chair Ector County Ind. Sch. Dist., Odessa, 2001—04, social studies coord., 2005—. Cmty. outreach Kelview Heights Bapt. Ch., Midland. Recipient IMPACT Edn. grant, U. of Tex. of the Permian Basin, USDE, 2002—04, Carr Acad. scholarship, Angelo State U., 1995—99, Choir scholarship, 1996—99, FAME scholarship, Angelo State Friends of Art and Music, 1999, Randy Bell Meml. scholarship, Angelo State U., 1997—98, Charles Van Pelt Music sholarship, 1996—97, Choir Dir.'s award, Angelo State U. Concert Choir, 1999; named Oustanding Tchr. of the Yr., Ector County Ind. Sch. Dist., 2004, Outstanding New Vocalist, Angelo State U. Concert Choir, 1996. Mem.: Nat. Coun. for Social

Studies, Tex. Coun. for Social Studies, Tex. Social Studies Supr., West Tex. Regional Coun. for Social Studies (bd. dirs. 2005—06), Pi Kappa Lambda, Alpha Chi. Avocations: musician, hiking, fishing, reading.

ROARK, KEITH (R. KEITH ROARK), lawyer, political organization administrator; b. Salt Lake City, Apr. 10, 1949; BA, U. Utah, 1974, JD, 1977. Dep. prosecuting atty. Blaine County, Idaho, 1977—78, prosecuting atty. Idaho, 1979—85; founder, sr. & mng. ptnr. The Roark Law Firm, Twin Falls and Hailey, Idaho, 1985—; mayor City of Hailey, Idaho, 1990—93; chmn. Idaho Dem. Party, 2008—. With US Army, 1969—71. Mem.: ABA, Am. Inns of Ct., Criminal Justice Advisory Com., Idaho Supreme Ct. Civil Rules Com., Am. Trial Lawyers' Assn., Idaho Trial Lawyers Assn., Nat. Assn. of Criminal Defense Attys., Idaho State Bar Assn., Nat. Dist. Attys. Assn. (former mem. bd. dirs.), Idaho Prosecuting Attys. Assn. (past pres.). Democrat. Office: The Roark Law Firm 409 N Main St Hailey ID 83333 also: Idaho Dem Party PO Box 445 Boise ID 83701 Office Phone: 208-788-2427, 208-788-2427. Office Fax: 208-788-3918. E-mail: keith@roarklaw.com, keith@idahodemocrats.org.*

ROARK, ROBERT CAMERON, insurance agent; b. San Diego, Jan. 11, 1931; s. Alfred T. and Virginia J. Roark; m. Lois J. Maynard, July 19, 1952; children: Cynthia, Susan, Kellie, Robert. BA, San Diego State U., 1954. Life underwriter Mass. Mut. Life, San Diego, 1955-57; supr. John Hancock Mut., San Diego, 1957-59; gen. agt., mgr. Am. Mut. Life Ins., San Diego, 1959-65; regional v.p. Northwestern Life Ins., Seattle, 1965-68; broker, owner Roark Ins., Menifee, Calif., 1968—. Author: Good News Letter, 1991—. Divsn. capt. USCG Aux., 1990, flotilla comdr., 1987, vice capt., 1989, publs. officer, 1997. Mem. Mission Hills Homeowners Assn. (pres. 1970-73, bd. mem. 1991-92), Lions Internat. (zone chmn. 1972, club pres. 1971). Office: Roark Ins 28032 Whittington Rd Menifee CA 92584

ROARKE, MICHAEL CHARLES, medical educator, nuclear medicine physician; b. Albany, NY, May 8, 1959; s. Charles Augustus and Joan Ann Roarke; m. Maria Giuliani, June 25, 1988; 1 child, Michael Andrew. BS, SUNY, Albany, 1981, MS, 1982; MD, U. Rochester Sch. Medicine, NYC, 1990. Cert. Am. Bd. Radiology, 1995, Am. Bd. Nuc. Medicine, 1996. Chemistry tchr. Albany Acad. Boys, NY, 1982—86; intern internal medicine St. Mary's Hosp., Rochester, 1990—91; resident diagnostic radiology Mallinckrodt Inst. Radiology, St. Louis, 1991—95, fellow nuc. medicine, 1995—96; asst. prof. radiology U. Tex. Med. Ctr., Houston, 1996—97, Mayo Med. Sch., Scottdale, 1997—. Sect. head nuc. radiology Mayo Clinic Ariz., Scottsdale, Ariz., 1997—2007, med. dir. nuc. radiology, 1997—2007. Recipient Best Intern award, St. Mary's Hosp. Internal Medicine Program, 1991, Tchr. Recognition award, White House Commn. on Presdl. Scholars, 1985; named one of Best Doctors in Am., 2003—08, America's Top Physicians, Consumer's Rsch. Coun., 2005—08; Klingenstein Summer Tchg. fellow, Columbia U., 1983. Mem.: AAAS, Am. Roentgen Ray Soc., Acad. Molecular Imaging (assoc.), Soc. Nuc. Medicine (assoc.), Radiol. Soc. N.Am. (assoc.), Beta Beta Beta, Alpha Omega Alpha (life). Avocations: music, composing, mineral photography, coin collecting/numismatics. Office: Mayo Clinic Ariz 13400 East Shea Blvd Scottsdale AZ 85259 Personal E-mail: mroarke@aol.com.

ROBAINA, JULIO, mayor, state representative; b. Miami, Fla., Sept. 1, 1961; AA, Miami-Dade County CC, 1983. Real estate and mortgage broker; councilman City of Hialeah, Fla., 1997—2000, coun. pres., 2001—05, mayor, 2005—; mem. Dist. 117 Fla. House of Reps., Tallahassee, 2002—. Chmn. City of Hialeah Charter Rev. Bd.; rep. City of Hialeah Elected Officials Retirement Bd. Pres. Miami Dade League of Cities, 2002—03, Gold Coast League of Cities, 2004, Fla. League of Cities, 2005; bd. mem. Beacon Coun.; chmn. Fla. Mcpl. Investment Trust. Named Pub. Ofcl. of Yr., South Fla. Hispanic C. of C., 2007. Mem.: Northwestern Dade Assn. Realtors (pres.), Hands in Action (bd. dirs.). Republican. Office: 501 Palm Ave Hialeah FL 33010 also: Dist Office 6262 Bird Rd Ste 2E Miami FL 33155-4882 also: 410 House Office Bldg 402 S Monroe St Tallahassee FL 32399-1300 Office Phone: 305-883-5800, 305-442-6868, 850-488-6506. Business E-Mail: mayorjrobaina@hialeahfl.gov.*

ROBATCHKA-WALTERS, JANICE MARIE, medical/surgical and critical care nurse; b. Detroit, Apr. 8, 1958; d. John Robatchka and Marian M. Coatsworth; m. Mathew C. Walters, children: Shelaine Elizabeth, Vincent Thomas. AA, Wayne County Community Coll., Detroit, 1980; B in Applied Sci., Bus., Siena Heights Coll., 1986. Nursing supr. Heritage Hosp., Taylor, Mich.; RN supr. Associated Physicians Med. Ctr., Taylor, Mich.; clin. nurse staff asst. Sinai Hosp., Detroit. Nurse mgr. Henry Ford Hosp. Mem. Am. Heart Assn., Am. Assn. Office Nurses, ABWA. Home: 42263 Montroy Dr Sterling Heights MI 48313 Home Phone: 586-932-6264, 734-578-3061. Personal E-mail: janicerobatchka@yahoo.com.

ROBB, BABETTE, retired elementary school educator; b. St. Paul, Jan. 25, 1923; d. Roy F and Eda Johnson; m. David L Robb, July 23, 1945; children: Deborah G. Jankura, Pamela W. BA, So. Meth. U., Dallas, 1945; Elem. Educator, U. Wis., River Falls, 1948. Asst. to county auditor Washington County, Stillwater, Minn., 1945—46, county sch. tchr. Stillwater, 1947—53; elem. sch. tchr. Stillwater (Minn.) Dist. 834, 1953—81. Author: (elem.sch. text) St. Croix Valley Story, 1970; contbr. articles Childrens Mags., 1979. Chmn. Washington County Young Reps., Stillwater, 1946—50; mem. bd. dirs. Family Svc., Stillwater, Minn.; Grand Marshall of 4th of July Parade Afton (Minn.) Hist. Soc., 1973. Recipient Drama award, Minn. Regional Speech Contest, 1940; chosen to christen SS Ernie Pyle, U.S. Maritime Commn. Mem.: AAUW (life; Founder local chpt. 1946), St. Croix Valley Ret. Tchrs. Assn. (bd. dir.), Minn. Ednl. Assn. (sec. local br. 1953—), Delta Kappa Gamma (Sec. 1972—). Methodist. Achievements include first to introduce Spanish to Elementary Students in 1958. Avocations: modeling, photography, swimming, writing, water biking. Home (Summer): 2803 S St Croix Tr Afton MN 55001 Home (Winter): Apt 407-408 3500 S Ocean Blvd Palm Beach FL 33480

ROBB, CHUCK (CHARLES SPITTAL ROBB), law educator, former United States Senator from Virginia; b. Phoenix, June 26, 1939; s. James Spittal and Francis Howard (Wooley) R.; m. Lynda Bird Johnson, Dec. 9, 1967; children: Lucinda Desha, Catherine Lewis, Jennifer Wickliffe. BBA, U. Wis., 1961; JD, U. Va., 1973. Bar: Va. 1973, U.S. Supreme Ct. 1976. Law clk. to Hon. John D. Butzner U.S. Ct. Appeals (4th Dist.), 1973—74; atty. Williams & Connolly, 1974-77; lt. gov. State of Va., 1978—82, gov., 1982—86; ptnr. Hunton & Williams, 1986—88; US Senator from Va., 1989—2001; Disting. prof. law & pub. policy George Mason U., Fairfax, Va., 2001—. Chmn. Nat. Conf. Lt. Govs., 1979-80, Am. Coun. Young Polit. Leaders Dels. to Peoples Republic of China, 1979, Edn. Commn. of the States, 1984-85, Democratic Leadership Coun., 1986-88, Democratic Senatorial Campaign Com., 1991-93; vis. prof. pub. affairs George Mason U., spring 1987; co-chmn. Commn. on the Intelligence Capabilities of the US Regarding Weapons of Mass Destruction, 2004, mem. Iraq Study Group, 2006 Chmn. Jobs for Am.'s Grads. Inc., 1985-90; gov. Atlantic Inst. for Internat. Affairs, 1987. With USMC, 1961—70. Decorated Bronze Star, Vietnam Service medal with 4 Stars; Vietnamese Cross of Gallantry with Silver Star; recipient Raven award, 1973, Seven Soc. award U. Va. Mem. ABA, Va. Bar Assn., So. Govs. Assn. (chmn., 1983-85), Dem. Govs. Assn. (chmn., 1984-85), Coalition for Dem. Majority, Res. Officers Assn., USMC Res. Officers Assn., U.Fa. La. Alumni Assn. (bd. dirs. 1974-85), Am. Legion, Raven Soc., Navy League U.S., Coun. on Fgn. Rels., Omicron Delta Kappa. Democrat. Episcopalian. Office: George Mason U Sch Law 3301 N Fairfax Dr Rm 409 Arlington VA 22201-4498*

ROBB, GARY CHARLES, lawyer; b. Kansas City, Mo., May 17, 1955; m. Anita Candace Porte, Apr. 30, 1983. BA with distinction, U. Mo., Kansas City, 1977, MA in Econs., 1978; JD cum laude, U. Mich., 1981. Bar: Ill. 1981, U.S. Dist. Ct. (no. dist.) Ill. 1981, Mo. 1982, U.S. Dist. Ct. (we. dist.) Mo. 1982, U.S. Ct. Appeals (8th cir.) 1982. Assoc. Mayer, Brown & Platt, Chgo., 1981—82, Shughart, Thomson & Kilroy, Kansas City, Mo., 1982—84; ptnr. Robb & Robb LLC, Kansas City, Mo., 1984—. Adj. prof. law U. Mo., Kansas City; lectr., program chmn. Nat. Conf. on Products Liability Law, Chgo., 1983, lectr., 84. Contbg. author: Tort Law, Missouri Bar Handbook, 1982, Products Liability, 1984; editor: U. Mich. Jour. Law Reform, 1980—81; contbg. editor: Products Liability, 1983; mem. bd. editors: Products Liability Newsletter, 1982—, mem. bd. experts: Lawyers Alert Newsmag.; contbr. articles. Mem.: ATLA (tort and aviation sects.), ABA (tort and ins. practice 1981—, trial evidence com. 1981—, sect. litigation, chmn. future programs and projects subcom., products, liability and consumer law com., co-chmn.Aviation Litig. Com., Sect. of Litig., 2004-2005), Lawyers Assn. Kansas City, Mo. Bar Assn. (fed. practice com.), Kansas City Bar Assn., Mo. Assn. Trial Attys. (bd. govs. 1993—, pres. elect), Univ. Mo.-Kansas City Alumni Assn. (chmn. career planning com.), Pi Sigma Alpha (pres. 1977—78), Omicron Delta Epsilon, Phi Kappa Phi. Republican. Office: Robb & Robb LLC One Kans City Pl Ste 3900 1200 Main St Kansas City MO 64105-2100

ROBB, GEOFFREY LAWRENCE, plastic surgeon; b. El Paso, Tex., May 28, 1946; s. Giles Anthony and Mary Jo (Lawrence) R.; m. Cathy Jean Cross, May 31, 1974; children: Tiffany, Kimberly, Courtney, Carly, Melaney, Mary. BS, U. Miami, 1969, MD, 1974. Diplomate Am. Bd. Otolaryngology. Commd. ensign USNR, 1970-92; advanced through grades to capt., 1989; resident in otalaryngology, mem. staff US Naval Hosp., San Diego, 1974-79, otolaryngologist Orlando, Fla., 1979-83; plastic surgeon USN Sponsorship at U. Pitts., 1983-85, microvascular surgeon, 1985; plastic surgeon U.S. Naval Hosp., Portsmouth, Va., 1985-88; ret., 1992; chief plastic surgery U.S. Naval Hosp., Portsmouth, Va., 1988-92; vice chmn. plastic surgery M.D. Anderson Cancer Ctr., Houston, 1992-97, chmn. plastic surgery, 1997—, dep. chmn. divsn. surgery, 1994—, dir. postgrad. med. edn., 1992—, med. dir. plastic surgery clinic, 1992—, assoc. med. dir. skin cancer ctr., 1996. Contbg. author: Reconstructive Plastic Surgery for Cancer, 1995, Endoscopic Plastic Surgery, 1995, Advanced Skin Cancer of Head and Neck, 1995; contbr. articles to profl. jours. Fellow ACS, Am. Soc. Plastic Reconstructive Surgeons, Am. Soc. Reconstructive Microsurgeons, Am. Assn. Plastic Surgeons; mem. Internat. Soc. Reconstructive Microsurgery, Tex. Soc. Plastic Surgeons, Houston Soc. Plastic Surgeons, KC. Avocations: physical fitness, weightlifting, tennis, running. Office: MD Anderson Cancer Ctr 1515 Holcombe Blvd # 443 Houston TX 77030-4009 E-mail: grobb@mdanderson.org.

ROBB, JAMES ALEXANDER, retired lawyer; b. Huntingdon, Que., Can., May 3, 1930; s. Alexander George and Irma Mary (Martin) R.; m. Katherine Ann Teare, June 26, 1960; children: Laura, John, Andrew. BA, McGill U., 1951, B.C.L., 1954; postgrad., U. Montreal, 1961-63. Bar: Que. 1955, queen's counsel 1970. Lectr. comml. law and taxation Sir George Williams U., 1958-60; ptnr. Stikeman Elliott LLP and predecessor firm Stikeman, Elliott, Tamaki, Mercier & Robb, Montreal, 1967—2002, ret., 2003. Pres. Que-Japan Bus. Forum, 1993—95; bd. dirs. YKK Can. Inc., Western Life Assurance Co., Bank West. Mem. Protestant Sch. Bd. Greater Montreal, 1971-75; chmn. bd. trustees Martlet Found., 1967-69; v.p. Que. Liberal Party, 1976-79; mem. adv. com. McGill Ctr. for Study of Regulated Industries; bd. dirs. Montreal Mus. Fine Arts, 1987-90; bd. govs. McGill U., 1991-95. Mem.: Consumers Assn. Can. (past chmn. regulated industries program), Bar Que. (chmn. multidisciplinary com. 1998—2001), Can. C. of C. (internat. arbitration com.), McGill Alumni Assn. (pres. 1996—98), Hillside Tennis Club, Royal Montreal Curling Club (pres. 1999—2000), Kanawaki Golf Club (Que.), Univ. Club (pres. 1988—89), Can. Club Montreal (pres. 1990—91). Home: 9 Renfrew Ave Westmount PQ Canada H3Y 2X3 Office: 1155 Renè Lèvesque Blvd W 40th Fl Montreal PQ Canada H3B 3V2 Office Phone: 514-397-3086. Personal E-mail: jrobb@stikeman.com.

ROBB, JAMES WILLIS, Romance languages educator; b. Jamaica, NY, June 27, 1918; s. Stewart Everts and Clara Johanna (Mohrmann) R.; m. Cecilia Uribe-Noguera, 1972. Student, Inst. de Touraine, Sorbonne, 1937-38; BA cum laude, Colgate U., 1939; postgrad., U. Nacional de Mex., 1948; MA, Middlebury Coll., 1950; PhD, Cath. U. Am., 1958. Instr. romance langs. Norwich U., 1946-50; from asst. prof. to prof. romance langs. George Washington U., Washington, 1950-88, prof. emeritus, 1988—. Corr. mem. Academia Mexicana de la Lengua, 1998. Author: El Estilo de Alfonso Reyes, 1965, 78, Repertorio Bibliográfico de Alfonso Reyes, 1974, Prosa y Poesía de Alfonso Reyes, 1975, 84, Estudios sobre Alfonso Reyes, 1976, Por los Caminos de Alfonso Reyes, 1981, Imágenes de América en Alfonso Reyes y en Germán Arciniegas, 1990, Más Páginas Sobre Alfonso Reyes, 1996-97; contbr. articles to profl. jours. With USNR, 1942—44, Brazil, with USNR, 1944—46, PTO. Recipient Alfonso Reyes Internat. Lit. prize, 1978; Lit. Diploma of Merit, State of Nuevo León and City of Monterrey, Mex., 1979; OAS grantee, 1964; Am. Philos. Soc. grantee, 1977 Mem. MLA, Internat. Assn. Ibero-Am. Lit., Am. Assn. Tchrs. Spanish and Portuguese, Assn. Colombianistas, Phi Beta Kappa. Office: George Washington U Romance Langs Dept Washington DC 20052-0001

ROBB, JOHN DONALD, JR., lawyer; b. NYC, Jan. 11, 1924; s. John D. and Harriett (Block) R.; m. Peggy Hight, Feb. 8, 1946; children: John D., Celeste Robb Nicholson, Ellen, Bradford, George G., David. Student, Yale U., 1941—42, N.Mex.; BSL, U. Minn., 1948, LLB, 1949. Bar: N.Mex. 1950, U.S. Dist. Ct. N.Mex. 1950, U.S. Ct. Appeals (10th cir.) 1955, U.S. Supreme Ct. 1961. Pvt. practice, Albuquerque, 1950-51; assoc. Rodey, Dickason, Sloan, Akin & Robb PA, Albuquerque, 1951-56, ptnr., 1956-65, sr. dir., 1965-97, of counsel, 1997—. Nat. adv. com. legal svcs. program OEO, 1966-73; bd. dir. Christian Legal Soc., 1980-99, dir. legal aid, 1997-. Contbr. articles to profl. jours. Pres. Albuquerque Legal Aid Soc., 1957, bd. dirs., 1960-74; bd. dirs. Navajo Legal Svcs., 1967-68, United Cmty. Fund, 1962-64; chmn. Albuquerque Christian Legal Aid and Referral Svc., 1982-88; pres. Albuquerque Cmty. Coun., 1958-60, Family Consultation Svc. Albuquerque, 1965-67; chmn. bd. Drug Addicts Recovery Enterprises, 1974-79; bd. dirs. Pub. Ministries, 1997—; bd. dirs. N.Mex. Christian Legal Aid Inc., chmn., 1998—. Named Outstanding Man of Yr., Albuquerque Jr. C. of C., 1956; recipient Disting. Svc. award Albuquerque United Cmty. Fund, 1960, Hatton W. Sumners award Southwestern Legal Found., 1971. Fellow Am. Bar Found.; mem. ABA (nat. chmn. standing com. on legal aid and indigent defendants 1966-73), Nat. Legal Aid and Defendants Assn. (v.p. 1966-72), Albuquerque Bar Assn. (chmn. legal aid com. 1962-65), N.Mex. Bar Assn. (chmn. legal aid com.), Internat. Legal Aid Assn., Christian Legal Soc. (bd. dirs. 1982-2000), Albuquerque Christian Lawyers Assn. (chmn. 1979-2000), Am. Judicature Soc., Am. Bd. Trial Advs. Office: Rodey Dickason Sloan Akin & Robb PA PO Box 1888 Albuquerque NM 87103-1888 Home: 7200 Rio Grande Blvd NW Albuquerque NM 87107-6428 also: 201 3rd St NW Ste 2200 Albuquerque NM 87102-3380 Business E-Mail: jrobb@rodey.com.

ROBB, JOHN WESLEY, religion educator; b. LA, Dec. 1, 1919; s. Edgar Milton and Alta (Boger) R.; m. Ethel Edna Tosh, June 13, 1942; children: Lydia Joan Robb, Judith Nadine Robb Eggerman. AB, Greenville Coll., 1941; Th.M., U. So. Calif., 1945, PhD, 1952; L.H.D., Hebrew Union Coll.-Jewish Inst. Religion, 1977. Asst. prof. philosophy and religion Dickinson Coll., Pa., 1948-51; fellow Fund for Advancement Edn., 1951-52; asso. prof. U. So. Calif., LA, 1954-62, chmn. dept. religion, 1954-67, assoc. dean humanities Coll. Letters, Arts and Scis., 1963-68, Leonard K. Firestone prof., 1974-75, prof., 1962-87, prof. emeritus, 1987—, prof. Sch. Medicine, 1981-87; coun. mem. Inst. of Lab. Animal Resources Nat. Acad. Scis. Nat. Rsch. Coun., 1986-93. Vis. disting. prof. USAF Med. Ctr., Wilford Hall, Tex., 1985; mem. rev. com. NIH Guide for the Care and Use of Lab. Animals, NRC, NAS, 1993-96; advisor/tutor Med. Quality Assurance Commn., Dept. Health, State of Wash., 1994-2001; mem. ethics com. Swedish Med. Ctr., N.W. Hosp., Seattle, 1992-2002; adj. prof. bioethics Sch. Medicine, U. So. Calif., 1989-91, adj. prof. emeritus, 1991—. Author: Inquiry Into Faith, 1960; co-editor: Readings in Religious Philosophy; The Reverent Skeptic, 1979. Served as lt. (j.g.) USNR, 1945—47, o lt., 1952—54. Recipient award for excellence in tchg. U. So. Calif., 1960, 74, Dart award for acad. innovation, 1970, Raubenheimer Disting. Faculty award divsn. humanities, 1980, Robert Fenton Craig award Blue Key, 1980, Outstanding Faculty award Student Senate, 1981, Disting. Emeritus award, 1995, Educator of Yr. award Swedish Med. Ctr., Providence, Seattle, 2002. Fellow Soc. for Values in Higher Edn.; mem. Am. Acad. Religion (v.p. 1966, pres. 1967), Am. Philos. Assn., AAUP (v.p. Calif. Conf. 1977, pres. 1978-79), Phi Beta Kappa (hon.), Phi Kappa Phi, Phi Chi Phi. United Methodist. Home: 12507 Green Wood Ave N A-405 Seattle WA 98133

ROBB, SARAH RAINEY, biology professor; d. Elnora L. Nokes; m. Travis M. Robb, May 17, 2008. BS in Biology, Pitts. State U., Kans., MS in Biology, 2003. Dir. nature reach Pitts. State U., 2003—05; biology instr. Neosho County CC, Chanute, Kans., 2005—. Recipient Excellence Tchg. award, Nat. Inst. Staff & Orgnl. Devel., 2009; Tech. & Tchg. grant, Hewlitt Packard, 2008. Mem.: Kans. Nat. Edn. Assn.

ROBB, WALTER, food products executive; m. Emily Wilkins (div.); children: Ted, Abigail, Chris. BA in History, Stanford U., Calif., 1976. Pub. sch. tchr., Atlanta; almond farmer Calif.; owner, operator Mountain Marketplace, Trinity County, Calif., 1976—86; mgr. natural food store chain Calif.; store mgr. Whole Foods Market, Inc., Mill Valley, Calif., 1991—93, pres., Northern Pacific, 1993—2000, exec. v.p., 2000—04, COO, 2003—, co-pres., 2004—. Bd. dirs. Pot Belly Sandwich Works, Organic Trade Assn., The Organic Ctr. Office: Whole Foods Market Inc 5980 Horton St #200 Emeryville CA 94608 Office Phone: 510-428-7400.*

ROBB, WALTER LEE, retired electric and management company executive, consultant; b. Harrisburg, Pa., Apr. 25, 1928; s. George A. and Ruth (Scantlin) R.; m. Anne Gruver, Feb. 27, 1954; children: Richard, Steven, Lindsey. BS, Pa. State U., 1948; MS, U. Ill., 1950, PhD, 1951; DEng (hon.), Milw. Sch. Engring., 1994, Worcester Poly. Inst., 1988. With GE, 1951-93, mgr. R & D dept. silicone products Waterford, NY, 1966-68, venture mgr. med. devel. ops. Schenectady, NY, 1968-71, sr. v.p., group exec. med. sys. group Milw., 1973-86, sr. v.p. corp. R & D Schenectady, 1986-93; pres. Vantage Mgmt., Schenectady, NY, 1993—. Bd. dirs. Celgene Corp., Mech. Tech., Inc.; chmn. Capital Dist. Sports, Inc. Recipient Nat. Tech. medal, 1993, Indsl. Rsch. Inst. medal, 1994. Mem. NAE, Am. Philos. Soc. Achievements include patentee in field of membranes and gas separation; research in diagnostic imaging equipment. Home: 1358 Ruffner Rd Niskayuna NY 12309-2500 Office: Vantage Mgmt 3000 Troy-Schenectady Rd Schenectady NY 12309-1643 Office Phone: 518-782-0050. E-mail: waltrobb@nycap.rr.com.

ROBBINS, ALLEN BISHOP, physics professor; b. NB, NJ, Mar. 31, 1930; s. William Rei and Helen Grace (Bishop) R.; m. Shirley Mae Gernert, June 14, 1952 (div. 1978); children: Catherine Jean, Marilyn Elizabeth, Carol Ann, Melanie Barbara; m. Alice Harriet Ayars, Jan. 1, 1979. Student, Oberlin Coll., 1948—49; BS, Rutgers U., 1952; MS, Yale U., 1953, PhD, 1956. Rsch. fellow U. Birmingham (Eng.), 1957-58, lectr., 1960-61; instr. physics Rutgers U., New Brunswick, 1956-57, asst. prof. physics, 1957-60, assoc. prof., 1960-68, prof., 1968-97, prof. emeritus, 1997—, chmn. dept. physics and astronomy, 1979-95. Contbr. articles on nuc. physics to profl. jours. Recipient Lindbach Christian and Mary F. Lindbach Found., Rutgers U., 1975. Fellow Am. Phys. Soc.; mem. Am. Assn. Physics Tchrs., AAAS, Phi Beta Kappa, Sigma Xi. Office: Rutgers U Dept Physics and Astronomy 136 Frelinghuysen Rd Piscataway NJ 08854-8019 Home: 5 Meadow Lakes East Windsor NJ 08520 Personal E-mail: allenbrobbins@aol.com.

ROBBINS, ANNE FRANCIS See REAGAN, NANCY

ROBBINS, ARNIE, editor; m. Terrie Robbins. Grad., Northwestern U. Medill Sch. Journalism, 1975. Sports reporter & editor Suburban Tribune, 1975—78; copy editor, dep. sports editor Chgo. Sun-Times, 1978—84; exec. sports editor, asst. mng. editor, features & change editor Mpls. Star Tribune, 1984—97; dir. news staff & orgnl. devel. St. Louis Post-Dispatch, 1997, dep. editor, 1997—99, mng. editor, 1999—2005, editor, 2005—. Fellow: Transforming News Orgns. for the Digital Now Knight Digital Media Ctr. Office: St Louis Post-Dispatch 900 N Tucker Blvd Saint Louis MO 63101 Office Phone: 314-340-8130. E-mail: arobbins@post-dispatch.com.*

ROBBINS, CHRISTIANE PATRICIA, media director, artist, designer, educator; b. Montclair, NJ, Jan. 9, 1956; d. Frederick James Nabkey and Eleanor Maroon; m. Andrew Richard Magdanz (div. Feb. 1984); 1 child, Justin; m. K.C. Lambert, Oct. 5, 1987; 1 child, John. BA with honors, U. Wis., 1975; MFA with highest honors, Calif. Inst. Arts, 1989. Design prin. Western Influence Studios, Berkeley, Calif., 1976—80; assoc. curator Art Mus. Assn. of Am., San Francisco, 1977—81; prin. Max Almy Prodns., Oakland, Calif., 1981—84, Robbins Design, San Francisco, 1981—89; exec. editor, pub. G.A.S. Jour., Corning, NY, 1984—88; creative dir. Digifilm, Oakland, 1988—90; lectr. U. Calif., Berkeley, 1989; asst. prof. TFNM Sch. of Comm., San Diego State U., 1997—99; assoc. prof. Roski Sch. of Fine Art, U. Southern Calif., LA, 1999—; prin. Jetztzeit Studios, 1999—. Cons. fine arts and design, San Francisco, 1981—, Calif. Arts Coun., Sacramento, 1981—, Craft and Folk Art Mus., LA, 1985; vis. asst. prof. creative arts

San Francisco State U., 1990—96, Mills Coll., 1994—97; co-dir. ICATA, 1990; exec. co-dir. New Langton Arts, 1993—96, 1995. Numerous internat. pub. and pvt. collections, exhibitions, lectures, and publications, including SFMOMA, Banff Ctr. for the Arts, the Getty Mus., MOMA, NYC. Bd. dirs. New Langton Arts, CONSTRUCT; bd. advisors Session Gallery, San Francisco; chair, artist com. San Francisco Art Inst. Recipient 1st place Calif. State Art Exhibn., 1982, 1st place Women Design Internat., NYC, 1982-83, Best of Video, 27th SF Internat. Film Festival, 1984; Video Artist award, Long Beach Mus. of Art, 1991, Ind. Filmmaker award, Film Arts Found., 1991, Banff Ctr. fellowship, CAN, 1997; named Notable Alumni, CalArts, 2000-; Artist fellowship award, City of LA, 2002-03; Rsch. fellowship, Stanford U., 2006. Mem. AAUP, AAUW, AFI, BAVC, CAA, Film Arts Foundation, Norman Lear Center for the Study of Entertainment, Rhizome, X-Factor (co-founder), Glass Art Soc. (bd. dirs. 1984-88), Image Techs. (bd. advisors 1986-91), Commonwealth Club of Calif.

ROBBINS, CORNELIUS (VAN VORSE), educational administration educator; b. Wilmington, Del., Nov. 2, 1931; s. Cornelius V. and Irene (Tatman) R.; m. Janet Porter, Aug. 1953; children: Eva Robbins Burke, Laurel Robbins, Susan Robbins, Melissa Robbins Beegle. BA in Polit. Sci, U. Del., 1953, MEd in Social Scis, 1961; EdD in Ednl. Adminstrn, U. Pa., 1964. Asst. mgr. Robbins & Clark Hardware, 1953-57; asst. provost U. Del., 1957-58, 1964—65; tchr. Marshallton (Del.) Sch. Dist., 1958-60, Mt. Pleasant (Del.) Sch. Dist., 1960-62; asst. to dir. sch. study councils U. Pa., 1962-64; dir. mgmt. sys. U. Del., 1964—65; dean instrn. Ocean County Coll., 1965-67; dean of coll. C/C. of Delaware County, Pa., 1967-69; sr. assoc., coll. div. dir. McManis Assocs., Washington, 1969-70; pres. Genesee C.C., 1970-75; assoc. chancellor for community colls. SUNY, 1975-85; acting pres. Potsdam State Coll. (N.Y.), 1982-83; pres. Cobleskill (N.Y.) Coll. Agr. & Tech., 1985—2008; prof. edn. adminstrn. SUNY, Albany, NY, 1992—. Cons. Middle States Assn. Colls.; area liaison officer U.S. Mil. Acad., 1971-75; chmn. SUNY West Pres.'s Council and mem. Chancellor's Council, 1973-2007. Contbr. articles to profl. publs. Served with U.S. Army, 1954-56; maj. USAR ret. Recipient Outstanding Educator's award N.Y. State Assn. Jr. Colls., 1975, Disting. Svc. award Faculty Coun. Community Colls., 1988. Mem. Am. Assn. Higher Edn., State Dirs. of Community Colls. Assn., Phi Delta Kappa. Office: SUNY Albany Ed 322 Albany NY 12222-0001 Office Phone: 518-442-5085. Business E-Mail: crobbins@uamail.albany.edu.

ROBBINS, DAVID LEE, history professor, educator; b. Fairmont, W.Va., July 2, 1946; s. Charles Frank Robbins Jr. and Helen Dobbie Robbins; married; 1 child, Melissa Rachel. AB, Colgate U., Hamilton, NY, 1968; MPhil, Yale U., New Haven, 1972; PhD, Yale U., 1974. Assoc. dean, prof. history Suffolk U., Boston, 1974—, univ. historian, 1979—, univ. archivist, 1986—98, dir. Prague programs, 1990—. Assoc. dean Coll. Arts and Scis., Suffolk U., 1988—; chair Phi Beta Kappa Com., Suffolk U., 1988—, Dept. History and Dept. Philosophy, Suffolk U., 1987—89, NEASC, Suffolk U., 1989—92; pres. Internat. Edn. Orgn. InterFuture, 1989—; convenor U. Long Range Planning Com., Suffolk U., 1989—97; coord. Suffolk U. Madrid Programs, 1990—2002; grant dir. NAFSA, Boston, 1991—95; dir. USIA Coll. and U., Boston, 1997—2001; vis. prof. Am. studies Charles U., Prague, Czech Republic, 1994—; acad. dir. Suffolk U. Dakar Campus, Senegal, 1999—2002. Author (editor) four books; contbr. articles to profl. jours;, editor acad. jour. paralles. Grantee Fellowship, Danforth Found., 1968—74, Woodrow Wilson Found., 1968—74, Rsch. grant, Yale U., 1972—73; Fulbright Scholarship, US Govt., 1968—69, 1994—95. Mem.: Am. Hist. Assn., Boston Athenaeum. Home: PO Box 39 Reading MA 01867 Office: Suffolk Univ 41 Temple St Boston MA 02114 Office Fax: 617-557-2051. Business E-Mail: drobbins@suffolk.edu.

ROBBINS, DOROTHY ANN, retired foreign language educator; b. Little Rock, Mar. 17, 1947; d. W. E. and Ina (Spencer) Robbins. BA in Sociology, U. Ark., 1971; cert., U. Heidelberg, Germany, 1975; PhD, U. Frankfurt, Germany, 1981. Cert. state translator, Germany. Prof. Ctrl. Mo. State U., Warrensburg, 1999—2009. Author: (introduction) Collected Works of L. S. Vygotsky, 1999, Vygotsky's Psychology-Philosophy: A Metaphor for Language Theory and Learning, 2001, Voices within Vygotskian Non-Classical Psychology: Past, Present and Future, 2002, L.S. Vygotsky's and A.A. Leontiev's Russian Educational Semiotics and Psycholinguistics: Applications for Second Language Theory, 2003; editor: A.R. Luria and Contemporary Psychology, 2005; guest editor Jour. Russian and East European Psychology; contbr. articles to profl. jours., chapters to books; editor: International Perspections Non-Classical Psychology. Fulbright-Hays Travel fellow to Russia, 1994, sr. level Fulbright fellow to Moscow, 1999. Mem. Internat. Vygotsky Soc. (exec. bd.), Phi Beta Delta (campus pres. 1994-95). Avocations: travel to russia, russian language and literature, writing prose, trips to the sea, candlelight meals. Home: 4801 N Hills Blvd # 1207 North Little Rock AR 72116 Personal E-mail: dot.robbins@gmail.com.

ROBBINS, ELIZABETH, pediatric hematologist, oncologist; b. Palo Alto, Calif., 1951; Attended, Stanford U., Calif.; BA in English, U. Calif. Berkely; MD, U. Calif. Davis, 1978. Diplomate Am. Bd. Pediat., Am. Bd. Pediat. Hematology-Oncology. Intern pediat. Boston City Hosp., 1978—79; resident pediat. Mass. Gen. Hosp., Boston, 1979—80, resident hematologic oncology, 1980—81, fellowship, 1981—83, staff, 1986—92; rsch. fellow Inst. Maladies du Sang Hosp., Paris; staff U. Calif. San Francisco Children's Cancer and Blood Disorder Prog., 1992—; assoc. clin. prof. pediat. U. Calif. San Francisco. Contbr. articles to profl. jours. Mem.: Children's Oncology Grp., Am. Soc. Hematology. Mailing: U Calif Hosp 400 Parnassus Ave San Francisco CA 94143 Office Phone: 415-476-3831. Office Fax: 415-502-4372. Business E-Mail: robbinse@peds.ucsf.edu.

ROBBINS, FRANKIE, civil engineer; b. Enid, Okla., Dec. 7, 1945; children: Christian, Joshua. BS in Civil Engring., Okla. State U., 1969. Registered profl. engr., Kans., 1973. Forest transp. program mgr. USDA Forest Svc., 1990—99, regional transp. planner, 1999—2005. Chmn. bd. dirs. Ptnrs.-Mentoring Kids at Risk, 1989—90; mem. Medford C. of C., 2007—08; past mem. Wakita First Bapt. Ch.; mem., choir mem. Medford United Meth. Ch. Democrat. Methodist. Office: 119 N Main St Medford OK 73759 Office Phone: 580-395-2500. Office Fax: 580-395-2510. Business E-Mail: campaign@robbinsforcongress2008.com.

ROBBINS, HULDA DORNBLATT, artist, printmaker; b. Atlanta, Oct. 19, 1910; d. Adolph Benno and Lina (Rosenthal) Dornblatt. Student, Phila. Mus's. Sch. Indsl. Art, 1928-29, Prussian Acad., Berlin, 1929-31, Barnes Found., Merion, Pa., 1939. Poster designer and maker ITE Circuit Breaker Co. Inc., Phila., 1944; instr. serigraphy Nat. Serigraph Soc. Sch., NYC, 1953-60; instr. creative painting Atlantic County Jewish Cmty. Ctrs., Margate, Atlantic City, NJ, 1960-67. Represented by William P. Carl, Fine Prints, Boston, Picture Store, Boston. One-woman shows include Lehigh U. Art Galleries, 1933, ACA Galleries, Phila., 1939, 8th St. Gallery, N.Y.C., 1941, Serigraph Gallery, 1947, Atlantic City Art Ctr., 1961, 1971, exhibited in group shows at 2d Nat. Print Ann. Bklyn. Mus., Carnegie Inst., Libr. of Congress, LaNapoule Art Found., Am. Graphic Contemporary Art, Represented in permanent collections Met. Mus. Art, N.Y.C., Mus. Modern Art, Biblioteque Nationale, Smithsonian Instn., Art Mus. Ont., Can., Victoria and Albert Mus., London, U.S. embassies abroad, Lehigh U., Princeton Print Club, 6 prints, Phila. Mus. Art. Recipient Purchase prize, Prints for Children, Mus. Modern Art, N.Y.C., 1941, prize, 2d Portrait Am. Competition, 1945, 2d prize, Paintings by Printmakers, 1948. Mem.: Serigraph Soc. (mem. founding group, charter sec., Ninth Ann. prize 1948, 1949), Graphics Soc., Print Club, Am. Color Print Soc. Home: 11 Lenwood Ct Egg Harbor Township NJ 08234-5342 Office Phone: 609-823-7314. *To cherish and express living through devotion to art.*

ROBBINS, JANET LINDA, language and citizenship educator; b. LaJunta, Colo., Jan. 16, 1947; d. Richard Carl and Ruth Janet Robbins. B in Music Edn., Drake U., Des Moines, Iowa, 1969; BA, U. Minn., Mpls., 1974. Cert. life office mgmt. ins. cos., Iowa, 1970, tchg. music K-12, psychology 9-12 Iowa, 1969. Acctg. clerk Ctrl. Life Assurance Co., Des Moines, 1970; reader, tutor, intern Minn. State Svcs. for the Blind, St. Paul, 1973—74, 1975; tng. asst. psychology Mankato State U., Minn., 1974—75; intern mentally retarded St. Peter State Hosp., Minn., 1975; tchr. bi-lingual (Spanish and English) So. Minn., 1976; substitute tchr. pvt. students St. Louis Park Pub. Schs., Minn., 1977—81; care of aged and child care Okaloosa, Iowa, 1981—; instr. ESL Indian Hills CC, Okaloosa, 1987—. Intern pvt. co., Washington, 1977; tchr. Sunday Sch. Presbyn. Friends, Meth. Chs.; owner Janet L. Robbins Bookkeeping and Ednl. Svcs., 1987—. Violinist: Des Moines Symphony, 1965—69; author: numerous newspaper articles and poetry. Mem. League of Women Voters, Friends of Mpls. Pub. Libr., Willian Penn. U. Alumni Assn., Audubon Soc., Iowa chpt. UN Assn., YMCA; vol. some Dem. Party campaigns; youth asst. 1st Bapt. Ch., Okaloosa, 1987—88. Recipient Vol. award, Gov. Iowa, 1993, 2000, Ten County Literacy Tutor award, IHCC, 2001. Mem.: Friends Com. on Nat. Legis., Physicians for Social Responsibility, Iowa Life Long Learning Assn., U. Minn. Alumni Assn., Drake U. Alumni Assn., Nat. Wildlife Club, Sierra Club, Peale Ctr. Positive Thinkers Club, Peale Ctr. Bible Club. Democrat. Methodist. Avocations: piano, writing, tutoring, composing music, organ. Mailing: PO Box 576 Oskaloosa IA 52577 Personal E-mail: mittensiii1990@yahoo.com.

ROBBINS, JERRY HAL, educational administration educator; b. DeQueen, Ark., Feb. 28, 1939; s. James Hal and Barbara I. (Rogers) R. BA in Math, Hendrix Coll., 1960; M.Ed., U. Ark., 1963, Ed.D., 1966. Tchr. math. and music Clinton (Ark.) pub. schs., 1960-61; prin. Adrian (Mo.) High Sch., 1961-63; exec. sec. Ark. Sch. Study Council, Fayetteville, 1963-65; mem. faculty U. Miss., University, 1965-74, prof. ednl. adminstrn., 1970-74, chmn. dept. ednl. adminstrn., 1970-74; dean Coll. Edn., U. Ark., Little Rock, 1974-79; asso. v.p. for acad. affairs Ga. State U., Atlanta, 1979-84, dean Coll. Edn., 1984-90, prof. ednl. adminstrn., 1990-91; dean. Coll. Edn. Ea. Mich. U., Ypsilanti, 1991—2004, prof. ednl. leadership, 2004—05. Co-author: (with S. B. Williams Jr.) Student Activities in the Innovative School, 1969, School Custodian's Handbook, 1970, Administrator's Manual of School Plant Administration, 1970. Mem. NEA, Am. Assn. Sch. Adminstrs., Am. Assn. Colls. Tchr. Edn. (dir. 1979-82, 2000-04), Nat. Assn. Secondary Sch. Prins., So. Regional Council Ednl. Adminstrn. (pres. 1970-71), Tchr. Edn. Coun. State Colls. and Univs. (pres. 1998-99), Phi Delta Kappa, Kappa Delta Pi (v.p. chpt. devel. 1978-80, pres. elect 1980-82, pres. 1982-84, past pres. 1984-86) Mem. United Meth. Ch. Home and Office: 3384 Bent Trail Dr Ann Arbor MI 48108-9316 E-mail: jerry.robbins@emich.edu.

ROBBINS, JOHN CLAPP, management consultant; b. Cleveland, Jan. 22, 1921; s. John Clapp and Esther Turner (Holland) R.; m. Louise Severance Nash, Jan. 10, 1951 (div. Oct. 1974); children: Anne Millikin, Julia Severance, John Nash; m. Beatrice Blair, Aug. 2, 1975 (dec. July 1994); m. Sylvia Hordosch, Dec. 20, 2000. AB, Harvard U., 1942. Copy boy, reporter, writer, promotion editor Cleve. Press, 1946-57; exec. internat. div. Mobil Oil Corp., NYC, Istanbul, 1957-70; chief exec. officer Planned Parenthood/World Population, NYC, 1970-75; prin. mgmt. cons. Stanford Research Inst., 1976-83; v.p. GPA Inc., NYC, 1983—; pres. John Robbins Assocs. Spl. fin. cons. Internat. Helsinki Fedn., Vienna, Parkinson Disease Found., N.Y.C., Alan Guttmacher Inst., N.Y.C. Author: Too Many Asians, 1959. Bd. dirs., pres. Am. Hosp. Istanbul; treas. Harvard Libr. in N.Y.C. Capt. AUS, 1942-45. Decorated Bronze Star, Purple Heart; Reid fellow, 1953 Mem. Internat. Planned Parenthood Fedn. London, N.Y. State Rep. Pro-Choice Alliance. Unitarian Universalist. Home and Office: 115 E 87th St New York NY 10128-1136 Office Phone: 212-369-9800. Personal E-mail: johnrobbin2007@gmail.com.

ROBBINS, LANNY ARNOLD, chemical engineer; b. Wahoo, Nebr., Apr. 3, 1940; s. Earl Willard and Mildred Irene (Hanson) R.; m. Connie Lou Polich, Feb. 24, 1962; children: James Alan, Debra Renea. BS, Iowa State U., 1961, MS, 1963, PhD, 1966. Rsch. engr., project leader Dow Chem. Co., Midland, Mich., 1966-73, rsch. specialist, 1973-76, assoc. scientist, 1976-83, rsch. scientist, 1983-88, sr. rsch. scientist, 1988-97, rsch. fellow, 1997—2003; cons. Larco Techs., LLC, Midland, Mich., 2003—, GANTEC Inc. Adj. prof. Va. Poly. Inst., Blacksburg, 1973—76, Mich. State U., Lansing, 1983; mem. indsl. adv. bd. Iowa State U., Ames, 1994—2000. Author (chpt.) Schweitzer's Handbook of Separation Techniques, 1997, Perry's Chemical Engineer's Handbook, 1997. Recipient H.H. Dow medal, 1993. Mem.: NAE, AIChE. Republican. American Baptist. Achievements include patents for AquaDetox Aqueous Purification stripping devices and process, Sorbathene pressure swing adsorption vent emission control processes, liquid distributors for packed distillation, distillation process control and optimization. Home: 4101 Old Pine Trl Midland MI 48642-8892

ROBBINS, LAWRENCE M., hedge fund manager; BS in Econs., U. Pa. Wharton Sch. Bus.; BS, U. Pa. Moore Sch. Engring. Ptnr., portfolio mgr. Omega Advisors LLC; founder, portfolio mgr., CEO Glenview Capital Mgmt., LLC, 2000—. Bd. dirs. Robin Hood Found., NYC. Office: Glenview Capital Mgmt 767 Fifth Ave New York NY 10153 Office Phone: 212-812-4700. Office Fax: 212-812-4701.*

ROBBINS, MARY, concert pianist; b. Shelby, NC, Feb. 14, 1950; d. Clyde Hugh and Hazel Marguerite (Lovett) Robbins; m. Carl Brockman, Jan. 16, 1983. Student, Converse Coll., Spartanburg, SC, 1968-71; BMusic, U. Tex., 1973, MMusic, 1975, D Musical Arts, 1992. Concert coord. Austin (Tex.) Virtuosi, 1980-82; piano clinician Alfred Music Pub., Van Nuys, Calif., 1991-94; pianist various chamber org., Austin, 1976-91; pvt. piano instr. for adults and children Austin, 1971—; tchg. asst., instr. piano U. Tex., Austin, 1971-75; founder, prin. pianist A. Mozart Fest, Austin, 1991—, artistic dir., 1991—2008; founder, prin. pianist A. Mozart Fest Kidskonzerts, Austin. Accompanist U. Tex., Austin, 1971-84; invited lectr. Mozart Internat. Bicentennial Congress, Salzburg, Austria, 1991. Composer music and cadenzas following Mozart's style for his piano concertos, 1989—; composer, performer CD, A. Mozart Fest, 1998, CD with Austrian pianist Paul Badura-Skoda, 2002, CD with pianist Anton Nel, 2005. Presenter, Music Tchr. Nat. Assoc. Conf., 2003. (Presenter of session on stylistic issues of interpretation in Mozart). Vol. music class tchr. First English Luth. Ch., Austin, 1992; founder combined groups Classical Music Consortium, Austin, 1997. Grantee Tex. Commn. on Arts, 1991, 93, 2004—, City of Austin, 1992—. Mem. Austin Dist. Music Tchrs. Assn. (v.p. 1997-98, chair adult programs 1997—, chair festivals 1997-98, Pre-Coll. Tchr. of Yr. 1998), Mu Phi Epsilon. Lutheran. Avocations: cooking, entertaining, dance, outdoor sports, visual arts. Home: 2600 La Ronde St Austin TX 78731-5924 Personal E-mail: mozart4@peoplepc.com.

ROBBINS, MICHAEL J., cardiologist; MD, Cornell U. Med. Coll., NYC, 1981. Assoc. clin. prof. Mt. Sinai Sch. Medicine, NYC, 1987—. Fellow: ACP, Am. Heart Assn., Am. Coll. Cardiology. Office: Michael J Robbins MD 94-36 58th Ave Ste G4 Rego Park NY 11374

ROBBINS, N. CLAY, foundation administrator; b. Indpls., May 30, 1957; m. Amy Robbins; 3 children. BA, Wabash Coll., Crawfordsville, Ind., 1979; JD, Vanderbilt U. Sch. Law, Nashville, 1982; LLD (hon.), Ind. State U., 2004; LHD (hon.), Rose-Hulman Inst. Tech., Terre Haute, Ind., 2006. Assoc. Baker & Daniels, 1982-85, ptnr., 1988—92; exch. assoc. European Econ. Cmty. law dept. Rycken Burlion Bolle & Houben, Brussels, 1985-86; v.p. cmty. devel. Lilly Endowment Inc., Indpls., 1993-94, pres., 1994—, bd. dirs., 1999—. Mem. drafting com. Ind. Nonprofit Corp. Act, 1991. Active North United Meth. Ch. Indpls.; bd. dirs. United Way Ctrl. Ind.; bd. dirs., mem. exec. com. Ctrl. Ind. Corp. Partnership; past bd. dirs. Indpls. Chamber Orch., Greater Indpls. Progress Com. Mem.: Indpls. C. of C., Ind. State Bar Assn. Methodist. Office: Lilly Endowment Inc 2801 N Meridian St PO Box 88068 Indianapolis IN 46208-0068 Office Phone: 217-924-5471. Business E-Mail: robbinec@lei.com.*

ROBBINS, OREM OLFORD, insurance company executive; b. Mpls., Feb. 5, 1915; s. Douglas Ford and Grace (Rorem) R.; m. Annette Strand Scherer, May 17, 1992; children: Ford M., Ross S., Gail R. Tomei, Cynthia R. Rothbard. BBA with distinction, U. Minn., 1936; BS in Law, William Mitchell Coll. Law, 1946, JD, 1948. Comml. rep. NW Bell Telephone Co., Mpls., 1936-48; dep. dir. US Treas. Dept., Mpls., 1948-49; sales rep. Conn. Gen. Life Ins. Co., Mpls., 1949-56; founder, chmn. Security Life Ins. Co. Am., Mpls., 1956—. Bd. dirs., past pres. Family and Children's Svcs., Mpls., 1968—; bd. govs., past chmn. Meth. Hosp., Mpls., 1960-90; past treas., bd. dirs. Goodwill/Easter Seals, St. Paul, 1958-68, 75-88; life trustee Hamline U., St. Paul, 1979—, chmn. bd. trustees, 1990-91. Col. US Army, 1941-46. Decorated Legion of Merit; recipient Outstanding Achievement award U. Minn., 2001; named Disting. Eagle Scout, 2000. Fellow Life Mgmt. Assn.; mem. Am. Soc. CLU (pres. Mpls. chpt. 1959), Health Underwriters Assn., Chartered Fin. Cons., Am. Legion, Skylight Club (Mpls.), Naples Yacht Club, Mpls. Club, Officer's Club, Masons. Republican. Methodist. Office: Security Life Ins Co Am 10901 Red Circle Dr Minnetonka MN 55343-9304 Home Phone: 239-261-4295. E-mail: oorobbins@securitylife.com.

ROBBINS, RACHEL F., lawyer; b. Trenton, NJ, Oct. 30, 1950; 2 children. BA, Wellesley Coll., 1972; JD, NYU, 1976. Bar: N.Y. 1977. Assoc. Milbank Tweed Hadley & McCloy, 1976—80; atty. J.P. Morgan & Co., Inc., NYC, 1981—96, gen. counsel, corp. sec., 1996—2001; founding ptnr. Blaqwell, Inc., 2001—03; gen. counsel Citigroup Internat., 2003—04; strategic adv. Axiom Legal Solutions, 2004—06; exec. v.p., gen. counsel NYSE Group, Inc., NYC, 2006—07, NYSE Euronext, NYC, 2007—08; v.p., gen. counsel Internat. Fin. Corp. (IFC), Washington, 2008—. Mem. Fed. Regulation Com. Securities Industry Assn., 1987—2001, Legal Adv. Com. on NYSE, 1992—95, Exec. Com. Securities Regulation Inst., 1994—2001, US Treasury Adv. Com. on Fin. Services, 1996; chmn., pres Am. Bankers Assn. Securities Assn., 1997—2000. Mng. editor Ann. Survey Am. Law. Bd. trustees NYU Sch. Law. Named a Woman of Achievement, YMCA, 2003; named one of 100 Most Influential Lawyers, Nat. Law Jour., The 50 Most Influential Women Lawyers in Am., 2007. Mem. Coun. Fgn. Rels., ABA, Assn. of the Bar of the City of N.Y., N.Y. State Bar Assn., Order of the Coif. Office: Internat Fin Corp 2121 Pennsylvania Ave, NW Washington DC 20433 Office Phone: 202-473-1000.*

ROBBINS, RICHARD JAMES, endocrinologist, researcher; b. Danbury, Conn., Sept. 21, 1948; s. James Bernard and Ann Patricia Robbins; m. Anne Kathleen Schmiesing, Aug. 29, 1970; children: Andrew Richard, Heather Kathleen Kollar. MD, Creighton U., Omaha, Nebr., 1975. Cert. internal medicine and endocrinology Am. Bd. Internal Medicine, 1978. Dir. neuroendocrine unit Yale Med. Sch., New Haven, 1985—94; chief, endocrine svc. Meml. Sloan-Kettering Cancer Ctr., NYC, 1994—2005; prof., chmn. dept. medicine Meth. Hosp., Houston, 2005—. Recipient Alpha Omega Alpha, Creighton U., 1975, Henry Christian award, Am. Fedn. Clin. Rsch., 1993, Disting. Svc. award, Pituitary Soc., 1995, William Lees Lectureship, Johns Hopkins U., 2004, Best Doctors in NYC, 2005, Top Doctors in Cancer, Castel Connolly Med., Ltd., 2005—07, Charles and Anne Duncan Disting. Chair, Meth. Hosp., 2006, Best Doctors in Am., 2007. Fellow: ACP. Achievements include research in the synthesis of neuropeptides in mammalian cerebral cortex; first human to human neural transplantation for Parkinson's Disease; discovery of selective loss of inhibitory somatostain interneurons in human epilepsy; use of recombinant human TSH for treatment of thyroid cancer; prognostic value of PET scanning in metastatic thyroid cancer.

ROBBINS, ROBERT CLAYTON, surgeon; b. Laurel, Miss., Nov. 20, 1957; AA in Chemistry, Jones Jr. Coll., Ellisville, Miss., 1977; BS in Chemistry, Millsaps Coll., Jackson, Miss., 1979; MD, U. Miss. Med. Ctr., Jackson, Miss., 1983. Cert. cardiothoracic surgery Am. Bd. Thoracic Surgery, gen. surgery Am. Bd. Surgery. Intern, gen. surgery U. Miss. Med. Ctr., Jackson, 1983—84, resident, gen. surgery, 1984—85, chief resident, gen. surgery, 1988—89; postdoctoral fellow, cardiothoracic transplantation, dept. surgery Columbia-Presbyn. Med. Ctr., 1986; clin. assoc., cardiothoracic surgery, surgery br., Nat. Heart Lung Blood Inst. NIH, Bethesda, Md., 1986—88; resident, cardiothoracic surgery Stanford U. Hosp., Calif., 1989—91, chief resident, cardiothoracic surgery Calif., 1991—92, co-dir., Cardiac Clin. Ctr. Calif., 2002—, dir., Stanford Inst. for Cardiovascular Medicine Calif., 2004; pediat. fellow, congenital heart surgery Emory U. Sch. Medicine, Atlanta, 1992, Royal Children's Hosp., Melbourne, Australia, 1993; dir., cardiothoracic transplantation lab. Stanford U. Sch. Medicine, 1993—, acting asst. prof., cardiothoracic surgery, 1993—95, asst. prof., cardiothoracic surgery, 1995—2001, dir., heart, heart-lung, and lung transplant program, 1998—, assoc. prof., cardiothoracic surgery, 2001—05, chmn., dept. cardiothoracic surgery, 2005, prof., cardiothoracic surgery, 2005—. Dir., clin. cardiothoracic surgery tchg. conf., 1993—2006; mem. expert panel on minimally invasive surgery Health Tech. Ctr., 2001; bd. dirs. Calif. Transplant Donor Network, 1997—2005, Cohesion Technologies, Palo Alto, 2000—; mem. scientific adv. bd. Cardica, Inc., Menlo Park, Calif., 1997—, bd. dirs., 2000—; mem. scientific adv. bd. Cytograft Tissue Engring. Inc., Novato, Calif., 2000—, bd. dirs., 2003—; mem. scientific adv. bd. Transvascular, Inc., Menlo Park, Calif., 1995—2000, Embol-X, Inc., Sunnyvale, Calif., 1995—98, ArthroCare, Corp., Sunnyvale, Calif., 1997—2000, Cardio Vention, Inc., Palo Alto, 1997—99, A-med, Inc.,

Sacramento, 1997—2000, Microheart, Inc., Sunnyvale, Calif., 1999—2001, Radiant Med., Redwood City, Calif., 2000—, Curis, Inc., Cambridge, Mass., 2001—, Paracor Surgical, Inc., Sunnyvale, Calif., 2001—; mem. clin. adv. bd. Xoma, LLC, Berkeley, Calif., 2002—, Afmedica, Inc., Kalamazoo, 2005, Theregen, Corp., San Francisco, 2005—; mem. physician adv. panel Cardiac Surgery Technologies, Medtronic, Inc., Mpls., 2001—. Ad hoc reviewer Nat. Inst. Neurological Disorders and Stroke Study Sect., NIH, 1996, manuscript reviewer Jour. Thoracic and Cardiovascular Surgery, 1996—, mem. editl. bd., 2001—, manuscript reviewer Annals Thoracic Surgery, 1995—, New Eng. Jour. Medicine, 1996—, abstract reviewer Internat. Soc. Heart and Lung Transplantation, 1996—, mem. editl. bd. Cardiac Surgery Digest, 2001—, Jour. Heart and Lung Transplantation, 2003—, Innovations, 2005—, guest editor, surgical supplement Circulation, 2002—05; contbr. several articles to peer-reviewed jours. Mem. Thoracic Organ Transplantation Com. United Network for Organ Sharing, 1999—2002, Region 5 Thoracic Organ Rep. and Review Bd. Chamn., 1999—2002; rsch. com. mem. Thoracic Surgery Found. for Rsch. and Edn., 2000—; mem. Calif. Transplant Donor Network-Med. Affairs Com., 1996—. Fellow: Am. Coll. Cardiology, Am. Heart Assn. (Vivien Thomas Young Investigator award selection com. 1997—, mem. exec. com., coun. on cardiothoracic and vascular surgery 1997—, mem. program com. 1999—), ACS; mem.: Bay Area Soc. Thoracic Surgeons (founding mem.) (pres. 2006, bd. dirs. 2000—), Soc. U. Surgeons, Am. Soc. Transplantation, Am. Soc. Transplant Surgeons, 21st Century Cardiac Surgical Soc., Transplantation Soc., AAAS, Internat. Soc. Heart and Lung Transplantation (co-chair, ventricular assist device coun. 2000—02, bd. dirs. 2000—, program chair 2001—02, mem. program com. 2003, pres. 2006), San Francisco Surgical Soc., Assn. Academic Surgeons (vice-chair, cardiovascular surgery and anesthesia coun. 2005—, mem. strategic planning com. 2006), Soc. Thoracic Surgeons (mem. workforce on clin. edn. 2004—, workforce on surgical treatment end-stage cardiopulmonary disease 2004—), Western Thoracic Surgical Assn., Am. Assn. Thoracic Surgery (membership com. 2003—06, mem. edn. com. 2003—, chair. membership com. 2005—06), Cardiothoracic Surgery Network, James D. Hardy Soc., Andrew G. Morrow Soc., Alpha Omega Alpha (Resident award 1989). Achievements include patents in field. Office: Dept Cardiothoracic Surgery Falk Cardiovasc Rsch Ctr Stanford U Sch Medicine 300 Pasteur Dr CVRB MC 5407 Stanford CA 94305-5407 Office Phone: 650-725-3828, 650-723-5771. Fax: 650-725-3846. E-mail: robbins@stanford.edu.

ROBBINS, STEPHEN J. M., lawyer; b. Seattle, Apr. 13, 1942; s. Robert Mads and Aneita Elberta (West) R.; m. Nina Winifred Tanner, Aug. 11, 1967; children: Sarah E.T., Alicia S.T. AB, UCLA, 1964; JD, Yale U., 1971. Bar: D.C. 1973, U.S. Dist. Ct. D.C. 1973, U.S. Ct. Appeals (D.C. cir.) 1973, U.S. Ct. Appeals (3d cir.) 1973, U.S. Dist. Ct. (ea. and no. dists.) Calif. 1982, U.S. Dist. Ct. (cen. dist.) Calif. 1983, Supreme Ct. of Republic of Palau, 1994. Pres. U.S. Nat. Student Assn., Washington, 1964-65; dir. scheduling McGovern for Pres., Washington, 1971-72; assoc. Steptoe & Johnson, Washington, 1972-75; chief counsel spl. inquiry on food prices, com. on nutrition and human needs U.S. Senate, Washington, 1975; v.p., gen. counsel Straight Arrow Pubs., San Francisco, 1975-77; dep. dist. atty. City and County of San Francisco, 1977-78; regional counsel U.S. SBA, San Francisco, 1978-80; spl. counsel Warner-Amex Cable Communications, Sacramento, 1981-82; ptnr. McDonough, Holland and Allen, Sacramento, 1982-84; v.p. Straight Arrow Pubs., NYC, 1984-86; gen. legal counsel Govt. State of Koror, Rep. of Palau, Western Caroline Islands, 1994-95; pvt. practice law, 1986—. Adj. prof. govt. Calif. State U., Sacramento, 1999-05. Staff sgt. U.S. Army, 1966-68. Fellow Acad. Polit. Sci.; mem. ABA (sect. urban, state and local govt.), DC Bar, State Bar Calif., Am. Hist. Assn., Supreme Ct. Hist. Soc. Democrat. Unitarian. Avocations: theater, art, hiking. Office: PO Box 85567 Seattle WA 98145

ROBBINS, SUSAN PAULA, social work educator; b. Bklyn., Aug. 15, 1948; d. Harold Jess and Rose (Bernstein) R. AA, Manhattan C.C., 1972; BA summa cum laude, Hamline U., 1974; MSW, U. Minn., 1976; PhD, Tulane U., 1979. Adj. instr. dept. sociology and social work Augsburg Coll., Mpls., 1975-76; part-time instr. women's studies program U. Minn., Mpls., 1976; rsch. and grant cons. Seminole Tribe of Fla., Hollywood, 1978-79, child and adolescent caseworker, program planning cons., 1979-80; coord. criminal justice/corrections program St. Mary's Dominican Coll., New Orleans, 1979-80; asst. prof. social work New Orleans Consortium, 1978-80, U. Houston, 1980-86, assoc. prof., 1986—, assoc. dean acad. affairs, 1998-2000. Cons. ABA Multi Door Program, Houston, Cmty. Svc. Option Program, Houston; mediator Dispute Resolution Ctrs., Houston, 1982—; trainer Tex. Dept. Protective Svcs. Tng. Inst., 1995—. Author (with others): Encyclopedia of Social Work, Social Workers' Desk Reference; contbr. articles and book chpts. to profl. jours. Women's Club of Mpls. fellow, 1975, Nat. Inst. of Mental Health fellow, 1976-78; recipient Nat. Faculty Excellence award Univ. Continuing Edn. Assn., 1998. Mem. NASW, Coun. on Social Work Edn., Social Welfare Action Alliance, Assn. for Cmty. Orgn. and Social Adminstrn., So. Sociol. Soc., Phi Kappa Phi (sec. Houston chpt. 1984—). Democrat. Jewish. Office: Univ Houston 4800 Calhoun Rd Houston TX 77204-4013 Office Phone: 713-743-8103. Business E-Mail: srobbins@uh.edu.

ROBBINS, THOMAS LANDAU, researcher, editor; b. NYC, Oct. 13, 1943; s. Manuel Lee and Elly (Landau) R. AB, Harvard U., 1965; MA, U. N.C., 1968, PhD in Sociology, 1973. Instr., asst. prof. Queens Coll., 1971-78; instr. Cen. Mich. U., 1982-83; NIMH postdoctoral trainee in sociology Yale U., New Haven, 1979-81; sr. rsch. assoc. Santa Barbara (Calif.) Ctr. for Humanistic Studies, 1990—. Author: Cults, Converts and Charisma, 1988; co-editor: In Gods We Trust, 1981, 2d edit., 1990, Cults, Culture and the Law, 1985, Church-State Relations, 1987, Millennium, Messiahs and Mayhem, 1997, Misunderstanding Cults, 2004, New Religious Movements in the 21st Century, 2000; assoc. editor Sociol. Analysis, 1984-90; editl. cons. Nova Religio, 1997—; contbr. articles to profl. jours. Mem. Soc. for the Sci. Study of Religion (exec. coun. 1988-91), Assn. for the Sociology Religion, (exec. coun. 1985-87), Am. Sociol. Assn., Soc. for the Study of Social Problems. Meher Baba. Home: 936 41st St NW Apt 109 Rochester MN 55901-1305 Personal E-mail: tomrobbins427@aol.com. *I am becoming concerned these days about threats to freedom of religion in the United States and Europe.*

ROBBINS, TIM (TIMOTHY FRANCIS ROBBINS), actor, film director; b. West Covina, Calif., Oct. 16, 1958; s. Gil Robbins; life ptnr. Susan Sarandon; children: John Henry, Miles 1 stepchild, Eva Maria. BA with honors, UCLA, 1981. Founder, artistic dir. The Actor's Gang, 1981—. Actor: (films) No Small Affair, 1984, Toy Soldiers, 1984, Fraternity Vacation, 1985, The Sure Thing, 1985, Howard the Duck, 1986, Top Gun, 1986, Five Corners, 1987, Bill Durham, 1988, Tapeheads, 1989, Eric The Viking, 1989, Miss Firecracker, 1989, Cadillac Man, 1990, Twister, 1990, Jacob's Ladder, 1990, Jungle Fever, 1991, The Player, 1992 (Best Actor award Cannes Film Festival 1992), Short Cuts, 1993, The Hudsucker Proxy, 1994, The Shawshank Redemption, 1994, Ready to Wear (Prêt-à-Porter), 1994, I.Q., 1994, Nothing to Lose, 1997, Arlington Road, 1999, Austin Powers: The Spy Who Shagged Me, 1999, Mission to Mars, 2000, High Fidelity, 2000, Antitrust, 2001, Human Nature, 2001, The Truth About Charlie, 2002, The Day My God Died (voice), 2003, Mystic River, 2003 (Golden Globe for best supporting actor in a drama, 2004, SAG Award for best supporting actor, 2004, Acad. Award for best supporting actor in a drama, 2004), Code 46, 2004, Anchorman: The Legend of Ron Burgundy, 2004, War of the Worlds, 2005, The Secret Life of Words, 2005, Zathura: A Space Adventure, 2005, Catch a Fire, 2006, Tenacious D: The Pick of Destiny, 2006, The Lucky Ones, 2008, City of Ember, 2008; (TV movies) Quarterback Princess, 1983, Malice in Wonderland, 1985; (TV appearances) St. Elsewhere, 1982, Legmen, 1984, Hardcastle and McCormick, 1984, Hill Street Blues, 1984, Moonlighting, 1985, Amazing Stories, 1986, (voice) The Simpsons, 1999, Jack & Bobby, 2005; actor, dir., writer, composer: Bob Roberts, 1992; dir., writer, prodr.: Dead Man Walking, 1995 (Golden Globe nomination for best dir. of film 1996, Acad. Award nomination for best dir. 1996), The Cradle Will Rock, 1999; exec. prodr., The Typewriter, the Rifle, and the Movie Camera, 1994, The Spectre of Hope, 2000; dir. (plays) Ubu Roi (L.A. Weekly Dir. award), A Midsummer's Night Dream, Methusalem, the Eternal Bourgeois, The Good Woman of Setzuan (LA Drama Critics Circle nominee), and others, (TV series) Queen's Supreme, 2003; co-writer: (plays) Alagazam...After the Dog Wars, Violence: The Misadventures of Spike Spangle, Farmer, Carnage, a Comedy, Embedded, and others. Recipient Tribute to Ind. Vision Award, Sundance Film Festival, 1997, Star on Hollywood Walk of Fame, 2008. Office: ICM c/o Elaine Goldsmith Thomas 40 W 57th St New York NY 10019*

ROBBINS-WILF, MARCIA, educational consultant; b. Newark, Mar. 22, 1949; d. Saul and Ruth (Fern) Robbins; 1 child, Orin. Student, Emerson Coll., 1967-69, Seton Hall U., 1969, Fairleigh Dickinson U., 1970; BA, George Washington U., 1971; MA, NYU, 1975; postgrad., St. Peter's Coll., Jersey City, 1979, Fordham U., 1980; MS, Yeshiva U., 1981, EdD, 1986; postgrad., Monmouth Coll., 1986. Cert. elem. tchr., N.Y., N.J., reading specialist, N.J., prin., supr., N.J., adminstr., supr., N.Y. Tchr. Sleepy Hollow Elem. Sch., Falls Church, Va., 1971-72, Yeshiva Konvitz, NYC, 1972-73; intern Wee Folk Nursery Sch., Short Hills, NJ, 1978-81, dir. day camp, 1980-81, tchr., dir., owner, 1980-81; adj. prof. reading Seton Hall U., South Orange, NJ, 1987, Middlesex County Coll., Edison, NJ, 1987-88; asst. adj. prof. L.I. U., Bklyn., 1988, Pace U., NYC, 1988—. Ednl. cons. Cranford High Sch., 1988; presenter numerous workshops; founding bd. dirs. Stern Coll. Women Yeshiva U., N.Y.C., 1987; adj. vis. lectr. Rutgers U., New Brunswick, N.J., 1988. Chairperson Jewish Book Festival, YM-YWHA, West Orange, N.J., 1986-87, mem. early childhood com., 1986—, bd. dirs., 1986—; vice chairperson dinner com. Nat. Leadership Conf. Christians and Jews, 1986; mem. Hadassah, Valerie Children's Fund, Women's League Conservative Judaism, City of Hope; assoc. bd. bus. and women's profl. divsn. United Jewish Appeal, 1979; vol. reader Goddard Riverside Day Care Ctr., N.Y.C., 1973; friend N.Y.C. Pub. Libr., 1980—; life friend Millburn (N.J.) Pub. Libr.; pres. Seton-Essex Reading Coun., 1991-94. Co-recipient Am. Heritage award, Essex County, 1985; recipient Award Appreciation City of Hope, 1984, Profl. Improvement awards Seton-Essex Reading Council, 1984-86, Cert. Attendance award Seton-Essex Reading Counci, 1987. Mem. N.Y. Acad. Scis. (life), N.J. Council Tchrs. English, Nat. Council Tchrs. English, Am. Ednl. Research Assn., Coll. Reading Assn. (life), Assn. Supervision and Curriculun Devel., N.Y. State Reading Assn. (council Manhattan), N.J. Reading Assn. (council Seton-Essex), Internat. Reading Assn., Nat. Assn. for Edn. of Young Children (life N.J. chpt., Kenyon group), Nat. Council Jewish Women (vice chairperson membership com. evening br. N.Y. sect. 1974-75), George Washington U. Alumni Club, Emerson Coll. Alumni Club, NYU Alumni Club, Phi Delta Kappa (life), Kappa Gamma Chi (historian). Clubs: Greenbrook Country (Caldwell, N.J.); George Washington Univ. Avocations: reading, theater. Home: 242 Hartshorn Dr Short Hills NJ 07078-1914 also: Claridge House I PH22 1 Claridge Dr Verona NJ 07044 E-mail: dr.mrw349@aol.com.

ROBBOY, STANLEY J., pathologist, educator; s. John and Sarah (Shapiro) R.; m. Anita Wyzanski, July 21, 1968 (div. 1981); children: Elizabeth, Caroline; m. Marion Meyer, June 14, 1990. Student, U. Mich., 1958-61, MD, 1965. Diplomate Am. Bd. Pathology, Am. Bd. Med. Mgmt. Intern Mt. Sinai Hosp, Cleve., 1965-66; resident to chief in pathology Mass. Gen. Hosp., 1966-70, asst. in pathology, 1972-73, asst. pathologist, 1973-76, assoc. pathologist, 1976-84; resident in pathology Boston Hosp. for Women, 1970; instr. Tufts Med. Sch., 1968-69; asst. prof. pathology Harvard Med. Sch., Boston, 1972-76, assoc. prof., 1976-84; prof. pathology U. Medicine and Dentistry N.J.-N.J. Med. Sch., Newark, 1984—92, chmn. dept., 1984-89, prof. ob-gyn, 1990—92, pathologist-in-chief, 1984-89, dir. faculty practice service, 1985-89; prof., vice chmn. dept. pathology Duke U., 1992—, prof. ob-gyn., 1993—. Cons. pathologist St. Joseph Hosp., Paterson, NJ, 1985—92, St. Barnabas Hosp., Livingston, NJ, 1985—92, Beth Israel Hosp., Newark, 1985—92, VA Med. Ctr., Durham, 1992-, Durham Reg. Hosp., 2003-, Raleigh Com. Hosp., 2003-; pathologist (DES) Registry Rsch. Transplacental Hormonal Carcinogenesis (formerly Clear-Cell Adenocarcinoma Registry), 1972-83; pathologist, prin. investigator Nat. Collaborative Diethylstilbestrol project, 1974-82; vis. scientist New Eng. Primate Ctr., 1973-84; vis. prof. U. Shiraz Med. Sch., Iran, 1976; commr. NJ Commn. on Cancer Rsch., 1987-92; sr. advisor East Asia Cons. Group, Boston, LA and Tokyo, 1984-85; reference panel for diagnostic and therapeutic tech. AMA, 1982—99; mem. nat. med. com. Planned Parenthood Fedn. Am., 1990-93, vice chmn. com. on oncology, 1993; mem. DES steering com. Nat. Cancer Inst., 1995—; mem. exec. editl. bd. ArchPathhab Med, 2005-; bd. dir. Pamet Sys. Inc., 1991. Mem. editl. bd. Human Pathology, 1980-90, Cervix and the Low Female Genital Tract, 1983-94, Internat. Jour. Gynecologic Pathology, 1985-; sect. editor Functional Biomarkers in Disease, 2005-; editor: Informatics in Pathology, 1985-88, Pathology Rsch. and Practice, 1990-2000, Gynecologic Oncology, 1997-2004, InsScight, 1998-; sect. editor Functional Biomarkers in Disease, 2005-; editor-in-chief, Pathology the Female Reproductive Tract, edits. 1 & 2; contbr. articles to profl. jours. Trustee Am. Pathology Found., 1984—86; NJ commn. Cancer Rsch., 1987—92; co-pres. Chapel Hill Kehillah, 2005—08, Triangle Jewish Film Festival, 2007—, chair, 2007—. Maj. US Army, 1970—72. Recipient Jr. Faculty award Am. Cancer Soc., 1972-75, Found. prize Am. Coll. Ob-Gyn, 1975, Coll. Am. Pathologist Pres. award, 2005; Sara & Mutt Evans Outstanding Cmty. Svc. award, Durham-Chapel Hill, 2005; Pardee fellow U. Mich., 1961, Lederle Lab. fellow, 1962, Eliza Howell fellow, 1964, Ford Found. fellow, 1964-65; clin. fellow Am. Cancer Soc., 1967-68. Fellow Am. Soc. Clin. Pathologists (chmn. pathology telecommunications network com. 1983, task force on computers 1980-83, council on med. informatics 1983-84, planning and scope com. 1983-84, co-chmn. pathology communication network 1983-87, coun. anat. pathology, 1995-2001, future directions, 1995-98), Coll. Am. Pathologists (alt. Mass. del. to house dels. 1981-84, co-chmn. pathology comm. network 1983-85, alt. NJ del. to house dels. 1985-92, exec. com. and advisor nomenclature and classification of disease 1975-80, editl. bd. Systematized Nomenclature Medicine 1976-80, gov. 1999-2005, mem. reimbursement com., 1992-94, profl. and econ. affairs com., 1995-97, outcomes com., 1999-2000, vice chmn. coun. on pub. affairs 1999-2005, coun. of govt. prof. affairs, 2000-2004, credentials com., 2000-04, spokesperson, 2001—, performance measurement com. 2000, nat. meeting planning com. 2003—, vice chmn. election oversight com. 2006—, leadership devel. com. 2006-; strategic planning com., 2008-), Soc. Gynecologic Oncologists Assocs.; mem. Arthur Purdy Stout Soc. Surg. Pathology (membership com. 1980-86, treas. 1993-2001, pres.-elect 2001-03, pres. 2003-05), Internat. Acad. Cytology, Internat. Acad. Pathology (edn. com. 1979-83), Internat. Soc. Gynecologic Pathologists (chmn. membership com. 1982-84), Mass. Soc. Pathology (3d party relations 1978-84, chmn. computer com. 1981-84), NC Med. Soc., NC Soc. Pathology, NJ Med. Soc., NJ Soc. Pathology (edn. and profl. rels. coms. 1984-92, exec. com. 1985-92), Chapel Hill Kehillah (co-pres. 2004—). Jewish. Office: Duke U Med Ctr PO Box 3712 Durham NC 27710-0001 Home Phone: 919-968-9773; Office Phone: 919-684-3656. Business E-Mail: stanley.robboy@duke.edu.

ROBE, THURLOW RICHARD, retired engineering educator, dean; s. Thrulow Scott and Mary Alice (McKibben) R.; m. Eleanora C. Komyati, Aug. 27, 1955; children: Julia, Kevin, Stephen, Edward. BSC.E., Ohio U., 1955, MS in Mech. Engring., 1962; PhD in Applied Mechanics, Stanford U., 1966. Engr. Gen. Electric Co., Niles, Ohio, Cleve., Erie, Pa., Evendale,Ohio, 1954-60; acting instr. to instr. Ohio U., Athens, 1960-63, dean Russ Coll. Engring. and Tech., 1980-96, Cruse W. Moss prof. Engring. Edn., 1992-96, founding dir. T. Richard and Eleanora K. Robe Leadership Inst., 1997—2005, dir. Innovation Ctr. Authority, 1983-96; asst. prof to prof., assoc. dean, spl. asst. to pres. U. Ky., Lexington, 1965-80; rsch. fellow Postgrad. Sch. Applied Dynamics U. Edinburgh, Scotland, 1973; dean emeritus, Moss prof. emeritus Russ Coll. Engring. and Tech., Ohio U., Athens, 1996—; pres., chmn. bd. Q.E.D. Assocs., Inc., Lexington, 1975-83. Trustee Engring. Found. Ohio, 1988-94; bd. trustees Ohio Aerospace Inst. 1990-96, bd. govs. Edison Materials Tech. Ctr., 1987-96; mem. adv. bd. Robe Leadership Inst., 2005—; liaison engring. accreditation commn. Accreditation Bd. Engring. and Tech., 1989-91; mem. Russ Prize Selection Com., NAE, 2000—. Contbr. articles to profl. jours.; patentee trailer hitch. Bd. dirs. Athens County Cmty. Redevel. Corp., 1980-86; treas. South Lexington Little League, 1976-80; vice chmn. Thoroughbred dist., Boy Scouts Am., 1975-77; mem.-at-large Oconee Dist. Boy Scouts Am., 2007—; pres. Tates Creek H.S. PTA, Lexington, 1975-76; bd. dirs. U. Ky. Athletics Ass.n, 1975-80; bd. trustees Assn. Ohio Commodores, 1995-97; trustee Ohio U. Found., 1998-2007, trustee emeritus, 2007—. Maj. USAFR, 1955—85, officer, jet fighter pilot USAF, 1956—59. Recipient Alumni medal of merit Ohio U., 1993; named Am. Coun. on Edn. Adminstrn. fellow, 1970-71, Ohio U. Alumnus of Yr., 1996, inductee Acad. Disting. Grads., Russ Coll. Engring. & Tech., 2001. Mem. ASME, NSPE (profl. engring. in edn. exec. bd., ctrl. region vice-chmn. 1987-89), Am. Soc. Engring. Edn. (Outstanding Contbn. in Rsch. award 1966), Athens Running Club, Athens Symposiarchs, Rotary, Sigma Xi, Tau Beta Pi, Omicron Delta Kappa, Alpha Lambda Delta Avocations: reading, golf, tennis. Personal E-mail: robe@ohio.edu.

ROBEAU, SALLY GARWOOD, secondary school educator; b. Corpus Christi, Tex., Nov. 19, 1933; d. Robert B. and Hazel V. (Priour) Garwood; m. Joseph Ruel Robeau, June 5, 1954; children: James, Stephen, David, Catherine, Cheri. BS in Edn., Tex. A&I U., Kingsville, 1973, MS in Edn., 1979. Cert. secondary tchr. Tex. Rep. Southwestern Bell Tel. Co., Dallas, Houston, 1954—55; sec. A.G. Edwards & Co., Houston, 1955—56; tchr. Calallen Ind. Sch. Dist., Corpus Christi, 1973—98; ret., 1998. Author: Of Pride and Pioneers, 1964. Sponsor Jr. Historians, 1974—; chmn. Nueces County Hist. Commn., Corpus Christi, 1984—86; exec. dir. Nuecestown Schoolhouse Hist. Ctr., Corpus Christi, 1986—. Recipient Daniel Kilgore Local History award, Nueces County Hist. Soc., 2005; named Tchr. of the Yr., Daus. Rep. of Tex., DAR. Mem.: PTA (life), Nueces County Hist. Soc., Tex. State Hist. Assn. (co-sponsor Calallen Jr. Historians). Methodist. Avocations: research, historical center restoration. Home: 14233 Fairway Dr Corpus Christi TX 78410-5612

ROBECK, MILDRED COEN, retired education educator, writer; b. Walum, ND, July 29, 1915; d. Archie Blain and Mary Henrietta (Hoffman) Coen; m. Martin Julius Robeck, Jr., June 2, 1936; children: Martin Jay Robeck, Donna Jayne Robeck Thompson, Bruce Wayne Robeck. BS, U. Wash., 1950, MEd, 1954, PhD, 1958. Ordnance foreman Sherman Williams, U.S. Navy, Bremerton, Wash., 1942-45; demonstration tchr. Seattle Pub. Schs., 1946-57; reading clinic dir. U. Calif., Santa Barbara, 1957-64; rsch. cons. State Dept. Edn., Sacramento, 1964-67; prof., head early childhood edn. U. Oreg., Eugene, Oreg., 1967-86; vis. scholar West Australia Inst. Tech., Perth, 1985; v.p. acad. affairs U. Santa Barbara, Calif., 1987-95; ret., 1989. Vis. prof. Victoria Coll., B.C. Can., summer 1958, Dalhousie U., Halifax, 1964; trainer; evaluator US Office Edn. Head Start, Follow Thru, 1967-72; cons., evaluator Native Am. Edn. Programs, Sioux, Navajo, Umatilla, 1967-86; cons. on gifted Oreg. Task Force on Talented and Gifted, Salem, 1974-76; evaluator Early Childhood Edn., Bi-Ling. program, Petroleum and Minerology, Dhahran, Saudi Arabia, 1985. Author: Materials Kindergarten Evaluation Learning Progress, 1967, Infants and Children, 1978, Psychology of Reading, 1990, Oscar: His Story, 1997, 2d edit., 2000; contbr. articles to profl. jours. Evaluation cons. Rosenburg Found. Project, Santa Barbara, 1966-67; faculty advisor Pi Lambda Theta, Eugene, Oreg, 1969-74; guest columnist Oreg. Assn. Gifted and Talented, Salem, Oreg., 1979-81; editorial review bd. ERQ, U.S. Calif., L.A., 1981-91. Recipient Nat. Dairy award 4-H Clubs, Wis., 1934, NYA and U. Wis. scholar, Madison, 1934-35, Faculty Rsch. grant U. Calif., Santa Barbara, 1958-64, NDEA fellow Retraining U.S. Office Edn., U. Oreg., 1967-70. Mem. APA, Am. Ednl. Rsch. Assn., Internat. Reading Assn., Phi Beta Kappa, Pi Lambda Theta. Democrat. Achievements include research in high IQ children who had severe difficulties learning to read and then doing a follow up study of them as 30-40 year olds; updating and promoting kindergarten evaluation of learning progress. Avocations: historical research, writing. Home: 95999 Highway 101 S Yachats OR 97498-9714 Office Phone: 541-547-3967. Personal E-mail: mrobeck@casco.net.

ROBEK, MARY FRANCES, business education educator; b. Superior, Wis., Jan. 30, 1927; d. Stephen and Mary (Hervert) R. BE, U. Wis., Whitewater, 1948; MA, Northwestern U., 1951; MBA, U. Mich., 1962, PhD, 1967. Tchr. Bergland (Mich.) High Sch., 1948, Tony (Wis.) High Sch., 1948-50, Sch. Vocat. and Adult Edn., Superior, 1950-58; prof. bus. edn. and office tech. Ea. Mich. U., Ypsilanti, 1958-93; instr. Jazyckova Gymnasium, Banská, Stiavnica, Slovakia, 1994. Author: Information and Records Management, 1995. Assn. of Records Mgrs. and Adminstrs. fellow, 1992. Mem. Assn. Records Mgrs. and Adminstrs. (life), Inst. Cert. Mgrs. (pres. 1980-81, Emmett Leahy award 2000), Cath. Daus. Am., Delta Pi Epsilon, Delta Kappa Gamma, Pi Lambda Theta. Republican. Roman Catholic. Home: 515 Clough Ave Superior WI 54880 Home Phone: 715-394-5400. Personal E-mail: RobekMary@aol.com. *Opportunity to do creative and innovative things without infringing on the rights of others is limited only by priorities set considering people and technology.*

ROBEL, CHUCK (CHARLES J. ROBEL), computer software company executive; BS in Acctg., Ariz. State U., Tempe. Ptnr. PricewaterhouseCoopers; mng. mem., COO Hummer Winblad Venture Ptnrs.,

2000—05; chmn. bd., chmn. audit com. McAfee, Inc., 2006—. Dir., chmn. audit com. Borland Software, Adaptec, Inc.; dir., mem. audit com. Informatica Corp. Office: McAfee Inc 3965 Freedom Cir Santa Clara CA 95054

ROBEL, LAUREN, dean, law educator; b. Dec. 1953; BA with high honors, Auburn U., 1978; JD summa cum laude, Ind. U., 1983, postgrad., 1985. Bar: US Supreme Ct., Ind., Ill. Law clk. to Hon. Jesse Eschbach, U.S. Ct. Appeals (7th cir.), 1983—85; assoc. dean Ind. U. Sch. Law, Bloomington, Ind., 1991—2002, Val Nolan prof. law, 1999—, acting dean, 2002—03, dean, 2003—. Vis. faculty U. Panthenon-Assas, Paris; reporter rules com. U.S. Dist. Ct. (so. dist.) Ind.; mem. rules com. Ind. Supreme Ct. Author: Les États des Noirs: Federalisme et question raciale aux États-unis, 2000, Federal Courts: Cases and Materials on Judicial Federalism and The Lawyering Process, 2005; contbr. articles to profl. jours. Recipient Leon Wallace Teaching Award, 1997, Teaching Excellence Recognition Award, Ind. U. Sch. Law, 1997, 1999, Leonard D. Fromm Public Interest Award, 1999, 2002. Mem.: Ind. State Bar Women (Law Recognition award 2000), Ind. Bar Found. (Pro Bono Publico award 1997), Order of Coif. Office: Ind Univ Sch Law 211 S Indiana Ave Bloomington IN 47405 Home Phone: 812-334-8844; Office Phone: 812-855-8885. Business E-Mail: lrobel@indiana.edu.*

ROBERDS, RICHARD MACK, professor emeritus; b. Lawrence, Kans., June 22, 1934; s. Wesley Milton and Dorothy Dean (McBroom) R.; m. Marian Marchena Lanyon, Aug. 8, 1958; children: Michael R., Catherine M., Wendy M. AB in Physics, U. Kans., 1956, MA, 1963; PhD in Nuclear Engring., Air Force Inst. Tech., Wright-Patterson AFB, Ohio, 1975. Commd. 2d lt. U.S. Air Force, 1956, advanced through grades to col.; dep. chief tech. div. Air Force Weapons Lab., Kirtland AFB, OH, 1973-76, chief applied physics br., 1976-77; div. chief Air Force Avionics Lab., Wright Patterson AFB, 1977-80; ret. U.S. Air Force, 1980; head dept. engring. tech. Clemson (S.C.) U., 1980-84; dean Sch. Engring. U. Tenn., Martin, 1984-86; assoc. dean for acad. affairs U. Tenn. Space Inst., Tullahoma, 1986-89, acting dean, 1989-91, prof. engring. sci., 1991-93; prof. and head integrated sci and tech. James Madison U., Va., 1993—2005, prof. emeritus, 2005—. Assoc. exec. dir. U. Tenn.-Calspan Ctr. for Aerospace Rsch., Tullahoma, 1989-91; bd. dirs. U. Tenn. Rsch. Corp., Knoxville, 1989-91, Tenn. Valley Aerospace Region, Tullahoma, 1989-91. Contbr. articles to profl. jours. Chmn. bd. First Christian Ch., Tullahoma, 1989. Decorated Silver Star Legion of Merit, D.F.C. with bronze oak leaf cluster, Air medal (8), Meritorious Svc. Medal, Air Force Commendation Medal. Fellow AIAA (assoc.); mem. Am. Nuclear Soc., Am. Phys. Soc., Am. Soc. for Engring. Edn., Tenn. Conf. Grad. Schs. (pres. 1989-90), Sigma Xi. Presbyterian. Avocations: flying, tennis, golf. Home: 536 Milano Rd Kissimmee FL 34759-4052

ROBERSON, CAROLYN A., counseling administrator; b. McComb, Miss., Jan. 12, 1950; d. Vernon and Christine (Alexander) Williams; m. Sylvester Roberson, June 17, 1975; 1 child, Carol Syleste. BS, Abilene Christian U., 1972; MS with honors, Chgo. State U., 1978, MS in Guidance and Counseling, 1987; PhD, Loyola U., Chgo., 1993. Cert. spl. educator, bus. eucator, phys. edn. instr., elem. counselor Ill. Tchr. phys. edn. and health Waukegan (Ill.) Sch. Dist., 1972—75; phys. edn. coord., asst. activities dir. Hamlin House, Chgo., 1975—76; mental health therapist Ridgeway Hosp., Chgo., 1976—77; adaptive phys. tchr. phys. therapy dept. Spalding H.S., Chgo., 1977—78; tchr. emotionally and mentally handicapped Blue Island (Ill.) Sch. Dist., 1978—79; tchr. emotionally disturbed Ray Graham Assn., Des Plaines, Ill., 1980; tchr. EMH, TMH, phys. edn., health Spalding H.S., Chgo., 1980—, learning disability dept. chair, 1997—2000, acting asst. prin. in charge of discipline, 1983—84, discipline counselor, 1984—85, sch. disciplinarian, Phys. Edn. dept., 1985—86; from tchr. handicapped to guidance counselor H.S. Chgo. Bd. Edn., 1985—2004, guidance counselor H.S., 2004—. Grantee tchg. sci. to handicapped, U. Chgo., 1984—85. Mem.: NAACP, Ill. Assn. Health, Phys. Edn. and Recreation, Coun. Exceptional Children, Am. Assn. Counseling and Devel., Coun. Basic Edn., Assn. Supervision and Curriculum Devel., Phi Delta Kappa. Church Of Christ. Office: Kelly High School 4136 S California Chicago IL 60632 Home: PO Box 289268 Chicago IL 60628 Office Phone: 773-535-4900 ext. 7325. Personal E-mail: doccal@hotmail.com. Business E-Mail: caroberson@cps.edu.

ROBERSON, DAWNLEE, engineering educator; b. Tex. d. Roberson and Marschino. PhD, U. Tex., Austin, 1998. Asst. prof. U. Tex., San Antonio, 2001—. Vice chair IEEE Ctrl. Tex. Sect., San Antonio. Mem.: IEEE. Office: Univ Tex 1 UTSA Cir San Antonio TX 78249 Business E-Mail: dawnlee.roberson@utsa.edu.

ROBERSON, JAMES O., foundation executive; m. Rita Quinn; children: Melanie Merrill, Sharyl, James Jr., Trisha, Joel. AB in Journalism, Baylor U., 1956; student Indsl. Devel. Inst., U. Okla.; student Inst. Orgnl. Mgmt., U. Houston. Cert. econ. developer. Dir. info. West Tex. C. of C., Abilene, 1956-59; area devel. mgr. Mo.-Kans.-Tex. R.R., 1959-63; exec. dir. Albuquerque Indsl. Devel. Svc., 1963-65; dir. N.Mex. Dept. Devel., Santa Fe, 1965-69; mgr. Forward Metro Denver, 1969-72; dir. R.I. Dept. Econ. Devel., Providence, 1972-77; v.p., dir. new bus. devel. Howard Rsch. and Devel. Corp. subs. Rouse Co., Columbia, Md., 1977-79; sec. Md. Dept. Econ. and Community Devel., Annapolis, 1979-83; pres. Louisville C. of C., 1983-88; pres., CEO Rsch. Triangle Found. N.C., 1988—. Chmn. bd. dirs. Charlotte br. Fed. Res. Bank Richmond; cons., speaker in field. Editor West Tex. Today mag., 1956-59. Trustee, vice chmn. Wake Tech. C.C.; bd. dirs. N.C. Biotech. Ctr. Fellow Am. Econ. Devel. Coun. (past chmn.); mem. Indsl. Devel. Rsch. Coun., Nat. Assn. State Devel. Agys. (past pres.), Assn. Univ. Related Rsch. Parks (pres.).

ROBERSON, JANET, registrar; MBA, Averett U., Danville, Va., 1999. Cert. in mastery in prior learning assessment CAEL, 2001. Dir. ideal program Averett U., 1995—2005, registrar, 2008—. Bd. mem. Adult Edn. (GED) Bd., Danville, Va., 1997—2008. Mem.: AACIS, NCTE. Office: Averett Univ 420 W Main St Danville VA 24541 Business E-Mail: roberson@averett.edu.

ROBERSON, MICHAEL LEE, lawyer; b. Cleve., July 28, 1955; s. Arden E. and Alice Frances Roberson; m. Mary Christy Roberson, Dec. 20, 1980; children: Ty Michael, Lee Arden, Will Cotter. BA, Ohio No. U., Ada, 1977; MS, U. Tenn., Knoxville, 1980; JD, Wake Forest U., Winston-Salem, NC, 1983. Bar: Ohio 1984. Residence hall dir. U. Tenn., Knoxville, 1977—78; asst. dir. admissions Ohio No. U., Ada, 1978—80; atty. Bloom & Green LPA, Cin., 1986—89; sr. corp. counsel Owens Corning Fiberglass, Toledo, 1989—93; asst. gen. counsel Carlisle Co. Inc., Syracuse, NY, 1993—. Mem. parish coun. Immaculate Conceptions Cath. Ch., Fayetteville, 1996—; pres. Ohio No. U. Alumni Assn., 1990—95; dir. and pres. Fayetteville-Manlius Youth Lacrosse, NY, 1995—; bd. dir. Boys & Girls Club Ctrl. N.Y., Syracuse, 2000—06. Lt. comdr. JAG USN, 1983—86. Mem.: ABA, Ohio Bar Assn., Corp. Counsel Assn. Independent. Roman Catholic. Home: 111 Old Farm Rd Fayetteville NY 13066 Office: Carlisle Co Inc 250 S Clinton St Syracuse NY 13202 Office Phone: 315-477-9107. Office Fax: 315-474-2008. E-mail: mroberson@carlisle.com.

ROBERSON, ROBERT S., investment company executive; b. Mt. Kisco, NY, 1942; m. Barbara Drane, 1967; children: Elizabeth de V., Merritt B., Barbara D. BS, NYU, 1964; Postgrad., NYU Grad. Sch. Bus. Adminstrn., 1964; postgrad., Wash. & Lee U. Law Sch., 1966; MBA, Coll. William and Mary, 1973. Various positions in fin. and bldg. industries, 1964—67; mem. NY Produce Exchange, 1965—66; with Weaver Bros., Inc., Newport News, Va., 1967—, now pres., dir.; bd. dirs. First Peninsula Bank & Trust Co., Hampton, Va., 1977—78. Former dir. Peninsula unit Am. Cancer Soc., Newport News; former dir. Heritage Coun. Girl Scouts USA, Hampton; former trustee Newport News Pub. Libr., former trustee Va. Living Mus., Newport News; former trustee, chmn. com. on devel. Hampton Roads Acad., Newport News; former mem. bd. visitors to George Washington's Mt. Vernon Nat. Shrine; hon. dep. chief NYC Fire Dept.; trustee, pres., chief curator Golf Mus., Newport News; former commr. chmn. Newport News Arts Commn.; former trustee pres. Va. War Mus. Found., Newport News; former mem. bd. visitors, mem. exec. com., chmn. com. on devel. and alumni affairs Coll. William and Mary, Williamsburg, Va.; trustee, former vice chmn. NY Geneal. and Biog. Soc., NYC; former mem. bd. visitors, mem. exec. com. Richard Bland Coll., Petersburg, Va. Decorated officer Order of St. John (England); recipient Patrick Henry award Commonwealth of Va., 2001. Mem. Newcomen Soc. US, Hon. Fire Officers Assn., US Golf Assn. (former nat. com. mem. mus. and libr.), Gen. Soc. Colonial Wars, St. Nicholas Soc. City NY, Colonial Order Acorn, Sovereign Mil. Order Temple of Jerusalem (knight comdr.), Squadron A Assn., Pilgrims US/UK, Union Club, The Brook (libr. and arts com.), Church Club (NYC), Southampton Club (NY), Farmington Country Club (Charlottesville, Va.), Cypher Soc. of William and Mary (exec. com.), James River Country Club, Hampton Roads German Club (past pres.), Hampton Roads Assembly, The Hundred Club (Newport News, Va.), NY Yacht Club (libr. com.), Fishers Island Yacht Club (NY), Rotary Internat. (Paul Harris fellow), Blue Key, Delta Sigma Pi. Republican. Episcopalian. Home: PO Box 3 Williamsburg VA 23187-0003

ROBERT, BATES D., archaeologist, educator; s. Gary D. and Julia May Bates. AS, Pacific Union Coll., Angwin, Calif., 1985; BA, Loma Linda U., Calif., 1987, MA, 1990; PhD, Andrews U., Berrien Springs, Mich., 2004. Tchr. San Francisco Jr. Acad., 1990—92, Mesa Grande Acad., Calimesa, Calif., 1992—94, Golden Gate Acad., Oakland, Calif., 1994—98; asst. to dir. publs. Andrews U., Berrien Springs, Calif., 1999—2005; postdoc. rschr. U. Chgo., 2004—06; asst. prof. nr. east archaeology and history antiquity La Sierra U., Riverside, Calif., 2006—. Book rev. editor Nr. East Archeol. Soc. Bull., Berrien Springs, Mich., 2001—; adminstrv. dir. Madaba Plains Project, Umayri, Riverside, Calif., 2006—08. Mem.: Adventist Soc. Religious Studies, Egyptian Antiquities Soc., Am. Rsch. Ctr. Egypt, Am. Schs. Oriental Rsch., Soc. Bibl. Lit., Nr. East Archaeology Soc. Office: La Sierra Univ 4500 Riverwalk Pky Riverside CA 92515 Business E-Mail: rbates@lasierra.edu.

ROBERT, HERFKENS JOHN, medical educator; married. MD, Loyola Stritch Sch. Medicine, Maywood, Ill. Diplomate in nuc. medine Am. Bd. Radiology, 1980. Prof. Stanford U., Calif., 1989—. Fellow: Internat. Soc. Magnetic Resonance. Office: Stanford Univ Lucas MR Ctr P263 Stanford CA 94305

ROBERT, JACKSON L., education professor, literature and language professor; b. Ames, Iowa, July 9, 1968; s. Jerry Jackson and Linda Lundquist; m. Heidi Schaefer, Aug. 7, 1993; children: Anna Jackson, Zachary Jackson, Wesley Jackson, Gabriel Jackson. PhD in Edn., Fla. State U., Tallahassee, 1999. Asst. dir., CIES Fla. State U., 1995—99; dir. haggerty ELP SUNY, New Paltz, 1999—2001; assoc. prof. english & edn. King's Coll., NY, 2001—. Mem.: Nat. Assn. Scholars, Intercollegiate Studies Inst. Office: King's Coll 350 5th Ave Ste 1500 New York NY 10118 Business E-Mail: rjackson@tkc.edu.

ROBERTO, J. PETER, state agency administrator; ACSW. Dir. Dept. Mental Health and Substance Abuse, Guam; spl. asst. health initiatives and policies Office the Lt. Gov., Guam, 2007; dep. dir. Dept. Health and Social Services, Guam, dir., 2008—. Office: Dept Pub Health & Social Services 123 Chalan Kareta Rt 10 Mangilao GU 96923 Office Phone: 671-735-7102. Office Fax: 671-734-5910.*

ROBERTS, ANDREW C., air transportation executive; married; 2 children. Grad. with honors in Engring. Prodn., U. Birmingham, Eng.; grad. in Mfg., Coventry City Poly., Eng. Various engr. and maintenance positions Lucas Industries; gen. mgr. engine repair Aviall, Inc., Dallas; gen. mgr. Columbus engine ctr. Pratt & Whitney, Columbus, Ga.; mng. dir. Mpls./St. Paul engine ops. Northwest Airlines Corp., 1997, v.p. materials mgmt. ops., sr. v.p. tech. ops., 2001—04, exec. v.p. ops., 2004—. Chmn. bd. Aeroxchange. Bd. mem. Spl. Olympics Minn. Office: Northwest Airlines Corp 2700 Lone Oak Pky Eagan MN 55121 Office Phone: 612-726-2111.

ROBERTS, BILL GLEN, retired protective services official; b. Deport, Tex., June 2, 1938; s. Samuel Westbrook and Ann Lee (Rhodes) R.; m. Ramona Ryall, June 1, 1963 (dec. Nov. 1988); 1 child, Renee Ann; m. Johana R. Caines, Oct. 14, 2000. Student, So. Meth. U., 1968, North Tex. State U., 1974; grad. paramedic course, U. Tex. Southwestern Med. Sch., 1974; grad. Exec. Program for Fire Service, Tex. A&M U., 1978; AAS, El Centro Jr. Coll., Dallas, 1980; grad. exec. fire officer program, Nat. Fire Acad., 1989. With Dallas Fire Dept., 1958-82, lt., 1964-67, capt., 1967-71, div. fire chief, 1971-79, asst. fire chief, 1979-83; fire chief Austin (Tex.) Fire Dept., 1983-94. Tech. bd. dirs. Found. Fire Safety, Washington, 1982-85; adj. faculty Nat. Fire Acad., 1981-86; aft. State Life of Indpls., Dallas, 1962; owner Personnel Testing Lab., Dallas, 1963; real estate salesman Dale Copus Realtor, Dallas, 1963-66; salesman intercommunications equipment Chandler Sound, Dallas, 1966-67; field engr. IBM Corp., Dallas, 1968; cons. U. Tenn., 1974, Ga. Inst. Tech., 1974, Tex. Dept. Health Resources, 1973-78, Rand Corp., Washington, Mission Rsch., Santa Barbara, Calif., Macro Author: EMS Dallas, 1978; (with others) Anesthesia for Surgery Trauma, 1976, EMS Measures to Improve Care, 1980; contbr. articles to periodicals. Com. chmn. Dallas Jaycees, 1962-65; mem. task force Am. Heart Assn., Austin, 1973-83; bd. dirs. Brackenridge Hosp., 1989, Rehab. Hosp. Austin, 1992-94, Austin Police Pensions Bd., 1989, Capitol Area coun. Boy Scouts Am., 1989-92. Recipient John Stemmons Service award Dallas Fire Dept., 1979; Internat. Assn. Fire Chiefs scholar, 1967. Mem. Internat. Assn. Fire Chiefs, Am. Heart Assn., North Tex. Coun. of Govts. (regional emergency svc. adv. coun. 1973-79), Found. Fire Safety (tech. bd. dirs. 1982-85), Tex. Assn. Realtors, Rotary. Methodist. Home: 192 Hunter's Ridge Rd Canton NC 28716 Office Phone: 828-648-4345. E-mail: bglenrob@aol.com.

ROBERTS, BRIAN L., communications executive; b. Phila., June 28, 1959; s. Ralph J. and Suzanne F. Roberts; m. Aileen Kennedy, Dec. 28, 1985; children: Sarah, Tucker, Amanda. BS, U. Pa., 1981. V.p. ops. Comcast Cable Communications, Inc., Phila., 1985-86; exec. v.p. Comcast Corp., 1986-92, pres., 1992—97, pres., CEO, 1997—2004, chmn., pres., CEO, 2004—. Bd. dirs. The Bank of NY; bd. trustees Simon Wiesenthal Ctr.; founding co-chair Phila. 2000; dir., exec. com. CableLabs, 1999, now chmn. bd. dir. Vice chmn. The Walter Katz Found. Recipient Steven J. Ross Humanitarian award, UJA Fedn NY, 2003, Humanitarian Award, Simon Wiesenthal Ctr., 2004; named one of Am. Top CEOs, Inst. Investor mag., 2004—07, The Most Influential People in the World of Sports, Bus. Week, 2007; named to Cable TV Hall of Fame, 2006. Mem.: Nat. Cable & Telecommunications Assn. (chmn. 1995—96, 2005—). Avocation: squash (All-American, silver medal with U.S. team 1981, 85 and 97). Office: Comcast Corp Fl 35 East Twr 1500 Market St Fl 33 Philadelphia PA 19102-2100*

ROBERTS, BRONWYN L., lawyer; b. Boston, Feb. 14, 1971; BS, Tufts U., 1993; JD cum laude, Suffolk U., 1997. Bar: Mass. 1997, NH, US Dist. Ct. (Dist. Mass.), US Ct. Appeals (1st Cir.). Assoc. Lane Altman & Owens LLP, Boston, 1997—2000, Duane Morris LLP, Boston, 2000—06, ptnr., 2007—. Spkr. in field. Contbr. articles to law jours. Mem.: ABA, Women's Bar Assn. of Mass., Boston Bar Assn. (labor and employment law sect., comml. litig. sect.). Office: Duane Morris LLP Ste 500 470 Atlantic Ave Boston MA 02210 Office Phone: 857-488-4218. Office Fax: 857-401-3019. E-mail: BLRoberts@duanemorris.com.*

ROBERTS, BURTON BENNETT, lawyer, retired judge; b. NYC, July 25, 1922; s. Alfred S. and Cecelia (Schanfein) R.; m. Gerhild Ukryn. BA, NYU, 1943, LL.M., 1953; LL.B., Cornell U., 1949. Bar: NY 1949. Asst. dist. atty., New York County, 1949-66; chief asst. dist. atty. Bronx County, Bronx, NY, 1966-68, acting dist. atty., 1968-69, dist. atty., 1969-72; justice Supreme Ct. State NY, 1973-98, adminstrv. judge criminal br. Bronx County 12th Jud. Dist., 1984-98, adminstrv. judge civil br. Bronx County 12th Dist., 1988-98; ret., 1998; counsel Fischbein, Badillo, Wagner & Harding, 1999—2005, Dreier LLP, 2005—. Pres. Bronx div. Hebrew Home for Aged, 1967-72. With US Army, 1943-45. Decorated Purple Heart, Bronze Star with oak leaf cluster, Combat Infantry badge Mem. Assn. Bar City NY, Am. Bar Assn., NY Bar Assn., Bronx County Bar Assn., NY State Dist. Attys. Assn. (pres. 1971-72) Jewish (exec. bd. temple). Home: 215 E 68th St Apt 19A New York NY 10021-5727 Office: Dreier LLP 499 Park Ave New York NY 10022 Business E-Mail: broberts@dreierllp.com.

ROBERTS, CARL GEOFFREY, lawyer; b. Boston, June 17, 1948; s. Simon Matthew and Ruth (Gorfinkle) Roberts; m. Sharon Ash, Mar. 24, 1979 (div. June 19, 2002); 1 child, Dennis; m. Susan Busch, Dec. 28, 2002. BA, Harvard U., 1970; JD, U. Pa., 1974. Bar: Pa. 1974, U.S. Dist. Ct. (ea. dist.) Pa. 1974, U.S. Ct. Appeals (3d cir.) 1978, U.S. Supreme Ct. 1980, U.S. Ct. Claims 1980, U.S. Dist. Ct. (mid. dist.) Pa. 1986. Law clk. U.S. Dist. Ct. (ea. dist.) Pa., Phila., 1974-76; assoc. Dilworth, Paxson, Kalish & Kauffman, Phila., 1978-82, ptnr., 1982-92, Ballard, Spahr, Andrews & Ingersoll, Phila., 1992—. Bd. dirs. Phila. Chamber Ensemble, sec., 1977-92, pres., 1992-95; mem. Hillel com. U. Pa., 1999—, chair 2001-05; bd. dirs. Hillel of Greater Phila., 2000-06. Mem.: ABA (law practice mgmt. sect. sec. 2002—03, vice chmn. 2003—04, chmn.-elect 2004—05, SCOTIS 2004—07, chmn. 2005—06, SCOTIS 2008—), Phila. Bar Assn. (bd. govs. 2007, co-chair law practice mgmt. divsn. 2007). Office: Ballard Spahr Andrews & Ingersoll 1735 Market St Fl 51 Philadelphia PA 19103-7599 Office Phone: 215-864-8120. Business E-Mail: cgroberts@ballardspahr.com.

ROBERTS, CECIL EDWARD, JR., labor union administrator; b. Oct. 31, 1946; s. Cecil Edward and Evelyn Roberts; m. Carolyn Sue Stewart; children: Kyle Edward, Melissa Dawn. Grad., W.Va. Tech. Coll., 1987; HHD (hon.), W.Va. U. Tech. Gen. inside laborer, shuttle car operator, unitrack operator, greaser, beltman & mechanic Carbon Fuels Mine, Winifred, W.Va., 1971—77; v.p. dist. 17 United Mine Workers of America (UMWA), 1977—82, v.p. UMWA, 1982—95, pres., 1995—. Mem. Com. Employer Support Vet. Employment, 1985—86; pres. Nat. Coun. Holmes Safety Assn., 1985; mem. W. Va. Employment Opportunities & Econ. Devel. Commn.; mem. exec. coun. AFL-CIO, 2001—, apptd. exec. com., 2005. Gen. v.p. Nat. Coun. Sr. Citizens; mem. adv. bd. W.Va. U. Inst. Labor Studies & Rsch., 1996; mem. adv. com. Black Lung Prog.; bd. dirs. Am. Income Life Ins. Co., Cabin Creek Clinic, W.Va., Blue Cross Blue Shield So. W.Va. With US Army, 1966—67, Vietnam. Recipient Martin Luther King award, Rainbow Coalition. Mem.: Vietnam Vets. of America, Am. Legion, VFW (life). Office: UMWA 8315 Lee Hwy Fairfax VA 22031-2215 Office Phone: 703-208-7200.*

ROBERTS, CELIA ANN, librarian; b. Bangor, Maine, Feb. 6, 1935; d. William Lewis and Ruey Pearl (Logan) Roberts. AA, U. Hartford, 1957, BA, 1961; postgrad., So. Conn. State Coll., 1963—. With catalog, acquisition and circulation depts. U. Hartford Libr., 1956-65; libr. Simsbury Free Libr., Simsbury, Conn., 1965-69; reference libr. Simsbury Pub. Libr., 1969—. Tchr. ballet, 1965—66; tchr. genealogy, 1977—; ballet mistress Ballet Soc. Conn., Inc., 1968—70; with corps de ballet Conn. Opera Assn., 1963—64; active in prodns. Simsbury Light Opera Assn., 1964—69. Contbr. articles to profl. jours. Vol. Family History Ctr., 1970—. Mem.: DAR (Abigail Phelps chpt. regent 2007—), AAUW (past pres. Greater Hartford br.), ALA, Simsbury Hist. Soc., Conn. Libr. Assn., Denison Soc., Inc., Daus. of Scotia, Simsbury Geneal. and Hist. Rsch. Libr., Chateauguay Valley Hist. Soc., New Brunswick Geneal. Soc., Conn. Hist. Soc., Dance Masters Am. (Conn. Dance Tchrs. Club chpt.), Soc. Mayflower Descs. Conn., Conn. Soc. Genealogists (registrar Hartford 1983), Pro Dance, New Eng. Historic Geneal. Soc., Ont. Geneal. Soc. Unitarian Universalist. Office: Simsbury Public Libr 725 Hopmeadow St Simsbury CT 06070-2243 Business E-Mail: croberts@simsburylibrary.info.

ROBERTS, CHARLES MURRAY, retired publishing executive, writer; b. New Haven, Conn., Mar. 30, 1937; s. Samuel S. and Bertha L. Roberts; m. Sally Miller, June 19, 1960; children: Susan Hilary, Julie Handel. BA, U. Pa., 1958. V.p. field sales dir. western region Simon & Schuster, NYC, 1960—2002; pres. Author Escort & Media Svcs., Houston, 2002—. PBR Mag. Bd. trustees Congregation Beth Israel, Houston, 1972—74. With Air N.G., 1961—64. Mem.: Houston Forum. Avocations: tennis, travel, walking. Home: 49 Briar Hollow Ln #1002 Houston TX 77027 Home Fax: 713-572-5785. Personal E-mail: charles@authortours.net.

ROBERTS, CHARLES PATRICK (PAT ROBERTS), United States Senator from Kansas; b. Topeka, Kans., Apr. 20, 1936; m. Frankie Fann, 1969; children: David, Ashleigh, Anne-Wesley. BA in Journalism, Kans. State U., 1958. Pub. Litchfield Park, Ariz., 1962-67; adminstrv. asst. to U.S. Senator Frank Carlson, U.S. Senate, Washington, 1967-68; adminstrv. asst. to U.S. Congressman Keith Sebelius U.S. House Reps., Washington, 1968-80; mem. 97th to 104th Congresses from Kans. 1st Dist., Washington, 1980-96; US Senator from Kansas, 1997—. Com. agr. US Senate, com. armed services, com. health, edn., labor and pensions, select com. ethics, chmn. select com. intelligence. Served with USMC, 1958—62. Recipient Am. Farmer award, Future Farmers of Am., 1986, Disting. Leadership award, Prodn. Credit Assn., Disting. Svc. award, Kans. Farm Bur., Wheat Man of Yr., Assn. Wheat Growers, 1993, Public Svc. award, Am. Chem. Soc., 2001, John H. Chafee award public svc., Rep. Main Street Partnership, 2003. Republican. Methodist. Office: US Senate 109 Hart Senate Off Bldg Washington DC 20510-1605 also: District Office Ste 203 100 Military Plz Dodge City KS 67801 Office Phone: 202-224-4774, 620-227-2244. Office Fax: 202-224-3514, 620-227-2264. E-mail: pat_roberts@roberts.senate.gov.*

ROBERTS, CHARLES STEWART, surgeon; b. Washington, June 23, 1960; s. William Clifford and Carey Cansler Roberts; m. Mary Lydia Warren, July 11, 1997; children: Amelia, Carey Camille, William Warren, Charles Stewart Roberts II; m. Pamela Jo Yadro, July 1, 1988 (div. Apr. 13, 1994). BA, Vanderbilt U., Nashville, 1981; MD, Emory U., Atlanta, 1986. Cert. in surgery Am. Bd. Surgery, 1994, in thoracic surgery Am. Bd. Thoracic Surgery, 1997. Sect. chair, thoracic and cardiovasc. surgery Winchester Med. Ctr., Valley Health, Va., 2004—. Author: (biography) Life and Writings of Stewart R. Roberts, MD: Georgia's First Heart Specialist, (poetry book) An Olive Branch for the Conquered, Stoking The Fire: A Surgical Memoir of London. Fellow: ACS; mem.: Soc. Thoracic Surgeons, Am. Osler Soc., Nat. Honor Soc., Kappa Alpha Order. R-Conservative. Protestant Episcopal. Avocations: book collecting, geneology. Office: Winchester Med Ctr Valley Health Suite 410 190 Campus Boulevard Winchester VA 22601 Office Fax: 540-536-6724. Personal E-mail: csrwinchester@hotmail.com.

ROBERTS, CHRISTOPHER WAYNE, psychologist, educational consultant; b. Richmond, Va., June 5, 1974; s. Eddie Donald and Patricia Walker Roberts; m. Robin Lee Reinert, Aug. 14, 2005; 1 child, Tatum Grace. BS in Psychology cum laude, Va. Poly. Inst. and State U., 1996; MS in Psychology, Radford U., Va., 1998, EdS in Sch. Psychology, 1999; postgrad., Ariz. State U., 2002—. Nat. cert. sch. psychologist, cert. sch. psychologist Ariz. Dept. Edn., Calif. Dept. Edn., NC Dept. Edn., Va. Dept. Edn. Tchr. The Children's Ho., Chesterfield, Va., 1991—96; svc. provider New River Valley Cmty. Svcs., Radford, 1996—98; sch. psychologist Cumberland County Pub. Schs., Fayetteville, NC, 1998—2000; psychologist, diagnostician Piedmont Psychol. Svcs., Farmville, Va., 2000—01; sch. psychologist Dept. Correctional Edn., Richmond, 2001—02; contract sch. psychologist Phoenix 1 Elem. Sch. Dist., 2002—, Whittier Area Coop. Spl. Edn. Program, Calif., 2002—, Balsz Elem. Sch. Dist., Phoenix, 2004—05, Ariz. Dept. Juvenile Corrections, Phoenix, 2004—; pres. Valley Ednl. Specialists, Phoenix, 2004—. Camp counselor, svc. provider Camp Baker, Chesterfield, Va., 1995—96; substitute tchr. Montgomery County Pub. Schs., Christiansburg, Va., 1996—97, Chesterfield County Pub. Schs., 2000; intern Montgomery County Pub. Schs., 1997—98; mem. local arrangements com. 19th Internat. Conf. on Learning Disabilities, Washington, 1997; grad. counselor Disability Resource Office, Radford U., 1997—98; adj. prof. gen. psychology, developmental psychology and behavior modification Fayetteville Tech. CC, 1998—2000; evaluator Maricopa County Juvenile Probation/Vocat. Rehab. Program, Ariz. State U., Phoenix, 2002, 03; mem. conf. com. 26th Ann. Conf. on Severe Behavior Disorders of Children and Youth, Tempe, Ariz., 2002; rsch. asst. Nat. Ctr. on Edn., Disability and Juvenile Justice, Ariz. State U., Tempe, 2002—03; intern, co-instr. Ariz. State U., 2003, instr., 2003—05; presenter in field. Recipient Tara Reilly Meml. Scholarship award, Behavioral Inst. for Children and Adolescents, 2004. Mem.: Tchr. Educators for Children with Behavior Disorders, Nat. Assn. Sch. Psychologists (nat. cert.), Coun. Exceptional Children (divsn. learning disabilities, coun. for children with behavioral disorders), Pi Lambda Phi. Avocations: racing, exercise, movies, football. Home: Valley Educational Specialists 418 E Beth Dr Phoenix AZ 85042-7661 Office Phone: 602-690-1502. Fax: 602-304-9332. E-mail: skoolpsyco@aol.com.

ROBERTS, COKIE (CORINNE BOGGS ROBERTS), newscaster; b. New Orleans, Dec. 27, 1943; d. Thomas Hale and Corinne Morrison (Claiborne) Boggs; m. Steven V. Roberts, Sept. 10, 1966; children: Lee Harriss, Rebecca Boggs. BA in Polit. Sci., Wellesley Coll., 1964; degree (hon.), Amherst Coll., Columbia Coll., Loyola U. of the South, Manhattanville Coll., Gonzaga U., Boston Coll., Hood Coll., Chestnut Hill Coll., Miss. Women's U., Notre Dame U., Duke U. Assoc. prodr., host Altman Prodns., Washington, 1964—66, prodr. LA, 1969—72; reporter, editor Cowles Comm., NYC, 1967; prodr. Sta. WNEW-TV, NYC, 1968, Sta. KNBC-TV, LA, 1972—74; reporter CBS News, Athens, Greece, 1974—77; sr. news analyst. Nat. Pub. Radio, Washington, 1977—; corr. MacNeil/Lehrer Newshour, Washington, 1984—88; spl. Washington corr. ABC News, Washington, 1988—92; interviewer, commentator This Week With David Brinkley, Washington, 1992—96; co-anchor This Week with Sam Donaldson & Cokie Roberts, 1996—2002; chief congrl. analyst ABC News, 1998—; polit. commentator, analyst ABC News, World News Tonight and other ABC News broadcasts. Lectr. in field. Co-host weekly pub. TV program on Congress The Lawmakers, 1981—84, prodr., host pub. affairs program Sta. WRC-TV, Washington; prodr.: Sta. KNBC-TV Serendipity (award for excellence in local programming, Emmy nomination for children's programming); author: We Are Our Mother's Daughters, 1998, Founding Mothers: The Women Who Raised Our Nation, 2004; contbr. articles to newspapers, mags.; writer of a weekly column along with husband for newspapers around the country by United Media; contbg. editor (with husband): USA Magazine; co-author: From this Day Forward. Bd. dir. Presidential Commn. on Service and Civic Participation, Dirksen Ctr., Pekin, Ill., 1988—95, Fgn. Students Svc. Ctr., Washington, 1990—, Manhattanville Coll., Purchase, NY, 1991—99, Children's Inn at NIH, Bethesda, Md., 1992—. Recipient Broadcast award, Nat. Orgn. Working Women, 1984, Disting. Alumnae Achievement award, Wellesley Coll., 1985, Everett McKinley Dirksen disting. reporting of Congress award, 1987, Weintal award, Georgetown U., 1987, Corp. Pub. Broadcasting award, 1988, Edward R. Murrow award, 1990, Broadcast award, Nat. Women's Polit. Caucus, 1990, David Brinkley Comm. award, 1991, Mother of Yr. award, Nat. Mother's Day Com., 1992, Emmy award for news and documentary, 1991; named one of 50 Greatest Women in the History of Broadcasting, Am. Women in Radio & TV; named to Broadcasting Hall of Fame, Cable Hall of Fame. Mem.: Radio-TV Corrs. Assn. (pres. 1981—82, bd. dirs. 1980—94), US Capitol Hist. Soc. Roman Catholic. Mailing: 1717 DeSales St NW Washington DC 20036*

ROBERTS, CRAIG A., legislative staff member; b. Alton, Ill., 1962; BA, Western Ill. U., Macomb, 1984. Staff dir., rep. staff issues devel. Ill. State House Rep., 1985—90; asst. Office of Lt. Gov. State of Ill., 1990; exec. asst. programs & policy devel. Ill. Sec. of State, 1991—96; chief of staff for Rep. John Shimkus US House of Reps., 1997—. Co-author: Almanac of Illinois Politics, 1990, 1992, 1994, 1996. Mem.: House Chiefs Staff Assn. (region 4 rep.), Sigma Pi. Office: Office of Congressman John Shimkus 2452 Rayburn House Office Bldg Washington DC 20515 Office Phone: 202-225-5271. Business E-Mail: craig.roberts@mail.house.gov.*

ROBERTS, DAVID A., manufacturing executive; b. Dec. 8, 1947; m. Susan Roberts; 2 children. BS, Purdue Univ., 1974; MBA, Indiana Univ., 1978. Mgmt. positions Budd Co., Detroit, 1969—83; v.p., gen. mgr. Pitney Bowes, Stamford, Conn., 1983—93; div. gen. mgr. FMC Corp., Chgo., 1993—95; pres. AM Internat., Mt. Prospect, Ill., 1995—96; group v.p. Marmon Group, Chgo., 1996—2001; pres., CEO Graco Inc., Mpls., 2001—07, chmn., 2006—07; chmn., pres., CEO Carlisle Companies Inc., Charlotte, NC, 2007—. Bd. dir. Franklin Elec. Co., Arctic Cat Inc. Served USMC, 1967—69. Office: Carlisle Companies Inc Ste 400 13925 Ballantyne Corp Pl Charlotte NC 28277

ROBERTS, DAVID E., JR., oil industry executive; BS in Min. Engring., Univ. Alabama, Tuscaloosa, Ala. Engr., oil and gas ops. Texaco No. Am., 1983—96, regional mgr., 1997, dir. strategic mgmt., worldwide ops., 1999—2001; adv. to vice-chmn. Chevron Texaco Corp., 2001—03; exec. v.p., mng. dir. BG Group, 2003—06; sr. v.p. bus. devel. Marathon Oil Corp., Houston, exec. v.p. upstream, 2008—. Office: Marathon Oil Co 5555 San Felipe St Houston TX 77056*

ROBERTS, DAVID GLEN, prospector, investor, ceo; b. Plainview, Tex., Feb. 8, 1952; s. Doris Glen and Anna Grace (Mathis) R. Student, Tex. A&M U., 1970-71, Dallas Bapt. Coll., 1971-75; BA in Comm., U. Tex. Permian Basin, 1987. Lic. minister Bapt. Ch.; cert. profl. landman. Profl. stuntman, actor, 1972-76; mgr. Channel 100, Midland, Tex., 1976-78; pub., owner Basin Voice newspaper, 1987—; owner Diamond Developers Fire and Enviro-Safety Co., Midland, 1989—; regional mktg. dir. Nochar Inc.-Region 11, Midland, Tex., 1990-96; owner D.G. Roberts Land Mgmt., Midland, Tex., 1978—2004; CEO Heart of Tex. Quik Internet., Inc., 2004—07, Permian Basin Diamond Developers, Inc., 2006—07, Skelly Oil and Land Co., Inc., 2006—; mng. ptnr. Dutch's Pumpjack Svc., LLC, 2008—. Cons. EPA, Indpls., 1991—. Appeared in film Giovanni & Ben, 1974, Drive In, 1976; theatre appearance at Globe Theatre, Odessa, Tex., 1975, Shakespeare in the Park, Dallas, 1976. Past chair Midland County Libertarian Party; past mem. exec. com. Dist. 31 Tex. Libertarian Party; organizer Sons of Liberty, Midland, 1990—; candidate US Congress Dist. 21, Tex., 2002. Mem. Am. Assn. Petroleum-Landmen (cert. Prof. Landman by Am. Assn. Petroleum-Landmen), Five Aces, MC, NRA, Tex. State Rifle Assn., Permian Basin Landman's Assn., Denver Petroleum Landman's Assn., Houston Petroleum Landman's Assn, N.O.R.M.L., Rep. Nat. Com. (libertarian), Harley Owner's Group, Danver Assn. Pet. Landmen, Houston Assn. Pet. Landmen, Marijuana Policy Project, Col. Commemorative AF (life). Avocations: golf, motorcycling, travel, shooting, poker. Home Phone: 432-897-4788; Office Phone: 432-520-0012, 432-230-8423. Business E-Mail: dgroberts@skellyoil.com.

ROBERTS, DENNIS WILLIAM, retired construction executive; b. Chgo., Jan. 7, 1943; s. William Owen and Florence Harriet (Denman) R. BA in Journalism, U. N.Mex., 1968; MA in Legal Studies, Antioch U., 1982; MA, St. John's Coll., 1984. Gen. assignment reporter Albuquerque Pub. Co., 1964, sports writer, 1960-64, advt. and display salesman, 1967-68; dir. info. N.Mex. bldg. br. Asso. Gen. Contractors Am., Albuquerque, 1968-79, asst. exec. dir., 1979-82, dir., 1982—2008. Adj. prof. civil engring. U. N.Mex., 2004—. Active United Way, Albuquerque, 1969-78; chmn. Albuquerque Crime Prevention Coun., 1982; bd. dirs. Rio Grande chpt. ARC, 1992-95, Albuquerque Lit. Coun., 1998-2004, Luth. Campus Ministry, U. N.Mex., 2003-08; mem. cmty. adv. coun. Albuquerque Jobs Corps. Recipient Pub. Rels. Achievement award Assoc. Gen. Contractors Am., 1975, 78. Mem. N.Mex. Pub. Rels. Conf. (chmn. 1975, 82-83), Pub. Rels. Soc. Am. (accredited, pres. N.Mex. chpt. 1981, chmn. S.W. dist. 1984, chmn. sect. 1988), Constrn. Specifications Inst. (Outstanding Industry Mem. 1974, Outstanding Com. Chmn. 1978), Am. Soc. Safety Engrs., Toastmasters Club (dist. gov. 1977-78, Disting. Dist. award 1978, Toastmaster of Yr. 1979-80), Masons, Shriners, Sigma Delta Chi (pres. N.Mex. chpt. 1969). Republican. Lutheran. Office: Assn Gen Contractors 1615 University Blvd NE Albuquerque NM 87102-1717 Home: Apt 1-B 3700 Aspan Ave NE Albuquerque NM 87110 Office Phone: 505-974-6838. Personal E-mail: dennisroberts3708@comcast.net. Business E-Mail: dennisr@agcnm.org. *Personal philosophy: Set your priorities in life, then your goals. In pursuing your goals, visualize their accomplishment. Be persistent, and you will accomplish what you set out to accomplish. Learn to be fair to others and empathetic.*

ROBERTS, SIR DENYS (TUDOR EMIL), judge; b. London, Jan. 19, 1923; s. William David and Dorothy Elizabeth (Morrison) R.; m. Brenda Marsh, Jan. 1, 1949 (div. July 1973); children: Nigel Charles Emil, Amanda Karen Patricia; m. Fiona Alexander, Feb. 20, 1985; 1 child, Henry David Alexander. MA, Oxford U., 1948, BCL, 1949. Bar: London, 1950. Crown counsel, Nyasaland, 1953-59; atty. gen. Gibraltar, Hong Kong, 1960—62; solicitor gen. Hong Kong, 1962-66; atty. gen., 1966-73; chief sec., 1973-78; chief justice, 1979—88, Brunei, 1979—2001; mem. Ct. Final Appeal, Hong Kong, 1997—2003. Pres. Ct. of Appeals Bermuda, 1989-94; pres. Ct. of Appeal, Brunei, 2002-03; mem. exec. and legis. couns., Gibraltar, 1960-62, Hong Kong, 1966-78. Author of 9 books. Served to capt. Royal Arty., 1942-46. Decorated knight Order of Brit. Empire; SPMB (Sultan of Brunei); hon. fellow Wadham Coll., Oxford U.; hon. bencher Lincoln's Inn, London, pres. MCC, 1989-90. Mem. Royal Commonwealth Soc. (London). Avocations: walking, tennis, cricket, music, writing. Home: The Grange North Green Rd Pulhm St Mary Norfolk IP21 4QZ England Home Phone: 01379-608-700. E-mail: Roberts.Leithen@BTInternet.com.

ROBERTS, DONALD JOHN, economics, business professor, consultant; b. Winnipeg, Man., Can., Feb. 11, 1945; came to U.S., 1967; s. Donald Victor and Margaret Mabel R.; m. Kathleen Eleanor Taylor, Aug. 26, 1967 (dec. 2006), Jayne Marie Lange, Mar. 23, 2009. BA with honors, U. Man., 1967; PhD, U. Minn., 1972; LLD honoris causa, U. Winnipeg, 2007. Instr. dept. managerial econs. and decision scis. J.L. Kellogg Grad. Sch. Mgmt., Northwestern U., Evanston, Ill., 1971—72, asst. prof., 1972—74; assoc. prof. J. L. Kellogg Grad. Sch. Mgmt., Northwestern U., Evanston, Ill., 1974—77; prof. J.L. Kellogg Grad. Sch. Mgmt., Northwestern U., Evanston, Ill., 1977—80, Grad. Sch. Bus., Stanford (Calif.) U., 1980, Jonathan B. Lovelace prof., 1980—2001, assoc. dean, dir. rsch., 1987—90, dir. exec. program in strategy and orgn., 1992—, dir. global mgmt. program, 1994—, sr. assoc. dean, 2000—, John H. Scully prof., 2001—; dir. Ctr. for Global Bus. and the Economy, 2003—. Prof. (by courtesy) dept. econs. Stanford U., 1986—; vis. rsch. faculty U. Catholique de Louvain, Belgium, 1974-75; inaugural Clarendon lectr. mgmt. studies Oxford U., 1997; cons. bus., econs. and antitrust, 1976—; vis. fellow All Souls Coll., Oxford U., 1995, Nuffield Coll., Oxford U., 1999-00; vis. acad. fellow in leadership and orgn. McKinsey & Co., London, 1999-00. Author The Modern Firm: Organizational Design for Performance and Growth, 2004; co-author: Economics, Organization and Management, 1992; assoc. editor Jour. Econ. Theory, 1977-92, Econometrica, 1985-87, Games and Economic Behavior, 1988-; mem. edit. bd. Am. Econ. Rev., 1991-95, Jour. Econs. and Mgmt. Strategy, 1991-98, Orgns. and Markets Abstracts, 1996-; contbr. articles to profl. jours. NSF grantee, 1973-93; rsch. fellow Ctr. Ops. Rsch. and Econometrics, Heverlee, Belgium, 1974, fellow Ctr. for Advanced Study in the Behavioral Scis., 1991-92. Fellow Am. Acad. Arts and Scis., Econometric Soc. (coun. 1994-96); mem. Am. Econ. Assn., Beta Gamma Sigma. Home: 835 Santa Fe Ave Stanford CA 94305-1022 E-mail: roberts_john@gsb.stanford.edu.

ROBERTS, DORIS, actress; b. St. Louis, Nov. 4, 1930; d. Larry and Ann (Meltzer) R.; m. Michael E. Cannata, June 21, 1950; 1 child, Michael R.; m. William Goyen, Nov. 10, 1963 (dec.). Student, NYU, 1950-51; studies with, Sanford Meisner, Neighborhood Playhouse, NYC, 1952-53, Lee Strasberg, Actors' Studio, 1956. Ind. stage, screen and TV actress, 1953—. Profl. stage debut, Ann Arbor, Mich., 1953; appeared in summer stock Chatham, Mass., 1955; Broadway debut in The Time of Your Life, 1955; other Broadway and off-Broadway appearances include The Desk Set, 1955, The American Dream, 1961, The Death of Bessie Smith, 1961, The Office, 1965, The Color of Darkness, 1963, Marathon 33, 1963, Secret Affair of Mildred Wilde, 1972, Last of the Red Hot Lovers, 1969-71, Bad Habits, 1973 (Outer Circle Critics award 1974), Cheaters, 1976, Fairie Tale Theatre, 1985, The Fig Tree, 1987, It's Only a Play, 1992, Bye Bye Birdie, 2004; movie debut Something Wild, 1961, film appearances include: Barefoot in the Park, 1968, No Way to Treat a Lady, 1973, A Lovely Way to Die, 1969, Honeymoon Killers, 1969, A New Leaf, 1970, Such Good Friends, 1971, Little Murders, 1971, Heartbreak Kid, 1972, Hester Street, 1975, The Taking of Pelham, One, Two, Three, 1974, The Rose, 1979, Good Luck, Miss Wyckoff, 1979, Rabbit Test, 1979, Ordinary Hero, 1986, #1 with a Bullet, 1987, For Better or for Worse-Street Law, 1988, National Lampoon's Xmas Vacation, 1989, Used People, 1992, The Night We Never Met, Momma Mia, 1994, Walking to Waldheim, 1995, The Grass Harp, 1995, A Fish in the Bathtub, 1997, My Giant, 1998, All Over the Guy, 2001, Dickie Roberts-Child Star, 2003, Lucky 13, I Can See You.Com, Grandma's Boy, 2005; TV debut on Studio One, 1958, Mary Hartman, Mary Hartman, 1975, Mary Tyler Moore Hour, 1976, Soap, 1978-79, Angie, 1979-80, Remington Steele, 1984-88, Lily Tomlin Comedy Hour, Barney Miller, Alice, Full House, Perfect Strangers, Sunday Dinner, A Family Man, The Fig Tree (PBS), 1987, (TV films) The Story Teller, 1979, Ruby and Oswald, 1978, It Happened One Christmas, 1978, Jennifer: A Woman's Story, 1979, The Diary of Anne Frank, 1982, A Letter to Three Wives, Blind Faith, 1989, A Mom For Christmas, 1990, The Sunset Gang, 1990, Crossroads, 1993, Dream On, 1993, The Boys, 1993, A Time To Heal, 1994, A Thousand Men and a Baby, 1997, One True Love, 2000, Sons of Miseltoe, 2001, A Time to Remember (Hallmark channel) 2003, Raising Waylon, (CBS) 2003, Lucky 13, 2004, (Hallmark channel) Our House, 2005, Grandma's Boy, 2005, Keeping Up With The Sterns, 2006; (TV series) include St. Elsewhere, 1982 (Emmy award best sup. actress drama) Murder She Wrote, 1990, Step By Step, 1994, Burk's Law, 1994, Walker Texas Ranger, 1995, High Society, 1996, Everybody Loves Raymond, 1996-05 (Amer. Comedy award, 1999, Emmy award outstanding supporting actress in a comedy series, 2001, 02, 03, 05, Gracie Allen award, 2004), Law and Order, Criminal Intent, 2007. Recipient People's Choice award, 2006. Mem. SAG (Ensemble award 2002), AFTRA, Actors Equity Assn., Dirs. Guild Am.

ROBERTS, DWIGHT LOREN, engineer, writer; b. San Diego, June 3, 1949; s. James Albert and Cleva Lorraine (Conn) Roberts; m. Phyllis Ann Adair Roberts, Mar. 29, 1969; children: Aimee Renee, Michael Loren, Daniel Alexandr. BA, U. San Diego, 1976, MA, 1979. Engring. aide Benton Engring. Inc., San Diego, 1968—73; pres., subs. Robert's Tech. Research Co.; pres. Rsch. Technique Internat., 1978—; freelance writer, 1979—; owner Agrl. Analysis, 1985—88; constrn. mgr. Homestead Land Devel. Corp., 1988—92; sr. engr. cons. Morrison Knudson, 1992—95; sr. soils analyst Geotechnics, Inc., 1995—98; offsite field supt. coastal divsn. Kaufman & Broad, 1998—. Author: (book) Geological Exploration of Alaska, Alfred Hulse Brooks, Alaskan Trailblazer, Papaveraceae of the World, Arid Regions Gardening, Visions of Dame Kind: Dreams, Imagination and Reality, Antal's Theory of the Solar System, Common Ground: Similarities of the World Religions; book, Black Sheep-Scientific Discoveries From the Fringe; contbr. articles to profl. jours. Served with USAR, 1969—71. Mem.: AAAS, ASTM, Soil & Found. Engr. Assn., Nat. Inst. Cert. Engring. Techs., NY Acad. Scis., Nat. Inst. Sci., Phi Alpha Theta. Office: 3111 E Victoria Dr Alpine CA 91901-3679 *Personal philosophy: Honesty and ethical behavior at all times. Trueness of being throughout my life. Love of my wife and children makes my life worth living and is always a light when there is darkness. God watches over my shoulder.*

ROBERTS, E. F., law educator; b. 1930; m. Alice A. Dunn, July 4, 1955; children: Martha, Ernest III, Michael, Marianne. BA, Northeastern U., Boston, 1952; LL.B., Boston Coll., 1954. Bar: Mass. 1954. Asst. prof. law Villanova U., Pa., 1957-59, assoc. prof. law Pa., 1959-60, prof. law Pa., 1960-64, Cornell U., Ithaca, NY, 1964-96, Edwin H. Woodruff prof. law, emeritus prof., 1996. Vis. prof. Nottingham U., Eng., 1962-63, Harvard U., 1983. Author: Public Regulation of Title Insurance, 1960, Land Use Planning, 2d edit., 1975, Law and the Preservation of Agricultural Land, 1982, (with Broun et al) McCormick on Evidence, 6th edit., 2006. Mem. Am. Law Inst. (life). Office: Cornell U Sch Law Ithaca NY 14853 Home Phone: 607-257-6298; Office Phone: 607-255-2356. Business E-Mail: efr4@cornell.edu.

ROBERTS, EDWARD GRAHAM, librarian; s. Samuel Noble and Frances Johnson (Boykin) R.; m. Anna Jean Walker, Nov. 12, 1949; children: Galer Walker, Edward Graham, John Boykin. BA, U. South, 1943; BA in Library Sci., Emory U., 1948; PhD, U. Va., 1950. Curator manuscripts Duke U., Durham, NC, 1948-52; dir. libraries (Drake U.), Des Moines, 1952-56; dir. Southeastern Interlibrary Research Facility, Atlanta, 1956-59; asst. prof. info. sci. Ga. Inst. Tech., Atlanta, 1963-66, assoc. prof., 1966-69, prof., 1969-73, assoc. dir. libraries, 1966-71, dir. libraries, 1971-84, dir. emeritus, 1984—. Chmn. info bank com. Ga. Tech. Service Program, Atlanta, 1965-67; mem. exec. bd. Southeastern Library Network, Atlanta, 1973-74; library cons. So. Regional Edn. Bd., Atlanta, 1958-59 Compiler, editor: Southeastern Supplement to the Union List of Serials, 1959; author: Literature of Science and Engineering, 1966, 2d edit.,1969. Served with U.S. Army, 1942-43. Mem. ALA, Southeastern Library Assn., Ga. Library Assn. Democrat. Episcopalian. Home: 1639 Adelia Pl NE Atlanta GA 30329-3807 Home Phone: 404-634-5523.

ROBERTS, EDWIN ALBERT, JR., editor, journalist; b. Weehawken, NJ, Nov. 14, 1932; s. Edwin Albert and Agnes Rita (Seuferling) R.; m. Barbara Anne Collins, June 14, 1958; children: Elizabeth Adams, Leslie Carol, Amy Barbara, Jacqueline Harding. Student, Coll. William and Mary, 1952-53, NYU, evenings 1955-58; AA in Coll. & Cmty. Svc., St. Petersburg Jr. Coll., 1994. Reporter N.J. Courier, Toms River, 1953-54, Asbury Park (N.J.) Press, 1954-57; reporter Wall Street Jour., NYC, 1957, editorial writer, 1957-63; news editor Nat. Observer, Silver Spring, Md., 1963-68, columnist, 1968-77; editorial writer, columnist Detroit News, 1977-78, editorial page editor, 1978-83; editor editorial page Tampa Tribune, 1983—2003, ret., 2003. Author: Elections, 1964, 1964, Latin America, 1965, The Smut Rakers, 1966, Russia Today, 1967; Editor anthology: America Outdoors, 1965. Recipient Disting. Reporting Bus. award U. Mo., 1969; Pulitzer prize for distinguished commentary, 1974 Business E-Mail: ededitor@tampabay.rr.com.

ROBERTS, ELIZABETH H., Lieutenant Governor of Rhode Island, former state legislator; b. Washington, Apr. 17, 1957; m. Thomas H. Roberts; children: Kathleen, Nora. BA, Brown U., 1978; MBA, Boston U., 1984. Mem. RI Senate, Dist. 11, Providence, 1996—2006; lt. gov. State of RI, 2007—. Mem. fin. com. RI State Senate, health, edn. and welfare com. Mem. bd. dirs. Childrens Mus. RI, Southside Cmty. Land Trust. Democrat. Office: Lieutenant Governor State House Rm 115 Providence RI 02903 Office Phone: 401-222-2371. Office Fax: 401-222-2012.

ROBERTS, EMMA ROSE, actress; b. Rhinebeck, NY, Feb. 10, 1991; d. Eric Roberts and Kelly Cunningham, Eliza Roberts (Stepmother). Brand amb. Neutrogena, 2009. Model nat. ad campaign Dooney & Bourke, 2006. Actress (films) BigLove, 2001, Blow, 2001, Grand Champion, 2002, Spymate, 2006, Aquamarine, 2006, Nancy Drew, 2007, Hotel for Dogs, 2009, (TV series) Drake & Josh, 2004, Unfabulous, 2004—07, appearances include The Late Show with David Letterman, 2004, The Ellen DeGeneres Show, 2005, Teen Choice Awards, 2005, Live with Regis and Kelly, 2005—07, Nikelodeon Kids' Choice Awards, 2006—07; singer: (albums) Unfabulous and More: Emma Roberts, 2005. Named Female Star of Tomorrow, ShoWest, 2007. Office: Sweeny Mgmt 8033 Sunset Blvd Ste 1048 Los Angeles CA 90046*

ROBERTS, ERNST EDWARD, marketing consultant; b. Wheeling, W.Va., Dec. 19, 1926; s. Charles Emmitt and Virginia Mae (Stephenson) R.; m. Donna Clare Davis, Dec. 27, 1949; children: Ernst Edward II, Carol Lee Roberts Gaydac. BS, U.S. Mil. Acad., 1949; MBA, Xavier U., Cin., 1954; MS in Mech. Engring., U. So. Calif., 1957; grad. with distinction, Air War Coll., 1970. Commd. 2nd lt. U.S. Army, 1949, advanced through grades to brig. gen., 1971, served as officer in combat Korea, 1950-52; prof. mil. sci. Xavier U., 1952-54; mgmt. asst. to asst. comdt. U.S. Army Air Def. Sch., Fort Bliss, Tex., 1957-60; admissions officer U.S. Mil. Acad., West Point, NY, 1961-62, asst. to supt. (pres.), 1962-64, dir. admissions, 1964-65; comdg. officer 3d Missile Bn., 71st Arty., Fed. Republic of Germany, 1965-67; staff officer Gen. Staff U.S. Army, Washington, 1968-70; commdg. officer NATO Air Def. Arty. Group, Germany, 1970-71; commdg. gen. 38th Air Def. Arty. Brigade, Korea, 1971-72; dep. commanding gen. U.S. Army Air Def. Sch. and Ctr., Fort Bliss, 1972-74; ret. U.S. Army, 1974; v.p. bldg. and property mgr. El Paso (Tex.) Nat. Bank and Corp., 1974-79, sr. v.p., dir. pers. and tng., 1979-83, exec. v.p., dir. mktg., 1983-92; mktg. cons., 1992—. Mem. exec. mgmt. com. Tex. Commerce Bank, El Paso, 1983-92; vis. lectr. mktg. Webster U. Mem. bd. advisors SBA; mem. mayor's Citizens Com. on Police Dept. Matters, El Paso; mem. Task Force to Evaluate Mgmt. of Sheriff's Dept.; head bond-issue campaign, El Paso; adv. dir. Armed Svcs. YMCA, past pres.; adv. dir. nat. bd. dirs. Armed Svcs. YMCA, El Paso Cmty. Found.; past pres. U. Tex.-El Paso Eldorados; mem. bd. dirs., trustee Found. Lighthouse for Blind; chmn. adv. bd. dirs. El Paso Bus. Com. for Arts; chmn. capital fund drive com. Rio Grande Girl Scouts Am., Plz. Theatre-Plz. Park Restoration bd.; past mem. campaign cabinet United Way El Paso County; chmn. Capital Fund Drive, Air Def. Arty. Mus., Ft. Bliss; bd. dirs. City of El Paso, mem. steering com. Safe 2000; bd. dirs. Crimestoppers of El Paso. Decorated D.S.M., Legion of Merit, Silver Star, Meritorious Svc. medal; recipient Pro Eclesio Et Pontifice, Vatican, 1971; Conquistator award City of El Paso, Liberty Bell award Legal Cmty. El Paso, 1988. Mem. Am. Inst. Banking, Assn. U.S. Army (Gen. Army Omar N. Bradley chpt.), El Paso C. of C. (mem. armed forces com., chmn. spl. task force to evaluate chamber mgmt.), Mil. Order World Wars (chpt. chmn. citizen of yr. award 1996-2001), U.S. Army Air Def. Arty. Assn. (past pres., named Disting. Korean War Vet. 2004), El Paso Club (past pres., bd. dirs.), Rotary (past pres.). Republican. Roman Catholic. Home: 8212 Antero Pl El Paso TX 79904-2401

ROBERTS, FRANCIS STONE, advertising executive; b. Scranton, Pa., Aug. 15, 1944; s. Gordon Link and Eleanor Swartz (Stone) R.; m. Julie Ann Dolan; children: Francis Stone, Link McGregor. BA, Grove City Coll., Pa., 1966; A.M.P., U. Chgo., 1984. With media dept., then account exec. Compton Advt. Inc., NYC, 1966-69; account exec. Tatham-Laird & Kudner Advt., NYC, 1969-70; account supr., v.p. SSC&B Advt. Inc., NYC, 1970-78, sr. v.p., mgmt. supr., 1994; group exec. v.p. SSC&B: Lintas Advt. Worldwide, 1987-89; COO, pres. Lintas, NY, 1990-94; mem. policy and ops. coms., chmn. strategy rev. bd. Lintas N.Y.; also dir. Lintas N.Y. and U.S.A.; CEO, chmn. The CEO-Gotham Grp., NYC, 1994-95; chmn., CEO Gotham Inc., NYC, 1995—2004; mng. dir. Gotham Ltd., London, 1996—2004; CEO, pres. Carlson & Ptnrs., NYC, 2004—05, Roberts & Tarlow, NYC, 2005. Mem. bd. dirs. Am. Assn. Advertising Agencies, Am. Advertising Fedn., The Ad Coun.; bd. trustees Pro Ad PAC. Alumni coun. Grove City Coll., 1999—. Mem. William Penn Charter Alumni Assn., Ad Club N.Y., The Union League N.Y. Clubs: New Canaan Field, New Canaan Winter, New Canaan Country, Congl. Country, Ardsley Country Club. Republican. Presbyterian. Home: 28 Landing Dr Dobbs Ferry NY 10522 Office: Roberts and Tarlow 437 Madison New York NY 10022 Office Phone: 646-289-7301. Business E-Mail: stone@robertsntarlow.com.

ROBERTS, GARY, retired professional hockey player; b. North York, Ont., Can., May 23, 1966; Left wing Calgary Flames, 1987—97, Carolina Hurricanes, 1997—2000, Toronto Maple Leafs, 2000—05, Fla. Panthers, 2005—07, Pitts. Penguins, 2007—08, Tampa Bay Lightning, 2008—09; ret., 2009. Player NHL All-Star Game, 1992, 93, 2004. Recipient Bill Masterton Trophy, NHL, 1996; named to NHL All-Star team, 1992, 1993, 2004. Achievements include being a member of Stanley Cup Champion Calgary Flames, 1989.

ROBERTS, GARY RAYMOND, dean, law educator; b. Owatonna, Minn., Apr. 24, 1948; s. Ronald Raymond and Evelyn Mary (Halverson) R.; m. Nancy Louise Crnkovich, Sept. 30, 1983; 1 child, Andrew August. BA, Bradley U., 1970; JD, Stanford U., 1975. Tchr. Limestone HS, Bartonville, Ill., 1970-72; instr. Bradley U., Peoria, Ill., 1971-72; law clk. US Ct. Appeals (9th cir.) Calif., San Francisco, 1975-76; assoc. Covington and Burling, Washington, 1976-83; prof. law Tulane U. Law Sch., New Orleans, 1983—2007, vice dean, 1990—95, dep. dean, 2001—07; Gerald L Bepko prof. law Ind. U Sch. Law Indpls., 2007—, dean, 2007—. Sports law cons. to athletes, leagues and univs.; faculty rep. NCAA; mem. pres.'s adv. com., ad-hoc com. on men's basketball, univ. senate Tulane U.; chmn. athlete career counseling and agt. screening com. Tulane U. Author: Cases and Materials on Sports and the Law, 1993; editor-in-chief The Sports Lawyer; contbr. articles to numerous univ. law revs. Recipient Felix Frankfuter Tchg. award, 2001. Mem. ABA (mem. antitrust sect., litigation sect., forum com. on sports and entertainment), Am. Assn. Law Schs. (past chmn. law and sports sect.), Sports Lawyers Assn. (v.p., bd. dirs., officer, pres. 1995-97). Democrat. Office: Ind U Sch Law Indpls Lawrence W Inlow Rm 227 530 W New York St Indianapolis IN 46202-3225 Office Phone: 317-274-2581. Office Fax: 317-274-3955. Business E-Mail: robertsg@iupui.edu.*

ROBERTS, GEORGE BERNARD, JR., management and government relations consultant, former state legislator; b. Andover, Mass., June 13, 1939; s. George Bernard and Helene F. (Eversen) R.; m. Margaret Fay Edmunds, Aug. 26, 1967; children: Abigail Emerson, Jessica Swift. BS, U. N.H., 1964, M.P.A., 1967. Ptnr. Roberts Real Estate Assocs., Gilmanton, NH, 1966—; mem. N.H. Ho. of Reps., 1967-80, majority leader, 1971-74, speaker, 1975-76, 77-78, 79-80; pres. Policy Mgmt. Assocs., Concord, NH, 1980—. Pres. and treas. Concord, Concord Coach Soc. Del. Nat. Rep. Conv., 1972-76; mem. N.H. Constl. Conv., 1974, 84, N.H. Rep. Party Fin. Com.; pres. Nat. Conf. State Legislatures, 1979-80; chmn. exec. com. 1st Congl. Soc. Gilmanton. Mem. Nat. Rep. Legislators Assn. (founding, past pres.), Masons, Shriners, Scottish Rite, Historic Dist. Commn. Gilmanton, Sigma Alpha Epsilon. Republican. Office: Concord Policy Mgmt Assocs 4 Park St Ste 100 Concord NH 03301-6313

ROBERTS, GEORGE R., investment banker; b. Houston, Tex., 1945; m. Leanne Bovet Roberts (dec.); children: Eric, Mark, Courtney. BA, Claremont McKenna Coll., 1966; JD, U. Calif. Hastings Law Sch., San Francisco, 1969; LLD (hon.), Claremont McKenna Coll., 2003. Joined corp. fin. dept. to partner Bear Stearns & Co., New York, 1969—79; founding sr. ptnr. Kohlberg, Kravis, Roberts, San Francisco, 1976—. Dir. Accel-KKR, Safeway, Inc., DPL, Inc., KinderCare Learning Centers, Inc., Owens-Illinois, Inc. and PRIMEDIA Inc. Bd. San Francisco Symphony, San Francisco Ballet, Fine Arts Mus., San Francisco, Claremont McKenna Coll. Recipient Man of Yr. award, Culver Ednl. Found., 2006; named one of Forbes' Richest Americans, 2006. Achievements include historic billion dollar buyout of Wometco Companies in 1984; $25 billion RJR Nabisco buyout in 1989. Office: Kohlberg Kravis Roberts & Co 2800 Sand Hill Rd Ste 200 Menlo Park CA 94025-7055

ROBERTS, HARRY MORRIS, JR., lawyer; b. Dallas, June 10, 1938; s. Harry Morris and La Frances (Reilly) R.; m. Nancy Beth Johnson, Mar. 7, 1964; children: Richard Whitfield, Elizabeth Lee. BBA, So. Meth. U., 1960; LLB, Harvard U., 1963. Bar: Tex. 1963, U.S. Dist. Ct. (no. dist.) Tex. 1964, U.S. Ct. Appeals (5th cir.) 1972, U.S. Supreme Ct. 1971. Assoc. Thompson & Knight, Dallas, 1963-69, ptnr., 1970-75, sr. ptnr., 1975—. Chmn. real estate, probate and trust law sect. State Bar Tex., 1984-85; vis. scholar U. Tex. Law Sch., 1986; adj. prof. Southern Meth. U. Law Sch., 2007-09. Contbr. articles to profl. jours. Trustee Shelter Ministries of Dallas, 1982—, chmn. bd. trustees, 1992-95, 2004-05. Mem. ABA, Dallas Bar Assn. (chmn. real estate sect. 1981), Am. Bar Found., Tex. Bar Found., Dallas Bar Found., Am. Coll. Real Estate Lawyers, Tex. Coll. Real Estate Attys., Salesmanship Club (Dallas), Dallas Country Club. Episcopalian. Office: Thompson & Knight 1722 Routh St Ste 1500 Dallas TX 75201-2533 Office Phone: 214-969-1616. Business E-Mail: harry.roberts@tklaw.com.

ROBERTS, HILDA R., business educator; d. Harold Martin and Rose Sivell; m. David Moleod, June 28, 1958; children: Lorraine Rauch, Christina Hower, Dave. MS, Pepperdine U., LA, 1982. Tchr. North Am. Rockwell, LA, 1960—63, sec., 1960—63; tchr. Dorsey HS, LA, 1960—64; developer trainer Aerospace Corp., El Segundo, Calif., 1964—66; prof. Santa Ana Coll., Calif., 1972—2000, dean bus. and engring., 2000—. Contbr. articles to profl. jours. Named Adminstr. of Yr., Southern Sect. Calif. Bus. Edn. Assn., 2005—06. Mem.: Nat. Bus. Edn. Assoc. Home: 18329 Santa Lauretta Fountain Valley CA 92708 Office: Santa Ana Coll 1530 West 17th St Santa Ana CA 92706

ROBERTS, IAN See KWEI-ARMAH, KWAME

ROBERTS, J. SCOTT, psychologist, educator; BA in English, Duke U., 1992; MA in Clinical Psychology, U. Mich., 1996, PhD in Clinical Psychology, 1999. Lic. clinical psychologist, cert. geropsychology. Fellow Ann Arbor VA Health Svcs. Rsch. & Devel. Ctr., Harvard Med. Sch. Dept. Psychiatry; asst. prof. dept. neurology Boston U. Sch. Medicine; co-dir. edn. core Boston U. Alzheimer's Disease Ctr.; asst. prof. health behavior & edn. U. Mich. Sch. Pub. Health. Mem.: Nat. Coalition for Health Profl. Edn. in Genetics, Gerontological Soc. America, Am. Soc. Bioethics & Humanities, Am. Pub. Health Assn., Am. Psychological Assn. Office: 1420 Washington Heights Rm M5065 Ann Arbor MI 48109 Office Phone: 734-369-3283. Office Fax: 734-763-7379. E-mail: jscottr@umich.edu.*

ROBERTS, JAMES ALLEN, retired urologist, educator; b. Beach, ND, May 31, 1934; s. Earl Fernando and Maria Ellen Roberts; m. Hilda Peachy Roberts, Nov. 29, 1986; children from previous marriage: Jennifer Lou Roberts Walsh, Mary Ellen Roberts Wargo, Thomas Jay. MD, U. Chgo., 1959. Diplomate: Am. Bd. Urology. Intern U. Chgo. Sch. Medicine, 1959-60, resident in urology, 1961-65; from mem. faculty to prof. Tulane U. Med. Sch., New Orleans, 1971-99, prof. urology, 1999—, assoc. chmn., 1986—99; sr. research scientist, head dept. urology Tulane Regional Primate Research Center, Covington, 1972-99; prof. emeritus, 1999—; fellow Fogarty Sr. Internat. NIH, 1984; ret., 2005. Mem. editorial bd. Am. Jour. Kidney Diseases and Urol. Rsch.; contbr. articles to profl. jours. Bd. dirs. Highland Park Hosp., 1985-87. With USN, 1965—67. Recipient grants NIH, Original Rsch. award Southern Med. Assn., 1990, Cert. Achievement Am. Urological Assn., 1997; Fulbright Sr. scholar, 1999-2000. Fellow ACS; mem. St. Tammany Parish Med. Soc. (pres. 1979), Soc. Rsch. on Calculous Kinetics, La. Urol. Soc., Am. Urol. Assn., Soc. Univ. Urologists, Nat. Kidney Found., Soc. Exptl. Biology and Medicine, Nat. Inst. Health (SAT study sect. 1995-99), Sigma Xi. Office: 83 Towne Place Dr Hendersonville NC 28792 Personal E-mail: jrhr285@mchsi.com.

ROBERTS, JAMES BRIAN, engineer; b. Milw., Aug. 25, 1954; s. Phillip Wallace and Betty Ann Roberts, Walter Punko (Stepfather); m. Julie Joanne Wenzler, Aug. 5, 1978; children: Phillip Carl, Jamie Joanne. BS, U. Wis., Madison, 1976. Hull designer and test driver Ski Boats Inc. -Cobra Jet Divsn., Menomonee Falls, Wis., 1976—77; mgr. fleet operation Sherwin Williams Automotive Divsn., Chgo., Afghanistan, 1977—79; v.p. customer svcs. W.B. Combustion Inc., Milw., 1980—85; mgr. application engring. Eclipse Combustion Inc., Rockford, Ill., 1985—99, dir. global metals accts., 1999—. Charter mem. Penn State Ctr. Advanced Materials, Ctr. Heat Treating Excellence, Worcester Poly Tech. Inst., Mass. Contbr. articles to profl. jours. Named to Hall of Fame, Am. Gas Assn., 1998. Mem.: Metal Treating Inst. (assoc.; trustee, bd. dirs. 2005—), Sigma Chi (life). Liberal. Avocations: skiing, golf, writing, sports. Office: Eclipse Combustion Inc 1665 Elmwood Rd Rockford IL 61103 Business E-Mail: jroberts@eclipsenet.com.

ROBERTS, JAMES HAROLD, III, lawyer; b. Omaha, Aug. 11, 1949; s. James Harold Jr. and Evelyn Doris (Young) R.; m. Marilyn Novak, June 29, 1974; children: Jessica Noël, Meredith Caitlin. BA, U. Notre Dame, 1971; JD, St. Louis U., 1974. Bar: Iowa 1974, U.S. Ct. Mil. Appeals 1974, U.S. Supreme Ct. 1979, D.C. 1981. US govt. atty. US Army, Kans., 1974—78, Ala., 1974—78, Washington, 1978-83; govt. contract atty. US Dept. Treasury, Washington, 1983-88; pvt. practice Van Scoyoc Kelly PLLC, Washington, 1988—. Editor St. Louis U. law rev., 1973-74. Lt. col. JAGC, U.S. Army, 1974-78, USAR/NG, 1978-99. Mem. ABA (pub. contract law sect.), D.C. Bar Assn., Fed. Bar Assn. Roman Catholic. Home: 308 N Monroe St Arlington VA 22201-1736 Office: Van Scoyoc Kelly PLLC Ste 665E 101 Constitution Ave NW Washington DC 20001-1737 Office Phone: 202-898-1898. Business E-Mail: jroberts@vsklaw.com.

ROBERTS, JEANETTE C., dean, pharmacy educator; BS in Biochemistry, Albright Coll., Reading, Pa., 1979; PhD in Medicinal Chemistry, U. Minn., Mpls., 1986; MPH, U. Utah, 2001. Quality control chemist Warner-Lambert Co., Rockford, Ill., 1979; chemist minerals divsn. Dept. Natural Resources, St. Paul, 1980—81; rsch. fellow isotope/nuc. chemistry divsn. Los Alamos Nat. Lab., N.Mex., 1986—88; asst. prof. medicinal chemistry U. Utah Coll. Pharmacy, Salt Lake City, 1988—94, assoc. prof., 1994—2001, prof., 2001—03, adj. prof., 2003—, adj. asst. prof. pharmacology/toxicology, 1992—94, adj. assoc. prof., 1994—2001, adj. prof., 2001—, interim chair dept. medicinal chemistry, 1995—96, adj. assoc. prof. foods/nutrition, 2000—01, adj. prof., 2003—, assoc. dean academic affairs, 2000—03; prof. divsn. pharm. scis., dean U. Wis. Sch. Pharmacy, Madison, 2003—. Vis. prof. dept. pediat. U. Vienna, 1998; cons. Jean Brown Assoc., Salt Lake City, 1999, Utah Health Informatics, Salt Lake City, 1999—2000, Protein Solutions, Inc., Salt Lake City, 1999—2000. Co-author: Drugs and Justice, 2005. Recipient Disting. Tchg. award, U. Utah Coll. Pharmacy, 1995, 2003. Mem.: AAAS, Utah Pub. Health Assn., Mountain West Region Soc. Toxicology, Am. Soc. Pharmacognosy, Am. Assn. Cancer Rsch., Am. Chem. Soc. (sec. 1990—92), Am. Assn. Colleges of Pharmacy, Delta Omega, Phi Kappa Phi, Rho Chi. Achievements include patents in field. Office: U Utah Coll Pharmacy Rennebohm Hall 1126B 777 Highland Ave Madison WI 53705 Office Phone: 608-262-1414. Office Fax: 608-262-3397. Business E-Mail: jroberts@pharmacy.wisc.edu.*

ROBERTS, JEANNE ADDISON, retired literature educator; b. Washington; d. John West and Sue Fisher (Nichols) Addison; m. Markley Roberts, Feb. 19, 1966; children: Addison Cary Steed Masengill, Ellen Carraway Masengill Coster. AB, Agnes Scott Coll., 1946; MA, U. Pa., 1947; PhD, U. Va., 1964. Instr. Mary Washington Coll., 1947-48; instr., chmn. English Fairfax Hall Jr. Coll., 1950-51; tchr. Am. U. Assn. Lang. Center, Bangkok, Thailand, 1952-56; instr. Beirut (Lebanon) Coll. for Women, 1956-57, asst. prof., 1957-60, chmn. English dept., 1957-60; instr. lit. Am. U., Washington, 1960-62, asst. prof., 1962-65, assoc. prof., 1965-68, prof., 1968-93. Dean faculties Am. U., 1974; lectr. Howard U., 1971-72; seminar prof. Folger Shakespeare Libr. Inst. for Renaissance and 18th Century Studies, 1974; dir. NEH Summer Inst. for HS Tchrs. on Tchg. Shakespeare, Folger Shakespeare Libr., 1984-86; dir. NEH summer inst. Va. Commonwealth U. 1995-96 Writings By and About Women In The English Renaissance; study group leader Inst. Learning in Retirement, Am. U., 1999-, mem. study groups.;Founder and leader, Shakespeare Discussion Group, Cosmos Club, 2004-08 Author: Shakespeare's English Comedy: The Merry Wives of Windsor in Context, 1979, The Shakespearean Wild: Geography, Genus and Gender, 1991, Literacy Criticism as Dreams Analysis, 2009; editor: (with James G. McManaway) A Selective Bibliography of Shakespeare: Editions, Textual Studies, Commentary, 1975; (with Peggy O'Brien) Shakespeare Set Free, vol. 1, 1993, vol. 2, 1994, vol. 3, 1995, (with Georgianna Ziegler) Shakespeare's Unruly Women, 1997; contbr. articles to profl. jours. and scholarly collections. Danforth Tchr. grantee, 1962—63, Folger Sr. fellow, 1969—70, 1988. Mem. MLA (chmn. Shakespeare divsn. 1981-82), Renaissance Soc. Am., Milton Soc., Shakespeare Assn. Am. (trustee 1978-81, 87-89, pres. 1986-87), AAUP (pres. Am. U. chpt. 1966-67), Southeastern Renaissance Conf. (pres. 1981-82), English Speaking Union (bd. dirs. 2005-07), Mortar Board, Phi Beta Kappa, Phi Kappa Phi. Episcopalian. Home: 4931 Albemarle St NW Washington DC 20016-4359 Personal E-mail: jeannerobe@aol.com.

ROBERTS, JEFFREY OWAYNE, builder, renovator, consultant; b. Greensboro, NC, May 24, 1969; s. Jeffrey Wayne Roberts and Kimberly Ann Bailey; 1 child, Jaden George Bailey. Degree in psychology with honors, U. NC, Greensboro. Lic. in masonry, carpentry, CAD, PMP, NC Dept. Cmty. Colls., 2001. CEO Sunshineblue Svcs., Greensboro, 2001—; sales rep. Tidewater M.E.R.C., Greensboro. Cons. Aniz, Inc., Atlanta. Recipient Editor's Choice award. Mem.: SAG (hon.). Freedom. Avocations: swimming, weightlifting. Office: Sunshineblue Svcs 3403 Lenox Ct Greensboro NC 27408 also: Sunshineblue Svcs 310 E Victory Greensboro NC 27401 Home Fax: 336-288-4302. Business E-Mail: jeffreyroberts@sunshineblue.biz.

ROBERTS, JO ANN WOODEN, school system administrator; b. Chgo., June 24, 1948; d. Tilmon and Annie Mae (Wardlaw) Wooden; m. Edward Allen Roberts Sr. (div.); children: Edward Allen Jr., Hillary Ann. BS, Wayne State U., 1970, MS, 1971; PhD, Northwestern U., 1977. Speech, lang. pathologist Chgo. Bd. Edn., 1971—78, adminstr., 1987—88; project dir. Ednl. Testing Svc., Evanston, Ill., 1976—77; instr. Chgo City C.C., 1976—77; exec. dir. Nat. Speech Lang. and Hearing Assn., Chgo., 1984—86; dir. spl. svcs. Rock Island (Ill.) Pub. Schs., 1988—90; supt. Muskegon Hts. (Mich.) Pub. Schs., 1990—93; dep. supr. Chgo. Pub. Schs., 1993—96; supt. of schs. Hazel Crest (Ill.) Sch. Dist. #152 1/2, 1996—98; cons. Chgo. Pub. Schs., 1998—2000, dep. accountability svcs., 1999—, InterVention officer, 2000—01, chief troubleshooter, 2001—. Hon. guest lectr. Gov.'s State U., U. Pk., Ill., 1983—86; cons. in field. Author: Learning to Talk, 1974. Trustee Muskegon County Libr. Bd., 1990, Mercy Hosp. Bd., Muskegon, 1990, St. Mark's Sch. Bd. Dirs., Southborough, Mass., 1989, United Way Bd., Muskegon, 1990; mem. Mich. State Bd. Edn. Systematic Initiative in Math and Sci., 1991, Gov. John Engler Mich. 2000 Task Force, 1991, Chpt. II Adv. Commn., 1991. Recipient Leadership award Boy Scouts Am., 1990; named finalist Outstanding Young Working Women, Glamour Mag., 1984, Outstanding Educator, Blacks in Govt., 1990. Mem. Am. Assn. Sch. Adminstrs., Nat. Alliance Black Sch. Educators, Mich. Assn. Sch. Adminstrs., Assn. Supervision & Curriculum Devel., Phi Delta Kappa. Avocations: creative writing, peotry, modern dance, theater, drawing. Address: Chgo Pub Schs 125 S Clark St Chicago IL 60603-5200

ROBERTS, JOHN, news anchor; b. Toronto, Ont., Nov. 15, 1956; naturalized, USA; Attended, U. Toronto. Anchor, corr. several broadcasts City TV, Toronto, 1979—89; anchor, corr. WCIX TV (now WFOR-TV), Miami, Fla., 1989—90; co-anchor Can. A.M., 1990—92, CBS Morning News, 1992, WCBS-TV, NYC, 1994—95; anchor CBS Evening News Sunday, NYC, 1995—2006; chief White House corr. CBS News, NYC, 1999—2006; sr. nat. corr. CNN, Washington, 2006—07, anchor, American Morning NYC, Washington, 2007—. Recipient Emmy awards, NATAS, NY Press Club award, Nat. Headliner award, 2006. Office: CNN Bldg 820 First St NE Washington DC 20002

ROBERTS, JOHN CHARLES, law educator; b. Aberdeen, SD, Feb. 29, 1940; s. Jacob John Schmitt and Leona (Blethen) Blake; m. Kathleen Kelly (div. 1985); children: Katherine, John Charles Jr.; m. Lynn Dale Friedman, Dec. 22, 1985; 1 child, Emily Sara. BS, Northwestern U., 1961; LL.B., Yale U., 1968. Bar: U.S. Dist. Ct. D.C. 1969, Mich. 1981. Assoc. Covington & Burling, Washington, 1968-71; assoc. dean, lectr.

Yale U. Law Sch., New Haven, 1971-77; gen. counsel U.S. Senate Com. on Armed Services, 1977-80; adj. prof. law Washington Coll. Law, Am. U., 1978-80; dean, prof. law Wayne State U. Law Sch., Detroit, 1980-86; prof., dean Law Sch. DePaul U., Chgo., 1986-96, v.p. for univ. advancement, 1996-97, prof. law, 1997—. Mem. exec. com. Inst. for Continuing Legal Edn., Chgo., 1988-91. Mem. adv. com. Mich. Psychiat. Soc., 1980-86; bd. dirs. Constl. Rights Found., 1992-96. Lt. USN, 1961-65. Mem. ABA, Assn. Am. Law Schs. (mem. exec. com., chmn. sect. instn. advancement 1987-88, chmn., sec. adminstrn. law schs. 1993-94), Order of Coif. Democrat. Avocation: collecting modern first editions. Office: DePaul U Coll Law 25 E Jackson Blvd Chicago IL 60604-2289 Office Phone: 312-362-8776. Business E-Mail: jroberts@depaul.edu.

ROBERTS, JOHN D., chemist, educator; b. LA, June 8, 1918; s. Allen Andrew and Flora (Dombrowski) Roberts; m. Edith Mary Johnson, July 11, 1942; children: Anne Christine, Donald William, John Paul, Allen Walter. AB, UCLA, 1941, PhD, 1944; D in Natural Scis. (hon.), U. Munich, 1962; DSc (hon.), Temple U., 1964, Notre Dame U., 1993, U. Wales, 1993, Scripps Rsch. Inst., 1996. Instr. chemistry UCLA, 1944—45; NRC fellow chemistry Harvard U., 1945—46, instr. chemistry, 1946, MIT, 1946, asst. prof., 1947—50, assoc. prof., 1950—52; vis. prof. Ohio State U., 1952, Stanford U., 1973—74; prof. organic chemistry Calif. Inst. Tech., 1953—72, inst. prof. chemistry, 1972—88, inst. prof. chemistry emeritus, lectr., 1988—, dean of faculty, v.p., provost, 1980—83, lectr., 1988—, chmn. divsn. chemistry and chem. engring., 1963—68, acting chmn., 1972—73. Bd. dirs. Huntington Med. Rsch. Insts., 1984—99, Organic Syntheses Inc.; Robert Noyce vis. prof. sci. Grinnell Coll., 2001. Author: Basic Organic Chemistry Part I, 1955, Nuclear Magnetic Resonance, 1958, Spin-Spin Splitting in High-Resolution Nuclear Magnetic Resonance Spectra, 1961, Molecular Orbital Calculations, 1961; author: (with M.C. Caserio) Basic Principles of Organic Chemistry, 1964, 2d edit., 1977, Modern Organic Chemistry, 1967; author: (with R. Stewart and M.C. Caserio) Organic Chemistry-Methane To Macromolecules, 1971; author: At The Right Place at the Right Time, 1990, ABCs of FT-NMR, 2000; contbg. editor: McGraw-Hill Series in Advanced Chemistry, 1957—60; editor: Organic Syntheses, Vol. 41, 1961; Spectroscopy, mem. editl. bd.: Organic Magnetic Resonance in Chemistry. Trustee L.S.B. Leakey Found., 1983—92; bd. dirs. Coleman Chamber Music Assn.; adv. com. Calif. Competitive Tech., 1989—92. Recipient Alumni Profl. Achievement award, UCLA, 1967, Nichols medal, 1972, Tolman medal, 1975, Michelson-Morley award, 1976, Norris award, 1978, Pauling award, 1980, Theodore Wm. Richards medal, 1982, Willard Gibbs Gold medal, 1983, Golden Plate award, Am. Acad. Achievement, 1983, Priestley medal, 1987, Madison Marshall award, 1989, Nat. Medal Sci., NSF, 1990, Glenn T. Seaborg medal, 1991, Award in nuclear magnetic resource, 1991, Svc. to Chemistry award, 1991, History Maker award, Pasadena Hist. Soc., 1994, Pauling Legacy award, 2006; co-recipient Robert A. Welch award, 1990; named Hon. Alumnus, Calif. Inst. Tech., 1990, SURF dedicatee, 1992; named one of Most Influential Chemists of Last 75 yrs., Chem. and Engring. News, 1998;, Guggenheim fellow, 1952—53, 1955—56. Mem.: AAAS (councillor 1992—95), NAS (councillor 1980—83, com. on sci. and engring. pub. policy 1983—87, Chem. Scis. award 1999, award for chemistry in svc. to soc. 2009), Royal Soc. Chemistry, Am. Acad. Arts and Scis., Am. Philos. Soc. (coun. mem. 1983—86), Am. Chem. Soc. (chmn. organic chemistry divsn. 1956—57, award pure chemistry 1954, Harrison Howe award 1957, Roger Adams award in organic chemistry 1967, Arthur C. Cope award 1994, Chem. Pioneer award 1994, Nakanishi prize 2001, Auburn Kosolapoff award 2003), Phi Lambda Upsilon, Sigma Xi. Office: Calif Inst Tech 358 Crellin Lab Mail Code 164-30 Pasadena CA 91125-0001 Office Phone: 626-395-6036. Business E-Mail: robertsj@caltech.edu.*

ROBERTS, JOHN DERHAM, lawyer; 1 child. Cert., Richmond Coll., Va., 1960; BS, Hampden-Sydney Coll., Va., 1964; LLB, Washington & Lee U., 1968. Bar: Va. 1968, Fla. 1969, U.S. Supreme Ct. 1969, U.S. Ct. Customs and Patent Appeals 1970, U.S. Tax Ct. 1970, U.S. Ct. Appeals (5th cir.) 1970, U.S. Ct. Appeals (9th cir.) 1974, U.S. Supreme Ct. 1969. Law clk. U.S. Dist. Ct., Jacksonville, Fla., 1968-69; assoc. Phillips, Kendrick, Gearhart & Aylor, Arlington, Va., 1969-70; asst. U.S. Atty. mid. dist. Fla. U.S. Dept. Justice, Jacksonville, 1970-74, Dist. of Alaska, Anchorage, 1974-77, U.S. magistrate judge, 1977—. Bd. dirs. Teen Challenge Alaska, Anchorage, 1984-93; chmn. Eagle Scout Rev. Bd., 1993-2008; bd. dirs. Alaska Youth for Christ, 1993-96; govs.'s Prayer Breakfast Com., 1994—, vice-chair, 1998—. Recipient Citizenship award DAR, Anchorage, 1984, plaque, U.S. Navy, Citizen Day, Adak, Alaska, 1980, Silver Beaver award, 2004. Mem. ABA, Nat. Conf. Spl. Ct. Judges (exec. bd. 1985-92), 9th Cir. Conf. Magistrate Judges (exec. bd. 1982-85, chmn. 1984-85, 2005-07), Alaska Bar Assn., Anchorage Bar Assn., Chi Phi, Psi Chi, Phi Alpha Delta. Republican. Office: US Magistrate Judge 222 W 7th Ave Unit 46 Anchorage AK 99513-7504 Office Phone: 907-677-6255.

ROBERTS, JOHN GLOVER, JR., United States supreme court chief justice; b. Buffalo, Jan. 27, 1955; s. John Glover and Rosemary (Podrasky) Roberts; m. Jane Marie Sullivan, July 27, 1996; children: Jack, Josie. AB summa cum laude, Harvard U., 1976, JD magna cum laude, 1979. Bar: DC 1981, US Ct. Claims 1982, US Ct. Appeals (fed. circuit) 1982, US Supreme Ct. 1987, US Ct. Appeals (DC, 5th and 9th circuits) 1988, US Ct. Appeals (3rd, 7th, and 10th circuits) 1996. Law clk. to Honorable Henry Friendly US Ct. Appeals (2nd cir.), NYC, 1979-80; law clk. to Assoc. Justice William H. Rehnquist US Supreme Ct., Washington, 1980-81; spl. asst. to US Atty. Gen. William French Smith US Dept. Justice, Washington, 1981-82; assoc. counsel to Pres. Ronald Reagan The White House, Washington, 1982-86; assoc. Hogan & Hartson, LLP, Washington, 1986-87, ptnr., 1988—89, 1993—2003; prin. dep. solicitor gen. US Dept. Justice, Washington, 1989-93; judge US Ct. Appeals (DC Cir.), Washington, 2003—05; chief justice US Supreme Ct., Washington, 2005—. Named one of The World's Most Influential People, TIME mag., 2006, 2007. Fellow: American Acad. Arts & Sciences; mem.: Supreme Ct. Historical Soc., Edward Coke Appellate Inn of Ct., American Acad. Appellate Lawyers, American Law Inst., Robert Trent Jones Golf Club, Met. Club, Lawyers Club, Phi Beta Kappa. Republican. Office: US Supreme Ct One First St SE Washington DC 20543*

ROBERTS, JOHN ROBERT, cardiothoracic surgeon, consultant; b. Athens, Tenn., Apr. 5, 1959; s. Doyle Ford and Frankie Howard Roberts; children: Amanda, Timothy, John Anthony, Thomas. AB summa cum laude, Duke U., 1981; MD with honors, Yale U., 1985; MBA, Auburn U., 2003. Bd. cert. gen. surgery Am. Bd. Surgery, bd. cert. thoracic surgery Am. Bd. Thoracic Surgery, lic. med. practice Tenn. Resident surgeon Johns Hopkins Hosp., Balt., 1986—92, fellow in surg. oncology, 1992—93; fellow in thoracic surgery Brigham and Women's Hosp., Boston, 1993—95; asst. prof. U. Pa., Phila., 1995—97; chief gen. thoracic surgery Vanderbilt U., Nashville, 1997—2003; thoracic surgeon The Surg. Clinic, Nashville, 2003—; with Southeastern Rsch. Assocs., 2008—. Ingram Prof. Cancer Rsch. Vanderbilt U., 1997; Richard Wilsen vis. prof. surg. oncology Harvard Med. Sch.; lectr. in field. Reviewer: jours. CHEST, Annals of Thoracic Surgery, Jour. Thoracic and Cardiovasc. Surgery; contbr. articles to profl. jours. Capt. USAR, 1999—2003. Recipient Resident Rsch. award, Johns Hopkins Hosp., 1986, grants in field. Master: Am. Coll. Chest Physicians (Alfred Soffler award); fellow: ACS (scholarship for health policy 2004); mem.: Am. Coll. Surgeons Workforce on Health Policy, Reform and Advocacy, So. Thoracic Surg. Assn., Soc. Thoracic Surgeons, Am. Soc. Clin. Oncology, So. Assn. for Oncology, Soc. Cell and Tissue Kinetics, Alpha Omega Alpha, Phi Kappa Phi. Achievements include mentoring the winner of the Alfred Soffler Award from the American College of Chest Physicians in 2008. Avocation: Tae Kwon Do. Office: The Surg Clinic #356 24th Ave Nashville TN 37203 Office Phone: 615-329-7887. Personal E-mail: johnbob999@msn.com, robertshame@comcast.net. Business E-Mail: jroberts@tsclinic.com.

ROBERTS, JOHN S., process engineer, researcher; b. Dayton, Ohio, Aug. 9, 1969; s. Edwin Stuart Roberts, III and Janet Rae Roberts; m. Michelle L. Rizzella, Oct. 11, 2002; children: Emma Lenore Rizzella-Roberts, Michael Edwin Rizzella-Roberts. BS (hon.), U. Fla., Gainesville, 1993, MS, 1994; PhD, Rutgers, State U. NJ, New Brunswick, 1999. Asst. prof. Cornell U., NYSAES, Geneva, NY, 1999—2005; rsch. food technologist USDA-ARS, WRRC, Albany, Calif., 2005—07; process engr. Rich Products Corp., Buffalo, 2008—. Lectr. Rutgers State U. NJ, 1998; cons. Birds-Eye, Green Bay, Wis., 2000—02; chair Western NY IFT, Geneva, 2002—03; assoc. editor Internat. Jour. Food Properties, 2008—. Contbr. chapters to books. Recipient Internat. Young Food Engr. award, Icef 9, 2004, Ency. Agr. and Biol. Engring.; Student fellowship, USDA, 1995—98, NRI Competive grant, 2000—03. Mem.: Inst. Food Technologists, Phi Kappa Phi Honor Soc., Golden Key Nat. Honor Soc., Gamma Sigma Delta Honor Soc. Achievements include design of high UV intensity short time treatment of mushrooms with vitamin D; low temperature short time microwave processing of fruits and vegetables; simultaneous multi-unctional microwave processing, evaporation-concensation as governing mechanism in hygroscopic porous materials and development of onionkraut and spicy sourkraut. Avocations: hiking, model building, reading, guitar, gardening. Office: Rich Products Corp One Robert Rich Way Buffalo NY 14213 Business E-Mail: jsrob25@hotmail.com.

ROBERTS, JOHN W., historian, federal agency official; b. NJ, 1954; s. Walter I. and Lucile K. Roberts. BA, Coll. of N.J., Trenton, 1976; MA, U. Md., 1979, PhD, 1992. Instr., rschr. U. of Md., College Park, 1976—82; archives technician Nat. Archives, Washington, 1978—82; dir. devel. svcs. Trinity Coll., Washington, 1982—85; archivist Nat. Archives, Washington, 1985—87; chief of archives Fed. Bur. of Prisons, Washington, 1987—98; sr. historian, archivist History Assocs. Inc., Rockville, Md., 1998—2002; chief mus. mgmt. Nat. Pk. Svc., Washington, 2002—05, chief Nat. Register of Hist. Places and Nat. Hist. Landmarks program, 2005—. Author: (book) Escaping Prison Myths: Selected Topics on the History of Federal Corrections, Putting Foreign Policy to Work: The Role of Organized Labor in American Foreign Relations, 1932-1941, Reform and Retribution: An Illustrated History of American Prisons; co-author (with Richard Phillips): Quick Reference to Correctional Administration; contbr. articles to profl. jours. and encys. Mem.: Am. Assn. of Mus., Soc. of Am. Archivists, Soc. for History in the Fed. Govt. (exec. coun. 2002—04, v.p. 2005—06, pres. 2006—). Office: Nat Park Svc 1201 I St NW Washington DC 20005 Business E-Mail: john_w_roberts@nps.gov.

ROBERTS, JON, pulmonologist; b. Rockville Ctr., NY, Feb. 23, 1975; s. Alfred Roberts and Bonnie Brooks; m. Adriana Dyurich, Feb. 23, 2001; children: Rebeka, Diego. BS, Sophie Davis Sch., City U., Harlem, 1998; MD, NY Med. Coll., Valhalla, NY, 2000. Cert. Pediat. Am. Bd. Pediat., 2003. Pediatric pulmonologist Winthrop Pediatric Assocs., Mineola, NY, 2006—. Rsch. grant, Medimmune Corp., 2005. Fellow: Am. Acad. Pediat.; mem.: Nassau Pediat. Soc., European Respiratory Soc., Am. Thoracic Soc., Am. Coll. Chest Physicians. Office: Winthrop Pediatric Assocs 120 Mineola Blvd ste 210 Mineola NY 11501 Office Fax: 516-663-3826. Business E-Mail: jroberts@winthrop.org.

ROBERTS, JONATHAN, dancer; b. Apr. 20, 1974; m. Anna Trebunskaya. Profl. dancer, 1994—; winner USA Rising Star Am. Ballroom championship, 1997, Blackpool Rising Star Latin championship, 2003, USA Rising Star Latin championship, 2004, USA Pro-Am 10 Dance championship, USA Pro-Am Latin championship, USA Pro-Am Am. Ballroom championship; profl. dancer Dancing with the Stars, ABC, 2005—.

ROBERTS, JONATHAN C., pharmaceutical executive; Grad., Sch. Pharmacy Va. Commonwealth Univ. Area v.p. stores CVS Pharmacy Inc., 1997—2002, sr. v.p. store ops., 2002—05; sr. v.p., CIO CVS Caremark Corp., 2006—09, exec. vp. Rx purchasing pricing & network rels., 2009—. Mem. SureScripts Exec. Adv. Coun., eHealth Initiatives Leadership Coun. Bd. dir. ALS Therapy Alliances. Office: CVS Caremark COrp 1 CVS Dr Woonsocket RI 02895*

ROBERTS, JULIA FIONA, actress; b. Smyrna, Ga., Oct. 28, 1967; d. Walter and Betty Roberts; m. Lyle Lovett, June 25, 1993 (div. Mar. 22, 1995); m. Daniel Moder, July 4, 2002; children: Hazel Patricia, Phinnaeus Walter, Henry Daniel. Actress (films) Blood Red, 1986, Satisfaction, 1987, Mystic Pizza, 1988, Steel Magnolias, 1989 (Golden Globe award for Best Supporting Actress, Acad. award nominee), Pretty Woman, 1990 (Golden Globe award for Best Actress, Acad. award nominee), Flatliners, 1990, Sleeping With the Enemy, 1991, Hook, 1991, Dying Young, 1991, The Player, 1992, The Pelican Brief, 1993, I Love Trouble, 1994, Ready to Wear (Prêt-à-Porter), 1994, Something To Talk About, 1995, Mary Reilly, 1996, Everybody Says I Love You, 1996, Michael Collins, 1996, My Best Friend's Wedding, 1997, Conspiracy Theory, 1997, Stepmom, 1998, Notting Hill, 1999, Runaway Bride, 1999, Erin Brockovich, 2000 (Academy award for Best Actress, Golden Globe award fro Best Actress, SAG award for outstanding performance by a female actor in a leading role, BAFTA award), The Mexican, 2001, America's Sweethearts, 2001, Ocean's Eleven, 2001, Full Frontal, 2002, Confessions of a Dangerous Mind, 2002, Mona Lisa Smile, 2003, Closer, 2004, Ocean's Twelve, 2004, The Ant Bully (voice only), 2006, Charlotte's Web (voice only), 2006, Charlie Wilson's War, 2007, Fireflies in the Garden, 2008, Duplicity, 2009, (Broadway plays) Three Days of Rain, 2006, (TV films) Baja Oklahoma, 1988; exec. prodr.: (films) Kit Kittredge: An American Girl, 2008; narrator (TV spl.) Before Your Eyes: Angelie's Secret, 1995, TV appearances Crime Story, 1987, Miami Vice, 1988, Friends, 1996, Murphy Brown, 1998, Sesame Street, 1998, AFI's 100 Years...100 Movies, 1998, In the Wild, 1998, Law & Order, 1999. Involved with UNICEF; lent celebrity name to help raise money for research to develop a cure for Rett Syndrome. Recipient People's Choice awards, Favorite Motion Picture Actress, 1991, 1998, Favorite Comedy/Dramatic Motion Picture Actress, 1992, Favorite Dramatic Motion Picture Actress, 1994, Woman of Yr. award, Hasty Pudding Theatricals, 1997, Spl. Internat. Star of Yr. award, ShoWest Conv., 1998, Am. Cinematheque award, 2007; named Female Star of Yr., Nat. Assn. Theatre Owners, 1991, Best Actress (for Erin Brockovich), Broadcast Film Critics Assn., Chgo. Film Critics Assn., LA Film Critics Assn., San Diego Film Critics Soc., Nat. Bd. Rev.; named one of 50 Most Beautiful People in the World, People Mag., 1990, 1991, 50 Most Beautiful People (USA), 2000, 2002, 25 Most Intriguing People, 2001, 50 Most Powerful People in Hollywood, Premiere mag., 2002—06, 100 Most Powerful Celebrities, Forbes.com, 2007. Achievements include recognition as the highest paid actress in film history, as well as one of the most popular and sought-after talents in Hollywood. Office: c/o Hirsch Wallerstein Matlof and Fishman LLP 10100 Santa Monica Blvd Los Angeles CA 90067-1722*

ROBERTS, KARLENE ANN, education educator; b. San Francisco, June 12, 1937; d. Carl Joachim and Doris Elizabeth (Hosman) Hahn; m. Sept. 7, 1963 (div. June 1981); 1 child, Donald Brett. BA, Stanford U., 1959; PhD, U. Calif., Berkeley, 1967. Rsch. assoc. Stanford (Calif.) U., 1967-69; lectr. U. Calif., Berkeley, 1967-70, asst. prof., 1970-73, assoc. prof., 1973-78, prof., 1978—. Cons. in field; reviewer in field. Mem. editorial bd. Acad. Mgmt. Jour., 1976-81, Jour. of Applied Psychology, 1977-87, Jour. of Vocat. Behavior, 1974-76, Orgnl. Behavior and Human Decision Processes, 1978-87, Calif. Mgmt. Rev., 1981-88, Acad. Mgmt. Exec., 1987; author: Comparative Studies in Organizational Behavior, 1972, Communication in Organizations, 1977, Toward an Interdisciplinary Science of Organizations, 1978, New Directions in Methodology: Aggregation Issues in Organizational Science, 1980, Organizational Behavior, 1991, New Challenges to Understanding Orgns., 1993.

ROBERTS, KATHARINE ADAIR, retired bookkeeper; b. Columbus, Ga., June 4, 1930; d. William Lynn and Ella Miller (Adair) R. BA, U. Redlands, 1955; postgrad., San Bernardino Valley Coll., 1971—74, Calif. State U., San Bernardino, 1975—78. Bookkeeper Rettig Machine Shop, Inc., Redlands, Calif., 1970-97, ret., 1997. Pres. Dem. Study Club, San Bernardino, 1967-68, Redlands Dem. Club, 1976, Wilsonian Club, San Bernardino, 1986; chair Redlands/San Bernardino chpt. Citizens for Global Solutions, 1987—, San Bernardino leader ptnrs. for global change program; active San Bernardino County Dem. Ctrl. Com., treas. 1977-80. Recipient Citizen Achievement award, LWV, 1989; named one of 63 Women of Distinction, 63rd Assembly Dist., Calif., Assemblyman Bill Emmerson, 2005. Mem. Dem. Luncheon Club (George E. Brown Amb. of Peace award 2000), Humane Soc. of San Bernardino Valley, Redlands Humane Soc., Redlands Dem. Club (treas.), LWV, Inland Empire Debating Soc. (treas.). Democrat. Home: Po Box 622 Redlands CA 92373-0201

ROBERTS, KATHLEEN JOY DOTY, technology staff developer, educational consultant, supervisor; b. Jamaica, NY, Apr. 19, 1951; d. Alfred Arthur and Helen Caroline (Sohl) Doty; m. Robert Louis Roberts, Nov. 24, 1974; children: Robert Louis, Michael Sean, Kathleen Meagan. BA in Edn., CUNY, 1972, MS in Spl. Edn., 1974; cert. advanced study in ednl. adminstrn., Hofstra U., 1982; Ednl. Specialist, Nova Southeastern U., 2003, PhD Computing Tech. in Edn., 2004. Cert. sch. adminstrn., tchr. math., N.Y.; cert. N.Y. Dept. Mental Hygiene; lic. spl. edn. supr., ednl. adminstr., N.Y. Tchr. health conservation Woodside (N.Y.) Jr. H.S., 1973-77; coord. spl. edn. dept. Ridgewood (N.Y.) Jr. H.S., 1977-81; adminstrv. asst., health, compliance and mainstream coord., grant writer Grover Cleveland H.S., Ridgewood, 1981—2004, also coord. transition linkage, resource tchr. mentor, 1981—2004; tech. staff developer Region 4, N.Y.C. Dept. Edn., 2004—06; collaborative team tchr. Queens H.S. of Tchg., 2006—07, distance learning facilitator; supr. tchg. fellows Empire State Coll. SUNY, 2008—. Instr. Grad. Sch. U. Phoenix, 2004—; title II D tech. staff developer Queens Office Instrnl. Tech., NYC-DOE, 2008—, PBS online instr., 2008—; supr. teaching fellows prog. Empire State Coll., SUNY, 2008—. Author: Closed Circuit TV and Other Devices for the Partially Sighted, 1971, Nat. Soc. Colonial Daughters of the Seventeenth Century Lineage Book (Centennial Remembrance edit.), 1999, Infusing Online Components Into the Academic Coursework of High Schools in the State of New York Using HSTOR-E, 2003; contbr. articles to profl. jours. Mem.: ACM, DAR, NEA, NY State Assn. Computing & Tech. Edn., Internat. Soc. Tech. in Edn., N.Y. State Tchrs. Assn., Colonial Dames of the XVII Century (pres., LI Chpt. 2009—), Colonial Daus. of the XVII Century (pres. 1985—91, nat. chmn. hist. activities com. 1988—91, registrar, historian Founders chpt. 1991—94, nat. councillor, publicity chmn. 1991—94, centennial com. 1994—96, registrar gen. nat. soc. 1997—2000, pres. 2000—), Pilgrim Edward Doty Soc. Republican. Home: 52 Hicksville Rd Massapequa NY 11758-5843 Personal E-mail: kathyroberts19@msn.com. Business E-Mail: kathyjdoty@aim.com.

ROBERTS, KEN, electrical engineer, director; married. MS in Elec. Engring., Va. Tech, Blacksburg, 1990. CET, Electronics Certification, 2001. Elec. engr. Reliance Electric Co., Athens, Ga., 1987—95; computer specialist Mgmt. Tech. Inc., Athens, 1996—2000; dir., electronics tech. Athens Tech. Coll., 2000—. Owner, engr. AIS Co., Athens, 1995—2000. Contbr. scientific papers. Mem.: ISCET, ETA. Achievements include development of control theory software; AutoLISP programming tools for AutoCAD; design of control systems object oriented programming; research in total harmonic distortion and IEEE Standards. Office: Athens Tech Coll 800 US Hwy 29 N Athens GA 30601

ROBERTS, KENNETH BARRY, pediatrician; b. Macon, Ga., Feb. 27, 1944; MD, Johns Hopkins U., Baltimore, 1969. Cert. in pediat. Am. Bd. Med. Specialties. Intern in pediat. Johns Hopkins Hosp., 1969—70, resident in pediat., 1970—71, resident, 1973—76; dir. pediat. tchg. programs Moses H. Cone Meml. Hosp., Greensboro, NC; prof. pediat. U. NC, Chapel Hill. Mem.: Fedn. Pediat. Orgns. Office: Moses H Cone Meml Hosp 1200 N Elm St Greensboro NC 27401 Office Phone: 336-832-8064. Office Fax: 336-832-7893. Business E-Mail: kenneth.roberts@mosescone.com.

ROBERTS, KENNETH BOYETT, pharmacy educator, former dean; b. Sharon, Tenn., Nov. 7, 1944; s. James Russell and Blanche (Boyett) Roberts; m. Kittye Louise Rice, Oct. 20, 1968; children: Millicent Boyett, LouAnne Rice. BS in Pharmacy, U. Tenn., Memphis, 1964-67; MBA in Mktg., U. Tenn., Knoxville, 1973; PhD in Health Care Adminstrn., U. Miss., Oxford, 1975. Tchg. asst. U. Miss. Sch. Pharmacy, Oxford, 1973-75, prof., dean, 1989—2000; asst. prof. U. Tex., Austin, 1975-77; exec. dir. Mo. Found. Pharm. Care, St. Louis, 1977-79; prof. pharmacy U. Tenn., Memphis, 1979-89, assoc. dean, 1984-89; exec. dir. Am. Coll. Apothecaries, Memphis, 1981-85; dean U. Ky. Coll. Pharmacy, 2000—09, dean emeritus, 2009—. Cons. Chapman Drug Co., 1985—92, Cardinal Health, 1992—96; pres. West Tenn. Health Edn. Ctr., Memphis, 1987—88. Author: Establishing a Professional Pharmacy Practice, 1980, Managing Support Personnel in Community Pharmacy, 1982, Guidelines for Marketing a Pharmacy Practice, 1983, Guidelines for Pharmacy Management by Self Study, 1984, Guidelines for Establishing Pharmacy Services for Hospice, 1987. Asst. dir. pharmacy US Naval Hosp., Great Lakes, Ill., dir. pharmacy Taipei, Taiwan; mem. Ky. Pharmacy Leadership Coun.; appt. mem. Ky. Innovations Commn., 2000. Recipient Profl. Promotions award, Ky. Pharmacists Assn., 2002, Pres.'s award, Ky. Soc. Hosp. Pharmacists, 2003, Outstanding Dean award, Am. Pharmacists Assn. Student Acad., 2009; named a Charles R. Walgreen Meml. fellow, Am. Found. Pharm. Edn., 1974—75. Fellow: Am. Coll. Apothecaries (Dean's Recognition award 1998); mem.: Tenn.

Pharmacists Assn., Miss. Soc. Hosp. Pharmacists, Miss. Pharmacists Assn., Am. Assn. Colleges of Pharmacy (bd. dirs. 1997—99), Am. Soc. Hosp. Pharmacists, Am. Pharm. Assn., Internat. Fedn. Pharmacists, Am. Assn. Pharm. Scientists, Phi Lambda Sigma, Phi Kappa Phi, Rho Chi, Kappa Psi (nat. pres. 1987—89, Citation of Appreciation 1989), Pi Kappa Alpha, Sigma Xi. Office: U Ky 327 Coll Pharmacy 725 Rose St Lexington KY 40536 Address: 701 The Grance Ln Lexington KY 40511-9577 Office Phone: 859-323-7601. E-mail: krobe2@email.uky.edu.

ROBERTS, KEVIN, advertising executive; b. Lancaster, Eng., Oct. 20, 1949; s. John and Jean (Lambert) Roberts; m. Barbara Beckett; 1 child, Nicola Jane; m. Rowena Joan Honeywill, Dec. 31, 1974; children: Ben, Rebecca, Dan. D (hon.), Waikato U., Hamilton, New Zealand, 1998. With Mary Quant, London, Gillette, Procter & Gamble; CEO Pepsi-Cola Middle East, 1987—89; COO Lion Breweries, New Zealand, 1989—96; worldwide CEO Saatchi & Saatchi, NYC, 1997—. Prof. sustainable enterprise U. Waikato Mgmt. Sch., New Zealand, 2003, U. Limerick, Ireland, 2003; CEO in residence Judge Inst. Mgmt., Cambridge U.; mem. Global Bus. Policy Coun. A.T. Kearney; mem. judging panel Fast Co.'s "Fast 50" Competition. Co-author: (book) Peak Performance: Business Lessons from the World's Best Sporting Organizations, 2000. Bd. mem. New Zealand Rugby Football Union; coach, mentor Turn Your Life Around Trust, Auckland, New Zealand. Avocations: rugby, tennis, art, travel, music. Office: Saatchi & Saatchi 375 Hudson St New York NY 10014-3520 Office Phone: 212-463-2000. Office Fax: 212-463-2367.*

ROBERTS, KURT ERIC, medical educator, director; b. New Haven; s. Dennis and Theresia Roberts; m. Annette Roberts; children: Eric, Lukas. MD, Innsbruck Med. Sch., Austria, 1997. Diplomate Am. Bd. Surgery, 2006. Surg. resident Innsbruck Med. U., 1998—2000, Johns Hopkins Hosp., Balt., 2000—03, U. Wash., Seattle, 2003—05; minimally invasive surgery fellow Yale U., New Haven, 2005—06, asst. prof., 2006—, dir., surg. endoscopy, 2006—, assoc. dir., surg. skills and simulation ctr., 2006—, asst. dir., surg. clerkship, 2007. Contbr. numerous articles to profl. jours. Grantee, Yale U., 2005—07. Mem.: ACS, Austrian Soc. Surgery, Soc. Am. Gastrointestinal and Endoscopic Surgeons, Soc. Laparoendoscopic Surgeons (Best Sci. Paper award 2006, 2007), U. Wash. Alumni. Achievements include patents pending for surgical retraction device; first to introduce total transvaginal and single port appendectomy. Office: Yale Univ Temple St Ste 7B New Haven CT 06510 Office Fax: 203-764-9066. Business E-Mail: kurt.roberts@yale.edu.

ROBERTS, LARRY SPURGEON, biological science educator, zoologist; b. Texon, Tex., June 30, 1935; s. E. Fowler and Frances Wray (Huggins) R.; m. Maria Elek, Feb. 7, 1962; children: Gregory Lorinc, Bruce Tibor, Teresa Margit, Eric Miklos. BS, So. Meth. U., Dallas, 1956; MS, U. Ill., Urbana, 1958; DSc, Johns Hopkins U., Balt., 1961. Cert. scuba instr. Nat. Assn. Underwater Instrs. From asst. prof. to prof. zoology U. Mass., Amherst, 1963-79; prof. biol. scis. Tex. Tech U., Lubbock, 1979-90, chmn. dept., 1979-84. Adj. prof. biol. scis. U. Miami, 1990-99, Fla. Internat. U., 1990-93, 99—, adj. prof., molecular microbiology & infectious diseases, 2008-. Author (with others): Foundations of Parasitology, 1977, 8th edit., 2009; author: Integrated Principles of Zoology, 1979, 14th edit., 2008, Biology of Animals, 1982, 7th edit., 1998, The Underwater World of Sport Diving, 1991, Animal Diversity, 5th edit., 2009. Mem. Amherst Dem. Town Com., 1968-79, vice chmn., 1972-76; mem. Amherst Town Meeting, 1966-76; mem. Amherst Zoning Bd. Appeals, 1972-75, vice chmn., 1972-75; recorder West Tex. Dems., 1985-86; mem. Dade County Dem. Exec. Com., 1991—. NIH postdoctoral trainee, 1961-63; NSF fellow, 1958, NIH fellow, 1969-70; recipient Disting. Svc. cert. Mass. Tchrs. Assn., 1979. Mem. AAAS, ACLU (vice chmn. Hampshire County chpt. 1966-68, bd. dirs. Lubbock chpt. 1985-89, vice chmn. 1988-89, bd. dirs. Miami, Fla. chpt. 1991—, 1st v.p. 1998-00, treas. 2000-06, Fla. State bd. dirs., treas. 2006-09), Am. Soc. Parasitologists (Henry Baldwin Ward medal 1971, coun. mem. at large 1980-83, v.p. 1984-85, 96-97, pres. 1998-99), Am. Micros. Soc. (v.p. 1974-75, exec. com. 1978-81), Mass. Soc. Profs. (pres. 1977-78), Soc. Protozoologists, Am. Soc. Tropical Medicine and Hygiene, Southwestern Assn. Parasitologists (v.p. 1982, pres. 1983), Southeastern Soc. Parasitologists (pres.-elect 1993, pres. 1994), Internat. Soc. Reef Studies, Crustacean Soc., Am. Acad. Underwater Scis., Sigma Xi. Home: 27700 SW 164th Ave Homestead FL 33031-2846 E-mail: Lroberts1@compuserve.com.

ROBERTS, LAWRENCE GILMAN, telecommunications industry executive; b. Conn., Dec. 21, 1937; s. Elliott John and Elizabeth (Gilman) R.; m. June Ellen Stuller, 1959 (div. 1973); children: Paul, Kenny. BSEE, MIT, 1959, MSEE, 1960, PhD, 1963. Dir. info. proc. Advanced Rsch. Projects Agy. U.S. Dept. Def., Arlington, Va., 1969-73; pres., CEO, GTE Telenet Corp., Vienna, Va., 1973-82; pres. DHL, Redwood City, Calif., 1982-83; chmn., CEO, NetExpress, Inc., Foster City, Calif., 1983-93; pres. ATM Systems, Santa Clara, Calif., 1993-98; founder, chief tech. officer Caspian Networks, San Jose, Calif., 1998—2004; founder, CEO Anagran Inc., Woodside, Calif., 2004—. Recipient L.M. Ericsson award for comms., 1981, Prince of Asturias award, 2002, NEC Computer Comms. award, 2005. Mem.: AAAS, IEEE (W. Wallace McDowell award 1992, Internet award 2000), NAE (Draper award 2001), Assn. Computing Machinery (SIGCOM award 1998), Am. Fedn. Info. Processing, IEEE Computer Soc., Sigma Xi. Office Phone: 408-701-0880. E-mail: lroberts@packet.cc.

ROBERTS, LEIGH MILTON, psychiatrist; b. Jacksonville, Ill., June 9, 1925; s. Victor Harold and Ruby Harriet (Kelsey) R.; m. Marilyn Edith Kadow, 1946 (dec. 1995); m. Ellen Rabenhorst, 2003; children: David, Carol Troxell, Paul, Nancy Mills. BS, U. Ill., 1945, MD, 1947. Diplomate Am. Bd. Psychiatry and Neurology. Intern St. Francis Hosp., Peoria, Ill., 1947-48; gen. practice medicine Macomb, Ill., 1948-50; resident in psychiatry U. Wis. Hosps., Madison, 1953-56; staff psychiatrist Mendota (Wis.) State Hosp., 1956-58; mem. faculty U. Wis. Med. Sch., Madison, 1959-89, prof. psychiatry, 1971-89, acting chmn. dept., 1972-75. Cons. in psychiatry, 1989-; mem. spl. rev. bd. Wis. Parole Bd. Sex Crimes Law, 1962-88, forensic cons., 1988—; mem. Dane County Devel. Disabilities Bd., 1962-66, Wis. Planning Com. Mental Health, 1963-65, Wis. Planning Com. Health, 1969-71, Wis. Planning Com. Vocat. Rehab., 1966-68, Wis. Planning Com. Health Centers, 1967-71, Wis. Mental Health Adv. Com., 1973-78; bd. dirs. Methodist Hosp., Madison, Dane County Rehab. House, Dane County Assn. Mental Health; cons. in field. Editor: Community Psychiatry, 1966, Comprehensive Mental Health, 1968; contbr. articles profl. jours. Pres. Wis. Coun. Chs., 1976-78; bd. dirs. Madison Campus Ministry, St. Benedict Center; trustee North Central Coll., Naperville, Ill. Served with USNR, 1943-45, 50-53. Decorated Bronze Stars, Purple Heart. Fellow Am. Psychiat. Assn. (trustee 1981-84), Wis. Psychiat. Assn. (pres. 1967) Methodist. Home and Office: 33 S Midvale Blvd Madison WI 53705 *Life is a precious gift whose journey is molded and shaped by cumulative experiences and relationships. Religious belief and practice which provides future-oriented hope, disciplined accountability and living service are balanced by professional psychiatric vistas on the uniqueness and worth of each human person.*

ROBERTS, LEONARD H., retail executive; b. Chgo., Feb. 19, 1949; s. Jack and Goldie (Solomon) R.; m. Laurie Susan Osser, Aug. 20, 1967; children: Dawn, Adina, Melissa. BS in Chemistry and Mktg., U. Ill., 1971; JD, DePaul U., 1974. Food scientist Armour Foods, Chgo., 1968-71, Cen. Soya, Chgo., 1971-74; govt. lobbyist Ralston Purina Co., St. Louis, 1974-76, dir. mktg., 1976-78, mng. dir. Raltech Madison, Wis., 1978-81, v.p. food service ops. St. Louis, 1981-85; pres., CEO Arby's Inc., Atlanta, 1985-89; chmn. bd., CEO Shoney's Inc., 1989-93; pres. Radio Shack, Fort Worth, Tex., 1993—99, Tandy Corp., Fort Worth, Tex., 1996—99; chmn., pres., CEO RadioShack Corp., Fort Worth, 1999—2005, exec. chmn., 2005—06. Bd. dirs. Ghirardelli Chocolate Co., Tandy Corp. Holder numerous patents on Soya protein research. Active United Way Met. Tarrant County, 1994, Nat. Crime Prevention Coun., 1994, Clark U. Students in Free Enterprise, Girl Scouts U.S., Harris Meth. Bd.; mem. exec. com. Fort Worth Symphony. Recipient Pvt. Sector Initiative award Office Pres. of U.S., Washington, 1987, Disting. Achievement award B'nai B'rith, Restaurant Bus. Leadership award, 1991, Golden Plate award Nations Restaurant News, 1991, Wall St. Bronze Critics award, 1992. Mem. ABA, Ill. Bar Assn. Home: 3516 Briarhaven Rd Fort Worth TX 76109-3128

ROBERTS, LILLIAN, retired principal; b. Albuquerque, Dec. 1, 1927; d. John Wagner and Mattie Rebecca (Beaty) Thomas; m. Vernie Roberts, Aug. 28, 1953 (dec. Sept. 13, 1980); children: Albert, Kenneth, Constance Marie. BA, Calif. State U., Stanislaus, 1964; MA, Fresno Pacific Coll., Calif., 1979. Cert. elem. tchr., Calif. Mgr., co-owner Vernie's Barber Shop and Cocktail Lounge, Merced, Calif., 1955-66; tchr. Merced City Sch. Dist., 1962-72, resource tchr., 1972-77, coord. consolidate programs, 1977-92, preschool prin., 1981-92; ret., 1992. Pvt. music tchr., Merced, 1960-65; adult edn. tchr. Merced Union High Sch. Dist., 1965-66; chief attendance officer Merced City Sch. Dist., 1981-92, affirmative action officer, title IX officer, 1981-86, mem. blue ribbon boundary task force, 1990-91; adj. instr. Merced Community Coll., 1983-86, seminar leader Early Childhood Devel., 1985, Early Childhood Edn., 1989- 90. Mem. Muir Trail Coun. Girl Scouts U.S.A., 1979-80, 15th Congl. Dist. Constituents Adv. Com., 1987—, Merced Cmty. Concerts, 1972-79; mem. acad. adv. coun. Calif. State U., Stanislaus, 1980; mem. Merced Masterworks Chorale, 1980-85; proctor Merced County Acad. Decathalon; mem. com. Children's Svc. Network Merced County, 1983-2003, chmn., 1986, also bd. dirs.; exec. dir. Spl. Advs. for Children Merced County, 1992-96; bd. dirs. ct. appointed spl. advocates for Abused, Neglected, Abandoned Children (CASA), cons., 1993-96. Named an honoree, Merced County Hist. Soc. Mus. Exhibit, 2007. Mem. NEA, Calif. Tchrs. Assn. Merced City Tchrs. Assn., Assn. Calif. Sch. Adminstrn. (charter ret. mems. region IX 1993), Merced Sch. Employees Fed. Credit Union (credit com. 1972-77, bd. dirs 1977-84), Nat. Assn. for the Edn. Young Children, Calif. Assn. for the Edn. Young Children, Merced Coll. Cmty. Chorale, Kiwanis Club of Merced. Democrat. Avocations: reading, piano and organ playing, swimming, exercise, singing.

ROBERTS, LORIN WATSON, botanist, educator; b. Clarksdale, Mo., June 28, 1923; s. Lorin Cornelius and Irene (Watson) Roberts; m. Florence Ruth Greathouse, July 10, 1967; children: Michael Hamlin, Daniel Hamlin, Margaret Susan. BA, U. Mo., 1948, MA, 1950; PhD in Botany, U. Mo.-Columbia, 1952. Asst. prof., then assoc. prof. botany Agnes Scott Coll., Decaur, Ga., 1952-57; vis. asst. prof. Emory U., 1952-55; mem. faculty U. Idaho, 1957—, prof. botany, 1967-91, prof. botany emeritus, 1991—; Fulbright research prof. Kyoto (Japan) U., 1967-68; research fellow U. Bari, Italy, 1968; Cabot fellow Harvard, 1974; Fulbright teaching fellow North-Eastern Hill U., Shillong, Meghalaya, India, 1977; Fulbright sr. scholar and fellow Australian Nat. U., Canberra, 1980; sr. researcher U. London, 1984; pres. botany sect. 1st Internat. Congress Histochemistry and Cytochemistry, Paris, 1960; Alexander von Humboldt vis. fellow Australian Nat. U., 1992. Author: Cytodifferentiation in Plants, 1976; author: (with J. H. Dodds) Experiments in Plant Tissue Culture, 1982, 3d edit., 1995; author: (with P. B. Gahan and R. Aloni) Vascular Differentiation and Plant Growth Regulators, 1988; contbr. articles to profl. jours. With USAAF, 1943—46. Decorated chevalier de l'Ordre du Merit Agricole France; Alexander von Humboldt fellow, 1992. Fellow: AAAS; mem.: Idaho Acad. Scis., Am. Inst. Biol. Scis., Internat. Assn. Plant Tissue Culture, Am. Soc. Plant Physiologists, Bot. Soc. Am., N.W. Sci. Assn. (pres. 1970—71), Sigma Xi, Phi Sigma, Phi Kappa Phi. Home (Winter): 920 Mabelle St Moscow ID 83843-3834

ROBERTS, MARGARET HAROLD, editor, publisher; b. Aug. 18, 1928; AB, U. Chattanooga, Tenn., 1950. Editor, pub. series Award Winning Art, 1960-70, New Woman mag., Palm Beach, Fla., 1971-84; editor, pub. BONKERS mag., 1992—2001. Author: juvenile book series Daddy is a Doctor, 1965.

ROBERTS, MARILYN GOTTLIEB, artist, educator; b. Rome, Ga., Apr. 18, 1939; d. John Treadwell and Mary Georgina (Crichton) Roberts; m. Norman Lee Gottlieb, May 6, 1964 (div. Sept. 1975); children: Eric Inness, Karla Lewis. AB in Painting and Lit., Goddard Coll., 1975; MFA, U. Miami, 1977. Prof. Miami Dade Coll., Fla., 1980—2006, R.W. Greenfield Endowed chair, 1993—96, 1996—99. Exhibns. include Carpenter Ctr. Arts Harvard U., Mass., Currier Gallery Art, NH, Clocktower, NYC, Exit Art, NYC, Fleming Mus. U. Vt., New Gallery U. Miami, Birmingham Mus. Art, Ala., Columbus Mus. Art, Ga., Mus. Contemporary Art, Fla., others. Trustee Miami Beach Devel. Corp., 1992—. Fulbright scholar U. Jos, Nigeria, 2000-02. Business E-Mail: m427@bellsouth.net.

ROBERTS, MARKLEY, economist, educator; b. Shanghai, Sept. 3, 1930; s. Donald and Frances Charlotte (Markley) Roberts; m. Jeanne Addison, Feb. 19, 1966; children: Addison, Ellen. AB, Princeton U., 1951; MA, Am. U., 1960, PhD, 1970. Reporter Washington Star newspaper, 1952-57; legis. asst. Office of Senator Hubert Humphrey of Minn., Washington, 1957-62; legis. asst., economist AFL-CIO, Washington, 1962-96, asst. dir. econ. rsch. dept., 1989-96. Bd. dirs., vice-chmn. Econ. Edn. Found. Clergy, 1972—80; chmn. labor rsch. adv. coun. Bur. Labor Stats., Dept. Labor, 1972—96; adj. prof. econs. U. Md., 1966—, George Washington U., 1972—96; bd. dirs., chair Inst. Learning Retirement, 2002—. Contbr. articles to profl. jours.; author: monographs in field. Mem. DC Dem. Ctrl. Com., 1964—68; ward III coord. Washington Mayor Walter Washington, 1974—78; bd. dirs. Laymen's Nat. Bible Com. Inc., NYC, 1972—82. Mem.: Newspaper Guild, Nat. Consumers League (bd. dirs. 1991—99), Am. Statis. Assn., Assn. Evolutionary Econs., Nat. Acad. Social Ins., Am. Polit. Sci. Assn., Indsl. Rels. Rsch. Assn. (exec. bd. 1975—77), Am. Econ. Assn., Social Dems. USA, UN Assn. (bd. dirs. labor chair nat. capitol area chpt. 1996—, mem. exec. com. nat. coun. orgns. 2007—09, arms control chair), Ams. Dem. Action (exec. bd. 1992—), Cosmos Club. Democrat. Episcopalian. Home: 4931 Albemarle St NW Washington DC 20016-4359

ROBERTS, MELVILLE PARKER, neurosurgeon; b. Phila., Oct. 15, 1931; s. Melville Parker and Marguerite Louise (Reimann) R.; m. Sigrid Marianne Magnusson, Mar. 27, 1954; children: Melville Parker III, Julia Pell, Erik Emerson. BS, Washington and Lee U., 1953; MD, Yale U., 1957. Diplomate: Am. Bd. Neurol. Surgery. Intern Yale Med. Ctr., 1957, neurosurgical resident, 1958-60, 62-64, Am. Cancer Soc. fellow in neurosurgery, 1962-64, instr., 1964; asst. prof. surgery Sch. Medicine U. Va., Charlottesville, 1965-69; practice medicine specializing in neurol. surgery Hartford, Conn., 1970-1998; mem. staff Hartford Hosp.; asst. prof. surgery Sch. Medicine U. Conn., Farmington, 1970-71, assoc. prof., 1972-75, assoc. prof. neurology, 1974-77, chmn. divsn. neurosurgery, 1971-84, prof. surgery, 1975—, acting chmn. dept. neurology, 1973-77, acting chmn. dept. surgery, 1974-77, William Beecher Scoville prof. neurosurgery, 1976-98, prof. emeritus, 1998—. James Hudson Brown rsch. fellow Yale U., 1957. Author: Atlas of the Human Brain in Section, 1970, 2d edit., 1987, The Brain Atlas, 1998; mem. editl. bd.: Conn. Medicine, 1973-98; contbr. articles to profl. jours. Capt. MC, US Army, 1960-61. Fellow Royal Soc. Medicine London (life); mem. Am. Assn. Neurol. Surgeons, Soc. Neurol. Surgeons, Congress Neurol. Surgeons (bd. dirs. joint spinal sect. with Am. Assn. Neurol. Surgeons, chmn. ann. meeting 1987, sci. program chmn. ann. meeting 1988), Assn. for Rsch. in Nervous and Mental Diseases, New Eng. Neurosurg. Soc. (bd. dirs. 1976-79, pres. 1989-91), Yale Surg. Soc., Sigma Xi (hon.), Lambda Chi Alpha, Soc. Brit. Neurol. Surgeons, Rsch. Soc. Neurol. Surgeons, Soc. Rsch. into Hydrocephalus and Spina Bifida, Conn. Acad. Arts and Sci., Vereingung Schweizer Neurochirugen, Mory's Assn., Beaumont Med. Club (pres. 1988, New Haven), Yale Club NY, Sloane Club (London). Episcopalian.

ROBERTS, MICHAEL G., lawyer; b. 1956; BA with high honors, Mich. State U., 1977; jd cum laude, Am. U., 1982. Bar: DC 1983, Fla. 1984. Law clerk DC Superior Ct., 1983; maritime atty. Washington; from corp. counsel to v.p., govt. rels. Crowley Maritime Corp., 1991—2000; with Thompson Coburn LLP, Washington, 2000—04; ptnr., transp. law Venable LLP, Washington, 2004—. Adj. prof., bus. law Am. Univ. Mem. Navy League US; bd. gov. Propeller Club US, 1994—2003; founding chmn. CoastWise Coalition. Mem.: Maritime Adminstrv. Bar Assn. (pres. 1999—2000), Nat. Def. Transp. Assn. (life). Office: Venable LLP 575 Seventh St NW Washington DC 20004 Office Phone: 202-344-4350. Office Fax: 202-344-8300. Business E-Mail: mgroberts@venable.com.

ROBERTS, MICHAEL T., lawyer, educator; Attended, Drake U., Des Moines; BS, U. Utah, 1986, JD, 1989; LLM, U. Ark. Sch. Law, 2001. Bar: Utah. Judicial clk Utah Ct. of Appeals, 1989—90; atty. Van Cott Bagley Cornwall & McCarthy, Ogden, Utah; rsch. assoc. prof. U. Ark. Sch. Law, 2001—06, dir. Nat. Agrl. Law Ctr., 2003—06; of counsel Venable LLP, Washington, 2006—. Past chmn., Agribusiness Practice Group Lex Mundi. Contbr. articles to law jours. Mem.: ABA, Food Safety Consortium, Inst. of Food Technologists, Food and Drug Law Inst., Am. Law Sch. Assn., Am. Agrl. Law Assn. Office: Venable LLP 575 7th St, NW Washington DC 20004 Office Phone: 202-334-4684. Office Fax: 202-344-8300. E-mail: mtroberts@venable.com.

ROBERTS, MICHELE A., lawyer; b. NYC, Sept. 14, 1956; BA, Wesleyan U., 1977; JD, Boalt Hall Sch. Law, U. Calif., Berkeley, 1980. Bar: Wash. DC 1980. Atty. Pub. Defender Svc., Washington, 1986—92; ptnr. Rochon & Roberts, 1992—2001, Shea & Gardner, 2001—04; ptnr., civil/white collar litig. Akin Gump Strauss Hauer & Feld LLP, Washington, 2004—. Former mem. adj. faculty George Wash. U. Sch. Law; former lectr. Pub. Defender Svc. Tng. Program; past instr. Nat. Inst. Trial Advocacy; mem. adj. faculty Harvard Law Sch.; serves on DC Adv. Commn. on Sentencing. Named First Among Washington's Top 75 Lawyers, Washingtonian mag. survey, 2002; named one of 75 Best Lawyers in Washington, 2004, Am. Top Black Lawyers, Black Enterprise Mag., 2003, Washington's 10 Leading Criminal Def. Lawyers, Legal Times, 2006; named to Best Lawyers in America, 2006. Fellow: Am. Coll. Trial Lawyers; mem.: Nat. Assn. Criminal Def. Lawyers, Nat. Bar Assn., ABA, DC Bar. Office: Akin Gump Strauss Hauer & Feld LLP Robert S Strauss Bldg 1333 New Hampshire Ave NW Washington DC 20036-1564 Office Phone: 202-887-4306. Business E-Mail: mroberts@akingump.com.

ROBERTS, MONTY, horse trainer, writer; b. Calif., 1935; m. Pat, 3 children, 47 foster children. D (hon.), Univ. Zurich. Stuntman, Hollywood; owner, operator, thoroughbred breeding, training facility Flag Is Up Farms, Solvang, Calif.; owner, operator Monty Roberts Equestrian Acad., Join Up Internat. Inc., Solvang, Calif. Creator Join Up method for non-violent equine training. Author: The Man Who Listens to Horses, 1997 (NY Times Bestseller list), Shy Boy: The Horse that Came in from the Wild, 1999 (NY Times Bestseller list), Horse Sense for People, 2001, From My Hands to Yours, 2002, The Horses in My Life, 2005; subject, with Shy Boy, the mustang (PBS/BBC documentary) Monty Roberts: The Real Horse Whisperer. Achievements include being invited by Queen Elizabeth II to teach Join Up method to her equestrian team, London. Home and Office: Flag Is Up Farms 901 E Hwy 246 PO Box 1700 Solvang CA 93464 Office Phone: 805-688-6288. Office Fax: 805-688-2242. Business E-Mail: admin@montyroberts.com.

ROBERTS, NORA (ELEANOR MARIE ROBERTSON), writer; b. Silver Spring, Md., Oct. 10, 1950; m. Ronald Aufdem-Brinke, 1970 (div. 1983); children: Dan, Jason; m. Bruce Wilder, 1985. Author: (novels) Hot Ice, 1987, Promise Me Tomorrow, 1984, Brazen Virtue, 1988, Sweet Revenge, 1989, Public Secrets, 1990, Genuine Lies, 1991, Carnal Innocence, 1992, Divine Evil, 1992, Honest Illusions, 1992, Private Scandals, 1993, Hidden Riches, 1994, Born in Fire, 1994, Born in Ice, 1995, True Betrayals, 1995, Born in Shame, 1996, Daring to Dream, 1996, Montana Sky, 1996, Holding the Dream, 1997, Finding the Dream, 1997, Sanctuary, 1997, Rising Tides, 1998, Once Upon a Castle, 1998, Homeport, 1998, Sea Swept, 1998, The Reef, 1998, Inner Harbor, 1999, Jewels of the Sun, 1999, River's End, 1999, Heart of the Sea, 2000, Tears of the Moon, 2000, Carolina Moon, 2001, Heaven and Earth, 2001, The Villa, 2002, Three Fates, 2002, Chesapeake Blue, 2002, Key of Knowledge, 2003, Key of Light, 2003, Once Upon a Midnight, 2003, Birthright, 2003, Blue Dahlia, 2004, Once Upon a Moon, 2004, Northern Lights, 2004, A Little Fate, 2004, Key of Valor, 2004, Black Rose, 2005, Blue Smoke, 2005 (Quill award for romance, 2007), First Impressions, 2006, Tribute, 2008 (Quill award for romance, #1 Publishers Weekly bestseller, 2008), The Pagan Stone, 2008 (#1 Publishers Weekly bestseller), Vision In White, 2009 (#1 Publishers Weekly bestseller), Black Hills, 2009 (#1 Publishers Weekly bestseller), (under pseudonym J.D. Robb) Naked in Death, 1995, Glory in Death, 1995, Immortal in Death, 1996, Rapture in Death, 1996, Ceremony in Death, 1997, Vengeance in Death, 1997, Holiday in Death, 1998, Loyalty in Death, 1999, Conspiracy in Death, 1999, Judgment in Death, 2000, Witness in Death, 2000, Betrayal in Death, 2001, Seduction in Death, 2001, Interlude in Death, 2001, Purity in Death, 2002, Reunion in Death, 2002, Imitation in Death, 2003, Portrait in Death, 2003, Visions in Death, 2004, Survivor in Death, 2005, Origin in Death, 2005, Memory in Death, 2006, Dance of the Gods, 2006, Creation in Death, 2007, High Noon, 2007, Angels Fall, 2007 (Quill award for romance, 2006, Quill award for Book of Yr., 2006), Blood Brothers, 2007, The Hollow, 2008, Strangers in Death, 2008 (Publishers Weekly bestseller), Salvation in Death, 2008 (Publishers Weekly bestseller);: Promises in Death, 2009. Recipient Lifetime Achievement award, Waldenbooks, 1991; named one of The World's Most Influential People, TIME mag., 2007. Mem.: Novelists, Inc., Crime League America, Sisters in Crime, Mystery Writers America, Romance Writers America (charter mem. Washington chpt., 7 Golden Medallion awards 1983—89, Lifetime Achievement award 1997, Centennial award, Hall of Fame inductee, 14 Rita awards 1992—2006). Achievements include having 124 out of over 150 novels ranked on the NY Times bestseller list, including 29 that debuted in the number-one spot for a combined 90 weeks. Office: GP Putnams Sons 375 Hudson St New York NY 10014-3658*

ROBERTS, NORM, men's college basketball coach; b. Queens, NY, July 21, 1965; m. Pascale Roberts; children: Nicholas, Justin. BS in Health and Phys. Edn., CUNY: Queens Coll., Flushing, 1987. Freshman team head basketball coach, varsity team asst. Archbishop Molloy HS, Queens, 1987—90; head basketball coach Queens Coll. Knights, 1991—95; team asst., men's basketball Oral Roberts U. Golden Eagles, 1995—97, U. Tulsa Golden Hurricane, 1997—2000; asst. coach U. Ill. Fighting Illini, 2000—02, assoc. head coach, 2002—03, U. Kans. Jayhawks, 2003—04; head basketball coach St. John's U. Red Storm, Queens, 2004—. Active Coaches vs. Cancer. Mem.: Black Coaches Assn., Nat. Assn. Basketball Coaches. Office: St Johns Univ 8000 Utopia Pky Jamaica NY 11439*

ROBERTS, PATRICIA LEE, education educator; b. Coffeyville, Kans. d. Philip Lee Brighton and Lois Ethel Wortham; m. James E. Roberts, Oct. 5, 1953; children: James Michael, Jill Frances. BA, Calif. State U., Fresno, 1953, MA, 1964; EdD, U. Pacific, Stockton, Calif., 1975. Lifetime tchg. diploma; sch. adminstrn. cert. Prof. edn. Calif. State U., Sacramento, 1969—. Cons. in field. Author: (textbooks) Alphabet: A Handbook of ABC Books and Book Extensions for the Elementary Classroom, 2d edit., 1994, Integrating Language Arts and Social Studies for Kindergarten and Primary Children, 1996, Literature-Based History Activities for Children, Grades 4-8, 1997, Taking Humor Seriously in Children's Literature, 1997, Multicultural Friendship Stories and Activities for Children Ages 5-14, 1997, Language Arts and Environmental Awareness, 1998, Literature-Based History Activities for Children, Grades 1-3, 1998, Family Values Through Children's Literature, Grades K-3, 1999, Family Values Through Children's Literature, Grades 4-6, 2005, A Guide for Developing an Interdisciplinary Thematic Unit, 4th edit., 2008, A Resource Guide for Elementary School Teaching. Named Disting. Alumnae of Yr., U. Pacific, 1975-76. Mem. Internat. Reading Assn., Nat. Coun. Rsch. on English.

ROBERTS, PAUL CRAIG, III, economics professor, writer, columnist; b. Atlanta, Apr. 3, 1939; s. Paul Craig and Ellen Lamar (Dryman) R.; m. Becky B. Bickerstaff, 1959 (div. 1968); m. Linda Jane Fisher, July 3, 1969 (div. 1994); children: Becky Ellen, Stephanie Bradford, Pendaran Struan Sherman. BS, Ga. Inst. Tech., 1961; postgrad., U. Calif., Berkeley, 1962—63, Merton Coll., Oxford U., Eng., 1964—65; PhD, U. Va., 1967. Asst. prof. econs. Va. Poly. Inst., 1965-69; assoc. prof. U. N.Mex., 1969-71; rsch. fellow Hoover Instn., Stanford U., 1971-77, sr. rsch. fellow, 1978—2004; mem. U.S. Congl. Staff, 1975-78; asst. sec. of treasury for econ. policy Dept. Treasury, Washington, 1981-82; William E. Simon prof. polit. economy Georgetown U. Ctr. for Strategic and Internat. Studies, Washington, 1982-93; chmn. Inst. for Polit. Economy, 1985—, John M. Olin fellow, 1994—2004; rsch. fellow Ind. Inst., 1990—. Disting. adj. scholar Ctr. Strategic and Internat. Studies, Washington, 1993-96; adj. scholar Cato Inst., 1987-93, disting. fellow, 1993-96; assoc. editor, columnist Wall St. Jour., N.Y.C., 1978-80; columnist Bus. Week, 1983-98, Fin. Post, Can., 1988-89, Liberation, Paris, 1988-89, Erfolg, Fed. Rep. of Germany, 1988, Washington Times, 1988—, San Diego Union, 1988-92, Le Figaro, Paris, 1992-96, Investors Bus. Daily, 1998-2005; nationally syndicated columnist Scripps Howard News Svc., 1989-97, Creators Syndicate, 1997—; contbr. editor: Nat. Rev., 1993-2003, Reason Mag., 1993-95, World Trade mag., 1997-98; mem. Pres.-elect Reagan's Task Force on Tax Policy, 1980; dir. Value Line Investment Funds, N.Y.C., A. Schulman, Akron, Ohio; cons. Morgan Guaranty Trust Co., Lazard Freres Asset Mgmt., 1983-97; pres. Econ. & Communication Svcs. Inc.; cons. Dept. Commerce, 1983, Dept. Def., 1983-84; mem. adv. bd. Marvin and Palmer, 1986-96, Am. studies program Harding U.; mem. ad. com. Ctr. for the Am. Founding; mem. Wright Investors' Svc. Internat. Bd. Econ. and Invesmtent Advisors; bd. dirs. Com. on Present Danger; trustee Intercollegiate Studies Inst., Com. on Developing Am. Capitalism; mem. selection com. Frank E. Seidman disting. award in Polit. Economy; pres. Inlet Beach Water Co., 2000-06. Author: Alienation and the Soviet Economy, 1971, new edit., 1990, Marx's Theory of Exchange, 1973, new edit., 1983, The Supply-Side Revolution: An Insider's Account of Policymaking in Washington, 1984, The Cost of Corporate Capital in the U.S. and Japan, 1985, Meltdown: Inside the Soviet Economy, 1990, The New Color Line: How Quotas and Privilege Destroy Democracy, 1995; The Capitalist Revolution in Latin America, Oxford U. Press, 1997, The Tyranny of Good Intentions, 2000, new edit., 2008, Chile: Dos Visiones-la Era Allende-Pinochet, 2000; mem. editl. bd. Modern Age, Intercollegiate Rev.; contbg. editor Harper's Mag. Drafted original Kemp-Roth Bill, 1976. Recipient Meritorious Svc. award Dept. Treasury, 1982, Pub. Svc. award GSA, 1991, Warren Brookes award for Excellence in Journalism, 1992; Am. Philos. Soc. grantee, 1968; named to Chevalier de la Légion d'Honneur, 1987, Gridiron Secret Soc., U. Ga.; Earhart fellow U. Va., 1966-67, Nat. Chamber Found. fellow, 1984-85. Mem. Mont Pelerin Soc., Beethoven Soc., Am. Soc. French Legion of Honor, U.S. C. of C. (taxation com.), Polanyi Soc., Sierra Club, Fla. Wildlife Fedn., Am. Civil Liberties Union, Amnesty Internat. Home and Office: 169 Pompano St Panama City FL 32413-7245

ROBERTS, PAUL DALE, state agency administrator, writer; b. Fresno, Calif., Jan. 17, 1955; s. Paul Marceau and Rosemarie Roberts; divorced; 1 child, Jason Randall Porter. AA, Sacramento City Coll., Calif., 1977; diploma in pvt. investigations, Ctrl. Investigation & Security, 1984. Office asst. I, Dept. Benefit Payments, Sacramento, 1976-77; firefighter Calif. Divsn. Forestry, Colfax, 1977; key data operator Dept. Justice, Sacramento, 1977-78; intelligence analyst, spl. forces instr. US Army Mil. Intelligence, Seoul, Republic of Korea, 1979-84; office asst. 1 Calif. State Lottery Commn., 1987-89; law libr. Employment Devel. Dept., Sacramento, 1989-92; office asst. II, Calif. Dept. Health Svcs., Sacramento, 1992-98, chief cert. support, 1992-93; supervising program technician II Dept. Cmty. Svcs. and Devel., State Calif., Sacramento, 1998-2000; divsn. supr. polit. reform Sec. of State, Sacramento, 2000—07; office mgr. Calif. Dept. Fish and Game, Sacramento, 2007—. Office asst I, Calif. Lottery Commn., 1987-89; disaster courier dept. social svcs. Gov.'s Office of Emergency Svcs., LA, 1994. Author: Organization of D.E.A.T.H. (Destroy Evildoers and Teach Harmony), 1984, The Cosmic Bleeder, 1991, Madam Zara, Vampiress, 1993, People's Comic Book Newsletter, 1996, The Legendary Dark Silhouette, 1997, Vacationing in Dublin, Ireland and Newry, Northern Ireland, 1997, (comic book) The Legendary Dark Silhouette, 1997, Jazma Universe Online!, 1998, Jazma League of Justice, 1999, Jazma Man/Jazma Girl, 2000, My Adventures in Brazil, 2001, My Adventures in Thailand/Burma, 2003, My Adventures in Moscow, Russia, 2004, Nicole Mila Phengaroune Growing Up Years, 2005, My 50th Birthday on Catalina Island, 2005, My Crazy Adventure to Spain, Gibralter, Portugal and Tangiers/Morocco- North Africa, 2005, The Amsterdam/Belgium/Berlin Romp!, 2006, Ghost Hunting with Haunted and Paranormal Investigations, 2007, HPI Chronicles: HPI Meets Dracula, 2008, My Adventure to Aruba & the Territorial Waters of Venezuela, 2009; (TV documentaries): Mysteries of Angels & Demons by Ives Street Entertainment, 2008, The Mayan Prophesy of 2012 by Showtime's Penn & Teller, 2008, Conversations with a Serial Killer-Richard Trenton Chase by Two Four Productions, 2008. Sgt. U.S. Army Mil. Police, 1973-76. Republican. Roman Catholic. Avocations: flying, tennis, photography, ballooning, skydiving. Home: 5606 Moonlight Way Elk Grove CA 95758-6837 Office: 1500 11th St Rm 495 Sacramento CA 95814 Personal E-mail: pauld5606@comcast.net.

ROBERTS, R. MICHAEL, animal scientist, biochemist, educator; b. U.K., 1941; BA in Botany, Oxford U., PhD in Plant Physiology and Biochemistry; doctorate (hon.), U. Liege, Belgium, 1998. Prof. animal scis. and biochemistry U. Mo., Columbia, 1985—, curators' prof., 1996—, dir. Life Scis. Ctr., 2004—. Vice-chmn. Gordon Conf. on Mammalian Genital Tract Plymouth State Coll., 1986; chmn. Gordon Conf. on Reproductive Tract Biology Brewster Acad., 1988; fgn. specialist Nat. Inst. Animal Industry, Japan, 1998; chief scientist Nat. Rsch. Initiative Competitive Grants Program/Coop. State Rsch., Edn., Extension Svc./USDA, 1998—2000. Contbr. articles to profl. jours. Recipient Rsch. award, Soc. for Study of Reproduction, 1990, Merit award, NIH, 1990—2000, Milstein award, Internat. Soc. Interferon and Cytokine Rsch., 1995, Alexander von Humboldt award for agr., 1996, Wolf prize in agr., Wolf Found., Israel, 2003; named Disting. Scientist, USDA, 1992. Mem.: NAS. Office: U Mo Columbia Divsn Animal Scis 158 Animal Sci Rsch Ctr Columbia MO 65211

ROBERTS, RALPH JOEL, telecommunications industry and cable broadcast executive; b. NYC, Mar. 13, 1920; s. Robert and Sara (Wahl) Roberts; m. Suzanne Fleisher, Aug. 23, 1942; children: Catherine, Lisa, Ralph Jr., Brian, Douglas. BS in Econs., U. Pa., 1941; LHD (hon.), Holy Family Coll., 1994; HHD (hon.), Arcadia U., 2004; LLD (hon.), U. Pa., 2005. Account exec. Aitken Kynett Advt., Phila., 1946-48; v.p. Muzak Corp., NYC, 1948-50; pres., chief exec. officer Pioneer Industries, Inc., Darby, Pa., 1950-61; pres. Internat. Equity Corp., Bala Cynwyd, Pa., 1961-83; chmn., chief exec. officer Sural Corp. (merger with Internat. Equity Corp. 1983); chmn. Comcast Corp., Phila., 1997—2002, chmn. exec. com., 2002—. Trustee, chmn. conflict interest com. Albert Einstein Med. Ctr.; bd. dirs. Phila. Electric Co., Phila. Nat. Bank, Corestates, Penn Medicine; bd. trustees U. Pa. Health Sys., 2002. Bd. dirs. regional NCCJ; trustee Brandywine Mus. and Conservancy, charter mem. World Bus. Coun.; past mem. mentor program and Benjamin Franklin assocs. U. Pa.; bd. dirs. Phila. Orch., 1993; past v.p. Family Svc. Phila.; past bd. dirs., mem. budget and fees com. State Coll. and Univ. Dirs.; mem. re-regulation and legis. affairs coms. Nat. Cable TV Assn.; past mem. Gov.'s Rev. of Govt. Mgmt., Inc. Lt. USNR, 1942-45. Reipient Americanism award Anti-Defamation League of B'nai B'rith, Brotherhood award NCCJ, 1989, award for outstanding svc. to cable TV industry Walter Kaitz Found., 1990, Acres of Diamonds Entrepreneurial Excellence award Entrepreneurial Inst. Temple U., 1991, Disting. Vanguard award for leadership Nat. Cable TV Assn., 1993, Golden Plate award Am. Acad. Achievement, 1994, PAL award Police Athletic League Phila., 1995, Edward Powell award for cmty. svc. City of Phila., 1995, Joseph P. Wharton award U. Pa., 1995, Whitney M. Young Jr. Leadership award Urban League Phila., 1997, Disting. Cmty. Leadership award Operation Understanding, 1997, Cable TV Hall of Fame award, 2000, Mensa Achievement award, 2000, Heroes of Liberty award Liberty Mus., 2000, William Penn award Greater Phila. C. of C., 2002, Am. Horizon award for Visionary Leadership, Media Inst., Washington, 2002, Humanitarian award United Jewish Appeal Fedn. of NY, 2003, Trustee award NATAS, 2003, Excellence in Leadership award Temple U., 2005, Partnership for Drug Free Am. hon., 2005; named to Broadcasting and Cable Hall of Fame, 1993. Avocations: tennis, travel. Home: Sural Farm 505 Fairview Rd East Fallowfield Township PA 19320-4451 Office: Comcast Corp One Comcast Ctr 1701 J7K Blvd Philadelphia PA 19103-2838 Office Fax: 215-981-7790. Business E-Mail: rroberts@comcast.com.*

ROBERTS, RICHARD CHARLTON, III, lawyer; b. Jackson, Miss., Mar. 18, 1951; BA, U. Miss., 1973, JD with distinction, 1976. Bar: Miss. 1976, U.S. Dist. Ct. (no. and so. dists.) Miss. 1976, U.S. Ct. Appeals (5th cir.) 1976, U.S. Ct. Appeals (11th cir.) 1981, U.S. Supreme Ct. 1989. Pvt. practice, Jackson, Miss. Assoc. editor Miss. Law Jour., 1976. Named Middle South Super Lawyers, 2006; named one of Best Lawyers in Am., Outstanding Lawyers Am. Fellow: Nat. Conf. Bar Pres., Miss. Bar Found.; mem.: ABA (sect. on family law, gen. practice, solo and small firm practice), Nat. Lawyer's Assn., Bar Assn. 5th Fed. Cir., Miss. Bar (chmn. solo and small firm practitioner's task force 1993—94, exec. com. family law sect. 1994—95, chmn. 1996, bd. bar commrs. 1996—99, nominating com. 1998—99, bench-bar liaison standing com. 2001—, bd. bar commrs. 2002—05, pres. 2003—04), Hinds County Bar Assn. (bd. dirs. 1990—96, sec.-treas. 1992—93, pres. 1994—95, chmn. long range planning com. 1995—97), Fed. Bar Assn. (pres. Miss. chpt. 1987—88, nat. coun. 1988, jud. liaison for U.S. Dist. Cts.-So. Dist. Miss. 1989), Am. Inss of Ct., Phi Kappa Phi. Office: PO Box 55882 Jackson MS 39296-5882 Office Phone: 601-607-4144.

ROBERTS, RICHARD JOHN, molecular biologist, consultant, research director; b. Derby, Eng., Sept. 6, 1943; arrived in US, 1969; s. John Walter and Edna Wilhelmina (Allsop) Roberts; m. Elizabeth Dyson, Sept. 21, 1965 (dec.); children: Alison, Andrew; m. Jean E. Tagliabue; children: Christopher, Amanda. BS, Sheffield U., 1965, PhD, 1968. Rsch. fellow Harvard U., Cambridge, Mass., 1969—70, rsch. assoc., 1971—72; sr. staff investigator Cold Spring Harbor Lab., NY, 1972—87, asst. dir., 1987—92; cons. New Eng. Biolabs., Ipswich, Mass., 1974—92, rsch. dir., 1992—. Sci. adv. bd. Genex., Rockville, Md., 1977—85; chief sci. officer Molecular Tool, Balt., 1994—. Contbr. articles to profl. jours. Recipient Nobel prize in physiology or medicine, Nobel Found., 1993, Honor of Knight Bachelor, 2008; fellow, John Simon Guggenheim Found., 1979. Fellow: Royal Soc.; mem.: Am. Soc. Microbiology. Office: New Eng Biolabs 240 County Rd Ipswich MA 01938-2723 Office Phone: 978-380-7405. E-mail: roberts@neb.com.

ROBERTS, ROBIN, newscaster; b. Nov. 23, 1960; d. Lawrence Roberts and Lucy Marion. BA in Comms. cum laude, Southeastern La. U., 1983. Sports dir. WHMD/WFPR Radio, Hammond, La., 1980-83; spl. assignment sports reporter KSLU-FM, 1982; sports anchor, reporter WDAM-TV, Hattiesburg, Miss., 1983-84, WLOX-TV, Biloxi, Miss., 1984-86, WSMV-TV, Nashville, 1986-88, WAGA-TV, Atlanta, 1988-89; with WVEE-FM, Atlanta; host. Sunday SportsDay, contbr. NFL Prime Time, reporter, interviewer ESPN, Bristol, Conn., 1990-95, host, anchor SportsCenter, host In the SportsLight, 1995—2005; host Wide World of Sports ABC, 1995—2001; co-anchor Good Morning Am., 2005—. Mem., adv. bd. Fedn. Internat. Football Assn., 1999. Author: From the Heart: Seven Rules to Live By, 2007. Apptd. adv. bd. Women's Sports Found., 1991; spkr. charity, civic functions. Recipient DAR T.V. Award of Merit, 1990, Women at Work Broadcast Journalism award, 1992, Excellence in Sports Journalism award Broadcast Media Northeastern U. Ctr. Study of Sport in Society and Sch. Journalism, 1993, Disting. Achievement award, DiGamma Kappa, U. Ga., 1996, Media award, New England Women's Fund, 1998, Pres. award, Women's Sports Found., 2001; named Journalist of Yr., Ebony mag., 2002 named to Inst. Sport and Edn. Found., Hall of Fame, 1994; named one of Five Most Intriguing People in Coll. Basketball, Basketball Times, 1997, Named one of The 50 Most Powerful Women in NYC, NY Post, 2008. Office: Good Morning America 147 Columbus Ave New York NY 10023

ROBERTS, RUSSELL L. (RUSTY ROBERTS), legislative staff member; Attended, Western Carolina U., Cullowhee, NC, 1972, St. Petersburg Jr. Coll., Fla., 1973—75, U. South Fla., Tampa, 1976—77. Adminstrv. asst. Fla. House of Reps., Tallahassee, 1976—79; fed. liaison Metro-Dade County, Fla., 1988—89; pub. affairs dir. Capital Bank, Miami, Fla., 1988—89; dist. rep. for Rep. Sen. Paula Hawkins US House of Reps., Washington, 1981—86, adminstrv. asst. for Rep. Ileana Ros-Lehtinen, 1989—93, chief of staff for Rep. John L. Mica, 1993—. Office: Office of Rep John L Mica 404 Cannon House Office Bldg Washington DC 20515 Office Phone: 202-225-4035. Business E-Mail: rusty.roberts@mail.house.gov.*

ROBERTS, RYAN M., librarian, educator, webmaster; b. Springfield, Ill., Nov. 17, 1973; s. Dan L. Roberts and Karen L. Zimmerli; m. Tricia Hardway, June 7, 2003. MS in Libr. & Info. Sci., U. Ill., Champaign, 1997, CAS in Libr. & Info. Sci., 1999. Faculty libr. Lincoln Land CC, Springfield, 2000—; editl. asst. Between the Lines, London, 2002—. Webmaster Julian Barnes Website, 1998—, Ian McEwan Website, 2002—, James Fenton Website, 2005—, Hermione Lee Website, 2006—, Ian Hamilton Website, 2009—. Co-editor (with Vanessa Guignery): Conversations with Julian Barnes; editor: Conversations with Ian McEwan. Recipient Disting. Svc. award, Lincoln Land CC, 2008; Mellon Rsch. fellowship, Harry Ransom Humanities Rsch. Ctr., 2003—04, 2009—. Office: Lincoln Land CC 5250 Shepherd Rd Springfield IL 62794-9256 Business E-Mail: ryan.roberts@llcc.edu.

ROBERTS, SAMUEL SMITH, television news executive; b. Port Chester, NY, Feb. 8, 1936; s. Robert M. and Lillian (Smith) R.; m. Harriet Rubin, 1975; children: Rachel, David; children by previous marriage: Nancy, Pamela. BS, Northwestern U., 1957. With UPI, NYC, 1961, Capital Cities Broadcasting, Providence, 1962, CBS News, 1962-95; sr. prodr. CBS Evening News, NYC, 1978-81, nat. editor, 1982-84, fgn. editor, 1984-87; exec. prodr. CBS News Prodns., 1992-95; pres. Roberts Media Internat., NYC, 1995-96; v.p., gen. mgr. TV programming Electronic Media Co., N.Y. Times, 1996-99; Frances L. Wolfson chair U. Miami, Coral Gables, Fla., 1999—2008. Served to lt. USN, 1957-61.

ROBERTS, SIDNEY, biological chemist; b. Boston, Mar. 11, 1918; s. Samuel Richard and Elizabeth (Gilbert) R.; m. Clara Marian Szego, Sept. 14, 1943. BS, MIT, 1939; postgrad., Harvard U., 1939-41; MS, U. Minn., 1942, PhD, 1943. Instr. physiology U. Minn. Med. Sch., 1943-44, George Washington U. Med. Sch., 1944-45; rsch. assoc. Worcester Found. Exptl. Biology, Shrewsbury, Mass., 1945-47; asst. prof. physiol. chemistry Yale U. Med. Sch., 1947-48; mem. faculty U. Calif. Med. Sch., Los Angeles, 1948—, prof. biol. chemistry, 1957—; chmn. acad. senate UCLA, 1989-90; mem. adv. panel regulatory biology NSF, 1955-57, adv. panel metabolic biology, 1957-59; mem. metabolism study sect. NIH, 1960-63; basic sci. study sect. Los Angeles County Heart Assn., 1958-63. Cons. VA Hosp., Long Beach, Calif., 1951-55, Los Angeles, 1958-62, UCLA Pew Fin. Biomed. Scholar Program, 1992-2007; air conservation tech. adv. com. Los Angeles County Lung Assn., 1972-76 Author articles, revs.; editor med. jours. Served to 2d lt. AUS, 1944-48. MIT Nat. Entrance scholar, 1935; Guggenheim fellow, 1957-58. Fellow AAAS; mem. Am. Physiol. Soc., Endocrine Soc. (v.p. 1968-69, Ciba award 1953), Brit. Biochem. Soc., Soc. Neurosci., Am. Chem. Soc. (exec. com. div. biol. chemistry 1956-59), Am. Soc. Biol. Chemists, Am. Soc. Neurochemistry, Internat. Soc. Neurochemistry, Phi Beta Kappa, Sigma Xi (pres. UCLA chpt. 1959-60). Home: 1371 Marinette Rd Pacific Palisades CA 90272-2627 Office: UCLA Sch Med Dept Biol Chemistry Los Angeles CA 90095-1737 Office Phone: 310-825-6997. Business E-Mail: sr@ucla.edu.

ROBERTS, SUZANNE CATHERINE, artist; b. San Antonio, Oct. 27, 1953; d. Thomas Simons and Marceline Margaret (Conrady) Garrett; m. Ted Blake Roberts, May 22, 1976; 1 child, Elizabeth. BS Radio-TV-Film, U. Tex., 1975, B Journalism, 1977; MA Interdisciplinary Studies, Corpus Christi State U., Tex., 1982; MS Gen. Counseling, Corpus Christi State U., 1989; MA Polit. Sci., S.W. Tex. State U., 1995. News announcer Sta. KIXL Radio, Austin, Tex., 1976, Sta. KSIX Radio, Corpus Christi, 1977—78; news anchor Sta. KZTV-TV, Corpus Christi, 1979, news reporter, 1977—80; news announcer, reporter Sta. KRYS-AM-FM, Corpus Christi, 1983—87; freelance reporter UPI, Austin, 1989—94, Tex. State Network, Austin, 1995—97, Des Moines, 1997—2000; artist, 1998—; adj. instr. Des Moines Area CC, West Campus, 2004—.

ROBERTS, TERI ALANE, finance educator, volunteer; b. Mission Hills, Calif., Oct. 25, 1963; d. Alan Lewis and Barbara Ann (Taylor) R. BA in Speech Comm., Calif. State U., Northridge, 1990, BA in Polit. Sci. with honors, 1993, MA in Polit. Sci., 1997. Peer educator on rape Discovering Alternatives to Today's Encounters, Northridge, 1996-97; dir. Save the Animals Fund, Pasadena, Calif., 1997. Vol. Ga. Mercer for City Coun., Encino, Calif., 1997; mem. planning com., presenter at workshop Ending Violence Against Women Conf., Northridge, 1997; mem. planning com. Rainbow Sisters Project, L.A., 1999. Recipient Commendation for Rainbow Sisters Project, L.A. County, 1999. Mem. Polit. Sci. Club Calif. State U. (dir. fundraising 1992-93, dir. graduation com. 1992-93), Student Speech Comm. Assn. Calif. State U. (dir. social activities 1987-88), Delta Sigma (life). Democrat. Avocations: reading, dance, church activities. Home: 7233 Kelvin Ave Apt 218 Winnetka CA 91306-2763 Personal E-mail: terialaneroberts@yahoo.com.

ROBERTS, THOMAS GEORGE, retired physicist; b. Ft. Smith, Ark., Apr. 27, 1929; s. Thomas Lawrence and Emma Lee (Stanley) R.; m. Alice Anne Harbin, Nov. 14, 1958 (dec. 1994); children: Lawrence Dewey, Regina Anne; foster child, Marcia Roberts Dale; m. Betty Howard McElyea, July 28, 1995. AA, Armstrong Coll., 1953; BS, U. Ga., 1956, MS, 1957; PhD, N.C. State U., 1967. Rsch. physicist U.S. Army Missile Command, Huntsville, Ala., 1958-85; cons. industry and govt. agys., 1970—, SAIC, Huntsville, Ala., 1997-2001; owner Technoco, Huntsville, 1985-96. Contbr. articles to profl. jours.; patentee in field. Sgt. USAF, 1948-52. Fellow Am. Optical Soc.; mem. Am. Phys. Soc., IEEE, Huntsville Optical Soc. Am. (pres. 1980, 92), Toastmaster Internat. (pres. 1963), Phi Beta Kappa, Phi Kappa Phi (Wheatly Physics award). Episcopalian. Achivements include research in laser physics, optics, particle beams and instrumentation; diagnostic devices and techniques development; 70 patents. Home Phone: 256-828-3333. Personal E-mail: robertsbetty@bellsouth.net.

ROBERTS, VIRGIL PATRICK, lawyer, judge; b. Ventura, Calif., Jan. 4, 1947; s. Julius and Emma D. (Haley) R.; m. Brenda Cecilia Banks, Nov. 10, 1979; children: Gisele Simone, Hayley Tasha. AA, Ventura Coll., 1966; BA, UCLA, 1968; JD, Harvard U., 1972. Bar: Calif. 1972. Assoc. Pacht, Ross, Warne Bernhardt & Sears, LA, 1972-76; ptnr. Manning, Reynolds & Roberts, LA, 1976-79, Manning & Roberts, 1980-81; mng. ptnr. Bobbitt & Roberts, 1995—; exec. v.p., gen. counsel Solar Records, LA, 1981—; pres. Dick Griffey Prodns., LA, 1982—, Solar Records, 1988—; judge pro tem L.A., Beverly Hills Mcpl. Cts., 1975—. Bd. mem. The Bridgespan Consulting Group, 2004—, Broadway Fed. Bank, 2003—, Cmty. Build, 1994—; chmn. bd. Families Schs.; bd. mem. Alliance Coll. Ready Pub. Schs., Hilliance Hvtists and Record Co. Past bd. dirs. LA Black Leadership Coalition, LA Mus. African Am. Art, Beverly Hills Bar Assn., LA Legal Aid Found.; bd. dirs. Coro Found., 1984-90, LA Ednl. Alliance Restructuring Now, Cmty. Build; bd. dirs. Calif. Cmty. Found., 1991-99, chmn. bd., 1999-02; past pres. Beverly Hills Bar Scholarship Found.; commr. Calif. Commn. Tchr. Credentialing, 1980-83; chmn. LA Ednl. Partnership, 1989—, v.p. 1983-89; vice-chmn. Nat. Pub. Edn. Fund Network; chmn. bd. dirs. LA Annenberg Met. Project; trustee Com. Econ. Devel., 1991—, Occidental Coll., Marlborough Sch. (trustee 1994-03); mem. bd. councillors UCLA; trustee Claremont Grad. Sch., 2006-. Recipient NAACP Legal Def. Fund Equal Justice award, 1988, Rose award U. So. Calif., 1998, Lifetime Achievement award, LHEP, named to Hall of Fame, BLACK, Entertainment Sports Lawyers, ASSOS. Mem. Recording Industry Assn. Am., Black Entertainment and Sports Lawyers (treas., bd. dirs. 1982—). Lead atty. for NAACP in Crawford vs. Bd. Edn. desegregation case, L.A., 1979-80. Address: 4820 Vista De Oro Ave Los Angeles CA 90043-1611 Office: Bobbitt & Roberts 400 Corporate Painte Ste 300 Culver City CA 90230 Office Phone: 310-645-4100, 424-750-3073. Business E-Mail: vroberts@bobroblaw.com.

ROBERTS, WALTER RONALD, retired diplomat; b. Waltendorf, Austria, Aug. 26, 1916; arrived in U.S., 1939, naturalized, 1944; s. Ignatius and Elizabeth (Diamant) R.; m. Gisela K. Schmarak, Aug. 22, 1939; children: William M., Charles E., Lawrence H. MLitt, Cambridge U., Eng., 1940, PhD, 1980. Rsch. asst. Harvard U. Law Sch., 1940-42; writer, editor Voice of Am., 1942-49; press officer U.S. del. to Austrian Treaty talks, 1949, 55; fgn. affairs officer Dept. State, 1950-53; dep. asst. dir. USIA, 1954-60; counselor of embassy for pub. affairs Am. Embassy, Belgrade, Yugoslavia, 1960-66; diplomat-in-residence Brown U., Providence, 1966-67; counselor U.S. Mission to Internat. Orgns., Geneva, 1967-69; dep. assoc. dir. USIA, Washington, 1969-71, assoc. dir., 1971-74; dir. diplomatic studies Ctr. Strategic and Internat. Studies Georgetown U., Washington, 1974-75; exec. dir. Bd. Internat. Broadcasting, Washington, 1975-85; diplomat-in-residence George Washington U., Washington, 1986-96. Author: Tito, Mihailovic and the Allies, 1941-45, 73, paperback, 1987, (with Terry L. Deibel) Culture and Information: Two Foreign Policy Functions, 1976; contbr. articles to profl. pubs. Apptd. mem. U.S. Adv. Commn. on Pub. Diplomacy, 1991-97, sr. advisor, 1998-2003; bd. dirs. Salzburg Seminar, 1993-97, Coun. Sr. Fellows, 1998—, Oxford and Cambridge com., 1975-, Pub. Diplomacy Coun., 1996—, mem. emeritus bd. dirs. 2005—; bd. dirs. Pub. Diplomacy Inst., George Washington U., 2001-2004, sr. advisor 2006—. Recipient Disting. Honor award USIA, 1974. Mem. Washington Inst. Fgn. Affairs, Coun. Fgn. Rels., Oxford-Cambridge Com., USIA Alumni Assn. (bd. dirs. 1995-98), Met. Club. Home: 700 New Hampshire Ave Apt 1002 Washington DC 20037

ROBERTS, WILLIAM B., lawyer; b. Detroit, Aug. 23, 1939; s. Edwin Stuart and Marjorie Jean (Wardle) R.; m. Cathleen Anne Thompson, Sept. 1, 1962; children: Bradford William, Brent William, Katrina Marjorie. BA, Mich. State U., East Lansing, 1961; JD with distinction, U. Mich., Ann Arbor, 1963; China law diploma, U. East Asia, Macau, 1989. Bar: Mo. 1964, Fla. 1983, US Dist. Ct. (ea. dist.) Mo. 1964, US Dist. Ct. (mid. dist.) Fla. 1993. Mem. firm Thompson & Mitchell, St. Louis, 1963-67; atty. Monsanto Co., 1967-70; sr. exec. v.p. adminstrn., sec., gen. counsel Chromalloy Am. Corp. (successor Segua Corp. NY), St. Louis, 1970—78, exec. v.p.-adminstrn., gen. counsel, sec. Clayton, Mo., 1978—82; pvt. practice, 1983-87, St. Louis and Naples, 1989-90, Naples, 1994—, Kansas City, Mo., 1999—; mng. ptnr., corp. bus. counselor and broker Fairborne Group, Ltd., 1986—89; mng. ptnr. Roberts and Nordahl, St. Louis and Naples, Fla., 1988-89, Darrow & Roberts, P.A., Naples, 1992-93. Pres., mng. dir. The Fairborne Group, Ltd., St. Louis and Naples, 1988-91, Kansas City, 1999-2007, William B. Roberts & Assocs. Co., Merger and Acquisitions Specialists, 1982—; mem. exam. com. of policyowners Northwestern Mut. Life Ins. Co., Milw., 1978; del. to US-China Joint Session on Trade Investment and Econ. Law, Beijing, 1987; sports rep. Steve Carlton, St. Louis Cardinals, Phila. Phillies baseball clubs, 1987-89; pres., CEO Tropical Tracks, Inc., Naples, 1994—, BBB Arbitration, 2004—; owner Security K.C. Royals, 2000-01; internat. bus. and legal adviser, 1982—. Mem. ABA, Fed. Bar Assn. (Mid. Dist. Fla.), Mo. Bar Assn., St. Louis Bar Assn. (chmn. antitrust sect. 1973, spl. assignments law & counsel corp. and internat.), Fla. Bar Assn., Collier County Bar Assn., Delta Theta Phi. Methodist.

ROBERTS, WILLIAM EVERETT, lawyer; b. Pierre, SD, May 12, 1926; s. Everett David and Bonnie (Martin) R.; m. Cynthia Cline, July 18, 1953; children: Catherine C. Roberts-Martin, Laura M., Nancy F., David H. BS, U. Minn., 1947; LLB, Yale U., 1950. Bar: Ind. 1950, U.S. Supreme Ct. 1964. Employee, ptnr. Duck and Neighbours, Indpls., 1950-58; ptnr. Cadick, Burns, Duck & Neighbours, Indpls., 1958-60, Roberts, Ryder, Rogers & Scism, Indpls., 1960-85, Barnes & Thornburg, Indpls., 1986-93, of counsel, 1994—. Pres., bd. dirs. Park-Tudor Sch., Indpls., 1982-83; elder Second Presbyn. Ch., Indpls., 1962—; trustee Indpls. Mus. Art, 1978—; pres. New Hope of Ind., Indpls., 1986-87. Fellow Am. Bar Found.; mem. ABA, Ind. Bar Assn., Indpls. Bar Assn., Rotary Club, Meridian Hills Country Club (pres. 1983-84). Republican. Home: 10466 Spring Highland Dr Indianapolis IN 46290-1101 Office: Barnes & Thornburg 11 S Meridian St Ste 1313 Indianapolis IN 46204-3535 Office Phone: 317-231-7520.

ROBERTS, WILLIAM H., lawyer; b. Buffalo, June 14, 1945; s. Esther C. Roberts and William H. Roberts, Jr. JD, U. Pa., Phila., 1970; AB, Harvard Coll., Cambridge, MA, 1967. Bar: Pa. 1970, U.S. Ct. Appeals (3d cir.) 1972, U.S. Supreme Ct. 1974, U.S. Ct. Appeals (11th cir.) 1982, U.S. Claims Ct. 1986, U.S. Ct. Appeals (4th cir.) 1987, U.S. Ct. Appeals (9th cir.) 2000. Ptnr. Blank Rome LLP, Phila., 1977—. Co-author: (book) Com. Free Speech, 1985. Trustee Phila. Chamber Music Soc., 2008—, The Curtis Inst. of Music, Phila., 1997—; trustee, pres. Chamber Orch. of Phila., Phila., 1988—; trustee Harvard Rev. of Philosophy, Cambridge, Mass., 1993—, Marlboro Music Sch., 2004—. Named Disting. Honoree, Nat. Assn. of Fundraising Execs., 2002. Mem.: Phila. Chamber Music Soc. (trustee 2008—), Phila. Bot. Club, Harvard Club NYC. Avocations: violin, botany, salmon fishing. Office Phone: 215-569-5632.

ROBERTS-BROWN, ARLENE MARIA, executive assistant; b. East St. Louis, Ill., May 30, 1939; d. Joe Roberts and Elizabeth Smith; children: Johnny Purchase Jr., Francena Purchase-Owens, Darlene Pleas-McLemore, Regenia Pleas, Rodney Brown. Student, Jordan Coll., Grand Rapids, Mich., 1987—89. Cert. long-term care facility nurse aid, State of Mich. Dept. Pub. Health, 1990. Nurse aide Raybrook Nursing Home, Grand Rapids, 1990—91; asst. Grand Rapids Pub. Schs., 1994—95; tchg. asst. New Branches Sch., Grand Rapids, 1992—93; exec. asst. Francena Purchase Consulting Svcs., Grand Rapids, 2004—; pastoral asst. First Missionary Baptist Ch., Grand Rapids, Mich. TV appearance, Grand Rapids Cmty. Media TV, 2007; contbr. articles to profl. jours. Mem. Rev. Popov Ministries, Grand Rapids, 1994—; choir bd. mem. East Paris Christians Reformed Ch., Grand Rapids, 2008—. Recipient cert. of recognition, Grand Rapids Pub. Schs., 1994, Francena Purchase Consulting Svcs., 2006—09. Mem.: West Mich. Postal Customer Coun. Avocation: reading. Office: Francena Purchase Consulting Svcs PO Box 88304 Kentwood MI 49518

ROBERTS-MAMONE, LISA A., lawyer; BA magna cum laude, Grove City Coll., 1985; JD magna cum laude, Case Wester Res. U., 1988. Bar: Ohio 1988. With Jones Day, Cleve., 1988—, ptnr., 2000—. Trustee The Laub Found.; mem. Estate Planning Coun. of Cleve., Estate Planning Discussion Group, Cleve., Case Western Reserve U. Estate Planning Adv. Coun.; mem. diamond adv. group U. Hosps. Cleve.; mem. Am. Red Cross Cleve. Profl. Adv. Bd.; mem. nominating com. Girl Scouts NE Ohio. Mem.: Cleve. Met. Bar Assn. (estate planning, probate and trust law sect.), Ohio State Bar Assn. (estate planning, trust and probate sect.). Office: Jones Day North Point 901 Lakeside Ave Cleveland OH 44114-1190 Office Phone: 216-586-7172.

ROBERTSON, A. HAEWORTH, actuary, foundation executive, benefits consultant; b. Oklahoma City, May 10, 1930; s. Albert Haeworth and Bonnie Tennessee (Duckett) R.; m. Mary Adeline Kissee, Feb. 3, 1952 (div. July 1979); children— Valerie Lynn, Alan Haeworth, Mary Kathryn. BA in Math., U. Okla., Norman, 1951; MA in Actuarial Sci., U. Mich., 1953. Actuary Wyatt Co., Washington and Dallas, 1955-58; actuary Bowles, Andrews & Towne, Dallas, 1958-60; v.p., actuary W. Alfred Hayes & Co., St. Louis, 1960-63; pres. First Am. Security Life Ins. Co. Mo., St. Louis, 1964-68; pvt. practice internat. cons. actuary Barbados and Ghana, 1969-72; sr. actuary ILO, Geneva, 1973-75; chief actuary US Social Security Adminstrn., Balt., 1975-78; mng. dir. William M. Mercer, Inc., Washington, 1978-88; pvt. practice, internat. cons., actuary Washington, Kuwait, Turkey, Guyana, Zimbabwe, China, The Philippines, 1988—. Chmn. Retirement Bd. Actuaries, Dept. Def., 1984-95; mem. Edn. Benefits Bd. Actuaries, 1985-95; pres., founder Retirement Policy Inst. Inc., 1986—. Author: The Coming Revolution in Social Security, 1981, Social Security: What Every Taxpayer Should Know, 1992, The Big Lie: What Every Baby Boomer Should Know About Social Security and Medicare, 1997. Served to 1st lt. USAF, 1953-55 Recipient Commrs. citation, Social Security Adminstrn., Washington, 1976, Arthur J. Altmeyer award, HEW, Washington, 1978, Disting. Alumni award, Ctrl. HS, Oklahoma City, 1997, Wynn Kent Comm. award, Actuarial Found., Chgo., 2007. Fellow Soc. Actuaries (bd. govs. 1979-81, v.p. 1985-87), Conf. Cons. Actuaries; mem. Am. Acad. Actuaries (Robert J. Myers Pub. Svc. award 2004), Internat. Actuarial Assn., Internat. Assn. Cons. Actuaries, U.K. Inst. Actuaries (assoc.), Cosmos Club, Phi Beta Kappa, Phi Eta Sigma, Phi Kappa Sigma. Republican. Methodist. Personal E-mail: haeworth@aol.com.

ROBERTSON, ABEL L., JR., pathologist; b. St. Andrews, Argentina, July 21, 1926; came to U.S., 1952, naturalized, 1957; s. Abel Alfred Lazzarini and Margaret Theresa G. (Anderson) R.; m. Irene Kirmayr Mauch, Dec. 26, 1958; children: Margaret Anne, Abel Martin, Andrew Duncan, Malcolm Alexander. BS, Coll. D.F. Sarmiento, Buenos Aires, Argentina, 1946; MD suma cum laude, U. Buenos Aires, 1951; PhD, Cornell U., 1959. Fellow tissue culture div. Inst. Histology and Embryology, Sch. Medicine Inst. Histology and Embryology, 1947-49; surg. intern Hosp. Ramos Mejia, Buenos Aires, 1948-50; fellow in tissue culture research Ministry of Health, Buenos Aires, 1950-51; resident Hosp. Nacional de Clinicas, Buenos Aires, 1950-51; head blood vessel bank and organ transplants Research Ctr. Ministry of Health, Buenos Aires, 1951-53; fellow dept. surgery and pathology Sch. Medicine Cornell U., NYC, 1953-55; asst. vis. surgery U. Hosp. N.Y., NYC, 1955-60; asst. prof. research surgery Postgrad. Med. Sch. NYU, NYC, 1955-56; asst. vis. surgeon Bellevue Hosp., NYC, 1955-60; assoc. prof. research surgery NYU, 1956-60, assoc. prof. pathology Sch. Medicine and Postgrad Med. Sch., 1960-63; staff mem. div. research Cleve. Clinic Found., 1963-73, prof. research, 1972-73; assoc. clin. prof. pathology Case Western Res. U. Sch. Medicine, Cleve., 1968-72, prof. pathology, 1973-82, dir. interdisciplinary cardiovascular research, 1975-82; exec. head dept. pathology Coll. Medicine, U. Ill., Chgo., 1982-88; prof. pathology Coll. Medicine U. Ill., 1982-93, prof. emeritus, 1993—; vis. prof. emeritus cardiovascular med. Core Analysis Lab., Stanford U. Coll. Medicine, 1995—, cardiac pathologist, 2000—. Rsch. fellow N.Y. Soc. Cardiovasc. Surgery, 1957-58; mem. rsch. study subcom. of heart com. N.E. Ohio Regional Med. Program, 1969—. Mem. internat. editl. bd. Atherosclerosis, Jour. Exptl. and Molecular Pathology, 1964—, Lab. Investigation, 1989—, Acta Pathologica Japonica, 1991—; contbr. articles to profl. jours. Recipient Rsch. Devel. award NIH, 1961-63, Disting. Alumnus award Grad. Sch. Med. Sci. Cornell U., 2003. Fellow AAAS, Am. Coll. Cardiology, Am. Coll. Clin. Pharmacology, Am. Heart Assn. (established investigator 1956-61, nominating com. coun. on arteriosclerosis 1972), Royal Microscopical Soc., Royal Soc. Promotion Health (Gt. Britain), Am. Geriat. Soc., N.Y. Acad. Scis., Cleve. Med. Library Assn.; mem. AMA, AAUP, Am. Soc. for Investigative Pathology, Am. Inst. Biol. Scis., Am. Judicature Soc., Am. Soc. Cell Biology, Am. Soc. Pathologists, Am. Soc. Nephrology, Assn. Am. Physicians and Surgeons, Assn. Computing Machinery, Electron Microscopy Soc. Am., Assn. Pathology Chmn., Internat. Acad. Pathology, Soc. Cardiovasc. Pathology, Internat. Cardiovasc. Soc., Internat. Soc. Cardiology (sci. council on arteriosclerosis and ischemic heart disease), Internat. Fed. on Genetic Engring. and Biotechnology, Internat. Soc. for Heart Rsch., Internat. Soc. Nephrology, Internat. Soc. Stereology, Pan Am. Med. Assn. (life, councillor in angiology 1966), Ill. Registry Anatomical Pathology (treas. 1985-87), Chgo. Pathology Soc., Reticuloendothelial Soc. Leucocyte Biology, Soc. Cryobiology, Tissue Culture Assn., Ohio Soc. Pathologists, Electron Microscopy Soc. Northeastern Ohio (pres., trustee 11966-68), Heart Assn. Northeastern Ohio, N.Y. Soc. Cardiovasc. Surgery, N.Y. Soc. Electron Microscopists, Cuyahoga County Med. Soc., Cleve. Soc. Pathologists, The Oxygen Soc., Sigma Xi. Home: PO Box 3125 452 Belleville Blvd Half Moon Bay CA 94019 Office Phone: 650-712-0357. Office Fax: 650-712-0357. Personal E-mail: abelrobertsonmd@yahoo.com.

ROBERTSON, ALONZO MORRELL, lawyer, educator; s. Clarence Alonzo and Mable Williams Robertson; m. Shelia Henry, Apr. 29, 1989; children: Ashley, Lauren. BA in History, Morehouse Coll., Atlanta, 1990; JD with honors, Howard U., DC, 1994. Spl. asst. Def. Base Closure Commn., DC, 1990—91; atty. CIA, McClean, Va., 1995—98; legis. atty. Nat. Security Agy., Ft. Meade, Md., 1998—2008; atty. Joint Intelligence Commn., DC, 2002; assoc. gen. counsel Nat. Geospatial-Intelligence Agy., Bethesda, Md., 2008—; with Fed. Comm. Comn., Portugal, 1991—95, Internat. Trade Comn., 1992. Prof. law Bowie State U., Md., 2001—. Pres. Baden Elem. PTA, Md., 1998—2000; gen. counsel Worldview Early Learning Ctr., Upper Marlboro, Md., 1995—2000; chmn. Cornerstone Peaceful Bible Bapt. Ch., Upper Marlboro, 1998—2009. Sgt. US Army, 1994, DC. Decorated Army Achievement award 210 Mil. Law; recipient Intelligence Cmty. award, Office of Dir. on Nat. Intelligen, 2007. Mem.: ABA (assoc.), Phi Alpha Theta (assoc.), Phi Alpha Delta (assoc.), Alpha Phi Alpha (assoc.; chmn., go to HS, go to coll. com. 2007—09). D-Conservative. Baptist. Avocation: running. Home: 15909 Baden Westwood Rd Brandywine MD 20613 Office: Nat Security Agency 9800 Savage Rd Fort George G Meade MD 20755 Personal E-mail: amrob28@yahoo.com.

ROBERTSON, ANDREW J., advertising executive; b. Zimbabwe, Nov. 17, 1960; m. Susan Robertson; 3 children. Degree in Economics, London U. Joined as media planner Ogilvy & Mather, London, 1982, account mgr., bd. dirs., 1986—89, mgmt. supr., new bus. dir., 1989; group account dir. J. Walter Thompson, London, 1989—90; CEO WCRS, London, 1990—95; mng. dir. Abbott Mead Vickers, London, 1995—99; CEO Abbott Mead Vickers BBDO, 1999—2000; pres., CEO BBDO N.Am., NYC, 2001—04; pres. BBDO Worldwide, NYC, 2002—, CEO, dir., 2004—. Bd. mem. Spl. Olympics, Ctr. Media & Child Health, Autism Speaks. Mem.: Am. Assn. Advt. Agencies (bd. mem.), Advt. Coun. (bd. mem.). Office: BBDO Worldwide Inc 1285 Ave of the Americas New York NY 10019-6028*

ROBERTSON, ANNE WALTERS, music educator, music historian; MusB, U. Houston, 1974, MusM in Chamber Music, 1976; MusM in Music Theory, Rice U. Shepherd Sch. Music, 1979; MPhil in Musicology, Yale U., 1981, PhD, 1984. With U. Chgo., 1984—, appointed asst. prof. musicology, 1984, appointed full prof. musicology, 1996, chair, music dept., 1992—98, dep. provost for rsch. and edn., 2001—04, Claire Dux Swift Disting. Svc. prof. music, 2004—, full prof. musicology, 1996—2004. Served on committees for NEH, Am. Coun. Learned Societies. Author: The Service Books of the Royal Abbey of St. Denis: Images of Ritual and Music in the Middle Ages, 1991 (John Nicholas Brown prize, Medieval Acad. Am., 1995), Guillaume de Machaut and Reims: Context and Meaning in his Musical Works, 2002 (Otto Kinkeldey award, Am. Musicological Soc., 2003, Haskins medal, Medieval Acad. Am., 2006). Recipient Van Courtlandt Elliot prize, Medieval Acad. Am., 1987, Wilbur Lucius Cross medal, Yale Grad. Sch. Alumni Assn., 2007; John Simon Guggenheim Meml. Found. Fellowship, 1995, George A. and Eliza Gardner Howard Found. Fellowship, 1996. Fellow: Am. Acad. Arts & Scis.; mem.: Am. Musicological Soc. (bd. dirs., Alfred Einstein award 1989, H. Colin Slim award 2007). Office: U Chgo Dept Music Goodspeed 209 1010 E 59th St Chicago IL 60637 Office Phone: 773-834-0882. Business E-Mail: awrx@uchicago.edu.

ROBERTSON, BEVERLY CARRUTH, retired steel company executive; b. Texarkana, Ark., May 16, 1922; s. Glenn C. Robertson (dec.); m. Ruth Mulcare, Oct. 31, 1945 (dec. Oct. 1993); children: Glenn J., Beverly R. Dodds, Rebecca A. Robertson Deans; m. Charlotte Doty Lawler, June 2, 1995. In sales Nat. Supply Co., Laurel, Miss., 1941-51; purchasing agt. Kirby Petroleum Co., Houston, 1951-54; exec. v.p. mktg. Lone Star Steel Co., Dallas, 1954-85, exec. v.p., 1985-86; pres., dir., chief exec. officer LSSCO Trading Corp., 1985-86; owner BSEER Enterprises, Dallas, 1986—; ptnr. Clayton Equipment Co., Dallas, 1992-97; ret., 1997. Chmn. Sir Alec Inc., 1985-94; cons. Pipeco, Inc., Houston, 1986-88; exec. v.p. mktg. and procurement Nat. Pipe and Tube Co., Houston, 1988-89; pres., CEO Tex. Am. Pipe & Supply Co., Inc., Dallas, 1989—; cons. Ipsco Steel, Inc., Camanche, Iowa, 1991-92. Served to capt. USAF, 1943-46, ETO. Named Supplier of Yr. Petroleum Industry Buyers group Nat. Assn. Purchasing Mgmt., 1982 Mem.: Dallas Petroleum Club, Dallas Country Club. Republican. Episcopalian. Home: PO Box 12688 Dallas TX 75225-0688 Personal E-mail: bcrobby@sbcglobal.net.

ROBERTSON, CAREY JANE, musician, educator; b. Culver City, Calif., Apr. 18, 1955; d. Robert Bruce and Marjorie Ellen (Greenleaf) Coker;l m. Brian Collins Robertson, June 28, 1975 (div. July 1985); 1 child, Sean Kalen. BMus, Calif. State U., Northridge, 1977; MMus, U. So. Calif., LA, 1979, PhD of Mus. Arts, 1987. Organist/choir dir. Village Meth. Ch., North Hollywood, Calif., 1972-75, St. Bede's Episcopal Ch., Mar Vista, Calif., 1975-79; organist interim St. Alban's Episcopal Ch., Westwood, Calif., 1985; organist Covenant Presbyn. Ch., Westchester, Calif., 1985-90; organist/choir dir. St. David's United Ch., West Vancouver, B.C., Can., 1990-91; prin. organist Claremont United Ch. of Christ, Calif., 1991—; music educator Fontana Unified Sch. Dist. Prof. organ Claremont Grad. U., 1991—, New Calif. Conservatory, Buena Park, Calif., 2002—; concert organist Am. Guild of Organists, throughout U.S. and Can., 1974—; cons. Sch. Theology, U. B.C., 1990. Bd. dirs. Ruth and Clarence Mader Found., Pasadena, Calif., 1993—. Recipient Music Tchrs. Nat. Assn. Wurlitzer Collegiate Artist award, 1980; Irene Robertson scholar, 1977, 78. Mem. Am. Guild Organists (historian, sec. 1985-92, exec. com. 1983-85, sub-dean Pasadena chpt., 1998-99), Pi Kappa Lambda (Scholastic award 1987). Avocation: scuba diving instructor. Home: 3319 N Live Oak Ave Rialto CA 92377 Business E-Mail: carey.robertson@cgu.edu.

ROBERTSON, CHARLES JAMES, museum director emeritus; b. Houston, Sept. 12, 1934; s. Charles James and Felide Corinne (O'Brien) R. BA, U. Va., Charlottesville, 1956; MA, Harvard U., 1958; student, U. London Courtauld Inst., 1960; JD, George Washington U., 1964. Atty. Dow, Lohnes & Albertson, Washington, 1964-69; adminstr. Richard H. Chamberlain, M.D. & Assoc., Phila., 1969-75; assoc. dir. N.C. Mus. Art, Raleigh, 1975-77; deputy dir. Smithsonian Am. Art Mus., Washington, 1977—2001. Treas. Am. Assn. Mus., Washington, 1982-84, mem. exec. com., 1982-84; mem. adv. com. Octagon House Mus., Washington, 1989-97, chmn. 1993-96; bd. dirs. Victorian Soc. Am., Phila., 1990—, v.p., 1994-2000, 06—; mem. Hist. Preservation Rev. Bd. of DC, 1992-2004; bd. regents Am. Archtl. Found., Washington, 1993-96; trustee Cosmos Club Historic Preservation Found., Washington, 1993—, treas., 1999—2003, sec., 2007-. Author: Temple of Invention: History of a National Landmark, 2006; contbr. articles to profl. jours. Pres. Dupont Circle Conservancy, Washington, 1978-92; v.p., bd. mem., Dupont Circle Citizens Assn. Washington, 1980-83, 86; mem. com. 100 Fed. City Washington, 2005—, trustee, 2006—. Recipient Rumrill fellowship Harvard U., Cambridge, Mass., 1956-57. Mem. Cosmos Club, Phi Beta Kappa, Phi Pi Theta, Delta Theta Phi.

ROBERTSON, CLIFF (CLIFFORD PARKER ROBERTSON III), actor, writer, director; b. La Jolla, Calif., Sept. 9, 1925; s. Clifford Parker II and Audrey (Willingham) Robertson; m. Cynthia Stone, 1957 (div. 1959); 1 child, Stephanie; m. Dina Merrill, Dec. 22, 1966 (div. 1986); 1 child, Heather. DFA (hon.), Bradford Coll., 1981, MacMurray Coll., 1986, Susquehanna U., 1988. Stage appearances include Late Love, Wisteria Trees, Orpheus Descending; films include Picnic, 1956, Autumn Leaves, 1956, The Naked and the Dead, 1958, The Girl Most Likely, 1958, Gidget, 1959, All in a Nights Work, 1961, The Big Show,

1961, Under-World, U.S.A., 1961, As the Sea Rages, 1961, The Interns, 1962, PT 109, 1963, Sunday in New York, 1964, The Best Man, 1964, 633 Squadron, 1964, Love Has Many Faces, 1965, Masquerade, 1965, Up From the Beach, 1965, The Honey Pot, 1967, The Devil's Brigade, 1968, Charly, 1968, (Academy award for Best Actor, 1968), The Great Northfield Minnesota Raid, 1972, Ace Eli and Rodger of the Skies, 1973, Too Late the Hero, 1970, Man on a Swing, 1974, 3 Days of the Condor, 1975, Out of Season, Obsession, 1976, Shoot, 1976, Star 80, 1983, Brainstorm, 1983, Malone, 1987, Wild Hearts Can't Be Broken, 1991, Wind, 1992, The Sunset Boys, 1995, Escape from L.A., 1996, Assignment Berlin, 1997, Family Tree, 1999, (star, co writer) Curse of the 13th Child, 2002, Spider-Man, Spider-Man 2, 2004, Riding the Bullet, 2004, Spider-Man 3, 2007; TV films and miniseries appearances include The Days of Wine and Roses, 1958, The Sunshine Patriot, 1968, The Game, 1968 (Emmy award) The Man Without a Country, 1973, A Tree Grows in Brooklyn, 1974, My Father's House, 1975, Return to Earth, 1976, Washington: Behind Closed Doors, 1977, Overboard, 1978, Two of a Kind, 1982, The Key to Rebecca, 1985, Dreams of Gold, 1986, Ford: The Man and The Machine, 1987, Dead Reckoning, 1990, Dazzle, 1995, Pakten, 1995, Melting Pot, 1997, Assignment Berlin, 1998, "With God on Our Side: the Rise of the Religious Right in America," (T.V. Mini Series), 1996, The Last Best Place, Outer Limits, 1998; appeared in TV series Falcon Crest; writer, dir.: play The V.I.P.'s, 1981; J. W. Coop.; contbr. articles to various publs. Served to lt. (j.g.) USNR. Recipient Wallace award Am. Scottish Found., 1984, Sharples aviation award AOPA, 1983, Theatre World award, 1970, award Advt. Age, 1985, E.A.A. Freedom of Flight award, 1986, USAF Outstanding Supporter award, 1997, Nat. Aviation Henderson award, 1995 World Aviation Conf., India, Nat. Soaring Mus. award Expts. Aviation Assn., 1996, I.C.A.S. Aviation award, 1998; holder of Nev. state distance soaring record, 1996. Mem.: SAG, Writers Guild America, Dirs. Guild, Brook Club (NYC), River Club (NYC), Maidstone Club (East Hampton), Bath & Tennis Club Palm Beach. Presbyterian. Avocations: flying, skiing, soaring, tennis.*

ROBERTSON, DAVID, physician, pharmacologist, educator; b. Sylvia, Tenn., May 23, 1947; s. David Herlie and Lucille Luther (Bowen) R.; m. Rose Marie Stevens, Oct. 30, 1976; 1 child, Rose. BA, Vanderbilt U., 1969, MD, 1973. Diplomate Am. Bd. Internal. Medicine, Am. Bd. Clin. Pharmacology. Intern Johns Hopkins U., Balt., 1973-74, asst. resident, 1974-75, asst. chief svc. in medicine, 1977-78; fellow in clin. pharmacology Vanderbilt U., Nashville, 1975-77, asst. prof. medicine and pharmacology, 1978-82, assoc. prof., 1982-86, prof., 1986—, prof. neurology, 1991—, Elton Yates prof. autonomic disorders, 1998—, dir. clin. rsch. ctr., 1987—; dir. Ctr. Space Physiology and Medicine, 1989—, Med. Sci. Tng. Program, 1993—2003; mem. staff Vanderbilt Hosp., Burroughs Wellcome scholar in clin. pharmacology, 1985-91. Author: (with B.M. Greene and G.J. Taylor) Problems in Internal Medicine, 1980, (with C.R. Smith) Manual of Clinical Pharmacology, 1981, (with Italo Biaggioni) Disorders of the Autonomic Nervous System, 1995, (with Italo Biaggioni, Geoffrey Burnstock and Phillip A. Low) Primer on the Autonomic Nervous System, 1996, 2d edit., 2004, Robertson's Autonomic Neuroscience, Japanese, 2007, (with Gordon H. Williams) Clinical and Translational Science: Principles of Human Research, 2009; editor-in-chief: Drug Therapy, 1991-94; assoc. editor, Jour. Pharmacol. Exptl. Therapy, 1998—; mem. editl. bd. Am. Jour. Medicine, Autonomic Neuroscience, Clin. Pharm. and Therapeutics, Clin. Autonomic Rsch., Am. Jour. Med. Sci., Current Topics in Pharmacology. Logan Clendening fellow, Reykjavik, Iceland, 1969; Adolph-Morsbach grantee Bonn, Germany, 1968; recipient Rsch. Career Devel. award NIH, 1981, Grant W. Liddle award for leadership in rsch., 1991, 1995-99 NASA Neurolab prin. investigator, Tchg. award Nat. Program Dir.'s Assn., 2003, Rschr. of Yr. award Nat. Dysautomia Rsch. Found., 2001, PhRMA award for Excellence in Pharmacology, Earl Sutherland prize, 2007. Fellow Am. Heart Assn. Coun. Hypertension and Circulation, ACP (tchg. and rsch. scholar 1978-81), Am. Autonomic Soc. (pres. 1992-94); mem. Am. Acad. Neurology, Soc. Neurosci., Am. Inst. Aeronautics and Astronautics, U.S. Pharmacopeial Conv., Nat. Bd. Med. Examiners, Aerospace Med. Assn. (space sta. sci. and applications com.), NASA (microgravity human rsch. com.), FDA Consortium Rare Disorders, Rare Disorder Network, Am. Fedn. Med. Rsch., Am. Soc. Clin. Investigation, Assn. Am. Physicians, Assn. Patient-Oriented Rsch. (bd. dirs., pres.), So. Soc. Clin. Investigation, Am. Soc. Clin. Pharmacology and Therapeutics, Phi Beta Kappa, Alpha Omega Alpha (hon., bd. dirs. 1995—. William Darby award 2000). Baptist. Home: 4003 Newman Pl Nashville TN 37204-4308 Office: Vanderbilt U Clin Rsch Ctr 21st Ave S Nashville TN 37232-2195 Business E-Mail: david.robertson@vanderbilt.edu.

ROBERTSON, DAVID, conductor, music director; b. Santa Monica, Calif., July 19, 1958; m. Orli Shaham; 2 children. Studied French horn, composition, and conducting, Royal Acad. Music, London; D (hon.), Maryville U., St. Louis, 2007. Resident condr. Jerusalem Symphony Orch., 1985—87; music dir. Ensemble Intercontemporain, Paris, 1990—2000, Orchestre Nat. de Lyon, France, 2000—04; artistic dir. Lyon Auditorium, 2000—04; music dir. St. Louis Symphony Orch., 2005—; prin. guest condr. BBC Symphony Orch., 2005—. Guest condr. Minn. Orch., Phila. Orch., Chgo. Symphony, Boston Symphony, San Francisco Symphony, NDR Symphony Orch. Hamburg, Germany, Royal Concertgebouw Orch., Orch. del Maggio Musicale Fiorentino, London Symphony Orch., Halle Orch., Bayerisches Staatorchester, Munich, Berlin Staatskapelle, La Scala Philharm., Boston Symphony, NY Philharm., LA Philharm. Recipient Condr. award, Seaver Inst./NEA, 1997, Ditson Conductor's award, Columbia U., 2006, ASCAP Morton Gould award, Am. Symphony Orch. League, 2006; named Condr. of Yr., Musical America, 2000. Mailing: St Louis Symphony Orch 718 N Grand Blvd Saint Louis MO 63103 Office Fax: 33 4 78 60 13 08.*

ROBERTSON, DAVID ALAN, museum director, educator; b. Jefferson City, Mo., Oct. 10, 1950; s. Roy Victor and Mary Jane (Buford-Threlkeld) R. BA in English, U. Mo., 1973, MA in Art History, 1976; PhD in Art History, U. Pa., 1983. Mus. asst. U. Mo. Mus., Columbia, 1975-76; rsch. asst. Victoria and Albert Museum, London, 1976; curatorial asst. Yale Ctr. for Brit. Art, New Haven, 1977-78; tchg. fellow U. Pa., Phila., 1978-81; staff supr. Rosenbach Mus. and Libr., Phila., 1980-82; dir. Dickinson Coll., Carlisle, Pa., 1982—2002, U. Oregon, Mus. Art, 1996—2000, Loyola U., D'Arcy Gallery, 1992—96; assoc. dir. Smart Mus., U. Chgo., 2000—02; Ellen Philips Katz dir. Mary and Leigh Block Mus Art Northwestern U., Evanston, Ill., 2002—, lectr. art history dept., 2003—. Fulbright prof. U. Munich, Germany, 1989-90; mem. selection com. Fulbright Commn., Bonn, Germany, 1989; grant reviewer Inst. Mus. Svcs., Washington, 1989-91. Penfield fellow U. Pa., Vienna, Austria, 1981-82, Kress fellow Kress Found., London, 1976, Vienna, 1980. Mem. Am. Assn. Mus.(peer reviewer accreditation and mus. assess program), Coll. Art Assn., Assn. Coll. and U. Mus. and Galleries (pres. 2008-). Office: Mary and Leigh Block Mus Art Northwestern U 40 Arts Circle Dr Evanston IL 60208 Office Phone: 847-491-2562. Business E-Mail: d-robertson@northwestern.edu.

ROBERTSON, DAVID STUART, art educator; b. Calgary, Alberta, Canada, Nov. 26, 1966; m. Dana Robertson. PhD, U. Okla., Norman, 2001. Assoc. prof. SUNY Geneseo, NY, 2000—08. Author: (book) Hard as the Rock Itself: Place and Identity in the American Mining Town (Fred B. Kniffen Book award, 2008).

ROBERTSON, DAWN H., former retail executive; b. Birmingham, Ala., June 28, 1955; m. Thomas A. Robertson; 2 children. BA in Fashion Merchandising, Auburn U., Ala., 1976. Buyer, exec. trainee Davidson's (divsn. R.H. Macy & Co.), Atlanta, 1977; various positions The May Co., 1983—96; pres., CEO McRae's (divsn. Saks Inc.), Jackson, Miss., 1997—98; exec. v.p. men's/children's/home Fed. Merchandising Group, 1998—2000; pres., chief merchandising officer Federated Stores Direct, NYC, 2000—02; mng. dir. Coles Meyer, Australia, 2002—06; pres. Old Navy divsn. Gap Inc., San Francisco, 2006—08. Named one of 50 Most Powerful Women, Fortune mag., 2005. Home: 40 Deepwoods Ln Old Greenwich CT 06870-1450

ROBERTSON, DONNA VIRGINIA, architect, educator, dean; b. Richmond, Va., Feb. 26, 1952; d. Charles Henry and Florence (Givens) R.; m. Robert M. McAnulty, May 24, 1986; 1 child, Robertson. Cert. theater arts studies, Webster Coll., St. Louis, 1972; BA, Stanford U., 1974; MArch, U. Va., 1978. Registered arch., N.Y. Asst. prof. Harvard U., Cambridge, Mass., 1983-84; asst. prof. Barnard Coll. Columbia U., NYC, 1984-92; dean Sch. Arch. Tulane U., New Orleans, 1992-96; dean Coll. Arch., prof. Ill. Inst. Tech., Chgo., 1996—; ptnr. Robertson McAnulty Archs., Chgo., 1986—; owner Donna V. Robertson Archs., NYC, 1982-86; sr. designer Kohn Pedersen Fox Archs., NYC, 1980-82, Mitchell Giurgola Archs., NYC, 1979-80. Adj. asst. prof. Barnard Coll., Columbia U., N.Y., 1982-83, dir. arch. program, fall 1985-92; vis. critic in design Harvard U., Cambridge, fall 1990, U. Va., Charlottesville, fall 1991; organizer, panelist Arch. and Lit. Symposium, N.Y.C., 1985; jury chair Am. Collegiate Schs. Arch., Boston, 1996; mem. bd. dirs. Nat. Archtl. Accrediting Bd., 2000-03; profl. advisor Ford Calumet Environ. Ctr. Competition, City of Chgo., 2004. Prin. arch. Fishback residence, New Orleans, Sunkel residence, New Orleans, Pisar residence, N.Y.C., Dachs residence, N.Y.C.; pres. Nat. Archtl. Accrediting Bd., 2002-03; profiled in Archtl. Record May 2004. Juror invitational competition Seoul Performing Arts Ctr., Republic of Korea, 2006. Recipient Honor award, Chgo. Landmarks Commn., 2005, Education award, Arch. Constrn. Engring. Mentor Program, Chgo., 2007; named one of Most Influential Women in Chgo., Crain's Chgo. Bus., 2004. Mem. AIA (juror annual design hons. awards 1996, Educators and Practitioners Network, co-chair tchrs. seminar 2006, mem. Chgo. bd.), Coll. Fellow of AIA, Am. Coll. Sch. Arch. (co-chair 2006, Endowed Chair Arch., John and Jeanne Rowe, 2007), Chgo. Network-Internat. Women's Forum, Raven Soc. (U. Va.), Arts Club (Chgo.), Nat. Trust His. Preservation, Phi Beta Kappa. Office: Ill Inst Tech Coll Architecture 3360 S State St Chicago IL 60616 Office Phone: 312-567-3263. E-mail: robertson@iit.edu.

ROBERTSON, EDWIN DAVID, lawyer; b. Roanoke, Va., July 5, 1946; s. Edwin Traylor and Norma Burns (Bowles) R.; m. Anne Littelle Ferratt, Sept. 7, 1968, 1 child, Thomas Therit. BA with honors, U. Va., 1968, LLB, 1971. Bar: N.Y. 1972, U.S. Ct. Appeals (2d cir.) 1972, U.S. Dist. Ct. (ea. and so. dists.) N.Y. 1973, U.S. Supreme Ct. 1975, U.S. Dist. Ct. (ea. dist.) Mich. 1986. Assoc. Cadwalader, Wickersham & Taft, NYC, 1971—80, ptnr., 1980—. Author: Brethren and Sisters of the Bar, 2008. Bd. dirs. Early Music Found. N.Y.C., 1983-99, chmn., 1993-99; bd. dirs. Oratorio Soc. of N.Y.C., 1988—2004, sec., 1991—2004; judge Ct. of Rev., Episcopal Ch., 2001-03. 1st lt. USAF, 1971-72. Echols scholar. Mem. ABA (ho. of dels. 2004-07), Nat. Conf. Bar Presidents, Fed. Bar Coun., NY County Lawyers Assn. (chmn. bankruptcy com. 1983-87, chmn. fin. com. 1999, bd. dirs. 1985-88, 95-99, 2000—, investment com. 1992-2007, exec. com. 1996-2008, treas. 2001-02, v.p. 2002-04, pres. 2006-07), NY State Bar Assn. (house dels. 2001-, nominatng com. 2002-07), Assn. Bar City NY, Soc. Colonial Wars, Jefferson Soc., Sons of Revolution, Order of Coif, Phi Beta Kappa, Phi Kappa Psi, NY State Ind. Jud. Screen Commn. 1st Jud. Dist. Republican. Episcopalian. Home: 10 Liberty St Apt 21C New York NY 10005 Office: Cadwalader Wickersham & Taft OneWorld Fin Ctr New York NY 10281 Office Phone: 212-504-6000. Business E-Mail: darob@cwt.com.

ROBERTSON, EDWIN MALCOLM, psychology educator; s. Ronald and Elizabeth Robertson. BA, U. Cambridge, UK, 1994; DPhil, U. Oxford, UK, 1998; BM BChir, House Physician & House Surgeon,Oxford Med. Sch., 2000—01. Rsch. fellow Harvard Med. Sch., 2001—03, instr., 2003—05, asst. prof., 2005—. Editor PLoS ONE, San Fransisco, 2006—. Contbr. multiple rsch. articles to profl. jours. Recipient R01, NIH, 2005—. Office: Harvard Med Sch 330 Brookline Ave Boston MA 02215

ROBERTSON, GLEN A., aerospace engineer; m. Elena A. Robertson; children: Melissa A. Le, Veronica Sclyarenko. MSE, U. Ala., Huntsville, 1993. Aerospace engr. NASA-Marshall Space Flight Ctr., Huntsville, Ala., 1987—; pres. Inst. Advance Studies Space, Propulsion & Energy Sci., Madison, Ala., 2008—. Contbr. scientific papers. E-5 US Army, 1974—78, Va. Beach. Recipient Invention Disclosures award, NASA-Marshall Space Flight Ctr., 1992, Outstanding Paper award, Space Tech. Application & Internat. Forum, 2005. Achievements include patents for piezoelectrostatic generator; electromagnetic meissner effect launcher; spiral fluid separator; pressure-driven magnetically coupled conveyance. Office: Inst Advanced Studies 265 Ita Ann Madison AL 35757 Business E-Mail: gar@ias-spes.org.

ROBERTSON, GREGORY B., lawyer; b. Sandusky, Ohio, Apr. 2, 1951; BA, Washington & Lee Univ., 1973; JD, Univ. Richmond, 1976. Bar: Va. 1976. Ptnr., co-chmn. labor, employment practice group Hunton & Williams LLP, Richmond, Va. Mem.: ABA, Va. Bar Assn., Energy and Mineral Law Found. (past pres.), Va. CofC (bd. dir., counsel), Phi Delta Phi, Pi Sigma Alpha. Office: Hunton & Williams LLP Riverfront Plz East Tower 951 E Byrd St Richmond VA 23219-4074 Office Phone: 804-788-8526. Office Fax: 804-788-8218. Business E-Mail: grobertson@hunton.com.

ROBERTSON, HORACE BASCOMB, JR., retired law educator; b. Charlotte, NC, Nov. 13, 1923; s. Horace Bascomb and Ruth (Montgomery) R.; m. Patricia Lavell, Aug. 11, 1947; children— Mark L., James D. BS, U.S. Naval Acad., 1945; JD, Georgetown U., 1953; MS, George Washington U., 1968. Commd. ensign U.S. Navy, 1945, advanced through grades to rear adm., 1972; line officer, 1945-55; law specialist, 1955-68; spl. counsel to sec. Navy, Washington, 1964-67, judge adv., 1968-76; spl. counsel to chief naval ops. Washington, 1970-72; dep. judge adv. gen. Navy Dept., Washington, 1972-75, judge adv. gen., 1975-76; prof. law Duke U., 1976-89, sr. assoc. dean, 1986-89, ret., 1990; Chas H. Stockton chair of internat. law Naval War Coll., Newport, R.I., 1991-92. Decorated D.S.M. Mem. ABA, Am. Soc. Internat. Law. Home: 9 Silver Maple Ct Durham NC 27705-5642 Office: Duke U Sch Law Durham NC 27708 Office Phone: 919-613-7038. Business E-Mail: hbr@law.duke.edu.

ROBERTSON, HUGH (ELIHU F.), lawyer; b. Annapolis, Md., 1953; BA, Yale Univ., 1976; JD, Univ. Va., 1979. Bar: N.Y. 1980. Atty. Milbank Tweed Hadley & McCloy, London, Hong Kong, ptnr. Global Fin. Dept. NYC, 1987—. Mem.: ABA, N.Y. State Bar Assn. Office: Milbank Tweed Hadley & McCloy 1 Chase Manhattan Plz New York NY 10005-1413 Office Phone: 212-530-5187. Office Fax: 212-530-5219. Business E-Mail: erobertson@milbank.com.

ROBERTSON, JACK CLARK, accounting educator; b. Marlin, Tex., Apr. 27, 1943; s. Rupert Cook and Lois Lucille (Rose) R.; m. Caroline Susan Hughes, Oct. 23, 1965; children: Sara Ellen, Elizabeth Hughes. Student, Rice U., 1961-63; BBA with honors, U. Tex., Austin, 1965, M in Profl. Acctg., 1967; PhD, U. N.C., 1970. CPA, Tex. Tax acct. Humble Oil and Refining Co., Houston, 1964-65; auditor Peat, Marwick, Mitchell & Co., Houston, 1965-66; acct. Wade, Barton, Marsh CPAs, Austin, Tex., 1966-67; from asst. prof. to prof. emeritus U. Tex., Austin, 1970—2003, C.T. Zlatkovich Centennial prof. emeritus, 2003—. Acad. assoc. Coopers & Lybrand, N.Y.C., 1975-76; acad. fellow U.S. Securities and Exchange Commn. Office of the Chief Acct., Washington, 1982-83; Erskine fellow U. Canterbury, Christchurch, New Zealand, 1988; tng. the trainers instr. Vilnius, Lithuania, 1993; lectr. in field. Contbr. articles to profl. jours. Lay reader St. Matthews Episcopal Ch., Austin, 1972-75, mem. vestry, 1973-75, 77-79, 84-86, treas., 1974-75, 77-96, chmn. bldg. fund, 1976-87, chmn. everymen. canvass, 1980, sr. warden, 1986; del. Diocese of Tex. Coun., 1993-95, Usher Guild, 2006-; Trompetista El Grupo Chinampa, 2000—, lector laico, 2000-03, Miembro comite del obispo Iglesia San Francisco de Asis, 2000-03, treas., 2002-03; dir., treas. Austin Chamber Music Ctr., 2003-07; mem. New Horizons Band, 2006-; ofcl. U.S.A Track and Field, 1996—; bd. dirs. Episcopal Province VII Ctr. for Hispanic Ministries, 2006—; mem. Austin Fine Woodworkers Assn., 2003-; adminstr. Jovences Episcopales Coll. Scholarship Fund, 2001-. Mem. AICPA, Am. Acctg. Assn. (sec.-treas. auditing sect. 1976-77, v.p. auditing sect. 1977-78, pres. auditing sect. 1978-79, chmn. auditing stds. com. 1980-81, chmn. SEC liaison com. 1983-84, historian auditing sect. 1999-2001), Tex. Soc. CPAs (vice-chmn., profl. ethics com. 1986-94, 95-97, Presdl. citation 1994), Assn. Cert. Fraud Examiners (regent emeritus, cert.), Kosse Heritage Soc. (Tex.) (dir. devel. 2008-), Phi Kappa Phi, Beta Gamma Sigma, Beta Alpha Psi.

ROBERTSON, JAMES, federal judge; b. Cleve., May 18, 1938; s. Frederick Irving and Doris Mary (Byars) R.; m. Berit Selma Persson, Sept. 19, 1959; children: Stephen Irving, Catherine Anne, Peter Arvid. AB, Princeton U., 1959; LLB, George Washington U., 1965. Bar: D.C. 1966, U.S. Supreme Ct. 1969. Assoc. Wilmer, Cutler & Pickering, Washington, 1965-69, ptnr., 1973-94; judge US Dist. Ct. (DC dist.), 1994—, Fgn. Intelligence Surveillance Ct., 2002—06. Chief counsel, Lawyers Com. for Civil Rights Under Law, 1969-70, dir., 1970-72, co-chmn., 1982-84; mem. com. on grievances U.S. Dist. Ct., 1988-92, vice chmn., 1989-92; bd. dirs. South Africa Legal Svcs. and Edn. Project, Inc., 1987-01, pres., 1989-94; bd. dirs. D.C. Prisoners Legal Svcs., Inc., 1992-94. Editor in chief George Washington Law Rev., 1964-65. Lt. USN, 1959-64. Fellow Am. Coll. Trial Lawyers, Am. Bar Found.; mem. ABA, D.C. Bar (bd. govs. 1986-93, pres.-elect 1990-92, pres. 1991-92), Am. Law Inst. Home: 3318 N St NW Washington DC 20007-2807 Office: US Courthouse Rm 4903 333 Constitution Ave NW Washington DC 20001-2854

ROBERTSON, JAMES HENRY, history professor; b. Phila., Nov. 21, 1945; s. J. Hamilton and Edna C. Robertson; 1 child, Karyn Alison Davis. BA in History, Grove City Coll., Pa., 1967; MA in Modern Eur. History, Wash. State U., Pullman, 1972; AA in Com Sci., Acctg & Bus. Adminstrn., Montgomery Co. Cmty. Coll., Blue Bell, Pa., 1984. Cert. secondary tchr. Pa., 1968, in Portuguese Def. Lang. Inst., 1972. Purchasing coord. Wendy's Internat., Columbus, Ohio, 1984—88; tchr. CAP, Phila., 2003—05; adj. prof. history Del. Co. Cmty. Coll., Media, Pa., 2005—. Councilman Schwenksville Boro, Pa., 1987—89. Capt. USAF, 1968—76. Decorated Disting. Mil. Grad. award GCC; recipient Disting. Scholar Seminar award, U. Del., 2005. Mem.: Pa. Holocaust Edn. Coun. (corr.), So. Poverty Law Ctr. (corr.), Phi Kappa Phi, Phi Alpha Theta. Independent-Republican. Avocations: travel, painting, reading, writing. Home: 916 Rydal Rd PO Box 416 Jenkintown PA 19046 Office: Del Co Cmty Coll Media Line Rd Media PA 19063 Personal E-mail: jamesr2235@aol.com. Business E-Mail: jroberts@dccc.edu.

ROBERTSON, JAQUELIN TAYLOR, architect, educator; b. Richmond, Va., Mar. 20, 1933; s. Walter Spencer and Mary Dade (Taylor) Robertson; m. Marianne Neese, Sept. 15, 1962. BA cum laude, Yale U., New Haven, 1955, MArch, 1961; BA, Oxford U., 1957. Archtl. designer Sir Leslie Martin, Cambridge, England, 1961—62, Edward Barnes Assocs., NYC, 1963—66; lectr. architecture Yale U., 1964—65, Columbia U., NYC, 1965—67; prin. urban designer NYC Planning Commn., 1967—69; dir. Office Midtown Planning and Devel., NYC, 1969—72; lectr. The New Sch., NYC, 1973; city planning commr. NYC, 1973—75; v.p. Arlen Realty Devel., NYC, 1974—75; mng. dir. Llewelyn-Davies Va Shoraka, Tehran, Iran, 1975—77; chmn. Llewelyn-Davies Assocs., NYC, 1977—78; prin. Jaquelin Taylor Robertson FAIA, NYC, 1978—80, Design Devel. Resources, NYC, 1980—88, Eisenman-Robertson Archs., NYC, 1980—88; dean Sch. Architecture U. Va., Charlottesville, 1980—88, Commonwealth prof. architecture, 1985—90; ptnr. Cooper, Robertson & Ptnrs., NYC, 1988—. Vis. faculty mem. Salzburg Seminar, Austria, 1974; vis. prof. archtl. design RI Sch. Design, Providence, 1979; William Henry Bishop prof. Yale U., 1980, William B. and Charlotte Shepherd Davenport prof., 2004. Contbr. articles to profl. jours., mags.; exhibitions include Mus. Modern Art, NYC, 1967, Archtl. League and Mcpl. Arts Soc., 1969, Inst. Architecture and Urban Studies, NYC, 1975. Chmn. policy panel Design Arts Program Nat. Endowment for Arts, 1979—83; mem. art and architecture rev. coun. State of Va., 1982—88; mem. vis. com. Harvard Grad. Sch. Design, 1983—88; advisor Aga Khan Program for Study of Islamic Art & Architecture Harvard U. and MIT, 1983—90; trustee Inst. Architecture and Urban Studies, NYC, 1984—85, Va. Mus. Fine Arts, 1985—90; founder Jeffersonian Restoratiorn Adv. Bd. U. Va., 1985; founder Mayor's Inst. City Design, Washington, 1986; mem. Congress for New Urbanism, 1993; bd. dirs. Pks. Coun., NYC, 1971—75, Mcpl. Arts Soc., NYC, 1971—75, Archtl. League NY, 1972—75, 1979—81; bd. dirs. Ctr. for Study of Am. Architecture Columbia U., 1984—87. Recipient Thomas Jefferson Found. Medal in Architecture, 1998, Seaside Inst. prize, 2002, Richard H. Driehaus Prize for Classical Architecture, 2007, award, Patks Coun., 1973, Batd, 1973; Rhodes scholar, U. Oxford, 1955—57. Fellow: AIA, Am. Inst. Cert. Planners; mem.: Am. Planning Assn., Maidstone Club, Easthampton, NY, Pundits, U. Yale, Bullingdon Club, U. Oxford, Knickerbocker Club, NYC (bd. govs. 2004—), St. Anthony Hall, U. Yale, Torch. Hon. Soc., U. Yale. Episcopalian. Office: Cooper Robertson & Ptnrs 311 W 43rd St New York NY 10036 Office Phone: 212-247-1717, 631-329-7387. Office Fax: 212-245-0361.

ROBERTSON, JEAN ELIZABETH, sociology educator; b. Galashiels, Scotland, Sept. 20, 1956; arrived in U.S., 1998; d. Frank Robertson and Jean Isabella Connochie; m. Mohan Narayanasamy; children: Sonja

Jean Lowit, Simon David Lowit, Nicholas Ian Lowit. MA, U. Aberdeen, Scotland, 1995. ESOL tchr. Spanish Cath. Ctr., Gaithersburg, Md., 1999—2001; adjuct faculty mem. Strayer U. Online, Newington, Va., 2002—, cons. course development, 2006—; faculty mem. Northwest AF U., Yangling, Shaanxi, China, 2008—09. Vol. Easter Seals Balt., Wash., Montgomery County Dept. Health and Human Svcs., Rockville, Md. Home: 19105 Plummer Dr Germantown MD 20876 Office: Strayer U Online Newington VA Home Fax: 301-515-1337. Personal E-mail: jerliz56@yahoo.com.

ROBERTSON, JOEL THOMAS, railroad executive; b. Milo, Maine, Aug. 30, 1947; s. Paul Russell Robertson and Denice Luella Stevens; m. Bonita Louise Hosford, July 29, 1966 (div. Nov. 1968); m. Patricia Rae Willinski, Mar. 14, 1970 (div. May 1990); children: Jason Thomas, April Dawn Robertson Bishop; m. Marie Paulette Melvin, Dec. 31, 1994; 1 child, Stuart Spencer Stratton. BS, W.Va. State U., 1982; MS, Marshall U., 1986. Cert. safety mgr. World Safety Orgn., 85. Agt. Bangor (Maine) & Aroosook R.R., 1966—70, Can. Pacific Rwy., St. John, NB, 1970—80; hazardous materials inspector Fed. RR Adminstrn., Washington, 1980—2001, hazardous materials specialist, 2001—02; ptnr. Robertson & Assocs., LLC, 2002—; regulatory specialist Am. Honda Co. Inc., 2004—. Transp. cons. Union Carbide Corp., Danbury, Conn., 1989—90; expert witness/accident investigator Collins, Collins & Dinardo, Buffalo, 1989—; bus. devel. cons. Brothers Coal Cons., Charleston, W.Va., 1989—90, TransMar Inc., Spokane, Wash., 1994, Coal Tech. Corp., Bristol, Va., 1989—97; appearance on nat. news program ABC Wide World News Tonight, 1985; interviewed by Tass Soviet News Agy., 89; owner Guest Nat. Soc. of Profl. Engrs., Nat. Press Club, Washington, 1989; founder, devel. dir. Stuart Spencer Stratton Meml. Found., unit of Nat. Heritage Found., 2002—; regional sci. fair judge and scholarship founder for environ. scis. INTEL N.W., 2000—; adj. tech. faculty Marshall U., Transp. Safety Inst., 1987—; adv, U.S. Senate Murray U.S. Dept. State, Volpentest Hammer Tng. Inst., Transportation Safety Security, Richland, Wash.; leader, organizer Multi-Agy. Internat. Transp. Safety-Security Strike Force, 2000; internat. trade and devel. cons. Govt. Cameroon, West Africa; loaned exec. Combined Fed. Campaign, 2001—02; assoc. Oreg. Fed. Bd., 2001—02; mem. exec. potential program USDA Grad. Sch. Leadership, 2002; internat. lectr. and citizen amb. China Assn. of Sci. and Tech., 1989; acting regional adminstr., acting staff dir. U.S. Hazardous Materials, 1994—2002. Contbr. articles to profl. publs. Organizer, master of ceremonies First Joint Chem. Industry/Rwy. Safety Symposium, W.Va., 1985, Celebration of Engring. Career Day, Huntington, W.Va., 1989; sci. advisor Bush White House Space Coun., Washington, 1989. Recipient Commendation, Gov. of W.Va., 1985, Superior Achievement award, U.S. DOT-FRA. Mem.: Am. Soc. Metals, Am. Inst. Hygiene Assn., Soc. Mechanical Engrs., AIChE, Am. Soc. Quality Control, Am. Soc. Safety Engrs., Am. Soc. Profl. Engrs. (exec. affiliate 1983—89), Engrs. Club of Huntington (pres. 1987—88), Kiwanis (pres. West Huntington chpt. 1989—90). Republican. Mem. Lds Ch. Avocations: fund-raising activities, event organizing, photography, travel, writing. Address: 16505 A SE 1st St Ste 285 Vancouver WA 98684 Home: 16505 SE 1ST ST STE A Vancouver WA 98684-9299 Office Phone: 360-873-2329. E-mail: joel@safety.specialist.com, cameroon313@aol.com.

ROBERTSON, JOHN ARCHIBALD LAW, nuclear scientist; b. Dundee, Scotland, July 4, 1925; arrived in Can., 1957, naturalized, 1963; s. John Carr and Ellen (Law) R.; m. Betty-Jean Moffatt, June 26, 1954 (dec. Feb. 10, 2007); children: Ean Stuart, Clare Deborah, Fiona Heather. BA, Cambridge U., Eng., 1950, MA, 1953. Sci. officer UK Atomic Energy Authority, Harwell, England, 1950-57; rsch. officer Atomic Energy Can. Ltd., Chalk River, Ont., Canada, 1957-63, head reactor materials br., 1963-70, dir. fuels and materials div., 1970-75, asst. to v.p., 1975-82; dir. program planning Atomic Energy Can. Ltd. (Rsch. Co. Head Office), 1982-85; cons., 1985—. Mem. Atomic Energy Control Bd.'s Adv. Com. on Nuc. Safety, 1988-97. Author: Irradiation Effects in Nuclear Fuels, 1969, Decide the Nuclear Issues for Yourself: Nuclear Need Not Be Unclear, 2000; editor: Jour. Nuclear Materials, 1967-71. Capt. Royal Engrs. Brit. and Indian Armies, 1943—47. Recipient W.B. Lewis medal Can. Nuc. Assn., 1987, W.J. Kroll Zirconium medal W.J. Kroll Inst. for Extractive Metallurgy, 1993, Queen's Golden Jubilee medal, 2004, Edn. and Comm. award Can. Nuc. Assn., 2005. Fellow Royal Soc. Can. Personal E-mail: jalrober@magma.ca.

ROBERTSON, JOSEPH EDMOND, grain processing company executive; b. Brownstown, Ind., Feb. 16, 1918; s. Roscoe Melvin and Edith Penina (Shields) R.; m. Virginia Faye Baxter, Nov. 23, 1941; 1 son, Joseph Edmond, Jr. BS, postgrad., Kans. State U., 1940. Cereal chemist Ewing Mill Co., 1940—43, engr. flour milling, 1946—50, feed nutritionist, 1951—59; v.p., sec. Robertson Corp., Brownstown, Ind., 1960—80, pres., 1980—97, chmn., 1997—. Author: On Kilroy's Trail, 1998. Mem. Kans. State U. Varsity Basketball Team, 1937-40; pres. Jackson County Welfare Bd., Ind., 1948-52; mem. Ind. Port Commn., 1986-91; mem. Ind. Gov.'s Coun. of Sagamores of the Wabash. Served with USAAF, 1943-45. Named to Hon. Order Ky. Cols.; recipient Brownstown (Ind.) First Lifetime Achievement award, 1999. Mem. Hardwood Plywood Mfrs. Assn. (v.p. affiliate div. 1971-73, 87-88, internat. lectr. forest products industry 1973-97), Am. Assn. Cereal Chemists, Assn. Operative Millers, Am. Legion, Brownstown C. of C. (dir. All Am. city program 1955), Kans. State U. Alumni Assn. (life), Blue Key, Phi Delta Theta, Phi Kappa Phi, Alpha Mu. Clubs: Internat. Travelers Century (LA), Circumnavigators Club (NYC), Elks. Presbyterian. Home: Lake and Forest Club 1268 E Lake Shore Dr PO Box A Brownstown IN 47220

ROBERTSON, JULIAN HART, JR., hedge fund manager; b. Salisbury, NC, 1932; s. Julian Hart and Blanche (Spencer) Robertson; m. Josephine Robertson; 3 children. BBA, U. NC, Chapel Hill, 1955. Various sales positions Kidder, Peabody & Co., 1957—66, v.p. & stockbroker, 1966—74, chmn., CEO Webster Mgmt. Corp., 1974—78; founder, chmn., CEO Tiger Mgmt. Corp., 1980—2000. Owner Kauri Cliffs Lodge, Kerikeri, New Zealand, The Farm, Cape Kidnappers, New Zealand; bd. visitors Kenan-Flagler Bus. Sch. U. NC, mem. bd. dirs. Gen. Alumni Assn.; co-founder The Robertson Found., 1996. Mem. nat. bd. advs. Children's Scholarship Fund; founder Robertson Scholars Prog. Duke U./ U. NC; bd. trustees Cathedral Ch. St. John the Divine, Wildlife Conservation Soc., Rockefeller U., Cancer Rsch. Inst., NYC; mem. exec. com. Lincoln Ctr. Performing Arts. Served with USN, 1955—57. Recipient Davie award, U. NC Bd. Trustees, 1992, Oliver R. Grace award for disting. svc. in advancing cancer rsch., Cancer Rsch. Inst., 2006; named one of Forbes Richest Americans; named to 'The World's Billionaires' list, Forbes mag. Republican. Office Phone: 212-984-2500. Office Fax: 212-984-8807.*

ROBERTSON, LAVERNE, minister; MS, Nova Southeastern U., 1995; DD, Miracle Theol. Coll. Pastor Mansion Ave. Triumphant Bapt. Ch., Richmond, Va., 2001—04; founder, pres. Va. Triumphant Coll. and Seminary, 2006. Singer: (songs) Freedom Day Has Come. Gospel music writer and performer, Richmond, 1980—99. Named 3rd runner up, Miss Black Richmond Pageant. Personal E-mail: laverroberts@aol.com.

ROBERTSON, LEON H., management consultant, educator; b. Atlanta; s. Grady Jospeh and Pearline (Chandler) R. BS in Indsl. Mgmt., Ga. Inst. Tech., 1957, MS, 1959; postgrad., U. Okla.-Norman, 1958, U. Mich., 1961; PhD in Bus. Adminstrn., Ga. State U., 1968. Mgr. mgmt. cons. divsn. Arthur Andersen & Co., Atlanta, 1960-65; prof. bus. adminstrn. Ga. State U., 1965-75; corp. v.p. Tex. Gas Corp., Owensboro, Ky., 1975-78, sr. v.p., 1982-83; chmn., CEO Am. Carriers, Inc., Overland Park, Kans., 1978-88; chmn. bd. dirs. Midwest Coast Transport, Overland Park, 1988-89; prof. mgmt., dir. divsn. bus. adminstrn. U. Mo., Kansas City, 1990-96, prof. Internat. Acad. Programs, 1996-98, dir. Ctr. for Internat. Bus., 1998—2006; emeritus prof., 2009—. Office: Univ of Mo-Kansas City Henry W Bloch Sch Bus & Pub Admn 5110 Cherry St Kansas City MO 64110-2426 Business E-Mail: robertsonl@umkc.edu.

ROBERTSON, LESLIE EARL, structural engineer; b. LA, Feb. 12, 1928; s. Garnett Roy and Tina (Grantham) R.; m. Saw-Teen See, Aug. 11, 1982; children: Jeanne, Christopher Alan, Sharon Miyuki, Karla Mei. BS, U. Calif., Berkeley, 1952; D in Engring. (hon.), Rensselaer Polytech. Inst., 1986; DSc (hon.), U. Western Ont., Can., 1988; DEng (hon.), Lehigh U., 1991. Lic. arch., Japan; registered profl. engr., Calif., other states; chartered structural engr., U.K. Structural engr. Kaiser Engrs., Oakland, Calif., 1952-54, John A. Blume, San Francisco, 1954-57, Raymond Internat. Co., NYC, 1957-58; mng. ptnr. Skilling, Helle, Christiansen, Robertson, NYC, Seattle and Anchorage, 1958-82; chmn. Robertson, Fowler & Assocs., P.C., NYC, 1982-85, Leslie E. Robertson Assocs., structural engrs., 1986—. Past chmn. Coun. on Tall Bldgs. and Urban Habitat; mem. Com. on Natural Disasters; commr., mem. US Nat. Com. for Decade for Natural Disasters Reduction; chmn. Wind Engring. Rsch. Coun.; lectr. Rensselaer Poly. Inst., 1984, Johns Hopkins U., 1985, Nat. Bur. Stsa, 1986, Cornell U., Hong Kong U., 1986, Technischische U., Delft, Holland, 1991, 93, Waseda U., Japan, Musashi Inst. Tech., 1993, others; James L. Sherard lectr. U. Calif., Berkeley, 1991; Frank Howard Disting. lectr. George Washington U., 2002; Felix Cardela lectr. MIT, Mus. Modern Art, NY, Princeton U., 2002-03, prof., 2002-; Gordon Smith lectr. Yale U., 2003; Inaugural Y.K. Cheung lectr., Hong Kong, 2005; mem. adv. bd. Coll. Engring., U. Calif., Berkeley; prof. honoris causa U. de Architectura Si Urbanism ion Mincu, Bucuresti, Romania, 2005; Lichtenstein Disting. lectr. Ohio State U., 2007; bd. dirs. MacDowell Colony, Archs., Designers, Planners for Social Responsibility, Skycraper Mus.; com. on fed. constrn. design criteria Commn. on Engring. and Tech. Sys. Author papers in field. Bd. dirs. Architects/Designers/Planners for Social Responsibility; mem. Japan Structural Cons. Assn.; fellow human rights of scientists com. N.Y. Acad. Scis.; mem. U.S. Nat. Com. for Decade for Nat. Disaster Reduction; mem. engring. coll. coun. Cornell U. Served with USNR, 1944-46. Recipient Inst. Honor award AIA, 1989, Mayor's award for excellence in sci. and tech. Mayor of City of N.Y./N.Y. Acad. Scis., 1993, John R. Parmer award, 1991, Disting. Engring. Alumnus award U. Calif., Berkeley, 1991, Prof. Gengo Matsui prize, Japan, 1993, World Trade Ctr. Individual Svc. medal, 1993, Citation of Excellence, ENR, 1993, 98, J. Lloyd Kimbrough award AISC, 2001, 1st recipient of Henry C. Turner award for innovation in constrn. tech., 2002, 1st recipient of Fazlur Rahman Kahn medal, 2004; named Constrn. Man of Yr., 1989. Fellow ASCE (hon., Raymond C. Reese Rsch. prize 1974, Outstanding Projects and Leaders award for lifetime contbns. in design 2003), Singapore Structural Steel Soc., Instn. Structural Engrs. (London, hon., medal), Instn. Engrs. Ireland; mem. AIA (hon., NY chpt.), Nat. Acad. Engring. Archtl. League NY (bd. dirs.), NY Acad. Scis. (Mayor Excellence award in Sci. and Tech. 1993, 95), Tokyo Soc. Architects (Disting. Hon. fellow), Instn. Structural Engrs. (UK, Gold medal 2004), Nat. Soc. Romanian Engrs., Structural Engrs. Assn. NY (hon.), Arch. Inst. Japan. Home: 100 Riverside Blvd Apt 18d New York NY 10069-0423 Personal E-mail: xxlerxx@yahoo.com.

ROBERTSON, LINDSAY GORDON, law educator; b. Takoma Park, Md., Nov. 16, 1959; s. James Cole and Pauline Taylor Robertson; children: Eliza W., John B. AB, Davidson Coll., NC, 1981; JD, U. Va., Charlottesville, 1963, MA, 1986, PhD, 1997. Bar: Va. 1986, DC 1987, Okla. 1998. Assoc. Ober, Kaler, Grimes & Shriver, Washington, 1986—89, Lichtman, Trister, Singer & Ross, Washington, 1989—90; atty. McGuire, Woods, Battle & Boothe, Charlottesville, 1992—93; jud. clk. Hon. Sue L. Robinson, US. Dist. Judge, Wilmington, Del., 1994—96; atty. McGuire Woods, Charlottesville, Va., 1996—97; vis. assoc. prof. U. Okla. Coll. Law, Norman, 1997—98, assoc. prof., 1998—2003, prof., 2003—; lectr. U. Va., Sch. Law, 1990—94, 1996—97. Pvt. sector advisor US Del. to the Working Group on the U.N. Draft Declaration on the Rights of Indigenous Peoples, Geneva, 2004—06, US Del. OAS Draft Am. Declaration on the Rights Indigenous People, Washington, 2004—07, US Del. to UN CERD, Geneva, 2008; faculty dir. Ctr. Study Am. Indian Law and Policy, Norman, 1997—; spl. counsel Gov. of Okla. on Indian Affairs, 2000—; spl. justice Supreme Ct. of the Cheyenne and Arapaho Tribes, Concho, Okla., 2004—. Author: (book) Conquest by Law (PSP award, 2005). Bd. dirs. Okla. Indian Legal Svcs., Okla. City, 1998—2004; mem. NAIC, Norman, 2004—. Recipient Sam K. Viersen Jr. Presdl. award, U. Okla., 2002—, Orpha and Maurice Merrill award, U. Okla. Coll. Law, 2005—09, Brandt award, U. Okla., 2008—09, Judge Haskell A. Holloman award, 2009—; Vis. fellowship, Phila. Ctr. Early Am. Studies, 1992—94, Governor's fellowship, U. Va., 1993. Mem.: ABA, Am. Soc. Legal History, Okla. Indian Bar Assn. Episcopalian. Office: Univ OK Coll Law 300 Timberdell Rd Norman OK 73019 Business E-Mail: lrobertson@ou.edu.

ROBERTSON, MARIAN ELLA (HALL), small business owner, handwriting analyst; b. Edmonton, Alta., Can., Mar. 3, 1920; d. Orville Arthur and Lucy Hon (Osborn) Hall; m. Howard Chester Robertson, Feb. 7, 1942; children: Elaine, Richard. Student, Willamette U., 1937-39; BS, Western Oreg. State U., 1955. Cert. elem., jr. high. tchr., supt. (life) Oreg.; cert. graphoanalyst. Tchr. pub. schs., Mill City, Albany, Scio and Hillsboro, Oreg., 1940-72; cons. Zaner-Bloser Inc., Columbus, Ohio, 1972-85, assoc. cons., 1985-89; pres. Write-Keys, Scio, 1980-90; owner Lifelines, Jefferson, Oreg., 1991-94. Tchr. Internat. Graphoanalysis Soc., Chgo., 1979; instr. Linn-Benton CC, 1985-89; del. Oreg. Water Resources Congress at Seaside, 2002; mem. Ptnrs. of the Ams., Costa Rica, 2003. Master gardener vol. Marion County Oreg. State U. Extension Svc., 1992; floriculture judge Marion County Fair, 1992; master gardener clinic Oreg. State Fair, 1992; sr. intern 5th Congl. Dist. Oreg., Washington, 1984, mem. sr. adv. coun., 1984; mem. precinct com, Rep. Ctrl. Com., Linn County, 1986, alt. vice chair, 1986, parliamentarian, 1988—; candidate Oreg. State Legislature, Salem, 1986; del. NW Friends Yearly Meeting, Newberg, Oreg., 1990—92; clk. Marion Friends Monthly Meeting, 1992—93. Mem.: Ptnrs. of Ams.-Costa Rica., Port Orford Heritage Soc. (hon.). Republican. Mem. Soc. Of Friends. Avocations: piano, organ, violin, gardening, writing. Home: 2757 Pheasant Ave SE Salem OR 97302-3170 Office Phone: 503-371-5940.

ROBERTSON, MARY AMOS, mathematics educator; b. Fairmont, W.Va., Apr. 10, 1963; d. Robert Newton and Martha Evelyn Amos; m. W Scott Robertson, July 6, 1989. B in Math Edn., Fairmont State U., Fairmont, W.Va., 1984; M in Ednl. Leadership, Nova Southeastern U., Ft. Lauderdale, Fla., 1993. Cert. profl. tchg. Fla., 1986. Tchr. Mononghalia County Sch., Morgantown, W.Va., 1985—86, Sch. Dist. Lee County, Ft. Myers, Fla., 1986—. Mem. Matlacha (Fla.) Hookers, 1998—2006. Named Math Tchr. of Yr., Lee County Sch., 2004—05. Mem.: Lee County Math Coun. (pres. 1996—97), Floridia Coun. Tchrs. Math. (regional dir. 1998—99), Nat. Coun. Tchrs. Math. Methodist. Office: Ft Myers High Sch 2635 Cortez Blvd Fort Myers FL 33901 Office Fax: 239-334-3095. E-mail: maryar@leeschools.net.

ROBERTSON, MELANIE ANNE, oil industry executive; b. Lubbock, Tex., Mar. 5, 1982; d. Jonathan Stuart Robertson and Anne Louise McNaughton. BS in Cellular & Molecular Biology, Biochemistry magna cum laude, Tex. Tech. U., Lubbock, 2005. Ind. landman, Midland, 2005—08; landman Bold Energy II LLC, Midland, 2008—. Treas. Fellow Svc. Orgn. Tex. Tech U. Med. Vol., Lubbock, 2002—04. Rsch. fellowship, Howard Hughes Med. Inst., 2003—05. Mem.: Permian Basin Landman Assn. Office: Bold Energy II LLC 600 N Marienfeld Ste 1000 Midland TX 79701 Office Fax: 432-686-1104. Personal E-mail: melanie.robertson@boldenergy.com.

ROBERTSON, MERLE GREENE, art historian, academic administrator; b. Miles City, Mont., Aug. 30, 1913; d. Darrel Irving and Ada Emma (Foote) McCann; m. Wallace McNeill Greene, Dec. 2, 1936 (div. Sept. 1950); children: Barbara Merle Greene Metzler, David Wallace Greene; m. Lawrence William Robertson, Dec. 19, 1966 (dec. May 1981). Student, U. Washington, 1933-35; BA, U. San Francisco, 1952; MFA, U. Guana Guato, Mex., 1963; LHD, Tulane U., 1987. Cert. tchr., Calif. Camp dir. Camp Tapawingo, Sequim, Wash., 1951-53; tchr. San Rafael Mil. Acad., 1952-64; camp dir. Marin County Camp Fire Girls, San Rafael, Calif., 1954-56; expedition dir. Tulane U., New Orleans, 1962—; tchr. Monterey (Calif.) Penninsula Coll., 1974-76, Robert Louis Stevenson Sch., Pebble Beach, Calif., 1967-76; exec. dir. Pre-Columbian Art Rsch. Inst., San Francisco, 1971—. Adj. curator H.M. de Young Meml. Art Mus., San Francisco, 1991—, com. mem. pre-Columbian art, 1990—; rsch. assoc. Middle Am. Rsch. Inst./Tulane U., New Orleans, 1976—, U. Calif. Archaeol. Rsch. Facility, Berkeley, 1982—, Calif. Acad. Scis., San Francisco, 1985—; dir. Archaeol. Recording Maya Art in Mex., Gualemala, Belize, Honduras, 1962—. Author: Sculpture of Palenque, 4 vols., 1983-91, Ancient Maya Relief Sculpture, 1967 (Best Design 1967), (CD-ROMS) Merle Greene Robertson's Rubbings of Maya Sculpture; editor: Palenque Round Table, 10 vols., 1973-95; prin. works include over 4500 rubbings of Maya Sculpture, Merle Greene Robertson Rare Manuscript Archives, Tulane U.; exhbns. including rubbings in most major mus. in US and Europe. Merle Greene Robertson Sch. named in her honor, Chiapas, Mex., 1981; recipient Order of the Aztec Eagle award Mexican Govt., 1994, Orden del Pop award, Guatemala, 2004, Reconocimento Especial "TOH", Merida, Yue, 2004. Fellow AAAS, The Explorers Club, Soc. for Am. Archaeology; mem. 47th Internat. Cong. Americanists (hon. v.p. 1992), Am. Anthropol. Assn., Assn. de Artistes Mougins. Avocations: travel to exotic countries, painting, hiking. Home and Office: 1100 Sacramento St Apt 1004 San Francisco CA 94108-1918 Personal E-mail: parimerle@mindspring.com.

ROBERTSON, MICHAEL, Internet company executive; B in Cognitive Sci., U. Calif. San Diego. Founder MR Mac Software, 1994—95, Media Minds, Inc., 1995—96; founder, pres. The Z Co., 1996; founder, CEO, chmn. MP3.com, San Diego, 1998—2001; founder, CEO Linspire, Inc., San Diego, 2001—; CEO SIPphone, 2003—. Cons. San Diego Super Computer Ctr.; cons. in field. Founder Robertson Educational Empowerment Found. (REEF), San Diego, 2002—. Named one of 100 most influential individuals in the music industry BAM Mag. Achievements include established Filez and Websitez.

ROBERTSON, MICHAEL JOHN, internist, research scientist, educator; b. Morrison, Ill., Sept. 13, 1958; s. Donald L. and Doris M. (Burch) R. AB in English summa cum laude, U. Ill., 1980; MD with honors, U. Chgo., 1984. Diplomate Am. Bd. Internal Medicine, Am. Bd. Med. Oncology. Intrn in internal medicine U. Chgo. Med. Ctr., 1984-85, resident, 1985-87; fellow in med. oncology Dana-Farber Cancer Inst., Boston, 1987-90, fellow in tumor immunology, 1990-94, attending physician, 1991—; instr. medicine Harvard U. Med. Sch., Boston, 1991-93, asst. prof., 1994-96; asst. prof. medicine Ind. U. Sch. Medicine, Indpls., 1996—2002, assoc. prof., 2002—08, prof., 2008—. Contbr. articles to med. jours. Mem. ACP, Soc. for Natural Immunity, Am. Soc. for Blood and Marrow Transplantation, Internat. Soc. for Hemototherapy and Graft Engring., Am. Soc. Clin. Oncology, Am. Soc. Hematology, Am. Assn. Immunologists, Phi Beta Kappa, Alpha Omega Alpha. Office: Ind Univ Med Ctr Hematology Oncology Sect 535 Barnhill Ave Indianapolis IN 46202

ROBERTSON, MICHAEL SWING, minister; b. Boston, July 20, 1935; s. Charles Stuart and Elizabeth (Swing) R.; m. Margaret Filoon, Sept. 17, 1960 (dec. Oct. 1996); children: Michael Swing, Ashlee Whipple, Christopher Filoon, Andrew Stuart; m. Emily Erickson, Feb. 22, 1998. AB, Harvard U., 1957, grad. Advanced Mgmt. Program, 1979. With Robertson Factories, Inc., 1957-80, exec. v.p., 1968-73, pres., 1973-79, chmn. bd., 1979-80; dir. Robertson-Swing Co., 1980—; pres. The Berkley Co. Inc., 1981-90, Reactions Inc., 1985-90; treas. Falmouth Marine Inc., 1981-88; pres., treas. Orchard Computer Inc., 1984-91, chmn., treas., 1991-93; exec. sec. Nat. Assn. Congl. Christian Chs., Oak Creek, Wis., 1991-97; minister Pilgrim Congl. Ch., Taunton, Mass., 2000—02; ch. coord. Cmty. Faith Alliance, Milw., 1997-2000; exec. dir. Cmty. Village, Ltd., 1998-2000, 2003—; pastor Pilgrim Congrl. Ch., Taunton, 2001—02, Urban Ministry Cmty. Bapt. Ch., Milw., 2003, Union Congl. Ch., Braintree, Mass., 2004—06, First Ch. of Squantum, Quincy, Mass., 2006—. V.p. adv. coun. Coll. of Bus. and Industry, Southeastern Mass. U., North Dartmouth, Mass., 1979-91; selectman, Town of Berkley, Mass., 1974-80, chmn. 1979-80; mem. Pres.'s Adv. Com. for Trade Negotiations, 1983-86; bd. dirs. Mass. Easter Seal Soc., 1977-91, pres. 1982-83; bd. dirs. Nat. Easter Seal Soc., 1985-91, Wis. Easter Seal Soc., 1994-95; bd. dirs. Trips for Kids, New Bedford, 2005-, treas., 2007, chmn., pres., 2008; chmn. Berkley Rep. Town com., 1977-91; Rep. nominee U.S. Senate from Mass., 1976, nominee for Mass. state auditor, 1982; co-chmn. Mass Reagan for Pres. Com., 1980; Bristol County coord. Reagan/Bush campaign; co-chmn. Mass. Dole for Pres. Commn., 1987; chmn. Southeastern Mass. campaign Harvard Coll., 1981; chmn. Friends of Harvard Track, 1986-91; trustee Barnstable County Hosp., 1985-90, chmn., 1988. Mem. Harvard Varsity Club, Harvard Club of Boston, Harvard Bus. Sch. Assn. Boston, Squantum Yacht Club. Congregationalist. Office: 164 Bellevue Rd Squantum MA 02171 Home: 7 Camden Pl Cambridge MA 02138 Office Phone: 617-328-6649. Office Fax: 617-328-3391. Personal E-mail: emmyandmike@verizon.net. *Accept responsibility with enthusiasm and gratitude. Our individual freedom is unmatched in history, compelling us to remain true to our heritage and our God.*

ROBERTSON, NED, dentist; b. Rumford, Maine, Mar. 3, 1950; s. Edward Norris and Edith Louise (Kirk) Robertson; m. Susan Elizabeth Valentine, July 24, 2004; 1 child, Olivia; children: Christie Portia, Juliet Melissa(dec.), Jenni Celia, Edward Noah, Jessica Edith. BS in Biology,

Antioch Coll., Yellow Springs, Ohio, 1973; MS in Epidemiology, Ohio State U., 1977; DDS, Case Western Res. U., 1983, DMD, 2004. Faculty adv. to med. students Ohio State U., Columbus, 1975-77; rsch. cons. Ohio Dept. Health, Columbus, 1976-77; rsch. assoc. UCLA, 1977; epidemiologic/statis. cons. LA, 1977; medic J & L Steel Corp., Cleve., 1979-84; pvt. practice Cleveland Heights, Ohio, 1983-94, Lyndhurst, Ohio, 1995-2000. Mem. adj. faculty Cuyahoga C.C., Cleve., 1986-88; assoc. prof. Sch. Dentistry Case Western Res. U., 1991-96; asst. prof. Case Western Res. U. Sch. Dentistry, Cleve., 1997-2003; pvt. contractor Indian Health Svc. Dental Clinic, Pine Ridge, S.D., 1999-2000; clin. instr. U. Md. Dental Sch., 1999-00. Pres. Robertson Family Assn. of N.Am., 1986-88. Recipient numerous rsch. grants; named one of Best Dentists in Am., No. Ohio Live mag., 2007. Mem.: ADA, Internat. Congress Oral Implantologists, Am. Acad. Craniofacial Pain, Internat. Assn. for Study of Pain, Greater Cleve. Dental Soc., Ohio Dental Assn., Acad. Gen. Dentistry, Midwest Pain Soc., Acad. Laser Surgery, U.S. Dental Inst., Am. Chronic Pain Assn., Ohio Acad. Gen. Dentistry, Am. Pain Soc., Am. Acad. Pain Mgmt. Avocations: scuba diving, cross country skiing, camping, canoeing, bicycling. Office: 24755 Chagrin Blvd Ste 145 Beachwood OH 44122-5692 Office Phone: 216-468-0041. Business E-Mail: dentalned@aol.com.

ROBERTSON, PAT (MARION GORDON ROBERTSON), religious broadcasting executive, university president and chancellor; b. Lexington, Va., Mar. 22, 1930; s. A. Willis and Gladys (Churchill) R.; m. Adelia Elmer; children: Timothy, Elizabeth, Gordon, Ann. BA, Washington and Lee U., 1950; JD, Yale U., New Haven, 1955; MDiv, NY Theol. Sem., 1959; ThD (hon.), Oral Roberts U., Tulsa, Okla., 1983. Ordained minister So. Bapt. Conv., 1961-87. Founder, CEO, chmn. Christian Broadcasting Network, Virginia Beach, Va., 1960—; host 700 Club, 1968—; founder, chancellor, pres. Regent U. (formerly CBN U.), 1977—; founder, chmn. Operation Blessing Internat. Relief and Devel. Inc., 1978—; founder, pres. The Christian Coalition, 1989—; founder, pres., chmn. The Am. Ctr. for Law and Justice, 1990—; founder, chmn. Internat. Family Entertainment, Inc., 1990-97, Asia Pacific Media Corp., 1993—; chmn. Starguide Digital Networks, Inc., 1995—, Porchlight Entertainment, Inc., 1995—. Bd. dirs. United Va. Bank, Norfolk; mem. Pres. Task Force on Victims of Crime, Washington, 1982. Author: (with Jamie Buckingham) Shout It From the Housetops: The Story of the Founder of the Christian Broadcasting Network, 1972, My Prayer for You, 1977, The Secret Kingdom, 1982, Answers to 200 of Life's Most Probing Questions, 1984, (with William Proctor) Beyond Reason: How Miracles Can Change Your Life, 1984, America's Dates with Destiny, 1986, The Plan, 1989, The New Millennium: 10 Trends that Will Impact Your Family by the Year 2000, 1990, The New World Order, 1991, The Turning Tide: The Fall of Liberalism and the Rise of Common Sense, 1993, The End of the Age, 1995, Six Steps to Spiritual Revival: God's Awesome Power in Your Life, 2002, Bring It On: Tough Questions. Candid Answers, 2002, The Ten Offenses: Reclaim the Blessings of God's Eternal Truth, 2003, Courting Disaster: How the Supreme Court Is Usurping the Power of Congress and the People, 2004, Miracles Can Be Yours Today, 2005 Candidate for Rep. nomination for Pres. U.S., 1988. Served in USMC, 1950—52. Recipient Disting. Merit citation NCCJ, Knesset medallion Israel Pilgrimage Com., Faith and Freedom award Religious Heritage Am., Bronze Halo award So. Calif. Motion Picture Council, Humanitarian award Food for the Hungry, 1982, George Washington Honor medal Freedoms Found. at Valley Forge, 1983, Defender of Israel award Christians Israel Pub. Action Campaign, 1994, John Connor Humanitarian Svc. award Operation Smile Internat., 1994, Cross of Nails award, 2000, The State of Israel Friendship award, Zionist Org. of Am., 2002; named Internat. Clergyman of Yr. Religion in Media, 1981, Man of Yr. Internat. Com. for Goodwill, 1981. Mem. Nat. Religous Broadcasters (bd. dirs. 1973—2006), Kentucky Colonels. Office: The Christian Broadcasting Network 977 Centerville Tpke Virginia Beach VA 23463-7701 also: Regent U 1000 Regent U Dr Virginia Beach VA 23464

ROBERTSON, PAUL FRANCIS, mathematician, educator, technologist, entrepreneur; b. Galveston, Tex., Aug. 23, 1953; s. Gilfred and Wilda Robertson; m. Ana Cecilia Moreno, May 17, 1988 (div. Nov. 1993); m. Cynthia Arnet Gilford, June 3, 1978 (div. Dec. 1980); children: Chiquita Monique, Paul Alexander, Andrea Celeste. BA in Math., Tex. So. U., Houston, 1975. Cert. tchr. Tex., 1997. Instr. data processing Houston C.C. Sys., 1981; tchr. math., computer literacy Galveston Ind. Sch. Dist., Tex., 1997—99; adj. prof. math. Galveston Coll., Tex., 1999, 2004; tchr. math., tech. applications Galveston Cath. Sch., Tex., 1999—2004; sub. tchr. Tex. City Ind. Sch. Dist., 2004—05. Recipient Unsung Hero award, Galveston County - The Daily News, 2002, Cert. of Appreciation, Communities in Schs. Galveston, Inc., 2002, Cert. for Outstanding Support, Big Bros. Big Sisters of Gulf Coast, 2002; Four Yr. Acad. Scholarship award, The Moody Found., 1971. Mem.: Nat. Sheriffs Assn., Golden Key Internat. Honour Soc., Nat. Crime Prevention Coalition, Assn. Pub. Safety Comm. Ofcls. Internat., Nat. Assn. Indsl. Tech., Sheriffs Assn. of Tex., Phi Delta Kappa. Democrat. Roman Catholic. Avocations: reading, tutoring, poetry. Office: 8801 Palmer Hwy 2205 Texas City TX 77591 Home Phone: 409-908-0649. E-mail: education_8875@earthlink.net.

ROBERTSON, PAUL JOHN, music educator; MusB in Applied Percussion, U. Del., Newark, 2005; MusM in Classical Percussion, NJ City U., Jersey City, 2007. Adj. prof. music NJ City U., 2007—, Essex County Coll., Newark, 2007—. Prin. percussion Pk. Ave. Chamber Symphony, NYC, 2008—. Recipient award, Concerto Competition, U. Del., 2002, 2005; finalist, Young Artist Competition, Cynthia Woods Found., 2004. Business E-Mail: probertson@njcu.edu.

ROBERTSON, PAULINE DURRETT, publishing executive; b. Amarillo, Tex., Apr. 17, 1922; d. Walter Lucius and Mary Eddie (Jones) Durrett; m. Roy Lewis Robertson, Dec. 18, 1940; children: Kay Linda Robertson Savage, Kent Lewis, Robyn M. Robertson Turner, Paula Jo Robertson Pierce, Roy Durrett, Laurel Annette Robertson Gibson, Virginia Lee Robertson-Baker, Ellen Robertson Green, Neil Thomas, Carrie Beth Robertson Meyer. AA, Amarillo Coll., 1969; BA in English Writing, St. Edward's U., Austin, Tex., 1992. Editor project history U.S. Reclamation Bur., Amarillo, 1942-43; editor post newspaper U.S. Army Air Force, Amarillo, 1943-44; freelance writer, 1944-73; writer books of history Staked Plains Press, Canyon, Tex., 1973-77; writer books of history and poetry Paramount Pub. Co., Amarillo, 1977—, pub. house pres., editor, 1977—; tchr. poetry writing and history Amarillo Coll., 1971—2002. Tchr. poetry writing Elderhostel, U. Tex., Austin, 1988-89; writer book revs. Amarillo Globe News, 1968-2005; editor books, articles, newspapers, 1985-; spkr. in field. Author: (with R.L. Robertson) Panhandle Pilgrimage: Illustrated Tales Tracing History in the Texas Panhandle, 1976, 77, 81, 85, 90, Tascosa: Historic Site in the Texas Panhandle, 1978, 2d edit., 1995, Mystery Woman of Old Tascosa: The Legend of Frenchy McCormick, 1979, 2d edit., 1995, Cowman's Country: Fifty Frontier Ranches in the Texas Panhandle 1876-1887, 1981, 2d edit., 1995, (poetry) Fringe Benefits: Light Verse From Living, 1985, Borrowed Moccasins: Poems From Other Viewpoints, 1986, Field Notes: Poems on Late Light, 1987; editor and designer: Austin Originals: Chats With Colorful Characters by Robyn Turner, 1982, Long Shadows: Indian Leaders Standing in the Path of Manifest Destiny 1600-1900 (by Jack Jackson), 1985; designer, editor: (poetry) Bootsteps: Poems of the West-Then and Now (by Mildred C. Speer), 1978, 83, coauthor, editor: Eve's Version: 150 Women of the Bible, 1983; featured in documentary Story Of A Family on NBC-TV, 1960; mem. writing team Ch. Women United U.S.A., 2001—. Co-founder, sec. Cerebral Palsy Treatment Ctr., Amarillo, 1948-60, Opportunity House, Amarillo, 1970-87; founder, pres. Children's Cottage, Amarillo, 1964-84, Women's Coalition for Change: Focus on Poverty, Amarillo, 1989-95; founder, dir. for underprivileged children Camp Friendship, Ceta Glen, Tex., 1971-74; vol. tutor neighborhood pub. schs., 1992-; chair of elders First Christian Ch., 1979-81; host family Internat. Christian Youth Exch., 1963-64, sending family, 1968, 78; active Potter County Hist. Commn., Tex., 1988-96; pres.-elect Ch. Women United of Tex., 1996-98, pres., 1998-2000; chair Amarillo Mayor's Commn. on Early Childhood Nurture/Neglect, 1997—; nat. del. Christian Ch. Named Amarillo's Family of the Yr., Amarillo Globe-News, 1957, Tex. Merit Mother, Am. Mothers Assn., Boston, 1991, 1995 Woman of the Yr. in Amarillo, Beta Sigma Phi, Amarillo, 1995, Yellow Rose Tex., Gov. Anne Richards, 1991, Mayor's Friend of Young Children, 1999, Tex. Mother of Yr., Am. Mothers Assn., Boston, 2003; named to Amarillo HS Hall Fame, 1998; recipient Tex. Panhandle Disting. Svc. award West Tex. A&M U., Canyon, 1977, Lifetime Career Achievement award Amarillo Women's Network, 1996, Woman of Distinction award Girl Scouts Tex. Plains Coun., 2002. Mem. AAUW, LWV (v.p., Amarillo program chair), Western Writers Am., Acad. Am. Poets, Amarillo Photog. Soc. (Salon awards 1961-), Panhandle Profl. Writers (pres. 1978-80, bd. mem.), Poetry Soc. Tex. (founder. area chpt. 1972, pres. area chpt. 1979-81, Tex. state councilor 1973—), Tex. Tchrs. of Creative Writing, Common Cause (area rep. 1971—). Democrat. Avocations: photography, travel, reading, walking. Home: 124 Wayside Dr Amarillo TX 79106-6425 Office: Paramount Pub Co Amarillo TX Home Phone: 806-355-1040. E-mail: pdr-rlr@suddenlink.net.

ROBERTSON, ROBERT GRAHAM HAMISH, physicist; b. Ottawa, Ont., Can., Oct. 3, 1943; arrived in US, 1971, naturalized, 1993; s. Hugh Douglas and Alice Madeleine (Bell) R.; m. Peggy Lynn Dyer, July 4, 1980; 1 child, Ian. BA, Oxford U., Eng., 1965, MA, 1969; PhD, McMaster U., Can., 1971. Rsch. assoc. Mich. State U., East Lansing, 1971-72, asst. rsch. prof., 1972-73, asst. prof., 1973-78, assoc. prof., 1978-81, prof., 1981-82; mem. staff Los Alamos (N.Mex.) Nat. Lab., 1981—, fellow, 1988—; prof. U. Washington, Seattle, 1994—; sci. dir. Ctr. for Exptl. Nuc. Physics and Astrophysics, 2000—, Boeing disting. prof., 2008—. Rsch. assoc. Princeton U., NJ, 1975—76; vis. scientist Argonne Nat. Lab, Ill., 1979, Chalk River Nuc. Labs., Ont., Canada, 1980; dir. Sudbur Neutrino Obs., 2003. Contbr. over 80 articles to profl. jours. Alfred P. Sloan Found. fellow Mich. State U., 1976; Trevelyan scholar Eng., 1962-65, NRC scholar McMaster U., 1965-69, Oriel Coll. scholar, 1962-65. Fellow Am. Phys. Soc. (chair divsn. nuclear physics 2000, Tom W. Bonner prize 1997), Inst. Physics of Eng., Am. Acad. Arts and Scis.; mem. NAS, Can. Assn. Physicists. Achievements include first observation of nuclear isobaric quintet; development of technique for precise measurement of neutrino mass; determination of Lithium-6 synthesis in early universe; demonstration of neutrino mass, oscillations with Sudbury Neutrino Obs. Home Phone: 425-743-7468. E-mail: rghr@u.washington.eu.

ROBERTSON, SAMUEL HARRY, III, transportation safety research engineer, educator; b. Phoenix, Oct. 2, 1934; s. Samuel Harry and Doris Bryl (Duffield) R.; m. Nancy Jean Bradford, 1954 (div. 1989); children: David Lyle, Pamela Louise; m. Linda Faye O'Neill, 1999. BS, Ariz. State U., 1956; D in Aviation Tech. (hon.), Embry-Riddle Aero. U., 1972. Registered profl. engr.; cert. comml. pilot--fixed wing, rotary wing, glider and balloon. Chief hazards divsn. Aviation Safety Engring. and Rsch., Phoenix, 1960-70; pres. Robertson Rsch. Engrs., 1960-70; rsch. prof., dir. Safety Ctr. Coll. Engring. and Applied Scis., Ariz State U., Tempe, 1970-79; pres. Robertson Rsch. Inc., 1970-86, Robertson Aviation Inc., 1977—86, Internat. Ctr. for Safety Edn., 1982-96; pres., CEO Robertson Rsch. Group, Inc., Tempe, 1986—, Robertson Aviation, LLC, Tempe, 1995—2006. Airplane design and accident investigator, 1961—; instr. aircrash investigation Internat. Ctr. Safety Edn., 1960-2003, inst. aerospace safety U. So. Calif., 1962-70, Armed Forces Inst. Pathology, 1970-90, Dept. Transp. Safety Inst., 1970-89; pres. Pine Springs Ranch, Inc, 1976—; adv. bd. Rio Salado Bank, Tempe, 1985-94; mem. adv. coun. Ctr. Aerospace Safety Edn., Embry-Riddle Aero. U., Daytona Beach, Fla., 1986—, trustee, 1992—; pres. Devil Dog Rsch., Inc., 1990—, Robertson Land & Cattle Inc., 1990—; comml. pilot, 1957—. Contbr. over 85 articles to profl. jours.; patentee applying plastic to paper, fuel system safety check valves, crash resitant fuel system, safety aircraft seats; holder FAA STC's various fuel systems, fuel system components; designer, developer, mfr. crash resistant fuel systems for airplanes, helicopters, championship racing cars. Pilot USAF, 1956-60, Ariz. Army NG 1960-61, 70-74, Ariz. Air NG, 1961-69. Recipient Contbns. Automotive Racing Safety award CNA, 1976, Adm. Luis De Florez Internat. Flying Safety award, 1969, Cert. Commendation Nat. Safety Coun., 1969, Gen. W. Spruance award, SAFE Soc., 1982; holder Nat. Speed Record for one class of drag racing car, 1955-62, 5 nat. records for flying model aircraft, 1950-56; named to Ariz. Aviation Hall of Fame, 1996, OX5 Aviation Pioneers Hall of Fame, 1996, U.S. Army Aviation Hall of Fame, 2001; candidate Nat. Aviation Hall of Fame. Mem. AIAA, Internat. Soc. Air Safety Investigators (Jerome Lederer Aircraft Accident Investigation award, 1981), Aerospace Med. Assn., Soc. Automotive Engrs., Soc. Exptl. Test Pilots, Am. Helicopter Soc., Nat. Fire Protection Assn., Aircraft Owners and Pilots Assn., Exptl. Aircraft Assn., Air Force Assn., Army Aviation Assn., U.S. Automobile Club. Home: 5994 E Orange Blossom Ln Phoenix AZ 85018 Home Phone: 480-946-0651.

ROBERTSON, SAMUEL LUTHER, JR., psychotherapist, educator; b. Houston, Apr. 28, 1940; s. Sam L. and Portia Louise (Burns) R.; children: Samuel Luther IV, Sean Lee (dec.), Ryan William, Susan Elizabeth (dec.), Henry Philmore. BS, McMurry U., 1969; MA, Hardin-Simmons U., 1973; PhD, U. Tex., 1993. Cert. tchr., adminstr., counselor, Tex.; lic. chem. dependency counselor, Tex., lic. clin. mental health counselor, N. Mex. Instr., coach, athletic dir. Tex. and La. schs., 1969-94; social worker, supr. Children's Protective Svcs., Abilene, Tex., 1978-79; instr., adminstr. Harlandale Sch. Dist., San Antonio, 1980-84, 87-90; adminstr. night sch. Harlandale Ind. Sch. Dist., San Antonio, 1988-89; instr. Edgewood Ind. Sch. Dist., San Antonio, 1985-87; developer, instr., integrated unit program San Antonio, 1990—; CEO The Educative Inst., San Antonio, 1992—. CEO Educative Therapeutic Processes, 1972—; co-founder, dir. Inst. Orgnl. Personal Devel.; mem. faculty writing program U. Tex., San Antonio, 2000—, founder, dir. Recovery Ctr., 2004-05. Author: (play) The Challenged, 1965, Dream Poems, 1998; (poem) Trains in the Night, 1969; (screenplay) Tom & Jane, 2000; dir. (film) Tom & Jane, 2003. State co-chmn. Youth for Kennedy-Johnson, Tex., 1960; mem. W. Tex. Dem. Steering Com., Abilene, 1962-63; founding dir. Way Off Broadway Cmty. Theater, Eagle Pass, Tex., 1971-72; founding bd. dirs. Battered Women's Shelter, Abilene, 1978-79; v.p. bd. dirs. Mental Health Assn., San Antonio, 1980-83, Palmer Drug Abuse Program, San Antonio, 1985-87; pres., bd. dirs. Alcoholic Rehab. Ctr., 1985-86, 1987-92; bd. mem., v.p. Woman at the Well, 2006—; vice-chmn. Civilian and Mil. Addictive Programs, San Antonio, 1991-92; author, implementer Cmty. Vitalization Program, 1994—; mem. vestry St. George Episc. Ch., mem. day sch. bd., 1999-02; stds. chair com. Tex. Certification Bd. Addiction Profls., chmn. 1999-01. Named Tchr. of Yr. Southside Ind. Sch. Dist., San Antonio, 1970-71, Harlandale Alternative Ctr., San Antonio, 1987-88; Vol. of Yr., Mental Health Assn., San Antonio, 1982, Alcoholic Rehab. Ctr., San Antonio, 1992-93; Businessman of Yr., 2003. Mem. ACA, NEA, Am. Mental Health Counseling Assn., Tex. State Tchrs. Assn., Am. Ednl. Rsch. Assn., Am. Assn. Sch. Adminstrs. (mem. exec. com.), Internat. Consortium Reciprocity Commn. Nat. Alcoholism and Drug Abuse Counselors, N.Mex. Mental Health Counselors Assn., N.Mex. Profl. Counselors Assn., Phi Kappa Phi, Kappa Delta Pi. Episcopalian. Avocations: reading, writing, travel, theater, sports. Office: Educative Therapeutic Processes 339 E Hildebrand Ave San Antonio TX 78212-2412 Office Phone: 210-828-9919. Personal E-mail: samdr9@yahoo.com. *I have participated in my life, my family's life, and my community's life in a responsible fashion through the Grace of God.*

ROBERTSON, SARA STEWART, investor, entrepreneur; b. NYC, Feb. 4, 1940; d. John Elliott and Mary Terry (Schlamp) Stewart; m. James Young Robertson, Nov. 29, 1975 (dec. Mar. 1988). BA, Conn. Coll., 1961; MBA, Am. U., 1969. From trainee to officer First Nat. Bank/First Chgo. Corp., 1969-75, v.p., 1975-92; prin. Royall Enterprises, Chgo., 1992—; prin., dir. Zeppelin Press, Inc., Miami, Fla., 1995—2002. Chair individuals fundraising, exec. com., dir. Youth Guidance, Chgo., 1982-85, 93-95. Bd. dirs. Harbor House Condominium Assn. Chgo., 1990-92; trustee Sherwood Conservatory Music, 1993-2005, chair bd. devel., 1993-95, 97-99; mem. allocations com. and family priority grants com. United Way-Chgo., 1992-95; co-founder, v.p., sec.-treas., dir. Animal Support Kindness and Kinship, Inc., 1999-2005, v.p., sec., 2001-05. Mem.: So. States Mastiff Fanciers (treas. 2007—), Club 13 Palm Beach (pres. 1996—98, v.p. 2003—05, pres. 2005—07). Home Phone: 904-845-7389. Personal E-mail: saisairob@aol.com.

ROBERTSON, STEVE, political organization administrator; Commr. Gov.'s Office for Local Devel., Ky., 2006. Former polit. dir., orgnl. dir. Rep. Party of Ky., chmn., 2007—. Republican. Office: Rep Party of Ky PO Box 1068 Frankfort KY 40602 Office Phone: 502-875-5130. Office Fax: 502-223-5625. E-mail: steve@rpk.org.*

ROBERTSON, THOMAS SINCLAIR, dean, marketing educator; b. Scotland, Nov. 16, 1942; s. Thomas C. and Ann Gorman (Mundie) R.; m. Diana S. Conway, June 18, 1966; children: Brian, Ashley, Alexandra BA, Wayne State U., Detroit, 1963; MA, PhD, Northwestern U., 1966. Asst. prof. mktg. UCLA, 1966-68, Harvard U., 1968-71; prof. mktg. Wharton Sch., U. Pa., 1971, Pomerantz prof. mktg., chmn. mktg. dept., 1978-84, assoc. dean, 1984—88, dean, 2007—; assoc. dean London Bus. Sch., 1994-98; dean Goizueta Bus. Sch., Emory U., Atlanta, 1998—2004, Asa Griggs Candler prof. mktg.; spl. asst. to pres. for internat. strategy Emory U., Atlanta, 2005, exec. dir. Inst. Devel. Nations. Author: Innovative Behavior and Communication, 1971, Televised Medicine Advertising and Children, 1979, Consumer Behavior, 1984, Handbook of Consumer Behavior, 1991. Grantee NSF NIH. Mem. Am. Mktg. Assn., Assn. Consumer Rsch., Cherokee Town Club. Republican. Office: Wharton Sch U Pa Office of Dean 3620 Locust Walk Philadelphia PA 19104-6306 Home: 2117 Delancey St Philadelphia PA 19103-6511 Office Phone: 215-898-4715. E-mail: robertson@wharton.upenn.edu.*

ROBERTSON, TIMOTHY JOEL, statistician, educator; b. Denver, Oct. 4, 1937; s. Flavel P. and Helen C. (Oliver) Girdner; m. Joan K. Slater, Aug. 18, 1959; children— Kelly, Jana, Doug, Mike BA in Math., U. Mo., 1959, MS in Math., 1961, PhD in Stats., 1966. Asst. prof. Cornell Coll., Mt. Vernon, Iowa, 1961-63; prof. stats. U. Iowa, Iowa City, 1965—2004, prof. emeritus, 2004—. Vis. prof. U. N.C., Chapel Hill, 1974-75, U. Calif.-Davis, 1983-84; Eugene Lukacs Disting. vis. prof. Bowling Green State U., 1991-92; vis. lectr. Com. Pres. Statis. Soc., 1971-74. Author: (with F.T. Wright and R.L. Dykstra) Order Restricted Statistical Inference; assoc. editor Am. Math. Monthly, 1977-81; mem. editl. bd. Comms. in Stats., 1981-92; assoc. editor Jour. Am. Statis. Assn., 1990-96; contbr. numerous articles to profl. jours. Recipient Collegiate Teaching award U. Iowa, 1990. Fellow Am. Statis. Assn. (council 1974-75), Inst. Math. Stats., Internat. Statis. Inst.; mem. Math. Assn. Am., Sigma Xi, Sierra Club Democrat. Avocations: canoeing, camping, bicycling, walking. Home: 673 Garfield Rd West Branch IA 52358-8574 Office: Univ Iowa Dept Stats/Actuarial Sci Iowa City IA 52242 Home Phone: 319-643-3118; Office Phone: 319-335-2019. Personal E-mail: tincity@lcom.net.

ROBERTSON, WILLIAM WRIGHT, JR., orthopedist, educator; b. Mayfield, Ky., Dec. 26, 1946; m. Karel Virginia Dierks, Jan. 26, 1974. BA, Rhodes Coll., 1968; MD, Vanderbilt U., 1972; MBA, Geo Washington U., 2000. Intern U. Calif., San Diego, 1972-73, resident in orthop. surgery, 1975-76, Vanderbilt U., Nashville, 1976-79; asst. prof. orthop. Tex. Tech U., Lubbock, 1979-86; assoc. prof. U. Pa., Phila., 1986-90; prof. orthop. surgery George Washington U., Washington, 1990-2000; chmn. pediat. orthop. Children's Nat. Med. Ctr., Washington, 1990-99. Field rep. accreditation coun. grad. med. edn. Fellow Am. Acad. Orthop. Surgeons, Am. Orthop. Assn., Pediat. Orthop. Soc. (bd. dirs. 1993-96—). Avocations: gardening, music. Office: Accreditation Coun Grad Med Edn 515 N State St Chicago IL 60610 Home Phone: 301-718-7867. Business E-Mail: wrobertson@acgme.org.

ROBESON, TERRY LAZUK, elementary school educator, priest; b. Denver, Sept. 29, 1953; d. Alex and Florence Gertrude Lazuk; m. Thomas A. Robeson, July 5, 1980; children: Mary Heather Babb, Sasha Lena. BA, U. No. Colo., Greeley, 1975. Tchr. Colo. BOCES, 1975—76, Sedgewick Elem., Colo., 1976—78; spl. edn. tchr., elem. tchr. Fremont County Sch. Dist. # 1, Lander, Wyo., 1978—. Critical friends coach West Elem., Lander, 2004—. Mem.: Nat. Reading Assn. Episcopalian. Avocations: travel, gardening, cooking. Office: Fremont County Sch Dist # 1 350 Smith Ct Lander WY 82520 Office Phone: 307-332-6967.

ROBICHAUD, CAROLYN WOMMACK, retired secondary school educator; b. Gilbertsville, Ky., Feb. 24, 1941; d. Joel Benjamin and Amy Vergie (Stockton) Wommack; m. John Cedric Robichaud, Apr. 1, 1943; children: Nicole Robichaud Fann, Shawn Chadwick. BA, David Lipscomb U., Nashville, 1963; MA, Murray State U., Ky., 1983. Sec. Vanderbilt U., Nashville, 1963-64; tchr. English Sharpe (Ky.) Elem. Sch., 1964-74, North Marshall Jr. H.S., Calvert City, Ky., 1974-88, Marshall County H.S., Benton, Ky., 1988—2003, ret., 2003. Copresenter writing workshops; mem. dean coll. edn. search com. Murray State U., 1984; selected participant Purchase Area Writing Project, Murray State U., 1988; mem. State Mid. Sch./Jr. High Indicators Com., State Sec. Sch. Recognition Com. Sec., mem. Assoc. Ladies of Lipscomb, Benton, 1994—. Recipient Outstanding Ky. Tchr. award Murray State U., 1996. Mem. NEA, Ky. Edn. Assn. (sch. based decision making coun. 1996-98), Marshall County Ednl. Assn. (tchr. rep. negotiating team 1967, 76-84), Nat. Coun. Tchrs. English (chair showing and telling stories 1993), Ky. Coun. Tchrs. English (participant panel 1989), Alpha Delta Kappa. Ch. of christ. Avocations: gardening, reading, flowers, yard work, lake activities. Home: 343 Tatumsville Hwy Benton KY 42025-7195

ROBIDAS, STEPHANE, professional hockey player; b. Sherbrooke, Que., Can., Mar. 3, 1977; m. Marie-Eve Robidas; children: Justin, Lexie. Defenseman Montreal Canadiens, 2000—02, Dallas Stars, 2002—03, 2005—, Chgo. Blackhawks, 2003—04. Named to NHL All-Star Game, 2009. Office: Dallas Stars 2601 Avenue of the Stars Frisco TX 75034 also: Am Airlines Ctr 2500 Victory Ave Dallas TX 75201*

ROBIE, DANIEL CARDIGAN, chemist; b. Bethesda, Md., Jan. 26, 1954; BA, Reed Coll., Portland, Oreg., 1975; PhD, U. Ill., Chgo., 1987. Postdoctoral rsch. assoc. SRI Internat., Menlo Park, Calif., 1987-89, U. So. Calif., LA, 1989-92; asst. prof. Barnard Coll., NYC, 1992—. Mem. Am. Chem. Soc., Am. Phys. Soc. Office: Barnard Coll Dept Chemistry New York NY 10027

ROBILLARD, JEAN EUGENE, academic administrator; b. Montreal, 1943; m. Renee Robillard. BA, U. Montreal, 1964, MD, 1968. Pediat. residency Saint Justine Hosp., Montreal, 1969—72; pediat. nephrology fellowship UCLA Med. Ctr., Los Angeles, 1972—73, U. Iowa Med. Ctr., Iowa City, 1973—74; asst. prof., dept. pediat. U. Montreal Coll. Med., 1975—76; asst. prof. Dept. Pediat., Coll. Med., U. Iowa, 1974—75, 1976—78, assoc. prof., 1978—82, dir. nephrology div., 1976—96, prof., 1982—96, vice chmn.; chief pediat. U. Mich., Ann Arbor, 1996—2003; physician-in-chief C.S. Mott Children's Hosp., 1996—2003; dean Roy J. and Lucille A. Carver Coll Medicine, U. Iowa, 2003—08; v.p. med. affairs U. Iowa, 2007—. Editl. bd. Jour. Pediat., 2001—; bd. dirs. Am. Bd. Pediat., 2001—, chmn. bd. dirs., 2006—07. Author of over 220 sci. papers. Recipient Disting. Alumni Award for Achievement, U. Iowa, 2002. Fellow: Coun. for High Blood Pressure Rsch., Am. Heart Assn., Royal Coll. Physicians & Surgeons; mem.: Iowa Bus. Coun., Climatologically Assoc., Am. Clin., Nat. Med. Assoc., Am. Soc. Transplant Physicians, The Perinatal Rsch. Soc, Soc. for Gynecologic Investigation, Am. Physiol. Soc., Am. Assn. for Advancement Sci. (fellow 1999), Am. Soc. Pediat. Nephrology (pres. 1994—95), Soc. Pediat. Rsch., Am. Heart Assn., Am. Soc. Nephrology, Internat. Soc. Nephrology, Internat. Pediat. Nephrology Assn., Midwest Soc. Pediat. Rsch. (Founder's Award 2002), Am. Acad. Pediat., Am Pediat. Soc. Office: Roy J & Lucille A Carver Coll Med 312 CMAB Iowa City IA 52242

ROBIN, CLARA NELL (CLAIRE ROBIN), English language educator; b. Harrisonburg, Va., Feb. 19, 1945; d. Robert Franklin and Marguerite Ausherman (Long) Wampler; m. Phillip Camden Branner, June 10, 1967 (div. May 1984); m. John Charles Robin, Nov. 22, 1984 (div. Dec. 1990) BA English, Mary Washington Coll., 1967; MA English, James Madison U., 1974; postgrad., Jesus Coll., Cambridge, Eng., 1982, Princeton U., 1985—86, Auburn U., 1988, U. No. Tex., 1990—91. Cert. tchr. English, French, master cert., Tex. Tchr. 7th grade John C. Myers Intermediate Sch., Broadway, Va., 1967—68; tchr. 10th grade Waynesville H.S., Mo., 1968—70; tchr. 6th, 7th, 8th grades Mary Mount Jr. H.S., Santa Barbara, Calif., 1970—72; tchr. 9th grade Forest Meadow Jr. H.S. Richardson Ind. Sch. Dist., Tex., 1972—78, tchr. 10th grade Lake Highlands H.S., 1972—84; tchr. 11th, 12th grades Burleson H.S. Burleson Ind. Sch. Dist., Tex., 1986—2003; tchr. 9th and 10th grade English Ft. Worth Country Day Sch., 2003—, tchr. 9th and 12th grade English, 2007—09, tchr. 9th and 11th grade English, 2009—. Instr. composition Hill Coll., 1989-90 Contbg. author: (book revs.) English Jour., 1989-94, (lit. criticism) Eric, 1993 Vol. Dallas Theater Cir., 1990—96; active Kimbell Art Mus., Ft. Worth, 1990—, Modern Art Mus., Ft. Worth, 1992—, KERA Pub. TV, Dallas, 1990—, Amon Carter Mus., Ft. Worth, 2001—. Fellow NEH, 1988, 89, 92, 95, Fulbright-Hays Summer Seminar Abroad, 1991; ind. study grantee Coun. Basic Edn., 1990; recipient Chpt. Achievement award Epsilon Nu Delta Kappa Gamma, 1993, Hon. Mention Tex. Outstanding Tchg. of Humanities award, 1995, Burleson Ind. Sch. Dist., Campus Ednl. Improvement Com., 1997-2000, Dist. Ednl. Improvement Com., 1998-2001 Mem.: Tex. State Reading Assn., Nat. Coun. Tchrs. English (spring conf. presenter 2000, 2002), Epsilon Nu of Delta Kappa Gamma (1st v.p. 1988—94, v.p. 1992—94, profl. affairs com. 1996—98, comms. chair 1998—). Avocations: bicycling, travel, reading, writing, landscaping. Home: 4009 W 6th St Fort Worth TX 76107-1619 Office: Ft Worth County Day Sch 4200 Country Day Ln Fort Worth TX 76109-4299 Office Phone: 817-302-3203 ext. 102. Personal E-mail: crbkrd@aol.com. Business E-Mail: crobin@fwcds.org.

ROBINETTE, GARY OMER, landscape architect, educator; b. Mankato, Kans., Feb. 11, 1932; s. Harry Clinton and Ruby Permelia Robinette; m. Margaret Ann Roth, June 28, 1952. BS in Landscape Architecture, Mich. State U., East Lansing, 1962, MS in Landscape Architecture, 1963. Lic. landscape architect, State Tex., 1983. Asst. chief landscape arch. Andrews and Clarke, Inc., NYC, 1963—65; asst. prof. U. Wis., Madison, 1965—68; assoc. exec. dir. Am. Soc. Landscape Architects, Wash., 1968—76; exec. dir. Landscape Architecture Found., Wash., 1970—76, Ctr. Landscape Archtl. Edn. and Rsch., Reston, Va., 1977—81; dir. mktg. Myrick, Newman, Dahlberg & Ptnrs., Dallas, 1982—83; pres. AGORA Comm., Plano, Tex., 1983—2008; prof. U. Tex., Arlington, 1988—. Contbr. articles to numerous profl. jours. (Merit award, 1983, Honor award, 1988). Sp3 US Army, 1955—57, Ft. Sill, Okla. Fellow: ASLA. Office: Univ of Tex at Arlington UTA Box 19108 Arlington TX 76019 Business E-Mail: grobnet@uta.edu.

ROBINETTE, JOSEPH ALLEN, playwright; b. Rockwood, Tenn., Feb. 8, 1939; s. Paul Henry and Willie Merle (Ghormley) R.; m. Helen Marie Seitz; children: John, Anne, Michael, Christopher, Andrew. BA, Carson-Newman Coll., 1960; MA, So. Ill. U., 1966, PhD, 1972. Tchr. Bearden H.S., Knoxville, Tenn., 1962-63; instr. Arkansas City (Kans.) Jr. Coll., 1963-64, U. Hawaii, Hilo, 1968-69, So. Ill. U., Carbondale, 1965-68, 69-71; prof. theatre arts Rowan U., Glassboro, NJ, 1971—2005; ret. Author 51 pub. plays and musicals; authorized dramatizer Charlotte's Web, Stuart Little, The Lion, The Witch and the Wardrobe, The Paper Chase, A Rose for Emily, others. Founding mem. Opera for Youth, 1978—. Recipient ASCAP awards, 1975—; recipient Charlotte Chorpenning cup for outstanding writing of children's plays, Children's Theatre Assn. Am., 1976, medal Children's Theatre Found. Am., 2006. Mem. Am. Alliance for Theatre and Edn. (Best Play of Yr. award 2004). Home: PO Box 11 Richwood NJ 08074-0011 Business E-Mail: robinettej@rowan.edu.

ROBINOV, JEFF (JEFFREY STEPHEN ROBINOV), film company executive; b. Portland, ME, Nov. 8, 1958; s. Gerald Scott and Jacqueline (Bookbinder) Robinov; m. Sharon Morrill; 1 child, Reece Charles. Agent Writers & Artists; literary agent Internat. Creative Mgmt., 1992—97; sr. v.p. prodn. Warner Bros. Pictures, 1997—2000, exec. v.p. prodn., 2000—02, pres. domestic prodn., 2002—08; pres. Warner Bros. Pictures Group, 2008—. Exec. prodr.: (films) On Deadly Ground, 1994. Office: Warner Bros Pictures Group 4000 Warner Blvd Burbank CA 91522*

ROBINOWITZ, CAROLYN BAUER, psychiatrist, educator, director; b. Bklyn., July 15, 1938; d. Milton Leonard and Marcia (Wexler) Bauer; m. Max Robinowitz, June 10, 1962; children: Mark, David AB, Wellesley Coll., 1959; MD, Washington U., 1964. Diplomate Am. Bd. Psychiatry and Neurology. Chief physician tng. NIMH, Bethesda, Md., 1968-70; dir. pediatric liaison U. Miami Sch. Medicine, Fla., 1970-72, dir. child psychiatry tng., 1971-72; dir. edn. George Washington U. Sch. Medicine, Washington, 1972-74; project dir. Psychiatrist as Tchr., Washington, 1973-75; dep. med. dir. Am. Psychiat. Assn., Washington, 1976-86, dir. Office Edn., 1976-87, sr. dep. med. dir., 1986-94, COO, 1986-94, treas., 2004—05, sec.-treas., 2005—06, pres.-elect, 2006—07, pres., 2007—. Assoc. dean Georgetown U. Sch. Medicine, 1995—98, dean, 1998—2000, lectr., 1976—82, professorial lectr., 1982—94, prof., 1995—2000, clin. prof., 2000—; dir. Am. Bd. Psychiatry and Neurology, Evanston, Ill., 1979—86, sec., 1984, v.p., 85, pres., 86; clin. prof. psychiatry and behavioral scis., child health and devel. George Washington U., 1984—98, 2001—; professorial lectr. Uniformed Svcs. U. of Health Scis., 1986—. Editor: Women in Context, 1976; contbr. articles to jours., chpts. to books Admissions com. Wellesley Coll. Club, Washington, 1983-84. Served with USPHS, 1966-69. Recipient NIMH Mental Health Career Devel. award, 1966-70, NIMH grantee, 1974-94. Fellow Am. Psychiat. Assn. (Disting. Svc. award 1991, Vestermark award 1995, Adminstrv. Psychiatry award 1999), Am. Coll. Psychiatrists (bd. dirs. 1993-96, 1st v.p. 1996-97, pres. 1999-00, past pres. 2000-04, sec. gen. 2005—07, Bowis award 1994, Disting. Svc. award 2001); mem. AMA (coun. psychiatry sect. 2000-, coun. on sci. affairs 2001-05, coun. on sci. and pub. health 2005—), Assn. for Acad. Psychiatry (disting. life fellow, pres. 1994-95, dir. 1992-96, 03-06, Lifetime Achievement award 2003), Group for Advancement of Psychiatry (dir. 1982-84, pres. 1989-91), Coun. Med. Splty. Socs. (dir. 1977-82, pres. 1981-82). Office: #514 5225 Connecticut Ave NW Washington DC 20015 Home Phone: 301-229-9252, 202-270-9252; Office Phone: 202-237-1466. E-mail: cbrobinowitzmd@usa.net.

ROBINS, LINDA CAROL, language educator; d. Aaron Arthur and Jeanette Rose Robins. BA, Barnard Coll., Columbia U., NYC, 1963; MA, Middlebury Coll. Grad. Sch. French, Paris, 1964, Montclair State U., NJ, 1988; MPhil, NYU, 1965. Cert. reflexologist Bergen CC, Paramus, NJ, 2002. Ballrm. dance instr. John Clancy Dance Studio, NYC, 1962—63; instr. French Can. Acad., Kobe, Japan, 1964—65, Suffolk County CC, Selden, NY, 1965—67, Queensborough CC, Queens, NY, 1967—68; events prodr. Bergen CC, 1968—; prof. World langs. Cultures Founder Nat. Am. Day Celebrat, 1996—2001, cert. reflexologist, 2002. Contbr. articles to profl. jours. Penfield fellowship, NYU, 1971—72. Mem.: Am. Coun. Tchrs. Fgn. Langs. (sec. Fla. sig 1999—2000), Am. Assn. Tchrs. French (bd. dir. 1969—79). Liberal. Avocations: painting, dance, travel, guitar, piano. Office Phone: 201-447-9283. Business E-Mail: lrobins@bergen.edu.

ROBINS, MORRIS JOSEPH, chemistry professor, researcher; b. Nephi, Utah, Sept. 28, 1939; s. Waldo George and Mary Erda (Anderson) R.; m. Jerri Johnson, June 11, 1960 (div. July 1972); children: Dayne M., Diane, Douglas W., Debra, Dale C.; m. Jackie Alene Robinson, Aug. 24, 1973; children: Mark K., Janetta A., Tiffany A. BA, U. Utah, 1961; PhD, Ariz. State U., 1965. Cancer rsch. scientist Roswell Park Meml. Inst., Buffalo, 1965-66; rsch. assoc. U. Utah, Salt Lake City, 1966-69; from asst. prof. to prof. chemistry U. Alberta, Edmonton, Can., 1969-86; prof. chemistry Brigham Young U., Provo, Utah, 1987—. Vis. prof. medicinal chemistry U. Utah, Salt Lake City, 1981-82; adj. prof. medicine U. Alberta, Edmonton, 1988-2000; grant evaluation panel Am. Cancer Soc., N.Y.C., 1977-80, Nat. Cancer Inst. Can., Toronto, 1983-86; mem. AIDS & Related Rsch. Study Sect. 4, NIH, Washington, 1995-2000; cons. in field. Mem. editl. bd. Nucleic Acids Rsch., 1980-83; contbr. articles to profl. jours., chpts. to books; patentee in field. NSF fellow, 1963-64; Rsch. grantee Nat. Cancer Inst. Can., Natural Scis. and Engring. Rsch. Coun. Can., 1969-87, Am. Cancer Soc., NIH, 1987-2007; named J. Rex Goates prof. Brigham Young U., 1989—; recipient medal for sci. and tech. award Gov. Utah, 1996, Galien Can. Rsch. award, 1998. Mem. Am. Assn. for Cancer Rsch., Am. Chem. Soc. (Utah award 1997), Internat. Soc. for Antiviral Rsch., Internat. Soc. Nucleic Acids Chemistry (mem. adv. bd. 1995-1998), Internat. Soc. Nucleosides Nucleotides and Nucleic Acid (adv. bd. mem. 2001-2002, Imbach-Townsend award 2008). Mem. Lds Ch. Avocations: fishing, reading, games. Office: Brigham Young Univ Dept Chemistry/Biochemistry Provo UT 84602-5700 Office Phone: 801-422-6272. Business E-Mail: morris_robins@byu.edu.

ROBINS, PERRY, dermatologist, educator, foundation administrator; MD, U. Heidelberg, 1961. Intern Orange Meml. Hosp., 1961—62; resident in dermatology, syphilology Bronx VA Med. Ctr., 1962—64; clin. fellow in dermatology, syphilology NYU Med. Ctr., 1965—67, prof. emeritus dermatology, clin. prof., chief, Mohs micrographic surgery unit; founder, pres. Internat. Soc. Dermatologic Surgery, The Skin Cancer Found. Author: Sun Sense: A Guide to the Prevention and Early Detection of Skin Cancer, Understanding Basal Cell Carcinoma: What You Need to Know, Understanding Squamous Cell Carcinoma: What You Need to Know, Play it Safe in the Sun; co-author (with M. Perez): Understanding Melanoma: What You Need to Know; contbr. articles to profl. jours. Recipient Presdl. Citation, Internat. Soc. Dermatologic Surgery. Fellow: Am. Acad. Dematology (hon. Award Excellence in Edn., Golden Triangle award, Presdl. Citation); mem.: Am. Soc. Dermatol. Surgery (past pres.), Am. Coll. Mohs Micrographic Surgery (founder, past pres.). Office: 345 E 37th St Ste 209 New York NY 10016 also: Skin Cancer Found 149 Madison Ave Ste 901 New York NY 10016 Office Phone: 212-263-7222. Office Fax: 212-686-5842.*

ROBINS, ROBERT SIDWAR, political science professor, department chairman; b. Spangler, Pa., Apr. 20, 1938; s. Sydney and Katherine (Sidwar) R.; m. Marjorie McGann, Nov. 25, 1959; children: Anthony P., Nicholas A. BA, U. Pitts., 1959; MA, Duke U., 1961, PhD, 1963. Prof. polit. sci. Tulane U., New Orleans, 1965—, chmn. dept. polit. sci., 1979-90, dep. provost, 1991-98. Acad. visitor Inst. Commonwealth Studies, U. London, 1969-70, 78-79, mem. 1987-88; sr. assoc. mem. St. Antony's Coll., Oxford, Eng., 1972-73; vis. scholar Hastings Ctr., 1982; vis. scientist Tavistock Clinic, London, 1987-88. Author: Political Institutionalization and the Integration of Elites, 1976 (Carnegie Commn. report) Legislative Attitudes Toward Higher Education in Louisiana, 1968, Psychopathology and Political Leadership, 1977, Disease and Political Leadership, 1990; co-author: When Illness Strikes the Leader, Political Paranoia; contbr. articles to profl. pubs. Vice-chmn. Elections Integrity Commn., State of La., 1981-82; active Conn. Bd. Govs. Higher Edn., Stamford Urban Redevel. Commn., Conn. Recipient Excellence in Tchg. award Tulane U., 1978; Fulbright scholar, 1961-62. Mem. Am. Polit. Sci. Assn., Internat. Soc. Polit. Psychology, Conn. Bd. Govs. Higher Edn., Stanford Urban Re-Devel. Commn. Avocations: carpentry, gardening. Home: 64 Pond Rd Stamford CT 06902 Personal E-mail: robins_06902@yahoo.com.

ROBINSON, ADAM MAYFIELD, JR., career military officer, surgeon; b. Louisville, Nov. 9, 1950; s. Adam Mayfield and Addie Hilda (Brown) Robinson; m. Judith Schevtchuk, Dec. 29, 1973 (div. Aug. 1982); m. Yuko Sakurai, Aug. 30, 1984. AB in Polit. Sci., Ind. U., 1972; MD, Ind. U. Sch. Medicine, Indpls., 1976; MBA, U. South Fla., 1994. Diplomate Am. Bd. Surgery, Am. Bd. Colon & Rectal Surgery. Commd. ensign USN Med. Corps, 1977, advanced through grades to capt., 1990, then vice adm., gen. med. officer Ponce, PR, 1977-78, gen. surgery resident Bethesda Naval Hosp. Md., 1978-82, staff gen. surgeon Yokosuka Naval Hosp. Japan, 1982-84, ship's surgeon USS Midway Yokosuka, 1982-84, head divisn. colon-rectal surgery Bethesda Naval Hosp., 1985-90, asst. head gen. surgery, 1987-90, chmn. dept. gen. surgery Portsmouth Naval Hosp. Va., 1990—95, acting med. dir., 1994—95, force surgeon, comdr. Naval Surface Force, US Atlantic Fleet Norfolk, Va., 1995—97, exec. officer Naval Hosp. Jacksonville, Fla., 1997—99, dir. readiness Bur. Medicine & Surgery, 1999—2000, prin. dir. clin. & prog. policy, acting dep. asst. sec. of def. for health affairs, 2000—01, cmdg. officer Naval Hosp. Yokosuka, 2001—04, acting chief Med. Corps, dep. chief med. support ops. Bur. Medicine & Surgery, 2004, comdr. Nat. Naval Med. Ctr. Bethesda, 2004—05, comdr. Navy Medicine Nat. Capital Area Region, 2005—07, surgeon gen., chief Bur. Medicine & Surgery, 2007—. Fellow colon-rectal surgery Carle Clinic, U. Ill., Champaign, 1984—85. Contbr. articles to profl. jours. Fellow: ACS, Am. Soc. Colon & Rectal Surgeons; mem.: AMA, Assn. Program Dirs. in Surgery (bd. dirs. 1990), Assn. Mil. Surgeons US, Nat. Med. Assn., Beta Gamma Sigma. Avocations: ballroom dancing, golf, singing. Office: USN Navy Pentagon Washington DC 20503*

ROBINSON, ADELBERT CARL, lawyer, judge; b. Shawnee, Okla., Dec. 13, 1926; s. William H. and Mayme (Forston) R.; m. Paula Kay Settles, Apr. 16, 1988; children from previous marriage: William, James, Schuyler, Donald, David, Nancy, Lauri. Student, Okla. Bapt. U., 1944-47; JD, Okla. U., 1950. Bar: Okla. 1950. Pvt. practice, Muskogee, Okla., 1956-97; with legal dept. Phillips Petroleum Co., 1950-51; adjuster U.S. Fidelity & Guaranty Co., 1951-54, atty., adjuster-in-charge, 1954-56; ptnr. Fite & Robinson, 1956-62, Fite, Robinson & Summers, 1963-70, Robinson & Summers, 1970-72, Robinson, Summers & Locke, 1972-76, Robinson, Locke & Gage, 1976-80, Robinson, Locke, Gage & Fite, 1980-83, Robinson, Locke, Gage, Fite & Williams, Muskogee, 1983-95, Robinson, Gage, Fite & Williams, Muskogee, 1995-97. Police judge City of Muskogee, 1963—64, mcpl. judge, 1964—70; prin. justice 84Temp. Divsn. 36 Okla. Ct. Appeals, 1981—84, spl. dist. judge, 1997—; pres., dir. Wall St. Bldg. Corp., 1969—78, Three Forks Devel. Corp., 1968—77, Rolo Leasing Inc., 1971—97, Suroya II Inc.1, 1977—99; mng. ptnr. RLG Ritz, 1980—97; ptnr. First City Real Estate Partnership, 1985—94; dir. First City Bank, Tulsa, Okla., 1985—92; del. to U.S./China Jt. Session on Trade, Investment and Econ. Law, Beijing, 1987; dir. First Bankshares of Muskogee, 1980—95, First of Muskogee Corp., 1980—95; adv. dir. First Nat. Bank and Trust Co. of Muskogee, 1978—95. Chmn. Muskogee County (Okla.) Law Day, 1963, Muskogee Area Redevel. Authority, 1963, Muskogee County chpt. Am. Cancer Soc., 1956; pres., bd. dirs. United Way of Muskogee Inc., 1980-88, v.p., 1982, pres., 1983; bd. dirs. Muskogee Cmty. Concert Assn., Muskogee Tourist Info. Bur., 1964-68; bd. dirs., gen. counsel United Cerebral Palsy Eastern Okla., 1964-68; trustee Connors Devel. Found., Connors Coll., 1981-99, chmn., 1987-89; active Muskogee Housing Authority, 1992-95. With inf. AUS, 1945-46. Mem. ABA, Okla. Bar Assn. (chmn. uniform laws com. 1970-72, chmn. profl. coop. com. 1965-69, past regional chmn. grievance com.), Muskogee County Bar Assn. (pres. 1971, mem. exec. coun. 1971-74), Okla. Assn. Def. Counsel (dir. 1970-74), Okla. Assn. Mcpl. Judges (dir. 1968-70), Muskogee c. of C., Delta Theta Phi., Rotary (pres. 1971-72). Methodist. Office: Muskogee County Courthouse PO Box 1350 Muskogee OK 74402-1350 Home: 3405 Park Pl N Muskogee OK 74403-1815

ROBINSON, ALLAN RICHARD, oceanography educator; b. Lynn, Mass., Oct. 17, 1932; married, 1955; 3 children. BA, Harvard U., 1954, MA, 1956, PhD in Physics, 1959; Dr. honoris causa, U. Liege, Belgium, 1988. NSF fellow in meteorology and oceanography Cambridge U., 1959-60; asst. prof. to assoc. prof. Harvard U., Cambridge, Mass., 1960-68, dir. Ctr. Earth and Planetary Physics, 1972-75, Gordon McKay prof. geophys. fluid dynamics, 1968—, chmn. com. oceanography, 1972-87. Co-chmn. Mid-Ocean Dynamics Expdn. I Sci. Coun. NSF, 1971-74; U.S. chmn. U.S.-USSR Polymode Expdn., 1973-81; co-chmn. Phys. Ocean East Mediterranean, Intergovernmental Oceanographic Commission-UNESCO, 1983—; guest investigator Woods Hole (Mass.) Oceanographic Inst., 1979-80; CNOC prof. Naval Postgrad. Sch., 1982; vis. scientist Applied Physics Lab. Johns Hopkins U., Laurel, Md., 1986—; Slichter vis. prof. UCLA, 1987; Franqui vis. prof. U. Liege, Belgium, 1988. Editor-in-chief: Dynamics of Atmospheres and Oceans, 1976—. Guggenheim fellow Cambridge (Eng.) U., 1972-73. Fellow AAAS, Am. Acad. Arts and Scis. Office: Harvard U Schl of Engg & Applied Sci Pierce Hall 29 Oxford St Cambridge MA 02138-2901

ROBINSON, BARBARA PAUL, lawyer; b. Oct. 19, 1941; d. Leo and Pauline G. Paul; m. Charles Raskob Robinson, June 11, 1965; children: Charles Paul, Torrance Webster. AB magna cum laude, Bryn Mawr Coll., 1962; LLB, Yale U., 1965, Order of the Coif. Bar: N.Y. 1966, U.S. Dist. Ct. (so. and ea. dists.) N.Y. 1975, U.S. Tax Ct. 1972, U.S. Ct. Appeals (2d cir.) 1974. Assoc. Debevoise & Plimpton LLP, NYC, 1966-75, ptnr., 1976—2006, with Trusts and Estates Dept., of counsel, 2007—. Bd. dirs. Am. Arbitration Assn., 1997—2003. Mem. bd. editors: Chase Jour., 1997—2001; contbr. articles to profl. jours. Mem. adv. coun., bd. vis. CUNY Law Sch., Queens, 1984—90; active Coun. on Fgn. Rels.; mem. commn. women's issues Mayor, 2002—; trustee Trinity Sch., 1982—88, pres., 1986—88; bd. dirs. Found. for Child Devel., 1988—2000, 2001—07, chmn., 1991—2000; bd. dirs. Catalyst, 1993—2006, treas., 1993—2006; bd. dirs. Fund for Modern Cts., 1994—2003, Wave Hill, 1994—, Garden Conservancy, 1996—2002, Lawyers Com. for Civil Rights Under Law, 1997—2003, William Nelson Cromwell Found., 1993—, Irish Legal Rsch. Found. Inc., 1996—2002, Citizens Union Found. Inc., 1996—2004, Am. Friends Brit. Mus., 2003—, The Ocean Conservancy, 2004—, Teagle Found., 2005—, The Greenwall Found., 2006—, The John A. Hartford Found., 2006—; trustee Bryn Mawr Coll., 2000—. Recipient Laura Parsons Pratt award, 1996, Lifetime Achievement award, The Am. Lawyer mag., 2008 Fellow Am. Bar Found., N.Y. Bar Found.; mem. ABA (commn. on women in profession 1999-2002), N.Y. State Bar Assn. (vice chmn. com. on trust adminstrn., trusts and estates law sect. 1977-81, ho. of dels. 1984-87, 90-92, com. ann. award 1993-94), Assn. of Bar of City of N.Y. (chmn. com. on trusts, estates and surrogates cts. 1981-84, judiciary com. 1981-84, coun. on jud. adminstrn. 1982-84, chair nominating com. 1984-85, 99-2000, exec. com. 1986-91, chair 1989-90, v.p. 1990-91, chair com. on honors 1993-94, com. on long-range planning 1991-94, co-chair coun. on childen 1997-98, pres. 1994-96), Assn. of Bar of City of N.Y. Fund Inc. (bd. dirs. 2000-03, pres. 1994-96), Women's Forum, Yale Coun., Yale Law Sch. Assn. N.Y. (devel. bd., exec. com. 1981-85, 93—, pres. 1988-93), The Century Assn., Yale Club, Washington Club. Office: Debevoise & Plimpton LLP 919 Third Ave New York NY 10022 Home Phone: 212-222-4160; Office Phone: 212-909-6325. Business E-Mail: bprobinson@debevoise.com.

ROBINSON, BEATRIZ GONZALEZ, academic administrator; b. Havana, Cuba, Mar. 3, 1964; d. Jose V. and Josefina C. Gonzalez; m. John T. Robinson, Oct. 7, 1989; 1 child, Sean T. BA in English, Barry U., Miami, Fla., 1987, MS in Guidance & Couseling, 1991, PhD in Leadership, 1998. Lic. mental health counselor Fla. Dept. Health, 1998. Prof. St. Thomas U., Miami, 1997—, self-study dir., 2000—03, planning & evaluation officer, 2002—05, interim dean undergrad. studies & programs, 2004—05, v.p. planning, chief staff, 2005—. State coord. women higher edn. Am. Coun. Edn., Miami, 2000—; external evaluator commn. So. Assn. Colls. and Schs. Recipient Grad. Student Rsch. award, Nat. Career Devel. Assn., 1999, Outstanding Svc. award, St. Thomas U., 2001, Faculty Scholarship award, 2002; grantee, Am. Coun. Edn., 2004—05; fellow Fellow, Hispanic Serving Insts., 2005. Office: St Thomas Univ 16401 NW 37th Ave Miami Gardens FL 33054

ROBINSON, BOB LEO, retired international investment service executive; b. Franklin, Tenn., Sept. 9, 1933; s. W.A. and Cornelia Irene (Lampley) R.; m. Carolyn Overton, Dec. 18, 1955; children: Richard Glenn, Leigh Ann, Elizabeth Lynne. BS in Indsl. Mgmt, Tenn. Tech. U., 1955. Cert. property mgr. Quality control engr. Gates Rubber Co., Nashville, 1960; tech. rep. Home Ins. Co., 1961-65; civilian staff adminstrv. asst. Dept. Army, Nashville, 1965; exec. asst. to pres. Sullivan's Dept. Stores, Nashville, 1966-69; dir. engring. and devel. Venture Out in Am., Knoxville, Tenn., 1969; v.p., then exec. v.p. Hosp. Corp. Am., Nashville, 1970-79; pres., chief exec. officer Real Estate Group Inc., Nashville, 1974—, Fidelity Title Co., Nashville, 1974-83; now ret. Pres. Internat. Bus. and Investment Services, Orlando, 1978—; gen. partner Union Sq. Ltd., Jacksonville, Fla., 1973-79; dir. Am. Travel Service, World Health Cons.; chmn. bd. emeritus Arnold Palmer Devel. Co., Orlando, Fla., 1988—; past vice chmn. bd. dirs., chief exec. officer Clin. Diagnostic Systems, Inc., Orlando, 1988-89; past vice chmn. Space Rail Corp., Orlando, 1991; speaker patriotic Christian events. Mem. Mayor Nashville Blue Ribbon Com., 1975-77; commr. City of Brentwood, Tenn., 1969-71, vice mayor, 1969-71, mayor, 1971, mem. planning commn., 1970-71; bd. dirs. Goodwill Industries Ctrl. Fla., exec. com., chmn. ops. com.; chmn. bldg. fund St. Cecilia Acad., Nashville, 1978; vice chmn. Audubon council Boy Scouts Am., 1968; founder Tenn. Tech. ROTC Gen.'s Cup Scholarship Found., 1986; aide U.S. Com. for Normandy Meml. Mus., Caen, France, 1987—; parachutist Israeli Def. Forces, 1989, Royal Thai Spl. Warfare Command, 1990; campaign dir. Drage for County Chmn., Orange County, Fla., 1990; bd. dirs. Camp Blanding Mus. Found., 1995—, Camp Blanding Mus. and Hist. Assocs. Inc., 1996—, chmn. new mus. bldg. com., 1997—. Served as officer, master army aviator, parachutist, U.S. Army, 1955-60, USAR, 1960-83; maj. gen. (brevet) USAR, 1990. Decorated Army Commendation medal, Meritorious Service medal; recipient numerous public service awards; named to Tenn. Tech. ROTC Hall of Fame, 1988. Mem. Internat. Inst. Hosp. Cons., Inst. Real Estate Mgmt., Army Aviation Assn. Am., Res. Officers Assn., Internat. Assn. Airborne Vets., 82d Airborne Divsn. Assn. Republican. Baptist.

ROBINSON, CARRIE, pastor; b. Balt., Jan. 11, 1945; d. Charles Dingle and Anna Lemmon; m. Bill Robinson, Nov. 26, 1977 (dec. June 2, 2003); children: Michael Stukes, Maurice Johnson, Monica Johnson. Doctorate, Interdenominational Coll.; degree in Christian edn., Theol. Sem. and Coll. Notary pub. With Verizon Tel. Co., 1968—; pastor Prayer and Faith Ministries Bapt. Ch., Balt., 1987—. Sec. United Bapt. Conf., Balt., 1990—, v.p., 2000—. Mem.: Internat. Women Ministerial Alliance (v.p. 2000—), Order of Ea. Star (Helen Benton House # 34). Avocations: singing, reading, computers, drumming. Office: Prayer and Faith Ministries Bapt Ch Inc 1865 N Gay St Baltimore MD 21213 Home: 2705 Hamilton Ave Baltimore MD 21214-1912 Office Phone: 410-675-0047. E-mail: bishopcrobinson3@aol.com.

ROBINSON, CHARLES WESLEY, boat design company executive; b. Long Beach, Calif., Sept. 7, 1919; s. Franklin Willard and Anna Hope (Gould) R.; m. Tamara Lindovna, Mar. 8, 1957; children: Heather Lynne, Lisa Anne, Wendy Paige. BA in Econs. cum laude, U. Calif., Berkeley, 1941; MBA, Stanford U., 1947. Asst. mgr. mfg. Golden State Dairy Products Co., San Francisco, 1947-49; v.p., then pres. Marcona Corp., San Francisco, 1952-74; undersec. of state for econ. affairs Dept. State, Washington, 1974-75; dep. sec. of state, 1976-77; sr. mng. ptnr. Kuhn Loeb & Co., NYC, 1977-78; vice chmn. Blyth Eastman Dillon & Co., NYC, 1978-79; chmn. Energy Transition Corp., Santa Fe and Washington, 1979-82; pres. Robinson & Assocs., Inc., Santa Fe, 1982—. Pres. CBTF Co., San Diego, 1992—, M Ship Co., San Diego, 1998; dir. emeritus NIKE, Inc. Patentee slurry transport and both sail and power boat designs, Brookings Instn., Washington, 1977—; mem. Pres.'s Cir. NAS. Lt. USN, 1941-46. Recipient Disting. Honor award Dept. State, 1977, Lifetime Achievement award, N.Mex., 2007. Republican. Methodist. Office: Robinson & Assocs Inc PO Box 2224 Santa Fe NM 87504-2224 Office Phone: 505-988-5589.

ROBINSON, CHARLOTTE HILL, artist; b. San Antonio, Nov. 28, 1924; d. Lucius Davis and Charlotte (Moore) Hill; m. Floyd I. Robinson, Mar. 1943; children: Floyd I. Jr., Laurence H., Elizabeth H. Student, Incarnate Word Coll., 1942—45, NYU, 1947-48, Corcoran Sch. Art, 1951-52. Painting instr. Art League No. Va., Alexandria, 1967-75. Condr. Art World Seminar Washington Women's Art Ctr., 1975-80, drawing workshop Smithsonian Instn. Resident Assocs. Program, Washington, 1977; program dir. Nat. Women's Caucus for Art, 1979; project coord., exhbn. curator The Artist and the Quilt, nat. mus. traveling exhbn., 1983-86; vis. artist S.W. Craft Ctr., San Antonio, 1983-85; lectr. WFUV 90 FM, Fordham U., NYC, 1990, San Antonio Art Inst., 1991, Nat. Mus. for Women in Arts, Washington, 1991, Iowa State U., Ames, 1991; panelist Nat. Mus. Women in Arts, 1997, Woman and the Arts, Douglass Coll./ Rutgers U., 1998, Washington Women's Caucus for Art at the Millenium Art Ctr., 2001. Editor: The Artist & The Quilt, 1983; one-person shows include Thames Sic. Ctr., New London, Conn., 1991, Brunner Gallery & Mus., Iowa State U., 1991, 92, San Antonio Art. Inst., 1991, Fordham U., 1991, de Andino Fine Arts, Washington, 1992, Masur Mus. Art, Monroe, La., 1993, 96, 2001, Lee Hansley Art Gallery, Raleigh, NC, 1993, 97, 2001, Sol Del Rio, San Antonio, 1995, 97-98, 1812 Artic Gallery, Virginia Beach, Va., 1995, Savannah Coll. Art and Design, 1997, Duke U. Sch. Law, 1998, No. Va. CC, 1999, McLean Project for the Arts, 2002, Southwest Sch. Art & Craft, San Antonio, 2003, Chavlotte Probiason:A Retrospective Lee Hansley Gallery, Raleigh, NC, 2007, Charlotte Robinson:Crosswords to the Pond, Georgetown U. Wash., 2009; exhibited in group shows at Franklin Square and Watkins Gallery, Washington, 1992, Rutgers U., New Brunswick, NJ, 1992, 96, 98, Brody's Gallery, Washington, 1992, Lee Hansley Art Gallery, Raleigh, 1993, 96, 98-2001, 02, 03, 05, 06, 07, Emerson Gallery, McLean, 1993, 95, 99, No. Va. CC, 1994, 99, Harvard U., 1996, Ceres Gallery, NYC, 1999-2000, Millennium Art Ctr., Washington, 2001, Am. Ctr. Physics, 2003. Trustee Bronx Mus., NY, 1977; bd. dirs. Washington Women's Art Ctr., 1977, New Art Examiner, 1985-86; nat. bd. dirs. Women's Caucus for Art, 1983-84. Recipient Concourse award Corcoran Sch. Art, 1952; Telfair Acad. Art scholar, Savannah, Ga., 1959; Nat. Endowment for Arts grantee, 1977-81; fellow Va. Ctr. for Creative Arts, Sweet Briar, Va., 1985. Address: Lee Hansley Gallery 225 Glenwood Ave Raleigh NC 27603 Home Phone: 703-941-3865; Office Phone: 703-941-3865. E-mail: bjohnb@mchs1.com, chardyrob@cox.net.

ROBINSON, CHESTER HERSEY, retired dean; b. Yonkers, NY, Nov. 8, 1918; s. Sherman Alexander and Alice (Hersey) R.; m. Marguerite Davis, Dec. 14, 1945 (div. Oct. 1976); children— Barry, Roslyn; m. Heidemarie Höfler, Dec. 30, 1976. AB, Union Coll., Schenectady, 1940; PhD, Stanford U., 1950. Asst. registrar Stanford U., 1949-50; dir. div. extension and summer session Miami U., Oxford, Ohio, 1950-54; assoc. dir. Sch. Gen. Studies, Hunter Coll., 1954-60; dir. Sch. Gen. Studies, Bronx campus, 1960-66, dean, 1966-68; dean Sch. Gen. Studies, Herbert H. Lehman Coll. CUNY, 1968-82, dean Continuing Edn., 1982-86; prof. emeritus, 1986—. Served to lt. USNR, 1942-46. Mem. NEA, Beta Theta Pi, Phi Delta Kappa. Lodges: Elks. Presbyterian. Home: Bldg 500 Apt 216 4920 Locust St NE Saint Petersburg FL 33703 Home Phone: 727-528-9116.

ROBINSON, DANIEL N., psychology and philosophy professor; b. NYC, Mar. 9, 1937; s. Henry S. and Margaret R.; children: Tracey, Kimberly; m. Francine Malasko, 1967. BA, Colgate U., 1958; MA, Hofstra U., 1960; PhD, CUNY, 1965. Rsch. psychologist, electronics rsch. labs. Columbia U., 1960-65, asst. dir. sci. honors program, 1964-68, sr. rsch. psychologist, electronics rsch. labs., 1965-68, asst. dir. of life scis. electronics rsch. labs., 1967-68; asst. prof. dept. psychology Amherst Coll., 1968-70, assoc. prof., 1970-71; dir. grad. program dept. psychology Georgetown Univ., 1981-83, chmn. dept. psychology, 1973-76, 85-91, assoc. prof., 1971-74, prof., 1974—, adj. prof. philosophy Washington, 1996—, disting. rsch. prof. and prof. psychology, 1998—2001, disting. prof. emeritus, 2002—. Vis. lectr. psychology Princeton U., 1965-68; vis. prof. Folger Shakespeare Inst., 1977; vis. sr. mem. Linacre Coll., vis. lectr. philosophy Oxford (Eng.) U., 1991—, faculty fellow, 1999—, philos. faculty, 2002—; vis. prof. Princeton U., 2001; adj. prof. Columbia U., 2002-2005; cons. NIH, 1967-70, NSF, 1965-75, PBS, 1978-84, 1985-88, MacArthur Found., 1985, Atty. Gen's. Task Force on Crime, 1980, HHS, NIH, 1988. Author: Psychology: A Study of Its Origins and Principles, 1972, The Enlightened Machine: An Anlytical Introduction to Neuropsychology, 1973, 80, Psychology: Traditions and Perspectives, 1976, An Intellectual History of Psychology, 1976, The Mind Unfolded: Essay's on Psychology's Historic Texts, 1978, Systems of Modern Psychology: A Critical Sketch, 1979, Psychology and Law: Can Justice Survive the Social Sciences?, 1980, An Intellectual History of Psychology-Revised Edition, 1981, 3rd edit., 1995, Toward A Science of Human Nature: Essays on the Psychologies of Hegel, Mill, Wundt, and James, 1982, Philosophy of Psychology, 1985, Aristotle's Psychology, 1989, (with William R. Uttal) Foundations of Psychobiology, 1983, (with Sir John Eccles) The Wonder of Being Human: Our Mind and Our Brain, 1984; editor Heredity and Achievement, 1970, Readings in the Origins and Principles of Psychology, 1972, Significant Contributions to the History of Psychology, 1977-78, Annals of Theoretical Psychology, 1990, Social Discourse and Moral Judgment, 1992, Wild Beasts and Idle Humours: Legal Insanity from Antiquity to the Present, 1996, Consciousness and Mental Life, 2008; editor Jour. Theoretical and Philosophical Psychology, 1997-2002; contbr. chpts. to books, reference books, articles to profl. jours. Recipient Inst. for Advanced Study in the Humanities fellow, U. Edinburgh, 1986-87; Pres's. medal Colgate U., 1986, Pub. Svc. award Gen. Svcs. Adminstrn., 1986. Fellow APA (past pres. divsns. 24 and 26, Lifetime Achievement award Divsn. History of Psychology 2001, Disting. Contbn. award Divsn. Theoretical and Philos. Psychology 2001), Witherspoon Inst. (Sr.); mem. Sigma Xi, Psi Chi. Home: 300 E Main St Middletown MD 21769 Office Phone: 301-371-7600, 301-676-0015. Personal E-mail: dnmrobinson@msn.com. Business E-Mail: dan.robinson@philosophy.ox.ac.uk.

ROBINSON, DAVID, manufacturing executive; b. Huntington, NY, Nov. 21, 1961; B in acctg. cum laude, The Ohio State U., Columbus, 1984; MA in Theol. Studies, Chgo. Theol. Sem., 1991; PhD, Emory U. Divsn. Religion, Theology & Psychology, Atlanta, 2002. Acctg. intern Lancaster Colony, Deloitte Haskins & Sells; mktg. intern City of Columbus; rsch. analyst, asst. to the pres. Mgmt. Horizons, 1985—88; English tchr. Presbyn. Ch. Communities, Taiwan, 1991—92; v.p. Marcy Enterprises, Inc., 1994—. Presenter V.P. Al Gore's Climate Project Initiative, 2007. Author: Conscience and Jung's Moral Vision, 2005. Founder, organizer Ride for Reason, 1988; mem. First Cmty. Ch. Mem.: Jung Assn. Ctrl. Ohio, Sigma Chi. Democrat. Office: Marcy Adhesives 2977 Lamb Ave Columbus OH 43219 Office Phone: 614-471-5200. Office Fax: 614-471-9176.

ROBINSON, DAVID BROOKS, retired naval officer; b. Alexandria, La., Oct. 26, 1939; s. Donald and Marion (Holloman) R.; m. Gene Kirkpatrick, Aug. 1, 1964; children: Kirk, David. Student, Tex. A&M U., 1958—59; BS, U.S. Naval Acad., 1963; MS in Physics, Naval Postgrad. Sch., Monterey, Calif., 1969. Commd. ensign USN, 1963, advanced through grades to vice adm., 1993; commdg. officer USS Canon and USS Ready, Guam, 1969-71; adminstrv. aide to Chmn. Joint Chiefs Staff, Washington, 1971-74; commdg. officer USS Luce, Mayport, Fla., 1976-78; surface comdr. assignment officer. and dir. fiscal mgmt. and procedural control divsn. Naval Mil. Pers. Command, 1979-81; mem. Fgn. Svc. Inst. Exec. Seminar, Washington, 1982; commdg. officer USS Richmond K. Turner, Charleston, SC, 1983-84; chief of staff, comdr. Naval Surface Force, Atlantic Fleet, Norfolk, Va., 1984; exec. asst. and sr. aide to vice chief Naval Ops., Washington, 1985, dir. Manpower and Tng. divsn., 1986, dir. Surface Warfare divsn., 1987-88; comdr. cruiser destroyer group 8, 1988-89; vice dir. and subsequently dir. operational plans and inter-operability directorate Joint Staff, Washington, 1989-91; dep., chief of staff to comdr. U.S. Pacific Fleet, 1991-93, comdr. naval surface force, 1993-96; ret. USN, 1996. Decorated Navy Cross, Def. D.S.M., D.S.M., Legion of Merit with 4 gold stars, Bronze Star, Purple Heart. Mem. Optimists (pres. Oakton, Va. 1986-87). Methodist. Avocations: golf, bicycling, stamp collecting/philately, reading. Home Phone: 972-763-0760; Office Phone: 703-902-5001, 214-800-2681. Personal E-mail: drobinson022@tx.rr.com. Business E-Mail: drobinson1963@tx.rr.com.

ROBINSON, DAVID M., dentist; m. Tammy Robinson; 2 children. DDS cum laude, Ohio State U.; atteneded, Las Vegas Inst. for Advanced Dental Studies. Gen. dentist Kenwood Cosmetic Dentistry, Cin. Mem.: ADA, Ohio Dental Assn., Cin. Dental Soc., Am. Acad. Cosmetic Dentistry, Western Ohio Acad., Northern Hills Dental Study Club, Phi Kappa Phi, Omicron Kappa Upsilon. Avocations: skiing, tennis, travel. Office: Kenwood Cosmetic Dentistry 7615 Kenwood Rd Cincinnati OH 45236 Office Phone: 513-791-6262. Office Fax: 513-791-0599. E-mail: smiles@kenwoodcosmeticdentistry.com.

ROBINSON, DAVID M., ambassador; b. Hartford, Conn., 1955; m. Donna Lewis; children: David Malcolm, Casey. BA, U. Notre Dame; MA in Theology, Christ the King Sem.; MA, Nat. Def. U. With US Fgn. Svc., 1985—, served in Dominican Republic, El Salvador, Iceland, Bolivia,and Paraguay; fgn. affairs adv. to Senator Joseph Lieberman US Senate, 1996; nat. performance review analyst to V.P. The White House; dep. chief of mission US Embassy, Asuncion, Paraguay, 2000—03, La Paz, Bolivia, 2003—06; US amb. to Guyana US Dept. State, Georgetown, 2006—08, spl. coord. for Venezuela, Bur. We. Hemisphere Affairs, 2008—. Office: US Dept State Bur We Hemisphere Affairs 2201 C St NW Washington DC 20520*

ROBINSON, DAVID ZAV, not-for-profit consultant; b. Montreal, Que., Sept. 29, 1927; s. Benjamin and Antonia (Seiden) R.; m. Nan Senior, Sept. 6, 1954; children: Marc, Eric. AB, Harvard U., 1946, AM, 1947, PhD, 1950. Asst. dir. rsch. Baird-Atomic Inc., Cambridge, Mass., 1949-59, 60-61; sci. liaison officer Office Naval Rsch., London, 1959-60; sci. advisor staff Office of Pres., Washington, 1961-67; v.p. acad. affairs NYU, 1967-70; v.p. Carnegie Corp. NY, NYC, 1970-80, exec. v.p., 1981-85, exec. v.p., treas., 1986-88; exec. dir. Carnegie Commn. on Sci Tech. and Govt., 1988-97; cons., 1997—. Dir. Urban Research Corp., Chgo., 1968-75; cons. Congressional Office of Tech. Assessment, 1975-78; mem. com. women in sci. NRC, 1975-82, chair com. on tchr. testing, 1999-2000; mem. vis. com. dept. chemistry Harvard U., 1977-83; physics dept. Princeton U., 1970-76 Mem. NY Energy Rsch. and Devel. Authority, 1971-77; trustee CUNY, 1976-81, Amideast, 1983-88, Citizens Union Found., 1985-2007, Inst. Schs. of the Future, 1986-, NC Sch. Sci. and Math., 1989-97, Santa Fe Inst., 1987-2008, Prep for Prep, 1989-98, Actors Ctr., 1996—, Inst. Current World Affairs, 2005-08. Mem. AAAS, Optical Soc. Am., Coun. on Fgn. Rels., Am. Contract Bridge League, Fedn. Am. Scientists, Harvard Club (NYC). Office Phone: 212-675-1277. Personal E-mail: dzrobinson@aol.com.

ROBINSON, DAVIS ROWLAND, lawyer, international arbitrator; b. NYC, July 11, 1940; s. Thomas Porter and Cynthia (Davis) R.; m. Suzanne Walker, June 11, 1966; children: Christopher Champlin II, Gracyn Walker. BA magna cum laude, Yale U., 1961; LLB cum laude, Harvard U., 1967. Bar: N.Y. 1968, D.C. 1971, U.S. Supreme Ct. 1972. Fgn. svc. officer U.S. Dept. State, Washington, 1961-69; assoc. Sullivan & Cromwell, NYC, 1969—71; assoc., then ptnr. Leva, Hawes, Symington, Martin and Oppenheimer, Washington, 1971-81; the legal adviser U.S. Dept. State, Washington, 1981-85; ptnr. Pillsbury, Madison & Sutro, Washington, 1985-88, Le Boeuf, Lamb, Greene & MacRae LLP, Washington, 1988—2002, ret., 2002—; sr. mng. dir. Richard C. Breeden & Co., LLC, 2003—08; mem. Brock Capital Group, 2008—. Dir. Mid. East Policy Coun., Washington, 1999—. Pres. Harvard Legal Aid Bur., 1966-67. Mem. Am. Law Inst. (adviser fgn. rels. law of U.S.), Am. Soc. Internat. Law, Internat. Centre for Settlement of Investment Disputes (U.S. panel, 2002-08), Coun. on Fgn. Rels., Phi Beta Kappa. Office Phone: 202-669-3270. Personal E-mail: davisrrobinson@verizon.net.

ROBINSON, DENNIS R., state agency administrator; b. Apr. 21, 1957; BA, Wesleyan U., 1979; MA in Sports Mgmt., U. Mass.; MBA, Harvard U. With U. Houston, NFL; asst. commr. S.W. Athletic Conf.; with NJ Sports & Exposition Authority, 1990—98, pres., CEO, 1998—99, 2007—; sr. v.p. bus. & league ops. NBA, NYC, 1999—2007. Office: NJ Sports & Exposition Authority 50 State Rt 120 East Rutherford NJ 07073

ROBINSON, DEVETTE LORRAINE, music educator; d. Horace Edward and Cassie Jones; m. Claude Robinson, Oct. 10, 1992; 1 child, Clarisa. MusB, MA, Prairie View A&M U., Tex., 1981. All-level music cert. Tex. Edn. Agy. Choir dir., Houston, 1994—96; band and percussion dir., 1996—2000; choir dir., 2000—03; choir dir., aux. dir., 2000—03; choir dir., 2003—04, Sheldon Ind. Sch. Dist., Houston, 2004—. Singer: (jazz ensemble) Salute to Martin Luther King and Mahalia Jackson. Named Tchr. of Yr., Sch. Campus and Adminstrv. Office, 2000—01. Mem.: Tex. Music Educators Assn., Iota Phi Lambda (assoc.), Delta Sigma Theta (assoc.). Democrat. Baptist. Avocations: travel, walking, Karate.

ROBINSON, DONALD LEONARD, social scientist, educator; b. Buffalo, Dec. 28, 1936; s. Sidney Smith and Marion Esther (Hershiser) R.; m. Molly McCaslin Jahnige, Jan. 1, 1983; children: John Samuel, David Wynn; stepchildren: Katherine Jahnige Mathews, Paul Jahnige. BA, Yale U., 1958; MDiv, Union Theol. Sem., 1962; PhD, Cornell U., 1966. Instr. govt. Cornell U., Ithaca, N.Y., 1965-66; asst. prof. Smith Coll., Northampton, Mass., 1966—71, assoc. prof., 1971—78, prof., 1978—2004, Sylvia Dlugasch Bauman chair Am. studies, 1990—93, dir. Am. studies, 1979—85, chmn. dept. govt., 1997—2000, Charles N. Clark prof., 1998—2004. Cons. Ford Found., 1986-88, 91-92, Media and Society, 1986-87, Comm. on Operation of U.S. Senate, 1976; dir. Project '87, 1977-78; vis. prof. Doshisha U., Kyoto, Japan, 1989; vis. fellow polit. sci. Yale U., 1999, St. Antony's Coll., Oxford, 1999. Author: Slavery in the Structure of American Politics, 1765-1820, 1971, To the Best of My Ability: The Presidency and the Constitution, 1987, Government for the Third American Century, 1989; co-author: Partners for Democracy: Crafting the New Japanese State under MacArthur, 2002; mem. editl. bd. Presdl. Studies Quar., 1987—; editor: Reforming American Government: The Bicentennial Papers of the Committee on the Constitutional System, 1985; co-editor: The Constitution of Japan: A Documentary History of Its Framing and Adoption, 1998, The History of Ashfield, Vol. III, 1960-2010. Adminstr. New Eng. Regional Commn., 1973; chmn. Dem. City Com., 1978-80, Northampton Planning Bd., 1980-82; warden St. John's Episcopal Ch., 1981-85, 2003-06; trustee Diocese of Western Mass., 1988—; mem. select bd., Ashfield, Mass., 1992-2001; columnist Daily Hampshire Gazette, 2007-. Rockefeller Bros. fellow, 1958-59; Kent fellow, 1962-66; Project '87 fellow, 1980; fellow Ctr. for Study Democratic Insts., 1971; Phi Beta Kappa vis. scholar, 1988-89; recipient Anisfield-Wolf award, 1971 Mem. Am. Polit. Sci. Assn., Phi Beta Kappa. Home: 38 Norton Hill Rd Ashfield MA 01330-0378 Office: Smith Coll Dept Govt Northampton MA 01063-0001 Home Phone: 413-628-3361. E-mail: drobinso@smith.edu.

ROBINSON, DONALD PETER, musician, retired electrical engineer; b. Phila., Jan. 27, 1928; s. Warren Frederick and Marcella Theresa (Derry) R.; m. Beatrice Graves, Sept. 22, 1951 (dec.); children: Donald, Stephen, Sharon Robinson-Byrd, Michael; m. Mary Katherine Robertson, June 9, 1990. A.A., Temple U. Sch. Tech., 1956. Sr. engr./technician Gen. Electric Co., Utica, N.Y., 1956-89, ret., 1989; organist emeritus St. Joseph-St. Patrick's Ch., Utica, 1983—; minister music/organist St. Paul's Baptist Ch., Utica, 1961-88; organist Utica Council K.C., 1969—; organist/choir dir. 4th degree assembly Central N.Y. dist. K.C., 1985—; producer, host Organ Loft radio program WLFH, Little Falls, N.Y., 1962-90; pipe organ cons. Served with AUS, 1948-54. Mem. Am. Guild Organists (past dean central N.Y. chpt.), Am. Theatre Organ Soc., Nat. Assn. R.R. Passengers (bd. dirs.), K.C. (past faithful navigator 4th degree assembly). Roman Catholic. Home: 715 Garfield Ave Rockford IL 61103-6023

ROBINSON, DOROTHY K., lawyer; b. New Haven, Feb. 18, 1951; children: Julia R., Alexandra T. BA in Econs. with honors, Swarthmore Coll., 1972; JD, U. Calif., Berkeley, 1975; MA (hon.), Yale U., 1987. Bar: Calif. 1975, N.Y. 1976, Conn. 1981, U.S. Ct. Appeals (2d cir.) 1975, U.S. Dist. Ct. (so. dist.) N.Y. 1981. Assoc. Hughes Hubbard & Reed, NYC, 1975-78; asst. gen. counsel Yale U., New Haven, 1978-79, assoc.

gen. counsel, 1979-84, dep. gen. counsel, 1984-86, gen. counsel, 1986—95, dir. fed. rels., 1986-88, acting sec., 1993, v.p., gen. counsel, 1995—. Mem. Calif. Law Rev., 1973-75. Trustee Hopkins Grammar Day Prospect Hill Sch., New Haven, 1983-88, sec., 1986-88; trustee Wenner-Gren Found. Anthrop. Rsch., 1991-2003, Newark Pub. Radio, Inc., 2006-, Tchrs. Ins. and Annuity Assn. (TIAA), 2007—; bd. dirs. Cold Spring Sch., New Haven, 1990-95; mem. adv. bd. Conn. Mental Health Ctr., New Haven, 1979-89; bd. dirs. Nat. Assn. Ind. Coll. and Univs., 1995-98; mem. alumni coun. Swarthmore Coll., 1999-2002. Fellow Ezra Stiles Coll. Yale U., Am. Bar Found.; mem. ABA, Nat. Assn. Coll. and Univ. Attys. (bd. dirs. 1987-90), Conn. Bar Assn., Calif. Bar Assn., Assn. Bar City N.Y., Phi Beta Kappa. Office: Yale U Office of VP and Gen Counsel PO Box 208255 New Haven CT 06520-8255 Office Phone: 203-432-4949.

ROBINSON, E. GLENN, lawyer; b. Charleston, W.Va., Jan. 1, 1924; s. Elmer George and Eva Elena (Rexrode) Robinson; m. Emma Lou Legg, Dec. 23, 1947; children: Richard G., Martha L., William E., Ann K. BSc, Ohio State U., 1948; JD, W.Va. U., 1950. Bar: W.Va. 1950, U.S. Ct. Appeals (4th cir.) 1953, U.S. Ct. Appeals (3d cir.) 1980, U.S. Supreme Ct. 1982. Ptnr. Shannon & Robinson, Charleston, 1950—52, James, Wise, Robinson, & Magnuson, Charleston, 1952—76, Love, Wise, Robinson & Woodroe, Charleston, 1976—83, Robinson & McElwee, Charleston, 1983—91, of counsel, 1991—. With AUS, 1942—45. Fellow: W.Va. Bar Found., Am. Coll. Trial Lawyers, Am. Bar Found.; mem.: Am. Bd. Trial Advocates, Kanawha County Bar Assn. (pres. 1968—69), W.Va. Bar Assn. (pres. 1982—83), W.Va. State Bar (pres. 1972—73), Rotary. Republican. Home: 507 Superior Ave South Charleston WV 25303-2024 Office: 400 Fifth Third Ctr 700 Virginia St E Charleston WV 25301 Home Phone: 304-744-2812; Office Phone: 304-347-8334. E-mail: egr@ramlaw.com.

ROBINSON, EARL, JR., nanotechnologist, marketing, transportation executive, educator, retired air force officer; b. St. George, Bermuda, Nov. 5, 1954; s. Willie Earl and Jeanette (Wilson) Robinson; m. Indera Rodgers, Dec. 11, 1999; children: Aiyana Spring, Jasmine Summer, Earl III. BA in Radio and TV, U. Detroit, 1976; MS in Mgmt., Troy State U., 1986; postgrad., Old Dominion U., 1986—, North Ctrl. U.; MS in Computer Info. Sys., U. Detroit, 1998; PhD in Legal Letters, Nanotech., Sunbelt Paralegal Inst., 1999. Commd. lt. USAF, 1976, advanced through grades to lt. col., 1992, gen. officer aide, adminstrv. staff officer Sembach, Germany, 1982-85, with tactical air command Hampton, Va., 1986-88, mem. faculty Air Command and Staff Coll. Montgomery, Ala., 1989-92, comdr. recruiting squadron Clinton Twp., Mich., 1992-94, ret., 1994; pres. Power-Base USA, 1994—; chief advisor solar energy co., 1994—; exec. dir. Detroit Tranist Authority, 1994-95, 1995—. Maj. prof. Spring Arbor (Mich.) Coll., 1992—; adj. prof. Faulkner U., Montgomery, 1991—; pres., CEO ERJ Corp. Ltd., Hampton, Va., 1986-88; pres. Paddle King Corp., Zaragoza, Spain, 1980-82; cons. Inst. Def. Analysis. Inventor info. resource mgmt. system. Mem. Nat. Tech. Assn. (publicity chmn. 1984-85), Urban Youth Action (case worker 1984-85), Housing Opportunity, Inc., Hampton Host Lions Club, Tuskegee Airmen (past chpt. pres.). Avocations: computers, reading, table-trennis, team sports, fishing, golf. Home: 1035 Roslyn St Mount Clemens MI 48043-2934 Office Phone: 313-492-0845. Personal E-mail: earlpower1@yahoo.com. Business E-Mail: erobinson@powerbaseusa.us.

ROBINSON, EDWARD LEE, retired physics professor, consultant; b. Clanton, Ala., Nov. 6, 1933; s. Alonzo Lee and Ollie Sarah (Mims) R.; m. Shirley Anne Burnett (div. Sept. 1972); children: Edward Lee Jr., James Allan, Paul David; m. Linda G. Moon, 1990. AB with honors, Samford U., 1954; MS, Purdue U., 1958, PhD, 1962. Dir. Cyclotron Lab. Samford U., Birmingham, Ala., 1961-67, asst. prof. physics, chmn. dept., 1961-62, assoc. prof., chmn. dept., 1962-66, prof., chmn. dept., 1966-67; assoc. prof. U. Ala., Birmingham, 1967-77, co-radiation safety officer, 1967-85, dir. Van de Graaff Accelerator Lab., 1970-91, acting chmn. dept., 1973-74, prof. physics, 1977-91, adj. prof. forensic sci., 1983-91, cons. in applied physics and accident reconstrn., 1991—; prin., owner Robinson & Assocs., LLC, 1998—2008; sr. reconstructionist Vista Engring. Accident Reconstrn., Inc., 2008—. Cons. Hayes Internat. Corp., Birmingham, 1963-68, So. Rsch. Inst., Birmingham, 1968-69; rschr. Oak Ridge Nat. Lab., Tenn., 1968, 74-75, 82, U. Md., College Park, 1966, 67; bd. overseers Samford U., 1999—; adv. com. to dean Howard Coll. of Arts and Scis. of Samford U., 2002—. Active Birmingham YMCA; mem. at large nat. coun., chmn. sci. adv. com. for explorer scouting Boy Scouts Am., 1999—2002. Mem. Am. Phys. Soc., Soc. Automotive Engrs., AAAS, Ala. Acad. Sci. (life, v.p. 1964-65), Tex. Assn. Accident Reconstrn. Specialists (bd. dirs. 1999-2003), numerous other nat. and internat. profl. assns. Baptist. Achievements include discovery, co-discovery of six radioisotopes. Home: 233 Oakmont Rd Birmingham AL 35244-3264 Home Phone: 205-408-1692; Office Phone: 205-307-6543.

ROBINSON, ENDERS ANTHONY, geophysicist, educator, writer; b. Boston, Mar. 18, 1930; s. Edward Arthur and Doris Gertrude (Goodale) Robinson; m. Eva Arborelius, Sept. 9, 1962 (div. 1973); children: Anna, Erik Arthur, Karin; m. Joyce McPeake, Aug. 8, 1992. BS in Math., MIT, 1950, MS in Econs., 1952, PhD in Geophysics, 1954. Dir. geophys. analysis group MIT, Cambridge, Mass., 1952-54, instr. math., 1955-56; geophysicist Gulf Oil Corp., Pitts., 1954-55; petroleum economist Standard Oil Co. NJ, NYC, 1956-57; asst. prof. stats. Mich. State U., East Lansing, 1958; asst. prof. math. U. Wis., Madison, 1958-61, assoc. prof. math. (with tenure), 1961-62; dep. prof. stats. Uppsala (Sweden) U., 1960-64; v.p., dir. Digicon Inc., Houston, 1965-70; pres. Robinson Rsch. Inc., Houston, 1970-82; vis. prof. theoretical and applied mechanics Cornell U., Ithaca, NY, 1981-82; McMan prof. geophysics U. Tulsa, 1983-93; Maurice Ewing and J.L. Worzel prof. geophysics Columbia U., NYC, 1993—2000, prof. emeritus, 2000—. Author: (book) Seismic Inversion and Deconvolution, Dual Sensor Technology, 1999, 31 other books on sci., tech. and history; editor: Internat. Jour. Imaging Sys. & Tech., 1988—; mem. editl. bd.: Multidimensional Sys. and Signal Processing, An Internat. Jour., 1990—. 2d lt. US Army, 1950—51. Recipient Medal award in recognition of outstanding contribr. to the digital processing of seismic data, Soc. Exploration Geophysicists, 1969, Conrad Schlumberger award, European Assn. Exploration Geophysicists, 1969, Donald G. Fink Prize award, IEEE, 1984, Achivement award, Thayer Acad. Alumni, 1997, Alexander von Humboldt Rsch. award for sr. U.S. scientists, 1999, Maurice Ewing Gold medal Lifetime Achievement, 2001, Blaise Pascal medal Earth Scis., European Acad. Scis., 2003. Fellow: European Acad. Scis.; mem.: Nat. Rsch. Coun. (com. undiscovered oil and gas resources), Nat. Acad. Engring. (petroleum and mining sect.), Soc. Exploration Geophysicists (hon. Classic Paper award 1953, 1957, Best Paper award 1964, Reginald Fessenden medal 1969, father of deconvolution 1983, Best Paper award 2001, Maurice Ewing Gold medal 2001), European Assn. Geoscientists and Engrs. (Conrad Schlumberger award 1969), Renaissance Inst. Washington, NY Athletic Club, MIT Club NY. Known as the "Father of Digital Geophysics". Office: 8 Dorothy E Lucey dr Newburyport MA 01950-1781 Office Phone: 978-465-2053. E-mail: endersrobinson@comcast.net.

ROBINSON, EUGENE H., journalist, newspaper columnist; b. Orangeburg, SC, 1955; m. Avis Robinson; 2 children. Student, U. Mich. Staff writer San Francisco Chronicle, 1976; city hall reporter Washington Post, 1980—81, asst. city editor, 1981—84, city editor, 1984—87, S.Am. corr. Buenos Aires, 1988—92, London bur. chief, 1992—94, fgn. editor Washington, 1994—99, asst. mng. editor, 1999—2005, assoc. editor, columnist, 2005—. Syndicated columnist Washington Post Writers Group. Author: (books) Coal to Cream: A Black Man's Journey Beyond Color to an Affirmation of Race, 1995, Last Dance in Havana: The Final Days of Fidel and the Start of the New Cuban Revolution, 2004; appearances as polit. analyst (MSNBC) Race for the White House, Countdown with Keith Olbermann, Hardball with Chris Matthews. Recipient Pulitzer prize for Commentary, 2009; Nieman Fellow in Journalism, Harvard U., 1987—88. Mem.: Coun. Fgn. Rels., Nat. Assn. Black Journalists. Mailing: Washington Post Writers Group 1150 15th St NW Washington DC 20071*

ROBINSON, EVELYN ETTA, principal; b. Pocatello, Idaho, Nov. 5, 1946; d. Luther Nelson Robinson and Marian Rose Smith. Tchr. diploma, Bapt. Bible Coll., 1968; BA, U. Ill., Springfield, 1978, MA, 1979; edn. specialist, Idaho State U., Boise, 1988. Cert. elementary tchr., sch. prin., superintendent. 1st grade tchr. Villa Christian Sch., Broadview, Ill., 1968—74, North Jacksonville Elem., Jacksonville, Ill., 1978—79, Bonneville Elem., Pocatello, Idaho, 1979—88; edn. supr. Grace Acad., Springfield, Ill., 1977—78; prin. Westfair Acad., Jacksonville, 1977—84, Lewis & Clark Elem., Pocatello, Idaho, 1988—. Instr. Idaho Sate U. Coll. Edn., Pocatello, 1987—, Dist. 25 Tech. Portfolio, 1997—; curriculum instr. Integration of Tech. into Idaho history, 1999—; in-svc. instr. Dist. 25, Pocatello, 1988—; mentor Dist. 25 Tech. Mentor Program, 1996—; mem. Dist. 25 Curriculum Com., 1996—2000, Leadership for the 21st Century Com., 1997—, Home Page Devel. Com., 1999—, Tchr. Evaluation Com., 2000—01, Sch. Improvement Criteria Com., 2000—01, Enhancement Learning Project Com., 2000—; commr. Idaho State Bd. Edn. Accountability Commn., 2003—; presenter in field. Author: Lewis & Clark School Improvement Profile, 1988—2005. Tchr. children's program Idaho State Mus. Natural History, Pocatello, 1984; mem. Salvation Army Canned Food Drive Com., Pocatello, 1994—, Neighborhood Watch Program, Pocatello, 1994—, Neighborhood Support Group for the Elderly, Pocatello, 1996—, Ross Park Zoological Soc., Pocatello, 2003—; tchr. Sunday Sch. Workshop Nazarene Ch., Pocatello, 1985—; bd. dirs. Pocatello Zoo, 2003—. Recipient Outstanding Svc. award, Messiah Baptist Ch., 1972, Outstanding Leadership award, Am. Assn. Sunday Schools, 1977, Sunday Sch. Leadership award, Westfair Baptist Ch., 1979, Dedication to Youth award, Ctr. for Leadership, Edn., and Devel., 1989, 8 Who Make a Difference award, Idaho Channel 8, Pocatello, 1997, Woman of Achievement award, ZONTA Internat., 2005, Excellence in Edn. award, Northwest Regional, 2006, Idaho's Excellence in Edn. award, Alpha Delta Kappa, 2006, Internat. Excellence Edn. award, 2007; named Tchr. of Yr., Bonneville Elem. Parent-Tchr. Assn., 1982—83, Bonneville Elem., 1988—89, Idaho Nat. Disting. Prin., 2005; nominee Idaho Tchr. of Yr., 1982—83, Outstanding Adminstr., Pocatello Edn. Assn., 1994. Mem.: ASCD, SE Idaho Reading Assn. (bldg. rep. 1983—88, chair newspsaper in edn. week 1984—88), Internat. Reading Assn. (chair newspaper in edn. 1986—87, chair Idaho Honors coun. 1987—88), Assn. Elem. Sch. Prins. (v.p. 1989—90, pres. 1990—91, dist. 25, region V), Idaho Assn. Sch. Adminstrs., Idaho Assn. Elem. Sch. Prins. (Idaho Gem award 1990—91, Idaho's Nat. Disting. Prin. award 2005), Nat. Assn. Elem. Sch. Prins., Internat. and Portneuf Valley Audubon Assn., Phi Delta Kappa (chair program com. 1987—88, v.p. program com. 1988—89, v.p. membership 1989—90, pres. 1990—91), Alpha Delta Kappa (sgt. at arms 1982—84, chair altruistic com. 1986—88, chair courtesy com. 1990—92, historian 1992—94, Idahos Excellence in Edn. award 2006). Avocations: gardening, hunting, fishing, birdwatching, hiking. Office: Lewis & Clark Elem 800 Grace Dr Pocatello ID 83201 Business E-Mail: robinsev@d25.k12.id.us.

ROBINSON, FLORINE SAMANTHA, marketing executive; b. Massies Mill, Va., Feb. 4, 1935; d. John Daniel and Fannie Belle (Smith) Jackson; m. Frederick Robinson (div. 1973); children: Katherine, Theresa, Freda. BS, Morgan State U., 1976; postgrad., U. Balt., 1977-81, Liberty U., 1987. Writer, reporter Phila. Independent News, 1961-63; freelance writer, editor Balt., 1963-71; asst. mng. editor Williams & Wilkins Pubs. Inc., Balt, 1971-76; mktg. rep., then mktg. mgr. NCR Corp., Balt., 1977-93; assoc. minister, trustee Christian Unity Temple, Balt., 1976—; pres. ABCOM, Inc., Balt., 1993—. Bd. dirs. Armstrong & Bratcher, Inc., Balt. Editor: Stedman's Medical Dictionary, 1972; contbr. articles to profl. jours. Active PTA, Balt., 1963-65; bd. dirs. Howard Pk. Civic Assn., Balt., 1967—, pres. 1991—; leader, cons. Girl Scouts USA, 1970-73. Recipient Excellence in Rsch. award Psi Chi, 1976, Citizen citation Mayor of Balt. Mem. NAFE, Mid-Atlantic Food Dealers Assn., Am. Soc. Notaries, Internat. Platform Assn., Edelweiss Club, Order of Eastern Star. Democrat. Avocation: piano. Home: 3126 Howard Park Ave Baltimore MD 21207-6715

ROBINSON, FRANK, former professional baseball manager, retired professional baseball player; b. Beaumont, Tex., Aug. 31, 1935; s. Frank and Ruth (Shaw) R.; m. Barbara Ann Cole, Oct. 28, 1961; children: Frank Kevin, Nichelle. Student, Xavier U., Cin. Outfielder Cin. Reds, 1956-65, Balt. Orioles, 1966-71, LA Dodgers, 1972, Calif. Angels, 1973-74, Cleve. Indians, 1974-76, mgr., 1975-77; coach Calif. Angels, 1977, Balt. Orioles, 1978-80, 85-87, mgr., 1988-91, asst. to gen. mgr., 1991-95; mgr. San Francisco Giants, 1981-84; batting coach Milw. Brewers, 1984; dir. baseball ops. Arizona Fall League Major League Baseball, 1997—99, v.p. on-field operations, 1999—2002, spl. asst. to v.p. baseball ops., comm. office, 2006—; mgr. Wash. Nationals (formerly Montreal Expos), 2002—06. Author: (with Al Silverman) My Life is Baseball, 1967, (with Barry Steinbach) Extra Innings, 1989, Frank the First Year, 1976. Named Rookie of Yr., Nat. League, 1956, Most Valuable Player, 1961, Am. League, 1966, Am. League Mgr. of Yr., 1982, 89; mem. World Series Championship Team, 1966, 70, Nat. League All-Star Team, 1956-57, 59, 61-62, 65, Am. League All-Star Team, 1966-67, 69-71, 74; inducted into Baseball Hall of Fame, 1982; recipient Presdl. Medal of Freedom, The White House, 2005, Beacon of Life award Maj. League Baseball, 2008.

ROBINSON, FRANKLIN WESTCOTT, museum director, art historian; b. Providence, May 21, 1939; s. Charles Alexander Robinson Jr. and Celia (Sachs) Stillwell; m. Margaret Dredge, Aug. 14, 1967; 1 child, John Alexander. BA, Harvard U., 1961, MA, 1964, PhD, 1970. Instr. Wellesley Coll., 1968-69; asst. prof. Dartmouth Coll., 1969-75; assoc. prof. Williams Coll., 1975-79; dir. Williams Coll. Mus., 1976-79, Mus. of Art, R.I. Sch. Design, Providence, 1979-92, Herbert F. Johnson Mus. Art, Cornell U., Ithaca, N.Y., 1992—. Author: Gabriel Metsu, 1975, Seventeenth Century Dutch Drawings from American Collections, 1977, Dutch and Flemish Paintings from the Ringling Mus, 1980. Fulbright fellow, 1961-62; recipient Claiborne Pell award R.I. State Coun. Arts, 1992. Mem. Assn. Art Mus. Dirs., Coll. Art Assn. Clubs: Century, Hope. Office: Herbert F Johnson Mus Art Cornell University Ithaca NY 14853-4001 Office Phone: 607-255-6464. Office Fax: 607-255-9940. Business E-Mail: fwr1@cornell.edu.

ROBINSON, FRED COLSON, language educator; b. Birmingham, Ala., Sept. 23, 1930; s. Emmett Colson and Morwenna Hope (Bennett) R.; m. Helen Caroline Wild, June 21, 1959; children: Lisa Karen, Eric Wild. BA, Birmingham So. Coll., 1953; MA, U. N.C., 1954, PhD, 1961; DLitt (hon.), Williams Coll., 1985; MA (hon.), Yale U., 1989. Instr. Stanford (Calif.) U., 1960-61, asst. prof., 1961-65, assoc. prof., 1967-71, prof. English philology, 1971-72; asst. prof. Cornell U., Ithaca, NY, 1965-66, assoc. prof., 1966-67; prof. Yale U., New Haven, 1972-83, Douglas Tracy Smith prof., 1983—2000, prof. emeritus, 2000—, chmn. medieval studies, 1975-78, 80. Vis. prof. Harvard U., Cambridge, Mass., 1983; pub. com. Medieval Acad. Monographs, Cambridge, 1987-90. Author: Old English Literature: Select Bibliography, 1970, Beowulf and the Appositive Style, 1985, The Tomb of Beowulf, 1993, The Editing of Old English, 1994; co-author: A Bibliography...on Old English Literature, 1980, Old English Verse Texts from Many Sources: A Comprehensive Collection, 1991, A Guide to Old English, 7th edit., 2007, Beowulf: An Edition with Relevant Shorter Texts, 1998, rev. edit., 2006; English in Print: From Caxton to Shakespeare to Milton, 2008, editor Old English Newsletter, 1966-73, Early English MSS in Facsimile, 1971-2002, Jour. English Linguistics, 1971—, Anglo-Saxon England, 1972-2008, Anglistica, 1981—; contbr. over 100 articles to profl. jours. Trustee Yale Univ. Libr. Assocs., New Haven, 1986-89, 91-95, 97-2000, 03-06. With U.S. Army, 1954-56. Recipient Disting. Vis. Scholar award U. Ala., 1999, William Clyde DeVane medal, 1999; fellow Guggenheim Found., 1974-75, Am. Coun. Learned Socs., 1968-69, Inst. Social and Econ. Rsch., Rhodes U., 1978, Japan Soc. Promotion of Sci., 1989; grantee NEH, 1976, 79, 81, 85, Am. Philos. Soc., 1973, 85; named Professore solo per ricerca Univ. di Roma "La Sapienza", 2000. Fellow AAAS, Medieval Acad. Am. (pres. 1983-84, Haskins medal 1984), Brit. Acad. (corr., Sir Israel Gollancz prize 1997), Meddeleeue-verenigung van Suidelike Afrika (corr.); mem. Finnish Acad. of Sci. and Letters (fgn. mem.), New Eng. Medieval Conf. (pres. 1982-83), Conn. Acad. Arts and Scis. (pres. 1980-85), Internat. Soc. Anglo-Saxonists (elected hon.), Elizabethan Club (bd. govs. 1986-88, v.p. 1989-90, pres. 1990-92), Manuscript Club (v.p. New Haven chpt. 1990-92), Phi Beta Kappa. Episcopalian. Office: Yale Univ Dept English New Haven CT 06520 Business E-Mail: fred.robinson@yale.edu.

ROBINSON, GAIL PATRICIA, retired mental health counselor; b. Medford, Oreg., Dec. 31, 1936; d. Ivan T. and Evelyn H. (Hamilton) Skyrman; m. Douglas L. Smith; children: Shauna J., James D. BS in Edn., Oreg. State U., 1958, PhD in Counseling, 1978; MS in Counseling, Western Oreg. State Coll., 1974. Tchr. Monterey (Calif.) Pub. Schs., 1958-59, Corvallis (Oreg.) Pub. Schs., 1959-62, 69-75, counselor, 1977-81; pvt. practice Corvallis, 1977-95. Vol. therapist Children's Svcs. divsn., Linn and Benton Counties, 1982-83; asst. prof. Western Oreg. State coll., 1977, counselor, 1982-83; mem. grad. faculty Oreg. State U., Corvallis, 1978-95; presenter workshops, lectr. in field. Contbr. articles to profl. jours. Mem. Benton County Mental Health Citizens Adv. Bd., 1979-85, chair, 1982-83; trustee WCTU Children's Farm Home, 1978-84, chair child welfare com., 1982-83, pres., 1984; adv. bd. Old Mill Sch., 1979-85, chair, 1979-81; bd. dirs. Cmty. Outreach, 1979-83; mem. Benton Com. for Prevention of Child Abuse, 1979-85, v.p., 1982; mem. Oreg. Bd. Lic. Profl. Counselors and Therapists, 1989-95, chair, 1989-90, Aurora Colony Historical Soc., vol., 2000-, bd. dirs., 2005-, sec., 2006—08, pres. 2008-. Mem. ACA (govt. rels. com. 1988-91, professionalization com. 1988-92, pres. 1996-97), Am. Mental Health Counselors Assn. (chair consumer and pub. rels. com. 1988-91, bd. dirs. Western region 1989-91, chair strategic planning com. 1994-95, pres. 1992-93), Oreg. Counseling Assn. (chair licensure liaison com. 1985-91, exec. bd. 1985-88, steering com. 1986-87, register editorial com. 1985-86, Disting. Svc. award 1985, 87, Leona Tyler award 1989), Oreg. Mental Health Counselors Assn. Personal E-mail: robinsgp@comcast.net.

ROBINSON, GEOFFREY LAURENCE, lawyer; s. Russell Joseph and Marjorie Reed Robinson; m. Verna Alane Haas, June 29, 1985; children: Samantha Elizabeth, Kayla Michelle, Lauren Emily. Attended, Diablo Valley Coll., Pleasant Hill, Calif., 1975; BA in History, U. Calif., Berkeley, 1978; BA, U. Va. Law Sch., Charlottesville, 1980; JD cum laude, U. Calif., Hastings, San Francisco, 1983. Bar: Calif. 1983, cert.: US Dist. Ct. (ea. dist.), Sacramento 1983, bar: US Ct. Appeals (9th Cir.), San Francisco 1999, US Supreme Ct., DC 1995. Law clk. to Hon. Thomas McBride US Dist. Ct., Sacramento, 1983—84; extern to Hon. Joseph Sneed US Ct. Appeals, San Francisco, 1984; assoc. Bronson, Bronson & McKinnon, San Francisco, 1984—86, McCutchen, Doyle, Brown & Enersen, Walnut Creek, Calif., 1986—91, ptnr., 1991—2003, Bingham McCutchen, Walnut Creek, 2003—. Judge pro tem Contra Costa Superior Ct., Martinez, Calif., 1987—92; chair lang. access com. Calif. Commn. on Access to Justice, San Francisco, 2002—, co-chair, 2003—05; bd. mem. Calif. State Bar Found., 2002—06. Dir. Contra Costa Sr. Legal Svcs., Richmond, Calif., 1992—2007, pres., 2001—04; mem. Calif. State Bar Found., San Francisco, 2002—06. Recipient Pres. Pro Bono award, State Bar Calif., 1996, John J. Curtin Pub. Svc. award, Bingham McCuthan, 2006; named No. Calif. Super Lawyer, Law & Politics Mag., 2004—07; named to Best Lawyers in Am., Woodward Whyte, 2007—08. Mem.: ABA, Calif. Assn. Realtors.

ROBINSON, GLENIECE ARMSTRONG, library director; m. Harry Robinson. BS, Ala. State U., 1973; MLS, U. Mich., 1976, PhD in Libr. Sci., 1982. With Libr. Congress, Washington, Dallas Pub. Libr., 1988, asst. dir. pub. svcs.; dir. Ft. Worth Pub. Libr., 1999—. Mem. Tex. Hist. Records Adv. Bd. Ex officio mem. bd. dirs. Ft. Worth Pub. Libr. Found. Recipient Women of Spirit award, Am. Jewish Congress SW Region's Commn. Women's Equality, 1999. Mem.: Tex. Libr. Assn. (mem. exec. bd. 1997, pres.-elect 1998). Office: Ft Worth Pub Libr Adminstrv Offices 500 W 3rd St Fort Worth TX 76102 Office Phone: 817-871-7706. E-mail: gleniece.robinson@fortworthgov.org.

ROBINSON, GWENDOLYN NIEMA, elementary school educator; d. John Henry and Beatrice Robinson; children: Wadiya K., Zakia N., Niemah G. BA, Coll. New Rochelle, NY, 1985; MA, CUNY, 2000; MS, Touro Coll., NYC, 2006. Tchr. Gates Acad., Bronx, 1988—89, Cmty. Elem. Sch. 114X, 1989—90, Macombs Hr. HS 82X, 1990—95, CES 64X, 1995—99, Sisulu Children's Acad., NYC, 1999—2000, Mosholu Montefiore Daycare, Bronx, 2000—01, CES 124X, 2001—. Tchr., co-chair Sch. Leadership Team, Bronx, 2005—; advisor Bronx Arts Ensemble, 2005—06. Mem.: NAACP, Alumni Assn. City Colls. Baptist. Office: Bd Edn 175 W 166th St Bronx NY 10452

ROBINSON, HAROLD GILBERT, retired military officer, civilian military employee; b. NYC, Jan. 21, 1935; s. Mark Joseph and Millie Nmi Robinson; m. Renee Joy Robinson, Mar. 5, 1990; children: Ricky Lee, Gay Lee, John Lee, Robin Kiyoshi, Soontorn Nmi Leoni-Robinson, Marc Allan, Jasmine Sangwan. AA, Leeward CC, Pearl City, Hawaii, 1978; BS summa cum laude, Chaminade U., Honolulu, 1980; MA with honors, Ctrl. Mich. U., 1981; PhD, U. Libre de Terapias Psicobionergeticas, Salvador-Bahia, Brazil, 2006; PhD (hon.), U. Manila, 2004, U. Martial Arts, Arak, Iran, 2004, Internat. U. Martial Arts and Scis., 2006, Internat. Council Higher Martial Arts Sci Edn., Frankfurt,Germany, 2009. Spl. ops. escape and evasion instr. Dept. of USAF, Randolph AFB,

Tex., 1952—76, gen.'s aide for BGEN C.T. Edwinson Bergstrom AFB, Tex., 1962—67, presdl. support: L.B. Johnson Austin, Tex., 1964—67, ret. res., 1976—86; dir., pers. and cmty. activities Dept. of Army, Republic of Korea, 1989—96, chief cmty. recreation divsn. Bamberg, Germany, 1998—2000; dir. cmty. activities Def. Fgn. Lang. Ctr., Monterey, Calif., 1996—98; chief cmty. recreation and bus. ops. HQ 98th Area Support Group, Wuerzburg, Germany, 2000—03; SE Asia exec. liaison McCoskrie/Threshhold Found., Bangkok, 2002—; sr. exec. officer Armed Services Judo, Naval Air Station Pensacola, Fla., 2005—. US rep. degree rev. and adjudication U. of Therapeutic Psychodynamics, Salvador-Bahia, Brazil, 2004—. Entertainer WOR Radio, NYC. Master sgt. USAF, 1952—76. Decorated Dept. of USAF, Royal Thai Air Force, Govts. Vietnam and South Korea; recipient Platinum Life award, World Organizer of Martial Arts Assns., 2005, Hall of Fame award, Internat. Kempo Assn., 2006, Martial Arts Hall of Honors and Spirit award, Action Martial Arts Mag., 2007, Hall of Fame and Hall of Honor award, Am. Fedn. Martial Arts Assns., 2007, US Presdl. award, 1989; named to Hall of Fame, Elite Grandmaster of Honor, Internat. Hall of Honor/Hall of Champions Assn., 2006, 10th Internat. Black Belt Martial Arts Hall of Fame, World Martial Arts League, 2007, Hall of Fame, Shihan of Yr. award judo, US Universal Martial Arts Hall of Fame, 2002, Hall of Fame, Platinum Pioneer Over 50 Years Tchg., Sang Kim Celebrity Hall of Fame, 2005, Hall of Fame, Am. Pioneer award, Legends of Champion Martial Arts Assn., 2005, Hall of Fame, Elite Man of Honor Close Quarter Combat, US Head of Family Martial Arts Assn., 2005, Hall of Fame, Brasilian Traditional, US and World Kick Boxing Fedn., 2007. Master: US Martial Arts Assn. (internat. armed services dir. devel. 2001, brotherhood martial arts, Golden Life award 2000, Most Disting. Master 2001, Disting. Humanitarian of Yr. 2003, Hall of Fame, Founder's Lifetime Achievement award 2006, Four Diamond Lifetime Achievement award), US Judo Assn. (master judo rank examiner and certifier 1996—, benefactor), US Ju-jitsu Fedn. (former nat. program dir. US traditional Kodokan judo 2005); mem.: World Martial Art Leage, Internat. Kempo Fedn. (grandmaster Kokusai Kempo Tokukai 2003—), SE Asia Martial Arts Internat. Fedn. (commr. 2005—), Martial Arts Internat. Fedn. (founding bd. dirs. 2005—), US Martial Arts Fedn. (charter gold life founder, bd. dirs. 2005—). Republican. Buddhist. Avocations: physical fitness training, Kodokan judo training, fishing, travel. Home: 569 Batten Blvd Pensacola FL 32507 Office Fax: 850-492-6382; Home Fax: 850-492-6382. Personal E-mail: robin0305@aol.com.

ROBINSON, HERBERT HENRY, III, psychotherapist, educator; b. Leavenworth, Wash., Mar. 31, 1933; s. Herbert Henry II and Alberta (Sperber) R.; m. Georgia Murial Jones, Nov. 24, 1954 (div. 1974); children: Cheri Dean Asbury, David Keith, Peri Elizabeth Layton, Tanda Rene Graff, Gaila Daire. Grad. of Theology, Bapt. Bible Coll., 1959; BA in Philosophy/Greek, Whitworth Coll., 1968; MA in Coll. Teaching, Ea. Wash. U., 1976; PhD, Gonzaga U., 2002. Cert. psychotherapist, perpetrator treatment program supervision; nat. bd. cert. counselor. Choir dir. Twin City Bapt. Temple, Mishawaka, Ind., 1959-61; min. Inland Empire Bapt. Ch., Spokane, Wash., 1961-73; tchr. philosophy Spokane C.C., 1969-72; dir. Alternatives to Violence, Women in Crisis, Fairbanks, Alaska, 1985-87; tchr. pub. rels. U. Alaska, Fairbanks, 1986-87; dir. Alternatives to Violence Men Inc., Juneau, 1988-89; tchr. leadership mgmt. U. Alaska S.E., Juneau, 1988-89; min. Sci. of Mind Ctr., Sandpoint, Idaho, 1989-92; dir., therapist Tapio Counseling Ctr., Spokane, 1991—; cert. psychotherapist, supr. perpetrator treatment program Wash. Cons. Lilac Blind/Alpha Inc./Marshall Coll., Spokane, 1975-85, Alaska Placer Mining Co., Fairbanks, 1987; tchr. Spokane Falls C.C., Spokane, 1979-85; seminar, presenter Human Resource Devel., Spokane and Seattle, Wash., Pa., 1980; guest trainer United Way/Kellogg Found. Inst. for Volunteerism, Spokane, 1983. 1st trombone San Diego Marine Band, 1953-56, Spokane Symphony, 1961; bd. dirs. Tanani Learning Ctr., Fairbanks, 1987; mem. consensus bldg. team Sci. of Mind Ctr., Sandpoint, 1989-92. Cpl. USMC, 1953-56. Mem. ACA, Assn. for Humanistic Edn. and Devel., Assn. for Religious Values in Counseling, Internat. Assn. Addictions and Offender Counselors, Internat. Assn. Marriage and Family Counselors, Am. Assn. Profl. Hypnotherapists, Masterson Inst. Office: Tapio Counseling 5325 E Sprague Ave Spokane WA 99212-0820 Home Phone: 509-927-9825; Office Phone: 509-534-5028. E-mail: peace@herb-robinson.com.

ROBINSON, HOBART KRUM, management consulting company executive; b. Quincy, Mass., Oct. 8, 1937; s. Hobart Krum and Charlotte Elizabeth (Hall) R.; m. Gerd Ingela Janhede, Oct. 17, 1964; children: Steven Whitney, Karina Jill, Peter Danforth. BA, Williams Coll., 1959; MBA, Columbia U., 1964. Market analyst Mobil Chem. Co., Richmond, Va., 1964-67; mgr. program analysis and control Polaroid Corp., Cambridge, Mass., 1967-69; exec. v.p., dir. Simplex Wire and Cable, Inc., North Berwick, Maine, 1969-73; sr. engagement mgr. McKinsey and Co., Inc., NYC, 1973-76, prin. Copenhagen, 1977-81, NYC, 1985-89, Stockholm, 1989-95, dir. adminstrn. Eastern Europe, 1993-95, dir. adminstrn. NYC, 1995-98; pres., CEO Brink's Inc., Darien, Conn., 1981-84; ret., 1998. Dir. Burlington No. Air Freight, Inc., Newport Beach, Calif., 1982-84; partner Pursuit Consulting Group, 2008- Pres. Am. Club in Copenhagen, 1980-81; dir. Fulbright Commn., Copenhagen, 1980-81; vice chair Williams Coll. Alumni Fund, 1999—2004. Lt. USNR, 1959-62. Mem. Tournament Players Club (Ponte Vedra, Fla.), Taconic Golf Club (Williamstown, Mass.), Sawgrass Country Club (Ponte Vedra). Republican. Episcopalian. Home (Summer): 94 Ide Rd Williamstown MA 01267-2815 Personal E-mail: hkrobinson59@gmail.com.

ROBINSON, HOWARD ARTHUR, JR., minister; s. Howard Arthur Sr. and Mary Hairston Robinson; children: Dionne Carol, Angela Marie, Howard Arthur III. MDiv, Morehouse Sch. of Religion / Interdenominational Theol. Ctr., 1976. Cert. advanced marriage and family therapy Puget Sound Counseling Ctr., 1979, consecrated as Bishop Full Gospel Bapt. Ch. Fellowship Internat., 2000. Pres. Berean Kingdom Ctr., Renton, Wash., 1995—2002; adj. prof. N.W. Coll. Assemblies God, Kirkland, 1999—2001; provost Sunday sch. curriculum Full Gospel Bapt. Ch. Fellowship, Seattle, 1999—2003, aux. bishop New Orleans, 2000—03, bishop for Wash. and Oreg. states Seattle, 2000—03; pres. Berean Acad. Christian Devel., Renton, 1995—; presiding bishop and chief apostle Agape Christian Fellowship Internat., Seattle, 2002—; pres. Howard A. Robinson, Jr. Ministries, Kent, Wash., 2002—. Pres. Black United Clergy for Action Pacific N.W., Seattle, 1995—2000; moderator Macedonia Dist. Bapt. Assn.; pres. pastors conf. Nat. Bapt. Conv. Am., Inc., v.p. congress of christian workers, Shreveport, La., 1998—99; sec. Gen. Bapt. Conv. N.W., Portland, Oreg. Author: Changing the 21st Century Ch., 2003. Adv. bd. mem. Wells Fargo Bank, Seattle, 1995—96, First Interstate Bank, Seattle. Maj. USAFR, 1967—90. Decorated Am. Spirit Honor Medal U. S. Army, Trainee of the Cycle; M. L. King scholar, Coun. Chs. Seattle Wash., 1974—76. Avocations: swimming, travel, photography.

ROBINSON, HUGH GRANVILLE, consulting management company executive; b. Washington, Aug. 4, 1932; s. James Hill and Wilhelmina (Thomas) R.; 1 stepchild, Mia; children by previous marriage: Hugh Granville, Susan K. Student, Williams Coll., 1949-50; BS, U.S. Mil. Acad., 1954; MS, MIT, 1959; LLD, Williams Coll., 1983. Commd. 2d lt. U.S. Army, 1954, advanced through grades to maj. gen., 1983; platoon leader, co. comdr. Co. B, 185th Engrs. Bn., Korea, 1955; platoon leader, ops. officer 74th Engr. Co., Korea, 1955-56; br. chief Engr. Supply Control Office, St. Louis, 1956-58; chief Catalog and Authorization div. Engr. Supply Control Agy., Orleans, France, 1960-62; co. comdr. 553d Engr. Bn., Orleans, 1962-63; chief combat br. War Plans divsn. Engr. Strategic Studies Group, Washington, 1963-65; Army asst. to armed forces aide to Pres. Washington, 1965-69; comdr. 39th Engr. Bn., Vietnam, 1969-70; br. chief war plans divsn. Office Dep. Chief Staff for Ops., Washington, 1970-71; assigned Nat. War Coll., 1972; comdr. 3rd regt. U.S. Corps Cadets, West Point, NY, 1973-74, U.S. Army Engr. Sch. Brigade, Fort Belvoir, Va., 1974-76; dist. engr. U.S. Army Engr. Dist., LA, 1976-78; dep. dir. civil works office Chief of Engrs., Washington, 1978-80; comdr. Southwestern Divsn., U.S. Army C.E., 1980-83; ret., 1983; v.p. Southland Corp., Dallas, 1983-88; pres. Cityplace Devel. Corp.; sr. v.p. Grigsby Brandford Powell, Inc., 1988-94; chmn., CEO The Tetra Group, Inc., Dallas, 1989—2002; chmn. Granville Cons. and Devel. Co., Inc., 2001—03, Global Bldg. Sys., Dallas, 2004—05. Mem. Mississippi River Commn., 1980-83, bd. engrs. for rivers and harbors, 1980-83, Coastal Engring. Rsch. Bd., 1980-83; bd. dirs. Carmax, Inc., Guaranty Bank, Aleris Internat., New Market Tech.; chmn. Dallas Fed. Res. Bd., 1991; adv. bd. TXU, 2007; with Tex. Pub. Broadcasting, LBJ Found., 1989—. Mem. nat. bd. dirs. Keep Am. Beautiful, 1981-85; bd. dirs. Dallas Symphony, 1981-85, Dallas United Way, 1984-92, Baylor U. Med. Ctr. Found., 1983-91, Dallas Opera, 1983-90, Dallas Citizens Coun., 1987-91, Greater Dallas C. of C., 1986-91, Vietnam Vets Meml. Fund Tex.; chmn. African Am. Mus., Dallas Youth Svcs. Corp.; trustee Dallas Mus. Fine Arts, 1988-93; mem. adv. coun. U. Tex. Engring. Fedn., 1991—. Mem. Am. Soc. Mil. Engrs. (past sec. Orleans chpt., regional v.p. Tex., pres. Dallas chpt.), Assn. U.S. Army, Dallas Black C. of C., ASCE Methodist. Home Phone: 972-223-5873. Personal E-mail: general2star@aol.com.

ROBINSON, IRWIN JAY, lawyer; b. Bay City, Mich., Oct. 8, 1928; s. Robert R. and Anne (Kaplan) R.; m. Janet Binder, July 7, 1957; children: Elizabeth Binder Schubiner, Jonathan Meyer, Eve Kimberly Wiener. AB, U. Mich., 1950; JD, Columbia U., 1953. Bar: N.Y. 1956. Assoc. Breed Abbott & Morgan, NYC, 1955-58; asst. to ptnrs. Dreyfus & Co., NYC, 1958-59; assoc. Greenbaum Wolff & Ernst, NYC, 1959-65, ptnr., 1966-76; sr. ptnr. Rosenman & Colin, NYC, 1976-90; of counsel Pryor, Cashman, Sherman & Flynn, 1990-92; sr. ptnr. Phillips, Nizer, Benjamin, Krim & Ballon, NYC, 1992-99; pvt. practice NYC, 1999—. Asst. treas. Saarsteel, Inc., Whitestone, N.Y., 1970—. Bd. dirs. Henry St. Settlement, N.Y.C., 1960-85, Jewish Cmty. Ctr. Assn. N.Am., N.Y.C., 1967-94, mem. adv. bd., 1998—; bd. dirs. Heart Rsch. Found., 1989-94, pres., 1991-93. Mem. ABA, Assn. Bar City of NY, Thai-Am. C. of C. (founder, bd. dirs. 1992-95, pres. 1992-95), Vietnam-Am. C. of C. (founder, bd. dirs. 1992-95, pres. 1992-95), Philippine-Am. C. of C. (bd. dirs. 1960-98), Sunningdale Country Club (Scarsdale, NY), Desert Mountain Club (Scottsdale, Ariz.). Jewish. Home: 365 West End Ave New York NY 10024 Personal E-mail: ijrjbr@aol.com.

ROBINSON, J. PATRICK, consumer products company executive; B, Wharton Sch. Univ. Pa.; MBA, Loyola Univ. CPA. Acct. KPMG, Balt.; fin. mgmt. positions through v.p. fin. Black & Decker, 1982—2000; CFO AirClic Inc.; v.p., contr. Newell Rubbermaid Inc., Atlanta, 2001—03, exec. v.p., CFO, 2003—. Office: Newell Rubbermaid 10B Glenlake Pky Atlanta GA 30328

ROBINSON, JACK ALBERT, retail executive; b. Detroit, Feb. 26, 1930; s. Julius and Fannie (Aizkowitz) Robinson; m. Aviva Freedman, Dec. 21, 1952; children: Shelby, Beth, Abigail. B in Pharmacy, Wayne State U., 1952. Founder, chief exec. officer, chmn. bd. Perry Drug Stores, Inc., Pontiac, Mich., 1957-95; founder, chmn., pres. JAR Group LLC, Bloomfield Hills, Mich., 1996—. Chmn. Wayne State U. Fund, Detroit, 1986, Concerned Citizens for Arts Mich., 1990, 1991—; chmn. ann. fund Detroit Symphony Orch.; bd. dirs. United Way Pontiac, Mich., 1986, United Found. Detroit, 1986, Pontiac Area Urban League, Cmty. Found., S.E. Mich., Detroit Svc. Group, Save Orch. Hall, Inc., Cranbrook Inst. Sci., Jewish Fedn. Apts., Wetzman Inst. Sci., Holocaust Meml. Ctr., Harper-Grace Hosp., Detroit; past dir. Pontiac Symphony, Boys Club, Detroit Osteo. Hosp.; pres. United Jewish Found. Met. Detroit, 1992—94; co-chmn. Greater Detroit Interfaith Round Table NCCJ, 1986—92, v.p., 1994—95; pres. Jewish Fedn. Met. Detroit, 1992—94. Recipient Disting. Alumni award, Wayne State U. Coll. Pharmacy, 1975, Eleanor Roosevelt Humanities award, State of Israel, 1978, Youth Svcs. Am. Tradition award, B'nai B'rith, 1982, Gt. Am. Traditions award, 1991, Disting. Alumni award, Wayne State U., 1985, Corp. Leadership award, 1985, Tree of Life award, Jewish Nat. Fund, 1985, Disting. Citizen award, Pontiac Boy Scouts Am., 1985, Brotherhood award, Booker T. Washington Bus. Assn., 1986, Humanitarian award, March of Dimes, 1987, Variety Club, 1988, award, Weizmann Rsch. Inst., 1987, Fred M. Butzel award, Jewish Fedn. Met. Detroit, 1991, Cmty. Svc. award, Am. Arabic and Jewish Friends, 1995, Outstanding Philanthropic award, Nat. Soc. Fundraising Execs., 1999, Mich. Hall of Fame award in Real Estate and Retailing, Internat. Coun. Shopping Ctrs., 2001, Gov.'s Arts award Spl. Recognition, 2003; named Entrepreneur of the Yr., Harvard Bus. Sch., Detroit, 1982; named to Heritage Hall of Fame Inductee, Internat. Inst. Found., 2007. Mem.: Econ. Club (bd. dirs. Detroit chpt.), Am. Found. for Pharm. Edn. (bd. dirs.), Am. Pharm. Assn., Nat. Assn. Chain Drug Stores (chmn. 1987, Lifetime Achievement award 1995, Robert B. Begley award 1995). Avocations: skiing, jogging, photography, classical music, glass collecting. Office: JAR Group LLC Ste 3100 4190 Telegraph Rd Bloomfield Hills MI 48302-2082

ROBINSON, JAMES ARTHUR, political scientist; b. Blackwell, Okla., June 9, 1932; s. William L. and Ethel Bell (Hicks) R.; children: Adelaide, Luke; m. Andrea C. Hatcher, Jan. 20, 2006 AB, George Washington U., 1954, DPS (hon.), 1977; MA, U. Okla., 1955; PhD, Northwestern U., 1957. Congl. fellow Am. Polit. Sci. Assn., 1957-58; Instr. polit. sci. Northwestern U., 1958-59, asst. prof., 1959-62, assoc. prof., 1962-64; prof. polit. sci. Ohio State U., Columbus, 1964-71; dir. Mershon Center, 1967-70, v.p. acad. affairs, provost, 1969-71; pres., prof. polit. sci. Macalester Coll., St. Paul, 1971-74; pres. U. West Fla., Pensacola, 1974-88, pres. emeritus, 1988—, Regents prof., 1988—2002. Author: (with R. C. Snyder) National and International Decision Making, 1961, Congress and Foreign Policy Making, rev. edit, 1967, House Rules Committee, 1963, (with J. Baum) Party Primaries in Taiwan, 1999, (with D. Brown and E. Moon) Appraising Steps in Democratization: Elections in Taiwan, 1986-2000, 2000. Mem.: Cosmos (Washington).

ROBINSON, JAMES D., III, venture capitalist; b. Atlanta, Nov. 19, 1935; m. Bettye Bradley (div.); 2 children; m. Linda Gosden, 1984; 2 children. BS, Ga. Inst. Tech., 1957; MBA, Harvard U., 1961. Officer various depts. Morgan Guaranty Trust Co. of N.Y., NYC, 1961-66, asst. v.p., staff asst. to chmn. bd. and pres., 1967-68; gen. ptnr. White, Weld & Co., 1968-70; exec. v.p. American Express Co., NYC, 1970-75, pres., 1975-77, chmn., CEO, 1977-93; pres., CEO American Express Internat. Banking Corp., 1970—73; chmn. American Express Credit Corp., 1973—75; pres. J.D. Robinson Inc., 1993—; co-founder, gen. ptnr. RRE Ventures, 1994—; chmn. RRE Investors, LLC; non-exec. chmn. The Bristol-Myers Squibb Co., 2005—08, bd. dirs., 1976—2008. Bd. dirs. The Coca Cola Co., 1975-, First Data Corp., 1992-2007, Novell, Inc., 2001-09. Author: Inflation Overkill, 1994, Full Steam Ahead, 2000. Active Bus. Coun., Coun. on Fgn. Rels., U.S. Japan Bus. Coun., Dean's Adv. Coun. Roberto C. Goizueta Sch. Bus. Emory U., Exec. Adv. Bd., Ivan Allen Coll.; hon. chmn. bd. Meml. Sloan-Kettering Cancer Ctr.; hon. mem. The Brookings Instn.; mem. bd. dirs. Nat. Acad. Found.; mem. Pres.' Cir. The Asia Soc.; bd. dirs., chair emeritus Partnership of N.Y.C.; chair emeritus World Travel & Tourism Coun.; former chair Internat. Trade and Investment Task Force of the Bus. Roundtable, former chair svcs. policy adv. com.; former chmn. adv. com. on trade and policy negotiations United Way of Am.; former mem. Coun. on Competitiveness; former trustee Alfred P. Sloan Found., Coun. on Econ. Devel.; former mem. Dewitt Wallace Found. Lt. USNR, 1957-59. Mem. Econ. Club (N.Y.C.). Office: RRE Ventures 130 E 59 St 17TL New York NY 10002-3613 Office Phone: 212-418-5100.

ROBINSON, JAMES SIDNEY, public health service officer; b. Lake Arthur, La., Feb. 18, 1947; s. James Sidney and Vernita Robinson; m. Yvonne Victoria Jones; children: Samantha Ann, Curtis James Abernathy, Talliferro Jones, Derrick James, Tiana Nasatja Collazo. MPA in Human Resources Mgmt., Golden Gate U., San Francisco, 1985. Cert. in addiction treatment Calif. Assn. Alcohol, Drug Educators, 2003. Supt. maintenance USAF, 1965—85; supervising caseworker St. John's Sch., Whitewater, Calif., 1985—86; supervising officer San Bernardino County Probation Dept., 1986—2001. Dir., student asst. program San Bernardino Valley Coll., 1996—2006. Decorated Numerous award US Air Force. Mem.: Calif. Assn. Alcohol, Drug Educators (grievance rep., chair 1998—). Democrat. Methodist. Avocations: fishing, camping, reading, travel. Office: San Bernardino Valley Coll 701 S Mt Vernon Ave San Bernardino CA 92410-2705 Office Fax: 909-889-0702. Business E-Mail: jrobinso@valleycollege.edu.

ROBINSON, JAMES WILLIAM, chemistry professor; b. Kidderminster, Eng., July 12, 1923; arrived in U.S., 1955, naturalized, 1958; s. James William and Eva Robinson; m. Winifred Gladys Nixon, Jan. 8, 1946; children: James William, Linda Juanita, Sandra Jacqueline. BSc with hons., U. Birmingham, England, 1949, PhD, 1952, DSc, 1978. Sr. sci. officer Brit. Civl Svc., Birmingham, England, 1952—55; from rsch. assoc. to prof. emeritus La. State U., Baton Rouge, 1955—93, prof. emeritus, 1993—; sr. chemist Esso Rsch. Labs., Baton Rouge, 1956—63; tech. advisor Ethyl Corp., Baton Rouge, 1963—64. Mem. rsch. grants adv. com. EPA, 1969—75; vis. prof. U. Colo., 1970, U. Sydney, 1983; lectr. in field. Author: Atomic Absorption Spectroscopy, 1966, 2d edit., 1975, Undergraduate Instrumental Analysis, 1970, 6th edit., 2005, Atomic Spectroscopy, 1990, 2d edit., 1996; editor: Analytica Chemica Acta, 1956—80, Spectroscopy Letters, 1966—98, Environl. Sci. and Health, 1971—97, Monograph Series Analysis Environ. Control, 1977—85, Applied Spectroscopy Revs., 1977—90, Jour. Applied Spectroscopy, 2003, Handbook of Spectroscopy, Vol. I, 1974, Vol. II, 1974, Vol. III, 1981, Practical Handbook of Spectroscopy, 1991; contbr. articles to profl. jours., chapters to books. Recipient Gold medal, N.Y. Soc. Applied Spectroscopy, 2000; fellow, Guggenheim Found., 1975. Fellow: Royal Chem. Soc. Avocations: gardening, travel, snorkeling. Office: Dept Chemistry La Sate Univ Baton Rouge LA 70803 Home Phone: 225-766-6420; Office Phone: 225-578-3025. Business E-Mail: jrobi24@tigers.lsu.edu.

ROBINSON, JANET L., publishing executive; b. Fall River, Mass, June 11, 1950; d. Louise Robinson. BA in English cum laude, Salve Regina Coll., Newport, RI, 1972; diploma in Exec. Edn., Dartmouth U., 1996; DBA (hon.), Salve Regina U., Newport, RI, 1998. Tchr., reading specialist, 1972—83; account exec., Tennis Mag. The NY Times Co., 1983—85, nat. resort and travel mgr., Golf Digest/Tennis, 1985—87, advt. dir., Tennis Mag., 1987—90, v.p. advt. sales and mktg., The Women's Mag. Group, 1990—92, group sr. v.p., advt. sales and mktg., The Women's Mag. Group, 1992—93, v.p., dir. advt., 1994, sr. v.p. advt., 1995, pres., gen. mgr., NY Times newspaper, 1996—2004, sr. v.p. newspaper ops., 2001—04, exec. v.p., COO, 2004, pres., CEO, 2004—. Cons. Dept. Edn., Mass., 1977—83; chair. Advertising Council, 2004—; bd. dirs. The NY Times Co., 2004—, Newspaper Assn. America, New England Sports Ventures. Mem. Literacy Vols. NY; mem. adv. bd. Salve Regina Coll.; trustee, chmn. planning and fin. com. Carnegie Corp. NY; vice chair bd. dirs. Liberty Sci. Ctr.; mem. leadership com. Lincoln Ctr. Consolidated Corp. Fund. Named Outstanding Newspaper Exec., Frohlinger's Mktg. Report, 1994; named one of 100 Most Powerful Women in World, Forbes Mag., 2005—09, The 100 Most Influential Women in NYC Bus., Crain's NY Bus., 2007. Mem.: Women in Comm., Advt. Women NY, Advt. Club NY. Office: The New York Times 620 8th Ave New York NY 10018*

ROBINSON, JAY (THURSTON), artist; b. Detroit, Aug. 1, 1915; s. Carter Boston and Marie Rose (Steger) R.; m. Dorothy June Whipple, Sept. 15, 1937 (dec. 1968); children: Theodore Carter, Thomas Whipple, James Jay; m. Anne Frances Helen Posch, Nov. 5, 1970 (dec. 1999). BA, Yale U., New Haven, Conn., 1937; MFA, Cranbrook Acad. Art, Bloomfield Hills, Mich., 1943. One-man shows include, Guggenheim Mus. Non-Objective Painting, NYC, 1947, Milch Galleries, NYC, 1948, 51, 53, 54, 55, 56, J.B. Speed Art Mus., Louisville, 1953, Dayton Art Inst., 1953, Phila. Art Alliance, 1957, Monede Gallery, NYC, 1961, 62, Raymond Burr Galleries, Beverly Hills, Calif., 1963, xxth Century West Gallery, NYC, 1968, E. Kuhlik Gallery, NYC, 1971, New Canaan Soc. for Arts, 1983, Broome St. Gallery, NYC, 1994, Ga. Mus. Art, Athens, 2006; group shows include, Guggenheim Mus., 1947, 49, Carnegie Inst., Pitts., 1949, Des Moines Art Center, 1950, Butler Inst., Youngstown, Ohio, 1953, also Audubon Artists, NYC, Corcoran Gallery, Washington, Mich. Artists, Detroit, NAD, NYC, Pa. Acad., Phila., Provincetown Annual, Mass., Va. Biennial, Richmond; represented in permanent collections, including, Detroit Inst. Art, Houston Mus. Fine Art, Witte Meml. Mus., San Antonio, Philbrook Art Center, Tulsa; Berea Coll., Goucher Coll., Fisk U.; represented also in corp. collections, including, IBM; Republic Steel Co., Bristol-Myers Squibb, portrait painter, designer china and textiles; illustrator: Seventeenth Summer (Maureen Daly), 1948, The New York Guide Book, 1964; contbr. illustrations to other books. Served with OSS, 1943; Served with USN, 1943-46. Louis Comfort Tiffany Found. award, 1950; various purchase awards Am. Acad. Arts and Letters, 1951-64; Outstanding Alumnus award Detroit Country Day Sch., 1966 Home: 305 E Landing Williamsburg VA 23185-8254 *I have always been drawn to the theme of Man in His Environment. By extension to our own, I love jazz music, many of whose players I have painted; classic cars; Japanese gardens; good company and active social life. Travel enables me to see what others have done and are doing.*

ROBINSON, JEFFERY P., lawyer; b. Memphis, Aug. 30, 1956; BA cum laude, Marquette U., 1978; JD, Harvard U., 1981. Bar: Wash. 1981, US Dist. Ct. (we. dist. Wash.) 1981, US Ct. Appeals (9th cir.) 1986. Pub. defender state, fed. courts, 1981—88; atty. criminal def. Schroeter,

Goldmark & Bender, P.S., Seattle. Instr. trial advocacy prog. U. Wash. Sch. Law, 1988—; faculty Nat. Criminal Def. Coll., Macon, Ga.; mem. trial advocacy workshop Harvard Law Sch., 1990—. Contbr. articles to law jours. Named Lawyer of Yr., King County Bar Assn., 2003; named one of Am. Top Black Lawyers, Black Enterprise Mag., 2003. Fellow: Am. Coll. Trial Lawyers; mem.: Nat. Inst. Trial Advocacy, NACDL (former mem. bd. dirs.), Wash. Assn. Criminal Def. Lawyers (past pres.), Wash. State Trial Lawyers Assn., Wash. State Bar Assn. (mem. criminal law exec. com. 1989). Office: Schroeter Goldmark & Bender PS 810 Third Ave Ste 500 Seattle WA 98104 Office Phone: 206-622-8000. Office Fax: 206-682-2305.

ROBINSON, JENNIFER META, senior lecturer, consultant; b. Boston, 1962; d. Samuel Sachs and Catherine Greenacre Robinson; m. J. A. Hartenfeld, 1946; 1 stepchild, Sarah Meghan Hartenfeld. PhD in Am. Lit., Ind. U., 2001. Dir., campus instrnl. cons. Ind. U., Bloomington, 2002—08. Coord. scholarship of tchg. and learning Ind. U., 2003—08; adj. lectr. Ind. U. Dept. Comm. and Culture, 2006—08. Contbr. chapters to books, articles to profl. jours; author: Kate Douglas Wiggin:Bibliography of American Fiction, 1866 to 1918, 1993, A Question of Authority: Dealing With Disruptive Students," In Our Own Voice: Graduate Students Teach Writing, 1999, The Farmers' Market Book: Growing Food, Cultivating Community, 2007; editor (with Reynolds & Brondizio): Teaching Environmental Literacy, 2009 (Teagle Found. grant, 2008), author poems. Institutional coord. Carnegie Acad. Advancement Scholarship Tchg. & Learning Leadership, 2003—09; treas. People and Animal Learning Svcs., Bloomington, Ind.; 2000—08; mem. dir. com. Big Ten Tchg. Ctr., 2002—08. Recipient Tchg. Excellence Recognition award, Ind. U., 1997, Hesburgh award for a faculty devel. program, TIAA-CREF, 2003, Wagner award, Ind. U., 2005; Noyes fellowship, 1995. Mem.: Internat. Soc. Scholarship of Tchg. and Learning (founding com. 2003—05, conf. exec. com. 2004, interim exec. com. 2004—05, v.p. 2005—, chair, going public com., mem. vision and planning com., conf. and covening com., pres. 2009—), Hoosier Folklore Soc. Office: Indiana Univ 800 E Third St Bloomington IN 47405 Business E-Mail: jenmetar@indiana.edu.

ROBINSON, JERI, museum program director; Grad., Wheelock Coll., 1967—71. With Boston Children's Mus., 1973—, v.p. early childhood programs, 2006—. Founder Boston Cultural Collaborative for Early Learning; co-founder Families First-parenting programs, CountDown to Kindergarten, Boston. Author: Activities for Anyone. Anytime. Anywhere, 1982, Playspace: Creating Family Spaces in Public Spaces, 1984. Named to Centennial Honor Roll, Am. Assn. Museums, 2006. Office: Boston Children's Mus 300 Congress St Boston MA 02210 Office Phone: 617-426-6500 ext. 219. Business E-Mail: earlychild@BostonChildrenMuseum.org.

ROBINSON, JOANNE ADELE, retired secondary school educator, volunteer; b. Alameda, Calif., May 9, 1936; d. Herbert William and Jeanne Adele (Stoddard) Justin; m. William Grant Robinson, Aug. 26, 1961; children: Deann Adele, Scott William, Paul Justin. BS in Physical Edn./Bio. Sci., San Francisco State U., 1958. Cert. secondary tchr. Calif., 1959. Phys. edn. tchr. San Mateo Union High Dist., Menlo Park, Calif., 1959—64, Alameda Unified Sch. Dist., 1964—66; program dir. Girls Club Am., Alameda, 1975—80, Camp Fire Boys & Girls, Inc., Oakland, Calif., 1980—85; phys. edn. tchr. Alameda Adult Sch., 1990—2004; ret., 2004. Vol. 1st aid/CPR instr. ARC, Alameda, 1960—2007, tech. leadership coord., 1978—2007. Pres., fundraiser bd. mem. Alameda Girls Club, 1967—89; mem. UN Assn. E. Bay Chpt., Alameda, 1968—2007; active summer faire Alameda Welfare Coun., 1981—2007, past pres., bd. mem.; area rep. Youth For Understanding Internat. Exchange, Alameda, 1986—91; vol. coord. food distribution to low-income families SHARE No. Calif., 1988—98; v.p., program coord. Ch. Women United, Alameda, 1985—2007. Recipient Gulick award, Camp FIre Boys & Girls, Inc., 1982, Woman of Yr. award, City of Alameda, 1996. Mem.: Key Women Educators (Zeta Phi chpt.) (past pres., corr. sec.), Philanthropic Ednl. Organ. (corr. sec. 1999—), Womans Nat. Sports Assn. (nat. acquatics judge 1959—67), Calif. Assn. Health, Phys. Edn., Recreation & Dance (life), Delta Kappa Gamma Internat. Avocations: hiking, bicycling, kayaking, drawing. Home: 2857 Lincoln Ave Alameda CA 94501

ROBINSON, JOE SAM, neurosurgeon, educator; b. Atlanta, July 21, 1945; s. Joe Sam and Nell (Mixon) R.; m. Elizabeth Ann Moate, Apr. 3, 1982; children: Joe Sam III, Edward Richard, Thomas McRae. AB cum laude, Harvard Coll., 1967; MD, U. Va., 1971; MS, Northwestern U., 1976. Surg. intern Emory U., 1971-72, resident in surgery, 1972-73; resident in neurosurgery Northwestern U., 1973-78; instr. U. Ill., 1978-79, Yale U., 1979-81; pres. Ga. Neurosurg. Inst. P.A., Macon, 1981—. Prof., chief neurosurgery Mercer U. Sch. Medicine, Macon, 1986; chief surgery Med. Ctr. Ctrl. Ga., Macon, 1989—, vice chmn. surgery, 1991-97, chmn. dept. surgery, 1996—; vis. neurosurgeon China, 1992, Konaus Acad. Neurosurgery Inst., Lithuania, 1992; clin. prof. Med. Coll. Ga., 2002; vice chmn. Ga. Bd. Physicians Workforce, 2007. Lt. col. USANG, 1972-95. Fellow Internat. Coll. Surgeons (vice regent 1983-93); mem. Am. Assn. Neurol. Surgeons, Congress Neurol. Surgeons, AAAS, Ga. Neurosurg. Soc., Alpha Omega Alpha. Republican. Methodist. Office: Ga Neurosurg Inst PA 840 Pine St Ste 880 Macon GA 31201-7525 Business E-Mail: vickie@ganeurosurg.org.

ROBINSON, JOHN BECKWITH, development management consultant; b. Portland, Oreg., May 23, 1922; s. Jewell King and Arvilla Agnes (Beckwith) R.; m. Dilys Walters, Sept. 8, 1945; children— John Gwilym, David Gwyn. BA, U. Oreg., 1944; postgrad., U. Shrivenham, Eng., 1945, U. Oxford, 1946, Am. U., 1947. Staff U.S. Bur. Budget, 1947—48; sr. program and budget officer UNESCO, 1948—51; mem. staff U.S. Bur. Budget, 1951—52; chief personnel policy Mut. Security Agy., Washington, 1952-54, program officer Guatemala, 1954-59, planning officer, later acting asst. dep. dir. for program and planning AID Washington, 1959-61; dep. U.S. rep. devel. assistance com. OECD, 1961-64, asst. dir. devel. policy Pakistan, 1964-68; dep. dir. North Coast Affairs, AID, State Dept., Washington, 1969-71; dep. mission dir. U.S. Econ. Aid Program, Colombia, 1971-73, mission dir. Dominican Republic, 1973-76, mission dir. Honduras, 1976—79; privatization adviser Gov. of Costa Rica, 1986-88; prin. assoc. J.B. Robinson & Assocs. (devel. mgmt. cons.), 1979—. Mem. faculty, fellow Harvard U., 1968-69; cons. NATO, 1951, UN, 1951. Served to 1st lt., inf. AUS, 1943-46, ETO. Recipient Knight Commdr., Order Morazan, Republic Honduras, 1979. Mem. Oriental Club (London), DACOR BACON House (Washington), Minchinhampton Probus Club (pres. 1983-84). Episcopalian. Address: Anglezarke The Hithe Rodborough Common Stroud GL5 5BN Gloucestershire England also: 2323 SW Park Pl Portland OR 97205 Office Phone: 00-44-1453-873346. Business E-Mail: jackanddilys@gmail.com. *Summary: always do more than what is asked for the task at hand. The extra effort always leads to unexpected opportunities for career advancement. Helping others to realize their potential has its own rewards and their success helps to realize your own hopes and aspirations, and improve your own quality of life and satisfaction in a life well-spent. Never underestimate the contribution of your wife and family.*

ROBINSON, JOHN HAYES, law educator; b. Providence, Apr. 4, 1943; s. William Philip and Dorothy Frances (Hayes) R.; m. Deborah Ann Deery, Aug. 15, 1981; children: Gena, John. BA, Boston Coll., 1967; MA, Notre Dame U., Ind., 1972, PhD, 1975; JD, U. Calif., Berkeley, 1979. Bar: RI 1980. Asst. prof. U. San Francisco, 1973-76; instr. law U. Miami, Coral Gables, Fla., 1979-80; jud. clk. US Dist. Ct., Hartford, Conn., 1980-81; asst. prof. law and philosophy U. Notre Dame, 1981-96, assoc. prof. law, 1996—, assoc. dean acad. affairs, 2002—04, exec. assoc. dean, 2005—09. Office: U Notre Dame Law Sch Box 780 Notre Dame IN 46556 Office Phone: 574-631-6980. Business E-Mail: robinson.1@nd.edu.

ROBINSON, JOHN M., federal agency administrator; BA, Brown Univ.; M, Tuskegee Univ. Various adminstrv. positions through sr. dean Brown Univ., 1973—90; dir. RI Dept. Employment & Training, 1991—93; dep. asst. sec. Employment & Training Adminstrn., US Dept. Labor, Washington, 1994—99; sr. policy adv. to sec. US Dept. Energy, Washington, 1999—2001; chief of EEO & diversity IRS, Washington, 2002—06; chief of EEO Office of Dir. Nat. Intelligence, Washington, 2006—08; dir. office of civil rights & chief diversity officer US State Dept., Washington, 2008—. Office: US State Dept 2201 C St NW Washington DC 20520*

ROBINSON, JOHN WILLIAM, IV, lawyer; b. Atlanta, Apr. 29, 1950; s. J. William III and Elizabeth (Smith) R.; m. Ellen Showalter, Dec. 28, 1976; children: William, Anna. BA with honors, Washington & Lee U., 1972; JD, U. Ga., 1975. Bar: Fla., Ga., U.S. Dist. Ct. (no., so. and mid. dists.) Fla., U.S. Ct. Mil. Appeals, U.S. Ct. Appeals (5th and 11th cirs.), U.S. Supreme Ct.; cert. labor & employment law, Nat. Bd. Trial Advocacy, civil trial and bus. litigation lawyer, Fla. Trial atty. Nat. Labor Rels. Bd., New Orleans, 1975—76; trial def. counsel 8th infantry U.S. Army, Mainz, Germany, 1977—78, trial counsel 8th infantry, 1979; law clk., commr. Ct. Mil. Rev., Washington, 1980; atty. Fowler, White, Boggs, PA, Tampa, Fla., 1980—, head labor and employment law dept., 1993—, dir., 1998—, sec./treas., 2001—. Mem. faculty U. Md., 1977-79; arbitrator U.S. Dist. Ct. (mid. dist.) Fla.; mem. Leadership Fla., 2004— Editor-in-chief: Employment & Labor Relations Law, 1991-95; editor: Developing Labor Law, 1982—, Model Jury Instructions for Employment Litigation, 1994—; editor: Employment Litigation Handbooks, 1998, 2007. Chmn. Tampa Bay Internat. Trade Coun., 1990-91, Rough Riders Dist. Boy Scouts Am., 1990; legal counsel, chair Drug Free Workplace Task Force, 1999-00; legal counsel, chair, gen. counsel, bd. dirs., 1996, 04-, Greater Tampa C. of C., 1996, 05-; trustee U. Tampa, bd. fellows, chair bus. symposia, 2006-. Capt. U.S. Army, 1976-80. Named one of Best Lawyers in Am. for labor and employment law, Top Ten Super Lawyers in Fla., Fla. Legal Elite. Fellow: Am. Bar Found., Coll. Labor and Employment Lawyers (Founding fellow); mem.: ABA (chmn. employment and labor rels. com. 1993—96, divsn. dir. 1996—2000, mem. coun. 2000—03, chmn. com. on multijurisdictional practice 2000—, task force on electronic discovery 2003—04, litigation sect.), Acad. Fla. Mgmt. Attys. (pres., founding mem. 1993—, chair 2008, charter mem.), Leadership Tampa (chmn. 2006), Hillsborough County Bar Assn. Trial Lawyers (bd. dirs. 1996—, chmn. 2003—), Comml. Bar Assn. (hon.), Am. Inn of Ct. (pres., dir. and master barrister, trustee Am. Inns of Ct. Found., exec. com. Am. Inns of Ct. Found.), Washington & Lee U. Bd. (pres. nat. alumni bd. 1990—91, trustee 1995—2005), Fla. Bar Assn. (chmn. labor and employment law sect. 1992—93), Rotary (bd. 1984—, exec. com. 1984—, bd. dirs. Tampa Bay History Ctr. 2006—, past pres. Tampa Bay chpt.). Avocations: tennis, history. Office: Fowler White Boggs PA 501 E Kennedy Blvd Tampa FL 33602-5237

ROBINSON, JOSEPH EDWARD, geology educator, petroleum engineer, consultant; b. Regina, Sask., Can., June 25, 1925; came to US, 1976. s. Webb Gabriel Wilton and Blanche Marion (Schiefner) R.; m. Mary Corrine Maclaughlin, Nov. 1, 1952 (div. 1977); children: Joseph Christopher, John Edward, Timothy Webb. B.Eng., McGill U., 1950, M.Sc., 1951; PhD, U. Alta., 1968. Registered profl. engr., Que., Can. Geophysicist Imperial Oil Ltd., Can., 1951-68; sr. geologist Union Oil Co. Can., Calgary, Alta., Can., 1968-76; cons. geologist J.E. Robinson & Assocs., Syracuse, N.Y., 1976—; prof. geology Syracuse U., 1976-91, prof. emeritus, 1991—. Author: Computer Applications in Petroleum Geology, 1982. Served with Can. Navy, 1943-46, ETO. Mem. Am. Assn. Petroleum Geologists, Soc. Exploration Geophysicists, Can. Assn. Petroleum Geologists, Internat. Assn. Math. Geology (assoc. editor 1976-78). Home: 837 Ackerman Ave Syracuse NY 13210-2906 Office: Syracuse U Dept Geology Syracuse NY 13244-0001 Office Phone: 315-472-8255. Personal E-mail: joerobinson1@peoplepc.com.

ROBINSON, JOSH, legislative staff member; BS in Fin., Tex. A&M U., 2007. Chief of staff for Rep. Bill Cassidy, US House of Reps., Washington, 2009—. Office: Office of Congressman Bill Cassidy 506 Cannon House Office Bldg Washington DC 20515 Office Phone: 202-225-3901. E-mail: josh.robinson@mail.house.gov.*

ROBINSON, JOYCE MCPEAKE, academic administrator, consultant; b. Newark, July 28, 1941; d. Salvatore and Wilhelmina (Cervetto) Guinta; m. John David McPeake, June 15, 1963 (div. Aug. 1974); children: John Paul, David Samuel; m. Enders Anthony Robinson, Aug. 8, 1992. BA in English, Tufts U., 1962; MA in English, Boston U., 1965, EdD, 1979. Adminstr. Boston U., 1962—67; reading specialist Hingham Pub. Schs., Mass., 1963—64; reading and learning specialist Manter Hall Sch., Cambridge, Mass., 1964—67; reporter Patriot Ledger, Quincy, Mass., 1967—69; dir. Christ Luth. Sch., Scituate, Mass., 1971—74; prin. and reading specialist Scituate Pub. Schs., 1974—80; chair English, dir. reading programs St. Andrew's Sch., Boca Raton, Fla., 1980—88; chair English, learning specialist Broadwater Acad., Exmore, Va., 1988—89; dir. learning resources, English Fountain Valley Sch., Colorado Springs, Colo., 1989—91; asst. prin. Islamic Saudi Acad., Alexandria, Va., 1991—93; chair English Masters Sch., Dobbs Ferry, NY, 1995—96, Dwight Sch., NYC, 1994—96, head of sch., 1994—2004, head of sch., emeritus, 2004—; dir. reading programs Mass. Pub. Schs., 2004—, ednl. cons., 2005—. Prof. Nova Southeastern U., Ft. Lauderdale, Fla., 1984-88, St. Thomas U., Miami, Fla., 1987-88; sch. evaluator Fla. Coun. Ind. Schs., 1985-88; cons. in field. Author: Teaching Study Skills, 1987, Wordworks, 1990, Stress-Proofing Your Child, 1996, Portfolio of a School, 1998, Fostering Creativity in Children, K-8: Theory and Practice, 2001; editor: How to Double Your Child's Grades in School, 1997. Coord. Am. Inst. Fgn. Study, Boston, 1987; parent agt. Hamilton Coll. Parents Fund, Clinton, N.Y., 1986—; mem. town adv. com. Scituate Town Com., 1975-80. Recipient Tchr. award, English Speaking Union, 1987, Achievement award, Nat. League Am. Pen Women, 1988. Mem.: MLA (mem., Com. on Instn.-Wide Accreditation 2000—), Treasure Time Prodns. (bd. mem. 2004—), Cum Laude Soc. Children's Progress (bd. mem. 2000—04), Nat. Mus. Women Arts, Shakespeare Soc., Fitzgerald Soc., Nat. Acad. Ednl. Rsch., Assn. for Advancement Ednl. Rsch. (pres. 2006—09, exec. bd. 2009—), Coun. Exceptional Children, Internat. Reading Assn., Ea. Ednl. Rsch. Assn. (membership chair 1993—95), Fla. Coun. Librs., Nat. Assn. Ind. Schs., Am. Acad. Poets, Nat. Coun. Tchrs. English (internat. women's rev. bd. mem. 2008, award 2002, Woman of Yr. 2005), Hemingway Soc. Home: 8 Dorothy Lucey Dr Newburyport MA 01950 Business E-Mail: joycerobinson@comcast.net.

ROBINSON, JUNE KERSWELL, dermatologist, educator; b. Phila., Jan. 26, 1950; d. George and Helen S. (Kerswell) R.; m. William T. Barker, Jan. 31, 1981. BA cum laude, U. Pa., 1970; MD, U. Md., 1974. Diplomate Am. Bd. Dermatology, Nat. Bd. Med. Examiners, Am. Bd. Mohs Micrographic Surgery and Cutaneous Oncology. Intern Greater Balt. Med. Ctr., Hanover, NH, 1974, resident in medicine, 1974—75; resident in dermatology Dartmouth-Hitchcock Med. Ctr., Hanover, 1975—78, chief resident, clin. instr., 1977—78, instr. in dermatology, 1978; fellow Mohs; chemosurgery and dermatologic surgery NYU Skin and Cancer Clinic, NYC, 1978—79; instr. in dermatology NYU, NYC, 1979; asst. prof. dermatology Northwestern U. Med. Sch., Chgo., 1979, asst. prof. surgery, 1980—85, assoc. prof. dermatology and surgery, 1985—91, prof. dermatology and surgery, 1991—98; prof. medicine and pathology, dir. divsn. dermatology Cardinal Bernardin Cancer Ctr., Loyola U. Med. Ctr., 1998—2004, program leader skin cancer clin. program, 1998—2004; prof. medicine Med. Sch. Dartmouth U., 2004—05, chief Dermatology Sect. Hitchcock Med. Ctr., 2004—05; prof. clin. dermatology Feinberg Sch. Medicine, Northwestern U., Chgo., 2006—. Mem. consensus devel. conf. NIH, 1992; mem. panel on use of sunscreens Internat. Agy. for Rsch. on Cancer, WHO, 2000; lectr. in field. Author: Fundamentals of Skin Biopsy, 1985, also audiovisual materials; editor: (textbooks) Atlas of Cutaneous Surgery, 1996, Cutaneous Medicine and Surgery: An Integrated Program in Dermatology, 1996, Surgery of the Skin, 2005; mem. editl. bd. Archives of Dermatology, 1988-97; sect. editor The Cutting Edge: Challenges in Med. and Surg. Therapeutics, 1989-97, editor, 2004—; contbg. editor Jour. Dermatol. Surgery and Oncology, 1985-88; mem. editl. com. 18th World Congress of Dermatology, 1982; contbr. numerous articles, abstracts to profl. publs., chpts. to books. Bd. dirs. Northwestern Med. Faculty Found., 1982-84, chmn. com. on benefits and leaves, 1984, nominating com. 1988. Grantee Nat. Cancer Inst., 1985-91, 2004—, Am. Cancer Soc., 1986-89, Skin Cancer Found., 1984-85, Dermatology Found., 1981-83, Northwestern U. Biomed. Rsch., 1981, Syntex, 1984. Fellow: Am. Coll. Mohs Chemosurgery (chmn. sci. program ann. meeting 1983, chmn. publs. com. 1986—87, chmn. task force on ednl. needs 1989—90, co-editor bull. 1984—87, Frederic E. Mohs Career Achievement award 2008); mem.: Chgo. Dermatol. Soc., Women's Dermatol. Soc. (pres. 1990—92, Wilma Bergeld, MD Visionary and Leadership award 2002), Soc. Investigative Dermatology, Am. Soc. Dermatol. Surgery (pres. 1994—95, Samuel J. Stegman award disting. svc. 2006), Dermatology Found. (trustee 1995—98), Am. Acad. Dermatology (asst. sec.-treas. 1995—98, sec.-treas. 1998—2001, bd. dirs. 1993—95, Stephen Rothman Lectr. award 1992, Presdl. citation 1992, 2000), Am. Dermatol. Assn., Am. Cancer Soc. (pres. Ill. divsn. 1996—98, St. George Disting. Svc. medal 2004). Office: Northwestern U Feinberg Sch Med Dept Dermatology 132 E Delaware Pl #5806 Chicago IL 60611 E-mail: wtbjkr@rcn.com.

ROBINSON, KAREN VAJDA, dietician; BS in Home Econs., Montclair State Coll., 1980; MS in Health Scis./Dietetics, James Madison U., 1992. Cert. food svc. sanitation mgr., N.J. 1984. Dietician Roosevelt Hosp., Edison, NJ, 1980-85; asst. mgr. UVA (U. Va.) Dining Svcs., Charlottesville, 1985-86; temp. sales sec., mem. banquet prep. staff Boar's Head Inn, Charlottesville, 1986-88; head diet counselor Diet Ctr., Charlottesville, 1986-90; dietetic intern VA Med. Ctr., Hampton, Va., 1991; pub. health nutritionist Ctrl. Shenandoah Health Dist., Waynesboro Health Dept., Va., 1993-97. Grad. dietetic intern mentor, 1993—97; cons. dietitian Hebrew Hosp. Home, Bronx, NY, 1998; food svc. mgr. Sodexho Marriott Svcs., Morningside House Nursing Home, Bronx, 1998—99; clin. dietitian Yonkers (NY) Gen. Hosp., 1999—2001; cmty. svcs. instr. Westchester C.C., Valhalla, NY, 2001; inpatient/outpatient dietitian Park Care Pavilion (formerly Yonkers Gen. Hosp.), 2001—; clin. dietitian St. John's Riverside Hosp., Yonkers, 2002—, mentor student dietetics, 2006; outpatient dietitian St. John's Riverside, Valentine Lane Family Practice, Yonkers, 2005, 2007—08. Contbr. articles to local newspapers. Mem. Charlottesville Health Promotion Coalition, 1993-97. Mem.: Westchester Rockland Dietetic Assn. (health fairs chair 1998—2001, scholarship com. mem. 2000, pub. rels. co-chair 2000—01, sec. 2001—08, chmn. nominating com. 2003—04, health fairs com. 2005—07, mem. com. 2008—09, scholarship com. mem. 2006, 2009, grantee 2000), Va. Dietetic Assn. (exec. bd. 1996—97), Blue Ridge Dietetics Assn. (nat. nutrition month coord. 1993—95, editor newsletter 1993—96, mem. exec. bd. 1993—97, pres.-elect 1995—96, scholarship com. 1996, pres. 1996—97), Va. Pub. Health Assn. (sec. 1995, awards chair 1996—97), Healthy Aging Practice Group, Cons. Dietitians in Health Care Facilities, Am. Dietetic Assn. (registered). Home: 10-02 Hunter Ln Ossining NY 10562 Office Phone: 914-964-4216. Personal E-mail: kvrobinson@aol.com.

ROBINSON, KAYNE B., lobbyist, former political organization officer; m. Donna R. Robinson. B, Drake U. With Des Moines Police Dept., 1968—99; dep. Iowa chmn. Dole Presdl. campaign, 1988; Iowa chmn. Gramm Presdl. campaign, 1996; chmn. Iowa Rep. Party, 1999—2001; 1st v.p. NRA, Fairfax, Va., 1997—2003, pres., 2003—. With USMC. Named Police Officer of the Yr. Iowa Assn. Women Police. Office: NRA 11250 Waples Mill Rd Fairfax VA 22030

ROBINSON, KENNETH PATRICK, lawyer, electronics executive; b. Hackensack, NJ, Dec. 12, 1933; s. William Casper and Margaret Agnes (McGuire) r.; m. Catherine Esther Lund, Aug. 26, 1961; children: James, Susan. BS in Elec. Engring., Rutgers U., 1955; JD, NYU, 1962. Bar: N.Y. 1962, U.S. Ct. Appeals (fed. cir.) 1990. With Hazeltine Corp., Greenlawn, N.Y., 1955-88, patent counsel, 1966-69, gen. counsel, 1969-88, sec., 1971-88; v.p. Hazeltine Rsch. Inc., Chgo., 1966-88; of counsel Brumbaugh, Graves, Donohue & Raymond, NYC, 1989-92; prin. Kenneth P. Robinson, Huntington, N.Y., 1992—. Dir. Hazeltine Ltd., London, 1973-80; dir. Imlac Corp., Needham, Mass., 1978-83. Served to 1st lt. USAF, 1955-57. Mem. ABA, IEEE, Am. Intellectual Law Assn., Licensing Execs. Soc. Roman Catholic. Home: 137 Darrow Ln Greenlawn NY 11740-2923 Office: PO Box 0328 Greenlawn NY 11740-0328

ROBINSON, KENNETH S., pastor, former state agency administrator, physician; b. Nashville, Tenn. m. Marilynn Sasportas Robinson, 1979; children: Maisha Tamar, Nuriya Desta. BA cum laude, Harvard Univ., MD; MDiv, Vanderbilt Univ.; D (hon.), Meharry Med. Coll. Diplomate Am. Bd. Internal Medicine. Physician & prof. Vanderbilt Univ. Sch. Med., 1982—91; asst. dean admissions & student affairs Univ. Tenn. Sch. Med., Memphis, 1991—2003; commr. Tenn. Dept. Health, Nashville, 2003—07; dir. GTX, Inc., Memphis, 2008—. Past pres. & CEO The Works Inc. Pastor, chief exec. St. Andrew AME Ch., 1991—. Recipient Cmty. Leadership award, U.S. Dept. Health & Human Svcs., Cmty. Builder award, United Way Am., 2000; named a Cmty. Health Leader of the Yr., Robert Wood Johnson Found., 1998. Office: St Andrew AME Ch 867 S Parkway E Memphis TN 38106 Office Phone: 901-948-3441.*

ROBINSON, LARRY CLARK, professional hockey coach, retired professional hockey player; b. Winchester, Ont., Can., June 2, 1951; m. Jeannette Robinson; children: Jeffery, Rachelle. Defenseman Montreal Canadians, 1971—89, LA Kings, 1989—92; asst. coach NJ Devils, 1993—95, 1999—2000, 2007—08, head coach, 2000—02, 2005, spl. assignment coach, 2002—05, 2006—07, 2008—; head coach LA Kings, 1995—99. Mem. Team Can., Can. Cup, 1976, 81, 84. Recipient James Norris Meml. Trophy, 1977, 1980, Conn Smythe Trophy, 1978; named to NHL All-Star game, 1974, 1976—78, 1980, 1982, 1986, 1988, 1989, 1992. Achievements include being a member of Stanley Cup Champion Montreal Canadians, 1971, 1973, 1976, 1977, 1978, 1979; being inducted into the Hockey Hall of Fame, 1995; being the head coach of Stanley Cup Champion New Jersey Devils, 2000; having his number, 19, retired by Montreal Canadians, 2007. Avocations: polo, boating. Office: NJ Devils Prudential Ctr 165 Mulberry St Newark NJ 07102

ROBINSON, LAURIE OVERBY, federal agency administrator; b. Washington, July 7, 1946; d. Kermit and Ethel Esther (Schlasinger) Overby; m. Craig Baab, Oct. 22, 1977 (div. 1991); 1 child, Teddy Baab; m. Sheldon Krantz, Dec. 8, 1991. BA in Polit. Sci. magna cum laude, Brown U., 1968. Desk editor Cmty. News Svc., NYC, 1968-71; asst. staff dir. sect. criminal justice ABA, Washington, 1972-74, dir. sect. criminal justice, 1979-93; assoc. dep. atty. gen. US Dept. Justice, Washington, 1993-94, asst. atty. gen. Office Justice Programs, 1994-2000, prin. dep. asst. atty. gen. Office Justice Programs, 2009—, acting asst. atty. gen. Office Justice Programs, 2009—; sr. fellow program on crime policy U. Pa. Jerry Lee Ctr. Criminology, 2001—09, exec. dir. Forum Crime & Justice; dir. Master of Sci. in Criminology program U. Pa., 2004—09. Mem. ex-officio, bd. regents Nat. Coll. Dist. Attys., Houston, 1979—93; adv. bd. Fed. Sentencing Reporter, NYC, 1990—; chair Nat. Forum Criminal Justice, Washington, 1991—93; bd. dirs. Nat. Ctr. Victims of Crime. Mem. advisory bd. George Mason U. Adminstrn. of Justice Adv. Program.; Clinton transition com. US Dept. Justice, 1992; trustee Vera Inst. Justice, 2001—; bd. dirs. Police Found. Mem.: ABA, Phi Beta Kappa. Democrat. Office: US Dept Justice 950 Pennsylvania Ave NW Washington DC 20530 E-mail: laurieorob@aol.com.*

ROBINSON, LINDA GOSDEN, communications executive; b. LA, Jan. 10, 1953; d. Freeman Fisher and Jane Elizabeth (Stoneham) Gosden; m. Stephen M. Dart (div. June 1977); m. James Dixon Robinson III, July 1984. Student, UCLA, 1970-72; BA summa cum laude in Psychology, U. So. Calif., 1978. Dep. press sec. Reagan Presdl. Campaign, LA, 1979; press sec., dir. pub. relations Rep. Nat. Com., Washington, 1979-80; dir. pub. affairs US Dept. Transp., Washington, 1981-83; sr. v.p. corp. affairs Warner Amex Cable Communications, NYC, 1983-86; chmn. Robinson Lerer & Montgomery, LLC, NYC, 1986—, CEO, 1986—2002. Dir. BlackRock, Inc., NYC. Trustee NYU Langone Med. Ctr., The Chapin Sch.; del. Rep. Nat. Conv., 1985. Mem.: Phi Beta Kappa. Avocations: tennis, horseback riding.

ROBINSON, LOGAN GILMORE, lawyer; b. Cin., Dec. 26, 1949; s. Landon Graves and Alis (Rule) R.; m. Edrie Baker Sowell, Sept. 22, 1983; children: Leyland G., Landon G., Linden G., Lane G. BA in Econ. and History magna cum laude, Cornell U., 1972; JD, Harvard U., 1976; Cert. Competence in German, Goethe Inst., Freiburg, Germany, 1978. Bar: Ohio 1977, N.Y. 1979, Mich. 1989, U.S. Ct. Internat. Trade 1983. Rsch. faculty Leningrad State U., Russia, 1976-77; rsch. officer U. Leiden, Netherlands, 1977-78; assoc. Wender, Murase & White, NYC, 1978-81, Coudert Bros., NYC, 1981-83; sr. counsel TRW Inc., Cleve., 1983-87; asst. gen. counsel Chrysler Corp., Highland Park, 1987—96; sec., v.p., gen. counsel ITT Automotive, Auburn Hills, Mich., 1996—98; v.p., gen. counsel Delphi Corp., Troy, Mich., 1998—2006; exec. v.p., gen. counsel, govt. rels. Metaldyne Corp., Plymouth, Mich., 2006—08; prof. law U. Detroit Mercy, 2008—. Author: An American in Leningrad, 1982, paperback, 1984, Evil Star, 1986, paperback, 1987. Mem. Assoc. Gen. Counsels, Internat. Bar Assn. (former co-chair corp. counsel forum), Mich. State Bar (former chmn. internat. sect., Outstanding Contbn. award), German Am. C. of C. Mich. (pres. chair), Coun. US and Italy, Phi Beta Kappa. Mailing: 4131 Echo Rd Bloomfield Hills MI 48302-1942

ROBINSON, LOIS HART, retired public relations executive; b. Freeport, Ill., Aug. 9, 1927; d. Seril N. and Cora (Stabenow) Hart; m. Noel M. Henze, Nov. 15, 1947 (div. 1964); children: Susan Bentley, Cynthia Berkeley, Charles Henze; m. Jack Fay Robinson, July 16, 1968; stepdau.: Alice Dungey. Student, Oakton C.C., 1976-77, Northwestern U., 1977-81. Med. sec. Freeport Meml. Hosp., 1945-47; sec. No. Ill. Corp., 1947-49; adminstrv. asst. to supt. schs. Cmty. Sch. Dist. 303, St. Charles, Ill., 1962-68; exec. sec. Bell & Howell Co., Chgo., 1969-73, supr. corp. rels., 1973-79, mgr. corp. comm., 1979-85, mgr. corp. comm. svcss., 1985-88; pres., dir. Bell & Howell Found., 1983-88; freelance writer Evanston, Ill., 1989-91. Bd. dirs. Evanston Ecumenical Action Coun., 1991-93, Tri-Village United Way, 1996-97, Friends of Judson Coll., 1998-2003, Friends Bartlett Libr., 1997-2002, 2006-07; trustee Elgin Symphony Orch., 2006—. Recipient Effie award Am. Mktg. Assn., 1983. Mem. United Ch. of Christ. Home: 2771 Cascade Falls Cir Elgin IL 60124-3116

ROBINSON, MARGUERITE STERN, anthropologist, educator, consultant; b. NYC, Oct. 11, 1935; d. Philip Van Doren and Lillian (Diamond) Stern; m. Allan Richard Robinson, June 12, 1955; children: Sarah Penelope, Perrine, Laura Ondine. BA, Radcliffe Coll., 1956; PhD, Harvard U., 1965. Assoc. scholar Radcliffe Inst. for Advanced Studies, Cambridge, Mass., 1964-65; asst. prof. anthology Brandeis U., 1965-72, assoc. prof., 1972-78, prof., 1978-85, dean Coll. Arts and Scis., 1973-75; assoc. fellow Inst. Internat. Devel. Harvard U., Cambridge, 1978—79, fellow Inst. Internat. Devel., 1980-85, inst. fellow Inst. Internat. Devel., 1985-2000, inst. fellow emeritus Inst. Internat. Devel., 2000—; dir. Cultural Survival Inc., 1981-99, Am. Inst. Indian Studies, Chgo., 1977—2000, chmn., 1983-84; faculty mem. Microfinance Tng. Program, Boulder, Colo. and Turin, Italy, 1995—2009. Bd. dirs. MasterCard Found., 2006—, Equity Bank Found., Kenya, 2006—, Boulder Inst. Microfinance, 2008—; coun. advisors Ctr. Fin. Inclusion, Accion Internat.; cons. in field. Author: Political Structure in a Changing Sinhalese Village, 1975, Local Politics: The Law of the Fishes, 1988, Pembiayaan Pertanian Pedesaan, 1993, The Microfinance Revolution, Vol. 1: Sustainable Finance for the Poor, 2001, Vol. 2: Lessons from Indonesia, 2002, Mobilizing Savings from the Public: Basic Principles and Practices, 2005, The Future of the Commercial Microfinance Industry in Asia, 2005, Commercial Microfinance and Employment in Developing Countries, 2005; contbg. author: Cambridge Papers in Social Anthropology 3, 1962, Cambridge Papers in Social Anthropology 5, 1968, Enterprises for the Recycling and Composting of Municipal Solid Waste, 1993, The New World of Microenterprise Finance, 1994, New Perspectives on Financing Small Business in Developing Countries, 1995, Assisting Development in a Changing World, 1997, New World of Microfinance, 1997, Agricultural Development in the Third World, 1998, Strategic Issues in Microfinance, 1998, Microfinance: Conversations with the Experts, 1999, Microbanking: Creating Opportunities for the Poor Through Innovation, 2005, Transforming Microfinance Institutions, 2006; The Mzanzi Bank Account Initiative in South Africa, 2009; contbr. articles to profl. jours. Mem. internat. coun. advisors Calmeadow Found., 1996-2000; pres. Greatest Gift Corp. Fellow NIH, 1964-65; grantee NSF, 1966-70, Ford Found., 1972-74, 79, Calmeadow Found., 1994; fellow Indo-Am. Fellowship Program-Indo-U.S. Subcommn. on Edn. and Culture, 1976-77, Am. Inst. Indian Studies, 1976-77; grantee Calmeadow Found., 1994. Fellow Am. Anthrop. Assn., Soc. Bunting Inst. Fellows; mem. Assn. Asian Studies, India Internat. Centre. Personal E-mail: MRobinso1@aol.com.

ROBINSON, MARIETTA S., lawyer; b. Platteville, Wis., Dec. 26, 1951; BA, U. Mich., 1973; JD, UCLA, 1978. Bar: Calif. 1978, Mich. 1979, U.S. Dist. Ct. (ea. dist.) Mich. 1979, U.S. Ct. Appeals (6th cir.) 1983, U.S. Supreme Ct. 1989. Data processing mktg. rep. IBM Corp., Flint, Mich., 1973-75; assoc. The Bank of Bermuda Legal Dept., Hamilton, 1978-79; from assoc. to ptnr. Dickinson, Wright, Moon, VanDusen & Freeman, Detroit, 1979-94; ptnr. Sommers, Schwartz, Silver & Schwartz, P.C., Southfield, Mich., 1985-89; pvt. practice Detroit, 1989—. Adj. prof. U. Detroit Sch. of Law, 1982-83, Wayne State U., Detroit, 1983-84; mem. Rep. of State Bar Rep. Assembly, 1984-85; Dem. nominee for Mich. Supreme Ct., 2000; lectr. in field. Contbg. author: Evidence in America, The Federal Rules in the States, 1987, Introducing Evidence, A Practical Guide for Michigan Lawyers, 1988; contbr. articles to profl. jours. Trustee Dalkon Shield Claimants Trust, 1989-97; appointee Gov. James Blanchard, State of Mich. Bldg. Authority, 1985-89; appointee Transition Team of Wayne County Exec. Robert Ficano, 2002, appointee adv. com. to senators Coal Levin & Debbie Stab; bd. dirs. Life Raft Group, cancer patient advocacy group Mich. Women's Found., 2003-06. Named one of ten Mich. Lawyers of Yr., Lawyers Weekly, 2000. Fellow ABA, Internat. Soc. Barristers (bd. govs., 1st v.p.), Am. Bar Found., Mich. State Bar Found.; mem. State Bar Mich., State Bar Calif., ATLA, Mich. Trial Lawyers Assn., Women Lawyers Mich., Am. Bd. of Trial Advocates, Detroit Bar Assn., Oakland Bar Assn., U.S. Ct. Appeals (6th cir.) Jud. Conf. (life). Democrat. Avocations: running, biking, tennis, boating, skiing, reading, horseback riding. Office: 436 S Broadway St Ste C Lake Orion MI 48362 Office Phone: 248-693-6245. Personal E-mail: mariettarobinson@gmail.com.

ROBINSON, MARILYNNE, writer; b. Sandpoint, Idaho, Nov. 26, 1943; d. John J. and Ellen (Harris) Summers; children: James, Joseph. BA, Brown U., 1966; PhD in English Lit., U. Wash., 1977. Mem. faculty Writer's Workshop U. Iowa, 1991—. Vis. prof. Amherst Coll., Mass., U. Kent, England, U. Mass. MFA Prog. Poets & Writers; spkr. in field. Author: (novels) Housekeeping, 1981 (Hemingway Found./PEN award, 1981), Gilead, 2004 (Nat. Book Critics Cir. prize for fiction, 2004, Pulitzer Prize for fiction, 2005, Ambassador Book award, 2005, Publishers Weekly bestseller), Home, 2008 (Orange prize for fiction, 2009), (non-fiction) Mother Country: Britain, the Welfare State and Nuclear Pollution, 1989, The Death of Adam: Essays on Modern Thought, 1998. Recipient Mildred & Howard Strauss Living award, AAAL, 1998, Richard & Hinda Rosenthal award. Office: Farrar Straus & Giroux 18 W 18th St New York NY 10011-4607*

ROBINSON, MARY BETH, educational administrator; b. Hinsdale, Ill., Sept. 2, 1943; d. Lee Fulton and Freda Margaret (Doehle) Higman. BA, UCLA, 1965; MA, Stanford U., 1974; PhD, Ohio State U., 1978; cert. sch. adminstr., Calif. State U., Long Beach, 1988. Secondary tchr. Berkeley Unified Sch. Dist., Calif., 1966-75; tchg. evaluator Ohio State U. Sch. Vet. Med., Columbus, 1975-78; lectr., curriculum evaluator Calif. State Poly. U., Pomona, 1978-80; fed. program evaluator Sch. Dist. Phila., 1980-81; coord. field edn., tchr. edn., sch. edn. Stanford U., Calif., 1982-86; reading specialist East Side Union HS Dist., San Jose, Calif., 1986-87; chair dept. fgn. lang., sch. program evaluation instrnl. coach for beginning tchrs. Centinela Valley Union HS Dist., Lawndale, Calif. Instnl. program evaluator Commn. on Tchr. Credentialing, Sacramento, 1987—; advocate County of LA Commn. on Human Rels.; vol. mentor to first generation coll. applicants Mem. ASCD, Calif. Coun. on Tchr. Edn., Stanford Club Los Angeles County, Phi Delta Kappa. Democrat. Episcopalian. Avocations: stamp collecting/philately, football, opera. Office: Leuzinger High Sch 4119 Rosecrans Lawndale CA 90260 Home: 512 Ave G #109 Redondo Beach CA 90277-6023 Personal E-mail: mrobi97705@aol.com.

ROBINSON, MARY ELIZABETH GOFF, retired historian, researcher; b. East Providence, RI, Jan. 3, 1925; d. Newell Darius and Eva Agnes (Crane) Goff; m. Charles Albert Robinson, July 30, 1954; 1 child, Thomas Goff (dec.). BA, Wheaton Coll., Norton, Mass., 1947. Cataloger, fine arts, trustee Chadds Ford Hist. Soc., Pa., 1973—80. Cataloger artifacts Chester County Hist. Soc., Chadds Ford, Pa., 1973—80. Co-author: (monograph) Ada Clendenin Williamson, 1983, (history) The Ingalls and the Hoyts, The Crane Sawmill, The Ingalls-Crane House, 1995; author: (monograph) The Life of a Young Entrepreneur at the Turn of the Twentieth Century, 1992; editor: A Quiet Man from West Chester (Pa.), 1974. Mem. Jr. League, Providence, 1957-62, Providence Athenaeum, 1955-63, Providence Preservation Soc., 1959-63, Brandywine Conservancy, Del. Symphony Orch., Winterthur Mus.; donor Newell D. Goff Fund Chester County Cmty. Found.; founder Chester County Artists Register, Chester County Art Assn., acting libr., 1994-2000. Donor T. Morris Longstreth Libr. endowment West Chester U., Greater Lewes (DE) Found., Friends of Lewes Pub. Libr. Mem. AAUW, R.I. Hist. Soc. (trustee 1994-99, founder Newell D. Goff Edn. Ctr.), Danville (Vt.) Hist. Soc., Hershey's Mill Country Club, Hope Club (Providence, RI). Avocations: writing, reading, hiking, travel.

ROBINSON, MARY JO, pathologist; b. Spokane, Wash., May 26, 1954; d. Jerry Lee and Ann (Brodie) R. BS in Biology, Gonzaga U., 1976; DO, Des Moines U., 1987. Diplomate Nat. Bd. Osteo. Med. Examiners, Am. Osteo. Bd. Pathology; cert. anatomic pathology, lab. medicine and dermatopathology. Med. technologist Whitman Cmty. Hosp., Colfax, Wash., 1977—81, Madigan Army Med. Ctr., Ft. Lewis, Wash., 1981—83; intern Des Moines Gen. Hosp., 1987—88; resident in pathology Kennedy Meml. Hosp., Stratford, NJ, 1988—92; asst. prof. pathology Sch. Medicine U. Medicine & Dentistry NJ, Stratford, 1992—2008; staff pathologist Kennedy Meml. Hosp., Cherry Hill, NJ, 1995—2008; fellow in dermatopathology Jefferson Med. Coll., Phila., 1994—95; assoc. pathologist Pacific North-west Pathology Assoc., Kent, Wash., 2008—. Fellow Coll. Am. Pathologists; mem. AMA, Am. Osteo. Assn., Am. Soc. Clin. Pathologists, Am. Osteo. Coll. Pathologists (pres. 2003-04, 1st prize resident paper 1992), N.J. Assn. Osteo. Physicians and Surgeons, Am. Osteo. Bd. Pathologists (chmn. 2003-09). Avocations: astronomy, antiques, science fiction. Personal E-mail: mrobin7403@aol.com.

ROBINSON, MOLLY JAHNIGE, statistician, educator; b. Cleve., July 8, 1936; d. John White and Mary Tayler (Sullivan) McCaslin; m. Thomas Paul Jahnige (dec.); m. Donald Leonard Robinson, Jan. 1, 1983; children: Katherine Jahnige Mathews, John Samuel, David Wynn, Paul John Jahnige. Student, Swarthmore Coll., Pa., 1954—56; BA, Pomona Coll., Claremont, Calif., 1958; MA, Claremont U., 1962. Tchr. 4th, 7th, and 8th grades Claremont Sch. Dist., 1958—63; instr. stats. Smith Coll., Northampton, Mass., 1973—2004. Leader Girl Scouts US, 1957—; vol. Cmty. Found. We. Mass., 2000—05, Ashfield Youth Commn., 1995—2005; Sunday sch. dir., youth leader St. John's Episcopal Ch., Northampton, 1973—75, 2002—04; coord. Episcopal Relief and Devel. We. Mass., 2005—; mem. sch. bd. Mohawk Region, Ashfield, Mass., 2003—06; edn. chair Wells Trust Fund, Greenfield, Mass., 1996—; chair Town Common Com., Ashfield, 2003—05. Recipient World Friendship medal, Girl Scouts USA. Democrat. Avocations: writing, working with children.

ROBINSON, MURIEL COX, psychiatrist; d. Henry Willard and Veola Garry Cox; m. Julius Ceasar Robinson (div.); children: Julius W., Rosalyn P. Student, Ohio State U., 1945—48; MD, Meharry Med. Coll., 1952. Psychiatry resident Homer Phillips Hosp./Washington U., St. Louis, 1953—56; staff psychiatrist St. Louis Child Guidance Ctr., St. Louis, 1956—57, Napa (Calif.) St. Hosp., 1958, Cmty. Mental Health Centers, Richmond, Calif., 1958—75; pvt. practice psychiatry Calif., 1960—79; staff psychiatrist East Oakland Mental Health Ctr., Calif., 1976—79, Calif. Youth Authority, Sacramento, 1979—92; with Locum Tenens Physicians Group, 1992—94. Mem. mental health adv. com. Contra Costa County, Martinez, Calif., 1960—64. Bd. dirs. North Richmond Neighborhood Ho., Calif., 1961—63. Mem.: AAAS, AMA, NAACP, Am. Psychiat. Assn. (life). Avocations: block flute, keyboards. Home: PO Box 292148 Sacramento CA 95829-2148 E-mail: mcrobinson@webtv.net.

ROBINSON, NATE (NATHANIEL ROBINSON), professional basketball player; b. Seattle, May 31, 1984; s. Jacque Robinson and Renee Busch; 1 child, Nahmier. Attended, U. Wash., Seattle, 2002—05. Guard NY Knicks, 2005—. Named 1st Team All-Conf., PAC 10 Conf., 2004, 2005. Achievements include winning the NBA All-Star Slam Dunk Contest, 2006, 2009. Office: NY Knicks 2 Pennsylvania Plz 14th Fl New York NY 10121-0091*

ROBINSON, NATHANIEL DAVID, JR., physician, consultant; b. Kansas City, Mar. 6, 1941; s. Nathaniel David Robinson and Dorothy Mae McLaughlin; m. Joanne Marie Kaleida, July 7, 1979; children: Donelle, Nathaniel David Robinson III. BSEE, U. RI, 1963; MD, U. Bologna, 1975. Cert. bd. cert. ins. medicine. Intern Roger Williams Gen. Hosp. Brown U., Providence, 1975—76; resident St. Francis Hosp. and Med. Ctr. U. Conn., Hartford, 1976—77; resident Hamot Med. Ctr., Erie, Pa., 1977—79, Mt. Sinai Med. Ctr., Miami Beach, Fla., 1981—82; med. officer USPHS Hosp., Seattle, 1979—81, VA, Nashville, 1982—85; med. dir. CNA, Nashville, 1985—95, v.p., med. dir., 1997—2004; asst. med. dir. Am. United Life, Indpls., 1995—97; med. cons. AIG Am. Gen., Nashville, 2005—. Cons. in field. Contbr. articles to profl. jours. Mem.: IEEE, AMA, Fla. Med. Assn., Midwest Med. Dirs. Assn., Providence Engrng. Soc., Nashville Acad. Medicine, Tenn. Med. Assn., Am. Acad. Ins. Medicine, Am. Radio Relay League. Avocation: amateur radio. Home: 1304 Choctaw Trail Brentwood TN 37027-7422 Office: AIG Am Gen American General Ctr Nashville TN 37250-0001 Office Phone: 615-749-1171. Personal E-mail: djdrobinson@comcast.net. Business E-Mail: k1ant@ieee.org.

ROBINSON, NEIL CIBLEY, JR., lawyer; b. Columbia, SC, Oct. 25, 1942; s. Neil C. and Ernestine (Carns) R.; m. Judith Ann Hunter, Sept. 4, 1971 (div. Nov. 1979); 1 child, Hunter Leigh; m. Vicki Elizabeth Kornahrens, Mar. 2, 1985; children: Neil C. III, Taylor Elizabeth. BS in Indsl. Mgmt., Clemson U., 1966; JD, U. SC, 1973. Bar: SC 1974, US Ct. Appeals (4th cir.) 1974, US Dist. Ct. SC 1976. Asst. to dean U. SC Law Sch., Columbia, 1973-74; law clk. to Hon. Charles E. Jr. Simons Jr. US Dist. Ct. SC, Aiken, 1974-76; assoc. Grimball & Cabaniss, Charleston, SC, 1976-78; ptnr. Grimball, Cabaniss, Vaughan & Robinson, Charleston, 1978-84; ptnr., pres. Robinson, Wall & Hastie, P.A., Charleston, 1984-91; ptnr., exec. com. Nexsen, Pruet, Jacobs, Pollard & Robinson, Charleston, 1991—2003; mem. exec. com. Nexsen Pruet, LLC, 2004—, real estate practice group leader, 2006—. Permanent mem. 4th Cir. Jud. Conf., 1982—; pres. Coastal Properties Inst., Charleston, 1981—. Co-founder, chmn. Charleston Planning Project Pub. Edn., 1996; pres. Clemson Advancement Found., 2003—06; mem. SC Edn. Oversight Com., 2005—; mem. devel. coun. SC Homebuilders Assn.; mem. Gov. Sanford's Quality of Life Task Force, 2003; bd. dirs. SC Tourism Coun., Columbia, 1991—2000, Charleston Maritime Festival, 1993—99; bd. dirs Charleston Edn. Found., Clemson U. Humanities Found., 2000—03, Charleston Edn. Network, chmn. bd. dirs, 2000—03; bd. dirs. Clemson U. Found., 2007—, bd. visitors, 2007—; bd. dirs. Southeastern Wildlife Expn. Found., 1987—, pres., 2003—; bd. dirs. Clemson Real Estate Devel. Found., 2006—, Parklands Found. of Charleston County, pres., Southeastern Wildlife Expn., 1994—99; edn. adv. bd. Coll. of Charleston; pres. Charleston Maritime Festival, 1994—98; bd. dirs. Clemson U. Found., 2003—05. Cpl. USMCR, 1960—66. Recipient Order of Palmetto, Gov. David Beasley, SC, 1996, Disting. Svc. award Clemson U., 2009. Mem. Urban Land Inst. (recreational devel. coun.), SC Bar Assn., Fed. Bar Assn., Hibernian Soc. (mgmt. com. 1984—98, sec. 1998-2000, chmn. 2000-02, v.p. 2002-04, pres. 2004-06), Kiawah Club, Haig Point Club, Country Club of Charleston, Carolina Yacht Club, Phi Delta Phi. Presbyterian. Avocations: golf, boating. Home: PO Box 121 Charleston SC 29402-0121 Office: Nexsen Pruet LLC 205 King St Ste 400 Charleston SC 29401 Office Phone: 843-577-9440. Personal E-mail: nrobinson@nexsenprenet.com, nrobinson@npsp.com. Business E-Mail: nrobinson@npjp.com, nrobinson@nexsenpruet.com.

ROBINSON, NEWELL BRUCE, cardiothoracic surgeon; b. Columbus, Miss., Mar. 31, 1951; s. Jo Newell and Virginia (Henderson) Robinson; m. Victoria Margaret Genovese, Apr. 27, 1986; children: Ruth, Sarah, Bryce, Hunter. BS, Davidson Coll., Charlotte, NC, 1973; MD, U. Miss. Sch. Med., 1977. Diplomate Am. Bd. Surgery, Am. Bd. Thoracic Surgery, lic. physician, Miss., NY, Wash. Intern surgery NY Hosp., Cornell U. Med. Ctr., 1971—79, resident surgery, 1978-79, 81-83, chief resident surgery, 1983-84, resident, chief resident cardiothoracic surgery, 1984-86; trauma fellow burn/trauma rsch. Harborview Med. Ctr., U. Wash., 1979-81; sr. resident surg. oncology Meml. Sloan Kettering Cancer Ctr., 1982-84, fellow thoracic surg. oncology, 1984; asst. attending cardiothoracic surgery St. Francis Hosp., Roslyn, N.Y., 1986—. Instr. dept. surgery NY Hosp., Cornell U. Med. Ctr. Contbr. articles to profl. jours. Recipient NIH rsch. award, Harborview Med. Ctr., U. Wash., 1979—81. Fellow: ACS, Internat. Coll. Surgeons, Am. Coll. Cardiology, Coll. Chest Physician; mem.: AMA, Soc. Thoracic Surgeons., NY Thoracic Surg. Soc., Nassau County Med. Soc., NY Acad. Scis., Nassau County Med. Soc., Am. Burn Assn. Avocations: computer science, sailing, skiing, tennis, weight and aerobic training. Office: Cardiothoracic Surgery PC 100 Port Washington Blvd Roslyn NY 11576-1353 Office Phone: 516-627-2173. Office Fax: 516-365-5813.

ROBINSON, NICHOLAS ADAMS, law educator, department chairman; b. NYC, Jan. 20, 1945; s. Albert Lewis and Agnes Claflin (Adams) R.; m. Shelley Miner, Jan. 5, 1969; children: Cynthia M., Lucy A. BA cum laude, Brown U., 1967; JD cum laude, Columbia U., 1970. Bar: N.Y. 1971, U.S. Dist. Ct. (so. and ea. dists.) N.Y. 1972, U.S. Supreme Ct. 1974, U.S. Ct. Appeals (2d and 7th cirs.) 1972. Law clk. to U.S. dist. judge So. Dist. Ct., NY, 1970-72; assoc. Marshall, Bratter, Greene, Allison & Tucker, NYC, 1972-78, counsel, 1978-82; assoc. prof. Pace U.

Sch. Law, White Plains, NY, 1978-81, prof., 1981-99, Gilbert and Sarah Kerlin Disting. prof. environ. law, 1999—; vis. prof. Pace U., 2009—; counsel Winer, Neuburger & Sive, NYC, 1982-83; dep. commr., gen. counsel NY State Dept. Environ. Conservation, Albany, 1983-85; counsel Sive, Paget & Reisel, 1985-92, Sidley & Austin, NY and London, 1992-96; legal advisor Internat. Union Conservation of Nature and Natural Resources, 1996—2004; counsel to Internat. Union Conservation of Nature and Natural Resources Observer Mission to UN, 2002—05, legal advisor to Asian African Consultative Orgn., 2005—09; chair Internat. Union Conservation of Nature Acad. Environ. Law, 2004—08. Co-dir. Ctr. Environ. Legal Studies, Pace U., 1982—; mem. environ. adv. coun. European Bank for Reconstron. and Devel., 2005-; del. U.S.A. environ. law meetings with USSR, 1974-92; chmn. Environ. Adv. Bd. to Gov. Mario Cuomo, 1985-94; mem. environ. adv. coun. European Bank Reconstruction and Devel., London, 2004-. Contbr. articles to profl. jours. Nat. bd. dirs. UN Assn. U.S.A., 1966-76, 79-84, U.S. Com. for UNICEF, 1970-80, World Environment Ctr., 1981—, chmn., 1993-96; bd. dirs. Westchester County Soil and Water Conservation Dist., 1976-83; chmn. N.Y. State Freshwater Wetlands Appeals Bd., 1976-83; chmn. planning bd. Village of Sleepy Hollow, N.Y., 1999—2008; bd. edn. Union Free Sch. Dist., Tarrytown, 1981-83, 85. Recipient NY State Gov.'s Citation for Hist. Preservation, 1983, Eliz Haub prize Free U., Brussels, 1992, Nat. Environ. Quality award Natural Resources Coun. Am., 2002. Fellow Am. Bar Found.; mem. Internat. Coun. Environ. Law (gov. 1993—), Commn. Environ. Law (chmn. 1996-04), Am. Soc. Internat. Law, ABA, ALI, N.Y. State Bar Assn. (chmn. environ. law sect. 1979-80, Environ. Law award 1981), Assn. Am. Law Schs. (chair sect. on postgrad. legal edn. 1999-00, chair sect. environ. law 1987-88), Assn. Bar City N.Y. (chmn. environ. law com. 1977-78, internat. law com. 1985-88, internat. environ. law com. 1990-92, Russian law com. 1992-95), Westchester County Bar Assn., Sierra Club (nat. bd. dirs. 1979-83, hon. v.p. 2004-), Phi Beta Kappa. Democrat. Unitarian Universalist. Home: 258 Kelbourne Ave Sleepy Hollow NY 10591-1322 Office: Pace U Sch Law 78 N Broadway White Plains NY 10603-3710 Office Phone: 914-422-4244. Business E-Mail: nrobinson@law.pace.edu.

ROBINSON, OLIVER DALE, counselor, pastor; b. Mound Bayou, Miss., Dec. 8, 1939; s. Commodore Perry and Ada Mae Robinson; m. Drucilla C. Robinson, May 3, 1964; children: Oliver A. Jr., Andrew L. BTh, Miss. Bapt. Sem., 1968; BMA, St. Leo Coll., Fla., 1978; MA, Northwestern U., Oklahoma City, 1978; PsyD, Neotarian Coll., Kansas City, Mo., 1980; BA in Bus. Adminstrn., Ctr. Distance Learning, 1981; postgrad., La. State U. Pastor Beautiful New Hope Ch., Mound Bayou, 1969—; dir. counseling Urban Life Ctr. Inc., Mound Bayou, 1984—. Scoutmaster sch. troop 302 Boy Scouts Am., Mound Bayou, 1964—66. Recipient Band Booster Club award, Mound Bayou, 1989—2007. Mem.: NAACP, Mound Bayou Alumni Assn. Democrat. Baptist. Mailing: PO Box 205 Mound Bayou MS 38762 Personal E-mail: beauthope@nexband.com.

ROBINSON, PAUL ARNOLD, historian, educator, writer; b. San Diego, Oct. 1, 1940; s. Joseph Cook and Beryl Marie (Lippincott) R.; m. Ute Brosche, Aug. 3, 1964 (div. Aug. 1967); 1 child, Susan Marie; life ptnr. Stephen Dunatov. BA, Yale U., 1962; postgrad., Free U. Berlin, 1962-63; PhD, Harvard U., 1968. Asst. prof. history Stanford U. (Calif.), 1967-73, assoc. prof., 1973-80, prof. history, 1980—2007, Richard W. Lyman prof. in the humanities, 1994—2007; Lyman prof. emeritus, 2007—. Author: The Freudian Left, 1969, The Modernization of Sex, 1976, Opera and Ideas: From Mozart to Strauss, 1985, Freud and His Critics, 1993, Ludwig van Beethoven: Fidelio, 1996, Gay Lives: Homosexual Autobiography from John Addington Symonds to Paul Monette, 1999, Opera, Sex, and Other Vital Matters, 2002, Queer Wars: The New Gay Right and Its Critics, 2005; editor: Social Thought in America and Europe, 1970; contbg. editor The New Republic, 1979—85. Guggenheim fellow, 1970-71, Stanford Humanities Ctr. fellow, 1984-85, 96-97, Inst. for Advanced Study fellow, 1990-91, Ctr. for Advanced Study in the Behavioral Scis. fellow, 2002-03. Mem. Am. Acad. Arts and Scis., Am. Hist. Assn. Home: 671 Santa Ynez St Stanford CA 94305-8542 Office: Stanford Univ Dept History Stanford CA 94305 Business E-Mail: paulr@stanford.edu.

ROBINSON, PAUL DAVID, literature and language educator; b. Newburgh, NY, Dec. 26, 1955; s. Abraham and Natalie Dorothy Robinson; life ptnr. Santo LoGiudice. BA in Spanish and French cum laude, SUNY, Cortland, 1977; MA in Spanish, Middlebury Coll., Vt., 1980; study abroad program, Neuchâtel, Switzerland, 1974, Salamanca, Spain, 1975, Madrid, 1979—80. Cert. Spanish tchr. grades 7-12 NY, 1979, French tchr. grades 7-12 NY, 1979, TESOL grades K-12 NY, 1983, diploma Básico de la Lengua Española como lengua extranjera Govt. Spain, 1992. Long term substitute Spanish and Latin tchr. Wappingers Ctrl. Sch. Dist., Wappingers Falls, NY, 1983—84, ESL tchr., 1984—87, 1990—, tchr. Spanish and Italian, 1987—89, tchr. Spanish, French, ESL, 1989—90. Curriculum writer Wappingers Ctrl. Sch. Dist., 1990, tchr. in-svc. courses, 1997—2000. Mem.: TESOL, NY State TESOL, Nat. French Honor Soc., Pi Delta Phi. Office: Wappingers Ctrl Sch Dist 167 Myers Corners Rd Wappingers Falls NY 12590 Office Phone: 845-298-5260. Personal E-mail: pdr296@yahoo.com.

ROBINSON, PAULA LEKATZ, artist; b. Thermopolis, Wyo., Jan. 26, 1953; m. Thomas Tucker Donovan (dec.); 1 child, Bonnie Lynn Larsen; m. Everett Lawson Robinson, Oct. 3, 1998 (dec.); 1 child, Equezance Fawn Marie. BA in History & Sociology, U. Minn., 1976; BA in English, St. CLoud State U.; MA in Tchg., Webster U., 1983; MA in English, St. Cloud State U., 1994. Painter U. Minn., Morris, 1973; intern Mille Lass Co., Milacg, 1974; adminstrv. asst. St. Cloud State U., 1983—94; owner, printer Ostby Printing, Duluth, 1981—89, Crosby Printing, Crosby, 1981—89; owner, quilter Waboos Enterprises, Ironton, 1989—2005. Author: Arapaho Tribal Culture, 1985, (plays) Feather, 1993, (children's book) Maggie the Moocher, 2007. Vol. Hellett Meml. Libr., Crosby. Mem.: Am. Legion Aux. (mem. Ironton aux. 2005). Democrat. Roman Catholic. E-mail: waboos1985@yahoo.com, waboos1985@emily.net.

ROBINSON, PETER J., retired dean, periodontal educator, pathologist; b. St. Louis, May 31, 1941; s. Hamilton Burrows-Greaves and Katherine (Long) R.; m. Letticia Schumacher, July 18, 1964; children: Elizabeth Haskins Vance, Emily Hamilton. BA, Drake U., Des Moines, 1963; DDS, U. Mo., Kansas City, 1966; PhD, U. Pa., Phila., 1972. Dental intern U.S. Army, Washington, 1966-67; asst. prof. U. Pa., Phila., 1973-75; prof., chmn. periodontics Northwestern U., Chgo., 1975-88, chmn. stomatology, 1988-97; dean, prof. periodontology U. Conn. Sch. Dental Medicine, 1997—2006; sr. policy fellow Am. Dental Edn. Assn., 2007—. Co-author: Transplantation for Dental Specialties, 1980. Pres. Dist. 38 Sch. Bd., Kenilworth, Ill., 1985-87. Capt. U.S. Army, 1966-69. Recipient Procter & Gamble Guest Scientist award Am. Dental Assn. Rsch. Inst., Chgo., 1983, Fogarty award NIH, Washington, 1984. Mem. ADA (sr. scientist Rsch. Inst.), Internat. Assn. Dental Rsch. (pres. periodontal rsch. group 1990-92), Midwest Soc. Periodontology (pres. 1986-87), Ill. Soc. Periodontology (pres. 1985-86). Achievements include patent on Northwestern periodontal probe. Office: U Conn Sch Dental Medicine 263 Farmington Ave Farmington CT 06030

ROBINSON, PETER M., business association executive; BA, U. Del., 1977; MA in Internat. Affairs, Columbia U., 1979. Dir. Inbound Div. Am. Inst. Fgn. Study, 1986—89; mng. Trade and Transport Policy US Coun. Internat. Bus., v.p. memberships, pres. and CEO, 2005—. Bd. dirs. AFS-USA, 1990—96, WAND, Inc., NAFSA: Assn. Internat. Educators; mem. internat. bd. trustees Am. Field Svc. Intercultural Programs, 1997—2004. Fellow: Fgn. Policy Assn.; mem.: Econ. Club of NY. Office: US Coun for Internat Bus 1212 Ave of Americas New York NY 10036 Office Phone: 212-354-4480. Office Fax: 212-575-0327. E-mail: probinson@uscib.org.

ROBINSON, PREZELL RUSSELL, academic administrator; b. Batesburg, SC, Aug. 25, 1922; s. Clarence and Annie (Folks) R.; m. Lulu Harris, Apr. 9, 1950; 1 dau. AB in Econs. Social Sci., St. Augustine's Coll., 1946; MA in Sociology, Econs., Cornell U., 1951, EdD in Sociology-Ednl. Adminstrn., 1956; degree (hon.), St. Augustine's Coll.; DCL (hon.), U. South, 1970; LHD, degree, Cuttington U. Coll., Monrovia, Liberia; LHD (hon.), Voorhees Coll., 1981, degree (hon.); LHD (hon.), Episcopal Theol. Sem., 1982; LLD (hon.), Bishop Coll., 1979; DCL (hon.), Columbia U., 1980, degree (hon.); DHL (hon.), Kenyon Coll., 1988; degree (hon.), Va. Theology Sem., Alexandria, Barton Coll., Campbell U., NC State U., Shaw U. Tchr. social sci., French Bettis Jr. Coll., Trenton, SC, 1946-48; sucessively registrar, tchr., acting prin. high sch., acting dean jr. coll., instr., dir. adult edn. Voorhees Jr. Coll., Denmark, SC, 1948-56; prof. sociology, dean coll. St. Augustine's Coll., Raleigh, NC, 1956-64, exec. dean, 1964-66, acting pres., 1966-67, pres., 1967-95, pres. emeritus, 1995—. Pres. United Negro Coll. Fund, Inc., 1978-81, Nat. Assn. Equal Opportunity Higher Edn., 1981-84, N.C. Assn. Coll. & U., Cooperating Raleigh Colls., 1981, 86—; bd. dirs. Learning Inst. N.C.; scholar-in-residence Nairobi (Kenya) U., 1973; vis. lectr. Dept. State del. to African nations, 1971, 73, 78; dir. Wachovia Bank & Trust Co.; vice chmn. N.C. State Bd. Edn., mem., 1973-99, vice-chmn., 1994-99. Contbr. articles to profl. publs. Exec. com. N.C. Edn. Com. on Tchr. Edn.; active N.C. Bd. Edn.; chmn. bd. Assn. Episcopal Colls.; mem. Mayor's Community Relations Com.; vice-chmn. Wake County divsn. Occoneechee coun. Boy Scouts Am., 1959-67; chmn. Wake Occoneechee coun., 1963-66, exec. com., 1965—; vice-chmn. Wake County chpt. ARC; chmn. edn. divsn. United Fund of Raleigh, budget com., 1965—; exec. com. Wake County Libraries; trustee Voorhees Coll. Fulbright fellow to India, 1965; appointed US alt. rep. or public mem. amb. Gen. Assembly UN, by Pres. George Bush, 1992, by Pres. Clinton, 1996. Served with AUS, 1942. Recipient Distinguished Alumni award Voorhees Coll., 1967, Silver Anniversary award N.C. Community System, 1989; decorated Star of Africia Liberia; recipient numerous service awards and citations; named one of the most effective coll. pres.s in U.S. Coun. for Advancement and Support of Edn., Washington, 1986; Univ. fellow Cornell U., 1954, rsch. fellow, 1955-56; Fulbright fellow, 1965. Mem. AAAS, Nat. Assn. Collegiate Deans and Registrars, Am. Acad. Polit. and Social Sci., Am. Sociol. Soc., N.C. Sociol. Soc. (exec. com.), Ctrl. Intercollegiate Athletic Assn. (exec. com.), N.C. Assn. Ind. Colls. and Univs. (dir.), Raleigh C. of C. (A.E. Finley Disting. Svc. award 1989), So. Sociol. Assn., Am. Acad. Polit. Sci., N.C. Lit. and Hist. Soc., N.C. Hist. Soc., Delta Mu Delta, Phi Delta Kappa, Phi Kappa Phi, Alpha Kappa Mu, Phi Beta Lambda. Protestant Episcopalian (lay reader). Home: 821 Glascock St Raleigh NC 27604-2317 Office: St Augustine's Coll 1315 Oakwood Ave Raleigh NC 27610-2247

ROBINSON, RALPH W., lawyer; b. San Francisco, Mar. 26, 1947; BA, U. Calif., Berkeley, 1968; JD, Golden Gate U., 1971. Bar: Calif. 1972, US Supreme Ct., Supreme Ct. Calif. Mng ptnr. San Francisco office Wilson, Elser, Moskowitz, Edelman & Dicker LLP, head San Francisco trial practice area. Mem.: ABA, Alameda County Bar Assn., Bar Assn. San Francisco. Office: Wilson Elser Moskowitz Et Al Sten 1700 525 Market St San Francisco CA 94105-2725 Office Phone: 415-433-0990 ext. 3001. Office Fax: 415-434-1370. Business E-Mail: robinsonr@wemed.com.

ROBINSON, RAYMOND EDWIN, conductor, music educator, writer; b. San Jose, Calif., Dec. 26, 1932; s. Elam Edwin and Zula Mai (Hatley) R.; m. Ruth Aleen Chamberlain, Mar. 12, 1954; children: Cynthia Rae, Greg Edwin, David L., Brent Steven, Jeffrey Vernon. BA, San Jose State U., 1956; MMus, Ind. U., 1958, D in Mus. Edn., 1969; LHD, Westminster Choir Coll., 1987; postdoctoral study, Jagiellonian U., Poland, 1995, Cambridge U., 1987—89, postdoctoral study, 2002—03. Instr. music Ind. U., Bloomington, 1958-59; music critic Portland Reporter, 1962-63, Balt. Evening Sun, 1964-68, Palm Beach (Fla.) Post, 1991—, Palm Beach Daily News, 2003—04; founder, tchr. seminar for music adminstrs., 1972—; chmn. divsn. fine arts Cascade Coll., Portland, Oreg., 1959-63; dean Peabody Inst., Balt., 1963-69; pres. Westminster Choir Coll., Princeton, NJ, 1969-87; vis. fellow Wolfson Coll. U. Cambridge, England, 1987—89, 2002—03; disting. prof. choral studies, choral condr. Palm Beach Atlantic U., West Palm Beach, Fla., 1989—; pres. Prestige Publs., Inc., 1978—; prof. Sch. Ch. Music Knox Theol. Sem., Ft. Lauderdale, Fla., 1989—; vis. prof. U. Miami, 2001—02. Choral condr. Palm Beach CC, Lake Worth, Fla., 1992-93; condr.-in-residence, dir. music First Presbyn. Ch., West Palm Beach, 1989-97; dir. music Coral Ridge Presbyn. Ch., Ft. Lauderdale, Fla., 1997, music dir., conductor Palm Beach Symphony Orch., 2004—; spl. guest choral condr. Palm Beach Opera, 1990—; interim condr. Choral Soc. Palm Beaches, 1992; condr. Ray Robinson Chorale, 1994—, Cambridge (Eng.) U., Cambridge, Eng., 1987-89, 2002-03, Kiev, Ukraine, 1997, Budapest, 1997, Cracow, 2002, Coral Ridge Presbyn. Ch., 1997; vis. prof. U. Miami, Fla., 2001-2002. Author: The Choral Experience, 1976, Choral Music, 1978; Krzysztof Penderecki, A Guide to His Works, 1983, A Study of the Penderecki St. Luke Passion, 1983, John Finley Williamson: A Centennial Appreciation, 1987, Postcards from Cambridge, 2005, A Bach Tribute: Bach Essays in Honor of William H. Scheide, 1993; co-author, editor: Studies in Penderecki, 1998, 2003; editor: Labyrinth of Time: Five Addresses for the End of the Millenium, 1998; The Choral Tradition Series, Hinshaw Music Inc., 1978—. Bd. dirs. Balt. Symphony Orch., 1967-69, Am. Boy Choir Sch., 1970-73, N.Y. Choral Soc., 1972—, Palm Beach Atlantic U. choral series Hinshaw Music Inc., 1990—; bd. dirs. Palm Beach County Coun. Arts, chmn. profl. artists com., mem. task force for master plan, 1990-92; mem. cultural plan com. Palm Beach County Cultural Coun., 1992; mem. task force for edn. Fla. Philharm. Orch., 1994-95; mem. art in pub. places com. West Palm Beach, Fla. 2004—. Recipient Disting. Alumni Merit award Ind. U., 1975, Disting. Alumni award Sch. Music Ind. U., 1973, Disting. Alumni award San Jose State U., 1990. Mem. Coll. Music Soc. (life), Am. Choral Dirs. Assn. (life, chmn. rsch. and publs. com. 1986—), Internat. Heinrich Schütz Soc. (chmn. Am. sect. 1984-87), Univ. Club N.Y., Nassau Club Princeton, Govs. Club West Palm Beach. Presbyterian. Home: 2413 Medina Way West Palm Beach FL 33401-8019 Business E-Mail: ray_robinson@pba.edu.

ROBINSON, REBECCA LYNNE, medical researcher; b. Evansville, Ind., Dec. 9, 1967; d. Sherman Joseph and Joyce Jeane Black; m. Robert Wayne Robinson, Aug. 8, 1992; children: Calder Luke, Mary Helen Ellie. BA, U. So. Ind., 1990; MS, Purdue U., 1995. Tchg. asst. Ind. U.-Purdue U., 1990—92; rsch. asst. Osgood Lab. for Cross-Cultural Rsch., Indpls., 1990—93; rsch. analyst Regenstrief Inst./Bowen Rsch. at Ind. U. Sch. Medicine, Indpls., 1993—98; rsch. scientist St. Vincent Hosp., Indpls., 1996—98; health outcomes rsch. cons. U.S. Med. Divsn., Eli Lilly and Co., Indpls., 1998—. Cons. Osgood Lab. for Cross-Cultural Rsch., 1993—98, Ind. Hand Ctr., Indpls., 1996—98, Ind. State Dept. Health, Indpls., 1996—98; presenter in field. Contbr. articles to profl. jours. Facilitator, team leader, participant Ministry of Moms, Nativity Ch., Indpls., 2001—05. Recipient Outstanding Grad. Student award, Purdue U., 1992, Best Author Presentation award, 17th World Congress on Psychosomatic Medicine, 2003, Rsch. award, Marketscan, 2005; grantee Agy. for Health Care Policy and Rsch., 1990—95. Mem.: DAR. Office Fax: 317-277-7444. E-mail: rlrobinson@lilly.com.

ROBINSON, RICHARD, publishing executive; b. Pitts., May 15, 1937; s. Maurice Richard and Florence (Liddell) Robinson; children: John Benham, Maurice. BA in English, magna cum laude, Harvard U., 1959; student, St. Catharines Coll., Cambridge U., Columbia U. Tchr. English, Evanston Twp. HS, Ill., 1960-62; asst. editor Lit. Cavalcade Scholastic Inc., NYC, 1962-63, editor Scholastic lit. units, 1963-64; founder, editor Scope mag., 1964, editorial dir. English, 1967-71, pub. sch. divsn., 1971-74; pres. Scholastic Inc., 1974—, CEO, 1975—, chmn. bd., 1982—. Recipient Cleveland E. Dodge medal, Columbia U. Tchrs. Coll., Best Friend award, LA's BEST After Sch. Enrichment Program, For Love of Reading award, UJA Fedn., Spotlight award, Creative Coalition; named Corp. Citizen of Yr., Robin Hood Found., 1999, Publisher of Yr., UJA Fedn. NY, 2000; named to EdPress Hall of Fame, Assn. Ednl. Publrs. Mem.: Assn. Am. Pubs. (chmn. 1996—98, exec. com., bd. dirs. 1989—, LMP Publ. of Yr. 1998), Nat. Assn. Bilingual Edn. (Corp. Citizen of Yr. 1996), Nat. Coun. Tchrs. English, Century Assn., University Club NYC, Pubs. Lunch Club, Phi Beta Kappa. Office: Scholastic Inc 557 Broadway New York NY 10012-3919 Office Phone: 212-343-6705. E-mail: drobinson@scholastic.com.

ROBINSON, ROBERT BLACQUE, foundation administrator; b. Long Beach, Calif., Apr. 24, 1927; s. Joseph LeRoi and Frances Hansel R.; m. Susan Amelia Thomas, Jan. 21, 1960; children: Victoria, Shelly, Blake, Sarah. Student, Oreg. State Coll., 1946; BA, UCLA, 1950; student, U. Hawaii. Partner, Pritchard Assocs. (Mgmt. Cons.), Honolulu, 1956-58; asst. dir. Econ. Planning and Coordination Authority, Hawaii, 1959; dep. dir. dept. econ. devel. State of Hawaii, 1960-63; asst. mgr. Pacific Concrete and Rock Co., Ltd., Honolulu, 1963-66, exec. v.p. and gen. mgr., 1966-68, pres. and gen. mgr., 1968-75, chmn., 1976-77; pres. C. of C. of Hawaii, Honolulu, 1977—. Bd. govs. Hawaii Employers Coun., 1969-74, mem. exec. com., 1969-74, vice chmn., 1973-74; bd. dirs. Pacific Aerospace Mus., 1982-86; mem. Hawaii Tourism Conf., 1977, chmn., 1981-82; bd. dirs. Aloha United Fund, 1970-76, sec., 1972, v.p., 1973-76; bd. dirs. Oahu Devel. Conf., 1970-75; treas., bd. dirs. Crime Stoppers Hawaii, 1981—; mem. Hawaii Joint Coun. on Econ. Edn., 1985—; bd. dirs. Jr. Achievement Hawaii, 1967-73, pres., 1969; bd. dirs. Hawaii Ednl. Coun., 1974-75, Health and Community Services Coun. Hawaii, 1982-84; mem. exec. com. Hawaii Conv. Ctr. Coun., 1984—, Interagency Energy Conservation Coun., State of Hawaii, 1978—; trustee Cen. Union Ch., 1983-86; bd. dirs. Waikiki Improvement Assn. Inc., 1986—; mem. Ctr. for Tropical and Subtropical Aquacultute industry Adv. Coun., 1987—; chmn. Mayor's Adv. Com. on Pacific Nations Ctr., 1988-89. Lt. comdr. USNR, 1945-46, ret. Mem. Japan-Am. Conf. of Mayors and C. of C. Pres. (mem. Am. exec. com. 1974—), Am. Soc. Assn. Execs. (past dir. Hawaii chpt.), Hawaii Execs. Coun. (found., Young Pres. Assn. (past mem.), Aloha Soc. Assn. Execs., C. of C. Hawaii (dir. 1972-75, chmn. 1975), Coun. of Profit Sharing Industries (past dir. Hawaii sect.), Cement and Concrete Products Industry of Hawaii (pres. 1968), Hawaii Mfrs. Assn. (past dir.), Navy League of U.S. (Hawaii council), Engring. Assn. Hawaii, Pacific Club, Rotary, Sigma Chi. Home: 1437 Kalaepohaku St Honolulu HI 96816-1804 Office: C of C Hawaii 735 Bishop St Ste 220 Honolulu HI 96813-4816 Business E-Mail: robinson@hawaii.rt.com.

ROBINSON, ROBERT L., retired diversified financial services company executive, lawyer; b. Ridgeway, Va., Feb. 22, 1936; s. Gerald L. and Annie (McBride) R.; m. Audrey M. Allen, July 30, 1960; children: Robert, Diane, Kelly. BA, Va. State Coll., 1957; LL.B., Harvard U., 1960; MBA, U. Conn., 1976. Bar: N.Y. 1961, Pa. 1978. Atty. N.Y. Central Ry. Co., NYC, 1960-63; asst. gen. counsel Crane Co., NYC, 1963-71; counsel Xerox Corp., Stamford, Conn., 1971-77; v.p., asst. gen. counsel and sec. INA Corp., Phila., 1977-82; sr. v.p., gen. counsel investment group CIGNA Corp., Bloomfield, Conn., 1982-84, sr. v.p., asst. gen. counsel, corp. sec., 1984-87, sr. v.p., gen. counsel property & casualty group Phila., 1987-88, sr. v.p., chief counsel litigation and ins., 1988-2000; ret., 2000. Dir. Phila. Reinsurance Corp., Am. Arbitration Assn., CPR Inst. for Dispute Resolution. Served to lt. U.S. Army, 1957. Mem. ABA, Pa. Bar Assn., Westchester-Fairfield Corp. Counsel Assn. (founder, bd. dirs. pres. 1976-77), Great Oak Yacht Cub, Harvard Club (N.Y.C.), Merion Cricket Club, Phila. Club., Phila. Cricket Club. Republican. Office: 451 Moreno Rd Wynnewood PA 19096 Office Phone: 610-896-0758. Personal E-mail: rlrobinson@verizon.net.

ROBINSON, ROGER, actor, director; b. Seattle, Wash., May 2, 1940; s. Roger and Naomi Letitia Robinson; children: Kia Koutsialis, Dana Davis. Actor: (Broadway prodns.) Drowning Crow, Seven Guitars (Tony award nomination, Outer Critics Cir. award, Drama League award, Image award), The Iceman Cometh, Amen Corner - The Musical, Ain't Supposed to Die a Natural Death, The Miser, Does a Tiger Wear a Necktie?, Talent 64, Joe Turner's Come and Gone (Tony Award for Best Featured Actor in a Play, 2009), (off-Broadway prodns.) Of Mice and Men, The Middle of Nowhere, Sty Farm, To Die for Havana; (films) Vig, Bunzy's Last Call, Meteor, Willie Dynamite, It's My Turn, The Lonely Guy, Believe in Me, Who's the Man, Real Estate, Brother to Brother, 2004; (TV series) ER, NYPD Blue, Law & Order, Homocide Life on the Streets, The Hoop Life, The Education of Max Bickford, NY Undercover, The Cosby Show; (films) On the One. Fellow: Fox Found. (hon. Fox Found. Study Grant 2000). Achievements include film and television acting credits. Office: Terri Kelly & Associates # 809 1443 Washington St Pasadena CA 91104*

ROBINSON, RONALD ALAN, manufacturing executive; b. Louisville, Mar. 23, 1952; s. J. Kenneth and Juanita M. (Crosier) R.; m. Joan Parker, 1986; children: Rex, Jay. BS, GA Inst. Tech., 1974; MBA, Harvard U., 1978. Staff engr., asst. to exec. v.p. ops. Dual Drilling Co., Wichita Falls, Tex., 1978-80; v.p. Dreco, Inc., Houston, 1980-84, pres., dir. subs. Triflo Industries Internat., Inc.; pres., COO Ramteck Sys., Inc., 1984-87; chmn., CEO Denver Techs. Inc., 1988-95; pres. Svedala Industries, Inc., 1996-99; pres., CEO Alamo Group Inc., Seguin, Tex., 1999—. Recipient Optimist Internat. Citizenship award, 1970; Gardiner Symonds fellow, 1977. Mem. Harvard Alumni Assn. Home: 18 Pourtales Colorado Springs CO 80906 Office: Alamo Group Inc 1627 E Walnut St Seguin TX 78155-5202

ROBINSON, RONALD GENE, military officer, political science professor; b. Detroit, June 13, 1952; s. John Henry and Linnie (Mattingly) R.; m. Cheryl Lee Robinson, Aug. 27, 1982 (div. July 2000); children: Ronald Jr., Lindee Marie, Ryan John; m. Dee Robinson, May

6, 2001. AA, Schoolcraft Coll., 1972; B in Gen. Studies, U. Mich., 1974; MA, Western Mich. U., 1977. Cert. govt. contracting level III. Prof. polit. sci. Schoolcraft Coll., Livonia, Mich., 1976—; contract negotiator U.S. Army, Warren, Mich., 1981—. Pres. R&B Advt. Agy., Warren, 1996-98; former mem. So. Polit. Sci. Assn. Author: Judicial Character, 1977; columnist The County Line, Warren, 1990-96, The Warren Examiner, 1996-97. Candidate Warren City Coun., 1991, nominee, 1995, 2003, 07; chmn. Hartsig Pk. Homeowners Assn., Warren, 1990-97; precinct del. Livonia Rep. Party, 1974-81; mem. Oakland County Young Reps., 2000—; bd. dirs. Warren-Centerline Right to Life, 1991—2001. Avocations: swimming, travel, dance, playing stratego, playing pool. Personal E-mail: rgr11897@aol.com.

ROBINSON, ROXANA BARRY, writer, art historian; b. Pine Mountain, Ky., Nov. 30, 1946; Attended, Bennington Coll., 1964—66; studied with Bernard Malamud and Howard Nemerov; BA in English Lit., U. Mich., 1969. Art cataloguer Sotheby's, NYC, 1970-74; exhbn. dir. Terry Dintenfass Gallery, NYC, 1974-76; freelance writer, 1976—. Instr. creative writing dept. U. Houston, 2001, Wesleyan U., 2002—03, instr. Wesleyan Writers' Conf.; lectr. Bennington Coll., U. Southern Ind., George Mason U. Author: (novels) Summer Light, 1987 (Washington Irving Book award Westchester Libr. Assn., 1988), This is My Daughter, 1998 (Washington Irving Book award Westchester Libr. Assn., 1999), Sweetwater, 2003, Cost, 2008, (short story collections) A Glimpse of Scarlet and Other Stories, 1991, Asking for Love, 1996 (Washington Irving Book award Westchester Libr. Assn., 1997, ALA Notable Book of Yr., 1997), A Perfect Stranger and Other Stories, 2005, (biography) Georgia O'Keeffe: A Life, 1989 (Washington Irving Book award Westchester Libr. Assn., 1990). Trustee Eugene Lang Coll., NY, Nat. Humanities Ctr., NC, 1995—, PEN Am. Ctr., NY, 1998—. Named a Lit. Lion, NY Pub. Libr., 1991; Creative Writing fellowship, Nat. Endowment Arts, 1987, fellowship, MacDowell Colony, 1999, Guggenheim Found., 2000. Avocation: gardening. Office: c/o Lynn Nesbit Janklow-Nesbit 445 Park Ave New York NY 10022

ROBINSON, SALLY SHOEMAKER, lay associate; b. NYC, Dec. 31, 1931; d. Samuel M. and Helen Dominick Smith S.; m. James Courtland Robinson, Dec. 31, 1931; children: Samuel Shoemaker, W. Courtland, A. Alexander, Ellen Whitridge Robinson Mihalski. BA cum laude, Bryn Mawr Coll., 1953; postgrad. studies, Yonsei U. Lang. Inst., Korea, 1960-62, Children's Theatre Assn., 1964; MA, Towson State U., 1974. Ordained elder Brown Meml. Presbyn. Ch., 1985. Commd. missionary to Korea United Presbyn. Ch., Republic of Korea, 1959-71; dir. Brown Meml. Tutorial Program, 1974-84; exec. dir. Episcopal Social Ministries Diocese of Md., Balt., 1984-97; canon for social ministry Episcopal Diocese of Md., Balt., 1985-96; chair, global bd. United Bible Societies, 2001. Trustee Am. Bible Society. Met. chmn. 10th Decade Campaign Bryn Mawr Coll., 1974-76, nat. chmn. Centennial Campaign. 1980-85, trustee, 1985—; trustee Am. Bible Soc., 1988—, v.p., 1993—, chmn. bd., 1996-2001; chmn. global bd. United Bible Socs., 2001—; trustee United Bd. for Christian Higher Edn. in Asia, 1990-95; trustee emeritus Bryn Mawr Coll., 1997—. Home: 10522 Burnside Farm Rd Stevenson MD 21153-2024 Office: Brown Meml Ch 1316 Park Ave Baltimore MD 21217-4185

ROBINSON, SALLY WINSTON, artist; b. Detroit, Nov. 2, 1924; d. Harry Lewis and Lydia (Kahn) Winston; m. Eliot F. Robinson, June 28, 1949; children: Peter Eliot, Lydia Winston, Sarah Mitchell, Suzanne Finley. BA, Bennington Coll., 1947; postgrad., Cranbrook Acad. Art, 1949; grad., Sch. Social Work, Wayne U., 1948, MA, 1972; MFA, Wayne State U., 1973. Psychol. tester Detroit Bd. Edn., 1944; psychol. counselor and tester YMCA, NYC, 1946; social caseworker Family Svc., Pontiac, Mich., 1947; instr. printmaking Wayne State U., Detroit, 1973—. Tchr. children's art Detroit Inst. Art, 1949-50, now artistic advisor, bd. dirs. drawing and pring orgn. One-woman shows include, U. Mich., 1973, Wayne State U., 1974, Klein-Vogel Gallery, 1974, Rina Gallery, 1976, Park McCullough House, Vt., 1976, Williams Coll., 1976, Arnold Klein Gallery, 1977, exhibited in group shows, Bennington Coll., Cranbrook Mus., Detroit Inst. Art, Detroit Artists Market, Soc. Women Painters, Soc. Arts and Crafts, Bloomfield Art Assn., Flint Left Bank Gallery, Balough Gallery, Detroit Soc. Woman Painters, U. Mich., U. Ind., U. Wis., U. Pitts., Toledo Mus., Krannert Mus., Represented in permanent collections. Bd. dirs. Planned Parenthood, 1951—, mem. exec. bd., 1963—; bd. dirs. PTA, 1956-60, Roeper City and Country Sch., U. Mich. Mus. Art, 1978; trustee Putnam Hosp. Med. Rsch. Inst., 1978; mem. Gov.'s Commn. Art in State Bldgs., 1978-79; mem. art and devel. coms. So. Vt. Art Ctr., 1987-88; mem. vol. com. Marie Selby Gardens; patron Graphic Art Studio, U. So. Fla., Tampa; patron, benefactor Clark Mus., Williamstown, Mass.; vol. Shelburne Art Ctr., Vt. Fellow: Williams Coll. Mus. Art (mem. visiting com.); mem.: Bloomfield Art Assn. (program co-chmn. 1956), Birmingham Soc. Women Painters (pres. 1974—76), Detroit Soc. Women Painters, Detroit Artists Market (dir. 1956—, hon. bd. mem.), Founders Soc. Detroit Inst. Art, Bennington Coll. Alumnae Assn. (regional co-chmn. 1954), Harvard Club (Sarasota, Fla.), Williams College Club (NYC), Cosmopolitan Club (NYC), Founders Garden Club (Sarasota), Garden Club Am. (selby gardens herbarium vol. 2006—), Oaks Club (Fla.), Women's City Club (coord. art shows Detroit 1950), Village Women's Club (Birmingham, Mich.). Unitarian Universalist. Home: 209 Hills Point Rd Charlotte VT 05445-9698 also: 639 Eagle Watch Ln Osprey FL 34229 Personal E-mail: sallyrobinsonflorida@msn.com.

ROBINSON, SARA CURTIS, arts administrator; b. Amarillo, Tex., Jan. 6, 1967; d. Don Teel Curtis and Suzanne (Stokes) Brent; m. Benjamin Rowland Robinson, Oct. 5, 1991; children: Rowland Wyatt, Tristan Rodman, Spalding Rhys. BA, Pine Manor Coll., 1989. Asst. to curator Asiatic art Mus. Fine Arts, Boston, 1990-91; from devel. officer to dir. devel. Bank of Boston Celebrity Series, 1992—96. Mem. Women in Devel., Boston, 1993-96, Boston Arts Mktg. Group, 1992-94. Mem. Jr. League Boston, 1990-95, com. chair, 1993; mem. Mass. Advocates for the Arts, Boston, 1993-96, Cultural Diversity Com. for the Arts, Boston, 1993-96; com. Newbury St. League Auction, Boston, 1989. Mem. Internat. Soc. Performing Arts Adminstrs., Nat. Soc. Fundraising Execs., Palm Beach Day Acad. (parent coun. pres., bd. dirs. 2007-09, assoc. dir. 2009). Episcopalian.

ROBINSON, SHARON PORTER, educational association administrator; b. Louisville, 1944; B in Edn., English and Psych., U. Ky., 1966, M in Edn., Curriculum and Instrn., 1976, D in Ednl. Adminstrn. and Supervision, 1979; D (hon.), U. Louisville. Tchr., Lexington, Ky., US AFB, Bitburg, Germany; assoc. dir. Jefferson County Edn. Consortium, Ky.; dir. instrn. and profl. devel. NEA, 1980—89, dir. Nat. Ctr. Innovation, 1989—93; asst. sec. edn. Office Ednl. Rsch. and Improvement US Dept. Edn., 1993—96; v.p. tchg. and learning for state and fed. rels. Ednl. Testing Svc., Washington, 1997—98, sr. v.p., COO, 1998, exec. v.p., pres. Ednl. Policy Leadership Inst., 2002—04; interim dep. dir. Progs. and Legis. Office PTA; pres., CEO Am. Assn. Colls. for Tchr. Edn., Washington, 2005—. Cons. Nat. Bd. Profl. Tchg. Stds.; head tchr. edn. initiative Nat. Ctr. Innovation. Bd. trustees Alfred Harcourt Found. Recipient Award of Appreciation, Nat. Head Start Found., Founders award, Nat. Commn. African Am. Edn., Pinnacles of Excellence award, Helping Hands Enrichment & Leadership Found., Tchr. for Am. award, Girl Scouts' Woman of Distinction award. Office: Am Assn Colls for Tchr Edn 1307 New York Ave NW Ste 300 Washington DC 20005-4701 E-mail: srobinson@aacte.org.*

ROBINSON, STEPHANIE NICOLE, education educator; b. Chgo., July 8, 1974; d. Thomas Earl and Lola Jean Robinson; m. Melvin Douglas Burch. BA, U. Ill., Champaign, 1996, MA, 2000, PhD, 2002. Rsch. asst. U. Ill., 1997—2000, tchg. asst., 2000—02; substitute tchr. Champaign Pub. Schs., 1998—2002; asst. prof. Ball State U., Muncie, Ind., 2002—04; substitute tng. instr. Dept. Def., Camp Lejeune, NC, 2005; faculty mentor Western Govs. U., Salt Lake City, 2005—. Contbr. to book: Greenwood Dictionary of Education, 2003; author: History of Immigrant Female Students, 2004. Vol. ARC, NC, 2005; mem. com. Martin Luther King Sch., 2005. Mem.: Nat. Coun. Social Studies, Nat. Assn. Multicultural Edn., Officers Wives Club. Roman Catholic. Avocations: tennis, golf, crafts.

ROBINSON, STEPHEN MICHAEL, mathematician, educator; b. Columbus, Ohio, Apr. 12, 1942; s. Arthur Howard and Mary Elizabeth (Coffin) R.; m. Chong-Suk Han, May 10, 1968; children: Diana Marie Oestreich, James Andrew. BA, U. Wis., 1962, PhD, 1971; MS, NYU, 1963; Diploma, U.S. Army War Coll., 1986; Dr. honoris causa, Univ. Zürich, 1996. Adminstr. U. Wis., Madison, 1969-72, asst. prof., 1972-75, assoc. prof., 1975-79, prof. indsl. and sys. engring. and computer scis., 1979—2007, prof. emeritus indsl. sys. engring. and computer scis., 2008—, chmn. dept. indsl. engring., 1981-84. Cons. to various agys. Dept. Def., 1971—. Author: (with Jagdish Chandra) An Uneasy Alliance: The Mathematics Research Center at the University of Wisconsin, 1956-1987, 2005; editor: Math. of Ops. Rsch., 1981-86, assoc. editor, 1975-80, Jour. Ops. Rsch., 1974-86, Math. Programming, 1986-91; mem. bd. editors Annals Ops. Rsch., 1984-99, Set-Valued Analysis, 1992-99, Jour. Convex Analysis, 1994—2002; adv. editor Math. of Ops. Rsch., 1987—, Ops. Rsch. Letters, 2002-; mem. editl. bd. Springer Series in Ops. Rsch. and Fin. Engring., 1996—, Set Valued & Variational Analysis, 2009-; contbr. numerous articles to profl. jours. Trustee Village of Shorewood Hills, Wis., 1974-76, mem. fin. com., 1973-87; bd. on math. scis. and their applications NRC, 2001-07, bd. overseers Simon's Rock Coll., Great Barrington, Mass., 1991-02. Served to capt. US Army, 1963—69, Korea, Vietnam, col. AUS, ret. Decorated Legion of Merit, Bronze star, Air medal, Army Commendation medal with 2 oak leaf clusters; recipient John K. Walker Jr. award, Mil. Ops. Rsch. Soc., 2001. Fellow Inst. Ops. Rsch. and Mgmt. Scis. (mem. Ops. Rsch. Soc. Am. coun. 1991-94, sec. 2000-03, treas. 2007—), Soc. Indsl. and Applied Math.; mem. Inst. Indsl. Engrs. (sr.), Math. Programming Soc. (mem.-at-large of coun. 1991-94, George B. Dantzig prize 1997), Nat. Acad. Engring. (elected mem. 2008-), Madison Club, Nat. Rsch. Coun.(Assoc., 2008) Home: 1014 University Bay Dr Madison WI 53705-2251 Office: U Wis Dept Indsl and Sys Engring 1513 University Ave Rm 3015 Madison WI 53706-1539 Home Phone: 608-231-3065; Office Phone: 608-263-6862. Business E-Mail: smrobins@wisc.edu.

ROBINSON, THOMAS CHRISTOPHER, health science educator; b. Buffalo, Oct. 16, 1944; s. Christopher Sidney and Eleanor Florence (Martin) R.; m. Rena H. Robinson; children: Diane Dunn, Kristen O'Melia. BA, SUNY, Buffalo, 1966, EdM, 1968, PhD, 1971; grad. mgmt. devel. program, Harvard U., Cambridge, Mass., 1989. Admissions officer, office of admissions and records SUNY, Buffalo, 1966-72, assoc. dean Sch. Health Related Professions, 1975-78; asst. dir. Erie County Lab., Buffalo, 1972-75; assoc. dean Coll. Allied Health Professions, U. Ky., Lexington, 1978-84, dean Coll. Health Scis., 1984—2004, prof., 1984—2008, dean emeritus, 2005—, prof. emeritus, 2008—. Cons. MDS Labs., Hamilton, Ont., Can., 1973-75, Joint US-Arabian Commn. on Econ. Cooperation, 1986-87, West Sussex Inst. Higher Edn., Bogner Regis, U.K., 1987, U. Wis. Sys. Ctrs. of Excellence Program, 1988, Pub. Health Svc. Health Resources Adminstrn., 1983, 90-91; mem. exec. com. Nat. Practitioner Data Bank, 1992-94, cons. 1994-95; hon. mem. faculty Khabarovsk (Russia) Med. Inst., 1996; bd. dirs. Health Ky. Contbr. articles to profl. jours. Mem. Health Sys. Agy. Coun., Buffalo, 1977-78, Western NY Hemophilia Soc. Bd. Buffalo, 1977-78, Lexington-Fayette County Bd. Health, Lexington, 1987-91, program excellence project Ohio Bd. Regents, United Way of Bluegrass Healthcare Devel. Bd., 1991; cons. La. Bd. Regents, 1995, 98, 2001, 04, 06, 07, Univ. Wolverhampton fellow, UK, 1991; bd. dirs. Ky. HealthCare Improvement Authority, 2006—; mem. leadership coun. Am. Diabetes Assn., Lexington, 2007-09. Sgt. NY Army N.G., 1968-74. Recipient Svc. award, Jour. Allied Health, 1986; Internat fellow, Hatfield Coll., Un. Durham, Eng., 2005. Mem. Assn. Schs. Allied Health Professions (bd. dirs. 1985-87, Svc. award 1987, Fellow award 1988, pres. 1991-94, past pres. 1994-95, Outstanding Mem. award 1995), Ky. Allied Health Consortium (bd. dirs. 1985-93, chair 1995-96), So. Assn. Allied Health Deans (sec. 1986-88, chmn. 1988-90), Assn. Schs. Allied Health Professions (pres. 1991-94), Ky. Hosp. Assn., Ky. Assn. Healthcare Facilities, So. Assn. Colls. and Schs. (chair and accreditation evaluator), Sigma Phi Epsilon. Avocations: golf, travel, genealogy, gardening. Business E-Mail: tcrobi@uky.edu.

ROBINSON, TONYA LOUISE, nursing educator, director; b. Springfield, Ohio, July 13, 1963; d. Gary Johnson and Sharon Lee Walls; m. Arthur Richard Robinson, June 18, 1988; children: Bruce, Shocka, Adrianna. AS in Nursing, San Joaquin Delta Coll., Stockton, Calif., 2008, AA in Natural Scis., 2008. Nursing clin. instr. Modesto Jr. Coll., Calif., 2005—08; dir., nursing Casa Modesto, 2008—. Home: 3605 Bellwood Ct Modesto CA 95356 Office: Casa Modesto 1745 Eldena Way Modesto CA 95350 Personal E-mail: trobi618@netzero.com.

ROBINSON, V. GENE (THE RIGHT REVEREND V. GENE ROBINSON), bishop; b. Lexington, Ky., May 29, 1947; life ptnr. Mark Andrew; children: Jamee, Ella. BA in Am. Studies and History, U. South, 1969; MDiv, Gen. Theol. Sem., 1973. Curate Christ Ch., Ridgewood, NJ, 1973—75; youth ministries coord. Province 1 Episcopal Province New England, 1978—85, exec. sec. Province I, 1983—2003; canon to the ordinary (asst. to bishop) Episcopal Diocese NH, 1988—2003, bishop, 2003—. Bd. trustees Gen. Theol. Sem., 2001—; co-owner, dir. Girl's Summer Camp and Horse Farm, 1975—78; founding dir. Sign of the Dove Retreat Ctr., Temple, NH; mem. Nat. Youth Ministries Devel. Team. Author: In the Eye of the Storm: Swept to the Center by God, 2008. Founder Concord Outright; trustee Church Pension Fund; bd. mem. NH Children's Alliance. Avocations: cooking, gardening, music, running. Office: Episcopal Diocese of NH 63 Green St Concord NH 03301-4243 Office Phone: 603-224-1914. E-mail: grinn@nhepiscopal.org.*

ROBINSON, W. LEE, lawyer; b. Rome, Ga., Sept. 24, 1943; m. Irene Scales, 1966; children: Christine, Jacquelyn. BS, Ga. Inst. Tech.; MBA, JD, Mercer U., 1985. With Robinson Hardware Store, Macon, Ga., 1954-86; mem. Ga. Senate, Atlanta, 1975-83; mayor City of Macon, Macon, 1987—91; pvt. practice Macon, 1985—2004; circuit pub. defender Macon Jud. Circuit, 2005—. Judge mcpl. ct. (part time), Macon. Bd. dirs. Cherry Blossom Festival, 2006—, chmn., 2008—. 2d lt. US Army, col. USAR. Decorated Bronze Star with two oak leaf clusters, Legion of Merit with oak leaf cluster; recipient Justice Robert Benham award for Cmty. Svc., 2007; named to U.S. Army Officer Candidate Sch. Hall of Fame. Mem. Ga. Assn. Criminal Def. Lawyers, Macon C. of C. (former bd. dirs.), Macon Bar Assn, Alzheimer's Assn. (chmn., bd. govs. Ga. chpt. 2005-07) Address: 3824 Overlook Ave Macon GA 31204-1325 Office: 201 2nd St Ste 550 Macon GA 31201-8282 also: PO Box 4852 Macon GA 31208-4852 E-mail: wlrmcnlaw@aol.com.

ROBINSON, WILKES COLEMAN, retired federal judge; b. Anniston, Ala., Sept. 30, 1925; s. Walter Wade and Catherine Elizabeth (Coleman) R.; m. Julia Von Poellnitz Rowan, June 24, 1955 (dec.); children: Randolph C., Peyton H., Thomas Wilkes Coleman; m. Dorothy Anne LaVictoire, Jan. 17, 2004. BA with honors, U. Ala., 1948; JD, U. Va., 1951. Bar: Ala. 1951, Va. 1962, Mo. 1966, Kans. 1983; cert. mediator, Fla., Ala. Assoc. Bibb & Hemphill, Anniston, 1951-54; city recorder City of Anniston, 1953-55; judge Juvenile and Domestic Rels. Ct. of Calhoun County, Ala., 1954-56; atty. legal dept. GM&O R.R., Mobile, Ala., 1956-58; commerce counsel, asst. gen. atty. Seaboard Air Line R.R., Richmond, Va., 1958-66; chief commerce counsel Monsanto Co., St. Louis, 1966-70; gen. counsel, v.p. Marion Labs., Inc., Kansas City, Mo., 1970-79; pres. Gulf and Gt. Plains Legal Found., Kansas City, Mo., 1980-85, also bd. dirs.; atty. Howard, Needles, Tammen & Bergendoff, Kansas City, 1985-86, also bd. dirs.; v.p. S.R. Fin. Group, Inc., Overland Park, Kans., 1986-87; judge U.S. Ct. Fed. Claims, Washington, 1987-97, sr. judge, 1997—2003; of counsel Morris, Cary, Andrews, Talmadge, Jones & Driggers, Dothan, Ala., 2006—. Bd. govs. Kansas City Philharm. Orch., 1975-77. Served with USNR, 1943-44. Mem. Indian Bayou Golf Club, Destin Health & Fitness Club, Scottish Rite, Phi Beta Kappa (past treas. Kansas City, Mo. chpt.), Phi Eta Sigma, Phi Alpha Theta, Kappa Alpha. Episcopalian. Home: 12 Weekewachee Cir Destin FL 32541-4426 Office Phone: 850-654-9137. E-mail: wilkescrob@cox.net.

ROBINSON, WILLIAM ANDREW, retired health service executive, physician; b. Phila., Pa., Jan. 31, 1943; s. Colonial Washington and Lillian Dorothy Robinson; m. Jacqueline Ellen Garcia, Mar. 28, 1980; 1 child, David Alan; 1 child by previous marriage, William Andrew Jr. BA, Hampton U., 1964; MD, Meharry Med. Coll., 1971; MPH, Johns Hopkins U., 1973. Diplomate Nat. Bd. Med. Examiners; lic. physician, Md. Rotating intern George W. Hubbard Hosp., Nashville, 1971-72, emergency room physician, 1972; med. officer gastrointestinal drug sect., bur. drugs FDA USPHS, HEW, Rockville, Md., 1973-75; dep. dir. office health resources opportunity USPHS, HHS, Rockville, Md., 1975-80, dep. dir. bur. health professions health resources adminstrn., 1980-87, chief med. officer health resources and svcs. adminstn., 1987-89, dep. asst. sec. minority health, dir. office minority health Washington, 1989-91, acting adminstr. health resources and svc. adminstrn. Rockville, Md., 1993-94, chief med. officer health resources and svc. adminstrn., 1991—2007, dir. Office Pub. Health Affairs, 1996-97, dir. Ctr. for Quality, 1997—2006, dir office Min. Health and Health Disparities, 2006—07. Chmn. sr. execs. performance rev. bd. Office of Asst. Sec. for Health, 1990-91; pub. health svc. rep. 2d Internat. Conf. on Health Promotion, Adelaide, South Australia; health cons. com. on interior and insular affairs U.S. Ho. of Reps., Washington, 1982-83; appointed field faculty dept. family and cmty. health Meharry Med. Coll., 1979; U.S. rep. to WHO Primary Health Care Conf., Alma Ata, Kazakhstan. Mem. nat. editl. bd. Jour. Health Care for the Poor and Underserved, 1991. Capt. U.S. Army, 1964-67. Recipient Nat. Urban Coalition Comty. Health Svc. award, 1972, Letter of Appreciation, Chmn. Congl. Black Caucus Health Braintrust, U.S. Ho. of Reps., 1988. Mem. AMA, APHA, Am. Acad. Family Physicians, Blacks in Govt., Fed. Physicians Assn., Nat. Med. Assn., Sr. Execs. Assn., Delta Omega (Alpha chpt., pres., 2005-07).

ROBINSON, WILLIAM H., engineering educator; PhD in Elec. & Computer Engring., Ga. Inst. Tech., Atlanta, 2003. Asst. prof. elec. engring. Vanderbilt U., Nashville, 2003—. Recipient award, Nat. Sci. Found. Mem.: Alpha Phi Alpha Frat., Inc. Office: Vanderbilt Univ VU Stn B 351824 2301 Vanderbilt Pl Nashville TN 37235-1824 Office Fax: 615-343-6702.

ROBINSON, WILLIAM PHILIP, III, state supreme court justice; b. Providence, Jan. 30, 1940; s. William Philip and Dorothy Frances (Hayes) R. BA, U. de Louvain, Belgium, 1962; MA, U. RI, 1966; PhD, U. Conn., 1971; JD, Boston Coll., 1975. Bar: RI 1975, Mass. 1985, US Ct. Appeals (1st cir.) 1977, US Supreme Ct. 1989. Instr. U. Conn., Storrs, 1967-71; law clk. U.S. Ct. Appeals, Boston, 1975-77; assoc. Edwards & Angell, Providence, 1977-81, ptnr., 1981—2004; justice RI Supreme Ct., 2004—. Bd. trustees Providence Country Day Sch., East Providence, 1991-97. Mem. East Greenwich Sch. Com., 1988-96, vice chmn., 1990-94; mem. exec. com. RI Assn. Sch. Coms., 1990-96; mem. East Greenwich Dem. Town Com., 1988-2004; mem. Fed. Bd. Bar Examiners, RI, 1994-2004; mem. RI Jud. Performance Evaluation Com., 1993-2004, RI Bd. Govs. for Higher Edn., 2000-03. Mem. Boston Coll. Law Sch. Alumni Assn. (v.p. RI chpt. 1990-93, pres. 1993-97, nat. del. 1997—), Order of Coif, Phi Beta Kappa. Avocations: reading, literary translation, swimming. Office: RI Supreme Ct Frank Licht Jud Complex 250 Benefit St Providence RI 02903 Office Phone: 401-222-3775. Business E-Mail: wrobinson@courts.ri.gov.*

ROBINSON, WILLIAM T., III, lawyer; b. Covington, Ky., Jan. 6, 1945; s. William T. Jr. and Hilda C. (Tatermann) R.; m. Joan Mary Wernersbach, Aug. 2, 1969; children: William Taylor IV, Todd Arthur. AB, Thomas More Coll., 1967; JD, U. Ky., 1971. Bar: Ohio 1971, Ky. 1972, Tenn. 1999, U.S. Dist. Ct. (ea. dist.) Ky. 1972, U.S. Dist. Ct. (so. dist.) Ohio 1971, U.S. Dist. Ct. (we. dist.) Ky. 1993, U.S. Dist. Ct. (so. dist.) Ind. 1996, U.S. Ct. Appeals (6th cir.) 1972, U.S. Supreme Ct 1978. Ptnr. Robinson, Arnzen, Parry & Wentz, P.S.C., Covington, Ky., 1971—; mem. in charge, Greater Cincinnati & No. Ky., exec. comm. Greenebaum Doll & McDonald, Covington, Ky.; mem.-in-charge Florence office Frost Brown Todd, Florence. Found. bd. mem. Appellate Judges Edn. Inst., 2003; adj. prof. No. Ky. U., 1977—; lectr. numerous seminars. Bd. of trustees Redwood Sch. and Rehabilitation Ctr., 1971-81, 83—, sec., 1972-73, 1st v.p., 1973-75, pres., 1975-78, bd. of overseers, 1981-83; bd. of trustees, chmn. Dorothy Wood Found., 1980—, bd. mem. emeritus 2003-; bd. dirs. Cin. chpt. ARC, 1979-85; sust. atty. mem. Product Liability Adv. Council 1997-; Coll. Law Univ. Ky. Lafferty Soc. 1981-, mem. visiting comm. 1988- (chmn. 1995 & 1998), commencement speaker 1988, Hall of Fame 2004; bd. mem. Boy Scouts Am. Powder Horn dist. 1994-; bd. mem. Cincinnati Inst. Fine Arts 1999-2004; bd. dir. Cincinnati/No. Ky. Internat. Airport 1998-, vice chmn. 2004-; bd. trustees Cincinnati Symphony 1998-2004; found. bd. mem. Cincy-Tech USA, 2002-; found. bd. mem. Forward Quest 1997-; policy bd. mem. Partnership for Greater Cincinnati 1999-, chmn. 1999-2003; bd. mem. Greater Cincinnati C. of C. 1994-, exec. comm. 1999-2003; bd. mem. Greater Cincinnati Scholrship Assn. 1994-; bd. mem. Kentuckians for Better Transp. 1996-2004; bd. mem. Ky. C. of C. 1987-93, chmn. 1992-92, Dunlevy frontiersman Comm. Svc. award 1991; mem. Legatus Cincinnati chptr. 1996-2004; bd. trustees Mt. St. Joseph Coll. 1997-; bd. mem. Nat. Conf. Community & Justice 1986-97, treas. 1990-97, co-chmn. 1995-97, emeritus bd. 1997-, Disting. Svc. Citation 2004; adv. trustee Nat. Underground Railroad Freedom Ctr. 2001-; found. bd. mem. & sec./treas. Tri-County Econ. Dev. Corp. 1987-; co-found. & charter bd. mem. Tri-County Econ. Devel. Found. 1996-, charter sec./treas. 1996-2000, treas. 2000-; life mem. Univ. Ky. Alum. Assn., fellow 1981-. Recipient Covington award, Friends of Covington, 1998, Judge Learned Hand Human Rels. award, Am. Jewish Comm., 1998, Governor's Econ. Devel. Leadership award, Ky., 1997, Knight of Malta, 1992. Fellow Am. Acad. Appellate Lawyers 1998, Internat. Soc. Barristers 1988; Mem. ABA (bd. govs. 2000-, exec. com. 2002-03, treas.-elect 2004-2005, treas. 2005-2008, chmn. fin. comm. 2002-03), Ohio Bar Assn., Fed. Bar Assn. (mem. steering comm. 2002-), Ky. Bar Assn. (past pres., Outstanding Lawyer award, 1989), Am. Bar Found. (life fellow, fellows chmn Ky. 2000-2004), Am. Law Inst., Sixth Cir. Jud. Conf. (life mem.), Ky. Bar Found. (pres. 1988-89, charter life fellow 1986-), No. Ky. Bar Assn., Louisville bar Assn., Cincinnati Bar Assn. (Themis award 2003), Kenton County Bar Assn. (mem. exec. com. 1973-75, chmn. legal-med. com. 1978-83, Ann. Merit award 1973), Ky. Def. Counsel Assn., Internat. Assn. Ins. Counsel, Internat. Assn. Def. Counsel, Salmon P. Chase Am. Inn Ct. (co-founder & pres. 1993-94, master 1993-), Acad. Trial Lawyers Am., So. Conf. Bar Pres., Nat. Conf. Bar Pres.s', U. Ky. Alumni Assn. (bd. dirs. 1981—), No. Ky. C. of C. (vice chmn. 1985-86, bd. dirs. 1980—, Profl. of Yr. 1980), Thomas More Coll. Alumni Assn. (bd. dirs. 1972—, pres. 1974-75, chmn. alumni fund drive 1974-75, Disting. Alum. award 1982), Phi Alpha Theta, Alpha Delta Gamma, Phi Delta Phi. Office: Frost Brown Todd 7310 Turfway Rd Ste 210 Florence KY 41042 Office Phone: 859-817-5901. Office Fax: 859-283-5902. E-mail: wrobinson@fbtlaw.com.*

ROBINSON, WYNNELLE ANN, counseling administrator; d. William H. Battles and Jeanette A.; children: Wendy, Lance, Cody. BS in Phys. Edn., Jacksonville U., Ala., 1971; MA in Phys. Edn., U. Ala., Tuscaloosa, 1981, EdS in Guidance/Counseling Adminstrn., 1998; PhD in Counselling & Supervision, U. Argosy, 2009. Phys. edn. tchr. Gadsden City Bd. Edn., Ala., 1973—99; counselor Etowah County Bd. Edn., Gadsden, Ala., 1999—2001, Trion City Sch., Ga., 2001—. Gymnastic coach Baton, 1960—. Mem.: GSA, NEA, Family Connections (bd. mem.), NBTA, Am. Sch. Counselor Assn., Am. Econ. Assn. Office: 919 Allgood St Trion GA 30753 Home Phone: 256-413-0100; Office Phone: 706-734-2530. Personal E-mail: wynnrobinson1@yahoo.com. Business E-Mail: wynn.robinson@trionschools.org.

ROBINSON-GUSTIN, BRENDA SUE, retired art educator, painter; b. Kenosha, Wis., July 22, 1949; d. Ralph Burt and Alene Margaret Robinson; m. John Julius Gustin, Mar. 25, 1972; children: Amy Beth Farr, John Andrew Gustin, Daniel Adam Gustin. BA, U. Wis. Parkside, Kenosha, 1971. Cert. unltd.life cert. State of Wis. Dept. Pub. Instrn., 1977, art tchr. grades K-8, secondary sch. tchr. grades 7-12. Art tchr. Kenosha Unified Sch. Dist. 1, 1974—2006, coord. art exhibit elem. children, 1991—2006; ret., 2006. Art coord., advertiser Animal Rehab. Kinship, Racine, Wis., 1987—91; coord. art exhibit Anderson Art Ctr., Kenosha, 2004, Bose Elem. Sch. Artist (exhibitions) local restaurants, Kenosha, 1969—71, U. Wis., Racine, Parkside Art Gallery, Kenosha, 1987, 1991, 1997, 1999—2000, 2005, Anderson Art Ctr.; permanent collection, Legacy Mus. and Vets. Ctr., Racine. Recipient Blue Ribbon, Kenosha County Fair, Wilmot, Wis., 1976, Cert. of Appreciation, Kenosha Unified Sch. Dist., 1999. Mem.: Kenosha County Ret. Educators Assn., Wis. Edn. Assn. Coun., Kenosha Edn. Assn., Wis. Ret. Educators' Assn. (life), Kenosha Unified Twenty-Five Yr. Club. Independent. Lutheran. Avocations: collecting vintage dog figurines, travel, visiting Southwestern art galleries. Home: 1802 83rd St Kenosha WI 53143-1652 Home Phone: 262-658-2118.

ROBINSON-ODOM, JUNE FRANCES MARGARET A., art educator; m. David Leonard Odom, July 4, 1993. BA in History of Art, Birkbeck Coll., London, 1968; diploma in Design, Croydon Coll. Art, 1965. Cert. tchr. Dept. Edn. and Sci., 1965, examiner in art and design Midland Exam. Group, 1988. Vis. lectr. art and design Cambridgeshire Coll. Art and Tech., Cambride, England, 1966—73; lectr. drawing and painting, Inst. Edn. U. Cambridge, 1970—79, lectr. drawing and painting, Grad. Soc., 1970—81, examiner art and design, 1987—89, Midland Exam. Group, Birmingham, England, 1988—90; asst. head art dept. Comberton Coll., Cambridge, 1988—89; adj. lectr. art history Lorain County CC, Elyria, Ohio, 1992—. Examiner Cambrige Examinations Syndicate, 1987—89. Painting and drawing, Lorain County CC, various art exhbns.in London and Cambridge; illustrator (childrens book) Super Kids, shoe designer H M Rayne the Queen of England's Shoe. Home: 2490 Brownhelm Station Rd Vermilion OH 44089 Office: Lorain County CC Abbe Rd Elyria OH 44035 Personal E-mail: odoms@centurytel.net.

ROBINSON-ZAÑARTU, CAROL A., psychology professor, department chairman; d. Montgomery Scott and Doris Little Robinson; m. Juan Pablo Zanartu, July 1989; children: Felipe Reymundo Robinson-Zanartu, Federico Lautaro Robinson-Zanartu. BA, W.Va. Wesleyan U., 1966; MS, Boston U., 1967; PhD, U. Pitts., 1981. Cert. sch. psychologist Calif. Counselor Allegheny County CC, Pitts., 1968—70; dir. Learning Founds., Inc., San Diego, 1971—74; prin. Found. Elem. Sch., San Diego, 1973—74; sch. psychologist Grossmont Union HS Dist., La Mesa, Calif., 1977—79; edn. specialist Nat. Coun. Alcoholism, San Diego, 1974—75; co-director Interdisciplinary Devel. Ctr., La Mesa, 1975—77; sch. psychologist Lakeside Union Sch. Dist., Calif., 1979—80; prof., chair Dept. Counseling & Sch. Psychology San Diego State U., 1980—. Prin. investigator San Diego State U. Found., 1990—; pres. Calif. Assn. Mediated Learning, San Diego, 1996—97; standing panel reviewer Office Spl. Edn. U.S. Dept. Edn., DC, 2000—; panel reviewer U.S. Office Indian Edn., DC, 2000; dir., Native Am. Scholars & Collaborators Project Office Spl. Edn. U.S. Dept. Edn., DC, 2003—. Author: (book) Handbook of Psychological Assessment, Dynamic Assessment: Prevailing Models and Applications, (textbook) Manual de Evaluaction Psicologica, Handbook of Psychological Evaluation, The Psychology of Multiculturisation In the Schools. Grantee Tchg. fellow, U. Pitts., 1978-1979. Mem.: NASP (folio reviewer 1992—), APA, Calif. Assn. Sch. Psychologists, Calif. U. Educators Sch. Psychologists (chair, tng. standards & innovations com. 1992—98), Calif. Assn. Mediated Learning (pres. 1996—97). D-Liberal. Avocations: sailing, reading, writing. Office: San Diego State U 5500 Campanille Dr San Diego CA 92182-1179 Office Phone: 619-594-7725.

ROBISON, EMILY BURNS, musician; b. Pittsfield, Mass., Aug. 16, 1972; d. Paul and Barbara Burns; m. Charlie Robison, May 1, 1999 (div. Aug. 6, 2008); children: Charles Augustus, Julianna Tex, Henry Benjamin. Performer Blue Night Express, 1984—89; banjo player, guitarist, vocalist Dixie Chicks, 1989—. Musician: (albums) Thank Heavens for Dale Evans, 1990, LIttle Ol' Cowgirl, 1992, Shouldn't a Told You That, 1993, Wide Open Spaces, 1998 (Maximum Vision Clip of Yr., Billboard, 1998, Best New Country Artist Clip of Yr., Billboard, 1998, Best Country Album, Grammy Awards, 1998, Album of Yr., Acad. Country Music, 1998, Best Selling Album, Can. Country Music Awards, 1999, Song of Yr., WB Radio Music Award, 1999, Album of Yr., ACM, 1999), Fly, 1999 (Best Country Album, Grammy Awards, 1999, Best Selling Album, Can. Country Musc Awards, 2000, Internat. Album, British Country Music Award, 2000, Country Album of Yr., Billboard Awards, 2000, Album of Yr., ACM, 2000, Album of Yr., CMA, 2000), Home, 2002 (Favorite Country Album, Am. Music Awards, 2002, Best Recording Package, Grammy Awards, 2002, Best Country Album, Grammy Awards, 2002), Top of the World Tour: Live, 2003 (Best Country Group Vocal Performance, Grammy Awards, 2005), Taking the Long Way, 2006 (Album of Yr. and Best Country Album, Grammy Awards, 2007), (songs) Not Ready to Make Nice, 2006 (Record of Yr., Song of Yr., Best Performance by a Duo or Group with Vocal, Grammy Awards, 2007); performer: (documentary) Dixie Chicks: Shut Up and Sing, 2006. Recipient Horizon award, CMA, 1998; named Most Significant New Country Act, Country Monitor, 1998, Top New Country Artist, Billboard, 1998, Top Vocal Group, Acad. Country Music, 1998, Country Artist of Yr., Rolling Stone, 1999, Top Country Artist, Billboard, 1999, Internat. Rising Star, British Country Music Awards, 1999, Artist of Yr. (Country), WB Radio Music Award, 1999, Favorite New Artist (Country), AMA, 1999, Vocal Group of Yr., CMA, 1999, Country Artist of Yr., Billboard, 1999, 2000, Entertainer of Yr., CMA, 2000, ACM, 2000, Vocal Group of Yr., 2001, Entertainer of Yr., 2001, Favorite Musical Group or Band, People's Choice Award, 2002, Vocal Group of Yr., Country Music Assn., 2002, others; named one of 100 Most Influential People, Time Mag., 2006.

ROBISON, MATTHEW L., legislative staff member; B, Swarthmore Coll., Pa.; M in Pub. Policy, Harvard U. Kennedy Sch. Govt., Boston. Legis. asst. to congressman John Baldacci US House of Reps., 2001—02, legis. dir. dep. chief of staff to congressman Michael Michaud, 2003—07, chief of staff to congressman Paul Hodes, 2007—. Democrat. Mailing: US House Reps 1317 Longworth House Office Bldg Washington DC 20515 Office Phone: 202-225-5206. Office Fax: 202-225-2946. Business E-Mail: matt.robison@mail.house.gov.*

ROBISON, OLIN CLYDE, political science educator, former college president; b. Anacoco, La., May 12, 1936; s. Audrey Clyde and Ruby (Cantrell) R.; div.; children: Gordon Reece, Blake Elliott, Mark Edward. BA, Baylor U., 1958, LLD, 1979; D.Phil., Oxford U., Eng., 1963; LHD (hon.), Ehrenburger-Johannes Gutenberb U., Mainz, Fed. Republic Germany, 1977, Monterey Inst. Internat. Studies, 1982, Hofstra U, 1988; LLD (hon.), U. Vt., 1989, Middlebury Coll., 2000. Dean students San Marcos (Tex.) Acad., 1963-64; regional officer Peace Corps, Washington, 1964-65, dir. univ. affairs, 1965-66; spl. asst. dep. under-sec. for polit. affairs Dept. State, Washington, 1966-68; asso. provost for social scis. Wesleyan U., Middletown, Conn., 1968-70; provost, dean faculty, sr. lectr. govt. and legal studies Bowdoin Coll., Brunswick, Maine, 1970-75; prof. polit. sci. Middlebury (Vt.) Coll., 1975-95, pres., 1975-90, pres. emeritus, 1990—, prof. emeritus, 1995—; pres. Salzburg Seminar, 1991—. Chmn. Am. Collegiate Consortium, 1987-94; cons. State Dept., 1968-72, 77-88; bd. dirs. Investment Co. Am., Am. Mut. Fund, Bank of Vt., 1989-92, The Noel Group, N.Y.C, 1989-91, AMCAP, ACMAP Mut. Fund; cons. Paine Webber Mitchell Hutchins Inc., Am. Coun. Life Ins., 1968-81, Washington Forum, Met. Life Ins. Co. Bd. dirs. Atlantic Info. Center for Tchrs., London, 1970-77, Am. Com. on U.S.-Soviet Rels., Washington; chmn. Vt. com. Rhodes Scholarship Trust, 1976-77; bd. dirs. Am. Coun. Young Polit. Leaders, 1968-78, 81-90, Inst. East-West Security Studies, N.Y.C., Nat. Spinal Cord Injury Assn., Washington, Atlantic Coun. U.S., 1973-78, 81-91, U.S. Commn. for United World Coll. Schs.; mem. U.S. Adv. Commn. on Public Diplomacy, 1978-83, chmn., 1978-81, visiting comm. Harvard Div. Sch., Cambridge, Mass., 1980-86, adv. comm. Harvard U., Ctr for Middle Ea. Studies, Cambridge, 1992-96; adviser U.S. del. Conf. on Security and Coop. in Europe, Belgrade, 1977-78; U.S. del. Conf. on Security and Coop. in Madrid, 1980, in Vienna, 1986-87; bd. dirs. Nat. Endowment for Democracy, 1984-92; bd. dirs., chmn. Chatham House Found., 1985-93. Named Ehrenburger Johannes Gutenberg Universität, Mainz, Fed. Republic Germany, 1977; Rockefeller Found./Aspen Inst. fellow, 1978-79; Presdl. fellow Aspen Inst. Humanistic Studies, 1979-80, Harry Luce fellow Aspen Inst., 1982-83. Mem. Internat. Inst. Strategic Studies (London), Soc. Values in Higher Edn., Council Fgn. Rels., Royal Inst. Internat. Affairs (bd. dirs. 2000—). Clubs: Federal City (Washington); Century (N.Y.C.); United Oxford and Cambridge (London). Baptist. Office: Salzburg Seminar The Marble Works PO Box 886 Middlebury VT 05753-0886

ROBISON, PAULA JUDITH, flutist; b. Nashville, June 8, 1941; d. David Victor and Naomi Florence R.; m. Scott Nickrenz; Dec. 29, 1971; 1 child, Elizabeth Hadley Amadea Nickrenz. Student, U. So. Calif., 1958-60; BS, Juilliard Sch. Music, 1963; MusD honoris causa, San Francisco Conservatory Music, 2008. Founding artist, player Chamber Music Soc., NYC, 1970-90; co-dir. chamber music Spoleto Festival, Charleston, SC, 1978-88; Filene artist-in-residence Skidmore Coll., Saratoga Springs, NY, 1988-89; mem. faculty New Eng. Conservatory Music, 1972—76, 1991—, Donna Heiken flute chair 1st occupant, 2005—; co-dir. Gardner Chamber Orch., Boston, 1995—; artist-in-residence Gardner Mus., 2005; Hans and Thelma Lehman disting. lectr. music U. Wash., 2009. Mem. faculty Juilliard Sch., NYC, 1978—82; annual concert series Met. Mus. Art, NYC, 1990—; With Art series PS 1 Art Gallery, NY, 2000, Mass. Mus. Contemporary Art, 2001; dir. Vivaldi in the Courtyard, Gardner Mus., Boston, 2002—; founder Pergola Recs., 2006; collaboration with Sol Le Witt, Variations on a Theme, Gardner Mus., 2005; mem. Robison Lubambo Baptista Trio, 2000—09. Soloist with various major orchs., including N.Y. Philharm., London Symphony Orch.; player, presenter Concerti di Mezzogiorno, Spoleto (Italy) Festival, 1970-2003; commd. flute concertos by Leon Kirchner, Toru Takemitsu, Oliver Knussen, Robert Beaser, Kenneth Frazelle; premiered works by Pierre Boulez, Elliott Carter, William Schuman, Thea Musgrave, Carla Bley, John Tavener, Michael Tilson Thomas, William Bolcom; premiered Rio Days Rio Nights, Music Theatre Group prodn. in N.Y.C., 1998; participant Marlboro Music Festival, 1999-05; founder Pergola Recs., 2005; author: The Paula Robison Flute Warmups Book, 1989, The Andersen Collection, 1994, Paula Robison Masterclass: Paul Hindemith, 1995, The Sidney Lanier Collection, 1997, Frank Martin: Ballade, 2002, To a Wild Rose, 2003, MasterClass Series, Diller-Quaile Sch. of Music, 2004-; recs. on CBS Masterworks, Music Masters, Vanguard Classics, New World Records, Omega, Arabesque, Sony Classical, King Recs., Mode Recs., Artemis Recs.; two person show Gardner Mus., Boston, 2005; featured in PBS documentary and book: Juilliard; collaborator project with visual artist Jim Schantz and Pucker Gallery of Boston: Places of the Spirit, 2003, Places of the Spirit II-The Holy Land, 2007, Amazing Grace, 2009. Recipient Disting. Svc. award, Music Tchrs. Nat. Assn., 1989, Laurence Lesser Presdl. award, 1999, Lifetime Achievement award, Usdan Ctr. for Creative and Perfomring Arts, 2000, Hon. Citizen for Life award, City of Charleston, S.C., 2002, Lifetime Achievement award, Nat. Flute Assn., 2004, 1st prize, Geneva Internat. Competition, 1966, Adelaide Ristori prize, 1987; named Musician of Month, Musical Am., 1979, Ho. Musician for Isamu Noguchi Garden Mus., NYC, 1988; grantee, Nat. Endowment for Arts, 1978, 1986, Fromm Found., 1980; Martha Baird Rockefeller grantee, 1966, Housewright Eminent scholar, Fla. State U., 1990—91. Mem. Sigma Alpha Iota (hon.).

ROBISON, SARA ANNE, middle school educator, band director; d. Arthur Charles and Sherry Louise Harbison; m. Van Henry Robison, June 6, 2003. MusB, U. Tex., Austin, 2003. Cert. music edn. tchr. K-12 Tex. State Bd. Educator Cert., 2003. Asst. band dir. Weslaco East HS, Tex., 2003—04, Kealing Mid. Sch., Austin, Tex., 2004—. Steel drums player Inside Out Cmty. Steel Band, Austin, 2006; faculty Campus Adv. Coun., Austin, 2006—08. Musician Grace Covenant Ch., Austin, 2005—07. Music Edn. Devel. Fund scholarship, U. Tex., 2003. Mem.: Tex. Bandmasters Assn., Tex. Music Educators Assn., Ho. Rabbit Resource Network. Avocations: reading, scrapbooks, exercise, travel. Business E-Mail: srobison@austinisd.org.

ROBISON, SHANE V., computer company executive; BS in Computer Sci., MS in Computer Sci., U. Utah. With Apple Computer Co., 1988, v.p., gen..mgr., 1994—95; exec. v.p. rsch. & develop., pres. design productivity grp. Cadence Design Systems; exec. v.p. AT&T, 1995—97, pres. design productivity grp., 1997—99, pres. internet tech. and devel., 1999—2000; sr. v.p., chief tech. officer strategy and tech. Compaq Computer Corp., 2000—02; exec. v.p., chief strategy and tech. officer Hewlett-Packard Co., Palo Alto, Calif., 2002—. Cons. database systems architecture U. Utah. Office: Hewlett-Packard Co 3000 Hanover St Palo Alto CA 94304*

ROBISON, VICTOR JAMES, JR., retired naval officer; b. Youngstown, Ohio, Apr. 29, 1920; s. Victor James Robison and Babe Albert. BS, Case We. Res. U., 1942, MA, 1948; Qualified Comms. Officer, U.S. Naval Acad. Grad. Sch., 1943; student, Sorbonne U., Paris, 1949—50, Columbia U., 1950—51. Commd. ensign USN, 1943, advanced through grades to comdr., comm. officer USS Taylor Pacific PTO, 1943—45, tng. officer U.S. Naval Res. Tng. Ctr. Balt., 1952—55, asst. ops. officer USS Worcester Mediterranean and Pacific, 1955—56; U.S. Naval attaché and U.S. Naval attaché for air U.S. Embassy, Warsaw, 1957—58, Brussels, 1962—65; officer in charge Navy Liaison Group and Chief Plant Engrng and Maintenance Divsn. Joint Commns. Ctr., Ft. Ritchie, Md., 1958—61; asst. curator for Navy Dept., Office Chief of Naval Ops. USN, Washington, 1966—69, ret., 1969; tchr. English Corcoran Coll. Art, Washington, 1969—70; pvt. practice appraiser Navy artifacts and memorabilia Washington and Annapolis, Md., 1970—84. Author: (biography) 500 Greatest Geniuses of the 21st Century, 2009. Decorated Order of Leopold II, 1966, Navy Unit Commendation, 13 Battle Stars, USN, Asiatic Pacific Campaign medal, others, Named to Hall of Fame Am. Biog. Inst., 2008. Mem. VFW, Am. Legion, Fleet Res. Assn., Smithsonian Instn., Beta Theta Pi, US Navy League Avocations: stamp collecting/philately, jogging, poetry, learning. Home: 423 7th St SE Washington DC 20003-2756

ROBITAILLE, CAROLYN ANN, music educator; b. Ft. Wayne, Ind., Nov. 25, 1930; d. Edgar Herman and Della Katharina Neuenschwander; m. Anthony McLeon Robitaille, June 29, 1957; children: Beth Ann Smyth, Robert Scott; children: Melody Joy Berryhill, Douglas Eric. Student, St. Louis Inst. Music, 1948—50, Washington U., 1948—49. Pvt. piano tchr., Compton, Calif., 1946—48; piano tchr. Brea, Calif., 1968—2009, Del Burg's Music Store, South Gate, Calif., 1946—48; exec. sec. Sears, Roebuck and Co., LA, 1953—68; pianist Faith Bapt. Ch., Yorba Linda, Calif., 1969—83, Crossroad Ch., Fullerton, Calif., 1983—2008, Temple Bapt. Ch., Fullerton, 2008—. Piano tchr. Nat. Piano Guild, Austin, Tex., 1984—2004, evaluator, 2004—; adjudicator Assn. Christian Schs. Internat. Piano Festivals, La Habra, Calif., 1999—; pianist Gideon State Convs., 2000—05, Rep. State Convs., 2000—05. Pianist North Intermediate Sch., Saginaw, Mich., 1942—45, Christian and Missionary Alliance Ch., Saginaw, 1942—45, Huntington Park (Calif.) H.S., Calif., 1945—48; pianist, Sunday sch. tchr. Lynton Village Chapel, Lynwood, Calif., 1947—48, 1950—68; chaplain Gideon Internat. Aux., 2005—. Piano scholar, St. Louis Inst. Music, 1948—50. Mem.: Music Tchrs. Assn. Calif. (treas. Orange County br. 2004—06), Gideons Internat. Aux. (sec.-treas. 2001—05). Republican. Baptist. Avocations: tennis, croquet, swimming, badminton, board games.

ROBITAILLE, LUC, professional sports team executive, retired professional hockey player; b. Montreal, Que., Can., Feb. 17, 1966; Left wing Hull Olympiques Major Jr. Hockey League, Que., 1983—84, LA Kings, 1984—94, 1997—2001, 2003—06, Pitts. Penguins, 1994—95, NY Rangers, 1995—97, Detroit Red Wings, 2001—03; owner, pres. Omaha Lancers, US Hockey League, 2006; asst. to gov. and alt. gov. LA Kings, 2006—07, pres. bus. ops., 2007—. Guest appearance (films) D2: The Mighty Ducks, 1994, Sudden Death, 1995, H-E Double Hockey Sticks, 1999. Recipient Guy LaFlleur Trophy, 1985—86, Can. Hockey Player of Yr. award, 1985—86, Calder Meml. Trophy; named NHL Rookie of Yr., 1986—87; named to NHL All-Star Team, 1987, 1988, 1990—91, 1992—93, Quebec Major Junior Hockey League Hall of Fame, 2007. Achievements include scoring the winning goal for the national team of Canada at the 1994 World Hockey Championship; being a member of Stanley Cup Champion Detroit Red Wings, 2002; having his number, 20, retired by LA Kings, 2007. Office: LA Kings Suite 3100 1111 S Figueroa St Los Angeles CA 90015 also: Omaha Lancers Mid-Am Ctr One Arena Way Council Bluffs IA 51501

ROBLES, DARLINE P., school system administrator; AA in History, East L.A. Coll., 1968; B in History, Calif. State U., LA, 1972; MEd, Claremont Grad. Sch., 1976; D in Edn. Policy and Adminstrn., U. So. Calif. Cert. tchr., adminstr. Tchr. Montebello Intermediate Sch., Calif., 1973—79; dir. bilingual program Montebellow Unified Sch. Dist., Calif., 1979—81; prin. Washington Elem., Montebello, Calif., 1981—85, Montebello Intermediate, Montebello, Calif., 1985—88; asst. supt. Montebello Unified Sch. Dist., Montebello, Calif., 1988—91, acting supt., 1991—92, supt., 1992—95, Salt Lake City Sch. Dist., 1995—2002; county supt. schs. L.A. County Office of Edn., 2002—. Office: LA County Office of Edn Rm EC 109 9300 Imperial Hwy Rm EC109 Downey CA 90242-2890 Office Phone: 562-922-6127. Business E-Mail: Robles_Darline@lacoe.edu.

ROBLES, FÉLIX, retired language educator, dean; b. Santa María de los Angeles, Jalisco, Mex., Jan. 28, 1945; s. José María Robles and Amalia de los Santos; m. Harriett J. Joyner; children: Jessica Leigh, Analisa Alexandra. MA in Spanish, San José State U., Calif., 1974. Spanish instr. Cabrillo Coll., Aptos, Calif., 1972—2006, divsn. chair, 1996—99, divsn. dean, 2000—03. Trustee Santa Cruz City Schs., Calif., 1996—2008. Democrat. Avocation: travel. Home: 21 Mill Rd Santa Cruz CA 95060 Office: Cabrillo Coll 6500 Soquel Dr Aptos CA 95003 Office Fax: 831-479-5717; Home Fax: 831-420-1021. Business E-Mail: ferobles@cabrillo.edu.

ROBLES, JOSUE, JR., insurance company executive; b. Rio Piedras, PR, Jan. 24, 1946; B in Acctg., Kent State U., Ohio, 1972; MBA, Ind. State U., Terre Haute, 1979. Exec. v.p., chief adminstrv. officer, CFO, corp. treas. USAA (United Svcs. Automobile Assn.), San Antonino, Tex., 1994—2007, pres., CEO San Antonio, 2007—. Mem. Def. Base Closure and Realignment Commn., 1995; bd. dirs. DTE Energy Co., 2003—. Advanced through grades to maj. gen., comdr. 1st Infantry Div. US Army, 1966—94, ret. US Army, 1994. Office: USAA 9800 Fredericksburg Rd San Antonio TX 78288-0002 Office Phone: 210-498-2211.*

ROBO, JAMES L., utilities executive; BA summa cum laude, Harvard Coll.; MBA, Harvard Bus. Sch. V.p. Strategic Planning Assocs.; various positions including gen. mgr. distbn. ops. GE Lighting, gen. mgr. Six Sigma GE Lighting, pres. and CEO GE Mex. GE, pres., CEO Capital TIP/Modular Space; pres. FPL Energy, 2002—06; v.p. corp. devel. and strategy FPL Group Inc., 2002—06, pres., COO, 2006—. Bd. dirs. J.B. Hunt Transport Svcs., Inc., Lowell, Ark., 2003—. Mem.: Phi Beta Kappa. Office: FPL Group Inc 700 Universe Blvd Juno Beach FL 33408-0420

ROBOCK, ALAN, meteorology professor; b. Boston, Sept. 7, 1949; s. Stefan Hyman and Shirley Robock; m. Sherri Robock, May 12, 1990; children: Brian, Daniel. BA, U. Wis., Madison, 1970; SM, MIT, Cambridge, Mass., 1974, PhD, 1977. Vol. Peace Corps, The Philippines, 1970-72; rsch. scientist Lawrence Livermore Lab., Calif., 1973; asst. prof. dept. meteorology U. Md., College Park, 1977-82, assoc. prof., 1982-96, prof., 1996-97; prof. dept. environ. scis. Rutgers U., New Brunswick, NJ, 1998—2003, prof. II, 2003—. Dir. Ctr. Environ. Prediction Rutgers U., 2001-05; snow forecaster Montgomery County Pub. Schs., Md., 1980-81; state climatologist State of Md., 1991-97; vis. rsch. scientist Princeton U., NOAA/Geophys. Fluid Dynamics Lab., 1994-95 Editor: Jour. Climate and Applied Meteorology, 1985—87, Jour. Geophys. Rsch-Atmospheres, 2000—05; assoc. editor Jour. Geophys. Rsch-Atmospheres, 1998—2000, Revs. Geophysics, 1994—2000, 2006—; contbr. articles to profl. jours., chapters to books. Fellow AAAS (congl. sci. fellow 1986-87, chair-elect, atmosphere and hydrospheric scis. sec., 2009-), Am. Meteorol. Soc., Am. Geophys. Union (pres. elect, atmospheric sci. sect., 2006-08; pres. 2008-). Avocations: tennis, Bob Dylan music, travel, politics. Office: Rutgers U Dept Environ Scis 14 College Farm Rd New Brunswick NJ 08901-8551 E-mail: robock@envsci.rutgers.edu.

ROBOCK, STEFAN HYMAN, retired economics professor; b. Redgranite, Wis., July 31, 1915; s. Samuel and Elizabeth (Kushner) R.; m. Shirley Bernstein, June 17, 1946 (div. Mar. 1980); children: Alan David, Jerry, Lisa (Mrs. Stephen Shaffer); m. Hanne Miree, June 13, 1998. BA, U. Wis., 1938; MA (Adminstrn. fellow), Harvard U., 1941, PhD, 1948; Prof. Honoris Causa, U. Recife, Brazil, 1956; M. Honoris Causa, E.S.T.E., San Sebastian, Spain, 1974. Economist Nat. Resources Planning Bd., Washington, 1940-41; antitrust div. U.S. Dept. Justice, Washington, 1941-42, Boston, 1948-49; chief economist TVA, Knoxville, 1949-54; devel. adviser UN, Brazil, 1954-56, tech. asst. missions India, 1959, Bolivia, 1963; with Midwest Rsch. Inst., 1956-58, Com. Econ. Devel., 1958-60; prof. internat. bus. Ind. U., Bloomington, 1960-67; with World Bank, Philippines, 1961, Ford Found., Pakistan, 1964; R.D. Calkins prof. internat. bus. Columbia U., NYC, 1967-84, prof. emeritus, 1984—. Internat. economist Dept. Commerce, 1975-76; trustee Inst. Current World Affairs, 1981-86; cons. fgn. countries, 1959—; bd. dirs. Econs. Inst., Boulder, Colo., 1984-89; adv. bd. World Trade Inst., 1974-95; mem. bd. sci. and tech. NAS, 1969-72; vis. prof. Beijing Mgmt. Inst., 1985, U. Internat. Bus. and Econ., Beijing, 1989, Internat. Mgmt. Ctr., Budapest, Hungary, 1992. Author: Brazil's Developing Northeast, 1963, Brazil: A Study in Development Progress, 1975, International Business and Multinational Enterprises, 4th edit., 1989; Editorial bd.: Columbia Jour. World Bus, 1975-85. Served with USNR, 1942-46. Mem. Soc. Internat. Devel. (mem. council 1966-69), Am. Econ. Assn., Acad. Internat. Bus. (v.p. 1983-85), Harvard Club NYC, Phi Kappa Phi, Beta Gamma Sigma, Phi Eta Sigma. Clubs: Columbia Tennis. Home: 560 Riverside Dr Apt 21J New York NY 10027-3237

ROBOL, RICHARD THOMAS, lawyer; b. Norfolk, Va., Feb. 8, 1952; s. Harry James and Lucy Henley (Johnson) R. BA, U. Va., 1974; JD, Harvard U., 1978. Bar: Va. 1979, Ohio 1996, U.S. Dist. Ct. (ea. dist.) Va. 1979, U.S. Ct. Appeals (4th cir.) 1979, U.S. Dist. Ct. (we. dist.) Va. 1981, U.S. Supreme Ct. 1982, D.C. 1991, U.S. Ct. Appeals (4th, 6th and 9th cirs.) 1995. Law clk. to presiding justice U.S. Dist. Ct. (ea. dist.) Va., 1978-79; ptnr. Seawell, Dalton, Hughes & Timms, Norfolk, 1979-87, Hunton and Williams, Norfolk, 1987-92; exec. v.p., gen. counsel Columbus Am. Discovery Group, Inc., 1992—. Adj. prof. U. Dayton Law Sch.; asst. prof. mil. sci. Capital U.; pro bono counsel Nat. Commn. for Prevention Child Abuse, Norfolk, 1983, Tidewater Profl. Assn. on Child Abuse, 1983, Parents United Va., 1981-82, Sexual Abuse Help Line, 1983-86; mem. Boyd-Graves Conf. on Civil Procedure in Va., 1981-87. Contbr. articles to law revs.; contbg. editor: International Law for General Practitioners, 1981. Bd. dirs. Va. Opera Assn. Guild, Norfolk, 1983-87, Tidewater br. NCCJ, 1991-92; deacon Ctrl. Bapt. Ch., Norfolk, 1980-83. Maj. USAR, 1992—. Fulbright scholar, 1974. Mem. Va. State Bar Assn. (bd. dirs. internat. law sect. 1984-87, chmn. 1982-83), Va. Young Lawyers Assn. (cir. rep. 1984-88), Va. Assn. Def. Attys., Maritime Law Assn., Norfolk-Portsmouth Bar assn. (chmn. speakers bur. 1987-88), Assn. Def. Trial Attys. (chmn. Va. 1987), Def. Rsch. Inst., 1982-88. Avocations: camping, rowing, scuba diving. Home: 60 Kenyon Brook Dr Worthington OH 43085-3629 Office: Robol Law Office LPA 433 W Sixth Ave Columbus OH 43201 Office Phone: 614-737-3739. Business E-Mail: rrobol@robollaw.com.

ROBOTTOM, DAVID T., lawyer, energy executive; m. Bonnie Robottom; 2 children. B of Commerce with distinction, MBA; LLB, U. Alta., 1979. Bar: Alta. 1980. Nat. mng. ptnr., CEO Fraser Milner Casgrain LLP; sr. ptnr. Stikeman Elliott LLP, Calgary, Alta., Canada, 2004—06; grp. v.p. corp. law Enbridge Inc., 2006—. Bd. trustees Enbridge Comml. Trust; dir. Noverco, Inc., Gaz Métro Inc. Office: Enbridge Inc 3000 5th Ave Pl 425 1st St SW Calgary AB T2P 3L8 Canada Business E-Mail: david.robottom@enbridge.com.*

ROBRAN, CONRAD JOHN, retired education educator; s. Forrest Woodrow Wilson and Ruth Lillian Robran; m. Hela Beth Robran, Aug. 11, 1990; children: Carolyn Sue Kochis, Karen Lee Downs, Kelly Jean Phelan. BS, U. Hawaii, Honolulu, 1976; MS, Chapman U., Orange, Calif., 1994. Cert. in secondary edn. Colo., 2009. Adj. prof. Pikes Peak CC, Colo. Springs, Colo., 1998—, UCCS, Colo. Springs, 2003—. Pres. Home Owners Assn., Colo. Springs, 2005—09. Recipient Tchr. of Yr., Lawrence Senich award, 1984; Fulbright fellowship, US Govt., 1990—98. Independent. Roman Catholic. Avocations: travel, hiking, fishing, reading, skiing. Home: 8427 Grand Carriage Grove Colorado Springs CO 80920

ROBSON, DONALD, physics professor; b. Leeds, Eng., Mar. 19, 1937; came to U.S., 1963; s. Albert and Rose Hannah (Parbutt) Robson; m. Joy Olivia Burkitt Findlay, Aug. 1960 (div. May 1971); children: Donald Peter, David Ian, Karen Joy; m. Martha Breitenlohner, Aug. 26, 1971 (div. Sept. 1999); m. Kimberly G. Kitchen, Dec. 18, 1999; 1 child, Nadirah Berge. BSc, U. Melbourne, Australia, 1959, MSc, 1961, PhD, 1963. Rsch. assoc. Fla. State U., Tallahassee, 1963-64, asst. prof. physics, 1964-65, assoc. prof., 1965-67, prof., 1967—, chmn. dept. physics, 1985-91, Disting. prof., 1990—2003, emeritus prof., 2003—. Editor: (with J.D. Fox) Isobaric Spin in Nuclear Physics, 1966, Nuclear Analogue States, 1976; assoc. editor Nuclear Physics A., 1972-96; contbr. more than 100 articles to profl. jours. Chmn. bd. trustees Southeastern Univ. Rsch. Assn., 1996-98. Fulbright scholar, 1963-64; A.P. Sloan fellow, 1966-67; Alexander Von Humboldt sr. scientist, 1976-77. Fellow Am. Phys. Soc. (co-recipient Tom W. Bonner prize 1972). Avocations: chess, golf, running. Office: Fla State U Dept Physics Tallahassee FL 32306 Office Phone: 850-644-1767. Business E-Mail: robson@csit.fsu.edu.

ROBSON, MARK GREGORY, agriculturist, educator; b. Trenton, NJ, Apr. 24, 1955; s. Arthur John and Joan Catherine Robson; m. Patricia Ann Mykalosky, June 30, 1979; 1 child, Christina Anastasia. BS, Rutgers U., New Brunswick, NJ, 1977, MS, 1979, PhD, 1988; MPhil, U. Medicine and Dentistry NJ, Piscataway, 1995. Cert. sci. tchr. State NJ, 1977, agr. tchr. 1977. Rsch. scientist NJ Dept. Environ. Protection, Trenton, 1985—89; divsn. dir. NJ Dept. Agr., Trenton, 1989—91; exec. dir. EOHSI Rutgers, New Brunswick, 1991—2000; dept. chmn. U. Medicine and Dentistry NJ, Sch. Pub. Health, 2000—06; dir. NJAES Rutgers, New Brunswick, 2006—08, prof., 2006—08; ext. specialist Rutgers U., 1980—85, prof., 2008—, dean agr. programs, 2008—. Firemen Wrightstown Vol. Fire Dept., NJ, 1973; landuse com. chmn. North Hanover Twp., Wrightstown, 2007; lector and eucharistic min. Holy Cross Ch., Trenton, 1985. Recipient George Hammell Cook Disting. Alumni award, Rutgers U., 2005, Disting. Tchrs. award, Pfizer Pharma., 2007, Jesse B. Leslie award, NJ Assn. Mosquito Control Execs., 2008; named Master Educator, U. Medicine and Dentistry NJ, Sch. Pub. Health, 2001; fellow, Acad. Toxicological Sci., 2002, 2003. Fellow: Am. Coll. Toxicology; mem.: New Solutions, Jour. Environ. and Occupl. Health Policy, Jour. Environ. Health, Internat. Jour. Occupl. and Environ. Health, NJ Pub. Health Inst., NJ Mosquito Control Assn. Bd. Trustees, Mid-Atlantic Soc. Toxicology, Ctrl. Atlantic States Assn. Food and Drug Officials, Nat. Environ. Health Assn. Democrat. Roman Catholic. Achievements include research in evaluate the risk of agriculture chemicals in rural communities in Thailand. Home: 569 Sch House Rd Wrightstown NJ 08562 Office: Rutgers Univ 88 Lipman Dr New Brunswick NJ 08901 Office Fax: 732-932-8955; Home Fax: 609-758-2750. Business E-Mail: robson@aesop.rutgers.edu.

ROBUSTO, DINO E., insurance company executive; With Chubb Corp., 1986—, comml. lines underwriter, field ops. officer Chubb Comml. Ins., mng. dir. Multinational Resource Group, sr. v.p., NY brokerage zone officer, exec. v.p., worldwide claims officer Chubb & Son, exec. v.p., chief adminstrv. officer, 2008—. Office: Chubb Corp 15 Mountain View Rd Warren NJ 07059 Office Phone: 908-903-2000. Office Fax: 908-903-2027.

ROBY, PAMELA ANN, sociologist, educator; b. Milw., Nov. 17, 1942; d. Clark Dearborn and Marianna (Gillman) Roby; m. James Peter Mulherin, July 15, 1977 (div. 1987). BA, U. Denver, 1963; MA, Syracuse U., NYC, 1966; PhD, NYU, 1971. Instr. ednl. sociology NYU, NYC, 1966; asst. prof. George Washington U., Washington, 1970—71; asst. prof. sociology and social welfare Brandeis U., Waltham, Mass., 1971—73; assoc. prof. U. Calif., Santa Cruz, 1973—77, prof. sociology and women's studies, 1977—2007, emerita prof. sociology and women's studies, 2007—, chair cmty. studies bd., 1974-76, 79, dir. sociology doctoral program, 1988—91, 2006—07, chair sociology dept., 1998—2001, prof. emerita, 2007—, prof. recalled. Mem. social sci. rsch. rev. com. NIMH, Washington, 1976—80; vice chair Nat. Commn. Working Women, Washington, 1977—80; cons. James Irvine Found., San Francisco, 1986; mem. sociology program rev. com. Northeastern U., Boston, 1990; mem. anthropology, linguistics and sociology panel NSF, Washington, 1993; assessor Social Scis. and Humanities Rsch. Coun. Can., Toronto, 1993; mem. postdoc. and dissertation fellowship evaluation panel Ford Found., 2005—09; mem. commn. women in higher edn. coun. edn. U. Calif., Santa Cruz, 1973—76. Co-author: The Future of Inequality, 1970; editor: Child Care: Who Cares? Foreign and Domestic Infant and Early Childhood Development Policies, 1973—75, The Poverty Establishment, 1974; author: Women in the Workplace, 1981; adv. editor: Social Quar., 1990—93, Gender and Society, 1986—89, mem. editl. bd.: Contemporary Sociology, 2006—07; mem. editl. bd. Sage Studies in International Sociology, 1978—82. Vis. scholar, Indian Coun. Social Sci. Rsch., 1979, U. Wash., Seattle, 1991—92; Andrew W. Mellon Sr. scholar, Wellesley Coll., 1978—79. Mem.: Alpha Kappa Delta, Re-Evaluation Counseling (coll. and univ. faculty reference person 1980—), Eastern Sociol. Assn. (exec. coun. mem.-at-large 1973—74), Pacific Sociol. Assn. (v.p. 1996—97), Internat. Sociol. Assn. (rsch. coun. mem.-at-large 1978—82), Am. Sociol. Assn. (chair sect. sex and gender 1974—78, exec. coun. mem.-at-large 1975—78), Sociologists Women in Soc. (pres. 1978—80), Soc. Study Social Problems (pres. 1996—97), Phi Beta Kappa. Avocations: camping, hiking, painting, swimming, pen and ink drawing. Office: U Calif Dept Sociology C8 Santa Cruz CA 95064

ROCARD, MICHEL LOUIS LÉON, French politician; b. Courbevoie, France, Aug. 23, 1930; s. Yves Rocard and Renée Favre; m. Sylvie Pélissier, 2002; children: Sylvie, Francis, Olivier, Loic. Student, U. Paris, Ecole Nat. Adminstrn. Nat. sec. Parti Socialiste Unifié, 1967-73; dep. to Nat. Assembly, Paris, 1969-73, 78-81; mem. Parti Socialiste, 1974, mem. exec. bur., 1975-81, nat. sec. in charge of pub. sector, 1975-79; mayor Conflans-Sainte-Honorine, 1977-94; min. state, min. planning, regional devel. France, Paris, 1981-83, min. agr., 1983-85, prime min., 1988-91; 1st sec. Parti Socialiste, 1994—; mem., chmn. culture, edn. com. European Parliament, 1994—, senator, 1995-97. Address: 266 Blvd St Germain 75007 Paris France Office Phone: 33 1 47052500. E-mail: mrocard.paris@noos.fr, mrocard@europarl.eu.int, michel@rocard.fr.

ROCCA, CHRISTINA B., ambassador, former federal agency administrator; b. Washington, 1957; m. Gordon L. Rocca; 2 children. BA in History, King's Coll., London, 1980. Staff ops. officer, Directorate of Ops. CIA, Washington, 1982—97; fgn. affairs advisor to Senator Sam Brownback US Senate, Washington; asst. sec for South Asian Affairs US Dept. State, Washington, 2001—06; US perm. rep. & amb. UN Conf. on Disarmament, Geneva, 2006—.

ROCCHI, ROBIN HENNING, financial and automotive company executive; BA, Dartmouth Coll., 1983; MBA, Northwestern U., 1988. Lending officer Manufacturers Hanover, NYC, 1983-86; fin. analyst, treas.' office GM, NYC, 1988-91, mgr., 1991-94, dir., 1994-2000; dir. internat. strategy Promark Global Advisors (formerly GM Asset Mgmt.), NYC, 2000—01, dir. global equity strategy, 2001—04, gen. dir., 2004—05, v.p. investment programs, 2005—. Office: Promark Global Advisors 767 5th Ave Fl 16 New York NY 10153-0023

ROCCO, NIKKI, film company executive; m. Joseph Rocco. Sales dept. Universal Pictures, 1967, asst. to gen. sales mgr., 1981—84, v.p. distbn., 1984—90, sr. v.p. distbn. and mktg., 1990—95, exec. v.p., distbn., 1995—96, pres., distbn., 1996—. Bd. dirs. Will Rogers Motion Picture Pioneers Found. Recipient Crystal award, Women in Film, 2000; named one of The 100 Most Powerful Women in Entertainment, Hollywood Reporter, 2004, 2005, 2006, 2007. Office: Universal Pictures 100 Universal City Plaza Universal City CA 91608

ROCEK, JAN, retired chemist; b. Prague, Czech Republic, Mar. 24, 1924; came to U.S., 1960, naturalized, 1966; s. Hugo and Frida (Loebl) Robitschek; m. Eva Trojan, June 26, 1947; children: Martin, Thomas. MS, Tech. U., Prague, 1949, PhD, 1953. Scientist Czechoslovak Acad. Sci., Prague, 1953-57, sr. scientist, 1957-60; vis. scientist U. Coll., London, 1958; research fellow Harvard U., 1960-62; asso. prof., then prof. Cath. U. Am., 1962-66; prof. chemistry U. Ill., Chgo., 1966-95, acting head dept., 1980-81, head dept., 1981-93, vice chancellor rsch., dean grad. coll. Chgo., 1993-95, acting dean Grad. Coll., 1969-70, dean Grad. Coll., 1970-79, asso. mem. Ctr. for Advanced Studies, 1968-69; ret., 1995. Vis. scholar Stanford U., 1979-80, Cambridge U., 1980 Contbr. articles to profl. jours. Mem. Am. Chem. Soc., AAAS, Czechoslovak Soc. Arts and Scis. in Am., AAUP, Sigma Xi (pres. chpt. 1976-77, 85-86), Phi Kappa Phi. Home: 4031 Kennett Pike # 24 Greenville DE 19807 Personal E-mail: rocek@uic.edu.

ROCH, LEWIS MARSHALL, II, ophthalmic surgeon, medical entrepreneur; b. Mineola, Tex., Aug. 13, 1934; s. Lewis Marshall and Gladys Irene (Hoover) R.; m. Lois Afton Price; children: Lewis Marshall Roch III, Katrina Ann Seitz. BA, U. Tex., Austin, 1955; MD, U. Tex. Southwestern, Dallas, 1959. Diplomate Am. Bd. Ophthalmology. Intern USPHS Hosp., Boston, 1959-60, resident in ophthalmology New Orleans, 1960-63, dep. chief ophthalmology, 1963-64, chief ophthalmology Seattle, 1964-67; attending ophthalmic surgeon Ball Meml. Hosp., Muncie, Ind., 1967—, chmn. dept. surgery, chmn. clin. staff, 1975, chmn. exec. com., 1984—87, bd. dirs., 1984—90, mem. fin. com., 1984—87; founder, CEO, med. dir. The Eye Ctr. Group, Muncie, 1985—, The Surgi Ctr. Group, Muncie, 1985—. Mem. exec. com. Ind. Acad. Ophthalmology, 1978-82; bd. dirs. Cardinal Health Ventures, Paragent, LLC, Cardinal Ethanol, LLC, Cardinal Health Found., Inc., 1999-, Ball Meml. Found., 1998-; clin. asst. prof. Ind. U. Sch. Medicine, 1978—. Chmn. Muncie-Delaware Devel., 2000-03; active Ball State U. Bus. Forecasting Roundtable, 2000—; exec. v.p. Muncie-Delaware Econ. Devel., 2000-02; trustee Minnetrista Cultural Ctr., 2002—; bd. dirs. United Way Delaware County, 2003-06. Fellow ACS, Am. Acad. Ophthalmology; mem. AMA, Ind. State Med. Assn., Muncie Acad. Medicine (pres. 1981-82), Am. Soc. Cataract and Refractive Surgeons, Am. Coll. Physician Execs., Muncie-Delaware C. of C. (bd. dirs. 1999-2003), Rotary. Republican. Achievements include first to work in outpatient ambulatory surgery; innovation in intraocular lens implantation in cataract surgery; integration of physician's practices with hospital health care delivery systems. Home: 2006 E Robinwood Dr Muncie IN 47304-2857 Office: The Eye Ctr Group LLC 200 N Tillotson Ave Muncie IN 47304-3988 Office Phone: 765-289-7073. E-mail: lmroch@comcast.net.

ROCHE, CATHY, energy executive; m. Terry Roche; 2 children. BA in Journalism, U. NC, Chapel Hill. Reporter AP, Charlotte News; self-employed pub. rels. cons., 1980—83; dir. publs. Duke Power Co., 1983—89; v.p. pub. and industry comm. Nuc. Energy Inst., Washington, 1989—96; v.p. corp. comm. Entergy Corp., New Orleans, 1996—99; dir. external rels. pub. affairs dept. Duke Energy, Charlottle, NC, 2000—03, v.p. corp. comm., 2003—06, sr. v.p., chief comm. officer, 2006—. Bd. visitors U. NC Sch. Journalism; bd. visitors Carolina Environ. Prog. U. NC, Chapel Hill. Office: Duke Energy 526 S Church St Charlotte NC 28202-1904 Office Phone: 704-594-6200.

ROCHE, GAIL CONNOR, editor; b. Phila., Aug. 14, 1953; d. Donald Russell Connor; m. Richard Roche, Nov. 21, 1981; children: Alex James, Clare Evelyn. AB cum laude, Franklin & Marshall Coll., Lancaster, Pa., 1975; MA with distinction, Rider U., 1988. Cert. tchr., Pa. Tchr. Pennsbury Schs., Fallsington, Pa., 1975-76, Cen. Bucks Sch., Doylestown, Pa., 1977-79; reporter Trenton Times, NJ, 1979-82; editor Dow Jones & Co., Princeton, NJ, 1982-95; mem. adv. bd. Dow Jones Women's Network, Princeton, 1990-95; tech. editor Bloomberg News, Princeton, 1995-2000; sr. editor, letters editor Bloomberg Markets, 2000—. Contbr. articles to mags. Mem. Phi Beta Kappa. Home: 23 Jericho Run Washington Crossing PA 18977-1027 Office Phone: 609-394-0738. Personal E-mail: groche@bloomberg.net.

ROCHE, GERARD RAYMOND, management consultant; b. Scranton, Pa., July 27, 1931; s. Joseph Arthur and Amelia Jane (Garcia) R.; m. Marie Terotta, Apr. 27, 1957; children: Mary Margaret, Anne Elizabeth, Paul Joseph. BS in Acctg., U. Scranton, 1953; MBA, NYU, 1958. Mgmt. trainee AT&T, Phila., 1955-56; account exec. ABC-TV, NYC, 1956-58; sales and mktg. positions Kordite Corp. subs. Mobil Oil Co., Macedon, NY, 1959-63; assoc. Heidrick & Struggles, Inc., NYC, 1964-68, ptnr., 1968—, mgr. N.Y., 1968-73, mgr. East, 1973-77, pres., chief exec. officer, 1978—81, chmn., 1981-2000, sr. chmn., 2000—. Former trustee Cath. U. Am., U. Scranton; mentor Nat. Mentoring Partnership. Served to lt. USN, 1953-55. Mem.: Cmty. Anti-Drug Coalitions of am. (bd. dirs.), Knights of Malta, Loblolly Pines Country Club, Blind Brook Club, Sleepy Hollow Country Club, Univ. Club, Yale Club, Alpha Sigma Nu (past treas.). Roman Catholic. Office: Heidrick & Struggles Inc 1114 Ave of the Americans New York NY 10036 Office Phone: 212-551-0505.

ROCHE, JAMES RICHARD, pediatric dentist, university dean; b. Fortville, Ind., July 17, 1924; s. George Joseph and Nelle (Kinnaman) R.; m. Viola Marie Morris, May 15, 1949; 1 child, Ann Marie Roche Potter. DDS, Ind. U., 1947, MS in Dentistry, 1983. Diplomate Am. Bd. Pediat. Dentistry, 1959. Prof. Ind. U. Sch. Dentistry, Indpls., 1968—88, chmn. divsn. grad. pediat. dentistry, 1969-76, asst. dean faculty devel., 1976-80, assoc. dean faculty devel., 1980-87, assoc. dean for acad. affairs, 1987-88, prof. emeritus, 1988—. Cons. Coun. Dental Edn., Hosp. Dental Svc. and Commn. Accreditation, Am. Dental Assn., Chgo., 1977-1983; pres. Coll. Diplomates, Am. Bd. Pediat. Dentistry, 1968; chmn. Am. Bd. Pediat. Dentistry, 1980-81, exec. sec.-treas., 1982-2002. Capt. U.S. Army, 1952-54. Recipient Disting. Teaching Recognition award Ind. U., 1976, Experience Excellence Recognition award Ind. U., Purdue U., Indpls., 1984, Outstanding Svc. award Ind. Optometric Assn., 1989. Fellow Internat. Coll. Dentists, Am. Coll. Dentists (named Fund Recipient, 2007, Ind. Sect. Ethics award, 2009), Am. Acad. Pediat. Dentistry (bd. dirs. 1967-70), Pierre Fauchard Acad.; mem. ADA (cons. Bur. Dental Health Edn. 1977-87, Coun. Dental Edn., Hosp. Dental Svc. and Commn. Accreditation, chgo., 1977-83), Am. Soc. Dentistry for Children (award of excellence 1993), Ind. Dental Assn. (v.p. 1973-74, chmn. legis. com. 1968-77, lobbyist 1970-77, honor dentist 2008), Indpls. Dist. Dental Assn. (pres. 1967-68), Ind. U.-Purdue U. Indpls. Sr. Acad. (charter), Masons, Scottish Rite, Omicron Kappa Upsilon (pres. Theta Theta chpt., 1967), Ind. U. Sch. Dentistry Alumni Assn. (Disting. Alumnus award, 2003), Ind. U. Pediat. Dentistry Alumni Assn. (Disting. Alumnus award 2005). Office Phone: 317-574-9769.

ROCHE, MARK A., lawyer, consumer products company executive; b. 1954; m. Barbara Roche. BA, U. Va.; JD, Cornell U. Bar: NY 1980. Assoc. to counsel Chadbourne & Park, LLP, NYC, 1981-88; group gen. counsel Fortune Brands Inc., Deerfield, Ill., 1988-91, Lincolnshire, Ill., 1991-96, v.p., assoc. gen. counsel, 1996-98, v.p., gen. counsel, 1998-99, sr. v.p., gen. counsel, 1999—2000, sr. v.p., sec., gen. counsel Deerfield, Ill., 2002—. Office: Fortune Brands Inc 520 Lake Cook Rd Deerfield IL 60015-5611 Office Phone: 847-484-4400.

ROCHE, MICHAEL J., insurance company executive; BS in math., No. Ill. U., MBA. Various info. tech. positions Continental Ill. Nat. Bank, Heller Fin.; v.p. info. tech. Allstate Ins. Co., Northbrook, Ill., 2002—03, group v.p. protection tech., 2003—05, chief info. officer, 2003—05, sr. v.p. protection tech. and adminstrn., 2005—06, sr. v.p. property & casualty claims svc. org., 2006—. Mem. bd. trustees Rosary High Sch., Aurora, Ill.; mem. bd. dir. One Economy. Named one of Premier 100 IT Leaders, Computerworld, 2006. Office: Allstate Corp 2775 Sanders Rd Northbrook IL 60062 Fax: 847-402-2351.*

ROCHE, PAULINE JENNIFER, artist; b. London, Sept. 22, 1961; arrived in U.S., 1995; d. Walter Daniel and Doreen Molly Roche; m. Hany Massarany, Feb. 27, 1986; children: Thomas Daniel, Natalie Jane. BS, Monash U., Melbourne, Australia, 1982. Rsch. physiology dept. physiology Monash U., Melbourne, 1983—86; rsch., policy and planning officer Victorian State Govt. Dept. Edn./Pub. Svc. Bd., Melbourne, 1986—92; artist, 1989—. Exhibitions include Sherbrooke Art Award exhbns., 1991—97, Victorian Artists Soc. Ann. Exhbns., 1992—2001, 2009, Alice Bale Ann. Nat. Exhbns., 1993—98, Camberwell Rotary Ann. Juried Art Exhbn., 1992—98, 1993, 2000, Kew Gallery Invitational Exhbn., 1994, Victorian Artists Soc. Artist of Yr. Invitational Exhbn., 1997, Salmagundi Club 20st Ann. Open Exhbn., Salmagundi Club, 1997—98, Catherine Lorillard Wolfe Art Club Exhbn., 1997, Am. Artists Profl. League 69th Grand Nat. Exhbn., 1997, Newbury Fine Arts, Boston, 1998—2007, Newbury Fine Arts Figurative Art Group Exhbn., 2000, Celebrate! Exhbn., Tucson, 2002, Catherine Lorillard Wolfe Art Club 109th Art Exhbn., 2004, Catherine Lorillard Wolfe Art Club 112th Open Juried xhbn., 2008, El Presidio Gallery, Tucson, 2005—07, Australian Guild of Realist Artists Summer Mem. Exhbn., 2006, Alice Bale Art Award Exhbn., 2006, Am. Artist Profl. League 79th Grand Nat. Exhbn., 2007, Am. Artist Profl. League 80th Grand Nat. Exhbn., 2008, Am. Women Artists Juried Exhbn. and Master Signature Show, 2007, Art Renewal Ctr. Internat., 2007, ARC Salon, 2007, Settlers West 26th Ann. Am. Miniatures Exhbn., 2008, Newbury Fine Arts Ann. Figurative Exhbn., 2008, Newbury Fine Figurative Show, 2009, Munger-Chadwick Found. Art Show, 2008, Salmagundi Club Annual Non-Member Exhbtn., 2008, A. M. E. Bale Art Award Exhbn., 2008, Australian Art Excellence Awards Exhbn., 2008, Tucson Plein Air Painters, 2009, Settlers West 27th Ann. Am. Miniatures Exhbn., 2009, Oil Painters America Western Regional Exhbn., 2009, one-woman shows include Cato Gallery, Victorian Artists Soc. Galleries, Melbourne, 1994, Ventana Med. Sys. Nat. Hdqs., Tucson, 2003, 39th Ann. Mountain Oyster Club Art Show, 2008, Empire 100 Western Art Show, 2009, Victorian Artists Soc. Portrait Exhbn., 2009. Recipient Gold Medal of Honor, Audubon Artists 55th Ann. Exhn., 1997, Hans Heysen award, Sherbrooke Art Soc., 1992, 2nd prize for Oil Painting, Alice Bale Nat. Art Awards, 1994, Mavis Hill Acquisitive Award, Sherbrooke Spring Exhbn., 1995, Gordon Moffat award, Victorian Artists Soc., 1997, Highly Commended, Victorian Artists Soc. Dep. Lord Mayor's Exhbn., 1999, N.J. Chpt. award for artistic excellence, Am. Artists Profl. League, 1997, Pres. award, Salmagundi Club, 1997, Artist Showcase award, Manhattan Arts Internat., 1997, 1998, Leonard J. Meiselman Meml. award, Catherine Lorillard Wolfe Art Club, 1997, Sharon and Danielle Ortlip Meml. award, Salmagundi Club, 1998, Highly Commended award, Australian Guild Realist Artists, 2006, 2008, 2009, Top 100 Finalist, Art Renewal Internat. Salon, 2007, Helen G. Oehler Meml. award, Am. Artists Profl. League, 2007, Bale Nat. Art award, AME, 2008, award, Australian Art Excellence, 2008. Mem.: Oil Painters Am., Tucson Plein Air Painters Soc., Australian Guild Realist Artists, Portrait Soc. Am., Victorian Artists Soc. (signatory mem., Gordon Moffat award 1997). Office Phone: 520-219-2902. Personal E-mail: paulineroche@comcast.net.

ROCHE DE COPPENS, PETER GEORGE, sociologist, educator; b. Vevey, Switzerland, May 24, 1938; s. George Sebastian and Alice Emmanuela (De Coppens) Roche de C.; m. Marian Karpacz, May 27, 1977 (dec. 1991); m. Marie Teresa Crivelli, Sept. 16, 2002. BS, Columbia U., 1965; MA, Fordham U., 1966, PhD, 1973; MSW, U. Montreal, 1978. Prof. sociology, anthropology East Stroudsburg U., Pa., 1970—2005; prof. emeritus. Instr. sociology Fordham U., NYC, 1968-69, tchg. fellow, 1965-68; cons. UN, NYC, 1997; v.p. Internat. Inst. Integral Human Studies, Montreal, 1977-97; cons. UN; adv. prof. faculty edn. McGill U., Montreal, 1998—. Author: The Development of the New Man, 1989, 98, The Art of Joyful Living, 1991, The Sociological Adventure, 1991, 96, Divine Light and Fire, 1992, Divine Light and Love, 1994, The Initiatory Path for the Year 2000, 1994, The Levels of Human Counciousness, 1996, Love Vitamins, 1998, Prayer, the royal Path of the Spiritual Tradition, 2003, La Priére la Voie royale de la Tradition Chretienne, 2003, Medicina e Spiritualita, 2003, La Preghiera, Strumento di Guarigione, 2004, Medicine and Spirtuality, 2004, What are Life and Death, 2004, La Scintilla Divina: Il piu' grande Mistero e Tesoro, 2004, Il Perdono: Chiave essenziale della Salute e della Guarigione, 2005, Il Perdono, 2005, Il Destino, 2005, La Famille Spirituelle au 21e Siecle, 2005, The Spiritual Family in the 21st Century, 2005, La Sagesse, 2005, Il Pellegrinaggio: Risveglio alla Realta', 2006, L'Incontro con Santi e Saggi, 2006, Religion, Spirituality and Health Care, 2007, Medicina Differenziale e Qualitativa, 2007, La Natura Umana, lo Sforzo e la Grazia, 2007, Le Pouvoir et la Volonté, 2007, La Motivazione, Linguaggio del Cuore, 2008, La Reincarnazione ed il Karma, 2008, LIllumininazione Nella Pratica Medica, 2009, Religion et Spiritualite, 2009, Essential Encounters Vols. I, 2006, II, 2007, III, 2008, IV, 2009, The Great Theory of Human and Spiritual Evoilution, 2009, Medicina e Spiritualita: Sintesi Teorica e Pratica, 2009; contbr. articles to mags.; host (TV) Soul Sculpture. Office Phone: 570-422-3276. Business E-Mail: proche@esu.edu.

ROCHELLE, LUGENIA, academic administrator; b. Maple Hill, NC, July 14, 1943; d. John Edward and Ruby Lee (Holmes) R. BA, St. Augustine's Coll., 1965; MS, N.C. A & T State U., 1969; D of Pedagogy, Barbar-Scotia Coll., 1993. Cert. tchr., N.C. Tchr. French, English Butler High Sch., Barnwell, SC, 1965-67; instr. English N.C. A & T State U., Greensboro, 1970-77, St. Augustine's Coll., Raleigh, NC, 1977-86, dir. freshman studies program, 1986-91, dean lower coll., 1991-95, asst. to v.p. acad. affairs, 1991-92; dir. gen. studies, asst. prof. English Voorhees Coll., Denmark, SC, 1996-98, spl. asst. to pres. external affairs, 1999—2002, dir. Hons. Coll., 1999—, dean, Coll. of General Studies, 2002—. Dir. Mellon program St. Augustine's Coll., Raleigh, 1980-83; adv. bd. cooperating Raleigh Colls., 1986—, Off to Coll., Montgomery, Ala., 1993—; mem. profl. practices commn. N.C. Dept. Pub. Instrn., 1994-96; coord. Title III, 1999-00, coord. Bd. Trustees Rels., 1999-02; dir. Ctr. Excellence in Humanities, Vorhees Coll., April 2000-02; Hostess for Radio Talk Show, Views and News from Voorhees Coll., Sept. 2001-03. Author: English Manual of Writing, 1980, (with others) Off to College, 1997, 98, reprinted, 1999, 2000, 01; editor: Can't Nobody Do You Like Jesus, 1998. Judge oratorical contests, Optimist Club, Raleigh, 1985-93; chair pro tem Raleigh Bicentennial Hist. Com., Raleigh, 1991-92; initiated, effected chartering of Phi Eta Sigma St. Augustine's Coll., 1995; bd. dirs. Garner Rd. YMCA, Raleigh, 1994-1996; coord. Honda Campus All-Star Challenge, 1996—; lay min., sec. vestry St. Philip's Episcopal Ch., 1997—; instnl. rep. S.C. Women in Higher Edn., Voorhees Coll., 1998—. Nat. teaching fellow N.C. A & T State U., Greensboro, 1968-70. NCTE Fellow Nat. Coun. Tchrs. English; mem. ASCD (assoc.), Am. Assn. U. Women (pres. Denmark Br.), Cardinal Club. Avocations: reading, collecting antique birds, travel. E-mail: rochelle@voorhees.edu.

ROCHELSON, BURTON L., obstetrician; MD, U. Mich., 1978. Cert. Maternal Fetal Medicine Am. Coll. Ob-Gyn, 1988. Dir. obstetrics and maternal fetal medicine North Shore U. Hosp., Manhasset, NY, 1999—. Contbr. numerous articles to profl. jours. Office: North Shore Univ Hosp 300 Community Dr Manhasset NY 11030 E-mail: brochels@nshs.edu.

ROCHESTER, ANDREW LAWRENCE, lawyer; b. Columbus, Ohio, Sept. 2, 1969; BS in Indsl. and Labor Rels., Cornell U., Ithaca, NY, 1991; JD, Boston U., 1994. Bar: NJ 1994, Pa. 1995, US Dist. Ct. NJ 1994, US Dist. Ct. (ea. dist.) Pa. 1995. Assoc. Dalsemer & Assocs., Phila., 1995—97, McLafferty, Cohen & Stein, Phila., 1996—97; sr. assoc. Adinolfi & Spevak, PA, Haddonfield, NJ, 1997—2004; assoc. McDonough, Korn, Eichhorn & Schorr, Springfield, NJ, 2004—06; ptnr. Morgenstern & Rochester, Cherry Hill, NJ, 2006—. Mem. Camden County Matrimonial Early Settlement Panel, Burlington County Matrimonial Early Settlement Panel. Mem.: Thomas Forkin Family Law Inns of Ct., Camden County Bar Assn. (mem. family law com.), NJ State Bar Assn. (mem. family law com.). Office: Morgenstern & Rochester 1874 Rt 70 East Ste 4 Cherry Hill NJ 08003 Office Fax: 856-424-6977. Business E-Mail: rochesterlaw@comcast.net.

ROCHESTER, MICHAEL GRANT, geophysics educator; b. Toronto, Ont., Can., 1932; s. Reginald Rochester and Ruth Rochester Konrad; m. Elizabeth Manser, 1958; children: Susan, Fiona, John. BA with honors, U. Toronto, 1954, MA, 1956; PhD, U. Utah, 1959. Aerodynamicist A. V. Roe Can. Ltd., Malton, Ont., 1954-55; lectr. geophysics U. Toronto, 1959-60, asst. prof., 1960-61, U. Waterloo, Ont., 1961-65, assoc. prof., 1965-67, Meml. U. Nfld., St. John's, Canada, 1967-70, prof., 1970-98, univ. research prof., 1986—, prof. emeritus, 1998—. Officer Nat. Spiritual Assembly of Baha'is of Can., 1963—92. Grantee, NRC, Natural Scis. and Engring. Rsch. Coun. Can, 1961—2002. Fellow Royal Soc. Can.; mem. Internat. Union Geodesy and Geophysics (Can. nat. com. 1971-75, 84-88), AAAS, Am. Geophys. Union, Can. Assn. Physicists, Can. Geophys. Union (Tuzo Wilson medal, 1986), Internat. Astron. Union (commn. rotation of the Earth 1973—), Royal Astron. Soc. London, Sigma Xi Avocations: hiking, swimming, history. Office: Meml Univ Nfld Dept Earth Scis Saint John's NL Canada A1B 3X5 Office Phone: 709-737-7565. E-mail: mrochest@mun.ca.

ROCHETTE, LOUIS, water transportation executive; b. Quebec City, Que., Can., Feb. 19, 1923; s. Evariste and Blanche (Gaudry) R.; m. Nicole Barbeau, Oct. 12, 1968; children: Louise (dec.), Anne, Guy. M. Commerce, Laval U., Que., 1948. Chartered acct., Que. Chief auditor Sales Tax Govt. Que., Quebec City, 1952—55; treas. Davie Ltd., Lauzon, Que., 1955—65; chmn., CEO Davie Ltd., Lauzon, Que., 1976—81; exec. v.p. Marine Industries, Ltd., Montreal, 1965—76; pres., CEO Soconav Inc., Quebec, 1976—86; pres. Gesconav Inc., 1986—. Past chmn. Lloyd's Com. for Can. Author: Le Reve Separatiste, 1969. Bd. dirs. Gov. Coun. for Can. Unity; gov. Laval U. Found, Quebec Opera Found. Pilot RCAF, 1943-45, ETO. Fellow Inst. Chartered Accts. Can., Can. Inst. Mgmt. Accts. Home and Office: 2500 Pierre Dupuy 508 Montreal PQ Canada H3C 4L1 Home Fax: 514-875-6094. *Whatever success I have met with throughout my career was mainly achieved through perseverance in the face of what often looked like insurmountable obstacles.*

ROCHLIN, PAUL R., lawyer; b. Balt., Dec. 14, 1934; s. Jack and Sara (Levin) Rochlin; m. Lois David, Oct. 25, 1962 (div. 1969); children: Greg, Jennifer; m. Joyce Tretick, July 12, 1973; children: Keith Sopher, Maura Sopher. JD, U. Balt., 1958. Bar: Md. 59, U.S. Dist. Ct. Md. 59. Assoc. Milton Talkin, Balt., 1959—61, Rochlin & Settleman, Balt., 1961—63, ptnr., 1963—78; pres., sr. ptnr. Rochlin Settleman & Dobres, P.A., Balt., 1978—2001, of counsel, 2001—06; pres., sr. ptnr. Rochlin & Goldman, P.A. Bd. dirs. Balt. Jewish Coun., 1979. Mem.: Balt. City Bar Assn., Md. Trial Lawyers Assn. (bd. dirs. 1988—92), Md. State Bar Assn., Suburban Club (pres. 2003—05). Jewish. Office: 100 Church Ln Baltimore MD 21208 Office Phone: 410-602-0222.

ROCHON, THOMAS RICHARD, academic administrator; b. Wash., DC, July 29, 1952; s. Lawrence Charles and Elizabeth Rochon; m. Amber Rochon. BA, U. Mich., 1973, MA, 1976, PhD, 1980. Asst. prof. Princeton U., 1980—87; assoc. prof. Claremont Grad. U., Calif., 1987—96, prof., dean, 1996—2000, interim provost, 1997—98; fulbright scholar Kobe U., Japan, 1992—93; exec. dir., grad. record examination Ednl. Testing Svc., Princeton, 2000—03; exec. v.p., chief academic officer U. St. Thomas, St. Paul, 2003—08; pres. Ithaca Coll., NY, 2008—. Author: Mobilizing For Peace, 1988 (Choice award, 1988), Culture Moves, 1998 (Sociology award, 2000), The Netherlands, 1999. Roman Cath. Avocation: tennis. Office: Ithaca Coll 300 Job Hall 953 Danby Rd Ithaca NY 14850 Office Phone: 607-274-3111. Office Fax: 607-274-1500. Business E-Mail: presidentrochon@ithaca.edu.

ROCK, ALLAN MICHAEL, academic administrator, lawyer, former Canadian government official; b. Ottawa, Ont., Can., Aug. 30, 1947; s. James Thomas and Anne (Torley) R.; m. Deborah Kathleen, June 24, 1983; children: Jason, Lauren, Andrew, Stephen. BA, U. Ottawa, 1968, LLB, 1971; degree (hon.), U. Windsor, 1997. Certified specialist in civil litigation. Sr. ptnr. Fasken Campbell & Godfrey, Toronto, Ont.; min. justice, atty. gen. Govt. of Can., 1993—97, min. health, 1997—2002, min. industry and infrastructure, 2002—03; Can. amb. to UN, New York, 2004—06; atty. Sutts, Strosberg LLP, Windsor, Canada, 2006—08; pres., vice chancellor U. Ottawa, 2008—. Treas. Law Soc. Upper Can., 1992-93; bencher Law Soc., 1983, 87, 91; former chmn. discipline and legal edn. coms.; past chmn. litigation dept. Fasken Campbell Godfrey. Recipient Meritas-Tabaret Disting. Alumnus Award, U. Ottawa, 2007. Fellow: Am. Coll. Trial Lawyers; mem.: Law Soc. of Upper Can. (former treas.). Office: Office of Pres / U Ottawa Tabaret Hall 550 Cumberland, Rm 212 Ottawa ON K1N 6N5 Canada Office Fax: 617-562-5103.

ROCK, ARTHUR, venture capitalist; b. Rochester, NY, Aug. 19, 1926; s. Hyman A. and Reva (Cohen) Rock; m. Toni Rembe, July 19, 1975. BS, Syracuse U., 1948; MBA, Harvard U., 1951. Gen. ptnr. Davis & Rock, San Francisco, 1961-68, Arthur Rock & Assocs., San Francisco, 1969-80. Mem. exec. com. Teledyne, Inc., L.A., 1961-94; dir. emeritus, founder, past chmn., chmn. exec. com., lead dir. Intel Corp., Santa Clara, Calif.; bd. dirs. Echelon Corp., San Jose, Calif.; bd. govs. Nasdaq Stock Market, Inc. Trustee Calif. Inst. Tech.; pres. Basic Fund; bd. dirs. San Francisco Opera Assn., 1970-92, San Francisco Mus. Modern Art; mem. vis. com. Harvard U. Bus. Sch., 1982-88. Recipient Medal of Achievement Am. Electronics Assn., 1987, Am. Acad. Achievement, 1989, Lifetime Achievement in Entrepreneurship and Innovation award U. Calif., 1999; named to Jr. Achievement Hall of Fame, 1990, Calif. Bus. Hall of Fame, 1990, Bay Area Bus. Coun. Hall of Fame, 1995, Arents Pioneer medal Syracuse U., 1997, Outstanding Dir., Corp. Am., 1999, SDForum Visionary award, 2001, Bus. Leader of Yr. award Harvard Bus. Sch. Assn. No. Calif., 2002. Fellow Am. Acad. Arts & Scis. Office: 1 Maritime Plz Ste 1220 San Francisco CA 94111-3502

ROCK, CHARLES PATRICK, economics professor, researcher; s. Vincent Patrick and Alice Mortenson Rock; children: Kerry Robertshaw, Alexander Vincent. BA, Williams Coll., Mass.; MA, Ohio U., Athens, 1979; PhD, Cornell U., Ithaca, NY, 1984. Vol. & staff Action-Peace Corps, Mochudi, Wash., Botswana, 1970—74; prof. Rollins Coll., Winter Pk, Fla., 1984—. Vol. cons. Nonprofit Fin. Instns., Orlando, Fla., 1985—2008. Econ. advisor Cmty. Devel. Credit Unions, Orlando, 1985—2008. Peace Corps Grad. Fellowship, Ohio U., Internat. Affairs Program, 1977—78, Cornell Internat. Studies Grant, Cornell U., Internat. Studies Program, 1983—84, IREX Rsch. Fellow, IREX, 1991—92, Velux Fellow, Velux Found., 1998—99. Mem.: Internat. Assn. Econs. Participation (bd. mem. 2008—). D-Liberal. Achievements include research in financial aspects of democratic businesses. Avocations: biking, travel, history. Office: Dept Econs Rollins Coll 1000 Holt Ave Winter Park FL 32789-4499 Office Fax: 407-646-2485. Business E-Mail: crock@rollins.edu.

ROCK, CHRIS, actor, comedian; b. Bklyn., Feb. 7, 1965; s. Julius and Rose Rock; m. Malaak Compton, Nov. 23, 1996; children: Lola Simone, Zahra Savannah. Actor: (films) Beverly Hills Cop II, 1987, I'm Gonna Git You Sucka, 1988, New Jack City, 1991, Boomerang, 1992, Panther, 1995, The Immortals, 1995, Sgt. Bilko, 1996, Beverly Hills Ninja, 1997, (voice) Doctor Dolittle, 1998, Lethal Weapon 4, 1998, Dogma, 1999, Torrance Rises, 1999, Spin Doctor, 1999, Nurse Betty, 2000, (voice) Artificial Intelligence, 2001, Pootie Tang, 2001, (voice) Osmosis Jones, 2001, Jay and Silent Bob Strike Back, 2001, Bad Company, 2002, Paparazzi, 2004, (voice) Madagascar, 2005, The Longest Yard, 2005, (voice) Bee Movie, 2007, You Don't Mess with the Zohan, 2008, (voice) Madagascar: Escape 2 Africa, 2008, actor, writer, dir. I Think I Love My Wife, 2007, actor, writer, exec. prodr. Down to Earth, 2001, actor, dir., prodr. Head of State, 2003, actor, writer, prodr. (with Nelson George) CB4, 1993; actor: (TV series) Saturday Night Live, 1990-93, Def Comedy Jam, 1992, In Living Color, 1993-94; (TV appearances) Miami Vice, 1987, The Fresh Prince of Bel-Air, 1995, Martin, 1996, Homicide: Life on the Street, 1996, (voice) King of the Hill, 1998, Chappelle's Show, 2003; actor, writer, exec. prodr. (TV series) The Chris Rock Show, 1997-2000 (Emmy for Outstanding Writing for a Variety or Music Program, 1998), Everybody Hates Chris, 2005-09; exec. prodr. (TV series) The Hughleys, 1998; writer, exec. prodr. (comedy specials) Chris Rock: Big Ass Jokes, 1993, Chris Rock: Bring the Pain, 1996 (Emmy for Outstanding Variety, Music or Comedy Special), Chris Rock: Bigger and Blacker, 1999 (American Comedy award for Funniest Male Performer in a TV Special, 2000), Chris Rock: Never Scared, 2004 (Grammy award, Best Comedy Album, 2006), Chris Rock: Kill The Messenger, 2008, writer, prodr. Best of Chris Rock, 1999; (voice) Whatever Happened to Michael Ray?, 2000; performer (comedy albums) Born Suspect, 1991, Roll with the New, 1997 (Grammy award for Best Spoken Comedy Album, 1997), Bigger & Blacker, 1999 (Grammy award for Best Spoken Comedy Album, 1999), Never Scared, 2004; Author Rock This!, 1998. Recipient Star, Hollywood Walk of Fame, 2003; named one of The 100 Most Influential People in the World, TIME mag., 2008. Office: c/o Mosaic Media Group 9200 West Sunset Blvd 10th Fl Los Angeles CA 90069

ROCK, DAVID PETER, history professor; b. Great Harwood, Lancashire, Eng., Apr. 8, 1945; s. William and Elsie Rock; m. Rosalind Louise Farrar, Aug. 3, 1968; children: Edward David, Charles John(dec.). BA, U. Cambridge, Eng., 1967, PhD, 1971. Rsch. officer U. Cambridge; asst. sec. U. London, England, 1974—77; prof. history U. Calif., Santa Barbara, 1977—. Contbr. articles to hist. jours. (Guggenheim fellowship, 1989); author: (book) State Formation and Political Movements in Argentina, 1860-1916 (NEH fellowship, 1992), Politics in Argentina, 1890-1930. The Rise and Fall of Radicalism. (Herbert E. Bolton prize, 1976). Home: 820 Tye Rd Santa Barbara CA 93105 Office: Dept History Univ Calif Santa Barbara CA 93106 Business E-Mail: rock@history.ucsb.edu.

ROCK, DOUGLAS LAWRENCE, manufacturing executive; b. Glen Cove, NY, Jan. 25, 1947; s. Herb and Beatrice (Vyse) R.; m. Cindy Pegoraro, May 11, 1967 (div. Apr. 1973); 1 child, Jason; m. Mary Sue Bell, Mar. 23, 1991 (div. Jan. 1996). BS in Psychology and Chemistry, Pa. State U., 1968; postgrad., U. Chgo., 1971-73. Rsch. chemist FMC Corp., Princeton, NJ, 1968-69; mfg. system project leader A.O. Smith Corp., Erie, Pa., 1969-71; dir. materials and info. systems Joy Mfg., Michigan City, Ind., 1971-74; dir. info. systems Smith Tool div. Smith Internat. Inc., Irvine, Calif., 1974-75, dir. materials, 1975-77, v.p. mfg., 1977-80, sr. v.p. ops., 1980-82, pres., 1985-87, Drilco div. Smith Internat. Inc., Houston, 1982-85; pres., CEO Smith Internat. Inc., Houston, 1987—91, chmn., pres., CEO, 1991—2008, chmn., pres., CEO, COO, 2008, chmn., 2009—. Bd. dirs. Viad Corp. Named Golden Knight, Nat. Mgmt. Assn., 1983. Mem. Internat. Assn. Drilling Contractors, Am. Petroleum Inst., Petroleum Equipment Suppliers Assn. (bd. dirs. Houston chpt. 1987—, 1st v.p. 1996), Nat. Offshore Industries Assn. (fin. com. 1988, audit com. 1989), Greenspoint Club. Avocations: golf, racquetball, reading. Office: Smith Internat PO Box 60068 16740 Hardy Rd Houston TX 77205*

ROCK, HAROLD L., lawyer; b. Sioux City, Iowa, Mar. 13, 1932; s. Harold L. and Helen J. (Gormally) R.; m. Marilyn Beth Clark Rock, Dec. 28, 1954; children: Michael, Susan, John, Patrick, Michele, Thomas. BS, Creighton U., 1954, JD, 1959. Bar: Nebr., N.Y., Wyo. Law clk. to judge Woodrough U.S. Ct. Appeals 8th Circuit, Omaha, 1959-60; assoc. law clk. Fitzgerald Hamer Brown & Leahy, Omaha, 1960—65; of counsel Kutak Rock, Omaha, 1965—. Chmn. Nebr. Bd. Bar Examiners, 1989-96; bd. dirs. Mid City Bank, Omaha. Bd. dirs. Douglas County Hist. Soc., 1992-99, Nat. Equal Justice Libr., 1995—, Nebr. Nebr. Humanities Coun., 1996-2002. Served to 1st lt. U.S. Army, 1954-56. Recipient Alumni Achievement award Creighton U., 1995. Mem. ABA (ho. of dels. 1970-96, bd. govs. 1992-95), Nebr. Bar Assn. (ho. of dels., bd. dirs. 1985—, pres. 1988, Nebr. Bar found. bd. dirs., 1982-2003), Omaha Bar Assn. (pres. 1972-73), Omaha Legal Aid Soc. (pres. 1969-72), Nebr. State Bd. Pub. Accts. (bd. dirs. 1981-85). Roman Catholic. Office: Kutak Rock The Omaha Bldg 1650 Farnam St Omaha NE 68102-2186

ROCKAS, LEO, English educator; b. Rochester, NY, Oct. 12, 1928; s. John Constantine and Crystal (Tsychlas) R.; m. Virginia Louise Rouvina, June 25, 1960; children: Nia, Anastasia. AB, AM, U. Rochester; PhD, U. Mich. Instr. Wayne State U., Detroit, 1957-60; asst. prof. Rochester Inst. Tech., 1960-61; asst. to full prof. SUNY, Geneseo, 1961-67; prof. English Briarcliff Coll., Briarcliff Manor, N.Y., 1967-71, U. Hartford, West Hartford, Conn., 1971—2006; ret., 2006. Author: Modes of Rhetoric, 1964, Ways In, 1984, A Creative Copybook, 1989, Style in Writing, 1992, Mice Make War, 2007. With U.S. Army, 1946-48. Home: PO Box 414 West Simsbury CT 06092-0414

ROCKAWAY, EYTAN, film producer, director; b. Tel Aviv, Dec. 23, 1976; s. Robert and Betty Rockaway. BFA, Tisch Sch. Arts NYU, NYC, 2003. Co-founder & CEO Matter Substance Entertainment, NYC, 2000—; co-founder & pres., programming & content Amos TV, NYC, 2006—. Dir.: (short film) Human (Grand Festival award, 2006), (music video) B&J (Music Video of Yr. award, 2006).

ROCKBURNE, DOROTHEA GRACE, artist; b. Montreal; naturalized; Student, Black Mountain Coll.; PhD (hon.), Coll. of Creative Studies, Detroit, 2002. Milton and Sally Avery Disting. prof. Bard Coll., 1986. Trustee Ind. Curators Inc., N.Y., Art in Gen.; artist in residence Am. Acad. in Rome, 1991; vis. artist Skowhegan Sch. Painting and Sculpture, 1984; Rockefeller Found. resident Bellagio (Italy) Conf. and Study Ctr., 1997. One-woman shows at Sonnabend Gallery, Paris, 1971, New Gallery, Cleve., 1972, Bykert Gallery, NYC, 1970, 72-73, Galleria Toselli, Milan, Italy, 1972-74, Galleria D'Arte, Bari, Italy, 1972, Lisson Gallery, London, 1973, Daniel Weinberg Gallery, San Francisco, 1973, Galerie Charles Kriwin, Brussels, 1975, Galleria Schema, Florence, Italy, 1973, 75, 92, John Weber Gallery, NYC, 1976, 78, Galleria la Polena, Geona, Italy, 1977, Tex. Gallery, Houston, 1979-81, Xavier Fourcade Gallery, NYC, 1981-83, 85-86, David Bellman, Toronto, 1980-81, Margo Leavin, Calif., 1982, Arts Club Chgo., 1987, André Emmerich Gallery, NYC, 1988-89, 91-92, 94-95, Rose Art Mus., 1989, P. Fong & Spratt Galleries, San Jose, Calif., 1991, Sony Music Hdqs., NYC, 1993, Frederick Spratt Gallery, San Jose, 1994, Guild Hall Mus., Easthampton, N.Y., 1995, Portland Mus. Art, Maine, 1996, Ingrid Raab Gall., Berlin, 1997, Art in Gen., NY, 1999, Greenberg, Van Doren, NYC, 2000, Dieu Donné Papermill, NYC, 2003, Jan Abrams Fine Art, NY, 2003, Beard Gallery, Wheaton Coll., Norton, Mass., 2009, Black Mountain Coll. Mus. & Arts Ctr., Asheville, NC, 2009; group exhbns. at Leo Castelli Gallery, NYC, 1966, Whitney Mus. Am. Art, 1970, 73, 77, 79, 82, 05, Mus. Modern Art, NYC, 71, 73, 81, 84, 86, 91, 93-94, 05, Buenos Aires, 1971, Kolner Kunst Market, Cologne, Germany, 1971, Stedelijk Mus., Holland, 1971, Spoleto (Italy) Festival, 1972, Palazzo Taverna, Rome, 1973, Nat. Gallery Victoria, Melbourne, Australia, 1973, Art Gallery NSW, Sydney, 1973, Auckland (New Zealand) City Art Gallery, 1973, Inst. Contemporary Art, London, 1974, Mus. d'Arte de la Ville, Paris, 1975, Galerie Aronowitsch, Stockholm, 1975, Stadtiches Mus., Manchengladbach, Germany, 1975, Galleria D'Arte Moderna, Bologna, Italy, 1975, Art Gallery Ont., Toronto, Can., 1975, Mus. Fine Art, Houston, 1975, Contemporary Arts Ctr., Cin., 1973, 75, 81, Mus. Contemporary Art, Chgo., 1971, 77, 86, Corcoran Gallery of Art, Washington, 1975, 87, Städtisches Mus., Leverkusen, Germany, 1975, Cannaviella Studio d'Arte Rome, 1976, Phila. Coll. Art, 1976, 83, New Mus., NYC, 1977, 80, 84, 83, Renaissance Soc. of U. Chgo., 1976, Lowe Art Mus., U. Miami, Fla., 1976, Inst. Contemporary Art, Boston, 1976, Seibu Mus. Art, Tokyo, 1976, NY State Mus., Albany, 1977, Drawing Ctr., 1977, Kansas City (Mo.) Art Inst., 1977, Smithsonian Inst., Washington, 1977, Kassel, Fed. Republic Germany, 1972, 77, Ackland Art Ctr., Chapel Hill, NC, 1979, 84, Milw. Art Ctr., 1978, 81, Biblioteca Nacional, Madrid, 1980, Gulbenkian Mus., Lisbon, Portugal, 1980, Bklyn. Mus., 1981, 89, Guggenheim Mus., 1982, 88-89, 2004, Albright Knox Art Gallery, Buffalo, 1979-80, 88-89, Kuustforeningen Mus., Copenhagen, 1980, Venice Biennale, 1980, Cranbrook (Mich.) Acad. Art, 1981, Mus. Fine Arts, Boston, 1983, Contemporary Arts Mus., Houston, 1983, Norman Mackenzie Art Gallery, U. Regina, Sask., Can., 1983, Galleriet, Sweden, 1983-84, Seattle Art Mus., 1979-84, Nat. Mus. Art., Osaka, Japan, 1984, Fogg Art Mus., Cambridge, Mass., 1984, Am. Acad. and Inst. Arts and Letters, NYC, 1984, 87, LA County Mus. Art, 1984, 86, Wadsworth Atheneum, Hartford, Conn., 1981, 84, Evehart Mus., Pa., 1984, Grey Art Gallery, NYU, 1977, 84, 87, Avery Ctr. Arts, Bard Coll., N.Y., 1985, 87-88, Stamford (Conn.) Mus., 1985, Aldrich Mus., Conn., 1979, 82, 95, Bronx Mus. Arts, N.Y.C., 1985, High Mus., Atlanta, 1975, 81, Phila. Mus. Art, 1986, Nat. Gallery Art, Washington, 1984, 94, 97, Mus. Art, Ft. Lauderdale, Fla., 1986, Nat. Mus. Women in Art, Washington, 1987, Xavier Fourcade Gallery, 1982, 83, 86-87, LA County Mus. Modern Art, 1986-87, The Hague, The Netherlands, 1986, Carnegie-Mellon Art Gallery, Pitts., 1979, 87, Balt. Mus. Art, 1975-76, 88, Ctr. for Fine Arts, Miami, 1989, Milw. Art Mus., 1989, Cin. Art Mus., 1989, New Orleans Mus., 1989, Denver Art Mus., 1989, Parrish Art Mus., South Hampton, NY, 1990-91, 99, Margo Leavin Gallery, LA, 1991, Guild Hall Mus., East Hampton, NY, 1991, Am. Acad., Rome, 1991, Mus. Contemporary Art, LA, 1991, 99, Hunter Coll., NY, 1991, CentroCultural/Arte Contemporanea, MexicoCity, 1991, Hilton, San Jose, Calif.,1992, Hillwood Art Mus., L.I., NY, 1992, Am. Acad. and Inst. Arts and Letters, 1992, Neuberger Mus., 1992, 00, Kohn-Abrams Gallerie, LA, 1993, Gallery at Bristol Myers Squibb, NJ, 1993-94, Found. Art and Preservation in Embassies, NYC, 1993, Andre Emmerich Gallery, NYC, 1993, Fred Spratt Gallery, San Jose, Calif., 1994, Raab Galarie, Berlin, 1994, NY Studio Sch., NYC, 1995, 02, Rose Art Mus., Brandeis U., 1996, Addison Gallery Am. Art, Andover, Mass., 1997, 04, Fine Arts Mus. San Francisco, 1997, Wexner Ctr., Columbus, 1997, Dieu Donne Papermill, Inc., NYC, 1998, Pub. Sch. 1, Long Island City, NYC, 1999, Gemini G.E.L., 1998, Am. Acad. Arts and Letters, 1999, 01, Parsons Sch. Design, NYC, 1999, David Dorsky Gallery, NY, 2000, Greenberg Van Doren Fine Art, NYC, 2000, 02, 04, 05, 06, NAD, NYC, 2002, Armory Show, NYC, 2002, Nat. Gallery of Art, 2001, Krannert Art Mus., 2002, Selby Gallery, Fla., 2002, Geffen Contemporary, LA, 2002, Marcus Ritter, NYC, 2002, Bowdoin Coll. Mus. Art, 2002, Reina Sophia Mus., Madrid, 2003, Cleve. Mus. Art, 2003, New Britain (Conn.) Mus. Am. Art, 2003, Mus. New Zealand, 2003, Guggenheim Mus., NYC, 2004, ACA Galleries, NYC, 2004, Bruce Mus., Greenwich, Conn., 2004, MOCA at Calif. Plz., L.A., 2004, Boca Raton Mus. Art, 2005, Betty Cunningham Gallery, 2005, Spanierman Gallery, East Hampton, NY, 2005, Black Mtn. Coll. Mus., Asheville, NC, 2005, Mus. Modern Art, NYC, 2006, Nat. Acad. Design, NYC, 2006, Yellow Bird Gallery, Newburgh, NY, 2005, Pa. Acad. Fine Arts, Phila., 2006, Cleve. Mus. Art, 2006, Weatherspoon Mus., Greensboro, NC, 2006, Morgan Libr., 2006, David Nolan Gallery, NYC, 2007, Arte Contemporanea, Madrid, Yale U. Art Gallery, New Heaven, Nat. Acad. Mus., NYC, 2007, Mus. Modern Art, NYC, 2007-09, Mus. Contemporary Art, LA, 2007-08, High Times, Hard Times: New York Painting, 1965-75, Am. U., Washington, Tamayo Mus., Mexico City, New Gallery Graz, Austria, ZKM, Ctr. Art and Media Karlsruhe, Germany, Drawing Connections: Baselitz, Kelly, Penone, Rockburne and the Old Masters, 2007-08, Multiplex: Directors in Art, Bjorn Ressle Gallery, NY, 2008-09, Black Mountain Coll. Mus. & Arts Ctr., Asheville, NC, 2008-09, Bowman Art Adv., Chgo., 2009, Hood Mus. Art, Dartmouth Coll., NH, 2009-, others; print exhbns. at Nat. Gallery, Washington, 1994, 97, 2001, Kate Ganz, Ltd., NYC, 2000, David Adamson Gallery, Washington, 2000, Fine Arts Mus. San Francisco, 1997, Bklyn. Mus., 1989, Mt. Holyoke Coll. Art Mus., 1987, Harcus Gallery, Boston, 1985, Xavier Fourcade Gallery, NYC, 1982, Mus. Modern Art, NYC, 1981, 91, Yale U. Art Gallery, New Haven, 1981, New Gallery Contemporary Art, Cleve., 1978, Art Gallery Ont., Toronto, 1978, Stadtiches Mus., Monchengladbach, Germany, 1971, Mus. New Zealand Te Papa Tongarewa, Wellington, 2003, Ralls Collection, Washington, 2004, Addison Gallery Am. Art, Mass., 2004, Mus. Fine Arts, Boston, 2003, 04, 05; represented in permanent collections Milw. Art Ctr., Mus. Modern Art NYC, Fogg Mus., Cambridge, Mass., Phila. Mus. Art, High Mus. Art, Atlanta, Houston Mus. Fine Arts, Corcoran Gallery, Washington, Mpls. Art Inst., Mpls. Art Mus., Met. Mus. Art, NYC, Guggenheim Mus., NYC, Nat. Acad. Design, NYC, J. Paul Getty Trust, LA, Ludwig Mus., Aachen, Fed. Republic Germany, Holladay, Washington, Saatchi, London, Bard, Albright-Knox Art Gallery, Buffalo, Whitney Mus. Am. Art, NYC, U. Mich., Ann Arbor, Ohio State U., Columbus, Gilman Paper Co., NY, Auckland (New Zealand) City Art Mus., Portland (Oreg.) Art Mus., Aaken Art Mus., Oberlin, Ohio, Highhold Internat., South Africa, U. Ohio Art Gallery, Columbus, HHK Charitable Found., Milw., Art Gallery Ont., Nat. Mus. Women in Art, Washington, Chase Manhattan Bank, NYC; installations: Hilton Hotel, San Jose, Calif., Sony Music Hdqrs., Aldridge Mus., Conn., Edward T. Gignoux Courthouse, Portland, Maine. Recipient Witowsky prize, Art Inst., Chgo., 1976, Creative Arts award, Brandeis U., 1985, Bard Coll., 1986, Alliance for Young Artists and Writers Inc. award, 1997, Jimmy Ernst Lifetime Achievement award in art, Am. Acad. Arts and Letters, 1999, Pike award, Nat. Acad. of Art and Design, 2002, Adolph and Clara Obrig prize, Nat. Acad. Design, 2002, Pollock Krasner award, 2002, 2004, Omi Internat. Francis J. Greenberger award, 2003, Lifetime Achievement award, Nat. Acad. Mus., NY, 2009; grantee, Nat. Endowment Arts, 1974, Am. Acad. Rome, 1991; fellow, Guggenheim fellow, 1972. Mem.: AAAL. Personal E-mail: drockburne@gmail.com.

ROCKEFELLER, DAVID, banker; b. NYC., June 12, 1915; s. John Davison Jr. and Abby Greene (Aldrich) R.; m. Margaret McGrath, Sept. 7, 1940 (dec. Mar. 1996); children: David, Abby A., Neva, Margaret D., Richard G., Eileen M. BS, Harvard Coll., 1936; student, London Sch. Econs.; PhD, U. Chgo., 1940; LLD (hon.), Columbia U., 1954, Bowdoin Coll., 1958, Jewish Theol. Sem., 1958, Williams Coll., 1966, Wagner Coll., 1967, Harvard U., 1969, Pace Coll., 1970, St. John's U., 1971, Middlebury, 1974, U. Liberia, 1979, Rockefeller U., 1980, Am. U., 1987, U. Miami, 1988; DEng (hon.), Colo. Sch. Mines, 1974, U. Notre Dame, 1987. Sec. to Mayor Fiorello H. La Guardia, 1940-41; asst. regional dir. Office Def., Health and Welfare Services, 1941-42; asst. mgr. for. dept. Chase Nat. Bank, NYC, 1946-47, asst. cashier, 1947-48, 2d v.p., 1948-49, v.p., 1949-51, sr. v.p., 1951-55; exec. v.p. Chase Manhattan Bank (Chase Nat. Bank merged with Bank of Manhattan), 1955-57; vice chmn. bd. Chase Manhattan Bank, 1957-61, pres., chmn. exec. com., 1961-69, chmn., 1969-81, CEO, 1969-80. Chmn. Chase Internat. Adv. Com., 1981-99, Rockefeller Group, Inc., 1981-95, N.Y. Clearing House, 1971-78, Ctr. for Intern-Am. Rels., 1966-70, Overseas Devel. Coun., U.S.-USSR Trade and Econ. Coun. Inc.; chmn. Internat. Exec. Svc. Corps., 1964-68; chmn. Rockfeller Ctr. Properties Trust, Inc., 1996-2000 Author: Unused Resources and Economic Waste, 1940, Creative Management in Banking, 1964. Active Urban Devel. Corp., N.Y. State Bus. Adv. Coun., 1968-72, U.S. Adv. Com. on Reform on Internat. Monetary System, 1973-77, U.S. exec. com. Dartmouth Conf. Bd. Inst. Internat. Econs., Am. Friends of LSE, U.S. Hon. Fellows LSE, Bus. Com. for Arts; founding mem. Commn. on White House Fellows, hon. mem., 1964-65; exec. com., chmn. Downtown Lower Manhattan Assn., 1958-75; trustee Rockefeller U., 1940-95, Carnegie Endowment Internat. Peace, Hist. Hudson Valley, 1981-95; chmn. Rockefeller Bros. Fund, 1981-87, vice-chmn., 1968-80; hon. trustee Rockefeller Family Fund; life trustee U. Chgo.; trustee, chmn. emeritus, Mus. Modern Art, N.Y.C.; bd. overseers Harvard Coll., 1954-60, 62-68; co-founder Trilateral Commn., 1973-91, N.Am. chmn. 1981-92, hon. chmn., 1992; hon. chmn. Internat. House, 1940—, dir., 1940-63; pres. Morningside Heights, Inc., 1947-57, chmn., 1957-65; chmn. Am. Soc., 1981-92, hon. chmn., 1992—, N.Y.C. Partnership, 1979-88. Capt. AUS, 1942-45, NATOUSA, ETO. Decorated Legion of Honor France, Order of Arts and Letters; Order of the Liberator San Martin, Argentina, Order of Valor, Rep. of Cameroun, Order of Boyaca, Colombia, Order of Christopher Columbus, Domincan Republica, Nat. Order of Merit, Ecuador, Knight Comdr.'s Cross of the Order of Merit, Germany, Order of the Republic, Guinea, Gwengha Medal of the Rep. of Korea, Order of the Aztec Eagle, Mexico, Order of the Throne, Morocco, Hilal-i'Quaid-e-Azam, Pakistan, Order of Vasco Nunez de Balboa, Panama, Order of Manuel Amador Guerrero, Panama, Nat. Order of Merit/Grand Cross, Paraguay, Order of Merit, Italy, Order of Southern Cross, Brazil, Order of the White Elephant and Order of Crown, Thailand, Order of the Cedars, Lebanon, Order of the Sun, Peru, Nicholas Copernicus award, Porland, Order of Prince Henry the Navigator, Portugal, Nat. Order of the Lion, Rep. of Senegal, Order of Francisco de Miranda, Venezuela, Order of the Humane African Redemption, Liberia, Order of the Crown, Belgium, Nat. Order of Ivory Coast, Grand Cordon Order of Sacred Treasure, Japan, Order Bernardo O'Higgins, Chile, others; recipient Merit award N.Y. chpt. AIA, 1965, Gold medal Nat. Inst. Social Scis., 1967, AIA medal of Honor for City Planning N.Y.C., 1968, Charles Evans Hughes award NCCJ, 1974, World Brotherhood award Jewish Theol. Sem, 1953, C. Walter Nichols award NYU, 1970, Regional Planning Assn. award, 1971; Hadrian award, World Monuments Fund, 1994, U.S. Presdl. Medal of Freedom, 1998; named one of Top 200 Collectors, ARTnews Mag., 2004, Forbes' Richest Americans, 2006. Mem. Council Fgn. Relations (dir. 1949-51, v.p. 1951-70, chmn. 1970-85), Japan Soc. (hon. chmn.), Internat. House (hon. chmn.), Bilderberg Conf., Harvard Club, Univ. Club, Century Club, The Links, The Knickerbocker. Avocations: sailing, collecting 19th-century Am. art, impressionism and modern art, porcelain. Address: 30 Rockefeller Plz Rm 5600 New York NY 10112-0002

ROCKEFELLER, EDWIN SHAFFER, lawyer; b. Sept. 10, 1927; s. Edwin and Nancy Rhea (McCullough) R.; m. Marilie Gould Wallace, Dec. 22, 1952; children: Ben Wallace, Edwin Palmer. AB, Yale U., 1948, LLB, 1951; M in Internat. Pub. Policy, Johns Hopkins U., 1989. Bar: Conn. 1951, D.C. 1956, U.S. Supreme Ct. 1957. Atty. FTC, 1956—61, asst. to gen. counsel, 1958—59, exec. asst. to chmn., 1960—61; pvt. practice Washington, 1961; chmn. adv. bd. bna.antitrust rept., 1961—. Mem. USIA Inspection Team, Pakistan, 1971; adj. prof. Georgetown U. Law Ctr., Washington, 1987. Author: Antitrust Questions & Answers, 1974, Desk Book of FTC Practice & Procedure, 3d edit., 1979, Antitrust Counseling for the 1980s, 1983, (book) The Antitrust Religion. Mem.: ABA (chmn. sect. antitrust law 1976—77, ho. of dels. 1979—82), Met. Club, Chevy Chase Club. Office: Ste 1024 2801 New Mexico Ave NW Washington DC 20007-3940

ROCKEFELLER, JAY (JOHN DAVISON ROCKEFELLER IV), United States Senator from West Virginia; b. NYC, June 18, 1937; s. John Davison III and Blanchette Ferry (Hooker) R.; m. Sharon Percy, Apr. 1, 1967; children: John, Valerie, Charles, Justin. Student, Japanese lang. Internat. Christian U., Tokyo, 1957-60; BA in Far Eastern Languages and History, Harvard U., 1961, MA, 1954—57; postgrad. in Chinese, Yale U., 1961-62. Mem. nat. adv. council Peace Corps, 1961, spl. asst. to dir. corps, 1962, ops. officer in charge work in Philippines, until 1963; desk officer for Indonesian affairs, Bur. Ea. Affairs US Dept. State, 1963; cons. Pres.'s Commn. on Juvenile Delinquency and Youth Crime, 1964; mem. W.Va. Ho. of Delegates, 1966-68; sec. state State of W.Va., Charleston, W.Va., 1968-72, gov., 1977—85; pres. W.Va. Wesleyan Coll., Buckhannon, 1973-75; US Senator from W.Va., 1985—; mem. US Senate Fin. Com., Joint Com. on Taxation, US Senate Veterans Affairs Com., chmn., 1993—95, 2001, 2001—03; mem. US Senate Select Com. on Intelligence, chmn., 2007—09, US Senate Commerce, Sci. & Transp. Com., 2009—. Contbr. articles to mags. including N.Y. Times Sunday mag. Trustee U. Chgo., 1967—; chmn. The White House Conf. Balanced Nat. Growth & Econ. Devel., 1978, Pres.'s Commn. on Coal, 1978-80, White House Adv. Com. on Coal., 1980 Recipient Excellence in Public Svc. award, Am. Acad. Pediatrics, 1990, Congressional Adv. of Yr. award, Child Welfare League of Am., 1997, Langer Chip award, Sci. Coalition, 1999, Award Excellence in Public Svc., Consortium Sch. Networking, 2002, Wellstone award, United Steelworkers of America, 2003; named one of Top 200 Collectors, ARTnews Mag., 2004—08. Mem.: Nat. Gov. Assn. Democrat. Presbyn. Avocation: collecting 19th-century Am. art and Am. impressionism. Office: US Senate 531 Hart Senate Bldg Washington DC 20510-0001 also: District Office Ste 308 405 Capitol St Charleston WV 25301-1786 Office Phone: 202-224-6472, 304-347-5372. Office Fax: 202-224-7665, 202-228-4656, 304-347-5371. Business E-Mail: senator@rockefeller.senate.gov.*

ROCKEFELLER, SHARON PERCY, broadcast executive; b. Oakland, Calif., Dec. 10, 1944; d. Charles H. and Jeanne (Dickerson) Percy; m. John D. (Jay) Rockefeller IV; children: John, Valerie, Charles, Justin. BA cum laude, Stanford U., 1966; DPS (hon.), Alderson-Broaddus Coll., 1977; LLD (hon.), U. Charleston, 1977, Beloit Coll., 1978; LHD (hon.), West Liberty State Coll., 1980, Hamilton Coll., 1982, Wheeling Coll., 1984. Founder, chmn. Mountain Artisans, 1968—78; teacher's asst., Head Start Head Start program, Coal Branch Heights, W.Va.; chmn. Corp. Pub. Broadcasting, Washington, 1981—84; bd. dirs. Stas. WETA-TV-FM, Washington, 1987—89, pres., CEO, 1989—. Former chmn. Va. Assn. Pub. TV Stas.; bd. dirs. Pub. Broadcasting Svc., W.Va. Edn. Broadcasting Authority, Corp. for Pub. Broadcasting, PepsiCo, Smithsonian Instn., Nat. Gallery of Art, Nat. Cathedral, Stanford Univ., Chgo. Univ., George Washington Univ., Phillips Collection, Colonial Williamsburg Found., Rockefeller Bros. Fund, Rockefeller Family Office, NYC; trustees coun. Nat. Gallery of Art. Adv. bd. Nat. Women's Polit. Caucus, 1975—; adv. bd., bd. dirs. Women's Campaign Fund, 1975—81; co-chairwoman ERAmerica, 1972—82; mem.-at-large Dem. Nat. Conv., del., 1976, 1980, 1984; mem.-at-large Dem. Nat. Com., 1980—; trustee Fed. City Coun.; bd. mem. Day Care and Child Devel. Coun. America, 1969—72; former mem. bd. dir. Sunrise Mus., W.Va.; bd. mem. Sotheby's, NYC, Colonial Williamsburg Found; mem. internat. coun. Mus. Modern Art, NYC, 1973—81; former chmn. Va. Assn. Pub. TV Stas. Recipient Charles Frankel Prize, Nat. Endowment for the Humanities, 1994, Distinguished Broadcaster Award, 1994, Woman of Vision Award, Women in Film & Video, CINE Lifetime Achievement Award; named Washingtonian of Yr., Washingtonian Mag., 1994; named one of Top 200 Collectors, ARTnews Mag., 2004—08. Fellow: Am. Acad. Arts & Sciences, Smithsonian Am. Art Commn. (bd. mem.); mem.: Stanford-in-Washington Coun. (former chmn.). Avocation: collecting 19th-century Am. art and Am. impressionism. Office: Sta WETA-FM 2775 S Quincy St Arlington VA 22206-2236

ROCKENSIES, JOHN WILLIAM, mechanical engineer; b. NYC, May 30, 1932; s. John William and Wilma (Mercz) R.; m. Marion Pauline Peachman, Sept. 16, 1956; children: Kenneth John, Karen Martha Rockensies Steinbeck. B of Mech. Engring., CCNY, 1954, M of Mech. Engring., 1960; postgrad., Bklyn. Poly. Inst., 1955, Columbia U., 1956. Registered profl. engr., NY. Jet engine performance and compressor devel. Curtiss Wright Corp., Woodridge, NJ, 1954—56; product devel. engr. Sperry Gyroscope Corp., Lake Success, NY, 1956—60; sr. exptl. test engr. Pratt & Whitney Corp., East Hartford, Conn., 1960—62; project engr. Stratos Corp., Bayshore, NY, 1962; prin. propulsion engr. Republic Aviation Corp., Farmingdale, NY, 1963—64; power plant design engr., group and project leader, project engr., engr. specialist and mgr. Grumman Aerospace Corp., Bethpage, NY, 1964—95; ret., 1995; contract staff engr. Northrop-Grumman Corp., Bethpage, 1996—98. Mem. SAE E-32 Engine Condition Monitoring com., 1983; lt. comdr. Smithtown Bay Power Squadron, instr. navigation. Author tech. papers in field; co-author chpt. in book. Deacon, trustee, elder First Presbyn Ch. Smithtown; docent Cradle of Aviation Mus., Garden City, NY, 2002-. Recipient Apollo Achievement award NASA, Washington, 1970. Assoc. fellow AIAA (mem. air breathing propulsion tech. com. 1996-2009, mem. coun. LI sect. 2002—, Chmn.'s award 2003, 06, instr. air breathing propulsion design course, Sustained Svc. award 2009); mem. NSPE, ASME, US Power Squadrons (sr. navigator). Avocations: sailing, boating, jogging, camping, travel, model aircraft. Home: 65 Parnell Dr Smithtown NY 11787-2428 Personal E-mail: jrock8@optonline.net.

ROCKETT, D. JOE, lawyer, director; b. Drumright, Okla., May 3, 1942; s. Gordon Richard and Hazel Peggy (Rigsby) R.; m. Mary Montgomery, Aug. 31, 1963; children: David Montgomery, Ann Morley. BA, U. Okla., 1964, JD, 1967. Bar: Okla. 1967, U.S. Dist. Ct. (we. dist.) Okla. 1968. Assoc. Kerr, Davis, Irvine & Burbage, Oklahoma City, 1967-69, Andrews Davis Legg Bixler Milsten & Price, Oklahoma City, 1969—, mem., 1973—, also bd. dirs., pres., 1986-90, 96-00. Securities law advisor Oil Investment Inst., Washington, 1984-87. Bd. dirs. Myriad Gardens Found., Oklahoma City, 1987—, chmn., 1991-92. Mem. ABA (fed. regulation of securities and partnership coms. of bus. law sect. 1984), Okla. Bar Assn. (securities liaison com. 1983, chmn. bus. assocs. sect. 1985, securities adminstr.'s select com. 1986—). Avocations: sailing, fishing, skiing. Office: Andrews Davis 100 N Broadway Ste 3300 Oklahoma City OK 73102-8812 Business E-Mail: djrockett@andrewsdavis.com.

ROCKEY, PEGGY ANN, pre-school educator; b. New Orleans, Aug. 29, 1955; d. Sidney E. and Bonnie L. Clavijo; m. David L. Rockey, June 12, 1976; children: Robert, Randy. AAS, Tyler Jr. Coll., Tex., 1975; degree in Child Devel. Assoc., 2002. Presch. instr. 1st Meth. Ch., Ashbury Meth. Ch., Odessa, Tex., 1983—93; presch. tchr. Good Shepherd Presbyn. Ch., Bartlesville, 1993—. Canteen chmn. Svc. League Bartlesville, 1998; mem. disaster team ARC, Bartlesville, 2005. Recipient Dist. award of merit, Boy Scouts Am. Mem.: Nat. Assn. Edn. Young Children, Assn.Childhood Edn. Internat. Avocations: cooking, reading, fishing, hiking. Home: 2425 Kensington Way Bartlesville OK 74006

ROCKEY, SALLY JEAN, federal agency administrator; PhD in Entomology, Ohio State U., 1985. Postdoc. fellow U. Wis.; prog. officer Coop. State Rsch. Edn. & Extension Svc. (CSREES), US Dept. Agr., 1986, dep. adminstr. competitive rsch. grants & award Mgmt. unit, then chief info. officer CSREES, 2002—05; dep. dir. Office Extramural Rsch. (OER), NIH, Bethesda, Md., 2002—08, acting dep. dir. extramural rsch., interim dir. OER, 2008—. Recipient Presdl. Rank award, 2004. Office: NIH OER Bldg 1 Shannon Bldg 144 1 Ctr Dr Bethesda MD 20892 Office Phone: 301-496-1096. Business E-Mail: sr393d@nih.gov.*

ROCKHILL, MARSHA, special education educator; AA, Gulf Coast CC, Panama City, Fla., 1976; BA in Music Edn. - Choral, Fla. State U., Tallahassee, 1978; M in Social Sci. Edn., Fla. State U., Panama City, 2002; student, Fla. State U., Tallahassee, 2003—. Cert. art tchr. Fla. Dept. Edn., Tallahassee, 2000, art & music 2000. Spl. edn. tchr. Rosenwald Mid. Sch., Panama City, 1988; music/art tchr. St. Andrew Sch. Ctr. for Exceptional Students, Panama City, 1989—; music tchr., physically handicapped Margaret K. Lewis, Panama City, 1993—98. Founder, coord. Very Spl. Art Festival, Bay County, 1990—; charter mem. Fla. League Arts Tchrs., Tallahassee, 1999—; bd. mem. Svc. Learning Coun., Bay County, 2002—; artist in residency Fla. Dept. Very Spl. Arts, Tampa, 2004—; historian St. Andrew Waterfront Project, 1989—2007; oral history project coord. St. Andrew Sch., 2005—; state chmn. Advocacy Svc. Learning Edn., 2008—; presenter in field; judge Fla. Svc. Learning, 2009; bd. mem. USA Arts Fla., 2009—. Recipient Tchr. of Yr. award, St. Andrew Sch., Panama City, 1995, 2006—07, Bay Dist. Sch., 2007—08, Golden Spike award, Bay Arts Alliance, Panama City, 2001; grantee scholarship, Bay Edn. Found., 2004, 2005, John David Jones ABCD scholarship, 2005; Arts grant reviewer, US Dept. Edn., 2008—. Mem.: Garnet and Gold Honor Soc., Pi Lambda Theta. Avocations: singing, writing plays, travel. Office: St Andrew Sch 3001 W 15th St Panama City FL 32401

ROCKLAND, LAWRENCE HOWARD, psychiatrist, educator; b. NYC, Apr. 13, 1932; s. Milton and Bess Sherry Rockland; m. Charlotte Francis Roberts, June 29, 1957; children: Nancy, Thomas, Peter. BS, Union Coll., 1952; MD, Albany Med. Ctr., 1956. Diplomate Am. Bd. Psychiatry and Neurology. Rsch. psychiatrist NIMH, Bethesda, Md., 1959—61; pvt. practice Scarsdale, Larchmont, NY, 1961—; instr. psychiatry Georgetown Med. Coll., Washington, 1961—63; asst. prof. psychiatry Albert Einstein Coll. Medicine, NYC, 1967—76; assoc. prof. clin. psychiatry Cornell U. Med. Coll., NYC, 1982—99; assoc. prof. psychiatry emeritus Weill/Cornell Med. Coll., NYC, 1999—; assoc. prof. clin. psychiatry U. Mass. Med. Coll., Worcester, 1999—2002. Cons. Montgomery County Child Clinic, Rockville, Md., 1962—66, US Peace Corps, Washington, 1963—66, Carson Adult Family Clinic, Westfield, Mass., 1999—2002. Contbr. articles to profl. jours., chapters to books; author: Supportive Therapy, 1989, Supportive Therapy for Borderlines, 1992, La Terapia di Sostegno, 1994. Surgeon USPHS, 1959—2005. Fellow: Am. Psychoanalytic Assn. (exec. coun. 1976—79, 1985—2005), Am. Psychiat. Assn. (disting. life fellow); mem.: Group for Advancement Psychiatry, Sigma Xi, Phi Beta Kappa, Alpha Omega Alpha. Avocations: music, hiking, physical exercise, reading. Home and Office: 7 East Drive Larchmont NY 10538 Office Phone: 914-834-7601.

ROCKLEN, KATHY HELLENBRAND, lawyer; b. NYC, June 30, 1951; BA, Barnard Coll., NYC, 1973; JD magna cum laude, New England Sch. Law, 1977. Bar: NY 1978, US Dist. Ct. (so. and ea. dists.) NY 1982, US Dist. Ct. (no. dist.) Calif. 1985. Interpretive counsel NY Stock Exchange, NYC; 1st v.p. E.F. Hutton & Co. Inc., NYC; v.p., gen. counsel, sec. S.G Warburg (USA) Inc., NYC; mem. Proskauer Rose LLP, NYC. Adj. prof. Fordham Sch. Law. Vice-chair, mem. exec. com. NY lawyers Pub. Interest; mem. exec. com. lawyers divsn. Am. Friends Hebrew U.; mem. lawyers' divsn. exec. com. ADL Mem. NY State Bar Assn., Assn. Bar City NY (v.p., chmn. exec. com., chmn. drugs law com., chmn. fed. legis. com., chmn. libr. com., securities law com., sec. 2d century com., sex law com., young lawyers' com., corp. law com.). Office: Proskauer Rose LLP 1585 Broadway New York NY 10036 Office Phone: 212-969-3755. E-mail: krocklen@proskauer.com.

ROCKOFF, MARK ALAN, pediatric anesthesiologist; b. Jersey City, Apr. 13, 1948; s. Aaron and Rose Rockoff; m. Elizabeth Sceery, Aug. 6, 1978; children: Benjamin, Jillian, Michael. BS, MIT, 1969; MD, Johns Hopkins U., 1973. Diplomate Am. Bd. Pediatrics, Am. Bd. Anesthesiology. Pediatric intern and resident Mass. Gen. Hosp., Boston, 1973-75, anesthesia resident, 1975-77, assoc. dir. pediatric ICU, 1979-81; neuroanesthesia fellow U. Calif., San Diego, 1978-79; assoc. dir. ICU Children's Hosp., Boston, 1981-89, assoc. anesthesiologist-in-chief, 1988—; med. dir. operating rm., 1992-99; prof. anaesthesia Harvard Med. Sch., Boston, 1999—. Editor jours. Survey of Anesthesiology, 1984-94, Jour. Neurosurg. Anesthesiology, 1994-98. Fellow: Soc. Critical Care Medicine, Am. Acad. Pediats., Am. Soc. Anesthesiologists; mem.: Soc. Pediat. Anesthesia (pres. 1996—98), Am. Bd. Anesthesiology (dir. 2000—). Office: Children's Hosp 300 Longwood Ave Boston MA 02115-5737

ROCKOFF, S. DAVID, radiologist, physician, educator; b. Utica, NY, July 21, 1931; s. Samuel and Sarah (Rattinger) R.; m. Jacqueline Garsh; children— Lisa E., Todd E., Kevin D. AB, Syracuse U., 1951; MD, Albany Med. Coll., 1955; M.Sc. in Medicine, U. Pa., 1961. Diplomate: Am. Bd. Radiology. Intern U.S. Naval Hosp., Bethesda, Md., 1955-56; resident and fellow in radiology, USPHS trainee dept. radiology p. of U. Pa., Phila., 1958-61; staff radiologist NIH, Bethesda, Md., 1961-65; asst. prof. radiology Yale U. Sch. Medicine, New Haven, 1965-68, assoc. prof., 1968; asst. attending radiologist Yale-New Haven Med. Center, 1965-68; assoc. prof. radiology Washington U. Sch. Medicine, St. Louis, 1968-71; asst. radiologist Barnes and Allied Hosps., St. Louis, 1969-71; cons. radiologist VA Hosp., St. Louis, 1969-71, Homer G. Phillips Hosp., St. Louis, 1968-71; prof. radiology George Washington U. Sch. Medicine, Washington, 1971—, chmn. dept. radiology, 1971-77, head pulmonary radiology, 1978—, interim chmn. dept. radiology, 1989-90, prof. emeritus radiology, 1993—. Cons. NIH, 1972—; vis. prof. Hadassah U., Beersheba U., Rambam Hosp., Israel, 1977; cons. in radiology VA Hosp., Washington, 1972-77, U.S. Naval Med. Center, Bethesda, 1973-77; mem. diagnostic radiology adv. com. NIH, 1973-76; mem. Cancer Research Manpower Rev. Com., NIH, 1978 Editor-in-chief: Investigative Radiology, 1965-76; editor-in-chief emeritus, 1976—; editor Jour. Thoracic Imaging, 1985; reviewer Jour. Computed Tomography, 1997—; contbr. articles to profl. jours. Served with USN, 1955-58; Served with USPHS, 1961-63. Recipient numerous USPHS grants. Fellow Am. Coll. Radiology (pres.-elect DC chpt. 1976), Am. Coll. Chest Physicians; mem. Am. Fedn. Clin. Rsch., DC Med. Soc. (med.-legal com. 1975-78), AMA, Radiol. Soc. N.Am. (roster of disting. sci. advisors Rsch. and Edn. Found. 1999), Assn. Univ. Radiologists, Soc. Thoracic Radiology (pres. 1983-84, exec. dir. 1984-87, Gold medal 2007). Home: PO Box 675650 Rancho Santa Fe CA 92067-5650 E-mail: drockoff@cox.net.

ROCKS, PATTI TEMPLE, marketing executive; m. Bob Rocks; 3 children. Grad., Albion Coll., 1981. Exec. v.p. GolinHarris, Cleve., Chgo., 1999—2006; v.p. global comm. and reputation Dow Chemical Co., Midland, Mich., 2006—. Named one of Best Marketers, BtoB Mag., 2006—08. Office: Dow Chemical Co Dow Ctr Midland MI 48674 Office Phone: 800-232-2436, 989-832-1426.*

ROCKWELL, DAVID, architectural firm executive; b. Chgo., July 21, 1956; m. Marcia Kirkley; children: Sam, Lola. Attended Syracuse U. Founder, CEO Rockwell Architecture, Planning & Design, P.C., NY, 1984—. Author: Pleasure: The Architecture Design of Rockwell Group, 2002; co-author (with Bruce Mao): Spectacle. Chmn. bd. Design Industries Found. Fighting AIDS (DIFFA); bd. dir. The Public Theater, City Meals on Wheels. Recipient Lifetime Achievement award, Interiors Mag., Presidential Design award for Grand Central Terminal Renovation; named one of Magnificent Seven Gurus of Innovation, BusinessWeek, 2005; named to Hall of Fame, Interior Design Mag. Projects include the new theatre for the Academy of Motion Picture Arts and Sciences in LA, renovation of Radio City Music Hall, interiors on the Disney Cruise ships, the Mohegan Sun Casino, the Cirque du Soleil theatre in Orlando, and the Loew's Theatre at E-Walk in Manhattan. Office: Rockwell Architecture Planning & Design PC 5 Union Sq W New York NY 10003 Office Phone: 212-463-0334. Office Fax: 212-463-0335.*

ROCKWELL, DON ARTHUR, retired psychiatrist; b. Wheatland, Wyo, Apr. 24, 1938; s. Orson Arthur and Kathleen Emily Rockwell; m. Frances Pepitone-Arreola, Dec. 23, 1965; children: Grant, Chad. BA, Wash. U., 1959; MD, U. Okla., 1963; MA in Sociology, U. Calif., Berkeley, 1967. Diplomate Am. Bd. Psychiatry and Neurology. Intern in surgery San Francisco Gen. Hosp., 1963-64; resident in psychiatry Langley-Porter Neuropsychiatric Inst. U. Calif. Med. Ctr., San Francisco, 1964-67; instr. dept. psychiatry U. Calif. Sch. Medicine, Davis, 1969-70, asst. prof., 1970-74, assoc. prof., 1974-80, acting. assoc., dean curricular affiars, 1979-80, acting assoc. dean student affairs, 1980, assoc. dean student affairs, 1980-82, prof., 1980-84; career tchr. NIMH, 1970-72; assoc. psychiatrist Sacramento Med. Ctr.; med. dir. U. Calif. Med. Ctr., Davis, 1982-84; prof., vice chmn. dept. psychiatry and biobehavioral sci. UCLA, 1984-96; dir. UCLA Neuropsychiat. Hosp., 1984-95; chief profl. staff Neuropsychiat. Inst., UCLA, 1984-85, also dir. outpatient svc. Chmn. U. Calif. Hosp. Dir. Council, 1988-89; cons. Nat. Commn. on Marijuana, Washington, 1971-73; mem. Santa Barbara County Civil Grand Jury, 2001-02. Co-author: Psychiatric Disorders, 1982; contbr. chpts. to books; articles to profl. jour. Mem. bd. visitors U. Okla. Sch. Medicine; chmn. hosp. dirs. coun. U. Calif. Hosp.; mem. governing coun. AHA Psychiat. Hosp.; mem. County of Santa Barbara Civil Grand Jury, 2001—02; bd. dir. Bereavement Outreach, Sacramento, 1974—84, Suicide Prevention, Yolo County, 1969—84. Fellow APA (disting. life), Am. Coll. Psychiatrists, Am. Coll. Mental Health Adminstr.; mem. AMA (gov. coun. psych. hosp.), Am. Sociologic Assn., Calif. Med. Assn. (med. staff survey com.), Cen. Calif. Psychiat. Assn. (sec.-pres. 1977-78), U. Okla. Alumni Assn. (trustee 1981-86), Alpha Omega Alpha. Home: 2293 Ginger Hill Loop Lincoln CA 95648

ROCKWELL, JOHN SARGENT, critic, writer, former arts administrator; b. Washington, Sept. 16, 1940; s. Alvin John and Anna Sargent (Hayward) Rockwell; m. LInda Mevorach; 1 child, Sasha Eve. BA, Harvard U., 1962; postgrad., U. Munich, 1962-63; MA, U. Calif., Berkeley, 1964, PhD, 1972. Music and dance critic Oakland Tribune, Calif., 1969; asst. music and dance critic LA Times, 1970-72; freelance music critic NY Times, 1972-74, staff music critic, 1974-91, European cultural corr. and prin. classical recordings critic Paris, 1992-94, editor Arts & Leisure sect., 1998—2002, sr. cultural corr., 2002—05, chief dance critic, 2005—06; dir., Lincoln Ctr. Festival Lincoln Ctr. Festival, NYC, 1994—98; arts review program Sta. WNYC-FM. Lectr. in field. Author: All American Music: Composition in the Late 20th Century, 1983, Sinatra: An American Classic, 1984, The Idiots, 2003, Outsider: John Rockwell on the Arts 1967-2006, 2006. Named Chevalier, French Ordre des Arts et Lettres; Harvard-German Govt. fellow, 1962—63, Woodrow Wilson fellow, 1963—64. Mem.: Dance Critics Assn., Century Assn., Music Critics Assn., Phi Beta Kappa. Office Phone: 212-941-1875. Office Fax: 212-334-5073.

ROCKWELL, THEODORE, nuclear engineer; b. Chgo., June 26, 1922; s. Theodore G. and Paisley (Shane) R.; m. Mary Juanita Compton, Jan. 25, 1947 (dec.); children: Robert C. (dec.), W. Teed, Lawrence E., Juanita C. BS in Engring, Princeton U., 1943, Chem.E. (MS), 1945; grad. courses, Oak Ridge, 1944-49; D.Sc. (hon.), Tri-State U., 1960. Registered profl. engr., D.C. 1964-1990. Process improvement engr. Manhattan Project, Oak Ridge, 1944-45; head shield engring. group Oak Ridge Nat. Lab., 1945-49; nuclear engr., naval reactors br. AEC, also nuclear propulsion divs. Navy Bur. Ships, 1949-55, tech. dir., 1955-64; founding officer, dir. MPR Assos., Inc., Washington, 1964—; rsch. assoc. Johns Hopkins U. Sch. Advanced Internat. Studies, 1965—66. Chmn. Atomic Indsl. Forum Reactor Safety Task Force, 1966-72; mem. adv. group artificial heart program NIH, 1966; cons. to Joint Congl. Com. on Atomic Energy, 1967; founding officer, dir. Radiation, Sci. and Health, Inc., 1996—; Disting. lectr. World Nuc. U., 2006-07. Author: The Rickover Effect: How One Man Made a Difference, 1992, Creating the New World, 2003 (First Place award non-fiction JADA Pub. Ann. Book Competition, 2005, Ind. Publishers award, 2005), The Virtual Librarian: A Tale of Alternative Realities, 2007 (finalist Best Books award USA Book News, 2008, Nat. India Excellence award, 2009); co-author: Shippingport Pressurized Water Reactor, 1958, Arms Control Agreements/Designs Verification, 1968; co-founder Princeton Engr.; editor: Reactor Shield Design Manual, 1956; contbg. editor: New Realities, 1988—92; contbr. sci. articles to profl. publs., non-tech. articles to nat. mags. Mem. adv. council dept. chem. engring. Princeton U., 1966-72. Recipient Disting. Civilian Svc. medal USN, 1960, Disting. Svc. medal AEC, 1960, Lifetime Contbn. award Am. Nuclear Soc. (1st, now known as Rockwell award), 1986, Edward Teller award Drs. for Disaster Preparedness, 2006. Fellow Am. Nuclear Soc., Am. Soc. Psychical Rsch. (life); mem. AAAS (rep. of Parapsychol. Assn. to AAAS 1975-87), N.Y. Acad. Scis., Soc. for Sci. Exploration, U.S. Psychotronic Assn. (dir. 1988-91), Nat. Inst. for Discovery Sci. (sci. adv. bd. 1995—), Nat. Acad. Engring. (Sigma Xi disting. lectr. 2003—), Authors Guild, Writers Ctr., Washington Ind. Writers, Philos. Soc. Washington (life), Cosmos Club (Washington), Nat. Press Club. Presbyterian (elder). Achievements include patent applications for neutron-absorbing cermets and plastics; patents in field. Address: 3403 Woolsey Dr Chevy Chase MD 20815-3924 Home Phone: 301-652-9509. Personal E-mail: tedrock@starpower.net.

ROCKWOOD, IRVING E., JR., publisher; b. Norwood, Mass., Dec. 13, 1944; s. Irving E. and Cassie A. (Richardson) R.; m. Nancy E. Wilcox, June 14, 1969; children: Catherine Anne, Margaret Elaine. BA in Polit. Sci., No. Ill. U., 1967, MA in Polit. Sci., 1969. Sales rep. Coll. Divsn. Houghton Mifflin Co., Geneva, Ill., 1970-72, maths. editor Coll. Divsn. Boston, 1972-74; editor, math. and econs. Coll. Divsn. D.C. Heath, Lexington, Mass., 1974-76; gen. editor U. Wis. Press, Madison, 1976-79; exec. editor Longman, Inc., NYC, 1979-85; pres. Irving Rockwood & Assocs., Inc., Chappaqua, NY, 1985-89; pub. Dushkin Pub. Group, Guilford, Conn., 1989-95; editor and pub. Choice, Middletown, Conn., 1995—. Mem. rsch. libr. delegation Citizen Amb. Program People to People, S. Africa, 1997; mem. N.Am. chpt. Assn. Learned and Profl. Soc. Pubs. Mem. ALA, Assn. Coll. and Rsch. Librs. Mem. Ch. of Christ. Avocations: reading, hiking, do-it-yourself projects, choral singing. Office: Choice 100 Riverview Ctr Ste 298 Middletown CT 06457-3401 Home Phone: 203-445-0688; Office Phone: 860-347-6933. Business E-Mail: irockwood@ala-choice.org.

ROCQUE, VINCENT JOSEPH, lawyer; b. Franklin, NH, Nov. 27, 1945; s. Francis Albert and Mary Helen R.; m. Emily Adams Arnold, May 31, 1969; children: Amanda Adams, Peter O'Connor, Caroline Quin. BA magna cum laude, Georgetown U., 1967; JD, Columbia U., NYC, 1970. Bar: D.C. 1971, U.S. Supreme Ct., 1973. Assoc. Hogan & Hartson, Washington, 1970-73; counsel, spl. asst. to Commr. Barbara Franklin, U. S. Consumer Product Safety Commn., Washington, 1973-77; asst. dir. bur. trade regulation U.S. Dept. Commerce, Washington, 1977-80; ptnr. Sullivan & Worcester, Washington, 1980-90; pvt. practice law Washington, 1990—. V.p., co-pres. Janney Pub. Elem. Sch. PTA, Washington, 1982-84; vol. coord. homeless shelters Cath. Charities, Washington and Silver Spring, Md., 1984-90. Staff sgt. USAR, 1969-75. Mem. ABA (adminstrv. law and regulatory practice sect. and internat. law and practice sect.), D.C. Bar (internat. law sect. and adminstrv. law and agy. sect.), Mid-Atlantic Literary Edification Soc., Phi Beta Kappa. Catholic. Avocations: reading, travel, American Civil War history. Office: Ste 1000 1155 Connecticut Ave NW Washington DC 20036-4306

RODALE, ARDATH HARTER, publishing executive; 5 children. B in Art Edn., Kutztown U., LLD (hon.), 1995; LHD (hon.), DeSales U., 1994, Lehigh U., 1994; HHD (hon.), New Coll. of Calif., San Francisco, 2006. Chmn. Prevention Mag., Rodale Press, Inc., 1990—2007; owner, CEO Rodale Press Inc., Emmaus, Pa., 1990—2002, chief inspiration officer, 2007—. Chmn. emeritus on the bd. Rodale Inst. Author: Climbing Toward the Light, 1989, Gifts of the Spirit, 1997, Reflections: Finding, Love, Hope and Joy in Everyday Life, 2002. Mem. internat. adv. com. Harvard AIDS Inst. Recipient Outstanding Alumni award, Kutztown U., 1990, Human Rels. award, Allentown Human Rels. Commn., 1995, Extraordinary Voices award, Mothers' Voices, 1996, Woman of Distinction award, Great Valley Girl Scout Coun., 1998, Friend of Lehigh award, Lehigh U., 2002, Lifetime Cmty. Achievement award, Boys & Girls Club of Allentown, 2002, Shining Star award, St. Luke's Hosp., Allentown, 2003, Life & Breath award, Am. Lung Assn., 2003, Exceptional Woman award, Women in Periodical Pub., 2004, LifePath's Cmty. Svc. award, Pa. Inst. of CPA's, 2004, Cir. of Excellence - Enlightened Media award, Internat. Furnishings & Design Assn., 2005, Lehigh Valley Coalition for Alt. Transp. award, 2006; named a Disting. Daughter of Pa., Gov. Tom Ridge, 1997; named one of 50 Best Women in Bus. in Pa., Ctrl. Pa. Bus. Jour., 1996, Top 50 Women Bus. Owners in the US, Working Woman mag., 1997, 50 Leading Women Entrepreneurs in the World, Star Group, 1999. Office: Rodale Press Inc 33 E Minor St Emmaus PA 18098-0099

RODALE, MARIA, publishing executive; b. 1962; d. Ardath and Robert Rodale; 1 child, Maya. BA in Art & Comm., Muhlenberg Coll., 1985. With Rodale Inc., Emmaus, Pa., 1987—96, 1998—, dir. strategy, 1998, dir. Organic Living divsn., vice chmn., 2001—07, chmn., 2007—09, chmn., CEO, 2009—. Bd. dirs. Rodale Inc., 1991—. Editor: Organic Gardening, 1999—2001, Organic Style, 2001—05; author: Maria Rodale's Organic Gardening, 1998, Maria Rodale's Organic Gardening Companion, 1999, Betty's Book of Laundry Secrets, 2001; co-author: It's My Pleasure, 2005. Bd. mem. NY Restoration Project, Lehigh Valley Health Network. Recipient Rachel Carson award, Nat. Audubon Soc., 2004, Spl. Citizen award, Arts for Healing & Children's Health Environ. Coalition, 2005, Award for the Health & Dignity of Women, UN Population Fund, 2007; co-recipient Exceptional Women in Pub. award, Women in Periodical Pub., 2004. Office: Rodale Inc 33 E Minor St Emmaus PA 18098-0099 Office Phone: 610-967-5171. Office Fax: 610-967-8963.*

RODAMAKER, MARTI TOMSON, bank executive; m. Bill Rodamaker; children: Mackenzie, Meeghan. BA in Econs., U. No. Iowa; MBA in Fin., U. St. Thomas. Credit analyst Marquette Bank, Mpls., 1984—87; field examiner Norwest Bank, 1987—93; from mem. staff to pres. First Citizens Nat. Bank, Mason City, Iowa, 1993—2000, pres., CEO, 2000—. Mem. adv. coun. Fed. Res. Iowa. Chmn. Hosp. Found.; treas. campaign YMCA; bd. regents Luther Coll., 2003—. Named one of 25 Women to Watch, US Banker mag., 2003, 2007. Mem.: Iowa Ind. Bankers Assn. (pres. 2001), Mason City C. of C. (bd. dir.). Office: First Citizens National Bank 2601 Fourth St SW Mason City IA 50401-1708

RODAY, LEON E., lawyer, finance company executive; BA, U. Calif., Santa Barbara; JD, Brooklyn Law Sch. Assoc. LeBoeuf, Lamb, Greene & MacRae, LLP, 1982—91, ptnr., 1991—96; sr. v.p., gen. counsel, sec. GE Financial, 1996—2004, Genworth Financial, Inc., Richmond, Va., 2004—. Chmn. Ins. Marketplace Standards Assn., 2005. Mem.: NY Bar Assn. Office: Genworth Financial, Inc 6620 W Broad St Richmond VA 23230 Office Fax: 804-281-6000.

RODBELL, CLYDE ARMAND, retired distribution executive; b. Atlanta, Aug. 16, 1927; s. Joseph Hirsch and Fannie (Turetzky) R.; m. Cecile Rosenson, Mar. 27, 1949 (div.); children: Marsha, Jeffrey, Keith, Kim; m. Robin Graham McKenzie Rodbell, Dec. 15, 1974; 1 child, Lindsey. BBA, Emory U., 1949. Chmn. Apex Supply Co. Inc., Atlanta, 1949—2002. Co-chmn. George Bush Presdl. Fund Raising, Ga., 1988-89; mem. State of Ga. Electoral Coll., 1989, exec. commr. Am. Bicentenial Pres. Inaugural Bus. Adv., 1989, Pres' Commn. on White House Fellowships, 1989-92. With U.S. Army, 1945. Mem. Wholesale Assn. Ga., Southern Wholesalers Assn., Am. Supply Assn., Standard Club, Rotary Club. Republican. Jewish. Avocations: reading, gardening, antiques, politics. Personal E-mail: rrodbell@aol.com.

RODDICK, ANDY STEPHEN, professional tennis player; b. Omaha, Aug. 30, 1982; s. Jerry and Blanche Roddick; m. Brooklyn Decker, Apr. 17, 2009. Profl. tennis player ATP, 2000—; winner jr. Grand Slam titles Australian Open and US Open, 2000; quarter-finalist Roland Garros, 2000; singles titles, Atlanta, Houston, Washington US Clay Court Championships, 2001, singles titles, Memphis, Houston, 2002; runner up US Open, 2002, winner Grand Slam title, 2003; quarterfinalist Indian Wells TMS, 2003; semifinalist Paris TMS, Basel, Tennis Masters Cup, Wimbledon, Australian Open, Washington, 2003; finalist Houston, Memphis, 2003; winner Raiffeisen Internat. Grand Prix, 2003, Stella Artois Championships, 2003, RCA Championships, 2003, Montreal Masters, 2003, Cin. Masters, 2003, 2006, Artois Championship, London, 2007, Legg Mason Tennis Classic, 2007, Davis Cup, 2007, SAP Open, San Jose, Calif., 2008, Dubai Tennis Championships, 2008, Regions Morgan Keegan Championships, 2009, ATP World Tour Masters 1000 Indian Wells, 2009. Mem. US Olympic Tennis Team, Athens, 2004. Host: Saturday Night Live, 2003. Founder The Andy Roddick Found. Recipient Espy Award for Best Male Tennis Player, 2004, Arthur Ashe Humanitarian award, ATP, 2004; named to President's Coun. of Sports and Fitness, Pres. George W. Bush, 2006. Achievements include finishing the year as the youngest player at 18 years, 3 months in the top 200 and as the No. 1 junior in the world, 2000. Avocations: movies, music, skydiving. Office: Andy Roddick Found 5458 Town Center Rd #13 Boca Raton FL 33486*

RODDICK, DAVID BRUCE, construction company executive; b. Oakland, Calif., Oct. 31, 1948; s. Bruce Ergo and Hortensia Cabo (Castedo) R.; m. Sharon Ann Belan, May 25, 1975; children: Heather Marie, Christina DeeAnn. BSCE, U. Calif., Davis, 1971. Engr. Bechtel Corp., San Francisco, 1971-77, contract specialist, 1977-78; subcontract adminstr. Boecon Corp., Richland, Wash., 1978-79; constrn. mgr. BE&C Engrs., Inc., Vancouver, Wash., 1979-81; contracts mgr. Boecon Corp., Tukwila, Wash., 1981-83; sr. constrn. mgr. BE&C Engrs., Inc., Wichita, Kans., 1983-84; project mgr., v.p. ops. Carl Holvick Co., Sunnyvale, Calif., 1984-88, also corp. sec. bd. dirs.; v.p., gen. mgr. Brookman Co. div. B.T. Mancini Co., Inc., Milpitas, Calif., 1988-92; v.p., sec., CFO B.T. Mancini Co., Inc., 1992-98, sr. v.p. ops., CFO, corp. sec., 1998-2000, exec. v.p., CFO, corp. sec., 2000—. Mem. devel. com. San Jose (Calif.) Mus. Assn., 1993—95; pres. Reed Sch. PTA, San Jose,

1985—88, San Jose Coun. PTAs, 1988—89; trustee, deacon Heart of Valley Bapt. Ch., 2003—04; treas. Ch. of the Chimes, 2005—08, deacon, 2006—08; bd. dirs. Vinehill Homeowners Assn., 1975—77. Lt. col. C.E. USAR, 1969—99. Decorated Army Achievement medal, 1988, Commendation medal, 1991, 96, 98, meritorious svc. medal, 1998, 99; recipient Calif. State PTA Hon. Svc. award, 1988, Bronze de Fluery medal Army Engr. Assn., 1998. Mem. Am. Soc. Civil Engrs., Constrn. Fin. Mgmt. Assn. (mem., dir. 1995—, pres. Silicon Valley chpt. 1999-2000, 01-02, 04-05, 07-08, dir.-at-large 2005-07), Nat. Strategic Planning Com., 2007-09, Res. Officers Assn. (life), Am. Arbitration Assn. (mem. panel arbitrators), Am. Subcontractors Assn., Engr. Regimental Assn. (life), Calif. Aggie Alumni Assn., Ill. State Geneal. Soc., Floor Covering Installation Contractors Assn., Santa Maria Valley Geneal. Archtl. Engring. Inst. (founding mem.), Soc., Army Engr. Assn. (de Fleury medal 1998), U. Calif.-Davis Century Club, Sigma Nu. Republican. Office: B T Mancini Co Inc 876 S Milpitas Blvd Milpitas CA 95035-6311

RODDY, CAROL LYNN, library director; b. Detroit, May 31, 1947; d. James A. and Bernadette F. (Bruley) Murray; m. Gregory Ambrose Roddy, July 26, 1969; children: Jennifer Catherine Spector, Rachel Maria, Joel F. BA in Hist., Ohio State U., 1972; MLS, Kent State U., Ohio, 1981. Pub. svcs. libr. Westerville Pub. Libr., Ohio, 1981—84; info. specialist Linc Resources, Columbus, Ohio, 1984—87; documentation specialist Online Computer Libr. Ctr., Columbus, 1987-88, software support mgr., 1988-90; support svcs. mgr. Ameritech Info. Svc., Columbus, 1990-93; mgr. bus. customer svcs. CompuServe, Inc., Columbus, 1993-96, bus. line mgr., 1996-97; exec. dir. Ohio Pub. Libr. Info. Network, Columbus, 1997—2005; project mgr. Ohio State U. Prior Health Scis. Libr. & Ctr. Knowledge Mgmt., Columbus, 2007—09, asst. dir. tech., 2008—09; exec. dir. Ctrl. Libr. Consortium, Lithopolis, Ohio, 2009—. Pres. bd. dirs. Compas Post-Adoption Program, Columbus, 1994—95. Mem.: ALA, Ohio Libr. Coun. Office: Ctrl Libr Consortium 122 E Columbus St Canal Winchester OH 43110 Office Phone: 614-837-8533. E-mail: croddy@oplin.lib.oh.us.*

RODDY, CHRISTOPHER, academic administrator, educator; b. Glens Falls, NY, Mar. 31, 1958; s. Clarence and Dorothy Roddy; children: Christina, Jonathan. MS in Physics, NC State U., Raleigh, 1987. Dir. demonstrations instr. NC State U., 1982—90; sci. enrichment ctr., sch. outreach coord. Purdue U., West Lafayette, Ind., 1990—92; dept. chair sci. and landscape gardening Sandhills CC, Pinehurst, NC, 1992—2003; assoc. dean phys. sci. and wellness Broward Coll., Davie, Fla., 2003—. Dir. Regional, Internat. Sci. and Engring. Fair, West Lafayette, 1990—92; physics tchr. Am. Assn. Physics Tchrs., Coll. Pk., Md., 1992; chair Am. Inst. Physics, Com. Sci. Writing Children, Coll. Pk., Md., 1997—99. Author: (textbook ancillary) Instructors Manual for Ohanian's Principles of Physics. Recipient Outstanding Ext. Svc. award, NC State U., 1988—89, Black Belt - Tae Kwon Do, Imperial Martial Arts, 2007. Mem.: Am. Assn. Physics Tchrs. Office: Broward Coll 3501 SW Davie Rd Davie FL 33314 Office Fax: 954-201-6847. Personal E-mail: roddy.chris@gmail.com. Business E-Mail: croddy@broward.edu.

RODDY, HARRY LOUIS, JR., language educator; b. Groves, Tex. PhD, U. Tex., Austin, 2004. Lectr. German Rice U., Houston, 2001—05; asst. prof. German U. South Ala., Mobile, 2005—. Mem.: AATG. Office: Univ South Ala Humb 322 Mobile AL 36688

RODDY, KATHLEEN, literature and language professor; d. Francis John and Ann Marie Roddy; m. Martin Lee Roll, Dec. 27, 1986; children: Katie Lee Roll, Connor Martin Roll. BA, Fla. State U., Tallahassee, 1978, Ph.D, 1991; MA, Austin Peay State U., Clarksville, TN, 1984. Tchg. asst. Austin Peay State U., 1982—84, Fla. State U., 1986—91; assoc. prof. English Ga. Perimeter Coll., Dunwoody, 1996—. Co-advisor drama club Ga. Perimeter Coll., Dunwoody, 1991—96, fiction editor Chatahoochee Rev., 1994—97. Author: (play) That the Night Come, The Walled Garden. Recipient Outstanding New Faculty award, Ga. Perimeter Coll., 1997, Chancellor's award, Ga. Bd. Regents, 1998. Mem.: NCTE, MLA, South Atlantic MLA. Office: GA Perimeter Coll 2101 Womack Rd Dunwoody GA 30338 Business E-Mail: kroddy@gpc.edu.

RODE, DANIEL L., engineering educator; s. Louis L. and Veronica Rode; m. Giovana Matias Matias, Jan. 9, 1970. PhD, Case Western Res., Cleve., 1968. Tech. group supr. Bell Tel. Lab., Murray Hill, NJ, 1968—79; prof. elec. engring. Wash. U., St. Louis. Tech. cons. Pendragon Corp., St. Louis. Recipient Disting. Svc. award, GaAs Mantech, 2003.

RODE, MEREDITH EAGON, artist, educator; b. Delaware, Ohio, Mar. 27, 1938; d. Gilbert Frend and Ruth Odah (Hopwood) Eagon; m. Alex Rode Redmountain, Aug. 31, 1958 (div. 1984); m. Arthur Michael Diness, Oct. 6, 1988 (dec. Sept. 2002); children: Cecily Diness, Jordan Rode, Marnie Rode, Ethan Diness. BA, George Washington U., 1958; MFA, U. Md., 1974; PhD, Union Inst., Cin., 1994. Head art program Colo. Acad., Denver, 1959-62; asst. instr. Corcoran Sch. Art, Washington, 1962-68; art instr. Walden Sch., Washington, 1963-68; assoc. prof. art Fed. City Coll., Washington, 1968-77; prof. art U. DC, 1977—, chair, mass media, visual and performing arts; adj. prof. art U. Md., College Park, 1996—. V.p. Women's Caucus Art, 1974-75. Exhibitions include US Dept. State Art in Embassies, 1977—; contbr. (logo) 20th Ann. March on Washington, 1983, (illustration) Earth Day Publ., 1990. Vice-chair U. DC/Advocates Plus, 1996—. Recipient Sussman award Union Inst., 1994, Excellence in Acad. award NEA, 2000; named Disting. Educator, U. DC, 2009; rsch. grantee U. DC, 1983, 85. Mem. Founds. in Art Theory and Edn., Art Conf. African Art Studies Assn., Coll. Art Assn., Southeastern Coll. Art Assn. Avocations: reading, walking, travel. Home: 5114 Battery Ln Bethesda MD 20814-2406 Office: Univ DC 4200 Connecticut Ave NW Washington DC 20008-1175 Home Phone: 301-654-1378; Office Phone: 202-274-5548. E-mail: mrode@udc.edu.

RODECKER, STEPHEN BAILEY, science specialist, secondary school educator; b. San Bernardino, Calif., July 10, 1953; s. Charles and Merilyn Rodecker; m. Jelen Gonzales, July 24, 1993. BA in German, San Diego State U., 1975, BA in Biology, 1977, MA in German, 1977, MS in Biology, 1987. Cert. tchr. Calif., 1978. Tchr. San San Diego (Calif.) Office Edn., 1983—84; instr. Upward Bound San Diego (Calif.) State U., 1990; tchr. Sweetwater Union H.S. dist., Chula Vista, Calif., 1985—, specialist sci. curriculum, 1999—. Prin., owner Spectrum Pubs., Bonita, Calif., 1990—; bd. dirs. Greater San Diego (Calif.) Sci. and Engring. Fair; cons. in field. Author: Laboratory Experiments and Activity in Physical Science, 1995, Biological Experiments and Activities Integrating Math, 1999. Named Tchr. of Yr., Tandy Tech., 1995, Nat. Sci. Tchr. of Yr., Disney, 1995; grantee, Tapestry, 1995, Gen. Telephone and Electronics, 1996, Dept. of Def., 1996, Calif. Tchr. Appreciation and Advancement Program, 1996, 2000. Master: San Diego (Calif.) Sci. Educators Assn. (pres. 2005—); mem.: Calif. Sci. Tchrs. Assn. (bd. dirs. 1990—91). Avocations: tennis, gardening, collecting porcelain.

RODEN, CAROL LOONEY, retired language educator; b. Boston, Jan. 10, 1939; d. William Vincent and Margaret Carey Delaney; m. Vincent James Looney, Feb. 11, 1961 (div. Nov. 1995); children: Vincent J. III Looney, Kara A. Putnam, Douglas B. Looney, John W. Looney; m. Thomas Edward Roden, July 7, 1997. BA, Emmanuel Coll., 1960; postgrad., SUNY, Albany, 1974. Spanish tchr. Hingham (Mass.) H.S., 1960—61, Kennedy H.S., Utica, NY, 1974—80, Waterville (N.Y.) Cen. Sch., 1983—94, Archbishop Carroll H.S., Wayne, Pa., 1995—96; ret., 1996. Author (numerous poems); photographer. Pres. PTA, Whitesboro, NY, 1971; v.p. Newcomers Group, Utica, NY, 1970; vol. Puerto Rican Cmty. House, Boston, 1959. Fellow, U. Kans., 1960; scholar Gov. Furcolo scholar, State of Mass., 1956. Mem.: AAUW (v.p. membership 1995—99, Gift honoree 1999, Outstanding Woman of Yr. 2000), Alpha Mu Gamma. Democrat. Roman Catholic. Home: 119 Sawgrass Dr Blue Bell PA 19422

RODENBERG, JOHANNA KRISTINE, education educator, consultant; d. Edward Ellis and Francess Irene Rodenberg; m. Andrew Thomas Myers, Sept. 3, 1994; children: Justin Grant, Jeffrey Richard Myers, Jakob Edward Myers. AA in Fine Art, Mesa C.C., 1980; BA in Linguistics, San Diego State U., 1982; MA in Ednl. Psychology, U.S. Internat. U., San Diego, 1987; postgrad., U. San Diego/San Diego State U., 2000—. Cert. Nat. Bd. Profl. Tchg. Stds. English lang. tchr. EF Internat. Sch., San Diego, 1983—90; reading specialist San Diego Unified Sch. Dist., 1996—99, peer coach/staff developer, 1999—2002, peer assistance and support consulting tchr., 2002—. Ednl. cons. Nat. Ctr. on Edn. and the Economy, Washington, 1998—2002; ind. ednl. cons., faculty devel., 2003—; faculty San Diego State U., 2000—; spkr., presenter in field. Rm. mom Holmes Elem. Sch., San Diego, 2003. Mem.: ASCD, Internat. TESOL, Nat. Coun. Tchrs. of English, Internat. Reading Assn. Avocations: cooking, reading, gardening. Office: San Diego Unified Schs/SDSU San Diego CA Personal E-mail: jkr1007@earthlink.net.

RODENBERGER, CHARLES ALVARD, aerospace engineer, consultant; b. Muskogee, Okla., Sept. 11, 1926; s. Darcy Owen and Kathryn Martha (Percival) R.; m. Molcie Lou Halsell, Sept. 3, 1949; children: Kathryn Sue Wilcox, Charles Mark. Student, U. Ark., 1944—45; BS in Gen. Engring., Okla. State U., 1948; MSM.E., So. Meth. U., 1959; PhD in Aero. Engring., U. Tex.-Austin, 1968. Registered profl. engr., Tex. Petroleum engr. Amoco Oil Co., Levelland, Tex., 1948-51; chief engr. McGregor Bros., Odessa, Tex., 1953; petroleum engr. Gen. Crude Oil Co., Hamlin, Tex., 1954; sr. design engr. Gen. Dynamics, Ft. Worth, 1954-60; aerospace engr. NASA, Houston, summer 1962; prof. aerospace engring. Tex. A&M U., College Station, 1960-82, prof. emeritus, 1982—; chmn. bd. Meiller Research, Inc., College Station, 1967-82; pres. JETS, Inc., NYC, 1977-79; cons. Southwest Research Inst., Gen. Motors Corp., Gen. Dynamics. Patentee hypervelocity gun and orthotic device; newspaper columnist: Livestock Weekly, 1986—; mag. columnist, Santa Gertrudis, Tex., 2002. Bd. dirs. Cross Plains Pub. Libr., 1986—, pres., treas.; meth. Sunday sch. tchr., 1984—. Served with USAAF, 1945, served with USAF, 1951—53. NSF fellow, 1964-65; recipient Disting. Teaching award Tex. A&M U., 1962 Fellow AIAA (assoc.); mem. ASME, NSPE (v.p. 1980-81), Tex. Soc. Profl. Engrs., Am. Soc. for Engring. Edn., Croatian Rsch. Soc., Sigma Xi, Kiwanis Club (pres. Cross Plains chpt. 2002-03). Methodist. Home: 8377 FM 2228 Baird TX 79504-4813 Office Phone: 254-725-6816. Personal E-mail: crodenberg@aol.com. Business E-Mail: car926@aol.com.

RODES, ROBERT EMMET, JR., law educator; b. NYC, May 29, 1927; s. Robert Emmet and Marjorie (Reid) R.; m. Jeanne Emily Cronin, Aug. 29., 1953; children: Anne, Robert, John, David, Peter, Paul, Mary. Student, Middlebury Coll., Vt., 1944-45; AB, Brown U., 1947; LLB, Harvard U., 1952. Bar: Mass. 1953, Ind. 1957, U.S. Dist. Ct. (no. dist.) Ind. 1983. Atty. Liberty Mut. Ins. Co., Boston, 1952-54; asst. prof. Sch. Law Rutgers U., Newark, 1954-56, Notre Dame (Ind.) U., 1956-58, assoc. prof., 1958-63, prof., 1963—. Atty. Kaufman & Harris, Pitts., 1977, Legal Svc. Program No. Ind., South Bend, 1982. Author: The Legal Enterprise, 1976, Ecclesiastical Administration in Medieval England, 1977, Lay Authority and Reformation in the English Church, 1982, Law and Liberation, 1986, Law and Modernization in the Church of England, 1991, (with Howard Pospesel) Premises and Conclusions, 1997, Pilgrim Law, 1998, Classic Problems of Jurisprudence, 2005, On Law and Chastity, 2006. Ensign USN, 1947-49. Roman Catholic. Home: 846 Park Ave South Bend IN 46616-1338 Office: U Notre Dame Sch Law Notre Dame IN 46556 Home Phone: 574-233-3623; Office Phone: 574-631-6573.

RODEWALD, HEIDI, musician, composer; b. Pomona, Calif. Band mem. Wednesday Week, The Negro Problem, 1997—; co-prodr., arranger Stew, 1999—. Musician: (albums) (with The Negro Problem) Joys and Concerns, 1999, Welcome Black, 2002, (Stew albums) Guest Host, 2000 (Album of Yr., Entertainment Weekly), The Naked Dutch Painter and Other Songs, 2002 (Album of Yr., Entertainment Weekly), Something Deeper Than These Changes, 2003; composer, musical dir. (plays) Passing Strange, 2004, (Broadway plays), 2008 (NY Drama Critics' Cir. Best Musical, 2008, Drama Desk awards for Oustanding Musical and Outstanding Music, 2008, Obie award for Best New Theater Piece, 2008). Office: c/o William Craver Paradigm 360 Park Ave S 16th Fl New York NY 10010

RODGERS, BRADLEY MORELAND, pediatric, thoracic surgeon; b. Montclair, NJ, Jan. 16, 1942; BA, Dartmouth Coll., Hanover, NH, 1963, BS, 1964; MD, Johns Hopkins U., Balt., 1966. Diplomate Am. Bd. Surgery, Am. Bd. Pediat. Surgery, Am. Bd. Thoracic Surgery. Intern Duke U., Durham, NC, 1966-67, resident cardiovasc. surgery, 1967-68, resident thoracic surgery, 1970-73; fellowship Nat. Inst. Health, 1968-70; chief resident pediat. surgery Montreal Children's Hosp., 1973-74; asst. prof. pediat. & surgery U. Fla., Gainesville, 1974-81; prof. surgery & pediat., chief div. pediatric surgery U. Va., Charlottesville, 1981—. Contbr. articles to profl. jours. Mem.: So. Thoracic Surg. Assn. (chmn. 1993, Osler Abbott award 1989), Am. Acad. Pediat., Am. Pediat. Surgical Assn. (pres. 2002). Mailing: U Va Dept Pediat Surgery PO Box 800709 Charlottesville VA 22908 Office Fax: 434-924-2656. Business E-Mail: bmr@virginia.edu.

RODGERS, BRUCE ALAN, government agency administrator, psychologist; s. Bernice Junior and Louise Andreason Rodgers; m. Angela Lei Lani Wiseman; children: Diana Louise, Sarah Brooke, Daniel Alan, Hartley Elizabeth, Alexus Lei Lani Maldonado. BS, Tex. State U., 1989; PhD, U. Denver, 2000. Undersheriff Park County Sheriff's Office, Fairplay, Colo., 1996—98; dir. Ea. Colo. Plains Drug Task Force, Yuma, 1998—2000; immigration adjudication officer US Dept. Homeland Security, Dallas, 2000—. Author: The Psychological Aspects of Police Work: An Officer's Guide to Street Psychology. Mem.: APA, Soc. Police and Criminal Psychology, Soc. for Theoretical and Philos. Psychology, Sovereign Mil Order of Temple of Jerusalem. Personal E-mail: rodgersbruce@sbcglobal.net.

RODGERS, DANIEL TRACY, historian, educator; b. Darby, Pa., Sept. 29, 1942; s. Oliver Eliot and Dorothy (Welch) R.; m. Irene Wylie, 1971; children: Peter Samuel, Dwight Oliver. AB, BS in Engring., Brown U., 1965; PhD in History, Yale U., 1973. Instr. history U. Wis., Madison, 1971-73, asst. prof., 1973-78, assoc. prof., 1978-80; assoc. prof. history Princeton U., NJ, 1980-86, prof., 1986-98, chair, 1988—95, 1997—98, Henry Charles Lea prof. history, 1998—. Fulbright lectr., Frankfurt, Fed. Republic Germany, 1983-84; Pitt prof., Cambridge Univ., 2003-04. Author: The Work Ethic in Industrial America, 1860-1920 (Frederick Jackson Turner award 1978), 1978, Contested Truths: Keywords in American Politics since Independence, 1987, Atlantic Crossings: Social Politics in a Progressive Age, 1998 (Ellis W. Hawley award 1979, George Louis Beer prize 1979). Recipient Chancellor's award U. Wis., Madison, 1978, Behrman award for disting. achievement in humanities, Princeton U., 2008; Am. Coun. Learned Socs. fellow, 1976, NEH fellow, 1987-88, Ctr. for Advanced Study in Behavioral Scis. fellow, 1991-92; Woodrow Wilson Ctr. fellow, 1999-2000; Guggenheim fellowship, 2007-08. Fellow: Am. Acad. Arts and Sciences. Office: Princeton U Dept History Princeton NJ 08544-0001 E-mail: drodgers@princeton.edu.

RODGERS, FRANK, librarian; b. Darlington, Eng., July 28, 1927; came to U.S., 1956; s. Charles Bede and Frances (Page) R.; m. Sarah Louise Edelson, Dec. 18, 1971; children: Hilda Marie, Norah Frances. BA with honors, King's Coll., U. Durham, 1947; diploma librarianship, London U., 1952. Libr. Poplar Tech. Coll., London, 1951-53, St. Martin's Sch. Art, 1953-56; sr. libr. adult svcs. divsn. Akron (Ohio) Pub. Libr., 1956-59; asst. reference libr. U. Ill., 1959-64; chief reference libr., then asst. dir. pub. svcs. Pa. State U. Librs., 1965-69; dir. Portland (Oreg.) State U. Libr., 1969-79; dir. librs. U. Miami, Fla., 1979-97. Mem. Oreg. adv. coun. librs., 1973-74; bd. dirs. Pacific N.W. Bibliog. Ctr., 1973-77; tech. adv. com. librs. Columbia Regional Assn. Govts., 1976-79; vis. fellow U. Southampton Eng., 1975-76; pres. Oreg. Libr. Assn., 1974-75; mem. nominating com. Southeastern Libr. Network, 1984-85; bd. dirs. S.E. Fla. Libr. Info. Network, 1984-97, pres. 1991-92; mem. exec. coun. Assn. Caribbean U. Rsch. and Instl. Librs., 1985-88; chmn. local organizing com. for 1981 and 1987 confs. in Miami; mem. Fla. Libr. Network Coun., 1985-91; NEH challenge grant rev. panel, 1987, Howard U. ann. inspection team, 1989, Reaffirmation com., Tex. Christian U., 1993. Author, editor various libr. publs., guides. Patron Jerome K. Jerome Soc., 1986—. Sr. fellow Grad. Sch. Libr. and Info. Sci. UCLA, 1983; grantee Coun. Libr. Resources, 1975-76. Fellow Libr. Assn. U.K.; mem. ALA, Assn. Rsch. Librs. (office mgmt. studies adv. com. 1981-83, stats. and measurements com. 1993-96), Assn. Specialized and Coop. Libr. Agys. (membership promotion com. 1994-96, chair 1990 program com.), Assn. Southeastern Rsch. Librs. (chmn. membership com. 1982-97). Address: 7a Avenida Norte #25 Antigua Guatemala E-mail: frodgers@conexion.com.gt.

RODGERS, FREDERIC BARKER, judge; b. Albany, NY, Sept. 29, 1940; s. Prentice Johnson and Jane (Weed) R.; m. Valerie McNaughton, Oct. 8, 1988; 1 child: Gabriel Moore. AB in Polit. Sci., Amherst Coll., Mass., 1963; JD, Union U., Albany, 1966. Bar: NY 1966, US Ct. Mil. Appeals 1968, Colo. 1972, US Supreme Ct. 1974, US Ct. Appeals (10th cir.) 1981, US Ct. Appeals (fed. cir.) 2001. Chief dep. dist. atty., Denver, 1972-73; magistrate Denver Juvenile Ct., 1973—79; mem. Mulligan Reeves Teasley & Joyce, P.C., Denver, 1979-80; pres. Frederic B. Rodgers, P.C., Breckenridge, Colo., 1980-89; ptnr. McNaughton & Rodgers, Central City, Colo., 1989-91; county ct. judge Gilpin County Combined Cts., Colo., 1987—; probate judge Jefferson County Dist. Ct., 2005—07. Presiding mcpl. judge cities of Breckenridge, Blue River, Black Hawk, Central City, Edgewater, Empire, Idaho Springs, Silver Plume and Westminster, Colo., 1978-96; chmn. com. on mcpl. ct. rules of procedure Colo. Supreme Ct., 1984-96; mem. Colo. Supreme Ct. Task Force Probate Protective Procs., 2006—; mem. Colo. Supreme Ct. jud. Conf. Planning Com., 2007—; mem. gen faculty Nat. Jud. Coll. U. Nev., Reno, 1990—, mem. faculty coun., 1993-99, chair 1999, trustee, 2004—, sec., 2007-, chair of bd. elect for 2009-10, 2008. Author (with Dilweg, Fretz, Murphy and Wicker): Modern Judicial Ethics, 1992; contbr. articles to profl. jours., chapters to books; author: The Improvement of The Administration of Justice 7th edit., 2001. Mem. Colo. Commn. on Children, 1982-85, Colo. Youth Devel. Coun., 1989-98, Colo. Family Peace Task Force, 1994-96. Served with JAGC, US Army, 1967-72; to maj. USAR, 1972-88. Decorated Bronze Star with oak leaf cluster, 1969, 1970, Air medal, 1969, Army Commendation medal with silver oak leaf cluster, 1969-1972; recipient USAR Achievement Medal, 1986, Am. Spirit Honor medal, 1966, Outstanding County Judge award Colo. 17th Judicial Dist. Victim Adv. Coalition, 1991; Spl. Cmty. Svc. award Colo. Am. Legion, 1979, Lifetime Achievement award Denver Law Club, 2003; USAID grant, 2002-2003, Anthony Greco award Colo. Cts. Judges Exemplary Achievement 3rd Leadership, 2008, Franklin N. Flaschne award Nat. Conf. Ct Judges, 2009. Fellow Am. Bar Found. (life, Colo. state chair 2005—, Outstanding State Chair award 2009), Colo. Bar. Found. (life); mem. ABA (jud. div. exec. coun. 1989-2000, vice-chair 1996-97, chair-elect 1997, chair 1998-99, mem. House of Dels. 1993-2004, jud. divsn. del. to ABA nominating com. 2000-01, bd. govs. Dist. 11 2001-04, chair traffic ct. program com. 2005-06), Colo. Bar Assn. (bd. govs. 1986-88, 90-92, 93-99, 2002-05, 2007-, sr. v.p. 2004-05), Continental Divide Bar Assn., Denver Bar Assn. (trustee 1979-82), First Jud. Dist. Bar Assn. (trustee 2000-02), Nat. Conf. Spl. Ct. Judges (chmn. 1989-90), Colo. County Judges Assn. (pres. 1995-96, Anthony Greco award 2008), Colo. Mcpl. Judges Assn. (pres. 1986-87), Colo. Trial Judges Coun. (v.p. 1994-95, sec. 1996-97, 2006-07), Denver Law Club (pres. 1981-82), Colo. Women's Bar Assn., Am. Judicature Soc. (bd. dirs. 2003—), Nat. Coun. Juvenile and Family Ct. Judges, Nat. Coll. Probate Judges, Federalist Soc. for Law and Pub. Policy Studies, Judge Advs. Assn., Univ. Club (Denver), Arlberg Club (Winter Park), Marines Meml. Club (San Francisco), Rotary (charter pres. Peak to Peak 2000-01, Paul Harris fellow 1996). Episcopalian. Avocations: bicycling, skiing, hiking, music, writing. Office: First Judicial Dist Courts Gilpin County Justice Ctr 2960 Dory Hill Rd Black Hawk CO 80422 Office Phone: 303-582-5323 ext. 16. Personal E-mail: fbr@q.com. Business E-Mail: frederic.rodgers@judicial.state.co.us.

RODGERS, GEORGE MARION, hematologist; s. George Marion and Martha Virginia Rodgers. BS in Biochemistry, LSU; MD, Tulane U., New Orleans, 1976, PhD in Pharmacology, 1974. Diplomate Am. Bd. Internal Medicine, 1979, hematologist Am. Bd. Internal Medicine, 1982. Prof. Univ. Utah Med Ctr., Salt Lake City, 1997—; internal med. residency baylor Coll. Medicine, Houston, 1976—79; hematology fellowship UCSF, 1979—82. Office: Univ Utah Div Hematology 30 N 1900 East Salt Lake City UT 84132

RODGERS, GRIFFIN PLATT, federal agency administrator, researcher; b. New Orleans, Nov. 4, 1954; BS, Brown U., Providence, 1976, MD, 1979; MBA, Johns Hopkins U., Balt., 2005. Cert. Internal Medicine, Emergency Medicine, Hematology. Intern Barnes Hosp., Wash. U. Sch. Medicine, St. Louis, resident internal medicine; fellowship hematology/oncology George Washington U. and Washington Vets. Adminstrn. Med. Ctr.; dep. dir. Nat. Inst. Diabetes and Digestive and Kidney Diseases (NIDDK), NIH, Bethesda, Md., 2001—07, acting dir., 2006—07, dir., 2007—. Gov. Am. Coll. Physicians, 1994—97; chair

Hematology Subspecialty Bd.; bd. dirs. Am. Bd. Internal Medicine. Contbr. articles to profl. jours., chapters to books. Recipient Richard & Hinda Rosenthal Found. award, 1998, Arthur S. Fleming award, 2000, Legacy of Leadership Award, 2002. Mem.: Assn. Am. Physicians, Am. Soc. Clin. Investigation, Am. Soc. Hematology. Office: NIDDK Bldg 31 Rm 9A06 31 Ctr Dr MSC 2560 Bethesda MD 20892-2560 Office Phone: 301-496-3583.*

RODGERS, JAN A., social work educator; b. Pa. m. Mark E. Rodgers; 1 child, Luke. MSW, U. Pa., Phila., 1980; MLIS, Dominican U., River Forest, Ill., 2008. Cert. LCSW Pa., NJ. Specialist prof. Monmouth U., West Long Branch, NJ, 2000—04; vis. asst. prof. Dominican U., 2005—09, lectr., 2009—. Editor-in-chief Jour. Global Social Work Practice. Office: Dominican Univ GSSW 7200 West Divsn St River Forest IL 60305 Business E-Mail: jrodgers@dom.edu.

RODGERS, JOHN HUNTER, lawyer; b. Lubbock, Tex., Jan. 18, 1944; s. James O'Donnell Rodgers and Dorothy (Ulin) Carpenter; m. Anne C. Smith, Nov. 29, 1969; children: Anne Elizabeth, Catherine Hunter. BA, Tex. A&M, 1966; JD, U. Tex., 1969. Bar: Tex. 1969, U.S. Supreme Ct. 1973. Atty. The Southland Corp., Dallas, 1973-79, gen. counsel, 1979-91, sec., 1987-95, sr. v.p., chief adminstrv. officer, 1991-93, exec. v.p., chief adminstrv. officer, 1993-95; pres. Clairemead Corp., Dallas, 1996-2000; sr. v.p., gen. counsel, sec. Am. Pad & Paper Co., Dallas, 1998-2000, pres., 2000—04; prin. J. Hunter & Assocs., Dallas, 2003—. Mem. visual arts com. Tex. A&M U., 1985-94, bd. dirs. student fund enrichment bd., 1986-94; mem. exec. com. Jr. Achievement Dallas, 1988-93; mem. Dallas Citizens Coun., 1992-95; bd. dirs. Boys and Girls Clubs of Greater Dallas, 1998—, vice chmn., 2003-04, chmn., 2005—07; nat. chair Tulane U. Parents Coun., 1997-98; trustee Goals for Dallas, 1991-92; bd. trustees The Sci. Pl. Mus., 2004-06, Dallas Mus. Nature and Sci., 2006-; nat. bd. dirs. Boys and Girls Clubs Am., 1993-98; mem. mktg. com. Dallas Mus. Art, 1994-97. Capt. JAGC, US Army, 1969-73, Vietnam. Mem. ABA, Tex. Bar Assn. (coun. mem. corp. counsel sect. 1988), Dallas Bar Assn., Southwestern Legal Found. (adv. bd. Internat. and Comparative Law Ctr., rsch. fellow 1986-94), Nat. Assn. Convenience Stores (bd. dirs. 1993-95). Roman Catholic. Office: 4655 Insurance Ln Ste 100 Dallas TX 75205 Office Phone: 214-219-7771. E-mail: Jhunterlp@sbcglobal.net.

RODGERS, JOHNATHAN, broadcast executive; b. San Antonio, Jan. 18, 1946; s. Marion Alford and Barbara (Merriwether) Rodgers; m. Royal Graves Kennedy, Sept. 27, 1976; children: David, Jamie. BA, U. Calif., Berkeley, 1967; MA, Stanford U., 1972; PhD (hon.), Columbia Coll., Chgo., 1991. Writer-reporter Sports Illustrated, NYC, 1966—68; assoc. editor Newsweek, NYC, 1968—72; prodr. WNBC-TV, NYC, 1972—73; reporter WKYC-TV (NBC), Cleve., 1973—74; sta. mgr., news dir. KCBS-TV, LA, 1978—83; exec. prodr. CBS News, NYC, 1983—86; v.p., gen. mgr. WBBM-TV (CBS), Chgo., 1986—90; former pres. CBS TV Stas., Chgo.; pres. Discovery Networks, US, Bethesda, Md., 1996—2003; pres., CEO TV One, LLC, Silver Spring, Md., 2003—. Bd. dirs. Procter & Gamble. Trustee U. Calif., Berkeley, 2000—. With US Army, 1969—71, Korea. Named to Power 150, Ebony mag., 2008. Mem.: NIKE, Inc. (bd. dirs.), Nat. Assn. Black Journalists. Home: 3120 Newark St NW Washington DC 20008-3343 Office: TV One, LLC 1010 Wayne Ave Silver Spring MD 20910

RODGERS, LANA LORETTA LUSCH, retired elementary school educator; b. Lehighton, Pa., Jan. 26, 1943; d. Charles Norman and Loretta Margaret (Gaumer) Lusch; m. Harold Eugene Rodgers, Aug. 15, 1964; children: Jacqui Rodgers Kirchner, Travis Dustin. BS in Elem. Edn., Kutztown U., Pa., 1964, BS in Blind and Partially Sighted Edn., 1967, M in Elem. Edn., 1968. Cert. reading specialist Kutztown U., 1983. Tchr. Honey Brook Elem. Sch., Twin Valley Sch. Dist., Elverson, Pa., 1964—67, 1986—2000, Berkshire Bldg., Wilson Sch. Dist., Reading, Pa., 1967—68; substitute tchr. Robeson Elem. Sch., Twin Valley Sch. Dist., 1981—83, reading tchr., 1985; ret., 1985. English tchr. Reading Area CC. Sec. Twin Valley Sch. Dist. Tchr.'s Orgn., Elverson, 1966; leader Girl Scouts USA, Wyomissing, Pa., 1966—68; vol. Ct. Apptd. Spl. Advocates, Reading Ct., 2000—; mem. Lit. Coun., 1977—79; min. West Lawn United Meth. Ch. Recipient CASA Cert. Recognition, Cert. Recognition, West Lawn United Meth. Ch., 1998, Tutor award, Reading Area CC, 2004. Mem.: AAUW, Colonial Hills Gym. Republican. Avocations: piano, painting, surfing, motorcycling, ice skating. Home: 106 Halsey Ave Reading PA 19609-2110

RODGERS, LAWRENCE RODNEY, internist, educator; b. Clovis, N.Mex., Mar. 9, 1920; s. Samuel Frank and Lillian (O'Connor) R.; m. Ivy Lorna Piper, Aug. 6, 1943; children: Lawrence Rodney (dec.), Ivy Elizabeth, George Piper. BS, West Tex. State U., 1940; MD, U. Tex., 1943. Diplomate Am. Bd. Internal Medicine. Intern Phila. Gen. Hosp., 1943-44, resident in medicine, 1946-49; assoc. internist Tumor Inst., U. Tex. M.D. Anderson Hosp., Houston, 1949—; chmn. dept. medicine Hermann Hosp., Houston, 1966-71; assoc. prof. clin. medicine Baylor U., 1949—; prof. clin. medicine U. Tex., 1972—. Editor: Harris County Physician, 1976-80. Bd. dirs. Tex. Med. Found.; trustee Houston Mus. Med. Sci., 1981. Maj. M.C. AUS, 1944-46. Decorated Bronze Star with two oak leaf clusters; recipient Ashbel Smith Disting. Alumnus award U. Tex. Med. Br.-Galveston, 1993, Mastership award Am. Coll. Physicians, 1996. Fellow ACP (gov. for Tex. 1979-83, Laureate Internist Tex. award 1994); mem. AMA (del. 1975-94), Tex. Med. Assn. (elected emeritus), Harris County Med. Soc. (exec. bd. 1978-82, v.p. 1984), Am. Heart Assn., Houston Soc. Internal Medicine (pres. 1974), Houston Acad. Medicine (pres. 1981), Houston Philos. Soc. (pres. 1993-94), Doctor's Club Houston (bd. govs. 1984-88, pres. 1986). Personal E-mail: rod3920@aol.com.

RODGERS, MARY COLUMBRO, literature educator, writer, academic administrator; b. Aurora, Ohio, Apr. 17, 1925; d. Nicola and Nancy (DeNicola) Columbro; m. Daniel Richard Rodgers, July 24, 1965; children: Robert, Patricia, Kristine. AB, Notre Dame Coll., 1957; MA, Western Res. U., 1962; PhD, Ohio State U., 1964; postgrad., U. Rome, 1964-65; EdD, Calif. Nat. Open U., 1975, DLitt, 1978. Tchr. English Cleve. elem. schs., 1945-52, Cleve. secondary schs., 1952-62; supr. English student tchrs. Ohio State U., 1962-64; asst. prof. English U. Md., 1965-66; assoc. prof. Trinity Coll., 1967-68; prof. English D.C. Tchrs. Coll. U. D.C., 1968—2000; pres. Md. Nat. U., 1972—2006; founder, chancellor Open U. Am., 1965—; dean Am. Open U. Acad.; ret., 2000; ind. rschr., writer, 2000—. Author: A Short Course in English Composition, 1976, Chapbook of Children's Literature, 1977, Comprehensive Catalogue: The Open University of America System, 1978-80, Open University of America System Source Book, V, VII, VII, 1978, Essays and Poems on Life and Literature, 1979, Modes and Models: Four Lessons for Young Writers, 1981, Open University Structures and Adult Learning, 1982, Papers in Applied English Linguistics, 1982, Twelve Lectures on the American Open University, 1982, English Pedagogy in the American Open University, 1983, Design for Personalized English Graduate Degrees in the Urban University, 1984, Open University English Teaching, 1945-85: Conceptual History and Rationale, 1985, Claims and Counterclaims Regarding Instruction Given in Personalized Degree Residency Programs Completed by Graduates of California National Open University, 1986, The American Open University, 1965 to 1985: History and Sourcebook, 1986, New Design II: English Pedagogy in the American Open University, 1987, The American Open University, 1965 to 1985: A Research Report, 1987, The American Open University and Other Open Universities: A Comparative Study Report, 1988, Poet and Pedagogue in Moscow and Leningrad: A Travel Report, 1989, Foundations of English Scholarship in the American Open University, 1989, Twelve Lectures in Literary Analysis, 1990, Ten Lectures in Literary Production, 1990, Analyzing Fact and Fiction, 1991, Analyzing Poetry and Drama, 1991, Some Successful Literary Research Papers: An Inventory of Titles and Theses, 1991, Catalogue for the Mary Columbro Rodgers Literary Trust, 1992, A Chapbook of Poetry and Drama Analysis, 1992, Convent Poems, 1943-1961, 1992, Catholic Marriage Poems 1962, 1979, 1993, Catholic Widow with Children Poems 1979-1993, 1994, First Access List to the Mary Columbro Rodgers Trust by Year, 1994, Nicola Columbro: A Brief Biography, 3d edit., 1994, Biographical Sourcebook I: Mary Columbro Rodgers 1969-1995, 1995, Catholic Teacher Poems, 1945-1995, 1995, Fables and Farm Stories for Fiction Analysis, 1995, Second Access List to the Mary Columbro Rodgers Literary Trust by Alphabet, 1995, Third Access List to the Mary Columbro Rodgers Literary Trust by Subject, 1996, Fourth Access List to the Mary Columbro Rodgers Literary Trust for K-PhD Open Learning-Open University Methods with Data Batches Delineated, 2002, Journals: Reflections and Resolves 1992-2002, 03, 04, 16 vols., 2002, Fifth and Final Access List to the Mary Columbro Rodgers Literary Trust with Annotations, 2004, Journals: Reflections and Resolves, 2005, Catholic Open University of America System Poems, 1962-2005, 2005, Joursnals: Reflection and Resolves, 2006, 07, 08, Catholic Faith Poems, 2007, A Family Book for Benjamin: Poems and Vignettes, 2008, Jezu My Beloved: Jezu Ufam Tobie, Autobiography, 1st edit, 2009; contbr. articles to profl. jours. Fulbright scholar U. Rome, 1964-65. Fellow Cath. Scholars; mem. U.S. Distance Learning Assn., Poetry Soc. Am., Nat. Coun. Tchrs. English, Am. Ednl. Rsch. Assn., Am. Acad. Poets, Pi Lambda Theta. Home: 1 Meadowgate Cir Gaithersburg MD 20877-3774 Office Phone: 301-779-0220. Personal E-mail: openuniv@aol.com.

RODGERS, MICHAEL OWEN, civil engineer, educator; s. Paul Owen and Martha Marie Rodgers; m. Susan Virginia Updegrove, Oct. 20, 1984; children: Gwendolyn Virginia, Vivian Marie. BS in Physics, Ga. Inst. Tech., Atlanta, 1976, MS in Physics, 1978, PhD, 1985. Engr. Electromagnetic Scis., Inc., Norcross, Ga., 1976—78; rsch. scientist, sr. rsch. scientist Earth & Atmospheric Scis., Ga. Inst. Tech., Atlanta, 1978—88, dir., air quality lab., 1988—98; adj. prof. & prin. rsch. scientist Civil & Environ. Engring., Ga. Inst. Tech., 1998—; prin. Avatar Environtech, Inc., Marietta, Ga., 1998—; chief engr. Aerospace, Transp. & Advanced Systems Lab., Ga. Tech Rsch. Inst., Atlanta, 2005—08. Mem., bd. dirs. Ga. Conservancy, 1998—2004; mem., mobile source tech. adv. bd. US EPA, Washington, 1998—. Contbr. scientific papers (Monie A. Ferst award, 1986, Pyke Johnson award, 2006). Recipient Achievement award, NASA, 1998; named one of Profl. of the Yr., Am. Lung Assn.,Ga., 1993; Inst. fellow, Ga. Inst. Tech. Mem.: Alpha Epsilon Pi. Achievements include development of photofragmentation laser-induced fluorescence detection method for atmospheric trace gases; research in southeastern regional oxidant network, georgia tech air quality laboratory and NASA pacific exploratory mission. Home: 2230 Piedmont Forest Dr Marietta GA 30062 Office: Civil & Environmental Engineering Georgia Institute Technology Atlanta GA 30332 Business E-Mail: michael.rodgers@ce.gatech.edu.

RODGERS, RICHARD MALCOLM, management accountant; b. Montgomery, Ala., June 23, 1949; s. Charles Malcolm and Betty Jean (Gilbert) R.; m. Linda Joyce Meeks, Dec. 9, 1966 (div. Mar. 1970); 1 child, Angela Christina Rodgers Bolin; m. Sharon Lynn Thomas, May 10, 1992. Student, Emory U., 1967-69; BBA magna cum laude, Ga. State U., 1988. Cert. mgmt. acct.; ordained deacon, Ecumenical Cath. Ch., 1999, oblate Order St. Benedict, Southern Cross Abbey, Acworth, Ga., 2009-. Staff acct. Charter Enterprises, Inc., College Park, Ga., 1971-72; contr. Royal Arts & Crafts, Inc., Atlanta, 1972-73; justice of peace Justice's Ct. Dist. 531, Decatur, Ga., 1973-76; chief cost acct. Gen. Assembly Mission Bd., Presbyn. Ch. U.S., Atlanta, 1974-80; internal audit mgr. Waffle House, Inc., Norcross, Ga., 1980-87; acctg. mgr. W.L. Thompson Cons. Engrs., Inc., Atlanta, 1988-90; contr. Hudson Everett Simonson Mullis & Assocs., Inc., Atlanta, 1990-96. Freelance cons. and writer, 1995—; instr. Gwinnett Coll. Bus., Lilburn, Ga., 1997-99. Poet, contbg. editor Archon mag., 1968-70 (Anthology award 1970); composer, lyricist: (musical play) Many a Glorious Morning, 1971; playwright, composer, lyricist: (musical play) Take the Money and Run!, 1979, 91; contbr. articles Heritage of Chambers County, Ala, Heritage of Fayette County, Ga. Exec. com. mem. DeKalb County Rep. Party, Decatur, 1969-76; v.p. Ga. Assn. Justices of the Peace and Constables, Warner Robbins, Ga., 1973-74; treas., founding dir. Ga. Bus. Com. for Arts, Inc., Atlanta, 1981-86; sec. Ga. State Poetry Soc., Inc., Atlanta, 1986 (Judge for Chapbook award 1991, 96, 98); pres. Emory Garden Condominium Assn., Decatur, Ga., 2006-. Stipe scholar Emory U., 1968. Mem. Inst. Mgmt. Accts., ACLU, Sierra Club, The Dramatists Guild, Acad Am. Poets, Union Concerned Scientists, Amnesty International, Golden Key Nat. Honor Soc. (charter), Beta Gamma Sigma, Phi Kappa Phi. Democrat. Avocations: field archeology, geophysical rsch., genealogy, American history, playing jazz on trumpet. Home and Office: 1111 Clairemont Ave Apt K-2 Decatur GA 30030-1216 Office Phone: 404-636-4854.

RODGERS, ROBERT HOWARD, ancient language educator; b. Alexandria, La., May 24, 1944; s. Lynn Carl Rodgers and Elsie Eleanor Mae Leach; m. Barbara Saylor Rodgers, Aug. 25, 1973; children: Eleanor Farnsworth Hagopian, Cyrus Holland. AB, Harvard U., Cambridge, Mass., 1966, PhD, 1970. Cert. Bd. Cert. Genealogists, 1992. Asst. lectr. U. Coll., London, 1967—68; asst. and assoc. prof. classics U. Calif., Berkeley, 1970—80; prof. classics U. Vt., Burlington, 1979—. Editor: Palladius De agricultura, Frontinus De aquaeductu, Columella Res rustica. Fellow, Am. Coun. Learned Socs., 1977, John Simon Guggenheim Meml. Found., 1987, Dumbarton Oaks, 1996. Mem.: Am. Philol Assn., Vt. Hist. Soc., New Eng. Hist. Geneal. Soc. (Pub. 1992—96). Home: 2284 South St New Haven VT 05472-4047 Office: Univ Vt 481 Main St Burlington VT 05405-0218 Business E-Mail: robert.rodgers@uvm.edu.

RODGERS, RONALD L., federal agency administrator, lawyer; Grad., US Navel Acad., 1977; JD summa cum laude, U. Dayton, 1983; attended, US Marine Corps Command and Staff Coll., 1989—90. Cir. and dep. chief mil. judge Navy-Marine Corps Trial Judiciary, 1995—99; joined Drug Intelligence Unit, Criminal Divsn. US Dept. Justice, Washington, 1999, dir., 2005—08, US pardon atty., 2008—. Officer USMC, 1977—99. Office: US Dept Justice Office Pardon Atty 1425 New York Ave, NW, Ste 11000 Washington DC 20530 Office Phone: 202-616-6070. Office Fax: 202-616-6069.*

RODGERS, SUZANNE HOOKER, physiologist, consultant; b. Rochester, NY, Dec. 26, 1939; d. John Ashmead and Priscilla May (Bodman) Rodgers AB, Vassar Coll., 1961; PhD, U. Rochester Med. Ctr., 1967. Postdoctoral fellow USPHS Middlesex Hosp., London, 1966—68; ergonomist Eastman Kodak Co., Rochester, 1968—82; ind. cons. in ergonomics Rochester, 1982—. Author: Working With Backache, 1985; tech. editor, prin. author Ergonomic Design for People at Work, 1983, 86, co-editor, contr. Kodak's Ergonomic Design for People at Work 2d edit., 2003 Bd. dirs., chmn. com., v.p. Rochester Philharm. Orch. Inc., 1969-75; bd. dirs. Opera Theatre Rochester, 1969-75; bd. dirs., chmn. com., pres. Monroe County Bd. Health, Rochester, 1979-88 Mem. Human Factors and Ergonomics Soc., (pres. We. N.Y. chpt. 1971-72), Am. Coll. Sports Medicine Avocations: photography, gardening, reading, silent films. Home and Office: 169 Huntington Hls Rochester NY 14622-1121 Office Phone: 585-544-3587. Personal E-mail: shrodgers@aol.com.

RODGERS, T(HURMAN) J., semiconductor company executive; AB in physics and chemistry, Dartmouth Coll., 1970; MS in electrical engring., Stanford U., 1973, PhD in electrical engring., 1975. Managed MOS memory design group Am. Microsystems Inc., 1975—80; managed static RAM product group Advanced Micro Devices, 1980—82; founder, pres., CEO Cypress Semiconductor Corp., San Jose, Calif., 1982—. Bd. dirs. Silicon Light Machines, Bloom Energy (formerly Ion Am.), SunPower Corp., Cypress MicroSystems, Provina. Bd. trustees Dartmouth Coll., 2004—. Recipient Encore award entrepreneurial company of the year, Stanford U. Bus. Sch., 1988, Entrepreneur of the Year award, Ernst & Young, 1991; named CEO of the Year, Financial World mag., 1996; named one of 100 People Who Changed Our World, Upside mag., 2001, Top 100 Chief Executives, Chief Executive mag., 2002, 100 Best Corporate Citizens, Business Ethics mag., 2005. Mem.: Semiconductor Industry Assn. Achievements include patents in field. Avocations: cooking, movies, collecting wines, jogging. Office: Cypress Semiconductor Corp 198 Champion Ct San Jose CA 95134

RODGMAN, ALAN, chemist, consultant; b. Aberdare, Wales, Feb. 7, 1924; came to U.S. from Canada, 1954, naturalized, 1961; s. Arch and Margaret (Llewellyn) R.; m. Doris Curley, June 7, 1947; children: Eric, Paul, Mark. BA in Chemistry, U. Toronto, 1949, MA in Organic Chemistry, 1951, PhD in Organic Chemistry, 1953. Rsch. asst. med. rsch. dept. U. Toronto, 1947-51, rsch. assoc., 1951-54; tchr., courses in organic chemistry, phys. chemistry, math. Chem. Inst. Can., 1951-54; sr. rsch. chemist R.J. Reynolds Tobacco Co., Winston-Salem, N.C., 1954-65, head smoke rsch. sect., 1965-75, mgr. analytical rsch., 1975-76, dir. rsch., 1976-80, dir. fundamental rsch. and devel., 1980-87; cons. in field, 1987—. Co-author: (T. A. Perfetti) The Chemical Components of Tobacco and Tobacco Smoke, 2009; mem. editl. bd. Tobacco Sci., 1963-67 (Vol. 31 Tobacco Sci. dedicated in his name 1987), Beitrage zur Tabakforschung Internat., 1978-87. Mem. Tobacco Working Group, Nat. Cancer Inst., 1976-77, Tech. Study Group on Cigarette and Little Cigar Fire Safety, 1984-87, Sci. Commn. Cooperation Ctr. for Sci. Rsch. Relative to Tobacco, 1982-84. With Royal Can. Navy, 1942-45. Recipient Tobacco Sci. Rsch. Conf. Inaugural Lifetime Achievement award, 2005. Mem. Coun. Tobacco Rsch. (industry tech. com. 1956-62), Chem. Inst. Can., Can. Chem. Soc., Am. Chem. Soc. Episcopalian. Home: 2828 Birchwood Dr Winston Salem NC 27103-3410

RODI, THOMAS JOHN, archbishop; b. New Orleans, Mar. 27, 1949; BA, Georgetown U., 1971; JD, Tulane U. Law Sch., 1974; MDiv, Notre Dame Sem., 1978; JCL in Canon Law, Cath. Am. U., Washington, 1986. Ordained priest Archdiocese of New Orleans, 1978; assoc. pastor St. Ann, Metairie, Miss., St. Christopher, Metairie, St. Agnes, Jefferson, Miss.; judge Met. Tribunal; prof. canon law Notre Dame Sem., 1986—95; ordained bishop, 2001; bishop Diocese of Biloxi, Miss., 2001—08; archbishop Archdiocese of Mobile, Ala., 2008—. Dir., Office Religious Edn. Notre Dame Sem., 1988—89, exec. dir., dept. pastoral svcs., 1989—96. Named a Prelate of Honor, 1992. Office: Archdiocese of Mobile PO Box 1966 400 Government St Mobile AL 36633 Office Phone: 334-434-1585. Office Fax: 334-434-1588.

RODIMER, FRANK JOSEPH, bishop emeritus; b. Rockaway, NJ, Oct. 25, 1927; s. Frank Grant and Susan Elizabeth (Hiler) Rodimer. Attended, St. Charles Coll., Catonsville, Md., 1944-45, Immaculate Conception Sem., Darlington, NJ, 1947-50; BA, St. Mary's Coll.-Sem., Balt., 1947; STL, Cath. U. Am., 1951, JCD, 1954. Ordained priest Diocese of Paterson, NJ, 1951; asst. chancellor, 1954-64; chancellor, 1964-77; apptd. papal chaplain, 1963; ordained bishop, 1978; bishop Diocese of Paterson, 1978—2004, bishop emeritus, 2004—. Roman Catholic. Office: 777 Valley Rd Clifton NJ 07013-2205

RODIN, EUGENE, aerospace scientist, researcher, engineering educator; b. Moscow, Feb. 20, 1937; arrived in U.S., 1993; s. Ivan Fedotovich Rodin and Maria Ivanovna Rodina; m. Bella Medvedeva, Jan. 15, 1981; children: Oleg Medvedev, Karmela Medvedeva. MS, Bauman State Tech. U., Moscow, 1960, PhD, 1969. Instr. Bauman State Tech. U., Moscow, 1960—64, asst. prof., 1964—70, assoc. prof., 1970—93; head sci. lab. Suffolk U., Boston, 1995—2005, asst. prof., 2005—. Sci. rschr. Inst. Spl. Mech. Engring., Moscow, 1970—93, Heat Engring. Rsch. inst., Moscow, 1972—93. Author: Heat Exchanges in Cryogenic Engineering, 1988, Heat Calculation of Cryogenic System, 1990; contbr. articles to profl. publs. Recipient Gold medal, Ministry Spl. Engring., Moscow, 1985, Jubilee Gagarin's medal, NASA, Russia, 2001, Jubilee Tereshkova's medal, 2002. Avocations: travel, reading, sailing, skiing.

RODIN, HOWARD ALAN, periodontist; b. Bronx, NY, Oct. 21, 1942; s. David and Edna (Fialkow) R.; m. Gail Sandra Stein, July 8, 1967; children: Dennis, Stephanie. BS, Fairleigh Dickinson U., 1964, MS in Physiology, 1966; DDS, Howard U., 1970; cert. in periodontics, Columbia U., 1973. Intern Sydenham Hosp., NYC, 1970-71; staff dept. virology Mt. Sinai Hosp., 1964-66; postdoctoral fellow Fairleigh Dickinson U., Teaneck, NJ, 1971; pvt. practice Babylon, 1973-82, Smithtown, 1978—; staff dept. spl. surgery St. John's Hosp., 1979-81, 85-91. Cons. NYU Med. Ctr./Goldwater Meml. Hosp., 1995-97; planning com. Greater L.I. Dental Meeting, 1973-97, gen. chmn., 1985; asst. clin. prof. periodontics Columbia U., 1986-88; pres. L.I. Acad. Periodontists, 1986-90; mass disaster forensic identification team TWA Flight 800; mem. forensic identification team World Trade Ctr., 2001. Contbr. articles to profl. jours. Fellow Am. Coll. Dentists (chmn. NY sect. 2002), Am. Soc. Forensic Odontology, Internat. Coll. Dentists, Pierre Fauchand Acad., Acad. Dentistry Internat., NY Acad. Dentistry, Suffolk Acad. Medicine (pres. 1992-93, trustee 1990-95), Am. Acad. Osseointegration, Am. Acad. Forensic Scis.; mem. ADA (del., alt. del. 1989-2001), Internat. Assn. Dental Rsch. (periodontal rsch. com. 1984—2008, implantology rsch. com. 1995—2008, Hatton award competition 1968), Am. Acad. Periodontology, Suffolk County Dental Soc. (bd. dels. 1981—, pres. 1991, Robert Raskin Meml. award 2007), NY State Soc. Periodontists (bd. dirs.), NY Acad. Scis., Suffolk Soc. Forensic Dentistry (exec. com. 1995-2004), Columbia U. Periodontal Alumni Assn. (trustee 1996—2008, Disting. Alumnus award), Nat. Acads. Practice, Sigma Xi, Alpha Omega (pres. 1985-87), Omicron Kappa Upsilon. Office Phone: 631-360-0090.

RODIN, JUDITH SEITZ, foundation administrator, former academic administrator; b. Phila., Sept. 9, 1944; d. Morris and Sally R. (Wilson) Seitz. AB in Psychology, U. Pa., Phila., 1966; PhD in Psychology, Columbia U., NYC, 1970. Asst. prof. psychology NYU, 1970—72, Yale U., New Haven, 1972—75, assoc. prof. psychology, 1975—79, prof. psychology, 1979—83, Philip R. Allen prof. psychology, 1984—94, prof. medicine & psychiatry, 1985—94, dir. Health Psychology Training Prog., 1982—89, chmn. dept. psychology, 1989—91, dean Grad. Sch. Arts & Scis., 1991—92, provost, 1992—94; pres. U. Pa., Phila., 1994—2004, pres. emerita, 2004—, prof. psychology, medicine & psychiatry, 1994—2007, Fox leadership prof., 2000—07; pres. Rockefeller Found., NYC, 2005—. Chmn. John D. & Catherine T. MacArthur Found. Rsch. Network on Determinants & Consequences of Health-Promoting and Health-Damaging Behavior, 1983—93; mem. Ind. Panel Review Safety Procedures, The White House, Washington, 1994—95; chair adv. com. Robert Wood Johnson Found., 1994—; mem. Pres. Clinton's Com. Advisors Sci. & Tech., 1994—95; mem. Coun. Competitiveness, 1997—; bd. dirs. Aetna Inc., 1995—2004, AMR Corp., 1997—, Comcast Corp., 2002—, Citigroup Inc., 2004—. Co-author: Obese Humans and Rats, 1978, Exploding the Weight Myths, 1982, Body Traps, 1992, The University & Urban Renewal: Out of the Ivory Tower and Into the Streets, 2007, others; editor: Appetite Jour., 1979—92; contbr. articles to profl. jours. Mem. Pa. Task Force Higher Edn. Funding, 1994; bd. dirs. Catalyst, NYC, 1994—; trustee Brookings Inst., Washington, 1995—; pres. steering com. America Reads, 1997—2000. Recipient Wilbur Lucius Cross medal, Yale Grad. Sch. Alumni Assn., 1992, Golden Plate award, Am. Acad. Achievement, 1994, Woman of Inspiration award, Am. Anorexia Bulimia Assn., 1995, Glass Ceiling award, ARC, 1995, Sara Lee Frontrunner award, 1999, Disting. Daughters of Pa. award, 2000, Beacon award, Trustees Coun. of Penn Women, 2001; named one of The 100 Most Influential Women in NYC Bus., Crain's NY Bus., 2007; grantee NSF, 1973—82, NIH, 1981—; Woodrow Wilson fellow, 1966—67, Columbia U. Disting. Faculty fellow, 1967—70, Yale U. Jr. Faculty fellow, 1974—75, John Simon Guggenheim Found. fellow, 1986—87. Fellow: APA (bd. sci. affairs 1979-82, Disting. Sci. award 1977, Outstanding Contbn. award 1980, Lifetime Achievement award 2005), AAAS, Acad. Behavioral Medicine Rsch., Soc. Behavioral Medicine; mem.: Am. Philosophical Soc., Conn. Acad. Sci. & Engring., Am. Psychosomatic Soc., Soc. Experimental Social Psychology, NY Acad. Scis., Inst. Medicine, Am. Acad. Arts & Scis., Sigma Xi (pres. Yale chpt. 1986-87), Phi Beta Kappa. Achievements include being the first women to be named president of an Ivy League institution, 1993. Office: Rockefeller Found 420 Fifth Ave New York NY 10018 Office Phone: 212-869-8500. Office Fax: 212-764-3468. Business E-Mail: president@rockfound.org.*

RODIN, MIRIAM B., medical educator; PhD, U. Ill., Urbana; MD, U. Ill., Chgo., 1986. Cert. Am. Bd. Internal Medicine, 1989, in added qualifications geriatrics Am. Bd. Internal Medicine, 2001, Am. Assn. Hospice and Palliative Medicine, 200. Assoc. prof. At. Louis U. Med. Sch., 2007—. Office: St Louis Univ 1402 S Grand Blvd Rm M238 Saint Louis MO 63104

RODITTI, ESTHER C(LAIRE), lawyer, writer; b. LA, Feb. 7, 1933; d. David and Lucy Roditti; m. Oscar H. Schachter, Aug. 8, 1957 (div. Oct. 1992); children: Charles David, Susan Dayana. BA, UCLA, 1954; JD, Harvard U., 1957. Bar: N.Y. 1959. Assoc. Stickles, Hayden and Kennedy, NYC, 1957-62; asst. dir. Legis. Drafting Fund Columbia U., NYC, 1962-65, cons., 1965-67, N.Y.C. Air Pollution Control Dept., 1965-67; instr. and cons. New Sch. for Social Rsch., NYC, 1968-70; cons. Internat. League for Rights of Man, NYC, 1969, Rand Inst., NYC, 1969, U.S. Soviet Environ. Studies Program, UN Assn., NYC, 1969; sr. rsch. assoc. Ctr. for Policy Rsch. Columbia U., 1970-73; sr. program officer Ford Found., NYC, 1972-78; pres. Esther Roditti Schachter, P.C., NYC, 1978-83; ptnr. Schachter & Froling, NYC, 1983-85, Schachter, Courter, Purcell & Kobert, NYC, 1985-92; pres. Esther C. Roditti, P.C., 1992—. Spkr., lectr., panelist profl. assn. confs., forums, workshops, U.S., Can., Tokyo, London. Author: N.Y.C. Air Pollution Control Code Annotated, 1965, Enforcing Air Pollution Controls, 1979, Financial Support of Women's Programs in the 1970's, 1979, Computer Contracts Reference Directory, 1979-83, Hiring and Firing Knowledge Workers, 1995, Tax and Business Handbook for Consultants and Clients, 1998; co-author: Charities and Charitable Foundations, 1974; author, co-author articles in field; legal editor: Computer Economics, 1983-89; editor Computer Law & Tax Report, 1984-86, pub., editor, 1986-2000; author, editor Computer Contracts-Negotiating Drafting Treatise, 1992—. Nat. governing bd. Common Cause, 1979-82, mem. state governing bd., N.Y., 1982-84; mem. com. on urban environ. Citizens Union, N.Y.C., 1969-73; mem. West Side Dem. Club, 1958-63. Recipient Outstanding Svc. award Brandeis U., Nat. Women's Com., 1973; grantee Ford Found., 1970, NSF, 1971. Mem. ABA (lectr. 1987), Assn. Bar City NY (founder, chmn. com. on computer law 1980—), NY State Bar Assn., Computer Law Assn. (lectr. 1985, bulletin editor 1998-, bd. dirs. 2000-), Am. Arbitration Assn. (chair com. for computer disputes 1985-), Phi Beta Kappa. Office Phone: 212-879-3322. Personal E-mail: ecroditti@aol.com.

RODKIN, GARY M., food products executive; BA in Econs., Rutgers U., NJ; MBA, Harvard Bus. Sch. Various mktg. and gen. mgmt. positions up to pres. Yoplait-Colombo yogurt unit Gen. Mills; pres. Tropicana N.Am., 1995—98, pres., CEO, 1998—99, PepsiCola N.Am., 1999—2002; pres. PepsiCo, Beverages and Foods N.Am., 2002—03, CEO, 2002—05, chmn., 2003—05; pres., CEO ConAgra Foods, Inc., Omaha, 2005—. Office: ConAgra Foods Inc 1 ConAgra Dr Omaha NE 68102-5001 Office Phone: 402-595-4000.*

RODLEY, CAROL ANN, United States Ambassador to Cambodia; b. Mass., 1954; married; 3 children. Grad., Smith Coll. Dep. chief of mission Am. Embassy, Phnom Pehn, Cambodia, 1997—2000; dep. exec. sec. US Dept. State, Washington, 2001—03, prin. dep. asst. sec. Bur. Internat. Orgn. Affairs, 2003—06, acting asst. sec. Bur. Intelligence and Rsch., 2005—06; counselor polit. mil. affairs US Embassy, Kabul, Afghanistan; faculty adv. Fgn. Svc. Inst.; US amb. to Cambodia US Dept State, Phnom Pehn, 2008—. Recipient Christian A. Herter award, Am. Fgn. Svc. Assn., 2000, Sr. Performance award, US Dept. State, Human Rights & Democracy award, James Clement Dunn award for Leadership, Dir. Ctrl. Intelligence Exceptional Humint Collector award, Intelligence Community Seal Medalion. Office: US Embassy 4540 Phnom Penh Washington DC 20521*

RODMAN, ALPINE C., arts and crafts company executive, photographer; b. Roswell, N. Mex., June 23, 1952; s. Robert Elsworth and Verna Mae (Means) R.; m. Sue Arlene Lawson, Dec. 13, 1970; 1 child, Connie Lynn; m. Graham L. Jackson. Student, Colo. State U., 1970—71, U. No. Colo. Ptnr. Pinel Silver Shop, Loveland, Colo., 1965-68, salesman, 1968-71; real estate salesman Loveland, 1971-73; mgr. Traveling Traders, Phoenix, 1974-75; co-owner Deer Track Traders, Loveland, 1975-85; pres. Deer Track Traders, Ltd., Loveland, 1985—. Spkr., lectrs. at seminars in field, 2004—. Author: The Vanishing Indian: Fact or Fiction?, 1985. Mem. Civil Air Patrol, 1965-72, 87-92, dep. comdr. for cadets Greeley, Colo., 1988-90; cadet comdr. Ft. Collins, Colo., 1968, 70, Colo. rep. to youth tng. program, 1969, U.S. youth rep. to Japan, 1970. Mem. Western and English Salesmen's Assn. (bd. dirs. 1990), Indian Arts and Crafts Assn. (bd. dirs. 1988-94, exec. com. 1989-92, v.p. 1990, pres. 1991, market chmn. 1992), Compassion Internat.(sponsor), Crazy Horse Grass Roots Club, Crazy Horse Dreamkeepers Soc. Office: Deer Track Traders Ltd PO Box 448 Loveland CO 80539-0448 *Personal philosophy: I believe that most good and bad in the world comes out of respect or lack of respect for one's self, fellow man, environment and creator.*

RODMAN, LEIBA, mathematician; b. Riga, Latvia, June 9, 1949; arrived in U.S., 1985; s. Zalman and Haya Rodman; m. Ella Levitan, Feb. 2, 1983; children: Daniel, Ruth, Benjamin, Naomi. Diploma in maths., Latvian State U., 1971; MA in Statis., Tel Aviv U., 1976, PhD in Maths., 1978. Instr. Tel Aviv U., 1976-78, sr. lectr., 1981-83, assoc. prof., 1983-85; postdoctoral fellow U. Calgary, Can., 1978-80; from assoc. to full prof. Ariz. State U., Tempe, 1985-87; prof. math. Coll. William and Mary, Williamsburg, Va., 1987—. Author: Introduction to Operator Polynomials, 1989, (with others) Matrix Polynomials, 1982, Matrices and Indefinite Scalar Products, 1983, Invariant Subspaces of Matrices with Applications, 1986, Interpolation of Rational Matrix Functions, 1990, Algebraic Riccati Equations, 1995, Indefinite Linear Algebra and Applications, 2005; co-editor: Contributions to Operator Theory and Its Applications, 1988, Current Trends in Operator Theory and its Applications, 2004. Mem. Am. Math. Soc., Internat. Linear-Algebra Soc., Soc. Indsl. and Applied Math. Office: Coll of William & Mary Dept Math PO Box 8795 Williamsburg VA 23187-8795 Office Phone: 757-221-2027. E-mail: lxrodm@math.wm.edu.

RODMAN, SUE A., wholesale company executive, artist, writer; b. Ft. Collins, Colo., Oct. 1, 1951; d. Marvin F. Lawson and Barbara I. (Miller) Lawson Shue; m. Alpine C. Rodman, Dec. 13, 1970; 1 child, Connie L. Rodman; m. Graham L. Jackson. Student, Woodbury Bus./Arts Coll., Calif., 1969, Colo. State U., 1970—73. Silversmith Pinel Silver Shop, Loveland, Colo., 1970-71; asst. mgr. Traveling Traders, Phoenix, 1974-75; co-owner, co-mgr. Native Am. arts and crafts company Deer Track Traders, Loveland, 1975-85; v.p. Deer Track Traders, Ltd., Loveland, 1985—. Author: The Book of Contemporary Indian Arts and Crafts, 1985, short stories; contbr. articles to popular mags. Mem. U.S. Senatorial Club, 1982-87, Rep. Presdl. Task Force, 1984-90; mem. Civil Air Patrol, 1969-73, 87-90, pers. officer, 1988-90. Mem.: Arbor Day Found., Indian Arts and Crafts Assn., Western and English Sales Assn., Compassion Internat. (sponsor), Nat. Wildlife Fedn., Crazy Horse Grass Roots Club. Mem. Am. Baptist Ch. Avocations: museums, piano, recreation research, fashion design.

RODMAN, SUMNER, insurance company executive; b. Malden, Mass., Aug. 5, 1915; s. Nathan Markel and Sara Ruth (Slater) Rodman; m. Helen Rhoda Morris, July 2, 1942; children: Peter Warren, John Slater. AB cum laude, Harvard U., 1935. CLU. Ins. broker, employee benefits specialist Aetna Life Ins. and Annuity Co., Boston, 1935-98; with Rodman Ins. Agy., Inc., Needham, Mass.; life ins. adviser, 1953—. Pres. Boston Life Ins. and Trust Coun., 1958—59. Bd. dirs. Boston Estate Planning Coun., 1960—85, pres., 1958; mem. Anti-Defamation League B'nai Brith, World Affairs Coun. Boston; chmn. class com. Harvard, 1935; bd. dirs. Jewish Family and Children's Svc., Boston, 1953—85; active Am. Jewish Com.; hon. trustee Temple Israel, Boston; bd. dirs. Youth Tennis Found. New Eng., 1963—85, Simons-Gutman Found., 1965—, Alzheimers Assn. Ea. Mass., 1990—97; hon. trustee Combined Jewish Philanthropies of Greater Boston, 1967—. Served to capt. AUS, 1941—46, ETO. Fellow CLU Inst., 1952, 1961. Mem.: New Eng. Tennis Assn. (bd. dirs. 1966—68, Hall of Fame 1992), Am. Soc. CLUs (pres. 1972—73), Boston Life Underwriters Assn. (pres. 1965—66), Am. Coll. (trustee 1971—74), Million Dollar Round Table (life), Club Hall Fame, Newton Squash and Tennis Club, Harvard Varsity Club (Boston), Harvard Club (Boston), Newton Club (Mass.), Wightman Tennis Ctr. Club (Weston, Mass.), Boston Latin Sch. Varsity (Hall of Fame), Masons, Golden Key Soc. Jewish. Office: Rodman Ins Agy Inc 145 Rosemary St Needham MA 02494-3238 Home Phone: 617-527-8745; Office Phone: 781-247-7835. Business E-Mail: srodman@rodmanins.com.

RODNICK, AMIE BOWMAN, lawyer; b. Paris, Nov. 4, 1953; d. David and Elizabeth (Amis) Rodnick; m. Lawrence Mark Smith, June 20, 1975. Student, Sarah Lawrence Coll., 1972; BA (with honors), U. Tex., 1975, JD, 1978. Bar: Tex. 1979, U.S. Dist. Ct. (no. dist.) Tex. 1979, U.S. Dist. Ct. (so. dist.) Tex. 1981, U.S. Dist. Ct. (we. dist.) Tex. 1985, U.S. Ct. Appeals (5th cir.) 1981; cert. in family law Tex. Bd. Legal Specialization. Asst. attorney gen. Attorney Gen. Office, Austin, 1979-84; ptnr. Cox & Rodnick, Austin, 1984—2001; pvt. practice Law Office of Annie Rodnick, 2001—. Pres. Ctrl. Tex. Collaborative Lawyers, 2001—; spkr. in field. Mem. Rollingwood City Coun., Tex., 1984-88; bd. dirs. United Action for Elderly, Inc., pres., 1987-89. Fellow Tex. Bar Found. (life); mem. Austin Bar Assn. (chair family law sect., 2000-01), Travis County Bar Assn., Travis County Women Lawyers (v.p., treas. Scholarship Trust, Inc. 1984—). Democrat. Home: 3017 Hatley Dr Austin TX 78746-4652 Office: Law Office 507 W 7th St Austin TX 78701-2817 Office Phone: 512-477-2226.

RODNING, CHARLES BERNARD, surgeon; b. Pipestone, Minn., Aug. 4, 1943; s. Selmer Bernard and Ida Amanda (Selness) R.; m. Mary Elizabeth Lipke, June 15, 1968; children: Christopher Bernard, Soren Piers, Kai Johannes. BS, Gustavus Adolphus Coll., St. Peter, Minn., 1965; MD, U. Rochester, 1970; PhD, U. Minn., 1979. Diplomate Am. Bd. Med. Examiners, Am. Bd. Surgery. Intern, asst. resident dept. surgery U. Rochester Sch. Medicine and Dentistry, 1970-72; assoc. resident to chief resident, med. fellow dept. surgery U. Minn. Health Scis. Ctr., Mpls., 1972-79; prof. dept cell biology and neurosci. U. South Ala., Mobile, 1981—, prof. dept. surgery, 1981—, vice chmn. dept. surgery, 1981—2006, chmn. dept. surgery, 2006—, dir. gen. surgery, 1996—. Field liaison physician Commn. on Cancer-ACS, Chgo., 1984—; mem. med. adv. bd. Ala. Organ & Tissue Ctr., Birmingham, 1988—; mem. Bd. Health County of Mobile, pres., 2007. Author: Elan Vital, 1988, Wode and Ston, 1988, Sorrowful Wheel, 1989, Ponderings, 1990, The Sea Rises in the West, 1991, Stepping Stones, 1991, Snowbound Below the Firn Line, 1991, Love Knot, 1994, Papering Dreams, 1994, Carry Onward, 1996, Swaying Grass, 1998, Tradition of Excellence: Pictorial History of Surgical Education at the Mobile General Hospital and University of South Alabama College of Medicine and Medical Center, 1999; reviewer: Jour. Histochem. Cytochem., 1988—; contbr. (articles) Clin. Anatomy, Surg. Endoscopy, Pharos, Jours. Thoracic Cardiovasc. Surgery, So. Med. Jour., others. Bd. dirs. Mobile Mental Health Ctr., Mental Health Found. of South Ala., Mobile Med. Mus., Christian Med. Ministry of South Ala., bd. trustees; sec.-treas. bd. censors Med. Soc. Mobile County, 2006. Comdr. USN, 1974-81. Recipient Physicians Recognition award AMA, 1980, 85, 88, 91, 95, 99, 02, Bacaner Rsch. award Minn. Med. Found., 1979, Humanism in Medicine award Arnold P. Gold Found., Healthcare Found. N.J., 2002, Howard L. Holley award Med. Assn. State Ala., 2002. Fellow ACS (mem, exec. coun., Ala. chpt., sec.-treas. 2008, pres.-elect 2009), Internat. Coll. Surgeons (vice regent Ala. chpt. 1989—); mem. Iota Delta Gamma, Alpha Omega Alpha, Phi Kappa Phi, Gold Humanism Honor Soc, Med. Soc. County Mobile, (sec.-treas. 2007, mem. bd. censors, 2006, 08, v.p. 2008, pres.-elect 2009), Ala. Chapter Am. Coll. Surgeons (sec., treas., 2008). Office: U South Ala Coll Med Allied Health Professions Mobile AL 36617-2293 Office Phone: 251-471-7034. Business E-Mail: crodning@usouthal.edu.

RODNUNSKY, SIDNEY, lawyer, educator; b. Edmonton, Alta., Can., Feb. 3, 1946; s. B. and I. Rodnunsky; m. Teresita Asuncion; children: Naomi, Shawna, Rachel, Tevie, Claire, Donna, Sidney Jr. BEd, U. Alberta, 1966, LLB, 1973; MEd, U. Calgary, 1969, grad. diploma, 1990; BS, U. of State of N.Y., 1988; MBA, Greenwich U., 1990. Served as regional counsel to Her Majesty the Queen in Right of the Dominion of Can.; former gov. Grande Prairie Regional Coll.; now prin. legal counsel Can. Nat. exec., Alta. coord. for gifted children, ombudsman, SIG coord. Mensa Can.; past pres. Grande Prairie and Dist. Bar Assn., Alta Tchrs. Assn., Aspenview. Author: Breathalyzer Casebook; editor: The Children Speak. Decorated knight Grand Cross Sovereign and Royal Order of Piast, knight Grand Cross Order of St. John the Baptist; knight Hospitaller Order St. John of Jerusalem; Prince of Kiev, Prince of Trabzon, Prince and Duke of Rodari, Duke of Chernigov, Count of Riga, Count of St. John of Alexandria; named to Honorable Order of Ky. Colonels; named adm. State of Tex.; recipient Presdl. Legion of Merit. Mem. Law Soc. Alta., Law Soc. Sask., Can. Bar Assn., Inst. Can. Mgmt., Phi Delta Kappa. E-mail: wonderfulschool@hotmail.com.

RODOPOULOS, PANTELEIMON EVAGGELOS, clergyman; b. Athens, Greece, Mar. 26, 1929; s. Alexander and Eleni (Santamouri) R. Degree in Theology, U. Athens, 1952, ThD, 1959; LittB, Oxford U., Eng., 1957; ThD (hon.), Holy Cross Theol. Sch., Brookline, Mass., 1982; PhD (hon.), U. Sibiu, Romania, 1998, U. Presov, Slovakia, 2008. Ordained to Orthodox Christian ministry, 1952. Deacon Ch. of Greece, Athens, 1952-54; archimandrite Ecumenical Patriarchate, Oxford, 1954-57, Frankfurt, Germany, 1957-58; vicar gen. Metropolis of Thessaloniki (Greece), 1958-63; asst. prof. U. Thessaloniki, 1960-68, assoc. prof., 1968—70, prof. theology, 1970—; dean Holy Cross Theol. Sch., Brookline, 1963-66, St. John of Damascus Theol. Sch., Tripoli, Lebanon, 1972-79; metropolitan of Tyroloe Ecumenical Patriarchate, 1974—. Mem. Nat. Coun. Chs. US, 1963-66, senator U. Thessaloniki, 1976-77, dean Theol. Sch., 1977-78, vice rector, 1981-82, rector, 1982-83; observer II Vatican Coun., 1964; mem. cen. com. World Coun. Chs., 1974-75; co-chmn. Commn. Theol. Dialogue Between Orthodox and World Alliance of Reformed Chs., 1985—; pres. Patriarchal Inst. Patristic Studies, 1985-89; v.p. Patriarchal Inst., 1989—; abbot Thessaloniki Vlatadon Monastery, 1985—. Author books and articles on canon law, liturgy and inter-ch. rels. Ednl. leader Ellenikon Phos, Thessaloniki, 1968—; pres. annual conf. organizing com. Municipality of Thessaloniki, 1987—; hon. mem. bd. Pro-Oriente, Vienna, Austria, 1985. Recipient St. Demetrius Cross, Metropolis of Thessaloniki, 1980, medal St. Peter and St. Paul, Patriarchate of Antioch, Damascus, 1986, medals Municipality of Thessaloniki, 1988, Patriarchate of Moscow, 1990. Mem. Soc. for Law of Eastern Chs. (pres. 1983—). Greek Orthodox. Avocations: music, swimming. Home: Anapauseos 11 Panorama 55236 Thessaloniki Greece Office: U Thessaloniki Royal Patriarchal Monastery of Vlataday 54634 Thessaloniki Greece Office Phone: 30 2310 209913. Business E-Mail: vlatadon_monastery@yahoo.com.

RODOWSKY, LAWRENCE FRANCIS, retired state judge; b. Balt., Nov. 10, 1930; s. Lawrence Anthony and Frances (Gardner) R.; m. Colby Fossett, Aug. 7, 1954; children: Laura Rodowsky Ramos, Alice Rodowsky-Seegers, Emily Rodowsky Savopoulos, Sarah Jones Rodowsky, Gregory, Katherine Rodowsky O'Connor. AB, Loyola Coll., Balt., 1952; LLB, U. Md., 1956. Bar: Md. 1956. Ct. crier, law clk. U.S. Dist. Ct. Md., 1954-56; asst. atty. gen. Md., 1960-61; assoc., ptnr. firm Frank, Bernstein, Conaway & Goldman, Balt., 1956-79; judge Ct. Appeals Md., Annapolis, 1980-2000, mem. rules com., 1969-80; sr. status judge Ct. of Spl. Appeals Md., Annapolis, 2001—. Lectr., asst. instr. U. Md. Law Sch., 1958-68, 87-91; reporter jud. dept. Md. Constl. Conv. Commn., 1966-67. Chmn. Gov. Md. Commn. Racing Reform, 1979. Fellow Am. Coll. Trial Lawyers; mem. Md. Bar Assn., Balt. Bar Assn. Roman Catholic. Home: 6614 Walnutwood Cir Baltimore MD 21212-1213 Office: 620 CM Mitchell Jr Courthse 100 N Calvert St Baltimore MD 21202 Office Phone: 410-333-4374. Business E-Mail: lawrence.rodowsky@mdcourts.gov.

RODRÍGUEZ, AGUSTÍN ALEJO ROMÁN, bishop emeritus; b. San Antonio de los Banos, Cuba, May 5, 1928; came to U.S., 1966; s. Rosendo and Juana (Rodriguez) R. BA, Sem. for Fgn. Missions, Montreal; M in Divinity, St. Vincent de Paul Regional Sem., Boynton Beach, Fla.; MA in Religious Studies, Barry U., Miami; MA in Human Resources, Biscayne Coll., Opa Locka, Fla. Ordained priest Diocese of Matanzas, Cuba, 1959, pastor parishes, 1959-61, spiritual dir. youth; expelled by Cuban Govt., 1961; pastor Holy Spirit Parish, Temuco, Chile, 1962-66; spiritual dir., prof. Inst. Humanities, 1962-66; spiritual dir. Cursillo Movement Diocese of Temuco, 1962-66; asst. pastor St. Mary's Cathedral, Miami, 1966-67, St. Kieran's Parish, Miami, 1967-68; chaplain Mercy Hosp., Miami, 1967-73, Shrine of Our Lady of Charity, Miami, 1967; named monsignor Archdiocese of Miami, 1974, named vicar for Hispanics, 1976, aux. bishop, 1979—2003, aux. bishop emeritus, 2003—; ordained bishop, 1979. Mem. Nat. Conf. Cath. Bishops (mem. ad hoc com. on migration and tourism 1980—, mem. ad hoc com. for hispanic affairs 1980—). Roman Catholic. Office: Archdiocese of Miami 9401 Biscayne Blvd Miami FL 33138-2970

RODRIGUEZ, ALEX (ALEXANDER EMMANUEL RODRIGUEZ), professional baseball player; b. NYC, July 27, 1975; s. Victor Rodriguez and Lourdes Navarro; m. Cynthia Scurtis, Nov. 2, 2002 (div. Sept. 18, 2008); children: Natasha Alexander, Ella Alexander. Shortstop Seattle Mariners, 1994—2000, Tex. Rangers, 2001—03; third baseman NY Yankees, 2004—. Mem. US nat. team World Baseball Classic, 2006, mem. Dominican Republic nat. team, 09. Author: (children's book) Out of the Ballpark, 2007; co-author (with Greg Brown): Hit a Grand Slam, 1998. Founder Grand Slam for Kids, 1996—, Alex Rodriguez Found., 1998—. Recipient Silver Slugger award, 1996, 1998—2003, 2005, 2007, 2008, Hank Aaron award, 2001—03, 2007, Gold Glove award, 2002—03, Hitter of Yr. award, MLB.com, 2007, Oscar Charleston Legacy award, Negro Leagues Baseball Mus., 2008, ESPY award, Best Baseball Player, ESPN, 2008; named Maj. League Player of Yr., 1996, 2002, 2007, Am. League Batting Champion, 1996, Am. League MVP, 2003, 2005, 2007; named one of The Most Influential People in the World of Sports, Bus. Week, 2007, 2008, The 100 Most Powerful Celebrities, Forbes.com, 2008; named to Am. League All-Star Team, 1996—98, 2000—08. Achievements include leading the Am. League in: batting average: 1996; runs scored, 1996, 2001, 2003, 2005, 2007; doubles, 1996; hits, 1998; home runs, 2001-03, 2005, 2007; RBI, 2002, 2007; becoming the first player in MLB history to hit at least 35 home runs 11 consecutive seasons, 1998-2008; youngest player in MLB history to hit 500 home runs, August 4, 2007; recording his 2,500th hit, September 2, 2009. Office: NY Yankees Yankee Stadium One E 161st St Bronx NY 10451*

RODRIGUEZ, ANNABELLE, territorial supreme court justice, former attorney general; b. Santurce, PR, 1953; m. Francisco de Jesus-Schuck; children: Ricardo Enrique Candle, Fernando Manuel Vela. BA in history magna cum laude, U. PR, JD, 1985. From asst. solicitor gen. to solicitor gen. PR Dept. Justice, 1986—93; ptnr. Martino, Odell & Calabria, Hato Rey, PR, 1993—96; judge US Dist Ct. (PR dist.), 1996; sec. justice PR, 2001—04; assoc. judge PR Supreme Ct., 2004—. Democrat. Office: Tribunal Supremo de PR PO Box 2392 San Juan PR 00902*

RODRIGUEZ, ANTONIO JOSE, lawyer; b. New Orleans, Dec. 7, 1944; s. Anthony Joseph and Josephine Olga (Cox) R.; m. Virginia Anne Soignet, Aug. 23, 1969; children: Henry Jacob, Stephen Anthony. BS, U.S. Naval Acad., 1966; JD cum laude, Loyola U. of the South, New Orleans, 1973. Bar: La. 1973, U.S. Dist. Ct. (ea. dist.) La. 1973, U.S. Ct. Appeals (5th cir.) 1973, U.S. Dist. Ct. (mid. dist.) La. 1975, U.S. Dist. Ct. (we. dist.) La. 1977, U.S. Ct. Appeals (11th cir.) 1981, U.S. Supreme Ct. 1987, U.S. Dist. Ct. (so. dist.) Miss. 1991, U.S. Ct. Appeals (4th cir.) 1991, U.S. Ct. Appeals (1st cir.) 1997, U.S. Ct. Internat. Trade, 1991. Assoc. Phelps, Dunbar, Marks, Claverie & Sims, New Orleans, 1973-77; ptnr. Phelps Dunbar, New Orleans, 1977-92, Fowler Rodriguez & Chalos, New Orleans, 1992—. Prof. law Tulane U., New Orleans, 1981—; mem. nat. rules of the road adv. coun. U.S. Dept. Transp., Washington, 1987-90, chmn. nat. navigation safety adv. coun., 1990-94, mem., 2000—; spkr. on admiralty and environ. Co-author: Admiralty-Limitation of Liability, 1981—, Admiralty-Law of Collision, 1990—; author: (chpt.) Benedict on Admiralty, 1995—; assoc. editor Loyola Law Rev., 1971-73; contbr. articles to profl. maritime and environ. jours. Bd. dirs. Greater New Orleans Coun. Navy League, 1988—, Propeller Club of New Orleans, 1997—. Lt. USN, 1966-70; capt. USNR, 1970-95. Decorated Navy Commendation medal; recipient Disting. Pub. Svc. award U.S. Dept. Transp., 1993. Fellow La. Bar Found.; mem. ABA, La. State Bar Assn., La. State Law Inst., Maritime Law Assn. U.S. (proctor 1975—), New Orleans Bar Assn., Southeastern Admiralty Law Inst., Assn. Average Adjusters U.S., Assn. Average Adjusters U.K., Naval Res. Assn. (chpt. pres. 1982-84), U.S. Naval Acad. Alumni Assn. (chpt. pres. 1981-83), Bienville Club, Phi Alpha Delta, Alpha Sigma Nu. Republican. Roman Catholic. Home: 4029 Mouton St Metairie LA 70002-1303 Office: Fowler Rodriguez & Chalos Texaco Ctr 400 Poydras St 30th Fl New Orleans LA 70130-1000 Home Phone: 504-455-9388; Office Phone: 504-523-2600. Business E-Mail: ajr@frc-law.com.

RODRIGUEZ, ARTURO SALVADOR, labor union official; b. San Antonio, June 23, 1949; s. Arthur Salvador and Felice (Quintero) Rodriguez; m. Linda Fabela Chavez, Mar. 1974 (dec. Oct. 9, 2000); children: Olivia, Julie, Arthur; m. Sonia Hernandez, 2006. BA in Sociology, St. Mary's U., San Antonio, 1971; MSW, U. Mich., Ann Arbor, 1973. Various positions United Farm Workers of America (UFW), Keene, Calif., 1973-90, v.p., 1981-93, pres., 1993—. Chief instr. union organizers training sch. UFW La Paz hdqs., 1978—79. Coord. Edward Kennedy Presdl. dr., Tex., 1980. Office: UFW Nat Hdqs PO Box 62 La Paz 29700 Woodford Tehachapi Rd Keene CA 93531*

RODRIGUEZ, CIRO DAVIS, United States Representative from Texas; b. Piedras Negras, Mex., Dec. 9, 1946; m. Carolina Pena; 1 child. BA, St. Mary's U., San Antonio, 1973; MSW, Our Lady of the Lake U., San Antonio, 1978. Mem. Harlandale Ind. Sch. Dist. Bd., 1975-87; faculty assoc., Worden Sch. Social Work Our Lady of the Lake U., 1987-96; mem. Tex. Ho. of Reps., 1987-97, US Congress from 28th Tex. dist., 1997—2005, US Congress from 23rd Tex. dist., 2007—, mil. readiness subcom. house nat. security com., health subcom. house vets. affairs com. Vice chair, health care task force chair Congrl. Hispanic Caucus, 2004—05. Democrat. Roman Catholic. Office: US Congress 2458 Ho Rayburn Office Bldg Washington DC 20515*

RODRIGUEZ, DANIEL B., law educator; b. 1962; BA, Calif. State U., Long Beach, 1984; JD, Harvard U., 1987. Law clk. to Hon. Alex Kozinski U.S. Ct. Appeals (9th cir.), Pasadena, Calif., 1987-88; acting prof. U. Calif., Boalt Hall Sch. Law, Berkeley, 1988—94, prof., 1994—98; dean, prof. law U. San Diego Sch. Law, 1998—2005, Warren Disting. prof. law, 2005—07; Minerva House Drysdale regents chair in law U. Tex., Austin, 2007—. Vis. scholar Hoover Inst., Stanford U.; vis. prof. McGeorge Sch. Law-Govt. Affairs Program, U. So. Calif., U. Tex., Austin, U. Ill.; John M. Olin Fellow in Law and Econs. U. Va.; adj. prof. U. Calif., San Diego Sch. Internat. Rels. and Pacific Studies. Contbr. articles to profl. jours. Mem.: Am. Bar Found., Am. Law Inst. Office: Univ Tex Austin Sch Law 727 E Dean Keeton St Austin TX 78705 Office Phone: 512-232-1090. Business E-Mail: drodriguez@law.utexas.edu.*

RODRIGUEZ, DAVID M., career military officer; b. 1954; BS, US Mil. Acad., West Point, 1976; MMAS in Mil. Art and Sci., US Army Command and Gen. Staff Coll.; MA in Nat. Security and Strategic Studies, US Naval War Coll. Commd. 2d. lt. US Army, 1976, advanced through grades to lt. gen., 2008; rifle platoon leader A Co. 1st Battalion, 61st Infantry, 5th Infantry Divsn., Fort Polk, La., 1977—78, scout platoon leader Combat Support Co., 1978—79, motor officer, 1979, exec. officer Combat Support Co., 1979—80; comdr. B Co. 1st Batalion, 52d Infantry, 1st Armored Divsn., US Army Europe and Seventh Army, Germany, 1981—83, asst. S-3, 3d Brigade, 1st Armored Divsn., 1983, S-3, 1st Battalion, 52d Infantry, 1st Armored Divsn., 1983—84; asst. S-3 75th Ranger Regiment, Fort Benning, Ga., 1984—85, liaison officer 3d Battalion, 1985—86, comdr. B Co., 3d Battalion, 1986—87; chief doctrine devel. G-3, XVIII Airborne Corps, Fort Bragg, NC, 1989—90; S-3 than exec. officer 1st Battalion, 505th Parachute Infantry Regiment, Fort Bragg, NC, 1990—92, Operation Desert Shield/Storm, Saudi Arabia, 1990—92; joint exercise officer than exec. officer Exercise Divsn., C-3/J-3/G-3, UN Command/Combined Forces Command/US Forces Korea, 1992—94; comdr. 2d Battalion, 502d Infantry Regiment, 101st Airborne Divsn., Fort Campbell, Ky., 1994—96, 2d Brigade, 82d Airborne Divsn., Fort Bragg, NC, 1997—99; asst. chief staff G-3, XVIII Airborne Corps, Fort Bragg, NC, 1999—2000; dep. commdg. gen./asst. commandant US Army Infantry Ctr. and Sch., Fort Benning, Ga., 2000—02; asst. divsn. comdr. 4th Infantry Divsn., Fort Hood, Tex., 2002—03, Operation Iraqi Freedom, Iraq, 2002—03; dep. dir. regional ops. (J-3) The Joint Staff, Washington, 2003—05; comdr. Multi-Nat. Divsn.-N.W. Operation Iraqi Freedom, 2005—06, spl. asst. to comdr. Multi-Nat. Corps-Iraq, 2006; commdg. gen. 82d Airborne Divsn., Fort Bragg, NC, 2006—08, Combined Joint Task Force-76, Operation Enduring Freedom, Bagram Air Field, Afghanistan, 2007—08; sr. mil. asst. to sec. US Dept. Defense, Washington, 2008—09; dep. comdr. US Forces Afghanistan (USFOR-A), 2009—. Decorated Disting. Svc. Medal, Defense Superior Svc. Medal, Legion of Merit (with 4 Oak Leaf Clusters), Bronze Star Medal (with Oak Leaf Cluster), Defense Meritorious Svc. Medal, Meritorious Svc. Medal (with 4 Oak Leaf Clusters), Joint Svc. Commendation Medal, Army Commendation Medal (with 2 Oak Leaf Clusters), Joint Svc. Achievement Medal, Combat Infantryman Badge, Expert Infantryman Badge, Master Parachutist Badge, Air Assault Badge, Ranger Tab, Joint Chiefs of Staff Identification Badge. Office: ISAF-Kabul (AFG) Pub Info Office Feldpost 64298 Damsatadt Germany*

RODRIGUEZ, ENRIQUE, computer software company executive; BS, Tech. Inst. Monterrey, Mex., 1982. Exec. v.p. broadband access products Thomson/RCA, sr. v.p. multimedia products; v.p. Xbox partnerships Microsoft Corp., 2003—06, corp. v.p. Microsoft TV divsn., 2006—09, corp. v.p. TV, music and video bus., 2009. Office: Microsoft Corp Microsoft TV Divsn 1 Microsoft Way Redmond WA 98052-6399

RODRÍGUEZ, FÉLIX M., oil industry executive; Grad. in Petroleum Engring., U. Oriente, Venezuela; student in Sys. Analysis, Harvard U., Columbia U. With Corporación Venezolana de Petróleo, Exxon Rsch., ELF Aquitaine; v.p. Petróleos de Venezuela, S.A. (CITGO's ultimate parent co.); dep. pres. CITGO Petroleum Corp., 2004—05, pres., CEO, 2005—. Prof. math. and stats. Ctrl. U. of Venezuela Sch. Geography. Office: CITGO Petroleum Corp 1293 Eldridge Pky Houston TX 77077

RODRÍGUEZ, FERDINAND, chemical engineer, educator; b. Cleve., July 8, 1928; s. José and Concha (Luís) R.; m. Ethel V. Koster, July 28, 1951; children: Holly Edith, Lida Concha. BS, Case Western Res. U., 1950, MS, 1954; PhD, Cornell U., 1958. Devel. engr. Ferro Corp., Bedford, Ohio, 1950-54; asst. prof. chem. engring. Cornell U., 1958-61, asso. prof., 1961-71, prof., 1971—. On sabbatic leave at Union Carbide Corp., 1964-65, Imperial Chem. Industries, Ltd., 1971, Eastman Kodak Co., 1978-79; cons. to industry. Author: Principles of Polymer Systems, 5th edit., 2003; contbr. articles; songwriter:. Served with U.S. Army, 1954-56. Recipient Excellence in Teaching award Cornell Soc. Engrs., 1966, Edn. Achievement award Hispanic Engr. Mag., 1991. Fellow Am. Inst. Chem. Engrs.; mem. Am. Chem. Soc., Soc. Plastics Engrs. Lutheran. Office: Cornell U 267 Olin Hall Ithaca NY 14853 Business E-Mail: FR13@cornell.edu.

RODRIGUEZ, FRANCISCO JOSE, professional baseball player; b. Caracas, Venezuela, Jan. 7, 1982; Relief pitcher LA Angels of Anaheim (formerly Anaheim Angels), 2002—08, NY Mets, 2008—. Mem. Venezuelan nat. team Pan-Am. Youth Championship, Mexico, 1998, World Baseball Classic, 2006, 09. Recipient Am. League Rolaids Relief award, 2006; named to Am. League All-Star Team, Maj. League Baseball, 2004, 2007, 2008, Nat. League All-Star Team, 2009. Achievements include being a member of the World Series Championship winning Anaheim Angels, 2002; being the youngest pitcher in MLB history to win a World Series game (20 years old), 2002; leading the American League in: saves, 2005, 2006, 2008; setting Major League Baseball's all-time record for saves in a single season (62), 2008. Office: NY Mets Citi Field 126th St & Roosevelt Ave Flushing NY 11368*

RODRIGUEZ, IRMINA BESTARD, science educator; b. Havana, Cuba, Apr. 29, 1945; came to U.S., 1961; d. Gaspar and Ester Antonia (Bas) Bestard; m. Luis Felipe Rodriguez, June 8, 1968; children: Damien Brandon, Leslie Christina. BA in Chemistry, Coll. of New Rochelle, 1967; postgrad., U. Bridgeport, 1969-71, Barry U., Fla. Internat. U. Cert. tchr. Fla. Rsch. technician in pharmacology N.Y. Med. Coll., NYC, 1967-70; rsch. chemist Clairol, Inc., Stamford, Conn., 1970-74; pre-sch. instr. Happi-tymes, Miami, 1981-84; educator St. John Neumann Sch., Miami, 1984-92; sci. educator Carrollton Sch., Miami, 1992—. Coord. sci. dept. Carrollton Sch., 2004—. Contbr. articles to profl. jours. Mem. ways/means chmn. Stamford Women's Rep. Club, 1975-79, v.p. 1979. Mem. AAUW, Nat. Sci. Tchrs. Assn., Fla. Sci. Tchrs. Assn., Dade County Sci. Tchrs. Assn. Republican. Roman Catholic. Avocations: swimming, biking, reading, art collecting, ecology club advisor. Office: Carrollton Sch of the Sacred Heart 3747 Main Hwy Miami FL 33133-5907 Office Phone: 305-446-5673. Business E-Mail: irodriguez@carrollton.org.

RODRIGUEZ, IVAN TORRES, professional baseball player; b. Vega Baja, PR, Nov. 30, 1971; m. Maribel Rivera, June 20, 1991; 3 children. Catcher Tex. Rangers, 1991—2002, Fla. Marlins, 2003, Detroit Tigers, 2004—08, NY Yankees, 2008, Houston Astros, 2009, Tex. Rangers, 2009—. Mem. Puerto Rican nat. team World Baseball Classic, 2009. Co-founder Ivan Pudge Rodriguez Found., 1993. Recipient Gold Glove award, 1992—2001, 2004, 2006—07; named Am. League MVP, 1999, Nat. League Championship Series MVP, 2003; named to Am. League All-Star Team, 1992—2001, 2004—07, Am. League Silver Slugger Team, The Sporting News, 1994—99, 2004. Achievements include member of World Series Championship winning Florida Marlins, 2003; setting Major League Baseball's record for most games caught (2,227), 2009. Office: Tex Rangers 1000 Ballpark Way Arlington TX 76011*

RODRIGUEZ, JAI, television personality; b. Brentwood, NY, June 22, 1977; Actor: (films) The New Guy, 2002; (Broadway plays) Rent, Spinning into Butter, (off broadway plays) Zanna, Don't!, 2003; co-author: (books) Queer Eye for the Straight Guy: The Fab 5's Guide to Looking Better, Cooking Better, Dressing Better, Behaving Better, and Living Better, 2004; culture specialist (TV series) Queer Eye for the Straight Guy, 2003, host Groomer Has It, 2008; actor, actor: (Broadway plays) The Producers, 2005.

RODRIGUEZ, JAMES G., city councilman; m. Wendy Montoya, June 30, 2007. B in Bus. Adminstrn., U. Houston, 1998. Former staff mem. PaperCity Mag., Houston; mktg. dir. Entech Civil Engrs., Inc., Houston; councilman, Dist. I Houston City Coun., 2007—. Campaign mgr., chief of staff to councilwoman Carol Alvarado Houston City Coun., 2002—06; cons. Tony Sanchez for Gov. Campaign, Mayor Lee P. Brown Campaign. Vol. Al Gore Presdl. Campaign, Houston, 2000; coord. Houston Ind. Sch. Dist.'s Rebuild 2002 Bond Campaign; active Our Lady of Mt. Carmel Ch.; bd. dirs. El Centro de Corazon, Houston. Mem.: Tejano Assoc. Cmty. Concerns (bd. dirs.), Houston Hispanic Architects & Engrs., Harris County Tejano Dems., Greater East End C. of C., U. Houston Young Alumni Connection (adv, bd. mem.), Houston Alumni Orgn., Garden Villas Civic Club. Democrat. Office: City Hall Annex 900 Bagby 1st Fl Houston TX 77002 Office Phone: 832-393-3011. Office Fax: 713-247-3067. Business E-Mail: districti@cityofhouston.net.*

RODRIGUEZ, JOHN M., physics professor; b. Berkeley, Calif., June 10, 1964; s. V. Louis Franks (Stepfather), Michael Rodriguez and Patricia A. Franks. MS in Physics, UC Berkeley, 1996. Physics prof. Laney Coll., Oakland, 1998—2007. Mem.: Am. Phys. Soc. Office: Diablo Valley Coll 321 Golf Club Rd Pleasant Hill CA 94523 Business E-Mail: jrodriguez@dvc.edu.

RODRIGUEZ, JORGE JACINTO, psychiatrist; b. Moron, Ciego de Avila, Cuba, Jan. 28, 1950; s. Nicolas Mercedes Rodriguez and Fela Julia Sánchez; m. Miriam L. de León, Apr. 0, 2005; 1 child, Elisabet. MD, U. Camaguey, Cuba, 1972; PhD, U. Havana, Cuba, 1991. Cert. psychiatry Ministry Health Cuba, 1978. Prof. psychiatry U. Camaguey, 1973—88; head psychiatry dept. U. Hosp. Calixto Garcia, Havana, 1988—97, prof., 1973—88; temp. internat. advisor mental health Pan Am. Health Orgn., Regional Office WHO, 1996—2004, mental health advisor Guatemala, 1997—2004, mental health advisor ctrl. Am. countries Panamá, 2004—06, mental health program coord. Washington, 2006—. Mental health coord. Ministry Health, Havana, 1989—97, psychiatrist and mental health advisor, Sao Tome, 1980—81, several mgr. and academic posts, Camaguey and Havana, 1973—96; coord. academic bd. social psychiat. ms course Med. U. Havana, 1994—97, chmn., 1994—97. Contbr. articles to numerous profl. jours. Master: Assn. Psiquiátrica Guatemalteca (hon.). Home: 2501 Q St NW Apt 223 Washington DC 20007 Business E-Mail: rodrigjo@paho.org.

RODRIGUEZ, JOSE L., neurosurgeon, educator; s. Loretta Kirchner; m. Angela V. Vega, July 2, 1976; 1 child, Tonatzin V. MD, U. Calif., Irvine, 1981. Diplomate Am. Assn. Neurol. Surgeons, 1992. Clin. instr., dept. surgery Marshall U. Sch. Medicine, Huntington, W.Va.; asst. prof., dept. neurosurgery U. Ky., Lexington, 1990—93; asst. clin. prof., dept. surgery Coll. Osteopatic Medicine of the Pacific, Pomona, Calif., 1995—. Bd. mem. Geiger Easter Seal Speech and Hearing Ctr., Ashland, Ky., 1991—93. Contbr. articles to profl. jours. Contbr. local funds Found. for the Tristate Cmty., Bus. and Profl., Ashland, Ky., 1990—93. Fellow: Congress Neurol. Surgeons; mem.: Calif. Assn. Neurol. Surgeons (bd. dirs. 2001—05), Calif. Med. Assn., AMA, ACS, Am. Assn. Neurol. Surgeons. R-Consevative. Avocations: fly fishing, scuba diving. Office: LDR Neurosurgery 255 E Bonita Ave Bldg #9 Pomona CA 91767 Office Fax: 909-450-0366. Personal E-mail: jrodriguezmd@earthlink.net.

RODRIGUEZ, JOSEFA NIEVES, special education and language educator; b. Mantanzaz, Cuba, Nov. 7, 1942; d. Basilio Gonzalez Santana and Edelmira Margarita Escalona; m. Manuel B. Rodriguez, June 17, 1972; children: Josie, Aimee, Manuel Jr. B in Secretarial Sci., Barry U., Miami Shores, Fla., 1965, BS, 1980, MS, 1992. Profl. educator's cert. Fla., cert. ESOL, Spanish, specific learning disabilities, mentally handicapped, tchr. birth-4 Fla. Dept. Edn., trainer of trainers State of Fla. Child Care Child Devel. Assoc. Program. Sales agt. Eastern Airlines, Inc., Miami, Fla., 1965—90; pre-sch. tchr. Archdiocese Miami, 1994—96; ESOL tchr. adult edn. Dade County Pub. Schs., Miami, 1996—, spl. edn. tchr., 2000—08, tchr. of students with phys. impairments, 2005—08; trainer of child care trainers State Fla. Dept. Children and Families, Dade County Pub. Schs., 2006—. Substitute tchr. Dade County Pub. Schs., Miami, 1992—2000; adj. prof. Miami Dade CC, Miami, 1997, ESOL instr., 2000; facilitator U. Miami Reading Inst.; ESOL tutor adult edn. Dade County Pub. Schs., Miami, 2005—06. Mem.: AFT, NEA, Dade Art Educators Assn., Coun. for Exceptional Student Edn., Fla. Edn. Assn., United Tchrs. Dade, Barry U. Alumnae Assn. Republican. Roman Catholic. Avocations: opera, piano, painting, tennis, languages. Office: Dade County Pub Schs 1500 Biscayne Blvd Miami FL 33132

RODRIGUEZ, JUAN, physics professor; PhD, U. Ark., Fayetteville, 1986. Postdoc. rsch. assoc. Wash. U., St. Louis, 1986—90; prof. physics Centenary Coll., Shreveport, La., 1990—. Office: Centenary Coll Dept Physics Shreveport LA 71134 Business E-Mail: jrodrigu@centenary.edu.

RODRIGUEZ, JUAN ALFONSO, information technology executive; b. Santiago, Cuba, Feb. 10, 1941; came to U.S., 1953; s. Alfonso and Marie Madeleine (Hourcadette) R. BEE, CCNY, 1962; MEE, NYU, 1963. Engr. IBM, Poughkeepsie, NY, 1963—66, Boulder, Colo., 1966—69, engring. mgr., 1968-69; dir. tech. Storage Tech. Corp., Louisville, Colo., 1969-74, v.p. engring., 1974—76, v.p., gen. mgr. disk, 1976—80, v.p., gen. mgr. optical disk Longmont, Colo., 1980—85; pres., CEO Exabyte Corp., Boulder, 1985-87, CEO, 1987-90, chmn., 1987-92; pres. Sweetwater Corp., 1992-93, chmn., 1992-95, also bd. dirs.; prof. elec. and computer engring. and engring. mgmt. U. Colo., 1992—2001, co-exec. dir. Deming Ctr. Entrepreneurship, 1994-2000; mem. adv. coun., 1994—; chmn. Datasonix, 1992-96, Vixel, 1995-99; chmn., CEO Ecrix Corp., 1996—2001; chief technologist, bd. dirs. Exabyte Corp., 2001—03, interim CEO, pres., 2002, chmn., 2003—06; connectivity ptnr. Appian Ventures, 2002—. Mem. devel. coun. Coll. Engring. U. Colo., 1990-92, mem. tech. transfer office adv. bd., 2000-, adv. bd. Boulder grad. sch., 2007-; Decisionism Corp.; bd. dirs. Maxtor Corp., 1992-94, HiveLive Corp., 2005-; mem. engring. adv. bd. CCNY, bd. dirs. Colo. Advanced Tech. Enterprise, 1994-98; Robert J. Appel Disting. lectr. law and tech. Law Sch. U. Denver, 1990. Patentee in field. Bd. dir. Boulder YMCA, 1982-87, U. Colo. Artist Series, 1988-92; mem. bd. govs. Boulder County United Way, 1989-93, chairperson campaign, 1992; commr. Colo. Advance Tech. Inst., 1988-92; co-chmn. Colo. Innovation Coun., 2008-. Recipient Ind. Quality award, Am. Soc. Quality Control (Rocky Mountain sect.), 1990, Gen. Palmer award Outstanding Engr. in Industry, Am. Cons. Engrs. Coun. Colo., 1995, Career Achievement award, Engring. Sch. Alumni CCNY, 2002, Townsend Harris medal, Alumni Assn. CCNY, 2003, Sprit Visionary award, Boulder C. of C., 2004, Hispanic Engr. of Yr., Entrepreneur Hispanic Engr. Nat. Achievement Awards Coun., 1995; named Boulder Spirit Entrepreneur of Yr., 1989, Entrepreneur of the Decade, 1994; named one of Top 50 Tech. Innovators, VAR Bus., 2004; finalist Entrepreneur of Yr., Arthur Young & Inc Mag., 1989. Fellow IEEE (life); mem. Computer Soc. of IEEE (mem. steering com. on mass storage 1981-93), Soc. Photo-Optical Instrumentation Engrs., Boulder C. of C. (chmn. entrepreneurs support program 1989), Greater Denver C. of C. (bd. dirs. 1990-91); mem. Beta Gamma Sigma (medallion of Entrepreneurship 2003). Office: Appian Ventures 1512 Larimer St Ste 200 Denver CO 80202 Personal E-mail: jar@ieee.org.

RODRIGUEZ, JUSTIN, Councilman; m. Victoria Rodriguez; children: Miranda, Aidan, Olivia. BBA, U. Incarnate Word; JD, U. Wis. Law Sch., 2000. Pvt law practice; juvenile prosecutor Bexar County Dist. Atty. Office, 2001, asst. dist. atty.; councilman, Dist. 7 San Antonio City Coun., 2007—. Trustee San Antonio Ind. Sch. Dist. Bd. Edn., 2004, chmn. Govt. Affairs Com., chmn. Student Adv. Panel; mem. Coun. Urban Bds. Edn. Vol. Cmty. Justice Program, Meals on Wheels; former bd. mem. San Antonio Children's Shelter. Recipient Bruce F. Beilfus award, U. Wis. Law Sch., Congl. award for Outstanding Svc. to Cmty.; named one of 40 under 40 Rising Stars, San Antonio Bus. Jour. Mem.: Jefferson Neighborhood Assn. (pres.), Latino Law Students Assn. (former v.p.), Boys & Girls Club San Antonio. Office: City Hall PO Box 839966 San Antonio TX 78283 also: 2712 Hillcrest San Antonio TX 78228 Office Phone: 210-207-7044, 210-733-7525. Business E-Mail: district7@sanantonio.gov.*

RODRÍGUEZ, LILIANA CRISTINA, mathematics educator; b. Valencia, Carabobo, Venezuela, May 19, 1975; d. Rodolfo Rodríguez and Ana Rosa Sanabria de Rodriguez; m. Harold Enrique Torrence, Dec. 22, 1999; children: Jonathan Enrique Torrence, Susana Andreina Torrence. BS in Math and Learning Disabilities (hon.), U. of Carabobo/Nat. Open U., Valencia, 1999. Cert. 7-12 Mathematics tchr. Minn. Dept. of Edn., 2002. Bilingual Spanish-English tchr. Aurora Charter Sch., Mpls., 2000—03; secondary math tchr. Hazel Pk. Acad. (St. Paul Pub. Sch.), St. Paul, 2003—. Music tchr. Aurora Charter Sch., Mpls., 2000—03. Musician (singer): (music writer) Mensaje de Hermandad. Chorus dir. Holy Rosary Ch., Mpls., 2000—06. Scholar Cum laude scholar, U. of Carabobo -Venezuela, 1999—2003. Mem.: Nat. Coun. of Tchrs. of Math. (assoc.). Achievements include development of Spanish curriculum for children. Avocations: swimming, music, travel, drawing, painting. Home: 6145 Courtly Alcove Unit C Woodbury MN 55125 Office: Saint Paul Public School 360 Colborne St Saint Paul MN 55102 Personal E-mail: lilianac75@hotmail.com. E-mail: liliana.rodriguez@spps.org.

RODRIGUEZ, LOUIS JOSEPH, academic administrator, economist, educator; b. Newark, Mar. 13, 1933; m. Ramona Dougherty, May 31, 1969; children: Susan, Michael, Scott. BA, Rutgers U., 1955; MA, La. State U., 1957, PhD, 1963. Dean, Coll. Bus. Adminstrn., Alcee Fortier Disting. prof. Nichols State U., Thibodaux, La., 1958-71; dean Coll. Bus. U. Tex.-San Antonio, 1971-72, v.p. acad. affairs, dean faculty, 1972-73; dean Sch. Profl. Studies U. Houston-Clear Lake City, 1973-75, vice-chancellor, provost, 1975-80; pres. Midwestern State U., Wichita Falls, Tex., 1981—2000, Hardin Found. prof., 1994—2000; ret., 2000. Vice chmn. Coun. Tex. Pub. Univ. Pres. and Chancellors, 1992-93; mem. formula and health professions edn. adv. coms. Tex. Higher Edn. Coordinating Bd. Author 4 books; contbr. over 50 articles to profl. jours. Chmn. bd. Tex. Council on Econ. Edn., Houston, 1981-83; bd. dirs. Joint Council on Econ. Edn., N.Y.C., 1981-83, Goodwill Industries Am., Washington, 1976-82, Robert Priddy Found., 1993-96, Wichita Falls Met. Y.M.C.A., 1999-2000, 4A Economic Devel. Bd., 2000-2003, Wichita Falls Area Cmty. Found., 1999-2001; pres. Wichita Falls Bd. Commerce and Industry, 1988-89, Clear Lake City Devel. Found., Houston, 1976-77, Goals for Wichita Falls, Inc., 1983; mem. internat. adv. com. Tex. Higher Edn. Coordinating Bd.; pres. United Way Greater Wichita Falls, 1998-99. Recipient Tchr. Edn. Supportive Pres. award Am. Assn. Colls. Tchr. Edn., 1991, Disting. Citizen award N.W. coun. Boy Scouts Am., 1998; named Wichitan of the Yr., 1987; Ford Found. grantee, 1964; Fulbright fellow, 1976 Mem. Am. Assn. State Colls. and Univs. (bd. dirs.), So. Assn. Colls. and Schs. (Commn. on Colls.), Assn. Tex. Colls. and Univs. (pres. 1988-89), Rotary (pres. Downtown Wichita Falls club 1990-91). Mem. Ch. of Christ.

RODRÍGUEZ, MARÍA ISABEL, literature and language professor; d. Antonio Rodríguez and Jesús Rodríguez María. BA, U. Salamanca, Spain, 1988; MA, U. Rochester, NY, 1992, U. Calif., Davis, 1993. Lectr. U. Mich., Residential Coll., Ann Arbor, 1995—. Author: (spanish textbook) Palabra Abierta; contbr. articles to profl. jours. Mem. Migrant Resource Coun., Adrian, Mich., 2000—08. Recipient Mich. Campus Compact (MCC) Faculty award, U. Mich., 2007, LS&A Excellence Edn. award, 1999, 2003, 2008; CRLT Faculty Devel. grant, 2003, grant, 2004, Lecturers' Profl. Devel. grant, 2006, grant, 2008. Office: Univ Mich 701 E University Ann Arbor MI 48109-1245 Office Fax: 734-763-7712. Business E-Mail: mrodri@umich.edu.

RODRIGUEZ, NARCISO, fashion designer; b. NJ, 1961; Studied, Parsons Sch. Design, NY. With Anne Klein, Calvin Klein; design dir. TSE, 1995, Cerruti, Paris, Loewe leather, Madrid, 1997—2001; owner Narciso Rodriguez, NYC, 1997—. Released signature fragrance Musc for Her. Women's ready-to-wear signature collection debuted in 1998 in Milan. Recipient Best New Designer, VH1 Fashion Awards, 1997, Perry Ellis award, Coun. of Fashion Designers Am., 1998, Womenswear Designer of Yr., 2002, 2003, Hispanic Designer of Yr., 1997, Spl. Achievement in Fashion, Am. Latino Media Arts, 2008; named one of 25 Most Influential Hispanics, Time Mag., 2005. Achievements include becoming a household name after designing Carolyn Bessette's wedding dress for her marriage to John F. Kennedy, Jr. Office: PR Consulting 50 Bond St New York NY 10012 also: 9th fl 30 Irving Pl New York NY 10003 Office Phone: 212-677-2989.

RODRIGUEZ, PLACIDO, bishop; b. Celaya, Mex., Oct. 11, 1940; came to US, 1953; s. Eutimio and Maria Concepcion (Rosiles) Rodriguez. STB, STL, Cath. U., Washington, 1968; MA, Loyola U., 1971. Ordained priest Missionary Sons of the Immaculate Heart of Mary, 1968; pastor Our Lady Guadalupe Ch., Chgo., 1972-75, Our Lady of Fatima Ch., Perth Amboy, N.J., 1981-83; ordained bishop, 1983; vocat. dir. Claretians, Chgo., 1975-81; bishop aux. Archdiocese of Chgo., 1983-94; bishop Diocese of Lubbock, Tex., 1994—. Roman Catholic. Office: The Catholic Ctr PO Box 98700 Lubbock TX 79499-8700

RODRIGUEZ, RENÉ F., orthopedic surgeon; MD, Salamanca Univ., Spain; postgrad study, NY Polyclin. Hosp., Queens Hosp. Ctr., Jewish Cronic Diseases Hosp., Health Policy Inst. at George Washington Univ. Cert. Am. Bd. Orthopedic Surg. Chief Veterans Adminstrn. Med. Ctr., Miami; and orthopedic staff Jackson Meml. Med. Ctr., Cedars Med. Ctr., Univ. Miami Sch. Med. Bd. sci. counselors, Nat. Ctr. for Health Statistics CDC, Atlanta, 2003—. Founder, editor-in-chief Medico Interamericano, Medico Familia. Co-founder, co-chmn. Nat. Hispanic Youth Initiative. Recipient Officer of the Cross, Spain, Knight of the Order of Jerusalem, Knight of Malta, Freddie award in recognition of pub. svc. as an Adv. to the underserved in Am., MediMedia USA, 2004. Fellow: Soc. Med. Cons. to Armed Forces, Cuban Orthopaedic Soc. in Exile, Am. Coll. internat. Physicians, Internat. Coll. Surgeons, Am. Fracture Assn., Am. Coll. Surgeons, Am. Trauma Soc. (founding mem.), NY Acad. Medicine.; mem.: Nat. Confederation of Hispanic-Am. Med. Assns. (founder, chmn.), Interamerican Coll. Physicians and Surgeons (pres.). Office: Orthoped Surg Sect VA Med Ctr 1201 NW 16th St Miami FL 33125 E-mail: rrr@icps.org.*

RODRIGUEZ, RICH, college football coach; b. Grant Town, W.Va., May 24, 1963; m. Rita Rodriguez; children: Rhett, Raquel. BS in Phys. Edn., W.Va. U., 1986. Secondary coach, spl. teams coord. Salem Coll., 1986—87, asst. head coach, defensive coord., 1987—88, head coach, 1988; asst. coach W.Va. U., 1989; head coach Glenville State Coll., 1990—96; offensive coord., quarterbacks coach Tulane U., 1997—98; offensive coord., assoc. head coach Clemson U., 1999—2000; head coach W.Va. U., 2001—07, U. Mich., 2008—. Athletic dir. Glenville State Coll., 1995—95; mem. bd. trustees Am. Football Coaches Assn., 2005—. Named WVIAC Coach of Yr., 1993—94, NAIA Coach of Yr., 1993, W.Va. State Coll. Coach of Yr., 1993, Big East Coach of Yr., 2003, 2005, Dist. I Coach of Yr., Am. Football Coaches Assn., 2003, AFCA Region I Co-Coach of Yr., 2007; named to Glenville Sports Hall of Fame, 2003. Achievements include winning 4 Big East Conf. Championships with W.Va. U., 2003, 2004, 2005, 2007. Office: U Mich Football Athletic Dept 1000 S State St Ann Arbor MI 48109-2201

RODRIGUEZ, RICHARD L., transportation executive; BA in Sociology & Comm., Loyola U., Chgo.; JD, Chgo. Kent Coll. Law; grad., Met. Leadership Inst., 2005. Staff lawyer Office of Solicitor Gen., Guam, 1997; field atty. Fed. Emergency Mgmt. Agency (FEMA), Washington, 1999; procurement policy mgr. Chgo. Pub. Schs.; mng. dir. ops. Chgo. Housing Authority, 2000; mng. dep. commr. real estate planning Chgo. Dept. Aviation, 2005; exec. dir. Chgo. Dept. Construction and Permits, 2007—08; commr. Chgo Dept. Bldgs., 2007—08, Chgo. Dept. Aviation, 2008—09; pres. Chgo. Transit Authority (CTA), 2009—. Mem. Catholic Charities of the Archdiocese. Office: Chgo Transit Authority 567 W Lake St Chicago IL 60661*

RODRIGUEZ, RICK, former executive editor; b. Salinas, Calif., Apr. 5, 1954; m. Emelyn Cruz Lat Rodriguez, July 25, 1998. Grad., Stanford U., 1976, Guadalajara, Mex. Newspaper intern Salinas Californian; reporter Fresno Bee, Sacramento Bee, asst. mng. editor, mng. editor, 1993—98, exec. editor & sr. v.p., 1998—2007. Mem. Pulitzer Prize juries 1994, 95. Mem. Am. Soc. Newspaper Editors (bd. dirs. 1997-2001, treas. designate 2001-02, treas. 2002-03, sec. 2003-04, v.p. 2004-2005, pres. 2005-06), Calif. Chicano News Media Assn. (co-founder Sacramento chpt., past bd. dirs.). Office Phone: 916-321-1007. E-mail: rrodriguez@sacbee.com.

RODRIGUEZ, ROBERT, filmmaker; b. San Antonio, June 20, 1968; s. Cecilio and Rebecca Rodriguez; m. Elizabeth Avellan, July 9, 1990 (separated), 5 children. Student, U. Tex. Dir. (films) Bedhead, 1991, El Mariachi, 1992, Desperado, 1995, Four Rooms (segment The Misbehaviors), 1995, From Dusk Till Dawn, 1995, The Faculty, 1998, Spy Kids, 2001, Spy Kids II: Island of Lost Dreams, 2002, Spy Kids 3-D: Game Over, Once Upon A Time in Mexico, 2003, Sin City (co-directed with Frank Miller & Quentin Tarantino), 2005, The Adventures of Shark Boy & Lava Girl in 3-D, 2005, Grindhouse, 2007, prodr. From Dusk Til Dawn II: Texas Blood Money, 1999, writer, prodr. From Dusk Til Dawn 3: The Hangman's Daughter, 2000, Once Upon A Time in Mexico, 2003, writer, dir. Shorts, 2009; prodr. (TV films) Roadracers (also writer), 1994; TV appearances: Nash Bridges, 1997, Deadline, 2000. Named one of 25 Most Influential Hispanics, Time Mag., 2005, 50 Most Powerful People in Hollywood, Premiere mag., 2005. Office: c/o Troublemaker Studios 4900 Old Manor Rd Austin TX 78723*

RODRIGUEZ, ROBERTO MIGUEL, investment company executive, educator; arrived in US, 1977; s. Jose Rodriguez and Onelia R. Diaz; m. Lourdes Maria Rodriguez, Nov. 9, 1968; children: Jose Enrique, Mayra. B in Bus. Adminstrn., The Havana Bus. U., 1961; MBA in Mktg., Acctg. and Fin., U. Minn., 1981, MBT, 1992, BA, 1995, MA in Ednl. Policy and Adminstrn., 1995, M in Pub. Health, 1993, MLA, 1997, PhD in Ednl. Policy and Adminstrn., 1998, M in Agrl., 2005, MEd, 1994; BS in Social Scis. cum laude, Colo. State U., 2001; M in Software Sys., U. St. Thomas, 2002; M in Agrl., Iowa State U., 2002; M in Liberal Studies, U. State NY, 2003; M in Humanities, Calif. State U., Dominguez Hills, 2004; JD, Northwestern Calif. Sch. Law, 2006; MS in Econs., Americus U., 2003; MA in Integrated Studies, Athabasca U., Can., 2004; M in Liberal Arts, Tex. Christian U., 2006; MSA, Ctr. Mich. U., 2007; D in Laws, Canterburg U., 2007; PhD, Commonwealth U., British Virgin Islands, 2007; LLM summa cum laude, Novus Law Sch., 2007; MS in Environ. Sci., U. Ala., 2007; M diploma in internat. Relations (hon.), World Acad. Letters, 2007; MA in Internat. Rels, Troy U., 2008; MA in Polit. Sci., Am. Mil. U., 2008; D in Jud. Scis., Northwestern Calif. Sch. Law, 2008; MA in Internat. Rels., Am. Mil. U., 2009; MA in Conflict Resolution, Negotiation and Peace Bldg., Calif. State U., 2009; D in Diplomacy & Internat. Affairs, Euclid U., 2009. Pres. RMR Real Estate Co., Blaine, Minn., 1979—; sr. acct. Palm Beach Beauty Products, 1997—98; fin. analysis Conwed Plastics, Mpls., 1998—2002; pres. AHR Properties, Inc., 2000—, Shoreview Investments LLC, 2002—, Blaine Investments Inc., 2004—, AHR Constrn., Inc., 2004—. Mgr. fin. analysis, forecasting Tennant Co., Golden Valley, Minn., 1977—92; contr. J and M Properties, Inc., Mpls., 1992—97; asst. prof. John Jay Sch. Diplomacy and Internat. Affairs, 2007—; adj. prof. Novus Law Sch., 2007—; pres. First Equity Group Bloomington, Minn. Sec. Latin Am. affairs Christian Solidarity Internat., Zurich, 1988—98. Mem.: Assn. Trial Lawyers Am., Inst. Mgmt. Accountants, Nat. Ctr. Missing Youth (hon.), Nat. Narcotics Officers Assn. (hon.). Republican. Roman Catholic. Avocations: travel, reading. Home: 11916 Davenport Ct NE Minneapolis MN 55449 Office: AHR Constrn Inc 5840 Hodgson Rd Saint Paul MN 55126 Office Phone: 763-754-2932. Personal E-mail: rbrtrod@earthlink.net.

RODRIGUEZ, ROSEMARY E., former municipal official, federal agency administrator; BS, Metro State Coll., 1977. Dir. scheduling City of Denver, 1992-95, dep. dir. art, culture and film, 1995-96, clk., recorder, 1997—2002; dir. bd. and commissions Office of Mayor, Denver, 2002—03; pres. City Coun., Denver, 2005—06; vice-chair US Election Assistance Commn., 2007, chair, 2008—. Co-founder Latina Initiative; co-chair Colo. Voter Initiative. Mem. Internat. Assn. Clks. and Recorders. Office: US Election Assistance Commn 1225 NY Ave Ste 1100 Washington DC 20005*

RODRIGUEZ, TIMOTHY ALLEN, language educator; b. Fond Du Lac, Wis., July 11, 1958; s. Donald William and Margaret Ann Rodriguez; m. Kathryn Marie Hébert, July 9, 1988; children: William Joseph, Kathryn Ann, Bryan Allen. BS, Western Ill. U., 1982, MS, 1984; PhD, U. Iowa, 1995. Tchr. bilingual edn. Danville (Ill.) Sch. Dist. 118, 1982-83, Houston Ind. Sch. Dist., 1984-86; ESL tchr. Palm Beach (Fla.) County Sch. Dist., 1986-88, 95-97, Martin County Sch. Dist., Stuart, Fla., 1988-91, 98-99; asst. prof. Western Ill. U., Macomb, 1993-95; adj. prof. Nova Southeastern U., Ft. Lauderdale, Fla., 1996-2000; asst. prof. U. Findlay, Ohio, 2001—03; lectr. Ohio State U., Lima, 2003—. Vis. prof. Fla. Atlantic U., 2000-01, Port St. Lucie; validator Nat. Bd. for Profl. Tchg. Stds.; keynote spkr. Ala.-Miss. TESOL Conf., 2007. Contbr. articles to profl. jours.; presenter Internat. TESOL Conf., 1996. Recipient Outstanding Tchg. award, Ohio State U., 2005; named Excellence in Edn., Ohio Mag., 2005. Mem. Internat. TESOL, Internat. Reading Assn., Nat. Assn. Bilingual Edn., Sunshine State TESOL (bd. dirs. 1998-2001). Home Phone: 419-873-1753; Office Phone: 419-495-8250. Business E-Mail: rodriguez.238@osu.edu.

RODRIGUEZ, VINCENT ANGEL, lawyer, director; b. Cayey, PR, 1921; s. Vicente and Maria (Antongiorgi) R. BS, Harvard U., 1941; LLB, Yale U., 1944. Bar: N.Y. 1947. Assoc. Sullivan & Cromwell, NYC, 1944-56, ptnr., 1956—. Mem. Council Fgn. Relations, ABA, Assn. Bar City N.Y., Am. Soc. Internat. Law Clubs: River (N.Y.C.). Home: 3400 Southwest 27th Ave Apt 902 Coconut Grove FL 33133 Office: Sullivan & Cromwell 125 Broad St Fl 28 New York NY 10004-2489

RODRIGUEZ-CAMBERO, RAFAEL LUIS, project manager; s. Rafael Rodriguez-Hernandez and Luisa Argelia Cambero-Gonzalez; m. Annette Milagros Marrero-Oliveras, Jan. 3, 2007. BS, U. PR, Mayaguez, 2000; M in Engring., U. Md., Coll. Pk., 2007. Lic. profl. engr., PR, 2004. Rsch. asst. U. Mass., Amherst, 2000; quality and validation engr. Merck Sharp and Dohme Quimica PR, Barceloneta, 2000—01, DePuy Casting, Inc. A Johnson and Johnson Co., Las Piedras, PR, 2002; chem. engr. US Nuc. Regulatory Commn., Rockville, Md., 2002—07, project mgr., 2007—. Mem. Hispanic Employment Program Adv. Com., US Nuc. Regulatory Commn., 2003—05, sec., 2005—07, co-chair, 2008—; emergency response data sys. analyst Emergency and Incident Response Team, US Nuc. Regulatory Commn., 2008—. Mem. Animal Welfare League Montgomery County Md., 2008—; cmty. svc. Cath. Ch., Mayaguez, 1997—99. Mem.: AIChE, Animal Welfare League Montgomery County(Md.), Coll. Engrs. Land Surveyors PR, Phi Kappa Phi, Tau Beta Pi, Golden Key Honor Soc. Democrat. Roman Catholic. Achievements include development of the U.S. Nuclear Regulatory Commission's decommissioning lessons-learned program; leading and completing the regulatory review and issuance of the first-ever 40 years license renewal for a nuclear facility in the US; completion of research for the University of Maryland on the influence of Hydraulic Retention Time (HRT) vs. Sludge Retention Time (SRT) on the nitrogen removal efficiency of a membrane bioreactor; research found that the SRT is more dominant than the HRT when it comes to the performance of membrane bioreactors. Avocations: reading, travel, physical fitness. Office: US Nuc Regulatory Commn Mail Stop E2C40M 6003 Executive Blvd Rockville MD 20852 Office Fax: 301-492-3363.

RODRIGUEZ-CAMILLONI, HUMBERTO LEONARDO, architect, historian, educator; b. Lima, Peru, May 30, 1945; came to U.S., 1963; s. Alfonso and Elda (Camilloni) R.; m. Mary Ann Alexanderson, July 1, 1972; children: Elizabeth Marie, William Howard. BA magna cum laude, Yale U., 1967, MArch, 1971, MPhil, 1973, PhD, 1981. Rsch. asst. Sch. Architecture Yale U., 1964-70, teaching fellow dept. history art, 1971-72, 74-75; chmn. research dept. Centro de Investigacion y Restauracion de Bienes Monumentales Instituto Nacional de Cultura, Lima, 1973; restoration architect OAS, Washington, 1976—; prof. Sch. Architecture Tulane U., New Orleans, 1975-82; prof., dir. Henry H. Wiss Ctr. Theory and History of Art and Architecture, Coll. Architecture and Urban Studies Va. Poly. Inst. and State U., Blacksburg, 1983—, dir. Ctr. for Preservation and Rehab. Tech., Coll. Architecture, 1986—. Vis. prof. U. Ill., Chgo., 1982-83; reviewer, cons. Choice, 1975—; interim bd. dirs. Ctr. Planning Handbook Latin-Am. Art, 1978-87; cons., adviser Internat. Exhbn. and Symposium Latin-Am. Baroque Art and Architecture, 1980; adv. bd. Mountain Lake Symposium on Art and Architecture Criticism, 1985—, Internat. Symposium Luis Barragan, 1990; coord., advisor exhbn. Tradition and Innovation: Painting, Architecture and Music in Brazil, Mex. and Venezuela between 1950-80, 1991, Internat. Art History Colloquium, 1993, Internat. Congress of Americanists, 1994, 97, 2006, 09, Frank Lloyd Wright: An Architect in America, 1995, Congress Internat. Union Architects, 1996, European Assn. for Archtl. Edn./Archtl. Rsch. Ctrs. Consortium Conf., 2000, The Jesuits, Conf. II: Cultures, Scis. and the Arts, 1540-1773, 2002, Internat. Congress on Constrn. History, 2003, 06-09, III Internat. Copan Maya Congress, 2007, 5th Internat. Congress ICOMOS Sci. Coun. 20th Architecture, 2008. Author: (with Walter D. Harris) The Growth of Latin American Cities, 1971; (with Charles Seymour, Jr.) Italian Primitives, The Case History of a Collection and its Conservation, 1972, Religious Architecture in Lima of the Seventeenth and Eighteenth Centuries: The Monastic Complex of San Francisco el Grande, 1984; contbg. editor Handbook of Latin American Studies, 1987—, The Retablo Facade as Transparency: A Study of the Frontispiece of San Francisco, Lima, 1991, Tradición e Innovación en la Arquitectura del Virreinato del Perú, Constantino de Vasconcelos y la Invención de la Arquitectura de Quincha en Lima Durante el Siglo XVII, 1994, (with Graziano Gasparini) Arquitectura Iberoamericana, 1997, Manuel de Amat y Junyent y la Navona de Lima: un ejemplo de diseño urbano barroco del siglo XVIII en el virreinato del Perú, 1999, (with Mehdi Setareh) Monticello's Dome: Development of an Integrated Resource for the Study of Thomas Jefferson's Architecture, 2000, Quincha Architecture: The Development of an Antiseismic Structural System in Seventeenth Century Lima, 2003, The Rural Churches of the Jesuit Haciendas in the Southern Peruvian Coast, 2004, The Survival of Gothic Rib Vaulting in the Viceroyalty of Peru, 2006, Rethinking Bamboo Architecture as a Sustainable alternative for Developing Countries: Juvenal Baracco and Velez, 2009; contbg. editor: The Dictionary of Art, 1991-96, Encyclopedia of Twentieth Century Architecture, 1999. Named Ellen Battell Eldridge fellow, 1970-72, Robert C. Bates Jr. fellow Jonathan Edwards Coll., Yale U., 1970-71, Social Sci. Rsch. Coun. fellow, 1972-74, Yale Concilium Internat. Studies fellow, 1972-73, Giles Whiting fellow, 1974-75, NEH fellow Columbia U., 1983, Hobart and William Smith Colls. fellow, 1987, U. Ill. fellow, 1990, Edilia De Montequin fellow, 1991, NEH fellow U. N.Mex., 1992. Mem.: KC, Ctr. Palladian Studies America, Construction Hist. Soc. America, Constrn. His. Soc. Am., Ctr. Palladian Studies in Am., Preservation Resource Ctr. (past bd. dirs.), Inter-Am. Inst. Advanced Studies in Cultural History (bd. dirs. 1998—), Blacksburg Regional Art Assn., Assn. for Preservation Tech., Save Our Cemeteries (past bd.dirs.), Nat. Trust Hist. Preservation, New River Valley Preservation League (bd. dirs. 1987—), Assn. Preservation Va. Antiquities, Coll. Art Assn. Am., S.E. section Soc. Archtl. Historians, Soc. Archtl. Historians (bd. dirs. 1977—80, past pres., past sec. South Gulf chpt.), Internat.Archive of Women in Architecture (treas. 1999—2002), Assn. Latin Am. Art, S.E. Coll. Art Conf., Latin Am. Studies Assn., Phi Beta Delta, Sigma Delta Pi, Tau Sigma Delta. Roman Catholic. Office: Va Poly Inst and State U Coll Architecture & Urban Studies Blacksburg VA 24061-0205 Home Phone: 540-961-1296; Office Phone: 540-231-5324. E-mail: hcami@vt.edu. *As an educator across the years, I have come to realize that the true art of teaching consists of reaching both the human mind and the human heart.*

RODRIGUEZ-CINTRON, WILLIAM, pulmonologist; b. San Juan, Dec. 26, 1959; s. Ramon Rodriguez and Felicita Cintron; m. Lissette Jimenez; children: William Alfonso Rodriguez, Lissette Maria Rodriguez, Roberto Sebastian Rodriguez. MD, U. PR Sch. Medicine, San Juan, 1983. Diplomate Am. Bd. Internal Medicine, 2007, Am. Bd. Sleep Medicine, 2007. Fellow Baylor Coll. Medicine, Houston, 1988—91, pulmonologist, 1991—92. Chief, pulmonary diseases VA San Juan, 1994—2000; chief, pulm ccm VA Caribbean Healthcare Sys., 2001—. Fellow: ACP (gov. 2004—08, evergreen award), Am. Coll. Chest Physicians, Am. Coll. Critical Care Medicine.

RODRIGUEZ-DIAZ, JUAN E., lawyer; b. Ponce, PR, Dec. 27, 1941; s. Juan and Auristela (Diaz-Alvarado) Rodriguez de Jesus; m. Sonia de Hostos-Anca, Aug. 10, 1966; children: Juan Eugenio, Jorge Eduardo, Ingrid Marie Rodriguez. BA, Yale U., 1963; LLB, Harvard U., 1966; LLM in Taxation, NYU, 1969. Bar: N.Y. 1968, P.R. 1970. Assoc. Baker & McKenzie, NYC, 1966-68, McConnell, Valdes, San Juan, P.R.; undersec. Dept. Treasury P.R., 1971-73; mem. Sweeting, Pons, Gonzalez & Rodriguez, 1973-81; pvt. practice San Juan, 1981-94, Totti & Rodriguez-Diaz, 1994—. Bd. dirs. Triple S Vida, Inc., Industrias Vassallo, Inc., Luis Ayala Colon Sucres., Inc., Triple S Salud Inc., Triple S Mgmt., Inc., PR Govt. Devel. Bank. Bd. govs. Aqueduct and Sewer Authority P.R., 1979-84; mem. adv. com. collective bargaining negotiation of P.R. elec. Power Authority to Gov. P.R., 1977-78; bd. govs. P.R. coun. Boy Scouts America, mem. transition com., 1984-85, 2008-09; mem. adminstrv. coun. Ballajá, 1993-00. Mem. N.Y. State Bar Assn., P.R. Bar Assn., AFDA Club, Berwind Country Club, Palmas de Mar Country Club. Office: Ste 1200 416 Ave Ponce De Leon Hato Rey San Juan PR 00918-3418 Office Phone: 787-753-7910. Business E-Mail: JERD@TRDLAW.com.

RODRIGUEZ-TORRES, JOSE GERMAN, retired veterinarian; b. Caracas, Distrito Federal, Venezuela, July 27, 1940; m. Margarita Hilda Soto Schmal, Oct. 17, 1986. Cert. veterinarian Ctrl. U. Venezuela, Aragua, 1965, diplomate animal health planning Pan Am. Health Orgn., 1971. Dir. Pan Am. Foot & Mouth Ctr. Paho, Rio de Janeiro, 1998—2000, chief tech. coop., 1963—97; rural veterinarian Ministry Agr., Temblador, Monagas, Venezuela, 1965—71, dir. quarantine sta. Cardon, Falcon, Venezuela, 1966—72, chief animal def. svc. Caracas, Distrito Federal, Venezuela, 1970—73; advisor animal health planning Zoonoses Ctr., Buenos Aires, Capital Federal, 1973—79; vet. advisor

Pan Am. Health Orgn., El Paso, Tex., 1980—83, Mex., Distrito Federal, 1983—85, Kingston, Jamaica, 1986—93, a.i rep. Mex., 2005. Cons. Screw Worm Eradication Program, Tuxtla Gutierrez, Chiapas, Mexico, 2005—06. Com. mem. Utep, Ctr. Life Long Learning, El Paso, Tex., 2001—02. Recipient James Steel Award, Inter Am. Vet. Epidemiology Soc., 2000, USDA, Animal & Plant Health Inspection Svc., 2000, S. Am. Commn. Foot & Mouth Eradication, 2000, Sec. Health Mex. Avocations: jogging, swimming, travel. Home: 3529 Tierra Vergel El Paso TX 79938-4338 Personal E-mail: jgelpaso@gmail.com.

RODRIGUEZ-VELEZ, ROSA EMILIA, prosecutor; Grad., U. Sacred Heart, 1973; M in Criminal Justice, Interamerican U., PR, JD, 1977. Bar: PR 1977. Asst. dist. atty. PR Dept. Justice, 1979—88, asst. US atty. dist. PR, 1988—94; violent crime coord. dist. PR US Atty.'s Office, 1994—2002, exec. asst., 1994—2992, acting chief civil divsn., 1995—97, first asst. US atty., 2002; US atty., PR US Dept. Justice, 2006—. Coord. High Intensity Drug Trafficking Area, 1994—96, chair, 2006. Recipient Dir. Commendation Letter, FBI, 1987. Office: US Attys Office Torre Chardon Ste 1201 350 Carlos Chardon Ave San Juan PR 00918 Office Phone: 787-766-5656. Office Fax: 787-766-6219.*

RODWELL, JOHN DENNIS, biochemist; b. Boston, Oct. 9, 1946; s. William Joseph and Lillian Catherine (Cunningham) R.; m. Ellen M. McCaffrey, Dec. 18, 1971; children: Elizabeth Ann, Sarah Catherine. BA in Chemistry, U. Mass., 1968; MS in Organic Chemistry, Lowell Technol. Inst., 1971; PhD in Biochemistry, UCLA, 1976. Postdoctoral fellow Sch. Medicine U. Pa., Phila., 1976—80; rsch. asst., prof. U. Pa. Sch. Medicine, 1980—81; with Cytogen Corp., Princeton, NJ, 1981—99, v.p. discovery rsch., 1987—88, v.p. R&D, 1989—96, sr. v.p., chief sci. officer, 1996—99; CEO, pres., bd. dirs. eMetagen LLC, Madison, Wis., 2004—06. Adj. asst. prof., then adj. assoc. prof. Sch. Medicine, U. Pa., 1981—; series editor Marcel Dekker, Inc., NYC, 1988—98; treas., bd. dirs. Biotech. Consortium, 1994—98; pres., bd. dirs. AxCell Bioscis. Corp., Newtown, Pa., 1996—2002; pres. Rodwell Consulting, New Hope, Pa., 2003—04. Patentee, antibody conjugates for compound delivery, antibody metal ion complexes; editor: Antibody Mediated Delivery Systems, 1988; co-editor: Covalently Modified Antigens and Antibodies in Diagnosis and Therapy, 1989. Recipient Nat. Rsch. Svc. award NIH, 1978-80, Thomas Alva Edison Patent award, 1993. Mem. AAAS, Am. Assn. Immunologists, Am. Chem. Soc. (assoc. editor 1989-93), N.Y. Acad. Scis., Soc. Nuc. Medicine. Democrat. Achievements include 85 patents worldwide. Avocations: gardening, photography, flying, sports. Office: EMetagen Corp 3591 Anderson St Madison WI 53704 Home: 28 Hillside Ln New Hope PA 18938-1703 Office Phone: 608-310-9531. E-mail: jrodwell@eMetagen.com.

ROE, BONNIE JEAN, lawyer; b. NYC, June 8, 1953; d. Robert A. Roe and Ruth Ann Perkins; m. Paul Harris Freedman, Aug. 15, 1982. AB, Smith Coll., Northampton, Mass., 1975; MA, U. Calif., Berkeley, 1979; JD, NYU, NYC, 1982. Bar: NY 1983, Tenn. 1993, Conn. 2002. Assoc. Fried Frank Harris Shriver & Jacobson, NYC, 1982—91; assoc. then ptnr. Bass Berry & Sims, Nashville, 1992—97; sr. counsel Proskauer & Rose LLP, NYC, 1997—2000; ptnr. Day Berry & Howard LLP, Stamford, Conn., 2000—06, NYC, 2000—06, Davies Ward Phillips & Vineberg LLP, NYC, 2006—. Mem. adv. bd. Soc. Corp. Secs. & Governance Profls., 2003—. Contbr. chapters to books. Mem.: ABA, Assn. Bar City NY. Office: Davies Ward Phillips & Vineberg 625 Madison Ave New York NY 10022

ROE, BYRON PAUL, physics professor; b. St. Louis, Apr. 4, 1934; s. Sam S. and Gertrude Harriet (Claris) R.; m. Alice Susan Krauss, Aug. 27, 1961; children: Kenneth David, Diana Carol. BA, Washington U., St. Louis, 1954; PhD, Cornell U., 1959. Instr. physics U. Mich., Ann Arbor, 1959-61, asst. prof., 1961-64, assoc. prof., 1964-69, prof., 1969—. Guest physicist SSC Lab., 1991. Author: Probability and Statistics in Experimental Physics, 1992, 2d edit., 2001, Particle Physics at the New Millennium, 1996 (Libr. Sci. Book Club selection). CERN vis. scientist Geneva, 1967, 89; Brit. Sci. Rsch. Coun. fellow, Oxford, 1979; recipient inventor's prize CDC Worldtech, Edina, Minn., 1982, 83. Fellow Am. Phys. Soc. Home: 3610 Charter Pl Ann Arbor MI 48105-2825 Office: U Mich Physics Dept 500 E University Ave Ann Arbor MI 48109-1040 E-mail: byronroe@umich.edu.

ROE, CHARLES BARNETT, lawyer; b. Tacoma, June 25, 1932; s. Charles Brown and Gladys Luvena (Harding) Roe; m. Marilyn Marie Quam, July 31, 1954; children: Sharon Lynn Roe De Groot, Jeannine Carole Roe Dellwo. BA, U. Puget Sound, 1953; postgrad. Boalt Hall, U. Calif. Law Sch., Berkeley, 1957—58; JD, U. Wash., 1960. Bar: Wash. 1960, U.S. Dist. Ct. (ea. and we. dists.) Wash. 1960, U.S. Ct. Appeals (9th cir. 1963, U.S. Supreme Ct. 1963, U.S. Ct. Appeals (D.C. cir.) 1964, Oreg. 2007. Asst. atty. gen. depts. natural resources, conservation, water resources and pollution control commn. State of Wash., Olympia, 1960—70, asst. dir. dept. water resources, 1967—69, sr. asst. atty. gen., 1970—90; of counsel Perkins Coie, Olympia, 1991—2008. Chief counsel Dept. Ecology, 1970—85, Nuclear Waste Bd., 1983—90; counsel natural resources com. Wash. Ho. of Reps., Olympia, 1970; supr. sea grant trainees U. Wash. Law Sch., 1970—72; adj. prof. Gonzaga U. Sch. Law, Spokane, 1973—76, U. Puget Sound Law Sch., 1985—90; contr. Nat. Water Commn., Washington, 1970—71; environ. aide Gov. Daniel J. Evans, 1969—77. Spl. asst. atty gen. State of Mont, Helena, 1983; rep. Western States Water Coun., Salt Lake City, 1970—90; sec. Olympia Audubon Soc., 1962—63; chmn. bd. mgrs. United Chs., 1967—68. 1st lt. USAF, 1954—57. Mem.: SAR, ABA (chmn. water resources com. natural resources sect. 1981—83), Wash. Cts. Hist. Soc. (bd. dirs. 1998—), Wash. State Bar Assn. (chmn. environ. law sect. 1971—72), Rotary, Am. Legion, Masons, Phi Delta Phi, Kappa Sigma. United Ch. Of Christ. Home: 2400 Wedgewood Dr SE Olympia WA 98501-3841

ROE, JAMIE A., legislative staff member; Chief of staff to congresswoman Candice Miller US House of Reps., Washington, 2003—. Republican. Mailing: US House Reps 228 Cannon House Office Bldg Washington DC 20515 Office Phone: 202-225-2106. Office Fax: 202-225-1169. Business E-Mail: jamie.roe@mail.house.gov.*

ROE, KATHRYN JANE, elementary school educator; b. Indpls., July 25, 1958; d. Max Richard and Marthana Jane Kidwell; m. Patrick Allen Dawson, June 14, 1980 (div. Jan. 15, 1996); 1 child, Gregory Scott Dawson; m. William R. Roe, Jr., July 24, 2006. BS, Ball State U., 1987, MA in Edn., 1992. Cert. tchr. NC. Aide Blue River Valley Schs., Mt. Summit, Ind., 1987—88; grad. asst. Ball State U., Muncie, Ind., 1988—92, adj. faculty, 1992—97; tchr. Muncie Cmty. Schools, 1997—2005, Cumberland County Schs., Fayetteville, NC, 2005—. Article reviewer Ind. Reading Quar., Muncie, 1994—97; presenter in field. Author: (textbook) Academic Survival Skills: Batteries Not Included. Active lit. walk-a-thon Cumberland County Schs., Fayetteville, NC, 2005—07; active Habitat for Humanity, Ball State U., Muncie, 1994—96; mem. walk-a-thon Longfellow Student Coun., Muncie, 2002—03; mem. neighborhood clean-up Whitely Assn., Muncie, 2004. Named Longfellow Tchr. of Yr., Muncie Cmty. Schools, 2003, Tchr. Vol. of Yr., Longfellow PTA, 2003, Student Body Tchr. of Yr., Longfellow Student Coun., 2003; named one of Outstanding Am. Tchrs., 2006; grantee, Florence Rogers Charitable Trust, 2005, Armed Services Sci. Tchg. award, 2005, 2006, Buddy Project, 2003—04, Arts Coun., 2006, 2007; Buddy grantee, Buddy Writing Project, 1999—2005. Mem.: Internat. Reading Assn. (assoc.). Independent. Pentecostal. Avocations: travel, reading, writing, choral singing. Office: Cumberland County Schs 3876 Sunnyside School Rd Fayetteville NC Home: 7141 Canary Dr Fayetteville NC 28314 Office Fax: 910.483.5711. Personal E-mail: kidiewell@yahoo.com, kathy@roesolutions.com. Business E-Mail: kathrynroe@ccs.k12.nc.us.

ROE, LESA B., federal agency administrator; b. 1963; m. Ralph Roe. B. in elec. engring., U. Fla., Gainesville; M. in elec. engring., U. Ctrl. Fla., Orlando. Satellite comm. analyst Hughes Space & Comm., El Segundo, Calif.; with NASA, 1987—, comm. engr. Space Shuttle Engring. Directorate Kennedy Space Ctr., Fla., 1987, payloads office mgr. Internat. Space Sta. (ISS) Program Office, Johnson Space Ctr. Houston; assoc. dir. bus. mgmt. Langley Rsch. Ctr., NASA, Hampton, Va., 2003—04, dep. dir., 2004—05, dir., 2005—. Office: Bldg 1219 Rm 213 Mail Stop 106 Hampton VA 23681-2199 also: Langley Rsch Ctr 100 NASA Rd Hampton VA 23681 Office Phone: 757-864-4111. E-mail: lesa.b.roe@nasa.gov.

ROE, MARY ANN, retired postmaster; b. Greenwich, Conn., Jan. 10, 1945; d. Frederick Johnston and Doris Irene Capp; m. Robert Andrew Roe, June 17, 1966; children: Jeffrey Brian, Jennifer Yvonne. Student, S.W. Mo. State U., 1969, N.E. Mo. State U., 1970. Clk. U.S. Postal Svc., Brookfield, Mo., 1977-82, supt. postal ops., 1983-93, postmaster, 1993—2007; ret., 2007. Author: Roe's Reference, 1987; contbr. articles to mags. Sec.-treas. Busy Women's Club, Brookfield, 1990—; asst. leader Girl Scouts U.S.A., Brookfield, 1990-99. Recipient Best Column award Show Me Postmaster, 1997. Mem. Nat. Assn. Postmasters U.S. (instr. conv. 1996, 97, 2001,& 2002. Mo. Career Devel. com. 1996-98, state editor 1999-2002). Methodist. Avocations: reading, sewing, travel.

ROE, PHIL (DAVID PHILLIP ROE), United States Representative from Tennessee, former vice-mayor; b. Clarksville, Tenn., July 21, 1945; m. Pam Roe; children: David, Whitney, John. BS in Biology, Austin-Peay State U., 1967; MD in Ob-Gyn., U. Tenn., Memphis, 1973. Obstetrician, gynecologist State of Franklin Health Care, 1974—2008; chmn. of bd. and med. staff Johnson City Splty. Hosp.; planning commr. Johnson City, 1997—2003; commr. Johnson City, 2003—05; vice-mayor, 2005—07; mem. US Congress from 1st Tenn. Dist., 2009—. Past pres. Tri-County Med. Soc.; del. Tenn. Med. Assn. Mem. East Tenn. U. Found. Bd., 2006—; pres. Austin-Peay State U. Found. Bd., 2008, Austin-Peay State U. Nat. Alumni; mem. Munsey United Meth. Ch. Maj. US Army Med. Corps, 1974. Recipient King Pharm. Health Care Hero award, award for Excellence in Philanthropy, Tenn. Bd. Regents. Republican. Methodist. Office: US Congress 419 Cannon House Office Bldg Washington DC 20515-4201 also: Dist Office 1609 College Park Dr Ste 4 Morristown TN 37813 Office Phone: 202-225-6356, 423-317-7459. Office Fax: 202-225-5714, 423-317-7562.*

ROE, SHARON LOUISE, architect, educator; b. St. Cloud, Minn., Oct. 28, 1945; d. Richard Harbaugh and Eunice Johnson Roe; children: Christopher Chilgren, Sarah Chilgren Piard, Susan Duffy. BA, Coll. Liberal Arts, U. Minn., Mpls., 1969; BArch, Inst. Tech., U. Minn., 1982; MArch, U. Calif., Berkeley, 1992. Registered arch., State of Minn., 1984. Asst. prof. Miss. State U., Starkville, 1992—93, NC State U., Raleigh, 1993—98; adj. asst. prof. U. Minn., Sch. Architecture, 1998—2002, Cass Gilbert vis. scholar, 1998, sr. lectr., 2002—. Co-author (with Lance LaVine and Mary Fagerson): (book) Five Degrees of Conservation: A Graphic Analysis of Energy Alternatives for a Northern Climate; author: Las Vegas: Genuinely Inauthentic. Recipient Ralph Rapson Tchg. award, Coll. Architecture and Landscape Architecture, U. Minn., 2006. Mem.: AIA. Office: Univ Minn 89 Church St SE Minneapolis MN 55455 Office Fax: 612-624-5743. Business E-Mail: roexx007@umn.edu.

ROE, THOMAS COOMBE, former utility company executive; b. Dover, Del., Sept. 22, 1914; s. John Moore and Elizabeth Lindale (Cooper) R.; m. Emma Lillian Scotton, Oct. 16, 1937 (dec.); children: Thomas C., Margaret Ruth (dec.); m. Carolyn Scotton, May 4, 2002. BS in Elec. Engring, U. Del., Newark, 1935; DHL (hon.), Wesley Coll., Dover, Del., 1987. With Eastern Shore Public Service, 1936-43; with Delmarva Power & Light Co., 1943—; pres. subs. Delmara Power & Light Co., 1971-76, chmn. bd., 1976-79, dir., 1971-80, ret., 1980. Hon. trustee Peninsula Regional Med. Ctr., Salisbury, Md.; hon. trustee, former chmn. Wesley Coll., Dover, Del.; former trustee Wesley Theol. Sem., Washington. Served with AUS, 1941-45. Mem.: Rotary (past pres.). Republican. Methodist.

ROE, THOMAS LEROY WILLIS, retired pediatrician; b. Bend, Oreg., Sept. 1, 1936; MD, U. Oregon Health Scis. U., Portland, 1961. Diplomate Am. Bd. Pediatrics. Intern U. Calif., San Francisco, 1961-62, resident, 1962-64; physician Sacred Heart Med. Ctr., Eugene, Oreg.; pvt. practice Peace Health Med. Group, Eugene, 1969—2006; clin prof. pediatrics U. Oreg., Portland, 1985—2006; ret., 2006. Fellow Am. Acad. Pediatricians; mem. AMA, North Pacific Pediatrics Soc. Office: Peace Health Med Clinic 1162 Willamette St Eugene OR 97401-3568 Office Phone: 541-687-6061. Business E-Mail: troe@peacehealth.org.

ROEBUCK, JUDITH LYNN, retired secondary school educator; b. Huntington, W.Va., Jan. 1, 1946; d. Russell Vance and Janice Lee (Adams) Dickey; m. William Benjamine Roebuck Jr., Mar. 28, 1970; children: Lisa, Paul. AB, Marshall U., 1968; MA, W.Va. U., 1973; postgrad., Marshall U., 1973—, W.Va. U., 1973—. Cert. tchr., adminstr., W.Va. Tchr. art, English Vinson High Sch., Huntington, 1967-68; tchr. art Wayne (W.Va.) and Crockett Elem. Sch., 1968-69; tchr. art, speech Ona (W.Va.) Jr. High/Mid. Sch., 1969-91; tchr. speech, debate Huntington H.S., 1991-92; tchr. art Barboursville (W.Va.) H.S., 1992-94, Cabell Midland H.S., Ona, W.Va., 1994—96, ret., 1996; chair related arts team Ona Mid. Sch., 1988-91, sch. improvement team, 1990-91; ret., 1996. Adv. bd. Teen Inst., Huntington, 1990—, W.Va. Teen Inst., 1995, leader, 1990—; mem. drama and debate program, Huntington, 1991-92, Invitationalism Coun., Huntington, 1990—, Cabell County Curriculum Coun., Huntington, 1991-92, Cabell County Reading Coun., 1991-92, Cabell County Tchrs. Acad., Tchr. Expectancy Student Achievement, W.Va. Health Schs. Program, 1998; mediator, trainer Helping Improve Peace, 1994; mentor, tchr. Impact. Contbr. articles to profl. jours. Counselor, Coll. Scouts Program, 1994—; vol. nat. disaster ARC, 1996—, human rels. liaison officer, 1996—; mem. citizen's emergency response team Homeland Security, 2004-, skywatch team Nat. Weather Bur., 2004; mem. Nat. Critical Incident Stresss Mgmt. Team., 2000—. Mem. NEA, DAR (sec. 1988—), Nat. Art Edn. Assn. (curriculum coun., art chair 1993-96, county del. 1994), W.Va. Edn. Assn., Cabell Edn. Assn. (membership chair 1989-91), Horizons, Phi Delta Kappa (pres. 1998—). Avocations: crafts, sewing, reading, diet and health, walking. E-mail: mickeyjmouse@verizon.net.

ROECKNER, MICHAEL G., mathematics professor; Habil, Bielefeld U., NRW, Germany, D in Math. Prof. Bielefeld U., 1994—; adj. prof. Purdue U., West Lafayette, Ind., 2006—. Recipient Heinz Maier Leibnitz prize, German Rsch. Found., 1990, Sir Edmund Whittaker Meml. prize, Edinburgh Math. Soc., 1990, Rsch. prize, Max-Planck Soc. & Alexander Von Humboldt Soc., 1992. Mem.: Acad. Scis. & Lit. (Mainz). Office: Bielefeld Univ Math Universitaetsstrasse 25 Bielefeld NRW D-33615 Germany

ROEDDER, WILLIAM CHAPMAN, JR., lawyer; b. St. Louis, June 21, 1946; s. William Chapman and Dorothy (Reifeiss) R.; m. Gwendolyn Arnold, Sept. 13, 1968; children: William Chapman, Barcley Shane. BS, U. Ala., 1968; JD cum laude, Cumberland U., 1972. Bar: Ala. Law clk. to chief justice Ala. Supreme Ct., Montgomery, 1972; ptnr. McDowell Knight Roedder & Sledge, L.L.C., Mobile, Ala., 1997—. Comments editor Cumberland-Samford Law Rev.; contbr. articles to legal publs. Bd. dirs. Def. Rsch. Inst., 1999—2002; mem. Bd. Lawyers for Civil Justice. Named to Best Lawyers in Am. Mem.: ABA (vice chair com. trial tactics, torts and ins. practice 1995—96), Lawyers for Civil Justice (pres. 2006—07, bd. dirs), Def. Rsch. Inst. (bd. dirs. 1999—2002), Ala. Def. Lawyers Assn., Fedn. Def. and Corp. Counsel (chmn. products liability sect. 1990—93, bd. dirs. 1993—2000, regional v.p. 1994—96, exec. com. 1997—, sec.-treas. 1999—2000, pres.-elect 2000—01, pres. 2001—02, chmn. bd. dirs. 2002—03), Mobile County Bar Assn. (sec., chmn. ethics com. 1988—90, grievance com. 1994—96), Ala. State Bar Assn., Order of Barristers, Curia Honoris, Phi Alpha Delta (pres. 1971—72). Home: 211 Levert Ave Mobile AL 36607-3219 Office: McDowell Knight Roedder & Sledge LLC PO Box 350 Mobile AL 36601-0350 E-mail: broedder@mcdowellknight.com.

ROEDER, GLORIA JEAN, civil rights specialist, retired private investigator; b. Des Moines, Dec. 4, 1945; d. Gerald Arthur and Dorothy Jean (Pardekooper) R. BA, Simpson Coll., Indianola, Iowa, 1970; postgrad., Iowa State U., Ames, 1991. Examiner Disability Determination Divsn. State Iowa, Des Moines, 1970—75; owner, pres. Aaron Investigations, Des Moines, 1975-98; pvt. investigator Des Moines; ret., 2001. Cons. All Area Detective Agy., Des Moines, 1965-78. Civil rights specialist Iowa Civil Rights Commn., Des Moines, 1978—2001, local liaison; vol. Luth. Social Svcs., 1988—, eucharistic min., 1996—98. Recipient Achievement award, 2009, Internat. Pres. award, 2009, Ambassador award, World Congress Arts Sci. & Commerce. Mem. Nat. Assn. Human Rights Workers, Nat. Assn. Prevention Child Abuse (bd. dirs. 1988-91), Iowa Assn. Pvt. Investigators (chair constn. com. 1994-95, sec. bd. dirs. 1996). Avocations: poetry, drawing, painting, swimming, reading.

ROEDER, RICHARD KENNETH, business owner, lawyer; b. Phila., Oct. 11, 1948; s. Walter August and Gloria (Miller) R.; 1 child, William Frederick; m. Allison Nunn Roeder, June 12, 1999. AB, Amherst Coll., 1970; JD, U. Calif., Berkeley, 1973, Cambridge U., 1973-74. Assoc. Paul, Hastings, Janofky & Walker, LA, 1974-81, ptnr., 1981-90; founding ptnr. Aurora Capital Group, LA, 1990—2007; ptnr. Vance St. Capital, 2007—. Office: Vance Street Capital Ste 750 11150 Santa Monica Blvd Los Angeles CA 90025 Business E-Mail: rroeder@vancestreetcapital.com.

ROEDER, ROBERT GAYLE, biochemist, molecular biologist, educator; b. Boonville, Ind., June 3, 1942; s. Frederick John and Helene (Bredenkamp) Roeder; m. Suzanne Himsel, July 11, 1964 (div. 1981); children: Kimberly, Michael; m. Cun Jing Hong, June 2, 1990; 1 child, Maxine. BA summa cum laude (Gilbert scholar), Wabash Coll., 1964, DSc (hon.), 1990; MS, U. Ill., 1965; PhD (USPHS fellow), U. Wash., 1969; DSc (hon.), Washington U., 2005. Am. Cancer Soc. fellow dept. embryology Carnegie Instn. Washington, Balt., 1969-71; asst. prof. biol. chemistry Washington U., St. Louis, 1971-75, assoc. prof., 1975-76, prof., 1976-82, prof. genetics, 1978-82, James S. McDonnell prof. biochem. genetics, 1979-82; prof. lab. biochemistry and molecular biology Rockefeller U., NYC, 1982—, Arnold O. and Mabel S. Beckmann prof. molecular biology and biochemistry, 1985—. Cons. USPHS, 1975-79, Am. Cancer Soc., 1983-86. Recipient Dreyfus Tchr.-Scholar award Dreyfus Found., 1976, molecular biology award NAS-U.S. Steel Found., 1986, outstanding investigator award Nat. Cancer Inst., 1986-2002, Dickson prize in medicine, 2001, Albert Lasker award for Basic Med. Rsch., Lasker Found., 2003; co-recipient Lewis S. Rosensteil award for disting. work in basic med. scis. Brandeis U., 1995, Passano award Passano Found., Inc., 1995, Alfred P. Sloan prize GM Cancer Rsch. Found., 1999, Louisa Gross Horowitz award Columbia U., 1999, Gairdner Found. Internat. award, 2000, ASBMB-Merck Award, 2002; grantee NIH, 1972-, NSF, 1975-79, Am. Cancer Soc., 1979-85. Fellow AAAS, Am. Acad. Arts and Scis., Am. Acad. Microbiology, NY Acad. Scis.; mem. NAS, Am. Chem. Soc. (Eli Lilly award 1977), Am. Soc. Biol. Chemists, Am. Soc. Microbiologists, Am. Soc. Immunologists, Am. Diabetes Assn., European Molecular Biology Orgn. (assoc.), Harvey Soc. (pres. 1994), Phi Beta Kappa. Office: Rockefeller U 1230 York Ave New York NY 10065-6399 Office Phone: 212-327-7600. Business E-Mail: roeder@rockefeller.edu.

ROEDERER, JUAN GUALTERIO, retired physics professor; b. Trieste, Italy, Sept. 2, 1929; came to US, 1967, naturalized, 1972; s. Ludwig Alexander and Anna Rafaela (Lohr) R.; m. Beatriz Susana Cougnet, Dec. 20, 1952; children: Ernesto, Irene, Silvia, Mario. PhD, U. Buenos Aires, 1952. Research scientist Max Planck Inst., Gottingen, W.Ger., 1952-55; group leader Argentine Atomic Energy Commn., Buenos Aires, 1953-59; prof. physics U. Buenos Aires, 1959-66, U. Denver, 1967-77, U. Alaska, Fairbanks, 1977-93, prof. emeritus, 1993—, dir. Geophys. Inst., 1977-86, dean Coll. Environ. Scis., 1978-82. Vis. staff Los Alamos Nat. Lab., 1969-81; chmn. US Arctic Research Com., 1987-91; sr. adviser Internat. Ctr. Theoretical Physics, Trieste, Italy, 1998—2002. Author: Dynamics of Geomagnetically Trapped Radiation, 1970, Physics and Psychophysics of Music, 1973, 4th edit., 2008, Mecanica Elemental, 2002, Information and Its Role in Nature, 2005; contbr. articles to profl. jours Nat. Acad. Sci. NASA sr. rsch. fellow, 1964—66. Fellow AAAS, Am. Geophys. Union (Edward A. Flinn III award, 2000); mem. Assn. Argentina de Geodestas y Geofisicos (hon.), Nat. Acad. Sci. Argentina (corr.), Nat. Acad. Sci. Austria (corr.), Third World Acad. Scis. (assoc.), Internat. Assn. Geomagnetism and Aeronomy (hon.), Sci. Com. on Solar-Terrestrial Physics (hon.). Lutheran. Achievements include research in plasma and energetic particles in earth's and Jupiter's magnetosphere, policy issues for Arctic, perception of music, information theory. Office: Univ Alaska Geophys Inst Fairbanks AK 99775-7320 Business E-Mail: jgr@gi.alaska.edu.

ROEDIGER, HENRY L., III, psychology educator; b. Roanoke, Va, July 24, 1947; s. Henry L. Jr. and May Wertz; children: Kurt, Rebecca. BA, Washington & Lee U., 1969; PhD, Yale U., 1973; D Social Svcs. (hon.), Purdue U., 2004. Asst. prof. Purdue U., 1973-76, assoc. prof., 1978-82, prof., 1982-88; Lynette S. Autrey prof. psychology Rice U., 1988-96; J.S. McDonnell Disting. univ. prof. Washington U., St. Louis, 1996—, chmn., 1996—2004, dean acad. planning in Art and Scis., 2004—. Vis. asst. prof. U. Toronto, 1976-78, vis. assoc. prof., 1981-82; spkr. in field. Co-editor: Varieties of Memory and Consciousness, 1989,

Psychology, 1996, The Nature of Remembering:Essays in Honor of Robert G. Crowder, Perspectives on Human Memory and Cognition: Essays in Honor for Fergus I.M. Craik, 2002, Compleat Academic: A Career Guide, 2004, Experimental Psychology: Understanding Psychological Research, 2009, Rsch. Methods in Psychology, 2006, Critical Thinking in Psychology, 2007, Science of Memory, Concepts, 2007; contbr. articles to profl. jour. Rsch. grantee NSF, Purdue U., Nat Inst. Child Health and Human Devel., Nat. Inst. of Aging, Inst. Edn. Sci., J.S. McDonnell Found.; Air Force Office Sci. Rsch.; NSF Rsch. fellow, 1967-69, Yale U. fellow, 1972-73, Guggenheim fellow, 1994-95. Fellow AAAS, APA, Am. Psychol. Soc. (pres. 2003-04), Can. Psychol. Assn., Am. Acad. Arts and Scis., Am. Edn. Res. Assoc.; mem. Midwestern Psychol. Assn. (pres. 1992-93), Soc. Exptl. Psychologists, (chair, 2002-2003), Memory Disorders Rsch. Soc., False Memory Syndrome Found. (scientific adv. bd.), Psychonomic Soc. (chair governing bd. 1989-90), Phi Beta Kappa, Sigma Xi. Avocation: squash. Home: 18 Ridgemoor Dr Clayton MO 63105 Office: Washington U 1 Brookings Dr Saint Louis MO 63130-4899 Office Phone: 314-935-4307.

ROEG, NICOLAS JACK, film director; b. London, Aug. 15, 1928; s. Jack Nicolas and Mabel Getrude (Silk) R.; m. Susan Rennie Stephen, May 12, 1957; children: Joscelin Nicolas, Nicolas Jack, Lucien John, Sholto Jules; m. Theresa Russell, 1985; children: Maximilian Nicolas Sextus, Statten Jack. Student Brit. schs.; LittD honoris causa, Hull U., Eng., 1995; DFA (hon.), CUNY, 2004. Cinematographer films The Caretaker, 1963, Masque of Red Death, 1964, Fahrenheit 451, 1966, A Funny Thing Happened on the Way to the Forum, 1966, Far from the Madding Crowd, 1967, Petulia, 1968; co-dir. film Performance, 1970; dir. films Walkabout, 1970, Don't Look Now, 1973, Glastonbury Fayre, 1973, The Man Who Fell to Earth, 1976, Bad Timing, 1980, Eureka, 1982, Insignificance, 1985, Castaway, 1986, 89, Track 29, 1987, Aria, 1987, The Witches, 1988-89, Cold Heaven, 1990, Heart of Darkness, 1994, Two Deaths, 1994, Hotel Paradise, 1995, Full Body Massage, 1995, Samson & Delilah, 1996, Puffball, 2006; dir. TV films: Sweet Bird of Youth, 1989, Heart of Darkness, 1994; exec. prodr. Without You I'm Nothing, 1989, Young Indy, 1991, The Sound of Claudia Schiffer, 1999-; co-prodr. Rock Concert, 2002; writer (screenplays) Night Train, 2000, Ivanhoe, 2000, History Play, 2004. Decorated comdr. Brit. Empire. Fellow Brit. Film Inst.; mem. Dirs. Guild Am., Dir. Guild Gt. Britain, Acad. Motion Picture Arts and Scis., Assn. Cinematograph, TV and Allied Technicians. Office Phone: 02072578723.

ROEHL, JERRALD J., lawyer; b. Austin, Dec. 6, 1945; s. Roehl Joseph E. and Jeanne Foster (Scott) R.; m. Nancy J. Meyers, Jan. 15, 1977; children: Daniel J., Katherine C., J. Ryan, J. Taylor. BA, U. N.Mex., 1968; JD, Washington and Lee U., 1971. Bar: N.Mex. 1972, U.S. Ct. Appeals (10th cir.) 1972, U.S. Supreme Ct. 1977. Practice of law, Albuquerque, 1972—; pres. Roehl Law Firm P.C. and predecessors, Albuquerque, 1976—. Lectr. to profl. groups; real estate developer, Albuquerque. Bd. advs. ABA Jour. 1981-83; bd. editors Washington and Lee Law Rev., 1970-71. Bd. dirs. Rehab. Ctr. of Albuquerque, 1974-78; mem. assocs. Presbyn. Hosp. Ctr., Albuquerque, 1974-82; incorporator, then treas. exec. com. Ctr. City Coun., 1991-98, law coun. Washington & Lee U. Law Sch., 2002—08. Recipient award of recognition State Bar N.Mex., 1975-77. Mem. ABA (award of achievement Young Lawyers divsn. 1975, coun. econs. of law practice sect. 1978-80, exec. coun. Young Lawyers divsn. 1979-81, fellow divsn. 1984—, coun. tort and ins. practice sect. 1981-83), N.Mex. Bar Assn. (pres. young lawyers sect. 1975-76), Albuquerque Bar Assn. (bd. dirs. 1976-79), N.Mex. Def. Lawyers Assn. (pres. 1983-84), Albuquerque Country Club, Albuquerque Petroleum Club, Sigma Alpha Epsilon, Sigma Delta Chi, Phi Delta Phi. Roman Catholic. Office: 300 Central Ave SW Ste 2500e Albuquerque NM 87102-2320 Office Phone: 505-242-6900.

ROEHM, JULIE ANN, marketing executive; b. Sept. 1970; m. Michael S. Roehm; children: Nicholas, Luke. BS in Civil Engring., Purdue U., Ind., 1993; MBA in Mktg., U. Chgo. Booth Sch. Bus., 1995. Mktg. comm. mgr. Ford Motor Co., Detroit, 1995—2001; dir. mktg. comm. Chrysler, Jeep, Dodge divsns. DaimlerChrysler, Detroit, 2001—04; dir. mktg. Chrysler Group, Detroit, 2004—06; sr. v.p. mktg. comm. Wal-Mart Stores, Inc., Bentonville, Ark., 2006; founder, mktg. cons. Backslash Meta LLC, 2007—. Bd. dirs. BIAP Inc., 2007—; contbr. Fox Bus. News. Recipient Disting. Alumni award, U. Chgo., 2006; named Mktg. All-Star for 2004, Automotive News, Automotive Marketer of Yr., Brandweek, 2004; named one of Top 25 Women of 2004, Working Mothers mag., Top 100 Most Influential Women in Automotive Industry, 2005; named to Advt. Hall of Achievement, Am. Advt. Fedn., 2004, Automotive Hall of Fame, 2005.*

ROEHRIG, C(HARLES) BURNS, internist, consultant; b. Brookline, Mass., Jan. 21, 1923; s. Gilbert Haven and Helen (Burns) R.; m. Patricia Joan Orme, July 22, 1952 (dec. 2002); children: Joan Russell Roehrig Vater, Jennifer Orme Roehrig Munn, Charles Burns, Jr. Student, Amherst Coll., 1941-43, Vanderbilt U., 1943-44; MD, U. Md., 1949; cert. in internal medicine, U. Pa., Phila., 1953. Diplomate Am. Bd. Internal Medicine. Intern Boston City Hosp., 1949-50; resident in internal medicine and diabetes Joslin Clinic, New Eng. Deaconess Hosp., Boston, 1952-54; practice medicine specializing in internal medicine and diabetes Boston, 1954-91; chief of staff, pres. med. adminstrv. bd. New Eng. Deaconess Hosp., Boston, 1972-75; dir., mem. exec. com. Blue Shield of Mass., Inc., Boston, 1977-88; exec. com. Met. Boston Hosp. Coun., 1982-86; physician adv. coun. Mass. Hosp. Assn., Burlington, 1982-86. Editor: Today's Internist, Washington, 1987-99; contbr. articles to profl. jours. Bd. dirs. Camping Svcs. Bd., Greater Boston YMCA, 1966—; mem. physician adv. group Health Care Financing Adminstrn., Washington, 1983-88; mem. adv. panel on physician payment and med. tech. Office of Tech. Assessment, U.S. Congress, Washington, 1984-85; chmn. Federated Coun. for Internal Medicine, Washington, 1985-86; trustee New Eng. Deaconess Hosp. Capt. (flight surgeon) USAF, 1949-52. Master ACP (pres. emeritus); mem. AMA (chmn. coun. on long range planning and devel., Chgo.), New Eng. Diabetes Assn. (pres. 1963-64), Mass. Soc. Internal Medicine (pres. 1971-72), Am. Soc. Internal Medicine (pres. 1984-85), Country Club of Hilton Head, Wellesley (Mass.) Country Club. Republican. Episcopalian. Office: 5 Summer Breeze Ct Hilton Head Island SC 29926-2536 Personal E-mail: burnsroehrigmd@aol.com.

ROEHRS, CHRISTOPHER SCOTT, lawyer; b. King of Prussia, Pa., Oct. 20, 1963; s. Anthony Gair and Jean Affleck Asch. BA, U. BC, 1991, LLB, 1994. Bar: BC 1995, NY 1999. Collections field auditor Revenue Can. Taxation, Vancouver, BC, Canada, 1982—86; assoc. atty. Baker and McKenzie, NYC, 1999—2004; sr. assoc. gen. counsel corp. reporting & comm. Am. Internat. Group, Inc., NYC. Mem.: Travelers Century Club. Avocation: photography. Office: Am Internat Group Inc 80 Pine St 8th Fl New York NY 10005 Office Phone: 212-770-2720. E-mail: csr212@hotmail.com.

ROELANDTS, WILLEM P., data processing executive; b. Jan. 4, 1945; came to U.S., 1982; BEE, Rijks Hogere Technische Sch., Belgium, 1965. Various position including sr. v.p. Hewlett-Packard, 1966—96; CEO, pres. Xilinx Inc., San Jose, 1996—2008, chmn., 2003—. Spkr. in field. Mem.: Fabless Semiconductor Assn. (pres.), Tech. Network (bd. dirs.), Semiconductor Industry Assn. (bd. dirs.). Office: Xilinx Inc 2100 Logic Dr San Jose CA 95124-3400

ROELL, STEPHEN A., manufacturing executive; b. 1949; BS in Acctg., St. Ambrose U., 1971. Cert. Mgmt. Devel., Northeastern U. Acct. Arthur Young & Co., 1971—75; divsn. contr. FMC Corp., 1975—82; mgmt. positions Johnson Controls, Inc., Milw., 1982—91, v.p., CFO, 1991—98, sr. v.p., CFO, 1998—2004, exec. v.p., CFO, 2004—05, exec. v.p., vice chmn., 2005—07, pres., CEO, 2007, chmn., pres., CEO, 2008—. Bd. dirs. Johnson Controls, Inc., 2004—, Covenant Healthcare Sys., Inc., Interstate Battery Svc. America, Inc. Office: Johnson Controls Inc 5757 W Green Bay Ave Milwaukee WI 53201*

ROELLER, HERBERT ALFRED, biology professor; b. Magdeburg, Germany, Aug. 2, 1927; came to U.S., 1962; s. Alfred H. and Elfriede (Wartner) R.; m. Manuela R. Buresch, Dec. 20, 1957. Abiturium, Christian Thomasius Schule, Halle/Saale, 1946; PhD, Georg August U., Goettingen, 1962; MD, U. Muenster, 1955. Project assoc. zoology U. Wis., Madison, 1962-65, asst. prof. pharmacology, 1965-66, rsch. assoc. zoology, 1966-67, assoc. prof. zoology, 1967-68; prof. biology Tex. A&M U., 1968-83, prof. biochemistry and biophysics, 1974-83, dir. Inst. Devel. Biology, 1973-83, Disting. prof., 1977—, Alumni prof., 1980-85. V.p. rsch. Zoecon Corp., Palo Alto, Calif., 1968-72, sci. adv., 1972-85, chief scientist, Zoecon Rsch. Inst., Palo Alto, 1985-88; sci. advisor Syntex Rsch., Palo Alto, 1966-68, European Cmty., 1988—, Affymax Rsch. Inst., Palo Alto, 1989-96; corp. advisor Symyx Techs., Sunnyvale, Calif., 1996—; mem. adv. panel regulatory biology, divsn. biol. and med. scis. NSF, 1969-72; mem. Internat. Centre Insect Physiology and Ecology, Nairobi, Kenya, 1970—, dir. rsch., 1970-75. Mem. editl. bd. Jour. Chem. Ecology, 1974—; Contbr. articles to profl. jours. Recipient Disting. Achievement award for research Tex. A&M U., 1976. Fellow Tex. Acad. Sci.; mem. German Acad. Naturforscher Leopoldina, AAAS, Am. Soc. Zoologists, Entomol. Soc. Am., Am. Soc. Devel. Biology, Sigma Xi.

ROELLIG, DAWN M., research scientist; BA in Biol. Sci., Agnes Scott Coll., Decatur, Ga., 2004; MS in Biology, Ga. So. U., Statesboro, 2006; attending, U. Ga., Athens, 2006—. Grad. rsch. asst. SCWDS, UGA, CVM, Athens, Ga., 2006—. Office: Univ Ga Wildlife Health 589 DW Brooks Dr Athens GA 30602 Business E-Mail: droellig@uga.edu.

ROELLIG, LEONARD OSCAR, physics professor; b. Detroit, May 17, 1927; s. Oscar Otto and Laura K. (Rutz) R.; m. B. Pauline Cowdin, June 20, 1952; children: Thomas Leonard, Mark Douglas, Paul David. AB, U. Mich., 1950, MS, 1956, PhD, 1959. From asst. prof. to prof. physics Wayne State U., Detroit, 1958-78, dean, 1971-72, asso. provost, 1972-76; pres. Central Solar Energy Research Corp., Detroit, 1977; prof. physics CCNY, 1978-96, prof. emeritus, 1996—; vice chancellor acad. affairs CUNY, 1978-83. Vis. prof. Univ. Coll., London, 1968-69, Tata Inst. Fundamental Rsch., Bombay, India, 1973, Paul Scherrer Inst., Villigen, Switzerland, 1991-92; chmn. bd. advisers Midwest Regional Solar Energy Planning Venture, 1977. Co-author: Positron Annihilation, 1967; contbr. articles to profl. jours. Bd. dirs. Luth. Publicity Bur., 1981-91, v.p., 1984-85, pres., 1985-89; v.p. Grosse Pointe (Mich.) Human Rels. Coun., 1969-70. With USN, 1945-46, U.S. Army, 1950-52. Recipient Wayne State U. Fund Research Recognition award, 1963, Probus Club award for acad. achievement, 1968, Probus Club award for acad. leadership, 1977 Mem. Am. Phys. Soc. Home: 4520 Sioux Dr Boulder CO 80303-3733 Office: U Colo Dept Physics Boulder CO 80302 Office Phone: 303-492-8707. Personal E-mail: loroellig@aol.com.

ROELLIG, MARK D., lawyer, insurance company executive; BS in Applied Maths. with highest distinction, U. Mich., 1976; JD, George Washington U., 1979; MBA, U. Washington, 1988. Assoc. Perry & Smity, Seattle, Reed, McClure, Moceri & Thonn, Seattle; litigation and regulator atty. law dept. Pacific Northwest Bell Telephone Co., Seattle, 1983-92, v.p. law and litigation sect. Denver, 1992-95, v.p. law and human resources, asst. sec. corp. sect., 1995, exec. v.p. pub. policy and regulatory law, 1996-97, exec. v.p. pub. policy, human resources, law, gen. counsel, 1997—2000; dir., sec., consultant Bulletin News Network, Inc., 2000—02; v.p., gen. counsel, sec. StorageTek, Louisville, Colo., 2002—05, Fisher Scientific Internat. Inc., Hampton, NH, 2005; exec. v.p., gen. counsel Mass. Mut. Life Ins. Co., Springfield, 2005—. Mem. Beta Gamma Sigma. Office: MassMutual Fin Group 1295 State St Springfield MA 01111-0001*

ROELOFS, LYLE DEAN, academic administrator, physics professor; b. Grand Rapids, Mich., Dec. 19, 1953; s. Harlan Ray and Cynthia Clara (Van Dyke) Roelofs; m. Lauren Beth Mulder, June 14, 1975; children: Christopher Dean, Brian Alexander. BS with honors in Physics and Math., Calvin Coll., 1975; MS in Physics, U. Md., 1978, PhD in Physics, 1980. Instr. Calvin Coll., Grand Rapids, 1977; rsch. asst., instr. U. Md., College Park, 1977-80; rsch. assoc. Brown U., Providence, 1980-82; asst. prof. physics Haverford Coll., Pa., 1982-87, assoc. prof. physics Pa., 1987-93, prof. physics Pa., 1993—2004, assoc. provost Pa., 2001—04; provost and dean faculty, prof. physics Colgate U., NY, 2004—, interim pres. NY, 2009—. Author: Electricity and Magnetism Simulations, 1995, Handbook of Surface Science; contbr. articles to profl. jours. Democrat. Office: Colgate U 13 Oak Drive 301 James B Colgate Hall Hamilton NY 13346 Office Phone: 315-228-7222. E-mail: lroelofs@colgate.edu.*

ROELOFS, WENDELL LEE, biochemistry professor, consultant; b. Orange City, Iowa, July 26, 1938; s. Edward and Edith (Beyers) Roelofs; m. Joanna Roelofs, Jan. 13, 2005; children: Brenda Jo, Caryn Jean, Jeffrey Lee, Kevin Jon. BS, Central Coll., Pella, Iowa, 1960; PhD, Ind. U., 1964; DSc (hon.) (hon.), Central Coll., Pella, Iowa, 1985, Ind. U., 1986, Hobart and William Smith Colls., 1988; DSc (hon.), U. of Lund, Sweden, 1989, Free U. Brussels, 1989. Predoctoral fellow NIH, 1962—64; NIH postdoctoral fellow MIT, 1964; asst. prof. Dept. Entomology Cornell U., Geneva, NY, 1965—69, assoc. prof. Dept. Entomology, 1969—76, prof., 1976—, Liberty Hyde Bailey prof. insect biochemistry, 1978—, chmn. dept., 1991—2007. Contbr. articles to sci. jours. Recipient Alexander von Humboldt award in agr., 1977, Outstanding Alumni award, Central Coll., 1978, Wolf prize for agr., Wolf Found., Israel, 1982, Disting. Alumnus award, Ind. U., 1983, Nat. Medal of Sci., 1983, Disting. Svc. award, USDA, 1986, Silver medal, Internat. Soc. Chem. Ecology, 1990. Fellow: Entomol. Soc. Am. (J. Everett Bussart Meml. award 1973, Founder's Meml. award 1980, Disting. Achievement award Ea. br. 1983), AAAS; mem.: Am. Acad. Arts and Sci., Am. Chem. Soc. (Sterling B. Hendricks award 1994, Spencer award 2001), NAS, Sigma Xi (Outstanding Faculty award 2007). Republican. Presbyterian. Achievements include patents in field. Home: 4 Crescence Dr Geneva NY 14456-1302 Office: Cornell Univ Dept Entomology Barton Lab Geneva NY 14456

ROEMER, ELIZABETH, retired astronomer, educator; b. Calif., 1929; d. Richard Quirin and Elsie Roemer. BA with honors, U. Calif., Berkeley, 1950, PhD (Lick Obs. fellow), 1955. Tchr. adult class Oakland pub. schs., 1950-52; lab technician U. Calif. at Mt. Hamilton, 1954-55; grad. research astronomer U. Calif. at Berkeley, 1955-56; research asso. Yerkes Obs. U. Chgo., 1956; astronomer US Naval Obs., Flagstaff, Ariz., 1957-66; asso. prof. dept. astronomy, also in lunar and planetary lab. U. Ariz., Tucson, 1966-69, prof., 1969-97; prof. emerita, 1997—; astronomer Steward Obs., 1980-97, astronomer emerita, 1997—. Chmn. working group on orbits and ephemerides of comets commn. 20 Internat. Astron. Union, 1964-79, 85-88, v.p. comm. 20, 1979-82, pres., 1982-85, v.p. commn. 6, 1973-76, 85-88, pres., 1976-79, 88-91; adv. panel Office Naval Rsch., Nat. Acad. Scis.-NRC, NASA. Recipient Dorothea Klumpke Roberts prize U. Calif., Berkeley, 1950, Mademoiselle Merit award, 1959; asteroid (1657) named Roemera, 1965; Benjamin Apthorp Gould prize Nat. Acad. Scis., 1971, NASA Spl. award, 1986. Fellow AAAS (council 1966-69, 72-73), Royal Astron. Soc. (London); mem. Am. Astron. Soc. (program vis. profs. astronomy 1960-75, council 1967-70, chmn. div. dynamical astronomy 1974), Astron. Soc. Pacific (publs. com. 1962-73, Comet medal com. 1968-74, Donohoe lectr. 1962), Internat. Astron. Union, Am. Geophys. Union, Brit. Astron. Assn., Phi Beta Kappa, Sigma Xi. Achievements include research in astrometry and astrophysics of comets and minor planets including 79 recoveries of returning periodic comets, visual and spectroscopic binary stars, computation of orbits of comets and minor planets. Office: U Ariz PO Box 210092 Lunar & Planetary Lab Tucson AZ 85721-0092

ROEMER, JAMES ANTHONY, retired university director; b. South Bend, Ind., Jan. 15, 1930; s. William F. and Carmelita (Luther) R.; m. Mary Ann Earle, Jan. 31, 1953; children: Michael, Timothy, Daniel, Patrick, Kathryn. BA, Notre Dame, 1951, JD, 1955. Bar: Ind., 1955. Contracts mgr. Curtis Wright Aircraft, South Bend, 1955-59; subcontracts mgr. Lockheed Aircraft, Sunnyvale, Calif., 1959-69; ptnr. Roemer, Sweeney & Roemer, South Bend, 1969-73; city atty. City of South Bend, 1973-76; univ. atty. Notre Dame, South Bend, 1973-76, dean of students, 1976-84, dir. cmty. rels., 1984—2002, adj. prof. Law Sch., 1975-2002, adj. prof. Bus. Sch., 1983, ret., 2002. Bd. dirs. Neighborhood Study Help, Inc., Holy Cross Assocs., Neighborhood Housing Services, Friends of the Unemployed, Good Will Industries, Dismas, Inc., Shamrock Bus. Assn., Northeast Neighborhood Assn., Internat. Spl. Olympics Adv. Com.; com. mem. United Religious Cmty., Ctr. for the Homeless, Snite Mus.; chmn. United Way, Notre Dame; adv. bd. for founds. administered Wells Fargo Trust; pres. VIP bd. dirs.; v.p. Martin Luther King Found.; co-founder cmty. leaders program; dir. Nat. Youth Sports Program City Kids; former dir. United Negro Coll. Fund, Urban League; bd. mem. South Bend Alzheimers Bd, Mayors Com. for Racial Equality; founder Irish Connection. Recipient Granville Clark award U. Notre Dame, John O'Hara award. Mem. Ind. Bar Assn., South Bend/Mishawaka C. of C. (bd. dirs.). Democrat. Roman Catholic. Home: 430 Lake Dr #111 New Buffalo MI 49117-1088 Business E-Mail: jroemer@nd.edu.

ROEMER, MICHAEL E., insurance company executive; BS in Acctg., St. John's U., 1984. Auditing profl. JP Morgan Chase, sr. v.p. gen. audit dept.; dir. internal audit, sr. v.p. Am. Internat. Group, Inc. (AIG), 2005—. Republican. Office: Am Internat Group Inc 70 Pine St New York NY 10270*

ROEMER, NILS H., history professor; b. Hamburg, Germany, July 3, 1966; children: Jonas, Max. PhD, Columbia U., NYC, 2000. Assoc. prof. U. Tex. Dallas, Richardson, 2006—. Office: Univ Tex Dallas Arts and Humanities JO 31 PO Box 8306 Richardson TX 75083-0688

ROEMER, TIMOTHY JOHN, United States Ambassador to India, former United States Representative from Indiana; b. South Bend, Ind., Oct. 30, 1956; m. Sally Lee Johnston, 1989; children: Patrick, Matthew, Sarah, Grace. BA in Polit. Sci, U. Calif., San Diego, 1979; MA, PhD in Internat. Rels., U. Notre Dame, 1986. Staff asst. to Rep. John Brademas US Congress; def., trade and fgn. policy advisor to Senator Dennis DeConcini US Senate; mem. US Congress from 3rd Ind. dist., 1991—2003; ptnr. Johnston & Associates, Washington, 2003; pres. Ctr. for Nat. Policy, Washington, 2003—09; US amb. to India US Dept. State, New Delhi, 2009—. Adj. prof. Am. U.; commr. The Nat. Commn. on Terrorist Attacks Upon the U.S. (The 9-11 Commn.), 2002—04; bd. dirs. Oshkosh Corp., 2007—09. Democrat. Roman Catholic. Office: US Embassy 9000 New Delhi Pl Washington DC 20521*

ROEMMICH, DALONNES KAY, music educator; b. Bismarck, ND, Sept. 14, 1951; d. Edmund and Verna Roemmich. MusB in Music Composition, Dickinson State U., ND, 1972; MusM, U. ND, Grand Forks, 1987. Nat. registered music tchr., nat. cert. music tchr. 1st-12th grade vocal/instrumental music tchr. Sykeston (N.D.) Pub. Sch., 1972—77; 5th-12th grade instrumental music tchr. Hazen (N.D.) Pub. Schs., 1977—80; K-6th grade gen. music tchr. Carrington (N.D.) Pub. Sch., 1980—99; 5th-12th grade vocal music tchr. Bottineau (N.D.) Pub. Schs., 1999—. Dir. N.D. Gov.'s Choir, 2004—05. Contbr. articles to profl. jours. Piano accompanist Women's Cmty. Choir, 2001—05; clarinet player N.D. Centennial Band, 1989; piano accompanist Bethel Chapel Ch., Carrington, ND, 1972—99, Grace Lutheran Bretheran Ch., 2001—. Recipient Golden Apple award, 2004—05. Mem.: NEA, Soc. Gen. Music (N.D. chmn. 1985), Am. Choral Dirs. Assn., Bottineau (N.D.) Edn. Assn., Music Educators Nat. Conf., Music Educator Assn., N.D. Music Educator Assn. (15 Yr. Career Achievement, 25 Yr. Career Achievement), N.D. Music Edn. Assn. (N.E. bd. mem. 1990—98). Office: Bottineau Pub Schs 301 Brandon St Bottineau ND 58318 Home: 601 W Pine Cir Bottineau ND 58318

ROENICK, JEREMY, retired professional hockey player; b. Boston, Jan. 17, 1970; m. Tracy Roenick; children: Brandi, Brett. Center Chgo. Blackhawks, 1988—96, Phoenix Coyotes, 1996—2001, Pheonix Coyotes, 2006—07, Phila. Flyers, 2001—05, LA Kings, 2005—06, San Jose Sharks, 2007—09; hockey analyst TSN, Canada, 2007. Mem. US Olympic Hockey Team, Nagano, Japan, 1998, Salt Lake City, 2002; player NHL All-Star Game, 1991—94, 1999, 2000, 2002—04. Named NHL Rookie of Yr., Sporting News, 1990. Achievements include being a member of silver medal winning USA Hockey Team, Salt Lake City Olympics, 2002.

ROEPENACK, DWIGHT ELMER, public health service officer; b. Chgo., May 23, 1947; s. Elmer Henry and Hazel Ethel Roepenack; m. Carol Ann Jasica, Oct. 11, 1980. AA, Wilbur Wright Jr. City Coll., Chgo., 1968; BS in Biology, Northland Coll., Ashland, Wis., 1970; postgrad. in Pub. Policy and Adminstrn., Northwestern U., Chgo., 2009. Lic. environ. health specialist 1981, cert. swimming pool operator 1984, lic. environ. health practitioner 1996, cert. scuba diver, lic. amateur radio, cert. emergency preparedness FEMA, 2002, hazardous materials awareness Ill, 2002, emergency repsonse tng. cert. 2004. Quality assurance auditor Wyler Foods, Northbrook, Ill., 1971—72; engr. product supr. NPC Pronto Foods, Inc., Chgo., 1972—75; with Baxter Travenol Lab., 1975—76; dept. head sanitation salerno Megownen Biscuit Co., Niles, Ill., 1976—78; plant sanitarian Revere Sugar Corp.,

Chgo., 1978—82; health dept. inspector Evanston North Shore Health Dept., Ill., 1983—88; health and lic. officer Village Niles, 1988—. Self employed contract sanitarian pest control, 1982—89. Weather spotter Nat. Weather Svc., 1992—; mem. zoning bd. appeals, planning commr. Villiage Morton Grove, Ill., 1993—; water safety instr. ARC, first air instr.; mem. Morton Grove Traffic Safety Commn., Morton Grove, Ill., 1984—92; theatre adv. bd. Loyola U., 1992—93. Mem.: Nat. Orgn. Am. Radio Relay League, Chgo. Art Inst., Chgo. Field Mus., Interlochen Nat. Music Camp, Nat. Environ. Health Assn., Ill. Environ. Health Assn. Independent. Lutheran. Office: Village Niles Cmty Devel 1000 Civic Center Dr Niles IL 60714 Office Phone: 847-588-8045. Business E-Mail: der@vniles.com.

ROESCH, CLARENCE HENRY, banker; b. Egg Harbor City, NJ, Aug. 22, 1925; s. Joseph Aloysius and Bertha (Heumann) R.; m. Helen Regina Owens, Sept. 25, 1954; children: Kathleen Marie, Helena Patricia, Maryanne Cornelia. BBA, Rutgers U., 1949, postgrad., 1961; cert., Am. Inst. Banking, Atlantic City, 1961; grad. Trust Sch., Bucknell U., Lewisburg, Pa., 1971. Cert. internal auditor, data processing auditor. Bookkeeper, teller, head teller, asst. sec., trust officer, auditor Egg Harbor Bank & Trust Co., 1949-61; bank examiner Phila. Fed. Res. Bank, 1962-65; chief auditor Am. Bank & Trust Co. of Pa. (name changed to Meridian Bancorp Inc. 1985), Reading, 1966-88, v.p. audit dept., 1968-88, ret. officer, 1988; parish sec. St. Benedict Ch., Plowville, 1989-99; sr. staff auditor Nat. Penn Bank, Boyertown, 1990-97. Census enumerator, 2000; mem. faculty Berks County chpt. Am. Inst. Banking, 1966-68; instr. bank auditing Bank Adminstrn. Inst., U. Richmond, 1968; pres., past mems. chpt. Am. Banking Inst., Atlantic County, NJ, 1958-59. Budget com. Berks County chpt. United Way, 1967-73; bd. dirs. Berks Reading Coun. Camp Fire, 1966-93, chmn. fin. com., 1973, 75, treas., 1974-84; instr. 55 Alive Program AARP, 1989-93; mem. Garden Spot Village Retirement, New Holland, Pa.; vol. trolley driver Welcome Desk Vol., 2007, 08. Recipient John Johnston award as outstanding banker NJ, 1955; award U.S. Savs. Bond Com., 1961; Luther Halsey Gulick award for vol. services Camp Fire, 1975; John C. Collier award for outstanding bus. and fin. services, 1981, Blue Ribbon award for vol. services Camp Fire, 1984, award for corp. vol. of yr. Meridian Bancorp Inc., 1984, 85, Outstanding Svc. in Fin. Mgmt. award Camp Fire, 1988. Mem. Inst. Internal Auditors (dir. ctrl. Pa. chpt.), Berks County Bankers Assn., Travelers Protective Assn., Berks Reading C. of C., Bank Administration Inst. (past pres., dir. Penn-Jersey chpt.), Spring Lawn Optimist Club (bd. dirs. 1992, Key Mem. award 1992, chmn. fin. and budget com. 1992-94), St. BEnedict Ch. Prime Timers Srs. Home: 433 S Kinzer Ave #212GN New Holland PA 17557

ROESER, ANDY, professional sports team executive; m. Anne Roeser; 2 children. Grad., Mich. State U., East Lansing. Assoc. LA Clippers, 1981—84, exec. v.p., 1986—2007, NBA alt. gov., pres., 2007—. Mem. adv. com. Grad. Prog. Sport Mgmt. Calif. State U., Long Beach; bd. dirs. LA Sports Coun. Pres., CEO LA Clippers Found. Office: LA Clippers 1111 S Figueroa St Ste 1100 Los Angeles CA 90015*

ROESIJADI, GURITNO, toxicology educator; b. Tokyo, Apr. 4, 1948; s. Chizuko (Kitamura) Roesijadi; m. Pamela Jaekel, June 6, 1970; children: Tanya K., Dalen H., Marissa L. BS, U. Wash., 1970; MS, Humboldt State U., 1973; PhD, Tex A&M U., 1976. Rsch. scientist Battelle N.W. Labs., Sequim, Wash., 1976-80, sr. rsch. scientist, 1980-84; assoc. prof. Pa. State U., State College, 1984-86, U. Md., Solomons, 1986-93, prof., 1993—. Vis. prof. U. Zurich, 1996-97; Fogarty sr. internat. fellow NIH, 1996-97. Mem. editl. bd., U.S. editor Marine Environ. Rsch., 1980—, editor, 1986-93; contbr. articles to profl. jours. Mem. AAAS, Soc. Toxicology, Soc. Environ. Toxicological Chemistry, Sigma Xi. Achievements include research on cellular regulation of toxic metals in marine animals. Office: U Md CBL PO Box 38 Solomons MD 20688-0038

ROESKY, HERBERT WALTER, chemistry professor; b. Laukischken, Germany, Nov. 6, 1935; s. Otto and Lina (Hublitz) R.; m. Christel Glemser, July 24, 1964; children: Rainer, Peter. Diploma, U. Göttingen, Fed. Republic Germany, 1961, PhD, 1963; degree (hon.), Nankai U., Tienjin, China, 1990; PhD (hon.), U. Bielefeld, Germany, 1992, U. Brno, Czech Republic, 1994, U. Bucharest, Romania, U. Paul Sabatier, Toulouse, France, U. Toulouse, Columbia U., 2005, U. Brodeaux, 2005. Postdoctoral fellow DuPont Co., Wilmington, Del., 1965-66; docent U. Göttingen, 1968-71, dir. Inst. Inorganic Chemistry, 1980—, prof. inorganic chemistry, 1980—2004, prof. emeritus, 2004—. Vis. prof. Tokyo Inst. Tech., 1987, Kyoto U. Elsevier: Rings, Clusters and Polymers of Main Group and Transition Elements, 1990, Verlagsgesellschaft: Chemische Kabinettstuecke, 1994, Chemical Curiotities, 1996, Chemie en miniature, 1998, Glanzlichter Chemischer Experimentierkunst, 2006, Spectacular Chemical Experiments, 2007, Experiments in Green and Sustainable Chemistry, 2009; contbr. articles to profl. jours. Recipient Dozenten prize Fonds der Chemischen Industrie Frankfurt, 1970, Alfred-Stock-Gedächtnis prize Gesellschaft Deutscher Chemiker, 1990, Grand Prix de la Fondation de la Maison de la Chimie, 1998, ACS Fluorine award, 1999, Wilkinson prize, ACS Inorganic award, 2004, Wittig-Grignard prize, 2005. Fellow Nat. Indian Acad. (hon.), Royal Soc. Chemistry (hon.); mem. Acad. Scis., Akademie der Naturforscher Leopoldina, Austrian Acad. Scis. (corr.), Berlin Brandenburgische Akademie (corr.), Russian Acad. Scis., French Acad. Scis., Third World Acad. Scis., Romanian Acad. (hon.) Achievements include 12 patents in field. Home: Emil-Nolde-Weg 23 37085 Göttingen Germany Office: Inst Anorganische Chemie Tammannstrasse 4 37077 Göttingen Germany E-mail: hroesky@gwdg.de.

ROESLER, ROBERT HARRY, media consultant; b. Hammond, La., Oct. 5, 1927; s. Albert N. and Hilda (Schwartz) R.; m. Cloe Alferez, May 7, 1955; children: Kim, Bob, Toby. Student, Tulane U. Mem. sports staff Times Picayune, New Orleans, 1949-94, sports editor, 1964-80; exec. sports editor Times Picayune and States-Item, 1980-94; sports coord. New Orleans Met. Conv. and Visitors Bur., 1994—99; CEO Roesler Media Cons. Chmn. faculty coun., Student Publs. Bd., U. New Orleans, 1998-2001. Author: Fair Grounds: Big Shots and Long Shots, 1998. Vice-chmn. Navy Recruiting Dist.; mem. assistance coun., New Orleans, 1992-96. With USN, WWII, Korean conflict. Mem. Profl. Football Writers Assn. Am. (pres. 1976-77, PFWA McCAnn Meml. award NFL Hall of Fame, 1997), Nat. Turf Writers Assn., Football Writers Am., Am. Legion, Navy League U.S., New Orleans Press Club (pres. 1959-60, sports writing awards). Home and Office: 982 Robert E Lee Blvd New Orleans LA 70124 Home Phone: 504-304-9266. Personal E-mail: bobroesler@gmail.com.

ROESNER, LARRY AUGUST, civil engineer; b. Denver, Mar. 14, 1941; s. Walter George and Sarah Jane (Merrick) R.; m. Kathleen Ann Fahrenbruch, Dec. 13, 1964; children: David John, Kevin Walter, Nathan August, Melissa Jane. BS in Civil Engring, Valparaiso U., Ind., 1959—63; MS in Civil Engring, Hydrology, Colo. State U., 1963—65; PhD, U. Wash., Seattle, 1969. Registered profl. engr., Calif., Colo., hydrologist. From assoc. engr. to prin. engr. Water Resources Engrs., Inc., Walnut Creek, Calif., 1968-77; from assoc. to v.p. Camp Dresser & McKee Inc., Annandale, Va., 1977-85, sr. v.p., dir. water resources Maitland, Fla., 1985-92, chief tech. officer, 1992-98; dean Camp Dresser & McKee Corp. U., 1998-99; Harold H. Short prof. urban water infrastructure systems Colo. State U., Ft. Collins, 1999—, interim head dept. civil engring., 2000. Guest lectr., cons. urban hydrology and surface water quality; NRC exec. com. Wastewater Mgmt. in Urban Coastal Areas, 1992; chair Engring. Found. Conf. Stormwater Mgmt.-Sustainable Urban Water Resources in the 21st Century, 1997, NRC study panel Oil in the Sea, 2001; urban wet weather adv. Water Environ. Rsch. Found. Contbr. articles to profl. jours. Recipient Water Resource Planning and Mgmt. Divsn. Svc. to the Profession award 1999. Fellow ASCE (life, chmn. 1995 water resources planning and mgmt. divsn. splty. conf., nat. Walter L. Huber civil engring. rsch. prize 1975); mem. NAE (elected mem. 1990), Am. Acad. Water Resource Engrs. (diplomate), Am. Water Resources Assn., Water Environ. Fedn., Tau Beta Pi (eminent engr.). Democrat. Lutheran. Achievements include development of mathematical models for U.S. government agencies including QUAL-II stream quality model for the EPA; an urban stormwater management model, the dynamic hydraulics model SWMMEXTRAN for storm drainage and sewer systems. Home: 5926 Huntington Hills Dr Fort Collins CO 80525-7118 Office: Colo State U Dept Civil Engring Fort Collins CO 80523-1372 Business E-Mail: larry.roesner@colostate.edu. *An environmental engineer is a caretaker in God's garden, the earth. The challenge for the environmental engineer is to maintain a balance between the needs of people and those of nature so that we may both use and enjoy the garden. It is the responsibility of the environmental engineer to leave the garden a little nicer than he found it.*

ROESNER, PETER LOWELL, manufacturing executive; b. Winchester, Ind., July 3, 1937; s. Lowell LeClair and Martha Christine (Overmyer) R.; children: Peter Lowell II, David Brandon, John Franklin. Student, Durham U., Eng., 1957-58; BA, DePauw U., 1959; JD, U. Mich., 1962; MBA, Harvard U., 1964. Bar: Ind. 1962, N.J. 1992. Asst. to pres. Overmyer Corp., Muncie, Ind., 1964-65, corp. sec., 1965-69, pres., 1969-84, also dir.; pres. Clinitemp Inc., Indpls., 1985-88; pres., owner Middletown (N.J.) Interiors Inc., 1993—. Dir. Mchts. Nat. Bank, 1974-84 Trustee Purdue U., 1978. Mem. Ind. Mfrs. Assn. (dir. 1970-82, pres. 1975, chmn. Phoenix Award com. 1974), Glass Packaging Inst. (trustee 1981-84), ABA Episcopalian.

ROETHENMUND, OTTO EMIL, finance company and bank executive; b. Thun, Switzerland, Sept. 1, 1928; came to U.S., 1951, naturalized, 1957; s. Franz and Berta (Dallenbach) R.; m. Ermina Grassi, May 7, 1955; children— Robert, Denise. MA, U. Neuchatel, 1948. Mgmt. trainee Kantonalbank, Bern, 1948-51; exec. trainee J. Henry Schroeder Banking and Trust Corp., NYC, 1951-56; with Deak-Perera Group, NYC, 1956—, vice chmn., group partner, 1962—; v.p., then sr. v.p. Deak & Co. (holding co.), 1962-74, exec. v.p., 1974-80, pres., chief exec. officer, 1980-86; pres., dir. Inter-Nation Capital Mgmt. Corp., 1986—. Lectr. internat. monetary and investment seminars; emeritus trustee Dickinson Coll., Carisle, Pa.; bd. trustees Mercy Coll., Dobbs Ferry, NY. Served to lt. Swiss Army, 1948-51. Decorated knight Mil. Order Sts. Salvador and Brigitta (Sweden). Mem. Explorers Club, Met. Club (N.Y.C.), Westchester Country Club. Home: 2 Shore Rd Rye NY 10580-1031 Office: Inter-Nation Capital Mgmt Corp 230 Park Ave Rm 1536 New York NY 10169-0699 E-mail: oeratincm@aol.com.

ROETHLISBERGER, BEN, professional football player; b. Findlay, Ohio, Mar. 2, 1982; s. Ken and Brenda Roethlisberger (Stepmother). BA, Miami U. of Ohio, 2004. Quarterback Pitts. Steelers, 2004—. Named Offensive Rookie of the Yr., AP, 2004. Achievements include setting the NFL record for wins by a rookie quarterback (15), 2004; holding the highest compeletion percentage by a rookie quarterback (66.1%), 2004; member of Super Bowl Championship winning Pittsburgh Steelers, 2006, 2009. Office: c/o Pittsburgh Steelers 3400 S Water St Pittsburgh PA 15203*

ROFF, J(OHN) HUGH, JR., energy executive; b. Wewoka, Okla., Oct. 27, 1931; s. Hugh and Louise Roff; m. Ann Green, Dec. 23, 1956; children— John, Charles, Andrew, Elizabeth, Jennifer AB, U. Okla., 1954, LL.B., 1955. Bar: Okla., Mo., N.Y. Law clk. to presiding justice U.S. Ct. Appeals (10th cir.), 1958; atty. Southwestern Bell Telephone Co., St. Louis, 1959-63, AT&T, NYC, 1964-68; v.p., gen. atty. Long Lines, NYC, 1969-73, gen. atty., 1973-74; chmn., pres., chief exec. officer United Energy Resources, Houston, 1974-86; chmn. PetroUnited Terminals Inc., Houston, 1986-98, Roff Resources LLC, Houston, 1998—. Past chmn. Cen. Houston Inc.; mem. adv. bd. Ctr. for Strategic and Internat. Studies, Washington; trustee Baylor Coll. Medicine; past chmn. adv. bd. The Salvation Army, Houston; dir., Inasmuch Found., Ethics and Excellence in journalism Found.; 1st lt. U.S. Army, 1955-58. Mem. Order of Coif, Phi Beta Kappa, Beta Theta Pi. Clubs: Houston Country, Coronado, Houstonian. Office: 333 Clay St Ste 4300 Houston TX 77002-4103 Office Phone: 713-655-5310. Business E-Mail: hughroff@roffresources.com.

ROFF, WILLIAM ROBERT, historian, educator, writer; b. Glasgow, Scotland, May 2, 1929; arrived in U.S., 1969; s. Robert Henry William and Isabella (Anderson) R.; m. Susanne Rabbitt, Aug. 2, 1978; children: Sarah, Emily. BA, U. New Zealand, 1957, MA, 1959; PhD, Australian Nat. U., 1965. Lectr. history Monash U., Australia, 1963-66; lectr., sr. lectr. U. Malaya, Malaysia, 1966-69; assoc. prof. Columbia U., NYC, 1969-73, prof., 1973-90, prof. emeritus, 1990—. Vis. prof. Yale U., 1971, L'Ecole des Hautes Etudes en Scis. Sociales, Paris, 1985; vis. fellow Australian Nat. U., 1974; hon. fellow Edinburgh U., Scotland, 1992—2009, hon. prof. fellow Author: The Origins of Malay Nationalism, 1967, Bibliography of Malay and Arabic Periodicals, 1972, (with others) The Emergence of Modern Southeast Asia, 2004; author, editor: Kelantan: Religion, Society and Politics, 1973; editor: Islam and the Political Economy of Meaning, 1987, Studies on Islam and Society in Southeast Asia, 2009 Guggenheim Found. fellow 1973; Rockefeller Found. fellow, 1982. Mem. Royal Asiatic Soc. (life), Assn. for Asian Studies, Asian Studies Assn. Australia, Brit. Soc. for Mid. East Studies, Mid. East Studies Assn. Avocation: parenting. Home: 29 Shore St Cellardyke Fife KY10 3BD Scotland Personal E-mail: william.roff@btinternet.com.

ROGACHEFSKY, ARLENE SANDRA, dermatologist; b. Rochester, NY, June 29, 1970; d. Hymen Rogachefsky and Deanna Rogachefsky Luntz; m. David Black, Oct. 27, 2001; children: Mitchell Harris Black, Ellie Rachel Black. BA with honors, Brown U., Providence, 1992; MD magna cum laude, SUNY, Buffalo, 1996. Diplomate Am. Bd. Dermatology, cert. Am. Coll. Mohs Micrographic Surgery and Cutaneous Oncology. Intern in internal medicine Cleve. Clinic Found., 1996—97, resident in dermatology, 1997—2000; fellow Mohs and cosmetic laser surgery Office of Dr. David Goldberg, Westwood, NJ, 2000—01; assoc. Skin Laser and Surgery Specialists NY and NJ, Hackensack and Westwood, NJ, 2001—03, Affiliated Dermatologists and Dermatol. Surgeons, Morristown, NJ, 2005—. Program dir. procedural dermatology fellowship Affiliated Dermatologists and Dermatol. Surgeons, 2006—. Contbr. articles to profl. jours. Home: 160 Myrtle Ave Millburn NJ 07041 Office: Affiliated Dermatologists and Dermatologic Surgeons 182 S St Ste 1 Morristown NJ 07960 Office Phone: 973-267-0300. E-mail: arogachefsky@hotmail.com.

ROGAL, GARY JEFFREY, cardiologist; b. Newark, Nov. 20, 1952; s. David and Bert Shane Rogal; m. Camille Elizabeth Rogal, Oct. 18, 1981; children: David, Jennifer, Sarah. BA, George Washington U., 1974, MD, 1978. Diplomate Am. Bd. Internal Medicine, Am. Bd. Cardiovasc. Disease. Resident in internal medicine L.I. Jewish-Hillside Med. Ctr., 1978-81; resident in cardiology U. Rochester-Strong Meml. Hosp., 1981-84; asst. prof. medicine Albany Med. Coll., NY, 1984-86; chief cardiology St. Barnabas Med. Ctr., Livingston, NJ, 1998—, dir. cardial rehab.; pvt. practice gen. and invasive cardiology, spl. interest complementary medicine and cardiology, 1986—. Fellow Am. Coll. Cardiology; mem. Am. Heart Assn. (bd. dirs.), Hertiage Affiliation (bd. dirs.), Phi Beta Kappa Avocations: photography, skiing, resistance/aerobic training. Office: Diagnostic and Clin Cardiology PA 769 Northfield Ave West Orange NJ 07052-1198 Office Phone: 973-731-9442. E-mail: grogal@sbhcs.com.

ROGALSKI, LOIS ANN, speech and language pathologist; b. Bklyn. d. Louis J. and Filomena Evelyn (Maro) Giordano; m. Stephen James Rogalski, Jun e 27, 1970; children: Keri Anne, Stefan Louis, Christopher James, Rebecca Blair, Gregory Alexander. BA, Bklyn. Coll., 1968; MA, U. Mass., 1969; PhD., NYU, 1975. Lic. speech and lang. pathologist, N.Y.; cert. Nat. Acad. Sports Medicine; cert Powerhouse Pilates; cert. for yoga, profl. trainer Yogafit, Nat. Acad. Sports Medicine, yoga instr., pilates fitness instr., 2003-, cert. silver sneakers instr., 2005-. Speech, lang. and voice pathologist Rehab. Ctr. of So. Fairfield County, Stamford, Conn., 1969, Sch. Health Program-P.A. 481, Stamford, 1969-72, pvt. practice speech, lang. and voice pathology Scarsdale, NY, 1972—. Cons. Bd. Coop. Ednl. Svcs., 1976-79, Handicapped Program for Preschoolers for Alcott Montessori Sch., Ardsley, N.Y., 1978—; rsch. methodologist Burke Rehab. Ctr., 1977. Mem. profl. adv. bd. Found. for Children with Learning Disabilities, 1978—; bd. dirs. United Way of Scarsdale-Edgemont, 1988-89; instr. religious instr. CCD Immaculate Heart of Mary Ch., Scarsdale, 1991—; bd. dirs. Scarsdale Teen Ctr., Inc., 1998—. Fellow Rehab. Svcs. Adminstrn., 1968-69; N.Y. Med. Coll., 1972-75. Mem. N.Y. Speech & Hearing Assn., Westchester Speech & Hearing Assn., Am. Speech, Hearing & Lang. Assn. (cert. clin. competence), Coun. for Exceptional Children, Assn. on Mental Deficiency, Am. Acad. Pvt. Practice in Speech Pathology & Audiology (bd. dirs., treas. 1983-87, pres. 1987-89), Internat. Assn. Logopedics & Phoniatrics, Sigma Alpha Eta. Avocations: yoga, pilates. Office Phone: 914-723-6721.

ROGAN, BRIAN G., bank executive; b. 1957; BA in Economics, U. Rochester, 1979; MBA, UCLA, 1988. Joined The Bank of NY, 1981, head capital markets, global markets, credit restructuring, securities lending, CEO issuer, treasury & broker-dealer svcs., 2003—07; CEO issuer, treasury and broker-dealer svcs. The Bank of NY Mellon, 2007—08, chief risk officer, mem. exec. com., 2008—. Office: The Bank of NY Mellon One Wall St New York NY 10286

ROGAN, ELEANOR GROENIGER, oncologist, educator; b. Nov. 25, 1942; d. Louis Martin and Esther (Levinson) G.; m. William John Robert Rogan, June 12, 1965 (div. 1970); 1 child, Elizabeth Rebecca. AB, Mt. Holyoke Coll., 1963; PhD, Johns Hopkins U., 1968. Lectr. Goucher Coll., Towson, Md., 1968-69; rsch. assoc. U. Tenn., Knoxville, 1969-73, U. Nebr. Med. Ctr., Omaha, 1973-76, asst. prof., 1976-80, assoc. prof. Eppley Inst., dept. pharm. scis., 1980-90, prof. dept. pharm. scis. and dept. biochem. & molecular biol, 1990—2007, chair, dept. environ. agrl. and occupl. health, 2007—. Contbr. articles to profl. jours. Predoctoral fellow USPHS, Johns Hopkins U., 1965-68; recipient Linus Pauling Functional Medicine award, 2006, UNMC Disting. Scientist award, 2007. Mem. AAAS, Am. Assn. Cancer Rsch., Soc. Toxicology. Democrat. Roman Catholic. Home: 8210 Bowie Dr Omaha NE 68114-1526 Office: U Nebr Med Ctr Eppley Inst 986805 Nebr Med Ctr Omaha NE 68198-6805 Home Phone: 402-397-7342; Office Phone: 402-559-4095. Business E-Mail: egrogan@unmc.edu.

ROGAN, ELIZABETH A., professional society administrator; BA in Acctg., U. of Conn.; exec. bus. program, Wharton Sch., U. of Pa. CPA. Various positons in corp., non-profit and govt.; asst. contr. John F. Kennedy Ctr. for Performing Arts, Washington, 1987—92; various positions, including CFO and COO Optical Soc. of Am., Washington, 1992—2002, exec. dir., 2002—. Former staff mem. Senator Patrick Leahy's Re-election Campaign. Office: OSA 2010 Massachusetts Ave NW Washington DC 20036 Business E-Mail: oed@osa.org.

ROGAN, JOSEPH P., special education educator; b. Peckville, Pa., Feb. 18, 1947; s. Jean and John Rogan; m. Elaine L. Serafini, July 27, 1968; children: David, Lenore. BA, Kutztown U., Pa., 1968; MA, Marywood U., Scranton, Pa., 1974; EdD, Lehigh U., Bethelehem, Pa., 1983. Cert. tchr. Pa. Dept. Edn., 1968, profl. developer Kans. U., 1983. Spl. edn. tchr. Northeastern Intermediate Unit, Scranton, Pa., 1968—79; prof. spl. edn. Misericordia U., Dallas, Pa., 1979—2009. SIM trainer Kans. U., Lawrence, 1983—. Spl. edn. appeals panel mem. Pa. Dept. Edn., Harrisburg, 1983—2008; pres. Pax Christi NEPA, Clarks Summit, Pa., 2005—09; chairperson, mem. Gov.'s Spl. Edn. Adv. Panel, Harrisburg. Mem.: Am. Assn. U. Profs. (pres. 2003—08). Home: 711 Fourth St Eynon PA 18403 Office: Misericordia Univ 301 lake St Dallas PA 18612 Office Fax: 570-675-2441. Business E-Mail: jrogan@misericordia.edu.

ROGAN, MICHAEL P., lawyer; BA, Oberlin Coll., 1970; JD, U. Conn., 1974. Joined Skadden, Arps, Slate, Meagher & Flom LLP, Washington, 1980—, ptnr., 1984—, head, DC corp. mergers and acquisitions, 1994—2009, DC office leader, 1998—2009, global co-head trans. practice, 2009—. Office: Skadden Arps Slate Meagher & Flom LLP 1440 New York Ave NW Washington DC 20005 Office Phone: 202-371-7550. Office Fax: 202-661-8200. Business E-Mail: michael.rogan@skadden.com.

ROGAN, RICHARD A., lawyer; b. LA, Sept. 6, 1950; AB with honors, Hamilton Coll., 1972; JD, U. Calif., 1975. Bar: Calif. 1975. Ptnr. Broad, Schulz, Larson & Hastings, Wineberg, 1978-94, chmn., 1991-93; ptnr. Jeffer, Mangels, Butler & Marmaro, San Francisco, 1994—, mng. ptnr., San Francisco office, 2002—. Editorial assoc. Hastings Law Jour., 1974-75. Trustee Bentley Sch., 1989-92. Mem. ABA (mem. corp., banking, and bus. sect.), Bar Assn. of San Francisco (mem. comml. law and bankruptcy sect.), Calif. Receivers Forum (bd. dirs. Bay Area chpt.), Delta Sigma Rho. Office: Jeffer Mangels Butler Marmaro-JMBM 2 Embarcadero Ctr 5th Fl San Francisco CA 94111-3823 Office Phone: 415-398-8080. E-mail: rrogan@jmbm.com.

ROGANTE, MASSIMO, nuclear scientist, researcher; b. Macerata, Italy, Oct. 2, 1958; s. Dante and Maria (Ninonà) R.; m. Natalija Miltakyte, Sept. 28, 1995; children: Lorenzo, Francesco. Diploma di pianoforte, Conservatoire G. Rossini, 1983; student mech. engring., U. Ancona, Italy, 1984; PhD in Nuclear Engring., U. Bologna, Italy, 1999.

Cert. profl. engr. Gen. mgr. Rogante D&C Shipowners, Civitanova Marche, Italy, 1978—; dir. Rogante Engring. Office, Civitanova Marche, 1996—; rschr. in nuc. engring. U. Bologna, 1999—; rschr. materials sci. U. Ancona, 1994-98. Tech. cons. Tribunal of Macerata, 1998—; expert evaluator European Commn., Brussels, 1999—; non destructive testing expert, 2000—; mem. internat. sci. adv. com. Budapest Neutron Ctr. Contbr. articles to sci. and profl. jours. With Italian Army, 1986-87. Mem. Neutron Scattering Soc. of Am., Swiss Soc. for Neutron Scattering, Can. Inst. for Neutron Scattering, Italian Soc. for Neutron Spectroscopy, World Directory Crystallographers, Acad. Catenati, Acad. Ga. Achievements include research in neutron techniques and their industrial applications; stress-corrosion; materials processing. Office: Rogante Engring Office Contrada San Michele 61 PO Box 189 62012 Civitanova Marche MC Italy Office Phone: 39-0733-775248. Office Fax: 39-0733-1941197. E-mail: engineering@interfree.it.

ROGATZ, PETER, retired physician; b. NYC, Aug. 5, 1926; s. Julian and Sally (Levy) Rogatz; m. Marjorie Plaut, June 10, 1949; children: Peggy Joy, William Peter. BA, Columbia Coll., 1945; MD, Cornell U., 1949; M.P.H., Columbia U., 1956. Cert. Am. Bd. Preventive Medicine 1958. Intern Lenox Hill Hosp., NYC, 1949-50, resident, 1950-51, VA Hosp., Bronx, NY, 1951-52, N.Y. Hosp., NYC, 1952-53; dep. dir. Montefiore Hosp., NYC, 1960-63; dir. L.I. Jewish Med. Center, 1964-68, Univ. Hosp., SUNY, Stony Brook, 1968-71; sr. v.p. Blue Cross/Blue Shield of Greater N.Y., 1971-76; prin., founding ptnr. RMR Health and Hosp. Mgmt. Cons., Inc., Roslyn Heights, NY, 1976-84; v.p. med. affairs Vis. Nurse Service, NY, 1984-91; med. dir. Staff Builders, Inc., 1992-98. Prof. cmty. medicine SUNY, Stony Brook, 1968—94; mem. N.Y.C. Mayor's Commn. on Delivery of Health Svcs., 1967; v.p. Health and Welfare Coun. of Nassau County, 1968—72; bd. dirs. Cmty. Coun. Greater N.Y., 1974—77; mem. Task Force on N.Y.C. Crisis, 1976—81; chmn. bd. dirs. Cmty. Health Program affiliated with L.I. Jewish Med. Ctr., 1989—94; chmn. bd. dirs. Managed Health Inc., 1990—94. Author: Organized Home Medical Care in New York City, 1956; co-author (with Eli Ginzberg): Planning for Better Hospital Care, 1961; mem. editl. bd. Preventive Medicine, 1975—81; contbr. articles to profl. jours. Bd. dirs. Choice in Dying, 1994—2000, Compassion and Choices of N.Y., 1998—. Recipient Dean Conley award, Am. Coll. Hosp. Adminstrs., 1975; fellow, Commonwealth Fund, 1955. Fellow: ACP, Am. Coll. Preventive Medicine, N.Y. Acad. Medicine, APHA; mem.: N.Y. County Med. Soc., N.Y. State Med. Soc., N.Y. Pub. Health Assn., Am. Hosp. Assn., AMA. Home and Office: 299 E Overlook Port Washington NY 11050 Home Phone: 516-767-0189; Office Phone: 516-767-0189. Personal E-mail: rogatz2@aol.com.

ROGEN, SETH, actor; b. Vancouver, Canada, Apr. 15, 1982; s. Mark and Sandy Rogen. Actor: (films) Donnie Darko, 2001, Anchorman: The Legend of Ron Burgundy, 2004, Wake Up, Ron Burgundy: The Lost Movie, 2004, You, Me and Dupree, 2006, (voice) Shrek the Third, 2007, The Spiderwick Chronicles, 2008, Horton Hears a Who!, 2008, Kung Fu Panda, 2008, Zack and Miri Make a Porno, 2008, Fanboys, 2008, (voice) Monsters vs. Aliens, 2009, Observe and Report, 2009, Funny People, 2009, Paper Heart, 2009; actor, co-prodr. (films) The 40 Year Old Virgin, 2005, actor, exec. prodr. Knocked Up, 2006, actor, exec. prodr., writer Superbad, 2007, writer Drillbit Taylor, 2008, writer, actor Pineapple Express, 2008; actor: (TV films) North Hollywood, 2001, Early Bird, 2005; (TV series) Freaks and Geeks, 1999—2000, Undeclared, 2001—02, (appearances) Dawson's Creek, 2003, Help Me Help You; staff writer (TV series) Da Ali G Show. Named one of Top 25 Entertainers of Yr. (with Apatow Gang), Entertainment Weekly, 2007. Office: c/o Principal Entertainment 1964 Westwood Blvd Ste 400 Los Angeles CA 90025*

ROGENESS, MARY SPEER, retired state legislator; b. Kansas City, Kans., May 18, 1941; d. Frederic A. and Jeannette (Hybskmann) Speer; m. Dean Rogeness, Aug. 31, 1964; children: Emily, James, Paul. BA, Carleton Coll., 1963. Computer analyst Dept. Def., Ft. Meade, Md., 1963-66; freelance writer, editor Longmeadow, Mass., 1982-91; mem. Mass. Ho. of Reps., Boston, 1991—2009, asst. minority leader, 2003—09. Editor: Reflections of Longmeadow, 1983. Active Longmeadow Rep. Town Com., 1983—; com. mem. Longmeadow Sch., 1982-88; corp. trustee Trustees of Reservations. Mem. Am. Legis. Exch. Coun., World Affairs Coun. of Western Mass.

ROGERS, ALAN VICTOR, former career officer; b. Hannibal, Mo., Nov. 13, 1942; s. Julian Alan and Gladys Cuneo R.; m. Linda Rae Peterson, May 8, 1966; children: Kimberly Rae, Krista Anne, Peter Alan. BS in Mil. Sci., USAF Acad., 1964; MBA with distinction, Harvard Bus. Sch., 1972; grad. with distinction, Air War Coll., 1980. Commd. 2d lt. USAF, 1964, advanced through grades to maj. gen., 1989, ret., 1993; combat fighter pilot 355th Tactical Fighter Wing, Takhli, Thailand, 1966-67; jet pilot instr. Flying Tng. Wing, Williams AFB, Ariz., 1967-69; student Harvard Bus. Sch., Cambridge, Mass., 1970-72; pers. officer Cols. Group USAF Pentagon, Washington, 1972-75; student Air War Coll., Maxwell AFB, Ariz., 1980; wing comdr. 5th Bomb Wing, Minot AFB, ND, 1982-84, 96th Bomb Wing (1st B-1 Wing), Dyess AFB, Tex., 1984-86; dir. ops. SAC, Offutt AFB, Nebr., 1986-89; asst. chief of staff ops. Supreme HQ Allied Powers Europe NATO, Mons, Belgium, 1989-91; dir. J-7 Joint Staff, Pentagon, Washington, 1991-93; assoc. Burdeshaw Assocs., Ltd., Bethesda, Md., 1993-94; prin. Gemini Consulting, Morristown, NJ, 1994-97; sr. v.p., gen. mgr. Fed. Defense Group, Am. Mgmt. Sys., Inc., Fairfax, Va., 1997—2002; exec. v.p. CACI Internat., 2003—07, AV Rogers Assoc., LLC, 2007—. Mem. Active Angel Investors, Vienna, 2003—; mem. adv. bd. Infodata, Inc., 2003—06; bd. dirs. RGS & Assocs., Inc., 2003—06. Mem., mil. adviser C. of C., Minot, N.D., 1982-84, Abilene, Tex. 1984-86; trustee The Falcon Found., Colorado Springs, 2003—; mem. bd. advisors Our Mil. Kids, 2006-; dir. XeDar Inc. Decorated Defense Disting. Svc. Medal, Legion of Merit, D.F.C. with two oak leaf clusters, Purple Heart, Def. Superior Svc. medal, Disting. Svc. medal, Def. Disting. Svc. medal; recipient Am. U. Leadership award, 2000. Mem.: Nat. Assn. Corp. Dirs., Nat. Def. Industry Assn. (bd. dirs.), Potomac Officers Club, Daedalians (chpt. pres. 1986), Nat. Eagle Scout Assn., Red River Valley Fighter Pilots Assn., Sabre Soc., USAF Acad. Assn. Grads. (bd. dirs. 1999—2007), Air Force Assn. Republican. Lutheran. Avocations: skiing, travel, antiques, Fitness. Home: 4600 32nd Rd N Arlington VA 22207-4406 Office Phone: 703-795-3802. E-mail: alanvrogers@aol.com.

ROGERS, BARBARA J., musician; b. Teaneck, NJ, June 7, 1951; m. Richard D. Weis. MusB with highest distinction, Eastman Sch. Music, 1973; MusM in Piano Accompanying, U. So. Calif., 1974; D Mus. Arts in Piano Performance, U. Cin., 1992. Choir dir. Westminster United Presbyn. Ch., Ontario, Calif., 1980-84; instr., staff accompanist U. La Verne, Calif., 1981-85; grad. tchg. asst. U. Cin. Conservatory Music, 1985-88; pvt. piano tchr. and vocal coach, Ontario, Calif., 1977-85, N.Y., N.J., 1988-99; dir. music The Presbyn. Ch., New Brunswick, N.J., 1994-99, founding dir. summer music day camp, 1996-99. Freelance performer, N.Y. and N.J. met. area, 1988-99, Twin Cities Minn. area, 1999—; dir. music Cmty. Presbyn. Ch. Sand Hills, Kendall Park, N.J., 1988-93; accompanist Cantabile Chamber Chorale, Bound Brook, N.J., 1992-99; piano faculty Northwestern Coll., St. Paul, 2000—; cons. and presenter in field. Co-composer: children;s bibl. music It's Good!, 1993, composer choral anthems Opera Ruth Operas, songs, works for organ, chamber music. Mem. Music Tchrs. Nat. Assn., Internat. Alliance for Women in Music, Choristers Guild, Soc. for Am. Music, Am. Guild Organists, Am. Composers Forum, Minn. Music Tchrs. Assn. Office Phone: 651-631-5485. Business E-Mail: bjrogers@nwc.edu. E-mail: momcatdma@earthlink.net.

ROGERS, BENJAMIN FRANKLIN, retired history professor; b. St. Paul, Minn., Dec. 10, 1917; s. Benjamin Franklin and Ruth De Coster Rogers; m. Peggy Louise Brodrick, Sept. 9, 1972; children: Ruth, Benjamin, Karl, David, Susan, Sara, Clay. AB, Harvard U., 1940, MA, 1941; PhD, U. Minn., 1951. Prof. history Fla. State U., Tallahassee, 1950—60; v.p. Jacksonville U., Fla., 1960—64; dean Coll. Humanities Fla. Atlantic U., Boca Raton, Fla., 1964—66; head Dept. History Parsons Coll., Fairfield, Iowa, 1966—73; prof. history Ottumwa Heights Coll., Iowa, 1973—80, ret., 1980. Lt. USNR, 1942—45. Decorated Air medal Three Stars Presdl. Unit. Mem.: Fla. Hist. Soc. (bd. dirs., mem. editl. bd.), Am. Hist. Assn. Democrat. Episcopalian. Home: PO Box 877 Fairfield IA 52556

ROGERS, BENJAMIN TALBOT, mechanical engineer, consultant; b. Cleve., Oct. 4, 1920; s. Benjamin Talbot and Marie Aline (Miller) Rogers; m. Dale Hays, Sept. 11, 1961 (dec. Nov. 1975); children: Leslie, Phyllis. BSME, U. Wis., 1944. Registered profl. engr., N.Mex, Colo., Ariz., Tex. Mech. engr. Black & Veatch, Kansas City, Mo., 1946-49; staff mem. U. Calif., Los Alamos, N.Mex., 1949-76; cons. engring. Los Alamos, N.Mex., 1949-76, Embudo, N.Mex., 1976-80, 81-2000; ret., 2000. Vis. prof. Ariz. State U., 1980—81, 1984; v.p. Barkmann & Rogers Cons. Engrs., Santa Fe, 1964—70. One-man shows include Millicent Rogers Mus., Taos, N.Mex, 1994, Roller Mill Mus., Cleveland, N.Mex, 1995, Ariz. State U. Coll. Architecture, Tempe, 1996, First State Bank Taos, 1997 (Artist of the Month, 1997), Johnson Gallery, Madrid, N.Mex, 1998—99; contbr. articles to tech. and profl. jours. Commr. Rinconada Cmty. Acequia, Embudo, 1961—70; v.p. adv. bd. Embudo Presbyn. Hosp., 1972; pres. Embudo Valley Health Found., 1974. 1st lt. C.E. US Army, 1942—46. Recipient Solar Design award, HUD, Dept. Energy, Solar Energy Rsch. Inst., 1978, Peter van Dresser award, N.Mex Solar Energy Assn., 1983, Maharishi award, Maharishi Found., 1984; grantee, Graham Found. Advanced Studies Fine Arts, 1992, 1995. Fellow: ASHRAE; mem.: NSPE (life), ASME (life), Nat. Assn. Scholars, Am. Soc. Materials (life), Celtic Confederation (founding sec. 2000—03). Republican. Achievements include patents in field. Home: 9911 S Spring Hill Pl Highlands Ranch CO 80129-4343

ROGERS, BETSY, elementary school educator; b. Birmingham, Ala., Mar. 2, 1952; children: Alan, Rick. BA in Elem. Edn., Samford Univ., 1974, MA, 1998, PhD, 2002. Cert. generalist/early childhood Nat. Bd. Profl. Tchg. Standards, 2000. Tchr. Hewitt Elem. Sch., 1974—76; kindergarten tchr. Leeds First Baptist Church, 1982—85; first grade tchr. Leeds Elem. Sch., Ala., 1985—2004; tchr., curriculum coord. Brighton Sch., Ala., 2004—. Chair Governor's Task Force on Tchr. Quality. Named Nat. Tchr. of Yr., 2003. Mem.: Ala. Conf. of Educators (past pres.).

ROGERS, BRIAN CHARLES, investment company executive; b. Beverly, Mass., June 27, 1955; s. Charles E. and Margaret A. (Sweeney) R.; m. Mary Jo Skayhan, Oct. 7, 1979; children: Hilary, Peter, Sydney. AB, Harvard U., 1977, MBA, 1982. Chartered fin. analyst, investment counselor. Asst. treas. Bankers Trust Co., NYC, 1977-80; portfolio mgr. T. Rowe Price Equity Income Fund, Balt., 1985—; mng. dir. T. Rowe Price Group, Inc., Balt., 1982—2004, chief investment officer, 2004—, chmn., 2007—. Bd. dirs. T. Rowe Price Group, Inc., 1997—. Bd. dirs. Balt. County Econ. Devel. Commn., 1988—, Fund for Ednl. Excellence, Batl. 1988-92. Home: 1708 Ruxton Rd Baltimore MD 21204-3505 Office: T Rowe Price Group, Inc 100 E Pratt St Fl 4 Baltimore MD 21202-1090 Office Phone: 410-547-5758. Office Fax: 410-752-3477.*

ROGERS, BRYAN LEIGH, dean, artist, educator; b. Amarillo, Tex., Jan. 7, 1941; s. Bryan Austin and Virginia Leigh (Bull) R.; m. Cynthia Louise Rice; 1 child, Kyle Austin Rogers. BE, Yale U., 1963; MS, U. Calif., Berkeley, 1966, MA, 1969, PhD, 1971. Design engr. Monsanto Co., Texas City, Tex., 1962; research engr. Rocketdyne, Canoga Park, Calif., 1963-64; research scientist Lawrence Livermore (Calif.) Lab., 1966; lectr. U. Calif., Berkeley, 1972-73; fellow Akademie der Bildenden Künste, Munich, 1974-75; prof. art San Francisco State U., 1975-88; head, prof. sch. art Carnegie Mellon U., Pitts., 1988-99, dir. Studio for Creative Inquiry, 1989-99; dean, prof. Sch. of Art and Design U. Mich., Ann Arbor, 2000—. Fellow Ctr. Advanced Visual Studies MIT, Cambridge, Mass, 1981. Editor Leonardo Jour., San Francisco, 1982-85. One-man shows include: Laguna Beach (Calif.) Mus. Art, 1974, DeSaisset Art Gallery U. Santa Clara, Calif., 1974, San Francisco Mus. Modern Art, 1974, Baxter Art Gallery Calif. Inst. Tech., Pasadena, 1979, Contemporary Crafts gallery, Portland, Oreg., 1987; group exhbns. include: Berkeley (Calif.) Art Ctr., 1969, Hansen-Fuller Gallery, San Francisco, 1970, San Francisco Arts Commn. Gallery, 1984, Clocktower Gallery, N.Y.C., 1984, Otis-Parsons Gallery, L.A., 1985, P.P.O.W. Gallery, N.Y.C., 1985, 18th Internat. Bienal, São Paulo, Brazil, 1985, MIT, Cambridge, 1990, Objects Gallery, Chgo., 1992, ARTEC 93 Internat Biennale, Nagoya, Japan, 1993, Chgo. Cultural Ctr., 1993, Am. Iron and Steel Expo., Pitts., 1993, Pitts. Ctr. for Arts, 1994, Allegheny Coll. Gallery, Meadville, Pa., 1997, Aichi Art Ctr., Nagoya, Japan, 1997. Fellow NEA, Washington, 1981, 82, Deutscher Akademischer Austauschdienst, Fed. Republic of Germany, 1974, NSF, Washington, 1965-69; recipient SECA award San Francisco Mus. Modern Art, 1974. Office: Sch Art & Design Univ Michigan Ann Arbor MI 48109 Office Phone: 734-763-4093. Business E-Mail: blrogers@umich.edu.

ROGERS, C. B., lawyer; b. Birmingham, Ala., July 10, 1930; s. Claude B. Rogers and Doris (Hinkley) Rogers Lockerman; m. Patricia Maxwell DeVoe, Dec. 22, 1962; children: Bruce Lockerman, Evelyn Best, Brian DeVoe. AB, Emory U., 1951, LL.B., 1953. Bar: Ga. 1953. Adj. prof. litigation Emory U., 1968-70; assoc., then partner firm Powell, Goldstein, Frazer & Murphy, 1954-76; founding partner Rogers & Hardin, Atlanta, 1976—. Recipient A. Sherman Christensen award, Am. Inns of Ct., 2005. Fellow Am. Coll. Trial Lawyers; mem. Am. Law Inst., Atlanta Bar Assn., State Bar Ga., Capital City Club (Atlanta). Democrat. Episcopalian. Home: 1829 W Wesley Rd NW Atlanta GA 30327-2019 Office: Rogers & Hardin 2700 International Tower 229 Peachtree St NE Atlanta GA 30303-1638 Office Phone: 404-520-4606. Office Fax: 404-525-2224. E-mail: cbr@rh-law.com.

ROGERS, CARLETON CARSON, JR., trade show and convention executive; b. Chgo., Nov. 5, 1935; s. Carleton Carson and Eleanor (Lowell) Rogers; m. Loretta Zirkel; children: Kirsten Ann, Mark, Brett. BS in Bus. Adminstrn., Am. U., 1957; postgrad., Northwestern U., 1957, Chgo.-Kent Coll. Law, 1957—58. Mgmt. trainee Ill. Bell Telephone Co., Chgo., 1959-61; sales mgr. Programs Internat., Chgo., 1961-64, pres., 1964-71; show mgr. Indsl. & Sci. Conf. Mgmt., Chgo., 1975-78; pres. Expo Mgmt., Inc., Chgo., 1978-82, Trade Expositions and Assoc. Mgmt. Ltd., Chgo., 1982-92, Expn. Mmgt., Inc., Elgin, 1992-99, National Show Mgmt., Inc., Elgin, 1999—. Adj. prof. Roosevelt U., Chgo. Pres. Kane County, Ill., Young Republican Club, 1962-64; trustee Gail Borden Pub. Libr., Elgin; bd. dirs. Area C Coun. on Aging for Ill., Upper Kane County chpt. Am. Heart Assn., Chgo. Conv. and Tourism Bur.; mem. adminstrv. bd., pres. bd. trustees First United Meth. Ch., Elgin.; sec.-treas. found. pres. Ctr. for Exhbn. Industry Rsch. Mem. Internat. Assn. Exhibit Mgmt. (chmn. bd., recipient Disting. Svc. award), Masons, Shriners, Omicron Delta Kappa, Alpha Tau Omega. Home: 11n937 Almora Ter Elgin IL 60124-4705 Office: Nat Show Mgmt Inc PO Box 6282 Elgin IL 60121-6282 Office Phone: 847-695-5330. Personal E-mail: expomgmt@juno.com.

ROGERS, CARMEN VILLEGAS, language educator; d. Jesús Villegas and Leonor Narváez; m. Elia V. Eschenazi, Sept. 10, 1989; 1 child, David Eschenazi. EdD, U. Ga., Athens, 1984. Asst. prof. langs. U. Tenn., Knoxville, 1984—89; asst. prof. French La. State U., Baton Rouge, 1989—93; assoc. prof. langs. Xavier U. La., New Orleans, 1994—2006, Chestnut Hill Coll., Phila., 2007—. Contbr. articles to profl. jour. Scholarship, French Govt., 1972. Office: Chestnut Hill Coll 9601 Germantown Ave Philadelphia PA 19118 Business E-Mail: rogersc@chc.edu.

ROGERS, CARTON (H. CARTON ROGERS III), library director; BA in History, Marietta Coll., Ohio, 1970; MLS, Drexel U., 1973. Joined libraries staff U. Pa., Phila., 1975; head reference & tech. services Biomedical Libr., 1975—79; sr. bus. officer U. Libr., 1979—85; Patricia and Bernard Goldstein Dir. Info. Processing U. Pa. Libraries, 1985—2003, acting dir. collections devel. & mgmt., 2003; interim vice provost & dir. libraries U. Pa., 2003—04, vice provost & dir. libraries, 2004—. Office: Van Pelt-Dietrich Libr Ctr 3420 Walnut St Philadelphia PA 19104-6206 Office Phone: 215-898-7091. Office Fax: 215-898-0559. Business E-Mail: rogers@pobox.upenn.edu.

ROGERS, CHARLES EDWIN, physical chemistry and polymer science professor; b. Rochester, NY, Dec. 29, 1929; s. Charles Harold and Maybelle (Johnson) R.; m. Barbara June Depuy, June 12, 1954; children: Gregory Newton, Linda Frances, Diana Suzanne. BS in Chemistry, Syracuse U., 1954; PhD in Phys. Chemistry, SUNY at Syracuse U., 1957. Rsch. assoc. dept. chemistry Princeton U., 1957-59, Goodyear fellow, 1957-59; mem. tech. staff Bell Telephone Labs., Murray Hill, NJ, 1959-65; assoc. prof. macromolecular sci. Case Western Res. U., Cleve., 1965-74, prof., 1974-98, prof. emeritus, 1998—. Sr. vis. fellow Imperial Coll., U. London, 1971; assoc. dir. Ctr. for Adhesives Sealants Coatings, Case Western Res. U., 1984-88, dir., 1988-91; co-dir. Edison Polymer Innovation Corp., Ctr. for Adhesives, Sealants and Coatings, 1991-97; cons. to polymer and chem. industries; devel. overseas ednl. instns. Editor: Permselective Membranes, 1971, Structure and Properties of Block Copolymers, 1977; contbr. numerous articles to profl. jours.; patentee in field. Staff sgt. 82nd airborne divsn. US Army, 1946—49, staff sgt. USAR, 1949—53, commd. officer USAR, 1953—63. Mem.: Am. Phys. Soc., Am. Chem. Soc. Home: 8400 Rockspring Dr Chagrin Falls OH 44023-4645 Office: Case Western Reserve U Dept Macromolecular Sc Cleveland OH 44106-7202 Office Phone: 216-368-6376. Business E-Mail: cer@case.edu.

ROGERS, CHASE THEODORA, state supreme court chief justice; b. Conn., Nov. 12, 1956; BA, Stanford U., 1979; JD, Boston U. Sch. Law, 1983. Atty. Cummings & Lockwood, ptnr., 1991—98; judge Conn. Superior Ct., 1998—2006, presiding judge, juvenile matters Bridgeport, judge, regional child protection session Middletown, judge, complex litig. docket Stamford, 2001—05, presiding judge, civil matters, Stamford-Norwalk dist., 2005—06; judge Conn. Appellate Ct., 2006—07; chief justice Conn. Supreme Ct., 2007—. Office: Conn Supreme Ct 231 Capitol Ave Hartford CT 06106*

ROGERS, DALE CRAIG, finance company executive; b. Wichita Falls, TX, Jan. 21, 1945; s. Moral W. and Opal Davlin Rogers; m. Judy Carole Coburn, Sept. 11, 1965; children: Lori Alyssa Rogers-Williams, Craig Coburn. Cert. pension cons. Am. Soc. Pension Cons. & Actuaries Wash., DC, 1989. Ins. & securities agt. Penn Mut. Life Ins. Co., Wichita Falls, Tex., 1966—68; divsn. mgr. Jefferson-Pilot Equity Co., Fort Worth, Tex., 1968—73; chmn., CEO Rogers Co., Fort Worth, 1973—, Rogers & Associates- Pension Cons., Fort Worth, 1973—, Rogers Capital Mgmt., Inc., Fort Worth, 1990—. Author: The First Time Investor, How to Build, Protect & Maintain Your 401(k) Plan. Pres., bd. trustees Keller Ind. Sch. Dist., Tex., 1983—89; bd. dirs. Keller Youth Assn., 1980—88. Mem.: Am. Soc. Pension Actuaries & Cons. (licentiate). Republican. Baptist. Avocations: travel, boating. Home: 6905 Old Homestead Rd Fort Worth TX 76132 Office: Rogers Co 1330 Summit Ave Fort Worth TX 76102 Business E-Mail: dcrogers@rogersco.com.

ROGERS, DAVID, playwright, actor; b. NYC; s. George and Deborah (Samuels) Rosenberg; m. June Lois Walker, Oct. 14, 1962; children: Dulcy Dru, Amanda Brooke. Student, Am. Theatre Wing Sch., 1948-49. Author (N.Y.C. prodns.): Ziegfeld Follies, 1957, Vintage '60, 1960, New Faces of 1962, Fun City, 1967, Charlie and Algernon, 1980 (Tony award nomination); author: (London prodns.) Jubilee Girl, 1956, Young at Heart, 1961, Flowers for Algernon, 1979, Killing Jessica, 1986; pub. plays Tom Jones, 1964, Flowers for Algernon, 1969, Brave New World, 1970, F.L.I.P.P.E.D., 1971, Here and Now, 1973, Soft Soap, 1982, Rehearsal for Murder, 1983, pub. musicals Best of Broadway, 1961, Cheaper by the Dozen, 1969, The Hobbit, 1972, The Truth About Cinderella, 1974, The Dream on Royal Street, 1981; author: (tv) The Hero, 1966, (TV series) Opera, 1966 (winner Prix d'Italia Concorso Internat. Per Opera Radiofoniche e Televisive), The Carol Burnett Show, 1970, (novels) Oh Eden, 1974, The Bedroom Set, 1976, Somewhere There's Music, 1977, The Great American Alimony Escape, 1979, The In-Laws, 1979; actor: (Broadway plays) Doubles, 1985, George Abbott's Broadway, 1987, A Funny Thing Happened On the Way to the Forum, 1997, (Off Broadway Play) Down the Garden Paths, 2000, Jewtopia, 2006, internat. tour Grand Hotel, 1991, (regional theatre appearances): Players Theatre, 1992,: Birmingham Theatre, 1993, Jupiter Theatre, 1993, Great Lakes Theatre Festival, 1994, Phoenix Theatre, 1995, Denver Ctr. Theatre Co., 1996, Repertory Theatre of St. Louis, 1998, Cin. Playhouse in the Park, 1998, Westport Playhouse, 1998, San Jose Repertory Theatre, 1999 (Dean Goodman Choice award), Va. Stage Co., 2000, Fla. Studio Theatre, 2002, Two Rivers Theatre Co., 2002, Merrimack Repertory Theatre, 2003, 2005, 2007, Rich Forum, 2004, 2005, Conn. Repertory, 2005; writer, performer: (one-man show) Naked on Broadway, 2004; actor: Ivoryton Playhouse, 2006, (TV guest appearances): Law and Order, 2000, Law and Order: Criminal Intent, 2001, 2005, Law and Order: Special Victims Unit, 2003. With US Army, 1951—52, Korea. Mem.: AFTRA, SAG, Actors Equity, Broadcast Music Inc., Writers Guild Am. East, Dramatists Guild, Theatre Artists Workshop Westport (bd. dirs. 1985).

ROGERS, DAVID FREEMAN, aerospace engineering educator; b. Theresa, NY, Sept. 3, 1937; s. Lewis Freeman and Gladys Marion Zoller; m. Nancy Ann Nuttall, Sept. 5, 1959; children: Stephen David, Karen Nanci, Ransom Robert. B in Aero. Engring., Rensselaer Poly. Inst., 1959, MS in Aero. Engring., 1960, PhD, 1967. From asst. prof. to prof. U.S. Naval Acad., Annapolis, Md., 1964—2003, dir. aeronautics, 1999—2003, prof. emeritus, 2004—. Fujitsu Rsch. prof. Royal Melbourne Inst. Tech.; hon. rsch. scholar U. Coll. London, 1977-78. Author: Mathematical Elements for Computer Graphics, 1976, 2d edit. 1990; Procedural Elements for Computer Graphics, 1985, 2d edit., 1997, Laminar Flow Analysis, 1992, Flying Adventures, Vols. 1-2, 1999, An Introduction to NURBS: with Historical Perspective, 2001; editor Meml. edit. for P. Bezier, CAD Jour., 2001; mem. editl. bd. Visual Computer, CAD, the Computer Aided Design Jour.; contbg. editor World Beechcraft Soc. Mag., 1995—; contbr. articles to profl. jours. David F. Rogers Chair in Aerospace Engineering named in his honor, 2000. Avocations: flying, photography, sailing. Office: US Naval Acad Aerospace Engring Dept Annapolis MD 21402

ROGERS, DAVID HUGHES, banking and financial service professor, dean, real estate company executive; b. Chgo., May 21, 1947; s. Joseph Gordon and Viola Winifred (Hughes) R.; Bonnie Hope Sinai, 1997; children: Kirsten Morgan, Loren Avery, Daniel Jay. BA, U. Mich., 1968; PhD, Columbia U., 1975. Economist Fed. Res. Bank of Cleve., 1974-75; asst. treas. B.F. Goodrich Co., Akron, Ohio, 1975-82; exec. v.p., chief fin. officer First Tex. Savs. Assn., Dallas, 1982-83; sr. exec. v.p., chief operating officer PriMerit Bank, Las Vegas, 1984-87, pres., dir., 1987-91, vice chmn., 1991-92; COO, The Baird Cos., Las Vegas, 1992-99; v.p., chief fin. officer Norall Labs., Las Vegas, 1999—2001; v.p., relationship mgr. Wells Fargo Bank, Las Vegas, Nev., 2001—04; CFO Lloyd Cos., Sioux Falls, SD, 2004—06; prof. banking and fin. svcs., asst. dean external programs No. State U., 2006—. Adj. prof. econs. C.C. So. Nev., 1998-2004. Author: Consumer Banking in New York, 1975; also articles. Bd. dirs. Boulder Dam Area coun. Boy Scouts Am., 1986—2004; bd. dirs. Nev. Sch. Arts, 1988-98; chmn. Las Vegas Bus. Bank, 1995-99. Office: No State U 2205 Career Ave Rm 268 D Sioux Falls SD 57107 Home Phone: 605-271-1103; Office Phone: 605-376-4319. Personal E-mail: dhrogers14@aol.com. Business E-Mail: dhrogers@northern.edu.

ROGERS, DESIREE GLAPION, federal official, former insurance company executive; b. June 16, 1959; d. Roy and Joyce Glapion; 1 child, Victoria. B in Polit. Sci., Wellesley Coll., 1981; MBA, Harvard U., 1985. Customer svc. mktg. mgr. AT&T Corp., NJ, 1985-87; dir. devel. Levy Orgn., Chgo., 1987-89; founder, pres. Mus. Ops. Consulting Assocs., Chgo., 1989-91; dir. Ill. State Lottery, Chgo., 1991-97; chief mktg. officer Peoples Energy Corp., Chgo., 1997—2004; pres. Peoples Gas and North Shore Gas, 2004—08; pres. social networking Allstate Fin., 2008—09; spl. asst. to Pres., social sec. The White House, Washington, 2009—. Bd. dirs. Equity Residential, Blue Cross Blue Shield Ill. Bd. dirs. Mus. Sci. and Industry, Ravinia; trustee Lincoln Park Zoo. Named a Woman to Watch, Crain's Chgo. Bus., 2007. Mem. Com. of 200, Young Pres.' Orgn., The Econ. Club, Execs. Club, Comml. Club Chgo. Democrat. Office: The White House 1600 Pensylvania Ave NW Washington DC 20500*

ROGERS, DEWITT RALPH, lawyer; b. Durham, NC, Sept. 26, 1952; s. Ralph P. and Elizabeth (Stutts) R.; m. Claire Hamby, Sept. 25, 1982; children: DeWitt Ralph Jr., Elizabeth Lee, Laura Alice. BA, Emory U., 1974, JD with distinction, 1986; MS in Journalism, Columbia U., 1975. Bar: Ga. 1986. Staff writer The Atlanta Constn., 1975-77, bus. editor, 1977-79, city editor, 1979-82; asst. mng. editor The Atlanta Jour. & Constn., 1982-83; assoc. Troutman Sanders LLP, Atlanta, 1986-93, ptnr., regulatory grp., 1994—. Bd. dirs. So. Inst. Bus. and Profl. Ethics, 1998-2006, bd. govs. Ga. State U. Ctr. Ethics & Corp. Responsibility, 2007-. Editor-in-chief Emory Law Jour. Mem.: Order of Coif. Office: Troutman Sanders LLP 600 Peachtree St NE Ste 5200 Atlanta GA 30308-2216 Office Phone: 404-885-3412. Office Fax: 404-962-6671. Business E-Mail: dewitt.rogers@troutmansanders.com.

ROGERS, DONALD L., music educator, department chairman, animal breeder; b. Bayshore, NY, Jan. 22, 1945; s. Donald Hampton and Laura Rogers; m. Bonnie L. Nieman, June 25, 1967; 1 child, Rebecca L. B.S, SUNY, Fredonia, 1966. Tchg. cert. Bd. of Regents State of NY, 1966. H.s. band dir. Attica (NY) Ctrl. Sch. Dist., 1966—. Music dept. chmn. Attica Ctrl. Sch., 1980—. Dir.: (band performance) Tournament of Roses Parade, 2003. Pres. Western NY Pheasant & Waterfowl Assn., NY, 1985—. Sgt. U.S. Army, 1969—72. Decorated Army Commendation U.S. Army; recipient Service award, Wyoming County Youth Bd., 2001, Lifetime Achievement award, Wyo. County Arts Coun., 2006; named Tchr. of Yr., U. Rochester, 1993, Educator of Yr., Phi Delta Kappa, 2001. Mem.: Music Educators Nat. Conf., NY State Sch. Music Assn., Am. Pheasant & Waterfowl Assn., Western NY Pheasant and Waterfowl Assn. (life; pres. 1985—). Home: 2338 Chick Rd Darien Center NY 14040 Office: Attica Senior High Sch 3338 East Main St Attica NY 14011 Personal E-mail: wildwingedhaven2@aol.com.

ROGERS, E. KENNEDY, dentist; DDS, Indiana U. Pvt. practice, Overland Park, Kans. Fellow: Am. Coll. Dentists; mem.: ADA, Kans. Dental Assn., Am. Acad. Cosmetic Dentistry, Fifth Dist. Dental Soc.

ROGERS, EDWARD MAURICE, JR., lobbyist, lawyer; b. Birmingham, Ala., Nov. 22, 1958; s. Edward Maurice and Peggy (Williams) Rogers; m. Edwina M. Clifton, Nov. 4, 1989; children: Haley, Sabra. JD, U. Ala., Tuscaloosa, 1984. Press sec. Ala. Rep. Party, Birmingham, 1980-81; advance man The White House, Washington, 1981-83; S.E. regional polit. dir. Reagan-Bush campaign, Washington, 1984; dep. sgt. at arms 1984 Rep. Nat. Conv., Dallas, 1984; pvt. practice Birmingham, 1984-85; spl. asst. to the Pres. of U.S. The White House, Washington, 1985-87, dep. asst. to the Pres., exec. asst. to chief staff, 1989—91; sr. dep. to campaign mgr. Bush-Quayle Campaign, 1987-88; co-founder, chmn. Barbour Griffith & Rogers, LLC, 1991—; of counsel Balch & Bingham. Vis. prof. U. Ala. Law Sch.; mem. pres. cabinet, nat. adv. bd. U. Ala. Named one of 50 Top Lobbyists, Washingtonian mag., 2007. Mem.: ABA, DC Bar Assn., Ala. Bar Assn. Home: 600 Estates Dr Alexandria VA 22310-1867 Office: Barbour Griffith & Rogers, LLC 601 13th St NW Ste 1100N Washington DC 20005-3868 Office Phone: 202-333-4963. Office Fax: 202-833-9392. E-mail: Ed_Rogers@bgrdc.com.*

ROGERS, EDWARD WILLIAM, engineering company executive; s. William A. and Dorothy E. Rogers; m. Mary Elizabeth Hopley, June 21, 1980; children: Yasmin R. Amis, Jumana L., Jesse E., Julia M.n. BS, Ohio State U., Columbus, 1980; MIB, U. SC., Columbia, 1991; PhD, Cornell U., Ithac, NY, 2000. Asst. prof. U. Ala., Huntsville, 2000—03; chief knowledge officer NASA-Goddard Space Flight Ctr., Greenbelt, Md., 2001—. Home: 513 Evergreen Rd Severna Park MD 21146 Office: NASA Goddard Space Flight Ctr 8800 Greenbelt Rd Greenbelt MD 20771 Business E-Mail: ewr5@cornell.edu.

ROGERS, ELIZABETH (BETTY) CARLISLE, educator, consultant; d. Charles Bunyan and Maggie Era (Little) Carlisle; children: Kellie Elizabeth, Sean Lewis. BS, U. Miss., 1972, MS, 1974; PhD, U. Ga., 1997. Chair divsn. sci. and math. Truett-McConnell Coll., Cleveland, Ga., 1974—84; chair dept. math. Lakeview Acad., Gainesville, Ga., 1984—89; prof. math. and edn. Piedmont Coll., Demorest, Ga., 1989—; prin. R&H Analytics, 2004—. Pres. BCR Inc., Gainesville, Ga., 1990—; ptnr. The Ednl. Solutions Task Force, Washington, 2000—. Author: (profl. book) A Study of Curriculum and Pedagogy, 1997; editor (contbg. author): Cooperative Learning In Undergraduate Mathematics, 2001; author: (textbook) Mathematics for Agriculture, 2000. Chair, ceremonies and events Spl. Olympics of Ga., 2001—04. Grantee Faculty Devel. in Ga., State of Ga., 1992—95; scholar Carrier Scholarship, Carrier Found.; Tchg. Fellow, U. of Miss., 1971—73. Mem.: Women in Math., Math. Assn. of Am., Alpha Delta Pi (Dorothy Shaw Leadership award), Alpha Lambda Delta (pres.), Kappa Delta Phi (pres.), Phi Kappa Phi. Achievements include research in advantages of coop. learning for undergraduate math. students; history of math. in Ctrl. and South Am. Home: 4733 Highland Rd Gainesville GA 30506 Office: Piedmont Coll Ctrl Ave Demorest GA 30535 Personal E-mail: b.rogers@prodigy.net. Business E-Mail: brogers@piedmont.edu.

ROGERS, ELIZABETH LONDON, retired geriatrics services professional; BA, Mt. Holyoke Coll., St. Hadley, Mass., 1967; MD, Jefferson Med. Sch., Phila., 1971. Lic. internal medicine, gastroenterology, and geriatrics Am. Bd. of Internal Medicine. Chief of staff Balt. VA Med. Ctr., 1982—93; prof. dept. of medicine U. of Md. Med. Sch., Baltimore, 1990—93; assoc. dean for clin. medicine Duke U. Med. Sch., Durham, NC, 1993—96; acting chief of staff VA Healthcare Sys., New Haven, 1996—2002; chief ambulatory and primary care Yale New Haven VA Med. Ctr., 1996—2002; ret., 2002. Pres. Bradmer Biotech, Miami, 2002—05; dir. Cardiome Pharma, Vancouver, B.C., Canada, 2003—04; assoc. prof. med. sch. Yale U., 1996—2002. Chmn., pres. London Charitable Found., Miami, Fla. Recipient Geriat. scholarship, Hartford Found., 1984—85. Fellow: ACP.

ROGERS, ERNEST MABRY, lawyer; b. Demopolis, Ala., Sept. 22, 1947; s. James B. and Ernestine B. (Brewer) R.; m. Jeanne Edwards, Dec. 15, 1979; children: Gilbert B., Katherine B., Mary C. BA, Yale U., New Haven, Conn., 1969; JD, Harvard U., Cambridge, Mass., 1974. Bar: Ala. 1974, US Dist. Ct. (no. dist.) Ala. 1975, US Ct. Appeals (5th cir.) 1976, US Ct. Appeals (11th cir.) 1981, US Supreme Ct. 1981, US Ct. Claims 1983, US Ct. Appeals (6th cir.) 1987. Law clk. to judge U.S. Dist. Ct. (no. dist.) Ala., 1974—75; ptnr. Bradley Arant Rose & White LLP, Birmingham, Ala., 1981—2008, Bradley Arant Bonlt Cummings LLP, 2009—. Contbr. articles to profl. jours. Mem. Jefferson County Bd. of Code Appeals, Ala., 2001—, City of Birmingham Bd. of Code Appeals. Fellow: Am. Coll. Constrn. Lawyers; mem.: Am. Arbitration Assn. (bd. dirs. 2001—05), Kiwanis. Episcopalian. Office: One Federal Pl 1819 5th Ave N Birmingham AL 35203-2104 Office Phone: 205-521-8225. Business E-Mail: emr@babc.com.

ROGERS, EUGENE JACK, retired medical educator; b. Vienna, June 13, 1921; came to U.S., 1937; s. Louis and Malvina (Haller) R.; m. Joyce M. Lighter, Feb. 9, 1952; children: Jay A., Robert J. BS, CCNY; M.B., Chgo. Med. Sch., 1946, MD, 1947. Diplomate Am. Bd. Phys. Medicine and Rehab. Intern Our Lady of Mercy Med. Ctr. and Cabrini Meml. Hosps., NYC, 1946-48; resident Madigan Hosp., Tacoma, 1951, Mayo Clinic, Rochester, Minn., 1951, N.Y. Med. Coll. Met. Med. Ctr., 1953-55; USPHS fellow, 1955-56; ship's surgeon U.S. Lines, Grace Lines, NYC, 1948-49; indsl. physician Abraham & Strauss Stores, Bklyn., 1949-51; practice medicine specializing in phys. medicine and rehab. Bklyn., 1956-73; dir. rehab. service, attending physician N.Y. City Hosp. Dept., 1955-73; prof., chmn. dept. rehab. medicine Chgo. Med. Sch., North Chicago, Ill., 1973—2005, prof. emeritus dept. rehab. medicine, 2005—, Rosalind Franklin U. Medicine & Sci., 2005. Cons. N.Y.C. Mayor's Adv. Com. for Aged, 1957; asst. prof. SUNY Downstate Med. Sch., Bklyn., 1958-73; med. dir. Schwab Rehab. Hosp., Chgo., 1973-75; acting chief rehab. service VA Center, North Chicgo, 1975-77; chmn. Ill. Phys. Therapy Exam. Com., 1977-78; examiner Am. Bd. Phys. Medicine and Rehab., 1983; sec., dir. Microtherapeutics, Inc., 1972 Editor: Total Cancer Care, 1975; contbr. articles to med. jours.; contbg. editor Ill. Med. Jour., 1983-89 Served to capt. US Army, 1951—53. Recipient Bronze medal Am. Congress Rehab. Medicine, 1974 Fellow: ACP, Am. Acad. Phys. Medicine and Rehab. (Cert. Appreciation 1993); mem.: Chgo. Med. Sch. Alumni Assn. (asst. treas. 1983—93, treas. 1993—95, sec. 1995—97, 1st v.p. 1999, pres. 2001—03, exec. com., Disting. Alumnus award 1980, Presdl. plaque Greater N.Y. chpt.), Chgo. Med. Sch. Faculty Assembly (spkr. 1978—80), Ill. Soc. Phys. Medicine and Rehab. (pres. 1983—84), Ill. Med. Soc. (chmn. workmen's compensation com. 1980—83), Odd Fellows (pres. 1961—62), Phi Lambda Kappa (trustee 1980), Alpha Omega Alpha. Home: 1110 N Lake Shore Dr Chicago IL 60611-5248 Home Phone: 312-266-7494. Personal E-mail: eugenerogers@att.com. *To render good medical care: Prevent disease, evaluate the patient, treat the condition, educate patient and family, restore function, support group referral, on-line medical knowledge maintenance, never neglect or lie to or for patients, never divulging patient med. info. without consent.*

ROGERS, FRED BAKER, medical educator; b. Hamilton, NJ, Aug. 25, 1926; s. Lawrence H. and Eliza C. (Thropp) R. AA, Princeton U., 1947; MD, Temple U., 1948; MS in Medicine, U. Pa., 1954; MPH, Columbia U., 1957; spl. student, Johns Hopkins U., 1962. Diplomate: Am. Bd. Preventive Medicine. Intern Temple U. Hosp., Phila., 1948-49, chief resident physician, 1953-54; USPHS fellow Temple U. Sch. Medicine, 1954-55, asst. prof. preventive medicine, 1956-58, assoc. prof., 1958-60, prof., 1960-90, prof. emeritus, 1991—, chmn. dept., 1970-77. Lectr. epidemiology Columbia U. Sch. Pub. Health, 1957-68, Sch. Nursing, U. Pa., 1964-67; cons. USN Hosp., Phila., 1964-73 Author: A Syllabus of Medical History, 1958, Help-Bringers: Versatile Physicians of N.J, 1960, Epidemiology and Communicable Disease Control, 1963, Studies in Epidemiology, 1965, (with A.R. Sayre) The Healing Art, 1966, (with M.E. Cashel) Your Body is Wonderfully Made, 1974; mem. editorial bd. Am. Jour. Pub. Health, 1967-73; contbr. articles to profl. jours. With M.C. USNR, 1950-53, Korea, capt. (ret.) USNR. Recipient Chapel of Four Chaplains award, 1982. Fellow ACP; mem. AMA (past chmn. sect. preventive medicine), Am. Pub. Health Assn., Royal Soc. Medicine of London (hon.), Sigma Xi, Alpha Omega Alpha, Phi Rho Sigma. Clubs: Campus (Princeton); Franklin Inn (Phila.); Charaka (N.Y.C.); Osler (London). Home: 333 W State St Apt 6K Trenton NJ 08618-5722 Office: Temple U Sch Med Philadelphia PA 19140

ROGERS, FREDERIC HALSEY, economist; s. Stephen H. and Kent B. Rogers; m. Song-ae Aromie Noe, 1995; children: Tajin, Tayae. AB, Princeton U., NJ, 1986; MPP, Harvard U., Cambridge, Mass., 1989; PhD in Economics, U. Calif., Berkeley, 1996. Vis. rschr. Korea Devel. Inst., Seoul, Republic of Korea, 1986—87; project asst. trade policy Harvard Inst. Internat. Devel., Jakarta, Indonesia, 1989—90; staff economist Coun. Econ. Advisors White House, Washington, 1994—95; economist Econ. Devel. Inst., World Bank, Washington, 1996—97, World Bank, Washington, 1997—2000, advisor chief economist, 1997—2000, 2000—02, sr. economist, 2000—02, sr. economist, devel. rsch. group, 2002—. Author: (book) Growth and Empowerment: Making Development Happen (MIT Press); contbr. articles to profl. jours. Elder First Presbyn. Ch., Arlington, Va., 2005—07.

ROGERS, HAROLD DALLAS (HAL), United States Representative from Kentucky; b. Barrier, KY, Dec. 31, 1937; BA, U. Ky., 1962, LLB, 1964. Bar: La. 1964. Assoc. Smith & Blackburn, 1964—67; pvt. practice Somerset, Ky., 1967-69; Commonwealth atty. Pulaski and Rockcastle counties, Ky., 1969-80; mem. US Congress from 5th Ky. dist., 1981—, mem. appropriations com., subcom. homeland security, transp., commerce, justice and state. Mem. Congressional Horse Caucus, Tenn. Valley Authority Caucus. Founder So. Ky. Economic Council. With KY and NC Nat. Guard, 1957—64. Mem.: Ky. Commonwealth Atty. Assn. (past pres.). Republican. Office: US Ho Reps 2406 Rayburn Ho Office Bldg Washington DC 20515-1705 Office Phone: 202-225-4601. Business E-Mail: talk2hal@mail.house.gov.*

ROGERS, HAYDEN, legislative staff member; BA in Politics, Princeton U., NJ, 1995. Owner & pres. Saplings, Inc., Knoxville, Tenn., 2001—05; campaign mgr. Office Heath Shuler for Congress, 2006; chief of staff for Rep. Heath Shuler US House of Reps., Washington, 2007—. Baptist. Office: Office of Congressman Heath Shuler 422 Cannon House Office Bldg Washington DC 20515 Office Phone: 202-225-6401. Business E-Mail: hayden.rogers@mail.house.gov.*

ROGERS, HOWARD H., retired chemist; b. NYC, Dec. 26, 1926; s. Julian Herbert and Minnie (Jaffa) R.; m. Barbara Kniaz, Mar. 27, 1954 (div. 1978); children: Lynne, Mark David, Susan; m. Maureen Dohn, Dec. 28, 1978. BS in Chemistry, U. Ill., 1949; PhD in Inorganic Chemistry, MIT, 1953. Research group leader Allis-Chalmers Mfg. Co., West Allis, Wis., 1952-61; sr. tech. specialist Rocketdyne div., Rockwell, Canoga Park, Calif., 1961-70; chief research scientist Martek Instruments, Newport Beach, Calif., 1970-73; scientist Boeing Satellite Systems, Torrance, Calif., 1973—2002; ret., 2002. Contbr. sci. papers to profl. publs. in field. With USN, 1944—46. Recipient Lawrence A. Hyland Patent award Hughes Aircraft Co., 1987. Mem. Electrochem. Soc. (chmn. So. Calif./Nev. sect. 1976-78), Am. Chem. Soc. Achievements include development of nickel-hydrogen battery; 27 US patents. Avocation: amateur radio. Home: 18361 Van Ness Ave Torrance CA 90504-5309 Personal E-mail: howard.rogers@alum.mit.edu. *In my 80 plus years of living experience I have found that these two items are vital: focus on what you intend to do, not what you have already done; complete honesty to yourself and to others in interpreting and reporting results is mandatory.*

ROGERS, HUGH DANIEL, electrical engineer, educator; s. Emmett Earl and Violet Maxwell Rogers; m. Rita Susan Lanier; children: Hugh Dustin, Jacob Daniel, Matthew Buchanan, Joshua Caine. Degree in Elec. Installation, James Sprunt Coll., Kenansville, NC, 1971, A in Gen. Edn., 1995. Lic. elec. contractor's Elec. Bd., NC, 1993, cert. elec. instr. NCCER, 2006, core curriculum instr. 2006. Farm owner and mgr. Roger's Bros. Farms, Pink Hill, NC, 1972—89; elec. technician Carolina Turkeys, Mt. Olive, NC, 1989—93; sys. technician Guilford East, Kenansville, 1993—94; elec. instr. Pitt CC, Greenville, NC, 1994—97, James Sprunt Coll., 1997—2005; prof., elec. tech. San Jacinto Coll., Houston, 2005—. Tech. advisor Rogers Elec. Svc., Pink Hill, 1994—97. Mem. Sch. Bd. Com., Albertson, NC, 1974—76, Duplin Airport, Kenansville, 1976—78. Recipient Citizenship award, Vets. Assn., 1964. Achievements include design of theft proof vapor recovery gas despenser. Avocations: boating, fishing, golf, travel. Personal E-mail: hrogers53@yahoo.com.

ROGERS, JACK DAVID, plant pathologist, educator; b. Point Pleasant, W.Va., Sept. 3, 1937; s. Jack and Thelma Grace R.; m. Belle C. Spencer, June 7, 1958. BS in Biology, Davis and Elkins Coll., 1960; MF, Duke U., 1960; PhD, U. Wis., 1963. From asst. prof. to prof. Wash. State U., Pullman, 1963-72, chmn. dept. plant pathology, 1986-99, Regents prof., 2007—. Contbr. articles to profl. jours. Recipient Eminent Faculty award, Wash. State U., 2006. Mem. Mycol. Soc. Am. (pres. 1977-78, William H. Weston Tchg. Excellence award 1992, Disting. Mycologist award 2004), Am. Phytopathol. Soc., Bot. Soc. Am., Brit. Mycol. Soc. Office Phone: 509-335-9541.

ROGERS, JAMES DEVITT, judge; b. Mpls., May 5, 1929; s. Harold Neil and Dorothy (Devitt) R.; m. Leanna Morrison, Oct. 19, 1968. AB, Dartmouth Coll., 1951; JD, U. Minn., 1954. Bar: Minn. 1954, U.S. Supreme Ct. 1983. Assoc. Johnson & Sands, Mpls., 1956-60; sole practice Mpls., 1960-62; judge Mpls. Municipal and Dist. Ct., 1959-91. Mem. faculty Nat. Judicial Coll. Bd. dirs. Mpls. chpt. Am. Red Cross, chmn. service to mil. families and vets. com.; bd. dirs. Minn. Safety Coun., St. Paul, 1988-91; founding dir., sec. Forest Landowners Tax Coun. Served sgt. U.S. Army, 1954-56. Mem. ABA (chmn. nat. conf. spl. ct. judge, spl. com. housing and urban devel. law, traffic ct. program com., chmn. criminal justice sect., jud. adminstrn. div.), Nat. Jud. Coll. (bd. dirs.), Nat. Christmas Tree Grower's Assn. (pres. 1976-78), Mpls. Athletic Club. Congregationalist. Office: 14110 Prince Pl Minnetonka MN 55345-3027

ROGERS, JAMES EUGENE (JIM ROGERS), energy executive; b. Birmingham, Ala., Sept. 20, 1947; s. James E. and Margaret (Whatley) R.; m. Robyn McGill (div.); children: Chrissi, Kara, Ben; m. Mary Anne Boldrick, Oct. 28, 1977. BBA, U. Ky., 1970, JD, 1974; LLD (hon.), Ind. State U.; DHL (hon.), Queens Univ., Charlotte NC. Reporter Lexington (Ky.) Herald Leader, 1967—70; asst. atty. gen. Commonwealth Ky., Louisville; asst. chief trial atty. Fed. Energy Regulation Commn., Washington, dep. gen. counsel litigation and enforcement; law clk. to presiding justice Supreme Ct Ky., Louisville; ptnr. Akin, Gump, Strauss, Hauer & Feld LLP, Dallas, Akin Gump Strauss Hauer & Feld LLP, Houston, 1985-86; exec. v.p. Enron Gas Pipeline Group, 1986—88; pres., CEO, chmn. PSI Resources, Inc, 1988—94, Cinergy Corp. (formerly PSI Resources, Inc.), Cin., 1994—2006; pres., CEO Duke Energy Corp., Charlotte, NC, 2006—07, chmn., pres., CEO, 2007—. 2nd vice chmn. Edison Electric Inst., 2004—05, vice chmn., 2005—06, chmn., 2006—; bd. dirs. Chesapeake Corp., 1999—2004, Duke Energy Corp., 2006—, Applied Materials Inc., 2008—, Fifth Third Bancorp, Fifth Third Bank, Am. Gas Assn., US C. of C., Bus. Roundtable, Nat. Coal Coun.; bd. dir., mem. exec. com. Nuclear Energy Inst. Trustee Nat. Symphony Orch.; bd. dirs. Cin. Mus. Assn., The Nature Conservancy-Ind. chpt., U. Ky. Bus. Partnership Found. Recipient Disting. Svc. Citation, NCCJ, 2004, Keystone Ctr. in Leadership in Industry award, 2005, Ronald McDonald House Lifetime Achievement award, 2005, Human Rels. award, Am. Jewish Com., 2006, Ellis Island Medal of Honor, Nat. Ethnic Coalition of Org., 2007; named CEO of Yr., Platts Global Energy awards, 2007; named one of The Global Elite, Newsweek mag., 2008; named to Hall of Fame Gatton Coll. Bus. & Econ., Univ. Ky., Hall of Fame Coll. Law, Univ. Ky. Mem. Ky. Bar Assn., D.C. Bar Assn., Meridian Hills Country Club, Crooked Stick Golf Club, Queen City Club, Met. Club. Baptist. Avocations: tennis, bicycling, skiing, golf. Office: Duke Energy Corp 526 S Church St Charlotte NC 28202 also: Edison Electric Inst 701 Pennsylvania Ave NW Washington DC 20004*

ROGERS, JAMES FREDERICK, banker, management consultant; b. Centerville, Iowa, June 27, 1935; s. John W. and Mildred Holly (Morris) R.; m. Janet L. Marsden, July 27, 1957; children: Jennifer Burke, John William. AB, U. Mo., 1957; postgrad., Rutgers U. Grad. Sch. Banking, 1970-72. With Am. Security and Trust Co., Washington, 1959-85, exec. v.p., 1980-83. Bd. dirs., pres. Am. Security Corp., 1983-85; cons. B.E.I.-Golembe Assoc., 1985-93; chmn. Nat. Bank of No. Va., 1988-89. Commr. Arlington County Planning Commn., 1979-80; asst. treas. Kennedy Ctr. Performing Arts; pres., trustee Leonard Wood Found.; trustee Friends of Nat. Zoo, Greater Washington Rsch. Ctr., Washington Dulles Task Force, Arena Stage, Sch. Commerce U. Va. Officer AUS, 1958-59; dir. Conococheague Inst. Mem. D.C. Bankers Assn. (pres. 1984-85), Davenport Soc., U. Mo., Met. Club (Washington), Chevy Chase Club. Presbyterian. Home: 4201 38th Rd N Arlington VA 22207-4554 Personal E-mail: jroger@comcast.net.

ROGERS, JAMES GORDON, JR., art educator; b. Dec. 16, 1944; AB in English, U. Mo., 1967, MA in Art History and Archaeology, 1983, PhD, 1989. Asst. prof. art history William Woods Coll., Fulton, Mo., 1989-90; prof. art history Savannah Coll. Art & Design, Ga., 1990-92, Fla. So. Coll., Lakeland, Fla., 1992—. Adj. prof. Sch. Arch. and Cmty. Design, U. S. Fla., 1995—2002; cons. Design Ctr., 1977—84, chair dept. art and art history; dir. art & art history program Melvin Art Gallery, 1999—2006; chair divsn. fine, applied and performing arts Fla. So. Coll., 2007—; lectr. in field. Contbr. articles to profl. jours. Active Nat. Holocaust Meml. Mus.; past bd. dirs. Mid-Mo. chpt. Am. Heart Assn.; past bd. dirs. Sta. KBIA Pub. Radio, Columbia, Mo., Columbia Art League, co-chmn. fin. com.; past mem. peer rev. com. Fla. Arts Coun. Mem.: AAUP, Hist. Lakeland Inc. (bd. dirs.), Coll. Art Assn., Soc. Archtl. Historians, Am. Soc. Hispanic Art Hist. Studies. Office: Fla So Coll Lake Hollingsworth Dr Lakeland FL 33803 Home Phone: 863-619-5494; Office Phone: 863-680-4223. E-mail: jrogers@flsouthern.edu.

ROGERS, JAMES P., chemicals executive; b. Bethesda, Md., Mar. 23, 1951; BA in Psychology, U. Va., 1973; MBA, U. Pa., 1983. Corp. fin. calling officer Morgan guaranty Trust Co., 1983-87; treas. LPL Techs., Inc., 1987-92, GAF Corp./INternat. Specialty Products, Inc.; exec. v.p., CFO GAF, 1992-99; exec. v.p. fin. Internat. Specialty Products, Inc., 1992-99; sr. v.p., CFO & COO Eastman div. Eastman Chem. Co., Kingsport, Tenn., 1999—2003, exec. v.p., 2003—06, pres., head chemicals & fibers bus. group, 2006—09, pres., CEO, 2009—. Lt. USN, 1973-80. Office: Eastman Chem Co 100 N Eastman Rd Kingsport TN 37660*

ROGERS, JIM (JAMES BEELAND ROGERS JR.), retired investment company executive; b. Balt., Oct. 19, 1942; s. James Beeland and Ernestine Barbara (Brewer) Rogers; m. Paige Parker, Jan. 1, 2000; children: Hilton Augusta, Beeland Anderson. BA cum laude, Yale U., 1964; BA with honors, Balliol Coll., Oxford U., Eng., 1966, MA in Politics, Philosophy, Econs. Investment analyst Bache & Co., NYC, 1968-69, R. Gilder & Co., NYC, 1969-70; asst. to chmn. Neuberger & Berman, NYC, 1970-71; with Arnhold and S. Bleichroeder Inc., 1971—73; co-founder Quantum Fund, 1973—80; exec. v.p. Soros Fund Mgmt., NYC, 1973-80; chmn. bd. dirs. Rogers Holdings, 1980—; founder Rogers Internat. Cmty. Index, 1998. Adj. prof. Columbia U. Sch. Bus., 1983—85, prof. fin., 1986—90, vis. prof., 1994—96. Moderator (TV series) The Dreyfus Roundtable, 1989—90, host The Profit Motive with Jim Rogers, 1989—90, Guinness Record Motorcycle Trip Around World, 1990—92; author: Investment Biker: On the Road with Jim Rogers, 1994, Adventure Capitalist: The Ultimate Road Trip, 2003, Hot Commodities: How Anyone Can Invest Profitably in the World's Best Market, 2004, A Bull in China: Investing Profitably in the World's Greatest Market, 2007, A Gift to My Children: A Father's Lessons For Life And Investing, 2009—. With US Army, 1966—68. Achievements include being listed 3 times in Guinness Book of World Records for Henley Regatta Race, for 100,000 mile motorcycle trip across six continents in 1990-92, for automobile trip around world, 1999-2001. Office: 150 W Flagler St Miami FL 33130

ROGERS, JOEL, biology professor; married. MA in Kinesiology, Exercise Sci., Calif. State U., Fresno, 2000; EdD student, Walden U., 2008—. Biology, kinesiology instr. West Hills Coll. Lemoore, Calif., 2005—. Recipient Excellence award, NISOD, 2008; named Instr. of Yr., West Hills Coll. Lemoore Student Body, 2008. Office: West Hills Coll Lemoore 555 College Ave Lemoore CA 93245

ROGERS, JOHN MARSHALL, federal judge; b. Rochester, NY, June 26, 1948; s. Harry Lovejoy III and Virginia Kathryn (Meyers) R.; m. Ying Juan Xiong, 1990. BA, Stanford U., 1970; JD, U. Mich., 1974. Bar: DC 1975, Ky. 1980, US Ct. Appeals, US Supreme Ct. Commd. USAR, 1970; appellate atty. civil div. US Dept. Justice, Washington, 1974-78; asst. prof. U. Ky., Lexington, 1978-81, assoc. prof., 1981-86, prof., 1986—2002, prof. emeritus, 2002—; cir. judge US Ct. Appeals (6th cir.), 2002—. Vis. prof. Civil Divsn. US Dept. Justice, Washington, 1983-85; Fulbright lectr. Fgn. Affairs Coll., Beijing, 1987-88, Zhongshan U., Guangzhou, People's Republic of China, 1994-95; spl. counsel impeachment com. Ky. Ho. of Reps., 1991. Author: Internat. Law and U.S. Law, 1999; contbr. articles to profl. jours. Mem. Coun. on Fgn. Rels., Am. Law Inst., Order of Coif, Phi Beta Kappa. Office: 532 Potter Stewart US Courthouse 100 E 5th St Cincinnati OH 45202-3988 also: Cmty Trust Bank Bldg 100 E Vine St Lexington KY 40507*

ROGERS, JOHN W., JR., investment company executive; b. Chgo., Mar. 31, 1958; s. John W. Sr. and Jewel (Mankarious) R.; m. Desiree Glapion, 1988 (div.) m. Sharon Fairley; 1 child, Victoria AB in Econs., Princeton U., NJ, 1980. Broker William Blair & Co.; founder, chmn., CEO Ariel Capital Mgmt., LLC, Chgo., 1983—. Bd. dirs. Aon Corp., Exelon Corp., McDonald's Corp., Ariel Capital Mgmt., LLC, and Ariel Mutual Funds. Columnist: Forbes mag. Trustee U. Chgo.; dir. Chgo. Urban League; alumnus Leadership Greater Chgo. Recipient Disting. Fellow award, Leadership Greater Chgo., 2000, Most Influential Black Americans, Ebony mag., 2005; named one of 50 for the Future, Time mag., 1994; named to Power 150, Ebony mag., 2008. Office: Ariel Capital Mgmt # 2900 200 E Randolph St Chicago IL 60601-6436*

ROGERS, JUDITH ANN WILSON, federal judge; b. NYC, 1939; AB cum laude, Radcliffe Coll., 1961; LLB, Harvard U., 1964; LLM, U. Va., 1988; LLD (hon.), DC Sch. Law, 1992. Bar: DC 1965. Law clk. Juvenile Ct. DC, 1964-65; asst. U.S. atty. DC, 1965-68; trial atty. San Francisco Neighborhood Legal Assistance Found., 1968-69; atty. assoc. atty. gen.'s office US Dept. Justice, 1969-71, atty. criminal divsn., 1969-71; gen. counsel Congl. Commn. on Organization of D.C. Govt., 1971-72; coordinator legis. program Office of Dep. Mayor DC, 1972-74, spl. asst. to mayor for legis., 1974-79, corp. counsel, 1979-83; assoc. judge DC Ct. Appeals, 1983-88, chief judge, 1988-94; judge US Ct. Appeals (DC cir.), 1994—. Mem. DC Law Revision Commn., 1979-83; mem. grievance com. US Dist. Ct. DC, 1982-83; mem. exec. com. Conf. Chief Justices, 1993-94. Bd. dirs. Wider Opportunities for Women, 1972-74; mem. vis. com. Harvard U. Sch. Law, 1984-90; trustee Radcliffe Coll., 1982-88. Recipient citation for work on DC Self-Govt. Act, 1973, Disting. Pub. Svc. award DC Govt., 1983, award Nat. Bar Assn., 1989; named Woman Lawyer of Yr., Women's Bar Assn. DC, 1990. Fellow ABA; mem. DC Bar, Nat. Assn. Women Judges, Conf. Chief Justices (bd. dirs. 1988-94), Am. Law Inst., Phi Beta Kappa. Office: US Ct Appeals Fed Cir 717 Madison Pl NW Washington DC 20001-2866 also: US Courthouse 333 Constitution Ave NW STE 5800 Washington DC 20001*

ROGERS, JUSTIN TOWNER, JR., retired utility company executive; b. Sandusky, Ohio, Aug. 4, 1929; s. Justin Towner and Barbara Eloise (Larkin) R. AB cum laude, Princeton U., 1951; JD, U. Mich., 1954. Bar: Ohio 1954. Assoc. Wright, Harlor, Purpus, Morris & Arnold, Columbus, 1956-58; with Ohio Edison Co., Akron, 1958-93, v.p., then exec. v.p., 1970-79, pres., 1980-91, chmn. bd., 1991-93; ret., 1993. Past mem. coal adv. bd. Internat. Energy Agy. Past pres., trustee Akron Cmty. Trusts, Akron Child Guidance Ctr.; past chmn. Akron Assoc. Health Agys., U. Akron Assocs., Ohio Electric Utility Inst.; past chmn., trustee, Akron Gen. Health Sys.; trustee Sisler McFawn Found.; former trustee Stan Hywet Hall & Gardens, VNS-Hospice Found.; past dir. Edison Elec. Inst., Elec. Power Rsch. Inst., Assn. of Edison Illuminating Co.'s. Mem. Portage Country Club, Mayflower Club, Rockwell Springs Trout Club (Castalia, Ohio), Columbus Beach Club, Phi Delta Phi, Beta Gamma Sigma.

ROGERS, KENNY (KENNETH SCOTT ROGERS), professional baseball player; b. Savannah, Ga., Nov. 10, 1964; m. Rebecca Lewis; children: Jessica Lynn, Trevor. Pitcher Tex. Rangers, 1989-95, 2000—02, 2004—05, NY Yankees, 1996—97, Oakland A's, 1998—99, NY Mets, 1999, Minn. Twins, 2003, Detroit Tigers, 2006—. Active Habitat for Humanity. Recipient Am. League Gold Glove award, 2000, 2002, 2004-06; named to Am. League All-Star Team, 1995, 2004-06. Achievements include becoming the 14th pitcher in Major League history to pitch a perfect game, 1994; being a member of the World Series Championship winning New York Yankees, 1996; becoming the oldest starting pitcher (41 years old) to earn his first career postseason win, 2006. Avocations: golf, fishing. Office: c/o Detroit Tigers Comerica Pk 2100 Woodward Ave Detroit MI 48201

ROGERS, LAWRENCE E., education educator; b. Chgo., Apr. 26, 1942; s. Edwin J. and Margaret V. Rogers; m. Ruth E. Harper, Feb. 14, 1988; 1 child, Margaret E. Harper-Rogers; m. Janice M. Kopp, Aug. 8, 1969 (div. Feb. 25, 1987); 1 child, Elizabeth K. BA, U. Nebr., Lincoln, 1964; PhD, U. Nebr.-Lincoln, 1975. Social studies tchr. Lincoln Pub. Sch., 1969—72, Omaha Pub. Sch., Nebr., 1976—84; editor U. Nebr.-Lincoln, 1985—92; asst. prof. edn. Sioux Falls Coll., SD, 1992—95; prof. edn. SD State U., Brookings, 1995—. Trustee Brookings Libr. Bd., 2008—. SP5 US Army, 1966—68, 8th Army HQ, Seoul, Korea. Mem.: Nat. Coun. Social Studies, Phi Kappa Phi. Democrat. Mem. Ucc. Home: 522 Deer Pass Brookings SD 57006 Office: SD State Univ Box 507 209 Wenona Brookings SD 57007 Office Fax: 605-688-6074. Business E-Mail: larry.rogers@sdstate.edu.

ROGERS, LEE FRANK, radiologist; b. Colchester, Vt., Sept. 24, 1934; s. Watson Frank and Marguerite Mortimer (Cole) R.; m. Donna Mae Brinker, June 20, 1956; children: Michelle, Cynthia, Christopher, Matthew. BS, Northwestern U., 1956, MD, 1959. Commd. 2d lt. U.S. Army, 1959, advanced through grades to maj., 1967; rotating intern Walter Reed Gen. Hosp., 1959-60; resident radiology Fitzsimons Gen. Hosp., 1960-63; ret., 1967; radiologist Bapt. Meml. Hosp., San Antonio, 1967-68, U. Tex. Med. Sch., San Antonio, 1968-71, dir. residency tng., radiologist Houston, 1972-74; prof., chmn. dept. radiology Northwestern U. Med. Sch., Chgo., 1974-95; editor-in-chief Am. Jour. Roentgenology, Winston-Salem, NC, 1995—2003; prof. radiology U. Ariz. Health Scis. Ctr., 2003—. Fellow Am. Coll. Radiology (past pres.), Am. Roentgen Ray Soc. (past pres.); mem. Assn. Univ. Radiologists (past pres.), Radiol. Soc. N.Am., Am. Bd. Radiology (past pres.), Alpha Omega Alpha. Episcopalian. Home: 8235 N Fairway View Dr Tucson AZ 85742 Home Phone: 520-544-0807; Office Phone: 520-626-6794. Personal E-mail: lfrogers@comcast.net. *The source of most problems is previous solutions.*

ROGERS, LINDA L., middle school educator; b. Watertown, Minn., Feb. 2, 1947; d. Bernard and Lucille Pearson; children: Jessica J., Julia J. Martin. BA in Child Psychology, U. Minn., Mpls., 1969; MEd in ESL Curriculum & Instrn., U. Fla., Gainesville, 2003. Cert. elem. tchr. Fla. Dept. Edn., 1990, tchr. ESL Fla. Dept. Edn., 2003. Tchr. preschool Westbrook Coll. Children's Ctr., Portland, Maine, 1984—85; tchr. title 1 reading South Portland Pub. Schs., 1985—86; dir. New Beginnings Christian Day Care, 1986—88; tchr. Duval County Pub. Schs., Jacksonville, Fla., 1988—89, 1993—; prog. coord. YMCA, Jacksonville, 1990—93. Curriculum writer Duval County Pub. Schs., 2001—, profl. devel. trainer, 2003—07. Author: Community Re-entry Project Student Text, 1972, ESL Test Prep Trainer's Manual, 2004. Mem. Compassion Tour Israel, 2008—; participant English Lang. Del. to South Africa, 2006. Named Tchr. of Yr., Ft. Caroline Mid. Sch., 1997, Justina Rd. Elem. Sch., 2004. Mem.: ASCD, TESOL, Duval Reading Coun., Sunshine State TESOL, Internat. TESOL. Avocations: reading, swimming, travel. Home: 12301 Kernan Forest Blvd Condo 1706 Jacksonville FL 32225 Office: Landmark MS Duval County Public Schools 101 Kernan Blvd Jacksonville FL 32225 Business E-Mail: rogersl1@duvalschools.org.

ROGERS, MALCOLM AUSTIN, museum director, art historian; b. Scarborough, Yorkshire, Eng., Oct. 3, 1948; s. James Eric and Frances Anne (Elsey) R. BA in English Lang. & Lit., Oxford U., Eng.; MA, Magdalen Coll., U. Oxford, 1976; DPhil, Christ Ch., Oxford U., 1976. Asst. keeper Nat. Portrait Gallery, London, 1974-83, dep. dir., 1983—85, dep. keeper, 1985—94; Ann and Graham Gund dir. Mus. Fine Arts, Boston, 1994—. Noted authority on 16th, 17th & early 18th century portraits. Author: Blue Guide: Museums and Galleries of London, 1983; contbr. articles to profl. publs. Mem. Harvard overseers' com. Visit the Art Mus.; trustee Found. for the Arts, Nagoya, Japan, Wednesday Evening Club of 1777, Club of Odd Volumes. Comdr. British Empire, 2004, Commendatore al Merito Della Repubblica Italiana, 2009. Fellow Soc. Antiquaries; mem. Thursday Evening Club of 1846, Chevalier de L'Ordre des Arts et Lettres. Avocations: wine and food, travel, opera. Office: Mus Fine Arts 465 Huntington Ave Boston MA 02115-5597 Business E-Mail: mrogers@mfa.org.

ROGERS, MARGARET ELLEN JONSSON, civic worker; b. Dallas, Aug. 7, 1938; d. John Erik and Margaret Elizabeth (Fonde) Jonsson; m. Robert D. Rogers; children: Emily, Erik, Laura. Student, Skidmore Coll., 1956—57, So. Meth. U., 1957—60. Civic worker, Dallas. Dir. Sta. KRLD radio, Dallas, 1970-74; dir. 1st Nat. Bank, Dallas, 1976-85, vice-chmn. dirs. trust com.; trustee Meth. Hosps., 1972-82, mem. exec. com., 1977-82, corp. bd. mem., 1990-94, mem. fin. com., 1990-93; bd. dirs. Lamplighter Sch., 1967—; past mem. vis. com. dept. psychology MIT; mem. vis. com. Stanford U. Librs., 1984-90; bd. dirs. Callier Ctr. Communication Disorders, 1967-90, Winston Sch., 1973-85; bd. dirs., mem. exec. com. Episc. Sch., 1976-83; chmn. Crystal Charity Ball; co-chmn. nat. major gifts com. Stanford Centennial Campaign; bd. dirs. Children's Med. Ctr., Hope Cottage Childrens' Bur., Baylor Dental Sch., Dallas Health and Sci. Mus., Dallas YWCA, Day Nursery Assn.; mem. devel. bd. U. Tex., Dallas, 1988-90; bd. govs. The Dallas Found., 1988-95, chmn. investment com. 1991-92; trustee So. Meth. U., mem. investment com., 1988—, chmn. investment com., 1992-99; mem. vis. com. Dedman Coll., 1989-90; life trustee Dallas Mus. Art, mem. investment com.; mem. collectors com. Nat. Gallery Art; bd. dirs. Dallas Arboretum, 1991-92; trustee, mem. fin. com. Monterey Bay Aquarium, 1995—, chair devel. com., 1995-2000, mem. fin. com., 2000—. Mem. internat. coun. Mus. Modern Art; pres. MJR Fund, Jonsson Found. Margaret Jonsson Charlton Hosp. of Dallas named in her honor, 1973. Mem.: The Lamplighter Sch. (life).

ROGERS, MICHAEL ALAN, writer; b. Santa Monica, Calif., Nov. 29, 1950; s. Don Easterday and Mary Othilda (Gilbertson) R.; m. Donna Rini, Oct. 9, 2000. BA in Creative Writing, Stanford U., Calif., 1972. Assoc. editor Rolling Stone Mag., San Francisco, 1972-76; editor-at-large Outside mag., San Francisco, 1976-78; vis. lectr. fiction U. Calif., Davis, 1980; sr. writer Newsweek mag., San Francisco, 1983—; mng. editor Newsweek InterActive, San Francisco, 1993-97; exec. prodr. broadband divsn. The Washington Post Co., 1995-96; v.p. Washingtonpost.Newsweek Interactive, 1996—2004. Editor, gen. mgr. Newsweek-.MSNBC.com, NYC, 1998-2004, columnist, MSNBC.com, 2005—; prin. Practical Futurist, 2005-08; futurist-in-residence NY Times Co., 2006-08. Author: Mindfogger, 1973, Biohazard, 1977, Do Not Worry About The Bear, 1979, Silicon Valley, 1982, Forbidden Sequence, 1988; contbr. articles to mags., newspapers. Recipient Disting. Sci. Writing award AAAS, 1976, Best Feature Articles award Computer Press Assn., 1987, MIN Mag. Digital Hall of Fame, 2007. Mem. Author Guild, Sierra Club. Achievements include patents for for multimedia storytelling technology. Avocations: travel, hiking. Address: 535 Dean St # 704 Brooklyn NY 11217 Business E-Mail: mr@practicalfuturist.com.

ROGERS, MICHAEL BRUCE, orthodontist; b. Augusta, Ga., Aug. 25, 1945; s. Bruce Latimer and Dorothy (Baird) R.; m. Elizabeth Bennett, Dec. 21, 1968; children: Bruce, Kay, Alison, Lisa. Student, Emory U., 1963-65, DDS, 1969; cert. in orthodontics, Med. Coll. Ga., 1973. Diplomate Am. Bd. Orthodontists. Pvt. practice orthodontia, Augusta, 1973—. Part-time asst. clin. prof. Sch. Dentistry, Med. Coll. Ga., Augusta, 1973—. Capt. Dental Corps U.S. Army, 1971-73. Decorated Army Commendation medal; named John F. Mac Meritorous Svc. award, Emory Dental Alumni Assn., 2009. Fellow: Ga. Acad. Dental Practice, The Internat. Acad. Dentists, Pierre Fauchard Acad., Internat. Acad. Dental Studies, Ga. Dental Assn. (hon.; spkr. ho. of dels. 1999—2004, v.p. 2004—05, pres.-elect 2005—06, pres. 2006—07), Am. Coll. Dentists; mem.: Med. Coll. Sengia Steering Com., Ea. Dist. Dental Soc. (pres. 1982—83), Med. Coll. Ga. Orthodontic Alumni Assn. (pres. 1981—83), Ga. Assn. Orthodontists (v.p. 1983—84, pres. 1984—85, exemplary svc. award), So. Assn. Orthodontists (spokesperson, sec.-treas. 1993—95, dir. 1995, pres. 2000, Disting. Svc. award 2001—06), Am. Assn. Orthodontists (Ga. del., chmn. mem., ethics and jud. conderns, spkr. of house 1995—97, trustee 2002—, sec., treas.), ADA (del.), Omicron Kappa Upsilon, Psi Omega (pres. 1967—68). Roman Catholic. Home: 3214 Candace Dr Augusta GA 30909-3259 Office: 3545 Wheeler Rd Augusta GA 30909-6517

ROGERS, MICHAEL BRUCE, physics professor; b. Teaneck, NJ, Oct. 16, 1965; BA in Physics, SUNY, Geneseo, NY, 1994; MS in Physics, Oreg. State U., 1999, MA in Archaeology, 2001, PhD in Physics, 2003. Grad. tchg. fellow Oreg. State U., Corvallis, Oreg., 2000—03; asst. prof. Ithaca (N.Y.) Coll. Physics, 2003—. Cpl. US Army, 1988—91. Decorated 2 Achievement medal US Army, Commendation medal, Good Conduct medal, Nat. Def. Svc. medal; recipient Conspicuous Svc. cross, NY State, 1996. Mem.: Am. Phys. Soc. (mem. exec. com. 2005—), Am. Assn. Physics Tchrs., Soc. Am. Archaeologists, Am. Geophys. Union, Soc. Physics Students, Am. Phys. Soc., Sigma Pi Sigma, Sigma Xi. Office: Ithaca College Physics 265 Center for Natural Sciences Ithaca NY 14850 Business E-Mail: mrogers@ithaca.edu.

ROGERS, MIKE (MICHAEL J. ROGERS), United States Representative from Michigan; b. Livonia, Mich., June 2, 1963; m. Diane Rogers; 1 child. BA in Sociology and Criminal Justice, Adrian Coll., Mich., 1985. Spl. agt. FBI, 1989—94; small bus. owner; mem. Mich. Senate from 26th dist., 1995-2000; vice chmn. judiciary com. Mich. Senate, mem. fin. svc., human resources, labor and vet affairs coms., mem. reappropriations com., mem. tech. and energy commn., mem. banking and fin. com.; mem. US Congress from Mich. 8th dist., Washington, 2001—; mem. fin. svcs. and transp. coms.; mem. Com. on Energy and Commerce. Bd. trustees Cleary Coll., Mich. Served as 2nd Lt. rapid deployment US Army, 1985—88. Recipient Nextel Prepared award, Nextel Comm. Inc., 2004, ITS Congl. Champion awrad, Intelligent Transp. Sys. America, 2005, Joseph M. Magliochetti Industry Champion award, Motor and Equipment Mfrs. Assn., 2005. Mem.: Soc. Former Spl. Agents for FBI, Livingston County Home Builders Assn., Am. Heart Assn. Republican. Methodist. Office: US Congress 133 Cannon House Office Bldg Washington DC 20515-2208 also: District Office 1327 E Michigan Ave Lansing MI 48912 Office Phone: 202-225-4872, 517-702-8000. Office Fax: 202-225-5820, 517-702-8642.*

ROGERS, MIKE D., United States Representative from Alabama; b. Hammond, Ind., July 16, 1958; m. Beth Rogers; children: Emily, Evan, Elliot. BA in Polit. Sci., Jacksonville State U., 1981, MPA, 1985; JD, U. Birmingham, 1991. Dir., dislocated worker's project United Way of Etowah County; community rep., psychiatric counselor Northeast Ala. Regional Med. Ctr.; atty. Bolt, Isom, Jackson and Bailey; assoc. then ptnr. Rogers, Young, Wollstein and Hughes; mem. Ala. Ho. of Reps., 1994—2002, US Congress from 3rd Ala. Dist., 2003—. Mem. Calhoun County Commn., 1987—91; active State Rep. Exec. Com., 1990—. Republican. Baptist. Office: US House of Reps 324 Cannon House Office Bldg Washington DC 20515-0103 Office Phone: 202-225-3261.*

ROGERS, NANCY HARDIN, law educator, former dean, former state attorney general; b. Lansing, Mich., Sept. 18, 1948; d. Clifford Morris and Martha (Wood) Hardin; m. Douglas Langston Rogers, Jan. 30, 1970; children: Lynne, Jill, Kim. BA with highest distinction, U. Kans., 1969; JD, Yale U., 1972. Bar: D.C. 1975, Ohio 1972, U.S. Ct. Appeals (6th cir.) 1973, U.S. Dist. Ct. (no. dist.) Ohio 1974, U.S. Dist. Ct. (so. dist.) Ohio 1975. Law clk. U.S. Dist. Judge Thomas D. Lambros, Cleve., 1972-74; staff atty. Cleve. Legal Aid Soc., 1974-75; vis. asst. prof. Coll. of Law Ohio State U., Columbus, 1975-76, asst. prof., 1976-78, 83-89, assoc. prof., 1989-92, prof., assoc. dean acad. affairs, 1992-97, prof., 1992—, Joseph S. Platt, Porter, Wright, Morris & Arthur prof. law, 1995—2001, vice provost acad. adminstrn., 1999—2001, dean Michael E. Moritz Coll. Law, 2001—08, Michael E. Moritz chair in alternative dispute resolution, 2001—; acting atty. gen. State of Ohio, 2008—09. Adj. prof. Ohio State Coll., 1981-83; vis. prof. law Harvard Law Sch., 2000. Author (with Frank E.A. Sander, Sarah R. Cole, Stephen B. Goldberg): (Book) Dispute Resolution: Negotiation, Mediation and Other Processes), 2007; author: (book with Craig A. McEwen and Sarah R. Cole) Mediation: Law, Policy, Practice, 2nd edit., 1994; mem. (adv. bd.) World Arbitration and Mediation Report, 1991—, Alternatives, 1992—, co-chair (editl. bd. with Frank E.A. Sander) Dispute Resolution mag.,

1994—2002; contbr. chapters to books, articles to profl. jours. Bd. dirs. Assn. for Developmentally Disabled, Columbus, 1980-85; Legal Svcs. Corp. 1995-2003. Recipient Book prize, Ctr. Pub. Resources for A Student's Guide to Mediation and the Law, 1987, Ctr. Pub. Resources for Mediation: Law, Policy, Practice, 1989, Peacemaker of Yr. award, Comty. Mediation Svcs. Ctrl. Ohio, 1990, Disting. Svc. Recognition, Soc. Profls. in Dispute Resolution, 1990, Whitney North Seymour sr. medal, Am. Arbitration Assn., 1990, Svc. Recognition award, Legal Aid Soc. Columbus, 1996, Ritter award, Ohio State Bar Found for outstanding contbns. to adminstrn. of justice, 1998, Ohio Bar medal, 2008, Pres. award, Columbus Bar Found., 2008; named Outstanding Prof., Ohio State U. Coll. Law Alumni Assn., 1996; grantee Exxon Edn. Found., 1986, William and Flora Hewlett Found., 1990, Ohio State U. Interdisciplinary Seed, 1990, Ohio State U. Symposium, 1992, William and Flora Hewlett Found., 1992—96, Nat. Sci. Found., 1993—95, State Justice Instn., 1994, Fund for Improvement Post-Secondary Edn., U. Mo., 1996—97, William and Flora Hewlett Found., 1997—2003. Mem. ABA (chair, standing com. dispute resolution 1988-91, D'Alemberte-Raven award sect. on dispute resolution 2002), Assn. Am. Law Schs. (pres. 2007), Phi Beta Kappa. Office: Ohio State U Coll Law 55 W 12th Ave Columbus OH 43210-1306 Office Phone: 614-292-0574. Business E-Mail: rogers.23@osu.edu.*

ROGERS, NANCY MARIE, music educator; d. Joseph Wood and Margaret Anne Rogers; m. Michael Howard Buchler, Aug. 4, 1991. BA, Northwestern U., Evanston, IL, 1987; MusB, Northwestern U., 1987; MusM, U. Mich., Ann Arbor, 1989; PhD, U. Rochester, Eastman Sch. Music, NY, 2000. Lectr. Northwestern U., 1994—96; asst. prof. music theory U. Iowa, 1996—2000, Lawrence U., Appleton, Wis., 2000—02; assoc. prof. music theory Fla. State U., Tallahassee, 2002—. Faculty cons., reader, auther Coll. Bd. Ednl. Testing Svc., Princeton, NJ, 2002—. Co-author: (book) Music for Sight Singing. Mellon fellow, Woodrow Wilson Nat. Fellowship Found., 1987. Mem.: Coll. Music Soc., Music Theory SE (pres. 2008—), Soc. Music Perception & Cognition, Soc. Music Theory (sec. 2004—08), Sigma Alpha Iota, Pi Kappa Lambda, Phi Beta Kappa. Office: FL State Univ Coll Music Tallahassee FL 32303-1180 Personal E-mail: nancy_m_rogers@yahoo.com.

ROGERS, PATRICIA LOUISE, education educator, consultant, dean; b. St. Paul, Apr. 16, 1956; life ptnr. W. S. Larson. BS, U. Minn., Twin Cities, 1979, MA, 1982, PhD, 1997. Lic. tchr. art and theatre Minn., 1979. Tchr. St. Paul Schs., 1979—82; cancer rschr. U. Minn. Sch. Pub. Health, Mpls., 1984—95; prof. Bemidji State U., Minn., 1996—2006, dean Coll. Social and Natural Scis., 2007—08, dean Coll. Health Scis. and Human Ecology, Sch. Grad. Studies, 2008—; dean Sch. Edn. and Grad. Studies Valley City State U., ND, 2006—07. Cons. and trainer for online tchg. Minn. State Colls. and Univs., Twin Cities, cons., 1998—; spkr. in field. Editor: (book) Designing Instruction for Technology-Enhanced Learning, Ency. of Distance Learning, Teaching, Technologies and Applications; contbr. articles to profl. jours. Vice chair Minn. Online Coun., 2003—04, chair, 2004—06. Recipient 1st Ann. Pioneer award, Minn. Online Coun.; grantee, Minn. State Colls. and Univs. under a FIPSE Grant, 2001—02; scholar, Fulbright, Coun. for Internat. Exch. Scholars, 2000—01; Dissertation fellow, Getty Ctr. for Arts in Edn., 1996. Mem.: ND Assn. Colls. Tchr. Edn., Nat. Art Edn. Assn., Assn. Ednl. Comm. and Tech., Rotary Internat. (assoc.). Dfl. Office: Bemidji State Univ Coll Health Scis and Human Ecology Sch Grad Studies 1500 Birchmont Dr NE Bemidji MN 56601 Office Phone: 218-755-2965. Business E-Mail: progers@bemidjistate.edu.

ROGERS, PAULLETO, researcher, writer, delegate; b. Washington, Mich., Aug. 22, 1961; s. Paulleto Rogers I and Dorothy L.R. Rogers; children: Alexis R. Roycia July, Ambre L. Majasticaa. Student, Wayne County CC, 1984—85; cert. computer ops., Mother Waddles Sch., 1990—91. Cert. paralegal. Pres. C.C.OA, LA, 1983; gen. operator CBOU, 1983—; regent agent Security MGN, 1984; collector Nat. Credit Corp., LA, 1985; craftman Vinyl Indsl. Products, Chgo., 1986; field insp. Mortgage Svcs. Assoc., Inc., 1995; sales cons. Swepo, 1996; legal tech. cons. Probone Legal Svcs., 1997; directorate Prousa Internat. Projects 2001, 1998. Substaining member Rep. Platform Commn., 1986; substaining sponsor Ronald Reagan Presdl. Found., Libr., and Ctr. Pub. Affairs, Ventura County, Calif., 1988; sponsor Statue of Liberty Ellis Island Centennial Commn., 1985, Ronald Reagan Congressional-Vicotry Fund, 1987; advisorate Senate Adv. Coun., 1997; co-founder Justice Inst.; vol. Mother Waddles-Petr. Mission Support; del. at large Del. Adv. Coun.; legal adv. Alexis, Ambre, Dorthy-Lewis, Paul, Paulleto, Rogers, Sutton, Profl. Corp., 2001, adv. Stampout Hunger, 2000-08. Creator, founder The Collectionals Survey. At-large-del. Rep. Presdl. Task Force, 1992—, lobbyist, 1994—; activist US Def. Com., 1985; lobbyist Prousa Legal Corpsusa, 1999; del. Wayne County Clk. Office; Mich. state advisor Rep. Senatorial Com.; active GOPAC, congl. VIP, 1984; GOP Victory Fund sponsor NRCC, 1984; supporter Kidsfirst YESMI, 2000; assoc. mem. Ch. Tae Adv., 2000—. Decorated Rogers Coat of Arms, Medieval Knight, Chevron, 2000; recipient Cert. Recognition, NRCC, 1990, Cert. Appreciation, Presdl. Commn. A.A., 1990, Presdl. award Rep. Presdl. Legion of Merit, 1994. Mem. Oahspe (assoc.), World Peace Tonite/Freedom Inst. (assoc.), 2nd Ch. of Tae. Avocations: copyrights, activism, lobbying, community reinvesting. Home: PO Box 27473 Detroit MI 48227-0473 Office: Paulleto Rogers & Assoc PLLC EDM Rogers & Rogers LLC 315 W Allegan St Ste A PO Box 13203 Lansing MI 48901 Personal E-mail: rogerspaulleto@yahoo.com.

ROGERS, PETER PHILLIPS, environmental engineer, educator, urban planner; b. Liverpool., England, Apr. 30, 1937; arrived in U.S., 1960, naturalized, 1970; s. Edward Joseph and Ellen (Duggan) R.; m. Suzanne Ogden, Oct. 24, 1998; children: Christopher, Justin. B in Engring., Liverpool U., 1958; MS, Northwestern U., 1961; PhD, Harvard U., 1966. Asst. engr. Sir Alfred McAlpine & Sons Ltd., Cheshire, Eng., 1958-60; mem. faculty Harvard U., 1966—, Gordon McKay prof. environ. engring., 1974—, prof. city planning, 1974—. Mem. Ctr. for Environment Harvard U., 2002—; cons. World Bank, UN, U.S. Agy. for Internat. Devel., Govt. India, Govt. Pakistan, Govt. Bangladesh, Govt. Nepal, Govt. Italy, Govt. Costa Rica, Commonwealth P.R. Co-author: Urbanization and Change, 1970, Land Use and The Pipe: Planning for Sewerage, 1975, Resource Inventory and Baseline Study Methods for Developing Countries, 1983, Systems Analysis for River Basin Management, 1985, Evaluacion de Projectos de Desarrollo, 1990, America's Waters, 1993, Water in the Arab World, 1994, Measuring Environmental Quality in Asia, 1997, Science with a Human Face, 1997, Water Crisis: Myth or Reality, 2006, Introduction to Sustainable Development, 2006. Mem. World Commn. for Water in 21st Century. Gordon McKay tchg. fellow 1961; Radley rsch. student, 1962-64; doctoral dissertation fellow Resources for Future 1964-65; recipient Clemens Herschel prize Harvard U., 1964; Guggenheim fellow, 1973, 20th Century Found. fellowship, 1989, Maass-White fellow U.S. Army C.E., 2003.Warren Hall medal US Domestic Coun. Water Resources, 2008. Fellow: AAAS; mem.: ASCE, U. Coun. Water Resources (Warren Hall medal 2008), Third World Acad. Scis. (corr.), Indian Inst. Agrl. Engring. (life), Cambridge Tennis Club. Home: 20 Berkeley St Cambridge MA 02138 Office: Harvard U 116 Pierce Hall Cambridge MA 02138 Home Phone: 617-547-7473; Office Phone: 617-495-2025. Business E-Mail: rogers@seas.harvard.edu.

ROGERS, RALPH A., JR., insurance company executive; BBA, Tenn. Technol. U., Cookeville. CPA. Sr. v.p. fin. resources UnumProvident Corp.; sr. v.p. fin. svcs. AFLAC Inc., Columbus, Ga., 2000—02, sr. v.p., fin. svcs. acctg. officer, 2002—. Mem.: AICPA, Inst. Mgmt. Accts., Fin. Execs. Internat., Tenn. Soc. CPAs. Office: AFLAC Inc 1932 Wynnton Rd Columbus GA 31999 Office Phone: 706-323-3431.

ROGERS, RAYMOND JESSE, retired federal railroad associate administrator; b. Eugene, Oreg., Mar. 1, 1941; s. Raymond Everett and Virginia Elaine (Simpkins) R.; m. Joan Katherine Peterson, June 6, 1964 (div. Aug. 1974); 1 child, Virginia Arlene; m. Kim Lien Nguyen, Dec. 26, 1974; children: Kim Lan, Vincent Minh. Student, Santa Rosa Jr. Coll., Calif., 1960-61, U.S. Army Non-commd. Officer Acad., Anchorage, Alaska, 1963, U. Md., 1967-74, Fed. Exec. Inst., Charlottsville, Va., 1981. Lic. real estate agt., Va. Sr. asst. mgr. Household Fin. Corp., Md., 1964-67; contract specialist Dept. Navy, Washington, 1967-71; contract svcs. officer AID, Saigon, Vietnam, 1971-76; contracting officer Dept. Transp., Fed. R.R. Adminstrn., Washington, 1976-80, dir. fin. svcs., 1980-84, assoc. adminstr. for adminstrn., 1984—2002, CFO, CIO, 1994—2002, ret., 2002. Leader local group Boy Scouts Am., Vienna, Va., 1987-92, Izaac Walton League of Am., Am. Legion, Am. Assn. of Retired Persons. Sgt. U.S. Army, 1961-64. Decorated Vietnam Civilian Svc. medal. Mem. U.S. Sr. Exec. Svc., Fed. Exec. Inst. Alumni Assn. Avocations: fishing, hiking, camping, waterskiing. Home: 102 Yeonas Dr SW Vienna VA 22180-6557 Personal E-mail: Rayvin78@aol.com.

ROGERS, RICHARD DEAN, federal judge; b. Oberlin, Kans., Dec. 29, 1921; s. William Clark and Evelyn May (Christian) R.; m. Helen Elizabeth Stewart, June 6, 1947; children— Letitia Ann, Cappi Christian, Richard Kurt. BS, Kans. State U., 1943; JD, Kans. U., 1947. Bar: Kans. 1947. Ptnr. firm Springer and Rogers (Attys.), Manhattan, Kans., 1947-58; instr. bus. law Kans. State U., 1948-52; partner firm Rogers, Stites & Hill, Manhattan, 1959-75; gen. counsel Kans. Farm Bur. & Service Cos., Manhattan, 1960-75; judge U.S. Dist. Ct., Topeka, Kans., 1975—. City commr., Manhattan, 1950-52, 60-64, mayor, 1952, 64, county atty., Riley County, Kans., 1954-58, state rep., 1964-68, state senator, 1968-75; pres. Kans. Senate, 1975. Served with USAAF, 1943-45. Decorated Air medal, Dfc. Mem. Kans., Am. bar assns., Beta Theta Pi. Clubs: Masons. Republican. Presbyterian. Office: US Dist Ct 444 SE Quincy St Topeka KS 66683 Office Phone: 785-295-2735.

ROGERS, RICHARD HILTON, hotel executive; b. Florence, SC, May 26, 1935; s. Leslie Lawton and Bessie (Holloway) R.; m. Evelyn Pasciuto; children: Richard Shannon, Leslie Anne. Student, U. N.C., 1953-55; BA in Bus. Adminstrn. cum laude, Bryant U., 1961; postgrad., Memphis State U., 1964; DHL (hon.), Schiller Internat. U., Dunedin, Fla., 2003. Innkeeper Helmsley Spear, NYC, 1961—62; v.p. Holiday Inns of Am., Memphis, 1963—73; exec. v.p. First Hospitality Corp., Hackensack, NJ, 1974—77; v.p., chief oper. officer Cindy's Inc., Atlanta, 1978—82; v.p. 1982 World's Fair, Knoxville, Tenn.; pres., chief exec. officer Hospitality Internat., Atlanta, 1982—92; dir. franchise devel. Baymont Inns, 1992, 2000. Developer, operator The Warehouse Restaurant, Oxford, Miss., 1973-75, Beauregard's Restaurant, Hattiesburg, Miss., 1975-78. Contbr. to profl. jours. Mem. adv. bd. U. South Fla. With USN, 1954-58, Korea. Mem. Am. Hotel/Motel Assn. (mktg. com. 1986-92, adv. coun. 1987-92, industry adv. bd., chmn.), Economy Lodging Coun. Avocations: sailing, photography. Home and Office: 8525 Hope Vine Roswell GA 30076 Personal E-mail: innkpr@charter.net.

ROGERS, RICHARD LEE, academic administrator, educator; b. NYC, Sept. 17, 1949; s. Leonard J. and Beverly (Simon) R.; m. Susan Jane Thornton, Aug. 14, 1976; children: Caroline, Meredith. BA, Yale U., 1971, MA in Religion, 1973; postgrad., U. Chgo., 1977-80; MS in Edn., Bank St. Coll. Edn., NYC, 1989. Tchr. Foote Sch., New Haven, 1974-77; devel. assoc. U. Chgo., 1980-81, spl. asst. to v.p. planning, 1981-82; spl. asst. to pres. New Sch. Social Rsch., NYC, 1982-83, sec. of corp., then v.p., sec., 1983-94; pres. Coll. for Creative Studies, Detroit, 1994—. Office: Coll for Creative Studies 201 E Kirby St Detroit MI 48202-4048 Office Phone: 313-664-7474. Business E-Mail: rrogers@collegeforcreativestudies.edu.

ROGERS, ROBERT ERNEST, medical educator; s. Jessie H. and Willie L. (Bahr) Rogers; m. Barbara Ann Hill, May 16, 1950; children: Robert E., Jr., Stephanie Ann Thompson, Cheri Lee Heck. BS in Biology, John B. Stetson U., 1949; MD, U. Miami, 1957. Diplomate Am. Bd. Ob-Gyn. Commd. 1st lt. M.C., U.S. Army, 1952, advanced through grades to col., 1971—74; ret. U.S. Army, 1974; intern Brooke Gen. Hosp., San Antonio, 1957-58, chief resident ob-gyn, 1960-61; resident in ob-gyn Jackson Meml. Hosp., Miami, Fla., 1958-60; fellow gynecology M.D. Anderson Hosp., Houston, 1965-66; asst. chief ob-gyn Tripler Army Med. Ctr., Honolulu, 1966-69; chmn. ob-gyn Walter Reed Med. Ctr., Washington, 1969-70, Madigan Army Med. Ctr., Tacoma, 1970-74; prof. Ind. U. Sch. Medicine, Indpls., 1974—, also chief gynecol. div., 1974—; chief ob-gyn svd. Wishard Meml. Hosp., Indpls., 1983-87. Contbr. articles to profl. jours.; editl. bd. Jour. Am. Coll. Surgeons, 2003—. Bd. dirs. Lake Stonebridge Homeowner's Assn., 2000—03, sec., 2000—03. Recipient Army Commendation medal, 1969, Army Meritorious Service Medal, 1971, Army Legion of Merit, 1974, Army Surgeon General's "A" Prefix for Profl. Excellence, 1974. Mem.: ACS, ACOG (chmn. gynecol. practice com., commr. practice, Sci. Exhibit award Armed Forces dist. 1971, Zimmerman Cons. award Armed Forces dist.), AMA (Certificate Merit for Sci. Exhibit 1971), Felix Rutledge Soc. (pres. 1981, historian), Internat. Soc. Advancement Humanistic Studies Medicine (pres. 1997—98), Soc. Gynecol. Oncologists, Soc. Gynecol. Surgeons (pres. 1983—84). Avocations: gardening, photography. Office: Ind U Sch Medicine 550 University Blvd Indianapolis IN 46202-5149 Home Phone: 317-849-4330; Office Phone: 317-849-4026. Personal E-mail: boberogers@gmail.com. Business E-Mail: reroger@iupui.edu.

ROGERS, ROY STEELE, III, dermatologist, educator, dean; b. Hillsboro, Ohio, Mar. 3, 1940; s. Roy S. Jr. and Anna Mary (Murray) R.; m. Susan Camille Hudson, Aug. 22, 1964; children: Roy Steele IV, Katherine Hudson. BA, Denison U., 1962; MD, Ohio State U., 1966; MS, U. Minn., 1974. Cert. dermatologist, dermatopathologist and immunodermatologist. Intern Strong Meml. Hosp., Rochester, NY, 1966—67; resident Duke U. Med. Ctr., Durham, NC, 1969—71, Mayo Clinic, Rochester, Minn., 1972—73, cons., 1973—, prof. dermatology, 1983—, dean Sch. Health Related Scis., 1991—99. Adv. coun. Rochester Community Coll., 1991-2000; citation of appreciation Internat. League Dermatologic Soc., 2007. Contbr. over 250 sci. articles to publs. Mem. Rochester Planning and Zoning Comm., 1980—88; bd. dir. Casabella Assn., 2006—08. Capt., flight surgeon USAF, 1967—69. Recipient Alumni Achievement award Ohio State U. Coll. Medicine, 1991, Alumni citation Denison U., 1993, Faculty Svc. award Mayo Med. Sch., 1993, Gold medal 2d Med. Sch., Charles U., Prague, 2002; named Disting. Educator, Mayo Clinic, 2004, Thomas G. Pearson Meml. Edn. award, 2004, Everett J. Fox Lectureship, 2005, Paul A. O'Leary Lectureship, 2005. Mem. Am. Acad. Dermatology (hon., bd. dirs. 1987-91, v.p. 1999, Everett C. Fox lectureship 2005, Gold Triangle award 2004, Thomas G. Pearson Meml. Edn. award 2005), Am. Soc. Dermatologic Allergy and Immunology (sec.-treas. 1988-2000), Am. Dermatologic Assn. (v.p. 2002-03), Soc. Investigative Dermatology, Assn. Schs. Allied Health Professions, Dermatology Found. (Annenberg Circle 2002). Avocations: travel, reading, walking. Office: Mayo Clinic 200 1st St SW Rochester MN 55905-0002 Home: 10101 N Arabian Tail No 1006 Scottsdale AZ 85258 Home Phone: 480-991-4197; Office Phone: 507-284-2555. Business E-Mail: rogers.roy@mayo.edu.

ROGERS, RUTH FRANCES, retired microbiologist; b. Chgo., Nov. 5, 1925; d. Frank Joseph and Ruth Elizabeth (Abbott) Kucera; m. James Alvin Rogers, June 17, 1950; children: Kenneth James, David Wayne. BS, U. Ill., 1948. Microbiologist No. Rsch. Ctr., Nat. Ctr. for Agrl. Utilization Rsch., Peoria, Ill., 1963—85; ret., 1985. Contbr. articles to profl. jours. Recipient Sustained Superior Performance award USDA, 1984. Methodist.

ROGERS, RUTHERFORD DAVID, librarian; b. Jesup, Iowa, June 22, 1915; s. David Earl and Carrie Zoe (Beckel) R.; m. E. Margaret Stoddard, June 4, 1937; 1 child, Jane Shelley; m. Bernette W. Barton, Feb. 28, 2002. BA, U. No. Iowa, 1936, Litt.D., 1977; MA, Columbia, 1937, BS (Lydia Roberts fellow), 1938; D.Library Adminstrn. (hon.), U. Dayton, 1971. Asst. N.Y. Pub. Library, 1937-38; reference librarian Columbia Coll. Library, Columbia U., 1938- 41, acting librarian, 1941-42, librarian, 1942-45; research analyst Smith, Barney & Co., NYC, 1946-48; dir. Grosvenor Library, Buffalo, 1948-52, Rochester Pub. Library, 1952-54; chief pers. office N.Y. Pub. Libr., 1954-55; chief reference dept., 1955-57; chief asst. librarian of Congress, Washington, 1957-62, dep. librarian of, 1962-64; dir. univ. libraries Stanford U., 1964-69; univ. librarian Yale U., 1969-85, univ. librarian emeritus, 1985—. Founder, chmn. bd. dirs. Rsch. Librs. Group, Inc.; mem. Exam. Com. for Pub. Librarians' Certs., N.Y. State, 1951-54; mem. U.S. Adv. Coun. Coll. Libr. Resources; bd. govs. Yale U. Press; bd. dirs., v.p. H.W. Wilson Found., 1969-98; chmn. program mgmt. com. Internat. Fedn. Libr. Assns. Author: Columbia Coll. Library Handbook, 1941, (with David C. Weber) University Library Administration, 1971; also articles in profl. jours. Served from pvt. to 1st sgt. Air Transp. Command USAAF, 1942-43; from 2d lt. to capt., planning officer, chief, spl. Planning Div., Office Asst. Chief Staff, Plans, Air Transport Command 1943-46. Decorated officier de L'Ordre de la Couronne Belge; recipient U. No. Iowa Alumni Achievement award, 1958, Disting. Alumni award Columbia U. Sch. Libr. Svc., 1992, medal Internat. Fedn. of Libr. Assns., 1977. Fellow Am. Acad. Arts and Scis.; mem. A.L.A. (chmn. com. Intellectual Freedom 1950-51), (1950-60), (2d v.p. 1965-66), (mem. exec. bd. 1961-66), (trustee endowment fund), Assn. Research Libraries (dir., pres. 1967-68), N.Y. Library Assn., AAUP, Bibliog. Soc. Am., Assn. Coll. and Reference Libraries, Blue Key, Kappa Delta Pi, Sigma Tau Delta, Theta Alpha Phi. Clubs: Grolier; N.Y. Library (N.Y.C.), Columbia U. (N.Y.C.), Yale (N.Y.C.); Cosmos (Washington), Kenwood Country (Washington); Roxburghe (San Francisco); Book of Calif. Home (Winter): 1081 Lakemont Ct Winter Park FL 32792-5025

ROGERS, SAMUEL SHEPARD See SHEPARD, SAM

ROGERS, STEPHEN HITCHCOCK, retired ambassador; b. Flushing, NY, June 21, 1930; s. Francis Walker and Julia (Wheeler) R.; m. Kent Brain, June 23, 1956; children: Kryston R. Fischer, F. Halsey, Julia L., John H. BA, Princeton U., 1952; MA, Columbia U., 1956; MPA, Harvard U., 1962. Fgn. svc. officer Dept. of State, 1956-93; econ. counselor Am. Embassy, London, 1970-72; counselor U.S. Mission to OECD, Paris, 1972-75; office dir. Bur. Inter.-Am. Affairs Dept. of State, Washington, 1975-78; econ. counselor Am. Embassy, Mexico City, 1978-82; prof. Nat. Def. U., Washington, 1982-85; econ. counselor Am. Embassy, Pretoria, South Africa, 1986-90, amb. Mbabane, Swaziland, 1990-93; ret., 1993. Bd. dirs. Cen. Atlantic Conf., United Ch. of Christ, 2000-03; v.p. Princeton U. Class 1952, 2002-07, pres., 2007—. Lt. (jg) USN, 1952-55. Recipient Outstanding Civilian Svc. award Dept. of Army, 1985. Mem. Am. Fgn. Svc. Assn., Diplomatic and Consular Officers Ret., Nassau Club (Princeton, N.J.). Mem. United Ch. Of Christ. Home: 3803 Ivydale Dr Annandale VA 22003-2006

ROGERS, STEVEN A., energy executive; B in Econs./Acctg., Coll. Holy Cross, Worcester, Mass., 1983. Contr.-treas. Rehab Mgmt. Inc.; with Deloitte & Touche; mgr. internal audit Dominion Resources, Richmond, Va., 1996—97, v.p., contr. OptaCor Fin. Svcs. Co. subs. of Dominion Capital Inc., 1997—98, corp. contr. Dominion Energy Inc., 1998—2000, v.p., contr., 2000—06, sr. v.p., contr., 2006, sr. v.p., chief acctg. officer, 2007, sr. v.p., chief adminstrv. officer, subsidiary pres., 2007—. Mem. acctg. exec. adv. com. Edison Electric Inst., 2002—, chmn. acctg. exec. adv. com., 2005—06. Bd. mem. Crisis Pregnancy Ctr. Met. Richmond, 2003—, chmn. bd. Office: Dominion PO Box 26532 Richmond VA 23261-6532

ROGERS, T. GARY, apparel company executive, former food products company executive; b. 1943; BSME, U. Calif., 1963; MBA, Harvard U., 1968. Assoc. McKinsey & Co., San Francisco; founder, pres. Vintage Ho. Restaurants, Calif. and Tex.; chmn., CEO Dreyer's Grand Ice Cream, Inc., Oakland, Calif., 1977—2007; chmn. Levi Strauss & Co., 2008—. Bd. dirs. Levi Strauss & Co., 1998—, Shorenstein Co., L.P., Stanislaus Food Products, Gardonjim Farms, The Friends of Calif. Crew, Fed. Res. Bank San Francisco, 2004-, dep. chmn., 2006- Mem. Bay Area Coun. Mem. Internat. Dairy Foods Assn. (bd. dirs.). Office: Levi Strauss & Co 1155 Battery St San Francisco CA 94111

ROGERS, THEODORE COURTNEY, investment company executive; b. Lorain, Ohio, Aug. 25, 1934; s. William Theodore and Leona Ruth (Gerhart) Rogers; m. Elizabeth B. Barlow, June 28, 1984; children from previous marriage: Pamela Anne Rogers Harmon, Theodore Courtney Jr. BS in Social Sci., Miami U., Oxford, Ohio, 1956, LHD (hon.), 2001; postgrad., Johns Hopkins U., 1957; MBA summa cum laude, Marquette U., 1968; MALA, St. John's Coll., Annapolis, Md., 2004. With Armco Inc., 1958-80; pres. Olympic Fastening Sys., 1970-74; with Bathey Mfg. Co. subs., 1970, group v.p. indsl. products, 1971-74; exec. v.p. Nat. Supply Co. subs., Houston, 1974-76, pres., 1976-80, v.p. parent co., 1976-79, group v.p. parent co., 1979-80; pres., COO NL Industries, Inc., NYC, 1980-82, pres., CEO, 1982-83, chmn., pres., CEO, 1983-87; chmn. Am. Indsl. Ptnrs., NYC, 1987—. Chmn. Bucyrus Internat.; vice chmn. bd. trustees St. John's Coll. Nat. coun. Theatre Comm. Group; bd. dirs. Lincoln Ctr. Peforming Arts, City Ctr. Music and Drama; chmn. bd. dirs. Theatre for New Audience; former chmn. Ctr. Cmty. Interests; emeritus chmn. N.Y.C. Ballet; bd. dirs., trustee Ballet Rev. Qur. Lt. USN, 1956—58. Mem.: Am. Acad. Arts & Scis., Film Forum (bd. dirs.), Poets and Writers (bd. dirs.), NY Soc. Libr. (trustee), Grolier Club, Union Club (Cleve.), Econs. Club (N.Y.), Achilles Track Club (founder, bd. dirs.), Century Assn. (N.Y.), Links

Club, Met. Club (Washington), Univ. Club (Milw.), Kappa Phi Kappa, Sigma Chi (Significant Sig, Sigma Chi Hall of Fame 2005), Beta Gamma Sigma (bd. dirs.). Office: Am Indsl Ptnr 551 5th Ave Ste 3800 New York NY 10176-0001

ROGERS, THEODORE OTTO, JR., lawyer; b. West Chester, Pa., Nov. 17, 1953; s. Theodore Otto and Gladys (Bond) R.; children: Helen Elliot, Theodore Scott, Robert Montgomery Bond. AB magna cum laude, Harvard U., 1976, JD cum laude, 1979. Bar: NY 1980, US Ct. Appeals (2nd cir.) 1984, US Dist. Ct. (so. and ea. dists.) NY 1980, DC 1981, US Ct. Claims, 1982, US Supreme Ct. 1983, US Ct. Appeals (6th and 10th cirs.) 1983, US Ct. Appeals (1st cir.) 1984, US Ct. Appeals (fed. cir.) 1986. Assoc. Sullivan & Cromwell, NYC, 1979—87, ptnr., 1987—, and coord. labor and employment practice area. Co-author: (books) Employment Litigation in New York, 1996, Employment Law Desk-Book for Human Resources Professionals, 2001. Mem. US Presdl. Transition Team, 1980. Named one of Two Leading Labor and Employment Lawyers in NYC, Global Counsel Handbooks 2003-08 guides, Ten Leading Mgmt. Side Attys. in Country, Human Resources Exec., 2008, Six Leading Defense Employment Lawyers, Chambers Guide, NY, 2009; named to Best Lawyers in America, 2006, 2007, 2008. Fellow Coll. Labor and Employment Lawyers; mem. ALI, NY State Bar Assn. (labor and employment law sect.), Assn. Bar City NY (labor and employment law). Republican. Office: Sullivan & Cromwell 125 Broad St Fl 28 New York NY 10004-2489 Office Fax: 212-558-3588. Business E-Mail: rogerst@sullcrom.com.

ROGERS, THOMASINA VENESE, commissioner; b. 1951; m. Gregory M. Gill; 1 child, Cleo. BS in Journalism, Northwestern U., 1973; JD, Columbia U. Chmn. Adminstrv. Conf. U.S., Washington, 1994-95; presdl. pers. staff The White House, Washington; dep. legal counsel, then legal counsel EEOC, Washington; commr. Occupl. Safety & Health Rev. Commn. (OSHRC), Washington, 1998—2003, 2003—09, 2009—, chmn., 1999—2002, acting chmn., 2009. Bd. dirs. Children's Nat. Med. Ctr. Mem. Am. Arbitration Assn. (bd. dirs.) Office: Occupl Safety and Health Review Commn One Lafayette Ctr 1120 20th St NW Washington DC 20036-3457*

ROGERS, WANDA FAYE, vocalist; b. Oct. 24, 1929; d. John Riley and Bessie Louise Narmore; m. Weldon Nelson Rogers Sr., Feb. 27, 1959 (div. 1967); 1 child, Weldon Nelson. Student, Modesto Jr. Coll. Lic. radio broadcast. Author: (song book) Wanda Faye Song Book, 2004; singer: (CD) UFO, recorded with Jewel Records, 1958-64, Germanys Bear Import Records, 1998, Columbia Records, 1965, The Sunset Westerners, Sta. KGFL, 1946—53, Sta. WBAP, Ft. Worth, Tex., 1954—57. Named to, Cowgirl Mus. Hall of Fame, 2002, Hall of Fame, Western Swing Soc., Sacramento, 2003. Avocations: music, writing songs.

ROGERS, WILLIAM H., JR., bank executive; Exec. v.p. SunTrust Securities, Inc., Atlanta; sr. v.p. fin. SunTrust Banks, Inc., Atlanta, corp. exec. v.p. wealth and investment mgmt., mortgage, comml. and corp. and investment banking lines of bus., pres., 2008—. Office: SunTrust Banks Inc PO Box 4418 Atlanta GA 30302-4418 Office Phone: 404-588-7711. Office Fax: 404-827-6173.*

ROGERS, WILLIAM RAYMOND, retired academic administrator, psychologist, educator; b. Oswego, NY, June 20, 1932; s. William Raymond and A. Elizabeth (Hollis) R.; m. Beverley Claire Partington, Aug. 14, 1954; children: John Partington, Susan Elizabeth Apple, Nancy Claire Glassman. BA magna cum laude, Kalamazoo Coll., 1954; BD, U. Chgo. and Chgo. Theol. Sem., 1958; PhD, U. Chgo., 1965; MA (hon.), Harvard U., 1970. Cons., staff counselor Counseling and Psychotherapy Rsch. Ctr., U. Chgo., 1960-62; tchg. fellow, counselor to students Chgo. Theol. Sem., 1961-62; asst. prof. psychology and religion, dir. student counseling Earlham Coll., Richmond, Ind., 1962-68, assoc. prof. psychology and religion, assoc. dean of Coll., 1968-70; vis. lectr. pastoral counseling Harvard U. Div. Sch., Cambridge, Mass., 1969-70, prof. religion and psychology Div. and Edn. Schs., 1970-80, faculty chmn. clin. psychology and pub. practice, 1970-72, chmn. counseling and cons. psychology, 1979-80; prof. psychology and religious studies Guilford Coll., Greensboro, NC, 1980—, pres., 1980-96, pres. emeritus, 1996—. Bd. dirs. Moses Cone Health Sys., 1984-96, Moses Cone-Wesley Long Cmty. Health Found., 1996-2002, chmn. 1996-2002; bd. dirs. BB&T, Kendal Corp., chmn. 2005-09. Author: The Alienated Student, 1969, Project Listening, 1974, Nourishing the Humanistic in Medicine, 1979; Contbr. articles to profl. jours. Bd. dirs. Greensboro Symphony Soc.; mem. Cemala Found, Mary Reynolds Babcock Found. Danforth Found. fellow, Blatchford Traveling fellow U. Chgo. and Chgo. Theol. Sem. Mem.: Islesboro Hist. Soc. (pres. 1999—2002), So. Assn. Colls. and Schs., Nat. Assn. Ind. Colls. and Univs., Friends Com. on Nat. Legislation (mem. policy com.), Friends Assn. Higher Edn., Soc. Values in Higher Edn., Tarratine Club of Dark Harbor (bd. govs.), Rotary (past pres.). Mem. Soc. Of Friends. Home: 4212 B Trillium Ln Greensboro NC 27410-8871

ROGERS-DILLON, ROBIN, sociologist, educator; b. NYC, Oct. 2, 1968; d. Donald Warren and Kay Rogers; children: Nicholas Warren, Dashiell Ellis. PhD in Sociology, U. Pa., Phila., 1998. Robert Wood Johnson scholar health policy rsch. Yale U., New Haven, 1998—2000; assoc. prof. sociology CUNY Grad. Ctr., 2000—, Queens Coll., NYC, 2000—, dir. honors social sci. Flushing, NY, 2005—07; rsch. fellow Princeton U., Ctr. Study Religion, 2007—08. Author: (book) The Welfare Experiments: Politics and Policy Evaluation; contbr. articles to profl. jour. Congl. fellow women and pub. policy US House Representatives, Washington, 1995—96. Recipient Pres. award, Queens Coll., 2003. Mem.: Women's Studies Quarterly (editl. bd. mem.). Office: Queens Coll 65-30 Kissena Blvd Flushing NY 11367-1597 Office Fax: 718-997-2820. Business E-Mail: robin.rogers-dillon@qc.cuny.edu.

ROGERSON, CRAIG ALLAN, manufacturing executive; b. Detroit, July 4, 1956; s. William Durie and Eunice Clara (Richert) R.; m. Carina Joy Ballato, Sept. 11, 1982; children: Scott Allan, Kristen Joy, Colin William. BS in Chem. Engring., Mich. State U., 1979. Tech. rep. Water Mgmt. Chemicals div. Hercules Inc., Charlotte and Wilmington, N.C., 1979-82, sales rep. Fibers div. Atlanta, 1982-85, market devel. supr., 1985-87, product mgr., 1987-88, nat. sales mgr., 1989-90, dir. ops. Oxford, Ga., 1991-92, bus. dir. Wilmington, Del., 1992-94, sales dir. paper tech. divsn., 1995-96, v.p., gen. mgr. fibers divsn., 1996—97; pres., CEO Wacker Silicones Corp., 1997—2000; v.p., Betz Dearborn Div. Hercules Inc., 2000, pres., Betz Dearborn Div., 2000—02, pres., FiberVisions, 2002—03, pres., Pinova, 2002—03, v.p., Global Procurement, 2002—03, acting pres., COO, 2003, pres., CEO, 2003—08; chmn., pres., CEO Chemtura Corp., Middlebury, Conn., 2008—. Bd. dirs. PPL Corp., First State Innovation. Mem. Del. Bus. Roundtable (bd. dirs.), Am. Chemistry Coun. (bd. dirs.). Republican. Lutheran. Avocations: golf, travel, fishing. Home: PO Box 702 Gwynedd Valley PA 19437-0702 Office: Chemtura Corp 199 Benson Rd Waterbury CT 06749 Office Phone: 203-573-2000.*

ROGGE, RENA WOLCOTT, librarian; b. Bklyn., Nov. 3, 1920; d. Ralph Stratton and Mona Florence (Shannon) Wolcott; m. Carl Frederick Rogge Jr., Aug. 4, 1942; 1 son, Carl Frederick Rogge. B.A., Elmira Coll., 1941; M.L.S., Rutgers U., New Brunswick, N.J., 1966; M.A.L.S., New Sch. Social Research, N.Y.C., 1972, D. Info. Services, Nova Univ., 1987. Sec. Sch. Dist. South Orange, Maplewood, N.J., 1958-65; head reference librarian Cranford (N.J.) Pub. Library, 1966-68; readers' advisor Jersey City, 1968-69; reference librarian Newark State Coll., Union, N.J., 1969—; reference coordinator, asst. dir. for info. services Kean Coll. Library, sec. faculty senate, 1978-79, archivist faculty senate, 1979—, chmn. constn. revision, 1982—, grad. research com. 1983—. Recipient Outstanding Pub. Employee award, State of N.J., 1972, merit Award, 1983; online research grantee, Kean Coll. N.J., 1979. Mem. N.J. Library Assn., Am. Soc. Indexers, N.J. State Coll. Librarians' Assn., Kean Coll. Fedn. Tchrs. (exec. com.). Club: Elmira Coll. Home: 27 Bodwell Ter Millburn NJ 07041-1201 Office: Kean Coll Nancy Thompson Library Morris Ave Union NJ 07083-7117

ROGGENSACK, PATIENCE DRAKE, state supreme court justice; b. Joliet, Ill., 1941; BA, Drake U., 1962; JD, U. Wis. Law Sch., 1980. Atty. Dewitt Ross and Stevens, 1980—96; judge Wis. Ct. of Appeals, 1996—2003; justice Wis. Supreme Ct., 2003—. Mem.: ABA, Wis. Bar Assn. Office: Wis Supreme Ct PO Box 1688 Madison WI 53701-1688*

ROGGENTHEN, WILLIAM, geologist, educator; b. 1947; m. Eileen Roggenthen; 1 child, Michael. BS, SD Sch. Mines Tech., Rapid City, 1971; MS, U. Colo., Boulder, 1971; PhD, Princeton U., NJ, 1980. Cert. profl. geologist Wyo., 2008. Prof. SD Sch. Mines Tech., 1977—. Rschr. deep underground sci. and engring. lab. DUSEL Collaboration, Lead, SD, 2002—. Office: Dept Geology Geo Engring SD Sch Mines 501 E Saint Joseph St Rapid City SD 57701 Business E-Mail: wroggen@silver.sdsmt.edu.

ROGGIO, BOB, retired manufacturing executive; b. Phila., Feb. 7, 1947; m. Jeannie Roggio; children: Dax, Lia, Kate. BA in Am. Studies, Pa. State U., 2003. Various positions including sr. v.p. Zenith Products, 1969—99; ret., 1999; campaign staff Senator John Kerry, 2004; campaign cons. Senator Bob Casey, 2006, regional field rep., 2007—08. Vol. Am. Red Cross; pres. Berwyn-Paoli Little League; founder Great Valley Citizens Forum; mem. Charlestown Open Space Commn., Charlestown Parks & Recreation Bd.; v.p. Charlestown Civic Assn. Served with USAR, 1968—74. Democrat. Mailing: 9 Old Lincoln Hwy Ste 101 Malvern PA 19355 Office Phone: 610-251-0550. Office Fax: 610-251-0559.

ROGIDO, MARTA RAQUEL, medical educator; b. Villa Elisa, Entre Rios, Argentina, Aug. 13, 1957; d. Juan Rogido and Irma Dora Joannaz; m. Augusto Sola, Dec. 22, 1995. MD, U. Buenos Aires, 1981. Lic. in pediatrics Am. Bd. Pediat., 1998, in neonatal perinatal medicine Am. Bd. Pediat., 1999. Asst. prof. pediat. U. Buenos Aires, 1987—91; clin. instr. pediat. U. Calif., San Francisco, 1995—97, asst. prof. pediat., 1999—2001, Emory U., Atlanta, 2001—05, assoc. prof. pediat., 2005—06; assoc. prof. neurology U. Medicine and Dentistry NJ, Newark, 2006—. Nat. dir. resuscitation program Argentinian Acad. Pediat., Buenos Aires, 1990—91. Grantee Rsch. grant, William Tooley Meml. Fund, 1993, Wyeth Pediatric Rsch. Fund, 1994, Emory Egleston Children's Rsch. Ctr., 2002—03, United Cerebral Palsy Found., 2004—06. Fellow: Am. Acad. Pediat.; mem.: SIBEN Neonatal Ibero-Am. Soc., European Soc. Pediatric Rsch., Soc. Pediatric Rsch. Office: Morristown Meml Hosp 100 Madison Ave Morristown NJ 07960 Office Fax: 973-290-7175. Business E-Mail: marta.rogido@atlantichealth.org.

ROGILLIO, KATHY JUNE, musician, director, small business owner, educator; b. Baton Rouge, Nov. 4, 1950; d. David Hunter and Thelma Ruth (Tucker) R. MusB, La. State U., 1972, MusM, 1974. Organist Plains Presbyn. Ch., Zachary, La., 1963-73; teacher's aid Gifted/Talented East Baton Rouge Parish, 1974-75; staff accompanist La. State U., Baton Rouge, 1975-76; music enrichment tchr. Episc. HS, Baton Rouge, 1976-77; organist, choirmaster Grace Episc. Ch., St. Francisville, La., 1977-82; piano-technician So. U., Baton Rouge, 1977-84; apprentice in piano rebuilding and concert tuning with G.L-.Burton, 1978—81; music tchr., organist, choirmaster St. Patrick's Episc. Day Sch. and Ch., Zachary, La., 1985-86; vis. organist, dir. Numerous Chs., La. and Miss., 1982—; piano rebuilder pvt. practice, Zachary, La., 1986—. Ind. contract work Santi Falcone, Falcone Piano Co., Haverhill, Mass., 1987-88, part time organist/choirmaster St. Patrick's Episcopal Ch., Zachary, La., 1999-2000; pvt. piano tchr. La. Sch. for Visually Impaired, 2000-04; recitalist, vis. organist.; music dir., organist Faith Presbyn. Ch., Baton Rouge, La., 2002-07, aff. mem., 2004; guest artist First Bapt. Ch., Baker, La., 2003; music dir., organist, choir master Grace Meml. Episcopal Ch., Hammond, La., 2007—. Arranger: Piano-Trio Arrangement Brahms Intermezzo Opus 118, #2, 1986 (2d pl. Composer's Guild Farmington, Utah, 1986). Treas. Beulah Plains Cemetery Assn., Zachary, La., 1987; mem. Landowners for Equitable Flood Control, Zachary, La., 1994—; Dem. candidate for U.S. Ho. of Reps. from 6th Dist. La., 2000. Mem. Am. Guild Organists, Baton Rouge Musicians' Assn. (exec bd. 1990-92, v.p. 1992-94. pres. 1994-96), La. Endowment for the Humanities, La. Pub. Broadcasting, Order Ea. Star, Better Bus. Bur., Pi Kappa Lambda (profl. mus. hons. frat.). Democrat. Episcopalian. Avocations: needlework, cooking. Home and Office: Artist Pianos 18153 Barnett Rd Zachary LA 70791-8114 Home Phone: 225-654-4654; Office Phone: 225-654-8555.

ROGIN, GILBERT LESLIE, editor, author; b. NYC, Nov. 14, 1929; s. Robert I. and Lillian Carol (Ruderman) R. Student, State U. Iowa, 1947-49; AB, Columbia, 1951. Editor-at-large Miller Pub., LA, 1955—. Author: The Fencing Master, 1965, What Happens Next?, 1971, Preparations for the Ascent, 1980. Served with AUS, 1952-54. Recipient award for creative work in lit. Am. Acad. Inst. Arts and Letters 1972 Home: 21 W 10th St New York NY 10011

ROGOFF, JEROME HOWARD, psychiatrist, psychoanalyst, forensic expert; b. Detroit, Dec. 21, 1938; s. Abraham Solomon and Sarah Riva (Epstein) R.; (div. 1983); m. Erika Kathleen Keller, Sept. 25, 1983. BA cum laude, Harvard Coll., Cambridge, Mass., 1960; MD, Case Western Res. U., Cleve., 1965. Diplomate Am. Bd. Psychiatry and Neurology. Physician Peace Corps USPHS, Kathmandu, Nepal, 1966-68; clin. fellow psychiatry Harvard Med. Sch., Boston, 1975-79; staff psychiatrist Westwood (Mass.) Lodge Hosp., 1972-74; assoc. clin. prof. psychiatry Tufts Med. Sch., Boston, 1977-86; assoc. chief, psychiatry and dir., inpatient Psychiatry, day hosp. Faulkner Hosp., Boston, 1975-94; pvt. practice psychiatry, psychoanalysis and forensic psychiatry, 1994—. Cons. psychiatrist Mass. Parole Bd. Probate Ct. Plymouth County, Mass., LEAA, Washington, 1971-78; med. psychiat. dir. ct. diversion program Boston TASC-A, 1974-75; treas. Guild for Continuing Edn., Boston, 1981-95; founding dir. Law and Psychiatry Resource Ctr., Boston, 1983-2005; adj. prof. Simmons Sch. Social Work, Boston, 1981-85; lectr. psychiatry Harvard Med. Sch., Boston, 1986-94, 2001-. Chmn. psychiatry team Combined Jewish Philanthropies, Boston, 1978—83, assoc. chmn. med. team, 1984—87, social planning and allocations com., 1991—98, cmty. svcs. com., 1998—2007, chmn. chronic mental illness com., 1999—2000, disabilities com., 2000—04; bd. dirs. Jewish Vocat. Svc., Boston, 1987—91. Fellow: Am. Psychiat. Assn. (life; Disting., pub. affairs rep. 1988—94, budget com. 1996—2002, assembly rep. 2000—07, chmn. corr. com. on confidentiality 2003—07, task force to revise code of ethics 2005—, area dep. rep. 2007—09, mem. assembly exec. com. 2007—, area rep. 2009—); mem.: APA, AMA, Am. Assn. Pvt. Practice Psychiatrists, Am. Acad. Psychiatry and Law, Mass. Psychiat. Soc. (chair pub. affairs com. 1988—92, councillor 1988—94, chair nominating com. 1990, chair pub. affairs com. 1993—94, pres.-elect 1998—99, pres. 1999—2000, chair nominating com. 2000, Mass. rep. to Assembly 2000—07). Democrat. Avocations: cabinetry, carpentry, cooking, classical music, languages. Home and Office: 659 Chestnut St Waban MA 02468-2035 Office Phone: 617-964-1805. *Two guiding principles, both from my father: "When in doubt, do the right thing." Sounds trite and naive, but turns out in the event to be profound; one almost always knows deep down what the right thing is. "When you are born, you cry, and everyone around you laughs. So live your life that when you come to leave it, you laugh, and everyone around you cries." On my profession of psychiatry and psychoanalysis: psychotherapy adds insight to injury.*

ROGOFF, KENNETH SAUL, economics professor; b. Rochester, NY, Mar. 22, 1953; s. Stanley Miron and June Beatrice (Goldman) R.; m. Evelyn Jane Brody, Aug. 18, 1979 (div. 1989); m. Natasha Lance, June 25, 1995; children: Gabriel, Juliana. BA/MA in Econs., Yale U., 1975; PhD in Econs., MIT, 1980. Economist Internat. Monetary Fund, Washington, 1983; economist, sect. chief Internat. Fin. divsn., Bd. Govs. of the Fed. Res. Sys., Washington, 1979-84; assoc. prof. econs. U. Wis., Madison, 1985-89; prof. econs. U. Calif., Berkeley, 1989-92; prof. econs. and internat. affairs Princeton U., 1992—, Charles and Marie Robertson prof. of internat. affairs, 1995-98; prof. econs. Harvard U., 1999—, Thomas D. Cabot prof. pub. policy, 2004—, dir. Ctr. Internat. Devel., 2003—04; econ. counselor, dir. rsch. IMF, 2001—03. Vis. scholar San Francisco Fed. Res., 1990-92, World Bank, Washington, 1989, IMF, Washington, 1988-94. Author books and contbr. articles to profl. jours. Alfred P. Sloan Rsch. fellow, 1986-87, Hoover Instn. Nat. fellow, 1986-87, NSF fellow, 1985—, John Simon Guggenheim fellow, 1998. Fellow World Econ. Forum, Econometric Soc., Am. Acad. Arts and Scis., World Econ. Forum; mem. Am. Econ. Assn.(mem. trilateral com., v.p., 2007), Gsap of Thirty, Coun. on Fgn. Rels., Internat. Grandmaster Chess. Office: Harvard U Econs Dept Littauer Ctr Cambridge MA 02138-3001 Home: 11 Hillside Ave Cambridge MA 02140 Office Phone: 617-495-4022. Business E-Mail: krogoff@harvard.edu.

ROGOFF, PAULA DRIMMER, English and foreign language educator; b. NYC; d. George and Florence (Levine) Drimmer; m. Arnold Stevan Rogoff; children: Jeffrey Scott, Eric Todd, Brian Craig. BA cum laude, Hunter Coll., 1961; MEd summa cum laude, William Paterson Coll., 1979. Cert. elem. tchr., ESL tchr., supr., N.J. Tchr. handicapped Herricks Bd. Edn., Williston Park, NJ, 1965—68; tchr. reading compensatory edn. Oakland Bd. Edn., Oakland, NJ, 1981—84; tchr., coord. gifted-talented program North Haldeon Bd. Edn., NJ, 1984—85; ESL adult tchr., h.s. students Passaic County Tech. Inst., Wayne, NJ, 1989—2004. Presenter Children's Libr. programs. Named Tchr. of Yr., Passaic County Tech. Inst., 1999-2000. Mem. ASCD, NEA, TESOL, Internat. Platform Assn., N.J. Edn. Assn., Phi Beta Kappa, Phi Lambda Theta, Kappa Delta Pi. Home: 11 Furman Dr Wayne NJ 07470-5304 Office: Passaic County Tech Inst 45 Reinhardt Rd Wayne NJ 07470 Office Phone: 973-790-6000.

ROGOFF, PETER M., federal agency administrator; b. 1960; BA in Am. Studies, Amherst Coll., 1983; MBA with honors, Georgetown U., 2001. Staff mem. US Senate Appropriations Com., Washington, Dem. staff dir. Transp. Subcom.; adminstr. Fed. Transit Adminstrn. (FTA) US Dept. Transp., Washington, 2009—. Recipient US Coast Guard Disting. Pub. Svc. Award, Lester P. Lamm Meml. Award. Office: Fed Transit Adminstrn East Bldg 1200 New Jersey Ave SE Washington DC 20590 Office Phone: 202-336-4040.*

ROGOFF, TAMAR, choreographer; Choreographer, tchr. P.S. 122, NYC, NYU Exptl. Theater Wing; arts coord., artistic dir. Solar One, NYC. Choreographer Angle of Ascent, Lincoln Ctr., 1989, In Deep, 1991, The Ivye Project, Belarus, 1994, Demeter's Daughter, East Village, NYC, 1997, Daughter of a Pacifist Soldier, 2002, Christina Olson: America Model, 2005, Edith & Jenny, 2007, Anatomy Theatre, 2009. Fellow NY Found. Arts, 1988, 2003, John Simon Guggenheim Meml. Found., 2009. Office: Solar 1 2421 FDR Dr Svc Rd E New York NY 10010*

ROGOL, ALAN DAVID, pediatric endocrinologist; b. New Haven, Mar. 9, 1941; s. Oscar and Bess (Halperin) R.; m. Joanne Schoderbek, Nov. 2,1968; children: Ian, Babette. BS, MIT, 1963; PhD, MD, Duke U., 1970. Diplomate Am. Bd. Pediat., 1975, pediat. sub-bd. endocrinology. Prof. U. Va., Charlottesville, 1975—, prof. clin. pediatrics, 2002—; clin. prof. internal medicine Med. Coll. Va., Richmond; pres. ODR Consulting, Charlottesville, Va., 2002—. Prin. clin. scientist INSMED Pharmaceuticals, Inc., 1999—2001. Lt. comdr. USPHS, 1972-74. Fellow Am. Coll. Sports Medicine, Am. Acad. Pediats.; mem. Lawson Wilkins Pediatric Endocrine Soc. (sec. 2004—), Endocrine Soc., Am. Pediat. Soc. Office: U Va Health Sys Dept Pediat PO Box 800386 Charlottesville VA 22908-0386 Business E-Mail: arogol@estone.net. E-mail: adr@virginia.edu.*

ROGOSKI, PATRICIA DIANA, corporate financial executive; b. Chgo., Dec. 29, 1939; d. Raymond Michael and Bernice Rose (Konkol) R. BS in Acctg. and Econs., Marquette U., 1961, postgrad., 1965-66, NYU, 1966-68, St. John's U., NYC, 1975-76; cert. mgmt. acct., 1979. Sr. fin. analyst Blackhawk Mfg. Co., Milw., 1961-66; mgr., sr. analyst Shell Oil Co., NYC, 1966-71; mgr. data processing Bradford Nat./Penn Bradford, Pitts., 1971-75; asst. mgr. fin. controls ITT, NYC, 1975-79; v.p., comptr. ITT Consumer Fin. Corp., Mpls., 1979-80; sr. v.p. fin. ITT Fin. Corp., St. Louis, 1980-84; v.p., exec. asst., group exec. ITT Coins, Secaucus, NJ, 1984-85; pres. Patron S., Ltd., Wilmington, Del., 1986—; CFO, sr. v.p. Guardsmark, Inc., Memphis, 1989-94; sr. v.p. Peoplemark, Inc., Memphis, 1989-94. Bd. dirs. St. Louis Repertory Theater, 1983-84. Named to Acad. Women Achievers, YWCA, N.Y.C., 1980. Mem. Fin. Execs. Internat., Inst. Mgmt. Acctg., Econ. Club, Memphis Symphony Chorus. Avocation: duplicate bridge. Office: Patron S Ltd 2711 Centerville Rd Ste 400 Wilmington DE 19808- Personal E-mail: patrons@msn.com.

ROGOVIN, LAWRENCE H., lawyer; b. NYC, June 10, 1932; s. Abraham and Laura R.; m. Saundra Schwartz, Aug. 11, 1957; children: Jayne Lina, Wendy Renee, Evan Lewis. BS in Econ., Wharton Sch. U. Pa., 1953; LLB cum laude, NYU Law Sch., 1956. Bar: NY 1956, Fla. 1971. Dep. asst. atty. gen. State of N.Y., 1956-57, asst. atty. gen., 1960-61; assoc. Squadron, Gartenberg, Ellenoff & Plesent and predecessors, NYC, 1962-67, ptnr., 1967-72; pvt. practice Miami, Fla., 1972—74, Lawrence H. Rogovin Pa., 1983—98, Lawrence H. Rogovin, P.A., Miami, 2002—; ptnr. Squadron, Ellenoff, Plesent & Lehrer, NYC, 1974-75, Cohen, Angel & Rogovin, North Miami, Fla., 1978-82, Cohen,

Rogovin, Reed & Ivans, Miami, 1982-83; v.p., gen. counsel Rare, Inc., Miami, 1998—2002. 1st lt. JAGC, USAFR, 1957-60. Recipient NYU Founders Day award, 1956. Mem.: ABA, Fla. Bar Assn. Office: Ste 265 South 4000 Hollywood Blvd Hollywood FL 33021 Office Phone: 954-367-0666. Office Fax: 954-272-0225. Business E-Mail: lrogovin@bellsouth.net.

ROH, HEUI-SEOL, research scientist, educator; PhD, Ind. U., Bloomington, 1995. Rsch. scientist Stevens Inst. Tech., Hoboken, NJ, 2006—; adj. prof. Manhattan Coll., Riverdale, NY, 2008—. Contbr. articles to profl. jours. Achievements include patents in field. Office: Stevens Inst Tech Castle Point on Hudson Hoboken NJ 07030

ROH, MYUNG HWAN, medical educator; b. Busan, Republic of Korea, Aug. 8, 1961; s. Weon Bo Roh and Sang Inn Park; m. Eun Joo Hwang, Jan. 17, 1987; children: Seung Yoon, Hee Yoon. MD, Busan Nat. U., 1987; PhD, Dong-A U. Grad. Sch. Medicine, Busan, 2005. Cert. med. dr. Korean Ministry for Health, Welfare, 1987, Korean Soc. Internal Medicine, 1995, Korean Soc. Gastroenterology, 1997, Korean Soc. Gastrointestinal Endoscopy, 1998. Instr. Coll. Medicine, Dong-A U., 1997—99, asst. prof., 1999—2002, assoc. prof., 2002—, prof., 2009—; chief instr. endoscopic ctr. Dong-A U. Hosp., Busan, 2003—08. Contbr. articles to profl. jours. Master: Pancreatobiliary Disease Com. (Busan) (pres. 2009—); mem.: Korean Soc. Gastrointestinal Endoscopy, Korean Soc. Gastroenterology, Korean Soc. Internal Medicine, Korean Med. Assn., Gastrointestinal Endoscopic Assn. (com. mem. 2009—), Internal Med. Assn. (Busan) (com. mem. 2007—), Korean Soc. Gastrointestinal Cancer (ethical com. mem. 2008—), Korean Soc. Pancreatobiliary Disease, Korean Soc. Neurogastroenterology, Am. Gastroent. Assn (internat. mem. 2001—). Office: Dong-A Univ Hosp 3ga1 Dong Dae Shin Dong Seo Gu Busan 602-103 Republic of Korea Office Fax: 82 51-242-5852. Business E-Mail: mhnho@dau.ac.kr.

ROHACK, JOHN JAMES, cardiologist; b. Rochester, NY, Aug. 22, 1954; s. John Joseph and Margaret Elizabeth (McLaughlin) R.; m. Charlotte (Charli)McCown, Dec. 7, 1980; 1 child, Elisha Monique Feigle. BS with highest honors, U. Tex., El Paso, 1976; MD with honors, U. Tex. Med. Branch, Galveston, 1980. Diplomate Am. Bd. Internal Medicine. Intern U. Tex. Med. Br. Hosps., Galveston, 1980—81, resident internal medicine, 1981-83, chief resident internal medicine, 1983-84, fellow cardiology, 1984-86; instr. medicine U. Tex. Med. Br., Galveston, 1983-86; asst. prof. medicine to assoc. prof. Tex. A&M Coll. Medicine, College Station, 1986—2002, prof., 2002—, sect. chief cardiology, 1989-97, prof., 2002—. Assoc. med. dir. Scott and White Health Plan Bryan Coll. Sta., 1995-97; assoc. med. dir. for med. ops. Scott and White Clinic, Temple, Tex., 1997-2000, med. dir. Health Plan, 2000-04, med. dir. sys. improvement, 2004-, dir. healthcare policy, 2004-, sr. staff cardiologist; bd. dirs. Health for All Clinic, v.p., 1994-96; mem. Accreditation Coun. on Continuing Med. Edn., 1995-99, Liaison Com. on Med. Edn., 1999-2001; med. dir. Fitlife Ctr. Tex. A&M U., College Station, 1990-97; mem. bd. commrs. Joint Commn. on Accreditation of Healthcare Orgns., 2002—. Bd. dirs. Am. Heart Assn., Brazos Valley College Station, 1987-97, Tex. affiliate Austin, 1991-98, 1st v.p., 1994-95, pres.-elect, 1995-96, pres., 1996-97. Named Disting. Alumnus, U. Tex., El Paso, U. Tex., Galveston; named one of 50 Most Powerful Physician Executives in Healthcare, Modern Healthcare and Modern Physician, 2009. Fellow ACP, Am. Coll. Cardiology (bd. dirs. Tex. chpt. 1992-97); mem. AMA (alt. del. house of dels. 1984-93, del. 1993-2001, coun. on med. edn. 1995-2001, chair elect 1996-97, chair 1997-98, bd. trustee 2001-, pres.-elect 2008-, exec. com. 2003-06, chair 2004-05, pres.-elect 2008-2009, pres. 2009-), Tex. Med. Assn. (exec. coun. med. student sect. 1981-82, chair, coun. on med. edn., house of dels. 1982—, trustee 1994-2002, pres.-elect 1999-2000, pres. 2000-2001). Avocations: golf, gardening, reading, ranching. Office: Scott and White Clinic 2401 S 31st St Temple TX 76508-0001

ROHAM, MASOUD, biomedical researcher; b. Tabriz, Azarbaijan, Iran, Aug. 23, 1979; m. Hanieh Ghasemi, Sept. 14, 1986. MSc, Sharif U. Tech., Tehran, 2005; PhD, Case Western Res. U., Cleve, 2006—. Rsch. asst. Case Western Res. U., 2006—. Achievements include design of wireless integrated circuits for in-vivo recording of chemical and electrical activity inside brain. Office: Case Western Reserve Univ 10900 Euclid Ave Glennan 808 Cleveland OH 44106 Business E-Mail: masoud.roham@cwru.edu.

ROHAN, KAREN S., insurance company executive; BS, Boston Coll., 1984; MBA, Boston U., 1999. CPA. With CIGNA Corp., 1991—, contr., sr. v.p. underwriting CIGNA HealthCare, v.p., bus. fin. officer CIGNA HealthCare, 2000—02, chief underwriting officer CIGNA HealthCare, 2003—04, pres. CIGNA Specialty Cos., 2004—05, pres. CIGNA Dental & Vision Care, 2004—, pres. CIGNA Group Ins., 2005—. Office: CIGNA Corp Two Liberty Pl 1601 Chestnut St Philadelphia PA 19192-1550

ROHAN, KELLY J., psychology professor, researcher; b. Binghamton, Oct. 29, 1970; d. Betty J. and John, Jr. F. Rohan; m. Steven C. Cooley, Aug. 22, 1998; 1 child, Liam S. Cooley. PhD, U. Maine, Orono, 1998. Lic. psychologist Vt. Bd. Psychology, 2005. Asst. prof. Uniformed Svcs. U., Bethesda, Md., 2000—05; assoc. prof. psychology U. Vt., Burlington, 2005—. Contbr. scientific papers to profl. jours. (SLTBR Young Investigator award, 2003). Roman Catholic. Office: Univ VT Psychology Dept John Dewey Hall 2 Colchester Ave Burlington VT 05405-0134

ROHAN, THOMAS E., epidemiologist, educator; MD, U. Adelaide, Australia, 1975, PhD in Epidemiology, 1986; M.Sc in Epidemiology, U. London, 1981, M.Sc. in Med. Statistics, 1996. Intern Broken Hill Hosp., Australia, 1976—77; resident Flinders Med. Ctr., Australia, 1977; rsch. fellow U. Melbourne, 1979—80, CSIRO Divsn. Human Nutrition, 1981—86; sr. lectr. dept. environ. & preventive medicine St. Bartholomew's Hosp., 1986—87; epidemiologist MRC Epidemiology & Med. Care Unit, London, 1987—88; asst. prof. dept. preventive medicine & biostatistics U. Toronto, 1989—90, assoc. prof. dept. preventive medicine & biostatistics, 1990—97, dir. NCIC Epidemiology Unit, 1995—96, prof. dept. pub. health sciences, 1997—2000; adj. prof. dept. oncology McGill U., 1996—; prof. & chmn. dept. epidemiology & population health Albert Einstein Coll. Medicine, 2000—, assoc. dir. population rsch., 2000—. Recipient Terry Fox Cancer Rsch. Scientist award, Nat. Cancer Inst. Canada, 1996. Fellow: Australasian Faculty of Pub. Health Medicine, Am. Coll. Epidemiology, Royal Australian Coll. General Practitioners; mem.: Am. Assn. Cancer Rsch., Soc. Epidemiologic Rsch. Office: Albert Einstein College of Medicine Belfer Bldg Rm 1301 1300 Morris Park Ave Bronx NY 10461 Office Phone: 718-430-3355. Office Fax: 718-430-8653. E-mail: rohan@aecom.yu.edu.*

ROHATGI, PRADEEP KUMAR, engineering educator; BS, Banaras U., 1961; MS, MIT, 1963, DSc in Metallurgy, 1964. Rsch. metallurgist Merica Rsch. Lab., Suffern, NY, 1964—68; vis. faculty Indian Inst. Tech., Kanpur, 1968—69, prof. Bangalore, 1972—77; rsch. engr. Homer Rsch. Lab., Bethlehem, Pa., 1969—72; founder dir. regional rsch. lab. Coun. Sci. and Indsl. Rsch., Trivandrum, India, 1977—86; prof. Materials Dept., Milw., 1986—. Author (editor): State of the Art in Cast Metal Matrix Composites, Processing, Properties and Applications of Cast Metal Matrix Composites, Friction, Wear and Lubrication of Metal Matrix Composites. Recipient Nat. Metallurgists' Day award, Ministry, India, 1976, Gold Medal award, Indian Rsch. Ctr., 1981, UWM Outstanding Svc. award, 1992, Hall Heroult Sci. Merit award, Am. Foundrymens Soc., 2000, Award of Excellence, NRI, 2004, Hon. medal, Motor Trasport Inst., Warsaw, 2006, Bharat Gaurav award, 2007; named Wis. Disting. professorship, U. Wis., Milw., 1996; fellowship, ASME, 2007, grant, Coll. Engring. and Applied Sci., UWM, 2008. Mem.: Wis. Coalition Asian Indian Orgns. (bd. mem. 2002—), Milw. Ethnic Coun. (mem. steering com. 2002—).

ROHATYN, DENNIS, philosopher, educator; b. NYC, Apr. 21, 1949; children: Heather Pargament, Naomi. PhD, Fordham U., Bronx, NY, 1972. Asst. prof. philosophy Roosevelt U., Chgo., 1972—77; prof. philosophy U. San Diego, 1977—. Author: (book) The Reluctant Naturalist, 1986, Philosophy History Sophistry, 1997. Mem.: Philosophers Social Responsibility (sec. 1988—2007, treas. 1988—2007). Office: Univ San Diego 5998 Alcala Pk San Diego CA 92110-2492 Office Phone: 619-260-4704. Office Fax: 619-260-7950. Business E-Mail: drohatyn@sandiego.edu.

ROHATYN, FELIX GEORGE, diversified financial services company executive, former ambassador; b. Vienna, May 29, 1928; came to U.S., 1942, naturalized, 1950; s. Alexander and Edith (Knoll) R.; m. Jeannette Streit, June 9, 1956; children: Pierre, Nicolas, Michael; m. Elizabeth Fly, May 31, 1979. BS, Middlebury Coll., Vt., 1948; LLD (hon.), Adelphi U., Bard Coll., Hofstra U., 1981, L.I. U., 1981, Middlebury Coll., 1982, Fordham U., 1983; LLD (hon.), Columbia U., 2007; LLB (hon.), NYU, 1979, Brandeis U., 1987. With Lazard Freres & Co., LLC, NYC, 1948—97, mng. dir., 1960—97; US amb. to France US Dept. State, Paris, 1997—2001; pres. Rohatyn Assocs., NYC, 2002—06; sr. adv. to chmn. Lehman Brothers Inc., NYC, 2006—. Bd. dirs. Publicis Group, Lagardere Group, LVMH, Inc.; mem. bd. govs. N.Y. Stock Exch., 1968—72. Served with AUS, 1951—53, Korea. Office: Lehman Brothers Inc 745 7th Ave 31st Fl New York NY 10019 Office Phone: 212-526-5000. Business E-Mail: felix.rohatyn@lehman.com.

ROHDE, JAMES VINCENT, medical devices company executive; b. O'Neill, Nebr., Jan. 25, 1939; s. Ambrose Vincent and Loretta Cecillia Rohde; children: Maria, Sonja, Daniele, Olga. B of Comml. Sci., Seattle U., 1962. Chmn. bd. dirs., pres. Applied Telephone Tech., Oakland, Calif., 1974; v.p. sales and mktg. Automation Electronics Corp., Oakland, 1975-82; founder, pres., CEO, chmn. Am. Telecorp, Inc., Redwood City, Calif., 1982-99; founder, vice-chmn., bd. dirs. Ceon Corp., Redwood City, 1999—2008; co-founder & CEO BirthBuddies, Inc., 2009—. Chmn. exec. com., chmn. emeritus Pres.'s Coun. Heritage U., Toppenish, Wash., 1985—; chmn. bd. dirs. Calif. chpt. Coun. Growing Cos., 1990—93. Bd. dirs. Ind. Colls. No. Calif., 1991—93. With aux. USCG, 2005—. Recipient Export Exec. of Yr., US Dept. Commerce, Northern Calif., 1993. Mem.: Am. Electronics Assn. (bd. dirs. 1992—94, vice-chmn Northern Calif. Coun. 1992—93, chmn. 1993—94). Republican. Roman Catholic. Personal E-mail: jvrohde@aol.com.

ROHLF, F. JAMES, biologist, educator; b. Blythe, Calif., Oct. 24, 1936; BS, San Diego State Coll., 1958; PhD in Entomology, U. Kans., 1962. Asst. prof. biology U. Calif., Santa Barbara, 1962-65; assoc. prof. statis. biology U. Kans., 1965-69; assoc. prof. biology SUNY, Stony Brook, 1969-72, prof., 1972—2004, chmn. dept. ecology and evolution, 1975—80, 1990—91, disting. prof., 2004—, grad. program dir., 2005—06. Statis. cons. N.Y. Pub. Svc. Commn., 1975-78, IBM, 1977-81, U.S. EPA, 1978-80, TMT, 2006-; vis. scientist IBM, Yorktown Heights, N.Y., 1976-77, 80-81; vis. prof. U. Rome, 1997, 99; guest prof. U. Vienna, 2004. Fellow: Am. Acad. Arts and Scis., AAAS; mem.: Internat. Fedn. Classification Socs. (coun. 2005—07), Classification Soc. N.Am. (pres. 1975—78, editl. bd. 1984—, bd. dirs. 1994—97, fin. com. 2004—06, rep. to coun. 2004—07, election com. 2006—07, bd. dirs. 2006—), Soc. Systematic Biologists, Biometric Soc. Achievements include research and development of statistical methods and software for geometric morphometrics and applications of multivariate analysis to systematics and population biology. Office: Stony Brook U Dept Ecology And Evolution Stony Brook NY 11794-5245

ROHLFING, FREDERICK WILLIAM, lawyer, retired judge, political scientist; b. Honolulu, Nov. 2, 1928; s. Romayne Raymond and Kathryn (Coe) R.; m. Joan Halford, July 15, 1952 (div. Sept. 1982); children: Frederick W., Karl A., Brad (dec.); m. Patricia Ann Santos, Aug. 23, 1983. BA, Yale U., 1950; JD, George Washington U., 1955. Bar: Hawaii 1955, Am. Samoa 1978. Assoc. Moore, Torkildson & Rice, Honolulu, 1955-60; ptnr. Rohlfing, Nakamura & Low, Honolulu, 1963-68, Hughes, Steiner & Rohlfing, Honolulu, 1968-71, Rohlfing, Smith & Coates, Honolulu, 1981-84; pvt. practice Honolulu, 1960-63, 71-81, Maui County, Hawaii, 1988—; dep. corp. counsel County of Maui, Wailuku, Hawaii, 1984-87, corp. counsel, 1987-88; land and legal counsel Maui Open Space Trust, 1992-97, also bd. dirs. Polit. cons., 1996, 98, 2002; magistrate judge U.S. Dist. Ct. Hawaii, 1991-96. Active Hawaii Ho. Reps., 1959-65, 80-84, Hawaii State Senate, 1966-75; US alt. rep. So. Pacific Commn., Noumea, New Caledonia, 1975-77, 1982-84; mem. adv. coun. State Reapportionment Commn., Maui, Hawaii, 2001, mem. salary commn. Maui (Hawaii) County, 2005-08, Statewide Health Coordinating Coun., 2008-; hon. chmn. Maui coms. George W. Bush for Pres., 2000, 2004, Maui coord., John McCain for pres., 2008. Mem. Hawaii Bar Assn., Maui Country Club, Naval Intelligence Profls. Avocations: golf, swimming. Home: 2807 Kekaulike Ave Kula HI 96790

ROHM, ROBERT HERMANN, sculptor, educator; b. Cin., Feb. 6, 1934; s. Hermann George and Anna Katherine (Sager) R.; m. Patricia Jean Cutlip, Dec. 6, 1959 (div. 1978); children: Hans Tobin, Kyle Curtis. B in Indsl. Design, Pratt Inst., 1956; MFA in Sculpture, Cranbrook Acad. Art, 1960. Instr. Columbus (Ohio) Coll. Art and Design, 1956-59, Pratt Inst., Bklyn., 1960-65; prof. art U. R.I., Kingston, 1965-95, pres. emeritus, 1996—. One-man shows include O.K. Harris Gallery, N.Y.C., 1970, 72, 73, 75, 77, 80, 83, 84, 86, 89, 92, 94, 97, 99, 2002, 05, 09, Parker St. 470 Gallery, Boston, 1970, 72, Univ. Rochester, N.Y., 1971, N.S. Coll. Art, Halifax, 1970, Worcester Art Mus. (Mass.), 1978, Univ. R.I., 1981, 88, 94, Nielsen Gallery, Boston, 1985, 86, 92, 93, 2001, Wheaton Coll., Norton, Mass., 2002, La Jolla Mus. Contemporary Art, Calif., 1985, Lenore Gray Gallery, Providence, 1990, 93, 95, Wheeler Gallery, Providence, 1996, R.I. Coll., Providence, 1998, Salve Regina U., Newport, R.I., 2003; group shows include Boston Mus., 1974, Whitney Mus., N.Y.C., 1962, 64, 69, 70, 73, 83, Va. Mus., Richmond, 1970, Fogg Mus., Cambridge, Mass., 1971, Seattle Art Mus., 1969, Vancouver Art Mus., B.C., Can., 1970, N.J. State Mus., Trenton, 1969, R.I. State Coun. on Arts, 1973, 82, Vassar Coll., 1971, Inst. Contemporary Art, Boston, 1975, Miss. Mus. Art, Jackson, 1979-80, Grey Art Gallery, NYU, 1980, Montclair (N.J.) Art Mus., 1978, Aldrich Mus. Contemporary Art, Ridgefield, Conn.,1981, 82, SUNY-Plattsburgh, 1981, Zone Gallery, Springfield, Mass., 1982, Cumberland Gallery, Nashville, 1986, 93, Allan Frumkin Gallery, N.Y.C., 1985, Beitzel Fine Arts Inc., N.Y.C., Addison Gallery Am. Art, Andover, Mass., 1989, Nielsen Gallery, Boston, 1990-91, 99, 2004, 2007, Soma Gallery, San Diego, 1993, Palo Alto (Calif.) Cultural Ctr., Centre Coll., Danville, Ky., Harn Mus., U. Fla., Gainesville, 2004, Brevard Mus. Art & Sci., Melbourne, Fla., 2004; represented in permanent collections Columbus Gallery Fine Art, Finch Coll., N.Y.C., Pa. State U., Kunsthalle, Zurich, Va. Mus. Fine Arts, Mus. Modern Art, N.Y.C., U. N.Mex., Albuquerque, Albright-Knox Gallery, Buffalo, Whitney Mus. Am. Art, N.Y.C., Met. Mus. Art, N.Y.C., Rose Art Mus., Brandeis U., Waltham Mass., Mus. Fine Art, Boston, Mus. of Contemporary Art, Chgo., Newport (R.I.) Art Mus., Tucson Mus. of Art, Ariz., Flint Inst. Arts, Mich., Butler Inst. Am. Art, Youngstown, Ohio, Munson-Williams Proctor Arts Inst. Mus. Art, Utica, N.Y., Harn Mus., U. Fla., Gainesville, Amarillo Mus. Art, Tex., Erie Art Mus., Pa. Grantee Guggenheim Found., 1964, R.I. State Council on Arts, 1973, 82, 93, NEA, 1974, 86; recipient Cassandra Found. award, 1967, award Boston 200 Bicentennial Commn., 1975. Achievements include subject of numerous articles in jours. and catalogues. Home: PO Box 1679 Charlestown RI 02813-0909 Personal E-mail: robertrohm@hughes.net.

ROHNER, RALPH JOHN, lawyer, educator, dean; b. East Orange, NJ, Aug. 10, 1938; AB, Cath. U. Am., 1960, JD, 1963. Bar: Md. 1964. Teaching fellow Stanford (Calif.) U., 1963-64; atty. pub. health div. HEW, 1964-65; prof. law Cath. U. Am. Sch. Law, Washington, 1965—, acting dean, 1968-69, assoc. dean, 1969-71, dean, 1987-95; staff counsel consumer affairs subcom. U.S. Senate Banking Com., 1975-76; cons. Fed. Res. Bd., 1976-83, chmn. consumer adv. council, 1981; cons. FDIC, 1978-80; spl. counsel Consumer Bankers Assn., 1984—. Cons. U.S. Regulatory Coun., 1979-80. Co-author: Consumer Law: Cases and Materials, 1979, 3d edit., 2007; co-author, editor The Law of Truth in Lending, 1984, republished, 2000. Bd. dirs. Migrant Legal Action Program, Inc., Washington, Automobile Owners Action Coun., Washington, Credit Rsch. Ctr., Georgetown U., Am. Fin. Svcs. Assn. Edn. Found. Conf. on Consumer Fin. Law. Mem. ABA, Am. Law Inst., Coll. of Consumer Fin. Svcs. Lawyers. Home: 10909 Forestgate Pl Glenn Dale MD 20769-2047 Office: Cath U Sch Law 3600 John Mccormack Rd NE Washington DC 20064-0001 Office Phone: 202-319-5140. Business E-Mail: rohner@law.edu. *We learn from those we teach, we are inspired to write by those who read, and we should serve as examples to those who aspire.*

ROHNER, RONALD PRESTON, anthropology educator, psychologist; b. Calif., Apr. 17, 1935; BS in Psychology, U. Oreg., 1958; MA in Anthropology, Stanford U., 1960, PhD in Anthropology, 1964. Prof. emeritus family studies and anthropology U. Conn.; dir. Ctr. for Study Interpersonal Acceptance and Rejection, U. Conn. Author 12 books; contbr. numerous articles to profl. jours., chpts. to books. Pres.& exe. dir. Internat. Soc. Interpersonal Acceptance & Rejection; pres. bd. dirs. Natchaug Psychiat. Hosp.; bd. dirs. Conn. Assn. for Prevention Child Abuse and Neglect. Fellow APA, Am. Psychol. Soc., Am. Anthropol. Assn.; mem. Soc. Cross-Cultural Rsch. (pres. 1983), Internat. Assn. Cross-Cultural Psychology (exec. coun. 1976-78), Soc. Psychol. Anthropology. Home: 255 Codfish Falls Rd Storrs Mansfield CT 06268-1425 Office: U Conn Ctr Interpersonal Acceptance Storrs Mansfield CT 06269-0001

ROHR, DAVID MALCOLM, geologist, educator; b. Sept. 9, 1947; BS, Coll. William Mary, 1969; PhD, Oreg. State U., 1977. Vis. asst. prof. geology U. Oreg., 1977—79, U. Wash., 1979—80; asst. prof. geology Sul Ross State U., Alpine, Tex., 1980—, chair dept. earth and phys. scis., 1994—. Home: 1908 N 5th St Alpine TX 79830-1916

ROHR, DAVIS CHARLES, aerospace consultant, retired military officer; b. Burlington, Wis., Oct. 29, 1929; s. Charles Davis Rohr and Dorothy Elizabeth (Hahn) Rohr Larson; m. Gayle Lynn White, Aug. 22, 1959; children— Ellen Louise, Jean Elizabeth Student, Northwestern U., 1947-48; B.Sc., U.S. Mil. Acad., 1952; MA, U. Wash., 1960. Commd. 2d lt. USAF, 1952, advanced through grades to maj. gen, 1980, fighter pilot Ohio, Korea, Japan, 1954-58; asst. prof. history USAF Acad., Colo., 1960-64; fighter pilot, squadron ops. officer Idaho and, Fed. Republic Germany, 1965-69; fighter squadron comdr. Vietnam, 1969-70; country dir. S.Am. Office of Sec. of Def., Washington, 1970-73; exec. officer, dep. dir. maintenance Hdqrs. Tactical Air Command, 1973-75; tactical fighter wing comdr. Tex., Utah, 1976-79; chief Office of Mil. Coop., Cairo, 1979—81; dir. plans and policy U.S. European Command, Stuttgart, Fed. Republic Germany, 1981-84; dep. comdr. in chief U.S. Cen. Command, MacDill AFB, Fla., 1984-87, ret.; aerospace cons., 1988—. Adj. prof. history Paradise Valley C.C., 1991-94; real estate broker, 1991—. Decorated Def. D.S.M., 2 Def. Superior Service medals, Legion of Merit with cluster, D.F.C., Meritorious Service medal, Air medal with 14 clusters, Air Force Commendation medal, Purple Heart

ROHR, DONALD GERARD, history professor; b. Toledo, Oct. 10, 1920; s. Lewis Walter and Marie (Pilliod) R.; m. Joan Willis Michener, Sept. 14, 1948 (dec.) Apr. 07, 2007; children: Karen, Kristin. BA, U. Toronto, Ont., Can., 1943, MA, 1949; PhD, Harvard U., 1958. Instr., then asst. prof. Williams Coll., 1953—59; mem. faculty Brown U., 1959—, prof. history, 1963—86, prof. history emeritus, 1986—, chmn. dept., 1960—65, 1966—69, 1972—74, sec. faculty, 1969—72, assoc. dean faculty and acad. affairs, 1976—81; adminstrv. dir. Howard Fedn., 1989—92. Author: The Origins of Social Liberalism in Germany, 1963, (with Robert Ergang) Europe Since Waterloo, 1967; editor: The Young John Carter Brown in Europe, 2005. Served with AUS, 1943-46, ETO. Mem. Providence Com. Fgn. Rels. (sec. 1968-81, chmn. 1981-92), Thomas Becket Fedn. (v.p. 1983-84, pres. 1984-86), English Speaking Union (pres. Providence br. 1986-88), U. Club, Faculty Club (Providence, pres. 1981-83). Roman Catholic. Home: 71 Grotto Ave Providence RI 02906

ROHR, DWIGHT MASON, news director, radio marketing consultant; b. Covington, Va., July 18, 1952; s. Edward Mason and Betty (Eppling) R.; m. Betty Erwin, Aug. 1, 1977; children: Christopher Mason, Joseph Michael. AAS in Bus. Mgmt., Dabney S. Lancaster CC, Clifton Forge, Va., 1997. Cert. radio operator; cert. radio mktg. cons. Audio engr. WJBR, Wilmington, Del., 1971-72; announcer WASA/WHDG, Havre de Grace, Md., 1972-73; news dir. mktg. WKEY Inc., Covington, 1974—2005; assoc. Wal-Mart Inc. Active Stonewall Jackson Area coun. Boy Scouts Am., 1990-99; dir. cmty. rels. ARC, Covington, 1975-98; mem. adv. bd. Salvation Army, Covington, 1995-2001, Alleghany County chpt. March of Dimes, 2001-, Alleghany Heart Unit, Potts Valley Singers; city coucilman, Covington, 1997-98; mountaineer Amateur Radio Emergency Svc. Recipient Scouter of Yr. awrd VFW Post 1033, 1994, Dist. award of merit Boy Scouts Am., 1995, Silver Beaver, 1998; named to Outstanding Young Men of Am., 1980. Mem. Soc. Profl. Journalists, Radio TV News Dirs. Assn., Masons, Scottish Rite, Eastern Star, Va. Mountain Amateur Radio Club, Covington Ruritan Club, Natural Bridge Dist. Ruritan Gov., Highland Toastmasters. Avocations: amateur radio, broadcasting, coin collecting/numismatics. Home: 347 E Gray St Covington VA 24426-2109 Office Phone: 540-962-1133. Personal E-mail: w4spj@ntelos.net.

ROHR, JAMES EDWARD (JIM ROHR), bank executive; b. Cleve., Oct. 18, 1948; s. Charles E. and Loretta (Kramer) R.; m. Sharon Lynn Chambers, Dec. 29, 1970; children: Julie, James, Kristen. BA, Notre Dame U., 1970; MBA, Ohio State U., 1972. From comml. banking officer to pres. Pitts. Nat. Bank, 1974-89, chmn., CEO, 1989-93, pres., CEO, 1993—; vice-chmn. PNC Bank Corp., 1989-92, pres., 1992—98, pres., COO, 1998—2000; pres., CEO PNC Fin. Services Group, Inc., Pitts., 2000—01, chmn., CEO, 2001—. Bd. dirs. PNC Fin. Services Group, Inc., 1990-, Allegheny Technologies Inc., 1996-, EQT Corp., 1996-, Black Rock, Inc., 1999-, Fed. Reserve Bank Cleve., 2008- Bd. dirs. Greater Pitts. coun. Boy Scouts Am., Carnegie-Mellon U.; chair Cultural Trust. Recipient Banker of Yr. award, Am. Banker mag., 2007. Mem. Am. Bankers Assn., Internat. Monetary Conf., Fin. Svcs. Roundtable, Allegheny Conf., Pa. Bus. Roundtable. Roman Catholic. Office: PNC Financial Services Group Inc 249 5th Ave Pittsburgh PA 15222-2709*

ROHR, MARK C., chemicals executive; BS, Miss. State Univ., 1975, B in chem. engring., 1977. Sr. v.p. Occidental Chem. Corp.; exec v.p. ops. Albemarle Corp., Richmond, Va., 1999, pres., COO, 2000—02, pres., CEO, 2002—08, chmn., pres., CEO, 2008—. Bd. dir. Ashland Corp., Celanese Corp., Am. Chem. Council; mem. exec. com. NAM; sec. Synthetic Organic Chem. Mfr. Assn. Office: Albemarle Corp 330 S 4th St Richmond VA 23219 Mailing: Albemarle Corp PO Box 1335 Richmond VA 23218 Office Phone: 804-788-6000. Office Fax: 804-788-5688. Business E-Mail: mark_rohr@albemarle.com.

ROHRABACHER, DANA T., United States Representative from California; b. Coronado, Calif., June 21, 1947; s. Donald and Doris Rohrabacher; m. Rhonda Carmony, Aug. 1997; 3 children. Student, LA Harbor Coll.; BA in Hist., Long Beach State Coll., 1969; MA in Am. Studies, U. So. Calif., 1976. Reporter City News Svc./Radio News West, LA; editl. writer Orange County Register, 1979-80; asst. press. sec. Reagan/Bush Com., 1980; speechwriter, spl. asst. to Pres. Reagan White House, Washington, 1981-88; mem. US Congress from 46th Calif. dist., Washington, 1988—, mem. fgn. affairs com., internat. rels. com., sci. & tech. com. US del Young Polit. Leaders Conf., Russia; disting. lectr. Internat. Terrorism Conf., Paris, 1985. Recipient Disting. Alumnus award, LA Harbor Coll., 1987. Republican. Baptist. Avocations: surfing, white water rafting. Office: US House Reps 2300 Rayburn House Office Bldg Washington DC 20515-0546 Office Phone: 202-225-2415.*

ROHRBACH, HEIDI A., lawyer; b. Buffalo, Jan. 25, 1953; d. William R. and A.T. R.; m. Leonard Lance, Aug. 9, 1996; 1 child, Peter R. Frank. BA, Northwestern U., 1974; JD, Vanderbilt U., 1977. Bar: NY, 1978. V.p., asst. gen. counsel J.P. Morgan Chase & Co., NYC, 1985—2004. Home Phone: 908-236-7502.

ROHRER, HEINRICH, physicist; b. Buchs, Switzerland, June 6, 1933; m. Rose-Marie Egger, 1961; children: Doris, Ellen. Diploma in physics, Swiss Inst. Tech., Zurich, 1955, PhD in Physics, 1960; D. Sci. (hon.), Rutgers U., 1987, Marseilles U., France, 1988, Madrid U., 1988, Tsukuba U., Japan, 1994, Frankfurt U., Germany, 1996, Tohoku U., Japan, 2000. Rsch. asst. Swiss Inst. Tech., Zurich, 1960-61; postdoctoral Rutgers U., New Brunswick, NJ, 1961-63; with IBM Rsch. Lab., Zurich, 1963-97; rschr. CSIC, Madrid, 1997-2000, RIKEN, Waco, Japan, 1998, Tohoku U., Sendai, Japan, 1998—99. Vis. scholar U. Calif., Santa Barbara, 1974-75. Co-recipient King Faisal Internat. prize for sci., 1984, Hewlett Packard Europhysics prize, 1984, Nobel prize for Physics, 1986, Cresson medal Franklin Inst., Phila., 1987; IBM fellow, 1986; named to Nat. Inventors Hall of Fame, 1994. Fellow Royal Microscopical Soc. (hon.); mem. NAS (fgn. assoc.), Swiss Acad. Tech. Scis., Swiss Phys. Soc. (hon.), Swiss Assn. Engring. and Architecture (hon.), Zurich Phys. Soc. (hon.). Achievements include invention of the first scanning tunneling microscope (STM) that allowed for the first images of individual atoms on the surface of materials. E-mail: h.rohrer@gmx.net.*

ROHRICH, ROD(NEY) JAMES, plastic surgeon, educator; b. Eureka, SD, Aug. 5, 1953; s. Claude and Katie (Schumacher) R.; m. Diane Louise Gibby, July 3, 1990; children: Taylor Rodney, Rachel Nicole. BA summa cum laude, ND State U., 1975; MD with honors, Baylor Coll., 1979; LittD (hon.), U. ND, 2006. Diplomate Am. Bd. Plastic Surgery, Nat. Bd. Med. Examiners. Instr. surgery Harvard Med. Sch. Mass. Gen. Hosp., Boston, 1985-86; asst. prof. U. Tex. Southwestern Med. Ctr., Dallas, 1986-89, assoc. prof., 1989-91, prof., chmn. dept. plastic surgery, 1991—, Betty and Warren Woodward chair in plastic surgery, 1999; chief plastic surgery Parkland/Zale Univ. Med. Ctr., Dallas, 1989-99. Pres., faculty senate U. Tex., crystal charity ball disting. chair in plastic surgery. Mem. editl. bd. Selected Readings in Plastic Surgery, The Cleft Palate and Craniofacial Jour.; editor Plastic and Reconstructive Surgery, 2005—; contbr. articles to med. jours. Bd. dirs. Save-the-Children Found., Dallas, March of Dimes, Dallas, Dallas for Children; class mem. Leadership Dallas, 1989-90; mem. Adopt-A-Sch., Dallas Summer Mus. Guild, Dallas Mus. Art, Dallas Symphony Assn., Tex. Health Found., Youth Leadership Dallas. Grantee Urban Rsch. Fund, 1982, United Kingdom Ltd. Ednl. Rsch. Fund, 1983, Oxford Cleft Palate Found., 1983, Am. Assn. Plastic Surgeons, 1985, Plastic Surgery Ednl. Found., 1985, 89, 90, U. Tex. Health Sci. Ctr. Dept. Surgery, 1986, Howmedica, 1989, ConvaTec-Squibb, 1989, 91, ConvaTec, 1991; recipient Disting Svc. award Plastic Surg. Ednl. Found., 1997, Alumni Achievement award, N.D. State U., 1997. Mem. AAAS, AMA (Thomas Cronin award 1988, 90, Clifford C. Snyder award 1990), fellow, ACS, Am. Assn. Hand Surgery, Am. Burn Assn., Am. Cleft Palate Assn., Am. Soc. Law and Medicine, Am. Soc. Maxillofacial Surgeons, Am. Soc. for Surgery the Hand, Am. Soc. Plastic and Reconstructive Surgeons, Am. Trauma Soc., British Med. Assn., Nat. Vascular Malformations Found. Inc. (med. and sci. adv. bd.) Tex. Med. Assn., Tex. Soc. Plastic Surgeons, Mass. Gen. Hosp. Hand Club, Dallas County Med. Soc., Assn. Acad. Chmn. Plastic Surgery (pres.), Dallas Soc. Plastic Surgeons, Harvard Med. Sch. Alumni Assn., Inst. for Study of Profl. Risk, Plastic Surgery Rsch. Coun., Reed O. Dingman Soc. Plastic Surgeons, So. Med. Assn., Am. Soc. Plastic Surgeons (pres. 2004), Assn. Academic Chairmen Plastic Surgery (pres. 2008). Republican. Roman Catholic. Office: UT Southwestern Med Ctr Dept Plastic Surgery 5323 Harry Hines Blvd Dallas TX 75390-9132 Office Phone: 214-645-3119. Business E-Mail: rod.rohrich@utsouthwestern.edu.

ROHSENOW, WARREN MAX, retired mechanical engineer, educator; b. Chgo., Feb. 12, 1921; s. Fred and Selma (Gorss) R.; m. Katharine Towneley Smith, Sept. 20, 1946 (dec. Sept. 18, 2001); children— John, Brian, Damaris, Sandra, Anne. BS, Northwestern U., 1941; M.Eng., Yale, 1943, D.Eng., 1944. Teaching asst., instr. mech. engring. Yale, 1941-44; mem. faculty Mass. Inst. Tech., 1946-85, prof. mech. engring., 1955-85, dir. heat transfer lab., 1954-85. Co-founder, chmn. bd. dirs., prof. emeritus, Dynatech Inc., 1985, Thermal Process System. Author: (with Choi) Heat Mass and Momentum Transfer, 1961; Editor: Developments in Heat Transfer, 1964, (with Hartnett) Handbook of Heat Transfer, 1973, 3d edit., 1998. Served as lt. (j.g.) USNR, 1944-46; lt. comdr. USNR, ret. 1956. Recipient Pi Tau Sigma gold medal ASME, 1951; award for advancement sci. Yale Engring. Assn., 1952; merit award Northwestern Alumni, 1955; named hon. alumnus MIT, 2004. Fellow Am. Acad. Arts and Scis., Nat. Acad. Engring., ASME (hon. mem., Heat Transfer Meml. award 1967, Max Jakob Meml. award 1970, ASME medal 2001, Classic Paper award 2003); mem. Sigma Xi, Tau Beta Pi, Pi Tau Sigma. Home: 32 Carroll St Falmouth ME 04105-1908

ROHWEDDER, CHRISTOPHER, elementary school educator; b. Colorado Springs, Colo., May 1, 1973; m. Rhonnetta Stewart, Sept. 21, 1999 (div. Aug. 1, 2006); children: Destiny, Diamond, Kaiyelle. BA, Western Ill. U., Macomb, 1996. Sch. suspension coord. Steger Sch. Dist. 194, Ill., 1996—. Home: 78 W 30th PL Apt 2R Chicago Heights IL 60411 Personal E-mail: zmnupechris@tmo.blackberry.net.

ROI, ALICE (ROY BLUMENTHAL), apparel designer; b. 1976; m. Marc Beckman, 2005. BA in Fine Arts, NYU; grad., Parson's Sch. of Design. Former fashion consultant Elle mag., Fashion Group Internat.; designer Alice Roi Collection, 1999—. Recipient Perry Ellis award nomination, Council of Fashion Designers of Am., 2001. Office: c/o Designer Mgmt Agy 446 Broadway New York NY 10013*

ROIGER, DEBORAH, physiologist, educator; d. Corinne Payne; m. David Roiger, June 15, 2002; children: Katherine Bischoff, Nicholas Bischoff, Nadine Holland, Ben. MEd, St. Mary's U. Minn., Mpls., 1997. Anatomy & physiology instr. St. Cloud State U., Minn., 1997—2001, St. Cloud Tech. Coll., 2001—. Author: Anatomy and Physiology Digital Atlas (Excellence award, 2007, League Innovation award, 2009). Recipient Educator of Yr. award, Minn. State Coll. & U. Bd. Trustees, 2009. Mem.: Human Anatomy & Physiology Soc. Office: Saint Cloud Tech Coll 1540 Northway Dr Saint Cloud MN 56303 Business E-Mail: droiger@sctc.edu.

ROITBERG, BEN ZION, neurosurgeon, educator; b. Moscow, July 30, 1963; s. Michael and Svetlana Roitberg; m. Anat Tambur, Nov. 22, 1987; children: Tal, Shirley. MD, Hebrew U.-Hadassah Med. Sch., Jerusalem, 1987. Cert. physician Israel, physician and surgeon Ill., Ind., diplomate Am. Bd. Neurol. Surgery. Asst. prof. neurosurgery U. Ill., Chgo., 2000—06, assoc. prof. neurosurgery, 2006—08; assoc. prof. surgery, neurosurgery U. Chgo. Med. dir. neurosurg. ICU U. Ill. Hosp., 2001—08; editor, spl. issues Jour. Neurol. Rsch.; assoc. editor Jour. Surg. Neurology. Contbr. articles to multiple sci. journs. Mem.: Congress Neurol. Surgeons, Am. Assn. Neurol. Surgeons. Office: Univ Chgo Sect Neuros 5841 S Maryland MC 3026 Chicago IL 60637

ROITMAN, JUDITH, mathematician, educator, poet; b. NYC, Nov. 12, 1945; d. Leo and Ethel (Gottesman) R.; m. Stanley Lombardo, Sept. 26, 1978; 1 child, Ben Lombardo. BA in English, Sarah Lawrence Coll., 1966; MA in Math., U. Calif., Berkeley, 1971, PhD in Math., 1974. Asst. prof. math. Wellesley (Mass.) Coll., 1974-77; from asst. prof. to prof. math. U. Kans., Lawrence, 1977—. Author: Introduction to Modern Set Theory, 1990, No Face, 2008; contbr. articles to profl. jours. Grantee, NSF, 1975—87, 1992—95. Mem. Assn. Symbolic Logic, Am. Math. Soc., Assn. Women in Math. (pres. 1979-81, Louise Hay award 1996), Kans. Assn. Tchrs. Math., Nat. Assn. Tchrs. Math. Avocation: poetry. Business E-Mail: roitman@math.ku.edu.

ROIZEN, MICHAEL F., anesthesiologist, medical educator, writer; b. NY, Jan. 7, 1946; m. Nancy J. Roizen; children: Jeffery, Jennifer. AB in Chemistry with honors, Williams Coll., Williamstown, Mass., 1967; MD, U. Calif. Sch. Medicine, San Francisco, 1971. Cert. Am. Bd. Internal Medicine, Am. Bd. Anesthesiology. Intern, medicine Beth Israel Hosp., Boston, 1971—72, resident, medicine, 1972—73; rsch. assoc. in pharmacology NIH, Bethesda, Md., 1973-75; resident, anesthesia U. Calif., San Francisco, 1975—77, asst. prof., 1977-81, assoc. prof., 1981-85; prof. internal medicine U. Chgo., 1985, prof. and chair dept. anesthesia and critical care, 1985; prof., anesthesiology SUNY Upstate Med. Ctr. and Univ., Syracuse, NY; chmn., divsn. anesthiology, critical care medicine and comprehensive pain mgmt. Cleve. Clinic. Panel mem. FDA, past chmn. adv. com.; co-founder RealAge,Inc., chmn. scientific adv. bd; invited lectr. in field. Author: Essence of Anesthesia Practice, 1997, RealAge: Are You As Young as You Can Be?, 1999(#1 NY Times bestseller, Best Wellness Book, Books for a Better Life awards, 1999); co-author (with John La Puma) The RealAge Diet: Make Yourself Younger with What You Eat (NY Times bestseller), RealAge Way, The RealAge Makeover, 2004, (with Tracy Hafen) The RealAge Workout, (with Mehmet C. Oz) YOU: The Owner's Manual: An Insider's Guide to the Body That Will Make You Healthier and Younger (#1 Publishers Weekly bestseller, NY Times bestseller), 2005, YOU: The Smart Patient: An Insider's Handbook for Getting the Best Treatment, 2006, YOU: On a Diet-The Owner's Manual for Waist Management, 2006, YOU: Staying Young: The Owner's Manual for Extending Your Warranty, 2007(Publishers Weekly bestseller), YOU: Being Beautiful: The Owner's Manual to Inner and Outer Beauty, 2008, (compact disc) YOU: On a Walk, 2007, YOU: Breathing Easy: Meditation and Breathing Techniques to Help You Relax, Refresh and Revitalize, 2008; former editor of several med. jours.; reviewer numerous anesthesia and med. jours.; contbr. of articles to peer-reviewed jours., chpt. to books, med. books; guest appearances on Oprah Winfrey Show, Today Show, 20/20, CBN, CNN, CBS, Good Morning America, Montel Williams Show and PBS; featured in magazines including Fortune, Glamourm Cosmopolitan, Good Housekeeping, Ladies' Home Journal, Reader's Digest, Men's Health and Prevention. Named an Best Doctors in Am., 1989—. Mem. Am. Bd. Anesthesiology (assoc.), Am. Bd. Internal Medicine (assoc.), Am. Soc. Anesthesiologists, Soc. of Cardiovascular Anesthesiologists (pres. 1995-97), U.S. Squash Racquets Assn., Alpha Omega Alpha, Phi Beta Kappa. 12 US patents and several fgn. patents. Office: RealAge Inc 10675 Sorrento Valley Rd Ste 200 San Diego CA 92121 also: RealAge Inc 555 Fifth Ave 14th Fl New York NY 10017 Office Phone: 858-812-3800. Office Fax: 858-812-3801. Business E-Mail: roizenm@upstate.edu. E-mail: mrzz@airway2.bsd.uchicago.edu.*

ROIZMAN, BERNARD, virologist, educator; b. Chisinau, Rumania, Apr. 17, 1929; arrived in US, 1947, naturalized, 1954; s. Abram and Liudmilla (Seinberg) Roizman; m. Betty Cohen, Aug. 26, 1950; children: Arthur, Niels. BA, Temple U., Phila., 1952, MS, 1954; ScD in Microbiology, Johns Hopkins U., Balt., 1956; DHL (hon.), Gov.'s State U., 1984; MD (hon.), U. Ferrara, Italy, 1991; DSc (hon.), U. Paris, 1997, U. Valladolid, Spain, 2001. From instr. microbiology to asst. prof. Johns Hopkins Med. Sch., 1956—65; from mem. faculty Divsn. Biol. Scis. to prof. U. Chgo., 1965—69, prof., 1969—, chmn. dept. molecular genetics and cell biology, 1985—88, Joseph Regoustein Disting. Svc. prof., 1984—. Co-founder Aviron, Inc., 1992; convener herpes virus workshop, Cold Spring Harbor, NY, 72; lectr. Am. Found. for Microbiology, 1974—75; mem. spl. virus cancer program devel. rsch. working group Nat. Cancer Inst., 1967—71; mem. steering com. human cell biology program NSF, 1971—74; mem. adv. com. cell biology and virology Am. Cancer Soc., 1970—74; chmn. herpes virus study group Internat. Commn. Taxonomy of Viruses, 1971—73; mem. Internat. Microbiol. Genetics Commn. Internat. Assn. Microbiol. Scis., 1974—81; mem. sci. adv. coun. NY Cancer Inst., 1971—88; mem. adv. bd. Leukemia Rsch. Found., 1972—77; mem. herpes-virus working team WHO/FDA, 1978—81; mem. bd. sci. cons. Sloan Kettering Inst., NYC, 1975—81; mem. study sect. exptl. virology NIH, 1976—80; mem. task force on virology Nat. Inst. Allergy and Infectious Disease, 1976—77; mem. com. to establish vaccine priorities Nat. Inst. Medicine, 1983—85; chmn. sci. adv. bd. Tampa Bay Rsch. Inst., 1983—, chmn. bd. trustees, 1991—97; cons. in field. Editor: (book) Herpes Viruses, Vol. 1, 1982, Herpes Viruses, Vol. 2, 1983, Herpes Viruses, Vols. 3 and 4, 1985, The Human Herpesviruses, 1993, Infectious Diseases in an Age of Change, 1995; editor-in-chief: Jour. Infectious Agts. and Disease, 1992—96, mem. editl. bd.: Infectious Diseases, 1965—69, Jour. Virology, 1970—, Jour. Intervirology, 1972—85, Archives of Virology, 1975—81, Virology, 1976—78, Microbiologica, 1978—, Cell, 1979—80, Virology, 1983—, Jour. Hygiene, 1985—91, Gene Therapy, 1994, Wiley Encyclopedia of Molecular Medicine, 2002; contbr. scientific papers, chapters to books. Trustee Goodwin Inst. Cancer Rsch., 1977—2004. Recipient Lederle Med. Faculty award, 1960—61, Career Devel. award, USPHS, 1963—65, Pasteur award, Ill. Soc. Microbiology, 1972, Esther Langer award for Achievement in Cancer Rsch., 1974, Outstanding Alumnus in Pub. Health award, Johns Hopkins U., 1984, ICN Internat. prize in Virology, 1988, J. Allyn Taylor Internat. prize in Medicine, 1997, Bristol-Myers Squibb award for Disting. Infectious Disease Rsch., 1998, Abbott-ASM lifetime achievement award, 2008; named hon. prof., Shandong Acad. Med. Scis., China, 1985; grantee Facutly Rsch. Assoc., Am. Cancer Soc., 1966—71, USPHS/NIH, 1958—, Am. Cancer Soc., 1962—90, NSF, 1962—79; fellow Travelling, Internat. Agy. Rsch. Against Cancer, Karolinska Inst., Stockholm, 1970; scholar Am. Cancer Soc., Pasteur Inst. Paris, 1961—62. Fellow: AAAS, Japanese Soc. for Promotion of Sci., Am. Acad. Arts and Scis.; mem.: NAS, Johns Hopkins U. Soc. Scholars, Chinese Acad. Engring. (fgn.), Hungarian Acad. Scis. (fgn.), Brit. Soc. Gen. Microbiology, Am. Soc. Molecular Biology and Biochemistry, Am. Soc. Virology, Am. Soc. Microbiology, Am. Assn. Immunologists, Am. Acad. Microbiology, Inst. Medicine, Quadrangle Club (Chgo.). Home: 5555 S Everett Ave Chicago IL 60637-1968 Office Phone: 773-702-1898. Business E-Mail: bernard.roizman@bsd.uchicago.edu.

ROJAHN, JOHANNES, psychology professor; b. Vienna, May 23, 1948; s. Rudolf and Johanna Rojahn; life ptnr. Linda Joyce Muniz; children: Helene, Rudolf Johannes. Dr. Phil., U. Vienna, 1976. Rsch. assoc. U. NC, Chapel Hill, 1978—79; asst. prof. psychology Philipps U., Marburg, Germany, 1979—84; assoc. prof. psychology and psychiatry Ohio State U., Columbus, 1987—95, prof. psychology, 1995—2001, George Mason U., Fairfax, Va., 2001—; asst. prof. psychiatry U. Pitts. Med. Sch., Western Psychiat. Inst. and Clinic. Contbr. articles to profl. jours. Fulbright-Hayes Postdoc. fellowship, 1976—77. Fellow: APA (pres., divsn. 33 2005—06), Am. Assn. Intellectual and Devel. Disabilities. Office: George Mason Univ 10340 Democracy Ln Fairfax VA 22030 Business E-Mail: jrojahn@gmu.edu.

ROJAS, CARLOS, literature and language educator; b. Barcelona, Aug. 12, 1928; s. Carlos and Luisa (Vila) R.; m. Eunice Anne Mitcham, Mar. 19, 1966; children: Carlos, Eunice Anne. MA, U. Barcelona, 1951; PhD, U. Cen., Madrid, 1955; PhD (hon.), U. Simón Bólivar, Barranquilla, Colombia, 1985. Teaching asst. U. Barcelona, 1951-52; fgn. asst. U. Glasgow, Scotland, 1952-54; asst. prof. Rollins Coll., Winter Park, Fla., 1957-60, Emory U., Atlanta, 1960-63, assoc. prof., 1963-68, prof., 1968-80, Charles Howard Candler prof. Spanish lit., 1980-96, Charles Howard Candler prof. emeritus, 1996. Author: Auto de fe, 1968 (Premio Nacional de Literatura 1968), Azana, 1973 (Planeta award 1973), El Igenioso Hidalgo y Poeta F.G. asciende a los infiernos, 1980 (Nadal award 1980), El Sueno de Sarajevo, 1982, El Jardin de las Hespèrides, 1988, El Jardin de Atocha, 1990, Yo, Goya, 1990, Proceso A Godoy, 1992, Salvador Dali, or the Art of Spitting on Your Mother's Portrait, 1993, Alfonso de Borbón Habla Con El Demonio, 1995, !Muera La Inteligencia! !Viva La Muerte! Salamanca, 1995, The Garden of Janus, 1996, Crónica de la Guerra Civil Española, 1996; co-author, contbg. editor Spanish Civil War documents, Momentos estelares de la guerra de España, 1996, La Vida y la Época de Carlos IV, 1997, Los Borbones Destronados, 1997, El bastardo del Rey, 1999, The Garden of the Hesperides, 1999, Puneta La Espaneta, 2000, Despiada Memoria: Memorias, 2002, Diez Crisis del Franquismo, 2003, Por Que Perdimos la Guerra, 2006, El Enigma de la Vie, 2007. Recipient Premio Espejo de España award, Madrid, 1984, Encomienda al Mérito Civil, King of Spain, 1986, Univ. Scholar/Tchr. award Emory U., 1987, Arts and Scis. award of Distinction, Emory U., 2001; honoree of yr. Philol. Assn. of Carolinas, 1987, Llave de Barcelona, 2003. Mem. MLA, Am. Assn. Tchrs. Spanish and Portuguese (Premio a la Lealtad Republicana Madrid 2004), Assn. Doctores y Licenciados Españoles en los Estados Unidos (bd. dirs.), South Atlantic MLA (hon.). Avocation: painting. Home: 1378 Harvard Rd NE Atlanta GA 30306-2413 Home Phone: 404-378-0678. Personal E-mail: crojas49@gmail.com. Business E-Mail: crojas@emory.edu.

ROJAS, JESUS JON, health products executive, researcher; b. Havana, Cuba, Oct. 29, 1970; s. Bienvenido Amado Rojas and Edelmira Nena Caballero; 1 child, Jonathan Richard-Alexander. Clin. rsch. coord. SFBC Internat., Miami, Fla., 1996—97, dir. pharmacy, 1997—99, assoc. dir. clin. ops., 1999—2004, dir. clin. ops., 2004—06; v.p. project mgmt. OmniComm Sys., Inc., Ft. Lauderdale, Fla., 2006—. Clin. rsch. cons., Miami, 1998—. Dir. activities abused children Cath. Ch., Miami, 1994—2006. Named Best New Artist, 1994. Mem.: Project Mgr. Inst. (licentiate; mem. 1996), Assn. Clin. Rsch. Profls. (assoc. cert. clin. rsch. coord.). Avocations: martial arts, surfing, reading, running. Office: OmniCom Sys Inc 2101 W Commercial Blvd Fort Lauderdale FL 33309 Office Fax: 954-473-1256; Home Fax: 954-473-1256. Personal E-mail: rojasjonn@aol.com, rijasjonn@aol.com. Business E-Mail: jrojas@omnicomm.com.

ROJAS, MARIO AUGUSTO, pediatrician, director; b. Bogota, Colombia, July 9, 1955; s. Mario and Judy Rojas; m. Monica Chovil; children: Santiago, Nicolas. MD, Fund. U. Juan N Corpas, Colombia, 1980; MPH, U. NC, Chapel Hill, 2007. Cert. pediatrician Hosp. Infantil Lorencita Villegas de Santos, 1986, pediatrics St. Joseph's Hosp. & Med. Ctr., Phoenix, 1994, in neonatology Yale U., 1997. Dir. Servicio de Salud del Meta, Vistahermosa, Colombia, 1981—82; pediatric attending neonatology Caja Nacional de Prevision, Bogota, Colombia, 1986—90; pediatric attending, out patient svcs. Inst. del Seguro Social, Bogota, 1986—90; attending neonatologist U. NC, 1997—2003, Vanderbilt U., Nashville, 2003—; co-dir. Colombian Neonatal Rsch. Network, Bogota, 1997—. Contbr. scientific papers. Recipient Outstanding Fellow Tchg. award, Pediatric Housestaff, Yale U., 1994—97, Fitzbutler Humanitarianism In Medicine, U. Louisville, 2007. Mem.: AAP, Perinatal Sect. Am. Acad. Pediat., Soc. Pediatric Rsch., Am. Acad. Pediat., Colombian Neonatal Soc. Independent. Achievements include invention of the colombian neonatal research network. Avocations: rock climbing, writing, hiking, bicycling, photography. Office: Vanderbilt Univ 2200 Children's Way Nashville TN 37232-9544 Office Fax: 615-343-1763. Business E-Mail: mario.a.rojas@vanderbilt.edu.

ROJAS, MAURICIO, research scientist, educator; b. Bogota, Colombia, Aug. 8, 1963; s. Gloria Rosa Roa and Humberto Rojas; m. Ana Lucia Mora, Mar. 17, 1990; 1 child, Maria Paula. MD, Nat. U.

Colombia, Bogota, 1987. Instr. Vanderbilt U., Nashville, 2000—02; asst. prof. Emory U., Atlanta, 2002—. Contbr. articles to profl. jours. (Start award, 2007). Com. mem. Am. Thoracic Soc., 2005—. Rsch. grant, NIH, 2007. Mem.: Internat. Soc. Stem Cell Rsch. Achievements include patents for intracelular delivery of proteins. Office: Emory Univ 615 Michael St Atlanta GA 30322

ROJAS, VICTOR HUGO MACEDO, retired vocational education educator; b. Mollendo, Peru, Jan. 11, 1923; came to U.S., 1944; s. Mariano A. and Maria Santos (Macedo) R.; m. Mary Emily Bush, Apr. 28, 1945 (dec. 1984). AA, Miami-Dade CC, 1982; BS in Vocat. Edn., Fla. Internat. U., 1986. Cert. tchr., Fla.; personal computer repair tech., Penn Foster Career Sch., 2006. Engine tech. Nat. Sch., 1943; automotive mechanic various Ford dealerships, Miami, Fla., 1945-60; automotive technician East Tenn. Motors, Knoxville, 1960-63; car and truck salesman Ford Mktg. Inst., 1963; automotive technician Tally-Embry Ford, Inc., Miami, 1964-66, shop foreman, then mgr., 1966-75, master technician, automotive instr., 1973-75; instr. automotive tech. Dade County Pub. Schs., Miami, 1975-91; bus. exec. Internat. Correspondence, 1976; ret., 1991. Adviser, sponsor Vocat.-Indsl. Clubs Am., Miami, 1988-91. Contbr. articles to newspapers. With Armada Peruana, 1940-44, USN, 1945. Recipient Cert. of Achievement Motor Age mag., 1961, 62, St. Mary's Cathedral, Miami, 1988, Automotive Svc. Excellence award Nat. Inst. Automotive Svc., 1975, Hon. award Prefect of Arequipa, Peru, 2005. Mem. Am. Legion (historian 1989), Elks. Democrat. Roman Catholic. Avocations: music, ballroom dancing, reading, writing, photography. Personal E-mail: vicbullfighter@aol.com.

ROJAS-GONZÁLEZ, MARCELA, language educator; d. Mario Rojas and Sandra Ledezma-Rojas; m. Valentin González, Oct. 12, 1984; children: David González-Rojas, Andrew González-Rojas. BFA in Painting, Escuela de Artes Plásticas, San Juan, 1994, Calif. State U., LA, 2000; MFA in Art, U. Calif., Irvine; MA in Spanish Lit., Calif. State U., LA, 2003; PhD in Spanish Lit., U. Calif., Irvine. Spanish instr. Maranatha HS, Pasadena, Calif., 1997—2004, Biola U., La Mirada, Calif., 2004—06, Azusa Pacific U., Calif., 2006—, UCI, Irvine, Calif., 2006—. Youth counselor Panorama Bapt. Ch., Arleta, Calif., 1997—. Youth adviser Panorama Bapt. Ch., Artela, Calif., 1997—2008. Office: Azusa Pacific Univ 901 E Alosta Ave Azusa CA 91702-7000 Business E-Mail: mrojas@apu.edu.

ROJAS-PRIMUS, CONSTANZA, language educator; b. Santiago, Chile, Sept. 13, 1972; d. Leonidas Edgardo Rojas Albornoz and Reya del Carmen Primus Correa; m. Jeffrey Daniel McCarville, June 3, 2005. BA in French Pedagogy, U. Met. Ciencias de la Edn., Santiago, 1995; MA in Sociolinguistics, U. Alta., Edmonton, Can., 2000, PhD in Spanish and L.Am. Studies, 2007. Lectr. prof., Spanish Mt. St. Vincent U., Halifax, Nova Scotia, Canada, 2002—04; instrnl. faculty, Spanish Pima CC, Tucson, 2006—08; faculty prof., Spanish Kwantlen Poly. U., Metro Vancouver, BC, Canada, 2008—. Rschr. U. Alberta, Canada, U. Holguin, Cuba, 2004—05. Author: (short story) La iniciación; contbr. articles to profl. jours. (Lit. Author Recognition award, 2002, Author Recognition award, 2004). Recipient Faculty Standar Tchg. award, Pima County CC, 2005, 2007. Personal E-mail: constanza.rojas-primus@kwantlen.ca.

ROJER, OLGA ELAINE, German studies educator, translator; b. Curaçao, Netherlands Antilles, Mar. 29, 1953; came to U.S., 1972; BA cum laude, Mt. Holyoke Coll., 1976; MA with distinction, The Am. U., 1978; PhD, U. Md., 1985. Vis. asst. prof. German and Spanish St. Mary's Coll. Md., St. Mary's City, 1986-87; asst. prof. German Studies The Am. U., Washington, 1987—. Translator Nat. Geog. Soc., Washington, 1985—. Author: Exile in Argentina 1933-1945, 1990, Founding Fictions of the Dutch Caribbean, 2007; contbr. chpts. to books. Mem. MLA, South Atlantic MLA, Am. Assn. Tchrs. German, Soc. for Exile Studies, Women in German, Mid. Atlantic Coun. Latin Am. Studies, Am. Translators Assn. Office: Am U Dept Lang & Fgn Studies 4400 Massachusetts Ave NW Washington DC 20016-8003

ROJO, RUTH M., nutritionist, consultant, director; D in Naturopathy, US Sch. Naturopathy, Harvard Med. Sch., Clayton Coll. Natural Health, Birmingham, Ala., 1996; PhD in Nutrition, Am. Holistic Coll. Nutrition, Birmingham, 1996. Diplomate Nationally Bd. Naturopath, Am. Naturopathic Med., Accreditation Bd. Cons. Dept. Consumer Regulatory Affairs, Bus. Profl. Licensing Adminstrn.; pres. emeritus Tex. State Naturopathic Med. Assn. Author: Priority 1--A Guide to Natural Health. Hon. chmn. Physicians Adv. Bd. - NRCC, 2006. Recipient Legacy award, Global Edit., 2005—06, Congl. medal distinction, 2006; named Businesswoman of Yr., Nat. Rep. Congrl. Com., 2006. Mem.: Am. Naturopathic Med. Assn. (bd. mem.). Avocations: painting, walking, cross stitch, sports. Office: PO Box 1583 Helotes TX 78023 Personal E-mail: rrojo@drrojo.com. Business E-Mail: drrojo@togetwell.com.

ROKER, AL, newscaster; b. Queens, NY, Aug. 20, 1954; m. Alice Bell, Dec. 22, 1984 (div. 1994); m. Deborah Roberts, Sept. 16, 1995; 3 children. Grad., SUNY, Oswego. Weathercaster, graphic artist WTVH-TV, Syracuse, N.Y., 1974-76; weathercaster WTTG-TV, Washington, 1976-78, WKYC-TV, Cleve., 1978-83, WNBC-TV, NYC, 1983—; weatherman NBC News Today Show, NYC, 1995—; founder Al Roker Entertainment, Inc., 1994—. Exec. prodr.: (TV series) Roker on the Road, 2003; actor: (TV films) Broadway on Broadway, 2000, (voice): (films) Wholey Moses, 2003, Robots, 2005; author (non-fiction): Don't Make Me Stop this Car: Adventures in Fatherhood, 2000, Big Shoes: In Celebration of Dads and Fatherhood, 2005; author: (cookbooks) Al Roker's Big Bad Book of Barbecue: 100 Easy Recipes for Backyard Barbecue, 2002, Al Roker's Hassle-Free Holiday Cookbook, 2003. Named Best Weatherman, N.Y. mag., 1985. Mem. Am. Meteorol. Soc. (recipient Seal of Approval). Office: NBC News 30 Rockefeller Plz Rm 1420 New York NY 10112-0002

ROKER, CHRISTOPHER A., microbiologist, photographer; arrived in US, 1986; s. John A. T. and LueElla Roker; m. Elizabeth Moxey, Apr. 14, 1984; children: Krislar, Kwame, Kofi. BS in Med. Tech., LI U., 1996, post graduate, 2003—; student, NY Inst. Photography, 1975—78; student in Commercial Photography, Germain Sch. Photography, 1980—82. Cert. clin. lab. scientist Nat. Certify Agy. Lab. Profls. Profl. photographer, studio owner Esquire Photography Studio, Nassau, The Bahamas, 1983—88; photographic retoucher Color Wheel Inc., NYC, 1986—95; microbiologist Shield Med. Lab., Bklyn., 1995—99, Sherman-Abrams Med. Lab, Bklyn., 1999—2006, Analytical Diagnostic Labs Inc., Bklyn., 1999—. Photographer (exhibitions), NYC, Nassau, Bahamas, Down by the Sea, Body Works, New York After Dark. Mem.: Am. Soc. Clin. Lab. Sci., Am. Soc. Microbiology (mem. sub-com. 2002—). Avocations: sports, poetry, writing, jazz. Office: Analytical Diagnostic Labs Inc 2115 Ave X Brooklyn NY 11235 Home and Studio: 6119 Braidwood Lane NW Acworth GA 30101 Office Phone: 718-646-6000. Office Fax: 718-646-0820. Business E-Mail: carokers@msn.com.

ROKICKI, PHILLIP S., career planning administrator, educator; s. Felix S. and Rose N. Rokicki; m. Nancy S. Sallie, Jan. 26, 1990; children: Annette L. Squires, Milissa A. Hines. BS, Ctrl. Mo. U., Warrensburg, 1968, MEd, 1969; PhD, St. Louis U., 1981. Cert. global career devel. facilitator Ctr. Credentialing & Edn., Greensboro, NC, 1997. V.p. adminstrn. Deerfield Design, Pompano Beach, Fla., 1990—91; v.p. Rokicki and Assocs., Inc., Harrison, Tenn., 1991—; rsch. analyst Workforce One, Ft. Lauderdale, Fla., 1991—93; exec. dir., Fla. Inst. Career and Employment Tng. Fla. Atlantic U., Ft. Lauderdale, 1993—2002, exec. dir., Fla. Inst. Applied Rsch. and Evaluation, 2002—03; adj. prof. Nova Southeastern U., Ft. Lauderdale, 2003—. Contbr. articles to scholarly publs. Dir. Joachim-Plattin Ambulance Dist., Festus, Mo., 1975—79. Mem.: Adv. Bd., House Hope, Broward Alliance, Edn. and Tng. Com., Greater Ft. Lauderdale C. of C., Edn. and Tng. Com., Nat. Career Devel. Assn., Nat. Assn. Workforce Profls. Liberal. Roman Catholic. Home: 6554 River Stream Dr Harrison TN 37341 Office: Rokicki and Assocs Inc PO Box 427 Harrison TN 37341-0427 Personal E-mail: rokicki-associates@att.net. Business E-Mail: rokicki@nsu.nova.edu.

ROKITA, TODD, Secretary of State, Indiana; b. Chgo., Feb. 9, 1970; m. Kathy Rokita. BA in Polit. Sci., Wabash Coll., 1992; JD, Ind. U. Sch. Law, 1995. Atty.; gen. counsel to sec. state State of Ind., Indpls., 1997, dep. sec. state, 1997—2003, sec. state, 2003—. Mem.: Indiana Coun. for Economic Edn. (Director's Circle), St. Thomas More Parish, Indiana State Bar Association's Aviation Law Com. (past chair). Republican. Catholic. Office: Office Sec of State 201 State House Indianapolis IN 46204 Office Phone: 317-232-6531, 317-232-6536. Office Fax: 317-233-3283. Business E-Mail: aa@sos.state.in.us.

ROKKE, ERVIN JEROME, military officer, academic administrator; b. Warren, Minn., Dec. 12, 1939; s. Edwin K. and Joan (Ivery) R.; m. Pamela Mae Patterson, June 6, 1962; children: Lisa Mae, Eric Scott. Student, St. Olaf Coll., 1957-58; BS, USAF Acad., 1962; MPA, Harvard U., 1964, PhD in Polit. Sci., 1970. Commd. 2d lt. USAF, 1962, advanced through grades to lt. gen., 1994; intelligence officer Pacific Air Forces, Hawaii, Japan, 1965-68; assoc. prof. dept. polit. sci. USAF Acad., Colorado Springs, Colo., 1968-73, permanent prof., 1976-80, dean of faculty, 1982-86, chmn. characterand leadership devel., 2007—; plans officer NATO Hdqrs., Brussels, 1973-76; air attache Am. Embassy, London, 1980-82, def. attache Moscow, 1987-89; sr. staff Nat. Security Agy., Ft. Meade, Md., 1989-91; dir. intelligence Hdqrs. European Command, Stuttgart, Fed. Republic Germany, 1991-93; assigned to Hdqs. USAF, Washington, 1993-94; pres. Nat. Def. U., Ft. Lesley J. McNair, DC, 1994-97, Moravian Coll. and Moravian Theol. Sem., 1997—2006; pres. emeritus Moravian Coll., Bethlehem, Pa., 2007—. Cons. Dept. State, 1969. Editor: American Defense Policy, 1973. Chair character and leadership devel. USAF Acad., Colo. Decorated Def. Disting. Svc. medal, Disting. Svc. medal, Def. Superior Svc. medal, Legion of Merit. Mem. Coun. on Fgn. Rels., Falcon Found. Lutheran. Avocations: reading, skiing, squash. Home: 810 Dolan Dr Monument CO 80132-2219 Office Phone: 719-333-4510. Personal E-mail: chaos01@comcast.net.

ROLAND, J. THOMAS, surgeon, researcher; b. Lancaster, Pa., May 14, 1957; s. John and Geraldine Roland; m. Betsy Pfeffer, June 15, 1985; children: Jillian, Allison. MD, Temple U. Sch. Medicine, Phila., 1983. Cert. Am. Bd. Otolaryngology, 1993. Assoc. prof. NYU Sch. Medicine, 2003—, prof. otolaryngology and neurosurgery, dir. otology, neurotology, 2004—, co-dir. cochlear implant ctr. Editor: (text book) Cochlear Implants. Lt cmdr USPHS, 1986—88, Fort Yuma PHS Indian Hosp. Fellow: Am. Acad. Otolaryngology (com. memberships 2006—08). Independent. Luthern. Achievements include development of multiple cochlear implant electrodes. Avocations: skiing, tennis, travel. Office: NYU Sch Medicine 550 First Ave Ste 8S New York NY 10016 Office Fax: 212-263-2019; Home Fax: 212-263-2019. Business E-Mail: tom.roland@med.nyu.edu.

ROLANDO, FREDRIC V., labor union administrator; m. Jolene Rolando; 4 children. BS in Criminology & Psychology, Fla. Internat. U. Mem. br. 1071 Nat. Assn. Letter Carriers (NALC), steward, 1979—84, pres. br. 2148, 1988—99, part-time regional adminstrv. asst., 1992—99, dir. edn. Fla. State Assn., 1993—99, full-time regional adminstrv. asst. Atlanta, 1999, dir. city delivery, 2002—06, exec. v.p. NALC, 2006—09, pres., 2009—. Office: NALC 100 Indiana Ave NW Washington DC 20001-2144 Office Phone: 202-393-4695.*

ROLATER, J. RICK, science association director; BBA in Acctg., U. North Tex., Denton. CPA, fin. advisor Arthur Young & Co.; founder, CEO Rolater, Ducote & Co. CPAs, Paragon Communication Systems, Provident Bancorp Tex., Discovery Channel Stores; owner Splendor of Nature Gallery, 1996—, By Nature Gallery, Beaver Creek, Colo., 2004—; exec. dir. AIME, Littleton, Colo., 2003—. Office: AIME PO Box 270728 Littleton CO 80127-0013 Office Phone: 303-948-4255. Office Fax: 303-948-4260. E-mail: Rolater@aimehq.org.

ROLDAN, KENNETH ARROYO, executive recruiter, lawyer; married; 2 children. BA, Cornell U., 1986; JD, Touro Law Ctr. Atty. No. Manhattan Coalition for Immigrant Rights, NYC; asst. atty. gen. Civil Rights Bur. State of NY, Albany, 1995—98; gen. counsel Wesley, Brown & Bartle Co., Inc., NYC, 1998—2003, CEO, 2003—07; ptnr., head diversity practice Battalia Winston Internat., 2007—. Mem.: Cornell Latino Alumni Assn. (former pres.). Avocation: gardening. Office: Battalia Winston Internat 19th Fl 555 Madison Ave New York NY 10022

ROLDAN-FIGUEROA, RADY, philosopher, educator; s. Manuel A. Roldan and Mercedes Figueroa-Ruiz; m. Kretcha M. Rodriguez Cerezo, Aug. 7, 1993. BA, U. PR, Rio Piedras, 1993; MDiv, NB Theol. Sem., New Brunswick, NJ, 2000; ThD, Boston U., 2004. Asst. prof. Baylor U., Waco, Tex., 2004—; lilly tchg. fellow, philosophy and religion Claflin U., Orangeburg, SC. Contbr. articles to profl. jours. Baptist. Office: Baylor Univ One Bear Pl 97284 Waco TX 76798-7284

ROLEN, SCOTT BRUCE, professional baseball player; b. Jasper, Ind., Apr. 4, 1975; m. Niki Warner, Feb. 2, 2002; 1 child, Raine Tyler. Third baseman Phila. Phillies, 1996—2002, St. Louis Cardinals, 2002—07, Toronto Blue Jays, 2008—09, Cin. Reds, 2009—. Founder Enis Furley Found. Recipient Nat. League Gold Glove award, 1998, 2000—04, 2006, Nat. League Silver Slugger award, 2002; named Nat. League Rookie Player of Yr., The Sporting News, 1997, Baseball Writers Assn. of Am., 1997; named to Nat. League All-Star Team, 2002—06. Achievements include member of the World Series championship winning St. Louis Cardinals, 2006. Office: Cin Reds 100 Main St Cincinnati OH 45202*

ROLETT, ELLIS LAWRENCE, cardiologist, educator; b. NYC, July 10, 1930; s. Daniel Meyer and Mary Elaine (Warshaw) R.; m. Virginia Ann Vladimir, Mar. 25, 1956; children: Roderic Lawrence, Barry Vladimir, Daniel Alfred. BS, Yale U., 1952; MD cum laude, Harvard U., 1955. Diplomate: Am. Bd. Internal Medicine, Am. Bd. Cardiovas. Disease. Intern, resident in medicine Mass. Gen. Hosp., Boston, 1955-56, 59-61; asst. resident N.Y. Hosp.-Cornell U. Med. Ctr., NYC, 1956-57; Am. Heart Assn. research fellow Peter Bent Brigham Hosp., Boston, 1961-63; mem. faculty U. N.C., Chapel Hill, 1963-74, then prof., 1971-74; prof. UCLA, 1974-77; chief cardiology VA Wadsworth Hosp., LA, 1974-77, Dartmouth-Hitchcock Med. Ctr., Hanover, NH, 1977—87; prof. Dartmouth Med. Sch., Hanover, 1977-97, prof. medicine active emeritus, 1997—. Vis. scientist August Krogh Inst., Copenhagen, 1984; mem. merit rev. bd. Cardiovasc. studies VA, 1976-79, chmn., 1978-79; mem. regional rsch. rev. com. New Eng. Am. Heart Assn., 1978-83; mem. sci. bd. Stanley J. Sarnoff Endowment for Cardiovasc. Sci., 1992-97, chmn., 1994-95, bd. dirs., 1997-2000; mem. lit. sect. rev. com. Nat. Libr. Medicine, 1995-99, chmn., 1998-99; dir. Vt.-Karelia (Russia) Med. Project, St. Petersburg Univ. Global Fund. Bd. dirs. N.H. affiliate Am. Heart Assn., 1978-85; pres. N.H. affiliate Am. Heart Assn., 1983-85. Served to capt. M.C. USAF, 1957-59. Recipient Lederle Med. Faculty award, 1965-68, USPHS Career Devel. award, 1967-72; grantee USPHS/NIH, 1964-76, VA Merit Rev. Rsch. Program, 1975-77, Mathers Found., 1984-86, 93-96, Am. Heart Assn., 1989-91. Mem. AAAS, Am. Physiol. Soc., Internat. Soc. Heart Rsch., Phi Beta Kappa, Alpha Omega Alpha Home: 4 Balch Hill Ln Hanover NH 03755-1622 Office: Dartmouth Med Sch Hanover NH 03755 Office Phone: 603-650-1360. Business E-Mail: ellis.rolett@dartmouth.edu.

ROLF, HOWARD LEROY, mathematician, educator; b. Laverne, Okla., Nov. 25, 1928; s. James Walter and Edith (Yoho) R.; m. Anita Jane Ward, June 24, 1961; children: James Scott, Jennifer Jane, Stephanie Kaye, Rhonda Mary. BS, Okla. Baptist U., 1951; MA, Vanderbilt U., 1953, PhD, 1956. Instr. math. Vanderbilt U., 1954-56, asst. prof., dir. computer ctr., 1959-64; asst. prof. Baylor U., 1956-57, prof., 1964-98, dir. acad. computing, 1968-70, chmn. dept. math., 1971-97. Assoc. prof. Georgetown Coll., Ky., 1957—59. Author: (with William C. Brown) Mathematics, 1982, Finite Mathematics, 1988, 91, 94, 99, 02, 05, 08, (with Brooks-Cole) Mathematics for Management, Social and Life Sciences, 1991. Mem. Math. Assn. Am. (chmn. Tex. sect. 1977), Sigma Xi, Pi Mu Epsilon, Golden Key. Baptist. Home: 4096 Speegleville Rd Waco TX 76712-4033

ROLFE, CHRISTOPHER C., energy executive; BS in Mech. Engring., NC State U. Registered profl. engr., NC, SC. Engring. asst. design engring. dept. Duke Energy (formerly Duke Power Co.), 1972, v.p. corp. performance, 1992—97, v.p. corp. human resources, 1997—2000, v.p. human resources, 2000, group exec., chief human resources officer, group exec., chief adminstrv. officer, 2006—. Chmn. NC Commn. Workforce Devel. Recipient Jack Callahan Cornerstone award, Goodwill Industries of So. Piedmont of NC, 2007. Office: Duke Energy 526 S Church St Charlotte NC 28202-1904 Office Phone: 704-594-6200.

ROLFE, ELLEN MARY, retired music educator; b. South Bend, Ind. d. John Philip and Edna Deveraux Gallagher; m. George Obediah Rolfe, Oct. 24, 1964; children: John Joseph, Katherine Elizabeth. MusB, Eastern Mich. U., 1960. Tchr. Lapeer St. Home Tng., Mich., 1960—63; music/spl. edn. tchr. Seaside Regional Ctr., Waterford, Conn., 1963—64; spl. edn. tchr. Valley Regional H.S., Deep River, Conn., 1964—67; music tchr. Torrington Pub. Schools, 1972—2006, ret., 2006. Mentor/tchr. Conn. Bd. Edn. Bd. dirs. Girl Scouts Northest; mem., past pres. Litchfield County Choral Union, 1972—; v.p. Girl Scouts Northest. Recipient Thanks pin, Nat. Coun. Girl Scouts Am., 2006. Mem.: Conn. Music Educators Assn. (Mid. Sch. Educator of the Yr. 1997), Am. String Teachers Assn., Music Educators Nat. Assn., Torrington Symphony Orch. (bd. dirs.). Episcopalian. Home: 172 Wedgewood Dr Torrington CT 06790

ROLFE, ROBERT MARTIN, lawyer; b. Richmond, Va., May 16, 1951; s. Norman and Bertha (Cohen) R.; children: P. Alexander, Asher B., Joel A., Zachary A. BA, U. Va., 1973, JD, 1976. Bar: Va. 1976, NY 1985, US Dist. Ct. (ea. and we. dists.) Va. 1976, US Ct. Appeals (4th cir.) 1976, US Ct. Appeals (2d cir.) 1979, US Dist. Ct. (ea. dist.) Mich. 1985, US Ct. Appeals (DC cir.) 1985, US Dist. Ct. (so. and ea. dists.) NY 1985, US Ct. Appeals (7th cir.) 1995, US Ct. Fed. Claims, 1997, US Supreme Ct. 1979. Assoc. Hunton & Williams, Richmond, 1976—83, ptnr., 1983—, co-head litig., intellectual property and antitrust team, 1995—2007, gen. counsel, 1995—, exec. com., 1998—2004. Editorial bd. Va. Law Rev., 1976; contbr. articles to profl. jours. Trustee, pres. bd. trustees Jewish Family Supporting Found., chmn. of bd. trustees, 2005-; bd. dirs. Jewish Family Svcs., Richmond, pres., 1993-95; bd. mgrs., 2d v.p. Congregation Beth Ahabah, 1995-97, 1st v.p., 1997-99, United Way of Greater Richmond Action Coun. Children Youth and Families, 2008-. Fellow Am. Bar Found.; mem. ABA (litig. sect.), Va. Bar Assn., Va. State Bar, Richmond Bar Assn., Order of Coif (Alumni award for acad. excellence U. Va. 1976), United Way Richmond Children, Youth and Families Action Coun. Home: 18 Greenway Ln Richmond VA 23226-1630 Office: Hunton & Williams Riverfront Plz East Tower PO Box 1535 Richmond VA 23218-1535 also: 200 Park Ave New York NY 10166-0005 Office Phone: 804-788-8466. Office Fax: 804-343-4568. Business E-Mail: rrolfe@hunton.com.

ROLFE, RONALD STUART, lawyer; b. NYC, Sept. 5, 1945; s. Nat and Florence I. (Roth) R.; m. Yvonne Quinn, Sept. 1, 1979 (div. Apr. 2002); m. Sara Darehshori; children; Andrew, Dare. AB, Harvard U., 1966; JD, Columbia U., 1969. Bar: N.Y. 1969, U.S. Ct. Appeals (2d cir.) 1970, U.S. Dist. Ct. (so. and ea. dists.) N.Y. 1971, U.S. Supreme Ct. 1973, U.S. Dist. Ct. (no. dist.) Calif. 1982, U.S. Ct. Appeals (6th and 5th cirs.) 1982, U.S. Ct. Appeals (9th cir.) 1983, U.S. Dist. Ct. (ea. dist.) Ky. 1984, U.S. Ct. Appeals (7th and 10th cirs.) 1989, U.S. Ct. Appeals (fed. cir.) 1991, U.S. Ct. Appeals (3d cir.) 1992, U.S. Ct. Appeals (4th cir.) 1991. Law clk. to judge US Dist. Ct. (so. dist.) NY, 1969-70; assoc. Cravath, Swaine & Moore LLP, 1970-77, ptnr., litig., 1977—. Trustee Allen-Stevenson Sch., 1980—, pres., 1992—; trustee Lawrenceville Sch., 1987—, v.p., 2001—05; bd. visitors Law Sch. Columbia U., emeritus bd. adv. Ctr. Corp. Governance, dean's coun. Law Sch. Trustee DeLaSalle Acad., 2002—. Fellow: NY Bar Found., Am. Bar Found.; mem.: ABA, Am. Law Inst., Fed. Bar Coun. (trustee 1989—94), Assn. Bar City NY, NY State Bar Assn., Century Assn., The Bridge (Noyac, NY), Stanwich Club, Univ. Club, Union Club. Office: Cravath Swaine & Moore LLP Worldwide Plz 825 8th Ave 40th Fl New York NY 10019-7475 Office Phone: 212-474-1714. Office Fax: 212-474-3700. Business E-Mail: rrolfe@cravath.com.

.ROLIN, DANIEL WAYNE, JR., military officer; b. San Antonio, Aug. 9, 1981; s. Dan Rolin, Sr. and Diane Higginbotham; m. Judy Galvan; 1 child, Alexis Renee Rolin. Grad. H.S., La Vernia, Tex., 2000. Special Reaction Team Phase 1 Entry Team: US Army Mil. Police Sch. 2004, Special Reaction Team Phase 2 Marksman/Observer: US Army Mil. Police Sch. 2004, Multiport Distraction Device Course: Def. Tech. 2005, User/Instructor Certification Course: Taser Internat./ Ga. 2005, Basic/Advanced Sniper Course: Wackenhut Security Services/South Carolina 2005, SWAT Marksman/Observer Course: SC. Tactical Officers Assn./South Carolina 2005, Tactical Team Operations: Team One Network / Fla. 2005, Advanced Close Quarters Shooting: Team One Network/ Fla. 2005, Officers Survival Course: Team One Network/ Fla.

2005, SWAT Level 1 Course: Richmond County Sheriffs Dept./ Ga. 2005, Traffic Accident Investigator Level 1-2 Course: Richmond County Sheriffs Dept./ Ga. 2005, Police Cyclist Course: Richmond County Sheriffs Dept./ Ga. 2005. Sgt. US Army, 2002—, spl. reaction team entry team mem. 35th Mil. Police Detachment Ft. Gordon, Ga., 2003—04, traffic accident investigator 35th Mil. Police Detachment, 2003—05, spl. reaction team marksman/teamleader 35th Mil. Police Detachment, 2004—05, mil. police 204th Mil. Police Co. Ft. Polk, La., 2005—. Decorated Army Achievement medal US Army, Iraqi Campaign Svc. medal, Combat Action Badge, Army Commendation medal; recipient Honor award, Assn. US Army, 2003. Mem.: VFW. Home: 8354 Tavern Pt San Antonio TX 78254-5579

ROLL, TODD M., library director; s. James and Sandra Roll; m. Kathryn Lemmer; 1 child, Max Lrl. MLS, U.Wis, Madison, 1990. Academic libr., Marathon county U. Wis., Wausau, 1991—2008, dir. libr. Richland Ctr., 2008—. Contbr. articles to profl. jour. (Kaplan award, 2002). V.p. Friends Brewer, Richland Ctr., 2008—.

ROLLA, MAUREEN J., museum director; BA in English, Carnegie Mellon U.; MA in English and comparative lit., Columbia U. Adminstrv. dir. Getty Leadership Inst. Mus. Mgmt., LA; asst. dir. Carnegie Mus. Art, Pitts., 1999—2006, dep. dir., 2006—08, co-dir., 2008—. Office: Carnegie Mus Art 4400 Forbes Ave Pittsburgh PA 15213-4080 Office Fax: 412-622-3122. E-mail: rollam@carnegiemuseums.org.*

ROLLAND, ALAIN P., pharmaceutical executive; b. Landivisiau, France, Oct. 26, 1959; s. Alexandre and Gabrielle (Bizien) R.; m. Corine Lhuissier, July 11, 1981; children: Gabriel, Alix, Benjamin. BA in Math, Physics, Landerneau, France, 1976; Pharm D., Rennes U., France, 1981, DEA in Pharmacokinetics, 1983, PhD, 1987. Scientist Ciba-Geigy Pharms., Horsham, U.K., 1987-88; head formulation rsch. group CIRD Galderma, Sophia Antipolis, France, 1989-93; dir. gene delivery GeneMedicine, Inc., The Woodlands, Tex., 1993-96, v.p. gene delivery scis., 1996-97, v.p. rsch., 1997-98; v.p. R & D, The Woodlands Ctr. Head, Valentis Inc., 1999—. Reviewer for several scientific jours.; mem. editl. bd. Advanced Drug Delivery Revs., Jour. of Controlled Release, Jour. of Pharmacy and Pharmacology; editor books in field; patentee in field; contbr. articles to profl. jours. Recipient prize Found. of French Pharm. Industry for Rsch., 1987, Claude Bernard Assn., 1987, French Acad. of Pharmacy, 1987. Mem. Am. Controlled Release Soc., Internat. Soc. for Gene Therapy, Am. Chem. Soc., European Working Group on Human Gene Transfer and Therapy, Am. Assn. Pharm. Scientists, n.Y. Acad. Sci., Am. Soc. Gene Therapy. Achievements include devel. of delivery system to target anti-cancer drugs to the liver for treatment of hepatoma and creation of gene medicine for the prevention and treatment of human diseases. Home: 10696 Edenoaks St San Diego CA 92131-3222

ROLLAND, JANNICK P., medical educator; d. Roger and Emilienne Rolland; life ptnr. Kevin P. Thompson; children: Yvan N. Scher, Roman A. Scher. Diplome sup optqiue, Inst. d'Optique, 1984; PhD, U. Ariz., Tucson, 1990. Postdoc fellow U. NC, Chapel Hill, 1990—92, dir. vision group, 1992—96; prof. optics U. Ctrl. Fla., Orlando, 1996. Assoc. editor j. optical engring. SPIE, Bellingham, Wash., 1999—2004. Recipient Young Investigator award, Office Naval Rsch., 1995—98, First award, NIH-NLM, 1997—2002, Disting. Rsch. award, U. Ctrl. Fla., 2001, Tchg. Incentive Program award, 2001—06; grant, NSF, 1998, OSA, 2004. Fellow: SPIE (fellow 2008—).

ROLLAND, LUCIEN GILBERT, paper company executive, director; b. St. Jerome, Que., Can., Dec. 21, 1916; s. Olivier and Aline (Dorion) R.; m. Marie de Lorimier, May 30, 1942; children: Nicolas, Natalie, Stanislas, Dominique, Christine, Etienne, David. Student, Coll. Jean de Brebeuf, Montreal, U. Montreal, BA, BASc., C.E., also D.C.Sc. (hon.), 1960. Registered profl. engr. With Rolland Paper Co. Ltd. (name changed to Rolland inc. 1979), 1942—, v.p., gen. mgr., 1952, pres., gen. mgr., 1952-78, pres., CEO, 1978—, chmn., pres., CEO, 1984, chmn., CEO, 1985, chmn., 1991. Cons. in field, 1995; chmn. bd. Tarascon, Inc. Bd. govs. Notre-Dame Hosp., Montreal Children's Hosp., Montreal Gen. Hosp., Hôpital Marie Enfant. Decorated Knight Comdr. Order St. Gregory, officer Order of Can. Mem. Can. Pulp and Paper Assn. (hon.), Corp. Profl. Engrs., Montreal Bd. Trade, Province of Que., C of C, Montreal C. of C., Engring. Inst. Can. Home: Apt B-60 1321 Sherbrooke St W Montreal PQ Canada H3G 1J4 Office: Tarascon Inc 1200 McGill College #1100 Montreal PQ Canada H3B 4G7 Office Phone: 514-393-9928.

ROLLAND, PETER GEORGE, landscape architect; b. Frankfurt, Germany, July 2, 1930; came to U.S., 1936; s. Curt Henry and Lise (Kahn) R.; m. Wendy Diana Altschul, Dec. 26, 1955; children: David, Seth, Janna. B.Sc., Delaware Valley Coll., 1952; M.L.A., Harvard U., 1955. Registered landscape architect, N.Y., Conn., Coun. Landscape Archtl. Rev. Bds. Chief site planner Perkins & Will Architects, White Plains, NY, 1955-60; project landscape architect Lawrence Halprin & Assocs., San Francisco, 1960-63; prin. Peter G. Rolland & Assocs., Rye, NY, 1963—81, Canberra, Australia, 1963—81; ptnr. Rolland/Towers, Rye, New Haven, 1981—97. Andrew Mellon vis. prof. Yale U. Sch. Forestry, 1979; faculty Sch. Architecture, Yale U., 1973-94; vis. prof. Harvard Grad. Sch. Design, 1990; mem. Office Bldg. Ops., architecture adv. bd., US Dept. State, 2000-05, design jury US Dept. State Beijing Embassy, 2005, London Embassy, 2009; disting. prof. landscape architecture, Sch. Architecture, CCNY, 2004. Prin. landscape architect, New Parliament House, Canberra, Australia, 1980, SUNY, Coll. at Purchase, 1964-75. Mem., chmn. N.Y. State Bd. Landscape Architects, 1972-82; mem. N.Y. State Coun. on Arts, 1979-82, Rye Archtl. Bd. Rev., 1973-78; trustee Delaware Valley Coll., 1991-2003; mem. grad. coun. Grad. Sch. Design, Harvard U., Cambridge, Mass., 1978-88; trustee Am. Acad. in Rome, 1992-96, pres. Soc. Fellows, 1992-96. Served with U.S. Army, 1956-58. Recipient Arthur Brown award Del. Valley Coll., 1978, Pres.'s award, 2003; Design award AIA, 1975, 78, 85, 90, 92, 94, Inst. Honors award, 1990; Tucker award for IBM Conf. Ctr., 1982; Sir Zelman Cowens award Royal Australian Inst. Archs., 1989; Tucker award for New Parliament Ho., Canberra, Australia, 1990; Rome Prize fellow Am. Acad. in Rome, 1978, Pierson Coll. fellow Yale U., 1982-92. Fellow Am. Soc. Landscape Architects (ann. design awards 1972-85, 92, award of Excellence, 1991); mem. NAD (Academician), Australian Inst. Landscape Architects (Landmarks award for New Parliament House, Canberra, 1988). Office: 731 Milton Rd Rye NY 10580

ROLLE, ANDREW, historian, writer; b. Providence, Apr. 12, 1922; m. Frances Squires, Dec. 1945 (div.); children: John Warren, Alexander Frederick, Julia Elisabeth.; m. Myra Moss, Nov. 1983. BA, Occidental Coll., 1943; MA, UCLA, 1949, PhD, 1953; grad., So. Calif. Psychoanalytic Inst., 1976. Am. vice consul, Genoa, Italy, 1945-48; editorial asso. Pacific Hist. Rev., 1952-53; from asst. prof. to Cleland prof. history Occidental Coll., 1953-88; rsch. scholar Huntington Libr., San Marino, Calif., 1988—. Author: Riviera Path, 1946, An American in California, 1956, reprinted, 1982, The Road to Virginia City, 1960, reprinted, 1989, Lincoln: A Contemporary Portrait, 1961, (with Allan Nevins, Irving Stone) California: A History, 1963, rev. edits., 1963, 69, 78, 87, 98, 2002, 08, Occidental College: The First Seventy-Five Years, 1963, The Lost Cause: Confederate Exiles in Mexico, 1965, 1992, The Golden State, 1967, rev. edit., 1978, 1989, 2000, California, A Student Guide, 1965, Los Angeles, A Student Guide, 1965; Editor: A Century of Dishonor (Helen Hunt Jackson), 1964, Life in California (Alfred Robinson), 1971, Voyage to California (Jour. of Lucy Herrick), 1998; The Immigrant Upraised, 1968, The American Italians: Their History and Culture, 1972, Gli Emigrati Vittoriosi, 1973, reprinted, 2003; (with George Knoles others) Essays and Assays, 1973, (with others) Studies in Italian American Social History, 1975, (with others) Los Angeles: The Biography of a City, 1976, 2d edit., 1991; (with Allan Weinstein and others) Crisis in America, 1977, The Italian Americans: Troubled Roots, 1980, 2d edit. 1985, Los Angeles: From Pueblo to Tomorrow's City, 1981, 2nd edit., 1995, Occidental College: A Centennial History, 1986, John Charles Frémont: Character as Destiny, 1991, Henry Mayo Newhall and His Times, 1992, Westward the Immigrants, 1999, The Victorious Immigrants, 2005. Served to 1st lt. M.I. AUS, 1943-45, 51-52. Decorated Cavaliere Ordine Merito Italy; recipient silver medal Italian Ministry Fgn. Affairs; Commonwealth award for non-fiction; Huntington Libr.-Rockefeller Found. fellow; resident scholar Rockefeller Found. Ctr., Bellagio, Italy. Fellow Calif. Hist. Soc.; mem. Phi Beta Kappa. Office Phone: 626-405-2100 ext 2321.

ROLLE, MYRA MOSS See MOSS, MYRA

ROLLER, PAMELA JO, elementary school educator; b. Logansport, Ind., Mar. 22, 1952; d. Glen B. Roller and Clara Evelyn Sizemore. BS, Ind. U., Kokomo, 1974; MS, Ind. U./Purdue U. Indpls., 1976. Cert. CFG Coach for Nat. Sch. Reform Faculty 2004. Tchr. 5th and 6th grade Southeastern Sch. Corp., Logansport, 1974—76, tchr. 1st grade, 1976—79, tchr. 2d grade, 1979—82, tchr. 1st grade, 1982—88, readiness tchr. 1st grade, 1988—94, tchr. 2d grade, 1994—. Founder/coord., mentoring program K-12 Tender Loving Care, 1989—; coord. Young Astronauts, 1988—; founder/coord. Sch. on Sat., Galveston, Ind., 1994—; third grade tchr., Bolivia, 2004; mem. faculty Challenger Learning Ctr., 1996; workshop presenter Ind. Dept. Edn., 1989—91, Nature's Classroom; response to intervention team mem. Galveston Elem., 2007—08. Flight dir. Mission Possible, Galveston, 1996—; pres. Southeastern Edn. Assn., 1981—82; team mem. Response to Intervention, Galveston Elem.; dist. lay spkr. United Meth., Logansport, Ind., 1992—. Recipient NASA/NSTA Newest award, 1993, Good Neighbor award, 2001, Disney's Am. Tchr. Awards Honoree, Calif., 2003, Make a Difference Day honoree award, USA Weekend Mag., 2006, 2007; named Jaycee's Outstanding Young Educator, 1981, Tchr. of Yr., Cass County Soil and Water Dist. Conservation, 1997, WalMart Tchr. of Yr., 2008; scholar, Japan Fulbright Meml. Fund, 2005. Mem.: NEA, NSTA, People to People Amb. to China (sci. edu. del. 2008), Ind. State Tchrs. Assn., Southern Edn. Assn., Profl. Assn. in Edn., Hoosier Assn. Sci. Tchrs. Inc. (workshop presenter 1994—2008, workshop presenter 1994—2007), Pharos-Tribune NIE (local hero 2007), Pi Lambda Theta. Democrat. Methodist. Achievements include development of classroom business called Chocolate Lollipops, Inc., which earned over $5,000, given to numerous charities. Office Phone: 574-699-6687. Personal E-mail: proller1@msn.com. Business E-Mail: proller1@verizon.net.

ROLLE-RISSETTO, SILVIA, foreign languages educator, writer, artist; b. Rosario, Argentina, Apr. 19, 1967; d. Dante and Gladys Rolle. BA in Spanish, Calif. State U., Long Beach, 1987, BA in French and Italian, 1987, MA in Spanish, 1990; PhD in Spanish, U. Calif., Riverside, 1996. Assoc. prof. Spanish, grad. coord. and fgn. lang. assessor of Spanish and Italian, dept. world langs. and lit. Calif. State U., San Marcos, 1996—, chair, world lang. & hispanic lit., 2000—. Participant numerous confs. Author: La Obra de Ana Maria Fagundo: Una Poetica Fememino-Feminista, 1997, Plazas: un lugar de encuentro para la hispanidad (lab manual); contbr. articles to profl. jours.; translator. Recipient Patrons of Italian scholarship U. degli Studi di Siena, 1987. Mem. MLA, Nat. Hispanic Soc., Asociacion de Literatura Fememina Hispanica, Hispanic Assn. of the Humanties, Letra Femeninas, Mairena, Assn. Internat. Hispanistas. Democrat. Office: Calif State U San Marcos World Langs & Hispanic Lit 333 S Twin Oaks Valley Rd San Marcos CA 92096-0001 Business E-Mail: srolle@csusm.edu.

ROLLERSON, COREY L., professional basketball coach; b. NYC, Aug. 12, 1974; m. Shon Rollerson, June 30, 2001; children: Andre Johnson, Jacarey, Caleb. BA, Claflin U., Orangeburg, SC, 1997. Tchr., basketball coach West Port HS, Ocala, Fla., 2004—. Office: West Port HS 3733 SW 80th Ave Ocala FL 34481 Office Fax: 352-291-4001. Business E-Mail: corey.rollerson@marion.k12.fl.us.

ROLLIN, MICHAEL FREDRICK, history professor; b. Laredo, Tex., Apr. 25, 1975; s. Michael William and Maria Farias Rollin. BA in Polit. Sci., St. Mary's U., San Antonio, 1996; MA, U. Tex., San Antonio, 2002. Adj. instr., history St. Philip's Coll., San Antonio, 2003—05; lectr. U. Tex., San Antonio, 2004—. Mem.: The Sons of the Republic of Tex. Republican. Roman Catholic. Home: 13122 Brook Garden Ln San Antonio TX 78232-5155 Office: Univ Texas 6900 N Loop 1604 W San Antonio TX 78249-0652 Personal E-mail: mrollin75@sbcglobal.net. E-mail: michael.rollin@utsa.edu.

ROLLING, LINCOLN CURTIS, history professor; b. Houston, Sept. 12, 1950; s. Lincoln Curtis and Laurel Rolling; m. Jacquelyne Jones, Feb. 26, 1972; children: Jacquelyn Michelle, Lincoln Curtis III. BA, Sam Houston State, 1971, MA, 1975; PhD, U. Tex., Austin, 1992. Prof. history Cedar Valley Coll., Lancaster, Tex., 1977—; tchr. Windham Sch. Dist., Huntsville, Tex. Fulbright curriculum specialist Eastfield Coll., Mesquite, Tex. Pres. So. Hills Assn., Dallas. Home: 942 Brookwood Dallas TX Office: Cedar Valley Coll 3030 N Dallas Ave Lancaster TX 75134 Office Fax: 972-860-2988. Personal E-mail: aka1808@aol.com. Business E-Mail: linc@dcccd.edu.

ROLLINGER, MARY ELIZABETH, retired school counselor, clinical director; b. Jamestown, NY, May 12, 1950; d. Ernest and June Furlow, BS, Edinboro U., 1974; MEd, St. Bonaventure U., 1994. Cert. secondary edn. and elem. edn., NY, adv. cert. in counseling, 1996; advanced tng. in critical incident stress debriefing, 1996; mental health counseling lic., NY State, 2005. English tchr. Bemus Point (N.Y.) Ctrl. Sch., 1974—2000; part-time clothing buyer Good Morning Farm, Stow, N.Y., 1976-84; part-time GED instr. Erie 2 BOCES, Fredonia, N.Y., 1979-84; sch. counselor Bemus Point Ctrl. Sch. Dist., 2000—06; ret., 2006. Creative writing tchr. Chautauqua County Sch. Bd., Fredonia, 1986—; adj. prof. SUNY, Fredonia, 1994-96; turnkey trainer for N.Y. State syllabus N.Y. State Dept. Edn., Albany, 1985. Vol. Reg Lenna Civic Ctr., Jamestown, 1992, Critical Incident Stress Mgmt. Team, 1995-, clinical dir.; tchr. rep. Parent-Tchr.-Student Assn., Bemus Point, 1980-94; bd. dirs. Amicae-Hotline for Rape-Battering-Abuse, Jamestown, 1986-88, Mutuus Mime Theater, Jamestown, 1982-86; clin. dir. Chautauqua County Emergency Svcs. Stress Mgmt. Team, 2008 Mem. Am. Counseling Assn., Am. Sch. Guidance Counselors Assn., Chautauqua County Counselors Assn., NY State Sch. Counselors Assn., Delta Kappa Gamma (publicity chair 1985-90). Avocations: photography, reading, travel, walking, soaring. Home: PO Box 551 Bemus Point NY 14712-0551 Personal E-mail: merollinger@hotmail.com.

ROLLINGS, DALE LINN, lawyer; b. St. Louis, June 23, 1940; s. Jake Floyd and Ruby Ann Rollings; divorced; children: Mark, Matthew. BA, Washington U., St. Louis, 1962, JD, 1964. Bar: Mo. 1964, US Cir. Ct. (8th cir.) 1970, US Supreme Ct. 1970. Atty. Lincoln Haseltine Keet Forehand & Springer, Springfield, Mo., 1964—68; asst. pros. atty. Green County, Mo., Springfield, 1968—69; asst. atty. gen. Mo. Atty. Gen.'s Office, Jefferson City, 1969—71; past pres. Rollings, Shaw & Assocs. (and predecessors), St. Charles, Mo., 1971—. Owner Yellow Farmhouse Vineyard, Defiance, Mo.; dir. New Frontier Bank, St. Charles, 1999—. Author: (book) Exit Laughing, 1999. Bd. dirs. Lindenwood U., St. Charles, 1989—, mem. exec. com., 1989—, mem. gen. counsel, 1989—; chmn. Daniel Boone Home Governing Bd., 2005—. Office: Rollings Shaw & Assocs PC 1000 Fairgrounds Rd Ste 200 Saint Charles MO 63301

ROLLINGS, MICHAEL THOMAS, insurance company executive; Grad. in Fin., Georgetown U., Washington; grad., Northwestern U. Kellogg Sch. Mgmt. Head capital markets divsn. MassMutual Fin. Group, Springfield, Mass., 2001, sr. v.p., dep. CFO, interim CFO, 2006, exec. v.p., CFO, 2006—. Bd. mem. Bus. Friends of the Arts, Springfield. Office: MassMutual Fin Group 1295 State St Springfield MA 01111-0001 Office Phone: 800-767-1000.

ROLLINS, ALBERT WILLIAMSON, civil engineer, consultant; b. Dallas, July 31, 1930; s. Andrew Peach and Mary (Williamson) R.; m. Martha Ann James, Dec. 28, 1954; children: Elizabeth Ann, Mark Martin. BS in Civil Engring., Tex. A&M U., 1951, MS in Civil Engring., 1956, disting. grad. in Civil Engring., 2005. Registered profl. engr., Tex., La., Okla. Engring. asst. Tex. Hwy. Dept., Dallas, 1953-55; dir. pub. works City of Arlington, Tex., 1956-63, city mgr., 1963-67; ptnr. Schrickel, Rollins & Assocs., Land Planners-Engrs., Arlington, 1967—. Contbr. articles to profl. jours. Mem. Gov.'s Energy Adv. Coun.; chmn. Tex. Mass Transp. Commn.; bd. dirs. Tex. Turnpike Authority. Served as 1st lt. AUS, 1951-53. Mem. ASCE (Award of Honor Tex. sect. 2002), NSPE, Internat. City Mgmt. Assn., Am. Water Works Assn., Water Pollution Control Fedn., Sigma Xi, Phi Eta Sigma, Tau Beta Pi, Phi Kappa Phi, Chi Epsilon. Home: 3004 Yellowstone Dr Arlington TX 76013-1166 Office: Suite 200 1161 Corporate Dr W Ste 200 Arlington TX 76006-6819

ROLLINS, DIANN ELIZABETH, retired occupational health nurse, primary school educator, activist and advocator; b. Newark, Dec. 13, 1943; d. Lewis Paul and Letitia Lavinia Rollins. RN, Meth. Hosp. Sch. Nursing, Phila., 1964; postgrad., Howard U., 1966, Milton Coll., 1969—72, West Chester State Coll., 1972—79; cert. bldg. maintenance, John F. Kennedy Vocat. Tech., 1992; BSN, Thomas Jefferson U., 2000. RN Pa., N.J.; cert. religious sci. practitioner United Ch. Religious Sci., 2003. Nurse Meth. Hosp., Phila., 1964—66, 1967—69, Mercy Hosp., Janesville, Wis., 1969—72, Chester County Hosp., West Chester, Pa., 1972—74, Cheyney U., Pa., 1974—75, Embreeville State Hosp., coatesville, 1976—78; agy. nurse Norristown, Phila., 1978—86, Medox, Olsten, Kimberly, Phila., 1985-86; RN supr. New Ralston House, Phila., 1986-87, 88-89; agy. nurse Kimberly, Quality Care, Olsten, Medox, others, Phila., 1987-89; info. and referral specialist Nat. Mental Health Consumer Self Help Clearing House, Phila., 1992-93; intern ACT NOW Southeastern Mental Health Program, Phila., 1993-94; nursery sch. tchr. Bambino Gesu Child Devel. Ctr., Phila., 1994-99; primary instr. nursing assts. ARC, 2000—01, Clin. Pathways Educators Ins., 2001—02; supplemental staff nurse Breslin Learning Ctr., 2002—05, LPN instr., 2003—05; staff nurse Bayada Nurses, 2002—06; postal nurse (occupl. health nurse) US Post Office, 2003—07. Spkr. in field. Vol. instr. program Franklin Inst., Phila., 1973-74; vol. multimedia first aide instr. ARC, Wilmington, Del., 1975-83; vol. plan II nurse blood mobiles ARC, S.E. Pa., 1982-85, 2009. Recipient Stella M. Mummert maternal/child care award, Meth. Hosp., 1964. Mem. Alumnae Meth. Hosp. Sch. Nursing, Four Chaplains Legion of Honor. Avocations: reading, writing, walking, singing. Home Phone: 215-220-0389; Office Phone: 215-600-7667.

ROLLINS, EDWARD J., JR., political commentator; b. Boston, Mar. 19, 1943; s. Edward J. and Mary Rollins; m. Sherrie Rollins, 1987 (div. 1997); 1 adopted child, Lily; m. Shari Lois Scharfer, Nov. 15, 2003. AA, Solano Coll., Calif., 1964; BA in Polit. Sci., Calif. State U., Chico, 1968. Instr. Calif. State U., 1966-67; staff asst. assemblyman Ray Johnson, Calif., 1967-68; asst. vice chancellor, lectr. Washington U., St. Louis, 1969-72; asst. to minority leader Calif. State Assembly, 1968, 72; spl. asst. congl. affairs US Dept. Transp., 1973, dep. asst. sec. congl. and intergovernmental affairs, 1974-75, exec. asst. to fed. R.R. adminstrn., 1975-77; faculty dean Nat. Fire Acad. US Dept. Commerce, 1977-78; staff dir. Rep. Caucus Calif. Assembly, 1979-81; dep. asst. to Pres. for polit. affairs The White House, Washington, 1981-82, asst. to Pres. for polit. affairs, 1968-85; nat. campaign dir. Reagan-Bush, 1984; mem. cons. firm. Russo, Watts, Rollins & Reilly, Washington, 1985; co-mgr. Ross Perot Presdl. campaign, 1992; campaign mgr. Christine Todd Whitman NJ Gov., 1993, Katherine Harris US Senate Fla., 2006; national campaign chmn. Mike Huckabee Presdl. campaign, 2007—08. Bd. dirs. ASPSecure.com, 2000. Author: (memoir) Bare Knuckles and Back Rooms: My Life in American Politics, 1996. Republican.*

ROLLINS, FAYE LORRAINE, medical transcriptionist; b. Hallock, Minn., Dec. 12, 1940; d. Helmer Stenquist and Grace Evelyn Brown; children: John Wilkinson, Dean Wilkinson. Medical transcriptionist Eureka Family Practice, Calif., 1985—91, Faye's Secretarial Svc., Eureka, 1989—95, Humboldt Occpl. & Environ. Medicine, Eureka, 1991—95, Rollins Transcription Svc., Redding, Calif., 1995—. Mem.: Am. Assn. Medical Transcription. Avocation: piano.

ROLLINS, JIMMY (JAMES CALVIN ROLLINS), professional baseball player; b. Oakland, Calif., Nov. 27, 1978; s. James and Gigi Rollins. Shortstop Phila. Phillies, 2000—. Owner Bay Sluggas Inc.; mem. US nat. team World Baseball Classic, 2009. Hon. chmn. Easter Seals, 2004; active Phila. Action Team. Recipient Gold Glove award, 2007, 2008, Silver Slugger award, 2007, Oscar Charleston Legacy award, Negro Leagues Baseball Mus., 2008; co-recipient NL Cool Papa Bell award, Negro League Hall of Fame; named Nat. League MVP, 2007, Most Outstanding Pro Athlete, Phila. SportsWriters Assn., 2008; named to NL All-Star Team, 2001—02, 2005. Achievements include having the eighth longest hitting-streak in MLB history (38 games), 2005-2006; being a member of the World Series Championship winning Philadelphia Phillies, 2008. Avocation: travel. Office: Citizens Bank Park 1 Citizens Bank Way Philadelphia PA 19148*

ROLLINS, JOHN MAXWELL, business professor, disc jockey; b. Blakely, Ga., Jan. 2, 1959; s. Hursteen West and Miriam Christine Rollins; m. Donna Jean McDaniel, Apr. 20, 1991; children: Rebecca, Robert. BS in Math., Coll. Charleston, 1988; MA in Edn. Math., Citadel, 1990; MBA, Charleston So. U., 1995. Owner, disc jockey Jay Maxwell's Music by Request, Summerville, SC, 1982—; disc jockey Sta. WXLY, Charleston, SC, 1990—93; math. prof. Charleston Southern U., 1993—2007, bus. prof., 2007—. Weddiing cons. Jay Maxwell's Music by Request, Summerville, 1983—; chair admissions com. Charleston

So. U., 2004—, chair faculty senate, 1999—2000; mem. edn. com. Low Country Wedding Profls., Charleston, 1997—2000, pres., 2000—02, mem., 2002—04, edn. chair, 2007—. Author: (book) Play Something We Can Dance To, 1997; contbr. articles to Mobile Beat mag. With USN, 1977—83. Recipient Excellence in Tchg. award, Charleston So. U., 1999, Faculty of Yr. award, 1998. Republican. Baptist. Avocation: music. Home: 422 Eastover Cir Summerville SC 29483 Office: Charleston So U 9200 University Blvd Charleston SC 29423 E-mail: jay@jaymaxwell.com.

ROLLINS, KEN (QUINTON C. ROLLINS), museum director; BA, U. South Fla., 1964; MS in Ceramics and Sculpture, U. Tenn., 1973; grad., Getty Mus. Mgmt. Inst., U. Calif., Berkley. Asst. dir. DeLand Mus. Art, 1979—80, exec. dir., 1980—81, Polk Mus. Art, Lakeland, Fla., 1981—94, Gulf Coast Mus. Art (formerly Fla. Gulf Coast Art Ctr.), Largo, Fla., 1994—2005; interim exec. dir. Tampa Mus. Art, 2005—. Asst. program dir. U. South Fla., Tampa, 1965—66; program advisor U. Tenn., Knoxville, 1970—71, instr. ceramics, 1973—79; instr. Daytona Beach CC, Fla., 1979—80. Bd. mem. Clearwater Arts Found., 2002—04, 2002—04; adv. bd. Creative Tampa Bay, 2005—; mem. City of Tampa Pub. Art Com., 2005—. Lt. USN, 1966—69. Recipient Lifetime Achievement Award, Fla. Assn. of Mus., 2004. Mem.: Fla. Cultural Action and Edn. Alliance (state bd. mem. 1993—2000, chmn. membership com. 1994—96), Southeastern Mus. Conf., Fla. Assn. Mus. Found. (vice chmn. 1995—97, chmn. 1997—99, Lifetime Achievement Award 2007), Fla. Mus. Dirs. Assn., Am. Fedn. for Arts.

ROLLINS, LISA KAY, medical educator, director; PhD, U. Va., Charlottesville, 1992. Coord., generalist medicine U. Va., 1992—99, asst. prof., dept. family medicine, 1999—2008, assoc. dir., ctr. family, cmty. health rsch., 2003—05, dir., scholarship, dept. family medicine, 2007—, assoc. prof., dept. family medicine, 2008—. Grant, NIH NIAA STTR, 2005—06, Va. Tobacco Settlement Found., 2005—06, AAFP, 2006—07, NIH SBIR, 2006, Health Resources Svcs. Adminstrn., 2008—. Mem.: Assn. Am. Med. Colls., Soc. Tchrs. Family Medicine.

ROLLINS, SONNY (THEODORE ROLLINS), composer, musician; b. NYC, Sept. 7, 1930; s. Walter and Valborg (Solomon) R.; m. Dawn Finney, 1956 (div.); m. Lucille Pearson, Sept. 7, 1959 (dec. Nov. 2004). ArtsD, Bard Coll., 1992, Long Island U., 1998, Wesleyan U., 1998, Duke U., 1999; D of Music, New Eng. Conservatory of Music, 2002; MusD (hon.), Berklee Coll. Music, 2003; PhD (hon.), Colby Coll., 2007, Rutgers U., 2009. Tenor saxophonist, 1946—59, 1961—68, 1971—; mem. Max Roach-Clifford Brown Quintet, 1955—57, leader, 1956—57; co-founder Doxy Records, NYC, 2005—. Ann.concert tours in Europe and Asia; composer (songs) Airegin, Alfie's Theme, Blessing in Disguise, Blue 7, Doxy, East Broadway Run Down, He's Younger Than You Are, Movin' Out, Oleo, On Impulse, Pent-Up House, Sonnymoon for Two, St. Thomas, Tenor Madness, The Bridge, Freedom Suite, Way Out West; performer (albums) Sonny Rollins Quartet, 1951, Sonny & the Stars, 1951, Mambo Jazz, 1951, Movin' Out, 1954, Sonny Rollins Quintet, 1954, Taking Care of Business, 1955, Work Time, 1955, Saxophone Colossus, 1956, Sonny Rollins Plus Four, 1956, Three Giants, 1956, Tenor Madness, 1956, Sonny Boy, 1956, Tour de Force, 1956, Way Out West, 1957, Sounds of Sonny, 1957, Newk's Time, 1957, A Night at the Village Vanguard, 1957, Freedom Suite, 1958, Shadow Waltz, 1958, The Bridge, 1962, What's New?, 1962, Our Man in Jazz, 1962, Sonny Meets Hawk!, 1963, All the Things You Are, 1963, Now's the Time, 1964, There Will Never Be Another You, 1965, Alfie, 1966, East Broadway Run Down, 1966, Next Album, 1972, Horn Culture, 1973, Cutting Edge, 1974, Nucleus, 1975, The Way I Feel, 1976, Easy Living, 1977, Don't Stop the Carnival, 1978, Green Dolphin Street, 1978, Don't Ask, 1979, Love at First Sight, 1980, No Problem, 1981, Reel Life, 1982, Sunny Days, Stary Nights, 1984, Solo Album, 1985, G-Man, 1986, Dancing in the Dark, 1987, Falling in Love with Jazz, 1989, Here's to the People, 1991, Old Flames, 1993, The Meeting, 1994, Without a Song, 1995, Sonny Rollins Plus Three, 1996, Global Warming, 1998, Dearly Beloved, 1998, This is What I Do, 2000 (Grammy award for Best Instrumental Jazz Performance, 2001), Scoops, 2002, Solid, 2002, Without a Song: The 9/11 Concert, 2005 (Grammy award for Best Jazz Instrumental Solo: Why Was I Born?, 2006), Sonny Please, 2006, Soneymoon, 2007, Then and Now, 2008. Recipient Lifetime Achievement award, Nat. Acad. Recording Arts and Scis., 2004, Polar Music prize, Sweden, 2007, Golden Plate award, Acad. Achievement, 2006, numerous others; named to Big Band & Jazz Hall of Fame, 1999; Guggenheim fellow, 1972. Office: Doxy Records Parkwest Fin Sta PO Box 21063 New York NY 10025

ROLLINS, TREE (WAYNE MONTE ROLLINS), former professional basketball coach, retired professional basketball player; b. Winter Haven, Fla., June 16, 1955; 3 children. Student, Clemson U., SC. Ctr. NBA Atlanta Hawks, 1977—88, NBA Cleve. Cavaliers, 1988—90, NBA Detroit Pistons, 1990—91, NBA Houston Rockets, 1991—93; ctr., coach NBA Orlando Magic, Fla., 1993—95, asst. coach, 1996, NBA Washington Wizards, 1999—2000, NBA Ind. Pacers, 2000—02; head coach NBA Devel. League Greenville Groove, 2002; asst. coach WNBA Washington Mystics, 2006—07, head coach, 2007—08. Named to NBA All-Def. First Team, 1984. Avocations: deep sea fishing, movies.

ROLLINS-SMITH, LOUISE ANN, immunologist, educator; b. Wabash, Minn., Dec. 29, 1948; d. Leonard Henry and Louise Alice (Schleicher) Rollins; m. Bruce Douglas Smith, July 5, 1980; children: Pamela, Patricia. BA, Hamline U., St. Paul, 1969; MS, U. Minn., 1972, PhD, 1977. Postdoctoral fellow U. Rochester (N.Y.), 1977-81, instr. microbiology, 1981-83, scientist in microbiology, 1983-87; rsch. asst. prof. Vanderbilt U., Nashville, 1987—. Contbr. articles to profl. jours. Grantee, NSF, 1984—, NIH, 1981-85; recipient NIH Nat. Rsch. Svc. award, 1978-81. Mem. Am. Assn. Immunologists, Am. Soc. Zoologists, Internat. Soc. Development and Comparative Immunology. Office: D-3237 Mid Center N Vanderbilt Hospital Nashville TN 37232-1070

ROLLO, F. DAVID, healthcare company executive, cardiologist; b. Endicott, NY, Apr. 15, 1939; s. Frank C. and Augustine L. (Dumont) R.; m. Linda Wood, June 1, 1991; children: Mindee, Alex. BA, Harpur Coll., 1959; MS, U. Miami, 1965; PhD, Johns Hopkins U., 1968; MD, Upstate Med. Ctr., Syracuse, NY, 1972. Diplomate Am. Bd. Nuc. Medicine. Asst. chief nuc. medicine svcs. VA Hosp., San Francisco, 1974-77, chief nuc. medicine Nashville, 1977-79; sr. v.p. med. affairs Humana Inc., Louisville, 1980-92; dir. nuc. medicine div. Vanderbilt U. Med. Ctr., Nashville, 1977-81; prof. radiology Vanderbilt U., Nashville, 1979—; pres., CEO Metricor Inc., Louisville, 1992-95; sr. v.p. med. affairs HCIA, Louisville, 1995-96; sr. v.p. med. affairs, med. dir. Raytel Med. Corp., San Mateo, Calif., 1996-99; chief med. officer ADAC Labs., Milpitas, Calif., 1999—2002; internat. chief med. officer Philips Med. Sys., 2003—. Mem. med. adv. com. IBT, Washington, 1984—; mem. pvt. sector liaison panel Inst. of Medicine, Washington, 1983—; bd. dirs. ADAC Labs. Editor: Nuclear Medicine Physics, Instruments and Agents, 1977; co-editor: Physical Basis of Medical Imaging, 1980, Digital Radiology: Focus on Clinical Utility, 1982, Nuclear Medicine Resonance Imaging, 1983; mem. editorial adv. bd. ECRI, 1981—. Pres. bd. dirs. Youth Performing Arts Coun., Louisville, 1984-85; bd. dirs. Louisville-Jefferson County Youth Orch., 1983-85; sr. v.p., exec. com. USA Internat. Harp Competition, 1992-, chmn., 1994-. Fellow Am. Coll. Cardiology, Am. Coll. Nuc. Physicians (profl. Am. Coll. Radiology com. 1982-84, chmn. 1984); mem. AMA, Soc. Nuc. Medicine (trustee 1979-83, 84—, Cassen Meml. lectr. western region 1980, 84), Radiol. Soc. N.Am., NEMA (chmn. nuc. medicine sect., 2002-, bd. mem., 2002-, testimony medicine expert, 2003-), Am. Coll. Radiology, Ky. Sci. Tech. Coun. (exec. bd. 1987—), Advancement Med. Instrumentation (bd. dirs. 1986—), Louisville C. of C. (chmn. MIC com. 1987—). Avocations: racquetball, squash, golf. Home: 15735 Peach Hill Rd Saratoga CA 95070-6447

ROLLS, BARBARA JEAN, nutritionist, educator, director; b. Washington, Jan. 5, 1945; d. Howard Julian and Patricia Jane Simons; m. Edmund Thomson Rolls, Sept. 6, 1969 (div. Jan. 1983); children: Melissa May, Juliet Helen. BA, U. Pa., 1966; PhD, Cambridge U., Eng., 1970; MA (hon.), Oxford U., Eng., 1970. Mary Somerville rsch. fellow Oxford U., 1969—72, IBM rsch. fellow, 1972—74, jr. rsch. fellow Wolfson Coll., 1974—75, E.P. Abraham rsch. fellow Green Coll., 1979—82, fellow in nutrition, 1983—84; assoc. prof. psychiatry Johns Hopkins U. Sch. Medicine, Balt., 1984-91, prof., 1991-92; Jean Phillips Shibley prof. biobehavioral health Pa. State U., State College, 1992-94, nutritional scis., prof., nutritional scis. Helen A. Guthrie chair nutrition, 1994—; dir. lab Study Human Ingestive Behaviour, 1996. Mem. Nat. Diabetes and Digestive and Kidney Diseases Adv. Coun., 1994—98; cons. in field. Author: Thirst, 1982, Carbohydrates and Weight Management, 1998, Volumetrics: Feel Full on Fewer Calories, 2000, The Volumetrics Eating Plan, 2005; mem. editl. bd. Am. Jour. Physiology, 1985—99, Trends Food Sci. and Tech., 1991—93, Am. Jour. Clin. Nutrition, 1992—98, Obesity, 1992—2002, Nutrition Rev., 1993—97; contbr. articles to profl. jours. Recipient Merit award, NIH, 1997—, Internat. award for Modern Nutrition, 2001; grantee, NIH, 1987—, Med. Rsch. Coun. U.K., 1969—84; Thouron scholar, Cambridge U., 1966—69. Fellow: AAAS; mem.: Am. Soc. Nutrition (award in human nutrition 1995), Obesity Soc. (coun. 1991—93, v.p. 1994—95, pres.-elect 1995—96, pres. 1996—97), Soc. Study Ingestive Behavior (bd. dirs. 1986—90, pres.-elect 1990—91, pres. 1991—92), Am. Physiol. Soc., Am. Dietetic Assn. (hon.), Golden Key (hon.; Atwater lectr. 2007, Centrum Ctr. Nutrition Sci. award 2008). Office: Pa State U 226 Henderson Bldg University Park PA 16802-6501 Business E-Mail: bjr4@psu.edu.

ROLNIK, CLAIRE YVETTE, literature and language professor; b. NYC, Aug. 17, 1942; d. Michael and Solange Camille Rolnik; m. Pincus Aloof, Mar. 3, 1996 (div.); children: Emmet Abraham Bargraser, Ruth Elise Foss. BA in English and Romance Langs., Hebrew U. Jerusalem, 1966; MA in English Lit., Fed. U. Rio de Janeiro, Brazil, 1977; MEd in Curriculum and Instrn., Pa. State U., College Station, 1980; PhD in Iberian and Iberian-Am. Studies, U. Toulouse Le Mirail, France, 1985. Tchr. ESL Inst. Brazil-U.S., Rio de Janeiro, 1966—77; lang. specialist Nat. Open U., Caracas, Venezuela, 1978—89; prof. English lang. and lit. Cen. U. Venezuela, Caracas, Venezuela, 1989—92; grad. course prof. Pedagog. Inst. Caracas, Venezuela, 1990; instr. English Houston C.C., 1992—. Contbr. articles to profl. jours.; co-author: (instrnl. textbook) Ingles-English, 1980, 1995. Mem.: TESOL. Avocations: writing, singing, dance, painting. Office: Houston C C Sys 1010 W Sam Houston Pkwy N Houston TX 77043

ROLÓN, ROSALBA, performing company executive; Founder, artistic dir. Pregones Theater, Bronx, NY, 1979—. Chair, bd. dirs. Nat. Assn. Latino Arts and Culture; nat. bd. Theater Comm. Group. Named Outstanding Woman of the Yr., El Diario/La Prensa, 2008; Ford Visionaries fellow, 2006, US Artists Fontanals fellow, 2008. Office: Pregones Theater 571-575 Walton Ave Bronx NY 10451 Office Phone: 718-585-1202. E-mail: info@pregones.org.*

ROLSTON, BRIAN, professional hockey player; b. Flint, Mich., Feb. 21, 1973; m. Jennifer Rolston; children: Ryder, Brody, Stone. Attended, Lake Superior State U., 1991—93. Left wing NJ Devils, 1994—99, 2008—, Colo. Avalanche, 1999—2000, Boston Bruins, 2000—04, Minn. Wild, 2004—08. Mem. Team USA, Olympic Games, Lillehammer, Norway, 1994, Salt Lake City, 2002, Torino, Italy, 06, Team USA, World Cup of Hockey, 1996. Named to NHL All-Star Game, 2007. Achievements include invention of being a member of Stanley Cup Champion New Jersey Devils, 1995; being a member of World Cup Champion Team USA, 1996; being a member of silver medal USA Hockey Team, Salt Lake City Olympic Games, 2002. Office: NJ Devils Prudential Ctr 165 Mulberry St Newark NJ 07102

ROLSTON, HOLMES, III, theology studies educator, philosopher; b. Staunton, Va., Nov. 19, 1932; s. Holmes and Mary Winifred (Long) R.; m. Jane Irving Wilson, June 1, 1956; children: Shonny Hunter, Giles Campbell. BS, Davidson Coll., 1953; BD, Union Theol. Sem., Richmond, Va., 1956; MA in Philosophy of Sci., U. Pitts., 1968; PhD in Theology, U. Edinburgh, Scotland, 1958. Ordained ministry Presbyn. Ch. (USA), 1956. Asst. prof. philosophy Colo. State U., Ft. Collins, 1968-71, assoc. prof., 1971-76, prof., 1976—. Vis. scholar Ctr. Study World Religions, Harvard U., 1974-75; ofcl. observer UN Conf. on Environ. and Devel., Rio de Janiero, 1992; vis. prof. bioethics Yale U., 2005-06. Author: Religious Inquiry: Participation and Detachment, 1985, Philosophy Gone Wild, 1986, Science and Religion: A Critical Survey, 1987, new edit., 2006, Environmental Ethics, 1988, Conserving Natural Value, 1994, Genes, Genesis and God, 1999, Biography: Saving Creation, Christopher J. Preston, 2009; assoc. editor Environ. Ethics, 1979—; mem. editl. bd. Zygon: Jour. of Religion and Sci.; contbr. chpts. to books, articles to profl. jours. Recipient Univ. Disting. Prof., 1992; Disting. Lectr., Chinese Acad. of Social Scis., 1991, Disting. Lectr., Nobel Conf. XXVII, Gifford Lectr., U. Edinburgh, 1997; featured in Fifty Key Thinkers on the Environment, 2001, Templeton Prize in Religion, 2003, Gregor Mendel medal, Villanova Univ., 2005 Mem. AAAS, Am. Acad. Religion, Am. Philos. Assn., Internat. Soc. Environ. Ethics (pres. 1989-94), Phi Beta Kappa. Avocation: bryology. Home: 1712 Concord Dr Fort Collins CO 80526-1602 Office: Colo State U Dept Philosophy Fort Collins CO 80523-0001 Home Phone: 970-484-5883; Office Phone: 970-491-6315. Business E-Mail: rolston@lamar.colostate.edu.

ROMA, AIDA CLARA, artist; b. Phila., July 17, 1924; d. Carlo and Giustina S. R.; widowed; 7 children. Student, Camden County Coll., 1990-99. Dental Dr. Martin Apother, Runnemede, N.J., 1956-66; owner Rogers Auto Sales, Runnemede, N.J., 1966-90; tchr. St. Joseph's Sch., Camden, N.J., 1955-56. Author of poems, Jealousy, 1999, My 2 Best Friends, 2001, "Pal" My Pal, 2004, Dysfunctional Family. Art tutor, Haddenfield, N.J.; v.p. Girl Scouts Am., Runnemede, 1964; sec. Boy Scouts Am., 1960; mem. St. Teresa's Choir, 1993—, Atlantic City Choirs. Recipient Internat. Poet award, Artistic Artistry award, England, 2004. Mem. Sons of Italy. Republican. Achievements include invention of Rack on the Back auto addition. Avocation: singing. Home: PO Box 2076 Laurel Springs NJ 08021

ROMAGUERA, ALLAN E. (AL ROMAGUERA), credit manager; b. Queens, NY, June 20, 1955; m. Delores Romaguera; children: Christopher, Cassandra. Student in civil engring., Poly. Inst. NY, 1973—76; student in acctg., Pace U., NY, 1976—77. Security profl. Pinkerton, Wachenhut, NA, OCS Security, Credit Suisse First Boston, Fisher Brothers, Inc., 1973—80; sr. ops. specialist, 1980—87; correspondent and investigations mgr.; letter of credit reimbursement mgr. Bank of America, 1980—96; asst. v.p. Bank of America NT, SA, 1980—96; letter of credit specialist Holden Partners, Ltd., 1997—98, PNC Bank North America, 1998—. Candidate, dist. 51 NY State Assembly, 2004; candidate, NY dist. 12 US House of Representatives, 2006. Mem.: US Com. on Internat. Banking. Republican. Office: PNC Bank North America 505 Thornall St 4th Fl Edison NJ 08837 Office Phone: 732-632-6572.

ROMAINE, GRANT HIRSCH, retired protective services official; s. Hirschl Edward and Louise M. Romaine; m. Laura L. Harris, Sept. 17, 1990 (div. Apr. 1, 1993); 1 child, Diane V.L. AS in Electronics Tech., Gavilan Coll., Gilroy, Calif., 1981; student, U. Wash., Tacoma, 1992. Cert.: Wash. State Criminal Justice Tng. Commn. (Law Enforcement Officer) 1989, Wash. State Criminal Justice Tng. Commn. (Instr. Devel.) 2000, (crime scene analyst) 2007; Electronics Instr. USN, 1982. Electronics technician first class submarines USN, Pearl Harbor, Hawaii, 1975—88; electronics/computer technician Kachemak Gear Shed, Homer, Alaska, 1989; police detective Wash., 1989—2008; ret., 2008. Bd. mem. Spl. Assault Investigation & Victim Svcs., Port Orchard, Wash., 2000—08. Vol. Hilder Pearson Elem. Sch., Poulsbo, 1996—2001; bd. mem. United Way Kitsap County, Bremerton, Wash., 1991—92, Big Bros. & Big Sisters Kitsap County, Bremerton, Wash., 1992—95. With USN, 1975—88. Decorated Lifesaving Letter Commendation award USN; recipient Superior DUI Enforcement award, MADD, 1993, Lifesaving Letter Commendation award, Poulsbo Fire Dept., 1996. Master: Masons; mem.: Internat. Assn. for Identification, Am. Legion, MENSA. Jewish. Avocations: computer repair, motorcycling, camping, fishing. Home: 18661 10th Ave NE Poulsbo WA 98370 Personal E-mail: gromaine@msn.com.

ROMAN, ALFRED VICTOR, science education educator; b. Bronx, NY, Feb. 26, 1940; s. Alfred Ignatius and Helen Marie (Danin) R.; m. Patricia Jeanne Gardinier, Oct. 25, 1946; 1 child, Caroline Elizabeth. BA, Montclair State Coll., NJ, 1961; MA, NYU, 1963, D Edn, 1967. Speed reading specialist N.Y. Speed Reading Inst., NYC, 1965-67; teaching fellow NYU, NYC, 1965-67, instr., 1967; asst. prof. N.Y.C. Community Coll., Bklyn., 1965-67; dir. rsch. and devel. and edn1. adminstrn. Universal Edn. and Visual Arts, div. Universal City Studios, Calif., 1967-71; dir. div. media arts and tech. Potsdam Coll. SUNY, 1971-87, asst. prof. ednl. communications, 1988—, prof. sci. edn., 1987—. Film cons., N.Y.C., 1967—. Contbr. articles to profl. jours. Bd. mem. Ch. of the Nazarene, Potsdam, 1988-89; v.p. Potsdam Interfaith Community Svc. Coun., 1989, Nixa Area Arts Coun., 2002-06; supr. info. svcs. Olympic Village XIII Olympic Winter Games, Lake Placid, N.Y., 1980; adv. bd. Nixa Cmty. Found., 2004-06; Life Group leader The Bridge Ch., 2004-06. Recipient Pres. award Potsdam Coll., 1981; award NEH, 1980. Mem. Alexandria Bay Flotilla, U.S. Coast Guard Aux., Rotary, Masons, Shriners, Sigma Xi, Sigma Pi Sigma, Tau Epsilon Pi, Phi Delta Kappa, Kappa Delta Pi. Republican. Nazarene. Avocations: music, decorating, films. Personal E-mail: alpatroman@att.net.

ROMAN, JAMES WARREN, performing arts educator; s. Siegbert and Frieda Roman; m. Martha Lurman, Nov. 7, 1970; children: Matthew Steven, Joshua Albert, Heather Gail. EdD. Prof. Hunter Coll., NY, 1977—. Author: (book) Cablemania, the Cable Television Source, Love, Life and a Dream Television's Past, Present and Future, Bigger Than Blockbusters: Movies That Defined America.

ROMAN, KENNETH, business consultant, corporate communications executive; b. Boston, Sept. 6, 1930; s. Kenneth J. and Bernice (Freedman) Roman; m. Ellen L. Fischer, Mar. 27, 1953. BA, Dartmouth Coll., Hanover, NH, 1952. Asst. advt. promotion mgr. Interchem Corp., NYC, 1952-55; advt. sales promotion mgr. RCA Distbrs., Phila., 1955-56; advt. mgr. Allied Chem. Corp., 1956-63; account mgr. Ogilvy & Mather Worldwide, NYC, 1963-79, pres. US, 1979-85, chmn., pres., 1985-89; chmn., CEO The Ogilvy Group, 1988-89; exec. v.p. American Express Co., NYC, 1989-91; ind. cons., 1991—. Bd. dirs. Compaq Computer Corp., 1991—2001, Brunswick Corp., 1995—2001, Gartner Inc., 1999—2002; dir. Ames True Temper, 2004—. Author: The King of Madison Avenue: David Ogilvy and the Making of Modern Advertising, 2009; co-author: How to Advertise, 1977, Writing That Works, 1981. Vice-chmn. NY Bot. Garden; bd. dirs. Nat. Orgn. on Disability. Mem.: NYC Univ. Club, NYC Century Assn. Home Phone: 212-988-2824; Office Phone: 212-249-6641. E-mail: ken.roman@verizon.net.

ROMAN, NANCY GRACE, astronomer, consultant; b. Nashville, May 16, 1925; d. Irwin and Georgia Frances (Smith) R. BA (Joshua Lippincott Meml. fellow), Swarthmore Coll., 1946; PhD, U. Chgo., 1949; D.Sc., Russell Sage Coll., 1966, Hood Coll., 1969, Bates Coll., 1971, Swarthmore Coll., 1976. Asst. Sproul Obs., Swarthmore Coll., 1943-46; asst. Yerkes Obs., U. Chgo., at Williams Bay, Wis., 1946-48, research asso., 1949-52, instr. stellar astronomy, 1952-55, asst. prof., 1955; research asso. Warner and Swasey Obs., Case Inst. Tech., Cleve., summer 1949; physicist radio astronomy br. U.S. Naval Research Lab., Washington, 1955-56, astronomer, head microwave spectroscopy sect., 1956-58, astronomer cons., 1958-59; head observational astronomy program Office Space Flight Devel., NASA, Washington, 1959-60, chief astronomy and solar physics, geophysics and astronomy programs, 1960—79, chief astronomy and relativity programs, 1965—80, program scientist for space telescope, 1979-80; astronomy cons., 1980-89; prin. scientist Astronomical Data Ctr., NASA, 1981—97. With McDonnell Douglas Space Systems, 1988-94. Contbr. articles to sci. periodicals. Trustee Russell Sage Coll., 1973-78; bd. mgrs. Swarthmore Coll., 1979-83. Recipient Fed. Woman's award., 1962; citation for pub. service Colo. Woman's Coll., 1966; 90th Anniversary award Women's Ednl. and Indsl. Union, 1967; NASA Exceptional Sci. Achievement award, 1969; NASA Outstanding Leadership medal, 1978 Fellow AAAS, Am. Astronautical Soc. (William Randolf Lovelace II award 1980); mem. AAUW, Am. Astron. Soc., Internat. Astron. Union (editor symposia 1956-58), Astron. Soc. Pacific. Acheivements include rsch. on stellar clusters, high velocity stars, radio astronomy; 1st noted correlation of metallic lines in stars with their space velocity; asteroid named Roman, 1989. *This guiding principle sounds old fashioned but I have found it useful: "Forget that you are a woman but never forget that you are a lady.".*

ROMANI, JOHN HENRY, health science association administrator, educator; b. Milan, Mar. 6, 1925; s. Henry Arthur and Hazel (Pettengill) R.; m. Barbara A. Anderson; children: David John, Paul Nichols, Theresa A. Anderson. BA, MA, U. N.H., 1949; PhD, U. Mich., 1955. Instr. U. N.H., 1950-51; instr. U. Mich., Ann Arbor, 1954-55, assoc. prof., asst. to assoc. dean Sch. Pub. Health, 1961-69, assoc. v.p., 1971-75, chmn. health planning and adminstrn., 1975-80, prof., 1971-93, prof. emeritus pub. health adminstrn., 1993—, faculty assoc. program on the environment, 2004—; interim chair Pub. Health Policy and Adminstrn., 1991-92; faculty assoc. ERB Inst., 2008—. Asst. prof. W. Mich. U., 1956-57; assoc. dir. Cleve. Met. Svcs. Commn., 1957-59; assoc. prof. U. Pitts., 1959-61; vice chancellor, prof. U. Wis.-Milw., 1969-71; rsch. fellow Brookings Instn., 1955-56; mem. task force Nat. Commn. on Orgn. Cmty. Health Svcs., 1963-66; dir. staff Sec.'s Com. on Orgn. Health Activities, HEW, 1965-66; dir. Govtl. Affairs Inst., 1969-75, chmn., 1970-72; trustee Pub. Adminstrn. Svc., 1969-75, chmn., 1973-75; mem. Delta Dental Plan Mich., 1972-78, bd. dirs. 1972-78, chmn. consumers' adv. coun., 1975-77; bd. dirs. Ctr. for Population Activities, 1975-81, chmn., 1975-81; lifetime vis. prof. Capital U. Economics and Bus., Beijing, 1996—; vis. rschr. Human Scis. Rsch. Coun., Pretoria, South Africa, 1999—. Author: The Philippine Presidency, 1956; editor: Changing Dimensions in Public Administration, 1962; contbr. articles to profl. jours. Trustee Congregational Summer Assembly, 1982-85; commr. Accrediting Commn. on Edn. for Health Svcs. Adminstrn., 1989-95. Served with AUS, 1943-46, ETO. Fellow Am. Pub. Health Assn. (chmn. program devel. bd. 1975-77, exec. bd. 1975-80, governing coun. 1975—, pres. 1979, chmn. publs. bd. 1984-88), Royal Soc. Health (hon.), Am. Polit. Sci. Assn. (life); mem. ASPA (past mem. coun.), Population Assn. Am., Phi Kappa Phi, Pi Sigma Alpha, Pi Gamma Mu, Delta Omega. Home and Office: 2125 Nature Cove Apt 108 Ann Arbor MI 48104

ROMANO, CHARLENE BAUGHAN, music educator; b. Richmond, Va., July 30, 1969; d. John E. Baughan and Nancy G. Pierson; m. John Romano, July 10, 1993; children: Kevin, Lelia. MusB in Performance magna cum laude, Shenandoah Conservatory, Winchester, Va., 1991; MusM, San Francisco State U., 1995. Adj. prof. music Solano CC, Fairfield, Calif., 1998—2000; adj. asst. prof. flute and music theory Shenandoah Conservatory, Shenandoah U., 2003—. Faculty advisor Sigma Alpha Iota, Gamma Gamma Chpt., Winchester, 2007—. Vol. John Kerr Elem. Sch. PTO, Winchester, 2007—08. Avocations: reading, cooking, travel, exercise. Office: Shenandoah Univ 1460 University Dr Winchester VA 22601 Business E-Mail: cromano@su.edu.

ROMANO, DAVID GILMAN, archaeologist; b. Rochester, N.Y., Nov. 29, 1946; s. John and Miriam (Modisette) R.; Student Phillips Exeter Acad., 1965; AB, Washington U., St. Louis, 1969; MA with honors, U. Oreg., 1972; postgrad. Am. Sch. Classical Studies, Athens, 1976-80; Ph.D., U. Pa., 1981; m. Irene Frances Bald, Sept. 18, 1978; children: Katherine MacLeod, Elizabeth Scott, Sarah Gilman. Rsch. technician biol. rsch. Strong Meml. Hosp., U. Rochester Med. Ctr., summers, 1963, 64, 67; rsch. technician genetic rsch. U. Aarhus (Denmark), summers, 1965-66; apprentice tchr. The Shady Hill Sch., Cambridge, Mass., 1969-70; tchr. pub. schs., Eugene, Oreg., 1972-73; sec. sch. Am. Sch. Classical Studies, Athens, 1977-78; curatorial cons. Greek & Roman Collection, Glencairn Mus., Bryn Athyn, Pa., 1981—; lectr. classical archaeology dept. classical studies, U. Pa., 1982-87, adj. asst. prof. of classical archaeology, 1988—, keeper of the collection, Mediterranean sect. univ. mus., 1985—99, sr. rschr. scientist, 1999-2009, dir Greek Arch. Projects, 2009-, Corinth computer project, 1988-90, adj. assoc. prof. Classical Archaelogy, 1997, 2003, adj. prof., 2009-; Elizabeth Wit; Elizabeth Winstead vis. prof. Am. Sch. Classical Studies, Athens, 1994-95; dir Mt. Lykaion Excavation and Survey Project, 2004-. Recipient citation, Eliot Honors Day, Washington U., 1969, John Frederickn Lewis award Am. Philo. Soc., 1993; U. Oreg. fellow, 1973-74; Am. Sch. Classical Studies Eugene Vanderpool fellow, 1978-79; U. Pa. fellow, 1979-80; Olivia James travelling fellow, 1981. Mem. Archeol. Inst. Am., Am. Philological Assn., Univ. Mus. U. Pa. Unitarian, Arcadian Soc. Letter & Arts (Athens)(hon.) Contbr. articles to profl. jours. Home: 212 Valley Rd Merion Station PA 19066-1543 Office: Mediterranean Sect Univ Mus U Pa 33d and Spruce Sts Philadelphia PA 19104-6324 Business E-Mail: dromano@sas.upenn.edu.

ROMANO, FERNANDA (FEFA ROMANO), advertising executive; b. São Paulo, Brazil, 1972; BA in Bus. Mgmt. and Pub. Adminstrn., Fundação Getúlio Vargas, Brazil. With Carillo, Pastore EURO RSCG, São Paulo, Parlo.com, Starmedia, Tantofaz.net (Loquesea Inc.), iBest; dir. interactive comm. DM9DDB, 2002—04, dir. other medias/spl. projects, 2004—05; exec. creative dir. Lowe NY, 2005—07, Lowe Madrid, 2007—08; global exec. creative dir. JWT London, 2008—09; global exec. creative dir. digital/experiential advt. Euro RSCG Worldwide, London, 2009—. Tchr. interactive creative concepts & comm. Miami Ad Sch./ESPM São Paulo; jury mem. CCSP-Brazil, 2003, 05, London Internat. Awards, 2004, One Show Interactive Awards, 2005, London Advt. Awards, 2005. Columnist Radio Bandeirantes FM, Sao Paulo, (advt. newswire) BlueBus.com.br, (TV series) Qual é a Boa?. Recipient three Cannes CyberLions awards, 2004, seven Cannes CyberLions, 2005, Cannes CyberLions Grand Prix, 2005, Two Pencils, One Show Interactive, 2006; named a Woman to Watch, Advt. Age, 2007. Office: Euro RSCG Cupola House 15 Alfred Pl London WC1E 7EB England Office Phone: 212-605-8000. Office Fax: 212-605-8100.*

ROMANO, JOHN FRANCIS, dermatologist; b. SI, NY, July 4, 1948; BS, St. Peter's Coll., 1969; MD, Cornell U., 1973. Diplomate Am. Bd. Dermatology. Intern Einstein Hosps., NYC, 1973—74; resident in medicine St. Vincent's Hosp., NYC, 1974—76; resident in dermatology N.Y. Hosp., NYC, 1976—78; pvt. practice dermatology NYC, 1979—; attending physician St. Vincent's Hosp., NYC, 1979—; clin. asst. prof. dermatology Weill Hosp. Cornell U., 1979—; also asst. attending dermatologist N.Y. Presbyterian Hosp. Mem.: N.Y. State Dermatologic Soc., Am. Soc. for Laser Medicine and Surgery, Am. Soc. for Dermatologic Surgery, Am. Acad. Dermatology. Avocation: sailing. Office: 36 7th Ave New York NY 10011-6609 Office Phone: 212-242-5815. Business E-Mail: info@westvillagedermatology.com.

ROMANO, JOSEPH ANTHONY, healthcare education and marketing consultant; b. Bklyn., Sept. 5, 1946; s. Anthony Wilbur and Anne R.; m. Linda Rose Giacalone, Sept. 23, 1972; children: Nicholas Joseph, Christine Dianne. Student, Villanova U., 1964-66; BS Pharm. Sci., Columbia U., 1970, D Pharmacy, 1972. Clin. resident Lenox Hill Hosp., NYC, 1970-72; asst. dean, asst. prof. Columbia U., NYC, 1972-76, SUNY, Buffalo, 1976-78; assoc. dean, assoc. prof. U. Wash., Seattle, 1978-83; assoc. dir. medicine Pfizer Labs., NYC, 1983-85, product mgr., 1985, asst. to pres., 1985-87; sr. v.p., group dir. Hill & Knowlton, Inc., NYC, 1987-88; exec. dir. external affairs Sandoz (Novartis), NYC, 1988-89; pres., COO, Med. Mktg., NYC, 1989-92; vice chair Nelson Communications, Inc. Worldwide (divsn. Publicis), NYC, 1992—2002; chmn., CEO, SCIENS Worldwide Healthcare Comms., 1996—2002; co-chmn. Nelson Prof. Sales, 1998-2000; prin. May Flower Consulting, 2002—. Mem. U.S. Nat. Adv. Com. Health Profls., Washington, 1980-86. Co-author: Clinical Pharmacology, Pharmacy State Board Reviews, 1976, 78, 85, The Vitamin Book, 1985, 2000; contbr. articles to profl. jours. Fellow Royal Soc. Health London; mem. Am. Pharm. Assn., Am. Soc. Healthcare Pharmacists, Am. Assoc. Study Headaches, U.S. Golf Assn., Rho Chi. Avocations: photography, stamp collecting/philately, golf, music, cooking. Office Phone: 908-625-0014. Personal E-mail: jromano103@gmail.com.

ROMANO, STEPHANIE ANNE, education educator, consultant; d. Stephen Aloys and Josephine Eleanor Uivary; m. Paul William Romano, Sept. 2, 1972; children: Louis Frank, Jennifer Sue. BS in Edn., Shippensburg U., Pa., 1972; M in Reading, East Stroudsburg U., Pa., 1984; EdD in Reading, Lehigh U., Bethlehem, Pa., 1999. Tchr., reading specialist Stroudsburg Area Sch. Dist., 1984—2002; adj. prof. Marywood U., Scranton, Pa., 1994—2001, Lehigh U., 2000—01; assoc. prof. East Stroudsburg U., 2002—. Mem. midl. states steering com., featured spkr. Gov.'s Inst. English/Lang. Arts, Selinsgrove, Pa., 2000—05, LaPlume, Pa., 2006. Author: The Oral History Project: Connecting Students with the Community, Grades 4-8, 2006. Mem. Family Literacy Consortium, 2004—. Recipient Celebrate Literacy award, Colonial Assn. Reading Educators, 1994; named Outstanding Prof., Kappa Delta Pi, East Stroudsburg, 2004. Mem.: Orgn. Tchr. Educators Reading, Coll. Reading Assoc., Keystone State Reading Assn. (pres. 2002), Internat. Reading Assn. (com. chair 2005—06, 2008—). Avocations: reading, boating, travel. Office: East Stroudsburg U 200 Prospect St 112 Stroud Hall East Stroudsburg PA 18301

ROMANOFF, MARJORIE REINWALD, retired education educator; b. Chgo., Sept. 29, 1923; d. David Edward and Gertrude (Rosenfield) Reinwald; m. Milford M. Romanoff, Nov. 6, 1945; children: Bennett Sanford, Lawrence Michael, Janet Beth (dec.). Student, Northwestern U., 1941-42, 43-45, Chgo. Coll. Jewish Studies, 1942-43; BEd, U. Toledo, 1947, MEd, 1968, EdD, 1976. Tchr. Old Orchard Elem. Sch., Toledo, 1946-47, McKinley Sch., Toledo, 1964-65; substitute tchr. Toledo, 1964-68; instr. Mary Manse Coll., Toledo, 1974; instr. children's lit. Sylvania (Ohio) Bd. Edn., 1977; supr. student tchrs. U. Toledo, 1968—73, 1985—2001, instr. advanced comp., 1977, rschr., 1973-74; instr. Am. Lang. Inst., 1978—2002. Asst. prof. elem. edn. Bowling Green (Ohio) State U., 1978—88; chair rsch. com. Am. Lang. Inst., U. Toledo, 1985—94, asst. prof. elem. edn. in lang. arts, 1985—87, asst. prof. elem. edn., ESL specialist, 1978—2002; condr. workshop Internat. Conf./Teaching Langs., U. Cin., 1996; presenter in field. Author: Language and Study Skills: For Learners of English, Prentice Hall Regents, 1991. Trustee Children's Svcs. Bd., 1974-76; pres. bd. Cummings Treatment Ctr. for Adolescents, 1978-80; mem. Crosby Gardens Adv. Bd., 1976-82, Cmty. Planning Coun., 1980-84, Citizens Rev. Bd. of Juv. Ct., 1979—; allocations com. Mental Health and Retardation Bd., 1980-81; active Bd. Jewish Edn., 1976—, pres., 1982-84; active Jewish Family Svc., 1978-85, v.p., 1980-85; allocations com. Jewish Welfare Fedn., 1980, 89-91; bd. dirs. Family Life Edn. Coun., 1984-90, sec., 1988-90; budget and allocations com. Jewish Fedn., 1989-93; bd. dirs. Friends Toledo-Lucas County Librs., 1991—, bd. pres., 1991-93; program chair U. Toledo Women's Commn., 1991-93; bd. dirs. Ohio Friends of Pub. Librs., 1992-94. Named One of Ten Women of Yr., St. Vincent's Hosp., Guild, 1984, Outstanding Instructional Staff Woman, U. Toledo, 1990, Excellence award Citizen's Rev. Bd., 2003. Mem. Tchrs. English to Speakers Other Langs., Toledo Libr. Legacy Found., Orgn. Rehab. and Tng. (named Outstanding Woman in Cmty. Svc. 1987), Hadassah (chpt. pres. regional bd. 1961-64), Northwestern U. Alumni Assn., Phi Kappa Phi, Phi Delta Kappa, Kappa Delta Pi (pres., faculty adv. 1971-75, Point of Excellence award 1992), Pi Lambda Theta (chpt. pres. 1978-80, nat. com. 1979-84). Home: Stratford in the Hills 4343 W Bancroft St Apt 4B Toledo OH 43615

ROMANOFF, MILFORD MARTIN, retired building contractor; b. Cleve., Aug. 21, 1921; s. Barney Sanford and Edythe Stolpher (Bort) R.; m. Marjorie Reinwald, Nov. 6, 1945; children: Bennett S., Lawrence M., Janet Beth (dec.). Student, U. Mich. Coll. Arch., 1939-42; BBA, U. Toledo, 1943. Pres. Glass City Constrn. Co., Toledo, 1951-55, Milford Romanoff, Inc., Toledo, 1956—2003. Co-founder Neighborhood Improvement Found. Toledo, 1960; active Lucas County Econ. Devel. Com., 1979—, Childrens Svcs. Bd. Lucas County, 1981—97, Arthritis Bd. Dirs., Crosby Gardens Bd. Advisors, 1983—96, Toledo Met. Area Govt. Exec. Com., 1996—; citizens adv. bd. Recreation Commn. Toledo, 1973—86; campus adv. com. Med. Coll. Ohio, 1980—; trustee Cummings Treatment Ctr. for Adolescents, 1981—; pres. Toledo B'nai Brith Lodge, 1958—59, Cherry Hill Nursing Home, 1964—85; bd. dirs. Anti-Defamation League, 1955—60, Ohio Hillel Orgns., Lucas County Dept. Human Svcs., Arthritis Assn., 1995—, Comprehensive Addiction Svc. Sys., 1998, Kidney Found. Northwestern Ohio, 1986—, sec., 1989; chmn. Comprehensive Addiction Svc. Sys., 1999, Toledo Amateur Baseball and Softball Com., 1979—81; cons. U.S. Care Corp., 1985—; bd. govs. Toledo Housing for Elderly, 1982—84, sec., 1989, pres. bd. govs., 1990—, pres., 1991—; bd. adv. Ret. Sr. Vol. Program, 1987—89, chmn., 1988—90, 1993—, sec. adv. bd., 1990—, bd. dirs., 2000—; vice chmn. adv. bd. Salvation Army, 1986—87, chmn. adv. bd., 1988—90, ct. apptd. spl. advocate adv., bd. treas., 1988—; chmn. Mental Health Adv. Bd., 1983—84, sec., 1989; bd. dirs. Toledo Urban Forestry Commn., 1991—, pres., 1993, 1995, Lucas County Dept. Human Svcs. Bd.; adv. coun. Renaissance Sr. Apts., 1997, chmn. adv. coun., 1999; adv. bd. Lucas Co. Correctional Facility, 1999—; chmn. Compass Bd., 2002—; bd. dirs. Area Office on Aging of Northwest Ohio, 2001, Lucas County Mental Health, 2001; chair Compass Corp. for Recovery Svcs., 2002—; mem. Lucas County Mental Health Bd., 2002, Juvenile Correction Bd. Lucas County, 2004—; bd. dirs. Mental Health Lucas Co.; mem. Juvenile Correction Bd. Lucas County, 2003—; mem. adv. bd. ACLU, 2005—, 2005—; active Dem. Precinct Com., 1975—78; trustee Temple Brotherhood, 1956—58, bd. dirs., 1981—; pres. Ohio B'nai Brith, 1959—60; bd. mem. ACLU, 2005—. Recipient Toledo-Lucas County Jefferson awards, 2008—. Mem.: Friends Libr. Bd., Mental Health Bd. of Lucas County, U. Mich. Alumni Assn., Juvenile Justice (adv. bd.), Toledo Zool. Soc., Econ. Opportunity Planning Assn. Greater Toledo (adv. bd.), Nat. Coun. on Alcoholism & Drug Dependence, Toledo Mus. Art (assoc.), U. Toledo Alumni Assn., Am. Legion, Hadassah (assoc. Toledo chpt.), Masons (Outstanding Cmty. Svc. award of Lucas County 2001), Zeta Beta Tau. Home: Stratford in the Hills 4343 W Bancroft St Apt 4B Toledo OH 43615-3956

ROMANO GOMEZ, MIGUEL, bishop; b. El Paso, Tex., Dec. 11, 0959; Ordained priest Archdiocese of Guadalajara, Mexico, 1985; rector Archdiocesan Seminary of Guadalajara; ordained bishop, 2000; aux. bishop Archdiocese of Guadalajara, 2000—. Roman Catholic. Office: Archdiocese of Guadalajara Arzobispado Apartado 1-331 Calle Liceo 17 44100 Guadalajara Mexico

ROMANOS, JACK (JOHN ROMANOS JR.), retired publishing executive; b. Stamford, Conn., Nov. 1, 1942; s. John and Grace (Frano) R.; m. Mary Jane Veach, Jan. 29, 1972; 1 child, Cary Lynne. BS, U. Conn., 1965. Sales mgr. Fawcett Publs., Inc., Greenwich, Conn., 1966-73, Bantam Books, Inc., NYC, 1973-76, dep. to pres., 1976-78, v.p., dir. sales planning, 1978-79, dir. mktg., 1979-81, pub., 1981-85; pres. Simon and Schuster Trade Pub. Group, 1985-87, pres. Mass Market Pub., 1987-91; pres., CEO Simon & Schuster Consumer Pub. Group, NYC, 1991-93; pres., COO Simon & Schuster, NYC; pres., CEO Simon & Schuster (Viacom Entertainment Group), NYC, 2002—07; adv. to pres., CEO CBS Corp., 2008—. Bd. dirs. Periodicals Inst., N.Y.C., 1980-81 With Army N.G., 1967. Mem. Assn. Am. Pubs. (mem. heads of houses com.), Internat. Periodical Distbrs. Assn. (bd. dirs.), Country Club of Darien (Conn.), exec. com. The Quills. Republican. Greek Orthodox.

ROMANOSKY, LUANN, elementary school educator; d. Thomas Forese and Minnie Ann Bianchini Forese; m. David Charles Romanosky, May 20, 1978; children: David C. Jr., Maria. BS in Elem. Edn., West Chester State Coll., 1976; MS in Elem. Edn., West Chester U., 1983. Cert. middle sch. math. Pa. Dept. Edn., elem. instrnl. II Pa. Dept. Edn. Remedial math. tchr. Chester County Intermediate Unit, Downingtown, Pa., 1976—, chairperson math. program, 1996—. Workshop presenter Chester County Intermediate Unit, Downingtown, 1976—. Mem.: Math. Assn. Am., Nat. Coun. Tchrs. Math., ASCD. Avocations: reading, exercise. Office: Chester County Intermediate Unit 455 Boot Rd Downingtown PA 19335 Office Phone: 610-269-8675.

ROMANOV, VOLODYMYR ALEXEEVICH, computer science educator, researcher, computer science educator, researcher; b. Kamynino, Kursk, Russia, Jan. 23, 1960; s. Alexey Filippovich and Olga Sergeevna Romanov; m. Svitlana Chystova, Oct. 16, 1981; children: Olga Volodymyrivna, Volodymyr Volodymyrovych. MD, Nat. U., Kharkov, Ukraine, 1983, PhD, 1987. Cert. computer scis. and nuc. physics. Rschr. Nuc. Phys. Lab., Kharkiv, Ukraine, 1983-88; prof. State Tech. Univ. Agr., Kharkiv, 1988—2000, head Info. Tech. Ctr., 1996—2000; prof. Newton Coll., Montreal, Canada, 2000—05; sr. rsch. assoc. 3D Digital Corp., Newtown, Conn., 2005—06; rsch. assoc. Concordia U., Montreal, 2006—07; sr. rsch. scientist, project mgr. Phys. Optics Corp., Torrance, Calif., 2007—. Vice-head Coun. Young Rschrs., Kharkiv, 1984-91; editor Regional TV, Kharkiv, 1985-87 Author: (with S. Troubnikov) Nuclear Forces, 1992, (with I. Furman) Programmed Microcontrollers, 2000; contbr. articles to profl. jours. Mem. Can. Info. Processing Soc. Russian Orthodox. Avocations: russian literature, history, music. Office: 20600 Gramercy Pl Bldg 100 Torrance CA 90501-1821 Office Phone: 310-320-3088. Business E-Mail: vromanov@poc.com.

ROMANOVICH, PATRICIA M., parochial school educator; b. Akron, Ohio, Dec. 11, 1937; d. Joseph and Mary (Dorosz) Siwik; m. Paul Romanovich, Sept. 13, 1958; children: Paula Marie, Gregory Joseph, Jeffrey John, Martin Paul. BS in Edn., St. John Coll., Cleve., 1971; M.Curriculum and Instrn., Cleve. State U., 1988. Tchr. St. Josaphat Sch., Parma, Ohio, 1964—87, tchr., tech. coord., 1998—2004, tech. advisor, 2004—; tchr. St. Columbkille Sch., Parma, 1987—90; tchr., computer coord. St. Anthony Sch., Parma, 1990—93, Greenbriar Jr. HS, Parma Heights, Ohio, 1993—98. Tech. adv. bd. chair St. Josaphat Sch., 1998—2004, curriculum chair, 1998—2004, drama club dir., 1998—; creator, rschr. flip chart Sch. Crisis Mgmt. Plan, 1999—2003. Recipient Excellence in Tchg. award, Diocese of Cleve., 2001; named one of Outstanding Elem. Tchrs. of Am., 1974; grantee Tech. grantee, Sch. Net, Columbus, 2001. Mem.: Korean War Vets. Assn. Ukrainian Catholic. Avocations: reading, travel, country walks. Home: 5400 Sandy Hook Dr Parma OH 44134 Office Phone: 440-884-1812. Personal E-mail: sandyvalley@cox.net.

ROMANOVSKI, MIKHAIL REM, mathematician; b. Samara, Russia, June 22, 1952; s. Rem Vladimir and Lubov Mikhail (Volgina) R.; m. Elena Vladimir Kurtashina, Aug. 27, 1983 (div.); children: Victoria, Valeria. MS, Moscow Tech. U., 1975; PhD, Heat and Mass Transfer Inst., Kiev, Ukraine, 1982. Engr. Ctrl. Constrn. Bur., Moscow, 1975-78; head dept. math. Kriogenmash, Balashikha, Russia, 1978-93; head dept. CAD/CAE Point Ltd., Moscow, 1992—. Tcrh. math. modeling Chem. Industry Inst., Moscow, 1982-93. Contbr. articles to profl. jours. Mem. NY Acad. Sci. Avocations: sports, skiing. Home: Schelkovskoe Ave 79-1-334 107497 Moscow Russia Office: Point Ltd Lomonosovskiy pr 43/2 Moscow Russia Office Phone: 7(985)7683489. E-mail: mromanovski@netscape.net.

ROMANOW, JOSH, lawyer; b. 1964; BA, Brandeis U.; JD, Tulane U., 1991. Bar: Pa. 1992, DC 1993. Ptnr. Aviation practice, chmn. Travel Leisure & Hospitality practice Pillsbury Winthrop Shaw Pittman, Washington. Contbr. articles to profl. jours & newspapers; commentator (NPR, CNBC), mem. editl. bd. Gaming Law Rev. Office Phone: 202-775-9864. Office Fax: 202-833-8491. Business E-Mail: romanow@pillsburylaw.com.

ROMANOWICZ, BARBARA, geology and geophysics professor; married; 2 children. Maîtrise de Mathématiques Pures, Université Paris 6, 1972; MS in Applied Physics, Harvard U., 1975; Doctorat in Astronomy, Université Paris 6, 1975; Doctorat d'Etat, Université Paris 7, 1979. Postdoctoral assoc. MIT, Cambridge, Mass., 1979—81; attachée de recherches Nat. Coun. Sci. Rsch. Institut de Physique du Globe, Paris, 1978—79, chargée de recherches, 1981—86, directeur de recherches, 1986—90, dir. Geoscope program; prof. geophysics U. Calif., Berkeley, 1991—, chair Dept. Earth and Planetary Sci., 2002—; dir. Berkeley Seismological Lab. Recipient A. Wegener medal, European Union of Geosciences, 1999, Gutenberg medal, European Geophysical Soc., 2003. Fellow: Am. Acad. Arts & Sci., Am. Geophysical Union; mem.: NAS. Office: Univ Calif Berkeley 209 McCone Hall Berkeley CA 94720-4767 Office Phone: 510-642-1844, 510-643-5811. E-mail: barbara@seismo.berkeley.edu.

ROMANOWITZ, BYRON FOSTER, architect, engineer; b. Covington, Ky., Nov. 14, 1929; s. Harry Alex and Mildred (Foster) R.; m. Mildred Elaine Gize, June 15, 1957; children: Laura Ann, Mark Walter, Cynthia Ellen. BS in Civil Engring, U. Ky., 1951; M.F.A. in Architecture, Princeton, 1953. Instr. sch. architecture Princeton U., 1954; architect Brock & Johnson, Lexington, 1958-59, Johnson & Romanowitz, Architects, Lexington and Louisville, 1960-2000; ret., 2000. Pres. Ky. Bd. examiners and Registration of Archs., 1975-91; instr. U. Ky. Sch. Architecture, 1996, 2000; mem. Ky. Archtl. Svcs. Selection Com., 2006, 07, 08, 09. Prin. works include U. Ky. campus bldgs., 1959-96, Ea. Ky. U. campus bldgs., 1959-77, Centre Coll., Danville, Ky., campus bldgs., 1967-89, Georgetown (Ky.) Coll. campus bldgs., 1964-84, Asbury Coll., Wilmore, Ky., 1972-78, Asbury Theol. Sem., 1978-93, Berea Coll. bldgs., 1978-91, Transylvania U. bldgs., 1974-98, U. Louisville, 1990-98, 11 downtown Lexington office bldgs.; leader Men of Note Orch., 1986—, Jazzberry Jam Combo, 1993—; author: Jazz in Lexington, A Personal View, 2006, Issues & Images-Fifty Years as a Kentucky Architect, 2007. Mem. Lexington Urban Renewal Commn., 1963-69; chmn. adv. bd. Salvation Army, 1971-72; trustee Midway (Ky.) Coll., 1986-95; appt. architect svcs. sel. com. Commonwealth Ky., 20050172. With USNR, 1955-58; lt. comdr. Res. Recipient award of merit nat. archtl. competition AIA/Ednl. Facilities Lab., 1966 Fellow AIA (1st honor awards Ky. archtl. competition 1959, 61, 68, 70, 73, 78, 80, 81, pres. East Ky. chpt. 1965); mem. Ky. Soc. Architects (pres. 1966), Masons, Rotary, Lexington Club, Navy League, Tau Beta Pi, Phi Mu Alpha, Phi Sigma Kappa. Home: 2057 Lakeside Dr Lexington KY 40502-3016 Business E-Mail: mbromano@insightbb.com.

ROMANOWSKI, BILL (WILLIAM THOMAS ROMANOWSKI), nutrition company executive, retired professional football player, actor; b. Vernon, Conn., Apr. 2, 1966; m. Julie Romanowski; 2 children. BA, Boston Coll. Linebacker San Francisco 49ers, 1988—93, Phila. Eagles, 1994—95, Denver Broncos, 1996—2001, Oakland Raiders, 2002—03; founder, pres., CEO Nutrition 53, 2006—. Author: (autobiography) Romo, 2005; actor: The Longest Yard, 2005, Shooting Gallery, 2005, The Benchwarmers, 2006, Wieners, 2008, Get Smart, 2008, Bedtime Stories, 2008. Named to Am. Football Conf. Pro Bowl Team, NFL, 1996, 1998. Achievements include member of the Super Bowl Championship winning San Francisco 49ers, 1989, 1990; Denver Broncos, 1998, 1999. Office: Nutrition 53 3706 Mt Diablo Blvd Ste 200 Lafayette CA 94549*

ROMANOWSKI, THOMAS ANDREW, physicist, educator; b. Warsaw, Apr. 17, 1925; came to U.S., 1946, naturalized, 1949; s. Bohdan and Alina (Sumowski) R.; m. Carmen des Rochers, Nov. 15, 1952; children: Alina, Dominique. BS, MIT, Boston, 1952; MS, Case Inst. Tech., Cleve., 1956, PhD, 1957. Rsch. assoc. physics Carnegie Inst. Tech., 1956-60; asst. physicist high energy physics Argonne Nat. Lab., Ill., 1960-63, assoc. physicist, 1963-72, physicist, 1972-78; prof. physics Ohio State U., Columbus, 1964-92, prof. emeritus, 1992-98; sr. scientist Argonne Nat. Lab., 1992; physicist U.S. Dept. Energy, Washington, 1992-98; cons. in pvt. practice, 1998—. Contbr. articles to profl. jours. With high energy program U.S. Dept. Energy, 1993-98. Served with C.E. AUS, 1946-47. Fellow Am. Phys. Soc., AAAS; mem. Lambda Chi Alpha. Achievements include research in nuclear and high energy physics. Home Phone: 505-989-3784. Personal E-mail: romanowski@q.com.

ROMANS, DONALD BISHOP, manufacturing executive; b. Louisville, Apr. 22, 1931; s. Albert D. and Moneta (Bishop) R.; m. Marilyn Yvonne Neff, June 13, 1953 (dec. Aug. 2000); children: Rebecca Ann, Jennifer. BS, U. Louisville, 1953; MBA, Harvard U., 1958. Mgr. internal auditing and data processing, mem. contr. staff Container Corp. Am., Chgo., 1958-62; successively asst. to pres., asst. treas., treas., v.p. fin., sr. v.p. fin., exec. v.p. Trans Union Corp., Chgo., 1962-81; exec. v.p., chief fin. officer Sunbeam Corp., Chgo., 1981-82, Bally Mfg. Corp., Chgo., 1982-87; fin. cons. Chgo., 1987; pres. Romans and Co., Chgo., 1987—. Bd. dirs. Burnham Investment Trust, NYC, Cadogan Op. Alt. Inv. Fund; life trustee St. Mary of Nazareth Hosp. Capt. USMCR, 1953-56. Republican. Avocations: tennis, boating. Home: 39 S Sheridan Rd Lake Forest IL 60045-3269 Office Phone: 847-615-2537. Personal E-mail: dbromans@yahoo.com.

ROMANS, JAY, waste management executive; BS, Kent State U., Ohio; MS, Tex. A&M U., College Station. Corp. orgn. devel. specialist Firestone Tire & Rubber Co., 1974; mgr. orgnl. devel. Clark Equipment, 1979—81; mgr. tng. and devel. Union Pacific/Champlin Petroleum Co., 1981—88; supr. orgnl. devel. Amoco Pipeline Co., 1988—89; dir. orgn. devel. and staffing Ecolab/Chemlawn Svc. Corp.; mgr. tng. and devel. to dir. employee and orgn. devel. Amoco Oil Co., 1990—93; sr. ptnr. STS Internat., 1993—95; dir. orgn. effectiveness and learning to worldwide v.p. human resources for pre-analytical solutions bus. Becton Dickinson; founder, pres. Romans & Assocs.; sr. v.p. Std. Register Co., Dayton, Ohio, 2001—04; sr. v.p. human resources Hughes Supply, 2004; with St. Joe Co.; sr. v.p. people Waste Mgmt., Inc. Office: Waste Mgmt Inc 1001 Fannin Ste 4000 Houston TX 77002 Office Phone: 713-512-6200.

ROMANS, JOHN NIEBRUGGE, lawyer; b. Bklyn., May 23, 1942; s. John McDowell and Helen Pond (Niebrugge) R.; m. Caroline Ward; children: John A., Andrew C. BA, Williams Coll., 1964; LLB, Columbia U., 1967. Bar: N.Y. 1967, U.S. Dist. Ct. (so. and ea. dists.) N.Y. 1971, U.S. Ct. Appeals (2d cir.) 1971, U.S. Supreme Ct. 1971, U.S. Ct. Appeals (3rd cir.) 1976, U.S. Ct. Appeals (4th and 7th cirs.) 1987, U.S. Ct. Appeals (9th cir.) 1992, U.S. Ct. Appeals (11th cir.) 1996, U.S. Ct. Appeals (D.C. cir.), 2004. Ptnr. Curtis, Mallet-Prevost, Colt & Mosle, NYC, 1980—90, Katten Muchin & Zavis, NYC, 1990—98, Rosen Greenberg Blaha, LLP, NYC, 1998—. Lectr. on air law topics at various seminars. Contbr. articles to profl. jours. Trustee Summit (N.J.) Unitarian-Universalist Ch., 1978, Mamaroneck Pub. Libr. Dist., 1990-99; mem. budget com. Village of Mamaroneck, 2001-05, chmn., 2002-2005; dir. The Univ. Glee Club NYC, 1993-. Lt. USNR, 1968-71. Mem. Assn. Bar City N.Y. (aero. com. 1983-85, 2004-, chmn. 1986-89, 92-94, 2000, products liability com. 1989-91), Larchmont (N.Y.) Yacht Club. Avocation: sailing. Office: Rosen Greenberg Blaha LLP 40 Wall St 32d Fl New York NY 10005-1304 Office Phone: 212-530-4827.

ROMANSKI, JOYCE MARIE, secondary school educator, small business owner, instructor; b. Bklyn., July 15, 1936; d. Harold Joseph and Mildred Helen Grace (Mills) Culkin; m. Andrew Henry Romanski, Sept. 17, 1966 (dec. Nov. 1996). AA, Ctrl. Fla. C.C., 1976; BA in Psychology, U. Fla., 1979, M of English Edn., 1982, EdS in Curriculum and Instrn., 1985. Clk. Manhattan Savs. Bank, NYC, 1956-58, sec. ins. divsn., 1959-61, exec. sec. real estate, 1961-64, asst. sec. securities, 1966-70, dep. sec., asst. to pres., 1970-71, dep. sec., asst. to CEO, 1971-74; tutor North Marion Mid. Sch., Citra, Fla., 1979-80, tchr., 1980—2006; lectr. Ctrl. Fla. CC, 2008—, instr. Eng. Composition, 2008—, real estate licensee, 2008—. Cons. Abacuss Tng., Citra, FCAT Tng., Crown Region, Fla., Tech. for Educators, Citra, Connections Dept. of Edn., Tallahassee, 1999—, Grants for Great Ideas, Public Education Foundation, 2002-2003; panalist Nat. Bd. for Profl. Tchg. Stds., 1993; mem. Marion County Writing Prompt Com. for FCAT Student Preparation, 2003; mem. Marion county Final Lang. Arts Exam Devel. Com., 2004— Author: Redfield Alma Mater No More Teachers' Dirty Looks, Redfield Alma Master: No More Teachers Duty Looks, 2007; one-woman shows include Talk Show Participation, 2008. Mem. posse Marion County Sheriff's Dept., Ocala, 1986—89, lt. posse, 1989—92, capt. mounted posse, 1992—97; coord. US/USSR Exch. program, 1988—89, US/Latvia Student Exch. program, 1989—90; elected Marion County Exec. Com. Precinct Woman, 2004—, elected sec., 2007, Marion County Rep. Women Fedn., 2008—; reps. exec. com. precinct woman Merion County, 2004—; candidate Marion County Sch. Bd., 2006—. Butcher scholar Ctrl. Fla. CC, 1976; Marion County Sch. Sys., Tchrs. mini-grantee, 1988; grantee Dept. Edn. Tech., 1999, Grants for Great Ideas, 2002. Mem. Fla. Assn. Computers in Edn., Image Tech. Team, Ocala Ladies Golf Assn., Stride Dressage Club, Arredondo Dressage Soc. Republican. Lutheran. Avocations: horseback riding, dressage training and showing, golf, swimming, bowling. Home: Pegasus Farm PO Box 1059 Fairfield FL 32634-1059 Office: Pegasus Enterprises 15895 NW 115th Ct Reddick FL 32686 Office Phone: 352-816-1379. Personal E-mail: diamondpegasus_586@yahoo.com. Business E-Mail: diamondpegasus58@aol.com.

ROMANUCCI-ROSS, LOLA, anthropologist, educator; b. Hershey, Pa., June 13, 1928; d. Ignazio and Josephine (Giovannozzi) R.; m. John Ross Jr., Aug. 26, 1972; children: Deborah Lee, Adan Anthony. BA, Ohio U., 1948; MA, U. Minn., 1953; postgrad., Ecole des Hautes Etudes, Paris, 1961-63; PhD in Anthropology, Ind. U., 1963. Rsch. assoc. with Margaret Mead in field rsch., Admiralty Islands of Melanesia Am. Mus. Natural History, NYC, 1963-67; assoc. prof. U. Hawaii, Honolulu, 1967-68; from asst. prof. to prof. family and preventive medicine and anthropology Sch. Medicine U. Calif., San Diego, 1969—. Mem. study sect. HEW Maternal and Child Health, Bethesda, Md., 1973-75; cons. NSF, 1988-96. The Hierrchy Of Resort in curative Practices: The Admiralty Island, Melanesl in Qualitative Health Reasearch (ed. Robert Dingwall) Author: Conflict, Violence and Morality in a Mexican Village, 1973, 2d edit., 1986, Mead's Other Manus: Phenomenology of the Encounter, 1985, One Hundred Towers; an Italian Odyssey of Cultural Survival, 1991, When Law and Medicine Meet: A Cultural View, 2004, 2007; editor: Ethnic Identity, 1975, 4th edit., 2006, The Anthropology of Medicine, 1982, 3d edit., 1997; mem. editl. bd.: Anthropology and Humanism Quarterly, Interdisciplinary Jour. Study of Health, Illness and Medicine, 1997-81, contbr. articles to profl. jours., book chpts. Grantee Wenner-Gren Found. for Anthropol. Rsch., 1974-75. Fellow Am. Anthropol. Soc.; mem. Soc. Med. Anthropology, Soc. Psychol. Anthropology, Soc. Anthropology of Europe, Soc. Cultural Anthropology, Soc. Health and Human Values. Achievements include field research in New Guinea, South Pacific, Italy and Mexico. Avocations: music, hiking, literature, writing.

ROMAR, LORENZO, men's college basketball coach; b. Compton, Calif. m. Leona Romar; children: Terra, Tavia, Taylor. A, Cerritos CC, Calif., 1978; attended, U. Wash., Seattle, 1978—80; B in Criminal Justice, U. Cin., 1992. Guard Golden State Warriors, 1981—84, Milw. Bucks, 1984, Detroit Pistons, 1984—85; player, coach Athletes in Action, 1984—92; asst. coach UCLA Bruins, 1992—96; head basketball coach Pepperdine U. Waves, Malibu, Calif., 1996—99, St. Louis U. Billikens, Mo., 1999—2002, U. Wash. Huskies, 2002—. Asst. coach, USA under-22 nat. team World Championships, Melbourne, Australia, 1997; asst. coach, Team USA Pan Am. Games, 2003; head coach, USA under-18 nat. team FIBA Americas Championship, 2006. Named Coach of Yr., PAC-10 Conf., 2005, 2009. Office: Dept Intercollegiate Athletics Univ Wash Box 354070 Graves Bldg Seattle WA 98195*

ROME, TODD M., air transportation executive; m. Carole Oumano, 1993 (div. 2008); children: Jessica, Skylar; m. Vanessa Brahms, Aug. 21, 2008. Attended, U. Md. Broker Stratton Oakmont, 1990—94; co-founder Millennium Securities, 1994—2001; co-founder, pres. Blue Star Jets, Inc., 2001—. Office: 1 Drag Hammarskjold PLZ FL 16 New York NY 10017-2201 Office Phone: 212-446-9037. Office Fax: 212-446-9061.

ROMEO, ANTHONY ALBERT, orthopedic surgeon; b. Walnut Creek, Calif., Nov. 8, 1961; s. Sam J.W. and Patricia Ann (DeFilippo) Romeo; m. Laura Lee Sawicki, June 30, 1984; children: Brianna, Alyssa, Danielle, Christin, Sabrina. BS, U. Notre Dame, Ind., 1983; MD, St. Louis U. Sch. Medicine, 1987. Diplomate Am. Bd. Orthopedic Surgery, Nat. Bd. Med. Examiners, lic. Ill. Intern dept. gen. surgery Cleve. Clin. Found., 1987-88, resident dept. orthopaedic surgery, 1988-92; fellow shoulder/elbow svc., dept. orthopedic surgery U. Wash., Seattle, 1992-93; assoc. prof. dept. orthopaedics Rush Med. Coll., Chgo., 1993—; med. staff Rush-Presbyn.-St. Luke's Med. Ctr., 1993—, Oak Park Hosp., Ill., 1994—. Staff surgeon Univ. Hosp./Vet.'s Adminstrn Hosp./Harborview Med. Ctr./Children's Hosp. & Med. Ctr., Seattle, 1992—93. Contbr. articles to profl. jours. Recipient Disting. Alumni award, St. Louis U. Sch. Medicine, 1987; named a Top Doc., Chgo. Mag., 1997; named one of Best Doctors in America, Best Doctors, Inc., 1998. Fellow: Am. Acad. Orthopaedic Surgeons; mem.: AMA, St. Louis U. Med. Sch. Alumni Assn., Mid-America Orthopaedic Assn., Ill. State Med. Soc., Chgo. Med. Soc., Am. Shoulder & Elbow Soc. (assoc.), Ill. Orthopaedic Assn., Notre Dame Orthopaedic Soc., Am. Orthopaedic Soc. Sports Medicine, Arthroscopy Assn. N.Am., Alpha Sigma Nu, Alpha Omega Alpha (founder, pres.). Office: Rush Presbyn St Lukes Med Ctr 1725 W Harrison St Ste 1063 Chicago IL 60612-3836 Office Phone: 312-243-4244.*

ROMEO, JOANNE JOSEFA MARINO, mathematics educator, department chairman; b. Youngstown, Ohio, Nov. 21, 1943; d. Joseph James and Ann Marie (Bonamase) Marino; m. John Homer Romeo, Aug. 14, 1965; children: Christopher, Chrisanne, Jonathan; m. Harwood D. Schaffer, Apr. 25, 2003. BS, Ohio State U., 1965; postgrad., Youngstown State U., 1969-70; MS, Purdue U., 1974; postgrad. in computer sci., U. Tenn., Knoxville, 1982-91. Substitute tchr., Columbus, Ohio, 1964-65; tchr. geometry, math. and French Hamilton Sch. Dist., Columbus, Ohio, 1965-66; tchr. gifted children Bluegrass Elem. Sch., Knoxville, Tenn., 1976-77; tchr. math. and sci. Webb Sch., Knoxville, 1977-85, also developer computer sci. program, 1977-85; headmistress Greenbrier Acad., Sevierville, Tenn., 1985-86; instr. math. Pellissippi State Tech. Community Coll., Knoxville, 1986—; dir. religious edn. Sacred Heart Parish, Knoxville, 1987—2001; tchr. advanced math. Knox County Sch., Knoxville, 2000—02; math. dept. chair Washburn HS Grainger County Schs., Tenn., 2005—. Delegate to go to Russia and Lithuania Ministries of Edn., NCEA. Vol dir. religious edn. Sacred Heart Parish, Knoxville, 1979-87, lay pastoral minister, 1988-2004. Mem. Nat. Council Tchrs. Math., Nat. Cath. Edn. Assn., Nat. Council Parish and Religious Coordinators and Dirs., Nat. Sci. Tchrs. Assn., Nat. Assn. Exec. Females, Ohio State U. Alumni Assn., Tenn. Assn. Dirs. Religious Edn., Purdue U. Alumni Assn., Alpha Gamma Delta. Independent. Home: 1708 Capistrano Dr Knoxville TN 37922-6302 Office: Grainger County Schs Washburn HS 1725 Hwy 131 Washburn TN 37888 Personal E-mail: joannejmr@yahoo.com.

ROMEO, PETER JOHN, lawyer; b. Darby, Pa., Aug. 1, 1942; s. Joseph Paul and Rose Marie (Beckett) R.; m. Nancy Virginia Schmidt, July 15, 1972; children: Christopher, Jeffrey, Michael. BSBA, Georgetown U., 1964; JD, George Washington U., 1967, LLM, 1969. Bar: Va. 1968, U.S. Dist. Ct. D.C. 1969, U.S. Supreme Ct. 1972; CPA, D.C. Acct. Schumaker & Yates, Washington, 1964-69; atty. U.S. Securities and Exch. Com., Washington, 1969-72, spl. counsel, 1972-79, chief counsel divsn. corp. fin., 1980-84; ptnr. Hogan & Hartson LLP, Washington, 1984—. Author: The Registration Process, 2007; co-author: Section 16 Reporting Guide, 1989, Section 16 Forms and Filing Handbook, 1991, 7th edit., 2009, Section 16 Treatise and Reporting Guide, 1994, 3rd edit., 2008, Section 16 Deskbook (updated annually), 2009; contbr. articles to profl. jours. Mem. ABA (mem. fed. regulation securities com.), D.C. Bar, Va. State Bar. Roman Catholic. Office: Hogan & Hartson LLP 555 13th St NW Washington DC 20004-1161 Home Phone: 703-715-8320; Office Phone: 202-637-5805. Business E-Mail: pjromeo@hhlaw.com.

ROMER, CHRISTINA DUCKWORTH, federal official, economist; b. Alton, Ill., Dec. 25, 1958; d. Clifford Lee and Carol (Greer) Duckworth; m. David Hibbard Romer, Aug. 20, 1983; children: Katherine, Paul, Matthew. BA, Coll. William & Mary, Williamsburg, Va., 1981; PhD, MIT, Cambridge, Mass., 1985. Asst. prof. economics Princeton U., NJ, 1985—88; acting assoc. prof. economics U. Calif., Berkeley, 1988—90, assoc. prof., 1990—93, prof., 1993—97, Class of 1957 prof. economics, 1997—2009; co-dir. Monetary Econs. Program Nat. Bur. Econ. Rsch., Cambridge, Mass., 2003—09; chair Coun. Econ. Advisers, Exec. Office of the Pres., Washington, 2009—. Rsch. assoc. Nat. Bur. Econ. Rscsh., Cambridge, Mass., 1990—; mem. rsch. adv. bd. Com. for Econ. Devel., Washington, 1994—98; mem. editl. bd. Jour. Econ. History, 1994—97, Rev. Economics & Statistics. Editor: Reducing Inflation, 1997; contbr. articles to profl. jours. Recipient Presdl. Young Investigator award, NSF, 1989—94; fellow, John Simon Guggenheim Meml. Found., 1998—99. Fellow: Am. Acad. Arts & Sci.; mem.: Econ. History Assn. (nominating com. 2001—02), Am. Economics Assn. (exec. com. 2000—03, com. honors & awards 2004—, adv. com. editl. appointments 2002—04, chair, adv. com. editl. appointments 2003). Democrat. United Church Of Christ. Achievements include research in new statistical evidence of the effects of monetary policy on output, inflation and interest. Showed that historical macroeconomic indicators overstate the size of business cycles before World War II. Office: Council Economic Advisors 725 17th St NW Washington DC 20502*

ROMER, DANIEL, university official, psychologist, educator; b. Caracas, Venezuela, Apr. 19, 1947; arrived in U.S., 1948; s. Adolf and Eleanor (Rittermann) R.; m. Lauren B. Alloy, Jan. 4, 1985; 1 child, Adrienne. AB, Dartmouth Coll., 1969; PhD, U. Ill., Chgo., 1974. Rsch. fellow Dept Mental Health, Chgo., 1976-79; vis. asst. prof. Northwestern U., Evanston, Ill., 1979-81; adj. assoc. prof. U. Ill., 1981-89; assoc. rsch. dir. Leo Burnett Co., Chgo., 1982-89; sr. rschr. Annenberg Sch. for Comm., U. Pa., Phila., 1990—2000, sr. fellow Ctr. for Cmty. Partnerships, 1996—, rsch. dir. Inst. for Adolescent Risk Comm., 2001—. Mem. nat. expert panel on adolescent STD prevention Ctr. for Disease Control and Prevention, Atlanta, 2000-01; mem. rev. panels NIH, Washington, 1994-97, 98—. Mem. editl. bd. Jour. Exptl. Social Psychology, 1988-91, Youth and Society, 2001—; contbr. over 90 articles to psychol. and pub. health jours., chpts. to books, edited books. Grantee NIMH, 1992—, Ford Found., 1994. Mem. APA, APHA. Office: Annenberg Pub Policy Ctr 3535 Market St Ste 550 Philadelphia PA 19104 E-mail: dromer@asc.upenn.edu.

ROMER, DAVID, economics professor; AB, Princeton U., 1980; PhD, MIT, 1985. Jr. staff economist Coun. Economic Advisors, 1980—81; asst. prof. Princeton U., 1985—88; acting assoc. prof. U. Calif., Berkeley, 1988—90, assoc. prof., 1990—93, prof., 1993—2000, Herman Royer prof. polit. economy, 2000—. Vis. asst. prof. MIT, 1988; vis. assoc. prof. Stanford U., 1993, vis. prof., 95; vis. scholar Nat. Bur. Economic Rsch., 1987—88, faculty rsch. fellow, 1986—93, rsch. assoc., 1993—, mem. bus. cycle dating com., 2003—, co-dir. Monetary Economics program, 2003—; co-editor B.E. Journals in Macroeconomics, 2000—; adv. editor Economic Letters, 1992—2003; assoc. editor Jour. Money, Credit, and Banking, 1992—, Quarterly Jour. Economics, 1990—98; bd. editors Am. Economic Rev., 1996—2002. Author: Advanced Macroeconomics, 1996; co-editor (with N. Gregory Mankiw): New Keynesian Economics, 1991; co-editor: (with Christina D. Romer) Reducing Inflation, 1997; contbr. articles to profl. journals. Fellow: Am. Acad. Arts and Sciences. Office: Dept Economics Univ Calif Berkeley 549 Evans Hall #3880 Berkeley CA 94720-3880 Office Phone: 510-642-1785. E-mail: dromer@econ.berkeley.edu.

ROMER, FRANK E., literature and language professor, department chairman; s. Ira Francis Romer and Eleanor Lockwood Romer. BA, NYU; MA, PhD, Stanford U., Calif. Vis. asst. prof. classics Ohio State U., Columbus, 1977—78; asst. prof. classics Johns Hopkins U., Balt., 1978—86; asst. to assoc. prof., dept. classics U. Ariz., Tucson, 1991—2005; cardin disting. prof. humanities Loyola Coll. Md., Balt., 2002—03; prof. and chair, dept. fgn. lang. and lit. East Carolina U., Greenville, 2005—. Study tour leader Am. Mus. Natural History, NYC, 1997—2003, Stanford U., Calif., 2007, Archaeological Inst. Am., Boston, 2005—. Translator: (commentary) Pomponius Mela's Description of the World; editor: (book review) Am. Philosophy Jour., 1982—86. Recipient Maitland prize, NYU, 1968, Humanities Seminars Adv. Bd. award, U. Ariz., Coll. Humanities, 2004; grant, Am. Coun. Learned Soc., 1988, Fgn. Travel grant, U. Ariz., 1995, Distance Learning Course Devel. grant, 2002, Rsch. grants, 1993—94, 2004. Mem.: Modern Greek Studies Assn., Assn. Ancient Historians, Classical Assn. Atlantic States (chair, hahn scholarship com. 1986—94), Am. Philol Assn. (mem., ancient history com. 2002—05). Avocations: travel, bicycling. Office: East Carolina Univ Foreign Languages Bate 3324 Greenville NC 27858-4353 Office Fax: 252-328-6233. Business E-Mail: romerf@ecu.edu.

ROMER, PAUL MICHAEL, economics professor; b. Denver, Nov. 7, 1955; s. Roy R. and Beatrice A. (Miller) R.; m. Virginia K. Langmuir, Feb. 28, 1980; children: Geoffrey M., Amy J. BA in Math., U. Chgo., 1977, PhD in Econs., 1983. Asst. prof. economics U. Rochester, NY, 1982-88; prof. economics U. Chgo., 1988-90; fellow Ctr. for Advanced Study in Behavioral Sciences, Stanford, Calif., 1989-90; prof. economics U. Calif., Berkeley, 1990—; prof. Stanford U. Grad. Sch. Bus., 1996—; founder Aplia, Inc., 2000—; sr. fellow Hoover Instn.; Ralph Landau sr. fellow Stanford Inst. for Econ. Policy Rsch. (SIEPR). Recipient Disting. Teaching award, Stanford U., 1999, Horst Claus Rectenwald prize in Economics, 2002; named one of America's 25 Most Influential People, TIME mag., 1997. Fellow Econometric Soc.; mem. Am. Econs. Assn., Nat. Bur. Econ. Rsch., Am. Acad. Arts & Sciences Office: Stanford Institute for Economic Policy Research (SIEPR) Landau Economic Bldg 579 Serra Mall @ Galvez St Stanford CA 94305 Office Phone: 650-725-1874. Office Fax: 650-723-8611.*

ROMER, ROBERT HORTON, physicist, researcher; b. Chgo., Apr. 15, 1931; s. Alfred Sherwood and Ruth (Hibbard) R.; m. Diana Haynes, June 12, 1953 (dec. Feb. 1992); children: Evan James, David Hibbard, Theodore Haynes; m. Betty Steele, June 25, 1994. BA, Amherst Coll., 1952; PhD in Physics, Princeton U., 1955. Faculty Amherst (Mass.) Coll., 1955—, prof. physics, 1966—2001, prof. emeritus, 2001—. Research assoc. Duke, 1958-59; guest physicist Brookhaven Nat. Lab., 1963—; vis. prof. physics Voorhees Coll., 1969-70 Author: Energy—An Introduction to Physics, 1976, Energy Facts and Figures, 1984. NSF fellow Princeton, 1952-55, U. Grenoble, France, 1964-65 Fellow AAAS, Am. Phys. Soc.; mem. Am. Assn. Physics Tchrs. (asso. editor jour. 1968, book rev. editor 1982-88, editor 1988-2001), Phi Beta Kappa, Sigma Xi. Achievements include research in low temperature physics, solar energy, electromagnetic theory, history of slavery in Massachusetts. Home: 104 Spring St Amherst MA 01002-2332 E-mail: rhromer@amherst.edu.

ROMER, ROY R., educational association administrator, former Governor of Colorado; b. Garden City, Kans., Oct. 31, 1928; s. Irving Rudolph and Margaret Elizabeth (Snyder) R.; m. Beatrice Miller, June 10, 1952; children: Paul, Mark, Mary, Christopher, Timothy, Thomas, Elizabeth BS in Agrl. Econs., Colo. State U., 1950; LLB, U. Colo., 1952; postgrad., Yale U. Bar: Colo. 1952. Engaged in farming in Colo., 1942-52; ind. practice law Denver, 1955-66; mem. Colo. Ho. of Reps., 1958-62, Colo. Senate, 1962-66; owner, operator Arapahoe Aviation Co., Colo. Flying Acad., Geneva Basin Ski Area; engaged in home site devel.; owner chain farm implement and indsl. equipment stores Colo.; commr. agr. State of Colo., 1975, chief staff, exec. asst. to gov., 1975-77, 83-84, state treas., 1977-86, gov., 1987-98; chmn. Dem. Nat. Com., 1997—2000; supt. LA Unified Sch. Dist., 2000—06. Chmn. Gov. Colo. Blue Ribbon Panel, Gov. Colo. Small Bus. Coun.; mem. agrl. adv. com. Colo. Bd. Agr.; chmn., lead spokesman Strong Am. Schs., 2007—. Bd. editors Colo. U. Law Rev., 1960-62. Past trustee Iliff Sch. Theology,

Denver; mem., past chmn. Nat. Edn. Goals Panel; co-chmn. Nat. Coun. on Standards and Testing; mem. adv. bd. Ad Coun.; former chair Dem. Nat. Com., now chair Dem. Nat. Conv. Com. With USAF, 1952-53. Mem. Dem. Gov.'s Assn. (chmn.), Nat. Gov.'s Assn. (former chmn.), Colo. Bar Assn., Order of the Coif. Democrat. Presbyterian. Office: Strong Am Schs 1150 17th St NW, Ste 875 Washington DC 20036 Office Phone: 202-552-4560. Office Fax: 202-870-1093.

ROMERO, ANDRÉS, professional golfer; b. Tucuman, Argentina, May 8, 1981; Profl. golfer, 1998—, European Tour, 2006—, PGA Tour, 2008—. Named Rookie of Yr., PGA Tour, Golf Digest, 2008. Achievements include winning Cable and Wireless Masters Panama, 2003, Abierto de Medellin, 2003, Roberto de Vicenzo Classic, 2005, Morson Internat. Pro-Am Challenge, 2005, Torneo de Maestros Argentina, 2006; Deutsche Bank Players Championship Europe, 2007, Zurich Classic New Orleans, 2008. Office: PGA Tour 100 PGA Tour Blvd Ponte Vedra Beach FL 32082 also: PGA European Tour Wentworth Dr Virginia Water Surrey GU25 4LX England

ROMERO, ANTHONY D., legal association administrator; b. NYC, July 9, 1965; s. Demetrio and Coralie Romero. BA, Princeton U., NJ, 1987; JD, Stanford U., Calif., 1990. With Rockefeller Found., 1990—92; prog. officer for civil rights and racial justice Ford Found., 1992—96, prog. dir. for human rights and internat. cooperation, 1996—2001; exec. dir. ACLU, NYC, 2001—. Co-author (with Dine Temple-Raston): In Defense of Our America: The Fight for Civil Liberties in the Age of Terror, 2007. Named Stanford Pub. Interest Lawyer of Yr., Stanford U., 2003; named one of 25 Most Influential Hispanics, Time mag., 2005, 50 Most Influential Minority Lawyers in America, Nat. Law Jour., 2008; Cane scholar, Princeton U., Nat. Hispanic scholar, Stanford U., Dinkelspiel scholar. Mem.: Coun. Fgn. Rels., NY State Bar Assn. Office: ACLU 18th Fl 125 Broad St New York NY 10004*

ROMERO, DORA Y. MARRON, language educator; d. Luis and Dora Romillo Marrón; m. Raulise E. Romero, June 6, 1970; children: Luis R., Isabel Amina Villicaña. BA, Albright Coll., Reading, Pa., 1968; MA, U. Pitts., 1970; PhD, U. Miami, Fla., 2007. Cert. grad. gemologist Gemological Inst. Am., 1984. Assoc. prof. French & Spanish Camden County Coll., Blackwood, NJ, 1971—75; ptnr. & gen. mgr. Romero Jewelers, Ft. Lauderdale, Fla., 1975—92; sr. prof. French & Spanish Broward Coll., Ft. Lauderdale, 1992—. Dir. gemologist Romero Jewelers, 1992—2008. Advisor intervarsity Christian fellowship Broward Coll., North Campus, Coconut Creek, Fla., 1993—2006. Recipient Waste Mgmt. Corp. Endowed Tchg. Chair award, Broward Coll. Found., 2000—03, Bank of America Tchg. Chair award, 2009, Acad. Merit award, U. Miami, 2007; named Prof. of the Yr., Broward Coll., 1996; Tchg fellowship, U. Pitts., 1969—70, U. Miami, 1996—97. Mem.: Am. Assn. Tchrs. Spanish & Portuguese, Am. Assn. Tchrs. French, Am. Coun. Tchg. Fgn. Lags., U. Miami Alumni Assn. (life), GIA Alumni Assn. (life), Sigma Delta Pi, Pi Delta Epsilon, Phi Delta Sigma, Pi Delta Phi. United Methodist. Avocations: photography, reading. Office: Broward Coll 1000 Coconut Creek Blvd Coconut Creek FL 33066 Office Fax: 954-201-2387. Business E-Mail: dromero@broward.edu.

ROMERO, RAUL ENRIQUE, literature and language professor; PhD in Hispanic and Luso-Brazilian Studies, CUNY, 2007. Prof., Spanish and Luso-Brazilian lit. CUNY, 2003—08. Home: 101 Sherman Ave Apt 6-B New York NY 10034 Office: John Jay Coll Criminal Justice 619 West 54thst Rm 790 New York NY 10019 Business E-Mail: rromero@jjay.cuny.edu.

ROMERO, RICARDO VICENTE, gastroenterologist; b. Ponce, PR, Mar. 5, 1972; s. Vicente Romero and Ana Rosa Soler; m. Susana Lauraelena Dipp, June 23, 2001; 1 child, Sofia Gabriela. MD, Ponce Sch. of Medicine, Ponce, PR, 1999. Diplomate Am. Bd. Internal Medicine, 2002, Am. Bd. Internal Medicine Gastroenterology, 2005. Gastroenterology staff, clin. educator Baystate Med. Ctr., Springfield, Mass., 2005—; asst. prof. medicine Tufts U. Md. Sch. Dir. endoscopy Baystate Med. Ctr., 2005—. Recipient Samuel Floch award, Norwalk Hosp. Affiliated with Yale U., 2002. Mem.: ACP, Am. Soc. for Gastrointestinal Endoscopy, Am. Coll. Gastroenterology. Roman Catholic. Avocations: travel, painting, music. Office: Baystate Med Ctr 759 Chestnut St Springfield MA 01199 E-mail: ricardo.romero@bhs.org.

ROMERO, ROBERTO J., perinatologist, educator; b. Maracaibo, Venezuela, Sept. 19, 1951; MD magna cum laude, U. Nat. Zulia, Maracaibo, 1974. Cert. Ob-Gyn., 1984, Maternal-Fetal Medicine, 1987. Intern in ob-gyn. Hosp. Gen. del Sur, Maracaibo, Venezuela, 1975—76; resident in maternal fetal medicine Yale U., 1976—79, chief resident, 1978—79, fellow in gynecol. oncology, 1980—82, asst. prof., 1982; prof. ob-gyn. Wayne State U. Sch. Medicine, Detroit, 1992—; dir. perinatology rsch. br. NIH Nat. Inst. Child Health and Human Devel., Detroit, 1992—, prog. dir. for obstetrics and perinatology. Mem.: Inst. Medicine. Office: Nat Inst Child Health and Human Devel 4704 St Antoine Blvd Detroit MI 48201 Office Phone: 313-993-2700. Office Fax: 313-993-2694. E-mail: romeror@mail.nih.gov.*

ROMERO AGUERO, JULIO ENRIQUE, electrical engineer, educator; s. Julio Romero Casco and Mercedes Aguero Zeledon; m. Monica Felisa Enamorado Gomez, Jan. 5, 2002. BSEE, U. Nat. Autonoma, Tegucigalpa, Honduras, 1996; PhD in Elec. Engring. with honors, U. Nat. San Juan, Argentina, 2005. Registered profl. engr., Assn. Mech., Elec., and Chem. Engrs. of Honduras. Chief eastern area Empresa Nacional de Energía Eléctrica, Juticalpa, Honduras, 1996—97, chief southern area, 1997—98, asst. regional sys. dept. Tegucigalpa, Honduras, 1998—2000, chief ops. unit, 2000; cons. Comision Nacional de Energia, Tegucigalpa, 2005—06, commr., 2007—; advisor InfraSource Tech., Raleigh, NC, 2007—. Prof. U. Nat. Autonoma Honduras, Tegucigalpa, 2006—07. Contbr. articles to profl. jours. Scholar, German Acad. Exch. Svc., 2000—04. Mem.: IEEE (sr.; chmn. Honduras sect. 2007, Computational Intelligence Soc., Industry Apps. Soc., Power Engring. Soc.). Achievements include first application of type-2 fuzzy logic theory in power systems; development of fuzzy fault currents concept. Avocations: movies, music. Personal E-mail: jera@ieee.org.

ROMERO-GONZÁLEZ, MAURICIO, psychiatrist, educator, consultant; b. Santafe de Bogota, Colombia, Nov. 15, 1960; arrived in U.S., 2000; s. Carlos Guillermo Romero and Dora Cecillia Gonzalez. MD, Colegio Mayor del Rosario, Bogota, 1989, cert. in ednl. resources, 1984; Specialist in Psychiatry, U. Rosario, Bogota, 1989; MPH, U. Conn., Storrs, 2005. Med. intern Hosp. Univ. del Valle, Cali, 1983-84, Med. Social Svc./Primary Attention Unit, Planadas, 1985; emergency room med. coord. Hosp. San Blas, Bogota, 1986-87; med. resident in psychiatry Hosp. San Jose, Bogota, 1986-89; med. cons. in psychiatry Hosp. San Blas, Bogota, 1989-93; chief human rights dept. Mil. U., Bogota, 1995-97; psychotherapist, advisor mental health program Hispanos Unidos Inc., New Haven, 2002—07. Neurophysiology instr. K. Lorenz U., Bogota, 1988—89; mental health prof. Colegio Mayor del Rosario, Bogota, 1990—2009; mental health cons. Ministry of Health, Bogota, 1990—91; nat. health advisor for mental health, addiction behavior and HIV/SIDA program Ombudsman Office, Bogota, 1992—97; chief divsn. mental health Ministry of Health, 1997—2000; dir. of course: Human Rights Colegio Mayor del Rosario, dir. of course: HIV/AIDS, 1997—2000; invited asst. prof. psychiatry Yale U., New Haven, 2000—02, study coord. Dept. Psychiatry develop. medication against cocaine addiction, 2007—08, clin. study coord., 2009—; advisor Hispanos Unidos Mental Health Advisor Program, New Haven, 2002—06; participant World Health Conf. UCLA, 1998; founder, pres. CT Latino P.FLAG Inc., 2002—; pres. bd. dirs. Mapiripana Yurupari of New Eng. Inc., 2002—; psychotherapist Connection Inc., New Heaven, 2009—. Author: Psychotherapy, 1994, Special Mental Health Assistant in Special Case of Masacre de Trujillo-Valle, 1995, Nat. Policy of Mental Health of Colombia, 1997, Risk Reduction in Addiction Behavior, 1997; contbr. articles to profl. jours. including Rev. Colegio Mayor del Rosario. Tech. dir. Fundacion Connaccion, Bogota, 1987—88, exec. dir., 1988—94; sci. dir. Fundacion por La Salud, Bogota, 1994—2000. Rafael Pombo scholar, Colegio Mayor del Rosario, 1970—72, Hon. scholar, 1973—77. Mem.: Soc. Colombiana de Psiquiatria, Asociacion Medica Rosarista (hon.). Polo Democratico. Jewish. Avocations: music, beach volleyball, art. Personal E-mail: ganimedeszues@yahoo.com, maoct@yahoo.com. Business E-Mail: mauricio.romero-gonzalez@emayu.org.

ROMERSBERGER, SARA JANE, performing arts educator; b. Bloomington, Ill., Oct. 17, 1950; d. Richard George and Elaine Kerr Romersberger. BSc in Speech and Theatre, Ill. State U., Normal, 1972; MA in Dance, U. Ill., Urbana, 1975. Cert. mime theatre movement Ecole Jacques Lecoq, Paris, 1986. Dance instr. Ripon Coll., Wis., 1975—78; asst. prof., dance Ill. Wesleyan U., Bloomington, 1980—89; asst. prof., movement West Va. U., Morgantown, 1989—93; asst. prof., musical theatre Elon Coll., NC, 1996; assoc. prof., theatre Southern Meth. U., Dallas, 1998—. Choreographer (plays) The Wrestling Season (Theatre Critics and Leon Rabin award, 2005), Jackson Pollock: In the Painting; theatre, Hanna, A Run-On Odyssey, Man's Best Friend; dir.(asst.): (Operas) Hangman, Town of Greed, Madrid and Barcelona. Meadows Found. and Rsch. Grant, Southern Meth. U., 2002, 2005, 2006. Mem.: Assn. Theatre Higher Edn., Assn. Theatre Movement Educators (pres. 2006—08). Office: Southern Meth Univ 6101 Bishop Blvd Dallas TX 75205 Office Fax: 214-768-1136. Business E-Mail: sromer@mail.smu.edu.

ROMES, REKINA, psychologist; d. Veronica Ayers. MS, U. Ctrl. Ark., Conway, Specialist, 2002. Lic. tchr. Ark. Dept. Edn., 2002; cert. nationally sch. psychologist Nat. Assn. Sch. Psychologist, 2002, lic. specialist in sch. psychology Tex. State Bd. Psychologist, 2008. Sch. psychology intern Conway Pub. Sch. Dist., 2002—03; lic. specialist sch. psychology Klein Ind. Sch. Dist., Tex., 2005—, mentor, supr., 2008—. Hurricane victim relief mem. New Light Christian Ctr. Ch., Houston, 2008. Recipient Cert. of Achievement, U. Ctrl. Ark., 1997, Greek Steering Com. Co-Dir. award, 1999—2000, Greek Show awards, 2000, Outstanding Greek award, 2000, Program Com. Chair award, Order of Omega, 2000, Cert. of Achievement, Delta Sigma Theta Sorority, Inc., 1999—2000, Making a Difference award, St. Jude Children's Hosp., 2000; named Outstanding Com. Mem., U. Ctrl. Ark., 2000, Order of Omega, 2000, Ist Ann. Celebrating Women of Color, Alpha Phi Alpha Frat., Inc., 1999, 6th Ann. Tribute Black Woman, Phi Beta Sigma Frat. Inc., 2000. Business E-Mail: rromes@kleinisd.net.

ROMETTY, GINNY (VIRGINIA MARIA ROMETTY), information technology executive; b. 1957; BS in Computer Sci. & Elec. Engring. with high hon., Northwestern U., 1979. Applications, sys. devel. GM Corp.; bus., IT cons. IBM, 1985—91, supr. ops. ins. rsch., gen. mgr. strategy mktg., sales ops., gen. mgr. global services Am., mng. ptnr. bus. cons. services, 2002—05, sr. v.p., global sales & distbn., 2005—. Mem. bd. IBM Worldwide Mgmt. Coun., Sr. Leadership Team; bd. dirs. Am. Internat. Group (AIG), 2006—, APQC (formerly Am. Productivity Ctr.); spkr. in field. Recipient Carl Sloane award, Assn. Mgmt. Cons. Firms, 2006; named a Global Bus. Influential, Time Mag., 2002; named one of The 50 Most Powerful Women in Bus., Fortune mag., 2006, 2007, 2008, The Next 20 Female CEOs, Pink Mag. & Forté Found., 2006, The 100 Most Powerful Women, Forbes mag., 2008, 2009. Office: IBM One New Orchard Rd Armonk NY 10504*

ROMEU, JORGE LUIS, mathematics professor, writer; b. Havana, Cuba, Dec. 10, 1945; arrived in U.S., 1980; s. Manuel E. and Raquel (Fernandez) R.; m. Zoila Barreiro, July 25, 1970; children: Jorge Luis, Ricardo, Rafael. Lic. in Math., U. Havana, 1973; MS in Ops. Research, Syracuse U., 1981, M in Philosophy, 1987, PhD, 1990. Applied mathematician Cuban Inst. Petroleum, Havana, 1972-73, Ministry Pub. Works, Havana, 1974-76, Ministry Agr., Havana, 1977-79; rsch. engr. IIT Research Inst., Rome, NY, 1982—85; sr. engr. IIT Rsch. Inst., 1998—2007; assoc. prof. math. SUNY, Cortland, 1985-98, assoc. prof. emeritus, 1998—; rsch. prof. Syracuse U., NY, 2003—. Adj. prof. Syracuse U., 1988—; sr. svc. advisor, RIAC; dir. Juarez-Lincoln-Marti Internat. Edn. Project, 1994—; ednl. cons. Fundayacucho, Venezuela, 1998, Acad. Specialist, U.S. Dept. of State, Mex., 2000; rsch. assoc. USAF, 1992-93, 2007-08. Author: Los Unos Los Otros Etc., 1971, La Otra Cara de la Moneda, 1983, A Practical Guide to Statistical Analysis of Material Property Data, 1999; frequent contbr. Syracuse Post-Standard, Hispanic Link News Svc.; contbr. articles to Syracuse Herald, Miami Herald; prodr., dir., condr. (weekly radio program) Sobremesa, 1994-98; frequent panelist Mesa Redonda program, Radio Marti, host Entre Vecinos WSTM-TV monthly program, NBC, 2002-05; (panelist) Radio France Internat. Recipient Disting. Collaborator award Cuban Assn. Journalists, 1978, Dr. Nuala M. Drescher Minority Faculty award SUNY, 1989, Saaty award Am. Jour. Math. and Mgmt. Scis., 1997, Profl. Devel. award Mohawk Valley Exec. Engring. Coun., 2002; scholar French Govt., 1964, Spanish Govt., 1978, Fulbright scholar to Mexico, 1994; mem. Fulbright Spkr. Specialist Roster Program, 2001-07; Fulbright sr. specialist to Mex., 2000, 2003, to Dominican Republic, 2004, to Ecuador, 2006. Fellow Inst. Stats., Royal Stats. Soc. (chartered statis. fellow); mem. Am. Statis. Assn. (human rights nat. com. 1985-87), Am. Soc. Quality (sr., chmn. chpt., cert. reliability and quality engr.), Mgmt. and Ops. Rsch. Soc. Cen. N.Y. (past pres.), Internat. Assn. for Statis. Edn., Nat. Aassn. Cuban-Am. Edn. (past bd. dirs.), Assn. for Study of Cuban Economy (past bd. dirs.), Las Palmas Club (founder, pres. 1984-88). Democrat. Roman Catholic. Avocations: music, history, writing. Home: 201 Rugby Rd Syracuse NY 13203-1440 Office: Syracuse U Dept Mech and Aerospace Engring 151 Link Hall Syracuse NY 13244 also: PO Box 6134 Syracuse NY 13217 Business E-Mail: romeu@cortland.edu. E-mail: jlromeu@syr.edu.

ROMEY, WILLIAM DOWDEN, geologist, educator; b. Richmond, Ind., Oct. 26, 1930; s. William Minter and Grace Warring (Dowden) R.; m. Lucretia Alice Leonard, July 16, 1955; children: Catherine Louise Keener, Gretchen Elizabeth Tanzer, William Leonard. AB with highest honors, Ind. U., 1952; student, U. Paris, 1950—51, student, 1952—53; PhD, U. Calif., Berkeley, 1962. Asst. prof. geology and sci. edn. Syracuse (NY) U., 1962-66, assoc. prof., 1966-69; exec. dir. earth sci. ednl. program Am. Geol. Inst., 1969-72; prof., chmn. dept. geology and geography St. Lawrence U., Canton, NY, 1971-76, prof., 1976—93, prof., chmn. dept. geography, 1983-93, prof. emeritus, 1993—. Ednl. cons., 1962—; NAS visitor USSR Acad. Sci., 1967; vis. geoscientist Am. Geol. Inst., 1964-66, 71; earth sci. cons. Compton's Ency., 1970-71; adj. prof. Union Grad. Sch., 1974-2000; bd. rsch. advisors and readers Walden U., 1981-2000; prof. Grad. Sch. Am., 1993-99; travel writer and cruise ship lectr., 1990—. Author: (with others) Investigating the Earth, 1967, (with J. Kramer, E. Muller, J. Lewis) Investigations in Geology, 1967, Inquiry Techniques for Teaching Science, 1968, Risk-Trust-Love, 1972, Consciousness and Creativity, 1975, Confluent Education in Science, 1976, Plus Ça Change..., 1996, Illustrated Guide to the Geology of commonly visited sites on the Antarctic Peninsula, South Georgia, and the Falkland Islands, 2004, Norway Through a Geologist's Eyes, 2006, The Norman Conquest: How Normandy Conquered Us, 2007; co-editor: Geochemical Prospecting for Petroleum, 1959; assoc. editor: Jour. Coll. Sci. Tchg., 1972-74, Geol. Soc. Am. Bull., 1979-84, Jour. Geol. Edn., 1980—2003; editor-in-chief: Ash Lad Press, 1975—; contbr. articles to profl. jours. Bd. dirs. Onondaga Nature Ctrs., Inc., 1966—69. Served to lt. j.g. USNR, 1953—57, lt. comdr. res., 1957—66, Woodrow Wilson Found. fellow, 1959-60, 61-62; NSF sci. faculty fellow U. Oslo, 1967-68. Fellow AAAS, Geol. Soc. Am., Explorers Club; mem. Nat. Assn. Geology Tchrs. (v.p. 1971-72, Neil Miner award, 2006), NY Acad. Scis., Nat. Assn. Geology Tchrs. (pres. 1972-73), Assn. Am. Geographers, Am. Geophys. Union, Geol. Soc. Norway, Can. Assn. Geographers, Assn. for Can. Studies in US, Internat. Assn. Volcanology and Chemistry Earth's Interior, Phi Beta Kappa, Sigma Xi, Phi Delta Kappa. Home and Office: PO Box 294 East Orleans MA 02643-0294 Home Phone: 508-255-2590; Office Phone: 508-255-2301. Personal E-mail: romeywd@comcast.net.

ROMITA, MAURO CHARLES, plastic surgeon; b. NYC, Jan. 16, 1947; MD, U. Miami, 1973. Diplomate Am. Bd. Surgery, Am. Bd. Plastic Surgery. Resident, fellow NYU Med. Ctr., 1974—81; pvt. practice plastic surgery NYC, 1999—; founder, med. dir. Ajune Ctr. for Beauty Synergy, NYC. Attending physician St. Vincent Hosp. Med. Ctr., NYC; asst. clin. prof. surgery NY Med. Coll. Contbr. articles to numerous profl. jours. Mem. Boys Town of Italy; bd. govs. Sound Shore Med. Ctr. Mem.: Am. Bd. Plastic Surgery (diplomate), Am. Soc. Plastic Surgeons. Office: 853 5th Ave New York NY 10021-5802 also: Ajune 1294 Third Ave at 74th St New York NY 10021 Office Phone: 212-628-0044.*

ROMMEL, A. ROSS, JR., lawyer; b. Houston, 1947; BA, U. Va., 1969; JD, U. Houston, 1973. Bar: Tex. 1973, admitted to practice: US Dist. Ct. (No. Dist.) Tex., US Dist. Ct. (So. Dist.) Tex., US Dist. Ct. (Ea. Dist.) Tex., US Dist. Ct. (We. Dist.) Tex., US Ct. Appeals (5th Cir.), US Ct. Appeals (11th Cir.). Asst. dist. atty. Harris County, Tex., 1973-81; mcpl. judge West Univ. Place, Tex., 1984-87; gen. counsel Andrews & Kurth LLP, Houston. Lectr. - investigation of fraud in fin. inst. FBI Nat. Acad.; instr. U. Houston Law Ctr. (Trial Advocacy Inst.). Commr. Harris County Civil Svc. Commn., 1990—98; pres. bd. dir. AA White Dispute Resolution Inst., 1996—97; bd. arbitrators Nat. Assn. Securities Dealers. Mem.: Houston Bar Assn., State Bar Tex., ABA, Order of Barons, Phi Delta Phi. Office: Andrews Kurth LLP 600 Travis St Ste 4200 Houston TX 77002-3090 Office Phone: 713-238-3830. Office Fax: 713-238-7227. Business E-Mail: rrommel@andrewskurth.com.

ROMMEREIM, JOHN CHRISTIAN, music educator; b. Garden Grove, Calif., June 13, 1958; s. J. E. and Helen Jane Rommereim; life ptnr. Voos Angela; children: Helen Rachel Stuhr-Rommereim, Martin Samuel Stuhr-Rommereim. DMA, U. Kans., Lawrence, 1988. Prof. music Grinnell Coll., Iowa, 1988—. Composer: (choir, harp and string quartet) Convivencia. Home: 502 Tenth Ave Grinnell IA 50112 Office: Grinnell Coll Park St Grinnell IA 50112 Office Fax: 641-269-4420. Business E-Mail: rommer@grinnell.edu.

ROMNEY, CARL F., seismologist; b. Salt Lake City, June 5, 1924; m. Barbara Doughty; children: Carolyn Ann, Kim. BS in Meteorology, Calif. Inst. Tech., 1945; PhD, U. Calif., Berkeley, 1956. Seismologist U.S. Dept. Air Force, 1955-58; asst. tech. dir. Air Force Tech. Applications Center, 1958-73; dep. dir. Nuclear Monitoring Research Office, Def. Advanced Research Projects Agy., 1973-75, dir., 1975-79; dep. dir. Def. Advanced Research Projects Agy., 1979-83; dir. Ctr. Seismic Studies, 1983-91; v.p. Sci. Applications Internat. Corp., 1987—2001. Tech. adviser U.S. reps. in negotiations Test Ban Treaty; mem. U.S. del. Geneva Conf. Experts, 1958, Conf. on Discontinuance Nuclear Weapons Tests, 1959, 60; negotiations on threshold Test Ban Treaty, Moscow, 1974; mem. U.S. del. Peaceful Nuclear Explosions Treaty, Moscow, 1974-75 Contbr. articles to tech. jours. Recipient Exceptional Civilian Service awards Air Force, 1959, Exceptional Civilian Service awards Dept. Def., 1964, 79; Pres.'s award for Distinguished Fed. Civilian Service, for outstanding contbns. to devel. of control system for underground nuclear tests, 1967; Presdl. Rank of Meritorious Exec., 1980; inducted in Hall of Honor, Air Intelligence Agy., 1996. Achievements include research on earthquake mechanism, seismic noise; generation, propagation, detection seismic waves from underground explosions. Home: 4105 Sulgrave Dr Alexandria VA 22309-2629 E-mail: cromney@earthlink.net.

ROMNEY, MITT (WILLARD MITT ROMNEY), former Governor of Massachusetts; b. Detroit, Mar. 12, 1947; s. George W. and Lenore (Lafount) R.; m. Ann Davies, Mar. 21, 1969; children: Taggart, Matthew, Joshua, Benjamin, Craig. BA, Brigham Young U., 1971; JD, MBA, Harvard U., 1975. Cons. Boston Consulting Group, 1975-77, Bain & Co., Boston, 1977-78, v.p., 1978-84, chmn., CEO, 1991—2001; mng. ptnr., CEO Bain Capital, Inc., Boston, 1984—2001; pres., CEO Salt Lake Organizing Com. (Winter Olympics), Utah, 1999—2002; gov. Commonwealth of Mass., 2003—07. Bd. dirs. Staples Inc., Framingham, Mass., 1986-2001, Marriott Internat., Inc., Bethesda, Md., 1992-2002, 2009-. Author: Turnaround: Crisis, Leadership, and the Olympic Games, 2004. Pres. Boston Stake LDS Ch., 1986-1994; adv. bd. Brigham Young U. Sch. Bus., Provo, Utah, 1990—; vis. com. Harvard Bus. Sch., Cambridge, Mass; mem. nat. exec. bd. Boy Scouts Am.; trustee Belmont (Mass.) Hill Sch., 1989—. Baker scholar Harvard Bus. Sch., Cambridge, Mass., 1975. Mem. Belmont Hill Club. Republican. Lds Ch. Office: PO Box 55899 Boston MA 02205-5899 Office Phone: 857-288-5899.*

ROMNEY, PATRICIA ANN, psychologist, educator; b. NY, June 14, 1944; d. Hubert Forbes and Bernetta J (Taylor) R.; m. Joaquin Rosa, Aug. 25,1973 (div. 1980); children: Joaquin Maceo, Imani Romney; m. Paul Henry Wiley, June 2, 1984; 1 child, Maya Pacem. BA, Good Counsel Coll., White Plains, NY, 1966; PhD, CUNY, 1980. Lic. Clin. Psychologist. Coll. psychologist Mt. Holyoke Coll., South Hadley, Mass., 1981-86, vis. assoc. prof. psychology, 2001—; assoc. prof. psychology Hampshire Coll., Amherst, Mass., 1986—96; pres. Romney Assocs., Amherst, 1996—; pvt. practice Amherst, 1996—. Cons. Brown U., Phillips Acad., Smith Coll., U. Maine at Orono, 1988—. Contbr. articles to profl. jours. Mem. APA, Am. Family Therapy Acad. Avocations: reading, travel. Office: Romney Assocs 64 Carriage Ln Amherst MA 01002-3303 Office Phone: 413-253-5630. Business E-Mail: promney@romneyassociates.com.

ROMNEY, RICHARD BRUCE, lawyer; b. Kingston, Jamaica, Dec. 29, 1942; arrived in U.S., 1945, naturalized, 1956; s. Frank Oswald and Mary Ellen (Burton) Romney; m. Beverly Cochran, Sept. 11, 1965 (dec. 1984); children: Richard Bruce Jr., Stephanie Cochran; m. Lynthia H. Walker, Aug. 14, 1988; children: Alisa Dawn, Kristen Elizabeth. BA, U. Pa., 1964; JD, U. Va., 1972. Bar: N.Y. 1973, U.S. Ct. Appeals (2d cir.) 1975. Assoc. Dewey, Ballantine, Bushby, Palmer & Wood, NYC, 1972—80, ptnr., 1981—2004, of counsel, 2004—05. Mem. editl. bd. U. Va. Law Rev., 1970—72. Served to lt. USN, 1964—68. Fellow: Am. Bar Found.; mem.: ABA, Westchester County Bar Assn., Assn. Bar City of NY, NY State Bar Assn., Order of Coif. Home and Office: 35 Deerfield Rd Chappaqua NY 10514-1604 Home Phone: 914-238-2145; Office Phone: 914-238-3222. Personal E-mail: rromney@aol.com.

ROMNEY-MANOOKIN, ELAINE CLIVE, retired music educator, composer; b. Salt Lake City, July 11, 1922; d. Joseph Campbell Clive and Katie Winifred Gilroy; m. Eldon Brigham Romney, May 5, 1941 (dec. May 1998); children: Ruth Romney Powell, Frederic Clive Romney, Clive Jay Romney, Stanley Clive Romney, Eldon Clive Romney, Roslyn Kay Romney Reynolds, Rae Lynne Romney Johnson, Vincent Clive Romney; m. Stuart Midgley Manookin. Studied piano, violin and cello, Clive Music Studios, Salt Lake City, 1938; cert., U. Utah, 1941; studied organ, U. S.C., 1954; studied piano with Frederic Dixon, McCune Sch., 1938—42; studied paino with Alton O'Steen, Juilliard, 1936. Musician: Assembly Hall with McCune Symphony, 1941, author organ book for beginning organists; composer: (sch. song) South H.S., 1939, Skyline H.S., 1962, Wasatch Jr. H.S., 1964; organist Grandview Second Ward, 2001—; organist: Columbia (S.C.) Stake Ctr., 1953—54, East Millcreek 7th Ward and Stake, 1956—2001, Monument Pk. Stake, 1955—56. Bd. dirs. Utah Hemophlia Found., Salt Lake City, 1965—99; vol. specialist Welfare Employment; vice chmn. dist. Rep. Party, Salt Lake City, 1970—90. Recipient Dedicated Svc. award, Hemophilia Found., 1991. Mem.: Alpha Dorian Fine Arts Soc. (past pres.), AXO Luncheon Club (past pres.), Agalia Mu (past pres.). Avocations: travel, writing, volunteering. Address: 2987 Hartford St Salt Lake City UT 84106-3468

ROMO, TONY (ANTONIO RAMIRO ROMO), professional football player; b. San Diego, Apr. 21, 1980; BBA, Ea. Ill. U., Charlston, 2003. Quarterback Dallas Cowboys, 2003—. Co-host (radio show) Inside the Huddle, 2006. Recipient Walter Payton award, 2002; named Player of Yr., Ohio Valley Conf., 2000—02, 1st Team All-Conf., 2000—02; named to Nat. Football Conf. Pro Bowl Team, NFL, 2006, 2007. Mem.: Sigma Pi. Achievements include leading the NFL in: yards per pass attempt, 2006. Avocation: golf. Office: Dallas Cowboys 1 Cowboys Pky Irving TX 75063-4999*

ROMULO, ALBERTO G., Philippine government official; b. Camiling, Tarlac, Philippines, Aug. 7, 1933; m. Rosie Lovely Tecson; 5 children. BSc. in Acctg., De La Salle U., 1954; LLB, Universidad de Madrid, 1958; LLD, Universisdad de Madrid, 1963. CPA 1954. Sec. Budget and Mgmt., 1986—87; mem. Monetary Bd., 1986—87; chmn. Devel. Budget Coordinating Com., 1986—87; senator Philippine Govt., 1987—98; senate majority leader, 1992—96; chmn. Senate Com. on Banks, Currencies, and Fin. Inst., 1992—96, Senate Com. on Social Justice, Welfare and Devel., 1992—96, Senate Com. on Rules, 1992—96; sec. Fin., 2001; gov. World Bank Grp., 2001; exec sec., 2001—04; chmn. NEDA Board Exec. Com., 2001—04, Cabinet Oversight Com. on Internal Security, 2001—04; foreign sec., 2004—. Recipient Gintong Ama award, Philippines, Most Outstanding Senator, Philippine Free Press and Congressweek magazine, Order of Sikatuna award with the rank of DATU, Philippine Govt., 2005. Office: Office of Foreign Affairs 2330 Roxas Blvd 1300 Pasay City Philippines Office Phone: 834-3000 / 834-4000.

ROMULO, RICARDO J., lawyer; b. Philippines, Jan. 8, 1933; s. Carlos P. Romulo. BS cum laude, Georgetown Univ., DC; JD, Harvard Law Sch. Bar: Philippines 1960. Mem. Constitution Govt. Commn., 1986, Govt. Fact-Finding Commn., 1989; former bus. sector rep. Coun. of State Philippines; bar examiner in taxation Supreme Ct. Philippines, 1974—, examiner in comm. law, 1992—; advisory coun. mem. Pres. Gloria Macapagal-Arroyo; sr ptnr. Romul Mabanta Buenaventura Sayoc & De Los Angelos, Philippines. Chmn. Cebu Pacific Airlines, Digital Telecom. Philippines, InterPhil Labs., Sime Darby Phillipines; dir. Pfizer, Inc., IBM Philippines, Inc., mem. bd. trustees, Pension Funds; dir. Honda Philippines, Inc. Chmn. bd. Carlos P. Romulo Found., Found. Enhancement Legal Edn., Inc.; mem. fin. bd. Archdiocese of Manila. Mem.: Nat. Movement for Free Elections, Makati Bus. Club. Office: RMBSA 30th Fl Citibank Tower Citibank Plz 8741 Paseo De Roxas Makati Philippines Office Phone: 632-848-0114. Business E-Mail: ricardo.romulo@romulo.com.

RONALD, PAMELA C., plant pathologist, educator; m. Ronald Adamchak. Diploma in French Lang. Studies, U. Strasbourg, France, 1981; BA in Biology, Reed Coll., Portland, Oreg., 1982; MA in Biology, Stanford U., Calif., 1984; MS in Plant Physiology, U. Uppsala, Sweden, 1985; PhD in Molecular and Physiol. Plant Biology, U. Calif., Berkeley, 1985. Rsch. asst. dept. biology Stanford U., Calif., 1983—84; Fulbright fellow Inst. Botany U. Uppsala, Sweden, 1984—85; postdoctoral fellow dept. plant breeding Cornell U., 1990—92; asst. prof. dept. plant pathology U. Calif., Davis, 1992—97, assoc. prof., 1997—2002, prof. plant pathology, 2002—. Founder, CEO Tellus Genetics, Davis, Calif., 1998—2000; Guggenheim fellow Lab. Molecular Biology of Plant-Microorganism Interactions Nat. Ctr. Sci. Rsch., Nat. Inst. Agronomic Rsch., Castanet-Tolosan, France, 2000; hon. scientist Nat. Inst. Agrl. Biotechnology, Rural Develop. Adminstrn., Republic of Korea, 2002—05; chair plant genomics prog. U. Calif., Davis, 2004—, faculty asst. to Provost, 2004—07; external adv. Zhejiang U. Agrl. Inst., 2005—; dir., grass genetics Joint Bioenergy Rsch. Inst., Emeryville; chair U. Calif. David Disting. Women in Sci. seminar series; founder Genetics Resources Recognition Fund, U. Calif., Davis, 1996. Contbr. articles to sci. jours., including Nature and Science; also featured in New York Times, Wall Street Journal, Le Monde and on Nat. Pub. Radio; mem. editl. bd.: Planta, 1997—2002, Plant Molecular Pathology, 2002—; mem. editl. bd. Plant Physiology; assoc. editor: Transgenic Rsch., 2003—, sr. editor: Molecular Plant Microbe Interactions, 2003—; co-author (with husband): Tomorrow's Table: Organic Farming, Genetic and the Future of Food, 2008 (voted one of the best books of 2008, Seed Mag.). Co-recipient Consultative Group on Internat. Agrl. Rsch. Sci. award, 2007, USDA Nat. Rsch. Initiative Discovery award for work on submergence tolerant rice, 2008; fellow Davis Humanities Inst., Japan Soc. for the Promotion of Sci.; Fulbright Fellow, 1984—85, Guggenheim Fellow, 2000. Mem.: AAAS, Internat. Soc. Molecular Plant-Microbe Interactions, Am. Soc. Plant Biologists (chair, pub. affairs com. 2003—06), Am. Phytopathological Soc. Achievements include with colleagues genetically engineering rice for resistance to diseases and flooding. Office: Genome and Biomedical Scis Facility U Calif Davis 451 Health Sciences Dr Davis CA 95616-8816 Office Phone: 530-752-1654. Fax: 530-754-6940. E-mail: pcronald@ucdavis.edu.*

RONALD, PETER, utilities executive; b. Duluth, Minn., Aug. 26, 1926; s. George W. and Florence (Jones) R.; m. Mary Locke Boyd, Nov. 25, 1950 (dec. 2003); children: Peter Webb, Pauline Morton, Samuel Herschel; m. Anne H. Moore, Dec. 28, 2005. BA, U. Va., 1950. With Louisville Gas & Electric Co., 1950-88, treas., 1962—, v.p., 1969-82, sr. v.p., 1982-88, dir., 1979-89. Bd. dirs., mem. exec. com. Bus. Devel. Corp. Ky., 1967-75, pres., 1971-72; bd. dirs. Louisville Community Chest, 1967-72, v.p., 1969-72; bd. dirs., v.p. Louisville Rehab. Ctr., 1964-82, pres., 1970-71; bd. overseers Louisville Country Day Sch., 1967-70; trustee Children's Hosp. Found., 1978-81, sec.-treas., 1978-81; bd. govs. Captiva (Fla.) Civic Assn., 1990-94, v.p., 1992; commr. Captiva, Fla. Erosion Prevention Dist., 1996-98. With USNR, 1945-46. Mem. Louisville Country Club, Captiva Yacht Club, Zeta Psi. Home: 4710 Indian Hills Green Louisville KY 40207-1366 also: PO Box 877 Captiva FL 33924

RONALD, THOMAS IAIN, retired financial services executive; b. Glasgow, Scotland, Feb. 16, 1933; s. Newton Armitage and Elizabeth (Crawford) R.; m. Cristina de Yturralde, Aug. 30, 1962; children: Christopher, Isobel. B in Law, Glasgow U., 1956; MBA, Harvard U., 1963. Chartered acct. Pres., CEO Zellers, Inc., Montreal, Que., Canada, 1982-85; exec. v.p., dir. Hudson's Bay Co., Toronto, Ont., Canada, 1985-87; pres. Mgmt. Svcs. Group CIBC, Toronto, 1987-88, Adminstrv. Bank CIBC, 1988-92; vice chmn. CIBC, Toronto, 1992—95, ret., 1995. Past dir. Loblaw Co. Ltd., Leon's Furniture Ltd., Holt Renfrew & Co., Presidents Choice Bank, Strongco Inc.; trustee Allied Properties Income Trust, Transalta Power Ltd.; dir. emeritus. Sub. lt. Royal Navy, 1956-58. Fellow Inst. Chartered Accts. Ont.; mem. Inst. Chartered Accts. Scotland, Granite Club, Toronto Club, Toronto Hunt Club, Caledonian Club(London) Presbyterian. Avocations: music, golf, tennis. Office: 1 Chedington Pl Ste 6C Toronto ON Canada M4N 3R4 Business E-Mail: tinaronald@rogers.com.

RONALDINHO, (RONALDO DE ASSIS MOREIRA), professional soccer player; b. Porto Alegre, Brazil, Mar. 21, 1980; naturalized, Spain, 2007; s. João and Miguelina Moreira; 1 child, João. Player Gremio FC, Brazil, 1998—2001, Paris Saint Germain, France, 2001—03, FC Barcelona, Spain, 2003—08, AC Milan, Italy, 2008—. Mem. Brazil Nat. Team, 1999—, World Cup Champion, Brazil, 2002; mem. & capt. Confederations Cup Champion, Brazil, 2005; mem. Brazilian Olympic Team, Beijing, 2008. Recipient Bronze medal in men's soccer, Beijing Olympic Games, 2008; named World Soccer Player of World, 2004, 2005, FIFA World Player of Yr., 2004, 2005, FIFPro World Player of Yr., 2005, 2006, Best Forward, UEFA Champions League, 2005, European Footballer of Yr., 2005, UEFA Club Footballer of Yr., 2006, Best Soccer Player, ESPY Awards, 2006; named one of The 100 Most Powerful Celebrities, Forbes.com, 2008; named to FIFA 100, 2004, FIFPro World XI, 2005. Office: AC Milan Stadio Guiseppe Meazza Via Piccolomini 5 21051 Milan Italy

RONAN, LAURENCE JOSEPH, internist, pediatrician; b. Evanston, Ill., Jan. 11, 1954; MD, Harvard U., 1987. Intern, internal medicine Mass. Gen. Hosp., 1987, resident, 1988, staff physician; staff physician, Team 2 Internal Medicine Assocs. Team internist Boston Red Sox; internal medicine rep. Med. Alliance for Iraq. Vol. Project Hope. Named one of Best Doctors, Boston Mag., 2007. Office: Internal Medicine Assocs 15 Parkman St WAC 605 Boston MA 02114-3117

RONAN, WILLIAM JOHN, management consultant; b. Buffalo, Nov. 8, 1912; s. William and Charlotte (Ramp) R.; m. Elena Vinadé, May 29, 1939; children: Monica, Diana Quasha. AB, Syracuse U., 1934; PhD, NYU, 1940, LLD, 1969; certificate, Geneva Sch. Internat. Studies, 1933. Mus. asst. Buffalo Mus. Sci., 1928-30; with Niagara-Hudson Power Co., 1931; transfer dept. NYC R.R., 1932; Penfield fellow internat. law, diplomacy and belles lettres, 1935; Univ. fellow, 1936; editor Fed. Bank Service, Prentice-Hall, Inc., 1937; instr. govt. NYU, 1938, exec. sec. grad. div. for tng. in pub. services, 1938, asst. dir., 1940, asst. prof. govt., dir. grad. div. for tng. pub. service, 1940, assoc. prof. govt., 1946-47, prof., 1947, dean, grad. sch. pub. adminstrn. and social service, 1953-58; Cons. NYC Civil Service Commn., 1938; prin. rev. officer, negotiations officer US Civil Service Commn., 1942; prin. div. asst. US Dept. State, 1943; cons. Dept. State, 1948, Dept. Def., 1954; dir. studies NY State Coordination Commn., 1951-58; project mgr. NYU-U. Ankara project, 1954-59; cons. ICA, 1955, NY State Welfare Conf.; adminstrv. co-dir. Albany Grad. Program in Pub. Adminstrn.; 1st dep. city adminstr. NYC, 1956-57; exec. dir. NY State Temporary Commn. Constl. Conv., 1956-58; sec. to Gov. NY, 1959-66; chmn. interdept. com. traffic safety, commr. Port Authority NY and NJ, 1967-90, vice chmn., 1972-74, chmn., 1974-77; with UTDC Corp., West Palm Beach, Fla. Trustee Crosslands Savs. Bank; chmn. bd. LI R.R., 1966-74; chmn. Tri-State Transp. Com., NY, NJ, Conn., 1961-67; chmn. interstate com. New Haven R.R., 1960-63; chmn. NY Com. on LI R.R., 1964-65; mem. NY State Commn. Internstate Coop., 1961, NY State Com. Fgn. Ofcl. Visitors, 1961, NY State Coordination Commn., 1960; mem. NY Civil Svc. Commn., Temporary State Commn. on Constl. Conv., 1966-67; chmn. NY State Met. Commuter Transp. Authority, 1965-68, Met. Transp. Authority, 1968-74, Tri-Borough Bridge and Tunnel Authority, 1968-74, NYC Transit Authority, 1968-74, Manhattan and Bronx Surface Transit Operating Authority, 1968-74; chmn. bd., pres. 3d Century Corp., 1974-94; mem. Commn. Critical Choices for Am., 1973—, acting chmn., 1975—; mem. urban transp. adv. com. US Dept. Transp.; sr. adviser Rockefeller family, 1974-80; pres. Nelson Rockefeller Collection, Inc., 1977-80; trustee Power Authority of State of NY, 1974-77; cons. to trustees Penn Ctrl. Transp. Co.; vice chmn. bd. CCX, Inc.; sec.-treas. Sarabam Corp. N.V.; chmn., dir. UTDC (USA) Inc., 1987-88; chmn. UTDC Corp., 1989-94, Transit Svcs. Corp., 1989-94; cons. Herzog Transit Svcs., 1995-99, Dime Savs. Bank, Metal Powder Products Inc., Flomet Inc., 1997—, Teckna Seal, LLC, 2002—; Internat. Mining and Metals Inc., Quadrant Mgmt. Inc., 1990—, Ohio Highspeed Rail Authority, 1991-93; chmn. NY and NJ Inland Rail Rate Com.; dir. Nat. Mgmt. Coun., 1951. Author: Money Power of States in International Law, 1940, The Board of Regents and the Commissioner, 1948, Our War Economy, 1943, (with others), articles in profl. jours.; adviser: Jour. Inst. Socio-Econ. Studies. Mem. US FOA, Am. Public Health Assn.; staff relations officer NYC Bd. Edn.; Mem. Nat. Conf. Social Work, Nat. Conf. on Met. Areas, Citizens Com. on Corrections, Council on Social Work Edn.; bd. dirs. World Trade Club; adv. bd. World Trade Inst.; mem. 42d St. Redevel. Corp., chmn., 1980-94; mem. Assn. for a Better NY; bd. advisers Inst. for Socioecon. Studies, 1977—; dir. Nat. Health Council, 1980-86; dep. dir. policy Nelson Rockefeller campaign for Republican presdl. nomination, 1964; mem. NY State Gov.'s Com. on Shoreham Nuclear Plant, 1983-85, Nassau County Indsl. Devel. Authority, 1982-90, US Dept. Transp. Com. on Washington and Capital Dist. Airports, 1985-86; bd. dirs. Ctr. Study Presidency, 1986-90, Alcoholism Council of NY, 1986—; trustee NY Coll. Osteopathic Medicine, 1986-91; v.p. Am. Cancer Soc., Palm Beach. Served as lt. USNR, 1943-46. Mem. ASPA, NEA, Am. Polit. Sci. Assn., Am. Acad. Pub. Adminstrn., Civil Svc. Assembly of US and Can., Internat. Assn. Met. Rsch. and Devel., Nat. Mcpl. League, Mcpl. Pers. Soc., Citizens Union of NY, Nat. Civil Svc. League, Am. Acad. Polit. and Social Sci., LI Assn. Commerce and Industry (dir.), Internat. Inst. Adminstrv. Scis., Am. Fgn. Law Assn., Internat. Union Pub. Transport (mgmt. com., v.p.), Am. Pub. Transit Assn. (chmn. 1974-76), Nat. Def. Transp. Assn. (v.p. for Mass transit), English Speaking Union (bd. dirs. Palm Beach), Met. Opera Club, Maidstone Club, Devon Yacht Club, Knickerbocker Club, Hemisphere Club, Harvard Club, Creek Club, Wings Club, Traffic Club, Univ. Club, Am. Club Riviera, Beach Club (Palm Beach), Everglades Club. Home: 525 S Flagler Dr West Palm Beach FL 33401-5922 Address: Villa La Pointe Du Cap 29 Ave de La Corniche 06230 Saint Jean Cap Ferrat France Personal E-mail: w.j.ramp@aol.com.

RONCONE, JOHN EDWARD, health educator; s. John Edward and Carol Ann Roncone; m. Rachel Louise Stotsenburg, June 29, 1996; 1 child, Lauren Alexia. BA, Mount Union Coll., Alliance, Ohio, 1994; MS, Slippery Rock U., Pa., 1995; PhD, Kent State U., Ohio, 2005. Doctoral fellow Kent State U., 1996—99, adj. instr., 1999—2000; prevention specialist Townhall II, Kent, 1999—2000; coord. safe and drug free schs. N. Ctrl. Schs., Creston, Ohio, 2000—03; asst. prof. sport sci. & wellness edn. program coord. U. Akron, Orrville, 2009—; chair allied health Brown Mackie Coll., N. Canton, Ohio, 2003—09. Author: (book) Nonmative Beliefs Among Adolescent Cigarette Smoking, 2005. Mem.: Am. Sch. Health Assn., Ohio Alliance for Health, Physical Edn., Recreation and Dance (v.p. divsn. sport sci.), AAHPERD md west (v.p. health coun. 2009—). Republican. Roman Catholic. Avocations: reading, running, bicycling, swimming. Office: Va Wayne Coll 1901 Snucker Rd Orrville OH 44667 Business E-Mail: roncone@uakron.edu.

RONDEAU, ANN E., career military officer; b. San Antonio, 1951; Diploma in History, Eisenhower Coll., 1973; Grad., Officer Candidate Sch., 1974; D in Pub. Svc. (hon.), Carthage Coll. Commd. 2d lt. USN, 1974, advanced through grades to vice adm.; comdr. fleet communication US Pacific Fleet, 1974—76; air intelligence & ops. officer Patrol Squadron Fifty, 1976—80; mem. Navy Staff (Strategy & Policy/NATO-Europe Branch, 1982—83; spl. asst. for nat. security affairs to atty. gen. US Dept. Justice, 1985—87; various assignments to exec. officer Fast Sealift Squad. One, New Orleans, 1987-89; asst. for polit.-mil. analysis Office Chief Naval Ops., USN, 1989-90; battalion officer US Naval Acad., 1990—92; commdg. officer Naval Support Activity, La Maddalena, Italy, 1992—94; Chief Naval Ops. fellow Strategic Studies Group Naval War Coll., 1994—95; mil. asst. to prin. dep. under sec for policy US Dept. Def., 1995-96; mem. Navy's Quadrennial Def. Rev. Support Office, 1996—97; commdg. officer Naval Support Activity, Milington, Tenn., 1997—99; dep. chief of staff Shore Base Mgmt. N46/U.S. Pacific Fleet, 1999—2001; comdr. Naval Training Command & Naval Svc. Training Command, 2001—04, Naval Pers. Devel. Command, 2004—05; dir. Navy Staff Office Chief Naval Ops., USN, 2005—06; dep. comdr. US Transp. Command (USTRANSCOM), Scott AFB, Ill., 2006—, acting comdr., 2008. Decorated Def. Superior Svc. medal, Legion of Merit (4), Def. Meritorious Svc. medal (2 times), Navy Meritorious Svc. medal (2 times), Navy Commendation medal (3 times), Navy Disting. Svc. medal; recipient Groben award for Leadership Eisenhower Coll.; recipient Groben award for Leadership, Eisenhower Coll.; named Most Disting. Graduate, Eisenhower Coll., Woman of Yr., NYC USO, 2008 Office: US Transp Command (USTRANSCOM) Scott AFB Scott Air Force Base IL 62225

RONDO, RAJON PIERRE, professional basketball player; b. Louisville, Feb. 22, 1986; s. Amber Rondo. Attended, U. Ky., Lexington, 2004—06. Guard Boston Celtics, 2006—. Mem. USA Men's Under-21 Basketball Team, 2005. Achievements include member of the NBA Championship winning Boston Celtics, 2008. Office: Boston Celtics 226 Causeway St 4th Fl Boston MA 02114*

RONER, MICHAEL ROBERT, virologist, educator; b. Fla. s. Charles and Sylvia Roner; m. Lisa Roner; children: Meghan, Shannon. PhD, Miami U., Ohio, 1986. Postdoc. rsch. prof. Duke U. Med. Ctr., Durham, NC, 1986—96; asst. prof. Fla. Atlantic U., Boca Raton, 1996—2002, U. Tex., Arlington, 2002—. Mem.: ASV. Office: Univ Tex Arlington 501 S Nedderman Arlington TX 76019 Business E-Mail: roner@uta.edu.

RONEY, JOHN M., lawyer; b. Sept. 21, 1939; m. Barbara Kennedy; children: Christopher, Carley, Kristina. BA, Providence Coll.; JD, Cath. U. Am.; degree (hon.), Katherine Gibbs Sch., 2002. Senator R.I. State Senate, 1994—2002; sr. staff atty. R.I. Legal Svcs., 1970—75; assoc. Winograd Shine & Zacks, PC, 1975—78; ptnr. Mann & Roney, 1978—83, Roney & Labinger LLP, Providence, 1983—. Dep. majority leader, vice chair fin., health, edn. welfare RI State Senate, parliamentarian, 2005—; commr. Uniform Law Commn., 2006—. Mem. Leadership R.I.; pres. RI Coun. on Alcoholism, 1990—93, Narragansett Bay Commn., 1996—2003; bd. dirs. Sophia Acad., 2003—, Katherine Gibbs Sch., 2002—04, RI Philharmonic, 1996—2001, Family Svc., Inc., 1973—90, pres., 1987—89; mem. neighborhood coun. Mayor, 2003—; mem. R.I. Commn. Women, 2000—03, R.I. Retirement Bd., 1998—2003. Recipient Dorothy Lohmann Cmty. Svc. award, 1995, Unsung Hero award, R.I. Assn. Developmentally Disabled Children, 1999, Bronze Key award, Nat. Coun. Alcoholism, 1999, Disting. Alumni award, Cath. U. Am., 2004. Mem.: R.I. Bar Assn. (v.p. 1999—2002, sec. 2000—01, pres.-elect 2002—03, pres. 2003—04, exec. com.), Fox Point Citizens Assn. (mem. bd. 1988—, pres. 2002—). Democrat. Office: Roney & Labinger LLP 344 Wickenden St Providence RI 02903 Office Phone: 401-421-9794.

RONG, SHU, geophysicist, researcher; b. QingDao, ShanDong, China, Oct. 15, 1972; arrived in U.S., 1998; s. Yuexin Shu and Yong Li; m. Hua G Shu. MS in Computer Sci., U. Houston - Clearlake, 2002; PhD in Material Sci. with honors, China Acad.Sci U. Sci.Tech.China, Hefei, 1998. Rsch. engr. U. Science and Tech. China, Hefei, Anhui, China, 1994—98; cons RHIC, Houston, 2001; sr. rsch. engr. Rock Solid Images, Houston, 2001—. Contbr. articles to profl. jours. Mem.: AAAS, SEG, AAPG, Am. Phys. Soc. Office: Rock Solid Images 2600 S Gessner Ste 650 Houston TX 77099 Home: 827 Delford Dr Sugar Land TX 77479-1101

RONG, YONGWU, mathematician, researcher; b. Anqing, Anhui, People's Republic of China, May 14, 1964; came to U.S., 1984; s. Xian-Zhi and Geng-Xian (Tao) R. BS, U. Sci. and Tech. of China, Hefei, Anhui, 1983; PhD, U. Tex., Austin, 1989. Asst. instr. U. Tex., Austin, 1986-89, vis. postdoctoral fellow, 1990; rsch. instr. Mich. State U., East Lansing, 1989—. Contbr. articles to profl. jours. Recipient Chinese Math. Olympiad prize Chinese Math. Soc., Beijing, 1979. Mem. Am. Math. Soc. Office: Michigan State Univ Dept Of Math East Lansing MI 48824

RONG, YUE, environmental services administrator; s. Donggu Rong and Zi Zhuang Zhang; m. Felicia Liu; 1 child, Celina. BS, Beijing Normal U., 1982; MS, U. Wis., Green Bay, 1986; PhD, U. Calif., LA, 1995. Environ. scientist Calif. Regional Water Bd., LA, 1989—2002, environ. program mgr., 2002—. Chmn. UCLA Alumni Assn., nomination com., 2004; pres. Southern Calif. Chinese Am. Environ. Protection Assn., LA, 2006—. Environ. educator Southern Calif. Chinese Am. Environ. Protection Assn., 2001—. Recipient Outstanding Achievement award, Calif. Regional Water Quality Control Bd., 1998, Supervisory Performance award, 2001. Mem.: Assn. Environ. Health and Sci., Nat. Ground Water Assn., Southern Calif. Chinese Am. Environ. Protection Assn., UCLA Alumni Assn. Home: 320 W 4th St Ste 200 Los Angeles CA 90013 Office: Calif Regional Water Quality Bd 320 W 4th St Los Angeles CA 90013 Office Fax: 213-576-6700. Business E-Mail: yrong@waterboards.ca.gov.

RONNICK, MICHELE VALERIE, education educator; d. Albert Jacob and Elizabeth Ann Ronnick. PhD, Boston U., Mass, 1990. Prof. Wayne State U., Detroit, 1993—. Creator (photo installation) 12 Black Classicists; contbr. articles to profl. jour. Recipient Tchg. Excellence, Am. Philol Assn., 1997; grantee Incentive award, Classical and Modern Lit., 1994. Mem.: Classical Assn. Mid. West and South (Ovatio 2002). Democrat. Avocation: reading. Office: Wayne State Univ CMLLC 906 W Warren 487 Manoogian Hall Detroit MI 48202 Office Fax: 313-577-6243. E-mail: aa3276@wayne.edu.

RONSON, MARK DANIEL, recording industry executive, disc jockey; b. London, Sept. 4, 1975; Co-founder Allido Records, NYC, 2004—. Prodr. records including Blue Crush Original Soundtrack, 2002, Sean Paul's Dutty Rock, 2002, Honey Original Soundtrack, 2003, Macy Gray's Trouble With Being Myself, 2003, Hitch Original Soundtrack, 2005, Jamiroquai's Dynamite, 2005, Lily Allen's Alright, Still, 2006, Christina Aguilera's Back to Basics, 2006, Amy Winehouse's Back to Black, 2006, Rhymefest's Blue Collar, 2006, Half Nelson Original Soundtrack, 2006, Amy Winehouse's Rehab, 2006 (Grammy award for Record of Yr., 2008), Robbie Williams' Rudebox, 2006, Take the Lead Original Soundtrack, 2006, Amy Winehouse's You Know I'm No Good, 2006; musician: (albums) Here Comes the Fuzz, 2003, Version, 2007 (Best Album, Best Single, BRIT Awards, 2008). Recipient Non-Classical Prodr. of Yr. award, Grammy Awards, 2008, Best British Male Solo Artist award, BRIT Awards, 2008; named Alfred Dunhill Maverick of Yr., GQ Awards, 2008; named a Maverick, Details mag., 2008. Office: Allido Records 19 Mercer St New York NY 10013 Office Phone: 212-226-7320.

ROOBOL, NORMAN RICHARD, chemistry professor, consultant; b. Grand Rapids, Mich., Aug. 19, 1934; s. Pleune and Henrietta (Sietsema) Roobol; m. Joan Lois Ezinga, Aug. 15, 1957; children: Kerri Linda, Michael Eric, Victoria May, Sara Elizabeth Angelique. BS, Calvin Coll., Grand Rapids, Mich., 1958; PhD in Organic Chemistry, Mich. State U., East Lansing, 1962. Rsch. chemist Shell Oil Co., Emeryville, Calif., 1962-65; asst. prof. chemistry GMI Engring. Inst., Flint, Mich., 1965-68, assoc. prof., asst. head dept. math., sci., 1968-72, prof., 1972-89; pres. NR Painting Cons. Co., Peachtree City, Ga., 1989—. Rhodes prof., Russelsheim, Germany, 1980—81; tchr. short courses paint; cons. coatings application processes; spkr. indsl. painting methods; painting advisor Bombardier Can., 1988—; painting advisor, instr. Compaq-Asia, Singapore, 1991—, Harley-Davidson, 1992—, Metagal Comercie e Industri, San Paulo, Brazil, 1996—, Decometal S.A., Panama City, Panama, 1997—2001, J. R. McDermott Corp., Jebel Ali, 2000—; adj. prof. Kent State U., 1986—94, Okla. State U., 1994—98, U. Wis., 1992—2001, Peruvian Decorative & Protective Finishes Coun., 2005—. Author: (book) Painting Problems Solved, 1987, Industrial Paint and Powder Coating Principles and Practices, 3d edit., 2003; monthly columnist, tech. editor: Finishing Today Jour.; contbr. articles to profl. jours. With Signal Corps US Army, 1954—56. Fellow Johnson, 1957—58, NSF, 1960—62, Dow, 1961—62. Fellow: Am. Inst. Chemists; mem.: AAUP, Assn. Finishings Proc., Soc. Mfg. Engrs., Am. Sci. Affiliation, Atlanta Oenophilic Soc., Pi Tau Sigma (chpt. sr. adviser 1979—86), Alpha Tau Omega, Sigma Xi. Achievements include patents in field. Home and Office: Powder Coating & Painting Cons 507 Haddington Ln Peachtree City GA 30269-3340 Personal E-mail: drpaint@consultant.com.

ROOD, CYNTHIA HOOPER, landscape architect, consultant; b. Columbus, Miss., Jan. 22, 1944; d. James Fullerton and Virginia Fite Hooper; children: Virginia Rood Pates, Amelia Gordon. BS in Landscape Architecture, U. Ga., Athens, 1966. Registered landscape arch. Miss., 1974, landscape designer, horticultural supr. Ala., 2005. Landscape arch., assoc. Olmsted Assocs., Landscape Archs., Brookline, Mass., 1966—67; budget and design US Naval Air Systems Command, Adak, Alaska, 1968—69; landscape arch. C. H. Rood, Landscape Arch., Columbus, Miss., 1969—. Pres. AMD, Inc., Columbus, 1990—; pres. Miss. chpt. Am. Soc. Landscape Archs., Jackson, 1991—92, dep. chmn. residential design com., Washington, 2002—03. Author: (articles) Miss. Dental Assn. Jour. Dir. Nat. Assn. Jr. Auxs. Found., Greenville, Miss., 2007—, pres., 1984—85; mem. Nat. Assn. Colonial Dames Am., Washington, 1970—, Golden Triangle Regional Med. Ctr. Found., Columbus, 1986—90. Recipient E. C. Martin scholarship award, U. Ga., 1962—66, Award of Excellence, Nat. Coun. Tchrs. English, 1962, Scholarship award, Alpha Zeta chpt. U. Ga., 1963, Queen of Pilgrimage Ball, Columbus Jr. Aux., 1966, Award of Merit, Miss. chpt. Am. Soc. Landscape Archs., 1989, Merit award, Associated Builders and Contractors, 1994, Award of Merit, Main St. Columbus, Inc., 1996; finalist, Nat. Merit Scholarship Found., 1962; grantee, St. Clair County Ednl. Assn., 2007. Mem.: Magowah Country Club (life), Chi Omega (life; state pres. 1985—86, Outstanding Chi Omega in Miss. 1985). Office: C H Rood Landscape Architect 800 Eighth St N Columbus MS 39701 E-mail: abraco@aol.com, chr@amddesign.com.

ROOD, JOHN DARRELL, real estate developer, former ambassador; b. 1954; m. Jamie A. Rood; children: Jennifer, Christopher; 1 child, Holly. Founder, mng. ptnr. Vestcor Companies, Inc., Jacksonville, Fla., 1983—2004, chmn., 2007—, JDR Cos., Inc., 2007—; US amb. to Bahamas US Dept. State, Nassau, 2004—07. Housing/edn. com. chmn. Jacksonville Downtown Master Plan; vis. prof. U. North Fla.; founding bd. mem. First Coast Family & Housing Found.; apptd. adv. coun. on renewal communities US Dept. Housing & Urban Devel.; apptd. commr., chmn. Fla. Fish & Wildlife Conservation Commn., 2002—04. Former vol. Kesler Mentoring Connection, Jacksonville; hon. bd. dirs. Fla. Apartment Polit. Action Com.; bd. trustees Fresh Ministries; past bd. dirs. James Madison Inst., Jacksonville Symphony Assn., Jacksonville Housing Partnership. Named Entrepreneur of Yr., Ernst & Young, 2001. Mem.: Jacksonville C. of C., Rotary Club of Mandarin (past pres.). Office: Vestcor Companies Inc 3020 Hartley Rd Ste 300 Jacksonville FL 32257 Office Phone: 904-260-3030.*

ROODMAN, DAVID A., lawyer; b. St. Louis, Apr. 17, 1962; BSME, U. Mo., 1984, JD, 1990. Bar: Mo., Ill., U.s. Dist. Ct. (ea. dist.) Mo., U.S. Patent and Trademark Office, U.s. Ct. Appeals (fed. cir.), U.S. Dist. Ct. (so. dist.) Ill. Mech. design engr. Unidynamics Corp., St. Louis, 1985; sales engr. Reliance Elec. Co., Kansas City, Mo., 1985-87; assoc. Bryan Cave LLP, St. Louis, 1990, ptnr., group co-leader Intellectual Property. Assoc. editor-in-chief Mo. Law Rev. Mem. ABA (intellectual property law sect., patent legislation com., litigation sect.), Mo. Bar Assn. (civil practice and procedure com., tech. and computer law com., patent, trademark and copyright law com.), Order of Coif, Order of Barristers. Office: Bryan Cave One Metropolitan Sq 211 N Broadway Saint Louis MO 63102-2733 Office Phone: 314-259-2000. Business E-Mail: daroodman@bryancave.com.

ROOF, SALLY JEAN-MARIE, library and information scientist, educator; b. Cleve., Dec. 29, 1947; d. James William and Marie Monreal Roof; m. Christian John Hoffmann III, Sept. 22, 1973; children: Christian Graham Hoffmann, Joscelyn Nicole Hoffmann, Gavin Leigh Hoffmann. BA in English Lit., Dunbarton Coll. of Holy Cross, DC, 1969; MS in Libr. and Info. Sci., Cath. U. of Am., 1972; degree in Profl. Mgmt. (hon.), Miami U., 1976; MA in Elem. Edn., No. Ariz. U., 2001. Cert. tchr. in libr. media ctr. adminstrn. Nat. Bd. of Cert. Tchrs., 2004. Asst. libr. U.S.Postal Svc. Libr., Washington, 1971—72; head of acquisitions George Wash. U. Libr., Washington, 1972—74; libr. adminstr. and mgr. Calgon Corp. Libr. Merck Inc., Pitts., 1974—77; libr. info. specialist U. of Phoenix, 1979—81; reference libr. Grand Canyon U., Phoenix, 1990—91; reference libr. West Campus Libr. Ariz. State U., Phoenix, 1994—95; libr. tchr. info. specialist Madison Meadows Sch., Phoenix, 1998—. Libr. cons. U. of Phoenix, 1981—82; presenter Ariz. Libr. Assn., Scottsdale, 2003; mem., presenter People to People Amb. Program Children's Lit. Del., Spokane, Wash., 2004; participant rep., 04; cons. in field. Editor: Serial Titles in the Washington, D. C. University Consortium Libraries, No School Left Behind at Your Library. Librarians Meet Arizona Legislators, 2004; author: (pamphlet) Madison Meadows Library Media Center; designer (school website) Madison Meadows Sch. website. Chmn. grade level patroness Nat. Charity League, Phoenix, 1994—99; pres. Phoenix (Ariz.) Mus. of History, 1991—94. Mem.: ALA (assoc.), Ariz. Libr. Assn. (assoc.), Phi Kappa Phi, Beta Phi Mu, Jr. League of Phoenix. Democrat-Npl. Roman Catholic. Avocations: yoga, fast walking, reading, bicycling. Office: Madison Meadows School 225 W Ocotillo Rd Phoenix AZ 85013 Personal E-mail: sroofhoff@cox.net. E-mail: sroof@msd38.org.

ROOK, JUDITH RAWIE, television producer, writer; d. Wilmer Ernest and Margaret Jane (Towle) Rawie; m. Dr. John Holland, 1964 (div. 1978); children: Daryn Simons, Dawn Reinard; m. Tim Rook, 1993. BA, Loyola-Marymount Univ., 1964; postgrad., U. Calif., San Diego, 1978. Syndicated columnist Environ. Forum, 1971-74; dir. video IABC, San Francisco, 1982; dir. programming Westinghouse Cable, 1983-85; dir. devel. Embassy/Nelson Home Entertainment, 1985-87; ptnr. Real Magic, 1987-89; prodr., writer, ptnr. BrantHol Prodns., 1990-93; co-sponsorship Beetle Juice, The Last Emperor, 1987—89; founder, pres. R2 Group, 1990—. Assoc. dir.: (off-broadway play) Arms and the Man, 1967; The Man Who Came to Dinner, 1981; exec. prodr.: Neighborhood Without Bars (Emmy award, 1986); prodr., writer: PBS series Focus, 1980; Achieving, 1982 (Emmy award, ACE nominee, PBS nominee); NBC pilot Christmas Comes to Silverton, 1990—93; CNN pilot Clever Encounters, 1991; prodr.: One Creative Moment, 1992, Close up: The 60s, 1995—97; assoc. prodr.: Fox Latin Am. Billboard Music Awards, 1998—2000; (TV pilot) Fempresario; assoc. prodr. (documentary) Boots Across the Divide: A Love Story, 2005—09, (films) Somewhere in Between, 2005; playwright: Theatre 40 Writer's Workshop Anniversary for Three, 2003; assoc. prodr.: (films) Highway 101, 2005—. Mem. adv. bd. U. Calif. Irvine Screenwriting/Film Prodn., 1996-2000; mem. adv. bd. Univ. Art Mus., 1996-97, co-pres. contemporary coun., 1996-97; mem. exec. bd. Long Beach Mus. Art, 1995-96; bd. dirs. Counseling 4 Kids, 1998-2005, bd. sec., 2001-2005; editor, bd. LWV, Santa Monica, 2004-05, Getty Mus., 2005-. Mem. Am. Film Inst., Women in Film (dir. seminars on women in film), IFP West. Democrat. Episcopalian. Office Phone: 310-633-3292. Personal E-mail: judithjanerook@gmail.com.

ROOK, VICKI LYNN, safety specialist; b. Denton, Tex., Oct. 14, 1954; d. Lonzo Lester and Myrtle Jodelle Roberts; m. Rickey Hugh Rook, Jan. 27, 1979; children: Brandon Nicholas, Katy Lynn Student, Richland Jr. Coll., Dallas, 1974-75. Safety supr. United Parcel Svc., Dallas, 1975-81; pers., safety adminstr. Boeing Airport Equipment, Carrollton, Tex., 1981-83; safety rep. Loral Vought Sys. Corp., Grand Prairie, Tex., 1983-95; sr. safety specialist Fed. Express Corp., Dallas, 1995—. Mem. workers comp claims mgmt. various cos., Dallas, 1975—; mgr. union contract negotiation Boeing Airport Equipment, Dallas, 1983; com. mem. mgmt. safety program tng. Fed. Express, Memphis, 1997-2001 Tchr. Sunday sch. Walnut Ridge Bapt. Ch., Mansfield, Tex., 1997-2001, 1st Bapt. Ch., Grand Prairie, 1980-82, counselor ch. camp, 1980-82; vol. ednl. TV Loral Vought Sys., Dallas, 1993. Named Safety Specialist of Yr. Fed. Express, 1997. Mem. Am. Soc. Safety Engineers, Nat. Safety Coun. Republican. Office Phone: 469-524-4623. Business E-Mail: vlrook@fedex.com.

ROOKE, DAVID LEE, retired chemical company executive; b. San Antonio, Tex., May 2, 1923; s. Henry Levi, Jr. and Annie (Davidson) R.; m. Esthermae Litherland, June 2, 1945; children— Eugene, Mark, Paul, Bruce. BS in Chem. Engring, Rice Inst., Houston, 1944; postgrad., U. Houston. With Dow Chem., Midland, Mich., 1946-88, v.p. ops., 1977-78; pres. Dow U.S.A., 1978-82; v.p. Dow Chem. Corp., 1978-82, exec. v.p., 1982-83, sr. v.p., 1983-86, sr. cons., 1986-88, ret., 1988. Bd. dirs. Dow Corning Corp., James Avery Craftsman, Inc. Nat. exec. bd. Boy Scouts Am., 1979-86; bd. dirs. Meth. Mission Home, San Antonio. Served with USNR, 1944-46. Mem. AICE, United Meth. Reporter Found. (Dallas). Methodist.

ROOKLIDGE, WILLIAM CHARLES, lawyer; b. Portland, Oreg., Aug. 10, 1957; s. Chester Herbert and Barbara Kathryn (Dodson) R.; m. Kathryn Elaine Roosa, Aug. 20, 1983; children: Elizabeth Jill, Matthew Joseph. BS, U. Portland, 1979; JD, Lewis & Clark, 1984; LLM, George Wash. U., 1985. Bar: Oreg. 1985, US Patent Office 1985, US Ct. Appeals (fed. cir.) 1985, Calif. 1988, US Ct. Appeals (9th cir.) 1988, US Supreme Ct. 1993. Engr. Tube Forgings Am., Inc., Portland, 1978-82; jud. clk. US Ct. Appeals (fed. cir.), Washington DC, 1985-87; assoc. Knobbe, Martens, Olson & Bear, Newport Beach, Calif., 1987-89, ptnr., 1990-94; dir. Howard, Rice, Nemerovski, Canady, Falk & Rabkin, Newport Beach, Calif., 1995—2000. Contbr. articles to profl. jours. Recipient Joseph Rossman Meml. award Patent & Trademark Office Soc., 1988, Gerald Rose Meml. award John Marshall Law Sch., 1993. Mem. ABA (sect. intellectual property law, com. chair 1992-96), Am. Intellectual Property Law Assn. (com. chair 1988-93, dir. 1995-98, pres. 2005, Robert C. Watson award 1987), Orange County Patent Law Assn. (bd. dirs. 1990-93, pres. 1994). Republican. Presbyterian. Office: Howrey LLP 4 Park Plz Ste 1700 Irvine CA 92614-8557 Office Phone: 949-759-3904. Office Fax: 949-721-6910. Business E-Mail: rooklidgew@howrey.com.

ROOKS, GEORGE MALCOLM, writer, educator, small business owner; b. Anderson, SC, Mar. 5, 1951; s. George and Miriam (Bailey) R.; divorced, 1983; children: George, Brendan; m. Hila Zizov, Feb. 1, 1983; children; Kanon, Maayan. BA in English, U. Ga., 1973; MA in English, U. Calif., Davis, 1975. Mem. faculty U. Calif., Davis, 1976—; owner, CEO Teletext Corp., 1989—. Author: The Book of Losers, 1980, The Nonstop Discussion Workbook!, 1980, 2d edit., 1988, Can't Stop Talking, 1981, 2d edit., 1988, Share Your Paragraph, 1988, 2d edit., 1995, Paragraph Power, 1988, Beat the TOEFL: A Video-Workbook-Computer Series, 1990, videotape, 2006, Let's Start Talking, 1990, Power TOEFL Deluxe CD Rom and Workbook, 1998, Power 3000 Grammar Review CD rom, 2001, TOEIC Test Master CD Rom, 2001, Power TOEFL Listening CD Rom with Listening Scripts, 2001, The Ttext Word Frequency CD Rom Dictionary for the TOEIC Test, 2003, (DVD) Understanding the New TOEFL Test, 2005; (with others) Conversar Sin Parar, 1981, Conversations San Fin, 1982, Was Sagen Sie Dazu?, 1983, Japanese Listening and Grammar Exercises for TOEFL, 1996; editor: Vocabulary Enrichment for ESL Students (15 disks), 1994, Grammar Enrichment for ESL Students (9 disks), 1994; contbr. articles to profl. jours. Mem. Calif. Tchrs. ESL, Zionist Orgn. Am. Avocations: tennis, travel. Address: 10 Sara Emanu Tet Vav 77724 Ashdod Israel Office: 710 Valencia Ave Davis CA 95616-0153 Office Phone: 866-862-6420.

ROOKS, JOHN NEWTON, lawyer; b. Evanston, Ill., Jan. 7, 1948; s. R. Newton and Ruth D. Rooks; m. Mary Preston Noell, Sept. 15, 1973; children: John Newton, Thomas N. BA, DePauw U., 1970; JD, Washington U., 1973. Bar: Ill. 1973, U.S. Dist. Ct. (no. dist.) Ill. 1973. Corp. atty. No. Trust Co., Chgo., 1973—76; ptnr. Hynds, Rooks, Yohnka & Bzdill, Morris, Ill., 1976—. Chmn. bd. dirs. ARC, Morris, 1980-82, adv. com., 1996-97; adminstrv. coun. 1st United Meth. Ch., Morris, 1985-86; trustee, 1982-84; citizens adv. com. Morris Cmty. H.S., 1984-87; bd. dirs. Morris Elem. Sch. Dist. 54, 1987-91, 95; bd. dirs. Morris Downtown Devel. Partnership, Inc., 1996-2008, v.p., 1996-2000, pres., 2000-03; sec.-treas. Morris Progress, LLC, 1997-2004. Mem. ABA, Ill. Bar Assn., Chgo. Bar Assn., Grundy County Bar Assn. (pres. 1983-84), Grundy County C. of C. (chmn. bd. 1982). Office: Hynds Rooks Yohnka & Bzdill PO Box 685 Morris IL 60450-0685 Home: 1064 Forest View Dr Morris IL 60450 Office Phone: 815-942-0049. Business E-Mail: jnr@hyndsrookslaw.com.

ROOKS, LINDA, writer; d. Harold John and Marianna Wieck; m. Marvin Edward Rooks, Dec. 19, 1967; children: Juliana Wolf, Laura Katherine Voorhees. BA, San Francisco State U., 1965. Tchr. Seminole Jr. H.S., Fla., 1970—72; pro-life liaison for Paula Hawkins senatorial campaign Nat. Right to Life, Winter Park, Fla., 1986; asst. editor Ctr. Stage Mag., Maitland, Fla., 1987—89; office coord., newsletter editor Adoption by Shepherd Care, Orlando, Fla., 1994—2000; freelance writer Maitland, 2000—. Author: Broken Heart on Hold, 2006, (devotional) Tapestry; scriptwriter: radio and tv Testimony of An Unborn Child (Cammeo Award for Best of Show, 1987); contbr. articles to profl. jours., chapters to books. Pres. Ctrl. Fla. Right to Life, 1984—85, 1990—96; staff position state coord. for families Bob Dole Presdl. Campaign, Fla., 1995—96; pub. rels. co-chmn. Nat. Right to Life Conv., Orlando, 1983. Mem.: Word Weavers Writers Group (sec. steering com. 2002—07). Republican. Avocation: travel. Office: PO Box 241 Winter Park FL 32790-0241 Personal E-mail: linda@brokenheartonhold.com.

ROONEY, ANDREW AITKEN, writer, journalist; b. Albany, NY, Jan. 14, 1919; s. Walter S. and Ellinor (Reynolds) R.; m. Marguerite Howard, Mar. 21, 1942; children: Ellen, Martha, Emily, Brian. Student, Colgate U., 1942. Writer-producer CBS-TV News, 1959—; newspaper columnist Tribune Co. Syndicate, 1979—. Author: (with O.C. Hutton) Air Gunner, 1944, The Story of Stars and Stripes, 1946, Conquerors' Peace, 1947, The Fortunes of War, 1962, A Few Minutes with Andy Rooney, 1981, And More By Andy Rooney, 1982, Pieces of My Mind, 1984, Word for Word, 1986, Not That You Asked, 1989, Sweet and Sour, 1992, My War, 1995, Sincerely, Andy Rooney, 1999, Common Nonsense, 2002, Years of Minutes, 2003; TV programs include An Essay on War, Mr. Rooney Goes to Washington, Mr. Rooney Goes to Dinner; regular commentator-essayist: 60 Minutes, 1978—. Served with AUS, 1941-45. Decorated Air Medal, Bronze Star.; recipient awards for best written TV documentary Writers Guild Am., 1966, 68, 71, 75, 76, Emmy awards, 1968, 78, 81, 82

ROONEY, CAROL BRUNS, dietitian; b. Milw., Dec. 20, 1940; d. Edward G. and Elizabeth C. (Lemke) Bruns; m. George Eugene Rooney Jr., July 1, 1967; children: Steven, Sean. BS, U. Wis., 1962; MS, U. Iowa, 1965. Registered dietitian; cert. nutrition specialist; disting. health care food svc. adminstr.; cert. dietitian, Wis. Intern VA Med. Ctr., Hines, Ill., 1962-63, resident in nutrition and food svc. Iowa City, 1963-65, dietitian nutrition clinic Hines, 1965-67, 69-70, chief clin. dietetics, 1970-71, chief adminstrv. dietetics, 1971-73, clin. dietitian Memphis, 1967-68; asst. chief nutrition and food svc. Zablocki VA Med. Ctr., Milw., 1974-85, chief nutrition and food svc., 1985-96, divsn. mgr. cons. care, 1996-98, cons. nutrition and food svc. mgmt., 1995—, bus. enterprise mgr., 1998-2000. Adj. lectr. Loyola U. Coll. Dentistry, Maywood, Ill., 1969-72; investigator nutrition VA/Med. Coll. Wis., Milw., 1975-2000, co-dir. ann. clin. nutrition symposium, Milw., 1979-94; chmn. task force on ration allowance VA, Washington, 1977-84, nutrition and food svc. spl. interest users group, 1983-85, chmn. tech. adv. group region IV, 1986; mem. Dept. Vets. Affairs Mktg. Ctr. Subsistence Task Force, 1991-95, dietetic internship adv. bd. St. Luke's Hosp., Milw., 1983-87; mem. Dept. Vets. Affairs Nat. Cost Containment Ctr. Nutrition & Food Svc. Benchmarking Tech. Adv., 1995-96; nutrition and food svc. policy manual rev. task force, chiefs, food and nutrition svc, mentor group, 1992-96; lectr. in field Author: (videocassette) VA Ration Allowance as a Management Tool 1976; editor: Nutrition Principles and Dietary Guidelines for Patients Receiving Chemotherapy and Radiation Therapy, 1980; contbr. articles to profl. jours., 1978—. Profl. edn. com. Milw. South unit Am. Cancer Soc., 1976-86, bd. dirs. Milw. South unit, 1984-86, Milw. divsn., 1986-87, Wis. divsn., 1987-91, media spokesperson, 1983-91, del. to Milw. divsn., 1984-85, mem. orgnl. and expansion com. Milw. divsn., 1986-87, profl. edn. com. Milw. divsn., 1986-87, Wis. divsn., 1987-91, taking control Wis. divsn., 1987-91, chmn. nutrition Wis. divsn., 1989-91; med. adv. com. YMCA Met. Milw., 1985-2000; mem. Marquette U. HS Mothers Guild, 1990-94. Recipient Disting. Svc. award, Am. Cancer Soc. Milw. South unit, 1980, Women of Achievement award, Girl Scouts USA Milw. area, 1987, Leadership award, VA, 1989, Dept. Vets. Affairs Fed. Women's Program cert. merit for outstanding profl. leadership, 1994, commendation, Dept. Vet. Affairs, 2000, rsch. grantee, Paralyzed Vets. Am., 1981—83; named Dept. Vets. Affairs Dietitian of Yr., 1994. Fellow: FADA, Am. Dietetic Assn. (practice groups in gerontology nutrition 1980—2000, practice groups in mgmt. responsibilities in health care delivery 1980—2000, amb. nat. media spokesperson 1983—89, dietetics in phys. medicine and rehab. 1983—97, clin. nutrition mgmt. 1987—2001, Resource Amb. 1991—, registered, Outstanding Svc. award 1983—89); mem.: Am. Soc. Health Care Food Svc. Adminstrs. (dir.-at-large Wis. chpt. 1993—95, pres.-elect Wis. chpt. 1995—96, pres. 1996—97, immediate past pres. 1997—98, Disting. Health Care Food Svc. Adminstr. 1995—), Wis. Dietetic Assn. (co-chmn. divsn. mgmt. practice 1976—77, chmn. 1977—78, bd. dirs. 1981—83, coord. cabinet 1984—91, pres. 1988—89, legis. com. 1988—2000, chmn. long-range planning com. 1989—90, chmn. nominating com. 1989—90, Wis. Medallion award 1986), Milw. Dietetic Assn (cmty. nutrition and clin. dietetics and rsch. coms. 1975—76, chair ad hoc com. for nutrition and oncology patients 1976—79, clin. dietetics and rsch. study group 1981—90, pres. 1982—83, by-laws com. 1983—84, chair 1983—85, chair policies and procedures com. 1983—87, pub. rels. com. 1983—87, chair nominating com. 1984—85), Am. Cancer Soc., Fed. Execs. Assn., Leadership Vets. Affairs Alumni Assn. (life; charter), Coll. Endowment Assn., Kappa Delta, Milw. Kappa Delta Alumnae Assn. (rep. Milw. Panhellenic Coun. 1998—99, treas. 1999—2004), Kappa Delta Alumnae Assn., Phi Upsilon Omicron. Avocations: tennis, golf. Home: 18230 Le Chateau Dr Brookfield WI 53045-4922

ROONEY, DANIEL M., United States Ambassador to Ireland, professional sports team executive; b. Pitts., July 20, 1932; s. Arthur Joseph and Kathleen (McNulty) Rooney; m. Patricia Rooney; 9 children. BA in Acctg., Duquesne U., Pitts., 1955. Salesman advt., editor, other positions Pitts. Steelers Program, 1955—75; pres. to chmn. Pitts. Steelers, 1975—; US amb. to Ireland US Dept. State, Dublin, 2009—. Co-author (with Andrew E. Masich & David F. Halaas): Dan Rooney: My 75 Years with the Pittsburgh Steelers and the NFL, 2008. Bd. dirs. United Way of America, Am. Diabetes Assn.; vice chmn. Am. Ireland Fund; bd. dirs. Presbyn. U. Hosp., Pitts. History and Landmarks Found., Duquesne U. Recipient Reds Bagnell award for Outstanding Contbns. to the Game of Football, Maxwell Football Club, 1999, Allan H. Selig Mentoring award, Maj. League Baseball and McLendon Found., 2007; named one of The Most Influential People in the World of Sports, Bus. Week, 2008; named to The Pro Football Hall of Fame, 2000. Achievements include presented with Vince Lombardi Trophy for the winning team, Pittsburgh Steelers at Super Bowl XL in 2006. Office: US Embassy 5290 Dublin Pl Washington DC 20521 also: Pitts Steelers Three Rivers Stadium 3400 S Water St Pittsburgh PA 15203-2349 Office Phone: 412-323-1200.*

ROONEY, FRANCIS (LAURENCE FRANCIS ROONEY III), construction executive, former ambassador; b. Dec. 4, 1953; m. Kathleen Rooney; 3 children. AB, Georgetown U., 1975, JD, 1978. Bar: DC, Tex.; 100-Ton Master's Lic. U.S. Coast Guard. CEO Rooney Bros., Tulsa, Okla.; chmn., CEO Rooney Holdings, Naples, Fla.; US amb. to The Holy See US Dept. State, Vatican City, 2005—08. Bd. dirs. BOL Fin. Corp., NASDAQ, Helmerich and Payne, Inc., NY Stock Exch., Cimarex Energy Co.; vice chmn. Okla. Turnpike Authority; dir. Okla. Capital Investment Bd., 20/20 com., Wash. Advisory Coun. Ctr. for Strategic and Internat. Studies; transition team for gov. elect Brad Henry State of Okla.; bd. advisors Panama Canal Authority Republic of Panama. Mem. Sch. of Architecture Coun. U. of Notre Dame; mem. Sovereign Military Order of Malta (Fed. Assn.). Mem.: Young President's Org. (dir. 1992—98, internat. pres. 1997—98). Republican. Roman Catholic.

ROONEY, JOE DON, country musician; b. Baxter Springs, Kans., Sept. 13, 1975; s. Windell and Jo Rooney; m. Tiffany Fallon; 1 child, Jagger Donovan. Student, A&M Jr. Coll. (Northwestern Okla. A&M). Performer Printers Alley, Nashville, Chely Wright Band; guitarist Rascal Flatts, 2000—. Musician: (albums) East to West, 1993, Rascal Flatts, 2000, Melt, 2002, Feels Like Today, 2004 (Group/Duo Video of Yr., Country Music Television Music awards, 2005), Me and My Gang, 2006, Still Feels Good, 2007, Unstoppable, 2009, (songs) I'm Movin' On (Song of Yr., Acad. Country Music, 2002), Bless the Broken Road (Country Song of Yr., Radio Music Awards, 2005, Grammy award for Best Country Song, 2006), Skin (Sarabeth) (Group Video of Yr., Country Music TV, 2006), What Hurts the Most (Group Video of Yr., Country Music TV, 2007), Life is a Highway (Favorite Song from a Movie, People's Choice Awards, 2007), Take Me There (Group Video of Yr., Country Music TV, 2008). Recipient Vocal Group Yr., Country Music Assn., 2002, 2004—07, 2008, Top Vocal Group, Acad. Country Music Awards, 2003, 2005—07, 2008, 2009, Home Depot Humanitarian award, 2008, Favorite Country Band, Am. Music Awards, 2006, 2007, 2008, Favorite Group, People's Choice Awards, 2008, Favorite Country Song, 2008. Office: Lyric Street Records 1100 Demonbreun St Nashville TN 37203-3108 also: LGB Media 1228 Pineview Ln Nashville TN 37211 Office Phone: 615-963-4848.*

ROONEY, JOHN EDWARD, communications company executive; b. Evergreen Park, Ill., Apr. 24, 1942; s. John Edward and Margaret Wilma (Stolte) R.; m. Germaine Rose Dettloff, June 26, 1965; children: Kathleen, John, Colleen, 7 grandchildren. BS, John Carroll U., 1964; MBA, Loyola U., 1969. Credit analyst Fed. Res. Bank, Chgo., 1964-69, adminstrv. asst., 1969-70; asst. treas. Pullman Inc., 1970-73, asst. contr., 1973-78; v.p. fin. Pullman Standard, 1978-79; sr. v.p. fin. Trailmobile, Chgo., 1979-81; treas. Firestone Tire & Rubber Co., Akron, Ohio, 1981-87, v.p. retail fin. services, 1987-88, sr. v.p. MasterCare Svc. Ctrs., 1988-90; v.p., treas. Ameritech Corp., Chgo., 1990-92; pres. Ameritech Cellular Services, Chgo., 1992—97, Ameritech Consumer Services, Chgo., 1997—99; pres., CEO U.S. Cellular, Chgo., 2000—. Instr. fin. Ill. Benedictine Coll., 1975-80; bd. dir. First midwest Bancorp, Cellular Telecommunications & Internet Assn. Trustee Loyola Univ.; mem. adv. bd. Sch. Bus. Adminstrn. Loyola Univ.; mem. presidents' bd. Uhlich Children's Advantage Network; bd. dir. Chgo. Children's Advocacy Ctr.; mem. Mayor's Council of Tech. Adv., Chgo.; bd. mem. World Bus. Chgo. Mem. Ohio Mfrs. Assn. (trustee 1983-87), Ohio Pub. Expenditure Coun. (trustee 1986-87), Glen Oak Country Club (Glen Ellyn, Ill.), Boulders Club (Carefree, Ariz.), The Tavern Club (Chgo.). Office: US Cellular 8410 W Bryn Mawr Chicago IL 60631

ROONEY, JOHN PHILIP, law educator; b. Evanston, Ill., May 1, 1932; s. John McCaffery and Bernadette Marie (O'Brien) R.; m. Jean Marie Kliss, Feb. 16, 1974 (div. Oct. 1988); 1 child, Caitlin Mairin. BA, U. Ill, 1953; JD, Harvard U., 1958. Bar: Ill. 1958, Calif. 1961, Mich. 1975, U.S. Tax Ct. 1973, US Supreme Ct., 2000. Assoc. lawyer Chapman & Cutler, Chgo., 1958-60, Wilson, Morton, San Mateo, Calif., 1961-63; pvt. practice San Francisco, 1963-74; prof. law Cooley Law Sch., Lansing, Mich., 1975—. Author: Selected Cases (Property), 1985; contbr. articles to profl. jours. Pres. San Francisco coun. Dem. Clubs, 1970. 1st lt. U.S. Army, 1953-55. Recipient Beattie Teaching award Cooley Law Sch. Grads., 1979, 90, 92. Fellow Mich. Bar Found.; mem. ABA (real estate and fed. tax com., title ins. com.), Ingham County Bar Assn., Univ. Club. Democrat. Unitarian Universalist. Office: Cooley Law Sch 300 S Capitol Ave Lansing MI 48933-1586 Business E-Mail: rooneyj@cooley.edu.

ROONEY, KEVIN DAVITT, federal agency administrator; b. Springfield, Mass., June 23, 1944; s. Davitt Michael and Elizabeth Isabel (Wlodyka) R.; m. Annette Eloise Benevento, Nov. 11, 1972; children: Kathryn Denise, Mary Elizabeth. BA, St. Marys Coll., 1966; JD, George Washington U., 1975. Bar: Va. 1975, D.C. 1977. Computer systems analyst VA, Washington, 1967-68, 70-73; chief legal programs & budget US Dept. Justice, Washington, 1973-77, exec. asst. to assoc. atty. gen., 1977, asst. atty. gen. for adminstrn., 1977-84; prin. Rooney & Assocs, Washington, 1984-87, 90-94, Rooney & Barry, Washington, 1987-89; assoc. dir. Exec. Office for Immigration Rev. US Dept. Justice, Falls Church, Va., 1995-97, asst. dir. Fed. Bur. Prisons Washington, 1997-99, dir. Exec. Office for Immigration Rev. Falls Church, Va., 1999—, acting commr. Immigration and Naturalization Svc., 2001. Bd. dirs., v.p. Joint Action in Cmty. Svcs., Inc., Washington, 1988-94. With U.S. Army, 1968-70. Mem. ASPA, Fed. Bar Assn., Va. Bar Assn., D.C. Bar Assn. Office: Executive Office for Immigration Review 5107 Leesburg Pike Falls Church VA 22041

ROONEY, MATTHEW A., lawyer; b. Jersey City, May 19, 1949; s. Charles John and Eileen (Dunphy) R.; m. Jean M. Alletag, June 20, 1973 (div. Dec. 1979); 1 child, Jessica Margaret; m. Diane S. Kaplan, July 6, 1981; children: Kathryn Olivia, S. Benjamin. AB magna cum laude, Georgetown U., 1971; JD with honors, U. Chgo., 1974. Bar: Ill. 1975, U.S. Dist. Ct. (no. dist.) Ill. 1975, U.S. Ct. Appeals (7th cir.). 1990. Law clk. to cir. judge US Ct. Appeals (7th cir.), Chgo., 1974-75; assoc. Mayer, Brown, Chgo., 1975-80, ptnr., 1981—. Assoc. editor U. Chgo. Law Rev., 1973. Fellow Am. Coll. Trial Lawyers; mem. ABA, 7th Cir. Bar Assn., Order of Coif, Phi Beta Kappa. Democrat. Roman Catholic. Avocations: jogging, golf. Home: 2718 Sheridan Rd Evanston IL 60201-1754 Office: Mayer Brown LLP 71 S Wacker Dr Chicago IL 60606-4637 Office Phone: 312-702-7279. Business E-Mail: mrooney@mayerbrownrowe.com.

ROONEY, MICKEY (JOE YULE JR.), actor; b. Bklyn., Sept. 23, 1920; s. Joe and Nell (Carter) Yule; m. Ava Gardner, Jan. 10, 1942 (div. May 1943); m. Betty Jane Rase, Sept. 30, 1944 (div. 1949); children: Mickey Jr., Timothy (dec. 2006); m. Martha Vickers, June 3, 1949 (div.); m. Elaine Mahnken (div. 1958); m. Barbara Thomason, Dec. 1958; children: Kerry, Kyle, Kelly Ann, Kimmy Sue; m. Margie Lang, Sept. 1966 (div. 1967); m. Carolyn Hockett, (div.); 1 adopted child, Jimmy, 1 child, Jonell; m. Jan Chamberlin, July 28, 1978; stepchildren: Chris Aber, Mark Aber. Student, Pacific Mil. Acad. First appeared in vaudeville with parents; then appeared with Sid Gould, numerous TV programs; appeared in motion pictures Judge Hardy's Children, Hold That Kiss, Lord Jeff, Love Finds Andy Hardy, Boys Town, Stablemates, Out West With the Hardys, Huckleberry Finn, Andy Hardy Gets Spring Fever, Babes in Arms, Young Tom Edison, Judge Hardy and Son, Andy Hardy Meets Debutante, Strike Up the Band, Andy Hardy's Private Secretary, Men of Boystown, Life Begins for Andy Hardy, Babes on Broadway, A Yank at Eton, The Human Comedy, Andy Hardy's Blonde Trouble, Girl Crazy, Thousands Cheer, National Velvet, Ziegfeld Follies, The Strip, Sound Off, Off Limits, All Ashore, Light Case of Larceny, Drive A Crooked Road, Bridges at Toko-Ri, The Bold and Brave, Eddie, Private Lives of Adam and Eve, Comedian, The Grabbers, St. Joseph Plays the Horses, Breakfast at Tiffany's, Somebody's Waiting, Requiem For A Heavyweight, Richard, Pulp, It's a Mad, Mad, Mad, Mad World, Everything's Ducky, The Secret Invasion, The Extraordinary Seaman, The Comic, The Cockeyed Cowboys of Calico County, Skidoo, B.J. Presents, That's Entertainment, The Domino Principle, Pete's Dragon, The Magic of Lassie, Black Stallion, Arabian Adventure, Erik the Viking, My Heroes Have Always Been Cowboys, 1991, (voice) Little Nimo: Adventures in Slumberland, 1992, Long Road Home, 1996, Kings of the Court, 1997, Animals, 1997, Babe: Pig in the City, 1998, Internet Love, 1998, The First of May, 1999, (voice) Lady and the Tramp II: Scamps Adventure, 2001, Topa Topa Bluffs, 2002; starred in TV prodns. Pinocchio, 1957, Leave 'Em Laughing, 1981, Bill, 1981 (Emmy, Golden Globe), Senior Trip!, 1981, Bill on His Own, 1983, Little Spies (Acad. Hon. award 1982), It Came upon the Midnight Clear, 1984, Bluegrass, 1988, Legend of Wolf Mountain, 1992, That's Entertainment! III, 1994, Revente of the Red Baron, 1994, Radio Star-die AFN-Story, 1994, The Legend of O.B. Taggart, 1995; appeared on stage in Sugar Babies, 1979, The Will Rogers Follies, 1993; appeared in TV series A Year at the Top, The Mickey Rooney Show; author: I.E. An Autobiography, 1965, Life Is Too Short, 1991, Search for Sonny Skies, 1994, Brother's Destiny (T.V.), 1995, Michael Kael in Katango, 1997, Boys Will be Boys, 1997, Sinbad: The Battle of the Dark Knights, 1998, The First of May, 1998, The Face on the Barroom Floor, 1998, Babe: Pig in the City, 1998; fgn. films: Midsummer Nights Dream, 1937, Words and Music, 1946, Rachels, 1973, To Hong Kong with Love, 1975, Oddessy of the Pacific, 1979. With AUS, WWII. Recipient Spl. Acad. Award, 1940, Tony award for best mus. actor, 1980; named One of Top 10 Money-Making Stars, Herald-Fame Poll, 1938-43 Office: PO Box 3186 Thousand Oaks CA 91359-0186

ROONEY, PAUL C., JR., retired lawyer; b. Winnetka, Ill., Oct. 23, 1943; s. Paul C. and Mary K. (Brennan) R.; m. Maria Elena Del Canto, Sept. 6, 1980. BA, Harvard U., 1963, LLB, 1966. Bar: Mass. 1968, N.Y. 1972, Fla. 1980, U.S. Dist. Ct. (ea. and so. dists.) N.Y., U.S. Ct. Appeals (2d cir.). Ptnr. White & Case, NYC, 1983-98, ret., 1998. Served to lt. USNR, 1966-69. Mem. Fla. Bar Assn., Univ. Club (N.Y.C.), Mashomack Preserve (N.Y.), Sharon Country Club (Conn.). Home: 11 Lilac Ln PO Box 271 Sharon CT 06069-0271 Office: White & Case 1155 Avenue Of The Americas New York NY 10036-2787 Office Phone: 212-819-8200.

ROONEY, PAUL GEORGE, mathematics professor; b. NYC, July 14, 1925; s. Geoffrey Daniel and Doris Elizabeth (Babcock) R.; m. Mary Elizabeth Carlisle, June 20, 1950; children: Francis Timothy, Elizabeth Anne, Kathleen Doris, John Edward, James Carlisle. B.Sc., U. Alta., 1949; PhD, Calif. Inst. Tech., 1952. Asst. prof. math. U. Alta., 1952-55; asst. prof. U. Toronto, 1955-60, assoc. prof., 1960-62, prof., 1962-91, prof. emeritus, 1991—. Dir. Commonwealth Petroleum Co., Calgary, 1946-59 Editor in chief Can. Jour. Math. 1971-75; contbr. articles to profl. jours. Bd. dirs. Francis F. Reeve Found., 1954-85. Served with Can. Army, 1943-45. Fellow Royal Soc. Can.; Mem. Can. Math. Soc. (councillor 1960-64, 66-70, 76-78, v.p. 1979-81, pres. 1981-83), Am. Math. Soc., Math. Assn. Am. Office: U Toronto Dept Math 40 St George St Toronto ON Canada M5S 2E4 Business E-Mail: rooney@math.toronto.edu.

ROONEY, TERENCE JOSEPH (T.J.), political organization administrator, former state legislator; b. Garden City, NY, Dec. 9, 1964; s. Leo J. and Virginia R.; m. Kathleen Stilin, 1989; children: Leo J., Abeigeal C. Student, Catawba Coll. Realtor DW Kent, Caldwell, NJ, 1984-86; warehouse mgmt. and labor rels. All-Am. Metals, Inc., 1986-87; campaign dir. Fred Rooney for Judge Com., 1989-90; comml. ins. agt. TJ McHale & Co., Inc., 1990-93; mem. Dist. 133 Pa. House of Reps., Harrisburg, 1993—2006; chmn. Pa. Dem. Party, 2003—; mng. dir. Tri State Strategies PA, LLC. Democrat. Office: 4 East Wing Harrisburg PA 17120-2020 also: Pa Dem Party 8th Fl 300 N 2nd St Harrisburg PA 17101*

ROONEY, TOM, United States Representative from Florida, lawyer; b. Phila., Nov. 21, 1970; m. Tara Rooney; children: Tom Jr., Sean, Seamus. Student, Syracuse U., NY; BS in English Lit., Washington and Jefferson Coll., Pitts.; MA in Polit. Sci., U. Fla.; JD, U. Miami Sch. Law. Bar: Fla. 1999. Commd. officer JAG Corps, spl. asst. US atty. US Army, Fort Hood, Tex., 1999—2004; asst. atty. gen. State of Fla., 2004—06; apptd. bd. dirs. Children's Svcs. Coun. Palm Beach County, 2006—08; atty. Kramer, Sopko & Levenstein, P.A., Stuart, Fla., 2008—09; mem. US Congress from 16th Fla. dist., 2009—. Bd. dirs. Children's Place at Home Safe, South Lake Worth, Fla. Serves US Army Inactive Ready Reserves. Republican. Office: US Congress 1529 Longworth House Office Bldg Washington DC 20515-0916 also: Dist Office 226 Taylor St Ste 600 Punta Gorda FL 33950 Office Phone: 202-225-5792, 941-575-9101. Office Fax: 202-225-3132, 941-575-9103.*

ROOP, JAMES JOHN, public relations executive; b. Parkersburg, W.Va., Oct. 29, 1949; s. J. Vaun and Mary Louise (McGinnis) R.; m. Margaret Mary Kuneck (div. 1982); m. Susan Lynn Hoell (div. 1989); m. Daisy P. Billue, 1990 (div. 1999); m. Constance E. West, 2005. BS in Journalism, W. Va. U., 1971. Various account mgmt. postions Ketchum Pub. Rels., Pitts., 1972-77, v.p., 1977-79, Burson-Marsteller, Chgo., 1979-81; sr. v.p. Hesselbart & Mitten/Watt, Cleve., 1981-84, exec. v.p., 1984-86, pres., 1986-87, Watt, Roop & Co. (formerly Hesselbart & Mitten/Watt), Cleve., 1987-96; chmn., pres., CEO Roop & Co., Cleve., 1996—. Contbr. articles to profl. jours. Mem. Leadership Clevel.; bd. dirs. Malachi House, Home Repair Resource Ctr. Fellow Pub. Rels. Soc. Am. (chmn. investor rels. sect. 1984-85, chmn. honors and awards com. 1995); mem. Nat. Investor Rels. Inst. (pres. Cleve./Akron/Pitts. chpt., sr. investor rels. roundtable), Cleve. Skating Club, Mayfield Country Club, Hermit Club. Republican. Home: 2697 Scarborough Rd Cleveland Heights OH 44106-3241 Office: Roop & Co 650 Huntington Bldg 925 Euclid Ave Cleveland OH 44115-1408

ROOP, JOSEPH MCLEOD, economist; b. Montgomery, Ala., Sept. 29, 1941; s. Joseph Ezra and Mae Elizabeth (McLeod) R.; m. Betty Jane Reed, Sept. 4, 1965; 1 dau., Elizabeth Rachael. BS, Ctrl. Mo. U., Warrensburg, 1963; PhD, Wash. State U., Pullman, 1973. Economist Econ. Rsch. Svc., USDA, Washington, 1975-79; sr. economist Evans Econs., Inc., Washington, 1979-81; staff scientist Battelle Pacific N.W. Nat. Lab., Richland, Wash., 1981—. Adj. prof. dept. econs. Wash. State U., 1999—; with Internat. Energy Agy., Paris, 1990-91. Contbr. articles to profl. jours. With US Army, 1966—68. Grantee Rsch. grant, Dept. Agr. Coop. State Rsch. Svc., 1971—73. Mem. Am. Econ. Assn., Econometric Soc., Internat. Assn. Energy Econs., Am. Statis. Assn. Home: 715 S Taft St Kennewick WA 99336-9587 Office: PO Box 999 MSIN K6-05 Richland WA 99352-0999 Office Phone: 509-372-4245. Business E-Mail: joe.roop@pnl.gov.

ROORDA, JOHN FRANCIS, JR., manufacturing executive, consultant; b. Evanston, Ill., Jan. 16, 1923; s. John Francis and Sadie M. (Daley) R.; m. Elizabeth Mulcahy, July 2, 1949; children: Elizabeth Roorda Barker, John F., Ann Roorda Hollis. BSChemE, Purdue U., 1943, PhD, 1949. With Shell Oil Co., 1949-83; gen. mgr. combined oil products/chem. econs. dept., 1973-74; v.p. planning and econs., 1974-77; v.p. Shell Devel. Co., Houston, 1977-78; v.p. corp. planning Shell Oil Co., 1978-83; pres. John Roorda, 1983—. Coordinator Exec. Service Corps, Houston, 1985— Served to lt. (j.g.) USNR, 1943-46. Recipient Disting. Engring. Alumnus award Purdue U., 1976, Outstanding Chem. Engr. award Purdue U., 1993. Mem. Sigma Xi. Roman Catholic.

ROOS, CASPER, actor; b. NYC, Mar. 21, 1925; s. Jacob and Sabina (Uhlenbusch) R.; m. Shirley Anne Nicholson, June 27, 1953; 1 child, Pieter Nicholson. Student, N.Y. Coll. Music. Treas. Actors Equity Found., N.Y.C., 1982-88; co-chmn. research subcom. Nat. Theater Com., N.Y.C., 1983—; chair supv. com. Actors Fed. Credit Union, 1990-2001, 2003—. Prin. actor Shenandoah, N.Y.C., 1975-78, Brigadoon, N.Y.C., 1979-80, My One and Only, N.Y.C., 1982-85, Into the Light, 1986, Man of La Mancha, Zurich, 1988, (Broadway prodn.) Shenandoah Revival, 1989; numerous regional theater prodns. Served with U.S. Mcht. Marines, 1943-46. Mem. Actors Equity (treas. 1982-88, councilor 1964-79, 88-93). Home: 3 Cozzens Ct Newport RI 02840 *Don Quixote wanted to 'add a little grace to the world.' I, too, would like to add a 'little' to this world, whether it be grace or laughter or tears to an audience or service to my colleagues. If, like Don Quixote, I look a little foolish, so be it. I prefer a life of striving for the ultimate to the easier smug acceptance of the status quo.*

ROOS, DANIEL, engineering educator; b. Bklyn., Apr. 12, 1939; s. Sigmund and Anita (Sperling) R.; m. Eva Bonis, June 1, 1969; children— Richard Joseph, Linda Suzanne. BS in Civil Engring, MIT, Cambridge, Mass., 1961, MS, 1963, PhD, 1966. Mem. faculty MIT, 1963—, assoc. prof. civil engring., 1970—76, prof., 1976—, head transp. systems div., 1977—78, dir. Ctr. for Transp. Studies, 1978—85, dir. Ctr. Tech., Policy and Indsl. Devel., 1985—97, Japan Steel Industry prof., 1985—, mem. Commn. on Indsl. Productivity, 1987—89, assoc. dean engring. systems, 1997—2001, spl. asst. provost and chancellor, 1996—2003, co-dir. Ford Indsl. Ptnrships, dir. engring. sys. divsn., 1998—2004, dir. Portugal program, 2005—. Chair Council Engring. Sys. U.; founder, dir. Multisystems Inc., Cambridge, 1965—85; chmn. com. to assess advanced vehicle and hwy techs. NRC, 1990—91, mem. com. on fuel economy, 1991—92; dir. Internat. Motor Vehicle Program, 1980—99; co-dir. Lean Aircraft Initiative, 1992—97; mem. coun. indsl. relationships MIT, 1996—97. Author: ICES System Design, 1964; The Future of the Automobile, 1984, Auto Futures, 1990; co-author: Made in America, 1989, The Machine That Changed the World, 1990; contbr. articles to profl. jours. Mem. U.S. Task Force on Transp., 1969. Recipient Shingo Prize for Excellence in Mfg. Rsch., 1994. Mem. ASCE (Frank M. Masters Transp. Engring. award 1989), Assn. Computing Machinery, Ops. Research Soc. (treas. transp. sci. sect. 1970-71), Transp. Research Bd. (chmn. para-transit com. 1974-80, group coun. 1980-84), Coun. Univ. Transp. Ctrs. (pres. 1983), Coun. Engring. Sys. Univs. (founding pres. 1990—). Achievements include developing Dial-A-Ride transp. concept, 1965; dir. Internat. Motor Vehicle. Home: 44 Summit Rd Belmont MA 02478 Office: MIT Engring Sys Divsn 77 Massachusetts Ave Cambridge MA 02139-4307 Office Phone: 617-253-1661. Personal E-mail: roos@mit.edu.

ROOS, JOHN VICTOR, lawyer; b. San Francisco, Feb. 14, 1955; AB, Stanford U., 1977, JD, 1980. Bar: Calif. 1980. Ptnr. Wilson, Sonsini Goodrich & Rosati, San Francisco, 1988—, mng. dir. profl. services, CEO, 2005—, mem. exec. mgmt. com. & policy com. Mem.: Calif. Bar Assn., Order of the Coif. Office: Wilson Sonsini Goodrich & Rosati 650 Page Mill Rd Palo Alto CA 94304 Office Phone: 650-493-9300. Office Fax: 650-493-6811. E-mail: jroos@wsgr.com.

ROOS, SYBIL FRIEDENTHAL, retired elementary school educator; b. LA, Jan. 29, 1924; d. Charles G. and Besse (Weixel) Friedenthal; m. Henry Kahn Roos, May 8, 1949 (dec. Dec. 1989); children: Catherine Alane Cook, Elizabeth Anne Garlinger, Virginia Ann Bertrand. BA in Music, Centenary Coll., 1948; MEd, Northwestern State U., 1973. Cert. elem. edn. tchr., spl. edn. tchr. Tchr. Caddo Parish Schs., Shreveport, 1968-75, Spring Branch Ind. Schs., Houston, 1975-85; vol. Houston Grand Opera/Guild, 1979—, Houston Mus. of Fine Arts/Guild, 1990—, Houston Symphony Soc./Guild, 1997—. Pres. Nat. Coun. Jewish Women, Shreveport, 1958; life mem. Mus. Fine Arts; area coord. Spl. Olympics, Shreveport, 1974-75; bd. dirs. U. Houston Moore Sch. Music. With USN, 1944-46. Mem. AAUW (pres. Spring Valley Houston chpt. 1985-87), Houston Grand Opera Guild (pres. 1989-91), Spring Br. U. Women (corr.; sec., 2005-)Houston Symphony League, Houston Ballet Guild, Am. Needlepoint Guild, Delta Kappa Gamma (bd. dirs., treas. 1987-89), Phi Mu. Republican. Avocations: music, tennis, needlepoint, volunteering. Home: 10220 Memorial Dr Apt 78 Houston TX 77024-3227 Personal E-mail: s.roos@worldnet.att.net.

ROOSA, JAN BERTOROTTA, psychologist, writer; b. Champaign, Ill., Apr. 19, 1927; s. Walter Laidlaw and Giannina (Bertorotta) Roosa; m. Joan Herr. BS, U. Ill., 1950; MA, U. Denver, 1951, PhD, 1957. Coord., clin. psychologist Child Rsch. Coun., Kansas City, Mo., 1954-57, dir. neighborhood rsch. project, 1954—57; supr., psychologist State

Hosp., Fulton, Mo., 1957-59; chief of psychotherapy VA Hosp., Kansas City, 1959-63; pvt. practice clin. psychologist Kansas City, 1963—. Dir., co-founder Learning Resource Ctr., Kansas City, 1969—79; dir. Gestalt, Social Competence Inst., Kansas City, 1969—89, Competence and Coop. Group, 1992—. Author: Situation-Options-Consequences-Simulation: A Technique for Teaching Social Skills, 1973, Psychological and Social Competence Model and Skills, 1975, 1992, Pet Peeves of a Psychologist and Other Flights into Reality, 2005, Brainspire.com: Psychological Tools for a New Way of Life, 2006; creator SOCCSS and SOCCSS: A Decision Making Process, 1973, 1996, The Competence and Cooperation Based Program, 1995. With USNR, 1945—47, with USNR, 1951—52. Mem.: APA, Nat. Register Health Providers Psychology, Mental Health Profls., Kans. Assn. Profl. Psychologists, Mo. Psychol. Assn., Greater Kansas City Psychol. Assn. Office: 9237 Ward Pkwy Ste 103 Kansas City MO 64114-3334 Office Phone: 816-444-3366. E-mail: jbroosa@yahoo.com.

ROOSA, STEPHEN ALLEN, energy engineer; PhD, U. Louisville, Ky., 2004. Cert. energy mgr., AEE, 1984. Energy engr. LGE Enertech, Louisville, 1997—2002; acct. exec. ESG, Louisville, 2004—, performance engr., 2004—. Lectr. U. Louisville, 2003—06. Author: (book) The Sustainable Development Handbook (Energy Mgr.'s Hall of Fame, 2006). Chmn. AEE Cert. Sustainable Devel. Profl., Atlanta, 2006—08. Named Internat. Energy Mgr. of Yr., AEE, 1987. Mem.: AIA. Office Fax: 812-492-8428.

ROOSEVELT, JAMES, JR., insurance company executive, lawyer; b. LA, Nov. 9, 1945; s. James and Romelle (Schneider) R.; m. Ann M. Conlon, June 15, 1968; children: Kathy, Tracy, Maura. AB, Harvard U., 1968, JD, 1971. Bar. Mass. 1971, DC 1973, US Ct. Appeals (DC cir.) 1973, US Ct. Appeals (1st cir.) 1976, US Supreme Ct. 1975. Assoc. Winthrop, Stimson, Putnam & Roberts, NYC, 1971, Herrick & Smith, Boston, 1975-80, ptnr., 1981-86, Nutter, McClennen & Fish, Boston, 1986-88, Choate, Hall & Stewart, Boston, 1988-98; assoc. commr. for retirement policy Social Security Adminstrn., Washington, 1998-99; sr. v.p., gen. counsel Tufts Health Plan, Waltham, Mass., 1999—2005, pres., 2005—, CEO, 2005—. Mem. Dem. Nat. Com., Washington, 1980—, Dem. State Com., Boston, 1980—; trustee Emmanuel Coll., Boston, 1982-92, 95—; trustee Care Group, Inc., Boston, 1996-00, Mt. Auburn Hosp., Cambridge, Mass., 1984-2000, chmn., 1988-92, chmn. bd. overseers, 2000—06. Lt. JAGC, USN, 1972-75. Mem. ABA, Boston Bar Assn., Mass. Bar Assn., Am. Health Lawyers Assn. (pres. 2002-03), Mass. Hosp. Assn. (trustee 1987-99, chmn. 1996-97), Harvard Club. Roman Catholic. Avocation: public policy. Office: Tufts Health Plan 705 Mount Auburn St Watertown MA 02472 Office Phone: 617-972-9564. Business E-Mail: james_roosevelt@tufts-health.com.

ROOSEVELT, THEODORE, IV, investment banker; b. Jacksonville, Fla., Nov. 27, 1942; s. Theodore III and Anne Mason (Babcock) Roosevelt; m. Constance Lane Rogers, Aug. 1, 1970; 1 child, Theodore V. AB, Harvard U., 1965, MBA, 1972. Fgn. svc. officer U.S. Dept. of State, 1967—70; assoc. Lehman Bros., NYC, 1972-76; corp. v.p. Lehman Bros. Kuhn Loeb, NYC, 1976-82; sr. v.p. Lehman Comml. Paper Inc., NYC, 1982-85; mng. dir. Lehman Brothers, NYC, 1985—2008. Chmn., bd. dirs. Lehman Bros. Fin. Products, Inc.; chmn. Lehman Coun. Climate Change. Mng. dir. Barclay Capital Recreation & Hist. Preservation Commn. City NY; mem. Cultural Inst. Retirement Sys.; chmn. Pew Ctr. Global Change; trustee Allicance Climate Protection World Resources Inst. With underwater demolition team USN, 1965—67. Mem.: Fgn. Policy Assn. (gov.), Coun. Fgn. Rels., Trout Unlimited, Wilderness Soc., Somerset Club (Boston), Clove Valley Rod and Gun Club, Econ. Club N.Y., Harvard Club (N.Y.C.), Explorers Club, Heights Casino Club (Bklyn.), Edgartown Yacht Club, Links (N.Y.C.). Republican. Home: 1 Pierrepont St Brooklyn NY 11201-3302 Office: Barclays Capital 745 7th Ave 20th Fl New York NY 10019 Home Phone: 718-237-9172; Office Phone: 212-526-8363. E-mail: troosere@lehman.com.

ROOST, ALISA, theater educator; b. San Francisco, Nov. 9, 1971; d. Eric Robert-Tissiot Roost and Anna Lyons-Roost. BA, U. Calif., Santa Cruz, 1992; MA, U. Ill., Urbana, 1995; MPh, CUNY Grad. Ctr., 1998, PhD, 2001. Grad. tchg. fellow CUNY, 1997—98, writing fellow, 1999—2000; vis. artist acting and directing Winthrop U., 2001—02; asst. prof. theatre Monmouth Coll., Ill., 2002—06; asst. prof. John Jay Coll. Criminal Justice, NY, 2006—. Dir.: (staged reading) The Choice, 1997, (musical) Flahooley, 1998; (plays) Bloomer Girl, 2000; contbr. articles to profl. jours. Mem.: Middle Eastern Studies Assn., Am. Soc. Theatre Rsch., Assn. for Theater in Higher Edn. (conf. coord. 1999—2001, talent coord. 2005—07). Democrat. Episcopalian. Avocation: ice skating. Office Phone: 212-237-8180. Personal E-mail: flahooley@gmail.com.

ROOT, ALLEN WILLIAM, pediatrician, educator; b. Phila., Sept. 24, 1933; s. Morris Jacob and Priscilla R.; m. Janet Greenberg, June 15, 1958; children: Jonathan, Jennifer, Michael. AB, Dartmouth Coll., 1955, postgrad. Med. Sch., 1954-56; MD, Harvard U., 1958. Diplomate Am. Bd. Pediatrics (mem. bd. 1985—), Am. Bd. Pediatric Endocrinology (mem. bd. 1985-90, chmn. 1990). Intern Strong Meml. Hosp., Rochester, NY, 1958-60; resident in pediatrics Hosp. U. Pa., Phila., 1960-62; fellow in pediatric endocrinology Children's Hosp. of Phila., 1962-65; assoc. physician in pediatrics U. Pa. Sch. Medicine, 1964-66, asst. prof. pediatrics, 1966-69; assoc. prof. pediatrics Temple U. Sch. Medicine, Phila., 1969-73, prof., 1973; asst. physician in endocrinology Children's Hosp. Phila., 1965-69; chmn. divsn. pediatrics Albert Einstein Med. Center., Phila., 1969-73; prof. pediatrics U. South Fla. Coll. Medicine, Tampa, 1973—, prof. biochemistry, 1987—2007, assoc. chmn. dept. pediatrics, 1974-99, dir. sect. pediatric endocrinology, 1973-96. Dir. univ. tchg. svcs. All Children's Hosp., St. Petersburg, 1973-89; mem. Fla. Infant Screening Adv. Coun., 1979-06, chmn., 1994-06; mem. Hillsborough County Thyroid Adv. Com., 1980; mem. med. adv. com. Nat. Pituitary Agy., 1974-78, mem. growth hormone subcom., 1972-79, 81-85; chmn. Fla. Legis. Infant Screening Task Force, 2002. Author: Human Pituitary Growth Hormone, 1972; co-editor: (with C. La Cauza) Problems in Pediatric Endocrinology, 1980; mem. editl. bd. Jour. Pediats., 1973-81, Jour. Adolescent Health Care, 1979-95, Jour. Pediat. Endocrinology and Metabolism, 1985—, Jour. Clin. Endocrinology and Metabolism, 1993-96, 2001-04, Growth, Genetics and Hormones, 1993—, Pediat. in Rev., 1995-2001; assoc. editor Adolescent and Pediat. Gynecology, 1992-95, Current Opinion in Pediats., sect. editor, Endocrine and Metabolism, 1993-, mem. editl. bd. 2006-. USPHS grantee; Birth Defects Found. grantee. Mem. AAAS, Am. Pediatric Soc., Soc. Pediatric Rsch., Lawson Wilkins Pediatric Endocrine Soc. (treas. 1979-88, pres. 1988-89), Endocrine Soc., Am. Acad. Pediatrics, Am. Fedn. Clin. Rsch., Soc. Exptl. Biology and Medicine, Soc. Nuclear Medicine, N.Y. Acad. Sci., Phila. Coll. Physicians, Phila. Endocrine Soc. (bd. dirs. 1971-72, treas. 1973), Dartmouth Coll. Alumni Coun., Dartmouth Club. Office: 801 6th St S Saint Petersburg FL 33701-4816 Business E-Mail: roota@allkids.org.

ROOT, EDWARD LAKIN, education educator, academic administrator; b. Cumberland, Md., Dec. 5, 1940; s. Lakin and Edna Grace (Adams) Root. BS, Frostburg State U., Md., 1962, MEd, 1966; EdD, U. Md., 1970. Cert. tchr. Md. Tchr. Allegany County Bd. of Edn., Cumberland, Md., 1962—66; grad. fellow U. Md., College Park, 1966-67, fellow, 1967—69; with Frostburg State U., 1969—99, prof., head edn. dept., 1980—87, dean, 1987—95, prof., head EdM adminstrn., 1995—99; gubernatorial appointee Md. State Bd. Edn., 1999—2007, pres., 2003—07. Mem. Profl. Stds. Bd. Md., Balt., 1980—87, Balt., 1995—99, Cert. Rev. Bd. Md., Balt., 1987—90, Md. Task Force Adminstrn., Balt., 1985—88, Md. Task Force: Prisoners Time and Response, task force tchr. assessment, 1995—97, Md. Task Force Tchr. Quality, 2002—03, Md. Task Force Disadvantaged but Capable Students, 2000—02; chmn. Md. Tchr. Quality Task Group, 2002—03, Md. Tchr. Shortage Task Force, 2007—08. Mem. Allegany County (Md.) Planning and Zoning Bd. Appeals, 1995—96. Named Md. Ednl. Leader of Yr., 2003. Mem.: Mensa, Masons, Shriners, Phi Delta Kappa. Democrat. Methodist. Avocations: photography, travel. Home: 100 Pennsylvania Ave Cumberland MD 21502-4236 Office: Frostburg State U College Ave Frostburg MD 21532-1724 Home Phone: 301-724-2383.

ROOT, JAMES BENJAMIN, landscape architect; b. Detroit, Jan. 26, 1934; s. William Jehial and Helen Elizabeth (English) R. BBA, Memphis State U., 1960; B Landscape Architecture, U. Ga., 1966. Registered landscape architect; lic. real estate agt., Va. Asst. prof. W.Va. U., Morgantown, 1973-75, 93; pvt. practice Charlottesville, Va., 1976-85, 91—; site planner LBA, PH&R, Charles P. Johnson & Assocs., Fairfax, Va., 1986-90. Pvt. practice as golf course architect, Charlottesville, 1976—; instr. Parkersburg C.C., 1975, Piedmont Va. C.C., 1981. Author: Fundamentals of Landscaping and Site Planning, 1985, From Stardust to Insanity: The Moral Demise of a Troubled Nation, 2007; contbr. articles to profl. jours., also poetry. Mem. Planning Commn., Marietta, Ohio, 1972. Mem. Nat. Golf Found., Golf Course Builders Assn. Am. (assoc.), Va. Writers Club. Avocations: piano, drums. Office: PO Box 7017 Charlottesville VA 22906-7017 Office Phone: 434-971-4000. E-mail: jamesbroot@aol.com.

ROOT, NINA J., librarian, writer; b. 1934; d. Jacob J. and Fannie (Slivinsky) R. BA, Hunter Coll.; MSLS, Pratt Inst.; postgrad., USDA Grad. Sch., 1964-65, CUNY, 1970-75. Reference and serials libr. Albert Einstein Coll. Medicine Libr., Bronx, NY, 1958-59; asst. chief libr. Am. Cancer Soc., NYC, 1959-62; chief libr. Am. Inst. Aeros. and Astronautics, NYC, 1962-64; head ref. and libr. svcs. sci. and tech. divsn. Libr. Congress, Washington, 1964-66; mgmt. cons. Nelson Assocs., Inc., NYC, 1966-70; dir. libr. svcs. Am. Mus. Natural History, NYC, 1970—98; freelance mgmt. cons. and libr. planning, 1970-99; dir. emerita libr. svcs. Am. Mus. Natural Hist., NYC, 1999—. Trustee Barnard Found., 1984-91; mem. libr. adv. coun. N.Y. State Bd. Regents, 1984-89, trustee Metro, 1987-92; bd. dirs. Hampden/Booth Libr. Players, 1990-97, Sutton Area Cmty., 1997-2001; trustee Mercantile Libr. N.Y., 1993-95; dir. emerita Libr. AMNH, 1998—. Recipient Meritorious Svc. award Libr. of Congress, 1965, Founders medal SHNH, 1997. Mem. ALA (preservation com. 1977-79, chmn. libr./binders com. 1978-80, chmn. preservation sect. 1980-81, mem. coun. 1983-86), Spl. Librs. Assn. (sec. documentation group N.Y. chpt. 1972-73, 2d v.p. N.Y. 1975-76, treas. sci. and tech. group N.Y. 1975-76, mus. arts and humanities divsn. program planning chairperson-conf. 1977), Archons of Colophon (convener 1978-79), Soc. for Hist. of Natural History (N.Am. rep. 1977-85), N.Y. Acad. Scis. (mem. publs. com. 1975-80, 89-91, archives com. 1976-78, search. com. 1976), Explorers Club. Home: 400 E 59th St New York NY 10022-2342 Home Phone: 212-758-3805. Personal E-mail: n.root@rcn.com.

ROOT, STANLEY WILLIAM, JR., retired lawyer; b. Honolulu, Mar. 2, 1923; s. Stanley William and Henrietta E. (Brown) R.; m. Joan Louise Schimpf, Sept. 3, 1949; children: Henry, Louise. AB, Princeton U., 1947; LLB, U. Pa., 1950. Bar: Pa. 1950, U.S. Ct. Mil. Appeals 1951, U.S. Supreme Ct. 1971. Ptnr. Foley, Schimpf & Steeley, Phila., 1952-69, Ballard, Spahr, Andrews & Ingersoll, Phila., 1970-91, of counsel, 1992-97; ret., 1998. Lectr. Pa. Bar Assn., 1970-80; bd. dirs. Boardman-Hamilton Co., sec. 1980-98. Exec. v.p. Chestnut Hill Cmty. Assn., Phila., 1978; with Whitpain Farm Assn., Blue Bell, Pa., 1987, 90, pres., 1992-94; with St. Paul's Ch. Vestry, Phila., 1969-75; bd. dirs. Lansdale (Pa.) Med. Group, 1972-95, E.B. Spaeth Found. Wills Hosp., Phila., 1975-88, Chevalier Jackson Clinic, Phila., 1965-88; trustee Civil War Libr. and Mus., 1985-93, v.p., 1989, sec., 1992-93, mem. adv. bd., 1993-95; trustee Soc. Protestant Episc. Ch., Pa. Diocese, 1955-95. Lt. col. U.S. Army, 1942-45, ETO, 1950-52, Korea. Decorated Bronze Star; recipient Pa. Commendation medal State of Pa., 1962. Mem.: Mil. Order Fgn. Wars (comdr. Pa. Commandery 1970), Mil. Order Loyal Legion, Mil. Order World Wars (comdr. Phila. chpt. 1960—61), Union League Phila. (pres. 1983—85), Royal Poinciana Golf Club, Sunnybrook Golf Club. Republican. Episcopalian. Avocations: golf, tennis, fishing. Home: 2400 Gulf Shore Blvd N Apt 201 Naples FL 34103-4364 Home Phone: 239-262-8932; Office Phone: 215-864-8306. Personal E-mail: stanislaw16@aol.com.

ROOT, STUART DOWLING, lawyer, retired government agency administrator, banker; b. Chagrin Falls, Ohio, Oct. 14, 1932; s. Elton Albert and Virginia Saxton (Dowling) R.; m. Jean D. Youse, Dec. 28, 1957 (div. Jan. 1972); children: Bryan, Kathleen, Timothy, Todd; m. Patricia Stoneman Graff, Apr. 24, 1976. BA, Ohio Wesleyan U., 1955; JD, Columbia U., 1960. Bar: N.Y. 1960. Assoc. Cadwalader Wickersham and Taft, NYC, 1960-68, ptnr., 1969-81, 84-87; pres. Bowery Savs. Bank, NYC, 1981-82, vice chmn., 1982-83; exec. dir. Office Fed Savs. and Loan Ins. Corp., Washington, 1988-89; chmn. bd. Fin. Instn. Svcs. Corp., Washington, 1989. Lectr. ABA, Practicing Law Inst., Infocast, Am. Law Inst.; bd. dirs Bowest Corp., 1969-81. Contbr. articles to profl. jours. Chmn. bd. dirs. Harlem Sch. Arts, N.Y.C., 1974-83, trustee emeritus, 1984—; bd. dirs. Open Space Inst., 1976-80, 84-87, 89—, Nat. Choral Soc. N.Y.C., 1981-86, Canterbury Choral Soc., N.Y.C.; trustee N.Y. Geneal. and Biographical Soc., 1981-85; pub. interest dir. Fed. Home Loan Bank N.Y., N.Y.C., 1985-87. With U.S. Army, 1955-57. Mem. Century Assn. (N.Y.C.). Republican. Episcopalian. Avocations: liturgical music, fly fishing, golf. Home and Office: Beaverkill/Campsite Rd PO Box 417 Livingston Manor NY 12758-0417 Office Phone: 845-439-4255. E-mail: rootlaw32@aol.com.

ROOT, WAYNE ALLYN, entrepreneur, television producer, writer; b. Mt. Vernon, NY, July 20, 1961; s. David and Stella (Reis) R.; m. Victoria Payne, Sept. 9, 1986 (div. 1990); m. Debra Parks, Aug. 3, 1991; children: Dakota Skye, Hudson, Remington Reagan, Contessa Churchill. BA, Columbia U., 1983. Pres. Wayne A. Root & Assocs., Real Estate, White Plains, NY, 1983-86; account exec. Bixler Real Estate, Katonah, NY, 1986-88; owner Pure Profit Sport Analysis & Handicapping, White Plains, 1987-89; radio host NBC Source Radio Network, NYC, 1988; TV anchorman Fin. News Network, LA, 1989-91; author, pres. The Universal Frontier (renamed Power Principles), Las Vegas, Nev., 1991; pres., CEO WinningEDGE Internat., Las Vegas, Cool Hand ROOT Prodns., Las Vegas. Author: Root on Risk, 1989, Betting to Win on Sports, 1989, The Joy of Failure!: How to Turn Failure, Rejection, and Pain into Extraordinary Success, 1997, The Zen of Gambling: The Ultimate Guide to Risking It All and Winning at Life, 2004, Millionaire Republican, 2005, The King of Vegas' Guide to Gambling: How to Win Big at Poker, Casino Gambling & Life! The Zen of Gambling, 2006, The Conscience of a Libertarian: Empowering the Citizen Revolution with God, Guns, Gambling, & Tax Cuts!, 2009; contbg. sports editor Robb Report Mag., 1989—91; creator, exec. prodr., host: (TV and radio series) Wayne Root's WinningEDGE, 2000—; (TV series) King of Vegas, 2006; prodr.: Extreme Ghost Adventures, 2008; (documentaries) Entebbe. US vice presdl. candidate Libertarian Party, 2008. Named to Las Vegas Walk of Stars, 2006. Libertarian. Avocations: tennis, running, football, weightlifting, skiing, horseback riding. Office: Winning Edge Internat 5052 S Jones Blvd Ste 100 Las Vegas NV 89118 Office Phone: 702-967-6000. Office Fax: 702-967-6002.*

ROOTH, SIGNE ALICE, editor, consultant; b. NYC, Aug. 14, 1924; d. Gerhard Teodor and Florence Elizabeth (Miner) Rooth. BA summa cum laude, U. Miami, 1944; MA, U. So. Calif., 1945; PhD, U. Chgo., 1953. Translator IMF, Washington, 1954—56, UN Secretariat, NYC, 1956—58, editor Official Records Editing sect., 1958—69; translator/interpreter UN Mission to Congo, Leopoldville, 1962—63; editor/sr. editor divsn. Gen. Assembly Affairs UN Secretariat, NYC, 1969—84, cons. editor UN Devel. Programme, 1985—92, cons. editor trusteeship dept., dept. pub. info., dept. gen. assembly and conf. mgmt., 1993—2009. Editor Econ. and Social Commn. for Asia and the Pacific, Bangkok, 1999; bd. mem. Assn. Culturelle Francophone, UN Secretariat. Author: Seeress of the Northland: Fredrika Bremer's American Journey, 1849-1851, 1955; editor: Procs. of UN Congress on Pub. Internat. Law: International Law as a Language for International Relations, 1995; contbr. articles and essays to jours. Recipient Am. Swedish Woman of Yr., Woman's Auxiliary of Am. Swedish Hist. Mus., Phila., 1984. Mem.: French Inst./Alliance Francaise, Swedish Women's Ednl. Assn., Am. Scandinavian Soc., Am.-Scandinavian Found., Am. Swedish Hist. Found. (life), Southampton Hist. Mus., Rogers Meml. Libr., Parrish Art Mus., Paris Am. Club. Avocations: reading, travel, art, music, collecting F. Bremer autographs.

ROOZBEHANI, MARDAVIJ, research scientist; s. Houshang Roozbehani and Manijeh Zolfaghari; m. Mitra Osqui, 2004. BSc, Sharif U. Tech., Tehran, Iran, 2000; MSc in Mech. and Aerospace Engring., U. Va., Charlottesville, 2003; PhD in Aeronautics and Astronautics, MIT, Cambridge, 2008. Postdoc. rsch. assoc. MIT, 2008—, instr., 2008—. Organizer, weekly colloquia lids Lab. Info. and Decision Sys., MIT, 2005—06, mem. organizing com. lids student conf., 2007—08. Recipient Rsch. award, Am. Inst. Aeronautics and Astronautics, Best Paper Presentation award, Am. Control Conf. Portland, Oreg., 2005, Best Paper award, ACM, 2008. Mem.: IEEE. Office: MA Inst Technology 77 Massachusetts Ave 32-D714 Cambridge MA 02139

ROPE, WILLIAM FREDERICK, educator; b. NYC, Aug. 27, 1940; s. Frederick Thornton and Irene (King) R.; m. Priscilla Barnard, Feb. 18, 1967; children: Katherine Austin, Robert Whitney. BA in History, Yale U., 1962; MA in Govt., Georgetown U., 1970; postgrad., Nat. War Coll., 1977-78, Trinity Coll., Washington, DC, 1999—2000. Vice consul Am. Consulate Gen., Hong Kong, 1967-69, polit./econ. officer, 1971-73; econ./comml. officer U.S. Liaison Office, Beijing, 1973-75; chief N.E. Asia div. Bur. Intelligence and Rsch. U.S. Dept. State, Washington, 1975-77, dir. Ops. Ctr., 1978-80; dir. Office Internat. Security Policy, Washington, 1980-81; dir. Office Chinese and Mongolian Affairs Washington, 1981-83; dir. Office So. European Affairs, 1984-86; dep. chief of mission Am. Embassy, Ankara, Turkey, 1987-89; prin. dep. asst. sec. state for politic-mil. affairs. Dept. State, Washington, 1989-92; chargé d'Affaires Am. Embassy, Bandar Seri Begawan, Brunei Darussalam, 1993, Suva, Fuji, 1994; sr. adviser policy planning staff and to U.S. Mission to the U.N., 1993-95; ret. Fgn. Svc., 1995; Am. co-dir. Johns Hopkins U.-Nanjing U. Ctr. for Chinese and Am. Studies, Nanjing, China, 1995—96; pres. Ctr. Bus. Skills Devel., Am. Grad. Sch. Internat. Mgmt. (Thunderbird), 1997—98; elem. sch. tchr. DC Pub. Schs., 1999—. Mem. State Dept. Sr. Seminar, Rosslyn, Va., 1983-84. Lt. USN, 1962-66. Recipient Superior Honor award Dept. State, 1982, 89, Sr. Performance award, 1983, 84, 88-92. Office: Phoebe Hearst Elem Sch 3950 37th St NW Washington DC 20008 Personal E-mail: wfrope@aol.com.

ROPER, BERYL CAIN, writer, retired library director, publishing executive; b. Long Beach, Calif., Mar. 1, 1931; d. Albert Verne and Ollie Fern (Collins) Cain; m. Max H. Young, Aug. 22, 1947 (div. 1958); children: Howard, Wade, Debra, Kevin, John R., Christopher; m. George Albert Roper, Mar. 24, 1962 (dec. July 1978); children: Ellen, Georgianne; m. Jack T. Hughes, Sept. 21, 1993 (dec. May 2001). BA, West Tex. State U., 1986; MA, Tex. Womans U., 1989. Libr. clk. Cornette Libr., West Tex. State U., Canyon, 1981-87; dir. Clarendon (Tex.) Coll. Libr., 1988-96. Lectr. in history and archaeology; owner Aquamarine Publs. Editor, pub.: In the Light of Past Experience, 1989, Transactions of the Southwest Federation of Archaeological Societies, 1993, Greenbelt Site, 1996, Presbyterian Mission Work in New Mexico: Memoirs of Alice Blake, 1997; author, pub.: Trementina, 1990, Trementina Revisited, 1994, Seekers After Truth, 1998, The Queen of Sciences: Personal Ramblings in Anthropologia, 2006; author articles on women and history. Mem.: Biblical Archeology Soc., Internat. Soc. for Archeology and the Bible, Panhandle Archaeol. Soc., (newsletter editor), Archeology Conservancy, Phi Alpha Theta, Alpha Chi, Beta Phi Mu, Pi Gamma Mu. Republican. Mem. Lds Ch. Avocations: music, gardening, decorating, remodeling old houses, genealogy. Office: Aquamarine Publs 8001 Cattle Dr Canyon TX 79015 Personal E-mail: beryl01@midplains.coop.

ROPER, HARRY JOSEPH, lawyer; b. Bridgeport, Conn., Apr. 15, 1940; BEE, Rensselaer Poly. Inst., 1962; LLB, NYU, 1966. Assoc. Neuman, Williams, Anderson & Olson, 1966-70, ptnr., 1970-90, Roper & Quigg, 1990—2004, Jenner & Block, 2004—. Master: Richard Linn Am. Inn Ct.; fellow: Am. Bar Found., Am. Coll. Trial Lawyers; mem.: Chgo. Coun. Lawyers & Barristers of Patent Law, Chgo. Bar Assn., Intellectual Property Law Assn. Chgo., 7th Circuit Bar Assn., Fed. Circuit Bar Assn., Am. Intellectual Property Law Assn., Am. Bar Assn. (chmn., intellectual property com. sect. litig. 1982—86). Home: 611 W Fullerton Pky Chicago IL 60614-2613 Office: Jenner & Block 330 N Wabash Ave Chicago IL 60611-7603 Home Phone: 773-472-0983; Office Phone: 312-923-8303. Business E-Mail: hroper@jenner.com.

ROPER, RICHARD B., III, lawyer, former prosecutor; b. 1957; BA cum laude, U. Tex., Arlington, 1979; JD, Tex. Tech. U., 1982. Asst. dist. atty. Tarrant County, Tex., 1982—87; asst. US atty. (no. dist.) Tex. US Dept. Justice, Dallas, 1987—2004, interim US atty. (no. dist.) Tex., 2004, US atty. (no. dist.) Tex., 2004—08; ptnr. Thompson & Knight LLP, Dallas, 2009—. Recipient Jane Doe award, Dallas Genesis Women's Shelter; named a Disting. Alumnus, Tex. Tech. U. Sch. Law, 2007. Fellow: Tex. Bar Found.; mem.: State Bar of Tex. Office: Thompson & Knight LLP One Arts Plz 1722 Routh St Ste 1500 Dallas TX 75201 Office Phone: 214-969-1210. Office Fax: 214-880-3357. E-mail: Richard.Roper@tklaw.com.

ROPER, ROBERT, political organization administrator; b. Richmond, Va., July 15, 1968; m. Hilary Roper; 2 children. BA in English, Kenyon Coll., 1990. Copyrighter Young & Rubicam, NY, 1993—98; freelance writer Vt.; media rels. officer McMullen for Senate campaign, Vt., 2003; head FreedomWorks-Vt., 2005. State dir. Freedom Works, 2005—. Writer, editor Vt. Edn. Report. Bd. mem. Vermonters for Better Edn.; chmn. Vt. Rep. Party, 2007—; decon Stowe Cmty. Ch. Republican. Office: Vt Rep Party Ste 308 100 State St Montpelier VT 05601 Office Phone: 802-223-3411. Office Fax: 802-229-1864.

ROPER, SCOTT CHRISTOPHER, geographer, researcher; b. Quincy, Mass., Oct. 24, 1969; s. James Henry and Lynne Patricia (Dunlop) Roper; m. Stephanie Abbot, Aug. 3, 1991. BA, Clark U., Mass., 1991; MA, U. ND, 1993; PhD, U. Kans., 1997. Grad. tchg. asst. U. of ND, Grand Forks, ND, 1991—93, U. of Kans., Lawrence, 1993—96; adj. prof. Rivier Coll., Nashua, NH, 1999—2002; asst. prof. of geography West Tex. A&M U., Canyon, Tex., 2002—05, Castleton (Vt.) State Coll., 2005—. Co-president Lyndeborough Hist. Soc., NH, 1998—2001; book rev. editor Material Culture, Springfield, Ohio, 2003—07; rsch. cons., Lyndeborough, NH, 1997—2002. Co-author (nonfiction book) Citizen Soldiers: New Hampshire's Lafayette Artillery Company, 1804-2004; author: (nonfiction book) The Peterborough Savings Bank, 1847-1997, (monograph) Citizens' Hall: A History of Lyndeborough's 'Other' Town Hall, 1888-2000; co-editor (monograph) A Soldier's Life: Reminiscences of the Civil War; contbr. articles to profl. jours. Chmn. Lyndeborough Conservation Commn., 2006—08, Lyndeborough Meeting Ho., 2006—08, com. mem., 2006—; selectman Lyndeborough, NH, 1999—2002; chmn. bd. selectmen, 2001—02. Recipient Govs. Citation, Gov. of the State of NH., 2000, Award for Excellence in Geography, Assn. of Am. Geographers and Nat. Coun. for Geog. Edn., 1991, Ellen Churchill Semple Geography award, Clark U., 1991, Paul P. Vouras Social Scis. award, 1991; Summer scholar, ND State Bd. of Higher Edn., 1992. Mem.: Assn. for Gravestone Studies, Soc. for Am. Baseball Rsch., Assn. Am. Geographers, Pioneer Am. Soc. (life; editor Pioneer Am. Soc. Transactions 2006—), Phi Kappa Phi, Phi Beta Kappa, Gamma Theta Upsilon (chpt. pres. pro tem 1991). Home: 157 Pettingill Hill Rd Lyndeborough NH 03082 Office: Castleton State Coll Dept History, Geography, Econs and Polit Castleton VT 05735

ROPER, WAYNE R., legislative staff member; Newspaper reporter/editor Ohio, Tex. & Greenville, SC, 1982—96; owner pvt. mktg. firm Precept Comm., 1998—2005; dist. dir. then chief of staff to congressman Bob Inglis US House of Reps., Washington, 2005—. Republican. Mailing: US House Reps 100 Cannon HOB Washington DC 20515 Office Phone: 202-225-6030. Office Fax: 202-225-1177. Business E-Mail: wayne.roper@mail.house.gov.*

ROPER, WILLIAM LEE, dean, preventive medicine physician, administrator; b. Birmingham, Ala., July 6, 1948; s. Richard Barnard and Jean (Fyfe) R.; m. Maryann Roper, Jan. 14, 1978 AA, Fla. Coll., 1968; BS, U. Ala, 1970, MD, 1974, M.P.H., 1981. Diplomate Am. Bd. Pediatrics, Am. Bd. Preventive Medicine. Intern, resident in pediatrics U. Colo. Med. Ctr., Denver, 1974-77; health officer Jefferson County Dept. Health, Birmingham, 1977-82, 83; White House fellow Washington, 1982-83; spl. asst. to Pres. for health policy, 1983-86; adminstr., Health Care Finance Adminstrn. HHS, Washington, 1986-89; dep. asst. to pres. for domestic policy The White House, Washington, 1989-90; adminstr. Agy. for Toxic Substances and Disease Registry and dir. Ctrs. for Disease Control and Prevention, Atlanta, 1990-93; sr. v.p. Prudential Health Care, Roseland, NJ, 1994-97; pres. Prudential Ctr. for Health Care Rsch., Atlanta, 1993-95; dean, sch. pub. health, prof. medicine and health policy U. NC, Chapel Hill, 1997—2004, dean Sch. Medicine, 2004—, vice chancellor med. affairs, 2004—, CEO U. NC Health Care, 2004—. Mem. Inst. Medicine, Phi Beta Kappa, Alpha Omega Alpha Republican. Office: Office of Dean U NC Med School 125 MacNider Bldg CB #7000 Chapel Hill NC 27599 Office Phone: 919-966-4161.*

ROPPEL, MARK, lawyer; b. Calgary, Can., Aug. 29, 1963; arrived in U.S., 1989; s. Howard Ross and Karen Elaine Roppel. Student, U. Alta., Edmonton, Can., 1981—84; LLB, BCL, McGill U., Montreal, 1988; LLM, Columbia U., NYC, 1990. Bar: NY. With LeBoeuf, Lamb, Greene & MacRae, NYC, 1990—94, Shearman & Sterling, NYC, 1994—2000, ptnr., 2000—05, Cadwalader, Wickersham & Taft, NYC, 2005—08; mng. ptnr. Beijing office, 2006—08; ptnr. Allen & Overy, Hong Kong, 2008—. Author: Practical Law Handbook, 2005—06, Corporate Governance & Client Strategies, 2007; contbr. articles to profl. jours. Mem.: ABA, Bar Assn City NY. Office: Allen & Overy 3 Exchange Sq 10th Fl Central Hong Kong Home: 2603 9Old Peak Rd Central Hong Kong Office Phone: 85229747360. Business E-Mail: mark.roppel@allenovery.com.

ROPSKI, GARY MELCHIOR, lawyer; b. Erie, Pa., Apr. 19, 1952; s. Joseph Albert and Irene Stefania (Mszanowski) R.; m. Barbara Mary Schleck, May 15, 1982. BS in Physics, Carnegie-Mellon U., 1972; JD cum laude, Northwestern U. Sch. Law, 1976. Bar: Ill. 1976, US Patent and Trademark Office 1976, US Dist. Ct. (no. dist.) Ill. 1976, US Ct. Appeals (7th cir.) 1977, US Dist. Ct. (ea. dist.) Wis. 1977, US Ct. Appeals (3d cir.) 1981, US Ct. Claims 1982, US Ct. Appeals (fed. cir.) 1982, US Supreme Ct. 1982, US Dist. Ct. (ea. dist.) Mich. 1984, US Dist. Ct. (no. dist.) Calif. 1986, US Dist. Ct. (we. dist.) Wis. 2008. Assoc. Brinks Hofer Gilson & Lione, Chgo., 1976-81, shareholder, 1981—, pres., 2006—. Adj. prof. patents and copyrights Northwestern U. Sch. Law, Chgo., 1982-97. Contbr. numerous articles to profl. jours. Mem. ABA, Internat. Bar Assn., Internat. Trademark Assn., Am. Intellectual Property Law Assn., Ill. Bar Assn., Intellectual Property Law Assn. Chgo., Chgo. Bar Assn., Univ. Club, Chgo. Yacht Club. Roman Catholic. Office: Brinks Hofer Gilson & Lione Ste 3600 455 N CityFront Plaza Dr Chicago IL 60611-5599 Office Phone: 312-321-4216. Business E-Mail: gropski@brinkshofer.com.

ROQUE, ELIANA MENDES S. TEIXEIRA, social worker, educator; b. Monte Alto, Sao Paulo, Brazil, Aug. 30, 1952; d. Manoel Mendes de Souza and Iracema Salvador Mendes de Souza; m. Jose Cassio Teixeira Roque, Sept. 2, 1995. Degree Law, U. de Ribeirão Preto, Sao Paulo, 1985. Cert. pub. Utility and Svcs. NY U., 1980, domestic violence U. Sao Paulo, 1985, PhD in pub. Health U. Sao Paulo, 2006. Jud. social worker Sao Paulo state law ct., Jardinópolis, 1993—; prof. U. Ribeirao Preto, 2000—08. Organizer and current cons. PROMAR, Jardinópolis. Office: Univ de Ribeirao Preto Avenida Costábile Romano 2201 Sao Paulo Ribeirao Preto 14096-900 Brazil Office Fax: 55 16 36036756. Business E-Mail: jkroque@uol.com.br.

ROQUE, FRANCIS XAVIER, bishop emeritus; b. Providence, Oct. 9, 1928; s. Warren Edward Roque and Mary Loretta Gallagher BA, Saint John's Sem., 1950. Ordained priest Diocese of Providence, RI, 1953, parish priest, 1953-61; army chaplain US Army, 1961-83; ordained bishop, 1983; bishop Archdiocese for Mil. Svcs. USA, Washington, 1983—2004, bishop emeritus, 2004—. Served to col. US Army, 1961-83, Vietnam Decorated Bronze Star Roman Catholic. Home: 255 Lansdowne Rd Warwick RI 02888-5703 E-mail: froque@milarch.org.

RORER, JOHN WHITELEY, publisher, consultant; b. Phila., Aug. 4, 1930; s. Ronald Erle and Hazel (Whiteley) R.; m. Beverly Case, June 6, 1953. BS, U. Pa., 1952; MBA, Drexel U., 1956. Credit analyst Phila. Nat. Bank, 1954-56; with Curtis Pub. Co., Phila., 1956-68; dir. purchasing Chilton Pub. Co., Phila., 1968-70; founding pres. Focus Bus. Weekly, Bus. News, Inc., Phila., 1968—, pres., pub., 1974—; owner Pubs. Systems Assocs., Upper Darby, Pa., 1979—. Mem. Phila. World Affairs Council, 1979—. Served to capt. U.S. Army, 1952-54. Mem. Nat. Assn. Bus. Publs. (co-founder, bd. dirs. 1978-81), Nat. Assn. Indsl. Advt., Mktg. and Communications Execs. Assn., Union League Club, Engrs. Club (Phila.), Downtown Club. Republican. Episcopalian. Avocation: economics research. Office: 1015 Chestnut St Philadelphia PA 19107-4316

RORICK, WILLIAM CALVIN, portrait artist, retired librarian; b. Elyria, Ohio, June 23, 1941; s. Harold R. and Edythe E. (Harris) R.; m. Anne L. Sherbondy, Aug. 21, 1971. BA in Econs. and Bus. Adminstrn., Ohio Wesleyan U., 1963; MusB in Music History and Lit., U. Utah, 1968; MusM in Music History and Lit., Northwestern U., 1970; MLS, Pratt Inst., 1974; MA in Musicology, NYU, 1982; studied portraiture, various art schs., workshops. Curator orchestral-choral libr., reference asst., office mgr. Manhattan Sch. Music Libr., NYC, 1970-74; music reference libr. CUNY Queens Coll. Music Libr., Flushing, 1974-96, instr., 1974-79, asst. prof., 1979-96, asst. prof. emeritus, 1996—, mem. senate nominating com., del.-at-large arts divsn., 1984-86. Portrait painting demonstrator and instructor, show juror various art orgns. Corp., instnl., pub. and pvt. portrait commns.; contbr. articles and revs. to profl. jours. Bd. deacons South Britain (Conn.) Congl. Ch., 1998—2001, historian, 2002. With US Army, 1964—66. Grantee Rsch. Found. CUNY, 1981-84; recipient regional and nat. art awards including Best in Show Conn. Classic Arts Assn. Mem.: Conn. Pastel Soc., Kent Art Assn. (bd. dirs. 2003—07, elected artist, mem. exhbn. com.), Acad. Artists Assn. (artist mem.), N.Y. Soc. Portrait Artists (mem. leadership team 2001—02), Conn. Soc. Portrait Artists (founding mem. 2002—, sec. 2008—), Portrait Soc. Atlanta, Portrait Soc. of Am., Inc., Soc. Creative Artists of Newtown (corr. sec. 1999—2002), Conn. Classic Arts, Inc. (publicity chmn. 1996—99), Sonneck Soc., Am. Soc. Portrait Artists, Music Libr. Assn. (program chmn. Greater N.Y. chpt. 1977—79, mem. nat. subcom. on basic music collection 1977—79, sec.-treas. 1979—81, chmn. nat. membership com. 1979—82, chpt. chmn. 1983—85, mem. Music Pub. Assn. joint com. 1986—88), Libr. Assn. CUNY (chmn. grants com. 1978—80, mem. publ. com. 1979—81, editor Directory 1980—81, del. 1983—85), Internat. Assn. Music Libr., Assn. for Recorded Sound Collections, Am. Printing History Assn., Am. Musicological Soc., Portrait Clubs Am. (cert. leader-instr. 2003—, Greater Southbury chpt.), Beta Phi Mu, Phi Mu Alpha Sinfonia. Home and Studio: 63 Beacon Hill Dr Southbury CT 06488-1914 Office Phone: 203-264-4380. Personal E-mail: williamrorick@aol.com.

RORIG, KURT JOACHIM, chemist, science association director; b. Bremerhaven, Germany, Dec. 1, 1920; came to U.S., 1924, naturalized, 1929; s. Robert Herman and Martha (Grundke) R.; m. Helen Yonan, Mar. 20, 1949; children: James, Elizabeth, Miriam. BS, U. Chgo., 1942; MA, Carleton Coll., 1944; PhD, U. Wis., 1947. Lectr. Loyola U., Chgo., 1950-62; chemist to dir. Chem. Research G.D. Searle & Co., Chgo., 1947-87; pres. Chemo-Delphic Cons. Ltd., Chgo., 1987—. Adj. prof. chemistry U. Ill., Chgo., 1989—. Patentee in field. Mem. Sch. Bd., Wilmette, Ill., 1969-71. Mem. Am. Chem. Soc. (dir. Chgo. sect.), Am. Soc. Pharm. and Exptl. Therapeutics, N.Y. Acad. Scis., AAAS, Chgo. Chemists Club (past pres.) Presbyterian. Home and Office: 337 Hager Ln Glenview IL 60025-3329 Home Phone: 847-724-2808; Office Phone: 847-724-2808. E-mail: hrorig1@comcast.net.

RORKE-ADAMS, LUCY BALIAN, pathologist, educator; b. St. Paul, June 22, 1929; d. Aram Haji and Karzouhy (Ousdigian) Balian; m. Robert Radcliffe Rorke, June 4, 1960 (dec. Mar. 31, 2002); m. Boyce M. Adams, Apr. 16, 2004 (dec. June 21, 2006). AB, U. Minn., Mpls., 1951, MA, 1952, BS, 1955, MD, 1957. Diplomate Am. Bd. Pathology. Intern Phila. Gen. Hosp., 1957-58, resident anat. pathology and neuropathology, 1958-62, asst. neuropathologist, 1963-67, chief pediat. pathologist, 1967-68, chief neuropathologist, 1968-69, chmn. dept. anat. pathology and chief neuropathologist, 1969-73, chmn. dept. pathology, 1973-77, pres. med. staff, 1973-75; neuropathologist Children's Hosp., Phila., 1965—, pres. med. staff, 1986-88, acting pathologist-in-chief, 1995-2000. Cons. neuropathologist Wyeth Rsch. Labs., Radnor, Pa., 1961—87, Wistar Inst. Anatomy and Biology, Phila., 1967—93; assoc. prof. pathology U. Pa. Sch. Medicine, Phila., 1970—, prof. pathology, 1973—, clin. prof. neurology, 1979—, clin. prof. pediat., 1997—; forensic neuropathologist Office Med. Examiner, Phila., 1977—2004. Author: Myelinization of the Brain in the Newborn, 1969, Pathology of Perinatal Brain Injury, 1982; mem. editl. bd. Jours. Neuropathology Exptl. Neurology, 1980—85, 1993—98, Pediat. Neurosurgery, 1984—2002, Child's Nervous Sys., 1984—88, Brain Pathology, 1990—95; contbr. articles to profl. jours. Recipient Provost's award for excellence in tchg., U. Pa., 2003; NIH fellow, 1961—62, NIH grantee, 1963—68. Fellow: Coll. Am. Pathologists; mem.: AMA, Phila. Coll. Physicians (trustee 2002—04, treas. 2004—), Burlington County Med. Soc., Am. Neurol. Soc., Am. Soc. Neuroradiology (hon.), Am. Assn. Neuropathologists (exec. coun. 1976—85, v.p. 1979—80, pres. 1981—82, Meritorious Svc. award 1999), Phila. Neurol. Soc. (v.p. 1971—72, editor transactions 1973, pres. 1975—76, Richard D. Wood Disting. Alumina award 2007). Office: Childrens Hosp Phila 324 S 34th St Philadelphia PA 19104-4399 Home: 316 E Maple Ave Moorestown NJ 08057-2014 Business E-Mail: Rorke@email.chop.edu.

RORSCHACH, KIMBERLY, museum director; m. John Hart; 2 children. BA, Brandeis U.; PhD in art hist., Yale U. Curator Phila. Mus. Art, Rosenbach Mus. & Libr., Phila.; Dana Feitler dir. Smart Mus. Art, U. Chgo., 1994—2004; dir. Nasher Mus. Art, Duke U., Durham, NC, 2004—. Mem.: Assn. Art Mus. Dirs. (trustee). Office: Nasher Mus Art PO Box 90732 Durham NC 27708 Office Phone: 919-684-8420. E-mail: kim.rorschach@duke.edu.

RORSCHACH, RICHARD GORDON, lawyer; b. Tulsa, Aug. 9, 1928; s. Harold Emil and Margaret (Hermes) R.; m. Martha Kay King, Dec. 23, 1979; children by previous marriage: Richard Helm, Reagan Cartwright, Andrew Maxwell. BS, MIT, 1950; MS, U. Okla., 1952; JD, U. Houston, 1961. Bar: Tex. 1961; lic. prof. engr., Tex. Cons. civil engr. Freese & Nichols, Ft. Worth, 1955; cons. engr. Freese, Nichols & Turner, Houston, 1955-56; petroleum engr. Marathon Oil Co., Bay City, Tex., 1956-57, Houston, 1957-61, atty., 1961-64; ptnr. Broady, Kells & Rorschach, Houston, 1964-68, Ragan, Russell & Rorschach, Houston, 1968-80, R.G. Rorschach & Assocs., Kilgore, Tex., 1980—. Mem. exec. com. Colonial Royalties Co., Tulsa, 1970-77; officer Little River Oil & Gas Co., 1980-88; mng. ptnr. Pentagon Oil Co., 1988—; pres. Nat. Assn. Royalty Owners-Tex., 1993-96, trustee, 2004-05; chmn. Nat. Assn. Royalty Owners, Inc., 1996-99, bd. dirs., 1999-2000, adv. bd. dirs., 2004-05; mem. exec. com. Nat. Assn. Royalty Owners, Inc.; owner, breeder, exhibitor Arabian Horses Shadowbrook Farm, Kilgore, Tex., 1980—. Author: How to Protect Your Royalty Interests: Texas Perspectives, Vols. 1 & 2, 2002, The Ultimate Royalty Owner's Guide: A Manual of Procedure and Operation. 1st lt. CE US Army, 1952—54, Korea. Mem. ASME, ASCE, Tex. Bar Assn., Rotary Club (pres. Kilgore chpt. 1984-85), Sigma Xi, Sigma Alpha Epsilon. Republican. Presbyterian. Avocations: fly fishing, fly tying, golf, tennis. Home: 1893 CR 186 East Kilgore TX 75662-9023 Office: 1100 Stone Rd PO Box 1934 Kilgore TX 75663-1934

ROSA, EUGENE ANTHONY, sociologist, environmental scientist, educator, artist; b. Canandaigua, NY, Sept. 20, 1941; s. Louis Gastaldo and Flora Louise (Brevette) R.; m. Jody Ross, Sept. 7, 1985 (div. 1993). BS, Rochester Inst. Tech., 1967; MA, Syracuse U., 1975, PhD, 1976. Research assoc., instr. Stanford U., 1976-78; from asst. to prof. Wash. State U., Pullman, 1978—, prof., 1993—. Cons. Brookhaven Nat. Lab., Upton, N.Y., 1978—, Nuclear Regulatory Commn., Washington, 1978—; vis. prof. London Sch. Econs., 1988, U. Klagenfurt, 1996, 99, U. Stuttgart, 2002, IFF-Viena, 2008, U. Montesquieu - Bordeaux IV, 2009; adj. prof. Nat. Des Sci. Politiques, 2008; chmn. dept., 1996-2001, Edward R. Meyer Disting. prof. natural resources and environ. policy Wash. State U., Pullman, 1996—. Co-author: Risk, Uncertainity and Rational Action, 2001; editor: Public Reactions to Nuclear Power, 1984, Pub. Reactions to Nuclear Waste, 1993; bd. dirs. several profl. jours.; contbr. articles to profl. jours. Mem. nuc. waste adv. coun. Wash. State, 1987—92; mem. NAS Nuclear and Radiation Studies Bd., 2002—, Human Dimensions of Global Change Com., 2004—. Fellow: AAAS; mem.: Soc. Risk Analysis, Soc. for Human Ecology, Internat. Soc. Assn., Sociol. Rsch. Assn., Am. Sociol. Assn. (Disting. Contbn. award), Sigma Xi. Avocations: conceptual art, skiing, collecting native masks, collecting fine art, gardening. Home: 510 East C St Moscow ID 83843 Office: Wash State U Dept Sociology Pullman WA 99164-4020 Home Phone: 208-882-3411; Office Phone: 509-335-4163. Business E-Mail: rosa@wsu.edu.

ROSA, JOHN WILLIAM, academic administrator, career military officer; m. Donna Kangeter; children: Jonathan, Brad. BA in Bus. Adminstrn., The Citadel, 1973; M in Pub. Adminstrn., Golden Gate U., 1985. Commd. 2d. lt. USAF, 1973, advanced through grades to lt. gen., 2003; A-7D pilot, scheduler, weapons officer 353rd Tactical Fighter Fighter Squadron, Myrtle Beach AFB, SC, 1975-77; A-10 pilot 356th Tactical Fighter Squadron, Myrtle Beach AFB, 1977—78; weapons officer 353rd Tactical Figher Squadron, Myrtle Beach AFB, 1979—80; pilot Hunter and Jaguar Aircraft, RAF Lossiemouth, Scotland, 1980-81; weapons instr. RAF Lossiemouth, 1981-83; instr. pilot, weapons officer, flight comdr. 61st Tactical Fighter Tng. Squadron, MacDill AFB, Fla., 1983-86; programmer, dir. of programs and resources Hdqrs. USAF, Washington, 1987-90; comdr. 35th Tactical Fighter Squadron, Kunsan AB, Korea, 1991-92, 366th Ops. Support Squadron, Mountain Home AFB, Idaho, 1992, dep. comdr., 1992-93; dep. comdr. to comdr. 49th Ops. Group, Holloman AFB, N.Mex., 1994-95; comdr. 20th Fighter Wing, Shaw AFB, SC, 1995-97; inspector gen. Hdqrs. Pacific Air Forces, Hickman AFB, Hawaii, 1997-98; comdt. Air Command and State Coll., Air U., Maxwell AFB, Ala., 1998—2000; comdr. 347th Wing, Moody AFB, Ga., 2000—01, 347th Rescue Wing, Moody AFB, 2001; dep. dir. ops. Ops. Directorate, the Joint Staff, Washington, DC, 2001—03; supt. USAF Acad., Colorado Springs, 2003—05; pres. The Citadel, Mil. Coll. of SC, Charleston, 2005—. Decorated Def. Superior Svc. award, Meritorious Svc. medal with four oak leaf clusters, Air Force Commendation medal, Legion of Merit with oak leaf cluster, Combat Readiness medal with two oak clusters. Office: The Citadel Office of Pres 171 Moultrie St Charleston SC 29409 Office Phone: 843-225-3294.*

ROSA, RAYMOND ULRIC, retired banker; b. New Britain, Conn., Jan. 30, 1927; s. Kenneth E. and Regina (Chenette) R.; m. Irene M. Asselin, Feb. 5, 1949; children: R. James, David M., Cathryn P., Michael F., Nancy A., Kenneth E. AS, Hillyer Coll., 1949. CPA, Conn. Pvt. practice pub. accounting, Manchester, Conn., 1949-52; auditor Auditors of Pub. Accounts, State of Conn., Hartford, 1952-65; dir. Fed.-State Relations Dept. Finance and Control, Conn., 1965-69; dep. commr. Finance and Control, Conn., 1969-71; sr. v.p., auditor Soc. Savings, Hartford, 1971-90, ret., 1990. Mem. Windsor Locks (Conn.) Bd. Fin., 1973—81; pres. Savs. Bank Forum, 1981—82; trustee, sec.-treas. Mease Manor, Inc., Dunedin, Fla., 1995—2001, vice chmn., 2001—03, chmn., 2003—05. Treas. Mental Health Assn. Conn., 1974-77, v.p., 1977-80, pres., 1980-83; bd. dirs. Nat. Assn. Mental Health, 1977-85, v.p. region 1, 1982-83; bd. dirs. Combined Health Appeal of Greater Hartford, 1982-90. Served with USNR, 1944-46. Mem. AICPA, Conn. Soc. CPAs, Conn. Soc. Govtl. Accts., KC, Dunedin Country Club (bd. dirs. 1997-2000, v.p. 1998-99, pres. 1999-00), Suffield Country Club (bd. govs. 1984-91). Home: 2060 Golf View Dr Dunedin FL 34698-2330 Business E-Mail: rrosa1@tampabay.rr.com.

ROSA, ROBERT H., JR., ophthalmologist, medical educator, researcher; b. San Antonio, Oct. 27, 1964; s. Robert H. and Rosita L. Rosa; m. Maria B. Uryga; children: Zachary A., Matthew L., Cara Beth. BS, Tex. A&M U., College Station, 1986; MD, Tex. A&M Health Sci. Ctr., College Station, 1990. Diplomate Am. Bd. Ophthalmology, 1996. Intern internal medicine Scott & White Meml. Hosp., Tex. A&M Health Sci. Ctr., Temple, 1990—91; resident ophthalmology Bascom Palmer Eye Inst., U. Miami Sch. Medicine, Fla., 1991—94, asst. prof., clin. ophthalmology, 1996—2000, dir., ocular pathology lab., 1996—2000, dir., rsch. histology lab., 1997—99; fellow, ophthalmic pathology Wilmer Eye Inst., Johns Hopkins U., Balt., 1994—95; fellow, med. retina Moorfields Eye Hosp., U. London, 1995—96; assoc. prof., ophthalmology and surgery, Tex. A&M Health Sci. Ctr. Scott & White Eye Inst., Temple, 2000—08, dir., divsn. ophthalmic pathology, 2000—, asst. dir., ophthalmology residency program, 2002—, vice-chair rsch., dept. ophthalmology, 2008—; prof. ophthalmology and surgery Tex. A&M Health Sci. Ctr., 2008—. Med. dir. Fla. Lions Eye Bank, Miami, 1996—2000. Com. chair, BCSC sect. 4, ophthalmic pathology and intra-ocular tumors Am. Acad. Ophthalmology, 2004—08. Recipient First Yr. Resident Tchg. award, Bascom Palmer Eye Inst., U. Miami Sch. Medicine, 1998—99, Ross Carr Meml. award, Fla. Lions Eye Bank, 1999—2000, Chief's award, Scott & White Eye Inst., Tex. A&M Health Sci. Ctr., 2003—04, Physician FOCUS award, Scott & White Bd. Dirs., 2004—06, K08 award, Nat. Eye Inst., Nat. Insts. Health, 2007, Achievement award, Am. Acad. Opthalmology, 2008; named Tex. Super Drs., 2008—09; named one of America's Top Ophthalmologists, Consumers' Rsch. Coun. America, 2006—07. Fellow: Am. Acad. Ophthalmology; mem.: AMA, Tex. Ophthal. Assn., Tex. Med. Assn., Am. Assn. Ophthalmic Pathologists, Verhoeff Zimmerman Soc., Assn. Rsch. Vision and Ophthalmology. Achievements include research in retinal vasoregulation; macular degeneration; diabetic retinopathy. Office: Scott & White Eye Inst 2401 S 31st St Temple TX 76508

ROSADO, MARIA ARAYA, anthropologist, educator; b. Santiago, Chile, June 11, 1958; d. Hector Manuel Araya and Maria Palmina Trasatti; m. Victor Manuel Rosado, Apr. 9, 1983; children: James Michael, Victoria Helena Araya. PhD, Rutgers U., NB, NJ, 1994. Prof., anthropology Rowan U., Glassboro, NJ, 1993—. Adj. investigator Museo Arqueologico de La Serena, La Serena, Chile, 1991—. Contbr.

articles to profl. jours. Mem.: Paleopathology Assn., Archaeological Soc. NJ. Avocations: gardening, travel. Office: Rowan Univ 201 Mullica Hill Rd Glassboro NJ 08028 Business E-Mail: rosado@rowan.edu.

ROSADO, ROSSANA, publishing executive, editor-in-chief; b. Bronx, NY; married; 2 children. BA in Journalism, Pace U. Prodr. pub. affairs programming Sta. WPIX-TV, NYC, 1988, pub. svc. dir.; reporter El Diario/La Prensa, NYC, editor-in-chief, 1995—, gen. mgr., pub., 1999—. Prodr.: (TV series) Best Talk in Town; contbr. articles to mags. V.p. pub. affairs Health and Hosps. Corp., NYC, 1992. Recipient STAR award, N.Y. Women's Agenda, Emmy award, Broadcaster's award, N.Y. State, Folio award; named one of The 100 Most Influential Women in NYC Bus., Crain's NY Bus., 2007. Office: EL Diario La Prensa LLC 1 Metrotech CTR Brooklyn NY 11201-3831

ROSALDO, RENATO IGNACIO, JR., cultural anthropology educator; b. Champaign, Ill., Apr. 15, 1941; s. Renato Ignacio and Mary Elizabeth (Potter) R.; m. Michelle Sharon Zimbalist, June 12, 1966 (dec. Oct. 1981); children: Samuel Mario, Manuel Zimbalist; m. Mary Louise Pratt, Nov. 26, 1983; 1 child, Olivia Emilia Rosaldo-Pratt. AB, Harvard U., 1963, PhD, 1971. Asst. prof. cultural anthropology Stanford (Calif.) U., 1970-76, assoc. prof., 1976-85, prof., 1985—2003, Mellon prof. interdisciplinary studies, 1987-90, dir. Ctr. for Chicano Rsch., 1985-90, chair anthropology, 1994-96, Lucie Stern prof. social scis., 1993—. Author: Ilongot Headhunting 1883-1974, 1980, Culture and Truth, 1989, Prayer to Spider Woman/Rezo a la mujer araña, 2003, Remote Rosaldo:Eusayos de Antropoiogia Critica, 2006. Recipient Harry Benda prize Assn. for Asian Studies, 1983 Am. Book award, 2004; Guggenheim fellow, 1993. Fellow Am. Acad. Arts and Scis. Avocations: poetry, swimming, drawing, dance. Office: NYU Dept Anthropology 25 Waverly Pl New York NY 10003-6790 Home: 230 Ashland Pl Apt 12a Brooklyn NY 11217-1141 Business E-Mail: rr86@nyu.edu.

ROSALES, MONICA D., social studies educator; b. Hialeah, Fla., Oct. 24, 1974; d. Roberto F. and Maria A. Valdes; m. Ivan J. Rosales, Aug. 29, 1992; children: Ivan R., Marilyn I. AA in Secondary Edn., Miami Dade Coll., 1999; B Social Studies Edn., Fla. Internat. U., 2003, MA in History, 2006. Cert. grades 6-12 social studies tchr. Fla. Social studies tchr. Doral Mid. Sch., Miami, Fla., 2003—. Screenwriter Revolution. Mem. Fla. Media Market, 2007—08. Named Tchr. of Yr., Miami-Dade Coun. for Social Studies, Mid. Sch., 2007, Doral Mid. Sch., 2008, Daus. Am. Rev., 2008. Mem.: AFLCIO, NEA, Fla. Media Market, Fla. Edn. Assn., Am. Fedn. Teachers, United Teachers Dade (Doral Mid. Sch. Rookie Tchr. of Yr. 2004), Nat. Coun. Social Studies, Nat. Assn. Latino Ind. Producers (writers group coord. 2003—06).

ROSALES, VERONICA, language educator; b. Cuernavaca, Morelos, Mex., Apr. 13, 1969; arrived in US, 1992; d. Jose Francisco Rosales and Hermelinda Hernandez; m. Glenn D. Gonzalez (div.). AA, Moraine Valley CC, Palos Hills, Ill., 2002; BA, Northeastern Ill. U., Chgo., 2005; degree, U. Ill., Chgo., 2007; MS in Linguistic, TESOL Concentration, 2007. ESL tutor Chgo. Commons, 1994—95, ESL tchr., 1995—97; vocat. ESL instr. Summer Consulting, Chgo., 1997—99, Inst. Latino Progress, Chgo., 1999—2000; ESL tchr., coord. Chgo. Com., 2000—07, Assn. House Chgo., 2007—. Avocations: reading, bicycling, swimming, jogging, chess. Home: 2100 N Lamon Chicago IL 60639 Office: Assn House Chgo 1116 N Kedzie Ave Chicago IL 60651 Office Phone: 773-772-7170.

ROSALES HERRERA, RAÚL JOAQUIN, language educator; b. NYC, June 29, 1978; s. Jose Joaquin and Paula Rosales. BA, Drew U., 1999; MA, Columbia U., 2000, MPhil, 2001, PhD, 2007. Tchg. fellow Spanish Columbia U., NYC, 2000—05; asst. prof. Spanish Drew U., Madison, NJ, 2004—. Adj. instr. Spanish New Sch. U., NYC, 2003—05; mem. Columbia U., Lang. Program Com., Dept. Spanish, 2003—05. Summer Rsch. fellowship, Columbia U., 2002—05. Mem.: Popular Culture Assn., Am. Assn. Tchrs. Spanish and Portugese, Rocky Mt. Modern Lang. Assn., Modern Lang. Assn. Office: Drew U Dept Spanish 36 Madison Ave Madison NJ 07940 Home: 42 F Loantaka Way Madison NJ 07940 Office Phone: 973-408-3751. Personal E-mail: raulrh29@gmail.com.

ROSALSKY, BARBARA ELLEN, artist, community health nurse; b. NYC, Nov. 16, 1948; d. Ellis M. Rosalsky and Claire (Schwartz) Rosalsky Shapiro; m. Dennis Robinson (div.). BA, SUNY, Plattsburgh, 1970. Sales girl Cambridge Artist Art Supply Store, Mass., 1970—71; artist Pillar of Fire mag., Zarephath, NJ, 1977; home health aide CMR, Bound Brook, NJ, 1978—; designer New Brunswick Tomorrow, NJ, 1980—93; art therapist Middlesex Hosp., New Brunswick, 1981—83; vol. office Robert Wood Johnson Hosp., 1995—2008. One-woman shows include The Bird and Me, 1980, Highland Pk. Libr., N.J., The City, 2003, exhibited in group shows at Other Artists Other Art, Robeson Newark Gallery, N.J., 1983, Greeter State Theatre, 2007—09. Mem. Cultural Arts Commn., Piscataway, N.J., 1993-2007; mem. Ams. for the Arts Action Fund, 2006-09. SUNY Plattsburgh scholar, 1970. Mem.: Women's Caucus Art, Quality Inn Swim Club. Democrat. Avocations: piano, swimming, dance, print making. Home: 114 Woodland Rd Piscataway NJ 08854-4222

ROSAND, DAVID, art historian, educator; b. Bklyn., Sept. 6, 1938; s. Johan Herbert and Frieda (Grotenstein) R.; m. Ellen Fineman, June 18, 1961; children: Jonathan, Eric. AB, Columbia Coll., 1959; MA, Columbia U., 1962, PhD, 1965. Instr. art history Columbia U., NYC, 1964-67, asst. prof., 1967-69, assoc. prof., 1969-73, prof., 1973-95, chmn. Soc. of Fellows in the Humanities, 1979-83, Meyer Schapiro prof. art history, 1995—. Co-author (with Michelangelo Muraro): Titian and the Venetian Woodcut, 1976, Titian, 1978; author: Painting in Cinquecento Venice: Titian, Veronese Tintoretto, 1982, rev. edit., 1997; author: (with others) Places of Delight: The Pastoral Landscape, 1988; author: The Meaning of the Mark: Leonardo and Titian, 1988, Painting in Sixteenth-Century Venice, rev. edit., 1997, Robert Motherwell on Paper, 1997, Myths of Venice: The Figuration of a State, 2001, Drawing Acts: Studies in Graphic Expression and Representation, 2002, The Invention of Painting in America, 2004; editor: Titian: His World and His Legacy, 1982; editor: (with Robert W. Hanning) Castiglione: The Ideal and the Real in Renaissance Culture, 1983; editor: Interpretazioni Veneziane, 1984. Mem. bd. advisors CASVA Nat. Gallery Art., 1990-94. Fulbright Commn. fellow, 1962-63; NEH fellow, 1971-72, 85-86, 91-92; John S. Guggenheim Meml. Found. fellow, 1974-75. Mem.: Dedams Found. (bd. dirs.), Am. Acad. Arts and Scis., Renaissance Soc. Am. (mem. exec. bd. 1981—, Paul Oskar Kristeller award for lifetime achievement 2007), Coll. Art Assn. Am., Istituto Veneto di Scienze, Lettere ed Arti (fgn.), Ateneo Veneto (fgn.), Save Venice, Inc. (bd. dirs.). Home: 560 Riverside Dr New York NY 10027-3212 Office: Columbia U Dept Art History & Archaeology 826 Schermerhorn Hall Mail Code 5517 New York NY 10027 Home Phone: 212-222-9915; Office Phone: 212-854-4502. Business E-Mail: dr17@columbia.edu.

ROSANIO, SALVATORE, cardiologist, educator; b. Benevento, Italy, Nov. 23, 1962; 1 child, Ginevra Victoria. Prof. medicine in cardiology U. Tex. Med. Br., Galveston, Tex., 2003—. Fellow: Am. Coll. Cardiology, European Cardiologists. Achievements include research in cardiac pacing and primary prevention of sudden death. Office: The University of Texas Medical Branch 301 University boulevard Galveston TX 77553-0553 Office Fax: 409-772-4982. E-mail: sarosani@utmb.edu.

ROSARIO, BEDDA L., statistician; b. San Juan, Jan. 5, 1977; d. Osvaldo Rosario and Bedda Rivera; m. Emilio F. Zegarra, July 16, 2005. BS, U. PR, San Juan, 1999, MPhil, 2000; PhD, U. Pitts., 2008. Lectr. statis. analysis U. PR, Med. Scis. Campus, San Juan, 2000—01; bio statistician trainee, cancer inst. U. Pitts., 2003—04, grad. student rschr., med. ctr., 2004—08. Pastoral coun. mem. St. Regis Parish, Pitts., 2007—08; sec. Latin Am. Cultural Union, Pitts., 2003—05; mem. Soc. Hispanic Profl. Engrs., Pitts., 2004—06. Mem.: Am. Statis. Assn. Avocations: travel, movies, dance.

ROSARIO-OLMEDO, CARMEN GLORIA, principal; b. Mayaguez, PR, Jan. 4, 1940; d. Rafael and Emilia (Derieux) Rosario; m. William Galindo, Apr. 19, 1968 (div. 1974); m. Ruben Eduardo Olmedo, Dec. 25, 1976. BA, CCNY, 1963; MA, NYU, 1982; profl. diploma, L.I. U., 1987. Cert. elem. prin., asst. prin., sch. dist. adminstr., sch. adminstr. and supr., permanent tchg. cert., N.Y.C. Tchr. N.Y.C. Bd. Edn., 1963-89, asst. prin., 1989-95, prin. I.A., 1995-97, prin., 1997—2001. Curriculum designer Cmty. Sch. Dist. 17, Bklyn., 1965-66, tchr. trainer, 1967-70; exch. tchr. trainer, San Juan, P.R., 1970-71; founder, artistic dir. Children in the Arts, Bklyn., 1979-86; coord. sch. vol. program Pub. Sch. 316, Bklyn., 1988-95. Contbr.: The Mexican Family, 1979, The Chilean Family Structure, 1982. Mem. Puerto Rican Educator's Assn., NYC, 1979—, Atlas, NYC, 1972—93; mem. internat. com. YMCA, NYC, 2002—05, mem. global teens com., 2003—05; mem. Nat. Conf. Puerto Rican Women, 1998—. Recipient Women's Hist. Month award, Borough Pres. Office, 1986, McDonald cert. of appreciation, Anonymous Heroes of our Cmty., 1989, cert. of recognition, NYC Adminstrv. Women in Edn., 1989, NYC Coun. Proclamation award, 2002, Bklyn. Borough Pres. Citation, 2002, NY State Senate 20th Dist. award, 2002, NY State Exec. Chamber Cert. of Merit, 2002, Cmty. Dist. 17 Dedicated Svc. award, 2001, Admin. of Yr. award, Fordham U. chpt., Phi Delta Kappa, 2001; Fulbright scholar, Mex., 1972, Chile, 1982, NDEA grantee, U.S. Office Edn. Inst. for Tchg. Disadvantaged Children, 1965—66, Operation Understanding exch. program grantee, NYC Bd. Edn., 1970—71. Mem. ASCD, Counsel of Supervisors and Adminstrs., Nat. Assn. P.R. Women, Hispanic Orgn. Latino Actors, Fulbright Assn. (life). Achievements include benefactor to numerous animal welfare and humane causes. Avocations: acting, anthropology, artist, travel, writer, archaeology, gourmet cooking. Home: 176 Prospect Park W Brooklyn NY 11215-5285 Office: CGO Prop Corp Brooklyn NY Office Phone: 917-815-8424. E-mail: cgoprop@aol.com.

ROSASCHI, JIM, librarian; b. Alma, Mich., Apr. 4, 1949; s. Mary Henry and True Rosaschi; m. Gaylene Reynolds, Aug. 22, 1975; children: Nicole, Daniel, Michelle, Emma. MLS, Brigham Young U., 1979. Cert. K-12 tchrg. Calif., 1982. Dir. Nampa Pub. Libr., Idaho, 1979—82; mgr. Petaluma br. libr. Sonoma County Libr., Sana Rosa, Calif., 1982—85, mgr. ext. svcs. Santa Rosa, 1985—89, mgr. tech. svcs., 1989—2006, mgr. info. tech. divsn., 2007—08; project mgr. Yolo County Libr., Woodland, Calif., 2008—. Pres. Customers of Dynix, Inc., Salt Lake City, 2003; libr. tech. presentations, Melbourne, Australia, 03, Edinburgh, 04. Adult sunday sch. tchr. Ch. of Jesus Christ of Latter-Day Saints, Santa Rosa, 1998—2002. With US Army, 1969—72. Mem.: Calif. Libr. Assn., ALA, Mormon History Assn. Home: 925 Hyland Dr Santa Rosa CA 95404

ROSATO, ANTHONY DOMINICK, mechanical engineer, educator; b. Bklyn., Aug. 28, 1953; s. Michael Joseph and Betty (Rispoli) R. BME, Pratt Inst., 1975; MS in Theoretical and Applied Mechanics, Northwestern U., 1979; MS in Applied Maths., Carnegie Mellon U., 1981, PhD in Mech. Engring., 1985. Devel. engr. Green Fan Co., Beacon, NY, 1975—77; rsch. asst. dept. civil engring. Northwestern U., Evanston, Ill., 1977—79; tchg. asst. mech. engring. and maths. Carnegie Mellon U., Pitts., 1979—82, rsch. asst., 1981—84, rsch. assoc. dept. mech. engring., 1985—86; adj. faculty dept. exact scis. Carlow Coll., Pitts., 1986; asst. prof. mech. engring. NJ Inst. Tech., Newark, 1987—93, assoc. prof. mech. engring., 1993—2002, prof. mech. engring., 2002—, dir. Particle Tech. Ctr., 1995—99, coord. undergrad. rsch. in mech. engring., 2000—02, dir. Granular Sci. Lab., 2000—; vice chair faculty coun. NJIT, 2006—07, chair, 2007—. Faculty Gov.'s Sch. in Scis., Drew U., Madison, N.J., 1988; vis. faculty fellow, physicist dept. earth scis. Lawrence Livermore (Calif.) Nat. Lab., 1989, 90; Joliot professorship Ecole Superieure de Physique et de Chimie Industrielles, Laboratoire H.M.P., Paris, 1994; mem. nat. materials adv. bd. NRC, 1995; vis. scientist The Lovelace Insts., Albuquerque, 1995-96; vis. assoc. prof. mech. engring. Worcester Poly. Inst., 1995; assoc. chmn. mech. engring. grad. studies, N.J. Inst. Tech., 2001-2003; vice chair faculty coun. NJIT, 2006-07; vis. scholar Stanford U., 2003, organising com. mem. Powders and Grains, 2009, mem. J calandra Italian Am. Inst. Editor-in-chief Mechanics Rsch. Comms.; mem. editl. bd. Internat. Jour. Nonlinear Sci. and Numerical Simulation. Chair sci. com. IUTAM Symposium, Cape May, N.J., 1999. Vis. scholar mech. engring, Stanford U., 2003. Fellow ASME; mem. Am. Soc. Engring. Edn. (program chair elect grad. studes divsn. 1995), Am. Acad. Mechanics, ASCE Engr. Mechanics Inst., N.J. Inst. Tech. Ctr. for Applied Maths., Sigma Xi, Tau Beta Pi, Pi Tau Sigma. Roman Catholic. Office: NJ Inst Tech Mech Engring Dept University Heights Newark NJ 07102 Office Phone: 973-596-5829. Business E-Mail: rosato@njit.edu.

ROSAZZA, PETER ANTHONY, bishop; b. New Haven, Feb. 13, 1935; s. Aldo Massimiliano and Agatha Dolores (Dinneen) Rosazza. Student, Dartmouth Coll.; AA, St. Thomas Sem., Bloomfield, Conn., 1955; BA, St. Bernard Sem., Rochester, NY, 1957; postgrad., Seminaire Saint Sulpice, Paris; MA, Middlebury Coll., 1967. Ordained priest Archdiocese of Hartford, Conn., 1961; asst. pastor St. Timothy Ch., West Hartford, Conn., 1961-63; instr. modern langs. St. Thomas Sem., 1963-72; co-pastor Sacred Heart Ch., Hartford, Conn., from 1972; dir. Apostolate to Hispanics for Archdiocese of Hartford, 1972-78; ordained bishop, 1978; aux. bishop Archdiocese of Hartford, 1978—. Bd. dirs. Archdiocesan Office Urban Affairs. Mem. Nat. Conf. Cath. Bishops, US Cath. Conf. Roman Catholic. Office: Hosp of St Raphael 1450 Chapel St New Haven CT 06511-4440

ROSBE, KRISTINA W., pediatric otolaryngologist, surgeon; BA magna cum laude, Wellesley Coll., Mass., 1989; MD, Dartmouth Med. Sch., Hanover, NH, 1993. Diplomate Am. Bd. Otolaryngology-Head and Neck Surgery, lic. Calif. Resident gen. surgery U. NC Hosp., Chapel Hill, 1993—94, resident otolaryngology, 1994—98; fellowship pediat. otolaryngology Children's Hosp., Boston, 1998—2000; assoc. prof. U. Calif. San Francisco, dir. divsn. pediat otolaryngology, 2002—. Contbr. articles to profl. jours. Mem.: Am. Acad. Pediat., Soc. Ear, Nose, & Throat Advances in Children, Am. Soc. Pediat. Otolaryngology, Am. Acad. Otolaryngology— Head & Neck Surgery. Achievements include research in the association between neonatal upper airway symptoms and laryngopharyngeal reflux; sinus disease and hearing loss in patients with cystic fibrosis. Mailing: U Calif Pediat Otolaryngology 1300 S Eliseo Dr Ste 204 Greenbrae CA 94904 Office Phone: 415-353-2757. Business E-Mail: krosbe@ohns.ucsf.edu.

ROSCH, JOHN THOMAS (TOM), commissioner, lawyer; b. Council Bluffs, Iowa, Oct. 4, 1939; s. H.P. and Phebe Florence (Jamison) Rosch; m. Carolyn Lee, Aug. 18, 1961; children: Thomas Lee, Laura Lee. BA, Harvard U., 1961, LLB, 1965. Bar: Calif. 1966, US Dist. Ct. No. Dist. Calif. 1966, US Dist. Ct. Ea. Dist. Calif. 1967, US Ct. Appeals 9th cir. 1966. Assoc. McCutchen, Doyle, Brown & Enersen, San Francisco, 1965-72, ptnr., 1972-73, 75-93; dir. Bur. Consumer Protection FTC, Washington, 1973—75; ptnr. Latham & Watkins, San Francisco, 1994—2006, office mng. ptnr., 1994—99; commr. FTC, Washington, 2006—. Adv. bd. Antitrust and Trade Regulation Report, Bur. Nat. Affairs, 1976—2006, Practising Law Inst., NYC; bd. dirs. Eisenhower Inst., Washington, 2003—06. Contbr. articles to profl. jours. Knox Fellow, Cambridge U., 1962. Fellow Am. Bar Found., Am. Coll. Trial Lawyers; mem. ABA (chmn. antitrust sect. 1990), Calif. State Bar Assn. (past chair Antitrust and Unfair Competition Sect., Antitrust Lawyer of Yr. 2003) San Francisco Bar Assn. Republican. Episcopalian. Office: FTC 600 Pennsylvania Ave NW Rm 540 Washington DC 20580 Business E-Mail: trosch@ftc.gov.

ROSCH, PAUL JOHN, internist, educator; b. Yonkers, NY, June 30, 1927; s. Samuel Joseph and Mary (Gang) R.; m. Lorraine Marie Hunt, June 27, 1951; children: David Carl, Jonathan Hunt, Jane Ellen, Michael Edward, Richard Joseph, Donna Marie; m. Marguerite Delamater, Sept. 12, 1972. AB, Brown U., NYU, 1948, MA, 1950; MD, Albany Med. Coll., 1954. Diplomate Am. Bd. Internal Medicine. Fellow Inst. Exptl. Medicine and Surgery, U. Montreal, Que., Canada, 1951-52; intern, asst. resident in medicine Johns Hopkins Hosp., 1954-56; resident in medicine, then chief dept. metabolism Walter Reed Med. Ctr., 1956-58; physician-in-charge nuclear medicine St. John's Riverside Hosp., Yonkers, 1959-67, dir. endocrine clinic, sr. attending physician, 1959-96, vice chief of staff, 1977; chief endocrine clinic St. Joseph's Hosp., 1959, sr. cons. in medicine, 1980—; pres. Am. Inst. Stress, Yonkers, 1978—, sr. cons. in medicine, 1980—; clin. prof. medicine and psychiatry N.Y. Med. Coll., 1980—. Asst. clin. prof. medicine Mt. Sinai Hosp. Sch. Medicine, 1963-67; former adj. prof. medicine in psychiatry U. Md. Sch. Medicine. From asst. to assoc. editor Health Comm. and Informatics; editor-in-chief Stress Medicine, 1990—; mem. editorial bd. AMA Archives Internal Medicine, Folia Clinica Internat, Jour. Human Stress, Internat. Jour. Psychosomatics, Am. Jour. Health Promotion, Cardiovascular Revs. & Reports, Internat. Jour. Stress Mgmt., Comprehensive Therapy, Jour. Human Behavior; contbg. editor Creative Living; contbr. articles to profl. jours. Bd. govs. Jewish Community Ctr.; bd. dirs. Family Svc. Soc., Mensana Clinic, 1980—; chmn. bd. Internat. Found. Biosocial Devel. and Human Health, 1980—; mem. adv. bd. Image Inst., 1980—. Capt. AUS, 1956-58. Fellow ACP, Internat. Stress Mgmt. Assn. (hon. v.p. 1991—), Am. Coll. Cardiology, Internat. Acad. Medicine, Am. Coll. Angiology, NY Diabetes Assn.; mem. Westchester Diabetes Assn. (pres. 1968), Internat. Law Enforcement Stress Assn. (adv. bd. 1980—), Yonkers Acad. Medicine (bd. govs., pres. 1971), NY Cardiology Soc., Acad. Psychosomatic Medicine, Soc. Behavioral Medicine, NY Acad. Scis., Endocrine Soc., Am. Diabetes Assn., Westchester Soc. Internat. Medicine (past pres.), Stress Mgmt. Assn. (hon. v.p.), NY State Soc. Internal Medicine (pres. 1974), Soc. Nuclear Medicine (bd. dirs.), Am. Fedn. Clin. Rsch., Am. Soc. Internal Medicine, Am. Geriatrics Soc., Elmwood Country Club, Atlantis Golf Club, Breakers Golf Club, St. Andrews Golf Club. Home: 10 Old Jackson Ave Hastings On Hudson NY 10706-3203 Office Phone: 914-963-1200. Personal E-mail: stress124@optonline.net.

ROSCHKE, PAUL NORBERT, engineering educator; b. Murray, Utah, July 14, 1947; s. Norbert F. and Ruth E. Roschke; m. Kin Ming Roschke, July 8, 1979. BS in Civil Engring., Valparaiso U., Ind., 1969. Lic. profl. engr., Calif., Ariz., N.Mex, Tex. Prof. Zachry dept. civil engring. Tex. A&M U., College Station, 1986—. Mem.: ASCE. Achievements include invention of roadway soundwall and modules made from recycled plastic. Office: Texas A&M Univ Zachry Dept of Civil Engineering College Station TX 77843-3136

ROSCOE, KEVIN JAY, radiologist, physician; s. Michael and Beverly Roscoe; m. Melanie Anne Stillman; children: Darren Evan, Kellie Lynn, Benjamin Alexander, Brooke Elizabeth. BS, SUNY, Albany, 1989; MD, Albany Med. Coll., 1993. McChord AFB maj. USAF, Turkey, 1993—2001, family practician Tacoma, 1998—2001; radiologist Lahey Clinic, Burlington, Mass., 2004—; dir. Woodcreek Healthcare Convenience Care Clinic, 2001—04, Diagnostic Imaging Mason Gen. Hosp., Shelton, Wash., 2008—. Home Phone: 360-427-1060; Office Phone: 360-427-9590.

ROSCOPF, CHARLES BUFORD, lawyer; b. Marvell, Ark., Apr. 21, 1928; s. Emmett Lee and Sally Virginia (King) R.; m. Mary Anne Maddox, Aug. 22, 1954; children— Charles David; Ann Karen. Student, Hendrix Coll., 1948-50; JD, U. Ark., 1954. Bar: Ark. bar 1954, U.S. Dist. Cts 1955, 64, U.S. Supreme Ct. bar 1965. Pvt. practice, Helena, Ark., 1954—; assoc. firm Burke, Moore & Burke, 1954-58; ptnr. firm Burke & Roscopf, 1958-64; sr. ptnr. Roscopf and Roscopf, P.A., 1964—. Mem. Ark. Ho. of Reps., 1953-58; del. Ark. Constl. Conv., 1968; mem. Ark. Probate Drafting Com.; mem. Ark. State Bd. Law Examiners, 1973-79; spl. justice Ark. Supreme Ct. Served with USN, 1946-48; served with USAFR, 1962-68. Fellow Am. Bar Found., Ark. Bar Found. (pres. 1995-96); mem. ABA, Ark. Bar Assn. (pres. 1990-91), Am. Law Inst., Rotary (Paul Harris fellow), Masons, Shriners, Kappa Sigma. Methodist. Home: 117 Avalon Pl Helena AR 72342-1715 Office: Helena Nat Bank Bldg PO Box 610 Helena AR 72342-0610 Office Phone: 870-338-3438.

ROSE, ALBERT SCHOENBURG, lawyer, educator; b. Nov. 9, 1945; s. Albert Schoenberg Sr. and Karleen (Klein) Rose; m. Nancy K. Rose; children: Claudia, Micah Daniel. BSBA, U. Ala., 1967; JD, Washington U., St. Louis, 1970; LLM in Taxation, George Washington U., 1974. Bar: Mo. 1970, U.S. Dist. Ct. (ea. dist.) Mo. 1970, U.S. Tax Ct. 1970, U.S. Ct. Mil. Appeals 1970, U.S. Supreme Ct. 1970. Ptnr. Lewis Rice & Fingersh, St. Louis, 2001—. Adj. prof. law Washington U., 1979-98, Fontbonne Coll., 1993-96. Co-author: Missouri Taxation Law and Practice, 1986, supplement, 1989. Capt. U.S. Army, 1970-74, Korea. Mem.: Civic Entrepreneurs Orgn. (bd. dirs., sec.), Tax Lawyers Club, Mid.Am. Tax Conf. (chmn.). Office: Lewis Rice & Fingersh 500 North Broadway Ste 2000 Saint Louis MO 63102 Office Phone: 314-444-1300. E-mail: arose@lewisrice.com.

ROSE, ARON D., ophthalmologist, educator; b. Norwalk, Conn., Sept. 23, 1958; s. Gilbert and Anne Rose; m. Stacey L. Miller; children: Jenna, Lauren, Hannah. BA (hon.), Brown U., Providence, 1980; MD, NY Med. Coll., Valhalla, 1985; degree in ophthalmology, Mt. Sinai Sch. of Medicine, NYC, 1989. Fellow Am. Bd. Ophthalmology, 1989. Assoc. clin. prof. Yale U. Sch. Medicine, New Haven, 1989—, Yale U. Sch.

Nursing, New Haven, 1996—. Dir., residency tng. Yale U. Dept. Ophthalmology and Visual Scis., New Haven, 1992—94; cons. Advanced Med. Optics, Santa Ana, Calif., 2003—; sect. editor Techniques in Ophthalmology, 2004—. Composer: Quartet for Clarinet & Strings, 1980; contbr. articles various profl. jours. Advisor JusticeWorks Med. Humanitarian Assn., Newtown, Pa., 1994—99; bd. mem. New Haven Med. Assn., 1995—2004; strategic oversight New Haven Hunger & Relief, 1997—2006; invited faculty Project Orbis Internat., NYC, 1992—2006; advisor Yale China Health Adv. Com. Recipient Brand Music Premium for Excellence in Musical Composition, Brown U., 1980, Departmental Honors, 1980. Fellow: Am. Acad. Ophthalmology (life); mem.: European Soc. Cataract and Refractive Surgeons, Conn. Soc. Eye Physicians, Conn. Glaucoma Soc., New Eng. Ophthal. Soc., Conn. State Med. Soc., Am. Soc. Cataract and Refractive Surgeons. Office: Eye Care Group PC 40 Temple St 5B New Haven CT 06405

ROSE, ARTHUR, lawyer; b. NYC, June 25, 1930; s. Allan and Sybil (Kantrowitz) R.; m. Joan Elaine Markowitz, Aug. 21, 1960; children: Henry, Erwin, Allyn. BA, Rutgers U., 1951; JD, Harvard U., 1956. Bar: N.J. 1957, U.S. Dist. Ct. N.J. 1957, U.S. Supreme Ct. 1964. Assoc. Back, Nussman & Rose, Hackensack, NJ, 1957—61; ptnr. Rose & Gordon, Hackensack, NJ, 1961—67, Rose & Brod, Hackensack, NJ, 1967—70, Rose, Poley & DeFuccio, Hackensack, NJ, 1970—84, Rose & DeFuccio, Hackensack, NJ, 1984—. Mem. com. on character N.J. Supreme Ct.; pres. Leonia Neighborhood Men's Club, NJ, 1961—63, Jewish Fedn. Cmty. Svcs., Bergen County, NJ, 1972—74, Harvard Law Sch. Assn. NJ, past pres. Capt. USAF, 1951-53. Fellow: Internat. Acad. Matrimonial Lawyers, Am. Acad. Matrimonial Lawyers NJ Chpt. (pres. 1996—97); mem.: ABA, N.J. Bar Assn., Bergen County Bar Assn., Attys. Soc. Bergen County (pres. 1966—67). Jewish. Home: 1500 Palisade Ave Fort Lee NJ 07024 Office: Rose & DeFuccio 35 Essex St Hackensack NJ 07601-5418 Office Phone: 201-488-7800.

ROSE, BEATRICE SCHROEDER, harpist, educator; b. Ridgewood, NJ, Nov. 15, 1922; d. Henry William and Ida (LeHovey) Schroeder; m. William Harrison Rose, Apr. 10, 1954; 1 child, Daniel. Student, Inst. Musical Art, 1940—41, Mannes Coll. Music, 1942—44; studies with, Lucile Lawrence and Carlos Salzedo. Concert and radio debut NY World's Fair, NYC, 1939; soloist Damrosch Music Appreciation Hour broadcast, 1940, Duke of Windsor's Save the Children Fund, Nassau, The Bahamas, 1941; assoc. harpist Radio City Music Hall Orch., NYC, 1944-50; various radio and solo performances NY area, 1944-51; concert artist Italy, US and Can., 1952; prin. harpist Houston Symphony, 1953-84; prof. harp Moores Sch. Music, U. Houston, 1953—98. Soloist Contemporary Music Soc., 1959, 60, Houston Chamber Orch., 1969; dir. Christmas Festival of Harps, Houston Harp Ensemble, PBS, 1978, Harps of Gold, 1983; staff harpist Heritage Club, 1987-95, High Tea Ritz Carlton, 1996-97, St. Regis, 1998-2003. Author: The Harp in the Orchestra: A Reference Book for Harpists, Teachers, Composers and Conductors, 2003; composer works include Enchanted Harp, rev. edit., 1995; recs. for Houston Symphony, Stokowski, Everest, Capitol, Comissiona, Vanguard Records. Recipient 1st prize Federated Music Clubs Contest, 1936; NY Hour of Music award, 1945. Mem. Am. Harp Soc., Tex. Music Educators Assn. (adjudicator All-State competitions), Nat. Fedn. Music Clubs (harp adviser 1991), Phi Beta. Home: 1315 Friarcreek Ln Houston TX 77055-6714 Office: U Houston Sch Music Houston TX 77004

ROSE, CAROL MARGUERITE, law educator; b. Washington, Apr. 12, 1940; d. J. Hugh and Marie (Meenehan) R. BA, Antioch Coll., 1962; MA, U. Chgo., 1963, JD, 1977; PhD, Cornell U., 1970. Bar: Ill. 1977, Calif. 1978, D.C. 1978. Instr. history Ohio St. U., Columbus, 1969-73; assoc. dir. So. Govtl. Monitor Project, Atlanta, 1975-76; law clk. to judge U.S. Ct. Appeals (5th cir.), Austin, Tex., 1977-78; asst. prof. law Stanford U., 1978-80; acting prof. law U. Calif., Berkeley, 1980-82; prof. law Northwestern U., Chgo., 1982-88, Yale U., 1989—90, Fred A. Johnston prof. New Haven, 1990—94, Gordon Bradford Tweedy prof. of law and orgn., 1994—2005; emerita, 2005—06; Lohse prof. water and natural resource law U. Ariz., 2006—. Bd. editors Found. Press, Mineola, N.Y., 1986—. Mem. Am. Assn. Law Schs., Am. Acad. Arts and Scis., Order of Coif. Office: U Ariz Coll of Law PO Box 210176 Tucson AZ 85721-0176 Office Phone: 520-621-5544. E-mail: carol.rose@yale.edu.

ROSE, CHARLES P., lawyer; b. 1957; BA in Economics, Villanova U., Phila., 1979; JD, De Paul U., Chgo., 1982. Bar: Ill. In-house counsel Ill. Assn. Sch. Boards; ptnr. Vedder, Price, Kaufman & Kammholz; founding ptnr. & corp. sec. Franczek, Radelet & Rose, Chgo.; gen. counsel US Dept. Edn., Washington, 2009—. Adj. lectr. De Paul U. Coll. Law; adj. prof. Northeastern Ill. U. Adv. bd., Nat. Coll. Edn. Nat.-Louis U.; bd. dirs. Advance Ill.; Chgo. adv. bd. Facing History and Ourselves. Recipient Vision in Edn. award, ED-RED, 2006. Fellow: Coll. Labor & Employment Lawyers; mem.: Nat. Coun. Sch. Attorneys. Office: US Dept Edn 400 Maryland Ave SW Washington DC 20202*

ROSE, CHARLIE (CHARLES PEETE ROSE JR.), television journalist; b. Henderson, NC, Jan. 5, 1942; s. Charles Peete Sr. and Margaret Rose; m. Mary King (div. 1980). B in Hist., Duke U., Durham, NC, 1964; JD, Duke U. Sch. Law, 1968; student, NYU Stern Sch. Bus.; PhD (hon.), C.W. Post Coll., U. NC, Pembroke. Interviewer Sta. WPIX-TV, NYC, 1972; mng. editor Bill Moyers Internat. Report, 1974—75; exec. producer Bill Moyers Jour., 1975—76; corr. USA: People in Politics, PBS, 1976; polit. corr. NBC News, 1976-77; co-host A.M. Chgo., 1978; host The Charlie Rose Show Sta. KXAS-TV, Dallas, Ft. Worth, 1979-81, Sta. WRC-TV, Washington, 1981-83; host, interviewer CBS News Nightwatch, Washington, 1984—90; exec. prodr., exec. editor, host The Charlie Rose Show, 1991—; corr. 60 Minutes II, 1999—2005. Bd. dirs. Citadel Broadcasting Corp., 2003—. Recipient George Foster Peabody award, 1976, Emmy award, 1987, 1992, Cable ACE award, 1992, Futrell award, 2005, Lifetime Achievement award in Entertainment Journalism, Savannah Film Festival, 2007. Office: Rose Communications 499 Park Ave New York NY 10022-1240*

ROSE, DALE A.J., performing arts educator; b. Detroit, Sept. 5, 1946; s. Ora Henry Rose and Vida Blanche Birkett. BA, Mich. State U., 1966, MA, 1968. Performing arts coord. Mich. State Arts Coun. for the Arts, 1968—69; asst. prof. U. South Fla., Tampa, 1973—77; asst. prof. divsn. theatre So. Meth. U., Dallas, 1977—81, adj. prof., 1984—85, assoc. prof., 1985—88, Mo. Repertory Theatre/U. Mo., Kansas City, 1988—97, prof., 1997—2004; dir. Sch. Theatre and Dance U. South Fla., Tampa, 2004—05; dir. performance studies U. Conn., Storrs, 2005—; master tchr. acting The Actors Ctr., NYC, 2005—; assoc. artistic dir. Conn. Repertory Theatre, Storrs, 2005—. Artistic dir. Shakespeare Festival of Dallas, 1986—90, The Plaza Theatre, Dallas, 1983—84; acting tchr. George Morrison Studio and Warren Robertson Theatre Workshop, NYC, 1981—83; co-founder, dir. Stage #1, Dallas, 1979—85; artistic dir., founder The Alice People Theatre Co., Tampa, 1974—77; host, commentator The Bergman Films-WUSF-TV, 1975; co-host, theatre/film critic Variety, WTOG-TV, St. Petersburg, Fla., 1973—76; actor, NYC, 1970—73. Dir.: (plays) The Boys Next Door, 1991, Hydrophobia, 1993, The First Family of Africa, 1993, The Very First Family, 1994, The Belle of Amherst, 1996, Babes in Arms, 1996, Les Liaisons Dangereuses, 1998, Charley's Aunt, 2000; author: (plays) The Pearl, 1994; screenwriter Eye for Eye, 1996—98; dir.: (plays) numerous plays, As You Like It, 2006. Office: University of Connecticut 802 Bolton Rd Unit 1127 Storrs Mansfield CT 06269

ROSE, DAVE, men's college basketball coach; b. Houston; m. Cheryl Rose; 3 children. Attended, Dixie State Coll., St. George, Utah; B, U. Houston, 1983. Full-time mission The Church of Jesus Christ of Latter-day Saints, Manchester, England, 1977—79; head basketball coach Millard HS, 1983—86; asst. coach Pine View HS, 1986—87, Dixie State Coll. Rebels, 1987—90, head basketball coach, 1990—97; asst. coach Brigham Young U. Cougars, Utah, 1997—2005, head basketball coach, 2005—. Active Coaches vs. Cancer; hon. chmn. Children with Cancer Christmas Found.; youth group vol. coach. Recipient Game Pillar award, Nat. Assn. Basketball Coaches, 2008, Dale Rex Meml. award, 2008; named Dist. VIII Coach of Yr., US Basketball Writers Assn., 2006, Coach of Yr., Mountain West Conf., 2006, 2007, Citizen of Yr., St. George C. of C. Mem. Lds Church. Office: Brigham Young Univ Dept Athletics 2112 MC Provo UT 84602 Office Phone: 801-422-3612. Business E-Mail: dave_rose@byu.edu.*

ROSE, DAVID L., lawyer; b. Ft. Monmouth, NJ, Feb. 18, 1955; s. Llewellyn Paterson and Bebe (Faulk) R.; m. Karen M. Rose; children from previous marriage: Allison Michelle, Jessica Morgan, Ashley Elizabeth. BA in Comm., U. Colo., 1980; JD, Ariz. State U., 1991. Bar: Ariz. 1991, U.S. Dist. Ct. Ariz. 1991, U.S. Ct. Appeals (9th cir.) 1993, U.S. Supreme Ct. 1997, cert.specialist in family law, 2004. Law clk. Bonn & Anderson, Phoenix, 1988-91, Maricopa County Superior Ct., Phoenix, 1990-91; atty. Anderson, Brody, Levinson, Weiser & Horwitz, Phoenix, 1991-92, Brandes, Lane & Joffe, Phoenix, 1992-93, Rose & Hildebrand, P.C., 1997—2006, Rose and Huey, PLLC, 2007—; pvt. practice Phoenix, 2006—. Judge pro-tem Maricopa County Superior Ct., Maricopa County Justice Ct. Editor: Missive, 1992. Bd. dirs. Maricopa County Family Support Adv. Com., Phoenix; adv. coun. Washington Sch. Dist., Phoenix; mem. Ariz. State Legis., Domestic Rels. Reform Com., Phoenix. Mem. Maricopa County Bar Assn. (adv. family law com.), ABA (adv. family law sect.), Nat. Congress for Men (pres.), Father's for Equal Rights of Colo. (pres.). Avocations: aviation, computer systems. Office: 1440 E Washington St Phoenix AZ 85034-1109 Office Phone: 602-340-8400. Business E-Mail: davidlrose@arizonalaw.edu.

ROSE, DERRICK MARTELL, professional basketball player; b. Chgo., Oct. 4, 1988; s. Brenda Rose. Attended, U. Memphis, 2007—08. Guard Chgo. Bulls, 2008—. Named Third Team All-American, AP, Nat. Assn. Basketball Coaches, 2008, First Team All-Conference, Conf. USA, 2008, Freshman of Yr., 2008, Rookie of Yr., NBA, 2009, First Team All-Rookie, 2009; finalist John R. Wooden Player of Yr. award, 2008. Achievements include being the first overall pick in the NBA Draft, 2008. Office: Chgo Bulls 1901 W Madison St Chicago IL 60612*

ROSE, DORIS ANN, secondary school educator; b. MIddletown, Ohio, Apr. 10, 1947; d. Roy Patton and Anita Theresa Craft. AA, Temple Coll., Tex., 1971; BA, U. Mary Hardin Baylor, Belton, Tex., 1974. Cert. tchr. Tex. Social studies tchr. Galveston Ind. Sch. Dist., Tex., 1975—76; history and English tchr. Killeen Ind. Sch. Dist., Tex., 1978—. Grader Tex. Edn. Agy., Austin, 2006; co-chairperson profl. learning cmty. Eastern Hills Mid. Sch., Harker Heights, Tex., 2007—08. Editor: (newspaper) Ea. Hills Times, 2005—06; contbg. author: The Colors of Life, 2003, American Profiles Cookbook, 2007. Mem. Tex. Watch, Austin, 2006. Recipient Cert. of Merit, Nat. League Jr. Cotillions, 2005; named Tchr. of Month, Killeen Ind. Sch. Dist., 1995. Mem.: Am. Fedn. Tchrs. (rep. 1994—95), Killeen Fedn. Tchrs. (sec. 1994—95). Democrat. Avocation: domestic arts. Home: PO Box 385 Eddy TX 76524 Office: Ea Hills Mid Sch 300 Indian Tr Harker Heights TX 76548

ROSE, DWIGHT DEAN, music educator; b. Omaha, Nebr., Apr. 6, 1970; s. Marvin Alan Rose (Deceased) and Betty Jane Rose. BA, Midland Luth. Coll., Fremont, NE, 1993; MA Music Ed., Univ. Nebr., Omaha, NE, 2002. Music educator Laurel-Concord Schools, Laurel, Nebr., 1993—97, Lyons-Decatur Schools, Lyons, 1997—2003. Recipient Snider Young Band Dir., Nebr. State Bandmasters Assn., 1998. Mem.: Nebr. Choral Dirs. Assn., Am. Choral Dirs. Assn., Music Educators Nat. Conf., Nebr. Music Educators Assn., Nebr. State Bandmasters Assn. Office: Lyons-Decatur Public Schools PO Box 526 Lyons NE 68038 also: Conestoga Pub Schs 8404 42nd St PO Box 40 Murray NE 68409 Home Phone: 402-235-3249; Office Phone: 402-235-2271. E-mail: drose@esu3.org.

ROSE, ERIC ALLEN, cardiothoracic surgeon; b. Bronx, NY, Jan. 25, 1951; s. Herb and Myra (Morgenstern) Rose; m. Ellise Delphin; children: Adam, Sydney, Zachary, Gabriel. BA summa cum laude, Columbia Coll., NYC, 1971; MD, Columbia U. Coll. Physicians & Surgeons, NYC, 1975. Diplomate Am. Bd. Thoracic Surgery, Am. Bd.Surgery. Surg. rsch. fellow NIH, 1977; intern surgery NY Presbyn. Hosp., 1975—76, resident surgery, 1976—79, resident thoracic surgery, 1980—81, asst. attending surgeon, 1982—86, assoc. attending surgeon, 1982—93, attending surgeon, 1993—; dir. cardiac transplantation svc. Columbia Presbyn. Med Ctr., 1982—93, dir. surgical cardiac intensive care unit, 1982—86, dir. clin. perfusion svc., 1986—95, chief cardiothoracic surg. svc., 1990—96; chief surgeon NY Presbyn. Hosp./Columbia U. Med. Ctr., 1994—. Asst. prof. surgery Coll. Physicians and Surgeons, Columbia U., 1982—88, assoc. prof., 1988—93, prof., 1993—; dir. cardiothoracic svc. St. Michael's Med. Ctr., Newark, 1997—2001; assoc. dean translational rsch. Columbia U. Med Ctr., 2004—05; chmn. dept. surgery Columbia U. Coll. Physicians & Surgeons, 1994—; prof. surgery Johnson & Johnson, 1999—; bd. dirs. NY Regional Transplant Program; mem. com. on heart transplantation United Network for Organ Sharing. Contbr. articles to profl. jours.; author: (book) Management of End-Stage Heart Disease, 1998, Second Opinion: The Columbia Presbyterian Guide to Surgery, 2000; editl. bd. Jour. Heart Transplantation, 1982—86, Jour. Thoracic Cardiovascular Surgery, 1993—. Recipient William Cumming Meml. award in Experimental Psychology, Robert Loeb Meml. award in Internal Med., Allen O. Whipple Meml. award in Surgery. Fellow: Am. Coll. Cardiology; mem.: AMA, ACS, Soc. U. Surgeons, Soc. U. Surgeons, Soc. Thoracic Surgeons, NY Soc. Thoracic Surgery, NY Heart Assn., NY County Med. Soc., Internat. Soc. Heart & Lung Transplantation (bd. councilors, pres. 1993), Am. Surgical Assn., Am. Soc. Transplant Surgeons (com. on heart transplantation), Am. Heart Assn. (exec. com. of coun. cardiovascular surgery), Am. Coll. Physician Inventors, Am. Assn. Thoracic Surgery, Alpha Omega Alpha, Phi Beta Kappa. Achievements include research in mechanical alternatives to transplantation. Office: NY Presbyn Hosp Columbia Milstein Bldg Rm 7435 177 Fort Wash Ave New York NY 10032 also: Columbia U 622 W 168th St New York NY 10032 Office Phone: 212-305-9600. Office Fax: 212-305-3100. Business E-Mail: erose@mafgrp.com.

ROSE, ERNST, dentist; b. Oldenburg, Germany, July 22, 1932; came to U.S., 1940, naturalized, 1946; s. William and Elsie (Lowenbach) R.; m. Shirley Mae Glassman, Dec. 24, 1960 (div. Dec. 1997); children: Ruth Ellen, Michele Ann, Daniel Scot, Seth Joseph; m. Sally Rayen Dunn, Mar. 14, 1998; 1 stepchild, Toby Jugenheimer. BS, Georgetown U., DC, 1955; DDS, Case Western Res. U., Cleve., 1963. Intern Waterbury Hosp., Conn., 1964; pvt. practice dentistry Hubbard, Ohio, 1964-96. Pres., treas. Dr. Ernst Rose, Inc.; lab. instr. Ohio State U., Columbus, 1956-57; dental adviser Assoc. Neighborhood Ctr. Active Liberty Twp. Zoning Commn., 1967-74, 88-92, vice chmn., chmn., 1970-74, 90; chmn. Hubbard Urban Renewal Com., Ohio, 1968-74; mem. Brotherhood Bd., 1967—, treas., 1971-73, 88-90, pres. 1975-77, 90-92, 97-99, temple bd. dirs., 1975-84, 89-95, 1997-2003; bd. dirs. The Playhouse, 2000-01, Victorian Players, 2000-2003, Beth Israel SCC Men's Club. With AUS US Army, 1957—59, Eniwitok nuclear testing. Mem. ADA (life), Ohio Dental Assn. (life), Corydon Palmer Dental Soc. (life, mem. coun. 1983-87), Warren Dental Soc., Hubbard C. of C. (bd. dirs. 1967-97, v.p. 1995-97), Jewish Chatauqua Soc. (life), German Am. Club of Sun City Center, European Brass Band, Mil. Officers World Wars, Sun City Center Men's Club, Alpha Omega (coun. mem. 1968—2002, sec. 1970-71, v.p. 1971-72, pres. 1972-73, pres. 1989-90, 99-2000), B'nai B'rith (pres. 1970-71, trustee 1971—), Rotary (life, Paul Harris fellow, sec. 1999-2001, vice chmn. Kashrut com. 1983-85, Mikvah com. 1983-93, chmn. Kashrut com. 1985-94), Freedom Plaza Wood Worker Club (v.p. 2008-). Personal E-mail: dresrose@webtv.net.

ROSE, GEORGE ANDREW, Internet information systems specialist; b. Mt. Clemens, Mich., Dec. 17, 1950; s. George Hubert and Geraldine Katherine (Benoit) Rose. BA in Psychology and Biology, BSW in Psychology and Biology, Eastern Mich. U., Ypsilanti, 1973; MBA in Internat. Fin., George Wash. U., Washington, 1987. Inpatient substance abuse therapist St. Joseph's Hosp., Mt. Clemens, 1974—77; dep. twp. clk. Twp. of Clinton, Mich., 1977—79; social worker Bur. Rehab., Washington, 1979—84; sr. social worker Comprehensive Alcohol and Drug Abuse Ctr., Washington, 1984—88; health contract specialist UMWA Health and Retirement Funds, Washington, 1988—91; dir. software devel., info. svcs. United Seniors Health Coop., Washington, 1991—98; founder, pres., CEO Portsmouth Group, Inc., Washington, 1996—. Bd. mem. The Kennedy Ctr. for Performing Arts, Wash., DC, 2008—. Mem.: Kennedy Ctr. Performing Arts (Washington) (bd. mem.). Achievements include first to develop a web-enabled community-based health and human service organizations; developing internet services for community-based health and human service organizations; development of software to screen children and families for community resources and touch-screen benefit eligibility screening service and a web-based case management service; patents in field. Home: 2929 Connecticut Ave NW Washington DC 20008-1435 Office: The Portsmouth Group PO Box 11735 Washington DC 20008-0935 Office Phone: 202-261-6558. Business E-Mail: georgerose@portsmouthgroup.net.

ROSE, GREGORY MANCEL, neurobiologist; b. Eugene, Oreg., Feb. 3, 1953; s. Mancel Lee and Ilione (Schenk) R.; m. Kathleen Ann Frye, June 30, 1979; 1 child, Julian Mancel. BS cum laude, U. Calif., Irvine, 1975, PhD, 1980. Research fellow M.P.I. for Psychiatry, Munich, 1976; rsch. assoc. Miescher Labor, M.P.I., Tuebingen, Republic of Germany, 1980-81; regular fellow dept. pharmacology U. Colo. Health Sci. Ctr., Denver, 1981-84, asst. prof., 1984-89, assoc. prof., 1989-97; rsch. biologist VA Med. Ctr., Denver, 1981-97, co-dir. neurosci. tng. program, 1986-89, assoc. rsch. career scientist, 1989-97; dir. cognition program Bristol-Meyers Squibb Co., Wallingford, Conn., 1997-00; with Memory Pharm. Corp., New York, 2000—; dir. Vivo Pharm., 2004—07; neuroscientist Bristol-Myers squibb Co., Wallingford, Conn., assoc. dir., 1999—2002, dir., 2002—04; pres. Bonnie Crest Coop Assoc., 2003—05; dir. Ctr. Integrated Rsch. Cognitive & Neural Scis.; prof. anatomy Southern Ill. U. Achievements include discovery of importance of stimulus patterning for induction of hippocampal synaptic plasticity. Bd. dirs. Greater Park Hill Community, 1987-90. VA Rsch. Svc. grantee, 1984, 86, 89, 93, 97, NSF grantee, 1988, 90, NIMH grantee, 1989, 94, NIA grantee, 1991, 97. Mem. AAAS, Am. Aging Assn., Soc. Neurosci., Internat. Brain Rsch. Orgn., N.Y. Acad. Sci. Democrat. Episcopalian. Avocations: fine woodworking, fly fishing. Office: Ctr for Int Rsrch Cog & Neural Sci Southern Illinois U 600 Agriculture Dr Mail Code 6503 Carbondale IL 62901 Office Phone: 618-453-1451. E-mail: grose@siumed.edu.

ROSE, I. NELSON, lawyer, educator; b. LA, May 23, 1950; s. Bernard and Helen Mae (Nelson) Rose. BA, UCLA, 1973; JD, Harvard U., 1979. Bar: Hawaii 79, U.S. Dist. Ct. Hawaii 79, Calif. 80, U.S. Supreme Ct. 91. Pvt. practice, Honolulu, 1979—82; asst. prof. law Whittier Coll., LA, 1982—85, assoc. prof., 1985—89, tenured prof. law, 1989—2007, disting. sr. prof., 2007—. Cons. legal gaming; vis. scholar Inst. for Study of Gambling and Comml. Gaming, U. Nev., Reno. Author: Gambling and the Law, 1986; author: (with Robert A. Loeb) Blackjack and the Law, 1998; co-author (with Robert M. Jarvis, J. Wesley Cochran. Ronald J. Rychlak): Gaming Law: Cases and Materials, 2003; co-author: (with Martin D. Owens) Internet Gaming Law, 2005, 2nd edit., 2009; contbr. articles profl. jour. and books. Founder, counsel Hawaii Lions Eye Bank, Honolulu; founder, v.p., counsel Calif. Coun. on Compulsive Gambling; mem. Calif. Gambling Policy Adv. Com., 2002—04. Mem.: ABA, Internat. Masters Gaming Law, Internat. Assn. Gaming Advisors., Hawaii Bar Assn., Calif. State Bar Assn. Democrat. Jewish. Home and Office: 17031 Encino Hills Dr Encino CA 91436-4009 Office Phone: 818-788-8509. Personal E-mail: rose@sprintmail.com. Business E-Mail: rose@gamblingandthelaw.com.

ROSE, IRWIN A. (ERNIE), biochemist, educator; b. Bklyn., July 16, 1926; s. Harry and Ella Greenwald Royze; m. Zelda Budenstein; 4 children. BS, U. Chgo., 1948, PhD in biochemistry, 1952. Researcher Fox Chase Cancer Ctr., Phila., 1963—95; ret., 1995; specialist, Dept. Physiology and Biophysics, Sch. Med. U. Calif., Irvine, Calif., 1997—. Contbr. articles to profl. jour. Served with USN, World War II. Co-recipient Nobel Prize in Chemistry, 2004. Mem.: NAS. Achievements include discovery of ubiquitin-mediated protein degradation. Office: U Calif Dept Physiology and Biophysics Coll Medicine Irvine CA 92697*

ROSE, ISRAEL HAROLD, mathematics professor; b. New Britain, Conn., May 17, 1917; s. Abraham and Dora (Dubrow) R.; m. Pearl Nitzberg, Jan. 24, 1942 (div. Feb. 1956); 1 son, Steven Philip; m. Susan Ann Lazarus, Mar. 26, 1961; children: Dora, Eric. Student, CCNY, 1934-36; AB, Bklyn. Coll., 1938, A.M., 1941; PhD, Harvard, 1951. Tutor, instr. Bklyn. Coll., 1938-41; instr. Pa. State Coll., 1942-46; asst. prof. U. Mass., 1948-54, assoc. prof., 1954-60; faculty Hunter Coll., 1960-68, prof. math., 1965-68, chmn. dept., 1966-68; prof. math. Lehman Coll., CUNY, 1968-82, prof. emeritus, 1983—, chmn. dept., 1968-72, 80-82, resident prof., 1983—. Vis. asst. prof. Mt. Holyoke Coll., 1951-52, vis. assoc. prof., 1954-55, 58-59; sci. cons. AID, India, summer 1965 Author: A Modern Introduction to College Mathematics, 1959, Algebra: An Introduction to Finite Mathematics, 1963, Vectors and Analytic Geometry, 1968, Elementary Functions: A Precalculus Primer, 1973, (with Esther R. Phillips) Elementary Functions, 1978.

NRC predoctoral fellow Harvard, 1946-48; fellow Fund Advancement Edn., 1952-53 Mem. Am. Math. Soc., Math. Assn. Am. (chmn. Met. N.Y. sect. 1973-75), Nat. Council Tchrs. Math., Assn. Tchrs. Math. New Eng. (pres. Conn. Valley sect. 1956-57), Sigma Xi (pres. Hunter Coll. chpt. 1966-67) Home: 18 Floral Dr Hastings On Hudson NY 10706-1202 Office: Lehman Coll Bedford Park Blvd W Bronx NY 10468

ROSE, JALEN, sportscaster, retired professional basketball player; b. Detroit, Jan. 30, 1973; s. Jeanne R. Student, U. Mich. Guard Denver Nuggets, 1994-96, Ind. Pacers, 1996—2002, Chicago Bulls, 2002—04, Toronto Raptors, 2004—06, NY Knicks, 2006, Phoenix Suns, 2006—07; ret., 2007; studio analyst ESPN, 2007—. Named Honorable Mention All-Am., AP, 1991; set Michigan freshman scoring record, 1991; selected as All-Am., Parade Magazine, Third-Team All-Am., USA Today; set Nuggets' rookie record for assists, 1994-95 season; named to All-Rookie Second Team, NBA, 1995 Office: ESPN Plz Bristol CT 06010

ROSE, JAMES MCKINLEY, JR., lawyer, government official; b. NYC, 1927; m. Anne Louise Bourne, 1960; children: Anne Rose Williams, Louise aba Lee Rose Emery. Grad., Phillips Exeter Acad., 1946; BA, Princeton U., 1951; JD, Harvard U., 1954. Bar: N.Y. 1955, D.C. 1977. With Dewey, Ballantine, Bushby, Palmer & Wood, NYC, 1954-57; asst. U.S. atty. U.S. Dist. Ct. (so. dist.) N.Y., 1957-61; legal asst. to pres. Atlantic Mut. Ins. Co., 1961-65, sec., counsel, 1965-71; asst. fed. ins. adminstr. U.S. HUD, Washington, 1971-81; exec. asst. to adminstr. Fed. Ins. Adminstrn., Fed. Emergency Mgmt. Agy., Washington, 1981-93. Mem. men's com. Am. Mus. Natural History, 1968-71; sr. warden Episcopal ch. With AUS, 1946-47. Mem. D.C. Bar Assn., Assn. of Bar of City of N.Y., St. Nicholas Soc., Prouts Neck Assn. (pres. 1979-85), Prouts Neck Country Club, Chevy Chase Club. Republican. Home: 4913 Rodman St NW Washington DC 20016-3238

ROSE, JAMES TURNER, aerospace engineer, consultant; b. Louisburg, NC, Sept. 21, 1935; s. Frank Rogers and Mary Burt (Turner) R.; m. Daniele Raymond, Sept. 15, 1984. BS with high honors, N.C. State U., 1957. Aero. rsch. engr. NASA, Langley Field, Va., 1957-59; project engr. NASA (Mercury and Gemini), Langley Field, Va. and Houston, 1959-64; program sys. mgr. McDonnell Douglas Astronautics Co (MDAC), St. Louis, 1964-69; mgr. shuttle ops. and implementation (MDAC) McDonnell Douglas Astronautics Co., St. Louis, 1969-72, mgr. shuttle support (MDAC), 1972-74, mgr. space processing programs, 1976-83; dir. electrophoresis ops. in space McDonnell Douglas Astronautics Co (MDAC), St. Louis, 1983-86; dir. space shuttle engring. NASA, Washington, 1974-76, asst. adminstr. comml. programs, 1987-91; aerospace cons., 1992—. Chmn. Fla. Space Bus. Roundtable, 1995-98. Recipient Lindberg award for mgmt. leadership AIAA, 1983, Presdl. Meritorious Rank award, 1989, NASA Exceptional Svc. medal, 1990, Laurels award Aviation Week, 1990, Aerospace Contribution to Soc. award AIAA, 1993. Mem. Phi Kappa Phi. Episcopalian. Personal E-mail: jrose935@aol.com.

ROSE, JANE A., financial planner; b. Phila., Sept. 30, 1940; d. Maurice and Miriam (Blank) Auritt; divorced; children: Lynne C., Wendy J., Debora J. Rose-Stewart. Student, Pa. State U., 1958; BA, Rutgers U., 1975; MBA, Temple U., 1978, postgrad., 1978-80. CPA, N.J.; CFP; cert. mgmt. acct., personal fin. specialist. Asst. v.p. Data Control Ctr., Cherry Hill, N.J., 1966-70; statistician, sr. staff asst. I.U. Internat. Corp., Phila., 1970-72; ops. mgr. Bus. Data Ctr., Cherry Hill, N.J., 1972-75; instr. acctg. and mgmt. Rutgers U., Camden, N.J., 1975-80; cost acctg. supr., acctg. mgr. Phila. Nat. Bank, 1980-82; asst. dir. fiscal planning N.J. Dept. Higher Edn., Trenton, 1982-85; contr., CFO Essex County Coll., Newark, 1985-87; v.p. fin. Horizon House, Inc., Phila., 1987-89; v.p. RTD Fin. Advisors Inc., Phila., 1989—. Instr., advisor Cen. Mich. U., McGuire AFB, N.J., 1978-80; instr. MBA Program, Widener U., Chester, Pa., 1980-82; rsch. asst. Temple U. Sch. Bus., Phila., 1975-76. Singer: Choral Arts Soc. Phila., 2003—06, NJ Master Chorale, 2006—, Peter Nero & Philly Pops Holiday Chorus, 2007—. Trustee Contact Cmty. Helpline, Cherry Hill, N.J., 1987-97, v.p., 1988-89, pres., 1989-94, mem. fin. com., 1995—; chair planned giving com. Women's Way, 2001-07. Fellow Temple U. Sch. Bus., Phila., 1976-78. Fellow N.J. Soc. CPAs (chair subcom. 1985-89); mem. AICPA (grader CPA exam. 1987), Am. Woman's Soc. CPAs, Inst. Mgmt. Accts. (sec. South Jersey chpt. 1971-73, v.p. 1982-84, bd. dirs. 1971-75, 84-85, 91-93; grader, cons. CMA exam. 1986-99), Fin. Planning Assn., Am. Soc. Women Accts. (sec. Phila. chpt. 1972-74, bd. dirs. 1970-75), Choral Arts Soc. Phila. (singer, 2003-06). Office: RTD Fin Advisors Inc 30 S 17th St Ste 1720 Philadelphia PA 19103-1752 Home Phone: 856-795-4235; Office Phone: 215-557-3800. E-mail: jrose@rtdfinancial.com.

ROSE, JEFFREY RAYMOND, retired economist, public servant, trade unionist; b. Toronto, Ont., Can., 1946; s. Albert and Thelma R.; m. Sandra Black; 1 child, Adam. BA with honors, U. Toronto, 1968, M.Indsl. Relations, 1983; postgrad., London Sch. Econs., 1968-69. Planner planning dept. City of Toronto, 1976-80; pres. local 79 Can. Union Pub. Employees, Toronto, 1980-83, nat. pres. Ottawa, Ont., 1983—91, nat. pres. emeritus, 1991—; dep. min. intergovtl. affairs Govt. of Ont., Toronto, 1991-95; sr. fellow Harrowston program in conflict mgmt.-negotiation U. Toronto, 1995—2002. Gen. v.p. Can. Labour Congress, 1983—91. Exec. mem. Ont. New Dem. Party, 1982-91; bd. dirs. Inst. for Rsch. on Pub. Policy, 1988-91; mem. fed. coun. New Dem. Party, 1988-91; co-chmn. Ont.-Que. Commn. for Cooperation, 1991-95. Home: 55 Sunnydene Crescent Toronto ON Canada M4N 3J5

ROSE, JESSICA, medical educator; d. Menko and Marjorie DeWitt Rose; children: Will Jackson Agramonte, Thomas Grant Agramonte. BS in Zoology, U. C. Davis, Calif., 1980; PhD in Physiology, Stanford U., Calif., 1991. Cert. phys. therapist Phys. Therapy Bd. Calif., 1982. Phys. therapist Children's Hosp., Stanford, Palo Alto, Calif., 1982—88; sr. rsch. scientist, dept orthop. Surgery Stanford U., 1994—2003, asst. prof., dept orthop. Surgery, 2003—; dir., motion & gait analysis lab Lucile Packard Childrens Hosp., Palo Alto, 1989—. Taskforce mem. Nat. Ctr. Med. Rehab. Rsch., 1998—99; adv. bd. botulinum toxin b Elan Pharms, San Francisco, 2000—02; faculty adv. bd. Clayman Inst. Studies Gender, Stanford U., 2003—08; editl. reviewer Archives Phys. Medicine & Rehab., 2006—07; sci. rsch. reviewer NSF, 2007—08; taskforce mem. NIH, Pediats Motor Disorders, 2001—; course dir., anatomy movement Stanford U., 2004—; editl. reviewer Devel. Medicine & Child Neurology Jour., London, 2005—, Jour. Applied Biomechanics, 2009; primary investigator Nat. Rsch. Network Artificial Walking Cerebral Palsy, 2008—. Editor: (book) Human Walking. Bd. mem. Com. Green Foothills, Palo Alto, 1999—2006. Recipient Harman Neuroscis. Clin. Endowment award, Stanford U., 2005—07; Dean's Postdoc. fellowship, Stanford U. Sch. Medicine, 1992, Ednl. fellowship, Am. Lung Assn., 1986—87. Fellow: Am. Acad. Cerebral Palsy and Devel. Medicine. Achievements include research in neonatal brain abnormalities and motor deficits in preterm children and neuromuscular mechanisms of cerebral palsy. Office: Dept Orthopedic Surgery Stanford Univ 770 Welch Rd Ste 400 Palo Alto CA 94304 Office Phone: 650-497-8084. Office Fax: 650-498-7521. Business E-Mail: jessica.rose@stanford.edu.

ROSE, JESSICA LEE, actress; b. Salisbury, Md., Apr. 26, 1987; Student, Mount Maunganui Coll., New Zealand, 2000—01; student makeup, Acad.Film and TV, Auckland, New Zealand, 2004; graduate acting for film program, NY Film Acad., Universal City, Calif., 2005—06. Actor: (films) Dearly Beloved, I Know Who Killed Me, 2007, Perfect Sport, 2008, (internet video series) The Children of Anchor Cove (as lonelygirl15), 2006—07 (Best Actress film and video cat., Webby Awards, 2007); (TV series) Greek, 2007—08. Named to ad campaign to promote antipoverty cause, United Nations, 2006; named one of Top 25 Web Celebs, Forbes mag., 2006. Mailing: care of United Talent Agy 9560 Wilshire Blvd Ste 500 Beverly Hills CA 90212-2401

ROSE, JOANNA SEMEL, volunteer; b. Orange, NJ, Nov. 22, 1930; d. Philip Ephraim and Lillian (Mindlin) Semel; m. Daniel Rose, Sept. 16, 1956; children: David S., Joseph B., Emily, Gideon G. Cert., Shakespeare Inst., UK, 1951; BA summa cum laude, Bryn Mawr Coll., Pa., 1952; postgrad., St. Hilda's Coll., Oxford U., 1953. Mem. exec. com. Am. Friends St. Hilda's Coll., former chmn.; bd. dir., former pres. Paper Bag Players, NYC; former bd. dir., current mem. adv. coun. Poets and Writers, Inc., NYC; former chmn. adv. bd. Partisan Rev., NYC; mem. adv. coun. Nat. Dance Inst., NYC; bd. mem. NY Coun. for Humanities. Bd. dir. Bay St. Theatre, Sag Harbor; adv. coun. Am. Friends Jewish Mus. Greece; assoc. fellow Berkeley Coll. Yale U.; mem. NY Inst. for Humanities; bd. dirs. Ctr. for Humanities CUNY Grad. Ctr. Former bd. dirs. Eldridge St. Project, NYC. Hon. fellow, St. Hilda's Coll. Oxford. Mem. Cosmopolitan Club, Bryn Mawr Club of NY, LVIS East Hampton. Home: 895 Park Ave New York NY 10021-0327 also: 1 Lily Pond Ln East Hampton NY 11937

ROSE, JOEL ALAN, legal consultant; b. Bklyn., Dec. 26, 1936; s. Edward Isadore and Adele R. Rose; m. Isadora Fenig, Apr. 12, 1964; children: Susan, Terri Angstriech. BS in Econs., NYU, 1958; MBA, Wharton Grad. Sch., U. Pa., 1960. Asst. purchasing agt. Maidenform Inc., NYC, 1960-62; personnel dir. E.J. Korvette Inc., NYC, 1962-66; mgmt. cons. Daniel J. Cantor & Co. Inc., Phila., 1966—, sr. v.p., 1987—; mgmt. cons. to legal profession. Coord. Ann. Conf. on Law Firm Mgmt. and Econs. Author: NY law Jour., NJ Law Jour. & numerous others, editl. adv. bd. Corp. Counsel's Guide to Law Dept. Mgmt. With U.S. Army, 1960, Res., 1960-66. Fellow Coll. of Law Practice Mgmt.; mem. ABA (chmn. acquisition and mergers com., practice mgmt. sect., large law firm interest group), Inst. Mgmt. Cons., Am. Arbitration Assn. (nat. panel), Adminstrv. Mgmt. Soc. (past chpt. pres.), Am. Mgmt. Assn., Assn. Legal Adminstrs., NY State Bar Assn. (com. law practic mgmt., com. continuing legal edn., spl. com. age discrimination in professions, chair). Office: Joel A Rose & Assoc Inc PO Box 162 Cherry Hill NJ 08003-0162 Office Phone: 856-427-0050. Business E-Mail: jrose63827@aol.com.

ROSE, JOHN THOMAS, finance educator; b. Ft. Worth, Aug. 20, 1943; s. Paul Pittman and Francis Nan (White) R.; m. Sandra Kaye Rolen, Sept. 5, 1969; children: Melanie Ann, Leah Nan, Lynnelle Renee. BA with honors, Tex. A&M U., 1965; MA, Washington U., St. Louis, 1968, PhD, 1976. Economist Bd. Govs. of FRS, Washington, 1972-82, sr. economist, 1982-84; prof. fin., Harriette L. & Walter G. Lacy, Jr. chair banking Baylor U., Waco, Tex., 1984—, acting chmn. dept. fin. ins. and real estate, 1996-97, chmn. dept., 1997—2006. Contbr. articles to profl. jours. Bd. visitors Abilene Christian U., Tex., 1989-92. Capt. US Army, 1969—71. Decorated Bronze Star; recipient Disting. Bus. Prof. award Baylor U., 1988, Alpha Kappa Psi Favorite Prof. award Hankamer Sch. Bus. Baylor U., 2004; Econ. Devel. Adminstrn. US Dept. Commerce fellow, 1968-69; Ernst & Young Found. Rsch. grantee, 1991. Mem. So. Fin. Assn., Southwestern Fin. Assn., Fin. Mgmt. Assn., Omicron Delta Epsilon, Beta Gamma Sigma. Mem. Ch. of Christ. Office: Baylor U Hankamer Sch of Bus Dept Fin Ins and Real Estate One Bear Pl # 98004 Waco TX 76798-8004 Home Phone: 254-776-6038. Business E-Mail: jt_rose@baylor.edu.

ROSE, JONATHAN CHAPMAN, lawyer; b. Cleve., June 8, 1941; s. Horace Chapman and Katherine Virginia (Cast) R.; m. Susan Anne Porter, Jan. 26, 1980; 1 son, Benjamin Chapman. AB, Yale U., 1963; LL.B. cum laude, Harvard U., 1967. Bar: Mass. 1968, D.C. 1972, U.S. Supreme Ct. 1976, Circuit Ct. Appeals 1977, Ohio 1978. Law clk. Justice R. Ammi Cutter, Mass. Supreme Jud. Ct., 1967-68; spl. asst. to U.S. pres., 1971-73; gen. counsel Coun. on Internat. Econ. Policy, 1973-74, The White House; assoc. dept. atty. gen. U.S. Dept. Justice, 1974-75; dept. asst. atty. gen. U.S. Dept. Justice (Antitrust Div.), 1975-77, asst. atty. gen. Office of Legal Policy, 1981-84; ptnr. firm Jones Day, Washington, 1977-81, 84—. Prin. Ctr. for Excellence in Govt.; pres. Yale Daily News Found.; bd. govs. Yale Alumni Assn., 1996-99, Yale Inaugural Leadership Exchange, 2008, Yale Global Alumni Leadership Exchange, 2009, 1st lt. U.S. Army, 1969-71. Mem. ABA, D.C. Bar Assn., Mass. Bar Assn., Ohio Bar Assn., Fed. Bar Assn., Am. Law Inst. Clubs: Met, Chevy Chase, Union, Yale, Harvard. Republican. Episcopalian. Office: Jones Day 51 Louisiana Ave NW Washington DC 20001-2113 Office Phone: 202-879-3888. Business E-Mail: jcrose@jonesday.com.

ROSE, (ROBERT) KEVIN, Internet company executive, blogger; b. Calif., Feb. 21, 1977; Grad. in Computer Sci., U. Nev., Las Vegas. Tech. advisor Dept. Energy, Nev.; tech. prodn. asst. TechTV; co-founder Revision3 Corp., 2005, Megatechtronium, 2007; founder Digg.com, 2004, chief arch., 2004—. Contbr. (TV series) The Screen Savers, 2000—04, co-host, 2004—05, host (podcast) Diggnation, 2005—, blog writer: kevinrose.com, digg.com. Named a Maverick, Details mag., 2008; named one of Most Important People on the Web, PC World, 2007, Top 25 Web Celebs, Forbes mag., 2007. Avocation: rock climbing.

ROSE, (M.) LYNN, history professor; BA in History, U. Minn., Mpls., 1985, PhD in History, 1995. Asst. prof. history Truman State U., Kirksville, Mo., 1995—2000, assoc. prof., 2000—. Guest lectr. Institut für Klassische Altertumswissenschaften Martin Luther Universität Halle-Wittenberg, 2003—04. Author: The Staff of Oedipus: Transforming Disability in Ancient Greece, 2003; contbr. articles to profl. publs., chapters to books. Recipient US Prof. of Yr. award, Carnegie Found. for Advancement of Tchg. and Coun. for Advancement and Support of Edn., 2006; named Outstanding Tchr. of Yr., Mo. Coun. Pub. Higher Edn., 2006. Mem.: Women's Classical Caucus, Soc. Disability Studies, Internat. Assn. for Sci. Study of Intellectual Disabilities, Classical Assn. of Midwest and South, Am. Classical League, Assn. Ancient Historians. Office: Divsn Social Sci Truman State U Kirksville MO 63501 E-mail: lynnrose@truman.edu.

ROSE, MARK ALLEN, humanities educator; b. NYC, Aug. 4, 1939; s. Sydney Aaron and Rose (Shapiro) R.; m. Ann (Bermingham); 1 son, Edward Gordon. AB (hon.), Princeton U., NJ, 1961; LittB, Merton Coll., Oxford, Eng., 1963; PhD, Harvard U., Cambridge, Mass., 1967. Instr. to assoc. prof. in English Yale U., 1967-74; prof. English U. Ill., 1974-77; prof. U. Calif., Santa Barbara, 1977—2008, emeritus prof., 2008—, chmn. dept. English, 1987-89; dir. U. Calif., Humanities Rsch. Inst., Santa Barbara, 1989-94, chmn. dept. English, 1997—2001, assoc. vice chancellor, 2002—06. Author: Heroic Love, 1968; (fiction) Golding's Tale, 1972; Shakespearean Design, 1972; Spenser's Art, 1975; Alien Encounters, 1981; Authors and Owners, 1993; editor: Twentieth Century Views of Science Fiction, 1976; Twentieth Century Interpretations of Antony and Cleopatra, 1977, (with Slusser and Guffey); Bridges to Science Fiction, 1980; Shakespeare's Early Tragedies, 1994; (CD-ROM) Norton Shakespeare Workshops. Woodrow Wilson Fellow, 1961; Henry Fellow, 1961-62; Dexter Fellow, 1966; Morse Fellow, 1970-71; NEH Fellow, 1979-80, 90-91. Mem. MLA, Renaissance Soc. Am., Shakespeare Soc. Am., Phi Beta Kappa. Office: U Calif English Dept Santa Barbara CA 93106 Business E-Mail: mrose@english.ucsb.edu.

ROSE, MARYA MERNITZ, lawyer; b. Sept. 1962; m. Anthony J Rose. BA, Williams College, Williamstown, Mass.; JD, Ind. U. Corp. counsel Cummins Inc, 1997—98, corp. counsel & dir. public relations, 1998—99, corp. counsel & dir. public relations & comm. strategy, 1999—2000, v.p., gen. counsel, sec., 2001—. Office: Cummins Inc 500 Jackson St Columbus IN 47202*

ROSE, MATTHEW K., rail transportation executive; BS in Mktg., U. Mo. With Mo. Pacific RR; various positions Schneider Nat., Internat. Utilities; v.p. transp. Triple Crown Svcs. (Norfolk So. RR subs.); various v.p. positions Burlington No. Santa Fe Corp., 1993—96, sr. v.p. mdse. bus. unit, 1996—97, sr. v.p., COO, 1997—99, pres., COO, 1999—2000, pres., CEO, 2000—, chmn., 2002—. Bd. dirs. AMR Corp., Ctr. Energy & Econ. Devel., Centex Corp., Dallas, 2006—; mem. Tex. Gov.'s Bus. Coun., Bus. Roundtable. Trustee Tex. Christian U.; mem. exec. bd. Boy Scouts of Am. Mem.: Assn. Am. RRs (bd. dirs.). Office: Burlington No Santa Fe Corp PO Box 961056 Fort Worth TX 76161-0056 Office Phone: 817-867-6100.

ROSE, MICHAEL DAVID, hotel company executive; b. Akron, Ohio, Mar. 2, 1942; s. William H. and Annabel L. (Kennedy) R.; children: Matthew Derek Franco, Gabrielle Elaine Franco, Morgan Douglas BBA, U. Cin., 1963; LL.B., Harvard U., 1966. Bar: Ohio 1966. Lectr. U. Cin., 1966-67; atty. Strauss, Troy & Ruehlmann, Cin., 1966-72; exec. v.p. Winegardner Internat., Cin., 1972-74; v.p. hotel group Holiday Inns, Inc., Memphis, 1974-76, pres. hotel group, 1976-78, corp. exec. v.p., 1978-79, pres., 1979, CEO, 1981, chmn. bd. dirs., 1984; chmn., CEO Promus Cos. Inc., 1990—95; chmn. Promus Hotel Corp., 1995—97, Harrah's Entertainment Inc., 1995—96; chmn. exec. com., bd. dirs. Gaylord Entertainment, Nashville, 2001—. Bd. mem. Darden Restaurants, FelCor Lodging Trust, First Tenn. Nat. Corp., SteinMart. Bd. dirs. Memphis Arts Coun., from 1979; mem. Future Memphis, from 1979; mem. bd. advisors U. Cin., from 1979; hon. chmn. bd. trustees Jr. Achievement, Memphis. Named one of Corp. Am.'s Ten Outstanding Dirs. for 2000, Dir.'s Alert. Mem. Ohio Bar Assn., Young Pres.' Orgn. Office: Gaylord Entertainment One Gaylord Dr Nashville TN 37214 Office Phone: 615-316-6000.

ROSE, MICHAEL DEAN, retired lawyer, educator; b. Johnstown, Pa., Oct. 22, 1937; BA, Ohio Wesleyan U., 1959; JD, Case Western Res. U., 1963; LLM, Columbia U., 1967. Bar: Ohio 1963. Assoc. firm Porter, Stanley, Treffinger & Platt, Columbus, Ohio, 1963-66; asst. prof. law Ohio State U., Columbus, 1967-69, assoc. prof., 1969-72, prof., 1972-99, Lawrence D. Stanley prof. law, 1987-99, prof. emeritus, 1999—. Staff asst. to chief counsel IRS, Washington, 1970-71. Author: (with Leo J. Raskind) Advanced Federal Income Taxation: Corporate Transactions, 1978, (with Joseph S. Platt) A Federal Taxation Primer, 1973, Hornbook on Federal Income Taxation, 3d edit., 1988; editor Selected Federal Taxation Statutes and Regulations, 1973-99, Ohio Will Manual, 1986-2002. Mem.: Am. Law Inst.

ROSE, MICHAEL IAN, plastic surgeon; b. NYC, Sept. 29, 1968; MD, NY Sch. Med., 1994. Cert. Am. Bd. Plastic Surgery, Am. Bd. Surgery. Intern, plastic surgery NYU/Bellevue Med. Ctr., NYC, 1994—95, resident, 1995—2000; fellow, plastic and reconstructive surgery Emory U., Atlanta, 2000—02; clin. instructor NYU Sch. Medicine, NYC, 1999—2000; private practice The Plastic Surgery Ctr. (NJ/NY); bus. ptnr. Smoothmed, NYC, 2007—. Contbr. articles to profl. jours.; featured on WPIX News, Good Morning America, ABC News, CBS News, Discovery Channel, News 12 NJ and Asbury Park Press. Fellow: Am. Coll. Surgeons. Office: The Plastic Surgery Ctr 535 Sycamore Ave Shrewsbury NJ 07702 Address: The Plastic Surgery Ctr 308 E 79th St New York NY 10021 Office Phone: 732-741-0970, 212-421-6725. Office Fax: 732-747-2606.

ROSE, MITCH, lobbyist; BA in Polit. Sci., U. Wash., 1985; JD, Washington Coll. Law, 1993. Chief of staff to Senator Ted Stevens US Senate; v.p. govt. rels. The Walt Disney Co., 2000—06; pres. Mitch Rose Strategic Cons., Washington, 2006—. Office: Mitch Rose Strategic Cons 1431 Cola Dr Mclean VA 22101

ROSE, NOEL RICHARD, immunologist, microbiologist, educator; b. Stamford, Conn., Dec. 3, 1927; s. Samuel Allison and Helen (Richard) R.; m. Deborah S. Harber, June 14, 1951; children: Alison, David, Bethany, Jonathan. BS, Yale U., 1948; MA, U. Pa., 1949, PhD, 1951; MD, SUNY, Buffalo, 1964; MD (hon.), U. Cagliari, Italy, 1990; ScD (hon.), U. Sassari, Italy, 1992; Order of the First Class (hon.), Ctrl. U. Venezuela, 1997. From instr. to prof. microbiology SUNY Sch. Medicine, Buffalo, 1951-73, dir. Center for Immunology, 1970-73, dir. Erie County Labs., 1964-70; dir. WHO Collaborating Center for Autoimmune Disorders, 1968—; prof. immunology and microbiology, chmn. dept. immunology and microbiology Wayne State U. Sch. Medicine, 1973— 82; prof., chmn. dept. immunology and infectious diseases Johns Hopkins U. Sch. Hygiene and Pub. Health, Balt., 1982-93, prof. medicine and environ. health scis., 1982—, prof. molecular microbiology and immunology, 1993—; prof. pathology Johns Hopkins U. Sch. Medicine, 1994—; dir. Johns Hopkins Autoimmune Disease Rsch. Ctr., 1998; chmn. NIP Auto-Immune Diseases Coordinating Com., 2004—06. Cons. in field. Editor: (with others) International Convocation on Immunology, 1969, Methods in Immunodiagnosis, 1973, 3d, 4th rev. edit., 1986, The Autoimmune Diseases, 1986, 2d edit., 1992, 3d edit., 1998, 4th edit., 2007, Microbiology, Basic Principles and Clinical Applications, 1983 Principles of Immunology, 1973, 2d rev. edit., 1979, Specific Receptors of Antibodies, Antigens and Cells, 1973, Manual of Clinical Laboratory Immunology, 1976, 6th edit., 2002, Genetic Control of Autoimmune Disease, 1978, Recent Advances in Clinical Immunology, 1983, Clinical Immunotoxicology, 1992, Manual of Human Immunology, 1997; editor in chief Clin. Immunology and Immunopathology, 1988-98; contbr. articles to profl. jours. Recipient award Sigma Xi, 1952, award Alpha Omega Alpha, 1976, Lamp award, 1975, Faculty Recognition award Wayne State U. Bd. Govs., 1979, Pres.'s award for excellence in teaching, 1979, Disting. Service award Wayne State U. Sch. Medicine, 1982, U. Pisa medal, 1986, U. Venezuela medal, 1998, AESKU Lifetime Achievement award, 2004, Keystone Lifetime Achievement award, 2006, Nicolaus Copernicus medal 2009; named to Acad. Scholars Wayne State U., 1981; Josiah Macy fellow, 1979. Fellow AAAS (coun. 2004—), APHA, Am. Acad. Allergy and Immunology, Am. Acad. Microbiology, Assn. Med. Lab Immunologists; mem. Acad. Clin. Lab. Physicians and Scientists, Am. Assn. Immunologists, Am. Soc. Investigative Pathology, Am. Soc. Clin. Pathologists, Am. Soc.

Microbiology (hon.; Abbott Lab. Clin. and Diagnostic Immunology award 1993, Profl. Achievement award 2003), Brit. Soc. Immunology, Coll. Am. Pathologists, Sociètè Française d'Immunologie, Can. Soc. Immunology, Polish Acad. Sci. (fgn. mem.), Soc. Exptl. Biology and Medicine Coun., Clin. Immunology Soc. (sec., treas., pres. 1993), Austrian Immunology Soc. (hon. mem.), Sigma Xi (pres. Johns Hopkins U. chpt. 1988), Alpha Omega Alpha, Delta Omega. Office: Johns Hopkins U 615 N Wolfe St Baltimore MD 21205-2103

ROSE, NORMA LOUISE, retired human services manager; d. Elzie Mars and Hattie Mae Rose. MBA, Chapman U., Orange County, Calif., 1979. With Hewlett-Packard Co., San Diego, 1959—98, prodn. worker, 1959—78, order processing clk., prodn. supr., pers. rep., coll. recruiting mgr., human resources mgr.; ret., 1998. Mem. Smithsonian Inst. Mem.: Hewlett Packard Retiree Club, Sierra Club. Home: 24218 Via Llano Murrieta CA 92562-5581 Personal E-mail: normar15@verizon.net.

ROSE, PATRICIA, artist, educator; 1 child, Nicholas Flores. BA, U. Calif., Berkeley, 1968; MA, Roosevelt U., 2002. Cert. elem., secondary tchr. Ill. Tchr. Cook and Lake Counties, Ill., 1991—95; dir. Ravenswood Gallery and Studios, Chgo., 1995—96; founder, dir. Art Odyssey, Wilmette, Ill., 1997—; tchr. Muslim Cmty. Ctr. Full Time Sch., Morton Grove, Ill., 1999—2000; instr. gifted edn. and arts Sch. of Art Inst., Chgo., 2001. One-woman shows include Union League Club, Chgo., 1999, Rush Presbyn. St. Lukes Med. Ctr., Core Gallery, 2005—06, exhibited in group shows at Montserrat Gallery, N.Y.C., 2000, Chgo. Art Open, 2000, Art Odyssey, Willmette, 2002—04, Represented in permanent collections Chgo. Bd. Edn. Office Langs. and Culture. Mem.: Nat. Assn. Profl. and Exec. Women, Am. for the Arts, Nat. Mus. Women in Arts, Art Alumni Group U. Calif. Berkeley, Ill. Assn. Gifted Children, Nat. Assn. Gifted Children. Avocations: theater, social science. Office Phone: 312-286-7422. Personal E-mail: artodyssey@comcast.net, patrose253@comcast.net.

ROSE, PAUL EDWARD, systems administrator, educator; b. Denver, Oct. 14, 1978; s. Robert Ferguson and Kathleen Marie Rose; life ptnr. Shontience Nicole Morris; 1 child, Imani Brianna-Lee. Cert. A+ CompTia, Network+ CompTia, Security+ CompTia, Server+ CompTia, i-Net+ CompTia, CIW cert. instr. ProSoft, cert. master CIW adminstr. ProSoft, CIW assoc. ProSoft, CIW profl. ProSoft, master CIW site designer ProSoft, CIW security analyst ProSoft, ITCAP designated instr., MCP Microsoft, MCSA Windows 2000 Microsoft, MCDST Windows XP Microsoft, MCSA Windows 2003 Microsoft, MCSE Microsoft, Security Microsoft, Microsoft cert. trainer Microsoft. Migration cons. Oxford Global Resources, Mountain View, Calif., 2000; owner RoseNet Solutions, Oakland, Calif., 2000—; sr. instr. TechSkills, San Francisco, 2003—; chief tech. officer Computer Svcs. Group, San Jose, Calif., 2004—. Cons. Young Cmty. Developers, San Francisco, 2005—. Bd. dirs. African-American.com, San Jose, 2003—06. With USMC, 1996—99. Decorated Good Conduct medal USMC, Meritorious Mast. Master: Masons (3d degree). Democrat. Avocations: travel, baseball, football, softball. Personal E-mail: paul@paulrose.net. Business E-Mail: prose@techskills.com.

ROSE, PETER ISAAC, sociologist, writer, editor; b. Rochester, NY, Sept. 5, 1933; s. Aaron E. and Lillian (Feld) R.; m. Hedwig Hella Cohen, Mar. 25, 1956; children: Elisabeth Anne, Daniel Eric. AB, Syracuse U., 1954; MA, Cornell U., 1957, PhD, 1959. Mem. faculty Smith Coll., Northampton, Mass., 1960—2003, sr. fellow Kahn Inst., 2000—, Sophia Smith prof. emeritus, 2003—; mem. grad. faculty U. Mass., 1961—. Fulbright prof. U. Leicester, Eng., 1964-65, Kyoto (Japan) Am. Studies Inst., Flinders U., Australia, 1970, U. Vienna, 2004, Roosevelt Acad. Utrecht U., Netherlands, 2008; vis. prof. Wesleyan U., Middletown, Conn., 1966-67, U. Colo., 1968, Yale U., 1970, Clark U., 1970-71, Doshisha U., Kyoto, Japan, fall 1999, Göteborgs U., Sweden, 2007; vis. scholar Harvard U., 1983, 84-85, vis. prof., spring 1984; vis. scholar Chinese Acad. Social Sci., Beijing, 1986; resident scholar Rockefeller Study Ctr., Bellagio, Italy, summer 1987; vis. fellow St. Catherine's Coll., Oxford, spring, 1995, Stanford U., 1996, 2005, 2007, 08 Liguria Study Ctr., Bogliasco, Italy, spring 1998, fall 2001. Author: They and We, 1964, 6th edit., 2006, The Subject is Race, 1968, Strangers in Their Midst, 1977, Mainstream and Margins, 1983, Tempest-Tost, 1997, Guest Appearances and Other Travels in Time and Space, 2003, With Few Reservations, 2009; co-author: Sociology, 1977, 2d edit., 1982, Understanding Society, 1978, 3d edit., 1986; editor: The Study of Society, 1967, 4th edit., 1977, The Ghetto and Beyond, 1969, Americans From Africa, 1970, Nation of Nations, 1972, reissued, 1981, Seeing Ourselves, 1972, rev. edit., 1975, Through Different Eyes, 1973, Socialization and the Life Cycle, 1979, Working With Refugees, 1986, Interminority Relations in the U.S., 1993, Professorial Passions, 1998, The Dispossessed, 2005, SoGoNow.com Travel Mag., 2007—. Mem. Am. Sociol. Assn. (mem. coun. 1974-77), Mass. Sociol. Assn. (pres. 1967-68), Soc. Study of Social Problems (v.p. 1968-69), Ea. Sociol. Soc. (v.p. 1970-71, pres. 1991-92), Am. Soc. Journalists & Authors, Soc. Profl. Journalists. Home: 96 Round Hill Rd Northampton MA 01060-2907 Office Phone: 413-585-3515. Business E-Mail: prose@smith.edu.

ROSE, PETER J., delivery service executive; V.p. air divsn. The Harper Group, San Francisco, 1969-81; exec. v.p. Expeditors Internat. Wash. Inc., Seattle, 1981-88, pres., CEO, 1988—, chmn., 1996—. Office: Expeditors Internat Wash Inc 1015 3rd Ave Seattle WA 98104

ROSE, RICHARD LOOMIS, lawyer; b. Long Branch, NJ, Oct. 21, 1936; s. Charles Frederick Perrott and Jane Mary (Crotta) R.; m. Marian Frances Irons, Apr. 1, 1960; children: Linda, Cynthia, Bonnie. BA, Cornell U., 1958; JD, Washington and Lee U., 1963. Bar: N.Y. 1963, Conn. 1966, U.S. Dist. Ct. (so. dist.) N.Y. 1964, U.S. Dist. Ct. Conn. 1966, U.S. Ct. Appeals (2d cir.) 1965, U.S. Supreme Ct. 1970. Ptnr. Cummings & Lockwood, Stamford, Conn., 1965—91, Kleban & Samor, P.C., Southport, 1991-93; counsel Whitman Breed Abbott & Morgan, Greenwich, Conn., 1993—95; prin. Roberts, Rose & Bates, P.C., Stamford, Conn., 1995—2005, Murtha Cullina LLP, 2005—. Mem. adv. com. Conn. Banking Commr. on Conn. Securities Laws, 1982—; bd. dirs. Conn. World Trade Assn. Editor: Washington and Lee Law Rev. Chmn. Fgn. Trade Zone Com. to Mayor of City of Bridgeport, Conn., 1988-90; mem. fgn. trade awareness com. S.W. Area Industry and Commerce Assn., Task Force, 1987-88; bd. dirs. German Sch. of Conn., Inc., 1992—, New Canaan Preservation Alliance, Inc., 2007-; commr. New Canaan (Conn.) Hist. Dist. Commn., 1995—. 1st lt. U.S. Army, 1958-60, Korea. Mem. ABA, Conn. Bar Assn. (exec. com. corp. sect.), Internat. Bar Assn., New Canaan Country Club, Gridiron Club New Canaan, Poinsettia Club New Canaan, Phi Delta Phi, Omicron Delta Kappa, Phi Delta Theta. Republican. Office: Murtha Cullina LLP 177 Broad St Stamford CT 06901

ROSE, ROBERT DIDIER, neurophysiologist; b. Washington, Oct. 10, 1954; s. Richard Contee and Mary Estill (Martin) R. AB, Transylvania U., 1976; MS, Emory U., 1981; PhD, SUNY, Stony Brook, 1986. Tchg. asst. Emory U., 1977-81, SUNY, Stony Brook, 1981-82, NIMH predoctoral rsch. fellow, 1982-84, rsch. asst., 1984-86; rsch. assoc. prof. dept. pharmacology U. Pitts. Med. Sch., 1987-88; clin. neurophysiologist dept. neurosurgery U. Pitts. Med. Ctr., 1992; clin. fellow Ctr. Clin. Neurophysiology U. Pitts. Sch. Medicine, 1992-97; asst. prof. dept. biol. sci. Duquesne U., Pitts., 1988-90; asst. prof. dept. biology Slippery Rock U., Pa., 1991-92; vis. prof. dept. anatomy and histology U. Pitts. Dental Sch., 1998—; COO Neurex, Inc., 1999—. Pres., CEO Neuro-Resource, 1998—; cons. Computational Diagnostics, Inc., Pitts., 1992—; cons. dept. otolaryngology Children's Hosp. of Pitts., 1994—, NuVasive, Inc., 2000—; adj. faculty C.C. Allegheny County, Pitts., 1988—; trainee activities com. Ctr. for Neurosci., U. Pitts., 1988—; naturalist-cons. Queens Coll. Ctr. for Environ. Edn., 1982-84; grant reviewer US-Israel Bination Sci. Found., Tel Aviv, 1990—; mem. panel NSF, Washington, 1990, 92; exec. dir. Childrens Rights Inst., 1999—; bd. dir. Child & Family Advocates; clin. dir. EMG Group, 2000—; bd. dir., PT Works, 2003-; Neurophysiology Program Dir. Integrative Med. Ctr., Atlantic City, 2003-; lectr., reviewer in field. Contbr. articles, chpts., abstracts to profl. publs. Fellow Marine Biol. Lab., Woods Hole, Mass., 1978, Luft-Brückendank fellow Inst. Tierphysiologie und Angewandte Zoologie, Arbeitsgruppe Neurobiologie, Freie U. Berlin, 1979, Deutscher Akademischer Austauschdienst fellow, 1979, NIMH/NRSA fellow SUNY-Stony Brook, 1982-84; grantee Emory U., 1978-81, Freie U., 1979, Hunkele Devel. Fund, 1988, State of Pa., 1989, NSF, 1989-91, Copeland Found., 1992-94, Children's Hosp. of Pitts., 1994, 94-95. Mem. AAAS, Am. Soc. Neurophysiol. Monitoring, Soc. Neurosci. Avocations: white water kayaking, fishing, skiing, rugby. Office: 440 Broadway Pitcairn PA 15140-1447

ROSE, ROBERT EDGAR, retired state supreme court justice; b. Orange, NJ, Oct. 7, 1939; BA, Juniata Coll., Huntingdon, Pa., 1961; LL.B., NYU, 1964. Bar: Nev. 1965. Dist. atty. Washoe County, 1971-75; lt. gov. State of Nev., 1975-79; judge Nev. Dist. Ct., 8th Jud. Dist., Las Vegas, 1986-88; justice Nev. Supreme Ct., Carson City, 1989—2006, chief justice, 1993-94, 1999—2000, 2006, sr. justice, 2007—. Office Phone: 775-684-1540.

ROSE, ROBERT GORDON, lawyer; b. Newark, June 25, 1943; s. Harry and Ann Shirley (Gordon) R.; m. Ellen Nadley Berkowitz, July 2, 1966; children: Lisa Pauline, Michael Allan. BA, SUNY, Buffalo, 1965; MA, Columbia U., 1969; JD, Seton Hall U., 1974. Bar: NJ 1974, US Dist. Ct. NJ 1974, US Ct. Appeals (3rd cir.) 1974, US Ct. Appeals (2nd cir.) 1975. Law clk. to Hon. John J. Gibbons US Ct. Appeals (3rd cir.), Newark, 1974-75; assoc. Day Pitney LLP, Morristown, NJ, 1975-80, ptnr., 1980—. Mem. com. on unauthorized practice of law NJ Supreme Ct., 1989-2001, apptd. com. chair, 2000-2001; apptd. lawyers adv. com. US Dist. Ct., Dist. NJ, 2002—; trustee Legal Svcs. NJ, 2001—. Contbr. articles to profl. jours. Recipient Disting. Grad. award Seton Hall U. Law Sch., 2000. Mem. ABA, NJ Bar Assn., Morris County Bar Assn. (trustee 1989-90). Avocations: travel, stamp collecting/philately. Office: Day Pitney LLP PO Box 1945 Morristown NJ 07962-1945 Office Phone: 973-966-8070. Business E-Mail: rrose@daypitney.com.

ROSE, ROBERT JOHN, bishop emeritus; b. Grand Rapids, Mich., Feb. 28, 1930; s. Urban H. and Maida A. (Glerum) Rose. Student, St. Joseph Sem., 1944-50; BA, Seminaire de Philosophie, Montreal, Que., Can., 1952; S.T.L., Pontifical Urban U., Rome, 1956; MA, U. Mich., 1962. Ordained priest, 1955; dean St. Joseph Sem., Grand Rapids, 1966-69; dir. Christopher House, Grand Rapids, 1969-71; rector St. John's Sem., Plymouth, Mich., 1971-77; pastor Sacred Heart Parish, Muskegon Heights, Mich., 1977-81; ordained bishop, 1981; bishop Diocese of Gaylord, Mich., 1981-89, Diocese of Grand Rapids, Mich., 1989—2003, bishop emeritus, 2003—. Mem. Nat. Conf. Cath. Bishops Roman Catholic.

ROSE, ROBERT M., consultant interdisciplinary research netwoks; s. Henry and Anne Blossom Rose, Eve Feldsott Rose (Stepmother); m. Kay Weinstock, May 31, 1992; children: Alyssa Anne, Ariana Jane Komaroff, Jeff Weinstock. BA, Bard Coll., Annandale-on-Hudson, NY, 1957; MD, Harvard Med. Sch., Boston, 1961. Cert. in pyschiat. residency Mass. Mental Health Ctr., 1964, diplomate psychiatry & neurology ABPN, 1971. Asst. chief dept neuroendocrinology Walter Reed Army Inst. Rsch., Washington, 1965—68, chief dept. psychiatry, 1968—71; chief dept. psychosomatic medicine Boston Univ. Sch. Medicine, 1971—77; dir. air traffic contr. health change study BU Sch. Medicine, Boston, 1973—77; chair, dept. psychiatry & behavioral scis. Univ. Tex. Med. Br., Galveston, Tex., 1977—89; fellow, ctr. advanced study behavioral scis. Stanford U., Palo Alto, Calif., 1988—89; dir. health program John D. and Catherine T. MacArthur Found., Chgo., 1990—2005; scholar residence Inst. Med. Humanities, UTMB, Galveston, 2005—. Dir., rsch. network mind body interactions MacArthur Found., 1989—99; founder and chair, Mind Brain Body & Healthlinitiative, Chgo., 2001—. Contbr. scientific papers to sci. jours. Bd. mem. Personality Disorder Rsch. Found., NYC, 2000—03. Capt. MC US Army, 1965—68, Walter Reed. Grant, FAA, 1973—78, NIMH, 1971—77, 1976—78, NASA, 1990—91, Kohlberg Found., 2000—02, NIH, 1980—86, 2004—07. Fellow: Am. Assn. Advancement Sci., Am. Psychiat. Assn.; mem.: Psychiat. Rsch. Soc. (pres. 1981—82), Am. Psychopathological Assn. (pres. 1985—86), Am. Coll. Neuropsychopharmacology, Am. Psychosomatic Soc. (pres. 1981). Avocations: boating, fishing, aquariums. Home: 2860 Dominique Galveston TX 77551 Office: Robert M Rose MD Consulting 2860 Dominique Galveston TX 77551 Business E-Mail: brose@urbancom.net.

ROSE, ROBERT MICHAEL, materials engineering educator; b. NYC, Apr. 15, 1937; s. Lawrence Lapidus and Lillian (Rosen) R.; m. Martha Gibbs, Oct. 15, 1961; children: Cynthia J., James L., Joshua S. BS, MIT, 1958, DSc, 1961. Registered profl. engr., Mass. Asst. prof. materials sci. and engring MIT, Cambridge, 1961-66, assoc. prof., 1966-72, prof., 1972—2003, prof. emeritus, 2003—, dir. MIT Concourse program, 1988—; prof. health scis. and tech. Harvard Med. Sch.-MIT, 1978-90; dir. Cryoelectro Assocs., Wenham, Mass., 1978-90. Author: Structure and Properties of Materials, 1964, Practical Biomechanics for the Orthopedic Surgeon, 1979, 92, The Chicken From Minsk, 1995. Recipient Kappa Delta prize Am. Acad. Orthop. Surgeons, 1973. Mem. Am. Soc. Metals (vice chmn. 1971-72, Bradley Stoughton prize, chmn. 1972-73), Metal Soc. AIME, Boston Yacht Club. Jewish. Home: 18 Morgan St Wenham MA 01984-1114 Office: Rm 8 031 MIT 77 Massachusetts Ave Cambridge MA 02139-4301 Business E-Mail: rose@mit.edu. *I would share my thoughts with you if I were satisfied with what I am. But I submit to you that anyone who is truly satisfied with his personal success doesn't understand the nature of his own achievement.*

ROSE, ROBERT NEAL, investment banker; b. Chgo., Feb, 27, 1951; s. James Allan Rose and Hazel (Gordon) Kaufman; m. Anna Yvette Trujillo, Aug. 23, 1981; children: David James, Michelle Elizabeth, Daniel Jonathan. BS, Georgetown U., 1973; MPA, Harvard U., 1995. Trader Salomon Bros., NYC, 1974-75; regional coord. Latin Am. Merrill Lynch Govt. Securities, NYC, 1975-76; dir. fed. govt. affairs Pub. Svc. of N.Mex., Albuquerque, 1977-78; exec. dir. Gov. Jerry Apodaca, Washington, 1979-80; expert cons. U.S. Dept. Commerce, Washington, 1980-81; asst. treas. Am. Express Internat. Bank, NYC, 1981-82; sr. v.p. Refco, Inc., NYC, 1982-84; v.p., mgr. Thomson McKinnon Securities, NYC, 1984-88; sr. v.p. Lehman Bros., NYC, 1988-92; mng. dir. Credit Agricole Futures Inc., NYC, 1992-95; sr. mng. dir. Bear Stearns, NYC, 1995—2008; mng. dir. JP Morgan, NYC, 2008—. Cons. BDM Corp., McLean, Va., 1981-88; Presdl. appointee J. William Fulbright Fgn. Scholarship Bd., 1993-97; bd. adv. Shenandoah U. Sch. Bus., 2001—. Exec. com. Conn. Yankee Coun. Boy Scouts Am., 2000—, v.p. exec. com., 2003—; mem. arrangements com. Dem. Nat. Conv., San Francisco, 1984, mem. site selection com., 1989—90, alt. del. Boston, 2004, mem.rules com. LA, 2000; chmn. nat. fin. coun. Dem. Nat. Com., 1998—2005; fin. chmn. Conn. Dem. State Ctrl. Com., 1993, 2003—05; trustee Conservative Synagogue of Westport, 2000—02. Wexner Heritage Found. fellow, 1992-94; recipient Disting. Citizen award Conn. Yankee Coun. Boy Scouts Am., 2004. Jewish. Avocation: skiing. Home: 326 Bayberry Ln Westport CT 06880-1315 Office: 383 Madison Ave New York NY 10179 Office Phone: 212-272-2822. E-mail: robrose@att.net.

ROSE, SELWYN H., chemicals executive; b. NYC, May 1, 1933; s. Rubin and Ruth Rosenthal; m. Helen Diana De Mov, July 25, 1957; children: Michelle, Wendy, Suzanne. BS, CCNY, 1954; MS, Ohio State U., 1958, PhD, 1961; MBA with honors, U. Chgo., 1979; CFP, Coll. Fin. Planning, 1994. Sr. rsch. chemist Pennwalk Corp., King of Prussia, Pa., 1961-65; dept. mgr. Horizons Inc., Beachwood, Ohio, 1965-72, dir. rsch., 1972-74; mgr. long range rsch. De Soto Inc., Des Plaines, Ill., 1974-79; dir. rsch., cen. rsch. lab. Borg-Warner Chems., Des Plaines, 1979-85; v.p. tech. Parker Chem. Co., Madison Heights, Mich., 1985-88; gen. mgr. rsch. and devel. Himont Inc., Wilmington, Del., 1988-91, v.p. product devel., 1991-93; pres. SHR Fin. Advisors, Wilmington, 1993—. Contbr. articles to profl. jours.; patentee in field. 1st lt. U.S. Army, 1954-56. Recipient IR 100 award Indsl. Rsch. mag., 1971, award Roon Found., 1979. Mem. Am. Chem. soc., Nat. Assn. Personal Fin. Advisors, Fin. Planners Assn. Achievements include development of polyphosphazene polymers. Home: 1503 Evergreen Ln Wilmington DE 19810-4431

ROSE, SHIRLEY KELLY, retired language educator; b. Marianna, Fla., Jan. 22, 1939; d. James William and Alice Elizabeth Kelly; children: William Timothy Livingston, Kelly Livingston Carlton. BA, Fla. State U., Tallahassee, 1960; MS in Adult Edn., Troy State U., Montgomery, Ala., 1979, MS in English, 1990. English tchr. Bay County HS, Panama City, Fla., 1960—62, St. James HS, Montgomery, 1972—73, Patterson State Tech. Coll., Montgomery, 1973—2000, chmn. gen. edn., 1990—2000; ret., 2000. Tech. coll. rep. State Policy Adv. Comm., Montgomery, 1986—99, Postsecondary Exec. Com., Montgomery, 1985—99. Coord. edn. divsn. United Way, Montgomery; organizer, pres. Jr. Woman's Club, Mobile, Ala., 1965—67; co-chmn. March of Dimes, Montgomery, 1965—68; bd. dirs. Cystic Fibrosis, Montgomery. Recipient Davenport Meml. award, Nat. Coun. Higher Edn., 1996; named Disting. Young Woman, Montgomery Jaycettes, 1969, Outstanding Clubwoman, Montgomery Jr. Woman's Club, 1969, Outstanding Faculty Mem., Ala. Coll. Sys., 1992. Mem.: Ala. Edn. Assn. (pres. postsecondary divsn. 1986—87, Outstanding Postsecondary Mem. 1995, Rose award), Wynlakes Women's Club. (v.p.). Methodist. Avocations: travel, reading, bridge, exercise. Home: 8620 Lillian Pl Montgomery AL 36117

ROSE, STEPHEN, medical researcher; Chief rsch. officer Found. Fighting Blindness. Office: 11435 Cronhill Dr Owings Mills MD 21117-2220 Office Phone: 410-568-0150. E-mail: info@FightBlindness.org.*

ROSE, STEPHEN F., columnist; b. Kansas City, Mo., Nov. 5, 1947; s. Stanley J. and Shirley Rose; m. Carol S. Brady, May 31, 1970; children: Joshua Scott, Melissa Rose Faulkner, Rebecca Kathryn. BJ, U. Mo., Columbia, 1966—70. Chmn. Sun Publs., Overland Park, Kans., 1977—. Vice-chmn. Greater Kans. City C. of C., Kansas City, 1995—2003; chmn. U. Kans. Sch. Nursing, Kansas City, 1997—99, UMB Scout Mut. Funds, 1990—2005, dir., 1990—2005; pres. Suburban Newspapers Am., Chgo., 1998—99; dir. Metcalf Bank, Overland Park, Kans., 1986—99; roundtable panelist Sta. KCPT-TV, Kansas City, 1995—2003, weekly Sta. PBS-TV program host. Specialist 4th class/corr. US Army, 1968—69, Vietnam. Recipient Johnson Countian of Yr., Johnson County CC Found., 1999. Achievements include co-chairing the first bi-state cultural initiative in America. Home: 2110 Stratford Rd Mission Hills KS 66208 Home Fax: 913-722-5353. Personal E-mail: srose@kc.rr.com.

ROSE, SUSAN ANN, psychology professor, consultant; b. Brockton, Mass., June 27, 1939; d. George and Pessie (Task) Lazarus; m. Israel H. Rose, Mar. 26, 1961. BA, U. Mass., 1961; PhD, NYU, 1969. Lic. psychologist, N.Y. NIMH predoctoral fellow NYU, NYC, 1963-67; NIH postdoctoral fellow Albert Einstein Coll. Medicine, Yeshiva U., Bronx, N.Y., 1969-72, instr. psychiatry, 1972-74, asst. prof., 1974-77, assoc. prof., 1978-83, prof. psychiatry, 1983—, prof. pediatrics, 1985—. Mem. rev. com. NIMH, 1987-91; invited prof. Sorbonne, U. Paris, 1983; vis. scientist B.J. Wadia Hosp. for Children, Bombay, 1984; Flora Stone Mather Disting. Vis. prof. Case Western Res. U., Cleve., 1990. Co-author: The Language of Learning, 1978, (tests) Preschool Language Assessment Instrument, 1978, Spanish version, 1983; mem. editorial bd. Infant Behavior and Devel., 1980—, Child Devel., 1982-83, Devel. Psychology, 1986-93, 98—; contbr. over 90 articles to profl. jours., chpts. to books. Indo-Am. fellow Coun. for Internat. Exch. of Scholars, 1984; grantee NIH and Nat. Found. March of Dimes, 1974—. Fellow APA; mem. Soc. for Behavioral Pediatrics (exec. coun. 1988-91), Internat. Soc. for Infant Studies (steering com. 1986-91, exec. bd. 1992-98, sec. 1998—). Avocations: reading, tennis, piano, cooking. Home: 18 Floral Dr Hastings On Hudson NY 10706-1202 Office: Albert Einstein Coll Medicine Dept Pediatrics 1300 Morris Park Ave Bronx NY 10461-1926 Office Phone: 718-430-3042. Business E-Mail: srose@aecom.yu.edu.

ROSE, SUSAN PORTER, management and governmental affairs consultant; b. Cin., Sept. 20, 1941; d. Elmer Johnson and Dorothy (Wurst) Porter; m. Jonathan Chapman Rose, Jan. 26, 1980; 1 child, Benjamin Chapman. BA, Earlham Coll., 1963; MS, Ind. State U., 1970; HDL (hon.), Rose-Hulman Inst. Tech., 2002. Staff asst. Congressman Richard L. Roudebush, Washington, 1963-64; asst. dean George Sch., Bucks County, Pa., 1964-66; asst. dir. admissions Mt. Holyoke Coll., South Hadley, Mass., 1966-71; asst. dir. correspondence First Lady Pat Nixon The White House, 1971-72, dir. of scheduling to First Lady Pat Nixon, 1972-74, to First Lady Betty Ford, 1974-77; spl. asst. to asst. atty. gen. Office Improvements in Adminstrn. Justice, Washington, 1977-79; spl. asst. to dep. asst. atty. gen. Justice Mgmt. divsn. U.S. Dept. Justice, Washington, 1978-81; chief of staff to Barbara Bush, asst. to U.S. v.p. Washington, 1981—89; chief of staff to First Lady Barbara Bush, dept. asst. pres. of U.S. The White House, 1989—93; commr. U.S. Commn. Fine Arts, 1993-98. Bd. dirs. Barbara Bush Found. for Family Literacy, 1993—2002; trustee Bush Presdl. Libr.; mem. alumni coun. Earlham Coll., 1975—78, pres. alumni assn., 1978—81; partcipant Yale Inaugural Alumni Leadership Exchange program, 2008, Yale Global Alumni

Leadership Exchange program, 2009. Recipient Disting. Alumni award, Earlham Coll., 1992, Ind. State U., 1991. Mem.: Ind. Acad. Home: 5955 Ranleigh Manor Dr Mc Lean VA 22101-2428

ROSE, TESSIE E., special education educator, consultant; b. Galveston, Tex., Aug. 13, 1974; d. Carolyn and Kenneth Rose; m. Tom Nay, July 7, 2001. BS in Outdoor Recreation for Spl. Populations, Ferrum Coll., Va., 1993—96; MS in Therapeutic Recreation, U. Utah, Salt Lake City, 1996—98, PhD in Spl. Edn., 2001—05; Post Doctorate - Spl. Edn., Lehigh U., Bethlehem, Pa., 2005—06. Lic. Spl. Edn. Severe Disabilities Endorsement Utah Bd. Edn., 2002, cert. Spl. Edn. Mild/Moderate Utah Bd. Edn., 2004, AIMSweb Trainer Edformation, Inc., 2005. Spl. edn. tchr. Murray Sch. Dist., Utah, 2002—05; adj. faculty, dept. spl. edn. U. Utah, Salt Lake City, 2003—05; rsch. assoc. Ctr. for Promoting Rsch. to Practice, Bethlehem, Pa., 2005—. Trainer AIMSweb- Edformation, Inc., Minn., 2005—; project coord., mp3 model demo grant Lehigh U., 2005—, project coord., tchr. study group, 2005—; mgr., transition and assessment Lehigh U. & Pocono Mountain Sch. Dist., Pocono, Pa., 2005—; edn. cons., Salt Lake City, 1999—. Author: (rsch. and presentation) Effectiveness of Personalized Level Systems (Outstanding Profl. Performance award, CCBD, 2005); contbr. chapters to books, articles to profl. jours. Trip coord. YouthLINC, Holliday, Utah, 2003—05; fund raising com. Nat. Ability Ctr., Park City, Utah, 1998—2003; scholarship com. Lehigh Women's Group, Bethlehem, 2005—06. Recipient Tchr. of Yr. Nomination, Key Bank, Utah, 2004, The Rose award, Grant Elem., 2005; grantee Leadership grant, U. Utah, 2001—04. Mem.: AAHPERD, Coun. for Exceptional Children. Avocations: rock and ice climbing, travel. Personal E-mail: queentessie@yahoo.com.

ROSE, THOMAS ALBERT, artist, educator; b. Washington, Oct. 15, 1942; s. Francis John and Ann Elizabeth (Voelkel) R.; m. Mary Melinda Moyer, Aug. 21, 1965; children: Sarah, Jessica. BFA, U. Ill., 1965; MA, U. Calif., Berkeley, 1967; postgrad., Lund U., Sweden, 1967-68. Instr. U. Calif., Berkeley, 1968-69, N.Mex. State U., Las Cruces, 1969-72; faculty mem. U. Minn., Mpls., 1972—, prof. art, 1983—, Fesler-Lampert chair in humanities, 2001—. Author: Winter Book, 1995, Where Do We Start?, 2003, 1018 W. Scott St., 2005, Time Frames, 2008; one-man shows include Clock Tower, N.Y.C., 1977, Truman Gallery, N.Y.C., 1977-78, Rosa Esman Gallery, N.Y.C., 1979, 81, 82, Marianne Deson Gallery, Chgo., 1984-86, Robert Thomson Gallery, Mpls., 1986, 91, 92, 95, Deson Saunders Gallery, Chgo., 1989, Mpls. Inst. Art, 1992, Weisman Art Mus., Mpls., 1994, Tweed Mus., Duluth, Minn., 1995, Steinbaum/Krauss Gallery, N.Y.C., 1996, 99, Brevard Mus. Art, Melbourne, Fla., 1997, Gensler Arch., Washington, 1999, 2004, Flanders Gallery, Mpls., 2000, 05, Bernice Steinbaum Gallery, Miami, Fla., 2001, 03, 05, Intermedia Arts, Mpls., 2003, Flanders Gallery, Mpls., 2005, Kent Mueller Gallery, Milw., 2005, solo PNG YAO Photography Festival China 2009; exhibited in group shows at Walker Art Ctr., Mpls., 1974, 76, 77, Whitney Mus. Downtown, N.Y.C., P.S. #1, N.Y.C., 1978, Wave Hill, Bronx, N.Y., 1981, Hirshhorne Mus., Washington, 1981, Am. Ctr. in Paris, 1982, Harvard U. Sch. Architecture, 1983, Cultural Ctr., Chgo., 1983, Hal Bromm Gallery, N.Y.C., Sheldon Mus., Lincoln, Nebr., 1989, Tampa (Fla.) Mus., 1988, MCAD, Mpls., 1996, Minn. Mus. Art, 1996, Socrates Sculpture Park, N.Y.C., Fla. Internat. U., Miami, 1997, Gallerie Lipanjepuntin, Trieste, Italy, 2006, Luxan Acad. Art, Shenyang, China, 2006, Beijing Film Acad., 2006, Tehran Mus. Contemporary Art, Iran, 2007, Korean Culture Ctr., Beijing, 2009, Beijing Film Acad. 2009; represented in permanent collections Whitney Mus., N.Y.C., Columbia U. Lib. NYC 2009, Lib. Congress Washington 2009, Getty Inst. L.A., Walker Art Ctr., Joslyn Mus., Omaha, Park St. Lofts, Springfield, Mass., U. Minn., Mpls., Am. Lung Assn. Target Ctr., Mpls., St. Lukes Episcopal Ch., Mpls., Wonkwang U., Republic of Korea, Mpls. Inst. Art, Weisman Mus. Art, Mpls., Stanford U. Libr., Sch. of the Art Inst., Chgo., Milw. Pub. Libr.; set designer: Fool for Love, Cricket Theater, Mpls., 1985, Circus, Theater de Jeune Lune, 1986; project dir. Works of Art in Pub. Places for Humphrey Inst. Pub. Affairs, Mpls., 1988; prin. works include Minn. Zoo, Marine Edn. Ctr., Sacred Heart U., Fairfield, Conn., Berniece Steinbaum Gallery, Miami, 1999, Steinbaum residence, 2002, Bennett Meml., Mpls., 2002. Recipient McKnight Artist fellow, 1995, travel fellow, Dayton-Hudson/Jerome, 1990, 1995, Jerome Found. Arts, 1993—94, Mellon Found., 1993, Fesler-Lampert Chair in Humanities, 2002; named Rockefeller resident, Bellagio, Italy, 1993; grantee, Arts Bd. Opportunities, 1993; fellow, Nat. Endowment for Arts, 1977, 1981, Bush Found., 1979, Minn. State Arts Bd., 1979, 1984, McKnight Found., 1981, McKnight Found. Rsch., 1993—96, McKnight Photography, 2002. Home: 91 Nicollet St Minneapolis MN 55401-1513 Office: Univ Minn 208 Studio Arts 23D S Avenue Minneapolis MN 55425 Office Phone: 612-889-9871. Personal E-mail: rosex001@umn.edu.

ROSE, WILLIAM N. (BILL ROSE), museum administrator; PhD in Plant Ecology, Mich. State U. Pres., CEO Kalamazoo Nature Ctr., Mich., 1989—. Mem.: Assn. Nature Centers Adminstrs. (tres. bd. dirs., mem. nat. bd.). Office: Kalamazoo Nature Ctr 7000 N Westnedge Ave Kalamazoo MI 49009 Office Phone: 269-381-1574.

ROSE, WILLIAM SHEPARD, JR., lawyer; b. Columbia, SC, Mar. 9, 1948; s. William Shepard and Meta Cantey (Boykin) R.; m. Frances John Hobbs, Aug. 11, 1973; children: Katherine Cummings, William Shepard, III, Whitaker Boykin. BA in English, U. South, 1970; JD, U. S.C., 1973; LLM in Taxation, Georgetown U., 1976. Bar: S.C. 1973, Ohio 1977, D.C. 1974, U.S. Dist. Ct. D.C. 1976, U.S. Tax Ct. 1976, U.S. Supreme Ct. 1976, U.S. Ct. Claims Ct. 1978, U.S. Ct. Appeals (10th cir., 5th cir., 4th cir.) 1987, U.S. Ct. Appeals (3d, 6th, 7th, 8th, 9th and 11th cirs.) 1988. Trial atty. Office of Chief Counsel IRS, Washington, 1973-77; assoc. Frost & Jacobs, Cin., 1977-80, McNair Law Firm PA, Hilton Head Island, SC, 1981—83, ptnr., 1983—87, 1989—2008, of counsel, 2008—. Asst. atty. gen., tax divsn. U.S. Dept. Justice, Washington, 1987-89; chmn., dir. Sea Pines Montessori Sch., 1983-86, Hilton Head Broadcasting, 1983-87, MBR Corp., Adwell Corp., and subsidiaries, Links Group, Inc., 1989-2000, The Dye Preserve, LLC, Hilton Head Prep. Sch., 1986-87, 89-93; bd. dir. Contbr. articles to profl. jours. Asst to chmn. bus. fundraising Beaufort County United Way, Hilton Head Island, 1984; vice chmn. Beaufort County Rep. Party, 1991-92, 93, chmn., 1992-93, vice chmn., 1993-95; mem. Beaufort County Transp. Com., 1994-95; commr. Sea Pines Pub. Svc. Dist., 2003-06, South Island Pub. Svc. Dist., 1995-2006; S.C. aquarium dir. Carolinian Ball, 2004-2007. Fellow Am. Coll. Tax Counsel; mem. ABA (past co-chmn. subcom. tax sect.), Beaufort County Bar Assn., S.C. Yacht Club (bd. govs. 1989-94, exec. com. 1993-94, rear commodore 1993-94), Low Country Citizens Com. Jud. Qualifications (dir. vols. medicine clinic 2009-). Republican. Episcopalian. Office: PO Drawer 3 23-B Shelter Cove Ln Ste 400 Hilton Head Island SC 29928-3588 E-mail: rrose@mcnair.net.

ROSE-ACKERMAN, SUSAN, law and political economy educator; b. Mineola, NY, Apr. 23, 1942; d. R. William and Rosalie Rose; m. Bruce A. Ackerman, May 29, 1967; children: Sybil, John. BA, Wellesley Coll., 1964; PhD, Yale U., 1970. Asst. prof. U. Pa., Phila, 1970-74; lectr. Yale U., New Haven, 1974-75, asst. prof., 1975-78, assoc. prof., 1978-82; prof. law and polit. economy Columbia U., NYC, 1982-87; Ely prof. of law and polit. econ. Yale U., New Haven, 1987-92, co-dir. Ctr. Law, Econ. and Pub. Policy, 1988—. Henry R. Luce prof. jurisprudence law and polit. sci., 1992—. Vis. rsch. fellow World Bank, 1995-96. Author: (with Ackerman, Sawyer and Henderson) Uncertain Search for Environmental Quality, 1974 (Henderson prize 1982); Corruption: A Study in Political Economy, 1978, (with E. James) The Nonprofit Enterprise in Market Economies, 1986; Rethinking the Progressive Agenda: The Reform of the American Regulatory State, 1992, Controlling Environmental Policy: The Limits of Public Law in Germany and the United States, 1995, Corruption and Government: Causes, Consequences and Reform, 1999 (translated into 13 languages) (Levine Prize 2000), From Elections to Democracy: Building Accountable Government in Hungary and Poland, 2005 editor: The Economics of Nonprofit Institutions, 1986, (with J. Coffee and L. Lowenstein) Knights, Raiders, and Targets: The Impact of the Hostile Takeover, 1988, (with Janós Kornai) Building a Trustworthy State in Post-Socialist Transition, 2004, (with Kornai and B. Rothstein) Creating Social Trust in Post-Socialist Transition, 2004, International Handbook on the Economics of Corruption, 2006, Economics of Administrative Law, 2007; contbr. articles to profl. jours.; mem. editl. bd. Jour. Law, Econs. and Orgn., 1984—, Internat. Rev. Law and Econs., 1986—, Polit. Sci. Quar., 1988—. Bd. dirs. Transparency Internat., 1994—. Guggenheim fellow 1991-92, Fulbright fellow, Free U. Berlin, 1991-92; fellow Ctr. for Advanced Study in the Behavioral Scis., Stanford, Calif., 2002, Collegium Budapest, 2002. Mem. Am. Law and Econs. Assn. (bd. dirs. 1993-96, 2002-04), Am. Econ. Assn. (mem. exec. com. 1990-93), Am. Polit. Sci. Assn., Assn. Am. Law Schs., Assn. Pub. Policy and Mgmt. (policy coun. 1984-88, treas. 1998-2000). Democrat. Office: Yale U Law Sch PO Box 208215 New Haven CT 06520-8215 Office Phone: 203-432-4891. Business E-Mail: susan.rose-ackerman@yale.edu.

ROSEBERRY, EDWIN SOUTHALL, retired state agency administrator; b. Roanoke, Va., July 4, 1925; s. Edwin Alexander and Gladys Edmonia (Southall) R.; m. Mary Louise Sprengel, Sept. 2, 1949 (dec. 1978); children: Edwin Jr., David, Kevin; m. Alice Proffit Boger, Dec. 27, 1980; 1 stepdaughter, Elizabeth Leigh Boger. BS in Commerce, U. Va., 1949. Registered sanitarian, Hawaii, Va. Store mgr. Allied Arts, Charlottesville, Va., 1949-51; retail credit sales mgr. B.F. Goodrich Co., Charlottesville, 1951-53; environ. health specialist Dept. of Health, Charlottesville, 1953-84, Dept. of Labor, Honolulu, 1987-2000; ret., 1999. Freelance photographer, Charlottesville, 1949-85, Honolulu, 1985—. Contbr. photographs: The Inward Eye, 1986. Election ofcl. State of Hawaii, Honolulu, 1988—. With USN, 1944-46. Recipient Nat. awards Eastman Kodak Co., nat. newspapers, and photography mags., 1951-69. Mem. VFW (life), Am. Indsl. Hygiene Assn., Austrian Hawaiian Club (v.p., bd. dirs. 1985), Antique Auto Assn. (pres. Piedmont region 1964), Hawaii Photo Soc. (v.p. 1989), Elks (tiler and inner guard 1985, officer Honolulu chpt. 1985-2001), Am. Legion (dept. historian, VFW jr. vice commdr.), Mason (32 degree), Shriners (sojourners, heroes of '76, eastern star), Pi Delta Epsilon. Episcopalian. Avocations: photography, stamp collecting/philately, antique automobiles, figure skating. Home: Carriage Hill Apts #302 820 Beverly Dr Charlottesville VA 22911 Personal E-mail: uvaflashed@comcast.net.

ROSEBERRY, JAMES ALAN, retired science educator; b. Chico, Calif., June 11, 1946; s. Richard Dickinson and Margaret Ann Roseberry; m. Susan Jane O'Leary, July 28, 1979; children: Nathan James, Nora Elizabeth, Atoras Finnian. AB, U. Calif., Berkeley, 1968; MA, U. Wis., Madison, 1975, ABD, 1979. Tchr. Madison Area Tech. Coll., Wis., 1980—2003, part time instr., 2003—. Author: All of Us Went to Vietnam. Bd. mem. Crossing, Mafison, Wis., 2004—08. With US Army, 1969—71, US, Vietnam. Avocations: baking, hiking, reading, writing, bicycling. Home: 2220 West Lawn Ave Madison WI 53711 Personal E-mail: jim.roseberry@gmail.com.

ROSEBOROUGH, TERESA WYNN, lawyer; b. Iowa City, Nov. 28, 1958; d. Robert Larry Wynn Jr. and Ethel (Crawford) Wynn; m. Joseph Anthony Roseborough, May 24, 1980. BA, U. Va., 1980; MEd, Boston U., 1983; JD with high honors, U. N.C., 1986. Bar: Ga. 1987, U.S. Ct. Appeals (4th cir.) 1987, U.S. Dist. Ct. (no. dist.) Ga. 1989, U.S. Ct. Appeals (11th cir.) 1989, U.S Ct Appeals (5th, 6th and 7th cir.), U.S. Supreme Ct. Counselor U.S. Dept. of Army, Giebelstadt, Fed. Republic of Germany, 1980-83; law clk. to hon. Judge J. Dickson Phillips U.S. Ct. Appeals (4th cir.), 1986-87; law clk. to hon. Justice John Paul Stevens U.S. Supreme Ct., Washington, 1987-88; assoc. Sutherland, Asbill & Brennan, Atlanta, 1988-93; dep. asst. atty. gen. office legal counsel U.S. Dept. Justice, Washington, 1994—96; ptnr. Sutherland Asbill & Brennan LLP, Atlanta. Adj. prof. litig. Emory U. Sch. Law, 1996—98. Editor in chief U. N.C. Law Rev., 1985-86. Bd. dirs. Howard Schs., Atlanta, 1990—, Neighborhood Justice Ctr., 1993—, Nat. Assn. for Pub. Interest Law, The Children's Sch.; chair pro bono com. Atlanta Coun. Younger Lawyers, 1990-92, bd. dirs., 1990-93. Named to Am.'s Top Black Lawyers, Black Enterprise mag., 2003. Mem. ABA (vice chair young lawyers sect. pro bono com. 1990-92, vice chair water quality com. sect. on natural resources energy and environment 1992—), Am. Constn. Soc. (chair, 2004-), State Bar Ga., Gate City Bar Assn., Ga. Assn. Black Women Attys., Order of Coif. Avocations: skiing, golf. Office: Sutherland Asbill & Brennan LLP 999 Peachtree St NE Atlanta GA 30309-3996 Office Phone: 404-853-8100. E-mail: teresa.roseborough@sablaw.com.

ROSEBUSH, JAMES SCOTT, financial services company executive, former government official; b. Flint, Mich., June 1, 1949; s. Kenneth F. and Jacqueline (Porter) R.; m. Nancy Paull, May 18, 1974; children: Claire Haisley, Lauren Culver. BA, The Principia, Elsah, Ill., 1971; MA, Boston U., 1973. Cons., Boston, 1972-76; v.p. Nat. Chamber Found., Washington, 1976-79; assoc. dir. corp. contbn. Std. Oil Co., Cleve., 1979-81; dir. Office Bus. Liaison, U.S. Dept. Commerce, Washington, 1981, spl. asst. to pres. for pvt. sector initiatives, Washington, 1981-82; dept. asst. to Pres., chief staff for First Lady The White House, Washington, 1982-86; pres. James Rosebush & Co., 1986—; CEO Growth Strategy, Inc., OurfamilyManager.com. Lectr. Georgetown U., Washington, 1977-79, George Washington U., Washington, 1977-79; presdl. appointee Nat. Mus. Svcs. Bd. Author: First Lady, Public Wife, 1987; contbr. articles to profl. jours. Mem. rev. com. United Way, Cleve., 1979; mem. cmty. rels. com. Cleve. Orch., 1979; bd. dirs. Phillips Collection Mus., SDC, Inc.; art adv. panel Fed. Res. Bd.; mem. adv. bd. Boston U. Recipient Internat. award Rotary Internat., 1970 Republican. Avocations: tennis, skiing, reading, travel. Office: 1250 24th St NW Ste 350 Washington DC 20037-1124 Office Phone: 202-835-1695. Personal E-mail: jsrosebush@aol.com.

ROSEDALE, PHILIP E., computer software company executive; b. San Diego, 1968; m. Yvette Rosedale. BS in Physics, U. Calif., San Diego. V.p., chief tech. officer RealNetworks; entrepreneur-in-residence Accel Partners, San Francisco, 1999; founder, CEO Linden Lab, San Francisco, 1999—2008, chmn., 1999—. Recipient Rave award for bus., WIRED mag., 2006; named one of The World's Most Influential People, TIME mag., 2007, 50 Who Matter Now, Business 2.0, 2007, 50 Most Important People on the Web, PC World, 2007. Achievements include development of Second Life computer game software. Office: Linden Lab 945 Battery St San Francisco CA 94111-1305

ROSEFSKY, JONATHAN BENENSOHN, pediatrician; b. Johnson City, NY, June 28, 1939; s. I. J. and Elsie S. Rosefsky; m. Sue Perel, 1964 (div. 2005); children: Katherine, Douglas, Matthew. AB, Cornell U., 1960; B in Med. Sci., Dartmouth U., 1962; MD, Harvard U., 1964. Diplomate Am. Bd. Pediat., lic. Pa., Va. Intern in surgery Vanderbilt Univ. Hosp., Nashville, 1964-65; resident in pediatrics Children's Hosp. Med. Ctr., Boston, 1965-67; pediatrician USAF Med. Corps, Langley AFB, Va., 1967-69; dir. neonatal ICU United Health Svcs. Hosp., Johnson City, NY, 1969-74; pvt. practice Binghamton, NY, 1969-86; pres. Notation Systems, Inc., Binghamton, 1981-89; asst. dir. clin. devel. McNeil Consumer Products Co., Ft. Washington, Pa., 1986-89; dir. med. svcs., sr. dir. med. affairs Wyeth-Ayerst Labs., St. David's, Pa., 1989—99; pres. Fluidmotive, Inc., Haverford, Pa., 2000—, Simulatrix, Inc., Wynnewood, Pa., 2004—, HydroCoil Power, Inc., Wynnewood, Pa., 2006—08, chmn., CTO, 2009—; cons., primary clin. leader Mature Products, Johnson & Johnson PRD, 2008—09. Cons. pediat. N.Y. State Dept. Social Svcs., Albany, 1976—86; FDA adv. com. Gen. Hosp. and Personal Use Devices, Rockville, Md., 1986; industry rep. FDA Adv. Com. on Immunology Devices, Rockville, 1987—93; asst. prof. Pediat. Jefferson Med. Sch., Phila., 1987—2008; chmn. com. on ethics in clin. trials Pharm. Rsch. & Mfrs. Assn., 1998; pharm. device cons. Rapid Pathogen Screening Corp., 2004—08. Contbr. articles to profl. jours. Chmn. Citizen's Adv. Com. to Mayor of Binghamton, NY, 1971. Capt. USAF, 1967—69. Recipient Physician's Recognition award, AMA, 2007. Fellow: Am. Coll. Nutrition, Am. Acad. Pediat.; mem.: Mainline YMCA (bd. dirs. 2005—08), Harvard Club NYC. Achievements include invention of back wedge, mole marker, DecTRR electronic camouflage, ribbon drive: propulsion, pump, hydrocoil low head hydroelectric turbine. Avocations: skiing, swimming, photography, languages, travel. Home: 1359 Arbordale Rd Wynnewood PA 19096 Office Phone: 877-790-7972. Business E-Mail: hydrocoilpower.inc@att.net.

ROSELL, KAREN J., art history professor; b. Ithaca, NY; d. Joan N. Rosell; m. James R. Donaldson. PhD, Ohio U., Athens, 1986. Prof. art history Juniata Coll., Huntingdon, Pa., 1986—, chair, dept. art and art history, 1988—. Recipient Beachely award, Juniata Coll., 1996. Mem.: Coll. Art Assn. Office: Juniata Coll 1700 Moore St Huntingdon PA 16652 Office Fax: 814-641-3695. Business E-Mail: rosell@juniata.edu.

ROSELL, KURT F., lawyer; b. Ithaca, NY, May 12, 1960; BS magna cum laude, Wake Forest U., NC, 1982; JD, Columbia Law Sch., 1985; LLM in Taxation, NYU, 1993. Bar: NY 1986. Atty. Cravath, Swaine & Moore, NYC; hiring ptnr., recruiting com. Schulte Roth & Zapel LLP, NYC. Spkr. in field, sr. editor Columbia Law Rev., 1983—85; contbr. articles to profl. jour. Harlan Fiske Stone Scholar. Mem.: Assn. Bar City NY, Phi Beta Kappa. Office: Schulte Roth & Zapel LLP 919 Third Ave New York NY 10022 Office Phone: 212-756-2099. Office Fax: 212-593-5955. Business E-Mail: kurt.rosell@srz.com.

ROSELL, SHARON LYNN, physics and chemistry professor; b. Wichita, Kans., Jan. 6, 1948; d. John E. and Mildred C. (Binder) Rosell. BA, Loretto Heights Coll., 1970; postgrad., Marshall U., 1973; MS in Edn., Ind. U., 1977; MS, U. Wash., 1988. Cert. profl. educator, Wash. Assoc. instr. Ind. U., Bloomington, 1973-74; instr. Pierce Coll. (name formerly Ft. Steilacoom CC), Wash., 1976-79, 82, Olympic Coll., Bremerton, Wash., 1977-78; instr. physics, math. and chemistry Tacoma CC, Wash., 1979—89; instr. physics and chemistry Green River CC, Auburn, Wash., 1983—86; rschr. Nuc. Physics Lab., U. Wash., Seattle, 1986-88; asst. prof. physics Cen. Wash. U., Ellensburg, 1989—. Faculty senate senator Ctrl. Washington U., 1992-98; alt. senator 2006-07, 2008-09. Senator St. Andrew's Ch., Ellensburg, Wash., 1992—98, lector & dir., Rite of Christian Initiation Adults, 1993-, mem. parish coun., 1995-2000. Mem.: Soc. Physics Students (councilor zone 17 1998—2004, com. judging Nat. Outreach and Rsch. awards 2000—01, 2003—05, nat. nominating com. 2005—07), Pacific NW Assn. Coll. Physics (bd. dirs. 1997—99, 2001—, treas. 2002—, pres. 2009—, chmn. bd. dirs. 2009—), Internat. Union Pure and Applied Chemistry (affiliate), Am. Chem. Soc., Am. Assn. Physics Tchrs. (rep. com. on physics for 2-yr. colls. Wash. chpt. 1986—87, v.p. 1987—88, pres. 1988—89, v.p. 1994—95, pres. 1995—96, past pres. 1996—97), Am. Phys. Soc. Democrat. Roman Catholic. Avocations: leading scripture discussion groups, reading, poetry, needlecrafts. Home: 1100 N B St Apt 7 Ellensburg WA 98926-2570 Office: Ctrl Wash U Physics Dept Ellensburg WA 98926 Office Phone: 509-963-2757. Business E-Mail: rosells@cwu.edu. *Personal philosophy: Every human being is born with a unique set of talents and gifts with which to serve the Lord and other people; the greater the gift, the greater the obligation to serve.*

ROSELLE, DAVID PAUL, retired academic administrator, mathematician, educator; b. Vandergrift, Pa., May 30, 1939; s. William John and Esther Suzanne (Clever) R.; m. Louise Helen Dowling, June 19, 1967; children— Arthur Charles, Cynthia Dowling BS, West Chester State Coll., 1961; PhD, Duke U., 1965; LLD (hon.), West Chester U., 1994; degree (hon.), Westchester U., Soka U., Japan. Asst. prof. math. U. Md., College Park, 1965-68; assoc. prof. math. La. State U., Baton Rouge, 1968-73, prof., 1973-74, Va. Poly. Inst. and State U., Blacksburg, 1974-87, dean grad. sch., 1979-81, dean research and grad. studies, 1981-83, provost, 1983-87, chmn. Commn. on Rsch., 1981-83, chmn. Commn. on Grad. Studies, 1983-87; prof. U. Ky., 1987-90, pres., 1987-90; pres., prof. math. U. Del., 1990—2007. Pres. COMAP, Inc., Lexington, Mass., 1986-95; bd. dirs. Wilmington Trust Corp., VTLS, Inc. Editor: Proc. of the First Louisiana Conf. on Combinatorics, Graph Theory and Computing, 1970, Proc. of the Second Louisiana Conf. on Combinatorics, Graph Theory and Computing, 1971; mem. editorial bd. The Bicentennial Tribute to American Mathematics, 1977; contbr. numerous research articles to profl. jours. Mem. Del. Roundtable, 1990—, Bus.and Pub. Edn. Coun., 1990—; trustee Winterthur Mus., 1991—; bd. dirs. Del. Acad. Medicine, 1991—, Med. Ctr. Del., 1991—, OCLC, Inc., 2004-; mem. USAID adv. com. vol. fgn. aid, 2000-04. Named Outstanding Alumnus West Chester State Coll., 1979; Westinghouse Coop. scholar, 1957; NSF grantee, 1965-75; Teaching Excellence Cert., 1978; Digital Equipment grant, 1984; Nat. Coun. Tchrs. Math. Cert. of Appreciation, 1984; founding fellow of Inst. for Combinatorics and Its Applications, 1990; numerous invited addresses at univs. and profl. soc. meetings. Mem. Am. Math. Soc., Math. Assn. Am. (sec., fin. com., exec. com., com. on publs. 1975-84; com. on spl. funds 1985—; chmn. com. on accreditation 1985; numerous other coms.). Home: 14 Laurel Ridge Ln Wilmington DE 19807-1322 Business E-Mail: roselle@udel.edu.

ROSELLE, WILLIAM CHARLES, librarian; b. Vandergrift, Pa., June 30, 1936; s. William John and Suzanne Esther (Clever) R.; m. Marsha Louise Lucas, Aug. 2, 1959; 1 child, Paul Lucas. BA, Thiel Coll., 1958; MLS, U. Pitts., 1963. Lic. profl. guide State of Mont., 1978. Mem. faculty Milton Hershey (Pa.) Sch., 1960-62; trainee Pa. State Library, 1962-63; asst. catalog librarian Pa. State U., 1963-65; engring., math. librarian U. Iowa, 1965-66, library adminstrv. asst., 1966-69, asst. dir.

libraries, 1969-71; prof., dir. library U. Wis.-Milw., 1971-89; dir. univ. library system U. Pitts., 1989-90; pvt. cons. Thiensville, Wis., 1991—. Chmn. Morris Fromkin Meml. Lectr. Com., 1972-89; chmn. planning task force on computing U. Wis. System, 1973-74, mem. library planning study com., 1978-79, co-chmn. library automation task force, 1983-85; chmn. computing mgmt. rev. team U. Wis.-Stout, 1976; chmn. Council for U. Wis. Libraries, 1981-82; library cons. Grambling (La.) State U., Viterbo Coll., LaCrosse, Wis., N.C. A&T U., Greensboro, Mt. Mary Coll., Milw., U. Ill. at Chgo., Milw. Sch. Engring., Bklyn. Coll., U. South Ala., Concordia Coll., Milw., Metrics Rsch. Corp., Cardinal Stritch Coll., Milw., N.Y. Inst. Tech., Indiana U. of Pa., Med. Coll. Wis., Wis. Luth. Coll., Milw.; participant Library Adminstrs. Devel. Program, U. Md., 1973, micrographics seminar Nat. Microfilm Assn., 1973, Mgmt. Skills Inst., Assn. Rsch. Libraries, Kansas City, Mo., 1977, Meadowbrook Symposium Midwest Library Network, 1976; mem. sect. geography and map libraries Internat. Fedn. Library Assns. and Instns., 1978-83; mem. bldg. com. Ctr. for Rsch. Libraries, 1980-82. Editorial cons. The Quest for Social Justice, 1983, Current Geographical Publications, 1978-89; contbr. articles to profl. jours. Pres. Thiensville (Wis.) Village Bd., 1987; bd. dirs. Charles Allis Art Mus., 1979-84. Served with AUS, 1958-60, panel mem. Gallup Poll, 2005-. Named Disting. Alumnus, Thiel Coll., 1985, recipient Ernest Spaights award, U. Wis. Milw., 2007, Samuel F. B. Morse medal, Am. Geographical Soc., 2009 Hon. fellow Am. Geog. Soc.; mem. Spl. Libraries Assn. (spl. citation 1979), ALA (life), Iowa Library Assn. (chmn. audit com. 1968-70, chmn. intellectual freedom com. 1969-70), Wis. Library Assn., Midwest Acad. Librarians Conf. (chmn. 1969-71), AAUP (treas. U. Iowa chpt. 1969-70), Coun. Wis. Libraries (chmn. 1973-74), Soc. Tympanuchus Cupido Pinnatus, Internat. CBX Owners Assn., Milw. Civil War Round Table, Ozaukee Corvette Club, Beta Beta Beta, Beta Phi Mu, Phi Alpha Theta, Phi Kappa Phi, Phi Delta Kappa. Lutheran. Home: 324 Sunny Ln Thiensville WI 53092-1334

ROSELLI, RICHARD JOSEPH, lawyer; b. Chgo., Mar. 2, 1954; s. H. Joseph and Dolores Roselli; m. Lisa McNelis; children: Nicholas Joseph, Christiana Elise, Alexandra Grace, Michaela Luciana, Anthony Santino. BA, Tulane U., 1976, JD, 1980. Bar: Fla. 1981, U.S. Dist. Ct. (so. dist.) Fla. 1981, U.S. Ct. Appeals (5th and 11th cirs.); Bd. Cert. Civil Trial Lawyer. Ptnr. Krupnick, Campbell, Malone, Roselli et al, Ft. Lauderdale, 1981—2002, Roselli & Roselli Trial Lawyers, Boca Raton, Fla., 2002—05, Roselli & McNelis, PA, Boca Raton, Fla., 2005—. Adj. asst. prof., mem. bd. advisors Physician Asst. Program, Nova Southeastern U., 2005. Trustee Fla. Dem. Party. Mem. Am. Assn. Justice (pres.' coun. 1996-97), Am. Bd. Trial Advocates, Am. Soc. Law and Medicine, So. Trial Lawyers Assn. (founder), Acad. Fla. Trial Lawyers (bd. dirs. 1987—, exec. com. 1990-97, sec. 1993, treas. 1994, pres. elect. 1995, pres. 1996, chmn., Fla. Lawyers Action Group-PAC 1996, Golden Eagle award, 1989, 1996, 98, Silver Eagle award, 1990, Crystal Eagle award 1995, named one of Best Lawyers in America, Top 100 Lawyers in Fla., Fla. Super Lawyers), Broward County Trial Lawyers (bd. dirs.), Fla. Justice Assn., Trial Lawyers for Pub. Justice, Lawyer Pilots Bar Assn., Am. Assn. for Justice, Fla. Justice Assn., Palm Beach Trial Lawyers Assn, Fla. Grand Opera. Democrat. Roman Catholic. Office: 4800 N Federal Hwy Ste 202E Boca Raton FL 33431 Office Phone: 561-826-0826. Business E-Mail: rroselli@rosellimcnelis.com.

ROSELLINI, ALBERT D., former governor; b. Tacoma, Wash., Jan. 21, 1910; s. John and Annunziata Pagni Rosellini; m. Ethel McNeill, 1937 (dec. 2002); children: John M., Janey, Sue, Lynn, Albert D. Jr. Student, U. Wash., U. Wash. Law Sch. Dep. prosecutor King County, Wash., 1935—41; mem. Wash. State Senate from 33rd dist., 1939—57; spl. asst. atty. gen. State of Wash., 1941—46, gov., 1957—65; atty., polit. consultant Seattle. Del. Dem. Nat. Conv., 1968; chmn. US Olympic Com., Wash., Wash. State Transp. Commn.; bd. dirs. Wash. State Conv. Ctr. Mem.: Wash. Bar Assn., Sons of Italy, Italian Club, K. of C., Eagles, Kiwanis, Moose, Elks, Tau Kappa Epsilon, Phi Alpha Delta. Democrat. Roman Catholic. Office: 5930 6th Ave S Seattle WA 98108-3318 Office Phone: 206-763-7110. Office Fax: 206-762-9367. Personal E-mail: govadr@nwlink.com.

ROSELLINI, JAY JULIAN, language educator; b. Chgo., May 11, 1947; s. Julian and Julia Rosellini; m. Eleanor D. Florence, Aug. 16, 1969; children: Alissa, Stefan. BA, U. Ill., Urbana Champaign, 1969; MA, U. Ill., 1972; PhD, Ind. U., Bloomington, 1976. Asst. prof. German Haverford Coll., 1976—77, MIT, Cambridge, Mass., 1978—86; prof. German Purdue U., West Lafayette, Ind., 1986—2001, chair German, 1992—97; chair, dept. humanities & modern lang. Suffolk U., Boston, 2001—07, prof. German & humanities, 2001—. Vis. prof. German U. Hamburg, Germany, 1989—90. Recipient Book Award, DAAD, 2002; Postdoc. Fellowship, Mellon Found. Wash. U., 1977—78, Grant, German Acad. Exch. Svc., 1980, 1989, Fellowship, Am. Coun. Learned Socs., 1981, Rsch. grant, NEH, 1997, Fulbright, Fulbright Commn., 1999. Mem.: MLA, Am. Assn. Tchrs. German, German Studies Assn. Avocation: tennis. Office: Suffolk Univ HUML Dept 41 Temple St Boston MA 02114-4280 Office Fax: 617-367-5965. Business E-Mail: jroselli@suffolk.edu.

ROSEMAN, CHARLES SANFORD, lawyer; b. Jersey City, Feb. 26, 1945; s. Leon and Edith (Neidorf) R.; children: Rochelle Lynn, Loren Scott. BA, Calif. State U., Northridge, 1968; JD, U. San Diego, 1971. Bar: Calif. 1972, U.S. Dist. Ct. (so. dist.) Calif. 1972, U.S. Dist. Ct. (cen. dist.) Calif. 1975, U.S. Supreme Ct. 1980, U.S. Claim Ct. 1990. Assoc. Greer, Popko, Nickoloff & Miller, San Diego, 1972-73; ptnr. Roseman & Roseman, San Diego, 1973-78, Roseman & Small, San Diego, 1978-82, Frank, Roseman, Freedus & Mann, San Diego, 1982-86, Roseman and Mann, 1986-92; pvt. practice San Diego, 1992—; judge pro tem San Diego County Superior Ct., 1975—; also arbitrator, mediator, 1977—; founding ptnr. i2i Resolutions, 2001. Bd. dirs. Glenn Aire Cmty. Devel. Assn., San Diego, 1972-73, Big Bros. San Diego County, 1973-81,; bd. dirs. San Diego County Anti-Defamation League, 1985—; chmn. exec. com. 1984-85, assoc. nat. commr., 1995—; bd. dirs. San Diego County Legal Aid Soc., 1988-89, Tifereth Israel Synagogue, pres. 1982-84, Homeys Youth Found., 2002-06. Mem. ABA, Am. Assn. for Justice, Fed. Bar. Assn., Consumer Attys. of Calif. (Recognition of Experience award 1985), Calif. Bar Assn., Am. Arbitration Assn. (arbitrator, panel 1985-86), San Diego Bar Assn., Consumer Attys. of San Diego (bd. dirs. 1982-84), U. San Diego Sch. Law Alumni Assn. (bd. dirs. 1972-73), B'nai B'rith (pres. 1978). Democrat. Office: Law Offices Charles S Roseman & Assocs 1761 Hotel Cir S Ste 250 San Diego CA 92108 Office Phone: 619-544-1500. Business E-Mail: csroseman@rosemanlaw.com.

ROSEMAN, JACK, computer services company executive; b. Lynn, Mass., June 13, 1931; s. Abraham and Bessie (Guz) Roseman; m. Judith Ann Rosenthal, Feb. 21, 1960; children: Laura, Alan, Shari. BA, Boston U., 1954; MS, U. Mass., 1955. Instr. U. Mass., 1958—60; dir. info. processing CEIR, Inc., Washington, 1960—66; v.p. KMS Tech. Ctr., Washington, 1966—70; pres., bd. dirs. On-Line Systems, Inc., Pitts., 1970—79; pres., chmn. United Computing Internat. subs. of SPRINT, 1979—80; pres., bd. dirs., later chmn. Actronics, 1981—85; pvt. investor, ptnr. J.R. Assocs., Pitts., 1988—92; chmn. of bd. dirs. Omega Systems, 1994—96; CEO/dir. Roseman Inst., 2001—. Disting. adj. prof. Donald H. Jones Ctr. Entrepreneurship, 1992—2000, assoc. dir., 1992—2001; John Thorne prof. entrepreneurship Carnegie Mellon U., 2000—01; dir. emeritus Pitts. High Tech. Coun.; chmn. Cerebellum, Inc., 1997—2000; bd. dirs. Roseman Inst., Collaborate, Inc., 2001—05, MIT Forum; advisor Donald H. Jones Ctr. for Entrepreneurship, Carnegie Mellon U., Echo Internat., 2001—06; internat. CEO Energy Chasec, Ill. Co-author: Outrageous Optimism: Wisdom for the Entrepreneural Journey. Adv. Kobold Found.; chmn. Nat. Found. Tchg. Extrepreneurships. Recipient Judges' award, Ernst & Young, and Merrill Lynch Inc. mags., 1991. Office Phone: 412-369-5306. Business E-Mail: rosemanj@rosemaninstitute.com.

ROSEMAN, SAUL, biochemist, educator; b. Bklyn., Mar. 9, 1921; s. Emil and Rose (Markowitz) R.; m. Martha Ozrowitz, Sept. 9, 1941; children: Mark Alan, Dorinda Ann, Cynthia Bernice. BS, CCNY, 1941; MS, U. Wis., 1944, PhD, 1947; MD (hon.), U. Lund, Sweden, 1984. From instr. to asst. prof. U. Chgo., 1948-53; from asst. prof. to prof. biol. chemistry, also Rackham Arthritis Research Unit, U. Mich., 1953-65; Ralph S. O'Connor prof. biology Johns Hopkins U., Balt., 1965—, chmn. dept., 1969-73; dir. McCollum-Pratt Inst., 1969-73, chmn. dept. biology, dir., 1988-90. Cons. NIH, NSF, Am. Cancer Soc., Hosp. for Sick Children, Toronto; sci. counselor Nat. Cancer Inst.; Lynch lectr. U. Notre Dame, 1989; Van Niel lectr. Stanford U., 1992. Author articles on metabolism of complex molecules containing carbohydrates and on solute transport.; former mem. editorial bd.: Biochemistry, Jour. Biol. Chemistry. Served with AUS, 1944-46. Recipient Sesquicentennial award U. Mich., 1967, T. Duckett Jones Meml. award Helen Hay Whitney Found., 1973, Rosenstiehl award Brandeis U., 1974, Internat. award Gairdner Found. award, 1981, Townsend Harris award CUNY, 1987, Spl. award 11th Internat. Symposium on Glycoconjugates, 1991, Karl Meyer award Soc. Glycobiology, 1993. Fellow Am. Acad. Microbiology; mem. Am. Soc. Biol. Chemists, Am. Soc. Cell Biology, Am. Acad. Arts and Scis., Nat. Acad. Scis., Am. Chem. Soc., Am. Soc. Microbiologists, Biochem. Soc. Japan (hon.). Office: Johns Hopkins U 34th Charles St Baltimore MD 21218 Office Phone: 410-516-7333.

ROSEMARIN, CAREY STEPHEN, lawyer; b. Englewood, NJ, Aug. 19, 1950; s. Jack L. and Muriel Ruth (Gordon) R.; m. Joan Maxine Lafer, June 17, 1973; children: Benjamin Joseph, Meryl Ruth. BS, U. Mich., 1972; MS, Pa. State U., 1974; JD, U. Tenn., 1978. Bar: Tenn. 1978, Ill. 1982, U.S. Dist. Ct. (ea. dist.) Tenn. 1978, U.S. Dist. Ct. (no. dist.) Ill. 1982. Rsch. assoc. Union Carbide Corp., Oak Ridge Nat. Lab., 1974-80; asst. regional counsel U.S. EPA, Chgo., 1980-86; ptnr. Katten, Muchin, & Zavis, Chgo., 1986-90, Jenner & Block, Chgo., 1990-99; prin. Law Offices of Carey S. Rosemarin, P.C., Northbrook, Ill., 1999—. Mem. ABA, Tenn. Bar Assn., Chgo. Bar Assn. (chmn. environ. law com. 1985-86), Environ. Law Inst. (assoc.), North Suburban Bar Assn. (pres. 2009-), Congregation Beth Judea (bd. dirs.), Jewish Nat. Fund Chgo. Region (bd. dirs.). Jewish. Avocations: licensed glider pilot, bicycling. Office: Law Offices of Carey S Rosemarin PC 500 Skokie Blvd Ste 510 Northbrook IL 60062-2893 Office Phone: 847-897-8000. Fax: 312-896-5786. Business E-Mail: csr@rosemarinlaw.com.

ROSEN, ABY JACOB, real estate developer; b. Frankfurt, Germany, 1960; m. Elizabeth Wechsler (div. 2004); children: Charlie, Gaby; m. Sammantha Boardman, 2005; children: Alexander Baker, Vivian Munn. With Jones Lang Wootton, NYC, 1987—90; co-founder RFR Holding LLC, NYC, 1991—; works with Ian Schrafer. Helped develop properties at 390 Park Ave., NYC, 400 Park Ave., NYC, 516 Fifth Ave., NYC, 521 Fifth Ave., NYC, 275 Madison Ave., NYC, 636 Madison Ave., NYC, many other commercial and residential properties. Recipient Man of Yr. award, Spring Ahead Gala, Jeffrey Modell Found., 2000; named one of Top 200 Collectors, ARTnews mag., 2006—08. Avocation: collecting modern and contemporary art and contemporary photography. Office: RFR Holding LLC 60 E 55th St New York NY 10022 Office Phone: 212-759-7011.*

ROSEN, ADRIENNE, artist, educator; b. St. Louis, Dec. 18, 1940; d. Charles and Rena Gallop; m. Alex Paul Tucker, June 21, 1961 (dec. June 1965); 3 children; m. Martin M. Rosen, Feb. 1967; 1 child; 3 stepchildren. BFA, Washington U., St. Louis, 1972. Illustrator, designer Internat. Shoe Co., St. Louis, 1961; owner, illustrator, graphic designer A.R. Art Studio, St. Louis, 1961—; painter portraits of people and pets St. Louis, 1995—. Art tchr. St. Louis Artist Guild; art tchr. Coll. for Kids program Meramec C.C.; pvt. instr. Adrienne's Acad. Art; juried mem. The Best of Mo. Hands, 2005, 06, 07, 2008—. Designer, illustrator (dolls) Bethany Farms Inc., 1990—. Vol. artist Leukemia Soc. Am., St. Louis, 1999, Animal Aid, St. Louis, 1975, Am. Med. Ctr., St. Louis, Cystic Fibrosis Found.; vol. St. Louis Showstoppers for Breast Cancer Rsch., chair advt. and promotion, 2006—08. Recipient 2d pl. award, Jewish Cmty. Ctrs. Assn., St. Louis, 1997, Univ. City Art Assn., St. Louis, 1999, award of mention, South County Art Assn., St. Louis, 1998, Recognition award, Art Happening, 2001—02, 1st pl. award profl. watercolor, Jewish Cmty. Ctrs. Assn., 2002, 2003, Hon. Mention, Mo. Art Tchrs. Exhibit, William Woods Coll., Fulton, 2005, Jewish Cmty. Ctr., 2005, 2006, 2007, 2008, 1st place profl. watercolor, Sr. Olympics Art Show, 2006; named Artist of Month, Ballwin, Mo., 2004. Mem.: Artists Boutique (publicity chair 2005—06, 2009), Greater St. Louis Art Assn. (publicity dir. 1994—99, sec. 1995—98, v.p. 1998—2000, pres. 2000—02, exhibits chair 2002—03, publicity chair 2004—05, pres. 2006, 2007, publicity 2008—09), St. Louis Watercolor Soc. (signature mem.), St. Louis Artist Guild (bd. dir. 1993—94), Art World Art Assn., St. Louis Track Club. Avocations: dance, photography, running. Home and Office: AR Art Studio 1717 Seven Pines Dr Saint Louis MO 63146-3713 Office Phone: 314-576-7137. Personal E-mail: arosen3125@aol.com.

ROSEN, ALLEN DAVID, plastic surgeon; b. Bklyn., Mar. 5, 1957; MD, SUNY-Buffalo, 1983. Diplomate with subspecialty in hand surgery Am. Bd. Plastic Surgery, cert. advanced edn. in cosmetic surgery Am. Soc. Aesthetic Plastic Surgery, diplomate Nat. Bd. Med. Examiners. Intern Columbia-Presbyn. Med. Ctr., NYC, 1983—84, resident in surgery, 1984—86, resident in plastic surgery, 1986—88, fellow in hand surgery, 1987; pvt. practice plastic surgery, 1987—; founding ptnr., med. dir. The Plastic Surgery Group, Montclair, NJ, 1995—; med. dir. North Fullerton Surgery Ctr., Montclair. Attending plastic surgeon, former chief divsn. plastic surgery Gen. Hosp. Ctr. Passaic, NJ; attending plastic surgeon, former chief dept. plastic surgery Mountainside Hosp., Montclair, NJ; attending plastic surgeon St. Barnabas Med. Ctr.; clin. asst. prof. U. Medicine and Dentistry NJ, Newark; spokesperson Am. Soc. Plastic and Reconstructive Surgery, 1990—. Active IRAQ STAR, Inc.; mem. grant com. Found. Diabetes Rsch. Recipient Sergio award, Healing the Children, Nat. Leadership award, Physician Adv. Bd. Fellow: ACS; mem.: NJ Soc. Plastic and Reconstructive Surgery, Am. Cancer Soc. (past pres.), Alpha Omega Alpha. Office: Plastic Surgery Group 37 N Fullerton Ave Montclair NJ 07042 Office Fax: 973-233-1933, 973-233-1934.*

ROSEN, ANDREW W., apparel executive; b. Feb. 19, 1964; s. Carl Rosen; m. Adrian Mottola (div.); 1 child, Ashely. Attended, U. Miami. Pres. Puritan Fashions, Calvin Klein Sport; pres., COO Ann Klein; co-founder, pres. Theory, 1997—2003; dir., pres., co-CEO Link Theory Holdings, 2003—. Office: Link Theory Holdings Inc 38 Gansevoort St New York NY 10014*

ROSEN, ARTHUR MARVIN, advertising executive; b. NYC, Dec. 28, 1930; s. Joseph and Cornelia (Grob) R.; m. Maureen Elizabeth Reilly; children: Ellen Jessica, Deborah Lynn, Daniel Joshua. BA, CUNY, 1952; MA, Yale U., 1953; postgrad., Columbia U., 1955-57. Analyst research Dancer-Fitzgerald-Sample, NYC, 1955-56; supr. research Benton and Bowles, NYC, 1956-61; account exec. Young and Rubicam, NYC, 1961-66; v.p. account supr. Grey Advt., NYC, 1966-69; pres. Met. Diagnostic, NYC, 1969-73; v.p. group mgmt. Grey Advt., NYC, 1973-81; exec. v.p. Sudler and Hennessey, NYC, 1981-94; mktg. cons. Himmel Nutrition, Inc., 1994-95, Martin Himmel, Inc., 1994-95. Spkr. in field. Contbr. articles to profl. jours. Pres. Temple Beth Or, Washington Twp., N.J., 1973-74; chmn. Soc. Families, Colgate U., 1983-84; chmn. curriculum com., mem. exec. coun., study leader ILEAD, 2004-05, Dartmouth Coll.; pres.,study leader Adventures in Learning, Colby-Sawyer Coll.; past pres. Country Squires of New London, NH; mem. Jewish-Christian Interfaith Partnership., mem. Kearsarge Inter Faith Coun. Cpl. U.S. Army, 1953-55. Republican. Jewish. E-mail: ponderosen@tds.net.

ROSEN, CAROL MENDES, artist; b. NYC, Jan. 15, 1933; d. Bram de Sola and Mildred (Bertuch) Mendes; m. Elliot A. Rosen, June 30, 1957. BA, Hunter Coll., 1954; MA, CUNY, 1962. Tchr. art West Orange (N.J.) Pub. Schs., 1959—85. Co-curator exhibit Printmaking Coun. N.J., Somerville, 1981; exhibit curator 14 Sculptors Gallery, NYC, 1988; guest curator Hunterdon Mus. Art, 2009; collection: Nat. Collection of Fine Arts, Smithsonian Instn., Newark Mus., N.J. State Mus., Bristol-Myers Squibb, AT&T, Noyes Mus., N.Y. Pub. Libr., Zimmerli Art Mus., Mus. of Modern Art, Whitney Mus., Libr. Collection Bklyn. Mus., Victoria & Albert Mus., Nat. Art Gallery, London, Mus. of Tolerance, LA, Hunterdon Mus. Art, Nat. Mus. Women in Arts, Tel Aviv U. and The Jewish Nat. & U. Libr., Jerusalem, Houghton Libr., Harvard U., Yale U., Clark Art Inst., Skidmore, Williams Coll. Mus. Art, Oberlin Coll., William Paterson U., Stanford U., Smith Coll., Wellesley Coll., Tate Britain, Kreitman Rsch. Ctr., Ackland Art Mus., U. NC, U. Wis., Milw.; collections: Elias Sourasky Libr., Tel Aviv U. Contbr. articles to arts mags. Recipient Hudson River Mus. award, Yonkers, 1983; fellow, N.J. State Coun. Arts, 1980, 1983. Jewish. Avocations: gardening, reading. Home: 10 Beavers Rd Califon NJ 07830-3433 Personal E-mail: earosen@earthlink.net.

ROSEN, CHARLES, II, retired lawyer; b. New Orleans, Jan. 29, 1925; s. Louis Leucht and Nita (Silverstein) R.; m. Mary Alice Waldauer (div. 1976); children: Charles III, Virginia, Jane, James Louis; m. Sandra Reed (div. 1995); m. Emily Hart, 1995. BA, Tulane U., 1948, LLB, 1951. Bar: La. 1951. Assoc. Rosen, Kammer, Wolff, Hopkins & Burke, New Orleans, 1951-55, Jones, Walker, Waechter, Poitevent, Carrere & Denegre, New Orleans, 1955-58, ptnr., 1958-90; spl. counsel Locke, Purnell, Rain, Harrell (now Locke Liddell & Sapp), New Orleans, 1990-97; of counsel Sullivan Stolier & Resor, New Orleans, 1997—2005; ret. Past chmn. and mem. exec. com. Golf & Sports Attractions, Inc., ret. mem. fore kids Found. Past trustee Touro Synagogue; hon. trustee Touro Infirmary; chmn. lawyers div. Jewish Fedn. Greater New Orleans, 1969; past chmn. lawyers div. United Fund. 1st lt. U.S. Army, 1944-46, PTO. Mem. ABA, La. Bar Assn., New Orleans Bar Assn., Am. Coll. Real Estate Attys., Anglo Am. Real Property Inst., So. Golf Assn. (past bd. dirs.), New Orleans Golf Assn. (past pres., past bd. dirs.), Tulane Green Wave Club (past bd. dirs.), Lakewood Country Club (past pres., bd. dirs.). Republican. Avocation: golf. Home: 140 E Oakridge Park Metairie LA 70005 Business E-Mail: charlie2121@bellsouth.net.

ROSEN, DAVID M., law educator; m. Victoria P. Potts, Dec. 7, 1986; 1 child, Sarah Maya. PhD, U. Ill., Urbana-Champaign, 1966—73; JD, Pace U. Sch. Law, White Plains, NY, 1987. Bar: NY 1988. Lectr. Ben Gurion U., Beersheba, Israel, 1978—81; prof. anthropology and law Fairleigh Dickinson U., Madison, NJ, 1981—. Author: (book) Armies of the Young: Child Soldiers in War and Terrorism; contbr. articles to profl. publs. Recipient Disting. Faculty award, Fairleigh Dickinson U., 2008. Mem.: Law and Soc. Assn., African Studies Assn., Am. Anthrop. Assn. Office: Fairleigh Dickinson Univ 285 Madison Ave Madison NJ 07940 Business E-Mail: rosen@fdu.edu.

ROSEN, DAVID MICHAEL, public relations administrator, public affairs consultant; b. Cambridge, Mass., Mar. 26, 1945; s. Maynard S. and Irma (Leavitt) R.; m. Nina J. Glick, Apr. 8, 1967; children: Michelle, Elisabeth. BA, Boston U., 1967, MS, 1977. Reporter The Day, New London, Conn., 1968-69, Boston Herald, 1969-73; polit. writer UPI, Boston, 1973-76, State House bur. chief, 1976-77; polit. commentator WGBH-TV, Boston, 1975-77; pub. affairs cons. Boston, 1977-79; pub. info. dir. U.S. Commodity Futures Trading Commn., Washington, 1979-80; dir. pub. rels. Harvard U., Cambridge, Mass., 1980-84, assoc. v.p., 1984-85, U. Chgo., 1986-88; v.p. Nicolazzo Assocs., Boston, 1988; chief of staff Office of Lt. Gov., Boston, 1988-89; v.p. Brandeis U., Waltham, Mass., 1989-93; cons. David Rosen Assocs., Boston, 1993, 2009—; dir. pub. rels. Yeshiva U., NYC, 1993-99; v.p. pub. affairs Emerson Coll., Boston, 1999—. Cons. U.S. GAO, Washington, 1977-79, Mass. Ins. Divsn., Boston, 1977-78, Harvard U., 1977-80, Radcliffe Coll., 1993, New Eng. Bd. Higher Edn., 1993, Clark U., 1993, Pilgrim Health Care, 1993; substitute tchr. Boston Pub. Schs., 1967-68. Author: Protest Songs in America, 1977. Avocations: piano, running. Home: 157 Bishops Forest Dr Waltham MA 02452-8800 Office: Emerson Coll Pub Affairs 120 Boylston St Boston MA 02116-4624 Home Phone: 781-893-6138; Office Phone: 617-824-8541, 781-330-9040. Business E-Mail: david_rosen@comcast.net, david_rosen@emerson.edu, david_rosen@verizon.net.

ROSEN, ERIC S., state supreme court justice; b. Topeka, May 25, 1953; BA, MA, U. Kansas; JD, Washburn U., 1984. Former social worker Topeka Public Sch.; former ptnr. Hein, Ebert and Rosen; former asst. dist. atty. & asst. public defender Shawnee County; judge State Dist. Ct., Third Dist., Shawnee County, Kans., 1993—2005; justice Kansas Supreme Ct., 2005—. Former assoc. gen. counsel Kans. Securities Commn.; former adjunct prof. Washburn U. Sch. of Law; mem. Koch Crime Commn., 1994; lecturer Menninger Sch. of Law and Psychiatry; mem. Kans. Sentencing Commn., 2004—. Recipient Atty. General's Victim's Svc. award, 2000, Martin Luther King Living the Dream Humanitarian award, 2002. Mem.: ABA, Kans. Bar Assn., Kans. Dist. Judges Assn., Am. Judicature Soc., Am. Judges Assn. Office: Kans Supreme Ct 301 W 10th Topeka KS 66612 Office Phone: 785-233-8200 ext. 4303, 785-296-6290. Office Fax: 785-296-1028.*

ROSEN, FRED, travel company executive; b. Windsor, Ont., Can., May 19, 1926; arrived in U.S., 1946; s. Harry and Dora Rosen; m. Gertrude Rush, May 13, 1952; 1 child, Robert Martin. Cert. Elec. Tech.,

Washington U., St. Louis, 1964; AA in Tourism, Forest Park C.C., St. Louis, 1993; Cert. Microcomputers, Meramec C.C., St. Louis, 2000. X-ray maint. staff Keleket X-Ray, Covington, Ky., 1953—54; whse. mgr. Western Shoe Jobbers, St. Louis, 1954—64, prodn. supr., 1977—92; owner Vanity Shoes, Kirkwood, Mo., 1964—77; travel cons. Hausler Travel, St. Louis, 1995—97; owner Accessible Travel, St. Louis, 1997—. Contbg. editor: the Independence, 1997—98; author: (guidebook) How to Travel - A Guidebook for Persons with a Disability, 1997, How to Travel in Canada - A Guidebook for a Visitor with a Disability, 2000, How to Travel To and In Britain and Northern Ireland, Accessibility Around the World-A Guidebook for a Travellers with a Disability, 2003. Pres. Kirkwood Noonday Optimist Club, 1971—72; commr. Kirkwood Disabled Commn., 1984—91, Kirkwood Housing Authority, 1977—83, Kirkwood Human Rights, 1974—77; bd. dirs. Mo. Assn. Retarded Citizens, Jefferson City, 1962—65, St. Louis Assn. Retarded Citizens, 1962—89, mem. recreation com., 1962—89. Sgt. 1st class US Army, 1946—53, ETO. Mem.: Masons (worshipful master 1990—91, Achievement award 1991). Jewish. Avocations: dance, cruising. Home: 144 Oakside Ln Saint Louis MO 63122-1211

ROSEN, GEORGE, economist, educator; b. St. Petersburg, Russia, Feb. 7, 1920; s. Leon and Rebecca (Rosenoer) Rosen; m. Sylvia Vatuk; 1 child, Mark. BA, Bklyn. Coll., 1940; MA, Princeton U., NJ, 1942, PhD, 1949. Prof. econs. Bard Coll., Annandale-on-Hudson, NY, 1946-50; economist Dept. State, Washington, 1951-54, Council Econ. Indsl. Research, Washington, 1954-55, MIT, CENIS, Cambridge, 1955-59, UN, NYC, 1959-60, Ford Found., NYC, Nepal and India, 1960-62, Rand Corp., Santa Monica, Calif., 1962-67; chief economist Asian Devel. Bank, Manila, Philippines, 1967-71; prof. econs. U. Ill.-Chgo., 1972-85, prof. econs. emeritus, 1985—, head dept., 1972-77; fellow Woodrow Wilson Internat. Ctr., Washington, 1989-90. Adj. prof. Johns Hopkins U.-Nanjing U. Ctr. Chinese-Am. Studies, 1986—87; cons. USAID, Egypt, 1994; trustee Am. Com. Asian Econ. Studies, 1990—2000; Golden Jubilee spkr. dept. commerce Osmania U., Hyderabad, India, 1999; disting. spkr. Ctr. Advanced Study Internat. Devel., Mich. State U., East Lansing, 1999. Author: Industrial Change in India, 1958, Some Aspects of Industrial Finance in India, 1962, Democracy and Economic Change in India, 1966, 1967, Peasant Society in a Changing Economy, 1975, Decision-Making Chicago-Style, 1980, Western Economists and Eastern Societies, 1985, Industrial Change in India 1970-2000, 1988, Contrasting Styles of Industrial Reform: China and India in the 1980s, 1992, Economic Development in Asia, 1996; co-author: The India Handbook, 1997, Globalization and Some of Its Contents: The Autobiography of a Russian Immigrant, 2005; book rev. editor: Econ. Devel. and Cultural Change, 1988—2004. Grantee, U. Ill., 1977—78, Social Sci. Rsch. Coun. and Am. Inst. Indian Studies, 1980—81, Am. Inst. Indian Studies, 1983—84, 1987—88, Rockefeller Found. Bellagio Study Ctr., 1984; Ford Found. fellow, NYU, 1971—72. Home: 5830 S Stony Island Ave Apt 11A Chicago IL 60637-2024 Office: 5830 S Stony Island Ave (IIA) Chicago IL 60637-2024

ROSEN, GERALD ELLIS, federal judge; b. Chandler, Ariz., Oct. 26, 1951; s. Stanley Rosen and Marjorie (Sherman) Cahn; m. Laurie DeMond; 1 child, Jacob DeMond. BA, Kalamazoo Coll., 1973; JD, George Washington U., 1979. Researchist Swedish Inst., Stockholm, 1973; legis. asst. U.S. Senator Robert P. Griffin, Washington, 1974-79; law clk. Seyfarth, Shaw, Fairweather & Gerardson, Wash., 1979; from assoc. to sr. ptnr. Miller, Canfield, Paddock and Stone, Detroit, 1979-90; judge U.S. Dist Ct. (ea. dist.) Mich., Detroit, 1990—, chief judge, 2009—. Mem. Jud. Evaluation Com., Detroit, co-chmn. 1983-88; adj. prof. law Wayne State U., 1992—, U. Detroit Law Sch., 1994-98, Cooley Law Sch., 2005-; mem. U. Mich. Law Sch., 2008-, U.S. Jud. Conf. Com. on Criminal Law; lectr. CLE confs., 1996-05, others. Co-author: Federal Civil Trials and Evidence, 1999, Michigan Civil Trials and Evidence, 2001, Federal Employment Litigation, 2006; contbr. articles to profl. jours. Rep. candidate for U.S. Congress, Mich., 1982; chmn. 17th Congl. Dist. Rep. Com., 1983-85; mem. Mich. Criminal Justice Commn., 1985-87; mem. Birmingham Athletic Club; bd. visitors George Washington U. Law Sch., 2000—; bd. dirs. Focus Hope, 2000—. Fellow Kalamazoo Coll. (sr. 1972); recipient Career Achievement award Rolex/Intercollegiate Tennis Assn. Mem. Fed. Judges Assn. (bd. dirs.). Jewish. Office: US Courthouse 231 W Lafayette Blvd Rm 730 Detroit MI 48226-2707 Office Phone: 313-234-5135.

ROSEN, GERALD HARRIS, physicist, consultant, educator; b. Mount Vernon, NY, Aug. 10, 1933; s. David A. and Shirley (Schapiro) R.; m. Sarah Louise Sweet, June 8, 1963; children: Lawrence A., Karlyn Rosen Aires. BSE, Princeton U., 1955, MA, 1956, PhD, 1958. Rsch. assoc. dept. aero. engring. Princeton U., 1958-59, NSF predoctoral fellow, 1956, Inst. Theoretical Physics, Utrecht, Netherlands, 1957-58, NSF postdoctoral fellow Stockholm, 1959-60; tech. cons. weapon sys. evaluation divsn. The Pentagon, 1960; prin. scientist Martin-Marietta Aerospace divsn., Balt., 1960-63; cons. to a tech. v.p. Southwest Rsch. Inst., 1963-66; prof. physics Drexel U., Phila., 1966-73, M.R. Wehr prof. physics, 1973-98, prof. emeritus, 1998—. Cons. fin., indsl. and govt. agys., 1966—. Author: Formulations of Classical and Quantum Dynamical Theory, 1969, A New Science of Stock Market Investing, 1990; assoc. editor Bull. Math. Biology, 1982-98; contbr. over 300 articles to profl. jours.; patentee in field. Sponsor San Antonio Chamber Music Soc., 1963-66; mem. Franklin Inst., 1967—; mem. publ. bd. Soc. Math. Biol., 1983—. Guggenheim Jet Propulsion scholar, Princeton U., 1955, Whiton Engring.-Physics scholar, 1955. Fellow Am. Phys. Soc., AAAS; mem. Am. Math. Soc. Home and Office: 415 Charles Ln Wynnewood PA 19096-1604 Office Phone: 610-896-8727. Personal E-mail: gr@geraldrosen.com. *The meaning of life has transcended human understanding up to the present time, but there are reasons to believe that future discoveries in science will illuminate the significance of life in nature. We must break completely free of non-rational dogma and illusion, and attempt to solve this mystery with factual clues revealed by scientific progress.*

ROSEN, GERALD ROBERT, editor; b. NYC, Nov. 17, 1930; s. Sol and Essie (Shapiro) R.; m. Lois Lehrman, May 9, 1958; 1 son, Evan Mark. BS, Ind. U., 1951, MA, 1953. Intelligence analyst Dept. Def., NYC, 1955-58; assoc. editor Challenge: The Mag. of Econ. Affairs, NYC, 1959-61, mng. editor, 1961-64, 65-66; sr. editor Dun's Rev., NYC, 1964-65, nat. affairs editor, 1967—; exec. editor Dun's Rev. (now Bus. Month), 1978-90; editor IMF survey Washington, 1990-93; mng. dir. Global Insights Svcs., Washington, 1993—. Fin. corr. Westinghouse Broadcasting Co. Served with CIC U.S. Army, 1953-55. Mem. Soc. Am. Bus. and Econ. Writers, N.Y. Fin. Writers Assn., White House Corrs. Assn. Clubs: Nat. Press. Home: 1625 31st St NW Washington DC 20007-3628 Office Phone: 202-337-7748. Personal E-mail: gerry308@aol.com.

ROSEN, HAROLD, medical association administrator; b. Bronx, NY; married. MD, Albert Einstein Coll. Medicine, Bronx, 1985. Cert. in endocrinology ABIM, 1991, 2000. Dir., osteoporosis prevention and treatment Beth Israel Deaconess Med. Ctr., Boston, 1999—. Office: Beth Israel Deaconess Med Ctr 330 Brookline Ave Boston MA 02215 Office Fax: 617-667-7060.

ROSEN, JACOB, engineering educator; BSc in Mech. Engring., Tel-Aviv U., Israel, 1987, MSc in Biomedical Engring., 1993, PhD in Biomedical Engring., 1997. Tech. officer, test and evaluation unit. Israel Def. Forces, Ordnance Hdqrs., 1987—91; rsch. asst., biomechanics lab., dept. biomedical engring., faculty engring. Tel-Aviv U., Israel, 1993—97, tchg. asst., dept. biomedical engring., faculty engring., 1994—95; rsch. assoc., biorobotics lab., dept. elec. engring. and dept. bioengineering U. Wash., Seattle, 1997—2000, asst. rsch. prof., dept. elec. engring., 2000—06, assoc. rsch. prof., dept. elec. engring., 2006—. Cons. RAMOT, U. Authority for Applied Rsch. & Indsl. Develop., Ramat-Aviv, Israel, 1993—97, NAYOT-ORTIM, Ltd., 1993—97, NAYOT-MPRS, Ltd., 1993—97; co-private investigator The Blue Dragon (Asys. for monitoring the kinematics and the dynamics of endoscopic tools in minimally invasive surgery for objective laparoscopic skill assessment), 2000—, Mini Robot Design for Mil. Telesurgery in the Battlefield: Breaking the Size Barrier for Surgical Manipulators, Dept. Def., Dept. Army, US Army Med. Rsch. Acquisition Activity, 2002—06, Patient Safety Ctr. Orgn., Dept. Def., Dept. Army, US Army Med. Rsch. Acquisition Activity, 2004—07, Implementing Simulation and Skills to Improve Patient Safety, 2005—07, High Altitude Platforms Mobile Robotic Telesurgery, Dept. Def., Dept. Army, US Army Med. Rsch. Acquisition Activity, 2007; adj. position, dept. surgery U. Wash., Seattle, 2002—, adj. position, dept. mech. engring., 2005—; chair, tutorials and spl. sessions, organizing com. ICAR2005 Seattle, 2003—05; mem. rsch. com. Inst. Surgical Intervention and Simulation, U. Wash., 2004—; mem. organizing com. BioRob Pisa Italy, 2006; invited presenter in field. Contbr. articles to profl. jours., chapters to books; ad hoc reviewer for several jours. Recipient award and spl. recognition of creative contbn. to a new human engring. mil. standard, Israel Def. Force, 1990, Best paper award finalist, Internat. Conf. Robotics and Automation, Washington, DC, 2002; co-recipient Winning Poster, Control Sys. Arch. for a Minimally Invasive Surgical Robot Proceedings of Medicine Meets Virtual Reality, Long Beach, Calif., 2006. Mem.: IEEE. Achievements include patents pending in field. Office: Dept Elec Engring Office EE Bldg M410 Box 352500 University of Washington Seattle WA 98195-2500 Office Phone: 206-685-1600. Office Fax: 206-221-5264. Business E-Mail: rosen@u.washington.edu.

ROSEN, JEFFREY ADAM, lawyer; b. Boston, Apr. 2, 1958; m. Kathleen Nichols, May 29, 1982. BA in Econs., Northwestern U., Ill., 1979; JD magna cum laude, Harvard U., Cambridge, Mass., 1982. Bar: DC 1982, US Dist. Ct. DC 1983, US Ct. Appeals (fed. cir.) 1983, US Supreme Ct. 1986, US Ct. Appeals (11th cir.) 1988, US Ct. Appeals (6th cir.) 1990, US Ct. Appeals (3rd cir.) 1996, US Dist. Ct. (ea. dist.) Mich., US Dist. Ct. (no. dist.) Ill., US Ct. Appeals (4th cir.). Assoc. Kirkland & Ellis LLP, Washington, 1982-88, ptnr., 1988—2003, 2009—; gen. counsel US Dept. Transp., Washington, 2003—06; gen. counsel, sr. policy adv. Office Mgmt. & Budget (OMB), Exec. Office of the Pres., Washington, 2006—09. Mem. Arlington County Hist. Affairs & Landmark Rev. Bd., Va., 1991—93; adj. prof. Georgetown U. Law Ctr., 1996—2003. Mem.: Va. Hist. Soc., US Supreme Ct. Hist. Soc., Am. Law Inst. Office: Kirkland & Ellis LLP 655 15th St NW Fl 12 Washington DC 20005-5793 Office Phone: 202-879-5000. Office Fax: 202-879-5200. E-mail: jeffrey.rosen@kirkland.com.

ROSEN, JEFFREY J., lawyer; b. NYC, May 13, 1949; s. Fred and Jane (Krieger) R. BA, Harvard U., 1971, JD, 1978. Bar: D.C. 1980. Reporter, columnist Rocky Mountain News, Denver, 1971-75; law clk. to presiding justice U.S. Ct. Appeals, Washington, 1978-79; law clk. to justice William J. Brennan U.S. Supreme Ct., Washington, 1979-80; spl. asst. to sec. US Dept. Treasury, Washington, 1980-81; assoc. Paul, Weiss et al, Washington, 1981—84, O'Melveny & Myers, Washington, 1985-87, ptnr., 1987—2001, Debevoise & Plimpton, 2001—. Supreme Ct. editor Harvard Law Rev. Named a Dealmaker of the Yr., The Am. Lawyer mag., 2004, 2007, 2009. Mem. ABA (tax sect.), D.C. Bar Assn. Office: Devevoise & Plimpton 919 3rd Ave New York NY 10022 E-mail: jrosen@debevoise.com.*

ROSEN, JEFFREY MATTHEW, law educator, journalist; b. NYC, Feb. 13, 1964; s. Sidney and Estelle Rosen. AB summa cum laude, Harvard U., 1986; BA, Oxford U., Eng., 1988; JD, Yale U., 1991. Bar: Pa. 1992, D.C. 1992. Law clk. to Hon. Abner J. Mikva US Ct. Appeals (DC Cir.), Washington, 1991-92; legal affairs editor The New Republic, Washington, 1992—; staff writer The New Yorker, Washington, 1997-99; assoc. prof. George Washington U. Law Sch., 1997—2003, prof., 2004—. Guest commentator NPR, Washington, 1998—; nonresident sr. fellow Brookings Inst., 2008-. Author: The Unwanted Gaze: The Destruction of Privacy in America, 2000, The Naked Crowd: Reclaiming Security and Freedom in an Anxious Age, 2004, The Most Democratic Branch: How the Courts Serve America, 2006, The Supreme Court: The Personalities and Rivalries That Defined America, 2007. Marshall scholar Balliol Coll., Oxford, 1986-88. Mem. Harvard Club, Cosmos Club, Phi Beta Kappa. Office: George Washington U Law Sch 2000 H St NW Washington DC 20052-0001 E-mail: jrosen@law.gwu.edu.

ROSEN, JON HOWARD, lawyer; b. Bklyn., May 20, 1943; s. Eli and Vera Horowitz Rosen; m. Patricia R. Marshall; children: Jason Marc, Hope Terry. BA, Hobart Coll., 1965; JD, St. John's U., 1968; postgrad. in bus., CCNY, 1969—71. Bar: N.Y. 1969, Calif. 1975, Wash. 1977. Atty. FAA, NYC, 1968-71; regional atty., contract adminstr. Air Line Pilots Assn., NYC, Chgo., L.A., San Francisco, 1971-77; pvt. practice Seattle, 1977-80; ptnr. Frank and Rosen, Seattle, 1981-98, Frank Rosen Freed Roberts LLP, Seattle, 1999—2002, The Rosen Law Firm, 2002—. Instr. labor studies Shoreline C.C., 1978-90; bd. dirs. Music of Remembrance, Seattle Symphony Orch.; bd. trustee, Union for Reform Judaism. Chair Ward Springs Pk. Steering Com.; active mem. Commn. Social Action; mem. Seattle Arts Commn., 2009—; trustee Temple DeHirsch Sinai, 1992—98, v.p., 1998—2000, pres.-elect, 2000—01, pres., 2001—03; active mem. Union Reform Judaism Commn. Outreach. Fellow: Am. Bar Found., Coll. Labor and Employment Lawyers; mem.: ABA (union co-chmn. com. on employee rights and responsibilities 1992—96, union co-chmn. regional programs subcom. 1998—2000, union co-chmn. nat. programs. subcom. 2000—02, union co-chmn. ADR in labor and employment law com. 2002—05, co-regional EEOC liaison), Coun. Am.-Islamic Rels. (Humanitarian award 2008), Wash. State Trial Lawyers Assn. (past chair employment law com.), Nat. Employment Lawyers Assn. (state steering com. 1990—95, founding state chair), King County Bar Assn. (past chmn. aviation and space law sect., past chmn. Pacific Coast Labor and Employment Law Conf., past chmn. labor law sect.). Office: Rosen Law Firm 705 2nd Ave Ste 1200 Seattle WA 98104-1729 Office Phone: 206-652-1464. Business E-Mail: jhr@jonrosenlaw.com.

ROSEN, JUDAH BEN, computer scientist; b. Phila., May 5, 1922; s. Benjamin and Susan (Hurwich) R.; children: Susan Beth, Lynn Ruth. BSEE, Johns Hopkins U., 1943; PhD in Applied Math., Columbia U., 1952. Rschr. Manhattan (N.Y.) Project, 1944—46, Brookhaven (N.Y.) Nat. Lab., 1946—48; rsch. assoc. Princeton (N.J.) U., 1952-54; head applied math. dept. Shell Devel. Co., 1954-62; vis. prof. computer sci. dept. Stanford (Calif.) U., 1962-64; prof. dept. computer sci. and math. rsch. ctr. U. Wis., Madison, 1964-71; prof., head dept. computer sci. U. Minn., Mpls., 1971-92, fellow Supercomputer Inst., 1985—2007; sr. fellow Supercomputer Ctr., San Diego, 1993—2007; adj. rsch. prof. dept. computer sci. and engrin. U. Calif. San Diego, La Jolla, 1992—2007, bioinformatics grad. program faculty, 2001—07; ret. Fulbright prof. Technion, Israel, 1968-69, Davis vis. prof. 1980; invited lectr. Chinese Acad. Sci., Peking, 1980, Guilin, 1996, Samos, Greece, 2000; lectr., cons. Argonne (Ill.) Nat. Lab.; mem. Nat. Computer Sci. Bd. Author: Topics in Parallel Computing, 1992; editor: Nonlinear Programming, 1970, Supercomputers and Large-Scale Optimization, 1988; assoc. editor Global Optimization, 1990—, Annals of Ops. Rsch., 1984—; contbr. articles to profl. jours. and procs. Grantee, NSF, 1995—, ARPA/NIST, 1994—97. Mem. Assn. Computing Machinery, Soc. Indsl. and Applied Math., Math. Programming Soc., European Acad. Scis. Achievements include research in supercomputers and parallel algorithms for optimization, computation of molecular structure and drug design by energy minimization and homology models, algorithms for structured approximation in signal processing. Business E-Mail: jbenr55@yahoo.com.

ROSEN, LESLIE SMITH, humanities educator, director; arrived in US, 1971; d. Michael Brackett and Nancy Hodgson Smith; life ptnr. Jodi E. Fishman; children: Marielle, Alyssa, Samuel. BA in Classic, Liberal Arts, St. John's Coll., Annapolis, 1982; MA in Edn. and Jewish Studies, The Am. U., Washington, DC, 1988; PhD student, Balt. Hebrew U. English, history and math. tchr. The Barrie Day Sch., Silver Spring, Md., 1983—84; history and math. tchr. The Canterbury Sch., Accokeek, Md., 1985—89; prin., founding head The Aleph-Bet Jewish Day Sch., Annapolis, 1989—95; prin. Adat Reyim Fryiar Religious Sch., Fairfax, 1989—90, Adat Reyiar Fryiar Religious Sch., 1990—91; faculty, adminstrn. The Krieger Schechter Mid. Sch., Balt., 1995—2003; dir. integrated studies an humanities The Shoshana S. Cardin Sch., 2003—. Faculty evening program Netivon HS, Balt. Recipient Grinspoon award, Coun. Jewish Edn., 2005. Democrat. Jewish. Avocations: literature, philosophy, gardening. Office: The Cardin Sch 7310 Park Heights Ave Pikesville MD 21208

ROSEN, MARK DANIEL, chemist; b. Washington, Dc, Jan. 11, 1967; s. Hyman and Inge Rosen; m. Kathryn Nguyen, Oct. 7, 2007. BS, U. Calif., San Diego, 1997; PhD, U. Calif., Irvine, 2002. Rsch. assoc. Signal Pharms., San Diego, 1995—97; grad. rschr. U. Calif., 1997—2002; sr. rsch. scientist Johnson & Johnson, San Diego, 2002—. Contbr. scientific papers. Parabotanist, San Diego native plant atlas project San Diego Natural History Mus., 2008. Mem.: ACS Divsn. Medicinal Chemistry, ACS Divsn. Organic Chemistry, Am. Chem. Soc. Achievements include patents for preparation of aryl sulfonamide compounds. Avocations: surfing, kayaking, fishing, botany. Office: Johnson & Johnson 3210 Merryfield Row San Diego CA 92121 Office Fax: 858-784-3267. Personal E-mail: markdrosen@gmail.com. Business E-Mail: mrosen1@its.jnj.com.

ROSEN, MATTHEW STEPHEN, retired botanist; b. NYC, Oct. 7, 1943; s. Norman and Lucille (Cass) R.; m. Deborah Louise Mackay, June 16, 1974 (div. Feb. 1983); children: Gabriel Mackay, Rebecca Mackay; m. Kay Eloise Williams, July 11, 1987. MFSc, Yale U., New Haven, Conn., 1972; BS, Cornell U., Ithaca, NY, 1967. Instr. ornamental horticulture SUNY-Farmingdale, 1968-69; landscape designer Manhattan Gardener, NYC, 1969-70; instr. ornamental horticulture McHenry County Coll., Crystal Lake, Ill., 1972-74; coord. agrl. studies, asst. prof. biology, chemistry Mercer County Community Coll., West Windsor, NJ, 1974-79; adminstr. Des Moines Botanical Ctr., 1979—96; horticulture divsn. mgr. City of DeMoines, 1996—2007; ret., 2007. Cons. dir. West Mich. Hort. Soc., 1993; nat. judge Communities in Bloom, 2001-, Winter Lights, 2002-04, Am. in Bloom, 2002, sr. nat. judge, 2004-05, 2007-08; cons. in field. Contbr. articles to profl. jours. Com. chmn. United Way Cen. Iowa, 1982, divsn. chmn. 1983-86, 88-89, 91, 2000, group chmn. 1987, chmn. arts adv. com. 1985-86, pres. 1986, bd. dirs. Arts and Recreation Coun., 1985-86, com. chmn., 1992; career vocat. com. Des Moines Indsl. Sch. Dist., 1986, co-chmn., 1987, ptnrs. for progress com., 1988-90, sci. monitoring program, 1991-92; chmn. Two Rivers Festival, 1987-88; active Des Moines Sister City Program, Kofu, Japan, 1984, delegation, 1989, Naucalpan, Mexico, 1986, 87, Shijiazhuang, China, 1986, 90, 92, 95, 97; vice-chmn. Greater Des Moines Sister City Commn., 2004-05, chmn., 2005—; mem. edn. com. Am. Assn. Bot. Gardens and Arboretum, membership com., conservation com., bd. dirs., 1997-2001. Mem. Am. Assn. Bot. Gardens and Arboreta (edn. com.), Greater Des Moines C. of C. (team leader 1984—, chmn. new mem. sales, chmn. 8 O'clock new, Pres. Cabinet award 1983-85, bd. dirs., exec. com. 1995—, Achievement award C. of C. Fedn. 1986, exec. com. 1995-97), East Des Moines C. of C. (bd. dirs. 1992—, v.p., sec. 1993—, pres.-elect 1994, pres. 1995-96, sister cities commn. 1994, china chair 1995—, treas. 1995—, vice chair 2003, 04, chair 2005—), Greater Des Moines Conv. and Visitors Bur. (chmn. new mem. sales com. 1988-89), Iowa Advt. Rev. Coun., Affiliate Pres.'s Coun. of Chambers (chair 1995, 97), bd. dirs. DM Gen. Hosp., 1994-97, Bd. Coun. Internat. Trade, Latinos Unidos (bd. dirs. 1996-97), Rotary, Phi Kappa Phi, Pi Alpha Xi. Democrat. Jewish. Avocations: photography, reading, model trains, collecting old books, writing. Home: 1042 22nd St West Des Moines IA 50265-2219 Personal E-mail: m.rosen@mchsi.com.

ROSEN, MEYER ROBERT, chemical engineer; b. Bklyn., Mar. 9, 1943; s. Philip and Jeanne (Rosenzweig) R.; children: Carrie, David; m. Selma Schwartz Mirman. BS, Poly. Inst. Bklyn., 1964, MS, 1966. Diplomate, Am. Bd. Forensic Engring. and Tech., cert. forensic examiner, profl. chemist, profl. chem. engr.; fire and explosion investigator Nat. Cert. Bd., Nat. Assn. Fire Investigators. Rsch. engr. Union Carbide Corp., Tonawanda, NY, 1966-73, project scientist, 1973-79, devel. scientist Tarrytown and Boundbrook, NJ, 1979-92; dir. chemistry and fire investigation Inter-City Testing and Cons. Corp., Mineola, NY, 1993—2003; pres. Interactive Cons. Inc., 1993—. Cons. Brookfield Engring. Labs., Stoughton, Mass., 1979-81; cons. to chem. industry; course dir. Ctr. for Profl. Advancement, East Brunswick, N.J., 1994; adj. prof. chemistry Westchester C.C., 1970-84; exec. advisor Am. Bd. Forensic Engring. and Tech.; Vaaler Awards judge Chem. Processing Mag., 2003; chief sci. advisor HBA Global Expo Tech. Confs.; editl. adv. bd. mem. Knovel Corp.; forensic litigation expert in field; spkr. in field. Co-author: Rheology Modifier Handbook: Practical Use & Application, 2000; editor: Delivery System Handbook for Personal Care and Cosmetic Products Technology, Applications, Formulations, 2005; series editor Breakthroughs in Personal Care and Cosmetic Technology; contbr. articles to profl. jours. Fellow Am. Coll. Forensic Examiners, Royal Soc. Chemistry London (chartered chemist), Am. Inst. Chemists (dir., exec. bd. dirs.); mem. ASTM (mem. various subcoms.), Am. Inst. Chem. Engrs., Am. Chem. Soc. (divsn. colloid and surface chemistry, mem. noise com., organizer, session leader nat. mtgs. 2002—, chmn. and organizer first and second health beauty Am. regulatory summit 2006, cheif scientific advisor health & beauty expo), Am. Indsl. Hygiene Assn. (cons. spl. interest group), Am. Soc. Safety Engrs. (v.p.), Assn. Cons. Chemists and Chem. Engrs., Am. Assn. Colorists and Textile Chemists, Am. Med. Writers Assn., Nat. Assn. Sci. Writers, Soc. de Chimie Industrielle (Am. sect.), Nat. Fire Protection Assn., Soc. Indsl. Chemistry (Am. sect.), Am. Assn. Acupuncture and Oriental Medicine, Acupuncture Soc. Pa., Nat. Dental Acupuncture Soc. (exec. bd.), Nat. Alliance Acupuncture and Oriental Medicine (bd. cert. in pain mgmt.), Nat. Hearing Conservation Assn. Achievements include 21 patents for process for fire fighting foams, antifoams; flocculation of phosphatic slimes, high molecular weight water soluble polymers and flocculating method, process for producing polymer water-in-oil emulsion, process for agglomerating ore concentrate utilizing clay and dispersions of polymer binders or dry powder binders, removal of residual ethylene oxide from poly(ethylene oxide); development of treatment of previously incurable ear disorder, seminar leader in Reflex-Correspondence Training. Publications include Polyox R Water Soluble Resin Worldwide Technical Literature; Rheology of Non-Newtonian Fluids; Energy Medicine; Auriculotherapy; Korean Hand Therapy. Office: Interactive Cons Inc PO Box 66 East Norwich NY 11732-0066 Office Phone: 516-922-2167. Office Fax: 516-922-3830. Business E-Mail: meyer.rosen@chemicalconsult.com.

ROSEN, MICHAEL HOWARD, real estate executive; b. NYC, May 22, 1943; s. Irving Edward and Lilyan Ruth (Ruttenberg) R.; children: Daniel Matthew, Lenise Gayle. AB, Tufts U., 1965. Lic. real estate broker, N.Y., Md. Exec. v.p., dir. Rosen Orgn., Inc., NYC, 1971-75; v.p. apt. ops. Monumental Properties, Inc. & Monumental Properties Trust, Balt., 1975-79; exec. v.p. Town and Country Mgmt. Corp., Balt., 1979-93; exec. v.p., chief oper. officer Town & Country Trust, Balt., 1993—2001; pres. MH Rosen Enterprises LLC, 2001—. Office Phone: 443-987-8201. Personal E-mail: micharos4@aol.com.

ROSEN, MICHAEL JOSHUA, surgeon; b. Alexandria, Va., Jan. 5, 1970; m. Debra Ann Widman, Aug. 8, 1998; children: Samantha, Alexandra, Zachary. MD, U. Southern Calif., LA, 1997. Diplomate Am. Bd. Surgery, 2004. Chief divsn. gastrointestinal and gen. surgery Case Western Res. U., Cleve., 2005—08. Home: 32460 Wintergreen Dr Solon OH 44139 Personal E-mail: michael.rosen@uhhospitals.org.

ROSEN, MICHAEL N., lawyer; AB, Princeton U., 1962; LLB, Harvard U., 1965. Bar: NY 1966, US Dist. Ct., So. Dist NY 1974. Chmn. Robinson Silverman Pearce Aronsohn & Berman LLP, NYC; ptnr., mem. exec. com. Bryan Cave LLP, NYC. Sec., dir., counsel GameStop Corp., 2000—; bd. dirs. Barnes & Noble & Barnes & Noble.com. Office: Bryan Cave LLP 1290 Ave of the Americas New York NY 10104 Office Phone: 212-541-2200. E-mail: mnrosen@bryancave.com.

ROSEN, MOISHE, religious organization founder; b. Kansas City, Mo., Apr. 12, 1932; s. Ben and Rose (Baker) R.; m. Ceil Starr, Aug. 27, 1950; children: Lyn Rosen Bond, Ruth. Diploma, Northeastern Bible Coll., 1957; DD, Western Conservative Bapt. Sem., 1986. Ordained to ministry Bapt. Ch., 1957. Missionary Am. Bd. Missions to the Jews, NYC, 1956, minister in charge Beth Sar Shalom Los Angeles, 1957-67, dir. recruiting and tng. NYC, 1967-70; leader Jews for Jesus Movement, San Francisco, 1970-73, exec. dir., 1973-96, founder, 1973—. Speaker in field. Author: Sayings of Chairman Moishe, 1972, Jews for Jesus, 1974, Share the New Life with a Jew, 1976, Christ in the Passover, 1977, Y'shua, The Jewish Way to Say Jesus, 1982, Overture to Armageddon, 1991, The Universe is Broken: Who on Earth Can Fix It?, 1991, Demystifying Personal Evangelism, 1992, Witnessing to Jews, 1998. Trustee Western Conservative Bapt. Sem., Portland, Oreg., 1979-85, 86-91, Bibl. Internat. Coun. on Bibl. Inerrancy, Oakland, Calif., 1979-89; bd. dirs. Christian Advs. Serving Evangelism, 1987-91. Named Hero of the Faith, Conservative Bapt. Assn. Am., 1997. Office: Jews for Jesus 90 Miraloma Dr San Francisco CA 94127-1641 Office Phone: 415-661-2263. Personal E-mail: MityMo@aol.com, moishe.rosen@gmail.com.

ROSEN, PAUL PETER, pathologist; b. Bklyn., Aug. 16, 1938; s. George and Beate (Caspari) R.; m. Mary Sue, Aug. 7, 1994; children: Susan Deborah, Jonathan Daniel. BS, Swarthmore Coll., 1960; MD, Columbia U., 1964. Asst. attending pathologist Meml. Hosp., NYC, 1970-73; asst. prof. pathology Cornell U. Med. Sch., NYC, 1972-78; assoc. attending pathologist Meml. Hosp., NYC, 1973-78, attending pathologist, 1978-98; assoc. prof. pathology Cornell U. Med. Sch., NYC, 1978-84, prof. pathology, 1984—; assoc. mem. Sloan Kettering Inst., NYC, 1980-84; mem. tenure title Meml. Sloan-Kettering Cancer Ctr., NYC, 1984-98; sr. cons. pathologist Dickstein Cancer Treatment Ctr., White Plains, NY, 1998-99; attending pathologist, chief of breast pathology NY Presbyn. Hosp., NYC, 1999—2009, sr. cons. breast pathology, 2009. Adj. prof. pathology N.Y. Med. Coll., Valhalla, N.Y., 1996-99. Author: Rosen's Breast Pathology, 1996, 2d edit., 2001, Breast Pathology: Diagnosis by Needle Core Biopsy, 1999; co-author: 2d edit., 2005; co-author: Tumors of the Mammary Gland, 1993; co-editor Pathology Annual, 1977—95, Revs. Pathology, 1996—98; contbr. more than 300 articles to profl. jours. Mem. Internat. Acad. Pathology, Am. Soc. Clin. Pathologists, Soc. Surg. Pathologists, N.Y. Acad. Medicine.

ROSEN, RHODA, museum director; Asst. prof. art history U. Witwatersrand, Johannesburg; Rockefeller Inst. residency fellowship Inst. Advanced Rsch. and Study, African Humanities, Northwestern U., Evanston, Ill., 1994; dir. Spertus Mus., Chgo. Prin. for a Day Lawndale Cmty. Acad., Chgo.; mem. Arab Jewish Partnership for Peace. Office: Spertus Mus 610 S Michigan Ave Chicago IL 60605 Office Phone: 312-322-1785. Office Fax: 312-922-3934. Business E-Mail: rrosen@spertus.edu.

ROSEN, RICHARD A. (RICK ROSEN), agent; s. Bob and Claire Rosen. Grad., U. Southern Calif. Talent agent Internat. Creative Mgmt.; founding ptnr. Endeavor Agy., Beverly Hills, 1995—. Office: Endeavor Agy 9601 Wilshire Blvd Beverly Hills CA 90211 Office Phone: 310-248-2000. Office Fax: 310-248-2020.

ROSEN, RICHARD LEWIS, lawyer, real estate developer; b. NYC, Mar. 6, 1943; s. Morris and Lorraine (Levy) R.; m. Doris Ellen Bloom, Aug. 28, 1983. BA, Cornell U., 1965; JD, N.Y. Law Sch., 1968; cert., NYU Real Estate Inst., 1980. Bar: NY 1968, US Dist. Ct. (so. and ea. dists.) NY 1972, US Ct. Appeals (2d cir.) NY 2008; lic. real estate broker. Pvt. practice, NYC, 1971-73; ptnr. Rosen, Wise, Felzen & Salomon, NYC, 1973-79, Rosen & Felzen, NYC, 1979-84, Rosen, Rudd, Kera, Graubard & Hollender, NYC, 1985-88, Bell, Kalnick, Klee and Green, NYC, 1989-90; shareholder Rosen, Einbinder & Dunn, P.C., NYC, 1990—2005; pvt. practice The Richard L. Rosen Law Firm, PLLC, NYC, 2005—. Contbg. author: Franchising 101, The Complete Guide to Evaluating, Buying and Growing Your Franchise Business; author: Renewal of Your Franchise: Some Solutions, Franchise Times. Named one of America's 100 Best Franchise Lawyers, Franchise Times; named to Best Lawyers in Am., Super Lawyers, Best of US; recipient Total Quality Franchising Lifetime Achivement award, Am. Assn. Franchisees & Dealers, 2008; NY State Regents scholar. Mem.: ABA (mem. forum com. on franchising), Am. Assn. Franchises and Dealers (former chmn. legal steering com., bd. dirs., past chmn. fair franchising stds. com., chmn. alternate dispute resolution com.), NY State Bar Assn. (founding mem. franchise law com., exec. com. bus. law sect., chmn. mission statement com. of franchise law com.), Am. Franchise Assn., Nat. Franchise Mediation Program (mem. steering com., disting. panel neutrals), Assn. Bar City NY (panel mem. com. on franchising, panel mem. com. on corp. law), Red Key Hon. Soc. (Cornell U.), Sphinx Head Hon. Soc. (Cornell U.), Spiked Shoe Soc. (Cornell U., NY State Track Champion, Sprint Medley Relay 1960, Pa. Relays Gold medalist 1964), Ea. Intercollegiate Athletic Assn. (named Lightweight Football All Ea. Selection 1963, 1964, named Eastern States Lightweight Weightlifting Champion 1968, LI Masters Sprint Champion). Avocations: guitar, reading, coaching youth soccer and track, masters track competition. Home: 1 Old Jericho Tpke Jericho NY 11753-1205 Office: Richard L Rosen Law Firm PLLC 110 E 59th St 23rd FL New York NY 10022 Home Phone: 516-931-0771; Office Phone: 212-644-6644. Business E-Mail: rlr@rosenlawpllc.com.

ROSEN, ROBERT ARNOLD, management consultant, real estate owner, manager, developer, investor, farmer; b. NYC, June 19, 1936; s. Louis and Helen (Weiss) R.; m. Florence Cohen, Oct. 23, 1960; children: David S., Kenneth A., Mark A., Emily B. BBA, CUNY, 1957, MBA, 1960; postgrad. (Ford Found. scholar), NYU, 1961; grad., Indsl. Coll. Armed Forces, Air War Coll., 1960, U.S. Air Force U.; various courses, Naval Edn. and Tng. Command. Sales promotion mgr. Leipzig & Lippe, Inc., 1956-58; advt. and sales promotion mgr. Zenith Radio, 1957-62; chmn., pres., founder Am. Bus. Resources Corp., 1963-64; v.p., dir. Royal Bus. Funds Corp., 1964-68; chmn., CEO Rosen Assocs. Mgmt. Corp., Jericho, NY, 1983—; chmn. Lakeside Farms Assoc. Inc.; Mng. mem. Livingston Farms LLC. V.p. corp. finance div., dir. Brand Grumet & Siegel, Inc., 1969-70; pres. Brand Grumet & Siegel Equities, Inc., 1970; former pres., chief oper. officer Bell TV, Inc., N.Y.C.; pres., former chmn. bd. Holmes Protection, Inc.; former chmn. bd., pres. Union Small Bus. U.Investment Co., 1968-77, Skyway-Laguardia Corp.; dir. past chmn. bd. Okuraya Davos Internat., Inc.; chmn. bd., pres., chief exec. officer, treas. Suburban Broadcasting Corp., 1970-80; chmn., pres. Affiliated Comms. Corp.; vice chmn., pres. Comm. Svcs. Corp.; pres. Wescom Corp.; pres. Androse Corp., 1983—; cons. Asian Devel. Bank, Albert Einstein Coll. Medicine, Nat. Housing Bank of Brazil, 1972-76; mem. U.S. Senatorial Bus. Adv. Bd.; lectr. Baruch Coll. Grad. Sch. Bus., CUNY, 1960-63; adj. prof. Fairleigh Dickinson U. Grad. Sch. Bus., 1968-75; ret. pres., ret. dean Internat. Inst. Real Estate Studies Ltd.; dir. Ctr. for Real Estate Studies, Adelphi U.; adj. prof. mgmt. NYU; mem. faculty New Sch. for Social Rsch.; guest lectr., mem. bd. advs. Fordham U.; prin. owner, developer shopping ctrs., comml. real estate throughout, U.S.; chmn. UN Trade and Tech. Adv. Mission to Israel, 1972, Econ. Devel. Com./UJA Fedn.; active Nat. Builder Mktg. Bd.; former owner, investor seat on N.Y. Stock Exch, US NY Commissioning (com. mem.), NYS Trooper Found. (bd. trustee), Shields LI Inc. (hon.). Chmn. Borough Pres.'s of Manhattan Com. on Narcotics Addiction Control, 1970—75; NY mem. adv. coun. USAF Acad.; mem. editl. policy com. Internat. Property Investment Jour. of Hofstra U. Law Sch.; mem. Navy Recruiting Dist., NY Assistance Coun., NY State Gov.'s Bus. Adv. Coun.; chmn. Navy Task Force to Study Navy Budgeting, Acquisition and Procurement; former mem. Pres.'s Pvt. Sector Survey on Cost Control (Grace Commn.); former trustee Zachary and Elizabeth M. Fisher Found.; trustee North Shore-LI Jewish Health Sys.; chmn. econ. devel. com., former bd. dirs. United Jewish Appeal/Fedn.; former mem. corp. adv. bd. Queens Coll.; mem. adv. bd. Roundabout Theatre; advisor Disaster Preparedness Commn.; sr. advisor NY State Senate for Homeland Security, Vets. Affairs and the Mil.; advisor to adjutant gen. State of NY Divsn. Mil. and Naval Affairs for Homeland Security; co-chmn. Florence & Robert A. Rosen Family Wellness Ctr. Law Enforcement and Millitary Pers.; ex-officio bd. mem. NY Bot. Gardern; bd. dirs. The Film Forum, 1979—86, NYC Housing Partnership, Housing Partnership Devel. Corp., Fed. Law Enforcement Found.; bd. dirs., trustee emeritus Intrepid Sea, Air, Space Mus. With USAFR and USNR, 1959—90, ret. as capt. USNR, 1990, rear adm. ret. upper half NY Naval Militia, former comdr. Divsn. Mil. and Naval Affairs, naval aide to the Gov. Mem. Soc. Internat. Devel., Internat. Inst. Valuers (SCV designation), NRA, Nat. Def. Exec. Res., Chief Execs. Orgn., Nat. lPres.'s Orgn., Young Pres.'s Orgn. (past chmn. Met. chpt.), Real Estate Bd. N.Y., Assn. for Better N.Y., Internat. Coun. Shopping Ctrs., Property Cons. Soc., Nat. Assn. Rev. Appraisers (cert. rev. appraiser), Air Force Assn., Res. Officers Assn., Nat. Guard Assn. (life), Naval Res. Assn. (life), U.S. Naval Inst., Navy League U.S., Naval War Coll. Found. (assoc.), Am. Legion, Jewish War Vets. U.S., Wine Inst. Group Stony Brook State U. N.Y., chmn. emeritus Naval Militia Assn. Inc. and commr. NYC Korean War Veterans 50th anniversary Commemorative Commn., U.S. Navy Pub. Affairs Assn., Alpha Delta Sigma, Phi Sigma Delta, Sigma Alpha. Home: 60 Apple Lake Ln PO Box 8 Rhinebeck NY 12572 Office: Rosen Associates Mgmnt Corp 33 South Service Rd Jericho NY 11753-1006 Office Phone: 516-333-2000. Business E-Mail: rar@rosenmgmt.com.

ROSEN, SANFORD JAY, lawyer; b. NYC, Dec. 19, 1937; s. Alexander Charles and Viola S. (Grad) R.; m. Catherine Picard, June 22, 1958; children: Caren E. Andrews, R. Durelle Schacter, Ian D., Melissa S. AB, Cornell U., 1959; LLB, Yale U., 1962. Bar: Conn. 1962, Calif. 1974, U.S. Supreme Ct. 1966. Law clk. to Hon. Simon E. Sobeloff US Ct. Appeals, Four Cirs., Balt., 1962—63; prof. sch. law U. Md., Balt., 1963-71; assoc. dir. Coun. on Legal Edn. Opportunity, Atlanta, 1969-70; vis. prof. law U. Tex., Austin, 1970-71; asst. legal dir. Nat. ACLU, NYC, 1971-73; legal dir. Mex.-Am. Legal Def. Fund, San Francisco, 1973-75; ptnr. Rosen, Remcho & Henderson, San Francisco, 1976-80, Rosen & Remcho, San Francisco, 1980-82; prin. Law Offices of Sanford Jay Rosen, San Francisco, 1982-86; sr. ptnr. Rosen & Phillips, San Francisco, 1986-89; prin. Rosen & Assocs., San Francisco, 1990; sr. ptnr. Rosen, Bien & Asaro, San Francisco, 1991—2006, Rosen, Bien & Galvan LLP, San Francisco, 2006—. Mem. Balt. Cmty. Rels. Commn., 1966-69; mem. com. Patuxent Instn., Md., 1967-69; ad hoc adminstrv. law judge Calif. Agrl. Labor Rels. Bd., San Francisco, 1975-80; interim monitor U.S. Dist. Ct. for no. dist. Calif., San Francisco, 1989, early neutral evaluator, 1987—, mediator, 1993—; mediator Calif. Ct. Appeal 1st dist., 2004—; permanent atty. del. Jud. Conf. U.S. Ct. Appeal for 4th Cir.; atty. del. Jud. Conf. U.S. Ct. Appeals 9th cir., 1996-98. Contbr. articles to profl. jours. Mem. Com. on Adminstrn. of Criminal Justice, Balt., 1968; mem. adv. com. HEW, Washington, 1974-75. Mem. ABA, Am. Assn. Justice, Calif. Bar Assn., Bar Assn. San Francisco. Avocations: reading, travel, movies. Office: Rosen Bien & Galvan LLP 315 Montgomery St 10th Fl San Francisco CA 94104 Home Phone: 415-563-5707; Office Phone: 415-433-6830. Business E-Mail: srosen@rbg-law.com.

ROSEN, SARAH PEREL, social worker; b. Russia, Sept. 19, 1946; arrived in U.S., 1961; married, Apr. 8, 1970; children: Esther, Bayla, Yehoshua, Yakov, Levi, Nechoma, Menachem, Chana, Rochel. BA, Hunter Coll., NYC, 1969; MA, Columbia U., NYC, 1974; MSW, Hunter Coll., NYC, 1997. LCSW, lic. Acad. Cert. Social Workers, cert. group therapist Ctr. Advancement Group Studies. Social worker Maimondes Hosp., Bklyn., 1995—97, North Shore Children and Family Svcs., Roslyn, NY, 1997—, supr., 1997—; pvt. practice psychotherapist Bklyn., 2002—. Provider Luth. Elem. Sch., Bklyn., 2005—. Grantee, United Jewish Appeal, 1996; scholar, Jewish Found. Edn. Women, 1995. Mem.: NASW, Nat. Assn. Advancement Psychoanalysis, Am. Group Psychoanalytic Assn., Acad. Clin. Social Workers. Jewish. Avocations: exercise, literature, dance. Home: 423 Kingston Ave Brooklyn NY 11225 Office: North Shore Child and Family 480 Old Westbury Roslyn NY 11577

ROSEN, STANLEY HOWARD, humanities educator; b. Warren, Ohio, July 29, 1929; s. Nathan A. and Celia (Narotsky) R.; m. Francoise Harlepp, Sept. 5, 1955; children: Nicholas David, Paul Mark, Valerie. BA, U. Chgo., 1949, PhD, 1955; postgrad., Am. Sch. Classical Studies, Athens, Greece, 1955-56; D honoris causa, New U. Lisbon, 1997. Mem. faculty Pa. State U., 1956-94, prof. philosophy, 1966-94; Fulbright research prof. U. Paris, 1960-61; research fellow Humanities Research Inst., U. Wis., 1963-64; Inst. Arts and Humanities research sr. fellow Pa. State U., 1972—, Evan Pugh prof. philosophy, 1985-94; Bowne prof. philosophy Boston U., 1994—, univ. prof., 2000—. Vis. prof. U. Calif., San Diego, 1978, U. Nice, 1981, Scuola Superiore Pisa, 1989; vis. lectr. U. Barcelona, Spain, 1992; Priestly lectr. U. Toronto, 1997; Cardinal Mercier lectr. Louvain U., 1998; Gilson lectr. Institut Catholique, Paris, 2003. Author: Plato's Symposium, 1968, Nihilism, 1969, G.W.F. Hegel, 1974, The Limits of Analysis, 1980, Plato's Sophist: The Drama of Original and Image, 1983, Hermeneutics as Politics, 1987, The Quarrel Between Philosophy and Poetry, 1988, The Ancients and the Moderns, 1989, The Question of Being, 1993, Plato's Statesman: The Web of Politics, 1995, The Mask of Enlightenment, 1995, Metaphysics in Ordinary Language, 1999; editor: The Examined Life: A Treasury of Western Philosophy, 2000, The Elusiveness of the Ordinary, 2002, La Production Platonicienne, 2005, Plato's Republic, 2005 Rsch. grantee Am. Philos. Soc., 1961, Earhart Found., 1971, 73, 81, 2000. Mem. Metaphys. Soc. Am (pres. 1990-91). Home: 117 Brook St Wellesley MA 02482-6632 Office: 745 Commonwealth Ave Boston MA 02215-1401 E-mail: srosen@bu.edu.

ROSEN, STEVEN O., lawyer; b. NYC, Jan. 11, 1949; s. Albert I. and Yvette (Sterenbuch) R. BS Aerospace Engring., SUNY, 1970; MS System and Control Engring., Case Western Reserve, 1975; JD, Lewis & Clark Coll., 1977. Bar: Ill. 1977, Oreg. 1978, Wash. 2004. Assoc. Lord, Bissell & Brook, Chgo., 1977-79, Miller, Nash, Wiener, Hager & Carlsen, Portland, Oreg., 1979-84, ptnr., 1984-97; pvt. practice Rosen Law Firm, 1997—. Disting. adj. prof. Lewis & Clark Law Sch., 1986. Named one of Best Lawyers in America, 2009. Mem. ABA (dir. divsns. sect. of litigation 1996-97, chmn. aviation litigation com. 1990-93), Am. Bd. Trial Advocates, Oreg. State Bar Assn. (exec. com. aviation sect. 1984-2001, chmn. 1994-95), Washington State Bar Assn. Avocations: skiing, bicycling. Address: The Rosen Law Firm 620 SW Main St Ste 702 Portland OR 97205-3030 Home: 1330 SW 3rd Ave Apt Portland OR 97201 Office Phone: 503-525-2525. Business E-Mail: rosen@rosenlawfirm.com.

ROSEN, STEVEN TERRY, medical professor, oncologist, hematologist; b. Bklyn., Feb. 18, 1952; MB, Northwestern U. Med. Sch., Evanston, Ill., 1972, MD, 1976. Diplomate Am. Bd. Internal Medicine, cert. in med. oncology, hematology. Resident internal medicine McGaw Med. Ctr./Northwestern U., 1976—79; fellow med. oncology Nat. Cancer Inst., NIH, 1979—81; Genevieve Teuton prof. medicine, divsn. hematology/oncology Northwestern U. Feinberg Sch. Medicine, 1989—, dir. Robert H. Lurie Comprehensive Cancer Ctr., 1989—. Dir. clin. programs Northwestern Meml. Hosp., 1989—. Editor: Contemporary Oncology, 1990—95, Cancer Treatment & Rsch., 1995—, In Touch, 1998—2002; contbr. articles to profl. jours. Recipient Alumni Achievement award, Northwestern U. Med. Sch., 1994, Martin Luther King Humanitarian award, Northwestern Meml. Hosp., 1995, Marv Samuel award, Chgo. Baseball Cancer Charities, 1996. Mem.: AMA, ACP, AAAS, Ctrl. Soc. Clin. Rsch., Am. Soc. Clin. Oncology, Am. Soc. Hematology. Office: Northwestern U Divsn Hematology/Oncology 676 N St Clair St Ste 850 Chicago IL 60611-3093 Office Phone: 312-908-5250. Business E-Mail: s-rosen@northwestern.edu.

ROSEN, WILLIAM WARREN, lawyer; b. New Orleans, July 22, 1936; s. Warren Leucht and Erma (Stich) R.; m. Eddy Kahn, Nov. 26, 1965; children: Elizabeth K., Victoria A. BA, Tulane U., 1958, JD, 1964. Bar: La. 1964, US Dist. Ct. (ea. dist.) La. 1965, US Ct. Appeals (5th cir.) 1965, US Supreme Ct. 1984, US Dist. Ct. (mid. dist.) La. 1985, Colo. 1989. Assoc. Dodge & Friend, New Orleans, 1965-68, Law Office of J.R. Martzell, New Orleans, 1968-70; pvt. practice New Orleans, 1970-79, 89-90; ptnr. Lucas & Rosen (and predecessor firm), New Orleans, 1979-87, Herman, Herman, Katz & Cotlar, New Orleans, 1987-88, Rosen and Samuel, New Orleans, 1990-95; of counsel Rittenberg & Samuel, New Orleans, 1996-99; ptnr. Rosen & Lundeen, LLP, New Orleans, 1999—2002; pvt. practice New Orleans, 2002—05; founder & dir. Litigation Consultation Svcs., New Orleans, 1996—; pvt. practice Franklin, Tenn., 2005—. Adj. prof. trial advocacy Law Sch. Tulane U., 1988-2006, mem. adv. com. paralegal studies program, 1977-86, instr. bus. orgns., 1978, instr. legal interviewing, 1980-81; mem. adv. com. Paralegal Inst. U. New Orleans, 1990-2006, instr. legal interviewing and investigations, 1986-87; lectr. legal and paralegal fields; lectr. real and demonstrative evidence Nat. Edn. Network, 1993; lectr. new judges seminar La. Jud. Coll., 2000, 01, 02, 03. Author: (with others) Trial Techniques publ. La. Trial Lawyers Assn., 1981; columnist Briefly Speaking publ. New Orleans Bar Assn., 1993-2000; Photographer: Immersion: A Katrina Rm. Photo Instalation, Parthenon Mus., Nashville, Tn. Mem. budget and planning com. Jewish Welfare Fedn., 1970-73; mem. adv. coun. on drug edn. La. Dept. Edn., 1973; mem. profl. adv. com. Jewish Endowment Found., 1982—2006; mem. exec. com. US Olympic Com., La., 1982-84; bd. dirs. Planned Parenthood La., 1994-2001, Hillel Found. New Orleans, 2003-05, Dad's Club, Isidore Newman Sch., 1984-85, Uptown Flood Assn., 1982-85; bd. dirs. Jewish Children's Home Svc., 1973-76, Met. Crime Commn. New Orleans, 1976-82. Spl. agt. Office Spl. Investigations USAF, 1958—61. Fellow, Inst. of Politics. Loyola U. Mem. ABA, ATLA (keyperson com. 1986-89, vice chmn. paralegal com. 1986-89, mem. family law adv. com. 1989-90, sec. family law sect. 1990-91, lectr. legal edn. 1979, 81, 83, 86, 88); mem. La. Bar Assn. (vice chmn. pub. rels. com. 1970-73, 88-89, past chmn. state youth drug abuse edn. program, vol. lawyers for arts 1986-96, chmn. sr. counsel com. 1995-96), Am. Arbitration Assn., Nat. Fedn. Paralegal Assn. (adv. coun. 1989-1998), Assn. Atty. Mediators (pres. La. chpt. 1995), Nat. Choice in Dying (legal adv. com. 1992-96), Nat. Edn. Network (lectr. legal edn. 1993), New Orleans Bar Assn. (CLE com. 1990-91, chmn. 1991-92, mem. alternative dispute resolution com. 1996-2000, panel moderator 1997), Inn of Ct. (master 1992-2004), Tenn. Trial Lawyer Assn., Rotary Club New Orleans (bd. dirs. 1996-98, 2003-05, chmn. legal com. 1996—2005), Franklin Rotary Club, Audubon Park Tennis Club (pres. 2004-06), Audubon Pub. Tennis Assn., Inc. (v.p. 2006-), Nashville Pub. Television (pub. adv. comm. 2009-). Avocation: photography. Office: 704 Wild Timber Ct Franklin TN 37064 Office Phone: 615-649-8192. Office Fax: 615-673-7351. Personal E-mail: lcsno@aol.com.

ROSENAU, JAMES NATHAN, political scientist, educator, writer; b. Phila., Nov. 25, 1924; s. Walter Nathan and Fanny Fox (Baum) R.; m. Norah McCarthy, Aug. 5, 1955 (dec. July 1974); 1 child, Heidi Margaret; m. Pauline Vaillancourt, June 14, 1987 (div. 1993); m. Hongying Wang,

Dec. 11, 1993; children: Fan Elizabeth, Patrick Rosenau (adopted). AB, Bard Coll., 1948; AM, Johns Hopkins U., 1949; PhD, Princeton U., 1957. From instr. to prof. Rutgers U., New Brunswick, NJ, 1949-70; prof. Ohio State U., Columbus, 1970-73; prof. polit. sci. U. So. Calif., LA, 1973-92; prof. internat. affairs George Washington U., 1992—. Rsch. asst. Inst. Advanced Study, Princeton, NJ, 1953-54; rsch. assoc. Princeton U., NJ, 1960-70; dir. Sch. Internat. Rels. U. So. Calif., LA, 1976-79; dir. Inst. for Transnat. Studies, U. Southern Calif., LA, 1973-92. Author: Public Opinion and Foreign Policy, 1961, National Leadership and Foreign Policy, 1963, The Dramas of Politics, 1973, Citizenship between Elections, 1974, The Scientific Study of Foreign Policy, 1980, Turbulence in World Politics, 1990, The United Nations in a Turbulent World, 1992, Along the Domestic-Foreign Frontier, 1997, Distant Proximities, 2003, The Study of World Politics: Vol. 1, Theoretical and Methodological Challenges, Vol. 2, Globalization and Governance, 2005; (play) Kwangju: An Escalatory Spree, 1991; co-author: American Leadership in World Affairs, 1984, Global Voices, 1993, Thinking Theory Thoroughly, 1995, 2nd edit., 2000, International Political Economy, 1995, Understanding Globalization, 1998, On the Cutting Edge of Globalization, 2005, People Count!, 2008; co-editor: Journeys through World Politics, 1989, Global Changes and Theoretical Challenges, 1989, Governance without Government, 1992, Strange Power, 2000, Information Technologies and Global Politics, 2002, Globalization, Security and the Nation State, 2005, Governance and Sustainability, 2005. Trustee Bard Coll., Annandale-on-Hudson, 1968-70, Odyssey Theater Ensemble, LA, 1987-88. With US Army, 1942-46. Ford Found. fellow, 1958-59, Guggenheim fellow, 1987-88; Rsch. grantee NSF, 1970, 73, 78-79, 83, 88, 92, 96, NEH grantee, 1976. Fellow World Acad. Art and Sci.; mem. Internat. Studies Assn. (pres. 1984-85), Am. Polit. Sci. Assn. (exec. coun. 1975-77). Democrat. Office: 2130 H St NW Washington DC 20052-2521 Business E-Mail: jnr@gwu.edu.

ROSENBAUM, ARTHUR L., ophthalmologist; b. St. Louis, Aug. 20, 1940; s. Harry David and Evelyn Levy Rosenbaum; m. Sandra Dine Rosenbaum, May 28, 1985; 1 child, Steven. BA, U. Mich., 1962; MD, Washington U., St. Louis, 1966. Diplomate Am. Bd. Ophthalmology, lic. physician Calif. Intern Mt. Zion Hosp., San Francisco, 1966—67; resident Jules Stein Eye Inst.-UCLA, 1969—73; chief divsn. pediat. ophthalmology UCLA-Jules Stein Eye Inst., 1985—, vice chmn. dept. ophthalmology, 1990—. Editor: Clinical Strabismus Management, 1999. Maj. USPHS, 1967—69. Mem.: Am. Assn. Pediat. Ophthalmology and Strabismus (pres. 1987—88), Am. Acad. Ophthalmology (Sr. Honor award 1995). Office: Jules Stein Eye Inst UCLA 200 Stein Plz Los Angeles CA 90024 Home Phone: 310-470-3355; Office Phone: 310-825-2872. E-mail: rosenbaum@jsei.ucla.edu.

ROSENBAUM, DAVID MARK, engineering executive, consultant, educator; b. Boston, Feb. 11, 1935; s. Frederick and Elizabeth (Gelman) R.; m. Karen Jeanne Smith, Dec. 27, 1964; children: Benjamin Micah, Shoshana Elizabeth. BSc, Brown U., 1956; MS, Renessaler Poly. Inst., 1958; PhD, Brandeis U., 1964. Asst. rsch. prof. Boston U., 1964-65; assoc. prof. Poly. U., Bklyn., 1969-70; pres. Network Analysis Corp., Glen Cove, NY, 1970-72; asst. dir. Office of Nat. Narcotics Intelligence, Washington, 1973-74; cons. to comptr. gen. GAO, Washington, 1975-78; dir. Office of Radiation Programs EPA, Washington, 1978-81; pres. Tech. Analysis Corp., McLean, Va., 1981—. Cons. Dir. of Licensing, AEC, Washington, 1972-73. Author: Super Hilbert Space and the Quantum Time Operator, 1969, Liquefied Energy Gases Safety, 1978, A Statistical Procedure for Testing Pacemakers, 1978, Health Effects of Low-Level Radiation, 1981, A Statistical Procedure for Cluster Recognition with Application to Atlanta Leukemia Data, 1983. Mem. IEEE (sr.), Am. Phys. Soc. Office: Tech Analysts Corp # 202 6723 Whittier Ave Mc Lean VA 22101-4533 Personal E-mail: dmrose@radix.net.

ROSENBAUM, GREG ALAN, merchant banker, consultant; b. Toledo, Aug. 7, 1952; s. Marvin and Ida Edith (Millman) R.; m. Martha Jane Radlo, Sept. 3, 1978; children: Eli Samuel, Eve Hannah, Elliott Jacob. AB, Harvard U., 1974, M in Pub. Policy, 1978, JD, 1978. Bar: Ohio 1978, Ill. 1980, US Supreme Ct. 2006. Summer assoc. Jones, Day, Reavis & Pogue, Cleve., 1977; tchg. fellow in govt. and social scis. Harvard U., Cambridge, Mass., 1976-78; cons. Boston Consulting Group, Boston and Chgo., 1978-82; v.p. Dyson-Kissner-Moran Corp., NYC, 1982-87; mng. dir. Carlyle Group, Washington, 1987-88; pres. Palisades Assocs., Inc., Bethesda, Md., 1988—. Debating coach Harvard U., 1976-79; dir. Varlen Corp., Naperville, Ill., 1985-99, Richey Electronics, Inc., Garden Grove, Calif., 1993-99, McLaren/Hart Inc., Rancho Cordova, Calif., 1995-2000, Expressions Furniture, Inc., Anaheim, Calif., 1992-97, AMCO Corp., Chgo., 1993-97, The Whaler on Kaanapali Beach, 1999-2005, PlayCore Holdings, Inc., 2000-07, Nations Rent, Ft. Lauderdale, Fla., 2003-06, TVC Commns., Annaville, Pa., 2003-, Empire Kosner Poultry, Mifflintown, Pa., 2003-. Co-author: The Crime of Poverty, 1973, Beyond Politics, 1974, World Without Plenty, 1975. Dir. Lifeline, A Mental Retardation Partnership, Washington, 1993-98; baseball coach Potomac (Md.) Boys' Club, 1992-96; co-chair Harvard Debate Centennial, 1991—; mem. Harvard Law Sch. 30th Reunion gift com., 2006-07, Harvard Coll. 30th Reunion gift com., 2003-04; chair Dean's Alumni Leadership Coun., Kennedy Sch., Harvard, mem.; mem. com. on univ. resources, Harvard U., 2003-. Winner Ames Moot Ct. competition Harvard Law Sch., 1976. Mem. ABA, Am. Forensic Assn. (nat. intercollegiate debate champion 1974, coach nat. intercollegiate debate champion 1979), Am. Acad. Polit. and Social Scis., Ctr. for Study of Presidency, Toledo Bar Assn., Chgo. Bar Assn., Phi Beta Kappa. Democrat. Jewish. Avocations: major league baseball, golf, computers, sports memorabilia. Office: Palisades Assocs Inc 9140 Vendome Dr Bethesda MD 20817-4021 Business E-Mail: greg@palisadesassociates.com.

ROSENBAUM, HERBERT EDWIN, neurology educator; b. Los Angeles, Dec. 11, 1924; s. Samuel P. and Rebecca (Goldberg) R.; m. Dorothy Goldner, Nov. 2, 1944 (div. Aug. 1972); children: Robert, Barbara, Nancy; m. Velma Rosenbaum, Nov. 5, 1988. BS, U. Oreg., 1947, MD, 1949. Prof. neurology Washington U. Sch. Medicine, St. Louis, 1978—. Served to 1st lt. USAF, 1952-53. Fellow Am. Acad. Neurology (counselor 1970-74); mem. Am. Psychiat. Assn. (life mem., pres. Mo. chpt. 1964-65), Soc. Clin. Neurologists (pres. 1974-75). Avocation: golf. Office: Wash U Sch Medicine Campus Box 8111 660 S Euclid Ave Saint Louis MO 63110-1010 Home: 13 Sackston Woods Ln Creve Coeur MO 63141-8228

ROSENBAUM, JACOB I., retired lawyer; b. Cleve., Oct. 4, 1927; s. Lionel C. and Dora (Heldman) R.; m. Marjorie Jean Arnold, Apr. 20, 1952; children: Laura Rosenbaum, Alexander, Judith Bartell. JD, U. N.Mex., 1951. Bar: N.Mex. 1951, Ohio 1952. Pres. Ohio Savs. Bank., Cleve., 1955—60, sr. v.p., 1960—92, also dir., 1995—2009; ptnr. Burke, Haber & Berick, 1955-79, Arter & Hadden, 1979-94, of counsel, 1994—2003, Tucker Ellis & West, 2003—05; ret., 2005. Active Judson Retirement Cmty., Cleve. Heights, Ohio, 1990—, trustee, 1994—2003, 2006—, pres., 1992, Cleve. Nat. Air Show, 1994—, pres. Found., 1995—2003, trustee, 1981—, found. trustee, 2007—; life trustee Cleve. Zool. Soc., 1983—2009; trustee Golden Age Ctrs. of Cleve., 1996—, Judson Found., 2007—; pres. Cleve. Nat. Air Show, 1987—90, Temple Emanu El, Orange Village, Ohio, 1965—67, 1995—. Mem.: Cleve. Execs. Assn. (pres. 1989, chmn. 1990, pres. 2003), Greater Cleve. Bar Assn., Ohio Bar Assn. (chmn. aviation law com. 1981—84), Lawyer-Pilots Bar Assn. (pres. 1981—82, editor jour. 1982—97), Kiwanis Club of Cleve. (pres. 1970—71, pres. found. 1999—). Democrat. Jewish. Home: 28050 N Woodland Rd Cleveland OH 44124-4521 Office: Tucker Ellis & West 1150 Huntington Bldg 925 Euclid Ave Cleveland OH 44115-1475 Office Phone: 216-696-2480. Personal E-mail: jirmir@aol.com. Business E-Mail: jrosenbaum@tuckerellis.com.

ROSENBAUM, JAMES MICHAEL, federal judge; b. Ft. Snelling, Minn., Oct. 12, 1944; s. Sam H. and Ilene D. (Bernstein) Rosenbaum; m. Marilyn Brown, July 30, 1972. BA, U. Minn., 1966, JD, 1969. Bar: (Minn) 1969, (Ill.) 1970, (U.S. Supreme Ct.) 1979. Atty. VISTA, 1969—70, staff atty., Leadership Coun. Met. Open Cmtys. Chgo., 1970—72; assoc. Katz, Taube, Lange & Frommelt, Mpls., 1972-77; ptnr. Rosenbaum & Rosenbaum, Mpls., 1977-79, Gainsley, Squier & Korsh, Mpls., 1979-81; US dist. atty. US Dept. Justice, Mpls., 1981-85; judge US Dist. Ct., Minn., 1985—, chief judge Minn., 2001—08. 8th cir. rep. Jud. Conf. U.S., 1997—2005, mem. exec. com., 1999—2001. Author: (booklet) Guide to Practice Civil Rights Housing, 1972; co-author: U.S. Courts Design Guide, 1991—96; contbr. In Defense of the Hard Drive. Campaign chmn. People for Boschwitz, Minn., 1978; bd. vis. U. Minn. Law Sch. (pres. 1996-97). Mem.: FBA (bd. dirs.). Jewish. Office: US Courthouse 300 S 4th St Minneapolis MN 55415-1320

ROSENBAUM, JOAN HANNAH, museum director; b. Hartford, Conn. d. Charles Leon and Lillian (Sharasheff) Grossman; m. Peter S. Rosenbaum, July 1962 (div. 1970). AA, Hartford Coll. for Women, 1962; BA, Boston U., 1964; student, Hunter Coll. Grad Sch., 1970-73; cert., Columbia U. Bus. Sch. Inst. Non Profit Mgmt., 1978; DHL (hon.), Jewish Theol. Sem., 1993. Curatorial asst. Mus. Modern Art, NYC, 1966-72; dir. mus. program NY Council on Arts, NYC, 1972-79; cons. Michal Washburn & Assocs., NYC, 1979-80; Helen Goldsmith Menschel dir. The Jewish Mus., NYC, 1981—. Bd. dirs. Creative Time.2000-2008 Bd. dirs. Artists Space, 1980-93; mem. coun. Am. Jewish Mus., 1981-90; mem. policy panel Nat. Endowment Arts, 1982-83. Created knight (Denmark), 1984; recipient Disting. Alumni award Boston U. Coll. Libera Arts, 1994, Woman of Distinction award Hadassah, 1997, diploma Chevalier of Order of Arts and Letters (France), 1999 Mem. Am. Assn. Mus. (cons. 1979—), Assn. Art Mus. Dirs., NY State Assn. Mus. (mem. coun. 1981-90), Art Table. Office: Jewish Mus 1109 5th Ave New York NY 10128-0118

ROSENBAUM, MARK E., health products executive; BBA, Univ. Tenn. Sales & mgmt. positions Am. Hosp. Supply, Baxter Healthcare, 1981—89; v.p., gen. mgr. Amsco Internat., 1989—96; regional v.p. Cardinal Health, Dublin, Ohio, 1996—98, exec. v.p. health sys. sales & mktg., 1998—2002, exec. v.p. corp. sales & mktg., 2002—05, pres. integrated provider solutions, 2005—. Office: Cardinal Health 7000 Cardinal Pl Dublin OH 43017*

ROSENBAUM, MARY LOUISE, elementary school educator; b. Wayzata, Minn., Sept. 10, 1942; d. Elmer and Helen Louise (Foote) Quam; m. Mitchell Dale Rosenbaum, Oct. 28, 1976; children: Shauna Lee, Brent Mitchell. BS, U. Minn., Mpls., 1965. Cert. in elem. edn. Ariz., 1976. Tchr. State Alska, Anchorage, 1965—67, US Dept. Def., 1967—72, Dysart Unified Schs., Peoria, Ariz., 1973—99, Fletcher Heights Elem., Glendale, Ariz., 1999—2003; 4th grade tchr. Carden Traditional Sch., Surprise, Ariz., 2003—. Office: Carden Traditional Sch 15688 W Acoma Rd Surprise AZ 85379 Personal E-mail: mmtworoses@cox.net. Business E-Mail: mary.rosenbaum@learningmatters.org.

ROSENBAUM, MICHAEL A., pediatrician, educator; b. NYC, Dec. 7, 1956; s. Salo Rosenbaum and Vivian Fromberg; m. Nina J. Chertoff, Oct. 16, 1983; children: Matthew, Amanda. BA in Neuroscience, Amherst Coll., 1978; MD, Cornell U., 1982. Diplomate Am. Bd. Pediatrics, Am. Bd. Pediatric Endocrinology. Intern in pediat. Columbia Presbyn. Hosp., NYC, 1982—83, resident in pediat., 1983—85; fellow in pediatric endocrinology NY Hosp., NYC, 1985-88; rsch. assoc. Rockefeller U., NYC, 1988-92, asst. prof., 1993—97; ptnr. W. End Pediat., NYC, 1989—; assoc. prof. clin. pediat. and medicine Columbia Presbyn. Med. Ctr., NYC, 1997—; attending physician NY Presbyn. Hosp., NYC, 1997—. Recipient Ethan Sims Young Investigator award N.Am. Assn. Study Obesity, 1987; named to America's Top Doctors, 2006, NY Mag. Best Doctors, 2006; John Woodruff Simpson fellow Amherst Coll., 1978, Norman and Rosita Winston fellow Cornell U., 1982-85; Amparo Rugarcia scholar Rockefeller U., 1981-91. Fellow Am. Acad. Pediat.; mem. AMA, Am. Diabetes Assn., Nat. Obesity and Weight Coun. Inst. (advisor 1993—), NY County Med. Soc. Avocations: reading, theater. Office: Columbia Presbyn Med Ctr 1150 Saint Nicholas Ave New York NY 10032-3822 also: West End Pediatrics 450 W End Ave New York NY 10024 Office Phone: 212-305-9949, 212-469-3070. Office Fax: 212-851-5306. E-mail: mr475@columbia.edu.

ROSENBAUM, RANDALL, arts association administrator; b. Phila., Dec. 29, 1954; s. Israel J. and Berta (Lesla) Rosenbaum; m. Claire Marie Hennessy, Oct. 23, 1954; children: Jane Marie, Hannah Margaret. BA in Music Edn., Temple U., 1976. Intern Am. Symphony Orch. League, Washington, 1979; asst. to mgr. Jacksonville Symphony, Fla., 1979; gen. mgr. Asheville Symphony, NC, 1979—81, Rome Symphony Orch., Ga., 1980, Ohio Chamber Orch., Cleve., 1981; dep. dir., dir. dance and presenting organs. programs Pa. Coun. on Arts, 1984—95; exec. dir. RI State Coun. on Arts, 1995—. Site visitor, panelist Nat. Endowment for Arts; panelist Mid-Atlantic Arts Found., Heinz Endowment of Pitts.; bd. mem. New England Found. for Arts. Mem.: Orgn. Ohio Orchestras, Am. Symphony Orchestra League. Democrat. Jewish. Office: RI State Coun on Arts One Capitol Hill, 3rd Fl Providence RI 02908 Office Phone: 401-222-3880. Office Fax: 401-222-3018. E-mail: randy@arts.ri.gov.

ROSENBAUM, RICHARD MERRILL, lawyer; b. Oswego, NY, Apr. 8, 1931; s. Jack M. and Shirley (Gover) R.; m. Judith Kanthor, June 1, 1958; children: Amy, Jill, Matthew, Julie. BA, Hobart Coll., 1952; JD, Cornell U., 1955. Bar: N.Y. 1956. Ptnr. Rosenbaum, Agnello, Agnello & Levine, Rochester, N.Y., 1955-70; justice Supreme Ct. N.Y. State, 1970-73; ptnr. Nixon, Hargrave, Devans & Doyle, Rochester, 1977-84, 88-98; counsel to chmn. of bd., dir. govt. rels. and pub. affairs. Integated Resources, Inc., 1984-88, also bd. dirs. Dir. Integrated Resources, Inc.; past mem. econ. adv. bd. U.S. Dept. Commerce; bd. dirs., sec. Jonathan Inst.; mem. mediation arbitration panel JAMS/Endispute, 1997, Am. Arbitration Assn., 1998, Empire Mediation, 1998; jud hearing officer, 1997; chmn. N.Y. State Unemployment Ins. Bd., 1998-2006; sr. counsel Nixon Peabody, 2006-. Author political insiders memoir No Room for Democrat, The Triumph of Ego over Common Sense, RIT Pub.; contbr. writings in fields of politics and public affairs, legal opinions to pubs., 1984-88. Trustee Hobart Coll., 1971-89; nat. committeeman N.Y. State Rep. Nat. Com., 1977—, rules rev. com., subcom. chmn. conv. procedures, 1977—; del.-at-large Rep. Nat. Conv., 1980, 84, 88, congl. dist. del., 1968, chmn. N.Y. State del., 1976; chmn. Monroe County Rep. Com., 1968-70, N.Y. Rep. State Com., 1973-77, Northeastern Rep. State Chairmen's Assn., 1973-76, Nat. Rep. State Chairmen's Assn., 1975-77; justice of peace Town of Penfield (N.Y.), 1962-66; mem. and asst. majority leader Monroe County Legislature, 1966-68; former mem. coun. SUNY, Brockport; dep. counsel U.S. Senate Majority, 1988; apptd. by Pres. Ronald Reagan, U.S. Holocaust Meml. Coun., reapptd. by Pres. George Bush; apptd. by U.S. Senate to Bd. of Fed. Jud. Ctr. Found., 1989—; bd. dirs. Cardozo Sch. Law Yeshiva U.; bd. dirs. Rochester Mus. & Sci. Ctr., 1978—, gen. chmn. devel. fund drive, 1977—; trustee Rochester Area Colls., 1979—; mem. coun. of governing bds. of Ind. Colls. of State of N.Y., 1979—; apptd. mem. N.Y. Mental Hygiene Council, 1973-77, Nat. Citizens Adv. Com. on Environ. Quality, 1977; past bd. dirs. Jewish Home for Aged, Rochester, bd. dirs. Rochester Philharmonic Orchestra; exec. com. Cornell Law Sch; Rep. candidate for nomination for N.Y. state gov., 1994. Recipient Congl. Medal Honor Ellis Island, 1992, Hobart Coll. Alumni citation. Mem. ABA, N.Y. State Bar Assn. Clubs: Royal Order of Jesters, Masons, Shriners. Jewish. Home: 19 Denonville Rdg Rochester NY 14625-1611 Office: Nixon Peabody Clinton Sq Po Box 31051 Rochester NY 14603

ROSENBAUM, ROBERT A., lawyer; s. Irwin L. and Marilyn E. Rosenbaum; m. Maggie A. Gilbert, May 1, 1994; m. Peggy A. Daly, Nov. 1982 (div. May 1991); children: Jacob A., Samuel A., Benjamin P. BA, Princeton U., 1978; JD, Harvard Law Sch., 1981. Bar: Calif. 1982, Minn. 1987. Assoc. atty. Latham & Watkins, LA, 1982—87; law clk. to chief justice Minn. Supreme Ct., St. Paul, 1981—82; ptnr., corp. securities law, corp. governance and compliance, and mergers and acquisitions groups Dorsey & Whitney LLP, Mpls., 1987—, and group head, corp., mem., mgmt. com. Mem., bd. dirs. Guthrie Theatre, Mpls., 2001—04. Named Am.'s Leading Bus. Lawyers, Chambers USA, 2003-2004, Minn. Superlawyer in M&A, Minn. Law and Politics, 1998-2004. Mem.: ABA, Minn. State Bar Assn. (ch. 302a subcommittee), Calif. Bar Assn., Hennepin Bar Assn., Mpls. Club. Office: Dorsey & Whitney LLP 50 South Sixth St Minneapolis MN 55402-1553 Office Fax: 612-340-2868. E-mail: rosenbaum.robert@dorsey.com.

ROSENBAUM, SIDNEY J. (JERR ROSENBAUM), legislative staff member; s. Sidney and Diane Rosenbaum. Legis. counsel, Rep. Virgil Goode US House of Reps., Washington, 2003—04, chief of staff to Rep. Virgil Goode, 2004—08, asst., appropriations com., 2007—08, chief of staff to Jack Kingston, 2009—. Republican. Office: 2368 Rayburn House Office Bldg Washington DC 20515 Office Phone: 202-225-5831. Office Fax: 202-225-2269.*

ROSENBERG, AARON GLEN, orthopedist, educator; BS, Rensselaer Polytechnic Inst., 1974; MD, Albany Med. Coll. Union Univ., 1978. Diplomate Am. Bd. Orthopedic Surgeons, 1986, cert. in Orthopaedic Surgery 1995. Instr., orthopedic surgery Harvard Med. Sch., 1983—84, Rush Univ. Med. Ctr., Chgo., 1979—83, adj. attending in orthopedic surgery, 1981—83, clin. instr., 1983—85, asst. attending in orthopedic surgery, 1983—92, asst. prof., dept. orthopedic surgery, 1985—92, assoc. prof., 1992—96, sr. attending in orthopedic surgery, 1996—, prof., 1996—. Mem. adv. bd. Zimmer Inst.; bd. dirs. Am. Acad. Orthopaedic Surgeons, dir., instr., Orthopaedic Learning Ctr. Editor: (instructional CD-ROM) The Arthritic Knee; co-editor: (textbook) The Adult Hip-Lippincott, 2000, The Adult Knee-Lippincott, 2002; contbr. articles to numerous profl. jours. Fellow: Am. Acad. Orthopedic Surgeons; mem.: The Hip Soc., The Knee Soc., The Internat. Hip Soc. Achievements include design of several joint replacement devices including the VerSys Hip System, Nex Gen Knee System, and ZMR Revision Hip System. Office: Rush Univ Med Ctr Profl Bldg Ste 1063 1725 W Harrison St Chicago IL 60612*

ROSENBERG, ALAN, actors guild executive; b. Passaic, NJ, Oct. 4, 1950; m. Robin Bartlett (div.); m. Marg Helgenberger, Sept. 9, 1989; 1 child. Actor: (Broadway plays) Lost in Yonkers; (films) The Wanderers, 1979, Happy Birthday, Gemini, 1980, Not for Publication, 1984, Stewardess School, 1986, White of the Eye, 1987, The Last Temptation of Christ, 1988, Miracle Mile, 1988, After Midnight, 1989, Impulse, 1990, The Bum, 2002, (voice) Robots, 2005,: (TV films) Kojak: The Belarus File, 1985, Promise, 1986, The King of Love, 1987, The Revenge of Al Capone, 1989, The Preppie Murder, 1989, Parker Kane, 1990, The Boys, 1991, Partners, 1993, On Hope, 1994, Witch Hunt, 1994, Freaky Friday, 1995, On Seventh Avenue, 1996, Undue Influence, 1996, Breaking Through, 1996, Cloned, 1997, Bronx County, 1998, Giving Up the Ghost, 1998, The Temptations, 1998, A Touch of Hope, 1999, A Mother's Fight for Justice, 2001, On the Edge, 2001; (TV series) Civil Wars, 1991—93, L.A. Law, 1993—94, Cybill, 1995—98, The Guardian, 2001—04, (guest appearances) Barnaby Jones, 1978, The Days and Nights of Molly Dodd, 1987, Coach, 1989, Empty Nest, 1989, ER, 1994, Murphy Brown, 1998, Touched by an Angel, 1999, Chicago Hope, 1999, 2000, NYPD Blue, 2005, CSI, 2005, Numb3rs, 2005. Mem.: SAG (pres. 2005—). Office: SAG 5757 Wilshire Blvd Los Angeles CA 90036*

ROSENBERG, ALAN DAVID, accountant; b. Mt. Vernon, NY, Apr. 11, 1946; s. Benjamin Bernard and Miriam (Nierenberg) R.; m. Wendy Patricia Cutler, May 25, 1975; children: Kerri L., Joshua Z., Brian S. BS in Acctg., NYU, 1967; MBA in Taxation, Baruch Coll., 1970. CPA NY. Sr. acct. Ernst & Ernst, NYC, 1967-70; dir. acctg., CFO various firms, NYC, 1970-75; pres. Alan D. Rosenberg, CPA, P.C., NYC, New Rochelle, N.Y., 1975—. Mem. AICPA (mem. tax practice mgmt. com. 1992—), N.Y. State Soc. CPAs, Inst. Mgmt. Accts., Nat. Conf. CPA Practitioners, Alliance of Practicing CPAs, Estate Planning Coun. Westchester County, Tax Soc. NYU. Jewish. Avocations: sports, reading, family activities. Office: 2 W 45th St Ste 1208 New York NY 10036-4212

ROSENBERG, ALAN GENE, editor; b. Chgo., Sept. 14, 1957; s. Earl David and Lorraine Faith (Blum) R.; m. Avis Beth Gunther-Rosenberg, Apr. 8, 1984; children: Ethan Elijah, Rebecca Greer, Jacob Sigmund. BS in Journalism, Northwestern U., 1978. From state staff reporter to asst. mng. editor breaking news Providence Jour., 1978—. Tchr. Temple Beth-El Religious Sch., Providence, 1998—, Emerson Coll. Profl. Students Program, 2007—. Recipient Goldberg Tchr. Creativity award, Bur. Jewish Edn., 2003, Jenny Klein Religious Tchr. of Yr. award, 2006. Office: Providence Jour 75 Fountain St Providence RI 02902-0050 Home Phone: 401-885-0768; Office Phone: 401-277-7409. Business E-Mail: alan_rosenberg@projo.com.

ROSENBERG, ALAN STEWART, lawyer; b. NYC, Mar. 29, 1930; s. Louis and Sadye (Knobler) R.; m. Ilse Rosenberg/Klein, Aug. 15, 1963; children: Gary, Robert. BA, Stanford U., 1949; LLB, Columbia U., 1952; LLM, NYU, 1960. Bar: N.Y. 1955. Assoc. Wolf Haldenstein Adler & Freeman, NYC, 1955-56; ptnr., chmn. tax dept. Proskauer Rose LLP, NYC, 1957—92. Contbr. articles to profl. jours. Mem. exec. com., bd. visitors Stanford (Calif.) U. Law Sch., 1982-85, Jewish studies program, 1986—; chmn. bd. NY Alliance for the Pub. Sch., 1988-91; mem. adv. com. on pub. issues Advt. Coun., 1991-94; bd. dirs., sec. Univ.-Urban Schs. Nat. Task Force Inc., 1981-96; mem. bd. visitors Columbia U. Law Sch., 1991-96; trustee Ctr. Ednl. Innovation Pub. Edn. Assn., 2000—; mem. bd advisors Spl. Music Sch Am., 1999—; bd. dirs., treas. Justice

Resource Ctr., 1994-97; bd. dirs., The Abraham Fund, 2000-; chmn. bd. dirs. Richalan Found., 1996-2003. Lt (jr. grade) USNR, 1952—55. Jewish. Avocation: singing. Home: 115 Central Park W New York NY 10023-4153 Home Phone: 212-877-7471. Personal E-mail: aandi98@aol.com.

ROSENBERG, ALEX JACOB, art appraiser and dealer, educator; b. NYC, May 25, 1919; s. Israel and Lena (Zar) R. Student, Albright Coll., 1935-37, Sch. Phila. Mus. Art, 1937-40; BS, Phila. U., 1948; DHL (hon.), Hofstra U., 1989; DSc in Art, Inst. Superior Art, Havana, Cuba, 2003. completed Personal Property courses, levels I, II, III and IV, Am. Soc. Appraisers, Uniform Standards of Profl. Appraisal Practice, 1994, 2000, 06. Pres. Anserphone, 1959-66, Transworld Art Inc., Alex Rosenberg Gallery and Alba Edits., NYC, 1968—89, The Abbot Group, 1987-89, Ardmore Affiliates Ltd., Alex Rosenberg Fine Art, 1985—, Neikrug-Rosenberg Assocs., 1989-97. Lectr. Parsons Sch. Design, NYC, 1979—88; instr. appraising modern art NYU, 1992—95, adj. asst. prof. appraising, 1995—; vis. prof. fine art Inst. Superior Art, Havana, Cuba, 1993—; organizer Henry Moore exhbn. Mus. Budapest, Bratislava and Prague, Hungary, 1993; co-author Appraisers Assn. America, 1994; co-curator Leonoid Sokov, Albright Coll., Reading, Pa., 2002; guest lectr. CUNY, NYC, 2000—03; organizer Henry Moore Exhbn., Havana, 1998; chmn. Salvadore Dali Rsch. Ctr., 2006—. Curator An American Portrait, 1976—78, Mus. Fine Art, Havana, 1992—93, co-curator Romare Bearden as Printmaker, 1992—97, Henry Moore Mother and Child Exhbn., 1987—88, assoc. editor exhbn. catalogue; exhibitions include Alex Rosenber Collection, Albright Coll., 2008—09; author: (book) The Art, Science and Business of Appraising in English, 1999, The Art, Science and Business of Apprasing in Spanish, 2008, Advanced Problems in Apprasing, 2009. Trustee Alice Baber Art Fund, 1991-93, Phila. Coll. Textiles and Sci., 1992-95; mem. internat. bd. dirs. Tel Aviv Mus. Art, 1999-, bd. dirs., 2000-06, 2007-; bd. dirs. Artists' Rights Today, 1974-80; mus. adv. bd. Hofstra Mus., Hempstead, N.Y., 1987-92; mem. collection and exhbn. com. Parrish Art Mus., Southhampton, N.Y., 1989-95; mem. adv. com. Pollock-Krasner House and Study Ctr., 2000—; trustee Guttman Inst., 1979-92; mem. exec. bd. Nat. Emergency Civil Liberties Com., 1970-98, treas., 1981-98; trustee Nat. Emergency Civil Liberties Found., 1964-98, chmn., 1992-98; nat. bd. dirs. and bd. dirs. local coun. SANE, 1974-83, bd. trustees Ctr. for Constitutional Rights, 1998—, v.p. 2003—; trustee, treas. New Lincoln Sch., 1968-71; trustee Givat Haviva Ednl. Found., N.Y.C., 1969—, chmn. exec. com., 1992-99, v.p., 1998—; trustee Stephen Wise Free synagogue, 1967-70, 73-76, 99-2000, Mus. Borough Bklyn., 1986-89; del. 28th World Zionist Congress, Jerusalem, 1972; mem. Cmty. Planning Bd. # 7, 1965-67, 70-72; mem. Lower West Side Anti-Poverty Bd., 1965-66, Lincoln Ctr. Cmty. Coun., 1968-74, Com. for Ind. Civilian Police Rev. Bd., 1967; mem. steering com. Com. Pub. Edn. and Religious Liberty; chmn. Am. Israel Civil Liberties Coalition, 1988-89; Dist. leader Am. Labor Party, 1949-1950, dem. dist. leader, 1964-74, state committeeman, 1970-73, mem. county exec. com., 1964-74; del. Dem. Nat. Convs., 1968, 72; bd. dirs. Raoul Wallenberg Commn. of U.S., 1986-90, chmn., 1990-92; mem. print and drawing coun. Israel Mus., 1980-85; assoc. dir. Snug Harbor Cultural Ctr., S.I., 1982-88; mem. AAA del. to Pres. Coun. of Appraisal Orgns., 1995-96; bd. mem. Ludwig Found. of Cuba, 1995—; mem. Assn. Governing Bds. of Univs. and Colls., 1994-96; hon. fellow Tel. Aviv Mus. Art, 2002. Recipient Spl. prize Grenschen Triennial, Switzerland, 1976, Cuban Order of Culture, 1995, Cert. of Commendation, Am. Soc. Appraisers, 1993, Cert. for Disting. Svc., Appraisers Assn. of Am., 1993, Graham J. Littlewood III award for profl. excellence Phila. Coll. of Textiles and Sci., 1996, Alex and Carole Rosenberg Collection, Savannah Coll. of Art and Design, 1999, Alex Rosenberg Gallery Hofstra U., 1996—, Alex and Carole Rosenberg Collection Albright Coll., Reading, Pa.; named to Silver Cir., Pres.'s Coun., Albright Coll., 2007, Diploma for Service, Nat. Mus. of Fine Art, Havana, Cuba, 2003. Mem. Am. Soc. Appraisers (sr., bd. examiners 1987-95, personal property com. 1987-89), Appraisers Assn. Am. (cert. mem., bd. dirs. 1990-96, v.p. 1992-94, 1st v.p. 1994, pres. 1994-96, Pres.' award 2005), Fine Art Pubs. Assn. (v.p., bd. dirs. 1981-83, pres. 1983-86, treas. 1986-89), Nat. Arts Club (Lifetime Achievement Gold medal 2004). Home and Office: 3 E 69th St New York NY 10021-4943 Fax: 212-628-4969.

ROSENBERG, ALISON P., retired public policy officer; b. Miami, Fla., Sept. 5, 1945; d. Mortimer I. and Gail (Sklar) Podell; m. Jeffrey Alan Rosenberg, May 4, 1969; 1 child, Robert Aaron. BS in Econs., Smith Coll., 1967. Mng. officer Citibank, NYC, 1967-69; legis. aide Senator Charles Percy, Washington, 1969-80; profl. staff mem. Senate Fgn. Rels. Com., Washington, 1981-85; assoc. asst. adminstr. Agy. for Internat. Devel., Washington, 1985-87; dir. African affairs Nat. Security Coun., Washington, 1987-88; dep. asst. sec. for Africa State Dept., Washington, 1988-92; asst. admnstr. for Africa Agy. for Internat. Devel., Washington, 1992-93; lead partnerships specialist (Africa) The World Bank, Washington, 1993—2007, partnership cons. (Africa), 2007—. Personal E-mail: alirosenb@gmail.com.

ROSENBERG, BRIAN C, academic administrator; BA in English, Cornell U.; MA in English, PhD in English, Columbia U. Tchg. asst. Columbia U., NYC, 1979—80; English instr. Queens Coll., NY, 1980—82; asst. prof. The Cooper Union, NYC, 1982—83; asst. prof. to assoc. prof. to prof. to chmn., dept. of English Allegheny Coll., Meadville, Pa., 1983—98; chief acad. officer to dean of faculty and prof. English Lawrence U., Appleton, Wis., 1998—2003; pres. Macalester Coll., 2003—. Pres. fellowship Columbia U., 1977—78, 1980—81; bd. trustees The Dickens Soc., 2000—. Author: (book) Mary Lee Settle's Beulah Quintet: The Price of Freedom, 1991, Little Dorrit's Shadow's: Character and Contradiction in Dickens, 1996. Mem.: Phi Beta Kappa. Office: Office of the Pres, Macalester Coll 208 Weyerhaeuser Hall 62 Macalester St Saint Paul MN 55105 Office Phone: 651-696-6207. Office Fax: 651-696-6500. E-mail: rosenbergb@macalester.edu.*

ROSENBERG, CHARLES ERNEST, historian, educator; b. NYC, Nov. 11, 1936; s. Bernard and Marion (Roberts) R.; m. Carroll Ann Smith, June 22, 1961 (div. 1977); 1 child, Leah; m. Drew Gilpin Faust, June 7, 1980; 1 child, Jessica. BA, U. Wis., 1956, DHL, 1997; MA, Columbia U., 1957, PhD, 1961. Fellow Johns Hopkins U., Balt., 1960-61; asst. prof. U. Wis., 1961-63; assoc. prof. U. Pa., Phila., 1965-68, prof. history, 1968—, chmn. dept., 1974—75, 1979—83, 1991—95; prof. history of sci. Harvard U., 2001—, chmn. dept. history of sci., 2003—04. Author: The Cholera Years: The United States in 1832, 1849 and 1866, 1962, The Trial of the Assassin Guiteau: Psychiatry and Law in the Gilded Age, 1968, No Other Gods: On Science and Social Thought in America, 1976, The Care of Strangers: The Rise of America's Hospital System, 1987, Explaining Epidemics and Other Studies in the History of Medicine, 1992, Our Present Complaint: American Medicine Then and Now, 2007; editor Isis, 1986-89. Bd. dirs. Mental Health Assn. Southea. Pa., 1973—76, Libr. Co. of Phila., 1980—, Ctr. Advanced Study Behavioral Scis., 1999—2005. Nat. Inst. Health Research grantee, 1964-70; Guggenheim Found. fellow, 1965-66, 89-90; Nat. Endowment Humanities fellow, 1972-73; Rockefeller Found. humanities fellow, 1975-76; fellow Inst. Advanced Study, 1979-80, Ctr. Advanced Study in Behavioral Scis., 1982-83. Fellow: Am. Philos. Soc. (coun. 2006—), Am. Acad. Arts and Scis.; mem.: Orgn. Am. Historians (exec. bd. 1985—88), Soc. Social History of Medicine (pres. 1981), History of Sci. Soc. (coun. 1972—75, George Sarton medal 1995), Am. Assn. History of Medicine (coun. 1974—76, pres. 1992—94, William H. Welch medal 1969), Inst. Medicine of NAS. Office: Harvard U Dept History of Sci Cambridge MA 02138 Home: 33 Elmwood Cambridge MA 02138 Office Phone: 617-495-9953. Business E-Mail: rosenb3@fas.harvard.edu.

ROSENBERG, CHUCK (CHARLES P. ROSENBERG), lawyer, former prosecutor; b. 1960; married; 2 children. BA, Tufts U., 1982; MA in Pub. Policy, Harvard U., 1985; JD, U. Va., 1990. Legal analyst NBC TV; ptnr. Hunton & Williams LLP, McLean, Va., 2000—02; spl. asst. US atty. (ea. dist.) Va US Dept. Justice, Alexandria, Va., 1991—94, asst. US atty., 1994—2000, counselor to FBI Dir. Robert S. Mueller III Washington, 2002—03, counselor to atty. gen. John Ashcroft, 2003—04, chief of staff to dep. atty. gen., 2004—05, interim US atty. (so. dist.) Tex. Houston, 2005—06, interim US atty (ea. dist.) Va. Alexandria, Tex., 2006, US atty., 2006—09; ptnr. Hogan & Hartson LLP, Washington, 2009—. Office: Hogan & Hartson LLP 555 Thirteenth St NW Washington DC 20004 Office Fax: 202-637-5910. E-mail: crosenberg@hhlaw.com.*

ROSENBERG, DAN YALE, retired plant pathologist; b. Stockton, Calif., Jan. 8, 1922; s. Meyer and Bertha (Naliboff) R.; m. Marilyn Kohn, Dec. 5, 1954; 1 son, Morton Karl. AA, Stockton Jr. Coll., 1942; AB, Coll. of the Pacific, 1949; MS, U. Calif., Davis, 1952. Jr. plant pathologist State of Calif. Dept. Agr., Riverside, 1952-55, asst. plant pathologist Sacramento, 1955-59, assoc. plant pathologist, 1959-60, pathologist IV, 1960—63, program supr., 1963—71, chief exclusion and detectin, divsn. plant industry, 1971—76, chief nursery and seed svcs. divsn. plant industry, 1976-82, spl. asst. divsn. plant industry, 1982-87; pres. Health Inc., 1972-73. Agrl. cons., 1988—; mem. Citrus Rsch. Adm. Com., U. Calif., Riverside, 1992-07; mem. Gov.'s Interagy. Task Force on Biotech., 1986-87; agrl. cons. Calif. Avocado Commn., 1994-07. Contbr. articles to profl. jours. Served with AUS, 1942-46, ETO. Mem. Am. Phytopath. Soc. (fgn. and regulatory com. 1975—, chmn. 1978, grape diseases and pests 1977-98), Calif. State Employees Assn. (pres. 1967-69), Sacto. Met. C. of C. (internat. trade com. 1993-97), N.Am. Plant Protection Orgn. (industry adv. group), Plant Patents Fruit Trees and Ornamental Trees, Olive Trees and Grapevines Achievements include research in grape genetics; new olive varieties; patents for grapevines, fruit, ornamental, and olive trees. Home and Office: 2328 Swarthmore Dr Sacramento CA 95825-6867 Office Phone: 916-929-4620.

ROSENBERG, DAVID ALAN, military historian, strategic analyst; b. NYC, Aug. 30, 1948; s. Sidney and Fay (Breitman) R.; m. Deborah Lee Haines, July 1, 1973; 1 child, Rebecca Haines. BA in History, Am. U., 1970; MA in History, U. Chgo., 1971, PhD in History, 1983. Asst. historian, cons. Lulejian & Assocs., Inc., Falls Church, Va., 1974-75; instr. history U. Wis., Milw., 1976-78; pvt. practice cons., rschr. Chgo., Washington, 1978-82; asst. prof. history U. Houston, University Park, 1982-83; sr. fellow Strategic Concepts Devel. Ctr., Nat. Def. U., Washington, 1983-85; prof. strategy and ops. U.S. Naval War Coll., Newport, RI, 1985-90; assoc. prof. history Temple U., Phila., 1990-2000, professorial lectr., 2001—; Adm. Harry W. Hill prof. maritime strategy Nat. War Coll., Washington, 1996—2003; sr. prof. U.S. Naval War Coll., 1998—2006, asst. to vice chief naval ops., 1996—2004; dir. Task Force History for chief naval ops. Operation Iraqi Freedom, Global War on Terror, 2003—04; rsch. staff mem. intelligence studies Inst. for Defense Analyses, 2006—. US exec. com. four Nation Nuc. History Program, project dir. Berlin Crisis, 1989-95; cons. Office of Sec. Def., 1991-93, Office Chief of Naval Ops., 1991-2005, Office Sec. of Navy, 1992-2003; chair Sec. Navy's Adv. Subcom. Naval History, 1995-2005 Co-author: The Admiral's Advantage U.S. Navy Operational Intelligence in World War II and the Cold War, 2005; co-editor: (15 vol.) U.S. Plans for War, 1945-1950, 1990; contbr. articles to profl. jours., chpts. to books. With USNR, 1982—. Recipient Meritorious Pub. Svc. award Dept. of Navy, 1995, Superior Civilian Svc. medal, 2000; Advanced rsch. scholar U.S. Naval War Coll., 1974-79; Ford Found grantee, 1985-86, MacArthur rsch. grantee 1987-88; MacArthur fellow 1988-93. Mem. Orgn. Am. Historians (Binkley-Stephenson article prize), Soc. for Historians of Am. Fgn. Rels. (Bernath article prize), Soc. for Mil. History, U.S. Naval Inst., Internat. Inst. for Strategic Studies. Jewish.

ROSENBERG, DONALD JAY, communications company executive, lawyer; b. Feb. 19, 1951; BS in Math., SUNY, Stony Brook, 1972; JD, St. John's U. Sch. Law, 1975. Bar: NY 1976. Atty. CHQ IBM Corp., 1976—80, lab counsel data systems divsn., 1981—83, sr. atty., 1983—85, sr. counsel, 1985—86, divsn. counsel DSD, 1986—92, assoc. gen. counsel CHQ/L, 1992—97, asst. gen. counsel, 1997—98, v.p., asst. gen. counsel litig., 1998—2006, sr. v.p., gen. counsel, 2006; sr. v.p., gen. counsel, sec. Apple Inc. (formerly Apple Computer Inc.), Cupertino, Calif., 2006—07; exec. v.p., gen. counsel, corp. sec. Qualcomm Inc., San Diego, 2007—. Adj. prof. law Pace U. Sch. Law, NY. Contbr. chapters to books; editor: St. John's Law Rev. Chmn. bd. visitors Pace U. Sch. Law. Office: Qualcomm Inc 5775 Morehouse Dr San Diego CA 92121

ROSENBERG, ELI IRA, physicist, educator; b. Bklyn., Feb. 19, 1943; s. Milton and Beatrice Rosenberg; m. Wendy Jean Harrod, July 23, 1990; m. Eileen Ewig, Aug. 29, 1965 (div. Dec. 1, 1987); children: Elliot Michael, Evan Robert. BS, CCNY, 1964; MS, U. Ill., 1966, PhD, 1971. Enrico Fermi postdoctoral fellow U. Chgo., 1971—72, instr., 1972—74, asst. prof., 1974—79; assoc. physicist Ames (Iowa) Lab., U.S. Dept. Energy, 1979—81, program dir., 1988—93, physicist, 1981, sr. physicist, 1987—93; asst. prof. Iowa State U., Ames, 1979—81, assoc. prof., 1981—87, prof., 1987—, chmn. dept. physics and astronomy, 2002—08; program mgr. US Dept. Energy, 2008—. Contbr. articles to profl. jours. Grantee, U.S. Dept. of Energy, 1979—2008. Fellow: Am. Phys. Soc. (life); mem.: Sigma Xi, Phi Beta Kappa.

ROSENBERG, HARRY, biochemist, natural product chemist; b. USSR, Feb. 14, 1940; came to U.S., 1964; s. Ben and Marcia (Waltstein) R.; m. Miriam Grace Lappin; children: Faye Lisa, Jason, Aubrey. BS, U. Toronto, 1961; BS in Pharmacy, U. Mich., 1968, PharmD, 1968, MS, 1970, PhD, 1972. Asst. prof. U. Nebr. Coll. Pharmacy, Lincoln, 1972-75; assoc. prof. U. Nebr. Med. Ctr., Omaha, 1975-80, prof., 1980-86; prof., chmn. pharm. scis. Campbell U., Buies Creek, N.C., 1986—; dean N.D. State U. Coll. Pharmacy, Fargo, 1987—. Patentee in field; contbr. articles to profl. jours. Recipient Outstanding Tchr. award U. Nebr. Med. Ctr., 1982, Teaching award Campbell U. Sch. Pharmacy, 1987. Mem. Am. Assn. Colls. Pharmacy, Am. Pharm. Assn., Am. Assn. Pharm. Scientists. Office: ND State U Dept of Pharm Scis Fargo ND 58105

ROSENBERG, JEROME LAIB, chemist, educator; b. Harrisburg, Pa., June 20, 1921; s. Robert and Mary (Katzman) R.; m. Shoshana Gabriel, Sept. 15, 1946; children— Jonathan, Judith. AB, Dickinson Coll., 1941; MA, Columbia U., 1944, PhD, 1948. Rsch. chemist S.A.M. Labs., 1944-46; Instr. chemistry Columbia U., 1946-48; rsch. assoc. (asst. prof.) inst. Radiobiology and Biophysics, U. Chgo., 1950-53; mem. faculty U. Pitts., 1953-91, chmn. dept. biophysics and microbiology, 1969-71, prof. biol. scis., 1976-91, dean faculty arts and scis., 1970-86, vice provost, 1978-89, chmn. biol. scis., 1989-90, interim chmn. communication, 1991, assoc. dean faculty arts and scis., 1991-92, rsch. integrity officer, 1992—, prof. emeritus biol. scis., 1991—, dir. Jewish studies program, 1991-99. Author: Photosynthesis, 1965; editor, reviser: Outline Theory and Problems of College Chemistry (Schaum), 1949, 58, 66, 80, 90, 97; contbr. articles to profl. jours. NSF sr. fellow Technion Israel Inst. Tech., 1962-63, AEC fellow U. Chgo., 1948-50; recipient Pitts. award Am. Chem. Soc., 1987. Mem. AAUP (nat. coun. 1968-69, pres. Pa. div. 1968-69). Home: 1029 S Negley Ave Pittsburgh PA 15217-1045 Office Phone: 412-624-3007. Business E-Mail: jrosenb@pitt.edu.

ROSENBERG, JOAN I., psychologist, educator; PhD, U. Mo., Columbia, 1986. Lic. psychologist Calif., 1989. Pvt. practice, LA, 1989—; adj. prof. grad. psychology Pepperdine U., LA, 2005—. Bd. mem. Global Assn. Interpersonal Neurobiology Studies, LA, 2007—. Maj. USAFR, 1985—88, Dayton, Ohio. Recipient Socrates Tchg. award, U. Southern Calif., 2001. Office: 1663 Sawtelle Blvd Ste 250 Los Angeles CA 90025 Business E-Mail: dr.jrosenberg@gmail.com.

ROSENBERG, LEE, lawyer; m. Jennifer Rosenberg, 2004. BA, SUNY, Stony Brook, 1983; JD, Touro Coll., NY, 1986. Ptnr. Saltzman Chetkof McLoughlin & Robinson, Garden City, NY, 1995—96, Saltzman Chetkof & Rosenberg LLP, Garden City, 1996—. Arbitrator-attorney client fee dispute panel State of NY Unified Ct. Sys., Mineola, 1993—. Editor: NY Family/Matrimonial Practice Insights, 2005—; mem. editl. bd.: NY Family Law Monthly, 2005—; contbr. articles to profl. publs. Fellow: Am. Acad. Matrimonial Lawyers; mem.: ABA (family law sect.), Suffolk County Bar Assn. (matrimonial law com.), NY Family Law Am. Inn of Ct. (lectr.), Nassau County Bar Assn. (vice chair matrimonial com. 2006—), NY State Bar Assn. (asst. editor family law rev. 2005—, family law sect., lectr.). Office: Saltzman Chetkof & Rosenberg LLP 300 Garden City Plaza Garden City NY 11530

ROSENBERG, LUCILLE GLICKLICH, retired physician, child psychiatrist; b. Fond du Lac, Wis., Jan. 10, 1926; d. Peter and Freda (Pevnick) Barash; m. Marvin Glicklich, Sept. 12, 1948 (div. Apr. 1983); children: Daniel, Anne, Peter, Lynn, Barry; m. John A. Rosenberg, Aug. 12, 1984. BA, U. Wis.-Madison, 1947, MD, 1950. Diplomate Am. Bd. Pediatrics, Am. Bd. Psychiatry and Neurology, Am. Bd. Child Psychiatry. Intern, Youngstown Hosp. Assn., Ohio, 1950-51; resident in pediatrics Milw. Children's Hosp., 1951-53, practice medicine specializing in psychiatry Marquette Med. Sch. Associated, Wis., 1967-69; child psychiatry fellow Marquette and Milw. Childrens Hosp., 1969-71; med. dir. children's div. Curative Workshop, Milw., 1959-63, Easter Seals Child Devel. program, 1963-67; chief med. cons. Milw. Pub. Schs., 1964-67; asst. prof. pediatrics Med. Coll. U. Wis., Milw., 1965-85, clin. prof., 1985—, prof. psychiatry, 1971-85, prof. psychiatry, 1995—; dir. liaison psychiatry Milw. Children's Hosp., 1975-85; dir. Child-Family Psychiatry Program, assoc. prof., vice chmn. dept. psychiatry U. Wis. Med. Sch., Milw. Clin. Campus, 1985—; med. dir. child and adol. psychiat. clinic Sinai Samaritan, 1985—; hosp. staff appointments Milw. Children's Hosp., Milw. Psychiatric Hosp., Milw. County Med. Comples, Mt. Sinai Med. Ctr.; lectr. various colls. and univs.; cons. in field. Contbr. articles to profl. publs. Active mem. N'Shei group, Jewish Parenting, Communication for the 80's; Jewish Fedn. Women's div., Milw. Childrens Hosp. Jr. Aux. Target M.D. program U. Wis., Milw., 1981, congl. Emmanuel Yom Hashoah, 1982, Milw. Neonatal Nursing Consortium, Marquette U. panel Survivors of Holocaust, 1984; bd. dir. Milw. Bd. of Jewish Edn. Bd., 1971-78, pres. 1974-76, Milw. Jewish Fedn., 1977-84; bd. trustees Congl. Beth Israel, 1975-77, youth commn. 1971-77; mem. Kesher Jewish Woman's network; mem. task force on teen pregnancies Planned Parenthood, 1984; bd. dirs. Wis. State Med. Soc. Found., 1996—, Milw. Jewish Coun. Cmty. Rels., 1997—. Fellow Am. Acad. Child and Adolescent Psychiatry (mem. com. 1988—), Am. Psychiat. Assn., Am. Acad. Pediatrics (Wis. Br.); mem. Am. Soc. Adolescent Psychiatry, Wis. Council Adolescent and Child Psychiatry (sec. 1981-82, pres.-elect 1982-83, pres. 1983-85), Am. Orthopsychiatric Assn., Am. Acad. Child and Adolescent Psychology (alt. regional assembly del. 1989—), Milw. Pediatric Soc., Soc. Adolescent Medicine, AMA, Wis. State Med. Soc. (del. 1978—, bd. dirs. 1985—, reference com. 1982—), Milw. County Med. Soc. (sec. treas. 1981, pres.-elect 1984, pres. 1985), Am. Med. Women's Assn. (Southeastern Wis. chpt. vice-dir. 1977-79), Women in Medicine in Wis. (bd. dirs. 1979-82, pres. 1979-80), Wis. Council Child and Adolescent Psychiatry (pres. 1984-86), Wis. Psychiat. Assn. (pres.-elect 1993-95, pres. 1995-97, coun. mem. 1989—), Strengthening Wis. Families (legis. coun. com. mem. 2008-), Art At Large (adv. bd. mem. 2008-). Avocations: travel, bicycling, tennis, walking, reading. Home: 3431 N Lake Dr Milwaukee WI 53211-2919

ROSENBERG, MARC STEVEN, lawyer; b. NYC, June 15, 1958; s. Marvin and Bette Rosenberg; m. Tina Rosenberg; children: Brett, James, Katherine. AB, Princeton U., 1980; JD, Harvard U., 1983. Bar: NY 1984. Assoc. Cravath Swaine & Moore LLP, NYC, 1985-90, ptnr., corp., 1990—. Named one of Best Lawyers in Am., Securities Law, 2008. Mem.: Assn. Bar of NYC. Office: Cravath Swaine & Moore LLP 825 8th Ave Fl 47 New York NY 10019-7475 Office Fax: 212-474-3700. Business E-Mail: mrosenberg@cravath.com.

ROSENBERG, MARK B., academic administrator; b. Athens, Ohio, Aug. 15, 1949; married; 2 children. BA, Miami U., Oxford, Ohio, 1971; PhD in Polit. Sci., U. Pitts., 1976. Prof. polit. sci. Fla. Internat. U., Miami, 1976—, chmn. Caribbean L.Am. studies coun., 1977-79, founding dir. L.Am. and Caribbean Ctr., 1979—, founding/acting dean Coll. Urban and Pub. Affairs, 1994-97, vice provost for internat. studies, 1996-98, provost, acting pres., 1998—, acting pres., 1999-2000, provost, exec. v.p. acad. affairs, 2000—05, pres., 2009—; chancellor State Univ. Sys. of Fla., Tallahassee, 2005—09; vis. rsch. prof. Vanderbilt U., 2009. Mem. exec. com. OLAM; mem. articulation coordination com. Fla. Bd. Edn.; mem. Coun. of Fgn. Relations, Pacific Coun. on Internat. Realtions. Author, editor, co-editor 6 books; former bd. editors Fla. Trend, Latin Trade; contbr. articles to profl. jours. Presdl. appointee U.S. Customs Dist. Export Coun.; mem. exec. com. OLAM, the Jewish Leadership Inst./Jewish Fedn. Miami; mem. statewide articulation coordination com. Fla. Bd. Edn. Mem. Greater Miami C. of C. (vice chair exec. com. for internat. econ. devel. 1992-94), Coun. Fgn. Rels., Pacific Coun. in Internat. Rels. Office: Fla Internat U Office of Pres University Park Pc 526 Miami FL 33199-0001 Office Phone: 850-245-0466. Office Fax: 850-245-9685. E-mail: Chancellor@flbog.org.*

ROSENBERG, MARK L., health facility administrator; b. Newark, July 30, 1945; m. Jill Alison Dimond; children: Julie, Ben. BA in Biology magna cum laude, Harvard Coll., 1967, MD cum laude, 1972, M of Pub. Policy, 1972. Diplomate Am. Bd. Internal Medicine, Am. Bd. Psychiatry and Neurology. Intern Mass. Gen. Hosp., Boston, 1972—73, resident in medicine, 1973—74; resident in preventive medicine Ctrs. for Disease Control, Atlanta, 1975—76; resident in psychiatry Beth

Israel Hosp., Boston, 1980—83; clin. prof. dept. cmty. medicine and family practice Morehouse Sch. Medicine, Atlanta, 1984—93; clin. prof. psychiatry Emory U. Sch. Medicine, Atlanta, 1994—99; exec. dir. Task Force for Child Survival and Devel., 1999—; dir. sci. devel., dir. programs Ctr. for Child Well-being, 1999—. Dir. Nat. Ctr. for Injury Prevention and Control, Atlanta, 1994—99, acting assoc. dir. for pub. health practice, 1992—93; dir. divsn. injury control Ctr. for Environ. Health and Injury Control, 1989—92; spl. asst. for behavioral sci., office of dep. dir. CDC, Atlanta, 1989, advisor to dep. dir., 88, asst. dir. for sci. divsn. injury epidemiology and control, 1986—88, liaison officer office program planning and evaluation, 1979—80; assoc. dir. office extramural health programs Harvard Sch. Pub. Health, Boston, 1979—80; clin. fellow in psychiatry Harvard Med. Sch., Boston, 1980—83; vis. prof. dept. cmty. health Emory U. Sch. Medicine, Atlanta, 1984—91, clin. asst. prof. psychiatry, 1985—87, clin. assoc. prof., 1988—93; adj. prof. Emory U. Sch. Pub. Health, Atlanta, 1991—; clin. prof. dept. cmty. health and preventive medicine Morehouse Sch. Medicine, Atlanta, 1993—; staff physician Women's Med. Clinic, Atlanta, 1974—76, Harvard St. Neighborhood Health Ctr., Boston, 1976—77, Winchester (Mass.) Hosp., 1978—83; emergency rm. physician Burbank Hosp., Fitchburg, Mass., 1976—77, Harrington Hosp., Southbridge, Mass., 1976—77; vis. physician dept. psychiatry Grady Meml. Hosp., Atlanta, 1985—; lectr. and cons. in field. Author: Patients: The Experience of Illness, 1980, Violence in America: A Public Health Approach, 1990; mem. editl. bd. Violence and Victims, 1985—88, Violence, Aggression and Terrorism, 1986—; contbr. articles to profl. jours. Active Calif. Wellness Found., 1993—; bd. dirs. southeastern divsn., sci. adv. coun. Am. Suicide Found., 1990—. Recipient Coulter Lecture award, Am. ongress Rehab. Medicine, 1991, William S. one award, Am. Trauma Soc., 1991, Outstanding Achievement award, 1994, World Health Day award, Am. Assn. for World Health, 1993, Disting. Svc. award, Ga. Assn. Family and Marital Therapists, 1994, Disting. Achievement award, Disability Wellness Assn., 1998, Outstanding Svc. medal, USPHS, 2000, Meritorious Svc. medal, 2000, DSM, 2000; fellow, Mass. Gen. Hosp., 1977—78, Mead-Johnson, 1982; scholar, John Harvard, 1964. Mem.: Alpha Omega Alpha, Inst. of Medicine of NAS, Phi Beta Kappa. Avocation: photography. Home: 972 Oakdale Rd NE Atlanta GA 30307-1272 Office: 750 Commerce Dr Ste 400 Decatur GA 30030

ROSENBERG, MICHAEL, lawyer; b. NYC, Oct. 13, 1937; s. Walter and Eva (Bernstein) Rosenberg; m. Jacqueline Raymonde Combe, Apr. 29, 1966; children: Andrew James, Suzanne Jennifer. AB in Econs. with honors, Ind. U., 1959; LLB, Columbia U., 1962. Bar: NY 1963, US Ct Appeals (2d cir) 1975, US Dist Ct (ea dist so div) Mich 1989. From. dep. asst. atty. gen. to asst. atty. gen. N.Y. State Dept. Law, NYC, 1963-66; assoc. Hellerstein, Rosier & Rembar, NYC, 1966-73; assoc. gen. counsel Gen. Instrument Corp., NYC, 1973-78; from assoc. gen. counsel to dep. gen. counsel U.S. Filter Corp., NYC, 1978-82; v.p., gen. counsel, sec. Alfa-Laval Inc., Ft. Lee, NJ, 1982-88; counsel Becker Ross Stone De Stefano & Klein, NYC, 1988-89; ptnr. Rosenberg & Rich, White Plains, NY, 1989-95, Quinn, Marantis & Rosenberg, LLP, White Plains, NY, 1995-97, Marantis, Rosenberg & van Nes, LLP, 1997-2001; atty. Law Offices of Michael Rosenberg, Armonk, 2001—. Mem Zoning Bd. Appeals Town of North Castle, NY, 1995—2006. Mem.: ABA, Westchester County Bar Assn., NY State Bar Assn. Office: Law Offices of Michael Rosenberg 3 Spruce Hollow Armonk NY 10504

ROSENBERG, PAUL I., lawyer; b. Newark, Feb. 26, 1937; BS in Econs., U. Pa. Wharton Sch., 1959; MBA, NYU, 1964, JD, 1970, LLM, 1975. Bar: NJ 1970, US Dist. Ct. NJ 1970, NY 1982, US Dist. Ct. (3rd dist.) NY 1982, US Tax Ct. 1983, US Supreme Ct. Ptnr. Fox and Fox LLP, Livingston, 1974—2006, Bressler, Amery & Ross, PC, 2006—. Mem. Essex Co. Probate Early Settlement panel. Fellow Am. Coll. Trust and Estate Counsel (nat. employee benefits in estate-planning, estate and gift tax com.); mem. ABA, Essex County Bar Assn., NJ State Bar Assn. Home: One Belgrade Terr West Orange NJ 07052 Office: Bressler Amery & Ross 325 Columbia Tpke Florham Park NJ 07932 Office Phone: 973-514-1200. Business E-Mail: prosenberg@bressler.com.

ROSENBERG, RAND L., utilities executive; B, Whitman Coll., Walla Walla, Wash.; MBA, U. Chgo. Engagement mgr. Marakon Assocs.; head corp. devel. Pacific Telesis Group; ptnr., founder media and telecom. group Montgomery Securities; sr. positions Goldman Sachs & Co.; mng. dir., head global telecom. investment banking Salomon Bros.; exec. v.p., CFO Infospace; sr. v.p. corp. strategy and devel. PG&E Corp., San Francisco. Office: PG&E Corp One Market Spear Tower Ste 2400 San Francisco CA 94105-1126 Office Phone: 415-267-7070. Office Fax: 415-267-7268.

ROSENBERG, RAYMOND DAVID, special education educator, consultant; b. Jersey City, Apr. 25, 1951; s. Fabulous Sam and Arlene (White) R.; m. JoAnn Simchera, June 10, 1984; 1 child, Anna Teresa. BA, Boston U., 1974; MEd in Spl. Edn., William Paterson Coll., 1978, MEd in Ednl. Adminstrn. and Supervision, 1994. Cert. tchr., N.J.; profl. recognized spl. educator in ednl. diagnosis, PRSE, 2005. Tchr. reading Passaic County Tech. Vocat. High Sch., Wayne, NJ, 1980-82; specialist learning disabilities North Jersey Devel. Ctr., Totowa, 1983-84; ednl. specialist Div. Devel. Disabilities, Totowa, NJ, 1984-85, North Jersey Devel. Ctr., Totowa, NJ, 1986—93; learning disabilities tchr., cons. Office of Edn., NJ, 1993-96; learning cons. child study team North Bergen HS, NJ, 1996-98; learning disabilities tchr., cons., 1997—2002; mem. child study team West NY Early Childhood Sch., 2002—03; staff Office of the Child Study Team, Garfield, NJ, 2003—05; learning disabilities tchr. cons., supr. child study team Morris Plains Elem. Sch. Dist., 2005—06; mem. bd. edn. child study team, learning disabilities tchr., cons. Bryant Hawthorne Elem. Schs., 2006—07; learning disabilities tchr. cons., mem. child study team Teaneck, 2006—07. Pres. Ednl. Assessment Svcs., Inc., 2008—. With ABA discrete trial learning with PDD autistic students, 2008—; lectr., applied behavior analysis. Mem. Nat. Assn. Special Edn. Tchrs., Nat. Assn. Edn. Young Children, Nat. Eagle Scout Assn., Pi Lambda Theta (Beta Chi chpt.), Assn. Learning Cons., Highland briar condominiums(pres., 2004-, bd. dirs.) Episcopal. Lodge: Order of Arrow. Office Phone: 201-694-4579. Personal E-mail: cstadvocate@nj.rr.com. Business E-Mail: rayjoanna@nj.rr.com.

ROSENBERG, RICHARD MORRIS, banker; b. Fall River, Mass., Apr. 21, 1930; s. Charles and Betty (Peck) R.; m. Barbara K. Cohen, Oct. 21, 1956; children: Michael, Peter. BS, Suffolk U., 1952; MBA, Golden Gate U., 1962; LLB, Golden Gate Coll., 1966. Publicity asst. Crocker-Anglo Bank, San Francisco, 1959-62; banking services officer Wells Fargo Bank, N.A., San Francisco, 1962-65, asst. v.p., 1965-68, v.p. mktg. dept., 1968, v.p., dir. mktg., 1969, sr. v.p. mktg. and advt. div., 1970-75, exec. v.p., from 1975, vice chmn., 1980-83, Crocker Nat. Corp., 1983-85; pres., chief operating officer Seafirst Corp., 1986-87, also dir.; pres., chief operating officer, also bd. dirs. Seattle First Nat. Bank, 1985-87; vice chmn. bd. BankAm. Corp., San Francisco, 1987-90, chmn., CEO, 1990-96. Bd. dirs. ABX Air, Inc., Pacific Life, Exigen Group, Health Care Property Investors, Inc.; past chmn. Mastercard Internat.; past. pres. Fed. Res. Adv. Coun. Bd. dirs. San Francisco Symphony, United Way, Buck Inst. for Age Rsch., Am. Ctr. for Wine, Food and the Arts; trustee Calif. Inst. Tech. Jewish. Office: Bank of Am CA5-705-11-01 555 California St San Francisco CA 94104- E-mail: richard.rosenberg@bankofamerica.com.

ROSENBERG, ROBERT ALLEN, psychology professor; b. Phila., July 31, 1935; s. Theodore Samuel and Dorothy (Bailes) R.; m. Geraldine Bella Tishler, Sept. 3, 1961; children: Lawrence David, Ronald Joseph. BA, Temple U., 1957, MA, 1964; BS, Pa. Coll. Optometry, 1960, OD, 1961. Lic. optometrist, psychologist, Pa. Instr. Pa. Coll. Optometry, Phila., 1962-65, asst. prof., 1965-67; asst. prof. psychology Community Coll. Phila., 1967-76, assoc. prof., 1976—. Pvt. practice optometry, Roslyn, Pa., 1965-95; assoc. in practice optometry, Huntingdon Valley, Pa., 1995-98. Contbr. articles to profl. jours. Named Humanitarian Chapel of Four Chaplains Bapt. Temple, 1980. Fellow Am. Acad. Optometry; mem. Am. Optometric Assn., Pa. Optometric Assn., Bucks-Montgomery Optometric Assn., Alumni Assn. Pa. Coll. Optometry (v.p. 1992-98, sec. 1991-2006, bd. mem. 2006—). Avocations: singing, acting, photography, writing, public speaking. Home: 970 Corn Crib Dr Huntingdon Valley PA 19006-3304 Office: Community Coll Phila 1700 Spring Garden St Philadelphia PA 19130-3991 Business E-Mail: rrosenberg@ccp.edu.

ROSENBERG, ROBERT BRINKMANN, information technology executive; b. Chgo., Mar. 19, 1937; s. Sidney and Gertrude (Brinkmann) Rosenberg; m. Patricia Margaret Kane, Aug. 1, 1959 (dec. Feb. 1988); children: John Richard, Debra Ann; m. Maryann Bartoli Manrot, June 25, 1989. BSChemE with distinction, Ill. Inst. Tech., 1958, MS in Gas Tech, 1961, PhD in Gas Tech, 1964. Registered profl. engr., Ill. Adj. asst. prof. Ill. Inst. Tech., 1965-69; mem. staff Inst. Gas Tech., Chgo., 1962-77, v.p. engrng. rsch., 1973-77; v.p. R & D Gas Rsch. Inst., Chgo., 1977-78, exec. v.p., sr. v.p., 1978-84, v.p., 1984-96; pres. RBR Vision, Burr Ridge, Ill., 1996—; bd. dirs. IEA Internat. Ctr. Gas Tech. Info. Tech. program dir. World Energy Congress, 1996—98. Pres. Triangle Frat. Edn. Found., 1974—96, bd. dirs., 1996—2001, dir. emeritus; bd. dirs. Hinsdale Arts Coun., 1977—85, dir. emeritus, 1985—95; mem. adv. coun. U. Tex. Coll. Natural Scis. Found., 1990—95; mem. giving com. Morton Arboretum, 2004—; mem. Hinsdale Home Rule Ad Hoc Com., Ill., 1975—77; mem. vis. com. dept. chemistry U. Tex.; bd. advisors Chgo. 502, 2004—07; pres. Lake Ridge Club Homeowners Assn., 2001—08; v.p. Condominium Assn. Bd., 2009—. Recipient Gas Industry Rsch. award, 1985, Energy Exec. of the Yr. award, 1987, Profl. Achievement award, Ill. Inst. Tech. Alumni Assn., 1991. Mem.: AIChE, Triangle (Svc. Key and Outstanding Alumnus award 1987), Air Pollution Control Assn. (past sect. com. residential pollution sources), Gas Appliance Engrs. Soc. (past trustee), Internat. Gas Union, Atlantic Gas Rsch. Exch., Combustion Inst. (past treas. bd. dirs. ctrl. states sect.), Inst. Gas Engrs., Am. Gas Assn. (oper. sect. award of merit 1989). Achievements include patents for 13 patents in field. Avocations: cooking, gardening, travel. Home: 28 Lake Ridge Club Dr Burr Ridge IL 60527-7937 Office: RBR @ Vision 28 Lake Ridge Club Dr Burr Ridge IL 60527-7937 Office Phone: 630-654-3213. Personal E-mail: RBR3@comcast.net.

ROSENBERG, ROBERT CHARLES, housing corporation executive; b. Bronx, NY, Oct. 21, 1934; s. Bernard L. and Flora (Popiel) R.; m. Diane Stricof, Jan. 29, 1962 (dec.); children: Andrew, Scott; m. Frances Kaufman, Sept. 11, 1976; stepchildren: Michael Kaufman, Benjamin Kaufman. BS, NYU, 1955, JD (hon.), 1995; LLB, Columbia U., 1958. Bar: N.Y. 1959. Adminstrv. asst. N.Y. State Dept. Law, NYC, 1957-58; assoc. firm Barron Rice & Rochmore, NYC, 1959-62, Carro Spanbock & Londin, NYC, 1962-68; 1st dep. commr. for devel. dept. N.Y.C. Housing and Devel. Adminstrn., 1968-73; 1st sr. v.p., dir. Starrett Corp., NYC, 1973-97; gen. mgr. Starrett City; pres., chmn. bd. Grenadier Realty Corp., 1976-97; pres. Rosenberg Housing Group, 1997—. Lectr. Practicing Law Inst., Real Estate Bd. N.Y.C., Harvard U. Kennedy Sch. of Govt., Beijing Inst. of Design, U. Nancy (France), Columbia U., NYU, others; fed. receiver Chester (Pa.) Housing Authority, 1994—; adj. prof. dept. urban affairs Hunter Coll., N.Y.C., 1998—. Author N.Y. acts for residential constrn., rent. Candidate for N.Y. State Assembly, 1958, 65; sec. N.Y. State Assn. Young Rep. Clubs, 1959-61; bd. dirs., chmn. emeritus Bklyn. Philharm.; bd. dirs. Bklyn. Acad. Music, 1978-99; v.p. Citizens Housing and Planning Coun.; dir. Nat. Housing Conf. Served with USAF, 1958. Mem. ABA, N.Y. State Bar Assn., N.Y. County Lawyers Assn., Nat. Assn. Housing and Renewal Ofcls., Urban Land Inst., N.Y.C. Assn. Builders and Owners (v.p.). Home: 201 E 79th St New York NY 10021-0830 Office: 3 Park Ave Ste 2800 New York NY 10016-8410 E-mail: bob@rhgcommunities.com.

ROSENBERG, ROGER NEWMAN, neurologist, educator, department chair; b. Milw., Mar. 3, 1939; s. Sol J. and Cora D. (Newman) R.; m. Adrienne Turick, June 24, 1962; children: Jennifer, Lara Student, Tufts U., 1957-60; BS, Northwestern U., 1961, MD with distinction, 1964. Diplomate Am. Bd. Psychiatry and Neurology. Intern Harvard Med. Service, Beth Israel Hosp., Boston, 1964-65; resident in neurology Neurol. Inst., Columbia U., NYC, 1965-67, instr. neurology, 1967-68; research assoc. Lab. of Biochem. Genetics, NIH, Bethesda, Md., 1968-70; clin. instr. Howard U. Med. Sch., Washington, 1969-70; asst. prof. neuroscis. Sch. Medicine, U. Calif.-San Diego, 1970-71; assoc. prof. neuroscis. and pediatrics, attending neurologist Univ. Hosp., U. Calif.-La Jolla, 1971-74; prof., chmn. dept. neurology U. Tex. Southwestern Med. Ctr., Dallas, 1973-91, prof. physiology, 1976—, Zale Disting. chair, prof. neurology, 1990—, dir. Alzheimer's Disease Rsch. Ctr., 1989—. Attending neurologist Parkland Meml. Hosp. and Children's Med. Ctr., Dallas, 1974—, Zale Lipshy Univ. Hosp., 1990—; mem. staff Presbyn. Hosp., Dallas, 1974—, St. Paul's Hosp., Dallas, 1974—; cons. staff VA Hosp., Dallas, 1974—; mem. nat. med. adv. bd. Nat. Ataxia Found., Mpls., 1971—, Myasthenia Gravis Found., 1973; chmn. med. adv. bd., dir. med. sci. research Internat. Joseph Diseases Found., Livermore, Calif., 1977—; lectr. Japanese Soc. Neurology, 1987, 94, Chinese Neurol. Soc., 1987, Spanish Neurol. Soc., 1992; chmn. bd. sci. councilors NINDS/NIH, 1984-86; pres. (hon.), Intl. French Soc. of Neurology Charcot Centenary Symposium, 1993. Editor Jour. Neurogenetics; mem. editl. bd. Neurology, 1977-82, 91-97, Trends in Neurosci., 1980-86, Current Opinion in Neurology & Neurosurgery, 1990—, Jour. of AMA, 1997—; chief editor Archives of Neurology, 1997—; contbr. articles to profl. jours. Bd. dirs. Winston Sch., Dallas, 1974-80; trustee World Fedn. Neurology, 2005. 1st Woody Guthrie scholar, 1971; USPHS grantee; recipient Disting. Alumnus award Neurol. Inst., N.Y., 1994, Nancy R. McCune Alzheimer's Rsch. award Alzheimer's Ass., 2005, Lifetime Achievement award Tex. Neurol. Soc., 2005. Fellow AAAS; mem. Am. Neurol. Assn. (hon.), Am. Acad. Neurology (chmn. sci. program com. nat. meetings 1979-84, elected councillor exec. bd. 1984-89, pres. 1991-93), Am. Neurochem. Soc., Tissue Culture Soc., Soc. Neurosci., Am. Fedn. Clin. Rsch., Soc. Pediat. Rsch., Internat. Child Neurology Assn., Am. Neurol. Assn. (hon., 1st v.p. 1987), Ctrl. Soc. Neurol. Rsch., Can. Congress Neurol. Scis. (hon.), Spanish Neurol. Soc. (hon.), Sigma Xi, Alpha Omega Alpha (Merit award Northwestern U. Alumni Assn. 1986). Home: 4425 Wildwood Rd Dallas TX 75209-2801 Office: U Tex Southwestern Med Ctr Dallas TX 75235 Business E-Mail: rogerrosenberg@utsouthwestern.edu.

ROSENBERG, RONALD J., radiologist, director; m. Patricia Sheehan Rosenberg; children: Erica, Laura, Stephanie, Caleb. BS, Pa. State U., State Coll., 1969; MD, Jefferson Med. Coll., Phila., 1971. Diplomate in internal medicine Am. Bd. Internal Medicine, 1974, in endocrinology & metabolism 1977, Am. Bd. Nuc. Medicine, 1976. Clin. assoc. prof. nuc. medicine U. Conn. Sch. Medicine, Farmington, 1994—2003, clin. prof. diagnostic imaging, therapeutics, 2003—; dir. Jefferson Radiology P.C., East Hartford, Conn., 2006—. Contbr. articles to med. jours. Mem.: Radiology Soc. N.Am., Am. Coll. Radiology, Soc. Nuc. Medicine (pres., New Eng. chpt. 1996—98). Office: Jefferson Radiology PC 85 Seymour St Ste 200 Hartford CT 06106-5509

ROSENBERG, RUDY, chemical company executive; b. Feb. 26, 1930; came to U.S., 1949, naturalized, 1954; s. Hilaire and Frieda Rosenberg; 1 child, Rudy. Student in classical studies, Atheneum Leon Lepage, Brussels, 1946. Buyer Lever Bros., Brussels, 1946-49; head biochem. divsn. Mann Rsch. Labs., NYC, 1954-61, Gallard-Schlesinger, Carle Place, NY, 1961-75; pres. Accurate Chem. & Sci. Corp., Westbury, NY, 1975—. Prin., v.p., Leeches U.S.A. Ltd. Author: (memoirs) And Somehow We Survive, 2007. Served with U.S. Army, 1951-53. Mem. Reticuloendothelial Soc. Internat. Clubs: Antique Automobile, Rolls Royce, Puppetry Guild Greater N.Y. Democrat. Personal E-mail: rudyrr@att.net.

ROSENBERG, RUTH HELEN BORSUK, lawyer; b. Plainfield, NJ, Feb. 23, 1935; d. Irwin and Pauline (Rudich) Borsuk; children: Joshua Cohen, Sarah, Rebecca, Daniel, Miriam, Tziporah, Isaac AB, Douglass Coll., 1956; JD, U. Pa., 1963. Bar: Pa. 1964, N.Y. 1967, D.C. 1986, Md. 1987, Va. 1994, Mass. 1995, U.S. Ct. Appeals (3d cir.) 1969, U.S. Supreme Ct. 1969, U.S. Ct. Appeals (4th cir.) 1994. Law clk. Ct. Common Pleas, Phila., 1963-64; assoc. Blank, Rudenko, Klaus & Rome, Phila., 1964-67; atty. Office Corp. Counsel, City of Rochester, 1967-68; assoc. Nixon, Hargrave, Devans & Doyle, Washington, 1968-74, ptnr., 1975-99, Nixon Peabody LLP, Washington, 1999—2003. Vice chairperson character and fitness com. Appellate divsn. 4th dept. 7th Jud. Dist. N.Y. Supreme Ct., 1976-80, mem. grievance com., 1981-84. Bd. dirs. Soc. Prevention Cruelty to Children, 1976-77, N.Y. Civil Liberties Union, 1972-85, v.p. 1976-85; bd. dirs. Jewish Home and Infirmary, 1978-83, pres., 1980-83; v.p. Jewish Fedn. Rochester, 1983, Yachad, Inc., Jewish Cmty. Housing Devel. Corp., 1990-94; bd. dirs. Jewish Cmty. Coun., Greater Washington, 1989-93, Leadership Washington, 1990-91, Libr. Theatre, 1994-97, Op. Understanding, D.C., 1994-95. Mem. ABA, D.C. Bar Assn., Md. Bar Assn., Va. Bar Assn., Phi Beta Kappa. Office: Nixon Peabody LLP 401 9th St NW Ste 900 Washington DC 20004-2128 E-mail: rrosenberg@nixonpeabody.com.

ROSENBERG, SAMUEL NATHAN, French and Italian language educator; b. NYC, Jan. 19, 1936; s. Israel and Etta (Friedland) R. AB, Columbia U., 1957; PhD, Johns Hopkins U., 1965. Instr. Columbia U., NYC, 1960-61; lectr. Ind. U., Bloomington, Ind., 1962-65, asst. prof., 1965-69, assoc. prof., 1969-81, prof. dept. French and Italian, 1981-99, prof. emeritus, 2000—. Chmn. dept. French and Italian Ind. U., Bloomington, 1977—84; editor ENCOMIA jour. of Internat. Courtly Lit. Soc., 2005—. Author: Modern French CE, 1970, (with others) Harper's Grammar of French, 1983, (with W. Apel) French Secular Compositions of the 14th Century, 3 vols., 1970-72, (with H. Tischler) Chanter m'estuet: Songs of the Trouveres, 1981; translator: (with S. Danon) Ami and Amile, 1981, rev. edit., 1996, Lyrics and Melodies of Gace Brulé, 1985; (with H. Tischler) The Monophonic Songs in the Roman de Fauvel, 1991, Lancelot-Grail Cycle, vol. 2, 1993, Chansons des trouvères, 1995, Songs of the Troubadours and Trouvères, 1997; (with others) Early French Tristan Poems, 2 vols., 1998; (with C. Callahan) Les Chansons de Colin Muset, 2005, (with E. Doss-Quinby) The Old French Ballette, 2006; (with Patricia Terry) Lancelot and the Lord of the Distant Isles, 2007. Pres. Mid-Am. Festival of the Arts, Inc., Bloomington, Ind., 1984-85. Woodrow Wilson Found. fellow, 1959-60; Fulbright fellow, 1960-61; Lilly Faculty fellow, 1986-87. Mem MLA, Am. Assn. Tchrs. French; mem. Medieval Acad. Am., Internat. Courtly Lit. Soc. (editor Encomia 2005—), Am. Lit. Translators Assn. (bd. dirs. 2002-06), Romance Philology Adv. Bd., Phi Beta Kappa. Home: PO Box 1164 Bloomington IN 47402-1164 Business E-Mail: srosenbe@indiana.edu.

ROSENBERG, SARAH ZACHER, retired cultural organization administrator; b. Kelem, Lithuania, Jan. 10, 1931; came to U.S., 1938; d. David Meir Zacher and Rachel Korbman; m. Norman J. Rosenberg, Dec. 30, 1950; children: Daniel, Alyssa. BA in History, U. Nebr., 1970, MA in Am. History, 1973. Rsch. historian U. Mid-Am., Lincoln, Nebr., 1974-78, program developer dept. humanities, 1978-79, asst. dir. div. acad. planning, 1980-81, dir. program devel., 1981-82; exec. dir. Nebr. Humanities Coun., Lincoln, 1982-87, Nebr. Found. for Humanities, Lincoln, 1984-87, Am. Inst. for Conservation Hist. and Artistic Works, Washington, 1987-97, exec. dir. found., 1991-97; program officer, spl. cons. mus. div. NEH, Washington, 1987, external reviewer, 1981, 89; pvt. practice Potomac, Md., 1997—2004; ret., 2004. Lay participant long-range planning conf. Nebr. Bar Assn., Hastings, 1986. Co-editor: The Great Plains Experience: Readings in the History of a Region, 1978; contbr. articles to profl. jours. Action mem. Hadassah, Lincoln, 1961—87, Tifereth Israel Synagogue, Lincoln, 1961—87, Beth El Congregation, Besthesda, Md., 1988—2001, Kol Shalom Congregation, 2001—; bd. dirs. Sta. KUCV, affiliate Nat. Pub. Radio, Lincoln, 1986—87, Lincoln Cmty. Playhouse, Lincoln, 1986—87. NEH grantee, 1981, 86, merit awards, 1983, 87; Humanities Resource Ctr. grantee, Peter Kiewit Found., 1984. Mem. Am. Hist. Assn., Western Hist. Assn., Alpha Theta. Democrat. Home: 8102 Appalachian Ter Potomac MD 20854-4050 Personal E-mail: srosenb435@aol.com.

ROSENBERG, SAUL ALLEN, oncologist, educator; b. Cleve., Aug. 2, 1927; BS, Western Res. U., 1948, MD, 1953. Diplomate Am. Bd. Internal Medicine, Am. Bd. Oncology. Intern Univ. Hosp., Cleve., 1953—54; resident in internal medicine Peter Bent Brigham Hosp., Boston, 1954—61; research asst. toxicology AEC Med. Research Project, Western Res. U., 1948—53; asst. prof. medicine and radiology Stanford (Calif.) U., 1961—65, assoc. prof., 1965—79, chief divsn. oncology, 1965—93, prof., 1970—95; prof. emeritus, 1995—; Am. Cancer Soc. prof. Stanford (Calif.) U., 1983—89, assoc. dean, 1989—92. Chmn. bd. No. Calif. Cancer Program, 1974—80. Contbr. articles to profl. jours. Served to lt. M.C. USNR, 1954—56. Master: ACP; fellow: Am. Coll. Radiology (hon.); mem.: Western Assn. Physicians, Western Soc. Clin. Rsch., Radiation Rsch. Soc., Calif. Acad. Medicine, Assn. Am. Physicians, Am. Soc. Clin. Oncology (pres. 1982—83), Inst. Medicine NAS, Am. Assn. Cancer Rsch., Am. Soc. Therapeutic Radiotherapy Oncology (hon.). Office: Stanford U Sch Medicine Div Oncology 269 Campus Dr Stanford CA 94305

ROSENBERG, SEYMOUR, psychologist, educator; b. Newark, Sept. 7, 1926; s. Morris and Celia (Weiss) R.; children: Harold Stanley, Michael Seth. BS, The Citadel, 1948; MA, Ind. U., 1951, PhD, 1952. Rsch. psychologist USAF, San Antonio, 1952-58, U. Kans., Lawrence, 1958-59, Bell Tel. Labs., Murray Hill, NJ, 1959-65; vis. prof. psychology Columbia U., NYC, 1965-66; prof. psychology Rutgers U., New

Brunswick, NJ, 1966—2000, chmn. dept. psychology, 1981-83, 94-95, prof. emeritus psychology, 2001—. Adj. prof. Rutgers U. Med. Sch., 1974—2000; vis. scholar U. Leuven, Belgium, 1983, Belgium, 92, Univ. de Provence, France, 1990; panel mem. NSF, 1970—72. Cons. editor Jours. Personality Social Psychology, 1968-69; assoc. editor, 1970-73; contbr. articles to profl. jours. With USN, 1945—46. Grantee, NSF, 1965—90, NIMH, 1966—68; Rsch. scientist grantee, 1968—73, Social Sci. Rsch. Coun. fellow, 1973—74. Fellow APA; mem. Soc. Exptl. Social Psychology, Psychometric Soc., Classification Soc., NY Acad. Sci., Ea. Psychol. Assn. Home and Office: 689 Canal Rd Somerset NJ 08873-7327

ROSENBERG, SHELI ZYSMAN, retired finance company executive; b. NYC, Feb. 2, 1942; d. Stephen B. and Charlotte (Laufer) Zysman; m. Burton X. Rosenberg, Aug. 30, 1964; children: Leonard, Marcy. BA, Tufts U., 1963; JD, Northwestern U., 1966. Bar: Ill. 1966. Ptnr. Schiff, Hardin & Waite, Chgo., 1973-80; exec. v.p., gen. counsel Equity Fin. Mgmt., Chgo., 1980-90, Equity Group Investments, Inc., Chgo., 1988-94, pres., CEO, 1994—99, Equity Group Investments, LLC, Chgo., 1999—2000, vice chmn., 2000—03; prin. Rosenberg & Liebentritt, P.C., Chgo., 1980—97. Adj. prof. Northwestern U., 2000—03, J.L. Kellogg Grad. Sch. Bus., 2003—; bd. dirs. CVS/Caremark Corp., Capital Trust, Cendant Corp., Manufactured Home Communities, Inc., Equity Residential Properties Trust, Equity Office Properties Trust, Ventas, Inc.; adv. bd. J.L. Kellogg Grad. Sch. Bus. N.W. Univ.; trustee Equity Residential, 1993—, lead trustee, 2002—. Trustee Rush Presbyn. St. Luke's Med. Ctr., exec. com.; co-founder, pres. Ctr. for Exec. Women, J.L. Kellogg Grad. Sch. Bus., 2001—.

ROSENBERG, SIMON, think-tank executive; Grad., Tufts U., 1985. Writer, prodr. ABC News; mem. Michael Dukakis Presdl. Campaign, 1987—88, Bill Clinton Presdl. Campaign, 1991—92; founder, pres. New Dem. Network, Washington, 1996—. Bd. dirs. Jonathan M. Tisch Coll. Citizenship and Pub. Svc., Democracy: A Journal of Ideas of the Roosevelt Inst.; mem. platform com. Dem. Nat. Com., 2004. Named one of The 50 Most Powerful People in DC, GQ mag., 2007; Henry Crown fellow, Aspen Inst., 2001. Office: New Dem Network 2nd Fl 729 Fifteenth St NW Washington DC 20005 Office Phone: 202-544-9200. Office Fax: 202-547-2929. E-mail: sdupont@ndn.org.*

ROSENBERG, STEVEN AARON, surgeon, medical researcher; b. NYC, Aug. 2, 1940; s. Abraham and Harriet (Wendroff) Rosenberg; m. Alice Ruth O'Connell, Sept. 15, 1968; children: Beth, Rachel, Naomi. BA, Johns Hopkins U., 1960, MD, 1963; PhD, Harvard U., 1968. Resident in surgery Peter Bent Brigham Hosp., Boston, 1963—64, 1968—69, 1972—74; resident fellow in immunology Harvard U. Med. Sch., Boston, 1969—70; clin. assoc. Immunology Br. Nat. Cancer Inst., NIH, Bethesda, Md., 1970—72, chief surgery, 1974—, assoc. editor Jour., 1974—. Mem. U.S.-USSR Coop. Immunotherapy Program, 1974—, U.S.-Japan Coop. Immunotherapy Program, 1975—; clin. assoc. prof. surgery George Washington U. Med. Ctr., 1976—; prof. surgery Uniformed Svcs. U. Health Scis. Contbr. articles to profl. jours.; author: The Transformed Cell: Unlocking the Mysteries of Cancer, 1992. Served with USPHS, 1970-72 Recipient Meritorious Svc. medal, US Pub. Health Svc., 1981, 1986, Armand Hammer Cancer prize, 1988, Friedrich Sasse prize, U. West Berlin, 1986, Nils Alwell prize, Stockholm, Sweden, 1987, Disting. Alumnus award, Johns Hopkins U., 1987, Simon Shubitz prize, U. Chgo. Cancer Rsch. Ctr., 1988, Griffuel prize, French Assn. Rsch. on Cancer, 1988, Cancer award, Milken Family Found., 1988, Ellis Island medal of honor, 1998, Heath Meml. award, MD Anderson Cancer Ctr., 2002, Richard V. Smalley, MD, Meml. award, Internat. Soc. Biological Therapy of Cancer, 2005; co-recipient Armand Hammer Cancer prize, 1985; named Scientist of Yr., R&D mag., 1990. Mem.: Inst. Medicine, Am. Soc. Clin. Oncology (bd. dirs., Karnofsky prize 1991, John Wayne award for clin. rsch. 1995), Am. Assn. Cancer Rsch., Am. Assn. Immunologists, Transplantation Soc., Halsted Soc., Surg. Biology Club II, Soc. Surg. Oncology, Am. Surg. Assn. (Flance-Karl award 2002), Soc. Univ. Surgeons, Alpha Omega Alpha, Phi Beta Kappa. Office: Nat Cancer Inst Bldg 10 Rm 3-3940 9000 Rockville Pike Bethesda MD 20892 Office Phone: 301-402-4164. Office Fax: 301-402-1738. E-mail: sar@nih.gov.*

ROSENBERG, WILLIAM MARK, chef, restaurant owner; b. North Miami, Fla., Sept. 30, 1967; s. Herman and Norma Rosenberg; m. Gina Marie Faranda, Oct. 2, 1994; children: Hannah Mae, Joseph Samson, Joshua Elijah. A in Culinary Arts, Culinary Inst. Am., Hyde Park, NY, 1991. Exec. chef Dome Restaurant, Greenwich, Conn., 1999—2001; owner, exec. chef F.i.s.h. Restaurant, Port Chester, NY, 2001—. With USAF, 1986—88. Home: 21 Irenhyl Ave Port Chester NY 10573 Office: Fish Restaurant 102 Fox Island Rd Port Chester NY 10573 Office Fax: 914-939-1594. Personal E-mail: wrosen7922@aol.com. Business E-Mail: fishies2@optonline.net.

ROSENBERGER, BRYAN DAVID, lawyer; b. Johnstown, Pa., Oct. 8, 1950; s. Clarence Haines and Ida Rae (Neiderheiser) Rosenberger; m. Barbara Leah Byer, July 4, 1977; children: Laura Michelle, Lisa Renee. BS, Juniata Coll., 1971; JD, Coll. of William and Mary, 1974. Bar: Pa 1974. Assoc. Eckert Seamans Cherin & Mellott, Pitts., 1974-82, ptnr., 1983—2006, chmn. corp. and bus. dept., 1992—98, mem. exec. com., 1994-98, also bd. dirs., chmn. bus. div., 2001—04, of counsel, 2006—. Mem. bd. dirs. Horsehead Holding Corp., 2007—. Active new leadership bd Pitts. Symphony Soc, 1990—98. Mem.: Allegheny County Bar Assn. Home: 1358 Oakledge Ct Upper Saint Clair PA 15241-3540 Office: Eckert Seamans Cherin & Mellott 600 Grant St Ste 4400 Pittsburgh PA 15219-2702 Home Phone: 412-221-1529; Office Phone: 412-566-6123. Business E-Mail: brosenberger@eckertseamans.com.

ROSENBLATT, ALBERT MARTIN, retired state appeals court judge; b. NYC, Jan. 17, 1936; s. Isaac and Fannie (Dachs) R.; m. Julia Carlson, Aug. 23, 1970; 1 child, Elizabeth. BA, U. Pa., 1957; JD, Harvard U., 1960. Bar: NY 1961. Dist. atty. Dutchess County, NY, 1969-75, county judge NY, 1976-81; supreme ct. justice NY State Supreme Ct., 1982-89, chief adminstrv. judge, 1987—89, assoc. justice, appellate divsn., second dept., 1989-98; assoc. judge NY State Ct. Appeals, Poughkeepsie, NY, 1998—2006. Instr. judge NY State, 1987-89; vis. prof., victorian studies dept., Vassar Coll., 1992-94; moderator NY State Fair Trial Free Press Conf., 2000-07; instr. newly elected state supreme ct. judges and county judges; asst. dist. attys., 1974, 75; instr. law tng. NY State Police Acad., 1997; lectr. Nat. Dist. Attys. Assn., 1968-74; tchg. team mem. trial advocacy workshop Harvard Law Sch., 1998, 99; chmn. State-Fed. Jud. Coun., 2005-06; jud. fellow NYU Law Sch., 2007-. Mem. bd. editors NY State Bar Jour., 1992-99; former editor, Baker Street Jour.; contbr. articles on law to profl. jours. and popular mags. Bd. dirs. United Way Cmty. Chest, 1970; bd. dirs. Bardavon 1869 Opera House, Dutchess County Hist. Soc.; mem. adv. bd. Jewish Cmty. Ctr., 1987—; pres. Hist. Soc. Cts. of State of N.Y., 2002—; mem. State-Fed. Jud. Coun., 2003—, chmn., 2005—; mem. U.S. Master's Maccabiah Team, 1997; With USAR, 1960-66. Mem. NY State Bar Assn. (named Outstanding Prosecutor 1974, Outstanding Jud. Svcs. award 1994), NY State Dist. Attys. Assn. (pres. 1974, Frank S. Hogan award 1987, Jud. Svcs. award 1994), Profl. Ski Instrs. Am. (cert. 1984—), Baker St. Irregulars Club (former assoc. editor Baker St. Jour.). Republican. Jewish. Avocations: cert. profl. assoc. ski instructor, squash. Home: 300 Freedom Rd Pleasant Valley NY 12569-5431 Office: 63 Washington St Poughkeepsie NY 12603 Office Phone: 845-486-6893.

ROSENBLATT, CYNTHIA SCHAFFER, lawyer; b. Alexandria, Minn., June 18, 1947; d. Frank H. and Helen Field Schaffer; m. Fredric T. Rosenblatt, Dec. 27, 1970 (dec. Sept. 22, 1993); 1 child Hart L. Rosenblatt; m. Burton G. Ross, Mar. 4, 1995 (dec. May 1, 2003). Student, U. Wis., 1965-66; BA magna cum laude, U. Minn., 1969, MA, 1971, JD cum laude, 1976. Bar: US Dist. Ct. Minn. 1976, US Tax Ct. 1977, US Ct. Appeals (11th cir.) 1985, US Supreme Ct. 1991. Rschr. & lectr. U. Minn., 1971—73, Met. State U., 1971—73; mng. editor law rev. vol. 60 U. Minn., 1975—76; assoc. atty. Doherty, Rumble & Butler, P.A., St. Paul, 1976-81, ptnr., 1981-84; founder, v.p. Ross, Rosenblatt, Ltd., Mpls., 1984—2002; of counsel Lindquist & Vennum, P.L.L.P., Mpls., 2002—. Chmn. bd. of visitors U. Minn. Law Sch., Mpls., 1984-93; bd. dirs. Children's Hosps. and Clinics, Mpls., St. Paul. Co-author (with Rubin, Roserblatt, Balow): Psychological and Educational Sequelae of Low Birth Weight, 1972. Bd. of advisors U. Minn. Art Mus., Mpls., 1989-95. Mem. ABA (taxation sect., generation-skipping bd. 1995). Office: Ste 4200 80 S 8th St Minneapolis MN 55402-2223 Office Phone: 612-371-3211. Business E-Mail: crosenblatt@lindquist.com.

ROSENBLATT, JASON PHILIP, literature and language professor; b. Balt., July 3, 1941; s. Morris D. and Esther (Friedlander) R.; m. Zipporah Marton, June 2, 1964; children: Noah David, Raphael Mark. BA, Yeshiva U., 1963; MA, Brown U., 1966, PhD, 1969. Asst. prof. English U. Pa., Phila., 1968-74, Georgetown U., Washington, 1974-76, assoc. prof., 1976-83, prof. English, 1983—, dept. chmn., 2008—09. Vis. lectr. English lit. Swarthmore (Pa.) Coll., 1972-73; cen. exec. com. Folger Inst./Folger Shakespeare Libr., Washington, 1976-88. Author: Torah and Law in "Paradise Lost", 1994, Renaissance England's Chief Rabbi: John Selden, 2006; co-editor: Not in Heaven: Coherence and Complexity in Biblical Narrative, 1991; mem. editl. bd. Milton Studies, 1992—; contbr. articles to scholarly publs. Recipient Virginia Graham Healey award, 1998-99; Guggenheim Found. fellow, 1977-78, NEH fellow, 1990-91, Folger Shakespeare Libr./NEH fellow, 1999-2000. Mem. MLA (del. assembly 1989-91, exec. com. div. religion and lit. 1982-86, exec. com. 17th century Eng. lit. 2002—), Milton Soc. Am. (exec. com. 1977-80, James Holly Hanford award 1989, John T. Shawcross award 2007, v.p. 1998, pres. 1999), Milton Seminar, Phi Beta Kappa. Democrat. Jewish. Avocations: talmud study, music, swimming. Office: Dept English Georgetown Univ Box 571131 Washington DC 20057-1131 Office Phone: 202-687-7577. E-mail: rosenblj@georgetown.edu.

ROSENBLATT, JOAN RAUP, mathematical statistician; b. NYC, Apr. 15, 1926; d. Robert Bruce and Clara (Eliot) Raup; m. David Rosenblatt, June 10, 1950. AB, Barnard Coll., 1946; PhD, U. N.C., 1956. Intern Nat. Inst. Pub. Affairs, Washington, 1946-47; statis. analyst U.S. Bur. of Budget, 1947-48; rsch. asst. U. N.C., 1953-54; mathematician Nat. Inst. Standards and Tech. (formerly Nat. Bur. Standards), Washington, 1955—, asst. chief statis. engring., 1963-68, chief statis. engring. lab., 1969-78, dep. dir. Ctr. for Applied Math., 1978-88; dep. dir. Computing and Applied Math. Lab., Gaithersburg, 1988-93, dir., 1993-95, guest rschr. Statis. Engring. Divsn., 1996—. Mem. com. on indsl. rels. Dept. Stats. Ohio State U., 1981-90; mem. adv. com. in math. and stats. USDA Grad. Sch., 1971—; mem. Com. Applied and Theoretical Stats., Nat. Rsch. Coun., 1985-88. Mem. editorial bd. Communications in Stats., 1971-79, Jour. Soc. for Indsl. and Applied Math., 1965-75, Nat. Inst. Stds. and Tech. Jour. Rsch., 1991-93; contbr. articles to profl. jours. Chmn. Com. on Women in Sci., Joint Bd. on Sci. Edn., 1963—64. Rice fellow, 1946, Gen. Edn. Bd. fellow, 1948-50; recipient Fed. Woman's award, 1971, Gold medal Dept. Commerce, 1976, Presdl. Meritorious Exec. Rank award, 1982. Fellow AAAS (chmn. stats. sect. 1982, sec. 1987-91), Inst. Math. Stats. (coun. 1975-77), Am. Statis. Assn. (v.p. 1981-83, dir. 1979-80, Founders award 1991), Washington Acad. Scis. (achievement award math. 1965); mem. AAUW, Royal Statis. Soc. London, Philos. Soc. Washington, Internat. Statis. Inst., Caucus Women Stats. (pres. 1976), Assn. Women Math., Exec. Women Govt., Phi Beta Kappa, Sigma Xi (treas. Nat. Bur. Standards chpt. 1982-84). Office: Nat Inst Stds and Tech 100 Bureau Dr Stop 8980 Gaithersburg MD 20899-8980 Home: 701 King Farm Blvd Apt 630 Rockville MD 20850 Business E-Mail: jrr@nist.gov.

ROSENBLATT, LIEF DOV, hedge fund manager; b. Sept. 28, 1953; s. Franklin D. and Florence Rosenblatt; m. Melinda Lande, Feb. 4, 1990. AB summa cum laude, Harvard U., JD; MA in Philosophy, Politics & Econs., Oxford U. Sr. v.p. risk arbitrage dept. Lehman Bros.; gen. ptnr. Plaza Securities Co.; mng. dir., head arbitrage, high yield & distressed securities dept. Soros Fund Mgmt. LLC; co-founder, sr. mng. ptnr. Satellite Asset Mgmt. LP, 1999—. Waynflete fellow Magdalen Coll., Oxford. Trustee Am. Hosp. in Paris Found., AVI CHAI Found.; chmn. Nat. Yiddish Book Ctr., Amherst, Mass.; bd. trustees Cancer Rsch. Inst., NYC, 2001—. Mem.: Phi Beta Kappa. Office: Satellite Asset Mgmt 623 5th Ave New York NY 10022-6842 Office Phone: 212-209-2000. Business E-Mail: lief.rosenblatt@satellite-ny.com.*

ROSENBLATT, MICHAEL, internist, dean, educator; b. Lund, Sweden, Nov. 27, 1947; s. Arthur Rosenblatt and Jean (Strosberg) Bialer; m. Patricia Ellen Regenbogen, Aug. 23, 1969; children: Anna Miriam, Adam Richard. AB summa cum laude, Columbia U., NYC, 1969; MD magna cum laude, Harvard U., Cambridge, Mass., 1973. Diplomate Am. Bd. Internal Medicine. Intern to resident Mass. Gen. Hosp., Boston, 1973-75, clin. rsch. fellow endocrinology and metabolism, 1975-77, chief endocrine unit, 1981-84; instr. medicine Harvard U., Boston, 1976-78, asst. prof. medicine, 1978-82, assoc. prof. medicine, 1982-85; v.p. for biol. rsch. Merck Sharp & Dohme Rsch. Labs., 1984-87, v.p. for biol. rsch. and molecular biology, 1987-89, sr. v.p. rsch., 1989-92; dir. divsn. health sci. and tech. Harvard-MIT, 1992-98; Ebert prof. molecular medicine Harvard Med. Sch., Boston, 1992-98; chief divsn. bone and mineral metabolism Beth Israel Hosp., Boston, 1992—2000, 2002—03; dean, prof. physiology and medicine Tufts U. Sch. Medicine, 2003—. Faculty dean acad. programs Beth Israel Deaconess Med. Ctr., Harvard Med., 1996—2000, George R. Minot prof. med., 1996—2003; exec. dir. Carl J. Shapiro Inst. Edn. and Rsch. at Harvard Med. Sch. and Beth Israel Deaconess Med. Ctr., 1996—2000, pres., 1999—2001. Editor: Atrial Natriuretic Factor Endocrinology and Metabolism Clinics of N.Am., 1987; contbr. numerous sci. articles on parathyroid hormone and calcium metabolism to leading sci. jours. Recipient Vincent du Vigneaud award Gordon Confs., Kingston, R.I., 1986, Fuller Albright award Am. Soc. for Bone and Mineral Rsch., 1986, citation Japan Endocrine Soc., Tokyo, Taiwanese Osteoporosis Soc., Tainan. Fellow AAAS, Am. Coll. Physicians; mem. The Endocrine Soc., Am. Soc. for Biochemistry and Molecular Biology, Am. Soc. for Clin. Investigation, Am. Soc. Bone and Mineral Rsch. (pres. 1997-98), Assn. Am. Physicians, Inter-Urban Clin. Club (pres. 1997-98). Office: Tufts U Sch Medicine 136 Harrison Ave Boston MA 02111-1800

ROSENBLATT, PETER RONALD, lawyer, former ambassador; b. NYC, Sept. 4, 1933; s. William and Therese (Steinhardt) Rosenblatt; m. Naomi Henriette Harris; children: Therese Sarah Sonenshine, Daniel Harris, David Steinhardt. BA, Yale U., 1954, LLB, 1957. Bar: NY 1959, DC 1969. Tchg. asst. history Yale U., New Haven, 1954—55; asst. dist. atty. NY County, 1959—62; assoc. Stroock & Stroock & Lavan, NYC, 1962—66; dep. asst. gen. counsel AID, Washington, 1966; mem. White House staff, Washington, 1966—68; jud. officer, chmn. bd. contract appeals US Post Office Dept., Washington, 1968—69; v.p., dir. EDP Technology, Inc., Washington, 1969—71; chmn. bd. Internat. Devel. Svcs., Washington, 1969—71; spl. cons. to Senator Edmund S. Muskie, 1970—72; practice law Washington, 1972—77, 1981—91; founding ptnr. Heller & Rosenblatt, Washington, 1991—. Personal rep. of Pres. with rank amb. to conduct negotiations on future polit. status of Trust Ter. of Pacific Islands, Washington, 1977-81; mem. Mid. East study group Dem. Adv. Coun. Elected Ofcls., 1974-76; bd. dirs. MediSense, Inc., 1983-96. Contbr. (anthology) Lyndon Johnson Remembered, 2003. Sec., chmn. exec. com. Coalition for a Dem. Majority, 1973-77, pres., 1983-93; bd. dirs. Com. on Present Danger, 1976-77, 82-93, 04-; mem. US Nat. Com. Pacific Econ. Cooperation, 1986, sec., 1987-03; bd. govs. Haifa U., Israel, 1990-94, 98—; sec.-treas. Fund for Democracy and Devel., 1991-94, pres., 1994—; mem. adv. coun. Nixon Ctr., 1994—; mem. task force on fgn. policy Dem. Policy Commn., 1986; bd. govs. Am. Jewish Com., 1998—, v.p. 2005-, pres. DC chpt. 2003-05, bd. dirs. UN Watch, 2000—, chmn., bd. govs. Koppelman Inst. on Am. Jewish-Israeli Rels., 1999-02, chmn. strategic policy group, 2007-; bd. advisors Jewish Inst. Nat. Security Affairs, 2000—; mem. Nat. Security Initiative, 2001—. 2nd lt. USAR, 1957—58, 1st lt. USAR, 1958—65. Recipient Superior Honor award, Dept. of State, 1981; postgrad. fellow, Tel-Aviv U., 1971. Mem. ABA, NY, DC Bar, Coun. Fgn. Rels. Jewish. Office: 1140 Connecticut Ave Nw Ste 702 Washington DC 20036-4009 Office Phone: 202-466-4700.

ROSENBLATT, ROGER, writer; b. NYC, Sept. 13, 1940; m. Virginia Rosenblatt; children: Carl, Amy, John. PhD in English and Am. Lit., Harvard U.; doctorate (hon.), U. Md., Claremont Grad. Sch., U. Utah, Pace U., Brigham Young U., Kenyon Coll. Briggs-Copeland prof. creative writing Harvard U., 1968-73; dir. edn. NEH, 1973-75; lit. editor The New Republic, 1975-78; columnist Washington Post, mem. editorial bd., 1976-79; essayist, sr. writer Time, 1980-88; essayist MacNeil/Lehrer News Hour, PBS, 1983—2006; columnist, editor-at-large Life mag., 1989-92; editor-at-large Time, Inc., 1999—2001. Disting. prof. English and writing Stony Brook U., 2007-. Author: Black Fiction, 1974, Children of War, 1983 (Robert F. Kennedy Book prize), Witness: The World Since Hiroshima, 1985, Life Itself: Abortion in the American Mind, 1992 (Melcher award), The Man in the Water, 1994, Coming Apart, 1997, Consuming Desires, 1999, Rules for Aging, 2000, Where We Stand, 2002, Anything Can Happen, 2003, (novels) Lapham Rising, 2006, Beet, 2008, (plays) Free Speech in America, 1991, And, 1992, Bibliomania, 1993, Ashley Montana Goes Ashore in the Caicos, 2005, Blueberry, The Oldsmobiles, 2008. Fulbright scholar, Dublin, Ireland, 1965; recipient numerous honors including two George Polk awards, George Foster Peabody award, Emmy award.

ROSENBLATT, STEPHEN PAUL, marketing and sales promotion company executive; b. NYC, Feb. 13, 1935; s. Jack Aaron and Ruth (Kloth) R.; m. Dorothy Freedman, Apr. 7, 1962; children: Gregg, Amy, Robert. BEd, NYU, 1957. Tchr. art N.Y.C. Schs., 1957-58; art dir. Morse Internat., NYC, 1958-65; v.p. L.C. Gumbinner Advt., NYC, 1966-71; group mktg. dir. Norcliff Thayer, Tarrytown, NY, 1971-75; pres. BMS Mktg. Services, Inc., NYC, 1975-89, The Promotion Group Inc. subs. Doctus PLC, NYC, 1989-91, SPQR Inc., Yorktown Heights, NY, 1991-93, ret., 1993. Home: 50 Watkins Dr Sandy Hook CT 06482

ROSENBLOOM, BERT, marketing educator, consultant, writer; b. Phila., Feb. 2, 1944; s. Max and Dora (Cohen) R.; m. Pearl Friedman, Aug. 18, 1968; children: Jack Alan, Robyn. BS, Temple U., 1966, MBA, 1968, PhD, 1974. Instr. mktg. Rider Coll., Trenton, NJ, 1968-72, asst. prof., 1972-74; asst. prof. mktg. Baruch Coll. CUNY, 1974-76; assoc. prof. Drexel U., Phila., 1976-80, prof., 1980-85, G. Behrens Ulrich prof. mktg., 1985-98, assoc. dean grad. programs, 1994-97, Rauth chair electronic commerce mgmt., 1999—2005, Rauth prof. mktg. mgmt., 2005—; external examiner Trinity Coll., U. Dublin, 2008—. Vis. scholar Higher Sch. Commerce Paris, 1993; cons. editor mktg. Random House, N.Y.C., 1977—; exec. dir. Safe Guard Sci. E-Commerce Mgmt. Ctr., 1999-2000, sr. rsch. fellow, 2000—; cons. in field; bd. dirs. Reality Landscaping Corp., McKee Real Estate Devel. Corp., RESHARE Corp.; vis. disting. prof. Hannon U., Japan, 2000; vis. disting. scholar U. St. Gallen, 2000; Disting. vis. fellow Sogang U., Korea, 2001; bd. dirs. Reshare Corp., 2004—; mem. adv. bd. Duttweiler Inst. Mktg. and Retailing. Author: Marketing Channels, 1978, 3d edit., 2003, Market Functions and the Wholesaler Distribution, 1987, Marketing Channels: A Management View, 5th edit., 1997, 6th edit., 1999, 7th edit., 2003, Retail Marketing, 1981, Direct Selling Channels, 1993, Wholesale Mktg. Channels, 1994; editor Jour. Mktg. Channels, 1989—, Jour. Consumer Mktg., Jour. Global Mktg., Jour. Acad. Mktg. Sci.; contbr. articles to profl. jours. Mem. E-Commerce Commn., Mayor Phila., 1999—. Named Disting. Erskine fellow U. Canterbury, New Zealand, 1986; recipient Outstanding Educator award Chapel of Four Chaplains, 1984, Nomura Fund Collaborative rsch. award U. Rykus, Japan, 1998; rsch. award Distbn. Rsch. and Edn. Found., 1986, rsch. award Direct Selling Found., 1986, 91, 96, Literati Club award for excellence, 2002; Nat. Assn. Wholesaler Distbrs. grantee, 1991; honored as disting. prof. Retail Mktg. Inst. of Australia, 1985. Fellow Acad. Mktg. Sci. (bd. govs. 1978-89); mem. Internat. Mgmt. Devel. Assn. (pres. 1992-94), Am. Mktg. Assn. (v.p. Phila. chpt. 1978-79), Beta Gamma Sigma. Office: Drexel U Sch Bus 32d and Market Sts Philadelphia PA 19104 Home Phone: 856-722-0142. Business E-Mail: rosenblb@drexel.edu.

ROSENBLOOM, DANIEL, investment advisor, lawyer; b. NYC, Feb. 11, 1930; s. Sol and Florence (Vogel) R. BA, U. Va., 1951, JD, 1954; LLM, NYU, 1960. Bar: Va. 1954, N.Y. 1956. Atty. Paskus, Gordon, and Hyman, NYC, 1956—61; v.p., sec., gen. counsel Phila. and Reading Corp., NYC, 1962—67; ptnr. First Manhattan Co., NYC, 1968—2002, sr. mng. dir., 2002—. Trustee Nat. Found. for Facial Reconstruction, N.Y. Univ. Med. Ctr., hon. trustee, Univ. Va. Law Sch. Found. 1st lt. AUS, 1954—56. Mem. Sunningdale Country Club, Farmington Country Club, Harmonie Club, Atlantic Golf Club, River Club, Phi Alpha Delta, Phi Epsilon Pi. Office: First Manhattan Co 437 Madison Ave New York NY 10022-7001 Office Phone: 212-756-3355.

ROSENBLOOM, DAVID HARRY, political science and law educator; b. NYC, Aug. 27, 1943; s. Jerome and Rita R. BA, Marietta Coll., 1964, LLD (hon.), 1994; MA, U. Chgo., 1966, PhD in Polit. Sci., 1969. Asst. prof. U. Kans., Lawrence, 1969-71; fellow Am. Soc. Pub. Adminstrn. U.S. Civil Svc. Commn., Washington, 1970-71; vis. sr. lectr. Tel Aviv (Israel) U., 1971-73; asst. prof. U. Vt., Burlington, 1973-75, assoc. prof., 1975-78; vis. assoc. prof. Syracuse (N.Y.) U., 1978-79, prof., 1979—88, disting. prof., 1988-90, Am. U., Washington, 1990—. Bd. trustees Marietta Coll., 2003—; guest prof. pub. adminstrn. People's U., Beijing, 2003—, Northwest U., Xi'an, China, 2005—. Author: (Books) Federal

Service and Constitution, 1971, Public Administration, 2004, 6th edit., Public Administration and Law, 1997, Building a Legislative-Centered Public Administration, 2000, Administrative Law for Public Managers, 2003. Mem. Clinton-Gore Transition Team, U.S. Office Pers. Mgmt., Washington, 1992; chair Am. U. Faculty Senate, 2004—05; acting chair Am. U. Dept. Pub. Adminstrn. and Policy, 2005—06. Recipient Charles Levine Meml. award for excellence and Disting. Rsch. award Am. Soc. for Pub. Adminstrn. and Nat. Assn. Schs. of Pub. Affairs and Administration, Washington, 1992, 93, Thomas Dye award for outstanding svc. Policy Studies Orgn., 1996, Dwight Waldo award for outstanding contbns. to lit. and leadership of Pub. Adminstrn., Am. Soc. Pub. Adminstrn., Washington, 1999, Louis Brownlow Book award Nat. Acad. Pub. Adminstrn., 2001, John Gaus award for exemplary scholarship in joint tradition polit. sci. and pub. adminstrn. Am. Polit. Sci. Assn., 2001. Fellow Nat. Acad. Pub. Adminstrn. Recipient John Gaus award for exemplary scholarship in joint tradition polit. sci. and pub. adminstrn. Am. Polit. Sci. Assn., 2001. Avocations: bicycling, motorcycling. Office: American U 4400 Massachusetts Ave NW Washington DC 20016-8070 Office Phone: 202-885-2361. Business E-Mail: rbloom313@hotmail.com, rbloom@american.edu.

ROSENBLOOM, H(ARRY) DAVID, lawyer; b. NYC, May 26, 1941; s. Milton M. and Rose (Gold) Rosenbloom; m. Carla L. Peterson, June 23, 1968; children: Sarah Alix, Julia Micol. AB, Princeton U., 1962; postgrad. (Fulbright scholar), U. Florence, Italy, 1962-63; JD, Harvard U., 1966. Bar: N.Y. 1967, DC 1968. Spl. asst. to Arthur J. Goldberg U.S. amb. UN, 1966-67; law clk. to Abe Fortas U.S. Supreme Ct., 1967-68; assoc. Caplin & Drysdale, Washington, 1968-72, ptnr., 1972-77, 81—; pres. Harvard Law Review, Vol. 79. Spl. asst. to dep. asst. sec. for tax policy Dept. Treasury, Washington, 1977, internat. tax counsel, 1978—81; lectr. Harvard U. Law Sch., 1984—87, 1990—93, 1995—96, 1999, Pub. Fin. Tng. Inst., Taipei, 1985—86, 1989, Stanford U. Law Sch., 1988, Inst. Tecnologico Autonomo d' Mex., 1993, 95, 97, Columbia U. Law Sch., 1997, U. Pa. Law Sch., 1998, U. Luigi Bocconi, Milan, 2001, 04, 05, 08, So. African Tax Inst., U. Pretoria, 2002, Petrobras U., Rio de Janeiro, 2006, Johannes Gutenberg U., Mainz, 2008, Ruprecht Karl U., Heidelberg, 2008, U. degli Studi Bergamo, 2008, U. Melbourne, 2009, NYU Law Sch., 2000—, dir. internat. tax program, 2002—; James J. Eustice vis. prof., taxation, 2007—; faculty law U. Sydney, 2001, 03, 2005—08, U. Melbourne, 2009. Home: 2948 Garfield Ter NW Washington DC 20008-3507 Office: 1 Thomas Cir NW Washington DC 20005-5802 Home Phone: 202-797-1215; Office Phone: 202-862-5037. Business E-Mail: hdr@capdale.com.

ROSENBLOOM, LEWIS STANLEY, lawyer; b. Ft. Riley, Kans., Feb. 28, 1953; s. Donald and Sally Ann (Warsawsky) R.; children: Micah, Shaina. BA, Lake Forest Coll., 1974; JD with high honors, DePaul U., 1977. Bar: Ill. 1977, US Dist. Ct. (no. dist.) Ill, 1977, US Ct. Appeals (7th cir.) 1979, US Supreme Ct. 1983, US Ct. Appeals (9th cir.) 1987, US Ct. Appeals (3rd cir.) 1993. Sr. acct. Gale, Takahasi & Channon (now Ernst & Young), Chgo., 1973-74; law clk. to Hon. Robert L. Eisen U.S. Bankruptcy Ct. (no. dist.) Ill., Chgo., 1976; assoc. Nachman, Munitz & Sweig, Ltd., Chgo., 1976-82, prin., 1982-87; ptnr., co-chmn. involvency, bankruptcy & bus. reorgn. dept. Winston & Strawn, Chgo., 1987-93; ptnr., sr. corp. reorgn. counsel, practice group head McDermott, Will & Emery, Chgo., 1993—2006; ptnr., chmn. dept. bankruptcy and reorganization LeBoeuf, Lamb, Green & MacRae, LLP NIKIA Deweg & LeBoeuf, Chgo., 2006—. Mem. bd. advisors to bankruptcy, comml. law advisor Bus. Laws, Inc., 1988—; lectr. in field. Contbr. articles to profl. jours. Mem. adv. com. and fin. subcom. Ill. Bd. Higher Edn., Springfield; mem. state edn. and legal aid subcom. Ill. Coun. on Children and Youth Welfare. Coll. Scholar Lake Forest Coll., 1973-74. Fellow Am. Coll. Bankruptcy (dir.); mem. ABA (bus. bankruptcy com. 1982—, chmn. new and pending bankruptcy legis. com. 1982-85, chmn. transp. reorganizations com. 1985-88), Chgo. Bar Assn. (bankrupcy reorganization com., co-chmn. subcom. on retention and fees 1987-88). Office: Dewey & Le Boauf Two Prudential Plz 180 N Stetson Ste 3700 Chicago IL 60601 Home Phone: 847-630-6943; Office Phone: 312-794-8090, 212-424-8049. Business E-Mail: lrosenbloom@llgm.com.

ROSENBLOOM, MOREY STEPHEN, lawyer; b. Phila., Aug. 26, 1944; s. Howard and Esther (Medvene) R.; m. Marsha Riffkin, May 26, 1968; children: Brett, Eric. BS in Acctg., Temple U., 1966, JD, 1969. Bar: Pa. 1970, US Tax Ct., 1975, US Supreme Ct., 1980, NY, 2001. Law asst. to chief justice Pa. Supreme Ct., 1969-70; ptnr. Blank Rome Comisly & McCauley, Phila., 1970—90; prin. CMS Co., 1990—95; ptnr. Blank Rome LLP, Phila., 1995—, chair, tax and fiduciary dept., 1996—2001, chmn., bus. dept., 2001—06. Adj. prof. law Temple U. Sch. Law, Phila., 1977-2000, Villanova Law Sch., 1999-2004; lectr., prof. Am. Coll., Bryn Mawr, Pa., 1978-90. Co-author: Tools and Techniques of Estate Planning, 13th edit., 1990, Funding Corporate Buy-Sell Agreements with Life Insurance, 1980, The Wait and See Buy Sell, 1978. Bd. visitors Temple U. Sch. of Law; bd. mem. Am. Friends of Hebrew U., Elwyn Jerusalem, Thomas Jefferson U. Cardiology Rsch. Found. Fellow Am. Coll. Trust and Estate Coun.; mem. ABA, Pa. Bar Assn. (past chmn. real property probate and trust law sect.), Phila. Bar Assn., Phila. Estate planning Coun. Office: Blank Rome LLP One Logan Sq Philadelphia PA 19103-6998 Office Phone: 215-569-5599. Office Fax: 215-832-5599. Business E-Mail: rosenbloom@BlankRome.com.

ROSENBLOOM, PAUL SIMON, computer scientist; b. Santa Monica, Calif., Dec. 13, 1954; s. Arnold and Florence Simon Rosenbloom; m. Sharon Elaine Lee, Sept. 5, 1986; 1 child, Michael Lee. BS, Stanford U., Calif., 1976; MS, Carnegie Mellon U., Pitts., 1978, PhD, 1983. Rsch. computer scientist Carnegie Mellon U., 1983—84; asst. prof. computer sci. and psychology Stanford U., 1984—87; rsch. asst. prof. computer sci. U. Southern Calif., LA, 1988—90, assoc. prof. computer sci., 1991—99, prof. computer sci., 1999—; dep. dir., intelligent sys. divsn. USC Info. Sci. Inst., Marina del Rey, Calif., 1993—2002, project leader, 1987—93, dir., new directions, 1998—2002, assoc. dir., 2002—07, dep. dir., 2007, USC Ctr. Rapid Automated Fabrication Techs., LA, 2005—; project leader USC Inst. Creativity Techs., 2009—. Chair ACM Spl. Interest Group Artificial Intelligence, 1987—89; councilor Assn. Advancement Artificial Intelligence, 1992—95, conf. chair, 1998—2001. Recipient Gary K. Poock award, AVIOS Jour., 1994; Grad. fellowship, NSF, 1976—79, IBM, 1981—82. Fellow: Assn. Advancement Artificial Intelligence (councilor 1992—95, Best Written Paper award 1984); mem.: AAAS, Cognitive Sci. Soc., ACM Spl. Interest Group Artificial Intelligence (chair 1987—89), Assn. Computing Machinery, Phi Beta Kappa, Sigma Xi. Office: Univ Southern Calif 941 W 37th Pl SAL 238 Los Angeles CA 90089-0781 Office Fax: 213-740-7285. Business E-Mail: rosenbloom@usc.edu.

ROSENBLUM, ESTELLE H., retired dean, nursing educator; b. Davenport, Iowa, Feb. 8, 1933; d. Dan and Cecil (Spiewak) Masters; m. Sidney Rosenblum, Aug. 30, 1953 (dec. 1988); children: Jay Douglas, Gail Rae, Paul Mitchell; m. Jack Grevey, Mar. 31, 1996; stepdaughter: Eileen Grevey Hillson. Student, U. Iowa, 1950—53; BSN, Wayne State U., Detroit, 1956; MA in Audiology, U. N.Mex., 1971, PhD, 1979; MSN, U. Tex., El Paso, 1981. Head nurse Northville (Mich.) State Hosp., 1956; head nurse, supr. Sister Kenny Polio/Rehab. Hosp., 1957-60; pub. health nurse Englewood County Health Dept., 1961-62; nursing supr. Bernalillo County Indian Hosp., Albuquerque, 1962-63, asst. dir. nursing, 1963-64; clin. tchr. U. N.Mex. Coll. Nursing, Albuquerque, 1964-65, inst. to prof., 1972-86, dean and prof. nursing, 1986-93, dean and prof. emerita, 1993—; sch. nurse West Mesa H.S., Albuquerque, 1967-69. Internat. nursing cons.; dir. ANA Approved CE program, Profl. Seminar Cons., 1979-89; spkr. Hong Kong Nurse Educators Soc., 1985; founder convenio U. N.Mex. and U. Mex., 1990, first nurse practitioner program at grad. level, 1987. Author: Fundamentals of Hearing for Health Professionals, 1981; contbr. articles to profl. jours., chpts. to books. Bd. dirs. U. N.Mex. Found., 1996—, bd. sec. 2000-04, Nancy Floyd Haworth Breast Cancer Found., 1995—; docent City of Albuquerque, 1996—; chair recognition com. Jewish Cmty. Ctr., 1998—; chair opening events N.Mex. Holocause Mus., 2006—. USPHS grantee, 1989; Albuquerque Rotary Charitable Found. Clinton P. Anderson fellow; recipient Centennial Disting. Alumni award, U. N.Mex., 1989, Helene Fuld award to Coll. Nursing, U. N.Mex., 1987, Sigma Delta Tau Nat. Disting. Alumni award, 1988, State N.Mex. Gov.'s Disting. Svc. award, 1993, Estelle H. Rosenblum Thesis award U. N.Mex. Coll. Nursing, 1995, Nurse of the Yr. Awards "Legend of Nursing" award March of Dimes, 2002, Myrtle K. Aydelotte Dean's award U. Iowa Coll. Nursing, 2004; Rosenblum-Weiss Ctr. for Nursing Excellence in women and children's health care established at U. N.Mex., 2000. Univ. Iowa Coll. of Nursing Alumni award, 2004. Fellow Am. Acad. Nursing; mem. Am. Assn. Colls. of Nursing (emeritus, exec. devel. series 1988-92), Am. Colls. Nursing (bd. dirs. 1990-92), N.Mex. Nurses Assn. (pres. 1975), N.Mex. Health Resources (bd. dirs. 1986-88), The Rotary Club of Albuquerque (Harvest ball fundraiser 1994—), Sigma Theta Tau (founding pres. Gamma Sigma chpt. 1974-76, Mentor award, Lifetime Achievement award 2008), Phi Kappa Phi.

ROSENBLUM, FRANK MICHAEL, civil engineer, consultant, surveyor; b. Calif., Nov. 12, 1961; s. Jerald and Lois Rosenblum; 1 child, Jane. BCE, Calif. Poly. State, San Luis Obispo, 1983. Profl. civil engr., Calif., 1987, profl.land surveyor, Calif., 1990. Prin. engr. and pres. Underwood & Rosenblum, Inc., San Jose, Calif., 1993—. Facility planning cons. Calif. Pub. Schs., Calif.; vol. profl. svcs. Calif. State Parks and U.S. Nat. Parks, Calif., 1999—2007. Mem.: ASCE (assoc.), Calif. Assn. Sch. Bus. Ofcls. (assoc.), Calif. Land Surveyors Assn. (assoc.), Am. Pub. Works Assn. (assoc.), Coalition for Adequate Sch. Housing (assoc.). Achievements include development of 9-step sch. traffic safety planning sys; digital mapping and planning system. Office: Underwood & Rosenblum Inc Ste A114 1630 Oakland Road San Jose CA 95131 Home Fax: 408-453-1207.

ROSENBLUM, JAY ALAN, neurologist; b. Newark, June 12, 1933; s. Irving and Peggy (Carpenter) R.; m. Judith Grandes, Sept. 1958 (div. 1965); children: Melissa, Shepherd, Todd; m. Sue Goldman Rosenblum, June 13, 1971; 1 child, Steven. AB with honors, U. Pa., 1954; MD, Wake Forest Med., 1958; GM, U. Pa., 1965. DIplomate Am. Acad. of Pain Mgmt., Am. Bd. Forensic Medicine; cert. neurorehabilitation physician. Dir. neurology Madison Ave Hosp., NYC, 1980, N.Y. Infirmary Hosp., NYC, 1980; clin. cons. in neurology N.Y. State Dept of Health, NYC, 1985; instr. in neurology N.Y. Med. Coll., 1985; clin. asst. prof. neurology NYU Med. Sch., 1965, 1970—. Asst. vis. neurologist Bellevue Hosp., NYC; bd. dirs. Am. Bd. Forensic Medicine, Spingifield, Mo., bd. adv. for profl. standing; dir. indsl. medicine seminar Coll. of Ins., NYC, 1988-89; moderator diagnosis and treatment back disorders Acad. of Medicine, NYC, 1991; lectr. in field; pres. med. bd. NY Infirmary-Beekman Downtown Hosp., 1982; mem. NY State Bd. for Profl. Med. Conduct, 2004. Contbr. articles to profl. publs. Task force of handicap vehicles Dept. Health, City of N.Y., 1985; impartial specialist-neurology U.S. Dept. Labor, 1985. Capt. U.S. Army, 1959-62. Fellow Am. Soc. Indsl. Medicine (pres. 1993), Am. Acad. of Infared Imaging (pres. 1995); mem. Am. Back Soc. (dir. neurothemograhy workshop 1989), NY County Med. Soc. (bd. dirs., chmn. bd. censors 2002). Office: 65 E 76th St New York NY 10021-1844 Office Phone: 212-249-7867. Personal E-mail: ps206@aol.com.

ROSENBLUM, MARTIN JEROME, ophthalmologist; b. NYC, Apr. 7, 1948; s. Philip and Rita (Steppel) R.; m. Zina Zarin, May 31, 1975; children: Steven David, Richard James. BS, Bklyn. Coll., 1968; MD, U. Ariz., 1973; postgrad., Columbia U., 1977. Diplomate Am. Bd. Ophthalmology, Nat. Bd. Med. Examiners. Intern Cornell U., NYC, 1973-74; resident N.Y. Med. Coll., 1975-78, instr., 1978-79; practice medicine specializing in eye surgery St. Petersburg, Fla., 1979—. Chief ophthalmology Edward White Hosp.; asst. clin. prof. ophthalmology, U. So. Fla.; attending surgeon St. Anthony's Bayfront Med. Ctr., Am. Soc. for Cataract and Refractive Surgery, Ctr. Spl. Surgery; med. dir. Suncoast Eye Clinic, Pa. Fellow ACS, Am. Acad. Ophthalmology; mem. AMA, Am. Soc. Ophthalmic Plastic and Reconstructive Surgery, Fla. Med. Assn., Fla. Soc. Ophthalmology, Pinellas County Med. Soc., Bayou Country Club. Republican. Jewish. Avocations: tennis, golf, travel, skiing. Office: 2200 16th St N Saint Petersburg FL 33704-3106 Home: 7676 Hunter Lane Pinellas Park FL 33782 Office Phone: 727-822-4729. E-mail: mjreye@aol.com.

ROSENBLUM, RICHARD MARK, utilities executive; b. NYC, Apr. 28, 1950; s. Victor Sigmund and Julia K. R.; m. Michele E. Cartier, Aug. 30, 1979; children: Gialisa, Jeremy Scott. BS, MS, Rensselaer Poly. Inst., 1973. Startup engr. Combustion Engring., Inc., Windsor, Conn., 1973-76; engr. So. Calif. Edison Co., Rosemead, 1976-82; project mgr. San Onofre Nuclear Generating Sta., 1982-83, tech. mgr., 1983-84, nuclear safety mgr., 1984-86, mgr. quality assurance, 1986-89, mgr. nuclear regulatory affairs, 1989-93, v.p. engring. and tech. svcs., 1993-95, v.p. distbn., 1996-98, sr. v.p. T&D, 1998—2005; sr. v.p. generation, chief nuc. officer Generation Bus. Unit, 2005—09; pres. & CEO Hawaiian Electric Co., 2009—. N.Y. State Regents scholar, 1968-73. Office: 900 Richards St Honolulu HI 96813

ROSENBLUM, SCOTT S., lawyer; b. NYC, Oct. 4, 1949; s. Harold Lewis and Greta Blossom (Lesher) R.; m. Barbara Anne Campbell, Oct. 29, 1977; children: Harold, Emma, Casey. AB summa cum laude, Dartmouth Coll., 1971; JD, U. Pa., 1974. Bar. US Dist. Ct. (so. dist.) NY 1975. From assoc. to ptnr. Stroock & Stroock & Lavan, NYC, 1974-91; ptnr. Kramer, Levin, Naftalis & Frankel, NYC, 1991—, mng. ptnr., 1994—2000, mem., exec. com., 2001—. Mem. NY bd. govs., Mid. East Forum, Phila., 1994—; bd. dirs. Dovenmuehle Mortgage, Inc., Lake Zurich, Ill., Temco Svc. Industries, Inc., NYC, Cinema City Internat. NV, Herzlia, Israel, Investec US Holdings Corp., NYC. Co-author: Public Limited Partnerships and Roll-Ups, Securities Law Techniques, The Practitioner's Guide to Transactions and Litigation, 1995. Trustee Village of Saltaire, NY, 1993-03, mayor, 2003-. Mem.: Phi Beta Kappa. Avocation: sailing. Home: 19 Wildwood Cir Larchmont NY 10538-3426 Office: Kramer Levin Naftalis Frankel 1177 Avenue of the Americas New York NY 10036-2714 Office Fax: 212-715-8411. Business E-Mail: srosenblum@kramerlevin.com.

ROSENBLUM, ZINA MICHELLE ZARIN, psychology professor, marketing professional, researcher; b. NYC, Mar. 4, 1949; d. Harry and Miriam (Bachrach) Zarin; m. Martin Jerome Rosenblum, May 31, 1975; children: Steven David, Richard James. BA magna cum laude, Queens Coll., 1971; MEd, Columbia U., 1973, MEd Counseling Psychology, 1973. Prof. psychology Marymount Manhattan Coll., NYC, 1971—73; addictions counselor Manhattan Vets. Hosp., NYC, 1971—73; project dir. BBD&O Advt., NYC, 1973—74, Grey Advt., NYC, 1974—75; supr. market rsch. Doyle Dane & Bernbach, NYC, 1975—77, SSC& B, NYC, 1977—78; dir. rsch. Hershey Co., Pa., 1978—79; adminstr. Suncoast Eye Clinic, St. Petersburg, Fla., 1979—97; prof. psychology St. Petersburg Coll., Seminole, Fla., 1997—. Sec. Nat. Coun. Jewish Women, Fla., 1980—81; docent Fla. Holocaust Mus., 2005—. Scholar, Columbia U., 1971; Nat. Merit acholar, Coll. Bd., 1970. Mem.: APA, Phi Beta Kappa. Office: Suncoast Eye Clinic Martin Rosenblum 2200 16th St North Saint Petersburg FL 33704 Personal E-mail: zcurl@aol.com.

ROSENBLUTH, FRANCES MCCALL, political scientist, educator; b. Osaka, Japan, Oct. 22, 1958; d. Robert Donnell McCall and Virginia Lancaster Montgomery; m. James Edward Rosenbluth, Oct. 5, 1985; children: Benjamin Lee, John Gabriel, William Lancaster. BA, U. Va., 1980; MIA, Colubia U., 1983, PhD, 1988. Asst. prof. U. Va., Charlottesville, 1988-89, U. Calif., San Diego, 1989-92, UCLA, 1992, prof., 1993, Yale U., New Haven, 1994—. Mem. editl. bd. Am. Polit. Sci. Rev., Washington, 1996-2000, Internat. Orgn., MIT Press, 1996-2000, Am. Asian Rev., 2000--. Author: Financial Policies in Japan, 1989; co-author: Japan's Political Marketplace, 1993, The Politics of Oligarchy, 1995 (Luebbert award 1997). Fellow Fulbright Found., 1985-86, Social Sci. Rsch. Coun., 1987-88, Coun. on Fgn. Rels., 1999-2000; NSF rschr., 1991; ABE fellow, 2000-02. Fellow Am. Acad. Arts & Scis.; mem. Am. Polit. Sci. Assn. Democrat. Presbyterian. Avocations: reading, hiking. Office: Yale U Dept Polit Sci New Haven CT 06520-8301 E-mail: frances.rosenbluth@yale.edu.

ROSENBLUTH, MORTON, periodontist, educator; b. NYC, Sept. 28, 1924; s. Jacob and Eva (Bigeleissen) R.; m. Sylvia Fradin, July 2, 1946; children: Cheryl Bonnie, Hal Glen. BA, NYU, 1943, grad. program in periodontia, oral medicine, 1946, DDS, 1946. Diplomate Am. Bd. Periodontology. Intern Bellevue Hosp., NYC, 1946-47, resident, 1947; individual practice dentistry NYC, 1947-59; individual practice periodontia North Miami Beach, Fla., 1960—; individual practice periodontia, TMJ, implantology Bay Harbor Islands, Fla., 1995—. Periodontist Mt. Sinai Hosp., N.Y., Polyclinic Hosp. and Med. Sch. N.Y., Mt. Sinai Hosp., Miami Beach, Fla., Parkway Gen. Hosp.; chief dental dept. North Miami Gen. Hosp.; chmn. periodontia sect. Dade County Rsch. Ctr.; clin. assoc. prof. divsn. oral and maxillofacial surgery U. Miami Sch. Medicine; assoc. clin. prof. Southeastern U. Health Scis.; assoc. prof. Nova Southeastern U. Coll. Dental Medicine; lectr. throughout U.S.A., Israel, Mexico, Rome, Teheran, Bangkok, Hong Kong, Tokyo, Honolulu, Jamaica, Paris, London, Sicily, Budapest, Berlin, Luxembourg, South Africa and others; vis. lectr. U. Tenn. Dental Coll., NYU Dental Coll.; cons. VA Hosp., Miami. Contbr. articles to profl. jours. Mem. adv. bd. U. Fla. Coll. Dentistry; mem. profl. adv. bd. North Dade Children's Ctr., Hope Sch. Mentally Retarded Children; mem. sci. adv. com. United Health Found.; chmn. Dental divsn. United Fund of Dade County, Combined Jewish Appeal; nat. chmn. Hebrew U. Sch. Dental Medicine; bd. dirs. Health Planning Coun. South Fla.; pres. Condominium Assn.; bd. dirs. and bd. overseers Am. Friends of Hebrew U.; mem. med. adv. bd. Dade-Broward Lupus Found.; trustee Jewish Congregation, 1961-64. With AUS, 1943-44, as capt. USAF, 1951-52. Recipient Maimonides award State of Israel, 1979. Fellow Am. Coll. Dentists, Internat. Coll. Dentists; mem. ADA, Am. Acad. Periodontology, Am. Assn. Hosp. Dental Chiefs, Am. Acad. Dental Medicine, Am. Soc. Advancement Gen. Anesthesia in Dentistry, Am. Soc. Periodontists, Fla. Soc. Periodontists, Northeastern Soc. Periodontists, Fla. Dental Soc. (chmn. coun. on legislation), Miami Dental Soc., Miami Beach Dental Soc., East Coast Dental Soc. (sec.-treas. 1968, pres. 1971-72), North Dade Dental Soc. (pres. 1963-64), Fedn. Dentaire Internat., Fla. Acad. Dental Practice Adminstrn., Alpha Omega (pres. 1978-78, internat. regent 1973-75, internat. editor 1975-77, internat. pres.-elect 1977-78, internat. pres. 1979, chmn. bd. Alpha Omega Found. 1985-90), Am. Dental Interfrat. Coun. (pres. 1981-82), Nocoma Club (pres. 1958-60), NYU Century Club (local chmn.), Jockey Club (bd. govs.), KP, Masons, Kiwanis (bd. dirs. 1965), Chaine Des Rotisseurs (Miami Beach charge de missions). Home: 20281 E Country Club Dr Apt # 1001 Aventura FL 33180 Personal E-mail: periomort@aol.com.

ROSENCRANTZ, LAWRENCE, holding company executive, lawyer; b. Portland, Oreg., May 21, 1945; s. Louis Meier and Blanche Faye (Lewis) R.; m. Gayle Schnitzer, Sept. 27, 1970 (div. Jan. 1981); children: Bryan, Laura. Student, U. Oreg., 1963-65; BS, U. Calif., Berkeley, 1967; JD, U. Calif., 1970. Bar: Oreg. 1970. V.p., gen. counsel Schnitzer Group/Lasco Shipping Co., Portland, 1970-75, sr. v.p., 1975-77, exec. v.p., dir., 1984-85; pres., chief exec. officer Softsource Computer, Portland, 1984-85; exec. v.p., treas. U.S. Bancorp, Portland, 1985-91; pres., chief exec. officer The Aspen Group, Portland, 1991—; chmn. & CEO Capital Pacific Bank, 2003—05. Mem. spl. mgmt adv. com. Multnomah County Govt. Ops.; chmn. transit subcom. West Side Light Rail Financing. Pres. bd. trustees Portland Repertory Theater; chmn. corp. campaign Doernbecher Children's Hosp.; mem. activities coun. Oregon Art Inst., steering com. Arts Plan 2000, adv. bd. Portland Festival Symphony Orch.; bd. dirs. Cen. City Concern, Portland Ctr. Visual Arts, Portland Devel. Commn. Transit Mall Extension Task Force, Beth Israel Sch.; pres. bd. dirs. Oreg. Bus. Com. Arts; bd. dirs. Am. Cancer Soc Oreg., co-chmn. Jail 'N Bail Campaign, 1988; chmn. Lake Oswego Planning Commn., bd. mem. Portland Ctr. Stage; past mem. Blue Ribbon Commn. East End Devel., Lake Oswego, grand opening task force Portland Ctr. Performing Arts, pub.-pvt. task force on transit fin. Recipient Gavel award Am. Cancer Soc., 1987, 88, White Charger award Portland Ctr. Visual Arts, 1987. Mem. Portland C. of C. (task force social issues and bus. devel.), City Club, Founder's Club, West Hills Racquet Club, Tower Club. Avocations: photography, boating, carpentry, skiing, tennis. Office: The Aspen Group 10822 NW Laurinda Ct Portland OR 97229 Office Phone: 503-746-5500.

ROSENDAHL, BILL, councilman; BA in Polit. Sci. and Economics, St. Vincent Coll., Latrobe, Pa.; MSW, U. Pitts. Psychiatric social worker US Army, spl. asst. to commanding gen., Ft. Carson Colo.; assoc. in philanthropic work for John D. Rockefeller, III; chief ops. US trade and devel. program US Dept. State; disting. prof. Cal State Dominguez Hills. Chair Southern Calif. Regional Airport Authority; mem. Santa Monica Bay Restoration Commn., Exposition Light Rail Constrn. Authority; councilman, Dist. 11 LA City Coun., 2005—. Prodr., host (TV series) Local Talk, Week in Review, Beyond the Beltway. Chair Calif. Commn. on Tax Policy in the New Economy. Served in US Army, 1969—71. Recipient Cable Ace award, Diamond award, Freedom of Info. award, Pub. Svc. award, LA League of Women Voters, Beacon award for Cable's Free Air Time Project. Mem.: Cable and Telecom. Assn. (chmn.), The Am. Legion, Post 283, LA Press Club (pres.). Office: Dist Office 1645 Corinth Ave Los Angeles CA 90025 also: City Hall 200 N Spring St Rm 415 Los Angeles CA 90012 Office Phone: 213-473-7011, 310-575-8461. Office Fax: 213-476-6926, 310-575-8305. Business E-Mail: councilman.rosendahl@lacity.org.*

ROSENDHAL, JEFFREY DAVID, federal agency administrator, educator, astronomer, consultant; b. Bklyn., June 21, 1941; s. Louis and Beulah (Goldsmith) R.; m. Sharon E. Katzman, Dec. 27, 1964 (div. Jan. 25, 1989); children: Martin Andrew, Rachel Lynn; m. Ellen R. Anderson, Feb. 14, 1992. BA, Williams Coll., 1962; MS, U. Ill., 1963; PhD, Yale U., 1968. Vis. asst. prof. astronomy U. Wash., Seattle, 1968-69; asst. prof. U. Wis., Madison, 1969-71, U. Ariz., Tucson, 1971-74; with NASA, Washington, 1974—2004, mgr. advanced programs and tech., astrophysics divsn., 1978-80, asst. assoc. adminstr. advanced planning Office Space Sci., 1980-81, asst. assoc. adminstr. sci. Office Space Sci., Applications, 1981-87, spl. asst. to assoc. adminstr. for space sci. and applications, 1987-89, 92-93, spl. asst. for policy Office Exploration, 1989-90, asst. dir. exploration (internat.) Office Aeronautics, Exploration and Tech., 1990-91, asst. dir. strategic planning Astrophysics Divsn. Office of Space Sci., 1993-96, asst. assoc. adminstr./edn. and outreach Office Space Sci., 1996-2001, edn. and pub. outreach dir. Office of Space Sci., 2001—04, asst. assoc. adminstr. for edn. programs Office of Edn., 2004. Vis. prof. internat. rels. George Washington U., 1988-89; mem. staff energy subcom. House Sci. Space and Tech. Com., 1992; vis. sr. scholar Nat. Air and Space Mus., 2005-06; cons., Jet Propulsion Lab., NASA, 2005-06, NRC, TERC, Boston Mus. Sci., De Paul U., 2007; dep. dir. U. Space Rsch. Assn. Nat. Ctr. Earth and Space Sci. Edn., 2006. Mem. editl. bd.: Jour. Brit. Interplanetary Soc., 1988—; contbr. articles to profl. jours. Recipient Team Achievement award European Space Agy., 1983, 85, 86, Presdl. award of Meritorious Exec. in Sr. Exec. Svc., 1987, 2001, Group Achievement award, NASA, 1982, 1986, 1995, 1996, Outstanding Leadership medal, NASA, 1984, 2003,; NSF grantee, 1971, 72-73; NASA fellow Yale U., 1966-68; hon. Woodrow Wilson fellow, 1962. Mem.: AIAA (assoc. fellow 1996), Sr. Execs. Assn., Internat. Astron. Union, Internat. Acad. Astronautics, Am. Astron. Soc. (divsn. planetary scis., hist. astronomy divsn., high-energy astrophysics divsn.), Astron. Soc. Pacific (adv. com. 2006—, Klumpke-Roberts prize 2006), Cosmos Club, Phi Beta Kappa. Achievements include discovery of the variability of the microturbulence in early-type high luminosity stars; direction of the selection of flight experiments for every major NASA scientific mission 1980-1988; development of strategic and implementation plans for incorporating education and the public understanding of science into space science research programs and missions; establishment of a national support network for space science education; creation of the largest single program in astronomy and space science education ever undertaken, an effort that, at it's peak, reached tens of millions of people every year. Home: 11446 Links Dr Reston VA 20190-4813 Home Phone: 703-437-6363. E-mail: jeffrosendhal@comcast.net.

ROSENE, PAUL EARL, music educator; b. Chgo., Ill., Mar. 26, 1930; s. Earl Nile and Dorothy Mae Rosene; m. Doris J. Mehrkens, Nov. 18, 1951; children: Richard, Cindy Mann. MusD Edn., U. of Ill., Champaign-Urbana, Illinois, 1968—76; Master degree in Edn. -Psychology and Music, Ill. State U., Normal, IL, 1955—57; BS in Music Edn., Ill. State Normal U., Normal, Illinois, 1951. Cert. master tchr. Ill., supr. student tchg. in music Ill., master tchr. Music Educators Nat. Conf. Dir. music edn. Saybrook Pub. Sch., Ill., 1951—52; supr. music, dir. bands Chenoa Pub. Schs., Ill., 1952—53; instructor band sch. USAF, Geneva, NY, 1953—54, bandsman French horn Dayton, Ohio, 1954—55, dir. men's glee club, 1954—55; dir. instrumental music Avon Pub. Schs., Ill., 1955—57; supr. music and dir. HS bands Pittsfield Pub. Schs., Ill., 1957—67; prof. music edn., supr. student tchg. music Ill. State U., Normal, 1967—90; music cons. handbells and choirchimes Malmark, Inc., Orlando, Fla., 1990—. USA pers. dir. Sch. Band/Chorus of Am., Bloomington, Ill., 1967—79. Author: (music book) Making Music With Choirchimes Instruments, 1982; author: (composer) (music techniques book) Making Music with Choirchimes Instruments - Advanced Method, 1986; composer (music for choirchimes): (music publ.) Pontifest, 1988; author: (techniques book) Special Effects for Choirchimes, 2003. Dir. of handbells Bethany Luth. Ch., Leesburg, Fla., 1990—2006; dir. Ctrl. Ill. Cmty. Band, Bloomington-Normal, 1979—90; dir. and founder Ill. State U. Handbells and Choirchime Ensembles, Normal, 1974—90. Staff sgt. band dir., instr. band sch. USAF, 1953—55. Mem.: Pittsfield Tchrs. Assn. (pres. 1960—67), Ill. Music Edn. Assn. (v.p. 1972—80, pres. dist. III 1972—84, Disting. Svc. Award 1991), Fla. Music Educators Assn., Nat. Assn. for Music Therapy (editor Gt. Lakes newsletter 1967—90), Music Educators Nat. Conf. (univ. contact Gt. Lakes divsn. 1979—84), Fla. Band Assn. (adjudicator 1994—). Republican. Lutheran. Avocations: Bible study, walking, reading, attending concerts, computer technology. Home: 822 Pinar Dr Orlando FL 32825-7822 Office: Music Edn Cons 822 Pinar Dr Orlando FL 32825-7822 Office Phone: 407-803-7861. Personal E-mail: rosenebell@aol.com.

ROSENFELD, ARTHUR F., federal official, lawyer; b. Allentown, Pa., 1944; m. Carla Toledo. BA, Muhlenberg Coll., 1970; MBA in Labor Rels., Lehigh U., 1974; JD, Villanova U., 1979. Bar: DC 1979, US Supreme Ct., US Ct. Appeals (4th, 5th and DC cirs.). Labor atty. U.S. C. of C., Washington, 1979—84; atty. Hansell & Post, 1984—86; numerous positions including counsel for regulations divsn. employee benefits, spl. asst. to solicitor of labor, assoc. dep. sec. U.S. Dept. Labor, 1986—97; sr. labor advisor to chmn. James M. Jeffords Senate Com. Health, Edn., Labor and Pensions, 1997—2001; gen. counsel NLRB, 2001—05, acting gen. counsel, 2005—06; dir. Fed Mediation & Concilation Svc., Washington, 2006—. Fellow: The Coll. of Labor and Employment Lawyers. Office: Fed Mediation & Concillation Svc 2100 K St NW Rm 900 Washington DC 20427*

ROSENFELD, EDWARD R., apparel executive; BA in Economics, cum laude, Amherst Coll., Mass. V.p. mergers and acquisitions group Peter J. Solomon Co., 1997—2005; joined exec. mgmt. team Steve Madden, Ltd., 2005, exec. v.p. strategic planning and fin., interim CEO, 2008, CEO, 2008—, chmn. bd. dirs., 2008—. Avocations: politics, tennis. Office: Steve Madden Ltd 52-16 Barnett Ave Long Island City NY 11104*

ROSENFELD, HARRY MORRIS, editor; b. Berlin, Aug. 12, 1929; arrived in US, 1939, naturalized; s. Sam and Esther Rosenfeld; m. Anne Hahn, Feb. 28, 1953; children: Susan, Amy, Stefanie. BA, Syracuse U., 1952; postgrad., NYU, 1954, Columbia U., 1955-59. With N.Y. Herald Tribune, 1954-66, fgn. editor, 1962-66; mng. editor Herald Tribune News Svc., 1959-62; with Washington Post, 1966-78, fgn. editor, 1969; asst. mng. editor Met. News, 1970-74, Nat. News, 1974-76, Outlook/Book World, 1976-78; editor Times Union and Knickerbocker News, Albany, NY, 1978—97, L.A. Herald Examiner, 1985, The Times Union and Sunday Times Union, 1978-96; editor-at-large, columnist L.C. Times Union, Albany, NY, 1996—97. Dir. daily Watergate coverage Washington Post; pres. NYS Assn. Assoc. Press, 1983; vice-chmn. NY Fair Trial Free Press Conf., 1985—98, vice chmn. emeritus, 1998—; co-chmn. NY State Reporters Com. Freedom Press; mem. adv. com. Harvard Journalism Fellowship Advanced Studies Pub. Health; Pulitzer juror, 1987—88, 1996, 97; mem. 3 commns. Cameras in Cts. Commr. NY State Regents Commn. Libr. Svcs.; chmn. Elder Network Capital Region. Recipient newspaper award Pulitzer Gold medal for pub. svc., Black United Front award, 1973, First Amendment award, Anti-Defamation League-B'nai B'rith, Oustanding Alumni award, Syracuse U. Coll. Arts and Scis., 1993, Media Responsibility award, NY State Martin Luther King Jr. Inst. Non-Violence, 1993, Dr. Morton Berger Meml. award, Malmonides Day Sch., 2005, Disting. Public Svc. award, U. Albany Sch. Social Welfare, 2008. Office: Times Union PO Box 15000 Albany NY 12212-5000 Office Phone: 518-454-5450. Business E-Mail: hrosenfeld@timesunion.com.

ROSENFELD, HOWARD H., lawyer; b. Chgo., Nov. 6, 1938; s. Edward M. and Eve R. (Lenetzky) R.; m. Honey B. Jordan, Apr. 14, 1962; children: Julie, Lisa. LLB, DePaul U., 1962. Bar: Ill. 1962, U.S. Dist. Ct. (no. dist.) Ill. 1962. Assoc. Gillen, Owens & Willens, Chgo., 1963-67; ptnr. Rosenfeld, Hafron & Shapiro, Chgo., 1967-81, Rosenfeld Hafron Shapiro & Farmer (formerly Rosenfeld, Rotenberg, Schwartzman, Hafron & Shapiro), Chgo., 1981—. Adj. prof. family law DePaul U. Served with U.S. Army, 1962-63. Fellow Am. Acad. Matrimonial Lawyers, Am. Trial Lawyers Assn.; mem. Ill. State Bar Assn., Chgo. Bar Assn. Office: Rosenfeld Hafron Shapiro & Farmer 221 N La Salle St Ste 1763 Chicago IL 60601-1422

ROSENFELD, IRENE B., food products company executive; b. Bklyn., 1953; m. Richard Illgen; 2 children. BA in Psychology, Cornell U, 1975, MS in Bus., 1977, PhD in Mktg. & Statistics, 1980. With Dancer, Fitzgerald Sample Advertising (now Saatchi and Saatchi), 1979—81, Kraft Foods Inc., 1981—2004, exec. v.p., gen. mgr., beverages divsn., 1991—94, exec. v.p., gen. mgr. desserts & snacks divsn., 1994—96; pres. Kraft Foods Canada, 1996—2004; group v.p. Kraft Foods Inc., 2000—04; pres. Kraft Food N. Am., 2003—04; chmn., CEO Frito-Lay Inc. (divsn. of PepsiCo Inc.), Plano, Tex., 2004—06; CEO Kraft Foods Inc., Northfield, Ill., 2006—07, chmn., CEO, 2007—. Bd. dirs. AutoNation, Inc., Grocery Mfrs. Assn. Mem. YWCA Acad. Women Achievers; bd. trustees Cornell U.; mem. Econ. Club Chgo. Recipient The Masters in Excellence award, Jewish Student Cmty. at Cornell Univ., 2005; named a Woman to Watch, Crain's Chgo. Bus., 2008; named one of 100 Most Powerful Women, Forbes mag., 2006—09, 50 Most Powerful Women in Bus., Fortune mag., 2006, 2007, 2008, 50 Women to Watch, The Wall St. Jour., 2006, 2008, Next 20 Female CEOs, Pink Mag. & Forté Found., 2006. Office: Kraft Foods Inc 3 Lakes Dr Northfield IL 60093*

ROSENFELD, ISADORE, cardiologist, educator; b. Sept. 7, 1926; arrived in U.S., 1958; s. Morris and Vera (Friedman) Rosenfeld; m. Camilla Master, Aug. 19, 1956; children: Arthur, Stephen, Hildi, Herbert. BS, McGill U., 1947, M.D.C.M., 1951, diploma in internal medicine, 1956, DSc (hon.), 1999; PhD (hon.), Tel Aviv U. Intern Royal Victoria Hosp., Montreal; resident Balt. City Hosp.; clin. asst. prof. medicine NY Hosp. Weil Cornell Med. Ctr., NYC, 1964—71, clin. assoc. prof., 1971—79, clin. prof., 1979—. Now hon. fellow; attending physician NY Hosp., NYC, 1989—, Meml. Sloan Kettering Cancer Ctr.; juror Lasker Sci. Awards, 1974—90; dir. Rsch. Am., 1990; Rossi Disting prof. clin. medicine NY Hosp. Weil Cornell Med. Ctr., 1993—; vis. prof. Baylor U. Coll. Medicine, 1982; mem. practicing physicians adv. coun. to U.S. Sec Health and Human Svcs., practicing physician, 1992—96; bd. overseers Cornell U. Med. Coll., 1980—; bd. vistors U. Calif. Sch. Medicine, Davis, 1983—; cons. NIH; invited lectr. Am. Coll. Physicians; lectr. in field; TV commentator in field; dr. Philosophiae Honoris Causa Tel Aviv U., 2002; trustee Nat. Health Mus., Washington, 2003; mem., Adv. Coun. Paul G. Rogers Soc. for Global health Research, 2006; mem. Lehman Coll. Sci. Faculty Adv. Com., 2006; chmn., bd. of trustee Sackler Sch. of Medicine, NYC, 2007. Author: EKG and X-Ray in Diseases of the Heart, 1963, The Complete Medical Exam, 1978, Second Opinion, 1981, Modern Prevention, 1986, Symptoms, 1988, The Best Treatment, 1991, Doctor, What Should I Eat?, 1995, Dr. Rosenfeld's Guide to Alternative Medicine, 1997, Love Now-Age Later, 1999, Power to the Patient: The Treatment to Insist on When You're Sick, 2002, Dr. Isadore Rosenfeld's Breakthrough Medicine, 2004, Healing Breakthroughs, 2004, Dr. Isadore Rosenfeld's Breakthrough Health, 2005; med. cons.: Vogue mag., 1993—97, FOX News Channel, 1996—; contbg. editor: Parade mag., 1997—; health editor:, 1998—. Pres. Rosenfeld Heart Found., NYC, 1974—; bd. dirs. N.Y. Heart Assn., 1979—82; mem. nat. adv. com. Harriman Inst. Advanced Study of Soviet Union, 1982—; mem. nat. adv. comm. increasing physical activity program Robert Wood Johnson Found. Recipient Vera award, The Voice Found., 1981, Inaugural award, N.Y. Heart Assn., Silver award for patient edn. and info., Nat. Health Info. Rsch. Chr., 1996, Citizen of the World award, U.N., 1999, Siver award, Nat. Health Info., 1999, Gold Triangle award, Am. Acad. Dermatology, Silver award, Nat. Mature Media awards, Dist. Med. Svc. award, Am. Physicians Fellowship, Merit award, Consumer Health Pub. Assn., Am. Consumer Publ. Assn. and Am. Consumer Publ. Corp, 2000, Advocacy award for impact on pub. opinion through the Media, Rsch. Am., 2001, Lifetime Achievement award, Found. Biomed. Rsch., Gold Triangle award, Am. Acad. of Dermatology, 2002, Silver award, Nat. Health Info. Rsch. Ctr., 2002, NPI Excellence in Immunization award, 2003, Maurice R. Greenberg Disting. Svc. award, NY Presbyn. Hosp., Well Cornell Med. Ctr., 2006. Fellow: Am. Physician's Fellowship for Israel (hon. nat. pres. 1975—), N.Y. County Med. Soc. (bd. censors 1979—83, v.p. 1983—84, pres. 1984—85, bd. trustees 1985—), Royal Coll. Physicians Can., Am. Coll. Chest Physicians, ACP, Cornell Alumni Assn. (hon.). Jewish. Achievements include research in hypertension; angina pectoris; sudden cardiac death; arteriosclerosis. Office: 125 E 72nd St New York NY 10021-4250 Home Phone: 914-251-0091. Personal E-mail: irmd@earthlink.net. E-mail: irmd@mac.com.*

ROSENFELD, JEFFREY VICTOR, neurosurgeon; b. Melbourne, Victoria, Australia, Nov. 19, 1952; s. Joseph Rosenfeld and Lorraine Behrend; m. Deborah Sarah Kipen, Oct. 23, 1988; children Hannah Elizabeth, Alexander Oscar, Gabriella Rebecca. MB, BS, U. Melbourne, Australia, 1976, MS, 1992, MD, 2006. Commd. lt. Royal Australian Army M.C., 1984, advanced through grades to maj. gen., 2009, sr. med. officer 4th Brigade, 2001—; registrar in neurosurgery Royal Melbourne Hosp., Parkville, Australia, 1985-88, asst. neurosurgeon, 1988-91, dep. dir. dept. neurosurgery, 1996—2000; registrar in neurosurgery Radcliffe Infirmary, Oxford, Eng., 1987; chief resident in neurosurgery Cleve. Clinic Found., 1987-88; head dept. neurosurgery Monash Med. Ctr., Clayton, Victoria, Australia, 1990-92; dir. dept. neurosurgery Royal Children's Hosp., Melbourne, 1993—; assoc. prof. pediat. and surgery U. Melbourne, 1997—; prof. neurosurgery U. Papua New Guinea, 2000—; staff officer grade 1 health adminstrn. Regional Health Support Agy., 1998; prof., dir. neurosurgery The Alfred Hosp. and Monash U., 2001—06; policy advisor to dir. gen. of Def. Health Svcs., Australian Def. Force, 2003—; dir. health res. Australian Army, 2005—06; prof., head dept. surgery Ctrl. Clin. Sch., 2006. Vis. rsch. fellow dept. surgery U. Melbourne, Parkville, 1981-91; vis. prof. Singapore Children's Hosp., 2002, Radcliffe Infirmary, Oxford, Eng., 2002, Sally Harrington Goldwater Meml. Barrow Neurol. Inst., Phoenix, 2003, others; adj. prof. Ctr. for Mil. and Vets. Health, U. Queensland, 2006—; hon. prof. dept. neurosurgery Capital Med. Scis. U., Beijing, China, 2006—. Author (with D.A.K. Watters): Neurosurgery in the Tropics, 2000; mem. editl. bd.: Jour. Clin. Neuroscience, Australian Def. Force Health Svcs. Jour., Am. Jour. Disaster Medicine; contbr. more than 170 articles to profl. jours. Corps surgeon St. John Ambulance, 1967—; commr. St. John Ambulance (Victoria), 2001—05. With Australian Mil. Decorated comdr. Order of St. John, Commendation medal USAF; recipient Geoffrey Harkness medal, RAAMC, 2001, medal, Centenary of Fedn., 2003, Michael E. DeBakey Internat. award, 2009; named Victorian of the Yr., 2002. Fellow: ACS, Royal Coll. Surgeons (Edinburgh) (Syme medal and Syme professorship 1991, King James IV professorship 2002), Australasian Coll. Tropical Medicine, Royal Australasian Coll. Surgeons (neurosurg. 1984—, Victoria road trauma com. 1991—, trauma com. 1993—, mem. bd. neurosurgery 1999—, Victorian state govt. trauma com. 2000—, gen. surg., John Mitchell Crouch Rsch. Fellowship award 2004); mem.: World Fedn. Neuro Socs. (mem. ethics com. 2006—), World Soc. Functional and Stereotactic Neurosurgery (pres. UN Assn. Australia, Victorian divsn. 2001—, v.p. UN Assn. Australia 2001—), Australasian Assn. Mil. Medicine, Internat. Soc. Pediat. Neurosurgery, Am. Assn. Neurol. Surgeons, Congress Neurol. Surgeons (USA), Neurosurg. Soc. Australasia (exec. com. 1999—, chmn. trauma com. 2001—), UN Assn. Australia (pres. Victorian divsn. 2001—04, nat. v.p. 2001—04). Avocations: music, wind instrumental performance. Office: Ste 5 4th Flr 517 St Kilda Rd Melbourne VIC 3004 Australia Business E-Mail: j.rosenfeld@alfred.org.au.

ROSENFELD, JOHN LANG, geology educator; b. Portland, Oreg., July 14, 1920; s. James Wendel and Gladys (Lang) R.; m. Juanita Baker, Oct. 22, 1943 (dec. Feb. 2004); children: Susan Jane, John Lang. AB, Dartmouth Coll., Hanover, NH, 1942; AM, Harvard U., Cambridge, Mass., 1949, PhD, 1954. Asst. prof. geology Mo. Sch. Mines, U. Mo., Rolla, 1949—55; vis. asst. prof. geology Wesleyan U., Middletown, Conn., 1955—57; from asst. prof. to prof. geology UCLA, 1957—91, prof. geology emeritus, 1991—. Commr. Geol. and Natural History Survey, State of Conn., 1955-57. Contbr. articles to profl. jours. Guggenheim fellow, 1963—64. Fellow Mineral. Soc. Am., Geol. Soc. Am.; mem. AAAS, Am. Geophys. Union, Nature Conservancy (life), Union Concerned Scientists. Office: UCLA Dept Earth And Space Scis Los Angeles CA 90095 Office Phone: 310-825-1505. Business E-Mail: rosenfel@ucla.edu.

ROSENFELD, ROBERT A., lawyer; BA in Pub. Affairs with highest distinction, George Wash. U., 1971; BA with first class honors, Oxford U., 1973; JD cum laude, Harvard U., 1976. Bar: Calif., US Ct. Appeals (7th and 9th cirs.), US Ct. Fed. Claims, US Supreme Ct. Law clerk for Honorable Marvin Frankel, 1976—77, Honorable Warren E. Burger, US Supreme Ct., 1977—78; atty., shareholder Heller Ehrmaer LLP, San Francisco, 1979—. Bd. dirs. Calif. Pacific Med. Ctr. Rhodes scholar, 1973. Office: Heller Ehrman 333 Bush St San Francisco CA 94104 Office Phone: 415-772-6609. Office Fax: 415-772-6268. Business E-Mail: bob.rosenfeld@hellerehrman.com.

ROSENFELD, STEVEN B., lawyer; b. NYC, Apr. 12, 1943; s. Eugene David and Laura (Sipin) R.; m. Naomi Eve Winkler, Aug. 21, 1965 (dec. Apr. 2006); children: Kathryn Anne, Elizabeth Jane; m. Joan Rappoport, June 3, 2007. BA, Columbia Coll., 1964; LLB, Columbia U., 1967. Bar: NY 1967, DC 1984, US Dist. Ct. (so. dist.) NY 1969, US Dist. Ct. (ea. dist.) NY 1970, US Ct. Appeals (2d cir.) 1971, US Ct. Appeals (3d cir.) 1974, US Ct. Appeals (Fed. cir.) 1978, DC 1979, US Supreme Ct. 1979, US Ct. Appeals (5th cir.) 1982, US Ct. Appeals (6th and DC cirs.) 1984, US Ct. Appeals (4th and 9th cirs.) 1987, US Ct. Appeals (1st cir.) 1989, US Ct. Appeals (10th cir.) 1991. Law clk. to Hon. Charles M. Metzner U.S. Dist. Ct. (so. dist.) NY, 1967-68; assoc. Rosenman & Colin, NYC, 1968-71; dep. gen. counsel NY State Commn. on Attica, NYC, Batavia, NY, 1971-72; assoc. Paul, Weiss, Rifkind, Wharton & Garrison, NYC, 1972-75, ptnr., 1976—. Lectr. Columbia U. Sch. Law, 1995—2002; chmn. Conflicts of Interest Bd. N.Y.C., 2002—. Contbr. articles to profl. jours. Bd. dirs. NY Assn. New Ams., NYC, 1973-95; trustee Dalton Sch., NYC, 1988-94; trustee Putney Sch. Putney, Vt., 1995-01, NY Theatre Workshop, 1996—; chair bd. visitors CUNY Law Sch., 2003—. Mem. NY State Bar Assn. (ho. of dels. 1996-98), Assn. Bar City NY (exec. com. 1992-96, v.p. 1998-99, past mem. various coms.), Legal Aid Soc. (pres. 1989-91, bd. dirs., exec. com. 1978-95). Democrat. Jewish. Avocations: opera music, chamber music, theater, tennis. Office: Paul Weiss Rifkind Et Al 1285 Ave of Americas New York NY 10019-6028

ROSENFELD, STEVEN IRA, ophthalmologist; b. NYC, Nov. 18, 1954; s. Frederick and Pearl (Stern) R.; m. Lisa Allyson Klar, June 24, 1978; children: Michael, Julie. BA, Johns Hopkins U., 1976; MD, Yale U., 1980. Diplomate Am. Bd. Ophthalmology, Nat. Bd. Med. Examiners. Intern Yale-New Haven Hosp., 1980-81; resident Barnes Hosp., St. Louis, 1981-84; fellow Bascom Palmer Eye Inst., Miami, Fla., 1984-85; ptnr. in pvt. practice Delray Eye Assocs., Delray Beach, Fla., 1985—. Clin. instr. Bascom Palmer Eye Inst., 1985-90, asst. clin. prof., 1990-96, assoc. clin. prof., 1996—; assoc. examiner Am. Bd. Ophthalmology, Phila., 1993—. Author: The Eye in Systemic Disease, 1990, Lens and Cataract, 1996; contbr. articles to profl. jours. Recipient Harry Rosenbaum Rsch. award Washington U. Sch. Medicine, 1984; named one of Best Doctors in Am., 1996—; Heed Ophthalmic Found. fellow, 1984. Fellow ACS, Am. Acad. Ophthalmology (chmn. B.C.S.C. section Lens and Cataract Surgery 2002-06, BCSC sect. Refractive Surgery 2006-, Honor award 1999, Sr. Achievement award 2007, Secretariat award 2007), Soc. Heed Fellows; mem. Castroviejo Corneal Soc., Eye Bank Assn. Am., Fla. Med. Assn., Fla. Soc. Ophthalmology, Assn. for Rsch. in Vision and Ophthalmology, Ocular Microbiology and Immunology Group, Phi Beta Kappa, Alpha Omega Alpha. Avocations: tennis, golf, fly fishing, lacrosse. Office: Delray Eye Assocs 16201 South Military Trail Delray Beach FL 33484-6503 Office Phone: 561-498-8100.

ROSENFELD, SUZANNE, pediatrician; b. NYC; d. Lester and Carol Rosenfeld; m. Henry Pollack, Aug. 24, 1986. BA, Sarah Lawrence Coll., Bronxville, NY, 1975; MD, Columbia U., NYC, 1980. Cert. in pediat. Am. Bd. Med. Specialties, 1986. Intern in pediat. Mt. Sinai Hosp., NYC, 1980—81; resident in pediat. Columbia U., 1981—83; resident Babies & Children Hosp. of NY; fellow Cornell U.-NY Hosp., 1983—84; clinical instr. pediat., asst. attending pediatrician NY-Presbyn. Hosp. Named to America's Top Doctors, 2006, NY Mag. Best Doctors, 2006. Office: 450 W End Ave New York NY 10024 also: 2 Fifth Ave New York NY 10021 Office Phone: 212-769-3070. Office Fax: 212-769-4703.

ROSENFELD, WALTER DAVID, JR., architect, writer; b. NYC, May 30, 1930; s. Walter David and Florence (Romann) R.; m. Marilyn Smith, Oct. 15, 1954; children: John W., Sarah E., Susannah, Elizabeth A. AB, U. Pa., 1952; postgrad., Ind. U., 1953-54, Yale U., 1954-55, 57-60. Registered architect, Mass.; cert. constrn. specifier. Draftsman, specifier Perry Dean Stewart, Boston, 1960-67; architect, specifier, v.p., prin. The Architects Collaborative, Cambridge, Mass., 1967-86, also dir., 1980-84; cons. architect Walter Rosenfeld CSI, Newton, Mass., 1986—. Author: The Practical Specifier, 1985; contbg. editor Progressive Architecture mag., 1980-94; contbr. articles to profl. jours. Pres. Friends of Newton Free Libr., Mass., 1970-72; chmn. Newton Ward 1 Dem. Com., 1974-80; vice chmn. designer sel. com. City of Newton, 1976-86; bd. dirs. Mass. Audubon Soc., 1987-99, Mass. Audubon Coun., 01—. Mem.

AIA, Constrn. Spcifications Inst. (bd. dirs. Boston chpt. 1980-86, pres. Boston chpt. 1987-88), Boston Soc. Architects. Office: Walter Rosenfeld CSI PO Box 568 Edgartown MA 02539-0568 Personal E-mail: walros@rcn.com.

ROSENFIELD, JAMES HAROLD, SR., communications executive; b. Boston, July 18, 1929; s. Harold and Beatrice (Garber) R.; m. Nancy Lee Stenbuck, Oct. 19, 1952; 2 children. BA, Dartmouth Coll., 1952; D of Comml. Sci. (hon.), St. John's U., 1981. TV network sales exec. NBC, NYC, 1954-57; advt. mgr. Polaroid Corp., Boston, 1956-59; v.p. mktg. Airequipt, Inc., New Rochelle, NY, 1959-65; TV account exec. CBS, Inc., NYC, 1965-67, dir. daytime sales, 1967-70, v.p. Ea. sales, 1970-75, v.p. network sales adminstrn., 1975-77, v.p., nat. sales mgr., 1977, pres. TV Network Div., 1977-81; exec. v.p. CBS/Broadcast Group, NYC, 1981-83, sr. exec. v.p., 1983-85; chmn., CEO John Blair Communications, Inc., NYC, 1987-93; pres. JHR Assocs., Consulting, NYC, 1993; mng. dir. Veronis, Suhler & Assocs., NYC, 1994-98; pres. JHR & Assocs., 1998—. Bd. dirs. Salon Interactive, Inc.; mem. adv. bd., instr., ptnr. Indycoast Ptnrs., 2008—; ptnr. Bluesky Entertainment Co., 2009—; chmn. Reisenbach Found. Emeritus nat. bd. dirs. Jr. Achievement, Inc.; past alumni trustee Roxbury (Mass.) Latin Sch.; bd. dirs., former chmn. Adv. Coun. With Signal Corps, AUS, 1950-53. Fellow: Internat. Acad. TV Arts (life); mem.: Internat. Radio TV Soc. (past pres.).

ROSENFIELD, LORNE KING, plastic surgeon; b. Winnipeg, Man., Can., Jan. 24, 1956; children: Lauren, Ian, Michael. BS in Medicine, U. Man., Winnipeg, 1976; MD, U. Man., 1980. Diplomate Am. Bd. Surgery, Am. Bd. Plastic Surgery. Resident in gen. surgery St. Mary's Hosp., San Francisco, 1985-87; intern. Mt. Zion, San Francisco; fellow in plastic surgery Baylor Coll. Medicine, 1987; tchr. U. Calif. San Francisco Med. Ctr., Stanford U. Hosps.; chmn. dept. plastic surgery Mills-Peninsula Hosp., Burlingame, Calif., 1995—, vice chmn. dept. surgery, 1997—. Past chmn. St. Mary's Hosp., San Francisco, 1992-95; expert cons. Med. Bd. Calif., 1997—. Mem. Burlingame/San Mateo C. of C. Fellow Am. Coll. Surgeons; mem. San Francisco Med. Soc. (mem. ethics com. bd. 1990-95), Rotary. Avocations: writing, photography, cooking. Office: Peninsula Plastic Surgery Inc 1750 El Camino Real Ste 405 Burlingame CA 94010-3217 Office Phone: 650-692-0467. Office Fax: 650-692-0110.

ROSENFIELD, ROBERT NORMAN, biology professor; b. Stillwater, Minn., Aug. 27, 1953; s. Harold and Louella Grace Rosenfield; m. Laura Jeanne Gissibl, Oct. 6, 2001; children: Alexandra Marie, Keeley McNeill. PhD, ND State U., Fargo, 1990. Contbr. articles. Achievements include research in description of natural history, population survey techniques and migratory biology of bird of prey species. Office: Univ Wis 800 Reserve St Stevens Point WI 54481 Office Fax: 715-346-3624.

ROSENGART, TODD KENNETH, cardiothoracic surgeon, researcher, neurosurgeon, consultant; b. Bklyn., Jan. 24, 1960; s. Martin Rosengart and Barbara Kodish; m. Debra Helen Rosengart, June 15, 1989; children: Michael, Eric. BS with distinction, Northwestern U., Evanston, Ill., 1981; MD with distinction, Northwestern U., Chgo., 1983. Diplomate Am. Bd. Surgery, Am. Bd. Thoracic Surgery. Intern in gen. surgery NYU Med. Ctr., NYC, 1983-84, resident in gen. surgery, 1984-85, resident and chief resident in gen. surgery, 1987-89; med. staff fellow NIH, Bethesda, Md., 1985-87; asst. thoracic surgeon N.Y. Hosp., 1989-90, thoracic surgeon, 1990-91; instr. Cornell U. Med. Coll., NYC, 1989-90, asst. prof. surgery, 1991-93, asst. prof. cardiothoracic surgery, 1993-97, assoc. prof. cardiothoracic surgeery, 1997—; assoc. prof. cardiothoracic surgery Weill Med. Coll. Cornell U., NYC, 1998—; assoc. attending cardiothoracic surgeon N.Y. Presbyn. Hosp., NYC, 1997-99; chief cardiothoracic surg. Evanston (Ill.) Hosp., 1999—; prof. surgery Northwestern U. Med. Sch., 1999—2006; head CT surgery Stony Brook U., SUNY, Stony Brook, NY, 2007—. Sr. registrar Hosp. for Sick Children, London, 1991; asst. Harley St. Clinic, London, 1991; tchg. asst. NYU Med. Ctr., 1988-89; asst. attending surgeon Jamaica Hosp., 1993-96; United Hosp. Med. Ctr., 1994—; attending physician N.Y. Hosp. Med. Ctr. of Queens, 1995—; mem. Ctr. for Vascular Biology, 1996—; assoc. attending cardiothoracic surgeon N.Y. Hosp., 1997, N.Y. Presbyn. Hosp., 1998—; vis. assoc. prof. surgery Columbia U., 1997—; vis. assoc. attending surgeon Presbyn. Hosp., 1997—; manuscript reviewer, presenter, cons. in field. Editl. bd. Cardiac and Vascular Regeneration: Angiogenesis and Myogenesis, Basic th Therapeutic, 1999—; contbr. numerous articles to profl. publs., chpts. to books; patentee gene transfer therapy delivery devide and method, perfusion and occlusion device and method. Nat. Merit scholar, 1977; recipient rsch. award A.G. Morrow Soc., 1987, 97; grantee miles Labs., 1992—, N.Y. Heart Assn., 1994-97, Datascope Corp., 1995—, Accu-Lase, Inc., 1995—, St. Jude Med., 1996—, Picower Found., 1996—, U.S. Surg. Corp., 1996—, Thoracic Surgery Found. Rsch. and Edn. 1997-99, OrthoBiotech, 1997—, Baxter Healthcare Corp., 1998—, NIH, 1998—. Fellow ACS, Am. Coll. Cardiology (Ill. chpt. alternate councilor 2002—), Am. Coll. Chest Physicians; mem. AAAS, Am. Fedn. Clin. Rsch., Am. Heart Assn. (sci. coun. on cardiothoracic and vascular surgery, met. Chgo. bd. dirs. 2002—, coun. cardiovascular surgery and anesthesia exec. com. 2002—, coun. cardiovascular surgery and anesthesia chmn. memership and comm. com. 2003—, coun. cardiovascular surgery and anesthesia program 2003—, mem., mktg. and comm. com. 2004—), Am. Soc. Gene Therapy (cardiovascular scientific com. 2003—), Nat. Assn. for Bloodless Medicine and Surgery (bd. dirs. 1997—), Andrew Morrow Soc. Cardiac Surgeons, N.Y. Soc. Thoracic Surgery (membership com. 1994-97, chmn. membership com. 1998—, program com. 1994—, chmn. program com. 1997-99), Soc. Thoracic Surgeons, Soc. Univ. Surgeons, N.Y. Acad. Scis., 21st Century Cardiac Surg. Soc. (pres. 1998-2000, membership chmn. 1995-96, v.p. 1996-98), N.Y. Soc. Thoracic Surgery (chmn., membership com. 2001-2002, workforse health policy, reform and advocacy 20003—), Chgo. Cardiac Surgery Soc. (chmn. orgn. com. 2002, pres. 2003-2004), Spencer Soc. Surgeons, Alpha Omega Alpha, Phi Rho Sigma. Office: Stony Brook Univ Med Ctr T19-030 Stony Brook NY 11794

ROSENGREN, ERIC S., bank executive; b. Ridgewood, NJ, June 3, 1957; BA in Econs., summa cum laude, Colby Coll., Waterville, Maine, 1979; MS in Econs., U. Wis., Madison, 1984, PhD. in Econs., 1986. Rsch. fellow Thomas Watson Found., Melbourne, Australia, 1979—80; teaching asst. U. Wis., 1981—84; dissertation fellowship gen. acctg. officer, Washington DC, 1984—85; economist, rsch. dept. Fed. Res. Bank Boston, 1985—89, asst. v.p., economist, rsch. dept., 1989—91, v.p., economist, rsch. dept., 1991—2000, sr. v.p., supervision and regulation dept., 2000—02, sr. v.p., supervision & regulation dept., chief discount officer, 2003—05, exec. sr. v.p., supervision & regulation dept., chief discount officer, 2005—07, pres., CEO, 2007—. Contbr. articles to profl. jours. Office: Fed Res Bank Boston 600 Atlantic Ave Boston MA 02210 Office Phone: 617-973-3090. E-mail: Eric.Rosengren@bos.frb.org.*

ROSENHAUS, DREW, professional sports agent; b. Oct. 29, 1965; BA, U. Miami, 1987; JD, Duke U., 1990. CEO Rosenhaus Sports Representation, Miami Beach, Fla. Co-author (with Don Yaeger): A Shark Never Sleeps: Wheeling and Dealing with the NFL's Most Ruthless Agent, 1988; film appearances include Jerry Maguire, 1996, Any Given Sunday, 1999. Office: Rosenhaus Sports Representation 6400 Allison Rd Miami Beach FL 33141 Office Phone: 305-936-1093. Fax: 305-864-3731.*

ROSENHEIM, DANIEL EDWARD, journalist, television news director; b. Chgo., Aug. 12, 1949; s. Edward W. and Margaret Morton (Keeney) R.; m. Christina J. Adachi, May 10, 1974 (div. 1979); m. Cindy Catherine Salans, June 20, 1980; children: Joseph Michael, James Salans, Nicholas Edward. BA, Wesleyan U., 1971. Factory worker, Pitts. and Chgo., 1972-77; reporter Sun-Jour., Lansing, Ill., 1977; bus./labor editor Hammond (Ind.) Times, 1977-80; bus. writer Chgo. Sun Times, 1980-82, spl. writer, 1982-84; bus. writer Chgo. Tribune, 1984-85; econs. editor San Francisco Chronicle, 1985-87, city editor, 1987-94, mng. editor, 1994-96; news dir. KRON-TV, San Francisco, 1996-2000, KPIX-TV, San Francisco, 2000—05, v.p. news, 2005—. Mem. adv. bd. News Lab, Project for Excellence in Journalism. Recipient Peabody award, 1997, James Batten award, 1997, RTNDA Regional award for Overall News Excellence, 2003. Mem. Soc. Profl. Journalists, Radio and TV News Dirs. Assn., San Francisco Tennis Club. Avocations: tennis, golf, book collecting. Office: KPIX-TV 855 Battery St San Francisco CA 94127 Office Phone: 415-765-8618. Personal E-mail: drosen7777@hotmail.com. Business E-Mail: rosenheim@kpix.cbs.com.

ROSENHEIM, DONALD EDWIN, electrical engineer; b. NYC, Mar. 23, 1926; s. Seymour Lawrence and Leah Rebecca (Rosenberg) R.; m. Judith Comfort Hyman, June 22, 1958; children— Micah Robert, Jay Aaron. BSEE magna cum laude, Poly. Inst. Bklyn., 1949; MS, Columbia U., 1957. Devel. engr. Servo Corp. Am., 1949-51; mem. rsch. staff IBM., 1951—, asst. dir. rsch. divsn., 1972-73. Dir. San Jose (Calif.) Rsch. Lab., 1973-83, dir. tech. coordination, 1983-84; asst. dir. Almaden Rsch. Ctr., San Jose, 1984-92 With USN, 1944—46. Fellow IEEE; mem. Sigma Xi, Tau Beta Pi, Eta Kappa Nu. Republican. Jewish. Home: 128 Smith Creek Dr Los Gatos CA 95030-2139 Personal E-mail: jdrosenheim@msn.com. E-mail: rosenheimjudydon@yahoo.com.

ROSENHOUSE, MICHAEL ALLAN, lawyer, editor, consultant, columnist; b. Chgo, Nov. 8, 1946; s. Seymour Samuel and Jeanne Mozette (Rosenthal) R. BA, Yale U., 1968; JD, U. Chgo., 1974. Bar: Ill. 1974, N.Y. 1982. Atty. pvt. practice, Rochester, NY. Mng. editor: Am. Jurisprudence, 2d edit., 1991—93, Am. Law Reports (Fed.), 1991—93; editor: (newsletter) Bank Employment Law Report, 1998—99; author: New York Pattern Jury Instruction Companion Handbook, 2008, Recent Ct. of Appeals Decisions Reflect Strict Interpretation of Procedure Requirements, 2003, Employment Law (Syracuse Law Rev.), 1998; columnist: The Daily Record, 2001—03. Chmn. bd. trustees Urban Choice Charter Sch., Rochester, NY, 2005; pres. Temple Beth El, Rochester, 2009—, trustee, 2008—. Mem.: ABA, N.Y. State Bar Assn., Monroe County Bar Assn. (co-chair Disability Labor and Employment Law Commn. 1998—99), U. Chgo. Club of Rochester (bd. dirs. 1999—2001), Yale Alumni Assn. (schs. com. 1997—), U. Chgo. Law Sch. Alumni Assn. (bd. dirs. 1977—80). Avocations: tennis, golf. Office: 16 W Main St Rochester NY 14614 Office Phone: 585-232-8500. E-mail: mar@rosenhouselaw.com.

ROSENKER, MARK VICTOR, former federal agency administrator; b. Balt., Dec. 8, 1946; s. Stanley and Irene (Moss) R.; m. Heather Beldon. BA in Communications, U. Md., 1969, postgrad., 1970-71; grad., USAF Air Command and Staff Coll., 1990, USAF Air War Coll., 1996, Air War Coll., Air Command and Staff Coll. Asst. to events producer, relief engr. ABC-TV News, Washington, 1968-69; dep. dir. radio and TV Com. Reelect Pres., Washington, 1972; staff asst. to sec. US Dept. Interior, Washington, 1972-73; account exec. Daniel Edelman Pub. Relations, Inc., Washington, 1973-75; dir. comm. Am. Moped/Motorized Bicycle Assn., Washington, 1975; dep. press sec. Pres. Ford Com., Washington, 1976; v.p. Electronic Industries Alliance, Washington, 1977—99; asst. exec. dir. for external affairs United Network for Organ Sharing, 1999—2001; dep. asst. to Pres. The White House, Washington, 2001—02, dir. Mil. Office, 2001—02; mem. Nat. Transp. Safety Bd. (NTSB), Washington, 2003—09, vice chmn., 2003—06, 2008—09, acting chmn., 2005—06, 2008—09, chmn., 2006—08; maj. gen. Air Force Res.; dep. asst. White House Mil. Office, 2001. Mem. bd. visitors Cmty. Coll. USAF, Maxwell, Ala., 1981-86; commr. Am. Battle Monument Commn., 1990-94.; bd. dirs. White House Mil. Office 2001, Sequa Corp. Active Campaign to Elect Reagan/Bush, Washington, 1980, 84, Campaign to Elect Bush/Quayle, 1988, 92—; sr. advisor Dole/Kemp Campaign, 1995-96, Bush/Cheney Campaign, 2000-01. 1st lt. USAF, 1969-72, maj. gen. USAFR, 1972-2006, ret. 2006., mem., bd. visitors Cmty. Coll. of the Air Force., v.p., Pub. Affairs Electronic Industries Alliance, mng. dir. Organ Sharing Washington. Decorated Air Force Disting. Svc. medal with oak leaf cluster, Legion of Merit, Meritorious Svc. medal with oak leaf cluster, Air Force Commendation medal, Joint Svc. Achievement medal, Air Force Achievement medal with oak leaf cluster, NASBLA Pres. award, 2007, Confluence award Am. Safe Boating Coun., 2005, 08; recipient Chuck Docekal Meml. award, 1987, Am. Battle Monuments Commn. Meritious Svc. medal, 1994. Mem. Res. Officers Assn. Club, Capitol Hill Club, Army Navy Club. Avocations: sailing, tennis, skiing, golf. Office: Sequa Corp 200 Park Ave New York NY 10166 Office Phone: 212-986-5500. Office Fax: 212-370-1969.*

ROSENKILDE, CARL EDWARD, retired physicist; b. Yakima, Wash., Mar. 16, 1937; s. Elmer Edward and Doris Edith R.; m. Bernadine Doris Blumenstine, June 22, 1963 (div. Apr. 1991); children: Karen Louise, Paul Eric; m. Wendy Maureen Ellison, May 24, 1992. BS in Physics, Wash. State Coll., 1959; MS in Physics, U. Chgo., 1960, PhD in Physics, 1966. Fellow Argonne (Ill.) Nat. Lab., 1966-68; asst. prof. math. NYU, 1968-70; asst. prof. physics Kans. State U., Manhattan, 1970-76, assoc. prof., 1976-79; physicist Lawrence Livermore (Calif.) Nat. Lab., 1979-93, lab. assoc., 1994-95, participating guest, 1995-97; chief scientist C.R. Sci., 1993-98; ret. Cons. Lawrence Livermore Nat. Lab., 1974-79; astronomy instr. Los Positas Coll., 1997; part-time instr. physics Bellarmine Coll. Prep., 1999-2000; full-time instr., 2000-04, Tchg. Opportunities Ptnrs. Sci., 2004—. Contbr. articles to profl. jours. Woodrow Wilson fellow, 1959-60. Mem.: NSTA, Math. Assn. Am., Accoustical Soc. Am., Am. Geophys. Union, Soc. Indsl. and Applied Math., Am. Astron. Soc., Calif. Math. Coun. C.C., Am. Assn. Physics Tchrs., Am. Phys. Soc., Sigma Xi, Phi Eta Sigma, Phi Kappa Phi, Phi Beta Kappa. Republican. Presbyterian. Achievements include research in nonlinear wave propagation in complex media, theoretical physics, fluid dynamics. Personal E-mail: carlrosenkilde@comcast.net.

ROSENKRANTZ, DANIEL J., computer science educator; b. Bklyn., Mar. 5, 1943; s. Harry and Ruth (Sirota) R.; m. Carole Jaffee, Aug. 2, 1969; children: Holly, Sherry, Jody, Andrew. BS, Columbia U., 1963, MS, 1964, PhD, 1967. With Bell Telephone Labs., Murray Hill, N.J., 1966-67; info. scientist GE Co. R & D Ctr., Schenectady, N.Y., 1967-77; prof. dept. computer sci. U. Albany-SUNY, 1977—2005, prof. emeritus, 2005—, dept. chair, 1993-99; prin. computer scientist Phoenix Data Systems, Albany, 1983-85. Author: (with P.M. Lewis II and R.E. Stearns) Compiler Design Theory, 1976. Fellow ACM (editor-in-chief jour. 1986-91, area editor for formal langs. and models of computation 1981-86, mem. spl. interest group on mgmt. of data, mem. numerous conf. coms., Sigmod Contbns. award 2001); mem. IEEE Computer Soc., ACM Spl. Interest Group on Automata and Computability Theory (sec. 1977-79). Office: U at Albany SUNY Dept Computer Sci Albany NY 12222-0001 Home: 6882 Milani St Lake Worth FL 33467-5902 Business E-Mail: djr@cs.albany.edu.

ROSENKRANTZ, STEVEN JAY, lawyer; b. NYC, Feb. 4, 1965; s. Michael and Rhona Sue (Dasheff) R. BA, Rutgers U., 1987, JD, 1991. Bar: Pa. 1994, DC 1996. Rsch. assoc. Fedn. Am. Scientists, Washington, 1993-94; rsch. asst. U.S. Dept. Justice, Washington, 1994-95; fgn. affairs specialist U.S. Arms Control & Disarmament Agy., Washington, 1995-99; spl. asst. office of undersec. state arms control U.S. Dept. State, Washington, 1998-2001, fgn. affairs officer Office of Missile Def. and Space Policy, 2001—. Mem.: Am. Constitution Soc., Mid. East Inst., Phi Beta Kappa. Avocations: history, classical music, fencing, reading, chess. Office: US Dept State Office Missile Def and Spa Washington DC 20520 Home: 1220 Blair Mill Rd Apt 1009 Silver Spring MD 20910 Office Phone: 202-647-8140. Business E-Mail: rosenkrantzsj@state.gov.

ROSENKRANZ, ROBERT BERNARD, military officer; b. Paterson, NJ, Sept. 26, 1939; s. Irving Morton and Lucille (Kane) R.; m. Barbara Jean Larson, May 17, 1970; children: Stephen Robert, Deborah Anne, Diana Rebecca, Susan Leslie. BS, U.S. Mil. Acad., 1961; MA, U. Pa., 1969. Commd. 2d. lt. U.S. Army, 1961, advanced through grades to maj. gen., 1992, officer Fed. Republic of Germany, 1962-65, bn. exec. officer Republic of Korea, 1973-74, battery comdr. Vietnam, 1966-67, bn. and brigade comdr. Germany, 1977-79, 83-85; assoc. prof. U.S. Mil. Acad., West Point, NY, 1969-72; dir. soviet studies U.S. Army War Coll., Carlisle, Pa., 1981-83; sr. mil. asst. under sec. of def. Pentagon, Washington, 1986-88; dep. dir. Army Ops., Readiness and Mobilization U.S. Army Pentagon, Washington, 1988-89, dir. force programs, 1989-92; comdr. U.S. Army Optec, Washington, 1992-95; sr. v.p. range and logistics svcs. Dyncorp, Reston, Va., also Ft. Worth, 1995-2001; v.p. force mgmt. and logistics MPRI, Alexandria, Va., 2001—04; sr. v.p., gen. mgr. BeamHit, Columbia, Md., 2004—05; v.p. bus. devel. KEI Pearson Inc., Arlington, Va., 2005; exec. v.p. Dyncorp Internat., Falls Church, Va., 2005—. Decorated Bronze Star, Air medal; recipient Superior Svc. medal U.S. Dept. Def., 1988, D.S.M., 1992, 95. Mem.: Nat. Def. Indsl. Assn., Internat. Test and Evaluation Assn., Assn. of the U.S. Army, Internat. Inst. Strategic Studies. Republican. Jewish. Avocations: jogging, reading, woodworking, golf, racquetball. Home: 3222 Wynford Dr Fairfax VA 22031-2828 Office Phone: 571-722-0238. E-mail: bob.rosenkranz@dyn-intl.com, rrosen007@aol.com.

ROSENMAN, KENNETH D., medical educator; b. NYC, Feb. 25, 1951; AB, Cornell U., 1972; MD, NY Med. Coll., 1975. Bd. cert. internal medicine; bd. cert. occupational and preventive medicine. Asst. prof. U. Mass., Amherst, 1979-81; dir. occupational and environ. health N.J. Dept. Health, Trenton, 1981-86; pvt. practice Plainsboro, NJ, 1986-88; assoc. prof. Mich. State U., East Lansing, 1988-93, prof., 1993—. Office: Mich State U 117 W Fee Hall East Lansing MI 48824-1316 Office Phone: 517-353-1846. E-mail: rosenman@msu.edu.

ROSENN, HAROLD, lawyer; b. Plains, Pa., Nov. 4, 1917; s. Joseph and Jennie (Wohl) R.; m. Sallyanne Frank, Sept. 19, 1948; 1 child, Frank Scott. BA, U. Mich., Ann Arbor, 1939, JD, 1941; LLD, Coll. Misericordia, Dallas, Pa., 1991. Bar: Pa. 1942, U.S. Supreme Ct. 1957. Ptnr. Rosenn & Rosenn, Wilkes Barre, Pa., 1948-54, Rosenn, Jenkins & Greenwald, Wilkes Barre, 1954-87, of counsel, 1988—. Mem. Pa. State Bd. Law Examiners, 1983-93, Pa. Gov.'s Justice Commn., 1968-73, Pa. Crime Commn., 1968-73, Fed. Jud. Nominating Com., Pa., 1977-79, Appellate Ct. Nominating Com., Pa., 1979-81; asst. dist. atty. Luzerne County, Pa., 1952-54. Chmn. United Jewish Appeal Campaign of Wyo. Valley, 1956, 1984, 2003, ARC, Wilkes-Barre, 1959, chair, 1963—65, life bd. dirs., 1991—; pres. Pa. Coun. on Crime and Delinquency, Harrisburg, 1969—71; chmn. United Way Campaign of Wyo. Valley, 1975, chmn. of bd., 1978—80; hon. mem., bd. dirs. N.E. Pa. Philharmonic, 2005; trustee mem. Wyoming Valley Vets. Hosp. Fund, 2002—; pres. Temple Israel of Wilkes Barre, 1972—74, chmn. bd., 1974—84, life bd. dir.; bd. dir. Coll. Misericordia, Dallas, Pa., 1976—86, emeritus, 1986—; bd. dir. Hoyt Libr., Kingston, Pa., 1971—78, Nat. Coun. on Crime and Delinquency, NYC, 1969—71, Jewish Cmty. Ctr., Wilkes-Barre, 1964—66, Keystone State Games, Jewish Fedn. Bd. of Greater Wilkes-Barre, St. Vincent de Paul Soup Kitchen, 1987—2000; trustee Wilkes-Barre and Wyoming Valley Vets. Hosp. Fund, 2003; comdr. Post 395 Am. Legion, Kingston, 1947—48. Capt. USAAF, 1942—45, ETO. Decorated Medal with Six Bronze Stars US Army Air Force, Eng., European Combatant Cross French Govt.; recipient Erasmus medal, Dutch Govt., Disting. Svc. award in trusteeship, Assn. Governing Bds., Univs. and Colls., 1990, Disting. Cmty. Svc. award, Greater Wilkes-Barre Soc. Fellows Anti-Defamation League, 1991, Clara Barton Honor award, Wyo. Valley Chpt. ARC, 1992, Lifetime Achievement award, United Way of Wyo. Valley, 1992, Outstanding Vol. Fundraiser award, Greater Pocono chpt. Nat. Soc. Fundraising Execs., 1995, honoree, Wyo. Valley Interfaith Coun., 1986, Ethics Inst. N.E. Pa., 2001, 11 Gallon Blood Donor award, ARC, inductee, Jr. Achievement Hall of Fame for N.E. Pa., 1997, Pres. award, Luzerne County Bar, 2003; named Golden Key Vol. of Yr., United Way of Pa., 1989; Presdl. Citation grant, Gen. Ira Eaker, 1944. Mem. ABA, Pa. Bar Assn., Am. Judicature Soc., The Pa. Soc., B'nai B'rith (pres. Wilkes Barre 1952-53, Cmty. Svc. award 1976), U. Mich. Club N.E. Pa. (pres. 1946-76), Westmoreland Club (Wilkes-Barre) Soc. U. Mich., Cavaedium Soc. U. Mich. Law Sch. Republican. Jewish. Office Phone: 570-826-5600. Office Fax: 570-831-7211. Business E-Mail: hrosenn@rjglaw.com. E-mail: hr@rjg.com.

ROSENOW, JOHN EDWARD, foundation executive; b. Lincoln, Nebr., Sept. 15, 1949; s. Lester Edward and Lucille Louise (Koehler) R.; m. Nancy Kay Hadley; children: Matthew, Stacy. BS in Agrl. Engring., U. Nebr., 1971. Dir. of tourism Nebr. Dept. Econ. Devel., Lincoln, 1971-79, interim dept. dir., 1985; founder Nat. Arbor Day Found., 1972, exec. dir. million-mem. Lincoln and Nebraska City, 1979-94, pres., 1994—. Co-author: (book) Tourism: the good, the bad, and the ugly, 1979. Democrat. Mem. United Ch. of Christ. Office: Nat Arbor Day Found 211 N 12th St Lincoln NE 68508-1422 Office Phone: 888-448-7337.

ROSENOW, MITCHELL PAUL, sound recording engineer, studio owner, musician, music producer; s. Richard Vernon and Norma Mae Rosenow; m. Ronette Shaleen Dizmang, Nov. 25, 1983; 1 child, Francis (Frank) Vernon. GED, Manhattan Vocat. Tech. Sch., Kans., 1971. Sound sys. design engr. Silvertrain Sound, Lawrence, Kans., 1974—76; self-employed audio engr. Interlace Video, Sunflower Cablevision, HBO, Cinemax, NBC, ABC, CBS, ESPN, Fox, Raycom, Time Warner Cable, various Fortune 500 teleconfs. nationwide, Lee's Summit, Mo., 1975—; sound engr. various local bands Kansas City area, Kans., 1975—80; monitor engr. Amazing Rhythm Aces, Memphis, 1976; audio engr., music show prodr. Columbine Cablevision, Ft. Collins, Colo., 1980—81; rec. engr. Little Apple Studio, Manhattan, Kans., 1981—83;

chief audio engr. Interlace Video, Lenexa, Kans., 1987—89. Cons. in rec. and live sound nationwide, 1987—; cons. in audio design TV remote facilities nationwide, 1987—. Rec. engr. (TV series) Bring It All Back Home (Cable Ace award, 1978); engineer: (DVD) Motivating Moves for People with Parkinson's (U. Continuing Edn. Assn. Nat. Outstanding Program award, 2004). Mem.: Broadcast Music, Inc., Soc. Electro-Acoustic Music US, Internat. Brotherhood Elec. Workers Local 53 radio and TV divsn., Audio Engring. Soc. Personal E-mail: info@bandedmoon.com.

ROSENSAFT, LESTER JAY, management consultant, lawyer; b. Leominster, Mass., Jan. 11, 1958; s. Melvin and Beatrice (Golombek) Rosensaft; m. Elizabeth Amanda Lahti, July 29, 1992 (div. 2004); 1 child, Mia Elisabeth. BS in Econs., Wharton Sch., U. Pa., 1978; JD, MBA, Case Western Res. U., 1981; LLM in Corp. Law with high honors, NYU, 1983. Bar: Ohio 1981, U.S. Dist. Ct. (no. dist.) Ohio 1982, U.S. Dist. Ct. (all dists.) N.Y. 1982, Mass. 1992. With Cons. to Mgmt., Inc., Cleve., NYC, Boston, Hong Kong, 1977—, v.p., 1977—80, pres., 1980—83, chmn., 1983—85; pvt. practice specializing in corp. and comml. law Ohio, 1981—. Mem. Hall, Rosensaft & Yen, Cleve., Singapore, 1981—90; reorganization law fed. cts., Ohio, 1982—, NY, 1982—; pres., CEO Eljay Devel. Corp., 1985—86; chmn., CEO Logistix Ltd., 1987—90; ptnr. Sanctuary Assocs., Boston, 1988—89; pres., CEO Union Meat Co., East Hartford, Conn., 1989—90, also bd. dirs.; pres. Golub Enterprises II, Inc., 1989—90, also bd. dirs.; COO CCC Fin. Orgn., Cleve., 1992—95, also bd. dirs.; pres., CEO ASA Comm., Inc., NYC, 1995—, also bd. dirs.; pres., CEO ASA Adminstrn., Inc., Chgo., 1999—, Greensboro, NC, 1999—, Toronto, 1999—, also bd. dirs.; mem. fin. and strategic planning com. ASA Acquisition Corp., also bd. dirs.; mem. ASA Mgmt. and Exec. Com., 1995—. ASA Investment Com., 1996—98; v.p. corp. devel. Paramount Sys. Design Group, Inc., NYC, also vice chmn. bd. dirs.; v.p., CFO Chipurnoi Inc., Long Island City, NY, also bd. dirs.; v.p., CFO Kinnerton Industries, NYC, London, 1983—85; vice chmn., gen. counsel GIOIA Couture, Inc., Akron, Ohio, 1984—86, also bd. dirs.; chmn., CEO Invictus Ventures, Boston, 2005—; mem., bd. dirs. Artcraft Co., 2005—, Insight Edn., 2005—; mem. exec. com. bd. dirs. The Soffer Orgn., Pitts., 2007—. Co-author: Industrial Development Survey for City of Leominster, 1978; contbr. articles to profl. jours. Active Combined Jewish Philanthropies; participant 40th Anniversary II Pres.'s Mission, 1987; chmn. Region V Outreach Mission, 1988; vice chmn. Regional Campaign Leadership Mission, 1991; mem. Russian Resettlement Com., 1988—91, Maj. Gifts Gala Com., 1989, Leadership Mission to Ukraine, 2006, Boston Leadership Coun., The Carbon Found., 2007—; ednl. cons., advisor indsl. devel. and strategic urbanism; cons. federally funded biomed rsch. projects; mem. exec. adv. coun. Keene State Coll., 1984—88; assoc. alumni trustee U. Pa., 1991—95, active secondary com. ctrl. Mass., bd. govs. Cleve., 1992—95; bd. overseers, mem. pres.'s soc. Beth Israel Deaconess Hosp., Boston, 2003—, mem. adv. bd. Transplant Ctr., mem. fin. and devel. com., bd. dirs., 2004—, mem. bd. overseers; mem. exec. and leadership com., bd. dirs. Horizon for Homeless Children, Boston, 2007—; mem. Boston Leadership Coun. Caron Found., 2007—. Recipient Grand award, APEX, 1999, Best of Show award, ESMA, 1999, numerous ACE awards, Silver and Gold Quill awards, 1996—99, Cronite Cup award. Mem.: ABA, Coll. Firm Prins., Coun. Cons. Orgns., Inst. Mgmt. Cons. (cert.), Soc. Profl. Mgmt. Cons., Internat. Soc. Strategic Planning Cons., N.Y.C. Reorganization Roundtable, Bankruptcy Lawyers Bar Assn., Assn. Bar City of N.Y., Ohio State Bar Assn., Greater Cleve. Bar Assn., Turnaround Mgmt. Assn., Assn. Corp. Growth, North Ctrl. Mass. C. of C. (indsl. devel. com. 1984—86), Belmont Country Club, Boca Pointe Golf and Racquet Club, Phi Alpha Delta (vice justice).

ROSENSAFT, MENACHEM ZWI, lawyer, writer, foundation administrator; b. Bergen-Belsen, Germany, May 1, 1948; arrived in U.S., 1958, naturalized, 1962; s. Josef and Hadassah (Bimko) Rosensaft; m. Jean Bloch, Jan. 13, 1974; 1 child, Joana Deborah (Jodi). BA, MA, Johns Hopkins U., 1971, Columbia U., 1975, JD, 1979. Bar: NY 1980. Adj. lectr. dept. Jewish studies CCNY, 1972-74, professorial fellow, 1974-75; rsch. fellow Am. Law Inst., 1977-78; law clk. to judge US Dist. Ct. (so. dist.) NY, NYC, 1979-81; assoc. Proskauer, Rose, Goetz & Mendelsohn, NYC, 1981-82, Kaye, Scholer, Fierman, Hays & Handler, NYC, 1982-89; v.p., sr. assoc. counsel Chase Manhattan Bank, NYC, 1989-93; spl. counsel Hahn & Hessen, NYC, 1994-95; sr. internat. counsel Ronald S. Lauder Found., NYC, 1995-97; exec. v.p. Jewish Renaissance Found., Inc., NYC, 1996-2000; ptnr. Ross & Hardies, NYC, 2000—03, McGuire Woods LLP, NYC, 2003; spl. counsel Van Der Moolen Specialists USA, LLC, NYC, 2004, sr. legal counsel, 2004—05, gen. counsel, 2005—07. Adj. prof. law Cornell Law Sch., 2008—. Author: Moshe Sharett Statesman of Israel, 1966, Not Backward to Belligerency, 1969, (poetry) Fragments, Past and Future, 1968; editor: Bergen Belsen Youth Mag., 1965, Life Reborn, Jewish Displaced Persons 1945-1951, 2001; book review editor Columbia Jour. Transnational Law, 1978—79; co-editor (with Yehuda Bauer): (book) Antisemitism: Threat to Western Civilization, 1988; contbg. editor: Reform Judaism, 1993—2002; contbr. articles to newspapers and profl. jours.; chmn. editl. bd.: Holocaust Survivors' Memoirs Project, 2000—. Chmn. Internat. Network Children Jewish Holocaust Survivors, 1981—84, founding chmn., 1984—; nat. pres. Labor Zionist Alliance, 1988—91; v.p. Am. Gathering of Jewish Holocaust Survivors and Their Descendants, 2007—; chmn. commn. human rights World Jewish Congress, 1986—, chmn. exec. com. Am. sect., 1986—90, gen. counsel, 2009—, 2009—; mem. Gen. Coun. World Zionist Orgn., 1987—92; mem. U.S. Holocaust Meml. Coun., 1994—2004, chmn. content com., 1994—2000, chmn. collections and acquisitions com., 1996—2000, chmn. task force on procs. for com. on conscience, 1996, mem. exec. com., 1996—2003, chmn. governance com., 2001—02; bd. dirs., exec. com. Nat. Com. for Labor Israel, 1988—91, 1995—2001; mem. Am. Zionist Tribunal, 1988—90, chmn., 1990; sec. Am. Zionist Fedn., 1990—93; bd. dirs. Am. Jewish Joint Distbn. Com., 1988—91; mem. exec. com. Nat. Jewish Cmty. Rels. Adv. Coun., 1994—97; organizer, leader demonstration in Germany against Pres. Reagan's visit to Bitburg Cemetery and Bergen-Belsen concentration camp, 1985; del. meeting on recognition of Israel between five Am. Jews and leaders of Palestine Liberation Orgn. Stockholm, 1988; mem. NYC Holocaust Meml. Commn., 1982—96, chmn. collections com., 1987—89; spl. counsel Elie Wiesel Found. Humanity, 2007—08; mem. NY County Dem. Com., 1981—85; mem. nat. adv. bd. United Synagogue Conservative Judaism, 1995—2002, also chmn. United Synagogue del. to Nat. Jewish Cmty. Rels. Adv. Coun., 1994—97; pres. Park Ave. Synagogue, NYC, 2003—08, hon. pres., 2008—, sec., 1988—2003, trustee, 1994—; chmn. Sherr Inst. Adult Jewish Studies, 1993—2002. Recipient Parker Sch. recognition of achievement with honors in internat. and fgn. law, 1979, Abraham Joshua Heschel Peace award, 1989, 40th Anniversary medal, City of Warsaw, 1999, commendation Jewish Heritage Week, Comptr. NYC, 1999, Elie Wiesel Holocaust Remembrance award, Israel Bonds, 2003, Simon Rockower award for excellence in feature writing, 2006; Harlan Fiske Stone scholar, Columbia U. Law Sch., 1977—79. Mem.: ABA, Phi Beta Kappa. Jewish. Home: 179 E 70th St New York NY 10021-5109 Office: World Jewish Congress 501 Madison Ave 17th Fl New York NY 10022 Office Phone: 212-755-5770. Personal E-mail: mzrosensaft@yahoo.com. Business E-Mail: mrosensaft@wjcmail.org.

ROSENSCHEIN, GUY RAOUL, pediatric and visceral surgeon, airline pilot; b. July 28, 1953; s. Maurice and Caroline (Meller) R. MD, Lariboisiere-St. Louis, Paris, 1977. Qualified airline transport pilot; FAA-approved aviation med. examiner, flight instr. Intern Hosp. St.-Louis, 1973-74, Hosp. Lariboisière, 1975-76; resident Hosp. de Paris, 1977-80, Hosp. Bretonneau, 1977-78, Hosp. Lariboisière, 1979-80, Hosp. de Monaco, Monte Carlo, 1980-81, Hosp. St. Vincent de Paul, Paris, 1981-82, attache, 1982-84, asst., 1984-86, asst. prof. pediat. surgery; chef de clinique U. Paris, 1984-86; attache Hosp. de Villeneuve St. Georges, 1987-94, C.H.S. Saine Anne, Paris, 1982-94; maitre de stage hospitalier Faculty Med. de Creteil, 1987-92; profl. transport instr., 1993; attending pediat. surgery Maimonides Med. Ctr., 1994-97, S.I. Univ. Hosp., 1994-2000, St. John's Regional Health Ctr., Springfield, Mo., 2000, N.W. Med. Ctr., Springdale, Ark., 2001—. Pilot, 1981; asst. clin. prof. of surger UAMS, U. Ark., 2003-, founder, ceo, instr. NY Helicopter Flight Svcs., Springdale, 2006. Author: Pancreatite non traumatique et non infectieuse de l'enfant, 1982. Capt., M.C., French Armed Forces, 1977. Mem. Nat. Assn. Flight Instrs., TE Flying Club (chief flight instr. 1995-2000). Home: PO Box 395 Springdale AR 72765-0395 Office: Minimal Access Surgery Clinic 5230 Willow Creek Dr Springdale AR 72762 Office Phone: 479-927-3100. Business E-Mail: guy.rosenschein@gmail.com.

ROSENSHINE, ALLEN GILBERT, retired advertising agency executive; b. NYC, Mar. 14, 1939; s. Aaron and Anna (Zuckerman) Rosenshine; m. Suzan Weston-Webb, Aug. 31, 1979; children: Andrew, Jonathan. AB, Columbia Coll., NY, 1959. Copywriter J.B. Rundle, NYC, 1962-65, Batten, Barton, Durstine & Osborn, NYC, 1965, copy supr., 1967, v.p., 1968, assoc. creative dir., 1970, sr. v.p., creative dir., 1975-77, exec. v.p., 1977-80, pres., 1980-82, CEO, 1981-86, chmn., 1983-86, also dir., mem. exec. com.; bd. dirs., pres., CEO BBDO Internat., NYC, 1984-86; pres., CEO Omnicom Group, NYC, 1986-88; chmn., CEO BBDO Worldwide, NYC, 1989—2004, chmn., 2004—07, chmn. emeritus, 2007—. Lectr. Bklyn. Coll., 1961—65. Office: BBDO Worldwide Inc 1285 Avenue Of The Americas New York NY 10019-6028 Business E-Mail: allen.rosenshine@bbdo.com.*

ROSENSON, ROBERT SIDNEY, cardiologist, researcher; b. Chgo., Oct. 31, 1956; s. Ronald Howard and Arlene Rosenson. BA, Drake U., 1978; MD, Tulane U., 1983. Intern Brigham and Women's Hosp., Boston, 1983-84, resident in medicine, 1984-86; fellow in cardiology U. Chgo., 1986-89, rsch. assoc., 1989-90; assoc. prof. Rush Med. Coll., Chgo., 1990—. Bd. dirs. Preventive Cardiology Ctr., Cardiac Rehab., Lipoprotein and Hemorheology Rsch. Facility. Contbr. articles to Jour. Physiology, Chest, Biochem. Biophys. Rsch., Am. Jour. Cardiology, Gastroenterology, Jour. Am. Coll. Cardiology, Archives Internal Medicine, Arteriosclerosis and Thrombosis, Lancet, Jour. of AMA. Mem. epidemiology and atherosclerosis couns. Am. Heart Assn., Dallas, 1990—. Fellow ACP, Am. Coll. Cardiology (mem. prevention cardiovascular disease com.), Am. Coll. Chest Physicians (fellowship grantee 1991—), Am. Coll. Physicians; mem. Mended Hearts (med. liaison). Office: Rush-Presbyn-St Lukes Med Ctr 1653 W Congress Pkwy Chicago IL 60612-3833

ROSENSTEEL, GEORGE THOMAS, nuclear physicist, professor; b. Balt., Sept. 30, 1947; s. Walter St. George and Marie Emily (White) R.; m. Tsetsa Dankova. BSc, U. Toronto, Ont., Can., 1973, PhD, 1975. Can. fellow NRC, 1976-78; prof. physics Tulane U., New Orleans, 1978—, chmn. dept., 1985-91. Vis. fellow Brit. Sci. and Engring. Coun., U. Sussex, Eng., 1986; vis. prof. Nat. Inst. Nuclear Theory, U. Washington, 1992, Inst. Theoretical Physics U. Gent, Belgium, 1999. Contbr. numerous articles to profl. jours. Delivered grad. sch. commencement address Tulane U., 1987; recipient 7 grants NSF, 1979—. Mem. Am. Phys. Soc., Am. Math. Soc., Sigma Xi (young scientist award 1987). Office: Tulane U Dept of Physics New Orleans LA 70118 Home Phone: 504-738-0160; Office Phone: 504-862-3174. Business E-Mail: george.rosensteel@tulane.edu.

ROSENSTEIN, BARRY, hedge fund manager; s. Herbert Rosenstein; m. Lizanne Teitelbaum, Dec. 20, 1986; 3 children. BA, Lehigh U., Bethlehem, Pa., 1981; MBA, U. Pa. Wharton Sch. Bus., 1984. CPA. Investment banker Merrill Lynch, NY; prin. corp. takeovers Asher Edelman's Plaza Securities Corp.; mng. ptnr. Reatta Partners; founder, head investment & banking group Genesis Merchant Group; founder, mng. ptnr. Sagaponack Partners LP, 1996, JANA Partners LLC, 2001—. Bd. dirs. Cobra Electronics Corp., 2003—05, Copart, Inc., 2007—, Convergys Corp., 2009—, Marisa Christina, Inc., Pacific Wireless, Inc., Princeton Photo Network Inc., Revtech, Inc., Signs USA, TestAmerica, Inc., Tuneup Masters, Inc., UST Liquidating Corp. Named an 'The World's Billionaires' list, Forbes mag. Mem.: Phi Beta Kappa. Office: JANA Partners 201 Post St Ste 1000 San Francisco CA 94108 also: JANA Partners 200 Park Ave New York NY 10166 Business E-Mail: barry@janapartners.com.*

ROSENSTEIN, JAMES ALFRED, lawyer, mediator, negotiation facilitator; b. Phila., Jan. 4, 1939; s. Louis Charles and Natalie Selma (Stern) R.; m. Linda Merle Lederman, Sept. 7, 1969; 1 child, Judith Esther AB, Harvard U., 1961, JD, 1968. Bar: Pa. 1968. Assoc. Wolf, Block, Schorr and Solis-Cohen, Phila., 1968-76, ptnr., 1976-97; prin. Rosenstein Assocs., Phila., 1997—; of counsel Fineman Krokstein & Harris, P.C., 2009—. Mem. adv. com. task force on condominiums Joint State Govt Commn., Pa. Gen. Assembly, 1977-79; mem. condominium-coop. steering com. Phila. City Planning Commn., 1980-81 Contbr. articles to profl. jours. Trustee Jewish Fedn. of Greater Phila., 1977—2005, 2007-, mem. exec. com., 1989-97, 98-2002, chmn. com. on local svcs., 1986-89, sec., 1987-88, v.p., 1988-94, chmn. com. on allocations and planning, 1989-92; v.p. jewish Cmty. Rels. Coun., 1982-85, 89-90, 96-2000, pres., 2000-2002; trustee United Way of Greater Phila., 1979-84, bd. dirs., 1982-85, 91-97; pres. Hillel Greater Phila., 1981-83; vice chmn. Synagogue-Fedn. Coun. Greater Phila., 1995-97, chmn., 1997-99. Lt. USN, 1961-65. Mem. ABA (chmn. devel. and financing of condominium projects 1993-97), Pa. Bar Assn. (chmn. common interest ownership com. 1980-93, chmn. real property divsn. 1993-95, chmn. real property, probate and trust law sect. 1995-96), Phila. Bar Assn. (co-chmn. legis. rels. com. 1996-97, co-chmn. ADR com. 2003—2004), Am. Coll. Real Estate Lawyers, Coll. Cmty. Assn. Lawyers, Soc. Profls. in Dispute Resolution (co-chmn. comml. sect. 1998-2000), Coun. Jewish Fedns. (bd. dirs. 1986-98, chmn. com. on svcs. to aging 1991-94, chair nat. funding coun. 1996-98, exec. com. 1997-98), United Jewish Cmtys. Fedn. N.Am. (chmn. N.E. region 1998-2001), Assn. Conflict Resolution (pres. 2008-, philos. chap. 2003-2004, bd. dir. 2006-); PA Coun. Mediators (bd. dir. 2005-); Am. Jewish Com. (pres. Phila. & S. Jersey chpt. 2007-). Office: Mellon Fineman Krekstem & Harris Bank Ctr 1735 Market St Ste 600 Philadelphia PA 19103 Office Phone: 215-893-8709. Business E-Mail: lawyers@finemanlawfirm.com.

ROSENSTEIN, ROD J., prosecutor; b. Phila., Jan. 13, 1965; s. Robert Jacob and Gerry M. (Stoloff) R. BS in Econ., U. Pa., Phila., 1986; JD, Harvard U., 1989. Bar: Pa. 1989, DC 1992, Md. 2002, US Ct. Appeals (DC cir.) 1990, US Ct. Appeals (5th cir.) 1991, US Ct. Appeals (9th cir.) 1992, US Ct. Appeals (4th cir.) 1998, US Ct. Appeals (8th cir.) 2003, US U.S. Tax Ct. 2003, US Ct. Appeals (1st, 2d, 10th and 11th cirs.) 2004, US Supreme Ct. 2002. Law clk. to Hon. Douglas H. Ginsburg US Ct. Appeals (DC cir.), Washington, 1989-90; trial atty. Pub. Integrity Sect., Washington, 1990-93; counsel to dep. atty. gen. US Dept. Justice, Washington, 1993-94, spl. asst. crminal divsn., 1994-95, asst. US atty. dist. MD, 1997—2001, dep. asst. atty. gen. criminal matters, 2001—02, prin. dep. asst. atty. gen. tax divsn., 2002—05, US atty. Dist. Md. Baltimore, Md., 2005—; assoc. counsel Office Ind. Counsel, Washington, 1995—97. Office: US Attys Office 36 S Charles St 4th Fl Baltimore MD 21201

ROSENSTOCK, ARTHUR RICHARD, plastic surgeon, educator; b. NYC, Feb. 4, 1947; MD, U. Libre de Bruxelles, 1976. Intern, gen. surgery Metro Hosp.-NY Med. Coll., NY, 1976—77; resident gen. surgery NY Med. Coll., Valhalla, NY, 1977—81; fellow plastic & reconstructive surgery Med. Coll. Va., Richmond, Va., 1981—83; hosp. appointment, surgery, admitting privileges Stamford Cmty. Hosp., 1983—; clin. instr. Columbia Presbyn. Coll. Physicians and Surgeons, NYC, 2005—; private practice Stamford, Conn., 1983—. Mem.: Am. Soc. Plastic Surgeons, Am. Soc. for Aesthetic Plastic Surgery. Avocations: painting, photography, architectural design, fly fishing. Office: 1290 Summer St Ste 3100 Stamford CT 06905 Office Phone: 203-359-1959. Office Fax: 203-359-9344. E-mail: arosenstockmd@aol.com, arr52@columbia.edu.

ROSENSTOCK, SUSAN LYNN, orchestra administrator; b. Bklyn., Nov. 2, 1947; BS, SUNY, Cortland, 1969; MBA, So. Meth. U., 1977, MFA, 1978. Neval mgr. Columbus (Ohio) Symphony Orch., 1978—82; grants program dir., info. officer Greater Columbus Arts Coun., 1982-83, asst. dir. grants and adminstrn., 1983-84; dir. ann. giving and spl. events Columbus Symphony Orch., 1984-86, dir. devel., 1986-90, orch. mgr., 1990-98, gen. mgr., 1998—. Panelist Ohio Arts Coun. Music Panel, 1986, 87, NEA, 2002, Challenge Grants Panel, 1991, J.C. Penney Gold Rule Award Judges Panel, 1993, 94. Mem. Am. Symphony Orch. League (devel. dirs. steering com. nat. conf. 1987, 88), Nat. Soc. Fund Raising Execs. (program com. Ctrl. Ohio chpt. 1988-94, chmn. program com. 1993, 94, bd. dirs. 1993-95, treas. 1995). Office: Columbus Symphony Orch 55 E State St Columbus OH 43215-4203 E-mail: susanr@columbussymphony.com.

ROSENSTREICH, DAVID LEON, medical educator, immunologist, allergist; b. NYC, Nov. 16, 1942; s. Joseph S. and Gertrude (Tankenbaum) R.; m. Victoria Abokrek, June 13, 1965; children: Jonathan, Peter, Rebecca. BS in Chemistry, CCNY, 1963; MD, NYU, 1967. Intern, resident Bronx (N.Y.) Mcpl. Hosp. Ctr., 1967-69; clin. assoc. NIAID, NIH, Bethesda, Md., 1969-72; sr. investigator NIDR, NIH, Bethesda, 1972-78; vis. assoc. prof. Rockefeller U., NYC, 1978-80; prof. medicine Albert Einstein Coll. Medicine, NYC, 1980—, dir. div. allergy and immunology, 1980—. Dir. Bronx Asthma Project. Editor: Mitogens in Immunobiology, 1975, Cellular Functions in Immunity and Inflamation, 1980; assoc. editor Clin. Revs. in Allergy, 1987—, Annals of Allergy, 1994—. Comdr. USPHS, 1969-78. Fellow Am. Soc. Clin. Investigation, Am. Acad. Allergy and Immunology, Am. Coll. Allergy, Am. Assn. Physicians. Avocation: winemaking. Office: Albert Einstein Coll Med 1635a Poplar St Bronx NY 10461-1926 Office Phone: 718-405-8075.

ROSENSWEIG, DANIEL L., video gaming company executive; b. 1961; BA in Polit. Sci., Hobart Coll., NY, 1983. Assoc. pub. PC Mag., 1992—94, v.p., pub. NYC, 1994—96; pres. Ziff-Davis Internet Pub. Group, 1996-97; pres., CEO ZDNet, Inc., NYC, 1997—2000; pres. CNET Networks, 2000—02; COO Yahoo!, Inc., Calif., 2002—06; operating principal Quadrangle Capital Partners, 2007—09; pres., CEO Guitar Hero unit Activision Blizzard Inc., Santa Monica, Calif., 2009—. Bd. dir. Adobe Systems Inc., San Jose, Calif., 2009—. Mem. adv. bd. DonorsChoose.org. Office: Activision Blizzard Inc 3100 Ocean Park Blvd Santa Monica CA 90405*

ROSENSWEIG, RONALD ELLIS, chemical engineer, consultant; b. Hamilton, Ohio, Nov. 8, 1932; s. Herman and Deana (Meisel) Rosensweig; m. Ruth Evelyn Cohen, Sept. 5, 1954; children: Scott Elliot, Beth Ellen, Perry Ethan. BSChemE, U. Cin., 1955; SM, MIT, 1956, ScD, 1959. Asst. prof. dept. chem. engring. MIT, Cambridge, 1959-62; prin. scientist Avco Corp., Wilmington, Mass., 1962-69; pres., tech. dir., co-founder Ferrofluidics Corp., Burlington, Mass., 1969-73, also dir., 1969-85; rsch. assoc. Exxon Corp., Annandale, NJ, 1973-78, sr. rsch. assoc., 1978-85, sci. advisor, 1985-95; internat. rsch. chair Blaise Pascal, Paris, 1996-98; rsch. affiliate MIT, 2004—. Vis. prof. U. Minn., Mpls., 1980, U. Chgo., 1990, Weizmann Inst. Sci., Israel, 1997, HEIG, Yverdon-les-Bains, Switzerland, 2007. Author: Ferrohydrodynamics, 1985; contbr. articles to profl. jours. Recipient IR-100 award, Indsl. Rsch. Pubs., 1968, 1969, 1971; named Young Engr. of the Yr., Avco Corp., 1966, Disting. Engring. Alumnus, U. Cin., 1986; fellow, NSF, MIT, 1955—56. Mem.: AIChE (Alpha Chi Sigma award for Rsch. 1985), Internat. Steering Com. (chmn. 1977—92), Magnetic Fluids Conf., Am. Phys. Soc., Nat. Acad. Engring. Jewish. Achievements include patents in field. Home: 34 Gloucester Rd Summit NJ 07901-3023 Home Phone: 908-277-2846. Business E-Mail: rerosen1@verizon.net.

ROSENTHAL, ABIGAIL LAURA, philosophy educator; b. NYC, Mar. 2, 1937; d. Henry M. and Rachelle Rosenthal; m. John B. Bacon, 1982 (div. 1987); m. Jerry L. Martin, 1999. AB, Barnard Coll., NYC, 1958; MA, Columbia U., 1962; PhD, Pa. State U., 1968. Grad. asst. dept. religion Columbia U., NYC, 1960-61, sec. Seminar on Hermeneutics, 1960-61; tchg. asst. dept. philosophy Pa. State U., State College, 1962-64; asst. prof. dept. philosophy SUNY, Stony Brook, N.Y., 1968-71, Bklyn. Coll./CUNY, NYC, 1971-85; rsch. affiliate dept. traditional and modern philosophy U. Sydney, Australia, 1982-83; assoc. prof. dept. philosophy Bkly. Coll./CUNY, NYC, 1986-88, prof., 1989—. Author: A Good Look at Evil, 1987, Conversions: A Philosophic Memoir, 1994; editor: The Consolations of Philosophy: Hobbes's Secret; Spinoza's Way (Henry M. Rosenthal), 1989. Fulbright scholar Sorbonne, Paris, 1958-59; recipient Tow award Bklyn. Coll., 1996-97. Mem. Am. Philos. Asssn. Avocations: cafés, museums. Office: Bklyn Coll CUNY Dept Philosophy Brooklyn NY 11210 Personal E-mail: alr.martin@verizon.net.

ROSENTHAL, ALAN SAYRE, government official, lawyer; b. NYC, Sept. 30, 1926; s. Morris S. and Elizabeth (Ralph) R.; m. Helen Miller, Sept. 8, 1951; children: Edward S., Susan L., Richard M., James M. AB, U. Pa., 1948; LL.B., Yale U., 1951. Bar: N.Y. 1952. Asst. in instrn. Yale U. Law Sch., 1950-51; law clk. to U.S. Circuit Judge Henry W. Edgerton, Washington, 1951-52; atty. appellate sect., civil div. Justice Dept., 1952-72, asst. chief, 1958-72; adminstrv. judge atomic safety and licensing appeal panel AEC (now Nuclear Regulatory Commn.), Washington, 1972-91, chmn., 1972-88; adminstrv. judge pers. appeals bd. GAO, Washington, 1991-96, chmn., 1992-94; adminstrv. judge atomic safety and licensing bd. panel Nuclear Regulatory Commn., Washington, 1999—. Mem. ethics panel Montgomery County Bd. Edn., 1987-93; lectr. law U. Pa., 1981-83, Am. U., 1991-92. Pres. Kensington Elem.

Sch. PTA, 1966-67; pres. North Chevy Chase Swimming Pool Assn., 1974-76; chmn. trustees Cedar Ln. Unitarian Universalist Ch., 1970-71; bd. dirs. Montgomery chpt. ACLU, 1967-69. Served with USAAF, 1944-46. Recipient John Marshall award Justice Dept., 1969, Disting. Svc. award Nuclear Regulatory Commn., 1988. Mem. Order of Coif, Phi Beta Kappa, Pi Gamma Mu, Delta Sigma Rho Home: 3203 Kent St Kensington MD 20895-3210 Personal E-mail: rsnthl@verizon.net.

ROSENTHAL, ALBERT LESTER, dermatologist, educator; b. New Bedford, Mass., July 25, 1926; s. Myer and Ruth Naomi (Gourse) R.; m. Carol Ash, July 30, 1969; children: Robert, Jill, Bruce. BA magna cum laude, Tufts U., 1946, MD, 1951. Diplomate Am. Bd. Dermatology. Intern RI Hosp., Providence, 1951-52, asst. resident surgery, 1952-53; asst. resident dermatology Mass. Gen. Hosp., Boston, 1955-56; asst. in dermatology NYU, 1958-60; practice medicine specializing in dermatology Trenton, NJ, 1958—; attending dermatologist Mercer Hosp., 1958—, chief dermatologist, 1958-93; chief dermatology Helene Euld Hosp., 1973-85; assoc. in dermatology U. Pa., Phila., 1969-73; assoc. prof. dermatology Hahnemann Med. Coll., Phila., 1973-87, clin. prof. dermatology, 1987—; mem. staff Grad. Hosp. Pa., 1969-73, Hamilton Hosp., chief dermatologist, 1972-76. Contbr. articles to profl. jours. Trustee Friend of the NJ State Mus., 1972—, chmn. bd. trustees, 1980-82, v.p. fine arts, 1978-80; gov. appointee adv. coun. NJ State Mus., 1994-2000, exec. com., 2001-; adv. bd. Princeton Sr. Resource Ctr., 1997—, exec. com.; adv. bd. Am. Art Newark Mus., 1998-2002; mem. Mercer County Cultural and Heritage Commn., 1982-2000, chmn., 1984-2000; mem. Mercer County Open Space Preservation Commn., 1992-2000; founding mem. Leader's Soc. Dermatology Found., 1988; gov. appointee Bd. Trustees NJ State Mus., 2000—, exec. com. sec. 2002—. Served to capt., M.C., USAF, 1953-55. Mem. Am. Acad. Dermatology, Pa. Acad. Dermatology, Noah Worcester Dermatology Soc., Phila. Dermatology Soc. (pres. 1984-85), NJ Dermatology Soc., NJ Med. Soc., Mercer Med. Soc., AMA. Jewish. Office: 74 Franklin Corner Rd Lawrenceville NJ 08648-2102 E-mail: carosentha@aol.com.

ROSENTHAL, AMNON, pediatric cardiologist; b. Gedera, Israel, July 14, 1934; came to U.S., 1949, naturalized, 1959; s. Joseph and Rivka Rosenthal; m. Prudence Lloyd, July 22, 1962; children: Jonathan, Eben, Nathaniel. MD, Albany Med. Coll., 1959. Intern Buffalo Children's Hosp., 1959-60; resident in pediatrics Children's Hosp. Med. Center, Boston, 1960-62, resident in pediatric cardiology, 1965-68; asso. prof. pediatrics Children's Hosp. Med. Center and Harvard U. Med. Sch., Boston, 1975-77; prof. pediatrics C.S. Mott Children's Hosp., U. Mich., Ann Arbor, 1977—2006, assoc. dir. dept. pediatrics, 1989-92, dir. pediatric cardiology, 1977-97, prof. emeritus pediatrics, 2006—. Served to capt. M.C. USAF, 1962-65. Recipient Outstanding Clinician award (Pediat.), U. Mich., 2002, Disting. Svc. award, 2003, Founders award, Am. Acad. Pediat., 2003, Humanitarian award, Jewish Fedn., 2007, Meritorious Achievement award, AHA, 2008; Amnon Rosenthal endowed professorship, U. Mich., 1994. Mem. Am. Acad. Pediatrics, Soc. for Pediatric Rsch., Am. Pediatric Soc., Am. Heart Assn., Am. Coll. Cardiology, Am. Bd. Pediatrics, Am. Bd. Pediatric Cardiology (chmn. 1987-88). Office: CS Mott Children's Hosp Ann Arbor MI 48109-0204 Business E-Mail: amnonr@umich.edu.

ROSENTHAL, ANDREW MARK, newspaper editor; b. New Delhi, 1956; s. Abraham Michael and Ann Marie (Burke) Rosenthal; m. Mary Beth Bierut, Jan. 15, 1994. BA in Am. History, U. Denver, 1978. Police reporter The Rocky Mountain News, Denver; Moscow bur. chief AP; Washington correspondent NY Times, 1987—92, Washington bur. editor, 1992—97, fgn. editor, 1997—2000, nat. editor, 2000—01, asst. mng. editor, 2001—03, dep. editl. page editor, 2003—07, editl. page editor, 2007—. Office: The NY Times 620 8th Ave New York NY 10018-1618

ROSENTHAL, BERNARD MICHAEL, small business owner; b. Munich, May 5, 1920; s. Erwin Rosenthal and Margherita Olschki; m. Ruth Schwab, Nov. 18, 1969; m. Lilli Bohnke, Oct. 10, 1950 (div. 1964). BA, U. Calif., Berkeley, 1941. CEO Bernard M. Rosenthal, Inc., NYC, 1953—70, San Francisco, 1970—. Pres. Antiquarian Books Assn. America, 1968—70. Contbr. articles to numerous profl. jours. With US Army, 1942—46. Recipient Hobert Howe Bancroft award, U. Calif., 2003, Medal, U. San Francisco, 2007. Mem.: Foxburohe Club, ABAA, Internat. Assn. Bbliophiles (hon.), The Old Book Table (hon.), Grolier Club. Avocations: skiing, hiking. Office: Bernard M Rosenthal Inc PO Box 5855 Berkeley CA 94705

ROSENTHAL, BERNICE GLATZER, history professor; b. Bronx, NY, Mar. 24, 1938; d. Morris and Frieda Glatzer; divorced; 1 child, Lara. BA, CCNY, 1959; MA, U. Chgo., 1960; PhD, U. Calif., Berkeley, 1970. Asst. prof. history Fordham U., Bronx, N.Y., 1970-76, assoc. prof., 1976-80, prof., 1980—. Editor, contbg. author: Nietzsche in Russia, 1986, Editor: Nietzsche and Soviet Culture, 1994, editor and contbg. author The Occult in Russian and Soviet Culture, 1997, East Europe Reads Nietzsche, 1998, New Myth, New World: From Nietzsche to Stalinism, 2002. Grantee NEH, NCESS, others. Mem. Am. Assn. for Advancement of Slavic Studies. Avocations: theater, dance, fine dining and cooking. Office: Fordham U Dept History 441 E Fordham Rd Bronx NY 10458-9993 Office Phone: 718-817-3936. E-mail: rosenthal@fordham.edu.

ROSENTHAL, DOUGLAS EURICO, lawyer; b. NYC, Feb. 12, 1940; s. Jacob and Edna Louise (Muir) R.; m. Erica Switzen Kremen, Nov. 12, 1967; children: Benjamin Muir, Rachel Elizabeth. BA summa cum laude, Yale U., 1961, LLB, 1966, PhD in Polit. Sci, 1970; postgrad., Oxford U., Eng., 1962; MA, Columbia U., 1963. Bar: NY 1968, DC 1980, US Dist. Ct. DC, US Dist. Ct. (so. and ea. dists.) NY, US Ct. Appeals (D.C. cir.), US Ct. Appeals (2d cir.), US Supreme Ct. 1976. Project dir. Russell Sage Found., NYC, 1968-70; assoc. Fried, Frank, Harris, Shriver & Jacobson, NYC, 1970-74; asst. chief fgn. commerce sect., antitrust divsn. Dept. Justice, Washington, 1974-77, chief, 1977-80; ptnr. Sutherland, Asbill & Brennan, Washington, 1980-88, Coudert Bros., 1989-94, Sonnenschein, Nath & Rosenthal, LLP, Washington, 1994—2005, Constantine/Cannon LLP, Washington, 2005—. Adj. prof. Tokyo U. Law Sch., 1992; spkr. USIA, Australia, France, England, Canada, Germany, Japan, Portugal. Author: Lawyer and Client: Who's in Charge?, 1972, 2d rev. edit.; co-author: (with Donald I. Baker) US Dept. Justice Antitrust Guide for International Operations, 1977, (with William Knighton) National Law and International Commerce: The Problem of Extraterritoriality, 1982; co-editor (with Carl J. Green) Competition Regulation in the Pacific Rim, 1996. mem. bd. advisors Antitrust and Trade Regulation Report, 1989-, George Washington Jour. Internat. Law and Econ.; mem. editl. bd. CCH Merger Notification and Clearance in Can.; contbr. articles to profl. publs. Mem. Sedona Conf. Working Group on econs. and antitrust Inst. for Consumer Antitrust Studies, Loyola U., Chgo.; committeeman Nassau County (N.Y.) Dem. Party, 1963—65; lifetime mem. corp. Culinary Inst. Am.; mem. Brookings Roundtable on Trade and Investment; mem. trade and competition com. Internat. C. of C. Recipient Edward S. Corwin Nat. Award Am. Polit. Sci. Assn., 1971; Henry Fellow Balliol Coll., Oxford U., 1962, Nobel Internat. and Woodrow Wilson Fellow Columbia U., 1963. Mem. ABA (antitrust sect.), Coun. Fgn. Rels., Am. Law Inst. (life, adv. com. law governing lawyers), Confrerie des Chevaliers du Tastevin, Mory's Assn., Phi Beta Kappa. Jewish. Achievements include being lead attorney in 19 major international antitrust litigations. Office: 1627 Eye St NW Washington DC 20006 Office Phone: 202-204-3510. Business E-Mail: drosenthal@constantinecannon.com.

ROSENTHAL, EDWARD CHARLES, management science educator; m. Bryony R.V. Kay; 2 children. BS in Math., SUNY, Albany, 1980; MS in Indsl. Engrng. and Mgmt. Sci., Northwestern U., 1981, PhD in Indsl. Engrng. and Mgmt. Sci., 1985. Asst. prof. Temple U., Phila., 1985—91, assoc. prof., 1991—. Contbr. articles to profl. jours.; author: The Era of Choice. Recipient Lindback award for disting. tchg. Mem.: Inst. for Ops. Rsch. and the Mgmt. Scis. Office: Fox Sch Bus and Mgmt Temple Univ Philadelphia PA 19122 Business E-Mail: edward.rosenthal@temple.edu.

ROSENTHAL, HOWARD GARY, psychotherapist, educator, author; b. St. Louis; s. Merle Lewis and Shirley (Partegyl) R.; m. Patricia Rosenthal, June 7, 1987. AA, Florissant Valley Coll., 1972; BA in Psychology, U. Mo., St. Louis, 1974, MEd in Counseling, 1976; EdD in Counseling, St. Louis U., 1981. Psychotherapist Mid-West Stress Ctr., St. Charles, Mo., 1987—. Psychotherapist Gen. Guidance Group, St. Louis, 1976—; prof., program dir. human svcs. St. Louis C.C., Florissant Valley, 1987—. Author: Not With My Life I Don't, 1988, Before Your See Your First Client, 1997, Favorite Counseling and Therapy Homework Techniques, 2001, Human Services Dictionary, 2003, Therapy's Best, 2006; (audio tapes) Audio Study Guide for Counselor Licensure, 1990, 2005; (video) Suicide Prevention Techniques That Work, 1991, The Encyclopedia of Counseling, 1993, 2002, spl. 15th anniversary edit., 2007; editor: Favorite Counseling & Therapy Techniques, 1997; contbr. articles to profl. jours. Recipient Mo. Juvenile Justice award, 1987, Emerson Excellence Tchg. award, 1998; named to Hall of Fame St. Louis C.C., 1988. E-mail: drhowardr@juno.com.

ROSENTHAL, HOWARD LEWIS, political science professor; b. Wilkinsburg, Pa., Mar. 4, 1939; s. Arnold Sidney R. and Elinor (Kaufman) (Rosenthal) Lewis; m. Annie Regine Lunel, June 30, 1960 (div. Nov., 1967); children: Illia Rebecca, Jean Laurent; m. Margherita Guastoni Spampinato, Feb. 6, 1968; 1 son, Gil Guastoni. BS, MIT, 1960, PhD, 1964. Asst. prof. polit. sci. U. Calif.-Irvine, 1965-66; asst. prof. and assoc. prof. polit. sci. Carnegie-Mellon U., Pitts., 1966-71, prof., 1971-93; Roger Williams Straus prof. social scis. Princeton U, NJ, 1993—2005; prof. polit. sci. NYU, 2005—; prof. emeritus Princeton U., 2005—. Vis. prof. Hebrew U., Jerusalem, 1968-69, U. Calif., San Diego, 1976-77, MIT, Cambridge, 1989-90, U. Paris I, 1990; Walras-Pareto lectr. U. Lausanne, Switzerland, 1996; vis. grad. lectr. Fondation Nat. des Scis. Politiques, Paris, 1972-73; disting. vis. prof. Brown U., 2003—05. Author: Prediction Analysis of Cross Classifications, 1977, Analysis of Ordinal Data, 1977, Partisan Politics, Divided Government and the Economy, 1995, Flexible Integration: Towards a More Effective and Democratic Europe, 1995, The Realignment of National Politics and Income Redistribution, 1997, Congress: A Political-Economic History of Roll Call Voting, 1997, Credit Markets for the Poor, 2005, Polarized America: The Dance of Ideology and Unequal Riches, 2006, Ideology and Congress, 2007; mem. editl. bd. Economics of Governance. Fellow NSF, 1969-92, 98-2003, 2006-, Ford Found., 1972-73, Social Sci. Rsch. Coun., 1964-65, nat. fellow Hoover Instn., Stanford U., 1979-80; Sherman Fairchild disting. scholar Calif. Inst. Tech., 1982-83; fellow Internat. Ctr. for Econ. Rsch., Turin, Italy, 1991-93, Ctr. for Advanced Study in Behavioral Scis., 1991-92, 98-99, ECARE U. Libre de Brussels, 1995, Russell Sage Found., 2002-03, 2005-, John Simon Guggenheim Meml. Found., 2002-03, 05-06. Fellow Am. Acad. Arts and Scis.; mem. Pub. Choice Soc. (Duncan Black award 1979), Am. Polit. Sci. Assn. (CQ Press award 1985). Office: NYU Politics Dept New York NY 10003 E-mail: hr31@nyu.edu.

ROSENTHAL, JACOB (JACK ROSENTHAL), foundation executive; b. Tel-Aviv, June 30, 1935; came to U.S., 1938, naturalized, 1943; s. Manfred and Rachel (Kaplan) R.; m. Holly Russell, Dec. 21, 1985; children by previous marriage: John, Annie; stepchildren: Christopher Russell, Andrew Russell. AB, Harvard U., 1956. Reporter, editor Portland Oregonian, Reporter, 1950-61; asst. dir., dir. public info. U.S. Dept. Justice, Washington, 1961-66; exec. asst. to Undersec. of State, 1966-67; Kennedy fellow Harvard Inst. Politics, 1967-68; nat. urban corr. Life Mag., NYC, 1968-69; urban corr. N.Y. Times, Washington, 1969-73, asst. Sun. editor, mag. editor NYC, 1973-77, dep. editor editl. page, 1977-86, editor editl. page, 1986-93; editor-in-chief N.Y. Times Mag., NYC, 1993-99; pres. N.Y. Times Co. Found., NYC, 2000—; chmn. ReServe, Inc., 2005—. Editor: Kerner Commn. Report on Urban Riots, 1968. Mem. Harvard Crimson Grad. Coun. Recipient Best Editl. award Internat. Labor Press Assn., 1961, Loeb award, 1973, Pulitzer prize for editls., 1982, Charles Loring Brace medal, 2002. Office: NY Times Co 229 W 41 St New York NY 10036-3959 Office Phone: 212-556-1092. E-mail: rosebud@nytimes.com.

ROSENTHAL, JAMES D., retired federal official, retired ambassador; b. San Francisco, Jan. 15, 1932; BA, Stanford U., 1954; student, Fgn. Svc. Inst., 1960—61, Nat. War Coll., 1974—75. With U.S. Fgn. Svc., 1956—90, adminstrv. officer Port of Spain, Trinidad and Tobago, 1958—60; polit. officer Saigon, Vietnam, 1961—65; mem. faculty U.S. Mil. Acad., 1965—67; internat. rels. officer Vietnam affairs Dept. State, 1967—70, dir. Vietnam, Laos and Cambodia affairs, 1975—77, dep. dir. mgmt. ops. Washington, 1986—90; mem. U.S. del. to Vietnam Peace Talks Paris, 1970—72; dep. chief of mission Bangui, 1972—74, Kuala Lumpur, Malaysia, 1977—79, Manila, Philippines, 1979—83; amb. to Guinea Conakry, 1983—86; exec. dir. Commonwealth Club of Calif., 1990—96. Lt. USMC, 1953—55. Personal E-mail: jrosent333@aol.com.

ROSENTHAL, JANE L., film company executive; b. Providence, Sept. 21, 1956; d. Martin and Ina; m. Craig Hatkoff; children: Juliana, Isabella. Student, Brown U.; BA, NYU, 1977. Rsch. staff CBS Sports, NY; editor program practices CBS Entertainment, 1977, program exec. miniseries LA, 1978, assoc. dir. motion pictures for TV, 1979; v.p. feature prodn. Universal Studios, 1984—85; v.p. in charge of motion pictures & TV The Walt Disney Co., 1985—87; v.p. in charge of movies and miniseries Warner Bros. TV, 1987—88; co-founder (with Robert DeNiro), ptnr. Tribeca Film Ctr., NYC, 1989—; co-founder Tribeca Film Festival, NYC, 2002. Prodr.: (films) Thunderheart, 1992, Night and the City, 1992, A Bronx Tale, 1993, Faithful, 1996, Marvin's Room, 1996, Wag the Dog, 1997, Analyze This, 1999, Entropy, 1999, Flawless, 1999, The Adventures of Rocky & Bullwinkle, 2000, Meet the Parents, 2000, Prison Song, 2001, Showtime, 2002, About a Boy, 2002, Analyze That, 2002, House of D, 2004, Stage Beauty, 2004, Meet the Fockers, 2004, Rent, 2005, The Good Shepherd, 2006, What Just Happened, 2008; (TV series) Tribeca, 1993; exec. prodr.: (films) Nine, 1996, The Repair Shop, 1998; (TV films) Witness to the Mob, 1998, Holiday Heart, 2000. Named one of The 100 Most Powerful Women in Entertainment, Hollywood Reporter, 2006, The 100 Most Influential Women in NYC Bus., Crain's NY Bus., 2007, The 50 Most Powerful Women in NYC, NY Post, 2007, 2008. Office: Tribeca Prodns 6th Fl 375 Greenwich St New York NY 10013*

ROSENTHAL, JOEL, chemist, researcher; b. NYC, Dec. 5, 1979; s. Peter Rosenthal and Christine (Giglio) Nanni. BS in Chemistry with honors, NYU, NYC, 2001; PhD, MIT, Cambridge, Mass., 2006. Undergraduate rsch. fellow NYU, NYC, 1998—2001; Fannie and John Hertz rsch. fellow MIT, Cambridge, 2001—06, postdoctoral NIH rsch. fellow, 2006—; rsch. asst. Cornell Med. Coll., NYC, 1995—98. Chemistry tchg. fellow NYU, NYC, 1999—2001. Editor: John W. Draper Chem. Soc.'s Ann. Jour.; contbr. articles to profl. jours. Recipient award for Sci. Achievement, NY Acad. Scis., 1997, Sustainable Chemistry award, MIT, 2006, Am. Inst. Chemists prize, 2001, Outstanding Tchg. award, NYU Coll. Arts and Sci., 2000—01, Harold Seidenstein award, 2000, Allison Huang Rsch. Conf. award, 2001, Dean's award for Scholarship, 2001; Trustee scholar, 1997-2001, Founders Day scholar, 2001, Nat. Def. Sci. and Engring. Grad. fellow, Dept. of Def., 2001, Myron Kove Rsch. grantee, NYU, 1999, Pfizer Summer Undergraduate Rsch. grantee, Pfizer Ctrl. Rsch., 2000. Mem.: Am. Chem. Soc. (assoc.), Phi Beta Kappa, Phi Lambda Upsilon. Achievements include research in role of the human gene CD36 in the development of aerteriosclerosis; photocycloaddition of cyclic enones to C60 and C70. Synthesized extended fullerine-triazine hybrids for the generation of long-lived photoinduced charge separated states; mechanistic role of Proton-Coupled Electron Transfer in small molecule activation and water splitting. Business E-Mail: jr330@mit.edu.

ROSENTHAL, LARRY W., cosmetic dentist; b. NYC, Feb. 14, 1948; m. Sandy Rosenthal; 1 child, Eric. DDS, NYU, 1972. Residency Montefiore Hosp.; dir. aesthetic continuum Baylor Coll. Dentistry, Dallas, U. Ky. Coll. Dentistry; dir. aesthetic continuum, Rosenthal Inst. NYU, Palm Beach CC, FMC/Eastman Dental Coll., London; dir. Aesthetic Advantage Inc., Rosenthal Group Aesthetic Dentistry, NY. Spkr. in field. Asst. editor: Am. Acad. Cosmetic Dentistry Jour., mem. editl. bd.: Compendium's CERP; featured in Vogue, Town & Country, W, Elle, Glamour, Forbes, NY Times, Wall St. Jour. and others; featured on: Inside Edit., The View, Vh1, Fox, CBS and others. Recipient Internat. Five-Star Diamond award, Am. Acad. Hospitality Sci., 2004; named one of Top Cosmetic Dentists in NY, NY Mag., 2004. Mem.: Am. Acad. Cosmetic Dentistry. Achievements include print features in Vogue Mag., Elle, Glamour, Town & Country, New York Times, and Wall Street Jour; TV appearances on Weekend Today, The View, Access Hollywood. Office: Rosenthal Group Aesthetic Dentistry 30 E 76th St Ste 5B New York NY 10021 Office Phone: 212-794-9600. Office Fax: 212-794-3644.

ROSENTHAL, LEE, electrical engineer, educator; b. Bklyn., Nov. 28, 1937; s. Louis Julius and Ida (Stern) R. BSEE, Poly. Inst. N.Y., 1958, PhD in Electrical Engring., 1967; MSEE, Calif. Inst. Tech., 1959. Asst. prof. Stevens Inst. Tech., Hoboken, N.J., 1966-70, Hofstra U., Hempstead, N.Y., 1970-72; prof. Fairleigh Dickinson U., Teaneck, N.Y., 1972—. Recipient Dow Outstanding Young Faculty award Am. Soc. Engring. Edn., 1973.

ROSENTHAL, LUCY GABRIELLE, writer, editor, educator; b. NYC; d. Henry Moses and Rachel (Tchernowitz) Rosenthal. AB, U. Mich., 1954; MS in Journalism, Columbia U., 1955; MFA, Yale Sch. Drama, 1961; postgrad. Writers Workshop, U. Iowa, 1965—68. Asst. editor Radiology mag., Detroit, 1955—57; free-lance editl. cons. various pub. houses, lit. agts. NYC, 1957—73; mem. admissions staff Writers Workshop U. Iowa, Iowa City, 1965—68; editor Book-of-the-Month Club, NYC, 1973—74, mem. editl. bd. judges, 1974—79, sr. editl. advisor, 1979—87. Mem. biography jury Pulitzer Prize, 1980; mem. bd. Am. Book Awards, 1981-82; adj. prof. English, NYU, 1986-2004; mem. guest faculty in writing Sarah Lawrence Coll., 1988-96, regular faculty writing, 1996—; lectr., adj. asst. prof. writing program Columbia U., 1990-96, Humanities faculty, 92nd St. YM/YWCA, 1987; fiction workshop The Writer's Voice, West Side YMCA, summer 1991; adj. prof. NYU Sch. Continuing Edn., 1988; mem. faculty Sarah Lawrence Ctr. for Continuing Edn., 1989, 90; instr. fiction writing course Art Workshop Internat., Assisi, Italy, summer 1993. Plays produced at Eugene O'Neill Meml. Theater Ctr., 1966, 1967; author: The Ticket Out, 1983; editor: Great American Love Stories, 1988, The World Treasury of Love Stories, 1995, The Eloquent Short Story: Varieties of Narration, 2004; contbr. fiction to Global City Rev.1995, 2008, articles and revs. to mags. and periodicals. Pulitzer fellow critical writing, 1968. Mem. Authors Guild, Authors League, Nat. Book Critics Circle, Women's Media Group (bd. mem. 1979-81), PEN Am. Ctr., Phi Beta Kappa, Phi Kappa Phi. Office: Sarah Lawrence Coll Bronxville NY 10708 Business E-Mail: lrosenth@slc.edu.

ROSENTHAL, LYOVA HASKELL See GRANT, LEE

ROSENTHAL, MICHAEL ROSS, retired academic administrator, consultant; b. Youngstown, Ohio, Dec. 2, 1939; s. Samuel Herman and Frances Vance (Schlesinger) R.; m. Linda Gabler, Sept. 6, 1963; children: Heidi, Erika, Nicolas Gabler. AB, Case Western Res. U., 1961; MS, U. Ill., 1963, PhD, 1965. Asst. prof. chemistry Bard Coll., Annandale, NY, 1965-68, assoc. prof. chemistry, 1968-73, prof. chemistry, 1973-84, assoc. dean acad. affairs, 1980-84; v.p. acad. affairs St. Mary's Coll. of Md., St. Mary's City, 1984-89; provost, dean faculty, prof. chemistry Southwestern U., Georgetown, Tex., 1989-96; dep. sec. Md. Higher Edn. Commn., Annapolis, 1996—99; spl. asst. to provost McDaniel Coll., Westminster, Md., 1999—2007, vis. prof., chair dept. chemistry, 2005—07; ret., 2007; cons., 2007—; adj. faculty mem. dept. sci. Mt. St. Mary's U., Md., 2008—. Contbr. articles to profl. jours. Chmn. Environ. Mgmt. Coun., Dutchess County, N.Y., 1978-84; founding chmn. Heritage Task Force for Hudson River Valley, 1980-84; pres., bd. dirs. Hudson River Heritage, N.Y., 1978-84; bd. dirs. Hudson River Rsch. Coun., 1976-84; teaching assoc. Danforth Found., 1980. Recipient Outstanding Cmty. Svc. award Dutchess County (NY) Legislature, 1980 Mem. Am. Chem. Soc., Hudson River Environ. Soc., Sigma Xi, Phi Beta Kappa, Phi Lambda Upsilon Democrat. Achievements include research in inorganic chemistry and chem. edn. Office Phone: 410-703-5743. Personal E-mail: chesdog@erols.com. *Those of us who spend our professional lives as educators are subject to many pressures and influences - financial influences, political influences, intellectual influences. I try to remember that in the usually chaotic world of education the only really important thing is the welfare of the student.*

ROSENTHAL, NAN, curator, educator, author; b. NYC, Aug. 27, 1937; d. Alan Herman and Lenore (Fry) R.; m. Otto Piene (div.); m. Henry Benning Cortesi, Sept. 5, 1990. BA, Sarah Lawrence Coll., 1959; MA, Harvard U., 1970, PhD, 1976. Asst. prof. art history U. Calif., Santa Cruz, 1971-77, assoc. prof., 1977-84, prof., 1985-86, chair dept. art history, 1976-80; curator 20th-century art Nat. Gallery Art, Washington, 1985-92; sr. cons. dept. modern art Met. Mus. of Art, NYC, 1993—2008; Lila Acheson Wallace vis. prof. fine arts NYU Inst. Fine Arts, NYC, 1996, 2000. Vis. prof. art history Fordham U., Lincoln Ctr.,

1981, 85; vis. scholar N.Y. Inst. for Humanities, NYU, 1982—83; vis. lectr. visual arts Princeton U., 1985, 88, 92; adj. prof. art history Columbia U., 2002. Author: George Rickey, 1977; also exhbn. catalogues, catalogue essays and articles; art editor Show, 1963-64; assoc. editor, then editor at large and contbg. editor Art in Am., 1964-70. Radcliffe Inst. fellow, 1968-69, scholar, 1970-71; travelling fellow Harvard U., 1973-74, rsch. fellow U. Calif., 1978, Ailsa Mellon Bruce curatorial fellow Nat. Gallery of Art, 1988-89; rsch. and travel grantee U. Calif., Santa Cruz, 1974, 77-80, 82-85. E-mail: nan.rosenthal@metmuseum.org.

ROSENTHAL, PHILIP, gastroenterologist; b. Bayshore, NY, Oct. 18, 1949; m. Sherrin Jean Packer; children: Seth, Aaron. BS, SUNY, Albany, 1971; MD, SUNY, Bklyn., 1975. Asst. prof. pediatrics Coll. of Physicians and Surgeons Columbia U., NYC, 1981-83; asst. prof. pediatrics U. So. Calif., LA, 1983-89, tenured assoc. prof. pediatrics, 1989; dir. pediatrics and nutrition, med. dir. pediatric liver transplant program Cedars-Sinai Med. Ctr., LA, 1989-95; assoc. prof. UCLA, 1989-95; prof. pediat. and surg. U. Calif. San Francisco Med. Ctr., 1995—. Vol. Am. Liver Found., Hepatitis Coun., Class Children's Liver Assn., Alagille Syndrome Alliance. Nat. Inst. Arthritis grantee, 1978-81, Children's Hosp. of L.A. grantee, 1984-86, 86-87, Abbott Labs. grantee, 1984-85, Children's Liver Found. grantee, 1985-86, numerous grants. Mem. Am. Acad. Pediatrics, N.Am. Soc. Pediatric Gastroenterology and Nutrition. Office: U Calif San Francisco Med Ctr MU4 East 500 Parnassus Ave San Francisco CA 94143-0136 Office Phone: 415-476-5892. Business E-Mail: prosenth@peds.ucsf.edu.

ROSENTHAL, ROBERT, psychology professor; b. Giessen, Germany, Mar. 2, 1933; came to U.S., 1940, naturalized, 1946. s. Julius and Hermine (Kahn) R.; m. Mary Lu Clayton, Apr. 20, 1951; children: Roberta, David C., Virginia. AB, UCLA, 1953, PhD, 1956; PhD (hon.), U. Giessen, 2003. Diplomate clin. psychology Am. Bd. Examiners Profl. Psychology. Clin. psychology trainee Los Angeles Area VA, 1954-57; lectr. U. So. Calif., 1956-57; acting instr. UCLA, 1957; from asst. to assoc. prof., coordinator clin. tng. U. N.D., 1957-62; vis. assoc. prof. Ohio State U., 1960-61; lectr. Boston U., 1965-66; lectr. clin. psychology Harvard U., Cambridge, Mass., 1962-67, prof. social psychology, 1967-95, chmn. dept. psychology, 1992-95, Edgar Pierce prof. psychology, 1995-99, Edgar Pierce prof. emeritus, 1999—; disting. prof. U. Calif., Riverside, 1999—, prof. univ. sys. wide, 2008—. Author: Experimenter Effects in Behavioral Research, 1966, enlarged edit., 1976; (with Lenore Jacobson) Pygmalion in the Classroom, 1968, expanded edit., 1992, Meta-analytic Procedures for Social Research, 1984, rev. edit., 1991, Judgment Studies, 1987; (with others) New Directions in Psychology 4, 1970, Sensitivity to Nonverbal Communication: The Pons Test, 1979; (with Ralph L. Rosnow) The Volunteer Subject, 1975, Primer of Methods for the Behavioral Sciences, 1975, Essentials of Behavioral Research, 1984, 3d edit., 2008, Understanding Behavioral Science, 1984, Contrast Analysis, 1985, Beginning Behavioral Research, 1993, 6th edit., 2008, People Studying People: Artifact and Ethics in Behavioral Research, 1997, (with Ralph L. Rosnow and Donald B. Rubin) Contrasts and Effect Sizes in Behavioral Research: A Correlational Approach, 2000; (with Brian Mullen) BASIC Meta-analysis, 1985; editor: (with Ralph L. Rosnow) Artifact in Behavioral Research, 1969, Skill in Nonverbal Communication, 1979, Quantitative Assessment of Research Domains, 1980, (with Thomas A. Sebeok) The Clever Hans Phenomenon: Communication With Horses, Whales, Apes and People, 1981, (with Blanck and Buck) Nonverbal Communication in the Clinical Context, 1986, (with Gheorghiu, Netter and Eysenck) Suggestion and Suggestibility: Theory and Research, 1989, (with Harrigan and Scherer) The New Handbook of Methods in Nonverbal Behavior Research, 2005. Recipient Donald Campbell award Soc. for Personality and Social Psychology, 1988, James McKeen Cattell Sabbatical award, 1995-96; co-recipient Golden Anniversary Monograph award Speech Comm. Assn., 1996; named Watson lectr. U. N.H., Lanzetta Meml. lectr. Dartmouth Coll., Bayer lectr. Yale Sch. Medicine, Foa lectr. Temple U., Disting. Alumni lectr. UCLA, Marschak lectr. UCLA; Guggenheim fellow, 1973-74, fellow Ctr. for Advanced Study in Behavioral Scis., 1988-89; sr. Fulbright scholar, 1972; recipient Gold Medal for Life Achievement in Sci. of Psychology Am. Psychol. Found., 2003. Fellow AAAS (co-recipient Sociopsychol. prize 1960, co-recipient Behavioral Sci. Rsch. prize 1993), Am. Acad. Arts & Scis., APA (divsn. evaluation, measurement, and stats., co-recipient Cattell Fund award 1967, co-chmn. Task Force on Statis. Inference, Disting. Sci. award for applications of psychology, 2002, Disting. Sci. Contbns. award, 2002, divsn. evaluation, measurement and stats., others), Am. Psychol. Soc. (charter, James McKeen Cattell award 2001); mem. Soc. Exptl. Social Psychology (Disting. Scientist award 1996), Ea. Psychol. Assn. (Disting. lectr. 1989), Mid-we. Psychol. Assn., Western Psychol. Assn. (Lifetime Achievement award, 2009), Mass. Psychol. Assn. (Disting. Career Contbn. award 1979), Soc. Projective Techniques (past treas.), Phi Beta Kappa, Sigma Xi. Office: Univ Calif Psychology Bldg Riverside CA 92521-0001 Office Phone: 951-827-4503.

ROSENTHAL, ROBERT JON, newspaper editor, journalist; b. NYC, Aug. 5, 1948; s. Irving and Ruth (Moss) R.; m. Inez Katherina von Sternenfels, Nov. 22, 1985; children: Adam, Benjamin, Ariella. BA, U. Vt., 1970. News asst. N.Y. Times, NYC, 1970-73; reporter Boston Globe, 1974-79, Phila. Inquirer, 1979-82, Africa corr., Nairobi, Kenya, 1982-86, fgn. editor, Phila., 1986-91, city editor, 1991-93, asst. mng. editor, daily, 1993-94, assoc. mng. editor, 1994-96, exec. editor, 1996-98, editor, exec. v.p., 1998—2001; mng. editor, v.p. San Francisco (Calif.) Chronicle, 2002—07; exec. dir. Ctr. Investigative Reporting, 2008—. Recipient Third World Reporting award Nat. Assn. Black Journalists, 1983, Mag. award Overseas Press Club, 1985, Disting. Fgn. Corr. award Sigma Delta Chi, 1985, Mag. Writing award World Population Inst., 1986. Avocations: ice hockey, gardening, fishing, cooking. Office: 1 Stevens Ct Belvedere Tiburon CA 94920-1549 Office Phone: 510-809-3162.

ROSENTHAL, SHIRLEY LORD, cosmetics magazine executive, novelist; b. London, Aug. 28; came to U.S., 1971; d. Francis J. and Mabel Florence (Williamson) Stringer; m. James Hussey; m. Cyril Lord; m. David Anderson; m. A. M. Rosenthal, June 10, 1987; children: Mark, Richard. Student, S.W. Essex Coll., London, 1948—50. Reporter London Daily Mirror; fiction editor Woman's Own, 1950-53; features editor Good Taste mag., 1953-56; features, fiction editor Woman and Beauty, 1956-59; women's editor Star Evening newspaper, 1959-60, London Evening Standard, 1960-63, London Evening News, 1963-68; beauty editor Harper's Bazaar, London, 1963-71, NYC, 1971-73; beauty, health editor Vogue mag., Condé Nast Publs., NYC, 1973-75; v.p. corp. rels. Colgate, Helena Rubinstein, NYC, 1975-80; beauty dir. Vogue mag., 1980—95, contbg. editor, 1995—. Chairwoman media coun. The Am. Acad. Dermatology, 1995—; corp. v.p. content iBeauty.com, 1999—2002; enrichment advisor Silversea Cruises, 2004—. Syndicated Field columnist on beauty, health; author 3 beauty books; also novels: Golden Hill, 1982; One of My Very Best Friends, (Lit. Guild Selection), 1985; Faces, 1989; My Sister's Keeper, 1993, The Crasher, 1998. City commr. Craigavon City, No. Ireland, 1963-68. Address: 131 E 66th St New York NY 10021-6129 E-mail: Shirlord3@aol.com.

ROSENTHAL, SOL, lawyer; b. Balt., Oct. 17, 1934; s. Louis and Hattie (Getz) R.; m. Diane Myra Sackler, June 11, 1961; children: Karen Abby, Pamela Margaret, Robert Joel. AB, Princeton U., 1956; JD, Harvard U., 1959. Bar: Md. 1959, Calif. 1961. Law clk. to chief judge U.S. Ct. Appeals, 4th cir., Balt., 1959-60; assoc. Kaplan, Livingston, Goodwin, Berkowitz & Selvin, Beverly Hills, Calif., 1960-66, ptnr., 1966-74, Buchalter Nemer, LA, 1974—96; of counsel Blanc, Williams, Johnston & Kronstadt, LA, 1996-2000, Arnold & Porter, 2000—. Bd. dirs. Playboy Enterprises, Inc., Chgo.; arbitrator Dirs. Guild Am., LA, 1976—, Writers Guild Am., LA, 1976—, Ind. Film and TV Alliance, 1989—, SAG, LA, 1992—; negotiator Writers Guild-Assn. Talent Agts., LA, 1978—; mem. entertainment and large complex case panels Am. Arbitration Assn., 1997—. Founder Camp Ronald McDonald for Good Times, LA, 1985; charter founder Mus. Contemporary Art, LA, 1988. Fellow: Coll. Comml. Arbitrators, Am. Bar Found.; mem.: ABA, Beverly Hills Bar Assn. (pres. 1982—83), Acad. TV Arts and Scis. (bd. govs. 1990—92), LA Copyright Soc. (pres. 1973—74), LA County Bar Assn. (trustee 1981—82), Calif. Bar Assn., Phi Beta Kappa. Office: Arnold & Porter 777 S Figueroa St Ste 4400 Los Angeles CA 90017-5844 Office Phone: 213-243-4000. Business E-Mail: sol_rosenthal@aporter.com.

ROSENTHAL, STEVEN SIEGMUND, lawyer; b. Cleve., May 22, 1949; s. Fred Siegel and Natalie Josephine Rosenthal; m. Ilene Edwina Goldstein, Oct. 1, 1983; children: Alexandra M., Eliana D. AB, Dartmouth Coll., 1971; JD, Harvard U., 1974. Bar: Fla. 1974, D.C. 1975, U.S. Supreme Ct. 1978, Calif. 1983. Law clk. judge Malcolm R. Wilkey U.S. Ct. Appeals (D.C. cir.), 1974-75; assoc. Covington & Burling, Washington, 1975-80, Morrison & Foerster, Washington, 1980-81, ptnr., 1981-97, Cooper, Carvin & Rosenthal, PLLC, Washington, 1998-2001, Holland & Knight LLP, Washington, 2001—02, Kaye Scholer LLP, Washington, 2002—, exec. com., 2005—. Lawyer rep. Jud. Conf. DC Cir., 1981-83, 2004—; mem. adv. com. on procedures U.S. Ct. Appeals DC Cir., 2003-09. Pres. Family and Child Svcs. Washington, 1986-88, trustee, 1978—. Mem. Am. Law Inst., Phi Beta Kappa. Republican. Office: Kaye Scholer LLP 901 Fifteenth St NW Ste 800 Washington DC 20005-2327

ROSENTHAL, SUSAN BARBARA, retired librarian; b. Elberon Park, NJ, Apr. 7, 1946; d. Joseph and Anna (Warar) Rosenthal. BA, Montclair State Coll., NJ, 1967; MEd in Libr. Sci., U. Miami, 1973. Cert. media specialist, tchr., Fla., NJ. Tchr. Manasquan Bd. Edn., NJ, 1967-71; tech. svcs. libr. Oakland Park Libr., Fla., 1978-92, asst. dir., 1992—93, acting dir., 1993, ret. Author: (mag.) Galumph, 1965-67; contbr. A Micro Handbook for Small Libraries and Media Centers, 1983, 2d edit., 1986, 3d edit., 1991. Mem. Humane Soc., Broward County, Fla., 1981, WPBT-TV PBS sta., 1975-2000, So. Mus. Flight, 1997—, Friends of the Oakland Park Libr., 1998—, mem. luncheon com., 1999, mem. planning com., 1999; charter mem. Mus. of Discovery and Sci., 1989-96, US Holocaust Meml. Mus., 1994—; donor Miami Book Fair Internat., 1990—, Cats Exclusive, Boca Raton Mus. Art, Fla., So. Poverty Law Ctr. Wall of Tolerance, Survivors of the Shoah Visual History Found., Martin Luther King Jr. Meml. Found., Poverello Ctr., thehungersite.com, freerice.com, Friends of the Oakland Park Libr., Sierra Club, WPBT-TV PBS Sta., ACLU, Am. Coming Together, Abandoned Pet Rescue, Becca's Closet, Black Box Voting, Broward House, Coconut Grove Arts Festival, Defenders of Wildlife, Delray Affair, others. Recipient St. Cloud Tchg. award Société d'Enseignement, St. Cloud, France, 1966, 2 awards Libr. Pub. Rels. Coun., winner, 1983, hon. mention, 1985, cert. appreciation U.S. Holocaust Meml. Mus., 1996, 2000. Mem. ALA, AARP, Nat. Alliance for Mentally Ill, Fla. Libr. Assn., Fla. Pub. Libr. Assn., Broward County Libr. Assn. (treas. 1981-83, continuing edn. com. 1980), Apple Libr. Users Group, Apple Computer Enjoyment Soc. (chpt. sec. 1984-87, corp. sec. 1985-89), Consumers Union, NFO Rsch., Wilderness Soc., World Wildlife Fund, Environ. Def. Fund, People for Ethical Treatment of Animals, Nat. Resources Def. Coun., Nature Conservancy, Nat. Wildlife Fedn., Mensa, actforchange.org, moveon.org, Procrastinators Club Am., Pi Delta Phi.

ROSENTHAL, TODD, set designer; BA in Eng. and Theater, cum laude, Colgate U., 1989; student, Moore Coll. Art, 1989, Art Students League NY, 1990; MFA in Set/Lighting Design, Yale. U., 1993. Scenic carpenter Stage West, Springfield, Mass., 1986; master carpenter Williamstown Theater Festival, Williamstown, Mass., 1988; student technical dir. Colgate U., Hamilton, NY, 1987—89; scenic artist Club MTV, 1989; scenic carpenter Am. Music Theater Festival, Phila., 1990; carpenter, welder, scenic artist Walnut St. Theatre, Phila., 1989—90; freelance set designer Chgo., 1993—; scenic carpenter, scenic artist Labrosse Ltd., Chgo., 1995; draftsman, scenic artist Fox Theatricals, Chgo., 1994—95; resident designer New Plays Lab, Steppenwolf Theatre, Chgo., 1995—96; draftsman, renderer Scenic View, Chgo., 1996; resident set designer Court Theatre, Chgo., 1997—98. Adj. prof. design DePaul U., Chgo., 1995—; vis. prof. Northwestern U., Chgo., 1999—, asst. prof. design, 2003—. Set designer: (plays) Still, 1994 (Best Set Design, Acad. Theater Artists and Friends, 1994); The Barber of Seville, 1996 (After Dark award for Best Set Design, 1997); Schoolgirl Figure, 2000 (New City Set Design of Yr., 2000); An Experiment with an Airpump, 2001 (After Dark award for Best Set Design, 2001); A Skull in Connemara, 2002 (After Dark award for Best Set Prodn., 2002); The Clean House, 2006 (After Dark award for Best Set Design, 2006); (Broadway plays) August: Osage County, 2007 (Tony award for Best Scenic Design of a Play, 2008, Laurence Olivier award for Best Set Design, 2009). Mem.: US Inst. Theater Technology, United Scenic Artists (examination com.). Mailing: 828 Davis St Ste 207 Evanston IL 60201 Office Phone: 312-515-7758. Fax: 847-869-6975. E-mail: toddAR@earthlink.net.*

ROSENTHAL, WILLIAM J., lawyer; b. Balt., Nov. 4, 1920; s. Justin J. and Ray Marian (Stern) Rosenthal; m. Margaret Irwin Parker, July 4, 1956; children: Adriane Leigh, Jacqueline Ray, John Justin. AB, Johns Hopkins U., Balt., 1941; LL.B., U. Balt., 1950. Bar: Md. 1950. Adminstrv. asst. Office Price Adminstrn., Washington, 1941-42; assoc. Earle K. Shawe, Balt., 1951-67; ptnr. Shawe & Rosenthal (formerly Earle K. Shawe), Balt., 1967—. Lectr. U. Balt., 1952—56; mem. regional adv. coun. NLRB; vets. rep. Md. Constrn. Adv. Coun., 1946—49; lectr. NYU Conf. Labor Rels., 1981, Boston U. Labor Law Seminar, 1985; expert witness on labor law, legis. and congl. coms. Author: D-Day Through V-E Day, WWII Veterans Archives, US Library of Congress, 2005; co-author: The Developing Labor Law, 1971; contbr. articles to profl. jours. Served to lt. USNR, 1942—46, ETO. Mem.: ABA, Balt. Bar Assn., Md. Bar Assn., Suburban Club (bd. govs., pres.), Spiked Shoe Soc., Pi Delta Epsilon, Omicron Delta Kappa. Home: 8207 Cranwood Ct Baltimore MD 21208-1823 Office: Shawe & Rosenthal 20 S Charles St Baltimore MD 21201 Home Phone: 410-486-1040; Office Phone: 410-752-1040. Business E-Mail: rosenthal@shawe.com.

ROSENZWEIG, CHARLES LEONARD, lawyer; b. NYC, Apr. 12, 1952; s. William and Frieda (Dechner) R.; m. Rya R. Mehler, June 14, 1975; children: Jessica Sara Newshel, Erica Danielle. AB cum laude, Princeton U., 1974; JD, NYU, 1977. Bar: NY 1978, US Dist. Ct. (ea. and so. dists.) NY 1978, US Ct. Appeals (7th cir.) 1980, US Ct. Internat. Trade 1981, US Ct. Appeals (2d cir.) 1985. Assoc. Graubard, Moskovitz et al, NYC, 1977-85; ptnr. Rand Rosenzweig Radley & Gordon LLP, NYC, 1987—. Mem. panel of neutrals comml. divsn. Supreme Ct. State NY. Editor NYU Jour. Internat. Law. and Politics. Chmn. bd. Jewish Cmty. Ctr., Harrison, 1998-2000. Mem. ABA (internat. law sect.), NY State Bar Assn. (co-chair internat. litig. com. 1995-98, mem. exec. com. comml. and fed. litig. sect. 1995-2005), Westchester County Bar Assn. (mem. ethics com.), NYU Alumni Assn. (chmn. jour. internat. law and politics alumni 1985-87), Assn. Comml. Fin. Attys. Avocations: skiing, bicycling, scuba diving, languages. Home: 9 Hadley Rd Armonk NY 10504-2417 Office: Rand Rosenzweig et al 800 3rd Ave New York NY 10022 also: 50 Main St 12th Fl White Plains NY 10606 Home Phone: 914-730-3132; Office Phone: 212-687-7070. Business E-Mail: crosenzweig@randrose.com.

ROSENZWEIG-LIPSON, SHARON JOY, pharmacologist; b. Queens, NY, July 8, 1966; d. Martin and Annette Nina (Epstein) Rosenzweig; m. Robert Steven Lipson, June 18, 1989; 1 child, Shelby Rachel. Student, Brandeis U., 1984-86; BA, U. Pa., 1988; MA, Harvard U., 1991, PhD, 1993. Grad. rsch. asst. Harvard Med. Sch., Southborough, Mass., 1989-92; postdoctoral rsch. scientist Am. Cyanamid Co., Pearl River, N.Y., 1992-94; sr. rsch. scientist Am. Home Products, Princeton, N.J., 1994—. Contbr. articles to profl. jours. William James Merit fellow Harvard U., 1988-90. Mem. Soc. for Neurosci., Soc. for the Stimulus Properties of Drugs, Behavioral Pharmacology Soc. Democrat. Jewish. Office: Wyeth-Ayerst Rsch Ridge Rd Princeton NJ 08543

ROSETT, ARTHUR IRWIN, lawyer, educator; b. NYC, July 5, 1934; s. Milton B. and Bertha (Werner) R.; m. Rhonda K. Lawrence; children: David Benjamin, Martha Jean, Daniel Joseph. AB, Columbia U., 1955, LL.B., 1959. Bar: Calif. 1968, N.Y. State 1960, U.S. Supreme Ct. 1963. Law clk. U.S. Supreme Ct., 1959-60; asst. U.S. atty. So. Dist. N.Y., 1960-63; practice law NYC, 1963-65; assoc. dir. Pres.'s Commn. on Law Enforcement and Adminstrn. Justice, 1965-67; acting prof. law UCLA, 1967-70, prof., 1970—. Author: Contract Law and Its Application, 1971, 6th edit. (with D.J. Bussell), 1999, (with D. Cressey) Justice by Consent, 1976, (with E. Dorff) A Living Tree, 1987. Served with USN, 1956-58. Mem. Am. Law Inst. Home: 641 S Saltair Ave Los Angeles CA 90049-4134 Office: UCLA Law Sch 405 Hilgard Ave Los Angeles CA 90095-1476 Business E-Mail: rosett@law.ucla.edu.

ROSETT, DANIEL J., film company executive; b. 1962; BS in bus. and econ., U. Calif., Santa Barbara, 1984. CPA. Mgr. KPMG Peat Marwick; with Walt Disney Co., exec. dir. studio ops.; v.p., corp. controller MGM Studios, 1994—95, sr. v.p. fin. ops., 1995—98, exec. v.p. studio fin. and ops., 1998—2001, exec. v.p. mktg. and distribution, 2001—04; pres. United Artists Corp., 2004—05; COO Overture Films, 2006—. Exec. prodr.: (films) Capote, 2005.

ROSHA, UZI, lawyer; b. Tel Aviv, Dec. 11, 1968; arrived in U.S., 1999; s. Rachel and Yossi Rosha; m. Jaehee Moon; 1 child, Uri Moon-Rosha. JD, Tel Aviv U., 1998; LLM, Columbia U., 2000. Bar: N.Y. 2004, Israel 1998. Clk. Supreme Ct., Chief Justice, Jerusalem, 1998—99, Ministry of Justice, Jerusalem, 1998; compliance officer Bear Stearns & Co., NYC, 2001—04; compliance mgr. Lehman Bros., NYC, 2004—05; chief compliance officer Fulcrum Global Ptnrs., NYC, 2005—06; cons. Fin. Svcs., 2006—07; chief compliance officer CarVal Investors LLC, 2007—. Contbr. of different articles regarding compliance obligations for hedge funds and broker dealers in US, Japan, UK and Singapore. Chmn. Orgn. for Democracy and Equality, Tel Aviv, 1996—99; mem. moot trial assoc. prof. sociology Tel Aviv U. Law Sch.; bd. dirs. ISEF, NYC, 2005. Lt. Israeli Paratroopers, 1987—91. Scholar, Columbia U., Sch. of Law, 1999, Tel Aviv U., 1994, 1995, 1996, 1997. Mem.: Israeli Bar Assn. (assoc.), N.Y. State Bar Assn. (assoc.).

ROSHEL, JOHN ALBERT, JR., orthodontist; b. Terre Haute, Ind., Apr. 7, 1941; s. John Albert and Mary M. (Griglione) R.; m. Kathy Roshel; children: John Albert III, James Livingston, Angela Kay. BS, Ind. State U., 1963; DDS, Ind. U., 1966; MS, U. Mich., 1968. Individual practice dentistry specializing in orthodontics, Terre Haute, 1968—. Mem. ADA, Am. Assn. Orthodontists, Terre Haute C. of C., Terre Haute Country Club, Lions, Elks, KC, Lambda Chi Alpha, Delta Sigma Delta, Omicron Kappa Upsilon. Roman Catholic. Home: 15 E Wedgeway Dr Terre Haute IN 47802-4983 Office: 4241 S 7th St Terre Haute IN 47802-4367 Office Phone: 812-238-2451. Personal E-mail: drjrosh@aol.com.

ROSHKIND, ROBIN, divorce lawyer; b. NY, Feb. 4, 1951; 2 children. BA in Comm., CUNY, 1972; JD, Nova Southeastern U., Ft. Lauderdale, Fla., 1996. Bar: Fla. 1998. Pvt. practice, West Palm Beach, Fla., 1998—. Fellow: Fla. Bar Found.; mem.: Palm Beach County Bar Assn., Palm Beach Yacht Club, Mar A Lago Club, NY Athletic Club. Office: 625 N Flagler Dr 509 West Palm Beach FL 33401

ROSHONG, DEE ANN DANIELS, dean, educator, counselor; b. Kansas City, Mo., Nov. 22, 1936; adopted d. Vernon Edmund and Doradell (Kellogg) Daniels, d. Ken Garner and Lucille Cronin Davidson; m. Richard Lee Roshong, Aug. 27, 1960 (div.). BMusEd., U. Kans., Lawrence, 1958; MA in Counseling and Guidance, Stanford U., Calif., 1960; postgrad., Fresno State U., U. Calif., Berkeley; EdD, U. San Francisco, 1980. Cert. in spiritual direction Claritas Inst., 2007, prayer chaplain Tri- Valley Unity Church, 2008. Counselor, psychometrist Fresno City Coll., 1961-65; counselor, instr. psychology Chabot Coll., Hayward, Calif., 1965-75, coord. counseling svcs. Livermore, Calif., 1975-81, asst. dir. student pers. svcs., 1981-89, Las Positas Coll., Livermore, Calif., 1989-91, assoc. dean student svcs., 1991-94, dean student svcs., 1991—2003, life coach, 2000—; counselor Experience Unltd., Pleasant Hill, Calif., 2004—; symposium organizer Calif. State U., East Bay, 2004—. Writer, coord. I, A Woman Symposium, 1974, Feeling Free to Be You and Me symposium, 1975, All for the Family Symposium, 1976, I Celebrate Myself Symposium, 1978, Person to Person in Love and Work Symposium, 1978, The Healthy Person in Mind and Spirit Symposium, 1980, Change Symposium, 1981, Sources of Strength Symposium, 1982, Love and Friendship Symposium, 1983, Self Esteem Symposium, 1984, Trust Symposium, 1985, Prime Time: Making the Most of This Time in Your Life Symposium, 1986, Symposium in Healing, 1987, How to Live in the World and Still Be Happy Symposium, 1988, Student Success is a Team Effort, Sound Mind, Sound Body Symposium, 1989, Creating Life's Best Symposium, 1990, Choices Symposium, 1991, Minding the Body, Mending the Mind Symposium, 1992, Healing through Love and Laughter Symposium, 1993, Healing Ourselves Changing the World Symposium, 1994, Finding Your Path Symposium, 1995, Build the Life You Want Symposium, 1996, Making Peace With Yourself and Your Relationships Symposium, 1997, Everyday Sacred Symposium, 1998, Wisdom of the Heart Symposium, 1999, Inner Wisdom Symposium, 2000, Second Half of Life Symposium, 2001, A Celebration of Life Symposium, 2003, Viewing Mental Health and Mental Illness From a Multi-Cultural Perspective Symposium, 2004, Promoting Mental Health in Multi-Cultural Settings Symposium, 2005, Building Bridges to Hope and Recovery: Healing Ourselves, Transforming the System Symposium,

2006; mem. cast TV prodns. Eve and Co., Best of Our Times, Cowboy; chmn. Falling Awake Symposium, 2002, Calif. C.C. Chancellor's Task Force on Counseling, Statewide Regional Counseling Facilitators, 1993-95, Statewide Conf. Emotionally Disturbed Students in Calif. C.C.s, 1982—, Conf. on the Under Represented Student in Calif. C.C.s, 1986, Conf. on High Risk Students, 1989; spiritual dir. Claritas Inst., 2005-07, Calif. State U., East Bay, 2007—. Author: Counseling Needs of Comunity College Students, 1980. Bd. dirs. Teleios Sinetar Ctr., Ctr. Cmty. Dispute Resolution, 1998—, Pleasanton Youth Collaborative Bd., 1997-2002, Pleasanton Youth Master Plan Bd., 1998—; choir dir., 1996-99; pres. bd. Tri-Valley Unity Ch., 1998-2005, v.p. 2005, lay minister 2005, Tri-Valley Haven bd., 2000—, Calif. State U. East Bay Inst. Mental Illness and Wellness Edn. bd., 2000—, Ellis Life Coach Tng., 1999—, Interspiritual Mentor Tng. Program, 2005; title III activity dir. Las Positas Coll., 1995-99, dir. pace program, 1999-2003, dir. quest program, 2000-03. Mem.: Spiritual Dirs. Internat., Calif C.C. Counselors Assn. (svc. award 1986—87, award for Outstanding and Disting. Svc. 1986—87, Pleasanton Mayor's award 2000—01, 2002), Calif. Assn. C. C. (chmn. commn. on students svcs. 1979—84), Assn. Counseling and Devel., Nat. Assn. Women Deans and Counselors, Western Psychol. Assn., Assn. Humanistic Psychologists. Home and Office: 1856 Harvest Rd Pleasanton CA 94566-5456 Personal E-mail: deeroshong@comcast.net.

ROSI, DAVID R., internist, oncologist, hematologist; b. Chgo. BS, Northwestern U., Evanston; MD, Northwestern U. Med. Sch., 1975. Cert. Internal Medicine, Med. Oncology. Internship and residency Cook County Hosp., Chicago, 1976—78; fellowship M.D. Anderson Hosp., Tex., 1978—80; staff mem. Rush Oak Park Hosp., Oak Park, 1980—, Gottlieb Meml. Hosp., Melrose Park, 1981—, Westlake Hosp., Melrose Park, MacNeal Hosp., Berwyn, Hematology Oncology Associates Ill. Asst. prof., dept. internal medicine Rush Med. Coll. Mem.: AMA, Ill. Med. Soc., Am. Coll. of Physicians, Am. Soc. of Clinical Oncology. Office: Hematology Oncology Associates 1200 S York Rd Ste 3280 Elmhurst IL 60126*

ROSICA, GABRIEL ADAM, retired manufacturing executive, electrical engineer; b. NYC, Jan. 9, 1940; s. Gabriel J. and Elma (P.) R.; m. Bettina R. Nardozzi, Sept. 8, 1962; children: Gregory A., Julie Ann, Mark A. BA in Math. and Physics, Columbia U., 1962, BSEE, 1963; MSEE, Rensselaer Poly. Inst., 1966; MBA, Boston U., 1971. Registered profl. engr., Mass. Rsch. engr. United Aircraft Research Labs., East Hartford, Conn., 1963-67; mgr. electronic devel. The Foxboro (Mass.) Co., 1967-75, gen. mgr. U.S. div., 1975-77, v.p., 1977-80; pres., COO Modular Computer Sys., Inc., Ft. Lauderdale, Fla., 1980-82, pres., chmn., CEO, 1982-88; pvt. practice bus. cons. Boca Raton, Fla., 1988-91; sr. v.p. Elsag Bailey Corp., Pepper Pike, Ohio, 1991-92; exec. v.p. Bailey Controls Co., Wickliffe, Ohio, 1993-94; COO Bailey Control Co., Wickliffe, Ohio, 1994-96; sr. v.p. Keithley Instruments, Solon, Ohio, 1996-2001, exec. v.p., 2001—05, ret.; ptnr. Glengery LLC, Venture Capital Firm, 2005—. Chmn. engring. adv. coun. U. Fla., Gainesville, 1987-90; chmn. hi tech adv. coun. Coll. Boca Raton, Fla., 1987-90. Mem. Pres.'s Coun. Fla. Atlantic U., Boca Raton, 1987-91; trustee Nova U., Ft. Lauderdale, Fla., 1987-94. Recipient Boston U. Chair, 1971, Outstanding Young Engr. of Year award Mass. Soc. Profl. Engrs., 1974. Mem. IEEE (sr. mem.), Am. Electronics Assn. (bd. dirs. 1987, chmn Fla. bd. dirs. 1987-88), Fla. High Tech. and Industry Coun. Home: 35640 Spicebush Ln Solon OH 44139-5063 Personal E-mail: gabe.rosica@att.net.

ROSICH, RAYNER KARL, physicist; b. Joliet, Ill., Aug. 28, 1940; s. Joseph F. and Gretchen (Cox) R.; m. Judy Louise Jackson, Aug. 20, 1966; children: Heidi Ann, Kimberly Ann, Dawn Ann. BS with distinction/honors in physics, U. Mich., Ann Arbor, 1962, MS in Physics, 1963; PhD, U. Colo., Boulder, 1977; MBA, U. Denver, 1982. Teaching fellow and rsch. asst. U. Mich., Ann Arbor, 1962-67; staff Argonne (Ill.) Nat. Lab. Applied Math. Div., summers, 1961-63; physicist, project leader Inst. for Telecommunication Sci. U.S. Dept. Commerce, Boulder, Colo., 1967-80; sr. scientist and program mgr. Electro Magnetic Applications, Inc., Denver, 1980-82; applications mgr. Energy Systems Tech., Inc., Denver, 1982-83, mgr. R&D, 1983; prin. scientist, program mgr. Contel Info. Systems, Inc., Denver, 1983-84, dir. tech. audits, 1985, dir. basic and applied R&D, 1986; lab. scientist for data systems engring. lab. Hughes Aircraft Co., Denver, 1986, lab. scientist for data systems lab., 1986-90, lab. scientist for systems lab., 1990-92; prin. engr. Advanced System Techs., Inc., Denver, 1992-95; project mgr. Evolving Systems, Inc., 1995—96; network planning engr., cons. engr., network arch. Galileo Internat., 1996-99; sr. network arch. Riverstone Networks subs. Cabletron Sys., Inc., 1999-2000; sr. consulting engr. Time0, Inc., Englewood, Colo., 2000-01; network engring. mgr. CQG, Inc., Denver, 2001—02; lead performance analyst Tanning Tech. Corp., Denver, 2002—03; sr. consulting engr. Martingale Corp., Denver, 2004; engr./scientist-5 Boeing Co., Denver, 2005—06; rsch. engr. Data Fusion Corp., 2006—07; sr. sys. engr. II Raytheon, Aurora, Colo., 2007—. Instr. math. Arapahoe Cmty. Coll., 1987-97. Vol. judo instr., county recreation dist., 1976-77. Recipient Spl. Achievement award U.S. Dept. Commerce, 1974, Outstanding Performance award, 1978, Sustained Superior Performance award, 1979; Libbey-Owens-Ford Glass Co./U. Mich. Phoenix Meml. fellow, 1964-66; NSF Summer fellow, 1965. Mem. AAAS, Am. Phys. Soc., IEEE (sr. mem.), Assn. Computing Machinery, Sigma Xi, Phi Kappa Phi. Home: 6613 S Gray St Littleton CO 80123-6880 Office: Raytheon MS:DN/S75/NG 16800 E Centre Tech Pkwy Aurora CO 80011-9046 Home Phone: 303-973-8652; Office Phone: 720-744-8086. Personal E-mail: rrosich@umich.edu.

ROSICKI, MARIA TRZETRZEWINSKA-TRETT, clinical psychologist; b. Warsaw, Dec. 13, 1925; d. Walter and Irena (Cywinska) T.; m. Tadeusz Rosicki, Nov. 26, 1960. BA summa cum laude, CUNY, 1956; MA, Fordham U., 1959, PhD in Clin. Psychology, 1969. Cert. psychologist, psychoanalyst, N.Y. Vocat. guidance counselor Archdiocese of N.Y., NYC, 1958-61; staff psychologist, supr. Cath. Guardian Soc., Bklyn., 1963-92; psychotherapist, supr. Advanced Inst. for Analytic Psychotherapy, Queens, N.Y., 1970-78; pvt. practice psychotherapy, psychoanalysis Glen Cove, N.Y., 1978—. Mem. Sigma Xi, Phi Beta Kappa. Roman Catholic.

ROSIER, DAVID LEWIS, retired investment banker; b. Sioux City, Iowa, Mar. 22, 1937; s. Orel Lewis and Jewell May (Palmer) R.; m. Jackie Dodd, July 1965 (div. 1973); 1 child, Michele, m. Carol Mary Byre, Nov. 25, 1982 (dec. Sept. 1997); m. Rosemarie Dimino, Sept. 9, 1999 (div. Jan. 2004). BSBA in Mktg., U. Denver, 1960. Registered rep. NASD 7, 62, 63, 22; registered investment advisor. V.p., mgr. mktg. Hertz Internat., Ltd., NYC, 1970-71; regional v.p. Amtrak, NYC, 1971-73; mng. ptnr. Rosier & Assocs., Ltd., San Diego, 1969—; sr. v.p. for strategic mktg. Am. Prins. Holdings, Inc., San Diego, 1979-84; v.p., registered prin. Am. Diversified Equity Corp., Costa Mesa, Calif., 1984-85; pres. Glen Eagle, Inc., 1986-87; sr. v.p. Western Region Cozad Investment Svcs. Inc., San Diego, 1987-88; dir. corp. fin. Brookstreet Securities Corp., Irvine, Calif., 1993—2005; ret.; dir. fixed asset group U.S. Euro Securities, Inc. Global Investment Bank, 2005—08. Spkr. in field. Co-author: Zip Code Sectional Center As It Applies to Direct Marketing, 1964. Bd. dirs. Nautical Heritage Soc. (Hamburg award 1988). Mem. Oceanside Rotary (Paul Harris fellow, benefactor, pres., founder Rotary Club of Oceanside Found.), Kona Kai Internat. Yacht Club (commodore 1987), Internat. Order of the Blue Gavel (founder, past chmn. bd. trustees Humanities Found.), Phone Charities Internat. (founder, mng. mem. 1996-98), Nat. Investment Banking Assn. (bd. dirs. 2001-04), Golf Club Calif. (bd. gov. 2005-07), Persimmon Country Club (mem. handycap com. 2008-), Sigma Alpha Epsilon. Avocations: skiing, golf, jazz. Office: Rosier & Assocs Ltd 38954 Proctor Blvd #275 Sandy OR 97055 Home: 16840 Hoffman Ln Sandy OR 97055 Office Phone: 760-310-2030. Business E-Mail: daverosier@verizon.net.

ROSINI, EDUARDO B., computer software company executive; b. 1968; married; 2 children. With Microsoft Corp., 1992—, gen. mgr. Microsoft Argentina, 1997—99, gen. mgr. worldwide enterprise group Redmond, Wash., 1999, regional v.p. home & office divsn. Europe, Middle East & Africa, 2003—04, v.p. Microsoft Asia-Pacific Singapore, 2004—06, corp. v.p. worldwide small & midmarket solutions & partners group Redmond, 2006—. Office: Microsoft Corp SMS&P Group 1 Microsoft Way Redmond WA 98052-6399

ROSINSKI, DAVID J., cardiovascular parfusionist; b. NEw Britain, Conn., Mar. 4, 1966; s. Thaddeus and Janice Elizabeth Rosinski; 1 child, Audrey. BS, Northeastern U., 1990. Staff parfusionist Llahey CLinic, Burlington, Mass., 1990—92, Hartford Hosp., Conn., 1992—95, dir. cardiovascular parfusion, 1995—2005, U. Conn. Health Ctr., Farmington, 2005—. Adj. faculty Quinnipiac U., Hamden, Conn., 2005—; pres. Conn. Sch. Parfusion, 1998—. Mem.: Am. Soc. Extracorporal Tech. Avocations: kayaking, hiking, golf, reading. Office: U Conn Health Ctr 263 Farmington Ave Farmington CT 06030-2023

ROSINSKI, EDWIN FRANCIS, medical educator; b. Buffalo, June 25, 1928; s. Theodore Joseph and Josephine M. (Wolski) R.; m. Jeanne C. Hueniger, Oct. 27, 1951; children: John T., Mary E., Sarah J. BS, SUNY, Buffalo, 1950; EdM, U. Buffalo, 1957, EdD, 1959. Prof. health scis. Med. Coll. Va., Richmond, 1959-66; dep. asst. sec. HEW, Washington, 1966-68; exec. vice chancellor U. Calif., San Francisco, 1968-72, prof., 1972-94; prof. emeritus medicine & pharmacy, 1994—. Adv. Rockefeller Found., N.Y.C., 1962-67, WHO, Geneva, 1962-78, Imperial Com. Health, Tehran, Iran, 1974-77; cons. Stanford Research Inst., Menlo Park, Calif., 1975-79. Author: The Assistant Medical Officer, 1965; contbr. over 100 articles to profl. jours. Served with USAF, 1950-54. Recipient spl. citation HEW, 1968, Merrell Flair award, 1991; named disting. prof. Australian Vice Chancellors Office, 1974, disting. vis. prof. Tulane U., New Orleans, 1983, Alumni of Yr. SUNY, Buffalo, 2006. Fellow AAAS; mem. Assn. Am. Med. Colls. (Merrel Flair award), Am. Ednl. Research Assn., Soc. Health and Human Values (founding mem.), Calif. Pharmacists Assn. (hon.), Phi Delta Kappa. Roman Catholic. Avocation: physical fitness. Home: 80 Sotelo Ave San Francisco CA 94116-1423

ROSKAM, JAN, aerospace engineer; b. The Hague, The Netherlands, Feb. 22, 1930; arrived in U.S., 1957; s. Kommer Jan and Agatha (Bosman) Roskam; m. Janice Louise Thomas-Barron, Dec. 21, 1994. MA in Aerospace Engring., Tech. U. Delft, 1954; PhD in Aeros. and Astronautics, U. Wash., 1965. Asst. chief designer Aviolanda Aircraft Co., Netherlands, 1954-57; sr. aerodynamics engr. Cessna Aircraft Co., Wichita, Kans., 1957-59; sr. group engr. Boeing Co., Wichita and Seattle, 1959-67; prof. emeritus aerospace engring. U. Kans., Lawrence, 1967—; cons. Design, Analysis and Rsch. Corp., 1991—. Cons. to govt. and industry. Author: Airplane Flight Dynamics and Automatic Flight Controls, 2 vols., 1979; co-author: Airplane Aerodynamics and Performance, 1981, Airplane Design, Part I-VIII, 1986, Roskam's Airplane War Stories, 2002. Served to 1st lt. Royal Netherlands Air Force, 1954—56. Fellow: AIAA, Soc. Automotive Engrs.; mem.: Exptl. Aircraft Assn., U.S. Chess Fedn., Koninklijk Instituut van Ingenieurs, Royal Aero. Soc., Air Force Assn., Aircraft Owners and Pilots Assn., Omicron Delta Kappa, Sigma Gamma Tau, Tau Beta Pi, Sigma Xi. Office: U Kans 2004 Lea Hl Lawrence KS 66045-0001 Personal E-mail: roskam@sunflower.com. Business E-Mail: roskam@darcorp.com.

ROSKAM, PETER JAMES, United States Representative from Illinois, former state legislator, lawyer; b. Hinsdale, Ill., Sept. 13, 1961; s. Verlyn Ronald and Martha (Jacobsen) Roskam; m. Elizabeth Andrea Gracey, June 18, 1988; children: Gracey, James(dec.), Frances, Stephen, Alec. BA, U. Ill., 1983; JD, Ill. Inst. Tech., 1989. Bar: Ill. 1989. Tchr. All Saints HS, St. Thomas, VI, 1984-85; legis. asst. to Rep. Tom Delay US Congress, Washington, 1985-86, legal asst. to Rep. Henry Hyde, 1986-87; exec. dir. Ednl. Assistance Ltd., Glen Ellyn, Ill., 1987-93; ptnr. Salvi & Roskam, Wheaton, Ill., 1994—2006; mem. Ill. Gen. Assembly from Dist. 40, Springfield, 1993—99, Ill. State Senate from Dist. 20, 2000—06, US Congress from 6th Ill. dist., 2007—, mem. fin. svcs. com. Legis. chmn. Ill. State Crime Commn. Named a Hero of Taxpayer, Americans for Tax Reform, 2005. Republican. Presbyterian. Office: 150 S Bloomingdale Rd Bloomingdale IL 60108 also: 507 House Office Bldg Washington DC 20515*

ROSKENS, RONALD WILLIAM, management consultant, retired academic administrator; b. Spencer, Iowa, Dec. 11, 1932; s. William E. and Delores A.L. (Beving) R.; m. Lois Grace Lister, Aug. 22, 1954; children: Elizabeth, Barbara, Brenda, William. BA, U. No. Iowa, 1953, MA, 1955, LHD (hon.), 1985; PhD, U. Iowa, 1958; LLD (hon.), Creighton U., 1978, Huston-Tillotson Coll., 1981, Midland Luth. Coll., 1984, Hastings Coll., 1981; LittD (hon.), Nebr. Wesleyan U., 1981; PhD (hon.), Ataturk U., Turkey, 1987; DSc (hon.), Jayewardenepura U., Sri Lanka, 1991; LHD (hon.), U. Akron, 1987, Am. Coll. Greece, Athens, 1994, Kent State U., 2005; LHD, U. Nebr., 2008; LLD, U. NE, 2009. Lic. min. United Ch. of Christ (Congl. and E&R). Tchr. Minburn (Iowa) High Sch., 1954, Woodward (Iowa) State Hosp., summer 1954; asst. counselor to men State U. Iowa, 1956-59; dean of men, asst. prof. spl. edn. Kent (Ohio) State U., 1959-63, assoc. prof., then prof., 1963-72, asst. to pres., 1963-66, dean for adminstrn., 1968-71, exec. v.p., prof. ednl. adminstrn., 1971-72; chancellor, prof. ednl. adminstrn. U. Nebr., Omaha, 1972-76; pres. U. Nebr. System, 1977-89, pres. emeritus, 1989; hon. prof. East China Normal U., Shanghai, 1985; adminstr. USAID, Washington, 1990-92; pres. Action Internat., Inc., Omaha, 1993-96, Global Connections, Inc., Omaha, 1996—. Interim exec. officer Omaha Pub. Libr., 1996-98; mem. Bus.-Higher Edn. Forum, 1979-89, exec. com., 1984-87; mem. govtl. relations com. Am. Council Edn., 1979-83, bd. dirs., 1981-86, vice chair, 1983-84, chair, 1984-85; chmn. com. on financing higher edn. Nat. Assn. State Univs. and Land Grant Colls., 1978-83, vice chmn. com. on financing higher edn., 1983-84, chmn. com. on fed. student fin. assistance, 1981-87; mem. nat. adv. com. on accreditation and instl. eligibility U.S. Dept. Edn., 1983-86, chmn., bd. dirs., 1986; exec. bd. North Cen. Assn., 1979-84, chmn. exec. bd., 1982-84, pres., 1989-90; active Environ. Ams. Bd., 1991-92, Strategic Command Consultation Commn., 1993-96, Nat. Exec. Res. Corps, Fed. Office Emergency Preparedness, 1968-88; chmn. Omaha/Douglas Pub. Bldg. Commn., 1996—. Co-editor: Paradox, Process and Progress, 1968; contbr. articles profl. jours. Mem. Kent City Planning Commn., 1962-66; bd. dirs. United Ch. of Christ Bd. Homeland Ministries, 1968-74, Met. YMCA, Omaha, 1973-77, Mid-Am. council Boy Scouts Am., 1973-77, Midlands United Community Services, 1972-77, NCCJ, 1974-77, Omaha Rotary Club, 1974-77, 93—, Found. Study Presdl. and Congl. Terms, 1977-89, First Plymouth Congl. Ch., 1989-90, Midland Luth. Coll., 1993-2000, Coun. Aid to Edn., 1985-89, ConAgra Foods, Inc., 1993—, Russian Farm Cmty. Project, Capitol Fed. Found., Topeka, Kans., 1999—, The Silverstone Group, 2004—; trustee Huston Tillotson Coll., Austin, Tex., 1968-81, chmn., 1976-78, Joslyn Art Mus., 1973-77, Nebr. Meth. Hosp., 1974-77, 1st Ctrl. Congregational Ch., Brownell-Talbott Sch., 1974-77, Harry S. Truman Inst., 1977-89, Willa Cather Pioneer Meml. and Ednl. Found., 1979-87; pres. Kent Area C. of C., 1966; mem. Met. Commn. Coll. Found., 1993-96; min.-in-residence Countryside Cmty. United Ch. Christ, Omaha, 2003—. Decorated comdr.'s cross Order of Merit (Germany); recipient Disting. Svc. award Kent, Ohio, 1967, Brotherhood award NCCJ, 1977, Americanism citation B'nai B'rith, 1978, Legion of Honor, Order of DeMolay, 1980, gold medal Nat. Interfrat. Coun., 1987, Agr. award Triumph Agr. Expn., Omaha, 1989, Disting. Alumni Achievement award U. Iowa, 2004, Order of Tower, U. Nebr., 2009; named Nat. 4-H Alumnus, 1967, Outstanding Alumnus, U. No. Iowa, 1974, Midlander of Yr., Omaha World Herald, 1977, King Ak-Sar-Ben LXXXVI, 1980; named to DeMolay Hall of Fame, 1993; named Hon. Consul Gen. of Japan, 1999, Order of Tower award, U. Nebr., Omaha. Mem. AAAS, APA, AAUP, Am. Coll. Pers. Assn., Assn. Urban Univs. (pres. 1976-77), Am. Ednl. Rsch. Assn., Coun. on Fgn. Rels., Chief Execs. Orgn., Young Pres. Orgn., Scottish Rite (bd. dirs. Omaha coun. 1999-), Lincoln C. of C. (bd. dirs. 1989-90), Masons (33 deg.), Rotary (bd. dirs. Omaha 1974-77, pres. Kent, Ohio chpt., 1970-71), Phi Delta Kappa, Phi Eta Sigma, Sigma Tau Gamma (pres. grand coun. 1968-70, Disting. Achievement award 1980, Disting. scholar 1981), Omicron Delta Kappa (nat. pres. 1986-90, Found. pres. 1986-96). Home: 10849 N 58th Plz Omaha NE 68152 Office Phone: 402-399-0928.

ROSKI, EDWARD P., JR., real estate developer, professional sports team executive; s. Edward P. Roski, III; m. Gayle Roski. BS in Fin. and Real Estate, U. So. Calif., 1962. Joined Majestic Realty Co., 1966, chmn., CEO; part owner Staples Ctr., LA Kings, LA Lakers; owner Silverton Hotel & Casino, Las Vegas, Nev. Bd. dirs. Comerica Bank, Calif., LA Sports & Entertainment Commn. Dir. Big Bros. of Greater L.A.; bd. govs. Natural History Mus. of L.A. County, Bowers Museum of Cultural Art; bd. trustees Loyola Marymount U., U. So. Calif.; bd. regents Loyola High School; founder Majestic Realty Found., 2002-. Served USMC, 1962—66. Recipient Partners with Youth award, Big Sisters of Greater Los Angeles and the Inland Empire, 2004, Woodrow Wilson award for Public Service, 2006; named a Champions of Industry, Calif. Bus. Properties Assn., 2004; named one of Forbes' Richest Americans, 2006. Mem. Explorers Club, Soc. Indsl. Realtors. Avocations: bicycling, mountain climbing. Office: Majestic Realty 13191 Crossroads Pkwy N 6th Fl City Of Industry CA 91746-3497 Office Phone: 562-948-4301. Business E-Mail: eroski@majesticrealty.com.

ROSKILL, JON, computer software company executive; m. Jennifer S. Roskill. BSS, U. Mass., Amherst, 1985; MBA, Boston U. Mktg. mgr. Digital Equipment Corp.; joined Microsoft Corp., 1993, gen. mgr. devel. & .NET enterprise server mktg., corp. v.p. US bus. & mktg., 2006—. Office: Microsoft Corp 1 Microsoft Way Redmond WA 98052-6399

ROSKIN, WILLIAM A., communications executive; BBA, City Coll. of NY, 1963; LLB, St. John's U. Sch. of Law, 1966; LLM, NY U. Grad. Sch. of Law, 1968. Staff, law dept. RCA Global Comm., Inc.; gen. counsel City NY Dept. Pers., City Svc. Commn., NYC, 1971—76; v.p., labor rels. Warner Comm., 1976—86; sr. v.p., human resources Coleco Industries, Inc., 1986—88; v.p. human resources, admin. Viacom, Inc., NYC, 1988—92, sr. v.p., human resources, admin., 1992—2004, exec. v.p., 2004—06, sr. advisor, 2006—. Office: Viacom Inc 1633 Broadway 8th Fl New York NY 10019 Office Phone: 212-258-6230. E-mail: bill.roskin@viacom.com.

ROSKO, MARYANN A., nurse; b. McKeesport, Pa., Sept. 22, 1930; d. George Rosko and Anna Makar. Grad. in Nursing, Homestead Hosp., Pa., 1951; postgrad. in Nursing, Chgo. Lying In, Ill., 1952—53. RN Pa. RN staff Homestead Hosp., Pa., 1951—55; RN supr. McKeesport Hosp., Pa., 1959—62, RN staff devel., 1963—68; RN insvc. edn. Magee Women's, Pitts., 1968—85. 1st lt. U.S. Army Nurse Corp, 1955—58. Home: 2605 Sunset Dr West Mifflin PA 15122-3564

ROSKOSKI, JOHN, religious studies educator, coach; b. Rahway, NJ, May 23, 1960; s. Charles Clement and Elaine Magdelene Roskoski; m. Tracy Ann Abrego, Apr. 23, 1995; children: Nicholas Thaddeus, Samuel John. BA in Religious studies, Seton Hall U., 1981, MA in Jewish-Christian studies, 1990; MA in Theology, New Brunswick Theol. Sem., 1986; MPhil in Theology, Fordham U., 2004; PhD in Bibl. Studies, Omega Bible Inst. and Sem., 2006. Cert. strength trng. instr. YMCA, catechist cert. Archdiocese Newark, 1986. Tchr. religion St. Michael's HS, Jersey City, 1982—83; instr. logic Middlesex CC, Edison, NJ, 1986; strength coach Bishop Ahr HS, Edison, 1984—89; tchr. religion Marist HS, Bayone, NJ, 1989—91; adj. prof. theol. St. Peter's Coll., Jersey City, 1992—. Adj. faculty theology Omega Bible Inst. Seminary; spkrs. bur. ThisAbled.com, 2008. Contbr. articles to profl. jours. Recipient Pres. award, Theology Omega Bible Inst. Seminary. Mem.: Home News Tribune (cmty. editl. bd. 2008—09), Assn. Bibl. Rsch., Nat. Honor Soc., Theol. Honor Soc. Roman Catholic. Avocations: chess, walking sticks, coin collecting/numismatics, powerlifting. Home: 23 Morse Ave Edison NJ 08817 Home Phone: 732-393-1960. Personal E-mail: sampson95@optonline.net.

ROSKOSKI, ROBERT, JR., biochemist, educator, author; b. Elyria, Ohio, Dec. 10, 1939; s. Robert and Mary R.; m. Laura Martinsek, Aug. 27, 1974. BS, Bowling Green State U., 1961; MD, U. Chgo., 1964, PhD, 1968. Asst. prof. U. Iowa, Iowa City, 1972-75, assoc. prof., 1975-79, vis. prof. Iowa City, 1993; prof. dept. biochemistry and molecular biology Health Scis. Ctr., La. State U., New Orleans, 1979—2006; Fred G. Brazda prof. Med. Ctr., La. State U., New Orleans, 1991—2006; founder, sci. dir. Blue Ridge Inst. for Med. Rsch., 2006—. Sr. investigator USAF Sch. Aerospace Medicine, 1967-69; assoc. dir. Med. Sci. Tng. Program, 1978-79; cons. biochemistry test com. Nat. Bd. Med. Examiners, 1981-84, 2003-06, Assn. Internat. Cancer Rsch., Royal Soc. New Zealand; mem. merit rev. bd. for basic scis. VA, 1992-95; mem. rev. com. biol. scis. U. South Fla., 1992, biochemistry St. George's U. Sch. Medicine, 1997, Kuwait U. Health Scis. Ctr., 2002. With USAF, 1966—69. NIH postdoctoral fellow U. Chgo., 1964-66; NIH spl. fellow Rockefeller U., 1969-71 Mem. Am. Chem. Soc., Am. Soc. Neurochemistry, Soc. for Neurosci., Am. Soc. Biol. Chemists, Am. Soc. Pharmacology and Exptl. Therapeutics, Internat. Soc. Neurochemistry, Assn. Med. and Grad. Depts. Biochemistry (sec. 1994-96, pres. 1997), Am. Assn. Med. Colleges (coun. Acad. socs., 1998-01), Greater New Orleans Soc. for Neurosci. (pres. 1982-83), Am. Med. Writers Assn. Achievements include research in signal transduction and cancer therapy. Home:

221 Haywood Knolls Dr Hendersonville NC 28791-8717 Office: 3754 Brevard Rd Ste 116 Box 19 Horse Shoe NC 28742-8814 Office Phone: 828-891-5637. Office Fax: 828-890-8130. Business E-Mail: rrj@brimr.org.

ROSKY, BURTON SEYMOUR, lawyer; b. Chgo., May 28, 1927; s. David T. and Mary W. (Zelkin) R.; m. Leatrice J. Darrow, June 16, 1951; children: David Scott, Bruce Alan. Student, Ill. Inst. Tech., 1944-45; BS, UCLA, 1948; JD, Loyola U., LA, 1953. Bar: Calif. 1954, U.S. Supreme Ct 1964, U.S. Tax Ct 1964; C.P.A., Calif. Auditor City of L.A., 1948- 51; with Beidner, Temkin & Ziskin (C.P.A.s), LA, 1951-52; supervising auditor Army Audit Agy., 1952-53; practiced law L.A., Beverly Hills, 1954—; ptnr. Duskin & Rosky, 1972-82, Rosky, Landau & Fox, 1982-93, Rosky, Landau & Stahl, Beverly Hills, 1993-99; pvt. practice Beverly Hills, 1999—. Lectr. on tax and bus. problems; judge pro tem Beverly Hills Mcpl. Ct., L.A. Superior Ct.; mem. L.A. Mayor's Community Adv. Council. Contbr. profl. publs. Charter supporting mem. Los Angeles County Mus. Arts; contbg. mem. Assocs. of Smithsonian Instn.; charter mem. Air and Space Mus; mem. Am. Mus. Natural History, L.A. Zoo; supporting mem. L.A. Mus. Natural History; mem. exec. bd. So. Calif. coun. Nat. Fedn. Temple Brotherhoods, mem. nat. exec. bd.; mem. bd. govs. Loyola Sch. Law, L.A.; regent Coll. Am. Assn. Atty.-CPAs. With USNR, 1945-46. Walter Henry Cook fellow Loyola Law Sch. Bd. Govs. Fellow Jewish Chautauqua Soc. (life mem.); mem. Am. Arbitration Assn. (nat. panel arbitrators), Am. Assn. Attys.-CPAs (charter mem. pres. 1968), Calif. Assn. Attys.-CPAs (charter mem., pres. 1963), Calif. Soc. CPAs, Calif., Beverly Hills, Century City, Los Angeles County bar assns., Am. Judicature Soc., Chancellors Assocs. UCLA, B'nai B'rith, Tau Delta Phi, Phi Alpha Delta. Jewish (mem. exec. bd., pres. temple, pres. brotherhood). Club: Mason. Office Phone: 323-655-9757.

ROSKY, THEODORE SAMUEL, insurance company executive; b. Chgo., Apr. 14, 1937; s. Theodore and Lora Marie (O'Connell) R.; m. Jacqueline Reed, Apr. 19, 1958; 1 child, Laura Marie. BA, State U. Iowa, 1959. Various actuarial positions Conn. Gen. Life Ins. Co., Hartford, 1959-66, assoc. actuary, 1967-70, controller, 1970-73, 2d v.p., actuary, 1973, v.p., 1973-78; exec. v.p. Capital Holding Corp., 1978-84, exec. v.p., CFO, 1984-91, exec. v.p., 1991-92; bd. dirs. Legend Funds, 1993-98, SBM Mut. Funds, 1995-97, SBM Certificate Co., 1996-98; fin. svcs. Dory L.P., 1998-99. Instr. State U. Iowa, 1958-59, U. Hartford, 1964-66, U. Conn., 1967-68. Active Mayor's Adv. Com. on Pub. Art, 1990—2005; mem. bd. pensions Evang. Luth. Ch. Am., 1974—82, 1984—87, 1989—95; bd. dirs. Hartford Coll. for Women, 1974—78, Macauley Theater, 1983—85, Louisville Fund for the Arts, 1980—97, Louisville Luth. Home, 1983—97, Louisville Orch., 1982—88, 1989—95, Ky. Opera, 1992—2001, Lincoln Found., 1992—2002, Actors Theatre of Louisville, 1995—, New Performing Arts, 1996—98, Oak and Acorn, 1995—2001, Glassworks Found., 2002—03, Pub. Radio Partnership, 2003—04, YMCA Safe Place, 2003—, Sch. Choice Scholarships, 2004—05. Recipient award Soc. Actuaries, 1958 Fellow Soc. Actuaries; mem. Am. Acad. Actuaries, Southeastern Actuaries Club. Republican. Lutheran. Home and Office: 2304 Speed Ave Louisville KY 40205-1642

ROS-LEHTINEN, ILEANA CARMEN, United States Representative from Florida; b. Havana, Cuba, July 15, 1952; arrived in US, 1959; d. Enrique Emilio and Amanda (Adato) Ros; m. Dexter Lehtinen; children: Amanda, Patricia stepchildren: Douglas, Katherine. AA, Miami-Dade Cmty. Coll., Fla., 1972; BA in Edn., Fla. Internat. U., Miami, 1975, MS in Ednl. Leadership, 1986; PhD in Higher Edn., U. Miami, 2004. Founder, chief adminstr. Eastern Acad., Miami-Dade County, 1978—; mem. Fla. Ho. of Reps., Tallahassee, 1983—86, Fla. State Senate, 1987—89, US Congress from 18th Fla. dist., 1989—, mem. govt. reform com., internat. rels. com., ranking mem. fgn. affairs com. Mem. Speaker's Task Force Drug Free America, Nat. Guard & Reserve Component Caucus, Travel & Tourism Caucus, Sunbelt Caucus, Human Rights Caucus, Horse Caucus, Fire Svcs. Caucus, Boating Caucus; co-chair Congl. Children's Caucus, Nat. Marine Sanctuary Caucus, 2008—, Congl. Vision Caucus, 2008—. Recipient Nat. Legis. award, LULACH, 1999, Edn. award, Hispanic Heritage Found., 2007; named Ofcl. of Yr., Youth Crime Watch America, 2001. Mem.: Bi-lingual Pvt. Sch. Assn. Republican. Episcopalian. Office: US House of Reps 2470 Rayburn House Office Bldg Washington DC 20515-0918 also: Ileana Ros Lehtinen Congress Woman 8660 W Flagler St Ste 131 Miami FL 33144-2035 Office Phone: 202-225-3931, 305-275-1800. Office Fax: 202-225-5620, 305-275-1801.*

ROSMAN, HOWARD S., cardiologist, educator; b. Detroit, Aug. 29, 1947; s. Carl and Mae S. Rosman; m. Sarine John-Rosman, Aug. 21, 1999; m. Nancy R Rosenhaus, Aug. 4, 1974 (div. Apr. 17, 1997); 1 stepchild, Akash D. Patel children: Sarah Z., Benjamin J., David A., John M. BA, Harvard Coll., Cambridge, Mass., 1969; MD, U. Mich., Ann Arbor, 1975. Resident in internal medicine Emory U., Ga., 1978; vis. fellow cardiology Royal Postgraduate Med. Sch., London, 1979; fellowship in cardiovascular disease Emory U., Ga., 1981; sr. staff physican Henry Ford Health Sys., Detroit, 1982—99; sr. staff physician St John Hosp. and Med. Ctr., Detroit, 1999—. Clin. asst. prof. of medicine U. of Mich., Ann Arbor, Mich., 1983—88; assoc. chief divsn. of cardiology Henry Ford Health Sys., Detroit, 1987—99; clin. assoc. prof. of medicine U. of Mich., Ann Arbor, Mich., 1989—94; program dir. cardiology fellowship Henry Ford Hosp., Detroit, 1987—99, dir. of undergraduate med. edn., 1992—99; prof. of internal medicine Case Western Res. U., Cleveland, Ohio, 1995—99; mem. bd. of governors Henry Ford Health Sys., Detroit, 1997—99; councilor Am. Coll. of Cardiology, Mich. Chpt., Mich., 1999—2005; cardiology program dir. St John Hosp. and Med. Ctr., Detroit, 1999—; prof. of medicine Wayne State U., Detroit, 1999—. Pres. Am. Heart Assn., Metro Detroit, 2004—06. Recipient Outstanding Faculty Tchr., U. Mich. Med. Students, 1982 - 1994 (11 awards), Henry Ford Hosp. Residents, 1983 - 1999 (6 awards), Instr. of the Yr., St John Hosp. Cardiology Fellows, 1999 - 2005 (3 awards), Dept. of Internal Medicine Tchg. award, Wayne State U. Med. Sch., Medicine Faculty, 2003. Fellow: Am. Heart Assn., Am. Coll. Cardiology (pres. Mich. chpt. 2008—, gov. 2008—). Office: 22101 Moross Rd 2nd Fl Vep Cardiology Grosse Pointe MI 48236 E-mail: howard.rosman@stjohn.org.

ROSMAN, MICHAEL E., lawyer; BA in Polit. Sci. and Econs. summa cum laude, U. Rochester, 1981; JD, Yale Law School, 1984. Assoc. Rosenman & Colin, New York City, 1984—93; gen. counsel Ctr. for Individual Rights, 1994—. Guest lecturer Washington Semester, American U. Office: Center for Individual Rights 1233 20th Street NW Suite 300 Washington DC 20036

ROSMAN, SAMANTHA L., pediatrician, emergency physician; m. David A. Rosman. BA magna cum laude, Bryn Mawr Coll.; MD with honors, Columbia U., 2004. Resident pediat. Children's Hosp. Boston.; fellow pediat. emergency medicine Boston Med. Ctr. Mem.: AMA (bd. trustees 2005—, chair Task Force on Health Sys. Reform), Med. Soc. of State of NY (former mem. House of Del.), Mass. Med. Soc., Am. Coll. Emergency Physicians, Am. Acad. Pediat. Office: Boston Med Ctr One Boston Medical Center Place Boston MA 02118*

ROSNER, INGRID K., pediatric allergist; b. 1947; MD, Wayne State U. Sch. Med., Detroit, 1972. Diplomate Am. Bd. Pediat., Am. Bd. Allergy & Immunology, lic. NY. Resident Boston Med. Ctr.; resident pediat. Boston City Hosp., 1973—77, Children's Hosp. Boston, 1977—78, fellowship, 1978—79; attending physician NY Presbyn./Weill Cornell Med. Ctr.; pvt. practice allergist, immunologist, 1991—. Contbr. articles to profl. jours. Mailing: Ingrid Rosner MD 301 E 66th St New York NY 10021 Office Phone: 212-650-9000.

ROSNER, JONATHAN LINCOLN, physicist, researcher; b. NYC, July 23, 1941; s. Albert Aaron and Elsie Augustine (Lincoln) R.; m. Joy Elaine Fox, June 13, 1965; children: Hannah, Benjamin. BA, Swarthmore Coll., 1962; MA, Princeton U., 1963, PhD, 1965. Research asst. prof. U. Wash., Seattle, 1965-67; vis. lectr. Tel Aviv U., Ramat Aviv, Israel, 1967-69; asst. prof. physics U. Minn., Mpls., 1969-71, assoc. prof., 1971-75, prof., 1975-82, U. Chgo., 1982—. Contbr. numerous articles to profl. and scholarly jours. Alfred P. Sloan fellow, 1971-73, Guggenheim fellow, 2002. Fellow Am. Phys. Soc. Democrat. Jewish. Avocations: fishing, hiking, skiing, amateur radio. Office: U Chgo Enrico Fermi Inst 5640 S Ellis Ave Chicago IL 60637-1433 Business E-Mail: rosner@hep.uchicago.edu.

ROSNER, LEONARD ALLEN, lawyer; b. NYC, Apr. 13, 1967; s. Arnold and Betty (Zimmerman) R.; m. Rachel Stein, Nov. 19, 1994; children: Andrew N., Leah Rose. AB in Polit. Sci. Pub. Rels., Syracuse U., 1989, JD cum laude, 1992. Bar: NY State Bar 1993, Dist. of Columbia Bar 1995, US Dist. Ct. (we. dist.), NY 1995. With Gallo & Iacovangelo LLP, Rochester, NY. Fin. editor Syracuse Jour. Internat. Law and Commerce, 1991—92. Bd. mem. Temple B'rith Kodesh, Rochester, NY; bd. mem. legal counsel Rochester Children's Theater; com. mem. J C C. Campership Golf Tournament. Mem.: Syracuse U. Alumni Club of Rochester, Monroe County Bar Assn. (mem., prof. performance com.), N.Y. Bar Assn. Avocations: golf, reading, television sports, nautilus, travel. Office: Gallo & Iacovangelo LLP Ste 700 39 State St Rochester NY 14614 Business E-Mail: leonardrosner@gallolaw.com.

ROSNER, ROBERT, astrophysicist, educator; b. Garmisch-Partenkirchen, Bavaria, Germany, June 26, 1947; came to U.S., 1959; s. Heinz and Faina (Brodsky) R.; m. Marsha Ellen Rich, Sept. 5, 1971; children: Daniela Karin, Nicole Elise. BA, Brandeis U., 1969; PhD, Harvard U., 1976; PhD (hon.), Ill. Inst. Tech., 2006, No. Ill. U., 2007. Asst. prof. Harvard U., Cambridge, Mass., 1978-83, assoc. prof., 1983-86; astrophysicist Smithsonian Astrophys. Observatory, Cambridge, 1986-87; prof. U. Chgo., 1987—, William E. Wrather prof., 1998—; chief scientist Argonne Nat. Lab., 2002—05, dir., 2005—09; pres. UChicago/Argonne LLC, 2006—09. Trustee Adler Planetarium, Chgo., 1989-98, chmn. dept. astronomy and astrophysics, 1991-97. Contbr. more than 200 articles to profl. jours. Woodrow Wilson fellow, 1969. Fellow Am. Phys. Soc., Am. Acad. Arts and Scis. (elected); mem. Am. Astron. Soc., Soc. Indsl. and Applied Math., Am. Geophys. Union, Norwegian Acad. Sci. and Letters (fgn. mem.). Home: 4950 S Greenwood Ave Chicago IL 60615-2816 Office: U Chicago Astrophysics 5640 S Ellis Ave Chicago IL 60637-1433 Business E-Mail: r-rosner@uchicago.edu.

ROSOFF, WILLIAM A., lawyer; b. Phila., June 21, 1943; s. Herbert and Estelle (Finkel) R.; m. Beverly Rae Rifkin, Feb. 7, 1970; children: Catherine D., Andrew M. BS with honors, Temple U., 1964; LLB magna cum laude, U. Pa., 1967. Bar: Pa. 1968, U.S. Dist. Ct. (ea. dist.) Pa. 1968. Law clk. to Hon. Abraham L. Freedman. U.S. Ct. Appeals (3d cir.), 1967-68; instr. U. Pa. Law Sch., Phila., 1968-69; assoc. Wolf, Block, Schorr & Solis-Cohen, Phila., 1969-75, ptnr., 1975-96, chmn. exec. com., 1987-88; also vice chmn. bd. dirs. Advanta Corp., Spring House, Pa., 1996—, pres., 1999—. Trustee RPS Realty Trust, 1990-96, Atlantic Realty Trust, 1996-2006; guest lectr. confs. and seminars on tax law; mem. tax adv. bd. Commerce Clearing House, 1983-94; mem. legal activities policy bd. Tax Analysts, 1978-95; mem. Little, Brown Tax Adv. Bd., 1994-96; chmn. bd. dirs. RMH Telesvcs., Inc., 1997-99. Editor U. Pa. Law Rev., 1965-67; mem. editl. bd. Jour. Partnership Taxation, 1983-2000; contbr. articles to profl. jours. Past mem. com. on law and social action Phila. coun. Am. Jewish Congress; bd. visitors Temple Fox Sch. Bus., 2005-. Fellow Am. Coll. Tax Counsel; mem. Am. Law Inst. (cons. taxation of partnerships 1976-78, assoc. reporter taxation of partnerships, 1978-82, mem. adv. group on fed. income tax project 1982-, cons. taxation of pass-through entities 1995-2000), Order of Coif, Beta Gamma Sigma, Beta Alpha Psi. Office: PO Box 918 Spring House PA 19477-0918 Mailing: PO Box 844 Spring House PA 19477

ROSOVSKY, HENRY, economist, educator; b. Danzig, Sept. 1, 1927; came to U.S., 1940, naturalized, 1949; s. Selig S. and Sophie (Rosovsky) R.; m. Nitza Brown, June 17, 1956; children— Leah, Judith, Michael. AB, Coll. William and Mary, 1949, LL.D., 1976; A.M. (John E. Thayer scholar), Harvard U., 1953, PhD, 1959; L.H.D. (hon.), Yeshiva U., 1977, Hebrew Union Coll., 1978, Colgate U., 1979, Brandeis U., 1984; PhD (hon.), Hebrew U. of Jerusalem, 1982; LL.D. (hon.), Queen's U., Ont., 1984, U. Hartford, 1984, CUNY, 1986, U. Mass., 1986, Harvard U., 1998; DHL (hon.), Hebrew Coll., Brookline, Mass., 1987, NYU, 1993; DL, St. Mary's Coll. Md., 1989, Jewish Theol. Sem., 1995; EdD with Honors, Williams U., 2008. From asst. prof. to prof. econs. and history U. Calif.-, Berkeley, 1958-65; chmn. Center Japanese and Korean Studies, 1962-65; prof. econs. Harvard U., 1965—, Walter S. Barker prof. econs., 1975-84, Geyser univ. prof., 1984-96, Geyser univ. prof. emeritus, 1996—, chmn. dept., 1969-72, dean Faculty Arts and Scis., 1973-84; assoc. dir. East Asia Research Center, 1967-69. Mem. Harvard U. Corp., 1985-97; vis. prof. Hitotsubashi U., Tokyo, 1957, Tokyo U., 1962, Hebrew U., Jerusalem, 1965; hon. dir. Japan Fund.; dir. emeritus Corning, Inc.; hon. prof. Centro U. Francisco, De Vitoria, Madrid, 1996. Author: Capital Formation in Japan, 1868-1940, 1961, Quantitative Japanese Economic History, 1961, (with K. Ohkawa) Japanese Economic Growth, 1973, The University: An Owner's Manual, 1990; editor: Explorations in Entrepreneurial History, 1954-56, Industrialization in Two Systems, 1966, Discord in the Pacific, 1972, (with H. Patrick) Asia's New Giant, 1976, (with P. Higonnet, D. Landes) Favorites of Fortune, 1991, (with S. Kumon) The Political Economy of Japan, Vol. 3: Cultural and Social Dynamics, 1992. Chmn. bd. trustees Am. Jewish Congress, 1975-88. Served to lst lt. AUS, 1946-47, 50-52. Jr. fellow Soc. Fellows, 1954-57; recipient Schumpeter prize Harvard, 1963, Clark Kerr medal U. Calif., Berkeley, 1992. Fellow Am. Acad. Arts and Scis., Am. Philos. Soc.; mem. Am. Econ. Assn., Econ. History Assn., Assn. Asian Studies, Chevalier, Legion of Honor, Order of Sacred Treasure, Star (Japan). Office: Harvard Univ Loeb House 17 Quincy St Cambridge MA 02138-3805 Home: 130 Mount Auburn St Apt 506 Cambridge MA 02138 Office Phone: 617-495-4151. Business E-Mail: hrosovsky@harvard.edu.

ROSOWSKY, ANDRE, chemist, educator; b. Lille, France, Mar. 3, 1936; came to the U.S., 1946; s. Vladimir and Tamara (Rajcyn) R.; m. Erlene Cohen, Aug. 26, 1962; children; David, Lisa, Jessica. BS, U. Calif., Berkeley, 1957; PhD, U. Rochester, 1961. Rsch. fellow Harvard U., Cambridge, Mass., 1961-62; rsch. assoc. Children's Cancer Rsch. Found., Boston, 1962-78; prin. assoc. Dana-Farber Cancer Inst., Boston, 1978-87; assoc. prof. Dana-Farber Cancer Inst., Harvard Med. Sch., Boston, 1987—. Cons. NIH Study Sect. Editorial adv. bd.: Jour. Medicinal Chemistry, 1974-79, Pteridines, 1988—; contbr. articles to profl. jours. and chpts. to books; patentee in field. Mem. Am. Chem. Soc. (alternate councilor 1972-74, councilor 1979-83), Am. Assn. for Cancer Rsch. Office: Dana Farber Cancer Inst 375 Longwood Ave Fl 7B Boston MA 02215-5395

ROSPUT REYNOLDS, PAULA GAIL, insurance company executive; b. RI, Oct. 2, 1956; m. Stephen P. Reynolds, Oct. 2004. BA with highest honors, Wellesley Coll., 1978. Economist consulting firm, Boston; sr. v.p. Pacific Gas Transmission Co.; pres. CEO Duke Energy N.Am., Houston; pres., COO AGL Resources, Atlanta, pres., CEO, 2000—05, chmn., 2002—05; pres., CEO Safeco Corp., Seattle, 2006—08, chmn., pres., CEO, 2008; vice-chmn., chief restructuring officer Am. Internat. Group (AIG), NYC, 2008—. Bd. dirs. Coca Cola Enterprises, 2001—, Delta Air Lines, Inc., 2004—, Safeco Corp., 2006—, Anadarko Petroleum Corp., 2007—. Bd. dir. United Way Met. Atlanta, Ga. Rsch. Alliance, Ga. C. of C., Commerce Club, Atlanta. Named one of 100 Most Powerful Women, Forbes Mag., 2006—09, 50 Most Powerful Women in Business, Fortune mag., 2006, Top 20 Nonbank Women in Fin., US Banker, 2007; named to Ga. State Univ. Bus. Hall Fame, 2004. Mem.: Am. Gas Assn. (bd. dir.). Office: AIG 70 Pine St New York NY 10270*

ROSS, ALEX, music critic; b. 1968; m. Jonathan Lisecki, 2005. BA, Harvard U., 1990. Music critic NY Times, 1992—96, New Yorker, 1996—. Author: The Rest is Noise: Listening to the Twentieth Century, 2007 (Nat. Book Critics Circle award, named one of Best Books of 2007, NY Times, LA Times, Washington Post, NY mag., Time, Newsweek, The Economist), (blog) The Rest is Noise, 2004—. Recipient ASCAP-Deems Taylor award for Music Criticism, 1996, 2004, letter of distinction, Am. Music Ctr., 2006; named a MacArthur Fellow, The John D. and Catherine T. MacArthur Found., 2008; Holtzbrinck fellow, Am. Acad. Berlin, 2002—03, Fleck fellow, Banff Ctr., 2006. Office: New Yorker 4 Times Sq New York NY 10036*

ROSS, AMANDA JOANNE, biology professor; b. Lafayette, Ind., Apr. 5, 1981; d. David Aaron and Angela Rose Zagorski; m. Matthew Donald Ross, Aug. 14, 2004; 1 child, Eloisa Abigail. MS in Environ. Sci., Taylor U., Upland, 2005. Environ. specialist Atwell-Hicks, Brighton, Mich., 2005—06; adj. faculty Saginaw Valley State U., Univ. Ctr., Mich., 2006—.

ROSS, AMI L., insurance and finance company executive; m. William Hyde. BS in Econs., U. Colo., Boulder. CLU long term care Calif., 2006. Fin. planner Prudential Fin., San Diego, 2003—06; pres. Ross Ins. & Fin. Svcs., LA, 2007—. Fin. cons., chairperson Tiny Stars - Charity, Malibu, Calif. Mem.: Nat. Assn. Ins. and Fin. Advisors, Mensa Internat. Office: Ross Insurance Financial Svcs 6219 Alta Ave Whittier CA 90601-3706 Office Fax: 866-449-5357; Home Fax: 866-449-5357. Business E-Mail: ami@ross-financial.com.

ROSS, ANNETTE LEE, educational consultant; b. Detroit, May 15, 1940; d. Jesse O. and Sylvia Irene Ross. BS Edn., Ctrl. Mich. U., Mt. Pleasant, 1963; M Edn., Wayne State U., Detroit, 1971. Cert. tchr. Mich. Tchr. Marian H.S., Bloomington, Mich., 1963—64, Macomb K-8 Sch., Mt. Clemens, Mich., 1964—71, Seminole K-8 Sch., Mt. Clemens, 1972—88; ednl. cons. Susan Kovalik & Assocs., Federal Way, Wash., 1988—2006, reflexologist Ctr. Integrative Therapy Spring Lake, Mich., 2006—. Girls basketball coach Seminole Middle Sch., 1978—88, girls volleyball coach, 1978—88, boys golf coach, 1978—88; varsity volleyball coach Mt. Clemens H.S., 1981—88; ptnr. Ctr. Reflexology Therapy, Spring Lake, 2005—. Author: The Way We Were The Way We Can Be, 1989, 2002. Recipient Slovak Republic award, Susan Kovalik & Assocs., 1997. Mem.: LWV. Home: 5970 Avalon Dr #211 Muskegon MI 49444

ROSS, ANNIE LEE, minister, counselor; b. Saluda, SC, Feb. 5, 1933; d. Alonzo and Daisy Bell (Stewart) Robinson; m. Robert L. Ross, Aug. 1957. Diploma, Washington Bapt. Sem., 1978, Automation Acad. Inc., Washington, 1979; DD (hon.), Gospel Ministry, Monicella, Ga., 1979; Doctrine in Ch., Bethany Baptist Ch., 2004. Ordained chaplain Nat. Chaplain Assn., 1979, lic. ministry lic. Christian Ch. Outreach, 1979. Minister New Bethany Bapt. Ch., Washington, 1966—, dir., Sunday sch. tchr., 1966—, tchr. Moments with the Children Sunday sch., 1992—2000; nurse asst. Jesuit Cmty. at Georgetown U., Washington, 1979—89; asst. Tobler Bookstore, Washington, 1986; owner Christian Books and Bibles, Washington, 1986—90. Author: The Works of Annie Lee Ross in the 90's to the Present, 2000. Chaplain Ward 6 Aging Planning Com., Washington, 1998—. Recipient Alumnus award, Washington Bapt. Sem., 1989. Mem.: Washington Bapt. Sem., So. Bapt. Assn. Women's Aux. (pres. Women's Aux. 1986, 1990), Abbey Place Block Club (chairperson 1985—). Democrat. Baptist. Avocations: writing, teaching, singing, preaching. Home: 1166 Abbey Place NE Washington DC 20002 Office: Christian Ch Outreach Ministry 1166 Abbey Place NE Washington DC 20002

ROSS, BARRY C., lawyer; BS, SUNY, Albany, 1971; JD magna cum laude, Brooklyn Law Sch. Bar: NY 1975. Ptnr., group co-leader Bryan Cave LLP, NYC. Office: Bryan Cave LLP 1290 Ave of the Americas New York NY 10104 Office Phone: 212-541-2255. E-mail: bcross@bryancave.com.

ROSS, BOBBY (ROBERT JOSEPH ROSS), retired college football coach; b. Richmond, Va., Dec. 23, 1935; s. Leonard Aloysius and Martha Isabelle (MMiller) R.; m. Alice Louise Bucker, June 13, 1959; children: Chris, Mary Catherine, Teresa, Kevin, Robbie. BA, Va. Mil. Inst., 1959. Tchr., head football coach Benedictine High Sch., Richmond, 1959-60; tchr., coach Colonial Heights (Va.) High Sch., 1962-65; asst. football coach Va. Mil. Inst., Lexington, 1965-67, Coll. William & Mary, Williamsburg, Va., 1967-71, Rice U., Houston, 1971-72, U. Md., College Park, 1972-73; head football coach The Citadel, Charleston, SC, 1973-77, U. Md., College Park, 1982-87, Ga. Tech., Atlanta, 1987-91; asst. coach Kansas City Chiefs, 1978-82; head coach San Diego Chargers, 1992-96, Detroit Lions, 1997-2001, U.S. Mil. Acad., West Point, NY, 2003—06. 1st lt. U.S. Army, 1960-62. Named Coach of Yr., Washington Touchdown Club, 1982, Kodak Coach of Yr., 1990, Bobby Dodd Coach of Yr., 1990, Bear Bryant Coach of Yr., 1990, Scripps-Howard Coach of Yr., 1990, Nat. Coach of Yr., CBS Sports, 1990, Coach of Yr., Walter Camp Football Found., 1990, NFL Coach of Yr. UPI, 1992, Pro Football Weekly, 1992, Pro Football Writers' Assn., 1992, Football News, 1992, Football Digest, 1992, Maxwell Football

Club, 1992, AFC Coach of Yr. Kansas City 101 Banquet. Mem. Am. Football Coaches Assn., Coll. Football Assn. (coaching com. 1988-92). Roman Catholic. Personal E-mail: abrjross@comcast.net.

ROSS, BRIAN ELLIOTT, chief investigative correspondent; b. Chgo., Oct. 23, 1948; s. Kenneth Earl and Shirley Louise (Johnston) R. BA, U. Iowa, 1971. Corr. KWWL-TV, Waterloo, Iowa, 1971, WCKT-TV, Miami, Fla., 1972-74; news corr. NBC News, Cleve. and NYC, 1974—94; chief investigative corr. ABC News, NYC, 1994—. Recipient Peabody award, 1974, 1991, 1999, 2001, 2006, duPont-Columbia U. award, 1975, 1985, 1986, 2002, 2004, 2009, Sigma Delta Chi award, 1976, Nat. Headliner award, 1976—78, 1987, 2004, 2005, Emmy award, 1980, 1985, 1988, 1992, 2004, 2006, Overseas Press Club award, 1988, 1990, 1992, 1994, 1998—2008, George M. Polk award, 1989, 1993, 1997, 1998, 2005, Sidney Hillman award, 1993, Outstanding Internat. Investigative Reporting award, Ctr. Pub. Integrity, 2005, Disting. Alumni award, U. Iowa, 2005; named to U. Iowa Journalism Sch. Hall of Fame, 1998. Office: ABC News 147 Columbus Ave New York NY 10023 Office Phone: 212-456-7612.

ROSS, BRUCE SHIELDS, lawyer; b. LA, Feb. 1, 1947; s. Floyd and Mary Louise (Shields) R.; m. Janet G. Ross, Jan 27, 1968 (div. Jan. 1977); 1 child, Stephanie; m. Carol Burlingame, Apr. 2, 1977; children: Andrew, Tiffany. AB cum laude, Oberlin Coll., 1968; JD, U. Calif., Berkeley, 1971. Bar: Calif. 1971, US Tax Ct. 1973, US Dist. Ct. (ctrl. dist. Calif.) 1977; cert. specialist in estate planning, trust, probate law, Calif. Assoc. Nossman & Krueger, LA, 1971-73; assoc. to ptnr. Poindexter & Doutre, LA, 1973-78; assoc. Alschuler & Grossman, LA, 1978, ptnr., 1979-84, Morrison & Foerster, LA, 1984—90, Ross, Sacks & Glazier, LA, 1991—2001; exec. ptnr. Holland & Knight, LLP, LA and Rancho Santa Fe, Calif., 2001—06; ptnr.-in-charge Luce, Forward, Hamilton & Scripps, LLP, LA, 2006—. Participant Temp. Judge Prog. LA Mcpl. Ct., 1989—95; mem. adv. bd. Philip E. Heckerling Inst. Estate Planning U. Miami, 2000—, adj. prof. law grad. prog. in estate planning, 2000—03; academician Internat. Acad. Estate and Trust Law; mem. panels, lectr. in field. Mem. U. Calif. Law Rev., 1969-71, note and comment editor 1970-71; author: Calif. Practice Guide: Probate, 1986-2004 (updated annually); co-editor Guidebook to the Calif. Rules of Profl. Conduct for Estate Planning, Trust and Probate Counsel, 1997; contbr. articles to profl. jours. Trustee Pacific Asia Mus., Pasadena, Calif., 1983-1991, pres., 1988-1991; fin. chmn. Boy Scouts Am., Glendale, Calif., 1984-85; gov. The Webb Schs. of Calif., Claremont, 1987—. Named one of Top 100 Attys., Worth mag., 2006. Fellow Am. Coll. Trust and Estate Counsel (sec., treas., v.p. and pres.-elect 2001-05, pres, 2005, mem. bd. regents 1995-2001, 02, mem. bd. exec. com. 2000-01, 02-).Mem. ABA (chair task force on state and local regulation, com. on exempt orgns., sect. taxation 1984-88, chair estate and trust litig. com. 1991-93, group chair litig. and controversy com. 1996-, mem. supervisory coun. 1997-2003, co-chair multijurisdictional practice com. 2000-02, sect. liasion to ethics 2000 commn. 1998-2000, real property, probate and trust law sect.), LA County Bar Assn. (exec. com. tax. sect. 1984-85, exec. com. estates and trusts sect. 1994-97, exec. com. alternative dispute resolution sect. 1996-97), State Bar Calif. (mem. 1987-89, vice-chair 1989-90, chair 1990-91, adv. 1991-1994. Democrat. Unitarian Universalist. Avocations: music, opera, swimming, stamp collecting/philately. Office: Luce Forward Hamilton & Scripps 601 S Figueroa Ste 3900 Los Angeles CA 90017 Office Phone: 213-896-2400, 213-892-4962. Office Fax: 213-452-8042. Business E-Mail: bruce.ross@hklaw.com. E-mail: bruce@luce.com.

ROSS, CARNE, international relations specialist, former diplomat; b. 1966; Grad. in econs. and politics, U. Exeter, England, 1989. Tchr. English lit and history, Zimbabwe; western European desk British Fgn. Office, London, 1989—91, 1995—98, fgn. policy tng. Bonn, Germany, 1992—95, speechwriter to the British fgn. sec., 1997—98; first sec., UK del. UN Security Coun., NYC, 1998—2002; strategy coord. UN in Kosovo, 2002—04; founder, dir. Ind. Diplomat, NYC, 2005—. Author: (plays) The Fox, 2001, (books) Independent Diplomat: Dispatches from an Unaccountable Elite, 2007. Office: Ind Diplomat 333 7th Ave 14th Fl New York NY 10001 Office Phone: 212-594-8295. Office Fax: 212-594-8430.

ROSS, CAROL, retired women's college basketball coach; b. Oakland, Miss. BA in Edn., U. Miss., 1982. Volunteer asst. Bellhaven Coll., Jackson, Miss., 1982—83; asst. coach Auburn U., 1984—90; women's basketball head coach U. Fla., 1991—2002, U. Miss., 2002—07. Head coach US Select Team, 1998. Recipient Coaches vs Cancer Champion award, 2000, Regional Coach Yr. award, Women's College Basketball Assn., 2001; named Coach of Yr., SEC Conf., 1994, 2001, co-Coach of Yr., 2003, Dist. 9 Coach of Yr., Women's College Basketball Assn., 1994, 1997, 2001; named one of The Top 50 Bus. Women in Miss., Miss. Bus. Jour.; named to U. Miss. Athletic Hall of Fame, 2001. Achievements include playing on US Women's Olympic Basketball Team, 2000.

ROSS, CATHERINE ELIZABETH, literature and language professor; b. Nurnberg, Germany, Sept. 23, 1950; d. Charles C. and Julia E. Ross; m. Calvin Mebane Ross, Dec. 21, 2003. PhD, U. Tex., Austin, 1998. Asst. prof. English U. Tex., Tyler, 1998—2003, assoc. prof. English, 2003—. Home: 3318 S Keaton Ave Tyler TX 75701 Office: Univ Tex 3900 University Blvd Tyler TX 75799 Business E-Mail: catherine_ross@uttyler.edu.

ROSS, CHARLES, artist; b. Phila., Dec. 17, 1937; s. Fred H. and Gertrude (Hill) R.; m. Elizabeth Ginsberg, 1977; m. Jill O'Bryan, 2007. AB in Math, U. Calif., Berkeley, 1960, MA in Sculpture, 1962. Adj. prof. dept. art Coll. Santa Fe. Exhibited in one-man shows: Dilexi Gallery, San Francisco, 1961, 65, 66, 68, Dwan Gallery, NYC, 1968, 69, 71, Daytons Gallery 12, Mpls., 1968, John Weber Gallery, NYC, 1972, 77, 79, 81, The Clocktower, NYC, 1974, Utah Mus. Fine Arts, Salt Lake City, 1975, Mus. Contemporary Art, La Jolla, Calif., 1976, Chgo., 1976, Inst. Contemporary Art, Phila., 1977, Susan Caldwell Gallery, NYC, 1977, MIT, 1977, Portland Center for Visual Arts, 1981, Sena Gallery, Santa Fe, 1991, Johnson Gallery U. N.Mex., 1992, Humphrey Gallery, NYC, 1995, Mus. de Arte y Diseno Contemporaneo, San Jose, Costa Rica, 1996, Braunstein/Quay Gallery, San Francisco, 2007; exhibited in group shows: Archtl. League of NY, 1967, Albright Knox Art Gallery, Buffalo, 1967, Finch Coll., NYC, 1967, Aldrich Mus., Ridgefield, Conn., 1967, Nelson Atkins Mus., Kansas City, 1968, Milw. Art Ctr., 1968, Whitney Mus., NYC, 1969, Art Inst. Chgo., 1969, Art Gallery of Ont., Toronto, 1969, Galeries-pilotes, Lausanne, Switzerland, 1970, Mus. Fine Arts, Boston, 1971, Indpls. Mus. Art, 1974, Neuberger Mus., SUNY, Purchase, 1975, Stadtisches Mus., Leverkusen, Germany, 1975, Phila. Coll. Art, 1977, Hirshhorn Mus., Washington, 1977, Old Customs House, NYC, 1977, Mus. Natural History, NYC, 1977, Leo Castelli Gallery, NYC, 1978, Yale U. Art Gallery, 1978, Dartmouth Coll. Gallery, 1978, Aspen Ctr. for Visual Arts, Colo., 1980, Centre Georges Pompidou, Paris, 1980, Renwick Gallery, Smithsonian Instn., Washington, 1980, Mus. Contemporary Art, Chgo., 1981, MIT, Cambridge, 1981, Bard Coll., 1984, Light Gallery, NYC, 1985, Venice Biennale, 1986, Differentes Natures la Defense, Paris, 1992, Anchorage Mus. History and Art, 1994, Richard Humphrey Gallery, NYC, 1995, Kunsthallen Brandts Klaedefabrik, Odense, Denmark, 1996, SITE Santa Fe, 1996, Ctr. Pompidou, Paris, 1997, NIT Intercomm. Ctr., Tokyo, 1997, Biennale de Lyon, France, 2000, Chiaroscuro Gallery, Santa Fe, 2004, Harwood Mus., Taos, N.Mex., 2005, Artempo, Palazzo, Fortuny, Venice, Italy, 2007; commns. include: prism/solar spectrum skylight sculpture for Fed. Bldg, Lincoln, Nebr., 1976, U. Pa., 1977, Dietrich Found., Phila., 1979, Spectrum Bldg, Denver, 1980, Grand Rapids Art Mus., Mich., 1982, Towson State U., Md., 1983, Cumberland Rapid Transit Sta., Chgo., 1983, Linay Corp., Kansas City, Mo., 1985, Plaza of the Americas, Dallas, 1985, Wells Fargo Bldg., San Diego, 1986, San Francisco Internat. Airport, 1987, Anchorage Internat. Airport, 1987, Naugatuck Higher Edn. Ctr., Conn., 1990, Harvard Bus. Sc. Chapel, 1992, French Ministry of Culture Chateau d'Oiron, 1993, Cook Inst., Grand Rapids, Mich., 1996, Dwan Light Sanctuary, United World Coll., Montezuma, N.Mex., 1996, US Fed. Courthouse, Tampa, 1998, Saitama U., 1999, Japan, Kauffman Found., Kansas City, 2001, Nat. Mus. of the Am. Indian, Smithsonian Inst., Washington, DC, 2004, Meiji U., Tokyo, 2004, Albuquerque Conv. Ctr., 2004, Highlands U., Las Vegas, 2005; represented in permanent collections Nelson Atkins Mus., Whitney Mus. Am. Art, Berkeley Art Mus., Indpls. Mus. Art, Butler Inst. Am. Art, Herbert F. Johnson Mus. Art Cornell U., GSA Art and Architecture Program, U. Pa., Dietrich Found., Grand Rapids Art Mus., Gen. Elec. Corp., City Chgo., Towson State U., Becton Dickinson Corp., Security Pacific Bank, Found. Ctr., N.Y.C., Wynne Jackson Inc., Albuquerque Mus., Linclay Corp., Witco Chem. Corp., City of San Diego, Walker Art Ctr., City of San Francisco, State of Alaska, Koll Co., Los Angeles County Mus. Art, Mus.de Arte y Diseno Contemporaneo, San Jose, Kunsthallen Brandts Klaedefabrik, Odense, Des Moines Art Ctr., French Ministry of Culture, Frederick A. Weisman Mus., Mpls., Harvard Bus. Sch., Mus. Fine Arts, Santa Fe, United World Coll., N.Mex., Saitama U., Japan, Kauffman Found., Kansas City, Meiji U., Tokyo, Nat. Mus. Am. Indian, Washington (Wash. Bldg. Congress award, 2005), Kramarsky Found.; works in progress include: Star Axis, architectonic earthwork/naked eye observatory atop a mesa in N.Mex. Author: Sunlight Convergence Solar Burn (Am. Inst. Graphic Arts award 1976); films Sunlight Dispersion, 1972, Solar Eclipse, 1972. Recipient Art and Architecture Collaborations award Boston Soc. Architects, 1993, Interfaith Forum on Religion, Art and Arch. Design award Harvard Bus. Sch. Chapel, 1993, award for distinction for artistic achievement Nat. Coun. Art Adminstrs., 1997. Office: Loïc Malle 167 Blvd Haussmann 75008 Paris France Business E-Mail: malle.loic@wanadoo.fr. E-mail: info@staraxis.org. *My work deals with the nature of light, time, and planetary motion.*

ROSS, CHARLOTTE PACK, social services administrator; b. Okla. City, Oct. 21, 1932; d. Joseph and Rose P. (Traibich) Pack; m. Roland S. Ross Ross, May 6, 1951 (div. July 1964); m. Stanley Fisher Ross, Mar. 17, 1991; children: Beverly Jo, Sandra Gail. Student, U. Okla., 1949—52, New Sch. Social Rsch., 1953. Cert. tchr. Exec. dir. Suicide Prevention & Crisis Ctr. San Mateo County, Burlingame, Calif., 1966—88, Death Dignity Edn. Ctr., San Mateo, Calif., 1994—; conf. coord. U. Calif., San Francisco, 1971—; pres., exec. dir. Youth Suicide Nat. Ctr., Washington, 1985—93; instr. San Francisco State U., 1981—83; pres. Calif. Senate Adv. Com. Youth Suicide Prevention, 1982—84; spkr. Menninger Found., 1983—84; cons. univs. & health svcs. Mem. edtl. bd. Suicide & Life Threatening Behavior, 1976—89; mem. regional selection panel Pres.'s Commn. White House Fellows, 1975—78; mem. CIRCLON Svc. Club, 1979—, Com. Child Abuse, 1981—85; founding mem. Women Responsible Govt., co-chmn., 1974—79. Group Counseling for Suicidal Adolescents, 1984, Teaching Children the Facts of Life and Death, 1985. Recipient Outstanding Exec. award, San Mateo County Coordinating Com., 1971, Koshland award, San Francisco Found., 1984. Mem.: Assn. County Contract Agys. (pres. 1982), Assn. United Way Agy. Execs., Am. Assn. Suicidology (sec. 1972—74, bd. govs. 1976—78, accreditation com. 1975—, chair region IX 1975—82, svc. award 1990), Internat. Assn. Suicide Prevention (v.p. 1985—), Wash. Acad. Scis., Peninsula Press Club.

ROSS, CHRISTOPHER WADE STELYAN, diplomat; b. Quito, Ecuador, Mar. 3, 1943; parents Am. citizens; s. Claude G. Anthony and Antigone Andrea R.; m. Carol Geraldine Canning, Nov. 30, 1968 (div.); 1 child, Anthony Gordon. AB summa cum laude, Princeton U., 1965; cert., Mid. East Ctr. Arab Studies, 1964; MA, Johns Hopkins U., 1967. Editl. asst. Mid. East Jour., Washington, 1965-68; instr. Arabic lang. Columbia U., NYC, 1966, Princeton U., NJ, 1967; pub. affairs trainee USIA, 1968-69; jr. officer trainee Am. Embassy, Tripoli, Libya, 1969-70; dir. Am. Cultural Ctr., Fez, Morocco, 1970-73; press attache Am. Embassy, Beirut, 1973-76, pub. affairs officer Algiers, 1976-79, dep. chief mission and charge d'affaires, 1979-81; pub. affairs advisor Bur. Nr. East & South Asian Affairs Dept. of State, Washington, 1981-82, spl. asst. to presdl. emissaries to Lebanon & Mid. East, 1982-84, dir. regional affairs Bur. Nr. East & South Asian Affairs, 1984-85; exec. asst. to Under Sec. State for Polit. Affairs Washington, 1985-88; amb. Algeria, 1988-91, Syria, 1991-98; coord. counterterrorism Dept. State, Washington, 1998; spl. coord. pub. diplomacy, 2001—03; sr. adv. Bureau Internat. Info. Programs, 2003—04; spl. adv. Iraq polit. affairs Bur. N.E. Affairs, 2005—; exec. dir. Search for Common Ground in Mid. East, 1999—2001; sr. advisor polit. affairs Coalition Provisional Auth., Baghdad, 2004; sr. adv. US del. UN Gen. Assembly, 2006—07; spl. envoy in the Western Sahara UN, 2009—. Chmn. bd. trustees Am. Sch. Algiers, 1978-80; hon. chmn., bd. trustees Damascus Cmty. Sch., 1991-98. Contbr. articles to profl. jour. Recipient Superior Honor award USIA, 1976, 83, Superior Honor award Dept. of State, 1988, Presdl. Meritorious Svc. award, 1983, 85, 89, 93, Disting. Honor award Dept. of State, 1997, Disting. Pub. Svc. medal Dept. Def., 2005. Mem. Coun. Fgn. Rels., Am. Fgn. Svc. Assn., Assn. Diplomatic Studies and Tng., Mid. East Inst., Mid East Studies Assn. N.Am., Royal Soc. Asian Affairs, Am. Inst. Maghrib Studies, Princeton Club. Greek Orthodox. Avocations: classic cars, bicycling. Office: MINURSO Hdqs Laayoune PO Box 5846 Grand Ctrl Station New York NY 10163-5864 Personal E-mail: cwsross@starpower.net.*

ROSS, COLEMAN DEVANE, accountant, insurance company executive; b. Greensboro, NC, Mar. 18, 1943; s. Guy Matthews and Nancy McConnell (Coleman) R.; m. Carol Louise Morde, Aug. 26, 1965; children: Coleman, Jonathan, Andrew. BSBA, U. NC, Chapel Hill, 1965; MA in Econs., Trinity Coll., Hartford, Conn., 2006; MSFS, Am. Coll., Bryn Mawr, Pa., 2008. CPA, CPCU, CLU. With Price Waterhouse, Tampa, Fla., Toronto, Can., Hartford, Conn., NYC, 1965—99, ptnr., 1977—99; chmn., mng. ptnr. Nat. Ins. Svcs. Group, 1988-94; exec. v.p., CFO Trenwick Group Ltd., Hamilton, Bermuda, 2000—02, Phoenix Cos., Inc., Hartford, Conn., 2002—03. Bd. dirs. NCCI Holdings, Inc., Boca Raton, Fla., 2004—, Pan-Am. Life Ins. Co., New Orleans, 2006—, Syncona Holdings Ltd., Hamilton, Bermuda, 2006—, Omega Ins. Holdings Ltd., Hamilton, 2009—. Exec. bd. Conn. Rivers coun. Boy Scouts Am., 1978—, pres., 1985-88, bd. dirs. N.E. Region, 1988—, v.p., 1993-96, 2002-07, pres. New England area, 1988-91, bd. dirs. Greater NY coun., 1994-2004; participant Leadership Greater Hartford, 1977; bd. visitors U. NC, 2001-05.; bd. advisors U. NC Rams Club, 2008-. Recipient Silver Beaver award Boy Scouts Am., 1987, Silver Antelope award, 1991. Mem. AICPA (reins. auditing and acctg. task force 1979-85, rels. with actuaries com. 1982-85, ins. cos. com. 1985-88, acctg. stds. exec. com. 2002-05, property and liability ins. co. task force 2005-), NC Assn. CPAs, Nat. Assn. Corp. Dirs., CFA Inst., Soc. Fin. Svc. Profls., CPCU Soc., Chartered Ins. Inst., Fin. Exec. Internat., Inst. Mgmt. Accountants, Inst. Internal Auditors, Polytechnic Club, Carolina Club. Avocation: running. Home: 318 W Univ Dr Chapel Hill NC 27516 Personal E-mail: coleman@colemanross.com.

ROSS, DANIEL R., lawyer; b. Stamford, Conn., Oct. 20, 1941; s. Adrian E. and Ruth (Hill) R.; m. Faye Zerwekh, Aug. 15, 1965; children: Kevin S., Eric D., David W. SB, MIT, 1963; LLB, U. Pa., 1966. Atty. adviser to Hon. Theodore Tannenwald, Jr. U.S. Tax Ct., Washington, 1966-68; assoc. Drinker, Biddle & Reath, Phila., 1970-77, ptnr., 1977-98, Commons & Commons, Phila., 1998—2005, Ross & McCrea, 2005—. Presenter in field. Pres. bd. trustees First United Meth. Ch. Germantown, 1984-2004; v.p. & dirs. Smith Playground and Playhouses, Inc, 2003—. Capt. U.S. Army, 1968-70, Vietnam. Mem. ABA (chair com. on income of estates and trusts 1985-87, com. on govt. subcoms. 1988-91, taxation sect.). Avocations: bicycling, skiing, tennis, computers. Office: 7169 Germantown Ave 2d Fl Philadelphia PA 19119 Home Phone: 215-247-8059; Office Phone: 215-247-3550. Personal E-mail: danrross@aol.com. Business E-Mail: dross@rossmccrea.com.

ROSS, DARRIN, composer; Pres. Bad Boi Studios; composer, sound engr. Jam on Prodns., 1984—. Collaborator: with Renee Harris Dance Party USA,: with Renee Harris 1 House Street. Recipient Philly's St. Buzz Producer of Yr. award, 1997.

ROSS, DAVID EDMOND, church official; b. Lewiston, Maine, Oct. 1, 1950; s. Rev. and Mrs. Lorne Arla Collins R.; m. Shirley Evelyn Godin, Aug. 19, 1972. BA in Theology cum laude, Berkshire Coll., 1973; MPA, U. Maine, 1989. Ordained to ministry Advent Christian Ch., 1975. Pastor State Road Advent Christian Ch., Presque Isle, Maine, 1973-91; exec. dir. Advent Christian Ch. Gen. Conf., Charlotte, NC, 1991—2003; sr. pastor Fellowship Advent Christian ch., Bethlehem, NC, 2003—. V.p. Maine State Conf. Advent Christian Chs., 1975-76, pres., 1976-81, 86-91; mem. exec. coun. Advent Christian Ch., 1981-90, long range strategy com., 1986—96; seminar leader Am. Festival of Evangelism, Kansas City, 1981; dir. Northern Lights Youth Choir, 1974-90. Pres. Piedment Conf. Advent Christian Chs., 2007—. Office: Fellowship Advent Christian Church 885 Icard Ridge Rd Taylorsville NC 28681 Office Phone: 828-495-8086. Personal E-mail: bethlehemshepherd@hotmail.com.

ROSS, DELMER GERRARD, historian, educator; b. Los Banos, Calif., Nov. 5, 1942; s. Elmer G. and Orva Beth (Dickinson) R.; m. Karen Ann Gibson, June 17, 1977; children: Michelle, Richard. BA, Pacific Union Coll., 1965; MA, U. Calif., Santa Barbara, 1967, PhD, 1970. Instr. Pacific Union Coll., Angwin, Calif., 1968-69; from asst. to assoc. prof. Oakwood Coll., Huntsville, Ala., 1970-76; from assoc. prof. to prof. history Loma Linda U., Riverside, Calif., 1976-91, chmn. dept. history and polit. sci., 1986-90; prof. history and polit. sci. La Sierra U., Riverside, 1991—. Author: Visionaries and Swindlers, 1975, Rails Across Costa Rica, 1976, Rails in Paradise, 1991, Gold Road to La Paz, 1992, Development of Railroads in Guatemala and El Salvador, 1849-1929, 2001, To End a Crooked Trail, 2002, Rockhounding the Wiley's Well District of California, 2006, Iner S. Ritchie, Medical Evangelist, 2007, The Bagdad Chase Mine & Its Ludlow & Southern Rialway, 2009; co-author: Hope...Not Ashamed, 2002, Reminiscences of Walter D. Scott, Desert Entrepreneur of the American West, 2003; mem. editl. bd. Adventist Heritage mag., 1987-90. Bd. dirs. Inst. for Research in Latin Am., Mobile, Ala., 1968-82. Mem. Am. Hist. Assn., Assn. 7th Day Adventist Historians (exec. sec. 1973-74, sec.-treas. 1974-75, pres. 1981-82), Assn. Western Adventist Historians, Nat. Railway Hist. Soc., Colo. Railroad Hist. Found. (life), Railway and Locomotive Hist. Soc. Republican. Avocations: reading, retracing historical trails and railroad routes, faceting gemstones. Office: La Sierra U Dept History Riverside CA 92515 Home Phone: 951-789-9384; Office Phone: 951-785-2067. E-mail: dross@lasierra.edu.

ROSS, DENNIS B., diplomat, writer; b. San Francisco, Nov. 26, 1948; m. Deborah Ross; children: Gabriel, Rachel, Ilana. Grad, UCLA, 1970; PhD (hon.), Amherst Coll., Jewish Theological Seminary, Syracuse U. Dep. dir. Office Net Assessment US Dept. Def., Washington, 1982—84, 1989—92; exec. dir. Berkeley-Stanford program on Soviet internat. behavior, 1984—86; dir. Near East and South Asian affairs NSC; dir. policy planning office US Dept. State, Washington, 1988—92, spl. Middle East coord., 1992—2001; counselor and Ziegler Disting. fellow Washington Inst. for Near East Policy, Washington, 2001—; spl. advisor for the Gulf & Southwest Asia US Dept. State, Washington, 2009—. Spkr. in field; fgn. affairs analyst Fox News Channel; commentator Washington Post, NY Times, LA Times; chmn. Inst. Jewish People Policy Planning; adj. lectr. pub. policy John F. Kennedy Sch. Govt. Harvard U., 2002—04; Fred & Rita Richman Disting. vis. prof. Brandeis U., 2003, 05; Allis-Chalmers Disting. prof. internat. affairs Marquette U., 2004—05; adj. prof. Georgetown U. Sch. Fgn. Svc., 2006—07; adj. prof. govt. Georgetown U., 2007. Author: The Missing Peace: The Inside Story of the Fight for Middle East Peace, 2004, Statecraft And How to Restore America's Standing in the World, 2007; contbr. articles to profl. jours. Recipient Presdl. Medal for Disting. Fed. Civilian Svc.; named Alumni of Yr., UCLA. Achievements include facilitation of Israeli-Jordan peace treaty; assisting the Israelis and Palestinians in reaching 1995 Interim Agreement; brokered Hebron Accord, 1997.*

ROSS, DENNIS E., retired automotive executive, lawyer; b. 1951; B, JD, U. Mich. Tax legis. counsel, dep. asst. sec. Office Tax Policy U.S. Treasury Dept., 1986—89; tax ptnr. Davis Polk and Wardwell, NY, 1989—95; chief tax officer Ford Motor Co., Dearborn, Mich., 1995—2000, v.p., gen. counsel, 2000—05, ret., 2005.

ROSS, DIANA, singer, actress, entertainer, fashion designer; b. Detroit, Mar. 26, 1944; d. Fred and Ernestine R.; m. Robert Ellis Silberstein, Jan. 1971 (div. 1976); children: Rhonda, Tracee, Chudney; m. Arne Naess, Oct. 23, 1985 (div. 2000, dec. 2004); children: Ross Arne, Evan Olaf. Pres. Diana Ross Enterprises, Inc., Anaid Film Prodns., Inc., RTC Mgmt. Corp., Chondee Inc., Rosstown, Rossville, music pub. Started in Detroit as mem. the Primettes; lead singer until 1969, Diana Ross and the Supremes; solo artist, 1969—; albums include Diana Ross, 1970, 76, Everything Is Everything, 1971, I'm Still Waiting, 1971, Lady Sings The Blues, 1972, Touch Me In The Morning, 1973, Original Soundtrack of Mahogany, 1975, Baby It's Me, 1977, The Wiz, 1978, Ross, 1978, 83, The Boss, 1979, Diana, 1981, To Love Again, 1981, Why Do Fools Fall In Love?, 1981, Silk Electric, 1982, Endless Love, 1982, Swept Away, 1984, Eaten Alive, 1985, Chain Reaction, 1986, Diana's Duets, 1987, Workin' Overtime, 1989, Red Hot Rhythm and Blues, 1987, Surrender, 1989, Ain't No Mountain High Enough, 1989, The Force Behind the Power, 1991, Stolen Moment: The Lady Sings... Jazz & Blues, 1993, Musical Memories Forever, 1993, The Remixes, 1994, A Very Special Season, 1994, Making Spirits Bright, 1994, Take Me Higher, 1995, Voice of Love, 1996, Gift of Love, 1996, The Greatest, 1998, The Real Thing, 1998, Every Day is a New Day, 1999, Love From...Diana Ross,

2001, The #1's, 2004, Complete Symphony, 2004, The Blue Album, 2006, I Love You, 2007; films include Lady Sings the Blues, 1972, Mahogany, 1975, The Wiz, 1978; NBC-TV spl., An Evening With Diana Ross, 1977, Diana, 1981, numerous others; TV movie Out of Darkness, 1994; author: Secrets of a Sparrow, 1993, Diana Ross: Going Back, 2002, Upside Down: Wrong Turns, Right Turns and the Road Ahead. Recipient citation V.P. Humphrey for efforts on behalf Pres. Johnson's Youth Opportunity Program, citation Mrs. Martin Luther King and Rev. Abernathy for contbn. to SCLC cause, awards Billboard, Cash Box and Record World as worlds outstanding singer, Grammy award, 1970, Female Entertainer Yr. NAACP, 1970, Cue award as Entertainer Yr., 1972, Golden Apple award, 1972, Gold medal award Photoplay, 1972, Antoinette Perry award, 1977, nominee as Best Actress Yr. Lady Sings the Blues Motion Picture Acad. Arts and Scis., 1972, Golden Globe award, 1972, BET (Black Entertainment Television) Walk Fame award, 1999, Heroes award, NARAS, NY Chpt., 2000, Kennedy Ctr. Honors, John F. Kennedy Ctr. for Performing Arts, 2007; named to The Rock & Roll Hall Fame, 1988. Office: c/o Motown Records 825 8th Ave New York NY 10019

ROSS, DONALD, JR., language educator, academic administrator; b. NYC, Oct. 18, 1941; s. Donald and Lea (Meyer) R.; m. Sylvia Berger (div.); 1 child, Jessica; m. 2d, Diane Redfern, Aug. 27, 1971; children—Owen, Gillian BA, Lehigh U., 1963, MA, 1964; PhD, U. Mich., 1967. Asst. prof. English U. Pa., Phila., 1967—70; prof. writing, studies and English U. Minn., Mpls., 1970—, dir. composition program, 1982—86, 2002—03, dir. Univ. Coll., 1984—89. Author: American History and Culture from the Explorers to Cable TV, 2000; co-author: Word Processor and Writing Process, 1984, Revising Mythologies: The Composition of Thoreau's Major Works, 1988; co-editor, contbr.: American Travel Writers, 1776-1865, 1997, American Travel Writers, 1850-1915, 1998; contbr. articles to profl. jours. Grantee Am. Coun. Learned Socs., 1976, 90, NSF, 1974, Fund for Improvement of Postsecondary Edn., 1982-85; recipient Disting. Teaching award U. Minn., 1992. Mem. MLA, Assn. for Computers and Humanities (exec. sec. 1978-88), Internat. Soc. for Travel Writing (exec. sec. 2001—). Office: U Minn Dept Writing Studies 180 Westbrook 77 Pleasant St SE Minneapolis MN 55455-0152 Business E-Mail: rossj001@umn.edu.

ROSS, DONALD KEITH, retired insurance company executive; b. Rochester, NY, July 1, 1925; s. Alexander L. and Althea G. (Granger) R.; m. Mary F. Fyffe, June 4, 1949; children: Catherine (Mrs. Charles P. Lesher), Susan (Mrs. William Gardner Morris, Jr.), Donald Keith, Deborah Anne Holt. B.E., Yale U., 1946; MBA, Harvard U., 1948. With N.Y. Life Ins. Co., NYC, 1948—, exec. v.p., 1974-79, vice chmn., 1979-80, pres., 1980-81, chmn. bd., CEO, 1981-90, chmn. exec. com., 1990-93; ret., 1996.

ROSS, DONALD L., rental and leasing company executive; m. Nancy Ross; 3 children. From mgmt. trainee to br. mgr. Enterprise Rent-A-Car, St. Louis, 1964—71, corp. v.p., 1980—92, sr. exec. v.p., COO, 1992—2001, pres., 2001—08, vice chmn., 2008—. Bd. dirs. Centric Group, BJC Health Care, Mo. Bapt. Hosp. Bd. dirs. Mcpl. Theatre Assn., St. Louis; past bd. dirs. DeSmet Jesuit HS, Boys Hope/Girls Hope. Mem.: Boone Valley Golf Club (bd. dirs.). Office: Enterprise Rent a Car 600 Corporate Park Dr Saint Louis MO 63105-4211

ROSS, DOUGLAS, lawyer; b. LA, July 12, 1948; s. Mathew and Brenda Butler (Boynton) R.; m. Lynne Rose Maidman, June 14, 1970. AB cum laude, Tufts U., 1970; JD with honors, George Washington U., 1973. Bar: Ohio 1973, D.C. 1980, U.S. Supreme Ct. 1976. Asst. atty. gen., antitrust sect. Office of Ohio Atty. Gen., Columbus, 1973-74; spl. asst. U.S. atty. Ea. Dist. Va., Alexandria, 1977; trial atty. antitrust divsn. U.S. Dept. Justice, Washington, 1975-82; atty. advisor Office of Legis. Affairs, 1984-86, Office of Legal Policy, 1987-89, Office Policy Devel., 1989-92; Supreme Ct. counsel Nat. Assn. Attys. Gen., 1982-91. Ran advocacy project for states to enhance their effectiveness before Supreme Ct., 1982—91; operated clearinghouse on state constl. law, 1987—91; civil divsn. Appellate Staff U.S. Dept. Justice, Washington, 1992—94, Office of Consumer Litigation, 1994—2000, spl. counsel for agr. antitrust divsn., 2000—. Recipient Meritorious award Dept. Justice, 1979, Spl. Achievement award, 1984, 96, 97. Mem. Supreme Ct. Hist. Soc., D.C. Bar Assn., Supreme Ct. Opinion Network (bd. dirs. 1989-91), Arlington County Sports Commn. (chair aquatics com. 2004—), Longbridge Park Master Plan Oversight Com. (chair indoor subcom. 2004—), Arlington Sports Found. (v.p. 2009-). Jewish. Home: 3153 19th St N Arlington VA 22201-5103 Office: US Dept Justice 950 Pennsylvania Ave NW Washington DC 20530-0001 Home Phone: 703-528-6386; Office Phone: 202-514-1874.

ROSS, EDWARD, cardiologist; b. Fairfield, Ala., Oct. 10, 1937; s. Horace and Carrie Lee (Griggs) R.; m. Catherine I. Webster, Jan. 19, 1974; children: Edward, Ronald, Cheryl, Anthony. BS, Clark Coll., 1959; MD, Ind. U., 1963. Diplomate Am. Bd. Internal Medicine; cert. specialist in clin. hypertension Am. Soc. Hypertension. Intern Marion County Gen. Hosp., Indpls., 1963; resident in internal medicine Ind. U., 1964-66, 68, cardiology rsch. fellow, 1968-70, clin. asst. prof. medicine, 1970; cardiologist Capitol Med. Assn., Indpls., 1970-74; pvt. practice medicine, specializing in cardiology Indpls., 1974—. Staff cardiologist Winona Meml. Hosp., Indpls., chief cardiovascular disease, 2000-04, med. dir. cardiovascular svcs., 2000-04, med. dir. cardiac cath lab, 2000-04, chief interventional cardiology, 2000-04; staff Meth. Hosp., Indpls., chmn. cardiovasc. sect., 1989-96; chmn. cardiovasc. sect., dir. cardiovasc. ctr. Meth. Hosp., 1990-92; bd. dirs. Meth. Hosp. Heart-Lung Ctr., med. dir. cardiovasc. svcs., 1991-98; med. dir. cardiovascular svcs. Methodist Hosp., Indpls., Ind., 2000-06, cardiac catheterization lab., 2000-06, cardiovascular programs, Clarian Health Indpls., 2000—, cardiovascular svcs., Cardicac Cath. Lab., cardiovascular programs, Clarian Health Ptnrs., 2000-, sr. cardiologist, Methodist Cardiology Physician, 2006-. Assoc. editor Angiology, Jour. Vascular Disease; sr. editor Jour. Vascular Medicine, 1983—. Mem. Ctrl. Ind. Health Planning Coun., 1972-73; bd. dirs. Ind. chpt. Am. Heart Assn., 1973-74, multiphasic screening East Side Clinic, Flanner Ho. of Indpls., 1968-71; med. dir. Nat. Ctr. for Health Svc. R&D, HEW, 1970; consumer rep. radiologic device panel health FDA, 1988-92; dir. hypertensive screening State of Ind., 1974; J.B. Johnson Cardiovasc. lectr. Nat. Med. Assn., 1991. Capt. MC, USAF, 1966-68. Recipient Lifetime Achievement award, Ctr. Leadership Devel., 2003, Leadership award, Indpls. Police Dept., 2005; scholar, Nat. Found. Health, 1955, Gorges Found., 1956; Woodrow Wilson fellow, 1959. Fellow Royal Soc. Promotion of Health (Eng.), Am. Coll. Angiology (v.p. fgn. affairs, sec. 1993—), Internat. Coll. Angiology, Am. Soc. of Angiology, Am. Coll. Cardiology, Assn. Black Cardiologists (mem. bd. dirs. 1990-94); mem. NAACP, AMA, Am. Soc. Contemporary Medicine and Surgery, Nat. Med. Assn. (coun. sci. assembly 1985-89), Ind. Med. Soc., Marion County Med. Soc., Am. Coll. Physicians, Am. Heart Assn., Ind. Soc. Internal Medicine (pres. 1987-89), Ind. State Med. Assn. (chmn. internal medicine sect. 1987-89), Ind. Med. Soc., Aesculapean Med. Soc., Hoosier State Med. Assn. (pres. 1980-84, 90-95), Urban League, Alpha Omega Alpha, Alpha Kappa Mu, Beta Kappa Chi, Omega Psi Phi. Methodist. Office: 1801 N Senate Blvd #310 Indianapolis IN 46202 Home Phone: 317-966-4848; Office Phone: 317-962-2500. Business E-Mail: eross@clarian.org.

ROSS, EDWARD JOSEPH, architect; b. Dec. 13, 1934; s. Miriam Ross; children: Linda Joy, Melissa Carol. Student, Boston Archtl. Ctr., 1952-55, 61-62, USAF Surveying Sch., 1955-56, Boston Soc. Civil Engrs., 1956-57, Carl Bolivar Structural Engr., 1962-63. Registered arch., Mass., Calif., NY, Fla., NH, Vt., cert. Nat. Coun. Archtl. Registration Bds.; lic. constrn. supr. Mass., expert witness constrn. law. Draftsman, assoc. William W. Drummey, Architect, Boston, 1952-59; job capt., designer Drummey-Rosane-Anderson, Boston, 1959-64; projects arch. Maginnis & Walsh & Kennedy, Boston, 1964-69; v.p. William Nelson Jacobs Assocs., Inc., Boston, 1969-73; staff arch. Robert Charles Assocs., Inc. Archs., Boston, 1973-74; office mgr. Charles F. Jacobs Assocs., Inc., Cambridge, Mass., 1974-76; cons. arch. Linenthal, Eisenberg & Anderson, Boston, 1976-77; staff arch. Eisenberg Haven Assocs., Inc., Boston, 1977-78; chief arch., chief insp. Boston Housing Authority, 1978-83; prin. Edward J. Ross, AIA/FARA, Randolph, Mass., 1983-84; arch., sr. assoc., dir. constrn. adminstrn. Stull and Lee, Inc., Boston, 1984-91; pvt. practice Randolph, Stoughton, Mass., West Palm Beach, Fla., 1963—2000; consulting arch., contrn. adminstr., expert witness, 2000—06. Mem. FCC Tech Plus. Mem. exec. bd. and ops. com. United Civic Orgn.; bd. dir. Linderhof Property Owners Assn., Knollsbrook Condominium Complex. Staff sgt. USAF, maj. Mass. Mil. Res. Fellow: Soc. Am. Registered Archs.; mem.: USO (New Eng. coun.), AIA, Boston Soc. Archs. (mem. housing com. 1982—86), Constrn. Specifications Inst., Mass. State Assn. Archs., Am. Arbitration Assn. (nat. panel 1965—2005), United Civic Orgn. (mem. exec. bd. and ops. com.), Assn. First Corps Cadets, Am. Assn. Ret. Persons, Air Force Assn. (pres. Boston chpt.), Mass. Air N.G. Hist. Assn., Mil. Hist. Soc. Mass., Oxford 100 Condominium Assn. (pres.), Linderhof Golf Course Site One Assn. (pres. 1980—86), Ancient and Hon. Arty. Co. Mass., Oxford Colony Club Century Village (v.p.), Ten of Us Club, Am. Legion, KP, Elks. Address: 201 Oxford 100 West Palm Beach FL 33417-1412 Home Phone: 561-512-2273; Office Phone: 561-615-6680. Office Fax: 561-686-6345.

ROSS, EDWIN WILLIAM, rubber company executive; b. Phila., May 28, 1938; s. Edwin Morrison and Frances Louise (Ort) R.; m. Dorothy Anne Reilly, Sept. 24, 1966; children: E. William Jr., Catherine Ross Conlin, James David. BS, Lehigh U., 1960. Chmn. bd., CEO Key Chems., Inc., Phila., 1965-87; pres., CEO Pelmor Labs., Inc., Newtown, Pa., 1989—; chmn. Pelseal Techs., LLC, Newtown, Pa., 1998—2005; shareholder Pelmor Thailand Co., Ltd., 2006—. Mem. adv. bd. Prime Bank, Ft. Washington, Pa., 1995—98. Deacon Bryn Mawr (Pa.) Presbyn. Ch., 1977-81, elder, 1985-91, trustee, 1997-2003, pres. bd. trustees, 2001-2003; bd. dirs. Main Line Adult Day Care Ctr., 1999. With US Coast Guard Reserve 1961-69. Recipient Alumni award Lehigh U. Alumni Assn., 1985. Mem. SAR, MidAtlantic Employers Assn. (chmn. 1995-96), Metal Finishing Suppliers Assn. (pres. 1986-88, 89-90, Munning award 1992), N.E. Phila. C. of C. (chmn. 1983), Lehigh U. Alumni Assn. (bd. dirs. 1997-2000), Swedish Colonial Soc., Sons. of the Revolution Soc., St. Andrew's Soc., Colonial Soc., Exch. Club (pres. Frankford-Phila. 1972), Phila. Country Club (pres. 1986-89). Republican. Avocations: downhill skiing, hunting, travel, golf. Office: Pelmor Labs Inc 401 Lafayette St Newtown PA 18940-0309 Office Phone: 215-968-3334. Personal E-mail: ewmross@hotmail.com.

ROSS, ELIZABETH, advertising executive; B in Advt., Mich. State U. Bus. devel., account mgmt. J. Walter Thompson, Chgo., NYC; head bus. devel. group Modem Media, San Francisco, Norwalk, Conn.; with Grey Advt., San Francisco; gen. mgr. Tribal DDB, San Francisco, 2004—06; pres. Tribal DDB West, Dallas, San Francisco, LA, 2006—08; pres. US, global chief mktg. officer Tribal DDB Worldwide, 2008—09; chief growth officer US Digitas, 2009—. Named a Woman to Watch, Advt. Age, 2007; named to Advt. Hall of Achievement, Am. Advt. Fedn., 2008. Office: Digitas 33 Arch St Boston MA 02110 Office Phone: 212-515-8600, 617-867-1000. Office Fax: 212-515-8660.*

ROSS, EUNICE LATSHAW, retired judge; b. Bellevue, Pa., Oct. 13, 1923; d. Richard Kelly and Eunice (Weidner) Latshaw; m. John Anthony Ross, May 29, 1943 (dec. Jan. 1978); 1 child, Geraldine Ross Coleman. BS, U. Pitts., 1945, LLB, 1951. Bar: Pa. 1952. Atty. Pub. Health Law Rsch. Project, Pitts., 1951-52; atty. jud. asst., law clk. Ct. Common Pleas Allegheny County, Pitts., 1952-70, dir. family divsn., 1970-72, judge, 1972-96, Commonwealth Ct. Pa., 1997—2004. Adj. law prof. U. Pitts., 1967-73; mem. Bd. Jud. Inquiry and Rev., Commonwealth of Pa., 1984-89, Gov's Justice Commn., 1972-78; mem. orphan's ct. rules com. Supreme Ct. Pa., 1998—2005. Author: (with others) Survey of Pa. Public Health Laws, 1952, Justice, 1995, Lötschers of Latterbach, Mennonite Heritage Mag., 2003; co-author: Will Contests, 1992; contbr. articles to law publs. Mem. exec. com. bd. trustees U. Pitts., 1980—86, bd. visitors Law Sch., 1985—, bd. visitors Sch. Health, 1986—98; mem. bd. Animal Friends, Pitts., 1973—; committeewoman for 14th ward, vice chmn. Pitts. Dem. com., 1972; bd. dirs. The Program, Pitts., 1983—87, Pitts. History and Landmarks Found., West Pa. Hist. Soc., West Pa. Conservancy. Recipient Disting. Alumna award, U. Pitts., 1973, Medal of Recognition, 1987, Alumni award, U. Pitts. Sch. of Law, 2001, Susan B. Anthony award, Women's Bar Assn. Western Pa., 1993, Probate and Trusts award, 1994, cert. of achievement, Pa. Fedn. Women's Clubs, 1975, 1977; named Girls Scouts Woman of Yr., Pitts. coun. Girl Scouts U.S.A., 1975, Alumni of Yr., U. Pitts. Law Sch., 2001. Mem.: ABA, Allegheny County Bar Assn. (vice chmn., exec. com. young lawyers sect. 1958—59), Scribes, Order of Coif. Home: 1204 Denniston Ave Pittsburgh PA 15217-1329 Personal E-mail: rossdent@comcast.net.

ROSS, FRANK HOWARD, III, management consultant; b. Charlotte, NC, Aug. 28, 1946; s. Frank Howard Jr. (dec.) and Alma (Richardson) R. (dec.); m. Beverly Hazel Ross, June 30, 1973 (dec.); children: Martha McCausland, Frank Howard IV; m. Barbara Rydz-Roth, July 9, 2005; children: Ingrid Rydz, Veronica Anne, Karl Vincent. BS in Engring., NC State U., Raleigh, 1968. Cons. Fails & Assocs., Inc., Raleigh, NC, 1968-73; ptnr. Ross-Payne & Assocs., Inc., Barrington, Ill., 1973—. Bd. dirs. Gilldorn Savs., Chgo., 1982-85, Brickman Industries, Inc., Chgo., 1980-90; CFO WRT, Inc., Chgo., 1993-95; pres., chmn. bd. dirs. Emerald Capital Investments, Inc., Barrington, 1993-97; adviser, spkr. on constrn. and fin.; bd. dirs. Sherman Plumbing, 1975-95. Author: More $ Through $ Management, 1975, MIS and You, 1978, Planning and Budgeting, 1979, Profit by Design, 1981, Pricing for Profit, 1983, Wealthbuilding, 1984, Equipment Cost Analysis, 1988, Survivial in a Tight Economy, 1988, Associated Landscape Contractors of America Operating Cost Survey, 1989, 91, Cash Flow, 1989, Dealing with the Competition of the 90's, 1990, Designing Your Accounting System, 1991, Bidding in a Tight Market, 1992, Industry's Wage and Benefit Study, 1992, Financing Your Business, 1993, Pricing, 1994, 2d edit., 1997, How Low Can You Go?, 1995, Valuing Your Business, 1998, Posturing for Growth and Prosperity, 1999, My Executive Dashboard, 2004, If You Can't Track It, You Can't Control It!, 2007. Active Presbyn. Ch. Barrington. Named to ANLA Contractors Hall of Fame, 2007. Mem. Inst. Mgmt. Cons., Barrington Hills Country Club, Haig Point Country Club, Sigma Alpha Epsilon. Home and Office: Ross Payne Assocs Inc 190 Kimberly Rd Barrington IL 60010-2017 Office Phone: 847-381-8939.

ROSS, GARY EARL, writing educator; b. Buffalo, Aug. 12, 1951; s. Earl Ross and Marlene (Edwards) Anderson; m. Katharyn Ellen Ketter, Dec. 23, 1970 (div. 1993); children: Colleen, Timothy, David; m. Patrice Lynette Cox, Aug. 14, 1999, (div. 2008); children: Cody, Madelynne. BA in English, SUNY, Buffalo, 1973, MA in Humanities, 1975. Cert. English tchr., N.Y. Secondary English tchr. Buffalo Pub. Schs., 1973-76, Canisius High Sch., Buffalo, 1976-77; writing instr. Ednl. Opportunity Ctr. SUNY, Buffalo, 1977—94, assoc. prof., 1994—2003, prof., 2003—. Writing instr. Upward Bound SUNY, Buffalo, summers 1980—, acting dir., summer 1984; presenter in field, U.S., Can., Europe, 1975—; reader various profl. fiction readings, 1985-; bd. dirs. Just Buffalo Literacy Ctr. Contbr. articles, short stories, poems, essays to profl. publs.; videographer Writers on Video, Buffalo Pub. Libr., 1989; author (book) Wheel of Desire, 2000, Dots, 2002, Shimmerville, 2002, Nickel City Nights, 2008, Blackbird Rising, 2009, (plays) Sleepwalker, 2002, Matter of Intent, 2005 (Edgar Allan Poe award, Mystery Writers Am., 2006), The Best Woman, 2007, Picture Perfect, 2007. Bd. dirs. Ujima Theatre Co., 2005—07. Local Incentive Funding Test fellow for fiction Buffalo Arts Coun., 1989; recipient Excellence award N.Y. State/United Univ. Professions, 1990, Artist of Yr. Arts Coun., 2003, Saltonstall Found. grant. Mem. Niagara Erie Writers (chmn. bd. dirs. 1987-89), Just Buffalo, Inc. (fiction resident 1987, 92, bd. dirs. 2003-), Mid-Atlantic Popular/Am. Culture Assn. (bd. mem., pres. 2006-07), United Univ. Professions, Assn. Tchg. Artists (bd. dirs. 2003-06). Avocations: computing, games, film history, contemporary literature. Office: SUNY EOC Buffalo 465 Washington St Buffalo NY 14203-1707 Office Phone: 716-849-6727 ext. 119. E-mail: geross@buffalo.edu.

ROSS, GERALD FRED, electrical engineering executive, researcher; b. NYC, Dec. 14, 1930; s. Samuel Henry and Jenny (Saltzman) Rozansky; m. Vivian Ida Turkish, Dec. 24, 1953; children: Jayne T. Ross Kaufman, Steven A., Helene B. Ross Joseph. BEE, CCNY, 1952; MEE, Poly. U., 1955, PhD, 1963; MBA, Harvard Bus. Sch., Boston, 1979. Registered profl. engr., N.Y., Mass., Fla. Rsch. asst. U. Mich., Ann Arbor, 1952-53; sr. engr. W.L. Maxson Corp., NYC, 1954-58; rsch. sect. head Sperry Gyroscope Co., Great Neck, L.I., NY, 1958-65; dept. mgr. Sperry Rsch. Ctr., Sudbury, Mass., 1965-81; chmn. Geospatial Sys. Inc. (formerlyANRO Engring.), Sarasota, Fla., 1981—, Ana Lux Corp., 2002—. Pres., v.p., treas. Adams Pool Corp., Lexington, Mass., 1968-81. Capt. USAFR, 1953—. Contbg. author 3 books, 1986, 90, 93; contbr. numerous articles to profl. jours.; patentee in field. Fellow Polytechnic U. Fellow IEEE (life; K.C. Black Nerem Best paper award 1974, Pioneer award 2004), Nat. Acad. Engring. (life); mem. Electromagnetics Acad., Lexington Golf Club, Longboat Key Club, Laurel Oak Country Club, Sigma Xi (sr.), Tau Beta Pi, Eta Kappa Nu. Republican. Jewish. Avocations: golf, bridge.

ROSS, GERALD HARVEY, family practice and environmental medicine physician; s. Henry Warburton and Norine Hazel (Bishop) Ross; m. Heather M. Pollett, Aug. 15, 1970; children: Graham D.P., Andrew W.J. BSc, Dalhousie U., Halifax, Can., 1969, MD, 1974. Diplomate Internat. Bd. Environ. Medicine, Am. Bd. Environ. Medicine; cert. Family Med. Bd., 1979. Family medicine practice, New Minas, Nova Scotia, Canada, 1974—87; med. fellow Environ. Health Ctr., Dallas, 1987—89, med. staff, 1989—99; med. dir. N.S. Environ. Medicine Clinic, Halifax, Canada, 1990—94; rschr. Gerald H. Ross, M.D., P.L.L.C., Bountiful, Utah, 1999—. Mem. adv. com. Environ. Hypersensitivites Ont. Dept. Health, Toronto, 1989—94; rsch. fellow Breakspeare Hosp. for Environ. Medicine, Kings Langley, Hertfordhsire, England, 1988—89. Co-author reports to Ont. Ministry of Health; contbr. chapters to books, articles to profl. jours., 30 sci. papers; mem. editl. bd. Internat. Jour. Hygiene and Environ. Health, 2001—03, Environ. Epidemiology and Toxicology, 1998—2001, mem. East Coast adv. com. The Med. Post, Toronto, 1978—94. Many leadership positions Ch. LDS, Dallas, 1988—99. Grantee, Innovations in Edn. Utah, 2003; Internat. Fellow in environ. medicine, NS Dept. Health, 1987—89. Fellow: Royal Soc. Medicine (UK), Am. Acad. Environ. Medicine (chair rsch. com. 1991—94, bd. dirs. 1993—98, pres. 1995—97, Award of appreciation for serving as Pres. 1997, Herbert Rinkel award for excellence in tchg. the principles of environ. medicine 2005); mem.: AMA, LDS, Utah Meth Cops Decontamination Project (med. dir. 2007—09), Assn. Am. Physicians and Surgeons, Am. Coll. Nutrition, Am. Coll. Occupl. and Environ. Medicine, Can. Soc. Environ. Medicine, Coll. Family Physicians Can., Am. Bd. Environ. Medicine (bd. govs. 1993—, 2007), Chem. Sensitivity Found. (bd. dirs.), Can. Med. Assn., Tex. Med. Assn. Mem. Lds Ch. Avocations: reading, movies.

ROSS, HUGH COURTNEY, electrical engineer; b. Dec. 31, 1923; s. Clare W. and Jeanne F. Ross; m. Sarah A. Gordon (dec.); m. Patricia A. Malloy; children: John C., James G., Robert W. Student, Calif. Inst. Tech., 1942, San Jose State U., 1946-47; BSEE, Stanford U., 1950, postgrad., 1954. Registered profl. elec. engr., Calif. Instr. San Benito (Calif.) High Sch. and Jr. Coll., 1950-51; chief engr. vacuum power switches Jennings Radio Mfg. Corp., San Jose, Calif., 1951-62; chief engr. ITT Jennings, San Jose, Calif., 1962-64; pres. Ross Engring. Corp., Campbell, Calif., 1964—. Contbr. articles to profl. jours. Fellow IEEE (life) (chmn. Santa Clara Valley subsect. 1960-61); mem. Am. Vacuum Soc., Am. Soc. Metals. Achievements include patents in field. Avocations: electronics, electric autos, camping, ranching, solar power. Office: 540 Westchester Dr Campbell CA 95008-5012 Office Phone: 408-377-4621. Office Fax: 408-377-5182.

ROSS, JAMES OWEN, education educator, researcher; b. Morganton, NC, Sept. 27, 1948; s. Owen and Vivian Chapman Ross; life ptnr. Charles Anthony Staley; 1 child, Juliana Adele. BFA, U. of NC at Greensboro, Greensboro, North Carolina, 1971; AM, Brown U., 1986, PhD, 2003. Prof. Ringling Sch. of Art and Design, Sarasota, Fla., 1974—75, Ctrl. Piedmont C.C., Charlotte, ND, 1976—80, Appalachian State U., Boone, NC, 1983—84, RISD, Providence, 1985—86, U. of Okla., 1987—88, Wentworth Inst. of Tech., Boston, 1990—91; tchg. fellow Brown U., 1990—92; prof. ND State U., 1991—92, Western Carolina U., 1992, U. of Memphis, 1995—96, East Tenn. State U., 1997—98. Building, Preliminary Design Windsor Locks Rapids Exhbn. Ctr. (Interior Design Educators Coun. Internat. Exhbn., Nashville, Tenn., 1995), building interior, Hynes Residence Libr. (Interior Design Educators Coun. Internat. Exhibit, Denver, Colo., 1996). Dem. nominee in NC state senate, 27th dist. NC Dem. Party, NC, 1996; vestry mem. St. Peter's Episcopal Ch., Charlotte, NC, 1981—82; represented bus. in hist. dist. Friends of Fourth Ward Hist. Dist., Charlotte, NC, 1979—82. Tchg. fellow, Brown U., 1990—91. Mem.: Internat. Interior Design Assn. (Presdl. Commendation 1999), AIA (assoc.), Soc. of Archtl. Historians (life). Democrat-Npl. Soc. Of Friends. Achievements include research in impact of nineteenth-century public health movement upon American architecture: Theories of Disease, Ventilation, and Sunlight,

1840-1944. Avocations: travel, back packing, swimming, gardening, cooking. Home: 132 Malbon's Mills Rd Skowhegan ME 04976 Personal E-mail: james.ross.g86@alumni.brown.edu.

ROSS, JEFFREY S., lawyer; b. NYC, Mar. 7, 1951; AB with highest honors, U. Mich., 1972; JD, Stanford U., 1975. Bar: Calif. 1975, US Dist. Ct. (Northern Eastern & Ctrl. Calif. dist.), US Ct. Appeals (9th cir.), US Supreme Ct. Atty., pres. Friedman Ross & Hersh PC; ptnr. Pillsbury Winthrop Shaw Pittman, San Francisco. Mem.: San Francisco Barrister Club (bd. dirs. 1981—83, pres. 1983), Nat. Assn. Bar Presidents, Bar Assn. San Francisco (bd. dirs. 1986—88, pres. 1997, Award of Merit 1990, 1998), Phi Beta Kappa, Phi Eta Sigma. Office: Pillsbury Winthrop Shaw Pittman 50 Fremont St San Francisco CA 94105 Office Phone: 415-983-1730. Office Fax: 415-983-1200. Business E-Mail: jeff.ross@pillsburylaw.com.

ROSS, JERROLD, music educator; b. NYC, Feb. 8, 1935; s. James Murray and Alice (Gubernick) R. BS, NYU, 1955, PhD, 1963; MS, Queens Coll., 1959; HHD, Emerson Coll., 1997. Music tchr., Syosset, NY, 1956-58, Great Neck, NY, 1958-61; instr. music edn. NYU, 1961-63; chmn. tchr. edn. dept. NY Coll. Music, 1963-65, pres., 1965-67; head divsn. music edn. NYU, 1967-74, head divsn. arts and arts edn., 1974-82, assoc. dean, 1982-95, acting vice dean, 1979, mem. senate, 1977-80, chmn. faculty coun., 1979-80, dir. Nat. Ctr. for Rsch. in Arts Edn., 1987-95; dean Sch. Edn. St. John's U., NY, 1995—. Dir. Town Hall of NYU, 1971-74; bd. dirs. Town Hall Found., 1973-75; asst. bd. examiners NYC Pub. Schs.; mem. Tchr. Edn. Certification and Practice Bd., State of NY, 1987-93; mem. charter bd. Tchr. Edn. Accreditation Coun., Coun. Ind. Colls., 1998-05; cons. to and mem. music com. NY State Edn. Dept. Coll. Proficiency Exam. Program; mem. adv. coun. on arts in edn.; mem. NY State Commr.'s Adv. Com. on Tchr. Edn., chair, Coun. U. Deans; mem. participant various confs.Nat. Endowment for Arts, US Office Edn., Am. Assn. Colls. Tchr. Edn., Getty Ctr. for Edn. in Arts; bd. dirs. various projects NY State Edn. Dept., Nat. Found on Arts and Humanities, NY State Council on Arts, Andrew W. Mellon Found., Rockefeller Found., Reimann Found., Henry and Lucy Moses Found., Pinkerton Found., Rubin Scholars Program in Israel. Author: Interpreting Music Through Movement, 1963. V.p. Concert Artists Guild NY, 1964-69; bd. dirs. Usdan Ctr. Arts, chmn. bd. dirs., 1972-80, 85-02; founding mem. Arts Edn. Group NY, 1998-; bd. dirs. Broadway Assn., Village Nursing Home, 1984-86; bd. dirs. Am. Assn. Music Therapists, pres., 1978-80; mem. citizens adv. bd. Sta. WNCN AM-FM, 1976-94, Tchr. Edn. Collaborative NY Comprehensive Ctr., 2008-; bd. dirs. Alumni LaGuardia Sch. Music and Arts, NYC, 1990-2008; mem. adv. bd. arts edn, NYC Dept. Edn., 2006-, NYC Sch. Chancellor's task force arts edn., 2007-, mem. Tchr. Edn. Collaborative, NY Comprehensive Ctr., 2008- Recipient Pres. medal, St. John's U., 2008. Mem. Music Educators Nat. Conf., Coll. Music Soc. (mem. coun. 1975-78), Nat. Assn. Schs. Music (mem. govtl. rels. com., mem. grad. commn. 1979-84), Lotos Club NY, Tchr. Edn. Collaborative, NY Comprehensive Ctr., Phi Delta Kappa (Disting. Eduator of Yr. 2008), Phi Mu Alpha Sinfonia (province gov. 1964-70). Home: 175 E 62nd St Apt 11C New York NY 10065-7626 Office Phone: 718-990-1305. Business E-Mail: rossj@stjohns.edu.

ROSS, JOHN, physical chemist, educator; b. Vienna, Oct. 2, 1926; arrived in U.S., 1940; s. Mark and Anna (Krcmar) Ross; m. Virginia Franklin (div.); 1 child, Robert K.; m. Eva Madarasz. BS, Queens Coll., 1948; PhD, MIT, 1951; D (hon.), Weizmann Inst. Sci., Rehovot, Israel, 1984, Queens Coll., SUNY, 1987, U. Bordeaux, France, 1987. Prof. chemistry Brown U., Providence, 1953—66, MIT, Cambridge, 1966—80, chmn. dept., 1966—71, chmn. faculty of Inst., 1975—77; prof. Stanford (Calif.) U., 1980—2001, chmn. dept., 1983—89, prof. emeritus, 2001—. Cons. to industries; mem. emeritus bd. govs. Weizmann Inst., 1971—. Author: Physical Chemistry, 1980, 2d edit., 2000; editor: Molecular Beams, 1966;: Determination of Complex Reaction Mechanisms, 2006, Thermodynamics and Fluctuations Far from Equilibrium, 2008; contbr. articles to profl. jours. 2nd lt. US Army, 1944—46. Recipient medal, Coll. de France, Paris, Presdl. Nat. Medal of Sci., 1999, Austrian Cross of Honor for Sci. and Art, 1st class, 2002. Fellow: AAAS, Am. Phys. Soc.; mem.: NAS, Am. Chem. Soc. (Irving Langmuir Chem. Physics prize 1992, Peter Debye award in phys. chemistry 2001, Theodore William Richards medal 2004), Am. Acad. Arts and Sci. Office: Stanford U Dept Chemistry Stanford CA 94305-5080 Home Phone: 650-858-2203; Office Phone: 650-723-9203. Business E-Mail: john.ross@stanford.edu.

ROSS, JOHN, JR., cardiologist, educator; b. NYC, Dec. 1, 1928; s. John and Janet (Moulder) R.; children: Sydnie, John, Duncan; m. Lola Romanucci, Aug. 26, 1972; children: Adan, Deborah Lee. AB, Dartmouth Coll., 1951; MD, Cornell U., 1955. Intern Johns Hopkins Hosp., 1955—56; resident Columbia-Presbyn. Med. Center, NYC, 1960—61, NY. Hosp.-Cornell U. Med. center, 1961—62; chief sect. cardiovascular diagnosis cardiology br. Nat. Heart Inst., Bethesda, Md., 1962—68; prof. medicine U. Calif., San Diego, 1968—2000, also dir. cardiovascular div., 1968—91, rsch. prof. medicine, 2000—, disting. prof. medicine, 2003—; prof. cardiovascular research Am. Heart Assn. Western States Affiliate, 1984—99. Mem. cardiology adv. com. Nat. Heart, Lung and Blood Inst., 1975-78, task force on arteriosclerosis, 1978-80, adv. council, 1980-84; bd. dirs. San Diego Heart Assn.; vis. prof. Brit. Heart Assn., 1990. Author: Mechanisms of Contraction of the Normal and Failing Heart, 1968, 76, Understanding the Heart and Its Diseases, 1976; mem. editorial bd. Circulation, 1967-75, 80-88, editor in chief 1988-93, Circulation Research, 1971-75, Am. Jour. Physiology, 1968-73, Annals of Internal Medicine, 1974-78, Am. Jour. Cardiology, 1974-79, 83-88, Jour. Clin. Investigation, 1992-97, Italian Heart Jour., 1998-99, Jour. Cardiac Failure, 2000-05, Circulation Jour. Japan, 2000—; cons. editor Circulation, 1993-03; contbr. chpts. to books, sci. articles to profl. jours. Served as surgeon USPHS, 1956—63. Decorated grande ufficiale Order of Merit of Republic of Italy, 1998; recipient Ing. Enzo Ferrari prize for Enzo Ferrari, Modena, Italy, 1989, James B. Herrick award Coun. Clin. Cardiology Am. Heart Assn., 1990, Academic Mentorship award Am. Heart Assn., 2004; Distinction award Weill Cornell Med. Coll. Alumni Assn., 2009. Master Am. Coll. Cardiology (v.p. trustee, pres. 1986-87, Disting. Scientist award 1990); fellow ACP; mem. Am. Soc. Clin. Investigation (councillor), Am. Physiol. Soc., Assn. Am. Physicians, Cardiac Muscle Soc., Assn. Univ. Cardiologists, Assn. West. Physicians (councillor), Japanese Circulation Soc. (hon.). Achievements include development of and application of transseptal left heart catherization for the diagnosis of heart disease; conceptualized "afterload mismatch" in the left ventricle of the heart and its application in the diagnosis and treatment of valvular heart disease and heart failure; demonstrated experimentally that reperfusion of a coronary artery after prolonged occlusion salvages heart muscle and partially restores heart function. Home: 8599 Prestwick Dr La Jolla CA 92037 Office: U Calif Dept Med M # 0613B San Diego CA 92093

ROSS, JOHN G., educator; b. Phila., July 20, 1967; s. John and Rosemary Ross; m. Anne M. Keane, Jan. 29, 1999; children: Victoria, Emily, Juliette. MEd. in Sch. Adminstrn., St. Peter's Coll., Jersey City. Registered prin., supr. NJ Dept. Edn., 2003. Social worker SJ Vol. Corps, Visalia, Calif., 1991—92; tchr. St. Stanislaus Coll. Prep, Bay St. Louis, Miss., 1992—95; prof. U. Latina, San Pedro, Costa Rica, 1995—97; dean jr. St. Anthony HS, Jersey City, 1997—99; site supr. Acad. I Mid. Sch., Jersey City, 2000—. Contbr. articles to travel jours. Independent. Roman Catholic. Home: 24 West Cedar Terrace Glenwood NJ 07418 Office: Acad I Mid Sch 209 Bergen Ave Jersey City NJ 07305 Personal E-mail: johngross87@hotmail.com. Business E-Mail: jross@jcboe.org.

ROSS, JOSEPH COMER, pulmonologist, educator, academic administrator; b. Tompkinsville, Ky., June 16, 1927; s. Joseph M. and Annie (Pinckley) R.; m. Isabelle Nevins, June 15, 1952; children: Laura Ann, Sharon Lynn, Jennifer Jo, Mary Martha, Jefferson Arthur. BS, U. Ky., 1950; MD, Vanderbilt U., 1954. Diplomate Am. Bd. Internal Medicine (bd. govs. 1975-81), with added qualifications in pulmonary disease. Intern Vanderbilt U. Hosp., Nashville, 1954-55; resident Duke U. Hosp., Durham, NC, 1955-57, rsch. fellow, 1957-58; from instr. medicine to prof. Ind. U. Sch. Medicine, Indpls., 1958-70; prof., chmn. dept. medicine Med. U. of S.C., Charleston, 1970-80; vis. prof. Vanderbilt U. Sch. Medicine, Nashville, 1979-80, prof. medicine, 1981-99, prof. medicine emeritus, 1999—, assoc. vice chancellor for health affairs, 1982-99, assoc. vice chancellor for health affairs emeritus, 1999—. Mem. cardiovascular study sect. NIH, 1966-70, program project com., 1971-75; mem. adv. coun. Nat. Heart, Lung and Blood Inst., 1982-86; mem. ad hoc coms. NAS, 1966, 67; mem. Pres.'s Nat. Adv. Panel on Heart Disease, 1972; mem. merit rev. bd. in respiration VA Rsch. Svc., 1972-76, chmn., 1974-76. Mem. editorial bd. Jour. Lab. and Clin. Medicine, 1964-70, Chest, 1968-73, Jour. Applied Physiology,1968-73, Archives of Internal Medicine, 1976-82, Heart and Lung, 1977-86; contbr. articles to profl. jours. Bd. dirs. Nashville Ronald McDonald Ho., past pres.; bd. dirs. Agape, Leadership Nashville, v.p.; mem. adv. com. Davidson County Cmty. Health Agy.; active Tenn. Lung Assn.; elder Ch. of Christ. With US Army, 1945—47. Fellow: ACP, Am. Coll. Cardiology, Am. Coll. Chest Physicians (gov. S.C. 1970—76, chmn. sci. program com. 1973, vice chmn. bd. govs. 1974—75, exec. coun. 1974—80, chmn. bd. govs. 1975—76, pres.-elect 1976—77, pres. 1977—78, chmn. by-laws com. 2002—04, bd. regents 2002—04); mem.: AMA (sect. on med. schs.), Am. Soc. Internal Medicine, So. Soc. Clin. Rsch., Am. Thoracic Soc. (nat. councillor 1972—76), S.C. Med. Soc., Ctr. Social Clin. Rsch., Assn. Profs. Medicine, Assn. Am. Physicians, Am. Soc. Clin. Investigatrion, Am. Physiol. Soc., Am. Fedn. Clin. Rsch. (chmn. Midwest sect.), S.C. Lung Assn. (v.p. 1974—75), Phi Beta Kappa, Alpha Omega Alpha. Office: Vanderbilt U Med Ctr Oxford House Ste 212 Nashville TN 37232-0001 Personal E-mail: joseph.ross@comcast.net.

ROSS, JOSEPH SOLOMON, physician investigator; b. Buffalo, 1974; MD, Albert Einstein Coll. Medicine, Bronx, NY, 2001; MHS, Yale U., New Haven, Conn., 2006. Robert Wood Johnson clin. scholar Yale U. Sch. Medicine, 2004—06; asst. prof. Mt. Sinai Sch. Medicine, NYC, 2006—. Office: Mount Sinai Sch Medicine One Gustave L Levy Pl Box 1070 New York NY 10029 Office Fax: 212-860-9737. Business E-Mail: joseph.ross@mssm.edu.

ROSS, JUNE ROSA PITT, biologist, educator; b. Taree, NSW, Australia, May 2, 1931; came to U.S., 1957; d. Bernard and Adeline Phillips; m. Charles Alexander, June 27, 1959. BSc with honors, U. Sydney, New S. Wales, Australia, 1953, PhD, 1959, DSc, 1974. Rsch. assoc. Yale U., New Haven, 1959—60, U. Ill., Urbana, 1960—65, Western Wash. U., Bellingham, 1965—67, assoc. prof., 1967—70, prof. biology, 1970—2003, prof. emeritus, 2004—, chair dept. biology, 1989—90. Pres. Western Wash. U. Faculty Senate, Bellingham, 1984-85; conf. host Internat. Bryozoology Assn., 1986. Author (with others): A Textbook of Entomology, 1982, Geology of Coal, 1984; editor (assoc.): Palaios, 1985—89; contbr. 166 articles to profl. jours. Recipient J. Wolfensohn Award of Excellence Sydney U. Grad. Union of N.Am., 1995, P. and R. Olscamp Outstanding Rsch. award Western Wash. U., 1986; NSF grantee. Mem.: Internat. Bryozoology Assn. (pres. 1992—95), The Paleontol. Soc. (councillor 1984—86, treas. 1987—93), Australian Marine Scis. Assn., U.K. Marine Biol. Assn. (life). Avocations: hiking, classical music. Office: Western Wash U Dept Biology Bellingham WA 98225-9160 Office Phone: 360-650-3634. E-mail: ross@fire.biol.wwu.edu.

ROSS, KAREN LEE HROMYAK, retired school psychologist; d. George Frank and Laina Dorothy (Luoma) Hromyak; m. Richard Ross (div.); m. William H. Uehlinger (div.); m. Carl Eugene Weiselberg (dec.); 1 child, Wendy Kay Weiselberg White. BS in Home Econs. Edn., Ohio State U., Columbus, 1961, postgrad., 1963—67; MS in Edn., Westminster Coll., New Wilmington, Pa., 1963; MS in Sch. Psychology, Kent State U., Ohio, 1973; postgrad., Walden U., Mpls., 1974, Youngstown State U., Ohio, 1976—88, Ashland U., 2001. Lic. profl. clin. counselor Ohio Counselor Bd. Home econs. tchr. Warren and Brookfield Schs., Ohio, 1961—63; prof. psychology Youngstown State U., 1968—78; owner antique and gift shop Karen's, Naples, Fla., 1989—2001; outpatient therapist David Lawrence Mental Health Ctr., Naples, 1990—91; psychologist Collier County Pub. Schs., Naples, 1990—2000, Erie, Huron, Ottawa Edn. Svc. Ctr., Sandusky, Ohio, 2000—01, Covington Schs., Covington, Ky., 2001—02; counselor Franklin County Schs., Frankfort, Ky., 2002—03; ret., 2003. Mem. Ohio Educators Polit. Action Com., 1986—90; co-chmn. Dukakis Presdl. Campaign Hdqrs., Warren, Ohio, 1988; del. Nat. Dem. Convention, Atlanta, 1988. Recipient Action award, Northeastern Ohio Tchrs. Assn., 1989, Svc. award, Ohio Sec. of State Sherrod Brown, 1989. Mem.: NASP (charter mem., nat. cert. sch. psychologist), NEA (del.), Trumbull Co. Retired Tchrs. Assn., Trumbull Meml. Hosp. Group, N.E. Ohio Edn. Assn. (exec. com., pres. Leadership award 1980—89), Warren Edn. Assn. (pres., past pres. negotiations), SW Fla. Assn. Sch. Psychologists (exec. com. 1998—2000, pres. 1999), Internat. Sch. Psychologist Assn. (del. conf. Riga, Latvia), Ohio Edn. Assn. (life; exec. com. 1984—89), Ohio State U. Alumni Assn. (chmn. exec. com. scholarship com. 1998—2000, Svc. award 1984—89), Lexington Women's Club (bd. dirs. kids com.), Phi Upsilon Omicron, Delta Kappa Gamma (pres., nat. del.), Psi Chi. Methodist. Avocations: antiques, growing orchids, travel, crafts. Home: 1156 Surrey Pointe Dr SE Warren OH 44484-2800

ROSS, KATHLEEN ANNE, academic administrator; b. Palo Alto, Calif., July 1, 1941; d. William Andrew and Mary Alberta (Wilburn) Ross. BA, Ft. Wright Coll., 1964; MA, Georgetown U., 1971; PhD, Claremont Grad. U., 1979; LLD (hon.), Alverno Coll. Milw., 1990, Dartmouth Coll., 1991, Seattle U., 1992, Pomona Coll., 1993, U. Notre Dame, 1999, Gonzaga U., 1999; LHD (hon.), Whitworth Coll., 1992, Coll. New Rochelle, 1998, Carroll Coll., 2003, Pacific Luth. U., 2004, U. Portland, Oreg., 2006, U. Puget Sound, 2007. Cert. tchr. Wash. Secondary tchr. Holy Names Acad., Spokane, Wash., 1964-70; dir. rsch. and planning Province Holy Names, Wash. State, 1972-73; v.p. acads. Ft. Wright Coll., Spokane, 1973-81; rsch. asst. to dean Claremont Grad. Sch., Calif., 1977-78; assoc. faculty mem. Harvard U., Cambridge, Mass., 1981; pres. Heritage U., Toppenish, Wash., 1981—. Cons. Wash. State Holy Names Schs., 1971-73; coll. accrediting assn. evaluator N.W. Assn. Schs. and Colls., Seattle, 1975—; dir. Holy Names U., Oakland, Calif., 1979—; cons. Yakama Indian Nation, Toppenish, 1975—; speaker, cons. in field. Author: (with others) Multicultural Pre-School Curriculum, 1977, A Crucial Agenda: Improving Minority Student Success, 1989; Cultural Factors in Success of American Indian Students in Higher Education, 1978. Chmn. Internat. 5-Yr. Convocation of Sisters of Holy Names, Montreal, 1981, 96; TV Talk show host Spokane Coun. of Chs., 1974-76; mem. Nat. Congl. Adv. Com. on Student Fin. Assistance, 2002-06. Recipient E.K. and Lillian F. Bishop Founds. Youth Leader of Yr. award, 1986, Disting. Citizenship Alumna award, Claremont Grad. Sch., 1986, Golden Aztec award, Wash. Human Devel., 1989, Harold W. McGraw Edn. prize, 1989, John Carroll award, Georgetown U., 1991, Holy Names medal, Ft. Wright Coll., 1981, Pres.'s medal, Estern Wash. U., 1994, First Ann. Leadership award, Region VIII Coun. Advancement and Support Edn., 1993, Wash. State Medal of Merit, 1995, Lifetime Achievement award, Yakima YWCA, 2001, numerous grants for projects in multicultural higher edn., 1974—; named Yakima Herald Rep. Person of Yr., 1987, MacArthur fellow, 1997. Mem. Nat. Assn. Ind. Colls. and Univs., Soc. Intercultural Edn., Tng. and Rsch., Sisters of Holy Names of Jesus and Mary-SNJM. Roman Catholic. Office: Heritage U Office of Pres 3240 Fort Rd Toppenish WA 98948-9562 Office Phone: 509-865-8600.

ROSS, KEN, state banking agency administrator; BA in Philosophy and Polit. Sci., U. Mich., Dearborn; JD cum laude, Thomas M. Cooley Law Sch. Asst. atty. gen. Tort Defense Divsn. Mich. Atty. Gen.'s Office; v.p. regulatory and legal affairs Mich. Credit Union League; chief of staff Mich. Office of Fin. and Insurance Svcs. (OFIS), 2003, dep. commr. policy, acting commr., 2007—08, commr., 2008—. Office: Mich Office of Fin and Insurance Regulation PO Box 30220 Lansing MI 48909-7720 Office Phone: 517-373-0220. Office Fax: 517-373-4870. E-mail: rossk1@michigan.gov.*

ROSS, KRISTEN ANN, school system administrator; d. Alexander William and Anna Marie Kalnes; m. James Allen Ruebush (div.); children: Julie Ann Lehman, Jennifer Louise Baltimore; m. Jesse Davis Ross, June 27, 1992. BS in Edn., Western Ill. U., Macomb, 1977; MEd, cert. reading specialist, No. Ill. U., DeKalb, 1988; EdD, Loyola U., Chgo., 1997. Jr. HS reading/lang. arts tchr. Dist. 303, St. Charles, Ill., 1977—90; reading/lang. arts coord. Ednl. Svc. Ctr. # 1, Rockford, Ill., 1990—92; asst. prin. Washington Mid. Sch. Dist. # 129, Aurora, Ill., 1992—93, asst. prin. for curriculum West Aurora HS, 1993—95, prin. Washington Mid. Sch., 1995, asst. supt. curriculum, 1998—2000; ind. cons., univ. instr. No. Ill. U., DeKalb, 2000—01; prin. Clinton Rosette Mid. Sch. Dist. # 428, DeKalb, 2001—04; prin. Kankakee Jr. HS Dist. # 111, Ill., 2004—05, asst. supt. curriculum and instrn., 2005—08; prin. Gombert Elem Sch., Indian Prairie Dist. 204, Aurora, Ill., 2008—. Cons. Ctr. for Best Practice, Chgo., 2000—01, Erickson Inst., Chgo., 2000—01; cons. for std. aligned classrooms DuPage County Regional Office of Edn., Wheaton, Ill., 2000—01; coord. Ill. Title I Conf., 1992; presenter confs. in field. Govtl. rels. chair Ill. Reading Coun., 1983. Named one of Kane County Honored Educators, Kane County Regional Office of Edn., Ill., 1989; grantee, NEH, 1984; fellow, IDEA, 1998; Literacy grantee, Fed. Govt., 2006, E2T2 Grant, 2006. Mem.: ASCD (del. US/Russian Edn. Conf. 1995), Internat. Reading Coun., Internat. Reading Assn. Avocations: hiking, creative writing, classes in personal development, book clubs. Office: Gombert Elem Sch 2707 Ridge Rd Aurora IL 60504 Office Phone: 630-375-3705. Business E-Mail: kris_ross@iqsd.org.

ROSS, LEONARD LESTER, retired academic administrator; b. NYC, Sept. 11, 1927; s. Aaron Theodore and Shirley (Smolen) R.; m. Marcella Gamel, June 23, 1951 (dec. Aug. 1995); children: Jane, Jill; m. Frances Robb, Nov. 12, 1998; 1 chld, Jennifer. AB, NYU, 1946, PhD, 1954. Asst. prof. U. Ala. Med. Coll., 1954-57; assoc. prof. Cornell U. Med. Coll., 1957-69, prof., 1969-73; vis. prof. Cambridge U., 1967-68; prof., chmn. dept. anatomy Med. Coll. Pa., Phila., 1973-89, exec. v.p., Annenberg dean, 1989-93, pres. and Annenberg dean, 1993-94, provost and Annenberg dean Phila., 1993-96; provost Allegheny U., Phila., 1996-98. Exec. v.p. Allegheny Health, Edn. and Rsch. Found. Assoc. editor: Anat. Record, 1976. Served with M.C., U.S. Army, 1946-47. Recipient Lindback award for teaching, 1976; NIH sr. research fellow, 1967-68 Mem. Am. Assn. Anatomists (exec. com. 1984-88), Soc. Neurosci., Soc. Cell Biology, N.Y. Soc. Electron Microscopists (pres. 1975-76), Assn. Anatomy Chairmen (pres. 1983-84), AAUP (nat. council 1974-77), Sigma Xi. Personal E-mail: rossll69@netscape.net.

ROSS, LESA MOORE, quality assurance professional; b. New Orleans, Jan. 25, 1959; d. William Frank and Carolyn West Moore; m. Mark Neal Ross, Nov. 30, 1985; children: Sarah Ann, Jacquelyne Caroline. BS in Engring., U. N.C., Charlotte, 1981; MBA in Quality and Reliability Mgmt., U. North Tex., 1991; MS in Reliability Engring., U. Md., 2004. Seismic qualification engr. Duke Power Co., Charlotte, N.C., 1981-82; quality assurance engr. Tex. Instruments Inc., Lewisville, Tex., 1982-91; compliance mgr. Am. Med. Electronics, Inc., 1992-93; owner Ross Quality Cons., 1993-95; customer quality assurance sect. mgr. Hitachi Semiconductor Inc., 1995-96; v.p. quality Ross Networking Cons. Inc., Flower Mound, Tex., 1996—. Bd. dirs. Greater Lewisville YMCA, 2000—03. Recipient Nat. Sci. Found. Rsch. Grant, U. N.C., Charlotte, 1980. Mem. Am. Soc. Quality Control (cert. quality engr., quality auditor, reliability engr., cert. quality technician, cert. quality mgr., sec. Dallas sect. 1994-95, chair-elect Dallas sect. 1995-96, chair 1996-97), Zeta Tau Alpha (pres. 1984-85). Avocations: crafts, cross-stitching, reading, travel. Home and Office: 4925 Wolf Creek Trl Flower Mound TX 75028-1955 E-mail: Lross@rnc-inc.com.

ROSS, LISA SIMS, special education educator; b. Jackson, Miss., Feb. 14, 1952; d. Johnie Mack and Elizabeth Crane Sims; m. Richard C. Ross, Aug. 16, 1974 (div. Mar. 1996); children: Jason Conn, Robert Sims. BS, U. So. Miss., 1974, EdM, 1996. Cert. tchr. Miss. Spl. edn. tchr. Jackson County Sch., Wade, Miss., 1974—75, Holly Springs (Miss.) Sch., 1975—76, Lanar County Schs., Purvis, Miss., 1976—93, Richton (Miss.) City Sch., 1995—99; educator Ellisville (Miss.) State Sch., 1999—. Mem.: Miss. Assn. Educators, Kappa Delta Alumnae (pres. 1998—99), U. So. Miss. Alumni Assn. Baptist. Avocations: reading, exercise, shopping. Home: 2309 Adeline St Hattiesburg MS 39401 Office: Ellisville State Sch 1101 Hwy 11 South Ellisville MS 39437 Office Phone: 601-477-6245.

ROSS, LORI A., lawyer; b. Cin., Apr. 14, 1975; BA in Psychology, Miami U., 1997, BA in Sociology, 1997; JD, U. Cin., 2000. Bar: Ohio 2000, US Dist. Ct. Southern Dist. Ohio 2000, Ky. 2001. Assoc. Strauss & Troy, Cin. Named one of Ohio's Rising Stars, Super Lawyers, 2006. Mem.: Ohio State Bar Assn., Ky. Bar Assn., Cin. Bar Assn., Order of Coif, Phi Beta Kappa, Phi Kappa Phi. Office: Strauss & Troy Federal Reserve Bldg 150 E Fourth St Cincinnati OH 45202-4018 Office Phone: 513-621-2120. Office Fax: 513-241-8259.

ROSS, MADELYN ANN, academic administrator, newspaper editor; b. Pitts., June 26, 1949; d. Mario Charles and Rose Marie (Mangieri) R. BA, Indiana U. of Pa., 1971; MA, SUNY-Albany, 1972. Reporter Pitts. Press, 1972-78, asst. city editor, 1978-82, spl. assignment editor, 1982-83, mng. editor, 1983-93, Pitts. Post-Gazette, 1993—2005; assoc.

vice chancellor U. Pitts., 2005—. Bd. dirs. PG Pub. Co.; instr. Community Coll. Allegheny County, 1974-81; Pulitzer Prize juror, 1989, 90. Mem. Task Force Leadership Pitts., 1985-92; v.p. Old Newsboys Charity Fund; bd. dirs. Dapper Dan Charity. Mem. Am. Soc. Newspaper Editors, Press Club of Western Pa., Internat. Women's Forum. Democrat. Roman Catholic. Avocations: tennis, piano, organ. Office: U Pitts 424 Craig Hall Craig St Pittsburgh PA 15260

ROSS, MALCOLM, minerals consultant; b. Washington, Aug. 22, 1929; s. Clarence Samuel and Helen Hall (Frederick) R.; m. Daphne Dee Virginia Riska, Sept. 1, 1956; children: Christopher A., Alexander MacC. BS in Zoology, Utah State U., 1951; MS in Chemistry, U. Md., 1959; PhD in Geology, Harvard U., 1962. Rsch. mineralogist U.S. Geol. Survey, Washington, 1954-5, 61-74, Reston, Va., 1974-95, scientist emeritus, 1996—; minerals and health cons., 1999—. Prin. investigator lunar sci. program NASA, 1969—74. Author: Asbestos and Other Fibrous Minerals, 1988; contbr. over 100 articles to profl. jours. First lt. US Army, 1952—54. Recipient Disting. Svc. award, U.S. Dept. Interior, 1986; grantee Fulbright Commn., Cyprus, 2000. Fellow Mineral. Soc. Am., Geol. Soc. Am., AAAS; mem. Am. Geophys. Union, Clay Minerals Soc., Can. Mineral Assn., Mineral Soc. Am. (bd. dirs. treas. 1976-80, v.p. 1990, pres. 1991, Pub. Svc. award, 1990). Republican. Congregationalist. Achievements include research in on asbestos and asbestos-related disease. Avocations: long distance bicycling, photography. Home: 1608 44th St NW Washington DC 20007-2025 Personal E-mail: mrdrr@earthlink.net.

ROSS, MARILYN J., language and communications educator; BA in Am. Studies, U. Miami, Fla., 1969, MA in Am. Studies, 1971, PhD in Higher Edn. Leadership, 1995. Asst. prof. English Fla. Meml. Coll., 1971-84, assoc. prof. English and mass comm. arts, 1985-94, prof. higher edn., 1995—. Founder mass comm. arts program Fla. Meml. Coll., 1980, coord. modern langs., 1999—; presenter Round Table Oxford U., Eng., 2005, others. Author: Success Factors of Young African American Males at a Historically Black College, 1998, Success Factors of Young African American Women at a Historically Black College, 2002; prodr. over 100 hrs. African Am., Caribbean and Hispanic programming, WLRN-TV. Recipient Outstanding Svc. award Vets. Club, 1979, Outstanding and Dedicated Svc. in Behalf of FMC award Miami Cable Access Corp., 1987, award Fla. Meml. Coll./Black Archives History and Rsch. Found. of South Fla., Inc., 1999. Mem. MLA, AAUW, Assn. Ednl. Leadership, Nat. Coun. Tchrs. English, Nat. Assn. African Am. Studies, Am. Studies Aassn., Epsilon Tau Lambda, Kappa Delta Pi, Phi Lambda Pi, Delta Theta Mu, Phi Kappa Phi, Phi Alpha Theta., Sigma Tau Delta (Advisor, Faculty), Alpha Lambda Gamma. Address: Unit F-602 1121 Crandon Blvd Apt F602 Key Biscayne FL 33149-2781 E-mail: ross1848@bellsouth.net.

ROSS, MARION, actress; b. Albert Lea, Minn., Oct. 25, 1928; children: Jim, Ellen. Grad., San Diego State U. Performed with Globe Theatre, San Diego, LaJolla Summer Theatre; Broadway debut in Edwin Booth; starred in touring prodns. of Never Too Late, Barefoot in the Park, The Glass Menagerie, Long Days Journey Into Night, Love Letter, Steel Magnolias, Over The River and Through The Woods, Barefoot in the Park, The Last Romance, film debut in Forever Female, 1953; on woman show A Lovely Light, 1988—; TV series include Life with Father, 1953-55, Paradise Bay, 1965-66, Happy Days, 1974-84, Love Boat, 1985-86 (2 Emmy nominations), Bklyn. Bridge, 1991-93 (Emmy nomination for lead actress in a comedy 1992, 93), Hidden in Silence, 1995, Evening Star, 1996, The Great War, 1996, The Third Twin, 1997, About Search, 1998, The Lake, 1998, Drew Carey Show, 1998, That 70's Show, 1998, Touched By an Angel, 1999 (Emmy nomination 1999), The Ladies and the Champ, 2001, The Gilmore Girls, A Family of Strangers, Brothers & Sisters, Flower Girl; voice of Sponge Bob's grandmother. Office: Dale Olson & Assocs 7420 Mulholland Dr Los Angeles CA 90046-1306 Office Phone: 323-876-9331. Business E-Mail: dolson2000@earthlink.net.

ROSS, MARK ALLEN, engineering educator, consultant; s. Bernard E. and Nancy Vivian Ross; m. Susan R. Carpenter. PhD, U. Fla., Gainesville, 1987. Cert. profl. engr., Fla., 1989. Prof. Dept. Civil and Environ. Engring., Tampa, Fla., 1987—. Pres. Hydrosystems Inc., Tampa, 1995—. Office: Univ South Fla 4202 E Fowler Ave Tampa FL 33620 Business E-Mail: mross@eng.usf.edu.

ROSS, MATTHEW, lawyer; b. NYC, Dec. 28, 1953; s. Harvey and Cecile (Shelsky) R.; m. Susan Ruth Goldfarb, Apr. 20, 1986; children: Melissa Danielle, Henry Max, Thomas Frank. BS in Econs., U. Pa., Phila., 1975; JD, U. Va., Charlottesville, 1978. Bar: NY 1979, US Dist. Ct. (so. dist.) NY 1979. Assoc. Cravath, Swaine & Moore, NYC, 1978-84; prin., assoc. gen. counsel KPMG LLP, NYC, 1984-90; prin., deputy gen. counsel Deloitte LLP, NYC, 1990—. Mem. ABA (corp. law sect.), NY State Bar Assn. (corp. banking and bus. law sect.), Assn. Bar of City of NY (corp. law com.), Beta Gamma Sigma. Avocations: golf, gardening. Home: 5 Barker Ln Scarsdale NY 10583-7507 Office: Deloitte LLP 1633 Broadway New York NY 10019-6708 Office Phone: 212-492-3898. Business E-Mail: mross@deloitte.com.

ROSS, MELVIN LEE, history professor; s. Melvin and Lorena Hill Ross. B, Ala. State U., Montgomery, 1966; M, Purdue U., West Lafayette, Ind., 1971; degree, Cornell U., Ithaca, NY, 1987. Coll. dean Long Beach City Coll., Calif., 1990—2000, coll. prof., 2000—. V.p. Cornell U. Sailing Club, Ithaca, 1984—85; pres. Long Beach City Coll. Adminstr. Assn., 1997—98, Cornell U. Black Grad. Student's Assn., Ithaca, NY, 1984—85, Maury County Youth Devel. Task Force, Columbia, Tenn., 1987—2000, Multicultural Edn. Productions, Long Beach, 2004—. Precinct capt., cmty. organizer Senator Barack Obama Presdl. Campaign, Long Beach, 2008. Mem.: Faculty Assn. Calif. Cmty. Coll., Calif. CC Tchrs. Assn., Assn. Study African Am. Life and History, Omega Psi Phi Frat. Liberal. Home: 4067 Hardwick St 382 Lakewood CA 90712 Office: Long Beach City Coll History Dept 4901 E Carson St Long Beach CA 90808 Personal E-mail: melvin.ross@att.net. Business E-Mail: mross@lbcc.edu.

ROSS, MICHAEL AARON, lawyer; b. Newark, Sept. 15, 1941; s. Alexander Ash and Matilda (Blumenthal) R.; m. Leslie Gordon, June 26, 1976; children: Christopher Gordon, Alan Gordon. BA, Franklin and Marshall Coll., 1963; JD, Columbia U., 1966; MS in Internat. Law, London Sch. Economics, 1967. Bar: N.Y. 1968. Assoc., then ptnr. Shearman & Sterling, NYC, 1967-93; dep. gen. counsel Citigroup, NYC, 1993—2001; gen. counsel Citibank, NYC, 1998—2003, Citigroup Internat., 2002—03; counsel Wilmer Cutler Pickering Hale and Dorr LLP, NYC, 2004—05; with Blaqwell Legal Consulting, NYC, 2006—. Mem. ABA, N.Y. State Bar Assn., Am. Law Inst., New York County Lawyers Assn., Assn. Bar City of N.Y., Univ. Club. Home Phone: 212-724-3839; Office Phone: 646-746-8083. Personal E-mail: mikeaross262@yahoo.com. Business E-Mail: michael.ross@blaqwell.com.

ROSS, MICHAEL FREDERICK, judge, lawyer; b. Coral Gables, Florida, Sept. 20, 1950; s. George Thomas and Frances (Brown) Skaro. BA, Yale U., 1973; JD, U. Conn., 1979; MLS, So. Conn. State U., 1981. Bar: Conn. 1979, Fla. 1979, N.J. 1983, Mass. 1984, U.S. V.I., 1985; U.S. Dist. Ct. Conn. 1979, N.J. 1983, Vt. 1984, U.S. V.I. 1985; U.S. Ct. Claims 1980; U.S. Tax Ct. 1980; U.S. Ct. Customs and Patent Appeals 1980; U.S. Ct. Mil. Appeals 1980; U.S. Ct. Appeals (1st, 2d and D.C. cir.) 1980, U.S. Ct. Appeals (5th, 9th and 11th cir.) 1981, U.S. Ct. Appeals (Fed. cir.) 1982, U.S. Ct. Appeals (3d, 4th, 6th, 7th, 8th and 19th cir.) 1983; Temp. Emergency Ct. Appeals 1985; Mashantucket Pequot Tribal Ct. 1995; U.S. Supreme Ct. 1982. Pvt. practice, New Haven, 1979—82; chief adjudicate Conn. Motor Vehicle Dept., Wethersfield, 1980—82; asst. atty. gen. State of Conn., Hartford, 1982—84; pvt. practice Madison, Conn., 1985—; adminstrv. law judge State of Conn. Motor Vehicle Dept., Wethersfield, 1985—; asst. atty. gen. Dept. of Law, St. Croix, U.S. V.I., 1984—85; magistrate Superior Ct. of Middlesex, New Haven, and New London Counties, Conn., 1988—. Faculty mem. Conn. Bar Assn. Acad. Profl. Devel. of Continuing Legal Edn. 1987, 91. Chmn. Madison Zoning Bd. Appeals, 1991-95. Mem. ABA, Am. Trial Lawyers Assn. (jud.), U.S. V.I. Bar Assn., Mensa, Conn. Def. Lawyers Assn., Conn. Magistrates Assn., Fence Club, Morys Assn. Club, Madison Men's Club. Democrat. Jewish. Office: 975 Sperry Rd Cheshire CT 06410-3732 Business E-Mail: mouthpiece@innocent.com.

ROSS, MICHAEL NEIL, publishing executive; b. Chgo., Feb. 5, 1952; s. Edward Louis and Muriel (Dlugach) R.; m. Naomi Manaka, Aug. 24, 1983 (dec. 1988); children: Monica Nina; m. Kathleen Schultz, June 14, 1992; children: Rachael Erin, Daniel Max. BA, U. Minn., 1974; MA, Brandeis U., 1977. Editor Time-Life Books, Tokyo, 1979-83; editorial dir. NTC Pub. Group, Lincolnwood, Ill., 1983-92; exec. v.p., pub. World Book, Inc., Chgo., 1992—2002; sr. v.p. Ency. Britannica, Chgo., 2003—. Bd. dirs. Indraweb, Inc., Smartpro3; cons. Ricsher Enterprises, Washington; bd. dirs., advisers, Ctr. for Reintegration. Author: Publishing without Borders, 2003; editor: Viva el Español!, 1987, World At Its Best, 1986, Everything Japanese, 1988, Early World of English, 1993, Wonderful World of English, 1994, Say It In English, 1995, Welcome to Reading, 1996, Ency. of Careers, 1997, Discoveries, 1998, Student Discovery Encyclopedia, 1999, Animals of the World, 2000, Tutor Link, 2001, Biographical Encyclopedia of Scientists, 2002, My First Britannica, 2003, Britannica Discovery Library, 2005. Named to, Print Media Prodn. Execs. Hall of Fame, 2002. Mem. Direct Selling Edn. Found., Am. Coun. Tchg. Fgn. Langs., Chgo. Coun. Fgn. Rels., Chgo. Book Clinic, Assn. Ednl. Publ. (elected bd. dirs. 1999—, pres. 2002-03). Avocations: photography, squash, tennis, reading, scuba diving. Home: 610 Kincaid St Highland Park IL 60035-5038 Office: 331 N LaSalle St Chicago IL 60654 Office Phone: 312-347-7392. E-mail: mross@eb.com, mrosspub@aol.com.

ROSS, MIKE, United States Representative from Arkansas; b. Texarkana, Ark., Aug. 2, 1961; m. Holly Ross; children: Sydney, Alex. BA in Polit. Sci., U. Ark., 1987. Owner Holly's Health Mart and Home Med. Equipment; area mgr. Fox Meyer Drug Co.; chief of staff to Lt Gov. Ark., 1985—89; mem. Ark. Senate, 1990-2001, chair children/youth com.; mem. US Congress from 4th Ark. dist., Washington, 2001—; mem. com. on energy/commerce US Ho. Reps. Democrat. Methodist. Office: US Ho Reps 314 Cannon Ho Office Bldg Washington DC 20515-0404 Office Phone: 202-225-3772. Office Fax: 202-225-1314. Business E-Mail: mross@arkleg.state.ar.us.*

ROSS, MOLLY OWINGS, small business owner, sculptor; b. Ft. Worth, Feb. 5, 1954; d. James Robertson and Lucy (Owings) R. BFA, Colo. State U., 1976; postgrad., U. Denver, 1978-79. Graphic designer Amber Sky Illustrators and Sta. KCNC TV, Denver, 1977—79; art dir. Mercy Med. Ctr., Denver, 1979-83, Molly Ross Design, Denver, 1983-84; co-owner Deltex Royalty Co., Inc., Castle Rock, Colo., 1981—, pres., 2007—; co-owner LMA Royalties, Ltd., Castle Rock, 1993—2007; pres. LMA Royalties Ltd., 2007—, Swift Wings Found., 2008—; art dir., account mgr. Schwing/Walsh Advt., Mktg. and Pub. Rels., Denver, 1984-87, prodn. mgr., 1987-88; jewelry designer Molly O. Ross, Gold and Silversmith, Denver, 1988—2002. Coun. mem. feminization of poverty critical needs area coun. Jr. League Denver, 1989—90, chmn. children in crisis/edn. critical needs area, 1990—91, chmn. project devel., 1991—92, co-chmn. Done in a Day Cmty. Project 75th Anniversary Celebration, 1991—93, bd. dirs., 1993—94, co-chmn. project IMPACT, 1994—95, exec. v.p. external affairs, 1995—96, co-chmn. cmty. coalitions com., 1996—98; mem. steering com. Denver Urban Resources Partnership, 1995—2002, steering com. chmn., 1996—99; pres.-elect Jr. League Denver, 1989—99, pres., 1999—2000; steering com. Internat. Conf. on Vol. Adminstrn., 2001—02; bd. dirs. Environ. Def. Regional Adv. Bd., 2003—06; nat. adv. bd. Am. Farmland Trust, 2005—; mem. Rachel's Network, 2005—, bd. dirs., 2008—; bd. trustees Am. Solar Energy Soc., 2006—; bd. dirs. Excelsior Youth Ctr., 2006—, ArtReach, 2001—, co-pres., 2007—09; pres. Four Mile Hist. Pk. Vol. Bd., 1985—86; bd. dirs. Four Mile Hist. Pk. Assn., 1985—86, Hist. Denver, Inc., 1986—87, Denver Emergency Housing Coalition, 1989—90; co-founder, bd. dirs. Ctr. Ethics and Social Responsibility/PREP, 1994—2001, pres. bd. dirs., 1997—99, treas. bd. dirs., 1999—2000; bd. dirs. Jr. League Denver Found., 1998—2002, Friends of Warren Village, 2000—01, Excelsior Youth Ctr. Found., 2001—, Sierra Club Found., 2009—. Named Vol. of Month (March), Jr. League Denver, 1990, Vol. of Yr., Four Mile Hist. Pk., 1988; recipient Gold Peak Mktg. award-team design Am. Mktg. Assn., 1986, Silver Peak Mktg. award-team design Am. Mktg. Assn., 1986, Gold Pick award-art dir. Pub. Rels. Soc. Am., 1980-81, cert. Appreciation USDA, 1999, 2001. Mem. Natural Resources Def. Coun., Physicians for Social Responsibility, Am. Farmland Trust, Nat. Trust for Hist. Preservation, Environ. Def., Rachel's Network. Avocations: horseback riding, bicycling, hiking, backpacking, pastel drawing.

ROSS, MURRAY DAVID, psychologist; b. Dec. 14, 1953; BA, State U. NY, Buffalo, 1972; MS, Syracuse U., NY, 1977; MA Cert. Advanced Grad. Study, U. Mass., Boston, 1995. Nat. Cert. Sch. Psychologist, cert. Sch. Psychologist Mass., Moderate Spl. Needs Mass., Secont Step Violect Prevention Cert. Trainer, cert. Social Studies NY, Spl. Edn. NY, Nursery, Elem. K-6 NY, Social Studies Mid. Sch. Mass. Social studies student tchr. West Hertel Mid. Sch., Buffalo, 1975; program dir. West Seneca Devel. Ctr., NY, 1973—76; tchr. Cmty. Sch., Syracuse, NY, 1976—77; tchr., diagnostician Bd. Coorp. Ednl. Svcs., Rochester, NY, 1977—84; tchr., cons. Cmty. Ctr. Sch., West Newton, Mass., 1984—94; psychology intern Wellesley Pub. Sch., Mass., 1994—95; sch. psychologist Bridgewater-Raynham Regional Sch. Dist., Raynham, Mass., 1995—2007; supr. sch. psychology intern U. Mass., 2006—07. Designer and presenter of workshops in field; vis. lectr. Bridgewater State Coll., Mass., 2008, adj. faculty. Illustrator Haiku Moment, an Anthology of Contemporary North American Haiku, 1993. Recipient Cmty. Svc. award, City of Buffalo, 1976; scholar, NY State Regents, 1972; fellowship and teaching assistantship, Syracuse U., 1976. Mem.: Nat. Assn. Sch. Psychologists, Mass. Sch. Psychologists Assn., Nat. Edn. Assn. Home: 154 Duffy Dr Taunton MA 02780 Personal E-mail: murraydross8@verizon.net. Business E-Mail: mross@bridge-rayn.org.

ROSS, NORMAN ALAN, publisher; b. Bklyn., Nov. 1, 1942; s. Robert E. and Bertha (Cohen) Ross; m. Leslie Ann Sandler, Oct. 10, 1969; children: Caroline Beth, Juliet Michelle. BBA, CCNY, 1964, postgrad., 1967-74. Prodn. mgr. Thomas Pub. Co., 1964-67; sys. analyst Reuben H. Donnelley Corp., 1968-70; project mgr. Holt Rinehart & Winston, 1971-73; pres. Clearwater Pub. Co., Inc., NYC, 1973-88, Video Strategies USA, Inc., NYC, 1981-84, Broadside Ltd. pub. Broadside Mag., 1983-87, Norman Ross Pub. Inc., 1987—2002, Acad. Microforms Inc., 1999—2003; exec. dir. Norman Ross Pub., subs. Proquest, 2003—; pres. Ross Pub., LLC, 2003—. Author: (book) Index to the Decisions of the Indian Claims Commission, 1973, Index to the Expert Testimony Before the Indian Claims Commission, 1973, Guide to Yiddish Children's Books from the Yivo Institute, 1989. Home: 392 Central Park W Apt 20-c New York NY 10025-5878 Office: Ross Pub Inc 250 W 57th St Ste 1329 New York NY 10107 Office Phone: 212-765-8200. Business E-Mail: norman@rosspub.com.

ROSS, PATTI JAYNE, obstetrics and gynecology educator; b. Nov. 17, 1946; d. James J. and Mary N. Ross; m. Allan Robert Katz, May 23, 1976. BS, DePauw U., 1968; MD, Tulane U., 1972. Diplomate Am. Bd. Ob-Gyn. Asst. prof. U. Tex. Med. Sch., Houston, 1976—82, assoc. prof., 1982—98, prof., 1998—2004, dir. adolescent ob-gyn., 1976—, dir. student edn., dir. devel. dept. ob-gyn. Cons. in field; spkr. in field; appeared on Lifetime TV network. Contbr. articles to profl. jours. Mem. Rape Coun.; vol. Children's Miracle Network/Hermann's Children's Hosp.; Olympic torch relay carrier, 1996; founder Women's Med. Rsch. Fund, U. Tex. Med. Sch., Houston; bd. dirs. Am. Diabetes Assn., 1982—, Susan Komen Found. Recipient Patti Jayne Ross Professorship, 2004. Mem.: Profl. Women Execs., Orgn. Women in Sci., Am. Women's Med. Assn., AAAS, Soc. Adolescent Medicine, Assn. Profs. Ob-Gyn., Houston Ob-Gyn. Soc., Harris County Med. Soc., Tex. Med. Assn., River Oak Breakfast Club, Sigma Xi. Roman Catholic. Office: 6431 Fannin St 3278 Houston TX 77030-1501 Office Phone: 713-500-6431. Business E-Mail: patti.j.ross@mth.tmc.edu.

ROSS, R. DALE, medical products executive; b. 1942; Sales mgmt. positions Am. McGaw Laboratories; founder, pres., CEO HMSS Inc., 1982—90; chmn., CEO Am. Oncology Resources, Houston, 1992—99, US Oncology, Houston, 1999—2008, exec. chmn., 2008—09. Former bd. dirs. US Oncology Holdings, Inc. Served USAF. Office: US Oncology 16825 Northchase Dr Houston TX 77060*

ROSS, RANDOLPH ERNEST, investor; b. NYC, Mar. 17, 1955; s. David Harvey and Pearl (Frandsen) R.; m. Joan Frances Healey, Apr. 2, 1982. AB in History, Brown U., 1977; MBA in Fin., Columbia U., 1981. CFA; comml. pilot FAA. Nat. editor Sta. WEAN Radio, Providence, 1977-79; rsch. analyst, asst. v.p. Kidder, Peabody & Co., Inc., NYC, 1981-85; rsch. analyst First Manhattan Co., NYC, 1985-86; portfolio mgr. Brundage, Story and Rose, NYC, 1986-92; sr. portfolio mgr., v.p. Bankers Trust Co., NYC, 1992-93; investment strategist, sr. v.p. Kidder, Peabody & Co. Inc., NYC, 1993-94; pvt. investor Bklyn., 1994-96; mng. dir. Morgan Hill Corp., NYC, 1996—2004; pvt. investor, 2004—. Mem. CFA Inst., N.Y. Soc. Security Analysts. Republican. Avocations: commercial pilot, sailing, trap and skeet shooting, architectural and urban history, fiction. Home: 111 Hicks St Ste 4A Brooklyn NY 11201-1638

ROSS, RICHARD FRANCIS, veterinarian, microbiologist, dean, educator; b. Washington, Iowa, Apr. 30, 1935; s. Milton Edward and Olive Marie (Berggren) R.; m. Karen Mae Paulsen, Sept. 1, 1957; children: Scott, Susan D.V.M., Iowa State U., 1959, MS, 1961, PhD, 1965. Rsch. assoc. Iowa State U., Ames, 1959—61, asst. prof., 1962—65, assoc. prof., 1966—72, prof., 1972—, assoc. dir., assoc. dean Coll. Vet. Medicine, 1990—92, interim dean, 1992—93, dean Coll. Vet. Medicine, 1993—2000, interim dean, dean Coll. Agr., dir. Agrl. Expt. Sta., 2000—02, prof. emeritus, 2004; oper. mgr. Vet. Lab. Inc., Remsen, Iowa, 1961—62; postdoctoral fellow NIAID, Hamilton, Mont., 1965—66. Sr. U.S. scientist Alexander von Humboldt Found., Bonn, Fed. Republic Germany, 1975-76; chmn. Internat. Rsch. Program on Comparative Mycoplasmology, 1982-86; pres. Iowa State U. Rsch. Found., Ames, 1984-86; Howard Dunne meml. lectr. Am. Assn. Swine Practitioners, 1984; mem. adv. bd. Sec. Agr., 1996-99; mem. strategic planning task force USDA, 1997-99, mem. safeguarding task force, 2001-02, mem. implementation team, 2003-04; bd. govs. ISU Found., 2004—. Contbr. numerous articles to profl. publs., 1963—. Vol. Union Sta. Homeless Shelter, Pasadena, Calif., 2007—. Named Disting. Prof., Iowa State U., 1982, Hon. Master Pork Producer, Iowa Pork Producers Assn., 1985; recipient faculty citation Iowa State U. Alumni Assn., 1984, Beecham award for rsch. excellence, 1985, Howard Dunne Meml. award Am. Assn. Swine Practitioners, 1988, Am. Feed Mfg. award for rsch., 1995, Sec. of Agr. award for personal and prof. accomplishment, 1996, Gamma Sigma Delta Merit award for disting. achievement in agr. 2002. Mem. Am. Coll. Vet. Microbiologists (diplomate, vice chmn. 1974-75, sec.-treas. 1977-83), ACVM(Pres. award of Excellence, 2007), Am. Soc. Microbiology (chmn. div. 1985-86), Internat. Orgn. Mycoplasmology (chair 1990-92, Bd. Dirs. award 2002), AVMA, AAAS, Osborn Research Club, Conf. Rsch. Workers in Animal Diseases (coun. mem., pres. 1992, Dedicatee, 2007), Assn. Am. Vet. Med. Colls. (pres. 1997-98), Rotary Club. Republican. Lutheran. Avocations: fishing, gardening, walking, reading, history, genealogy. Home: 4022 Stone Brooke Rd Ames IA 50010-2900 Personal E-mail: rfross@iastate.edu.

ROSS, RICHARD STARR, retired medical school dean, cardiologist, educator; b. Richmond, Ind., Jan. 18, 1924; s. Louis Francisco and Margaret (Starr) Ross; m. Elizabeth McCracken, July 1, 1950; children: Deborah Starr, Margaret Casad, Richard McCracken. Student, Harvard U., 1942—44, MD cum laude, 1947; ScD (hon.), Ind. U., 1981; LHD (hon.), Johns Hopkins U., 1994. Diplomate Nat. Bd. Med. Examiners, Am. Bd. Internal Medicine (subsplty. bd. cardiovasc. disease); cert. war cert. 1943. Successively intern, asst. resident, chief resident Osler Med. Service, Johns Hopkins Hosp., 1947—54; research fellow physiology Harvard Med. Sch., 1952—53; instr. medicine Johns Hopkins Med. Sch., 1954—56, asst. prof. medicine, 1956—59, assoc. prof., 1959—65, assoc. prof. radiology, 1960—71, prof. medicine, 1965—, Clayton prof. cardiovascular disease, 1969—75; dir. Wellcome Research Lab., Johns Hopkins; physician Johns Hopkins Hosp.; dir. cardiovascular div. dept. medicine, adult cardiac clinic Johns Hopkins Sch. Medicine and Hosp., dir. myocardial infarction research unit, 1967—75; dean med. faculty, v.p. medicine Johns Hopkins U., 1975—90, dean emeritus, 1990—. Sir Thomas Lewis lectr. Brit. Cardiac Soc., 1969; John Kent Lewis lectr. Stanford U., 1972; bd. dirs. emeritus Johns Hopkins Hosp., Francis Scott Key Med. Ctr.; mem. cardiovasc. study sect. Nat. Heart and Lung Inst., 1965—69, chmn. cardiovasc. study sect., 1966—69, mem. tng. grant com., 1971—73, chmn. heart panel, 1972—73, adv. coun., 1974—78; mem. Inst. Medicine, 1976—; chmn. vis. com. Harvard Med. and Dental Sch., 1979—86; bd. overseers Harvard U., 1980—86. Editor: Modern Concepts Cardiovascular Disease, 1961—65, The Principles and Practice of Medicine, 17th-22nd edits., 1968—88; mem. editl. bd.: Circulation, 1968—74, mem. editl. com.: Jour. Clin. Investigation, 1969—73; contbr. numerous articles to profl. jours. Capt. M.C. US Army, 1949—51. Recipient Flexner award, Assn. Am. Med. Coll., 1994, Pres.'s medal, Johns Hopkins U., 2005; named hon. fellow, UMDS, Guy's and

St. Thomas's Hosps., London, 1996. Master: ACP; fellow: Am. Coll. Cardiology (Convocation medal 1990); mem.: Heart Assn. Md. (pres. 1967—68), Am. Heart Assn. (chmn. sci. sessions program com. 1965—67, chmn. publs. com. 1970—73, pres. 1973—74, dir. 1974—77, Gold Heart award 1976, Connor lectr. 1979, James B. Herrick award 1982), Assn. Univ. Cardiologists (councillor 1972—75), Am. Clin. and Climatol. Assn. (pres. 1978—79, councillor 1979—83, Metzger lecture 1986), Am. Soc. Clin. Investigation (councillor 1967—69), Sociedad Peruana de Cardiologie (corr.), Brit. Cardiac Soc. (corr.), Cardiac Soc. Australia and New Zealand (corr.), Assn. Am. Physicians, Am. Physiol. Soc., Am. Fedn. Clin. Rsch., Boylston Med. Soc., Elkridge Club, Interurban Club (pres. 1978), Peripatetic Club, Alpha Omega Alpha, Sigma Xi. Home: 830 W 40th St # 851 Baltimore MD 21211-2181 Office: Johns Hopkins U 1830 E Monument St Baltimore MD 21287 E-mail: rross@jhmi.edu.

ROSS, ROBERT DONALD, library director; b. NYC, Mar. 28, 1931; s. William and Ceceile (Cross) Rosenfeld. BA, CCNY, 1954; postgrad., NYU, 1960—64, Columbia U., NYC, 1968; MLS, Rutgers U., New Brunswick, 1966. m. Madeleine Ladner, May 28, 1961; children: Jeffrey Laurence, Jodie Dianne. Ref. libr. Bklyn. Pub. Libr., 1965; reader svcs. libr., asst. prof. Suffolk County (N.Y.) C.C., 1966-69; dir. South Brunswick (N.J.) Pub. Libr., 1969-73, Ridgewood (N.J.) Pub. Libr., 1973-95. Adj. prof. Middlesex County C.C., NJ, 1973—76. Mem. exec. bd. South Brunswick Cmty. Coun., 1970-73, Human Rels. Coord. Coun., Ridgewood, 1988-94; mem. adv. com. Nat. Project Ctr. for Films and Humanities, N.Y.C., 1971-75; treas. Bergen-Passaic Regional Libr. Coop., 1987-88, mem. exec. bd., 1986-89; mem. Ridgewood Bicentennial Commn., 1975-76; treas. Temple Emanu-El, Reno, 1998-2000, bd. dirs., 2002-2003; bd. dirs. For the Love of Jazz, Reno, 1998-2000; docent Nev. Mus. Art, 2004—07. Mem. ALA (chmn. discussion group com. fundraising and fin. devel. sect. libr. adminstrn. and mgmt. divsn. 1984-85), N.J. Libr. Assn. (libr. devel. com. 1977-93, chmn. edn. for librarianship com. 1982-83, govt. rels. com. 1982, 100th ann. com. 1988-91), Librs. South Middlesex (chmn. 1970-73), North Bergen Fedn. Librs. (chmn. dirs. coun. 1975), Bergen County Coop. Libr. Sys. (pres., treas. 1982-83, 86-87, exec. bd. computer consortium 1987-89, budget com. 1989-94), Ridgewood C. of C. (bd. dirs. 1983-93, treas. 1988-93), Soc. Valley Hosp. Ridgewood, Ridgewood Kiwanis (pres. 1982-83, treas. 1987-88, Disting. Club. Pres. award 1983). Home: 4910 Deer Pass Dr Reno NV 89509-0577

ROSS, ROBERT K., foundation administrator, physician; B in Pub. Adminstrn., U. Pa., Phila., MPA, MD, U. Pa., Phila. Pediatrician Nat. Health Svcs. Corps, Camden, NJ, 1985—88; Robert Wood Johnson clin. scholar U. Penn. Sch. Medicine, 1988—90; commr. Phila. Dept. Pub. Health, 1990—93; dir. Health & Human Svcs. Agy., San Diego County, 1993—2000; pres., CEO The Calif. Endowment, 2000—. Chmn. Nat. Boost for Kids Initiative; mem. Nat. Vaccine Adv. Comm., Pres.'s Summit for America's Future; former cons. Phila. Sch. Dist. Children's Health Initiative; instr. clin. medicine Children's Hosp. Phila.; former mem. NJ Gov.'s Commn. Health Care Costs; med. dir. LINK Sch.-Based Clinic Prog., Camden; faculty San Diego State U. Sch. Pub. Health; bd. dirs. The Calif. Endowment, 1997—. Bd. dirs. Nat. Marrow Donor Prog., Grantmakers In Health, San Diego United Way, Jackie Robinson YMCA. Recipient Youth Advocacy Humanitarian of Yr. award, 1999, Outstanding Community Svc. award, Volunteers of America, 1999, Pub. Ofcl.'s of Yr. award, Governing Mag., 1999, Leadership award, Hosp. Coun. San Diego, 1999, Disting. Grantmaker of Yr. award, Coun. Foundations, 2008, Health Adminstr. of Yr. citation, Nat. Assn. Health Svc. Execs.; named one of Calif.'s Most Influential Civic Leaders in Health Policy, Capitol Weekly, 2006. Mem.: Am. Acad. Pediat. (diplomate). Office: Calif Endowment 21650 Oxnard St Ste 1200 Woodland Hills CA 91367 Office Phone: 818-703-3311. Office Fax: 818-703-4193.*

ROSS, RODERIC HENRY, retired insurance company executive; b. Jamestown, NY, July 14, 1930; s. Edwin A. and Mary (Dornberger) R.; m. Patricia Johnson, Aug. 6, 1955; children: Timothy, Amy, Jane, Christopher. BA, Hobart Coll., 1952, LLD (hon.), 1979. CLU, ChFC. Gen. agt. Phila. Life Ins. Co., 1957-70, sr. v.p. mktg., 1972-73, pres., 1973-83, vice chmn., 1983-84; chmn., CEO Keystone State Life Ins. Co., Phila., 1985-2000; ret., 2001. Bd. dirs. PMA Capital Corp., Phila., ret., 2008; past chmn. Ins. Fedn. Pa.; dir. Intergroup Svcs. Corp., Malvern, Pa. Rector's warden St. David's Ch., Radnor, Pa., 1989-90; hon. trustee Hobart-William Smith Colls., Geneva, N.Y., 1972—, chmn. bd., 1983-88. Sgt. U.S. Army, 1952-54. Mem. Am. Soc. CLUs, Nat. Assn. Nat. Assn. Life Underwriters, Million Dollar Round Table (life), Union League (former dir.), Orpheus Club, St. David's Golf Club (Wayne, Pa.), Penna Soc., Pine Valley Golf Club (Clementon, N.J.). Republican. Episcopalian. Avocations: golf, tennis. Home: 770 Pugh Rd Wayne PA 19087 Home Phone: 610-688-2763. Personal E-mail: rodnpatross@verizon.net.

ROSS, ROMAN, retail executive; BS, U. Oreg., Eugene; law degree, Willamette U., Salem, Oreg.; MBA, U. Tex., Austin. Trade mktg. mgr. sales merchandising Philip Morris USA; with Mexican affiliate Philip Morris Internat.; pres., CEO CompUSA, Dallas, 2006—. Office: CompUSA Inc 14951 North Dallas Pky Dallas TX 75254

ROSS, SHARON MARIE, communications educator; b. Cleve., Oct. 31, 1969; d. Lawrence James and Carol Marie Ross; m. Thomas James Skapes, Nov. 16, 2002; 1 child, Thomas James-Ross Skapes. BA, Cleve. State U, Ohio, 1994; M, Ohio State U., Columbus, 1997; PhD, U. Tex., Austin, 2002. TV dept, prof. Columbia Coll., Chgo., 2003—. Assoc. editor Internat. Digital Media Arts Assn. Jour., Chgo., 2005—. Author: (book) Beyond the Box: Television and the Internet; editor: Teen Television Essays on Programming and Fandom. Academic cons. Acad. TV Arts and Scis., Living History Archive, LA, 2006—; bd. mem. Soc. Cinema and Media Studies, TV and New Media Interest Group, 2008—; academic cons. Mus. Broadcast Comm., Chgo., 2007—. Faculty Devel. grant, Columbia Coll. Chgo., 2005. Fellow: NATPE; mem.: Internat. Digital Media Arts Assn. (assoc. editor jour. 2006—, outstanding achievement award 2008), Soc. Cinema and Media Studies (bd., tv and new media interest group 2008—). Democrat. Home: 2745 W Giddings 3 Chicago IL 60625 Office: Columbia Coll Chgo TV Dept 600 South Michigan Ave Chicago IL 60605 Business E-Mail: sross@colum.edu.

ROSS, STANFORD G., lawyer, government official; b. St. Louis, Oct. 9, 1931; m. Dorothy Rabin, June 9, 1958; children: John, Ellen. AB with honors, Washington U., 1953; JD magna cum laude, Harvard U., 1956. Bar: D.C. 1969, Calif. 1956, N.Y. 1959. Assoc. Irell & Manella, LA, 1956-57; tchg. fellow, rsch. asst. Harvard Law Sch., 1957-58; assoc. Dewey, Ballantine, Bushby, Palmer & Wood, NYC, 1958-61; asst. tax legis. counsel U.S. Dept. Treasury, 1961-63; prof. law N.Y. U., 1963-67; White House staff asst. to Pres. Johnson, 1967-68; gen. counsel U.S. Dept. Transp., 1968-69; ptnr. Caplin & Drysdale, Washington, 1969-78; commr. Social Security Adminstrn., Washington, 1978-79; ptnr. Califano, Ross & Heineman, Washington, 1980-82, Arnold & Porter, Washington, 1983—2002. Pub. trustee Social Security Trust Funds, Washington, 1990-95; chmn. Social Security Adv. Bd., 1997-2002. Editor: Harvard Law Rev, 1954-56. Mem. ABA, Fed. Bar Assn., Internat. Fiscal Assn., Nat. Acad. Social Ins. Office: Arnold & Porter 555 12th St NW Washington DC 20004-1206

ROSS, STEPHEN L., economics professor; b. Charlotte, NC, Aug. 3, 1961; s. Herbert and Patricia Ross; m. Margery Ross; children: Alexandra, Gwenyth. PhD, Syracuse U., NY, 1994. Prof. economics U. Conn., Storrs, 1994—. Cons. fair lending investigation NY State Atty. Gen.'s Office, NYC, 2005—07. Author: (acad. book) The Colour of Credit. Mem. State Conn. Anti-Predatory Lending Task Force, Hartford, 2006—08. Office: Univ Conn Economics Dept 341 Mansfield Rd U-63 Storrs Mansfield CT 06269-1063 Business E-Mail: stephen.l.ross@uconn.edu.

ROSS, STEPHEN MICHAEL, real estate company executive, professional sports team owner; b. Detroit, Mich., May 10, 1940; m. Kara Ross. BS, U. Mich., 1962; JD, Wayne State U., 1965; LLM in Taxation, NYU, 1966. Tax atty. Coopers & Lybrand, Detroit; dir. Insignia Fin. Group, Inc.; founder, dir. Charter Mcpl. Mortgage Acceptance Co.; founder, chmn., CEO The Related Cos. LP, NYC; co-owner Miami Dolphins, 2008—09, majority owner, 2009—. Chmn. Equinox Fitness Clubs, Real Estate Bd. NY. Trustee Juvenile Diabetes Rsch. Found., Solomon R. Guggenheim Mus., Jackie Robinson Found., Jewish Assn. for Svcs. for Aged, Lincoln Ctr., NY Presbyterian Hosp., Urban Land Inst., Levin Inst., Nat. Bldg. Mus.; chmn. bd. trustees Centerline Holding Co. Recipient Tree of Life award, 1998, "What NY Needs" award, The Dow Fund, 1999, Henry Pearce award, Jewish Assn. for Services for the Aged, 2001, Leadership in Tourism award, NYC & Co., 2002, Jack D. Weiler award, United Jewish Appeal, 2003, The Harry B. Helmsley Disting. New Yorker award, The Real Estate Bd. NY, 2005; named Housing Person of Yr., Nat. Housing Conf., Owner & Developer of the Yr., NY Construction News, 2000; named one of The 100 Most Influential Leaders in Bus., Crain's NY Bus., 2002, Forbes' Richest Americans, 2006. Mem.: Real Estate Board of NY (dir.). Office: The Related Cos LP 60 Columbus Cir New York NY 10023 Office Phone: 212-421-5333.*

ROSS, STEVEN ELLIOT, surgeon; b. Wilmington, Del., Sept. 12, 1951; s. Morris H. and Anita Selma (Luterman) R.; m. Carolyn Gross, June 13, 1981; children: Leah Jane, Asher Joshua, Tovah Jennifer. BA, U. Del., 1972; MD, Jefferson Med. Coll., Phila., Pa., 1976. Diplomate Am. Bd. Surgery, Am. Bd. Surg. Critical Care. Resident, general surgery York Hosp., York, Pa., 1976-81; fellow trauma and surgical critical care medicine Univ. Kansas Med. Ctr., Kansas City, 1981-82; attending surgeon Cooper Hosp., Camden, NJ, 1984—, head, divsn. trauma and emergency surgical services, vice chief, dept. surgery, fellowship dir. surg. critical care; prof. surgery Univ. Medicine Dentistry NJ/Robert Wood Johnson Med. Sch., Camden, NJ, 1984—. Contbr. several sci. articles to profl. jours. Chmn. NJ State Trauma Ctr. Coun., 1991-93, 97. Fellow Am. Coll. Surgeons (chmn. com. trauma NJ chpt. 1991-96, mem.), Am. Assn. Surgery Trauma, Soc. Critical Care Medicine, Western Trauma Assocs. (bd. dirs. 1993-95), Alpha Omega Alpha (faculty mem.), Am. Coll. Critical Care Medicine. Jewish. Office: Cooper Hosp Dept Surgery 3 Cooper Plz Rm 411 Camden NJ 08103 Address: 1 Cooper Plz Camden NJ 08103 Office Phone: 856-342-3041, 856-342-2657. Office Fax: 856-342-2817, 856-968-8306.

ROSS, TERENCE P., lawyer; b. 1958; BA with honors, Stanford U., 1980; JD, U. Va. Sch. Law, 1983; MA, George Masson U., 2008. Bar: Commonwealth Va., DC, NY, US Supreme Ct., US Ct. Appeals Fed. Circuit. Law clk. to Judge Roger Robb, US Ct. Appeals Dist. Columbia Circuit; assoc. Gibson, Dunn & Crutcher LLP, Washington, 1984—91, ptnr., 1991—. Adj. prof. George Mason U. Law Sch.; writer and spkr. in field on intellectual property topics; rsch. editor, mem. mng. bd. Va. Law Review. Author: Intellectual Property Law: Damages and Remedies, 2000. Mem. bd. visitors U. Va. Named to Magnificent Seven: IP's Best Young Trial Lawyers, IP Worldwide, 2002. Mem.: ABA (mem. steering com., mem. intellectual property lit. com.), DC Bar Assn. (chair annual develop. in intellectual property law forum). Office: Gibson Dunn & Crutcher LLP 1050 Conn Ave NW Washington DC 20036 Office Phone: 202-955-8664. Business E-Mail: tross@gibsondunn.com.

ROSS, THOMAS ALBERT, art educator; b. Jackson, Miss., Oct. 22, 1950; s. Thomas Albert and Andre Rosalind Ross; m. Gayle Megginson Ross, Nov. 27, 1971; 1 child, Arwen Lois Sharak. BA, Miss. Coll., Clinton, 1972; MFA, U. Ga., Athens, 1974. Vis. prof. Miss. Coll., Clinton, 1975; art instr., program coord. Copiah-Lincoln CC, Wesson, Miss., 1975—. One-man shows include paintings Arts and Crafts Nat. Exhbn., 1971, exhibited in group shows at Bryant Galleries in Jackson Miss., 1980, Miss. Arts Festival. Bd. mem. Brookhaven Animal Rescue League, Miss., 1997—2008. Named Outstanding Instr., Copiah-Lincoln CC, 1982, 1987, 1995. Mem.: Miss. Faculty Assn. Cmty. & Jr. Colls. (pres. 1986—87). Liberal. Methodist. Avocation: fishing. Office: Copiah-Lincoln CC PO Box 649 Wesson MS 39191-0641 Business E-Mail: tom.ross@colin.edu.

ROSS, THOMAS J., JR., personal financial adviser; b. NYC, Aug. 25, 1954; s. Thomas J. Sr. and Margaret (Byrne) R.; m. Elise Mary Bishop, Sept. 20, 1980; children: Kaitlyn Ann, John Patrick, Brendan Christopher. BA in English magna cum laude, Boston Coll., 1976; MBA in Fin., U. Pa., 1980. Cons. Wharton Applied Rsch. Ctr., Phila., 1978-80, CPA State NJ, 1980; part owner, v.p. Asset Mgmt. Group, Parsippany, NJ, 1980-86; dir. Coopers & Lybrand, Parsippany, 1986-89, ptnr., 1989-92, regional ptnr. personal fin. svcs. group, NY Metro Area, 1992—97; pres. Wealth Mgmt. Cons. LLC, Morristown, NJ, 1998—. Mem. nat. PFS steering com. Coopers & Lybrand, NYC, 1987-98; mem. investment policy com. Coopers & Lybrand Fin. Advs. LLC, 1996-97. Editor newsletter Growing Your Wealth, 1992-97; contbr. numerous tax and fin. articles to Chief Exec. Mag., Bottom Line Fin., NJ Law Jour. Mem. Boston Coll. Alumni Admissions Coun., Chestnut Hill, Mass., 1976—, Kickoff Classic Tix Com., Ind. Coll. Fund of NJ, Summit, 1990-98; bd. trustees Tri-County Scholarship Fund, 2001-, Mayo Ctr. for Performing Arts, 2007—; mem. exec. com. Boston Coll. Wall St. Coun., 1996—; soccer, baseball and basketball coach Mountain Lakes Youth Leagues, 1989-2001; mem. pre-cana team, Parish Fin. Coun., Parish Coun., St. Catherine of Siena. Recipient scholarships Boston Coll., Imaculate Heart Guild, others, 1972-76; named Fin. Coun. of Yr., Asset Mgmt. Group, 1983-85, one of Top 250 Fin. Advisors in Am., Worth Mag., 1997-99, one of Top 100 Advisors in Am., Worth Mag., 2004. Mem. AICPA, Callan Assn. Ind. Adv. Group, NJ Soc. CPAs (PFP com. mem. 1990-92), Wharton Bus. Club of NY, Rockaway River CC, Park Ave. Club, Boston Coll. Clubs of NJ and NYC, Wharton Club of NY, Buck Hill Golf Club. Avocations: golf, youth coaching, reading, running. Home: 140 Kenilworth Rd Mountain Lakes NJ 07046-1156 Office: Wealth Mgmt Cons The Abbey 355 Madison Ave Morristown NJ 07980 Office Phone: 973-401-1500. Business E-Mail: tross@wmcnj.com.

ROSS, THOMAS STUART, political organization administrator; Attended, U. Del.; grad., Del. State U. Co-chmn. New Castle County Republican Com., Del.; chmn. Wilmington Republican Com., Del., Republican State Com. of Del., Wilmington, 2008—. Republican. Office: Republican Party of Del 3301 Lancaster Ave Ste 4B Wilmington DE 19805 Office Phone: 302-651-0260 ext. 2. Office Fax: 302-651-0270. E-mail: tomross@delawaregop.com.*

ROSS, THOMAS WARREN, SR., academic administrator, former judge; b. Greensboro, NC, June 5, 1950; s. Charles Burdette and Mary Brownie (Franklin) R.; m. Susan Donaldson, June 17, 1972; children: Thomas Warren Jr., Mary Kathryn. BA in Polit. Sci., Davidson Coll., 1972; JD with honors, U. N.C., 1975; grad., Nat. Jud. Coll., 1985. Bar: N.C. 1975, U.S. Ct. Appeals (4th cir.) 1979, U.S. Supreme Ct. 1979. Asst. prof. pub. law Inst. Govt., U. NC, Chapel Hill, 1975-76; ptnr. Smith, Patterson, Follin, Curtis, James & Harkavy, 1976-82; adminstrv. asst. to Rep. Robin Britt US Congress, NC, 1983-84; judge NC Superior Ct., 1984—2000; dir. Adminstrv. Office of the Cts., 1999—2000; exec. dir. Z. Smith Reynolds Found., 2001—07; pres. Davidson Coll., NC, 2007—. Pres. Ctrl. Carolina Legal Svcs., Inc., 1981-82; mem. com. on sentencing and corrections Nat. Conf. State Trial Judges; chmn. N.C. Sentencing and Policy Adv. Commn., 1990-99, com. on probation and parole Conf. Superior Ct. Judges, 1988-94; mem. com. on professionalism N.C. State Bar, 1990-91. Deacon, elder 1st Presbyn. Ch., Greensboro; chmn. Guilford County Dem. Party, 1981-83, Ctr. for Creative Leadership Bd. Assocs., 1995—, Guilford County Substance Abuse Study Commn., 1987-88, Guilford County Corrections Commn., 1988-94; active campaign United Way, 1979-82, Greensboro Heart Fund, 1980-82, Greensboro Sports Coun., 1989-2000; trustee U. NC, Greensboro, 2001—07, chair, 2005—07; trustee Davidson Coll., 2003—; mem. N.C. Gov.'s Statewide Comprehensive Recreation Plan Policy, 1982-83; mem. exec. coun. Gen. Green coun. Boy Scouts Am., 1988-91, chmn. Eagle scout bd. rev., 1990-91, mem. exec. bd. Old North State coun., 1992-2000, chmn. Eagle scout bd. rev., 1992-2000; bd. dirs. Women's Residential Ctr., 1986-89; mem. steering com. Greensboro Coalition Substance Abuse, 1986-87, N.C. Open Govt. Coalition, 2004-06, Hispanics in Philanthropy, 2004-07, Southeastern Coun. Founds., 2005-07; chmn. bd. govs. Summit House, Inc., 1994-95. Recipient Silver Beaver award Boy Scouts Am., 1993, Pub. Ofcl. of Yr. Gov. Mag., 1994, Found. for the Improvement of Justice award, 1995, Disting. Alumni award, Davidson Coll., 2001, Disting. Alumni award, UNC-Chapel Hill Sch. Law, 2005, Chief Justice William H. Rehnquist award for Judicial Excellence, 2000; named Boss of Yr., Greensboro Legal Secs. Assn., 1981, Outstanding Young Man in Am., Greensboro Jaycees, 1984, N.C. Trial Judge of Yr., N.C. Acad. Trial Lawyers, 1996. Mem. ABA (jud. adminstrn. sect.), N.C. Bar Assn. (dispute resolution com. 1991-92, nominating com. 1991-92, v.p. 1997-98), Greensboro Bar Assn., U. N.C-Chapel Hill Law Alumni Assn. (bd. dirs. 2003-06). Office: Davidson Coll Office of Pres Box 7145 Davidson NC 28035*

ROSS, TRACEE ELLIS (TRACEE JOY SILBERSTEIN), actress, model, fashion editor; b. LA, Calif., Oct. 29, 1972; d. Diana Ross. BA, Brown U.; ed., William Esper Acting Studio. Fashion editor Mirabella, NY Mag.; contbg. editor Distinction Mag. Actress (TV series) The Dish, 1997, The Lyricist Lounge Show, 2000, Girlfriends, 2000—08 (BET Comedy award outstanding lead actress in a comedy series, 2000, Best Actress in a Comedy Series, NAACP Image award, 2007, 2009), (TV films) Race Against Fear: A Moment of Truth, 1998, Life Support, 2007, (films) Sue, 1997, A Fare to Remember, 1998, Hanging Up, 2000, In the Weeds, 2000, I-See-You.com, 2006, Daddy's Little Girls, 2007, (plays) Blackout, The Vagina Monologues. Named Vol. of Yr., LA Urban League, 2004. Mailing: c/o ICM 8942 Wilshire Blvd Beverly Hills CA 90211*

ROSS, TRACEY, actress; b. Bklyn., Feb. 27, 1959; 1 child, Bryce. Actress (TV series) Ryan's Hope, All My Children, Passions, NBC, 1999— (Outstanding Actess in Daytime Drama Series, NAACP Image Awards, 2007), guest apperances The Cosby Show, 1989, Doctor, Doctor, 1991, ROC, 1991, Baywatch Nights, 1996, Gregory Hines Show, actress (TV films) Mayflower Madam, 1987, Valley of the Dolls, (films) Unconditional Love, 1999. Achievements include winning Miss NJ Pageant, 1975; first $100,100 Star Search spokesmodel champion, 1984.

ROSS, VIOLET BICA, retired elementary school educator, psychologist; d. Ellie A. and Anna (Muresan) Bica; m. L. Clayton Ross, Oct. 23, 1976 (dec.). BS, Mount Union Coll., 1944; MA, Kent State U., 1952. Tchr. Alliance Bd. Edn., 1945—53; psychologist Maple Heights Bd. Edn., Ohio, 1954—56, Cleveland Heights Bd. Edn., 1956—61, Shaker Heights Bd. Edn., Ohio, 1961—76; ret., 1976. Psychologist chair Kent Area Sch., 1959—60, Cleve. Area Sch., 1962—63; editl. bd. Sch. Counselor Journal, 1962—64; del. nat. conventions. Sponser Ross Surg. Video Lectr. Svcs. Ophthalmologist Residents U. Hosps. Cleve. Named Dormitory at Mt. Union Coll. Bica-Ross Hall, 1999, Dormitory at Wash. Jefferson Coll. Bica-Ross Hall, 2004. Mem.: Nat. Assn. Sch. Psychologist, Ohio Edn. Assn. (life), Am. Coun. Assn. (life), Kappa Delta, Kappa Delta Pi, Delta Kappa Gamma. Achievements include donations of scholarships to Mount Union College, Washington and Jefferson College. Avocations: reading, travel, golf. Home: 112 Royal Oak Dr Aurora OH 44202

ROSS, WILBUR LOUIS, JR., investment banker; b. Weehawken, NJ, Nov. 28, 1937; s. Wilbur Louis and Agnes (O'Neill) R.; m. Judith Nodine, May 26, 1961 (div. 1995); children: Jessica, Amanda; m. Hilary Geary, Oct. 9, 2004. AB, Yale U., 1959; MBA with distinction, Harvard U., 1961. Assoc. Wood, Struthers and Winthrop, NYC, 1963-64; pres. Faulkner, Dawkins and Sullivan Securities Corp., NYC, 1964-76; sr. mng. dir. Rothschild, Inc., NYC, 1976-2000; CEO News Communications Inc., NYC, 1996-98; chmn., chief investment officer Rothschild Recovery Fund, NYC, 1997-2000; chmn., CEO W.L. Ross & Co. LLC, NYC, 2000—. Bd. dirs. Biocraft Labs Inc., Rutherford, NJ, FurVault Inc., NYC, Investors Ins. Co., Lawrence Harbor, NJ, Revere Copper and Brass Co., Stamford, Syms Corp., Secaucus, NJ, Am. Bankruptcy Inst., Washington, Allis Chalmers Corp., Milw., KTI Inc., RH Cement Co., Seoul, Korea, Tong Yang Life Ins. Co., Seoul, Kansai Sawayaka Bank, Osaka, Fresca Credit Card Co., Osaka; fin. advisor equity holders com. Texaco Co., A.H. Robins Co., Pub. Service NH; hon. econ. amb. from Korea to APEC Investment, Mont., 1999; chmn. Asia Recovery Fund L.P., WL Recovery Fund LP, Asia Co. Investment Ptnrs. L.P., Clarent Hosp. Corp., Compaigne Europeanee Wagan, Internat. Auto Computer Group, Internat. Steel Group, Inc., Cleve., 2002-04, Ohizumi Mfg. Co., Japan, 2003-, Burlington Industries, 2003-, Marquis Who's Who LLC, 2003-06, Marquis Who's Who Inc., 2004-06, Internat. Coal Group, 2004-, Internat. Textile Group, 2005—, Nikko Elec. Co., Japan, Miltal Steel Co., Nev., Internat. Steel Group, Japan Soc., Montpelier ReHoldings, Arcelor Mittal Steel Co., Wagon, PLC, Plascar Participacoes. Treas. NY State Dem. Com., 1980-83, Am. Fedn. Arts, 1993—, The New Mus., 1993—; vice chmn. Bklyn. Mus., 1981—; chmn. univ. coun. com. on art Yale U., 1983-88; chmn. NAD, NYC, 1985—, Am. Art Forum, Smithsonian Instn., 1987—; trustee, vice chmn. Nat. Mus. Am. Art, Washington, 1986-91, chmn., 1991—; trustee, Mus. Am. Fin. History, Gustave Hyde Ctr. Nat. Mus. Am. Indian, 2001—, Nat. Mus. Am. Fin. History, Whitney Mus. Am. Art, Preservation Found. of Palm Beach; trustee Sarah Lawrence Coll., 1986—, chmn. art gallery, 1984—; pres. Parrish Art Mus., 1991-95; chmn. NY Hist. Soc., 1993-94; bd. dirs.

Smithsonian Inst. Nat. Bd., 1994—, chmn. bd. 1995; nat. chmn. Smithsonian Bicentennial Celebration, 1996; bd. dirs. Turnaround Mgmt. Assn., 2001—; chmn. Absolute Recovery Hedge Fund, Ltd., Hamilton, Bermuda, Taiyo Fund, 2003-, Japan Real Estate Recovery Fund, 2003-; dir. Palm Beach Civic Assn., Yale U. Sch. Mgmt.; mem. com. on univ. rels., com. on capital markets regulation Harvard U.; mem. US India Bus. Coun., chmn. circle. With US Army, 1961—63. Recipient Legend in Leadership award, Yale Sch. Mgmt., 2005; named one of Forbes' Richest Americans, 2006. Fellow Jonathan Edward Coll. of Yale U., Met. Mus. Art; mem. Fin. Analysts Fedn. (chartered), Century Assn., The Bus. Round Table, Bath and Tennis Club, Everglades Club, Harvard Bus. Sch. Club NY (bd. dirs.), Beach Club. Avocation: collecting art. Office: 1166 Avenue Of The Americas New York NY 10036-2708 Office Phone: 212-826-2111. Business E-Mail: wlross@wlross.com.*

ROSS, WILLIAM JARBOE, lawyer; b. Oklahoma City, May 9, 1930; s. Walter John and Bertha (Jarboe) R.; m. Mary Lillian Ryan, May 19, 1962; children: Rebecca Anne Roten, Robert Joseph, Molly Kathleen Fritch. BBA, U. Okla., 1952, LLB, 1954; LHD (hon.), Oklahoma City U., 2005. Bar: Okla. 1954. Since practiced in, Oklahoma City; asst. mcpl. counselor, 1955-60; mem. firm Rainey, Ross, Rice & Binns, 1960—, ptnr., 1965-99, of counsel, 2000—; chmn. bd. Ethics and Excellence in Journalism Found., Inasmuch Found. Mem. bd. visitors U. Okla. Coll. Law; bd. dirs. Ethics and Excellence in Journalism Found., Inasmuch Found. Mem. Okla. Bar Assn., Okla. Heritage Assn., Okla. City Golf and Country Club, Econ. Club, Fortune Club, Phi Alpha Delta, Beta Theta Pi, KC Home: 6923 Avondale Ct Oklahoma City OK 73116-5008

ROSSEAU, GAIL L., neurosurgeon, educator; b. Nov. 30, 1956; m. Rick Rosseau; children: Natalie, Brendan. BS, U. Iowa, 1978; MD, George Washington Med. Sch., Washington, DC, 1981. Cert. Neurosurgery. Intern, gen. surgery George Washington U., Washington, 1985—86, resident, neurol. surgery, 1986—91; cranial base surgery fellow H.I.A. du Val-de-Grace Hosp., Paris, 1990; cranial base surgery and microvascular surgery fellow U. Pitts. Presbyn.-U. Hosp., Pa., 1991—92; staff mem., neurol. surgery Gottlieb Meml. Hosp., 1992—99, Columbus Hosp., 1992—2001, Ingalls Hosp., 1998—2000, Elmhurst Meml. Hosp., 1999, Neurologic & Orthopedic Inst. Chgo., 2001—; mem. Chgo. Inst. Neurosurgery and Neuroresearch (CINN), Neurologic & Orthopedic Inst. Chgo., 1992—, dir., cranial base surgery, 1992—; staff mem., neurol. surgery Rush Med. Coll., Rush U. Med. Ctr., Ill., 1998, asst. prof., neurol. surgery Ill., 1998—. Lectr. in field. Contbr. articles to profl. jours., chapters to books. Recipient Harry B. Zehner, Jr. Meml Traveling Fellowship award, ACS, Chgo. Women of Yr. Mentor award; Health Policy fellowship, Am. Coll. Surgeons. Mem.: Congress Neurol., Am. Assn. Neurol. Surgeons. Achievements include pioneering the use of endoscopic techniques in treating pituitary tumors; leadership in international neurosurgicals organisation such as CNS, AANS, FIENS and more. Office: Chgo Inst Neurosurgery and Neuroreseach Neurologic & Orthopedic Inst Chgo 4501 N Winchester Ave 2nd Fl Chicago IL 60640 Address: Chgo Inst Neurosurgery and Neuroreseach Med Group 1200 S York Rd Elmhurst IL 60126 Office Phone: 773-250-0400, 773-250-0500.*

ROSSELLI, DENISE LOUISE, literature and language professor, department chairman; b. St. Helena, Calif., Sept. 10, 1952; d. Joseph Eugene and Bernadette Marie Defilippis. BA in English, U. San Francisco, 1974, MA in Writing, 1989. Registered vet. technician Bd. Vet. Medicine, Calif., 1979. Hosp. mgr. Pet Emergency Clinic, Ventura, Calif., 1979—87; neurology and radiology technician Berkeley Dog and Cat Hosp., Calif., 1987—89; writing ctr. coord. Napa Valley Coll., Calif., 1996—2003, testing and tutoring ctr. coord., 1996—2006, mem. matriculation steering com., 1996—2007, English prof., dept. chair, 2007—. Judge Jessamyn West Writers' Contest, Napa, 2000—07. Sec. Napa Valley Coll. Faculty Assn., 2000—03, pres., 2003—06; philanthropist Napa Valley Writers' Conf., 1999. Recipient McPherson Disting. Tchr.'s award, 2006. Democrat. Roman Catholic. Avocations: writing, travel, walking. Home: 1076 Soda Canyon Rd Napa CA 94558 Office: 2277 Napa-Vallejo Hwy Napa CA 94558 Office Phone: 707-253-3172. Business E-Mail: drosselli@napavalley.edu.

ROSSELLINI, ISABELLA, actress, model; b. Rome, June 18, 1952; d. Roberto Rossellini and Ingrid Bergman; m. Martin Scorsese, Sept. 1979 (div. Nov. 1982); m. Jonathan Wiedemann (div.); 1 child, Elettra Ingrid. Student, Finch Coll., 1972, New Sch. for Social Research, NYC. Model for Lancôme cosmetics, 1982—95. Actor (films) A Matter of Time, 1976, Il Pap'occhio, 1980, The Meadow, 1982, White Nights, 1985, Blue Velvet, 1986, Siesta, 1987, Red Riding Hood, 1987, Tough Guys Don't Dance, 1987, Zelly and Me, 1988, Cousins, 1989, Wild at Heart, 1990, Les Dames Galantes, 1990, Death Becomes Her, 1992, The Pickle, 1992, Fearless, 1993, Wyatt Earp, 1994, Immortal Beloved, 1994, The Innocent, 1995, The Funeral, Crime of the Century, 1996, Big Night, 1996, The Real Blonde, 1998, Empire, 2002, Roger Dodger, 2002, The Tulse Luper Suitcases: The Moab Story, 2003, The Saddest Music in the World, 2003, The Tulse Luper Suitcases, Part 2: Vaux to the Sea, 2004, King of the Corner, 2004, Heights, 2004, The Feast of the Goat, 2005, The Architect, 2006; (TV films) The Last Elephant, 1990, Lies of the Twins, 1991, Don Quixote, 2000, Monte Walsh, 2003, Earthsea, 2004; (TV miniseries) The Odyssey, 1997, Merlin, 1998, The Impostors, 1998, Left Luggage, 1998; (TV series) Napoléon, 2002; (TV appearances) Friends, 1996, Chicago Hope, 1997, The Simpsons, 1999, Alias, 2004, 2005; writer (films) My Dad is 100 Years Old, 2005; Author: Some of Me, 1997, In the Name of the Father, the Daughter and the Holy Spirits: Remembering Roberto Rossellini, 2006 Office: United Talent Agy 9560 Wilshire Blvd Ste 500 Beverly Hills CA 90212

ROSSEN, JORDAN, lawyer; b. Detroit, June 13, 1934; s. Nathan Paul and Rebecca (Rizy) R.; m. Susan Friebert, Mar. 24, 1963 (div. June 1972); 1 child, Rebecca; m. M. Elizabeth Bunn, Jan. 3, 1981; children—N. Paul, Jordan David. BA, U. Mich., 1956; JD, Harvard U., 1959. Bar: Mich. 1959, N.Y. 1998, U.S. Dist. Ct. (ea. dist.) Mich. 1960, U.S. Dist. Ct. (ea. and so. dists.) N.Y. 1999, U.S. Ct. Appeals (6th cir.) 1966, U.S. Ct. Appeals (7th cir.) 1974, U.S. Ct. Appeals (D.C. cir.) 1984, U.S. Ct. Appeals (3rd cir.) 1987, U.S. Ct. Appeals (2d cir.) 2004, U.S. Supreme Ct. 1966. With US Army, 1959, Mich. Army-Res. & Mich. Nat. Guard, 1960—66; Assoc. Sullivan, Elmer, Eames & Moody, Detroit, 1960-62; assoc. Sugar & Schwartz, Detroit, 1962-64; asst. gen. counsel UAW, Detroit, 1964-74, assoc. gen. counsel, 1974-83, gen. counsel, 1983-98; of counsel Meyer, Suozzi, English and Klein, NYC, 1998—2008; prof. labor studies Wayne State U., 2000—04. Vice pres. N.P. Rossen Agy., Inc., Detroit, 1960-83; gen. counsel Mich. Health & Social Security Research Inst., Inc., Detroit, 1965-83; dir. UAW Job Devel. & Tng. Corp., Detroit, 1984-90; mem. 6th Cir. Jud. Conf. Editor: Mich. Bar Labor Section Publication, 1961-64. Contbr. articles to profl. jours. Pres. Young Democrats, Mich., 1963-65; chmn. Americans for Democratic Action, Mich., 1966-68; chmn. Voter Registration Dem. Party, Mich., 1967. Recipient Human Rights award, City of Detroit, 1978. Mem.: Natl. Bar Assn. (assoc. mem.), Nat. Assn. Adminstrv. Law Judges, Coll. Labor and Employment Lawyers (assoc. mem.), Fed. Bar Assn., N.Y. Bar Assn., Mich. Bar Assn. Jewish. Home: 207 E 30th St 2G New York NY 10016 Office: 207 E 30th St 2G New York NY 10016 Home Phone: 646-742-1220.

ROSSER, CHARLES J., chemistry professor; MD, Robert Wood Johnson Med. Sch., Piscataway, NJ, 1994. Cert. Fla. Med. Bd. U. Phoenix, 2008. Asst. prof. U. Fla., Gainesville, 2003—. Recipient Young Scientist award, Soc. Urologic Oncology. Fellow: ACS. Achievements include research in prostate and bladder cancer. Office: Univ Fla Coll Medicine 1600 SW Archer Rd Ste N215 Gainesville FL 32601 Office Fax: 352-392-8846. Business E-Mail: charles.rosser@urology.ufl.edu.

ROSSET, BARNET LEE, JR., publishing executive; b. Chgo., May 28, 1922; s. Barnet Lee and Mary (Tansey) R.; m. Joan Mitchell, 1950 (div. 1952); m. Hannelore Eckert, Aug. 1953 (div. 1957); 1 child, Peter; m. Cristina Agnini, Mar. 11, 1965 (div. 1979); children: Tansey, Beckett; m. Elisabeth Krug, 1980 (div. 1991; 1 child, Chantal; m. Astrid Myers, June 11, 2007. Ph.B., U. Chgo., 1947; BA New Sch. Social Research, NYC, 1952. Pub., editor Grove Press, Inc., 1951-86, Evergreen Rev., 1957-73, Blue Moon Books, Inc., NYC, 1987-98, Evergreen Rev. Inc., 1998—, Foxrock, Inc., 1995—. Served to 1st lt. Signal Corps AUS, 1942-46. Recipient Ninth Pub. citation PEN Am. Ctr., 1988, Poor Richard's award Small Press Ctr., 1999, Commandeur De L'Ordre Des Arts et Des Lettres, French Govt., 1999, Nat. Book Critics Cir. Lifetime Achievement award, 2001, Curtis Benjamin award Assn. Am. Pubs., 2001, 1st Ann. Hadada award Paris Rev., 2003. Mem. PEN, Overseas Press Club. Office: 61 4th Ave New York NY 10003-5204

ROSSETTI, GEORGE A., editor, director; b. Springfield, Mass., Apr. 13, 1958; s. Albert G. and Joan M. Rossetti; m. Donna Jean Ogilvie, Nov. 1, 1986. BA, Hunter Coll., CUNY, 1997; AOS, Am. Acad. Dramatic Arts, 1980. Editl. dir. PRR, Inc., Melville, NY, 1997—2001, Ross Comm. Assocs., Melville, 2001—; exec. editor Internat. Soc. Gastrointestinal Oncology, Melville, 2003—; sr. editor Sci. & Medicine, NY. Specialist US Army, 1987—89, Wiesbaden, Germany. Mem.: Am. Med. Writers Assn., Coun. Sci. Editors, Am. Soc. Clin. Oncology, Psi Chi, Golden Key Internat. Honour Soc., Phi Beta Kappa. Conservative. Lutheran. Avocations: flying, skeet shooting, cooking, photography. Office: Isgio 200 Broadhollow Rd Ste 207 Melville NY 11747 Office Fax: 631-393-5026. Business E-Mail: george.rossetti@isgio.org.

ROSSETTINI, TIMOTHY JAMES, music educator, director; b. Paterson, NJ, Nov. 20, 1980; s. Louis Joseph and Madeline Ruth Rossettini; m. Amanda J. West, May 20, 2006. MusB cum laude in Applied Percussion, James Madison U., 2003. Lic. tchr. music Va., 2003. Dir. bands Denbigh H.S., Newport News, Va., 2004—. Mem.: Va. Band and Orch. Dirs. Assn. (mem. all-state percussion audition com. 2005—06). Office: Denbigh High School 259 Denbigh Boulevard Newport News VA 23608 Office Fax: 757-872-6542. Business E-Mail: tim.rossettini@nn.k12.va.us.

ROSSI, ALICE S., sociology educator, writer; b. NYC, Sept. 24, 1922; d. William A. and Emma (Winkler) Schaerr; m. Max Kitt, Dec. 1941 (div. Sept. 1951); m. Peter H. Rossi, Sept. 29, 1951; children: Peter Eric, Kristin Alice, Nina Alexis. BA, Bklyn. Coll., 1947; PhD, Columbia U., 1957; 9 hon. degrees. Rsch. assoc. Cornell U., Ithaca, N.Y., 1951-52, Harvard U., Cambridge, Mass., 1952-55, U. Chgo., 1961-67, Johns Hopkins U., Balt., 1967-69; prof. sociology Goucher Coll., Balt., 1969-74, U. Mass., Amherst, 1974-91, prof. emerita, 1991—. Author/editor: 11 books; contbr. numerous articles to profl. jours. Founder, bd. mem. NOW, 1966-70; pres. Sociologists for Women in Soc., 1971-72. Career grantee NIMH, 1965-69, rsch. grantee Rockefeller Found., Ford Found., NIH, NSF, others; CommonWealth Disting. Scholarship award, 1988. Mem. Am. Sociol. Assn. (pres. 1983-84), Ea. Sociol. Soc. (pres. 1973-74). Avocations: design, sewing, gardening, creative writing. Home: 34 Stagecoach Rd Amherst MA 01002-3527

ROSSI, ANTHONY FRED, cardiologist; b. Bklyn., Sept. 17, 1957; s. Anthony and Josephine Rossi. MD, St. George's U., 1982. Cert. pediatric cardiologist AAP, 1992. Dir., pediatric cardiac intensive care and heart transplantation Mt. Sinai Med. Ctr., NYC, 1989—98; dir., cardiac intensive care program Miami Children's Hosp., Fla., 2000—08. Leader, cardiac surg. med. mission Healing Children, St. Petersburg, 1996—98. Achievements include goal directed therapy in congenital Heart surgery; SvO2 monitoring in hypoplastic left heart syndrome; arrhythmia management in cardiac intensive care patients. Office: Miami Children's Hosp 3200 SW 60 Ct Miami FL 33155 Office Fax: 305-662-8304. Business E-Mail: anthony.rossi@mch.com.

ROSSI, ANTHONY GERALD, lawyer; b. Warren, Ohio, July 20, 1935; s. Anthony Gerald and Lena (Guarnieri) R.; m. Marilyn J. Fuller, June 22, 1957; children: Diana L., Maribeth, Anthony Gerald III. BS, John Carroll U., 1957; JD, Cath. U. Am., 1961. Bar: Ohio 1961. Ptnr. Guarnieri & Secrest, Warren, 1961—; former acting judge Warren Municipal Ct. Mem. Mahoning-Shenango Estate Planning Coun., 1968—, past sec.; past pres. Warren Olympic Club; past bd. govs. Cath. U. Am. Law Sch. Coun.; past trustee Trumbull Art Guild, Warren Civic Music Assn. Capt. Transp. Corps, AUS, 1957-65. Mem. ABA, Ohio Bar Assn., Trumbull County Bar Assn. (exec. com. 1975—, pres. 1976-77), Am. Arbitration Assn., Ohio State Bar Found., Ohio Motorist Assn. (corp. mem., trustee 1980-86, 92-98), Wolf's Club, KC, Elks, Ohio Acad. of Trial Lawyers. Home: 2500 Hidden Lakes Dr NE Warren OH 44484-4159 Office: 151 E Market St Warren OH 44481-1102 Home Phone: 330-856-3774; Office Phone: 330-393-1584. E-mail: ganslaw@netdotcom.com.

ROSSI, ENNIO C., internist, educator; b. Madison, Wis., Apr. 3, 1931; s. Joseph and Esther (D'Amelio) R.; m. Anna Maria Bianchi, June 22, 1957; children: Roberta, Marco. BA, U. Wis., 1951, MD, 1954. Diplomate Am. Bd. Internal Medicine. Intern Ohio State U. Hosps., 1954-55; resident medicine U. Wis. Hosps., 1958-61, fellow, 1961-63; instr. medicine Marquette U., Milw., 1963-64, asst. prof. medicine, 1964-66; assoc. prof. medicine Northwestern U., Chgo., 1966-72, prof. medicine, 1972-96, prof. emeritus, 1996—, chief hematology, 1967-84, chief transfusion medicine, 1984-96. V.p. med. affairs Life Source Blood Ctr., Glenview, Ill., 1988-93; vis. scientist Mario Negri Inst., Milan, 1977. Co-editor: Haemostasis and the Kidney, 1989; sr. editor: Principles of Transfusion Medicine, 1991, 2d edit., 1996, 3rd edit., 2002, 4th edit., 2009 Capt. U.S. Army, 1956-58. Fulbright scholar, U.S. Dept. State, U. Rome, 1955; Nat. Heart, Lung Blood Inst. Transfusion Medicine Acad. awardee, 1983; WHO travelling fellow, 1985. Fellow ACP; mem. Am. Soc. Hematology, Am. Soc. Pharmacology and Exptl. Therapeutics, Am. Assn. Blood Banks (chmn. acad. transfusion medicine com. 1988-93), Internat. Soc. Blood Transfusion. Home: 812 Oak St Apt 302 Winnetka IL 60093-2560

ROSSI, FRANK DOMINICK, language educator; b. Pitts., Dec. 21, 1949; s. Frank Anthony and Anna Marie Rossi; children: Kimberly Ann, Michael Joseph, Christopher James. BS in Edn., Duquesne U., Pitts., 1971; MS, SUNY, Geneseo, 1972. Cert. in spanish NY, 1971, in social studies 1976, in French 1985, sch. dist. adminstr. 1985, in advanced study SUNY, Brockport, 1985. Tchr. Rush Henrietta Ctrl. Schs., NY, 1971—86; coord., instrn. Rochester City Sch. Dist., NY, 1986—2000, dir., fgn. lang., 2000—02; lectr. SUNY, 1989—; dir., youth advancement Cmty. Pl. Greater Rochester Inc., 2003—07. Lead cons. Tchg. & Tng. By Design, Rochester, 2005—. Contbr. articles. Recipient Golden Apple award, Rush Henrietta Educators Assn., 1985. Mem.: Nat. Assn. Secondary Sch. Prins., Fgn. Lang. Tchrs. Rochester Area (pres. 1984—86), NY State Assn. Fgn. Lang. Tchrs. (chair, instrnl. tech. com., Ramundo Cadeaux award 1993, Anthony Papalia award 1994). Avocations: photography, travel, walking. Home: 19 Jacaranda Ct Penfield NY 14526 Office: SUNY Brockport 350 New Campus Dr Brockport NY 14420 Home Fax: 585-388-0257. Personal E-mail: frossi@rochester.rr.com. Business E-Mail: frossi@brockport.edu.

ROSSI, GUIDO A(NTONIO), mathematics professor, researcher; b. Moretta, Cuneo, Italy, Jan. 17, 1944; s. Giulio Cesare and Anna Maria (Ferraris di Celle) R.; m. Maria Emilia Zucchi, Mar. 27, 1978. Dr. in Math., U. Torino, Italy, 1967. Asst. U. Torino, 1969-82; asst. prof. Facoltá di Economia e Commercio, 1969-82, assoc. prof. math., 1982-86, prof. math. social scis. and econs., 1986, full prof., 1986—, prof. math. for fin., 1996. Dir. Inst. Math Finanziaria, 1974-81, 83-85, 1992-94, dir. dept. stats. and applied math. human scis., 1995-2003, coord. rsch. projects, 1986—; pres. Sch. U. Mgmt d'Impresa, 2002—, pres.bd. tchrs. acturial scis., 2005-; prof. Scuola di Applicazione Italian Army, 1992—; mem. sci. bd. 3d A.F.I.R. Colloquium, 1993; mem. Internat. Sci. Com.; organizer FUR X conf.; bd. tchrs. doctorate program in math. for fin. markets joint Univs. Brescia, Milano, Torino, Pavia, 1991-2003, decision scis. U. Torino, 2003—. Contbr. articles to profl. and sci. jours. Served to lt. Italian Army, 1967-68, diplomated Sommelier, 1986. Decorated Knight of the Order of Civil Merit of Savoy, 1990, comdr., 1996, Knight of the Order of the S.S. Maurice and Lazarus, 2005. Mem. Unione Matematica Italiana, Assn. per la Matematica Applicata alle Scienze Economiche Sociali (auditor 1977-89, 2002—, adminstr. 1990—2001), Assn. Italiana di Ricerca Operativa (auditor 1990—), Italian Order of Actuaries, Assn. Italiana Sommeliers, Assn. Museo Ferroviario Piemontese (pres. 1986-2005, bd. mem. 2005—), Am. Math. Soc., European Math. Soc., Inst. Vienna Cir., Istituto Italiano dei Castelli-Internat. Burgen Institut, Fondo per l'Ambiente Italiano, Italian Fedn. Ferrovie Turistiche and Museali (co-founder, first pres. 1997-99), European Fedn. Mus. Tourist Railways (co-founder, bd. mem., 2003-); Clubs: I Neoteri (pres. 1990-92). Roman Catholic. Achievements include contributions to the foundations of probability, decision theory and financial decisions. Office: Dept Statistica & Matematica Applicata Piazza Arbarello 8 I-10122 Turin Italy E-mail: guido.rossi@unito.it.

ROSSI, JEROME R., retail executive; b. Boston, Aug. 12, 1943; m. Geraldine R.; children: Joseph, Jeffrey. Grad., Bentley Coll., 1966, Northeastern U., Boston, 1970. Sr. fin. analyst IT&T, 1966-68; supervising auditor Arthur Young & Co., 1968-72; v.p., contr. Dayton-Hudson Co., 1972-80; sr. v.p., CFO KDT Industries, 1980-82; sr. v.p. fin. G. Fox Co., 1982-85, chmn., 1985-89, Foley's, Houston, 1989; pres., COO Marshalls, 1990—96; exec. v.p. Marmaxx Group TJX Cos., Inc., 1996—2000, pres. HomeGoods, 2000—05, sr. exec. v.p., COO Marmaxx Group, 2005—07, sr. exec. v.p., group pres., 2007—. Office: TJX Cos Inc 770 Cochituate Rd Framingham MA 01701 Office Phone: 508-390-1000. Office Fax: 508-390-2091.

ROSSI, JOHN PATRICK, retired history professor; b. Phila., Apr. 7, 1936; s. Albert and Moroel Rossi; m. Frances Patricia Quinn, Jan. 22, 1966; 1 child, Monica Ellen Wilson. BA, La Salle Coll., Phila., 1958; MA in History, Notre Dame U., South Bend, Ind., 1960; PhD in History, U. Pa., Phila., 1965. Emeritus prof., history La Salle U., 1962—. Author: (book) A Whole New Game, 2000, The National Game, 2001, The 1964 Phillies, 2005, The Transformation of the British Liberal Party, 1873-1880, 1978, Tales of Lower Olney, 2009. Recipient Lind Back Disting. Tchg. award, 1977. Mem.: Soc. Am. Baseball Rsch. (MacMillan Baseball Rsch. Essay award 1999). Republican. Roman Catholic. Home: 500 Cheltena Ave Jenkintown PA 19046 Office: La Salle Univ Philadelphia PA 19141 Office Phone: 215-951-1121.

ROSSI, PATRICIO, radiologist; MD, U. Buenos Aires, 1997. Diplomate in Radiology Am. Bd. Radiology, 2004. Resident U. Miami, Sch. Medicine, Fla., 1999—2004; pres. Radiology Imaging Network, Inc., Miami, 2004—; med. dir. Larkin Hosp., South Miami, 2005—, dir., Radiology Edn. Program, 2005—; exec. dir. Radiology Inst. Fla., Miami, 2007—. Asst. prof. radiology Coll. Medicine Fla. Internat. U., 2008, mem. interview panel; pres. HCI Diagnostic Ctrs. Recipient JT Rutherford Internship Govt. Rels., Am. Coll. Radiology, 2003, Roentgen Resident Rsch. award, Radiol. Soc. N.Am., 2003, Robert Shapiro Resident award, Dept. Radiology, U. Miami, 2003, Disting. Physician, Fla. Med. Assn., 2005—07; named Resident of Yr., Fla. Radiol. Soc., 2004, Fla. Med. Bus., 2004, America's Top Radiologists, Consumers Rsch. America, 2007; Rsch. grant, Soc. Uroradiology, 2001. Mem.: AMA, Am. Roentgen Ray Soc., Dade County Med. Assn. (bd. dirs. 2002—04), Fla. Med. Assn. (com. strategic planning 2002—07, chair, resident-fellow sect. 2004—05), Fla. Radiol. Soc. (pres., resident-fellow sect. 2004—05), Am. Coll. Radiology. Office: Larkin Hosp 7031 SW 62nd Ave South Miami FL 33143 Personal E-mail: radusa@comcast.net.

ROSSI, PAUL, publishing executive; Mgr. advt. sales Middle East/Africa Economist Grp., London, 1984, advt. dir. Asia, advt. dir. N.Am., comml. dir. to pub. Economist.com, mng. dir., exec. v.p. Americas, N.Am. pub. The Economist, 2005—. Named a Top Innovator, BtoBonline, 2007; named one of MinOnline mag.'s Most Intriguing, 2008. Office: The Economist 25 St James's St London SW1A 1HG England Office Fax: 44 0 20 7839 2968.*

ROSSI, RONALD ALDO, sports association administrator, Olympic athlete; b. Bronx, NY, Dec. 2, 1956; s. Aldo D. and Jeanette (Morretta) R.; m. Susan Veltman, Mar. 26, 1983; children: Scott, Lauren. BEE, Manhattan Coll., 1978. Registered profl. engr., N.Y. Mem. computer ops. staff John Blair and Co., NYC, 1978-83, communications engr., 1984; sports program dir. US Luge Assn., Lake Placid, NY, 1984-85, exec. dir., CEO, 1985—. Com. mem. U.S. Luge Assn., 1978—, athlete's rep., 1980-83; com. mem. U.S. Olympic Com., Colorado Springs, Colo., 1989-90, 93-96. Mem. U.S. Olympic Luge Team, Sarajevo, Yugoslavia, 1984; mem. Olympic team staff, Calgary, Can., 1988, Albertville, France, 1992, Lillehammer, Norway, 1994, Nagano, Japan, 1998, Salt Lake City, 2002, Torino, Italy, 2006. Avocations: luge, golf, softball, movies, computers. Address: US Luge Assn 57 Church St Lake Placid NY 12946-1805

ROSSI, RUTH HARRIS, special education educator; d. Everett Tomlinson Harris and Clora Ethel Stanley; m. Raymond Anthony Rossi, Feb. 26, 1977; children: Hillary Niles, Tess Virginia, Anthony John. BA, U. R.I., 1967, postgrad., 1973; EdM, Seattle U., 1995. Spl. edn. tchr. Lakota Mid. Sch., Federal Way, Wash., 1989—, spl. edn. dept. chair, 2002—. Mem. post-secondary transition adv. com. Federal Way Sch. Dist.,

1999—2004. Treas. PTA, Woodmont Elementary Sch., Federal Way, 1982, 1996, 1997; leader, membership facilitator CampFire, Kent, Wash., 1982—86; mem. customer adv. com. Puget Sound Power, Renton, Wash., 1983, 1984. Grantee, Federal Way Edn. Found., 2003. Mem.: ASCD, ACLU, Audubon Soc. Avocations: reading, walking, gardening, cooking, needlepoint. Office: Lakota Mid Sch 1415 SW 314th St Federal Way WA 98023

ROSSIDES, EUGENE TELEMACHUS, lawyer, writer; b. NYC, Oct. 23, 1927; s. Telemachus and Anna (Maravel) R.; m. Elinor Burcham (div.); 1 child, Gale; m. Aphrodite Macotsin, Dec. 30, 1961; children: Michael, Alexander, Eleni. AB, Columbia U., 1949, JD, 1952. Criminal law investigator Office of Dist. Atty., NYC, 1952; assoc. Rogers & Wells, NYC, 1954-56, 61-66, ptnr., 1966-69, 73-92, sr. counsel, 1993—; asst. atty. gen. State of N.Y., NYC, 1956-58; asst. to undersec. Dept. Treasury, Washington, 1958-61, asst. sec., 1969-73. Bd. dirs. Sterling Nat. Bank, N.Y.C. Author: U.S. Import Trade Regulation, 2d edit., 1986, Foreign Unfair Competition, 3d edit., 1991, United States Import Trade Law, 1992, also articles; chief import editor Internat. Trade Reporter, Bur. Nat. Affairs, 1980—; editor: The Truman Doctrine of Aid to Greece: A Fifty-Year Retrospective, 1998, Doing Business in Greece, 1996, U.S. Rels. with Greece and Cyprus, 1990—. Mem. Grace Commn., Washington, 1981-82; chmn. nationalities div. Reagan Bush Com., Washington, 1980; campaign mgr. N.Y.C. Nixon for Pres. Com., 1968, Keating for Senator Com., N.Y. State, 1964; bd. dirs. Eisenhower World Affairs Inst., Washington, Am. Hellenic Inst. Inc. Capt. USAF, 1952-60. Recipient Medal for Excellence, Columbia U., 1972, Young Lawyer's award Columbia Law Sch. Alumni Assn., 1972, Silver Anniversary award NCAA, 1974, John Jay award Columbia Coll. Alumni Assn., 1994. Mem. ABA, N.Y. State Bar Assn., Fed. Bar Assn. Republican. Greek Orthodox. Avocations: tennis, photography. Home: 3666 Upton St NW Washington DC 20008-3125 Office: Clifford Chance Rogers & Wells LLP 2001 K St NW Washington DC 20006-1037

ROSSIDES, GALE D., federal agency administrator; b. 1955; BA, Wheaton Coll., Norton, Mass.; MPA, George Wash. U.; DC. 1st asst. dir. training Bur. Alcohol, Tobacco, & Firearms, 1994—2001, assoc. under sec. for tng. quality performance Arlington, Va.; chief support sys. officer Transp. Security Adminstrn. (TSA), US Dept. Homeland Security, 2002—04; sr. adv. to dep. sec., dir. bus. transformation US Dept. Homeland Security, Washington, 2004—05; assoc. adminstr. Bus. Transformation & Culture, 2005—06; acting dep. adminstr. Transp. Security Adminstrn. (TSA), US Dept. Homeland Security, 2007, dep. adminstr., 2008—, acting adminstr., 2009—; expert Orgnl. Tranformation & Leadership Devel. Office: TSA-1 Transp Security Adminstrn 601 S 12th St Arlington VA 22202-4220 Office Phone: 571-227-2800. Business E-Mail: gale.rossides@dhs.gov.

ROSSIGNOL, JEAN-FRANÇOIS ARMAND, research scientist, medical educator; b. Lyon, France, Sept. 5, 1943; s. Joseph René Rossignol and Marie Josèphe Odette Perrin; m. Patricia Ellen Gustafson, Jan. 7, 2000; m. Laure de Courtilloles, Oct. 21, 1967 (div. 1983); children: Celine, Guillaume. DSc, 1972; DM, U. Paris, 1980; MD with honors, U. Cajamarca, 2004. Rsch. asst. chemistry and microbiology U. Paris, 1965—82; asst. prof. medicine U. South Ala., 1982, assoc. prof. medicine, 1982—85; cons. acting dir., tropical medicine program SmithKline Beckman Corp., Phila., 1979—87; dir., product devel. Squibb Corp., Princeton, NJ, 1987—88; chmn., CEO Belmac Corp., Tampa, Fla., 1988—93; co-founder, chmn. and CSO Romark Lab., LC, Tampa, 1993—. Cons. tropical medicine WHO, Geneva, 1982—86, expert tropical medicine, 1987—91; cons. prof., Med. Divsn. Gastroenterology and Hepatology Stanford U., 2007—. Contbr. more than 80 sci. papers. Mem. Mayor's Global Bus. Com., Tampa, 2007; bd. trustees Admiral Farragut Acad., 2007—. First class pvt. French Air Force, 1970—71, France. Fellow: Royal Soc. Tropical Medicine & Hygiene, Royal Soc. Medicine, Colegio Medico del Peru (hon.), Royal Soc. Chemistry; mem.: Am. Assn. Study Liver Diseases, Am. Soc. Microbiology, Am. Soc. Tropical Medicine & Hygiene, Am. Chem. Soc. Independent. Roman Catholic. Achievements include 24 patents for new anti-infective drugs and their application; inventor of the thiazolides, a new class of kinases inducers antivirals; developer of anthelmintic albendazole (a WHO essential drug), the antimalarial halofantrine and the antiprotozoal nitazoxanide, all three marketed worldwide including in the US. Home: 510 Park St N Saint Petersburg FL 33710 Office: Romark Laboratories LC 3000 Bayport Dr Ste 200 Tampa FL 33607 Office Fax: 813-282-4910. Business E-Mail: jrossignol@romark.com, jfross@standford.edu.

ROSSIN, LAWRENCE GEORGE, ambassador; b. NJ, Nov. 3, 1952; m. Debra J. McGowan; children: Claire, Alec. BA in Economics, Claremont Men's Coll., Calif., 1975; student, NATO Def. Coll., Rome, 1988—89. Former dir. Office of South Cen. European Affairs, Dept. of State; US chief of mission in Kosovo US Embassy, Pristina, 1999—2000; US amb. to Croatia US Dept. State, Zagreb, 2001—03; spl. asst. to Pres., sr. dir. for strategic planning & S.W. Asia NSC, Washington, 2003—04; prin. dep. spl. rep. of sec. gen. for UN Adminstrv. Mission in Kosovo UN, Pristina, 2004—06, prin. dep. spl. rep. of sec. gen. for UN Stabilization Mission in Haiti Port-au-Prince, 2006—. Recipient Presdl. Disting. Svc. award, 2001, Award for Valour, US Dept. State, Superior Honor award (4), Meritorious Honor award, Order of Duke Branimir, Croatian Govt.

ROSSING, THOMAS D., physics professor; b. Madison, SD, Mar. 27, 1929; s. Torstein H. and Luella E. Rossing; children: Karen, Barbara, Erik, Jane, Mary. BA, Luther Coll., 1950; MS, Iowa State U., 1952, PhD, 1954. Rsch. physicist Univac div. Sperry Rand, 1954-57; prof. physics St. Olaf Coll., 1957-71, chmn. physics dept., 1963-69; prof. physics No. Ill. U., DeKalb, 1971—2003, prof. Emeritus, 2000—, disting. rsch. prof., chmn. dept., 1971-73. Rschr. Microwave Lab., Stanford (Calif.) U., 1961-62, Lincoln Lab., MIT, Cambridge, Mass., summer 1963, Clarendon Lab., Oxford (Eng.) U., 1966-67, physics dept. MIT, 1976-77; rsch. assoc. Argonne (Ill.) Nat Lab., 1974-76, scientist-in-residence, 1990-95; vis. lectr. U. New Eng., Armidale, Australia, 1980-81; vis. exch. scholar to China, 1988; guest rschr. Royal Inst. Tech., Stockholm, 1983, 84, 85, Inst. Perception Rsch., Eindhoven, The Netherlands, 1984, 85, Physikalisch-Technische Bundesanstalt, Braunschweig, Germany, 1988-89; guest rschr. Ecole Nat. Superiéure des Telecomm., Paris, 1996, Luleå U. Tech., Sweden, 1996, U. Calif., San Diego, 1998, Fraunhofer Inst., Stuttgart, Germany, 1998; vis. prof. U. Edinburgh, Scotland, 2003, Stanford U., 2005-, Seoul Nat. U., 2006. Contbr. articles to profl. jours.; author: (book) Heat Capacity Lag of Gaseous Mixtures, 1956, Musical Acoustics, 1976, Control of Environmental Noise, 1977, Environmental Noise Control, 1979, Science of Sound, 1982, 1990, 2002, Acoustical Laboratory Experiments, 1982, 2002, Acoustics of Bells, 1984, Acoustics and You, 1985, Musical Acoustics, 1988, Physics of Musical Instruments, 1991, 1998, Principles of Vibration and Sound, 1995, 2004, Light Science, 1998, Science of Percussion Instruments, 2000, Teaching Light and Color, 2002, Springer Handbook of Acoustics, 2007. Recipient Robert Millikan medal, 2000. Fellow AAAS, IEEE, Am. Phys. Soc., Acoustical Soc. Am. (Silver medal in mus. acoustics 1992, Gold medal 2009), Acoustical Soc. India (hon.); mem. Am. Assn. Physics Tchrs. (pres. 1991, Robert A. Milliken medal 2000), Sigma Xi (nat. lectr. 1984-87), Sigma Pi Sigma. Achievements include research in musical acoustics, psychoacoustics, speech and singing, vibration analysis, magnetic levitation, environmental noise conrol, surface effects in fusion reactors, spin waves in metals, physics education; 9 U.S. and 11 foreign patents in field. Office: Univ Stanford CCRMA Dept Music Stanford CA 94305 Business E-Mail: rossing@ccrma.stanford.edu.

ROSSINI, JOSEPH, contracting and development corporate executive; b. New Rochelle, NY, Nov. 25, 1939; m. Antonia Rossini; children: Katherine, Anthony, Andrew. Student, Fordham U., 1965—66, Iona Coll., 1972. Pres. Rossini Contracting Corp., Mt. Vernon, NY, 1963—; prin. Rossini Devel. Co., Monticello, NY, 1965—. Bd. dirs. Circuit Realty Corp., New Rochelle, 1970-71. Planning bd. City of New Rochelle, 1986-92, bldg. dept. adv. com., 1985; vol. instr. NY State Dept. Environ. Conservation, Albany, 1968-95; vice-chmn. New Rochelle Conservative Party, 1984-2001, chmn., 2001—; county committeeman Westchester County Conservative Party; pres., bd. trustees Beechwoods Cemetery, New Rochelle; dir. New Rochelle Neighborhood Revitalization Corp., 1993-96. With USN, 1959-61. Mem. NRA (benefactor life patron), Gen. Contractors Assn. N.Y., Constrn. Industry Coun. Westchester and Hudson Valley, Bldg. Trades Employers Assn., Soc. Explosives Engrs., Deep Founds. Inst., Young Ams. for Freedom, Am. Lauretana Assn., Mensa, Assoc. Gen. Contractors Am., Caths. in Constrn., Tin Can Sailors, Westchester County Firearm Owners Assn., N.Y. State Rifle and Pistol Assn., ASCE Constrn. Inst., Cath. League. Roman Catholic. Office: Rossini Contracting Corp 113 Edison Ave Mount Vernon NY 10550-5005 Office Phone: 914-664-4300. Personal E-mail: jr@rossinicontracting.com.

ROSSITER, ALEXANDER, JR., publishing executive, author; b. Elmira, NY, Mar. 2, 1936; s. Alexander H. and Eleanor (Howell) R.; m. Sylvia Lee Vanlandingham, June 11, 1960; children: Alexander H. III, Jill Rossiter Kerns. BA, Rutgers U., 1958; postgrad., Emory U., 1959. With UPI, 1959-92; newsman Atlanta, 1959-61, Richmond, Va., 1961-63; bur. mgr. Cape Canaveral, Fla., 1963-73; sci. editor Washington, 1973-87; exec. editor, 1987-88; exec. editor, sr. v.p., 1988-91; editor, exec. v.p., 1991-92; asst. v.p., dir. news svc. Duke U., Durham, NC, 1992—2001, dir. com. Pratt Sch. Engrs., 2001—02, assoc. dean pub. affairs, 2003—08. Mem. nat. adv. bd. Knight Ctr. for Specialized Journalism, Colleg Pk., Md., 1988-92; mem. adv. bd. Med. Journalism Program, U. N.C., Chapel Hill, 2000-04. Recipient Grady-Stack medal Am. Chem. Soc., 1987, other journalism awards. Mem. Nat. Assn. Sci. Writers. Office: Duke U 305 Teer Bldg Box 90271 Durham NC 27708 Office Phone: 252-946-8831. Business E-Mail: al.rossiter@duke.edu. *Enthusiasm is the key to success. Take on your education, your family responsibilities and your work with enthusiasm and good things will result.*

ROSSITER, BRYANT WILLIAM, chemistry consultant; b. Ogden, Utah, Mar. 10, 1931; s. Bryant B. and Christine (Peterson) R.; m. Betty Jean Anderson, Apr. 16, 1951; children: Bryant, Mark, Diane, Steven, Linda, Karen, Matthew, Gregory. BA, U. Utah, 1954, PhD, 1957. Researcher Eastman-Kodak Co., Rochester, NY, 1957-63, head color phys. chem. lab., 1963-70, dir. chemistry div., 1970-84, dir. sci., tech. devel., 1984-86; pres. Viratek Inc., Costa Mesa, Calif., 1986-89; sr. v.p. ICN Pharms., Costa Mesa, 1989-90; ret., 1990; pres., CEO WRECON, Inc., Laguna Hills, Calif., 1991-96, ret., 1996. Sr. editor John Wiley & Sons, N.Y.C., 1970—; chmn. bd. Nucleic Acid Rsch. Inst., Costa Mesa, 1987-88; trustee Eastman Dental Ctr., Rochester, 1973-93 (bd. pres. 1982-85); bd. dirs. Verax & Corp. Editor: (chem. treatises) Physical Methods of Chemistry (11 vols.), 1970-76, Physical Methods, (12 vols.), 1986—, Chemical Experimentation Under Extreme Conditions, 1979. Mem. rsch. adv. com. U.S. Agy. for Internat. Devel., Washington, chmn. rsch. adv. com., 1989-92; mem. panel on biosci. Pres.' Coun. Advisors on Sci. and Tech., 1991; mem. adv com. Cornell Internat. Inst. for Food, Agr. and Devel., 1991; presiding officer Ch. Jesus Christ Latter Day Saints, Ea. U.S. and Can., 1959-86, dir. cmty. rels. Orange County, 2004—; counselor presidency San Diego temple, 1998-2002, dir. cmty. rels. Orange county pub. affairs coun., 2005—. 1st lt. USAFR, 1951-58. Named Hon. Alumni Brigham Young U., Provo, Utah, 1982. Fellow AAAS, Am. Inst. Chemists (lectr., Fellows award 1988, Will Judy award Juanita Coll. 1978); mem. Internat. Union Pure and Applied Chemistry (chmn. U.S. nat. com., orignator, chmn. Chemical Rsch. Applied to World Needs com. 1975-87, chmn. Chemical Rsch. Applied to World Needs II The Internat. Conf. on Chemistry and World Food Supplies, 1982), Am. Chem. Soc. (chmn. internat. activities). Avocations: horseback riding, reading, fishing. Home and Office: 25662 Dillon Rd Laguna Hills CA 92653-5800 Personal E-mail: bwr@rossitess.com.

ROSSITER, ROBERT E., manufacturing executive; b. Detroit, 1946; BBA, Northwood U. With Lear Siegler Inc., 1971-87, pres. seating divsn.; COO Lear Corp., 1988—97, COO internat. ops., 1997—98, pres., COO, 1998—2000, pres., CEO, 2000—03, chmn., pres., CEO, 2003—. Bd. dirs. Detroit Renaissance, Focus: HOPE, Detroit. Office: Lear Seating Corp 21557 Telegraph Rd Southfield MI 48034*

ROSSKAMM, ALAN D., retail executive; b. Jan. 6, 1950; With Fabri-Ctrs. of Am., Inc., v.p., pres., CEO; chmn., pres., CEO Jo-Ann Stores, Inc., Hudson, Ohio, 1992—2006, bd. dirs., 1992—; chmn. Charming Shoppes, Bensalem, Pa., 2008—, interim CEO, 2008—09. Office: Charming Shoppes 450 Winks Ln Bensalem PA 19020*

ROSS-LEE, BARBARA, dean, educator; BS Biology and Chemistry, Wayne State U., M Tchr. Spl. Populations; grad., Mich. State U., 1973; DSc (hon.), N.Y. Coll. Osteo. Medicine; degree (hon.), Wilmington Coll., 2001. Legis. asst. Senator Bill Bradley; chmn. dept. family medicine, assoc. dean health policy Mich. State U. Coll. Medicine; dean Ohio U. Coll. Osteo. Medicine, 1993—2001; dean, v.p. health scis. and med. affairs N.Y. Coll. Osteo. Medicine, 2001—. Lectr. in field; dir. Osteo. Heritage Health Policy Fellowship Program; exec. dir. Inst. Nat. Health Policy and Rsch., NOMA (the osteo. affiliate NMA); mem. bd. dirs. Assn. Acad. Health Ctrs., Nat. Fund Med. Edn., Nat. Health Svs. Corps' Assn. Clinicians Underserved ; trustee Found. Appalachian Ohio; participant confs. Contbr. more than 30 scholarly articles med. and health-care issues. Recipient Magnificent 7 award, Bus. and Profl. Women/USA, 1993, Women's Health award, Blackboard African-Am. Nat. Bestsellers, Disting. Pub. Svc. award, Okla. State U. Coll. Osteo. Medicine, Walter F. Patenge medal pub. svc., Mich. State U. Coll. Osteo. Medicine, 2001; named to Ohio Women's Hall of Fame, 1998. Fellow: Am. Osteo. Bd. Family Physicians; mem.: NIH (adv. com. rsch. on women's health), Future Primary Care (Inst. Medicine's com.), U.S. Dept. Health and Human Svs. (nat. adv. com. rural health), Appalachian Health Policy (Appalachian regional commn.'s adv. coun.), AACOM Bd. Govs. (chair-elect exec. coun.), AOA Bur. Profl. Edn., Trilateral Internat. Med. Workforce Group. Achievements include first to be an osteopathic physician to participate in the prestigious Robert Wood Johnson Health Policy Fellowship. Office: NY Coll of Osteopathic Med Old Westbury No Blvd Rockefeller Bldg Rm 107 Westbury NY 11568-8000 Office Phone: 516-686-3747. E-mail: brosslee@nyit.edu.

ROSSMAN, MILTON DAVID, medical educator, director; b. Atlantic, Nj, July 17, 1944; s. Albert and Florence Rossman; m. Yvonne Jean Dubois, July 7, 1993; children: Dara Regainon, Tamara McGuire. BS, U. PA, Phila., 1966; MD, Jefferson Med. Coll., Phila., 1970. Cert. Am. Bd Internal Medicine, 1975, pulmonary diseases 1978. Prof. medicine Hosp. U. Pa., Phila., 1977—. Dir. Penn Lung Ctr., 2003—. Chair sci. adv. com. Found. Sarcodosis Rsch., 2003—. Lt. UPPHS, 1971—73, Atlanta. Achievements include research in lung cells. Office: Hosp Univ Pa 3400 Spruce St Philadelphia PA 19104

ROSSMAN, STEPHEN F., lawyer; b. Bklyn., Sept. 4, 1942; s. Samuel Jack and Sylvia Ulanoff Rossman; m. Karen Rossman, July 4, 1971; children: Adam, Karly, Rebecca, Danieik. BA, U. Fla., Gainesville, 1963; JD, U. Fla. Coll. Law, 1966. Bar: Fla. 1966, US Dist. Ct. (mid. dist.) 1978, US Supreme Ct 1981, US Dist. Ct. (so. dist.) 1983, US Ct. Appeals (11th cir.) 1983. Adj. faculty U. Miami Sch. Law, Fla., 1983—90; lawyer Colson & Hicks, PA, Miami, 1967—74, Rossman, Baumberger, Reboso, Spier & Connolly, Miami, 1974—. Contbr. articles to profl. jours. Bd. dirs. Ronald McDonald Children's Charities South Fla., 1988—89; bd. dirs., bd. sec., exec. com., 1st vice chair bd. Easter Seals, 2006—; legal adv. Miami Project Cure Paralysis; bd. mem. Miami Dade Easter Seals, 1987—, chmn. bd., 1999—2003; pres. Banyan Dr. Homeowners Assn., 1999—. With US Coast Guard Res., 1966—72. Fellow: Internat. Soc. Barristers, Am. Coll. Trial Lawyers; mem.: Fla. Lawyers Action Group (former trustee), U. Fla. Law Sch. Alumni Assn., Trial Lawyers Pub. Justice, Am. Bd. Trial Advocates, Am. Bar Assn., Dade County Bar Assn. (bd. dirs. youn lawyers section. 1970—74, jud. poll. com. chmn. 1974, cir. ct. mediation com. rep. 1988—89), Fla. Bar Assn. (bd. govs. young lawyers section 1977—79, young lawyers trial adv. seminar chmn. 1978, profl. ethics com. 1987, grievance com. 1997—99, former mem. civil procedure rules com., former mem. jud. nominating commn. com.), Assn. Trial Lawyers Am. (trial adv. program faculty mem. 1983, mem. bd. govs. 1983—90), Dade County Trial Lawyers Assn. (sec. 1980—81, treas. 1981—82, pres.-elect 1982—83, pres. 1983—84, founding bd. mem.), Acad. Fla. Trial Lawyers (bd. dirs. 1975—90, seminar chmn. 1977—79, treas. 1978—79, sec. 1979—80, pres.-elect 1980—81, pres. 1981—82, legis. adv. coun. chmn. 1986—, long range planning com. chmn. 1988—). Office: Rossman Baumberger Reboso Spier & Connolly PA Courthouse Tower 44 W Flagler St 23rd Fl Miami FL 33130

ROSSMANN, JACK EUGENE, psychologist, educator; b. Walnut, Iowa, Dec. 4, 1936; s. Wilbert C. Rossmann and Claire L. (Mickel) Walter; m. Marilyn Martin, June 14, 1958; children: Ann, Charles, Sarah. BS, Iowa State U., 1958, MS, 1960; PhD, U. Minn., 1963; MA (hon.), Macalester Coll., St. Paul, 2007. Asst. prof. Macalester Coll., St. Paul, 1964-68, assoc. prof., 1968-73, prof., 1973—2007, prof. emeritus, 2007—, v.p. acad. affairs, 1978-86, chair dept. psychology, 1990-2000. Cons.-evaluator North Ctrl. Assn., 1975—2008; cons. Pers. Decisions Internat., Mpls., 1989—2000, Bush Found., 1993—2006; sr. advisor Spencer Found., 2004—09. Author: (with others) Open Admissions at CUNY, 1975; contbr. articles to profl. jours. Bd. dirs. Twin City Inst. for Talented Youth, St. Paul, 1978-91; trustee United Theol. Sem., New Brighton, Minn., 1984-96; pres. Minn. Intercollegiate Athletic Conf., 2003-06. 2d lt. US Army, 1959. Recipient Thomas Jefferson award, Macalester Coll., 1990, Outstanding Svc. award, Minn. Intercollegiate Athletic Conf., 2007; Adminstrv. fellow, Am. Coun. on Edn., 1977—78. Mem.: AAUP (pres. Minn. conf. 1993—95, Robert Sloan award, Minn. Conf. 2003), APA, Minn. Psychol. Assn. (treas. 2001, pres. 2003), Assn. Instl. Rsch., Am. Psychol. Soc., Phi Kappa Phi, Phi Beta Kappa (hon.). Home: 99 Cambridge St Saint Paul MN 55105-1947 Office: Macalester Coll 1600 Grand Ave Saint Paul MN 55105-1801 Home Phone: 651-690-4370; Office Phone: 651-696-6110. Business E-Mail: rossmann@macalester.edu.

ROSSMANN, MICHAEL GEORGE, biochemist, educator; b. Frankfurt, Germany, July 30, 1930; s. Alexander and Nelly (Schwabacher) R.; m. Audrey Pearson, July 24, 1954; children: Martin, Alice, Heather. BSc with honors, Polytechnic, London, 1951, MSc in Physics, 1953; PhD in Chemistry, U. Glasgow, 1956; PhD (hon.), U. Uppsala, Sweden, 1983, U. Strasbourg, France, 1984, Vrije U., Brussels, 1990, U. Glasgow, 1993, U. York, Eng., 1994, U. Quebec, 1998. Fulbright scholar U. Minn., 1956-58; research scientist MRC Lab. Molecular Biology, Cambridge, Eng., 1958-64; assoc. prof. biol. scis. Purdue U., West Lafayette, Ind., 1964-67, prof., 1967-78, Hanley Disting. prof. biol. scis., 1978—, prof. biochemistry, 1975—. Mem. Nat. Sci. Bd., 2000—06. Editor: The Molecular Replacement Method, 1972; contbr. more than 477 articles to profl. jours. Grantee NIH, NSF, HFSP; recipient Fankuchen award Am. Crystallographic Assn., 1986, Horwitz prize Columbia U., 1990, Gregori Arminoff prize Royal Swedish Acad. Sci., 1994, Stein & Moore award Protein Soc., 1994, Ewald prize Internat. Union Crystallography, 1996, Cole award Biophys. Soc., 1998, Elion award Internat. Soc. for Antiviral Rsch., 2000, Ehrlich and Darmstaedter prize Paul Erhlich-Fedn., 2001, Paul Janssen Prize in Advanced Biotech. and Medicine, Ctr. for Advanced Biotech. and Medicine and Rutgers U., 2004, 3rd NIH Merit award, 2006; edited fellow, Am. Acad. Microbiology, 2007. Mem. Am. Soc. Biol. Chemists, Am. Chem. Soc., Biophys. Soc. (Cole award 1998), Am. Crystallographic Assn. (Fankuchen award 1986), Brit. Biophys. Soc., Inst. Physics., Chem. Soc. (U.K.), AAAS, NAS, Indian Nat. Sci. Acad., Royal Soc., Lafayette Sailing Club. Democrat. Home: 1208 Wiley Dr West Lafayette IN 47906-2434 Office: Purdue U Dept Biol Scis 915 W State St West Lafayette IN 47907-2054 Office Phone: 765-494-4911. Business E-Mail: mr@purdue.edu.

ROSS-NAZZAL, JAMES, history professor; married. PhD, Wash. State U., Pullman, 2001. Prof. history Houston CC, 2005—. Editor Jour. Internat. Women's Studies. Contbr. monograph. Sgt. USAR, 1983—90. Mem.: Soc. Historians Gilded Age and Prog. Era, Internat. Lion's Club. Avocations: gardening, cooking, writing.

ROSSO, KEVIN MICHAEL, geochemist, director; s. John Michael and Lorna Cecilia Rosso; m. Jodi Junta Rosso, Mar. 11, 1995; children: Ethan Michael, Natalie Morgan. BS in Geochemistry, Cal Poly Pomona, Calf., 1992; MS in Geochemistry, Va. Tech, Blacksburg, 1994, PhD in Geochemistry, 1998. Staff scientist Pacific NW Nat. Lab., Richland, 1998—2006, assoc. dir., chem. and materials scis. divsn., 2006—. Recipient award, Mineral. Soc. Am., 2004, Dir.'s award, Pacific NW Nat. Lab., 2004; Life fellowship, Mineral. Soc. Am., 2004. Mem.: Geochemical Soc.

ROSSO DE IRIZARRY, CARMEN (TUTTY ROSSO DE IRIZARRY), finance executive; b. Ponce, PR, Feb. 9, 1949; d. Jorge Ignacio and Carmen Teresa (Descartes) Rosso Castain; m. Alfredo R. Irizarry Sile, Aug. 29, 1967. BBA, U. P.R., Rio Piedras. Vice pres. Alcay Inc., San Juan, P.R., 1972—, also bd. dirs.; v.p. J.I.C. Corp., M.I.C. Corp. Bd. dirs., now pres. bd. Construcciones Urbanas Inc., Internat. Fin. Corp.; organizer Best of Saks Fifth Avenue 1990-2006. Troop leader Girl Scouts U.S.A., 1977-80; bd. dirs. PTA, San Juan, 1978-81, 86-88; activities coord. Colegio Puertorriqueño Niñas, San Juan, 1987-88; judge Miss P.R. Pageant, San Juan 1987-88, 93, 94, 95, Miss World P.R. Pageant, San Juan, 1987-88, Miss World of P.R., 1990; pres. fundacion dept. Oncologia Pediatrica Hosp. Universitario Dr. Antonio Ortiz, 1990-2004; organizer Best of Saks Fifth Avenue Benefit, 1991, 92, 93, 94, 95, pres. 1992, 94, 96, 2005; com. mem. Make a Wish Found. Colleccion Alta Moda, 1994; mem. com. Muceo Ponce Gala, 1994; mem. com. Museo Ponce Coala, 1994; luminaria J.C. Penney, 1994; destellos de la Moda, 1978-2006; pres. Best of Saks 5th Avenue Benefit, 1990-96; organizer Fundacion Oncologica Escada Spring and Summer, 2003. Named to Ten Best Dressed List, San Juan Star, 1986-87, Hall of Fame of Ten Best Dressed, 1989; recipient luminaria J.C. Penney, 1994, Club Damas Medal, 2005. Fellow Assn. Porcelanas; mem. Union Mujeres Americanas, Club de Leones (Garden Hills, P.R., Lady of Yr. award 1978), Club Avico Dama, Caparra Country Club (pres. 1985-86), Club de Presidentas, Altrusas, Bankers Club, Club Civicos Damas (judge hat show 1989, in charge spl. events 1992), Mu Alpha Phi. Republican. Roman Catholic. Avocations: china painting, boating, water-skiing. Office: Internat Fin Corp PO Box 8486 Santurce San Juan PR 00910-0486

ROSSOF, ARTHUR HAROLD, internal medicine educator; b. Chgo., Dec. 12, 1943; s. Jack and Libby (Gordon) R.; m. Rebecca Ann, Aug. 11, 1967 (div. 1983); children: Jacob Earl, Lizabeth Eva; m. Kristine Ann, Feb. 14, 1985. Student, Bradley U., 1961-64; MD, U. Ill., 1968. Diplomate Nat. Bd. Med. Examiners, Am. Bd. Internal Medicine, Am. Bd. Oncology, Am. Bd. Hematology. Fellow sect. neurobiology dept. neurology Presbyn.-St. Luke's Hosp., Chgo., 1965-68, intern straight medicine, 1968-69, resident dept. medicine, 1969-71, Eastern Coop. Oncology Group fellow sect. oncology, dept. medicine, 1971-72, asst. attending physician dept. internal medicine, 1976-80, assoc. attending physician, dept. internal medicine, 1980-82, sr. attending physician dept. internal medicine, 1982-90; med. dir. MacNeal Cancer Ctr., Berwyn, Ill., 1985-99; asst. medicine U. Ill. Coll. Medicine, 1969-71; clin. asst. prof. medicine U. Tex. health Sci. Ctr., San Antonio, 1973-76; instr. medicine Rush Med. Coll., 1971-72, asst. prof. medicine, 1976-81, assoc. prof. medicine, 1981-90, Loyola U. Med. Ctr., Chgo., 1990-91, attending physician, 1990-97, prof., 1991-97. Mem. resident selection com. Rush-Presbyn.-St. Luke's Med. Ctr., 1976-88, mem. ethics conf. planning group, 1981-90, tumor com., 1981-90; chmn. med. edn. com., continuing med. edn. subcom., 1982-90; mem. pharmacy and therapeutics com., chmn. instnl. rev. bd., chmn. cancer com. MacNeal Hosp. chmn. med. edn. com., continuing med. edn. subcom., 1993-97; cons. Cancer Info. Svcv., Ill. Cancer Coun., mem. clin. trials com. 1978-92, credentials rev. com.; mem. adv. com. Lincoln Park Zoo, 1978-2000; med. advisor Y-ME sci. adv. bd. Chgo. chpt. Israel Cancer Rsch. Found. Author: Lithium Effects on Granulopoiesis and Immune Function, 1980; contbr. articles in field to profl. jours.; patentee in field. Mem. exec. com. prevention com. Cancer Incidence and End Results com. Am. Cancer Soc.; mem. profl. adv. bd. Wellness House, Y-ME, Israel Cancer Rsch. Found. Fellow ACP; mem. AAAS, Internat. Soc. Exptl. Hematology, Am. Soc. Clin. Oncology, Am. Assn. Cancer Research, Am. Soc. Hematology, N.Y. Acad. Scis., Soc. Air Force Physicians, Soc. Med. History Chgo., Chgo. Soc. Internal Medicine, Assn. Community Cancer Ctrs., Sigma Xi, Phi Eta Sigma, Alpha Omega Alpha. Republican. Jewish. Avocation: tennis. Office: Hematology Oncology Assoc Il 715 W North Ave Melrose Park IL 60160-1612 Home Phone: 773-477-9465; Office Phone: 708-445-3150. E-mail: krisart2@rcn.com.

ROSSON, GLENN RICHARD, building products and furniture company executive; b. Galveston, Tex., Aug. 17, 1937; s. John Raymond and Elsie Lee R.; m. Edwina Lucille Hart, June 2, 1956; children— Darrell Richard, Alex Mark. BBA, Tex. Tech U., 1959. C.P.A., Tex. Supr., accountant Axelson div. U.S. Industries Inc., Longview, Tex., 1960-67, controller, 1968, group financial v.p. Dallas, 1969, group chmn., 1969-72, v.p., 1973-74, sr. v.p., 1974, exec. v.p., 1974-80, also dir.; pres. Rosson Investment Co., 1980—; chmn. bd. Yorktowne Inc., 1988—. Chmn. bd. dirs. Quality Product Finishing, Inc., 1998—. Mem. Am. Inst. C.P.A.s, Tex. Soc. C.P.A.s, Nat. Assn. Accts. (past nat. dir., past pres. E. Tex. chpt.), Assn. for Corp. Growth (past pres.). Clubs: Dallas Athletic, TBARM Raquet. Home: 11367 Drummond Dr Dallas TX 75228-1946 Office: 6060 N Central Expy Ste 526 Dallas TX 75206-5142 Office Phone: 214-891-6357. E-mail: rosson@gte.net.

ROSSUM, CONSTANCE, management and marketing educator, consultant; b. Hammond, Ind., Nov. 24, 1948; d. Thomas G. Brazina and Mary A. Buros; m. Ralph A. Rossum, Aug. 19, 1972; children: Kristin M., Brent C., Pierce E. BA, Ind. U., Bloomington, 1970; MA, Claremont Grad. U., Calif., 1989, PhD, 1998. Rsch. supr. Leo Burnett Advt., Chgo., 1980—81, account exec., 1981—83; restaurant divsn. manager-marketing, planning Marriott, Washington, 1983—85; dir. mktg. Marriott-Host Internat., Santa Monica, Calif., 1985—89; v.p., gen. mgr. Inland Bus. Media Group, Rancho Cucamonga, Calif., 1989—90; exec. v.p. Message Factors, Inc., Claremont, 1990—91; pres. Mgmt. Directives, Inc., Claremont, 1991—; assoc. prof. mktg. and mgmt. U. La Verne, Calif., 2004—. Plenary spkr. Asian Inst. Mgmt., Jakarta, Indonesia, 2005, workshop leader, Australian Inst. Mgmt., Sydney, 2007, spkr. Co-author (with Peter F. Drucker): Drucker Self Assessment Tool, 1993. Mem. Acme Markets Va., Richmond, 1991—96, Children's First Fund San Bernardino County, Calif., 1989—91, Acad. Lifelong Learning, Claremont Grad. U., 1994—96, Students Free Enterprise - La Sierra U., Riverside, Calif., 1995—97, Crossroads, Claremont, 2004—08, Mt. Baldy United Way Fund Distbn., Ontario, Calif., 1997—2004. Recipient Alumni award, Drucker Grad. Mgmt. Ctr., Claremont Grad. U., 1997. Mem.: Am. Mktg. Assn., Am. Mgmt. Assn. Home: 2687 San Angelo Dr Claremont CA 91711 Office: Univ La Verne Coll Bus 1950 Third St La Verne CA 91750 Business E-Mail: crossum@ulv.edu, crossum@laverne.edu.

ROSSUM, RALPH ARTHUR, political science professor; b. Alexandria, Minn., Dec. 17, 1946; s. Floyd Arthur and June Marion (Carlson) R.; m. Constance Mary Brazina, Aug. 19, 1972; children: Kristin, Brent, Pierce. BA summa cum laude, Concordia Coll., 1968; MA, U. Chgo., 1971, PhD, 1973. Instr. Grinnell (Iowa) Coll., 1972-73; asst. prof. Memphis State U., 1973-77, assoc. prof., 1977-80, Loyola U., Chgo., 1980-83, assoc. dean grad. sch., 1981-82; dep. dir. bur. justice stats. U.S. Dept. Justice, Washington, 1983-84; Alice Tweed Tuohy prof. govt. Claremont (Calif.) McKenna Coll., 1984-88, v.p. and dean of faculty, 1988-91; pres. Hampden-Sydney (Va.) Coll., 1991-92; Salvatori Vis. prof. Claremont (Calif.) McKenna Coll., 1992-93, Salvatori prof. Am. Constitutionalism, 1994—; Fletcher Jones Prof. of Am. Politics U. Redlands, Redlands, Calif., 1993-94. Mem. adv. bd. Nat. Inst. Corrections, U.S. Dept. Justice, 1988-91; mem. Robert Presley Inst. Corrections Rsch. and Tng., State of Calif., 1988-91; dir. Rose Inst. of State and Local Govt., 2000—; mem. nat. bd. dirs. FIPSE, U.S. Dept. Edn., 2002—. Author: Federalism, the Supreme Court and the Seventeenth Amendment, 2001, others, Antonin Scalia's Jurisprudence: Text and Tradition, 2006; co-author: The American Founding, 1981, American Constitutional Law, 1983, 1987, 1991, 1995, 1999, 2003—07, others; editor (sr.): Benchmark, 1983—86; book rev. editor:, 1986—91; contbr. 65 articles to profl. jours., chapters to books. Trustee Episcopal Theol. Sch., Claremont, 1987-91. Ford Found. fellow, 1968—72. Mem.: Am. Polit. Sci. Assn. Episcopalian. Office: Claremont McKenna Coll Dept Govt 850 Columbia Ave Claremont CA 91711-3901 Home Phone: 909-625-3802; Office Phone: 909-607-3392. Business E-Mail: ralph.rossum@claremontmckenna.edu.

ROST, THOMAS LOWELL, retired botany educator; b. St. Paul, Dec. 28, 1941; m. Ann Marie Ruhland, Aug. 31, 1963. BS, St. John's U., Collegeville, Minn., 1963; MA, Minn. State U., 1965; PhD, Iowa State U., 1971. Postdoctoral fellow Brookhaven Nat. Lab., Upton, NY, 1970-72; asst. to full prof. dept. botany U. Calif., Davis, 1972-82, faculty asst. to chancellor, 1982-83, prof., chmn. plant biology sect., 1994-96, assoc. dean divsn. biol. sci., 1996—2003, exec. assoc. dean, 2003—05, prof. emeritus, 2006—. Cons. faculty of agronomy U. Uruguay, 1979, 89, 2005; vis. fellow Rsch. Soc. Biol. Sci., Canberra, Australia, 1979-80; vis. prof. U. Wroclaw, Poland, 1987, U. Exeter, Eng., 1993, Copenhagen U., 2003, Aristotle U., Thessalaniki, Greece, 2005; spl. asst. to vice provost Internat. Programs, 2007; interim dir. FSNEP, 2008; US AID cons. Kabul U., Afghanistan, 2008. Co-author: Botany: A Brief Introduction to Plant Biology, 1979, Botany: An Introduction on Plant Biology, 1982; co-editor: Mechanisms and Control of Cell Division, 1977, Plant Biology, 1998, 2d edit., 2005; contbr. articles to profl. jours. Internat. pres. Gamma Sigma Delta, 2004—06. Served to capt. US Army, 1965—67. Fellow Japan Soc. Promotion of Sci.; mem. Bot. Soc. Am. (Edwin E. Bessey award 2007, Merit award, 2008, Soc. Exptl. Biology, Am. Inst. Biol. Sci. Democrat. Roman Catholic. Avocation: community theatre. Office: U Calif Sect Plant Biology Davis CA 95616-8537 Office Phone: 530-752-0628.

ROST, WILLIAM JOSEPH, chemist; b. Fargo, ND, Dec. 8, 1926; s. William Melvin and Christine Ruth (Hamerlik) R.; m. Rita Cincoski, Sept. 15, 1951; children— Kathryn, Patricia, Carol. BS, U. Minn., 1948, PhD, 1952. From asst. prof. to prof. pharm. chemistry Sch. Pharmacy U. Kansas City, Mo., 1952-63; prof. pharm. chemistry Sch. Pharmacy U. Mo., Kansas City, 1963—. Co-author: Principles of Medicinal Chemistry, 1974, 3d rev. edit., 1988; contbr. articles profl. jours. Mem. Am. Pharm. Assn., Am. Chem. Soc., Sigma Xi, Kappa Psi, Rho Chi, Phi Lambda Upsilon. Office: U Mo Sch of Pharmacy Kansas City MO 64110 Home: 709 W 100th Ct Kansas City MO 64114

ROSTER, MICHAEL, lawyer; b. Chgo., May 7, 1945; AB, Stanford U., 1967, JD, 1973. Bar: Calif. 1973, DC 1980. Ptnr. McKenna, Conner & Cuneo, LA, Washington, 1973—87, Morrison & Foerster, LA, Washington, 1987—93; gen. counsel Stanford (Calif.) U., 1993—2000; exec. v.p., gen. counsel Golden West Fin. Corp., Oakland, Calif., 2000—07. Bd. dirs. Silicon Valley Bancshares, vice chmn., 1995—98; chmn. Encirq, 1998—2000, Insert Therapeutics, 2000—04, Fed. Home Loan Bank, San Francisco, 2005—07, MDRC, 2009—. Contbr. articles to profl. jours. Bd. dirs. Pasadena Heritage, 1986—87; chmn. MDRC, 2009—. Lt. (j.g.) USN, 1969—71. Mem.: ABA (fin. svcs. com. 1981—, chmn. com. savs. instns. 1985—89, banking com. 1989—, vice chmn. 2005—08), Assn. Corp. Counsel Value Challenge (chmn. 2008—), Calif. Bankers Assn., Am. Corp. Counsel Assn. (chmn. 2000—01), Calif. Bar Assn. (chmn. banking com. 1978—79), Stanford U. Alumni Assn. (chmn. 1992), LA Athletic Club.

ROSTOW, CHARLES NICHOLAS, lawyer, educator; b. Geneva, Mar. 3, 1950; s. Eugene Victor and Edna (Greenberg) R.; m. Heyden White, Oct. 31, 1987; children: Theodore Isaac, Celia A.M. BA, Yale U., 1972, PhD, 1979, JD, 1982. Assoc. Shearman & Sterling, NYC, 1982-85; spl. asst. to legal adviser Dept. State, Washington, 1985-87; dep. legal adviser NSC, Washington, 1987, legal adviser, 1987—93; spl. asst. to Pres. Ronald Reagan, George H. W. Bush, 1987—93; assoc. prof. Coll. of Law U. Tulsa, 1993—95, disting. rsch. prof. Coll. of Law, 1995—98; exec. dir. Mass. Office Internat. Trade and Investment, 1995-98; counsel and dep. staff dir. House Select Comm. on Nat. Security & Mil./Comm. Concerns with the PRC, 1998; staff dir. Senate Select Com. on Intelligence, 1999-2000; Charles H. Stockton prof. internat. law U.S. Naval War Coll., Newport, RI, 2001; gen. coun. U.S. Mission UN, NYC, 2001—05; sr. counsel Rsch Found. of SUNY, 2005—06; univ. counsel, vice chancellor for legal affairs, univ. fellow, full prof. SUNY, 2006—. Author: Anglo-French Relations 1934-36, 1984; editor: Akten zur deutschen auswaertigen Politik: 1918-1945, vols. XIV-XXI, 1980-83; contbr. articles to profl. jours. Hon. dir. John Goodwin Tower Ctr. Polit. Studies, So. Meth. U.; nat. adv. bd. Am. Jewish Com.; dir. Toreador Resources, Am. Jewish Internat. Rels. Inst.; trustee Internat. House. Mem. Assn. Bar City of N.Y., Coun. Fgn. Rels., Phi Beta Kappa, Cosmos Club, Yale Club (N.Y.C.), Elizabethan Club (New Haven). Jewish. Office: SUNY State Univ Plz Albany NY 12246 Office Phone: 518-443-5400. Business E-Mail: nicholas.rostow@suny.edu.

ROSZKOWSKI, JOSEPH JOHN, lawyer; b. Pawtucket, RI, Aug. 11, 1938; s. Joseph J. and Anna T. Roszkowski; m. Geraldine J. Szpila, July 2, 1966. BA, Alliance Coll., 1960; JD, Marquette U., 1964. Bar: Wis. 1964, U.S. Dist. Ct. (ea. dist.) Wis. 1964, R.I. 1965. Ptnr. Zimmerman, Roszkowski & Brenner, Woonsocket, R.I., 1965—. Corporator Fogarty Hosp., North Smithfield, RI, 1976—88; counsel Landmark Med. Ctr., 1989—90; mem. R.I. Bd. Bar Examiners, 1994—2001; R.I. probate judge, 1996—2000, 2005—. Mem. Nat. Ski Patrol, RI, 1974—83; legal counsel R.I. Tuna Tournament, 1975—90, Commn. on Judicial Tenure and Discipline, 2006—; bd. dirs. R.I. Legal Svcs., Providence, 1974—87, Legal Aid Soc., Providence, 1985—; chmn. No. Rd Ct. House Task Force, 2004—. Mem. ABA (ho. of dels. 1996-2003, state del. 2000-2001, 2003—, bd. govs. 2001, 2002, commr. Interest on Lawyers' Trust Accounts 1986-90, 2002-2005), R.I. Bar Found. (pres. 1990-95), R.I. Bar Assn. (pres. 1985-86), Am. Law Inst., Am. Judicature Soc., Fed. Tax Inst. New England (adv. com. 1985-86), R.I. Med. Examiners, U.S. Jaycees (nat. dir. 1968), Am. Acad. Hosp. Attys. Lodges: Rotary (pres. Cumberland, R.I. 1987). Avocations: skiing, sailing, gardening, tennis. Home: 1o Little St Cumberland RI 02864-1101 Office: Zimmerman Roszkowski & Brenner 1625 Diamond Hill Rd Woonsocket RI 02895-1541 Office Phone: 401-769-3447. E-mail: jroskow@aol.com.

ROSZKOWSKI, MICHAEL JOSEPH, psychologist; b. Szczawno-Zdroj, Poland, July 20, 1950; s. Michael and Elaine (Sichler) R.; m. Maryann Theresa Carolan, Dec. 28, 1974; children: Daniel M., John T. BS, St. Joseph's U., 1973; MEd, Temple U., 1975, PhD, 1981. Cert. sch. psychologist Pa., N.J.; licensed psychologist, Pa. Inland marine ins. underwriter Gen. Accident Assurance Co., Phila., 1973-74; rsch. asst. Woodhaven Ctr., Phila., 1976-78, rsch. assoc., 1978-81; rsch. psychologist Am. Coll., Bryn Mawr, Pa., 1981-88, dir. mktg. rsch., 1988—. Test reviewer Buros Mental Measurements Yearbook. Cons. editor Jour. Genetic Psychology, 1984—, Genetic, Social and General Psychology Monographs, 1984—; contbr. articles to profl. jours. Mem. APA, Psi Chi. Home: 101 Cherry Tree Ln Cherry Hill NJ 08002-1006 Office: The Am Coll 270 S Bryn Mawr Ave Bryn Mawr PA 19010-2105

ROTA, MARCELLO, medical educator; b. Parma, Italy, June 1, 1972; s. Riccardo Rota and Pierina Calzi. Laurea in Natural Scis., U. Parma, 2000, PhD, 2004. Asst. prof. SUNY Med. Ctr. HSC, Bklyn., 2001—02; rsch. asst. prof. NY Med. Coll., Valhalla, 2003—05, asst. prof., 2005—07; lectr. Brigham & Woman's Hosp., Harvard Med. Sch., Boston, 2007—. Fellow: Am. Heart Assn. (Melvin Marcus Young Investigator award 2007). Achievements include research in stem cell and regenerative cardiology. Office: Brigham & Women's Hosp 75 Francis St Boston MA 02115 Office Fax: 617-264-6320. Business E-Mail: mrota@zeus.bwh.harvard.edu.

ROTBERG, EUGENE HARVEY, investment banker, lawyer; b. Phila., Jan. 19, 1930; s. Irving Bernard and Blanche Grace (Levick) R.; m. Iris Sybil Comens; children— Diana Golda, Pamela Lynn. BS, Temple U., 1951; LL.B., U. Pa., 1954; PhD (hon.), Salem-Teikyo U., 1992. Chief counsel Office Policy Research Securities and Exchange Commn., Washington, 1963-66; v.p., treas. World Bank, Washington, 1969-87; exec. v.p. Merrill Lynch & Co., NYC, 1987-90. Served with U.S. Army. Decorated King Leopold II medal (Belgium); recipient Disting. Svc. award Securities and Exch. Commn., 1968; named Alumnus of Yr., Temple U. Home: 7211 Brickyard Rd Potomac MD 20854-4808 Office: 1250 24th St NW Ste 350 Washington DC 20037-1124 Office Phone: 202-944-3810. E-mail: genebanker@aol.com.

ROTBERG, ROBERT IRWIN, historian, political scientist, educator, academic administrator; b. Newark, Apr. 11, 1935; s. Louis and Mildred S. R.; m. Joanna H. Henshaw, June 17, 1961, (dec. 2008); children: Rebecca T.H., Nicola S.D., Fiona J.Y. AB, Oberlin Coll., 1955; MPA, Princeton U., 1957; DPhil, U. Oxford, 1960. Asst. prof. history, rsch. assoc. Ctr. for Internat. Affairs Harvard U., 1961-68, rsch. assoc. Ctr. for Internat. Affairs, 1968-95; rsch. dir. Twentieth Century Fund, 1968-71; prof. polit. sci. and history MIT, 1968-87; acad. v.p. for Arts, Scis. and Tech. Tufts U., Medford, Mass., 1987-90; pres. Lafayette Coll., Easton, Pa., 1990-93, World Peace Found., Cambridge, 1993—; coord. Inst. for Internat. Devel. Harvard U., 1993-99, dir. program on intrastate conflict Kennedy Sch., 1999—. Adj. prof. Kennedy Sch. Govt., Harvard U., 1993—; mem. coun. NEH, 1993-99; cons. Dept. State, 1968-78, Commrs. of Middlesex County, Mass., 1976-77. Author: A Political History of Tropical Africa, 1965, The Rise of Nationalism in Central Africa, 1965, Protest and Power in Black Africa, 1970, Joseph Thomson and the Exploration of Africa, 1971, Haiti: The Politics of Squalor, 1971, Africa and Its Explorers, 1971, The Black Homelands of South Africa, 1977, Black Heart: Gore-Browne and the Politics of Multiracial Zambia, 1978, Conflict and Compromise in South Africa, 1980, Suffer the Future: Policy Choices in Southern Africa, 1980, Imperialism, Colonialism and Hunger, 1982, Namibia: Economic and Political Prospects, 1983, South Africa and its Neighbors, 1985, The Founder: Cecil Rhodes and the Pursuit of Power, 1988, rev. edit. 2002, Africa in the 1990s and Beyond: Policy Opportunities and Choices, 1988, From Massacres to Genocide: The Media, Public Policy, and Humanitarian Crises, 1996, Vigilance and Vengeance: NGOs Preventing Ethnic Conflict in Divided Societies, 1996, Haiti Renewed: Political and Economic Prospects, 1997, Burma: Prospects for a Democratic Future, 1998, War and Peace in Southern Africa, 1998, Creating Peace in Sri Lanka, 1999, Peacekeeping and Peace Enforcement in Africa, 2000, Truth v. Justice, 2000, Patterns of Social Capital, 2001, Ending Autocracy, Enabling Democracy, 2002, State Failure and State Weakness in a Time of Terror, 2003, When States Fail: Causes and Consequences, 2004, Crafting the New Nigeria, 2004, Battling Terrorism in the Horn of Africa, 2005; Building a New Afghanistan, 2007, A Leadership for Peace: How Edwin Ginn Tried to Change the World, 2007, Worst of the Worst: Dealing with Repressive and Rogue Nations, 2007, China into Africa: Trade, Aid & Influence, 2008, Corruption: Global Security & World Order, 2009, Index of African Governance (with Rachel Gisselquist), 2007, 2008, 2009; editor Jour. Interdisciplinary History, 1970—. Chmn. Middlesex County Govtl. Rev. Task Force, 1972; v.p. Cambridge Civic Assn., 1969-72; mem. Lexington Town Meeting, 1973-90, 94—, Lexington Sch. Com., 1974-77; mem. Ciskel Commn., 1979-80; trustee World Peace Found., 1980—, Oberlin Coll., 1983—, Coun. Internat. Exch. Scholars, 1991-95, Sec. of State, Africa's Policy Panel, 2003-04. Rhodes scholar U. Oxford, 1960; Guggenheim fellow, 1970-71; Hazen Found. fellow, 1976-77. Fellow Royal Geog. Soc., Am. Acad. Arts and Scis.; mem. Am. Hist. Assn., African Studies Assn., Coun. on Fgn. Rels., Oberlin Coll. Alumni Assn. (pres. 1981-82). Office: Belfer Ctr 79 John F Kennedy St Cambridge MA 02138-5758 Office Phone: 617-496-2258.

ROTELLA, STEPHEN J., former bank executive; BA, SUNY, Stony Brook, 1975; MBA, SUNY, Albany, 1978. Dir. mortgage products Shearson Lehman Bros.; with JP Morgan Chase, 1987—2005, COO Chase Home Fin., 1998—2001, exec. v.p., mem. exec. com., CEO Chase Home Fin., 2001—04; pres., COO Washington Mutual Inc., Seattle, 2005—08. Mem. exec. com. Housing Policy Council Fin. Services Roundtable; bd. dir., mem. residential bd. gov. Mortgage Bankers Assn. Bd. dir. St. Barnabas Med. Ctr., NJ. Office: Washington Mutual Inc Washington Mutual Tower 1201 Third Ave Seattle WA 98101*

ROTELLINI, FELECIA A., state banking agency administrator; b. Sheridan, Wyo., 1957; Grad. magna cum laude in Hist. and Polit. Sci., Rocky Mountain Coll., Billings, Mont., 1981; grad., Notre Dame Law Sch., 1986. Bar: Ariz. 1986, Wyo. Pvt. practice atty., Ariz., 1986—92; asst. atty. gen. State of Ariz., 1992—2005; asst. supt. Ariz. Dept. Fin. Instns., 2005—06, supt., 2006—. Trustee Boys and Girls Club Met. Phoenix Found., 1990—2002. Mem.: Wyo. State Bar, Ariz. State Bar (mem. adminstrv. law sect.). Office: Ariz Dept Fin Instns 2910 N 44th St Ste 310 Phoenix AZ 85018 Office Phone: 602-255-4421. Office Fax: 602-381-1225. E-mail: frotellini@azdfi.gov.*

ROTENBERG, MANUEL, physics professor; b. Toronto, Ont., Can., Mar. 12, 1930; came to U.S., 1946; s. Peter and Rose (Plonzker) R.; m. Paula Weissbrod, June 22, 1952; children: Joel, Victor. BS, MIT, 1952, PhD, 1956. Staff Los Alamos (N.Mex.) Nat. Lab., 1955-58; instr. physics Princeton (N.J.) U., 1958-59; asst. prof. U. Chgo., 1959-61; prof. applied physics U. Calif., San Diego, 1961-93, dean grad. studies and research, 1975-84, chmn. dept. elec. engring. and computer sci., 1988-93, rsch. prof., 1993—. Author: The 3-j and 6-j Symbols, 1959; founding editor: Methods of Computational Physics, 1963, Jour. of Computational Physics, 1962; editor: Biomathematics and Cell Kinetics, 1981. Fellow Am. Phys. Soc.; mem. AAAS, Sigma Xi. Office: U Calif San Diego La Jolla CA 92093-0407 Home Phone: 858-552-0415; Office Phone: 858-534-2726. Business E-Mail: rote@ucsd.edu.

ROTENBERG, SUSAN A., research scientist, educator; b. Providence, July 1, 1953; BA, Conn. Coll., New London, 1975; PhD, Brown U., Providence, 1984. Postdoc. rsch. Rockefeller U., NY, 1986—87, Columbia U., NY, 1987—90; prof., scientist and tchr. Flushing, NY, 1990—. Contbr. scientific papers. Grantee Cancer Rsch., NIH, 1994—99, 2001—03, 2007—; Postdoc. fellowship, 1985—86, grant, Elsa U. Pardee Cancer Rsch. Found., 1993—95, Gustavus and Louise Pfieffer Rsch. Found., 1996—99. Achievements include patents for dequalinium analogues in sunscreens. Office: Queens Coll 65-30 Kissena Boulevard Flushing NY 11367 Business E-Mail: susan.rotenberg@qc.cuny.edu.

ROTH, CAROLYN LOUISE, art educator; b. Buffalo, June 17, 1944; d. Charles Mack and Elizabeth Mary (Hassel) R.; m. Charles Turner Barber, Aug. 4, 1991. Student, Art Student's League N.Y., 1965, Instituto Allende, San Miguel de Allende, Mex., 1966; BFA, Herron Sch. Art, 1967; MFA, Fla. State U., 1969. Asst. prof. art U. Tenn., Chattanooga, 1969-72; lectr. art So. Ill. U., Carbondale, 1973-75; asst. prof. art U. Evansville, Ind., 1975-80; instr. art U. So. Ind., Evansville, 1984—. Exhbn. coord., gallery dir. Krannert Gallery, U. Evansville, 1977-79; exhbn. coord., conf. advisor Ind. Women in Arts Conf., Ind. Arts Commn., Evansville, 1978; reviewer in field. One-woman shows include Wabash Valley Coll., Mt. Carmel, Ill., 1994, So. Ind. Ctr. for Arts, Seymour, Ind., 1996, Zionsville (Ind.) Muncie Art Ctr., 1997, Oakland City (Ind.) U., 1998, Women's Inst. and Gallery, New Harmony, Ind., 2005; exhibited in group shows Liberty Gallery, Louisville, 1992, Artlink Contemporary Art Gallery, Ft. Wayne, Ind., 1994, S.E. Mo. Coun. on Arts, Cape Girardeau, 1994, Lexington (Ky.) Art League, 1996, Mills Pond Horse Gallery, St. James, N.Y., 1996, SOHO Gallery, Pensacola, Fla., 1996, Indpls. Art Ctr., 1996, Artemesia Gallery, Chgo., 1997, DelMar Coll., Corpus Christi, Tex., 1998, La. State U., Baton Rouge, 1998, Woman Made Gallery, Chgo., 2002; works appeared in various publs.; represented by Creative Art Gallery, St. Louis, the New Harmony Gallery of Contemporary Art, New Harmony, Ind. Malone fellow visitor to Morocco and Tunisia, 1996. Mem. Nat. Mus. Women in Arts, Met. Mus. Art, Evansville Mus. Arts and Sci., New Harmony Gallery of Contemporary Art, Golden Key Honor Soc. (hon.). Democrat. Mem. Unity Ch. Avocation: travel to study art works in museums and galleries in europe and mex. Home: 10801 S Woodside Dr Evansville IN 47712-8422 Office: U So Ind 8600 University Blvd Evansville IN 47712-3534 Business E-Mail: croth@usi.edu.

ROTH, DALE DAVIS, music educator, religious organization administrator; b. Williamston, SC, June 1, 1960; d. Carl Hampton and Marion Garrett Davis; m. Ronald D. Roth, June 11, 1988; children: Elizabeth, Garrett. MusB, Columbia Coll., 1982; MEd, Southern Wesleyan U., 2003. Tchr. cert. Columbia Coll., SC, 1982—, team evaluator SC, 1998; tchr. cert. Converse Coll., Spartanburg, SC, 1991. Piano, voice tchr. pvt. practice, 1982—; jv and varsity cheerleader coach Clinton H.S., 1982—, prom advisor, 1986—, spring musical music dir., 1990—. Bible sch. dir. First Baptist Ch., Joanna, SC, 2001—. Mem.: SC Music Educators (region chair coord. 1999—), Music Educators Nat. Conf. Baptist. Avocations: knitting, baking. Home: 707 E Ferguson St Clinton SC 29325 Office: Clinton HS 800 N Adair St Clinton SC 29325 Business E-Mail: ddroth@laurens56.k12.sc.us.

ROTH, DANIEL B., ophthalmologist, researcher; b. Montreal, Quebec, Can., Mar. 28, 1967; married. MD, Yale U., New Haven, Conn., 1994. Med. bd. cert. USMLE, bd. cert. Am. Acad. Ophthalmology. Physician Retina Vitreous Ctr., New Brunswick, NJ, 2000—. Mem.: AMA, Am. Soc. for Retinal Specialists, Assn. for Rsch. in Vision and Opthalmology, Am. Acad. Opthalmology. Achievements include patents pending for drug delivery. Office: Retina Vitreous Ctr 125 Paterson St New Brunswick NJ 08901 Office Phone: 732-235-6333.

ROTH, DARYL, theater producer; b. NJ; m. Steven Roth, 1969; children: Amanda, Jordan. Student, NYU. Prodr., owner Daryl Roth Prodns., NYC; owner Daryl Roth Theater, 1998—, DR2 Theater, 2002—. Co-anchor PBS show N.Y. Theatre Rev.; spkr. in field; guest lectr. Columbia U., NYU, Harvard Club, Women's Art Coalition. Prodr.: (N.Y. and London prodn.) Three Tall Women (Pulitzer prize, 1994), (Broadway prodn.) Twilight. Los Angeles.1992 (Tony nomination), Camping with Henry and Tom (Outer Critics Circle award, Lucille Lortel award), Defying Gravity, (off-Broadway) Snakebit, How I Learned to Drive (Best Play of Season, 1997, Pulitzer prize, 1998), Old Wicked Songs, 1996 (Pulitzer prize finalist for drama, 1996), Wit (Pulitzer prize for Drama, 1999), Bomb-itty of Errors; (plays) Closer Then Ever, 1987—1888, Nick & Nora, 1991, Proof, 2000—03 (Tony Award for Best Play, 2001), The Tale of the Allergist's Wife, 2000—02, Bea Arthur on Broadway, 2002, The Goat, or Who is Sylvia, 2002 (Tony Award for Best Play, 2002), Medea, 2002—03, Salome, 2003, Anna in the Tropics, 2003—04, Caroline, or Change, 2004—. Established (with husband) Roth Ctr. for Jewish Life, Dartmouth U., 1997; bd. dirs. Lincoln Ctr. Theater, Sundance Inst., Albert Einstein Coll. for Med. Rsch. Named award in her honor Daryl Roth Creative Spirit award, honored (with husband) with the Louis Marshall Award, Jewish Theological Seminary; named one of The 100 Most Influential Women in NYC Bus., Crain's NY Bus., 2007. Office: Daryl Roth Prodns 152 W 57th St Fl 21 New York NY 10019

ROTH, ERIC, screenwriter; b. NYC, Mar. 22, 1945; 6 children. Student, Columbia U., UCLA. Screenplays include: The Stranger in 7A, 1972, The Nickel Ride, 1975, The Concorde - Airport '79, 1979, Suspect, 1987, Memories of Me, 1988 (with Billy Crystal), Mr. Jones, 1993, Forrest Gump, 1994 (Acad. award Best Adapted Screenplay), the Postman, 1997, The Horse Whisperer, 1998, The Insider (nominated for Acad., Golden Globe 1999), Munich, 2005, The Good Shepherd, 2006, Lucky You, 2007, The Curious Case of Benjamin Button, 2008 (Best Adapted Screenplay, Nat. Bd. Review, 2008); co-writer: (with Michael Mann) Ali, 2001. Office: care Creative Artists Agy 9830 Wilshire Blvd Beverly Hills CA 90212-1804

ROTH, GEORGE STANLEY, biochemist, physiologist, researcher; b. Honolulu, Aug. 5, 1946; s. George Frederick and Laura Ann (Zembrzuski) Roth; m. Mary Jane Fletcher, Mar. 11, 1972; children: Susan Marie, George William. BS, Villanova U., 1968; PhD, Temple U., 1971. Fellow Fels Rsch. Inst., Phila., 1971-72; staff fellow Gerontology Rsch. Ctr. NIH, Balt., 1972-76, rsch. chemist, 1976—, chief molecular physiology and genetics sect., 1984-99, sr. guest scientist, 2000—04; CEO GeroScience, Inc. (formerly Gerotech Inc.), 2000—; exec. dir. Am. Aging Assn., 2002—03. Vis. prof. Mehary Med. Coll., Nashville, 1983; Alpha Omega Alpha prof. U. P.R. Med. Sch., San Juan, 1986; chmn. Gordon Rsch. Conf. Biology of Aging, Oxnard, Calif., 1985; rsch. cons. George Washington U., 1977—82; Ben Cohen Meml. lectr. U. Mich., 1998; lectr. Med. Sci. Ctr. Student Sci. program, 1980; Sandoz lectr. gerontology, Basel, Switzerland, 84, Basel, 86, Basel, 94. Contbr. articles to profl. jours.; editor: Exptl. Gerontology, Exptl. Aging Rsch., Proc. Soc.Exptl. Biology and Medicine; co-editor: Chem. Rubber Co. Press Series in Aging, 1981—; mem. editl. bd. Ency. of Aging, 1987—; author: The Truth About Aging: Can We Really Live Longer And Healthier, 2005. Co-dir. Ea. Harford County Civic Assn., Bel Air, 1981—88; v.p. Cmty. Coalition Harford County, Bel Air, Md., 1988—90, bd. dirs., 1990—92. Recipient Rsch. award, Am. Aging Assn., 1981, prize for gerontol. rsch., Sandoz Ltd., 1989, Third Age award, Internat. Assn. Gerontology, 1989, Spl. award, Balt. Longitudinal Study Aging, 1991, Equal Opportunity award, NIH, 1995, Merit award, 1996; Sigma Chi scholar, Miami U., Oxford, Ohio, 1989. Fellow: Gerontol. Soc. Am. (chair biol. scis. sect. 1975—76, chair rsch. com. 1978—79, chmn. fellowship com. 1986—87); mem.: Soc. Exptl. Biology and Medicine. Republican. Roman Catholic. Avocations: basketball, fishing, hiking, canoeing. Office: GeroSci Inc 1124 Ridge Rd Pylesville MD 21132

ROTH, HAROLD, architect; b. St. Louis, June 30, 1934; s. Samuel and Dorothy (Yawitz) R.; m. Dvora Feigon, Dec. 6, 1959; children: Elizabeth, David. AB, Washington U., St. Louis, 1956; MArch, Yale U., 1957. Designer Warner Burns Toan & Lunde, NYC, 1957; sr. designer Eero Saarinen & Assocs., Roche Dinkeloo & Assocs., Hamden, Conn., 1959-65; ptnr. Harold Roth—Edward Saad, Hamden, Conn., 1965-72; sr. ptnr. Roth & Moore Architects, New Haven, 1973—; critic archtl. design Yale U. Sch. Architecture, New Haven, 1964-98. Pres., trustee Perspecta, Yale Archtl. Jour. Trustee Long Wharf Theatre, New Haven, 1972-98, Conn. Trust for Hist. Preservation, 1983-90; pres. bd. trustees Conn. Architecture Found., 1990-93; bd. govs. Bldg. Stone Inst., 1999-2003; bd. regents Am. Arch. Found., 1999-2001; profl. advisor Western European Architecture Found., 2000-09. Officer U.S. Army, 1957-59, Korea. Recipient Design award Nat. Coun. Religious Arch., 1970, 96, Design award New Haven Preservation Trust, 1978, 88, Tucker award Bldg. Stone Inst., 1983, 88, Honor award Concrete Reinforcing Steel Inst., 1983, Design award Portland Cement Assn., 1984, Design award Archtl. Record, 1970, 80, Design award AIA/ALA, 1983, Faculty Design award Assn. Collegiate Schs. of Arch., 1988, Healthcare Facilities Design award Boston Soc. Archs., 1992, Preservation award, Conn. Trust Historic Preservation,2008; fellow Pierson Coll., Yale U., 1978—. Fellow: AIA (chmn. nat. com. on design 1990, bd. dirs. 1992—94, sec. Coll. of Fellows 1998—99, vice-chancellor 2000, chancellor 2001, Design award Conn. 1974, 1978, 1983, 1986, 1988, 1990, 1993, 1997, 1998, Design award New Eng. 1968, 1984, 1992, 2001, N.Y. State Design award of merit 2000). Home: 37 Autumn St New Haven CT 06511-2220 Office: Roth and Moore Architects 65 Audubon St New Haven CT 06510-1205 Office Phone: 203-787-1166. Business E-Mail: hroth@rothandmoore.com.

ROTH, HARVEY PAUL, retired publishing executive; b. NYC, Feb. 20, 1933; s. Lewis Theodore and Harriet (Wallow) R.; m. Tanya Cohen; children by previous marriage: Andrea Warriner, Matthew Jay; stepchildren: Laura Meryl Becker, Matthew Robert Turetzky. AB, Bklyn. Coll., 1954; LL.B., N.Y. U., 1957. Bar: N.Y. bar 1959. Editor West Pub. Co., NYC, 1959-61; pres. BFL Communications, Inc., Plainview, NY, 1961-76, Roth Pub., Inc., Great Neck, NY, 1976—2005, ret., 2005. Chmn. Alcove Press, London, 1970—75, Nash Pub. Corp., LA, 1971—75. With US Army, 1957—58. Personal E-mail: harveyproth@gmail.com.

ROTH, JAMES A., medical educator, director; m. Jeanne R. Roth; children: Claire Elizabeth, David William, Emily Marie. DVM, Iowa State U., Ames, 1975; MS Immunology, 1979, PhD, 1981. Diplomate Am. Coll. Vet. Microbiologists, 1982. Pvt. practice, Belle Plaine, Iowa, 1975—77; adjunt instr. to prof. Dept Vet. Microbiology & Preventive Medicine,Coll. Vet. Medicine,Iowa State U., Ames, 1977—95, disting. prof., 1995—; exec. dir., inst. internat. cooperation animal biologics Iowa State U., 1995—, asst. dean coll. vet. medicine, 2001—04, dir., Ctr. Food Security & Pub. Health, 2002—; adj. prof. dept. Epidemiology U. Iowa, 2006—. Bd. dirs. Vet. Resources, Inc., Ames, Iowa, 1993—2003; mem., fed. panel, 2003—04, White Ho. Office Sci. & Tech. Policy, 2003—04, Nat. Sci. Adv. Bd., 2005—. Contbr. numerous monographs. Recipient John G. Salsbury Endowed Chair award, Iowa State U., 1998—2001, Internat. Svc. award, 2001, Change Agt. of Yr., 2004, Clarence Hartley Couvalt Disting. Prof. award, 1995, Disting. Vet. Immunologist, 1997, AVMA 12th Internat. Congress Prize, 2001, AVMA Pub. Svc. award, 2006. Achievements include patents for vaccines for counteracting inhibition of neutrophil degranulation. Office: Ctr Food Security and Public Health 2156 Coll Veterinary Medicine ISU Ames IA 50011 Office Fax: 515-294-8259. Business E-Mail: jaroth@iastate.edu.

ROTH, JAMES FRANK, chemicals executive, chemist; b. Rahway, NJ, Dec. 7, 1925; s. Louis and Eleanor R.; m. Sharon E. Mattes, June 20, 1969; children by previous marriage: Lawrence, Edward, Sandra. BA in Chemistry, U. W.Va., 1947; PhD in Phys. Chemistry, U. Md., 1951. Research chemist Franklin Inst., Phila., 1951-53, mgr. chemistry lab., 1958-60; chief chemist Lehigh Paints & Chems. Co., Allentown, Pa., 1953-55; research chemist GAF Corp., Easton, Pa., 1955-58; with Monsanto Co., St. Louis, 1960-80, dir. catalysis research, 1973-77, dir. process sci. research, 1977-80; corp. chief scientist Air Products and Chems., Inc., Allentown, 1980-91; indsl. cons., 1991—. Contbr. articles to profl. jours.; mem. editl. bd. Jour. Catalysis, 1976-85, Catalysis Revs., 1973-93, Applied Catalysis, 1981-85; editor for Ams., 1985-88, assoc. editor, 1988-95. With USN, 1943-46. Recipient Richard J. Kokes award Johns Hopkins U., 1977, Chem. Pioneer award Am. Inst. Chemists, 1986, Perkin medal Soc. Chem. Industry, 1988. Mem. NAE, Am. Chem. Soc. (St. Louis sect. St. Louis award 1975, E.V. Murphree nat. award 1976, Indsl. Chemistry award 1991), Catalysis Soc. N.Am. (E.J. Houdry award 1991), Catalysis Club of Phila. (award 1981). Inventor process biodegradable detergents, for acetic acid; U.S., fgn. patents in field. Home: 8040 Frankford Rd Apt 432 Dallas TX 75252

ROTH, JANE RICHARDS, federal judge; b. Phila., June 16, 1935; d. Robert Henry Jr. and Harriett (Kellond) Richards; m. William V. Roth Jr., Oct. 9, 1965; children: William V. III, Katharine K. BA, Smith Coll., 1956; LLB, Harvard U., 1965; LLD (hon.), Widener U., 1986, U. Del., 1994. Bar: Del. 1965, US Dist. Ct. Del. 1966, US Ct. Appeals (3d cir.) 1974. Adminstrv. asst. various fgn. service posts US Dept. State, 1956-62; assoc. Richards, Layton & Finger, Wilmington, Del., 1965-73, ptnr., 1973-85; judge US Dist. Ct. Del., Wilmington, Del., 1985-91, US Ct. Appeals (3d cir.), Wilmington, Del., 1991—2006, sr. judge, 2006—. Adj. faculty Villanova U. Sch. Law. Hon. chmn. Del. chpt. Arthritis Found., Wilmington; bd. overseers Widener U. Sch. Law; bd. consultors Villanova U. Sch. Law; trustee Hist. Soc. Del. Recipient Nat. Vol. Service citation Athritis Found., 1982. Fellow Am. Bar Found.; mem. ABA, Del. State Bar Assn. Republican. Episcopalian. Office: US Court of Appeals 3rd Circuit Unit 12 5100 Fed Bldg 844 King St Wilmington DE 19801-1790*

ROTH, JEFFREY, geophysicist; b. Balt., June 17, 1979; s. Gary Arden and Eleanore Louise Roth; m. Tara Elizabeth Jones; 1 child, Madeleine Louise. BS, Dickinson Coll., Carlisle, 2001; MS, Ariz. State U., Tempe, 2008. Geology dept. technician Dickinson Coll., 2002—04; geophysicist ExxonMobil Exploration Corp., Houston, 2008—. Contbr. to profl. jours. Mem.: Soc. Exploration Geophysicists, Seismol. Soc. Am., Am. Geophys. Union, Houston ExxonMobil Club. Democrat. Avocations: travel, hiking, camping, flying, carpentry.

ROTH, JOHN REECE, electrical engineer, educator, researcher, inventor; b. Washington, Pa., Sept. 19, 1937; s. John Meyer and Ruth Evangeline (Iams) R.; m. Helen Marie DeCrane, Jan. 14, 1972; children: Nancy Ann, John Alexander. BS in Physics, MIT, 1959; PhD, Cornell U., 1963. Engring. aide Aerojet-Gen. Corp., Azusa, Calif., 1957, 1958; aerospace engr. N.Am. Aviation, Canoga Park, Calif., 1959; prin. investigator NASA Lewis Rsch. Ctr., Cleve., 1963—78; prof. U. Tenn., Knoxville, 1978—2004, prof. emeritus, 2004—06; hon. prof. Ul. Electronic Sci. and Tech. China, Chengdu, 1992—; ret.; prin. investigator Office Naval Rsch., Washington, 1980—89, Air Force Office Sci. Rsch., Washington, 1981—95, 2001—03, Army Rsch. Office, 1988—93, NASA Langley Rsch. Ctr., Hampton, Va., 1995—98, 2001—03, March Instruments, Inc., Concord, Calif., 1996—98, NSF, 2002—03. Cons. TVA, Chattanooga, 1982-84, BDM Corp., 1987-88, Tenn. Eastman, 1989-90, March Instruments, 1995-98, Procter & Gamble, 1996, 2000, Internat. Eco Scis., 1997-98, Environ. Elements Corp., 1997-00, Tetra Pak Suisse, 1998-00, Atmospheric Glow Techs., Inc., 1999-05, YTC-Am., Inc., 2005, Harrick Plasma, 2006; mem. NAS-NRC Com. on Aneutronic Fusion, 1986-87; hon. guest prof. Tsinghua U., Shenzhen campus, 2006-08; spkr. at profl. meetings Author: Industrial Plasma Engineering, Introduction to Fusion Energy; contbr. articles to profl. jours. Sloan scholar, 1955-59; Ford fellow, 1961-62; recipient B. Otto and Katherine Wheeley award for Excellence in Tech. Transfer, 1999, NASA Inventor's award, 2004, Gonzalez Family Lifetime Achievement award, 2006. Fellow IEEE, AIAA (assoc.); mem. Am. Phys. Soc., Am. Chem. Soc., Am. Nuc. Soc. (exec. com. No. Ohio sect. 1975-78), Nuc. and Plasma Scis. Soc., Am. Soc. Engring. Edn., Knoxville Mus. Art, East Tenn. Soc. Archaeol. Inst. Am., Sigma Xi (pres. U. Tenn. Knoxville chpt. 1985-86). Achievements include 11 US patents. Home (Winter): 12359 N Fox Den Dr Knoxville TN 37934-3755 Home (Summer): PO Box 181 Oakland ME 04963-0181 E-mail: jreeceroth@gmail.com.

ROTH, JONATHAN DAVID, pharmacist, researcher; s. Jerome E. and Beatrice Roth; children: Ellie Hannah, Solomon Isaac. PhD, U. Fla., Gainesville, 1999. Sci. investigator Amylin Pharmaceuticals Inc., San Diego, 2003—. Independent. Achievements include patents for methods for treating obesity and obesity related diseases and disorders. Office: Amylin Pharmaceuticals Inc 9360 Towne Ctr Dr San Diego CA 92121 Business E-Mail: jonathan.roth@amylin.com.

ROTH, KARL SEBASTIAN, retired pediatrician; b. NYC, Mar. 3, 1941; s. Victor and Ruth Leila (Fisher) R.; m. Beverly Rochelle, Apr. 16, 1967 (div. July 1984); children: Christopher Geordie, Marcus Amadeus; m. Lydia Carole Noland, July 28, 1984 (div. Jan. 2003); 1 child, Alexander Kristof Parham. BA, U. Rochester, NYC, 1963; MD, Wake Forest U., 1969. Pediatric intern Med. Coll. Pa., Phila., 1969-70; pediatric resident Thomas Jefferson U., Phila., 1970-72; fellow genetics/metabolism U. Pa., Phila., 1972-75, asst. prof. pediatrics, 1975-82; prof. pediatrics, biochemistry and molecular biophysics Med. Coll. Va., Richmond, 1982—2002; prof. and chair pediat. Creighton U., Omaha, 2002—08. Cons. state newborn screening program Commonwealth Va., Richmond, 1982—; mem. gov.'s genetics adv. bd. Commonwealth Va., Richmond, 1982—; mem. bd. Clin. Pediatrics, Cleve., 1988—; vis. prof. pediatrics U. Zurich, Switzerland, 1993. Author: (books) Metabolic Diseases: A Guide to Early Recognition, 1983, Biochemistry and Disease: Bridging Basic Science and Clincal Medicine, 1996; co-editor: Pediatric Endocrinology and Metabolic Diseases, 2008-09. Bd. mem. Agoraphobics Bldg. Ind. Lives, Richmond, 1987—, Gov.'s Coun. on Child Mental Health, Richmond, 1989—; participant Children's Miracle Network Telethon, Richmond, 1989—. Recipient Rsch. Career Devel. award NIH, 1978-83, Rsch. Grant, 1985-90; Daland fellow Am. Philos. Soc., 1976-78. Mem. Am. Pediatric Soc., Soc. Pediatric Rsch., Fedn. Am. Socs. Exptl. Biology, Soc. Inherited Metabolic Disorders, Sigma Xi. Lutheran. Achievements include development of prenatal therapy of an inborn error of metabolism for the second disease in medical history (Holocarboxylase Synthase Deficiency); establishment and characterization of (biochemically and physiologically) the first animal model for the human renal fanconi syndrome based upon use of a physiologically produced compound; discovered and characterized a unique inborn error of metabolism.

ROTH, KELLY, choreographer, educator; b. Carmel, Calif., Oct. 23, 1953; s. Joseph L. and Melba Roth; m. Leslie J. Creamer, Aug. 7, 1981; children: Kelsey Kremer Rogers, Tobias Kremer. BFA in Dance, Ariz. State U., Tempe, 1989, MFA in Choreography and Performance, 1993. Artistic dir. Keily Roth Dancers, Las Vegas, 1978—; coll. southern Nev. dance program head CSN Dept. Fine Arts, Las Vegas, 1995—. Dancer (dance theatre to mahler) Das Lied von der Erde, Cafe' Mahleria (1st prize, Choreography and Contemporary Dance, Danse Grand Prix Italia, 2003), choreographer (dance theatre) Lehi's Dream (2nd prize, Barcelona Dance awards, 2006), (pas de deux) Sentience (2nd prize: 5 senses competition, Haarmann & Reimer, 1989). Elder LDS Ch., Las Vegas, 1995—2008. Artist fellowship, Nev. Arts Coun., 2005. Mem.: Nikolais, Louis Alumni Assn. Avocations: hiking, composing. Office: Coll Southern Nev Dance 3200 E Cheyenne Ave J1A North Las Vegas NV 89030 Office Fax: 702-651-4765. Personal E-mail: rothdance@cox.net. Business E-Mail: kelly.roth@csn.edu.

ROTH, KENNETH, human rights advocate; b. Elmhurst, Ill., Sept. 23, 1955; BA magna cum laude, Brown U., 1977; JD, Yale U., 1980. Bar: N.Y. 1981. Law clk. to Judge Edward Weinfeld U.S. Dist. Ct. for So. Dist. N.Y., NYC, 1980-81; assoc. Paul, Weiss, Rifkind, Wharton & Garrison, NYC, 1981-83; from asst. U.S. atty. to chief appellate atty. criminal div. U.S. Atty.'s Office for So. Dist. N.Y., NYC, 1983-87; assoc. counsel Office Ind. Counsel for Iran/Contra, Washington, 1987; dep. dir. Human Rights Watch, NYC, 1987-93, exec. dir., 1993—. Editor, author numerous reports on human rights worldwide; contbr. articles to newspapers and mags. Mem. Coun. Fgn. Rels. Office: Human Rights Watch Floor 34 350 Fifth Ave New York NY 10118-3499

ROTH, LANE, communications educator; b. NYC, Apr. 10; BA with nat. honors in German, NYU; MA, Fla. State U., 1974, PhD in Mass Comm., 1976. Camera operator Sta. WFSU-TV, Tallahassee, 1973-74; broadcast engr., producer-creator, writer, performer Sta. WFSU-FM, Tallahassee, 1974-76; co-host Sta. WNIN-TV, Evansville, Ind., 1976—78; asst. prof. radio-TV-film U. Evansville, 1976-78; asst. prof. comm. Lamar U., Beaumont, Tex., 1978-82, assoc. prof., 1982—. Writer, performer fund-raising promos Sta. KVLU-FM, Beaumont, 1995—. Author: Film Semiotics, Metz, and Leone's Trilogy, 1983; sr. co-author: Analyzing Film: An Introduction, 2008; contbr. articles to profl. mags., jours., to acad. books. Bd. dirs. Mental Health Assn. Jefferson County, 1993—, pres. bd. dirs., 1997, 1998. Recipient Regents Merit award for excellence in tchg., 1980, Mental Health Assn. award for dedicated leadership, 1999. Mem. Popular Culture Assn. Roman Catholic. Avocations: Jungian psychology, analysis of popular film and tv, singer-impressionist-songwriter. Office: Lamar U Dept Communications Beaumont TX 77710 Office Phone: 409-880-8152.

ROTH, LAWRENCE MAX, pathologist, educator; b. McAlester, Okla., June 25, 1936; s. Herman Moe and Blanche (Brown) R.; m. Anna Berit Katarina Sundstrom, Apr. 3, 1965; children: Karen Roth Hart, David Josef. BA, Vanderbilt U., 1957; MD, Harvard U., 1960. Diplomate Am. Bd. Pathology. Rotating intern U. Ill. Research and Ednl. Hosps., Chgo., 1960—61; resident in anat. pathology Washington U. Sch. Medicine, St. Louis, 1961—64; resident in clin. pathology U. Calif. Med. Ctr., San Francisco, 1967—68; asst. prof. pathology Tulane U. Sch. Medicine, New Orleans, 1968—71; assoc. prof. pathology Ind. U. Sch. Medicine, Indpls., 1971—75, dir. divsn. surg. pathology, 1971—2001, prof., 1975—2001, prof. emeritus pathology, 2001—. Series editor: Contemporary Issues in Surgical Pathology; mem. editl. bd. Am. Jour. Surg. Pathology, Human Pathology, Seminars in Diagnostic Pathology, Internat. Jour. Gynecol. Pathology, Endocrine Pathology; contbr. articles to med. jours. Served to capt. US Army, 1965—67.

Recipient James Harshman award, Ind. Assn. Pathologists, 1989. Mem. Am. Assn. Pathologists, US and Can. Acad. Pathology, Am. Soc. Clin. Pathologists, Coll. Am. Pathologists, Internat. Soc. Gynecol. Pathologists, Arthur Purdy Stout Soc. Surg. Pathologists, Assn. Dirs. Anatomic and Surg. Pathology. Home: 7898 Ridge Rd Indianapolis IN 46240-2538 Office: 635 Barnhill Dr Indianapolis IN 46202-5120 Business E-Mail: lroth@iupui.edu.

ROTH, LOREN H., psychiatrist; b. May 9, 1939; m. Ellen A. Roth; children: Jonathan, Alexandra, Elizabeth. BA in Philosophy, Cornell U., 1961; MD cum laude, Harvard U., 1966, MPH, 1972; postgrad., Am. U., 1972-73. Diplomate Am. Bd. Psychiatry and Neurology; lic. physician, Conn., Md., Mass., Pa. Med. intern Univ. Hosps., Western Res. U., Cleve., 1966-67; resident psychiatry Yale U., New Haven, 1969-70, Mass. Gen. Hosp., Boston, 1970-72; staff psychiatrist Ctr. for Studies Crime and Delinquency, NIMH, Rockville, Md., 1972-74; co-dir., dir. law and psychiatry program Western Psychiat. Inst. and Clinic/U. Pitts., 1974—, chief adult clin. svcs., 1983-87, 88-89, chief clin. svcs., 1989-95, co-dir., dir. law and psychiatry program, 1974-94; vice-chmn. dept. psychiatry U. Pitts., 1988-97, asst. prof., 1974-78, assoc. prof., 1978-82, prof., 1982—; v.p. for managed care U. Pitts. Med. Ctr., 1993-97; assoc. vice chancellor for edn., health scis. U. Pitts. Sch. Medicine, 1995-97, assoc. sr. vice chancellor Health Scis., 1997—; sr. v.p., quality care U. Pitts. Med. Ctr. Health Sys., 2003—07, chief med. officer, 1997—2007, asst. special projects, office pres., 2007—. Med. staff Presbyn.-Univ. Hosp., Pitts., 1983—; gen. med. officer Fed. Penitentiary, Lewisburg, Pa., 1967-69; William E. Schumacher disting. lectr. Maine Dept. Mental Health and Mental Retardation, Portland, 1982; mem. commn. on mentally disabled ABA, Washington, 1987; cons. law and psychiatry Dept. Welfare, Commonwealth Pa., 1974; cons. reviewer, site visitor crime and delinquency sect. NIMH, 1977; examiner Am. Bd. Psychiatry and Neurology, 1985; spl. asst. to pres. UPMC, 2007-. Author: (with others) Informed Consent: A Study of Decision-making in Psychiatry, 1984; editor: (with others) Psychiatry, Social, Epidemiologic and Legal Psychiatry, Vol. 5, 1986; contbr. articles to profl. jours., chpts. to books; editorial bd. Criminology, 1974-78, Law and Human Behavior, 1980-85, Internat. Jour. Law and Psychiatry, 1980-88, Behavioral Scis. and the Law, 1987-95; assoc. editor Am. Jour. Psychiatry, 1982-90; cons. editor Criminal Justice and Behavior, 1982-85. Lt. comrd. USPHS Res., 1967—. Recipient Steve Allen award United Mental Health, Inc., 1990, Sr. Vice Chancellor's Extraordinary Svc. award, U. Pitts. Med. Ctr.; grantee NIMH, 1979, 80-81, 89, Founds. Fund for Rsch. in Psychiatry, 1980-82. Fellow Am. Psychiat. Assn. (Isaac Ray award 1988), Am. Coll. Utilization Rev. Physicians, Am. Coll. Psychiatrists; mem. AMA, Am. Acad. Psychiatry and Law (pres. 1983-84), Group for Advancement Psychiatry (com. on psychiatry and law 1979-80, chmn. 1981-84), Am. Soc. Criminology, Am. Soc. Law and Medicine (bd. dirs. 1982-85), Internat. Acad. Law and Mental Health (bd. dirs.), Am. Psychopath. Assn., Phi Beta Kappa, Phi Kappa Phi. Home: 6820 Edgerton Ave Pittsburgh PA 15208-2803 Office: U Pitts Med Ctr Forbes TWR 200 Lothrop St Ste 11016 Pittsburgh PA 15213-2546 Office Phone: 412-647-4860. Business E-Mail: rothlh@upmc.edu.

ROTH, MARGARET AGNES, child development educator; b. Rockford, Ill., Oct. 18, 1921; d. Otto Garfield and Agnes Marie (Anderson) Beckstrand; m. Robert Paul Roth, June 17, 1943; children: Erik, Maren, Maarja, John, Sonja. BA, Carthage Coll., Kenosha, Wis., 1943. Cert. elem. and preschool edn. Home and family child care instr. Luthergiri Seminary, Rajahmundry, India, 1947-48; dir. nursery sch. Ebenezer Luth. Ch., Columbia, S.C., 1954-58; head tchr. St. David's Episcopal Ch. Nursery Sch., Minnetonka, Minn., 1959-67; head tchr., dir. Jr. League Underpriviledged Sch., Mpls., 1963-67; tchr., adminstrv. asst. U. Minn. Lab. Nursery Sch., Mpls., 1967—. Cons. Midwest State Head Start, Chgo., 1965-68; tchr. Midwest Head Start, 1965-80, Kai Tak Refugee Sch., Hong Kong, 1983-84; tng. tchr. Minn. Migrant Schs., 1968-70; child devel. assoc. rep. Tchr. Assessments, Washington, 1974—. Author: Music for Young Children, 1973, Bible Times, 1973, Jesus Friend of Children, 1979; edit. asst. Areopagus Mag., 1990-91. Mem. Adv. Commn. for Preschool Edn., St. Paul, 1972-80, Gov.'s Commn. for Day Care, St. Paul, 1972, Commn. Com. for Childcare Lic. and Standards for Minn., Coun. for Childcare and Devel., St. Paul, 1972, Courage Ctr. Therapeutic Preschool Adv. Com., Mpls., 1979-82. Mem. Nat. Assn. for Edn. Young Children (bd. mem. 1977-81), Nat. Bd. Citation 1981), Midwest Assn. for Edn. Young Children (pres. 1976-79, Shirley Dean award 1984, Midwest Honor Citation 1986), Minn. Assn. for Young Children Edn. (pres., 1972-74, Evelyn House award 1982), World Orgn. for EArly Childhood Edn. Lutheran. Avocations: swimming, sewing, music. Home: 4194 Hillcrest Ln Wayzata MN 55391-3604 Office: U Minn-ICD 51 E River Rd Minneapolis MN 55455-0365 Home Phone: 952-473-3117.

ROTH, MARJORY JOAN JARBOE, special education educator; b. Ranger, Tex., May 24, 1934; d. James Aloysius and Dorothy Knight (Taggart) Jarboe; m. Thomas Mosher Roth, Jr., Dec. 22, 1959; children: Thomas Mosser III, James Jarboe. BA in English, Rice U., 1957; MEd in Ednl. Adminstrn., U. N.C., Greensboro, 1981. Cert. tchr.-specific learning disabilities, middle grades lang. arts and social studies, intermediate grades, adminstr.-prin., N.C. Tchr. 4th grade Houston Ind. Sch. Dist., 1957-60; specific lang. disabilities instr. Forsyth Tech. C.C., Winston-Salem, N.C., 1976-77; specific learning disabilities tchr. Forsyth Country Day Sch., Winston-Salem, 1977-80; tchr. 5th grade Winston-Salem/Forsyth County Schs., 1982-83, specific learning disabilities tchr. Mt. Tabor High Sch., 1983-86; part time instr. English and Learning Disabilities Forsyth Tech. C.C., 1986-90; founding pres., prin. Greenhills Sch., Winston-Salem, 1990—. Co-author, co-editor booklets. Sunday Sch. dir., tchr. Galloway Meml. Episcopal Ch., 1960-70, pres., treas., sec. Churchwomen, 1963-74; treas. Elkin Jr. Woman's Club, 1962; chmn. Elkin Heart Fund Drive, 1968; bd. dirs. Hugh Chatham Hosp. Auxillary, 1968, Friends of the Elkin Pub. Libr., 1968-74, chmn., 1970-72, chmn., exhibits chmn. summer reading program; pres. South Surry Heart Assn., 1969; mem. Churchwomen of St. Paul's Episcopal Ch., Winston-Salem, 1982—, Fiddle and Bow Folk Music Soc., Winston-Salem, 1992—. Recipient June Lyday Orton award for outstanding svc. in the field of dyslexia, 1997; Forsyth fellow NEH, 1985; grantee in field. Fellow Acad. Orton-Gillingham Practitioners and Educators; mem. ASCD, Children with Attention Deficit Disorder (profl. adv. bd. N.C. Triad chpt. 1990-96), Learning Disability Assn. N.C. (sec., bd. dirs. 1981-86), Internat. Dyslexia Assn. (sec., bd. dirs. Carolinas br. 1981-85, founding pres. N.C. br. 1987-91, bd. dirs. 1987-96, nat. nominating com. 1992-94), Internat. Multisensory Structured Lang. Edn. Coun., Inc. (bd. dirs. 2000-03, 05—; mem. coun. 1995—). Republican. Avocations: tennis, hiking, folk music. Home: 940 Fox Hall Dr Winston Salem NC 27106-4431 Office: Greenhills Sch 1360 Lyndale Dr Winston Salem NC 27106-9739 Office Phone: 336-924-4908.

ROTH, MARK, research scientist; b. 1957; BSc, U. Oreg., 1979; PhD, U. Colo., Boulder, 1984. Biomedical scientist, basic scis. divsn., prin. investigator Fred Hutchinson Cancer Rsch. Ctr., Seattle, 1989—; affiliate assoc. prof., dept. biochemistry U. Wash. Sch. Medicine, Seattle, 1996—. Contbr. articles to profl. jours., including Science, Proceedings of the NAS, and Journal of Cell Biology. Named a MacArthur Fellow, John D. and Catherine T. MacArthur Found., 2007. Achievements include pioneering research that ranges from molecular mechanisms of genetic regulation to whole-animal physiology to medical diagnostics. Office: Fred Hutchinson Cancer Rsch Ctr Divsn Basic Sciences Mailstop A3-015 1100 Fairview Ave N PO Box 19024 Seattle WA 98109-1024 Office Phone: 206-667-5602. Office Fax: 206-667-5939. Business E-Mail: mroth@fhcrc.org.

ROTH, MICHAEL, lawyer; b. NYC, July 22, 1931; s. Philip Arthur and Mollie (Breitenbach) R.; m. Jeanny Macoir, Nov. 24, 1957; 3 children BA, Yale Coll., 1953; JD, Columbia U., 1956, M. Internat. Affairs, 1964. Bar: NY 1956. Law assoc. Stroock & Stroock & Lavan, NYC, 1956-63; ptnr. Roth, Carlson, Kwit & Spengler, NYC, 1964-74; chmn. N.Y. State Liquor Authority, NYC, 1974-77; ptnr. Shea & Gould, NYC, 1979-89; of counsel Katten, Muchin, Rosenman, NYC, 1989—. Mem. U.S. del. to UN Population Commn., 1969; Rep.-Conservative candidate for N.Y. State atty. gen., 1978; mem. Pres.' Task Force on Internat. Pvt. Enterprise, 1983-84, Pres.' Commn. on Mgmt. AID Programs, 1991-92. Mem. Sunningdale Country Club (Scarsdale, N.Y.). Republican.

ROTH, MICHAEL I., marketing executive; b. Bklyn., Nov. 22, 1945; s. Harry A. and Sally (Kutin) Roth; m. Carole A. Snofsky, Aug. 10, 1968; children: Barrie, Marc, Andrew. BS, CCNY, 1967; JD, Boston U., 1971; LL.M., NYU, 1973. CPA NY, 1973, Conn., 1973; bar: NY 1971. With Coopers & Lybrand, NYC, 1969-76; ptnr. Stamford, Conn., 1976-82; exec. v.p. corp. fin., tax and adminstrn. Primerica Corp. (formerly Am. Can Co.), Greenwich, Conn., 1982-87, exec. v.p., 1987, chief fin. officer, 1987-88; exec. v.p., chief fin. officer MONY Fin. Svcs., NYC, 1989-91; pres., COO, MONY-Mut. Ins. Co., NYC, 1991-94, chmn. bd. dirs., CEO, 1994—2004; bd. dir. Interpublic Group, NYC, 2002—, chmn., 2004—, CEO, 2005—. Bd. dirs. Pitney Bowes Corp., Gaylord Entertainment, Advt. Coun. Mem. leadership com. Lincoln Ctr. for Performing Arts; bd. dirs. Baruch Coll. Fund, Enterprise Found., Partnership NYC; bd. dirs., Com. Encourage Corp. Philanthropy Nat. Ctr. Addiction, Substance Abuse, Columbia U. Mem.: Stamford Tax Assn. (pres. 1981—82), Conn. Soc. CPA's, Am. Inst. CPA's. Office: Interpublic Group 1114 Ave of the Americas New York NY 10036 Office Fax: 212-704-1200, 212-704-1201.

ROTH, MICHAEL S., academic administrator, historian; b. Bklyn. m. Kari Weil; 1 child, Sophie Weil-Roth. BA, Wesleyan U.; MA, Princeton U., Phd in history. H.B. Alexander Prof. Humanities & Cultural Studies Claremont Grad. Sch., Calif.; prof. humanities, founder Humanities Ctr. Scripps Coll., Claremont; assoc. dir. Getty Rsch. Inst., chmn. Rsch. & Edn. Dept.; pres. Calif. Coll. Arts, San Francisco, 2000—07, Wesleyan U., Middletown, Conn., 2007—. Author: Freud: Conflict & Culture, 1998; curator (exhibitions) Sigmund Freud: Conflict & Culture, Libr. Congress, 1998; author: Looking for L.A.: Architecture, Film, Photography & Urban Landscape, 2001, Disturbing Remains: Memory, History, & Crisis in Twentieth Century, 2001. Office: Wesleyan U Office of Pres Wesleyan Station Middletown CT 06459*

ROTH, PAUL BARRY, dean, educator, emergency medicine physician; b. Glen Ridge, NJ, Oct. 7, 1947; s. Jerome M. and Selma (Leitner) R. BS, Fairleigh Dickinson U., 1969, MS, 1972; MD, George Washington U., 1976; postgrad., U. N.Mex., Albuquerque, 1976-79. Resident in family practice U. N.Mex. Sch. Medicine, Albuquerque, 1976—79; owner, pres. EMS of N.Mex., Albuquerque, 1978-82; owner, mem. of bd. Heights Urgent Care Ctr., Albuquerque, 1980-82; dir. divsn. emergency medicine dept. family, cmty. and emergency medicine U. N.Mex. Sch. Medicine, Albuquerque, 1982-91, prof. emerg. med., 1991—, chair dept. emergency medicine, 1991-93, interim chief med. officer, 1992—93, interim dean, 1994—95, dean, 1994—; interim dir. U. N.Mex. Med. Ctr., Albuquerque, 1994—95; med. dir. disaster medicine Nat. Disaster Med. Sys.; exec. v.p. U. N.Mex. Health Sci. Ctr., 2005—. Chair disaster com. U. N.Mex. Med. Ctr. Contbr. articles to Annals of EM, Current Practice of EM-Disaster Medicine, Jour. of AMA. Recipient Outstanding Individual Svc. award Nat. Disaster Med. Sys., 1986. Fellow Am. Coll. Emergency Physicians (chair sect. on disaster medicine, 1991-92), Am. Acad. Family Practice; mem. AMA, Soc. for Acad. Emergency Medicine, Am. Coll. Physician Execs., Am. Acad. Family Physicians. Office: U NMex Sch Medicine Health Scis Svcs Bldg, Suite 302 MSC09 5300 Albuquerque NM 87131-0001 Office Phone: 505-272-5849. Business E-Mail: PRoth@salud.unm.edu.*

ROTH, PETER, broadcast executive; b. Larchmont, NY; m. Andrea Roth; 2 children. Student, U. Pa.; grad., Tufts U., 1972. From mgr. to dir. children's programs ABC TV Network, 1976, dir. current programs, 1979, v.p. current prime-time series, 1981; past pres. Stephen J. Cannell Prodns.; pres. prodn. Twentieth Network TV, 1992, pres., 1993, 20th Century Fox TV, 1994, Fox Entertainment Group, LA, 1996—98, Warner Bros. TV Production, Burbank, Calif., 1999—. Office: Office of President Warner Bros TV Production 400 Warner Blvd Burbank CA 91522*

ROTH, PHILIP MILTON, writer; b. Newark, Mar. 19, 1933; s. Herman and Bess (Finkel) Roth; m. Margaret Martinson, Feb. 22, 1959 (dec. 1968); m. Claire Bloom, Apr. 29, 1990 (div. 1994). Student, Rutgers U., NJ; AB in English, Bucknell U., Lewisburg, Pa., 1954; MA in English Lit., U. Chgo., 1955; LittD (hon.), Harvard U., 2003. English tchr. U. Chgo., 1956-58; faculty Iowa Writers Workshop, 1960-62; writer in residence Princeton U., 1962-64; adj. prof. comparative lit. U. Pa., 1967—91, ret., 1991. Disting. prof. CUNY Hunter Coll., 1989—92. Author: (novels) Goodbye, Columbus, 1959 (Daroff award, Jewish Book Coun. of America, 1960, Nat. Book award, 1960), Letting Go, 1962, When She Was Good, 1967, Portnoy's Complaint, 1969, Our Gang, 1971, The Great American Novel, 1973, My Life As a Man, 1974, Sabbath's Theater, 1995 (Nat. Book award, 1995), Everyman, 2006 (PEN/Faulkner award for Fiction, 2007), Indignation, 2008, (memoirs) The Facts: A Novelist's Autobiography, Patrimony: A True Story, 1991 (Nat. Book Critics Circle award, 1991), (Zuckerman novels) The Ghost Writer, 1979, Zuckerman Unbound, 1981, The Anatomy Lesson, 1983, The Prague Orgy, 1985, The Counterlife, 1986 (Nat. Book Critics Circle award, 1986), American Pastoral, 1997 (Prix du Meilleur Livre Étranger, France, 2000, Pulitzer Prize for Fiction, 1997), I Married a Communist, 1998, The Human Stain, 2000 (PEN/Faulkner award for Fiction, 2001, WH Smith Lit. award, 2001, Prix Médicis Étranger, France, 2002), Exit Ghost, 2007, (Roth novels) Deception: A Novel, 1990, Operation Shylock: A Confession, 1993 (PEN/Faulkner award for Fiction, 1994), The Plot Against America, 2004 (Sidewise award for Alt. Hist., 2005), (Kepesh novels) The Breast, 1972, The Professor of Desire, 1977, The Dying Animal, 2001, (story collections) Reading Myself and Others, 1976, A Philip Roth Reader, 1980, Shop Talk, 2001, numerous short stories, essays and narratives. Recipient Lit. Medal of Honor, Nat. Arts Club, 1991, Karel Capek prize, Czech Republic, 1994, Nat. Medal of Arts, The White House, 1998, Gold Medal in fiction, AAAL, 2001, Award for Disting. Contbn. to Am. Letters, Nat. Book Found., 2002, PEN/Nabokov award for lifetime achievement, 2006, PEN/Saul Bellow award for Achievement in Am. Fiction, 2007; grantee Guggenheim Found., 1959—60, Rockefeller Found., 1966.*

ROTH, ROBERT, lawyer, journalist; s. Andrew and Sarah Roth. BA cum laude, Bklyn. Coll., 1974; JD, Ind. U., 1977. Bar: NY 1980. V.p., gen. counsel Andrew Roth and Sons, Inc., Bklyn., 1980—; corr., contbg. photographer UPI, NYC, 1980—96; aviation analyst Fox News Channel, 1999—2000. Chair NY County Lawyers Assn. Continuing Legal Edn. Program. Photojournalist (news photograph) Statue of Liberty Centennial (UPI Pictures of the Yr., 1989), lead correspondent, Fox News Channel (series of television news reports on) Crash of Egyptair Flight 990. Mem. young fellows The Frick Collection, NYC, 2003. Recipient Sam Castan Meml. award Excellence Journalism, Bklyn. Coll., 1974. Mem.: ABA, NY County Lawyers Assn. Avocation: travel. Office: Andrew Roth and Sons Inc PO Box 190293 Brooklyn NY 11219-3736

ROTH, ROBERT EARL, ecologist, educator; b. Wauseon, Ohio, Mar. 30, 1937; s. Earl Jonas Roth and Florence Lena (Mahler) R.; m. Carol Sue Yackee, Aug. 8, 1959; children; Robin Earl, Bruce Robert. BS, Ohio State U., 1959, MS in Conservation Edn., 1960, BS in Secondary Sci. Edn., 1961; PhD in Environ. Edn., U. Wis., 1969. Supr. conservation edn. and elem. sci. tchr. Ethical Culture Schs., NYC, 1961—63; naturalist, sci. tchr. Lakeside Sch., Spring Valley, NY, 1963-65; instr. No. Ill. U., Oregon, 1965-67; asst. prof. Ohio State U., Columbus, 1969-73, assoc. prof., 1973-78, prof. environ. edn. and sci. edn., 1978-2001, prof. emeritus, 2001—, chmn. divsn., 1973-84, coord. office internat. affairs, 1985-89, asst. dir., sch. sec. Sch. Natural Resources, 1989-93, acting dir. Sch. Natural Resources, 1993-94, assoc. dir., 1994-2001, state extension specialist Environ. Edn., 1993-2001. Rsch. & devel. assoc. Mosely & Assocs., Columbus, 1986-89; project cons. NARMA project, U.S. Agy. internat. Devel., Santo Domingo, Dominican Rep., 1982-87; cons. Richard Trott & Assocs., 1988-90, Kinzelman & Kline, 1990-2001, Midwest consortium Internat. Activity, 1995; evaluator Montclair State U., N.J. Sch. Conservation, 1999; workshop leader Carribean Conservation Assn., Bridgetown, Barbados, 1981-83; vis. scholar Indonesian Second U. Devel. project, Jakarta, 1988; AID lectr., Thesolonika, Greece, 1992; bd. supr. Franklin Soil & Water Conservation Dist., 2003-05. Exec. editor Jour. Environ. Edn., 1974-91 (Pub.'s prize 1970); contbr. articles to profl. jours. Committeeman Boy Scouts Am., 1983-86; adv. coun. McKeever Environ. Learning Ctr., Pa., 1977-83. Recipient Pomerene Tchg. Enhancement award, Ohio State U., 1986, 1995, Environ. Edn. award, Ohio Alliance for the Enrivon., 1992, Outstanding Advising award, Coll. Food Agrl. and Environ. Scis., 1996; named vis. scholar, Uganda Makerere U., 1989, Pacific Cultural Found., Taipei, Taiwan, 1989, 1999, 2001. Mem.: Sch. Nat. Resource Alumni Assn. (inducted hon. 100), Nat. Sci. Tchrs. Assn. (life), N.Am. Assn. Environ. Edn. (life; bd. dirs. 1972—82, pres. 1977—78, Walt Jeske award 1988, Outstanding Contbns. to Rsch. award 2000). Avocations: swimming, fishing, travel. Home: 570 Morning St Columbus OH 43085-3775 E-mail: roth.3@osu.edu.

ROTH, ROBERT PAUL, seminary educator, writer; b. Milw., Dec. 8, 1919; s. Paul Wagner and Rose Marie (Schulzke) R.; m. Margaret Agnes Beckstrand, June 17, 1943; children: Erik, Maren, Maarja, John, Sonja. BA, Carthage Coll., Kenosha, Wis., 1941, DD (hon.), 2000; MA, U. Ill., 1942; MDiv, Northwestern Luth. Sem., 1945; PhD, U. Chgo., 1947; DD (hon.), Roanoke Coll., Salem, Va., 1958. Ordained to ministry Luth. Ch. in Am. Prof. Luthergiri Sem., Rajahmundry, India, 1946-48; pastor St. Paul Ch., Red Wing, Minn., 1949-53; prof. Luth. So. Sem., Columbia, S.C., 1953-61; dean Northwestern Luth. Sem., Mpls., 1968-76; dir. grad. studies Luther Northwestern Sem., St. Paul, 1976-83; pres. Minn. Consortium Sems., 1976-78; prof. Luth. Theol. Sem., Hong Kong, 1990-91; chmn. com. on worship Luth. Ch. Am., 1970-78; mem. Bd. Publ., Phila., 1978—86. Author: Meaning and Practice of the Lord's Supper, 1961, Story and Reality, 1973, Story and Reality, republished, 2005, The Theater of God, 1985, The Theater of God, republished, 2005, History of Northwestern Seminary, 1994, Shonyambisik Saga, 1995, Divine Disclosure, 2006, Freedom at Last: A Novel About the Birth of a New India, 2007; editor: New International Bible, 1978; editor-in-chief: Areopagus Mag., 1990—91. Rsch. fellow Am. Assn. Theol. Schs., 1966, Aid Assn. for Lutherans, 1976, 78, Luth. Brotherhood, 1983, Luth. Ch. Am. Div. for Profl. Leadership, 1983, Div. for Global Missions, 1983. Mem. Am. Acad. Religion. Avocations: painting watercolors, poetry, sailing. Home: 4194 Hillcrest Ln Wayzata MN 55391-3604 Home Phone: 203-814-8002; Office Phone: 952-473-3117. Personal E-mail: rothdragon@gmail.com.

ROTH, RONALD C., museum director; MA, George Washington U., 1976. Dir. Mus. of Nebr. Art, Kearney; dir., CEO Reading Pub. Mus. and Art Gallery, Pa., 2002—. Bd. dirs. Greater Reading Convention & Visitors Bureau. Office: Reading Pub Mus and Art Gallery 500 Museum Rd Reading PA 19611 Office Phone: 610-371-5850 ext. 222. Office Fax: 610-371-5632. Business E-Mail: ron.roth@readingpublicmuseum.org.

ROTH, RONALD LEE, engineering educator; b. Oakland, Calif., May 20, 1947; s. Howard Benjamin and Lillian Roth; m. Alma Hayes, July 7, 1984; children: Owen Howard, Adam Ronald. BS in Engring., Harvey Mudd Coll., Claremont, Calif., 1969; MS in Mech. Engring., Stanford U., Calif., 1971, PhD, 1976; MD, St. Georges U., Grenada, 1986. Engr. Westinghouse Corp., LA, 1969—70; lectr. Calif. State U., Fresno, Calif., 1975—76, U. Calif., Berkeley, 1977, 1979; vis. prof. U. Auckland, New Zealand, 1992—93, lectr., 1980—82, San Jose State U., Calif., 1979; postdoctoral rsch. affiliate Stanford U., 1976—77, lectr., 1973, 1980; assoc. prof. Calif. State U., Chico, 1986—90, prof., 1990—. Dept. chair Calif. State U., Chico, 2001—04, Chico, 2007—. Contbr. articles to profl. jours. Recipient Profl. Promise award, Calif. State U., 1987; John F O'Connell fellow, 1998—2000, NSF Traineeship fellow, Stanford U., 1970—74. Mem.: Am. Soc. Engring. Edn., Tau Beta Pi. Office: Calif State Univ Mech Engring and Mfg Tech Dept Chico CA 95929-0789 Office Fax: 530-898-4070.

ROTH, SANFORD IRWIN, pathologist, educator; b. McAlester, Okla., Oct. 14, 1932; s. Herman Moe and Blanche (Brown) R.; m. Kathryn Ann Corliss, Sept. 3, 1961; children: Jeffrey Franklin, Elisabeth Francyne, Gregory James, Suzannah Joan. Student, Vanderbilt U., 1949-52; MD, Harvard U., 1956. Intern Mass. Gen. Hosp., Boston, 1956-57, resident in pathology, 1957-60, pathologist, 1962-75, Armed Forces Inst. Pathology, 1960-62; asst. prof. Med. Sch. Harvard U., 1962-69, assoc. prof. Med. Sch., 1969-75; pathologist, prof., chmn. dept. Coll. Medicine U. Ark., Little Rock, 1975-81; prof. Med. Sch. Northwestern U., Chgo., 1981—2000, asst. dean admissions, 1998-2000, prof. emeritus, 2000—; chief lab. svc. VA Lakeside Med. Ctr., Chgo., 1981—84. Attending pathologist Northwestern U. Hosp., 1981-2000; vis. prof. pathology Harvard Med. Sch., 2001-06, lectr., 2007—; cons. in pathology Mass. Gen. Hosp., 2001—. With M.C. U.S. Army, 1960-62. Mem. AMA, AAAS, Coll. Am. Pathology, U.S.-Can. Acad. Pathology, Soc. for Investigative Dermatology, Mass. Med. Soc. Home: 169

Tisquantum Rd Chatham MA 02633-2578 Office: Mass Gen Hosp Warren 221 Fruit St Boston MA 02114 Office Phone: 508-945-2995. Personal E-mail: siroth@northwestern.edu. Business E-Mail: sroth@partners.org.

ROTH, SOL, rabbi; b. Rzeszow, Poland, Mar. 8, 1927; came to U.S., 1934, naturalized, 1939; s. Joseph and Miriam (Lamm) R.; m. Debra H. Stitskin, Nov. 26, 1957; children: Steven, Michael (dec.), Sharon. BA, Yeshiva U., 1948; MA, Columbia U., 1953, PhD, 1966; D in Divinity (hon.), Yeshiva U., 1977. Rabbi Yeshiva U. Theol. Sem., 1950. Ordained rabbi Orthodox Jewish Congregations, 1950; pres. Rabbinical Council Am., 1980-82, N.Y. Bd. Rabbis, 1976-79; chmn. Israel Commn. Rabbinical Council Am., 1976-78; dean Chaplaincy Sch., N.Y. Bd. Rabbis, 1976-79; Samson R. Hirsch prof. dept. philosophy Yeshiva U., NYC. Rabbi Jewish Ctr. Atlantic Beach, N.Y., 1956-86; rabbi Fifth Ave Synagogue, 1986-2003, rabbi emeritus, 2003—; pres. Rabbinical Coun. Am., 1980-82, Religious Zionists Am., 1991-94 Author: Science and Religion, 1967, The Jewish Idea of Community, 1977, Halakhah and Politics: The Jewish Idea of a State, 1988 (Samuel Belkin Meml. Lit. award 1989), The Jewish Idea of Culture, 1997, The Jewish Idea of Ethics and Morality, 2007; editor: Morasha. Recipient award Synagogue Adv. Council United Jewish Appeal, 1975; named Rabbi Dr. Sol Roth Chair in Talmud and Contemporary Halakha established at Yeshiva U., 1989. Jewish. Home: 201 E 62nd St New York NY 10065-8026 Office: Yeshiva U Dept Philosophy 500 W 185th St Dept New York NY 10033-3299 Office Phone: 212-421-0066. Personal E-mail: rothsol@aol.com.

ROTH, STEVEN, real estate company executive; m. Daryl Roth, 1969; children: Jordan, Amanda. AB, Dartmouth Coll., 1962, MBA with highest distinction, 1963. With Kenilworth Assoc., NJ, 1975—79; co-founder, mng. gen. ptnr. Interstate Properties, 1979—; chmn., CEO Vornado Realty Trust, NYC, 1989—2009, chmn., 2009—; CEO Alexander's Inc., 1995—, chmn., 2004—. Bd. dir. Amos Tuck Sch., Dartmouth Coll., 1981—87; trustee Whitney Mus. Am. Art, NYC, Intrepid Mus. Found., NYC; bd. dir. Jewish Theol. Seminary Am., NYU Sch. Med. Found. With USAR. Named one of Forbes' Richest Americans, 2006, The World's Thirty Most Respected CEO's, Barron's, 2005—07. Mem.: Nat. Assn. of Real Estate Investment Trusts (NAREIT) (chmn. 2002—03). Office: Vornado Realty Trust 888 Seventh Ave New York NY 10019 also: Alexander's Inc 210 Rte 4 E Paramus NJ 07652 Office Phone: 212-894-7000.*

ROTH, TIM, actor; b. London, May 14, 1961; m. Nikki Butler, 1993; children: Timothy, Cormac. With Glasgow Citizen's Theatre, The Oval House, The Royal Ct. Appeared in play Metamorphosis; films include The Hit, 1985, A World Apart, 1988, The Cook, the Thief, His Wife and Her Lover, 1990, Vincent and Theo, 1990, Rosencrantz and Guildenstern Are Dead, 1991, Jumpin' at the Boneyard, 1992, Reservoir Dogs, 1992, Bodies, Rest and Motion, 1993, Pulp Fiction, 1994, Rob Roy, 1995 (Acad. award nominee for best supporting actor 1996), Little Odessa, 1995, Four Rooms, 1995, No Way Home, 1996, Everyone Says I Love You, 1996, Hoodlum, 1997, Gridlock'd, 1997, Animals, 1997, Deceiver, 1998, The Legend of the Pianist on the Ocean, 1998, Vatel, 1999, Leggenda del pianista sull'oceano, 1998, The Million Dollar Hotel, 2000, Lucky Numbers, 2000, Planet of the Apes, 2001, Invincible, 2001, The Musketeer, 2001, Emmett's Mark, 2002, Whatever We Do, 2003, To Kill a King, 2003, With It, 2004, Silver City, 2004, New France, 2004, The Beautiful Country, 2004, Dark Water, 2005, Jumpshot, 2005, The Last Sign, 2005, Don't Come Knocking, 2005, Even Money, 2006, Youth Without Youth, 2007, Funny Games US, 2008, The Incredible Hulk, 2008; TV movies include Meantime, Made in Britain, Metamorphosis, Murder in the Heartland, 1993; dir.: The War Zone, 1998; TV guest appearance Tales From the Crypt, 1989. Office: c/o Ilene Feldman Agy 8730 W Sunset Blvd Ste 490 Los Angeles CA 90069-2248

ROTH, WILLIAM STANLEY, hospital foundation executive; b. NYC, Jan. 12, 1929; s. Sam Irving and Louise Caroline (Martin) Roth; m. Hazel Adcock, May 6, 1963; children: R. Charles, W. Stanley Roth'. AA, Asheville-Biltmore Jr. Coll., NC, 1948; BS, U. NC, Chapel Hill, 1950. Dep. regional exec. Nat. coun. Boy Scouts Am., 1953-65; exec. v.p. Am. Humanics Found., 1965-67; dir. devel. Bethany Med. Ctr., Kansas City, Kans., 1967-74; exec. v.p. Geisinger Med. Ctr. Found., Danville, Pa., 1974-78; found. pres. Bapt. Med Ctrs., Birmingham, Ala., 1978—. Sec. Western Med. Systems, Cherokee County Homes, Cullman Sr. Housing, Dekalb Sr. Housing, Limestone Sr. Housing, Oxford Sr. Housing. Editor: Torch and Trefoil, 1960—61. Mem.-at-large Nat. coun. Boy Scouts Am., 1972-86; chmn. NAHD Ednl. Fund, 1980-82; ruling elder John Knox Kirk, Kansas City, Mo., Grove Presbyn. Ch., Danville, Pa. Recipient Silver award United Meth. Ch., 1970, Mid-West Health Congress, 1971; Seymour award for outstanding hosp. devel. officer, 1983, 70 Yr. Vet. award Boy Scouts Am., 2006. Fellow Assn. for Healthcare Philanthropy (life; nat. pres. 1975-76); mem. Nat. Soc. Fund Raising Execs. (pres. Ala. chpt. 1980-82, nat. dir. 1980-84, mem. ethics bd. 1993-98, advanced cert fund raising exec., Outstanding Fund Raising Exec., Ala. chpt. 1983), Mid-Am. Hosp. Devel. Assn. (pres. 1973-74), Mid-West Health Congress (devel. chmn. 1972-74), Am. Soc. for Healthcare Mktg. and Pub. Rels., Ala. Soc. for Sleep Disorders, Ala. Heart Inst., Ala. Assn. Healthcare Philanthropy (pres. 1991-93, chmn. bd. 1993-94), Ala. Planned Giving Coun. (bd. dirs. 1991-2000, pres. 1994-95), Alpha Phi Omega (nat. pres. 1958-62, dir. 1950—, Nat. Disting. Scv. award 1962), Delta Upsilon (pres. NC Alumni 1963-65), Rotary (pres. club 1976-77), Relay House, Summit Club, Green Valley Club (bd. govs.), Elks, Order of the Arrow (Nat. Disting. Svc. award 1958), Order of Holy Grail, Order of Golden Fleece. Home: 341 Laredo Dr Birmingham AL 35226-2325 Office: 3500 Blue Lake Dr Ste 101 Birmingham AL 35243-1908 Office Phone: 205-979-8285. Personal E-mail: billroth1@aol.com.

ROTHBAUM, BARBARA OLASOV, psychologist, educator; b. Charleston, SC, July 4, 1960; d. Sanford Patla and Faye (Rabinowitz) Olasov; m. John Edel Rothbaum, June 19, 1988; children: Alex Olasov, Jake Olasov. BA with highest honors, U. N.C., 1982; MS in Psychology, U. Ga., 1984, PhD in Clin. Psychology, 1986. Behavior therapist Middlesex Hosp. Med. Sch., London, 1984—85; instr. psychiatry Med. Coll. Pa., Phila., 1986—88, asst. prof. psychiatry, 1988—90; from asst. prof. to prof. Sch. Medicine Emory U., Atlanta, 1990—2005, prof. Sch. Medicine, 2005—, dir. Trauma and Anxiety Recovery Program Sch. Medicine. Project coord. Rape and Crime Victim Program, Phila, 1986-90; pvt. practice psychology, Phila., 1986-90; mem. sci. adv. bd. Anxiety Disorders Assocs., 2002—; mem. DSM-III-R work group on post-traumatic stress disorder. Contbr. articles to profl. jours., chpts. to books. Mem. APA, Ga. Psychol. Assn., Assn. for Advancement Behavior Therapy, Internat. Soc. for Traumatic Stress Studies (bd. dirs., pres. 2004). Democrat. Jewish. Avocations: art, outdoors, reading, bicycling. Office: Dept Psychiatry 1841 Clifton Rd Atlanta GA 30329 Office Phone: 404-712-8866. Business E-Mail: brothba@emory.edu.*

ROTHBERG, ABRAHAM, writer; b. NYC, Jan. 14, 1922; s. Louis and Lottie (Drimmer) R.; m. Esther Conwell, Sept. 30, 1945; 1 son, Lewis Josiah. AB, Bklyn. Coll., 1942; MA, U. Iowa, 1947; PhD, Columbia U., 1952. Chmn. editorial bd. Stateside (mag.), NYC, 1947-49; instr. English, creative writing Columbia U., NYC, 1948; instr. English, humanities Hofstra Coll., Hempstead, NY, 1947-51; prof. English St. John Fisher Coll., 1973-83, chmn. dept. English, 1981-82; disting. writer-in-residence, vis. prof. Wichita State U., 1985. Editor-in-chief Free Europe Press, NYC, 1952—59, East Europe Mag., 1952—59; mng. editor George Braziller, Inc., NYC, 1959, New Leader mag., NYC, 1960—61; cons. editor New Jewish Ency., 1960—62; writer, editl. con.; European corr. Nat. Observer, Washington, Manchester (Eng.) Guardian, 1962—63; sr. editor Bantam Books, Inc., NYC, 1966—67; cons. editor The New Union Prayer Book, NYC, 1975. Author: Abraham, Eyewitness History of World War II, 1962, The Thousand Doors, 1965, The Heirs of Cain, 1966, The Song of David Freed, 1968, The Other Man's Shoes, 1969, The Boy and the Dolphin, 1969, The Sword of the Golem, 1971, Aleksandr Solzhenitsyn: The Major Novels, 1971, The Heirs of Stalin: Dissidence and the Soviet Regime, 1953-1970, 1972, The Stalking Horse, 1972, The Great Waltz, 1978, The Four Corners of the House, 1981, The Holy Warriors, 2005, A Beast in View, 2005, Pinocchio's Sister: A Feminist Fable, 2005, The Torii Gate, 2005, The Former People, 2006, Coming to Terms, 2006, numerous short stories, essays and poems; editor: U.S. Stories, 1949, Flashes in the Night, 1958, Anatomy of a Moral, 1959, A Bar-Mitzvah Companion, 1959, Great Adventure Stories of Jack London, 1967, No Traveler Returns, 2008; contbr. articles to profl. jours. Served with AUS, 1943-45. Recipient John H. McGinnis Meml. award for short story, 1970, John H. McGinnis Meml. award for essay, 1973—74, Lit. award, Friends of Rochester Libr., 1980; Ford Found. fellow, N.Y.C., 1951—52. Home: 340 Pelham Rd Rochester NY 14610-3355

ROTHBERG, GERALD, editor, publishing executive; b. Bklyn., Oct. 29, 1937; s. Abraham and Pauline Rothberg; m. Glenda Fay Morris, June 18, 1970 (div. 1988); children: Laura, Abigail. BA, Bklyn. Coll., 1960; postgrad., Dickinson Law Sch., 1962. Spl. projects editor Esquire, 1963-66; owner, editor, pub., founder Circus, NYC, 1966—; owner, founder, editor Sci. and Living Tomorrow, 1980—, Who's In, 1981; founder, editor Sports Mirror mag., 1983—, MGF mag., 1985—, Country Mirror mag., 1994—. Author: (novels) Composition 36, 1993, The Six Hour Song, 1994, Redeeming Esau, 1995, The Esau Swindle, 2004, Saturday Books, 2006, The Golem Code, 2007. Mem.: Periodical and Book Assn. Am. (pres.). Office: Ste 455 527 Third Ave New York NY 10016 Office Phone: 212-242-4902.

ROTHBERG, GERALD M., materials engineer, educator; b. Atlantic City, May 14, 1931; s. Harry Herman and Sarah Ada Rothberg; m. Elaine S. Williams, Jan. 25, 1954; children: S. Roshanna, Rei Williams. BS, MIT, Cambridge, 1952; PHD, Columbia U., NYC, 1958. Head, dept. materials sci. engring. Stevens Inst. Tech., Hoboken, NJ, 1974—88. Chair advanced materials Tokyo U., 1988. Fellow: Am. Phys. Soc.; mem.: Am. Soc. Engring. Edn. Achievements include patents for a ferromagnetic,semiconductor composite material whose magnetic and optical properties may be varied by means of an electric field; invention of photoemission extended X-Ray absorption fine structure spectroscopy (pexafs) to study surface structures. Office: Stevens Institute Technology Castle Point Sta Hoboken NJ 07030 Business E-Mail: gerald.rothberg@stevens.edu.

ROTHBERG, GLENDA FAY MORRIS, lawyer; b. Rome, Ga., Aug. 7, 1946; d. Glenn Howell and Fay (Givens) Morris; m. Gerald Rothberg, June 18, 1970 (div. Jan. 1989); children: Laura, Abigail. AB, Randolph-Macon Woman's Coll., 1968; JD, Benjamin Cardozo Law Sch., 1985. Bar: N.Y. 1986, U.S. Dist. Ct. (so. and ea. dists.) N.Y. 1987, U.S. Supreme Ct. 1990. Law guardian juvenile rights divsn. Legal Aid Soc., NYC, 1988-91; pvt. practice NYC, 1992—. Faculty dir. Inst. for not-for-profit Mgmt. Columbia Bus. Sch., N.Y.C., 1994-98. Vol. Manhattan Mediation Ctr., N.Y.C., 1996-99; chair legal com. N.Y.C. Comptr. Task Force on Open Adoption, 1999-2001 Fellow Am. Bar Found.; mem. ABA, Assn. of Bar of City of N.Y. (com. chair 1996-99, mem. coun. on children 1999-2002). Office: Ste 400 363 Seventh Ave New York NY 10001 E-mail: gmrlaw@aol.com.

ROTHBERG, JONATHAN M., medical products executive, researcher; b. New Haven, Conn., 1963; BSChemE, Carnegie Mellon U.; MS, MPhil, Yale U., PhD in Biology. Postdoctoral fellow Boyer Ctr. for Molecular Medicine, Howard Hughes Med. Inst.; founder Clarifi Corp., CuraGen Corp., Branford, Conn., 1991, CEO, pres., chmn., 1991—2005, bd. dirs.; founder 454 Life Sciences, Conn., 1999, chmn., 2005. Co-founder, chmn., bd. dir. RainDance Technologies, Inc.; founder Rothberg Inst. for Childhood Diseases; invited tech. pioneer World Econ. Forum, Davos, Switzerland; spkr. in field. Bd. trustee Carnegie Mellon U. Recipient Irvington Institute's Corporate Leadership award in Sci., Gold Winner, Wall Street Jour. Tech. Innovation award, 2005, Biotech-Med. Winner, 2005; named Ernst and Young Entrepreneur of Yr. Mem.: NAE, Conn. Acad. Sci. and Engring. Achievements include invention of new way to sequence DNA on a chip, called 454 sequencing; development of a series of new medicines, now in over 14 human clinical trials, for the treatment of a wide range of cancers; being the first person to sequence an individual human genome (that of James D. Watson) and initiated the Neanderthal Genome project; initiated the age of the personal genomics. Office: 454 Life Scis 20 Commercial St Branford CT 06405 Office Phone: 203-871-2300.

ROTHBERG, JUDITH, elementary school educator, researcher; b. NYC, Mar. 4, 1934; d. Louis and Esther (Charloff) Jablowsky; m. Lawrence Rothberg, Apr. 13, 1957; children: Richard, Loretta. BA, Bklyn. Coll., 1955, MS, 1960; cert. in guidance, L.I. U., 1969; cert. in adminstrn., Columbia U., 1988, PhD in Ednl. and Family Counseling, 1997. Tchr. grades 2 to 6, supr. Lindenhurst (N.Y.) Sch. System, 1955—. Pvt. practice ednl. counseling, Glen Cove, N.Y., 1990-92. Author: Meet Me in West Africa, 1992, Meet the Russian Historic Rivers Then and Now, 1992; co-host (cable program) Innersight; prodr. (cable program) Exploring Your Emotions. Mem., lectr. Bnai Zion, Glen Cove Chpt., 1989-93; bd. dirs. Innersight-Assn. for the Blind. Mem. Tchrs. Assn. Lindenhurst. Avocations: drama club, aerobics, writing, traveling to africa and asia, lecturing. Home: 1 Cedar Ln Glen Cove NY 11542-1320 Office Phone: 516-759-1779.

ROTHBERG, MOREY DAVID, historian, editor; b. Phila., Apr. 5, 1951; s. Herman Jacob and Dorothy Slotkin Rothberg. BA, U. Md., 1973; MA, PhD, Brown U., 1982. Pers. mgmt. specialist U.S. Office Pers. Mgmt., Washington, 1982—86; dir. John Franklin Jameson papers project Am. Hist. Assn., Washington, 1984—94; editor Comptr. Currency, Washington, 1999—. Editor: (documentary edit.) John Franklin Jameson and the Development of Humanistic Scholarship in America (3 vols.). Founding pres. Wash. Guitar Soc., Silver Spring, Md., 1992—94. J. Franklin Jameson fellow, Am. Hist. Assn. and Libr. of Congress, 1983—84. Mem.: Orgn. Am. Historians (assoc.), Am. Hist. Assn. (assoc.), Phi Beta Kappa. Home: Unit A 10801 Amherst Ave Silver Spring MD 20902

ROTHBERG-BLACKMAN, JUNE SIMMONDS, retired nursing educator, psychotherapist; b. Phila., Sept. 4, 1923; d. David and Rose (Protzel) Simmonds; m. Jacob Rothberg, Sept. 7, 1952 (dec. Feb. 2001); children: Robert Rothberg, Alan Rothberg; m. Stanley F Blackman, May 27, 2002 (dec. July 2005). Diploma in nursing, Lenox Hill Hosp., 1944; BS, N.Y. U., 1950, MA, 1959, PhD (NIH fellow), 1965; Diploma in Psychotherapy and Psychoanalysis, Adelphi U., Inst. for Advanced Psychol. Studies, 1987. USPHS traineeship N.Y. U., 1957-59; sr. public health nurse Bklyn. Vis. Nurse Assn., 1951-53; prin. investigator in nursing, homestead study project Goldwater Hosp. and N.Y. U., 1959-61; instr. N.Y. U., 1964-65, asst. prof., 1965-68, assoc. prof., 1968-69, project dir. grad. program rehab. nursing, 1964-69, prof., 1969-87, prof. emeritus, 1987—; dean Adelphi U., Garden City, NY, 1969-85, v.p. acad. adminstrn., 1985-86; pvt. practice West Hempstead, NY, 1993-97. Pres. David Simmonds Co. Inc., Med. Supply Co., 1982-89; dir., chmn. compensation com. Quality Care, Inc.; cons. region 2 Bur. Health Resources Devel., HHS.; audit com. Ipco Corp. (formerly Sterling Optical Corp.), 1991; cons., spkr. in field. Contbr. articles to profl. jours. Mem. pres's coun. N.Y. U. Sch. Edn., 1973-75; treas. Nurses for Polit. Action, 1971-73; trustee Nurses Coalition for Action in Politics, 1974-76; bd. visitors Duke Med. Ctr., 1970-74; mem. governing bd. Nassau-Suffolk Health Systems Agy., 1976-79; leader People-to-People Internat. med. rehab. del. to People's Republic of China, 1981; mem. com. for the study pain disability and chronic illness behavior Inst. Medicine, 1985-86, com. on ethics in rehab. Hastings Ctr., 1985-87; trustee Paget's Disease Found., 1987-89. Recipient Disting. Alumna award NYU, 1974, recognition award Am. Assn. Colls. Nursing, 1976, Achievers award Ctr. for Bus. and Profl. Women, 1980 Fellow Am. Acad. Nursing (governing coun. 1980-82); mem. Nat. League Nursing (exec. com. coun. of baccalaureate and higher degree programs 1969-73), Am. Nurses Assn. (joint liaison com. 1970-72), Commn. Accreditation of Rehab. Facilities, Am. Congress Rehab. Medicine (pres. 1977-78, chmn. continuing edn. com. 1979-86, 34th Ann. John Stanley Coulter Meml. lectr. 1984, Gold Key award 1984, Edward W. Lowman award 1990), Am. Assn. Colls. Nursing (pres. 1974-76), L.I. Women's Network (pres. 1980-81), Kappa Delta Pi, Sigma Theta Tau, Pi Lambda Theta. Achievements include having June S. Rothberg collection in Nursing Archives, Mugar Meml. Library, Boston U. Home and Office: 3941 Redondo Way Boca Raton FL 33487 Personal E-mail: stanleyb2@aol.com.

ROTHBLATT, DONALD NOAH, urban and regional planner, educator; b. NYC, Apr. 28, 1935; s. Harry and Sophie (Chernofsky) Rothblatt; m. Ann S. Vogel, June 16, 1957; children: Joel Michael, Steven Saul. BCE, CUNY, 1957; MS in Urban Planning, Columbia U., 1963; diploma in comprehensive planning, Inst. Social Studies, The Hague, 1964; PhD in City and Regional Planning, Harvard U., 1969. Cert. Am. Inst. Cert. Planners; registered prof. engr., NY. Planner NYC Planning Commn., 1960-62, NY Housing and Redevel. Bd., 1963-66; research fellow Ctr. for Environ. Design Studies, Harvard U., Cambridge, Mass., 1965-71; tchg. fellow, instr., then asst. prof. city and regional planning Harvard U., 1967-71; prof. urban and regional planning, chmn. dept. San Jose (Calif.) State U., 1971—. Lady Davis vis. prof. urban and regional planning Hebrew U., Jerusalem, 1978, Tel-Aviv U., 1978; vis. scholar Indian Inst. Architects, 1979, Shandong Province, China, 1996, U. Lodz, Poland, 2000, Paris Transp. Authority, 2002, Greater London Authority, 2003, Sydney Regional Orgn. Councils, 2004, Toronto Urban Devel. Svcs., 2005, NY Met. Transp. Coun., 2006, Phila., Del. Valley Regional Planning Commn., 2007, Guatemala City TransMetro Agy., 2008, St. Paul Met. Coun., Mpls., 2009; cons. to pvt. industry and govt. agys., 09. Author: Human Needs and Public Housing, 1964, Thailand's Northeast, 1967, Regional Planning: The Appalachian Experience, 1971, Allocation of Resources for Regional Planning, 1972, The Suburban Environment and Women, 1979, Regional-Local Development Policy Making, 1981, Planning the Metropolis: The Multiple Advocacy Approach, 1982, Comparative Suburban Data, 1983, Suburbia: An International Assessment, 1986, Metropolitan Dispute Resolution in Silicon Valley, 1989, Good Practices for the Congestion Management Program, 1994, Activity-Based Travel Survey and Analysis of Responses to Increased Congestion, 1995, An Experiment in Sub-Regional Planning: California's Congestion Management Policy, 1995, Estimating the Origins and Destinations of Transit Passengers from On/Off Counts, 1995, Changes in Property Values Induced by Light Transit, 1996, Comparative Study of Statewide Transportation Planning Under ISTEA, 1997, North American Metropolitan Planning Reexamined, 1999; actor: Government Performance Measures Linking Urban Mass Transportation with Land Use and Accessibility Factors, 2000, Best Practices in Developing Regional Transportation Plans, 2001, Comparative Study of U.S. Metropolitan Transportation Planning, 2004; editor: National Policy for Urban and Regional Development, 1974, Regional Advocacy Planning: Expanding Air Transport Facilities for the San Jose Metropolitan Area, 1975, Metropolitan-wide Advocacy Planning: Dispersion of Low and Moderate Cost Housing the San Jose Metropolitan Area, 1976, Multiple Advocacy Planning: Public Surface Transportation in the San Jose Metropolitan Area, 1977, A Multiple Advocacy Approach to Regional Planning: Open Space and Recreational Facilities for the San Jose Metropolitan Area, 1979, Regional Transportation Planning for the San Jose Metropolitan Area, 1981, Planning for Open Space and Recreational Facilities in the San Jose Metropolitan Area, 1982, Regional Economic Development Planning for the San Jose Metropolitan Area, 1984, Planning for Surface Transportation in the San Jose Metropolitan Area, 1986, Expansion for Air Transportation Facilities in the San Jose Metropolitan Area, 1987, Provision of Economic Development in the San Jose Metropolitan Area, 1989, Metropolitan Governance: American/Canadian Intergovernmental Perspectives, 1993, Metropolitan Governance Revisited, 1998; contbr. articles to profl. jours.; dir.: (TV series) Sta. KTEH, 1976. Mem. adv. coun. Bay Area Met. Transp. Commn., 1995—. Served to 1st lt. C.E. US Army Corps of Engrs., 1957—59. Recipient Innovative Tchg. award, Calif. State U. and Coll., 1975—79, award, Internat. Festival Films Architecture and Planning, 1983, Meritorious Performance award, San Jose State U., 1986, 1988, 1990, 1996—2001; co-recipient Best of West award, Western Ednl. Soc. Telecom., 1976; grantee, Nat. Inst. Dispute Resolution, 1987—88, Can. Studies Enrichment Program, 1992—93; Rsch. fellow, Harvard U., 1967—69, William F. Milton Rsch. fellow, 1970—71, Faculty Rsch. grantee, NSF, 1972—82, Calif. State U., 1977—78, Univ. Rsch. and Tng. Program grantee, Calif. Dept. Transp., 1993—97. Fellow: Am. Inst. Cert. Planners (inducted 2006); mem.: AAUP, Architecture and Urban and Regional Planning (chmn. 1973—75), Calif. Edn. Com. Architecture and Landscape, Internat. Fedn. Housing and Planning, Planners Equal Opportunity, Am. Planning Assn., Assn. Collegiate Schs. Planning (pres. 1975—76). Office: San Jose State U Dept Urban & Regional Planning San Jose CA 95192-0185 *My basic view is that we should try to develop ourselves fully and help others do the same, so that we will be able to live in harmony with, and contribute to, our world community.*

ROTHE, DESIDER J., gynecologist-obstetrician; b. Iger, Hungary, Dec. 24, 1936; came to U.S., 1969; s. Istvan Abonyi and Iren (Husi) R.; m. Nalda L. Findell, July 9, 1990; children: Suzanne, Stephan, Christopher. MD, U. Debrecen, Hungary, 1961. Diplomate Am. Bd. Ob-Gyn. Rsch. fellow U. Med. Scis. Debrecen, 1959-61, intern, 1960-61, resident in ob-stet., 1961-65; rsch. CNRS, Paris, 1966-69; rsch. assoc. N.Y. Blood Ctr., NYC, 1969-70; rsch. assoc. human genetics in pediats.

Cornell U. Med. Coll., 1970, chief resident in ob-stet., 1970-72, fellow in ob-stet., 1972; asst. ob-stet. N.Y. Hosp.-Cornell U., 1972; asst. attending in ob-gyn. Lenox Hill Hosp., 1974-78, N.Y. Hosp., 1978—. Clin. assoc. prof. ob-gyn. Cornell U. Med. Coll., N.Y. Hosp., 1978—. Contbr. articles to profl. jours. Recipient Young Scientist award Semmelweis Sci. Soc., 1976. Mem. AMA, ACOG, N.Y. Obstet. Soc., Semmelweis Sci. Soc. Avocations: running, skiing, waterskiing. Office: New York-Presbyterian Hosp 131 E 65th St New York NY 10065 Office Phone: 212-535-2175.

ROTHEMUND, PAUL W.K., research scientist; BS, Calif. Inst. Tech., 1994; PhD, U. So. Calif., 2001. Sr. rsch. fellow, computer sci. computation and neural sys. Calif. Inst. Tech., Pasadena, Calif., 2001—. Contbr. scientific papers articles to profl. jours., including Nature, Proceedings of NAS, PLos Biology. Named a MacArthur Fellow, John D. and Catherine T. MacArthur Found., 2007. Fellow: World Tech. Network (World Tech. award in Biotechnology 2006). Achievements include pioneering work with DNA origami in the field of synthetic biology. Office: Computer Sci Computation and Neural Sys Calif Inst Tech MS 136-93 Moore 216A Pasadena CA 91125 Office Fax: 626-584-0630. Business E-Mail: pwkr@dna.caltech.edu.

ROTHENBERG, ALAN DAVID, lawyer; b. Newark, Nov. 30, 1947; s. John F. and Ruth (Parent) R.; m. Karen Lynn (Jacobson) R.; m. May 17, 1970; children: Scott Michael, Kelli Brooke. BA, Franklin and Marshall Coll., 1970; JD, U. Md., 1975. Bar: D.C. 1976, Md. 1975, U.S. Dist. Ct. Md. 1976. Atty. I.C.C., Washington, 1975-96; pvt. practice Rockville, Md., 1975—. Bd. dirs. U.S. Premier Fed. Credit Union, Washington. Author: Landlord Tenant Handbook, 1974. With U.S. Army N.G., 1970-72. Mem. Md. Bar Assn., Md. Trial Lawyers Assn., Montgomery County Bar Assn. Jewish. Avocations: skiing, tropical fish. Home: 1721 Sunrise Dr Potomac MD 20854-2667 Office: 401 N Washington St Ste 500 Rockville MD 20850-2225 Office Phone: 301-424-7224. E-mail: adrothenberg@hotmail.com.

ROTHENBERG, ALAN I., lawyer, professional sports association executive; b. Detroit, Apr. 10, 1939; m. Georgina Rothenberg; 3 children. BA, U. Mich., 1960, JD, 1963. Bar: Calif. 1964. Assoc. O'Melveny & Myers, LA, 1963—66; ptnr. Manatt Phelps Rothenberg & Phillips, LA, 1968—90, Latham & Watkins, LA, 1990—2000; instr. sports law U. So. Calif., 1969, 1976, 1984, Whittier Coll. Law, 1980, 1984; pres., gen. counsel LA Lakers and LA Kings, 1967—79, LA Clippers Basketball Team, 1982—89; pres. U.S. Soccer Fedn., Chgo., 1990—98; founder, past chmn., trustee Maj. League Soccer, 1993—; chmn. Premier Partnerships, 1st Century Bank, LA, 2002—. Bd. dir. Calif. Pizza Kitchen Inc., 2006—, Arden Realty Inc., Zenith Nat. Corp.; mem. exec. com. CONCACAF. Bd. dirs., pres. Constl. Rights Found., 1987—90; soccer commr. 1984 Olympic Games; chmn., pres., CEO 1994 World Cup Organizing Com., 1990—94. Named to U.S. Nat. Soccer Hall of Fame, 2007. Mem.: NBA (bd. govs. 1971—79, 1982—89), ABA, N.Am. Soccer League (bd. govs. 1977—80, Major League Soccer mgmt. com. 1994—), LA Bar Assn., LA County Bar Assn., State Bar Calif. (pres. 1989—90), Order of Coif. Office: 1st Century Bank Ste 1400 1875 Century Park E Los Angeles CA 90067

ROTHENBERG, ALBERT, psychiatrist, educator; b. NYC, June 2, 1930; s. Gabriel and Rose (Goldberg) R.; m. Julia C. Johnson, June 28, 1970; children: Michael, Mora, Rina. AB, Harvard U., 1952; MD, Tufts U., 1956. Diplomate Am. Bd. Psychiatry and Neurology. Intern Pa. Hosp., Phila., 1956-57; resident in psychiatry Yale U., West Haven (Conn.) VA Hosp., 1957-58, Grace-New Haven Hosp., 1958-59, Yale Psychiat. Inst., New Haven, 1959-60, chief resident, 1960-61; practice medicine specializing in psychiatry New Haven, 1960-61, 1963-75; chief neuropsychiatry Rodriguez U.S. Army Hosp., San Juan, P.R., 1961-63; practice medicine specializing in psychiatry Farmington, Conn., 1975-79, Stockbridge, Mass., 1979-94, Chatham, NY, 1994—2006, Canaan, NY, 2006—, Great Barrington, Mass., 1994-98; dir. rsch. Austen Riggs Center, Stockbridge, Mass., 1979-94. Asst. dir. Yale Psychiat. Inst., 1963-64, sr. staff mem., 1964-83; mem. staff Yale-New Haven Med. Ctr., West Haven VA Hosp., U. Conn. Health Ctr., Farmington; cons., mem. editorial bd. various jours. in psychiatry and psychology; instr. dept. psychiatry Yale U. Sch. Medicine, 1960-61, 63-64, asst. prof., 1964-68, assoc. prof., 1968-74, clin. prof., 1974-84; prof. psychiatry U. Conn. Sch. Medicine, Farmington, 1975-79, dir. residency tng., 1976-78, dir. clin. svcs., 1975-78; prin. investigator Studies in the Creative Process, 1964—; vis. prof. Pa. State U., 1971, adj. prof., 1971-78; vis. prof. dept. Am. studies Yale U., 1974-76, U. Capetown Med. Sch., South Africa, 1999, Saltpêtrière Hosp., Paris, 1999; lectr. dept. psychiatry Harvard U. Med. Sch., 1982-86, clin. prof., 1986—; nominator, Nobel Prize in Medicine, 1990-. Author: (with B. Greenberg) Index of Scientific Writings on Creativity: Creative Men and Women, 1974, Index of Scientific Writings on Creativity: General 1566-1974, 1976; (with C.R. Hausman) The Creativity Question, 1976; The Emerging Goddess: The Creative Process in Art, Science and Other Fields, 1979; The Creative Process of Psychotherapy, 1988; Adolescence: Psychopathology, Normality, and Creativity, 1990; Creativity and Madness: New Findings and Old Stereotypes, 1990, Living Color, 2001; contbr. articles to profl. jours. Researcher on creativity in the arts, sci. and tech. Served with M.C. U.S. Army, 1961-63. Recipient Tufts Med. Alumni award 1956, Rsch. Scientist Career Devel. award NIMH 1964, 69, Golestan Found. award 1991, 92, Kovler award MESAB, 1999; Guggenheim Meml. fellow 1974-75, Ctr. Adv. Study in Behavioral Studies fellow 1986-87, Netherlands Inst. for Adv. Study in Humanities and Social Scis. fellow, 1992-93. Fellow Am. Psychiat. Assn.(disting. life), Am. Coll. Psychoanalysts; mem. AAAS, Mass. Psychiat. Soc., Am. Soc. Aesthetics, Rapaport-Klein Group, Sigma Xi. Democrat. Achievements include research in the creative process, schizophrenia, anorexia nervosa, and psychotherapy. Business E-Mail: albert_rothenberg@hms.harvard.edu.

ROTHENBERG, ELLIOT CALVIN, lawyer, writer; b. Mpls., Nov. 12, 1939; s. Sam S. and Claire Sylvia (Feller) R.; m. Sally Smalying; children: Sarah, Rebecca, Sam. BA summa cum laude, U. Minn., 1961; JD, Harvard U., Cambridge, 1964. Bar: Minn. 1966, U.S. Dist. Ct. Minn. 1966, D.C. 1968, U.S. Supreme Ct. 1972, N.Y. 1974, U.S. Ct. Appeals (2d cir.) 1974, U.S. Ct. Appeals (8th cir.) 1975. Assoc. project dir. Brookings Inst., Washington, 1966-67; fgn. svc. officer, legal advisor U.S. Dept. State, Washington, 1968-73; Am. Embassy, Saigon; U.S. Mission to the UN; nat. law dir. Anti-Defamation League, NYC, 1973-74; legal dir. Minn. Pub. Interest Rsch. Group, Mpls., 1974-77; pvt. practice law Mpls., 1977—. Adj. prof. William Mitchell Coll. Law, St. Paul, 1983—; faculty mem. several nat. comm. law and First Amendment seminars. Author: (with Zelman Cowen) Sir John Latham and Other Papers, 1965, The Taming of the Press: Cohen v. Cowles Media Co., 1999, The Taming of the Press, 1999; co-author: Defending the First, 2005, Whose First Amendment?, 2005, Dark Horse Chronicle; contbr. articles to profl. and scholarly jours. and books, newspapers, popular mags. State bd. dirs. YMCA Youth in Govt. Program, 1981-84; v.p. Twin Cities chpt. Am. Jewish Com., 1980-84; mem. Minn. Ho. of Reps., 1978-82, asst. floor leader (whip), 1981-82; pres., dir. North Star Legal Found., 1983—; legal affairs editor Pub. Rsch. Syndicated, 1986—; briefs and oral arguments published in full Landmark Briefs and Arguments of the Supreme Ct. of the U.S., Vol. 200, 1992; mem. citizens adv. com. Voyageurs Nat. Pk., 1979-81. Recipient Legis. Evaluation Assembly Legis. Excellence award, 1980, Vietnam Civilian Svc. medal U.S. Dept. State, 1970, North Star award U. Minn., 1961; Fulbright fellow, 1964-65. Mem. ABA, Minn. Bar Assn., Harvard Law Sch. Assn., Am. Legion, Mensa, Phi Beta Kappa. Jewish. Personal E-mail: ecrothenberg@gmail.com.

ROTHENBERG, JEROME, writer, literature educator; b. NYC, Dec. 11, 1931; s. Morris and Estelle (Lichtenstein) R.; m. Diane Brodatz, Dec. 25, 1952; 1 son, Matthew. BA, CCNY, 1952; MA, U. Mich., 1953; LittD (hon.), SUNY, Oneonta, 1997. With Mannes Coll. Music, NYC, 1961—70. Vis. prof. U. Calif., San Diego, 1971, 77-84, U. Wis.-Milw., 1974-75, San Diego State U., 1976-77, U. Calif., Riverside, 1980, U. Okla., Norman, 1984; vis. Aerol Arnold prof. English U. So. Calif., 1983; vis. writer in residence SUNY, Albany, 1986, prof. English SUNY, Binghamton, 1986-88; prof. visual arts and lit. U. Calif., San Diego, 1989—, chmn. visual arts, 1990-93; head, creative writing, 1994-95. Poet, freelance writer, 1956—; author: numerous books of poetry and prose including Between, 1967, Technicians of the Sacred, 1968, Poems for the Game of Silence, 1971, Shaking the Pumpkin, 1972, America a Prophecy, 1973, Revolution of the Word, 1974, Poland/1931, 1974, A Big Jewish Book, 1978, A Seneca Journal, 1978, Vienna Blood, 1980, Pre-Faces, 1981, Symposium of the Whole, 1983, That Dada Strain, 1983, New Selected Poems, 1986, Khurbn, 1989, Exiled in the Word, 1989, The Lorca Variations I-VIII, 1990, Apres le jeu de silence, 1991, The Lorca Variations (complete), 1993, Gematria, 1994, An Oracle for Delfi, 1995, Poems for The Millennium, vol. 1, 1995, Seedings, 1996, The Book, Spiritual Instrument, 1996, Poems for the Millennium, Vol. 2, 1998, A Paradise of Poets, 1999, A Book of The Book, 2000, The Case for Memory, 2001, Livre de Temoignage, 2002, A Book of Witness, 2003, María Sabina, 2003, Writing Through: Translations and Variations, 2004, A Book of Concealments, 2004, 25 Caprichos after Goya, 2004, The Burning Babe, 2005, China Notes & The Treasures of Dunhuang, 2006, Triptych, 2007, A Second Book of Concealments, 2007, Les Techniciens du Sacré, 2007, Three Poems after Images by Nancy Tobin, 2007, Homage to Goya, 2008, Poetics and Polemics, 2008, Poems for the Millennium, vol. 3, 2009, Gematria Complete, 2009; editor, pub. Hawk's Well Press., N.Y.C., 1958-65, Some/Thing mag., 1966-69, Alcheringa: Ethnopoetics, 1970-76, New Wilderness Letter, 1976-86. Served with AUS, 1953-55. Recipient award in poetry Longview Found., 1960, Am. Book award, 1982, PEN Ctr. USA West award, 1994, 02, PEN Oakland Josephine Miles award, 1994, 96, Alfonso el Sabio award for translation San Diego State U., 2004, Poetry in Transl. award PEN Am. Ctr., 2004, Lifetime Achievement award San Diego Authors, 2007; Wenner-Gren Found. grantee-in-aide for rsch. in Am. Indian poetry, 1968; Guggenheim fellow in creative writing, 1974; NEA poetry grantee, 1976. Mem. PEN Am. Ctr., New Wilderness Found., World Poetry Acad. Office: care New Directions 80 8th Ave New York NY 10011-5126 Office Phone: 760-436-9923. Personal E-mail: jrothenberg@cox.net. Business E-Mail: jrothenb@ucsd.edu.

ROTHENBERG, KAREN H., law educator, former dean; BA magna cum laude, Princeton U., 1973, MPA, 1974; JD, U. Va., 1979. Faculty mem. U. Md. Sch. Law, 1983—, founding dir. Law & Health Care Prog., 1983—99, Marjorie Cook Prof. Law, interim dean, 1999—2001, dean, 2001—09. Assoc. Covington and Burling, Washington, DC; pres. Am. Soc. Law, Medicine and Ethics; spl. asst. to dir. Office Rsch. on Women's Health, NIH, 1995—96. Co-editor-in-chief Jour. Law, Medicine, and Ethics; co-editor: Women and Prenatal Testing: Facing the Challenges of Genetic Technology; contbr. articles to profl. jours. Recipient Joseph Healey Health Law Tchr.'s award, Am. Soc. Law, Medicine and Ethics, 1996, Md. Leadership in Law Award, 2003; named one of Md. Top Women, Daily Record. Fellow: Md. Bar Found., Am. Bar Found.; mem.: ABA (coordinating group on bioethics and the law), NIH (sect. on prenatal care, recruitment & ret. of women in clin studies, sect. on ethical, legal and social implications of genetics), Am. Law Deans Assn. (bd. dirs.), Nat. Inst. Child & Human Develop. (adv. coun.), Nat. Action Plan Breast Cancer, Ethics in Reproduction (nat. adv. bd.), Inst. Medicine's Com. (sect. legal and ethical issues for inclusion of women in clin. stud.). Office: Univ Md Law Sch Office 244 500 W Baltimore St Baltimore MD 21201-1786 Office Phone: 410-706-2429. Office Fax: 410-706-0407. Business E-Mail: krothenberg@law.umaryland.edu.*

ROTHENBERG, LARAINE S., lawyer; b. Bklyn., Feb. 20, 1947; BA, U. Pa., 1967; JD, Columbia U., 1971. Bar: N.Y. 1972. Atty. Proskauer Rose LLP, 1974—90; ptnr. McDermott, Will & Emery, NYC, 1990—94, Fried Frank Harris Shriver & Jacobson LLP, NYC, 1994—. Contbr. articles to profl. jour. Bd. dir. Wallace Found., Pig Iron Theatre Co.; mem. bd. vis. Columbia Law Sch. Recipient Tax Mmgt. Disting. Author award, 1997, Women of Power and Influence award, NOW-NYC, 2002, DSM, Columbia U. Alumni Fedn., 2003, award for outstanding pro bono svc., Legal Aid Soc., 2005. Mem. N.Y. State Bar Assn. (mem. exec. com. 1981-89, co-chmn. continuing legal edn. 1988-89, problems of the profession 1987-88, chmn. employee benefits com. 1985-86, co-chmn. 1984-85, chmn. exempt orgns. com. 1982-84, mem.-at-large exec. com. 1981-82), Assn. Bar City N.Y. (mem. taxation of corporations com. 1990—, chmn. spl. com. on employee benefits 1987-88, mem. taxation com. 1979-82), Internat. Bar Assn., Internat. Fiscal Assn.; founding mem. Alumnae Columbia Law Sch. Office: Fried Frank Harris Shriver & Jacobson LLP 1 New York Plz New York NY 10004 Business E-Mail: rothela@friedfrank.com.

ROTHENBERG, ROBERT PHILIP, public relations counselor; b. NYC, June 5, 1936; s. Robert Edward and Lillian Babette (Lustig) R. BA, Cornell U., 1956; MS, Boston U., 1958. With publicity dept. Columbia Pictures Corp., NYC, 1959-60; asst. to pres., pub. rels. dir. Harry N. Abrams Pub. Co., NYC, 1960-62; press sec. to gubernatorial candidate William R. Anderson Tenn., 1962; with Rowland Co., NYC, 1963-70, v.p., 1965-67, sr. v.p., 1967-70; ptnr., exec. v.p. Robert Marston and Assocs., NYC, 1970-88, sr. exec. v.p., 1978-88, also bd. dirs.; ptnr., pres. Marston and Rothenberg Pub. Affairs, Inc., NYC and Washington, 1977-88; chmn., pres. Rothenberg Pub. Rels. Comms. Counsel, NYC, 1988—; v.p. Medbook Publs., Inc., 1995—2004; dir. pub. rels. BigChange Networks, LLC, Washington and NYC, 1998—2004. Sr. cons. The Lund Group, Inc. Trustee Mus. of Holography, N.Y.C.; bd. dir. Found. to Save African Endangered Wildlife, World Rehab. Fund, N.Y.C., 1982-98, Amas Musical Theatre, Inc., 2002-03; assoc. Nat. Park Found.; counselor Am. Bus. Cancer Rsch. Found., Southport, Conn.; fellow Met. Mus. Art, 1990—; pres., chmn., bd. trustees St. Bartholomew's Preservation Found., 1992-95; mem. Blue Hill Troupe, Ltd. With USAFR, 1959-65. Mem. Internat. Soc. Poets, Pride and Alarm Soc., Harriman Soc. of ARC, assoc. Media Rsch. Coun., English-Speaking Union, Anchor Soc. Morgan Libr. and Mus., DeWitt Clinton Soc. Mus. of City of NY, Players Club. Unitarian Universalist. Home and Office: 400 E 54th St Apt 29B New York NY 10022-5169

ROTHENBERG, STUART, political scientist, columnist; married; 2 children. BA, Colby Coll.; PhD in Polit. Sci., U. Conn. On-air polit. analyst CNN, 1992—2004; polit. analyst CBS News, 2006; editor, pub. The Rothenberg Polit. Report; columnist Roll Call. Tchr. Bucknell U., Lewisburg, Pa., Cath. U. of America, Washington; guest contbr. Political Wire. Contbr. articles to profl. jours. Office: The Rothenberg Polit Report 50 F St, NW, 7th Fl Washington DC 20001 Office Phone: 202-546-2822. Office Fax: 202-638-2120. E-mail: stu@rothenbergpoliticalreport.com.*

ROTHENBERGER, STEVEN JOHN, biology professor; b. Kans. City, Sept. 14, 1947; s. Milton E. and Kathryn E. Rothenberger; m. Judy Ann Runge, Mar. 27, 1970; 1 child, Jennifer Anne. BS, Kearney State Coll., Nebr., 1970, MS, 1973; PhD, ND State U., Fargo, 1978. Cert. in state tchg. Nebr., 1970. Sci. tchr. Marquette Consol. Schs., Nebr., 1970—74; asst. to full prof. Midland Luth. Coll., Fremont, Nebr., 1978—92; prof., biology U. Nebr., Kearney, 1992—. Editor: (book) A Prairie Mosaic (Book of Yr. award, 2000); contbr. numerous articles to publs. Mem., restoration & edn. Prairie Plains Resource Inst., Aurora, Nebr., 1998—2009; with, svc. orgn. United Campus Ministries, Kearney, 1998—2009; mem., prairie mgmt. bd. Willa Cather Meml. Found., Red Cloud, Nebr., 2007—09. Recipient Profiles Excellence award, U. Nebr., 1998; named to Nebr. Rock-n-Roll Hall of Fame, Nebr. Music Hall of Fame Found., 2000. Fellow: Ctr. Gt. Plains Studies (scholarship com. 2002—); mem.: Soc. Range Mgmt., Ecol. Soc. America, Nebr. Acad. Scis. (pres. 1995—96), Phi Kappa Phi. Office: Dept Biology Bruner Hall 905 W 25th St Kearney NE 68849-1140

ROTHER, JOHN, association executive, lawyer; b. Springfield, Mo., Apr. 18, 1947; s. Charles C. and Eleanor J. (Morrison) R. BA with honors, Oberlin Coll., 1969; JD with honors, U. Pa., 1975. Bar: Pa. 1975, D.C. 1977. Appellate litigator NLRB, Washington, 1975-77; counsel Senator Jacob Javits U.S. Senate labor & human resources commn., Washington, 1977-81; staff dir., chief counsel spl. commn. on aging U.S. Senate, Washington, 1981-84; policy and strategy dir. AARP, Washington, 1984—. Chair Generations United; vice chair Nat. Quality Forum; founding mem. Nat. Acad. Social Ins., Corp. for Nat. Service. Named One of 150 Who Make A Difference, Nat. Jour., Washington, 1986. Mem. D.C. Bar, Gerontol. Soc. Am. Office: AARP 601 E St NW Washington DC 20049-0001 Office Phone: 202-434-3701. E-mail: jrother@aarp.org.

ROTHERHAM, ANDREW J., educational association administrator; s. James A. Rotherham and Barbara M. LaRock, James LaRock (Stepfather) and Beverly Thierwechter (Stepmother); m. Julie Lynne Lusher, July 21, 2001; children: Elizabeth Rose, Susan Shenandoah. BA in Polit. Sci., Va. Tech. U., 1994; MEd., U. Va., 2000. Policy specialist Am. Assn. Sch. Administrs., Arlington, Va., 1996—98; dir. 21st Century Schs. Project Prog. Policy Inst., Washington, 1998—99, dir. edn. policy, 2000—05; spl. asst. to pres. domestic policy The White House, Washington, 1999—2000; co-founder, pub. Edn. Sector, Washington, 2005—. Chmn. bd. Nat. Coun. Tchr. Quality, Washington, 2003—05; bd. mem. Indianapolis Mind Trust, Democrats for Edn. Reform. Contbr. articles to profl. jours., newspapers and mags. Mem. prize review bd., vis. com. Havard Grad. Sch. Ednl., 2009; mem. Va. Bd. Edn., Richmond, Va., 2005—. Named Outstanding Young Alumni, Coll. Arts and Scis. Va. Tech. U., 2005; named one of 40 People Under 40 to Watch, Washingtonian Mag. Democrat. Home: 750 Montei Drive Earlysville VA 22936 Office: Education Sector 1201 Connecticut Ave Ste 850 Washington DC 20036 Office Fax: 202-544-5014. E-mail: arotherham@educationsector.org.

ROTHERT, MARILYN L., dean, nursing educator; b. June 4, 1939; married; 3 children. BSN cum laude, Ohio State U., 1961; MA in Ednl. Psychol., Mich. State U., 1979, PhD in Ednl. Psychol., 1980. RN, Mich. Staff nurse Univ. Hosp., Columbus, Ohio, 1961; instr. sch. nursing Hurley Hosp., Flint, Mich., 1961-66; asst. instr. sch. nursing Mich. State U., East Lansing, 1967-77, grad. asst. dept. community health sci., 1977-80, asst. prof. Coll. Human Medicine, 1980-82, asst. prof., dir. lifelong edn. Coll. Nursing, 1982-84, asst. prof. Coll. Human Medicine, 1982-84, assoc. prof., dir. lifelong edn. Coll. Nursing, 1984-88, assoc. prof. Coll. Human Medicine, 1984-86, prof., dir. lifelong edn. Coll. Nursing, 1988-92, prof., assoc. dean outreach and profl. devel., 1992-96, prof., dean Coll. Nursing, 1996—. Cons. No. Ill. U., Ohio State U., Mich. State Dept. Natural Resources, Can. Nurses Assn., Mich. Judicial Inst., Med. Coll. Va., U. Wash., Kirtland Coll., Anderson Coll. Contbr. articles to profl. jours. Co-chmn. Capitol Health Event, 1987-88; mem. worksite health subcom. Mich. Dept. Pub. Health; mem. State 4-H Health Com. Coop. Extension Svc., 1972-75, 82—; mem. med. adv. com. Mich. Civil Svc. Health Screening Unit, 1984. Mem. ANA (mem. coun. continuing edn., nurse researchers), Mich. Nurses Assn. (chmn. continuing edn. adv. com. 1989), Soc. for Med. Decision Making, The Brunswik Soc., Soc. for Judgment and Decision Making, Soc. for Rsch. in Nursing Edn., Midwest Nursing Rsch. Soc., Am. Pub. Health Assn., Nat. Ctr. for Health Edn., Nat. League for Nursing, Mich. State U. Faculty/Profl. Women's Assn. (bd. dirs. 1989—), Capitol Area Dist. Nurses Assn. (mem. nom. com. 1984-86, continuing edn. com. 1984), Phi Kappa Phi. Office: Mich State U Coll Nursing A-230 Life Sci Bldg East Lansing MI 48824

ROTHFELD, MICHAEL B., theatrical producer, investor; b. NYC, May 19, 1947; m. Ella M. Foshay, May 22, 1970; 2 children. BA, Columbia U., 1969, MS, MBA, Columbia U., 1971, cert. internatl fellows program, 1971. With Time, Inc., 1971-76, assoc. editor Fortune NYC, 1971-74; asst. to chmn. bd. dirs., CEO Time Inc., NYC, 1974-76; with Salomon Bros., NYC, 1976-83, v.p., 1979-83, The First Boston Corp., NYC, 1983-84, mng. dir., 1985-89; gen. ptnr. Bessemer Ptnrs. and Bessemer Holdings, 1989-97, ltd. ptnr., 1997-98. Chmn. bd. dirs. Graphic Controls Corp., 1995-98; bd. vis. Columbia Coll., 1998—, vice chmn. 2002-05, chair, 2005—, bd. adv. Knight-Bagheot program in fin. journalism Grad. Sch. Journalism, 1998—, trustee, 2005—; chmn. Redfields, LLC, Eagle Prodns., LLC, N.Y.C. Prodr. Gore Vidal's The Best Man, 2000 (winner Drama Desk award, Outer Critics Circle award, Tony nomination). Office: Eagle Productions LLC 200 E 69th St New York NY 10021

ROTHFIELD, LAWRENCE I., microbiology educator; b. NYC, Dec. 30, 1927; s. Joseph and Henrietta (Brown) R.; m. Naomi Fox, Sept. 18, 1953; children: Susan Anne, Lawrence, Jane, John. BA, Cornell U., 1947; MD, NYU, 1951. Intern, then resident Bellevue, Presbyn. hosps., NYC, 1951-53, 55-57; successively instr., clin. asst. prof., asst. prof. NYU Sch. Medicine, 1957-64; from asst. prof. to assoc. prof. Albert Einstein Coll. Medicine, NYC, 1964-68; prof. U. Conn. Sch. Medicine, Farmington, 1968—, chmn. dept. microbiology, 1968-80. Mem. molecular biology rev. panel NIH, 1970-75, microbiology and immunology adv. com. Pres.'s Biomed. Rsch. Panel, 1975, molecular biology rev. panel NSF, 1979-83; mem. microbial physiology and genetics rev. panel NIH, 1990-94, chairperson, 1991-93. Author: Structure and Function of Biological Membranes, 1972; mem. editorial bd. Jour. Membrane Biology, 1969-83, Jour. Biol. Chemistry, 1974-80. With M.C. U.S. Army, 1953-55. Mem. Am. Soc. Biol. Chemists, Am. Soc. Microbiology (chmn. microbial physiology div. 1975). Home: 540 Deercliff Rd Avon CT 06001-2859 Office: U Conn Health Center Farmington CT 06032 Office Phone: 860-679-3581. Business E-Mail: lroth@neuron.uchc.edu.

ROTHFIELD, NAOMI FOX, physician; b. Bklyn., Apr. 5, 1929; d. Morris and Violet (Bloomgarden) Fox; m. Lawrence Rothfield, Sept. 18, 1954; children: Susan, Lawrence, John, Jane. BA, Bard Coll., 1950; MD, NYU, 1955. Intern Lenox Hill Hosp., NYC, 1955-56; instr. NYU Sch. Medicine, 1956-62, asst. prof., 1962-68; assoc. prof. U. Conn. Sch. Medicine, Farmington, 1968-72, prof., 1972—, chief divsn. rheumatic diseases, 1972—99. Contbr. chpts. to books, articles to med. jours. Bd. dirs. Conn. Choral Artists, 1999—. Mem. Am. Soc. Clin. Investigation, Am. Rheumatism Assn., Assn. Am. Physics. Jewish. Home: 540 Deercliff Rd Avon CT 06001-2859 Office: U Conn Sch Medicine Divsn Rheumatic Diseases Farmington CT 06030-0001 Home Phone: 860-677-4781; Office Phone: 860-679-3604. E-mail: rothfield@nso.uchc.edu.

ROTHKOPF, ARTHUR J., business association executive; b. NYC, May 24, 1935; s. Abraham and Sarah (Mehlman) Rothkopf; m. Barbara Sarnoff, Dec. 25, 1958; children: Jennifer, Katherine. AB, Lafayette Coll., 1955; JD, Harvard U., 1958. Bar: N.Y. 1959, D.C. 1967. Atty. U.S. Dept. Treasury, NYC, 1958—60, SEC, Washington, 1960—63; assoc. tax legis. counsel U.S. Dept. Treasury, Washington, 1963—66; ptnr. Hogan & Hartson, Washington, 1967—91; gen. counsel U.S. Dept. Transp., Washington, 1991—92, dep. sec., 1992—93; pres. Lafayette Coll., Easton, Pa., 1993—2005, pres. emeritus, 2005—; sr. v.p. U.S. C. of C., 2005—. Bd. dirs. Ins. Svcs. Office, Inc., Jersey City; mem. Sec. of Edn.'s Commn. on Future of Higher Edn., 2005. Trustee Fed. City Coun., Washington, 1983—91, The Am. U.; past chair bd. dirs. Coun. Higher Edn. Accreditation; bd. dirs., past chmn. Assn. Ind. Colls. and Univs. Pa.; trustee Ednl. Testing Svc. Mem.: The Pa. Soc. (pres.), Univ. Club (N.Y.C.), Harvard Club of NYC, Chevy Chase Club, Met. Club of Washington. Jewish. Office: 1615 H St NW Washington DC 20062 Home Phone: 202-667-1373; Office Phone: 202-463-5359. Business E-Mail: ajrothkopf@uschamber.com.

ROTHKOPF, DAVID JOCHANAN, consulting firm executive, former federal agency administrator; b. Urbana, Ill., Dec. 24, 1955; s. Ernst Zacharias and Carol Louise (Zeman) R.; m. Jane Octavia Prelinger, Dec. 14, 1985; children: Joanna Susan, Laura Madeleine. BA, Columbia U., 1977, postgrad., 1977-78. Press sec. to Congressman Stephen J. Solarz US Congress, Washington, 1979-80; sr. v.p. Tilley, Marlieb & Alan, Inc., NYC, 1980-82; coord. prodr. TV Series-Omni: The New Frontier, NYC, 1980-82; exec. prodr. PBS Series-Flashpoint, Newark, 1984; v.p. Fin. World Mag., NYC, 1984-85; v.p., pub. spl. pubs. Instnl. Investor, Inc., NYC, 1985-87; chmn., CEO Internat. Media Ptnrs., Inc., NYC, 1987-93; dep. under sec. for internat. trade policy devel. US Dept. Commerce, Washington, 1993-95, acting under sec. for internat. trade, 1995-96; mng. dir. Kissinger Associates, Inc., NYC and Washington, 1996—98; founder, chmn., CEO Intellibridge, 1998—2005; chmn., CEO The Rothkopf Group, LLC, 2003—; chmn. Nat. Strategic Investment Dialogue, 2004—; co-founder, pres., CEO Garten Rothkopf, Washington, 2005—. Adj. prof. internat. affairs Columbia U. Sch. of Internat. and Pub. Affairs, 1996—; vis. scholar Carnegie Endowment for Internat. Peace, 1996—; CEO, chmn., The CEO Insts., N.Y.C., 1987-93; mem. adv. bd. US Inst. Peace, Johns Hopkins/Bloomberg Sch. Pub. Health Author: The Common Market: Uniting the European Community, 1978, Running the World: The Inside Story of the National Security Council and the Architects of American Power, 2005, Superclass: The Global Power Elite and the World They Are Making, 2008; editor Global Money Mgmt. Forum, 1986-87, Global Capital Markets Forum, 1986-87; editor-in-chief CEO/Internat. Strategies Mag., 1989-93, Emerging Markets Newspapers, 1987-93, World Market Outlook, 1991-93, Nat. Conv. News, 1992; co-editor: The Price of Peace: Emergency Economic Intervention and U.S. Foreign Policy, 1998, Cuba: The Contors of Change, 2000; prin. editor The Big Emerging Markets, 1996 Mem. Coun. Fgn. Rels., Columbia Club. Democrat. Jewish. Office: Garten Rothkopf 1330 Connecticut Ave NW Ste 500 Washington DC 20036 E-mail: david.rothkopf@gardenrothkopf.com.*

ROTHMAN, DAVID J., historian, educator; b. NYC, Apr. 30, 1937; s. Murray and Anne (Beier) R.; m. Sheila Miller, June 26, 1960; children: Matthew, Micol. BA, Columbia U., 1958; MA, Harvard U., 1959, PhD, 1964. Asst. prof. history Columbia U., NYC, 1964-67, assoc. prof., 1967-71, prof., 1971—, Bernard Schoenberg prof. social medicine, dir. Ctr. for Study of Society and Medicine. Fulbright-Hayes prof. Hebrew U., Jerusalem, 1968-69, India, 1982; vis. Pinkerton Prof. Sch. Criminal Justice, State U. N.Y., at Albany, 1973-74; Samuel Paley lectr. Hebrew U., Jerusalem, 1977; Mem. Com. for Study of Incarceration, 1971-74; co-dir. Project on Community Alternatives, 1978-82; chmn. adv. bd. on criminal justice Clark Found., 1978-82; mem. bd. advisors The Project on Death in Am., Open Soc. Inst., 1995-2000, trustee; mem. bd. trustees Open Soc. Inst., 1996—2008, pres. Inst. on Medicine as a Profession, 2003—. Author: Politics and Power, 1966, The Discovery of the Asylum, 1971; co-author: Doing Good, 1978, Conscience and Convenience: The Asylum and its Alternatives in Progressive America, 1980; (with Sheila M. Rothman) The Willowbrook Wars, 1984; Strangers at the Bedside, 1991, Beginings Count: The Technological Imperative in American Health Care, 1997; editor: The World of the Adams Chronicles, 1976, (with Sheila M. Rothman) On Their Own: The Poor in Modern America, 1972, The Sources of American Social Tradition, 1975, (with Stanton Wheeler) Social History and Social Policy, 1981, (with Norval Morris) The Oxford History of the Prison, 1995, (with Steven Marcus and Stephanie Kiceluk) Medicine and Western Civilization, 1995, (with Sheila M. Rothman) The Pursuit of Perfection, 2003, (with Sheila M. Rothman) Trust is Not Enough. Recipient Albert J. Beveridge prize Am. Hist. Assn., 1971. Mem. Am. Hist. Assn., N.Y. Acad. Medicine, Phi Beta Kappa. Office: Columbia U Coll Physicians and Surgeons Ctr Study Soc and Medicine 630 W 168th St New York NY 10032-3702

ROTHMAN, ELLIOTT, Mayor, Pomona, California; m. Pam Rothman; 1 child, Jason. Grad., U. La Verne. Councilman City of Pomona from Dist. 5, 1996—2008; mayor City of Pomona, 2008—. Rep. San Gabriel Valley Mosquito & Vector Control. Vol. Cat in the Hat Read Across America Program, Pomona Unified Sch. Dist. Reading Ranger Program, Boys & Girls Scouts America. Mailing: PO Box 660 Pomona CA 91769 Office: City Hall 505 South Garey Ave 2nd Fl Pomona CA 91766 Office Phone: 909-620-2376. Office Fax: 909-620-3707.*

ROTHMAN, ESTHER POMERANZ, social agency executive, psychologist; b. NYC, Nov. 25, 1919; d. Max and Anne (Reiner) Pomeranz; m. Arthur M. Rothman, Apr. 13, 1946; 1 dau., Amy. BA, Hunter Coll., 1942; MA, Columbia U., NYC, 1944; MA, CCNY, 1946; PhD, NYU, 1958. Cert. psychologist, NY Tchr., NYC Bd. Edn., 1944-57, prin., 1957-80; exec. dir. Glie Youth Program, NYC, 1980-85; exec. dir. Correctional Edn. Consortium, 1985—91; pres. Correctional Edn. Consortium, 1991—; research psychologist Tchrs. Hot Line, NYC, 1972-74. Author: Angel Inside Went Sour, 1972; Troubled Teachers, 1974; co-author: Disturbed Child, 1967. Mem. Citizens Com. for Children, NYC, 1972—. Recipient Valley Forge Freedom award, 1976; named to Hall of Fame Hunter Coll., 1972. Fellow Am. Assn. Orthopsychiatry (sec. 1976-79); mem. Am. Psychol. Assn. Home and Office: 200 E 16th St New York NY 10003-3707 Office: Correctional Edn Consortium 500 8 Ave New York NY 10018 Office Phone: 212-674-1973. Personal E-mail: esther.art@verizon.net.

ROTHMAN, HENRY ISAAC, lawyer; b. Rochester, NY, Mar. 29, 1943; s. Maurice M. and Golde (Nusbaum) R.; m. Golda R. Shatz, July 3, 1966; children: Alan, Miriam, Cheryl, Suri. BA, Yeshiva U., 1964; JD, Cornell U., 1967. Bar: NY 1967. Trial atty. SEC, NYC, 1967-69; ptnr. Booth, Lipton & Lipton, NYC, 1969-87, Parker, Chapin, Flattau & Klimpl, NYC, 1987-2000, Jenkens & Gilchrist Parker Chapin LLP, NYC, 2001—05, Troutman Sanders LLP, NYC, 2005—. Bd. dir. Camp Morasha, Lake Como, Pa., 1982-06, vice chmn., 1992-00; bd. dir. Assn. Jewish Sponsored Camps, Inc., 1986-00; bd. dir. Yeshiva U. High Schs., NYC, 1984-99, vice chmn. bd., 1990-91, chmn. bd., 1992-95; v.p. Manhattan Day Sch., NYC, 1985-96, bd. dir.; assoc. v.p. Orthodox Union, NYC, 1990-00, v.p., 2001-06, sr. v.p., 2006-; vice chmn. bd. dir. Azrieli Grad. Sch. Jewish Edn. and Adminstrn., 2000—. Mem.: ABA (com. on fed. regulation of securities), Yeshiva U. Alumni Assn. (pres. 1986—88, hon. pres. 1988—90). Office: Troutman Sanders LLP The Chrysler Bldg 405 Lexington Ave New York NY 10174-0002 Office Phone: 212-704-6000. Business E-Mail: henry.rothman@troutmansanders.com.

ROTHMAN, HOWARD JOEL, lawyer; b. NYC, July 10, 1945; BA, CCNY, 1967; JD, Bklyn. Law Sch., 1971; LLM, NYU, 1972. Bar: N.Y. 1972. From assoc. to ptnr. Marshall, Bratter, Greene, Allison & Tucker, NYC, 1972—82; ptnr. Rosenman & Colin LLP, NYC, 1982—97, Kramer, Levin, Naftalis & Frankel LLP, NYC, 1997—. Mem. adv. panel Commr. Fin. of City of N.Y., 1981-83. Author profl. books and articles. Mem. ABA (corp. tax. com. 1977-87, income from real property com. 1980—), Internat. Bar Assn., NY State Bar Assn. (exec. com. tax sect. 1999-2000, corp. tax com. 1979-, partnerships com. 1979—, NYC tax matters com. 1977—, income from real property com. 1987—), Bur. Nat. Affairs (real estate jour. 1984—, tax mgmt. adv. bd. 1979—), Alliance for Young Artists and Writers (bd. dirs.), Poetry Soc. Am. (bd. dirs.), NY Found. for Arts (bd. dirs.).

ROTHMAN, JAMES EDWARD, cell biologist, educator; b. Haverhill, Mass., Nov. 3, 1950; BA summa cum laude, Yale U., 1971; PhD in Biochemistry, Harvard U., 1976; D h.c., U. Regensburg, 1995, U. Geneva, 1997. Fellow MIT, Cambridge, 1976-78; asst. prof., dept. biochemistry Stanford U., Calif., 1978—81, assoc. prof., 1981—84, prof., 1984—88; E.R. Squibb prof. molecular biology Princeton U., NJ, 1988—91; Paul Marks chair Sloan-Kettering Inst., NYC, 1991—2003, chmn. program in cellular biochemistry and biophysics, 1991—2003, vice chmn., 1994—2003; prof. Dept. Physiology and Biophysics, dir. Genome Ctr. Coll. Physicians and Surgeons, Columbia U., NYC, 2003—08, Clyde and Helen Wu prof. chem. biology; chair Dept. Cell Biology, head Ctr. High-Throughput Cell Biology Yale U. Sch. Medicine, New Haven, 2008—. Editl. bd. Molecular and Cellulat Biology, 1982—84; chmn. Gordon Conf. on Molecular Membrane Biology, 1983; bd. editors Science, 1984—89; editl. com. Ann. Review Biochemistry, 1985—90, assoc. editor, 2003; editl. bd. Cell, 1984—94; study sect., Molecular Cytology NIH, 1990—94, coun., Nat. Inst. Digestive and Kidney Diseases, 1997—99; Devel. Therapeutics Review Group Nat. Cancer Inst., 1997—98; bd. sr. editors Jour. Clin. Investigation, 2002—. Recipient Eli Lily award for Fundamental Rsch. in Biol. Chemistry, 1986, Passano Young Scientist award, 1986, Alexander Von Humboldt award, 1989, Heinrich Wieland prize, 1990, Rosenstiel award in Biomedical Sciences, 1994, V.D. Mattia award, 1994, Fritz Lipmann award, 1995, Mayor's award for Excellence in Sci. and Tech., 1995, Gairdner Found. Internat. award, 1996, King Faisal Internat. prize in Sci., 1996, Harden medal, 1997, Feodor Lynen award, 1997, Jacobaeus prize, 1999, Heineken prize, 2000, Otto-Warburg medal, 2001, Albert Lasker award for Basic Medical Rsch., Lasker Found., 2002, Louisa Gross Horwitz prize of Columbia U., 2002; Fellow Andrew W. Mellon, 1979-1982; scholar Dreyfus Found. Teacher, 1981-86; commd. as a Kentucky Col., by Gov. State of Kentucky, 1997. Fellow: Am. Acad. of Arts and Sciences, NAS (Richard Lounsbery award 1997); mem.: European Molecular Biology Orgn. (foreign assoc. 1995), Inst. Medicine, NAS. Office: Yale U Cell Biology PO Box 208002 New Haven CT 06520-8002 E-mail: james.rothman@yale.edu.*

ROTHMAN, KENNETH JAY, epidemiologist; b. NYC, Nov. 2, 1945; s. Stephen and Lorraine (Lerner) R.; m. Diane Feinburg, June 1968 (div. July 1978); children: Emily, Margaret; m. Nancy Ann Dreyer, Aug. 30, 1980; 1 child, Samantha. AB in Phys. Sci., Colgate U., 1966; DMD, Harvard U., 1969, MPH, 1970, DrPH, 1972. Asst. prof. Harvard Sch. Pub. Health, Boston, 1972-75, assoc. prof., 1975-84; rsch. assoc. in cardiology Children's Hosp., Boston, 1973-85; cons. in epidemiology Mass. Gen. Hosp., Boston, 1975-85; sr. scientist Epidemiology Resources Inc., Newton, Mass., 1980—; prof. U. Mass. Med. Sch., Worcester, 1984-89; prof. pub. health Boston U. Sch. Medicine and Pub. Health, 1989—. Vis. epidemiologist Nat. Cancer Inst., Bethesda, Md., 1976-77. Author: Epidemiologic Analysis With a Programmable Calculator, 1980, Modern Epidemiology, 1986; editor: Causal Inference, 1988; editor Epidemiology, Newton, 1989—; editl. bd. New England Jour. Medicine, 1978-89. Recipient Adolph G. Kammer award Am. Occupational Med. Assn., 1983, Hist. Paper award Am. Jour. Epidemiology, 1995. Mem. Internat. Soc. Environ. Epidemiology, Internat. Epidemiol. Assn., Soc. Epidemiologic Rsch. (pres. 1984-85, Cassell lectr. 1995), Coun. Biology Editors, Am. Pub. Health Assn. (sect. coun. 1979-84), The Biometric Soc. Avocations: hiking, road racing, orienteering, sailing, backgammon.

ROTHMAN, LAURENCE SIDNEY, physicist; b. NYC, Jan. 20, 1940; s. Jules A. and May Lucy (Winston) R. BS, MIT, 1961; AM, Boston U., 1964, PhD, 1971. Rsch. physicist Block Assocs., Inc., Cambridge, Mass., 1961-64; teaching fellow Boston U., 1964-68; physicist Geophysics Lab. (Air Force), Bedford, Mass., 1968—; staff scientist Harvard-Smithsonian Ctr. for Astrophysics, Cambridge, Mass., 1995—. Co-chmn. working group Internat. Radiation Commn., 1990—; panel mem. Spectroscopy for NASA Satellites, 1986; panel mem. chlorofluorocarbon program Nat. Bur. Standards, Gaithersburg, Md., 1983; invited prof. U. Paris, 1985, 87, 90, 93, 95. Editor Procs. SPIE Critical Rev., 1988; co-author: Geophysics Handbook, 1985, Atmospheric Ozone, 1985; assoc. editor Jour. Quantitative Spectroscopy and Radiative Transfer; contbr. articles to profl. jours. Recipient AF Gunter Loeser award, 1996. Fellow Optical Soc. Am.; mem. Internat. Radiation Com. (officer), Soc. PhotoOptical Inst. Engring., Boston Computer Soc., Sigma Xi (local pres. 1985, 97). Avocations: tennis, music, travel, personal computers, gastronomy. Office: PL/GPOS 29 Randolph Rd Hanscom AFB MA 01731-3000

ROTHMAN, MICOL SARA, medical educator; b. NYC, Feb. 25, 1972; d. David J and Sheila M Rothman; m. Salim Haji, Aug. 13, 1971; children: Sierra Rothman-Haji, Anna Rothman-Haji. BA, Brown U., Providence RI, 1989—93; MD, Columbia Coll. of Physicians and Surgeons, New York, 1994—99. License CO, 2002, Endocrinology CO, 2005. Asst. prof. U. of CO-Denver, Aurora, Colo., 2005—. Office: University of Colorado Hospital Aurora CO 80045

ROTHMAN, PAUL A., publishing executive; b. Bklyn., June 26, 1940; s. Fred B. and Dorothy (Regosin) R.; m. Mary Ann Dalson, July 28, 1966 (div. 1992); m. Carol Ann Liske, Sept. 17, 1999; children: Deborah, Diana. BA, Swarthmore Coll., 1962; JD, U. Mich., 1965; LLM in Taxation, NYU, 1967. Bar: NY 1965. Assoc. Dewey, Ballentine, Busby, Palmer & Wood, NYC, 1965-67; v.p. Fred B. Rothman & Co., Littleton, Colo., 1967-85, pres., 1985-2000; chmn. bd. Colo. Plasticard, Littleton, 1983-95; owner LoDo Law Books, Denver, 1998—. Editor: Mich. Law Rev., 1963—65. Home: 1801 Wynkoop St Apt 708 Denver CO 80202-1196 Office: LoDo Law Books 1701 Wynkoop St Union Sta # 300 Denver CO 80202 Office Phone: 720-904-5145. E-mail: parothman@yahoo.com.

ROTHMAN, PAUL B., dean, medical educator; MD, Yale U., 1984. Resident Columbia-Presbyn. Med. Ctr., NYC; Richard J. Stock prof. immunology and microbiology, chief pulmonary allergy and critical care medicine divsn. Columbia U. Coll. Physicians and Surgeons, NYC, 1997; head, prof. internal medicine Roy J. and Lucille A. Carver Coll. Medicine, U. Iowa, 2004—08, dean, 2008—. Mem. Immunologic Scis. Study Sect., NIH, Israel Cancer Rsch. Fund Internat. Sci. Adv. Bd., Am. Acad. Allergy, Asthma and Immunology Grant Review Com., Am. Thoracic Soc. Asthma Immunology and Inflammation Program Com. Contbr. articles to profl. jours. Recipient James S. McDonnell Found. Career Devel. Award, Pfizer Scholars Award, Pew Scholars Award, Leukemia Soc. of America Scholar Award, Pharmacia Allergy Rsch. Found. Internat. Award. Fellow: Am. Coll. Physicians; mem.: Assn. Am. Physicians, Collegium Internationale Allergologicum, Am. Soc. for Clin. Investigation, Coun. of Assn. of Am. Physicians, Assn. Profs. of Medicine. Office: U Iowa Carver Coll Medicine 212 CMAB Iowa City IA 52242-2600 Office Phone: 319-384-4547. E-mail: paul-rothman@uiowa.edu.*

ROTHMAN, STEVEN R., United States Representative from New Jersey; b. Englewood, NJ, Oct. 14, 1952; 2 children. BA in Polit. Philos., Syracuse U., NY, 1974; JD, Washington U. Sch. Law, St. Louis, 1977. Bar: NJ 1977, NY 1984. Atty. Miller, Hochman, Meyerson and Schaeffer, Esquires, 1978—80, Steven R. Rothman, Esquire, Englewood, NJ, 1980—93; mayor Englewood, NJ, 1983—89; judge Bergen County Surrogate Ct., NJ, 1993-96; mem. US Congress from 9th NJ dist., 1997—, mem. appropriations, sci. & tech. and programs com. Gen. counsel NJ Young Dems., 1981—82; treas. Bergen County Dem. Party, 1982; bd. dirs. Palisades Jewish Cmty. Ctr., 1990—92, United Jewish Cmty. of Bergen/North Hudson. Recipient David Bodian Meml. award, Internat. Post-Polio Task Force, 2002, Human award, Am. Jewish Com.; named Legislator of Yr., Am. Humane Assn., 2000, Nat. Orgn. Insure Sound-Controlled Environ., 2001. Mem.: ABA, NJ Trial Lawyers Assn., Assn. Trial Lawyers Am., Bergen County Bar Assn., NJ Bar Assn. Democrat. Jewish. Office: US House Reps 2303 Rayburn House Office Bldg Washington DC 20515 Office Phone: 202-225-5061. Office Fax: 202-225-5851.*

ROTHMAN, TOM (THOMAS EDGAR ROTHMAN), film company executive; b. Balt., Nov. 21, 1954; s. Donald and Elizabeth (Davidson) R.; m. Jessica Randolph Harper, Mar. 11, 1989; children: Elizabeth, Nora. BA, Brown U., 1976; JD, Columbia U., 1980. Ptnr. Frankfurt, Garbus, Klein, NYC, 1982-87; exec. v.p. prodn. Columbia Pictures, Burbank, Calif., 1987-89; sr. v.p. prodn. Samuel Goldwyn Co., LA, 1989-91, pres. worldwide prodn., 1991—94; founder, pres. Fox Searchlight Pictures, 1994; pres. Twentieth Century Fox, Beverly Hills, 1995—99, Twentieth Century Fox Film Group, 1999—2000; co-chmn. Fox Filmed Entertainment, Inc., L.A., 2000—. Exec. prodr.: (films) The Program, 1993; co-prodr.: Down By Law, 1986. Trustee Sundance (Utah) Inst. Recipient Arthur B. Krim award, Columbia U.; named one of The 50 Most Powerful People in Hollywood, Premiere mag., 2004—06, The 50 Smartest People in Hollywood, Entertainment Weekly, 2007. Office: Fox Filmed Entertainment Inc 10201 W Pico Blvd Los Angeles CA 90035*

ROTHMEIER, STEVEN GEORGE, investment company executive; b. Mankato, Minn., Oct. 4, 1946; s. Edwin George and Alice Joan (Johnson) R. BBA, U. Notre Dame, 1968; MBA, U. Chgo., 1972. Corp. fin. analyst Northwest Airlines, Inc., St. Paul, 1973, mgr. econ. analysis, 1973-78, dir. econ. planning, 1978, v.p. fin., treas., 1978-82, exec. v.p., treas., dir., 1982-83, exec. v.p. fin. and adminstrn., treas., dir., 1983, pres., chief operating officer, 1984, pres., chief exec. officer, 1985-86, chmn., chief exec. officer, 1986-89, also bd. dirs.; pres. IAI Capital Group, Mpls., 1989-93; chmn., CEO Great No. Capital, St. Paul, 1993—. Bd. dirs. Arvin Meriter Inc., Precision Castparts, Waste Mgmt., Inc. Chmn. St. Agnes Found. Decorated Bronze Star. Mem. Mpls. Club, Chgo. Club. Republican. Roman Catholic. Office: Great Northern Capital 332 Minnesota St Ste W2900 Saint Paul MN 55101-1377 *Success is not an accident; it is a habit. Success is the result of desire, dedication, sacrifice, mental toughness, hard work— and prayer. And you are not successful until you can share your success with others.*

ROTHROCK, JOHN G., legislative staff member; Former USN recruiting liaison officer; chief of staff to congressman Gary Miller US House of Reps., Washington, 2000—. Recipient Navy & Marine Corps Achievement medal, 2001. Mem.: Reserve Officers Assn. Republican. Mailing: US House Reps 2349 Rayburn House Office Bldg Washington DC 20515 Office Phone: 202-225-3201. Office Fax: 202-225-6962. Business E-Mail: john.rithrock@mail.house.gov.*

ROTHROCK, LINDSEY NICHOLE, lawyer; b. Richmond, Ind., Nov. 19, 1978; d. Dale Ray Croley and Robin Lynn Lotich, Scott D. Lotich (Stepfather); m. Michael David Rothrock, July 16, 2005. BA in Psychology (hon.), Ind. U., Bloomington, 2001; JD, DePaul U. Coll. Law, Chgo., 2004. Law clk. Goldstein, Fishman, Bender & Romanoff, Chgo., 2002—04; atty. Burns, Figa & Will, PC, Greenwood Village, Colo., 2004—08, Moye White LLP, Denver, 2008—. Sr. law student DePaul Tech., Intellectual Property Clinic, Chgo., 2003—04; legal writing and analysis tchr. asst. DePaul U. Coll. Law, 2002—03. Project site mgr. Chgo. Cares, 2002—03; vol. judge U. Denver Sturm Coll. Law, 2005—; vol. coach Colo. HS Mock Trial Program, 2006—, Grad. Colo. Bus. Com. Arts., 2008—09, Leadership Arts Program. Recipient Ctr. for Computer-Assisted Legal Instrn. Legal Writing and Analysis award, DePaul U. Coll. Law, 2002. Mem.: ABA, Moot Court Soc., Denver Bar Assn., Colo. Bar Assn., Blue Key Hon. Frat., Golden Key Nat. Honor Soc., Nat. Honors Soc., Alpha Lambda Delta, Phi Eta Sigma, Order of Omega Greek Honor Frat. (life), Phi Beta Kappa (life), Alpha Xi Delta (life; pres. 1999—99). Office: Moye White LLP 1400 16th St 6th Fl Denver CO 80202 Office Phone: 303-292-2900. Business E-Mail: lindsey.rothrock@moyewhite.com.

ROTH ROGERS, SHERYL LYNN, marketing professional; b. Mpls, Aug. 20, 1955; d. Delbert Nicholas Roth and Esther Arlene (Wescoat) Olson; m. George J.R. Rogers Jr., Aug. 5, 1953; children: Jessica, Brianna. AB, Smith Coll., Northampton, Mass., 1977; MBA, Columbia U., 1979. Cons. Continental Group, NYC, 1978-79; mktg. mgmt. Gen. Mills, Mpls., 1979-86, Ragu Foods co., Trumbull, Conn., 1986--. Dir. Gold Medal Credit Union, Golden Valley 1984-85. Dir. Minn. Women's Network, 1983-86, participant Leadership Mpls., 1983-84. Mem. Columbia U. ALumni Fairfield (v.p., membership chmn.), Smith Coll. Club of Greenwich Stamford. Lutheran. Avocations: exercise, reading, real estate investments, learning new things. Office: Destinatin Maternity Corp 456 N 5th St Philadelphia PA 19123

ROTHSCHILD, AMALIE RANDOLPH, filmmaker, producer, director, photographer; b. Balt., June 3, 1945; d. Randolph Schamberg and Amalie Getta (Rosenfeld) R. BFA, R.I. Sch. Design, 1967; MFA in Motion Picture Prodn., NYU, 1969. Spl. effects staff in film and photography Joshua Light Show, Fillmore E. Theatre, NYC, 1969-71; artist-photographer Staley-Wise Gallery, NYC, 2004—, David Gallery, LA, 2007—. Still photographer TWA Airlines Pub. Rels. Dept., Village Voice newspaper, Rolling Stone mag., Newsweek mag., After Dark, N.Y. Daily News, others, 1968-72; co-founder, ptnr. New Day Films, distbn. coop., 1971—; owner operator Anomaly Films Co., N.Y.C., 1971—; mem., co-founder Assn. Ind. Video and Filmmakers, Inc., N.Y.C., 1974; bd. dirs., 1974-78; instr. in film and TV, NYU Inst. of Film and TV, 1976-78; cons. in field to various organizations including Youthgrant Program of Nat. Endowment for Humanities, Washington, 1973-76. Exhibitions include Soho Triad Fine Arts Gallery, 1997, 2000, 02, Gomez Gallery, 1998, 2000, VH-1 Mus. First Gallery, 1999, Govinda Gallery, 2001, Snap Galleries, Birmingham, Eng., 2005, SACI, Florence, Italy, 2005, 09, Tate Gallery, Liverpool, England, 2005, Holden Luntz Gallery, 2005, Redferns Music Picture Gallery, London, 2006, Tremaine Gallery, Conn., 2007, Staley Wise Gallery, NYC, 2007, Whitney Mus., NYC, 2007, Musee d'Arte Contemporaneo, Bologna, Italy, 2007, David Gallery, LA, 2007, Arts Co. Gallery, Nashville 2007, Michele Mosko Fine Art, Denver, 2009, Bonni Benrubi Gallery, NYC, 2009, Musée de la Musique, Paris, 2009, 9ft. high murals Allman Brothers Band Mus., Macon, Ga., 2009; (film): Woo Who? May Wilson, 1969, It Happens to Us, 1972, Nana, Mom and Me, 1974, Radioimmunoassay of Renin, Radioimmunoassay of Aldosterone, 1973, Conversations with Willard Van Dyke, 1981, Richard Haas: Work in Progress, 1984, Painting the Town: The Illusionistic Murals of Richard Haas, 1990 (Emily award Am. Film and Video Festival 1990); editor: Doing It Yourself, Handbook on Independent Film Distribution, 1977; author: Live at the Fillmore East: A Photographic Memoir, 1999; licensed photograph collections include Corbis/Bettmann Archive, 1994—, Star File Photo Agy., 1997-2006. Mem. Cmty. Planning Bd. 1, Borough of Manhattan, N.Y.C., 1974-86. Recipient spl. achievement award Mademoiselle mag., 1972; Ind. filmmaker grant Am. Film Inst. 1973; film grantee N.Y. State Coun. on the Arts, 1977, 85, 87, Nat. Endowment Arts, 1978, 85, 87, Md. Arts Coun., 1977, Ohio Arts and Humanities Couns., 1985. Mem.: AIVF, Ind. Documentary Assn., NY Women in Film, Univ. Film and Video Assn. Democrat. Address: 135 Hudson St New York NY 10013-2102 also: Via Carrand 22 Florence 50133 Italy E-mail: a.rothschild@agora.it.

ROTHSCHILD, DONALD PHILLIP, retired lawyer, arbitrator; b. Mar. 31, 1927; s. Leo and Anne (Office) R.; m. Ruth Eckstein, July 7, 1950; children: Nancy Lee, Judy Lynn Hoffman, James Alex. AB, U. Mich., 1950; JD summa cum laude, U. Toledo, 1965; LLM, Harvard U., Cambridge, Mass., 1966. Bar: Ohio 1966, DC 1970, US Supreme Ct. 1975, RI 1989. Tchg. fellow Harvard U. Law Sch., Cambridge, Mass., 1965—66; instr. solicitor's office U.S. Dept. Labor, Washington, 1966—67; prof. law George Washington U. Nat. Law Ctr., Washington, 1966—89, prof. emeritus, 1989; prof. law NY Law Sch., 1989—96; ret., 1996. Vis. prof. U. Mich. Law Sch., Ann Arbor, 1976; dir. Consumer Protection Ctr., 1971—, Inst. Law and Aging, Washington, 1973—89, Ctr. for Cmty. Justice, Washington, 1974—78, Nat. Consumers League, Washington, 1981—87; v.p. Regulatory Alternatives Devel. Corp., Washington, 1982—; cons. Washington Met. Coun. Govt., 1979—82; counsel Tillinghast, Collins & Graham, Providence, 1989—95, chair human resource group. Author: From the Cockpit of the Rubaiyat, 2002, Kiosks Keep the Devils Away: A Novel About Mental Health, 2006, Amazon Kindle Books, Recent Strides in Cancer Research Funding the Future, 2009; co-author: Consumer Protection Text and Materials, 1973, Collective Bargaining and Labor Arbitration, 1979, Fundamentals of Administrative Practice and Procedure, 1981; contbr. articles to profl. jours.; exhibitions include Koi Krane Gallery, Fort Heyens, Fla. Chmn. bd. dirs. D.C. Citizens Complaint Ctr., Washington, 1980; mayoral appointee Adv. Com. on Consumer Protection, Washington, 1979—80. Recipient Cmty. Svc. award, Television Acad., Washington, 1981. Mem.: ABA, D.C. Bar Assn., Am. Arbitration Assn., Fed. Mediation and Conciliation Svc., Nat. Acad. Arbitrators, Nat. Assn. Coll. and Univ. Attys. (Brown U.), Fed. Trade Commn. Adv. Coun., Phi Kappa Phi. Jewish. Office: Donald P Rothchild Esq 718 Durion Ct Sanibel FL 33957 Personal E-mail: dpchild@embargmail.com.

ROTHSCHILD, GITA F., lawyer; b. 1950; BA, George Washington U., 1971; MS, Boston U., 1972; JD cum laude, Temple U. Sch. of Law, 1977. Bar: NJ 1977, NY 1984, US Ct. of Appeals (2d and 3d cirs.), US Supreme Ct. Ptnr., ins. coverage, products liability groups McCarter & English, Newark. Chmn., dist. V fee arbitration com. NJ Supreme Ct., 1984—88; mem. Am. Law Inst., Defense Rsch. Inst.; faculty mem. Defense Trial Academy, 1996; ed. bd. mem. NJ Lawyer, 1996—99. Mem.: ABA, Internat. Assn. of Defense Counsel, Essex County Bar Assn., NJ State Bar Assn. Office: McCarter & English Four Gateway Ctr 100 Mulberry St Newark NJ 07102 Office Phone: 973-639-7969. Office Fax: 973-624-7070. Business E-Mail: grothschild@mccarter.com.

ROTHSCHILD, JENNIFER ANN, artist, educator; b. Mesa, Ariz., Aug. 16, 1948; d. Joe Dean and Frances Ann (McFarland) Johnston; m. Harry Ronald Rothschild, Feb. 14, 1981. Diploma, El Camino Jr. Coll., 1968; BA in Art Edn., Calif. State U., 1970. Cert. secondary sch. tchr., Calif. Arts and crafts specialist City of Hawthorne (Calif.) Parks and Recreation, 1966-67; portrait artist Disneyland, Anaheim, Calif., 1970-74; secondary sch. art tchr. Orange (Calif.) Unified Schs., 1972-80; freelance custom apparel designer Honolulu, 1982-94; sculptor, artist, 1994—. One woman show at Roy's Honolulu, 2001, Art Centre Gallery, Honolulu, 1997, Studio 1 Gallery, 2004; corp. artist Arts of Paradise Gallery, Honolulu, 1997—; exhibited in show at City of Manhattan Beach, Calif., 1966, Assn. of Hawaii Artists, 1996—, in book Encyclopedia of Living Artists, 10th edit., 1997. Bd. dirs. Hawaii Tennis Patrons, Honolulu, 1996—, Assn. of Hawaii Artists Show chairwoman, 2002. Recipient scholarship Chouinard Sch. Art Inst., 1965-66, 1st Place Stamp Design award Easter Seals, 1995-96, Hokele Artists award Hawaiian Airlines, 1996, Most Unique Art award Assn. of Hawaii Artists Aloha Show, 1997. Fellow Nat. Mus. Women in Arts; mem. AAUW, Honolulu Art Acad., Assn. Hawaii Artists (v.p. 1996-97, pres. 1999-2001), Hawaiian Pacific Tennis Assn. (rules chmn. 1997), mem. Windward Art Guild, 2002, Nat. League of Am. Pen Women, Hon., chapter, Alpha Omicron Pi. Republican. Presbyterian. Avocations: reading, writing, painting, sculpting, carving. E-mail: onoaloha@hawaii.rr.com.

ROTHSCHILD, MARY ANN, music educator; b. June 10, 1952; Student, U. N.W. Fla.; AA, Okallosa Walton, 1979; student, conservatory, Canberra, Australia, 1980—82; BA, U. N.Mex., 1985. Cert. (hon.) Calif. Music Tchrs. Assn. Music tchr. Composer Daughter of Zion I, 1990, Daughter of Zion II, 1994, La Chayim, 1997. Pres. Right to Life, Albuquerque, 1987-89. Mem. Music Tchrs. Nat. Assn. (sec. local chpt. Montgomery, Ala., 1981-88, Redlands, Calif., 1988-90, Palm Beach County, Fla., 1994-96, v.p. 1996-98, pres. 1998-99), Women's Algow (v.p. 1985-87, pres. 1987-89), Palm Beach County Music Tchr. Assn. (pres., 2007-08), Coast Music Tchr. Assn. (v.p. treas., 2002-2007). Republican. Home: 1433 SE Cambridge Dr Port Saint Lucie FL 34952-5410 Home Phone: 772-398-6808; Office Phone: 561-632-4952. Personal E-mail: csom@bellsouth.net.

ROTHSCHILD, MICHAEL ALAN, pediatric otolaryngologist, educator; b. Englewood, NJ, Mar. 26, 1962; s. Carl Eliot and Naomi Leah (Bloom) Rothschild; m. Jennifer Louise Hilmes, Aug. 1984; children: David Adrian, Dylan Frederick. BS cum laude, Yale U., New Haven, 1984; MD, Yale U. Sch. Medicine, 1988. Diplomate Am. Bd. Otolaryngology, Nat. Bd. Med. Examiners, lic. NY, NJ, Ohio. Resident gen. surgery Mt. Sinai Med. Ctr., NYC, 1988—90, resident otolaryngology, 1990-93; fellow pediat. otolaryngology Children's Hosp., Cin., 1993-94; attending physician Mt. Sinai Hosp., 1994—; asst. prof. otolaryngology and pediat. Mt. Sinai Sch. Medicine, 1994—98, assoc. prof. otolaryngology and pediat., 1998—2002, assoc. clin. prof. otolaryngology and pediat., 2003—. Instr. dept. otolaryngology U. Cin. Med. Ctr., 1993—94; cons. Englewood Hosp., NJ, 1995—, Mt. Sinai Cleft Palate & Craniofacial Team, 1995—. Editl. bd. (med. publs.) Archives of Otolaryngology-Head and Neck Surgery, Internat. Online Jour. of Otohrinolaryngology-Head and Neck Surgery, Virtual Reality in Medicine Jour.; contbr. articles to profl. jours. Mem. Bd. Health, Closter, NJ, 2003—. Recipient Faculty Tchg. award, Mt. Sinai Dept. Otolaryngology, 2000. Fellow: ACS, Am. Acad. Otolaryngology-Head and Neck Surgery (Honor award 1999), Am. Acad. Pediat.; mem.: Am. Med. Assn., NY Pediat Soc., Am. Med. Informatics Assn., Soc. Ear, Nose & Throat Advances in Children, Am. Broncho-Esophagological Assn., Am. Soc. Pediat. Otolaryngology (Charles F. Ferguson Clin. Rsch. award 2000). Office: Mt Sinai Med Ctr Dept Otolaryngology 1 Gustave L Levy Pl Box 1189 New York NY 10029 Office Phone: 212-241-5944. Office Fax: 212-996-2703.

ROTHSCHILD, RICHARD E., astrophysicist; b. St. Louis; PhD, U. Ariz., Tucson, 1971. Astrophysicist Goddard Space Flight Ctr., Greenbelt, Md., 1972—77; rsch. scientist U. Calif., San Diego, La Jolla, 1977—. Fellow: Am. Astron. Soc.; mem.: Am. Phys. Soc. Office: Univ Calif San Diego 9500 Gilman Dr La Jolla CA 92093-0424 Office Fax: 858-534-2294. Business E-Mail: rrothschild@ucsd.edu.

ROTHSCHILD, RICK, entertainment company executive; b. Santa Monica, Calif., Sept. 26, 1950; s. Wilfred A. and Janet W. Rothschild; m. Adrienne Rothstein, July 11, 1999; children: Elijah Aden, Mason Adler, Arin Isabel. BA in Theater Arts, Lawrence U., Appleton, Wis., 1971. Exec. show dir., sr. v.p. Walt Disney Imagineering, Glendale, Calif., 1978—. Dir.: (theme park attraction) Disney's Am. Adventure - EPCOT, Stitch's Great Escape!, Soarin' Over Calif.-Disney's Calif. Adventure (THEA award for outstanding acheivement, 2002), It's Tough to be a Bug!-Disney's Animal Kingdom (THEA award for outstanding acheivement, 1999), Honey, I Shrunk the Audience - EPCOT (THEA award for outstanding acheivement, 1996). Recipient Theodore F. Cloak award, Lawrence U., 1971, THEA Outstanding Achievement award, Finding Memo Submarine Voyage, Disneyland, 2008.

ROTHSTEIN, ANNE LOUISE, academic administrator, educator; b. Bklyn., Feb. 15, 1943; d. William and Rose Mary (Smith) R. BS, Bklyn. Coll., 1963; MA, Tchrs. Coll. Columbia, NYC, 1965, EdD, 1970. Tchr. Erasmus Hall High Sch., Bklyn., 1963-64, Fort Hamilton High Sch., Bklyn., 1964-64; lectr. Hunter Coll. in the Bronx, N.Y., 1965-68; instr., prof. Lehman Coll., Bronx, 1968—, dept. chair, 1980-83, assoc. dean, 1983-93, assoc. provost/dir. for sponsored program devel., 1993-98. Dir. Lehman Ctr. for Sch./Coll. Collaboratives, Bronx, 1988—; grant specialist for sch./coll. programs, 1985--; small sch. developer, 1999--. Editor, pub. Motor Skills: Theory into Practice, 1976-87; chair editorial bd. Strategies, 1986-92; author: Research and Statistics, 1985, Motor Learning: Basic Stuff, 1987. Grantee in field. Fellow Rsch. Consortium Am. Alliance, Am. Alliance for Health, Physical Edn., Recreation and Dance; mem. Nat. Assn. for Sport and Physical Edn., Nat. Assn. for Girls and Women in Sport, Assn. for Supervision and Curriculum Devel., Am. Edn. Rsch. Assn. Avocations: computers, grants consulting. Home: PO Box 3007 Newtown CT 06470-3007 Office: Lehman Coll Bedford Park Blvd W Bronx NY 10468 Office Phone: 718-960-8569. Personal E-mail: arothstein@aol.com. Business E-Mail: anne.rothstein@lehman.cuny.edu.

ROTHSTEIN, BARBARA JACOBS, federal judge; b. Bklyn., Feb. 3, 1939; d. Solomon and Pauline Jacobs; m. Ted L. Rothstein, Dec. 28, 1968; 1 child, Daniel BA, Cornell U., 1960; LL.B., Harvard U., 1966. Bar: Mass. 1966, Wash. 1969, U.S. Ct. Appeals (9th cir.) 1977, U.S. Dist. Ct. (we. dist.) Wash. 1971, U.S. Supreme Ct. 1975. Pvt. practice law, Boston, 1966-68; asst. atty. gen. State of Wash., 1968-77; judge Superior Ct., Seattle, 1977-80, Fed. Dist. Ct. Western Wash., Seattle, 1980—, chief judge, 1987-94, dir. Fed. Jud. Ctr., 2003—. Faculty Law Sch. U. Wash., 1975-77, Hastings Inst. Trial Advocacy, 1977, N.W. Inst. Trial Advocacy, 1979—; mem. state-fed. com. U.S. Jud. Conf., chair subcom. on health reform; bd. dirs. Inst. Jud. Adminstrn., NYU Sch. Law. Bd. mem. Inst. Jud. Adminstrn., NY U. La. Sch., Am. Law Inst.-Am. Bar Assn., Rule of Law Initiative-Am. Bar Assn., Nat. Hist. Pubs. and Record Commn., Am. Soc. Internat. Law, Jud. Adv. Bd.; bd. mem., physicians and lawyers Nat. Drug Policy Justice Edn. Adv. Com. Recipient Matrix Table Women of Yr. award Women in Communication, Judge of the Yr. award Fed. Bar Assn., 1989; King County Wash. Women Lawyers Vanguard Honor, 1995 Mem. Am. Judicature Soc. (mem. commn.), Nat. Assn. Women Judges, Fellows Am. Bar, Am. Law Inst., Wash. State Bar Assn., Phi Beta Kappa, Phi Kappa Phi. Office: Fed Jud Ctr 1 Columbus Cir NE Washington DC 20002-8003

ROTHSTEIN, FRED C., health facility administrator; b. Cleve. m. Jackie Rothstein; 2 children. BA, Miami U., Oxford, Ohio; MD, Chgo. Med. Sch. U. Health Scis., 1976. Bd. cert. pediatrics and pediatric gastroenterology. Pediat. intern Cleve. Metro Gen. Hosp., Ohio, 1976—77, Rainbow Babies & Children's Hosp., Ohio, 1976—77, pediat. resident Ohio, 1977—79, pediat. gastroenterology fellow Ohio, 1979—81, chief divsn. pediat. gastroenterology Ohio, practicing physician, pediat. gastroenterologist Ohio, pres., CEO; dir. dept. pediatrics, sr. v.p. med. affairs Mt. Sinai Med. Ctr., Cleve., 1989; sr. v.p. clin. integration U. Hosps. Health System, Cleve., 1990—96, acting pres., CEO, 2002—03; pres., CEO U. Hosps. Cleve., 2003—. Asst. prof. pediatrics Case Western Reserve U., Cleve., 1981—86; prof. pediatrics Case Western Res. U., Cleve., 2004—; bd. trustees Ctr. Health Affairs (CHA), 2004, Geauga Regional Hosp., Chardon, Ohio, 1997; bd. dirs. BioEnterprise. Contbr. more than 60 peer-reviewed abstracts, articles, and book chapters on issues concerning pediatric gastroenterology. Mem.: N.Am. Soc. Pediat. Gastroenterology and Nutrition, Am. Gastroenterological Assn., Am. Acad. Pediatrics, Am. Coll. Gastroenterology. Office: Univ Hosps Cleve 11100 Euclid Ave Cleveland OH 44106 Office Phone: 216-844-6217.*

ROTHSTEIN, GERALD ALAN, investment consultant; b. Bklyn., Oct. 18, 1941; s. Manuel and Gertrude (Buxbaum) R.; m. Cynthia Bea Pincus, June 11, 1967; children: Michael Neil, Lori Pamela, Meryl Patricia. BBA, City Coll. N.Y., 1962; MBA, U. Pa., 1965. 1st v.p. Shearson Hammill & Co., NYC, 1966-74, Shearson Hayden Stone, NYC, 1974-75; v.p. William D. Witter, Inc., NYC, 1975-76; from v.p. to managing dir. internat. investment banker Oppenheimer & Co., NYC, 1976—95, internat. investment banker, 1995—2004; mng. dir. internat. money mgmt. CIBC World Markets, NYC, 1998—2004; cons. Marshep-aug Advisors, 2004—; mem. Progressive Capital, LLC, 2006—. Trustee Ctr. Social and Emotional Edn., NYC. Mem. N.Y. Soc. Security Analysts, CFA Inst. Home Phone: 212-369-5828; Office Phone: 212-426-6002. Personal E-mail: gerald.rothstein@verizon.net.

ROTHSTEIN, LAURA, law educator, former dean; BA, U. Kans., 1971; JD, Georgetown U. Law Ctr., 1974. Asst. prof. law Ohio No. U., 1976—79, dir. admissions, 1978—79; assoc. prof. law W.Va U., 1980—84, prof. law, 1984—86, U. Houston, 1985—96, assoc. dean Student Affairs, 1988—93, Law Found. prof., 1996—2000, assoc. dean Grad. Studies and Spl. Progs., 1999—2000; prof. law Brandeis Sch. Law, U. Louisville, 2000—, dean, 2000—05, disting. univ. scholar, 2006—. Vis. asst. prof. law U. Pitts., 1979—80; staff atty. Dept. Justice, Antitrust Div., Washington, DC, 1974—75, Ohio State Atty. Gen., Antitrust Sec., 1975—76, Devel. Disabilities Law Project, U. Pitts. Sch. Law, 1979—80; affiliated Appalachian Rsch. & Defense Fund, Inc., Charleston, W.Va., 1980—85; assoc. dir. devel. Health Law and Policy Inst., U. Houston, 1997—2000. Editor: Health Law News, 1993—98; contbr. articles to law jours. Bd. mem. Urban Montessori Sch., Louisville, 2001—; adv. bd. mem. Children's Organ Transplant Assn., 2000—. Mem.: ABA (mem. Diversity Com. 2002—), Soc. Am. Law Tchrs., Brandeis Inns Ct., Ky. Bar Assn., Ky. Bar Found., Louisville Bar Assn.; River Oaks Women's Breakfast Club. Office: Louis D Brandeis Sch Law U Louisville Wilson W Wyatt Hall 2301 S Third St Louisville KY 40292 Office Phone: 502-852-6288. Office Fax: 502-852-0862. E-mail: laura.rothstein@louisville.edu.*

ROTHSTEIN, PAUL FREDERICK, lawyer, educator; b. Chgo., June 6, 1938; BS, Northwestern U., 1958, LLB, 1961. Bar: Ill. 1962, D.C. 1967, U.S. Supreme Ct. 1975. Instr. U. Mich. Law Sch., 1963; assoc. prof. law U. Tex., 1964-67; mem. Surrey, Karasik, Gould & Greene, Washington, 1967-70; prof. Georgetown U. Law Ctr., Washington, 1970—; spl. counsel U.S. Senate Jud. Com. Subcom. on Criminal Laws and Procedures, 1975-77; spl. counsel U.S. Ho. of Reps. Jud. Com. Subcom. on Criminal Law, 1980. Cons. Treasury, 1967-74, HEW, 1970, Commrs. on Uniform State Laws, 1969-75, Nat. Acad. Scis., 1976-77, 95-96, D.C. Law Revision Commn., 1976-78; spkr., coord. numerous legal edn. seminars for judges and lawyers, 1970—. Author: Evidence in a Nutshell, 1970, 2d edit., 1981, 3d edit., 1997, 4th edit., 2003, 5th edit, 2007; Understanding the New Federal Rules of Evidence, 1973, 74, 75, Federal Rules of Evidence with Practice Comments and Annotations, 1978, 2d edit., 1981, 3d edit., 2009, Cases, Materials and Problems in Evidence, 1986, 2d edit., 1998, 3rd edit., 2006; contbr. articles on various legal matters to profl. jours.; editor-in-chief Northwestern U. Law Rev., 1960-61. Recipient U. Iowa Legal Edn. award 1974, Disting. Pub. Svc. award Crime Victims Compensation Bd., 1978; other civic and profl. awards; Fulbright scholar, Oxford, Eng., 1962-63. Mem. Fed. Bar Assn. (chmn. fed. rules of evidence com. 1974-77, Disting. Svc. award 1975, nat. coun. 1976-80, chmn. continuing legal edn. com. 1980), D.C. Bar (continuing legal edn. bd. 1980—), ABA (chmn. rules of evidence and criminal procedure com., criminal justice sect. 1984-88), Assn. Am. Law Schs. (sec. evidence sect. 1976, chmn. 1977), Nat. Assn. Criminal Injuries Compensations Bds. (sec. 1977-80), Internat. Assn. Criminal Injuries Compensation Bds. Office: Georgetown U Law Ctr 600 New Jersey Ave NW Washington DC 20001-2022

ROTHSTEIN, RONALD, professional basketball coach; b. Bronxville, NY, Dec. 27, 1942; m. Olivia Pierorazio; children: David, Dana. Grad., U. RI, 1964; M, CCNY. Asst. coach Upsala Coll., 1974-75; HS coach, 1976-79; northeastern regional scout Atlanta Hawks, 1979-82; scout NY Knicks, 1982-83; asst. coach Atlanta Hawks, 1983-86, Detroit Pistons, 1986-88; head coach Miami Heat, 1988-91, Detroit Pistons, 1992-93; asst. coach Cleveland Cavaliers, 1993-99; head coach Miami Sol (WNBA), Miami, 1999—2002; asst. coach Ind. Pacers, 2003—04, Miami Heat, 2005—, interim head coach, 2007—. Office: The HEAT Group AmericanAirlines Arena 601 Biscayne Blvd Miami FL 33132

ROTHSTEIN, SAMUEL, librarian, educator; b. Moscow, Jan. 12, 1921; arrived in Can., 1922, naturalized, 1929; s. Louis Israel and Rose Rothstein; m. Miriam Ruth Teitelbaum, Aug. 26, 1951; children: Linda Rose, Sharon Lee. BA, U. B.C., 1939, MA, 1940, LLD, 2004; grad. student, U. Calif., Berkeley, 1941-42, grad. student, 1946-47, BLS, 1947; postgrad., U. Wash., 1942—43; PhD (Carnegie Corp. fellow 1951-54), U. Ill., 1954; DLitt, York U., 1971. Teaching fellow U. Wash., 1942-43; prin. libr. asst. U. Calif., Berkeley, 1947; mem. staff U. B.C. Libr., Vancouver, 1947-51, 54-62; acting univ. libr. U. B.C., Vancouver, 1961-62, prof. libr. sci., 1961—86, prof. emeritus, 1986—, dir. Sch. Librarianship, 1961-70. Vis. prof. U. Hawaii, 1969, U. Toronto, 1970, 79, Hebrew U., Jerusalem, 1973; mem. Commn. Nat. Plan Libr. Edn., 1963—; mem. assoc. com. sci. info. Nat. Rsch. Coun. Can., 1962-69; councillor B.C. Med. Libr. Svc., 1971; mem. exec. com. Pacific divsn. Can. Jewish Congress, 1962-69, Internat. House Assn. B.C., 1959-60; mem. Can. Adv. Bd. Sci. and Tech. Info.; mem. cabinet Combined Jewish Appeal of Greater Vancouver, 1992-95; pres. Vancouver Pub. Libr. Trust, 1987-88. Author: The Development of Reference Services, 1955, (with others) Training Professional Librarians for Western Canada, 1957, The University-The Library, 1972, Rothstein on Reference..., 1989; also articles.; co-editor: As We Remember It, 1970. Life mem. bd. dirs. Jewish Cmty. Ctr. of Greater Vancouver, 1977-, pres., 1972-74, 1997-98; bd. dirs. Jewish Fedn. of Greater Vancouver, 1993-2000. Recipient ALISE award Assn. Library Info. Sci. Edn., 1987, Beta Phi Mu award ALA, 1988. Mem. Can. Libr. Assn. (hon. life), Assn. Am. Libr. Schs. (pres. 1968-69), Can. Assn. Libr. Schs. (hon. life, pres. 1982-84), ALA (coun. 1963-69, Beta Phi Mu award 1988), B.C. Libr. Assn. (hon. life, pres. 1959-60, Helen Gordon Stewart award 1970), Pacific N.W. Libr. Assn. (pres. 1963-64, hon. life), Can. Libr. Assn. (hon. life, coun. 1958-60, Outstanding Svc. to Librarianship award 1986), Bibliog. Soc. Can. (coun. 1959-63), Can. Assn. Univ. Tchrs. Home: 1416 W 40th Ave Vancouver BC Canada

ROTHWELL, ELAINE B., artist; b. Mpls., May 8, 1926; d. Frederick Roscoe and Stella Frances (LaVallee) Bartholomew; m. William Stanley Rothwell, May 10, 1946; children: Suzanne, Amy Verrett, Wendy

Rothwell-Lopez, Bart. BFA, San Jose State U., 1966; pvt. study, Woodbury Graphic Studio, Los Altos, Calif., 1975-76, Amaranth Intaglio Workshop, Los Altos, 1985. One-woman shows include Triton Mus. Art, Santa Clara, Calif., 1976, Palo Alto Civic Ctr., Calif., 1977, Stanford Art Spaces, Stanford U., Calif., 1985, 1988, 1989, West Valley Art Mus., Surprise, Ariz., 1996, 2007, Roseville Arts Ctr., Calif., 2003, exhibited in group shows at Printwork '98, Barrett Ho., Poughkeepsie, N.Y., 1998, 73d Ann. Internat. Print Competition/Print Ctr., Phila., 1999, Manhattan Arts Internat., 1999, Chautauqua Nat. Exhbn. Am. Art, 1999, No. Colo. Ann. Nat. Exhbns., 1999, 2000, Stage Gallery, Merrick, N.Y., 2000, Pacific Prints, Palo Alto, Calif., 2006, Allied Artists Am., NYC, 2006, Gallery West, Alexandria, Va., 2007—08, Ctr. for Visual Arts, Wausau, Wis., 2007, 20th Parkside Nat. Small Print Exhbn., Kenosha, Wis., 2007—08, Red River Valley Mus. Internat., Vernon, Tex., 2007—09, Conn. Acad. Fine Arts 96th Exhbn., Mystic, 2007, Impact Artists, Buffalo, NY, 2007—09, Salmagundi Club, NYC, 2008, Am. Artists' Profl. League, NYC, 2008, Pen & Brush, Internat. Exhbn., NYC, 2009, Represented in permanent collections Newberry Libr., Chgo., Triton Mus. Art, Santa Clara, West Valley Art Mus., Brand Libr. Art Ctr., Glendale. Mem.: Am. Color Print Soc., Nat. Mus. Women in Arts (charter), Crocker Art Mus., Auburn Old Town Gallery, Triton Mus. Art. Home and Office: 3030 Eagles Nest Auburn CA 95603-5918

ROTHWELL, GEOFFREY SCOTT, economics educator; b. Longview, Wash., July 20, 1953; s. Michael and Dona (Adams) R. BAC, Francois Premier, Le Havre, France, 1972; BA, The Evergreen State Coll., Olympia, Wash., 1975; MA in Econs., U. Calif., Berkeley, 1981, MA in Jurisprudence, 1984, PhD, 1985. Postdoctoral fellow Calif. Inst. Tech., Pasadena, 1985-86; rsch. assoc. Stanford U. Econ. Rsch., Calif., 1986—89, sr. rsch. assoc., 1991—, sr. lectr. dept. econs., 1986—. Contbr. articles to profl. jours. Office: Stanford U Dept Econs Stanford CA 94305 Office Phone: 650-725-3456. Business E-Mail: rothwell@stanford.edu.

ROTHWELL, ROBERT ALAN, investing and consulting company executive, writer; b. Newark, May 13, 1939; s. Albert Robert and Rose Gloria (Cundari) Rothwell. BA in Philosophy, St. Francis U., Loretto, Pa., 1961; MS in Psychology, Seton Hall U., South Orange, NJ, 1962; MS in Fgn. Diplomacy, Georgetown U. Sch. Fgn. Svc., Washington, 1963; PhD in Existential Philosophy, Duquesne U., Pitts., 1965; DSc in Psychology, Georgetown U., 1968; DHL (hon.), Fribourg U., Switzerland, 1971. Prof. psychology & philosophy U. Steubenville, Ohio, 1966—73; dir. Edn. Dynamics, Las Vegas, 1973—76; pres. Robert's Investing & Cons., Las Vegas, 1976—, Muscle & Power Talent Mgmt., Inc., Las Vegas, 1988—; col. USMC, 1978—99; pres., owner Great Basin Mgmt. & Cons., Inc., Las Vegas, 1991—, Telluride Mktg. & Distbn., 1992—. Mem. presdl. commn. Russian Affairs US Govt., Washington, 1977—86; mem. Nev. Gov.'s Commn. Higher Edn., 1978—82, Presdl. Commn. Psychol. Warfare, Washington, 1977—82; spl. UN observer numerous countries, 1986—96. Author: (book) Existential Psychology, 1975, The Origin of Consciousness, 1977, The Bicameral Mind, 1980, Code Name: Grizzly, 1986. Decorated medal Navy DSM, Navy & Marine Corps medal, Bronze Star; recipient Disting. Service award, US Def. Dept., 1966, Superior Svc. Nat. Security award, 1968; named Mr. Nev. Masters Bodybldg. Champion, 1985, Mr. Silver State, State Masters Bodybldg. Champion, 1985. Mem.: AAUP, Am. Psychologists Assn., Internat. Assn. Psychologists, Nat. Physique Com., Assn. Advancement Psychology, Nat. Assn. Sch. Psychologists. Democrat. Roman Catholic. Personal E-mail: colrothwellusmc@aol.com.

ROTHWELL, TIMOTHY, pharmaceutical executive; b. London, Jan. 8, 1951; came to us., 1966; s. Kenneth Gordon Rothwell and Jean Mary (Stedman) Davey; m. Joanne Claire Fleming; children: Tiffany, Heather. BA, Drew U., 1972; JD, Seton Hall U., 1976; LLM, NYU, 1979, exec. MBA, 1983. With Sandoz Pharms., East Hanover, NJ, 1972—, patent atty., 1974-77, patent and trademark counsel, 1980-82, mng. ops. planning and adminstrn., 1982-84, dir. mktg. ops., 1984-85, exec. dir. field ops., 1985-86, v.p. field ops., 1986-87, pres. profl. bus. ops., 1987-88, corp. v.p., chief oper. officer, 1989—91; sr. v.p. sales and mktg. Squibb, Princeton, NJ, 1991; v.p. global mktg. and sales Burroughs-Wellcome, 1992; pres., CEO Sandoz Pharm. Corp., 1995; pres. pharm. op. Rhone-Poulenc Rorer Inc., 1996, pres., bd. dirs., 1996-97; exec. v.p., pres. pharm. ops. Pharmacia Corp., NJ, 1998—2003; pres., CEO Sanofi-Synthelabo N.Am., 2003—04, Sanofi-Aventis U.S., 2004—09, chmn., 2007. Bd. dirs. PhRMA; trustee Somerset Med. Ctr., Healthcare Inst. NJ; found. bd. dirs. U. Medicine and Dentistry of NJ. Mem. NJ State Bar Assn., NY State Bar Assn., Am. Soc. Pharmacy Law, Nat. Health Care Quality Coun., Am. Found. Pharm. Exec. (bd. dirs.), NJ Patent Law Assn. (pres. 1986), Health Inst. NJ. Avocations: stamp collecting/philately, soccer. Office: Antigenics Inc 162 Fifth Ave New York NY 10010 Office Phone: 212-994-8200. Office Fax: 212-994-8299.*

ROTI, THOMAS DAVID, judge; s. Sam N. and Theresa S. (Salerno) R.; m. Donna Sumichrast, 1972; children: Thomas S., Kyle D., Rebecca D., Gregory J BS, Loyola U., Chgo., 1967, JD cum laude, 1970. Bar: Ill. 1970, U.S. Dist. Ct. (no. dist.) Ill. 1971, U.S. Ct. Appeals (7th cir.) 1971. Sr. law clk. to Judge Frank McGarr, U.S. Dist. Ct. No. Dist. Ill., 1971-72; assoc. Arnstein, Gluck & Lehr, Chgo., 1972-73, Boodell, Sears et al, Chgo., 1973-75; asst. gen. counsel Dominick's Finer Foods, Inc., Northlake, Ill., 1975-77, v.p., gen. counsel, 1977-97; judge Cir. Ct. Cook County, 2000—, mentor. Mem. nat. conf. lawyers and econs. com. Food Mktg. Inst., Washington, 1987—97; trustee Nat. Conf. Cmty. and Justice, 1995—2000; legis. com. Ill. Retail Mchts. Assn., Chgo., 1987—97. Trustee Joint Civic Com. Italian Ams., Chgo., 1986-95; mem. Chgo. Coun. EDU-CARE Scholarship Program, 1988; dir. Chgo. Clean Streak, 1990-97. Maj., Qartermaster Corps, USAR, 1967-83 Recipient Am. Jurisprudence award, 1970, Alumni Assn. award Loyola U., 1970. Mem. ABA, Ill. Bar Assn., Ill. Judges Assn. (bd. dirs. 2005-), Ill. Judges Assn. Found. (bd. dirs. 2007-08), Nomination Com., 2007-, Chgo. Bar Assn., N.W. Suburban Bar Assn. (bd. govs. 2006-08, co-chair civil practice com.), Justinian Soc. Lawyers, Cath. Lawyers Guild Chgo. (bd. govs., dir. 2004—),Ill. Judges Assn. Found.(bd. trustees 2007-08), Phi Alpha Delta, Alpha Sigma Nu. Roman Catholic. Office: 2121 Euclid Ave Rolling Meadows IL 60008

ROTI ROTI, JOSEPH LEE, scientist, educator; b. Newport, RI, Oct. 12, 1943; s. Donald and Shirley Louise (Lemmer) Roti Roti; m. Linda L. Wotring, Mar. 16, 1968 (div.); m. Stephanie Pagano, Feb. 17, 1995. BS in Physics, Mich. Tech. U., 1965; postgrad., Oak Ridge Nat. Lab., 1966; PhD in Biophysics, U. Rochester, 1972; postdoctoral student, U. Fla., 1971-73. Rsch. isntr. U. Utah, Salt Lake City, 1973-76, asst. prof. dept. radiology, 1976-79, assoc. prof., 1979-85; assoc. prof. dept. radiology Wash. U. Med. Sch., 1985-87, prof. dept. radiology, chief sect. Cane biology, 1987—. Rsch. collaborator cancer biology Brookhaven Nat. Lab., Upton, N.Y., 1973-75; vis. sr. scientist Lawrence Livermore Lab., Livermore, Calif., 1980-81; vis. assoc. prof. U. Calif.-San Francisco, 1979-80. Creator computer game; assoc. editor Radiation Research, Oak Ridge, Tenn., 1983—. Grantee NIH-Nat. Cancer Inst., 1975-86; vis. scientist Flow Cytometry Svc. Villejuif, France, 1983, U. Paris, 1983. Mem. Radiation Rsch. Soc., Cell Kinetics Soc. (pres. 1984-85), AAAS, N.Y. Acad. Scis., N.Am. Hyperthernia Group, Sigma Xi, Phi Kappa Phi. Roman Catholic. Office: Wash U Sch Medicine Ste 411 4511 Froest Park Ave Saint Louis MO 63108-2138

ROTMAN, JOSEPH JONAH, mathematician, educator; b. Chgo., May 26, 1934; s. Ely and Rose (Wolf) R.; m. Marganit Weinberger, Aug. 25, 1978; children: Ella Rose, Daniel Adam. BA, U. Chgo., 1954, MA, 1956, PhD, 1959. Rsch. assoc. U. Ill., Urbana, 1959—61, asst. prof., 1961—63, assoc. prof., 1963—68, prof., 1968—2004, prof. emeritus, 2004—. Vis. prof. Queen Mary Coll., London, 1965-66, 1985-86, Hebrew U., Jerusalem, 1970; Lady Davis prof. Technion, Haifa, Israel, 1977-78, Hebrew U., 1977-78, Tel Aviv U., Israel, 1984, Oxford U., Eng., 1990. Author: Theory of Groups, 1965, 4th edit., 1995, Homological Algebra, 1970, 1979, 2d edit., 2008, Algebraic Topology, 1988, Galois Theory, 1990, 2d edit., 1998, Abstract Algebra, 1997, 3d edit., 2006, Advanced Modern Algebra, 2002, Journey into Math., 1998, 2007; editor: Proc. AMS, 1970, 1971; mng. editor Proc. AMS, 1972, 1973. Mem. Am. Math. Soc., Math. Assn. Am., London Math. Soc.

ROTMAN, MARVIN, radiation oncologist, radiologist, educator; b. Phila., Sept. 3, 1933; s. Herman Zelman and Edith (Solomon) R.; m. Marsha Vinson; children: David, Robert, Eve, Sydney. BS, Ursinus Coll., 1954; MD, Thomas Jefferson U., 1958. Asst. clin prof. radiology N.Y. Med. Coll., NYC, 1967-68, asst. prof. radiology, 1968-71, assoc. prof. clin. radiology, 1971-75, prof. radiology, 1975-79; prof., chmn. radiation oncology SUNY Health Sci. Ctr. at Bklyn., 1979—2003, Disting. Svc. prof., chair, 2003—; dir. radiation oncology Kings County Med. Ctr., NYC, 1979—, Long Island Coll. Hosp. Cons. Bklyn. VA Hosp., 1979—. Author textbook: (with others) Introduction to Radiotherapy, 1975, Genito-Urinary Malignancy, 1980; editor textbook: (with others) Clinical Applications of Continuous Infusion Chemotherapy and Commitant Radiation Therapy, 1986, others; contbr. more than 190 articles to profl. jours., textbooks. Bd. dirs. Young Concert Artists, N.Y.C., 1967—; nat. bd. dirs. Sante Fe Opera, 1987-93. Recipient Gold Medal award, Am. Soc. Therapeutic Radiology and Oncology, 2002, award of honor, Radiol. Soc. N.Am., 1991. Fellow Am. Coll. Radiology (counselor N.Y. State chpt. 1980—), Am. Coll. Radiation Oncology; mem. AMA (mem. radiology residency review com., Am. Bd. Radiology examiner on splty. bds.), Am. Radium Soc. (pres. 1994-96), Soc. Acad. Radiotherapy Programs (pres. 1984-86), N.Y. Cancer Soc. (pres. 1983-84), N.Y. Roentgen Soc. (chmn. radiotherapy sect. 1977-78), Med. Soc. Kings County (chmn. radiotherapy 1981—), Am. Soc. Therapeutic Radiology and Oncology (mem. exec. com., Gold medal), Kings Point Civic Assn. (pres. 2004—)Alpha Omega Alpha. Jewish. Avocations: tennis, piano, art. Home Phone: 516-482-5263.

ROTONDI, NICHOLAS JOHN, automotive executive; b. Hackensack, NJ, Aug. 15, 1976; s. Salvatore and Geraldine Rotondi. BA, Rutgers U., New Brunswick, NJ, 1998; MS, London Sch. Econs., 2001. Fin. asst. Ferrari N.Am., Englewood Cliffs, NJ, 1998—2000; distbn. specialist Nissan Divsn., Nissan N.Am., Inc., Somerset, NJ, 2002—06, sales ops. specialist, 2003—04; dist. parts and svc. mgr. Infiniti Divsn., Nissan N.Am., Inc., Somerset, NJ, 2004—06, regional tng. mgr., 2006—06; svc. dir. Pk. Ave. Infiniti, Englewood, 2006—. Mem.: Rutgers U. Alumni Assn., London Sch. Econs. Alumni Assn., Nat. Honor Soc., Mensa, Zeta Psi Frat. (life). Independent. Avocations: photography, poetry, guitar, golf, motorcycling. Office: Park Ave Infiniti 227 N Dean St Englewood NJ 07631 Home: 213 Phillips Ave # 1 South Hackensack NJ 07606-1624 Home Fax: 201-568-1840. Personal E-mail: nrotondi@yahoo.com.

ROTTENBERG, HAGAI, medical educator; s. Abraham Rottenberg and Fruma Tiger. PhD, Harvard U., Cambridge, Mass., 1969. Prof. Hahnemann Med. Sch., Phila., 1978—2001; adj. prof. Dartmouth Med. Sch., Hanover, NH, 2008—. Assoc. prof. Tel Aviv U., 1973—78.

ROTTER, ANDREW JON, history educator; b. Madison, Wis., June 13, 1953; m. Padma A. Kaimal, June 24, 1984; children: Sophie, Phoebe. BA in History, Cornell U., 1975; MA in History, Stanford U., 1976, PhD in History, 1981. Instr. Stanford U., Palo Alto, 1979; vis. asst. prof. Calif. State U., Chico, 1980-81; asst. prof. St. Mary's Coll. Calif., 1981-84, 85-86; vis. asst. prof. Colgate U., 1986-87, asst. prof., 1988-90, assoc. prof., 1990—98, prof., 1998—, Charles A. Dana prof., 2006—; asst. prof. Vanderbilt U., 1987-88. Author: The Path to Vietnam: Origins of the American Commitment to Southeast Asia, 1987, Comrades at Odds: The United States and India, 1947-1964, 2000, Hiroshima: The World's Bomb, 2008; editor: Light at the End of the Tunnel: A Vietnam War Anthology, 1999; Hiroshima: The World's Bomb, 2008; contbr. articles, rev. essays, book revs. to profl. jours. James Birdsall Weter fellow Stanford U., 1979-80, Stanford U. Ctr. for Rsch. Internat. Studies fellowship, 1980, Gandhi Peace Found. fellowship, 1984-85, Sr. Rsch. fellowship Am. Coun. Learned Socs., 1990-91, Picker Rsch. fellowship Colgate U., 1990-91; Albert J. Beveridge Rsch. grantee Am. Hist. Assn., 1984, Rsch. grantee Harry S. Truman Libr. Inst., 1987; recipient David M. Potter award Stanford U. Dept. History, 1978-79. Mem. Am. Hist. Assn., Orgn. Am. Historians, Soc. for Historians of Am. Fgn. Rels. (v.p. 2009). Home: 9 W Pleasant St Hamilton NY 13346-1203 Office: Colgate U Dept History 13 Oak Dr Dept History Hamilton NY 13346-1383

ROTTER, MARCEL PAUL, literature and language professor; PhD, U. Wis., Madison, 2004. Asst. prof. German U. Mary Wash., Fredericksburg, Va., 2004—. Mem.: AATG. Office: Univ Mary WA 1301 Coll Ave Fredericksburg VA 22401

ROTTLER, JUERGEN, computer software company executive; Grad. in Computer Sci. and Bus. Adminstrn., Fachhochschule Furtwangen, Germany; MBA, Bentley Coll., Waltham, Mass. Mng. dir. Delphi Consulting Group; various positions up to sr. v.p. pub. sector, healthcare and edn. customer segment Hewlett-Packard, 1986—2004; exec. v.p. Oracle customer svcs. Oracle Corp., Redwood City, Calif., 2004. Office: Oracle Corp 500 Oracle Pky Redwood City CA 94065 Office Phone: 650-506-0024.

ROTUNDA, ADAM MICHAEL, dermatologist; b. Mineola, NY, Aug. 2, 1974; s. Robert and Josephine Rotunda; m. Thuy Nguyen, July 20, 1997; 1 child, Tia Linh. BS in Nutritional Scis. summa cum laude with honors, Cornell U., Ithaca, NY, 1996; MD valedictorian, SUNY Downstate Med. Sch., Bklyn., 2001. Bd. Cert. Am. Bd. Dermatology, 2005. Intern St. Vincent's Hosp., NYC, 2001—02; resident, dermatology divsn. UCLA Sch. Medicine, 2002—05, asst. clin. prof. dermatology, 2006—; Mohs micrographic surgery and cutaneous oncology fellowship Bennett Surgery Ctr., Santa Monica, Calif., 2005—06; med. dir. dermatology R&D Allergan, Inc., 2006—08. Contbr. articles to profl. jours. Recipient Alumni Svc. award, SUNY Downstate Health Sci. Ctr., 2001, Lifetime Membership award, Downstate Student Ctr., 2001; named Review Article Incentive Program Competition winner, Dermatologic Surgery, 2006. Mem.: Am. Acad. Cosmetic Dermatology & Aesthetic Surgery (bd. dirs.), L.A. Met. Dermatologic Soc., Calif. Soc. Dermatology and Dermatologic Surgery, Pacific Dermatologic Assn., Am. Soc. Dermatologic Surgery, Am. Coll. Mohs Surgery, Am. Acad. Dermatology. Achievements include invention of Methods and related compositions for non-invasive reduction of fat and skin tightening. Office Phone: 949-760-0953.

ROTUNDA, DONALD THEODORE, public relations consultant; b. Blue Island, Ill., Feb. 14, 1945; s. Nicholas and Frances (Manna) R. BA, Georgetown U., 1967; MA, London Sch. Econs., 1968, PhD, 1972. Analyst NASA, Washington, 1972; lectr. in econs. U. DC, 1973; legis. asst. Ho. of Reps., Washington, 1974-76, economist budget com., 1977; mgmt. analyst Office Mgmt. and Budget, Washington, 1977-81; cons., 1981-82; mgr. editorial svcs. United Technologies Corp., Hartford, Conn., 1982-87, Pepsico, Inc., Purchase, NY, 1987-89, Union Carbide Corp., Danbury, Conn., 1989-90; dir. editorial svcs. Martin Marietta, Bethesda, Md., 1990-92; cons. pub. rels., 1992—. Contbr. numerous articles to Washington Post, New Republic, Saturday Rev. Roman Catholic. Home: 4431 Klingle St NW Washington DC 20016-3578 Home Phone: 202-966-4855; Office Phone: 202-966-4855. Personal E-mail: donaldrotunda@verizon.net.

ROTUNDA, RONALD DANIEL, law educator, consultant; b. Blue Island, Ill., Feb. 14, 1945; s. Nicholas and Frances (Manna) R.; children: Nora, Mark. AB magna cum laude, Harvard U., 1967, JD magna cum laude, 1970. Bar: N.Y. 1971, U.S. Ct. Appeals (2d cir.) 1971, U.S. Ct. Appeals (D.C. cir.) 1971, U.S. Ct. Appeals (7th cir.) 1990, U.S. Supreme Ct. 1974, Ill. 1975. Law clk. U.S. Ct. Appeals (2d cir.), 1970-71; assoc. Wilmer, Cutler & Pickering, Washington, 1971-73; asst. majority counsel Watergate Com., U.S. Senate, Washington, 1973-74; spl. cons. Office of Ind. Counsel, Washington, 1997-99; asst. prof. U. Ill. Coll. Law, Champaign, 1974-77, assoc. prof., 1977-80, prof., 1980-93, Albert E. Jenner, Jr. prof. of law, 1993—2002; spl. counsel Dept. Def., 2004—05; found. prof. law George Mason U., Arlington, Va., 2002—06, prof. law, 2006—08; Doy & Dee Hanley choir & disting. prof. jurisprudence Chapman U. Law Sch., Orange, Calif. Vis. prof. law European U. Inst., Florence, Italy, 1981, U. Ala., 1999; mem. profl. responsibility exam. com. Nat. Conf. Bar Examiners, 1980-87; constl. advisor Supreme Nat. Coun. Cambodia, 1993; cons. Supreme Ct. Moldova, 1996; vis. sr. fellow in constnl. studies Cato Inst., 2000. Author: (with Morgan) Problems and Materials of Professional Responsibility, 1976, 10th edit., 2008; (with Nowak and Young) Constitutional Law, 1978, (with Nowak) 2d edit., 1983, 8th edit., 2009, Modern Constitutional Law: Cases and Materials, 1981, 8th edit., 2007, (with Nowak) Treatise on Constitutional Law, 1992, 4th edit., 2007, Legal Ethics, 2002, 7th edit., 2009. Fulbright research scholar, Italy, 1981, Venezuela, 1986. Fellow Am. Bar Found. (life), Ill. Bar Found. (life); mem. Am. Law Inst. Roman Catholic. Office: Chapman Univ Law Sch Rm 406 One University Dr Orange CA 92866-1032 Office Phone: 714-628-2698. Business E-Mail: rrotunda@gmu.edu, rrotunda@capman.edu.

ROTZ, CAROL, retired theology studies educator; b. Sheldon, Iowa; m. Jim Rotz; children: Gary, Dav id. BA, NW Nazarene Coll., Nampa, Idaho; BTh, Nazarene U. Coll., Calgary, Alta., Canada; MA, U. Port Elizabeth, South Africa, Olivet Nazarene U., Bourbonnais, Ill.; D. Litt. et Phil., Rand Africaans U., Johannesburg. Cert. in ordination Ch. Nazarene. Lectr., libr. Nazarene Theol. Coll., Port Elizabeth, 1982—90, lectr. Jinja, Papua New Guinea, 2000—01, Africa Nazarene Theol. Coll., Muldersdrift; prof. Africa Nazarene U., 1994—99, NW Nazarene U., 2001—06. Mem.: Sociedad Wesleyana, Soc. Wesley, Soc. Bibl. Lit., Wesleyan Theol. Soc. Home: 2417 S Stonehedge Dr Nampa ID 83686

ROUB, BRYAN R(OGER), electronics executive; b. Berea, Ohio, May 1, 1941; s. Bernard Augustus and Pearl Irene (Koeblitz) R.; m. Judith Elaine Penman, June 19, 1965; children: Paul, Bradley, Michael. Student, Ohio Wesleyan U., 1959-62; BS, Ohio State U., 1966; MBA, U. Pa., 1978. Mem. audit staff Ernst & Ernst, Cleve., 1966-70; asst. contr. Midland-Ross, Cleve., 1970-73, contr., 1973-81, v.p., 1977-81, sr. v.p., 1981-82, exec. v.p. fin., 1982-84; sr. v.p. fin. Harris Corp., Melbourne, Fla., 1984-93, sr. v.p., CFO, 1993—2006. Bd. dirs. Fairchild Semicondr., 2004-; mem. fin. coun. II Machinery and Allied Products Inst., Washington, 1978-84, coun. I, 1984—2004, vice chmn., 1994-95, chmn., 1996-98; mem. conf. bd. coun. CFOs, 1993-96. Mem. adv. coun. Coll. Adminstrv. Scis., Ohio State U., 1978-81; mem. citizen's adv. coun. Westlake (Ohio) Schs., 1981-83; trustee Alcoholism Svcs. Cleve., 1982-84; mem. devel. bd. St. John's Hosp., 1983-84; pres. Westridge Homeowners' Assn., 1977; dir., treas. Tortoise Island Homeowners' Assn., 1988-90; bd. dirs. Easter Seal Soc. of Brevard County, 1993-98. Mem. AICPA, Ohio Soc. CPAs, Fin. Execs. Inst. (treas. N.E. Ohio chpt. 1976-78, bd. dirs. 1980-81, 83-84, v.p. 1981-82, pres. 1982-83, bd. dirs. Orlando chpt. 1984—, v.p. 1985-86, pres. 1986-87, nat. bd. dirs. 1987-90, area v.p. 1990-91, chmn. budget and fin. com. 1988-89, chmn. planning com. 1995-97, v.p. at large 1997-99, vice-chmn. 1999-2000, chmn. 2000-01, office of chmn. 1997-2002), Fin. Execs. Rsch. Found. (trustee 1994-97, 1999-2000, 2009-), Westwood Country Club, Eau Gallie Yacht Club (bd. govs., treas. 1990-92), Suntree Country Club. Address: 10280 S Tropical Trail Merritt Island FL 32952-6919 Personal E-mail: bryan@roub.net.

ROUBENOFF, RONENN, medical educator, researcher; b. Aug. 18, 1959; s. Robert R. and Dbora (Brandt) R.; m. Abby H. Shevitz. BSc, Northwestern U., Evanston, Ill., 1981, MD, 1983; MHS, Johns Hopkins U., 1990. Intern, then resident Johns Hopkins U., Balt., 1983-86, chief resident, 1986-87, fellow in rheumatology and epidemiology, 1988-90; fellow in nutrition Tufts U., Boston, 1990-92, asst. prof. medicine, 1992—, asst. prof. nutrition, 1994—. Sr. scholar Am. Coll. Rheumatology, 1990, nat. nutrition scholar PEN Found., 1990, fellow ACP, 1991. Office: USDA HNRC Tufts U 711 Washington St Boston MA 02111-1524

ROUBIDEAUX, YVETTE, federal agency administrator; b. Pierre, SD, Jan. 29, 1963; MD, Harvard Med. Sch., 1989; MPH, Harvard Sch. Pub. Health. Cert. Am. Bd. Internal Medicine. Intern/resident primary care internal medicine program Brigham & Women's Hosp., Boston, 1989—92; med. officer, clin. dir. San Carlos Indian Reservation, Ariz., Gila River Indian Cmty., Sacaton, Ariz.; asst. prof. Dept. Family & Cmty. Medicine, U. Ariz. Coll. Medicine; dir. Indian Health Svc. US Dept. Health & Human Services, Washington, 2009—. Apptd. sec.'s adv. com. on minority health HHS, 2000—02; dir. training program U. Ariz. Am. Indian Rsch. Ctr. Health; dir. U. Ariz. Indians Into Medicine Program (INMED); co-founder Native Rsch. Network, Inc. Co-editor: Promises to Keep: Public Health Policy for American Indians and Alaska Natives in the 21st Century. Mem. Rosebud Sioux Tribe, SD. Recipient Outstanding Am. Indian Faculty award, U. Ariz., 2002, Addison B. Scoville award for outstanding vol. svc., Am. Diabetes Assn., 2008; grantee Minority Health Policy Fellowship, Commonwealth Fund/Harvard U., 1997. Mem.: Assn. Am. Indian Physicians (pres. 1999—2000, Indian Physician of Yr. 2004). Office: US Dept Health & Human Services 200 Independence Ave SW Washington DC 20201*

ROUBINI, NOURIEL, economics professor; b. Istanbul, Turkey, Mar. 29, 1958; MA in Economics, Universita'L. Bocconi, 1982; PhD in Economics, Harvard U., 1988. Asst. prof. economics Yale U., New Haven, 1988—93, assoc. prof., 1993—95, NYU, NYC, 1995—. Vis. scholar Internat. Monetary Fund, Washington, 1987, 1993—94, 2001—03; rsch. fellow Ctr. Econ. Policy Rsch., London, 1991—; bd. govs. Fed. Reserve Sys., 1995; vis. economist Bank of Israel, Jerusalem, 1996; founder RGE Monitor, 1997—; sr. economist for internat. affairs Coun. of Econ. Advisors, Exec. Office of the Pres., 1998—99; rsch. fellow Nat. Bur. Econ. Rsch., Cambridge, Mass., 1998—; dir. Office Policy Devel. & Review US Dept. Treasury, 1999—2000, adv. to under sec. for internat. affairs, 2000. Author: Political Cycles and the Macroeconomy, 1997, Bailouts or Bail-ins? Responding to Financial Crisis in Emerging Economics, 2004. Named one of The Top 25 Market Movers, US News & World Report, 2009, The World's Most Influential People, TIME mag., 2009. Office: NYU Stern Sch Bus KMC 7-83 44 W 4th St New York NY 10012 Office Phone: 212-998-0886. Office Fax: 212-995-4218. E-mail: nroubini@stern.nyu.edu.*

ROUDEBUSH, LAWANDA CARPENTER, library director; d. James Arthur and Lois Elizabeth Carpenter; m. Peter V. Z. Roudebush; children: Elizabeth Michele, Robert Reid, Peter V. Z. II. BS in Edn., U. Ctrl. Mo., Warrensburg, 1966; MLS, Kent State U., Ohio, 1968. Libr. dir. Ft. Dodge Pub. Libr., Iowa, 2000—03, Davenport Pub. Libr., Iowa, 2003—; asst. dir. Indian Praire Pub. Libr., Darien, Ill., 1995—2000. Author: (lib. jours.) Movers and Shakers, 2002. Mem. Bi-State Literacy Coun., Bettendorf, Iowa, 2004—08. Mem.: Iowa Libr. Assn. (chair, LAMA chpt. 2007—08). Presbyterian. Home: 2250 E 48th St Davenport IA 52807 Office: Davenport Pub Libr 321 Main St Davenport IA 52801 Office Fax: 563-326-7809. Business E-Mail: lroudebush@davenportlibrary.com.

ROUECHE, JOHN EDWARD, II, education educator, director; b. Sept. 3, 1938; s. John Edward and Mary (Harris) R.; m. Suanne Davis; 1 stepchild, Robin Sue Maca; children by previous marriage: Michelle Renee, John Edward III. BA, Lenoir Rhyne Coll., Hickory, NC, 1960, LittD, 2001; LHD, Lenoir Rhyne Coll., 2001; MA, Appalachian Coll., Boone, NC, 1961; PhD, Fla. State U., 1964. Dean Gaston Coll., Gastonia, NC, 1964-67; assoc. rsch. educator UCLA, 1967-69; dir. jr. coll. divsn. Nat. Lab. Higher Edn., 1968-71; assoc. prof. edn. Duke U.; prof. edn., dir. c.c. leadership program U. Tex., Austin, 1971—, Sid W. Richardson regents chair, 1987—. Chancellor's coun. U. Tex. Sys., 1990—, U. Tex. Littlefield Soc., 1992—; lectr. Earl Pullias lectr. U. So. Calif., 1992, Coll. Bd. Disting. Lectr. NYC, 1993, Frances Crain Cook Disting. Lectr. U. Tex., 1994; chmn. nat. ednl. adv. bd. Gt. Am. Res. Ins. Co., 1988-94; co-chair Nat. Adv. Bd. for C.C.s, Invest Learning Corp., 1993-96; chair nat. adv. com. Kaplan Ednl. Partnerships, 1995-98; La Platica Disting. lectr. Ariz. State U., 1999; chmn. nat. adv. bd. 3-D Internat., 2000-. C.C. editor Jossey-Bass Publs., 1971-82; editor Creative Teaching Series, Media Systems Corp., 1980-85; mem. editl. bd. C.C. Times, C.C. Jour., 1990-94, others; author 35 books, including Profiles of Excellence in America's Schools, 1986, Access with Excellence, 1987, Shared Vision, 1989, Teaching as Leading, 1990, Underrepresentation: A Question of Diversity, 1991, Between a Rock and a Hard Place, 1993, The Company We Keep, 1995, Strangers in Their Own Land: Part Time Faculty, 1995, Embracing the Tiger: The Effectiveness Debate and the Community College, 1997, High Stakes, High Performance: Making Remedial Education Work, 1999, In Pursuit of Excellence: The Community College of Denver, 2001, Practical Magic: On the Front Lines of Teaching Excellence, 2003, Opting for Opportunity: Entrepreneurship in the Community College, 2005, The Creative CC, 2008; contbr. articles to profl. jours. Pres. Doss Sch. PTA, 1974-75; chmn. bd. N.W. Hills United Meth. Ch., 1973-76. Recipient Disting. Svc. award Nat. Coun. Univs. and Colls., 1984, Disting. Rsch. Publ. award, 1990, 93, 95, 97, Outstanding Alumnus award Appalachian State U., 1979, Disting. Grad. award Fla. State U., 1981, Mitchell Coll., 2009, Tchg. Excellence award U. Tex., 1982, Outstanding Rschr. award, 1985, Excellence award for outstanding learned article U.S. Edn. Press Assn., 1983, Disting. Rsch. award Nat. Assn. Devel. Edn., 1984-86, Disting. Rsch. Publ. award Nat. Coun. Student Devel., 1987, Disting. Rsch. award Nat. Coun. Staff, Program, and Orgn. Devel., B. Lamar Johnson Nat. Leadership award League for Innovation in the Cmty. Coll., 1988, Disting. Svc. & Leadership award CCP, INC., 1993, Disting. Faculty award U. Tex., 1994, Disting. Rsch. award Interassn. Student Devel. Orgns., 1995, Chancellor's Leadership award State of Ala., 1995, Career Rsch. Excellence award U. Tex., 1998, Disting. Grad. award Lenoir-Rhyne Coll., 2000; named lifetime amb. for N.C., 1978; Kellogg fellow, 1962-64, Disting. Internat. Leadership award Govt. of South Africa, 2000, 01, Disting. Nat. Svc. award Nat. Coun. Instrnl. Adminstrs., 2001, Disting. Leadership award Tex. Assn. Cmty. Colls., 2003 Star Leadership award Nat. Hispanic Border Inst., 2005, Mirabeau Lamar award Assn. Tex. Colls. and Univs., 2005, Disting. Grad. award., Mitchell CC, 2009 Mem. Am. Assn. Cmty. and Jr. Colls. (bd. dirs. 1989-94, Nat. Leadership award 1986, Disting. Rsch. award coun. colls. and univs. 1990, 94, 96, dist. rsch. sr. scholar award 1994, 96, nat. student devel. inter-assn. rsch. award 1995-96), Am. Assn. Higher Edn., Coun. Univs. and Colls. (past pres., bd. dirs.), Phi Beta Kappa, Phi Delta Kappa. Home: 4700 Lookout Mountain Cv Austin TX 78731-3654 Office: U Tex Austin One University Sta D5600 Austin TX 78712-0378 Office Phone: 512-471-7545. Business E-Mail: roueche@mail.utexas.edu.

ROUGHEAD, GARY, career military officer; b. 1951; m. Ellen Roughead. Grad., U.S. Naval Acad., 1973. Advanced through ranks to adm. USN, 2005; formerly with weapons dept. USS Josephus Daniels; former exec. officer USS Douglas & USS Tacoma; former commissioning chief engnr. USS O'Bannon, USS Spruance; former flag lt. to comdr. Naval Surface Force, US Atlantic Fleet; former surface warfare analyst, Office Program Appraisal USN, former adminstrv. aide to sec.; former exec. asst. to comdr.-in-chief US Pacific Command; former comdt. US Naval Acad.; chief legis. affairs USN; dep. comdr. US Pacific Command, Honolulu, 2004—05; comdr. US Pacific Fleet, Honolulu, 2005—07, US Fleet Forces Command, Norfolk, Va., 2007; chief naval ops. USN, Washington, 2007—. Decorated Defense Disting. Svc. Medal, Navy Disting. Svc. medal, Def. Superior Svc. medal, Navy Commendation medal, Legion of Merit; recipient Navy Achievement medal, Meritorious Svc. medal. Office: Office Chief Naval Ops 2000 Navy Pentagon Washington DC 20350 Office Phone: 703-695-4412.*

ROUHANI, SHAHROKH, civil engineering environmental educator, consultant; b. Tehran, Iran, Mar. 28, 1956; came to U.S., 1974; s. Aboutorab and Parirokh (Garakani) R.; m. Firouzeh Yekta, Aug. 18, 1983; children: Nina, Shiva. BSCE, U. Calif., Berkeley, 1978, BA in Econs., 1978; SM in Engring., Harvard U., 1980, PhD in Environ. Scis., 1983. Registered profl. engr., Ga. Asst. prof. Ga. Inst. Tech., Atlanta, 1983-90, assoc. prof. civil engring., 1990-96; sr. cons. Dames & Moore, Atlanta, 1990-95; pres. New Fields, Inc., Atlanta, 1995—. NSF vis. scientist Ctr. Geostats., Paris Sch. of Mines, 1987-88; expert mem. ASTM, EPA, U.S. Geol. Survey, Dept. Def. Geostats. Standardization Com., 1991-96. Co-author: Ground Water, 1991; contbr. articles to profl. publs., chpts. to books., also numerous reports, papers in field. Mem. ASCE (award 1991, chmn. nat. ground water hydrology 1991, chmn. task com. on geostatis. techniques in geohydrology 1987-89, sec. water resources com. Ga. sect. 1988, spl. session organizer 1989, 90, contact mem. task com. 1988-90, symposium organizer 1991), Am. Geophys. Union (assoc. editor Water Resources Rsch. 1989-94), Internat. Water Resources Assn., Am. Water Resources Assn., N.Am. Coun. on Geostats., Internat. Geostatis. Assn., Phi Beta Kappa, Tau Beta Pi, Chi Epsilon, Sigma Chi. Office: Newfields Inc 1349 W Peachtree St NW Ste 2000 Atlanta GA 30309-2926 Office Phone: 404-347-9050. Business E-Mail: srouhani@newfields.com.

ROUKEMA, LORAE TERESA, education educator, consultant; d. Mary Lorae and Ronald J Roukema. BA in Edn., U. NC, Chapel Hill, 1986, MEd, 1988; EdD, Fayetteville State U., NC, 2002. Cert. in education State NC, 1986, in adminstrn. and supervision 1998. Sch. adminstr. Moore County Schs., Carthage, NC, 1998—2004, tchr. mid. grades, 1988—2003; assoc. prof. edn. Campbell U., Buies Creek, NC, 2004—. Curriculum and design specialist Tailored Tng., Pinehurst, NC, 2005—. Recipient Governor's award for Tchg. Excellence, State NC, 1991, Golden Apple award, Moore County Schs., 1997, Dean's award for Tchg. Excellence, Campbell U., 2007, NC Young Educator of Yr.

ROULY, ELLIE ARCENEAUX, dancer, educator; b. New Iberia, La., Sept. 18, 1977; d. James and Paula Arceneaux; m. Karl Anthony Rouly, June 1, 2002; 1 child, Karrigan Elizabeth Andrea'. BA in Elem. Edn., U. La., Lafayette, 2001. Presch. tchr. ABC 123's Presch. Daycare, New Iberia, La., 1995—2001; dir., choreographer Dance Connection, 1998—; tchr. VB Glencoe Charter Sch., Franklin, 2001—. Lt. Mystic Krewe de Fou of Iberia, 1998. Scholar, Ladies Aux. Club, 1995. Office: VB Glencoe Charter School 4491 La 83 Franklin LA 70538

ROUMAN, JAMES CHRIST, anesthesiologist; b. Tomahawk, Wis., May 15, 1927; s. Christ John Rouman and Soteria Dendes. BS, Northwestern U., Evanston, Ill., 1949; MD, Northwestern U., Chgo., 1953. Diplomate An. Bd. Anesthesiology. Intern Meml. Hermann-Tex. Med. Ctr., Houston, 1953—54; resident Hartford Hosp./McGill U., Conn., 1956—59; attending staff Hartford Hosp., 1959—92; asst. prof. U. Conn., Sch. Medicine, Farmington, 1978—92. Author: (novels) Underwater Dreams, 2006. With USN, 1945—47. Recipient Disting. Svc. award, Conn. State Soc. Anesthesiologists, 1995. Greek Orthodox.

ROUMAN, JOHN CHRIST, classics educator; b. Tomahawk, Wis., May 1, 1926; s. Christ and Soteria (Dedes) R. BA in Greek, Carleton Coll., 1950; MA in Greek, Columbia U., 1951; student, Rutgers U., 1951-53, U. Kiel, Germany, 1956-57, U. Minn., Mpls., 1959-60; PhD in Classics, U. Wis., 1965. German tchr. Seton Hall Prep. Sch., South Orange, NJ, 1954-56; ancient history tchr. Malverne HS, NY, 1957-59; tchg. asst., ancient history U. Wis., Madison, 1960-61, rsch. asst., ancient history, 1961-65; rsch. asst., Greek epigraphy Inst. Advanced Study, Princeton, NJ, 1962-63; asst. prof., classics U. NH, Durham, 1965-71, assoc. prof., 1971-91, prof., 1991—, prof. emeritus, classics, 1999—, co-chmn., Spanish and classics depts., mem. adv. bd., Prof. John C. Rouman classical lectr. series, 1997—. Examiner NH State Bd. Edn. Latin and Greek, 1979-80; judge Warren H. Held Jr. Exam-Contests Latin and Mythology, 1988—; cons. Nat. Classical Greek Exam., 1980; mem. adv. bd. Christos and Mary Papoutsy Disting. Endowed Chair Bus. Ethics NH Coll./Southern NH U., 2000-03; mem. exec. bd. Hellenic Soc. PAIDEIA, NH, 2001; presenter, lectr. in field. Editor: (book) Smart-Start Learning System, 2000, (classical lectr. series) Tenth Ann. Celebration of John C. Rouman, 2007. Active Colovos Rd. Com., 1981-82. With USN, 1944—46. Fulbright scholar U. Kiel, 1956-57; recipient Disting. Tchg. award U. NH Alumni Assn., 1985, Pericles award Am. Hellenic Ednl. Progressive Assn. and Daus. of Penelope, 1993, Profile of Svc. award U. NH Aumni Assn., 2000. Mem. Am. Classical League (rep. to TCNE at ann. meeting 1978, mem. fin. com. 1981-82, treas. 1982-83, contbg. editor newsletter, 2005—), Am. Philol. Assn. (Nat. Excellence in Tchg. Classics award, 1991), Archaeol. Inst. Am., Classical Assn. Can., Classical Assn. New Eng. (mem. exec. com. at-large 1981-84, mem. nominating com. 1983-84, 86-87, pres. 1987-88, Barlow-Beach award 1991, mem. ad hoc com. on elections and appointments), Medieval Acad. Am., Modern Greek Studies Assn., Nat. Assn. Advisors Health Professions, NH Classical Assn. (mem. exec com. 1965—, chair nominating com. 1986—), Strafford County Greco-Roman Found. (pres. 1978—), Vergilian Soc. Am., Carleton Coll. Alumni Assn. (Alumni award for Dist. Achievement 2000), Phi Kappa Theta (faculty advisor, 1982—, chmn. nat. bd., 1993-94, nat. found. 1993—, Man of Achievement award 2000, Chpt. Advisor award 2002). Independent. Greek Orthodox. Achievements include having the Professor John C. Rouman Classical Lecture Series named in his honor. Home Phone: 603-868-2286. Personal E-mail: Jrouman@comcast.net.

ROUMBOS, MARIA K., elementary school educator; b. Flushing, NY, Nov. 22, 1970; d. Kostas J. and Alexandra K. Roumbos; m. Mark A. Cichon, July 2, 1995; children: Michael Roumbos Cichon, Marissa Roumbos Cichon, Matthew Roumbos Cichon. BS in Elem. Edn. summa cum laude, Adelphi U., 1991, MA in Secondary Edn. in Math. summa cum laude, 1993. Cert. tchr. early childhood edn., elem. edn., math. edn. Tchr. St. Nicholas Ch. Sch., Flushing, NY, 1986—, asst. dir., 1990—; tchr. Floral Park-Bellerose Sch. Dist., 1991—. Tutor in field, NY, 1991—2001. Recipient Pres.'s Achievement award, Queens Coll., 1989, Honors in Sci. and Math cert. merit, Soc. Women Engrs., 1991, Merit award, N.Y.C. Assn. Tchrs., 1988, Scholastic Achievement award, N.Y. Gov.'s Com., 1991, Merit award, Hellenic U. Club of N.Y., 1993, Outstanding Achievement award, Greek Lang. Inst., 1988, Internat. award for Striving for Peace on Earth, N.Y. Dist. of Kiwanis, 1987; Paul Douglas scholar, Empire State Challenger scholar, United Fedn. Tchrs. scholar, N.Y. State scholar. Mem.: Inst. for Math. and Sci. Studies (life), Internat. Baccalaureate Scholars (life), Nat. Honor Soc. (life; chpt. co-pres. 1987—88), Kappa Delta Pi (life). Democrat. Greek Orthodox. Avocations: reading, photography, painting, arts-n-crafts, gardening.

ROUNDS, MIKE (MARION MICHAEL ROUNDS), Governor of South Dakota; b. Huron, SD, Oct. 24, 1954; m. Jean Vedvei, 1978; children: Christopher, Lindsay, Brian, Carrie, John. BS in Polit. Sci., SD State U., Brookings, 1977. Ptnr. Fischer, Rounds & Assocs., Inc.; mem. SD State Senate from Dist. 24, 1991—2002, minority whip, 1993—94, majority leader, 1995—2002; gov. State of S.D., Pierre, 2003—. Bd. pres. Oahe YMCA; v.p. Home and Sch. Assn. St. Joseph Sch.; pres. Pierre-Ft. Pierre Exch. Club. Mem.: Midwestern Governors Assn. (chmn. 2008—), Ducks Unlimited, Knights of Columbus, Pierre Elks Lodge. Republican. Roman Catholic. Avocations: racquetball, hunting, boating, camping. Office: Office of Gov 500 E Capitol Ave Pierre SD 57501 Office Phone: 605-773-3212. Office Fax: 605-773-5844.

ROUNICK, JACK A., lawyer, clothing retail executive; b. Phila., June 5, 1935; s. Philip and Nettie (Brownstein) Rounick; m. Noreen A. Garrigan, Sept. 4, 1970; children: Ellen, Eric, Amy, Michelle. BBA, U. Mich., Ann Arbor, 1956; JD, U. Pa., Phila., 1959. Bar: Pa. 1960, US Dist. Ct. (ea. dist. Pa.) 1960. Ptnr. Israelit & Rounick, 1960-67, Moss & Rounick, 1968-69, Moss, Rounick & Hurowitz, Norristown, Pa., 1969-72, Moss & Rounick, Norristown, 1972-73, Pechner, Dorfman, Wolffe, Rounick and Cabot, Norristown, 1973-87; spl. asst. atty. gen., 1963-71; v.p., gen. counsel Martin Lawrence Ltd. Edits., Inc., 1987-93, dir., 1984—95; asst. sec. Deb Shops, Inc., 1974—2007, dir., 1974—2007; counsel to firm Wolf Block, Schorr & Solis-Cohen LLP, 1997—2006; of counsel Flamm, Boroff & Bacine, P.C., Blue Bell, Pa., 2006—. Author: Pa. Matrimonial Practice, 6 vols., 1982; editor: Pa. Family Lawyer, 1980—87; bd. editors Family Adv. Fin. chmn. Pa. Young Reps., 1964—66, treas., 1966—68, chmn., 1968—70. Recipient Boss of Yr. award, Montgomery County Legal Secs. Assn., 1970, cert. of appreciation, Pa. Bar Inst., 1980, Eric Turner award, Pa. Bar Family Law Sect., 2009; named one of Top 100 Attys., Worth mag., 2005. Fellow: Am. Acad. Matrimonial Lawyers (pres. Pa. chpt. 1982—84, gov. 1983—85, v.p. 1985—87, chmn. bd. rev. 1997—98), Internat. Acad. Matrimonial Lawyers; mem.: FLS, ABA (coun. family law sect. 1982—87, coun. 2000—03), Am. Coll. Family Trial Lawyers (diplomate), Scope and Correlation Com. (chmn. 2005—06), Family Adv. (bd. editors), Montgomery Bar Assn., Pa. Bar Assn. (past chmn. family law sect. 1978—80, Spl. Achievement award 1979—80), Friends of Hebrew U. (bd. dirs. 1987—93, nat. coun. trustees 1987—93, bd. trustees 1987—2006, pres. Phila. chpt. 1988—91, v.p. 1990—91). Republican. Jewish. Office: Flamm Boroff & Bacine PC 794 Penllyn Pike Blue Bell PA 19422-1669 Office Phone: 267-419-1504. Office Fax: 267-419-1560. Business E-Mail: jarounick@flammlaw.com.

ROUNSAVILLE, KEITH EUGENE, lawyer; b. Ancon, Panama, Aug. 6, 1945; s. William Russell Rounsaville and Dorothy Naletta Chambers; m. Linda Ann White, Feb. 14, 1976 (div. Oct. 1, 1994); m. Karla Rae Spaulding, May 24, 2000; children: Keith Chambers, David William. BA with honors, Yale U., 1967; JD cum laude, Columbia U., 1970. Cert.: Fla. Bar (in antitrust and trade regulation), bar: Calif. 1971, DC 1972, Fla. 1974. Assoc. O'Melveny & Myers LLP, LA, 1970; shareholder Trenam, Kemker, Scharf, Barkin, Frye, O'Neill & Mullis, P.A., Tampa, Fla., 1974—2000, Stearns Weaver Miller Alhadeff & Sitterson, P.A., Tampa, 2000—02, Litchford & Christopher, P.A., Orlando, 2007—; shareholder, chmn. antitrust dept. Akerman Senterfitt, Orlando and Tampa, Fla., 2002—06. Chmn. Rough Riders dist., Gulf Ridge coun. Boy Scouts Am., Tampa, 1991—92, dist. commr., 1990—91; pres. Rotary Club of Tampa Bay, Tampa, 1994—95, sec., 1993—94. Capt. JAGC USMC, 1971—73, Vietnam. Recipient Dist. award of Merit, Boy Scouts Am., 1991; named Rotarian of the Yr., Rotary Club of Tampa Bay, 1992; named one of America's Leading Lawyers Bus., Antitrust Law, Chambers USA, 2003—, The Best Lawyers in Am. Antitrust Law, Fla., 2005—, Fla. Super Lawyers Antitrust Law, 2006—; Harlan Fiske Stone scholar, Columbia U. Sch. of Law. Mem.: ABA (mem. Sherman Act com. sect. antitrust law 1974), Fla. Bar (chmn. and vice chmn. antitrust com. 1984—92, exec. coun., bus. law sect. 1984—92, chair antitrust law and trade cert. com. 2006—08), Am. Law Inst. Avocations: hiking, international travel. Office: Litchford & Christopher PA 390 N Orange Ave Ste 2200 Orlando FL 32801 Office Fax: 407-841-0325. Business E-Mail: krounsaville@litchfordchristopher.com.

ROUNTREE, ASA, lawyer; b. Birmingham, Ala., Aug. 9, 1927; s. John Asa and Cherokee Jemison (Van de Graaff) Rountree; m. Elizabeth Rhodes Blue, Aug. 11, 1951 (dec.); m. Helen Hill Updike, Oct. 10, 1998. AB, U. Ala., 1949; LLB, Harvard U., 1954. Bar: Ala. 1954, U.S. Dist. Ct. (no. dist.) Ala. 1954, U.S. Ct. Appeals (5th cir.) 1955, N.Y. 1962, U.S. Dist. Ct. (so. dist.) N.Y. 1963, U.S. Ct. Appeals (2d cir.) 1963, U.S. Supreme Ct. 1972. Assoc. Cabaniss & Johnston, Birmingham, Ala., 1954-60, ptnr., 1960-62; assoc. Debevoise & Plimpton, NYC, 1962-63, ptnr., 1963-91; spl. counsel Maynard, Cooper, & Gale, P.C., Birmingham, 1991—2006. Bd. dirs. U. Ala. Law Sch. Found. With US Army, 1945—46, lt. US Army, 1951—53. Mem.: ABA (chmn. litig. sect. 1980—81), Am. Coll. Trial Lawyers, Am. Law Inst., Assn. Bar City of N.Y., N.Y. State Bar Assn., Ala. Bar Assn., Am. Bar Found., Mountain Brook Club (Birmingham), River Club (N.Y.C.). Episcopalian. Home: 8 Cross Creek Dr Birmingham AL 35213

ROUPHAEL, NADINE G., physician; b. Ras Baalbeck, Bekaa, Lebanon, July 21, 1976; d. Georges Y. Rouphael and Marleine P. Saddy; m. Youssef W. Maakaroun, Aug. 16, 2008. MD, St. Joseph U., Beirut, 2001. Diplomate ABIM, 2005. Guest rschr. CDC, Atlanta, 2006—; staff physician Emory U., Atlanta, 2008—. Founder USJ sans frontieres, Beirut, 1998—2008. Recipient Fellow and Resident of Yr. award, Emory U., 2003—04, 2005—06. Mem.: IDSA. Achievements include research in vaccinology.

ROURKE, MICKEY (PHILIP ANDRE ROURKE JR.), actor; b. Schenectady, NY, Sept. 16, 1956; m. Debra Feuer, 1981 (div. 1989); m. Carre Otis, June 26, 1992 (div. Dec. 1998). Profl. boxer, 1991—95; gym owner Shapiro, West Hollywood. Actor: (films) Nineteen Forty-One, 1979, Heaven's Gate, 1980, Fade to Black, 1980, Body Heat, 1981, Diner, 1982 (Nat. Soc. of Film Critics award best supporting actor 1982), Rumblefish, 1983, The Pope of Greenwich Village, 1984, Year of the Dragon, 1985, Eureka, 1985, 9 1/2 Weeks, 1985, Angel Heart, 1987, A Prayer for the Dying, 1987, Barfly, 1987, Homeboy, 1988, Johnny Handsome, 1989, Wild Orchid, 1990, Desperate Hours, 1990, Harley Davidson and the Marlboro Man, 1991, White Sands, 1992, F.T.W., 1994, Fall Time, 1995, Exit in Red, 1996, Bullets, 1996, The Rainmaker, 1997, Love in Paris, 1997, Double Team, 1997, Buffalo '66, 1997, Thursday, 1998, Shergar, 1999, Shades, 1999, Out in Fifty, 1999, The Animal Factory, 2000, Get Carter, 2000, The Pledge, 2001, Spun, 2002, Masked and Anonymous, 2003, Once Upon a Time in Mexico, 2003, Man on Fire, 2004, Sin City, 2005, Domino, 2005, Stormbreaker, 2006, The Wrestler, 2008 (Best Actor Boston Soc. Film Critics, 2008, Best Performance by an Actor in a Motion Picture - Drama, Golden Globe award, Hollywood Fgn. Press Assn., 2009, Best Actor, Brit. Acad. Film and TV Arts, 2009, Ind. Spirit award for Best Male Lead, Film Ind., 2009), The Informers, 2009, Killshot, 2009; (TV movies) Act of Love, 1980, City in Fear, 1980, Rape and Marriage: The Rideout Case, 1980, Thicker Than Blood, 1998. Recipient Best Actor award, Elle Mag., 2009. Avocation: motorcycling. Office: c/o ICM LA 10250 Constellation Blvd Los Angeles CA 90067*

ROUS, BETH S., social studies educator, researcher; d. Robert D. and Ellen Mansfield Shanks; m. James D. Rous, Aug. 13, 1983; children: David A., Heather M. EdD, U. Ky., Lexington, 2001. Dir. cmty. edn., Human Devel. Inst. U. Ky., 1996—2007, assoc. prof. ednl. leadership studies, 2007—. Rschr. Nat. Early Childhood Transition Rsch. Inst. Author: (book) Tools for Transition. Recipient Merle Karnes Svc. award, Divsn. Early Childhood Coun. Exceptional Children, 2006. Mem.: Divsn. Early Childhood (pres. 2002—06). Democrat. Office: Univ Ky 111E Dickey Hall Lexington KY 40506-0017 Home Fax: 859-257-2769. Business E-Mail: brous@uky.edu.

ROUS, STEPHEN NORMAN, urologist, educator; b. NYC, Nov. 1, 1931; s. David H. and Luba (Margulies) R.; m. Margot Woolfolk, Nov. 12, 1966; children: Benjamin, David. AB, Amherst Coll., 1952; MD, N.Y. Med. Coll., 1956; MS, U. Minn., 1963. Diplomate: Am. Bd. Urology. Intern Phila. Gen. Hosp., 1956-57, resident, 1959-60, Flower-Fifth Ave. and Met. Hosp., NYC, 1957-59, Mayo Clinic, Rochester, Minn., 1960-63; practice medicine specializing in urology San Francisco, 1963-68; assoc. prof. urology N.Y. Med. Coll., NYC, 1968-72, assoc. dean, 1970-72; prof. surgery, chief div. urology Mich. State U., East Lansing, 1972-75; prof., chmn. dept. urology Med. U. S.C., Charleston, 1975-88; urologist-in-chief Med. U. S.C. and County hosps., Charleston, 1975-88; editorial dir. Norton Med. Books div. W.W. Norton and Co., 1988-94, editorial cons., 1994—; clin. prof. surgery Uniformed Svcs. U. of Health Scis., Bethesda, Md., 1992-2001; clin. prof. surgery, urology Brown U. Med. Sch., 2006—. Adj. prof. urology Med. U. S.C., 1988-99, prof. emeritus, 1999—; adj. prof. surgery Dartmouth Med. Sch., 1988-91, prof. surgery (urology), 1991-2001, prof. surgery emeritus, 2001—; staff urologist Dartmouth-Hitchcock Med. Ctr., 1991-99; cons. urologist Saginaw VA Hosp., 1971-75, Charleston VA Hosp., 1975-88; hon. cons. St. Peter's Hosp., London, 1981-82; sr. vis. fellow Inst. Urology, London, 1981-82; mil. cons. in urology USAF Surgeon Gen., 1982-85; chmn. alumni devel. com. Mayo Clinic, 1979-82; hon. staff The Exeter Hosp., N.H., 1988—; nat. bd. visitors N.Y. Med. Coll., 1988-97; chief urology VA Med. Ctr., White River Junction, Vt., 1991-2001; mem. reparative justice bd. Vt. Dept. Corrections, 2004; urologist VA Med. Ctr., Providence, 2005— Author: Understanding Urology, 1973, Urology in Primary Care, 1976, Spanish edit., 1978, Russian edit., 1979, Urology: A Core Textbook, 1985, 2d edit., 1996, The Prostate Book, 1988, latest rev. edit., 2001, (with Judge Hiller B. Zobel) Doctors and the Law: Defendants and Expert Witnesses, 1993, (with Dr. Pamela Ellsworth) The Little Black Book of Urology, 2001; editor Urology Ann., 1987-97, Stone Disease: Diagnosis and Management, 1987; mem. editl. bd. Mil. Medicine, 1984-94; contbr. articles to med. jours. Mem. East Lansing (Mich.) Planning Commn., 1974-75; vestryman, jr. warden All Saints Episcopal Ch., East Lansing, 1973-75, lay reader, mem. diocesan com. on continuing edn., 1975-86; vestryman St. Michael's Episc. Ch., 1979-82, Charleston, S.C., chmn. every mem. canvas, 1979-80, chmn. lay readers, 1983-86; mem. fin. com., lay reader Christ Episc. Ch., Exeter, N.H., 1989-91; lector St. Thomas Episc. Ch., Hanover, N.H., 1991-96, vestryman, 1992-96, stewardship chmn., 1992-94; jr. warden 1994-96; chalicist, lector, del. to diocesan conv. Trinity Ch., Newport, R.I, 2006—, jr. warden, 2009-; mem. selectman's alt. Hampton Falls Planning Bd., 1989-91; alt. mem. Zoning Bd. Adjustment, Hanover, 1997-2000; bd. trustees, Nat. Hypertension Assn., N.Y.C., 2001-; bd. dirs. Med. Sci. Techs. Inc., Newport News, Va., 2001—; Dept. Morale Welfare Recreation adv. bd., US Naval Station Newport, 2008-. Col. USAFR, 1981-85, col. USAR, 1985-2000, col. AUS, ret., 2001—. Recipient "A" designator in urology, U.S. Army Surgeon Gen., 1986. Fellow ACS, Am. Acad. Pediatrics; mem. AMA, Soc. Univ. Urologists, Internat. Soc. Urology, Am. Urol. Assn., Nat. Urologic Forum, Soc. Pediatric Urology, Brit. Assn. Urol. Surgeons, German Urol. Assn. (hon.), English Speaking Union (v.p. Newport County br. 2006-08, pres. 2008-), Newport Reading Room, Mayo Alumni Assn. (v.p. 1979-81, pres. 1983-85), Army and Navy Club (Washington), Lotos Club (N.Y.C.), Dartmouth Club of N.Y.C., Brown U. Faculty Club (bd. mgrs. 2006—), Sigma Xi, Alpha Omega Alpha. Home: 421 Bellevue Ave #2A Newport RI 02840 Personal E-mail: stephen.n.rous@dartmouth.edu.

ROUSE, CECILIA ELENA, federal official, economics and public affairs professor; b. Walnut Creek, Calif., Dec. 18, 1963; d. Carl Albert and Lorraine (Moxley) Rouse. BA, Harvard U., 1986, PhD in Economics, 1992. Asst. prof. economics & pub. affairs Princeton U., NJ, 1992—2009, Theodore A. Wells '29 prof. economics & pub. affairs, dir. Industrial Rels. Sect., founding dir. Edn. Rsch. Sect.; mem. Coun. Econ. Advisers, Exec. Office of the Pres., Washington, 2009—. Mem. Nat. Econ. Coun., The White House, 1998—99; mem. Rsch. Network on Transition to Adulthood MacArthur Found.; spkr. in field. Sr. editor The Future of Children; editor: Jour. Labor Econs.; contbr. articles to profl. jours. Vis. scholar, Russell Sage Found., 1994—95. Fellow: Nat. Bur. Assn. Econ. Rsch.; mem.: Am. Edn. Rsch. Assn., Am. Econ. Assn. Office: Council of Economic Advisors 725 17th St NW Washington DC 20502*

ROUSE, CHRISTOPHER CHAPMAN, III, composer, educator; b. Balt., Feb. 15, 1949; s. Christopher Chapman Jr. and Margery (Harper) Rouse; m. Ann Jensen, Aug. 28, 1983; children: Jillian, Alexandra, Adrian 1 stepchild, Angela. MusB, Oberlin Conservatory, 1971; MFA, DMA, Cornell U., 1977; DMus (hon.), Oberlin Coll., 1996, SUNY, Geneseo, 2000. Asst. prof. composition U. Mich., Ann Arbor, 1978—81, Eastman Sch. Music, Rochester, NY, 1981—85, assoc. prof. composition, 1985—91, prof. composition, 1991—2002; mem. faculty Juilliard Sch., 1997—. Composer-in-residence Balt. Symphony Orch., 1986—89, Schleswig Holstein Festival, 1989, Helsinki Bienniale, 1997, Tanglewood Music Ctr., 1997, Pacific Music Festival, 1998, Aspen Music Festival, 1999—; writer numerous musical subjects; historian rock music. Composer for numerous renowned soloists and ensembles, including Yo-Yo Ma, Evelyn Glennie, Emanuel Ax, Dawn Upshaw, Cho-Liang Lin, Charles Castleman, James VanDemark, Jan de Gaetani, Leslie Guinn, Sharon Isbin, Carol Wincenc, William Albright, Soc. New Music, Blackearth Percussion Group, Calder Quartet, Boston Pops, Boston Musica Viva, Aspen Music Festival, Chamber Music Soc. Lincoln Ctr., N.Y. Internat. Festival of Arts, Chamber Music Am., New Eng. Conservatory Music, Nonesuch Records, orchestral works programmed by Berlin, Helsinki, Stockholm, NYC, Israel, Netherlands, Buffalo, L.A., Rochester Philharms., Orch. Nat. de France, Orch. de Paris, Residentie, Concertgebouw, Vienna & Zurich Tonhalle, New Zealand, Philharmonia, also Vienna, BBC, Berlin, Montreal, Chgo., Boston, St. Louis, Detroit, Balt., Nat., Pitts., Houston, Denver, Milw., Cleve., Minn., Phila., Oakland, Cin., Atlanta, N.J., Utah, Indpls., Memphis, San Francisco, Dallas, Göteboro U., Bournemouth symphony orchs, also The Netherlands, Finnish, Frankfurt, Moscow, Austrian, Flemish, BBC and NHK Tokyo Radio Orchs., commd. composer Atlanta Symphony, Phila. Orch., N.Y. Philharm., L.A. Philharm., Balt. Symphony, Houston Symphony, Minn. Orch., London Symphony, Cleve. Orch., Detroit Symphony, St. Louis Symphony, Boston Pops, Rochester Philharm., Cleve. Quartet, NYC Ballet. Recipient awards, Guggenheim Found., League Composers/ISCM, NEA, Rockefeller Found., Am. Music Ctr., Warner Bros. Record Co., Koussevitzky Found., BMI and Pitney Bowes, Friedheim 1st prize, Kennedy Ctr., 1988, Pulitzer prize for music, 1993, Grammy award, 2002. Mem.: Am. Acad. Arts and Letters (Acad. award 1993). Office: Juilliard Sch 60 Lincoln Center Plz New York NY 10023

ROUSE, JACQUELINE ANNE, history educator, editor; b. Roseland, Va., Feb. 1, 1950; d. John Henry and Fannie (Thompson) R. B.A., Howard U., 1972; M.A., Atlanta U., 1973; Ph.D., Emory U., 1983. Sr. instr. Palm Beach Jr. Coll., Lake Worth, Fla., 1973-78; guest lectr. Ga. Inst. Tech., Atlanta, 1983; asst. prof. history Morehouse Coll., Atlanta, 1983—; guest lectr. Jackson State U., 1984; panelist NEH, Washington, 1985. Editorial intern Jour. of Negro History, 1979-83, asst. editor, 1983—. Smithsonian Instn. fellow 1982, 83; NEH fellow, 1984; grantee United Negro Coll. Fund, 1985, Mellon Found., 1985. Mem. Assn. Black Women Historians (regional dir. 1984—), Assn. Social and Behavioral Scientists (mem. exec. council 1984—), Assn. Study Afro-Am. Life and History, So. Hist. Assn., Nat. Women's Studies Assn., Howard U. Alumni Assn. Democrat. Baptist. Avocations: reading, spa-aerobics, writing, music. Home: 286 Forest Glen Cir Avondale Estates GA 30002-1204

ROUSE, JOHN WILSON, JR., technology consultant; b. Kansas City, Mo., Dec. 7, 1937; s. John Wilson and Gail Agnes (Palmer) R.; m. Susan Jane Davis, May 3, 1981; 1 son, Jeffrey Scott. A.S., Kansas City Jr. Coll., 1957; BS, Purdue U., 1959; MS, U. Kans., 1965, PhD, 1968. Registered profl. engr., Mo., Tex. Engr. Bendix Corp., Kansas City, Mo., 1959-64; rsch. coord. Ctr. for Rsch., U. Kans., Lawrence, 1964-68; prof. elec. engring., dir. remote sensing ctr. Tex. A&M U., College Station, 1968-78; Logan prof. engr., chmn. elec. engring. U. Mo., Columbia, 1978-81; dean engring. U. Tex., Arlington, 1981-87; pres. So. Rsch. Inst., Birmingham, Ala., 1987-97, The Rouse Group, Hoover, Ala., 1997—. Mgr. microwave program NASA Hdqrs., Washington, 1975-77. Contbr. articles to profl. jours. Recipient Outstanding Tchr. award Tex. A&M U., 1971; Outstanding Prof. award U. Mo., 1980; Engr. of Yr. Tex. Soc. Profl. Engrs., 1983 Mem. IEEE, Nat. Soc. Profl. Engrs., Am. Soc. Engring. Edn., Internat. Bus. Fellows, Internat. Union Radio Sci., Sigma Xi, Eta Kappa Nu., Tau Beta Pi Home: 39 Camden Cir San Antonio TX 78218 also: 39 Campden Cir San Antonio TX 78218-6055

ROUSE, PETER M., federal official; b. New Haven, Apr. 15, 1946; BA, Colby Coll., 1968; MA, London Sch. Econs., 1970; MPA, Harvard U., 1977. Legis. aide to Senator James Abourezk, Washington, 1973; chief of staff to Lt. Gov. Terry Miller, Alaska, 1979—83, Rep. Dick Durbin, 1984—85, Senator Tom Daschle, 1985—2004, Senator Barack Obama, 2004—08; co-chmn. Barack Obama Presdl. Transition Team, Washington, 2008—09; sr. adv. to Pres. The White House, Washington, 2009—. Named one of The 50 Most Powerful People in DC, GQ mag., 2007. Democrat. Office: The White House 1600 Pennsylvania Ave NW Washington DC 20500*

ROUSE, RICHARD HUNTER, historian, educator; b. Boston, Aug. 14, 1933; s. Hunter and Dorothee (Hüsmert) R.; m. Mary L. Ames, Sept. 7, 1959; children: Thomas, Andrew, Jonathan. BA, State U. Iowa, 1955; MA, U. Chgo., 1957; PhD, Cornell U., 1963. Mem. faculty UCLA, 1963—, prof. history, 1975—. Assoc. dir. Ctr. Medieval and Renaissance Studies, 1966-67, acting dir., 1967-68; dir. Summer Inst. in Paleography, 1978, chair grad. coun., 1989-90; adv. bd. Hill Monastic Microfilm Libr., St. John's U., Collegeville, Minn., Ambrosiana Microfilm Library, Notre Dame (Ind.) U., Corpus of Brit. Medieval Libr. Catalogues, Brit. Acad. Beinecke, 2009; vis. prof. paleography Dept. Classics, Yale U. Author: Serial Bibliographies for Medieval Studies, 1969, (with M.A. Rouse) Preachers, Florilegia and Sermons: Studies on the Manipulus Florum of Thomas of Ireland, 1979; (with others) Texts and Transmission, 1983; (with C.W. Dutschke) Medieval and Renaissance Manuscripts in the Claremont Libraries, 1986; (with M.A. Rouse) Cartolai, Illuminators and Printers in Fifteenth-Century Italy, 1988; (with L. Bataillon and B. Guyot) La Production du livre universitaire au moyen age, exemplar et pecia, 1988; (with others) Guide to Medieval and Renaissance Manuscripts in the Huntington Library, 1989; (with M. Ferrari) Medieval and Renaissance Manuscripts at the University of California, Los Angeles, 1991; (with M.A. Rouse and R.A.B. Mynors) Registrum de libris doctorum et auctorum veterum, 1991; (with M.A. Rouse) Authentic Witnesses: Approaches to Medieval Texts and Manuscripts, 1991; (with M.A. Rouse) Manuscripts and Their Makers: Commercial Book Producers in Medieval Paris 1200-1500, 2 vols., 2000, (with M.A. Rouse) Henry of Kirkestede, Catalogus de libris autenticis et apocrifis, 2004; co-editor: Viator: Medieval and Renaissance Studies, 1970-; mem. editorial bd. Medieval and renaissance manuscripts in Calif. libraries, Medieval Texts, Toronto; Medieval Texts, Binghamton, Library Quar., 1984-88, Speculum, 1981-85, Revue d'histoire des Textes, 1986-, Cambridge Studies in Paleography and Codicology, 1990-96, Catalogue of Medieval and Renaissance Manuscripts in the Beinecke Rare Book and Manuscript Library Yale University, 1984-92, Filologia MedioLatina, 1994-, Manuscripta, 2000—, Utrecht Studies in Medieval Literacy, 2000—, Litterae Caelestes, 2005— Am. Coun. Learned Socs. fellow, 1972-73, vis. fellow All Souls Coll., Oxford, 1978-79, Guggenheim fellow, 1975-76, Rosenbach fellow in bibliography U. Pa., 1976, NEH fellow, 1981-82, 84-85, 94-96, Inst. for Advanced Studies fellow Jerusalem, 1991; J.R. Lyell reader in bibliogrpahy U. Oxford, 1991-92; vis. fellow Pembroke Coll., U. Oxford, 1992, Pembroke Coll., U. Cambridge, 2000-01. Fellow Royal Hist. Soc., Medieval Acad. Am.; mem. Medieval Assn. Pacific (councillor 1965-68, pres. 1968-70), Medieval Acad. Am. (councillor 1977-80), Comité international de paléographie (treas. 1985-90), Comité international du vocabulaire des institutions et de la communication intellectuelles au moyen age, 1987—, Societa internazionale per lo studio del medioevo latino, 1988—. Home: 11444 Berwick St Los Angeles CA 90049-3416 Office: Dept History U Calif Los Angeles CA 90024 Office Phone: 310-825-4168. Business E-Mail: rouse@history.ucla.edu.

ROUSE, ROSCOE, JR., retired librarian, educator; b. Valdosta, Ga., Nov. 26, 1919; s. Roscoe and Minnie Estelle (Corbett) R.; m. Charlie Lou Miller, June 23, 1945; children: Charles Richard, Robin Rouse Wells. BA, U. Okla., 1948, MA in Libr. Sci., 1952; student (Grolier Soc. scholar), Rutgers U., 1956; AMLS, U. Mich., 1958, PhD, 1962. Bookkeeper C & S Nat. Bank, Valdosta, Ga., 1937-41; draftsman R.K. Rouse Co. (heating engrs.), Greenville, SC, 1941-42; asst. librarian Northeastern State Coll., Tahlequah, Okla., 1948-49, acting librarian, instr. library sci., 1949-51; circulation librarian Baylor U., 1952-53, acting univ. librarian, 1953-54, univ. librarian, prof., 1954-63, chmn. dept. library sci., 1956-63; dir. libraries State U. NY at Stony Brook, LI, 1963-67; dean libr. svcs., prof. Okla. State U., Stillwater, 1967-87, univ. libr. historian, 1987-92, chmn. dept. libr. edn., 1967-74; ret., 1987. Grolier Soc. scholar, Rutgers U., 1956; vis. prof. U. Okla. Sch. Library Sci., summer 1962, N. Tex. State U., summer 1965; acad. library cons.; pub. dir. Seretean Wellness Ctr., Okla. State U., 2002—07; mem. AIA-Am. Library Assn. Library Bldg. Awards Jury, 1976; bd. dirs. Fellowship Christian Libr. and Info. Specialists; in retirement, volunteers writing and photography for local newspaper. Author: A History of the Baylor University Library, 1845-1919, 1962; editor: Okla. Librarian, 1951-52; co-author: Organization Charts of Selected Libraries, 1973; A History of the Okla. State U. Library, 1992; contbr. articles, book revs., chpts. to publs. in field. Bd. dirs. Okla. Dept. Librs., 1989-92, chmn., 1990-92. 1st lt. USAAF, 1942-45. Sgt. USAF, 1942—45. Decorated Air medal with 4 oak leaf clusters; recipient citation Okla. State Senate, 1987, Rotary Outstanding Achievement award, 1996; named in 150 Prominent Individuals in Baylor's History. Mem. ALA (life, mem. coun. 1971-72, 76-80, 83-84, 84-88, chmn. libr. orgn. and mgmt. sect. 1973-75, planning and budget assembly 1978-79, coun. com. on coms. 1979-80, bldgs. and equipment sect. exec. bd. 1979-80, chmn. bldgs. for coll. and univ. librs. com. 1983-85, chmn. nominating com. libr. history roundtable 1993-94), AARP, (sec. local chpt. 1998-2000), Okla. Libr. Assn. (life, pres. 1971-72, ALA coun. rep. 1976-80, 83-84, OLA Disting. Svc. award 1979, Spl. Merit award 1987), S.W. Libr. Assn. (chmn. coll. and univ. div. 1958-60, chmn. scholarship com. 1968-70), Internat. Fedn. Libr. Assns. (standing com. on libr. bldgs. and equipment 1976-88), Assn. Coll. and Rsch. Librs. (chmn. univ. librs. sect. 1969-70, mem. exec. bd. and rep. to ALA Coun., 1971-72), U. Mich. Sch. Libr. Sci. Alumni Soc. (pres. 1979-80, Alumni Recognition award 1988), mem. Alumni Found. Com., 1992-94, Payne County Ret. Educators Assn. (v.p., pres. elect 1991-92, pres. 1992-93), Okla. State U. Emeriti Assn. (pres. 2000-01), Okla. Hist. Soc. (com. on Okla. Higher Edn. mus. 1985—, pub. dir. 2002—), Stillwater Rotary Club (pres. 1980-81, Rotarian of Yr. 1999, editor Rotary Weekly bulletin, various coms., pub. dir. 1998—), Beta Phi Mu, Archons of Colophon. Baptist (chmn. bd. deacons 1973). Personal E-mail: rouse74074@aol.com. *It is sometimes a hidden influence in our lives which drives us toward a set goal. We ourselves may not recognize the real source of that urge to fulfill a dream. Only after many years was I able to look back and discern the factors in my youth that pushed me toward my goal of attaining a good education. They grew out of the influence that the Great Depression had on my early life. Because of that experience the preparation for a career became my first goal in life, yet the ways and means for achieving it were virtually nonexistent. It was to be, however, and I was fortunate to realize that goal. It causes me to think now that perhaps the degree of determination and endurance one possesses is paced more by adverse condition than by times of comfort and ease.*

ROUSE, TERRIE SUZITTE, museum director; b. Youngstown, Ohio, Dec. 2, 1952; d. Eurad and Florence (Wilcox) Rouse; 1 child, Malcom Adam Rouse-West. BA, Trinity Coll., 1974; MS in Profl. Studies, Cornell U., 1977; cert. in internat. affairs, Columbia U., 1979, MA, 1979. Mgr., curator Adam Clayton Powell St. Office Bldg., NYC, 1979-81; sr. curator Studio Mus. Harlem, NYC, 1981-86; dir. mus. N.Y. Transit Mus., Bklyn., 1986—91; dir. Calif. Afro-Am. Mus., 1991—93; artistic exec. dir. Atlanta Ballet, 2002—03; exec. arts mgr., mus. dir. Union Sta., Kansas City, 2005—; CEO Capitol Visitor svc., United States Capitol. Advisor Bellevue Hosp. Art Bd., 1981—. Contbr. articles to profl. jours. Mem. Conf. Mil. Transp. Ofcls. Named Outstanding Young Women Am., 1981—83. Mem.: Am. Assn. Mus. (assessor 1981—). Avocations: sewing, reading, doll collecting. Office Phone: 202-593-1837. Personal E-mail: trouse3008@aol.com.

ROUSE, VIKI DASHER, literature and language professor; d. Victor Eugene Dasher and Ruth Made Wisenbaker-Dasher; m. W. F. Rouse, June 10, 1971; children: Benjamin William, Rebecca Victoria Rouse-Herring. MA in English, U. Tenn., Knoxville, 2003. Vis. asst. prof. English Tusculum Coll., Tenn., 2002—05; assoc. prof. English Walters State CC, Morristown, Tenn., 2005—. Coord. and dir. Mildred Haun Celebration Appalachian Lit., Culture, and Scholarship, Morristown, 2008—. Contbr. articles to profl. jours. Mem.: NCTE, TYCAT, Appalachian Studies Assn., TYCA-SE (state rep. 2008—), TE-TYC (mem. editl. bd. 2006—08). Office: Walters State CC 500 S Davy Crockett Pkwy Morristown TN 37813

ROUSH, JOHN A., academic administrator; b. Wis. m. Susie Miller Roush; children: Luke, Mark. B in English, Ohio U.; M, M, D, Miami U., Ohio. Grad. asst. football coach to exec. asst. to pres. Miami U., Ohio; exec. asst. to pres. U. of Richmond, 1982—90, v.p. planning, 1990—98; pres. Centre Coll., Danville, Ky., 1998—. Mem. Coun. of Pres., Assn. of Gov. Bds., Nat. Assn. Independent Coll. & Univ.; treas. Assn. Presbyn. Coll. & Univ., 2002—03. Contbr. articles to profl. jours. Capt. US Army. Office: Centre Coll 600 W Walnut St Danville KY 40422 Office Phone: 859-238-5200. E-mail: jroush@centre.edu.*

ROUSH, ROBERT WARREN, electrical engineer, director; b. Tulsa, Oct. 30, 1930; s. Ernest Edwin and Georgiana Roush; m. Emily Sinclair Knoblock, Sept. 2, 1956; children: Kathryn Elizabeth, Robert Mark. BSEE, Okla. A&M Coll., 1957. Lic. profl. engr., Okla., Fla., Colo., La., Tex., Calif., Ark., Iowa, N.C., Md., Va, D.C., Del., NH, Tenn. Field engr. Schlumberger Well Surveying Corp., Houston, 1957—65; aerosystems engr. Gen. Dynamics, Inc., Ft. Worth, 1966—69; elec. engr. Persons & Assocs., Oklahoma City, 1969—71; adj. assoc. prof., guest lectr. dept. environ. control, Sch. Arch. Okla. State U., 1978—82; from elec. engr. to sr. corp. v.p. The Benham Group, Oklahoma City, 1971—83; pres. Roush Engring. Co., Inc., Oklahoma City, 1983—87; elec. engring. dept. head Hansen Lind Meyer, Inc., Iowa City, 1987—89; mgr. elec. engring. dept. Gee & Jenson, Inc., West Palm Beach, Fla., 1989—92; chief elec. engr. FSB/Texas, Inc., Ft. Worth, 1992—2001; v.p. Setty & Assocs., Ltd., Fairfax, Va., 2001—06; dir. elec. engring. Calvin-Giordano & Assoc., Inc., 2006—. Lectr. in field. Contbr. articles to profl. jours. 1st lt. USAF, 1951—55. Recipient IES Lighting Design Award of Merit. Mem.: NSPE, IEEE (life; past chmn. ctrl. Okla. chpt., past chmn. bd. dirs. ctrl. Okla. chpt., Engr. of Yr. in mgmt. 1977—78), Am. Consulting Engrs. Coun. (cons. membership com.), Computer Soc., Industry Applications Soc. (past chmn.), Power Engring. Soc. (past chmn.), Okla. Soc. Profl. Engrs. (past state chmn. profl. engrs. in pvt. practice), Illuminating Engring. Soc. N.Am. (past pres. ctrl. Okla. chpt., mem. healthcare facilities com.). Republican. Home: 3572 Sahara Springs Blvd Pompano Beach FL 33069 Office: Calvin Giordano & Assocs Inc 1800 eller Dr Ste 600 Fort Lauderdale FL 33316 Office Phone: 954-921-7781. Personal E-mail: r_w_roush@bellsouth.net.

ROUSON, VIVIAN REISSLAND, alcohol/drug abuse services professional, consultant, journalist; b. New Orleans, July 18, 1929; d. Albert Isaac and Ophelia (Scott) Reissland; m. W. Ervin Rouson, June 22, 1953 (dec. May 1979); children: Lizette Hélène, Darryl Ervin, Brigette Maria, Janine Patrice, Damian William. BA, Xavier U., 1951; MS, Nova U., 1979; postgrad., U. Ky., 1965, U. South Fla., 1970. Tchr., cons. Gibbs Jr. Coll., St. Petersburg, Fla., 1958-60; tchr., cons. Pinellas County Schs., St. Petersburg, Clearwater, Fla., 1960-78; freelance opinion editorial columnist U.S. newspaper, 1976-82; columnist Evening Independent, Pinellas County, Fla., 1976-78, Palm Beach (County, Fla.) Post, 1979-82; tchr., cons. Palm Beach County Sch., Lake Worth, W. Palm Beach, Fla., 1978-82; editorial writer St. Petersburg Times, 1979, Cath. Standard, 1990—, Nat. Cath. Reporter, 1997—98, In a Word mag., 2000—; program coord., interim dir. Women's Resource Ctr. Normandale C.C., Bloomington, Minn., 1986-89; interim dir. Women's Resource Ctr., Normandale Community Coll., Bloomington, Minn., 1989; coord., internat. vol. program Inst. on Black Chem. Abuse, Mpls., 1989-90; alcohol-drug abuse svcs. profl., 1989—2000; assoc. editor Nat. Black Media Coalition, Washington, 1991—95. V.I.P. coord. Inst. on Black Chem. Abuse, Mpls., 1989-90; writing and fgn. lang. cons. Pinellas County and Palm Beach County, fla., 1960-82; bd. dirs. Carroll Pub. Co.; tchr. French, St. Peter's Interparish Sch., 1999; faculty Inst. Black Cath. Studies Xavier U., 2008-. Author: The Hummingbird Within Us, 1980, Like a Mighty Banyan, 1982, Alcohol and Drug Abuse in Black America, 1988; editor conf. proceedings, U. Minn.; editorial writer-columnist; editorial bd. St. Petersburg Times, 1979. Bd. dirs. St. Petersburg Cath. High Sch., 1976, Minn, divsn. Am. Cancer Soc., Mpls., 1983-90, Ind. Sch. Dist. 191, Burnsville, Eagan, Savage, Minn., 1984-87, Minn. Valley YMCA, Dakota County, Minn., 1987-90; dir. One Ch.-One Addict, 1990-2000; pres. D.C. chpt. Hook-Up Black Women, 1992-97; sec., bd. dirs. Ionia Whipper Home, Inc., 1992-, Nat. Urban League, initiator and co-founder Archdiocese of Wash. Sisters in the Spirit, 2001; vol. Dr. Porter & Gaston's Prime Time Health African American Woman Program. Named Outstanding Journalist South Atlantic Region Alpha Kappa Alpha, 1978, 79, 80; recipient Appreciation Pub. Svc. cert. Nat. Assn. Black Accts., 1992; DC honoree Experience Works, 2006; Tchg. scholar U. Notre Dame, 2006. Mem. AAUW, NAACP (life) Twin Cities Black Journalists (co-chair 1985-86, v.p. 1989-90), Minn. Polit. Congress Black Women (charter), Minn. Elected Women Ofcls., Dakota County Soc. Black Women (founder 1983, v.p.

1983-84), Pinellas County Fgn. Lang. Tchrs. (treas., pres.), Nat. Coun. Negro Women (life), The Links (alumna mem. Capital City chpt.), Washington Urban League (life), Alpha Kappa Alpha (life). Roman Catholic. Avocations: oratory, poetry, civic volunteerism, floral arrangements, walking. Home and Office: Seminars/Workshops 2311 N Capitol St NE Washington DC 20002

ROUSOS, LINDA, language educator; b. Rochester, NY, Mar. 12, 1953; d. Anthony Spiro Rousos and Martha Ellen Webster; 1 child, Joseph Rousos-Hammond. MA in English, U. Ill., Champaign-Urbana, 1979. Cert. CC Ariz. Dept. Edn. Faculty U. So. Calif., Madrid Ctr., 1979—80, Milw. Area Tech. Coll., 1986—88, Pima County CC, Tucson, 1996—; faculty, coord. U. Wis., Dept. Linguistics, Milw., 1980—86; project dir. Refugee Edn., Pima County Adult Edn., Tucson, 1989—96. Founder and mem., bd. dirs. Tucson Internat. Alliance Refugee Cmtys., 1996—; cons., English lang. program Banco Popular, Madrid, 1979—80. Author, creator (family history videos), author, dir. (numerous grant applications), 1989—2007. Mem.: Tchrs. English to Speakers Other Langs., Phi Beta Kappa. Achievements include development of community-based organization: Tucson International Alliance of Refugee Communities and adult education programs. Office: Pima County CC 5901 Calle Santa Cruz Tucson AZ 85709 Business E-Mail: lrousos@pima.edu.

ROUSSAKIS, PETER ELLWOOD, minister, publisher; b. Bridgeport, Conn., Oct. 16, 1946; s. Charles and Dorothy Roussakis; m. Phyllis Ann Berkshire, Oct. 31, 1970; children: Alex, Aaron. BSc, So. Conn. State U., 1968, MSc, 1973; M in Ch. Music, So. Bapt. Theol. Sem., 1973; D in Ministry, Austin Presbyn. Theol. Sem., 1986; MST, Boston U., 1991; PhD, Grad. Theol. Found., 1998. Elem. sch. tchr. Trumbull Pub. Schs., Conn., 1968—71; min. music and edn. Brethren Ch., New Lebanon, Ohio, 1973—75; assoc. pastor First United Meth. Ch., Shelby, Ohio, 1977—80; asst. prof. ch. music Southwestern U., Georgetown, Tex., 1980—86; pastor First Bapt. Ch., Hampton, NH, 1986—89; pastor, min. of music Cmty. Ch. Alton, NH, 1989—98; pastor First Brethren Ch., Burlington, Ind., 2000—. Editor Meetinghouse Press, Burlington. Author: (religion text) Classic Worship: With Brethren in Mind, 2005, Confessing the Compendium: Praying the Lord's Prayer as Confessing Faith, 2005. Mem.: Nat. Assn. Brethren Ch. Elders, Hymn Soc. of US and Can. Mem. The Brethren Church. Avocation: collecting antique records. Home and Office: PO Box 246 Burlington IN 46915 E-mail: jsbaklava@sbcglobal.net, meetinghousepress@sbcglobal.net.

ROUSSEAU, CHRISTINA JEANNIE, elementary school educator; b. Gardner, Mass., Jan. 18, 1951; d. Edward Patrick and Marjorie Forbes (Arey) O'Connor; m. Douglas Edward Rousseau, Aug. 11, 1973; children: Justin Douglas, Amanda Leigh. BSc, We. Conn. State U., Danbury, 1973, MSc, 1975; postgrad., L.I. U., Bklyn., 1986—88. Cert. tchr. Conn., 1973, N.Y., 1975. Tchr. Beacon City Sch. Dist., NY, 1973—. Sci. coord. Beacon Sch. Dist., 1987—88. Den mother Boy Scouts Am., Hopewell Junction, NY, 1984—85; participant holiday meal delivery Trinity Ch., Fishkill, NY. Named Sci. Tchr. of Yr., Ctrl. Hudson Corp., Poughkeepsie, N.Y., 1989; grantee, Area Fund Dutchess County, N.Y., 1990. Mem.: NEA, NSTA. Episcopalian. Achievements include selected for National Science Foundation program for exemplary teachers. Avocations: travel, exercise, reading, cooking, theater. Office: Beacon City Sch Dist Education Dr Beacon NY 12508 Personal E-mail: crousse44@optonline.net.

ROUSSEAU, DAVID R., state treasurer; b. Mercer County, NJ, 1960; m. Debra Rousseau; 2 children. BA cum laude, Temple U.; MBA, Rider U. With NJ Office Mgmt. & Budget; sr. policy adv. to Senate pres. NJ State Senate; sr. adv. to Gov. for budget & fiscal policy State of NJ, dep. state treas., 2002—06, acting state treas., 2008, state treas., 2008—. Democrat. Office: NJ Dept Treasury PO Box 002 Trenton NJ 08625-0002*

ROUSSEAU, EUGENE ELLSWORTH, musician, educator, consultant; b. Blue Island, Ill., Aug. 23, 1932; s. Joseph E. and Laura M. (Schindler) R.; m. Norma J. Rigel, Aug. 15, 1959; children: Lisa-Marie, Joseph. B of Mus Edn., Chgo. Mus. Coll., 1953; MusM, Northwestern U., 1954; student, Paris Conservatory of Music, 1960-61; PhD in Music Lit. and Performance, U. Iowa, 1962. Instr. Luther Coll., 1956-59; asst. prof. Cen. Mo. State Coll., 1962-64; prof. music Ind. U., Bloomington, 1964-88, disting. prof. music, 1988—; prof. U. Minn., 2000—. Guest prof. U. Iowa, 1964, Hochschule fur Musik, Vienna, Austria, 1981-82, Ariz. State U., 1984, Prague Conservatory Music, 1985, Showa Coll. Music, 1996, 98, Tokyo Coll. Music, 1997, Paris Conservatory, 1997, Munshino Acad. Music, Tokyo, 2000; tchr. U. Wis.-Ext., 1969—; R&D of saxophone mouthpieces; music arranger; svc. on numerous acad. coms.; tchr. 1st course in saxophone Mozarteum in Salzburg, Austria, 1991—; mem. jury Munich Internat. competitions, 1987, 90, 2001, pres. of juries, 1991-92; first solo saxophonist to perform on Prague Spring Festival, 1993; mem. jury Can. Nat. Music competition, 1994; juror Japan Wind and Percussion Competition, 1997; v.p. jury Adolphe Sax Internat. Competition, Belgium, 1998; guest artist prof. Villa Musica, Mainz, 1998, 2000; faculty saxophone Ticino Music, Lugano, 2001, 02, 03; chief cons. saxophone R&D Yamaha corp., 1972-92; soloist Hamamatsu Wind Instrument Festival; faculty ann. master class Vancouver C.C.; host World Saxophone Congress XIII, U. Minn., Mpls., 2003; recorded for Deutsche Grammophon, 1971; guest faculty Am. Band Coll., 2000, 03, 06; adjudicator Thailand Internat. Composition Competition, 2006; artist-in-residence U. Ga., 2007. Worldwide concert saxophonist; Carnegie Hall debut, 1965; author: Marcel Mule: His Life and the Saxophone, 1982, Saxophone High Tones, 1978, revised 2d edit., 2003, Method for Saxophone (2 vols.), 1975; performer 1st solo saxophone recitals, several European cities, 1st Am. solo saxophone performance in Japan, 1974; 1st to record concert saxophone on compact disc (Delos); radio broadcasts in Berlin, Bremen, London, Montreal, Ostrava, Paris, Prague, Toronto, Vienna; saxophone recs. for Deutsche Gramophon, Golden Crest, Coronet, Delos, Liscio, ALM, McGill, RIAX, and Jeanné; CD rec. with Belgian RAF Band; numerous world premieres of composition written for him. Instr., asst. band leader 25th Infantry Div. U.S. Army, 1954-56. Recipient Edwin Franko Goldman award, Am. Bandmasters Assn., 1995, Disting. Alumni award, U. Iowa, 1996; named Hon. Prof. Music, Prague Conservatory, 1993, Braga Inst., Italy, 2001; grantee, Fulbright Found., 1960—61, Rsch. and Exchange Bd., 1985, NEA, 1986. Mem. N.Am. Saxophone Alliance (pres. 1978-80), Comite Internat. de Saxophone (pres. 1982-85), Coll. Music Soc., Clarinet and Saxophone Soc. (U.K.), Music Tchrs. Nat. Assn. (Tchr. of Yr. award for Ind. 1993), Fulbright Assn. (life), World Saxophone Congress (co-founder 1969, pres. organizing com. 2000--). Home Phone: 812-332-3284; Office Phone: 612-624-3875. E-mail: rouss007@umn.edu.

ROUSSEAU, PAUL CHARLES, geriatrician, palliative care physician, educator; b. Charleston, SC; BS with cum laude, Urbana U., Ohio, 1974; MS, State U. NJ, Rutgers, Piscataway, 1980. Diplomate Am. Bd. Internal Medicine, 1983. Pvt. practice, Kissimmee, Fla., 1984; instr. geriatrics Edison C.C., Fort Myers, Fla., 1985; asst. prof. dept. medicine Meharry Med. Coll., Nashvillie, 1986—87; adj. prof., adult dev & aging Ariz. State U., Tempe, Ariz., 1987—2004; cheif, geriatrics VA Med. Ctr., Murfeesboro, Tenn., 1986—87, Prog. dir. Phoenix, 1998—2008; adj. asst. prof. Ariz. Coll. Osteopathic Med., Glendale, Ariz., 1999—2008; assoc. prof. dept. medicine palliative care program Gen. Internal Medicine & Geratrics, Med. U. SC, Charleston, 2008—. Contbr. scientific papers. Mem.: ACP, Ariz. Coalition Pain Mgmt., Ariz. Hospice & Palliative Care Orgn., Am. Acad. Hospice & Palliative Medicine (treas. bd. dirs. 2002—03, chairperson 1996—98, Disting. Svc. award 2007), Am. Acad. Healthcare Comm., Ariz. Geriatrics Soc. (sec. & treas. 1990—91, pres. 1992—93, Geriatrician of Yr. 1993), Am. Assn. Retired Persons, Nat. Geriatrics Soc. (sec. 1988—89, v.p. 1989—90). Office: 135 Rutledge Ave Box 591 Charleston SC 29425 Office Phone: 843-876-8986. Fax: 843-729-7283. Personal E-mail: palliativeDoctor@aol.com.

ROUSSEAU, RONALD WILLIAM, chemical engineering educator, researcher; b. Bogalusa, La., Sept. 28, 1943; s. Ivy John and Dorothy Dean (Talley) R.; m. Tess Marie McKinney, Aug. 5, 1963 (div. June 1978); children: Ronald William Jr., David Patrick, Brett Charles; m. Sandra Barbara Geller, Sept. 2, 1978. BS, La. State U., 1966, MS, 1968, PhD, 1969. Registered profl. engr., N.C. Prof. N.C. State U., Raleigh, 1969-86; prof., chair Sch. Chem. Biomolecular Engring. Ga. Inst. Tech., Atlanta, 1987—. Vis. prof. Princeton U., 1983-84; cons. numerous chem. cos., 1969—. Co-author: Elementary Principles of Chemical Processes, 1978, 2nd edit., 1986, 3rd edit., 2000; editor: Handbook of Separation Process Technology, 1987; contbr. over 190 articles to profl. publs. Fellow AIChE (bd. dirs. 1990-92, Outstanding Chem. Engr. award Ea. N.C. sect. 1986, Gerhold award, 1996, Lewis award, 2002), Am. Assn. Advancement Sci.; mem. Am. Chem. Soc., Coun. Chem. Rsch. (bd. govs. 1994-97, chmn. 1997). Democrat. Roman Catholic. Home: 4288 Conway Valley Ct NW Atlanta GA 30327-3602 Office: Sch Chem Engring Ga Inst Tech Atlanta GA 30332-0001

ROUSSEL, LEE DENNISON, economist; b. NYC, May 15, 1944; d. Ethan Allen and Frances Isabel (Ferry) Dennison; m. Andre Homo Roussel, Sept. 6, 1980; children: Cecilia Frances, Stephanie Anne. AB, Wellesley Coll., 1966; MA, Northeastern U., 1974. Mgmt. intern U.S. Dept. HEW, 1966-68; with Planning Office Commonwealth of Mass., 1968-70; exec. dir. Gov.'s Commn. Citizen Participation, Boston, 1973; with Boston area office U.S. Dept. HUD, 1970-78; fgn. svc. officer USAID, 1978-99, with housing and urban devel. office Washington and Tunis, 1978-82, chief housing and urban devel. office for C.Am. Honduras, 1982-87, asst. dir. office housing and urban programs Washington, 1987-91, country rep. for Czech and Slovak Fed. Rep., 1991-92, country rep. for Czech Rep., 1993-94; min. counselor, U.S. rep. to devel. assistance com. OECD, Paris, 1994-99; sr. advisor USAID, Panama, 1999—2002, chief, exec. mgmt. human resources, 2004—05, mgmt. advisor Office of Econ. growth, 2006—07; resident county dir. Millennium Challenge Corp., 2007—. Episcopalian. Office Phone: 202-216-6323. Personal E-mail: leeroussel@hotmail.com.

ROUSSELOT, PETER FRESE, lawyer, consultant; b. NYC, Jan. 7, 1942; s. Louis Marcel and Evelyn Valdez (Hastrup) R.; m. Mary Dumesnil, Cobb, Nov. 22, 1975; children: Laura Rodman, Richard Frese, Anne Stewart, Louise Dierks. BA summa cum laude, Yale U., 1963; LLB, Harvard U., 1966. Bar: US Dist. Ct. DC 1967, US Ct. Appeals (DC cir.) 1967, US Ct. Appeals (3d cir.) 1993, US Supreme Ct. 1970. Assoc. Hogan & Hartson, Washington, 1966-74, ptnr., 1975-94, mem. exec. com., 1986-88; mng. dir. corp. affairs So. Pacific Rail Corp., Washington, 1994-97; ind. internat. railroad cons., 1997—. Asst. to nat. co-chmn. Citizens for Robert F. Kennedy, Washington, 1968; del. Dem. Nat. Conv., 2004; chair Arlington County Dem. Com., Va., 2006-. Mem. Yale Club Washington, Phi Beta Kappa. Democrat. Episcopalian. Avocations: hiking, photography. Office: 3182 Key Blvd Arlington VA 22201-5065 Home Phone: 703-276-0341; Office Phone: 703-276-1584. Personal E-mail: peter.rousselot@gmail.com.

ROUSSELY, FRANCOIS, electric power industry executive; Grad. ENA. Sr. auditor Nat. Acctg. Office, 1978—81; prin. pvt. sec. Ministry Interior, 1981—86; adv. to chmn. parliamentary com. Assemblée Nationale, 1986—88; dir. gen. nat. police Ministry Interior, 1989—91; prin. sec., chief of staff Adminstrn. Ministry Def., 1991—97; gen. sec., mem. exec. com. SNCF (Nat. Rail Co.), 1997; prin. pvt. sec. Ministry Def., 1997—98; chmn., CEO Electricité de France, 1998—. Mem. Comité de l' Energie Atomique, 1998; mem. adv. bd. Banque de France, 1998; advisor internat. bus. leaders adv. coun. Mayor Beijing, 1998, Gov. Guangdong, 1998; pres. bd. dirs. l'Ecole Nationale des Ponts et Chaussées, 2000; mem. supervisory bd. DALKIA Holding, 2000; chmn. found. Electricité de France, 2001; adminstr. French Agency Internat. Investments, 2002. Office: Electricite De France 2230 Avenue de Wagram 75008 Paris France

ROUSSEY, ROBERT STANLEY, accountant, educator; b. NYC, July 20, 1935; m. Jeanne Archer, May 8, 1965; children: Robert Scott, John Stephen. BS, Fordham U., 1957. CPA, N.Y., Japan. Staff acct. Arthur Andersen & Co., NYC, 1957-63, mgr. NYC and Tokyo, 1964-69, ptnr. NYC and Chgo., 1969-92, dir. auditing procedures, 1977-92; prof. acctg. U. So. Calif., LA, 1992—. Adj. prof. auditing Northwestern U. Kellogg Grad. Sch. Mgmt., 1990, 91; mem. coll. bus. adminstrn. adv. bd. Fordham U., 1999—2006. Edit. cons. Handbook of Corporate Finance, 1986, Handbook of Financial Markets and Institutions, 1987; mem. editl. bd. Advances in Accounting, 1987—, Jour. Internat. Acctg. Auditing and Taxation, 1991—, Auditing: A Journal of Theory and Practice, 1994-2002; mem. adv. bd. Internat. Jour. Acctg., 1998—; contbr. articles to profl. jours. Treas., bd. dirs. Kenilworth (Ill.) Community House, 1979-81, Troop 13 Boy Scouts Am., Kenilworth, 1978-80, St. Joseph's Ch. Men's Club, Bronxville, N.Y., 1971-73. With U.S. Army, 1958, 61-62. Mem. AICPA (chmn. EDP auditing stds. com. 1978-81, auditing stds. bd. 1986-90, MAS practice stds. and adminstrn. com. 1990-93, internat. spl. strategy com. 1997-98, internat. auditing stds. subcom. 1998-2002, internat. strategy com. 1998—2004), Am. Acctg. Assn. (v.p. auditing sect. 1987-90, pubs. com. 1993-96), Info. Systems Audit and Control Assn. (stds. bd. 1986-96, v.p., mem. internat. bd. dirs. 1996—2007, mem. audit com. 2000-01, internat. pres. 2001-03), Info. Tech. Governance Inst. (internat. pres. 2001-03, mem. internat. bd. dirs. 1998-2007), Ill. State Soc. CPAs, N.Y. State Soc. CPAs, Inst. Internal Auditors (bd. rsch. advisors 1986-99), Internat. Fedn. Accts. (internat. auditing practices com. 1990-2000, chmn. 1995-2000, EDP audit com. 1980-88, mem. cons. adv. group to internat. auditing and assurance standards bd. 2001-), Met. Club (gov. 1977-78), Tokyo-Am. Club (life), Beaver Creek Club, Hammock Dunes Club, Beta Alpha Psi, Beta Gamma Sigma Republican. Roman Catholic. Avocations: skiing, sailing, tennis, Karate. Office: U So Calif Dept Acctg Los Angeles CA 90089-0441

ROUSSLANG, KENNETH W., retired chemistry professor; b. Portland, Oreg., Mar. 27, 1948; s. Arnold A. and Catherine E. Rousslang; m. Mary E. Magee; 1 child, Zachary Magee. BA, Portland State U., 1970; PhD, U. Wash., Seattle, 1976. Chemistry prof. U. Puget Sound, Tacoma, 1976—. Vis. asst. prof. U. Wash., Seattle, 1977, Johns Hopkins U., Balt., 1979; vis. assoc. prof. U. Calif., Berkeley, 1984; chmn., chemistry dept. U. Puget Sound, Tacoma, 1986—90, 2007; cons. analyst Boeing Aerospace, Kent, Wash., 1989—90. Contbr. articles to profl. jours. Recipient, NSF, 1984, 1987, 2000, ACS Petroleum Rsch. Fund Grant, 1997, President's Tchg. Excellence award, U. Puget Sound, 2002; grantee, NSF, 1977. Mem.: Am. Chem. Soc. Liberal. Avocations: bicycling, travel, gardening. Office: Univ Puget Sound Dept Chem 1500 N Warner Tacoma WA 98416 Personal E-mail: rousslang@harbornet.com.

ROUSSOS, CHRISTOPHER WAYNE, dental association administrator; b. Dec. 23, 1964; BS in Mgmt. and Mktg., Clarkson U., Potsdam, NY, 1986; MBA, U. Phoenix. Mgmt. position Newell Rubbermaid, Inc.; market mgr. Pepsico, Inc.; gen. mgr. Fleetwood Enterprises, Inc.; divsn. gen. mgr. Am. Homestar Corp.; pres., Matrix Outpatient Rehabilitation and Theraphysics Beverly Enterprises, Inc., pres., Ceres Purchasing Solutions, sr. v.p., Supply Chain Ops.; pres. AseraCare, Inc., 2004—07; CEO OCA, Inc., Metairie, La., 2007—. Cap. US Army, 1985—90. Office: OCA Inc 3850 N Causeway Blvd Ste 800 Metairie LA 70002

ROUTH, BRANDON, actor; b. Des Moines, Iowa, Oct. 9, 1979; s. Katie and Ron Routh; m. Courtney Ford, Nov. 24, 2007. Student, U. of Iowa. Actor: (TV series) Odd Man Out, 1999, Undressed, 2000, One Life to Live, 2001—02, (guest appearance) Gilmore Girls, 2001, Cold Case, 2003, Will & Grace, 2004, Oliver Beene, 2004, (voice only) The Batman, 2006,; (films) Superman Returns, 2006, Lie to Me, 2008, Zack and Miri Make a Porno, 2008. Office: PMK/HBH Public Relations c/o Simon Halls & Kacey Spies 700 San Vicente Blvd Ste G910 West Hollywood CA 90069

ROUTH, DONALD K(ENT), psychologist, educator; b. Oklahoma City, Mar. 3, 1937; s. Ross Holland and Fay (Campbell) R.; m. Marion Starbird Wendler, Sept. 10, 1960(Dec. Sept. 10, 2008); children: Rebecca Ann (dec.), Laura Diane. BA, U. Okla., 1962; PhD, U. Pitts., 1967; BA in History, Fla. Gulf Coast U., 2006. Diplomate Am. Bd. Profl. Psychology. Asst. prof. psychology and pediatrics U. Iowa, Iowa City, 1967-70, prof., 1977-85; assoc. prof. psychology Bowling Green State U., Ohio, 1970-71; assoc. prof. U. N.C., Chapel Hill, 1971-77; prof. psychology and pediat. U. Miami, Coral Gables, Fla., 1985—2002, prof. emeritus, 2002—. Chmn. behavioral medicine study sect. NIH, 1983-85 Editor Jour. Pediatric Psychology, 1976-82, Jour. Clin. Child Psychology, 1987-91, Jour. of Abnormal Child Psychology, 1992-98, Am. Jour. on Mental Retardation, 1998-2002, Internat. Clin. Psychologist, 2001—04; contbr. numerous articles to profl. jours., books Pres. Eno River Unitarian Universalist Fellowship, 1976-77; vol. faculty Fla. Gulf Coast U., 2002—05. Recipient award for disting. contbn. Soc. Pediatric Psychology, 1981, Presdl. award, 1988; Rsch. Psychologist of Yr. award Fla. Psychol. Assn., 1987, Reconocimiento, El Colegio Nacional de Psicologis de Mex., 1999, Disting. Alumni award Okla. Mil. Acad., 2004. Mem. APA (pres. div. child, youth and family svcs., 1984, pres. div. on mental retardation 1987, pres. divsn. clin. psychol. 1998), Internat. Soc. Clin. Psychology (founder, pres. 1998-99), Disting. Profl. Contbns. to Clin. Psychology (sect. on clin. child psychology 1989, div. clin. psychology, 1992, Nicholas Hobbs award div. child youth and family svcs., 1996, Edgar A. Doll award divsn. mental retardation and devel. disabiities 2001), Assn. Southwest Fla. (founder, 2003),Phi Beta Kappa. Democrat. Home: 20131 Seagrove St #402 Estero FL 33928 Personal E-mail: donaldrouth@mac.com.

ROUVELAS, EMANUEL LARRY, lawyer; b. Seattle, Sept. 10, 1944; s. Larry E. and Mary (Derezes) R.; m. Marilyn S. Edmunds, Jan. 23, 1967; children: Eleftherios, Mary. BA, U. Wash., 1965; JD, Harvard U., 1968, AMP, 1996. Bar: Ill. 1968, D.C. 1973. Assoc. Kirkland & Ellis, Chgo., 1968-69; counsel U.S. Senate Com. on Commerce, Washington, 1969-73; chief counsel U.S. Senate Mcht. Marine and Fgn. Commerce Subcoms., Washington, 1969-73; chmn., ptnr. Preston, Gates, Ellis & Rouvelas Meeds, Washington, 1974—2006; ptnr. K&L Gates, Washington, 2007—. Advisor to two Presdl. transitions and bi-partisan congl. caucus; bd. dirs. Am. Comml. Lines, 2005-, chmn. nominating governance com., 2005-. Regent Am. Architectural Found., 2005—. Office: K&L Gates 1601 K St NW Washington DC 20006 Office Phone: 202-778-9000.

ROUZE, JEFFREY ALAN, real estate executive; b. Rockford, Ill., Feb. 5, 1952; s. Robert Lloyd and Ellen Erma (Korpi) R. BBA in Real Estate Fin., U. Wis., 1974, MS in Bus. and Real Estate, 1977. Lic. real estate broker, Wis.; notary pub., Wis. Exec. mgmt. trainee Grootemaat Corp., Milw., 1977-79; real estate cons. CUNA Mut. Ins. Soc., Madison, Wis., 1979-84, real property and mortgage mgr., 1984-93, sr. asset mgr., 1994—2001; pres. Hollywood Econ. Alliance, 2002—; ptnr. Hollywood Devel. LLC, LA, 2001—. Treas. Strollers Theatre, Ltd., Madison, 1985-89; bd. dirs. Hollywood Entertainment Dist., Calif., 1998-99, 2005—, Hollywood Historic Trust, 2000—; treas. St. Paul's Luth. Ch., Santa Monica, Calif., 2002—; bd. dirs. Hollywood Neighborhood Coun., 2003—, Hollywood Heritage, 2003—; pres. Landmark Communities LLC, 2005—. Named Real Estate Pioneer, LA Bus. Jour., 2005. Mem. Nat. Assn. Corp. Real Estate Execs. (master corp. real estate), Inst. Real Estate Mgmt. (cert. property mgr.), Mortgage Bankers Assn. Am., Urban Land Inst., Coml. Investment Real Estate Inst., Hollywood C. of C. (treas. 2002—). Address: 530 S Barington Ave No 307 Los Angeles CA 90049 Home Phone: 310-440-3462; Office Phone: 310-451-6719. E-mail: jarouze@earthlink.net.

ROUZINE, IGOR M., microbiologist, educator; b. St. Petersburg, Russia, May 5, 1962; s. Martin I. Rouzine and Taisia N. Rouzina; m. Nina V. Rouzine, Feb. 28, 2005; 1 child, Denis I.; m. Ioulia F. Rouzina, June 1987 (div. Sept. 19, 1995); 1 child, Katerina I. Rouzina. PhD, A.F.Ioffe Phys. Tech. Inst., St. Petersburg, 1988. Cert. in theoretical physics A.F.Ioffe Phys. Tech. Inst., 1988. Rschr. A.F.Ioffe Phys. Tech. Inst., 1985—89; rsch. assoc. U. Minn., Mpls., 1990—92, UCLA, 1993—95, Tufts U., 1996—2000, rsch. asst. prof., 2001—06, rsch. assoc. prof., 2007—. Assoc. editor Jour. Math. Analysis and Applications, Amsterdam, 2007—. Fellowship, NIH, 2006—. Achievements include first to theory of multi-site genetic evolution of finite populations under selection; modeling of virus-host interaction by multiple-experiment match. Office: Tufts Univ Microbiology 136 Harrison Ave Boston MA 02111

ROVE, KARL CHRISTIAN, political analyst, former federal official; b. Denver, Dec. 25, 1950; s. Louis Claude (Jr.) and Reba Louise (Wood) Rove; m. Valerie Wainright Rove, July 10, 1976 (div. Jan. 1980); m. Darby Tara Hickson, Jan. 25, 1986; 1 child, Andrew Madison. Student, U. Utah, 1969—71, U. Md., 1972, George Mason U., 1973—75, U. Tex., 1977. Exec. dir. Coll. Rep. Nat. Com., Washington, 1971—73, chmn., 1973—77; spl. asst. to chmn. George Bush Nat. Com., Washington, 1973—75, exec. asst. to co-chmn. Richard Obenshain, 1975, also mem. RC exec. com., 1971—75; fin. dir. Va. Rep. Com., Richmond, 1976; dir. Fund for Ltd. Govt., Houston, 1977—79; dep. dir. Gov. William P. Clements Jr. Com., Houston, 1979—80; dir. Tex. Victory Com., Austin, 1980; spl. asst. for adminstrn., dep. exec. asst. to Gov. State of Tex., Austin, 1980—81; pres. Karl Rove & Co., Austin, 1981—99; polit. adv. & chief strategist George W. Bush gubernatorial and presdl. campaigns, 1993—2001; sr. adv. to pres. The White House, Washington, 2001—07, asst. & dep. chief of staff, 2005—07; contbr., polit. analyst FOX News Channel, 2008—; columnist Wall St. Jour., 2008—, Newsweek, 2008—. Pres. U.S. Youth Coun., Washington, 1975—77, selection panel, 1973—77; regent Tex. Woman's U., Denton, 1981—83, East Tex. State U., 1990—91; treas. Tex. Women's Employment and Edn. Program, Austin, 1981—83; mem. regional selection panel White House Fellows Commn., 1987—90. Mem. spl. com. on governance Tex. Higher Edn. Coord. Bd., 1989—91; bd. dirs. Tex. Bus. Hall of Fame, 1987—88; mem. Bd. for Internat. Broadcasting, 1991—94; bd. visitors McDonald Obs., 1993—2001. Named one of The 100 Most Influential People in the World, TIME mag., 2005, The 50 Most Powerful People in DC, GQ mag., 2007. Mem.: Barton Creek Country Club (Austin).

ROVELSTAD, MATHILDE V(ERNER), retired library and information scientist, educator; b. Germany, 1920; came to U.S., 1951. m. Howard Rovelstad, 1970. PhD, U. Tubingen, 1953; MLS, Cath. U. Am., Washington, DC, 1960. Prof. libr. sci. Cath. U. Am., 1960-90, prof. emeritus, 1990—; ret., 1990. Vis. prof. U. Montreal, 1969 Author: Bibliotheken in den Vereinigten Staaten, 1974; translator Bibliographia, an Inquiry into its Definition and Designations (R. Blum), 1980, Bibliotheken in den Vereinigten Staaten von Amerika und in Kanada, 1988; contbr. articles to profl. jours. Research grantee German Acad. Exch. Svc., 1969, Herzog August Bibliothek Wolfenbüttel, Germany, 1995. Mem. Internat. Fedn. Libr. Assns. and Instns. (standing adv. com. on libr. schs. 1975-81), Assn. for Libr. and Info. Sci. Edn. Office: Cath U Am Sch Libr & Info Sci Washington DC 20064-0001 Mailing: c/o Lisa Swei 6836 26th Ave NE Seattle WA 98115

ROVEN, ALFRED NATHAN, surgeon; came to the U.S., 1949. BA in Psychology, Calif. State U., Northridge, 1969; MD, U. So. Calif., 1977. Diplomate Am. Bd. Plastic and Reconstructive Surgery, Am. Bd. Otolaryngology. Resident in otolaryngology U. So. Calif., 1977-82; clin. chief plastic surgery Cedars Sinai Med. Ctr., LA, 1989-91; resident in plastic and reconstructive surgery U. N.C., 1982-84; clin. chief burns Cedars Sinai Med. Ctr., LA, 1990-92, clin. chief hands, 1990-92. Qualified med. examiner State of Calif., 1985. Contbr. articles to jours. Avocation: reading. Office: 5757 Wishire Blvd 6 Los Angeles CA 90036

ROVEN, ROBERT BOCHNER, cardiologist, educator; b. NYC, Oct. 28, 1932; AB, Columbia U., NYC, 1953, MD, 1957. Diplomate Am. Bd. Internal Medicine, Am. Bd. Cardiovasc. Disease. Intern St. Luke's Hosp., NYC, 1957-58, resident, 1958-59, St. Bartholomew Hosp., London, 1959-60; NIH fellow in cardiology St. Luke's Hosp., NYC, 1962-64; staff Lenox Hill Hosp., NYC; sr. attending physician St. Luke's-Roosevelt Hosp. Ctr., NYC; assistant attending physician Presbyn. Hosp., NYC; pvt. practice, NYC, 1964—. Asst. clin. prof. medicine Columbia U. Coll. Physicians and Surgeons (NYC) Office: 654 Madison Ave New York NY 10065-8404 Office Phone: 212-371-8516.

ROVER, EDWARD FRANK, foundation administrator, lawyer; b. Oct. 4, 1938; s. Frederick James and Wanda (Charkowski); m. Maureen Wyer, June 15, 1968; children: Elizabeth, Emily, William. AB, Fordham U., 1961; JD, Harvard U., 1964. Bar: N.Y. 1964, U.S. Tax Ct. 1968, U.S. Dist. Ct. (so. dist.) N.Y. 1975, U.S. Supreme Ct. 1994. Assoc. White & Case, NYC, 1964-71, ptnr., 1972—2004, of counsel, 2004—; pres. Dana Found., NYC, 2004—. Bd. dirs. Markel Found., NYC, Cranshaw Corp., Harvard-Mahoney Neurosci. Inst., Boston, Rumsey-Cartier Found., Geneva, Charles A. Dana Found., NYC, pres. Bd. dirs. Waterford Sch., Sandy, Utah, Dana-Farber, Boston, Norton Simon Art Mus., L.A.; sec. Solomon R. Guggenheim Found., NY. Mem.: Century Assn., Assn. Bar City NY, Univ. Club, Harvard Club, Scarsdale Golf Club. Home: 1111 Park Ave New York NY 10128-1234 Office: Dana Found 745 Fifth Ave Ste 900 New York NY 10151 Office Phone: 212-223-4040. Business E-Mail: erover@dana.org.

ROVINE, ARTHUR WILLIAM, international arbitrator; b. Phila., Apr. 29, 1937; s. George Isaac and Rosanna (Lipsitz) R.; m. Phyllis Ellen Hamburger, Apr. 7, 1963; children: Joshua, Deborah. AB, U. Pa., 1958; LLB, Harvard U., 1961; PhD, Columbia U., 1966. Bar: D.C. 1964, N.Y. 1984. Assoc. Curtis, Mallet-Prevost, Colt & Mosle, NYC, 1964—66; asst. prof. Cornell U., Ithaca, NY, 1966—72; editor Digest of U.S. Practice in International Law U.S. Dept. State, Washington, 1972—75, asst. legal adviser, 1975—81, first agt. of U.S. Govt. to Iran-U.S. Claims Tribunal The Hague, Netherlands, 1981—83; of counsel Baker & McKenzie, NYC, 1983—85, ptnr., 1985—2005. Adj. prof. law Georgetown U., Washington, 1977-81; vis. lectr. law Yale U., 1998; adj. prof. law Fordham U., 2005—; dir. internat. arbitration confs. Fordham Law Sch.; arbitrator in internat. disputes. Author: The First Fifty Years: The Secretary-General in World Politics, 1920-1970, 1970; editor: Digest of U.S. Practice in International Law, 1973, 74; co-editor: The Case Law of the International Court of Justice, 1968, 1972, 1974, 1976; bd. editors Am. Jour. Internat. Law, 1977-87; also articles on internat. law and arbitration, presenter and spkr. in field. Mem. panel on settlement of transnat. bus. disputes, N.Y. panel Ctr. for Pub. Resources; chmn. law subcom. of internat. adv. coun. on profl. edn. Coun. on Internat. Ednl. Exch.; mem. Coun. on Fgn. Rels. Mem. ABA (chmn. internat. law sect. 1985-86, del. to Ho. of Dels. 1988-90), Am. Soc. Internat. Law (cert. of merit 1974, exec. coun. 1975-77, v.p. 1998-99, pres. 2000-02), U.S. Coun. for Internat. Bus. (arbitration com.), Am. Arbitration Assn., Internat. Ctr. for Dispute Resolution (panel of arbitrators), Assn. Bar City NY (internat. arbitration com.), London Ct. Internat. Arbitration. Home: 215 East 68th St New York NY 10021 Office Phone: 212-891-3550. Business E-Mail: arthur.w.rovine@bakernet.com.

ROVINE, HARVEY, theater educator; m. Joyce Elaine Rovine, July 9, 1981; children: Samuel, Kaila. PhD, U. Ill., Urbana-Champaign, 1985. Chair dept. theatre West Chester U., Pa., 1992—96, prof. dept. theatre, 1996—, prof. honors coll., 2001—. Author: (book) Silence in Shakespeare: Drama, Power, and Gender. Office: West Chester Univ Theatre & Dance Dept West Chester PA 19383 Business E-Mail: hrovine@wcupa.edu.

ROVIRA, LUIS DARIO, state supreme court justice; b. San Juan, Sept. 8, 1923; s. Peter S. and Mae (Morris) R.; m. Lois Ann Thau, June 25, 1966; children: Douglas, Merilyn. BA, U. Colo., 1948, LL.B., 1950. Bar: Colo. 1950. Justice Colo. Supreme Ct., Denver, 1979-95, chief justice, 1990-95, ret., 1995. Mem. Pres.'s Com. on Mental Retardation, 1970-71; chmn. State Health Facilities Council, 1967-76; arbiter and mediator Jud. Arbiter Group, Denver. Trustee Temple Buell Found. With AUS, 1943-46. Mem. ABA, Colo. Bar Assn., Denver Bar Assn. (pres. 1970-71), Colo. Assn. Retarded Children (pres. 1968-70), Alpha Tau Omega, Phi Alpha Delta. Clubs: Athletic (Denver), Country (Denver). Home: 4810 E 6th Ave Denver CO 80220-5137 Office: Judicial Arbiter Group 1601 Blake St Denver CO 80202 Office Phone: 303-572-1919.

ROVISON, JOHN MICHAEL, JR., chemical engineer; b. North Tonawanda, NY, June 15, 1959; s. John Michael and Veronica Marie (Donat) R.; m. Janet Marie Konieczny, Apr. 27, 1991; 1 child, Kevin Michael (dec.). BA in Biology, BSChemE, Washington U., 1982; MS in Cancer Biology, Niagara U., NY, 1986. Physics tchr. North Tonawanda High Sch., 1985; assoc. process engr., Ag Chem. Group FMC Corp., Middleport, NY, 1982—90, tech. cons., Ag Chem. Group, 1985, process engr., 1990—92, prodn. mgmt., 1992—96, pxd, tech. mgmt., 1996—2006, mgr. comml. tech., peroxygens divsn., 2006—08, tech. mgr. product and applications, 2008—. Mem. new products evaluation bd. Chem. Engring. McGraw Hill, 1983-84. Contbr. articles to profl. jours. Mem. Resolve through Sharing Parents Group, Williamsville, NY, 1992-97. Recipient FMC Ag Chem Group Tech. award, 1988, FMC Corp. Environ. Achievement award, 1996, Safety Leadership Achievement award, FMC Corp., 2003. Mem. AIChE, Nat. Fire Prevention Assn., Am. Chem. Soc. Roman Catholic. Achievements include research in effects of alcohol on S1 endonuclease, reduction of thermal hazards associated with persulfates production; integrated approach to process improvements, risk benefit evaluation to minimize capital expenditures; leading effort to implement first unionized empowered work system within FMC; re-designed Brazilian insecticide formulating plant to remediate a dust explosion hazard to keep market profitable; addressing product hazards by multifunctional approaches; converting a waste stream into an environmental treatment product; leader supporting process safety and occupational safety initiatives; principle author of FMC corporate ammonia storage and handling standards; lead for Responsible Care training initiatives for customers with FMC AOD products; strategic technology studies; design based on material chemical characteristics; low risk plastic tote delivery systems for peracid; promotion of peracids/persulfates for decontamination of biological/chemical warfare agents mycosides and recreational water treatment chemicals; food processing sanitization and general disinfection products and delivery systems; environmental remediation treatment chemicals, oxidizer generation systems; engineered delivery systems for integrating chemistries to food processing units and other industries waste water treatment NOx/SOx/Hg emissions reductions. Home: 6066 Ward Rd Sanborn NY 14132-9366 Office: FMC Corp Sawyer Ave And River Rd Tonawanda NY 14150 Office Phone: 716-879-0468. Personal E-mail: jevanusa@aol.com.

ROVIT, RICHARD LEE, neurosurgeon; b. Boston, Apr. 3, 1924; s. Samuel and Frances (Ehrenberg) R.; m. Barbara Sayre Margolis, Mar. 29, 1953; children: Sandra Amy Golze, Adam John, Hugh Russel. Grad., U. Mich., 1944; MD, Jefferson Med. Coll., 1950; MSc, McGill U., 1961. Diplomate Am. Bd. Neurol. Surgery (dir. vice chmn. 1986-92). Intern in surgery Beth Israel Hosp., Boston, 1950-51; resident, then chief resident Mass. Gen. Hosp., Boston, 1951-58; USPH fellow in neurology The Nat. Hosp., London, 1956; sr. fellow in neurosurgery Lahey Clinic, Boston, 1957; fellow in neurophysiology and EEG Montreal (Can.) Neurol. Inst., 1958-59; prof. clin. neurosurgery NYU, 1967—; chmn. neurosurgery St. Vincent's Hosp. and Med. Ctr., NYC, 1967-92; prof. neurosurgery N.Y. Med. Coll., Valhalla, 1990—. Editor, author: Trigeminal Neuralgia, 1991; contbr. articles to profl. jours. Trustee Sarah Neuman divsn. Jewish Home and Hosps., N.Y.C., 2004-. Lt. USN, 1952-54. Fellow ACS (v.p. 1994-95), Am. Assn. Neurol. Surgeons (v.p. 1980-81); mem. N.Y. Soc. Neurosurgeons (pres. 1974-76, 79-80), Soc. Neurol. Surgeons, Fairview Country Club (Greenwich, Conn.), Harvard Club of N.Y. Avocations: golf, running. Home: 42 Brite Ave Scarsdale NY 10583-2309 Home Phone: 914-723-5936.

ROVNER, ILANA KARA DIAMOND, federal judge; b. Riga, Latvia, 1938; arrived in U.S., 1939; d. Stanley and Ronny (Medalje) Diamond. AB, Bryn Mawr Coll., 1960; postgrad., U. London King's Coll., 1961, Georgetown U., 1961—63; JD, Ill. Inst. Tech., 1966; LittD (hon.), Rosary Coll., 1989, Mundelein Coll., 1989; DHL (hon.), Spertus Coll. of Judaica, 1992. Bar: Ill. 1972, US Dist. (no. dist.) Ill. 1972, US Ct. Appeals (7th cir.) 1977, US Supreme Ct. 1981, Fed. Trial Bar (no. dist.) Ill. 1982. Jud. clk. US Dist. Ct. (no. dist.) Ill., Chgo., 1972—73; asst. US atty. US Atty.'s Office, Chgo., 1973—77, dep. chief of pub. protection, 1975—76, chief pub. protection, 1976—77; dep. gov., legal counsel Gov. James R. Thompson, Chgo., 1977—84; dist. judge US Dist. Ct. (no. dist.) Ill., Chgo., 1984—92; cir. judge US Ct. Appeals (7th cir.), Chgo., 1992—. Mem. Gannon-Proctor Commn. on the Status of Women in Ill., 1982—84; mem. civil justice reform act adv. com. 7th Cir. Ct., Chgo., 1991—95, mem. race and gender fairness com., 1993—; mem. fairness com. US Ct. Appeals (7th cir.), 1996—, mem. gender study task force, 1995—96; mem. jud. conf. US Com. Ct. Adminstrn. Case Mgmt., 2000—06. Ctrl. and East European law initiative vol. ABA, 1997—; trustee Bryn Mawr Coll., Pa., 1983—89; mem. bd. overseers Ill. Inst. Tech./Kent Coll. Law, 1983—; trustee Ill. Inst. Tech., 1989—; mem. adv. coun. Rush Ctr. for Sports Medicine, Chgo., 1991—96; bd. dirs. Rehab. Inst. Chgo., 1998—; bd. visitors No. Ill. U. Coll. Law, 1992—94; vis. com. Northwestern U. Sch. Law, 1993—98, U. Chgo. Law Sch., 1993—96, 2000—03; chair Ill. state selection com. Rhodes Scholarship Trust, 1998—2000. Recipient Spl. Commendation award, US Dept. Justice, 1975, Spl. Achievement award, 1976, Ann. Nat. Law and Social Justice Leadership award, League to Improve the Cmty., 1975, Ann. Guardian Police award, 1977, Profl. Achievement award, Ill. Inst. Tech., 1986, ORT Women's Am. Cmty. Svc. award, 1987—88, commendation def. of prisoners com., Chgo. Bar Assn., 1987, Svc. award, Spertus Coll. of Judaica, 1987, Ann. award, Chgo. Found. for Women, 1990, Louis Dembitz Brandeis medal for Disting. Legal Svc., Brandeis U., 1993, 1st Woman award, Valparaiso U. Sch. Law, 1993, Hebrew Immigrant Aid Soc. Chgo. 85th Anniversary honoree, 1996, Arabella Babb Mansfield award, Nat. Assn. Women Lawyers, 1998, award, Chgo. Attys. Coun. of Hadassah, 1999, First Woman award, Chgo. Bar Assn. Alliance for Women and Women's Bar Assn. Ill., 2000, Georgetown U. Law Ctr., 2001, Chgo. Hist. Soc. Trailblazers Award, 2003, Lifetime Achievement award, Decalogue Soc. Lawyers, 2004, Northwestern Univ. Jewish Law Students Assn., 2008, Vanguard award, Chgo. Bar Assn. and Lesbian and Gay Bar Assn. Chgo., 2004, Thurgood Marshall Career Achievement award, Assn. Corp. Counsel Chgo. chpt., 2005, Hero of Liberty award, Nat. Liberty Mus., 2005, Inaugural Judge Abraham Lincoln Marovitz Mentoring award, Chgo. Bar Assn. and Found. Lend-a-Hand Program, 2005, Professionalism award, Am. Inns Ct. Seventh Cir., 2008, Chgo. Legal Legends award, Am. Constn. Soc., 2008, Women of Valor award, B'nai B'rith Internat., 2008; named Today's Chgo. Woman of the Yr., 1985, Woman of Achievement, Chgo. Women's Club, 1986, Inaugural Spkr., Disting. Judge Series CLE Program Ill. Atty. Gen. Office, 2007; named one of 15 Chgo. Women of the Century, Chgo. Sun Times, 1999; named to Today's Chgo. Women Hall of Fame, 2002. Mem.: Chgo. Bar Assn. (Justice John Paul Stevens award 2005), Jewish Judges Assn. Ill. (Lifetime Achievement award 2004), Decalogue Soc. of Lawyers (citation of honor 1991, Merit award 1997), Chgo. Coun. Lawyers, Women's Bar Assn. Ill. (ann. award 1989, 1st Myra Bradwell Woman of Achievement award 1994, 1st Woman Award (in conjunction with Chicago Bar Assn. Alliance for Women) 2000), Fed. Judges Assn., Fed. Bar Assn. (mem. selection com. Chgo. chpt. 1977—80, treas. 1978—79, sec. 1979—80, 2d v.p. 1980—81, 1st v.p. 1981—82, pres. 1982—83, 2d v.p. 7th cir. 1983—84, v.p. 7th cir. 1984—85), Kappa Beta Pi, Phi Alpha Delta (hon.). Office: 219 S Dearborn St Ste 2774 Chicago IL 60604-1803*

ROVNYAK, STEVEN MICHAEL, engineering educator; b. Lafayette, Ind., July 4, 1966; s. James Leo and Virginia Garrett Rovnyak. AB in Math., Cornell U., Ithaca, NY, 1988, BS in Elec. Engring., 1988, MS in Elec. Engring., 1990, PhD in Elec. Engring., 1994. Postdoc. assoc. Cornell U., 1994—96; asst. prof. La. Tech U., Ruston, 1996—2003, Ind. U. Purdue U. Indpls., 2003—. Author jour. articles. Recipient Faculty Early Career Devel. award, NSF, 2000—06. Mem.: IEEE, Phi Kappa Phi, Phi Beta Kappa. Presbyterian. Achievements include research in pattern recognition for power system protection and control. Office: Ind Univ Purdue Univ Indpls 723 West Michigan St SL-160K Indianapolis IN 46202 Office Fax: 317-274-4493. Business E-Mail: srovnyak@iupui.edu. E-mail: rovnyak@ieee.org.

ROWAN, RICHARD G., former academic administrator; BS, Furman U.; MEd, EdS, Ga. State U.; D of Design (hon.), Nottingham Trent U., Eng. Pres., co-founder Savannah Coll. Art and Design, Ga., 1978—2000, chancellor Ga., 2000—01. Mem. Savannah adv. bd. Bank of Am. Recipient Oglethorpe award, Freedom award NAACP; named to Hon. Order Ky. Cols. Mem. Savannah C. of C. (pres., bd. dirs.). Office: Savannah Coll Art & Design Office of the Chancellor PO Box 3146 Savannah GA 31402-3146

ROWAN, STEVEN WILLIAM, history professor; b. Bremerton, Wash., Apr. 4, 1943; s. James Harvey and Dorothy Virginia Rowan; m. Marilyn Anne Schuster, July 6, 1966; children: Jonna Diane Rowan Needle, Austin Günther James. BA, U. Wash., Seattle, 1965; PhD, Harvard U., Cambridge, Mass., 1970. Prof. history U. Mo., St. Louis, 1970—. Vis. sr. lectr. King's Coll., London, 1975—76; rsch. fellow Alexander-von-Humboldt-Stiftung, Freiburg, Germany, 1979—80; Fulbright disting. chmn. Karl-Franzens-U., Graz, Austria, 2007; mem. Sch. Hist. Studies, Inst. Advanced Study, Princeton, NJ, 1989—90. Author: Ulrich Zasius: Jurist in German Renaissance, 1987; editor, translator: L. von Reizenstein, Mysteries of New Orleans, pub.: 16 books. Recipient Outstanding Achievement award, Soc. German-Am. Studies, Balt., 2003; fellow, NEH, 1971; rsch. fellow, Newberry Libr., Chgo., 1978—79. Fellow: Sixteenth Century Studies Conf. Lutheran. Avocations: travel, reading. Office: U Mo History Dept 1 University Blvd Saint Louis MO 63121

ROWAN, THOMAS BERNARD, III, political science professor; b. Nashville, Aug. 10, 1964; s. Thomas B. Jr. and Mary A. Rowan.; m. Min Yang BA with high honors, Vanderbilt U., Nashville, 1986; MA, U. York, Eng., 1987; PhD, U. Chgo., 1993. Asst. prof. Chgo. State U., 1996-99, assoc. prof., 1999—2004, prof., 2004—. Vis. fellow Asiatic Rsch. Ctr., Seoul, Republic of Korea, 2002; vis. prof. Hanyang U., Seoul, Republic of Korea, 2002; mem. Ctr. for Globalization of Korean Langs. and Culture, Seoul, Republic of Korea, 2004—; acting chair Chgo. State U., 2006—, chair, 2007—; peer reviewer North Ctrl. Higher Learning Commn., 2008—. Mem. editl. com. New Asia Rsch. Inst., Seoul, 2000—; guest columnist The Korea Times, 2002—; contbr. articles to profl. jours. Fellow, Rotary, 1986—87, U. Chgo., 1987—90, Korea Found., 2002. Mem. Am. Polit. Sci. Assn., Assn. Polit. Theory, UN Assn. USA, Phi Beta Kappa. Office: Chgo State U SCI 315 9501 S King Dr Chicago IL 60628 Office Phone: 773-995-2439. Office Fax: 773-821-2840. Business E-Mail: trowanii@csu.edu.

ROWARK, MAUREEN, fine arts photographer; b. Edinburgh, Midlothian, Scotland, Feb. 28, 1933; came to U.S., 1960, naturalized, 1970; d. Alexander Pennycook and Margaret (Gorman) Prezdpelski; m. Robert Rowark, May 3, 1952 (dec. 1974). 1 child, Mark Steven. Student, Warmington Bus. Coll., Royal Leamington Spa, Eng., 1950-51, Royal Leamington Spa Art Sch.; diploma, Speedwriting Inst., NYC, 1961; AS in Edn., St. Clair County C.C., Port Huron, Mich., 1977, AA, 1978. Supr. proof reading Nevin D. Hirst Advt., Ltd., Leeds, England, 1952-55; publicity asst. Alvis Aero Engines, Ltd., Coventry, England, 1955-57; adminstrv. asst. Port Huron Motor Inn, 1964-66; adminstrv. asst. pub. rels. dept. Geophysics and Computer Svcs., Inc., New Orleans, 1966-68; sales mgr. Holiday Inn, Port Huron, 1968-70; adminstrv. asst. Howard Corp., Port Huron, 1971-73; sales and systems coord. Am. Wood Products, Ann Arbor, Mich., 1973-74; systems coord. Daniels & Zermack Architects, Ann Arbor, 1974; systems coord., cataloger fine arts dept. St. Clair County Community Coll., Port Huron, 1976-79; freelance fine arts photographer Port Huron, 1978—. Photographer Patterns mag. front cover, 1978, Erie Sq. Gazette, 1979, Bluewater Area Tourism Bur. brochure, 1989, 92, 95, 97, 2000, 01, Corits Castle, Lexington, 2002, Port Huron, Can. Legion, Wyo., Ont. Br., 1987, 88—, Grace Episcopal Ch. Mariner's Day, Port Huron, 1987, 92-2001, Homes mag., 1989. Photographer (one-woman shows) Grace Episcopal Ch., 1995, Port Huron Mus., 1995, St. Clair River Remedial Action Plan, 1995 (Best in Landscape Category), Mich. Waterways Coun. Girl Scouts Exhibit, 1996; Exhibited in group shows at Ea. Mich. Internat. Juried Exhbn., 2000, 1981—98 (Award of Excellence, 1982, 1983, Best Photography award, 1995, 1996, 1997), Our Town Juried Exhbn., 1997, St. Clair County C.C., 1983, 1986 (Award of Excellence, 1986), Gallery Lambton, Sarnia, Ont., Can., 1983—92 (Best Photography, 1988), 1994, 1996—97, 2000, Bluewater Bridge, 1988, Kaskilaaksontie, Finland, 1991 (Par Excellence award), Swann Gallery, Detroit, 1996, St. Clair (Mich.) Art Gallery, Genesis Gallery, Lexington, Mich., others, Studio 1219, Port Huron, Mich., Represented in permanent collections Royal Can. Legion, Wyo. Br. Centaph, Capac State Bank, Grace Episcopal Ch., Thomas Edison Inn, Port Huron Hosp., Front Cover Good Health News; costume design, manufacture and modelling Bluewater Art Assn., 2000—01, photographer Bluewater Percussion Brochure, 2001;, author short stories. Cons., buyer interior decor Grace Episcopal Ch., 1994; active Port Huron Mus., 1978; founder Bluewater les Chapeaux Rouge chpt. Red Hat Soc., 2000—; prodr., dir. calendar We Can Still Make Waves, 2005, Waiting for Our Ship to Come In, 2007; prodr., designer parade float Rotary Internat., 2005 (1st pl. award). Recipient hon. mention Gallery Lambton, Sarnia, 1981, 2d pl. memoir writing women's history month St. Clair County C.C., 1999; winner 2d and 3d place awards Times Herald Newspaper, 1988, 1st place juried photography award Port Huron Art Festival, 1997, 1st place St. Patrick's Day Parade Float, 2006, 1st place Rotary Internat. Day Parade Float, 2005. Mem. St. Clair County CC Alumni Assn., Red Hat Soc., Internat. Club, Moose, Phi Theta Kappa, Lambda Mu. Democrat. Episcopalian. Avocations: interior decorating, travel, theater, writing. Home and Office: 521 Holland Ave Port Huron MI 48060 Home Phone: 810-989-9192. Personal E-mail: ha-penerth-of-tar@prodigy.net.

ROWBERG, KATHRYN L., chemistry professor; b. Spokane, Wash. m. Charles Schaefer. PhD, U. Ill. Chgo., 1990. Bar: Valparaiso Sch. Law (in jd) 2006. Asst. prof. chemistry Purdue U. Calumet, Hammond, Ind., 1996—2004, assoc. prof. chemistry, 2004—. Contbr. articles to profl. jours. Adv. bd. mem. CARE IDEM, Hammond, 2008—. Fulbright fellowship, Coun. Internat. Edn., 2004. Mem.: Am. Chem. Soc. Office: Purdue Univ Calumet 2200 169th St Hammond IN 46323 Business E-Mail: rowberg@calumet.purdue.edu.

ROWDEN, MARCUS AUBREY, lawyer, retired government agency administrator; b. Detroit, Mar. 13, 1928; s. Louis and Gertrude (Lifsitz) Rosenzweig; m. Justine Leslie Bessman, July 21, 1950; children: Gwen,

Stephanie. BA in Econs, U. Mich., Ann Arbor, 1950, JD with distinction, 1953. Bar: Mich. 1953, D.C. 1978. Trial atty. Dept. Justice, 1953-58; legal advisor U.S. Mission to European Communities, 1959-62; solicitor, assoc. gen. counsel, gen. counsel AEC, 1965-74; commr., chmn. U.S. NRC, Washington, 1975-77; ptnr. Fried, Frank, Harris, Shriver and Jacobson, Washington, 1977—. With US Army, 1946—47. Decorated officer Order Legion of Honor Republic of France; Recipient Disting. Service award AEC, 1972 Mem. ABA, Fed. Bar Assn., Mich. Bar Assn., DC Bar Assn., Internat. Nuc. Law Assn., Order of Coif. Home: 7937 Deepwell Dr Bethesda MD 20817-1927 Office: Fried Frank Harris Shriver and Jacobson 1001 Pennsylvania Ave NW Washington DC 20004-2505 Home Phone: 301-469-9318; Office Phone: 202-639-7070.

ROWE, BONNIE GORDON, music company executive; b. Buford, Ga, May 3, 1922; s. Bonnie Gordon and Alma (Poole) R.; m. Mary Wilburta Shidler; 1 child, Sharon Lynn; m. Gloria Lucille Fairfax, Feb. 17, 1962 (div.); 1 child, Susan Rebecca. Student, Ga. Evening Coll., 1939-41, U. Wichita, 1948-49, Ga. State Coll., 1949-52. Traffic mgr. Bonanza Air Lines, Las Vegas, 1946-48, music tchr., 1948-52; owner Rowe Accordion Distbg. Co., Rowe Accordion Ctr., Atlanta, 1952-56, Atlanta Music Pub. Co., 1956—, B. Rowe Music Co., Atlanta, 1957—. Pres.-treas. B. Rowe Enterprises, Inc., 1973—. Bd. dir. Sandtown Found., Atlanta. Lt. col. USAAF, World War II, ETO. Decorated Air medals with three oak leaf clusters. Mem.: Nat. Assn. Music Mchts., Atlanta Fedn. Musicians (life), The Mil. Order of the World Wars (past comdr. Atlanta chpt.), Internat. Platform Assn., Sandtown Civitan Club (pres., past pres. Met. Atlanta Coun., lt. gov.), Air Force Assn., Res. Officers Assn., Travelers Protective Assn., 781st Bomb Squadron Assn. (465th bomb group WWII), Atlanta C. of C., Mil. Officers Assn. Am., Southea. Accordion Assn. (past pres.), Dobbins AFB Officers Club, Elks (exalted ruler 1987, 1988, 1989, past pres. past exalted rulers assn., past state organist Ga. Elks Assn., trustee Union City), Am. Legion, Gamma Delta Phi. Home: 5085 Erin Rd SW Atlanta GA 30331-7810 Office: 6102 Mableton Pkwy Mableton GA 30126-4302 Personal E-mail: brga30331@aol.com.

ROWE, CHARLES ALFRED, artist, graphics designer, educator; b. Great Falls, Mont., Feb. 7, 1934; s. Alfred Lewis and Alice Lillian (Ledbetter) R.; m. Eugenia Dean, July 5, 1958; children: Allison Rene, Jon Garner, Dorian Leigh. Student, Mont. State U., 1952—53, So. Meth. U., 1956—57, U. Chgo., 1959—60; BFA, Sch. Art Inst., Chgo., 1960; MFA, Tyler Sch. Art, 1968. Prin. Charles Rowe Advt., Chgo., 1957-60; graphic designer Am. Can Co., Bellwood, Ill., 1960-62, Abrams-Bannister Engraving, Inc., Greenville, SC, 1962-64; prof. art U. Del., Newark, 1964-97, emeritus prof., 1997—. One-man shows include Tyler Sch. Art, Phila., 1968, Mickelson Gallery, Washington, 1970, 1974, C.M. Russell Mus., Great Falls, 1972—73, 1981, 1992, Pleiades Gallery, NYC, 1977, 1981, Vision of La Herradura, Almuñecar, Spain, 1988, USAF exhbn. Soc. Illustrators, NYC, 1991, 2004, West Chester U., Pa., 1992, Soc. Illustrators, NYC, 1993, 2004, exhibited in group shows at C.M. Russell Mus., 1974, 1976, 1978, 1980, 1982—83, 1986—91, Am. Painters in Paris, 1976, Monac-Western Art Exhibit, Spokane, Wash., 1977—78, Easton Waterfowl Festival, Md., 1981—82, USAF Nat. Collection, 1987, 1989, 1991, USAF exhbn. Soc. Illustrators, NYC, 1989, Our Own Show, Soc. Illustrators, 1990, 1991—96, 1998—2008, Atrium Gallery, 1995, 1996, One Small Step, NASA, U. Del., Newark, 1995, Art and Antiques, Wilmington, Del., 2005, Lower Del. Autism Found. Gala Exhbn., 2003—08, one-man shows include Howard Pyle Studio, Wilmington, DE, 2007, exhibited in group shows at over 220 other exhbns., Represented in permanent collections U. Del., Mont. State Collection, Mont. State U., Del. State Collection, Libr. Congress, Washington, Great Falls Pub. Schs., Michael Landon Prodns., Calif., Meredith Corp., Des Moines, Collection Knissel, Austria, Star Showers Found., Graveson-en-Provence, France, Archives Victoria and Albert Mus., London, artists USAF Nat. Collection, Washington, Jacqueline Pierson, Nice, France, artists USAF Nat. Collection, Washington, Banco de Granada, Spain, NASA Space Mus., Hauptman and Greenwood Collections, NYC, Vera Haas, Dallas, Jerry Pinkney, Croton-On-Hudson, Baker, Palm Springs, Calif., David Duncan, Spokane, Wash.; fabric designer Galleon Fabrics, Inc., NYC, Jones of NY, Saks Fifth Ave., Bush Collection, Swampscott, Mass., Steele Collection, Big Fork, MT, Jordan Baker, Kevin Kilner, Hollywood, Calif., 1987, Kevin Costner Collection, 1997, designer graphics Mont. State Arts Coun., Del. state duck stamp, 1981. With inf. U.S. Army, 1954-56. Ctr. for Advanced Study fellow, 1981-82; grantee U. Del., 1964-79, Nat. Endowment for Arts and Humanities, 1972-73, U. Del. Bicentennial, 1976. Mem. Soc. of Illustrators (N.Y.C.). Home: Chapel Hill 133 Aronimink Dr Newark DE 19711-3802 Home Phone: 302-738-0641; Office Phone: 302-584-2925. Business E-Mail: CharlesRoweStudio@comcast.net. *In my paintings and other artforms I strive for perfection, uniqueness, and a special inner beauty, but more than that, I try to create art that has a universal quality. This universality makes an artform communicate beyond a specific locale, continent or a limited time reference. All great works of art have this special element regardless of when they were created.*

ROWE, DAVID JOHN, physics professor; b. Totnes, Devonshire, Eng., Feb. 4, 1936; came to Can., 1968; s. Herbert Tyack and Marguerite Ella (Whitehead) R.; m. Una Mary Dawson, Oct. 4, 1959; children: Mark Jørgen Dawson, Jacqueline Amanda. BA, Cambridge U., Eng., 1959; MA, DPhil, Oxford U., Eng., 1959-62. Research assoc. U. Rochester, NY, 1966-68; assoc. prof. U. Toronto, Ont., Canada, 1968-74, prof. Ont., Canada, 1974—98, emeritus prof., 1998—. Author: Nuclear Collective Motion, 1970; editor: Dynamic Properties of Nuclear States, 1972; mem. editorial bd. (jour.) Phys. Rev., 1983-86, Jour. Phys. G., 1988-92, assoc. editor, 1992; contbr. articles to profl. jours. Dir. Mont Tremblant Internat. Summer Sch., 1971. Served to cpl. RAF, 1954-56. Ford Found. fellow, 1962-63, U.K. Atomic Energy Authority fellow, 1963-66, Sloan Found. fellow, 1972-74, Isaac Walton Killam rsch. fellow, 1990-92, C.A.P./C.R.M. prize for Theoretical and Mathematical Physics, 1999. Fellow Royal Soc. Can. (Rutherford Meml. medal and prize 1983); mem. Can. Assn. Physicists (chmn. theoretical physics div. 1970-71), Internat. Union Pure and Applied Physics (chmn. C18 commn. on math. physics 1999—2002), Internat. Assn. Math. Physics. Avocations: piano, hiking, travel, photography. Office: U Toronto Physics Dept Toronto ON Canada M5S 1A7

ROWE, DAVID WINFIELD, lawyer; b. Chgo., Nov. 7, 1954; s. Bernard John and Gertrude Katherine (Johnson) R.; m. Martha Lynn Plott, June 12, 1977; children: Daniel, Peter. BA in Psychology with honors, cum laude, Davidson Coll., NC, 1976; PhD in Psychology, U. Tenn., Knoxville, 1981; JD, U. Mich., Ann Arbor, 1987. Bar: Colo. 1987, Nebr. 1989, US Dist. Ct. Colo. 1987, US Dist. Ct. Nebr. 1989, US Ct. Appeals (10th cir.) 1987, US Ct. Appeals (8th cir.) 2004, US Supreme Ct. 2006. Post doctoral fellowship in law and psychology U. Nebr., Lincoln, 1989—91; vis. asst. prof. Davidson Coll., NC, 1981—82; mental health worker Peninsula Psychiat. Hosp., Louisville, Tenn., 1982-84; instr. dept. psychology U. Tenn., Knoxville, 1982-84; assoc. Gorsuch, Kirgis, Campbell, Walker & Grover, Denver, 1987-89; assoc. and ptnr. Kinsey, Ridenour, Becker & Kistler, Lincoln, Nebr., 1991—2005; ptnr. Kinsey, Rowe, Becker & Kistler, LLP, 2006—; cons. 3rd Coast Consultants, 2007—. Mem. interim study group on foster care Health and Human Svcs. com. Nebr. State Legislature, 1990-91; adj. prof. psychology U. Nebr., Lincoln, 1992-94; bd. dirs., past treas. Lincoln Attention Ctr. for Youth; mem. The Mediation Ctr., Detention Ctr. Adv. Bd., 2003-. Author: (with others) Dimensions of Child Advocacy: Advocating for the Child in Protection Proceedings, 1990, Children Under Three in Foster Care, 1991. Exec. com. Lancaster County Rep. Com., 1991-97, chmn., 1993-95; bd. dirs. Lincoln-Lancaster Mental Health Found., 1993-, v.p., 1995-96, pres., 1996-97; mem. Ctrl. Com. Nebr. Rep. Com., 1993-97; bd. dirs. The Arc of Lincoln Lancaster County, 2003-, Nebr. State Mus., 2008-; deacon Westminster Prebyn. Ch., 1996-99. Mem. ABA, Nebr. Bar Assn. (alternative dispute resolution com. 1990—2000), Cornhusker Kiwanis (pres. Lincoln 1997-98). Avocations: bicycle touring, bicycle racing. Office: Kinsey Rowe Becker & Kistler LLP 121 S 13th St#601 PO Box 85778 Lincoln NE 68501-5778 Home Phone: 402-488-3870; Office Phone: 402-438-1313. Business E-Mail: drowe@krbklaw.com.

ROWE, DEVONA POWELL, retired counseling administrator, director, social worker, secondary school educator; b. Bethesda, Md., Jan. 28, 1951; d. Julius Devon and Martha Ann (Molnar) Powell; m. Ralph Leon Rowe, June 11, 1971; children: Adam Powell, Reagan Powell. BA in History and Libr. Sci. magna cum laude, Fla. State U., 1971; MA in Edn. summa cum laude, U. North Fla., 1982; EdS in Counselor Edn., U. Fla., 1990; EdD, U. North Fla., 1999. Profl. tchg. lic., Fla.; cert. counselor, Nat. Bd. Cert. Counselors; cert. media specialist and guidance and adminstrn. tchr., Fla.; lic. mental health counselor; cert. Nat. Bd. Cert. Tchrs. Sch. libr. Most Holy Redeemer Sch., Tampa, Fla., 1972-74; asst. dir. N.E. Fla./S.E. Ga. divsn. Nat. Health Svcs., Palatka, Fla., 1981-83; guidance counselor St. Joseph Acad., St. Augustine, Fla., 1983-85; tchr. 8th grade social studies Putnam County Sch. System, 1985-86; county svcs. coord. Child Abuse Prevention Project, Palatka, 1986-92; guidance counselor E.H. Miller/Dist. Opportunity Ctr., Palatka, 1992-94; social worker Palatka HS, 1994—99, tchr., 1999—2004, Mandarin HS, Jacksonville, Fla., 2004—08; ret., 2008. Mem. Health Edn. Coun., 1986—, v.p., 1986, pres., 1987; workshop presenter in field. Mem. editl. bd.: World History Connected. Crucillo coord. St. Mark's Episcopal Ch., 1977-80; mem. Putnam Children's Task force, Children's Home Soc.; rep. Dist. Juvenile Justice Bd. Dept. Health and Rehab. Svcs. Dist. III, rep. State Coun. on Juvenile Justice; mem. Local Juvenile Justice Bd., Putnam County, 1993. Named Women Involved Today winner Palatka Daily News, 1988; grantee in field; Fla. Regent scholar. Mem. Am. Assn. Counseling and Devel., Nat. Com. Prevent Child Abuse, Fla. Ctr. Children and Youth, Fla. Com. Prevent Child Abuse, Child Welfare League, Adv. Network Severely Emotionally Disturbed Children, Jr. Woman's Club Palatka (hon., state jr. project chair 1975, leadership chair 1976, 1st v.p. 1977, pres. 1979, Outstanding Clubwoman 1978), Woman's Club Palatka (edn. chair 1988), Beta Sigma Phi (program chair 1987, cultural chair 1988), Chi Sigma Iota, Kappa Delta Pi. Democrat. Avocations: reading, duplicate bridge, doll making. Home Phone: 904-683-3819; Office Phone: 904-312-1100. Personal E-mail: devonaprowe@yahoo.com.

ROWE, G. STEVEN, former state attorney general; m. Amanda Rowe; 4 children. BS, US Mil. Acad.; MBA, U. Utah; JD, U. Maine. Mem. Dist. 30 Maine Ho. Reps., 1993-95, mem. Dist. 35, 1995—2001; litig. counsel UNUMProvident; atty. gen. State of Maine, 2001—09. Bd. mem. Pine Tree Legal Assistance, Inc. With US Army, with USAR. Mem.: NE Legis. Assn. on Prescription Drug Prices, Maine Econ. Growth Coun. Democrat. Office Phone: 207-626-8800.*

ROWE, HERBERT JOSEPH, retired trade association executive; b. Granite City, Ill., Mar. 25, 1924; s. Herbert Bernard and Maude (Klein) R.; m. Ann Muter, Dec. 2, 1950; children: Douglas H., Stephen F., James D., Edith L., Allen. Student, U. Tex., 1942—43, Purdue U., 1943—44; BS in Mktg., U. Ill., 1948; LittD (hon.), London Inst. for Applied Rsch., 1975. With Edward Valves, Inc. (subs. Rockwell Mfg. Co.), 1948—50, Muter Co., Chgo., 1952—71, v.p., 1957—64, pres., 1964—71, treas., 1964—67, chmn. bd., 1965—71, also dir., 1957—71; pres., treas., dir. Showell Co., 1964—66, Tri-Axial Corp., 1966—67; v.p., treas. Gen. Magnetic Corp., 1965—67, chmn. bd., dir., 1967—70, Pemcor, Inc., Westchester, Ill., 1971—75; assoc. adminstr. external affairs NASA, 1975—78; sr. v.p. Electronic Industries Assn., 1978—89; chmn. Famro Corp., 1989—90; pres. Internat. Electronics Fedn., 1989—90. Sec.-treas. Englewood Elec. Supply Wis., Inc., 1972-75, Rahr's Inc., 1972-75; pres. Enclave of Naples, Inc., 1992-94, treas., 1994-96; pres. Rowe Corp., 1994-97; treas. Quality wholesale Foods of S.W. Fla., 1994-96. Pres. Pokagon Trails coun. Boy Scouts Am., 1964-66, pres. Calumet coun., 1966-68, region 7 exec. com., 1966-72, vice chmn., 1971-72, bd. dirs. East Ctrl. region, 1972-75, nat. program com., 1970-78, 90-94, nat. Cub Scout com., 1970-80, chmn., 1990-94, S.E. regional exec. com., 1975-78, So. regional exec. bd., 1993—, bd. dirs. Nat. Capital Area coun., 1978-90, adv. bd., 1990-94, exec. bd. S.W. Fla. coun., 1992—, nat. exec. com., exec. bd., 1990-95, nat. adv. bd., 1995—; membership chmn. Nat. Eagle Scouts Assn., 1976-80; corp. campaign chmn. Chgo. Met. Crusade Mercy, 1964-68; chmn. Bd. Edn. Caucus, Flossmoor, Ill., 1962; bd. dirs. Flossmoor United Party, 1963-68; mem. U. Ill. Found., 1967—; adv. com. U. Ill. Coll. Commerce and Bus. Adminstrn., 1968-78, 97-2002; bd. dirs. Electronic Industries Found., 1974-94; adv. bd. Air and Space Mus., Smithsonian Inst., 1975-78; active Moorings Presbyn. Ch., Naples, Fla. With USMCR, 1942-46, 50-52; mem. Ernest Thompson Seton Inst., 1910 Soc. Boy Scouts Am. Recipient Silver Beaver award Boy Scouts Am., 1966, Silver Antelope award, 1969, Silver Buffalo award, 1994; NASA team award Bicentennial Expo on Sci. and Tech., Exceptional Svc. medal, 1978, Baden-Powell fellow World Scout Found., 1992. Mem. AIAA, AAAS, Electronic Industries Assn. (hon., bd. dirs. 1967-69, bd. govs. 1969-75, exec. com. parts divsn. 1966-75, vice chmn. parts divsn. 1970-74, chmn. 74-75, bd. dirs. consumer electronics divsn. 1972-75, chmn. world trade com. 1968-70, vice-chmn. 1970-73, chmn. membership and scope com. 1972-74, Disting. Svc. award 1989), Am. Loudspeaker Mfrs. Assn. (v.p., dir. 1967-68, pres., bd. dirs. 1968-70), Assn. Electronic Mfrs. (bd. dirs. 1970-73), Nat. Space Club, Nat. Space Inst., Am. Acad. Polit. Social Sci., Am. Soc. Assn. Execs. (vice chmn. internat. sect. 1986-87, chmn. 1987-88), US Naval Inst., Field Mus. Natural History, European Soc. Assn. Execs., Greater Washington Soc. Assn. Execs., Naples Coun. World Affairs (bd. dirs. 2003-05), Explorers Club, Travelers Century Club, Chgo. Art Inst., Am. Legion, Chaine des Rôtisseurs, L'Ordre Mondial, Internat. Wine and Food Soc. (pres. Naples br. 2001-07), English-Speaking Union (pres. Naples chpt. 1996—2007, chmn. 2007-, nat. dir. 1997—, chmn. fin.com. 2007-, regional vice chmn. 2000-03, Audit Com., 2003-06, Fin. Com., 2007-, Conservancy, S.W. Fla., Forum Club S.W. Fla. (bd. dirs. 2000-03), Naples Press Club (bd. dirs. 1998-2000), Royal Poinciana Golf Club, Naples Yacht Club, Circumnavigators Club, Traveler's Century Club, Beta Gamma Sigma, Alpha Phi Omega, Sigma Chi (dir. Kappa Kappa corp. 1954-75, sec. 1971-73, pres. 1973-75, Charles J. Kiler award 1975, Grand Consul's citation 1976, Significant SIG award 2006). Home: 4601 Gulf Shore Blvd N Apt 12 Naples FL 34103-2214 Personal E-mail: hrowe13@comcast.net.

ROWE, JOHN WILLIAM, utilities executive; b. Dodgeville, Wis., May 18, 1945; s. William J. and Lola R. (Rule) Rowe; m. Jeanne M. Rowe; 1 child, William John. BS, U. Wis., 1967, JD, 1970; D (hon.), DePaul U., Ill. Inst. Tech., Drexel U., U. Mass., Dartmouth, Bryant Coll. Bar: Wis. 1970, Ill. 1970, US Supreme Ct. 1979, Pa. 1982. Assoc. Isham, Lincoln & Beale, Chgo., 1970-77, ptnr., 1978-80; counsel to trustee Chgo. Milw. St. Paul & Pacific RR, Chgo., 1979-80; v.p. law Consol. Rail Corp., Phila., 1980-82, sr. v.p. law, 1982-84; pres., CEO Ctrl. Maine Power Co., Augusta, 1984-89, New Eng. Elecric Sys., Westboro, Mass., 1989-98, bd. dirs.; chmn., pres., CEO Unicom Corp. & Commonwealth Edison Co., 1998-2000; pres., co-CEO Exelon Corp., Chgo., 2000—03, chmn., pres., CEO, 2003—08, chmn., CEO, 2008—. Vice-chmn. Nuc. Energy Inst., 2006—07, chmn., 2007—; bd. dirs. Sunoco, No. Trust Co. Former pres. USS Constn. Mus., 1993—95; former chmn. Edison Electric Inst.; pres. Field Mus. Natural History; trustee Mechanics Hall, Pioneer Inst.; bd. trustees Art Inst. Chgo., Chgo. Hist. Soc., Wis. Alumni Rsch. Found., Am. Enterprise Inst.; bd. trustees Ill. chpt. Nature Conservancy; nat. trustee Northwestern U. Recipient World of Difference award, Anti-Defamation League, 2000, Citizen of Yr. award, City Club of Chgo., 2002, Corp. Leadership award, Spanish Coalition for Jobs, 2002, Civic Leadership award, Am. Jewish Com., 2004, Founder's award for Bus. Leadership, Union League Phila., 2005. Mem.: Comml. Club Chgo., Econ. Club Chgo., Order of the Coif, Phi Beta Kappa. Office: Exelon Corp 10 S Dearborn St 37th Fl PO Box 805398 Chicago IL 60680-5398 Office Phone: 800-483-3220.*

ROWE, KAREN D., literature and language professor; d. Abner Peter Rowe and Marjorie Burkhalter. B.A, Bob Jones U., Greenville, SC, 1985; MEd in English, Bob Jones U., 1987; PhD, Bowling Green State U., Ohio, 2005. Circulation supr. Mack Libr., Bob Jones U., 1987—89; prof. English Dept., Bob Jones U., 1989—. Cons. Bob Jones U. Press, 1990—2005, Mus. and Gallery, Inc., Greenville, 1999—2001; coord., composition and lit. Bob Jones U., 1995—; editor Alumni Assn., Greenville, 2007—08. Mem.: MLA, Victorians Inst., Pre Raphaelite Soc., Rhetoric Soc. Am. Conservative. Avocations: art, travel. Office: Bob Jones Univ 1700 Wade Hampton Blvd Greenville SC 29614 Business E-Mail: krowe@bju.edu.

ROWE, LARRY LINWELL, lawyer, former state senator; b. Bluefield, W.Va. m. Julia Beury; 2 children. BA, W.Va. U., 1970, MPA, JD, W.Va. U., 1976. Bar: W.Va. 1976, U.S. Dist. Ct. (so. dist.) W.Va. 1976, U.S. Ct. Appeals (4th cir.) 1978, U.S. Supreme Ct. 1992. Staff counsel W.Va. Housing Devel. Fund, Charleston, 1976-77; sr. law clk. to Hon. K. K. Hall U.S. 4th Cir. Ct. Appeals, Charleston, 1978-79; pvt. practice Charleston, 1980—. Adj. prof. law U. Charleston, 1980—81. Bd. dirs. W.Va. Artists & Craftsmen's Guild, Charleston, 1980—84, Cedar Lakes' Mountain State Arts & Crafts Fair, Ripley, 1981—82; chmn., mem. Legal Aid Soc. Charleston, 1981—84; pres. W.Va. Dance Theatre, Charleston, 1981—82; hearing examiner W.Va. Bd. Regents, Charleston, 1985—89, W.Va. Bd. Medicine, Charleston, 1987—88; mem. W.Va. Ho. of Del., 1997—2000, W.Va. Senate, 2001—05, W.Va. State Ethics Commn., 2005—. W.Va. Bd. Regents scholar, W.Va. U. Coll. Law, 1974—76, Cato scholar, 1974—76. Mem.: Phi Beta Kappa, Order of Coif. Democrat. Office: 4200A Malden Dr Charleston WV 25306-6442 Home Phone: 304-925-9382; Office Phone: 304-925-1333. Business E-Mail: larrylrowe@larrylrowe.com.

ROWE, LESLIE V., United States Ambassador to Papua New Guinea, Solomon Islands & Vanuatu; m. Theodore Dieffenbacher; 3 children. BA, Wash. State U., Pullman; MA, Tufts U. Fletcher Sch. Law and Diplomacy, Medford, Mass.; MEd, Northeastern U., Boston. Cert. Sorbonne, Paris. HS fgn. lang. tchr.; dir. internat. office Tufts U.; joined fgn. svc. US Dept. State, 1983—, consul gen. Bangkok, Lisbon, Portugal, dir. office children's issues Washington, country desk officer, Chile, prin. officer, US Consulate Recife, Brazil, fgn. svc. assignments San Jose, Costa Rica, Sao Paulo, Brazil, dep. chief of mission, US Embassy Nairobi, Kenya, US amb. to Papua New Guinea, Solomon Islands and Vanuatu, 2006—. Fulbright scholar, Germany. Office: DOS Amb 4240 Port Moresby Pl Washington DC 20521-4240*

ROWE, LOUIS E., Councilman; m. Brenda Kelly; 1 stepchild. BS in Elec. Engring., U. Tex, 1971. Registered profl. engr., Tex., 1976. Pres. Goetting & Assocs., 1991—; bd. dirs. Dist. 3 San Antonio River Authority, 1996—2007, chmn., 2005—08; councilman, Dist. 9 San Antonio City Coun., 2008—. Bd. mem. San Antonio Elec. Examining & Supervising Bd., 1989—90; mem. CPS Adv. Bd., 1998—2003, chmn., 1998—2003; mem. Bexar County Citizens Adv. Com. on Elected Officials Salaries, 2000—02, chmn., 2002. Mem. Greater San Antonio C. of C., 1975—, chmn., Govt. Affairs Coun., 2000, bd. dirs., 2000—07, chmn., 2005—07; mem. North San Antonio C. of C., 1990—, former chmn. Govt. Affairs Com.; mem. UTSA Pres. Coun., 1991—, UTHSC Pres. Coun., 1992—, Real Estate Coun. San Antonio, 1992—, former chmn., Govt. Affairs Com., pres., 1995; mem. UTSA Coll. Engring. Adv. Coun., 1995—2006, chmn., 2006—; mem. Leadership San Antonio XXII, 1996—97, class XXV steering com., 1999—2000; chmn. Christy's Hope for Battered Women & Children Golf Classic, 2000—07, Cystic Fibrosis Twilight Gala, 2003. Mem.: Alamo Area Coun. Govts. (bd. mem. 2006—, vice chmn. 2008—), San Antonio Econ. Devel. Found., Soc. Mktg. Profl. Svcs. (pres. 2005—06), Profl. Engrs. in Pvt. Practice (former pres.), Nat. Soc. Profl. Engrs., Urban Land Inst., Am. Heart Assn.-San Antonio Div. (bd. dirs. 2001—07, AHA Heart Walk chmn. 2002, chmn. 2006), March of Dimes (chmn. 1996—97), Boys Hope/Girls Hope (bd. mem. 1997—2003), Jr. Achievement South Tex. (bd. mem. 2005—06), Tex. Bus. Hall Fame Found. (bd. mem. 2002—), Downtown Rotary. Office: PO Box 839966 San Antonio TX 78283 also: 900 Isom Rd Ste 102 San Antonio TX 78216 Office Phone: 210-207-7325, 210-341-2390. Business E-Mail: district9@sanantonio.gov.*

ROWE, MIKE (MICHAEL GREGORY ROWE), television personality; b. Balt., Md., Mar. 18, 1962; Attended, Towson State U., Md. Singer: Baltimore Opera; writer (TV series) The Jamie Kennedy Experiment, 2002, announcer American Chopper: The Series, 2003—07, Ghost Hunters, 2004, Kevin and Drew Unleashed, 2004, Deadliest Catch: Crab Fishing in Alaska, 2005—, former host QVC, host (TV series) Worst Case Scenario, On-Air TV, The Most, No Relation, New York Expeditions, Your New Home, Evening Magazine, 2001—05, Egypt Week Live!, 2004, Dirty Jobs, 2005—; co-prodr.: (TV series) You Spoof Discovery, 2007. Office: Discovery Holding Co 12300 Liberty Blvd Englewood CO 80112*

ROWE, NANCIE E., director, minister; b. New Castle, Pa., Nov. 4, 1943; d. John Francis and Ellen Mae Gwin; m. Ronald Allen Rowe, June 10, 2001; m. Edward Dwight Sickels, Oct. 24, 1958 (div.); children: Teddy Edward Sickels, Terrie Ellen Wells. BA in Bus., Dallas Bapt. Coll., M in Psychology; PhD, Salt Lake Bapt. U., Dallas, 2001. Sch. adminstr. Calvary Christian Acad., Desoto, Tex., 1991—99; CEO, sch. adminstr., pastor Cmty. Christian Acad., Glenn Heights, 1999—. Assoc. pastor Victory Bapt. Ch., Desoto, 1997—2005; pastor Soulspiration Outreach Ch., Dallas, 1997—. Dir.(writer, editor, actor, singer): over 32 drama/mus. prodns. for children. Chairwoman ways & means Desoto BiCenntennial, 1973—76; prayer ptnr., support troops Presedential

Prayer Team, 2000—06. Fellow Assoc. Christian Sch. Internat., Am. Salesmasters, 1970—76. Mem.: Assn. Christian Sch. Adminstrs. (assoc.). Liberal. Achievements include commercial/residential Design Firm; development of hands on teaching program for at risk students; counseling program for trouble or at risk youth. Avocation: interior decorating. Office: Cmty Christian Acad PO Box 762 1931 S Hampton Rd Glenn Heights TX 75154 Office Fax: 972-274-0078. Personal E-mail: ccaacademy137@sbcglobal.net.

ROWE, PETER A., columnist; b. Walnut Creek, Calif., Sept. 7, 1955; s. Raymond Alan and Marion (Green) R.; m. Lynn Hanson, Aug. 13, 1977; children: Kyle, Reid, Alec. BA in History, U. Calif., Berkeley, 1977, BA in Journalism, 1977; MSJ, Northwestern U., 1981. Reporter Argus, Fremont, Calif., 1977-80, Va.-Pilot, Norfolk, 1981-84, San Diego Union, 1984-87, asst. features editor, 1987-88, features editor, 1988-92; columnist San Diego Union-Tribune, 1992—. Gannett fellow Northwestern U., 1980-81, Jefferson fellow, 2006; Fulbright scholar, 2003. Mem.: Nat. Soc. Newspaper Columnists (pres. 2000—02). Roman Catholic. Office: San Diego Union Tribune PO Box 120191 San Diego CA 92112-0191 Office Phone: 619-293-1227. Business E-Mail: peter.rowe@uniontrib.com.

ROWE, RICHARD HOLMES, lawyer; b. Waltham, Mass., Jan. 2, 1937; s. Robert C. Rowe and Roberta (Holmes) Hayes; m. Sylvia C. Barrow, Aug. 23, 1963; children: Elizabeth C., Dorothy H., Christopher H. AB, Bates Coll., 1957; JD, Harvard U., 1964. Bar: DC 1965, NY 1980. Atty., exec. SEC, Washington, 1964-69, 70-79; v.p. Shareholders Mgmt. Co., LA, 1969-70; ptnr. Proskauer Rose Goetz & Mendelsohn, Washington, 1979—. 1st lt. USMCR, 1957-60. Mem. ABA, FBA, DC Bar Assn., Assn. Bar City of NY Democrat. Office: Proskauer Rose LLP 1001 Pennsylvania Ave NW Ste 400 Washington DC 20004-2537 Office Phone: 202-416-6820. Personal E-mail: rrowe@proskavor.com.

ROWE, ROBERT C., bank executive; B in Econs., Boston Coll.; MBA, Ind. U., Bloomington. Corp. assoc. Nat. City Corp., Cleve., 1990, head equity sponsor group, 1999, chief credit officer Capital Markets Group, sr. v.p., chief credit officer, chmn. corp. credit com. Bd. dirs., treas. Positive Edn. Program, Cleve. Office: Nat City Corp Nat City Ctr 1900 E Ninth St Cleveland OH 44114-3484 Office Phone: 216-222-2000.

ROWE, SANDRA MIMS, editor; b. Charlotte, NC, May 26, 1948; d. David Lathan and Shirley (Stovall) Mims; m. Gerard Paul Rowe, June 5, 1971; children: Mims Elizabeth, Sarah Stovall. BA, East Carolina U., Greenville, NC, 1970; postgrad., Harvard U., 1991. Reporter to asst. mng. editor The Ledger-Star, Norfolk, Va., 1971-80, mng. editor, 1980-82, The Virginian-Pilot and The Ledger Star, Norfolk, Va., 1982-84, exec. editor, 1984-86, v.p., exec. editor, 1986-93; editor The Oregonian, Portland, 1993—. Mem. Pulitzer Prize Bd., 1994-2003, chair, 2003. Bd. visitors James Madison U., Harrisonburg, VA., 1991-95; chair journalism adv. bd. Knight Found.; mem. adv. bd. The Poynter Inst., Medill Sch. Journalism, Northwestern U.; chair bd. visitors Knight Fellowships, Stanford U. Recipient George Beveridge Editor of Yr. award Nat. Press Found., 2003; named Woman of Yr. Outstanding Profl. Women of Hampton Rds., 1987, Editor of Yr. Editor & Publisher mag., 2008; inducted into Va. Journalism Hall of Fame, 2000; named editor of yr. Edit. Pub. Mag., 2008. Mem. Am. Soc. Newspaper Editors (past pres., bd. dirs. 1992-99), Va. Press Assn. (bd. dirs. 1985-93). Episcopalian. Office: The Oregonian 1320 SW Broadway Portland OR 97201-3499 Office Phone: 503-221-8400. Office Fax: 503-294-4175. E-mail: srowe@news.oregonian.com.*

ROWE, SUNG MAN, university executive, educator; b. Kwangju, Korea, Apr. 26, 1939; parents Chun Eun Rowe and Kwang Sin Cha; m. Jo Ja Han, Mar. 20, 1968; children: Hye Gyung, Hye Won, Hye Eun, Young Hak. BSc, Chonnam Nat. U., Kwangju, 1964, MSc, 1967, PhD, 1974. Cert. Bd. Orthopedic Surgery, Bd. Rehab. From instr. to asst. prof. to assoc. prof. Chonnam Nat. U., Kwangju, 1973—85, prof., 1985—, supt. Chonnam U. Hosp., 1993—96, pres., 1996—2000. Inventor in field; contbr. articles to profl. jours. V.p. YMCA Bd. Com., Kwangju, 1996, Korean Hosp. Assn., Seoul; mem. Com. New Ednl. Comty., 1998; permanent mem. Adv. Com. of Dem. and Peaceful Unification, 1998; vice chmn. Korean Coun. of Pres. of Nat. and Public U., 1998-2000; v.p. Social Service Assn. of Korean U., 1999-2000. Maj. Korean Army, 1969-72. Decorated Order of Mil. Merit, Govt. Korea, 1972; named Best Citizen of Kwangju, Kwangju City, 1987; recipient Acad. Award of Mudung prize, 1992. Fellow SIROT, SICOT, We. Pacific Orthop. Assn.; mem. Korean Pediat. Orthop. Soc. (pres. 1991-92), Korean Orthop. Sports Medicine (pres. 1992-94), Korean Hip Soc. (pres. 1995-96), Korean Fracture Soc. (pres. 1995-96), Korean Orthop. Assn. (pres. 2002-2003, adv. com., soc. orgn. study com.), Assn. Orthop. Rsch. (bd.), Computer Assisted Orthopedic Surgery Korea (pres. 2004-). Home: 101-501 Hyundae Apt 270 Hak-dong Dong-gu Gwangju Republic of Korea Home Phone: 82-62-225-1177; Office Phone: 82-62-227-1640. Office Fax: 82 61 720 6363. Business E-Mail: smrowe@chonnam.ac.kr.

ROWE, THOMAS DUDLEY, JR., law educator; b. Richmond, Va., Feb. 26, 1942; s. Thomas Dudley and Georgia Rosamond (Stripp) R.; m. Susan Fletcher French, Jan. 5, 2001. BA, Yale U., 1964; MPhil, Oxford U., Eng., 1967; JD, Harvard U., 1970. Bar: D.C. 1971, N.C. 1976. Law clk. to assoc. justice Potter Stewart U.S. Supreme Ct., Washington, 1970-71; asst. counsel adminstrv. practice subcom. U.S. Senate, Washington, 1971-73; assoc. Miller, Cassidy, Larroca & Lewin, Washington, 1973-75; assoc. prof. Duke U. Sch. Law, Durham, NC, 1975-79, prof., 1979-96, Elvin R. Latty prof., 1996—2007, Elvin R. Latty prof. emeritus, 2008—, assoc. dean for rsch., 1981-84, sr. assoc. dean acad. affairs, 1995-96. Vis. prof. Georgetown U. Law Ctr., Washington, 1979—80, U. Mich. Law Sch., Ann Arbor, 1985, U. Va. Law Sch., Charlottesville, 1991, UCLA Law Sch., 2002, 04; Straus Disting. vis. prof. Pepperdine U. Sch. Law, 2006; atty. Munger, Tolles & Olson, LA, 1991; adv. com. on rules of civil procedure U.S. Jud. Conf., 1993—99. Co-author: Constitutional Theory: Arguments and Perspectives, 1993, 2000, 2007, Federal Courts in the 21st Century: Cases and Materials, 1996, 2002, 2007, Civil Procedure, 2004, 2008; contbr. articles to profl. jours. Fellow U.S. Dept. Justice, Washington, 1980-81; Rhodes scholar, 1964-67; recipient Disting. Teaching award Duke Bar Assn., 1985. Mem.: ABA, Am. Law Inst. (life). Democrat. Business E-Mail: trowe@law.duke.edu.

ROWE, WILLIAM JOHNSTON, JR., dentist; BA, Washington and Lee U.; DDS, U. Tenn. With Viral Immunology Rsch. Dept. Center for Disease Control and Prevention, Atlanta; cosmetic dentist Rowe & Rowe Smile Studio, Jonesboro, Ark. Named to IMHOTEP Leadership Soc. Mem.: ADA, N.E. Ark. Dist. Dental Soc., Ark. State Dental Assn., Hinman Dental Soc., Am. Acad. Cosmetic Dentistry, Crowley's Ridge Dental Study Club, Po Kappa Alpha Fraternity. Avocations: hunting, fishing, photography. Office: Rowe & Rowe Smile Studio 801-D Osler Dr Jonesboro AR 72401 Office Phone: 870-932-4126. Office Fax: 870-932-4042. E-mail: drrowe@suddenlink.net.

ROWE, ZANE CONRAD, air transportation executive; b. 1970; BSBA, Embry-Riddle Aero U., Daytona Beach, Fla., 1991; MBA in Fin., San Diego State U. With Continental Airlines, Inc., Houston, 1993—, mng. dir. fin. analysis, staff v.p. fin. planning & analysis, 2001—03, v.p. fin. planning & analysis, 2003—05, v.p. network strategy, 2005—06, sr. v.p. network strategy, 2006—08, exec. v.p., CFO, 2008—. Bd. dirs. ARINC. Mem. indsl. adv. coun. Embry-Riddle Aero. U. Office: Continental Airlines Inc PO Box 4607 Houston TX 77210 Office Phone: 713-324-5000. Office Fax: 713-324-2637.

ROWELL, BARBARA CABALLERO, retired academic administrator; b. New Orleans, Sept. 5, 1922; d. Ferdinand; Albert Henry Wischnewske (stepfather) and Antoinette (Angelo) Caballero; m. J.C. Rowell, Dec. 17, 1941; children: Jerrie Carlene, Kerry Gene, Ricky Ray. AA in Bus. Adminstrn., Okaloosa Walton. Coll., 1972; BA in Social Sci., U. West Fla., 1987. Exec. sec. Bishop Enterprises, Ft. Walton Beach; office mgr. and real estate property mgr. Fred Cooke Real Estate, Ft. Walton Beach, Fla.; adminstrv. sec. to v.p. Okaloosa Walton Coll., Niceville, Fla. Leader brownie scouts Girl Scouts U.S., Cub Scouts; bd. dirs. U. West Fla. Ctr. for Life Long Learning; chair univ svc. com., pres., began Writing Lab; originator, implementor U. West Fla. Tutor Program, Career Fair, started scholarship program, Proctor Program; curriculum com. U. West Fla.Ctr. for Lifelong Learning, presenter S.E. Conf. Insts. of Learning in Retirement, Charleston, S.C.; gov.'s campaign vol.; state legislature campaign vol.; active Ctr. for Life Long Learning, U. West Fla. Mem. AAUW, DAV Aux., Order of Ea. Star (past matron). Avocations: travel, reading, gardening, dance.

ROWELL, EDWARD MORGAN, retired foreign service officer, educator; b. Oakland, Calif., Oct. 13, 1931; s. Edward Joseph and Mary Helen (Mohler) Rowell; m. Lenora Mary Wood, Aug. 23, 1957; children: Edward Oliver, Karen Elizabeth Schuler, Christopher Douglas. BA in Internat. Relations, Yale U., 1953; postgrad., Stanford U., 1964-65, Stanford Bus. Sch., 1970-71. Fgn. service insp. U.S. Dept. State, Washington, 1971-74; dep. dir., econ. officer Office Iberian Affairs, Washington, 1974-75; dep. dir. Office West European Affairs, Washington, 1975-76, dir., 1977-78; minister-counselor U.S. Embassy, Lisbon, Portugal, 1978-83; dep. asst. sec. Bur. Consular Affairs, Washington, 1983-85; U.S. amb. to Bolivia La Paz, 1985-88; U.S. amb. to Portugal Lisbon, 1988-90; U.S. amb. to Luxemburg, 1990-94; sr. assoc. Global Bus. Access, Ltd., 1994—. Mem. adv. bd. Portuguese-Am. Leadership Coun. U.S.; mem. Cleveland Park Congregational Ch, Washington, 1956—; trustee Cleveland Park Ch., 2000—03; bd. dirs. Luso-Am Develop Found., 1988—90. With US Army, 1953—55. Decorated grand cross Bolivian Condor of the Andes, grand cross Luxembourg Oaken Crown; recipient State Dept. Superior Honor award, 1983, 1991, Presdl. Honor Award, 1988; grantee, Una Chapman Cox Found., 1984; Yale U. scholar, 1949—52, U. Calif. fellow, 1953. Mem.: Diplomatic & Consular Officers Ret. (gov. 2001—, treas. 2005—07, v.p. 2007—09, pres. 2009—), Arena Stage Assocs., Yale Univ. Alumni Assn., Stanford Univ. Alumni Assn., Wash. Inst. Foreign Affairs (membership com. 1999—2007), Assn. Diplomatic Studies & Training (pres. 1997—2001, treas. 2005—08), Am. Foreign Svc. Assn. (v.p. 1995—97), Am Acad. Diplomacy (bd. dirs. 2002—, chmn. audit com. 2006—), Cosmos Club. Avocations: photography, tennis, music. Home: 5414 Newington Rd Bethesda MD 20816-3316 Personal E-mail: edmrowell@aol.com.

ROWELL, LESTER JOHN, JR., retired insurance company executive; b. Cleve., Apr. 2, 1932; s. Lester John and Francis Laureen (Corbett) R.; m. Patricia Ann Loesch, Jan. 16, 1953 (div. Sept. 1970); children: Deborah, Cynthia, Gregory, Maureen, Diane; m. Carol Ann Jankowski, Sept. 26, 1970. BS, Pa. State U., 1955; grad. Advanced Mgmt. Program, Harvard U. Bus. Sch., 1971. CLU. Second v.p., field mgmt. Mut. Life Ins. Co. N.Y., NYC, 1969-70, v.p. agys., 1970-72, v.p. sales, 1972-78, sr. v.p., 1978-80; exec. v.p. Provident Mut. Life Ins. Co., Phila., 1980-84, pres., 1984-86, pres., chief oper. officer, 1987, pres., chief exec. officer, 1991-93, chmn., pres., chief exec. officer, 1993-96; ret. Bd. dirs. Pa. State U., The PMA Group. Capt. USMC, 1953-62. Recipient Alumni award Pa. State U., 1972, Disting. Alumni award Pa. State U., 1988; Alumni Fellow Pa. State U., 1987. Republican. Personal E-mail: budrowell@aol.com.

ROWELL, ROBERT, professional sports team executive; B in Broadcast Journalism, Calif. Poly. State U., San Luis Obispo, 1989, M in Bus. Adminstrn., 1993. Bus. mgr. intercollegiate athletics dept. Calif. Poly. State U., 1989—91, asst. athletics dir., 1992—94, assoc. athletics dir., 1994—95; asst. contr. Golden State Warriors, 1995—96, dir. fin., contr., 1996—98, v.p. bus. ops., 1998—2001, NBA chief mktg. officer, COO, 2001—03, pres., 2003—. Golden State Warriors rep. NBA Bd. Govs. Recipient Forty Under 40 award, St. & Smith's Sports Bus. Jour., 2001. Office: Golden State Warriors 1011 Broadway Oakland CA 94607*

ROWELL, VICTORIA, actress; b. Portland, Maine, May 10, 1960; m. Tom Fahey, 1989 (div. 1990); 2 children. Attended, Sch. Am. Ballet. Dancer Am. Ballet Theatre, Dance Theatre Harlem, Am. Ballet Theatre II. Actor: (TV series) The Young and the Restless, 1990—98, 2000, 2002— (Outstanding actress in daytime drama series, NAACP Image award, 2006), As the World Turns, 1988, The Cosby Show, 1989—90, The Fresh Prince of Bel-Air, 1990, Herman's Head, 1991, 1993, Deadly Games, 1995, Diagnosis Murder, 1993—2001, Family Law, 2001; (TV films) Full Eclipse, 1993, Secret Sins of the Father, 1994, Feast of All Saints, 2001, Without Warning, 2002, A Town Without Pity, 2002, Polly and Marie, 2007; (films) Leonard Part 6, 1987, The Distinguished Gentleman, 1992, Dumb and Dumber, 1994, One Red Rose, 1995, Barb Wire, 1996, Eve's Bayou, 1997, Dr. Hugo, 1998, Secrets, 1998, A Wake in Providence, 1999, Fraternity Boys, 1999, Black Listed, 2003, Motives, 2004, Midnight Clear, 2005, A Perfect Fit, 2005, Home of the Brave, 2006; author: (book) The Women Who Raised Me: A Memoir, 2008 (NAACP Image award for debut author, 2008, NAACP Image award for biography/auto-biography, 2008). Founder Rowell Foster Children's Positive Plan Fine Arts Scholarship Fund. Mem.: Sigma Gamma Rho. Mailing: c/o CBS Television City 7800 Beverly Blvd Los Angeles CA 90036

ROWE-MAAS, BETTY LU, real estate analyst; b. Apr. 2, 1925; d. Horace Dewitt and Lucy Belle (Spiker) Rowe; children: Terry Lee, Clifford Lindsay, Craig Harrison, Joan Louise. Real estate investor, Saratoga, Calif., 1968—. Mem. Nat. Trust Hist. Preservation, Smithsonian Instn., Archeol. Inst. Am., San Jose Symphony, San Jose Cleve. Ballet, San Francisco Symphony, San Francisco Ballet, M. H. de Young Meml. Mus., Santa Barbara Mus. Art, Calif. Palice of the Legion of Honor, Loberro Theatre Found., Arlington Theater Restoration Fund, Bishop Mus. Hawaii, Friends of Kawai Mus., Friends of Princeville Libr., others; bd. dirs. Valley Inst. Theatre Arts; mem. Saratoga Good Govt., 1970-89; mem. Rt 85 Task Froce, 1978—, treas., 1984-89; treas. Traffic Relief for Saratoga. Mem. LWV, NOW (mem. world affairs coun. No. Calif. chpt.), Commonwealth Calif. Club (life), Santa Barbara Rep. Club, Toastmasters (past treas. Santa Barbara Rep. club # 5).

ROWEN, ANDREW S., lawyer; b. Seattle, 1954; AB, U. Calif., Berkeley, 1976; JD, Harvard U., 1979. Bar: NY 1980. Assoc. Sullivan & Cromwell, NYC, now ptnr. fin. institutions and coord. insurance practice area. Mem.: ABA, NYC Bar Assn. (com. on insurance law). Office: Sullivan & Cromwell 125 Broad St Fl 28 New York NY 10004-2489 Office Phone: 212-558-3896. Office Fax: 212-558-3588. Business E-Mail: rowenas@sullcrom.com.

ROWEN, MARSHALL, radiologist; b. Chgo. s. Harry and Dorothy (Kasnow) R.; m. Helen Lee Friedman, Apr. 5, 1952; children: Eric, Scott, Mark. AB in Chemistry with highest honors, U. Ill., Urbana, 1951; MD with honors, U. Ill., Chgo., 1954, MS in Internal Medicine, 1954. Diplomate Am. Bd. Radiology. Intern Long Beach (Calif.) VA Hosp., 1955; resident in radiology Los Angeles VA Hosp., 1955-58; practice medicine specializing in radiology Orange, Calif., 1960—. Chmn. bd. dirs. Moran, Rowen and Dorsey, Inc., Radiologists, 1969—2002; asst. radiologist L.A. Children's Hosp., 1958; assoc. radiologist Valley Presbyn. Hosp., Van Nuys, Calif., 1960; dir. dept. radiology St. Joseph Hosp., Orange, 1961—2004, v.p. staff, 1972; dir. dept. radiology Children's Hosp. Orange County, 1964—2002, chief staff, 1977—78, v.p., 1978—83, v.p., trustee, 2008—09, 1993—98, 2000—06; asst. clin. prof. radiology U. Calif., Irvine, 1967—70, assoc. clin. prof., 1979—82, clin. prof. radiology and pediat., 1976—, pres. clin. faculty assn., 1980—81; trustee Choc. Padrinos; sec. Choco Health Svcs., 1987—89, v.p., 1990—93, trustee, 1995—. Found. Med. Care Orange County, 1972—76, Calif. Commn. Adminstrn. Svcs. Hosp., 1975—79, Profl. Practice Systems, 1990—92, Med. Splty. Mgrs., 1990—2004, St. Joseph Med. Corp., 1993—98; v.p. Found. Med. Care Children's Hosp., 1988—89; v.p., sr. v.p. St. Joseph Med. Corp. IPA, 1995—98; sr. v.p. Orange Coast Managed Care Svcs., 1995—98, Paragon Med. Imaging, 1993—2003, Calif. Managed Imaging, 1994—2009, Alliance Premier Hosps., 1995—96; chmn. bd. dirs. Children's Healthcare Calif., 1995—2002, hon. chmn., bd. dirs., 2003—09; corp. bd. Blue Shield Calif., 1995—2006; mem. physician's rev. com. Blue Cross Calif., 1996—2009, mem. Blue Shield coun. advisors, 2001—07; trustee Children's Hosp. at Mission, 2004—09, sec. bd. dir., 2008—09, vice chair, 2009; cons. Imaging Adminstrn., 2005—09, Choco realty vice chair, 2009; Calif. dept. mgr. health care Patient Advocate Improvement Program, 2008—09; real estate-vice chair Childrens Heart Care, 2009. Mem. editl. bd. Western Jour. Medicine; contbr. articles to med. jours. Founder Orange County Performing Arts Ctr., mem. Laguna Art Mus., Laguna Festival of Arts, Opera Pacific, South Coast Reportory, Am. Ballet Theater, World Affairs Coun. Served to capt. M.C., U.S. Army, 1958-60. Recipient Rea sr. med. prize U. Ill, 1953; William Cook scholar U. Ill., 1951, Friend of Children award Children's Hosp. Guild, 1995, Charley award Children's Hosp., 1996. Fellow Am. Coll. Radiology; mem. AMA, Am. Heart Assn., Soc. Nuclear Medicine (trustee 1961-62), Orange County Radiol. Soc. (pres. 1968-69), Calif. Radiol. Soc. (pres. 1978-79), Radiol. Soc. So. Calif. (pres. 1976), Pacific Coast Pediatric Radiologists Assn. (pres. 1971), Soc. Pediatric Radiology, Calif. Med. Assn. (chmn. sect. on radiology 1978-79), Orange County Med. Assn. (chmn. UCI liaison com. 1976-78), Cardioradiology Soc. So. Calif., Radiol. Soc. N.Am., Am. Roentgen Ray Soc., Am. Coll. Physician Execs., Soc. Chmn. Radiologists Children Hosp., Center Club, Sports Club (Irvine), Phi Beta Kappa, Phi Eta Sigma, Omega Beta Phi, Alpha Omega Alpha. Office: St Joseph Hosp 1100 W Stewart Dr Orange CA 92868 Home Phone: 714-349-8667. Personal E-mail: romarsh@aol.com.

ROWLAND, ARTHUR RAY, librarian; b. Hampton, Ga., Jan. 6, 1930; s. Arthur and Jennie (Goodman) R.; m. Jane Thomas, July 1, 1955; children: Dell Ruth, Anna Jane. AB, Mercer U., Macon, Ga., 1951; M. Librarianship, Emory U., 1952; postgrad., Oxford U., 1989. Circulation asst. Ga. State Coll. Library, 1952, circulation librarian, 1952-53; librarian Armstrong Coll., Savannah, Ga., 1954-56; head circulation dept. Auburn U. Library, 1956-58; librarian, assoc. prof. library sci. Jacksonville U., 1958-61, Augusta Coll., 1961-76, prof., libr., 1976-91, libr. emeritus, 1991—. Lectr. libr. edn. U. Ga., 1962-66; trustee Augusta-Richmond County Pub. Libr., 1980-93, pres. bd. trustees, 1983-85, v.p. bd., 1988-91; trustee Augusta Regional Libr., chmn., 1984-85; trustee East Cen. Ga. Regional Libr., 1987-93, chmn., 1988-91; chmn. Gov.'s Conf. on Ga. Librs. and Info. Svcs., 1977; del. White House Conf. on Librs. and Info. Sci., 1979; cons. on libr. mgmt. to Govt. of Indonesia, 1986. Author: Bibliography of the Writings of Georgia History, 1966, A Guide to the Study of Augusta and Richmond County, Georgia, 1967, (with Helen Callahan) Yesterday's Augusta, 1976, (with James E. Dorsey) A Bibliography of the Writings on Georgia History 1900-1970, rev. edit., 1978, (with Marguerite F. Fogleman) Reese Library Genealogical Resources, 1988, supplement, 1990, Goodman Cousins, 1988, Rowland Cousins, 1990, New Guide to the Study of Augusta, 1990, Index to City Directory of Augusta, Georgia, 1841-1879, 1991, More Goodman Cousins, 1993, My Fair Grandmother, 1994, Distant Cousins, The Huguenots Connecting Rowland, Bulloch, de Bourdeaux, DeVeaux and Roosevelt Families of S.C., N.C. and Ga., 1995, The Bessent Family of Georgia, 1995, Reeves Family of Georgia, 1996, Descendants of Wiley Reeves, 1996, Rowland-Huckaby Connections, 1996, Georgia Almanacs, 1996, Rowland Family of Virginia, North Carolina and Georgia and Beyond, 1998, Atkinson Family in Virginia, 1998, Ancestors of David Jackson, 1998, Ancestors of Rachael Hines Lewis, 1998, Ancestors of Elizabeth Proctor in Virginia and England, 1998, Ancestors of Martha Whitehead, 1998, Wiley Reeves, His Descendants and Ancestors, 1999, John Rowland, Immigrant, 2000, Reeves Family in England, Virginia, North Carolina, Georgia and Beyond, 2000, The Mississippi Branch of the Rowland Family, 2000, Ancestors and Connections of Dunbar Rowland, 2000, Printing in Louisville, 2000, Confederate Printing in Augusta, Ga., 2000, Goodman Family of N.C., Ga. and Beyond Their Cherokee Indian Heritage, 2000, Hillhouse Family of Wash., Ga., 2000, Printing in Wash., Ga., 2000, Jacob Martin Hugenot of Charleston, S.C., 2000, John Gensel of Charleston, S.C., 2000, Bessent Family, 2000, Rowland Family in Ga., 2000, Printers of Augusta, Georgia, 1786-1900, 2003, Printing in Milledgeville, Georgia, 2003, Preliminary Checklist of Penfield, Georgia Imprints, 2003, A Preliminary Checklist of Georgia Imprints, 1763-1860, 2003, Civil War Marriages Richmond County, Georgia, 2004, Grocers, Butchers, Baker and Others, 2004, 1890 Census of Augusta and Richmond County Georgia, 2004, 2d edit., 2006, Citizens of Augusta and Richmond County, Georgia During the Civil War, 2005, 2d edit., 2006, Confederate Soldiers From Augusta and Richmond County, Georgia, 2005, Name Index to Augusta Georgia City Directories 1880-1891, 2006, Business Directory of Augusta Georgia 1841-1901, 2006, Brides and Grooms: Marriage Licesnes and Certificates of Richmond County Georgia 1785-1890, 2006, China and Immigrants to Augusta and Richmond County Georgia, 2006, Citizens of North Augusta in Aiken County South Carolina, 2006, Black or Mulatto in Richmond County Georgia, 2006, Women in Business in Augusta Georgia 1841-1901, 2006, Ecclesiastical Index to Augusta Georgia 1736-1901, 2006, Foreign Born Citizens in Augusta and Richmond County Georgia 1850 and 1860, 2006, Hephzibah Georgia in Richmond County Georgia, 2006, Village of Summerville 1880-1910, 2006, Names Changed Legally in Georgia 1800-1856, 2007, List of Prisoners in Penitentiary, Convict Camps, Chain Gangs and Jails in Georgia, 2007, McPherson Barracks, 2007, Brides and grooms, Book, Richmond county, Georgia.,2007, Classified Business Directory August Georgia 1901-1930, 2007, Banker, Cashier, Teller, 2007, Index to Marriage Licences Book, 2008, Cross References to Personel Names, 2008, Public Buildings in August Georgia, 2008, others; co-author: (with Jane T. Rowland) Index to Marriage 1912-1942; editor: To New Book Titles, Reference Services, 1964, Historical Markers of Richmond County, Georgia, rev. edit., 1971, The Catalog and Cataloging, 1969, The Librarian and Reference Service, 1977, Reminiscences of Augusta Marines, 1985; supervising editor (with Heard Robertson) Jour. Archibald Campbell, 1981; contbr. to profl. jours. V.p. Ga. Libr. Assn. Trustees and Friends, 1989-91. With USN, 1948-49. Recipient Nix-Jones award for disting. service Ga. Library Assn., 1981, Town and Gown award Augusta Coll. Alumni Assn., 1985. Mem. ALA, Am. Assn. State and Local History, Bibliog. Soc. Am., Southeastern Libr. Assn. (hon. life, exec. bd. 1971-72), Ga. Libr. Assn. (hon. life, 2d v.p. 1965-67, 71-73, 1st v.p., pres.-elect 1973-75, pres. 1975-77, chmn. budget com. 1977-79, adv. to pres. 1979-83, 85-92), Ctrl. Savannah River Area Libr. Assn. (past pres., editor union list of serials 1967, contbn. local history and genecology, 2007), Duval County Libr. Assn. (past v.p.), Nat. Geneal. Soc., Ga. Geneal. Soc., N.C. Geneal. Soc., Va. Geneal. Soc., Augusta Geneal. Soc., Richmond County Hist. Soc. (curator 1964-91, pres. 1967-69, founder, editor Richmond County History), Huguenot Soc. S.C., Ga. Hist. Soc. (curator emeritus), Ga. Bapt. Hist. Soc., Nat., Young Men's Libr. Assn. (v.p. 1988-91), Ga. Trusts for Hist. Preservation, Hist. Augusta (trustee emeritus), Soc. Ga. Archivists, Kappa Phi Kappa. Baptist. Address: 334 Connor Cir Evans GA 30809 Personal E-mail: rrow999@comcast.net.

ROWLAND, ESTHER E(DELMAN), retired dean; b. NYC, Apr. 12, 1926; d. Abraham Simon and Ida Sarah (Shifrin) Edelman; m. Lewis P. Rowland, Aug. 31, 1952; children: Andrew, Steven, Joy Rosenthal. BA, U. Wis., 1946; MA, Columbia U., 1948, MPhil, 1984; cert. in bioethics, Columbia U./Albert Einstein, 1996. Instr. in polit. sci. CCNY, 1947-51, Mt. Holyoke Coll., South Hadley, Mass., 1948-49; dir. health professions adv. bd. U. Pa., Phila., 1971-73; adviser to pre-profl. students Barnard Coll., NYC, 1974-79, dean for pre-profl. students, 1980-93, assoc. dean studies, 1989-95; ret., 1995—. Proofreader Monthly Review, N.Y.C., 1997-2003. Mem. exec. com. Nat. Emergency Civil Liberties Com., N.Y.C., 1975-90; mem. exec. com. Women's Counseling Project, 1981-86. Mem. N.E. Assn. Health Professions Advisers (exec. com. 1973-74), N.E. Assn. Pre Law Advisors (exec. com. 1981-83, 85-86), Neurol. Inst. Aux., N.Y.C. Found. Sr. Citizens (ombudsman 1997-99), Aux. Am. Acad. Neurologists (exec. bd. 1999-2001). Home: 404 Riverside Dr New York NY 10025-1861 Personal E-mail: eerowland@gmail.com.

ROWLAND, FRANK SHERWOOD, chemistry professor; b. Del., Ohio, June 28, 1927; m. Joan Lundberg, 1952; children: Ingrid Drake, Jeffrey Sherwood. AB, Ohio Wesleyan U., 1948; MS, U. Chgo., 1951, PhD, 1952, DSc (hon.), 1989, Duke U., 1989, Whittier Coll., 1989, Princeton U., 1990, Haverford Coll., 1992, Clark U., 1996, U. East Anglia, 1996; LLD (hon.), Ohio Wesleyan U., 1989, Simon Fraser U., 1991, U. Calgary, 1997; laurea honoris causa, U. Urbino, Italy, 1998; DSc, Carleton Coll., 1998, Gustavus Adolphus Coll., 1997, Occidental Coll., 1998, Kanagawa U., Japan, 1999, LaTrobe U., Australia, 2000, U. Waterloo, Can., 2001, Ohio State U., 2002. Instr. chemistry Princeton (N.J.) U., 1952—56; asst. prof. chemistry U. Kans., 1956—58, assoc. prof. chemistry, 1958—63, prof. chemistry, 1963—64, U. Calif., Irvine, 1964—, dept. chmn., 1964—70, Aldrich prof. chemistry, 1985—89, Bren prof. chemistry, 1989—94, Donald Bren rsch. prof., chemistry, 1994—. Humboldt sr. scientist Fed. Republic Germany, 1981; chmn. Dahlem (Germany) Conf. on Changing Atmosphere, 1987; vis. scientist Japan Soc. for Promotion Sci., 1980; co-dir. western region Nat. Inst. Global Environ. Change, 1989—93; del. Internat. Coun. Sci. Unions, 1993—98; fgn. sec. NAS, 1994—2002; lectr., cons. in field; mem. ozone commn. Internat. Assn. Meteorology and Atmospheric Physics, 1980—88, hon. life mem., 1996, mem. commn. on atmospheric chemistry and global pollution, 1979—91; mem. acid rain peer rev. panel U.S. Office of Sci. and Tech., Exec. Office of White House, 1982—84; mem. vis. com. Max Planck Inst., Heidelberg and Mainz, Germany, 1982—96; ozone trends panel mem. NASA, 1986—88; chmn. Gordon Conf. Environ. Scis.-Air, 1987; mem. Calif. Coun. Sci. Tech., 1989—95; mem. exec. com. Tyler Prize, 1992—. Contbr. articles to profl. jours. Recipient numerous awards including, John Wiley Jones award, Rochester Inst. Tech., 1975, Disting. Faculty Rsch. award, U. Calif., Irvine, 1976, Profl. Achievement award, U. Chgo., 1977, Billard award, N.Y. Acad. Sci., 1977, Tyler World Prize in Environ. Achievement, 1983, Global 500 Roll of Honor for Environ. Achievement, UN Environment Program, 1988, Dana award for Pioneering Achievements in Health, 1987, Silver medal, Royal Inst. Chemistry U.K., 1989, Wadsworth award, N.Y. State Dept. Health, 1989, medal, U. Calif. Irvine, 1989, Japan prize in Environ. Sci., 1989, Dickson prize, Carnegie-Mellon U., 1991, Albert Einstein prize, World Cultural Coun., 1994, Nobel Prize in chemistry, 1995, Alumni medal, U. Chgo., 1997, Nevada medal, 1997, Gold medal, Acad. Athens, 2003; named to, GTE Acad. All-Am. Hall of Fame, 2000; fellow Guggenheim Found., 1962, 1974. Fellow: AAAS (pres.-elect 1991, pres. 1992, chmn. bd. dirs. 1993), Am. Geophys. Union (Roger Revelle medal 1994), Am. Phys. Soc. (Leo Szilard award for physics in pub. interest 1979); mem.: NAS (co-DATA com. 1977—82, com. atmospheric scis., solar-terrestial com. 1979—83, sci. com. on problems environment 1986—89, bd. environ. studies and toxicology 1986—91, com. on atmospheric chemistry 1987—89, Infinite Voyage film com. 1988—92, Robertson Meml. lectr. 1993, chmn. com. on internat. orgns. and programs 1993—2002, chmn. office of internat. affairs 1994—2002, coun. 1994—2002, co-chmn. interacad. panel 1995—2000, mem. exec. com. 2000—02, chair bd. atmospheric scis. and climate 2007—), Royal Soc. U.K. (fgn.), Academia Bibliotheca Alexandrinae, Inst. Medicine, Am. Philos. Soc., Am. Meteorol. Soc. (hon.), Korean Acad. Sci. Tech. (fgn. sec.), European Acad. Arts, Scis. and Humanities, Am. Chem. Soc. (chmn. divsn. nuclear sci. and tech. 1973—74, chmn. divsn. phys. chemistry 1974—75, E.F. Smith lectureship 1980, Orange County award 1975, Tolman medal 1976, Zimmerman award 1980, Environ. Sci. and Tech. award 1983, Esselen award 1987, Peter Debye Phys. Chem. award 1993), Am. Acad. Arts and Scis., Sigma Xi, Phi Beta Kappa. Office: Dept Chemistry U Calif Irvine 571 Rowland Hall Irvine CA 92697-2025 E-mail: rowland@uci.edu.*

ROWLAND, HERBERT, language educator; b. Little Rock, Aug. 5, 1943; s. Jesse Herbert and Myrtle May Rowland; m. Linda Adele Hill, Feb. 27, 1965; children: Stefanie Irene, Marc Van. BA in German and English with honors, U. Ark., Fayetteville, 1968; MA, U. Oreg., Eugene, 1971, PhD, 1973. Tchr. German, French and English Reedsport HS, Oreg., 1973—75; asst. prof. German Eastern Wash. U., Cheney, 1975—83; prof. German Purdue U., West Lafayette, Ind., 1983—. Contbr. chapters to books and articles numerous profl. jours. Radioman 3rd class USN, 1963—65, USS Kitty Hawk. Recipient Viet Nam, Armed Forces Expeditionary Svc. medal, USN, 1963—64, Nat. Def. medal, 1963—65, Dean's Alumni Achievement award, U. Oreg., 1990; named Outstanding Young Men of America, 1980; Fulbright scholarship, Fulbright Commn., 1968—69, Humboldt fellowship, Alexander von Humboldt Found., 1980, 1990, 1997. Mem.: MLA, Am. Assn. Tchrs. German, Am. Soc. Eighteenth-Century Studies, Matthias-Claudius-Gesellschaft, Lessing Soc., Goethe Soc. America, H. C. Andersen-Samfundet, Phi Kappa Phi, Phi Beta Kappa. Liberal. Roman Catholic. Avocations: reading, music. Home: 11 Elvernan Dr West Lafayette IN 47906

ROWLAND, JOHN ARTHUR, lawyer; b. Joliet, Ill., Mar. 6, 1943; s. John Fornof and Grace Ada (Baskerville) R.; m. Cher Rowland; children: Sean B., Keira L. BA, U. Notre Dame, 1965; JD, U. San Francisco, 1968. Bar: Calif. 1969, US Dist. Ct. (no. dist.) Calif. 1982, US Dist. Ct. (ctrl. dist.) Calif. 1998, US Dist. Ct. (so. dist.) Calif. 2006. Asst. dist. atty. San Francisco Dist. Atty.'s Office, 1971-81; assoc. Ropers, Majeski, Kohn and Bentley, San Francisco, 1982—, ptnr., 1985—. Pres., South of Market Boys, San Francisco, 1981. Served to capt. U.S. Army, 1969-70, Korea. Recipient Commendation San Francisco Bd. Suprs., 1981, Merit award Mayor of San Francisco, 1982. Mem.: Am. Bd. Trial Advocates. Roman Catholic. Office: Ropers Majeski Kohn and Bentley 201 Spear St Ste 1000 San Francisco CA 94105 Home Phone: 415-601-2424; Office Phone: 415-972-6311. Business E-Mail: jrowland@ropers.com.

ROWLAND, KELLY (KELENDRIA TRENE ROWLAND), singer; b. Atlanta, Feb. 11, 1981; With Destiny's Child, 1992—2005; solo career, 2005—. Singer (with Destiny's Child): (albums) Destiny's Child, 1998, The Writing's on the Wall, 1999, Survivor, 2001 (Am. Music award for Favorite Pop Album, 2002), 8 Days of Christmas, 2001, Destiny Fulfilled, 2004 (Am. Music award for Favorite R&B Album, 2005), (songs) No, No, No, 1997, Say My Name, 1999 (2 Grammy awards, 2001, MTV Video Music award for Best R&B Video, 2000), Get on the Bus, 1999, Bills Bills Bills, 1999, Bug-A-Boo, 1999, Jumpin' Jumpin', 2000, Independent Woman, 2000, Survivor, 2001 (Grammy award, Best R&B Performance, 2002, MTV Video Music award for Best R&B Video, 2001), Bootylicious, 2001, Emotion, 2001, Lose My Breath, 2004, Soldier, 2005; singer: (solo career) (albums) Simply Deep, 2002, Ms. Kelly, 2007, (songs) Stole, 2002, Can't Nobody, 2003, Train on a Track, 2003; singer: (with Nelly) Dilemma, 2002 (Grammy award for Best Rap/Sung Collaboration, 2003); actor: (films) Freddy vs. Jason, 2003; host (TV series) The Fashion Show, 2009—. Recipient Favorite R&B Group, Am. Music Awards, 2001, 2002, 2005, BET award for Best Female Group, 2001, NAACP Image award for Outstanding Duo or Group, 2001, 2005, 2006, Choice Pop Group, Teen Choice Awards, 2001, Brit award for Best Internat. Group, 2002, World's Best-Selling Group, World Music Awards, 2002, World's Best-Selling Pop Group, 2002, 2006, World's Best-Selling R&B Group, 2002, 2006, Best-Selling Female Group of All Time, 2006. Address: 1505 Hadley Houston TX 77002 Office Phone: 713-772-5175.*

ROWLAND, LANDON HILL, diversified holding company executive; b. Fuquay Springs, NC, May 20, 1937; s. Walter Elton and Elizabeth Carr (Williams) R.; m. Sarah Fidler, Dec. 29, 1959; children: Sarah Elizabeth, Matthew Hill, Joshua Carr. BA, Dartmouth Coll., 1959; LL.B., Harvard U., 1962. Bar: Mo. Assoc. Watson, Ess, Marshall & Enggas, Kansas City, Mo., 1962-70, ptnr., 1970-80; v.p. Kansas City So. Industries, Inc., 1980-83, pres., chief oper. officer, 1983-86, pres., CEO, 1987—2000, also bd. dirs.; pres., CEO Kansas City So. Ry. Co., 1990—91, chmn., 1990—2000. Lectr. antitrust law U. Mo. Kansas City; chmn. DST Sys., 1983-95. Co-author West's Mo. Practice Series. Trustee Midwest Rsch. Inst., Kansas City, Mo.; chmn. bd. dirs. Swope Ridge Health Care Ctr.; bd. dirs. Lyric Opera of Kansas City, Am. Royal, Jacob L. & Ella C. Loose Found.; chmn. Met. Performing Arts Fund. Mem. ABA, Mo. Bar Assn., Phi Beta Kappa. Clubs: Kansas City Country, Kansas City, River. Home: Ever Glades Farm 12717 NE Mt Olivet Rd Kansas City MO 64166-1236 Office: Ever Glades Fin 920 Main St #204 Kansas City MO 64105-2008

ROWLAND, LEWIS PHILLIP, neurology educator, editor, clinical investigator; b. Bklyn., Aug. 3, 1925; s. Henry Alexander and Cecile (Coles) Rowland; m. Esther Edelman Rowland, Aug. 31, 1952; children: Andrew Simon, Steven Samuel, Joy Rosenthal. BS, Yale U., 1945, MD, 1948; PhD (hon.), U. Aix-Marseilles, France, 1986, U. Padua, 1996. Diplomate Am. Bd. Psychiatry and Neurology. Intern New Haven Hosp., 1949-50; asst. resident NY Neurol. Inst., 1950-52, fellow, 1953; clin. assoc. NIH, Bethesda, Md., 1953-54; practice rsch. medicine, specializing in neurology NYC, 1954-67, Phila., 1967-73, NYC, 1973—; asst. neurologist Montefiore Hosp., NYC, 1954-57; vis. fellow Nat. Inst. Med. Rsch., London, 1956; from asst. prof. to prof. neurology Columbia Coll. Physicians and Surgeons, 1957-67, prof. dept. neurology, 1973—, chmn. dept. neurology, 1973-98; prof., chmn. dept. neurology U. Pa. Med. Sch., 1967-73; from asst. neurologist to attending neurologist Presbyn. Hosp., 1957-67; co-dir. Neurol. Clin. Rsch. Ctr., 1961-67, dir. neurology svc., 1973-98, attending neurologist, 1973—, pres. med. bd., 1991-94. Cons. Harlem Hosp., 1973—; mem. med. adv. bd. Myasthenia Gravis Found., pres., 1971-73; med. adv. bd. Muscular Dystrophy Assocs., Nat. Multiple Sclerosis Soc., NYC Multiple Sclerosis Soc., 1977-92, Com. to Combat Huntington's Disease; chmn. med. adv. bd. NYC Multiple Sclerosis Soc. 1977-92; pres. Parkinson's Disease Found., 1979-; mem. tng. grants com. Nat. Inst. Neurol. Disorders and Stroke, NIH, 1971-73, bd. sci. counselors, 1978-83, chmn., 1981-83, mem. nat. adv. coun., 1986-90, cons. to dir., 2000-01; hon. dir. Motor Neuron Rsch. Ctr., Columbia U., 2005-. Author: The Legacy of Tracy J. Putman and Houston Herrett Hodeck Neurology in the United States, Mem. editl. bd. Archives of Neurology, 1968-76, Advances in Neurology, 1969—, Italian Jour. Neurol. Sci., 1979—99, Handbook of Clin. Neurology, 1982—, New Eng. Jour. Medicine, 1990-2000, Med. Letter, 1990-97, Jour. Neurol. Sci., 1991—, Jour. Neuromuscular Disorders, 1991-97, Clin. Neurosci., 1995-98; editor-in-chief Neurology, 1977-87, Neurology Today, 2001—; assoc. editor Medlink, 1995—; editor Merritt's Neurology Textbook, 1995, 11th edit. 2005; author NINDS at 50: An Incomplete History Celebrating the Fiftieth Anniversary of the National Institute of Neurological Disorders and Stroke, 2001. With USNR, 1942—44, with USPHS, 1953—54. Forbes Norris award, 2001, Internat. Alliance of ALS/MND Assns.; Jerry Lewis award, Muscular Dystrophy Assn., 1993; named disting. tchr., Columbia P&S Class of 1975. Mem. Am. Neurol. Assn. (hon. mem. 1959—, pres. 1980; Soriano Lecture, 1991, Geroge W. Jacoby Award 1995), Inst. Medicine, Nat. Acad. Sci. (elected 1999), Am. Acad. Neurology (pres.-elect 1987-89, pres. 1989-91, hon. mem. 1997—), Phila. Neurol. Soc. (pres. 1972), Assn. Rsch. Nervous Mental Disease (pres. 1969, trustee 1976—, v.p. 1980, chmn. bd. trustees 1992-98), Assn. Univ. Profs. Neurology (sec. 1971-74, pres. 1978), Am. Acad. Neurol. Found. (pres. 1996, chair bd. trustees 1997-99, trustee 1999—), Am. Acad. Neurol. (Sheil Essey rsch. award 1998) Ea. Pa. Multiple Sclerosis Soc. (chmn. med. adv. bd. 1969-73); hon. mem. Neurol. Socs. France, Poland, Can., Europe, Italy, Gt. Britain, Spain, Japan. Home: 404 Riverside Dr New York NY 10025-1861 Office: Columbia U Med Ctr Neurological Inst 710 W 168th St New York NY 10032-2603 Office Phone: 212-305-8551. Business E-Mail: lpr1@columbia.edu.

ROWLAND, MARCUS C., energy executive; Grad., Wichita State U., 1975. CPA. CFO pvt. exploration co., Okla. City, 1981—85; owner, mgr. oil and gas co.; COO Anglo-Suisse, L.P., 1990—93; CFO Chesapeake Energy, 1993—, v.p. fin., 1993—97, sr. v.p., 1997—98, exec. v.p., 1998—. Office: Chesapeake Energy PO Box 18496 Oklahoma City OK 73154-0496*

ROWLAND, NEIL E., psychology professor, department chairman; PhD. Prof., dept. psychology U. Fla., Gainesville, chmn., dept. psychology, 2007—. Contbr. articles to profl. jours. Office: Univ Fla Dept Psychology 330 Psychology Bldg PO Box 112250 Gainesville FL 32611-2250 Office Phone: 352-273-2178. Business E-Mail: nrowland@ufl.edu.*

ROWLAND, PAUL STEPHEN, psychology professor; b. Phila., Feb. 4, 1945; s. Stanley Paul Rowland and Dorothy Catherine Schneider; m. Kathleen Lee Kinzie, Apr. 14, 1990; 1 child, Kachina L. PhD, U. Ark., Fayetteville, 1977. Lectr. U. Md., U. Coll., Germany, 1979—81, Japan, 1981—83; edn. rsch. analyst Def. Intelligence Coll., Washington, 1983—86; prof. Southern Oreg. U., Ashland, 1986—. Recipient Tchg. award, Southern Oreg. U., 2000, Roland H. Waters Grad. Tchg. award, U. Ark., 1975. Mem.: Coun. Tchrs. Undergrad. Psychology (coord. 2002), Soc. Tchg. Psychology, Western Psychol. Assn., Assn. Psychol. Sci., Psi Chi. Office: Southern Oreg Univ Psychology Dept 1250 Siskiyou Blvd Ashland OR 97520 Business E-Mail: rowland@sou.edu.

ROWLAND, RALPH THOMAS, retired architect; b. Elizabeth, NJ, Oct. 10, 1920; s. Thomas Aloysius and Anna Frances (McQuaid) R.; m. Bernice Barbara Cannizzo, Sept. 7, 1946; children: Glenn Thomas, Mark Louis, Roy Joseph, Lisa Rowland Majewski. Student, Manhattan Coll., 1937-38, Columbia U., 1945-49. Archtl. field supr., specifier Voorhees Walker Foley & Smith, NYC, 1945-50; specifier, project mgr. Sargent Webster Crenshaw & Folley, Watertown, N.Y., 1951-53; pvt. practice Hamden, Conn., 1958-65; field supr. Fletcher Thompson, Inc., Bridgeport, Conn., 1954-56, project mgr., 1957, 65-73, asso., 1969-73, v.p., 1973-81, dir. archtl. research, 1981-85, adv. coun., 1994-98. Chmn. Conn. Bldg. Code Standards Com., 1978-82; vice chmn. Conn. State Codes and Standards Com., 1982-86; cons. in field. Editorial chmn.: Conn. Architect Mag., 1966-74; project mgr. design, St. Vincents Med. Center, Bridgeport. Mem. Cheshire Planning Commn., 1966-72, chmn., 1967-68; pres. Hamden C. of C., 1964, New Eng. Bldg. Code Assn., 1989; mem. Cen. Naugatuck Valley Regional Planning Agy., 1966-74, chmn., 1969; mem. Cheshire Democratic Town Com., 1960-70, treas., 1963-69; mem. Conn. Archtl. Sch. Task Force, 1987-88. With USN, 1942-45. Fellow AIA; mem. AIA Conn. (past pres.), AARP (pres. Cheshire chpt. 1995-97), Conn. Bldg. Ofcls. Assn., Cheshire C. of C., Chesire Sr. Ctr. Assn. (vice chmn. bd. dirs., 2002-). Roman Catholic. Home: 201 N Rolling Acres Rd Cheshire CT 06410-2119

ROWLAND, ROBERT ALEXANDER, III, lawyer; b. McAllen, Tex., Apr. 27, 1943; s. Robert Alexander Jr and Marguerite (Gerry) Rowland; m. Victoria Nalle, Apr. 2, 1977; children: Julia Marie, Emily Nalle. BS, Tex. A&M U., 1966; JD, George Washington U., 1972. Bar: Tex. 1972, U.S. Dist. Ct. (so. dist.) Tex. 1973, U.S. Ct. Appeals (5th cir.) 1973, U.S. Supreme Ct. 1976, U.S. Dist. Ct. (no. dist.) Tex. 1979, U.S. Dist. Ct. (we. dist.) Tex. 1982, U.S. Dist. Ct. (ea. dist.) Tex. 1983. Law clk. U.S. Ct. Appeals (5th cir.), Houston, 1973-74; assoc. Vinson & Elkins, Houston, 1975-81; ptnr. Susman, Godfrey & McGowan, Houston, 1982—88; mng. dir. Johnson and Gibbs, Houston, 1988-91; ptnr. Hutcheson & Grundy, LLP, Houston, 1992-94; chmn., CEO Associated Counsel of Am., 1995—2007; ptnr. Roach & Rowland, Houston, 2003—07, Law Offices Robert A. Rowland III and Assocs., 2008—. Bd. dirs. Vol. Ctr., Houston, 1975—84, pres., 1982—83; founding mem., bd. dirs. Tex. Accts. and Lawyers for Arts, 1979—92, pres., 1989—91; devel. coun. Sch. Liberal Arts Tex. A&M U., 1992—2009, steering com., 1995—2007, devel. coun. George Bush Sch. Govt. and Pub. Svc., 2004—; trustee Houston Pks. Bd. Endowment Fund, 2002—; chmn. endowment com. Houston Audubon Soc., 2006—; endowment com. The Beacon, 2006—09; bd. dirs. Tex. Assn. Bus., 2008—09; bd. adv. US Pub. Svc. Acad., 2007—; co-chmn. Mayor's Transition Com. for Parks, City of Houston, 1992—94; candidate for State Rep., Tex. Legis. Dist. 134, Rep. Primary, 2002; fin. com. Harris County Rep. Party, 2003—07, chmn., 2005—07; bd. dirs. United Reps. of Harris County, 2002—; Rep. precinct chmn. Harris County Precinct, 2003—05, 2008—; mission outreach coun. Christ Ch. Cathedral, 2002—05, chmn., 2004—05, co-chmn., grants subcom., 2005—06, chmn. grants subcom., 2006—07, stewardship coun., 2006—, chmn., 2008—; bd. dirs. Houston Pks. Bd., 1993—2005, chmn., 2003—05; bd. dirs. Contemporary Art Mus. Houston, 1974—80, 1991—94; bd. dirs. Sarah Campbell Blaffer Gallery of Art U. Houston, 1989—94; bd. dirs. Tex. Opera Theater, 1988—89; bd. trustees Nat. Recreation and Pk. Assn., 1992—95; bd. dirs. Cultural Arts Coun., Houston, 1981—86, Pk. People Inc., 1979—2001, pres., 1991—92, endowment com. chmn., 1994—2004; bd. dirs. Compass, 2006—, v.p., 2008—09, pres., 2009—; with parks and open spaces com. Greater Houston Partnership, 2006—, chair, 2009—, quality of life adv. com., 2006—; bd. dirs. Houston Bot. Garden, 2007—, chmn. bylaws com., 2007—, sec., 2009—, chmn., pub. affairs com., 2009—. Capt. US Army, 1966—69, Vietnam. Fellow: Tex. Bar Found., Houston Bar Found.; mem.: State Bar Tex., Houston Bar Assn. (dir. 1979—88, sec., chmn. law and art com. 1984—85, 2d v.p. 1985—86), C Club (program chmn. 2005, exec. com. 2005—07, membership chmn. 2006, treas. 2007), Coronado Club, River Oaks Country Club, Phi Delta Phi. Republican. Episcopalian. Home: 2010 Chilton Rd Houston TX 77019-1502 Office: Associated Counsel Am Inc Ste 125 4605 Post Oak Pl Houston TX 77027-9744 Office Phone: 713-840-7100 ext. 234. Personal E-mail: rob@robrowland.com.

ROWLAND, THEODORE JUSTIN, physicist, educator, researcher; b. Cleve., May 15, 1927; s. Thurston Justin and Lillian (Nesser) R.; m. Janet Claire Millar, June 28, 1952 (div. 1967); children: Theodore Justin, Dawson Ann, Claire Millar; m. Patsy Marie Beard, Aug. 21, 1968 (div. 2007). BS, Western Res. U., 1948; MA, Harvard U., 1949, PhD, 1954. Rsch. physicist Union Carbide Metals Co., Niagara Falls, NY, 1954-61; prof. phys. metallurgy U. Ill., 1961-92, asst. dean Coll. Engring., acting assoc. dean Grad. Coll., 1990-91, prof. emeritus, 1992—; pres., dir. Materials Cons., Inc. Cons. physicist, 1961—; cons. metallurgist, 1976—. Editor 2 books; author monograph; contbr. articles to profl. jours. Fellow Am. Phys. Soc.; mem. AIME, AAAS, AAUP, Phi Beta Kappa, Delta Phi Alpha, Sigma Xi. Achievements include initial verification of charge density waves in dilute alloys; original contributions to theory and experiment in nuclear magnetic resonance in pure metals and alloys. Home: 805 Park Lane Dr Champaign IL 61820-7613 Office: U Ill Dept Materials Sci and Engring 1304 W Green St Urbana IL 61801-2920 Business E-Mail: trowland@uiuc.edu.

ROWLANDS, DAVID THOMAS, pathology educator; b. Wilkes-Barre, Pa., Mar. 22, 1930; s. David Thomas and Anna Jule (Morgan) R.; m. Gwendolyn Marie York, Mar. 1, 1958; children: Julie Marie, Carolyn Jane. MD, U. Pa., 1955. Diplomate: Am. Bd. Pathology, Am. Bd. Allergy and Immunology. Intern Pa. Hosp., Phila., 1955-56; resident Cin. Gen. Hosp., 1956-60; asst. prof. U. Colo., 1962-64, Rockefeller U.,

1964-66; assoc. prof. Duke U., Durham, NC, 1966-70; prof. pathology U. Pa., Phila., 1970-82, chmn. dept. pathology, 1973-78, prof. medicine, 1979-82; prof., chmn. dept. pathology U. So. Fla., Tampa, 1982-91, assoc. dean, 1983-84, prof. pediatrics, 1986-91; med. dir. Lifelink Tissue Bank, 1991-93. Mem. editorial bd.: Am. Jour. Pathology, 1971-81, Developmental and Comparative Immunology, 1977-79. Served with USNR, 1960-62. Recipient Lederle Med. Faculty award U. Colo., 1964, Jacob Ehrenzeller award Pa. Hosp., 1976 Mem. Am. Assn. Pathologists, Internat. Acad. Pathology, Am. Soc. Clin. Pathology, Am. Assn. Immunologists, Coll. Am. Pathologist, Arthur Purdy Stout Soc. Presbyterian. Home: 13804 Cypress Village Cir Tampa FL 33618-8406 Personal E-mail: drowl30@verizon.net. E-mail: drowl30@gte.net.

ROWLANDS, KATHLEEN DUDDEN, education educator; b. South Weymouth, Mass., Jan. 11, 1945; d. Arthur Power Dudden and Millicent Ruth (Hancock) Dillon; m. Dennis Earl Rowlands, July 5, 1997; children: Christopher J. Andrasick, Gregory O. Andrasick, Christopher, Jeffrey, Satia T-A. Wang, Jocelyn Vo, Jacquie Vo. AB in English, Conn. Coll., New London, 1966; MA in English, U. Hawaii, Honolulu, 1988; PhD in Composition, Indiana U. Pa., 2004. English tchr. Tottenville HS, NY, 1967—68, Weeks Jr. HS, Newton, Mass., 1969—71, St. Andrews Priory Sch., Honolulu, 1978—81; English tchr., chmn. dept. Iolani Sch., Honolulu, 1981—92; instr. Montgomery CC, Conroe, Tex., 1998, Sam Houston State U., Huntsville, Tex., 1999—2000; asst. prof. Calif. State U., Northridge, 2004—. Co-dir Hawaii Writing Project, Honolulu, 1982—96, dir. literature inst., 1992, Honolulu, 1997—2003; dir. Reading Inst. Acadm. Preparation, Northridge, 2004—. Author: (as Kathleen D. Andrasick) Opening Texts: Using Writing to Teach Literature, 1990; contbr. articles to profl. publs. Recipient Excellence in Tchg. English award, English Speaking Union, 1989, award for ednl. contbns. to state of Hawaii, Hawaii State Senate, 1992; named Master Tchr., Iolani Sch., 1990. Mem.: Nat. Coun. Tchrs. English, Phi Kappa Phi. Avocations: reading, cooking, golf, tennis. Office: Calif State Univ Dept Secondary Edn 18111 Nordhoff St Northridge CA 91330-8265 Office Phone: 818-677-2556. Business E-Mail: krowlands@csun.edu.

ROWLETT, RALPH MORGAN, archaeologist, educator; b. Richmond, Ky., Sept. 11, 1934; s. Robert Kenny and Daisy (Mullikin) R.; m. Elsebet Sander-Jorgensen, Aug. 25, 1963 (div. Jan. 1986); children: Rolf R. Arvid, Erik Kenneth; m. Elizabeth Helen Dinan, Apr. 21, 1989 (div. Oct. 1995); 1 child, Helen Holly; m. Magda Mircea, 2005. Student, U. Ky., 1952-53; BA summa cum laude, Marshall U., 1956; postgrad., U. London, 1962-63; PhD, Harvard U., 1968. Instr. anthropology U. Mo., Columbia, 1965-67, asst. prof., 1967-69, assoc. prof., 1969-75, prof., 1975—. Postdoctoral fellow Ghent U., 1969; vis. prof. Bucuresti U., 2005. Co-author: Neolithic Levels on the Titelberg, Luxembourg, 1981, Meeting Anthropology Phase to Phase, 2000; anthropology editor Random House Unabridged Dictionary of English, 1980—; editor: Horizons and Styles, 1993, Horizons and Styles in West Eurasiatic Archaeology; developer thermoluminescence dating of flint, 1972; co-developer electron spin resonance dating of flint, 1981.; designer Statue of Iron Age Warrior Arminius, Hermann, Mo. 1st lt. arty., U.S. Army, 1956-58, capt. civil affairs and mil. govt. Decorated officer Legion de Merit (Luxembourg); named Ky. col., 1976; grantee NSF, 1973-75, 76-79, 82-83, Earthwatch, 1985-88, Svc. Archeologique de Neuchatel, 1989, British Coun., 1993, Acad. of Romania, 1996, Internat. Rsch. and Exch. Bd., 1997. Fellow Am. Anthrop. Assn.; mem. AAAS, Archaeol. Inst. Am., Soc. Am. Archaeology, Societe Prehistorique de Luxembourg, Societe Archeologique Champenoise, English Heritage, Palomino Horse Breeders Assn., Sigma Xi. Green Party. Mem. Christian Ch. (Disciples Of Christ). Home: Hollywell Hill 1197 State Road WW Fulton MO 65251-5106 Office: Univ Mo Dept Anthropology Columbia MO 65211-0001 Office Phone: 573-882-4731.

ROWLETTE, HENRY ALLEN, JR., social worker, counseling psychologist; b. Phila., July 8, 1947; s. Henry Allen Sr. and Ophelia Alberta (Kilson) R.; m. Geraldine Lee Stevens, Mar. 1972 (div. Mar. 1986); children: Cessandra N., Deaeon D., Christiene A.; m. Carolyn Rowlette; 1 child, Janetta M.; m. Ann Laura Rowe, Mar. 19, 1989. BA, Cheyney State Coll., 1970; MEd, Boston U., 1981; MSW, Temple U., 1988; PhD, Suffield Coll. and U., 2003. Cert. sch. social worker, NJ; lic. clin. social worker; diplomate Am. Psychotherapy Assn., Nat. Bd. Cognitive Behavioral Therapists; ordained minister Bapt. Ch. Cardiac monitor technician Bapt. Med. Ctr., Little Rock, 1982-83; mental health technician The Horsham Clinic, Ambler, Pa., 1984; psychiat. technician The Lower Bucks Hosp., Bristol, Pa., 1984-90; mental health technician The Helene Fuld Med. Ctr., Trenton, NJ, 1988-90, psychiat. social worker, 1988-92; profl. sch. social worker The Willingboro Sch. Dist., NJ, 1990—96. Dist. crisis intervention team Willingboro Sch. Dist., 1994-96; therapist The NJ State Prison, Trenton, 1996-98, The Southwoods State Prison, Bridgeton, NJ; clinician Kennedy Meml. Health Ctr., Cherry Hill, NJ, 1998—, The Lumberton Schs./Sch. Social Worker, Lumberton, NJ, 1998; behavioral cons. Founds. Behavioral Health, Willow Grove, Pa., 1999; mental health technician The Children's Hosp. Phila., 1999-2000. Clin. social worker Phila. Prison System, 2000; mem. NAACP, Trenton, 1990. With US Army, 1971-79. Mem. NASW, Am. Assn. Christian Counselors, Omega Psi Phi (Delta Upsilon chpt.), Phi Delta Kappa (Trenton chpt.), Am. Psychotherapy Assn., Nat. Bd. Cognitive Behavioral Therapists, Nat. Bd. Addiction Examiners, Nat. Assn. Forensic Counselors. Democrat. Baptist. Avocations: fishing, reading, computer technology/games. Home: 18 Foxchase Dr Burlington NJ 08016-3044 Office Phone: 609-953-5608. Personal E-mail: drhrowlettejr@comcast.net.

ROWLEY, BEVERLEY DAVIES, sociologist; b. Antioch, Calif., July 28, 1941; d. George M. and Eloise Davies; m. Richard B. Rowley, Apr. 1, 1966 (div. 1983). BS, Colo. State U., 1963; MA, U. Nev., 1975; PhD, Union Inst., 1983. Social worker Nev. Dept. Pub. Welfare, Reno, 1963—65, Santa Clara County Dept. Welfare, San Jose, Calif., 1965—66; field dir. Sierra Sage coun. Camp Fire Girls, Sparks, Nev., 1966—70; program coord. divsn. health scis. Sch. Medicine U. Nev., 1976—78, program coord., health analyst office rural health, 1978—84, acting dir. office rural health, 1982—84; exec. asst. to pres. Med. Coll. of Hampton Rds., Norfolk, Va., 1984—87; rsch. mgr. Office Med. Edn. Info. AMA, Chgo., 1987—88, dir. dept. data systems, 1988-91; dir. med. edn. Maricopa Med. Ctr., Phoenix, 1991—99; pres. Med. Edn. and Rsch. Assocs., Inc., Phoenix, Chgo., 1999—, Med. Edn. & Rsch. Assocs., Tempe, Ariz., 1999—; vis. prof. Ariz. State U. East, Mesa, 1999—2000, profl. and personal coach, 2004—; pres., exec. dir. Maricopa Med. Found., Phoenix, 2004—. Various positions as adj. prof. and lectr. in health scis. U. Nev. Sch. of Medicine, 1972-75; lectr. dept. family and cmty. medicine U. Nev., 1978-84, asst. dir., evaluator Health Careers for Am. Indians Programs, 1978-84; cons. Nev. Statewide Health Survey, 1979-84; interim dir. Health Max, 1985-86; asst. prof. dept. family and cmty. medicine Med. Coll. of Hampton Rds., Norfolk, Va., 1985-87. Editor of five books; contbr. numerous articles to profl. jours. Mem. Am. Sociol. Assn., Nat. Rural Health Assn. (bd. dirs. 1986-88), Assn. Behavioral Sci. and Med. Edn. (pres. 1986), Assn. Am. Med. Colls. (exec. coun. 1993-95), Coun. Acad. Scis. (adminstrv. bd. 1992-97), Assn. Hosp. Med. Edn. (bd. dirs. 1997—), Delta Delta Delta. Achievements include development of three computer systems including AMA-FREIDA; four internet-based educational programs for physicians. Avocations: hiking, skiing, gardening, sewing, ceramics. Office: MERA Inc 1903 E Sarah Ln Tempe AZ 85284-3430 E-mail: BDR@MERAInc.com.

ROWLEY, CYNTHIA, apparel designer; b. Barrington, Ill., 1959; m. Bill Powers; 2 children. Grad., Art Inst. of Chicago. Designer Cynthia Rowley, Inc., 1983—; owner, designer Cynthia Rowley Boutiques, NYC, Chicago, Los Angeles and Japan, Swellco (subsidiary of Cynthia Rowley, Inc.). Work featured in Vogue, Elle, W, Harper's Bazaar, Glamour, New York Times, In Style, Elle Décor, French Vogue. Co-author: Swell: A Girl's Guide to the Good Life, 1999, Home Swell Home, 2002, Swell Holiday, 2003, The Swell Dressed Party, 2005; author: Slim: A Fantasy Memoir, 2007. Recipient Perry Ellis award for Womenswear, Coun. Fashion Designers of Am., 1994. Avocations: surfing, water-skiing, scuba diving. Office: Cynthia Rowley Inc 376 Bleecker St New York NY 10014*

ROWLEY, JANET DAVISON, physician; b. NYC, Apr. 5, 1925; d. Hurford Henry and Ethel Mary (Ballantyne) Davison; m. Donald A. Rowley, Dec. 18, 1948; children: Donald, David, Robert, Roger. PhB, U. Chgo., 1944, BS, 1946, MD, 1948; DSc (hon.), U. Ariz.; 1989, U. Pa., 1989, Knox Coll., 1991, U. So. Calif., 1992, St. Louis U., 1997, St. Xavier U., 1999, Oxford U., Eng., 2000, Lund U., Sweden, 2003, Dartmouth U., 2004; degree (hon.), U. Calif, San Francisco, 2008; DSc, Lake Forest Coll, Harvard, 2008. Diplomate Am. Bd. Med. Genetics. Rsch. asst. U. Chgo., 1949—50; intern Marine Hosp., USPHS, Chgo., 1950—51; attending physician Infant Welfare and Prenatal Clinics Dept. Pub. Health, Montgomery County, Md., 1953—54; rsch. fellow Levinson Found., Cook County Hosp., Chgo., 1955—61; clin. instr. neurology U. Ill., Chgo., 1957—61; USPHS spl. trainee Radiobiology Lab. The Churchill Hosp., Oxford, England, 1961—62; rsch. assoc. dept. medicine and Argonne Cancer Rsch. Hosp. U. Chgo., 1962—69, assoc. prof. dept. medicine, 1969—77, prof. dept. medicine and Franklin McLean Meml. Rsch. Inst., 1977—84, Blum-Riese Disting. Svc. prof., dept. medicine and dept. molecular genetics and cell biology, 1984—, Blum-Riese Disting. Svc. prof. dept. human genetics, 1997—, interim dep. dean for sci. biol. scis. divsn., 2001—02; vis. prof. World Class U. Project, Republic of Korea. Bd. sci. counsellors Nat. Inst. Dental Rsch., NIH, 1972—76, chmn., 1974—76; mem. Nat. Cancer Adv. Bd., Nat. Cancer Inst., 1979—84, Nat. Adv. Coun. for Human Genome Rsch. Inst., 1999—2004; adv. com. Frederick Cancer Rsch. Facility, 1983—84; bd. sci. counsellors Nat. Human Genome Rsch. Inst., NIH, 1994—99, chmn., 1994—97; adv. bd. Howard Hughes Med. Inst., 1989—94, MD Anderson Cancer Ctr., 1998—2005; vis. com. dept. applied biol. scis. MIT Corp., 1983—86; bd. sci. cons. Meml. Sloan-Kettering Cancer Ctr., 1988—90; adv. com. Ency. Britannica U. Chgo., 1988—96; Presdl. Symposium Am. Soc. Pediatric Hematology/Oncology, 1995; chmn. sci. adv. com. Translational Genomics Rsch. Inst., Phoenix., 2004—; med. adv. bd. Calif. Inst. Regenerative Medicine, 2005—; mem. sci. adv. coun. Children's Hosp., Boston, 2005—. Co founder co editor: Genes, Chromosomes and Cancer, mem. editl. bd.: Oncology Rsch., Cancer Genetics and Cytogenetics Leukemia Rsch., Internat. Jour. Hematology, Genomics, Leukemia; past mem. editl. bd. Internat. Jour. Cancer, Blood, Cancer Rsch., Hematol. Oncology, Leukemia Rsch.; contbr. chapters to books, articles to profl. jours. Adv. com. for career awards in biomed. scis. Burroughs Wellcome Fund, 1994—98; selection panel for Clin. Sci. award Doris Duke Charitable Found., 2000—02, 2006; mem. Pres.'s Adv. Coun. on Bioethics, 2001—09; mem. med. rsch. material command leukemia program U.S. Army, 2002—04; mem. selection com. Rosalind Franklin young investigator award, 2004, 2007—, 2009; nat. adv. com. McDonnell Found. Program for Molecular Medicine in Cancer Rsch., 1988—98; adv. bd. Leukemia Soc. Am., 1979—84; selection com. scholar award in biomed. sci. Lucille P. Markey Charitable Trust, 1984—87; trustee Adler Planetarium, Chgo., 1978—; med. adv. bd. G&P Charitable Found., 1999—. Recipient Esther Langer award, Ann Langer Cancer Rsch. Found., 1983, First Kuwait Cancer prize, 1984, A. Cressy Morrison award in natural scis., NY Acad. Scis., 1985, Past State Pres. award, Tex. Fedn. Bus. and Profl. Women's Clubs, 1986, Karnofsky award and lecture, Am. Soc. Clin. Oncology, 1987, Antoine Lacassagne Lique prize, Nat. Francaise Contre le Cancer prize, 1987, Katherine Berkan Judd award, Meml. Sloan-Kettering Cancer Ctr., 1989, Steven C. Beering award, U. Ind. Med. Sch, 1992, Robert de Villiers award, Leukemia Lymphoma Soc., 1993, Return of the Child award, 2005, Kaplan Family prize for cancer rsch. excellence, Oncology Soc. Dayton, 1995, Cotlove award and lecture, Acad. Clin. Lab. Physicians and Scientists, 1995, Nilsson-Ehle lecture, Mendelian Soc. and Royal Physiographic Soc., 1995, Gairdner Found. Internat. award, 1996, medal of honor, Basic Sci. Am. Cancer Soc., 1996, Nat. Medal of Sci., 1998, Lasker-DeBakey Clin. Med. Rsch. award, Lasker Found., 1998, Woman Extraordinaire award, Internat. Women's Assocs., 1999, Golden Plate award, Am. Acad. Achievement, 1999, Women Achieving Excellence award, YWCA of Met. Chgo., 2000, Philip Levine award, Am. Soc. Clin. Pathology, 2001, Emile M Chamot award, State Microscopy Soc. Ill., 2001, Mendel medal, Villanova U., 2003, Benjamin Franklin medal, Am. Philos. Soc., 2003, Dist. Alumni Award, U. Chgo., 2003, Norman McLean Mentorship award, 2006, Medal, Lake Forest Coll., Harvard, 2008, Award for Excellence, Assn. Molecular Pathology, 2007, Disting. Scientist award, Am. Assn. Cancer Inst., 2009, Peter & Patricia Gruhei Prize, 2009, Presdl. Medal of Freedom, The White House, 2009; co-recipient King Faisal Internat. prize in medicine, 1988, Charles Mott prize, GM Cancer Rsch. Found., 1989; named Chicagoan of Yr., Chgo. mag., 1998. Fellow: AAAS (nominating com. 1998); mem.: NAS (chmn. sect. 41 1995—99, mem. com. 2004), Chgo. Network (lectr. 2003—), Inst. Medicine (coun. 1988—90), Cancer Rsch. (G.H.A. Clowes Meml. award 1989, Charlotte Friend award 2003, Dorothy P. Landon award 2005), Am. Soc. Hematology (lectr. Millenium Symposium 1999, Presdl. Symposium 1982, Dameshek prize 1982, Ham-Wasserman award 1995, Henry M. Stratton medal 2003, Marion Spencer Fay Lifetime Achievement award 2006), Genetical Soc., Am. Soc. Human Genetics (pres.-elect 1992, pres. 1993, Allen award and lectr. 1991, Disting. Sci. lectr. 2003), Am. Philos. Soc., Am. Acad. Arts and Scis. (nominating com. 1998), Phi Beta Kappa (hon.), Sigma Xi (William Proctor prize for sci. achievement 1989), Alpha Omega Alpha (hon.). Episcopalian. Home: 5310 S University Ave Chicago IL 60615-5106 Office: U Chgo 5841 S Maryland Ave MC 2115 Chicago IL 60637-1463 Office Phone: 773-702-6117. Business E-Mail: jrowley@medicine.bsd.uchicago.edu.

ROWLEY, MAXINE LEWIS, education educator, retired academic administrator; b. Provo, Utah, Sept. 23, 1938; d. Max Thomas Lewis and Illa Lewis Sanford; m. Arthur William Rowley, Sept. 23, 1960; children: Anne, Jenefer. BA (Ford Found. scholar), Brigham Young U., 1960, PhD in Edn. Adminstrn., 1989; BS, U. Utah, 1974; MA, Utah State U., 1980. Promotion writer Sta. ABC KCPX-TV, 1960; extension home economist USDA, 1961; mgmt. trainee Deseret Book Co., Salt Lake City, 1969; dept. chair Patricia Stevens Career Coll., Salt Lake City, 1970; chair consumer and homemaking dept. Sand Ridge Jr. H.S. Weber Sch. Dist., Roy, Utah, 1975, learning experience designer, 1976-78; consumer and home econs. faculty Utah State U., Logan, 1978-79; spl. appointee to Utah State U. by the Utah State Bd. Edn., 1978-86; intern Gladys Chalkley Brannegan Am. Home Econ. Assn., 1993; chair dept. family life and home econs. Brigham Young U., 1988, 1999—2002, tchr., 2007—. Instrumental writer Utah State U. Found., 1979; mem. faculty Brigham Young U., 1979; women's legis. coun. State of Utah, 1992—; cons. Utah State Office Edn., 2005—. Author: NCFR Public Policy Handbook, 1997; (filmstrips, texts and tchrs. guide) CHECS, 1979; (curriculum guide) Operation: Free Enterprise, 1982, Curriculum of Food Sci., Nutrition, vol. I, 1990, vol. II, 1992, vol. III, 1993; co-author: Legacy, vol. I, 1998. Active ward, stake and region positions Ch. of Jesus Christ of Latter-day Saints; leader 4-H Club, coun. mem., adv. bd.; leader Girl Scouts U.S.A., Young Homemakers; active State Text Book Evaluation Com., 1978-86, U. Utah Evaluation Com., 1979; edn. and rsch. com. Am. Cancer Soc., State of Utah, 1993-94. Named Outstanding Leader Am. Edn., 1976, Nat. Tchr. of Yr., 1977, Outstanding Tchr. in Dept., Brigham Young U., 1984-94, Outstanding Voccat. Edn. Leader, State of Utah, 1996, Nat. Honor Roll in vocat. edn. Nat. Assn. Vocat. Family and Consumer Scis., 1999. Mem.: NAFE, NEA, Internat. Fed. Home Econ. (nat. officer), Am. Edn. Rsch. Assn. (Nat. chair, HERSIG 2001—03), Utah Assn. Family and Consumer Scis. (disting. svc. award 2003), Worldwide Orgn. Women (women's legis. coun. State of Utah 1998—2004, internat. bd. dirs. 1999—2003), Vocat. Home Econs. Tchrs. (nat. chmn. public rels. and legis. coms. 1978), Home Econs. Edn. Assn., Am. Edn. Rsch. Assn. (nat.chair Home Econs. Related Spl. Interest Group 2000—03, marriage, family & human devel. dept. 2002—), County Welfare Com., Utah Edn. Assn. (Womens Awareness Task Force Project award 1976), Utah Nutrition Coun. (chair 1995), Utah Coun. for Improvement Edn., Utah Vocat. Assn., Utah Home Econs. Assn., Am. Vocat. Assn., Am. Assn. Family and Consumer Scis. (nat. v.p., bd. dirs., chair ann. meeting, bd. liaison publs. 1995—97, nat. com. publs. 1999—, nat. treas. internat. fedn. home econ. 2007—), Am. Home Econs. Assn. (contbr., author yearbook 1984, Nat. Leadership award 1993), Nat. Assn. Vocat. Home Econs. Tchrs., Ellen H. Richards Cir., Spurs, White Key (pres. 1960), Alpha Delta Kappa, Gamma Phi Omicron, Phi Kappa Phi, Kappa Omicron Nu (advisor 1980—2005, nat. endowment honoree 1989, Nat. award of excellence 1999, nat. leadership endowment 2001).

ROWLEY, PATTI MITCHELL, psychology educator; d. Gordon Ben and Billie Maudine Mitchell; m. Geoffrey Alan Rowley, Oct. 16, 1970; 1 child, Tracy Lee Rowley Padon. BS in Academic Studies, Sam Houston State U., Huntsville, Tex., 1993, MEd in Counseling, 2003. Cert. tchr. Tex., 1993; in sch. counseling Tex., 2003. Kindergarten tchr. Madisonville CISD, Madisonville, 1993—2004, elem. sch. counselor, 2004—. Mem.: Alpha Delta Kappa (treas., sec., corr. sec.). Conservative. Office: Madisonville CISD 1000 Raney Ln Madisonville TX 77864 Office Fax: 936-349-8028. Personal E-mail: prowley@madisonvillecisd.org.

ROWLING, J.K. (JOANNE KATHLEEN ROWLING), writer; b. Gloucestershire, England, July 31, 1965; d. Peter and Anne Rowling; m. Jorge Arantes, Oct. 16, 1992 (div. Nov. 30, 1993); 1 child, Jessica; m. Neil Murray, Dec. 26, 2001; children: David, Mackenzie. BA in French and Classics, U. Exeter, Eng., 1986; LittD (hon.), Napier U., 2000, Dartmouth Coll., 2000, U. Exeter, 2000, Harvard U., 2008; degree (hon.), U. St. Andrews, 2000, U. Edinburgh, 2004; LLD (hon.), Aberdeen U., 2006. Former rschr. Amnesty Internat.; teacher Scotland, 1990—94. Author: (Harry Potter series) Harry Potter and the Philosopher's Stone (published in US as Harry Potter and the Sorcerer's Stone), 1997 (Smarties Book Prize Gold winner, 1997, British Book awards Children's Book of Yr., 1998, Premio Cento per la Letteratura Infantile, 1998, Anne Spencer Lindbergh Prize for children's lit., 1998, American Booksellers Assoc. ABBY award, 1999, Sorcieres Prix, 1999, Birmingham Cable Children's Book award, Young Telegraph Paperback of Yr., Sheffield Children's Book award), Harry Potter and the Chamber of Secrets, 1998 (Smarties Book Prize Gold winner, 1998), Harry Potter and the Prisoner of Azkaban, 1999, Harry Potter and the Goblet of Fire, 2000, Harry Potter and the Order of the Phoenix, 2003, Harry Potter and the Half-Blood Prince, 2005 (Quill award for Book of Yr., 2005, Brit. Book of Yr., 2006), Harry Potter and the Deathly Hallows, 2007, (supplement to Potter series) Quidditch Through the Ages, 2001, Fantastic Beasts & Where to Find Them, 2001, (children's stories) The Tales of Beedle the Bard, 2008. Numerous philanthropic donations and vol. work for various charities including Comic Relief, Multiple Sclerosis Soc. Great Britain, others; first amb. to pres. One Parent Families/Gingerbread, London, 2000—. Recipient Rave award for Bus., WIRED Mag., 2007, City of Edinburgh award, 2008; named No. 1 on Top 10 authors list, Amazon.com, 1995—2005, Entertainer of Yr., Entertainment Weekly, 2007; named an Officer of the Most Excellent Order of the British Empire (OBE), Prince of Wales, 2001, Hon. Knight Légion d'honneur, France, 2009; named one of Most Powerful Women, Forbes mag., 2005, The 100 Most Powerful Celebrities, Forbes.com, 2008, Brit. Top 50 Movers and Shakers, BBC 3. Office: Christopher Little Literary Agy 10 Eel Brook Studios 125 Moore Park Rd London SW6 4PS England*

ROWLINGSON, JOHN CLYDE, anesthesiologist, physician, educator; b. Syracuse, NY, Aug. 3, 1948; s. John Winthrop and Genevieve Estelle (Mahan) R.; m. Rosemary Colette Laney, Oct. 26, 1974 (div. 1992); children: Kristen, Andrew; m. Karen Wheeler, Aug. 4, 2001; stepchild, Isaac. BS, Allegheny Coll., 1970; MD, SUNY, Buffalo, 1974. Intern Millard Fillmore Hosp., Buffalo, 1974-75; resident in anesthesiology U. Va., Charlottesville, 1975-77; fellow in anesthesia pain mgmt. U. Va. Med. Ctr., 1977-78; asst. prof. anesthesiology U. Va. Sch. Medicine, Charlottesville, 1978-82, assoc. prof., 1982-86, prof., 1986—, Cosmo A. DiFazio prof. anesthesiology, 2005. Assoc. dir. Pain Mgmt. Ctr., U. Va. Health Sci. Ctr., 1978-79, dir., 1980-98, dir. acute pain svc., Acad. Disting. Educators, 1987-2007. Author: Regional Anesthesia, 1984; co-editor: Handbook of Critical Care Pain Management, 1993. Recipient Nils Lofgren award ASTRA, 1999; Nat. Inst. Handicapped Rsch. fellow, 1983-87, Pain fellow 1977-78. Fellow Am. Coll. Anesthesiology; mem. Am. Soc. Anesthesiologists, Am. Soc. Regional Anesthesia (rsch. grantee 1977, pres. 1996-97, recipient Disting. Svc. award 2007, Bonica Lectr., 2007), Am. Pain Soc., Internat. Assn. Study of Pain, Am. Acad. Pain Medicine (editl. bd. Anesthesia Analg 1996—, Reg. Anesthesia and Pain Medicine, 1997—), Va. Soc. Anesthesiology (sec, treas. 2005-07, pres. 2009-). Methodist. Avocations: running, tennis, skiing, biking. Home: 5006 Lake Tree Ln Crozet VA 22932 Office: U Va Hlth Sys Health Sci Ctr Anesthesiology PO Box 800710 Charlottesville VA 22908-0710 Home Phone: 434-823-9626; Office Phone: 434-924-2283. Business E-Mail: jcr3t@virginia.edu.

ROWSELL, JENNIFER, literature and language professor; m. Fred Wanklyn, Aug. 7, 1993; 1 child, Madeleine Wanklyn. PhD in Edn., U. London, 2000. Cert. in tchg. English as a fgn. lang. Rutgers U., Paris, 1993. Lectr. OISE, U. Toronto, Ont., Canada, 2001—05; asst. prof. literacy edn. Rutgers U., NB, NJ, 2005—. Contbr. to numerous academic literacy books. Achievements include research in literacy education to rethink in the 21st century. Home: 37 Jefferson Rd Princeton NJ 08540 Office: Rutgers Grad Sch Edn 10 Seminary Pl New Brunswick NJ 08901

ROWSON, SEBASTIAN, engineering executive; s. Norman William and Josette Eva Rowson. MS in Fundamental Physics, U. Paris Sud Orsay, 1995, MS in Elecs., Sensors, and Integrated Circuits, 1996, PhD in Physics, 2000. Rsch. engr. UCLA, 2000—00; sr. engr. Ethertronics, San Diego, 2000—02, dir. tech. transfer, 2002—04, dir. R & D, 2004—. Contbr. articles to profl. jours. Mem.: IEEE (assoc.). Achievements include patents for antenna technology. Office: Ethertronics Inc 9605 Scranton Rd Ste 300 San Diego CA 92121

ROY, ANURADHA, statistician, educator, researcher; d. Nirmal Chandra and Biva Roy. BSc in Math. with honors, Calcutta U., 1978; M Stat. in Advance Probability and Math. Stats. with honors, Indian Statis. Inst., Calcutta, 1981; PhD in Applied Stats., Oakland U., 2002. Rsch. scholar Indian Statis. Inst., Calcutta, 1982—86; rsch. officer Govt. of India, 1986—98; tchg. assoc. Oakland U., Mich., 1998—2002; assoc. prof. U. Tex., San Antonio, 2002—. Rsch. asst. Wayne State U. Sch. of Medicine, Detroit, 2000. Contbr. articles to profl. jours. Office: U Tex San Antonio Dept Mgmt Sci and Statistics San Antonio TX 78249 Business E-Mail: aroy@utsa.edu.

ROY, ASIM, business educator; b. Kolkata, India, May 5, 1948; arrived in U.S., 1975; s. Samarendra Nath and Chhaya (Mukherjee) R.; m. Suchandra Mukherjee, Feb. 10, 1974; 1 child, Sion Roy. BE, Calcutta U., 1971; MS (scholar), Case Western Res. U., 1977; PhD, U. Tex., 1979. Foreman, supr. Guest, Keen, Williams, Calcutta, 1972—74; mgr. optimization group Execucom Systems Corp., Austin, 1980-82; asst. prof. U. Nebr., Omaha, 1983, Ariz. State U., Tempe, 1983-89, assoc. prof., 1989-99, prof., 1999—. Vis. prof. Stanford U., Calif., 1991; cons. Mid-Am. Steel Corp., 1976-77; pres., CEO Decision Support Software, Inc., 1984-98, Autolearn, Inc., 2003—; founding ptnr. Laser Search, Inc. Author: (software) IFPS/Optimum, Maxima, Autolearn and Laser Search; contbr. articles to profl. jours. on new brain theory. Calcutta U. Merit scholar, 1967, U. Tex. Rsch. scholar, 1978-80; grantee NSF. Mem. IEEE, Inst. Mgmt. Sci. (program chmn. 1990), Ops. Rsch. Soc. Am. (gen. chmn. 1993), Internat. Neural Network Soc. Hindu. Achievements include patents in field. Home: 3340 E Ashurst Dr Phoenix AZ 85048 Office: Ariz State Univ Sch of Business Tempe AZ 85287

ROY, BISWADEV, environmental scientist; s. Mahadev Prasad and Aruna Roy; m. Saswati Datta, Dec. 29, 2000; children: Piyali, Arko. PhD, Jadavpur U., Calcutta, India, 1995; MSEE, U. Ctrl. Fla., 2000. Cert. in mapping scientist ASPRS. Sr. grad. rsch. asst. Sch. Elec. Engrng. and Computer Sci. U. Ctrl. Fla., Orlando, Fla., 1997—99; vis. scientist UMBC, 1999—2000; contractor NASA, Greenblet, Md., 2000—03; phys. scientist Nat. Exposure Rsch. Lab. US EPA, Rsch. Triangle Park, NC, 2003—07, environ. scientist, Sr. air quality modeler Region 6 Dallas, 2007—. Guest lectr. on remote sensing NC State U., Sch. of Marine, Earth and Atmospheric Sci., Raleigh, 2004—06. Recipient Group Achievement award, Nat. Aeronautics and Space Adminstrn., USA, 2002, USEPA Spl. Accomplishmen award, 2007, 2008. Mem.: IEEE Geoscience and Remote Sensing Soc., Am. Inst. of Aeronautics and Astronautics, Nat. Geog. Avocations: travel, music, cooking, aerospace. Office Fax: 919-541-1379. Personal E-mail: devroy2007@yahoo.com. Business E-Mail: roy.dev@epa.gov.

ROY, BRANDON DAWAYNE, professional basketball player; b. Seattle, July 23, 1984; Student in Am. ethnic studies, U. Wash., Seattle, 2002—06. Guard Portland Trail Blazers, Oreg., 2006—. Founder Brandon Roy Found., 2008—. Recipient Sportsmanship award, NBA, 2008; named Player of Yr., Pacific-10 Conf., 2006, 1st Team All-Conf., 2006, 1st Team All-Am., AP, 2006, NBA Rookie of Yr., 2007; named to All-Rookie First Team, NBA, 2007, Western Conf. All-Star Team, 2008, 2009. Office: Portland Trail Blazers Rose Quarter One Center Court Portland OR 97227*

ROY, DAVID TOD, literature educator; b. Nanking, China, Apr. 5, 1933; s. Andrew Tod and Margaret (Crutchfield) R.; m. Barbara Jean Chew, Feb. 4, 1967. AB, Harvard U., 1958, AM, 1960, PhD, 1965. Asst. prof. Princeton U., 1963-67; assoc. prof. U. Chgo., 1967-73, prof., 1973—99, prof. emeritus, 1999—, chmn. com. on Far Eastern Studies, 1968-70, chmn. dept. Far Eastern Langs. and Civilizations, 1972-75. Author: Kuo Mo-jo: The Early Years, 1971; contbr.: How to Read the Chinese Novel, 1990, Minds and Mentalities in Traditional Chinese Literature, 1999; co-editor: Ancient China: Studies in Early Civilization, 1978; translator: The Plum in the Golden Vase or Chin P'ing Mei, vol. 1, 1993, vol. 2, 2001, vol. 3, 2006. Served with U.S. Army, 1954-56. Ford Found. fellow, 1958-60, Jr. fellow Harvard Soc. Fellows, 1960-63, fellow Fulbright-Hays Commn., 1967, Chgo. Humanities Inst. fellow, 1994-95; grantee Am. Coun. Learned Socs., 1976-77, NEH, 1983-86, 95-96. Mem. Am. Oriental Soc., Assn. for Asian Studies. Clubs: Quadrangle (Chgo.). Democrat. Office: U Chgo 1050 E 59th St Chicago IL 60637-1559 Home: 5443 S Cornell Ave Chicago IL 60615-5603

ROY, ELMON HAROLD, minister; b. Russell Springs, Ky., Dec. 17, 1924; s. Leslie C. and Olza (Gosser) R.; m. Retha Adkins; children: Joel, Michael. BA in Theology, So. Missionary Coll., 1953; MA, Belin U., 1958, Spalding U., 1970; PhD in Theology, Pacific We. U., 1966; postgrad., Andrews Theol. Seminary, 1974; LLD, Coll. St. Thomas, 1982. Ordained to ministry, 1959. Assoc. pastor, Bucyrus, Ohio, 1955-56, Akron, Ohio, 1956-57; pastor East Liverpool, Ohio, 1957-60, Coudersport, Pa., 1960-64, Huntsville, Ala., 1964-65, Louisville, 1965-71; chaplain Pleasant Grove Hosp., Louisville, 1971—75; pastor Springfield, Ohio, 1975-85, Wooster, Ohio, 1985-88; chaplain Louisville, 1989—. Cons. religious liberty, 1983-88; chaplain Jefferson County Ct. Author: In Remembrance of Redemption, 1996, Courage for Hospital Days 1973, Earth's Coming Events, 1968, Israel's Early Leaders, 1984, Moments of Meditation, 1975, The Word for These Times, 1988, Morning is Coming, 1989, Something to Live By, 1958, Prescription for Personal Peace, 1995, Decisions Determine Destiny, 1994, Ships, Submarines and Kamikazes, 2000, Poems From a Pastor's Pen, 2003; contbr. numerous articles to mags. Pres. South Oldham Ch. Coun., 1971-72; mem. Ohio conf. bd. edn., 1985-88. With USN, 1943-46. Recipient Outstanding Cmty. Svc. award Pleasant Grove Hosp., 1974, Commrs. Commendation award Wayne County, 1987, Ohio Senate Commendation award, 1988, Gov.'s Outstanding Kentuckian award, 1985; decorated six battle stars, knight Sovereign Order of St. John of Jerusalem, Knights of Malta, Hospitallers, comdr. Star of Peace Fedn. des Combattants En Europe, Tenn. Col., Ky. Adm., Croix De Guerre, Croix du Combattant Volontaire, Cross of Valor, Royal Afghanistan Order of Crown of Amanullah, Order of Polonia Restituta, Orderu Virtuti Militari, Philippine Presdl. citation, Philipine Liberation medal, Order of Lafayette, Naval Order of US; named hon. citizen of Tenn., hon. sheriff Clark County, Ohio, hon. Ky. Sec. of State, Ky. Amb.; named to Order Ky. Cols. Fellow Philos. Soc. Gt. Britain, Huguenot Soc., Royal Soc. Arts; mem. SAR (chaplain Louisville-Thruston chpt. 1974-75), Am. Acad. Religion, Ky. Hist. Soc., Order Founders and Patriots of Am., East Liverpool Ministerial Assn. (sec., treas. 1960), Coudersport Ministerial Assn. (v.p. 1971-72), Soc. Ky. Pioneers, Mil. Order Fgn. Wars. Address: 2417 W Highway 22 Crestwood KY 40014-9481 Home Phone: 502-241-1939; Office Phone: 502-241-1939.

ROY, JAMES PARKERSON, lawyer; Children: John, James Jr., Christopher; m. Virginia R. Roy, 1990. BS, La. State U., 1973, JD, 1976; LLM, Georgetown U., 1977. Bar: La. 1976. Civil trial atty. Domengeaux, Wright, Roy & Edwards, Lafayette, 1976—. Fellow Internat. Acad. Trial Lawyers; mem. ABA, La. Trial Lawyers Assn. (pres. 1990-91), La. Bar Assn. Democrat. Episcopal. Avocations: hunting, boating, reading, travel. Office: Domengeaux Wright Roy & Edwards 556 Jefferson St Ste 500 Lafayette LA 70501-6979 Office Phone: 800-375-6186. Business E-Mail: jimr@wrightroy.com.

ROY, JANICE L., mathematics professor; d. Robert O. and Phyllis J. Surdam; m. James A. Roy, June 21, 1975; children: Jessica A., Julie K. BS, Ctrl. Mich. U., Mt. Pleasant, 1976, MA, 1983. Cert. tchr. Mich. Math. tchr. Saranac Cmty. Schs., Mich., 1977—86; math. instr. Montcalm CC, Sidney, Mich., 1986—. Recipient Faculty Recognition award, Montcalm CC, 1991, 1999. Mem.: Mich. Math. Assn. Two-Yr. Colls. (pres. elect, pres., past pres. 2002—06). Office: Montcalm CC 2800 College Dr Sidney MI 48885 Office Phone: 989-328-1235.

ROY, JULIANA W., music educator; b. Bandung, West Java, Indonesia, July 28, 1969; d. Yusak and Hanna Wiriasantosa; m. Dean P. Roy, June 4, 1994; 1 child, Jaden P. MusM, Southwestern Bapt. Theol. Sem., Ft. Worth, Tex., 1996. Cert. tchr. music Tex., 1999. Elem. sch. music tchr. Lubbock Ind. Sch. Dist., Tex., 1999—2001, 2003—. Ch. accompanist Calvary Bapt. Ch., Lubbock, 1995—. Recipient music scholarship, Calif. Bapt. U., 1992, Academic Music award, 1992. Mem.: Tex. Music Educator Assn. Office: Arnett Elem Sch 701 E Queens St Lubbock TX 79403 Business E-Mail: jroy@lubbockisd.org.

ROY, KEVIN, newscaster; b. Chgo. BA in Broadcast Journalism summa cum laude, U. Mo., Columbia, 1990. Anchor and reporter KCRG-TV, Cedar Rapids, Iowa, 1990—92; weekend anchor and reporter WHAS-TV, Louisville, 1992—93; Wash. corr. Belo Broadcasting Bur., 1993—95; weekend anchor and investigative reporter KGW-TV, Portland, Oreg., 1995—98; reporter WLS-TV, Chgo., 1998—, co-anchor Weekend Morning News, 2002—. TV journalist Son of Suicide, 2001 (Best News Series Emmy, 2001, Silver Dome award Best Series, 2001, nat. media award of Mental Health Assn. of Mentally Ill in Ill., 2001, Gold Bell Media award, Mental Health Assn. of Ill., 2001, Rosalynn Ctr. fellowship for Mental Health Journalism, 2007), AIDS in Africa: The Lost Generation, 2002 (Best Hard News Feature Emmy, 2002), (news segment) Frank Lloyd Wright, 2001 (AP Ill. honors, 2001). Vol. Loving Outreach to Survivors of Suicide Cath. Charities, Chgo.; bd. mem. Mental Health Assn. of Ill. Recipient Best Reporter Individual Excellence on Camera Emmy, NATAS, 2001, Individual Excellence in News Writing Emmy, 2002. Mem.: AFTRA, NATAS. Office: WLS-TV 190 N State St Chicago IL 60601 Home Phone: 773-928-5543; Office Phone: 312-750-7577. E-mail: krroy7@yahoo.com.

ROY, LORIENE, library and information scientist, association executive; Student, Coll. St. Benedict, St. Joseph, Minn., 1972; AS, BT, Oreg. Inst. Tech., Klamath Falls, 1977; MLS, U. Ariz., Tucson, 1980; student, Ariz. Western Coll., Yuma, 1979—81; PhD, U. Ill., Urbana-Champaign, 1987. Med. radiologic technologist extern Presbyn. Intercommunity Hosp., Klamath Falls, Oreg., 1976—77; med. radiologic technologist Yuma Regional Med. Ctr., Ariz., 1977—79; oral history coord. Century House Mus., Yuma, Ariz., 1981—82; reference libr. Yuma City-County Libr., 1981—82; instr. U. Ill. Grad. Sch. Libr. & Info. Sci., Urbana, 1985; rsch. assoc. U. Ill. Libr. Rsch. Ctr., Urbana, 1984—86; instr. U. Tex. at Austin Grad. Sch. Libr. & Info. Sci., 1987, asst. prof., 1987—93, assoc. prof., 1993—99, dir. If I Can Read,I Can Do Anything nat. reading club for native children, 1999—; prof. U. Tex at Austin Sch. Info., 1999—, U. Tex at Austin Ctr. for Women's & Gender Studies, 2002—; rsch. assoc. Four Directions, Pueblo of Laguna Dept. Edn., N.Mex., 1997—2001. Mem. steering com. U. Ariz. Sch. Info. Resources & Libr. Sci., 2001—05; mem. nat. envisioning com. Tribal Libr., Archives, and Museums: Preserving our Lang., Memory, and Lifeways: Nat. Conf., 2001—; adv. bd. for Peep & the Big Wide World & We Shall Remain WBGH-Boston, 2006—, adv. bd., We Shall Remain, 2006—; mem. Libr. Leadership Network, 2006—; invited co-presenter in field; cons. in field. Co-editor (with Dr. Brooke Sheldon): Library & Information Studies Education in the United States, 1998; co-editor: (with Antony Cherian) Getting Libraries the Credit They Deserve: A Festschrift in Honor of Marvin H. Scilken, 2002; manuscript reviewer Am. Indian Culture & Rsch. Jour., 1988, Jour. Edn. for Libr. & Info. Sci., 1998, Can. Jour. Native Studies, 2000, asst. editor Native Am. studies Counterpoise, 1996—98, bd. mem. reviews sect. Libr. Acquisitions: Practice & Theory, 1997—, mem. editl. bd. Librs. & Culture, 1987—97, editl. adv. bd. New Advocate: For Those Involved with Young People & Their Literature, 2000—, Electronic Libr., 2002—; contbr. articles and newsletters, chapters to books. Adv. bd. Sequoya Rsch. Ctr., 2001—, Internat. Children's Digital Libr., 2002—, Heart of the Cmty.: The Libraries We Lover, Berkshire Pub. Group, 2005—06; adv. com. El dia de los ninos, 2004—05, El dia de los libros, 2005—06, WebJunction.org, 2002—, Online Computer Libr. Ctr. (OCLC), 2002—, Bill & Melinda Gates Found., 2002—, Pub. Access Computing Portal, 2002—; mem. Freedom to Read Found., 1998—, trustee, 2006—; vol. Am. Diabetes Assn., 1990; vol. trainer Austin Free Net, 1997—98; mem., cultural awareness com. Fulmore Middle Sch., 2002; vol. Fulmore Middle Sch. Libr., 2003. Recipient Squibb award, Oreg. Inst. Tech., 1975, Tex. Excellence in Teaching award, U. Tex. at Austin Grad. Sch. Libr. & Info. Sci., 1988, 1991, James W. Vick Tex. Excellence award, 1992, Joe & Bettie Branson Ward Excellence award, 2001, Outstanding Alumna award, U. Ariz. Sch. Info. Resources & Libr. Sci., 2002, Texas Exes Teaching award, U. Tex. at Austin, 2005; named a Mover & Shaker, Libr. Jour., 2005; named an Hon. Tex. Citizen, 1990. Mem.: ALA (libr. rsch. roundtable 1987—92, libr. history roundtable 1987—92, continuing libr. edn. network and exchange round table 1987—94, reference and adult svcs. divsn. 1987—96, pub. libr. assn. 1987—, assn. for libr. svc. to children 1989—96, libr. rsch. roundtable 1995—, social responsibilities roundtable 1996—, reference and user svcs. assn. 1996—, nominating com. mem. 1999—, assn. for libr. svc. to children 2000—05, internat. rels. roundtable 2001—, ethnic & multicultural info. exch. roundtable 2001—, edn. assembly chair 2004—06, planning and budget assembly mem. 2004—06, pres. elect 2006—07, co-chair 2006—07, Allied Profl. Assn.:Orgn. Advancement Libr. Employees, pres.-elect 2006—07, pres.-elect 2006—07, ALISE liason 2006—, Am. Indian Libr. Assn. liason 2006—, players 2006—, exec. bd. mem. 2006—09, exec. com. mem. 2006—09, pres. 2007—08, and several other positions, Equality award 2006), Tex. State Libr. and Archives Commn. (TexShare Adv. Bd. mem. 2005—), Tex. State Historical Assn., Nat. Assn. Native Am. Studies, Tex. Oral History Assn., Assn. Coll. & Rsch. Librs., Am. Soc. for Info. Sci., Internat. Indigenous Librarians' Coun., Internat. Fedn. Libr. Assn. (mem. presdl. com. on indigenous matters 2006—), Am. Culture Assn., Reference & User Svcs. Assn., Am. Indian Libr. Assn. (v.p./pres. elect 1996—97, exec. bd. 1996—99, pres. 1997—98, and several other positions), Assn. Libr. & Info. Sci. Edn. (convener, libr. history spl. interest group 1988, govt. rels. com. 1988—90, mentor 2002), Libr. Leadership Network, Oral History Assn., REFORMA: Nat. Assn. to Promote Libr. and Info. Svcs. to Latinos and the Spanish Speaking, Tex. Libr. Assn. (pub. relations com. mem. 2001—, mem. cultural diversity com. 2006—, and several other positions), Wordcraft Cir. Native Writers & Storytellers, Tex. Libr. Legis. Hotline, Faculty Women's Orgn., U. Tex. Austin, Austin Songwriters Group (libr. 1995—96), Aboriginal and Torres Strait Islander Libr. Resource Network, Inc., Austin Book Workers, Beta Phi Mu, Phi Kappa Phi. Office: Sch Info U Tex at Austin 1 University Station D7000 Austin TX 78712-0390 Office Phone: 512-471-0390, 512-471-3959. Office Fax: 512-471-3971. E-mail: loriene@ischool.utexas.edu.

ROY, MATTHEW G., secondary school educator, social studies educator; b. Oct. 14, 1976; BA, U. Pa., Phila., 1998; MA in Tchg., Boston U., 2001; MA in Polit. Sci., Villanova U., 2009. Cert. tchr. secondary social studies, English Pa., 2005. Tchr. Chelsea H.S., Mass., 2001—05, Woodlynde Sch., Strafford, Pa., 2005—06, Sun Valley H.S., Aston, Pa., 2006—07, Conestoga HS, Berwyn, Pa., 2007—. James Madison fellow. Mem.: Nat. Educators Coun.- Nat. Constn. Ctr., Nat. Coun. Social Studies, Phi Delta Kappa, Pi Lambda Theta.

ROY, MICHELLE E., musician, information technology consultant; b. Lewiston, Maine, Dec. 15, 1969; d. Leonard A. and Joyce B. Roy; m. Andrew Jocuns, Aug. 15, 1997 (div. Mar. 8, 2007). BA, Swarthmore Coll., Pa., 1992; MusM, Ind. U., 1994. Data warehouse support analyst MIT, Cambridge, 1996—2000; tech. lead cons. Buchanan & Edwards, Inc., Alexandria, Va., 2000—06; lead network sys. and distributed sys. engr. MITRE Corp., 2006—, group leader, advanced tech. computing ctr., 2008—. Adj. prof. harpsichord Am. U., Wash., DC, 2008—. Musician (harpsichord soloist): J.S. Bach Brandenburg Concerto V, 2005; musician: (deuce, harpsichordist) The Bach Project, 2006; musician: (tresorino, harpsichordist) Il Voce d'Amor, 2006; musician: (harpsichord soloist) (CD) G.F. Handel Alexander's Feast, 2006. Active Planned Parenthood. Recipient Director's award, The MITRE Corp., 2008. Mem.: Chamber Music Am. (assoc.), Early Music Am. (assoc.). Democrat. Avocation: sewing. Personal E-mail: meroyinc@yahoo.com.

ROY, PATRICK, professional sports team executive, coach, retired professional hockey player; b. Quebec City, Que., Can., Oct. 5, 1965; m. Michèle Piuze (div.); children: Jonathan, Frederick, Jana. Goaltender Montreal Canadiens, 1984—95, Colo. Avalanche, 1995—2003; v.p. hockey operations Quebec Remparts, QMJHL, 2003—, owner, gen. mgr., head coach, 2005—. Recipient Conn Smythe Trophy as Playoff MVP, 1986, 1993, 2001, William M. Jennings Trophy, 1987—89, 1992, 2002, Vezina Trophy, 1989, 1990, 1992, Trico Goaltender award, 1989, 1990; named to All-Rookie Team, NHL, 1986, Second All-Star Team, 1988, 1991, First All-Star Team, 1989, 1990, 1992, Sporting News All-Star Team, 1989, 1990, 1992, Colo. Sports Hall of Fame, 2004. Achievements include being a member of Stanley Cup Champion Montreal Canadiens, 1986, 1993, Colorado Avalanche, 1996, 2001; being the first goaltender to record 500 NHL victories, 2001; holding the record for most NHL wins by a goaltender with 551, 2003-2009; setting the record for most NHL playoff wins by a goaltender with 151; having his number, 33, retired by Colorado Avalanche, 2003 & Montreal Canadiens, 2008; being inducted into the Hockey Hall of Fame, 2006. Office: Quebec Remparts Colisée Pepsi 250 boulevard Wilfrid-Hamel Quebec City PQ G1L 5A7 Canada

ROY, RACHEL, fashion designer; b. Seaside, Calif., Jan. 15, 1974; m. Damon Dash, July 15, 2005; children: Ava, Tallulah; 1 stepchild, Damon Dash Jr. BA in Comm., Columbia Union Coll., Takoma Park, Md. Stylist intern Rocawear, NYC, 1998, creative dir., children and women divsn.; founder, designer Rachel Roy collection, 2004—. Recipient Bollywood award for Outstanding Contribution to American Fashion, 2006. Achievements include having collections featured in various top fashion magazines and NY Fashion Week, 2007. Office: c/o HL Group, LLC 853 Broadway, 18th Fl New York NY 10003*

ROY, RALPH LORD, clergyman; b. St. Albans, Vt., Sept. 30, 1928; s. Howard Allen and Olive Lydia (Corliss) R.; m. Margaret Ellen Finlay, Feb. 12, 1960 (dec.); 1 child, Joyce Victoria. BA, Swarthmore Coll., 1950; MA, Columbia U. and Union, Theol. Seminary, 1952. Ordained to ministry United Meth. Ch. as deacon, 1952, as elder, 1961. Asst. minister Met. Community United. Meth. Ch., NYC, 1957-60; minister Grace United Meth. Ch., NYC, 1960-63, Greene Ave./Knickerbocker United Meth. Ch., Bklyn., 1964-68, Cuyler Warren St. Community Ch., Bklyn., 1968-70, United Meth. Ch., Clinton, Conn., 1970-74, Mary Taylor United Meth. Ch., Milford, Conn., 1974-79, First United Meth. Ch., Meriden, Conn., 1979-94, pastor Thomaston, Conn., 1994-99, United Meth. Ch., East Berlin, Conn., 2000—01, First and Summerfield United Meth. Ch., New Haven, 2001—02. Author: Apostles of Discord, 1953, Communism and the Churches, 1960; contbr. articles to profl. jours. Chaplain Meriden (Conn.) Police Dept., 1981-92; radio ministry, 1983-; newspaper columnist, 1999-; pastor South Congregational Ch., Hartford, Conn., 2004-05. Home: 697 S End Rd Unit 37 Plantsville CT 06479-1843 Home Phone: 860-620-1711. Personal E-mail: ralphlroy@aol.com. *When I consider the magnificence and vastness of the universe, I can be overwhelmed by childlike marvel. That's one key aspect of God's creation. Another is the almost infinite variety, complexity, and beauty of life on our planet, all of it interdependent, making it urgent that we dwell together in harmony, mutual respect and peace.*

ROY, RANJA, mathematician, educator; b. Kolkata, West Bengal, India, Aug. 13; d. Deba Prasanna and Dipali Roy; children: Sohini Upadhyay, Kushal Roy Upadhyay. PhD, Binghamton U., 1993—98. Vis. asst. prof. Millersville U., Pa., 1998—99, Union Coll., Schenectady, NY, 1999—2001; asst. prof. NY Inst. Tech., Old Westbury, NY, 2001—. Contbr. scientific papers. Mem.: Am. Math. Soc. (corr.). Home: 6 Lewis Ln Port Washington NY 11050

ROY, ROB J., biomedical engineer, anesthesiologist, educator; b. Bklyn., Jan. 2, 1933; m. Carole Ann Apmann, Aug. 1, 1959 (div.); children: Robert Bruce, David John, Bruce Glenn; m. Judith Anne Webb, Oct. 6, 1996. BSEE, Cooper Union, NYC, 1954; MSEE, Columbia U., 1956; DEngSc, Rensselaer Poly. Inst., 1962; MD, Albany Med. Coll., NY, 1976. Profl. engr., N.Y.; diplomate Am. Bd. Anesthesiology. Prof. elec. engrin. dept. Rensselaer Poly. Inst., Troy, N.Y., 1962, prof. elec. engrng. dept., 1980—, head biomed. engrng. dept., 1985-94; prof. anesthesiology Albany (N.Y.) Med. Ctr., 1979—. Author: State Variables for Engineers, 1965, 2d edit., 1998; author over 200 papers in field. Mem.: IEEE (life), Am. Soc. Anesthesiologists, Sigma Xi. Office: Albany Med Ctr Dept Anesthesiology 47 New Scotland Ave Albany NY 12208-3412 E-mail: royr@rpi.edu, robjroy@att.net.

ROY, ROBERT RUSSELL, toxicologist; b. Mpls., Sept. 14, 1957; s. Rudolph Russell and Arlene Charlotte (Miller) R.; m. Barbara Jane Richie, Oct. 10, 1987; children: Andrew, Katherine. BA cum laude, Augsburg Coll., 1980; MS, U. Minn., 1986, PhD, 1989. Bd. cert. in toxicology. Toxicologist, project mgr. Pace Labs., Inc., Mpls., 1989-90; toxicologist Minn. Dept. Health, Mpls., 1990-93, Minn. Regional Poison Ctr., St. Paul, 1990-97; team leader, toxicology specialist 3M, St. Paul, 1997—, sr. toxicology specialist, 2000—. Lectr. U. Minn., Mpls., 1986-90, Midwest Ctr. Occupl. Health and Safety, St. Paul, 1990—, instr., 1989; adj. assoc. prof. U. Minn., 1993—; grad. faculty toxicology and pub. health U. Minn.; adj. asst. prof. emergency medicine Oreg. Health Sci. U., Portland. Active Mt. Carmel Luth. Ch. Coun., Mpls., 1983-85. Mem. Soc. Toxicology, Am. Indsl. Hygiene Assn., Delta Omega. Home: 6301 Oxbow Bend Chanhassen MN 55317-9110 Office: Corp Toxicology 3 M Ctr Bldg 220-6E-03 Saint Paul MN 55144-1000 Business E-Mail: rroy@mmm.com.

ROY, RUSTUM, citizen scientist; b. Ranchi, India, July 3, 1924; came to U.S., 1945, naturalized, 1961; s. Narendra Kumar and Rajkumari (Mukherjee) R.; m. Della M. Martin, June 8, 1948; children: Neill, Ronnen, Jeremy. BSc with honors, Patna U., India, 1942, MSc, 1944; PhD, Pa. State U., 1948; DSc (hon.), Tokyo Inst. Tech., 1987, Alfred U, 1993. Research asst. Pa. State U., 1948-49, mem. faculty, 1950—, prof. geochemistry, 1957—, prof. solid state, 1968—, chmn. solid state tech. program, 1960-67, chmn. sci. tech. and soc. program, 1977-84, dir., 1984-89, dir. materials research lab., 1962-85, Evan Pugh prof., 1981—, Evan Pugh prof. solid state, geochemistry, sci. tech. & soc. emeritus, 1999; sr. sci. officer Nat. Ceramic Lab., India, 1950; mem. com. mineral sci. tech. Nat. Acad. Scis., 1967-69, com. survey materials sci. tech., 1970-74; exec. com. chem. div. NRC, 1967-70, nat. materials adv. bd., 1970-77, mem. com. radioactive waste mgmt., 1974-80, chmn. panel waste solidification, 1976-80, chmn. com. USSR and Eastern Europe, 1976-81. Mem. com. material sci. and engring. NRC, 1986-89; mem. Pa. Gov.'s Sci. Adv. Com.; chmn. materials adv. panel Gov.'s Sci. Adv. Com., 1965-80; mem. adv. com. on engring. NSF, 1968-72, adv. com. to ethical and human value implications sci. and tech., 1974-76, adv. com. div. materials rsch., 1974-77; Hibbert lectr. tech. and religion U. London, 1979; cons. to industry; mem. adv. com. Coll. Engring., Stanford U., 1984-86; internat. sci. lectr. NRC, 1991-92; rsch. prof. materials Ariz. State U., 1999—; vis. prof. medicine U. Ariz., 1999—. Author: Honest Sex, 1968, Crystal Chemistry of Non-metallic Materials, 1974, Experimenting with Truth, 1981, Radioactive Waste Disposal, Vol. 1, the Waste Package, 1983, Lost at the Frontier, 1985; founding editor-in-chief: Materials Rsch. Bull., 1966—, Jour. Materials Edn., 1980-2000, Bull. Sci. Tech. and Soc, 1981-2000, Materials Rsch. Innovations, 1997—; contbr. over 1000 articles to profl. jours., 25 patents in field. Chmn. bd. Dag Hammarskjold Coll., 1973-75; chmn. ad hoc com. sci., tech. and ch. Nat. Coun. Chs., 1966-68; bd. dirs. Kirkridge Retreat, 1958-80, chmn., 1978-80; founder, chmn. bd. Friends of Health; chmn. bd. Campaign for Better Health. Sci. policy fellow Brookings Instn., 1982-83; recipient Ellis Island medal of hon., 1996; named to Order of the Rising Sun with Gold Rays status in Japanese Emperor's birthday honors list, 2002. Fellow: AAAS (chmn. chemistry sect. 1985), Mineral. Soc. Am. (award 1957), Am. Phys. Soc., Indian Acad. Scis. (hon.), Am. Ceramic Soc. (Sosman lectr. 1975, Orton lectr. 1984, disting. life, Educator of Yr. 1993); mem.: U.S. Nat. Acad. Engring., Materials Rsch. Soc. (pres. 1976, founder & architect 1967—, co-chair 1973), Am. Soc. Engring. Educators (Centennial medal 1993, Hall of Fame 1993), Am. Chem. Soc. (Petroleum Rsch. Fund award 1960, Dupont award for Chem. of Materials 1993), Fine Ceramics Assn. Japan (Internat. award), Ceramic Soc.Japan (hon. Centennial award 1991), Mineral Soc. Am., Fedn. Materials Socs. (Nat. Materials Advancement award 1991), Russian Acad. Scis. (elected fgn.), Engring. Acad. Japan (elected fgn.), Indian Nat. Sci. Acad. (elected fgn.), Royal Swedish Acad. Engring. Scis. (elected fgn.). Home: 500 E Marylyn Ave Apt 124 State College PA 16801-5312 Office: 102 Materials Research Lab University Park PA 16802-4800 Office Phone: 814-865-3421. Business E-Mail: rroy@psu.edu. *My major responsibility to the increasingly unified world culture, as a scientist supported largely by the public, is to integrate into its emerging technology-shaped culture, a radically pluralist yet globally unifying Religion, the insights from Science and the impact of Technology on the human condition. As a Christian Radical Pluralist, I am committed to presenting to my fellow humans, scientists, and non-scientists, from Presidents and CEOs to the person in the street—an accurate picture of the whole truth about all scientific "advances" and their limited and ambivalent nature and their relatively minor position in the sum total of human concerns.*

ROY, SANJOY, health outcomes researcher; PharmB, Javadpur U., India, 1994; MS in Pharma. Sys. and Policy, W.Va. U., 2006, PhD. Mktg. svc. coord. Eli Lilly Asia Pacific, Singapore, 2000; mktg. mgr. Eli Lilly and Co., New Delhi, 2001; sr. mgr. bus. devel. Strategic Intelligence Rsch., Singapore, 2001—03; rsch. asst. W.Va. Medicaid, Charleston, 2005; mgr. global health economics and outcomes rsch. Abbott Labs., Ill., 2007—. Contbr. articles to numerous profl. jours. Recipient Rsch. Podium Presentation award, W.Va. U. Health Sci. Ctr., 2005, Poster Competition prize, 2006, Travel award, Drug Info. Assn., 2006, Immunology Peacock award, Abbott Labs, 2008; Academic Merit scholarship, State Govt., 1988, 1990. Mem.: Internat. Soc. Pharmacoeconomics and Outcomes Rsch. (chair 2005—06, pres. 2004—05, treas. 2003—04, Disting. Svc. award 2004—06), RHO Chi Pharmacy.

ROY, STEPHANIE, academic administrator, educator; b. Beloit, Wis., Oct. 6, 1977; d. Patrick and Irene Messer; m. Gerry Roy, Feb. 19, 2001; 1 child, Matthew. BS in Bus. Adminstrn., Mgmt. Emphasis, Acctg., Carroll Coll., Waukesha, Wis., 2000; MEd in Counseling & Psychology, U. Southern Miss., Hattiesburg, 2001, PhD in Higher Edn. Adminstrn., 2006. Area coord. U. Southern Miss., 2001—04, asst. dir. residence edn. & jud. affairs, 2004—07, assoc. dir. residence life, 2007—, higher edn. adj. instr., Gulfport, 2007—. Home: 40 Deerwood Dr Perkinston MS 39573 Office: Univ Southern Miss 118 College Dr #5064 Hattiesburg MS 39406 Office Fax: 601-266-4891. Business E-Mail: stephanie.roy@usm.edu.

ROY, SUZANNE SCULLY, reading specialist; d. Paul V. and Caroline A. Scully; 1 child, Robert W. MS in Edn., Duquesne U., Pitts., Pa., 1981. Cert. tchr. Pa., 1972. Reading specialist North Allegheny Sch. Dist., Pitts., 1983—. Participant Gov.'s Inst. for English Lang. Arts Educators: Oral History, Valley Forge, Pa., 1999, Gov.'s Inst. for English Lang. Arts Educators, Selingsgrove, Pa., 2005; Fulbright tchr. exch. US Dept. of State, Rapla, Estonia, 2006—07. Sec. North Allegheny Fedn. of Tchrs., Pitts., 1992—96, treas., 1996—2000. With USN, 1973—76. Mem.: Nat. Coun. Tchrs. English, Internat. Reading Assn., Am. Legion. Office: Marshall Mid Sch 5145 Wexford Run Rd Wexford PA 15090 Business E-Mail: sroy@northallegheny.org.

ROY, THOMAS FREDRICK, history professor; b. Guthrie, Okla., Aug. 11, 1953; s. Carroll Lew Roy and Mary Jane Lassiter; m. Celeste Jean, Mar. 11, 1994; children: Jennifer Lippoldt, Henry Kirkwood IV, Christopher Thomas, Lindsay Kirkwood. BA in Am. History and Native Am. Studies, MA in Am. History and Native Am. Studies, U. Okla., Norman, PhD in Am. History and Native Am. Studies, 2007. Grad. tchg. asst. U. Okla., 2001—07, lectr., 2007—. Contbr. articles to profl. jour. Mem.: Am. Hist. Assn., Phi Alpha Theta. Democrat. Roman Catholic.

ROY, TOM MCKIM, social worker; b. Cin., Feb. 21, 1941; s. John David and Clare McKim Roy; m. Susan Pauly, July 8, 1967; children: David Graham, Carter Pauly. BA, DePauw U., Greencastle, Ind., 1963; MA, U. Chgo., 1966. Prof. U. Mont., Missoula, chair, social work program, dir., environ. studies program, 1984—2006, prof., environ. studies program, 1984—2006. Founder various orgns., bd. mem. conservation-environ., social svc. Pres. YMCA; chair State Environ. Quality Coun., Northern Rockies Action Group, Helena, Murie Ctr., Moose, Wyo.; founder Friends to Youth, Missoula; chair Youth Homes, Missoula, Mont. Environ. Info. Ctr., Helena. Recipient Pantzer Humanitarian award, U. Mont., Tom and Ann Boone award, Outstanding Academic Adminstr. award, Alumni Cmty. Svc. award, DePauw U.; named Aldrin Conservationist of Yr., U. Mont., Leonardo & Sandy Sgt. Conservationist of Yr. Avocations: bicycling, hiking, skiing, camping. Home: 541 Evans Missoula MT 59801 Personal E-mail: tomandsue@bresnan.net. Business E-Mail: tom.roy@umontana.edu.

ROY, VALERIA ACOSTA, language educator; b. Montevideo, Uruguay, May 24, 1979; d. Jorge Demetrio Acosta and Graciela Martha Curbelo; m. Kyle Andrew Roy, Dec. 14, 2001; 1 child, Joaquin Samuel. AA in Spanish summa cum laude (hon.), SW TN CC, 2005; BA in Spanish summa cum laude (hon.), U. Memphis, 2007, BA (hon.) in ESL, 2007. Adminstrv. asst. Yarbrough's Music, 2003—06; native asst. U. Memphis, 2006—07, tchg. asst., 2007—08. Youth leader Bapt. Ch. Bellavista, 2003—08. Avocations: travel, music, languages, dance.

ROY, WILLIAM ROBERT, physician, lawyer, former congressman; b. Bloomington, Ill., Feb. 23, 1926; s. Elmer Javan and Edna Blanche (Foley) R.; m. Jane Twining Osterhoudt, Sept. 1947; children: Robin Jo, Randall Jay, Richelle Jane, William Robert, Renee Jan, Rise Javan. BS, Ill. Wesleyan U., 1946; MD, Northwestern U., 1949; JD with honors, Washburn U., 1970. Pvt. practice medicine, 1955-70, 79-89; mem. 92d-93d congresses from 2d Dist. Kans., 1971-75; exec. dir. Kans. Med. Edn. Found., 1976-94; newspaper columnist, 1989—. Former dir. Sentry Ins.; Democratic candidate for U.S. Senate, 1974, 78. Mem. Inst. Medicine of Nat. Acad. Scis. Democrat. Methodist. Home: 6137 SW 38th Ter Topeka KS 66610-1307

ROYAL, DARRELL K., university official, retired football coach; b. Hollis, Okla., July 6, 1924; s. Burley Ray and Katy Elizabeth (Harmon) R.; m. Edith Marie Thomason, July 26, 1944; children: Marian (Mrs. Abraham Kazen III) (dec.), Mack, David (dec.). BS in Bus, U. Okla., 1950. Former head football coach, then dir. athletics U. Tex., now asst. to univ. pres. Author: Darrell Royal Talks Football, 1963. Recipient Horatio Alger award, 1996, Contbns. to Coll. Football award Nat. Coll. Football Award Assn., 2002, Disting. Svc. award U. Tex., 2007; named Coach of Yr., Football Coaches Assn., 1963, 70, Tex. Sports Writers, 1961, 63, 69-70, Southwesterner of Yr., 1961-63, Coach of Decade for 1960's, ABC; named to U. Tex. Longhorn Hall of Fame, 1976, Tex. Sports Hall of Fame, 1976, Jim Thorpe Okla. Hall of Fame, 1977, Nat. Football Hall of Fame, 1983, Southwestern Bell Cotton Bowl Hall of Fame, 1998, Okla. Heritage Soc. Hall of Fame, 2000; Darrell K. Royal Meml. Football Stadium U. Tex. named in his honor, 1996; Named History Making Texan, 2008. Mem.: Delta Upsilon. Presbyterian.

ROYALL, MARY-JULIA C., church organist, historian; b. Donalds, SC, Dec. 30, 1925; d. John McCants Campbell and Cordelia Bearden; m. Jervey DuPré Royall, Sept. 18, 1949; children: Julia C., Anne DuPré. BA, Erskine Coll., 1945; MA, U. S.C., 1948, performers cert. in organ, 1953. Cert. in musical instrument supervision 1945. Attended Salem Coll. Organ Acad., 1979, 1984, 1986, 1987; mem. staff Brevard Music Ctr., 1946; music tchr. Montreat HS and Coll., NC, 1946—47; pvt. piano tchr., 1953—66; dir. glee club Moultrie HS, Mt. Pleasant, SC, 1960—62, Coll. Prep. Sch., Charleston, 1972—74; organist several Charleston Ch., 1950—2007; Erskine alumni bd. visitors., 1964—66. Author: Mt. Pleasant, SC: The Victorian Village, 1997, Mt. Pleasant, SC: The Friendly Town, 2001; musician: (concerts) St. Mary's NC, 1979—2006, Huguenot Ch. Tricentennial, 1980, St. Lukes Chapel, 1994—2009, Spolete Festival, 1977—78. Historian Town of Mt. Pleasant, 1996—; mem. com. Charleston County SC Nat. Heritage Corridor, 1995—98; mem. Mt. Pleasant Presbyn. Ch., 1950—; pres. Confederate Meml. Assn., Mt. Pleasant, 1984—; registered Charleston Tour Guide, 1968—78; pres. Christ Ch. Parish Preservation Soc., Mt. Pleasant, 1994—. Recipient Robert N. Pryor Svc. award, Confederation of Local Hist. Socs., S.C., 1997, Outstanding So. Citizen award, Sons of Confederate Vets., 2003, Parish Nurses Inst. (Musician), 1998—2008; named Tree Farmer of Yr., S.C., 1982—83; named to Order of the Gavel, Town of Mt. Pleasant, 1996. Mem.: Charleston Events Reporter Musical America, Charleston Preservation Soc. (competitions chmn.), Poetry Soc. SC, SC Hist. Soc., SC Forestry Assn., Organ Hist. Soc. (editor newsletter S.C. chpt. 1979—84), Am. Guild Organists (S.C. state chmn., mem. Charleston chpt. 1950—). Home: 349 Bay View Acres Mount Pleasant SC 29464

ROYBAL-ALLARD, LUCILLE, United States Representative from California; b. Boyle Heights, Calif., June 12, 1941; d. Edward Roybal; m. Edward T. Allard; 4 children. BA in Speech, Calif. State U., LA, 1965. Former employee United Way; asst. dir. Alcoholism Coun. East LA; mem. Calif. State Assembly, 1987—92, US Congress from 34th Calif. dist., 1993—; mem. appropriations com., standards of ofcl. conduct com. Mem. Livable Communities Task Force, Homeland Security Task Force, Congl. Children's Working Grp.; chair Congl. Hispanic Caucus, 1999—2000. Recipient Madre y Mujer award, Kimberly-Clark, 2006. Democrat. Roman Catholic. Office: Ho of Reps 2330 Rayburn Bldg Washington DC 20515-0534 also: 225 E Temple St Ste 1860 Los Angeles CA 90012 Office Phone: 202-225-1766, 213-628-9230. Office Fax: 202-226-0350, 213-628-8578.*

ROY-BURMAN, ARUP, pediatrician; s. Pradip and Sumitra Roy-Burman; m. Sheila Dianne Jenkins; children: Sophia Anjali, Sage Milan. BA, U. Calif., Berkeley; MD, U. Calif., San Francisco. Diplomate in pediat. critical care medicine Am. Bd. Pediat. Asst. clin. prof. pediat. U. Calif., San Francisco; pediat. intensivist Children's Hosp. & Rsch. Ctr., Oakland, Calif.; pres. Children's Critical Care Med. Group, Inc., Oakland; chair Northern Calif. Pediat. Intensive Care Network, Oakland. Co-founder and dir. Roatan Vol. Pediat. Clinic, Coxen Hole, Honduras. Chair Global Healing, Berkeley, Calif. Named Best Doctors in America. Fellow: Am. Acad. Pediat.; mem.: Soc. Critical Care Medicine, Phi Beta Kappa. Office: Children's Hosp & Rsch Ctr 747 52nd St Oakland CA 94609 Personal E-mail: arup.roy-burman@ucsf.edu.

ROY-BURMAN, PRADIP, molecular biology and virology educator; b. Comilla, Bengal, India, Nov. 12, 1938; came to U.S., 1963; s. Prafulla Nath and Mrinalini (Barman) Roy-Burman; m. Sumitra Ghosh, Nov. 26, 1963. BSc. with honors, Calcutta U., India, 1956, MSc., 1958, PhD, 1963. Rsch. assoc. dept. biochemistry Sch. of Medicine U. So. Calif., LA, 1963-66, Dernham sr. rsch. fellow in oncology Am. Cancer Soc., 1966-71, asst. prof. dept. biochemistry, 1967-72, assoc. prof. dept. pathology and biochemistry, 1972-78, prof. dept. pathology and biochemistry and molecular biology, 1978—, vice chmn. dept. pathology, 1987—2003. Interim chmn. dept. molecular microbiology and immunology, U. So. Calif., L.A., 1995-97, vis. prof. Med. U. Innsbruck, Austria, 2008; mem. pathology B study sect., NIH, 1990-94, 99-2003, reviewers res., 1994-98, 2005—, ad hoc mem. sci. tech. rev. bd. biomed. behavioral rsch. facilities NCRR, NIH, 1997—, prostate cancer rsch. program review panel, Dept. of Def., 2001—; chmn. NIH, ad hoc mem. TPM study seciton, 2006—, NCI Spl. Emphasis Rev. Panels, 1998—, European Comm. Program, 2006-05; symposium chmn. Internat. Congress Biochem. Molecular Biology, 1994; symposium co-chmn. Internat. Cancer Congess, 1994, chmn. workshop on pathogenesis of animal retrovirus, session immune interaction, 1996, 5th Internat. Symposium Hormonal Carcinegenesis, 2006; session chair Internat. Soc. Cell, Gene Therapy, 2007; spkr. in field. Author (with others) books; contbr. articles to profl. jours.; book reviewer; inventor novel transcription regulatory elements for gene transfer vectors, mouse models for human prostate cancer, others; mem. editl. bd. Hematological Oncology, 1987—97, Cancer Biology and Therapy, 2001—, Jour. Cell Comm. Sign, 2007-, Hormonal Oncogenesis, 2007-. Rsch. grantee Am. Cancer Soc., NIH, Am. Diabetes Assn., Wright Found., Martell Found. Mem. Am. Soc. Microbiology, Am. Soc. Biol. Chemists and Molecular Biology, Am. Assn. Cancer Rsch., Am. Soc. Investigative Pathology, Internat. Assn. Comparative Rsch. on Leukemia and Related Diseases. Democrat. Hindu. Avocations: writing, hiking, golf. Office: Keck Sch Of Medicine HMR 210B 2011 Zonal Ave Los Angeles CA 90033 Office Phone: 323-442-1184. Business E-Mail: royburma@usc.edu.

ROYCE, BARRIE SAUNDERS HART, physicist, researcher; b. Eng., Jan. 10, 1933; came to U.S., 1957, naturalized, 1978; s. Vincent Pateman Hart and Kathlene (Saunders) R.; m. Dominique J.M. Vallee, May 7, 1964; children: Vincent Rene Hart, Marc Edward Hart. BSc in Physics, King's Coll., U. London, 1954, PhD, 1957. Rsch. assoc. Carnegie Inst. Tech., 1957-60, Princeton U., 1960-61, mem. faculty, 1961—2003, prof. applied physics and materials scis., 1978—2003, prof. emeritus, 2003—, acting dean grad. affairs Sch. Engring. and Applied Sci., 2003—04; master of Dean Mathey Coll., 1986-94. Mem. editl. adv. bd. Jour. Photoacoustics, to 1984. Mem. Princeton Borough Zoning Bd. Adjustment, 1980-93, chair, 1993—. Grantee NSF, Air Force Office Sci. and Rsch., Army Rsch. Office. Mem. Am. Phys. Soc., Sigma Xi. Office: Princeton U J224 Engring Quadrangle Princeton NJ 08544-0001 Business E-Mail: bshroyce@princeton.edu.

ROYCE, ED (EDWARD RANDALL ROYCE), United States Representative from California; b. LA, Oct. 12, 1951; m. Marie Therese Porter. BA in Bus. Adminstrn., Calif. State U., Fullerton, 1977. Tax mgr. Southwestern Portland Cement Co.; mem. Calif. State Senate from Dist. 32, 1983—92, US Congress from 40th Calif. Dist. (formerly 39th), 1993—, asst. whip, 1993—, mem. fin. svcs. com., internat. rels. com., fgn. affairs com. Legis. author, campaign co-chmn. Proposition 15 Crime Victims/Speedy Trial Initiative; mem. Stop Corporate Welfare Coalition; co-chair Porkbusters Coalition. Bd. dirs. Calif. Interscholastic Athletic Found. Recipient Medal of Commendation, Veterans of Fgn. Wars, 1985, Taxpayers Friend award, Nat. Taxpayers Union, 1994, Taxpayers Hero award, Citizens Against Govt. Waste, 1994, Visionaries for Africa award, Africa Soc. (Nat. Summit on Africa), 2004; named Legislator of Yr., Orange County Republican Com., 1986, Child Adv. of Yr., Calif. Assn. Svc. for Children, 1987. Mem.: Anaheim C. of C., Fullerton C. of C., Literacy Volunteers of America. Republican. Roman Catholic. Achievements include writing nation's 1st felony stalking law; writing bill for Foster Family Home Insurance Fund, creating foster parent recruitment and training programs. Office: US Congress 2202 Rayburn Ho Office Bldg Washington DC 20515 also: 305 N Harbor Blvd Ste 300 Fullerton CA 92832 Office Phone: 202-225-4111, 714-992-8081. Office Fax: 714-992-1668.*

ROYCE, PAUL CHADWICK, healthcare administrator; b. Mpls., July 2, 1928; BA, U. Minn., 1948, MD, 1952; PhD, We. Res. U., 1959. Diplomate Am. Bd. Internal Medicine. Intern U. Chgo. Clinics, 1952-53; fellow We. Res. U., Cleve., 1953—54, 1956—59; resident internal medicine Bronx Mcpl. Hosp., NYC, 1959-61; asst. prof. of medicine Albert Einstein Coll. of Med., NYC, 1961-69; sr. staff endocrinologist Guthrie Clinic, Sayre, Pa., 1970-81; assoc. prof. of medicine Hahnemann Med. Sch., Phila., 1973-81; emeritus prof. medicine Med. Coll. Pa./Hahnemann U., 1996—; dean and prof. clin. sci. and physiology Sch. Medicine U. Minn., Duluth, 1981-87; sr. v.p., clin. dir. Monmouth Med. Ctr., Long Branch, NJ, 1987-94; med. dir. The Segal Co. N.Y., 1995-98; prin. Royce Assocs., 1995—; tutor Writing Ctr., Monmouth U., NJ, 2001—05. Producer, host TV prgram Doctors on Call, 1983-87 (Nat. Friends of Pub. Broadcasting Hill award 1987). Lt. Med. USNR, 1954-56. Fellow, NSF, 1953—54, 1956—58, Upjohn Found., 1958—59. Mem. Am. Physiol. Soc., Fedn. Am. Scientists, Physicians for Social Responsibility, Sigma Xi, Alpha Omega Alpha. Avocations: skiing, bicycling, canoeing. Personal E-mail: paul.royce1@verizon.net.

ROYCE, RAYMOND WATSON, lawyer, rancher, citrus grower, investor; b. West Palm Beach, Fla., Mar. 5, 1936; s. Wilbur E. and Veda (Watson) R.; m. Catherine L. Setzer, Apr. 21, 1979; children: Raymond, Steven, Nancy, Kathryn, Ryan. BCE, U. Fla., 1958, JD, 1961. Bar: Fla. 1961, U.S. Dist. Ct. (so. dist.) Fla. 1961, U.S. Ct. Appeals (5th cir.) 1961, U.S. Ct. Appeals (11th cir.) 1981. With Scott, Royce, Harris & Bryan P.A., Palm Beach, Fla., 1962-99; pres. Scott, Royce, Harris, Bryan, Barra and Jorgensen, P.A., Palm Beach Gardens, Fla., 1982-99; ptnr. Holland & Knight LLP, West Palm Beach, 1999—2009, Shutts & Bowen LLP, West Palm Beach, 2009—. Bd. suprs. No. Palm Beach Improvement Dist., 1995-99, pres. Palm beach Couty Bar Assn., 1973-74 Mem. Fla. Bar (bd. govs. 1974-78), Fla. Blue Key, Phi Delta Phi. Democrat. Presbyterian. Home: 5550 Whirlaway Rd Palm Beach Gardens FL 33418-7735 Office: Shutts & Bowen LLP 525 Okeechobee Blvd Ste 1100 West Palm Beach FL 33401-4027 Home Phone: 561-626-8246; Office Phone: 561-650-8536.

ROY CHOUDHURY, KAUSHIK, materials scientist; s. Dinesh and Sipra Roy Choudhury; m. Senjuti Gupta; 1 child, Srijan. PhD, SUNY, Buffalo, 2006. Rsch. asst. SUNY, Buffalo, 2001—06; rsch. scientist U. Fla., Materials Sci. and Engring., Gainesville, Fla., 2006—. Recipient Visionary Innovator award, SUNY, 2006; Mark Diamond Rsch. grant, U. Buffalo, 2004. Mem.: Internat. Soc. Optical Engrs., Materials Rsch. Soc., Am. Phys. Soc., Global Ambassadors U. Buffalo, Sigma Xi. Achievements include patents pending for nanocomposite devices; invention of organic & inorganic hybrid nanocomposites for high density energy storage; high density coupling of quantum dots to carbon nanotube surface for efficient photodetection; research in low temperature shape control of semiconductor nanocrystals using noble metallic nanoparticles; efficient photodetection and photorefractivity in an organic/inorganic hybrid polymeric nanocomposite at communication wavelengths. Avocations: travel, acting, photography, painting, movies. Home: 1825 SW 42 Way # F Gainesville FL 32607 Office: Univ Fla Materials Sci & Eng 237 Rhines Hall Gainesville FL Personal E-mail: kaushik.rc@gmail.com.

ROY CHOWDHURY, AYAN, engineer; s. Probir and Sabita Roy Choudhury; life ptnr. Eric Wolvovsky. BS in Electronics & Telecom., Jadavpur U., Kolkata, West Bengal, India, 1998; MS, U. Md., Coll. Pk., PhD, 2008. Sr. engr., software Wipro Technologies, Bangalore, Karnataka, India, 1998—2000; grad. rsch. asst. Inst. Sys. Rsch., Coll. Pk., Md., 2000—08; prin. engr. Cerona Networks Corp., Frederick, Md., 2008—09; rsch. assoc. Inst. Sys. Rsch., U. Md., 2009—. Contbr. scientific papers to profl. publs. Class rep., electronics & telecom.

engring. Jadavpur U., 1994—98, co-chairperson, organizing com. coll. engring., 1998; sec. U. Md. Students Coun. India, Coll. Pk., 2001—02; v.p. U. Md. Computer Engring. Grad. Student Assn., 2001—03; senator U. Md. Senate, 2004—05; mem., senate human rels. com. U. Md. Coll. Pk., 2004—05, mem., senate com., 2004—05, mem., senate nominations com., 2004—05; pres. U. Md. Grad. Lambda Coalition, 2005—06. Recipient Achievement award, Wipro Technologies, 1999. Mem.: AIAA, AAAS, IEEE, Assn. Computing Machinery, Sigma Xi, Golden Key Internat. Honor Soc. Achievements include invention of multicast communications in hybrid satellite, wireless networks. Avocations: travel, photography. Business E-Mail: ayan@umd.edu.

ROYCROFT, HOWARD FRANCIS, lawyer; b. Balt., Sept. 9, 1930; s. Howard F. and Bessie (Weaver) R.; m. Barbara Lee Seal, Mar. 20, 1954; children: Suzanne Carol Roycroft Soderberg, Nancy Lee Roycroft Branigan. BA, U. Md., 1953; LLB, Georgetown U., 1958. Bar: D.C. 1958. Mem. firm Hogan & Hartson, Washington, 1958, ptnr., 1965-87, exec. com., 1970-73, counsel, 1987—. Dir. United TV, Inc., 1982—2001, U TV San Francisco, Inc., 1983—2001; mng. ptnr., dir. WIJY, Inc., Hilton Head, SC, 1989—97; lectr. Howard U. Sch. Law, 1973—74; guest lectr. U. Tex., 1980; mem. Met. Washington Bd. Trade. Bd. dirs. YMCA Met. Washington, 1974-76. 1st lt. USMC, 1953-55. Mem. ABA, Va. Bar Assn., Fed. Comm. Bar Assn., Bar Assn. D.C., Nat. Broadcasters Club, Barristers, Aircraft Owners and Pilots Assn., Nat. Acad. TV Arts & Scis., Broadcast Pioneers, Alexandria Rotary Club, Bryce Mountain Ski and Country Club (dir., pres. 1974-87), Mt. Vernon Country Club, Old Dominion Boat Club, Washington Tennis Patrons Club, Army-Navy Club, Chaine des Rotisseurs Gastronome Club, Oysterville Yacht Club, Skull Creek Yacht Club, Kappa Alpha, Beta Kappa, Delta Theta Phi. Republican. Office: Hogan & Hartson 555 13th St NW Ste 800E Washington DC 20004-1161 Personal E-mail: roycroft@sheatel.net.

ROYE, DAVID P., JR., pediatric orthopaedic surgeon; b. Muskogee, Okla., Dec. 10, 1946; m. Carol Roye; 6 children. BA, U. Okla., Norman, 1971; MD, Columbia U. Coll. Physicians & Surgeons, 1975. Diplomate Am. Bd. Orthop. Surgery, AMA, Nat. Bd. Medicine, lic. NY, NJ, Conn., Ont., Can. Intern gen. surgery Roosevelt Hosp., NYC, 1975—76; resident orthop. surgery Columbia-Presbyn. Med. Ctr./NY Orthop. Hosp., 1976—78, jr. fellow orthop. surgery, 1978—79; fellowship pediat. orthop. surgery Hosp. for Sick Children, U. Toronto, 1979—80; St. Giles prof. pediat. orthop. surgery Columbia U. Coll. Physicians & Surgeons, 1980—; attending orthop. surgeon, dir. pediat. orthops. Children's Hosp. NY/Columbia-Prespyn. Med. Ctr., 1980—. Cons. med. staff, dept. orthop. surgery Helen Hayes Hosp., Greenwich Hosp., White Plains Hosp.; mem. alumni assn., awards com., devel. com. Columbia U. Coll. Physicians & Surgeons. Contbr. articles to profl. jours. Vol. cons. Healing the Children, Butler, NJ, Ea. Christian Children's Retreat, Wyckoff, NJ; vol. Children of China Pediat. Found., NY; vol. ops. com. Operation Smile, Norfolk, Va. Named one of America's Top Dr.'s, Castle Connolly Med. Ltd.; named to NY Mag.'s Best Dr.'s NY. Fellow: Orthop. Rsch. Soc., Scoliosis Rsch. Soc., Am. Acad. Cerebral Palsy and Devel. Medicine, Am. Acad. Pediat., NY Acad. Medicine, Am. Acad. Orthop. Surgeons (sec.); mem.: Am. Acad. Orthop. Surgeons Humanitarian of Leak, Pediat. Orthop. Soc. N. Am. (fin. com., Robert N. Hensiger Clin. Sci. award 2006), Am. Orthop. Soc., Am. Orthop. Assn., European Pediat. Orthop. Soc., Academic Orthop. Assn., Am. Bd. Orthop. Surgery (bd. examiners), Spine Club NYC, N. Am. Spine Soc., Pediat. Orthop. Club NY. Office: Childrens Hosp Columbia Presbyn Med Ctr 3959 Broadway Ste BHN 800 New York NY 10032 Office Phone: 212-305-5475. Office Fax: 212-305-8271.

ROYER, KATHLEEN ROSE, pilot; b. Pitts., Nov. 4, 1949; d. Victor Cedric and Lisetta Emma (Smith) Salway; m. Michael Lee Royer, June 6, 1971 (div. Aug. 1975). Student, Newbold Coll., 1968-69; BS, Columbia Union Coll., 1971; MEd, Shippensburg U., 1974; student, Lehigh U., 1974-75. Cert. tchr. Pa. Music. Music tchr. Harrisburg Sch. Dist., Pa., 1971-77; flight instr. Penn-Air, Inc., Altoona, Pa., 1977; capt., asst. chief pilot Air Atlantic Airlines, Centre Hall, Pa., 1977-80; capt., chief pilot Lycoming Air Svc., Williamsport, Pa., 1980-81; govs. pilot Commonwealth of Pa., Harrisburg, 1981-87; flight engr. Pan-Am, NYC, 1987-91; pilot, 1st officer B737 United Airlines, Chgo., 1992-96, 1st officer B767 NYC, until 1996, Washington, 1996-99; flight officer B747-400 JFK Internat. Airport, Jamaica, NY, 1999—2001, capt. Airbus 320, 2001—, airbus line check airman, 2005—. Frist woman pilot/engr. crew mem. on 747 Pan Am. Airlines, 1989—91, chief pilot, cons. Mem.: UAL-Airline Pilot Assn. (coord. critical incident stress program 1994—96), Flight Engrs. Internat. Assn. (scheduling rep. 1989, scheduling dir. 1990, 1st vice chmn., mem. bd. adjustments 1989, v.p. dir. scheduling 1991—92), Internat. Soc. Women Airline Pilots, Whirley Girls (Washington), 99's (local chair Ctrl. Pa. chpt. 1987—92). Republican. Avocations: owner/flying 1965 Cessna 180, golf, music, reading. Home: 34 Lazy Eight Dr Daytona Beach FL 32128 Office: San Francisco Intl Airport San Francisco CA Personal E-mail: royer17@bellsouth.net.

ROYER, THOMAS CLARK, physical oceanographer, educator; b. Battle Creek, Mich., Jan. 2, 1941; s. Clark Willard and Phyllis Adele (Hoisington) R.; m. Susan Elizabeth Burns, Aug. 31, 1968; children: Samantha Brewster, Heather North. A.B., Albion Coll., 1963; M.S., Tex. A&M U., 1966, Ph.D., 1969. Research asst. Woods Hole Oceanography Inst., Woods Hole, Mass., 1967; Tex. A&M U., College Station, 1966-69, vis. assoc. prof., 1977-81; asst. prof. U. Alaska, Fairbanks, 1969-74, assoc. prof., 1974-81, prof. oceanography, 1981—; cons. Gianotti & Assocs., Berkeley, Calif., 1982—; cons. NSF, 1984-86, mem. adv. com. ocean sci., 1986—. Assoc. editor Jour. Geophysical Research, 1983—. Contbr. articles to profl. jours. Grantee NSF, Office Naval Research, NOAA, NASA, Am. Meteorol. Soc., Am. Geophys. Union, Sigma Xi. Episcopalian. Home: 6212 Ocean Front Ave # 2 Virginia Beach VA 23451-2142 Office: U Alaska Inst Marine Sci Fairbanks AK 99775-1080

ROYHAB, RONALD, journalist, editor; b. Lorain, Ohio, Oct. 6, 1942; s. Halim Farah and Elizabeth Della (Naiser) R.; m. Roberta Lee Libb, Apr. 20, 1969; children: David Libb, Aaron Nicholas. Reporter Lorain Jour., 1966—69; reporter spl. assignment Scripps Howard Cin. Post, 1971—72; investigative reporter Scripps Howard Cleve. Press, 1972—75; chief bur. Scripps Howard Ohio Bur., Columbus, 1975—78; asst. mng. editor Scripps Howard News Svc., Washington, 1978—81; mng. editor Scripps Howard El Paso Herald Post, 1981—83; asst. mng. editor Scripps Howard Pitts. Press, 1983—92; assoc. editor Pitts. Post Gazette, 1992—93; mng. editor Toledo Blade, 1993—97, exec. editor, 1997—; v.p. Toledo Blade Co., 2004—. Bd. dirs. Toledo Blade Co. With USAR, 1964-70. Decorated Knight Order St. Ignatius of Antioch; recipient 7 awards for Excellence Cleve. Newspaper Guild, 1972-75, Spl. Sect. awards Pa. Newspaper Pubs. Assn., 1985, 86, 88, Benjamin C. Bradlee Editor of the Yr. award Nat. Press Found. 2005; named to DeMolay Legion of Honor, 1997; Am. Polit. Sci. Assn. fellow, 1970-71. Mem. Am. Soc. Newspaper Editors, AP Soc. Ohio (pres. 2000-01), Ohio Newspaper Assn., Toledo Press Club (pres. 2002-03). Eastern Orthodox. Home: 27262 Fort Meigs Rd Perrysburg OH 43551-1230 Office: Toledo Blade 541 N Superior St Toledo OH 43660-0002 Home Phone: 419-874-3142; Office Phone: 419-724-6161. Personal E-mail: royhab@theblade.com.

ROYO, SEBASTIAN, dean, finance educator; b. Madrid; s. Jose A. Royo and Maria Del Valle Medina; m. Cristina Del Sol, July 8, 2002; children: Andrea Cameron, Monica Dakota, Abigail Elisabeth. Degree in Law, U. Autonoma Madrid, 1989; MA in Internat. Rels., Boston U., 1993, MBA, 1993, PhD, 1997. Mktg. supporter Control Data, Madrid, 1989—91; dir. MBA IT svcs. Harvard Bus. Sch., Boston, 1996—97; assoc. prof. govt. Suffolk U., Boston, 1997—, dir., Madrid campus, 2003—, assoc. dean, 2006—; sr. program officer LASPAU Harvard U., 2001—03. 2nd lt. Spanish Army, 1988—89. Mem.: APSA. Office: Suffolk Univ 41 Temple St Boston MA 02114 Business E-Mail: sroyo@suffolk.edu.

ROYSTON, PAMELA JEAN, special education educator; b. Anchorage, Alaska, Sept. 26, 1958; d. Ralph Vedra Allen (Deceased) and Wilma Jean Daniels, Franklin Hicks Daniels (Stepfather); m. Randy Glenn Royston, June 23, 1977; children: Rusty Brandon, Bridgett Starr Vaughn. AA, Emmanuel Coll., Franklin Springs, Ga., 1991; BS in Edn., U. Ga., Athens, 1994. Severe/profound spl. edn. tchr. Madison County Mid. Sch., Danielsville, Ga., 1994—96; moderate/severe spl. edn. tchr. Hart County Mid. Sch., Hartwell, Ga., 1996—; program dir. Opportunity House Inc. Sch. beautification dir. Madison County Mid. Sch., Danielsville, 1994—96; peer tutor dir. Hart County Mid. Sch., Hartwell, Ga., 1996—, sch. beautification dir., 1996—, cmty.-based instrn. dir., 1996—; presenter in field. Contbr. articles to profl. jours., papers to profl. confs. and meetings. Assist in fundraising activities Congressman Charles Taylor, Asheville, NC, 2002—03. Recipient honor spl. edn. tchr. for state of Ga., Atlanta Jour.-Constitution, 2000. Mem.: Ga. Assn. Educators, Coun. for Exceptional Children, Assn. for Persons with Severe Handicaps (paper presenter ann. meeting), PA Ga. Educators, Golden Key, Kappa Delta Pi. Meth. Achievements include research in effectiveness of using constant time delay when teaching leisure skills to students who are intellectually disabled. Avocations: houseboating, painting, travel. Home: 196 Dove Hill Rd Royston GA 30662 Office: Opportunity House Inc PO Box 701 Carnesville GA 30521 Personal E-mail: proyston@bellsouth.net. Business E-Mail: proyston@hart.k12.ga.us.

ROZANSKI, MITCHELL THOMAS, bishop; b. Balt., Aug. 6, 1956; Grad., Cath. U. Am. Ordained priest Archdiocese of Balt., 1984; with St. Michael, Overlea, Md., 1984, Cathedral of Mary Our Queen, 1985; assoc. pastor St. Anthony, Balt., 1985, St. Isaac Jogues, Balt., 1990; adminstr. Holy Cross Parish, Balt., 1993, St. Mary Star of the Sea Parish, Balt., 1993, pastor, 1993; temp. adminstr. Immaculate Conception parish, Towson, Md., 2000, St. John the Evangelist, Severna Park, Md., 2000, pastor, 2000—; ordained bishop, 2004; aux. bishop Archdiocese of Balt., 2004—. Roman Catholic. Office: Archdiocese of Baltimore Catholic Ctr 320 Cathedral St Baltimore MD 21201

ROZANSKI, MORDECHAI, academic administrator; b. Lodz, Poland, July 4, 1946; arrived in US, 1968; s. Louis and Bertha Rozanski; m. Bonnie Gail Asher, May 30, 1970; 1 child, Daniel K. BA, McGill U., 1968; postgrad., Columbia U., 1970, New Asia Coll., 1971—72; PhD, U. Pa., 1974. Instr. history U. Pa., Phila., 1969—71; assoc. prof. Asian history Berry Coll., Rome, Ga., 1974—76; asst. prof. Asian history, dir. Office of Internat. Edn. and fgn. area studies program Pacific Luth. U., Tacoma, 1976—82; assoc. dean for internat. studies Adelphi U., Garden City, NY, 1982—84, assoc. provost, 1984—86; dean Coll. Liberal Arts Fairleigh Dickinson U., Teaneck, NJ, 1986—89, v.p. for acad. affairs, 1989—91; provost Wagner Coll., Staten Island, 1991—93; pres. U. Guelph, Ont., 1993—2003, Rider U., Lawrenceville, 2003—. Dir. programs Nat. Coun. on Fgn. Langs and Intermat. Studies, 1983—86. Author: Manual of World History, 1975, Guide to US State Papers on China, 1979; editor-in-chief: Am.-East Asian Rels. Newsletter, 1980—83; contbr. articles to profl. pubs. Trustee World Affairs Coun., Seattle, 1978—81; vice chmn. Nat. Com. on Internat. Studies and Program Adminstrs., 1979—80; chmn. Pacific N.W. Internat./Intercultural Edn. Consortium, 1979—82. Fellow, Que. Province, 1967, U. Pa., 1968—71, Am. Hist. Assn. Am.-East Asian Rels., Columbia U., 1970, Lilly Found., Stanford U., 1978; scholar, Wilson Meml., 1968; Doctoral fellow, Can. Coun., 1971—73, Rsch. grantee, Office of Edn., 1977. Office: Rider Univ 2083 Lawrence Rd Lawrenceville NJ 08648-3099

ROZANTINE, GAYLE STUBBS, psychologist; b. Atlanta, Dec. 1, 1944; d. William L. and Louise (Cash) Stubbs; children: Kathryn Patricia, Webb Black III, Gregory William, Benjamin Stubbs, John Paul; m. Barry Rozantine. BA in Psychology, Agnes Scott Coll., 1965; MA in Tchg., Emory U., 1966; MA in Clin. Psychology, Western Carolina U., 1990; PhD, U. Tenn., 1995. Lic. psychologist, Ga.; diplomate Am. Acad. Experts in Traumatic Stress; bd. cert. stress mgmt. Tchr. Fulton Co. Bd. Edn., Ga., 1967-68; psychology resident Med. Coll. of Ga., Augusta, 1994-95, clin. fellow, 1995-96; rsch. psychologist Pain Evaluation and Intervention Program Dept. of VA Med. Ctr., Augusta, 1995-98; staff psychologist Compass Health Systems, Miami Beach, Fla., 1998, Charter Savannah Bevioral Health System, Ga., 1999-2000; CEO Ctr. Health and Well-Being, 2000—. Mem. critical incident stress debriefing team Med. Coll. Ga.; disaster mental health response team ARC; presenter in field. Mem. APA, Coastal Area Psychologists, Ga. Psychol. Assn., Ga. Breast Cancer Coalition and Fund, Nat. Assn. Forensic Counselors, Nat. Register Health Svc. Providers in Psychology. Office: The Ctr for Health and Well-Being PC 400 Commercial Ct Savannah GA 31406 Office Phone: 912-352-9500 ext. 105. Personal E-mail: gaylerozantine@yahoo.com. Business E-Mail: gaylerozantine@quietawakening.com.

ROZBRUCH, S. ROBERT, orthopedist, researcher; b. Bklyn., Sept. 2, 1965; s. Max and Frieda Rozbuch; m. Yonina Jacobs, July 2, 1989; children: Jason, Elizabeth. BA magna cum laude, U. Pa., 1985; MD in Rsch. with honors, Cornell U. Weill Med. Coll., 1990. Resident orthop. Hosp. Spl. Surgery, NYC, 1990—95; fellow Internat. Ctr. Limb Lengthening, Balt., 1998—99; pres. S. Robert Rozbruch MD, PC, NYC, 1999—; now chief limb lengthening svc. Hosp. Spl. Surgery, NYC, dir. Inst. Limb Lengthening and Reconstruction, 2002—; assoc. prof. orthop. surgery Weill Med. Sch. Cornell U., 2002—. Treas. Limb Lengthening and Reconstruction Soc., 2002—, bd. dir., 2002; founder Limb Lengthening and Reconstruction Program Hosp. Spl. Surgery, NYC. Author: Fractures of the Knee in Clin. Orthop., 2000, Orthop. Knowledge Update-Trauma 3, 2003; contbr. articles to profl. jours. Bd. trustees Temple Israel Ctr., White Plains, NY, 2002—. Recipient Neer award, Am. Shoulder and Elbow Surgeons, 1991. Fellow: Am. Acad. Orthop. Surgeons; mem.: Orthop. Trauma Assn. Avocations: gardening, exercise. Office: Hosp Spl Surgery 535 E 70th St New York NY 10021 Office Phone: 212-606-1415. Business E-Mail: rozbruchsr@hss.edu.

ROZEN, JEROME GEORGE, JR., entomologist, curator, professor, researcher; b. Evanston, Ill., Mar. 19, 1928; s. Jerome George and Della (Kretchmar) R.; m. Barbara L. Lindner, Dec. 18, 1948; children: Steven George, Kenneth Charles, James Robert. Student, U. Pa., Phila., 1946-48; BA, U. Kans., Lawrence, 1950; PhD, U. Calif.-Berkeley, 1955. Entomologist in taxonomy U.S. Dept. Agr., 1956-58; asst. prof. entomology Ohio State U., 1958-60; assoc. curator dept. entomology Am. Mus. Natural History, NYC, 1960-65, curator hymenoptera, 1965—, chmn. dept. entomology, 1960-71, dep. dir. research, 1972-86. Field expdns. in U.S., Europe, Mex., Trinidad, Argentina, Chile, Brazil, Peru, Venezuela, Morocco, Pakistan, Republic of South Africa, Namibia, Israel, Egypt, Kyrgzstan, Turkey, Belize, Costa Rica; adj. prof. CUNY, 1968—; mus. assoc. Univ. Kans. Nat. History Mus. and Biodiversity Rsch. Ctr., 2004—. Contbr. articles to profl. jours. Fellow AAAS; mem. Am. Inst. Biol. Scis., Entomol. Soc. Am. (editor misc. publs. 1959-60), Soc. Study of Evolution, Soc. Systematic Biology, N.Y. Entomol. Soc. (pres. 1964-65), Washington Entomol. Soc., Pacific Coast Entomol. Soc., Kans. Entomol. Soc., Orgn. Biol. Field Stas. (pres. 1990), Internat. Soc. Hymenopterists (co-organizer, Bee Course, 1999-). Achievements include research in bees (Apoidea) and beetles (Coleoptera). Home: 55 Haring St Closter NJ 07624-1709 Office: Am Mus Natural History Central Park West New York NY 10024-5192 Office Phone: 212-769-5466. Business E-Mail: rozen@amnh.org.

ROZENBERG, LANA, cosmetic dentist; b. 1968; DDS, U. Pacific Sch. Dentistry, 1994. Founder, dir. Rozenberg Dental Day Spa, NYC. Named one of NY Top Cosmetic Dentists, NY Mag., 2002, 2004. Avocations: boating, golf, skiing, tennis, financial investments. Office: Rozenberg Dental Day Spa 45 W 54th St Ste 1B New York NY 10019 Office Phone: 212-265-7724. Business E-Mail: office@rozenbergdds.com.*

ROZENBERG, VALERIA, chemist, researcher; d. I. Rozenberg and M. Rainina. MS in Chemistry, Moscow State U., 1964, PhD, 1971. Cert. sr. sci. rschr. in organometallic chemistry Supreme Certifying Commn. Coun. Mins. USSSR, 1986. Jr. sci. rschr. A. N. Nesmeyanov Inst. Organoelement, Moscow, 1964—80, supr. grad. students, 1964—80, sr. sci. rschr., 1980—96, supr. grad. and PhD students, 1980—96, head rsch. group coordinated ligands, 1993—2003, leading sci. rschr., 1996—2003, cons. hon., 2003—; invited scientist Cornell U., Dept. Chemistry, Ithaca, NY, 1997. Contbr. articles to profl. sci. jours., chapters to books. Recipient European Sci. awards, Devel. New Asymmetric Catalysts Chem. Mfg., 2001, EU Descartes prize, 2001; grantee INTAS, Synthesis New Ligands Asymmetric Catalysis, 1995—97, INCO Copernicus, Devel. New Asymmetric Catalysts Chem. Mfg., 1998—2000; Russian Found. Basic Rschrs. grant, Fundamental Aspects Organometallic Chemistry, 1993—95, 1997—99, 2000—02. Achievements include patents for method of obtaining of film materials containing metal clusters. Avocations: art, poetry, walking, swimming. Personal E-mail: vroz2003@yahoo.com. Business E-Mail: lera@ineos.ac.ru.

ROZENCVAIG, PERLA, language educator; d. Simon and Leonor Rozencvaig; m. Roberto Aciar, Dec. 20, 1978; 1 child, Amelia Aciar. PhD, Columbia U., NYC, 1983. Asst. prof. Spanish Barnard Coll., NYC, 1986—93; lectr. Spanish Columbia U., 1994—. V.p. Cuban Cultural Ctr. NY, NYC, 2000—. Office: Columbia Univ 612W116th St New York NY 10027

ROZMAN, GILBERT FRIEDELL, sociologist, educator; b. Mpls., Feb. 18, 1943; s. David and Celia (Friedell) R.; m. Masha Dwosh, Jan. 25, 1945; children: Thea Dwosh Kendler, Noah Dwosh BA, Carleton Coll., Northfield, Minn., 1965; PhD (Woodrow Wilson fellow 1965-66), Princeton U., 1971. Mem. faculty Princeton U., 1970—, prof. sociology, 1979—, Musgrave prof. sociology, 1992—. Mem. com. studies Chinese civilization Am. Council Learned Socs., 1975-80; mem. U.S.-USSR Bi-Nat. Commn. Humanities and Social Scis., 1978-86, IREX Univ. Coun., 1998-2001. Author: Urban Networks in Ch'ing China and Tokugawa Japan, 1973, Urban Networks in Russia, 1750-1800, and Premodern Periodization, 1976, Population and Marketing Settlements in Ch'ing China, 1982, A Mirror for Socialism: Soviet Criticisms of China, 1985, The Chinese Debate About Soviet Socialism 1978-85, 1987, Japan's Response to the Gorbachev Era, 1985-1991: A Rising Superpower Views a Declining One, 1992, Northeast Asia's Stunted Regionalism: Bilateral Distrust in the Shadow of Globalization, 2004, Strategic Thinking about the Korean Nuclear Crisis: Four Parties Caught between North Korea and the United States, 2007; co-author: The Modernization of Japan and Russia, 1975; editor: The Modernization of China, 1981, Soviet Studies of Premodern China: Assessments of Recent Scholarship, 1984, Japan in Transition: From Tokugawa to Meiji, 1986, The East Asian Region: Confucian Heritage and Its Modern Adaptation, 1991, Dismantling Communism: Common Causes and Regional Variations, 1992, Russia and East Asia: The 21st Century Security Environment, 1999, Japan and Russia: The Tortuous Path to Normalization, 1949-1999, 2000, Korea at the Center: Dynamics of Regionalism in Northeast Asia, 2006, Russian Strategic Thought Toward Asia, 2006, Japanese Strategic Thought Toward Asia, 2007, South Korean Strategic Thought Toward Asia, 2008. Guggenheim fellow, 1979-80; grantee NSF, NEH, Social Sci. Rsch. Coun., Nat. Coun. for Soviet and E. European Studies, U.S. Inst. Peace, Woodrow Wilson Internat. Ctr. Mem. Assn. Asian Studies, Am. Sociol. Assn., Am. Assn. Advancement Slavic Studies. Home: 20 Springwood Dr Trenton NJ 08648-1048 Office: Princeton U 149 Wallace Hall Princeton NJ 08544-0001 Business E-Mail: grozman@princeton.edu.

ROZNOVSCHI, MIRELA, law librarian, writer; b. Tulcea, Romania, Apr. 10, 1947; d. Ianeu and Hrisula Roznovschi; 1 child, Maximilian Adrian Atanasiu. MA in Romance Langs., U. Bucharest, Romania, 1970; M of Info. Sci., Pratt Inst., NY, 1996. Cert. Internet Tech. NYU, 1997. Columnist, lit. editor Tomis lit. mag., Constanta, Romania, 1970—74; sr. columnist Magazin, Bucharest, Romania, 1979—89; sr. columnist, bd. dirs. Romania Libera, Bucharest, Romania, 1989—91; faculty, reference libr. internat. and fgn. law NYU Law Libr., New York, NY, 1996—. Cons. Ctrl. European U., Budapest, Hungary, 1999—2002; editor Globalex, 2005—. Author (as Mirela Roznoveanu): Always in the Autumn, 1988, Life on the Run, 1997, Platonia, 1999, Time of the Chosen, 1999, Toward a Cyberlegal Culture, 2001, 2d edit., 2002, Born Again - in Exile, 2004, The Life Manager and Other Stories, 2004, Elegies from New York City, 2008, The Civilization of the Novel: A History of the Fiction Writing form Ramaiyana to Don Quixote, 2008. Recipient Officer Nat. Order Faithful Svc. of Romania, Pres. of Romania, 2000. Mem.: Assn. Am. Law Schs., Romanian Writers' Guild, Am. Assn. Law Librs. (chair fgn. comparative and internat. law spl. interest sect. 2004—05), Am. Soc. Internat. Law, Beta Phi Mu Theta Chpt. Office: NYU Law Libr 40 Washington Square S New York NY 10012

ROZOVICS, MICHELLE JANEEN, lawyer; b. Chgo., Sept. 3, 1971; d. Ronald J. and Nancy Jean Rozovics. AB, U. Mich., Ann Arbor, 1993, JD, 1996. Bar: Ill. 1997, US Dist. Ct. (no. dist.) Ill. 2004. Vis. lectr. U. Slaski, Katowice, Poland, 1996—97, Novgorod State U., Russia, 1997—98; assoc. Cremer Kopon Shaughnessy & Spina, Chgo.,

Wheaton, 1999—2000; staff counsel Safeco Ins. Co. America, Chgo., 2000—04; assoc. Hinshaw & Culbertson LLP, Crystal Lake, Ill., 2004—06; mem. Rozovics Law Firm, LLC, Crystal Lake, 2006—. Spkr. in field. Contbr. chapters to books. Mem. Crystal Lake Hist. Preservation Commn., 2006—; vol. Epilepsy Found. Greater Chgo., 2006; pro bono atty. Lawyers for Creative Arts, Chgo., 2006. Mem.: ABA, Kane County Bar Assn., Ill. Assn. Def. Trial Counsel, McHenry County Bar Assn., Chgo. Bar Assn., Ill. State Bar Assn., Internat. Bar Assn. Avocations: humor writing, historical renovation, animal rescue. Office: Rozovics Law Firm LLC 263 King St Crystal Lake IL 60014 also: 10 S Riverside Plz Ste 1800 Chicago IL 60606 Office Phone: 815-479-9733.

ROZUMNYJ, JAROSLAV, literature educator; b. Honcharivka, Ukraine, Sept. 6, 1925; s. Hryhory and Anna (Parubocha) R.; m. Oksana Olha Hrycenko, Mar. 10, 1938; children: Larysa, Roman, Istan, Ruslan. BA with honors, Theol. Sem., Culemborg, Netherlands, 1950; MA, U. Ottawa, Ont., Can., 1958, PhD, 1968. Lectr. Laurentian U., Sudbury, Ont., 1960-63; asst. prof. Western Mich. U., Kalamazoo, 1963-64, U. Man., Winnipeg, Can., 1964-71, head dept., 1976-89, prof. lit., 1989—, sr. scholar, 1997. Vis. prof. U. Ottawa, 1972, Ukrainian Cath. U., Rome, 1987; dean Faculty of Philosophy, Ukrainian Free U., Munich, Germany, 1995-96; vis. rsch. scholar Macquarie U., Sydney, 1989; mem. internat. adv. bd. U. Kiev-Mohyla Acad., 1992—, hon. prof., 1996. Editor: New Soil--Old Roots: The Ukrainian Experience in Canada, 1983, I Was Nineteen... KM Academia, 2001, (compiler) Markian Shashkeuych in the West, 2007; editor & co-author: Yesterday, Today, Tomorrow: The Ukrainian Community in Canada, 2004; co-editor: Jubilee Collection of the Ukrainian Academy of Arts and Sciences, 1976; lit. editor: Anthology of Musical Compositions on the Poems of M. Shashkewych, 1992; editor Can. vol. Ency. of Ukrainian Diaspora, 7 vols.; editor-in-chief: Collection of Scholarly Papers, 1996; mem. editl. bd. Suchasnist, 1984-91. Pres. Ukrainian Cultural and Ednl. Ctr., Winnipeg, 1970-73; pres. Can. Friends of Rukh in Ukraine, Winnipeg, 1990-92; Can. rep. U. Kiev-Mohyla-Acad., 1992—; bd. govs. Man. Mus. Man and Nature, Winnipeg, 1976-80; pres. Markian Shashkevych Inst., Winnipeg, 1999—. Recipient Outreach Activities award U. Man., 1986, Order of the Eternal Flame in Silver World Conf. Ukranian Scouts, 1994, Taras Shevchenko medal Ukrainian Can. Congress, 1995, Petro Mohyla Silver medal Nat. U. Kyiv Mohyla Acad., 2003; honored Festschrift, Can. Inst. Ukranian Studies, 2000. Mem. Ukrainian Acad. Arts and Scis. in Can. (pres. 1977-80, v.p. 1995-01), Schevchenko Sci. Soc. US, Am. Assn. Ukrainian Studies, Ukrainian Am. Assn. U. Profs. Home: 801 Cambridge St Winnipeg MB R3M 3G3 Canada Office Phone: 204-474-9370. Personal E-mail: rozumnyj@cc.umanitoba.ca.

ROZWAT, CHARLES, computer software company executive; B in Fin. and Info. Systems, Marquette U., Milw. Mgmt. staff mem. Digital Equipment Corp.; with Oracle Corp., 1994—, v.p. New Eng. Devel. Ctr., exec. v.p. server techs. divsn. Redwood City, Calif. Office: Oracle Corp 500 Oracle Pky Redwood City CA 94085 Office Phone: 650-506-7000. Office Fax: 650-506-7200.

ROZZA, GIANLUIGI, mathematician, aerospace engineer; b. Sant'Angelo Lodigiano, Italy, Apr. 20, 1977; s. G. Rozza and R. Acerbi. MS in Aerospace Engring. cum laude, Politecnico di Milano, Italy, 2002; PhD in Numerical Analysis and Computational Engring. with honors, Ecole Polytechnique Federale de Lausanne, Switzerland, 2005. Registered Italian engr., Poly. Milan, 2004. Rsch. asst. Ecole Polytechnique Federale de Lausanne, 2001—06; post-doctoral assoc. MIT, Cambridge, Mass., 2006—08, rsch. affiliate, 2008—; lectr. EPFL, 2008—, rsch. scientist, 2008—. Contbr. chapters to books, sci. computing software, articles to profl. jours. Recipient Bill Morton Computational Fluid Dynamics prize, U. Oxford, 2004, Riconoscenza Civica Sant' Angelo Lodigiano award, Native Town Civic Adminstrn., 2005, PhD award Best Thesis, 2006, Computational Sci. And Engring prize, 2009; grantee, Politecnico di Milano Progetto Rocca, 2007; fellow, Sci. Com. MIT, 2005, Rsch. Commn. Ecole Polytechnique Fed. Lausanne, 2005—06; scholar, European Union, 2002—05. Mem.: Springer Computational Sci. & Engring. (CSE prize 2009), European Cmty. Computational Methods Applied Scis., Soc. for Indsl. and Applied Math., Ordine Ingegneri Provincia di Lodi (assoc.). Roman Catholic. Achievements include research in optimal control; reduced basis methods; shape optimization; computational haemodynamics. Office: EPFL CHCS Stat 8 MA B2 524 Lausanne CH 1015 Switzerland Office Phone: 41 21 693 4267. Business E-Mail: gianluigi.rozza@epfl.ch.

ROZZELL, SCOTT ELLIS, lawyer, energy executive; b. Texarkana, Tex., Apr. 12, 1949; s. George M. and Dora Mae (Boyett) Rozzell; m. Karen Brandstrader Rozzell; children: Stacey Rozzell Murphree, Kimberly Rozzell McVey. BA, So. Meth. U., 1971; JD, U. Tex., 1975. Bar: Tex. 1975, U.S. Dist. Ct. Tex. (so. dist), 1975, U.S. Dist. Ct. Tex. (no. dist.), 1977, U.S. Ct. Appeals (1st, 3d, 9th cirs.) 1977, U.S. Ct. Appeals (5th and D.C. cirs.) 1976. Assoc. BakerBotts, LLP, Houston, 1975-82, ptnr., 1983-94, sr. ptnr., 1995-2000; exec. v.p., gen. counsel, corp. sec. CenterPoint Energy, Inc., Houston, 2001—; exec. v.p., gen. counsel, corp. sec., bd. dir. Tex. Genco Holdings Inc., 2003—04. Bd. dirs. Houston Young Lawyers Assn. 1979-1982, pres. 1983-1984; mem. Tex. Commn. Lawyer Discipline, 2001-03, chair 2002-03. Bd. dirs. Manned Space Flight Edn. Found., Inc., 1997—2007, vice chair 2000-06, Tex. Aviation Hall of Fame, 2001-; vice-chmn., 2006—; mem. so. regional adv. bd. Inst. Internat. Edn., 2002—07; bd. dirs. Assn. Electric Cos. Tex., 2006-, chmn. 2006-07; bd. dirs. Cancer Counseling, Inc., 1984-88, State Tex. Aircraft Pooling Bd., 1997-2002, Houston Cmty. Coll. Found., 2006-, Southern Meth. U. Alumni Assn. 2007-, March of Dimes, Houston, 2007-, Alley Theater, 2008-. Mem. ABA, Houston Bar Assn. (bd. dirs. 1992-96, pres. 1996-97), Houston Bar Found. (bd. trustees 1990-92, chmn. 1992-93), State Bar Tex. (bd. dirs. 1997-2000, Outstanding Dir. 1999-2000), Texa. Bar Found. (bd. trustees 2007-, chmn. 2009-), Am. Bar Found., Experimental Aircraft Assn., Aircraft Owners and Pilots Assn., Commemorative Air Force, Coronado Club, Houstonian Club. Republican. Presbyterian. Avocation: flying vintage military aircraft. Office: CenterPoint Energy Inc 1111 Louisiana 47th Floor PO Box 4567 Houston TX 77210-4567 Home: 8 N West Oak Dr Houston TX 77056 Office Phone: 713-207-1502. Office Fax: 713-207-0894. Business E-Mail: scott.rozzell@centerpointenergy.com.

ROZZI, RICARDO, philosopher, ecologist; b. Santiago, Chile, Oct. 6, 1960; m. Francisca Massardo. BS in Biol. Scis. Ecology, U. Católica, Santiago, Chile, 1985; MS in Biol. Scis. Ecology, U. Chile, Santiago, 1990; MA in Philosophy, U. Conn., Storrs, 1998, PhD in Ecology, 2001. Assoc. prof. U. North Tex., Denton, 2004—; adj. rschr. Inst. Ecology and Biodiversity, Santiago, Chile; rschr. U. Magallanes, Punta Arenas, Chile. Rep. for S. Am. Internat. Soc. Environ. Ethics, 1998—; co-founder biocultural conservation, environ. ethics, and ecotourism grad. program U. Magallanes, Punta Arenas, Chile, 2003—; pres. Sci. Com. Cape Horn Biosphere Res., Punta Arenas, Chile, 2005—. Author: (book/audio cd) Multi-ethnic Bird Guide of the Austral Temperate Forests of South America; co-author: (textbook) Fundamentos de Conservación Biológica: Perspectivas latinoamericanas. Dir. Omora Ethnobotanical Pk., Cape Horn, 2000. Recipient Nat. prize, NSF, Chile, 2004, Sci. and Practice award, Ecology and Soc. Jour., 2008. Mem.: Ecol. Soc. Chile, Ecol. Soc. Am., Internat. Environ. Ethics. Achievements include invention of Tourism with a Hand-lens; development of Field Environmental Philosophy; Ecological Inquiry in the Everyday Environment - Chilean Ministry of Education. Office: Univ North Tex Po Box 310920 Denton TX 76203 Office Phone: 940-565-2266.

RSCH, HELMUT V. B., biology professor; s. Helmut and Eva Hirsch; m. Natalie Gans, June 13, 1966 (div.); 1 child, Paul D. Hirsch. BS in Math., U. Chgo., 1965; PhD, Stanford U., Calif., 1970. Disting. tchg. prof. U. Albany, SUNY, 1972—. Panelist, sci. forum WAMC Radio NPR, Albany; exec. steering com. Internat. Hormesis Soc., Amherst, Mass. Fellowship, Alfred P. Sloan Found., 1975—79, grant, DHEW Nat. Eye Inst., 1973—83, Nat. Inst. Drug Abuse, 1977—79, NSF, 1983—85, Whitehall Found., 1989—2000, Nat. Insts. Environ. Health Scis., 2002—. Office: Biology Univ Albany 1400 Washington Ave Albany NY 12222 Business E-Mail: hirsch@albany.edu.

RUAN, JIENING, language and literacy professor, director, writer; d. W. Ruan; m. D. Sun. BA in English, Xiamen U., China, 1989; MEd in Elem. Edn., Indiana U. Pa., 1995, MEd in Reading Edn., 1996; PhD, Purdue U., West Lafayette, Ind., 2000. Asst. prof. U. Okla., Norman, 2000—06, assoc. prof., 2006—, dir. reading cert. program, 2005—, dir. Reading Clinic, 2001—. Prin. Purdue Chinese Sch., West Lafayette, Ind., 1998—2000; affiliate US-China Issues Inst. U. Okla., Norman, 2006—; affiliate Confucius Inst. Translator: World Literature Today for Kids; mem. editl. rev. bd. Reading Tchr., 2002—05, mem. guest editl. bd., Reading Tchr., 2006—, mem. editl. rev. bd. World Lit. Today Kids, 2003—06, editl. cons. Jour. Action in Tchr. Edn., 2003—; contbr. articles to profl. jours., profl. book co-author. Recipient Jr. Faculty award, COE U. Okla., 2004; Purdue Rsch. Found. grantee, Purdue U., 1999, Jr. Faculty Rsch. grantee, U. Okla., 2003, COE Summer Rsch. grantee, 2005. Mem.: Assn. Tchr. Educators, Internat. Reading Assn., Nat. Reading Conf.

RUAN, LIAN JIN, library director; arrived in U.S., 1986; d. Yong-dong Jin and Jin-xiu Dai; m. Zhong-jin Ruan, June 24, 1987; children: Gordon J., George J. BA in World History, Peking U., 1984; MA in African History, UCLA, 1988; MLS, U. Ill., 1990. Rsch. info. specialist Ill. Fire Svc. Inst., Champaign, 1990—99, dir., head libr., 1999—. Newspaper cataloger Ill. State Hist. Libr., Springfield, 1990, manuscript cataloger, 90; libr. cons. Champaign Fire Dept., 1990—. Contbr. articles to profl. jours. Recipient Chancellor's Academic Profl. Excellence award, U. Ill. Mem.: ALA (mem. Illinet network adv. coun. 2003—), Spl. Libr. Assn. (downstate bd. dirs. Ill. chpt. 2002—04, Diversity Leadership Develop. award 2003), Chinese Heritage Assn. (vice prin. chinese sch. 1998—99, prin. chinese sch. 1999—2000, bd. dirs. 2000—03), Internat. Fire Libr. Consortium (adv. com. 1997—2001). Office: Ill Fire Svc Inst Univ Ill 11 Gerty Dr Champaign IL 61820 Office Phone: 217-265-6107. Business E-Mail: lruan@fsi.uiuc.edu.

RUANE, JAMES EDWARD, JR., engineering executive; b. Malden, Mass., July 22, 1954; s. James Edward and Marie Alice Ruane; m. Thelma Cahinde Ruane, Dec. 1, 1990; children: James Edward III, Katheryn Virginia. BSc in Physics, U. Mass., 1981. Test dir. Raytheon, Bedford, Mass., 1983—96; engring. mgr. Equimeter, Dubois, Pa., 1996—98; v.p. ops. Star Track, Morris Plains, NJ, 1998—99; program mgr. Com Tech Sys., Orlando, Fla., 1999—2001, Eaton Vorad, San Diego, 2001—03; dir. datalink applications Cubic Def. Applications, San Diego, 2003—. Platinum sponsor San Diego Telecom Coun., 2004—. Mem.: IEEE, Assn. UN Mannod Vehicle Sys. Internat., Air Force Assn. Avocation: Karate (black belt). Office: Cubic Defense Applications 9333 Balboa Ave San Diego CA 92123 Home: 17022 Martinal Rd San Diego CA 92127-1452

RUARK, GIBBONS, retired literature and language professor; b. Raleigh, NC, Dec. 10, 1941; s. Henry Gibbons and Sarah Elizabeth Ruark; m. Kay Stinson, Oct. 5, 1963; children: Jennifer, Emily Clarke. BA, U. NC, Chapel Hill, 1963; MA, U. Mass., Amherst, 1965. Instr. English UNC Greensboro, 1965—68, vis. writer, 1988—89; prof. English U. Del., Newark, 1968—2005. Recipient Saxifrage prize, 1984, Pushcart prize, 1989; fellowship, Nat. Endowment Arts, 1979, 1986, 1993. Home: 1805 Warwood Ct Raleigh NC 27612 Business E-Mail: gruark@udel.edu.

RUB, TIMOTHY F., museum director; b. NYC, Mar. 9, 1952; s. Louis Rub and Marguerite (Gustafson); m. Sally Rub; children: Peter, Katharine. BA in Art History, Middlebury Coll., 1974; MA in Art History, NYU, 1979; MBA, Yale U., 1987; postgrad., Harvard U., 1998. Curatorial intern Met. Mus. Art, 1983; lectr. art and archtl. history Cooper-Hewitt Mus./Parsons Sch. Design, Stevens Inst. Tech., 1979-84; guest curator Bronx Mus. Arts, NY, 1985-86; curator Cooper-Hewitt Mus., NYC, 1983-87; assoc. dir. Hood Mus. Dartmouth Coll., Hanover, NH, 1987-91, dir., COO, 1991-2000; dir. Cin. Art Mus., 2000—06; dir., CEO, Cleve. Mus. Art, 2006—. Avocation: gardening. Office: Cleveland Mus Art 11150 East Blvd Cleveland OH 44106 Office Phone: 216-421-7340, 216-707-2250. E-mail: info@clevelandart.org.

RUBALCAVA, MICAELA, education educator; b. San Jose, Calif., May 20, 1962; MA, Stanford U., Calif., 1987; PhD, U. Calif., Berkeley, 1995. Cert. in secondary edn. tchg. Calif., 1987. Prof. Truckee Meadows CC, Reno, 2000—. Exhibitions include Mandalas. Office: Truckee Meadows CC 7000 Dandini Reno NV 89512 Business E-Mail: mrubalcava@tmcc.edu.

RUBARDT, PETER CRAIG, conductor, educator; b. Oakland, Calif., Aug. 7, 1958; s. Kenneth and Betty (Maspero) R.; m. Hedi Salanki; children, Daniel, Vivienna. BA, U. Calif., Berkeley, 1981; M of Music, SUNY, Stony Brook, 1984; student, Hochschule fur Musik, Vienna, 1984-86; D Mus. Arts, Julliard Sch., 1989. Prof., conductor SUNY, Purchase, 1989-90, Rutgers U., New Brunswick, NJ, 1991-96; resident conductor N.J. Symphony, Newark, 1990-93; assoc. conductor Syracuse (N.Y.) Symphony, 1993-97; music dir., condr. Greater Pensacola (Fla.) Symphony Orch., 1997—. Guest conductor various orchs. Condr. rec. Bach Concerti, 1988. Fullbright fellow USIA, 1984-86; Bruno Walter scholar, Julliard Sch., 1986-88. Mem. Am. Symphony Orch. League, Condrs. Guild. Democrat. Home: 8774 Thunderbird Dr Pensacola FL 32514 Office: Pensacola Symphony Orch PO Box 1752 Pensacola FL 32598-1752 Office Phone: 850-435-2533.

RUBBERT, PAUL EDWARD, retired engineering executive; b. Mpls., Feb. 18, 1937; s. Adolf Christian and Esther Ruth Rubbert; m. Mary Parpart, Oct. 6, 1958 (div. 1985); children: Mark, David, Stephen. BS with high distinction, U. Minn., 1958, MS in Aero. Engring., 1960; PhD in Aerodyn., MIT, 1965. Rsch. engr. The Boeing Co., Seattle, 1960-62, 65-72, unit chief aerodyns rsch., comml. airplane group, 1972—, tech. fellow, 1989; ret. Cons. NASA, 1989—, aeronautics adv. com., aerospace rsch. and tech. subcoms.; corp. vis. com. MIT, 1990—; served on various coms. Nat. Rsch. Coun. Panel; aerodyns. cons. GM; speaker in field. Contbr. articles to profl. jours. Recipient Arch T. Colwell Merit award Soc. Automotive Engrs., 1968, Wright Brothers Lectureship in Aeronautics Am. Inst. of Aeronautics and Astronautics, 1994 Fellow AIAA (Outstanding Tech. Mgmt. award Pacific Northwest sect., disting. lectr., assoc. editor jour., past mem. fellow selection com., dir., chmn. various workshops and coms.), Royal Aero. Soc.; mem. NAE. Achievements include three patents in field.

RUBBIA, CARLO, physicist; b. Gorizia, Italy, Mar. 31, 1934; s. Silvio and Bice (Liceni) Rubbia; m. Marisa Rome, June 27, 1960; children: Laura, Andre. Diploma, Scuola Normale, Pisa, 1958; AM (hon.), Harvard U., 1970; degree (hon.), U. Geneva, 1983, Carnegie Mellon U., 1985, U. Genoa, Italy, 1985, U. Udine, 1985. Research fellow Columbia U., NYC, 1960—61; asst. prof. physics U. Rome, 1961—62; prof. physics Harvard U., Cambridge, Mass., 1970—88; sr. rsch. physicist European Orgn. for Nuclear Rsch., Geneva, 1960—, dir. gen., 1989—93; prof. Univ. Pavia, Italy. Dir. Internat. Ctr. for Theoretical Physics, Trieste, 1994; pres., dir. Italian Nat. Agency for New Technologies, Energy and Environment (Enea), 1999—2005. Recipient Nobel prize in Physics, 1984. Mem.: NAS (fgn. assoc.), Hungarian Acad. Scis., Polish Acad. Scis., Accademia dei Lincei, USSR Acad. Scis. (fgn.), Royal Soc. (fgn.), Pontifical Acad. Scis., Am. Physics Soc., European Physics Soc., Italian Com. for Control of Affirmations on Paranormal (CICAP) (hon.). Achievements include contributions to the project which led to the discovery of field particles W and Z, communicators of weak interaction. Office: Univ Pavia Strada Nuova 65 27100 Pavia Italy

RUBECK, FREDRICK JOHN, performing arts educator; b. Sycamore, Ill., Apr. 10, 1962; s. Jerome Evan and Linda Lee Rubeck. MFA, U. Nebraska-Lincoln, 1987. Rd. mgr. stage mgr. Nebr. Theatre Caravan, Omaha, 1986—88; dept. chair, prof. performing arts Elon U., NC, 1988—. Dir.: (theatre) Numerous Prodns. Mem.: Theatre Comm. Group, Southeastern Theatre Conf. (orgnl. liaison 2005—), NC Theatre Conf. (bd. dirs. 2007—), Assn. Theatre Higher Edn. (governing coun. 2008—), Alpha Psi Omega (chpt. advisor 2006—). Office: Elon Univ 2800 Campus Box Elon NC 27244 Business E-Mail: rubeck@elon.edu.

RUBEL, MATTHEW EVAN, retail executive; b. Ft. Lauderdale, Fla., Nov. 29, 1957; s. Stanley Bernard and Isabell Rubel. BS in Journalism, Ohio U., 1979; MBA, U. Miami, 1980. Pres. splty. store div. Revlon Inc., NYC, 1988; pres., CEO Pepe Jeans USA; exec. v.p. J. Crew Group, 1994—99, CEO Popular Club Plan, 1994—99; chmn., CEO Cole Haan, 1999—2005; chmn. pres., CEO Collective brands Inc. (Payless ShoeSource, Inc.), 2005—. Bd. dirs. Furniture Brands Internat., Inc., 2006—. Trustee Ballet Theatre Found., Inc./Am. Ballet Theatre. Avocations: tennis, boating. Office: Payless ShoeSource Inc 3231 SE 6th Ave Topeka KS 66607

RUBELL, DONALD, gynecologist, hotel executive, art collector; m. Mera Rubell; children: Jason, Jennifer. Named one of Top 200 Collectors, ARTnews Mag., 2004—08. Avocation: collector of contemporary art. Mailing: The Rubell Art Collection 95 NW 29th St Miami FL 33127

RUBELLO, DAVID JEROME, artist; b. Detroit, Sept. 3, 1935; s. Ludovico and Girolama (Trupiano) R.; m. Mary Anne Keithan, Oct. 14, 1978. BFA, Am. Acad. Art, Rome, 1961; MFA, U. Mich., 1972; cert., Acad. Fine Art, Copenhagen, 1966. Lect. art U. Mich., Ann Arbor, 1973—74; asst. prof. art Pa. State U., University Park, 1974-80; assoc. prof. art Towson (Md.) State U., 1980-81; assoc. prof. U. Mich., Ann Arbor, 1988-90. One man shows include Cade Gallery, Royal Oak, Mich., 1987, GM Design Ctr., Warren, Mich., 2007; exhibited in group shows at Detroit Inst. Art, 1987, GMB Gallery Internat., Bloomfield Hills, Mich., 1991, Kresge Art Inst., 1989, Kalamazoo Art Inst., 1990, 91, Photo Nat. 2, Ella Sharp Mus., Jackson, Mich., BBAA, Birmingham, Mich., Arts Coun., Traverse City, Mich., 1995-96, Patrimonio Invitational Wayne State U., Detroit, 1996, Ann. Celebrate Mich. Artists P.C. Art Ctr., Rochester, 1994, 95, 96, Art Ctr., Mt. Clemens, Mich., 1997, Crative Art Ctr., Pontiac, Mich., 1997, Paint Creek Art Ctr., Rochester, Mich., 2007, Denos Art Mus., Traverse City, Mich., 2007; exhibited Null Dimension, Fulda, Germany, 1988, Systematica Constructive Art, Madrid, 1989, B4 Pub. Invitational, London, 1990, Archive 90s, Amsterdam and London, Konkrete Miniatures Invitational, Amsterdam, 1991, Planet Art Gallery, Capetown, South Africa, 1999, Detroit Focus, 2000; author: Reflection and Form, 1984, My Sicilian Garden, Poetry & Photographs, 2004, Moment to Moment, Away at Home Story Poems & Photographs, 2007; contbr. articles to profl. jours. including The Structurist, 1999, 2002, 2005-06. Recipient awards for art work; featured professional artist profile B&W Fine Art Photography Mag., June 2001. Personal E-mail: drubello586@aol.com.

RUBEN, ALAN MILES, law educator; b. Phila., May 13, 1931; s. Maurice Robert and Ruth (Blatt) R.; m. Betty Jane Willis, May 23, 1965. AB, U. Pa., 1953, MA, JD, U. Pa., 1956. Bar: Pa. 1957, Ohio 1972. Law clk. Supreme Ct. Pa., 1956-58; pvt. practice Phila., 1958-65; assoc. counsel Aetna Life & Casualty Co., Hartford, Conn., 1965-69; corp. counsel Lubrizol Corp., Cleve., 1969-70; prof. Cleve.-Marshall Coll. Law, Cleve. State U., 1970—2003, prof. emeritus, 2003—; adv. prof. law Fudan U., Shanghai, People's Republic of China, 1993—; dep. to city solicitor Phila., 1958-61; dep. atty. gen. State of Pa., 1961-65; spl. counsel to U.S. Senate Subcom. on Nat. Stockpile, 1962; commentator Higher Edn. Issues Sta. WCLV-FM, Cleve., 1975-87. Mem. nat. panel labor arbitrators Nat. Acad. Arbitrators, Fed. Mediation and Conciliation Svc. and Am. Arbitration Assn., Ohio State Employment Rels. Bd.; lectr. law U. Conn. Law Sch., 1968; vis. prof. law FuDan U., Shanghai, Peoples Republic of China, 1988-89; cons. Shanghai Law Office for Fgn. Economy and Trade, Peoples Republic of China, 1991-94. Author: The Constitutionality of Basic Protection for the Automobile Accident Victim, 1968, Unauthorized Insurance: The Regulation of the Unregulated, 1968, Arbitration in Public Employee Labor Disputes: Myth, Shibboleth and Reality, 1971, Illicit Sex of Campus: Federal Remedies for Employment Discrimination, 1971, Model Public Employees Labor Relations Act, 1972, Sentencing the Corporate Criminal, 1972, Modern Corporation Law, supp. edit., 1978, An American Lawyer's Observations on the Inauguration of the Shanghai Stock Exchange, 1989, Ohio Limited Partnership Law, 1992-2002, Practice Guides, Ohio Limited Liability Company, Law, 1995-2006; co-editor: How Arbitration Works, 1997, editor-in-chief 6th edit., 2003, Supp, 2008; contbr.: With an Eye to Tomorrow: The Future Outlook of the Life Insurance Industry, 1968, The Urban Transportation Crisis: The Philadelphia Plan, 1961, Philadelphia's Union Shop Contract, 1961, The Administrative Agency Law: Reform of Adjudicative Procedure and the Revised Model Act, 1963, The Computer in Court: Computer Simulation and the robinson Patman Act, 1964. Bd. dirs. U.S. Olympic Com., 1968-73; chmn. U.S. Olympic Fencing Sport Com., 1969-73; pres. U.S. Fencing Assn., 1968-73; capt. U.S. Pan-Am. Fencing Team, 1971, U.S. Olympic Fencing Team, 1972; bd. dirs. Legal Aid Soc. Cleve., 1973-77; trustee Cleve.-San Jose Ballet, 1999-2001; Verb Ballet, 2009-. Winner Internat. Inst. Edn. Internat. Debate Championship, 1953; recipient Harrison Tweed Bowl and Am. Law Inst. prizes Nat. Moot Ct. Competition, 1955; named Guggenheim scholar, 1949-53, Fulbright scholar FuDan U., Shanghai, 1993-94. Fellow Coll. Labor and Employment Lawyers, Inc.; mem. ABA, Ohio Bar Assn. (corp. law and profl. responsibility com.), Cleve. Bar Assn. (Securities Law Inst. 1995-2002), Assn. Am. Law Schs. (chmn. sect. law and edn. 1976-78), Internat. Indsl. Rels. Rsch. Assn., Internat. Soc. Labor Law, Internat. Bar Assn., Union Internat. Des Avocats, Internat. Law Assn., AAUP (pres. Ohio conf. 1974-75), Rowfant Club, Phi Beta Kappa, Pi Gamma Mu. Home: 9925 Lake Shore Blvd Bratenahl OH 44108-1052 Office: Cleveland Marshall Coll Law Cleve State U 1801 Euclid Ave Cleveland OH 44115 Office Phone: 216-687-2310. Business E-Mail: alan.ruben@law.csuohio.edu.

RUBEN, LAWRENCE, real estate developer and company executive, lawyer; b. Bklyn., Sept. 28, 1926; s. Irving and Minnie (Sruelif) R.; m. Selma Belfer, Dec. 20, 1952 (dec. 2002); children: Richard Gordon, Lenore Denise, Rochelle Gail Ruben Kivell; m. Jan Gottlieb, Dec. 5, 2004. BA, NYU, 1949; LLB, Bklyn. Law Sch., 1951. Bar: N.Y. 1952. Gen. practice law, NYC, 1952-53; pres. Ru-Min Constrn. Co., NYC, 1953-54; exec. v.p. Belco Petroleum Corp., NYC, 1954-64, dir., 1954-85; v.p. Fundamental Bldg. Corp., 1952—; pres. Randall Devel. Co., Aragon Devel. Corp., Lawrence Ruben Co., Inc.; ptnr. Lexington Madison Co., Tower Plaza Assocs., Devonshire Assocs., Boylston Ptnrs., Devonshire Constrn. Co. Inc., Lawrence Assocs., Granite Ptnrs., Inc., Harper-Lawrence; pres. Washington Mgmt. Corp. Mem. adv. bd. NYU Real Estate Inst.; mem. Rockefeller U. Coun.; med. ctr. adv. bd. NY UJA; bd. Govs. Am. Jewish Com. Patron Albert Einstein Coll. Medicine; sponsor Grad. Sch. Sci.; bd. dirs. Cardoza Sch. Law at Yeshiva U.; chmn. United Jewish Appeal, Scarsdale, N.Y., 1974-75; mem. pres.'s coun. Meml. Sloan Kettering Cancer Ctr. With AUS, 1945-46. Mem. ABA, Fenway Golf Club, Boca Rio Golf Club, NY Weill Cornell Coun., Harmonie Club. Office: 600 Madison Ave New York NY 10022-1615

RUBEN, ROBERT JOSEPH, lawyer; b. NYC, Apr. 9, 1923; m. Audrey H. Zweig, Nov. 20, 1949; children: Pamela, James. BS, Columbia U., 1943; MA, Harvard U., 1948; LL.B., Fordham U., 1953. Bar: N.Y. 1954. Exec. trainee Chase Nat. Bank, NYC, 1948-49; economist, 1949-53; assoc. Milbank, Tweed, Hope & Hadley, NYC, 1953-55; assoc., then ptnr. Shea & Gould, NYC, 1955-90; sec. Gen. Battery Corp., Reading, Pa., 1963-73, Fiat Metal Mfg. Co., Inc., Plainview, N.Y., 1961-64, Filtors, Inc., East Northport, N.Y., 1961-64, Trans-Industries, Inc., 1969-2001, dir., 2001—06; asst. sec. Elgin Nat. Industries, 1975-88. Asst. Judge City Ct., Rye, N.Y., 1977-90; arbitrator Nat. Assn. Securities Dealers, 1990—, Pacific Stock Exch., 1992—, Am. Arbitration Assn., 1990—, N.Y. Stock Exch., 1994—. Trustee Rye Hist. Soc.; bd. dirs. Carver Center, Port Chester, N.Y., 1972-90. Served with AUS, 1943-46. Decorated Combat Inf. medal. Mem. ABA, N.Y. State Bar Assn., Assn. Bar of City of N.Y., Harvard Club (N.Y.C.), Harvard-Radcliffe Club So. Calif., Columbia U. Club So. Calif., Beta Gamma Sigma, Zeta Beta Tau. Home: 21285 Amora Mission Viejo CA 92692-4930

RUBENSKY, MITCHELL, band director; b. Bronx, Mar. 12, 1954; s. Herman H. and Norma Rubensky. MusB in Percussion, Manhattan Sch. Music, 1978; MusM, Herbert H. Lehman Coll., Bronx, 1984. Dir. music Frank D. Whalen Jr. HS, Bronx, 1982—2001; band dir. Bronx HS of Sci., 2001—. Chmn. student and tchr. programming Frank D. Whalen Jr. HS, 1995—2001. Recipient Prins. Pride of Music award, NYC Bd. Edn., Dist. 11, 1987, Ednl. Svc. award, Assn. Jewish Profls., 2001, Ednl. Leadership award, Jewish Tchrs. Cmty. Chest, 2004. Avocation: antique stereos. Office: Bronx HS Science 75 W 205th St Bronx NY 10468 Office Phone: 718-817-7700 ext. 517. E-mail: mir312@aol.com.

RUBENSTEIN, ARTHUR HAROLD, dean, internist, educator; b. Johannesburg, Dec. 28, 1937; arrived in U.S., 1967; s. Montague and Isabel (Nathanson) R.; m. Denise Hack, Aug. 19, 1962; children: Jeffrey Lawrence, Errol Charles. MB BCh, U. Witwatersrand, 1960, DSc (hon.) in Medicine, 2002. Diplomate Am. Bd. Internal Medicine. Intern, then resident Johannesburg Gen. Hosp., 1961, 63-65, 66-67; fellow in endocrinology Postgrad. Med. Sch., London, 1965-66; fellow in medicine U. Chgo., 1967-68, from asst. prof. to assoc. prof., 1968-74, prof., 1974-97, Lowell T. Coggeshall prof. med. sci., 1981-97, assoc. chmn. dept. medicine, 1975-81, chmn., 1981-97; attending physician Mitchell Hosp., U. Chgo., 1968-97; dean, Gustave L. Levy disting. prof. Mt. Sinai Sch. Medicine, NYC, 1997—2001; exec. v.p. U. Pa. Health Sys., Phila., 2001—; dean U. Pa. Sch. Medicine, Phila., 2001—. Mem. study sect. NIH, 1973-77, Hadassah Med. Adv. Bd., 1986-95, adv. coun. Nat. Inst. Arthritis, Metabolism and Digestive Diseases, 1978-80; chmn. Nat. Diabetes Adv. Bd., 1982, mem., 1981-83. Mem. editl. bd. Diabetes, 1973-77, Endocrinology, 1973-77, Jour. Clin. Investigation, 1976-81, Am. Jour. Medicine, 1978-81, Diabetologia, 1982-86, Diabetes Medicine, 1987-91, Annals of Internal Medicine, 1991-96, Medicine, 1992—; contbr. articles to profl. jours. Mem. Gov.'s Sci. Adv. Coun. State of Ill., 1989-96. Recipient David Rumbough Meml. award Juvenile Diabetes Found., 1978. Master: ACP (John Phillips Meml. award 1995); fellow: NY Acad. Medicine, Royal Coll. Physicians (London), South African Coll. Physicians; mem.: AAAS, Am. Clin. Climatology Assn., Assn. Acad. Health Ctrs. (bd. dirs. 2005—), Assn. Am. Med. Colls. (mem. coun. of deans adminstrv. bd. 2002—), Assn. Profs. Medicine (councillor 1991—94, v.p. 1994—95, pres. 1995—96, Robert Williams award 1997), Inst. Medicine (coun. 1991—96), Residency Rev. Com., Am. Bd. Internal Medicine (bd. govs. 1985—93, exec. com. 1990—93, chmn. 1992—93), Assn. Am. Physicians (treas. 1984—89, councillor 1989—94, v.p. 1994—95, pres. 1995—96), Ctrl. Soc. Clin. Rsch. (v.p. 1988, pres. 1989), Am. Fedn. Clin. Rsch., Endocrine Soc., Brit. Diabetes Assn. (Banting lectr. 1987), Am. Diabetes Assn. (Solomon Berson Meml. lectr. 1985, Eli Lilly award 1973, Banting medal 1983), Am. Soc. for Clin. Investigation. Office: U Penn School Med 295 John Morgan Bldg 3620 Hamilton Walk Philadelphia PA 19104 Office Phone: 215-898-6796.

RUBENSTEIN, ATOOSA BEHNEGAR, former editor-in-chief; b. Tehran, Iran, Jan. 13, 1972; arrived in U.S., 1978; d. Mansoor Behnegar; m. Ari Rubenstein, 1998. BA in Polit. Sci., Barnard Coll., 1993. Fashion asst., assoc. fashion editor, fashion edit to sr. fashion editor Cosmopolitan Mag., 1993—95; founding editor-in-chief CosmoGirl! mag., 1998—2003; editor-in-chief Seventeen Mag., 2003—06.

RUBENSTEIN, DAVID AARON, military officer, healthcare administrator; b. Rockville Centre, NY, Nov. 23, 1954; s. Robert R. and Mona Sydney (Feder) R.; m. Patricia Barrier, Mar. 18, 1978; children: Sarah Elizabeth, William Robert. BS in Health Edn., Tex. A & M U., 1977; MHA, Baylor U., 1989; M of Mil. Arts and Sci., Command and Gen. Staff Coll., 1990. Commd. 2d lt. U.S. Army, 1977, advanced through grades to maj. gen., 2008, med. platoon leader 3d inf. div. Germany, 1977—79, ops. officer 3d med. battalion, 1979—80, pers. officer 307th med. battalion Ft. Bragg, NC, 1981—82, co. comdr., 1982—83, mil. instr. Acad. of Health Scis. Ft. Sam Houston, Tex., 1984—87, grad. student, 1987—88, adminstrv. resident William Beaumont Army Med. Ctr. Ft. Bliss, Tex., 1988—89, grad. student Command and Gen. Staff Coll. Ft. Leavenworth, Kans., 1989—90; adminstrv. asst. Office of the Army Surgeon Gen. Army Med. Svc. Corps, Washington, 1990—92; chief coordinated care Army Hosp., Ft. Belvoir, Va., 1992—93; hosp. comdr. 18th Mobile Army Surg. Hosp., Ft. Lewis, Wash., 1994—96; grad. student Army War Coll., Carlisle Barracks, Pa., 1996—97; dep. comdr. Eisenhower Army Med. Ctr., Ft. Gordon, Ga., 1997—99; hosp. comdr. 21st Combat Support Hosp., Ft. Hood, Tex., 1999—2001, Bosnia-Herzegovina, 1999—2000; cmdr. Landstuhl Regional Med. Ctr., Germany, 2001—03; chief of staff Europe Regional Med. Commd., 2003—04; cmdr. 30th Med. Brigade, 2004; asst. surgeon gen., 2005—06; commanding gen. Europe Med. Commd., 2006—08; major general, army deputy surgeon general US Army, 2008—. Pres. Health Orgn. Network, El Paso, Tex., 1989, asst. surgeon gen. force sustainment, 2005; pres. Healthcare Execs. Ctrl. Savannah River Area, 1998-99; participant U.S. Army seminar Baylor U., Ft. Sam Houston, 1989. Author leadership seminar; reviewer books Lehigh U. Press, 1990, Mil. Rev. Jour., Mil. Medicine; contbr. articles to profl. jours. Religious lay leader Office of the Jewish Chapel, Ft. Bragg, 1982-83, Ft. Bliss, 1988-89, Ft. Leavenworth, 1989-90, Bosnia-Herzegovina, 1999-2000; fund drive coord. United Fund, Ft. Leavenworth, 1989; vol. Muscular Dystrophy Assn., Washington, 1990-91. Decorated Legion of Merit; recipient Fed. Healthcare Leadership award, 2003, Ray E. Brown award, Assn. Military Surgeons, US, 2006, Mentor of the Year award, U.S. Army Med. Svc. Corps., Federal Excellence in Healthcare Leadership award, Regent's healthcare Executive award, Am. Coll. Healthcare Executives. Fellow: Am. Coll. Healthcare Execs. (Regent's award 1993, regent 2000—02, gov. 2002—, chmn. elect 2007, Fed. Excellence in Healthcare Leadership award, Regent's Healthcare Exec. award); mem.: VFW, Assn. of U.S. Army, Am. Hosp. Assn., Assn. Mil. Surgeons of U.S. (Ray E. Brown 2006). Republican. Jewish. Avocations: flying, running, history, reading. Office Phone: 703-681-3002. Business E-Mail: david.rubenstein@us.army.mil.

RUBENSTEIN, DAVID M., investment company executive; b. Balt., 1949; m. Alice Rogoff; 3 children. BA, Duke U., 1970; JD, U. Chgo., 1973. With Paul, Weiss, Rifkind, Wharton & Garrison, NYC, 1973—75; chief counsel judiciary com. subcom. on constl. amendments U.S. Senate, Washington, 1975—76; dep. asst. to Pres. for domestic policy The White House, 1977—81; with Shaw, Pittman, Potts & Trowbridge (now Pillsbury, Winthrop, Shaw Pittman); co-founder, mng. dir. The Carlyle Group, 1987—. Mem. adv. bd. Stanford Inst. Econ. Policy Rsch.; mem. bus. coun. World Econ. Forum; mem. nat. adv. com. J.P. Morgan Chase. Vice chmn. Lincoln Ctr. Performing Arts; mem. bd. trustees Duke U., John Hopkins U., Meml. Sloan Kettering Cancer Ctr.; mem. vis. com. Kennedy Sch. Govt. Harvard U.; mem. bd. overseers Hoover Instn.; mem. trustees' coun. Nat. Gallery Art; mem. Madison Coun. Libr. Congress, Coun. Nat. Trust for Historic Preservation; mem. dean's coun. Woodrow Wilson Sch. Princeton. Recipient Golden Plate award, Acad. Achievement, 2006; named one of The 50 Most Powerful People in DC, GQ mag., 2007. Office: The Carlyle Group 1001 Pennsylvania Ave NW Washington DC 20004-2505 Office Phone: 202-729-5626. Office Fax: 202-347-1818.*

RUBENSTEIN, EDWARD, physician, educator; b. Cin., Dec. 5, 1924; s. Louis and Nettie Rubenstein; m. Nancy Ellen Millman, June 20, 1954; children: John, William, James. MD, U. Cin., 1947. House staff Cin. Gen. Hosp., 1947—50; fellow May Inst., Cin., 1950; sr. asst. resident Ward Med. Svc., Barnes Hosp., St. Louis, 1953—54; chief of medicine San Mateo County Hosp., Calif., 1960—70; assoc. dean postgrad. med. edn., prof. medicine Stanford (Calif.) U., 1971—, emeritus, active. Faculty Stanford Photon Rsch. Lab.; affiliated faculty Stanford Synchrotron Radiation Lab., 1971—; maj. materials facilities com. NRC, 1984—85, Nat. Steering Com. 6 GeV Electron Storage Ring, 1986—. Author (textbook): Intensive Medical Care; editor: Synchotron Radiation Handbook, 1988, vol. 4, 1991, Synchotron Radiation in the Biosciences, Molecular Medicine; mem. editorial bd.: Sci. Am., Inc., 1991—94; editor (textbook): Sci. Am. Medicine, 1978—94; editor: (series) Molecular Cardiovascular Disease, 1995, Molecular Oncology, 1996, Molecular Neuroscience, 1998. With USAF, 1950—52. Recipient Kaiser award for outstanding and innovative contbns. to med. edn., 1989, Albion Walter Hewlett award, 1993; named Disting. Scientist, SvrroMed, Inc., 2003. Master: ACP (Laureate 2002); fellow: AAAS, Royal Soc. Medicine; mem.: Am. Clin. and Climatol. Assn., Soc. Photo-Optical Engrs., Western Assn. Physicians, Calif. Acad. Medicine, Inst. Medicine, APS, Alpha Omega Alpha. Achievements include research in mechanisms of autoimmunity, dysfunction of the choroid plexus and cerebrospinal fluid circulatory system, synchrotron radiation, nonprotein amino acids, autoimmunity, molecular chirality; multiple sclerosis pathogenesis. Office: Stanford Med Ctr Dept Medicine Stanford CA 94305

RUBENSTEIN, HOWARD JOSEPH, public relations executive; b. NYC, Feb. 3, 1932; s. Samuel and Ada (Sall) R.; m. Amy Forman, Dec. 17, 1959; children: Roni, Richard, Steven. AB, U. Pa., 1953; student law, Harvard, 1953; LL.B. (Dean's scholar), St. Johns Sch. Law, 1959, LLD (hon.), 1990. Bar: NY 1960. Pres. Rubenstein Assocs., Inc. pub. rels. cons., NYC, 1954—; asst. counsel judiciary com. U.S. Ho. of Reps., 1960; cons. U.S. Fgn. Claims Commn., 1961-62; cons. joint legis. com. child care needs NY, 1965-66; adviser SBA, 1965-66. Mem. Gov.'s Com. on Sale of World Trade Ctr., 1981, Mayor's Com. on Holocaust Commemoration, 1981—, NY State Task Force on Energy Conservation, Dept. Housing, 1981-83, Mayor's Coun. Econ. Bus. Advisors, 1991-93; co-chmn. Holocaust Commn., 1993—; v.p. Jewish Cmty. Rels. Coun., 1988-94, advisor, 1995—; past dir. Brownsville Boys Club; bd. dirs. Provide Addict Care Today, Police Athletic League, NY chpt. March of Dimes; active U.S. Internat. Coun., 1977-81, Commn. on Status of Women, 1982-89, NYC Commn. Operation Welcom Home, 1991; mem. Mayor's Bus. Adv. Coun., 1996—; advisor NY Commn. on Status of Women, 1995—; comm. advisor Gov.'s Com. Jerusalem 3000, 1996-01; bd. dirs. Albert Einstein Coll. Medicine, 1997—; bd. govs. Jewish Cmty. Rels. Coun., 1999—; exec. com. Real Estate Bd. NY, 1985—, NYC & Co., 2001—, Partnership for NYC, 2004—. Mem. Assn. Better N.Y. (mem. exec. com. 1972—), Phi Beta Kappa, Beta Sigma Rho. Jewish (dir. congregation). Home: 993 5th Ave New York NY 10028-0105 Office: Rubenstein Associates Inc 1345 Avenue Of The Americas New York NY 10105-0302 Home Phone: 212-744-6333; Office Phone: 212-843-8080. Business E-Mail: hrubenstein@rubenstein.com.

RUBENSTEIN, HOWARD S., physician, writer; b. Chgo., June 14, 1931; s. Sidney Howard and Selma (Moldofsky) Rubenstein; m. Judith Ann Selig, May 26, 1968; children: Emily Rubenstein Engel, Adam Selig, Jennifer Rubenstein Zigun, John Stephen. BA, Carleton Coll., Northfield, Minn., 1953; MD, Harvard U., Boston, 1957. Intern and resident Los Angeles County Gen. Hosp., LA, 1957—60; rsch. fellow Harvard Med. Sch., Boston, 1960—64, rsch. assoc., 1964—68; physician, chief of allergy Harvard U. Health Svcs., Cambridge, Mass., 1968—89; med. cons. State of Calif., Dept. Social Svcs., Disability Program, San Diego, 1989—2000. Physician Albert Schweitzer Hosp., Deschapelles, Haiti, 1964. Author: (epic in free verse) Maccabee, 2004, (plays) Brothers All, 2006, The Golem, Man of Earth, 2007, Tony and Cleo, 2008; translator: Agamemnon: A Play by Aeschylus with Reconstructed Stage Directions, 1998, 2003, The Trojan Women: A Play by Euripides, 2002, Britannicus: A Play by Jean Racine, 2009; contbr. articles to profl. jours. Fellow, US Pub. Health Svc., 1960—62; Harold C. Ernst fellow, Harvard Med. Sch., 1962—64. Mem.: Harvard Med. Sch., Carleton Coll., Ezekiel Hersey Coun. (life), Joseph Heywood Soc. (life), Sigma Xi, Phi Beta Kappa (life). Jewish. Home: 8677 Villa La Jolla Dr # 1114 La Jolla CA 92037 Home Fax: 858-546-0406. Personal E-mail: hsrubenstein@yahoo.com.

RUBENSTEIN, JAY, history professor, writer; b. 1967; BA, Carleton Coll., 1989; MPhil, U. Oxford, St. John's Coll., 1992; PhD, U. Calif., Berkeley, 1997. Asst. prof. history U. N.Mex, 1999—2006; assoc. prof. history U. Tenn., Knoxville, 2006—. Author: Guibert of Nogent: Portrait of a Medieval Mind, 2002; co-editor: Teaching and Learning in Northern Europe, 1000-1200, 2007; contbr. articles to profl. jours. Recipient Koren Prize, Soc. for French Hist. Studies, 2005; named a MacArthur Fellow, The John D. and Catherine T. MacArthur Found., 2007; grantee Rhodes Scholarship, 1989—91, French-Am. Found. Bicentennial Fellowship, 1994—95, Am. Coun. of Learned Societies Fellowship, 2002—03, Burkhardt Fellowship, 2006—07, Nat. Endowment for Humanities Rsch. Fellowship, 2007. Office: U Tenn Dept History 915 Volunteer Blvd 6th Fl, Dunford Hall, #2629 Knoxville TN 37996-4065 Office Phone: 865-974-9870. E-mail: jruben1@utk.edu.

RUBENSTEIN, JEFFREY ELLIOT, prosthodontist, professor; s. Sam H. and Jennie Rubenstein; m. Hermine S. Schwartz, June 15, 1975; children: Ryan Scott, Lauren Michelle. DMD, Tufts U. Sch. Dental Medicine, Boston, 1975. Cert. in maxillofacial prosthetics M.D. Anderson Cancer Ctr., 1980. Resident and staff Lancaster Cleft Palate Inst., Pa., 1975—77; faculty Harvard Sch. Dental Medicine, Boston, 1980—89. Assoc. surgeon Children's Hosp. Med. Ctr., Boston, 1982—89; prosthodontist Arapahoe Native Am. Health Ctr., Riverton, Wyo., 2008. Author: (book) Osseointegration in Dentistry An Overview (Best Dentists Am., 2003). Fellow: Acad. Prosthodontics, Am. Coll. Prosthodontics, Wash. State Soc. Prosthodontists (pres. 2001—02), Am. Acad. Maxillofacial Prosthetics (pres. 2006—07); mem.: Acad. Osseointegration. Office: Univ Wash Sch Dentist/ divsn Prosthodontists 1959 NE Pacific St Seattle WA 98195

RUBENSTEIN, JEROME MAX, lawyer; b. St. Louis, Feb. 16, 1927; s. Jacob J. and Anne (Frankel) R.; m. Judith Hope Grand, July 31, 1954; children— Edward J., Emily Rubenstein Muslin, Daniel H. AB, Harvard U., 1950, LLB, 1955. Bar: Mo. 1956, U.S. Dist. Ct. (ea. dist.) Mo. 1956, U.S. Ct. Appeals (8th cir.) 1956. Mem. English lit. faculty U. So. Philippines, Cebu, 1950-51; law clk U.S. Dist. Ct., St. Louis, 1955-56; assoc. Lewis, Rice, Tucker, Allen & Chubb, St. Louis, 1956-64, Grand, Peper & Martin, St. Louis, 1964-65, ptnr., 1965-66; jr. ptnr. Bryan Cave, St. Louis, 1966-67, ptnr., 1968-97, of counsel, 1998—. Dir. Commerce Bank, N.A. Bd. dirs. Independence Ctr., St. Louis, 1985-88, The Arts and Edn. Coun. Greater St. Louis, 1991-99. Served with USN, 1945-46. Bd. dirs. Independence Ctr., St. Louis, 1985. Served with USN, 1945-46 Mem. ABA, Mo. Bar Assn., St. Louis Bar Assn., Mo. Athletic Club, Harvard Club of St. Louis (pres. 1982-83, bd. dirs. 1983-90). Jewish. Avocations: jogging, tennis. Home: 7394 Westmoreland Dr Saint Louis MO 63130-4240

RUBENSTEIN, JOSHUA SETH, lawyer; b. Bklyn., Aug. 5, 1954; s. Seth and Elaine (Freedman) Rubenstein; children: Mary-Jane, Kenan, Rebecca, Marlena, Isaac. BA in Greek and Latin magna cum laude, Columbia U., 1976; JD, Columbia Law Sch., 1979. Bar: NY 1980, NJ 1980, US Dist. Ct. (ea. and so. dist.) NY 1980, US Dist. Ct. NJ 1980, US Tax Ct. 1986. Assoc. Fried, Frank, Harris, Shriver & Jacobson, NYC, 1979—82, KMZ Rosenman LLP, 1982—88; ptnr. KMZ Rosenman LLP (now Katten, Muchin Rosenman, LLP), 1989—, mem. mgmt. com., 1994—98, chmn., 1998—2002, chmn. trusts and estates dept., 1995—; co-mng. ptnr. Katten Muchin Rosenman LLP, NYC, 2002—, mng. ptnr. Charlotte, NC, 2002. Mem. adv. com. surrogate's ct. Office Ct. Adminstrn., 1997—; mem. adv. coun. Law Sch. Trusts, Wills and Estate Planning Columbia U., 1997—; adj. prof. Bklyn Law Sch.; lectr. in field. Author: Answer Guide New York Surrogate's Court, 2004; featured in NY Times, Wall St. Jour., Wash. Post, NY Law Jour. and others; contbr. articles to legal publ. Dir., sec. Irvington Inst. Med. Rsch., 1991, treas., 1991—92, sec., 1992—93, co-pres., 1993—94, pres., 1994—2000, vice-chmn., 2000—; mem. legis. com., mem. devel. com., mem. bd. governance com., mem. Madeleine Borg com., chmn., mem. exec. com., 1994—; mem. profl. adv. com. Lincoln Ctr., NY Philharm., Mus. Modern Art, Met. Mus. Art, Columbia U., Columbia U. Law Sch., Mus. Art and Design; chmn. estates and trust splty. group, chmn. splty. group task force, mem. exec. com. lawyers divsn. United Jewish Appeal-Fedn., 1989—99; trustee Jewish Bd. Family and Children's Svc., 1991, v.p., 1998—. Recipient James H. Fogelson award, Lawyer's divsn. United Jewish Appeal Fedn., 1993, Trusts and Estate Lawyers award, 2001; named Best Lawyers in NY, NY Mag.; named one of Top 100 Attys., Worth mag., 2005. Fellow: NY State Bar Found. (regent), Am. Coll. Trusts and Estate Counsel (mem. state laws com.); mem.: ABA, Soc. Trust and Estate Practitioners, Internat. Acad. Estate and Trust Law (academician 1997—), Assn. Bar City of NY, NJ Bar Assn. (real property and probate sect., mem. adv. com. rels. legis. and exec. brs.), NY State Bar Assn. (vice chmn. legis. com. 1988, chmn. 1988—91, co-chmn. ad hoc com. rev. proposals EPTL adv. com. N.Y. State 1991—, mem.-at-large exec. com. 1992—95, liaison to legis. policy com. 1995—, treas. 1997—98, sec. 1998—99, chair elect 1999—, chair 2000—01, trust and estate law sect., Pres.'s Pro Bono Svc. award 1991, Exec. Com. award 1992, 1995, 1996), Practising Law Inst. (mem. estate adv. com., lectr. 1984—, Hadassah estate planning seminar faculty and adv. bd. 1993—), Phi Beta Kappa. Democrat. Jewish. Office: Katten Muchin Rosenman LLP 575 Madison Ave New York NY 10022-2585 Office Phone: 212-940-7150. Office Fax: 212-940-8545. Business E-Mail: joshua.rubenstein@kattenlaw.com.

RUBENSTEIN, JUDITH LOUISE, psychologist; b. N.Y.C., Aug. 13, 1940; d. Martin and Frances (Hoffs) Goldstein; A.B., Radcliffe Coll., 1961; M.A., Boston U., 1962, Ph.D., 1967; B.J.Ed., Hebrew Coll., 1959; m. Joel Rubenstein, June 24, 1962; children— Mark Howard, Lauren Elizabeth. Staff fellow NIH, Bethesda, Md., 1966-68, cons. psychologist, 1968-72; research psychologist Tufts New Eng. Med. Center, Boston, 1972-86; asst. prof. psychiatry Tufts U. Sch. Medicine, Boston, 1972-78, assoc. clin. prof., 1978-86; assoc. research prof. psychiatry (psychology) Boston U. Sch. Medicine, 1986—. William T. Grant Found. grantee, 1975-80; Spencer Found. grantee, 1977-79. Mem. APA, Mass. Psychol. Assn. Jewish. Author: (with L. Yarrow and F. Pedersen) Infant and Environment: Early Cognitive and Motivational Development, 1975; also articles, book chpts. Office Phone: 617-244-7132.

RUBENSTEIN, LEONARD, engineering company executive; b. NYC, June 18, 1931; s. William and Sylvia (Jaffe) R.; m. Reva Scharf, Jan. 1951 (div. 1960); m. Geraldine Marilyn Porper, Aug. 14, 1965 (dec. Sept. 2000); children: Alan, Elaine, Philip, Ruth, Jennie. BS in Physics, Poly. Inst. N.Y., 1964. Registered profl. engr. NY, NJ, Del., Ga. Equipment engr. We. Elec., NYC, 1957-66; elec. engr. Gibbs & Hill, NYC, 1966-69; chief engr. Kiegl Lighting, NYC, 1969-72; project mgr. Stone & Webster, NYC, 1972-87; pres., prin. Rubenstein Engring. PC, NYC, 1975—; v.p. engring. Laramore Douglas & Popham, NYC, 1988-90; v.p., dir. engring. Gibbs & Hill, NYC, 1990-92; pres., prin. David Internat., 1990—; markter NPS, Florham Pk., NJ, 1992-95.

Devel., pipeline project, Costanza, Romania, Trieste, Italy. Contbr. articles to profl. publs. Chmn. Walt Whitman Ind. Dems., Bklyn., 1966-68, chmn. West Bklyn. Ind. Dems., 1964-66; bd. dir. NY Gilbert & Sullivan Players, NYC, 1993—; chmn., bd. dirs. 450 West End Corp, 1984-88; mem. bd. mgr. McBurney YMCA, 1988-97. With US Army, 1951-53. Mem. IEEE (sr., chmn. NY sect. 1995-96, asst. editor Today's Engr. 1997-98, IEEE Region I award 1985, 94, 96), NSPE, Soc. Mfg. Engr. (charter mem. Vision Soc., sr. mem. Robotics Internat.), Power Engring. Soc. (chmn. NY/LI chpt. 1984-85). Achievements include project manager of first large scale waterless power plant; design of commercial power plant using compressed air stored in salt mines; suppervision and design of large piperack and power plant using robote for some construction; engineering project manager of savannah electric power plant. Avocations: handball, music. Home and Office: 8 W 65th St New York NY 10023 E-mail: repc@nyc.rr.com.

RUBENSTEIN, LISA V., medical association administrator, educator; MSPH, U. Calif.; MD, Albert Einstein Sch. Medicine. Dir. RAND Ctr. for the Study of Healthcare Provider Behavior VA Greater Los Angeles Med. Ctr., prof. medicine. Mem.: Soc. Gen. Internal Medicine (pres.). Office: 2501 M St NW Ste 575 Washington DC 20037 Office Phone: 310-393-0411 ext. 6303. E-mail: lisa_Rubenstien@Rand.org.*

RUBENSTEIN, PAMELA SILVER, manufacturing executive; b. Lansing, Mich., May 12, 1953; d. Neil M. and Leah Rebecca (Coffman) Silver; m. Alec Robert Rubenstein. BA in Linguistics, U. Mich., 1974; MA in teaching English to spkrs. of other langs., Columbia U. Tchrs. Coll., 1976; MA in Linguistics, U. Ill., 1978, doctoral studies in linguistics, 1978-80. Instr. Columbia U. Tchrs. Coll., NYC, 1976, U. Ill., Urbana, 1978, libr. Linguistic Dept., 1978-79; asst. libr. Ill. State Geol. Survey, 1979-80; tchr. Congregation Temple Israel, Springfield, Ill., 1980-81; adminstr., tchr. Springfield Bd. Jewish Edn., 1981-82; instr. Comm. Divsn. Lincoln Land C.C., Springfield, 1981-82; tchr. Cmty. Hebrew Sch., Charleston, SC, 1982-83; instr. The Citadel and Coll. of Charleston, 1983; legal sec. Gibbs & Holmes, Charleston, 1984, May, Oberfell & Lorber, South Bend, Ind., 1984-88; instr. U. Notre Dame, Ind., 1987; tchr. Triton Sch. Corp., Bourbon, Ind., 1988-89; v.p., asst. treas. Allied Splty. Precision, Inc., Mishawaka, Ind., 1989—2005, CEO, owner, 2005—. Contbr. articles to profl. jours. Mem. Temple Beth-El Sisterhood, South Bend, Ind., 1987—. Mem.: Nat. Tooling and Machining Assn. (bd. mem., Mich. chpt. 2004—07, mem. edn. team, audit team 2005—, edn. team leader 2008—), Hadassah (life). Office: Allied Splty Precision Inc 815 E Lowell Ave Mishawaka IN 46545-6480 Office Phone: 574-255-4718. Business E-Mail: pam.rubenstein@aspi-nc.com.

RUBESIN, STEOHEN E., radiologist; MD, Johns Hopkins U., Balt. Diplomate Am. Bd. Radiology. Radiologist Hosp. U. Pa., Phila., 1986—. Office: Hosp Univ Pa 3400 Spruce St Philadelphia PA 19104

RUBIN, ALAN, physician; b. Phila., 1923; s. Hyman and Miriam (Magil) R.; m. Helen Metz, May 1, 1947; children: Alan, Stephen, Blake. MD, U. Pa., 1947. Diplomate Am. Bd. Ob-Gyn. Intern Hosp. Pa., Phila., 1947-48, resident in ob-gyn., 1949-52; trainee Nat. Cancer Inst., Phila., 1950-51; fellow in pharm. U. Pa., Phila., 1948-49; mem. staff Grad. Hosp., Phila.; clin. prof. ob-gyn. Temple U., Phila. Clin. prof. ob-gyn. U. Pa., Phila. Contbr. more than 150 articles to profl. jours. Fellow ACS, Royal Soc. for the Promotion of Health; mem. Am. Coll. Ob-Gyn., Sigma Xi, Alpha Omega Alpha. Home Phone: 215-735-9979.

RUBIN, ALAN A., pharmaceutical and biotechnology consultant; b. NYC, July 10, 1926; s. Harry and Gertrude R.; m. Helen M. Feinstein; children: Jeffrey, Ronald, Howard. BS, NYU, 1950, MS, 1953, PhD, 1959. Pharmacologist Schering Corp., Bloomfield, N.J., 1954-64; dir. pharmacology Endo Labs., Garden City, N.Y., 1964-70, v.p. rsch., 1970-74; dir. rsch. DuPont Pharms., Wilmington, Del., 1974-82, dir. sci. info. and tech., 1982-87; dir. licensing tech. DuPont Merck Pharms., Wilmington, Del., 1987-91; pres. ARA Assoc., Rockland, Del., 1991—. Editor: Search for New Drugs, 1972, New Drugs: Discovery and Development, 1978; contbr. articles to profl. jours. With U.S. Army, 1944-46. Mem. AAAS, Am. Soc. Pharmacology and Exptl. Therapeutics, Soc. Exptl. and Biol. Medicine, N.Y. Acad. Sci. Home: 207 Hitching Post Dr Wilmington DE 19803-1914 Office: ARA Assoc PO Box 244 Rockland DE 19732-0244 Personal E-mail: alannar@verizon.net.

RUBIN, ALFRED PETER, law educator, educator; b. Bklyn., Oct. 13, 1931; s. Saul and Jeannette (Turberg) R.; m. Susanne Frowein, Sept. 2, 1960; children: Conrad P., Anna F., Naomi E. BA, Columbia U., 1952, LLB, 1957; MLitt, U. Cambridge, Eng., 1963. Bar: N.Y. 1960. Atty. U.S. Dept. of Def., Washington, 1961-66, dir. trade control, 1966-67; prof. of law U. Oreg., Eugene, 1967-73; prof. internat. law Fletcher Sch. Tufts U., Medford, Mass., 1973—, disting. prof., 1993—2000, disting. prof. emeritus, 2000—. Stockton chair Naval War Coll., Newport, R.I., 1981-82. Author: International Personality of the Malay Peninsula, 1974, Piracy, Paramountcy and Protectorates, 1974, The Law of Piracy, 1988, Ethics and Authority in International Law, 1997; contbr. articles to profl. jours. and newspapers. Lt. USN, 1952-55. Mem. Am. Soc. Internat. Law (exec. coun. 1982-85, chmn. coms. 1967-98), Internat. Law Assn. (chmn. com. on terrorism and extradition 1981-88, 92-98, exec. com. of Am. br. 1979—, pres. Am. br. 1994-2000). Avocation: bicycling. Office: Tufts U Fletcher Sch Law & Diplomacy Medford MA 02155 Business E-Mail: arubin@tufts.edu.

RUBIN, ANDREW E. (ANDREW E. RUBIN), technology product developer; b. Chappaqua, NY, 1963; BS in Computer Sci., Syracuse U. Develop. engr. Carl Zeiss, Inc., Thornwood, NY, 1985—88; software pyrotechnician Apple Computer, Inc., Cupertino, Calif., 1988—90, various positions, 1990—92; mnr., enterprise magic cup General Magic, Sunnyvale, Calif., 1992—95; with Artemis (acquired by Microsoft, Inc. in 1997); mgr., comm. engring. WebTV Networks, Palo Alto, Calif., 1995—99; co-founder, pres., CEO Danger, Inc., Palo Alto, Calif., 1999—2004; entrepreneur-in-residence Redpoint Ventures, 2004; founder, pres., CEO Android, Inc. (acquired by Google, Inc.), Palo Alto, Calif., 2005; dir., mobile platforms Google, Inc., Mountain View, Calif., 2005—. Adv. bd. Reatrix Media Systems, Inc. Named a Maverick, Details mag., 2008. Achievements include development of Google Phone. Office: Google Inc 1600 Amphitheatre Pkwy Mountain View CA 94043 E-mail: arubin@robot.net.

RUBIN, ARTHUR HERMAN, retired academic administrator; b. NYC, Aug. 14, 1927; s. Samuel and Bessie (Moritt) R.; m. Janice Levy, Apr. 9, 1950 (div. 1965); children: Renee Ellen, Linda Joy; m. Audrey M. Schmidt, July 1, 1973. BS, NYU, 1950, MA, 1951. Adminstrv. asst. to asst. dean Sch. Edn. NYU, 1947-54, lab. asst. bus. edn. dept., 1950-54, instr., 1954-56, program dir. grad. students orgn., 1954-63, dir. tours, 1955-58, coord. summer sessions activities, 1959-64, dir. Bur. Pub. Occasions, 1963-74, asst. v.p. pub. occasions, 1974-75, dir. extramural affairs Coll. Dentistry, 1976, assoc. dean adminstrn., 1976-80, adj. asst. prof. behavioral scis. and cmty. health, 1976-80, dir. alumni rels. Sch. of Med., 1980-95, dir. spl. events med. ctr., 1988-95; cons. to Office Alumni Rels. NYU Sch. Medicine, 1995-2000; cons. to Office Spl. Events, NYU Med. Ctr., 1995-2000, ret., 2000. Tchr. Patrick Henry Jr. High Sch., N.Y.C., 1949-58; acting asst. prin. Robert F. Wagner Jr. High Sch., N.Y.C., 1958-63; cons. in field. Trustee Agnew Found., 1967—2008; mem. Great Valley coun. Girl Scouts U.S., 2005—07; mem. exec. bd., sec. Harris York Condominium Assn., 1998—99, mem. exec. bd., treas., chmn. coms., 2001—. Recipient NYU Presdl. citation, 1971, GSO award, 1980, Ernest O. Melby award Sch. Edn. Alumni Assn., 1976, citation Bus. Edn. Assn. Met. N.Y., 1976, Sesquicentennial award NYU Alumni Fedn., 1982, Meritorious Svc. award, 1985, dir. Emeritus citation, 1992. Mem. Ea. Bus. Tchrs. Assn. (chmn. exhibits 1953-74, exec. bd. 1969-71, pres. 1972-73, award 1974), Bus. Edn. Assn. Met. N.Y. (exec. bd. 1962-83), Nat. Bus. Edn. Assn. (exec. bd. 1972-74, conv. mgr. 1974-92, Disting. Svc. award 1992, Cert. of Appreciation 1992), N.Y. Acad. Pub. Edn. (bd. dirs. 1979-98, pres. 1992-94), NYU Edn. Alumni Assn. (v.p. 1961-62, 64-67), NYU Club (bd. govs. 1972-78, 79-89, v.p. 1983-86, chmn. bd. 1986-87), Delta Pi Epsilon Rsch. Found. Inc. (bd. dirs. 1990-92), Delta Pi Epsilon (Svc. awards Alpha chpt. 1971, 81). Home: 2605 Houghton Lean Macungie PA 18062-9506 Home Phone: 610-966-2792.

RUBIN, BENJAMIN ARNOLD, microbiologist, immunologist, medical educator, researcher; b. NYC, Sept. 27, 1917; s. Eli and Helen Sarah (Arenoff) R.; m. Mae Koenig, Aug. 31, 1951. BS, CCNY, 1937; MS, Va. Polytech. Inst. & State U., 1938; PhD, Yale U., 1947. Asst. dir. Circle Analytical Lab., NYC, 1938-40; chief lab. and radiology U.S. Army C.E., Nfld., also Cen. Am., 1940-44; asst. chief microbiologist Scherly Rsch. Lab., Lawrenceburg, Ind., 1944; rsch. asst. Yale U., New Haven, 1944-47; chief microbiologist Broockhaven Nat. Lab., LI, 1947-52, Syntex, Mexico City, 1952-54; prof. pub. health and preventitive medicine Coll. of Medicine Baylor U., Houston, 1954-60; mgr. biol. rsch. Wyeth, Radnar, Pa., 1960-84; rsch. prof. Phila. Coll. Osteo. Medicine, 1984-95; ret. Cons. GE, Valley Forge, Pa., 1972-80, U.S. Congressional com. energy and commerce, 1976-80, biological applications of space. Contbr. over 150 articles to sci. jours. Named to Inventors Hall of Fame, 1992; recipient John Scott award and medal, 1982, Proctor medal Phila. Drug Exchange, 1993; named Inventor of Yr., 1985. Achievements include invention of bifurcated needle in Smallpox eradication program. Home: 50 Belmont Ave Apt 601 Bala Cynwyd PA 19004-2428 Office: Phila Coll Osteo Medicine 4150 City Ave Philadelphia PA 19131-1610*

RUBIN, BINYAMIN, aerospace engineer; b. Magnitogorsk, Russia, Aug. 9, 1977; married. PhD in Aerospace Engring., Technion - Israel Inst. Tech., Haifa, 2006. Sci. rschr. Keldysh Rsch. Ctr., Russian Space Agy., Moscow, 1998—2002; grad. rsch. asst. Technion - Israel Inst. Tech., 2002—06; postdoc. rschr. Colo. State U., Fort Collins, 2007—. Office: CO State Univ 1320 Campus Delivery Fort Collins CO 80523 Business E-Mail: brubin@engr.colostate.edu.

RUBIN, BRUCE KALMAN, medical professor, researcher; b. Miami Beach, Fla., May 8, 1954; s. Arnold and Dorothy Bella (Firtel) Rubin; m. Tomomi Tainaka, July 29, 1990; children: Noah David, Max Aaron, Sam Tainaka. BSc, Tulane U., New Orleans, 1975, MEngr in Biomed. Engring., 1977, MD, 1979; MBA, Wake Forest U. Babcock Sch. Mgmt., Winston-Salem, NC, 2004. Diplomate Am. Bd. Pediat., cert. in Pediatric Pulmonology. Intern pediat. Oxford U., England, 1979; resident Tulane U., 1980-81; respirology fellow Hosp. for Sick Children, Toronto, Ont., Canada, 1981-83; asst. prof., dir. pediat. ICU Queen's U., Kingston, Ont., 1983-87; asst. prof. pediat. U. Alberta, Edmonton, Canada, 1987-91; prof. pediat., dir. pulmonary medicine St. Louis U., Cardinal Glennon Hosp., 1991-97; prof., vice chair rsch., dept. pediat. Wake Forest U. Sch. Medicine, 1997—2009, chief pediat. pulmonology, 1999—2005; also prof. physiology and pharmacology, biomed. engring. Va. Tech.-Wake Forest U. Sch. Biomed. Engring., 1997—2009; Jessi Ball duPont prof. & chmn. dept. pediat. Va. Commonwealth U., 2009—; head Children's Hosp. Richmond, Va., 2009—. Pres. Internat. Congress Pediatric Pulmonology, 2004—06. Author: Therapy for Mucus Clearance Disorders (Lung Biology in Health and Disease), 2004, Antibiotics as Antiflammatory and Immunomodulatory Agents (Progress in Inflammation Research), 2005; contbr. articles to profl. jours., chapters to books. Recipient Achievement award for Excellence in Pulmonary Disease State Mgmt., Am Assn. Respiratory Care, 2007, Donald Ejan Meml. Lectr. award, 2009, Forrest M. Bird Lifetime Sci. Achievement award, Am. Respiratory Care Found. & Am. Assn. Respiratory Care, 2008; grantee Rhodes scholarship, Oxford U., 1980. Fellow: Am. Coll. Chest Physicians (Young Investigator award 1989, Critical Care Rsch. award 1990, Alfred Soffer award 2004), Am. Pediat. Assn., Royal Coll. Physicians Can.; mem.: Am. Pediatric Soc., Soc. Pediat. Rsch. Avocations: languages. Office Phone: 804-828-9602. Business E-Mail: brubin@vcu.edu.

RUBIN, CATHY ANN, secondary school educator; b. Denver, July 17, 1948; d. Harry Phillip and Charlotte Ruth (Brinig) R. BA, Colo. State U., 1970; MA, U. No. Colo., 1971. Cert. tchr. Colo. Tchr. Adams County Dist. 50 Schs., Westminster, Colo., 1971-72; tchr. educationally handicapped Jefferson County Pub. Schs., Golden, Colo., 1972-98. Typist, bookkeeper Kenmark-Shaw's Jewelers, Denver, 1966—. Sec.-treas. Hillel Found., Denver, 1979-81; fundraiser Women's Am. Orgn. for Rehab. through Tng., Denver, 1979—; bookkeeper Religious Coalition for Abortion Rights, Denver, 1982-90; vol. TV PBS sta., Denver, 1978, Muscular Dystrophy Assn., Colo. AIDS Project; vol. usher DCTC, 1999—; vol. for the blind and dyslexic, 2005-2007. Democrat. Jewish. Avocations: music, reading, sailing, knitting, needlepoint. Home: 3500 S Ivanhoe St Denver CO 80237-1123

RUBIN, CHUCK (CARL RUBIN), consumer products company executive; BA, Brandeis U., Waltham, Mass. Positions in merchandising and store mgmt. Federated Dept. Stores; ptnr. Accenture; exec. v.p., chief merchandising/mktg. officer Office Depot, Inc., Delray Beach, Fla., 2004—06, pres. North Am. retail, 2006—. Office: Office Depot Inc 6600 N Military Trl Boca Raton FL 33496-2434

RUBIN, DAVID LEE, humanities educator, critic, editor; b. Indpls., Sept. 30, 1939; s. Ira Bertram and Jeanne Iva (Gamso) R.; m. Carolyn Dettman, June 12, 1965; 1 child, Timothy Craig. BA, U. Tenn., 1962; cert., U. Paris, 1963; MA, U. Ill., 1964, PhD, 1967. Instr. French U. Ill., Urbana, 1966-67; asst. prof. U. Chgo., 1967-69, U. Va., Charlottesville, 1969-74, assoc. prof., 1974-82, prof. French, 1982-2001, mem. Fulbright selection com., 1996—, mem. com. on comparative lit., 1997-2001, prof. emeritus, assoc. univ. seminar program, 2001—; seminar dir. Folger Inst., 1989; academic and profl. writing program U. Va., 2007—. Chair poetry bd. Va. Quar. Rev., 2003—, Great Books discussion leader Jefferson Inst. Lifelong Learning, U. Va., 2001-08, Humanities Forum Moderator Charlottesville Sr. Ctr., 2008-; assoc. ctr. advanced studies U. Va., 1979, 80-81, 87, 93, 99-2000; pub., editor-in-chief Rookwood Press, 1992—; cons. PMLA Can. Coun., Etudes littéraires françaises, NEH, numerous univ. presses; lectr., spkr. in field. Author: Higher Hidden Order, 1972, The Knot of Artifice, 1981, A Pact with Silence, 1991; editor: The Selected Poetry and Prose of John T. Napier, 1972, La poésie française du premier 17e siècle, 1986, 2d edit., 2006, Sun King, 1991; co-editor: La Cohérence Intérieure, 1977, Convergences, 1989, The Ladder of High Designs, 1991, The Fulbright Difference, 1993; founding editor Continuum, 1989-93, EMF: Studies in Early Modern France, 1994-2002, EMF Critiques, 1994-2002, Rookwood Texts, 1997—, Rookwood Reprints, 2002—; mem. editl. bd. Purdue Studies in Romance Literatures, 1975-2001, Oeuvres et Critiques, 1976-2001, French Rev., 1986-94; Am. corr. Cahiers Maynard, 1973-2001, Cahiers Tristan L'Hermite, 1989-2001; contbr. articles to profl. jours., chpts. to books. U.S. State Dept. Fulbright fellow, 1963—64, fellow, Woodrow Wilson Found., 1963—64, Guggenheim Found., 1980—81, Hewlett fellow, summer, 1997, The Shape of Change: Studies in Honor of David Lee Rubin, 2002. Mem. MLA, ACLU, Phi Beta Kappa. Avocations: reading, exercise. Home: 520 Rookwood Pl Charlottesville VA 22903-4734 Personal E-mail: dlr93039@yahoo.com.

RUBIN, DAVID STUART, curator, art critic; b. LA, June 18, 1949; s. Allen Morris and Ruth Elinor (Persky) R. AB in Philosophy, UCLA, 1972; MA in Art History, Harvard U., 1974. Asst. dir. Galleries of The Claremont Colls., 1977-82; prof. Art Hist. Discussion Harvard U., 1973—75; prof. Topical Art Hist. Survey Sch. Visual Arts, 1976—77; asst. prof. art history Scripps Coll., 1977-82; art critic Art in America, NYC, 1981-89; adj. curator San Francisco Mus. Modern Art, 1983-85; dir. exhbns. San Francisco Art Inst., 1983-85; dir. Freedman Gallery, Albright Coll., 1986-90; assoc. dir., chief curator Cleve. Ctr. Contemporary Art, 1990-94; curator 20th Century Art Phoenix Art Mus., 1994—99; curator visual arts Contemporary Arts Ctr., New Orleans, 2000—06; Brown Found. curator contemporary art San Antonio Mus. Art, 2006—. Guest curator security Pacific Nat. Bank, LA, 1982; project dir. Artist/Architect collaboration between Mary Miss and Adele Santos, Albright Coll., Reading, Pa., 1988—90, Outside the Frame: Performance and the Object, 1991—93; juror nat. art exhibitions, 1991—; arts peer Art in Architecture Design Excellence Prog., US Gen. Svcs. Adminstrn., 2002—. Contbg. editor Arts mag., NYC, 1979-81; author exhbn. catalogues Black and White are Colors, 1979, Contemporary Triptychs, 1982, Jay De Feo, 1984, Wally Hedrick, 1985, Concerning the Spiritual, the 80's, 1985, Contemporary Hispanic Shrines, 1989, Cynthia Carlson, 1989, Donald Lipski, 1990, Cruciformed, 1991, Petah Coyne, 1992, O ld Glory, 1994, It's Only Rock and Roll, 1995, Phoenix Triennial, 1998, Photography Now, 2000, 2001 Entergy Louisiana Open, Chelsea Rising, 2001, Expanding Universe: The Recent Paintings of Al Held, 2002, 2003 Louisiana Biennial, Douglas Bourgeois, 2003, Birdspace: A Post-Audubon Artist's Aviary, 2004, The Culture of Queer: A Tribute to J.B. Harter, 2005, Celebrating Freedom: The Art of Willie Birch, 2006, Stuart Allen: Mapping Daylight, 2007, Playing with Time, 2008, Chocolate: A Photography Exhibition, 2008, Marcia Gygli King: Botanical Paintings, 2009, Ray Coader Uincent Valdez: Ei Chavez Ravine, 2009, John Hernondez Zoes Room, 2009, Waterflow, 2009, Culinary Delights: Photographs by David Halliday, 2009, Psychedelic: optical and Visionary Art, 1960-; contbr. articles to Arts, 1976-80, Art in Am. mag., 1981-89, Artweek, 1978-83; film appearances include Drapeau, 1998. Trustee Working Theatre, Cleve., 1993—94. Nat. Endowment Humanities M us. fellow, 1975-76, Northern Ohio LIVE award of Achievement in Visual Arts, 1992, 1994, Hon. Lifetime Docent, Phoenix Art Mus., 1999; S.R. Guggenheim Mus. summer fellow, 1976, Coll. Art Assn. fellow, 1976. Mem. Internat. Assn. Art Critics, Coll. Art Assn. Office: San Antonio Mus Art 200 W Jones Ave San Antonio TX 78215 Home Phone: 210-455-6154; Office Phone: 210-978-8115. Business E-Mail: david.rubin@samuseum.org.

RUBIN, DONALD BRUCE, statistician, educator, research and development company executive; b. Washinton, Dec. 22, 1943; s. Allan A. and Harriet Rubin. AB magna cum laude, Princeton U., 1965; MS, Harvard U., 1966, PhD, 1970. Rsch. statistician Ednl. Testing Svc., Princeton, NJ, 1971-75, chmn. stats., 1975-79, sr. statis. advisor, 1979-81; pres. Datametrics Rsch. Inc., 1981—2008; prof. U. Chgo., 1982-84, Harvard U., Cambridge, Mass., 1984—, chmn. stats., 1985—94, 2000—02, John L. Loeb Prof. Stats., 2002—. Author: Handling Nonresponse in Sample Surveys by Multiple Imputation, 1980, Multiple Imputation for Nonresponse in Surveys, 1987, classic edit., 2004; author: (with others) Incomplete Data in Sample Surveys (Vol. 2): Theory and Bibliography, 1983; co-author: (with R.J.A. Little) Statistical Analysis With Missing Data, 1987, 2d edit., 2002, (with A. Gelman, J. Carlin. H. Stern) Bayasian Data Analysis, 1995, 2d edit., 2003, (with R. Rosenthal and R. Rosnow) Contrasts and Effect Sites in Behavioral Research: A Correlational Approach, 2000, Matched Sampling for Causal Effects, 2006; co-editor: (with P.W. Holland) Test Equating, 1982; contbr. over 300 articles to profl. jours. Recipient Parzen prize for statis. innovation, 1996; Woodrow Wilson Grad. fellow, 1965; NSF Grad. fellow, 1965, 68, John Simon Guggenheim fellow, 1977-78. Fellow AAAS (chmn. stats. 1992), Am. Statis. Assn. (editor jour. 1980-82, dir. 1980-82, statistician of yr. Boston chpt. 1995, Chgo. chpt. 2000, S.S. Wilks medal 1995), Inst. Math. Stats. (coun. mem. 1990-92, 99-2001, Fisher lectr. 2004), Von Humbolt Found.; mem. NAS (com. on nat. stats. 1989-92, mem. panel on confidentiality data 1989-92, panel on bilingual edn. 1990-92, working group on statis. analysis of com. on basic rsch. in behavioral and social scis. 1985-86, panel statis. in 21st century 1995, other coms.), Am. Acad. Arts and Sci., Biometric Soc., Internat. Assn. Survey Statisticians, Internat. Statis. Inst., Psychometric Soc., Royal Statis. Soc. Office: Harvard U Dept Statistics Cambridge MA 02138 Business E-Mail: rubin@stat.harvard.edu.

RUBIN, DOROTHY MOLLY, language educator, writer; b. NYC, Feb. 11, 1932; d. Harry and Clara (Schweller) Schleimer; m. Arthur I. Rubin, Aug. 24, 1950; children: Carol Anne, Sharon Anne. Student, CUNY, 1949—51; BA, Rutgers U., 1959, MEd, 1961; PhD in Ednl. Psychology, Johns Hopkins U., 1968. Tchr. NJ pub. schs., 1959—62; asst. prof. Coppin State Coll., Md., 1962—63, Towson State Coll., Md., 1963—66; adj. prof. Rollins Coll., Fla., 1968—69; assoc. prof. Coll. NJ, 1969—73, prof., 1973—2004, prof. emeritus, 2004—. Cons.Harper & Row, 1983; cons., spkr., columnist. Author: Teaching Elementary Language Arts, 1975, 6th edit., 2000, Gaining Word Power, 1978, 7th edit., 2006, 8th edit., 2009, The Vital Arts-Reading and Writing, 1979, Reading and Learning Power, 1980, 3d edit., 1991, The Teacher's Handbook of Reading-Thinking Exercises, 1980, The Primary-Grade Teacher's Language Arts Handbook, 1980, The Intermediate Grade Teacher's Language Arts Handbook, 1980, Gaining Sentence Power, 1981, The Teacher's Handbook of Primary-Grade Reading/Thinking Exercises, 1982;: Vocabulary Expansion, 1982, A Practical Approach to Teaching Reading, 1982, 2d edit., 1993, Diagnosis and Correction in Reading Instruction, 1982, 4th edit., 2002, Teaching Reading and Study Skills in Content Areas, 1983;: 2d edit., 1991, Writing and Reading: The Vital Arts, 2d edit., 1983, Power English: Basic Language Skills for Adults, 1989, rev. edit., 1990, Power Vocabulary: Basic Vocabulary for Adults, 1992—93, Comprehension Strategies for an Integrated Language Arts Classroom, 1994, Mind Bind, Moon Master, Quick Scramble, ednl. video games, Comprehension Strategies for an Integrated Language Arts Classroom, 1994, Teaching Elementary Language Arts: An Integrated Approach, 1995, 5th edit., 2000, Power Reading: Reading and Thinking Strategies for Adults, 1995, Phonics: Skills and Strategies in a Balanced Reading Program, 1998, Levels 1-4, Comprehension Skills and Strategies in a Balanced Reading Program, 1998,

Vocabulary Skills and Strategies in a Balanced Reading Program, 1998, Your Child Can Succeed in School: 100 Common-Sense Answers to Frequently Asked Questions, 1999, Writing and Thinking Skills: Sentence Writing, 2000, Writing and Thinking Skills: Paragraphs and Composition, 2000, Word Meaning & Reasoning Levels 1-3, 2000, Writing and Thinking Skills: Fun With Writing, 2001, One Year of Words: College Vocabulary Enhancement, 2004, Grammar and Usage: Simplified, 2005, Diagnosis and Improvement in Reading Instrn., 2007, (audio) Passport to Power English, 1987; contbr. articles to profl. jours.; syndicated columnist Word Games, columnist The Times, Trenton, NJ, Asbury Park Press, NJ. Recipient profl. awards. Mem.: Phi Kappa Phi, Nat. Coun. Tchrs. English, Internat. Reading Assn., Pi Lambda Theta, Kappa Delta Pi. Home and Office: 917 Stuart Rd Princeton NJ 08540-1212 Personal E-mail: drdorothyrubin@aol.com.

RUBIN, EDWARD, law educator, former dean; AB, Princeton U., 1969; JD, Yale U., 1979. Curriculum planner NYC Bd. Edn., 1970—76; law clk. to Hon. Jon O. Newman US Ct. Appeals (2nd cir.), 1979—80; assoc. Paul, Weiss, Rifkind, Wharton & Garrison, NYC; acting prof. U. Calif. Sch. Law, 1982—87, assoc. dean, 1989—92, prof., 1987—96, Richard W. Jennings Professor, 1996—98; prof. U. Pa. Law Sch., Phila., 1998—2005, Theodore K. Warner, Jr. prof. law, 2003—05; dean & John Wade-Kent Syverud prof. law Vanderbilt U. Law Sch., Nashville, 2005—09, prof. law, 2009—. Contbr. articles to law jours.; author: Beyond Camelot: Rethinking Politics and Law for the Modern State, 2005; co-author (with Malcolm Feeley): Federalism: A Theoretical Inquiry, 2005. Mem.: ABA, Am. Assn. Law Sch. Office: U Vanderbilt Law Sch Room 246 131 21st Ave South Rm 290 A Nashville TN 37203-1181 Office Phone: 615-322-9800. Office Fax: 215-573-2025, 615-322-5151. E-mail: ed.rubin@vanderbilt.edu.*

RUBIN, ELLEN, education/access consultant; d. Jack and Mary Elizabeth Rubin; m. Rami Gertler, Oct. 4, 1979 (div.). MS in Spl. Edn., Bank St. Coll. Edn., NYC, 1976, MS in Museum Edn., 2002. Cert. spl. edn. N-6 NY, 1977. Asst. tchr. Helen Keller Services for the Blind (formerly Indsl. Home for the Blind), NYC, 1966—68; rehab. tchr. Lighthouse for the Blind, Haifa, Israel, 1969—70; ednl. program coord. George Simmons Rehab. Ctr. for the Blind, Ministry Welfare, Beersheva, Israel, 1970—79; ednl. counselor Ben Gurion U. of the Negev, Beersheva, 1979—80; ednl. programming counselor Assn. for the Advancement of the Blind and Retarded, Inc., Jamaica, NY, 1981—82; spl. educator Early Intervention Programs, Guild for Exceptional Children, Bklyn., 1982—83; instr., cons., advisor Computer Ctr. for Visually Impaired People, Baruch Coll., NYC, 1983—2004; coord. disability programs Ednl. Equity Concepts, Inc., NYC, 1983—2004; part-time coord. internat. exch. programs Mobility Internat. USA, Eugene, Oreg., 1996—; access cons. St. Louis Sci. Ctr., 1996—. Lectr. Sch. Occupl. Therapy, U. Hosp., Hadassah Med. Ctr., Jerusalem, 1974—79; team lectr. Haifa U., Natanya, Israel, 1977—78; lectr. Ministry Welfare, Beersheva, 1978—80; adv. panel mem. Commrs. Adv. Panel for the Office Spl. Edn. Svcs., NY State Edn. Dept., Albany, 1982—97; adv. com. mem. Quality Improvement Ctr. for Diabilities, NYU, NYC, 1984—2001; adv. coun. mem. Interagency Coordinating Coun., NY State Health Dept., Albany, NY, 1988—92; bd. dirs. Creative Adaptations for Learning, Great Neck, NY, 1990—; cons./adv. com. mem. Programs and Svcs. for People With Disabilities, Lincoln Ctr. for the Performing Arts, NYC, 1993—; testing coord. Touch Graphics, Inc., NYC, 1996—; trainer in accessibility features Assn. Sci. and Tech. Ctrs., Washington, 1998—2004; cons. Smithsonian Instn., Washington, 1999—2000; guest lectr. mus. edn. Bank St. Coll. Edn., NYC, 2001—; Ams. with Disabilities Act cons. Wildlife Conservation Soc., NY Aquarium, Bklyn., 2002—03. Contbr. articles to profl. jours. Advisor disability adv. com. Taxi and Limousine Commn., NYC, 1996—2006; cmty. liaison Beth Israel Methadone Clinic, NYC, 2000—04. Recipient Cmty. Svc. award, Jewish Guild for the Blind, 1993, Access Builder award, Baruch Coll., CUNY, 2003. Personal E-mail: ellenr5@verizon.net.

RUBIN, GARY ANDREW, entrepreneur, computer engineer; s. Budd Email and Joanne Lee Rubin. BA in Math., U. Calif., Berkeley, 1978; MS in Computer Sci. & Engring., Stanford U., Palo Alto, Calif., 1982. Cert. instr. Cisco Sys., 1993, network assoc. Cisco Sys., 1996. Software engr., fed. sys. divsn. IBM, Houston, 1978—80, software engr., comm. products divsn. Palo Alto, Calif., 1982—86; software engr., network engr., competitive analyst ROLM Comm., Santa Clara, Calif., 1986—91; pres., founder Advanced Network Info., Inc., Santa Clara, 1992—. Mem.: Inst. Nautical Archaeology, ROLMan Forum Toastmasters (forum v.p. 1990—91, Competent Toastmaster award 1992), Young Entrepreneurs' Orgn. (chpt. mentorship chair, forum moderator 2005—07), Mensa. Achievements include development of the digital auto-pilot for the NASA space shuttle; design of General Motors' manufacturing automation protocol, common application service elements. Avocations: travel, archaeology, scuba diving. Home: 3567 Benton St #248 Santa Clara CA 95051 Office: Advanced Network Info Inc 530 Lakeside Dr Ste 200 Sunnyvale CA 94085 Business E-Mail: grubin@ani-training.com.

RUBIN, GERALD MAYER, biochemistry researcher, educator; b. Boston, Mar. 31, 1950; s. Benjamin H. and Edith (Weisberg) R.; m. Lynn S. Mastalir, May 7, 1978; 1 child, Alan F. BS, MIT, 1971; PhD in Molecular Biology, Cambridge U., Eng., 1974, ScD, 2002. Helen Hay Whitney Found. fellow Stanford U. Sch. Medicine, Calif., 1974-76; asst. prof. biol. chemistry Sidney Farber Cancer Inst.-Harvard U. Med. Sch., Boston, 1977-80; instructor, embryology Marine Biol. Lab., Woods Hole, Mass.; staff mem., dept. embryology Carnegie Instn. of Washington, Balt., 1980-83; John D. MacArthur prof. genetics, dept. molecular & cell biology U. Calif., Berkeley, 1983—2000, head, divsn. genetics, dept. molecular and cellular biology, 1987—95, HHMI investigator, 1987—2000, dir. Drosophila Genome Ctr., 1992—2006, prof. genetic dept. molecular & cell biology, 2000—09; v.p. biomedical rsch. Howard Hughes Med. Inst., Chevy Chase, Md., 2000—01, v.p., dir. planning Janelia Farm Rsch. Campus, Ashburn, Va., 2002—03, v.p., dir., 2003—. Adj. prof. dept. biochemistry and biophysics U. Calif. Sch. Medicine, San Francisco, 1987-; assoc. faculty mem., cell and molecular biology divsn. Lawrence Berkeley Nat. Lab., Calif.; mem. sci. adv. bd. Athena Neurosci., Inc., Tularik, Inc.; co-founder, chair sci. adv. bd. Exelixis Pharm., Inc. Predoctoral fellow, NSF, Helen Hay Whitney Found. Fellow; Recipient Young Scientist award Passano Found., 1983, Eli Lilly award in biol. chemistry, Am. Chem. Soc., 1985; co-recipient Newcomb Cleveland prize, AAAS, 2000, George W. Beadle Medal, Genetics Soc. Am., 2003; named Scientist of Yr., R&D Mag., 2006. Mem. AAAS, NAS (US Steel Found. award in molecular biology, 1985), Inst. Medicine, Genetics Soc. Am. Med., Phi Beta Kappa, Phi Lambda Epsilon, Royal Soc. UK (fgn.); Fellow Am. Acad. Arts & Sciences, Am. Acad. Microbiology. Office: Janelia Farm Rsch Campus Howard Hughes Med Inst 19700 Helix Dr Ashburn VA 20147-2408 Business E-Mail: rubing@janelia.hhmi.org.

RUBIN, GRETCHEN CRAFT, author; b. Kansas City, Mo. married; 2 children. Grad., Yale U., New Haven; JD, Yale Law Sch. Former law clerk to justice Sandra Day O'Connor US Supreme Ct.; former chief adv. to chmn. Reed Hundt FCC. Lectr. Yale Law Sch., Yale Sch. Mgmt. Author: Power Money Fame Sex, 2000, (biographies) Forty Ways to Look at Winston Churchill: A Brief Account of a Long Life, 2003, Forty Ways to Look at JFK, 2005, (essays) Profane Waste, 2006; founder (daily weblog) The Happiness Project, spkr. various radio talk shows. Personal E-mail: grubin@gretchenrubin.com.*

RUBIN, HARRY MEYER, software industry executive; b. NYC, Dec. 21, 1952; s. Martin J. and Helene Rubin; m. Cathy Hemery, May 26, 1990; children: Gabriella, James. BA, Stanford U., 1974; MBA, Harvard U., 1976. Investment banker Wertheim & Co., Inc., NYC, 1976-77; fin. mgr. Am. Airlines, Inc., NYC, 1977-79; dir. fin. planning-entertainment, electronics groups RCA Corp., NYC, 1979-81; CFO RCA Videodiscs, RCA Home Video, RCA Cable RCA Entertainment Group, NYC; v.p. strategic planning RCA Corp., NYC, group v.p. fin. and bus. affairs RCA entertainment ops., 1981-86; gen. mgr. Home Video Gen. Electric Co., 1986-87; v.p., gen. mgr. home video div. NBC, Inc., 1988-93; exec. v.p. GT Interactive Software Corp., 1994-98; pres. GT Interactive Internat., 1998-2000; pres. internat. Infogrames, Inc., 2000-01; sr. exec. v.p. and head of worldwide pub. Atari Inc., 2001—05, COO, 2004—05; chmn. Henmead Enterprises, Inc., 2005—. Dir. Image-Metrics PLC, Synthesis Energy Sys., Inc.; dir., co-head exec. com. RCA/Columbia Pictures Worldwide Video; founding ptnr. Samuel Adams Beer; founding dir. Arts and Entertainment Network. Mem.: 22 Club, Phi Beta Kappa. Avocations: travel, foreign languages. Home: 784 Park Ave New York NY 10021-3553 Personal E-mail: harry.rubin@gmail.com.

RUBIN, HERBERT, lawyer; b. Lisbon, Conn., June 4, 1918; s. Simon and Rose (Berko) R.; m. Rose Luttan, July 6, 1941; children: Barbara, Caroline, Donald. AB, CCNY, 1938; JD, NYU, 1942. Bar: N.Y. 1942, U.S. Dist. Ct. (so. and ea. dists.) N.Y. 1951, U.S. Supreme Ct. 1956, U.S. Ct. Appeals (2d, 3d, 4th, 6th, 9th, 10th, 11th and D.C. cirs.). Assoc. Newman & Bisco, 1942; faculty NYU Law Sch., 1946-50, 57-62; prof. creditors' rights Rutgers U. Law Sch., 1949-57; pvt. practice, 1946-56; ptnr. Sereni, Herzfeld & Rubin, and successor Herzfeld & Rubin, NYC, 1956—, sr. ptnr., 1968—. Instr. mil. law U.S. Army, 1944-46; prof. constl. law L.I. U., 1963-68; trustee North Shore L.I. Jewish Hosp. Editor-in-chief NYU Law Rev., 1940-41; bd. editors N.Y. Law Jour., 1971—; contbr. articles to profl. jours. Mem. N.Y. State Banking Bd., 1975-85, N.Y. State Jud. Selection Com., 1975-83, Sen. Moynihan's Jud. Selection Com., 1982-2000, Sen. Schumer's Jud. Selection Com., 1999—, City Charter Revision Commn., 1998-2001; trustee Am. Assn. Jewish Lawyers and Jurists. 1st lt. Signal Corps, AUS, 1942-46. Recipient award, NCCJ, 1967, United Jewish Appeal, 1968, 1997, Israel Bonds, 1973, NYU Law Assn. award, 1987, Judge Weinfeld award, NYU, 1992, Vanderbilt award, 1999, Business award, NYU Joint Disease Hosp., 2007. Fellow Am. Bar Found.; mem. ABA (mem. coun. N.Y. state), N.Y. State Bar Assn., Queens County Bar Assn. (pres. 1970), Assn. Bar City Of N.Y., Fed. Bar Coun., Jewish Lawyers Guild (award 2001). Office: Herzfeld & Rubin 40 Wall St Fl 54 New York NY 10005-2301 Office Phone: 212-471-8500. Office Fax: 212-232-6610. Business E-Mail: hrubin@herzfeldrubin.com.

RUBIN, J. PETER, plastic surgeon; b. Manhasset, NY, May 6, 1966; s. Leonard R. Rubin and Annette R. Dales; m. Julie A. Hutton, Dec. 28, 1989; children: Eliana Justine, Liviya Johanna, Zachary Jacob. BA, Grinnell Coll., Iowa, 1988; MD, Tufts U., Boston, 1992. Cert. Am. Bd. Surgery, 2000, Am. Bd. Plastic Surgery, 2004. Asst. prof. surgery U. Pitts., 2002—08, assoc. prof. surgery, 2008—, dir. Surg. Body Contouring Program, 2002—. Editor: (text book) Aesthetic Surgery After Massive Weight Loss, 2007 (Brit. Med. Assn. book award, 2007). Bd.chmn. Internat. Fedn. for Adipose Therapeutics and Sci., Pitts., 2004—08. Recipient Presdl. Early Career award, 2007; grantee, NIH, 2006—. Fellow: ACS; mem.: Alpha Omega Alpha. Office: U Pitts 3380 Blvd of the Allies Pittsburgh PA 15213 Office Phone: 412-641-9670.

RUBIN, JAY, retired literature and language professor; b. Washington, Nov. 15, 1941; AB, U. Chgo., 1963, PhD, 1970. Prof. Japanese lit. U. Wash., Seattle, 1975—93, Harvard U., Cambridge, Mass., 1993—2006. Translator: (novels) Sanshiro, The Wind-Up Bird Chronicle.

RUBIN, JOEL EDWARD, theatre consulting executive; b. Cleve., Sept. 5, 1928; s. Morris and Pearl (Jacobs) R.; m. Lucille Schutmaat, Dec. 18, 1953; children: Brian G., Jennifer L., Rebecca R. BS, Case Inst. of Tech., 1949; MFA, Yale U., 1951; PhD, Stanford U., 1960. Exec. v.p. Kliegl Bros. Lighting, NYC, 1954-85; prin. cons. Joel E. Rubin & Assocs., NYC, 1985-93; prin. cons. theater planning Artec Cons. Inc., NYC, 1993—2005; prin. cons. Joel E. Rubin & Assoc., NYC, 2005—. Co-author: Theatrical Lighting Practice 1954; author: Technological Development of Stage Lighting 1960. Member Coll. of Fellows of Am. Theatre, John F. Kennedy Ctr. for the Performing Arts, Washington. Recipient Golden Triaga, Prague Quadrennial, 1987, Zlatou medal, 1991, 1st time award Bus. Com. for the Arts, Forbes Mag., 1987; recipient Founders' award US Inst. for Theatre Tech., 1972, 79, Nat. award, 1990, Lifetime hon. membership award, 1996, Spl. citation, 1996; Dr. Joel E. Rubin Founder's award named in his honor US Inst. Theatre Tchrs., 2000; Internat. Student Rsch. grants established in his honor US Inst. Theatre Tchrs., 2000; nominee Entertainment Design Lifetime Achievement in Lighting, 2005 Fellow Am. Theatre Assn. (v.p. 1961-63), US Inst. of Theatre Technology (pres. 1963-64); mem. Am. Nat. Theatre Acad. (bd. dirs. 1971-75), Internat. Theatre Inst. of the US (bd. dirs. 1975-79), Nat. Coun. of Arts and Govt. (bd. dirs. 1975-79), Internat. Orgn. Theatre Architects and Scenographers (US chmn., rep. 1968-98, pres. 1971-79, Gold medal award 1996), Illuminating Engring. Soc. Avocations: collecting books, stage design, lincolniana. Home: 24 Edgewood Ave Hastings On Hudson NY 10706-2024 Office: Joel E Rubin and Assoc 119 W 57th St Ste 820 New York NY 10019 Office Phone: 212-757-5646. Personal E-mail: booksjoel@aol.com.

RUBIN, KENNETH H., psychology professor, writer; s. Sonia and Jerry Rubin; m. Margo A Rubin; children: Amy, Joshua. BA, McGill U., Montreal, 1968; MS, Pa. State U., State Coll., 1969, PhD, 1971. Asst. prof. U. Windsor, Ontario, Canada, 1971—73; prof. U. Waterloo, Ontario, 1973—95, U. Md., Coll. Pk., 1995—. Author: (book) The Friendship Factor (Gold award, 2002, Nat. Parenting Publications awards, 2002); editor: L'isolamento sociale durante l'infanzia (Social withdrawal in childhood), Handbook of Peer Interactions, Relationships, and Groups, Social and Emotional Development (Critical Concepts in Psychology). Volumes 1-4, Children's play, Peer relationships and social skills in childhood, The play of children: Current theory and research, Children's peer relations: Issues in assessment and intervention. (Joan Kershaw Publ. award, 1987), The development and treatment of childhood aggression, Social withdrawal, shyness, and inhibition in childhood, The friendship factor (Gold award, 2002), Parental Beliefs, Parenting, and Child Development in Cross-Cultural Perspective; contbr. articles to profl. jours. Recipient Internat. Soc. Study Behavioral Devel. award, Disting. Contributions Internat. Advancement Rsch. and Theory Behavioral Devel., Disting. Contbn. Knowledge award, Ont. Psychol. Found.; Sr. Rsch. fellowship, Ont. Mental Health Found., Killam Rsch. fellowship, Can. Coun. Fellow: APA, Assn. Psychol. Sci., Can. Psychol. Assn.; mem.: Soc. Rsch. Child Devel., Internat. Soc. Study Behavioral Devel. (pres. 1998—2002). Office: Univ Maryland 3304 Benjamin Bldg College Park MD 20742

RUBIN, LEWIS JOSEPH, physician, researcher; b. NYC, Aug. 5, 1950; s. Theodore and Erna Rubin; 1 child. BA, diploma in Hebraic studies, Yeshiva U., NYC, 1972; MD, Albert Einstein Coll. of Medicine, 1972—75. Am. Bd. Internal Medicine ABIM/ Wash., DC, 1978, diplomate Nat. Bd. Med. Examiners. Internship and residency Duke U. Med. Ctr., 1975—78, Am. Bd. Internal Med Medicine, 1980; assoc. in medicine Duke U., Durham, NC, 1978—79; assoc. prof. medicine U. Tex. Health Sci. Ctr., Dallas, 1980—84, 1984—85, U. Md., Balt., 1985—89, prof. medicine, 1989—98, dir. divsn. pulmonary medicine, 1985—98; prof. medicine U. Calif. San Diego, 1999—. Cons. in field. Contbr. more than 200 articles to sci. publs.;, editor 6 textbooks. Fellow: ACP, Am. Coll. Chest Physicians (bd. govs. 1997), Am. Heart Assn., Royal Coll. Physicians UK; mem.: Am. Soc. Clin. Investigation. Achievements include basic and clinical research in cardiopulmonary diseases, leading to drug developments and new treatments. Avocations: classical music, opera, travel. Home: 6404 Avenida Wilfredo La Jolla CA 92037 Office: U Calif San Diego Med Ctr 9300 Campus Point Drive #7381 La Jolla CA 92037-7381 Business E-Mail: ljrubin@ucsd.edu.

RUBIN, LOUIS DECIMUS, JR., retired language educator, writer, publishing executive; b. Charleston, SC, Nov. 19, 1923; s. Louis Decimus and Janet (Weinstein) R.; m. Eva M. Redfield, June 2, 1951; children: Robert Alden, William Louis. Student, Coll. of Charleston, 1940-42, LittD (hon.), 1989; AB, U. Richmond, 1946, LittD (hon.), 1972; MA, Johns Hopkins U., 1949, PhD, 1954; LittD (hon.), Clemson U., 1986, U. of the South, 1991, U. N.C. at Asheville, 1993, U. N.C., Chapel Hill, 1995. Instr. Johns Hopkins U.; editor Hopkins Rev., 1950-54; fellow criticism Sewanee Rev., 1953-54; exec. sec. Am. Studies Assn., asst. prof. Am. civilization U. Pa., 1954-56; assoc. editor Richmond (Va.) News Leader, 1956-57; assoc. prof. English Hollins Coll., 1957-60, prof., chmn. dept., 1960-67; prof. English U. N.C., 1967-73, Univ. Disting. prof., 1973-89, prof. emeritus, 1989—. Editor Hollins Critic, 1963-68; vis. prof. history La. State U., 1957; Fulbright lectr. U. Aix-Marseille, 1960; lectr. Breadloaf Writer's Conf., 1961; vis. prof. U. N.C., 1965, Harvard U., 1969; lectr. Am. studies seminars Kyoto (Japan) U., 1979; founder, pub., editl. dir. Algonquin Books Chapel Hill, 1982-91. Author: Thomas Wolfe: The Weather of His Youth, 1955, No Place on Earth, 1959, The Golden Weather, 1961, The Faraway Country, 1963, The Teller in the Tale, 1967, The Curious Death of the Novel, 1967, George W. Cable, 1969, The Writer in the South, 1972, William Elliott Shoots A Bear, 1975, Virginia: A History, 1977, The Wary Fugitives, 1978, Surfaces of a Diamond, 1981, A Gallery of Southerners, 1982, The Even-Tempered Angler, 1983, The Edge of the Swamp, 1989, The Algonquin Literary Quiz Book, 1990, The Mockingbird in the Gum Tree, 1991, Small Craft Advisory, 1991, The Heat of the Sun, 1995, Babe Ruth's Ghost, 1996, Seaports of the South, 1998, A Memory of Trains, 2000, An Honorable Estate, 2001, My Father's People, 2002, Where The Southern Cross the Yellow Dog: On Writers and Writing, 2005, The Summer The Archduke Died, 2008; editor: Southern Renascence, 1953, The Lasting, South, 1957, Teach the Freeman: R.B. Hayes and the Slater Fund for Negro Education, 1959, The Idea of an American Novel, 1961, South: Modern Southern Literature in Its Cultural Setting, 1961, Bibliographical Guide to the Study of Southern Literature, 1969, The Comic Imagination in American Literature, 1973, The Literary South, 1978, The American South, 1980, The History of Southern Literature, 1985, An Apple for My Teacher, 1987, A Writer's Companion, 1995, The Quotable Baseball Fanatic, 2000; co-editor: So. Lit. Jour., 1968-89; contbr. articles to periodicals. Served with AUS, 1943-46. Guggenheim fellow, 1958-59, fellow Am. Coun. Learned Socs., 1964, Fulbright fellow, Oliver Max Gardner award, Mayflower award, Disting. Virginian award, NC award for Lit., 1992, R. Hunt Parker Meml. award for lifetime contributions to NC lit. heritage, Academy award in Lit., Am. Acad. of Arts and Letters, 2004, Ivan Sandrof Lifetime Achievement award, Nat. Book Critics Cir., 2005, John Tyler Caldwell award for the Humanities, 2005, Authors Guild award, 2008. Fellow So. Writers (chancellor 1991-93); mem. Soc. Study So. Lit. (pres. 1975-76), Phi Beta Kappa.

RUBIN, MARILYN MARKS, economics professor; d. Jacob and Rebecca Marks; m. A. Michael Rubin; children: Jennifer Tannenbaum, David. BA, Douglass Coll., New Brunswick, NJ; MA, NYU, 1973, PhD, 1976. Asst. prof. William Paterson U., Wayne, NJ, 1973—76, NYU, 1976—80; assoc. prof. New Sch. Social Rsch., 1980—86; prof. John Jay Coll. CUNY, 1987—. Cons. NYC Office Dept. Mayor Econ. Devel., 1976—80, NYC Office Mgmt. & Budget, 1980—84, Urbanomics, Wayne, NJ, 1984—. Contbr. articles to profl.jours. Recipient Outstanding Academic award, NY Chpt. ASPA, 1992, Disting. Rsch. award, Sect. Women Pub. Adminstrn. ASPA, 2008, Sr. Svc. Specialist award, Fulbright Coun. Internat. Exch. Scholars, 2009. Fellow: Nat. Acad. Pub. Adminstrn.; mem.: ASPA, Assn. Budgeting & Fin. Mgmt. (chairperson 1995—96). Liberal. Jewish. Avocations: travel, walking. Home: 25 Vale Rd Wayne NJ 07470 Office: John Jay Coll CUNY 445 W 59th St New York NY 10019 Home Fax: 973-694-2935. Personal E-mail: mmr2@optonline.net. Business E-Mail: mrubin@jjay.cuny.edu.

RUBIN, MELVIN LYNNE, ophthalmologist, educator; b. San Francisco, May 10, 1932; s. Morris and May (Gelman) R.; m. Lorna Isen, June 21, 1953; children: Gabrielle, Daniel, Michael. AA, U. Calif., Berkeley, 1951, BS, 1953; MD, U. Calif., San Francisco, 1957; MS, State U. Iowa, 1961. Diplomate Am. Bd. Ophthalmology, 1963. Intern U. Calif. Hosp., San Francisco, 1957-58; resident in ophthalmology State U. Iowa, 1958-61; attending surgeon Georgetown U., Washington, 1961-63; asst. prof. surgery U. Fla. Med. Sch., Gainesville, 1963-66, assoc. prof. ophthalmology, 1966-67, prof. ophthalmology, 1967—97, prof. emeritus, 1997—, chmn. dept. ophthalmology, 1978-95, eminent scholar, 1989-97, eminent scholar emeritus, 1997. Author: Studies in Physiological Optics, 1965, Fundamentals of Visual Science, 1969, Optics for Clinicians, 1971, 2d edit., 1974, 25th ann. edit., 1995, The Fine Art of Prescribing Glasses, 1978, 3d edit., 2004; editor: Dictionary of Eye Terminology, 1984, 5th edit., 2006, Eye Care Notes, 1989, revised edit., 2001, Taking Care of Your Eyes, 2003; cons. editl. bd. Survey Ophthalmology; contbr. more than 100 articles to profl. jours. Co-founder Citizens for Pub. Schs., Inc., 1965, ProArteMusica Gainesville, Inc., 1969, pres., 1971-73; mem. Thomas Ctr. Adv. Bd. for the Arts, 1978-84, nat. sci. adv. bd. Helen Keller Eye Rsch. Found., 1989-96; bd. dirs. Hippodrome State Theater, 1981-87, Friends of Photography Ansel Adams Ctr., 1991-97, Friends of Classic 89 public radio, 2002-08, U. Fla. Found., 2005-, Friends of Music; trustee U. Fla. Performing Arts Ctr., 1995—2008; chmn. nat. art coun. U. Fla. Harn Mus. Art, 2005—; With USPHS, 1961-63. Recipient Best Med. Book for 1978 award Am. Med. Writers Assn., 1979, Shaler Richardson award for svc. to medicine Fla. Soc. Ophthalmology, 1995; M.L. Rubin Ann. Lectureship established in his honor by Fla. Soc. of Ophthalmology, 1993. Fellow ACS, Am. Acad. Ophthalmology (sec., dir. 1978-92, pres. 1988, Sr. Honor award 1987. Guest of Honor 1992), Found. Am. Acad. Ophthalmology (bd. trustees, 1988-95, chmn., 1992-94), Joint Commn. on Allied Health Pers. in Ophthalmology (Statesman of Yr. award 1987); mem. Assn.

Rsch. in Vision and Ophthalmology (trustee 1973-78, pres. 1979), Retina Soc., Macula Soc., Club Jules Gonin, NY Acad. Sci., Fla. Soc. Ophthalmology, Am. Ophthal. Soc. (coun. 1998-2002, chmn. 2002), Pan Am. Soc. Ophthalmology, Ophthalmic Photographers Soc., Alachua County Med. Soc., Fla. Med. Assn., AMA (editorial bd. Archives of Ophthalmology 1975-85), Sigma Xi, Alpha Omega Alpha., Phi Kappa Phi. Office: U Fla Med Ctr PO Box 100284 Gainesville FL 32610-0284 Office Phone: 352-273-8790. Business E-Mail: melrubin@eye.ufl.edu.

RUBIN, MICHAEL HARRY, lawyer, educator; BA with honors, Amherst Coll., 1972; JD, La. State U., 1975. Bar: La., 1975; U.S. Ct. Appeals (5th Cir.) 1975; U.S. Dist. Ct. (Mid., Ea. and We. Dists.) La., 1976; U.S. Supreme Ct., 1982. Ptnr. McGlinchey and Stafford, Baton Rouge, 1993—. Adj. prof. La. State U. Law Sch., 1976—, Tulane Law Sch., 1976—. Co-author and author 12 books, numerous law rev. articles. Recipient Gold medal award, Atlanta Found. for the Improvement of Justice, Burton award, Libr. of Congress, 2003. Address: 301 Main St Baton Rouge LA 70825

RUBIN, PHYLLIS GETZ, health association executive; b. NYC, Aug. 6, 1937; d. Joseph and Sylvia (Rosenberg) Getz; m. James Milton Rubin, Oct. 28, 1961; children: Felicia Sue, Andrea Faith. BA, Syracuse U., 1959; MA, Columbia U., 1961, Adelphi U., 1975. Physical edn. tchr. Hicksville (N.Y.) Pub. Schs., 1959-93; bd. dirs., pres. Assoc. Am. Acad. Allergy, Asthma and Immunology; owner JP Med Fit, 1997—, Phyllis Rubin, Ltd., A Med. Exercise Tng. Co., 1998—. Producer: (video) Aerobic Dancercise for Children, 1987. Bd. dir. COPAY, Great Neck, N.Y., 1986-91; v.p., sec. Pierpont Condominium Bd., 1986-90. Recipient Founder's Day award PTA, 1986. Mem.: N.Y. State Alliance for Health, Phys. Edn., REcreation and Dance (program spkr. 1984, 85, 93, v.p. Nassau zone 1987—2000, Zone Svc. award 1993). Avocations: tennis, reading, meditation, golf. Office Phone: 516-972-2342. E-mail: jpmedfit@aol.com.

RUBIN, RHEA JOYCE, library consultant; b. Chgo., June 14, 1950; d. Harold and Edith (Botkin) B.; m. Lawrence Berman, June 7, 1975; 1 child, Hannah Rubin Berman. BA, U. Wis., 1972, MA, 1973. Dir. Oreg. Regional Library for The Blind and Handicapped, Salem, 1976—78; libr. Nat. Coun. Aging, Inc., Washington, 1978—80; cons. Rubin Cons., Oakland, Calif., 1980—. Author: Using Bibliotherapy, 1978, Bibliotherapy Sourcebook, 1978; (with others) Challenge of Aging, 1983, (with others) Let's Talk About It: A Planners Manual, 1984, Working With Older Adults, 1987, 2d edit., 1988, 3d edit., 1990, Of a Certain Age: A Guide to Contemporary Fiction Featuring Older Adults, 1990, Intergenerational Library Programs: A How to Do It Manual, 1993, (with others) Libraries Inside: A Practical Guide for Prison Librarians, 1995, Humanities Programming: A How to Do It Manual, 1997, Defusing the Angry Patron: A How to Do It Manual, 2000, Planning Library Services for People with Disabilities, 2001, Demonstrating Results: Using Outcome Measurement, 2006; book reviewer Libr. Jour.; contbr. articles to profl. jours. Recipient Shaw award, 1980, Monroe award, 1992, Exceptional Svc. award, Assn. Specialized and Coop. Libr. Agys., 1993, 2006. Mem. ALA (chair numerous coms. 1972). Office: 5860 Heron Dr Oakland CA 94618-2628 Office Phone: 510-339-1274. E-mail: rhea@rheajoycerubin.org.

RUBIN, RICHARD ALLAN, lawyer; b. NYC, June 19, 1942; s. Louis Max and Ruth Ann (Goldman) R.; m. Susan Deborah Levitt, June 18, 1966; children: Karen, Jill. BS, Queens Coll., 1964; JD, Bklyn. Law Sch., 1967; LLM, NYU, 1968. Bar: N.Y. 1967. Assoc. Schwartz and Frank, NYC, 1968—69, Javits and Javits, NYC, 1969—71; ptnr. Wolf Haldenstein Adler Freeman Herz & Frank, NYC, 1972—76, Parker Chapin LLP, NYC, 1977—2000, Jenkens & Gilchrist, Parker Chapin LLP, NYC, 2001—05, Troutman Sanders LLP, 2005—. Lectr. Am. Mgmt. Assn., N.Y. State Bar Assn., N.Y.C. Bar Assn. Mem. ABA. Office Phone: 212-704-6130. Business E-Mail: rrubin@troutmansanders.com.

RUBIN, RICK (FREDERICK JAY RUBIN), recording industry executive; b. Long Beach, NY, Mar. 10, 1963; s. Mickey and Linda (Tomberg) Rubin. BFA, NYU, 1985. Owner, founding pres. Def Jam Recordings, NYC, 1984—88, Am. Recordings (formerly Def Am. Recordings), LA, 1988—. Composer: (songs) I Need a Beat, 1985, Rock the Bells, 1985, I Can't Live Without My Radio, 1985, Can You Rock It Like This, 1985, Fight for Your Right, 1986, Brass Monkey, 1986, It's Tricky, 1986, My Adidas, 1986, New Style, 1986, No Sleep Till Brooklyn, 1986, She's On It, 1986, Bite the Bullet, 1986, Raising Hell, 1986, You & Me, 1987, Goin' Back to Cali, 1987, That's a Lie, 1988, Cold Chillin' in the Spot, 1989, Jack the Ripper, 1989, Hemp Rally, 1993, Kaught in da Ak, 1993, It's a New Style, 1996, 4,3,2,1, 1997, State to State, 1997, Nowhere to Run, 1998, Squirrels, 1999, Super Dee Jay, 1999, 99 Problems, 2004, Busted in the Hood, 2004, Chavas, 2004; prodr.: (albums) Beavis & Butthead Experience, 1993, Working Class Hero: A Tribute to John Lennon, 1995, Chef & Friends: The Songs of South Park, 1998, Chef Aid: The South Park Album, 1998, Mr. Hankey's Christmas Classics, 1999, Essential Roy Orbison, 2006, (Slayer) Hell Awaits, 1985, Reign in Blood, 1986, South of Heaven, 1988, Seasons in the Abyss, 1990, Decade of Aggression, 1991, Divine Intervention, 1994, Serenity in Murder, 1995, Undisputed Attitude, 1996, Diabolus in Musica, 1998, God Hates Us All, 2001, Soundtrack to the Apocalypse, 2003, (Run-D.M.C.) King of Rock, 1985, Raising Hell, 1986, Tougher Than Leather, 1998, Together Forever, 1991, Greatest Hits, 2002, (LL Cool J) Radio, 1985, Walking with a Panther, 1989, All World, 1996, (Beastie Boys) Licensed to Ill, 1986, Sounds of Science, 1999, Solid Gold Hits, 2005, (The Cult) Electric, 1987, Electric Mixes, 1989, Wildflower, 1990, Pure Cult, 1993, Love Removal Machine, 1994, High Octane Cult, 1996, Rare Cult, 2000, (Danzig) Danzig, 1988, Danzig II: Lucifuge, 1990, Danzig III: How the Gods Kill, 1992, Dirty Black Summer, 1992, Thrall: Demonsweatlive, 1993, Danzig 4, 1994, (Andrew Dice Clay) Andrew Dice Clay, 1990, Day the Laughter Died, 1990, Dice Rules, 1990, 40 Too Long, 1993, (Red Hot Chili Peppers) Blood Sugar Sex Magik, 1991, Give It Away, 1991, What Hits!?, 1992, Plasma, 1994, One Hot Minute, 1995, Under the Covers, 1998, Californication, 1999, Live Rare Remix Box, 1999, One Hot Minute, 1999, Road Trippin', 2001, By the Way, 2002, Greatest Hits, 2003, Phenomenon, 2006, Stadium Arcadium, 2006, (Mick Jagger) Wandering Spirit, 1993, (Tom Petty & the Heartbreakers) Greatest Hits, 1993, Playback, 1995, Songs & Music from She's the One, 1996, Anthology, 2000, (Tom Petty) Wildflowers, 1994, You Don't Know How it Feels, 1994, (Joan Jett & the Blackhearts) Flashback, 1994, (Johnny Cash) American Recordings, 1994, Unchained, 1996, American III: Solitary Man, 2000, Love, 2000, Murder, 2000, American IV: The Man Comes Around, 2002, Unearthed, 2003, My Mother's Hymn Book, 2004, Legend of Johnny Cash, 2005, American V: A Hundred Highways, 2006, (Johnny Cash & Willie Nelson) VH1 Storytellers, 1998, (Nine Inch Nails) Further Down the Spiral, 1995, Downward Spiral, 2004, (Donovan) Sutras, 1996, Try for the Sun, 2005, (Sheryl Crow) Globe Sessions, 1998, Sweet Child O'Mine, 1999, (System of a Down) System of a Down, 1998, Sugar, 1999, Chop Suey, 2001, Toxicity, 2001, Steal This Album!, 2002, Hypnotize, 2005, Mezmerize, 2005, (Rage Against the Machine) Renegades, 2000, Live at the Grand Olympic Auditorium, 2003, (Paloalto) Paloalto, 2000, Sonny, 2000, Heroes & Villains, 2003, (Aerosmith) Young Lust, 2001, O, Yeah!, 2002, Gold, 2005, (Krishna Das) Breath of the Heart, 2001, Door of Faith, 2003, (Audioslave) Audioslave, 2002, Doesn't Remind Me, 2005, Out of Exile, 2005, (Jay-Z) Black Album, 2003, (Jay-Z & Linkin Park) Collision Course, 2004, (Limp Bizkit) Eat You Alive, 2003, Results May Vary, 2003, Greatest Hitz, 2005, (The Mars Volta) De-Loused in the Comatorium, 2003, Intertiatic ESP, 2004, Televators, 2004, (Metallica) Death Magnetic, 2008, (Neil Diamond) 12 Songs, 2005, Home Before Dark, 2008, (Ozzy Osbourne) Prince of Darkness, 2005, (Dixie Chicks) Taking the Long Way, 2006 (Record of Yr. for Not Ready to Make Nice, Album of Yr., Grammy awards, 2007); exec. prodr. (Public Enemy) Yo! Bum Rush the Show, 1987, It Takes a Nation of Millions to Hold Us Back, 1988, Power to the People & the Beats, 2005, (Shakira) Don't Bother, 2005, Fijación Oral, Vol. 1, 2005, Oral Fixation, Vol. 2, 2005, (Sir Mix-A-Lot) Mack Daddy, 1992, Chief Boot Knocka, 1994, Jump On It, 1996, Return of the Bumpasaurus, 1996; prodr.: (soundtracks) Krush Groove, 1985, Less Than Zero, 1987, Marked for Death, 1990, Cool World, 1992, Wayne's World, 1992, Coneheads, 1993, Judgment Night, 1993, Last Action Hero, 1993, Party Girl, 1995, Mortal Kombat, 1996, Twister, 1996, I Know What You Did Last Summer, 1997, Jackie Brown, 1997, Private Parts, 1997, Can't Hardly Wait, 1998, Small Soldiers, 1998, Big Daddy, 1998, Human Traffic, 1999, Blair Witch 2, 2000, Heavy Metal 2000, 2000, Little Nicky, 2000, Scream 3, 2000, Jackass, 2001, Shallow Hal, 2001, Scorpion King, 2002, Spider-Man, 2002, Osbourne Family Album, 2002, Collateral, 2004, Kill Bill Vol. 2, 2004, Resident Evil: Apocalypse, 2004, Spider-Man 2, 2004, One Tree Hill, Vol. 2, 2006, Underworld: Evolution, 2006; actor: (films) Krush Groove, 1985, Men Don't Leave, 1990; writer, dir., actor (films) Tougher Than Leather, 1988. Recipient Joel Weber award, New Music Seminar, 1990, Best Visionary award, Esquire Esky Music Awards, 2006, Grammy award for Non-Classical Prodr. of Yr., 2007, 2009; named Hot Prodr. of Yr., Rolling Stone mag., 1988; named one of The World's Most Influential People, TIME mag., 2007. Office Phone: 818-223-8030.*

RUBIN, ROBERT EDWARD, former diversified financial services company executive, former United States Secretary of the Treasury; b. NYC, Aug. 29, 1938; s. Alexander and Sylvia (Seiderman) R.; m. Judith Leah Oxenberg, Mar. 27, 1963; children: James Samuel, Philip Matthew. AB in Econ. (summa cum laude), Harvard U., 1960; postgrad., London Sch. Econs., 1960-61; LLB, Yale U., 1964; DHL (hon.), Yeshiva U., 1996. Bar: N.Y. 1965. Assoc. Cleary, Gottlieb, Steen & Hamilton, NYC, 1964-66, Goldman, Sachs & Co., NYC, 1966-70, ptnr., 1971, mem. mgmt. com., 1980, vice chmn., co-COO, 1987-90, co-sr. ptnr., co-chmn., 1990-92; asst. to Pres. for econ. policy The White House, Washington, 1993-95; dir. The Nat. Econ. Coun., Washington, 1993—95; sec. US Dept. Treasury, Washington, 1995-99; chmn. exec. com. Citigroup, Inc., NYC, 1999—2008, interim chmn., 2007, sr. counselor, 2008—09; vice chmn. Coun. Fgn. Relations, Washington, 2003—. Mem. Pres.'s Adv. Com. for Trade Negotiations, Washington, 1980-82, mem. adv. com. on tender offers SEC, Washington, 1983, Gov.'s Commn. on Trade Competitiveness, 1987, regulatory adv. com. N.Y. Stock Exch., 1988-90, adv. com. internat. capital markets Fed. Res. Bank N.Y., 1989-93, Securities and Exch. Commn. Market Oversight and Fin. Svcs. Adv. Com., 1991-93, Gov.'s Adv. Panel on Fin. Svcs., 1988-89; ptnr., bd. dirs. N.Y.C. Partnership Inc., 1991-93; bd. dirs. Ctr. for Nat. Policy, 1982-93, vice chmn., 1984; bd. dirs. N.Y. Futures Exch., N.Y.C., 1979-85, Chgo. Bd. Options Exch. Inc., 1972-76, Citigroup Inc., 1999-2009, Ford Motor Co., 2000-06; bd. trustees Mt. Sinai Hosp., 1977, vice chmn., 1986; trustee Sta. WNET-TV, 1985-93, Carnegie Corp. of N.Y., 1990-93; mem. Mayor's Coun. Econ. Advisors, 1990, Gov.'s Coun. on Fiscal and Econ. Priorities, 1990-92; mem. advisory bd., Insight Venrure Partners, 2000- Author (with Jacob Weisberg): In an Uncertain World: Tough Choices from Wall Street to Washington, 2003 (named one of Ten Best Bus. Books, Bus. Week, 2003). Trustee Am. Ballet Theatre Found., Inc., N.Y.C., 1969-93, trustee Collegiate Sch., 1978-84; mem. bd. overseers' com. to visit econs. dept. Harvard U., 1981-87, com. on univ. resources, 1987-92; mem. fin. com. N.Y. campaign Mondale for Pres., 1983-84; mem. investment adv. coun. N.Y.C. Pension Fund, 1980-89; chmn. Dem. Congl. Dinner, Washington, 1982; Dems. for the 80s, 1985-89, Dems. for the 90s, 1989-90; chmn. N.Y.C. host com. 1992 Dem. Conv., 1989-92; mem. Commn. Nat. Elections. Recipient award Nat. Assn. Christians and Jews, N.Y.C., 1977, Disting. Leadership in Govt. award Columbia Bus. Sch., 1996, Euromoney Mag. award Fin. Min. Yr., 1996, Medal for High Civic Svc. award Citizens' Budget Com., 1997, Fgn. Policy Assn. medal, 1998, "Chmn." award Washington Greater Boys/Girls Clubs, 1998, Intrepid Sea Air Space Mus. award, 1998, Jefferson award Am. Inst. Pub. Svc., 1998, Award of Merit Yale U., 1998, Global Leadership award UN Assn., 1998, Paul Tsongas award, 1998. Mem. Phi Beta Kappa, Harvard Club (N.Y.C.), Century Country Club (Purchase, N.Y.). Democrat. Jewish.*

RUBIN, ROBERT JOSEPH, internist, nephrologist, consultant; b. Bklyn., Feb. 7, 1946; s. B. Norman and Suzanne (Fried) R.; m. Fran Auerbach, June 14, 1970; children: Elyse Beth, David Jon. AB, Williams Coll., 1966; MD, Cornell U., 1970. Diplomate Am. Bd. Internal Medicine, Nephrology. Intern New England Med. Ctr. Hosps., Boston, 1970-71, resident, 1971-72, 74-76; epidemic intelligence officer, respiratory disease and spl. pathogens, divsn. viral diseases Ctr. for Disease Control, 1972-74; asst. dean govt. affairs Tufts U., 1979-84, assoc. prof. medicine, 1981-84. Chief renal divsn. Lemuel Shattuck Hosp., Boston, 1979-81; asst. sec. planning and evaluation U.S. HHS, Washington, 1981-84; clin. assoc. prof. Georgetown U., Washington, 1984-95, clin. prof., 1995—; exec. v.p. ICF, Inc., 1984-88; pres. Health and Scis. Internat., 1988-92, Lewin ICF Inc., 1992, Lewin-VHI, Inc., 1992-96, Lewin Group, 1996-99, CEO, 1999-2001. Contbr. articles to profl. jours. With USPHS, 1972-74, asst. surgeon gen., 1981-84. Robert Wood Johnson Health Policy fellow, 1977 Mem. ACP, AMA, Am. Soc. Nephrology, Internat. Soc. Nephrology, Mass. Med. Soc., Kenwood Club, Potomac Club, Williams Club, Phi Beta Kappa. Republican. Jewish.

RUBIN, ROBERT SAMUEL, investment banker; b. Boston, Sept. 22, 1931; s. Jesse Abraham and Rose (Solomon) R.; m. Martha Lucy Adams, Dec. 15, 1956; children: Rebecca, David, James, Nathaniel. BA, Yale U., 1953; MBA, Harvard Coll., 1955. With Lehman Bros., 1958-70, ptnr., 1967-70; mng. dir., bd. dirs. Lehman Bros. Kuhn Loeb, Inc., NYC, 1970-84; mng. dir. Salomon Smith Barney, Inc., NYC, 1989—2001; sr. v.p. Bank One (now J.P. Morgan Chase), 2002—. Trustee Bklyn. Mus. 2d lt. US Army, 1955—58. Home: 218 Columbia Hts Brooklyn NY 11201-2105 Office: JP Morgan Chase 320 Park Ave New York NY 10022

RUBIN, ROBERT TERRY, psychiatrist, researcher, educator; b. LA, Aug. 26, 1936; s. Joseph Salem and Lorraine Grace (Baum) R.; m. Lynne Esther Mathews, Mar. 10, 1962 (div. Dec. 1980); children: Deborah, Sharon, Rachel; m. Ada Joan Mickas, Jan. 18, 1985. AB in premedical studies, UCLA, 1957; MD, U. Calif., San Francisco, 1961; PhD in physiology, U. So. Calif., 1977. Diplomate Am. Bd. Psychiatry and Neurology. Intern Phila. Gen. Hosp., 1961-62; resident in psychiatry Sch. Medicine UCLA, 1962-65, asst. prof. psychiatry, 1965-71, prof. psychiatry, 1972; prof. Pa. State U., Hershey, 1972-93; prof. neurosci. Coll. Medicine Drexel U., Pitts., 1992—2006, prof. psychiatry, dir. Ctr. Neurosci. Rsch. Allegheny Campus, 1992—2005; prof. psychiatry UCLA Sch. Medicine, 2005—; chief dept. psychiatry & mental health VA Greater LA Healthcare System, 2005—. Cons. Naval Health Rsch. Ctr., San Diego, 1969-70; mem. Brain Rsch. Inst. UCLA, 1969—89; assoc. dir. Pitts. Tissue Engring. Initiative, 1994-2004; trustee Kinsey Inst. Sex Rsch., Ind. U., 1986-90. Contbr. articles to profl. jours. With USNR, 1967—69. Recipient Rsch. Sci. Devel. awards NIMH, 1972-77, Rsch. Scientist award, 1982, 87, 93. Fellow: AAAS, Am. Coll. Psychiatrists, Am. Psychiat. Assn.; mem.: Internat. Soc. Psychoneuroendocrinology (pres. 1984—87). Avocations: swimming, bagpiping. Office: VA Greater LA Healthcare System Dept of Psychiatry 116A 11301 Wilshire Blvd Los Angeles CA 90073 Home Phone: 310-231-0380; Office Phone: 310-268-3319. Business E-Mail: robert.rubin@va.gov.

RUBIN, ROSE MOHR, economics professor; b. Montgomery, Ala., Nov. 20, 1939; d. Michael and Bernice (Solomon) Mohr; m. Richard M. Rubin, June 20, 1963; children: Mark, Debra. BS, Wellesley Coll., 1961; MA, Emory U., 1966; PhD, Kans. State U., 1968. Economist OEA, State of Kans., Manhattan, 1969-70; asst. prof. Miss. State U., Starkville, 1970-77; resident in pub. svc. NSF, Fort Worth, 1980-81; asst. prof. econs. U. North Tex., Denton, 1977-84, assoc. prof., 1984-90, prof., 1990-94; chair dept. econs. U. Memphis, 1994-96, prof. econs., 1996—. Faculty fellow Johns Hopkins U., Balt., 1986-87; vis. fellow Brookings Inst., Washington, 1987; rsch. fellow, Urban Child Inst., Memphis, 2007-. Bd. dirs. Vis. Nurses Assn., Ft. Worth, 1987-90, Temple Beth El, Ft. Worth, 1988-91, Plough Towers, Memphis, 1998-2004, 08-; adv. coun. Commn. Aging, 2008-. Assoc. Danforth Found., 1981-87; grantee Robert Wood Johnson Found., 1987-88, Andrus Found. grantee Am. Assn. Ret. Persons, 1990-94, Urban Child Inst., 2007-08. Mem.: Mo. Valley Econs. Assn. (bd. dirs. 1998—), Midsouth Acad. Econs. and Fin. (exec. bd. 1983—87, v.p. 1991—92), Assn. for Social Econs. (exec. coun. 1988—90), Southwestern Social Sci. Assn. (treas. 1990—93, v.p. 1998—, pres. 2000—01), Southwestern Econs. Assn. (treas. 1981—89, v.p. 1989—99, pres.-elect 1990—91, pres. 1991—92), Phi Kappa Phi, Omicron Delta Epsilon, Golden Key (hon.), Phi Chi Theta (hon.). Office: U Memphis Fogel Coll Bus Dept Econs Memphis TN 38152-0001

RUBIN, SAMUEL HAROLD, internist, consultant; b. NYC, July 24, 1916; s. Joseph and Esther (Goldfarb) R.; m. Audrey Arndt, Nov. 20, 1943; children: James E., David A. AB, Brown U., 1938; MD, St. Louis U., 1943; MS, U. Chgo., 1957; DSc (hon.), N.Y. Med. Coll., 1997. Diplomate: Am. Bd. Internal Medicine. Intern Jewish Hosp., St. Louis, 1943-44; resident St. Louis U. Group Hosp., 1944-45, St. Mary's Hosp., Kansas City, Mo., 1945-46; practice medicine Asbury Park, NJ, 1948-61; vol. faculty mem. N.Y. Med. Coll., 1948-61, assoc. prof. dept. medicine, 1962-65, prof., 1965—, dir. Inst. Human Values in Med. Ethics, 1984-86; chief med. service N.Y. Med. Coll.-Met. Hosp. Center, 1966-71, assoc. dean, 1971-72, exec. dean, 1972-74, dean, v.p. acad. affairs, 1975, provost, dean, 1977-83, provost, dean emeritus, 1983—, cons., 1983—. Mem. bd. trustees St. Clares' Hosp., N.Y.C., 1985-2000, N.Y. Med. Coll., 1988-94. Contbr. articles to med. jours. With M.C. AUS, 1946-48. NIH program dir. grantee, 1966-71 Fellow A.C.P.; mem. N.Y. Acad. Sci. Home: 425E Heritage Hills Dr Somers NY 10589-1912

RUBIN, SANDRA MENDELSOHN, artist; b. Santa Monica, Calif., Nov. 7, 1947; d. Murry and Freda (Atliss) Mendelsohn; m. Stephen Edward Rubin, Aug. 6, 1966. BA, UCLA, 1976, MFA, 1979. Instr. Art Ctr. Coll. Design, Pasadena, Calif., 1980, UCLA, 1981. One-woman exhbns. include LA Louver Gallery, 1982, 92, 2003, 07, LA County Mus. Art, 1985, Fischer Fine Arts, London, 1985, Claude Bernard Gallery, NYC, 1987; group exhbns. include LA County Mus. Art, 1977, 82, 83, LA Mcpl. Art Gallery, 1977, 83, 93, LA Contemporary Exhbns., 1978, LA Inst. Contemporary Arts, 1978, Newport Harbor Art Mus., Newport Beach, Calif., 1981, Odyssia Gallery, NYC, 1981, Nagoya City Mus., Japan, 1982, Long Beach Mus. Art, Calif., 1982, Brooke Alexander Gallery, NYC, 1982, Laguna Beach Mus. Art, Calif., 1982, Jan Baum Gallery, LA, 1984, San Francisco Mus. Art, 1986, Claude Bernard Gallery, NYC, 1986, Struve Gallery, Chgo., 1987, Boise Mus., Idaho, 1988, Judy Youen's Gallery, London, 1988, Tatistscheff Gallery, Inc., Santa Monica, Calif., 1989, Tortue Gallery, Santa Monica, 1990, Contemporary Arts Forum, Santa Barbara, Calif., 1990, San Diego Mus. Art, 1991, Fresno Met. Mus., Calif., 1992, Jack Rutberg Fine Arts, LA, 1993, San Jose Mus. Art, 2003, Pasadena Mus. Calif. Art, 2004, LA Louver at Art 38, Basel, Switzerland, 2007, Place in Time: Contemporary Landscape, Scripps Coll., 2008 Recipient Young Talent Purchase award LA County Mus. Art, 1980; Artist's Fellowship grant NEA, 1981, 91. Avocations: gardening, exercise, reading, singing. E-mail: smr@pacific.net.

RUBIN, STANLEY CREAMER, television producer, film producer; b. NYC, Oct. 8, 1917; s. Michael Isaac and Anne (Creamer) R.; m. Elizabeth Margaret von Gerkan (actress Kathleen Hughes), July 25, 1954; children: John, Chris (dec.), Angela, Michael. Student, UCLA, 1933-37, BA, 2006. Writer Universal Studios, Universal City, Calif., 1940-42, Columbia Pictures, Los Angeles, 1946-47; writer, producer NBC-TV, Burbank, Calif., 1948-49; theatrical film producer various studios, 1949-55, Rastar Prodns., Columbia Pictures, 1988-91; TV producer CBS-TV, Los Angeles, 1956-59, Universal Studios, Universal City, 1960-63, 20th Century-Fox, Los Angeles, 1967-71, MGM Studios, Culver City, Calif., 1972-77; pres. TBA Prodns., Los Angeles, 1978—. Producer theatrical films including The Narrow Margin, 1950, My Pal Gus, 1950, Destination Gobi, 1951, River of No Return, 1952, Promise Her Anything, 1966, The President's Analyst, 1967, Revenge, 1989; co-producer White Hunter, Black Heart, 1990; TV prodns. include G.E. Theatre, 1959-63, Ghost and Mrs. Muir, 1968-69, Bracken's World, 1969-71; writer, producer TV film The Diamond Necklace, 1948 (Emmy award 1949); producer TV films including Babe, 1975 (Hollywood Fgn. Press Golden Globe award, Christopher medal), And Your Name is Jonah, 1978 (Christopher medal 1979), The Story of Satchel Paige, 1980 (Image award 1981); exec. producer TV prodn. Escape from Iran: The Canadian Caper, 1981. Producer spl. programming Dem. Nat. Conv., San Francisco, 1984, Columbia Pictures and Rastar Prodns., 1988-91. 1st lt. USAAF, 1942-46. Mem. Writers Guild Am. (dir. 1941-42), Producers Guild Am. (bd. dirs. 1968-74, pres. 1974-79, v.p. 1987-94, bd. dirs. 1994-2000), Acad. Motion Picture Arts and Scis., Acad. TV Arts and Scis. (bd. govs. 1971, 73), Phi Beta Kappa. Home and Office: 8818 Rising Glen Pl Los Angeles CA 90069-1222 E-mail: tbaprez@aol.com. *I'm still too young to sum up my life, but here's a thought in progress: Stay curious.*

RUBIN, STEPHEN CURTIS, gynecologic oncologist, educator; b. Phila., May 24, 1951; s. Alan and Helen (Metz) R.; m. Anne Loughran, May 30, 1985; children: Michael, Elisabeth. BS, Franklin & Marshall U., 1972; MD, U. Pa., 1976. Diplomate Am. Bd. Ob-gyn. (dir. divsn. gynecol. oncology 2005—), Nat. Bd. Med. Examiners. Intern in ob-gyn. U. Pa. Hosp., Phila., 1976—77, residency in ob-gyn., 1977—80, fellow in gynecologic oncology, 1980—92; asst. prof. ob-gyn. Med. Coll. Pa., Phila., 1982-85, dir. surg. gynecology, 1982-85, chief gynecol. oncology, 1984-85; asst. mem. gynecol. staff Meml. Sloan-Kettering Hosp., NYC, 1985—90, assoc. mem., 1990—93; asst. prof. ob-gyn Cornell U. Med.

Coll., 1985—90, assoc. prof., 1990—93; prof. ob-gyn., chief gynecologic oncology U. Pa., Phila., 1993—, Franklin Payne prof., gyn. oncology, 2003—. Editor: Ovarian Cancer, Cervical Cancer, Chemotherapy of Gynecologic Cancer, Uterine Cancer; contbr. over 250 articles to profl. publs. Recipient Career Devel. award Am. Cancer Soc., 1987, Boyer award Meml. Sloan-Kettering; grantee Nat. Cancer Inst., 1991, 96, 98, 99. Mem. ACS, ACOG, Am. Soc. Clin. Oncology, Soc. Gynecol. Oncologists (Pres.'s award 1993), Am. Gynecol. and Obstet. Soc., Soc. Gynecologic Investigation, Soc. Pelvic Surgeons, Gynecol. Cancer Found. (Karin Smith award 1996), Am. Bd. Ob-gyn. (mem. exec. com. 2008-, chair, subspecialist com. 2008). Office: Univ Pa Med Ctr 3400 Civic Ctr Blvd Philadelphia PA 19104-4206 Office Phone: 215-662-3318.

RUBIN, STEVEN D., lawyer; b. June 1, 1960; BA in Econs., Tulane U., 1982; JD with honors, U. Fla., 1986. Bar: Fla. 1986. Assoc. Stearns, Weaver, Miller, Weissler, Alhadeff & Sitterson, 1986—91, shareholder, 1991—2000, dir., 1998—2000; sr. v.p., gen. counsel Telergy, Inc., 2000—01, Ivax Corp., Miami, 2001—. Office: Ivax Corp 4400 Biscayne Blvd Miami FL 33137 Office Phone: 305-575-6000. Office Fax: 305-575-6055. E-mail: steven_rubin@ivax.com.

RUBIN, STUART HARVEY, computer science educator, researcher; b. NYC, Mar. 18, 1954; s. Jack and Rhoda Rochelle Rubin. BS, U. R.I., 1975; MS in Indsl. and Systems Engrng., Ohio U., 1977; MS, Rutgers U., 1980; PhD, Lehigh U., 1988. Lectr. U. Cin., 1977—78; electronic engr. U.S. Army Rsch. Labs., Ft. Monmouth, NJ, 1980—83; assoc. prof. computer sci. Ctrl. Mich. U., Mt. Pleasant, 1988—2002, assoc. prof., 1996—, founder, dir. Ctr. Intelligent Sys., 1990—2002. Tech. cons. RCA, Princeton, N.J., 1982-83, Babcock and Wilcox Corp., Alliance, Ohio, 1990, Booz-Allen and Hamilton, Inc., San Diego, 1990-91, Adept Tech., San Jose, Calif., 1990-91; mem. rsch. coun. Scripps Clin.; cons. USAF, 1995. Contbr. articles to profl. jours.; inventor in field. Agt. United Fund Isabella County, Mt. Pleasant, 1988; supporting coach Mich. Spl. Olympics, Mt. Pleasant, 1990; event capt. San Diego Regional Sci. Olympic Competition, 1990, 92; judge 37th-51st, Ann. Greater San Diego Sci. and Engrng. Fairs, 1991-2009, judge 52nd, 2009. Recipient Am. Chem. Soc. award, 1972, U.S. Govt. Cert. Merit, Washington, 1987, Letter Appreciation, Gen. Charles C. McDonald, 1990; grantee NSF, Office Naval Tech., State of Mich., others, 1988—. Mem. IEEE (sr., founder, gen. chair Info. Reuse and Integration conf.), Am. Assn. Artificial Intelligence, Am. Soc. Engrng. Edn. (ONT post-doctoral fellow 1990-93), N.Y. Acad. Scis., Internat. Assn. Knowledge Engrs., Assn. for Computer Machinery. Avocations: boating, skiing, hiking and nature. Home: 1542 La Playa Ave # 4-208 San Diego CA 92109-6328 Office Phone: 619-553-3554. Business E-Mail: stuart.rubin@navy.mil.

RUBIN, THEODORE ISAAC, psychiatrist, writer; b. Bklyn., Apr. 11, 1923; s. Nathan and Esther (Marcus) R.; m. Eleanor Katz, June 16, 1946; children: Jeffrey, Trudy, Eugene. BA, Bklyn. Coll., 1946; MD, U. Lausanne, Switzerland, 1951; grad., Am. Inst. Psychoanalysis, 1964. Resident psychiatrist Los Angeles VA Hosp., 1953, Rockland State Hosp., NY, 1954, Bklyn. State Hosp., 1955, Kings County Hosp., NY, 1956; chief psychiatrist Women's House of Detention, NYC, 1957; mem. faculty Downstate Med. Sch., NY State U., 1957-59; pvt. practice NYC, 1956—. Tng. and supervising psychoanalyst Am. Inst. for Psychoanalysis of Karen Horney Clinic and Ctr.; mem. faculty Am. Inst. Psychoanalysis, 1962—; pres. emeritus bd. trustees Am. Inst. Psychoanalysis. Author: Jordi, 1960, Lisa and David, 1961, Sweet Daddy, 1963, In The Life, 1964, Platzo and the Mexican Pony Rider, 1965, The Thin Book by a Formerly Fat Psychiatrist, 1966, The 29th Summer, 1966, Cat, 1966, Coming Out, 1967, The Winner's Note Book, 1967, The Angry Book, 1969, Forever Thin, 1970, Emergency Room Diary, 1972, Doctor Rubin Please Make Me Happy, 1974, Shrink, 1974, Compassion and Self-Hate, An Alternative to Despair, 1975, Love Me, Love My Fool, 1976, Reflections in a Goldfish Tank, 1977, Alive and Fat and Thinning in America, 1978, Reconciliations, 1980, Through My Own Eyes, 1982, One to One, Understanding Personal Relationships, 1983, Not to Worry, The American Family Book of Mental Health, 1984, Overcoming Indecisiveness, 1985, Lisa and David, The Story Continues, 1986, Miracle at Bellevue, 1986, Real Love, 1990, Child Potential, 1990, Anti-Semitism: A Disease of the Mind, 1990, Little Ralphie and The Creature, 1998; mem. editl. bd. Am. Jour. Psychoanalysis; also articles, columns.; co-writer (TV movie) Lisa and David, 1998. Served as officer USNR, World War II. Recipient Adolf Meyer award, Assn. Improvement Mental Health, 1963. Fellow Am. Acad. Psychoanalysis; mem. NY County Med. Soc., Am. Psychiat. Assn., Assn. Advancement Psychoanalysis, Authors Guild, Contemporary Authors, Writers Guild East. Office: 141 E 55th St Ste 9B New York NY 10022 Office Phone: 917-301-4889.

RUBIN, ZICK, lawyer, writer, psychology professor; b. NYC, Apr. 29, 1944; s. Eli and Adena Rubin; m. Carol Moses, June 21, 1969; children: Elihu James, Noam Moses BA, Yale U., 1965; PhD, U. Mich., 1969; JD, Harvard U., 1988. Bar: Mass., 1988. Asst. to assoc. prof. Harvard U., Cambridge, Mass., 1969—76; Louis and Frances Salvage prof. social psychology Brandeis U., Waltham, Mass., 1976—89; law clk. chief judge U.S. Ct. Appeals (1st cir.), 1988—89; assoc. Palmer & Dodge, Boston, 1990—93, counsel, 1994—2001; of counsel Hill & Barlow, Boston, 2001—03; prin. Law Office of Zick Rubin, Boston, 2003—. Chmn. com. behavioral scis. Yale U. Coun., New Haven, 1981-86. Author: Liking and Loving, 1973, Children's Friendships, 1980; co-author: Psychology, 1993; editor: Doing Unto Others, 1974, Relationships and Development, 1986; contbg. editor: Psychology Today, 1980-85; mem. editl. bd. Harvard Law Rev., 1986-88. Recipient Socio-Psychol. prize AAAS, 1969, Nat. Media award Am. Psychol. Found., 1980; grantee NSF, NIMH, Ford Found., Social Sci. Research Council, Found. Child Devel. Mem. Nat. Assn. Coll. and Univ. Lawyers, Copyright Soc. USA, Boston Bar Assn., Soc. Exptl. Social Psychology, Soc. Personality and Social Psychology, Authors Guild, Mass. Hist. Soc. (mem. Adams Papers adminstrv. com. 2001-06, mem. pubs. com. 2007—), Phi Beta Kappa. Clubs: Elihu (New Haven). Jewish. Office Phone: 617-965-9425. Business E-Mail: zrubin@zickrubin.com.

RUBINFIEN, LEO H., photographer, writer; b. Chgo., Aug. 16, 1953; Student, Reed Coll.; BFA, Calif. Inst. Arts, 1974; MFA, Yale U., 1976. Instr. in photography Swarthmore Coll., 1977, Sch. Visual Arts, NYC, 1978-87; assoc. prof. art Fordham U., 1981-87; represented by Robert Mann Gallery, NYC; mem. faculty Gallatin Sch., NYU, 2001—. Mem. grad. faculty Sch. of Visual Arts, NYU, 2002—; vis. lectr. Cooper Union, 1982; vis. prof. Musashino Fine Arts U., Tokyo, 2002. One man shows include Castelli Gallery, N.Y., 1981, Fraenkel Gallery, San Francisco, 1982, 86, Robert Mann Gallery, N.Y.C. 2001, 1994, 2001, Met. Mus. Art, N.Y.C., 1992, Seibu Art Forum, Tokyo, 1993, Cleve. Mus. Art, 1994, Seattle Art Mus., 1994, Robert Mann Gallery, N.Y.C., Corcoran Gallery Art, 2008; exhibited in group shows at Internat. Ctr. Photography, N.Y., 1981, Inst. Contemporary Arts, London, 1981, San Francisco Mus. Modern Art, 1981, 2009, George Eastman House, Rochester, N.Y., 1981, Corcoran Gallery, Washington, 1981, Mus. Modern Art, N.Y., 1984, Met. Mus. Art, 2001, Tokyo Met. Mus. Photography, 2002; dir., co-author (film) The Money Juggler, 1988, My Bed in the Leaves, 1990; author: (books) A Map of the East, 1992, 10 Takeoffs 5 Landings, 1994, Shomei Tomatsu: Skin of the Nation, 2004,Wounded Cities, 2008, (essays) The Man in the Crowd, 1977, Love-Hate Relations, 1978, Investigations of a Dog, 1999, Guesses About the Work of Wu Yiming, 1999, The Poetry of Plain Seeing, 2000, Perfect Uncertainty, 2001, The Mask Behind the Face, 2004, Where Diane Arbus Went, 2005, Doomed Alleys, 2006, Another Trip Through The Americans, 2009. Fellow Guggenheim Found., 1982-83, Asian Cult Coun., 1984, Internat. Ctr. Advanced Studies, 1998—, Japan Found., 2002, Asian Cult. Coun., 2002 Home: 145 Nassau St Apt 11c New York NY 10038-1514 Personal E-mail: oscawana@earthlink.net.

RUBINO, JOELLE L., physical therapist, athletic trainer; b. Latrobe, Pa., Feb. 23, 1978; d. Dennis L. and Nancy D. Rubino. BA in Psychology, W.Va. Wesleyan Coll., Buckhannon, BS in Sports Medicine, 2000; D in Phys. Therapy, Creighton U., Omaha, 2003. Athletic trainer cert. NATABOC. Lab./tchg. asst. W.Va. Wesleyan Coll., 1997—2000; tchg. asst. Creighton U., Omaha, 2002; clinician Brown and Assocs. PT, Dover, Del., 2003—. Presenter Sideline Sports Medicine. Vol. Sr. Olympics, Dover, 2004—06; life mem., vol. Girl Scouts US, Dover, 1996—2006; com. mem. Wyoming United Meth. Ch., Del., 2006; vol. Habitat for Humanity, 2000—06; vol. med. coverage DFRC, Newark, 2004—06. Recipient Most Creative Nat. Award, Nat. Athletic Tng. Month. Mem.: Del. Athletic Trainers Assn. (presenter, traumatic brain injuries 2008, Del. Athletic Trainer of the Yr. 2005), Nat. Athletic Trainers Assn., Am. Phys. Therapy Assn., Kappi Phi (life; pres. 1999—2000). Republican. Office: Brown and Assocs Physical Therapy 1288 S Governors Ave Dover DE 19904 Personal E-mail: rubinoj_2000@yahoo.com.

RUBINO, RICHARD J., pharmaceutical executive; CPA. With Price Waterhouse & Co., Internat. Bus. Machines Corp., MedcoHealth Solutions Inc., 1993—, v.p. planning, 1995—98, contr., chief acctg. officer, 1998—2008, sr. v.p., 2005—, CFO, 2008—. Mem.: Am. Inst. Cert. Pub. Accountants. Office: MedcoHealth Solutions Inc 100 Parsons Pond Dr Franklin Lakes NJ 07417-2603 Office Phone: 201-269-3400. Office Fax: 201-269-1109.*

RUBINOFF, IRA, biologist, researcher, conservationist; b. NYC, Dec. 21, 1938; s. Jacob and Bessie (Rose) R.; m. Roberta Wolff, Mar. 19, 1961; 1 son, Jason; m. Anabella Guardia, Feb. 10, 1978; children: Andres, Ana. BS, Queens Coll., 1959; A.M., Harvard U., Cambridge, Mass., 1960, PhD, 1963. Biologist, asst. dir. marine biology Smithsonian Tropical Rsch. Inst., Balboa, 1964—70, asst. dir. sci., 1970—73, dir., 1973—2008, dir. emeritus and sr. staff scientist, 2008—. Assoc. in ichthyology Harvard U., 1965—; courtesy prof. Fla. State U., Tallahassee, 1976—; mem. sci. adv. bd. Gorgas Meml. Inst., 1964-88; trustee Rare Animal Relief Effort, 1976-85; bd. dirs. Charles Darwin Found. for Galapagos Islands, 1977—; chmn. bd. fellowships and grants Smithsonian Inst., 1978-79, acting under sec. sci., 2007-08; vis. fellow Wolfson Coll., Oxford U., Eng., 1980-81; vis. scientist Mus. Comparative Biology-Harvard U., 1987-88; dep. dir. US Nat. Mus. Natural History, 2001-02. Author Strategy for Preservation of Moist Tropical Forests; contbr. articles to profl. jours. Vice chmn. bd. dirs. Panama Canal Coll., 1989-93; bd. dirs. Internat. Sch. Panama, 1983-85, 90-93, Fundacion Natura, sec., bd. dirs., 1991—; bd. dirs. Ancon Panama, 1985-97, Earthwatch, 1995-97, City of Knowledge, 1996—, Charles Darwin Found. Inc., 2003-, Mpala Wildlife Found., 2003-; hon. dir. Instituto Latino Americano de Estudios Avanzados; dir. Biomusceo Panama. Awarded Order of Vasco Nunez de Balboa of Republic of Panama, Secs. Gold medal, 2008. Fellow Linnean Soc. (London), AAAS, Am. Acad. Arts & Scis.; mem. Am. Soc. Naturalists, Soc. Study of Evolution, NY Acad. Scis. Clubs: Cosmos (Washington).

RUBINSON, HOWARD ALAN, physician; b. Bklyn., Aug. 24, 1949; s. Samuel and Hilda (Cohen) R.; m. Carol Berman, May 16, 1976; children: Roger, Abby. AB, Cornell U., Ithaca, NY, 1971; MD, Hahnemann Med. Coll., Phila., 1975. Diplomate Am. Bd. Radiology. Radiology instr. Sch. Medicine U. Miami, Fla., 1979-81, asst. prof. radiology Fla., 1981-84; mem. attending staff North Beach Hosp., Ft. Lauderdale, Fla., 1984-89, North Ridge Med. Ctr., Ft. Lauderdale, Fla., 1989—2006, Hollywood Med. Ctr., Fla., 1998—2006, Parkway Regional Med. Ctr., 2001—05; attending staff Holy Cross Hosp., Ft. Lauderdale, Fla., 2004—, Mercy Hosp., Miami, Fla., 2005—. Contbr. articles to profl. jours. Mem. Am. Coll. Radiology, Am. Soc. Emergency Radiology, Soc. Breast Imaging, Radiol. Soc. N.Am., Am. Roentgen Ray Soc., Soc. Thoracic Radiology, South Fla. Radiol. Soc. (pres. 1996-97), Fla. Radiol. Soc., Fla. Med. Assn., Broward County Med. Assn. Office: 2929 E Commercial Blvd Ste 600 Fort Lauderdale FL 33308 Personal E-mail: hrubinson@comcast.net.

RUBINSTEIN, AARON, lawyer; b. NYC, Nov. 15, 1950; s. Jacob and Golda Rubinstein; m. Carri Sue Zogan, Mar. 3, 1974; children: David Michael, Jennifer Lauren. BA magna cum laude, Cornell U., 1972; JD, NYU, 1975. Bar: NY 1976, US Dist. Ct. (so. and ea. dists.) 1976, US Supreme Ct. 1986. Assoc. Kaye, Scholer LLP, NYC, 1975-84, ptnr., 1985—, chair Litig. Dept. and Securities and Derivatives Litig. Mem. ABA, NY State Bar Assn., Assn. of Bar of City of NY, Order of Coif. Office: Kaye Scholer LLP 425 Park Ave New York NY 10022-3506 Office Phone: 212-836-8412. Business E-Mail: arubinstein@kayescholer.com.

RUBINSTEIN, ARYE, pediatrician, microbiologist, immunologist, educator; b. Tel Aviv, Oct. 02; came to U.S., 1971; s. Reuven and Kathe (Samson) R.; m. Orna Eisenstein, Dec. 7, 1965 (div. 1982); children: Ran, Yair, Avner, Noam; m. Charline Nezri, Dec. 27, 1983; children: Reuven, Rena, Rachel. MD, U. Berne, Switzerland, 1962. Diplomate Am. Bd. Pediatrics; bd. cert. in pediatrics, Israel, Switzerland; Am. Bd. Allergy and Immunology cert. in allergy and immunology. Intern, pediatrics resident, fellow U. Tel Aviv, 1962-67; rsch. assoc. divsn. immunology Med. Sch. Harvard Coll., 1971-73; dir. divsn. immunology and bone marrow transplantation U. Berne, 1969-71; asst. prof. cell biology Albert Einstein Coll. Medicine, Bronx, 1973-80, asst. prof. pediatrics, 1973-77, assoc. prof., 1977-82, assoc. prof. microbiology and immunology, 1981-85, prof. pediatrics, 1982—, prof. microbiology and immunology, 1985—. Dir. divsn. clin. allergy and immunology Albert Einstein Coll. Medicine, dir. tng. program for allergy and immunology; dir. divsn. clin. allergy and immunology Albert Einstein Coll. Medicine, Montefiore Med. Ctr.; attending pediatrician Bronx Mcpl. Med. Ctr., Hosp. Albert Einstein Coll. Medicine; mem. study sect. on AIDS rsch. NIH; dir Focis affiliated Clin. Immunology Ctr. Albert Einstein Coll. Medicine Montegiare Med. Ctr. Mem. editl. bd. Annals of Allergy; reviewer New England Jour. Medicine, Jour. for Clin. Investigation, Jour. Pediatrics, Jour. Clin. Allergy and Immunology; contbr. over 175 articles to profl. publs. Lt. armed svcs., Israel, 1955-57. Recipient Lifetime award in Immunology, Humanitarian award DIFFA, Birch Svcs. for Children, Annual award U.S. Asst. Sec. of Health for excellence in AIDS rsch. and treatment, 1990, Bela Shick award for Pediatric Rsch., 1993, Ackerman award for Sci. and Humanity, 1995, Heroes in Medicine Internat. award, 2000; AIDS Rsch. Program grantee NIH, Bronx. Fellow Am. Acad. Allergy and Immunology, Am. Coll. Allergy & Immunology; mem. N.Y. Acad. Scis., Soc. Pediatric Rsch., The Harvey Soc., Am. Coll. Allergy, Clin. Immunology Soc., Clin. Immunology Soc. Office: Albert Einstein Coll Medicine 1625 Blondell Ave Bronx NY 10461-1926 Business E-Mail: rubinste@aecom.yu.edu.

RUBINSTEIN, ERNEST, librarian, educator; b. Queens, NY, July 11, 1952; s. Jack and Jeanne Rubinstein; life ptnr. Paul Glassman. BA, Brandeis U., 1974; AMLS, U. Mich., 1977; MTS, Harvard U., 1979; MA, Hebrew Union Coll., 1985; PhD, Northwestern U., Evanston, Ill., 1995. Indexer H.W. Wilson Co., Bronx, NY, 1984—88; editor Am. Theological Libr. Assn., Chgo., 1988—90; reference libr. North Park Coll., Chgo., 1990—94; libr. Interchurch Ctr., NYC, 1994—2005; libr. theol. Drew U., Madison, NJ, 2005—. Asst. adj. prof. humanities NYU, NYC, 1995—; adj. faculty New Sch., NYC, 2001—; book reviewer Publs. Weekly, NYC, 1999—2001. Author: (non-fiction) Episode of Jewish Romanticism, 1999; contbr. articles to mags.; author: (book) Religion and the Muse, 2007. Vol. peer counselor Horizons, Chgo., 1992—94, Aids Pastoral Care Network, Chgo., 1992—94. Mem.: Am. Acad. Religion. Jewish. Office: Drew Univ Libr Madison NJ 07940 Office Phone: 973-408-3472. Personal E-mail: ehr3@nyu.edu.

RUBINSTEIN, EVA (ANNA), photographer; b. Buenos Aires, 1933; d. Arthur and Aniela (Mlynarska) R.; m. William Sloane Coffin Jr., 1956 (div. 1968); children: Amy, Alexander (dec.), David. Ballet tng., Paris, NYC, Calif., 1938-53; student, Scripps Coll., Claremont, Calif., 1950-51, UCLA, 1952-53; student in photography, Lisette Model, 1969, Jim Hughes, 1971, Ken Heyman, 1970, Diane Arbus, 1971. Lectr. numerous workshops, seminars, confs.; instr. photo seminars Lodz Film Sch., Poland, 1986, 87. Dancer, actress: off-Broadway and Broadway, including original prodn. The Diary of Anne Frank, 1955-56; European dance tour, 1955; one-person shows of photographs include Underground Gallery, NYC, 1972, Dayton Art Inst., Ohio, 1973, Arles Festival, France, 1975, Canon Photo Gallery, Amsterdam, 1975, Neikrug Gallery, NYC, 1975, 79, 81, 82, 85, La Photogalerie, Paris, 1975, Friends of Photography, Carmel, Calif., 1975, Galerie 5.6, Ghent, Belgium, 1976, Gallery Trochenpresse, Berlin, 1977, Frumkin Gallery, Chgo., 1977, Galeria Sinisca, Rome, 1979, Hermitage Found. Mus., Norfolk, Va., 1982, Photographers Gallery, London, 1983, Galerie Forum Labo, Arles, France, 1983, Galerie Nicephore, Lyon, France, 1983, Image Gallery, Madrid, 1984, Muzeum Sztuki, Lodz, Poland, 1984, Il Diaframma/Canon Gallery, Milan, 1984, A.R.P.A. Gallery, Bordeaux, 1984, Chateau d'Eau, Toulouse, France, 1985, Galerie Demi-Teinte, Paris, 1985, Associated Artist Photographers galleries in Warsaw, Krakow, Lodz, Katowice and Gdansk, Poland, 1985-86, Foto/Medium/Art Gallery, Wroclaw, Poland, 1986, Visions Gallery, San Francisco, 1986, Canon Galerie, Paris, 1986, Salone Internat. SICOF, Milan, 1987, St. Krzysztof Gallery, Lodz, 1987, L'Image Fixe, Lyon, 1988, Artotheque, Grenoble, 1988, Neikrug Photographica, NYC, 1989, Heuser Art Ctr. Gallery, Bradley U., Peoria, Ill., 1989, 3-os Encontros da Imagem, Braga, Portugal, 1989, Bibliotheque Nat. Galerie Colbert, Paris, 1989, Galerie Picto-Bastille, Paris, 1989-90, Portfolio Gallery, London, 1990, Vaison-La-Romaine, France, 1990, Hist. Mus. of City of Lodz, 1990, Galerie Artem, Quimper, France, 1993, Galerie F.N.A.C. Etoile, Paris, 1994, other F.N.A.C. galleries (France, Belgium, Spain), 1994-97, Galerie Augustus, Berlin, 1995, L'Imagerie, Lannion, France, 1995, Zacheta Gallery, Warsaw, 1996, Salon of Modern Art B.W.A., Bydgoszcz, Poland, 1997, Galleries of Polish Insts., Sofia, Bulgaria, Berlin, Moscow, Bratislava, Slovakia, I. Beszkova Gallery, Plewen, Bulgaria, 1997, Hungarian Mus. Photographic Art, Budapest, 1997, LTF Gallery, Lodz, Poland, 1998, Konfrontacje Fotograficzne, Gorzow Wielopolski, Poland, 1998, Centrum Kultury Zamek, Poznan, Poland, 1998, Mus. Regionalny, Wrzesnia, Poland, 1998, Galeria Korytarz, Jelenia Gora, Poland, 1998, Galeria Foto-Medium-Art, Wroclaw, Poland, 1998, Galeria Pusta, Centrum Kultury, Katowice, Poland, 1998, Teatr Wielki, Lodz, Poland, 2000, Gallery Europa Club, NY, 2003, Château de la Petite, Malmaison, France, 2004, Alliance Française, NYC, 2006; Historical Mus. Lodz, 2007, Jan Krugier gallery, NYC 2008, 2009, In Camera Gallery, Paris, 2009, numerous group shows since 1971 including most recently Zacheta Gallery, Warsaw, 2002, Lodz Photographic Soc., 2002, Polish/Am.Photographers, Polish Consulate, NY, 2003, Gutman Libr., Harvard, 2003, Floating Found. Photography, NY, 2004, XL, La Collection Photographique du Musée d'Arles, 2005, Lisette Model and her Descendants, Aperture, NY, 2007, Musee Reattee Artes, 2009; represented: in permanent collections Library of Congress, Washington, Met. Mus. Art, NYC, Bibliotheque Nationale, Paris, Musee Reattu, Arles, France, Kalamazoo Inst. Arts, Israel Mus., Jerusalem, Fotografiska Museet, Stockholm, Muzeum Sztuki, Lodz, Poland, Histo Mus. of City of Lodz, National Mus. Warsaw, others; author: Eva Rubinstein, 1974, Eva Rubinstein, I Grandi Fotografi, 1983, 2 ltd. edit. portfolios with introductions by John Vachon andAndré Kertész, Lodz: Brief Encounters, 1998, Eva Rubinstein: Fotografie 1967-1990, 2003; contbr. photographs in various books, mags., profl. jours. *Making photographs is my way of exploring the questions that keep me alive by ever leading to further questions.*

RUBINSTEIN, JAVIER H., lawyer; b. Buenos Aires, 1963; m. Lisa Rubinstein; children: Stefanie, Jason. BA magna cum laude in Polit. Sci & Econs., U. Mich., 1984; MS in Pub. Policy, Harvard U., 1986; JD cum laude, Georgetown U., 1989. Bar: Ill. 1989, US Dist. Ct. (no. dist. Ill.) 1989, US Dist. Ct. (ea. dist. Wis.) 1992, US Dist. Ct. (dist. Ariz.) 1997, US Ct. Appeals (5th cir.) 1997, US Ct. Appeals (7th cir.) 1991, US Ct. Appeals (9th cir.) 1996, US Supreme Ct. 1993. Atty. Mayer, Brown, Rowe & Maw, Chgo., 1989—98, ptnr., 1998—2006; global gen. counsel PricewaterhouseCoopers Internat. Ltd., NYC, 2006—. Lectr. law U. Chgo Law Sch., 1996—. Contbr. articles in prof. law jours. Midwest Comm. Arbitration US Coun. Internat. Bus. Named one of 40 Ill. Attys. Under 40 to Watch, Chgo. Lawyer Mag., 2001, World's Leading Experts in Comml. Arbitration, Euromoney mag., 2006. Mem.: ABA (Midwest co-chmn. Bus. Torts Litig. com.), London Ct. Internat. Arbitration. Office: PricewaterhouseCoopers Internat Ltd 1177 Avenue of the Americas New York NY 10036

RUBINSTEIN, JONATHAN J., communications executive, former computer company executive; b. NYC, 1956; BSEE, Cornell U., 1978, MSEE, 1979; MS in Computer Sci., Colo. State U. Arch. HP 9000 series, mem. design team HP 9836 workstation Hewlett-Packard; mgr. processor devel. Titan graphics supercomputer family Stardent Computer, designer, arch. 3000 and 2000 computer sys.; v.p., gen. mgr. hardware, v.p. hardware engring. NeXT Computer; exec. v.p., COO FirePower Sys.; sr. v.p. hardware engring. Apple Computer, Inc., Cupertino, Calif., 1997—2004, sr. v.p. iPod divsn., 2004—06, cons., 2006—07; exec. chmn. Palm, Inc., Sunnyvale, Calif., 2007—09, exec. chmn., CEO, 2009—. Owner, cons. J.R. Ruby Consulting Corp.; bd. dirs. Immersion Corp., 1999—2007, Palm, Inc., 2007—. Contbr. articles to profl. jours. Mem.: NAE, IEEE, Assn. Computing Machinery. Achievements include patents in field. Office: Palm Inc 950 W Maude Ave Sunnyvale CA 94085*

RUBINSTEIN, JOSEPH HARRIS, education educator; b. NYC, Oct. 5, 1936; s. Morris M. and Anne (Roslofsky) R.; m. Heike Buechler, Aug. 12, 1968; children: Mark Philip, Sara Erika. AB, N.Y.U., 1960, MS, 1964, PhD, 1969. Assoc. rsch. scientist N.Y.U., 1969-71, asst. prof., biology, 1971-72; dir. maths. and sci. curriculum Open Court Publ. Co., La Salle, Ill., 1972-79, cons., 1979-84; prof. Coker Coll., Hartsville, S.C., 1984—, chmn. dept. edn., 1984-99. Author: Realmath, 1975, 2d edit. 1989, 3d edit. 1991, Math Explorations and Applications, 1998, 2d edit., 2003, Real Science, 1999, SRA Real Math, 2006, 2nd edit., 2009. With U.S. Army, 1955-58. Mem. Nat. Coun. Tchrs. Math., Nat. Sci. Tchrs. Assn., N.Y. Acad. Scis., Sigma Xi. Jewish. Home: 414 Laurel Oak St Hartsville SC 29550-3712 Office: Coll Ave Coker College Hartsville SC 29550-3797 Business E-Mail: jrubinstein@coker.edu.

RUBINSTEIN, KIM, theater educator; b. Cleve., July 29, 1954; d. Lee Irwin and Suzanne Rubinstein; m. Thomas Simpson, Oct. 9, 1983 (div. Apr. 10, 2005); children: Isaac Stein Simpson, Isaac Simpson. BS, Northwestern U., Evanston, Ill., 1977. Co-artistic dir. Bloomsburg Theatre Ensemble, Pa., 1982—85; dir., edn. Roundhouse Theatre, Silver Spring, Md., 1985—87; theatre tchr. U. Chgo., 1989—93; assoc. artistic dir. Northlight Theatre, Evanston, 1993—94, Long Wharf Theatre, New Haven, 2003—07; theatre prof. Northwestern U., 1993—2003, U. Calif. San Diego, La Jolla, 2009—. Dir.: (plays) Baby With The Bathwater (Helen Hayes award, 1987), Midsummer Night's Dream, Private Lives, Santaland Diaries, The Intelligent Design of Jenny Chow, The Cocktail Hour, Much Ado About Nothing, The American Plan, Romeo and Juliet, Beckett Shorts, Old Times (10 Best of Yr., 1997), Julius Caesar, Love's Labour's Lost (10 Best of Yr., 1999), Eloise and Ray, Pan and Boone (After Dark award, 2003), Guys and Dolls; co-dir.: Angels in America (Jeff award, 1996). Early Career Directing fellowship, Nat. Endowment Arts Theatre Comm. Group, 1993—94, Shakespeare Am. Cmtys. grant, 2005, Theatre Ednl. Video Project grant, Werth Family Found., 2004—07, Tchr. Edn. Confs. grant, 2006—07, grant, UCSD Academic Senate, 2008, Activating Dramatic Text grant, 2009. Mem.: Theatre Comm. Group, Soc. Stage Dirs. and Choreographers. Liberal. Jewish. Home: 12951 Caminito Bodega Del Mar CA 92014 Office: UCSD Dept Theatre and Dance 9500 Gilman Dr Galbraith Hall La Jolla CA 92093 Personal E-mail: kim.rubinstein@gmail.com. Business E-Mail: krubinst@ucsd.edu.

RUBINSTEIN, MOSHE FAJWEL, engineering educator; b. Miechow, Poland, Aug. 13, 1930; came to US, 1950, naturalized, 1965; s. Shlomo and Sarah (Rosen) Rubinstein; m. Zafrira Gorstein, Feb. 3, 1953; children: Iris, Dorit. BS, UCLA, 1954, MS, 1957, PhD, 1961. Designer Murray Erick Assos. (engrs. and archs.), LA, 1954-56; structural designer Victor Gruen Assos., LA, 1956-61; asst. prof. UCLA, 1961-64, assoc. prof. dept. engring., 1964-69, prof., 1969—, chmn. engring. sys. dept., 1970-75, program dir. modern engring. for execs. program, 1965-70. Cons. Pacific Power & Light Co., Portland, Oreg., Northrop Corp., US Army, NASA Rsch. Ctr., Langley, Tex. Instruments Co., Hughes Space System Divsn., US Army Sci. Adv. Com., Kaiser Aluminum and Chem. Corp., IBM Corp., TRW. Author: (with W.C. Hurty) Dynamics of Structures, 1964 (Yugoslavian transl. 1973), Matrix Computer Analysis of Structures, 1966 (Japanese transl. 1974), Structural Systems, Statics Dynamics and Stability, 1970 (Japanese transl. 1979), Patterns of Problem Solving, 1975, (with K. Pfeiffer) Concepts in Problem Solving, 1980, Tools for Thinking and Problem Solving, 1986; IEEE Press Videotapes; Models for People Driven Quality, 1991, Quality through Innovation, 1991, Creativity for Ongoing Total Quality, 1993, Relentless Improvement, 1993, (with I.R. Firstenberg) Patterns of Problem Solving, 2d edit., 1995, (with I.R. Firstenberg) The Minding Organization, 1999 (Portuguese/Japanese transl. 2000, Spanish/Chinese/Russian transls. 2001). Recipient Disting. Tchr. award UCLA Acad. Senate, 1964, Western Electric Fund award Am. Soc. Engring. Edn., 1965, Disting. Tchr. trophy Engring. Student Soc., UCLA, 1966; Sussman prof. for disting. visitor Technion-Israel Inst. Tech., 1967-68; named Outstanding Faculty Mem., UCLA Engring. Alumni award, 1979, Outstanding UCLA Civil Engring. Alumni award, 1990, Outstanding Faculty Mem., State of Calif. Command Coll., 1987-89, 94-95; Fulbright-Hays fellow, Yugoslavia and Eng., 1975-76; named one of UCLA's Top 20 Profs. of the Century. Mem. ASCE, Am. Soc. Engring. Edn., Seismol. Soc. Am., Sigma Xi, Tau Beta Phi. Achievements include research in use of computers in structural systems, analysis and synthesis; problem solving and decision theory; creativity and innovation in the orgn. Home: 10488 Charing Cross Rd Los Angeles CA 90024-2646 Office: UCLA Sch Engring and Applied Sci Los Angeles CA 90024 Office Phone: 310-825-7731. Business E-Mail: mrubinst@ucla.edu.

RUBINSTEIN, PETER J., rabbi; BA, Amherst Coll.; MHL, Hebrew Union Coll. - Jewish Inst. Religion. Ordained Rabbi Hebrew Union Coll.- Jewish Inst. Religion. Former rabbi Peninsula Temple Beth El, San Mateo, Calif., Woodlands Community Temple, White Plains, NY; sr. rabbi Ctrl. Synagogue Manhattan, NYC, 1991—. Vis. lectr. Manhattanville Coll., Colgate U. Author: Our Rabbis Taught, 1990, How Can I Find a God?, 1997. Rabbinic chmn. Commission on Rabbinic-Congregational Relations; chmn. bd. dir. Auburn Theological Seminary; mem. bd. UJA-Federation of New York, The Partnership of Faith, Plaza Jewish Community Chapel. Named one of The Top 50 Rabbis in America, Newsweek Mag., 2007. Office: Ctrl Synagogue 123 East 55th Street New York NY 10022-3566 Office Phone: 212-838-5122.

RUBLEE, DALE ALLAN, researcher; b. Ellington, NY, Feb. 27, 1951; s. Roger R. and Gladys L. (Anderson) R. BS, Slippery Rock Coll., 1973; PhD, Purdue U., 1980; MPH, Yale U., 1982. Grad. asst. Purdue U., Lafayette, Ind., 1976-80; asst. prof. Northeastern U., Boston, 1981-83, U. Ill., Urbana-Champaign, 1983-85; policy analyst AMA, Chgo., 1985—. Mem. adv. com. GAO, Washington, 1990—. Reviewer numerous jours.; contbr. articles to profl. jours. Office: AMA Ctr Health Policy Rsch 515 N State St Chicago IL 60610-4325

RUBNER, MICHAEL, international relations educator, university administrator; b. Tel Aviv, Aug. 3, 1940; came to U.S., 1956; s. Maurice and Eva Edith (Katz) R.; m. Audrey Ann Pfingst, Feb. 16, 1969; children: Daniel, Jessica. BA, Rockford Coll., Ill., 1962; MA, Marquette U., 1964; PhD, U. Calif., Berkeley, 1975. Instr. James Madison Coll. Mich. State U., East Lansing, 1970-75, asst. prof., 1975-80, assoc. prof., 1980-85, prof., 1985—2006; ret., 2006. Univ. faculty grievance ofcl. Mich. State U., 1989-2004 Co-author: The Palestinian Problem and U.S. Policy, 1986; contbr. articles to profl. jours. Pres. Jacob Schiff B'nai B'rith Lodge 694, Lansing, 1980-93; pres. Congregation Shaarey Zedek, East Lansing, 2002-04. Mem. Acad. Polit. Sci., Internat. Studies Assn. (governing coun. Midwest divsn. 1986-92), U.S. Arms Control Assn., Midwest Consortium for Internat. Security Studies, Phi Beta Kappa (pres. Epsilon of Mich. 1983-84), Alpha Sigma Nu, Phi Beta Delta. Democrat. E-mail: exfgomsu@aol.com.

RUBNITZ, MYRON ETHAN, pathologist, educator; b. Omaha, Mar. 2, 1924; s. Abraham Srol and Esther Molly (Jonich) R.; m. Susan Belle Block, Feb. 9, 1952; children: Mary Lu Rubnitz Roffe, Peter, Thomas (dec.), Robert. BSc, U. Nebr., 1945; MD, U. Nebr., Omaha, 1947. Diplomate Am. Bd. Pathology. Intern Mt. Sinai Hosp., Cleve., 1947-48, fellow NYC, 1948-49; resident in pathology Michael Reese Hosp., Chgo., 1949-51; pathologist VA Hosp., Hines, Ill., 1953-56, chief labs., 1956-93, cons., 1993—; assoc. prof. pathology Loyola U. Med. Sch., Maywood, Ill., 1963-70, prof., 1970-99, prof. emeritus, 1999—. Adj. prof. Ill. State U., Normal, 1979-96, 2003—, U. St. Francis, Joliet, Ill., 1989—, Ea. Ill. U. Charleston, 1991—, Western Ill. U., Macomb, 1991—; clin. instr. Augustana Coll., Rock Island, Ill., 1991—, med. dir. Myron Rubintz Sch. Med. Tech., 1974-. Chmn. candidates com. Village Caucus, Winnteka, Ill., 1969-70; bd. dirs. Chgo. Commons Assn., 1968—, North Shore Sr. Ctr., 19982009—; mem. New Trier High Sch. Caucus, Winnetka, 1972-74. With AUS, 1943-46, PTO; 1st lt. M.C., U.S. Army, 1951-53. Fellow Am. Soc. Clin. Pathologists, Coll. Am. Pathologists; mem. Internat. Acad. Pathology, Assn. VA Pathologists (pres. 1982-84), Chgo. Pathology Soc., Lake Shore Country Club (Glencoe, Ill.), Mich. Shores Club (Wilmette, Ill.). Avocations: electronics, tennis, travel. Home: 979 Sheridan Rd Winnetka IL 60093 Personal E-mail: susiebelle@sbcglobal.net.

RUBRIGHT, JAMES ALFRED, paperboard and packaging company executive; b. Phila., Dec. 17, 1946; s. James Alfred and Helen Lucille (Evans) R. (deceased); m. Mary Elizabeth Angelich, Dec. 30, 1987; children: Noah Michael, Benjamin James, Jami Anne, Nathaniel Drew, James McCurdy, William Angelich. BA, Yale U., 1969; JD, U. Va., 1972. Bar: Ga. 1972. Ptnr. King & Spalding, Atlanta, 1972-94; sr. v.p., gen. counsel Sonat Inc., Birmingham, 1994-97; pres. So. Natural Gas Co. subs. Sonat Inc., Birmingham, 1997-98; exec. v.p. Sonat Inc., Birmingham, 1998-99; chmn., CEO Rock-Tenn Co., Norcross, Ga., 1999—. Office: Rock-Tenn Co 504 Thrasher St Norcross GA 30071-1914

RUBY, NORMAN F., research scientist; s. Sr. Norman F. Ruby and Mary Augustine. PhD, U. Calif., Berkley, 1991. Postdoc. fellow Stanford U., Calif., 1991—97, rsch. scientist, 1997—99, sr. rsch. scientist, 1999—. Business E-Mail: ruby@stanford.edu.

RUBY, ROY HARRIS, academic administrator; b. Yazoo City, Miss., Jan. 22, 1939; s. Albert Roy and Jennie Louise (Harris) Ruby; m. Patricia Randle, Feb. 11, 1962; children: Mary, Robert Harris. BA in Polit. Sci., Miss. State U., 1961, MA in Polit. Sci., 1966, EdD, 1973. Program dir. univ. union Miss. State U., 1964—66, coord. student activities, 1966—67, asst. dean of men, 1967—69, acting dean of men, 1969—70, acting dean of students, 1970, asst. dean student devel., 1971—74, assoc. dean student devel., 1974, dir. Jackson Br., 1974—78, asst. to v.p. student affairs, 1978—81, dean student adminstrv. svcs., 1981—85, v.p. student affairs, 1985—2002, dean Coll. Edn., 2002—04, interim pres., 2008—. Lectr. in field. Trustee Starkville Separate Mcpl. Sch. Dist., 1980—84, pres., 1983. 2d lt. US Army, 1961—63, maj. USAR. Mem.: Miss. Counselors Assn., So. Assn. Coll. Student Affairs, Nat. Assn. State Univs. and Land Grant Colls., Nat. Assn. Student Pers. Adminstrs., Phi Delta Kappa, Pi Delta Epsilon, Phi Alpha Theta, Phi Kappa Phi. Methodist. Home: 104 Langston Ct Starkville MS 39759-4242 Office: Miss State U PO Box 6018 610 Allen Hall Mississippi State MS 39762 Office Phone: 662-325-3221. E-mail: president@msstate.edu.*

RUCCHIN, STEVE, professional hockey player; b. Thunder Bay, Ont., Can., July 4, 1971; BS, U. Western Ontario. Center Mighty Ducks of Anaheim, 1994—2005, NY Rangers, 2005—06, Atlanta Thrashers, 2006—. Office: Atlanta Thrashers Centennial Tower 101 Marietta St NW Ste 1900 Atlanta GA 30303

RUCCI, JOSEPH J., JR., lawyer; s. Joseph J. and Ida Mazza Rucci; m. Deborah B. Rucci, Feb. 4, 1967; children: David J., Marysue B., Joseph J. III, Theodore J. BS, Fairfield U., Conn., 1963; JD, Villanova U., Pa., 1966. Spl. agent FBI, 1966—70; mng. ptnr. Rucci, Burnham, Carta, & Carello, LLP, Darien and New Canaan, 1978—; with Conn. Bar, 1963, US Supreme Ct., US Dist. Ct., US Ct. Appeals First Ct. Founder New Canaan Bank & Trust Co., 1976—99; organizer Bank New Canaan, 1999—2000; founder Darien Rowayton Bank, 2002—. Mem. town coun. Town New Canaan, 1974—90, chmn. town coun., 1979—90; mem. exec. com. AmeriCares Found., Inc., Stamford, Conn., 2001—, bd. dirs., 2001—, AmeriCares Homefront, Inc., Stamford, 2004—, Pear Tree Point Sch. Found., Darien, 1996—; adv. trustee Fairfield U., Conn., 1994—2005. Mem.: Soc. Former Spl. Agents, Soverign Mil. Hospitaller Order Malta, Rotary. Achievements include invention of method and system for investment banking and financial services. Office: Rucci Burnham Carta & Carello, LLP 30 Old Kings Hwy S Darien CT 06820 Office Phone: 203-899-3341. Business E-Mail: jrucci@rucciburnham.com.

RUCCOLO, MARGARET ROSE ROEBKE, music educator, violinist; b. Concordia, Kans. d. Christian Martin and Dorothy Bertrand Roebke. MusB, KS State U.,Sorbonne U., Paris, France, 1965; MA, Columbia U., NYC, 1969; D of Musical Arts, U. Ariz., Tucson, 1971. 1st grade tchr. Sacred Heart Sch., Prescott, Ariz., 1972—74; 1st and 2d grade tchr. Phoenix Country Day Sch., 1974—77; elem. gen. music tchr. Cartwright Sch. Dist., Phoenix, 1974—75, dir. fine arts and gifted edn., 1974—2007; instr. Ariz. State U., 2001, No. Ariz. U., 2008—. Violinist Sun Cities Symphony, Sun City, Ariz., 1989—2005, Tempe Symphony, 2005—. Author: (poetry) Theater of the Mind, 2003; contbr. poetry: Best Poets of the 20th Century, 2000. Recipient award, Ariz. Alliance Arts Edn., 1994, Paul Harris Rotary award, Rotary, 1994, Outstanding Leadership Rotary award, 1999, Gen. Music Adminstrn. award, U. Ariz., 1995. Mem.: Ariz. Arts Standards State Assessment Com. (A2 dept. edn. 2007—), Ariz. Music Educators Assn. (pres. 1995—97, Outstanding Music Adminstr. award 1993, Ariz. Music Educator of Yr. award 1997), Ariz. String Tchrs. Assn. (pres. 1983—87), Phi Delta Kappa (v.p. 1989—91, Gerald Read Seminar scholar 1989, 1994, 1998, 2004).

RUCH, BARBARA, Japanese literature and culture educator emerita; b. Phila., Oct. 26, 1932; d. Harold H. and Anna A. (Kerr) R. BA, Earlham Coll.; MA, U. Pa., 1960; PhD, Columbia U., 1965. Lectr., instr. Harvard U., Cambridge, Mass., 1964-66; from asst. to assoc. prof. U. Pa., Phila., 1966-84; founder and dir. Inst. for Medieval Japanese Studies U. Pa., Phila., 1968-84; dir. Inst. for Medieval Japanese Studies Columbia U., NYC, 1984—; founder and dir. Donald Keene Ctr. of Japanese Culture Columbia U., NYC, 1985-89; prof. Japanese Lit. and Culture Columbia U., NYC, 1984—99; prof. emerita, 1999—. Dir. internat. rsch. project on Illustrated Medieval Japanese Literary Texts, London, Dublin, N.Y., Tokyo, 1978-79; vis. rsch. prof. Nat. Inst. Japanese Lit., Tokyo, 1993, dir. Internat. Rsch. and conservation project on Imperial Japanese Buddhist Convents, Kyoto, Nara, Japan, 1993—; bd. dirs. Urasenke, N.Y.C., 1996—. Author: Mo Hitotsu No Chu Sei Zo, 1991 (Aoyama Nao prize Tokyo Women's Christian U., 1992); editor: Kaigai Shozo Nara Ehon, 1979, Zaigai Nara Ehon, 1981, Otogi Zoshi No Sekai, 1982, Engendering Faith: Women and Buddhism premodern Japan, 2002. Minakata Kumagusu prize Minakata Kumagusu Assn., Tanabe, Japan, 1991; Aoyama Nas prize, 1992; Order Precious Crown Butterfly Crest Japanese Govt., 1999; Yamagata Banto prize, 2000; grantee, NEH, Japan Found., Ford Found., Social Sci. Rsch. Coun.; Outstanding Alumni award Eartham Coll., 2002, Cultural Bridge award, 2006; Bukkyo Dendo Cultural prize, 2008. Mem. Assn. for Asian Studies (bd. dirs. 1973-76), Assn. Tchrs. of Japanese (exec. com. 1974-77), European Assn. Japanese Studies, Japan Soc. N.Y., Setsuwa Bungakkai (Japan), Etoki Kenkyukai (Japan). Mem. Soc. Of Friends. Office: Columbia U 509 Kent Hall New York NY 10027

RUCK, ROSEMARIE ULISSA, retired social worker, freelance/self-employed writer; b. Buffalo, Aug. 24, 1939; d. Stanley Joseph Ren and Bertha Sosnowski; m. Donald Neal Ruck, Nov. 8, 1958; children: Theresa Dorene Ruck Novak, Donna Rose Ruck Seyler, Michael Donald. AS, Genesee C.C., 1970—72; BS, SUNY Brockport Coll., 1972—75. Chemical Dependency Counselor Pk. Ridge Unity Health Sys. & Brockport Coll., NY, 1999, Basic Reading and ESL Tutor Literacy Volunteers of Am., Inc., NY, 1984. Sr. caseworker/counselor Assn. for Retarded Citizens, Batavia, NY, 1975—79; dir. Literacy Volunteers of Am. - Genesee County Chpt., Batavia, NY, 1983—89. Exec. dir. Literacy Volunteers of Am. - Orleans County Chpt., Albion, NY, 1989—98; chem. dependency counselor Pk. Ridge- Unity Health Sys., Rochester, NY, 1998—99; social worker Lakeside Beikirch Care Ctr., Brockport, NY, 1999—2002; writer Freelance -, Holley, NY, 2002—. Mem. of Genesee c.c. steering com. Genesee County Legislature, Batavia, NY, 1967—68; mem. of com. responsible for devel. of Genesee county registry Genesee County Inter-Agy. Coun., Batavia, NY, 1975—77; grant writer & mem. of program com. for domestic violence program YWCA, Batavia, NY, 1980—81; mem. of steering com. for regional action phone Genesee County Inter-agency Coun., Batavia, NY, 1985—86; mem. of steering com. for vol. connection registry United Way of Genesee County, Batavia, NY, 1983—84; devel. Orleans County Adult Learning Svcs. United Way of Ea. Orleans County, 2006; founder Orleans County Adult Learning Svcs., 2006; program chair person YWCA, Batavia, NY, 1980—82; voluneer leadership chairperson Young Women's Christian Assn., Batavia, NY, 1983—84; strategic planning com. chairperson United Way of Ea. Orleans County, Albion, NY, 1999—2001. Recipient Friends of Edn., Albion Ctrl. Sch. Bd. of Edn., 1991, Recognition of Outstanding Leadership, Literacy Volunteers of Am. - Genesee County Chpt., 1989, Literacy Volunteers of Am. - Orleans County Chpt., 1992, 1993, 1994, 1995, 1996, 1997, 1998, Genesee County Chpt. of Assn. for Retarded Citizens, 1979, Quality Recognition award, Lakeside Beikirch Care Ctr., 2001. Mem.: Literacy Volunteers of Am., Holley's Writers Club. Catholic. Achievements include Revived rural literacy organization and became number one in national organizations from over 450 affiliates; development of first workplace literacy program in Western NY state; new literacy organization, Orleans County Adult Learning Services. Avocations: reading, writing, travel, art, exercise. Home: 5843 Byron Holley Rd Byron NY 14422-9522 Personal E-mail: ruruck@juno.com.

RUCKDESCHEL, JOHN CHARLES, health facility administrator; b. Newport, RI, Jan. 5, 1946; s. John Adam and Rita Frances (Riley) R.; m. Angela Stone, June 15, 2002; children: Daniel, Emily, Darby, Haley. BSc, Rensselaer Poly. Inst., Troy, NY, 1967; MD, Albany Med. Coll., NY, 1971; Found. for Advanced Edn. in the Scis., NIH, 1973, Found. for Advanced Edn. in the Scis., NIH, 1983—84. Lic. NY, Fla., Mich., cert. Am. Bd. Internal Medicine, Med. Oncology. Straight med. intern Johns Hopkins Hosp., Balt., 1971-72; staff assoc. Nat. Cancer Inst., Balt. Cancer Rsch. Ctr., Balt., 1972-75; sr. asst. resident, medicine Beth Israel Hosp., Boston, 1975-76; asst. prof. medicine Albany Med. Coll., NY, 1976-79, assoc. prof. medicine NY, 1979-85, prof. medicine, 1985-91, head div. med. oncology NY, 1987-91, dir. joint ctr. for cancer and blood disorders NY, 1999—2001; dir., CEO H. Lee Moffitt Cancer Ctr., Tampa, 1991—2002; pres. H. Lee Moffitt Cancer Hosp., 1991—2002, Moffitt Cancer Found., 1994—2002, Lifetime Cancer Screening, Inc., 1994—2002; prof. oncology and medicine U. South Fla. Coll. Medicine, 1991—2002; pres., CEO Barbara Ann Karmanos Cancer Inst., Detroit, 2002—; prof. medicine & oncology Wayne State U. Sch. Medicine, Detroit, 2002—, assoc. dean, cancer affairs, 2002—, interim chair, radiation oncology, 2002—03; sr. v.p., cancer Detroit Med. Ctr., 2002—05; pres. The Cancer Hosp., 2002—05. Vis. scientist Nat. Cancer Inst.-Navy Med. Oncology Branch, Bethesda, Md., 1983—84; vis. prof. Found. for Promotion of Cancer Rsch., Nat. Cancer Ctr., Tokyo, 1990; lung cancer steering com. Eastern Cooperative Oncology Group, 1977—2002, lung cancer steering com. chmn., 1982—84, chmn., toxicity com., 1987—89, prin. investigator, Albany Med. Coll., 1989—91, prin. investigator, H. Lee Moffitt Cancer Ctr. & Rsch. Inst., 1991—94, chmn., cancer prevention com., 2002—02; mem. Lung Cancer Study Group, 1982—90, exec. officer, 1986—90; co-chair Nat. Cancer Inst., Lung Cancer Progress Review Group, 2001; bd. dir. Mich. Cancer Consortium, 2002—, Nat. Comprehensive Cancer Network, 1998—2002, exec. com., 2000—02; Ctr. and Inst. adv. com. Wayne State U. Divsn. Rsch., 2004—; mem. adv. bd. Cancer Control Rsch. Adv. Coun. State of Fla., 1992—2002, chmn., 1994—96; site visitor, ad hoc reviewer Nat. Cancer Inst., 1978—2003; external advisor, reviewer for several organizations and programs, 1986—; bd. dir., physicians group U. Southern Fla., 1992—2002, mem. Dean's exec. coun., 1992—2002, bd. dir., rsch. found., 1992, 2002, mem. presdl. search com., 1993, 99, bd. dir., Health Scis. Ctr. Self-Insurance Programs Coun., leadership coun., 1994—2002, mem. Inst. on Aging, 1996—2002, mem. adv. bd., PhD program in applied physicis, 1999—2002, mem. steering com., Ctr. for Entrepreneurship and Global Mgmt. Tech., 2000—02. Co-editor: (textbook) Thoracic Oncology, 1989, 95; Lung and Mediastinum. sect. editor Current Opinion in Oncology, 1996-99; lead author (lung cancer chpt.) Clinical Oncology, 3rd edit., 2004; editor-in-chief Evidence-Based Oncology 1999-2002; mem. editl. bd. Current Treatment Options in Oncology, Oncology Spectrums, Medical Oncology, Social Marketing Quarterly, Journal Cancer Education, Cancer Control: Journal Moffitt Cancer Ctr.; reviewer Annals Internal Medicine, Annals Oncology, Cancer Chemotherapy and Pharmacology, Cancer Research, Chest, Journal Clinical Oncology, Journal Nat. Cancer Inst., Journal Neuro-Oncology, Investigational New Drugs, Preventative Medicine, Proceedings for NAS; contbr. articles to med. jours. Gen. chair capital campaign Sacred Heart Ch., 1998; staff physician People's Free Med. Clinic, Balt., 1972—75; pres., bd. dir. United Urban Ministry Troy, NY, 1976—80; mem. Sand Lake Ambulance, NY, 1984—91, bd. dir. NY, 1984—85, line officer NY, 1985—87, bd. pres. NY, 1989—91; pres. West Sand Lake Vol. Fire Dept., NY, 1981—83, line officer NY, 1982—83, NY, 1985—86; bd. trustee, Suncoast Chpt. Leukemia Soc. Am., 1995—98; bd. dir. Jesuit HS Found., 1998—2000; chair, health/bio-med. com. Tampa C. of C., 1999, mem. steering com., Com. of 100, 2001—02; bd. trustee Jesuit HS, 2000—02; bd. dir., trust com. bd. Sun Trust Bank, 2000—02; mem. cmty. adv. bd. Jr. League Tampa, 2002. US Pub. Health Srv., 1972—75. Recipient Physicians Recognition award, AMA, 1974—, Excel award for Excellence in Comm. Leadership, 1994, Rensselaer Alumni Assn. Fellows award-Biology, 1996, Bellwether award for Lifetime Achievement, 1997, Town and Gown Cmty. Svc. award, 1999, 11th Ann. Fla. Med. Bus. Healthcare Physician Bus. Leadership award, 2000, Exemplary Alumni award, Albany Med. Coll., NY, 2000, Disting. Southern Oncologist award, 2001; named Brooks Brothers Man of Yr., 1994; named one of Best Doctors in Am., Americas Top Doctors, 1993—, The Med. Bus. Top 25: The Most Influential Physicians in Tampa Bay, 1998, Tampa Bay Mag. Doctors Chosen by Doctors, 2001. Fellow ACP, Am. Coll. Chest Physicians; mem. AMA, Am. Assn. Cancer Insts. (bd. dir. 1997-99, legis. com. 2001-), U. Liggett Sch. Grosse Pointe Woods, NJ, 2007-, Greater Detroit Area Health

Coun., 2006-, Am. Cancer Soc. (jr. faculty clin. fellow, 1977-80, nat. adv. com. on psychosocial and behavioral rsch. 1986-89, chair, 1989, bd. dir. Greater Tampa, 1992-97, chair, rsch. com. fla. divsn., 1999-2000, bd. dir. Fla. divsn. 1997-2002, exec. com. Fla. divsn. 1998-2002, med. v.p., Fla. divsn. 1999-2000, pres. Fla. divsn., 2001-2002), Am. Assn. for Cancer Rsch. (mem. fin. com. 2001-), Am. Assn. for Cancer Edn., Am. Soc. Clin. Oncology (AJCC rep. 2000-), Am. Coll. Physician Execs., Am. Fedn. for Clin. Rsch. (coun., eastern sect. 1981-86), Internat. Assn. for the Study of Lung Cancer, Am. Assn. Med. Colls.(Coun. Tchg. Hosps. 1997-), Nat. Coalition for Cancer Rsch. (bd. dir. 1998-2002), US Nat. Com. for the Internat. Union Against Cancer Am. Joint Com. on Cancer, 2000-, Alpha Omega Alpha, Sigma Xi; hon. mem. U. South Fla. Golden Key Internat. Honour Soc. Office: Barbara Ann Karmanos Cancer Inst 4100 John R Detroit MI 48201 Office Phone: 313-576-8670, 313-993-7770. Business E-Mail: ruckdeschel@karmanos.org.

RUCKELSHAUS, WILLIAM DOYLE, investment company executive, former federal agency administrator; b. Indpls., July 24, 1932; s. John K. and Marion (Doyle) R.; m. Jill Elizabeth Strickland, May 11, 1962; children: Catherine Kiley, Mary Hughes, Jennifer Lea, William Justice, Robin Elizabeth. BA cum laude, Princeton U., 1957; LL.B., Harvard U., 1960. Bar: Ind. 1960. Atty. Ruckelshaus, Bobbitt & O'Connor, Indpls., 1960-68; dep. atty. gen. State of Ind., 1960-65, chief counsel Office of Atty. Gen., 1963-65; minority atty. Ind. State Senate, 1965-67; mem. Ind. Ho. of Reps., 1967-69, majority leader, 1967-69; asst. atty. gen. civil divsn. US Dept. Justice, Washington, 1969-70; adminstr. EPA, Washington, 1970-73, 1983-85; acting dir. FBI, Washington, 1973; dep. atty. gen. US Dept. Justice, Washington, 1973; ptnr. Ruckelshaus, Beveridge, Fairbanks & Diamond, Washington, 1974-76; sr. v.p. law & corp. affairs Weyerhaeuser Co., Tacoma, 1976-83; pres. William D. Ruckelshaus Assocs., 1985-88; ptnr. Perkins Coie, Seattle, 1985-88; chmn. bd., CEO Browning-Ferris Industries, Inc., Houston, 1988-95, chmn., 1995—99; founder, prin. Madrona Investment Group, LLC, 1996—; strategic dir. Madrona Venture Group, Seattle, 1999—; chmn. World Resources Inst., Washington D.C., 1999—. Bd. dirs. Cummins Engine Co., Nordstrom, Inc., Weyerhaeuser Co., Inc., Vykor, Inc. Rep. nominee for U.S. Senate, Ind., 1968; apptd. by Pres. Clinton to serve as U.S. envoy to Pacific Salmon Treaty with Can., 1997-98; mem., Pres. Council on Sustainable Devel., 1993-97; chmn. Salmon Recovery Funding Bd., Wash., 1999-, commr. Commn. on Ocean Policy, 2001-04 Recipient Outstanding First Year Legislator in House award, Ind. Broadcasters Assn., 1967; named Man of Yr., Indpls. Jaycess; named an Outstanding Republican Legislator in Ind. Ho. Representatives, Wyeking Press, 1967. Mem. World Resource Inst. (chmn. 1998—), Fed. Bar Assn., Ind. Bar Assn., D.C. Bar Assn., Indpls. Bar Assn. Republican. Roman Catholic. Office: Madrona Investment Group LLC 1000 2nd Ave Ste 3700 Seattle WA 98104-1053 Office Phone: 206-674-3008. E-mail: bill@madrona.com.*

RUCKENSTEIN, ELI, chemical engineering professor; b. Botosani, Romania, Aug. 13, 1925; arrived in U.S., 1969; m. Velina Rothstein, May 15, 1948; children: Andrei, Lelia. BSChemE, Poly. Inst., Bucharest, Romania, 1949, PhD, 1967; PhD (hon.), Tech. U., Bucharest, 1993. Prof. Poly. Inst., Bucharest, 1949—69; vis. prof. U. London, 1969; NSF sr. scientist Clarkson Coll. Tech., Potsdam, NY, 1969—70; prof. U. Del., Newark, 1970—73, SUNY, Buffalo, 1973—81, disting. prof., 1981—. Vis. Humbolt prof. Bayreuth U., Germany, 1986; Gulf vis. prof. Carnegie Mellon U., Pitts., 1988—89; disting. lectr. U. Waterloo, 1985, U. Mo., 1983; Fair Meml. lectr. U. Okla., 1987; Colburn Symposium lectr. U. Del., 1988, Robert L. Pigford meml. lectr., 99; Van Winkle lectr. U. Tex., 1989; Berkeley lectr., 97; Robert A. Welch Found. lectr., 97; Barnett F. Dodge disting. lectr. Yale U., 1998. Contbr. articles to profl. jours. Recipient Nat. award, Romanian Dept. Edn., 1958, 1964, Tchg. award, 1961, George Spacu award, Romanian Acad. Sci., 1963, Sr. Humbolt award, Alexander von Humbolt Found., 1985, Creativity award, NSF, 1985, Nat. Medal of Sci., 1998; named Merk Disting. lectr., Rutgers U., 1992. Mem.: AIChE (Alpha Chi Sigma award 1977, Walker award 1988, Founders award 2002), NAE (Founders award 2004), Am. Chem. Soc. (Kendall award 1986, Jacob F. Schoellkopf medal 1986, Langmuir Disting. Lectr. award 1994, E.V. Murphree award 1996). Office: SUNY Dept Chem Engring 303 Furnas Hall Buffalo NY 14260-4200 Home: 755 Renaissance Dr Apt 203 Buffalo NY 14221-8046 Office Phone: 716-645-1179. Business E-Mail: feaeliru@buffalo.edu.

RUCKER, BRONWYN, actress, writer, social worker; b. Ithaca, NY, Mar. 18, 1951; d. James Charles and Mary Elizabeth (Costello) R.; m. Rick Russo, Dec. 31, 1984. BA in Theatre Arts, Point Park Coll., Pitts., 1973; MSW, Hunter Coll., 1993. Cert. Social Worker NYU Edn. Dept., 1993. Profl. actress various theatres, N.Y., N.J., 1969-80; artistic dir./co-founder not-for-profit social svc. arts co. Meltdown Inc., Bklyn., 1983—; med. social worker Bklyn. Hosp. Ctr., 1993-95; therapist New Hope Guild, NYC, 1997; theatre dir. Madison Hamilton Settlement, NYC, 1997; prof. human svcs. N.Y.C. Tech. Coll., 1998—. Bd. dirs. Women in Limbo, N.Y.C., 1992—. Prodr. John Cage Meets Sun Ra Concert and album, Bklyn.-Coney Island, 1986; actress, writer (one-woman show) Subway Named Desire, 1980, (plays) Brooklyn Boys, 1980, Angela Plays, 1980, The Radon Daughters, 1984, The True Story, 1986, Voices of the Armory, 1992, Teen Scenes, 1993, (autobiography) White Lady, 1999; performer, songwriter (CD) Inclines, 1996. Vol. staff, dir. teen program, YWCA Bklyn., 1993—. Recipient Most Creative Painting award Associated Artists Pitts., 1979, Woman of Influence award YWCA Bklyn., 1993, commendation N.Y.C. Office Comptroller Violence Prevention Work, 1995, Racial Harmony and Diversity award Chase Manhattan Bank, N.Y.C., 1996, Dr. Harold Diner Meml. Lectr. award Albert Einstein Coll. Medicine, 1999; grantee N.Y.C. Mayor's Stop The Violence program, 1994. Mem. AFTRA, SAG, NASW, Actors Equity Assn., Assn. Advancement Social Work with Groups, The Players Club, Bklyn. C. of C. Democrat. d Office: Meltdown Inc 346 Flatbush Ave Brooklyn NY 11238-4902

RUCKER, FANON A., lawyer; b. Gary, Ind., Oct. 19, 1971; BA, Hampton U., 1993; JD, U. Cin., 1996. Bar: Ohio 1996, US Dist. Ct. (no. and so. dists.) Ohio 2000, US Ct. Appeals (6th cir.). Assoc. Santen & Hughes, Cin. Named one of Ohio's Rising Stars, Super Lawyers, 2006. Mem.: Ohio Mcpl. Attorney's Assn., Ohio Assn. Trial Attorneys, Black Lawyers Assn. Cin. (pres. 2001—03, trustee 2003—), Nat. Bar Assn., ABA, Ohio State Bar Assn., Cin. Bar Assn. (trustee 2002—), Lawyers Club. Office: Santen & Huges Ste 3100 312 Walnut St Cincinnati OH 45202 Office Phone: 513-721-4450. Office Fax: 513-721-0109.

RUCKER, KIM K.W., lawyer, cosmetics executive; BBA with high honors in Economics, U. Iowa, 1989; JD, Harvard Law Sch.; M in Pub. Policy, John F. Kennedy Sch. Govt., Harvard U., 1993. Ptnr., corp. & securities group Sidley Austin, LLP, Chgo., 1993—2001; coun. corp. affairs Kimberly-Clark Corp., Dallas, 2001—04; sr. v.p., sec., chief governance officer Energy Future Holdings Corp. (formerly TXU Corp.), 2004—08; sr. v.p., gen. coun. Avon Products, Inc., NY, 2008—, corp. sec. NY, 2009—. Named Honoree, Girls, Inc. NY Celebration Luncheon, 2009; Harry S. Truman Scholar, 1987. Office: Avon Products Inc 1345 Avenue of the Americas New York NY 10105-0196*

RUCKER, RICHARD DOUGLAS, JR., emergency physician; b. May 3, 1947; m. Helen Regina Mostue Hannula, Jan. 15, 1977; children: Brigit-Mary Irene Hannula, Seth Benjamin Hannula, Michael Jacob, Joshua Preiss. BA in Liberal Arts, U. Ariz., 1969, MS in Zoology, 1970; MD, George Washington U., Washington, 1975; PhD in Surgery, U. Minn., 1994. Diplomate Am. Bd. Emergency Medicine, Am. Bd. Surgery, Am. Bd. Thoracic Surgery, lic. Nat. Bd. Med. Examiners, Minn., Mo., Mass., N.D.; cert. BLS instr., ACLS instr., Pediat. Advanced Life Support instr., Advance Trauma Life Support instr. Intern in gen. surgery U. Minn., Mpls., 1975—76, resident in gen. surgery, 1976—83; resident in thoracic surgery Washington U., St. Louis, 1986—87, Boston U., 1987—88; emergency medicine physician Midway Hosp., St. Paul, 1978—81, St. John's Hosp., St. Paul, 1978—81, Divine Redeemer Hosp., St. Paul, 1983—86; trauma surgeon St. Paul Ramsey Hosp., St. Paul, 1983—86; cardiothoracic surgeon numerous hosps., St. Paul, 1989—92; emergency medicine physician hosps., Mpls., 1992; cardiovascular and thoracic surgeon Dakota Heartland Hosp., Fargo, ND, 1992—96; emergency medicine physician hosps., Bloomington, Minn., 1996—. From lab. asst. to grad. tchg. asst. U. Ariz., Tucson, 1968—71; physician with hosp. privileges Unity Hosp., Fridley, Minn., 1996—, Mercy Hosp., Anoka, Minn., 1996—, Fairview Ridges Hosp., Bloomington, Minn., 1999—, Meth. Hosp., St. Louis Park, Minn., 1996—, Healteast Hosps., 2002—; clin. asst. prof. surgery U. N.D. Sch. Medicine, 1993—96. Contbr. chpts. to books and articles to profl. jours. Lt. USAR, 1970—78. Recipient award, SAR, 1966, Res. Officers Assn., 1967, Assn. U.S. Army, 1968, Svc. award, Phi Delta Epsilon Med. Soc., 1973—74, Rsch. award, HEW, 1972, NIH, 1978—81, Resident Rsch. award, Assn. Acad. Surgeons, 1981; Rsch. grant, Washington Heart Assn., 1973. Fellow: Am. Acad. Emergency Medicine, Am. Coll. Emergency Medicine, Am. Coll. Cardiology, Am. Coll. Chest Physicians (assoc.), Am. Coll. Surgeons (assoc.); mem.: Am. Coll. Exec. Physicians, Aldo R. Castaneda Soc. Pediat. Cardiovascular Surgery, Ramsey County Med. Soc., Am. Coll. Emergency Physicians, Minn. Med. Soc., Alpha Epsilon Delta, Beta Beta Beta, Phi Eta Sigma. Office: Emergency Physicians Profl Assn 7301 Ohms Ln Ste 650 Edina MN 55439-4000 Home: 330 Woodlawn Ave Saint Paul MN 55105-1240 Office Phone: 952-835-9880. Office Fax: 952-835-4403. E-mail: RDRuckerJr@aol.com, RDRuckerJr@comcast.net.

RUCKER, ROBERT D., state supreme court justice; b. Canton, Ga. married; 3 children. BA, Ind. U., 1974; JD, Valparaiso Sch. of Law, 1976; LLM, U. Va., 1998. Dep. prosecuting atty., Lake County, Ind.; city atty. City of Gary, Ind.; pvt. practice East Chicago; judge Ind. Ct. of Appeals, 1991—99; justice Ind. Supreme Ct., Indpls., 1999—. Former vice chmn. Ind. Commn. for Continuing Legal Edn. Bd. dirs. Legal Svcs. of N.W. Ind. Decorated Vietnam Vet. Fellow: Indianapolis Bar Foundation; mem.: ABA, Nat. Bar Assn. (exec. com. mem. Judicial Council), Ind. Judges Assn., Am. Judicature Soc. Office: Ind Supreme Ct State House Rm 312 200 W Washington St Indianapolis IN 46204-2798*

RUCKERT, KYLE, legislative staff member; m. Lynnel Ruckert. BA in Polit. Sci. and History, Tulane U., New Orleans, 1996. Aide, Rep. Bob Livingston US House of Reps., Washington, legis. asst., Rep. Mac Thornberry, 1997—99, legis. dir., Rep. David Vitter, 1999—2003, chief of staff to Rep. David Vitter, 2003—05; chief of staff to Senator David Vitter US Senate, Washington, 2005—. Republican. Office: 516 Hart Senate Office Bldg Washington DC 20510-1805 Office Phone: 202-224-4623. Business E-Mail: kyle_ruckert@vitter.senate.gov.*

RUCKMAN, MARK WARREN, physicist; b. Rolla, Mo., Dec. 26, 1954; s. Homer Leslie and Audrey (Warren) R. BS in Physics, Pa. State U., 1977; PhD in Physics, Rensselaer Polytechnic Inst., 1984. Asst. physicist Brookhaven Nat. Lab., Upton, N.Y., 1985-87, assoc. physicist, 1987-91, physicist, 1991-93, physics assoc. I, 1993-2000; physicist Fusion UV Sys., Inc., Gaithersburg, Md., 2000—. Contbr. articles to profl. jours. Mem. Am. Phys. Soc., Am. Vacuum Soc., Am. Chem. Soc., Materials Rsch. Soc., Phi Beta Kappa, Phi Kappa Phi. Republican. Baptist. Office: Fusion UV Sys Inc 910 Clopper Rd Gaithersburg MD 20878-1357 Office Phone: 301-527-2660. Office Fax: 301-527-2661. Business E-Mail: mruckman@fusionuv.com.

RUCKMAN, ROGER NORRIS, pediatric cardiologist; b. Washington, Dec. 15, 1944; s. Norris Elliott and Eugenia (Campbell) R.; children: Robert, Karen, Stephen, Jonathan. BA in Chemistry, Williams Coll., Williamstown, Mass., 1966; MD, U. Va., 1970. Cert. in Pediat. 1976, in Pediatric Cardiology 1979. Intern Peter Bent Brigham Hosp., 1970-71; resident Med. Ctr. Hosp. of Vermont, 1973-75; fellow in cardiology Children's Hosp., Boston, 1975-77; asst. prof. pediatrics U. Nebr., Omaha, 1977-79, George Washington U., Washington, 1980-82, assoc. prof. pediatrics, 1982-90, prof. pediatrics, 1990—; pediatric cardiologist Children's Hosp. Nat. Med. Ctr., Washington, 1980—, chmn. cardiology, 1986-89. Contbr. articles to profl. jours. Served to capt. U.S. Army, 1971-73. Recipient Disting. Service award, Am.-Korea Found., 1972; NIH grantee, 1982—. Fellow Am. Acad. Pediatrics, Am. Coll. Cardiology; mem. Am. Heart Assn., Teratology Soc., Soc. Pediatric Research, Columbia Country Club (Chevy Chase, Md.). Republican. Presbyterian. Avocations: tennis, golf. Office: CNMC Dept Cardiology 111 Michigan Ave NW Washington DC 20010-2916 Office Phone: 202-476-2020. Business E-Mail: rruckman@cnmc.org.

RUDACILLE, SHARON VICTORIA, medical technician; b. Ranson, W.Va., Sept. 11, 1950; d. Albert William and Roberta Mae (Anderson) Rudacille. BS cum laude, Shepherd Coll., 1972. Med. technologist VA Ctr., Martinsburg, W.Va., 1972—. Instr. Sch. Med. Tech., 1972—76, assoc. coord. edn., 1976—77, edn. coord., 1977—78, quality assurance officer clin. chemistry, 1978—80, lab. svc. quality assurance and edn. officer, 1980—84, clin. chemistry sect. leader, 1984—86, staff med. technologist, 1986—94, supervisory med. technologist, 1994—95, sr. med. technologist, 1995—; adj. faculty mem. Shippensburg (Pa.) State Coll., 1977—78, Shepherd Coll., 1977—78. Mem.: Shepherd Coll. Alumni Assn., W.Va. Soc. Med. Technologists, Am. Soc. Clin. Pathologists, Am. Soc. Med. Tech., Sigma Pi Epsilon. Bapt. Home: PO Box 14 Ranson WV 25438-0014

RUDAKOV, DMITRY L., research scientist; b. Moscow, Feb. 25, 1966; s. Leonid I Rudakov and Olga V Kazakova. PhD in Physics, Australian Nat. U., Canberra, 1997. Assoc. project scientist U. Calif., San Diego, 2007—. Contbr. articles to profl. jours. Office: Univ Calif San Diego 9500 Gilman Dr Mail Code 0417 La Jolla CA 92093-0417 Business E-Mail: drudakov@ucsd.edu.

RUDAVSKY, DAHLIA C., lawyer; b. NYC, Sept. 9, 1951; d. Benjamin Zev and Malka B. (Liben) R.; m. Robert R. Jampol, Oct. 31, 1971; children: Malka, Noah. BA magna cum laude, Yale U., 1972; JD, U. Calif., Berkeley, 1978. Bar: Calif. 1979, Mass. 1980, U.S. Dist. Ct. (no. dist.) Calif. 1979, U.S. Dist. Ct. Mass. 1981, U.S. Ct. Appeals (1st cir.) 1984, U.S. Supreme Ct. 1990. Assoc. Angoff, Goldman, Manning, Pyle, Wanger & Hiatt, Boston, 1980-84, Avery & Friedman, Boston, 1984-86, McDonald Noonan & Kaplan, Newton, Mass., 1986-88; ptnr. Shilepsky, Messing & Rudavsky, P.C., Boston, 1988-93, Messing and Rudavsky, P.C., Boston, 1993—, Messing, Rudavsky & Weliky PC, Boston. Cons. in field; lectr. law Harvard Law Sch., 2006—07, 2007—08. Recipient Georgina Smith Award, AAUP, Washington, 1990; named one of top Boston lawyers, Boston Mag., 2004. Mem. AFL-CIO (lawyers coordinating com., nat. adv. bd. 1983-84), Nat. Employment Lawyers Assn., Mass. Bar Assn. Fluent in french & Hebrew. Office: Messing Rudavsky & Weliky PC 50 Congress St Boston MA 02109 Office Phone: 617-742-0004. E-mail: drudavsky@mrwemploymentlaw.com.

RUDAYEVA, YELENA, biology educator; married; children: Michail, Reena. MS in Biology, Odessa State U., 1985, PhD in Biology, 2006; MS in Holistic Nutrition, Clayton Coll. Natural Health, Alabama, 2003. Cert. Dept. Radiation Protection, Fla., 1997. Educator PBCC, Lake Worth, Fla., 2004—, South U., West Palm Beach, Fla., 2006—. Activist Animal Rescue League, West Palm Beach, 1990—. Office: PBCC Congress Ave Lake Worth FL 33461

RUDCZYNSKI, ANDREW B., academic administrator, medical researcher; b. Nottingham, England, Sept. 7, 1947; came to U.S., 1951; s. Richard B. and Krystyna Z. R.; m. Andrea Skalny, Oct. 16, 1976 (div. Oct. 1990); children: Christina, Thomas. BSc in Biology/Biochemistry, McGill U., 1969; PhD in Immunology, Syracuse U., 1974; MBA in Adminstrn., So. Ill. U., 1984. Prin. investigator scrub typhus project divsn. Rickettsiology U.S. Army Med. Rsch. Infectious Diseases, Ft. Detrick, Md., 1974—76; rsch. assoc. dept. biology Mich. Cancer Found., Detroit, 1976-77, rsch. scientist dept. immunology, unit chef immunology unit Breast Cancer Prognostic Study, 1977-80; asst. dir. Office Rsch. and Grants U. Md. Eastern Shore, Princess Anne, 1980-83; extramural assoc. Office Extramural Rsch. and Tng., Office of Dir. NIH, 1981-82; asst. dir. Office Rsch. & Sponsored Programs Rutgers U., Piscataway, NJ, 1983-84, dir., 1984-99, asst. v.p. rsch. adminstrn., 1985-93, assoc. v.p. rsch. policy and adminstrn., 1993-99; assoc. v.p. fin., exec. dir. rsch. svcs. U. Pa., Phila., 1999—. Field reader strengthening devel. instns. program U.S. Dept. Edn., 1990; mem. Chancellor's task force instrn. and rsch. infrastructure support N.J. Dept. Higher Edn., 1992. Contbr. articles, abstracts to profl. jours. Capt. U.S. Army Med. Svc. Corps, 1974-76. Recipient traineeship award NSF, 1969-71; predoctoral fellow NIH, 1973-74. Mem. AAAS, Nat. Coun. Univ. Rsch. Adminstrs. (profl. devel. com. 1988-90, region II program com. 1989-90, chmn. region II 1990-92, nat. program com. 1994-95), Coun. Govtl. Rels. (fed. mgmt. devel. com. 1989-90, bd. dirs. 1998-2003, tech. transfer and ethics com. 1998-99, chair rsch. compliance and adminstrn. com. 1999-2003), Beta Gamma Sigma, Sigma Xi. Roman Catholic. Office: Univ Pa Office Rsch Svcs 3451 Walnut St Ste P-221 Philadelphia PA 19104-6205 Home: 22 Fairway Dr Wallingford CT 06492-5459 Office Phone: 215-573-9249. Business E-Mail: abrude@pobox.upenn.edu.

RUDD, ANN TALTON, psychologist, artist; b. Raleigh, NC, Mar. 29, 1960; d. Fred Wesley and Margaret Baucom Talton; m. James Robert Rudd, Mar. 22, 1986; 1 child, Holden. BA Psychology, East Carolina U., Greenville, NC, 1982; MS Applied Psychology, Va. Tech, Blacksburg, 1984; postgrad., Art Inst. Charlotte, NC. Lic. Psychol. Assoc. N.C. Psychology Bd., 1985, cert. Psychologicst N.C. Psychology Bd., 1999. Staff psychologist Murdoch Ctr., Butner, NC, 1984—86; post-disaster counselor d Mental Health Roanoke Valley, Va., 1986; behavior cons. Behavior Therapy and Learning Ctr., Signal Hill, Calif., 1987—88; devel. disabilities specialist Mecklenburg County Area Mental Health/Devel. Disabilities Svcs., Charlotte, 1988—91; psychologist St. Marks Residential Svcs. and Luth. Family Svcs. Group Homes, Charlotte, 1989—94; staff psychologist Mecklenburg County Area Mental Health/Devel. Disabilities Svcs., Charlotte, 1994—99; psychologist Rudd Psychol. Svcs., Charlotte, 2003—. Mem.: Charlotte Art League, Psi Chi (sec. 1980—82), Chi Beta Phi Sci. Honor Soc. (sec. 1981—82), Mensa. Avocations: painting, drawing, graphic design, piano, reading.

RUDD, D(ALE) F(REDERICK), chemical engineering professor; b. Mpls., Mar. 2, 1935; m. Sandra C. Coryell, 1964; children: Karen, David. BS, U. Minn., 1956, PhD in Chem. Engring., 1960. Asst. prof. chem. engring. U. Mich., Ann Arbor, 1960-61; from asst. prof. to prof. U. Wis., Madison, 1961-94, Schlicter emeritus prof. chem. engring., 1994—. Co-author: Strategy of Process Enging., 1968, Process Synthesis, 1973, Strategy of Pollution Control, 1977, Petrochemical Tech. Assessment, 1981, Microkinetics of Heterogeneous Catalysis, 1993. Named J.S. Guggenheim fellow, 1970; recipient Allan P. Colburn award, 1971. Mem. Nat. Acad. Engring., 1978, Wash. State Acad. Sci. (founding mem. 2008). Achievements include contributions to the knowlege of process engineering. Personal E-mail: daleandsandy@yahoo.com.

RUDD, DAVID WILLIAM, management consultant, chemical engineer; b. Floral Park, NY, Dec. 31, 1931; s. Edward Lynn and Joanna (McSorley) Rudd; m. Harriet Fay Sart, Aug. 8, 1953; children: Rebecca, Rachel. BA in Chemistry, Colby Coll., 1953; MS in Phys. Chemistry, Northeastern U., 1962. Rsch. chemist Monsanto Chem. Co., Everett, Mass., 1956-58, Kendall Co., Walpole, Mass., 1958-60, Metal Hydrides, Beverly, Mass., 1960-62; sr. staff engr. Western Electric Co., North Andover, Mass., 1969-78; mem. rsch. staff Engring. Rsch. Ctr., Princeton, NJ, 1978-80; co-founder, dir. David W. Rudd Assocs., mfg. cons., 1985—. Iso-9000 auditor, 1993; co-owner cert. tree farm, Sumner, Maine. Vol. tutor program Mass. Pub. Sch., Lawrence, 1991. With 7th Cav. US Army, 1953—55. Recipient Engring. Excellence award, Western Electric Co., 1969, C. B. Sawyer Meml. award, 1974, Vol. Tutoring Program award, AT&T, 1991, Lucent Tech. Patent award, 1999; co-recipient Malcolm Baldrige Nat. Quality award, with AT&T's Transmission Divsn., 1992. Mem.: We. Electric Engring. Excellence Soc. (pres. 1977—83), Svc. Corp Ret. Execs., Tel. Pioneers Am. (life), Western Foothills Heritage Trust, McLaughlin Found., Sumner Hist. Soc. (bd. dirs. 1996—). Achievements include research in surface chemistry, permeability of metals to hydrogen, rocket propellant synthesis infrared method of Q evaluation synthetic quartz, crystal growth, printed circuit tech., metal joining; computer-integrated mfg. techniques, statis. quality control, soldering tech., environ. modifications of mfg. processes, ISO 9,000 auditor; patents for for growth of synthetic quartz; research in infra red analysis of quartz; computer control of symthetic quartz crystal growth process. Home: 489 Valley Rd Sumner ME 04292-3402 Home Phone: 207-388-2362; Office Phone: 207-388-2362. Personal E-mail: wiltay@hughes.net.

RUDD, LORETTA COOPER, education educator, researcher; b. Denver, Jan. 3, 1961; d. Kenneth Don and JoAnn Delfina Cooper; m. M. David Rudd, July 30, 1983; children: Nicholas Ryan, Emma Ashleigh. PhD, Baylor U., Waco, TX, 2003. Post-doctoral fellow Baylor U., Waco, Tex., 2004—06; asst. prof. Tex. Tech U., Lubbock, Tex. Deaf edn. tchr. Austin Regional Day Sch. for the Deaf, Austin, Tex., 1983—85, San Marcos Consol. Ind. Sch. Dist., San Marcos, Tex., 1985—87; pub. sch. educator Killeen Ind. Sch. Dist., Killeen, Tex., 1987—95, Killeen, 1989—95; spl. edn. tchr. Monterrey County Office of Edn., Monterey, Calif., 1987—89. Mem., steering com. Child Care Policy Rsch. Consortium, Washington, 2002—03; pres. Waco Montessori Sch., Waco, Tex., 2005—06; mem. Bill and Vera Daniels Heritage Village Mus., Waco, Tex., 2002—03; chairperson, publicity & recognition com. Smart

Start Child Care Assn., Waco, Tex., 2004—05. Mem.: Tex. Psychology Assn., Internat. Reading Assn., Nat. Assn. for Edn. Young Children, Am. Ednl. Rschrs. Assn. Avocations: travel, reading. Office: Texas Tech University Ms 41071 Lubbock TX 79409 Office Fax: 806-742-4132. Business E-Mail: loretta.rudd@ttu.edu.

RUDD, NICHOLAS, investor, consultant; b. NYC, Mar. 18, 1943; s. Emmanuel and Lucie Lia Rudd; m. Judith Carol Anderson, 1995; children: Alexis Henry, Kenneth Charles. BA, Columbia U., 1964, MBA, 1967. Mem. staff Ford Motor Co., NYC, 1964-65, Young & Rubicam Inc., NYC, 1968-99, sr. v.p. mgmt. svcs., 1980-90, chief info. officer, 1990-95; chief knowledge officer Wunderman Cato Johnson, NYC, 1996-99; prin. Venture Mgmt. Svcs., Inc., 1999—2003, Anderson Rudd Co., 2003—; mktg. chair Stamford Symphony Orch., 2003—. Dir. emeritus Nat. Choral Coun., chmn., 1993-95; bd. dirs. Columbia U. Club NY; adv. bd. A Better Chance of Westport; mem. com. TEAM Westport. Mem. Beta Gamma Sigma. Office: 20 Sea Spray Rd Westport CT 06880

RUDD, PAUL, actor; b. Passaic, NJ, Apr. 6, 1969; m. Julie Yaeger, Feb. 23, 2003; 1 child. BA, U. Kans.; Grad., Am. Acad. Dramatic Arts, Los Angeles. Actor: (films) A Question of Ethics, 1992, Clueless, 1995, Halloween: The Curse of Michael Myers, 1995, The Size of Watermelons, 1996, Romeo + Juliet, 1996, The Locusts, 1997, Overnight Delivery, 1998, The Object of My Affection, 1998, 200 Cigarettes, 1999, The Cider House Rules, 1999, Wet Hot American Summer, 2001, The Château, 2001, Reaching Normal, 2001, The Shapes of Things, 2003, Two Days, 2003, House Hunting, 2003, Anchorman: The Legend of Ron Burgundy, 2004, P.S., 2004, Tennis, Anyone...?, 2005, The Baxter, 2005, The 40 Year Old Virgin, 2005, The OH in Ohio, 2006, Diggers, 2006, Night at the Museum, 2006, The Ex, 2007, Reno 911!: Miami, 2007, Knocked Up, 2007, I Could Never Be Your Woman, 2007, Over Her Dead Body, 2008, Forgetting Sarah Marshall, 2008, I Love You, Man, 2009, (voice) Monsters vs. Aliens, 2009; actor, prodr. (films) The Ten, 2007, actor, writer Role Models, 2008; actor: (TV films) The Fire Next Time, 1993, Moment of Truth: Stalking Back, 1993, Runaway Daughters, 1994, Twelfth Night, or What You Will, 1998, The Great Gatsby, 2000; (TV series) Wild Oats, 1994, Sisters, 1993—95, Friends, 2002—04, Reno 911, 2006—07, (TV appearances) Deadline, 2000, Strangers with Candy, 2000, Cheap Seats: Without Ron Parker, 2004, Stella, 2005, Robot Chicken, 2006, The Naked Trucker and T-Bones Show, 2007, Veronica Mars, 2007. Named one of Top 25 Entertainers of Yr. (with Apatow Gang), Entertainment Weekly, 2007. Office: United Talent Agy 9560 Wilshire Blvd Ste 500 Beverly Hills CA 90212-2401

RUDDER, ERIC D., computer company executive, information technology executive; married; 2 children. Grad. with honors, Brown U., 1988. With Microsoft Corp., Redmond, Wash., 1988—, gen. mgr. visual studio, v.p. tech. strategy, sr. v.p. developer and platform evangelism, 2001—03, sr. v.p. servers and tools, 2003—05, sr. v.p. tech. strategy, 2005—. Spkr. in field. Office: Microsoft One Microsoft Way Redmond WA 98052-6399*

RUDDY, FRANK, lawyer, retired ambassador; b. NYC, Sept. 15, 1937; s. Francis Stephen and Teresa (O'Neil) Ruddy; children: Neil, David, Stephen. AB, Holy Cross Coll., 1959; MA, NYU, 1962, LLM, 1967; LLB, Loyola U., New Orleans, 1965; PhD, Cambridge U., Eng., 1969. Bar: D.C., N.Y., Tex., U.S. Supreme Ct. Faculty Cambridge U., 1967-69; asst. gen. counsel USIA, Washington, 1969-72, dep. gen. counsel, 1973-74; sr. atty. Office of Telecomm. Policy, White House, Washington, 1972-73; counsel Exxon Corp., Houston, 1974-81; asst. adminstr. AID (with rank asst. sec. state) Dept. State, Washington, 1981-84; U.S. ambassador to Equatorial Guinea, 1984-88; gen. counsel U.S. Dept. Energy, Washington, 1988-89; v.p. Sierra Blanca Devel. Corp., Washington, 1989-92; ptnr. Ruddy & Muir, Washington, 1998—2004, Sale & Quinn, Washington, 2004—. Vis. scholar Johns Hopkins Sch. Advanced Internat. Studies, 1990—94; dep. chmn. UN Referendum for Western Sahara, 1994. Author: International Law in the Enlightenment, 1975; editor: American International Law Cases (series); editor in chief Internat. Lawyer; contbr. articles to legal jours. Bd. dirs. African Devel. Found., Washington, 1983-84, Human Life Internat., 1999—; mem. Coun. of Am. Ambs., Washington, 1988—. Served with USMCR, 1956-61 Mem.: ABA (chmn. treaty compliance sect. 1991—93), Hague Acad. Internat. Law Alumni Assn., Internat. Law Assn., Am. Soc. Internat. Law, Dacor House, Cosmos Club (Washington), Knights of Malta. Republican. Roman Catholic. Office: Sale & Quinn Fifth Fl 910 16th St NW Washington DC 20006 Home Phone: 301-340-6325; Office Phone: 202-833-4170. Personal E-mail: fruddy@hotmail.com. Business E-Mail: globalltd@earthlink.net.

RUDDY, KATHY AAKRE, paralegal; d. Elmer Lawrence and Madge L. Aakre; m. Allen Clifford Ruddy, June 25, 1997. Assoc. Applied Scis. in Exec. Secretarial, Miles CC, Miles City, Mont., 1989, AAS in Legal Sec., 1989; cert. paralegal, Paralegal Inst. Phoenix, 1991. Enlisted US Army, 1992, advanced through ranks to staff sgt. group, 1992—2009; criminal law mil. paralegal battalion noncommissed officer in charge HHC, 7-158 Aviation Rgt., Fort Hood, Tex., 1992—. Decorated Army Acheivement medals US Army, Army Accomodation medals, Army Good Conduct medals, Mil. Overseas ribbons, Army Svc. ribbon, Operation Iraqi Freedom medal, NCOES Ribbons; recipient Global War on Terrorism medal, 2003—04, Combat Action Badge 2 Bars Iraq. Mem.: DAV, VFW. Republican. Roman Catholic. Avocations: yoga, pilates, reading, cooking, golf, aerobics. Personal E-mail: kathyruddy@hot.rr.com. Business E-Mail: kathy.ruddy@usar.army.mil.

RUDE, BRIAN DAVID, utilities executive; b. Viroqua, Wis., Aug. 25, 1955; s. Raymond and Conelee (Johnson) R.; m. Karen Thulin; children: Erik, Nels. BA magna cum laude, Luther Coll., 1977; MA, U. Wis., Madison, 1994. Mem. Wis. Assembly, Madison, 1982-84, Wis. Senate, Madison, 1984-2000; pres. Wis. State Sen., 1993-96, 98. With corp. comms. Trane Co., La Crosse, Wis., 1981-85; v.p. Dairyland Power Coop.; bd. dirs. Harris Bank of Westby, Riverfront, Inc. Mem. Lions, Sons of Norway, Norwegian-Am. Hist. Assn. (vice-chmn.), Gundersen Lutheran (trustee), State Agriculture Bd. Republican. Lutheran. Avocations: reading, travel, fishing, golf. Home: 307 Babcock St PO Box 367 Coon Valley WI 54623-0367 Office: 3200 East Ave S PO Box 817 La Crosse WI 54602 Office Phone: 608-788-4000. Personal E-mail: bdr@dairynet.com.

RUDE, ERIC JOHN, public health service officer, researcher; b. Chatham, NJ, Jan. 12, 1966; s. John Robert Rude. BA, U. Vt., Burlington, 1988; MSW, U. Denver, Colo., 2000. Cert. in epidemiology NYC Dept. Health, 2005. Dir. health programs Gay, Lesbian, Bisexual and Transgender Cmty. Ctr. Colo., Denver, 1998—2001; HIV prevention contract mgr. AIDS Inst., NY State Dept. Health, 2001—03; hepatitics planner NYC Dept. Health and Mental Hygiene, 2003—04, grad. student preceptor, 2003—, dir., office viral hepatitis coordination, 2004—. Scholar, New Eng. Pub. Health Leadership Inst., 2007. D-Liberal. Avocations: cycling, skiing, opera. Office: New York City Dept Health 125 Worth St Room 326 CN-22 New York NY 10013 Personal E-mail: erudenyc@gmail.com. Business E-Mail: erude@health.nyc.gov.

RUDEBECK, CAROL A., special education educator; d. Bernard Arthur and Cecilia Lucille Andrastek; children: Jaclyn Kate Semple, Megan Beth. BS in Communicative Disorders, U. Wis., Oshkosh, 1971; MS in Spl. Edn., U. Wis., Whitewater, 1977; cert. in elem. edn., Cardinal Stritch U., Milw., 1990. Tchr. Wis., 1971. Speech therapist Waukesha County Spl. Edn. Dist., Wis., 1971—73, Manitowoc County Handicapped Children's Edn. Bd., Wis., 1973—74; early childhood exceptional edn. needs tchr. Door County Regional Learning Ctr., Sturgeon Bay, Wis., 1974—76; tchr. trainer U. Wis., Whitewater, 1979—81; early chidlhood exceptional edn. needs tchr. Germantown Sch. Dist., Wis., 1985—90, 2d grade tchr., 1990—2000, instrnl. resource specialist, 2000—; early childhood exceptional edn. needs tchr., speech therapist Wauwatosa Sch. Dist., Wis., 1977—78. Grad. fellow, WI Dept. Pub. Instrn., 1976—77. Mem.: Wis. ASCD, ASCD, Wis. Assn. Tchrs. English, Nat. Coun. Tchrs. English, Nat. Assn. Gifted Children, Wis. Assn. Talented and Gifted. Conservative. Avocations: travel, reading, home decorating, scrapbooks. Office: Germantown Sch Dist W159 N9939 Butternut Rd Germantown WI 53022 Office Fax: 262-253-3491. Business E-Mail: crudebeck@germantown.k12.wi.us.

RUDEL, BARBARA ELIZABETH, elementary school educator; b. Chgo., Mar. 15, 1964; d. Alfred and Elizabeth Kocialkowski; m. Richard Rudel, Dec. 21, 1986; children: Anna, Cecylia. BA, Concordia U., River Forest, Ill., 1986. Cert. Standard Tchg. Ill. Primary tchr. Union Ridge Sch., Harwood Heights, Ill., 1986—. Mentor tchr. Union Ridge Sch., 2003—05, cooperating tchr., 1986—, yearly com. cons., 1986—. Tchr. rep. PTA, Sch. Dist. 86, 1987. Mem.: NEA (union treas. 1989), Nat. Coun. Tchrs. Math., Internat. Reading Assn., Phi Delta Kappa. Avocations: travel, reading, landscape design. Office: Union Ridge Sch 4600 Oak Pk Ave Harwood Heights IL 60706

RUDEL, JULIUS, conductor; b. Vienna, Mar. 6, 1921; came to US, 1938, naturalized, 1944; s. Jakob and Josephine (Sonnenblum) R.; m. Rita Gillis, June 24, 1942 (dec. May 1984); children: Joan, Madeleine, Anthony Jason. Student, Acad. Music, Vienna; diploma in conducting, Mannes Coll. Music, 1942; diploma hon. doctorates, U. Vt., 1961, U. Mich., 1971; doctorates hon. causa, Pace Coll., Manhattan Coll., 1994, Mannes Coll. Music, 1994, Manhattanville Coll., 1994, Manhattan Sch. Music, 1996. With NYC Opera, 1943-79, 2004, debut, 1944, gen. dir., 1957-79, 3rd St. Music Sch. Settlement, 1945-52, mus. dir. Chautauqua Opera Assn., 1958-59, Caramoor Festival, Katonah, NY, 1964-76, Cin. May Festival, 1971-72, Kennedy Ctr. Performing Arts, 1971-75; music advisor Wolf Trap Farm Pk., 1971, Phila. Opera, 1978-81; condr. Spoleto (Italy) Festival, 1962-63; music dir. Buffalo Philarm. Orch., 1979-85, debut as condr. Met. Opera, 1978, San Francisco Opera, 1979, Vienna State Opera, 1976, Royal Opera, Covent Garden, 1984, Rome Opera, 1987, Opera de la Bastille, 1992, Teatro Colon, Buenos Aires, 1992, Royal Danish Opera, Copenhagen, 1993, LA Opera, 1995; condr. Am. premiere of Braunfels's Die Vogel at Spoleto Festival USA, 2005; condr. Cosi fan Tatte, NYC Opera, 2006; dir. prodn.: Kiss Me Kate, Vienna Volksoper Opera, 1956; prin. guest condr. Palm Beach Opera, 2003; guest condr. Chgo. Symphony, Phila. Orch., NY Philharm., Boston Symphony, Detroit Symphony, Israel Philharm., Paris Opera, Munich Opera, Hamburg State Opera, Vienna State Opera, other symphonic, operatic orgns. in US and Europe. Decorated Croix du Chevalier in arts and letters, France; recipient gold medal, Nat. Arts Club, 1958, citation, Nat. Assn. Am. Composers and Conductors, 1958, citation, Nat. Fedn. Music Clubs, 1959, Ditson award, Columbia, 1959, Page One award in music, Newspaper Guild, 1959, hon. insignia for arts and sci., Govt. of Austria, 1961, Handel medallion for music, City of NY, 1965, citation, Nat. Assn. Negro Musicians, 1965, citation, Nat. Opera Assn., 1971, Comdr.'s Cross, German Order Merit, 1967, hon. lt., Israeli Army, 1969, Julius Rudel award for young condrs., Pan Am./Pan African award for humanism, 1981, Peabody award, 1985, Disting. Achievement award, Kurt Weill Found., 2000, Opera News award, 2008, Opera Index award & Nat. Endowment for the Arts Opera honor, 2009. Office: c/o Shuman Assocs 120 W 58th St Apt 8D New York NY 10019-2126 Office Phone: 212-315-1300. Personal E-mail: shumanpr@shumanassociates.net.

RUDELIUS, WILLIAM, marketing educator; b. Rockford, Ill., Sept. 2, 1931; s. Carl William and Clarissa Euclid (Davis) R.; m. Jacqueline Urch Dunham, July 3, 1954; children: Robert, Jeanne, Katherine, Kristi. BS in Mech. Engring., U. Wis., 1953; MBA, U. Pa., 1959, PhD in Econs., 1964. Program engr., missile and space vehicle dept. Gen. Electric Co., Phila., 1956-57, 59-61; sr. research economist North Star Research Inst., Mpls., 1966-66; lectr. U. Minn., Mpls., 1961-64, asst. prof. mktg. Coll. Bus. Adminstrn., 1964, assoc. prof., 1966-72, prof., 1972—. Co-author: (with W. Bruce Erickson) An Introduction to Contemporary Business, 1973, rev. 4th edit., 1985; (with Eric N. Berkowitz, Roger A. Kerin and Steven W. Hartley) Marketing, 1986, rev. 9th edit., 2009; (with Roger A. Kerin and Steven W. Hartley) Marketing: The Core, 2004, rev. 3rd edit., 2009; (with Krzysztof Przybytowski, Roger A. Kerin and Steven W. Hartley) Marketing na Przykładach, 1998; (with others) Mapketkht, 1st Russian edit., 2001; contbr. articles to profl. jours. Served USAF, 1954—55. Home: 1425 Alpine Pass Minneapolis MN 55416-3560 Business E-Mail: rudelius@umn.edu.

RUDEN, DOUGLAS MARK, science educator; b. Dayton, Ohio, Dec. 6, 1961; s. Donald Walter and Shirley G. Ruden; m. Xiangyi Lu; children: Ximena Lu, Tiger Lu. BS, Caltech, Pasadena, Calif., 1984; PhD, Harvard U., Cambridge, Mass., 2000. Asst. prof. biochemistry U. Kans., Lawrence, 1994—2000; assoc. prof. U. Ala., Birmingham, 2000—06, Wayne State U., Detroit, 2006—. Mng. editor Frontiers Bioscis., 2000—. Organizer Citizens Sci., Lawrence, Kans., 1999—2000. Rsch. grant, NIH, NIAAA, NIEHS, NCI, NIGMS, 2000—. Mem.: Genetics Soc. America. Democrat. Office: Wayne State Univ 2727 2nd Ave Detroit MI 48201 Business E-Mail: douglasr@wayne.edu.

RUDENSTINE, DAVID, law educator, former dean; BA, Yale U., 1963, MAT, 1965; JD, NY U., 1969. Staff atty. NY City Legal Services Program; dir. Citizen's Inquiry on Parole and Criminal Justice, Inc.; project dir., assoc. dir., acting exec. dir. NY Civil Liberties Union; adminstr. Benjamin N. Cardozo Sch. Law, Yeshiva U., NYC, 1979—, assoc. dean academic affairs, 1994—96, interim dean, 1996—97, Dr. Herman George and Kate Kaiser Prof. constitutional law, dean, 2001—09, Sheldon H. Solow prof. law. Inaugural fellow Program in Law and Public Affairs, Princeton U., 2000—01. Author: (book) The Day the Presses Stopped: A History of the Pentagon Papers Case. Vol. Peace Corps, Uganda, 1965—66. Office: Benjamin N Cardozo Sch Law 55 Fifth Ave, Ste 926 New York NY 10003 Office Phone: 212-790-0847. E-mail: rudenstn@yu.edu.*

RUDENSTINE, NEIL LEON, former academic administrator, educator; b. Ossining, NY, Jan. 21, 1935; s. Harry and Mae (Esperito) R.; m. Angelica Zander, Aug. 27, 1960; children: Antonia Margaret, Nicholas David, Sonya. BA, Princeton U., 1956; BA (Rhodes Scholar), Oxford U., 1959, MA, 1963; PhD, Harvard U., 1964. Instr. dept. English Harvard U., Cambridge, Mass., 1964-66, asst. prof., 1966-68; assoc. prof. English Princeton (N.J.) U., 1968-73, prof. English, 1973-88, dean of students, 1968-72, dean of Coll., 1972-77, provost, 1977-88, provost emeritus, 1988—; exec. v.p. Andrew W. Mellon Found., NYC, 1988-91; pres. Harvard U., Cambridge, Mass., 1991-2001, prof. English, 1991-2001, pres. emeritus, 2001—. Chair bd. ArtStor, 2001—. Author: Sidney's Poetic Development, 1967, Pointing Our Thoughts, 2001; (with George Rousseau) English Poetic Satire, 1972; (with William Bowen) In Pursuit of the PhD, 1992. Trustee Princeton U., 2002—06, N.Y. Pub. Libr., Courtauld Inst. Art, London, Goldman Sachs Found., 2002—08, The Barnes Found., J. Paul Getty Trust, 2007—; chair bd. Rockefeller Archieve Ctr. 1st lt. arty. US Army, 1959—60. Hon. fellow New Coll./Oxford U., Emmanuel Coll./Cambridge U., 1991. Fellow Am. Acad. Arts and Scis.; mem. Am. Philos. Soc., Coun. on Fgn. Rels., Com. for Econ. Devel. Office: ARTstor 151 E 61st St New York NY 10065 Office Phone: 212-500-2419.

RUDER, DAVID STURTEVANT, lawyer, educator, former federal agency administrator; b. Wausau, Wis., May 25, 1929; s. George Louis and Josephine (Sturtevant) R.; m. Susan M. Small; children: Victoria Chesley, Julia Larson, David Sturtevant II, John Coulter; stepchildren: Elizabeth Frankel, Rebecca Wilkinson. BA cum laude, Williams Coll., 1951; JD with honors, U. Wis., 1957, LLD, 2002. Bar: Wis. 1957, Ill. 1962. Of counsel Schiff Hardin & Waite, Chgo., 1971—76; assoc. Quarles & Brady, Milw., 1957—61; asst. prof. law Northwestern U. Sch. Law, Chgo., 1961—63, assoc. prof., 1963—65, prof., 1965—2005, William W. Gurley meml. prof. law, 1994—2005, prof. emeritus, 2005—, assoc. dean, 1965—66, dean, 1977—85; chmn. SEC, Washington, 1987—89; ptnr. Baker & McKenzie LLP, Chgo., 1990—94, sr. counsel, 1994—99. Cons. Am. Law Inst. Fed. Securities Code; planning dir. Corp. Counsel Inst., 1962-66, 76-77, com. mem., 1962-87, 90—; adv. bd. Ray Garrett Jr. Corp. and Securities Law Inst., 1980-87, 90—; vis. lectr. U. de Liege, 1967; vis. prof. law U. Pa., Phila., 1971; faculty Salzburg Seminar, 1976; mem. legal adv. com. bd. dirs. N.Y. Stock Exch., 1978-82; mem. com. profl. responsibility Ill. Supreme Ct., 1978-87; adv. bd. Securities Regulation Inst., 1978—, chmn., 1994-97; bd. govs. Nat. Assn. Securities Dealers, 1990-93, chmn. Legal Adv. Bd., 1993-96, Arbitration Policy Task Force, 1994-97; trustee Fin. Acctg. Found., 1996-2002, Internat. Acctg. Stds. Com. Found., 2000-05; mem. Internat. Acctg. Stds. Com. Strategy Working Party, 1997-99; chmn. Securities and Exch. Commn. Hist. Soc., 1999-04; chmn. Mut. Fund Dirs. Forum, 1999—; mem. Pub. Co. Acctg. Oversight Bd., 2002-09. Editor-in-chief: Williams Coll. Record, 1950-51, U. Wis. Law Rev, 1957; editor: Proc. Corp. Counsel Inst, 1962-66; contbr. articles to legal periodicals. Dir. Glen View Club Scholarship Found., 2000-07. 1st lt. US Army, 1951-54. Recipient William O. Douglass award, Assn. Securities and Exchange Comm. Alumni, 2007, Fund Directions Mutual Fund Lifetime Achievement award, 2008. Fellow Am. Bar Found.; ABA (sec. bus. law 1970—, coun. 1970-94, com. chmn., mem. various coms.), Chgo. Bar Assn., Wis. Bar Assn., Am. Law Inst., Order of Coif, Comml. Club of Chgo., Lawyers Club Chgo., Gargoyle Soc., Phi Beta Kappa, Phi Delta Phi, Zeta Psi. Home: 325 Orchard Ln Highland Park IL 60035-1939 Office: Northwestern U Sch Law 357 E Chicago Ave Chicago IL 60611 Office Phone: 312-503-8444.

RUDER, JOHN REGAN, physician; b. Colorado Springs, Colo., Oct. 23, 1947; s. Ralph Emerson and Rosemary Pierron (Regan) R.; m. Sheri Dee Rigby, July 6, 1985; children: Elizabeth, Lindsey, John. BA, Dartmouth Coll., 1969, MD, 1977. Intern in surgery U. N.Mex. & Affiliated Hosps., 1977-78; med. dir. Navajo Reservation, 1977-78; resident in surgery Dartmouth-Hitchcock Med. Ctr., 1978-81; resident in plastic and reconstructive surgery U. Utah, 1981-83, asst. clin. prof. plastic & reconstructive surgery Salt Lake City, 1986-90; chief plastic & reconstructive surgery VA Hosp., Salt Lake City, 1986-90; clin. instr. hand & upper extremity surgery Loma Linda (Calif.) U., 1990-91; v.p. Hand Surgery Assocs., Arlington Heights, Ill., 1991—. Co-author: (chpts.) Injuries and Rehabilitation of the Upper Extremity, 1998, Upper Extremity Compressive Neuropathies, 1998. Mem. ACS, Am. Soc. for Surgery of the Hand, Am. Soc. of Plastic and Reconstructive Surgery, Am. Assn. Hand Surgery, Alpha Omega Alpha. Office: Hand Surgery Assocs 515 W Algonquin Rd Ste 120 Arlington Heights IL 60005-4440

RUDER, TIA L., music educator; d. Judy K and Duane F Ruder. MusB cum laude in Edn., Wichita State U., 1992, MusB cum laude in Performance, 1992, BA cum laude, 1993, MusM in Edn., 1999. K-12 vocal and instrumental music Kans., 1992. Instrumental music tchr. Wichita Pub. Schs., Kans., 1992—, asst. dir. all-city band, 1993—2006, tchr. summer sch., 2000—04, summer instrument cleaner, repairer, 2000—05, dir. All-City Band, 2007. Summer sch. tchr. Oakley Pub. Schs., Kans., 1992—97; soprano soloist and instrumental music dir. Mt. Vernon Presbyn. Ch., Wichita, Kans., 1992—2001; pvt. music tchr., Wichita, 1992—2003. State forensics championships adjudicator Kans. State H.S. Activities Assn., Wichita, 1992—2005. Recipient Honors Program Grad., Wichita State U., 1992, Mortar Bd. Scholar, 1991; U. Leader Scholar, 1992—96. Mem.: NEA, Kans. Bandmasters Assn., Fedn. of Teachers, Kans. Music Educators Assn., Music Educators Nat. Conf. Avocations: cooking, home improvement, science fiction, theater. Personal E-mail: tia.ruder@cox.net.

RUDER, WILLIAM, public relations executive; b. NYC, Oct. 17, 1921; s. Jacob L. and Rose (Rosenberg) R.; m. Betty Cott, May 23, 1980; children: Robin Ann, Abby, Brian, Michal Ellen, Eric. BSS., City Coll., NYC, 1942. With Samuel Goldwyn Prodns., 1946-48; pres. Ruder & Finn, Inc., NYC, 1948-80, William Ruder Inc., 1981—. Asst. sec. commerce, 1961-62; Tobe lectr. Harvard Grad. Sch. Bus., 1962; mem. grad. adv. bd. City Coll. N.Y., Baruch Sch. Bus., N.Y.C.; cons. State Dept.; bd. dirs. W.P. Carey & Co., Inc.; trustee Continuum Health Ptnrs., Inc. Author: The Businessman's Guide to Washington. Bd. dirs. Bus. Com. for Arts, Jewish Bd. Guardians, Chamber Music Soc. Lincoln Ctr., Fund for Peace, Project Return Found.; exec. com. United Way Am.; trustee, chmn. Manhattanville Coll., Purchase, N.Y., 1974-75; trustee Com. for Econ. Devel., St. Lukes/ Roosevelt Hosp.; bd. overseers Wharton Sch. U. Pa.; mem. pres.'s coun. Meml. Sloan-Kettering Cancer Ctr.; chmn. bd. ACCESS. Capt. USAAF, 1941-45. Mem. UN Assn. U.S.A. (nat. policy panel dir., trustee com. for econ. devel.). Home: PO Box 230 East Hampton NY 11937 Office: Ruder Finn Inc 301 E 57th St New York NY 10022-2900

RUDI, LANGSTON CILIBRASI, software engineer; b. Bklyn., July 18, 1974; s. Salvatore Francis Cilibrasi and Theresa Pickett. BS, Calif. Inst. Tech., 1996; PhD in Computer Sci., Dutch Nat. Rsch. Inst. for Math. and Computer Sci., U. Amsterdam, Netherlands, 2007. Lead software arch. Idealab, Pasadena, Calif., 1994—97; chief tech. officer Weema Technologies Inc., Atlanta, 1999—2001; machine learning rschr. Centrum voor Wiskunde en Informatica, Amsterdam, Netherlands, 2002—. Computer cons. Rudi Cilibrasi, Amsterdam, 1992—. Contbr. articles to profl. publs. Recipient Rensselaer medal, Rensselaer Poly. Inst., 1991; scholar, Microsoft, 1993. Green Party. Achievements include invention of fast heuristic quartet (unrooted binary) tree search algorithm for use in bioinformatics, stemmatology, and other disciplines; development of novel music clustering algorithm; CompLearn: open source machine learning with data compressors; research in a new way to derive semantic meaning using the theoretical notion of Kolmogorov Complexity combined with Google's SOAP search engine interface; discovery of data compression based universal clustering technique; development of Linux kernel networking stack program, peer-to-peer distribution theorist. Avocations: computers, art, drawing. Personal E-mail: rudi@cilibrar.com.

RUDIGER, LANCE WADE, secondary school educator; b. Bklyn., Mar. 27, 1948; s. H.F. and Muriel Marie (Staudermann) R.; 1 child, Heidi. BS in Chemistry, SUNY, Albany, 1976; MEd, St. Lawrence U., 1982. Cert. tchr., N.Y. Tchr. chemistry Potsdam H.S., 1982—, chmn. dept. sci., 1992—. Adj. prof. Canton (N.Y.) Coll. Tech., Mater Dei Coll., Ogdensburg, N.Y., Empire Coll., Albany, 1986—; tchr. Inst. Chem. Edn.-Sci. demonstration; bd. dirs., treas. St. Lawrence Valley Tchrs. Learning Ctr., Canton; sci. coord. Upward Bound St. Lawrence U.; program com., bd. dirs. N.Y. Assn. State Computers & Tech. in Edn.; writer N.Y. State Regents chemistry core curriculum; mem. N.Y. State Part D Performance Regents Test Devel. Com.; reviewer chemistry tchr. cert. exam NY State; mem. SED Regents Benchmark Commn.; item writer NYS Chem. Regents; mem. NYSED-McGraw Hill Chemistry Regents Anchor Com.; mem. HS chemistry exam com. Am. Chem. Soc., 2005, reviewer NY State Tchr. Edn. Exam, instr. Johns Hopkins Ctr. Talented Youth, U. Calif. Santa Cruz, U. RI, Workshop Tchr. cons. Clarkson U. Nanoparticle. Co-author: Chemistry Environment, 1990; editor, reviewer Activ Chemistry. Bd. dirs. March of Dimes NY State, Syracuse, Potsdam Ctrl. NY State Tchr. Ctr., 2007—; NY State chemistry regional and state coord. mentor; mem. environ. mgmt. bd. St. Lawrence County, 1997-, edn. com. chair, 1999-, vice chair, 2003-; mem. bd. examiners Nat. Coun. Accreditation Tchr. Edn., 2001—; profl. devel. com. Potsdam Ctrl. Schs., 2005—. Recipient Newmast award NASA, 1987, Dreyfus Master Tchr. award, 1989, Fulbright Symposium award Australia, 2002; grantee NSTA-FDA, 2003, Am. Chem Soc., Woodrow Wilson Found., Binghamtom U. Step Program, St. Lawrence Valley Tchrs. Ctr., 1991-98, Sweetwater Found., Miami U. (Ohio), 1995, Johns Hopkins Space Grant Consortium, Wright Ctr. for Aerospace and Space Engring., Reynolds Metals Excellence in Edn., 1990-94, Cornell U. Sci. Workshop, IRIS; named solar sys. amb. Jet Propulsion Lab., NASA, STANYS Appreciation award, 2007. Mem. Nat. Sci. Tchrs. Assn. (local leader, manuscript review adv. panel The Sci. Tchr., sci. safety com. 2000, webwatchers 2001, Exxon BaP key leader and North Country liaison, mem. reports com.), Nat. Radio Astronomy Obs. (assoc., mentor astronomy workshop), Am. Astron. Soc. (tchr. resource agent 1996-98, Leadership Workshop award 1998), Sci. Tchrs. Assn. N.Y. State (bd. dirs. 1990—, chmn. sect. 1992—, fin. com. 2000—, grant com. chair, presenter at convs. 1988—, hospitality chair ann. conf. NYSC & TE 1996, 98, 2000, bd. dirs.), North Country Conservation Edn. Assn. (life), USCG Acad. Nat. Parents Assn. (bd. dirs. 1997-98), N.Y. State Tchr. Cert. Exam Adv. Com., Canton Club, Lions (past pres. Waddington, N.Y., Pres.'s award, bd. dirs. Canton, pres. 1997-98, treas. 1998-99, dir. 1999-2003), Potsdam Kiwanis (charter, bd. dirs. 1989-91), Phi Delta Kappa (rsch. dir., v.p. program 1999, v.p. membership, pres. 2001—, Phi Delta Kappan 2004, Gerald Read travel scholar 2004). Home: 54 Court St Canton NY 13617-1159 Office: Potsdam High School Leroy St Potsdam NY 13676-1798 E-mail: lrudiger@aol.com.

RUDIN, ANNE, retired mayor, nursing educator; b. Passaic, NJ, Jan. 27, 1924; m. Edward Rudin, June 6, 1948; 4 children. BS in Edn., Temple U., 1945, RN, 1946; MPA, U. So. Calif., 1983; LLD (hon.), Golden Gate U., 1990. RN, Calif. Mem. faculty Temple U. Sch. Nursing, Phila., 1946-48; mem. nursing faculty Mt. Zion Hosp., San Francisco, 1948-49; mem. Sacramento City Council, 1971-83; mayor City of Sacramento, 1983-92; ind. pub. policy cons. Pres. LWV, Riverside, 1957, Sacramento, 1961, Calif., 1969-71, Calif. Elected Women's Assn., 1973—; trustee Golden Gate U., 1993-96; mem. adv. bd. U. So. Calif., Army Depot Reuse Commn., 1992-94; bd. dirs. Sacramento Theatre Co., 1992-99, Japan Soc. No. Calif., Sacramento Symphony, 1993-96, Calif. Common Cause, 1993 -96, Sacramento Edn. Found., 1993-2006; v.p. Sacramento Traditional Jazz Soc. Found.; pres. bd. dirs. Natomas Basin Conservancy; foreman Sacramento County Grand Jury, 2000-01. Recipient Women in Govt. award U.S. Jaycee Women, 1984, Woman of Distinction award Sacramento Area Soroptimist Clubs, 1985, Civic Contbn. award LWV Sacramento, 1989, Woman of Courage award Sacramento History Ctr., 1989, Peacemaker of Yr. award Sacramento Mediation Ctr., 1992, Regional Pride award Sacramento Mag., 1993, Humanitarian award Japanese Am. Citizen's League, 1993, Outstanding Pub. Svc. award Am. Soc. Pub. Adminstrn., 1994, Cmty. Svc. Recognition award, Japanese Am. Citizens League, 1999, Contbr. to Pub. Art award Am. Soc. for Pub. Admin., 2004, Robert T. Matsui award Pub. Svc., Town & Country Dem. Club, 2005; named Girl Scouts Am. Role model, 1989; named to Sacramento Traditional Jazz Soc. Hall of Fame, 2000. Mem.: Calif. Med. Alliance (Mem. of Yr. 2005).

RUDIN, SCOTT, film and theatre producer; b. NYC, July 14, 1958; Prodn. asst., asst. to theatre prodrs. Kermit Bloomgarden and Robert Whitehead; casting dir. motion pictures and theatre, prodr. with Edgar Scherick, exec. v.p. prodn. 20th Century Fox, 1984-86, pres. prodn., 1986-87; founder Scott Rudin Prodns., 1990—. Prodr. (films) Mrs. Soffel, 1984, Pacific Heights, 1990, Regarding Henry, 1991, Little Man Tate, 1991, The Addams Family, 1991, Life With Mikey, 1993, The Firm, 1993, Searching for Bobby Fischer, 1993, Sister Act 2, 1993, Addams Family Values, 1993, I.Q., 1994, Nobody's Fool, 1994, Sabrina, 1995, Clueless, 1995, Up Close and Personal, 1996, Ransom, 1996, Marvin's Room, 1996, The First Wives Club, 1996, In and Out, 1997, Twilight, 1998, The Truman Show, 1998, A Civil Action, 1998. Wonder Boys, 1999, Rules of Engagement, 1999, Brokeback Mountain, 1999, Angela's Ashes, 1999, Bringing Out the Dead, 1999, Sleepy Hollow, 1999, Rules of Engagement, 2000, Zoolander, 2001, The Royal Tenenbaums, Changing Lanes, 2002, The Hours, 2002, The Stepford Wives, 2004, The Manchurian Candidate, 2004, The Village, 2004, I Heart Huckabees, 2004, Life Aquatic with Steve Zissou, 2004, Closer, 2004, Freedomland, 2006, Failure to Launch, 2006, No Country for Old Men, 2007 (Acad. award for Best Motion Picture, 2008), Margot at the Wedding, 2007, The Darjeeling Unlimited, 2007, The Other Boleyn Girl, 2008, Stop Loss, 2008; exec. prodr. (films) Flatliners, 1990, Sister Act, 1992, Jennifer Eight, 1992, South Park: Bigger, Longer and Uncut, 1999, Team America: World Police, 2004, Lemony Snicket's A Series of Unfortuante Events, 2004, Wild Tigers I Have Known, 2006, The Queen, 2006, Venus, 2006, Nothing Is Private, 2007, There Will Be Blood, 2007; (TV movies) Revenge of the Stepford Wives, 1980, He Makes Me Feel Like Dancing, 1983 (Outstanding Children's Program Emmy award 1982, Feature Documentary Acad. award 1984); (theatre) Passion, 1994 (Best Musical Tony award 1994), Indiscretions, 1995, Hamlet, 1995, Seven Guitars, 1995, Skylight, 1997, A Funny Thing Happened on the Way to the Forum, 1996, On the Town (with the N.Y. Shakespeare Festival), 1997, The Chairs, 1998, The Judas Kiss, 1998, (London) Closer, 1998, The Blue Room, 1998, Closer, 1999, Amy's View, 1999, Wide Guys, 1999, Copenhagen, 1999 (Tony Award); (off broadway) Stupid Kids, 1998, The Most Fabulous Story Ever Told, 1999, Shaft, 2000. Named one of 50 Most Powerful People in Hollywood, Premiere mag., 2002—06. Jewish. Office: Scott Rudin Prodns c/o Starr & Co 350 Park Ave 9th Fl New York NY 10022 also: Scott Rudin Prodns Inc c/o Star & Co LLC 850 Third Ave 15th Fl New York NY 10022

RUDING, HERMAN ONNO, banker, former cabinet minister; b. Aug. 15, 1939; m. Renee V.M. Hekking; 2 children. MA in Econs., Netherlands Sch. Econs., 1964; PhD in Econs. cum laude, 1969. Head divsn. internat. monetary affairs Treas. Gen. Ministry Fin., The Hague, 1965—70; joint gen. mgr. Amsterdam-Rotterdam Bank N.V., Amsterdam, 1971-76; bd. mng. dirs., 1981-82; exec. dir. IMF, Washington, 1977-80; min. of fin. Govt. of The Netherlands, The Hague, 1982-89; chmn. Netherlands Christian Fedn. Employers, The Hague, 1990-92; vice chmn., dir. Citicorp and Citibank, NYC, 1992—2003; pres. Internat. Christian Union of Bus. Execs., 2000—03; chmn. Amsterdam Inst. Fin., Ctr. European Policy Studies, Brussels, Nat. Mus. Palace, Het Loo, Netherlands. Contbr. articles to porlf. jours. Mem. Christian Dem. Alliance, Com. Monetary Union of Europe, Trilateral Commn., Am.-European Cmty. Assn., Pontifical Coun. Justice and Peace. Office: 545 Avenue Louise 1050 Brussels Belgium Office Phone: 32-2646 4729. Business E-Mail: rufinco@skynet.be.

RUDINSKY, NORMA LEIGH, English language educator, translator; b. Cedar City, Utah, Oct. 23, 1928; d. Wilford Webster and Anna Mae (Langford) Leigh; m. Julius A. Rudinsky, June 12, 1954 (dec. 1980); children: Helen Ann, Alexander John, Stephen Anthony, Paul Joseph, Michael Francis, Mary Louise. AB in English, Stanford U., Calif., 1950, AM in English, 1953; certs. in Slovak lang., Comenius U., Bratislava, Slovakia, 1981, 82, 84, 90. Sr. instr. English Oreg. State U., Corvallis, 1966—. Lectr. in field. Author: Incipient Feminists, 1991; translator: Seven Slovak Stories by Martin Kukucin, 1980, That Alluring Land: Slovak Stories By Timrava, 1992 (Heldt Prize for Transl. 1993). Internat. Rsch. & Exch. Bd. fellow, 1982, 84, 86-87, Humanities Ctr. fellow, 1988. Mem. Am. Assn. Advancement Slavic Studies, Czechoslovak History Conf., Slovak Studies Assn. (v.p. 1984-86), Slovak Inst. Roman Catholic. Office: Oreg State U Dept Of English Corvallis OR 97331 E-mail: normarudinsky@leigh.org.

RUDLEY, JOHN M., academic administrator; m. Docia Rudley. BA, U. Toledo; M.Ed. in Adminstrn. and Supervision, Tenn. State U., ED.D in Adminstrn. CPA Tenn. Accountant Coopers and Lybrand, LA, Seattle; internal auditor Tex. So. U., v.p. fiscal affairs, 1984; adminstr. U. Tenn., Chattanooga; sr. tech. advisor US Dept. Edn.; vice chancellor bus. and fin. Tenn. Bd. Regents, 1995—2002; vice chancellor adminstrn. and fin. U. Houston Sys., 2002—08, interim chancellor, 2007—08; v.p. adminstrn. and fin. U. Houston, 2002—08, interim pres., 2007—08; pres. Tex. So. U., Houston, 2008—. Mem.: Bioltonston Bd., 100 Black Men (Houston), Internat. Edn. Consortium (chmn.), Tex. Med. Ctr. (CEO, group mem.), Houston Tech. Bd., Greater Houston Partnership Bd., Tenn. Soc. of CPAs. Office: Tex So U Hannah Hall, Suite 220 3100 Cleburne St Houston TX 77004 Office Phone: 713-313-7011.

RUDLOFF, UDO, surgeon, researcher; b. Schweinfurt, Bavaria, Germany, Apr. 16, 1969; arrived in US, 2002; s. Herbert and Helga (Gall) Rudloff. PhD, German Cancer Rsch. Ctr., Heidelberg, 1994; MD, Ruprecht Karls U., Heidelberg, Germany, 1997. Rsch. fellow German Cancer Rsch. Ctr., Heidelberg, 1991—94, European Molecular Biology Labs., Heidelberg, 1993; ho. officer dept. surgery and orthop. Zomba Ctrl. Hosp., Malawi, 1997—98; ho. officer U. Hosp. Aintree, Liverpool, England, 1999, Leicester Gen. Hosp., England, 1999—2000, Hinchingbrooke Hosp., Huntington, England, 2000, Dewsbury Dist. Hosp., England, 2000—01; registrar Guy's and St. Thomas' Hosp., London, 2001—02; house officer North Shore - LI Jewish Health Sys., Manhasset, NY, 2002—05, NYU Sch. Medicine, NYC, 2005—07; fellow surg. oncology Meml. Sloan Kettering Cancer Ctr., NY, 2007—. Contbr. Archives Gynecology and Obstetrics, Basel, Switzerland, 2002—07. Contbr. articles to numerous profl. jours. Recipient Young Talent award, Soc. Advancements Rsch. in Molecular Biology, Heidelberg, Germany, 1995, Young Investigator award, Am. Soc. Clin. Oncology, 2008; scholar, German Acad. Scholarship Found., 1994—97, Scholarship Found. Roman Cath. Ch., 1994. Mem.: Am. Bd. Surgery, Royal Coll. Obstetricians and Gynecologists. Office: Meml Sloan-Kettering Cancer Ctr MSKCC Howard Bldg 1206/12 410 E 68th St New York NY 10021 Office Phone: 212-639-7537. Personal E-mail: udo_rudloff@hotmail.com. Business E-Mail: rudloffu@mskcc.org.

RUDMAN, JEFFREY B., lawyer; b. Cambridge, Mass., May 1, 1948; s. Stanley H. and Dorothy (Braidy) R.; m. Susan Victoria Fried, Aug. 25, 1986; children: Samuel Newland, Nicholas Braidy. AB, Columbia U., 1970; BA, Oxford U., Eng., 1972; JD, Harvard U., 1975. Bar: Mass. 1975, U.S. Dist. Ct. Mass. 1975, U.S. Ct. Appeals (1st cir.) 1977. Assoc. Hale and Dorr, Boston, 1975-80, jr. ptnr., 1980-83, sr. ptnr., 1983—2004; ptnr., co-chmn. Securities dept., mem. Litigation dept. Wilmer Cutler Pickering Hale and Dorr, Boston, 2004—. Trustee Boston Mus. Project; chmn. bd. trustees Boston Pub. Libr.; former sec. New Eng. & N.J. Rhodes Scholarship Selection Coms., 1985-; former mem. cmty. adv. bd. WGBH. Rhodes scholar, 1970-72. Mem. Mass. Bar Assn., Boston Bar Assn., Phi Beta Kappa, St. Botolph Club Home: 1 Adams St Charlestown MA 02129-3433 Office: Wilmer Cutler Pickering Hale and Dorr 60 State St Boston MA 02109-1816 Office Phone: 617-526-6912. Office Fax: 617-526-5000. Business E-Mail: jeffrey.rudman@wilmerhale.com.

RUDMAN, SOLOMON KAL, magazine publisher; b. Phila., Mar. 6, 1930; s. Benjamin and Lena (Holtzman) R.; m. Lucille Steinhauer, June 29, 1958; 1 child, Mitchell. BS in Edn., U. Pa., Phila., 1951; MS in Edn., Temple U., Phila., 1957; LHD (hon.), Holy Family U., Phila., 2002, U. Arts, 2003, LHD (hon.), 2005, PhD (hon.), 2006; HHD honoris causa (hon.), Drexel U., Phila., 1970. Chmn. dept. spl. edn. Franklin D. Roosevelt Sch., Bristol Twp., Pa., 1960-68; pub. premier record/ radio trade Fri. Morning Quarterback, Cherry Hill, Pa., 1968—. Bd. dirs. Variety Club, NARAS, Crime Commn., Pa., NJ, Del.; co-host Merv Griffin TV Show, 1981-82; music expert Today Show, 1981-82, Tomorrow Show, 1981-82, Tom Snyder TV Show; host Phila. Franklin Inst. Sci. and Fels Planetarium mobile sci. programs, entertainment shows to Phila.-NJ Sr. Citizens' homes, children's and vets. hosps.; co-host, talent booker Easter Seals Telethon; creator h.s. jazz piano competition U. the Arts, Phila.; created Kal and Lucille Rudman Inst. Drexel U.; fin. supporter Nat. Acad. TV Arts and Sci.; founder Media Ctr. & Fin. Digital TV Sta., Temple U. Pub.: (mag.) MQB (Modern QB); prodr. CD's of advance hits; launched music trade mag. Pro QB, launched Q-Beat; created 50 billboards for Mothers In Charge. Bd. dirs. Phila. Broadcast Pioneers; sponsor carillon bells Ave. of Arts, Phila., TV cameras Temple U. Sch. Comm., alert systems Phila. police dog cars, Franklin Inst. Travelling Sci. Show to Phila. elem. schs., Citizens' Crime Commn., 1st ann. classical piano HS competition, Chestnut Hill Coll., 100th Anniversary Jewish Fedn. Phila., Franklin Inst. Time Capsule, Phila., Jewish Fedn. Atrium, Phila.; co-sponsor purchase and distbn. of dictionaries to Phila. Elem. Sch. pupils, Robotics Competition Phila. HS, NJ United Cerebral palsy Marathon Dance, Rutgers U.; co-sponsor Succeeding By Reading Program; active Phila. Mid. Schs., Jewish Book week, Phila. Ave. of Arts., Newspapers In Edn., others; founder Kal and Lucille Rudman Inst. for Entertainment Studies, Drexel Hill. U. Coll. Media Arts and Design, Phila., 1974; grad. FBI Cmty. Outreach. Recipient Lifetime Achievement award Phila. Music Conf., Lifetime Music Achievement award Delaware Valley Music Poll., Presdl. Citation, Citizens Crime Com., Plaque on Walk of Fame, Ave. of the Arts, Enforcement award Nat. Marines, Radio Milestone award to Phila. Radio Legends, March of Dimes, T. Seddon Duke award, Bennell award; Top Civilian award, Phila Fire Dept., T.Seddon Duke award, Marshall award, Phila. Crime Commn. (1st Civilian to recieve it); Top Civilian award Phila./Del. Valley Crime Commn., Top award Citizen's Crime Commn., Phila.; named Penndelphia Humanitarian of Yr., Humanitarian of Yr. Nat. Sunshine Fedn., Hon. Dep. Commr., Phila. Police, Hon. Fire Commr., Person of Yr. Phila./Del/ Valley Broadcast Pioneers, Phila. Art CC, 1970, Philanthropist of Yr., 2007, Cmty. Philanthropic of Yr.; named to Broadcast Pioneers Hall of Fame Phila., Hon. Dep. Police Commr., Phila.; scholar Drexel U., Hahnemann Med. Sch., Phila.; Two Mini Med. Scholarships to Drexel Med. Sch. (Student of Masterman High, Phial.); 15th Yr. Scholarships from Olney High and Program, St. Christopher Hosp. Children. Mem. Phila. Music Alliance (bd. dirs.), Nat. Arthritis Found. (bd. dirs.), NARAS (bd. dirs.), Masons (cmty. svc. award, Grand Master), Phila. Police Commrs. Club (named hon. dep. police commr.). Roman Catholic. Achievements include helping to create Music Theater Dept. at U. Arts, Phila; creating the 1st Police Athletic League, Abington, Pa; donating dogs, billboard, motorcycles, plaques. Office: Friday Morning Quarterback 1930 Marlton Pike E Cherry Hill NJ 08003-2150 Home Phone: 856-424-0962; Office Phone: 856-424-7076.

RUDNER, SARA, dancer; b. Bklyn., Feb. 16, 1944; d. Henry Nathaniel and Jeannette (Smolensky) R.; 1 child, Edward Eli Rudner Marschner. AB in Russian Studies, Barnard Coll., 1964; MFA in Choreography, Bennington Coll., 1999. Dancer Sansardo Dance Co., NYC, 1964-65, Am. Dance Co. at Lincoln Ctr., NYC, 1965, Shakespeare Festival Touring Children's Show, NYC, 1966; featured dancer Twyla Tharp Dance Found., NYC, 1966-85; guest dancer Joffrey Ballet, NYC, 1973, Pilobolus Dance Theatre, NYC, 1975, Lar Lubovitch Dance Co., NYC, 1975-76; guest lectr., choreographer grad. dance dept. UCLA, 1975; artistic dir., dancer Sara Rudner Performance Ensemble, NYC, 1977—84. Dir. dance Sarah Lawrence Coll.; tchr. master workshop NYU Theater Program, 1988-90; pres., artistic dir. Heart Dance, Inc. Choreographer: Palm Trees and Flamingoes, 1980, Dancing for an Hour or So, 1981, Minute by Minute, 1982, Eight Solos, 1991, Heartbeats, Inside Out, 1993, Dancing-on-View St. Mark's Ch., NYC, 1999, Santa Fe Opera, Baryshnikov Arts Ctr., NYC, 2007, ICA Variations, Summer Stages Dance, Boston, 2008, This Dancing Life, Irish Modern Dance Theater, Dublin, Ireland, 2007; (with Jennifer Tipton and Dana Reitz) Necessary Weather, 1994; (with Rona Pondick, Robert Feintuch and Jennifer Tipton) Mine, 1996, Alley Theater-The Greeks part I and II, 1997, Heartbeat/mb with Christopher Janney and Mikhail Barysnikov, 1998. Grantee Creative Artists Pub. Svc. Program, N.Y., 1975-76, N.Y. State Coun. on Arts, 1975-78, Nat. Endowment for Arts, 1979-81, 91-92, 94-97; Guggenheim fellow, 1981-82; recipient N.Y. Dance and Performance award, 1984. Office Phone: 914-395-2628. Business E-Mail: srudner@slc.edu, srudner@sarahlawrence.edu.

RUDNICK, IRENE KRUGMAN, lawyer, educator, former state legislator; b. Columbia, SC, Dec. 27, 1929; d. Jack and Jean (Getter) Krugman; m. Harold Rudnick, Nov. 7, 1954 (dec.); children: Morris, Helen Gail. AB cum laude, U. S.C., 1949, JD, 1952. Bar: (S.C.) 1952. Individual practice law, Aiken, SC, 1954—; now ptnr. Rudnick & Rudnick; instr. bus. law U. S.C., Aiken, 1962—; tchr. Warrenville Elem. Sch., 1965-70; supt. edn. Aiken County, 1970-72; mem. S.C. Ho. of Reps., 1972—78, 1980—84, 1986—94. Pres. Adath Yeshurun Synagogue; active Aiken County Dem. Party, S.C. Dem. Party; hon. mem. Aiken Able-Disabled. Recipient Citizen of Yr. award, 1976-77, Bus. and Profl. Women's Career Woman of Yr., 1978, 94, Aiken County Friend of Edn. award, 1985, 93, Outstanding Legis. award Disabled Vets., 1991, Citizen of Yr. award Planned Parenthood, 1994, Sertoma Svc. to Mankind award, 1996, Pickens Salley So. Woman of Distinction award, 2005; named Aiken County C. of C. Woman of Yr., 2005. Mem. AAUW (life), Aiken Able-Disabled (hon.), Aiken Hist. Soc., Hist. Aiken Found., Alpha Delta Kappa, Order Eastern Star, Hadassah Sisterhood (life), Am. Legion Aux. Office: PO Box 544 135 Pendleton St NW Aiken SC 29802

RUDNICK, LEWIS G., lawyer; b. May 31, 1935; AB with honors, Univ. Ill., Urbana-Champaign, 1957; MBA, Columbia Univ., 1960; JD, Northwestern Univ., 1964. Bar: Ill. 1964, US Dist. Ct. (no. dist. Ill.) 1964. Of Councel, Franchise & Distribution practice group DLA Piper US LLP, Chgo. Former gen. counsel Internat. Franchise Assn. and Internat. Franchise Assn. Edn. Found.; mem., councel Ill. Franchise Adv. Bd.; mem. gov. com. ABA Forum on Franchising, 1977—84, chmn., 1981—83. Editor: Former Jour. of Internat. Franchising & Distribution Law; contbr. articles to profl. jours. Mem.: ABA, Internat. Franchise Assn. (counsel). Office: DLA Piper US LLP Suite 1900 203 N LaSalle St Chicago IL 60601-1293 Office Phone: 312-368-4055. Office Fax: 312-630-7312. Business E-Mail: lewis.rudnick@dlapiper.com.

RUDO, MILTON, retired manufacturing executive; b. Balt., Jan. 17, 1919; s. Saul E. and Bertha (Berkowitz) R.; m. Roslind Mandel, Mar. 27, 1943; children: Stephanie Ellen, Neil Dennis. BA, Johns Hopkins U., 1940; AMP, Harvard U., 1964. Various positions Brunswick Corp., Skokie, Ill., 1940-66, corp. v.p., pres. Bowling divsn. Chgo., 1966-74, group v.p. recreation bus., 1974-84, ret., 1984, cons. to the CEO, 1984-87; dir., cons. to the CEO Donlen Leasing Corp., Skokie, 1986-90. Pres. Nat. Bowling Hall of Fame and Mus., 1979. Capt. AUS, 1942-45, ETO. Recipient ann. award N.Y. Mktg. Club, 1960, Industry Svc. award, 1973; named to Bowling Hall of Fame, 1984; decorated with 3 Battle Star. Mem. Nat. Bowling Coun. (pres. 1972), Briarwood Country Club (Deerfield, Ill., pres. 1965-67), Hamlet Country Club (Delray Beach Fla.). Home (Summer): 1755 Lake Cook Rd Highland Park IL 60035 Home (Winter): 712 Pine Lake Delray Beach FL 33445

RUDOFF, SHELDON, lawyer; b. Bklyn., May 29, 1933; s. Raphael and Goldie (Gorelick) R.; m. Hedda Muller, Nov. 22, 1964; children: Shaindy, Sara, Simone. BA cum laude, Yeshiva Coll., 1954; JSD cum laude, NYU, 1958; ordination, RIETS, 1957. Bar: N.Y. 1958, U.S. Dist. Ct. (so. and ea. dists.) N.Y. 1958, U.S. Supreme Ct. 1978. Ptnr. Shatzkin, Cooper & Rudoff, NYC, 1970-84, Labaton Sucharow & Rudoff, NYC, 1984—2008, Phillip Vizo, LLP, 2008—; pres. Union Orthodox Jewish Congregation Am., 1990-94, hon. pres., 1994—; pres. Beth Din Am., 1996—2003, bd. chmn., 2003—. V.p. Yeshiva Coll. Alumni, N.Y.C., 1962-64; pres. Young Israel West Side, N.Y.C., 1969-72; sec. Orthodox Union, 1972-76, v.p., 1976-78, sr. v.p., 1978-84, chmn. bd., 1984-90, pres. 1990-94, hon. pres. 1954; trustee Fedn. Jewish Philanthropies, 1980-91, United Jewish Cmtys, chmn. Audit Com; material chmn. Conf. Governing 2005-. Recipient Pres.'s award Orthodox Union, N.Y.C., 1972, Nat. Leadership award Nat. Conf. Synagogue Youth, N.Y.C., 1974, Kesser Shem Tov award Ortohdox Union, 1995. Mem. ABA, N.Y. State Bar Assn., Assn. Bar City N.Y. (transp. com. 1976—). Office: Philhip Nizor LLP 666 Fifth Ave New York NY 10103 Office Phone: 212-907-0700, 212-841-0524. E-mail: srudoff@philhsnizor.com.

RUDOLPH, ABRAHAM MORRIS, pediatrician, educator; b. Johannesburg, Republic of South Africa, Feb. 3, 1924; s. Chone and Sarah (Feinstein) Rudolph; m. Rhona Sax, Nov. 2, 1949; children: Linda,

Colin, Jeffrey. MBBCh summa cum laude, U. Witwatersrand, Johannesburg, 1946, MD, 1951; MD (hon.), U. Witwatersrand, Johannesburg, S. Africa, 2006; D (hon.), Rene Descartes U., Paris, 1996. Instr. Harvard Med. Sch., 1955—57, assoc. pediat., 1957—60; assoc. cardiologist in charge cardiopulmonary lab. Children's Hosp., Boston, 1955—60; dir. pediatric cardiology Albert Einstein Coll. Medicine, 1960—66, prof. pediat., assoc. prof. physiology NYC, 1962—66; vis. pediatrician Bronx Mcpl. Hosp. Ctr., NYC, 1960—66; prof. pediat. U. Calif., San Francisco, 1966—94, prof. physiology, 1974—88, Neider prof. pediatric cardiology, prof. ob-gyn and reproductive scis., 1974—94, chmn. dept. pediat., 1987—91, prof. pediatr. emeritus, 1994—; practice medicine, specializing in pediatric cardiology San Francisco. Mem. cardiovasc. study sect. NIH, 1961—65; mem. nat. adv. heart coun., 1968—72; established investigator Am. Heart Assn., 1958—62; career scientist Health Rsch. Coun., NYC, 1962—66; Harvey lectr. Oxford (Eng.) U., 1984; inaugural lectr. 1st Nat. Congress Italian Soc. Perinatal Medicine, 1985. Editl. bd. Pediat., 1964—70, Circulation, 1966—74, 1983—88, assoc. editor Circulation Rsch., 1970, Pediatric Rsch., 1970—77; editor: Rudolph's Pediatrics, Congenital Diseases of the Heart: Clinical-Physiological Considerations, 2001, 2009, Rudolph's Fundamentals of Pediatrics; contbr. articles to profl. jours. Recipient Merit award, Nat. Heart, Lung and Blood Inst., 1986, Arvo Yllpo medal, Helsinki (Finland) U., 1987, Jonxis medal, Children's Hosp. Groningen, 1993, Nils Rosen von Rosenstein award, Swedish Pediat. Soc., 1999, Pollin prize for pediat. rsch., N.Y. Presbyn. Hosp., Columbia U. Coll. Physicians and Surgeons, 2005, award, FRCP(Edin.), 1965, FRCP(Lond.), 1985, E. Mead Johnson award, 1964, Borden Award, Am. Acad. Pediat., 1979, Howland award, Am. Ped. Soc., 1999, Arvo Yilpo award, U. Helsinki, 1987, JMP Jonxis Medal, U. Groningen, 1992, Rosen Von Rosentein award, U. Uppsala; named Disting. Scientist, Am. Heart Assoc., 2003. Fellow: AAAS, Am. Assn. Adv. Sci., Royal Coll. Physicians (London), Royal Coll. Physicians (Edinburgh); mem.: Am. Heart Assn. (Rsch. Achievement award 1991, Founding Disting. Scientist award 2003), Am. Pediatric Soc. (coun. 1985—92, v.p. 1992—93, pres. 1993—94, Howland award 1999), Soc. for Pediatric Rsch. (coun. 1961—64), Soc. for Clin. Investigation, Am. Phys. Soc., Am. Acad. Pediat. (past chmn. sect. on cardiology, E. Mead Johnson award for rsch. in pediat. 1964, Borden award 1979, Lifetime Med. Edn. award 1992, Joseph St. Geme leadership award Pediat. 1993, Founder award, cardiology sect. 2001, Pollin Pediatric Rsch. prize 2005), NAS Inst. Medicine. Office: U Calif Cardiovascular Rsch Inst Calif Rm HSE 1424 Box 0544 San Francisco CA 94143-0544 Home Phone: 415-665-6841. Business E-Mail: abraham.rudolph@ucsf.edu.

RUDOLPH, ANDREW HENRY, retired dermatologist, educator; b. Detroit, Jan. 30, 1943; s. John J. and Mary M. Rudolph; children: Kristen Ann, Kevin Andrew. MD cum laude, U. Mich., 1966. Diplomate Am. Bd. Dermatology. Intern Univ. Hosp., U. Mich. Med. Ctr., Ann Arbor, 1966-67, resident dept. dermatology, 1967-70; pvt. practice medicine specializing in dermatology, 1972—2007; ret., 2007. Asst. prof. dermatology Baylor Coll. Medicine, Houston, 1972-75, assoc. prof., 1975-83, clin. prof., 1983—; chief dermatology svc. VA Hosp., Houston, 1977-82; mem. staff Meth. Hosp. Mem. editl. bd. Jour. Sexually Transmitted Diseases, 1977-85; contbr. to med. publs. Served as surgeon USPHS, 1970-72. Regent's scholar U. Mich., 1966. Fellow Am. Acad. Dermatology; mem. AMA, Am. Dermatol. Assn., Tex. Med. Assn., Harris County Med. Soc., Houston Dermatol. Soc. (past pres.), Tex. Dermatol. Soc., Skin Cancer Found., Am. Venereal Disease Assn. (past pres.), Mich. Alumni Assn. (life), Alpha Omega Alpha, Phi Kappa Phi, Phi Rho Sigma, Theta Xi.

RUDOLPH, CONRAD, medieval art history educator; b. Rock Island, Ill., Jan. 26, 1951; s. Richard C. and Mary Alice (Potter) R.; m. Roberta Peterson, Sept. 10, 1980; children: Anna Katharina, John Caspar. PhD, UCLA, 1985. Mellon postdoctoral rsch. fellow U. Pitts., 1986-87; Getty postdoctoral fellow Getty Rsch. Ctr., LA, 1987-88; asst. prof. U. Notre Dame, Ind., 1988-91; assoc. prof. U. Calif., Riverside, 1991-97, prof., 1997—. Author: The Things of Greater Importance: Bernard of Clairvaux's Apologia and the Medieval Attitude Toward Art, 1990, Artistic Change at St.-Denis: Abbot Suger's Program and the Early Twelfth-Century Controversy Over Art, 1990, Violence and Daily Life: Reading, Art, and Polemics in the Citeaux Moralia in Job, 1997; contbr. articles to profl. jours. John Simmon Guggenheim fellow. Mem. Coll. Art Assn. (Millard Meiss Pub. fellow), Internat. Ctr. for Medieval Art, Medieval Acad. Am. Office: U Calif Riverside Dept History Of Art Riverside CA 92521-0001

RUDOLPH, FREDERICK, history professor; b. Balt., June 19, 1920; s. Charles Frederick and Jennie Hill (Swope) R.; m. Dorothy Dannenbaum, June 18, 1949; children: Marta R. MacDonald, Lisa R. Cushman. BA, Williams Coll., 1942, Litt.D., 1985; MA, Yale U., 1949, PhD, 1953; LHD, U. Rochester, 1994, Wilkes U., 1998. Instr. history Williams Coll., 1946-47; asst. instr. Yale, 1949-50; mem. faculty Williams Coll., 1951—, prof., 1961—, Mark Hopkins prof. history, 1964-82, emeritus, 1982—, chmn. Am. civilization program, 1971-80. Williams Coll. marshal, 1978-87; vis. lectr. history and edn. Harvard U., 1960, 61; vis. prof. Sch. Edn., U. Calif.-Berkeley, 1983; mem. commn. plans and objectives Am. Council Edn., 1963-66; mem. study group on postsecondary edn. Nat. Inst. Edn., 1980-83; mem. com. on baccalaureate degrees Assn. Am. Colls., 1981-85; vis. assoc. Ctr. Studies in Higher Edn., U. Calif.-Berkeley, 1983 Author: Mark Hopkins and the Log, 1956, rev. edit. 1996, The American College and University: A History, 1962, rev. edit., 1990 (Japanese translation, 2003), Curriculum: A History of the American Undergraduate Course of Study Since 1636, 1977, rev. edit., 1993; editor: Essays on Education in the Early Republic, 1965, Perspectives: A Williams Anthology, 1983; exec. editor: Change, 1980-84, cons. editor, 1985-92. Founding mem. Berkshire County Hist. Soc., 1962, v.p., 1962-66, pres., 1966-68, bd. dirs., 1974-76; trustee Hancock-Shaker Cmty. Inc., 1974-91, Wyoming Sem., 1976-79, Bennington Mus., 1985-95; bd. dirs. Armand Hammer United World Coll. Am. West, 1993-2005. Capt. AUS, 1942-46. Guggenheim fellow, 1958-59, 68-69; recipient Frederic W. Ness award Assn. Am. Colls., 1980, Rogerson cup Williams Coll., 1982, Disting. Svc. award Wyo. Seminary, 1986; Frederick Rudolph Professorship of Am. Culture established in his honor, Williams Coll., 2007. Mem. AAUP, Nat. Acad. Edn., Mass. Hist. Soc. (fellow), Am. Hist. Assn., Am. Studies Assn., Phi Beta Kappa. Democrat. Home: PO Box 515 Williamstown MA 01267-2800

RUDOLPH, GILBERT LAWRENCE, lawyer; b. LA, Aug. 23, 1946; BA, Ariz. State U., 1967; postgrad., Am. U., Washington, 1967-69; JD, U. Cin., 1973. Bar: D.C. 1973, U.S. Dist. Ct. D.C. 1974, U.S. Ct. Appeals (D.C. cir.) 1974, Ariz. 1975, U.S. Dist. Ct. Ariz. 1975, Calif. 1979. Assoc. Streich, Lang, Weeks & Cardon, P.A., Phoenix, 1975-78; ptnr. Gilbert L. Rudolph, P.C., Phoenix, 1978-87; sr. mem. O'Connor, Cavanagh, Anderson, Killingsworth & Beshears, P.A., Phoenix, 1987-99; shareholder, co-chair fin. instn. practice group Greenberg Traurig LLP, Phoenix, 1999—. Lectr. on lending issues. Bd. dirs. Temple Chai, 2002—08, pres., 2008; bd. dirs. Make-A-Wish Found. of Am., 1984—89, Aid to Adoption of Spl. Kids, Ariz., 1995—2003. Fellow Am. Coll. Consumer Fin. Svcs. Lawyers; mem. ABA (com. on consumer fin. svcs. bus. law sect. 1981—, com. on comml. fin. svcs. 1989—, mem. com. on uniform comml. code 1992—), Conf. on Consumer Fin. Law (governing com. 1986-, pres. 2009-). Republican. Jewish. Office: Greenberg Traurig LLP Ste 700 2375 E Camelback Rd Phoenix AZ 85016 Office Phone: 602-445-8206. E-mail: rudolphg@gtlaw.com.

RUDOLPH, JAMES ROBERT, psychologist; b. Albuquerque, Mar. 1, 1957; s. Anita Jean and Robert John Rudolph; life ptnr. John Chester Gonsiorek. BA in Psychology, Sociology, U. N. Mex, 1980, MA in Spl. Edn., 1981; PhD in Counseling Psychology, Lehigh U., 1988. Lic. psychologist Minn. Bd. of Psychology, 1990, registered Nat. Register of Health Svc. Providers in Psychology, 1999, Diplomate Am. Bd. of Profl. Psychology, 2000, cert. profl. qualification in psychology Assn. of State and Provincial Psychology Bds., 2001. Spl. edn. tchr. Albuquerque Pub. Schs., 1982—83; psychiat. crisis counselor Mt. Tom Inst. for Human Svcs., Holyoke, Mass., 1988; psychotherapist Constance Bultman Wilson Ctr. for Adolescent Psychiatry, Faribault, Minn., 1988—90, physician's assoc., 1990; adj. asst. prof. St. Mary's Coll. Grad. Ctr., Mpls., 1990—93; pvt. practice Mpls., 1992—2002; clin. dir., dir. of profl. tng. Carver County Mental Health Program, Waconia, Minn., 1991—; adj. faculty Capella U., Mpls., 2004. Clin. adj. faculty Minn. Sch. of Profl. Psychology, Mpls., 1992—99; practice sample reviewer. oral exam mentor, examiner counseling psychology Am. Bd. of Profl. Psychology, Mpls., 2001—. Contbr. articles to profl. jours., chapters to books. Recipient Certificates of Excellence in Clin. Supervision, Minn. Sch. of Profl. Psychology, 1990's. Mem.: APA, Chi Sigma Iota. Personal E-mail: jamesrrudolph@comcast.net.

RUDOLPH, KIMBERLY, legislative staff member; Chief of staff to Rep. Carolyn Kilpatrick US House of Reps., Washington, asst., appropriations com., 2007—. Democrat. Office: 2264 Rayburn House Office Bldg Washington DC 20515 Office Phone: 202-225-2261. Office Fax: 202-225-5730.*

RUDOLPH, LARRY, computer science educator, researcher; b. NYC, July 8, 1954; s. Morris and Helen Rudolph; m. Ainat Kalay, June 29, 1988; children: Hilla, Rogel, Noga Rogel. BA, Queens Coll., NYC, 1976; MA, Courant Inst., NYU, 1978, PhD, 1982. Postdoctoral fellow dept. computer sci. U. Toronto, 1981-82; asst. prof. dept. computer sci. Carnegie Mellon U., 1982-85; assoc. prof. Inst. Computer Sci. Hebrew U., Jerusalem, Israel, 1985—. Author: Parallel Evolution of Parallel Processor, 1993; patentee in optical computing. Avocations: juggling, clowning, magic and scientific tricks. Office: VMware Inc 5 Cambridge Ctr Cambridge MA 02142 Personal E-mail: rudolph@csail.mit.edu. Business E-Mail: rudolph@vmware.com.

RUDOLPH, LAVERE CHRISTIAN, library director; b. Jasper, Ind., Dec. 24, 1921; s. Joseph Frank and Rose (Stradtner) R. AB, DePauw U., 1948; B.D., Louisville Presbyn. Sem., 1951; PhD, Yale, 1958; student, U. Zurich, Switzerland, 1960; M.L.S., Ind. U., 1968. Ordained to Ministry Presbyn. Ch., 1950; pastor in Ind. and Conn., 1950-54; mem. faculty Louisville Presbyn. Sem., 1954-69, prof. ch. history, 1960-69; lectr. history U. Louisville, 1965-69; rare books bibliographer Van Pelt Library U. Pa.; head tech. services Lilly Library, Ind. U., 1970-78, curator of books, 1978-86, librarian emeritus, 1987—. Author: Hoosier Zion, 1963 (Thomas Kuch award Ind. U. Writers Conf. 1964), Story of the Church, 1966, Francis Asbury, 1966, Indiana Letters, 1979, Religion in Indiana, 1986, Hoosier Faiths, 1995. Served to capt. USAAF, 1940-46. Mem.: Am. Soc. Ch. History, Phi Beta Kappa. Democrat. Home: 2455 Tamarack Trail Apt 338 Bloomington IN 47408 Office: Ind U Library Bloomington IN 47405 Home Phone: 812-336-1751.

RUDOLPH, MAYA, actress, comedienne; b. Gainesville, Fla., July 27, 1972; d. Richard and Minnie (Riperton) Rudolph; one child (with Paul Thomas Anderson), Pearl BA in Photography, U. Calif., Santa Cruz, 1994. Former backup singer The Rentals. Actor: (TV series) Saturday Night Live, 2000—07, (TV apperances) Chicago Hope, 1996—97, City of Angels, 2000, (voice only) The Simpsons, 2007,: (TV films) The Devil's Child, 1997, True Love, 1999; (films) Gattaca, 1997, Chuck & Buck, 2000, Duets, 2000, Duplex, 2003, 50 First Dates, 2004, A Prairie Home Companion, 2006, Idiocracy, 2006, (voice only) Shek the Third, 2007, Away We Go, 2009. Office: c/o 3 Arts Entertainment 9460 Wilshire Blvd Beverly Hills CA 90212*

RUDOLPH, SCOTT, pharmaceutical executive; b. 1958; s. Arthur Rudolph. Dir., chmn. of bd., CEO NBTY, Inc., Bohemia, NY, 1986—. Past chmn. of bd. dirs. Dowling Coll., Long Island, NY, 1997—2000; vice chmn. Dowling Coll. Bd., 2004—. Office: NBTY PO Box 9001 Bohemia NY 11716-9001*

RUDOLPHSEN, WILLIAM M., retail executive; b. 1955; BS in Acctg., Marquette U., 1977; MBA, DePaul U., 1989. With Walgreen Co., Deerfield, Ill., 1977—, dir. 3d party acctg., 1995—98, divisional v.p. acctg., contr., 1998—2004, sr. v.p., CFO, 2004—08, sr. v.p., chief risk officer, 2008—. Office: Walgreen Co 200 Wilmot Rd Deerfield IL 60015

RUDY, BERNARDO, research scientist; s. Ruben Rudy and Bertha Chapiro; m. Olga L. Rodriguez, June 20, 1985. PhD in Physiology, Cambridge U., 1977; PhD in Biochemistry, Ctr. Rsch. and Advanced Studies, Mex., 1972. Lic. MD Mex., Ministry Health, Mex., 1971. Prof. NY U. Sch. Medicine, NYC, 1998—2009. Author: (book) Molecular and Functional Diversity of Ion Channels and Receptors; contbr. articles to rsch. jours. Achievements include discovery of DPPX. Office: NY Univ Sch Medicine 522 First Ave New York NY 10016 Office Fax: 212-263-9170. Business E-Mail: rudyb01@med.nyu.edu.

RUDY, DOROTHY LUCILLE, poet, educator; b. Hamilton, Ohio, June 27, 1924; d. William Herman and Marjorie Delma (Rammel) Richardson; A.B., Queens Coll., 1945; A.M., Columbia U., 1948; postgrad. Radcliffe Grad. Sch. Harvard U., 1949-50; PhD in Am. Civilization; m. Willis Rudy, Jan. 31, 1948; children— Dorothy Elizabeth, Willis Philip, Willa Catherine. Tchr. English and creative writing various schs., L.I., N.Y., Mass., N.Y. State, 1945-61; tchr. English, Worcester (Mass.) Jr. Coll., 1961-63, Tenafly (N.J.) High Sch., 1963-64; prof. English, Rutgers Evening Div., Newark, 1963-64; prof. English and creative writing Montclair State U., Upper Montclair, N.J., 1964-88; ret., 1988; lectr. Caldwell (N.J.) Coll., 1988-92, also coord. ind. study; lectr. N.Y. Poetry Forum, 1975-87, 1992-93, Bergen Poets, 1980-87, Fairleigh Dickinson U., Teaneck, NJ, 1993-2003; reader, lectr. in field. Composers, Authors, Artists Am., 1980, 81; reader original poetry Clifton Pub. Library, 1975, N.Y. Poetry Forum, Danbury State Coll., also N.J. Council Tchrs. English, New Eng. Small Press Assn., various N.Y. and N.J. locations; speaker N.Y. Press Women's Lit. Day, 1977, 78; judge various poetry contests. Am. Poets Fellowship Soc. grantee, 1970; Humanities scholar N.J. Cultural Coun. of the Arts, 1992-93. Mem. New Eng. Small Press Assn., N.Y. Poetry Forum, N.J. Council Tchrs. English, Poets and Writers, The Browning Soc., P.E.N. Women, Am. Pen Women, Centro Studi e Scambi Internazionali, Bergen Poets, Composers, Authors, Artists Am. (essay editor mag.). Club: Radcliffe Alumnae. Author: (poems) Quality of Small, 1971; Psyche Afoot and Other Poems, 1978; Grace Notes to the Measure of the Heart, 1979, Voices, 1993. Editor: Americana Anthology, 1976. Contbr. poems to various publs. Home: 161 W Clinton Ave Tenafly NJ 07670-1916 Home Phone: 201-569-7771.

RUDY, ELAINE KIM, elementary school educator; b. Meadville, Pa., Nov. 5, 1951; d. George David Matteson and Marie Alta Webster; m. Joseph G. Rudy, May 8, 1976; children: Angela Crawford, Julie Riley, Tamara Zwick. AS Early Childhood, Edinboro U., Pa., 1986; BS Edn., Edinboro U., 1987, M Edn. Reading, 1988. Tchr. Penncrest Sch. Dist., Townville, Pa., 1977—88, tchr. Title I, Reading Recovery Cambridge Springs, Pa., 1991—. Tchr. adult edn. Penncrest Sch. Dist., Townville, 1986—, coord. literacy, 2004—, mentor Title I, Cambridge Springs, mem. program improvement team, Saegertown, Pa., mem. strategic planning com.; leader Maplewood Elem. Literacy Leadership Team, 2004—. Named Outstanding Educator, Crawford County Headstart, 1990; named to Chancellor's List, Ednl. Comm. Inc., 2004—05, 2005—06. Avocations: reading, camping. Home: 31150 State Hwy 27 Guys Mills PA 16327 Office: Maplewood Elem Sch 32695 Hwy 408 Townville PA 16360

RUDY, FRANK R., pathologist; b. Harrisburg, Pa., Jan. 23, 1949; s. Burton B. and Blanch T. (Rhoads) R.; m. Debra R. Bromberg, Dec. 27, 1970; children: Allison, Nicole. BA, Franklin & Marshall Coll., 1970; MD, U. Pitts., 1974. From assoc. pathologist to chmn. lab. Polyclinic Hosp., Harrisburg, 1979-95; chmn. Pinnacle Health Lab., Harrisburg, 1996-99, vice-chmn., 2000—. Regional mem. Commn. for Lab. Accreditation, 1996—2002; pres. Pathology Assocs. Ctrl. Pa., Harrisburg, 1997—. Author: Uropathology, 1989, Principles and Practices of Surgical Pathology; contbr. articles to profl. jours. Fellow Coll. Am. Pathology, Am. Soc. Clin. Pathologists; mem. Internat. Acad. Pathology, Am. Pathology Found., U.S. Acad. Pathology, Canadian Acad. Pathology. Avocation: scuba diving. Office: Pinnacle Health Labs Med Scis Bldg 100 S 2d St PO Box 8700 Harrisburg PA 17105-8700 Business E-Mail: frudy@pinnaclehealth.org.

RUDY, KATHLEEN VERMEULEN, small business owner; b. Grand Rapids, Mich., Dec. 29, 1931; d. John Weston and Geneva (Swiet) Vermeulen; m. Fredrick Albers Yonkman, June 9, 1953 (div. Sept. 1980); children: Sara Yonkman Davis, Margriet Yonkman Finnegan, Nina Yonkman Tower; m. Raymond Bruce Rudy, Nov. 14, 1981. BA, Hope Coll., 1953. Owner Kate's Antiques, 1974—2000. Editor mag. Jr. League of Boston, 1960's, Scarsdale Jr. League, 1960's. Bd. dirs. Jr. League of Boston, 1960s, Greenwich Cmty. for Human Svcs., 1970s-80s, Neighbor to Neighbor, Greenwich, 1980-98; trustee Hope Coll., 1986-96; chmn. Mary Fund com. Ladies Golf Tournament, 1985; mem. Women's Nat. Rep. Club, N.Y.C., 1995—, bd. govs., 1997-2004, 06—; mem. Hope Coll. Pres.'s Task Force, 1997-99; treas. Women's Nat. Rep. Club, 2000-02, chmn. nominating com. 2000—, 2d v.p., 2002-04, 2008-. Mem. Jr. League of Phoenix, Greenwich Country Club, Boulders Golf Club (Scottsdale), Dorset Field Club, Doubles Club, Field Club Greenwich, Kappa Alpha Theta. Republican. Congregationalist. Avocations: tennis, golf, antiques, travel, art. Home and Office: 37 Lismore Ln Greenwich CT 06831-3741 Personal E-mail: kvrudy@optonline.net.

RUDY, PAUL, composer; BA, Bethel Coll., Kans., 1984; MusM in composition, U. Colo., Boulder, 1992; Doctor of Musical Arts in composition, U. Tex., Austin, 1997. Lectr. Bethel Coll., North Newton, Kans., 1988—89; tchg. asst. U. Colo., Boulder, 1989—93; tchg. asst., asst. instr. U. Tex., Austin, 1995—96; founder, dir. Amplified Music Performance Series, faculty composition technologist Aspen Music Festival, 1995—2001; vis. asst. prof. composition U. Mo., Kansas City, 1998—99, asst. prof. composition, 1999—2005, assoc. prof. composition, 2005—, coord. composition studies, 2005—, dir. Intermedia Music Prodn. and Computer Tech. Ctr. (iMPACT), 2005—. Bd. dirs. Columbine Chamber Players, Boulder, Colo., 1991—94, NewEar Ensemble, Kansas City, 2000—06; tutor New Zealand Young Composer's Workshop, 1998—99; composer-in-residence NYU New Music Ensemble, 2003; guest resident Lewis U., 2003; guest composer U. Colo., Boulder, 2004, Ball State U. Festival, 2006, MusicAcoustica, Ctr. Conservatory Music, Beijing, 2007, U. Aveiro, Portugal, 2007, Manchester U., England, 2007, DeMontfort U., Leicester, England, 2007, Cornell U. and Ithaca Coll., 2007; resident Helene Wurlitzer Found., Taos, N.Mex., 2007; guest tchr. Orford Sound Creation Workshop, Montreal, 2008. Composer: (albums) Parallax 2: Apparitions, ...and every island and mountain were moved from their place..., 2000, Degrees of Separation: Grandchild of Tree, 2002, Fantasie, 2003, Thema: Omaggio, 2004. Recipient Lead Grad. Tchr. in Music award, U. Colo., 1993, Dean Small Grant award, 1994, EMS prize for Thema: Omaggio, Stockholm, Sweden, 2002, Kaufmann award for Artistic Excellence, U. Mo. Kansas City Conservatory, 2008; fellow Fulbright Found., 1997, Guggenheim Found., 2008; Cecil Effinger grad. fellowship in composition, U. Colo., 1991, Robert Jeffry Womack endowed presdl. scholarship, U. Tex., 1994, continuing fellowship, 1996—97. Mem.: ASCAP (Spl. award 1996—), Electronic Music Found., Tex. Computer Music Network, Soc. Electroacoustic Music US, Living Music Found., Internat. Computer Music Assn., Soc. Composers, Inc., Music Associates of Aspen, Sonic Arts Network, Am. Composer's Forum, Nat. Assn. Jazz Educators (Oustanding Musicianship award 1983, 1984, Outstanding Musicianship in Arranging citation 1992), Mo. Music Teachers Assn. (Composer of Yr. 1998). Office: U Mo Kansas City Conservatory of Music 4949 Cherry Kansas City MO 64110-2229 Office Phone: 816-235-2940. Office Fax: 816-235-5265. E-mail: rudyp@umkc.edu.*

RUDY, RAYMOND BRUCE, JR., retired food company executive; b. LA, Apr. 24, 1931; s. Raymond Bruce and Wrena Margaret (Higgins) R.; m. Kathleen Vermeulen; children: Bruce Rudy, Alice M.R. Price, Barbara R. Frith. BS, UCLA, 1953; MBA, Xavier U., Cin., 1960. Brand mgr. Procter & Gamble, Cin., 1956-62; product mgr. Hunt-Wesson Foods, Fullerton, Calif., 1962-63; group v.p. Gen. Foods Corp., White Plains, NY, 1963-79; pres. Oroweat Foods Co. subs. Continental Grain Co., NYC, 1979-83; chmn., pres. Arnold Foods Co., Inc., Greenwich, Conn., 1984-86; pres. Affiliates of Best Foods subs. CPC Internat., Englewood Cliffs, NJ, 1987-89; ret., 1989; chmn., CEO, New Hampton, Inc., 1993-94; dep. chmn. Snapple Natural Beverages, Inc., 1992-94; mng. dir. J.W. Childs Assoc., 1995—; chmn. Personal Care Group, Inc., 1996-98. Chmn. Beltone Electronics Corp., 1997-2000, Internat. Diverse Foods, 1998-99, Empire Kosher Poultry, Inc., 1997-2000, Am. Safety Razor, 2000-05, Hartz Mountain Corp., 2001-04, The Meow Mix Co., 2002-03, The Sunny Delight Beverage Co., 2004—; bd. dirs. Widmer Bros. Brewing, Inc., 1993-2008; Advantage Sales and Mktg., 2007-. With US Army, 1954—56. Mem. Greenwich Country Club, Dorset Field Club, The Links, The Boulders. Congregationalist.

RUDY, RUTH CORMAN, former state legislator; b. Millheim, Pa., Jan. 3, 1938; d. Orvis E. and Mabel Jan (Stover) Corman; m. C. Guy Rudy, Nov. 21, 1956; children: Douglas G., Donita Rudy Koval, Dianna F. Degree in x-ray tech., Carnegie Inst., 1956; student, Pa. State U., 1968-71. Clk. of cts. County of Centre (Pa.), Bellefonte, 1976-82; rep. Pa. Gen. Assembly, Harrisburg, 1982-96. Mem. Dem. Nat. Com., 1980—, chair women's caucus, 1989-91; past pres. Pa. Fedn. Dem.

Women, Harrisburg; pres. Nat. Fedn. Dem. Women, 1987-89; mem. exec. com. Dem. Nat. Com., 1987-89; candidate U.S. Congress, 5th Dist., 1995-96; rep. Nat. Dem. Inst. for Internat. Affairs, 1997—; rep. to Yemen, 1997. Mem. Gov. Rendell's Transition Team on Agr., 2003. Named Woman of Yr. Pa. Fedn. dem. Women, 1982, Centre County Living Legend, 2000, PFDW Jeanette Riebman award, 2007. Methodist. Achievements include patent for hair spray face shield.

RUDZIK, LYNNE A., musician, educator; b. Concord, NH, June 28, 1963; d. Richard R. and Camille E. Ashland; m. John A. Rudzik, July 19, 1988; children: Thomas J., Michael R., Daniel R. MusB Edn., Fla. State U., Tallahassee, 1986. Profl. tchg. cert. Fla., 1986, cert. levels 1A, 1B, 2, 3 Suzuki Assn. of the Ams. Tchr. Orange County Pub. Schs., Orlando, Fla., 1986—2002; orch. dir. Gotha Mid. Sch., Windermere, Fla., 2002—. Musician St. Luke's United Meth. Ch., Windermere, 1990—2006. Mem.: Fla. Orch. Assn. (assoc.). Methodist. Avocations: reading, practicing instruments, swimming, camping. Office: Orange County Public Schools-Gotha Middl 9155 Gotha Rd Windermere FL 34786 Personal E-mail: jru1053016@aol.com. Business E-Mail: rudzikl@ocps.net.

RUDZINSKI, WALTER E., chemistry professor, department chairman; PhD, U. Ariz., Tucson, 1977. Prof. Tex. State U., San Marcos, 1979—2007, chemistry dept. chmn., 2007—. Sch. bd. mem. Hays CISD, Kyle, Tex., 1995—2001. Recipient Presdl. award. Office: Tex State Univ 601 University Dr San Marcos TX 78666-4684

RUEBENSON, GEORGE E., insurance company executive; BS, Bradley Univ. Mgmt. positions Allstate Ins. Co., Northbrook, Ill., 1970—90, v.p. fin. & planning bus. ins. div., internat. ops., 1990—97, v.p. procurement governance, 1997—2000, v.p. property & casualty claims svc. org., 2000—03, sr. v.p., 2003—06, pres. Allstate Protection, 2006—. Bd. mem. Bradley Univ.; St. Laurence HS. Office: Allstate Corp 2775 Sanders Rd Northbrook IL 60062*

RUEBHAUSEN, DAVID K., theater educator; s. Otto C. and Bonnie M. Ruebhausen. BA in Comm. and Theatre, William Jewell Coll., Liberty, Mo., 1987; MA in Theatre Arts, U. Minn., Mpls., 1991, PhD in Theatre Arts, 1996. Mng. dir. Minn. Centennial Showboat, St. Paul, 1994—95, U. Minn. Theatre, Mpls., 1994—95; assoc. prof. U. North Ala., Florence, 1996—. Scenic designer, cons. Ivy Green Helen Keller's Birthplace, Tuscumbia, Ala., 2002—; theatre arts chair State Ala. Articulation and Gen. Studies Com., Montgomery. Theatre, The Miracle Worker, 2002—, The Rocky Horror Show, 2003, The Little Prince, 2005, The Glass Menagerie, 2006; dir.(scenic designer): (theatre) Oedipus Tyrannus, 2007, Tartuffe, 2007, The Mouse Trap, 2005; Spring Awakening, 2008. Recipient theatre Festival Excellence in Design award, Kennedy Ctr., Am. Coll., 2007—08. Mem.: US Inst. Theatre Tech. Independent. Avocation: travel. Office: Univ N Ala 1 Harrison Plz UNA 5168 Florence AL 35632 Business E-Mail: druebhausen@una.edu.

RUEDENBERG, KLAUS, theoretical chemist, educator; b. Bielefeld, Germany, Aug. 25, 1920; came to U.S., 1948, naturalized, 1955; s. Otto and Meta (Wertheimer) R.; m. Veronika Kutter, Apr. 8, 1948 (dec. Jan. 2004); children: Lucia Meta(Wright), Ursula Hedwig, Annette Veronika, Emanuel Klaus. Student, Montana Coll., Zugerberg, Switzerland, 1938-39; licence es Scis., U. Fribourg, Switzerland, 1944; postgrad., U Zurich, Switzerland, 1948, U. Chgo., 1950; PhD, U. Zurich, Switzerland, 1950; PhD (hon.), U. Basel, Switzerland, 1975, U. Bielefeld, Germany, 1991, U. Siegen, 1994. Research assoc. physics U. Chgo., 1950-55; asst. prof. chemistry, physics Iowa State U., Ames, 1955-60, assoc. prof., 1960-62, prof., 1964-78, disting. prof. in sci. and humanities, 1978-91, disting. prof. emeritus, 1991—, sr. chemist Ames Lab., U.S. Dept. Energy, 1964-91, assoc., 1991—. Prof. chemistry Johns Hopkins, Balt., 1962-64; vis. prof. U. Naples, Italy, 1961, Fed. Inst. Tech., Zurich, 1966-67, Wash State U. at Pullman, 1970, U. Calif. at Santa Cruz, 1973, U. Bonn, Germany, 1974, Monash U. and CSIRO, Clayton, Victoria, Australia, 1982, U. Kaiserlautern, Germany, 1987; lectr. univs., rsch. instns. and sci. symposia, 1953—. Contbr. articles to profl. jours.; assoc. editor: Jour. Chem. Physics, 1964-67, Internat. Jour. Quantum Chemistry; Chem. Physics Letters, 1967-81, Lecture Notes in Chemistry, 1976-2003, Advances in Quantum Chemistry, 1987-2004; editor-in-chief Theoretica Chimica Acta, 1985-97; hon. editor Theoretical Chemistry Accounts, 1997—. Co-founder Octagon Center for the Arts, Ames, 1966, treas., 1966-71, also bd. dirs. Guggenheim fellow, 1966-67; Fulbright sr. scholar, 1982. Fellow: AAAS, Internat. Acad. Mathematical Chemistry, Internat. Acad. Quantum Molecular Scis., Am. Inst. Chemists, Am. Phys. Soc.; mem.: AAUP, Am. Chem. Soc. (Midwest award 1982, Nat. Award in Theoretical Chemistry 2002), Phi Lambda Upsilon, Sigma Xi. Office: Iowa State Univ Dept Chemistry and Ames Lab USDOE Ames IA 50011-0001

RUEDRICH, RANDY, political organization administrator; BS, Tex. A&M U., M in Engring., PhD. Commr., formerly Alaska Oil & Gas Conservation Commn., 2003—; gen. mgr. Doyon Drilling; sr. drilling engr. Arco's Alaska; pres. Arctic E&P Advisors; fin. chmn. Alaska Rep. Party, 1986—88, rules chmn., 1998—2000, asst. treas., 1999—2000, vice chmn., 2000, chmn., 2000—. Republican. Office: Alaska Rep Com 1001 W Fireweed Ln Anchorage AK 99503*

RUEGER, GEORGE EDWARD, bishop emeritus; b. Framingham, Mass., Sept. 3, 1930; AB, St. John's Sem., Brighton, Mass., 1954; MA, Boston Coll., 1957. Ordained priest Diocese of Worcester, Mass., 1958, pastor, headmaster, supt. of schools Mass.; ordained bishop, 1987; aux. bishop Diocese or Worcester, Mass., 1987—2005; aux. bishop emeritus Diocese of Worcester, Mass., 2005—. Roman Catholic.

RUEGSEGGER, DONALD RAY, JR., radiological physicist, educator; b. Detroit, May 29, 1942; s. Donald Ray and Margaret Arlene (Elliot) R.; m. Judith Ann Merrill, Aug. 20, 1965 (div.); children: Steven, Susan, Mark, Ann; m. Patricia Ann Mitchell, Oct. 16, 1999. BS, Wheaton Coll., 1964; MS, Ariz. State U., 1966, PhD (NDEA fellow), 1969. Diplomate Am. Bd. Radiology. Radiol. physicist Miami Valley Hosp., Dayton, Ohio, 1969—, chief med. physics sect., 1983—. Physics cons. X-ray dept. VA Hosp., Dayton, 1970-73; adj. asst. prof. physics Wright State U., Fairborn, Ohio, 1973-74, clin. asst. prof. radiology, 1976-81, clin. assoc. prof. radiology, 1981—, group leader in med. physics, dept. radiol. scis. Med. Sch., 1978-85. Mem. AAAS, Am. Assn. Physicists in Medicine (pres. Ohio River Valley chpt. 1982-83, co-chmn. local summer sch. arrangements com. 1986), Am. Coll. Radiology, Am. Phys. Soc., Ohio Radiol. Soc. Home: 6252 Donnybrook Dr Centerville OH 45459-1837 Office: Radiation Therapy Miami Valley Hosp 1 Wyoming St Dayton OH 45409-2722 Home Phone: 937-433-6668; Office Phone: 937-208-4058. E-mail: drruegsegger@mvh.org.

RUEHLE, CHARLES JOSEPH, pathologist, military officer; b. May 26, 1943; s. John Donald and Alta (Brown) R.; m. Nellie Backus, Aug. 5, 1972 (div.). DVM, Iowa State U., 1967; MD, U. Iowa, 1973; MS, 1973. Diplomate Am. Bd. Preventive Medicine, Am. Bd. Pathology. Commd. 2d lt. USAF, 1964; advanced through grades to col., sr. flight surgeon, 1984; chief flight surgeon, 1987; chief Vet. Svc., Grissom AFB, Ind., 1967-69; resident in aerospace medicine Brook AFB, Tex., 1973-75; resident in pathology Wilford Hall USAF Med. Ctr., Lackland AFB, Tex., 1975-79; with div. aerospace pathology Armed Forces Inst. Pathology, Washington, 1979-88; chief div. aerospace pathology, 1982-85; chmn. dept. forensic scis., 1985-88; sec. Joint COm. Aviation Pathology, 1984-88; exec. asst. to fed. air surgeon FAA, Washington, 1988—93, sr. aviation med. examiner, 1989—, mgr. appeals & special projects branch, 1993—2003, prin. liasion, 2004—; spl. asst. fed. Surgeon, 2003—. Adj. asst. prof. prevetive medicine Uniformed Services U. Health Scis. lectr. aerospace pathology; cons. USAF Sugeon Gen., 1987; chmn, Airliner Cabin Environ. Report Team, 2002- Fellow Am. Soc. Clin Pathologists, Aerospace Med. Assn.; mem. Am. Acad. Forensic Scis. AMA, USAF Flight Surgeons, Nat. Sojourners, Assn. Mil. Surgeons U.S., Internat. Soc. Air Safety Investigators, Air Force Assn., Alpha Zeta, Gamma Sigma Delta, Omega Tau Sigma (gov. 1967-75). Republican. Presbyterian. Home: 1000 Lower Pindell Rd Lothian MD 20711-2704 Office: Fed Air Surgeon FAA 800 Independence Ave SW Washington DC 20591-0001 Office Phone: 202-493-4580. E-mail: charles.ruehle@faa.gov.

RUEHSEN, MOYAA, political science professor, consultant; BA, Johns Hopkins Sch. Arts & Scis., Balt., 1984, Johns Hopkins Bloomberg Sch. Pub. Health, 1986; MA, Johns Hopkins Nietze Sch. Advanced Internat. Studies, Washington, 1988, PhD, 1992. Cert. anti-money laundering specialist Assn. Cert. Anti-Money Laundering Specialists, 2006. Postdoc. and lectr. U. Calif., Berkeley, 1993—94; assoc. prof. Monterey Inst. Internat. Studies, Calif., 1994—. Office: Monterey Inst Internat Studies 460 Pierce St Monterey CA 93940

RUEMMLER, KATHRYN H., lawyer, former prosecutor; b. Richland, Wash., 1971; BA cum laude, U. Wash., Seattle, 1993; JD, Georgetown U., 1996. Law clk. to Hon. Timothy K. Lewis US Ct. Appeals (3rd Cir.), 1996—97; assoc. Zuckerman Spaeder, LLP, Washington, 1997—2000; assoc. counsel to Pres. The White House, Washington, 2000—01; asst. US atty. DC US Dept. Justice, Washington, 2001—07; ptnr. Latham & Watkins LLP, Washington, 2001, 2007—. With Enron Task Force, US Dept. Justice, 2003—06, dep. dir., 2005—06. Recipient Atty. Gen's award for Exceptional Svc., US Dept. Justice, 2006; named one of Litigation's Rising Stars, The Am. Lawyer, 2007. Office: Latham & Watkins LLP 555 Eleventh St NW Ste 1000 Washington DC 20004

RUESCHEMEYER, MARILYN SCHATTNER, sociology educator; b. NYC, June 3, 1938; d. Julius Schattner and Bela Wax; m. Dietrich Rueschemeyer, June 14, 1962; children: Julia Yael, Simone Margalit. BA in Sociology, Queens Coll., 1959; MA in Sociology, U. Toronto, Can., 1965; PhD in Sociology, Brandeis U., 1978. Asst. prof. R.I. Sch. Design, Providence, 1981-87, assoc. prof., 1987-93, prof. sociology, 1994—. Fellow Russian Rsch. Ctr., Harvard U., Cambridge, Mass., 1986—; adj. prof. sociology Brown U., Providence, 1987—; chair European Policies Seminar Series Brown U. Watson Inst., Providence; adv. bd. Sociol. Analysis, 1998-2000; sr. assoc., mem. St. Anthony's Coll., Oxford U., 1979, 82, 97; vis. fellow dept. sociology Hebrew U. of Jerusalem, 1990, guest fellow Acad. Scis., Czech Republic, 1997, fellow Stockholm Inst. Soviet & E. European Econs., 1992, Wissenschaf & Zentrum, Berlin, 1994, Swedish Collegium Advanced Studies Social Scis., Uppsala, Sweden, 2000. Author: Profl. Work and Marriage: An East West Comparison, 1981; co-author (with Golomshtok and Kennedy): Soviet Emigré Artists, 1985; editor: Women in the Politics of Post Communist E. Europe, 1994, 1998; co-editor (with D. Rueschemeyer and B. Wittrock): Participation and Democracy East and West, 1998; co-editor: (with Linda Cook and Mitchell Orenstein) "Left Parties and Social Policy in Post Communist Europe", 1999; co-author (with V. Alexander): Art and the State: The Visual Arts in Comparative Perspective, 2005; co-editor: Woman in Power in Post-Communist Parliaments, 2009. Founding mem. Women's Polit. Caucus R.I.; active Reform Dems. R.I.; founder Friday Group, Providence, 1971—; bd. mem. RISD-Brown Hillel, 1990-. Rsch. grantee Internat. Rsch. and Exchs. Bd., Washington, 1984, 86, 91, 92, 97, Am. Coun. Learned Socs., 1987, 88. Mem.: Women East and West, German Studies Assn., Am. Sociol. Assn. (chair com. on internat. sociology 1993—96, rep. to Am. Assn. Advancement Slavic Studies), Am. Assn. Advancement Slavic Studies (bd. dirs. 1996—99, 2001—03, 2005—, editl. collective studies in comparative internat. devel.). Office: Watson Inst for Internat Studies Brown Univ Providence RI 02912-9042 E-mail: marilyn_rueschemeyer@brown.edu.

RUESINK, ALBERT WILLIAM, biologist, plant sciences educator; b. Adrian, Mich., Apr. 16, 1940; s. Lloyd William and Alberta May (Foltz) R.; m. Kathleen Joy Cramer, June 8, 1963; children: Jennifer Li, Adriana Eleanor. BA, U. Mich., 1962; MA, Harvard U., 1965, PhD, 1966. Postdoctoral fellow Swiss Fed. Inst. Tech., Zurich, 1966-67; prof. biology Ind. U., Bloomington, 1967—, spl. asst. to Pres. for Faculty Rels., 1999—2005. Recipient Amoco Teaching award Ind. U., 1980 Mem. AAUP (pres. chpt. 1978-79, 90-91), Am. Soc. Plant Physiologists, Bot. Soc. Am. Democrat. Mem. United Ch. of Christ. Home: 2605 E 5th St Bloomington IN 47408-4286 Office: Ind U Dept Biology 1001 E 3d St Bloomington IN 47405 Home Phone: 812-336-8366; Office Phone: 812-855-5555. Business E-Mail: ruesink@indiana.edu.

RUESTERHOLZ, VIRGINIA P., telecommunications industry executive; m. Kevin Ruesterholz; 2 children. B in Chem. Engring., Stevens Inst. Technology, 1983; MS in Telecom. Mgmt., Bklyn. Poly. Inst., 1991. Mgr. NY Tel., 1984, market area v.p., gen. mgr. svc. delivery and field ops., 1993; v.p. complex installation and maintenance for network svcs. Bell Atlantic, v.p. ops. assurance, sr. v.p. wholesale markets; pres. Verizon Ptnr. Solutions Verizon Comm., pres. Verizon Telecom, pres. Verizon Services Ops. Mem. bus. and tech. bd. Stevens Inst. Technology. Bd. dirs. Manhattan Theater Club. Recipient 40 Under 40 award, Crain's NY Bus., Rising Star award, NY Women's Agenda. Mem.: Edwin A. Stevens Soc. (chair). Office: Verizon Comm One Verizon Way Basking Ridge NJ 07920-1097 Office Phone: 908-559-1069. Office Fax: 908-696-2135. Business E-Mail: virginia.p.ruesterholz@verizon.com.*

RUFANOVA, VICTORIYA, medical researcher; b. Kharkov, Ukraine, May 11, 1974; children: Marina, Maxim. Sci. rschr. Inst. Clin. Cardiology, Russian Cardiology Rsch. Ctr., Moscow; rsch. scientist Med. Coll. Wis., Milw., 2001—. Grant, Am. Heart Assn., 2005—07. Achievements include discovery of level of protein named C3G is increased during kidney inflammation in glomerular epithelial cells; breast cancer protein BCAR3 expressed in kidney cells and regulated by hormone Endothelin. Personal E-mail: vikusik@pisem.net.

RUFE, LAURIE J., museum director; b. Pa. m. Mike Rufe. BA in Art History, Va. Commonwealth U., 1972. Intern Valentine Mus., Hist. Ho. Mus.; with Mercer Mus., Doylestown, Pa., 1973—80; Big Horn Basin Project Wyo., 1981—85; with Douglas County Coun. for the Arts and Humanities, Castle Rock; dir. Custer County Art Ctr., Mont., 1986—87; asst. dir. Roswell Mus. and Art Ctr., Roswell, 1987—98, dir., 1998—2002, exec. dir., 2005—; dir. Tucson Mus. Art, 2002—05. Office: Roswell Mus and Art Ctr 100 W 11th St Roswell NM 88201 Office Phone: 575-624-6744. Business E-Mail: rufe@roswellmuseum.org.

RUFE, ROGER T., JR., federal agency administrator; Grad., US Coast Guard Acad.; MBA, NYU; grad., Nat. War Coll., Naval War Coll. Vice chmn. Nat. Response Team US Coast Guard, chief congressional affairs office; dir. ops. US Dept. Homeland Security, 2006—. US Coast Guard rep. North Pacific and Mid-Atlantic Fisheries Mgmt. Councils; del. Marine Environ. Protection Com., Internat. Maritime Orgn.; pres., CEO The Ocean Conservancy. Capt. USCG, flag officer USCG, Pacific and Atlantic area, flag officer USCG, Alaska, Southeast US, and Caribbean, vice adm. USCG. Office: US Dept Homeland Security 12th & C St SW Washington DC 20024*

RUFEH, MARK, diversified financial services company executive; b. Oct. 31, 1958; BS, Mercy Coll., 1983; MBA, Manhattan Coll., 1991. V.p. ops. and risk mgmt. First Boston Corp.; head ops. taxable fixed income divsn. Lehman Bros., Inc., NYC, 1986, various sr. mgmt. positions mgmt. and corp. svcs., mng. dir., COO; CEO The Westchester Capital Group; chief adminstrv. officer investment banking divsn. Credit Suisse Group; chief adminstrv. officer, head productivity Citi Institutional Clients Group, NYC, 2008—. Republican. Office: Citigroup Inc 399 Park Ave New York NY 10043

RUFF, GARY KAY, lawyer; b. Lunwood, Calif., Dec. 9, 1959; BBA, Gonzaga Univ., 1981; JD, Pepperdine Univ., 1984; LLM in taxation, Georgetown Univ., 1985; M in mgmt., Northwestern Univ., 1992. Bar: Calif. 1985, Tex. 1995. Tax mgr. Deloitte & Touche; various Legal Dept. positions through v.p. & asst. gen. counsel Tenet Healthcare Corp., Dallas, 1992—2008, sr. v.p., gen. counsel, 2008—. Mem.: ABA, Tex. Bar Assn., State Bar Calif., Am. Health Lawyers Assn. Mailing: Tenet Healthcare Corp PO Box 809088 Dallas TX 75380-9088 Office: Tenet Healthcare Corp Ste 100 13737 Noel Rd Dallas TX 75240

RUFF, LINDY, professional hockey coach; b. Warburg, Alta., Canada, Feb. 17, 1960; m. Gaye Ruff; children: Brett, Eryn, Brian and Madeleine (twins). Defenseman Lethbridge Broncos, 1976—79, Buffalo Sabres, 1979-89, NY Rangers, 1989-91; player/asst. coach Rochester Americans, 1991-92, San Diego Gulls; asst. coach Fla. Panthers, 1993—97; head coach Buffalo Sabres, 1997—. Vol. Children's Hosp., Buffalo, Muscular Dystrophy Assn. Recipient Jack Adams Award, 2006; named Buffalo Sabre's Rookie of the Yr., 1980, NHL Coach of Yr., Sporting News, 2006. Avocations: fishing, boating, golf. Office: c/o Buffalo Sabres HSBC Arena 1 Seymour H Knox III Plz Buffalo NY 14203-3096

RUFF, ROBERT LOUIS, neurologist, physiologist, researcher; b. Bklyn., Dec. 16, 1950; s. John Joseph and Rhoda (Alpert) R.; m. Suzanne Ruff, June 7, 2003. BS summa cum laude, Cooper Union, 1971; MD summa cum laude, U. Wash., 1976, PhD in Physiology, 1976. Diplomate Am. Bd. Neurology and Psychiatry, Am. Bd. Phys. Medicine Rehab. Spinal Cord Medicine. Asst. neurologist N.Y. Hosp., Cornell Med. Sch., NYC, 1977—80; asst. prof. physiology and medicine U. Wash., Seattle, 1980—84; assoc. prof. neurology Case We. Res. Med. Sch., Cleve., 1984—92, prof. neurology and neuroscis., 1993—, residency dir., neurology dept., 1994—2003, vice chair neurology dept., 1995—2004; chief dept. neurology Cleve. VA Med. Ctr., 1984—2003, chief phys. medicine and rehab. svc., 1998—2000, 2006—, mgr. rehab. and spinal cord injury and disorder product line, 1999—2003; med. dir. Functional Elec. Stimulation Ctr., Cleve., 2000—; chief Spinal Cord Injury and Dysfunction Svc., Cleveland VA Med. Ctr., 2003—05; dir. neurology and acting rehab. rsch. svc. Office R & D Dept. VA Ctrl. Office, Washington, 2004—07; nat. dir. neurology Dept. Vet. Affairs, Washington, 2006—. Mem. adv. bd. for Neurology Dept. Vets. Affairs, 1989—, mem. study sect. for rehab. rsch. career devel. awards, 1998-, mem. merit rev. bd., rehab. rsch. devel. svc., 1999-2004; mem. NIH adv. couns. NINDS, 2006-, NICHD, 2006-08. Assoc. editor: Neurology, 1994—96, mem. editl. bd.:, 1996—97, Jour. Rehab. and Devel., 1999—, assoc. editor: Jour. Rehab. Rsch. and Devel., 2000—, ad hoc reviewer: various profl. and sci. jours., mem. editl. bd.: Muscle & Nerve, 2006—; contbr. articles to profl. jours., chapters to books. Advisor Child Devel. and Mental Retardation Ctr., Seattle, 1980-84, Burien Devel. Disability Ctr., Wash., 1982-84; med. adv. bd. Muscular Dystrophy Assn., Seattle, 1984, N.E. OH chpt. Multiple Sclerosis Soc.; chmn. med. adv. bd. N.E. OH chpt. Myasthenia Gravis Found., 1987—, mem. state bd. dirs., 1993-, nat. med. adv. bd., 1988-, nat. grant and fellowship com., 1990-2002, mem. nat. bd. dirs., 1990-2002, 2006-. Recipient Tchr. Investigator award NIH, Dr.'s award Periodic Paralysis Assn., 2005; NSF fellow, 1971; NIH grantee, Muscular Dystrophy Assn. grantee, Dept. Vets. Affairs, Rsch. Enhancement Advanced Ctr. awards, 1999—, Dr. award Myasthenia Gravis Found. Am., 2002; NY State Regents med. scholar, 1971. Fellow Am. Heart Assn. (stroke coun.), Am. Acad. Neurology (scientific issues com., legis. action com.); mem. AMA, IEEE, Am. Paraplegia Soc., Am. Soc. Neuro-Rehab., Am. Physics Soc., Neurosci. Soc., Biophys. Soc., Am. Neurol. Assn., N.Y. Acad. Sci., Am. Geriatrics Soc., Am. Physiol. Soc., Sigma Pi Sigma (v.p. 1970-71), Alpha Omega Alpha (v.p. 1975-76). Home: 935 Richmond Rd Lyndhurst OH 44124 Office: VA Med Ctr 10701 East Blvd Ste 128W Cleveland OH 44106-1702 Home Phone: 216-291-1643. Business E-Mail: robert.ruff1@va.gov.

RUFFA, ANTHONY ARMAND, mechanical engineer; s. Anthony R. and Joan R. Ruffa; m. Geraldine S. Skuches, June 30, 1984; children: Elizabeth C., A. Joseph. BS in mech. engring., U. Md., 1981; PhD, Yale U., 1990. Mech. engr. Elec. Boat Divsn. Gen. Dynamics, Groton, Conn., 1981—85; in-house lab. ind. rsch. program mgr. Naval Undersea Warfare Ctr., Newport, RI, 1985—. Adj. prof. physics U. R.I. Named NAVSEA Scientist of Yr., Naval Sea Sys. Command, 2000. Mem.: Am. Soc. Mech. Engrs., Assn. Scientists and Engrs. (Profl. Achievement award 2003). Achievements include 38 US Patents, with 10 pending and others in preparation. Office: Naval Undersea Warfare Center 1176 Howell Street Newport RI 02841 Business E-Mail: anthony.ruffa@navy.mil.

RUFFALO, MARK, actor; b. Kenosha, Wis., Nov. 22, 1967; s. Frank Lawrence and Marie Rose Ruffalo; m. Sunrise Coigney, June 2000; children: Keen, Bella, Odette. Actor: (films) Rough Trade, 1993, A Song For You, 1993, There Goes My Baby, 1994, Mirror, Mirror 2:Raven Dance, 1994, A Gift From Heaven, 1994, Mirror, Mirror III: The Voyeur, 1995, The Dentist, 1996, The Last Big Thing, 1996, Blood Money, 1996, Safe Men, 1998, 54, 1998, A Fish in the Bathtub, 1999, Ride with the Devil, 1999, You Can Count on Me, 2000, Committed, 2000, Life/Drawing, 2001, The Last Castle, 2001, XX/XY, 2002, Windtalkers, 2002, My Life Without Me, 2003, View From the Top, 2003, In the Cut, 2003, Eternal Sunshine of the Spotless Mind, 2004, 13 Going On 30, 2004, Collateral, 2004, Just Like Heaven, 2005, Rumor Has It..., 2005, All the King's Men, 2006, Zodiac, 2007; actor, actor: (films) Reservation Road, 2007, Blindness, 2008, What Doesn't Kill You, 2008, The Brothers Bloom, 2009; (TV films) On the 2nd Day of Christmas, 1997, Houdini, 1998; (TV series) The Beat, 2000; (films) The Destiny of Marty Fine, 1996; writer: films The Destiny of Marty Fine, 1996; exec. prodr., actor: (films) We Don't Live Here Anymore, 2004, Chicago, 2008; (Broadway plays) Awake and Sing!, 2006. Office: c/o Robert Stein 345 N Maple Dr Ste 317 Beverly Hills CA 90210 Office Phone: 310-550-2176. Business E-Mail: robertadamstein@aol.com.*

RUFFIN, HERBERT GEORGE, II, history professor; b. Sacramento, Aug. 17, 1969; s. Herbert George and Sadie Mae Ruffin; m. Veronia Tanya Ruffin, Dec. 18, 2004. AS in Social sci., San Jose City Coll., Calif., 1995; BA in Am. History, U. Calif., Santa Cruz, 1997; MA in Am. History, Claremont Grad. U., 2005, student in Am. History, 2003—; cert. in African Studies, Claremont U., 2004. Cert. computer numerical control machining specialist UAW-Labor Employment and Tng. Corp., Calif., 1991. Tchg. asst. San Jose City Coll., Calif., 1994—95, counseling asst., 1997, vis. prof., 1998—99; supply coord. Smithsonian Instn., Ctr. for Folklife and Cultural Heritage, Washington, 1998—99; web technician Claremont Grad. U., Calif., 1999—2003; tchg. asst. Pitzer Coll., Claremont, Calif., 2000; rsch. asst. Claremont Coll., Calif., 2001—04; vis. prof. Chaffey Coll., Rancho Cucamonga, Calif., 2002, Claremont McKenna Coll., Calif., 2003—05. Cons. folklife festival Smithsonian Instn., Ctr. for Folklife and Cultural Heritage, Washington, 1999—2000; intern Smithsonian Instn., Program in African Am. Culture, Nat. Mus. of Am. History, Washington, 2000, coord. and asst. program developer, 2000—01; cons. African Americans in West conf. Claremont Grad. U., Calif., 2001. Author: (multimedia) Africans on the North American Frontier, 1528-1864; multimedia, Priesthood and Ritual in Ghana: 10th MEHU Anniversary Celebration, 1987-1997, Priesthood and Ritual in Ghana: Musama Disco Christo Church Diamond Jubilee, 1922-1997; author: (multimedia cd) FundaMentals: Part One, A RUFF Assessment of Hip-hop History and Culture, 1965-1986; contbr. multimedia - smithsonian institution; rap album, Who Am I?: Songs From the Ruffunk Experience, multimedia, Ontario Community University Program (OCUP), for Ontario, Pitzer College, CGU, and HUD partnership, Black Graduate Students Association Online, multimedia - pomona college, Latin American Studies at Pomona College Online, multimedia, School of Politics and Economics at CGU; author: (multimedia) African Diaspora Central, (multimedia - smithsonian institution) A Quest for Freedom: The Black Experience in the American West; book reviewer: numerous books. Recipient Outstanding Social Sci./Family Studies Achiever award, San Jose-Evergreen C.C. Dist., 1994-1995, Martin Luther King scholarship, San Jose City Coll., 1994-1995, Leadership Opportunity Award scholarship, U. Calif., 1995-1997, Edn. Abroad award, U. Calif. Edn. Abroad Program, 1996-1997, Acad. Excellence award for African-Am. Student Life, U. Calif., 1996, 1997, Minority Student Internship Program award, Smithsonian Instn., 1997, 2000; Victor Atkins fellowship, Claremont Grad. U., 2001-2002, John McGuire fellowship, 2003-2004. Mem.: Black Grad. Students Assn. (sec. 2002—04), Western Hist. Assn., Assn. for Study of Afro-Am. Life and History, Am. Hist. Assn. Achievements include student activist leader instrumental in desegregating Claremont Graduate University and fighting hate crimes. Avocations: researching history and current affairs, working out, video gaming (sports and strategy games), multimedia production, rebuilding classic Mustang. Personal E-mail: herbert.ruffin@cgu.edu.

RUFFIN, JOHN, federal agency administrator, researcher; b. New Orleans, June 29, 1943; s. Wesley and Olivia Ruffin; m. Angela Beverly Ruffin, Aug. 24, 1968; children: John Wesley, Meeka Dionne, Beverly Alaina. BS, Dillard U., New Orleans, 1965; MS, Atlanta U., 1967; PhD in Systematic and Devel. Biology, Kans. State U., 1971; DSc (hon.), Spelman Coll., Atllanta, Tuskegee U., Ala., U. Mass., Boston. Instr. biology So. U., Baton Rouge, 1967-68; asst. prof. biology Atlanta U., 1971-74; assoc. prof. Ala. A&M U., Huntsville, 1974-75; prof., chmn. dept. biology NC Ctrl. U., Durham, 1978—90, dean Coll. Arts & Scis., 1986—90; assoc. dir. rsch. on minority health NIH, Bethesda, Md., 1990—2001, dir. Nat. Ctr. Minority Health & Health Disparities, 2001—. Recipient Samuel L. Kountz award, NIH Dir.'s award, Nat. Hispanic Leadership award, Beta Beta Beta Biol. Honor Soc. award, Presdl. Meritorious Rank award. Mem.: AAAS, Assn. Environ. & Exptl. Botany, Assn. Southeastern Biologists, NC Acad. Scis., Botanical Soc. of America. Office: NCMHD 6707 Democracy Blvd Ste 800 Bethesda MD 20892-5465 Office Phone: 301-402-1366. Office Fax: 301-480-4049. E-mail: ruffinj@ncmhd.nih.gov.*

RUFFIN, RICHARD A., orthopedic surgeon; b. Sept. 29, 1959; BS, U. Norte Dame, South Bend, Ind., 1981; MD, U. Okla., 1985. Cert. Am. Bd. Orthop. Surgery, Am. Bd. Orthop. Hand Surgery. Resident, orthop. U. iowa, Iowa City, 1985—90; fellow, upper extremity and microsurgery Kleinert Inst., Louisville, 1990—91; with Orthop. Assocs., Inc., Okla., 1991—. Named one of Golf Digest 2006 Top Golf Doctors in Am. Mem.: Arthoscopy Assn. N.Am., Am. Soc. for Surgery of the Hand, Am. Acad. Orthop. Surgeons. Office: Orthop Assocs Inc 3301NW 50th St Oklahoma City OK 73112 Office Phone: 405-947-0911. Office Fax: 405-942-5043.*

RUFFING, ANNE ELIZABETH, artist; b. Bklyn. d. John Paul and Ruth Elizabeth (Price) Frampton; m. George W. Ruffing, Mar. 29, 1967; 1 dau., Elizabeth Anne. BS, Cornell U., 1964; postgrad., Drexel Inst. Tech., 1966. One-woman exhbns. include, IBM, 1966, Hall of Fame, Goshen, NY, 1971, exhibited in group shows at Internat. Women's Arts Festival, World Trade Center, NYC, 1975-76, Berkshire Mus., Pittsfield, Mass., 1965, 76, Cooperstown Mus., NY, 1969; represented in permanent collections, Met. Mus. Art, Bklyn. Mus., Library of Congress, Harvard U., Smithsonian Instn., NY Hist. Soc. Johnston Hist. Mus., Atwater Kent Mus., Albany Inst. History and Art, Whitney Mus. Am. Art, Boston Public Library. Recipient 1st place Eric Sloane award, 1974, Internat. Women's Year award, Internat. Women's Art Festival, 1976. Address: 1031 Lewis Farm Rd Zebulon NC 27597

RUFFNER, COURTNEY JUDITH, literature and language professor; d. Michael and Patricia Ruffner; m. Jeffery C. Grieneisen, June 19, 2004. BA in English Lit., Penn State U., Erie, Pa., 1996; MA in English Lit., Clarion U., Pa., 1999; ABD, Ind. U. Pa., 2009. Prof. English Ringling Coll. Art & Design, Sarasota, Fla., 2000—06, State Coll. Fla. (formerly Manatee CC), Bradenton, 1999—. Co founder & co editor Fla. English, Bradenton, 2003—. Recipient Chancellor's List award, Grad. Instn., 2004—06, award, Nat. Scholars Honor Soc., 2008. Mem.: CEA, AWP, Italian Sons & Daughters America. Office: State Coll Fla 5840 26th St W Bradenton FL 34207 Office Phone: 941-752-5478. Business E-Mail: ruffnec@scf.edu.

RUFFNER, FREDERICK G., JR., book publisher; b. Akron, Ohio, Aug. 6, 1926; s. Frederick G. and Olive Mae (Taylor) R.; m. Mary Ann Evans, Oct. 8, 1954; children: Frederic G. III, Peter Evans. BS, Ohio State U., 1950. Advt. mgr. Jim Robbins Co., Royal Oak, Mich., 1950-52; research mgr. Gen. Detroit Corp., 1953-54; pres. Gale Research Co., Detroit, 1954-87, Omnigraphics, Inc., 1987—. Editor: Ency. of Assns, 1956-68, Code Names Dictionary, 1963, Acronyms and Initialisms Dictionary, 1965, Allusions Dictionary, 1985; pub. Gold Coast Mag., 1992—; patentee in field. Bd. dirs. Friends of Detroit Pub. Libr., pres., 1975-76; mem. exec. bd. Detroit coun. Boy Scouts Am., 1974—, v.p., 1976-82; pres. Coun. for Fla. Librs., 1979—; trustee Bon Secours Hosp., Grosse Pointe, Mich., 1980-81; v.p. Etruscan Found., Florence, Italy, 1980—; pres. Mich. Ctr. for the Book, 1990, Literary Landmarks Assn., Gold Coast Jazz Soc., Ft. Lauderdale, 1992—; bd. dirs., v.p. Ohio State U. Found., Bonnet House, Ft. Lauderdale, 1992. 1st lt. AUS, 1944-46. Decorated Bronze Star, Combat Inf. award; recipient Centennial award Ohio State U., 1970, Benjamin Creativity award Assn. Am. Pubs., 1985, Career medal Ohioana Libr. Assn., 1988, Lifetime Achievement award Am. Libr. Trustees Assn., 1992; named to Entrepreneurs Hall of Fame, Nova U. Mem. Am. Antiquarian Soc., ALA (hon. life), Am. Mgmt. Assn., Am. Assn. Mus., Detroit Hist. Soc., Am. Hist. Print Collectors Soc., Bibliog. Soc. Am., Sierra Club, Pres. Assn., Audubon Soc., Am. Name Soc., Early Am. Industries Assn., Nat. Press Club (Washington), Ephemera Soc., Johnny Appleseed Soc., Navy League, Newcomen Soc., Cen. Bus. Dist. Assn. Detroit (vice-chmn. 1985-87), Jazz Forum (Grosse Pointe Farms, Mich.), Nat. Trust Hist. Preservation, Fairfield Heritage Soc., Archives Am. Art, Pvt. Librs. Assn., Friends Ft. Lauderdale Pub. Libr. (pres. 1974-78), Phileas Soc. (pres. 1985—), Ohio State U. Club (pres. Detroit club 1958, nat. chmn. Ohio State U. campaign, 1985-88), Masons, Shriners, Book Club, Detroit Athletic Club, Econ. Club, Prismatic Club (pres. 1990), Fontenada Soc. (pres. 1990-91), Detroit Club, Country Club Detroit, Ocean Reef Club, Grosse Pointe Yacht Club, Coral Ridge Yacht Club, Lauderdale Yacht Club, Princeton Club, Salmagundi Club, Grolier Club, Century Assn., Marco Polo Club, Faculty Club Ohio State U., Old Club, Commonwealth Club (San Francisco), Gross Pointe Club, Wawetonong Club, Tau Kappa Epsilon. Republican. Presbyterian. Home: 17111 E Jefferson Ave Apt 18 Grosse Pointe MI 48230-1942 Address: Omnigraphics Inc PO Box 31-1640 Detroit MI 48231-1640: 936 Intracoastal Dr PH 1 Fort Lauderdale FL 33304

RUGA, WAYNE, architect; married. PhD, Manchester Met. U., England, 2005. Cert. architect, Calif., 1979. Pres. to ceo Ctr. Health Design, Martinez, Calif., 1992—99; founder to pres. CARITAS Project, Deerfield Beach, Fla., 1999—. Office: CARITAS Project PO Box 4309 Deerfield Beach FL 33442

RUGAI, VIRGINIA A. (GINGER RUGAI), alderwoman; b. Oct. 3, 1945; m. Ado Rugai; children: Michael, Robert, Karen. BS, Loyola U., Chgo., 1967; MPA, U. Ill., Chgo., 1991. English tchr. Queen Peace HS, Burbank, Ill., 1967-69; substitute tchr. Archdiocese of Chgo., 1969-76; asst. to the dir. Beverly Area Planning Assn., 1976—83; staff mem. Ill. State Senate, 1984—87, adminstrv. asst., State Senator Jeremiah Joyce, 1987—90; alderwoman, 19th ward Chgo. City Coun., 1991—. Chair energy, environ. protection & pub. utilities com. Chgo. City Coun., vice-chair police & fire com. Dir. Far Southwest Mental Health Coun., Beaver Family Ctr.; bd. dirs. Beverly Art Ctr., Brother Rice HS; mem. Ridge Park Adv. Coun., Little Co. of Mary Hosp. Found. Bd., St. Xavier U. Pres. Adv. Coun.; vol. Marist HS Mother's Club, Mt. Carmel Women's Club, St. Ignatius Mother's Club, Beverly Improvement Assn., Christ the King's Altar Guild; apptd. mem. Mayor Daley's Task Force on Women's Health, Cook County Women's Commn. Mem.: Irish Fellows Club Chgo. (v.p.), Kiwanis. Office: 10400 S Western Ave Chicago IL 60643 also: 3017 W 111th St Chicago IL 60643 also: City Hall 121 N La Salle St Rm 300 Chicago IL 60602 Office Phone: 773-238-8766, 312-744-3072. Office Fax: 773-238-9049. Business E-Mail: vrugai@cityofchicago.org.*

RUGEN, KAREN, retail executive, corporate communications specialist; Head corp. comm. Hyatt Hotels Corp., 1978—94; chief comm. officer Boston Chicken Co., Boston, 1994—99; sr. v.p. corp. comm. and pub. affairs Rite Aid Corp., Camp Hill, Pa., 1999—. Treas. Rite Aid Found. Office: Rite Aid Corp 30 Hunter Ln Camp Hill PA 17011 Office Phone: 717-730-7766.

RUGGERI, DIANNE ELLEN, music educator, band director; b. Elizabeth, NJ; d. Leo and Rose I. De Bartol; m. John C. Ruggeri, 0000; 1 child, Renee R. Veneziano. MusB in Vocal and Instrumental K-12, Newark State Coll. (now Kean U.), Union, NJ, 1971; MusM, NYU, 1974; MA in Spl. Edn., Georgian Court U., Lakewood, NJ, 1991. Vocal & instrumental music tchr. Deal Elem. Sch., NJ, 1985—; band dir. Maple Pl. Mid. Sch., Oceanport, NJ, 2000—. Mem. governing edn. com. NJ Performing Arts Ctr., NJ Symphony Orch., Newark, 1993—2006. Recipient Tchr. of Yr., 2008, gov.'s award, Maple Pl. Mem.: Region II Band Dirs. Assn., Shore Intermediate Band Dirs. Assn. (pres., v.p., sec.-treas. 1996—2008), Music Educator's Nat. Conf. (sec. 1971—72). Office: Maple Pl Mid Sch 2 Maple Pl Oceanport NJ 07757 Office Fax: 732-229-0961.

RUGGERO, MARIO ALFREDO, physiologist, educator; b. Resistencia, Argentina, Nov. 7, 1943; came to U.S., 1961; s. Juan M. and Carolina F. (Volpe) R.; m. Elsa L. Statzner, Apr. 2, 1973. BA, Cath. U. Am., 1965; PhD, U. Chgo., 1972. Rsch. assoc. U. Wis., Madison, 1975; asst. prof. otolaryngology U. Minn., Mpls., 1975-87, assoc. prof., 1987-92, prof., 1992-93; Hugh Knowles prof. hearing sci. dept. comm. scis. and disorders Northwestern U., Evanston, Ill., 1993—, head Audiology & Hearing Scis. Program, 1996-2000. Mem. comm. disorders rev. com. Nat. Inst. on Deafness and Other Comm. Disorders, NIH, Bethesda, Md., 1990-94. Assoc. editor Jour. of Neurosci., 1989-95; mem. editl. bd. Audiology and Neuro-Otology, 1998—; co-editor: The Mechanics and Biophysics of Hearing; contbr. articles to profl. jours. Grantee NIH, 1975—, NSF, 1983-87. Fellow AAAS, Acoustical Soc. Am.; mem. Assn. for Rsch. in Otolaryngology (mem. editl. bd. jour. 2005—), Am. Physiol. Soc. Achievements include research in relationship between submicroscopic vibrations of the middle and inner ears and the excitation of the auditory nerve. Home: 1209 Central St # A Evanston IL 60201-1611 Office: Northwestern U Dept Comm Scis and Disorders 2240 Campus Dr Evanston IL 60208-3550 Home Phone: 847-733-7248; Office Phone: 847-491-3180. Business E-Mail: mruggero@northwestern.edu.

RUGGERONE, GREGORY T., research scientist; s. Artemio P. and Kathryn E. Ruggerone; m. F. Joan Hardy, Nov. 10, 1989; children: Leah Kathryn Hardy, David Andrew Hardy. BS, U. Calif., Irvine, 1978; MS, U. Wash., Seattle, 1981, PhD, 1989. Rsch. scientist U. Wash., Seattle, 1984—93, grad. student advisor, 1989—; rsch. scientist, v.p. Natural Resources Cons. Inc., Seattle, 1993—. Fellow: Am. Inst. Fisheries Rsch. Biologists (dist. dir. 1990—92, Rsch. award 1992). Achievements include research in provided evidence that salmon species originating from adjacent continents intermingle in the ocean and compete for prey, leading to reduced growth and survival; evidence that climate change influenced salmon abundance and survival through greater growth during early marine life, leading to density-dependent growth during late marine life. Home: 6148 NorthEast 194th PL Kenmore WA 98028 Office: Natural Resources Cons Inc 4039 21st Ave W Ste 404 Seattle WA 98199 Office Fax: 206-283-8263. Personal E-mail: ruggerone@comcast.net. Business E-Mail: gruggerone@nrccorp.com.

RUGGIERI, MICHAEL RAYMOND, pharmacologist, educator; b. Quantico, Va., Mar. 2, 1954; s. Archie Raymond and Mary Louise (Walters) R.; m. Nicole Rose DeMicco, Sept. 12, 1981; 1 child, Michael Raymond Jr. BA, Temple U., Phila., 1976; PhD, U. Pa., Phila., 1984. Rsch. assoc. U. Pa., Phila., 1985-86, asst. prof., 1986-90; assoc. prof. pharmacology Temple U., Phila., 1990—, dir. urology rsch., 1990—. Dir. urology rsch. Grad. Hosp., Phila., 1987-90; adj. prof. Phila. Coll. Pharmacy and Sci., 1988-89; CEO Lifespan Tech., Inc., Phila., 1993—. Contbr. articles to profl. jours. Head coach King of Prussia Soccer Club. Recipient New Investigator award NIH, 1985, Investigator Initiated grant, 1988—. Mem. AAAS, Soc. Basic Urologic Rsch., Am. Urol. Assn. (award Jack Lapides Essay Contest 1989, 94), Am. Soc. Pharmacology and Exptl. Therapeutics. Achievements include identification of functional and cellular mechanism of muscarinic receptor subtype control of urinary bladder contraction, role of bacterial adherence in urinary tract infection. Office: Temple U Sch Medicine 3400 N Broad St Philadelphia PA 19140-5104

RUGGIERO, DAVID ARMAND, neuroscientist; b. NYC, May 2, 1949; s. Armand George and Margaret T. (Mirra) R.; m. Clara Tanya Ruggiero. BA in Biology, Queens Coll., 1972; MA/MPhil in Human Anatomy, Columbia U. Med. Coll., NYC, 1976, PhD in Human Neuroanatomy, 1977. Dir. and lectr. neurosci. and gross anatomy NY Coll. Podiatric Medicine, NYC, 1976-77; postdoctoral fellow dept. neurology Cornell U. Med. Coll., NYC, 1977-79, lectr. in neurosci., 1979-80, instr. dept. neurology, 1980-81, asst. prof. dept. neurology, 1981-88, assoc. prof. neurology and neurosci., 1988-97; prof. anatomy, cell biology and psychiatry Columbia U. Med. Coll., 1998—, staff continuing med. edn., 2000—. Dir. Neurol. Rsch. Inst. Lubec, Maine, 1993—; mem. instnl. animal care and use com., 1998—; cons. Vets. Health Svcs. and Rsch. Adminstrn., 1990—, NSF, 1990—; adv. com. Nat. Inst. Drug Abuse, 1990, Nat. Inst. Health, 1980-; adv. bd. Mayo Clinic, 1996—; instnl. animal care and use com. Cornell U. Med. Coll., 1988-97, med. sch. ethic and curriculum com.; mem. study sects. and site visit teams, NIH, Nat. Inst. Drug Abuse; biomed. rsch. rev. com., established investigator Am. Heart Assn., 1984-89; vis. prof. dept. physiology and pharmacology SUNY Health Sci. Ctr., 1998—. Author: The Human Nervous System, 6th edit., 2005; contbr. articles to profl. jours. and books. Dir. of judges Manhattan Sci. Fair, NYC, 1990, judge sci. fair NYC, 1980-2005. Recipient Harriet Ames award NY Heart Assn., 1979, Established Investigator award Am. Heart Assn., 1984-89, cert. honor NY State Westinghouse Talent Search, 1993, Neurosci. prize Am. Acad. Neurology, 1996, USAF Gold medal (mentor); grantee NIH, 1980-96, 97—, Am. Heart Assn., 1988-2007. Mem. Internat. Brain Rsch. Orgn., Am. Soc. Hypertension, Am. Assn. Anatomists, Am. Soc. Peripheral Nerve Injury, Soc. for Neurosci., Soc. for Neurosci. Rapid Response Network, Ea. Hypertension Soc., N.Y. Heart Assn., Columbia U. Coll. Physicians and Surgeons Alumni Assn., Am. Heart Assn. (Establish Investigator award, 1984-1989), Sigma Xi. Achievements include invention of novel multi-peptide regimen for treatment of autistic disorder. Office: Columbia U Coll Physicians and Surgeons 1051 Riverside Dr Unit 42 New York NY 10032-1013 Office Phone: 212-543-5574. Personal E-mail: tanyao@peoplepc.com. Business E-Mail: dr292@columbia.edu.

RUGGIERO, ERIC JOHN, mechanical engineer; b. Lawrence, Mass., Aug. 10, 1979; s. John J. and Nancy Jean Ruggiero; m. Jennifer Lee Vercoe, Aug. 4, 2001; children: Megan Lee children: Mason John. BSMechE, Va. Poly. Inst. and State U., 2001, MSMechE, 2002, PhD in Mech. Engring., 2005. Grad. rsch. fellow NSF, Blacksburg, Va., 2003—05; missile sys. engr. Raytheon, Andover, Mass., 2000—01; rsch. engr. Honeywell Space Sys., Glendale, Ariz., 2002; mech. engr. GE Global Rsch. Ctr., Niskayuna, NY, 2005—. Contbr. articles to profl. jours., chpts. to books. Student campus min. Newman Cmty. Cath. Campus Ministry at Va. Tech., Blacksburg, 1999—2000; young and engaged couples group leader St. Mary's Cath. Ch., Blacksburg, 2001—05. Recipient Gold Watch award, William Preston Soc. of Va. Tech, 2002; grantee, Va. Space Grant Consortium, 2005; fellow, 2002—05; Marshall Hahn Engring. scholar, Va. Poly. Inst. and State U., 1997—98, Faculty Honors scholar, 1997—2001, Seay scholar, 1998—2000, Hal L. Moses scholar, 2000—01, Litton Industries scholar, 2000—01, Pratt Engring. scholar, 2001—05. Mem.: ASME (mem. adaptive structures tech. com. 2006—, Elizabeth M. and Winchell M. Parsons scholar 2003—04, Best Paper award in Structural Dynamics and Control 2007, Old Guard Young Engrs. award 2008), AIAA (Gossamer spacecraft program com. mem. 2005—, Adaptive Structures Grad. Student award 2004), Golden Key Honor Soc., Nat. Soc. of Collegiate Scholars, Omicron Delta Kappa, Tau Beta Pi, Pi Tau Sigma (pres. 2000—01). Office: GE Global Rsch One Research Cir K1 3B17 A Niskayuna NY 12309 Business E-Mail: ruggiero@research.ge.com.

RUGGIERO, MATTHEW JOHN, bassoonist; b. Phila., Sept. 18, 1932; s. Pompeo and Theresa (Ciampa) R.; m. Nancy Cirillo, Apr. 2, 1961; children: Eleanor, Claudia, Lisa. Diploma, Curtis Inst. Music, 1957; AA, Harvard U., 1982, BA cum laude, 1984, MA, 1987; PhD, Boston U., 1993. Second bassoonist Nat. Symphony Orch., Washington, 1957-60; asst. prin. bassoonist Boston Symphony Orch., 1961-89; prin. bassoonist Boston Pops Orch., 1974-89; ret., 1989. Mem. faculty Boston U., 1963—, New Eng. Conservatory Music, 1963— Served with U.S. Army, 1954-57. Boston U. Profs. Program scholar and fellow, 1989.

RUGGLES, D. FAIRCHILD, writer; AB, Harvard U., Cambridge, 2000; PhD, U. Pa., Phila., 2001. Author: (book) Gardens, Landscape, and Vision in the Palaces of Islamic Spain; editor: Sites Unseen: Landscape and Vision, Cultural Heritage and Human Rights, Women, Patranoge and Self Representation in Islamic Societies; author: Islamic Gardens and Landscapes; contbr. articles to profl. jours. Recipient Eleanor Tufts award, Am. Soc. Hispanic Art Hist. Studies, 2002, J.B. Jackson Book prize, Found. Landscape Studies, 2009. Mem.: Historians Islamic Art and Architecture, Soc. Archtl. Historians, Internat. Ctr. Medieval Art, Coll. Art Assn. Office: Univ Ill Urbana-Champaign 101 Temple Buell 611 Taft Dr Champaign IL 61820

RUGGLES, RUDY LAMONT, JR., international security advisor; b. Evanston, Ill., Nov. 11, 1938; s. Rudy Lamont and Ruth (Cain) R.; m. Cecelia Ann Consorte, July 20, 1974 (div. 1996); m. Nancy Orbison, June 1965 (div. 1972); m. Sara Joyce Silbernagel, Feb. 3, 1998; children— Rudy, Christopher, Daniel, Andrew. BA, Harvard U., 1960, MBA, 1966. Sr. assoc. physicist IBM Rsch. Labs., Poughkeepsie, NY, 1960-64; corp. planning cons. corp. hdqrs. IBM, Armonk, NY, 1966-71; sr. mem. profl. staff Hudson Inst., Croton-on-Hudson, NY, 1971-75, pres., 1975-79, also dir.; prin. Cresap, McCormick & Paget, Inc., 1979-82; ptnr. The Phila. Mgmt. Cons. Group, Inc., 1982—; mng. dir. New China Group, Inc., 1982—. Chmn. residential solicitation United Fund, Pound Ridge, N.Y., 1969; mem. parents com. St. Paul's Sch., Concord, N.H.; dir. Danbury Hosp. and Danbury Hosp. Devel. Fund, Conn., 1978—, med. affairs com.; chmn. fin. com. Pound Ridge Community Ch., 1969-70; bd. dirs. Harry Frank Guggenheim Found., 1982—; bd. visitors Sch. Langs. and Linguistics Georgetown U.; trustee New Canaan Country Sch.; charter mem. bd. trustees The Newberry Libr., Chgo.; mem. coun. fellows Pierpont Morgan Libr., NYC; mem. Ridgefield (Conn.) Drug and Alcohol Commn.; mem. steering com. Ridgefield Coalition Against Alcohol and Substance Abuse; treas., bd. dir. Nat. Coun. Alcoholism and Drug Dependence; chmn. bd. dir. Midwestern Conn. Coun. on Alcoholism; adv. bd. Founders Hall, Ridgefield Sr. Ctr.; mem. bd. visitors Orgn. for Tropical Studies, Duke U. With C.E., U.S. Army, 1962. Recipient John Carroll Disting. medal, Georgetown U., 1986, hon. cert. Order of Lenin, Russian Nat. Acad. Sci., 1999. Fellow Explorers Club, Assn. Internat. Bibliophile (hon.); mem. Hudson Inst. (hon.), N. Am. Soc. Corp. Planning (dir. 1966-72),

Internat. Inst. Strategic Studies, Internat. Map Collectors Soc., James Caird Soc., Ends of the Earth (hon.), Hummingbird Soc. (life), Am. Antiquarian Soc. (hon.), Harvard Club N.Y.C., Carnegie Club at Skibo Castle (Scotland), Grolier Club, Sigma Xi (hon.)

RUGGLES, STEVEN, science educator; b. New Haven, May 8, 1955; s. Richard Frances and Nancy Doris Ruggles; m. Lisa Ann Norling; children: Abigail Norling-Ruggles, Rebecca Norling-Ruggles. PhD, U. Pa., Phila., 1984. Regents prof. U. Minn., Mpls., 1985—. Achievements include development of large-scale demographic databases. Office: Univ Minn 225 19th Ave S Minneapolis MN 55414 Business E-Mail: ruggles@umn.edu.

RUH, MICHAEL A., JR., lawyer; b. Ft. Mitchell, Ky., May 27, 1968; BBA, U. Ky., 1990, MBA, 1991; JD, U. Cin., 1996. Bar: Ohio 1996, Ky. 1997. Ptnr. Strauss & Troy, Cin. Named one of Ohio's Rising Stars, Super Lawyers, 2006. Mem.: ABA, Ky. Bar Assn., Ohio State Bar Assn., Cin. Bar Assn. Office: Strauss & Troy Federal Reserve Bldg 150 E Fourth St Cincinnati OH 45202-4018 Office Phone: 513-621-2120. Office Fax: 513-241-8259.

RUHANEN, TROY, advertising agency executive; married; 4 children. Account exec. BBDO Worldwide, Brisbane, Australia; from account supr. Chgo. to regional account dir. Asia Pacific Leo Burnett Worldwide, 1994—99, mng. dir. Sydney, 2000—04; exec. v.p., mng. dir. BBDO N.Am., 2004—. Active Autism Speaks. Named to Advt. Hall of Achievement, Am. Advt. Fedn., 2008. Office: BBDO Worldwide Hdqs 1285 Ave of Americas New York NY 10019 Office Phone: 212-459-5000.*

RUINA, JACK PHILIP, electrical engineer, educator; b. Rypin, Poland, Aug. 19, 1923; arrived in U.S., 1927, naturalized, 1932; s. Michael and Nechuma (Warshaw) R.; m. Edith Elster, Oct. 26, 1947; children: Ellen, Andrew, Rachel. BEE, CCNY, 1944; MEE, Poly. Inst. Bklyn., 1949, DEE, 1951. Rsch. fellow Microwave Rsch. Inst., Poly. Inst. Bklyn., 1948-50; from instr. to assoc. prof. elec. engring. Brown U., 1950-54; rsch. assoc. prof. coordinated sci. lab. U. Ill., 1954-59, rsch. prof., prof. elec. engring., 1959-63; prof. elec. engring. MIT, 1963—, v.p. for spl. labs., 1966-70. U.S. observer Antarctica, 1964; on leave to U.S. Govt., 1959-63, pres. Inst. Def. Analysis, 1964-66; dep. for rsch. to asst. sec. air force, 1959-60; asst. dir. for def. rsch. and engring. Office Sec. Def., 1960-61; dir. Advanced Rsch. Projects Agy., Dept. Def., 1961-63; mem. panel Presdl. Sci. Adv. Commn., 1963-72, sci. adv. bd. USAF, 1964-67, adv. bd. and panels for Dept. Def., HEW, Dept. Transp., ACDA, Office Tech. Assessment, NSF, NSC, 1963—; mem. gen. adv. com. ACDA, 1969-74; sr. cons. Office Sci. and Tech. Policy, The White House, 1977-80; chmn. com. on environ. decision making NAS, 1974-77; bd. dirs. Mitre Corp. Recipient Fleming award, 1962, Disting. Alumnus award Poly. Inst. Bklyn., 1970, One Hundred and Twenty Fifth Anniversary medal CCNY, 1973. Fellow IEEE, AAAS, Am. Acad. Arts and Scis.; mem. Internat. Sci. Radio Union. Office: MIT Dept Elec Engring 292 Main St Cambridge MA 02142-1014 Home: 130 Mount Auburn St Apt 409 Cambridge MA 02138-5779 E-mail: ruina@mitre.org.

RUIZ, CARLOS LEON, nuclear scientist, physicist; b. El Paso, Sept. 21, 1943; s. Pedro Luis and Maria Elida Ruiz; m. Cynthia Ann Stuart, Aug. 2; children: Christopher Leon, Theresa Ann. BS, U. Tex., El Paso, 1966; MS, U. Kans., 1969, PhD, 1975. Rsch. assoc. La. State U., Baton Rouge, 1974—76, sr. rsch. assoc., 1976—78; mem. tech. staff Sandia Nat. Lab., Albuquerque, 1981—96, prin. mem. tech. staff, 1996—. Vis. asst. prof. La. State U., Baton Rouge, 1979—81. Coach, referee Am. Youth Soccer Assn., Albuquerque, 1981—88. Recipient Nova award, Lockheed-Martin, Albuquerque, 2004. Mem.: Toastmasters Internat. Achievements include being an inventor in the field of nuclear physics. Avocation: guitar. Office: Sandia Nat Labs PO Box 5800 Albuquerque NM 87185 Home Phone: 505-293-6832; Office Phone: 505-845-7550. E-mail: clruiz@sandia.gov.

RUIZ, HECTOR DE JESUS, information technology executive; b. Piedras Negras, Mex. BS in Elec. Engring., MS in Elec. Engring., U. Tex., Austin; D in Electronics, Rice U., 1973. Various positions Tex. Instruments, Dallas; pres. Motorola's Semiconductor Products Sector; COO Advanced Micro Devices, Inc., Sunnyvale, Calif., 2000—02, pres., 2000—06, CEO, 2000—08, chmn., 2004—. Bd. dirs. Eastman Kodak Co., Semiconductor Indus. Assn. Apptd. by Pres. Adv. Com. Trade Policy and Negotiations; mem. Govs. Task Force Econ. Growth; apptd. by Gov. G.W. Bush Tex. Higher Edn. Coord. Bd.; mem. adv. coun. Coll. Engring. U. Tex.; mem. adv. bd. Tsinghua Sch. of Econ. and Mgmt.; Nat. Sec. Telecommunications Adv. Com. Named one of 50 Most Important Hispanics in Tech. & Bus., Hispanic Engr. & Info. Tech. mag., 2005; named to, Hispanic Engr. Nat. Awards Conf. Hall of Fame, 2000; fellow, Internat. Engring. Consortium, 2002. Mem.: Hispanic Profl. Engrs. (apptd. bd. dirs.). Office: Advanced Micro Devices Inc 1 AMD Pl Sunnyvale CA 94088

RUIZ, LUIS M., physical education educator; b. Logroño, La Rioja, Spain, Sept. 30, 1956; s. Luis Ruiz and Resurreccion Pérez; m. Catalina Amengual; children: Aixa, Aitana. MS in Phys. Edn., Poly. U., Madrid, 1978; PhD, Autonoumus U., Madrid, 1998, MS in Huge Performance Sports, 2001. Cert. in exercise and sport sci. Poly. U., 1981. Tenure prof. Faculty Sport Sci. UCLM, Toledo, Spain, 1998—2008; prof. Faculty Sport Sci. UPM, Madrid, 1984—98. Contbr. articles to profl. jour. Recipient Social Sci. prize, Internation U. Andalucia, 1994. Fellow: Spanish Assn. Sport Sci. Avocations: walking, reading, travel. Office: Univ Castilla Mancha Avda Carlos III S/n Toledo 45071 Spain Office Fax: 34-925-268846. Business E-Mail: luismiguel.ruiz@uclm.es.

RUIZ, MIRIAM, secondary school educator; b. San Lorenzo, Puerto Rico, May 15, 1968; d. Margaro Ruiz and Salvadora Vázquez; m. Pedro J. Mañón, Dec. 1995. B in Edn. and secondary Spanish (magna cum laude), U. Puerto Rico, 1992, M in Edn. Administrn. and Supervision, 2005. Lic. secondary edn. Tex. Tchr. Spanish Nuestra Senora la Providencia Acad., Rio Piedras, PR, 1992—94, Panamerica Lang. Inst., Guaynabo, PR, 1992—98, Caribbean Preparatory Sch., Hato Rey, PR, 1994—2004, Sam Rayburn HS, Pasadena, Tex., 2004—. Com. mem. sch. accreditation Middle State Assn., Hato Ray, PR, 2003—04. Mem.: Curriculum and Supr. Assn., Nat. Tchrs. Assn., Tex. State Tchrs. Assn., Fgn. Lang. Tchrs. Assn. Avocations: diving, reading, music, travel, writing. Home: 103 Marina Oaks Dr Kemah TX 77565 Office: Sam Rayburn HS 2121 Cherrybrook Pasadena TX 77502 Office Phone: 713-477-3601.

RUIZ, PEDRO JAVIER, education educator; b. San Juan, July 16, 1959; s. Pedro J. Ruiz and Carmen M. Gonzalez; life ptnr. Thomas G. Clark, Oct. 25, 1957. BS in Psychology, Cath. U. PR, Ponce, 1982; MS in Bilingual Spl. Edn., Adelphi U., Garden City, NY, 1993; PhD in Bilingual Edn., NYU, 2003; diploma, Administrn. Schs. Mgr., avp Citibank NA, Internat. Pvt. Banking, NYC, 1982—91; bilingual spl. edn. tchr. PS 94, Dist. 75/Citywide Programs, NYC, 1991—95; coord., project mas, title vii N.Y.C. Bd. of Edn.-Ctrl. Office, 1996—97; asst. dir. Dist. 75/Citywide Programs-Ctrl. Office, NYC, 1997—99; adminstr. k-12, bilingual, ESL Mt. Vernon City Sch. Dist., NY, 1999—2005; coord. NY State Edn. Dept., Office Bilingual Edn. and Fgn. Lang. Studies, Albany, 2005—; dirs. Nat. Counsel Title III, 2007—, elect pres., 2008—. Dir. Bilingual Spl. Edn. Acad., NYC, 1996—97; past-pres. NY State Assn. Bilingual Edn., NYC, 2001—02; exec. bd. mem. Nat. Assn. Bilingual Edn., Washington, 2004—, pres., 2005—, past pres., 2005—07; adv. bd. mem. Ctr. Instruction Issue Regarding English Langs. Learners, 2007—, Nat. Bd. Profl. Tchg. Standards, Nat. ESL Tchr. Standards, 2009—, Ctr. Equity & Excellence Edn. George Wash. U., 2009—. Recipient Svc. Excellence Award for Outstanding Performance, Citibank NA, 1985, Remunda Cadoux Leadership in Fgn. Lang. Supervision Award, NY State Assn. of Fgn. Lang. Tchrs., 2004, 2005 Dissertation award, Nat. Assn. for Bilingual Edn., 2005, Ednl. Leadership Scholarship Project award, Dr. Ramon S. Velez award, Nat. P.R. Day Parade, 2006; fellow Ph.D. - Fed. - Title VII Fellowship, NY U., NY, 1995-1998; scholar Masters Program in Bilingual Spl. Edn., NYC Bd. Edn., 1991-1993. Mem.: NY State Assn. Bilingual Edn., Nat. Assn. Bilingual Edn., Latino Children Ednl. Network, Coun. for Exceptional Children, Assn. Supervision and Curriculum Devel. Democrat. Roman Catholic. Avocations: furniture restoration, travel, reading, gardening. Home: 729 Belvidere Ave Plainfield NJ 07062 Personal E-mail: pedrojruiz@aol.com.

RUIZ, RAMÓN EDUARDO, history professor; b. Sessions Ranch, Calif., Sept. 9, 1921; s. Ramon and Dolores (Urueta) R.; m. Natalia Marrujo, Oct. 14, 1944; children: Olivia, Maura. BA, San Diego State Coll., 1947; MA, Claremont Grad. Sch., 1948; PhD, U. Calif., Berkeley, 1954. Asst. prof. U. Oreg., Eugene, 1955-57, So. Meth. U., Dallas, 1957-58; prof. Smith Coll., Northampton, Mass., 1958-69; prof. Latin Am. history U. Calif. at San Diego, 1969-91, prof. emeritus, 1991—, chmn. dept. history, 1971-76, chmn. divsn. humanities, 1972-74; mem. project grant com. NEH, 1972-73, 75-77, dir. pub. programs divsn., 1979-80; Ralph Chase lectr. San Angelo State U., 2000. Vis. prof. Facultad de Economia, Univ. de Nuevo Leon, Mexico, 1965-66, Coll. de Sonora, Mexico, summer 1983, Pomona Coll., 1983-84, Coll. de Michoacan, Mexico, summer 1986, 87, Univ. Nacional Autonoma de Mexico, fall 1992; scholar-in-residence Colegio de la Frontero Norte, Mexico, 1994-96; MacArthur Found. nominator, 1981-82; mem. project grant com. Ford Found. Author: Cuba: The Making of A Revolution, 1968 (One of Best History Books, Book World Washington Post 1968), Mexico: The Challenge of Poverty and Illiteracy, 1963, An American in Maximillians's Mexico, 1865-1866, 1959; (with James D. Atwater) Out From Under; Benito Juarez and Mexico's Struggle for Independence, 1969; (with John Tebbel) South by Southwest: The Mexican-American and His Heritage, 1969, Interpreting Latin American History, 1970, Labor and the Ambivalent Revolutionaries: Mexico, 1911-23, 1975, The Mexican War: Was it Manifest Destiny?, 1963, The Great Rebellion: Mexico, 1905-1924, 1980 (Hubert C. Herring prize), The People of Sonora and Yanqui Capitalists, 1988, Triumphs and Tragedy: A History of the Mexican People, 1992 (named One of Five Best History Books 1991-92, L.A. Times, Gold Medal award Commonwealth Club San Francisco 1993, History Book Club selection); (with Olivia Teresa Ruiz) Reflexiones Sobre la Identidad de los Pueblos, 1996, On the Rim of Mexico: Encounters of the Rich and Poor, 1998, Memories of a Hyphenated Man, 2003, Mexico: Why a Few are Rich and the People Poor, 2009. Served to lt. USAAF, 1943-46. William Harrison Mills traveling fellow in internat. rels., 1950; John Hay Whitney Found. fellow, 1950; Fulbright fellow Mex., 1965-66; fellow Ctr. for Advanced Study in Behavioral Scis., 1984-85, Rockefeller Resident, Bellagio Study Ctr., 2003, Ena H. Thompson lectureship, Pomona Coll., 1995; recipient Am. Philos. Soc. grant in aid, 1959, Nat. medal Humanities Pres. U.S., 1998. Mem. Am. Hist. Assn. (Beveridge prize com. 1974-76), Conf. Latin Am. History, Chicano-Latino Faculty Assn. U. Calif. (pres. 1989-91), Phi Beta Kappa, Sigma Delta Pi. Home: PO Box 1775 Rancho Santa Fe CA 92067-1775 Home Phone: 858-756-4370.

RUIZ, VANESSA, Associate Judge, DC Court of Appeals; b. San Juan, Mar. 22, 1950; d. Fernando and Irma (Bosch) Ruiz-Suria; married; m. David E. Birenbaum, Oct. 22, 1983; stepchildren: Tracy, Matthew. BA, Wellesley Coll., 1972; JD, Georgetown U., 1975. Bar: D.C. 1972. Assoc. Fried, Frank, Harris, Shriver & Kampelman, Washington, 1975—83; sr. mgr., counsel Sears World Trade Inc., Washington, 1983—87; founding ptnr. Sloan, Lehner & Ruiz, Washington, 1987—89; ptnr. Pepper, Hamilton & Scheetz, Washington, 1989—91; dep. corp. counsel, legal counsel div. DC, 1991—93; prin. dep. corp. counsel State of DC, 1993—94, corporation counsel, 1994; assoc. judge DC Ct. of Appeals, Washington, 1994—. Spkr. in field; adjunct prof. Georgetown U. Co-author: Europe Without Frontiers: A Lawyers' Guide, 1989. Trustee Carnegie Endowment for internat. Peace. Recipient Judge of the Yr. award, Hispanic Nat. Bar Assn., 2001. Mem.: Hispanic Bar Assn., DC, Am. Law Inst., Coun. Ct. Excellence, Nat. Assn. Women Judges (past pres.), Internat. Assn. Women (bd. mem.). Office: DC Ct of Appeals 500 Indiana Ave NW Fl 6 Washington DC 20001-2131 Office Fax: 202-626-8868.

RUIZ BRAVO, NORKA, federal agency administrator; BS in Biology, Goucher Coll., Towson, Md., 1975; MS in Biology, Yale U., New Haven, PhD in Biology, 1983. Postdoc. fellow physiol. chemistry Johns Hopkins U., Balt.; postdoc. fellow biochemistry & molecular biology U. Tex. MD Anderson Cancer Ctr., faculty, 1983—89, Baylor Coll. Medicine, Houston, 1983—89; joined NIH, 1990, various positions including sci. rev. adminstr., Nat. Inst. Gen. Med. Scis. (NIGMS), prog. dir. Divsn. Genetics & Biology, 1992, acting dep. dir. NIGMS Divsn. Minority Opportunities in Rsch., spl. asst. NIGMS Office Extramural Activities, sci. rev. adminstr., Nat. Ctr. Human Genome Rsch., then dep. dir. cancer biology divsn., Nat. Cancer Inst., 1997—98, acting dir. cancer biology divsn., 1998—99, dep. assoc. dir. extramural activities, NIGMS, 1999—2000, assoc. dir. extramural activities, 2000—03, dep. dir. extramural rsch., dir. Office Extramural Rsch., 2003—08, spl. adv. to dir., 2008—. Mem.: AAAS, Soc. Devel. Biology, Am. Soc. Cell Biology. Office: NIH 9000 Rockville Pike Bethesda MD 20892 Office Phone: 301-496-1096. Office Fax: 301-402-3469. E-mail: nb9b@nih.gov.*

RUIZ MADAS, YESENIA, educational counselor; b. Bklyn., Oct. 17, 1976; d. Federico and Margarita Ruiz, Adrian Feliciano (Stepfather); m. Timothy C. Madas, May 5, 2001; 1 child, Sonia G. Madas. BA, Mercy Coll., NY, 2000, MS, 2003. Job coach Lifespire, NY, 1994—99; social worker St. Christopher's Inc., NY, 2000; academic advisor Mercy Coll., Bronx, NY, 2001—04; student devel. specialist Brookdale C.C., Lincroft, NJ, 2004—. Mem. vol. rels. com. Habitat for Humanity. Recipient Humanitarian award, Jane Addams Vocat. H.S., 1994. Mem.: NJ Edn. Assn., NJ CC Counselors Assn. Roman Catholic. Avocations: reading, sewing, carpentry, bicycling, oragami. Office: Brookdale Community College 765 Newman Springs Rd Lincroft NJ 07738 Office Phone: 732-224-2556. Business E-Mail: ymadas@brookdalecc.edu.

RUIZ-VARGAS, YOLANDA, finance educator; b. Mayagüez, PR, Apr. 24, 1968; d. Samuel Ruiz and Isabel Vargas. BSBA cum laude, U. P.R., Mayagüez, 1990, MBA, 1994; PhD, U. of Tex., Edinburg, 2000. Acctg. officer Calzados HQ, Inc, Mayagüez, 1990—93; planner trainee Cutler Hammer of PR, Cabo Rojo, PR, 1994; tchg. asst. U. of Texas-Pan Am., Edinburg, 1996—99; instr. U. P.R., Mayagüez, 1994—96, asst. prof., 2000—03, assoc. prof., 2003—, assoc. dean for rsch. and grad. affairs, 2004—. Co-coordinator UPR- Ctr. for Profesional Enhancement, Mayagüez, PR, 2002—02; faculty rep. Grad. Coun. - UPR Mayagüez, Mayagüez, PR, 2001—03; faculty advisor 2002 Ph.D. Project Fin. Doctoral Students Assn. Conf., San Antonio, —, 2001 Ph.D. Project Fin. Doctoral Students Assn. Conf., Toronto, Canada; liaison 2000 PhD Project Fin. Doctoral Students Assn. Conf., Seattle; planning com. mem. 1999 PhD Project Fin. Doctoral Students Assn. Conf., Orlando; mem. 2002 FMA Ann. Meeting Program Com., San Antonio; vis. asst. prof. Tex. A&M Internat. U., Laredo, 1999—2000, Scholar acad. scholar, U. P.R., 1996—2000. Mem.: Am. Fin. Assn., Internat. Coun. for Small Bus., Fin. Mgmt. Assn. Internat., Alpha Delta Kappa, Beta Gamma Sigma. Avocations: reading, travel. Office: U PR COBA - PO Box 9009 Mayaguez PR 00681-9009 Business E-Mail: yruiz@caribe.net. E-mail: yruiz@uprm.edu.

RUKEYSER, M.S., JR., television consultant, writer; b. NYC, Apr. 15, 1931; s. Merryle Stanley and Berenice (Simon) Rukeyser; children: Jill Victoria, Patricia Bern. Student, U. Va., 1948-52. Reporter Albany (N.Y.) Times-Union, 1949, Internat. News Service, NYC, 1951; TV publicist Young & Rubicam, Inc., NYC, 1952-57; with NBC, 1958-80, 81-88, dir. news info. Washington, 1962, v.p. press and publicity NYC, 1963-72, v.p. corp. info., 1972-74, v.p. pub. info., 1974-77, exec. v.p. pub. info., 1977-80, 81-84, exec. v.p. corp. communications, 1984-88; v.p. comm. Newsweek Inc., 1980-81; sr. v.p. GTG Entertainment, 1988-90; pres. Rukeyser Communications, NYC, 1990—. Sr. fellow Freedom Forum Media Ctr., 1991-92. Author (with Grant Tinker): Tinker in Television: From General Sarnoff to General Electric, 1994. With US Army, 1953—54. Office: Ste 1213 616 Clearwater Park Rd West Palm Beach FL 33401-6250 Personal E-mail: budruk@gmail.com.

RUKEYSER, ROBERT JAMES, manufacturing executive; b. New Rochelle, NY, June 26, 1942; s. Merryle Stanley and Berenice Helene (Simon) R.; m. Leah A. Spiro, July 26, 1964; children: David Bern, Peter Lloyd. BA, Cornell U., Ithaca, NY, 1964; MBA with distinction, NYU, 1969. Bond analyst Dun & Bradstreet, NYC, 1964-65, Standard & Poors, NYC, 1965-66; mktg. rep. data processing div. IBM, NYC, 1967-72, regional mktg. staff, 1973-74, mktg. mgr., 1974-76, corp. mgr. internal comm. and editl. programs Armonk, NY, 1976-79, mgr. comm. ops. Franklin Lakes, NJ, 1979-81; pub. affairs dir., asst. to chmn. Fortune Brands, Inc. (formerly Am. Brands, Inc.), NYC, 1981-83, v.p. pub. affairs, asst. to chmn., 1983-85, v.p. office products Old Greenwich, Conn., 1986-87, v.p. ops., 1987-89, sr. v.p. corp. affairs, 1990-99. Bd. dirs. Fortune Brands (formerly Am. Brands Inc.); mgmt. cons. and author, 2000-. Vice chmn., chair fin. com., mem. exec. com. The Hole in the Wall Gang Camp; bd. dirs. Assn. Hole in the Wall Camps, treas., exec. com., chair budget and fin. com.

RUKEYSER, WILLIAM SIMON, journalist; b. NYC, June 8, 1939; s. Merryle Stanley and Berenice (Simon) R.; m. Elisabeth Mary Garnett, Nov. 21, 1963; children: Lisa Rukeyser Burn, James William. AB, Princeton U., 1961; rsch. student, Cambridge U., Eng., 1962—63; LittD (hon.), Maryville Coll., 2002. Copyreader Wall St. Jour., 1961-62, staff reporter Europe, 1963-67; assoc. editor Fortune mag., 1967-71, mem. bd. editors, 1971-72; founding mng. editor Money mag., NYC, 1972-80; mng. editor Fortune mag., 1980-86; dir. internat. bus. devel. Time Inc., 1986-88; editor in chief, exec. v.p. Whittle Communications, Knoxville, Tenn., 1988-91; chmn., CEO, Whittle Books, Knoxville, 1991-94; pres. William Rukeyser, Inc., Knoxville, 1994—; editl. dir. Corporate Board Member mag., 1998—2009; contbg. editor CNN, 1995-97; freelance book editor, 2007—. Commentator Good Morning America, ABC-TV, 1978-85, CBS Radio Stas. News Svc., 1979-86; mem. nat. adv. coun. Maryville Coll., Tenn., 1998-2007, chmn. nat. adv. coun., 2007-; mem. adv. bd. Ctr. of Inquiry in Liberal Arts Wabash Coll., Crawfordsville, Ind., 2001—. Editor: The Partnership: The Making of Goldman Sachs, 2008. Jud. com. Union County (NJ) Med. Soc., 1977-80; co-chair capital campaign Nat. Mental Health Assn., 1984-85; liaison com. U. Tenn. Med. Ctr., 1992-99; vice chmn. U. Health Sys. Inc., 1999—; chmn. bd. dirs. Knoxville Jazz Orch., 2001—09; mem. 2009-; mem. alumni adv. bd. Univ. Press Club, Princeton, 2005—, vice-chair alumni adv. bd., 2009-; mem. bd. dirs. Overseas Press Club Found., 2009-. Office: 1001 First Tennessee Plz Knoxville TN 37929 Personal E-mail: wsr@finehand.com.

RUKHADZE, IRMA, neuroscientist; b. Gali, Georgia, Apr. 14, 1972; d. Rusiko Rukhadze and Ketino jijelava. PhD (hon.), I. Beritashvili Inst. Physiology, Tbilisi, Ga., 1999. Cert. neurophysiologist Georgian Acad. Scis., 2002. Rsch. scientist Beritashvili Inst. Physiology, Tbilisi, Georgia, 2001—05; vis. scientist Max Planck Inst. Psychiatry, Miunchen, Germany, 2002—03; postdoc. fellow U. Pa., Phila., 2005—08, rsch. assoc., 2009—. Contbr. articles to profl. jours. Fellow German Academic Exch. Svcs., 2002—03; fellowship of Pres. of Ga., 2004—05. Office: Univ Pa 3800 Spruce St Philadelphia PA 19104 Office Fax: 215-573-5186. Business E-Mail: rukhadze@vet.upenn.edu.

RUKNUDIN, ABDUL M., health program administrator; BSc, MSc, U. Madras, Inida, PhD, 1982. Cert. in clin. rsch. assoc. CALGB, 2007. Adj. asst. prof. U. Md., Balt., 1998; health program mgr. UM Med. Ctr., Balt., 2007—. Contbr. articles to profl. jours. Nat. Postdoc. fellowship, Indo-French Cultural Com., 1984—85. Mem.: Am. Heart Assn. Achievements include research in ion trasporters and ion channels. Office: Univ Md Greenebaum Cancer Ctr 22 S Greene St Baltimore MD 21201 Office Phone: 410-328-8613. Office Fax: 410-328-8616. Business E-Mail: aruknudi@umaryland.edu.

RULAND, MILDRED ARDELIA, retired retail executive and buyer; b. Draketown, Ga., Aug. 11, 1918; m. Harry Morse Ruland, Aug. 19, 1947; children: Hal Morse, Judy Lee Ruland Rigas. BS, West Ga. Coll., 1966. Elem. tchr., New London, Conn., 1947-48, Atlanta, 1948-51, Rome, Ga., 1951-81; mgr. McBrayer Bros. Furniture Co., Rome, 1981—; ret., 2006. Rosenwald Found. scholar, 1941-42. Mem. NEA, Nat. Fedn. Ind. Bus. (corr. sec. 1975—), Ga. Edn. Assn. (del. 1964-74), Ga. Home Furnishings Assn., Twickham Garden Club, Rome Pride Assn., Rome C. of C., Alpha Delta Kappa. Republican. Baptist. Avocations: dance, swimming, bowling, hiking, singing.

RULAND, RICHARD EUGENE, literature educator, critic, historian; b. Detroit, May 1, 1932; s. Eugene John and Irene (Janette) R.; m. Mary Ann Monaghan; children: Joseph, Michael, Paul, Susan; m. Birgit Noll. BA, Assumption Coll. U. Western Ont., Can., 1953; MA, U. Detroit, 1955; PhD, U. Mich., 1960. Instr., then asst. prof. English and Am. studies Yale U., New Haven, 1960-67, Morse rsch. fellow, 1966-67; prof. English and Am. lit. Washington U., St. Louis, 1967—, chmn. dept. English, 1969-74; chmn. comparative lit. program, 1993-94. Vis. Bruern prof. Am. lit. Leeds (Eng.) U., 1964-65; vis. Fulbright prof. U. Groningen, The Netherlands, 1975, Sch. of English and Am. Studies U. East Anglia, Eng., 1978-79; vis. disting. prof. Am. lit. Coll. of William and Mary, 1980-81. Author: The Rediscovery of American Literature:

Premises of Critical Taste, 1900-1940, 1967, America in Modern European Literature: From Image to Metaphor, 1976, (with Malcolm Bradbury) From Puritanism to Postmodernism: A History of American Literature, 1991 (paperback 1992), translation into Czech and Hungarian, 1997; editor: Walden: A Collection of Critical Essays, 1967, The Native Muse: Theories of American Literature, Vol. I, 1972, 76, A Storied Land: Theories of American Literature, Vol. II, 1976; contbr. articles to profl. jours. Guggenheim Rsch. fellow, 1982-83. Mem. Assn. Depts. English (pres. 1974). Avocation: jazz musician. Office: Washington U Dept English Saint Louis MO 63130

RULE, ANN, author; 4 children. Degree in English, U. Washington, 1958, PhD in Humane Letters, Willamette U., 2004, postgrad. in police sci. Former policewoman, Seattle; speaker on subject of serial killers. Author (non-fiction books): The Stranger Beside Me, 1980, The I-5 Killer, Want-Ad Killer, Lust Killer, Beautiful Seattle, 1984, Small Sacrifices, 1987, If You Really Loved Me, 1991, Everything She Ever Wanted, 1992, (novel): Possession, 1983, A Rose for Her Grave, 1993, You Belong to Me, 1994, Dead by Sunset, 1995, A Fever in the Heart, 1995, Green River, Running Red, 2004, Kiss Me Kill Me: And Other True Cases, 2004; exec. prodr. ABC mini-series Small Sacrifices, 1989 (Peabody award), NBC mini-series Dead by Sunset, 1995, CBS mini-series And Never Let Her Go, 2000, USA Network mini-series The Stranger Beside Me, 2003; contbr. over 1400 articles to newspapers and mags. including True Detective, Cosmopolitan, and others. Vol. Seattle Crisis Clinic. Recipient: Washington State Governor's award. Address: PO Box 98846 Seattle WA 98198-0846

RULE, CHARLES FREDERICK (RICK), lawyer; b. Nashville, Apr. 28, 1955; s. Frederick Charles and Mary Elizabeth (Malone) R.; m. Ellen Friedland, May 13, 1976 BA, Vanderbilt U., 1978; JD, U. Chgo., 1981. Bar: U.S. Ct. Appeals. (D.C. cir.) 1983. Law clk. US Ct. Appeals (Fed. Cir.), Washington, 1981-82; spl. asst. to asst. atty. gen. Antitrust divsn. US Dept. Justice, Washington, 1982-83, dep. asst. atty. gen. policy planning, 1984-85, acting asst. atty. gen., then dep. asst. atty. gen. regulatory affairs, 1985-86, asst. atty. gen., 1986-89; ptnr. Covington & Burling LLP, Washington, 1989-2001, Fried, Frank, Harris, Shriver & Jacobson LLP, Washington, 2001—07, Cadwalder, Wickersham & Taft LLP, Washington, 2007—. Legal, econ. analyst Lexecon, Inc., Chgo., 1979-80 Mem. Bar of D.C. Ct. Appeals, Phi Beta Kappa, Phi Eta Sigma. Republican. Presbyterian. Office: Cadwalder Wickersham & Taft LLP 700 Sixth St NW Washington DC 20001 Office Phone: 202-862-2420. E-mail: rick.rule@cwt.com.

RULIS, CHRISTOPHER C., lawyer; b. Cheswick, Pa., Apr. 15, 1956; s. Casmer Rulis and Margaret Thimons; m. Lisa Ross, Sept. 26, 1992; children: Marisa, Amanda. BA, Indiana U., Pa., 1978; JD, U. Akron, 1981. Bar: U.S. Supreme Ct., Pa. Supreme Ct., U.S. Tax Ct., Allegheny County Ct. Common Pleas. Assoc. atty. Brandt, Milnes, Rea, Pitts., 1983—90, Rothman Gordon P.C., Pitts.; mng. ptnr. O'Brien, Rulis, Bochicchio, Sosso, LLC, Pitts., 1996—2005. Spl. master Allegheny County Ct. Common Pleas, 1996—. Mem. Gov.'s Club, Harrisburg, Pa., 1996—2000. Fellow, Million Dollar Advocate's Forum, 1997—. Fellow: Acad. Trial Lawyers; mem.: Pa. Def. Inst., Allegheny County Bar Assn., Pa. Bar Assn. Republican. Roman Catholic. Home: 2762 Brunton Ct Allison Park PA 15101 Business E-Mail: crulis@orbslaw.com.

RULIS, RAYMOND JOSEPH, manufacturing executive, consultant; b. New Britain, Conn., June 2, 1924; s. James Alexander and Eva (Ragauskas) R.; m. Thelma Pelchat, June 16, 1949 (dec.); children: Elaine, Jeffery, Catherine, Elizabeth, Amy, Daniel, Jean; m. Virginia Kleene, Oct. 9, 1999. BSME, U. Conn., 1949; postgrad., U. Conn., Ohio State U., Northeastern U., 1949-58; student, Fed. Exec. Inst., Charlottesville, Va., 1976. Devel. engr. Hamilton Standard, U.T.C., Windsor-locks, Conn., 1951-55; mgr. fuel controls Lycoming Textron, Stratford, Conn., 1955-59; mgr. controls and accessories GE, Lynn, Mass., 1959-62; successively program mgr. sert spacecraft, chief spacecraft engr., chief launch vehicle engr., chief engring design, program mgr. QCSEE program NASA Lewis Rsch. Ctr., Cleve., 1962-81; v.p. rsch. and. devel. Textron Turbocomponents Group, Walled Lake, Mich., 1981-92; cons., 1992—. Cons. Joint FAA/NASA Civil Aero Rsch. Document Study, 1972, Cruise Missile PRogram, 1977-78, C-17 Aircraft Source Selection Bd., 1978, Tri-Svcs. Propulsion Group, 1976-78; chmn. Conf. on Short Haul Systems, NASA, 1976; mem. exec. coun. Aerospace Industries Tech. Coun., 1988-89. Contbr. articles to profl. jours.; patentee in field. Chmn. Boy Scouts Am. Fund Drives, Cleve., 1976-78; mem. Coun. on World Affairs, Cleve., 1976-81. With US Army, 1943—46. Decorated Combat Infantryman's badge, Bronze Star medal, Purple Heart. Mem. Am. Helicopter Soc. (chmn. tech. session 1970), AIAA (chmn. tech. session 1965), Detroit Engring Soc., KC. Roman Catholic. Avocation: golf. Office: RJR Cons 9 Outpost Ln Hilton Head Island SC 29928-3820

RUMAKER, MICHAEL, writer, language educator; b. Phila., Mar. 5, 1932; s. Michael Joseph and Winifred Marvel Rumaker. Degree in writing (hon.), Black Mountain Coll., 1955; MFA, Columbia U., 1970. Lectr. writing New Sch. for Social Rsch., NYC, 1967-71; tchr. writer, mem. intellectual resources pool Tappan Zee H.S., Orangeburg, NY, 1965-69; instr. writing workshops Rockland Ctr. for Arts, West Nyack, NY, 1975-78; adj. lectr. Rockland C.C., Suffern, NY, 1978-87; writer-in-residence CCNY, CUNY, 1969-71, adj. prof., 1985—98. Author: (novels) The Butterfly, 1962, English edit., 1968, Russian edit., 2002, A Day and a Night at the Baths, 1979, German edit., 1997, My First Satyrnalia, 1981, To Kill a Cardinal, 1992, Pagan Days, 2000, (non-fiction) An Immodest Proposal, 2004, (short stories) Gringos and Other Stories, 1967, 2nd edit., 1991, German edit., 1968, English edit. (Exit 3), 1966, (memoir) Robert Duncan in San Francisco, 1996, Black Mountain Days, 2003, (poems) Pizza Selected Poems, 2005, The Fairies are Dancing All Over the World, 2006, (plays) Queers (Schwul), 1970, 2004, (poem) The Fairies Are Dancing All Over the World, 2006. Mem. Nat. Writers Union. Literary Agent: Harold Ober Assocs 425 Madison Ave Rm 1001 New York NY 10017-1183 Business E-Mail: mchlrumaker@gmail.com.

RUMAN, RENEE, principal; b. Warren, Ohio, Oct. 30, 1951; m. William S. Ruman, June 21, 1974. BS in Edn., Youngstown State U., Ohio, 1975, M in Ednl. Adminstrn., 1991. Tchr. Niles City Sch. Dist., Ohio, 1975—95, asst. prin., 1995—96, prin., 1996—98, lead prin. tchg. and learning, 1998—2002, lead prin. cip and title i, 2002—. Fin. com., lector, eucharistic min. St. Mary Ch., Mineral Ridge, Ohio, 1990. Recipient Ashland Oil Golden Apple Achiever, Ashland Oil, 1993; Martha Holden Jennings scholar, 1993—94. Mem.: Ohio Assn. Elem. Sch. Adminstrs. (assoc.), Reading Recovery Coun. N.Am. (assoc.), Ohio Assn. Adminstrs. State and Fed. Programs (assoc.), Phi Delta Kappa (assoc.). Roman Catholic. Avocations: cooking, needlecrafts, travel. Office: Niles City School District 100 West St Niles OH 44446 Office Fax: 330-652-3522. E-mail: renee.ruman@neomin.org.

RUMBAUGH, JEFFREY ARLIN, neurologist, neuroscientist; b. Lansing, Mich., Jan. 8, 1971; s. Stanley A. and Marcia L. Rumbaugh; m. Y. Nan Park, May 25, 1996; 1 child, Jonh J. A. BS, Haverford Coll., Pa., 1993; MS, U. Rochester, NY, 1996, PhD, 1998, MD, 2000. Lic. physician Md., 2004, diplomate Am. Bd. Psychiatry and Neurology, 2005. Intern Johns Hopkins U., Balt., 2000—01, resident neurology, 2001—03, chief resident neurology, 2003—04, asst. prof. neurology Divsn. Neuroimmunology and Neuro-Infectious Diseases, 2004—. Founder, dir. neuroimmunolgy, neuro-infectious disease consult svc. Johns Hopkins U., 2004—. Contbr. articles to profl. jours. Mem. humanism in medicine com., Rochester, 1999—2000; vol. outreach for AIDS awarenes Students Rochester, 1993—2000. Recipient Analytical Chemistry award, Am. Chem. Soc., 1993, Travel award, Am. Soc. Clin. Investigation, 2006, S. Weir Mitchell award, Am. Acad. Neurology, 2005; fellow, Elmer Stotz Found., 1995, Louis and Molly Wolk Found., 1996, NIH Genetics, 1996, E. H. Hooker, 1997; scholar, Phi Beta Kappa, 1992, Med. Scientist Tng. Program, 1993. Achievements include discovery of a possible new host defense mechanism involving matrix metalloproteinases and viral proteins; research in several new biochemical mechanisms involved in DNA replication and repair; a possible biochemical pathway involved in HIV replication. Avocation: running. Office: Johns Hopkins University 600 N Wolfe Street Baltimore MD 21287 Office Fax: 410-502-8075.

RUMBAUGH, MAX ELDEN, JR., professional society administrator; b. Ada, Okla., Dec. 11, 1937; s. Max E. and Gertrude (Gulker) R.; m. Joan E. Brockway; children: Maria Rumbaugh Gross, Max E. III. BS in Engring., U.S. Mil. Acad., 1960; MS in Engring. Scis., Purdue U., 1965, MBA, 1972. Instr. Purdue U., West Lafayette, Ind., 1964-65; corp. officer Midwest Applied Sci. Corp., West Lafayette, 1965-72; chief engr. advanced tech. Schwitzer div. Wallace-Murray Corp., Indpls., 1972-77, dir. research, 1977-81; mgr. engring. activities div. Soc. Automotive Engrs., Warrendale, Pa., 1981-84, v.p., asst. gen. mgr., 1984-86, exec. v.p., 1986—2002, exec. v.p. emeritus, 2002—; pres. Performance Rev. Inst., 1991—2001; cons. Ctr. Advanced Vehicular Sys., Miss. State U., 2007—. Pres. Soc. Rsch. Adminstrs. Internat., 1973-74; chmn. Ind. sect. Soc. Automotive Engrs., 1978-79; bd. dirs., exec. com. Am. Nat. Standards Inst., NYC, 1986-02; bd. dirs. Intelligent Transp. Soc. Am., 1992-04, mem. exec. com., 1998-04, v.p., 2009-; chair youth programs Scottsdale Sister Cities Assn., 2006-; internat. spkr. Automotive Engring., 1997-. Author mag. column Focus, 1986-2002. Bd. dirs. Jr. Achievement Western Pa., Pitts., 1986-98, YMCA, North Hills, Pitts., 1985-94, Scottsdale Sister Cities, 2006—, v.p., 2009-; chmn., Scottsdale HS Internat. Clubs, 2007-; sec. Intelligent Transp. Soc. Am. Bd. Dirs., 2000-04. 1st lt. US Army, 1960—63. Mem. ASME, Am. Soc. Assn. Execs., Coun. Engring. and Sci. Soc. Execs. (bd. dirs. 1990-97, sec. 1993-94, v.p. 1994-95, pres. 1995-96), Soc. Automotive Engrs. of China (hon.), Soc. Automotive Engrs. of India (hon.), Russian Internat. Acad. Engring., Intelligent Transp. Soc. Am. (bd. dirs. 1992-03, sec. 2000-03, chmn. fin. com. 2000-03), Russian Acad. Quality Problems, Rotary (bd. dirs. 1982-84, 93-97, v.p. 1994-95, pres. 1995-96, chmn. youth exch. 2003-). Avocations: skiing, photography. Home: 8731 E San Pablo Dr Scottsdale AZ 85258- Office: Soc of Automotive Engrs Inc 400 Commonwealth Dr Warrendale PA 15086-7511 Office Phone: 480-991-3059.

RUMBAUT, RUBÉN G., SR., social sciences educator; s. Rubén Darío Rumbaut and Carmen Riera; m. Irene Tienda-Rumbaut; 1 child, Rubén Darío Jr. PhD, Brandeis U., Waltham, Mass., 1973. Prof. sociology U. Calif., Irvine, 2002—. Office: Univ Calif Irvine 3151 Social Sci Plz Irvine CA 92697 Business E-Mail: rrumbaut@uci.edu.

RUMBOUGH, STANLEY MADDOX, JR., industrialist; b. NYC, Apr. 25, 1920; s. Stanley Maddox and Elizabeth (Colgate) R.; m. Nedenia Hutton, Mar. 23, 1946 (div. 1966); children: Stanley H., David P. (dec.), Nedenia Colgate; m. Margaretha Wagstrom, Dec. 21, 1967 (div. 1990); m. Janna Herlow, Mar. 8, 1990. AB, Yale U., 1942; postgrad. in bus. adminstrn., NYU, 1947-51. Vice pres., dir. Willis Air Service, Teterboro, NJ, 1946-47; v.p., dir. White Metal Mfg. Co., Hoboken, NJ, 1945-61, pres., 1960-61; pres., dir. Metal Container Corp., 1950-59, Am. Totalisator, Balt., 1956-58; chmn. bd. Extrusion Devel. Corp., 1959-61; co-founder, chmn. bd. Elec. Engring. Ltd., 1960-69; co-founder, dir. Trinidad Flour Mills, 1961-72; dir. Dart Industries, 1961—83; chmn. bd. Wallace Clark & Co., 1962—69; co-founder Jamaica Flour Mills, 1963-66. Spl. asst. to sec. Dept. Commerce, 1953; spl. asst. White House charge exec. br. liaison, 1953-55; founder Washington D.C. Tennis Patrons Found. Chmn. U.S. Com. for UN, 1957-58; co-founder Citizens for Eisenhower, 1951; vice chmn. Citizens for Eisenhower-Nixon Com., 1952; bd. dirs. Young Pres. Orgn., 1958-65, 69-80; trustee Young Pres. Found., 1957-70, pres., 1962-65; bd. dirs. N.Y. World's Fair Corp., 1961-70, Nat. Conf. on Citizenship, 1973-2003, Population Resource Ctr., 1978-92, Planned Parenthood of Palm Beach Area, 1979-95, Planned Parenthood Fedn. Am., 1981-84, life trustee Kravis Ctr. Performing Arts; bd. dirs. Palm Beach Civic Assn., chmn. 2005—09, chmn. emeritus 2009-, co-chmn., 1997-2005; trustee Libr. for Presdl. Papers, 1966-70, Fgn. Policy Assn., 1961-70, Am. Health Found., 1972-76; life trustee Internat. House 1959—. Capt. USMCR, 1942-46. Decorated Air medal (8), D.F.C. (2). Mem. Chief Execs. Orgn., World Pres.'s Orgn. (founding), Young Pres.'s Orgn. (founding), Def. Orientation Conf. Assn., Racquet and Tennis Club, Internat. Lawn Tennis Club, Maidstone Club, Seminole Club, Bath and Tennis Club, Everglades Club, Zeta Psi. Republican. Home: 655 Island Dr Palm Beach FL 33480-4744 Office: 44 Cocoanut Row Ste B103 Palm Beach FL 33480-4069

RUMFOLO, MARILU, financial analyst; b. Houston, July 19, 1953; d. Walter John and Lucille (Jones) R. Grad., Arrons Sch. Real Estate, 1978; student, U. Houston, 1979; BS in Bus. Adminstrn., Colo. Tech. U., 2007. Jr. acct. Gen. Leisure Corp., Houston, 1973-75; security cons. Burns Internat. Security, Houston, 1975-77; founder, dir. govt. affairs Time Energy Systems, Inc., Houston, 1977-83; founder, exec. dir., chmn. bd. trustees The Children's Drug Abuse Network, Houston, 1983—; founder, pres. Sun Am. Fin., LLC, 2000; general securities, principal, pres. founder Rumfolo & Assocs., Securities, LP, 2000—. Bd. dirs. Eliza Johnston Home for Aging, Houston, 1981-82; chmn. bd. Citizens United for Pub. Edn., Houston, 1980-82; candidate city council, Houston, 1981, 83; team capt. Am. Heart Assn. Houston, 1982. Recipient Drugbuster award Children's Drug Abuse Network, 1985; honoree ann. appreciation breakfast for outstanding work in community, County Commr. Houston, 1986; named Rep. of Yr., Tex., 2001. Mem.: Order Eastern Star (officer 1986-87). Republican. Avocations: swimming, reading, poetry, walking. Personal E-mail: rumfolo@comcast.net.

RUMLER, ROBERT HOKE, agricultural products executive, consultant, retired trade association administrator; b. Chambersburg, Pa., Apr. 4, 1915; s. Daniel Webster and Jennie (Sellers) R.; m. Frances Jeannette Montgomery, June 7, 1939 (dec. 1983); children: Craig M. (dec. 2006), Karen A. Loden; m. Hazel Miller-Karper, Aug. 23, 1986 (dec. 1998). BS, Pa. State U., 1936. Asst. county agt. U. Mo., 1936-37; county agrl. agt. Pa. State U., 1937-45; asst. mgr., editor agrl. promotion divsn. E. I. duPont de Nemours & Co., Inc., Wilmington, Del., 1945-48; asst. exec. sec., COO, Holstein-Friesian Assn. Am., 1948-53, 53-75, exec. sec., CEO, 1975-81, exec. chmn., 1981-82, chmn. emeritus, 1982—. Pres. Holstein-Assoc. USA, Inc., 1968-81; agribus. cons., 1982—; hon. mem. Holstein-Firesian de Mex. (C.A.); bd. dirs., chmn. Vt. Nat. Bank, Vt. Fin. Svcs., Inc., 1957-88; mem. U.S./USSR Joint Com. Agrl. Cooperation; past chmn. U.S. Agrl. Export Devel. Coun., FAS-USDA; mem. coordinating group Nat. Coop. Dairy Herd Improvement program USDA, 1964-80; mem. agrl. policy adv. com. USTR/USDA Multilateral Trade Negotiations, 1973-87, mem. agrl. tech. adv. com., 1987-95. Contbg. editl. writer Holstein World. Trustee Ea. States Expn., trustee emeritus, 1993—; trustee Assoc. Industries Vt.; past bd. dirs. Internat. Stockmans Ednl. Found.; chmn. adv. bd. Pa. State U., Mont Alto, 1988-98, chmn. 1990-94, emeritus 1998, Centennial fellow, 2004; bd. advisors Pa. State U., Harrisburg, 1990-94. Recipient Disting. award Nat. Dairy Herd Improvement Assn., 1974, Disting. Svc. award Nat. Agrl. Mktg. Orgn., 1977, Cert. of Appreciation, USDA, 1982, Disting. Svc. award Holstein Assn., 1985; named Disting. Alumnus, Pa. State U., 1978, Coll. Agr., 2000, Dairy Industry Man of Yr., World Dairy Expo, 1979, Headliner-of-Yr. Livestock Pubs. Coun., 1995, Internat. Person of Yr. World Dairy Expo, 1996, 1st Disting. Alumnus AZ Frat., Pa. State U., 1996; Centennial fellow Pa. State Mont Alto Campus, 20054; named to Internat. Livestock Hall of Fame, 1987; Robert H. Rumler scholarhip founded in his name. Fellow Agr. Adventures; mem. Purebred Dairy Cattle Assn. (dir., exec. com.), Nat. Soc. Livestock Record Assns. (past pres., dir., Disting. Svcs. award 1981), Am. Dairy Sci. Assn. (Disting. Svc. award 1977), Agri-Bus. Found. (All-Time Gt. award 1981), Nat. Dairy Shrine (Dairy Hall of Fame 1976), N.E. Master Farmers Assn. (hon. master farmer 1999, Pa. Farm Bur. Disting. Svc. to Agr. award 1999), U.S. Animal Health Assn., Kiwanis, Masons, Elks, Alpha Zeta (hon. roll 1997), Gamma Sigma Delta. Mem. United Ch. of Christ. Home: 937 Wallace Ave Chambersburg PA 17201-3884 Personal E-mail: bobrumler@pa.net.

RUMMAGE, JAMES MARK, history educator; b. Baldwyn, Miss., Oct. 10, 1963; s. James Clifton and Nellie Rue Rummage; m. Helen Deanna Stark, Nov. 17, 1989; 1 child, Ian Matthew. MA, U. Miss., Oxford, 1900. Grad. instr. U. Miss., 1986—91; history instr. Christian Bros. U., Memphis, 1992—93; history instr., dept. chair Holmes CC, Grenada, Miss., 1993—. Contbr. encyclopedia. Recipient Tchr. of Yr., Miss. Humanities Coun., 2006; named to Student Hall of Fame, NE Miss. CC, 1983. Mem.: Miss. Folklore Soc., North Am. Conf. Brit. Studies, Presdl. Studies Assn., Am. Hist. Assn., Phi Theta Kappa, Phi Kappa Phi. Office: Holmes CC 1060 Avent Dr Grenada MS 38901

RUMMAGE, STEPHEN MICHAEL, lawyer; b. Massillon, Ohio, Dec. 27, 1955; s. Robert Everett and Kathleen Patricia (Newman) R.; m. Elizabeth Anne Seivert, Mar. 24, 1979; children: Everett Martin, Carter Kevin. BA in History and English, Stanford U., 1977; JD, U. Calif., Berkeley, 1980. Bar: Wash. 1980, U.S. Dist. Ct. (we. dist.) 1980, U.S. Ct. Appeals (9th cir.) 1983, U.S. Supreme Ct. 1985, US Ct. Appeals (6th cir.), 2008. Assoc. Davis, Wright et al, Seattle, 1980-85; ptnr. Davis Wright Tremaine, Seattle, 1986—. Co-author: Employer's Guide to Strike Planning and Prevention, 1985. Mem. Wash. Athletic Club. Democrat. Roman Catholic. Office: Davis Wright Tremaine 1201 Third Ave Ste 2200 Seattle WA 98101-3045 Home Phone: 206-726-8433; Office Phone: 206-622-3150. Business E-Mail: steverummage@dwt.com.

RUMMEL, HAROLD EDWIN, construction executive; b. Youngstown, Ohio, Oct. 4, 1940; s. Harold Edward and Florence Louise (Hill) R.; children: Timothy B., Jonathan S., Briana. BS, U. Fla., 1963. Writer, editor, Fla., 1958—70; polit. campaign mgr. various state and congressional campaigns, Tallahassee, 1971-79; sr. v.p. Fla. Fed. Saving Bank, St. Petersburg, Fla., 1979-86; pres., CEO Rummel Co. including The Rummel Real Estate Group, Inc., HardwareUSA.net, St. Petersburg, Fla., 1986—2003, Woodland Bay Group Inc., Mobile, Ala., 1986—2003, Rummel Group Inc., St. Petersburg, Fla., 1986—2003, Global Quest, Inc., Sahara Quest. Active in civic and polit. orgns. Recipient Distinctive Imprint award, The Nat. Assn. U. Women, 2008, Against All Odds award, African Women Economic Consortium Alliance, 2008. Democrat. Avocations: nature, wildlife photography, travel. Home: 1002 Charleston St Mobile AL 36604 Office Phone: 727-204-1187. Business E-Mail: rumgroup@bellsouth.net.

RUMNEY, HELENE VOSBURGH, retired poet, peace activist; b. SI, NY, July 19, 1928; d. William Henry and Charlotte Louise (Roehrig) Vosburgh; m. Eward John Rumney, Jan. 27, 1948 (div. 1968); children: Bruce E., Marilyn Walenga, John E., William H., Stephen P., Kathleen Rinehart. Diploma, Grand Rapids C.C., Mich., 1972. Cert. Con-Edison cooking sch. cert. SI, 1948. Restaurateur Eddie's Pizza Palace, Grand Rapids, 1960—64; sales rep. Avon Cosmetics Co., Grand Rapids, 1965; distributor Amway Corp., Grand Rapids, 1966; membership dir. G.R. C. of C., Grand Rapids, 1967—74; adv. promoter Art Optical, Grand Rapids, 1980—86; contact lens mfr. H. & R Optical, Grand Rapids, 1987—93; ret. Author: (poetry books) Red Roses White Tears, 1977, Politics and Poetry, 2007, (poems) Timeless Verses, Centres of Expression, Favourite Memories, International Who's Who in Poetry, Best Poems and Poets, 2007. Mem., letter writer Amnesty Internat., NYC, 2000—; demonstrator Peace Presence, Grand Rapids, 2002—; supporter World Wildlife, Earth Justice, Maryknoll Missions, Paralyzed Vets., Vietnam Vets. Against War; vol. feed poor Cath. Svcs., Mich., 1990—. Served in Civil Air Patrol, 1946—48. Recipient Patriot Yr. award, Help Hospitalized Vets., 2007. Mem.: DAV (Bronze Leader award 2007), VFW, Union Concerned Scientists, Commander's Club, Internat. Aid and Drs. without Borders, Internat. Soc. Poets, Southern Poverty Law Ctr., Grand Rapids Art Museum, St. Alphonsus Found., St. Christopher's Inn, Sacred Heart League, Co-Redemptorist Assn., Friends Pub. Mus., Internat. Libr. Poetry (Editor's Choice award 2006), Greenpeace Soc. Propagation of Faith, Missionary Assn. Mary Immaculate, Soc. Little Flower, St. Jude League, Missionaries of Africa, Am. Lung Assn. Independent. Roman Catholic. Avocations: reading, writing, politics, needlecrafts. Home: 50 Ransom Ave NE Apt 913 Grand Rapids MI 49503

RUMPAKIS, E. JOHN, realtor emeritus; b. Portland, Oreg., Jan. 16, 1932; s. John E. Rumpakis and Fotini Komninos Rigopouli; m. Cleo Patra Adeline. BA in Bus., Econ., Edn., U. Portland, 1954. Cert. Indsl. War Coll. Exec. trainee Meier & Frank Co., Portland, 1954—58, group sales mgr.; owner, broker N.E.W.S., Portland, 1959—2009. Liaison to Sen. Mark O. Hatfield and Congresswoman Ron Wyden Nat. Assn. Realtors; past chmn. City of Portland Code Enforcement Adv. Com., Budget Review Com., Graffiti Task Force, Multnomah County Bds. of Equalization and Ratio Review; with S.A.F.E (working group regarding matters of the homeless); bd. mem. Metro's Solid Waste Bd. for Recycling; bd. dirs. Calaroga Terrace Tower, 1979—80; sr. advisor Peace Initiatives Grad. Program Sch. Liberal Arts and Scis., Portland State U., 2003—; trustee Oreg. Heritage Trust, 2006—07; founder Beaumont Bus. Assn.; mem. exec. bd. Irvington Cmty. Assn., Grant Park Neighborhood Assn.; bd. mem. Sullivan's Gulch Neighborhood Assn.; funded numerous cmty. projects. Recipient Plato award, 1995, Ellis Island Medal of Honor, NYC, 2003; named Realtor of Yr., 1971, 1995, Assn. Pres., 1974. Fellow: Rotary Internat.; mem.: Met. Property Assn. Oreg. (pres. 1993), Rho Epsilon Kappa (Oreg. pres.), Commercial Assn. Realtors (Oregon, SW Wash.) (life), Portland Met. Assn. Realtors (life),

Oreg. Assn. Realtors (life), Nat. Assn. Realtors Political Action Com. (life), State of Oreg. Heritage Commn. Avocations: community service, governmental affairs, foreign affairs.

RUMPF, ANN, psychologist; d. Melvin and Elizabeth Kasen; married; children: Arthur Rumpf IV, Kasen. M, U. Wis., Milwaukee, 1983. Cert. sch. psychologist 1983; lic. social worker Wis., 1995. Sch. psychologist Watertown Unified Sch. Dist., Wis., 1989—, Watertown Sch. Dist., 1983—89. Cert. trainer Framework Understanding Poverty, Highlands, Tex.; instr. Viterbo Coll., LaCrosse, Wis. Mem.: NASP, Suburban Sch. Psychologists Assn., Wis. Assn. Sch. Psychologists. Avocations: travel, sailing, gardening.

RUMPHO-KENNEDY, MARY ELLEN, plant biochemistry educator; b. Faribault, Minn., Aug. 12, 1956; d. Morris Palmer and Blanche Winifred (Miller) Rumpho; m. Robert Alan Kennedy, June 9, 1984; children: Bryce Robert, Curran Patrick; stepchildren: Caleb John, Alex E. BA in Biology, Winona State U., 1978; PhD in Horticulture, Wash. State U., 1982. Rsch. asst. Fed. Water Quality Lab. USDA Forest Svc., Winton, Minn., summer 1978; teaching asst. U. Iowa, Wash. State U., 1978, 79; rsch. asst. Wash. State U., 1979-82; postdoctoral rsch. assoc. Washington State U., 1982-84, asst. prof. courtesy, 1984-85; sr. rsch. assoc. Ohio State U., 1985-87, rsch. scientist, 1987-89; asst. prof. U. Md., 1990-92; assoc. prof. Tex. A&M, 1992—, mem. faculty plant physiology/plant biotechnology, 1993—. Vis. rsch. assoc. I.N.R.A. Lab. de Physiologie Vegetale, Bordeaux, France, 1982; vis. adj. lectr. Ohio State U., 1989; faculty rsch. assoc. U. Md., 1989; invited participant profl. seminars, 1979—; lectr. in field. Contbr. articles to profl. jours.; invited to participate in seminars, 1979-96; lectr. in field; reviewer agys. and jours. Sci. Fair judge, 1993-94; presentations at elem., jr. and sr. high schs., 1991. Recipient Sarah Bradley Tyson Found. fellowship, 1981-82, Am. Chem. Soc., NIH, NSF, USDA, Ohio State U., Wash. State U., Tex. A&M honors program grantee. Mem. AAAS, Am. Soc. Plant Physiologists, Phycological Soc., Assn. Women in Sci., Sigma Xi (Student Rsch. award 1990), Gamma Sigma Delta (historian Tex. A&M U. chpt. 1995-96, sec. 1996—). Avocations: gardening, bicycling, swimming. Office: Tex A&M U 522 HFSB Dept Horticultural Scis College Station TX 77843-2133

RUMSEY, VICTOR HENRY, electrical engineering educator emeritus; b. Devizes, Eng., Nov. 22, 1919; s. Albert Victor and Susan Mary (Norman) R.; m. Doris Herring, Apr. 2, 1942; children: John David, Peter Alan, Catherine Anne. BA, Cambridge U., 1941, DSc in Physics, 1972; DEng, Tohoku U., Japan, 1962. With U.K. Sci. Civil Service, 1941-48; asst. to asso. prof. Ohio State U., 1948-54; prof. U. Ill., 1954-57, U. Calif., Berkeley, 1957-66, prof. elec. engrng. and computer scis. San Diego, 1966-87, prof. emeritus, 1987—, dept. chmn., 1977-81. Author: 1 book in field; contbr. articles to profl. jours.; patentee in field. Guggenheim fellow, 1965-66; recipient George Sinclair award Ohio State U., 1982, John Kraus Antenna award IEEE Antennas and Propagation Soc., 2004. Fellow IEEE (Morris Liebman prize, John Kraus award Antennas and Propagation), Union Radio Scientifique Internationale, Internat. Astron. Union; mem. Nat. Acad. Engrng. Home: 1171 Bohemian Ln Occidental CA 95465-9115

RUMSFELD, DONALD HENRY, former United States Secretary of Defense; b. Chgo., July 9, 1932; AB, Princeton U., 1954; degree (hon.), De Paul U. Coll. Commerce, Ill. Coll., Lake Forest Coll., Park Coll., Tuskegee Inst., Nat. Coll. Edn., Bryant Coll., Claremont Grad. Sch., Calif., Ill. Wesleyan U., RAND Grad. Sch., Hampden-Sydney Coll. Adminstrv. asst. to Rep. David Dennison US Congress, 1957-59, mem. staff Rep. Robert Griffin, 1959; investment broker A.G. Becker & Co., Chgo., 1960-62; mem. US Congress from 13th Ill. dist., Washington, 1963—69; dir. Office of Econ. Opportunity & asst. to the Pres. The White House, Washington, 1969—70, counsellor to the Pres., 1970—73, dir. Cost of Living Coun., 1971—73; US amb. & permanent rep. to NATO US Dept. State, Brussels, 1973-74; chair transition to the presidency of Gerald R. Ford The White House, Washington, 1974, chief of staff to Pres., 1974-75; sec. US Dept. Def., Washington, 1975—77, 2001—06; pres., CEO G.D. Searle & Co., Skokie, Ill., 1977-85, chmn. CEO, 1985; spl. presdl. amb. to Mid. East The White House, 1983-84; sr. adv. William Blair & Co., Chgo., 1985-90; chmn., CEO General Instrument Corp., Chgo., 1990-93; chmn. Gilead Scis., Inc., Foster City, Calif., 1997—2001; disting. vis. fellow Hoover Instn. Stanford U., 2007—. Mem., Gen. Advisory Com. on Arms Control & advisor to the govt. on nat. security affairs, 1983-84, US Joint Advisory Commn. on US/Japan Relations, 1983-84, Nat. Commn. on Pub. Svc., 1987-90, Nat. Econ. Commn., 1988-89, Commn. on US/Japan Relations, 1989-91; spl. presdl. envoy on the Law of the Sea Treaty, 1982-83, sr. advisor to the Pres. panel on Strategic Systems, 1983-84, chmn. U.S. Commn. to Assess the Ballistic Missile Threat to the U.S., 1998; commr. U.S. Fed. Trade Deficit Rev. Commn., 1999-2000; U.S. Commn. to Assess Nat. Security Space Mgmt. & Orgn., 2000; bd. visitors, Nat. Def. U., 1988-92. Aviator, flight instructor USN, 1954—57 USNR, 1957—75. Recipient Disting. Eagle Scout award, 1975, Presdl. Medal of Freedom, The White House, 1977, Outstanding Chief Exec. Officer in the Pharmaceutical Industry award, 1980, George Catlett Marshall award, 1984, Woodrow Wilson award, 1985, Dwight David Eisenhower medal, 1993, James H. Doolittle award, 2003, Ronald Reagan Freedom award, 2003, Gerald R. Ford medal, 2004. Republican. the only person to hold the position of secretary of defense twice, 1975-77, 2001-06. Office: Hoover Instn 435 Galvez Mall Stanford U Stanford CA 94305

RUNCO, MARIO, JR., astronaut, meteorologist, researcher; b. Bronx, NY, Jan. 26, 1952; s. Mario and Filomena (Ragusa) Runco; m. Susan Kay Friess; 2 children. BS in Meteorology and Phys. Oceanography, CCNY, 1974, DSc (hon.), 1999; MS in Atmospheric Physics, Rutgers U., New Brunswick, NJ, 1976. Rsch. hydrologist US Geol. Survey, LI, NY, 1976—77; state trooper NJ State Police, 1977—78; commd. ensign USN, 1978; rsch. meteorologist Naval Rsch. Lab., Monterey, Calif., 1978—81; watch and meteorol. officer USS Nassau (LHA-4), 1981—83; lab. instr. Naval Postgrad. Sch., Monterey, 1984—85; commdg. officer Oceanographic Unit USNS Chauvenet, 1985—86; fleet environ. svcs. officer Naval Pacific Meterology and Oceanography Command, Pearl Harbor, Hawaii, 1986—87; astronaut NASA Johnson Space Ctr., Houston, 1987—; mission specialist Space Shuttles Atlantis (STS-44), 1991, Space Shuttle Endeavour (STS-54), 1993, Space Shuttle Endeavour (STS-77), 1996; space shuttle flight software avionics lab. test pilot Lyndon B. Johnson Space Ctr. NASA, Houston, 1987—92, capsule communicator Mission Control Ctr. (CAPCOM), 1989—94, lead sci. and utilization Internat. Space Sta. Sci. Window/Window Rsch. Facility, 1993—, Earth and planetary scientist, 1994—, project mgr. Lunar Habitation Sys. project, 2004—, lead spacecraft window optical requirements, 2005—. Decorated Def. Superior Svc. medal NASA, Def. Meritorious Svc. medal, Exceptional Svc. medal, Three Space Flight medals, Two Navy Sea Svc. Deployment Ribbons, Navy Battle Efficiency Ribbon, Navy Achievement medal, Navy Pistol Expert medal; recipient Class of 1938 Athletic Svc. award, CCNY, 1973, Townsend Harris medal, 1993, John Cardinal Spellman award, Cardinal Hayes HS, 1993. Achievements include three space flights, 551 hours in space and one 4.5 hour spacewalk, and designation as Naval Surface Warefare Officer. Avocations: ice hockey, antique cars, collecting toy trains, model railroads, baseball. Office: Human Exploration Sci Office NASA Lyndon B Johnson Space Ctr 2101 NASA Rd 1 Houston TX 77058-3696

RUND, DOUGLAS ANDREW, emergency physician; b. Columbus, Ohio, July 20, 1945; s. Carl Andrew and Caroline Amelia (Row) Rund; m. Sue E. Padavana, 1980; children: Carie, Emily, Ashley. BA, Yale U., 1967; MD, Stanford U., 1971. Lic. physician Ohio, diplomate Nat. Bd. Med. Examiners, Am. Bd. Family Practice, Am. Bd. Emergency Medicine. Intern U. Calif. San Francisco-Moffett Hosp., 1971—72; resident in gen. surgery Stanford U., 1972—74, Robert Wood Johnson Found. clin. scholar in medicine, 1974—76; med. dir. Mid-Peninsula Health Svc., Palo Alto, Calif., 1975—76; clin. instr. dept. medicine and preventive medicine Stanford U. Med. Sch., 1975—76; assoc. prof., dir. divsn. emergency medicine Ohio State Coll. Medicine, 1982—87, dir. emergency medicine residency program, assoc. prof. dept, 1976—87, prof., chmn. dept. preventive medicine, 1988—90, prof., chmn. dept. emergency medicine, 1990—, prof., interim chmn. dept. family medicine, 1994—95, assoc. dean, 2001—; pres. Ohio State Univ. Physicians, 2002—. Attending staff Ohio State U. Hosps., 1976—; med. dir. CSCC, Emergency Med. Svcs. Dept.; pres. Internat. Rsch. Inst. Emergency Medicine; sr. rsch. fellow NATO: Health and Med. Aspects of Disaster Preparedness, 1985—87; vis. epidemiology and injury control U. Edinburgh, Scotland, 1987; working group, emergency and critical care in space NASA, 2001—; bd. dirs. Am. Bd. Emergency Medicine, 1988—97, sr. editor in tng. exam., 1989—, pres., 1995—; pres., chmn. bd. dirs. Physicians of the Ohio State U. (POSU), 2002—; med. dir. Worthington Fire Dept. Author: Triage, 1981, Essentials of Emergency Medicine, 1982, 2d edit., 1986, Emergency Radiology, 1982, Emergency Psychiatry, 1983, Environmental Emergencies, 1985; editor: Emergency Medicine Ann., 1983—84, Emergency Medicine Survey, Annals of Emergency Medicine, Annals of Emergency Medicine Symposium, 1986; editor: (in chief) Ohio State Series on Emergency Medicine, Emergency Medicine Observer, 1986—87; mem. editl. bd.: Physician, Sports Medicine, Emergency Med. Svcs., Jour. Urgent Care Medicine; co-author: Family Medicine Priciples and Practice, 1978, 2d edit., 1983; contbr. articles to profl. jours. Recipient Faculty Tchg. award, Ohio State U., 1999, Douglas A. Rund Disting. Faculty award, Dept. Emergency Medicine, 2003. Fellow: Am. Coll. Emergency Physicians (task force on substance abuse and injury control, Outstanding Contbn. to Edn. award 1992); mem.: IAAA, Columbus Med. Review, Internat. Soc. for Emergency Med. Svcs. (med. dir.), Columbus Med. Forum (pres. 1993—), Soc. Acad. Emergency Medicine (chmn. internat. com. 1991—), Assn. Acad. Chairs Emergency Medicine (pres. 1992—93), Nat. Inst. on Alcohol Abuse and Alcoholism, Alpha Omega Alpha. Office: Ohio State U 146 Means Hall 1654 Upham Dr Columbus OH 43210-1240

RUNDALL, THOMAS GENE, medical educator; b. Cedar Rapids, Iowa, Sept. 13, 1948; s. Richard Earl Rundall and Georgiena Alice Serbousek; m. Jane Ellen Tiemann, May 24, 1975; 1 child, Owen Tiemann. AA, West Valley C.C., Campbell, Calif., 1968; BA, PhD, Stanford U., Calif., 1976. Asst. prof. med. care orgn. Cornell U., Ithaca, NY, 1976—80; prof. health policy and mgmt. U. Calif., Berkeley, 1980—. Exec. assoc. dean U.C. Berkeley Sch. Pub. Health, Berkeley, 2007—. Vol. VISTA, Honolulu, 1971—73; mem. Assn. U. Programs Health Adminstrn., Washington, 1999—2002; chair; mem. John Muir Physician Network, Walnut Creek, Calif., 1999—2008; mem. On Lok, San Francisco, 2006—, John Muir Health Sys., Walnut Creek, Calif., 2009—. Recipient Filerman award, Assn. U. Programs Health Adminstrn., 2005; Health Policy fellowship, Robert Wood Johnson Found., 1985—86. Fellow: Acad. Health. Avocations: travel, classical music, golf. Office: Univ Calif Berkeley 50 Univ Hall Berkeley CA 94720

RUNDIO, LOUIS MICHAEL, JR., lawyer; b. Chgo., Sept. 13, 1943; s. Louis Michael Sr. and Germaine Matilda (Pasternack) R.; m. Ann Marie Bartlett, July 10, 1971; children: Matthew, Melissa. BS in Physics, Loyola U., Chgo., 1965, JD, 1972. Bar: Ill. 1972, U.S. Dist. Ct. (no. dist.) Ill. 1972, U.S. Ct. Appeals (7th cir.) 1974, U.S. Dist. Ct. (ea. dist.) Mich. 1983. Assoc. McDermott, Will & Emery, Chgo., 1972-77, ptnr., 1978—. Served to 1st lt. U.S. Army, 1965-68, Vietnam. Mem. ABA, Chgo. Bar Assn. Home: 676 Skye Ln Barrington IL 60010-5506 Office: McDermott Will & Emery 227 W Monroe St Ste 3100 Chicago IL 60606-5096

RUNDQUIST, ELIZABETH ANN, art therapist; b. Bklyn., June 17, 1933; d. Carl Edgar and Margaret Langford Rundquist; children: Arthur L. Porter Jr., Karl L. Porter, Edward S. Porter, Laura Elizabeth S. Cohen. BS, CUNY, NYC, 1988; MA, NYU, NYC, 1991. Bd. cert. art therapist, cert. completion Edn. for Ministry, U. of the South, 2007. Art therapist supr. N.Y. City Health & Hosp. Corp., NYC, 1992—98; case mgr., art therapist Vantage Health System, Dumont, NJ, 2000—07, ptnr., 2000—; adj. child and adolescent faculty NJIPT. Psychotherapist pvt., Teaneck, NJ, 2003—. Contrbg. author Tuning the Therapeutic Instrument, 2000, designer (clergy vestments) St. Ann & The Holy Trinity Episc. Ch., Bklyn., N.Y.; prodr.: Not 1984 Film Festival, 2005; one-woman shows include paintings Witness, Fairleigh Dickinson U., Teaneck, NJ, 2009. Vol. Peace Corps., Malaysia, 1971—74; curator/prod. film festival St Ann & the Holy Trinity Episc. Ch., Bklyn., 1984. Scholar, Art Students League, 1978, Provincetown Art Assn., 1985, CUNY, 1988. Mem.: Salute Women in Arts, NJ Art Therapy Assn., Am. Group Psychotherapy Assn., Am. Art Therapy Assn. Office Phone: 201-741-2681. Personal E-mail: bluewater1020@aol.com.

RUNGE, CARLISLE FORD, trade and environmental policy educator; b. Madison, Wis., Mar. 7, 1953; s. Carlisle Piehl and Elizabeth (Eshleman) R.; m. Susan MacKenzie, July 3, 1982; children: Elizabeth Thayer Runge, Carlisle Piehl. BA, U. N.C., 1974; MA, Oxford U., Eng., 1977, U. Wis., 1980, PhD, 1981. Asst. prof. U. N.C., Chapel Hill, 1981-82, U Minn., St. Paul, 1983-86; spl. asst. U.S. Amb. to Gatt, Geneva, 1987-88, assoc. prof., 1986—, prof., dir., 1988-91. Author: Future of North American Grainary, 1984, Reforming Farm Policy, 1992, Freer Trade, Protected Environment, 1994. Spl. asst. Office of U.S. Trade Rep., Washington, 1987-88; chmn. Gov.'s Farm Crisis Commn., St. Paul, 1985. Named Rhodes scholar, 1975-77, AAAS fellow, 1982, Fulbright fellow, 1990—. Mem. Am. Econ. Assn., Am. Agrl. Econ. Assn., Assn. Am. Rhodes Scholars, Coun. on Fgn. Rels. Democrat. Avocations: fishing, tennis, french langauge, farming. Home: 901 Pine St W Stillwater MN 55082-5684 Office: U Minn 1994 Buford Ave Saint Paul MN 55108-6038

RUNGE, DONALD EDWARD, food wholesale company executive; b. Milw., Mar. 20, 1938; s. Adam and Helen Teresa (Voss) R.; divorced; children: Roland, Richard, Lori. Grad., Spencerian Coll., Milw., 1960. Fin. v.p. Milw. Cheese Co., Waukesha, Wis., 1962-69; dir. Farm House Foods Corp., Milw., 1966-89, pres., 1966-89, CEO, treas., 1984-89, chmn., pres., 1985-89; chmn., CEO Retailing Corp. Am., Milw., 1982-89; CEO, treas. Drug Sys. Inc., Milw., 1984-89; chmn. Drug Sys. Inc. (now Retailing Corp. of Am.), Milw., 1985-89; pres. TDC, 1987-89; chmn., pres. Runge Industries, Gen. Growth, Inc., 1989—. Bd. dirs. Convenient Food Mart, CasaBlanca Industries, Inc., City of Industry, Calif., Palm Beach Opera, 1992—; sec. The Diana Corp., Milw., 1985-86, treas. 1986—, pres. 1987-96; chmn. Economy Dry Goods Co. Inc.; treas. Fairbanks Farms Inc.; chmn., CEO Internat. Diamond Exch., LLC, 2006—. Adventist. Address: 111C Palm Point Cir Palm Beach Gardens FL 33418-4032 Office Phone: 561-625-4844. Personal E-mail: donald.runge@gmail.com. *I believe there is very little in life that cannot be accomplished if a person truly wants to attain the goal.*

RUNGE, JEFFREY WILLIAM, former federal agency administrator; b. Oct. 20, 1955; m. Ginny Runge; children: Emily, Will. BA, U. South, 1977; MD, U. S.C., 1981. Diplomate Am. Bd. Emergency Medicine. Resident Charlotte Meml. Hosp. and Med. Ctr., 1984; faculty emergency medicine residency Carolinas Med. Ctr., Charlotte, NC, 1984; dir. Carolinas Ctr. Injury Prevention and Control; adminstr. Nat. Hwy. Traffic Safety Adminstrn. US Dept. Transp., Washington, 2001—06; chief med. officer US Dept. Homeland Security, Washington, 2005—07, acting under sec. for sci. & tech., 2006, asst. sec. for health affairs & chief med. officer, 2007—09. Mem.: N.C. Med. Soc. (spkr.), N.C. Coll. Emerency Physicians (past pres.), Am. Coll. Emergency Physicians (trauma care and injury control com., rsch. com.). Office: US Dept Homeland Security Nebraska Ave Complex Washington DC 20528*

RUNGE, KAY KRETSCHMAR, library consultant; b. Davenport, Iowa, Dec. 9, 1946; d. Alfred Edwin and Ina (Paul) Kretschmar; children: Peter Jr., Katherine. BS in History Edn., Iowa State U., Ames, 1969; MLS, U. Iowa, Iowa City, 1970. Pub. svc. libr. Anoka County Libr., Blaine, Minn., 1971-72; cataloger Augustana Coll., Rock Island, Ill., 1972-74; dir. Scott County Libr. Sys., Eldridge, Iowa, 1974-85, Davenport (Iowa) Pub. Libr., 1985—2001, Des Moines Pub. Libr., 2001—07, KKRunge Assoc., 2007—. V.p. Quad-Cities Conv. and Visitors Bur., 1992—97, Quad-Cities Grad. Study Ctr., 1992—2001, Downtown Davenport Devel. Corp., 1992—2000, Hall of Honor Bd., Davenport Ctrl. H.S., 1992—95, Brenton Bank Bd., 1995—2001, Wells Fargo Bank Bd., 2001; steering com. Quad-Cities Vision for the Future, 1987—91, Humanities Iowa, 1993—2000, chair, 1998—99; bd. govs. Iowa State U. Found., 1991—; dean's adv. bd. Liberal Arts and Sci. Coll. Iowa State U., 2004—, citizens adv. coun., 1998—2000, Leadership Iowa, 1998—99; adv. bd. U. Iowa Sch. Libr. Sci., 1999—, chair, 2006—09, adj. prof., 2000—01; devel. bd. Iowa State U. Found., 2000—, Greater Des Moines Leadership, 2002—03; bd. regents Iowa Pub. Radio Exec. Coun., 2005—; chair Iowa Pub. Radio, 2008—; bd. dirs. Riverfront Devel. Comm., 2008—, River Ctr. for Performing Arts, Davenport, 1983—97, Iowa State U. Rsch. Pk., 1998—2000, Davenport One, Downtown Devel., 2000—01, Des Moines Operation Downtown, 2004—06; chmn. bd. dirs. Am. Inst. Commerce, 1989—98; mem. Quest Coll. Bd., 1998—2000, Kaplan U. Bd., 2000—, chair, 2008—; bd. dirs. Iowa State Alumni Assn., 2008—, Des Moines Partnership. Recipient Svc. Key award Iowa State U. Alumni Assn., 1979, ALA/ALTA Nat. Advocacy Honor Roll award, 2000, Des Moines Women of Influence award, 2004, Carrie Chapman Catt Pub. Advancement award Iowa State U. Alumni Assn., 2006; named Quad City Panhellenic Woman of Yr., 1998. Mem. ALA (chmn. libr. adminstrs. and mgrs. div., fundraising sect. 1988, bd. dirs., Exhibits Round Table 2003-09, councilor 2007-), Iowa Libr. Assn. (pres. 1983, Mem. of Yr. award 2000), Pub. Libr. Assn. (bd. dirs. 1990-99, pres. 2000-01, co-chair Nat. Conf., 2008-), Iowa Edn. Media Assn. (Intellectual Freedom award 1984), Alpha Delta Pi (alumni state pres. 1978). Lutheran. Home and Office: KKRunge Assoc 126 Forest Rd Davenport IA 52803 Office Phone: 515-669-1610. Business E-Mail: kkrunge@libraryconsulting.org.

RUNGE, MARSCHALL STEVENS, cardiologist, educator; m. Susan Runge; children: Thomas, Elizabeth, William, John, Mason. MD, Johns Hopkins U. Sch. Medicine, Baltimore, 1984; PhD, Vanderbilt U., Nashville, TN, 1979. Diplomate cardiovasc. diseases Am. Bd. Internal Medicine. Assoc. prof. medicine, cardiology Emory U., Atlanta, 1989—94; prof., internal medicine U. Tex. Med. Brance, Galveston, Tex., 1994—2000, john sealy disting. centennial chair, dir., divsn. cardiology, 1994—2000, dir., sealy ctr. molecular cardiology, 1994—2000; Marion Covington disting. prof. medicine U. NC Chapel Hill, NC, 2000—07, chair, dept. medicine, 2000—, Charles Addison & Elizabeth ann Sanders disting. prof. medicine, 2007—, pres., UNC physicians, 2004—, vice dean clin. affairs, 2006—. Mem., editl. bd. Circulation Rsch., Dallas, 2001—, Current Cardiology Reviews, Oak Park, Ill., 2004—; pres. Paul Dudley White Soc., Mass. Gen. Hosp., Boston, 2006—; editor chief eMedicine, NYC, 2007—; ad hoc reviewer NIH, Bethesda, Md., 2008—. Grantee Vasoactive agonists, oxidative stress atherosclerosi, NIH, 2002—07, Chaperones, ROS systems & IGF-1, 2004—. Fellow: ACP, Am. Soc. Internal Medicine, Am. Heart Assn. Coun., Am. Coll. Cardiology; mem.: Am. Heart Assn. Achievements include patents for mitochondrial DNA damage as a predictor of coronary atherosclerotic heart disease.

RUNGE, PAUL E., ophthalmologist, educator; b. Milw., June 7, 1946; m. Cheryl Runge; children: Sarah, Megan. AA in Liberal Arts, Orange Coast Coll., Costa Mesa, Calif., 1970; BS in Biology and Immunology, U. Calif., Irvine, 1972, MS in Cellular Immunology, 1974; B Medicine B Surgery, Flinders U., Adelaide, Australia, 1979. Diplomate Am. Bd. Pediat., Am. Bd. Ophthalmology. Rotating intern Flinders Med. Ctr., Adelaide, 1979—80; pediat. resident Hosp. Sick Children, Toronto, Ont., Canada, 1980—82; sr. pediat. resident U. Calif. San Diego Med. Ctr., Children's Hosp., 1982—83; pediat. ophthalmology fellow Hosp. Sick Children and Inst. Ophthalmology, London, 1983—85; resident in ophthalmology Cook County Hosp., Chgo., 1985—88; med. retina fellow U. Calif. Jules Stein Eye Inst., Harbor/UCLA Med. Ctr., LA, 1988—89; surg. retina and vitreous fellow U. Tenn. Ctr. Retina Vitresous Surgery, Memphis, 1989—90; assoc. Ctr. Retina Vitreous Surgery, Memphis, 1990—92; clin. instr. U. Tenn. Health Scis. Ctr., Memphis, 1992—93; clin. prof. So. Ill. U., Carbondale, 1993—96; ptnr. Ophthalmic Cons., Sarasota, Fla., 1996—; clin. asst. prof. dept. ophthalmology U. South Fla., Tampa, 1998—. Presenter in field. Contbr. articles to med. jours. With US Army, 1965—67, Vietnam. Scholar, Given Inst. Pathobiology, 1972; rsch. fellow, NIH, 1973, Brit. Retinitis Pigmentosa Soc., 1984, ARVO traveling fellow, Nat. Eye Inst., 1989. Fellow: ACS, Ont. Coll. Physicians and Surgeons, Am. Acad. Pediat., Am. Acad. Ophthalmology, Am. Ophthal. Soc.; mem.: Royal Coll. Ophthalmology London, Royal Soc. Medicine, Alpha Gamma Sigma. Office: 1700 S Tuttle Ave Sarasota FL 34239

RUNGE, VAL MURRAY, medical educator; b. Austin, Tex., Aug. 28, 1956; BS in Chemistry with honors, Stanford U., 1978, MD, 1982. Diplomate Am. Bd. Radiology. Chief magnetic resonance svcs. New Eng. Med. Ctr. Hosps., Boston, 1986-90; asst. prof. Tufts U. Sch. Medicine, Boston, 1986-88, assoc. prof., 1988-90; dir. Magnetic Resonance Imaging and Spectroscopy Ctr. U. Ky. Med. Ctr., Lexington, 1990—94; rosenbaum prof. diagnostic radiology U. Ky., Lexington, 1990—2001, prof. biomed. engrng., 1992—2001; centennial prof. diagnostic radiology Tex. A&M U., Scott & White Clinic and Hosp., 2002—. Editor: (textbook) Clinical Magnetic Resonance Imaging, 2002, The Physics of Clinical MR Taught Through Images, 2nd edit., 2009, Clinical 3 T Magnetic Resonance, 2007. Fellow Soc. Magnetic Resonance Imaging; mem. Am. Roentgen Ray Soc. (Exec. Coun. award 1984), Am. Soc. Neuroradiology (Dyke Meml. award 1984), Radiol. Soc. N.Am. (Magna Cum Laude award 1984).

RUNNER, JACK CHARLES, health facility executive; b. Sandusky, Ohio, Mar. 31, 1955; s. Kenneth Earl and Mary Margaret Runner; m. Kathleen Marie Kahle, July 15, 1978; children: Kristen Marie, Kelly Marie. BS in Microbiology, Bowling Green State U., 1977; MBA, Ashland U., 1984. Staff technologist Sandusky Meml. Hosp., 1978-84; supr. microbiology dept. Firelands Cmty. Hosp., Sandusky, 1984-86; adminstrv. dir. North Coast Clin. Lab. Inc., Sandusky, 1985—. Mem. Am. Soc. for Microbiology, Drug. Info. Assn., Assn. Clin. Rsch. Profls., Am. Assn. Clin. Chemistry, Clin. Lab. Mgrs. Assn., U.S. Power Squadron (dist. comdr. 1999—), Kiwanis Internat., Sandusky Yacht Club, Boat U.S. Office: North Coast Clin Lab Inc 2215 Cleveland Rd Sandusky OH 44870-4485 Office Phone: 419-626-6012. Business E-Mail: jack@northcoastlab.com.

RUNNICLES, DONALD, conductor; b. Edinburgh, Nov. 16, 1954; Student, Edinburgh U., Cambridge U., London Opera Ctr.; DMus (hon.), U. Edinburgh, 1995. Music dir., prin. condr. San Francisco Opera, 1992—; prin. condr. NY Orch. of St. Luke's. Prin. guest condr. Atlanta Symphony Orch., 2005—06. Repetiteur Nat. Theatre, Mannheim, Germany, 1980—, Kapellmeister, 1984—, prin. condr., Hanover, 1987—, numerous appearances with Hamburg Staatsoper, former gen. music dir. Stadtische Buhnen, Freiburg/Breisgau, appearances with Met. Opera include Lulu, 1988, The Flying Dutchman, 1990, The Magic Flute, condr. Vienna Staatsoper, 1990—91, Sonome, 1996, debut Don Giovanni, Glyndebourne, 1991, Salzburg Festival, 1996, condr. London Symphony Orch., La Scale Milan Freischutz, Orch. Paris, Israel Philharm., Rotterdam Philharm., Seattle Symphony, Pitts. Symphony, St. Louis Symphony, Chgo. Symphony, San Francisco Symphony, Cleve. Orch., New World Symphony, Bavarian Radio Symphony, Billy Budd and the Ring, Vienna State Opera, 2001, Katya Kabanova, San Francisco, 2002, Schoenberg's Gurrelieder, London Proms, 2002, Tristan und Isolde, BBC Symphony Orch., 2002—03, (world premier) Doctor Atomic, John Adams, 2005, rec. artist Hansel and Gretel, Gluck's Orphée with San Francisco Opera Orch., 1995, Tannhäuser-Bayreuth Festspick, 1995, Harvey Milk with San Francisco Opera, 1996, Mozart Requiem, 2005—, opened Edinburgh Festival, 1994, 1996. Recipient Officer of Brit. Empire. Office: San Francisco Opera War Meml Opera House 301 Van Ness Ave San Francisco CA 94102-4509

RUNOWICZ, CAROLYN DILWORTH, gynecologist, oncologist, researcher; b. Willimantic, Conn., May 1, 1951; d. S. Robert and Aline (Bergeron) Dilworth; m. Sheldon H. Cherry. BA, U. Conn., 1973; MD, Thomas Jefferson Med. Coll., Phila., 1977. Diplomate Am. Bd. Ob-Gyn., Am. Bd. Gynecologic Oncology. Resident ob-gyn. Mt. Sinai Sch. Medicine & Med. Ctr., NYC, 1977-81, fellow gynecol. oncology, 1981-83; instr., dir. divsn. ob-gyn. Albert Einstein Coll. Medicine, NYC, 1983-88, asst. prof. dept. ob-gyn., 1988-93, assoc. prof., 1993—98; dir. gynecologic & oncology Our Lady of Mercy, Bronx, NY, 1988; prof., dir. gynecol. oncology Montefiore Med. Ctr., NYC, 1998—2001; prof. clin. obstetrics & gynecology Columbia U. Coll. Physicians & Surgeons, 2001—03; vice chmn. ob-gyn. St. Luke's Roosevelt Hosp., NYC, 2001—03; dir. Carole & Ray Neag Comprehensive Cancer Ctr., prof. ob-gyn. U. Conn. Health Ctr., Famington, NY, 2003—. Presdl. appointee Nat. Cancer Adv. Bd., 2004—, chair, 2006—; lectr. in field. Author: To Be Alive: A Women's Guide to a Full Life After Cancer, 1995; co-author (with husband): Menopause Book: A Guide to Women's Health After 40, 1994, Answer to Cancer, 2004; co-author: (with Jeanne Petrek) Woman and Cancer: A Through and Compassionate Resource for Patients and Their Families, 1999; contbr. articles to profl. jours., chapters to books. Fellow: Am. Coll. Ob-Gyn.; mem.: AMA, Am. Soc. Clinical Oncology, Am. Gynecol. Club, Am. Cancer Soc. (pres. 2005—06), NY Obstet. Soc., Am. Gynecol. Obstetrics Soc., Soc. Gynecologic Oncologists (pres. 2000), Am. Med. Women's Assn. (Local Legend award), Alpha Omega Alpha, Phi Beta Kappa. Office: Carole & Ray Neag Comprehensive Cancer Ctr U Conn Health Ctr 263 Farmington Ave Farmington CT 06030-2875 Office Phone: 860-679-2809, 860-679-2100, 800-579-7822. Office Fax: 860-679-4815. Business E-Mail: crunowicz@uchc.edu.*

RUNQUIST, LISA A., lawyer; b. Mpls., Sept. 22, 1952; d. Ralf E. and Violet R. BA, Hamline U., 1973; JD, U. Minn., 1976. Bar: Minn. 1977, Calif. 1978, U.S. Dist. Ct. (ctrl. dist.) Calif. 1985, U.S. Supreme Ct. 1995. Assoc. Caldwell & Toms, LA, 1978-82; ptnr. Runquist & Flagg, LA, 1982-85; pvt. practice Runquist & Assocs., LA, 1985-99, 2005—, Runquist & Zyback LLP, LA, 1999—2005. Mem. adv. bd. Exempt Orgn. Tax Rev., 1990—, Calif. State U. L.A. Continuing Edn. Acctg. and Tax Program, 1995—. Mem. editl. bd.: ABA Bus. Law Today, 1994—2002; author: The ABCs of Nonprofits, 2005; editor: Nonprofit Resources, 2007; editor: (prin. author) Guide to Representing Religious Organizations, 2009; contbr. chapters to books. Recipient Outstanding Lawyer award, ABA Bus. Law Sect., 1999. Mem. ABA (bus. law sect. counsel 1995-99, com. on nonprofit corps. 1986—, chair 1991-95, subcom. current devels. in nonprofit corp. law 1989—, chair 1989-91, subcom. rels. orgns. 1989—, chair 1987-91, 95-98, subcom. legal guidebook for dirs. 1986—, partnerships and unincorp. bus. orgns. com. 1987—, state regulation of securities com. 1988-99, ad hoc com. info. tech. 1997-2003, chmn., 1997-98, co-chmn. 1998-2002, sect. liaison to tech. coun. 1997-2000, sec. of taxation exempt orgns. com. 1987—, subcom. religious orgns. 1989—, chair 1995-97, 2005—, subcom. model nonprofit corp. act, co-chmn. subcom. non-exempt orgns. 1997-2003, co-chair state and local regulation subcom. 2003-05, corp. laws com. 1999-2005, subcom. guidebook for dirs. of closely held corps. chair 2000-04, liaison ALI/ABA principles of law of nonprofit orgns. project 2003—, standing com. solo and small firm practitioners 2004-05, ABA liason to NCCUSL project to create legal framework for Unicorp. NP Assn. in N. Am., 2005-), Calif. Bar Assn. (bus. law sect., nonprofit and unincorp. orgns. com. 1985-92, 93-96, 97—, chair 1989-91, 2006—, exec. com. mem. 2008-), Christian Legal Soc., Ctr. Law and Religious Freedom, Christian Mgmt. Assn. (dir. 1983-89). Office: 17554 Community St Northridge CA 91325 Office Phone: 818-609-7761. Business E-Mail: lisa@runquist.com.

RUNTE, ROSEANN O'REILLY, academic administrator; b. Kingston, NY, Jan. 31, 1948; arrived in Can., 1971, naturalized, 1983; d. Robert B. and Anna Loretta O'Reilly. BA summa cum laude, SUNY, New Paltz, 1968; MA, U. Kans., Lawrence, 1969, PhD, 1974; DLitt (hon.), Acadia U., Wolfville, NS, Can., 1989, Meml. U., St. John's Newfoundland, 1990, U. Vest Timisoara, 1996, U. Arad, 2001, U. V. Goldis; Assoc. (hon.), Moraine Valley C.C., 2003. Lectr. Bethany Coll., W.Va., 1970—71, St. Mary's U., Halifax, NS, Canada, 1971—72, Dalhousie U., Halifax, NS, 1972—83, asst. dean, 1980—82, chmn. dept. French, 1980—83; pres. U. Sainte-Anne, Pointe-de-l'Eglise, NS, Canada, 1983—88; prin. Glendon Coll., Toronto, Canada, 1988—94; pres. Victoria U., 1994—2001, Old Dominion U., 2001—08; pres., vice chancellor Carleton U., Ottawa, 2008—. Bd. dirs. Banque Nat., Va. Advanced Carrier and Shipbldg. Integration Ctr., Va. Nat. Def. Indsl. Authority, 2009—; mem. hon. bd. Chesapeake Arts Coun., Va. Symphony; adv. bd. Sungard Sgt.; chair edn. com. Army ROTC, mem. Army edn. com. Author: Brumes Bleues, 1982, Faux-Soleils, 1984, Birmanie Blues, 1993; editor: Studies in 18th Century Culture, vols. VII, VIII, IX, 1977—79, A Canadian in Love, 2000, The Passionate Mind, 2000; lit. rev. editor: French Rev., 1988—94; editor: Lit. Rsch., 1994—97; co-editor: Man and Nature, 1982, Le Development Regional, 1986—87, From Orality to Literature, 1991, Lectures Canadiennes, 1993, Visions of Beauty, 1995, The Foundation for International Training: 25 Years of International Development, 2001; co-translator: Local Development, 1987; mem. editl. bd. Purdue Romance Lang. Series, 2001—. Can. commn. UNESCO, 1991—92, pres., 1992—96; vice-chair exec. bd. Found. for Internat. Tng., 1994—95, chair bd., 1995—2000; internat. adv. bd. Expo 2000, 1995—2000; v.p. Assn. Internat. des études québecoises, 1999—2001; mem. Internat. Women's Forum, 1998—; chair comm. internat. edn. Am. Coun. on Edn., 2004—06; chair accreditation com. visit NCAA, 2004, 2005, 2006, 2007; commr. Southeastern Accreditation Commn., 2004—06; chair Gottschalk Prize Com., 1994; chair publs. com. Hannah Found., 1989—92; vice-chair bd. Gardiner Mus., 1994—2001; mem. Commn. Langs. Instrn., Ontario, Canada, 1999—2001; chair prix du salon Livre Com., 1998; hon. life mem. UNESCO, 2003; adv. coun. Assn. Governing Bds.; bd. dirs. Assn. Med. Svcs., 1989—92; adv. bd. Nat. Libr., 1984—91; bd. dirs. Urban League, United Way, Va. Stage Co., Second Wind Dance Co., Hampton Roads Partnership, Greater Norfolk Corp. Decorated Order of Can., Ordre du Mérite France, Order Acad. Palmes, Disting. Civilian Svc. medal US Army; recipient Fr. Coppée award, French Acad., 1989, Queen Elizabeth Jubilee medal, 2002, Woman of Distinction award, Zonta Group, 2004, Environ. award, Norfolk Environment Commn., 2004, WFXN Trailblazer award, 2004, Lighthouse award, Elizabeth River Project, Women of Distinction award, YWCA, 2006, Humanitarian award, NCCJ, 2006, Billbro award Servant Leadership, 2006, Toast of Town award, Alpha Kappa Alpha, 2007, Peace and Dialogue award, Rumi Found., 2007, Wolfgary Pindur award, 2008; named Sportsperson of Yr., Norfolk Sports Club, 2007, Woman of Courage, Confidence & Character, Girl Scouts, 2008, Instl. Peace Leadership, 2008; Regents scholar, SUNY, 1965, Title IV grantee, NDEA, 1968. Fellow: Royal Soc. Can., Soc. Study Values in Edn., World Acad. Arts and Scis.; mem.: European Academy Arts & Scis., Royal Coll. Physicians and Surgeons (exec. com. 1998—2002), Soc. for Study Higher Edn. (bd. dirs. 1988—90), Royal CanLegion (hon.), Can. Legion Assoc. (hon.), Can. Soc. 18th Century Studies (pres. 1975—76), Atlantic Soc. 18th Century Studies (pres. 1972—76), Can. Fedn. Humanities (pres. 1982—84), Internat. Assn. of Comparative Lit. (treas. 1985—91, sec. 1991—94), Internat. Soc. 18th Century Studies (assoc. treas. 1983—87), World Parliament of Cultures, Club of Rome (exec. com. 1999—2006), Knights of Malta (grande dame 1991—), Phi Delta Kappa, Delta Kappa Gamma. Home: 8 Rideau Shore Ct Ottawa ON K2C 3Y8 Canada Office: Carleton Univ 1125 Colonel By Drive Ottawa ON KIS 586 Canada Office Phone: 613-520-3801. Office Fax: 613-520-4474. Business E-Mail: roseann_runte@carleton.ca.

RUNYAN, DESMOND KIMO, medical educator, researcher; b. Pasadena, Calif., Aug. 27, 1950; s. Raymond Albert and Patricia Alona (Collins) R.; m. Carol Sue Wolf, Dec. 23, 1972; 1 child, Alexander. BA, Macalester Coll., 1972; MD, U. Minn., 1976; DPH, U. N.C., 1983. Diplomate Am Bd. Pediat., Am. Bd. Preventive Medicine. Resident in pediat. U. Minn. Health Scis. Ctr., Mpls., 1976-79; Robert Wood Johnson clin. scholar U. N.C., Chapel Hill, 1979-81, from asst. to assoc. prof. social medicine and pediat., 1981-95, dir. preventive medicine residency, 1989-98, prof. social medicine and pediat., 1995—, chmn. dept. social medicine, 1999—. Mem. faculty Internat. Clin. Epidemiology Network, 1987—; mem. exec. com. Nat. Adv. Coun. Family Violence, Chgo., 1994—; med. dir. N.C. Child Med. Evaluation Program, Chapel Hill, 1986-98, Ctr. for Child and Family Health-N.C., Durham, 1996—; prin. investigator rsch. study of child abuse and neglect, Nat. Ctr. Child Abuse and Neglect, 1990—; co-prin. investigator nat. study child and adolescent well-being, U.S. Congress, 1997—. Mem. editl. bd. Internat. Jour. Child Abuse and Neglect, 1994—; bd. govs. Am. Journ. Preventive Medicine, 1996—. Soc. for Pediatric Rsch. fellow. Fellow Am. Coll. Preventive Medicine; mem. Internat. Soc. Prevention Child Abuse and Neglect, Ambulatory Pediat. Assn. Avocations: skiing, sailing. Office: U NC Dept Social Medicine PO Box 7240 Chapel Hill NC 27599-0001 Fax: 919-966-7499. E-mail: drunyan@med.unc.edu.

RUNYON, KEITH LESLIE, lawyer, editor; b. Louisville, Oct. 3, 1950; s. Leslie Thomas and Marjorie Fillmore (Fisher) R.; M. Amelia Payne Sweets, Dec. 29, 1979; children; Amelia Brown Payne, Keith Leslie Jr. Student, U. London, 1971; BA summa cum laude, U. Louisville, 1972, JD, 1982. Staff writer Courier-Jour., Louisville, 1972-77, staff atty., 1984-86; staff atty., assoc. editor Louisville Times and Courier Jour., 1977-86, forum editor, 1986-90; editl. page editor, 1990-92; editor opinion pages, 1992-96; opinion editor, 1996—. Moderator Ky. Author Forum, 1996-. Editor: The Forum and Book Editor, 2001—. Nat. bd. dirs. English-Speaking Union U.S., N.Y., 1976-79, pres. Ky. br., Louisville, 1986-87; pres., dir. U. Louisville Alumni Assn., 1987-93; mem. exec. com. Louisville com. on fgn. rels., 1985-87, Leadership Louisville, 1990-91; clk. Session Calvin Presbyn. Ch., Louisville, 1986-88; mem. St. Francis in the Fields Episcopal Ch., Harrods Creek, Ky.; bd. dirs. Walden Theatre, Louisville, 1999-2001; mem. alumni bd. U. Louisville Brandeis Sch. of Law, 2001—. Recipient William E. Leidt award The Episc. Ch. of U.S., 1975, Roy Howard award (shared) Scripps Howard Journalists Nat. for Pub. Svc., 1976; named Alumnus of Yr., U. Louisville, 1991, disting. alumnus U. Louisville Sch. Law, 1996; Ctr. Fgn. Journalists fellow, 1993, Bingham fellow, 1995-96. Mem. ABA, Ky. Bar Assn., Louisville Bar Assn., Nat. Conf. Edit. Writers (editor The Masthead, 1994-96), Soc. Profl. Jours. (Outstanding Editl. Writing award, 1983, 84, 85, Outstanding Criticism award 1997, 98). Home: Nitta Yuma Harrods Creek KY 40027 Office: Courier-Jour and Louisville Times Co 525 W Broadway Louisville KY 40202-2206 Home Phone: 502-228-5373. Business E-Mail: krunyon@courier-journal.com.

RUOCCO, JOE, manufacturing executive; BS in Indsl. and Labor Rels., Cornell U., Ithaca, NY; MBA, Syracuse U., NY. Joined human resources leadership prog. Gen. Electric Co., 1985, various positions aircraft engines, med. sys., plastics & corp. ops., sr. human resources mgr. lighting Cleve., 1999—2002, v.p. human resources indsl. sys., 2002, v.p. human resources consumer & indsl., 2003—08; sr. v.p. human resources Goodyear Tire & Rubber Co., 2008—. Office: Goodyear Tire & Rubber Co Hdqs 1144 E Market St Akron OH 44316 Office Phone: 330-796-2121. Office Fax: 330-796-2222.

RUOF, RICHARD ALAN, minister, poet, writer; b. Lancaster, Pa., Oct. 11, 1932; s. Robert Jacob and Geneva May (Devers) Ruof; m. Anne Margaret Demos; children: Mark Alan Demos Ruof, Anne Tracy Demos Ruof, Richard James Demos Ruof. AB, Franklin and Marshall Coll., 1954; MDiv, Lancaster Theol. Sem., Pa., Union Theol. Sem., Richmond, Va., 1960; STM, Luth. Theol. Sem., Gettysburg, Pa., 1974; DMin, McCormick Theol. Sem., 1981. Ordained to ministry United Ch. Christ, 1960. Pastor Harrisville (Va.) Charge of United Ch. Christ, 1959-62, Thurmont (Md.) Charge, 1962-67, First Congl. Ch., Cortland, NY, 1967-77, St. Paul's United Ch. Christ of Hamlin, Fredericksburg, Pa., 1977-82, St. John's United Ch. Christ, Egg Harbor City, NJ, 1982-87, Friedensburg, Pa., 1987-94, pastor emeritus, 1994. Author: (spiritual poems) Songs of the Lesser Servants, 2003, Melting World, 2004, Return of the Martyrs, 2005, Days of the Eagle, 2005, Departure of the Blossoms, 2006, Poems of the Bridge, 2008, Whispered Messages, 2008, How Still the Songbird Lies, 2009. Mem. Egg Harbor City Bd. Edn., 1984; registrar-treas. Susquehanna Assn. N.Y. Conf., United Ch. Christ, 1968—74. With USNR, 1954—56.

RUOFF, JANIS KAYE, human services administrator; b. Norman, Okla., Apr. 7, 1948; d. William Albert Ruoff and Georgia Ruth Curry Ruoff; m. Edward Dennis Schappell, Sept. 17, 1994; m. Grant Stephen Bouck, July 19, 1969 (div. Oct. 3, 1992); children: Jeffrey Stephen Bouck, Travis Joseph Bouck. PhD, Gallaudet U., Washington, 1995. Dir. Ctr. Edn. & Human Svcs. Acquired Brain Injury, George Washington U., 2001—, Md. State TBI Project, Md. Dept. Health & Mental Hygiene, Balt., 1997—99. Owner Ruoff & Assocs., LLC, Silver Spring, Md., 2000—. Bd. sec. Brain Injury Assn., Washington, 2007—; bd. mem. pres. Brain Injury Svcs., Inc., Springfield, Va., 1998—; adv. bd. mem. Traumatic Brain Injury Resource Optimization Ctr., Bethesda, Md., 2008—. Office: George Washington Univ 2134 G St NW Washington DC 20052 Personal E-mail: janiskr@aol.com. Business E-Mail: jruoff@gwu.edu.

RUOSLAHTI, ERKKI, cell biologist, cancer researcher; b. Puumala, Finland, Feb. 16, 1940; B. in Medicine, U. Helsinki, Finland, 1961, MD, 1965, PhD in Immunology, 1967; MD (hon.), U. Lund, Sweden, 1991. Rsch./teaching asst. dept. serology and bacteriology U. Helsinki, 1964-66; head blood group dept. State Serum Inst., Helsinki, 1966-68; NIH rsch. fellow Calif. Inst. Tech., 1968-70; asst. prof., acting assoc. prof. dept. serology and bacteriology U. Helsinki, Finland, 1970-75; prof. bacteriology and serology U. Turku, Finland, 1975-76; sr. rsch. scientist dept. immunology City of Hope, Nat. Med. Ctr., Duarte, Calif., 1976, dir. immunobiology divsn. immunology, 1976—79; assoc. sci. dir. Cancer Rsch. Found. (now The Burnham Inst.), La Jolla, Calif., 1979-80, scientific dir., 1980—95, v.p., COO, 1982-89, pres., CEO and dir. NCI Cancer Ctr., 1989—2001; disting. prof. The Burnham Inst., La Jolla, Calif., 2002—. Adj. prof. dept. pathology U. Calif., San Diego, 1980-2004, dept. bioengring., 2003-; mem. sci. adv. bd. Helen Keller Eye Rsch. Found., Birmingham, Ala., 1989—; mem. pathobiochemistry study sect. Nat. Cancer Inst., 1981-85; Robert and Estelle Stadtler lectr. U. Tex., Sys. Cancer Ctr., 1984, Burton L. Baker Meml. lectr. U. Mich., Ann Arbor, 1987, Harvey Soc. lectr., 1988, Jeanette Piperno Meml. lectr. Temple U., Phila., 1989, G.H.A. Clowes award and lectr. Am. Assn. Cancer Rsch., 1990, Karl H. Beyer lectr. U. Wis., 1990, Walter Hubert lectr. 33d Ann. Meeting, Brit. Assn. for Cancer Rsch., 1992. Contbr. over 300 articles to profl. jours.; editl. bd. mem. Matrix, 1991—, Internat. Jour. Cancer, 1979—, Ann. Rev. of Cell Biology, 1987-90, Jour. Cell Biology, 1987-89, Jour. Biol. Chemistry, 1985-88, Cancer Rsch., 1979-82; reviewing editor Science, 1989—; editor-in-chief Cell Regulation, 1989-91. Recipient Barbara Robert Meml. medal French Soc. of Connective Tissue, 1988, Outstanding Investigator award Nat. Cancer Inst., 1986-93, G.H.A. Clowes award, 1990, Robert J. and Claire Pasarow Found. award, 1991, Leila Gruber Cancer Rsch. award Am. Acad. Dermatology, 1993, Abbott award Internat. Soc. for Oncodevelopmental Biology and Medicine, 1995, Gairdner Found. Internat. award, 1997, Jacobaeus Internat. prize, 1998, Jubilee award, British Biomedical Soc., 2003; co-recipient Japan prize: Cell Biology, 2005; knight Order of the White Rose of Finland. Fellow Am. Acad. Arts and Scis.; mem. Finnish Acad. Scis., NAS, European Molecular Biology Orgn., Inst. of Medicine of the U.S. Nat. Academies; nobel fellow, Karolinska Inst., Stockholm. Office: The Burnham Inst 10901 N Torrey Pines Rd La Jolla CA 92037-1062

RUOTOLO, CHARLES J., orthopedist, department chairman; b. New London, Conn., Feb. 6, 1967; MD, NY Med. Coll., Valhalla, 1995. Pres. owner Total Orthops. & Sports Medicine, Massapequa, 2003—; chmn. Dept. Orthops., NUMC, East Meadow, 2004—. Recipient Attending Surgeon of Yr. award, SUNY Stony Brook Orthop. Residency, 2003. Fellow: Am. Acad. Orthop. Surgery; mem.: Arthroscopy Assn. N.Am. Conservative. Roman Catholic. Office: Total Orthops & Sports Medicine 5500 Merrick Rd Massapequa NY 11758 Office Fax: 516-795-3033. Business E-Mail: cruotolo@hotmail.com.

RUPERT, DONALD WILLIAM, lawyer; b. Clearfield, Pa., Oct. 15, 1946; s. Donald Donald Lee and Dorothy Mae (Bonsall) Rupert; m. Patricia A. Rupert, June 21, 1969. BS in Chemistry, Miami U., Ohio, 1968; JD, Washburn U., Topeka, 1976. Bar: Tex. 1976, Ill. 1978, US Ct. Appeals (Fed. cir.) 1978, US Supreme Ct. 1992, US Dist. Ct. (ctrl. dist.) Ill. 1999, US Dist. Ct. Minn. 2003, US Dist. Ct. Colo. 2007. Assoc. Arnold, White & Durkee, Houston, 1976—78, Kirkland & Ellis, Chgo., 1978—83, ptnr., 1983—86, Neuman, Williams, Anderson & Olson, Chgo., 1986—90, Mayer, Brown, Rowe & Maw, LLP, Chgo., 1996—2007, Marshall, Gerstein and Borun LLP, Chgo., 2007—. Founding ptnr. Roper & Quigg, 1990—93, ptnr. Keck, Mahin & Cate, Chgo., 1993—96; pvt. practice, Dayton, Ohio, 1974—81. Contbr. articles to profl. jours. Served to capt USAF, 1968—74. Miami U. Undergrad. Rsch. fellow, 1967, Grad. Rsch. fellow, 1968. Mem.: ABA, Tex. Bar Assn., Am. Intellectual Property Law Assn., Phi Kappa Phi. Democrat. Presbyterian. Home: 2310 Marcy Ave Evanston IL 60201 Office: Marshall, Gerstein & Borun LLP 233 S Wacker 6300 Sears Tower Chicago IL 60606

RUPERT, ELIZABETH ANASTASIA, retired dean; b. Emlenton, Pa., July 12, 1918; d. John Hamilton and Eva Blanche (Elliott) R. Diploma, Altoona Sch. Commerce, 1936; BS in Edn., Clarion State Coll., 1959; MSLS, Syracuse U., 1962; PhD, U. Pitts., 1970. Sec. Sterling Oil divsn. Quaker State Oil Refining Corp., 1939-56; tchr., libr. Oil City Area Schs., 1959-61; libr. Venango campus Clarion (Pa.) U., 1961-62, prof. Sch. Libr. Sci., 1962-70, dean Sch. Libr. Sci., Coll. Libr. Sci., 1971-85; prof. emeritus, 1994. Interim pres. Clarion U., spring, 1977; acct. William Rupert Mortuary, Inc., 1948—88. Author: Pennsylvania Practicum Program for School Librarians: An Appraisal, 1970; mem. ad hoc edit. com. Pa. Media Guidelines, Pa. Dept. Edn., 1976, author (with others) Encyclopedia of Library and Information Science, 1984. Bd. dirs. Knox Pub. Libr., 1991-97; mem. Abscurf; mem. numerous bds. and couns. Church of God. Recipient Disting. Faculty award, Clarion U. Alumni Assn., 1976, Disting. Svc. award, 1986, Disting. Alumni award, 1987, Leadership citation, Coun. of Deans Clarion U., 1985, Zonta Internat. Women of Achievement award, 1987. Mem.: Pi Gamma Mu, Beta Phi Mu. Republican. Home: PO Box H Knox PA 16232-0608

RUPERT, HOOVER, minister, writer; b. Madison, NJ, Nov. 3, 1917; s. Lynn Hoover and Hazel L. (Linabary) R.; m. Hazel Pearl Senti, June 22, 1941 (dec. Jan. 2007); children: Susan Newbry, Elizabeth Wright. AB, Baker U., 1938; A.M., Boston U., 1940, M.Div. cum laude, 1941; student (summers), Garrett Bibl. Inst. and Northwestern U., 1942, Union Theol. Sem., 1943; D.D., Adrian Coll., 1952, Baker U., 1966; L.H.D., Milliken U., 1974. Ordained to ministry Methodist Ch., 1940; asst.

pastor First Meth. Ch., Baldwin, Kans., 1936-38, St. Mark's Meth. Ch., Brookline, Mass., 1938-41; pastor Thayer-St. Paul, Kans., 1941-43, First Ch., Olathe, Kans., 1943-45; dir. youth dept. Gen. Bd. Edn. Meth. Ch., Nashville, 1945-50; pastor 1st Meth. Ch., Jackson, Mich., 1950-59, 1st United Meth. Ch., Ann Arbor, Mich., 1959-72, Kalamazoo, 1972-83; faculty dept. religion Fla. So. Coll., Lakeland, 1983-89; adj. faculty Wesley Theol. Sem., Washington, 1989-93. Dean Mich. Meth. Pastors Sch., 1959-65; mem. Jud. Coun. United Meth. Ch., 1968-88, sec., 1976-88, sec. emeritus, 1988; chaplain Epworth Summer Assembly, Ludington, Mich., 1984-98, chaplain emeritus, 1999; Bible lectr. Asbury Meth. Village, 1990-2004. Author: Prayer Poems on the Prayer Perfect, 1943, Christ Above All (editor), 1948, Youth and Evangelism, 1948, Youth and Stewardship, rev. edit., 1960, Your Life Counts (editor), 1950, What Methodists Believe, rev. edit., 1959, John Wesley and People Called Methodists, 1953, I Belong, 1954, And Jesus Said, 1960, Enjoy Your Teen-Ager, 1962, A Sense of What is Vital, 1964, The Church in Renewal, 1965, Divine Demands: God's Commandments, 1966, My People are Your People, 1968, Where is thy Sting?, Christian Perspectives on Death, 1969, What's Good About God?, 1975 God Will See You Through, 1976, An Instrument of Thy Peace, 1982, The High Cost of Being Human, 1986, Why Didn't Noah Swat Both Mosquitoes, 1993; writer, syndicated weekly mag. column Accent on Living; newspaper feature Talking to Teens; other publs., periodicals, and newspapers. Trustee Bronson Hosp., 1972-88, Adrian Coll., 1952-67, Asbury Meth. Village, 1996-2000; pres., bd. dirs. Youth for Understanding, 1970-83, Ann Arbor United Fund, YMCA-YWCA. Recipient Distinguished Alumnus award Boston U., 1969; Lucinda Bidwell Beebe fellow Boston U., 1941 Mem. World Meth. Council, Nat. Council Chs., Mark Twain Soc., Nat. Forensic League, Pi Kappa Delta, Alpha Psi Omega. Lodges: Mason, Rotary (Paul Harris fellow 1983), Chi Rho. Home Phone: 301-216-5415.

RUPLEY, LAWRENCE A., economics professor; b. Huntington, Ind., Dec. 1940; s. Clarence L. and Mary Darley Rupley; married. AB, Manchester Coll., Ind., 1962; PhD, U. Ill., Urbana, 1967. Sr. lectr. Ahmadu Bello U., Zaria, Nigeria, 1970—76; rep., Burkina Faso Mennonite Ctrl. Com., Akron, Pa., 1985—90; group travel coord. MTS Travel, Mennonite World Conf., Ephrata, Pa., 2001—04; adj. prof. economics Harrisburg Area CC, Lancaster, Pa., 2005—. Editor peace office newsletter Mennonite Ctrl. Com., Akron, 2005—. Contbr. articles to profl. jours. Bd. dirs. Ephrata Area Soc. Svc., Ephrata, Pa., 1991—96. Avocation: piano. Home: 918 Walnut St Akron PA 17501

RUPP, GEORGE ERIK, international relief organization executive; b. Summit, NJ, Sept. 22, 1942; s. Gustav Wilhelm and Erika (Braunoehler) R.; m. Nancy Katherine Farrar, Aug. 22, 1964; children: Katherine Heather, Stephanie Karin. Student, Ludwig Maximilians U., Munich, Germany, 1962-63; AB, Princeton U., 1964; BD, Yale U., 1967; post grad., U. Sri Lanka, Peradeniya, 1969-70; PhD, Harvard U., 1972; DD (hon.), Austin Coll., 1992; LittD (hon.), Columbia U., 1993; LHD (hon.), U. Redlands, 1994, Georgetown U., 2001; LLD (hon.), Hamilton Coll., 1995. Ordained to ministry Presbyn. Ch. USA, 1971; faculty fellow in religion, vice chancellor Johnston Coll., U. Redlands, Redlands, Calif., 1971-74; asst. prof. Harvard Div. Sch., Harvard U., Cambridge, Mass., 1974-76, assoc. prof., 1976-77, prof., dean, 1979-85; prof., dean acad. affairs U. Wis., Green Bay, 1977-79; prof., pres. Rice U., Houston, 1985-93, Columbia U., NYC, 1993—2002; pres. Internat. Rescue Com., NY, 2002—. Bd. dir. Bio-Ventures Pub. Health, Com. for Econ. Devel., Coun. Fgn. Rels., Harvard Bd. Overseers Vis. Com. Div. Sch., Inst. Internat. Edn., InterAction, Henry Luce Found., Josiah Macy Found. Author: Christologies and Cultures: Toward a Typology of Religious Worldviews, 1974, Culture Protestantism: German Liberal Theology at the Turn of the Twentieth Century, 1977, Beyond Existentialism and Zen: Religion in a Pluralistic World, 1979, Commitment and Community, 1989, Globalization Challenged: Conviction, Conflict, and Community, 2006; contbr. articles to profl. jour. Recipient Alexander Hamilton medal, Columbia U., 2002, Centennial medal for contbn. to soc., Harvard U. Grad. Sch. Arts and Scis., 2004, Gold medal, Nat. Inst. Social Scis., 2005, Woodrow Wilson award, Princeton U., 2006, Merit award, Bucknell U., 1997; Danforth Grad. fellow, 1964—71. Mem.: AAAS, Soc. Values in Higher Edn., Coun. Fgn. Rels., Am. Acad. Religion. Office: International Rescue Committee 122 East 42nd Street New York NY 10168

RUPP, JOSEPH D., metal products executive; BS in Metallurgical Engring., U. Mo. With Olin Corp., 1972—, v.p., manufacturing and engineering, 1985—96; pres. Olin Brass, Olin Corp., 1996—2001; v.p. Olin Corp., 1996—2001, exec. v.p., operations, 2001—02, pres. CEO, 2002—, chmn., 2005—. Office: c/o Olin 190 Carondelet Plaza Clayton MO 63105

RUPP, KATHERINE M., marketing executive; d. Lionel and Gloria Rupp. BA, St. Joseph's Coll., 1996. Cmty. affairs assoc. Suffolk AHRC, Bohemia, NY, 1998—2000; mktg. mgr. LI Works Coalition, Commack, NY, 2000—04; mktg. dir. North Shore Fin. Group, Hauppauge, NY, 2006—; dir. devel. Spl. Olympics NY, LI Region, Deer Park, NY, 2005—06. Bd. mem. Pub. Rels. Profls. LI, Hicksville, NY, 2005—. Candlelight ball steering com. Suffolk County chpt. Assn. for Help of Retarded Children, Bohemia, 2006. Mem.: GAMA Internat., St. Joseph's Coll. Alumni Bus. Networking Group (assoc.), LI Elite (assoc.), LI Assn. (assoc.). Home: 373 Nesconset Hwy Ste 290 Hauppauge NY 11788 Personal E-mail: kmrprofessional@gmail.com.

RUPP, SHERON ADELINE, photographer, educator; b. Mansfield, Ohio, Jan. 14, 1943; d. Warren Edmund Rupp and Frances (Hanson) Christian. BA in Sociology and Psychology, Denison U., Granville, Ohio, 1965; MFA in Photography, U. Mass., Amherst, 1982. Teaching asst. in photography Hampshire Coll., Amherst, Mass., 1981; instr. photography Northfield Mt. Hermon Sch., Mass., 1982-83, U. Mass., Amherst, 1984, Holyoke C.C., Mass., 1986, 87-88; vis. asst. prof. photography Hampshire Coll., 1985, 87; vis. lectr. photography Amherst Coll., Mass., 1994. Guest artist, lectr. Boston Mus. Sch., Portland Sch. Art, Maine, NYU, U. Mass., Hartford Sch. Art/U. Hartford-Conn., Springfield Mus. Fine Arts, Mass., Bard Coll, NY, Mass. Coll. Art, Boston, others; guest lectr. Carpenter Ctr., Harvard U., Cambridge, Mass., 2000. One-woman shows include Tisch Sch. Arts NYU, 1987, Portland Sch. Art, 1989, O.K. Harris Gallery, NYC, 1992, Cleve. Mus. Art, 2000, "Sheron Rupp: Dialogue with A Collection" U. Mass. Fine Arts Gallery, Amherst, 2009; two-person shows include Columbus Mus. Art, Ohio, 1997—98; Springfield Tech. C.C., Mass., 1997, exhibited in group shows at Mus. Modern Art, NYC, 1991, 1999—, Springfield Mus. Fine Art, 1993, U. Mass., Amherst, 1993, Dirs. Guild, LA, 1994, Manchester Inst. Arts and Scis., NH, 1995, Weber State U., Utah, 1995, Photog. Resource Ctr. 3d Biennial, Boston, 1995, DeCordova Mus., Lincoln, 2000—, Smithsonian Arts and Scis., Washington, 2001, Denison U. Art Gallery, Granville, Ohio, 2002, Around the House, A.N. Bush Gallery, Salem, Oreg., 2002, Boston Mus. Fine Arts, 2002—03, Guild Hall, East Hampton, N.Y., 2003, Smith Coll. Mus. Art, Northampton, Mass., 2004; photographer (group shows) Berman Collection, Getty Mus., LA, 2006—07, Sir Elton John Photography Collection; Exhibited in group shows at Der Garten in der Kunst seit 1900, Kunsthalle, Emden, 2007—08, Represented in permanent collections De Cordova Mus., Mus. Modern Art, NYC, Fogg Art Mus. at Harvard U., Hallmark Collection of Photography, Kansas City, Columbus Mus. Art, The J. Paul Getty Mus., L.A., Mus. Fine Arts, Boston, Rose Art Mus. Brandeis U., Mead Art Mus. Amherst Coll., Smith Coll. Mus. Art, Danforth Mus. Art, Springfield Tech. C.C. Found., Carpenter Ctr. for Visual Arts Harvard U., The Smithsonian, Corcoran Galley of Art, Washington; photographs (including cover photo) in Double-Take Mag., winter 1998; publ. and exhibit, Where We Live: Photographs of America from the Berman Collection, 2006, Garden Eden, 2007, publ., Emden, Germany, 2007. Recipient Mass. Fellowship award in photography Artist Found., 1984, 87; visual artist fellow Nat. Endowment for the Arts, 1986, 94, Guggenheim fellow, 1990. Home and Office: 3 The Lope Haydenville MA 01039 E-mail: sheron@crocker.com.

RUPPEL, EDWARD THOMPSON, geologist; b. Fort Morgan, Colo., Oct. 26, 1925; s. Henry George and Gladys Myrtle (Thompson) R.; m. Phyllis Beale Tanner; children: Lisa, David, Douglas, Kristin. BA in Geology, U. Mont., 1948, Doctorate (hon.), 1996; MA in Geology, U. Wyo., 1950; PhD in Geology, Yale U., 1958. Geologist U.S. Geol. Survey, Denver, 1950-68, rsch. geologist, 1968-86; dir., state geologist Mont. Bur. Mines and Geology, Butte, 1986-94; consulting geologist Twin Bridges, Mont., 1994—. Author and co-author of approximately more then 50 maps and reports; contbr. articles to profl. jours. Dir., v.p. Virginia City (Mont.) Preservation Alliance, 1997-98. Lt. (j.g.) USNR, 1943-50. Fellow Geol. Soc. Am. (sr.), Soc. Econ. Geologists; mem. Am. Inst. Profl. Geologists (cert. profl. geologist), Mont. Geol. Soc., Geol. Soc. Washington, Tobacco Root Geol. Soc. (Excellence in Field Work award 1993). Home and Office: 326 S Main St PO Box 402 Twin Bridges MT 59754-0402 Office Phone: 406-684-5565.

RUPPERSBERGER, CHARLES ALBERT, III, (DUTCH), United States Representative from Maryland; b. Balt., Jan. 31, 1946; s. Charles Albert Jr. and Margaret (Wilson) Ruppersberger; m. Kay Murphy, Dec. 28, 1968; 1 child, Charles Albert; 1 child, Jill Ann. BA, U. Md., 1967; JD, U. Balt., 1970. Bar: Md. 1972, US Supreme Ct. 1977. Social worker Balt. City Schs., 1967-69; claims adjuster US Fidelity and Guaranty Co., Balt., 1969-70; law clk. to presiding justice Balt. County Cir. Ct., Towson, 1970-72; asst. state's atty. Balt. County State's Atty., Towson, 1972-80; ptnr. Ruppersberger, Winter, Clark & Mister, Timonium, Md., 1980—94; mem. US Congress from 2nd Md. dist., 2003—. Chief investigation div. State's Atty.'s Office, Towson, 1972—80; liaison Balt. County Police Dept./Md. State Police, 1973—80. Legal coun. Balt. County Athletic League; pres. Topfield Condominium Assn., Cockeysville, Md., 1975—78; campaign mgr. Senator Francis X. Kelly, Annapolis, Md., 1980—85; councilman Balt. County Coun., 1985—94; coach, v.p Cockeysville Recreation Coun., 1978—; pres. Greater Timonium Cmty. Coun., Md., 1980—; bd. dirs. Timonium Meth. Ch., 1984—. Recipient Appreciation award, Balt. County Order Fraternal Police, 1977, 1979; named one of Outstanding Young Marylanders, Jaycees, 1979. Mem.: U. Md. Alumni Assn. (v.p.), Nat. Coll. Dist. Attys. (adv. 1974—80), Balt. County Bar Assn. (chmn. bench-bar com.), Md. Bar Assn. (grievance com.), Masons. Democrat. Methodist. Office: US Ho Reps 1630 Longworth Ho Office Bldg Washington DC 20515-2002*

RUPPERT, JOHN HUTCHINS, sculptor; b. Winchester, Mass., May 8, 1951; s. C. Farrell and June (Hutchins) R.; m. Sally Price, Mar. 20, 1952; children: June, Kimberly. BA in Art Edn., Miami U., Oxford, Ohio, 1974; MFA, Rochester Inst. Technology, 1977. Resident artist Wildcliff Mus., New Rochelle, N.Y., 1977-79; lectr. U. Wyo., Laramie, 1979; instr. Webster U., St. Louis, 1980-85; resident artist Liberty Foundry, St. Louis, 1985-87; asst. prof. U. Md., College Park, 1987-92, assoc. prof., 1992—, chair dept. art, 1998—. Chair dept. art U. Md., 1998—. One-man shows include Elliot Smith Gallery, St. Louis, 1984, George Ciscle Gallery, Balt., 1985, 87, Southeastern Ctr. for Contemporary Art, Open Air Gallery, Winston-Salem, N.C., 1988, Barbara Fendrick Gallery, N.Y.C., 1989, Franz Bader Gallery, Washington, 1991, 95, Va. Beach Ctr. for Arts, 1996, Cleve. Ctr. for Contemporary Art, 1996, Chgo. Cultural Ctr., 1996, C. Grimaldis Gallery, Balt., 1997, Art et Industrie, N.Y.C., 1997, Evanston (Ill.) Art Ctr., 1999, Contemporary Art Mus., Raleigh, N.C., 2000-01, Weatherspoon Gallery, Greensboro, N.C., Montavo Sculpture Park, Sarasota, Calif.; group shows include Corcoran Sch. of Art, Washington, 1994, Luminy-Marseille, France, 1995, Delaware Mus., Wilmington, 1996, C. Grimaldis Gallery, Balt., 1991-92, 94-96, 2000, Art Scape, Balt., 1992, 94, 96, others; work collected at Grounds for Sculpture, N.J., Balt./Washington Airport, Md., Am. Visionary Art Mus., Balt., Xerox Corp., Rochester, Contemporary Art Found., Marseille, Suwa Mcpl. Art Mus., Japan, Art Mus. We. Va., Roanoke, Stone Quarry Hill, Cazenovia, N.Y., 1998-2000, Yawkey Woodson Art Mus., Wausau, Wis., DeCordova Mus. and Sculpture Park, Boston, Kreeger Mus., Washington. Trustee Md. Art Place, 1956. Artist grantee Md. State Arts Coun., 1991, 95, 97, Baltimore City, 1991; Creative and Performing Arts award, U. Md., 1987, 89, 91, 97. Home: 532 Allegheny Ave Towson MD 21204-4232 E-mail: jr59@umail.umdiedu.

RUPPERT (METZGER), THOMAS ERICH, cell and molecular biologist, quality assurance and regulatory professional; b. Ulm/Donau, Germany, Mar. 4, 1966; s. Uwe and Monika Metzger; m. Kerstin Ruppert. Diploma in Biology, U. Bonn, 1989, U. Mainz, 1992, PhD magna cum laude, 1996. Lic. quality mgmt. profl. TÜV South Germany, 2000. Advt. profl. Wötzel Sci. Academic Books, Frankfurt Main, Germany, 1995—96; profl. application trainer SLAT Tng., 1997—99; head quality mgmt. SLAT IT-Consulting, Waldems-Esch, Germany, 2000—01; quality mgr. info. tech. Aventis Deutschland GmbH, Frankfurt Main, 2001—02; quality mgr. computerized sys. Sanofi-Aventis Deutschland GmbH, Frankfurt Main, 2003—06, quality assurance mgr., quality mgmt. sys., 2007—08; regulatory compliance mgr. Quality Regulatory, 2008—. Cons. info. tech. and biomed. software, 1998—2001; profl. auditor Pharma Validation Group, Berlin, 2003—08; lectr. computerized sys. validation Concept Heidelberg, 2003—04. Contbr. articles to profl. jours. Bd. dirs. Students' Reps., Düsseldorf, Bonn, Germany, 1983—84. Fellow, State of Rheinland-Pfalz, Germany, 1992—94. Mem.: German Assn. Regulatory Affairs (DGRA), Mainzer Wingolf (assoc.). Avocations: horseback riding, scooter, motorcycling, homeopathy, writing. Home: Klingenthaler Str 1 Taunusstein 65232 Germany Office Fax: +49 69 305 942450. Business E-Mail: thomas.ruppert2@sanofi-aventis.com.

RUS, TEODOR, computer scientist, educator; Mng. editor AMAST Series in Computing, Singapore, 1991—. Author: Systems Methodology for Software, 1994, Execution Support Environment, 1995; author (package of programs) TICS: Technology for Implementing Computer Software, 1982-98, software tools for computer users, 1998-2009; contbr. articles to profl. jours. on devel. of new computer tech. Office Phone: 319-335-0742. Fax: 319-335-3624. Business E-Mail: rus@cs.uiowa.edu.

RUSAW, SALLY ELLEN, librarian; b. Potsdam, NY, Apr. 24, 1939; d. Ralph Clinton and Marion Ellen (Jenack) R. BS in Edn., Potsdam Coll., 1964; MLS, SUNY, Albany, 1975. Cert. libr. media specialist, pub. libr., permanent tchr. N-6, N.Y. Tchr. grade 7th-9th Diocese Ogdensburg, NY, 1960-74, cons. office edn., 1975-78, archivist, vol. work, 2005—; assoc. libr. Mater Dei Coll., Ogdensburg, 1974-89, head libr., 1989-99, SUNY, Potsdam, 2000—04, vis. libr. Vol. Ogdensburg Correctional Facility, 1982-95, Riverview Correctional Facility, Ogdensburg, 1987—2006; lector, Eucharistic min. Rite for Christian Initiation of Adults catechist St. Mary's Cathedral; vol. Ogdensburg Cath. Ctrl. Sch., sch. bd., 1995-2000; commd. lay minister Diocese of Ogdensburg, 2005—. Named Vol. of Yr. Ogdensburg Correctional Facility, 1985, Outstanding Vol. Riverview Correctional Facility, 1991; Nat. Def. Edn. Act grantee, 1965. Mem. ALA, N.Y. Libr. Assn., North Country 3Rs Coun., North Country Ref. and Rsch. Resources Coun. (bd. dirs. 1994-99, 2008-). Roman Catholic. Avocations: music, reading, berrying, outdoor activities, swimming.

RUSCH, LISA MARIE, medical educator; b. New Britain, Conn., Aug. 20, 1964; d. Richard John and Beverly Theresa Stec; m. Douglas Miller Rusch, May 25, 1991; children: Brendon Kyle, Kendall Drue. BS, Duke U., Durham, North Carolina, 1986; MS, Wake Forest U., Winston-Salem, 1988. Clin. exercise specialist Am. Coll. Sports Medicine, 2005, cert. in exercise test tech. Am. Coll. Sports Medicine, 1987. Program coord. Hamilton Med. Specialists, NY, 1998—2000; program dir. Cmty. Wellness Ctr., Hamilton, 1998—2000; prof. Morrisville State Coll., NY, 2000—. Leader Saddleback 4H Club, Hamilton, 2006—09; Chair & mem. Eat Well Play Hard Initiative, Madison; chair Healthy Heart Coalition, Madison; mem. Livingwell Partnership, Madison; lector trainer St. Mary's Cath. Ch., Hamilton, 2007—09. Mem.: Am. Coll. Sports Medicine. Office: Morrisville State Coll PO Box 901 Morrisville NY 13408 Office Fax: 315-684-6392. Business E-Mail: ruschlm@morrisville.edu.

RUSCH, THOMAS WILLIAM, manufacturing executive; b. Alliance, Nebr., Oct. 3, 1946; s. Oscar William and Gwen Falerne (Middleswart) R.; m. Gloria Ann Sutton, June 20, 1968 (div. Oct. 1979); children: Alicia Catherine, Colin William; m. Lynn Biebighauser, Jan. 17, 1981. BEE, U. of Minn., 1968, MSEE, 1970, PhD, 1973; MS in Mgmt. of Tech., U. Minn., 1993. Sr. physicist cen. rsch. 3M Co., St. Paul, 1973-77, rsch. specialist cen. rsch., 1977-79; project scientist phys. electronics div. Perkin Elmer Corp., Eden Prairie, Minn., 1979-83, sr. project scientist phys. electronics div., 1983-85, lab mgr. phys. electronics div., 1985-87, product mgr. phys. electronics div., 1987-88, sr. product mgr. phys. electronics div., 1988-93; v.p. product devel. Chorus Corp., St. Paul, 1993-94; pres. Creekside Techs. Corp., Plymouth, Minn., 1994—; co-founder Xoft, Inc., Plymouth, 1998, chief tech. officer Fremont, Calif., 2001—02, prin. engr., 2002—07, chair, advanced tech., 2007—08, v.p. tech. outreach Sunnyvale, Calif., 2008—. Editor: X-rays in Materials Analysis, 1986; co-author: Oscillatory Ion Yields, 1977; patentee in field. Recipient IR100 award for transfer vessel Rsch. and Devel. mag., 1981, IR100 award for energy analyser, 1985. Office: 345 P Potrero Ave Sunnyvale CA 94085 Office Phone: 408-419-2300.

RUSCH, VALERIE WILLIAMS, thoracic surgeon; b. NYC, Oct. 16, 1951; AB in Biochemistry, Vassar Coll., 1971; MD, Columbia U., 1975. Diplomate Nat. Bd. Med. Examiners, Am. Bd. Surgery, Am. Bd. Thoracic Surgery. Intern in gen. surgery U. Wash., Seattle, 1975-76, resident in gen. surgery, 1975-80, resident in cardiothoracic surgery, 1980-82; faculty assoc. dept. of thoracic surgery M.D. Anderson Cancer Ctr., Houston, 1982-83; thoracic surgeon Harborview Med. Ctr., Seattle, 1983-86, assoc. staff mem., 1986-89; thoracic surgeon Group Health Coop. of Puget Sound, Seattle, 1983-84; chief cardiothoracic surgery VA Hosp., Seattle, 1986-87; thoracic surgeon Univ. Hosp., Seattle, 1983-89; mem. courtesy med. staff Pacific Med. Ctr., Seattle, 1987-89; assoc. attending surgeon thoracic svc. Meml. Sloan-Kettering Cancer Ctr., NYC, 1989-94, attending surgeon, 1994—, chief thoracic surgery, 2000—. Asst. prof. div. cardiothoracic surgery U. Wash., 1983-88, assoc. prof., 1988-89; asst. mem. divsn. clin. rsch. Fred Hutchinson Cancer Rsch. Ctr., Seattle, 1985-89; assoc. mem. Meml. Hosp., Meml. Sloan-Kettering Cancer Ctr., N.Y.C., 1989-94, mem., 1994—; assoc. prof. surgery Cornell U. Med. Coll., N.Y.C., 1989-95, prof. surgery Cornell U. Med. Coll., 1995—; mem. cancer clin. investigations rev. com. Nat. Cancer Inst., 1991-98. Mem. editl. bd. Jour. Thoracic and Cardiovasc. Surgery, 1992-2007, Jour. Clin. Oncology, 2004-, Annals of Surgery, 2007; contbr. articles to profl. publs.; author abstracts in field. Grantee NIH, 1985-89, Deknatel Corp., 1986-87, Bard Electro Med. Systems, 1989, NeoRx Corp., 1989-90, Pfizer Corp., 1995-98. Fellow ACS (mem. bd. govs. 2002-, pres. bd. govs. 2007-), Am. Coll. Chest Physicians; mem. Am. Assn. Thoracic Surgery (mem. coun. 2006-), Soc. Thoracic Surgeons, Assn. Acad. Surgery, Soc. Surg. Oncology (mem. com. tng. 1993-95, mem. edn. com. 1993-95), Am. Soc. Clin. Oncology, (mem. program com. 1993, 96, bd. dirs. 2002-05), Am. Thoracic Soc., NY Cancer Soc., Internat. Assn. Study of Lung Cancer, Am. Med. Women's Assn., Am. Bd. Thoracic Surgery (mem. bd. dirs. 2003-), Henry Harkins' Surg. Soc., M.D. Anderson Assocs., Gen. Thoracic Surg. Club, Alpha Omega Alpha. Office: Meml Sloan-Kettering Cancer Thoracic Surgery Svc 1275 York Ave New York NY 10021-6094 Office Phone: 212-639-8695. Business E-Mail: ruschv@mskcc.org.

RUSCH, WILLIAM GRAHAM, religious organization administrator; b. Buffalo, Dec. 23, 1937; s. William Godfrey and Hope (French) R.; m. Thora Joan Ellefsen, Sept. 2, 1967. BA, SUNY, Buffalo, 1959, MA in Classical Langs., 1960; MDiv, Luth. Theol. Sem., Phila., 1963; PhD, Oxford U., Eng., 1965; DD (hon.), Yale U., 1995. Ordained to ministry Evang. Luth. Ch., 1966. Assoc. pastor Evang. Luth. Ch. of the Holy Trinity, NYC, 1966-68; asst. prof., chmn. dept. classical langs. Augsburg Coll., Mpls., 1968-71; assoc. exec. dir. div. Theol. Studies Luth. Coun. in the USA, 1971-78; adj. prof. The Gen. Theol. Sem., NYC, 1978-82, 95; exec. dir., asst. to Bishop Evang. Luth. Ch. in Am., Chgo., 1987-96; dir. Commn. on Faith and Order Nat. Coun. of Chs. of Christ USA, NYC, 1996-2001; exec. dir. Found. for Faith and Order, NYC, 2001—06. Vis. lectr. Waterloo Luth. Theol. Sem., 1969; adj. prof. theology Fordham U., N.Y.C., 1984-86, Luth. Theol. Sem., Phila., 1998—, St. John's Disting. prof., 2002-03; prof. Angelicum Pontificia U. San Tommaso, Rome, 2005-; mem. cen. com. World Coun. Chs., 1991-98, mem. standing com. faith and order commn., 1991—; adj. faculty Yale Div. Sch., 1999—; scholar-at-large Graymoor Ecumenical Inst., 2002-03; Jean-Marie Tillard disting. prof. Angelicum Pontificia U., San Tommaso, Rome, 2005-06, vis. fellow, Mansfield Coll., Oxford. Author: The Trinitarian Controversy, Ecumenism: A Movement Toward Church Unity, Ecumenical Reception; contbr. articles to profl. jours. Samuel Trexler fellow of N.Y. Synod Luth. Ch. in Am., 1964, 65. Mem. Am. Acad. Religion, Am. Soc. Christian Ethics, Am. Soc. Ch. History, Internat. Assn. Coptic Studies. Lutheran. Avocations: book collecting, chess, tennis. Office: Found for Faith and Order 77 Park Ave New York NY 10016 Home Phone: 212-725-7435. Personal E-mail: ruschgrif@worldnet.att.net.

RUSCHA, EDWARD, artist; b. Omaha, Dec. 16, 1937; m. Danna Knego, 1967; children: Edward Joseph. Studied at, Chouinard Art Inst., Los Angeles, 1956-60. Numerous vis. artist positions including UCLA, 1969-70; US Rep., Venice Biennale, 2005. Author: Twentysix Gasoline Stations, 1962, Various Small Fires, 1964, Some Los Angeles Apartments, 1965, The Sunset Strip, 1966, Thirtyfour Parking Lots, 1967, Royal Road Test, 1967, Business Cards, 1968, Nine Swimming Pools, 1968, Crackers, 1969, Real Estate Opportunities, 1970, Records, 1971, A Few Palm Trees, 1971, Colored People, 1972, Hard Light, 1978; noted for numerous graphite, gunpowder and pastel drawings, over 200 limited-edit. prints; producer, dir.: films Premium, 1970, Miracle, 1974; began showing works, Ferus Gallery, LA, 1963; first internat. show Galerie Rudolf Zwirner, Cologne, Germany,1968; works include (paintings) Standard Station, Amarillo, Tex., 1963; Annie, 1963, Smash, 1963, Electric, 1964, (mural) Miami-Dade Pub. Library, Fla., 1985; one-man exhbns. include Minn. Inst. Arts, 1972, Nigel Greenwood Ltd., London, 1970, 73, 80, Leo Castelli Gallery, N.Y.C., (10 shows) 1973—, Albright-Knox Art Gallery, Buffalo, 1976, Stedelijk Mus., Amsterdam, 1976, Ft. Worth Art Mus., 1977, San Francisco Mus. Modern Art, 1982, Whitney Mus. Am. Art, 1982, Vancouver Art Gallery, 1982, Contemporary Arts Mus., Houston, 1983, Los Angeles County Mus. Art, 1983, James Corcoran Gallery, Los Angeles, 1985, Gagosian Galleries, Chelsea, 2002, Beverly Hills, 2003, also others; exhibited in group shows at 64th Whitney Biennial, 1987, Centre Pompidou, Paris, 1989, Mus. Boymans—van Beuningen, Rotterdam, The Netherlands, 1990, Ghislaine Hussenot, Paris, 1990, Fundacio Caixa, Barcelona, Spain, 1990, Serpentine Gallery, London, 1990, Mus. Contemporary Art, L.A., 1990-91, Robert Miller Gallery, N.Y.C., 1992, Thaddaeus Ropac, Salzburg, Austria, 1992; represented in permanent collections including Mus. Modern Art, Los Angeles County Mus. Art, Whitney Mus., Hirshhorn, Washington, Miami-Dade Pub. Libr., Denver Pub. Libr., J. Paul Getty Mus., L.A., also others; restrospective of works on paper J. Paul Getty Mus., L.A., 1998; paintings exhibited, Gagosian Gallery, Beverly Hills, 1999, Metro Plots, N.Y., 1999; retrospective of career Hirshhorn Mus., 2000, Sculpture Garden, Washington, D.C., 2000, Mus. Contemporary Art, Chgo., Miami Art Mus., Modern Art Mus., Ft. Worth, Tex. Trustee Mus. Contemporary Art, LA. Guggenheim fellow; Nat. Endowment Arts grantee. Fellow: Am. Acad. Arts & Sci.; mem.: Am. Acad. Arts and Letters (mem. dept. art). Office: Gagosian Gallery 980 Madison Ave New York NY 10021-1848 also: 35 S Venice Blvd Venice CA 90291

RUSCHE, MARK C., lawyer; b. Marietta, Ga., Jan. 19, 1959; BA, Furman Univ., 1981; JD cum laude, Univ. SC, 1985. Bar: Ga. 1986. Ptnr., leader, real estate, fin. and investment group Alston & Bird LLP, Atlanta. Bd. of editors Comml. Leasing Law & Strategy. Mem.: Order of Coif. Office: Alston & Bird LLP One Atlantic Ctr 1201 W Peachtree St NW Atlanta GA 30309-3424 Office Phone: 404-881-7281. Office Fax: 404-253-8798. Business E-Mail: mark.rusche@alston.com.

RUSCIC, BRANKO M., chemist, researcher; b. Rijeka, Croatia, Aug. 29, 1952; s. Irene Valeri-Gradisnik and Sime Ruscic; m. Lillian Dubravica, Nov. 16, 1974; 1 child, Katarina J. BSc, U. Zagreb, 1975, PhD, 1979. Sr. rsch. assoc. Rugjer Boskovic Inst., Zagreb, Croatia, 1973—88; sr. scientist Argonne Nat. Lab., Ill., 1988—. Contbr. articles to profl. jours. Achievements include research in spectroscopy and thermochemistry; patents in field. Office: Argonne National Laboratory 9700 S Cass Ave - CHM 200 Argonne IL 60439-4831 Home Phone: 630-964-6365; Office Phone: 630-252-4079. Business E-Mail: ruscic@anl.gov.

RUSCIO, KENNETH PATRICK, academic administrator, political science professor; b. Red Bank, NJ; BA, Washington and Lee U., 1976; MPA, Syracuse U., 1979, PhD, 1983. Asst. prof. social sci. and policy studies Worcester Polytechnic Inst., 1985—87; asst. prof. politics Washington and Lee U., 1987—94, dean Freshman, 1987—94, assoc. dean Williams Sch. Commerce, Econs. and Politics, 1991—98, assoc. prof., 1994—2000, prof., 2000—02, acting assoc. dean, 2001—02, pres., 2006—; dean Jepson Sch. Leadership Studies, U. Richmond, 2002—06. Contbr. articles to profl. jours. Mem.: Am. Conf. of Academic Deans, Assn. Am. Colls. and Univs., Internat. Leadership Assn., Am. Polit. Sci. Assn. Office: Washington and Lee U Office of Pres Lexington VA 24450-0303 Office Phone: 540-458-8400. Office Fax: 540-458-8945.*

RUSH, ANDREW WILSON, artist; b. Detroit, Sept. 24, 1931; s. Harvey Ditman and Mary Louise (Stalker) R.; m. Jean Cochran, Apr., 1957; children: Benjamin, Samuel, Joseph, Margaret; m. Ann Woodin, Oct., 1978. B.F.A. with honors, U. Ill., 1953; M.F.A., U. Iowa, 1958. Asso. prof. art U. Ariz., 1959-69; co-dir. Rockefeller Found. Indian Arts Project, 1960-64; vis. artist, artist-in-residence Ohio State U., 1970, U. Ark., 1972, Colo. Coll., 1973-74; resident mem. Rancho Linda Vista, Community of the Arts, Oracle, Ariz., 1969—; founder, dir. The Drawing Studio, Tucson, 1992—. One-man shows include Carlin Galleries, Ft. Worth, 1973, Graphics Gallery, Tucson, 1972, 75, Tucson Art Inst., 1984, Cruzitas Gallery, San Antonio, 1996, U. Ariz. Mus. Art, 2003, Davis-Dominguez Gallery, Tucson, 2003; exhibited in group shows at World's Fair, N.Y.C., 1964, USIS exhbns., Europe, Latin Am., 1960-65; represented in permanent collections Libr. of Congress, Uffizzi Mus., Dallas Mus., Ft. Worth Mus., Seattle Mus., Free Libr., Phila.; illustrator: Andrew Rush on Oliver Wendell Holmes, 1973, Rule of Two (Ann Woodin), 1984, Voice Crying in the Wilderness (Edward Abbey), 1990, Ask Marilyn, 1992 (pub. art winner 1995), Voice of the Borderlands, 2005; designer The Tucson Gateway Project, 1998. Served with USMC, 1953-55. Fulbright grantee, 1958-59; recipient Lifetime Achievement award Tucson-Pima Arts Coun., 2006. Home: Rancho Linda Vista 1955 W Linda Vista Rd Oracle AZ 85623 E-mail: awrush@earthlink.net.

RUSH, BOBBY L., United States Representative from Illinois; b. Albany, Ga., Nov. 23, 1946; m. Carolyn Ryan; 5 children. BA in Polit. Sci., Roosevelt U., Chgo., 1974; MA in Polit. Sci., U. Ill., 1992; MA in Theology, McCormick Theolocal Seminary, 1998. Fin. planner Sanmar Fin. Planning Corp.; assoc. dean Daniel Hale Williams U.; ins. agent Prudential Ins. Co.; city alderman Chgo., 1984-93; dem. committeeman Chgo. 2nd ward, 1984, 88, Central Ill., 1990; dep. chmn. Ill. Dem. Party, 1990; mem. US Congress from 1st Ill. Dist., 1993—; chmn. environ. protection, energy and pub. utilities com., budget/govt. ops. com., capitol devel. com., hist. landmark preservation com.; mem. commerce com. Past coord. Free Breakfast for Children, Free Med. Clinic; founder Ill. Black Panther Party. Served with US Army, 1963—68. Recipient Enterprise Zone award, Ill. Dept. Commerce and Cmty., Outstanding Young Man award, Operation PUSH, Outstanding Community Svc. award, Henry Booth House, Outstanding Bus. and Profl. Achievement award, South End Jaycees, Disting. Polit. Leadership award, Chgo. Black United Communities; named one of Most Influential Black Americans, Ebony mag., 2006, Power 150, 2008. Democrat. Office: US Ho Reps 2416 Rayburn Ho Office Bldg Washington DC 20515-1301 Office Phone: 202-225-4372. Office Fax: 202-226-0333.*

RUSH, CURT STEFAN, lawyer; b. 1955; BA in Philosophy, Hunter Coll., 1981; JD cum laude, Bklyn. Law Sch., 1984. Bar: NY 1985. Assoc. Shereff, Friedman, Hoffman & Goodman, P.A., NYC; corp. counsel Image Bank, Inc., 1990—93, Globe Comm. Corp., Boca Raton, Fla., 1993—96; gen. counsel Global DirectMail Corp., Port Washington, NY; gen. counsel, sec. Systemax, Inc., Port Washington, NY, 1996—. Office: Systemax Inc 11 Harbor Park Dr Port Washington NY 11050 Office Phone: 516-608-7000. Office Fax: 516-625-0038.

RUSH, DOMENICA MARIE, health facilities administrator; b. Gallup, N.Mex., Apr. 10, 1937; d. Bernardo G. and Guadalupe (Milan) Iorio; m. W. E. Rush, Jan. 5, 1967. Diploma, Regina Sch. Nursing, Albuquerque, 1958. RN N.Mex.; lic. nursing home adminstr.; cert. legal nurse cons., 2004. Charge nurse, house supr. St. Joseph Hosp., Albuquerque, 1958-63; dir. nursing Cibola Hosp., Grants, 1960-64; supr. operating room, dir. med. seminars Carrie Tingley Crippled Children's Hosp., Truth or Consequences, N.Mex., 1964-73; adminstr. Sierra Vista Hosp., Truth or Consequences, 1974-88, pres., 1989—90, adminstr., 1995—2003, CEO, 2008—; clin. nursing mgr. U. N.Mex. Hosp., 1990—94; adminstr. Nor-Lea Hosp., Lovington, N.Mex., 1990-94; with regional ops. divsn. Presbyn. Healthcare Svcs., Albuquerque, 1994—, regional ops., 1994—2003, regional adminstr., 2003—04, intern adminstrn. and spl. projects, 2004—06; founder Rush Health Consulting Svc., 2004—; CEO Trans Health, Inc., Balt., 2006—08; with Rush Consulting, LLC, 2009. Bd. dirs. N.Mex. Blue Cross/Blue Shield, 1977-88, chmn. hosp. relations com., 1983-85, exec. com. 1983—; bd. dirs. Region II Emergency Med. Svcs., CEO Truth Consequences Dissolved Rush Consultancy, LLC, Jera Vista Hosp., 2008 Originating bd. SW Mental Health Ctr., Sierra County, N.Mex., 1975; chmn. Sierra County Personnel Bd., 1983—. Recipient Frank Gabriel award N.Mex. Hosp. Health Sys. Assn., 2003, Govenor's award Emergency Med. Svcs., 2003, Govs.award for Outstanding Woman, N. Mex., 2004; Named Lea County Outstanding Woman, N.Mex. Commn. on Status of Women, Woman of Yr. for Lea County, N.Mex.; 1993. Mem. Am. Coll. Health Care Adminstrs., Sierra County C. of C. (bd. dirs. 1972, 75-76, svc. award 1973, Businesswoman of the Yr. 1973-74), N.Mex. Hosp. Assn. (bd. dirs., sec.-treas., pres.-elect, com. chmn., 1977-88, pres. 1980-81, exec. com., 1980-83, 84-85, recipient meritorius svc. award 1988), N.Mex. So. Hosp. Coun. (sec. 1980-81, pres. 1981-82), Am. Hosp. Assn. (N.Mex. del. 1984-88, regional adv. bd. 1984-88). Republican. Roman Catholic. Avocations: raising thoroughbred horses, cooking. Home: 1100 N Riverside Dr Truth Or Consequences NM 87901-9789 Office Phone: 575-740-2334. Personal E-mail: domrush@gmail.com.

RUSH, GEOFFREY, actor; b. Toowomba, Queensland, Australia, July 6, 1951; m. Jane Menelaus, Nov. 20, 1988; children: Angelica, James. diploma, LittD, U. Queensland. Actor: (plays) Wrong Side of the Moon, 1971, Lock Up Your Daughters, 1972, Assault With a Deadly Weapon, 1972, Twelfth Night, 1972, 1983, 1984, Ruling Class, 1972, You're a Good Man Charlie Brown, 1972, Puss in Boots, 1972, Juno and the Paycock, 1973, Expresso Bongo, 1973, National Health, 1973, The Imaginary Invalid, 1973, Suddenly at Home, 1973, Aladdin, 1973, Hamlet on Ice, 1973, Godspell, 1974, The Rivals, 1974, The Philanthropist, 1974, Present Laughter, 1974, Jack and the Beanstalk, 1975—77, King Lear, 1978, 1988, Point of Departure, 1978, Clowneroonies, 1978, Waiting for Godot, 1979, On Our Selection, 1979, Teeth and Smiles, 1980, Revenger's Tragedy, 1981, No End of Blame, 1982, You Can't Take It With You, 1981, A Midsummer Night's Dream, 1982, 1983, Mother Courage, 1982, Silver Lining, 1982, The Prince of Homburg, 1982, Royal Show, 1983, Blood Wedding, 1983, Netherwood, 1983, 1984, The Marriage of Figaro, 1983, Pal Joey, 1983, The Blind Giant is Dancing, 1983, Sunrise, 1983, Benefactors, 1986, On Parliament Hill, 1987, Shepherd on the Rocks, 1987, The Winter's Tale, 1987, Tristram Shandy-Gent, 1988, Les Enfants du Paradis, 1988, The Importance of Being Earnest, 1988, 1990—91, 1992, Troilus & Cressida, 1989, The Diary of a Madman, 1989, 1990, 1992 (Variety Club award for Stage Actor of Yr., 1989, Sydney Theatre Critics Cir. award for Most Outstanding Performance, 1989, Victorian Green Rm. award for Best Actor, 1990), Marat/Sade, 1990, The Comedy of Errors, 1990, The Government Inspector, 1991, Uncle Vanya, 1992, The Dutch Courtesan, 1993, Oleanna, 1993, Hamlet, 1994, 1995; (Broadway plays) Exit the King, 2009 (Drama Desk award for Outstanding Actor, 2009, Tony award for Best Performance by a Leading Actor in a Play, 2009); (films) Hoodwink, 1980, Starstruck, 1981, Twelfth Night, 1985, On Our Selection, 1994, Five Easy Pizzas, 1994, Children of the Revolution, 1996, Shine, 1996 (BAFTA award Best Actor, 1997, Golden Globe award for Best Performance in Motion Picture, 1997, Screen Actors Guild award for Outstanding Performance, 1997, Acad. award for Best Actor, 1997), Oscar & Lucinda, 1997, Les Misérables, 1998, Shakespeare in Love, 1998 (BAFTA award Best Supporting Actor, 1999), Elizabeth, 1998, Mystery Men, 1999, House on Haunted Hill, 1999, Quills, 2000 (NY Film Critics Online award for best actor, 2000), The Tailor of Panama, 2001, Lantana, 2001, Frida, 2002, The Banger Sisters, 2002, Swimming Upstream, 2003, Ned Kelly, 2003, Finding Nemo (voice), 2003, Pirates of the Caribbean: The Curse of the Black Pearl, 2003, Intolerable Cruelty, 2003, The Life and Death of Peter Sellers, 2004 (Golden Globe award for best actor miniseries or TV movie, 2005, Screen Actors Guild award for best actor in a TV movie or miniseries, 2005, Emmy award for outstanding lead actor in a miniseries or a movie, 2005), Munich, 2005, Candy, 2006, Pirates of the Caribbean: Dead Man's Chest, 2006, Pirates of the Caribbean: At World's End, 2007, Elizabeth: The Golden Age, 2007; (TV series) Consumer Capers, 1979—81, Menotti, 1980—81, The Burning Piano, 1992, Mercury, 1996; dir.: (plays) Clowneroonies, 1978—80, Animal Acts, 1984—86, Teen Ages, 1984—86, Carols-By-Lazerlight, 1984—86, The 1985 Scandals, 1986, Pearls Before Swine, 1986, Pell Mell, 1986, 1987, 1988, The Merry Wives of Windsor, 1987, The Popular Mechanicals, 1987, 1988, 1992, Les Enfants du Paradis, 1989, The Wolf's Banquet, 1989, Popular Mechanicals 2, 1992, Aristophane's Frogs, 1992; co-translator The Government Inspector, 1991, writer (with George Whaley) (TV film) Clowning Around, 1992, (with John Clarke) (play) Aristophane's Frogs, 1992, Call Me Sal, 1996, Children of the Revolution, 1997. Recipient Raymond Langford award, Australian Film Inst., 2009. Office: c/o Creative Artists Agy 9830 Wilshire Blvd Beverly Hills CA 90212-1804*

RUSH, HERMAN E., television executive; b. Phila., June 20, 1929; s. Eugene and Bella (Sacks) R.; m. Joan Silberman, Mar. 18, 1951; children: James Harrison, Mandie Susan. BBA, Temple U., 1950. With Ofcl. Films, 1951-57; owner Flamingo Films, 1957-60; with Creative Mgmt. Assocs., NYC, 1960-71, pres. TV divsn., 1964-71, exec. v.p. parent co., dir., 1964-71; ind. prodr., 1971-75; prodr. Wolper Orgn., 1975-76; pres. Herman Rush Assocs., Inc. (Rush-Flaherty Agy. subs.), 1977-78; CEO Marble Arch TV, LA, 1979—80; pres. Columbia Pictures TV, Burbank, Calif., 1980-87; chmn., CEO Coca-Cola Telecom., 1987-88, Rush Assocs., Inc., Burbank, 1988—, Katz/Rush Entertainment Group, Beverly Hills, Calif., 1990-96, New Tech. Entertainment, LLC, Beverly Hills, 1996—, Internet Content Provider Cap. Fin. Corp., chmn. emeritus; mng. ptnr. Media Consulting Assocs. CEO Infotainment Internat., Inc.; pres., chmn. Royal Animated Art, Inc.; co-owner, exec. prodr. The Montel Williams Talk Show, 1991-; mem. bd. advisors Smart Video Techs., Inc.; CEO Creative Content Providers, LLC Trustee Sugar Ray Robinson Youth Found., 1967-75; dir. Entertainment Industries Coun.; pres. Retarded Infant Svcs., N.Y.C., 1957-63; bd. dirs. U.S. Marshall's Svc. Found., Just Say No Found.; conferee White House Conf. for a Drug Free America, 1987, 88. Mem. Acad. TV Arts and Scis., Hollywood Radio and TV Soc., Producers Caucus. Clubs: Friars, Filmex. Office: 8871 Burton Way 305 Los Angeles CA 90048 Office Phone: 310-553-6145. Personal E-mail: hermanrush@aol.com.

RUSH, JULIA ANN HALLORAN (MRS. RICHARD HENRY RUSH), artist, writer; b. St. Louis, Oct. 25, 1927; d. Edward Roosevelt and Flavia Hadley (Griffin) Halloran; m. Richard Henry Rush, Aug. 15, 1956; 1 child, Sallie Haywood. Student Washington U., St. Louis, 1945-47; BA, George Washington U., 1949. Model John Robert Powers Agy., 1950; ptnr. Rush and Halloran, Inc., 1954-57, v.p. 1957-58; sec.-treas., dir. N.Am. Acceptance Corp., 1956-58; articles in Wall St. transcript, 1971—; research asst. bi-weekly newsletter Art/Antiques Investment Report, 1973—. One-woman shows: Fort Amador Officers Club, Panama Canal Zone, El Panama Hotel, Panama, George Washington U., Statler Hotel, Roosevelt Hotel, Washington, Newspaper Women's Club, Washington, Waukegan Library, Ill., Epworth Heights Hotel, Ludington, Mich.; exhibited in group shows: Panama Art League, Corcoran Gallery; represented in permanent collections: U. Panama; also pvt. collections; illustrator: Antiques As An Investment (author Richard H. Rush), 1968; research asst.: Investments You Can Live With and Enjoy (author: Richard H. Rush), 1974, 2d, edit., 1975, 3d edit., 1976; photographer: Automobiles as an Investment, 1982; Investing in Classic Cars, 1984. Recipient 1st prize (Panama) Newspaper Women's Club, 1953; First Prize Panama Art League, 1953. Mem. DAR, Nat. League Am. Penwomen, Florence Crittenton Circle (rec. sec. 1968-69), Kappa Kappa Gamma. Club: Washington, Royal Palm Yacht (No. Ft. Myers, Fla.), Boca West Golf and Country (Boca Raton, Fla.)

RUSH, LORETTA G., biology professor; d. Floyd Ray Head and Anna Pauline Carter; children: Annalee Caroline Parks, Kaite Gayle Parks, Micheal Sean Hood, Jennie Rayline Hood. MS, East Ctrl. U., Ada, Okla., MEd, 2004. Cert. LVN Calif., 1979. Sci. instr. Murray State Coll., Tishomingo, Okla., 2004—05; prof. life scis. Seminole State Coll., Okla., 2007—. Instr. upward bound prog. Chickasaw Nation, Tishomingo, 2000—04. Mem. The Nature Conservancy, Arlington, Va., 2001—. Avocation: travel.

RUSH, MICHAEL F., human services professor; b. Chadron, Nebr., Jan. 29, 1956; s. Bill David and Donna Mae Rush; m. Sherry L. Woodard, July 23, 2001. M, Kearney State Coll., Nebr., 1984. Lic. mental health practitioner Nebr., 1994. Mental health therapist South Ctrl. Counseling, Kearney, 1987—91; human svcs. instr. Met. CC, Omaha, 1991—. With Underwood Hills Presbyn. Ch., Omaha, 2007—. Recipient Tchr. Appreciation award, Phi Theta Kappa Honor Soc., 1999, 2000, Learning is our Purpose award, Met. CC, 2005. Mem.: ACA, APA, Nat. Orgn. Human Svcs. Liberal. Presbyterian. Avocations: reading, movies, music. Home: 810 N 74th St Omaha NE 68114 Office: Met CC PO Box 3777 Omaha NE 68103 Personal E-mail: mrush01_2@msn.com. Business E-Mail: mrush@mccneb.edu.

RUSH, RICHARD HENRY, finance company executive, educator, writer; b. NYC, Mar. 6, 1915; s. Henry Frederick and Bessie (Vreeland) R.; m. Julia Ann Halloran, Aug. 15, 1956; 1 dau., Sallie Haywood. BA summa cum laude, Dartmouth Coll., 1937, MCS, 1938; MBA with highest distinction, Harvard U., 1941, DCS (Littauer fellow), 1942. Chief economist, chmn. planning com. All Am. Aviation (U.S. Air), 1943—45; dir. aviation U.S. Bur. Fgn. and Domestic Commerce, 1945—46; dir. aircraft divsn. Nat. Security Resources Bd., 1948—51; Washington rep. to J. Paul Getty, 1951—52; ptnr. Rush & Halloran, 1953—58; pres., chmn. bd. N.Am. Acceptance Corp., Atlanta, Washington, 1956—59; owner Richard H. Rush Enterprises, Greenwich, Conn., Washington, 1953—73; prof., chmn. dept. finance and investments Sch. Bus. Adminstrn., Am. U., Washington, 1967—70, Sch. Bus. Adminstrn. Am. U., Washington, 1977—79. Author: Art as an Investment, 1961, A Strategy of Investing for Higher Return, 1962, The Techniques of Becoming Wealthy, 1963, Antiques as an Investment, 1968, The Wrecking Operation: Phase One, 1972, Investments You Can Live With and Enjoy, 1976, Techniques of Becoming Wealthy, 1977, Automobiles as an Investment, 1982, Selling Collectibles, 1982, Collecting Classic Cars for Profit and Capital Gain, 1984, Collector Cars: Classics for the New Century, 2001; contbr. over 700 articles to newspapers, mags. and profl. jours.; editor series of books on starting businesses for U.S. Dept. Commerce; contbg. editor Wall St. Transcript, 1971-97, Art/Antiques Investment Report, 1972-97. Trustee, exec. com. Finch Coll., 1968-72. Recipient Pres.'s med., CCNY, 1997. Mem. AAUP, Am. Mktg. Assn. (chmn. nat. com.), Am. Econ. Assn., Am. Statis. Assn., Internat. Platform Assn., Harvard Club N.Y.C., Royal Palm Yacht Club (Ft. Myers), Phi Beta Kappa, Phi Kappa Phi, Omicron Delta Kappa. Episcopalian. Achievements include Richard H. Rush Library at Edison State college, Fort Myers, Florida, named after him.

RUSH, RICHARD R., academic administrator; Pres. Calif. State U. Channel Islands, Camarillo. Office: Calif State U Channel Islands 1 University Dr Camarillo CA 93012 Business E-Mail: richard.rush@csuci.edu.

RUSH, SOPHIA A., law educator; b. Stroudsburg, Pa., Mar. 2, 1964; d. Robert and Karen Rush; m. Justin Bobby, Apr. 15, 1999; children: Eric Bobby, Thomas Bobby. BS in Criminal Justice, Pa. State U., Univ. Pk., 1982, JD, 1989; MS in Crime, Law and Justice, Louisville U., 1985. Bar: NY 1990, US Dist. Ct. (ea. dist.) NY 1995, US Ct. Appeals (8th cir.) 1992; diplomate Am. Bd. Surgery, 1995, TEST CHANGE. Asst. prof. law Queen's Coll., NY, 1985—88, Bklyn. Law Sch., 1989, assoc. prof. law, 1990—95; prof. law Pace Law Sch., NY, 1996—2002, Harvard U., 2002—. Vis. prof. Kingston Sch. Law, London, 1998, Preston Sch. Bus. and Adminstrn., England, 1999, Duke U., 2002; presenter in field. Author: (audio tape) How to Find and Keep a Mate, 1988 (First Nat. Prize of Natural Sciences, 1982), (video tape) How to Find a Mate, 1990, The Happiness of Pursuit, 1994, How to Deal with Difficult People, 1992, (books) Dealing With People You Can't Stand, 1994, 1994, Digital Publishing on e World, Discussions of Problem People and Happiness, 1995, Life By Design, 1999, Dealing with Relatives, 2002;: Love Thy Customer, 2005, Telecare: Exceptional Service on the Phone, 1998; co-author: (audio tape) How to Deal with Difficult People, 1987, video tape, (CD-Rom) The Leadership Series: Difficult People, 1997, Living Your Life by Design, 2003. Active PTA, 1996—2001; Sunday sch. tchr. Good Shepherd Ch., 1982—; bd. dirs. NY Hist. Soc., 1994—. Commdg. officer 9823 Squadron USAR, 1976—77. Recipient Disting. Prof. award, NYU, 2007; named to NYU Hall of Fame. Mem.: ASPCA (mem. vol. com. 2005), ABA (exec. dir. 2004—06), Kings County Bar Assn., NY Bar Assn. Conservative. Roman Catholic. Achievements include research in technological progress and its effects in the banking industry. Avocations: swimming, horseback riding, cliff diving, skydiving. Office Phone: 800-473-7020.

RUSH, W. MARVIN, trucking executive; children: W.M. (Rusty), Robin. CEO, chmn. Rush Enterprises Inc., San Antonio, 1965—2006, chmn., 2006—; founder World Wide Tires, several leasing companies, insurance agy., fin. co., hunting ranch. Office: Rush Enterprises Inc PO Box 34630 San Antonio TX 78265-4630

RUSH, W.M. (RUSTY), trucking executive; V.p. to exec. v.p. Rush Enterprises, New Braunfels, Tex., 1990—95, pres., 1995—2001, pres., COO, 2001—06, pres., CEO, 2006—. Office: Rush Enterprises 555 IH-35 S New Braunfels TX 78130

RUSHDI, AHMAD A., systems engineer; b. Jeddah, Saudi Arabia, 1981; BSc, Cairo U., 2002, MSc, 2004; PhD, U. Calif., Davis, 2008. Rsch. & devel. engr. Engring. Office Integrated Projects, Cairo, 2003; tchg. asst. Am. U. Cairo, 2003—04; hardware and signal integrity engr. Cisco Sys., Inc. Gigabit Sys. Bus. Unit, San Jose, Calif., 2008—. Recipient Best Tchg. Asst. award, Electronics Engring. Assn., Am. U. Cairo, 2003, Sci. Soc. Electronics & Elec. Comm., Cairo U., 2003—04, Acad. Achievement award, Cairo U., 1997—2002. Mem.: IEEE, Cal Aggie Alumni Assn., UC Davis, Soc. Indsl. & Applied Math. Achievements include research in multirate and statistical signal processing; wireless MIMO/OFDM communications; bioinformatics and genomic signal processing; development of signal and power integrity procedures; graphic design tools. Avocations: squash, swimming, soccer. Office: Cisco Sys Inc 170 West Tasman Dr San Jose CA 95134 Business E-Mail: aarushdi@ieee.org.

RUSHDIE, SIR SALMAN (AHMED SALMAN RUSHDIE), writer, educator; b. Mumbai, June 19, 1947; s. Anis Ahmed and Negin (Butt) Rushdie; m. Clarissa Luard, 1976 (div. 1987); 1 child, Zafar; m. Marianne Wiggins, 1988 (div. 1993); m. Elizabeth West (div.); 1 child, Milan; m. Padma Parvati Lakshmi, Apr. 17, 2004 (div. 2007). MA in Hist., with honors, King's Coll., Cambridge U., Eng., 1968; PhD (hon.), Chapman U., Orange, Calif. Freelance advt. copywriter Ogilvy & Mather, Ayer Barker; disting. writer in residence English Dept. Emory U., Atlanta, 2007—. Pres. PEN Am. Ctr., 2004—06; hon. prof. MIT. Author: (books) Grimus, 1975, Midnight's Children, 1981 (Booker prize for fiction, 1981, English Speaking Union Lit. award, 1981, James Tait Black Meml. prize, 1982, Booker of Bookers prize, 1993, Best of Booker prize, 2008), Shame, 1983 (Prix de Meilleur Livre Etranger, 1984), The Jaguar Smile: A Nicaraguan Journey, 1987, The Satanic Verses, 1988 (Whitbread Novel award, 1988, German Author of Yr. award, 1988), Haroun and the Sea of Stories, 1990 (Writer's Guild prize for children's fiction, 1991), Imaginary Homelands: Essays and Criticism, 1981-1991, 1992, Homeless by Choice (with R. Jhabvala and V. S. Naipaul), 1992, East, West, 1994, The Moor's Last Sigh, 1995 (Whitbread Novel award, 1995, Brit. Book awards Author of Yr., 1995), The Ground Beneath Her Feet, 1999, Fury, 2001, Step Across This Line: Collected Nonfiction 1992 - 2002, 2002, Shalimar the Clown, 2005, The Enchantress of Florence, 2008; editor: Best American Short Stories, 2008. Recipient Hutch Crossword Fiction prize, India, India Abroad Lifetime Achievement award, Outstanding Lifetime Achievement in cultural humanism, Harvard U., Kurt Tucholsky prize, Sweden, 1992, Prix Colette, Switzerland, 1993, State Prize for European Lit., Austria, 1994, Aristeion Lit. prize, European Union, 1996, Mantova Lit. prize, 1997, Budapest Grand prize lit., 1998, Commandeur de l'Ordre des Arts et des Lettres, 1999, Best of Booker award, 2008; named an Honorary Knight Comdr. Most Excellent Order of the Brit. Empire, Her Majesty Queen Elizabeth II, 2008. Fellow: Royal Soc. Lit.; mem.: AAAL (hon.). Address: Author Mail Random House UK 20 Vauxhall Bridge Rd London SW1V 2SA England Office: Emory U English Dept 1535-003-1AA 201 Dowman Dr Atlanta GA 30322 Business E-Mail: salman.rushdie@emory.edu.

RUSHER, WILLIAM ALLEN, writer, commentator, columnist; b. Chgo., July 19, 1923; s. Evan Singleton and Verna (Self) R. AB, Princeton U., 1943; JD, Harvard U., 1948; DLit (hon.), Nathaniel Hawthorne Coll., 1973. Bar: N.Y. 1949. Assoc. Shearman & Sterling & Wright, NYC, 1948-56; spl. counsel fin. com. N.Y. Senate, 1955; assoc. counsel internal security subcom. U.S. Senate, 1956-57; pub., v.p. Nat. Review mag., NYC, 1957-88, also bd. dirs.; Disting. fellow The Claremont Inst., 1989—. Mem. Adv. Task Force on Civil Disorders, 1972. Author: Special Counsel, 1968, (with Mark Hatfield and Arlie Schardt) Amnesty?, 1973, The Making of the New Majority Party, 1975, How to Win Arguments, 1981, The Rise of the Right, 1984, The Coming Battle for the Media, 1988; editor: The Ambiguous Legacy of the Enlightenment, 1995; columnist Universal Press Syndicate, 1973-82, Newspaper Enterprise Assn., 1982—; played role of Advocate in TV program The Advocates, 1970-74. Chmn.,bd. mem., bd. dirs. Media Rsch. Ctr., Washington, 2001-2008, Nat. Rev. Bd., 1957-88, 90-2008; bd. advisors Ashbrook Ctr., Ashland, Ohio, past chmn.; past vice chmn. Am. Conservative Union; past trustee Pacific Legal Found., Sacramento. Served as 2d lt. to capt., USAAF, 1943-45, India-Burma Theater. Recipient Disting. Citizen award NYU Sch. Law, 1973. Mem. ABA, Univ. Club (NYC), Met. Club (Washington). Anglican. Home and Office: 1661 Pine St Apt 933 San Francisco CA 94109

RUSHFORTH, ANN FAY, artist, educator; b. Tampa, Fla., July 17, 1944; d. Robert George Rushforth and Alla Petrovna Riordan; m. Reid Johnson Perryman, May 13, 2000; m. John William Semko, Nov. 11, 1971 (div.); 1 child, Tao Alexandre Semko. BA, George Wash. U., 1962—66; MFA, Antioch U., 1980. Asst. to dir. of film and broadcasting Smithsonian Instn., Washington, 1967—68; adminstrv. asst. Am. Craft Council-Bennington Exhbns., Bennington, Vt., 1972; asst. mgr. Am. Craft Council-Rhinebeck Exhbns., Rhinebeck, NY, 1973—74; dir. pub. rels. Scope Gallery, Torpedo Factory, Alexandria, Va., 1975, pres., 1976—77, bd. dirs., 1978; chmn. dept. art Stoneridge H.S., Bethesda, Md., 1981—84; v.p. Foundry Gallery, Washington, 1986; dir. Pavo Real Gallery, Washington, 1987—88; gallery dir. Arise Gallery of Asian Art and Antiques, Washington, 1988—90; spl. projects photographer Woodrow Wilson Ho. Mus., Washington; arts instr. Duke Ellington Sch. of Arts, Washington, 1990—91, Visual Systems, Rockville, Md., 1991, Fillmore Art Ctr., Washington, 1991; executive dir. The Art Barn Assn., Washington, 1991—93; freelance master paintings copyist Nat. Gallery of Art, Washington, 1993—94; arts instr., 2005—. Rep. Dupont Cir. Consortium of Galleries, Washington, 1986; art instr. Md. Coll. of Art and Design, Dept. Continuing Edn., Rockville, 1990—91; dir., devel. officer R St. Gallery, Washington, 1992—93; conservator, appraiser Artsserve, Ltd., Newnan, 1995—2008; co-founder Contemporary Arts Alliance, Newnan, 2003—; art instr. The Pottery Wheel, Newnan, Ga., 2005—. Dir.: Carrollton Arts Guild Exhbns.; art critic: Eyewash Newpaper, 1990—91; editor: (exhibition catalog) Sculpture to Touch: For the Sight Impaired, 1987, Md. Craft Coun. News, 1976—78; Wash. Post Mag., 1977, Woodrow Wilson House Mus. Annual Report, Nat. Trust Hist. Preservation, 1987, Greater Chattanooga Artists, The Bureau, 1999, CABIA Arts Calendar, 1999, one-woman shows include Everson Mus. Art Gallery, Syracuse, NY, 1978, Montpelier Cultural Ctr., Md., 1981, Foundry Gallery, Washington, DC, 1986, In Town Gallery, Chattanooga, 2000, exhibited in group shows at NE Juried Exhbn. 12, Rhinebeck, NY, 1974—77, Frederick Wholesale Fair 3, Md., 1975—77, Fairtree Gallery, NYC, 1976, Inc. Gallery, 1976, Concepts Gallery, Ridgewood, NJ, 1976, Scope Gallery, Alexandria, Va., 1976 (Best in Show), 1977, 1984, Montgomery Coll. Gallery, Rockville, Md., 1977, US Govt. Svc. Adminstrn. Invitational Exhbn., Washington, DC, 1977, Westlake Gallery, White Plains, NY, 1977, 1980, 1983, Coqui Galleries, Westport, Conn., 1977, 1978, 1979, Fredericksburg Gallery of Modern Art, Va., 1977, Jelly Mill Gallery, Manchester, Vt., 1981, Md. Nat. Capitol Park and Planning Commn., 1980, VAC Gallery, Columbia, Md., 1981, Visual Arts Ctr., 1982, WWAC Gallery, Washington, DC, 1982, 1985, 1985, 1986, Nat. Capital AMCCAP Festival, 1984 (Second Place, Hon. Mention in Sculpture), 1993, Design Ctr., 1984, Art League Gallery, Alexandria, 1985, Art Barn Gallery, Washington, DC, 1985, 1992, 1992, 1993, Signature Galleries Invitational, Boston and Hyannis, Mass., 1985, Concepts '85, Margate, NJ, 1985, Martin Luther King Libr. Gallery, Washington, DC, 1986, R St. Gallery, 1989, Rockland Ctr., Ellicott City, Md., 1989, Foundry Gallery, Washington, DC, 1989, Jackson Sch. Studios, 1990, 1991, 1992, 901 E St. Gallery, 1991, 1993, Capital Arts Inc. Georgetown Visitation Sch., 1992, 1993, Georgetown Holiday Inn, 1992, The Spy Club, 1993, Universal N. Gallery, 1993, 1993, Washington Project for the Arts, 1993, Jackson Art Ctr., Studio #21, 1993, Gallery West, Alexandria, 1993, Corcoran Sch. Gallery, Washington, DC, 1993, Avery Gallery, Atlanta, Ga., 1995, Blair Voltz Exhbns., Atlanta, 1997, The Stalls, Bennett St., 1997, Grandview Gallery, 1997, Waterhouse Pavilion, Chattanooga, 1998, AVA Gallery, 1998, 1999, Urban Art Inst., 2000, Panoply Showhouse, Newnan, Ga., 2001, Tenn. Valley Art Mus., Tuscumbia, Ala., 2002, Arts Clayton Gallery, Jonesboro, Ga., 2002, Atlanta Arts Club, 2002, Forum Gallery at Defoor Centre, Atlanta, 2002, 2004, Atlanta Coll. Art, Coweta County, Ga., 2003, Keptever Gallery, Peachtree City, Ga., 2004, Mandeville Gallery, Carrollton, Ga., 2004, Jackalope's Gallery, Carrollton, 2004, MECCA Festival for the Arts, 2004, Carrollton Artists Guild, 2004, one-woman shows include Roush Gallery, Carolton Cultural Arts Ctr., 2008, exhibited in group shows at Carrollton Arts Ctr., 2005, exhibitions include HMR Engring. Inc., Alexandria, 1993, Meml. Hosp. Foyer, Chattanooga, 1999, UTC Faculty Club, 1999, Ga. State Fair, Perry, 2001, prin. works include St. John the Wonderworker, Patron St. Altarpiece and Icon of St. Brigid, Abess & Healer, St. John the Wonderworker Ea. Orthodox Ch., Atlanta, 1996, Christus Rex, Ceramic Altarpiece, St. Paul's Episc. Ch., Newnan, 2006. Lector St.Paul's Episcopal Ch., Newnan, 2004—06. Mem.: US Nat. Com. UNIFEM (east Fla. chpt. 1st v.p.), Broward Art Guild (bd. mem.), Am. Ceramic Soc. Potter's Coun., Nat. Coun. Edn. for Ceramic Arts, Carrollton Artist Guild (exhbn. dir. 2005). Libertarian. Episcopalian. Avocations: physical fitness, travel, art history, art. Office Phone: 561-832-1776 ext. 23. Personal E-mail: annfayrushforth@hotmail.com. Business E-Mail: ann.rushforth@armoryart.org.

RUSHING, JOHN ALAN, business educator; s. Thomas Jefferson and Mary Emma Rushing; m. Sherre Lynn Garvin, Nov. 23, 1963; children: John Alan Jr., Laura Ann. M internat. bus. adminstrn., Nova U., 1990; D in Bus. Adminstrn., Nova Southeastern, 2001. Pres. Kiwi Rsch. and Devel., Ft. Lauderdale, Fla., 1987—89; adj. faculty Broward C.C., Davie, Fla., 1992—99; corp. sec. Geep Corp., Oxford, Miss., 1989—2005; asst. prof. Barry U., Miami Shores, Fla., 1989—2003, asst. dean for academic affairs, 2003—, regional dir., 2006—. Author: Adventure Capital, 2001. Chair bus. devel. Davie C. of C., Davie, Fla., 1997, chair edn. conf., 1999, mem., 1990—99. Mem.: Am. Soc. of Devel., Acad. of Internat. Bus., Sigma Beta Delta Internat. Bus. Honor Soc., Gold Key Honor Soc. Avocation: radio controlled boats and airplanes. Office Phone: 850-385-2279. Office Fax: 850-385-7576. Business E-Mail: jrushing@mail.barry.edu.

RUSHING, TONNIE AUSTIN PAGE, musician, educator; b. Hartwell, Ga., Mar. 6, 1940; d. George Wilson and Ruth Smith Page; m. Roger Kendall Vichery, June 18, 1960; children: George Kendall, Carol Page; m. Charles Maynard Rushing, Aug. 18, 1979; stepchildren: Joan E., Brian C., Susanne E. BS in Edn., Athens State Coll., Ga., 1973; cert. in Computer Tech., Trident Tech. Coll., 1992, Sylvan Learning Ctr., 1996; cert. in Sign Lang., Trident Tech. Coll., 1997. Musician, Ga., 1958—; prin., owner Opus 11 George Bed & Breakfast, 1988—97; afternoon activities dir. O'Quinn Preschool-Kindergarten, 2001; piano studio tchr., 2007. Dir. music Summer Stock Theater, Morristown, Tenn., 1969; music educator Covenant Sch. Fine Arts Enrichment, 1976—79; music dir. Young Charleston Theatre Co., 1988, 96; mem. founding com. Covenant Fine Arts Enrichment Sch., Decatur, 1976; mem. adv. com. Coun. Arts John C. Calhoun State Coll., Decatur; mem. Greater Anderson Musical Arts Consortium Concert and Chamber Choir, Anderson, SC, 2006. Singer: North Ala. Charleston Symphony, St. Micheal's Ch., Grace Episc. Ch., Choir Eng. Tour, 1981—2002; musician: French Protestant Ch., 1988—96; author: Huguenots and the Legacy, 1994; dir.: (recording) Huguenot Psalter, 1991; jacket cover, Huguenot Psalter, 1991. Pres. Decatur Civic Chorus; vol. Crisis Ctr. Mental Health Ctr., Decatur, 1971—79; mem. comprehensive planning com. City Hartwell, Ga., 2003; bd. dirs. Preservation Soc., 2004, Hart County Hist. Soc., 2004; with Hartwell Christmas Tour of Homes, 2006; chair Olde Time Singing, Hartwell Hist. Soc. Fundraiser, 2006; mem. Greater Anderson Musical Consortium Concert Choir, 2006—07, Greater Anderson Musical Consortium Chamber Choir, 2006—07; music asst. 2d Presbyn. Ch., Charleston, SC, 1988; sect. leader St. Michaels Ch., Charleston, 1998—2001; elder Hartwell 1st Presbyn. Ch., 2004; founder, dir. Youth and Sunshine Choir, Hartwell Presbyn. Ch., 2003, Organist Faith Lutheran Ch., 2007; bd. dirs. Charleston Symphony Orch. Chorus. Mem.: PTA, Gamac Concert Choir &Chamber Choir, Greater Anderson Musical Arts Consortium, Am. Guild Organists, Presbyn. Assn. Musicians, Nat. Assn. Mental Illness, Charleston County Med. Aux., Heartwell Historical Soc. Fundraiser (chair 2006), Hartwell Women's Club (v.p. 2006—07, pres. 2008), Sigma Alpha Iota. Republican. Home: 175 E Johnson St Hartwell GA 30643 Home Phone: 706-376-7342. Personal E-mail: cmandtpr@hartcom.net.

RUSHTON, ALAN R., physician, medical researcher, historian; b. Oak Park, Ill., Mar. 10, 1949; s. Raymond H. and D. Loree (Swan) R.; m. Nancy Spencer, May 5, 1973; children: Andrew, Daniel. AB in Chemistry, Earlham Coll., Richmond, Ind., 1971; PhD in Genetics, U. Chgo., 1975, MD, 1977. Diplomate Am. Bd. Pediatrics, Am. Bd. Med. Genetics. Resident, intern Yale U.-New Haven Hosp., Conn., 1977-80; physician Hunterdon Med. Ctr., Flemington, NJ, 1980—; assoc. clin. prof. pediatrics Robert Wood Johnson Med. Sch., New Brunswick, NJ, 1980—. Lectr. genetics Princeton U., NJ, 1980-84; adj. prof. Med. U. Ams., Nevis, West Indies. Author: Genetics and Medicine in the United States 1800-1922, 1994, Royal Maladies: Inherited Diseases In The Ruling House Of Europe, 2008, Genetics and Medicine in Great Britain 1600 to 1938, 2009. Fellow Am. Acad. Pediatrics, Am. Coll. Med. Genetics, NY Acad. Medicine, Royal Soc. Medicine; mem. Am. Assn. History Medicine, History Sci. Soc. Office: Hunterdon Pediatric Assocs 6 Sand Hill Rd Ste 202 Flemington NJ 08822-4600 Office Phone: 908-788-6468. Personal E-mail: arrdoc@aol.com.

RUSHTON, GERARD, geography professor, researcher; s. James and Alice Rushton; m. Carolyn Arnell Lucken, Sept. 21, 1963; children: Edward James, John Palmer. BA, U. Wales, Aberystwyth, 1959, MA, 1961; PhD, U. Iowa, 1964. Asst. prof. McMaster U., Hamilton, Ontario, Canada, 1964—67, Mich. State U., Lansing, 1967—69; full prof. U. Iowa, Iowa City, 1969—. Contbr. articles to profl. jours. Cons. Iowa City Cmty. Sch. Bd., 1990—. Mem.: Assn. Am. Geographers (editl. bd. mem. 2000—03). Achievements include research in methods of location analysis and their applications in health. Office: Univ Iowa Dept Geography 316 Jessup Hall Iowa City IA 52242 Office Fax: 319-335-2725. Business E-Mail: gerard-rushton@uiowa.edu.

RUSKELL, TIM, professional sports team executive; m. Linda Ruskell; children: Samantha, Jack. B in Comm., U. South Fla., Tampa. Scout Saskatchewan Roughriders, Can. Football League, 1983—85; dir. scouting Tampa Bay Bandits, US Football League, 1985—86; regional scout Tampa Bay Buccaneers, 1987—92, dir. coll. scouting, 1992—2000, dir. player pers., 2001—03; asst. gen. mgr. Atlanta Falcons, 2004; pres. football ops., gen. mgr. Seattle Seahawks, 2005—. Office: Seattle Seahawks 12 Seahawks Way Renton WA 98056*

RUSKIN, JOSEPH RICHARD, actor, director; b. Haverhill, Mass., Apr. 14, 1924; s. Ely and Betty Edith (Chaimson) Schlafman; m. Patricia Herd, 1959 (div. 1976); m. Barbara Greene; 1 child, Alicia Ruskin Bucklan. Grad., Carnegie Inst. Tech., 1949. Founder Rochester Arena Theatre, NY, 1949-52. Actor: NY stage plays, 1949—52; (plays) Theater Group, UCLA, Mark Taper Forum, 1959; (films) Fall of Legs Diamond, 1959, Magnificent Seven, 1960, Escape from Zahrein, 1963, Robin and the Seven Hoods, 1965, Prizzi's Honor, 1985, Longshot, 1987, Indecent Proposal, 1992, Spider-Man, 1994, (voice) Star Trek: Insurrection, 1998, King Cobra, 1999, The Scorpion King, 2002, The Streetsweeper, 2002, IceMaker, 2003, Smokin' Aces, 2006; (TV series) Untouchables, Land of the Giants, The Twilight Zone, Mission Impossible, Charlie's Angels, Knight Rider, Spider-Man, Star Trek, Alias; dir.: (plays) Houston Alley, 1965—69. With USNR, 1943—46. Mem.: SAG, AFTRA, Actors Equity Assn. (mem. nat. coun.). Home: 1326 Devon Ave Los Angeles CA 90024-5346

RUSKIN, ROBERT STERLING, educational association administrator; b. Washington, Nov. 27, 1945; s. Robert Edward and Thelma (Gipe) R.; m. Rebecca Lynne Wilson, Aug. 11, 1967; 1 child, Brant Edward. BA, Washington Coll., Chestertown, Md., 1967; MA, W.Va. U., 1969, PhD, 1971. Lic. psychologist Va., D.C. Prof. dept. psychology Georgetown U., Washington, 1971-86, chmn. dept. psychology, 1976-85, dir. Ctr. for Personalized Instrn., 1977-80; dir. Teaching Resource Ctr., 1985-86; chief psychol. assessor leadership devel. U. Md., College Park, 1984—; prin. investigator and project dir., consortium univs. rsch fellows program U.S. Army Rsch. Inst., Washington, Alexandria, 1985—; nat. rsch, fellow U.S. Dept. Edn., Washington, 1986-87; affiliate prof. psychology George Mason U., Washington, 1989—; prin. investigator Consortium & Office of Substance Abuse Prevention, Washington, 1990-93; dir. programs and rsch. Consortium of Univs. of Washington Metro. Area, 1987-88, v.p., 1989—. Psychol. cons. DuPont Corp., Seaford, Del., 1986-88; psychol. cons. Consortium of Univs. of D.C., 1984—; cons. in field; rep. of U.S. to UNESCO Planning Meeting, Paris, 1979. Co-author: Behavioral Instruction: An Evaluative Review, 1977; editor manuscript: Consortium Research Fellows Program; editor The Jour. of Personalized Instrn., 1975-81, Revista a Tecnologia Educativa, 1976-83. Battelle Inst. Disting. Acad. Rsch. fellow U.S. Army Rsch. Inst., 1984-86,Commendation for Meritorious Rsch. & Sci. award APA, 2008. Fellow APA, Am. Psychol. Soc. (charter); mem. AAAS, D.C. Psychol. Assn., Va. Psychol. Assn., Psi Chi. Methodist. Avocations: golf, fishing. Home: 309 W Alex Ave Alexandria VA 22302 Office: Consortium of Univs of Wash 1 Dupont Cir NW Washington DC 20036-1110 Office Phone: 703-998-7220. Personal E-mail: robertruskin@aol.com. Business E-Mail: robert.ruskin@consultiam_research_fellows.org.

RUSMISEL, STEPHEN RAYMOND, lawyer; b. NYC, Jan. 27, 1946; s. R. Raymond and Esther Florence (Kutz) R.; m. Beirne Donaldson, Sept. 6, 1980 (div. Jan. 1984); 1 child, Margo Alexander; m. Melissa J. MacLeod, Aug. 24, 1985 (div. Oct. 1996); children: Benjamin William, Eric Scot Kunze, Erin Lea Kunze; m. Teresa R. Paterniti, June 28, 1997; 1 child, Sarah J. Lamendola. AB, Yale U., 1968; JD, U. Va., 1971. Bar: NY 1972, US Ct. Appeals (2d cir.) 1974, US Dist. Ct. (so. dist.) NY 1975. Assoc. Winthrop, Stimson, Putnam & Roberts, NYC, 1971-80, ptnr., 1980-2000, Pillsbury Winthrop Shaw Pittman LLP, NYC, 2001—. Aux. officer Bedminster Twp. Police, NJ, 1976—. Mem. Practicing Law Inst., Am. Arbitration Assn. (arbitrator 1976—), Far Hills Polo Club (Annandale, NJ), Ausable Club (St. Huberts, NY), Phi Delta Phi. Republican. Avocations: flying, carpentry, gardening, poetry. Home: Shadowline Farm Bedminster NJ 07921 Office: Pillsbury Winthrop Shaw Pittman LLP 1540 Broadway New York NY 10036-4039 Home Phone: 908-722-6172; Office Phone: 212-858-1000. Business E-Mail: stephen.rusmisel@pillsburylaw.com.

RUSS, EDMOND VINCENT, JR., marketing professional; b. Washington, Feb. 14, 1944; s. Edmond V. and Thayer Kennedy (Thompson) R.; m. Tena Marie Loveland, Dec. 26, 1982; children: Jamie Russ Solanics, E.V. Russ III, Christina T. Russ, Cory S. Russ. BA, Kent State U., Ohio, 1966; MBA, U. Pitts., 1967. Dir. mktg. Borg-Warner Ednl. Systems, Niles, Ill., 1969-74; v.p. mktg. Rusty Jones Inc., Chgo., 1974-83; gen. mgr. Signed, Sealed and Delivered, Melrose Park, Ill., 1983-86; v.p. mktg. Merchant Network Inc., Chgo., 1986-90; dir. mktg. Am. Appraisal Assocs., Milw., 1990-93, Pricewaterhouse Coopers, 1993-2001; ptnr., chief mktg. officer Grant Thornton LLP, 2001—. Mem. Am. Mktg. Assn., Assn. Acctg. Marketers, Bus. Mktg. Assn., Strategic Mgmt. Assn., Vintage Sports Car Drivers Assn., Porsche Club Am. Avocations: tennis, community theater, sports car racing. E-mail: planetera@comcast.net.

RUSS, JAMES MATTHIAS, lawyer; b. Duluth, Minn., Sept. 20, 1929; s. Matthias James and Agnes Margaret (Jerina) R.; m. Nanelle Davis, June 27, 1953; children: Tanya, Robin, Sarah, Claudia, Janine, Monica, Matthias James, Kateri. AB cum laude, Spring Hill Coll., 1955; JD, Georgetown U., 1957. Bar: D.C., 1957, Fla., 1958, U.S. Dist. Ct. (no., so. and mid. dists.) Fla., U.S. Ct. Appeals (5th and 11th cirs.), U.S. Supreme Ct.; cert. criminal trial lawyer 1987, criminal appellate lawyer 1992. County solicitor Orange County, Fla., 1961-65; pvt. practice Orlando. Lectr. criminal law and legal ethics seminars. Contbr. articles to profl. jours. Trustee Orange County Legal Aid Soc.; chmn. The Chester Bedell Meml. Found., 1997-98. Recipient Tobias Simon Pro Bono Svc. award Fla. Supreme Ct., 1997, Joseph W. Durocher award Ctrl. Fla. Criminal Def. Lawyers Assn., 2003. Master, Am. Inns of Ct.; fellow Am. Coll. Trial Lawyers, Am. Bd. Criminal Lawyers; mem. ABA (criminal justice sect.-speedy trial com. 1976-77, com. on privacy 1982-83, def. function com. 1983-89, chmn. 1987-89), The Fla. Bar (chmn. criminal law com. 1964-65, 66-67, exec. coun. trial lawyers sect., 1967-68, mem. criminal law cert. com. 1988-91, recipient President's Pro Bono Svc. award, 9th jud. cir. 1993), Orange County Bar Assn. (exec. coun. 1967-70, sec. 1984-88), Nat. Assn. Criminal Def. Lawyers (2d v.p. 1992-93, 1st v.p. 1993-94, dir. 1984—, chmn. Lawyers' Assistance Strike Force 1987-89, Robert C. Heeney Meml. award 1988), Fla. Assn. Criminal Def. Lawyers (chmn. Lawyers' Assistance Strike Force 1988-89, Steven M. Goldstein Criminal Justice award 2002), Nat. Bd. Trial Advocacy (cert. 1982). Office: Tinker Bldg 18 W Pine St Orlando FL 32801-2612 Office Phone: 407-849-6050. E-mail: tinkerjmr@covad.net.

RUSS, JOANNA, author; b. NYC, Feb. 22, 1937; d. Evarett and Bertha (Zinner) R. BA high honors in English, Cornell U., Ithaca, NY, 1957; MFA in Playwriting and Dramatic Lit., Yale U., New Haven, Conn., 1960. Lectr. English Cornell U., 1967—70, asst. prof., 1970—72; asst. prof. English Harpur Coll. SUNY Binghamton, 1972—75; asst. prof. English U. Colo., 1975—77; assoc. prof. English, U. Wash., 1977—90, prof., 1984—90. Author: Picnic on Paradise, 1968, And Chaos Died, 1970, The Female Man, 1975, We Who Are About To, 1977, Kittatinny: A Tale of Magic, 1978, The Two of Them, 1978, On Strike Against God, 1980, The Adventures of Alyx, 1983, The Zanzibar Cat, 1983, How To Suppress Women's Writing, 1983, Extra (Ordinary) People, 1984, Magic Mommas, Trembling Sisters, Puritans and Perverts: Feminist Essays, 1985, (collection) The Hidden Side of the Moon, 1987, To Write Like a Woman, 1995, (nonfiction) What Are We Fighting For, 1998; also numerous short stories Mem. Sci. Fiction Writers Am. (Nebula award Best Short Story 1972, Hugo award for Best Novella 1983)

RUSS, RONALD STEVEN, librarian; b. Bklyn., Nov. 24, 1967; s. Manuel Leon and Beverly Selma Russ; m. Karen Madej, Feb. 21, 1995. MLS, U. Buffalo, 1993. Libr. Bklyn Pub. Libr., 1993—96; electronic and pub. svcs. libr. Ark. State U. Beebe, 1997—. Webmaster Ark. Libr. Assn., Benton, 1997—, reference and instrn. svcs. chair, 2008—, two yr. colls. round table chair, Little Rock, 2001—, pubs. com. chair, 2003—04. Contbr. articles to profl. jours. Recipient Suzanne Spurrier Academic Libr. award, Ark. Libr. Assn., 2007. Mem.: ALA, Ark. Libr. Assn., Ark. Outdoor Photographers Club (treas. 2005—08). Office: Ark State Univ-Beebe Abington Libr PO Box 1000 Beebe AR 72012 Office Phone: 501-882-8959. Office Fax: 501-882-8233. Personal E-mail: rsruss@comcast.net. Business E-Mail: rsruss@asub.edu.

RUSSACK, JOHN A., federal official; Grad., U. Kans., 1970, Nat. War Coll., 1991. Dep. to assoc. dir. of ctrl. intelligence for military support CIA, exec. asst. to dep. dir., military dep. dir. nonproliferation ctr., dep. asst. dir. for collection, dep. chief external ops., cover divsn. for counterintelligence; dir. office of intelligence US Dept. Energy, Washington, 2003—05; program mgr. Information-Sharing Environment Office Dir. Nat. Intelligence, Washington, 2005—.

RUSSAKOFF, NINA L., lawyer; b. New Haven, 1974; BA, Columbia Coll., NYC, 1996; M, St. Hilda's Coll., Oxford U., Eng., 1997; JD, Columbia U. Sch. Law, 2002. Bar: Pa. 2002, NJ 2002, US Dist. Ct. (ea. and mid. dists.) Pa., US Dist. Ct. (NJ), Supreme Ct. Pa., Supreme Ct. NJ. Legis. corr./mgr. to rep. Peter J. Visclosky, Ind., 1998—99; litig. assoc. Hangley Aronchick Segal & Pudlin, Phila., 2002—07; assoc. Duane Morris LLP, Phila., 2007—. Mem. human rights com. Anti-Defamation League. Contbr. articles to law jours. Active Phila. Reads Prog., 2002—05; gen. counsel PSC Partners Seeking a Cure Found., 2006. Recipient Pro Bono award, Phila. Ct. Common Pleas, 2006; named a Rising Star, Law and Politics Mag., 2005, 2006. Mem.: ABA, Am. Health Law Assn., Phila. Bar Assn., Pa. Bar Assn., Profl. Women's Roundtable (bd. dirs., co-chair mktg. com.). Office: Duane Morris LLP 30S 17th St Philadelphia PA 19103 Office Phone: 215-979-1937. Office Fax: 215-689-4945. Business E-Mail: nlrussakoff@duanemorris.com.*

RUSSEL, WILLIAM BAILEY, engineering educator; b. Corpus Christi, Tex., Nov. 17, 1945; m. 1972; 2 children. BA, Rice U., 1969, MS in Chem. Engring., 1969; PhD in Chem. Engring., Stanford U., 1973. NATO fellow applied math. Cambridge U., 1973-74; from asst. prof. to assoc. prof. chem. engring. Princeton U., NJ, 1974-83, prof. chem. engring. NJ, 1983—, chmn. dept. chem. engring. NJ, 1987-96, dir. Materials Sciences Inst. NJ, 1996-98, dean graduate sch. NJ, 2002—; faculty Princeton Inst. for the Sci. and Tech. of Materials. Olaf A. Hougen vis. prof. U. Wis., 1984, Debye vis. prof., U. Utrecht, 2001, coun. Grad. Schs., bd. dirs., 2004-, chair, 2007-08. Mem.: Am. Acad. Arts & Sciences, Materials Rsch. Soc., Am. Chem. Soc. (Colloid and Surface Chemistry award 2007), Soc. Rheology (pres. 2001—03, Bingham award 1999), NAE, AIChE (William H. Walker award 1992). Office: Princeton U A 225 Engring Quadrangle 205 Nassau Hall Princeton NJ 08544 Home Phone: 609-921-1863; Office Phone: 609-258-4590. Business E-Mail: wbrussel@princeton.edu. E-mail: graddean@princeton.edu.

RUSSELL, ALLAN DAVID, lawyer; b. Cleve., May 6, 1924; s. Allan MacGillivray and Marvel (Codling) R.; m. Lois Anne Robinson, June 12, 1947, m. Patricia A. Ellis, March 8, 2003; children: Lisa Anne, Robinson David, Martha Leslie BA, Yale U., 1945, LLB, 1951. Bar: N.Y. 1952, Conn. 1956, Mass. 1969, U.S. Supreme Ct. 1977. Atty. Sylvania Electric Products, Inc., NYC, 1951-56, div. counsel Batavia, NY, 1956-65, sr. counsel, 1965-71; sec., sr. counsel GTE Sylvania Inc., Stamford, Conn., 1971-76; asst. gen. counsel GTE Svc. Corp., 1976-80, v.p., assoc. gen. counsel, 1980—83; pvt. practice Redding, Conn., 1983—2004. Sec., dir. mktg. subs. Sylvania Entertainment Products Corp., 1961-67; sec. Wilbur B. Driver Co Dist. leader Rep. Party, New Canaan, Conn., 1955-56; sec. bd. dirs. Youth Found., Inc., 1981-83, bd. dirs., 1985-2001, pres., 2000-01; mem. planning commn., Redding, Conn., 1987-89; mem. Redding Bd. Ethics, 1990-96, chmn., 1992-96; warden Christ Ch. Parish, Redding, 1987-89; bd. dirs. Mark Twain Libr., 1988-94, 2002-2004, v.p., 1988-89, pres., 1990-92 With USAAF, 1943—46. Mem. SAR, Assn. of Bar of City of N.Y., Conn. Bar Assn. (exec. com. corp. counsel sect. 1986-90), Am. Soc. Corp. Secs., St. Nicholas Soc., Collie Club Am. Found., Inc. (v.p., dir. 1986-89, pres. 1989-90), Soc. Colonial Wars, Yale Alumni Assn. (sec. local chpt. 1953-56), Yale Club of Danbury (pres. 1990—), Phi Delta Phi Home: 33 Old Field Hill Rd Unit #32 Southbury CT 06488-3837

RUSSELL, ALLEN STEVENSON, retired metal products executive; b. Bedford, Pa., May 27, 1915; s. Arthur Stainton and Ruth (Stevenson) R.; m. Judith Pauline Sexauer, Apr. 5, 1941. BS, Pa. State U., 1936, MS, 1937, PhD, 1941. With Aluminum Co. Am., 1940-82, assoc. dir. rsch., 1973-74; v.p. Alcoa, Pa., 1974-78; v.p. sci. and tech. Pitts., 1978-81; v.p., chief scientist, 1981-82. Adj. prof. U. Pitts., 1981-86 Contbr. articles to profl. jours.; patentee in field. Named IR-100 Scientist of Yr., 1979; Pa. State U. alumni fellow, 1980; K.J. Bayer medalist, 1981; recipient chem. Pioneer award Am. Inst. Chemists, 1983 Fellow Am. Soc. Metals (Gold medal 1982), AIME (James Douglas gold medal 1987), Am. Inst. Chemists; mem. NAE (coun. 1978-84), Am. Chem. Soc., Sigma Xi. Republican. Presbyterian. Home: 27 Meadowlark Ln Hilton Head Plantation Hilton Head Island SC 29926 Home Phone: 843-682-3455. E-mail: russell2610@roadrunner.com.

RUSSELL, ANNE M., editor-in-chief; BA in Brit. Lit. magna cum laude, Yale U. Editor book divsn. Billboard Publ.; editor Photo Dist. News; reporter Adweek; assoc. editor Am. Photographer; sr. editor Working Women; exec. editor Folio: Pub. News, editor-in-chief, 1992—97, Living Fit, 1997—99, Vegetarian Times, 1999; editl. dir. Fox TV's Health Network; editl. dir. Shape mag. Am. Media Inc., 2001—03, editor-in-chief, 2003—06, Viv Mag. online, 2006—. Office: VIV Pub LLC El Cajon CA 92019 Office Phone: 858-832-1874.

RUSSELL, BEATRICE NIBIGIRA, performing arts educator; d. Firmin None Misigaro and Agnes None Nayigihugu; m. Dale Robin Russell, Mar. 23, 2007. PhD, U. Calif., Davis, 2004. Asst. prof. Calif. State U., Sacramento, 2004—; tchg. asst. U. Calif., 1998—2004, U. Ark., Fayetteville. Contbr. articles. Bd. mem. Ctr. African Peace Conflict and Resolution, Sacramento, 2005—08. Recipient appreciation cert., Cooper -Woodson Coll. Enhancement Program, 2006, Appreciation Cert., DigitalStream, 2008. Mem.: French Club (Calif. State U., Sacramento 2007—08), French Alliance Francaise. Avocation: reading, traveling.

RUSSELL, BELINDA, education educator; b. Columbia, Sc, May 29, 1951; d. Hermon Hansel and Ann Potts Hill; m. Gary Russell, June 23, 1994; m. Douglas Orr Pannell, Dec. 23, 1973 (dec. Nov. 21, 1989); children: Julia Rhea Douglas, Jason Douglas Pannell, Jessica Elizabeth Hanks, Jamie Elizabeth Baker. MEd, U. Miss., Oxford, 1980. Instr. W.P. HS, New Albany, Miss., 1974—85, NE Miss. CC, Booneville, Miss., 1985—. Prodr.: (podcasts itunes) Pub. Speaking Podcasts (award, 2008). V.p. Miss. Comm. Assn., Jackson, Miss., 2008. Recipient T.O.P. Tchg. award, NEMCC Devel. Assn., 2007—08. Mem.: New Albany Garden Club (former pres. 1976—79, State Life Membership award). Methodist. Avocations: travel, exercise. Office: Northeast Mississippi CC Cunningham Blvd Booneville MS 38829

RUSSELL, BILL (WILLIAM FELTON RUSSELL), former professional basketball team executive, retired professional basketball player; b. Monroe, La., Feb. 12, 1934; s. Charles and Katie Russell; m. Rosie Swisher, Dec. 9, 1956 (div. 1973); children: Karen Kenyatta, William Jr., Jacob; m. Dorothy Anstett, June 8, 1977 (div. 1980); m. Marilyn Nault, 1996 (dec. Jan. 25, 2009). BA, U. San Francisco, 1956. Ctr. Boston Celtics, 1956-69, head coach, 1966-69; sportscaster ABC-TV, 1969-80, CBS-TV, 1980-83; head coach Seattle Supersonics, 1973-77, Sacramento Kings, 1987-88, v.p. basketball ops., then exec. v.p., 1988-89. Appeared in: (TV series) Cowboy in Africa; co-host: The Superstars, ABC-TV, 1978-79; Co-author: (with Taylor Branch) Second Wind: Memoirs of an Opinionated Man, 1979, (with David Faulkner) Russell Rules: 11 Lessons on Leadership From the Twentieth Century's Greatest Winner, 2001, (with Alan Steinberg) Red and Me: My Coach, My Lifelong Friend, 2009 Recipient We Are Boston Leadership Award, 2008; named NBA MVP, 1958, 1961—63, 1965, First Team All-NBA, 1959, 1963, 1965, Second Team All-NBA, 1958, 1960—62, 1964, 1966—68, NBA All-Star Game MVP, 1963, Sportsman of the Year, Sports Illustrated, 1968, Athlete of the Decade, The Sporting News, 1970, Greatest Player in the History of the NBA, Profl. Basketball Writers Assn. America, 1980; named one of The 50 Greatest Athletes of the 20th Century, ESPN, 1999; named to The NBA All-Star Team, 1958—69, NBA All-Defensive Team, 1969, Naismith Pro Basketball Hall of Fame, 1974, The Bay Area Sports Hall of Fame, 1980, Nat. Collegiate Basketball Hall of Fame, 2006, The NBA 25th Anniversary Team, 1971, The NBA 35th Anniversary Team, 1980, The NBA 50th Anniversary Team, 1996. Achievements include being a member of 2 NCAA Championship teams with the University of San Francisco, 1955-56, winning a gold medal as captain of the US Basketball Team at the 1956 Summer Olypmics; winning 11 NBA Championship teams with the Boston Celtics, 1957, '59, '60-66, '68-69; becoming the first African American head coach in NBA history, 1966.*

RUSSELL, BRENDA L., psychology professor; d. Carlton J. and Janice A. Russell. PhD, St. Louis U., Mo., 1999. Assoc. prof., & forensic grad. program coord. Castleton State Coll., Vt., 1999—2005; program evaluator Tchg. Am. History, Castleton, 2004; assoc. prof. psychology Pa. State U., Reading, 2006—. Program evaluator State Ill. Treatment Alternatives Spl. Clients, St. Louis, 1995—96; program evaluation cons. Tapestry, a 21st Century Cmty. Learning Ctr., Rutland, Vt., 2002—06, State Pa. Rt. 222 Corridor, Reading, 2007—. Contbr. articles to publs. Mem.: APA. Office: PA State Univ Berks Tulpehocken Rd Reading PA 19610 Business E-Mail: blr15@psu.edu.

RUSSELL, CAROL ANN, city council member, retired company executive; d. Billy and Iris Koud; m. Victor Rojas (div.), Rosalind Katz, 2008. BA in English, CUNY-Hunter Coll., 1993. Registered employment cons. Various exec. positions in staffing/workforce devel. svcs., NYC, San Francisco Bay, 1964—82; v.p. Wollborg-Michelson, San Francisco, 1974-82; co-owner, pres. Russell Staffing Resources, Inc., San Francisco, Marin and Sonoma, 1983-98; ret.; elected mem. City Coun. Cloverdale, 2006. Media guest, spkr., workshop and seminar leader in field; host/cmty. prodr. Job Net program for TCI Cable T.V. Pub. Checkpoint Newsletter; feature writer/columnist The Slant; contbr. articles to profl. publs. Founding v.p. The Friends of the Frank Lloyd Wright Civic Ctr. Libr. Marin County; vice chair Sonoma County Commn. on Status of Women, 2003—06; mem. cmty. action com. Sonoma County Commn. on Human Rights; founding cmty. prodr. Northbay Pride Music Festival, 2005—06; elected city coun. mem. Cloverdale, Calif., 2006; vice mayor, 2008; bd. dirs. Sonoma County Libr. Found., 2003—. Named to Inc. 500, 1989—90. Mem. Am. Women in Radio and TV, No. Calif. Human Resources Coun., Soc. Human Resource Mgmt., Calif. Assn. Pers. Cons. (pres. Golden State chpt. 1984-85), Calif. Assn. Temp. Svcs., Bay Area Pers. Assn. (pres. 1983-84), Pers. Assn. Sonoma County, Scowrers and Molly Maguires (bd. dirs., editor The Herald), Sherlock Holmes Soc. London, Nat. Women's Polit. Caucus (comms. chair Marin chpt. 2002, pres. Marin chpt. 2003), Mayors and Coun. Mem.s Assn., Sherlockian Soc. (Scowers and Molly Maguires), Churchill Soc., Sisters in Crime, Cloverdale Performing Arts Ctr. (bd. mem. 2007-08), League of Calif. Cities (LGBT Cancus mem. 2007-, mem. employee rels. policy com. 2007-), Sonoma Marin Area Rail Transit (mem. bd. dirs., 2007-), Sonoma County Transp. Authority (mem. bd. dirs., 2008-), Health Action Coun. Sonoma County. Office Phone: 707-894-3451, 707-669-0009. Personal E-mail: incloverdale@comcast.net.

RUSSELL, CAROL ANN LAMKEN, special education educator; d. Jerome James Lamken and Mildred Mabel Lane; m. David Richard Russell, Jan. 8, 1966; 1 child, Ann Tabitha LaFontaine. BA in Gen. Edn., Glassboro State Coll., NJ, 1964; MA in Spl. Edn., Paterson State Coll., NJ, 1968; MEd in Tchr. Hanicapped, William Paterson Coll., NJ, 1981, MEd in Learning Disabilities Tchr. Cons., 1981; MA in Theology, Coll. St. Elizabeth, Convent Station, NJ, 2003. Chaplain Clin. Pastoral Supervisory Coll., 2006; gen. edn. K-8 NJ., 1964. Educator spl. edn. and grades first, fourth and sixth Paramus Bd. Edn., Paramus, NJ, 1964—, spl. edn. educator, 1964—; chaplain Hackensack U. Med. Ctr., Hackensack, NJ, 1997—. Pvt. practice, Ridgewood, NJ, 2000—; cons. in field. Contbr. articles to profl. jours. Mem. Mayor's Adv. Coun. Handicapped, Ridgewood, 1984—86; parish worker overnight shelter Annunciation Ch. St. Cecilia's shelter, Paramus, NJ, 1990. Recipient Governor's Tchr. award, Paramus, NJ, 1980, Staff Academic Scholarship award, Hackensack Med. and Dental Scholarship Com., 2002; numerous sch. innovative sch. projects grant, Paramus C. of C., 1998—99, 2002, 2004. Mem.: NEA, Lay Carmelities, ACPE Assn. Chaplains, Clin. Pastoral Supervisory Coll., NJ. Edn. Assn., Edn. Assn. Paramus. Roman Catholic. Avocations: reading, dance, movies, painting. Office: Memorial Sch Midland Ave Paramus NJ 07652 Business E-Mail: crussell@paramus.k12.nj.us.

RUSSELL, CATHY (CATHERINE M. RUSSELL), federal official; m. Thomas E. Donilon, Sept. 14, 1991. BA, Boston Coll.; JD, George Washington U. Assoc. dep. atty. gen. US Dept. Justice; sr. adviser Senate Fgn. Rels. Com.; staff dir. Senate Judiciary Com.; sr. counsel to Senator Patrick Leahy US Senate; counsel US Senate Commerce, Sci., and Transp. Subcommittee on Sci., Tech. and Innovation; chief of staff to Dr. Jill Biden The White House, Washington, 2009—. Chief of staff for Dr. Jill Biden Obama-Biden Presdl. Campaign, 2008. Office: The White House 1600 Pennsylvania Ave NW Washington DC 20500*

RUSSELL, CLARA B., information technology manager; b. Washington, Mar. 20; d. Gilbert L. Sr. and Emma Howard Bullock; m. William A. Russell. BA, Howard U., 1971. Cert. arbitrator. Info. tech. specialist U.S. Govt., Washington, 1971—. Arbitrator Better Bus. Bur., Atlanta. Mem. Am. Bus. Women's Assn., Am. Pub. Welfare Assn., Am. Arbitration Assn., Howard U. Alumni Assn., Order of Ky. Colonels. Avocations: travel, gardening. Office: US Gen Svcs Adminstrn Info Tech Dept 1800 F St NW Ste G 142 Washington DC 20405

RUSSELL, CLIFFORD SPRINGER, economics, public policy, educator; b. Holyoke, Mass., Feb. 11, 1938; s. Kenneth Clifford and Helen Alwilda (Springer) R.; m. Louise Pancoast Bennett, Feb. 3, 1965 (div. June 1985); m. Susan Vanston Reid, Sept. 7, 1985; stepchildren: Timothy Taylor Greene, Elizabeth Claussen Greene (dec.). BA, Dartmouth Coll., 1960; PhD, Harvard U., 1968. Sr. rsch. assoc. Resources for the Future, Washington, 1968-70, fellow, 1970-73, sr. fellow, 1973-85, div. dir., 1981-85; prof. econs. and pub. policy Vanderbilt U., Nashville, 1986—2002, prof. emeritus econs., 2002—, dir. Vanderbilt Inst. for Pub. Policy Studies, 1986—2002. Valfrid Paulsson vis. prof. environ. econs. Beijer Inst., Royal Swedish Acad. Scis., Stockholm, 1997; vis. prof. Local Govt. Rsch. Inst., Copenhagen, 2004-08. Author: Drought and Water Supply: Implications of the Massachusetts Experience for Municipal Planning, 1970, Residuals Management in Industry: A Case Study of Petroleum Refining, 1973, Steel Production: Processes, Products and Residuals, 1976, Environment Quality Management: An Application to the Lower Delaware Valley, 1976, Freshwater Recreational Fishing: The National Benefits of Water Pollution Control, 1982, Enforcing Pollution Control Laws, 1986, Applying Economics to the Environment, 2001; contbr. articles to profl. jours. Trustee, treas. Environ. Def. Fund, N.Y.C., and Washington, 1973-85; mem. Tenn. Gov.'s Energy Adv. Bd., Nashville, 1989-94; trustee Tenn. Environ. Coun., Nashville, 1989-96, Maine Maritime Mus. Bath, 2008-; sec., 2009-; pres. 1992-95; trustee, treas.Sheepscot VAlley Conservation Assn., 2004—. Lt. USN, 1960-63. Fellow: Assn. Environ. and Resource Econ. (bd. dir. 1983—85, chmn. workshop com., pres. 1993—94). Avocations: tennis, fly fishing, sailing, boat building. Home: 15 Head Tide Church Rd Alna ME 04535-3028 E-mail: cliff.russell@vanderbilt.edu.

RUSSELL, DAVID L., federal judge; b. Sapulpa, Okla., July 7, 1942; s. Lynn and Florence E. (Brown) R.; m. Dana J. Wilson, Apr. 16, 1971; 1 child, Sarah Elizabeth BS, Okla. Bapt. U., 1963; JD, Okla. U., 1965. Bar: Okla. 1965. Asst. atty. gen. State of Okla., Oklahoma City, 1968-69, legal adviser to gov., 1969-70; legal adviser Senator Dewey Bartlett, Washington, 1973-75; U.S. atty. for Western dist. Okla. Dept. Justice, 1975-77, 81-82; ptnr. Benefield & Russell, Oklahoma City, 1977-81; judge U.S. Dist. Ct. (we. dist.) Okla., Oklahoma City, 1982—, chief judge, 1994—2002. Lt. comdr. JAGC, USN, 1965-68. Selected Outstanding Fed. Ct. Trial judge Okla. Trial Lawyers Assn., 1988, The Jour. Record award Okla. County Bar Assn., 2005. Mem. Okla. Bar Assn., Fed. Bar Assn. (pres. Oklahoma City chpt. 1981), Order of Coif (alumnus mem.), Jud. Conf. US (mem. exec. com. 2003-06). Republican. Methodist. Office: US Dist Ct US Courthouse 200 NW 4th St Oklahoma City OK 73102-3026 Home Phone: 405-478-1990; Office Phone: 405-609-5100.

RUSSELL, DAVID WILLIAMS, lawyer; b. Lockport, NY, Apr. 5, 1945; s. David Lawson and Jean Graves (Williams) R.; m. Frances Yung Chung Chen, May 23, 1970; children: Bayard Chen, Ming Rennick. AB, Dartmouth Coll., 1967, MBA, 1969; JD cum laude, Northwestern U., 1976. Bar: Ill. 1976, Ind. 1983. English tchr. Talledega Coll., Ala., 1967; math. tchr. Lyndon Inst., Lyndonville, Vt., 1967-68; asst. to pres. for planning Tougaloo Coll., Miss., 1969-71, bus. mgr., 1971-73; law clk. Montgomery, McCracken, Walker & Rhoads, Phila., 1975; with Winston & Strawn, Chgo., 1976-83; ptnr. Klineman, Rose, Wolf & Wallack, Indpls., 1983-87, Johnson, Smith, Pence, Densborn, Wright & Heath, Indpls., 1987-99, Bose McKinney & Evans, Indpls., 1999—2004, Harrison & Moberly, Indpls., 2004—. Cons. Alfred P. Sloan Found., 1972-73; dir. Forum for Internat. Profl. Svcs., 1985—, sec., 1985-88, pres. 1988-89; U.S. Dept. Justice del. to U.S. China Joint Session on Trade, Investment & Econ. Law, Beijing, 1987; leader Ind. Products Trade Fair, Kawachinagano, Japan, 1996; lectr. Ind. law Ind. Gov.'s Trade Mission to Japan, 1986, internat. law Ind. CLE Forum, 1986-96, 2000-03, chmn., 1987, 89, 91, 2001-03; adj. prof. internat. bus. law Ind. U., 1993-95; nat. selection com. Woodrow Wilson Found. Adminstrv. Fellowship Program, 1973-76; vol. Lawyers for Creative Arts, Chgo., 1977-83; dir. World Trade Club of Ind., 1987-93, 2005-08, v.p., 1987-91, pres., 1991-92; dir. Ind. Swiss Found., 1991-2002; dir. Writer's Ctr., Indpls., 1999-2008, treas., 2001—07; dir. Asian Am. Alliance, 1999-2008, treas., 2006; dir. Indpls. Peace Games, Inc., 2000—, Friends of Taiwan Assn., Inc., 2001-, African U. Found., 2005-, vice chmn., 2006-; dir. Ind. Soviet Trade Consortium, 1991-99, sec., 1991-92; v.p., bd. dirs. Ind. Sister Cities, 1988—; dir. Internat. Ctr. Indpls., 1988-92, v.p. 1988-89; Ind. dist. enrollment dir. Dartmouth Coll., 1990-99; dir. Carmel Sister Cities, 1993—, v.p. 1995-96, pres. 1997-99, chmn., 1999—; v.p., gen. coun. Lawrence Durrell Soc., 1993—; internat. adv. bds. Supply Chain & Global Mgmt. Acad. Kelley Grad Sch. Bus., Ind. U., 2001—; mem. internat. adv. bd. Ind. U. Law Sch., 2003—, Ind. Econ. Devel. Corp, 2005-; bd. advisors Ctr. for Internat. Bus. and Rsch. Krannert Grad. Sch. Mgmt. Purdue U., 1995—; dir., v.p., gen. coun. Global Crossroads Found., Inc., 1995-2003; mem. bd. arbitrators FINRA, 1999—; dir. Ind. Dist. Export Coun., 1999—, chmn. 2005-. Named Hon. fellow, Ctr. for Internat. Legal Studies, 2002—, Internat. Bus. Person of Yr., World Trade Club of Ind., 2002, Sagamore of the Wabash, 2002, Ind. Super Lawyer, Ind. Monthly Mag. and Ind. Law and Politics, 2004, 2005, 2006, 2007; Adminstrv. fellow, Woodrow Wilson Found., 1969—72, David Williams Russell Day named in his honor, Jan. 15, 2002, Indpls. Mem. ABA, ACLU, Ill. Bar Assn., Ind. Bar Assn. (vice chmn. internat. law sect. 1988-90, treas., 2002-, chmn. 1990-92, 2002-04, co-chmn. written publs. com. 1997-99), Indpls. Bar Assn., Dartmouth Lawyers Assn., Indpls. Assn. Chinese Ams., Chinese Music Soc., Dartmouth Club of Ind. (sec. 1986-87, pres. 1987-88), Internat. Bar Assn., Zeta Psi. Presbyterian. Home: 10926 Lakeview Dr Carmel IN

46033-3937 Office: Harrison & Moberly LLP 2100 First Ind Plz 135 N Pennsylvania St Indianapolis IN 46204-2400 Home Phone: 317-514-4331; Office Phone: 317-639-4511, 317-639-4671. Business E-Mail: drussell@h-mlaw.com.

RUSSELL, DIANE ELIZABETH HENRIKSON, career counselor; b. Chgo., July 18, 1952; d. Arthur Allen and Lois Elizabeth (Wessling) H.; m. Darrell Lee Slider, May 31, 1975 (div. Dec. 1992); m. Thomas Lee Russell, July 27, 1999. BA in Spanish, U. Ill., 1974; MA in Counselor Edn., U. South Fla., 1996. Employment counselor Crown Personnel Inc., Mt. Prospect, Ill., 1974-75; bilingual tchr.'s aide Sch. Dist. #21, Wheeling, Ill., 1975; sec., asst. registrar Yale U., New Haven, 1975-77; asst. to personnel dir., personnel coord. Housing Authority New Haven, 1977-79; benefits specialist Profl. Pensions Inc., New Haven, 1980-81, Chloride Inc., Tampa, Fla., 1981-83; personnel technician II human resources dept. U. South Fla., Tampa, 1984-86, personnel technician III, personnel svcs. specialist, 1986-90, coord. human resources dept., 1990-96, career specialist Career Ctr., 1996—2002, 2004—, counselor, advisor honors coll., 2002—04. Mem. choirs St. Mark United Ch., Valrico, Fla., 1987-99, 2003-05, dir. Caregivers, 2001-2003; mem. chorus U. South Fla., 1986-88, women's chorale, 1993-95. Mem. AAUW (treas. 1976-78, 80-81), Am. Assn. Employment in Edn., Fla. Career Profls. Assn., Phi Kappa Phi, Phi Beta Kappa, Alpha Lambda Delta, Lambda Delta, Zeta Tau Alpha Soc. Avocations: singing, theater, going to theme parks, travel. Home: 723 Herlong Ct Brandon FL 33511-7920 Office: U South Fla Fla Career Ctr 4202 E Fowler Ave Stop SVC 2088 Tampa FL 33620-6930 E-mail: dhenrik718@aol.com.

RUSSELL, DOUG, manufacturing executive, former political organization administrator; BS in Bus. Adminstrn., U. Mo., Columbia. Pres. Durham Co., Lebanon, Mo., GEC Durham Industries, Inc., New Bedford, Mass.; chmn. Mo. Republican Party, 2005—09. Mem. U. Mo. Bd. Curators, Columbia, 1982—87, 2005—, v.p., pres., chair fin. and audit com., mem. exec. com., mem. academic and student affairs com., mem. external affairs com.; founding bd. mem., pres. Lebanon Edn. Found.; mem. bd. dirs. Am. Heartland Econ. Partnership; mem. bd. trustees Lifeway, Nashville. Sch. bd. mem. Lebanon R3; mem. Lebanon Ambassadors. Republican. Office: Durham Co PO Box 908 Lebanon MO 65536 also: 316 University Hall Columbia MO 65211 Office Phone: 417-532-7121.*

RUSSELL, FINDLAY EWING, physician; b. San Francisco, Sept. 1, 1919; s. William and Mary Jane (Findlay) R.; m. Janet Louise Thiel, Feb. 14, 1950; children: Christa Ann, Sharon Jane, Robin Emily, Constance Susan, Mark Findlay. BA, Walla Walla Coll., Wash., 1941; MD, Loma Linda U., Calif., 1950; postgrad. (fellow), Calif. Inst. Tech., 1951-53; postgrad., U. Cambridge, Eng., 1962—63; PhD, U. Santa Barbara, Calif., 1974, LLD (hon.), 1989. Intern White Meml. Hosp., Los Angeles, 1950-51; practice medicine specializing in toxinology and toxicology Los Angeles, 1953—; mem. staff Los Angeles County-U. So. Calif. Med. Center, Loma Linda U. Med. Center, U. Ariz. Med. Ctr.; physiologist Huntington Inst. Med. Research, 1953-55; dir. lab. neurol. research Los Angeles County-U. So. Calif. Med. Center, 1955-80; mem. faculty Loma Linda U. Med. Sch., 1955—2007; prof. neurology, physiology and biology U. So. Calif. Med. Sch., 1966-81; prof. pharmacology and toxicology U. Ariz. Health Scis. Coll. Pharmacy, 1981—. Cons. USPHS, NSF, Office Naval Rsch., WHO, U.S. Army, Walter Reed, USAF, Brooks AFB. Author: Marine Toxins and Venomous and Poisonous Marine Animals, 1965, Poisonous Marine Animals, 1971, Snake Venom Poisoning, 1980; co-author: Bibliography of Snake Venoms and Venomous Snakes, 1964, Animal Toxins, 1967, Poisonous Snakes of The World, 1968, Snake Venom Poisoning, 1983, Bibliography of Venomous and Poisonous Marine Animals and Their Toxins, 1984, Venomous and Poisonous Marine Invertebrates of the Indian Ocean, 1996; editor: Toxicon, 1962-70. Served with AUS, 1942-46. Decorated Purple Heart, Bronze Star; recipient award Los Angeles County Bd. Suprs., 1960; award Acad. Medicine Buenos Aires, 1966; Skylab Achievement award, 1974; Jozef Stefan medal Yugoslavia, 1978; U.S. State Dept. medallion, 2006, Disting. Citizen award, 1992. Fellow A.C.P., Am. Coll. Cardiology, Royal Soc. Tropical Medicine, N.Y. Acad. Scis.; mem. Internat. Soc. Toxinology (pres. 1962-66, Francisco Redi medal 1967), Royal Soc. Medicine, Am. Soc. Physiology, Western Soc. Pharmacology (pres. 1973) Office: U Ariz Health Scis Coll Pharmacy Pharm/Tox Tucson AZ 85721 Office Phone: 520-626-4047.

RUSSELL, FLORENCE L., elementary school educator; d. Helmer Russell, Jr. and Alma D. Russell. BS, Albany State Coll., Ga., 1972; MS, Nova U., Fort Lauderdale, Fla., 1995. Cert. tchr. Fla., 1972. Tchr. Lee County Sch. Dist., Fort Myers, Fla., 1972. Orgn. head Boy Scout #217, 2005—07; recording sec. St. Mary's Program M.B. Ch., 1980—2005; fin. sec. First Missionary Baptist Fellowship Assn., 1997—; grade level chmn./team leader Tanglewood Riverside Sch., Fort Myers, Fla., 1977—2003; dir. Tanglewood Riverside After Sch. Program, Fort Myers, Fla., 1988—96; pres. Tanglewood Riverside Sch. PTA, Fort Myers, Fla., 2002—04; chmn. sch. adv. com. Tanglewood Riverside Sch., Fort Myers, Fla., 2004—06, environ. edn. tchr. laison Fla., 1973—2006. Recipient Outstanding Vol. award, Tanglewood Riverside PTA, 2004. Mem.: Fla. PTA, Nat. PTA. Democrat. Personal E-mail: florenrss@aol.com. Business E-Mail: florencelr@leeschools.net.

RUSSELL, FRANCIA, retired ballet director, educator; b. LA, Jan. 10, 1938; d. W. Frank and Marion (Whitney) R.; m. Kent Stowell, Nov. 19, 1965; children: Christopher, Darren, Ethan. Studies with, George Balanchine, Vera Volkova, Felia Doubrouska, Antonina Tumkovsky, Benjamin Harkarvy; student, NYU, Columbia U.; degree (hon.), Seattle U., 2003. Dancer, soloist NYC Ballet, 1956-62, ballet mistress, 1965-70; dancer Ballets USA/Jerome Robbins, NYC, 1962; tchr. ballet Sch. Am. Ballet, NYC, 1963-64; co-dir. Frankfurt (Fed. Republic Germany) Opera Ballet, 1976-77; dir., co-artistic dir. Pacific N.W. Ballet, Seattle, 1977—2005; dir. Pacific N.W. Ballet Sch., Seattle, 1977—2005; ret., 2005. Affiliate prof. of dance U. Wash. Dir. staging over 100 George Balanchine ballet prodns. throughout world, including Russia and China, 1964—. Named Woman of Achievement, Matrix Table, Women in Comm., Seattle, 1987, Gov.'s Arts award, 1989, Dance Mag. award, 1996, Brava award Women's U. Club, 2003, ArtsFund Lifetime Achievement in the Arts award, 2004, Ernst & Young Entrepreneur of Yr. award, 2004, Seattle Mayor's Arts award for Lifetime Achievement, 2004. Mem. Internat. Women's Forum. Home: 2833 Broadway E Seattle WA 98102-3935 Office: Pacific NW Ballet 301 Mercer St Seattle WA 98109-4600

RUSSELL, FRANK ELI, retired newspaper publishing executive; b. Kokomo, Ind., Dec. 6, 1920; s. Frank E. and Maude (Wiggins) R.; children: Linda Carole Russell Atkins, Richard Lee, Frank E. III, Rita Jane Russell Eagle, Julie Beth Russell; m. Nancy M. Shover, Oct. 5, 1991 AB, Evansville Coll., 1942; JD, Ind. U., 1951; LLD (hon.), U. Evansville, 1985; HHD (hon.), Franklin Coll., 1989. Bar: Ind. 1951; CPA, Ind. Ptnr. George S. Olive & Co., Indpls., 1947—53; exec. v.p. Spickelmier Industries, Inc., Indpls., 1953—59; bus. mgr. Indpls. Star & News, 1959—77; v.p., gen. mgr. Ctrl. Newspapers, Inc., Indpls., 1977—79, pres., 1979—95, chmn., bd. dirs., 1996—98; ret., 1998; also bd. dirs. Ctrl. Newsprint; pres. Bradley Paper Co., also bd. dirs. Past chmn. adv. bd. Met. Indpls. TV Assn., Inc.; trustee retirement trust Ctrl. Newspapers, Inc.; chmn. retirement com. Hoosier State Press. Bd. dirs. Ariz. Cmty. Found., 1992-96, Eiteljorg Mus., 1994—; trustee, chmn. bd. Nina Mason Pulliam Charitable Trust, 1997— Recipient Disting. Alumni award Ind. U. Sch. Law, 1989, Life Trustee award U. Evansville, 1991, Ralph D. Casey award, 1997 Mem. ABA, AICPA, Ind. Bar. Assn., Indpls. Bar Assn. (past bd. dirs., past treas.), Ind. Assn. CPA (past dir.), Tax Execs. Inst. (past pres.), Ind. Assn. Credit Mgmt. (dir., v.p.), Inst. Newspaper Controllers and Fin. Officers (dir., past pres.), Ind. Acad. Ind. Assn. Colls., Midwest Pension Conf. (Ind. chpt.), Newspaper Advt. Bur. (bd. dirs.), Salvation Army (life, award 1989), Columbia Club, Meridian Hills Country Club, Masons, Shriners, Order of Coif, Phi Delta Phi, Sigma Alpha Epsilon Methodist. Office: Nina Mason Pulliam Charitable Trust 135 N Pennsylvania St Ste 1200 Indianapolis IN 46204-1956

RUSSELL, GEORGE HAW, video production company executive; b. Neosho, Mo., May 22, 1945; s. Kenneth L. and Marjorie (Haw) R.; m. Suzanne Bennett, June 1, 1967; children: Margaret Anne, Marjorie Jane, Karen Lee, George Andrew. BA, La. State U., 1967. Exec. Ednl. Video Network, Huntsville, 1990—; ptnr. Sam Houston Group Ltd. Liability Partnership, Huntsville, 1991—. Prodr. ednl. videos Nombres et Couleurs, 1988 (Silver Apple award 1988), Napoleon, 1989 (Silver Apple award 1989), Bullfight, 1990, The French Revolution, 1990; exec. prodr. Spain's Historic Cities, 1992, Munich's Oktoberfest, 1992, The New Nutriton Pyramid, 1992, The Visual Language of Design, 1992, Florence, 1993, Joan of Arc, 1993, New Food Guide Pyramid, 1993, Cleaning and Maintaining Your VCR, 1993, Arts and Crafts of Mexico, 1993, Understanding Geysers and Hot Springs, 1993, Thoreau at Walden Pond, 1993, French Markets, 1993, Great Zimbabwe, 1993, Longpig, 2008, Psycho Killer Attack, 2009. Bd. govs. Tex. Com. on Natural Resources, Dallas, 1979—; bd. dirs. Gibbs-Powell House Mus., Huntsville, Natural Area Preservation Assn., Dallas; chmn. forest practices Lone Star Sierra Club, Austin, Tex., 1984—; chmn. Fed. Forest Reform, Washington, D.C., 1991—; founder, bishop Universal Ethician Ch., 2000—; founder Ethician Family Cemetery; founder Talking Eagle Preserve, Russell Beaver Sanctuary, Russell River Otter Sanctuary, Russell Frog Sanctuary, 2000-2005. 1st lt. U.S. Army, 1971-74. Recipient spl. achievement award Sierra Club, San Francisco 1985, chpt. conservation award 1987, environ. heroes for centennial 1991; named Citizen of Month, Huntsville Item 1988. Democrat. Methodist. Avocations: environmental advocacy, historic building restoration, collecting antiques and folk art. Office: Ednl Video Network 1401 19th St Huntsville TX 77340-5057 Office Phone: 936-295-5767. Personal E-mail: ghr@cyberclone.net.

RUSSELL, JAMARCUS, professional football player; b. Mobile, Ala., Aug. 9, 1985; s. Bobby Lloyd and Zina Russell-Anderson. Attended, La. St. U., 2003—07. Quarterback Oakland Raiders, 2007—. Recipient Manning award, 2006; named Sugar Bowl MVP, 2007; named to First Team All-Southeastern Conference, 2006. Achievements include being the first overall selection in the NFL Draft, 2007. Office: Oakland Raiders 1220 Harbor Bay Pkwy Alameda CA 94502*

RUSSELL, JAMES ALVIN, JR., college administrator; b. Lawrenceville, Va., Dec. 25, 1917; s. Dr. James Alvin and Nellie M. (Pratt) R.; m. Lottye J. Washington, Dec. 25, 1943; children: Charlotte Justyne, James Alvin III. BA, Oberlin Coll., 1940; BS, Bradley U., 1941, MS, 1950, spl. insts.; EdD, U. Md., 1967; spl. insts., Wayne U., U. Mich., U. Ill., NSF. Prof., dir. div. engring., also prof. edn. div. grad. studies Hampton Inst., 1950-71; pres. St. Paul's Coll., Lawrenceville, 1971-81; dir. instructional programs and student services Va. C.C. System, 1981-82; chmn. div. profl. studies W.Va. State Coll., 1982-86, acting pres., 1986-87, exec. asst. to pres., 1987-88; pres. So. W.Va. C.C., 1988-89, ret., 1989. Pres. Peninsula Council Human Relations, 1961-65. United Negro Coll. Fund fellow, 1966-67. Mem. IEEE, Am. Soc. Engring. Edn., Am. Assn. Univ. Adminstrs., Am. Vocat. Assn., Am. Tech. Edn. Assn., Nat. Assn. Indsl. Tech., Am. Assn. for Higher Edn., Nat. Assn. for Equal Opportunity in Edn., Brunswick C. of C., Sigma Pi Phi, Alpha Kappa Mu, Iota Lambda Sigma, Omega Psi Phi. Home: 811 Grandview Dr Dunbar WV 25064-1175 E-mail: Drjarusdun@aol.com.

RUSSELL, JAMES EDWARD, physics professor; b. Fort Wayne, Ind., Sept. 27, 1931; m. Mary Carol Schalk, Sept. 17, 1977. BS, MS, Yale U., New Haven, PhD, 1958. Postdoc. fellow U. Va., Charlottesville, 1957—58; rsch. assoc. Ind. U., Bloomington, Ind., 1958—60; rsch. physicist Carnegie Mellon U., Pitts., 1960—62; vis. asst. prof. U. Padua, Italy, 1962—63; sr. rsch. officer U. Oxford, England, 1963—65; assoc. prof. U. Cin., 1965—74, prof. physics, 1974—. Contbr. scientific papers to profl. jours. Home: 12 Cypress Garden Cincinnati OH 45220 Office: Physics Dept Univ Cin Cincinnati OH 45221 Personal E-mail: jamarussell@fuse.net. Business E-Mail: james.russell@uc.edu.

RUSSELL, JAMES WEBSTER, JR., retired editor, columnist; b. Shreveport, La., Nov. 30, 1921; s. James Webster and Aline (Faulk) R.; m. Jean Buck, June 29, 1949 (dec. Sept. 2002); children: Nancy Russell Dearr, Eileen Russell Goure; m. Sylvia Swogger Sheldon, Aug. 17, 2004. BA, La. State U., 1942. Fla. mgr. Internat. News Service, 1946-51; bur. chief UPI, Tallahassee, 1951-52; regional editor U.P.I., Atlanta, 1953-57; asst. city editor Miami (Fla.) Herald, 1957-58, bus.-fin. editor, 1958-74, fin.-econ. columnist, 1974—99. Guest lectr. U. Miami, Fla. Internat. U., Miami-Dade Community Coll., La. State U. Contbr. articles to jours. and newspapers; author: (book) Out Of Ouachita. Trustee Fla. So. Coll. Served with USAAF, 1942-45. Recipient Eagle award Invest-in-Am. Nat. Coun., 1976; decorated Air medal with eleven oak leaf clusters; inducted La. State U. Sch. of Mass Comms. Hall of Fame, 1998. Mem. Soc. Am. Bus. Writers, Lambda Chi Alpha, Sigma Delta Chi. Republican. Methodist (chmn. ch. council on ministries 1971-72). Home: 4800 SW 64th Ct Miami FL 33155-6133

RUSSELL, JAMES WILLIAM, neuroscientist; b. Salisbury, Rhodesia, Jan. 1, 1960; s. William and Olive Russell; m. Jane, Nov. 3, 1990; 3 children. Student, U. Oxford, Eng., 1982-83; MB, ChB, U. Rhodesia, 1984; postgrad., Mayo Clinic, Rochester, Minn., 1991-93; MS, U. Mich., 2001. Diplomate in neurology and electrodiagnostic medicine Am. Bd. Am. Bd. Psychiatry and Neurology; diplomate Am. Bd. Electrodiagnostic Medicine; lic. physician, Iowa, Mich.; fellow Royal Coll. of Physicians, 2003. Intern in medicine and surgery U. Hosps. and Coll. Medicine U. Rhodesia, Salisbury, 1984-85; resident in internal medicine U. Hosps. and Coll. Medicine U. Zimbabwe, 1985-86; resident in internal medicine Pembury and Lewisham Hosps., London, 1986-88, S.E. Thames Regional Neurology Ctr., Brook Hosp., London, 1986-88; resident in neurology U. Iowa Coll. Medicine and Univ. Hosps., Iowa City, 1988-91; rsch. fellow in neuroscis. Mayo Postgrad. Med. Sch., Rochester, Minn., 1991-92; clin. peripheral nerve fellow Mayo Clinic, Rochester, 1992-93; clin. assoc. in electrophysiology and neuromuscular disease Nat. Insts. Neurologic Diseases and Stroke/NIH, Bethesda, Md., 1993-95; instr. residents and fellow dept. neurology U. Mich., Ann Arbor, 1995—, assoc. prof., 2003—; assoc. chief neurology Ann Arbor VA Med. Ctr., 1997—2006; assoc. prof. neurology, anatomy and neurobiology U. Md., 2006—, dir. neuromuscular divsn., 2006—. Lectr. med. student neurology rotation U. Iowa Coll. Medicine, 1989—91, lectr., organizer neurology residents' confs., 1988—91, lectr. phys. therapists grad. courses, 1989—91, mem. quality assurance com., 1989—91; organizer, presenter confs. Peripheral Nerve Ctr., electromyography residents and fellows Mayo Clinic, 1991—93, lectr. neurology grand rounds and postgrad. neurosci., 1991—93; lectr. electrophysiology and neuromuscular confs. Nat. Inst. Neurologic Diseases and Stroke, NIH, 1993—95, assoc., 1993—95, instr. electrophysiology and neuromuscular disease fellows and residents, 1994—; cons. NIH Intramural Program, 1996; grant reviewer NIH FDA Orphan Products Divsn., 1996—; grant reviewer Am. Diabetes Assn., 2002—, Juvenile Diabetes Rsch. Found., 2001—, NIH, 2002—, VA, 2004—; dir. Ann Arbor VAMC Neurology Electrophysiology Lab.; assoc. prof. U. Mich., 2003; assoc. chief neurology Md. Health Care Sys., 2007—; spkr. numerous confs. in field; dir. Md. Peripherial Neuropathy Ctr., 2007—; co-dir. Md. ALS Clinic, 2008—; dir. Neuromuscular Fellowship, 2009—. Contbr. numerous articles to profl. publs., confs.; ad hoc reviewer for neurology (Jour. AMA, diabetes and neurosci. jours.). Grantee NIH, Juvenile Diabetes Rsch. Found., Am. Diabetes Assn., VA. Fellow: Am. Acad. Electro-Diagnostic Medicine; mem.: European Assn. for Study Diabetes, European Assn. for the Study of Diabetes, Am. Diabetes Assn., Am. Neurological Assn., Am. Soc. Cell Biology, Soc. Neurosci., Am. Acad. Electrodiagnostic Medicine, Peripheral Nerve Soc., Am. Autonomic Soc., Juvenile Diabetes Rsch. Found., Am. Diabetes Assn., Am. Acad. Neurology, Royal Coll. Physicians (Edinburgh and Glasgow), Royal Coll. Physicians (London). Evangelical. Avocations: golf, equestrian activities. Office: Univ Md Dept Neurology 3S 129 110 S Paca St Baltimore MD 21201 Office Phone: 410-328-3100. Business E-Mail: jrussell@som.umaryland.edu.

RUSSELL, JEFFREY BURTON, historian, educator; b. Fresno, Calif., Aug. 1, 1934; s. Lewis Henry and Ieda Velma (Ogborn) R.; m. Diana Emily Mansfield, June 30, 1956; children: Jennifer, Mark, William, Penelope. AB, U. Calif., Berkeley, 1955, A.M., 1957; PhD, Emory U., 1960. Asst. prof. U. N.Mex., Albuquerque, 1960-61; jr. fellow Soc. of Fellows, Harvard U., Cambridge, Mass., 1961-62; mem. faculty U. Calif., Riverside, 1962-75, prof. dept. history, 1969-75, assoc. dean grad. div., 1967-72; dir. Medieval Inst.; Michael P. Grace prof. medieval studies U. Notre Dame, South Bend, Ind., 1975-77; dean grad. studies Calif. State U., Sacramento, 1977-79; prof. history U. Calif., Santa Barbara, 1979—, prof. religious studies, 1994—. Author: Dissent and Reform in the Early Middle Ages, 1965, Medieval Civilization, 1968, A History of Medieval Christianity: Prophecy and Order, 1968, Religious Dissent in the Middle Ages, 1971, Witchcraft in the Middle Ages, 1972, The Devil: Perceptions of Evil from Antiquity to Primitive Christianity, 1977, A History of Witchcraft: Sorcerers, Heretics, and Pagans, 1980, Medieval Heresies: a Bibliography, 1981, Satan: The Early Christian Tradition, 1981, Lucifer: The Devil in the Middle Ages, 1984, Mephistopheles: The Devil in the Modern World, 1986, The Prince of Darkness, 1988, Ruga in Aevis, 1990, Inventing the Flat Earth: Columbus and the Historians, 1991, Dissent and Order in the Middle Ages, 1992, A History of Heaven: The Singing Silence, 1997, Essays in Honor of Jeffrey B. Russell, 1998, Paradise Mislaid: How We Lost Heaven and How We Can Regain It, 2006, A New History of Witchcraft, 2007; contbr. articles to profl. jours. Fulbright fellow, 1959-60; Am. Council Learned Socs. grantee, 1965, 70; Social Sci. Research Council grantee, 1968; Guggenheim fellow, 1968-69; Nat. Endowment for Humanities sr. fellow, 1972-73 Fellow Medieval Acad. Am.; mem. Am. Soc. Ch. Histor Am. Acad. Religion, Astron. Soc. Pacific. Home: 4798 Calle Camarada Santa Barbara CA 93110-2053 Office: U Calif Dept History Santa Barbara CA 93106 Personal E-mail: gulielmus2000@yahoo.com. Business E-Mail: russell@history.ucsb.edu.

RUSSELL, JIM, application developer; b. NYC, Dec. 5, 1953; m. Patricia Russell; children: Marie, John, Megan. BA in Math., Fordham U., Bronx, NY, 1974, MA in the History of Christianity, 1976, PhD in Hist. Theology, 1990. Computer programmer, network adminstr. AT&T, White Plains, NY, 1979—2000; pvt. practice computer cons., 2000—. Lectr. in theology St. Peter's Coll. Dist. leader Conservative Party, 1972—79, Republican Party, 2000—; founder, Rep. dist. leader Westchester-Rockland Citizens Immigration Control, 2005—; mem. Holy Rosary Parish. Republican. Roman Catholic. Mailing: 288 Sherman Ave Hawthorne NY 10532

RUSSELL, JOHN FRANCIS, retired librarian; b. Mt. Carmel, Ind., Apr. 30, 1929; s. David Freeman and Bertha (Major) R.; m. Edith Raymond Hyde, June 27, 1953; 1 child, Anne Marie. BA, DePauw U., 1951; postgrad., Ind. U., 1951-52; MA, Johns Hopkins U., 1954; student, Cath. U. Am., summer 1955; MS, Grad. Sch. Libr. Sci./Drexel, U., 1977. Tchr. English Park Sch. Balt., 1954-75, chmn. dept., 1957-75; tchr. speech, dir. Ira Aldridge Players Morgan State Coll., fall 1965-66; tchr. drama Loyola Coll., 1964, 66. Editor: The Secondary School Theatre, 1972-74. Pres. Tchrs.'s Assn. Ind. Sch. Balt. Area, 1960-62, adv. bd., 1966-67, chmn. com. on English, 1966-68; exec. com. Assn. Ind. Md. Sch., 1967-68; dir., costumer Johns Hopkins U. Playshop, 1963-64; lectr. Lecture Group, Woman's Club Roland Park, others, 1964—; bd. dirs. Balt. area coun. World Federalists U.S.A., 1961-67, vice chmn., 1964-67, nat. exec. coun., 1963-65; bd. dirs. Ctr. Stage, 1964-77; dir. Blvd. Players, pres., 1960-67; dir. Pasadena Little Theatre, v.p., 1979-83, pres., 1983-85, 2d v.p., 1990-2007, hon. bd. chmn. 2006-; dir. Center Stage Players, New Image Theatre, Theatre Network of Houston, U.S.A. Theatre, Actors Conservatory Tex., v.p., 1990-91, Glenbrook United Meth. Ch. Drama Ministry; bd. dirs. Unicorn Sch. Acting, 1996-2003, v.p., 1997-2003; adv. com. Am. H.S. Theatre Festival, 1975; mem. adminstrv. bd. St. Mark's United Meth. Ch., 1957-67, Towson United Meth. Ch., 1967-77, First United Meth. Ch., Houston, 1980-89; adminstrv. coun., vice-chmn. Glenbrook United Meth. Ch., 1997, chmn. pastor-parish rels. com., 1998, lay del., 1999, 2000, 03, 04, lay leader 1999—; sec. Festival Angels, 1982-2001 (Outstanding Svc. award 1991); cmty. vol. svcs. com., ARC, 1985-90; comprehensive volunteerism adv. com., Sheltering Arms, 1986-89. Recipient Nat. Citation of Merit Am. Shakespeare Festival, 1961, Theatre Goddess award U.S.A. Theatre, 1998, Critics Choice award Houston Post, 1984; certs. of appreciation Sheltering Arms, 1986-89, cert. of recognition, 1988. Mem. Am. Assn. Cmty. Theatre, Harris County Heritage Soc., Am. Film Inst., Drama League, Am. Theatre Assn. (v.p. Mid-Atlantic dist. 1967-68, pres. 1968-69, nat. dir. 1970-73, Mid-Atlantic chpt. award for achievement and contbn. to theatre 1973), Secondary Sch. Theatre Assn. (v.p. devel. 1974-75), Tex. Non-Profit Theatre, Nat. (bd. dirs. 1969), Md. Coun. Tchrs. English (pres. 1969-70), Capital Area Media Educators Orgn. (exec. com. 1970-73, screening chmn. 1971-73), ALA, Tex. Libr. Assn. (audiovisual chmn. conv. planning com. 1981), Coun. Info. and Referral Svcs. (newsletter editor 1984-86), Tex. Alliance Info. and Referral Svcs. (conv. speaker 1981, 83, 84, 85), Alliance of Info. and Referral Svcs. (conv. speaker 1985), Houston Pub. Libr. Staff Assn. (pres. 1981-82), Literacy Vols. Am. (sec. Houston 1984-87, adv. bd. 1989-91, 95-96, bd. dirs. 1992-95, chmn. program com. 1991-93), Reading, Edn. and Devel. Coun. (recruitment chmn., exec. com. 1984-86), Cultural Arts Coun. of Houston/Harris County, Park Pl. Civic Club (exemplary svc. award 1991), AARP (bd.

dirs. chpt. 1172 1998—, v.p. 1999-2000, 01-02, pres. 2003-04), Phi Beta Kappa, Phi Eta Sigma, Beta Phi Mu. Home: 7817 Grove Ridge Dr Houston TX 77061-1405 Personal E-mail: jfrussell10@comcast.net.

RUSSELL, JOHN JOSEPH, English educator; b. Orange, NJ, Dec. 4, 1949; s. James Francis and Catherine Mary Russell. BA, Seton Hall U., 1973; MA, U. Chgo., 1979, Seton Hall U., 1982; PhD, Fordham U., 1991. Asst. prof. English Union County Coll., Cranford, NJ, 1991—97, assoc. prof. English, 1997—2005, sr. prof. English, 2005—. Author: (book) Hamlet and Narcissus, 1995. Office: Union County Coll 1033 Springfield Ave Cranford NJ 07016 Business E-Mail: russell@ucc.edu.

RUSSELL, JOHN WILLIAM, professional baseball team manager, retired professional baseball player; b. Oklahoma City, Jan. 5, 1961; m. Jamie Russell; children: Brooks, Steel, Stone. Attended, U. Okla., Norman. Catcher Phila. Phillies, 1984—88, Atlanta Braves, 1988, Tex. Rangers, 1990—93; mgr. Minn. Twins' Minor League Sys., Phoenix Desert Dogs, 2002, Peoria Chiefs, 2006—07, Pitts. Pirates, 2008—, third base coach, catching instr., 2003—05. Named Minor League Mgr. of Yr., Baseball Am., 2002. Office: c/o Pitts Pirates PNC Park 115 Federal St Pittsburgh PA 15212 Office Phone: 412-323-5000.

RUSSELL, JOYCE ANNE ROGERS, retired librarian; b. Chgo., Nov. 6, 1920; d. Truman Allen and Mary Louise (Hoelzle) Rogers; m. John VanCleve Russell, Dec. 24, 1942; children: Malcolm David, John VanCleve. Student, Adelphi Coll., 1937; BS in Chemistry, U. Ky., 1942; M.L.S., Rosary Coll., 1967; postgrad., Rutgers U., 1970-71. Research chemist Sherwin Williams Paint Co., Chgo., 1942-45; reference librarian Chicago Heights (Ill.) Pub. Library, 1959-61; librarian Victor Chem. Works, Chicago Heights, 1961-62; lit. chemist Velsicol Chem. Corp., Chgo., 1964-67; chemistry librarian U. Fla., Gainesville, 1967-69, interim assoc. prof., 1967-69; librarian Thiokol Chem. Corp., Trenton, N.J., 1969-73; supr. library operations E.R. Squibb Co., Princeton, N.J., 1973-80, sr. research info scientist, 1980-91. Mem. library adv. commn. Mercer Community Coll., 1979—; adv. asso. Rutgers U. Grad. Sch. Library and Info. Scis., 1978— Editor: Bibliofile, 1967—69; contbr. articles to profl. jours. Mem. PTA, 1950-66; den mother Cub Scouts, 1952-59. Mem. Spl. Libraries Assn. (sec., dir., v.p., pres. Princeton-Trenton 1971, 75-80), Am. Chem. Soc. (bus. mgr., sec., dir. Trenton sect. 1969-78), AAUW, Mortar Board, Beta Phi Mu, Sigma Pi Sigma, Chi Delta Phi, Pi Sigma Alpha. Home: 1189 Parkside Ave Trenton NJ 08618-2625 Office Phone: 609-883-6459.

RUSSELL, JUDITH, librarian, dean; BA cum laude, Dunbarton Coll. of Holy Cross; MLS, Cath. U. Am. Dir. Office of Electronic Info. Dissemination Svcs. US Govt. Printing Office, Washington, 1991—96, dir. Fed. Depository Libr. Program, supt. documents, 2003—06; dean univ. librs. U. Fla., Gainesville, 2007—. Former dep. dir. Nat. Commn. on Librs. and Info. Sci. (NCLIS). Mem.: ALA. Office: George A Smathers Librs U Fla PO Box 117001 Gainesville FL 32611-7001 Office Phone: 352-273-2505. E-mail: judruss@uflib.ufl.edu.

RUSSELL, KENNETH CALVIN, metallurgical engineering educator; b. Greeley, Colo., Feb. 4, 1936; s. Doyle James and Jennie Frances (Smith) R.; m. Charlotte Louise Wolf, Apr. 13, 1963 (div. 1978); children: David Allan, Doyle John. Met.E., Colo. Sch. Mines, 1959; PhD, Carnegie Inst. Tec., 1963. Engr. Westinghouse Rsch. and Devel. Ctr., 1959-61; NSF postdoctoral fellow Physics Inst., U. Oslo, 1963-64; asst. prof. metallurgy M.I.T., Cambridge, 1964-69, assoc. prof., 1969-78, prof. metallurgy, 1978—, prof. nuc. engring., 1979—. Contbr. articles to profl. publs. Served as 2d lt. U.S. Army, 1959-60. DuPont fellow, 1961-62; NSF fellow, 1962-63 Mem.: Metallurgical Soc. Am. Inst. Mining, Metallurgical and Petroleum Engrs., Am. Phys. Soc. Office: MIT Rm 13-5050 Cambridge MA 02139 Office Phone: 617-253-3328. E-mail: kenruss@mit.edu.

RUSSELL, KENT DUR, museum administrator; b. NYC, Mar. 5, 1952; m. Aisling Gaughan, Mar. 4, 1978; children: Christopher, Edward. BA, Trinity Coll., Dublin, 1975, MA, 1977; MA in Art History and Mus. Studies, CUNY, 1979. Cert. tchr., NY. Asst. curator Nat. Gallery Ireland, 1975-76; tchr. edn. Nat. Gallery Ireland and Mcpl. Gallery, 1977-78; chief curator, registrar collections Mus. Art, Sci. and Industry, Bridgeport, Conn., 1979-81; mng. dir. Newry (Northern Ireland) and Mourne Arts Ctr. and Theatre, 1982-83; vis. arts officer, dir. arts coun. Northern Ireland Gallery Contemporary Art, Belfast, 1982-88; project coord. The Decade Show Mus. Contemporary Hispanic Art, NYC, 1982-88; assoc. dir. for programs, curator edn. Parrish Art Mus., Southampton, NY; CEO Higgins Armory Mus., Worcester, Mass., 1995—2006; CEO, curator Mus. Russian Icons, Clinton, Mass., 2006—. Assoc. prof. mus. studies LI U., Southampton, 1992—; lectr. Bklyn. Mus., 1981; panelist visual arts Brit. Prix de Rome; mem. course devel. and adv. com. New U. Ulster Coll. Art, Belfast; assessment panelist NEH; mem. art in edn. panel Bd. Coop. Ednl. Svcs., Suffolk County, Conn.; mem. com. for minority edn. Southampton High Sch.; founder Internat. Com. of Museums, Assn. Internat. des Critiques d'art, Ireland, 1976. Curatorial scholar Nat. Gallery Ireland, 1976-77, Purser-Griffith scholar Trinity Coll., 1977. Mem.: Am. Assn. Mus. (chair coun. regions), New England Mus. Assn. (pres. 2006—), Soc. Mayflower Descendents, Worcester Club. Office: Mus Russian Icons 203 Union St Clinton MA 01510 Office Phone: 978-598-5000 12. Office Fax: 978-598-5009. Business E-Mail: krussell@rusiconsusa.org.

RUSSELL, KERI, actress; b. Fountain Valley, Calif., Mar. 23, 1976; d. David and Stephanie Russell; m. Shane Deary, Feb. 14, 2007; 1 child, River Russell. Actress: (films) Honey, I Blew Up the Kids, 1992, Eight Days a Week, 1997 Dead Man's Curve, 1998, Mad About Mambo, 2000, We Were Soldiers, 2002, The Upside of Anger, 2005, Mission Impossible III, 2006, Rohtenburg, 2006, Waitress, 2007, August Rush, 2007, Bedtime Stories, 2008; (TV series) MMC, 1989, Mickey Mouse Club, 1991-93, Emerald Cove, 1993, Daddy's Girls, 1994, Malibu Shores, 1996, Roar, 1997, Felicity, 1998-2002 (Golden Globe for Best Performan by an Actress in a TV series 1999); (TV films) MMC in Concert, 1993, Clerks, 1995, The Babysitter's Seduction, 1996, The Lottery, 1996, When Innocence Is Lost, 1997, Cinderelmo, 1999, The Magic of Ordinary Days; (TV mini-series) Into the West, 2005; (TV appearances) Boy Meets World, 1993, Married...with Children, 1987, 7th Heaven, 1996, Roar, 1997. Winner Golden Globe for best performance by an actress in a TV series for Felicity, 1999. Office: The Gersh Agy 232 N Canon Dr Beverly Hills CA 90210-5302*

RUSSELL, KURT, actor; b. Springfield, Mass., Mar. 17, 1951; s. Bing Oliver and Louise Julia (Crone) R.; m. Season Hubley, Mar. 17, 1979 (div. 1984), 1 child, Boston; 1 child (with Goldie Hawn), Wyatt Russell. Student, pub. schs. Profl. baseball player Calif. Angels-AA, 1971-73; co-head (with Goldie Hawn, Kate Hudson, Oliver Hudson) Cosmic Entertainment, 2003—. Actor: (films) The Absent Minded Professor, 1961, It Happened at the World's Fair, 1963, Guns of Diablo, 1964, Follow Me Boys!, 1966, Mosby's Marauders, 1967, The One and Only Genuine Original Family Band, 1968, The Horse in the Grey Flannel Suit, 1968, Guns in the Heather, 1969, The Computer Wore Tennis Shoes, 1970, The Barefoot Executive, 1971, Fools' Parade, 1971, Now You See Him Now You Don't, 1972, Charley and the Angel, 1972, Superdad, 1974, The Strongest Man in the World, 1975, Used Cars, 1980, (voice only) The Fox and the Hound, 1981, Escape from New York, 1981, The Thing, 1982, Silkwood, 1983, Swing Shift, 1984, The Mean Season, 1985, The Best of Times, 1986, Big Trouble in Little China, 1986, Overboard, 1987, Tequila Sunrise, 1988, Winter People, 1989, Tango and Cash, 1989, Backdraft, 1991, Unlawful Entry, 1992, Captain Ron, 1992, Tombstone, 1993, (voice only) Forrest Gump, 1994, Stargate, 1994, Executive Decision, 1996, Breakdown, 1997, Soldier, 1998, 3000 Miles To Graceland, 2001, Vanilla Sky, 2001, Interstate 60, 2002, Dark Blue, 2002, Miracle, 2004, Sky High, 2005, Dreamer: Inspired by a True Story, 2005, Poseidon, 2006, Grindhouse (Death Proof segment), 2007; actor, prodr., writer (films) Escape from L.A., 1996; actor (TV series) Travels with Jamie McPheeters, 1963-64, The New Land, 1974, The Quest, 1976; (TV movies) Dad, Can I Borrow the Car?, 1970, Search for the Gods, 1975, The Deadly Tower, The Quest, 1975, Christmas Miracle in Caulfield U.S.A., 1977, Elvis, 1979, Amber Waves, 1980; (TV appearences) Sam Benedict, 1963, The Eleventh Hour, 1963, Our Man Higgins, 1963, The Man from U.N.C.L.E., 1964, Gilligan's Island, 1965, The Virginian, 1964-65, The Legend of Jesse James, 1966, Laredo, 1966, Lost in Space, 1966, The F.B.I., 1966, The Fugitive, 1964-66, Daniel Boone, 1965-69, Then Came Bronson, 1969, Love, American Style, 1970, The High Cahaparral, 1970, Storefront Lawyers, 1970, The Road West, 1967, Room 222, 1971, Disneyland, 1967-72, Love Story, 1973, Gunsmoke, 1964, 1974, Hec Ramsey, 1974, The New Land, 1974, Harry O, 1975, Police Story, 1974-75, Hawaii Five-O, 1977; exec. prodr. (TV films) 14 Hours, 2005 Served with Calif. Air N.G. Recipient The Disney Legends award, 1998 Mem. Profl. Baseball Players Assn., Stuntman's Assn. Achievements include being the World championship Class Modified Stock, 1959 Race of Champions, Las Vegas.

RUSSELL, LIANE BRAUCH, retired geneticist; b. Vienna, Aug. 27, 1923; came to U.S., 1941; d. Arthur and Clara (Starer) Brauch; m. William Lawson Russell (dec.), Sept. 23, 1947; children: David Lawson, Evelyn Ruth. AB, Hunter Coll., 1945; PhD, U. Chgo., 1949; ScD (hon.), Hunter Coll., NYC, 1999; LHD (hon.), Berea Coll., 2005. Fellow U. Chgo., 1945-46, teaching asst., 1946-47; rsch. asst. Jackson Lab., Bar Harbor, Maine, 1945, 46; rsch. staff mem. Oak Ridge (Tenn.) Nat. Lab., 1947-75, sect. head., 1975-95, sr. rsch. fellow, 1988—2001; ret., 2002. Sci. advisor U.S. Del. at 1st Atoms for Peace Conf., Geneva, Switzerland, 1955; mem. numerous sci. bds. including Nat. Research Council com. on energy and environment, 1975-77, com. on biol. effects of ionizing radiation, 1977-80, bd. on environ. studies and toxicology, 1981-90, Nat. Council on Radiation Protection and Measurement Task Group, Washington, 1975-77, Genetox Program EPA, Washington, 1979—, Internat. Com. for Protection Against Environ. Mutagens and Carcinogens, Lausanne, Switzerland, 1977-83, Internat. com. on standardized genetic nomenclature for mice, 1977-91, office of tech. assessment, scientific adv. panel, 1985-86; mem. task group Internat. Agy. for Research on Cancer, Hanover, Fed. Republic of Germany, 1979, EPA review panel on mutagenicity guidelines, 1985-86; adj. faculty U. Tenn., 1980-. Assoc. editor Mutation Rsch., 1976-96, Environ. Mutagenesis, 1980-83; editor TCWP Newsletter, 1966—; editor: (book) Genetic Mosaics and Chimeras, 1979; contbr. more than 165 articles to profl. jours. Founder Tenn. Citizens for Wilderness Planning, Oak Ridge, 1966, pres. 1967-70, 86-87; active numerous environ. groups. Corp. fellow Union Carbide, 1983; corp. fellow Martin Marietta, 1985, sr. corp. fellow, 1988; recipient Merit award Mademoiselle, 1955, Roentgen medal City of Remscheid-Lennep, 1973, Disting. Assoc. award U.S. Dept. Energy, 1987; named to Hunter Coll. Hall of Fame, 1979, Sol Feinstone Environ. Achievement award SUNY, 1987, Lifetime Achievement award Tenn. Environ. Coun., 1990, Vocational Svc. award Oak Ridge Rotary, 1992, Marjorie Stoneman Douglas award Nat. Parks Conservation Assn., 1993, Enrico Fermi award U.S. Dept. Energy, 1993, Lifetime Conservation Achievement award So. Appalachian Forest Coalition, 1999, Lifetime Environ. Conservation award Tenn. Dept. Environment and Conservation, 2000; Tenn. Clean Water Network River Hero, 2008, River Network River Achievement award, 2009, YWCA Lifetime Achievement Honoree, 2009. Fellow AAAS, Environ. Health Inst.; mem. Nat. Acad. Scis., Environ. Mutagen Soc. (pres. 1984-85, EMS award 1993), Genetics Soc. Am., Tenn. Environ. Honor Soc. Avocation: environmental activism. Personal E-mail: lianerussell@comcast.net. Business E-Mail: russelllb@ornl.gov.

RUSSELL, LOUISE, retired education educator; b. Stratford, Okla., Aug. 9, 1931; d. Virgel Wylie and Louise J. (Hayden) R. BA magna cum laude, Oklahoma City U., 1953; MA, Northwestern U., 1955; PhD, Ind. U., 1977; postgrad., Colo. State U., 1981-82. Tchr. pub. schs., Sterling, Colo., 1958-59, Washington-Lee HS, Arlington, Va., 1959-62, John Handley HS, Winchester, Va., 1962-63, Weld Sch. Dist. No. 6, Greeley, Colo., 1963-68, 72-87, Colegio Internat., Valencia, Venezuela, 1968-69, Holmdel Schs., N.J., 1971-72; chmn. staff devel. team, English and basic skills Northland Pioneer Coll., Holbrook, Ariz., 1987-91, also subject specialist, 1987-91; instr. English humanitiea Ea. N.Mex. U., 1992-93; grant dir. Title V Indian edn. Dulce Ind. Sch. Dist., 1994-96; chmn. English dept. Santa Rosa Consol Schs., 1996-98, ret., 1998. Adj. faculty Otero Jr. Coll., La Junta, Colo., 1999-2000, Aims Cmty. Coll., 2006-. Author: Understanding Folklore, 1975, Understanding Folk Music, 1977; also articles. Named Tchr. of Yr., Masons. Mem. MLA, Am. Anthrop. Assn., Am. Folklore Soc., Nat. Coun. Tchrs. English, Phi Delta Kappa.

RUSSELL, LOUISE BENNETT, economist, educator; b. Exeter, NH, May 12, 1942; d. Frederick Dewey and Esther (Smith) B.; m. Robert Hardy Cosgriff, May 3, 1987; 1 child, Benjamin Smith Cosgriff. BA, U. Mich., 1964; PhD, Harvard U., 1971. Economist Social Security Adminstrn., Washington, 1968-71, Nat. Commn. on State Workmen's Compensation Laws, Washington, 1971-72, Dept. Labor, Washington, 1972-73; sr. economist Nat. Planning Assn., Washington, 1973-75; sr. fellow Brookings Instn., Washington, 1975-87; rsch. prof. Inst. for Health, Health Care Policy and Aging Rsch. Rutgers U., New Brunswick, N.J., 1987—, prof. econs., 1987—. Chmn. health care policy divsn. Rutgers U., 1988—. Author: Technology in Hospitals, 1979, The Baby Boom Generation and the Economy, 1982, Is Prevention Better Than Cure, 1986, Evaluating Preventive Care: Report on a Workshop, 1987, Medicare's New Hospital Payment System: Is It Working, 1989, Educated Guesses: Making Policy About Medical Screening Tests, 1994, (with MR Gold, JE Siegel and MC Weinstein) Cost-Effectiveness in Health and Medicine, 1996, (with M. Pignone, J. Wagner) Economic Models of Colorectal Cancer Screening in Average Risk Adults, 2005; contbr. over 100 articles to profl. jours.; assoc. editor Med. Decision Making, 2004—. Mem. U.S. Preventive Svcs. Task Force, 1984-88; co-chair Panel on Cost Effectiveness in Health and Medicine DHHS, USPHS, 1993-96. Mem. Inst. Medicine of NAS (elected 1983, com. to study future pub. health 1986-87, bd. on health scis. policy 1989-91, com. on clin. practice guidelines 1990-91, com. on setting priorities for practice guidelines 1994, nat. cancer policy bd. 2001-05). Office: Rutgers U Inst for Health Care Policy 30 College Ave New Brunswick NJ 08901-1293 Business E-Mail: lrussell@rci.rutgers.edu.

RUSSELL, MARK A., dermatologist; BS in Nutrition, Ohio State U., Columbus, MD. Dermatology resident Vanderbilt U., Nashville, 1994—97, mohs & dermatologic surgery fellow, 1998—99; dermatopathology fellow U. Va., Charlottesville, 1999—2000; mohs & dermatologic surgery dir., vice chair, dept. dermatology U. Va. Health Sys., Charlottesville, 2009—. Recipient Acad. Disting. Educators award, U. Va., 2006. Fellow: Am. Soc. Dermatopathology, Am. Soc. Dermatologic Surgery, Am. Coll. Mohs Surgery, Am. Acad. Dermatology. Office: Univ Va Box 800718 Charlottesville VA 22908 Office Fax: 434-924-5936.

RUSSELL, MARY RHODES, state supreme court judge; b. Hannibal, Mo., July 28, 1958; d. Cleveland Jerome and Mary Elisabeth (Stewart) Rhodes; m. James Lowell Russell, Nov. 25, 1995. BA in Mass. Comms., BS in Home Econs., Truman State U., 1980; JD, U. Mo., Columbia, 1983. Bar: Mo. 1983, Ill. 1984, U.S. Dist. Ct. (ea. dist.) 1984, U.S. Supreme Ct. 1992. Adminstrv. asst. Mo. Senate, Jefferson City, 1980-83, law clk., 1983-84; ptnr. Clayton & Rhodes, Hannibal, 1984-95; judge Mo. Ct. Appeals (ea. dist.), St. Louis, 1995—2004, Mo. Supreme Ct., 2004—. Author: Enforcement of Discovery Sanctions, 1994. Bd. dirs. Comm. on Ret., Removal and Discipline of Judges, St. Louis, 1994-95, Matthews-Dickey Boys & Girls Club; mem. urban campout project Girl Scouts USA, St. Louis, 1996; mem., past pres. PEO, Hannibal, 1993-95, Jefferson City, 1995—. Recipient Equal Justice award Legal Svcs. Ea. Mo., 1994, Citation of Merit award U. Mo. Sch. Law, 1997; Henry Toll fellow, 1997. Mem. Bar Assn. St. Louis (chair bench/bar rels. 1996-97), Woman Lawyers Assn. St. Louis, Nat. Assn. Women Judges, Kansas City Met. Bar Assn., Mo. Lawyer Trust Account Found. (vice chmn., bd. dirs. 1990-95), Rotary (program chmn. 1996-97). Episcopalian. Avocations: cardinal baseball, travel, cooking. Office: Supreme Ct Mo PO Box 150 Jefferson City MO 65102 Office Phone: 573-751-6880. Business E-Mail: mary.russell@courts.mo.gov.*

RUSSELL, MASON WEBSTER, economist, consultant; b. Beverly, Mass., July 28, 1956; s. Gordon Arthur and Elizabeth Mason (Webster) R.; m. Susanne Rachel Nadeau, Oct. 22, 1982. BA in Econs., Salem State Coll., 1978; MA in Polit. Economy, Boston U., 1981, postgrad., 1981-87. Lectr. econs. Boston U., 1979-82; asst. prof. econs. Bentley Coll., Waltham, Mass., 1982-85; sr. economist Policy Analysis Inc., Brookline, Mass., 1985-88, 94; exec. dir. White Mountain Health Svcs., Gorham, N.H., 1988-91; dir. corp. devel. North Care Corp., Berlin, N.H., 1991-92; dir., COO Mountain Health Svcs., Berlin, 1991-92; sr. economist Piedmont Group, Richmond, Va., 1992-94; sr. health economist Med. Rsch. Internat., Burlington, Mass., also London, 1994-98; dir. health econs. ICSL Healthcare Rsch., Burlington, Mass., also London, 1998-2000, v.p. outcomes rsch. Waltham, Mass., 2000—02; dir. global health econ., pricing, reimbursement strategy Biogen, Inc., Cambridge, Mass., 2002—04; v.p. rsch. Boston Health Economics, Inc., Waltham, 2004—06; v.p. exec. dir. registers, pricing reimbursement Abt Bio Pharma Solutions, Lexiston, Mass., 2006—. Faculty assoc. Sch. for Lifelong Learning, Univ. System N.H., Berlin, 1990-92; sec., dir. Gorham Devel. Corp., 1990-92; sr. adj. instr. Salem (Mass.) State Coll., 1995-2003; online faculty mem. U. Phoenix, 2005—. Contbr. articles to profl. jours. Pres., dir. United Way No. N.H., Berlin, 1990-92; vice chmn. gt. no. dist. Daniel Webster coun. Boy Scouts Am., 1990-92. Mem. Am. Coll. Healthcare Execs., Internat. Soc. Pharmacoecons. and Outcomes Rsch., Am. Coll. Clin. Pharmacy, Drug Info. Assn., Masons, Phi Kappa Phi. Democrat. Roman Catholic. Home Phone: 978-689-4792; Office Phone: 781-372-6515. Personal E-mail: masonwr@comcast.net. Business E-Mail: mason.russell@abtbiopharma.com.

RUSSELL, MICHAEL, chemistry professor; s. Ron and Bev Russell; m. Jill Russell, Aug. 0, 1999. PhD, Dartmouth Coll., Hanover, NH, 1995. Prof. chemistry Mt. Hood C.C., Gresham, Oreg., 1997—. Dir. DarkTo-Light Prodns., Gresham, 1995—. Office: Mt Hood Community College 26000 SE Stark Gresham OR 97030 E-mail: mike.russell@mhcc.edu.

RUSSELL, NAS'NAGA R., illustrator; b. Dayton, Ohio, Apr. 13, 1941; s. Willard Dudly and Kathryn Louise (Pangborn) R.; m. Harriet Ann Russell, June 1967 (div. 1973); 1 child, Jamie Noelle; m. Barbara Jane Mullins, Sept. 14, 1984. Grad. h.s. Mgr. AAAirlines, Ft. Worth, 1970-74; writer Harper & Rowe, NYC, 1974-75; owner, dir. Art Gallery, Kettering, Ohio, 1979-83. Dir., owner Nas'Naga Enterprises, Inc. Pro., Centerville, Ohio, 1980-83; lectr., spkr. in field. Author, illustrator: Indians' Summer, 1975, Western Writers of America, 1975-1980, Dayton's Society of Painters and Sculptors, 1978-1980, Faces Beneith The Grass, 1979, Darker Side of Glory, 2000; columnist Western Mag., Oslo, Norway, 1976-79; co-author: Poetry Anthology, 2004. Airlines rep. Okla. for Indian Opportunity, Tex., 1970—74; steering com. Newark state mound project Ohio Hist. Soc., 2000. With USN, 1959—63. Recipient Humanitarian Svc. award Oklahomians for Indian Opportunity, Norman, Okla., 1973, United Cerebeal Palsy, Dayton, 1984, Outstanding Artistic Achievement award Green County Ohio, Xenia, 1975. Avocations: archery, painting, research. Home: 3000 B E Main St #359 Columbus OH 43209

RUSSELL, PATRICK L., psychology educator; b. Windom, Minn., Jan. 30, 1961; s. Perry L. and Anne R. Russell; m. Kimberly A. Rudebusch, July 4, 1998; children: Claire C., Joseph P., Samuel A., Liam N. EdS, U. Wis., River Falls, 1990. Sch. psychologist Meeker and Wright Spl. Edn. Coop., Cokato, Minn., 1990—2001, Isd 742, St. Cloud, Minn., 2001—. Edn. specialist Minn. Dept. Health, Willmar, 1994—97. Worship leader United Meth. Ch., Litchfield, Minn., 2005—07. Independent. Office: Talahi Cmty Sch 1321 University Dr SouthEast Saint Cloud MN 56304 E-mail: patrick.russell@isd742.org.

RUSSELL, PAUL EDGAR, electrical engineering educator; b. Roswell, N.Mex., Oct. 10, 1924; s. Rueben Matthias and Mary (Parsons) R.; m. Lorna Margaret Clayshulte, Aug. 29, 1943; children: Carol Potter, Janice Russell Cook, Gregory. BSEE, N.Mex. State U., 1946, BSME, 1947; MSEE, U. Wis., 1950, PhDEE, 1951. Registered elec. engr., Ariz. From instr. to asst. prof. elec. engring. U. Wis., Madison, 1947-52; sr. engr., design specialist Gen. Dynamics Corp., San Diego, 1952-54; from prof. to chmn. elec. engring. dept. U. Ariz., Tucson, 1954-63; dean engring. Kans. State U., Manhattan, 1963-67; prof. Ariz. State U., Tempe, 1967-90; dir. engring. Ariz. State U. West, Phoenix, 1985-88; dir. Sch. Constrn. and Tech. Ariz. State U., Tempe, 1988-90. Cons. in field, 1954—; programs evaluator, mem. engring. commn. Accreditation Bd. for Engring. and Tech., N.Y.C., 1968-81. Contbr. articles to jours. and chpts. to books. Served as sgt. U.S. Army, 1944-46. Recipient Disting. Service award N.Mex. State U., 1965. Fellow IEEE (life, chmn. Ariz. sect. 1960), Accreditation Bd. Engring. and Tech.; mem. Am. Soc. Engring. Educators. Home: 5902 E Caballo Ln Paradise Valley AZ 85253 Office Phone: 480-948-0716.

RUSSELL, PAUL ELLIOTT, literature and language professor; b. Memphis, July 1, 1956; AB in English, Oberlin Coll., Ohio, 1978; MFA in Creative Writing, Cornell U., Ithaca, NY, 1982, PhD in English, 1983. Prof., english Vassar Coll., Poughkeepsie, NY, 1983—. Author: (novels) War Against the Animals, The Coming Storm (Ferro-Grumley award, 2000), Sea of Tranquillity, Boys of Life, The Salt Point, (book) The Gay

100: A Ranking of the Most Influential Gays and Lesbians, Past and Present. Home: 842 Elting Rd Rosendale NY 12472 Office: Vassar Coll 124 Raymond Ave Poughkeepsie NY 12604 Business E-Mail: russell@vassar.edu.

RUSSELL, PAUL GEORGE, lawyer; b. Akron, Ohio, Feb. 23, 1929; s. Paul George Russell and Fern Winter; m. Katherine Davis, Aug. 21, 1957 (div. 1972); m. Jinee Dunn, Sept. 20, 1980; 1 child, Camilla S.W. BA in Polit. Sci. with honors, Kenyon Coll., 1950; LLB, Harvard U., 1957. Bar: NY 1958. Assoc. Dewey, Ballantine, Bushby, Palmer & Wood, NYC, 1957-60; corp. sec. E.F. Hutton, Inc., NYC, 1960-62; ptnr. LeBoeuf, Lamb, Leiby & MacRae, NYC, 1972—86, Morgan, Lewis & Bockius, NYC, 1986—90; founder, mng. dir. Pacific Legal Group, Bangkok, 1990—2008; dir. regulatory affairs Tilleke & Gibbins Internat. Ltd., Bangkok, 2008—. Sec.-treas. US Korea Soc., NYC, 1980-85. V.p., coun. mem. Siam Soc., Bangkok, 1998-2004; founder, bd. mem. Am. C. of C. Thailand Charitable Fund, Bangkok, 2004-; Lt. USN, DC, 1950-54. Fellow Am. Coll. Investment Counsel; mem. ABA (coun. mem. pub. utility law sect. 1978-85, chmn. utility fin. com. 1978-85), Internat. Bar Assn. (vice chmn. utility com. 1983-85), Law Assn. for Asia and the Pacific, Harvard Law Sch. Assn., Am. C. of C. (founder, chmn. healthcare com. 2004-), Harvard Club Thailand (mem. exec. com.), Knickerbocker Club (NYC), Royal Bankok Sports Club Polo Club, Brit. Club, Heritage Club, Pacific City Club. Avocations: running, scuba diving, reading, travel. Home: Unit 5B 539 Prime Mansion Sukhumvit Soi 31 Bangkok Thailand 10110 Office: Supalai Grand Tower 26th Fl 1011 Rama 3 Rd Chongnonsi Yannawa Bangkok 10120 Thailand

RUSSELL, PAUL SNOWDEN, surgeon, educator; b. Chgo., Jan. 22, 1925; s. Paul Snowden and Carroll (Mason) R.; m. Allene Lummis, Sept. 24, 1952; children: Katherine Swift, Paul Snowden, Allene, Laura Rice. PhB, U. Chgo., 1944, BS, 1945, MD, 1947; MA (hon.), Harvard U., 1962. Diplomate Am. Bd. Surgery, Am. Bd. Thoracic Surgery. From surg. intern. to resident Mass. Gen. Hosp., 1948-56, asst. surgery, 1957-60, chief gen. surg. svcs., 1962-69, chmn. com. on rsch., 1973-76; postdoctoral fellow USPHS, 1954-55; from tchg. fellow to clin. assoc. surgery Harvard Med. Sch., 1956-60, John Homans prof. surgery, 1962-98, John Homans Disting. prof. surgery, 1998—; assoc. prof. surgery Columbia Coll. Phys. and Surg., 1960-62; assoc. attending surgeon Presbyn. Hosp., NYC, 1960-62; assoc. vis. surgeon Francis Delafield Hosp., NYC, 1960-62, 74-94. Mem. com. tissue transplantation NRC-Nat. Acad. Scis., 1963-71, com. trauma, 1963-68; ad hoc com. to study clin. investigation and edn. in USN, 1971-73; allergy and immunology study sect. USPHS, 1963-65, chmn. allergy and immunology study sect. B, 1965-67; mem. transplantation and immunology com. Nat. Inst. Allergy and Infectious Diseases, 1967-69, chmn., 1970; mem. com. on cancer immunotherapy Nat. Cancer Inst., 1974-79. Contbr. papers in field.; Editorial bd.: Archives Surgery, 1963-72, Surgery, 1963-71, Transplantation, 1965-79, Annals of Surgery, 1966—, Transplantation Procs, 1966—, Jour. Immunology, 1977-80. Trustee Pine Manor Coll., Chestnut Hill, Mass., 1963-76, Groton Sch., 1964-79, The Conservation Law Found., 1997—; bd. dirs. Boston Fulbright Com., 1968, pres., 1980—; vice chmn. bd. govs., trustee corp. Jackson Lab. With USAF, 1951-53. Recipient Roche Pioneer award, Am. Soc. Transplant Surgeons, 2005. Fellow AAAS, ACS, Royal Soc. Medicine, Am. Acad. Arts and Scis., Assn. Immunologists, NY Acad. Scis., Mass. Med. Soc., New Eng. Surg. Soc., Boston Surg. Soc. (pres. 1994), Soc. Univ. Surgeons, Soc. Exptl. Biology and Medicine, Halsted Soc., Whipple Soc., Internat. Soc. Surgery, Am. Surg. Assn., Transplantation Soc. (pres. 1970, Medawar Prize 2005), Polish Acad. Sci. (fgn.), Sigma Xi. Home: 10 Longwood Dr Apt 148 Westwood MA 02090 Office: Dept Surgery Mass Gen Hosp Boston MA 02114 Office Phone: 617-726-2801.

RUSSELL, RICHARD DONCASTER, geophysics educator, academic administrator; b. Toronto, Ont., Can., Feb. 27, 1929; s. Richard Douglas and Ada Gwennola (Doncaster) R.; m. Virginia Ann Reid Clippingdale, Aug. 11, 1951; children: Linda Jean, Morna Ann, Mary Joyce. BA, U. Toronto, 1951, MA, 1952, PhD, 1954. Asst. prof. physics U. Toronto, 1956-58, prof., 1962-63; assoc. prof. physics U. B.C., Vancouver, Canada, 1958-62, prof. geophysics, 1963-91, prof. emeritus, 1991—, head dept. geophysics, 1968-72, head dept. geophysics and astronomy, 1972-79, bd. govs., 1978-81, assoc. dean sci., 1980-83, assoc. v.p. acad., 1983-86. Sec.-gen. Inter-Union Commn. on Geodynamics, 1976—80; profl. geoscientist. Author (with John Arthur Jacobs and J. Tuzo Wilson): Physics and Geology International Series in the Earth Sciences, first edit., 1959, Physics and Geology McGraw-Hill International Series in the Earth and Planetary Science, 2d edit., 1973; author: (with Ronald McCunn Farquhar) Lead Isotopes in Geology Interscience, 1960. Fellow Royal Soc. Can.; mem. Am. Geophys. Union, Can. Geophys. Union (J. Tuzo Wilson medal 1992). Home: 226-4955 River Rd Delta BC Canada V4K 4V9

RUSSELL, RICHARD OLNEY, JR., retired cardiologist; b. Birmingham, Ala., July 9, 1932; s. Richard Olney and Louise (Taylor) R.; m. Phyllis Hutchinson, June 15, 1963; children: Scott Richard, Katherine Hutchinson, Meredith Cooper, Stephen Wilbon. AB cum laude, Vanderbilt U., Nashville, 1953, MD, 1956. Diplomate Am. Bd. Internal Medicine, 1964, Am. Bd. Cardiovascular Disease, 1967. Intern Peter Bent Brigham Hosp., Boston, 1956-57, resident, 1959-60, 63-64; fellow in cardiology Med. Coll. Ala., Birmingham, 1960-62, instr., 1962-63; instr. medicine U. Ala., Birmingham, 1964-65, asst. prof., 1965-70, assoc. prof., 1970-73, prof., 1973-81, clin. prof., 1981—2006; pvt. practice medicine specializing in cardiology Birmingham, 1981—2006; ret., 2006. Mem. Jefferson County Bd. Health, 1977—81, chmn., 1979. Author: (with Charles Edward Rackley) Hemodynamic Monitoring in a Coronary Intensive Care Unit, 1974, 2d rev. and enlarged edit., 1981, Coronary Artery Disease: Recognition and Management, 1979, (with others) Radiographic Anatomy of the Coronary Arteries: An Atlas, 1976, Acute Ischemic Syndromes in American College of Cardiology Self Assessment Program, 1993; mem. editl. bd. Circulation, 1976-80, Am. Jour. Cardiology, 1977-82, Heart and Lung, 1978-83, Chest, 1978-83, Ala. Jour. Med. Scis, 1977-80, Jour. Am. Coll. Cardiology, 1987-90; sect. editor for Case Studies for Cardiosource for Am. Coll. Cardiology, 2001-06, assoc. editor, 2006—; contbr. articles to profl. jours. Distbn. com. Greater Birmingham Found., 1984-90; exec. bd. Birmingham area coun. Boy Scouts Am., 1987-1998, v.p., 1990-96, coun. commr., 1996-98; vice chmn. Vulcan dist., 1988-89, chmn., 1989-91, bd. dirs. S.E. region, 1990-92, bd. dirs. southern region, 1992—; bd. dirs. Ctrl. Ala. United Way, 1988-92; mem. Newcomen Soc., 1988—; chmn. exec. com. Birmingham Bapt. Med. Ctr., Montclair, 1995, pres.-elect med. staff, 1998-99, pres. 1999-2000; chmn. Nat. Eagle Scout Assn. Scholarship Com. So. Region, 2001-03, chmn. area nine, 2009-; asst. coun. commr. Greater Ala. coun. Boy Scouts Am., 1998-2000, coun. commr., 2001-04, v.p. bd., 2006, pres., 2007; mem. Am. Bd. Cardiovasc. Disease, 1991-96. Capt. U.S. Army. Decorated Commendation medal; recipient Dist. Award of Merit, Boy Scouts Am., 1991, Silver Beaver award, 1990, Disting. Eagle Scout, 1999, Silver Antelope award 2001, Vigil Honor, 2007; NIH rsch. fellow, 1966-67. Fellow: ACP, Am. Coll. Cardiology (bd. govs. 1979—81, trustee 1984—85, 1989—94, ann. sci. session program chmn. 1994, disting. fellowship 2001, Ala. chpt. named lectureship in honor); mem.: Med. Assn. State Ala. (spkr. house counselors dels. 1989—94, Laureate award 1999), Birmingham Soc. Internists (pres. 2001—03), Birmingham Cardiovascular Soc. (pres. 1981), Jefferson County Med. Soc. (v.p. 1982, pres. 1984), So. Soc. Clin. Investigation, Am. Fedn. Clin. Rsch., Am. Coll. Chest Physicians (bd. regents 1985—91), Am. Heart Assn. (pres. Ala. affiliate 1975—76, v.p. so. region 1986—87, task force on practice guidelines 1998—2000), Royal Soc. Medicine, NY Acad. Scis., Kiwanis (Brimingham sec. 1984—85, disting. pres. 1994—95), Leadership Birmingham, Omicron Delta Kappa, Alpha Omega Alpha, Phi Beta Kappa. Home: 4408 Kennesaw Dr Birmingham AL 35213-1826 Personal E-mail: rorussell@charter.net.

RUSSELL, ROB, academic administrator; b. Knoxville, Tenn., Dec. 8, 1969; m. Tracey Russell; children: Kieran, Lucinda. BA in English/History, East Tenn. State U., 1991; MA in English, U. Tenn., 1993. Dir. Va. Intermont Coll. Writing Ctr., 1995—97, East Tenn. State U. Writing and Communication Ctr., 1997—; instr. NE State Tech. Cmty. Coll., 1993—95. Democrat. Unitarian Universalist. Office: PO Box 3413 Kingsport TN 37664-3413 Office Phone: 423-571-2515. Office Fax: 423-283-7600. Business E-Mail: rob@robrussellforcongress.com.*

RUSSELL, ROBERT A., legislative staff member; b. Camden, Ark., June 28, 1963; m. Amelia Mosley, Dec. 15, 1990; 3 children. BS, So. Ark. U., Magnolia, 1986; JD, U. Ark. Law Sch., Little Rock, 1990. Bar: Ark. 1990, US Dist Ct. 1990, US Ct. Appeals (8th cir.) 1992, US Supreme Ct. 1996, US Ct. Fed. Claims 2001. Atty. Bramhall, Duncan & Ohm, PA, 1990—91, Bramhall, Duncan & Russell, PA, 1991—93, Duncan & Rainwater, PA, 1993—98; chief dep. atty. State of Ark., 1999—2000; ptnr. Roberts, Roberts & Russell, PA, 2000—02; chief of staff to Senator Mark Pryor US Senate, Washington, 2003—. Democrat. Baptist. Office: 255 Dirksen Senate Office Bldg Washington DC 20510-0405 Office Phone: 202-224-2353. Business E-Mail: bob_russell@pryor.senate.gov.*

RUSSELL, ROBERT HILTON, Romance languages and literature educator; b. Oak Park, Ill., Dec. 26, 1927; s. Melvin Alvord and Gladys (Hilton) R.; m. June Adele Thayer, Oct. 27, 1956. AB, Knox Coll., 1949; A.M., Harvard U., 1950, PhD, 1963; A.M., Dartmouth Coll., 1968. Instr. Romance langs. and lits. Dartmouth Coll., 1957-61, asst. prof., 1961-63, assoc. prof., 1963-67, prof., 1967—93, prof. emeritus, 1993—. Vis. prof. Spanish, U. San Diego, 1989, 90, 91, Knox Coll., 1993; guest lectr. Trinity Coll., Dublin, 1967, U. Salamanca, 1977, U. Leeds, 1978, Oxford U., 1978, U. P.R., 1987. Author: The Christ Figure in Misericordia, 1968; translator: Our Friend Manso, 1987, Misericordia, 2007. Corporate mem. United Ch. Bd. Homeland Ministries, 1963-69; N.H. del. Gen. Synod, United Ch. Christ, 1973, 75; corporator Internat. Inst. in Spain. Mem. MLA, Asociación Internacional de Hispanistas, Asociación Internacional de Galdosistas, Phi Beta Kappa. Democrat. Home: 17 Willow Spring Cir Hanover NH 03755-2901 Office: 6072 Dartmouth Hall Hanover NH 03755-3511

RUSSELL, RODNEY E., school system administrator; b. Knoxville, Tenn., Feb. 3, 1964; s. Howard Wade and Lucille Annette Russell; m. Jamie Renee Humphrey, Apr. 7, 1990; 1 child, Daniel Thomas. BS, East Tenn. State U., 1986; EdS, Lincoln Meml. U., Harrogate, Tenn., 1997; EdD, Trevecca Nazarene U., Nashville, 2005. Supr. staff devel. and extended learning Knox County Schs., Knoxville, 2003—, evening alternative sch. prin., 2005—06. Non-daycare facility mgr. Boys Club of Knoxville, 1985—87; lang. devel. specialist Knox County Schs., 1987—97, tchr. 4th grade, 1989—96, sci. specialist, 1996—2003; min. of youth Smithwood Bapt. Ch., Knoxville, 1999—. Bd. dirs. Tenn. Staff Devel. Coun., Tenn., 2000—06. Recipient Beacon in the Classroom award, Apple Computers, 1994, 21st Century grant for computer tech., Knox County Schs., 1992; named Tchr. of the Yr. Bldg. Level, Tenn. Dept. of Edn., 1993; named to Leadership Edn. Class, Knoxville C. of C., 1993; grantee, Jr. League of Knoxville, 1995. Mem.: NEA (assoc.), NSTA (assoc.), Tenn. Staff Devel. Coun. (assoc.; bd. dirs. 2000—06), Nat. Staff Devel. Coun. (assoc.; co-chair conf. exhibits 2004—06), Phi Delta Kappa, Pi Lambda Theta. Baptist. Achievements include research in impact of content reading strategies impact on achievement; development of new teacher academy and mentor program for teachers in Knox County. Avocations: golf, swimming, skiing. Office: Sarah Simpson Prof Dev Center 810 Tipton Avenue Knoxville TN 37918 Home: 8072 Leclay Dr Knoxville TN 37938-3031 Office Fax: 865-579-8191; Home Fax: 865-579-8191. Personal E-mail: russell_rodney@bellsouth.net.

RUSSELL, SABIN, newswriter; m. Ashley Wolff; 2 children. Grad., Yale U., 1974. Writer Venture Mag., Electronic News, various cmty. newspapers Vermont and NH; med. writer San Francisco Chronicle, 1988—. Recipient Sci. in Soc. Journalism award, Nat. Assn. Sci. Writers, Inc., 2001; grantee Kaiser mini-fellowship, Kaiser Family Found., 2004. Primary responsibilities include coverage of science and health policy, focusing on topics such as HIV/AIDS, bioterrorism, SARS, West Nile virus, mad cow, and other infectious diseases. Office: San Francisco Chronicle 901 Mission St San Francisco CA 94103-2988 Office Phone: 415-777-8447. Office Fax: 415-896-1107. Business E-Mail: srussell@sfchronicle.com.

RUSSELL, STEFANIE LUISE, dental educator; d. Richard Paul and Rosemarie Elizabeth Russell; m. Robert Davidson, Aug. 10, 1996; 1 child, Sophie Ruth Russell-Davidson. DDS, U. Md., Balt., 1991; MPH, U. Conn., Farmington, 1997; PhD, Yale U., New Haven, 2004. Cert. in gen. dentistry SUNY, Stony Brook, 1992, periodontics U. Conn., 1997, in geriatric dentistry 1997. Asst. prof. NY U. Coll. Dentistry, NYC, 1996—. Grantee, NIH, 2007. Mem.: APHA, Internat. Assn. Dental Rsch. Liberal. Office: NY Univ Coll Dentistry 250 Pk Ave S 6th Fl New York NY 10003 Business E-Mail: slr6@nyu.edu.

RUSSELL, STELLA PANDELL, artist, author, educator; b. NYC, June 14, 1927; d. James C. and Dorothy (Ross) Pandell; m. George Russell, Aug. 10, 1951 (dec.); children: Janna, Jonathan, Loriann. BA, Hunter Coll., 1948; MA, Columbia U., 1950, PhD, 1972; M in Comml. Arts, NY Inst. Tech., 1986. Animator, Loucks and Norling Co., 1948; dir. art Alexander's Dept. Stores, NYC, 1948-51; tchr. art pub. schs., NYC, 1951-53; co-dir. Russell-Pandell Art Studies, NYC, 1953-61; lectr. art Hunter Coll., NYC, 1961-65; chmn. art Nassau CC, NY, from 1965; one-woman shows include: Oyster Bay Library, NY, 1962, 63, Huntington Library, 1970, Nassau CC, 1971, South Nassau Library, 1973, 83, Firehouse Gallery, 1975, 84, Country Art Gallery, 1977; group shows include: NY State U. traveling exhbn., 1969, St. John's U., 1975, Central Hall Gallery, 1976, C.W. Post Coll., 1977, Royal Acad., Stockholm, 1978, 82, Islip Mus., 1985, Fine Art Mus. of Lit., 1987; represented permanent collections Hunter Coll., Sallskapet Mus., Sweden, Zimmerli Coll., Rutgers U.; host Art in World sta. WHPC, Garden City, 1972—, Art and Religion, 2005-. Author: Art in the World, 1975, 84, 89, 94; contbr. articles to profl. jours. Winner Chancellor's award excellence in teaching, 1982. Mem. Profl. Artists Guild, NY State Ann. Jr. Colls., Nat. Assn. Women Artists, NY State African Studies Assn. Unitarian. Club: Mensa. also: 90 Lawton Rd Hilton Head Island SC 29928 Office: Stewart Ave Garden City NY 11530 Personal E-mail: drstellarrussell@aol.com.

RUSSELL, STEVE D., elementary school educator; b. Spring Valley, Ill., June 15, 1945; m. Kay A. Russell, Aug. 19, 1967; children: Tammy Syverson, Lori Templeman, Brad, Sarah Suhr. MS, U. Iowa, Iowa City, 1971. Tchr. Harding Mid. Sch., Cedar Rapids, Iowa, 1967—2002; tchr. math, sci. Cedar Valley Christian Sch., Cedar Rapids, 2002—09. Mem.: Profl. Educators Iowa. Conservative. Office: Cedar Valley Christian School 3636 Cottage Grove Ave SE Cedar Rapids IA 52402

RUSSELL, STUART DEAN, cardiologist, educator; BS in Cellular and Molecular Biology, U. Wash., Seattle, 1986, MD, 1991. Bd. cert. in cardiology and internal medicine. Resident Johns Hopkins Hosp., Balt., 1991—94, assoc. prof. medicine, 2004—, chief of heart failure and transplantation; fellow Duke U. Med. Ctr., 1994—97; transplant fellow UCLA Med. Ctr., 1997—98. Contbr. several articles to profl. jours. Office: Johns Hopkins Hosp Carnegie 568 600 N Wolfe St Baltimore MD 21287 Office Fax: 410-955-3478. E-mail: srusse14@jhmi.edu.

RUSSELL, SUE ANN, clinical psychologist; b. Connersville, Ind., Apr. 14, 1949; d. Hugh B. Russell and Martha Jane Meyer. BS, U. Colo., 1971; MDiv, Abilene Christian U., 1981; MS in Clin. Psychology, U. North Tex., 1984; PhD in Clin. Psychology, U. N.D., 1992. Intern Psychol. Svcs. Ctr. U. N.D., Grand Forks, 1986-92; intern Stone Ctr. Wellesley Coll., Wellesley, Mass., 1991-92; rsch. psychologist women's drinking project U. ND, Grand Forks, 1986-92; pvt. practice Grand Forks, 1993—. Founding fellow Jean Baker Miller Tng. Inst. of Wellesley Coll., 1996. Contbr. articles to profl. jours. Missionary to Tonga Tribe Africa, Zambia, 1972—74. Fellowship Nat. Inst. on Alcohol Abuse and Alcoholism Nat. Inst. of Mental Health, 1991-92, Nat. Rsch. Svc. award 1988-91; pre-doctoral rsch. fellow Stone Ctr. of Wellesley Coll., 1991-92. Mem. Am. Psychol. Assn., N.D. Psychol. Assn., Assn. of Prevention and Cruelty to Animals Avocations: American Eskimo dogs, creating wildlife sanctuary and natural prairie habitat on 290 acres. Office: 628 7th Ave S Ste B Grand Forks ND 58201-4854 Office Phone: 701-746-8737.

RUSSELL, TERRENCE JOSEPH, lawyer; b. Jacksonville, Fla., Sept. 26, 1944; AA, St. Leo Coll., 1964; BA, U. Fla., 1966; JD, Fla. State U., 1968. Bar: Fla. 1969. Law clk. to Hon. W.O. Mehrtens U.S. Dist. Ct. (so. dist.) Fla., 1969; atty. Ruden, McClosky, Smith, Schuster & Russell, P.A., Ft. Lauderdale, Fla. Mem. appellate restructure commn. Fla. Supreme Ct., 1985—86, mem. nominating com., 1994—, chmn. nominating com., 1997, 98; mem. Fed. Magistrate's merit selection panel, 1985; vice-chmn. 17th Jud. Cir. Nominating Com., 1982—84, chmn., 1985—86; mem. spl. com. representation of death sentenced inmates Fla. Bar, bd. govs., 1987—91, pres., 2001—02. Bd. govs. Nova U. Law Sch., 1981, chmn., 1993—97; bd. dirs. Broward County Legal Aid Svcs., 1985—86. Mem.: ATLA, ABA (ho. of dels. 2000—04, sects. litig., legal edn.), Fla. Jud. Qualifications Commn., Fla. Bar Found. (bd. dirs. 1992—98, pres. 2004—), Fla. State U. Law Sch. Alumni Assn. (pres. 1985), Am. Bd. Trial Advs., Am. Bar Found., Acad. Fla. Trial Lawyers (coll. diplomates), Broward County Trial Lawyers Assn., Broward County Bar Assn. (chmn. spl. com. legal malpractice ins. 1978, bar-bench liaison com. 1978, jud. selection and tenure com. 1978—79, exec. com. 1980, 1981, pres. 1984—85), Gold Key, Delta Theta Phi. Office: Ruden McClosky et al PO Box 1900 Fort Lauderdale FL 33302-1900 Home Phone: 954-753-1125; Office Phone: 954-527-2460. Business E-Mail: terrence.russell@ruden.com.

RUSSELL, THEODORE EMERY, diplomat; b. Madras, India, Nov. 21, 1936; s. Paul Farr and Phyllis Hope R.; m. Sara Mather Stedman, Sept. 3, 1960; children: Douglas Richmond, Richard Mather. BA, Yale U., 1958; MA, Fletcher Sch. Law & Diplomacy, 1960, MALD, 1961; sr. tng., Nat. War Coll., 1980—81. Fgn. svc. officer Dept. State, Italy, Czechoslovakia, Washington, 1963-80, dep. office dir. (EUR/RPE) Washington, 1981-83; dep. chief mission Copenhagen, 1983-87, Prague, Czechoslovakia, 1988-91; dep. asst. adminstr. for internat. activities EPA, Washington, 1992-93; amb. to Slovak Republic Bratislava, Slovakia, 1993-96; dep. comdt. internat. affairs Army War Coll., Carlisle, Pa., 1996-99; dir. internat. rels. MHz Networks, 2001—03; internat. security affairs cons., 2001—. Adj. fellow CSIS. Founding chmn. Friends of Slovakia. Mem. Washington Inst. Fgn. Affairs, Fgn. Svc. Assn., Nat. War Coll. Alumni Assn. Avocations: hiking, fishing, history. Home and Office: 1833 Briar Ridge Ct Mc Lean VA 22101-4233

RUSSELL, THOMAS ARTHUR, humanities educator, religious studies educator, researcher; b. Wash., DC, May 10, 1954; s. Donald Earle and Elizabeth Fowler Russell; m. Anne Elizabeth Holmes Russell, June 6, 1981; 1 child, Thomas Donald. BA in History, Furman U., Greenville, SC, 1976; MDiv, Gordon-Conwell Theol. Sem., S.Hamilton, Mass., 1980; MA in Religious Studies, Vanderbilt U., Nashville, 1992; PhD in Religious Studies, Vanderbilt U., 1999. Assoc. pastor 1st United Ch., Swampscott, Mass., 1977—81; min. christian edn. Ch. of Apostles, Fairfax, Va., 1982—85; tchg. asst. world religions and Hebrew bible Vanderbilt U., 1986—88; bibliographer world religions Vanderbilt Div. Sch. Libr., 1986—96; vis. asst. prof. religious studies, lectr. Western Ky. U., Bowling Green, 1988—2003, rsch. dir. so. migrations rsch. project, 2001—04; adj. instr. Belmont U., Nashville, 2003—, Palm Beach Cmty. Coll., Fla., 2003—, U. Md., Coll. Park, 2004—, Excelsior Coll., Albany, NY, 2004—, grad. thesis dir., 2007—; undergrad. and grad. instr. humanities U. Memphis, 2004—; chaplain Just Crumbs Ministry, Franklin, Tenn., 2007—. Cons. Christian edn. Diocese of Va., Richmond, 1982—84, organizer diocesan-wide christian edn. confs., 1982—84; faculty rep. Potter Coll. libr. com. Western Ky. U., 1999—2001, faculty rep. Asian studies minor com., 1999—2001, organizer spl. presentations, 2001—04, organizer spl. events, 2001, grant overseer, 2001—04; cons. various newspapers Bowling Green, Nashville, Owensboro, 2001—; del. to ann. conv. Episcopal Diocese Tenn., Nashville, 2005—07, diocesan christian edn. com. mem., 2008—; cons. Excelsior Coll., 2006; del. Diocese Tenn., 2006—07; spkr. in field. Contbr. articles to profl. jours. and manuscripts. Adult Sunday sch. tchr. St. Paul's Episcopal Ch., Franklin, 1995—2004, Ch. of Apostles, Franklin, 2004—07; guest bible tchr. Ch. of Resurrection, Franklin, 2007. Nominee Pres. Diversity award, Western Ky. U., 2001, Chaney Disting. Prof. award, Belmont U., 2006, Stanley J. Drazek Tchg. Excellence award, U. Md., 2007, Tchg. Recognition award, 2007; Rsch. grant, Pluralism Project of Harvard U., 1999, Louisville Inst., 2001—02, 2002. Mem.: Am. Soc. Missiology (founding mem. 1989—91, student officer 1989—91), Am. Acad. Religion. Avocations: swimming, travel, cooking. Home: 2378 N Berry's Chapel Rd Franklin TN 37069 Office: Univ Memphis Brister Hall 201 Memphis TN 38152 Personal E-mail: drtomrussell@yahoo.com. Business E-Mail: tarussel@memphis.edu.

RUSSELL, THOMAS R., medical association administrator; b. San Francisco; m. Nona Chiampi Russell, 1979; 2 children. BA in Zoology, U. Calif., Berkeley, 1962; MD, Creighton U. Med. Sch., Omaha, 1966. Intern San Francisco Gen. Hosp., 1966—67; resident gen. surgery U.

Calif, San Francisco, 1967, 1971—75; staff Calif. Pacific Med. Ctr., 1975—2000, chmn. dept. surgery, 1980—2000; exec. dir. ACS, Chgo., 2000—. Lt. cmdr., flight surgeon USN, 1968—70, Vietnam. Recipient Med. Exec. Achievement award, AMA, 2004. Fellow: ACS (bd. gov. 1990—93); mem.: Internat. Soc. Surgery, Soc. Am. Gastrointestinal Endoscopic Surgeons, Am. Soc. Colon & Rectal Surgeons. Office: ACS 633 N St Clair St Chicago IL 60611-3234 Office Phone: 312-202-5305. Business E-Mail: trussell@facs.org.*

RUSSELL, THOMAS WILLIAM FRASER, chemical engineer, educator; b. Moose Jaw, Sask., Can., Aug. 5, 1934; s. Thomas D. and Evelyn May (Fraser) R.; m. Shirley A. Aldrich, Aug. 1956; children: Bruce, Brian, Carey. BChe, U. Alta., Canada, 1956; MChe, U. Alta., 1958; PhD, U. Del., 1964. Registered profl. engr., Del. Rsch. engr. Rsch. Coun. of Alta., Edmonton, Alberta, Canada, 1956—58; process design engr. Union Carbide Can., Montreal, Quebec, Canada, 1958—61; Allan P. Colburn prof. of chem. engring. U. Del., Newark, Del., 1961—; acting dean Coll. of Engring., U. Del., 1978—79; dir. Inst. of Energy Conversion, U. Del., 1979—95; chmn. Dept. Chem. Engring., U. Del., 1986—91; vice provost for rsch. U. Del., 2000—05. Cons. E.I. duPont de Nemours & Co., Inc., Wilmington, Del., 1968—. Author 3 books; contbr. articles to profl. jours., patentee in field. Recipient award, NAE, 1990 to present, 3M Lectureship award, Am. Soc. of Engring. Edn., 1984, Thomas H Chilton award, AIChE, Wilmington Sect., 1988. Mem. NAE, Am. Inst. Chem. Engring. (Thomas H. Chilton award 1988, Chem. Engring. Practice award 1987), Am. Chem. Soc., Am. Soc. Engring. Edn. (3M Lecture award chem. engring. divsn. 1984). Achievements include patents for method for the manufacture of thin film solar cells; method for the continuous deposition by vacuum deposition; first to development of a continouus process for the manufacture of thin film solar modules. Avocations: hiking, skiing, windsurfing. Office: U DE Dept Chem Engring Newark DE 19716 Personal E-mail: twfr@udel.edu.

RUSSELL, WALTER DALLAS, JR., diversified financial services company executive; b. Culver City, Calif., Oct. 31, 1979; s. Walter Dallas and Leann Marie Russell. BBA in Fin., U. Houston, 2005. Sr. mgr. MRG, Inc., Houston, 2000—03; escrow officer Land Am. Ptnrs. Title, 2003—. Mem.: AARP (assoc.), Am. Mensa. Personal E-mail: drussell2028@yahoo.com.

RUSSELL, WAYNE DELANO, activist, educator, poet; s. Arthur Ismael and Edna Alberta Russell; children: Dayon Antoni Lorreen, Niani Simone, Taylor Audrey Delana, Nicholas Wayne Whittington. BS in Aerospace Engring., Poly. U., Bklyn., 1999, MS in Fin. Engring., 2002; postgrad., Walden U., Minn., 2004—. CEO World Youth Movement Global Peace, Bklyn., 1992—; lectr. math. CUNY, Bklyn., 2002—; exec. dir. LyricSurge, Bklyn., 2006—. Del. People To People Amb. Program, Bejing, 2007. Author: (poetry) Truly Pertinent Questions, In My Heart, On My Mind, To You-My Love. Recipient Spirit award, Nat. Soc. Black Engrs., 1997, 1998; grantee, The Sloan Found., 2006; fellow, Medgar Evers Coll. CUNY, 2005; scholar, Dept. Def., 1994—98, Lemelson Found. - Poly. U., 2001—02. Mem.: Soc. Econometrics, Global Assn. Risk Profls., Am. Inst. Aero. and Astronautics, Nat. Soc. Black Engrs., Inst. Ops. Rsch. and Mgmt. Scis., Am. Ednl. Rsch. Assn., Acad. Am. Poets, Bros. Acad. None. Achievements include research in metacognition, developmental mathematics; system theory analysis of schools and the prison industrial complex; minority polymer. Avocations: writing, travel, soccer, reading, painting. Office: Medgar Evers College - CUNY 1650 Bedford Ave Brooklyn NY 11225 Home: 965 E 94th St Brooklyn NY 11236-2023 Personal E-mail: wrusse01@aol.com. E-mail: wrussell@mec.cuny.edu.

RUSSELL, WILLIAM JOSEPH, educational association administrator; b. Boston, Sept. 23, 1941; s. Stanley Whiteside and Helen Rita R.; m. Frances Marie Chapdelaine, June 25, 1967; 1 son, Scott David. BS, Boston Coll., 1963; M.Ed., Northeastern U., 1966; PhD, U. Calif., Berkeley, 1971. Head math. dept. Oceana, Pacifica, Calif., 1966-71; asst. for fed. and profl. affairs Am. Ednl. Research Assn., Washington, 1971-73, dep. exec. dir., 1973-74, exec. dir., 1974—2002. Adv. bd. Edn. Resource Info. Center Ednl. Testing Center, Princeton, N.J., 1975-87; exec. officer Nat. Council on Measurement in Edn., Internat. Assn. Computing in Edn., 1987-89. Editor: Ednl. Researcher, 1979-90. Mem. Am. Ednl. Research Assn., Phi Delta Kappa. Roman Catholic. Home: 1443 Creekside Ct Vienna VA 22182-1701 Office: Aera 1430 K St NW Ste 1200 Washington DC 20005-2528 E-mail: bfrussell@gmail.com.

RUSSELL, WILLIAM STEVEN, finance executive; b. Evanston, Ill., Aug. 5, 1948; s. John W. and Lillian H. Russell; m. Susan M. Hanson, Aug. 20, 1972. BS, Southern Ill. U., 1970. CPA Ill. Sr. staff auditor Arthur Andersen & Co., Chgo., 1972—76; acctg. mgr., controller, asst. sec. and treas. Lawter Internat. Inc., Northbrook, Ill., 1976—86, treas. & sec., 1986—87, fin. v.p., treas. and sec., 1987—96; pvt. investor, 1996—. With US Army, 1970—72. Mem.: Am. Inst. CPAs, Beta Gamma Sigma, Beta Alpha Psi. Roman Catholic. Home and Office: 51 Park Lane Park Ridge IL 60068-2834

RUSSELL, WILLIAM TROWER, III, small business owner; b. Apr. 22, 1962; s. William Trower and Elizabeth Russell; m. Katarzyna Orzech; children: Anna Elizabeth, William Stanislaw. BA in Russian Studies, La. State U., Baton Rouge, 1985; grad. student in internat. rels., Inst. World Politics, Washington. Dock supr. Am. Freightways, Jackson, Miss., 1993; sr. rifle co. trainer Vinnell Corp., Riyadh, Saudi Arabia, 1995—96; owner, mgr. K&T Enterprises, Va. Served with US Army, Operation Desert Storm, Kosovo, Operation Iraqi Freedom, lt. col. (ret.) USAR. Mem.: KC. Republican. Mailing: PO Box 630 Johnstown PA 15907 Office: K&T Enterprises 1421 Jefferson Davis Hwy Arlington VA 22202 Office Phone: 703-463-4636.

RUSSELL-TYSON, PEARL LEONIE, elementary school educator; b. Kingston, Jamaica, July 10; d. Claudius Sylvester and Daisy Ann Cox; m. Kenneth Lee Tyson; children: Jermeth Angella Fothergill, Rosemary Tyson, Cheryl Andrea Russell, Laurel Emansea Robinson. BA, Mico U., Jamaica, 1977; BS, NSU, Davie, Fla., 1997, MS, 1999; EdD, Nova Southeastern U., Ft. Lauderdale, Fla., 2005. Cert. nurse, Fla. State Bd. Nursing, 1986; personnel mgmt. U. of Arts, Sci. & Tech., 1978. Literacy facilitator Palm Beach Schol Dist./ Belle Glade Elem. Sch., Fla., 1999—; pres. Tyson Ednl. & Cmty. Resources, Inc., Loxahatchee, Fla., 2000—. Tchr. Ministry Edn., Kingston, Jamaica, 1970—85; presenter in field. Pres. Home Owners' Assn., St Catherine, Jamaica, 1972—80; Cub Scout leader Jamaica, 1972—78; Sunday sch. tchr. Hope of the World Christian Ctr. Ministries, 1990—92; min. Hope of the World Christian Ministry, Pembroke Pines, Fla., Hope of the World Christian Ctr. Ministries, Loxahatchee, Fla. Recipient Distinction in Edn., Mico U., 1973—76. Mem.: Internat. Reading Assn. Conservative. Avocations: travel, evangelism, reading. Office: Tyson Ednl & Cmty Resources I 16218- 83 Pl N Loxahatchee FL 33470 Personal E-mail: leonie710@aol.com.

RUSSETT, BRUCE MARTIN, political science professor; b. North Adams, Mass., Jan. 26, 1935; s. Raymond Edgar and Ruth Marian (Martin) R.; m. Cynthia Margaret Eagle, June 18, 1960; children: Margaret Ellen, Mark David, Lucia Elizabeth, Daniel Alden. BA magna cum laude, Williams Coll., 1956; diploma in econs., Cambridge U., Eng., 1957; MA, Yale U., 1958, PhD, 1961; PhD (hon.), Uppsala U., 2002. Instr. MIT, Cambridge, 1961-62; asst. prof., then assoc. prof. Yale U., New Haven, 1961-68, prof., 1968—, Dean Acheson prof. internat. rels. and polit. sci., 1985—, chair dept. polit. sci., 1990-96, dir. UN studies, 1993—2006. Vis. prof. Columbia U., 1965, U. Mich., 1965-66, U. Libre Brussels, 1969-70, U. N.C., 1979-80, Richardson Inst., London, 1973-74, Netherlands Inst. Advanced Study, 1984, Tel Aviv U., 1989, U. Tokyo, 1996, Harvard U., 2001; prin. cons. pastoral letter on peace Nat. Conf. Cath. Bishops, Washington, 1981-83; co-dir., secretariat ind. working group Future of the UN, 1993-96. Author: World Handbook of Political and Social Indicators, 1964, What Price Vigilance?, 1970 (Kammerer award Amn. Polit. Sci. Assn. 1971), Interest and Ideology (with E. Hanson), 1975, Controlling the Sword, 1990, Grasping the Democratic Peace, 1993, The Once and Future Security Council, 1997, (with John Oneal) Triangulating Peace, 2001, (with Francis Oakley) Governance, Accountability, and the Future of the Catholic Church, 2004, (with Alex Mintz) New Directions for International Relations, 2005, Purpose and Policy in the Global Community, 2006, Internat. Security and Conflict, 2008, others; editor: Jour. Conflict Resolution, 1972-2009; contbr. articles to profl. jours. Grantee NSF, 1964, 65, 69, 77, 79, 85, 88, 89, 90, 95, 98, Ford Found., 1993, 94, 97, John and Catherine MacArthur Found., 1988, 91; Fulbright-Hays fellow, Belgium and Israel, 1969, 89; John Simon Guggenheim Found. fellow, 1969, 77; German Marshall Fund fellow, 1977. Fellow Am. Acad. Arts and Scis.; mem. AAUP, Am. Polit. Sci. Assn. (coun. 1984-86), Internat. Studies Assn. (pres. 1983-84), Peace Sci. Soc. Internat. (pres. 1977-79). Avocations: tennis, classical music, hiking. Home: 70 Martin Ter Hamden CT 06517-2333 Office: Yale U Dept Polit Sci PO Box 208301 New Haven CT 06520-8301 Home Phone: 203-248-2364; Office Phone: 203-432-5233. E-mail: bruce.russett@yale.edu.

RUSSIN, JONATHAN, lawyer, consultant; b. Kingston, Pa., Oct. 30, 1937; s. Jacob S. and Anne (Wartella) R.; m. Antoinette Stackpole, Oct. 6, 1962; children: Alexander, Andrew, Benjamin, Jacob. BA, Yale U., 1959, LLB, 1963. Bar: DC 1964. Guide interpreter Am. Nat. Exhibit, Moscow, 1959; rsch. asst. Law Faculty U. East Africa, Dar es Salaam, Tanganyika, 1961-62; regional legal adviser for Caribbean AID, 1967-69; ptnr. Kirkwood, Kaplan, Russin & Vecchi, Santo Domingo, Dominican Republic, 1969-74, Washington, 1974-78, Kaplan Russin & Vecchi, Madrid, 1978-81, Washington, 1981-92; ptnr., dir. Russian practice group Russin & Vecchi, Moscow, 1992—. Washington rep. Moscow Patriarchate of Russian Orthodox Ch., 1992-95; convener adv. coun. Inst. European, Russian and Eurasian Studies, George Washington U., 1990-96; mem. adv. bd. Caribbean Am. Directory, 1985-92; trustee St. Nicholas Cathedral, Washington, 1982-93, St. Vladimir's Orthodox Theol. Sem., Crestwood, NY, 1985-93; legal adviser Orthodox Ch. Am., 1985-2006. Contbr. articles to profl. jours. Bd. dirs. Nat. Coun. Internat. Visitors, Washington, 1987—93, Fund for Democracy and Devel., Washington, 1993—, MUCIA Global Edn. Group, Inc., 1996—2000, Delphi Internat., Washington, 1988—2000, Dominican Am. Cultural Inst., Santo Domingo, 1988—92. Recipient Order of St. Vladimir, Moscow Patriarchate, Russian Orthodox Ch., 1991. Mem.: Russian Assn. Internat. Law, DC Bar, Yale Club Washington, Yale Club NY, Inter-Am. Bar Assn., ABA, Cosmos Club, Washington. Office: 1000 Potomac St NW 5th Fl Washington DC 20007-3501 Office Phone: 202-822-6100. Business E-Mail: jonathan.russin@russinvecchi.com.

RUSSO, ALEXANDER PETER, artist, educator; b. Atlantic City, June 11, 1922; s. Peter Joseph and Lillian Mary (Soma) R.; 1 child, Eugenie. Student, Pratt Inst., 1940-42, Swarthmore Coll., 1946-47; S.S., Bard Coll., 1947; B.F.A. (Breevort-Eickenmeyer fellow), Columbia U., 1952; postgrad., Acad. Fine Arts, Rome, 1952-54, Inst. Advanced Fine Arts, 1977-79. Instr. New Orleans Acad. Art, 1948-49; asst. prof. art U. Buffalo, 1955-58; instr. in graphic design Parsons Sch. Design, 1958-60; chmn. dept. drawing and painting Corcoran Sch. Art, 1961-70, chmn. faculty, acting dean, 1967-70; lectr., thesis adv. George Washington U., 1961-70; prof. Hood Coll., Frederick, Md., 1970-90, prof. emeritus, 1990—, chmn. dept. art, 1970-87. Vis. guest prof. art Instituto Allende, San Miguel de Allende, Mexico, 1993-94; panelist Md. State Coun. Arts, Balt., 1981-82; reviewer art programs Md. State Bd. Edn., 1981—; guest art critic Southampton Press, N.Y., 1989, 91; cons. in field. One-man shows include Corcoran Gallery Art, Washington, 1946, 64, Chiurazzi Gallery, Rome, 1953, Cavallino Gallery, Venice, Italy, 1954, U. So. Ill., 1955, Frank Rehn Gallery, N.Y.C., periodic exhbns., 1954-74, Phoenix II Gallery, Washington, 1983, Ingber Gallery, N.Y.C., 1983, Washington Gallery Art, 1963, Franz Bader Gallery, Washington, 1967, Internat. Monetary Fund, Washington, 1968, 79, Agra Gallery, Washington, 1971, Benson Gallery, Bridgehampton, L.I., 1976, Phoenix Fine Arts, Frederick, 1981, Benton Gallery, Southampton, N.Y., 1985, 86, 88, 90-91, Arlene Bujese Gallery, East Hampton, N.Y., 1994-95, 97-98, to 2006, Hood Coll., Frederick, Md., 1991, Western Md. Coll., Westminster, 1991, Bell Gallery, Seattle, 1991-92, Gettysburg (Pa.) Coll., 1989, Nabi Gallery, N.Y.C., 2006; group exhbns. include Salon de la Marne, Paris, 1945, Met. Mus. Art, N.Y.C., 1948, Bordighera Internat., Italy, 1953-54, Mus. Modern Art, Madrid, 1953, Sala di Esposizione delle Biblioteca Americano, Rome, 1953, Whitney Mus. Am. Art, N.Y.C., 1960, Mus. Modern Art, N.Y.C., 1969, Guild Hall, East Hampton, N.Y., 1976, 2007, East Hampton Avant-Garde, A Salute to the Signa Gallery, 1990, NAS, Washington, 1984, Bell Gallery, Seattle, 1990, Illustrator's Club, N.Y.C., 1991, Armory Exhbn., N.Y.C., 1991, Inst. Alleude, San Niguel de Allende, Mex., 1994, Fulbright Assoc. 20th Anniv. Art Exhibition, 1997, Josh Kligerman Gallery, San Miguel de Allende, Mex., 1994, Spanierman Gallery, East Hampton, 2007, deCordova Gallery, Greenport, NY, 2007; represented in permanent collections Albright-Knox Gallery, Buffalo, Columbia U., N.Y.C., Delgado Mus. Art, New Orleans, Corcoran Gallery Art, Fiat Automobile Co., Rome, Nat. Collection Smithsonian Inst., Washington, Fed. Ins. Deposit Corp., Washington, Gettysburg Coll. Pa.; author: Profiles on Women Artists, 1985, The Challenge of Drawing, 1986, (poetry) Vignettes, 1996, Poems & Images, 2008. Served with USNR, 1942-46. Fellow Guggenheim Found., 1947-48, 49-50,Edward McDowell Found., 1956, Hood Coll. Hodson teaching fellow, 1983; Fulbright grantee for painting and research, Rome, 1952-54, U.S.-Indo Subcommn. on Edn. and Culture grantee, India, 1984. Office: PO Box 1377 Wainscott NY 11975-1377 also: Arlene Bujese Dealer 40 Whooping Hollow Rd East Hampton NY 11937-2400 Personal E-mail: cmdrusso@hotmail.com. *Success is an equivocal matter. "Outward success", no doubt, is meaningful and necessary to most people in terms of fulfilling goals or for some similar reason. "Interior success" is more difficult to achieve, for it means the labor of a developing soul, and, more often than not, the relinquishing of what most would consider to be "material success." Whatever I have achieved in the way of outward or material success, therefore, is but a minute reflection of that which I would wish to achieve on the spiritual level. There is a long way to go.*

RUSSO, ANTHONY JOSEPH, public relations professional; b. NYC, Oct. 23, 1953; s. Lucio and Tina (Iarossi) R. BA cum laude, Alfred U., 1974; MA, Columbia U., 1975; PhD, Claremont Grad. Sch., 1982. Asst. to chmn. Mocatta Metals, NYC, 1982-83; account exec. Gavin Anderson and Co., NYC, 1983-85; sr. account exec. Adams and Reinhart, NYC, 1985; dir. corp. rels. Geto and DeMilly, NYC, 1985-86; v.p. Cameron Assocs., NYC, 1986-88; chmn., CEO Russo Ptnrs. LLC, NYC, 1998—; chmn. Madison Life Scis., 1999—2003. Mem. editl. bd.: Jour. Comml. Biotech., Bio People. Bd. dirs. March of Dimes, Target Autism Genome. Mem. APA, Pub. Rels. Soc. Am., Psi Chi. Democrat. Office: 550 W C St Ste 2000 San Diego CA 92101 also: Maitland Russo Ptnrs 5 Upper St Martins Ln London WC2H 9EA England also: Russo Ptnrs Hdqts 75 Ninth Ave 2R New York NY 10011 Business E-Mail: tony.russo@russopatnersllc.com.

RUSSO, DONNA LEE, social worker; b. Suffern, NY, Sept. 9, 1963; d. Donald Ernest and Kathleen Helen D.; m. Kevin Frank Russo, Nov. 3, 1990. BS in Psychology, St. Lawrence U., 1985; MSW, Columbia U., 1987. LCSW. Child care relief worker St. Agatha's Home of N.Y. State Foundling Hosp., Nanuet, 1981-85; med. social worker, case mgmt. supr. Burke Rehab. Hosp., White Plains, NY, 1987—. Recipient Wholeness of Life award, N.Y. Healthcare Chaplaincy, 2001, Benjamin Osterhoudt vol. award, 1996. Mem. NASW, Acad. Cert. Social Workers, Brain Injury assn. of N.Y. (co-founder Westchester chpt.), Case Mgmt. Soc. Am. (cert. case mgr.). Office: Burke Rehab Hosp 785 Mamaroneck Ave White Plains NY 10605-2523

RUSSO, GILBERTO, engineering educator; b. Rome, Aug. 23, 1954; s. Guido and Maria (Mazzoni) R. Laurea, Poly. Inst. Turin, Italy, 1975; ScD, MIT, 1980; MD, U. Chgo. Pritaker Sch. of Medicine. Pres. Studio Russo, Inc. Engring. Cons., Turin, 1970; asst. prof. Poly. Inst. Turin, 1975-80; lectr. MIT, Cambridge, Mass., 1985-91; dr. dept. plastic and reconstructive surgery U. Chgo., 1992-95; mem. dept. surgery U. Calif., San Francisco, 1995—; asst. prof. vascular surgery U. Ala., Birmingham. Mem. designer selection bd. State of Mass., Boston, 1989. Contbr. articles to profl. publs., chpts. to books. Pres. Dante Alisheri Soc., Cambridge, 1986-88; treas. MIT/Poly. Alumni Assn., Turin, 1970. Fulbright fellow, 1978. Fellow Nat. Coun. Engring. Examiners; mem. Mass. Soc. Profl. Engrs. (v.p. 1991—), Tau Beta Pi (chpt. advisor 1985, Eminent Engr. 1985). Achievements include patents in solar energy collectors, development of computer aided therodynamics, computer methods for engineering, optimization of non-steady-state systems, compressible fluid flow with heat transfer, thermal dynamics models, diagnostics and surgical repair of electric/burn injuries. Address: Dept Surgery LIJ Med Ctr New Hyde Park NY 11004 Office: U Chgo Dept Plastic-Reconstrv Surg Chicago IL 60637 also: U Calif Dept Surgery Rm S-343 Box 0470 513 Parnassus Ave San Francisco CA 94122-2722 Home: 1130 E El Alameda Palm Springs CA 92262-5818 Office Phone: 760-969-6559. Personal E-mail: gilberto.russo.md.phd@gmail.com.

RUSSO, IRMA HAYDEE ALVAREZ DE, pathologist; b. San Rafael, Mendoza, Argentina, Feb. 28, 1942; came to U.S, 1972; d. Jose Maria and Maria Carmen (Martinez) de Alvarez; m. Jose Russo, Feb. 8, 1969; 1 child, Patricia Alexandra. BA, Escuela Normal MTSM de Balcarce, 1959; MD, U. Nat. of Cuyo, Mendoza, 1970. Diplomate Am. Bd. Pathology. Intern Sch. Medicine Hosps., Argentina, 1969-70; resident in pathology Wayne State U. Sch. Medicine, Detroit, 1976-80. Rsch. asst., instr. Inst. Histology and Embryology Sch. Medicine U. Nat. of Cuyo, 1963-71, assoc. prof. histology Faculty Phys., Chem. and Math. Scis., 1970-72; rsch. assoc. Inst. Molecular and Cellular Evolution U. Miami, Fla., 1972-73; rsch. assoc. exptl. pathology lab. divsn. biol. scis. Mich. Cancer Foun., Detroit, 1973-75, rsch. scientist, 1975-76, vis. rsch. scientist, 1976-82, asst. mem., pathologist, 1982-89, assoc. rsch. mem., 1989-91, co-dir. pathology reference lab., 1982-86, chief exptl. pathology lab., 1989-91; co-dir. Mich. Cancer Found. Lab. Svcs., 1986-91; mem. Fox Chase Cancer Ctr., 1991—, active staff mem. dept. surgery med. scis. divsn., 2004—; dir. anatomic pathology Am. Oncologic Hosp. Dept. Pathology, 1991-92; dir. Lab. Svcs., 1992-94; chief molecular endocrinology sect. Breast Cancer Rsch. Lab. Fox Chase Cancer Ctr., 1994—; chief resident physician dept. pathology Wayne State U. Sch. Medicine, 1978-80, asst. prof., 1980-82; mem. staff Harper-Grace Hosps., Detroit, 1980-82; adj. prof. Pathology and Cell Biology Jefferson Sch. Medicine/Thomas Jefferson U., 1992—, chairperson Basic Breast Biology Study Sect. U. Calif. Breast Cancer Program, 1997, mem. endocrinology panel peer rev. com. breast cancer rsch. program U.S. Army R & D Command, 1994, 95, 96, 2002, 03, chairperson endocrinology peer rev. com., 1996; ad-hoc mem. biochem. endocrinology study sect. NIH, DHHS, 1994, metabolic pathology study sect., 1996-97; mem. European Commn. Cancer Prevention, 1994—; mem. bd. sci. counselor, sec. health and human svcs. Nat. Toxicology Program Bd., 1994-98; mem. Internat. Life Scis. Inst.-Risk Sci. Inst. Mammary Working Group, 1992—; pres., founder League of Women Against Cancer, Rydal, Pa., 1994—; guest lectr. dept. obstetrics Sch. Medicine U. Nat. of Cuyo, 1965-71; mem. resource devel. subcommittee of the profl. advisory com., Latinas Living Beyond Breast Cancer, 2000—; mem. Breast Cancer Res. Sci. Review Panel, N.J.commr. on cancer rsch., Trenton, N.J., 1997, 2000. Editor-in-chief Jour. Women's Cancer, 1997—; contbr. articles to profl. jours. Rockefeller grantee, 1972-73; Nat. Cancer Inst. grantee, 1978-81, 84-87, 94-99, 2003—, Am. Cancer Soc. grantee 1988-89, 91-94, U.S. Army Med. R&D Command grantee, 1994-99, 2003—; recipient Shannon award Nat. Cancer Inst./NHHSS, 1992-94, Gold medal Inst. U. Dexeus, Barcelona, Spain, 2000. Mem. AAAS, Soc. Española Senología y Patología Mamaria, Nat. Cancer Inst. (breast cancer working group, breast cancer program 1984-88), Nat. Alliance Breast Cancer Orgns. (med. adv. bd. N.Y.C. chpt. 1986—), Ea. Coop. Oncology Group, Coll. Am. Pathologists, Am. Soc. Clin. Pathologists, Am. Assn. Cancer Rsch., Am. Assn. Clin. Chemistry, Internat. Coll. Physicians and Surgeons, Women in Cancer Rsch., The Endoctrine Soc., Internat. Assn. Against Cancer, Sigma Xi, Food Quality Protection Act, Sci. Review Bd., Fed. Insecticide Fungi and Rodenticide Act, Adivsory Panel, EPA. Roman Catholic. Office: Fox Chase Cancer Ctr 333 Cottman Ave Philadelphia PA 19111 Office Phone: 215-728-4781. Personal E-mail: Lowac@msn.com. Business E-Mail: Irma.Russo@fccc.edu.

RUSSO, JOSE, pathologist; b. Mendoza, Argentina, Mar. 24, 1942; came to US, 1971; s. Felipe and Teresa (Pagano) R.; m. Irma Haydee, Feb. 8, 1969; 1 child, Patricia Alexandra. BS, Agustin Alvarez Nat. Coll., 1959; MD, U. Nat. Cuyo, 1967. Instr. Inst. Gen. and Exptl. Pathology Med. Sch., Mendoza, 1961-66; asst. prof. Inst. Histology and Embryology, 1967-71; Rockefeller Found. postdoc. fellow Inst. Molecular and Cellular Evolution U. Miami, 1971—73; chief exptl. pathology lab. Mich. Cancer Found., Detroit, 1973-81; assoc. clin. prof. pathology Wayne State U., Detroit, 1979-91, chmn. dept. pathology, 1981-91; chmn. dept. pathology, sr. mem. Fox Chase Cancer Ctr., Phila., 1991-94, sr. mem., dir. Breast Cancer Rsch. and Environ. Ctr., 1994—, dir. med. outreach and minority affairs; sci. dir. League of Women Against Cancer. Mem. Mich. Cancer Found., 1982-91; adj. prof. pathology Jefferson Sch. Medicine, U. Pa. Sch. Medicine, Phila. Author: Tumor Diagnosis by Electron Microscopy, vol. 1, 1986, vol. 2, 1988, vol. 3, 1990, Immunocytochemistry in Tumor Diagnosis, 1985, Molecular Basis of Breast

Cancer, 2004; editor-in-chief Jour. of Women's Cancer; contbr. over 380 articles to profl. jours USPHS grantee, 1978, 80, 84, 88, 90, 93-95, 98, 2000, 02, grantee Am. Cancer Soc., 1982, Dept. of Def., 1999-2003; NRC Argentina fellow, 1967-71 Mem. Am. Assn. Cancer Rsch., Am. Soc. Cell Biology, Soc. Exptl. Biology and Medicine, Tissue Culture Assn., Am. Soc. Clin. Pathology, Internat. Acad. Pathology, Am. Coll. Pathology, Sigma Xi Roman Catholic. Office Phone: 215-728-4782. Business E-Mail: jose.russo@fccc.edu, j.russo@fccc.edu.

RUSSO, KELLY ANNE, secondary school educator; b. Buffalo, Oct. 4, 1977; d. Richard Joseph and Pamela Mae Panaro; m. Arthur Russo, III, Apr. 13, 2006; children: Nicholas, Arthur Julian, Avielle Marie. BA in English, Canisius Coll., Buffalo, 2000, MS in Secondary Edn., 2004. Cert. sch. dist./ bldg. adminstr. NY, 2007; tchr. NY, 2004. Tchr. English Bennett HS, Buffalo, 2002—05, Mid. Early Coll. HS, Buffalo, 2005—. Coach debate team Bennett H.S., 2002—04. Vol. Habitat for Humanity, Charleston, W.Va., 1998. Mem.: Sch. Adminstrs. Assn. NY State, Nat. Coun. Tchrs. English, Eta Sigma Phi. Democrat. Roman Catholic. Avocations: writing, poetry, reading, cooking. Home: 69 Crystal Ave Buffalo NY 14220

RUSSO, MARISA NATALINA, educational consultant; b. Fullerton, Calif., Mar. 4, 1969; d. Ralph and Nelia (Burdi) Russo. B, Calif. State U., 1992. Sales assoc. The Broadway, Brea, Calif., 1985—95; tchr. Bennett-Kew Sch., Inglewood, Calif., 1996—2000; regional cons. McGraw Hill, Calif., 2000—02, nat. cons. Calif., 2002—. Speaker various ednl. confs. Mem.: One, Internat. Reading Assn. Democrat. Roman Cath. Home: 11381 Parkfield Ct Riverside CA 92505

RUSSO, MARTIN A., lawyer, lobbyist, former congressman; b. Chgo., Jan. 23, 1944; s. Anthony and Lucille R.; m. Karen Jorgensen; children: Tony, Dan. BA, DePaul U., 1965, JD, 1967. Bar: Ill. 1967, U.S. Supreme Ct. 1974, DC 1977. Law clk. to presiding justice Ill. Appellate Ct., 1967-68; asst. state's atty. Cook County, Ill., 1971-73; sole practice law Chgo., 1973—; mem. from Ill. Dist. 3 US Ho. of Reps, 1975—93, mem. ways and means com., com. on budget, dep. whip; sr. vice chmn., CEO Cassidy & Assocs., Washington, 1993—. Mem. Joint Civic Com. of Italian-Ams., citizens bd. Ill. Masonic Med. Ctr., pres. Washington Golf Charities. Recipient Disting. Service award Pinta Neri KC, Appreciation award Vietnam Era Vets. in Congress, 1986, Michelangelo award Italo-Am. Nat. Union, 1986, Congl. Humanitarian award Coalition Suburban Bar Assn., 1985, Leadership award Greater Southwest Revitalization Program, 1982, Law Enforcement award Fraternal Order Police, 1982,; named Outstanding Legis. Leader, Soc. Little Flower, 1975, Man of Yr., Chgo. Chpt. Magen David Adom, 1977, One of Ten Outstanding Young People, Harvey (Ill.) Jaycees, 1977, Legislator of Yr., United Hellenic Voters of Am., 1981, Century Mem. of Boy Scouts Am., 1982-85, Legislator of Yr., United Irish-Am. soc. Ill., 1985-86, Man of Yr., New Hope Ctr., 1986. Mem. ABA, Fed. Bar Assn., Ill. Bar Assn., D.C. Bar Assn., South Suburban Bar Assn., Justinian Soc. Lawyers (Man of Year 1976), Alpha Phi Delta Alumni Assn. Lodges: KC, Elks, Order Sons of Italy. Roman Catholic. Office: Cassidy & Assocs 700 Thirteenth St, NW, Ste 400 Washington DC 20005 Office Phone: 202-347-0773. Office Fax: 202-347-0785.*

RUSSO, PATRICIA F., former telecommunications company executive; b. Trenton, NJ, June 12, 1952; m. Frank Russo. BA in Polit. Sci. & History, Georgetown U., 1973; Postgrad. in Advanced Mgmt., Harvard U., 1989; DEng (hon.), Steven Inst. Tech., 2003; D in Entrepreneurial Studies (hon.), Columbia Coll., SC. Sales and mktg. mgmt. exec. IBM, 1973-81; with AT&T (now Lucent Techs. Inc.), 1981; pres., Bus Comm. Sys. Unit AT&T (now Avaya Inc.), 1992-96; pres., COO Eastman Kodak Co., 2000—02; exec. v.p. strategy bus. devel. and corp. ops. Lucent Technologies Inc., Murray Hill, NJ, 1997-99, exec. v.p., CEO svc. provider networks Warren, NJ, 1999—2000, pres., CEO Murray Hill, NJ, 2002—03, chmn., CEO, 2003—06; CEO Alcatel-Lucent, Paris, 2006—08. Bd. dirs. Schering-Plough Corp., 1995—, Lucent Technologies Inc., 2002—06, Alcatel-Lucent, 2006—08, Alcoa Inc., 2008—, Gen. Motors Co., 2009—, Avaya Inc.; chair Nat. Security Telecom. Adv. Com., 2004—06. Bd. dirs. Georgetown U.; mem. Network Reliability Interoperability Coun.; mem. appointed by Gov. James McGreevey NJ Commn. on Jobs Growth and Econ. Develop. Named one of The 100 Most Powerful Women in Bus., Fortune mag., 1998—2006, The 100 Most Influential People, TIME mag., 2006, The 10 Most Powerful Women in NJ Bus., Newark Star-Ledger, 2006, The 50 Who Matter Now, CNNMoney.com Bus. 2.0, 2006, The 50 Women to Watch, The Wall St. Jour., 2006, The 100 Most Powerful Women, Forbes Mag., 2007. Office Phone: 908-582-9519. Personal E-mail: pfrusso2@aol.com.

RUSSO, RICHARD, writer; b. Johnstown, NY, July 15, 1949; s. James W. and Jean Findlay (LeVarn) Russo; m. Barbara Marie Russo; children: Emily, Kate. BA in English, U. Ariz., PhD in Am. Lit., 1980, MFA in Creative Writing, 1981. English dept. faculty So. Ill. U., Carbondale; prof. English Colby Coll., Waterville, Maine, 1991—96. Author: (novels) Mohawk, 1986, The Risk Pool, 1988, Nobody's Fool, 1993, Straight Man, 1997, Empire Falls, 2001 (Pulitzer Prize for Fiction, 2002, TIME mag.'s Best Novel of Yr., 2002), The Whore's Child and Other Stories, 2002, Bridge of Sighs, 2007, That Old Cape Magic, 2009 (#1 Publishers Weekly bestseller); writer (screenplays) Twilight, 1998, The Flamingo Rising, 2001, Brush with Fate, 2003, Empire Falls, 2005, Keeping Mum, 2005, writer, exec. prodr. The Ice Harvest, 2005.*

RUSSO, ROY LAWRENCE, retired electronics engineer; b. Kelayres, Pa., Nov. 6, 1935; s. Peter John and Mary (Fudge) R.; m. Elizabeth Jean Tautkus, Dec. 26, 1959; children: Mark, Keith, Aileen, Linda. BSE.E., Pa. State U., 1957, MSE.E., 1959, PhDE.E., 1964. Asst. prof. elec. engring. Pa. State U., University Park, 1964-65; mgr., staff mem. IBM Research, Yorktown Heights, NY, 1965-77, mem. research staff, 1983-85, mgr. design automation lab., 1985-94; sr. engr. Gen. Tech. div. IBM, Hopewell Junction, 1977-81, mgr. strategy, 1981-82; cons. prof. elec. engring Stanford U., 1982-83; retired, 1994. Editor-in-chief IEEE Computer Soc., 1983-85; co-inventor ink jet printer correction system. Treas. St. Patrick's Ch., Yorktown Heights, 1975-77. Recipient Invention Achievement award IBM, 1978, Outstanding Contbn. award IBM, 1968, 89, Outstanding Writing award Pa. State U., 1967 Fellow IEEE (dir. computer disvn. 1989); mem. IEEE Computer Soc. (pres. 1986-87, Svc. award, Centennial medal 1984, Richard E. Merwin award 1992), Eta Kappa Nu.

RUSSO, THOMAS ANTHONY, lawyer, former investment company executive; b. NYC, Nov. 6, 1943; s. Lucio F. and Tina (Iarossi) R.: m. Nancy Felipe, June 18, 1966 (div. 1974); m. Janice Davis, June 10, 1977 (div. 1979); m. Marcy C. Appelbaum, June 16, 1985; children: Morgan Danielle and Alexa Anne (twins), Tyler James. BA, Fordham U., 1965; MBA, JD, Cornell U., 1969. Bar: NY 1970, U.S. Ct. Appeals (2d cir.) 1971, U.S. Dist. Ct. (so. and ea. dists.) NY 1971, U.S. Ct. Appeals (7th cir.) 1982. Staff atty. Securities & Exchange Commn. (SEC), Washington, 1969—71; assoc. Cadwalader, Wickersham & Taft, NYC, 1971—75, ptnr., mem. mgmt. com., 1977—92; dir. divsn. trading and markets Commodity Futures Trading Commn. (CFTC), Washington, 1975—77; vice chmn., chief legal officer, mem. exec. com. Lehman Brothers Holdings, Inc., NYC, 1993—2008; sr. counsel Patton Boggs LLP, NYC, 2009—. Adj. prof. Columbia U. Grad. Sch. Bus. Author: Regulation of the Commodities Futures and Options Markets; co-author: Regulation of Brokers, Dealers and Securities Markets with Supplement; mem. editl. bd. Jour. Fin. Regulation and Compliance, Futures and Derivatives Law Report; practitioner bd. advs. Stanford Jour. Law, Bus. and Fin. Recipient Bond Market Assn. Chairman's Achievement award, Disting. Leadership award, Securities Industry Assn.; named one of The 100 Most Influential Lawyers in America, Nat. Law Jour.; named to Futures Industry Assn. Hall of Fame, 2003. Mem.: ABA, Fgn. Policy Assn., DC Bar Assn., Assn. Bar City NY (chmn. com. commodities regulations 1981—82, chmn. internat. law subcommittee of the com. on commodities regulation 1984—85), Econ. Club NY, Fellows of Phi Beta Kappa Soc. Office: Patton Boggs LLP 1185 Ave of the Americas 30th Fl New York NY 10036 Office Fax: 646-557-5101.

RUSSO, VINCENT JOSEPH, surgeon; b. Phila., Apr. 15, 1939; s. Joseph Vincent Russo and Yolanda Italia D'Ambrosio; m. Sheila Kay Roos, June 8, 1963; children: Teresa, Joseph, Katrina, Anita. AB, Columbia U., 1960; MD, Boston U., 1964, MPH, 1983. Diplomate Am. Bd. Surgery. Staff surgeon Anna Jaques Hosp., Newburyport, Mass., 1971-88; clin. instr. surgery Harvard Med. Sch., Boston, 1984-98; med. dir. Blue Cross/Blue Shield, Methuen, Mass., 1990-98; sr. staff surgeon Lawrence (Mass.) Gen. Hosp., 1990-2000; med. dir. Ea. Mass. Health Ctrs., 1999—2000; clin. instr. Sch. Medicine Boston U., 2001—04; seaterm ship's physician Mass. Maritime Acad., 2001—06. Cons. surgeon Manchester (N.H.) VA Med. Ctr., 1985-98; pres. Essex North Med. Soc., Newburyport, 1988-89, 2002-04; dist. 3 med. examiner Essex County, 1986-2007; ship's doctor Mass. Maritime Acad., 2001-06. Bd. trustees, corporator, mem. auditing com. Newburyport Savings Bank, 1987—; mem. UNICO, Andover, Mass., 1994-97. Lt. cmdr. USN, ships surgeon USS Forrestal Aircraft Carrier, 1969-71; chmn. bd. selectmen Town of Newbury, Mass, 2004—; field rep., surveyor Joint Commn. on Accreditation of Health Orgns., 2004—; commr. mosquito control Commonwealth of Mass., 2005—; chmn. auditing comm. Newburyport Five Cents Savings Bank, 2006-; corporator Anna Jaques Hosp., Newburyport, Mass., 1985—. Lt. col. U.S. Army, 1990-91, Desert Storm. Named Physician of Yr., Mass. Med. Soc. Essex North Dist., 2009. Fellow ACS (councilor Mass. chpt. 1995-98); mem. AMA, Soc. Am. Gastrointestinal Endoscopic Surgeons, Mass. Med. Soc. (legis. com. 1990—, del. 2000—), Boston Surg. Soc., Essex North Dist. Med. Soc. (exec. com. 1986—, pres. 2002-04), Rotary (sr. active), Mass. Med. Soc. (reference com. 2002-04, bd. trustees 2004—), U.S. Naval Inst. Roman Catholic. Avocations: theater, downhill skiing, automobiles, swimming, symphony. E-mail: vjrusso@massmed.org.

RUSSOM, JAMES RAYFORD, minister; b. Memphis, Dec. 9, 1949; s. Rayford Pinkney and Leola Jane (Briley) R.; m. Susan Theresa Smith, June 1, 1968; 1 child, Mark Stephen. AA in Biblical Lit., Nazarene Bible Coll., 1971; BA in Religion and Philosophy, Bethany Nazarene Coll., 1982; M Ministry, So. Nazarene U., 1988; postgrad., Western Sem., 1989. Ordained to ministry Ch. of the Nazarene, 1975. Youth minister Los Altos Ch. of Nazarene, Albuquerque, 1971-72; youth/assoc. pastor Buena park (Calif.) First Ch. of Nazarene, 1972-74; sr. pastor Long Beach (Calif.) Westside Ch. of Nazarene, 1974-78, Metroplex Fellow Ch. of Nazarene, Oklahoma City, 1978-86, Flagstaff (Ariz.) Ch. of Nazarene, 1986-92, San Jose (Calif.) Ch. of Nazarene, 1992—. Pres. Celebration At Sea, Inc., Oklahoma City, 1982-86; regional pres. S. Cen. Regional Nazarene Youth Internat., Oklahoma City, 1981-86; dist. pres. N.W. Okla. Nazarene Youth Internat., Oklahoma City, 1981-83; cons., pres. Eagle Bus. Cons., 1982—. Author: God's Plan for Marital Success, 1990, also youth program and curriculum in field. Founder Helping Hands, Oklahoma City, 1983. Mem. Eastside Businessmen's Alliance. Republican. Avocations: fishing, hunting, golf, piano, guitar. Address: PO Box 210925 Chula Vista CA 91921-0925

RUSSOMANNO, FRANK P., information technology executive; B in History, Seton Hall U., South Orange, NJ; grad. student, U. Okla., Norman, Monmouth Coll. Sales coord. to sales rep. Magnetic/Audio/Video Recording bus. 3M Co., 1973, European Bus. unit dir.; global sales and mktg. dir. Photo Color Products Imation Corp., Oakdale, Minn., various exec. and managerial positions including v.p. Data Storage Media and Svcs., gen. mgr. Advanced Imaging Program, corp. sales and mktg. dir., pres. Data Storage and Info. Mgmt. businesses, 2000—03, exec. v.p., COO, 2003—06, pres., COO, acting CEO, 2006—07, pres., CEO, 2007—09, vice-chmn., CEO, 2009—. Bd. dirs. Content Delivery & Storage Assn. Bd. mem. Merrick Cmty. Ctr., St. Paul. Artillery officer (rank of Capt.) US Army. Office: Imation Corp 1 Imation Pl Oakdale MN 55128*

RUSSONIELLO, JOSEPH PASCAL, prosecutor, lawyer; b. Jersey City, Oct. 12, 1941; s. Sabin G. and Justine B. (Terraciano) Russoniello; m. Moira F. Ward, Aug. 29, 1969. B in Social Sci., Fairfield U., 1963; JD, NYU, 1966. Bar: N.J. 1967, Calif. 1969. Spl. agt. FBI, Washington, 1966—67; dep. dist. atty. City and County San Francisco Dist. Atty. Offices, 1969—75; assoc. Cooley Godward Castro Huddleson & Tatum, San Francisco, 1975—78; ptnr. Cooley Godward L.L.P., San Francisco, 1978—82, 1990—2001; sr. counsel Cooley Godward Kronish L.L.P., San Francisco, 2002—08; US atty. US Dept. Justice (no. dist.) Calif., San Francisco, 1982—90, 2008—. Pres., bd. dirs. San Francisco Law Sch., 1996—2001, dean, 2002—07; analyst Sta. KTVU-Ch. 2, Oakland, 1994—2007. Pres. Northgate Cottages, Napa, Calif., 1988—; chmn. Silverado Property Owners Assn., 2004—07; v.p. Mid-Pacific region Nat. Italian Am. Fedn., 1996—99; mem. nat. rev. bd. U.S. Conf. Cath. Bishops, 2004—07; chmn. Caths. Truth and Justice, San Francisco, 1991—. Recipient Man of the Yr. award, NIAF, 1986, St. Thomas More Soc., San Francisco, 2000, Italian Am. Cmty. Svc. Agy., San Francisco, 2004, Assumpta award, Trustees St. Mary's Cathedral, 2000, Papal Pro Ecclesia medal, 2000, Landsman award, 2005; named Alumni of the Yr., Pub. Sector, NYU Law Sch., 1991. Fellow: Am. Coll. Trial Lawyers; mem.: Am. Law Inst., Am. Bd. Trial Lawyers (adv.), McFetridge Inn of Ct. (barrister). Republican. Avocations: tennis, golf, reading, saxophone. Office: US Atty Office 450 Golden Gate Ave Box 36055 San Francisco CA 94102

RUSSOTTO, PAUL, artist, educator; b. NYC, May 28, 1944; s. John and Margaret Russotto; m. Ellen Russotto, Aug. 30, 1969; children: Vita, Luca. Student, Art Students League, NYC, 1962-63. Painting and drawing instr., MFA program Parsons Sch. Design, NYC, 1978—80, N.Y. Studio Sch. Drawing, Painting and Sculpture, NYC, 1980—82, Vt. Studio Ctr., Johnson, 1985—, Internat. Sch. Art, Montecastello di Vibio, Italy, 1993, 94, Pa. Acad. Fine Arts, Phila., 1997, SUNY, Binghamton, 1997, Nat. Acad. Design, NYC, 1999—2000, painting instr., 2009. One-man shows include Forty-year Drawing Survey 1960-2000, traveling to U.N.C. and Italy, exhibited in group shows at Mus. Chateau de Rochefort-en-Terre, Brittany, France, 1995, Omaggio a Marino Marini, Venice, Florence, Rome, Paris, 2000, Heckscher Mus. Fine Art, Huntington, N.Y., 2000, 8 Artisti da New York, Florence, Rome, Montecatini Terme, Italy, 2001, Angeli, Rome, Florence, Montecatini Terme, Venice, Romania, 2001—02, Omaggio a Magnelli, Italy, France, Romania, 2005, Nat. Acad. Museum, NY, 2007—08, In Chartis Mevaniae, Bevagna, Italy, 2008, L'arte E Magia, Deruta, Italy, 2008, 1st Internationa Biennale, 2008, numerous others, Represented in permanent collections Met. Mus. Art, N.Y.C., Heckscher Mus. Fine Art, GE Corp., Novartis Corp., East Hanover, N.J., Mus. of Art, Bates Coll., Lewiston, Maine, N.Y. Pub. Libr., Tokai Bank, Chgo., Asheville (N.C.) Art Mus., Bklyn. Mus. Art, Accademia d'Arte Moderna Dino Scalabrino, Montecatini Terme, Italy, Circolo La Scaletta, Matera, Italy, City of Todi, Italy, Museo Della Ceramica Contemporanea, Deruta, Museo Palazzo Lepri, Bevagna. Recipient Purchase award, AAAL, N.Y.C., 1997, Found. award, Rochefort-en-Terre Found., 1995. Mem.: Nat. Acad. Design (cert. of merit 1996, Palmer Meml. prize 2000, Henry Ward Ranger award 2001). Office: P O Box 385 Canal St Sta New York NY 10013-0385

RUST, EDWARD BARRY, JR., insurance company executive, lawyer; b. Chgo., Aug. 3, 1950; s. Edward Barry Sr. and Harriett B. (Fuller) R.; m. Sally Buckler, Feb. 28, 1976; 1 child, Edward Barry III. Student, Lawrence U., 1968-69; BS, Ill. Wesleyan U., 1972; JD, MBA, So. Meth. U., 1975. Bar: Tex. 1975, Ill. 1976. Mgmt. trainee State Farm Ins. Companies, Dallas, 1975-76, atty. Bloomington, Ill., 1976, sr. atty., 1976-78, asst. v.p., 1978-81, v.p., 1981-83, exec. v.p., 1983-85, pres., CEO, 1985—87, chmn., pres., CEO, 1987—. Bd. dirs. Helmerich & Payne, Inc., 1997-, The McGraw-Hill Companies, Inc., 2001-, Caterpillar Inc., 2003- Trustee Ill. Wesleyan U., 1985—; mem. adv. coun. Grad. Sch. Bus. Stanford U., 1987-94; mem. bus. adv. coun. Coll. Commerce and Bus. Adminstrn. U. Ill. mem., pres. George W. Bush's Transition Adv. Team Com. on Edn. Mem. Am. Enterprise Inst., Bus. Roundtable (chmn. edn. task force), Tex. State Bar Assn., Ill. Bar Assn., Am. Inst. Property and Liability Underwriters (trustee 1986-96), Ins. Inst. Am. (trustee 1986-96), Ins. Inst. for Highway Safety (vice chmn.), Nat. Alliance of Bus. (chmn. 1998—), Ill. Bus. Roundtable (chmn. 1998—), Bus. Advisory Coun. Univ. Ill. Coll. Commerce and Bus. Admin. Office: State Farm Ins Cos 1 State Farm Plz E-12 Bloomington IL 61710-0001 Office Fax: 309-766-2311, 309-766-3621.*

RUST, GEORGE S., physician, educator; MD, Loyola U. Stritch Sch. Medicine, Maywood, Ill., 1981; MPH, U. Ill., Chgo., 1985. Diplomate in family practice Am. Bd. Family Medicine, 1984, Am. Bd. Preventive Medicine, 1993. Med. dir. West Orange Farm Workers Health Assn., Apopka, Fla., 1985—91; prof. family medicine Morehouse Sch. Medicine, Atlanta, 1991—; dir. Nat. Ctr. Primary Care, Morehouse Sch. Medicine, Atlanta, 2005—. Co-chair Ga. Minority Health Adv. Coun., Atlanta, 2008—. Recipient Physician Leadership award, Disease Mgmt. Assn. America, 2007; named Academic Family Physician of Yr., Ga. Acad. Family Physicians, 1994. Office: Nat Ctr Primary Care 720 Westview Dr Atlanta GA 30310

RUST, JOHN HOWSON, JR., lawyer, state legislator; b. May 21, 1947; s. John Howson and Laura Jeanne (Johnson) R.; m. Susan Byrne, Aug. 15, 1970; children: John W., Thomas A., Robert B. BA, U. Va., 1969, JD, 1972. Bar: Va. 1972, U.S. Dist. Ct. (ea. dist.) Va. 1973, U.S. Ct. Appeals (4th cir.) 1975, U.S. Supreme Ct. 1976. Mem. firm Rust & Rust, P.C. Mem. Ho. of Dels., Commonwealth of Va., 1980-82, 97-2001. Office: PO Box 460 10370 Main St Fairfax VA 22030-0460 Office Phone: 703-273-0583. E-mail: johnhr@erols.com.

RUSTAND, KAY, lawyer; Ptnr. Lawler, Felix & Hall, Arter & Hadden LLP, 1989—2001; v.p., gen counsel Reliance Steel & Aluminum Co., LA, 2001—. Office: Reliance Steel & Aluminum Co 350 S Grand Ave Ste 5100 Los Angeles CA 90071 Office Phone: 213-687-8792.

RUSTAY, JENNIFER BETH, lawyer; b. Kansas City, Mo., Jan. 30, 1973; m. Allen Harrington Rustay, Sept. 29, 2001. BA, Baylor U., 1995, JD, 1997. Bar: Tex. 1997, U.S. Dist. Ct. (all dists. Tex.), US Dist. Ct. (dist. Colo.), US Ct. Appeals (5th cir.). Law clk. Hon. Sam Johnson US Ct. Appeals (5th cir.), Austin, Tex., 1997—98; atty. Bracewell & Patterson, Houston, 1998—2000, Hagans Burdine Montgomery & Rustay P.C., Houston, 2001—. Notes and comments editor: Baylor Law Rev., 1996—97. Named a Rising Star, Tex. Super Lawyers mag., 2006—09. Fellow: State Bar Tex., Houston Bar Assn. Office: Hagans Burdine Montgomery & Rustay PC 3200 Travis 4th Fl Houston TX 77006 Office Phone: 713-222-2700.

RUSU, ADRIAN, engineering educator, director; b. Craiova, Dolj, Romania, May 7, 1973; s. Ioan and Olimpia Rusu; m. Amalia Rusu, Oct. 10, 1995; children: Alex, Andreea. PhD, SUNY, Buffalo, NY, 2003. Asst. prof. Rowan U., Glassboro, NJ, 2003—08, dir., software engring., graphics, and visualization rsch. group, 2004—, dir., FAA, Rowan air transp. rsch. lab., 2005—, assoc. prof., 2008—; adj. prof. St. John Fisher Coll., Rochester, NY, 2002—03; tchg. rsch. asst. SUNY; new faculty fellow NAE Ctr. Advancement Scholarship Engring. Edn., 2005. Contbr. articles to profl. jours. Recipient Innovative Ednl. Partnership award, Borough Glassboro, 2004, Industry Non Fed. Govt. U. award, Fed. Lab. Consortium Tech. Transfer NE Region, 2008; named Wall of Fame for Excellence in Tchg. and Advising, Rowan U., 2006; grantee, FAA, 2008. Mem.: Inst. Elec. and Electronic Engrs., Soc. Indsl. and Applied Math., Assn. Computing Machinery, Upsilon Pi Epsilon Computer Sci. Achievements include patents pending for area-efficient real-time synchronized tree-based web visualization and design. Office: Rowan Univ 201 Mullica Hill Rd Glassboro NJ 08028

RUTA, THOMAS V., professional sports team and accounting executive; married. BS summa cum laude, Fordham U., 1966; MBA with distinction, Pace U.; postgrad. in law, Fordham U. CPA, N.Y., N.J., Minn. Founding ptnr. Behan, Ling & Ruta CPAs, P.C., NYC, 1974, currently chmn., pres.; ltd. ptnr. Pitts. Penguins. Office: 475 Park Ave S 31st Fl New York NY 10016 Office Phone: 212-695-7003. Business E-Mail: truta@blrcpaspc.com.

RUTAN, BURT (ELBERT LEANDER RUTAN), aircraft designer, aircraft company executive; b. Portland, Oreg., June 17, 1943; s. George and Irene R. BS in Aero. Engring., Calif. State Polytech. U., 1965; attended, Space Tech. Inst., Calif. Inst. Tech.; attended academic portion of Aerospace Rsch. Pilots Sch., Edwards Air Force Base. Flight test project engr. Air Force Flight Test Ctr., Edwards AFB, Calif., 1965-72; dir. Bede Test Ctr., Kans., 1972-74; pres. Rutan Aircraft Factory, Mojave, Calif., 1974—; founder, CEO Scaled Composites Inc., Mojave, Calif., 1982—; v.p. Beech Aircraft, 1985. Designer more than 100 aircraft including BD-5J jet (world's smallest private jet aircraft), VariViggen, VariEze (a stall-proof kit airplane with a propeller at the back and winglets on the nose), Solitaire, Defiant, Raytheon Beechcraft Starship, Proteus (high altitude long endurance aircraft being used for everything from cellular communications to suborbital space launches), Boomerang, Virgin Atlantic GlobalFlyer (set a world record for the first solo, non-stop, non-refueled circumnavigation of the world, piloted by Steven Fossett, 2005), White Knight (an airborne launch aircraft) and other kits; designer Voyager aircraft (a superlight plane that could carry 10 times its weight in fuel, first to fly around-the-world without stopping, refueling in 1986); company made history with first private manned mission to space in SpaceShipOne (a two-passenger, high altitude research rocket); SpaceShipOne achieved two record flights (broke 62.5-mile barrier) and won the Ansari X prize on October 4, 2004; SpaceShipOne donated to Smithsonian Inst. on October 6, 2005; pilot for EZ-Rocket (XCOR), which made a record-setting point-to-point flight, departing from Mojave California Spaceport and gliding onto a neighboring airport in California City in 2005. Recip. Spirit of St. Louis medal, Am. Soc. Mech. Engrs., 1987, Best Design award, Exptl. Aircraft Assn.; Air medal, 1970, Stan Szik design contbn. trophy, 1972, EAA Outstanding New Design, 1975-76, 78; Dr. August Raspet Meml. award, 1976, ABC World News Tonight Person of the Week, 1986, Collier trophy for ingenious design and devel., Nat. Aeronautic Assn., 1986, Presdl. Citizens medal for design/develop. of the voyager "around-the-world" aircraft, 1986, FAI gold medal for Voyager Constrn., 1987, medal for the City of Paris, 1987, NASA langley Rsch. Ctr. dirs. award, 1987, Soc. of NASA Flight Surgeons, W. Randolph Lovelace award 1987, medal of Outstanding Achievement and disting. leadership, 1987, Soc. of exptl. test pilots, 1987, Aviation Man of the Yr, 1987, Lindbergh Eagle award, 1987, USAF 40th anniversary award, 1987, The City of Genoa, Italy, Christopher Columbus Internat. Communications medal, 1987, British gold medal, 1987, Outstanding Engring. achievement awards, 1988, Franklin medal, 1987, Disting. inventor award 1988, Meritorious Svc. award, 1988, Internat. Aerospace Hall of Fame Honoree, 1988, medal of achievement, 1989, Crystal Eagle award, 1989, Meritorious Civilian Svc. medal, 1989, Leroy Randle Grumman medal, 1989, Structures, Structural Dynamics and Materials award AIAA, 1991, Bus. Leader in Aerospace, Scientific Am., 2003, Ansari X prize, 2004, NAS Award in Aero. Engring., 2005, Breakthrough Leadership award, Popular Mechanics Breakthrough Awards, 2006; co-recipient with Paul Allen, Smithsonian's Nat. Air and Space Mus. Trophy, 2005; named Innovator of Yr., R&D Mag., 2004; named one of 100 Most Influential People of 2005, Time mag., Rave award in indsl. design, WIRED, 2005. Mem. NAE, Exptl. Aircraft Assn., Soc. Exptl. Test Pilots, Am. Inst. Aeronautics & Astronautics (recipient Reed Aeronautics award, 2001), Soc. Flight Test Engrs., Acad. Model Aeronautics, Internat. Order Characters, Aircraft Owners and Pilots Assn.; Fellow Am. Acad. Arts & Sciences Holds 3 US patents: Grizzly wide-chord flap suspension system; variable geometry high lift system incorporated in the Beech Starship (foreign patents also held); Rutan Model 115 Starship configuration (foreign patents also held). Office: Scaled Composites Inc Mojave Airport 1624 Flight Line Mojave CA 93501-1663 Office Phone: 661-824-4541. Office Fax: 661-824-4174.

RUTCOFSKY, BARRY, computer game company executive, lawyer; JD, Hofstra Univ., 1983. Ptnr. Tenzer Greenblatt LLP, 1987—99; pres. Take2 Interactive, NYC, 1999—2000, co-chmn., 2000—01, exec. v.p. mergers & acquisitions, strategic relationships, 2001—. Office: Take2 Interactive 622 Broadway New York NY 10012

RUTENBERG, MICHAEL ELLIOT, theater educator; s. Benjamin and Eva Rutenberg; m. Marietta Altarovici, Aug. 27, 1995; m. Anna Reinglass, Sept. 24, 1961 (div. 1985); children: Elana Beth Hayden, Melanie Hope de Hann, Brielle Joy. BA, Bklyn Coll., 1957; MFA, Yale Sch. Drama, New Haven, 1960, DFA, 1965. Prof. theatre Hunter Coll., NYC, 1965—; head Israel's Nat. Sch. Performing Art, Ram Gan, 1971—72. Author: (non-fiction) Edward Albee: Playwright in Protest, (play) Oedipus of Lucius Annaeus Seneca. Recipient Chancellor's award, NYC, 2004—05, Pres. award, Hunter Coll., 2006; Fulbright grant, US Govt., 2005—06. Mem.: Dramatist Guild, Soc. Stage Dirs. and Choreographers, Mystery Writers America, Actors Studio (life). Office: Dept Theatre Hunter Coll 695 Park Ave New York NY 10065 Office Phone: 212-772-5148.

RUTENBERG-ROSENBERG, SHARON LESLIE, retired journalist; b. Chgo., May 23, 1951; d. Arthur and Bernice (Berman) Rutenberg; m. Michael J. Rosenberg, Feb. 3, 1980; children: David Kaifel and Jonathan Reuben (twins), Emily Mara. Student, Harvard U., 1972; BA, Northwestern U., 1973, MSJ, 1975; cert. student pilot. Reporter-photographer Lerner Home Newspapers, Chgo., 1973—74; corr. Medill News Svc., Washington, 1975; reporter-newsperson, sci. writer UPI, Chgo., 1975—84; ret., 1984. Interviewer: exclusives White House chief of staff, nation's only mother and son on death row; others. Vol. Chgo.-Read Mental Health Ctr. Recipient Peter Lisagor award for exemplary journalism in features category, 1980, 81; Golden Key Nat. Adv. Bd. of Children's Oncology Svc. Inc., 1981; Media awards for wire svc. feature stories, 1983, 84, wire svc. news stories, 1983, 84, all from Chgo. Hosp. Pub. Rels. Soc. Mem. Profl. Assn. Diving Instrs., Nat. Assn. Underwater Instrs., Hon. Order Ky. Cols., Hadassah, Sigma Delta Chi, Sigma Delta Tau Home: 745 Marion Ave Highland Park IL 60035-5123

RUTER, RUTH EVELYN, elementary school educator; b. Louisville, Apr. 24, 1923; d. Thurston Lowell and Ida Lee (Shaw) Wise; m. Charles M. Ruter, Apr. 15, 1944. BA, We. Ky. U., Bowling Green, 1948; MA, George Peabody, Nashville, 1953. Tchr. elem. Bullitt County Pub. Schs., Sheperdsville, Ky., 1943, Jefferson County Pub. Schs., Louisville, 1943—79. Pres. 15th Dist. PTA, Louisville, 1981—83; pres. Fern Creek Women's Club, Ky., 1983—85, 1991—93, 2000—02; worthy matron Order Ea. Star, Louisville, 1962—63, 1984—85, 1987—88; coord. meals Ky. Fedn. Women's Club, Louisville, 1994—2006. Named to Hall of Fame, Heritage Festival, 2000, Fern Creek Traditional H.S., 2005. Presbyterian. Home: 9801 Hillock Dr Louisville KY 40291

RUTFORD, ROBERT HOXIE, geologist, educator; b. Duluth, Minn., Jan. 26, 1933; s. Skuli and Ruth (Hoxie) R.; m. Marjorie Ann, June 19, 1954; children: Gregory, Kristian, Barbara. BA, U. Minn., 1954, MA, 1963, PhD, 1969; DSc (hon.), St Petersburg State Tech U., Russia, 1994. Football and track coach Hamline U., 1958-62; rsch. fellow U. Minn., 1963-66; asst. prof. geology U. SD, 1967-70, assoc. prof., 1970-72, chmn. dept. geology, 1968-72, chmn. dept. physics, 1971-72; dir. Ross Ice Shelf Project U. Nebr., Lincoln, 1972-75, vice chancellor for research and grad. studies, prof. geology, 1977-82, interim chancellor, 1980-81; dir. divsn. Polar Programs NSF, Washington, 1975-77; pres., prof. geoscis. U. Tex., Dallas, 1982-94, Excellence in Edn. Found. prof. of geoscis., 1994—2007, pres. emeritus, 2007. US del. to Sci. Com. on Antarctic Rsch., 1986-02, v.p., 1996-98, pres., 1998-02, exec. com., 2002-04, hon mem, 2004—; chmn. NRC Polar Rsch. Bd., 1991-95; bd. trustees Geol. Soc. Am. Found., 2005—, vice chmn., 2006-07, chmn., 2007-; bd. govs. US Corp., 1988—, Arctic Inst. N.Am., mem. editl. bd. Issues in Sci. and Tech., 1991-94. Trustee Baylor Coll. Dentistry, 1989-96. 1st lt. U.S. Army, 1954-56. Recipient Antarctic Svc. medal, 1964, Disting. Svc. award NSF, 1977, Ernie Gunderson award for svc. to amateur athletics S.D. AAU, 1972, Outstanding Achievement award U. Minn., 1993, "M" Club Lifetime Achievement award, 1995, Commemorative medal Polish Acad. Scis., 2004. Fellow Geol. Soc. Am.; mem. Antarctican Soc. (pres. 1988-90), Arctic Inst. N.Am. (mem. bd. govs. US corp. 1996-), Explorers Club, Am. Polar Soc. (hon.), Philos. Soc. Tex., St. Petersburg Acad. Engring. (Russia), Tex. Acad. Sci., Sigma Xi. Lutheran. Office: Univ Tex Dallas Geosciences Program Richardson TX 75083-0688

RUTH, DIANNE, personal growth and prosperity coach, holistic counselor; b. Flint, Mich., Apr. 28, 1939; AA, L.A. City Coll., 1982; BA in Psychology, Antioch U., Marina Del Rey, Calif., 1983; MA in Counseling Psychology, Sierra U., Santa Monica, Calif., 1985; PhD in Clin. and Counseling Psychology, Union Inst. and U., Cin., 1989. Cert. life coach Ft. Collins, Colo., 2000, bd. cert. master clin. & med. hypnotist, hypotherapist, neurolinguist programmer. Founder, exec. dir. The Healing Tree, Inc., San Diego, Dynamic Resources Internat. Office: 4295 Gesner St Ste 3C San Diego CA 92117-6663 Office Phone: 619-275-2775. Personal E-mail: drruth@dynamicresources.net.

RUTH, JAMES PERRY, financial planner; b. Washington, Feb. 27, 1946; s. Robert Walker and Virginia Null Ruth; m. Kathleen McHugh, Aug. 10, 1968; children: Heather Lynn, Michael James. BS in Bus. and Public Adminstrn., U. Md., 1970; postgrad., Am. Coll., Bryn Mawr, 1971-83. CLU, CFP, chartered fin. cons. agt., Northwestern Mutual Life Ins. Co., Washington, 1967-74. Gen. agt. Indpls. Life, Rockville, Md., 1974-82; partner Fox, Ruth & Middledorf, Rockville, 1975-82; mgr. Mfrs. Fin. Svcs., Rosslyn, Va., 1982-84; pres. Potomac Fin. Group, 1984—. Contbr. articles to profl. publs.; quoted in N.Y. Times, U.S. News and World Report, USA Today, others. Past pres. Jelleff Boys' Club; past pres. Montgomery County Police Boys' and Girls' Club; past chmn. bd. dirs. Asbury Meth. Village Found. Named Outstanding Young Man Am., U.S. Jaycees, 1979. Mem. Nat. Assn. Ins. and Fin. Advisors (pres. Md. chpt. 1995-96), Nat. Assn. Securities Dealers, Suburban Md. Assn. Ins. and Fin. Advisors (past pres., H.L. Meyer Meml. award 1980), Fin. Planning Assn., Suburban Md. Estate Planning Coun. (past pres.), Million Dollar Round Table. Lutheran. Home: 508 Lawson Way Rockville MD 20850 Office: Ste 420 18310 Montgomery Village Ave Gaithersburg MD 20879-3553 Business E-Mail: jruth@pfgroup.org.

RUTH, RODNEY, musician, music consultant, contractor, educator; b. Robesonia, Pa., Sept. 12, 1934; s. Herbert J. and Pearl (Rentz) R.; m. Gloria Mae Kauffman, Nov. 14, 1953; 1 child, Tiffany Tunisia. MusB, Manhattan Sch. Music, 1960; MA, Columbia U., 1964. Freelance musician; music cons., contractor Meadowlands Sports Complex, various theaters and performing arts ctrs., individual conductors and performers, bands, orchs., festivals, NJ, NY, Pa., 1957—; tchr. Paterson (N.J.) Bd. Edn., 1961-98. Performed with USAF Band, 1953-57; music contractor for world premiers (musicals) Lucifer, Laugh a Little, Cry a Little, Shoemakers Holiday, Love Games, Las Vegas Laugh-In '75. Scholar Manhattan Sch. Music, N.Y.C., 1958-60. Mem. Nat. Edn. Assn., Music Educators Nat. Conf., Am. Fedn. Musicians, Air Force Musicians Assn. Avocations: travel, gardening, golf. Home and Office: Rod Ruth Music 129 Schuyler Rd Allendale NJ 07401-1836 Office Phone: 201-327-7374. E-mail: rodruthmusic@aol.com.

RUTHBERG, MILES N., lawyer; BA summa cum laude, Yale Univ., 1973; JD magna cum laude, Harvard Univ., 1976. Bar: DC 1979, Calif. 1979, NY 2006. Law clk. Judge Carl McGowan, US Ct. of Appeals, DC Cir., 1976—77, Justice Thurgood Marshall, US Supreme Ct., 1977—78; securities litigation and profl. liability practice group Latham & Watkins, 1998—99, nat. chair, 1999—2004, global dept. chair, litigation dept., 1999—2004, exec. com. mem., 2004—08. Bd. governors Assn. Bus. Trial Lawyers, 1994—98. Developments editor Harvard Law Rev., 1976; author: numerous articles in profl. publications. Mem.: ABA, NY State Bar Assn., DC Bar Assn., Calif. State Bar Assn. Office: Latham Watkins 355 S Grand Ave Los Angeles CA 90071-1560

RUTHCHILD, ROCHELLE GOLDBERG, education educator; b. Jersey City, Nov. 30, 1940; d. Samuel A. and Ruth (Raichelson) Goldberg; 1 child, Rafael A. BA, Hofstra U., 1962; MA, U. Rochester, 1964, PhD, 1976. Instr. Cardinal Cushing Coll., Brookline, Mass., 1969-72, Goddard-Cambridge Grad. Program, Cambridge, Mass., 1971-74, core faculty, 1974-79, Plainfield, Vt., 1979-81; asst. prof. Vt. Coll. of Norwich U., Montpelier, 1981-82, prof. grad. studies, 1988—2001; dir. Russian Sch. Norwich U., Northfield, Vt., 1988-94; assoc. Davis Ctr. for Russian Studies Harvard U., 1980—; prof. grad. studies Union Inst. and U., Montpelier, 2001—07, prof. emerita, 2007—. Author: (book) Women in Russian and the Soviet Union: An Annotated Bibliography, 1994; contbr. articles to profl. jours. Jewish Women's Archive mem. Temple Israel, Boston, 1996—. N.Y. State Regents scholar, 1958-62; grantee Internat. Rsch. and Exchs., Leningrad, Moscow, 1966-67, 78-79, 95, NEH, 1996, Dana Grant, 1997-98, others. Mem.: Assn. for Women in Slavic Studies (bd. dirs. 1990, pres./co-founder 1988—90, pres. 888 women's history project 2002—). Jewish. Office: 137 Coolidge St Brookline MA 02446-5807 Home Phone: 617-738-3381; Office Phone: 617-738-9524. E-mail: ruthchil@yahoo.com.

RUTHERFORD, BOYD KEVIN, political organization administrator, former federal agency administrator; b. Washington, 1957; BA, Howard U., 1979; MA, JD, U. So. Calif., 1990. Atty. analyst Bankers Trust Co., 1979—81; mktg. rep. Data Control Corp., 1981—86; sr. acct. exec. Telenet Comm. Corp., 1986—87; litigation assoc. Carlsmith Wickman Case Mukai & Ichiki, 1990—91; atty. Daihatsu Am., Inc., 1991—92; of counsel Mitsubishi Motor Sales of Am., Inc., 1992—94; assoc. Van Ness Feldman, P.C., 1994—98, Tydings & Rosenberg, LLP, 1998—2000; delegate Rep. Party Nat. Convention, 2000; dir. bus. devel. Kelly Law Registry, 2000—01; assoc. adminstr. office enterprise devel. Gen. Services Adminstrn. (GSA), 2001—03, assoc. adminstr. office performance improvement, 2002—03; acting sec. Md. Dept. Gen. Services, 2003, sec., 2003—06; asst. sec. for adminstrn. USDA, 2006—09; chief adminstrv. officer Republican Nat. Com. (RNC), 2009—. Mem. Baltimore City Brownfields Redevelopment Coun., 1998—2000. Office: Republican Nat Com (RNC) 310 First St SE Washington DC 20003*

RUTHERFORD, GEORGE WILLIAMS, III, public health association administrator, educator; b. San Diego, Apr. 6, 1952; s. George Williams II and Anna Gwyn (Dearing) Rutherford; m. Lisa Anderson, Aug. 24, 1974 (div. 1984); children: Alicia Gwyn, George Williams IV; m. Mary Workman, Feb. 23, 1985; children: Alexandra Catherine, Anne Elizabeth Martha, Hugh Thomas Gwyn, Amanda Frances Julia. AB in Classics, Stanford U., Calif., 1974, BS in Chemistry, 1975, AM in Hist., 1975; MD, Duke U., Durham, NC, 1978. Diplomate Am. Bd. Pediat., Am. Bd. Preventive Medicine, Nat. Bd. Med. Examiners. Intern pediat. U. Calif. Med. Ctr., San Diego, 1978-79; resident pediat. U. Calif. Med. Ctr./Hosp. for Children, San Diego, 1979-80; resident Hosp. Sick Children, Toronto, 1980-81; chief resident Children's Hosp. & Health Ctr., San Diego, 1981-82; EIS officer divsn. viral diseases, divsn. field svcs Epidemiology Office Ctrs. Disease Control, Atlanta, 1982-84; dir. divsn. immunization, acting dir. divsn. tropical disease NYC Dept. Health, 1983-85; med. epidemiologist AIDS program Ctrs. Disease Control, San Francisco Dept. Pub. Health, 1985-87; from med. dir. to dir. AIDS office San Francisco Dept. Pub. Health, 1986-90; chief, infectious disease br., state epidemiologist Calif. Dept Health, Berkeley, 1990-92; state epidemiologist Calif. Dept. Health, Berkeley, 1990—95; dep. dir. prevention svcs. Calif. Dept. Health, Berkeley, 1992-95, state health officer, 1993-95; assoc. dean adminstrn., prof. epidemiology/health adminstrn. U. Calif. Sch. Pub. Health, Berkeley, 1995-97; prof. epidemiology & preventive medicine U. Calif., San Francisco, 1997—, Salvatore Pablo Lucia prof. preventive medicine, head divsn. preventative medicine & pub. health, dir. Prevention & Pub. Health Group (formerly Inst. Global Health), 2004—. Transport physician Children's Hosp. & Health Ctr., San Diego, 1981; asst. clin. prof. pediat. Emory U., Atlanta, 1982—83, Cornell U., NYC, 1984—85, U. Calif., San Francisco, 1986—92, asst. clin. prof. epidemiology & biostats., 1987—92, assoc. adj. prof. epidemiology, biostats. & pediat., 1992—95, adj. prof., 1996—; assoc. clin. prof. cmty. health U. Calif., Davis, 1991—95; cons. Pan-Am. Health Orgn. S.Am., 1986—89, WHO, 1988—90, Ctrs. Disease Control, Atlanta. Editor: Calif. Morbidity, 1990—92; mem. editl. bd. Calif. AIDS Update, 1988—, Current Issues in Pub. Health, 1993—97; translator: cardiology teaching manual; contbr. numerous articles to profl. jours., chapters to books. Fellow: Am. Acad. Pediat.; mem.: APHA, Assn. State & Territorial Health Ofcls., Soc. Epidemiol. Rsch., Internat. AIDS Soc., No. Calif. Pub. Health Assn., Infectious Diseases Soc. of America, Calif. Med. Assn., Am. Soc. Tropical Medicine & Hygiene, Am. Assn. Hist. of Medicine, Bay Area Communicable Disease Exch. Republican. Episcopalian. Avocation: tennis. Office: UCSF Prevention & Pub Health Group Global Health Scis 50 Beale St Ste 1200 San Francisco CA 94105 Office Phone: 415-597-8200. Office Fax: 415-597-8299. Business E-Mail: grutherford@psg.ucsf.edu.*

RUTHERFORD, JIM, professional sports team executive; b. Beeton, Ont., Can., Feb. 17, 1949; 1 child, Andrea. Goalie Detroit Red Wings, 1970—71, 1973—80, 1982—83, Pitts. Penguins, 1971—73, Toronto Maple Leafs, 1980—81, LA Kings, 1981—82; dir. hockey ops Compuware Sports Corp., 1982-94; gen. mgr. Windsor Spitfires, Ont., 1984-88, head coach Ont., 1986-87; dir. hockey ops. Detroit Ambassadors, 1989-91, coach, dir. hockey ops., 1991-92, Detroit Jr. Red Wings (formerly Ambassadors), 1992-94; COO KTR Hockey Ltd. Partnership, Hartford, Conn., 1984—; pres., gen. mgr., COO Carolina Hurricanes (formerly Hartford Whalers), 1994—. Mem. Team Can. hockey world championships, Vienna, 1977, Moscow, 79; player rep. 5 seasons Red Wings. Named Exec. of Yr., Can. Hockey League, 1993, Ont. Hockey League, 1994, The Hockey News, 2002, NHL Exec. of Yr., Sporting News, 2006. Achievements include being the general manager of Stanley Cup Champion Carolina Hurricanes, 2006. Office: Carolina Hurricanes 1400 Edwards Mill Rd Raleigh NC 27607-3624

RUTHERFORD, JOHN SHERMAN, III, (JOHNNY RUTHERFORD), retired professional race car driver; b. Coffeyville, Kans., Mar. 12, 1938; s. John Sherman and Mary Henrietta (Brooks) R.; m. Betty Rose Hoyer, July 7, 1963; children: John Sherman Rutherford IV, Angela Ann Rutherford-Price. Student, Tex. Christian U., 1956. Profl. race car driver, 1959-94; ret., 1994; driver super-modified race cars, sprint cars, stock cars, midgets, sports cars, Indy cars, Trans-Am cars and formula 5000. Mem. Indy Car Racing Inc.; dir. spl. events Indy Racing League, 1995—; pace car driver for Championship Auto Racing Teams, 1992-95; auto racing cons. Pennzoil Products-Racing Divsn.; lectr. in field. Author: (autobiography) Lone Star J.R., 2000; host: TV show The Racers; race commentator TV show, NBC, ESPN, CBS, ABC; appeared in numerous TV commercials; art work included in traveling exhbn. Art and Athletes; TV and radio pub. services messages for Nat. Safety Council, Calif. Hwy. Patrol, U.S. Marines, Muscular Dystrophy Assn., Cystic Fibrosis Assn., Boy Scouts, Camp Fire, Jewel Charity, Shriner's Hosp., Tex. Soc. to Prevent Blindness, Air N.G. Hon. state chmn. Am. Cancer Soc., Tex., Tarrant County Soc. to Prevent Blindness, Emergency Medicine Found., Ft. Worth Kidney Assn., Ft. Worth Burn Ctr.; Ind. chmn. Am. Heart Assn.; hon. mem. bd. dirs. Tex. chpt. Speedway Children's Charities, 1998—. CARA Charities, 2000--; bd. dirs. Indy HOF and Oldtimers, 2002—. With USMC Res., 1955—61. Named Ft. Worth Newsmaker of Yr., 1974, Driver of Yr. Sport Mag., 1976, Driver of Yr. Auto Race Writers and Broadcasters Am., 1974, 80, Olsonite Driver of Yr., 1980, Corvette Challenge's Sportsman of Yr., 1988, Motorsports amb., 1993; recipient Jim Clark award, 1969, Extra Mile award, 1973, Jim Malloy award, 1974, Eddie Sachs award, 1975, Louie Meyer award, 1992; chosen for Internat. Race of Champions, 1974, 76-79, 84, chosen Fast Masters, 1993; named to Tex. Sports Hall of Fame, 1981, Indy 500 Hall of Fame, 1987, Boys Clubs Am.'s Celebrity Hall of Fame, 1987, Tex. Auto Racing Hall of Fame, 1988, Nat. Sprint Car Hall of Fame, 1995, Internat. Motorsports Hall of Fame, 1996, Tex. Motorsports Hall of Fame, 2003, Philanthropy Hall of Fame, 2006. Mem. Fedn. Internat. Automobile, Internat. Motors Sports Assn., Exptl. Aircraft Assn., Warbirds of Am., Confederate Air Force, Internat. Aerobatic Club, League Auto Racing (sec., bd. dirs.), Championship Drivers Assn. (bd. dirs.), Nat. Rifle Assn., Air Force Assn., Air Power Coun., Blue Angels Assn., Ft. Worth Boat Club, Shady Oaks Country Club, Speedway Club, Lions. Republican. Disciples Of Christ. Achievements include winning 27 championship car races; winner Indianapolis 500, 1974, 76, 80, second place, 1975; set new world's record for stock cars, Daytona Beach, Fla., 1963; set record at Indpls. 500, 1973; at Mich. Internat. Raceway, 1984; U.S. Auto Club Nat. Sprint Car champion, 1965; Nat. Driving champion USAC and CART, 1980; oldest driver (48) to win a 500 mile Indy Car Race, 1986. *I am a firm believer in the fact that a person can do anything in this world he or she wants to as long as you have desire. People have to set goals, things to achieve. No one ever remembers who finished second. Luck is where preparation meets opportunity.*

RUTHERFORD, PAUL HARDING, physicist; b. Shipley, Yorkshire, Eng., Jan. 22, 1938; came to U.S., 1965, naturalized, 1976; s. Joseph William and Annie (Harding) R.; m. Audrey Jones Irvine, Oct. 31, 1959; children— Andrea Christine, Julia Irvine. BA, Cambridge U., Eng., 1959, MA, PhD, Cambridge U., Eng., 1963. Research asso. Princeton (N.J.) U. Plasma Physics Lab., 1962-63, mem. research staff, 1965-68, research physicist, 1968-71, sr. research physicist, 1971-99, head theoretical div., 1972-80, dep. asso. dir. for research, 1978-80, asso. dir. research, 1980-95. Chair tech. adv. com. Internat. Thermonuclear Exptl. Reactor, 1992-99; rsch. assoc. U.K. Atomic Energy Authority Culham (Berkshire, Eng.) Lab., 1963-65; lectr. astrophys. scis. Princeton U. Co-author: (with R.J. Goldston) Introduction to Plasma Physics, 1995; mem. editl. bd. Physics of Fluids, 1973-75, Nuc. Fusion, 1980-99. Recipient E.O. Lawrence award U.S. Dept. Energy, 1983, Disting. Career award Fusion Power Assocs., 1998. Fellow Am. Phys. Soc. Home: 10 Burr Dr Princeton NJ 08540-1950 Office: Plasma Physics Lab PO Box 451 Princeton NJ 08543-0451 Business E-Mail: prutherford@pppl.gov.

RUTHERFORD, THOMAS TRUXTUN, II, state legislator, municipal official; b. Columbus, Ohio, Mar. 3, 1947; s. James William and Elizabeth Whiting (Colby) R.; m. Linda Sue Rogers, Aug. 28, 1965 (div.); 1 child, Jeremy Todd; m. Charlene Beth Smith, July 22, 2007. BBA, U. N.Mex., 1970, JD, 1982. Page, reading clk. N.Mex. State Legislature, 1960-65; mem. N.Mex. Atty. Gen. Environ. Adv. Commn., 1972; radio broadcaster Sta. KOB Radio and TV, 1963-72; mem. N.Mex. Senate, Albuquerque, 1972-96, majority whip, 1978-88. Chmn. rules com. N.Mex. State Senate, chmn. econ. devel. and new tech. interim. com., mem. sci. and new tech. oversight com., majority fl. leader, 1996; pres. Rutherford & Assocs., Albuquerque, 1978—83; pvt. practice, Albuquerque, 1983—; gen. counsel Nat. Fraternal Order of Police, 1996—2001; commr., chair Bernalillo County Commn., 1996—2004;

lobbyist The Rutherford Group, 1996—; bd. dirs. Hispano C. of C., Kirtland Partnership Com., Albuquerque Econ. Devel., Camp Sierra Blanca Youth Detention Ctr., N. Mex. Bus. Weekly Top 100 Power Brokers, 1996—2004; past chmn. Albuquerque Cable TV Adv. Bd.; mem. S.W. Regional Energy Coun., N.Mex. Gov.'s Commn. on Pub. Broadcasting; bd. dirs., v.p. Rocky Mountain Corp. for Pub. Broadcasting; mem. Am. Coun. Young Polit. Leaders; del. mission to Hungary, Austria, Greece, 1983; mem. Fgn. Trade Adv. Com. Bd. Econ. Devel. and Tourism; trade del. People's Republic of China, 1985; local govt. del. Switzerland, 2001. Mem. Leadership N.Mex. Class of 2004; bd. dirs. Nat. Assn. Counties, N.Mex. Assn. Counties. N.Mex. Broadcasting Assn. scholar, 1970. Office: 1016 monroe NE Albuquerque NM 87110-5822

RUTHERFORD, WILLIAM DRAKE, investment executive; b. Marshalltown, Iowa, Jan. 14, 1939; s. William Donald and Lois Esther (Drake) R.; m. Janice W. Rutherford, Feb. 4, 1965 (div. Mar. 1982); children: Wayne Donald, Melissa Drake; m. Karen Anderegg, Jan. 2, 1994. BS, U. Oreg., 1961; LLB, Harvard U., 1964. Bar: Oreg. 1964, U.S. Dist. Ct. Oreg. 1966. Assoc. Maguire, Kester & Cosgrave, Portland, Oreg., 1966-69; house counsel May & Co., Portland, 1969-70, pvt. practice, 1970-71, McMinnville, Oreg., 1971-84; mem. Oreg. Ho. of Reps., Salem, 1977-84; state treas. State of Oreg., Salem, 1984-87; chmn. Oreg. Investment Coun., Salem, 1986-87; exec. v.p., dir. U.S. and Australia ops. ABD Internat. Mgmt. Corp., NYC, 1987-88, pres., chief exec. officer, bd. dirs., 1988-89; pres., bd. dirs. Societé Gen. Touche Remnant, 1990-93; dir. spl. projects Metallgesellschaft Corp., NYC, 1994-95; mng. dir. Macadam Capital Ptnrs., Portland, 1995-96; CEO Fiberboard Asbestos Compensation Trust, Portland, 1997; prin. Rutherford Investment Mgmt. LLC, 1998—. Past chmn. bd. dirs. Metro One Telecomms. Author: Who Stole Goldilocks?, 2006. Trustee The Nature Conservancy, 2005—; bd. dirs. Portland Opera Assn., 1995—99; mem. investment bd. Oreg. Cmty. Found., 2006—. Recipient Contbn. to Individual Freedom award ACLU, 1981 Mem. Nat. Assn. State Treas. (exec. v.p. 1985, 86, pres. western region 1985, 86), Nat. Assn. State Auditors, Comptr. and Treas. (exec. com. 1987). Office: 10300 S W Greenburg Rd Ste 115 Portland OR 97223 Business E-Mail: WRutherford@rutherfordinvestment.com.

RUTHERFURD, LISA, school psychologist; b. Littleton, Colo., May 15, 1978; d. Hugo Rutherfurd, Jr. and Merika Aro Rutherfurd. BA in English, Colo. State U., Ft. Collins, 2000; EdS in Sch. Psychology, Lewis and Clark Coll., Portland, Oreg., 2006. Cert. nat. cert. sch. psychologist Nat. Assn. Sch. Psychologists, 2006. Coll. course facilitator Colo. State U., Ft. Collins, Colo., YMCA of the Rockies, Winter Park, Colo.; coord. outdoor leadership program Camp Chief Ouray, Winter Park; milieu counselor Hand Up Homes for Youth and Cornerstone Inc., Denver; applied behavior analysis therapist Home Program, Portland, Oreg.; ESL asst. Lincoln Park Elem., Portland. Vol. Larimer County Food Bank, Ft. Collins, Colo., 2006, Habitat for Humanity, Poudre River Clean-up, Nat. Pub. Lands Day, Boys and Girls Club; volleyball coach Littleton, Colo.; soccer coach Ft. Collins Soccer Club. Mem.: Autism Soc. Larimer County, Autism Soc. Am., Assn. Exptl. Edn., Colo. Soc. Sch. Psychologists, Nat. Assn. Sch. Psychologists. Office Phone: 970-613-6600. Business E-Mail: rutherfurdl@thompson.k12.co.us.

RUTKIN, AMY B., legislative staff member; Chief of staff to Rep. Jerrold Nadler US House of Reps., Washington. Democrat. Office: 2334 Rayburn House Office Bldg Washington DC 20515 Office Phone: 202-225-5635.*

RUTKOFF, ALAN STUART, lawyer; b. Chgo., May 31, 1952; s. Roy and Harriet (Ruskin) R.; m. Mally Zoberman, Dec. 22, 1974; children: Aaron Samuel, Jordana Michal, Robert Nathaniel. BA with high distinction, U. Mich., 1973; JD magna cum laude, Northwestern U., 1976. Bar: Ill. 1976, U.S. Dist. Ct. (no. dist.) Ill. 1976, U.S. Ct. Appeals (7th cir.) 1977, U.S. Ct. Appeals (3d cir.) 1978, U.S. Supreme Ct. 1981, U.S. Ct. Appeals (5th cir.) 1983, U.S. Ct. Appeals (8th cir.) 1990, U.S. Dist. Ct. (we. dist.) Wis. 1996, U.S. Ct. Appeals (6th cir.) 2003. Assoc. Altheimer & Gray, Chgo., 1976-80; ptnr. Kastel & Rutkoff, Chgo., 1980-83, Holleb & Coff Ltd., Chgo., 1983-84, McDermott Will & Emery LLP, Chgo., 1984—, gen. coun., 2005—; adj. prof. law-legal Northwestern U., 2008—. Pres. N. Suburban Synagogue Beth El, Highland Pk., Ill., 1999-2001. Mem. ABA, Chgo. Bar Assn., Order of Coif. Home: 801 Timberhill Rd Highland Park IL 60035-5148 Office: McDermott Will & Emery LLP 227 W Monroe St Ste 4400 Chicago IL 60606-5096 Home Phone: 847-432-2242; Office Phone: 312-984-7751. Business E-Mail: arutkoff@mwe.com.

RUTKOWSKI, DUANE JOSEPH, social studies educator; b. Phila., Aug. 20, 1956; s. Edward Joseph and Dorothy Lucille Rutkowski. BA, U. Pa., 1978; postgrad., U. Arts, 1978—82. Dean students, tchr. social studies Performing Arts Sch., Phila., 1978—89; dir. music, organist, dir. choir St. Laurentius Ch., 1968—, tchr. 7th grade social studies, music, lang. arts, 1990—. Asst. dir. Acad. Boys Choir, Phila., 1976—89; guest soloist, organist various area chs., 1990—. Chmn. pastoral coun., fundraiser St. Laurentius Ch., Phila., 1993—. Recipient Tchg. Excellence award, Phila. (Pa.) Flag Day Assn., 2005; named Tchr. of Yr., Fox 29 TV Sta. Phila., 1992, 1993, Celebrate Fishtown Assn., Phila., 1998, Fishtown Civic Assn., Phila., 2005. Mem.: Met. Opera Guild, Nat. Cath. Educators Assn., Phila. Flag Day Assn. Roman Catholic. Avocations: travel, gourmet cooking. Home: 2651 E Huntington St Philadelphia PA 19125 Office: St Laurentius Sch 1612 E Berks St Philadelphia PA 19125 Office Phone: 215-423-8834.

RUTKOWSKI, JOSEPH A., manufacturing executive; Mgr. Cold Finish Nucor Corp., Norfolk, Nebr., 1989-91, mgr. melting & casting steel divsn. Plymouth, Utah, 1991—92, gen. mgr. steel divsn. Darlington, SC, 1992—98, Hertford, NC, 1998, v.p., 1993—98, exec. v.p. steel mills Charlotte, NC, 1998—. Office: Nucor Corp 1915 Rexford Rd Charlotte NC 28211 Office Phone: 704-366-7000. Office Fax: 704-362-4208.

RUTKOWSKI, LAWRENCE, lawyer; b. Fall River, Mass., June 19, 1953; BA magna cum laude, Coll. of Holy Cross, 1975; JD, Columbia Univ., 1978. Bar: NY 1979. With Cadwalader, Wickersham & Taft, 1979—82, Hill, Betts & Nash, 1982—92; ptnr., maritime, aviation, corp. fin. Seward & Kissel, NYC, 1992—, co-head corp. fin. dept., and head, transp. fin. group. Mng. editor Columbia Jour. Law and Social Problems, 1977—78. Dir., pres. Holy Cross Coll. Lawyers Assn.; dir. Seafarers and Internat. House, NYC. Mem.: ABA, Maritime Law Assn. US (dir., sec. 2005—), Assn. Bar City NY (chair, maritime law com. 1994—97), Pi Sigma Alpha, Phi Beta Kappa. Roman Catholic. Office: Seward & Kissel LLP One Battery Park Plz New York NY 10004 Office Phone: 212-574-1206. Office Fax: 212-480-8421. Business E-Mail: rutkowski@sewkis.com.

RUTKOWSKI, SANDRA L., library director; d. Walter A. and Ethel Mae Rutkowski. BA, Mary Manse, Toledo; M in Libr. Sci., Wayne State, Detroit; EdS in Curriculum & Instrn., U. Toledo. Media specialist Cardinal Stritch HS, Oreg., Ohio; elem. prin. Aquinas Elem. Sch., Steubenville, Ohio; asst. libr. Lourdes Coll., Sylvania, Ohio, dir., libr. svcs., 2002—. Editor book; contbr. numerous conf. presentation. Mem. vocation awareness team. Mem.: ALA, Cath. Libr. Assn., Ohio Link, Ohio Pvt. Academic Libraries (vice chair and comm. coord. 2007—08). Office: Lourdes Coll 6832 Convent Blvd Sylvania OH 43560 Office Fax: 419-824-3511. Business E-Mail: srutkowski@lourdes.edu.

RUTLEDGE, CHARLES OZWIN, pharmacologist, educator; b. Topeka, Oct. 1, 1937; s. Charles Ozwin and Alta (Seaman) R.; m. Jane Ellen Crow, Aug. 13, 1961; children: David Ozwin, Susan Harriett, Elizabeth Jane, Karen Ann. BS in Pharmacy, U. Kans., 1959, MS in Pharmacology, 1961; PhD in Pharmacology, Harvard U., 1966. NATO postdoctoral fellow Gothenburg (Sweden) U., 1966-67; asst. prof. U. Colo. Med. Ctr., Denver, 1967-74, assoc. prof., 1974-75; prof., chmn. dept. pharmacology U. Kans., Lawrence, 1975-87; dean, prof. pharmacology Purdue U., West Lafayette, Ind., 1987—2002, exec. dir. Discovery Park, 2001—05, interim vice provost rsch., 2002—05, v.p. rsch., 2005—07. Contbr. articles on neuropharmacology to profl. jours. Grantee NIH, 1970-87. Mem. AAAS, Am. Soc. Pharmacology and Exptl. Therapeutics (councillor 1982 84, sec.-treas. 1990-93, pres. 1996-97), Am. Assn. Coll. Pharmacy (chmn. biol. scis. sect. 1983-84, chmn. coun. faculties 1986-87, chmn. coun. deans 1993-94, com. implement change pharm. edn. 1989-92, pres. 1996-97). Avocations: gardening, skiing, travel. Home: 40 Brynteg Est West Lafayette IN 47906-5643 Office: Purdue U Hovde Hall 610 Purdue Mall West Lafayette IN 47907-2040 Office Phone: 765-494-6209. Business E-Mail: chipr@purdue.edu.

RUTLEDGE, DAVID B., electrical engineer, educator; BA, Williams Coll., Williamstown, Mass., 1973; MA, U. Cambridge, Eng., 1975; PhD, U. Calif., Berkeley, 1980. Asst. prof. Calif. Inst. Tech., Pasadena, 1980—84, assoc. prof., 1984—89, prof., 1989—2001, exec. officer elec. engring., 1999—2002, Kiyo and Eiko Tomiyasu prof. elec. engring., 2001—, dir. Lee Ctr. Advanced Networking, chair Divsn. Engring. and Applied Sci., 2005—. Co-founder Wavestream Corp., San Dimas, Calif. Contbr. articles to sci. jours.; author: The Electronics of Radio, 1999. Recipient NSF Presdl. Investigator award, Doug DeMaw award, Am. Radio Relay League, Microwave prize, Microwave Theory and Techniques Soc., Disting. Educator award; grantee Japan Soc. for Promotion of Sci. fellowship. Fellow: IEEE (Millennium medal). Office: Calif Inst Tech MC 104-44 Pasadena CA 91125 Office Phone: 626-395-4806, E-mail: rutledge@caltech.edu.

RUTLEDGE, EDWARD K., mortgage broker; b. Winfield, Ill., Feb. 1, 1972; s. John K. and Nancy Ann D. Rutledge; m. Katherine Collins Horne, Nov. 13, 1999; children: Elizabeth Thorne, Eleanor Stone. BS, Miami U., 1994. Fin. mgr. LaSalle Nat. Trust, Chgo., 1994—96; global products coord. ABN AMRO Asset Mgmt., Amsterdam, 1996—99; mgr. Charter Cons., Chgo., 2000—03; v.p. Draper and Kramer, Chgo., 2003—. Mem. Trout Unlimited, Atlantic Salmon Fedn., Ruffed Grouse Soc., Chgo. Coun. on Fgn. Rels., Chgo.; steering com. Chgo. Opera Theater, Chgo., 2005. Recipient Eagle Scout, Boy Scouts of Am., 1986. Mem.: SAR, Friends of Downtown, No. Ill. Comml. Assn. Realtors (com. chair), CCIM, Mensa, Pinewood Club, Tavern Club (bd. dirs. 2005), U. Club Chgo., Casino, Phi Gamma Delta. Avocations: fishing, hunting, skiing, scuba diving, travel. Office: Draper and Kramer 33 W Monroe Ste 1900 Chicago IL 60603 Business E-Mail: rutledge@draperandkramer.com.

RUTLEDGE, JOANNE, retired artist consultant; b. Indpls., Dec. 17, 1941; d. Edward John and Dorothy Louise (Bachelor) Underwood; m. Kenneth Clay Smith, Sept. 7, 1963 (div. May 1990); children: Elizabeth, Kenneth Clay, Jr., Andrew; m. Mark Alan Rutledge, July 31, 1993. RN, St. Vincent's Sch. Nursing, Indpls., 1962; BSN, Ind. U., Indpls., 1979. RN Ind. Staff RN Children's Hosp., Washington, 1962—63, St. Vincent's Hosp., Indpls., 1963—64, Women's Hosp. Spl. Care Nursery, Indpls., 1990—97; nurse cons. Hosp. Care for Indigent Ind. State Program, Indpls., 1995—2007. Exhibitions include Ind. State Fair, Ind. Heritage Arts, Southside Art League Regional Show. Docent emeritus Indpls. Mus. Art, 1983—; reading tutor Kiwanis Project, 2002—; active various coms. Children's Mus. Guild, 1975—; v.p. Indpls. Athletic Club Art Bd. Found., 1990—. Recipient Billy Cothran Landscape award, Indpls. Art Ctr., 1985. Mem.: Ind. Plein Art Painters Assn., Stutz Artist's Assn., Ind. Artist's Club (assoc.), Proctor Club (pres. 1994—95). Roman Catholic. Avocations: travel, photography, hiking, attending concerts and theater. Home: 1019 W 75th St Indianapolis IN 46260-3408

RUTLEDGE, KATHERINE BURCK, artist; b. La., Mar. 16, 1949; d. Cyril Büsing and Sarah Marlette Burck; m. Clayton Fenton Rutledge, Apr. 24, 1982. BFA, La. State U., 1971; postgrad., New Orleans Acad. Fine Arts, 1988—90. Represented in permanent collections McIlhenny Collection of Natural Sci., La. State U., New Orleans Zoo. Fellow La. State Mus. Natural Sci., Baton Rouge, 1979—82. Scholar, Audubon Soc., Baton Rouge chpt., 1980. Mem.: The Pocahontas Found., Magna Carta Dames, Jamestown Soc. (life; historian-genealogist 2008—09). Republican. Avocations: gardening, birdwatching. Home: 238 Ship Dr Baton Rouge LA 70806

RUTLEDGE, THOMAS M., communications executive; b. 1955; BA in Econs., Calif. U., Pa., 1977; grad. advanced mgmt. prog., Harvard U., 1995. Mgr. trainee Am. TV & Comm., 1977, divsn. pres. Austin, Tex., Portland, Maine; sr. exec. v.p. Time Warner Cable, 1991—2001, pres., 2001; pres. cable & comm. Rainbow Media Holdings LLC, 2002—04; COO Cablevision Sys. Corp., 2004—, CSC Holdings Inc., 2004—. Bd. dirs. Nat. Cable Satellite Corp., Cable TV Labs., Inc.; chmn., mem. exec. com. Nat. Cable & Telecomm. Assn. Bd. dirs. CTAM Ednl. Found. Office: Cablevision Sys Corp 1111 Stewart Ave Bethpage NY 11714 Office Phone: 516-813-2300. Office Fax: 516-364-4913.*

RUTROUGH, JAMES E., insurance company executive; b. 1949; BA, U. Va. Various positions including asst. divsn. mgr. State Farm Ins., 1971—90, v.p. pers., 1990—92, regional v.p. Ill., 1992—94, sr. v.p., 1994—98, chief adminstrv. officer, 1998—, exec. v.p., 1998—2001, sr. exec. v.p., 2001—04, vice chmn., 2004—. Bd. dirs State Farm Ins., 2002—, chmn's coun. Bd. mem. Jr. Achievement USA, Colorado Springs, 2003—, chmn., 2008—. Office: State Farm Ins One State Farm Plz Bloomington IL 61710*

RUTSALA, VERN A., poet, writer, language educator; b. Feb. 5, 1934; s. Ray Edwin and Virginia Mae (Brady) R.; m. Joan Merle Colby, Apr. 6, 1957; children: Matthew, David, Kirsten. BA, Reed Coll., Portland, 1956; MFA, U. Iowa, Iowa City, 1960. Instr. Lewis and Clark Coll., Portland, 1961-64, asst. prof., 1964-69, assoc. prof., 1969-76, prof., 1976—2004. Vis. prof. U. Minn., Mpls., 1968-69, Bowling Green State U., Ohio, 1970; vis. writer Idaho, Moscow, 1988, Redlands U., Calif., 1979; chmn. English dept. Lewis and Clark, Portland, 1986-89, MWC/Pacific MFA program, 2005. Author: The Window, 1964, Laments, 1975, The Journey Begins, 1976, Paragraphs, 1978, Walking Home from the Icehouse, 1981, Backtracking, 1985, Ruined Cities, 1987, Selected Poems, 1991, Little-Known Sports, 1994, Greatest Hits: 1964-02, 2002, A Handbook for Writers, 2004, The Moment's Equation, 2004, How We Spent Our Time, 2006. With U.S. Army, 1956-58. Guggenheim Found. fellow, 1982-83, NEA fellow, 1975, 79, Masters fellow Oreg. Arts Commn., 1990; recipient Carolyn Kizer prize Western Oreg. State Coll., 1988, N.W. Poets prize N.W. Rev., 1975, Hazel Hall award Oreg. Inst. Lit. Arts, 1992, Juniper prize U. Mass. Press, 1993, Duncan Lawrie prize Arvon Found., 1994, Carolyn Kizer prize, 1997, Richard Snyder prize, 2004, Akron Poetry prize, 2004, Kenneth O. Hanson award, 2005; finalist Nat. Book award, 2005, Mississippi Review Poetry prize, 2009. Mem. AAUP, AWP, PEN, Acad. Am. Poets. Avocations: drawing, painting, sports.

RUTSKY, LESTER, retired textiles executive, writer; b. NYC, May 23, 1924; s. Samuel and Bess (Millman) Rutsky; m. Elaine Selesnik, Aug. 30, 1959. Student viola, Stuyvesant House, 1935—37, Christadora House, 1937—38. Co-writer (with Maceo Pinkard) (songs) You're Gonna Be Sorry (named to Songwriters Hall of Fame); contbr. articles to profl. jours., columns in newspapers; author: numerous poems. Recipient Paul Elliot Meml. award, Poetry Soc. Mich., 1982, 1st pl., Ind. State Poetry Soc., Poetry Clubs Ind. Democrat. Avocations: painting, violin, piano. Home Phone: 718-449-7011. Personal E-mail: llesrut@gmail.com.

RUTSTEIN, DAVID W., lawyer, food products executive; b. NYC, July 7, 1944; s. David and Mazie (Weissman) R.; m. Rena E. Bergsmann, July 19, 1967; children: Sara E., Charles B. BA, U. Pa., 1966; JD with honors, George Washington U., 1969. Bar: Pa. 1969, D.C. 1969. Dep. atty. gen., Pa., 1969-70; ptnr. firm Danzansky, Dickey, Tydings, Quint & Gordon, Washington, 1970-78; sr. v.p., gen. counsel Giant Food, Inc., Washington, 1978—2000; of counsel Bus. Transactions, Mergers & Acquisitions practices Venable LLP, Washington, 2001—. Bd. dirs., chmn., treas. Washington Met. Bd. Trade, Fed. City Coun. Bd. dirs., pres. Washington Hebrew Home for Aged (Hyman Goldman award), 1989-91; mem. exec. com. Fed. City Coun.; chmn. Agnes and Eugene Meyer Found., Wash. Met. Bd. Trade; trustee Greater Washington Rsch. Ctr. Recipient award for Disting. Svc. to Washington Theater Cmty., KPMG; named Washingtonian of the Year, Washingtonian Mag. Mem. D.C. Bar Assn., Washington Met. Area Corp. Counsel Assn. (pres. 1986). Jewish. Home: 9 Greentree Ct Bethesda MD 20817-1440 Office: Venable Law Firm 575 7th St NW Washington DC 20004-1601 Office Phone: 202-344-4000. Office Fax: 202-344-8300. Business E-Mail: dwrutstein@venable.com.

RUTSTEIN, SEDMARA ZAKARIAN, concert pianist, educator; b. Kazan, Russia, Oct. 18, 1937; came to U.S., 1974; d. Suren and Ekaterina (Todorovskaya) Zakarian; m. Alexander Rutstein, Aug. 29, 1958; 1 child, Alla. D in Music, Leningrad State Conservatory, USSR, 1961, diploma (hon.), 1959. Prof. Leningrad State Conservatory, 1961-73, Oberlin Conservatory, Ohio, 1976—; artist-in-residence Grinnell Coll., Iowa, 1974—76. Recording artist, classical piano music XVIII through XX centuries, 1972—. Grantee Oberlin Coll., 1984-98. Mem. Am. Music Tchrs. Assn. Avocations: reading, music, travel. Home: 226 N Prospect St Oberlin OH 44074-1035 Office: Oberlin Coll Conservatory of Music Oberlin OH 44074 Business E-Mail: sedrut@oberlin.edu.

RUTSTEIN, STANLEY HAROLD, apparel retailing company executive; b. Wilkes-Barre, Pa., July 1, 1941; s. Sydney D. and Bessie H. (Cohen) R.; m. Jo Ella Rutstein; children: Wendy Sue, Michael Scott, Lynne Elizabeth. Student, Wilkes Coll., 1959-61; grad., Advanced Mgmt. Program, Harvard U., 1975. Buyer Barbara Lynn Stores, Inc., NYC, 1961-63; buyer, then mdsg. mgr. Casual Corner div. U.S. Shoe Corp., Enfield, Conn., 1963-71, pres., 1971-76; pres., cons., dir. U.S. Shoe Corp., Cin., 1976-79; pres. Commonwealth Trading, Inc., Stoughton, Mass., 1979-85, Chadwick's of Boston Ltd., 1983-85; cons. Commonwealth Trading, Inc., 1985—; pres. Trim Trends, Inc., Boston, 1986-87, chmn., 1987-91; chmn., chief exec. officer, pres. Narragansett Clothing Co., Tiverton, RI, 1987-90, also bd. dirs.; bd. dirs. Reynolds Bros. Inc., 1989-95; pres., CEO S/J Designs Inc., 1989—2002, DBA, Northeast Knitters, Wagner Realty, Bradenton, Fla., 2002—; sales exec. Remax Alliance Realty, Bradenton, Fla., 2007—. Bd. dirs. The Icing, Inc., Sycamore Shops, Inc., Smapsota Ecosonic Devel. Corp., 2008-, Sampsota Film Position, 2008-, Sampsota Screson Scolptone Champion, 2009-. Bd. dirs. Ptnrs. for Disabled Youth, 1992. Mem. Young Pres. Orgn. Home: The Water Club 1281 Gulf of Mexico Dr #203 Longboat Key FL 34228 Office: Remax Alliance Realty 3007 Manatee Ave W Bradenton FL 34205 Office Phone: 941-758-7777. Personal E-mail: nextmoveboston@aol.com.

RUTTENBERG, CHARLES BYRON, lawyer; b. Reading, Pa., Nov. 16, 1922; s. Abraham David and Mollie Belle (Rabinowitz) Ruttenberg; m. Arden Honore Suk, July 29, 1955; children: Victoria Arden, Valerie Honore, Alexandra Anne. Student, Yale U., New Haven, Conn., 1941—42; BA, U. Va., Charlottesville, 1946; LLB, U. Pa., Phila., 1949. Bar: DC. With Covington & Burling, Washington; gen. counsel NSF, Washington, Nat. Found. Arts Humanities, Washington, 1949-69; ptnr. Arent, Fox, Kintner, Plotkin & Kahn, Washington, 1969—; fed. mediator US Dist. Ct., 1998—, DC Superior Ct., 2000—. Chmn. legis. bur., mem. exec. com., bd. dirs., gen. counsel Greater Washington Bd. Trade, 1983—92, Nat. Assn. Rec. Merchandisers, Video Software Dealers Assn., 1980—95. Editor, mem. mng. bd.: U. Pa. Law Rev., 1947—49. Gen. counsel Nat. Opera Inst., 1985—95; co-chmn. U. Pa. Law Sch. Alumni Fund, Washington, 1983—91; chmn. lawyers com. DC Commn. Arts, 1972—75; gen. counsel People to People Music Program, Washington, 1970—91; trustee, gen. counsel Wolf Trap Found. Performing Arts, Vienna, Va., 1981—91, Nat. Inst. Music Theatre, Washington, 1969—90; gen. counsel, bd. dirs. Am. Film Inst., 1969—91; trustee, mem. exec. com. U. DC, 1990—94; bd. dirs., pres. Cosmos Club Hist. Preservation Found., 1987—; bd. dirs., v.p., exec. com. Iona Sr. Svcs., 1997—; bd. dirs. Washington Area Lawyers for Arts, 1984—95, Greater Washington Rsch. Ctr., 1980—95; mem. adv. bd. DC Lottery, 2002—. With USAF, 1942—46, capt. USAFR, 1946—55. Recipient Outstanding Svc. awards, US Govt., 1967, 1968. Mem.: ABA, Arts Internat. (gen. counsel), U. Pa. Law Alumni Assn. (pres. 1967—71, bd. dirs. 1967—78), Washington Athletic Club (bd. govs. 1969—74), Mitchell Law Club, St. Alban's Club, Cosmos Club (bd. mgmt. 2000—03, gen. counsel 2003—06, v.p. 2006—07, pres. 2007—, Disting. Svc. award 2005), Phi Beta Kappa. Home: 4735 Butterworth Pl NW Washington DC 20016-4459 Office: Arent Fox Kintner Plotkin & Kahn 1050 Connecticut Ave NW Ste 500 Washington DC 20036-5303 Office Phone: 202-857-6082. Personal E-mail: cbruttenberg@aol.com. Business E-Mail: ruttenbc@arentfox.com.

RUTTENBERG, RUTH A., economist; b. Washington, Feb. 16, 1948; d. Stanley Harvey and Gertrude Leah Bernstein Ruttenberg; children: Estye Fenton, Jack Ross, Laila Fenton BA in Econs. with honors, U. Wis., Madison, 1969; M in City Planning, U. Pa., Phila., 1971, PhD in City Planning, 1981. Prof. Bradford Coll., 1972—73; sr. assoc. Ruttenberg, Kilgallon & Assocs., Inc., Washington, 1973-86; pres. Ruth Ruttenberg & Assocs., Berlin, Md., 1986—; prof. Nat. Labor Coll., 2001—. Sr. lectr. Am. U., Washington, 1973—75; asst. prof. Howard U.,

Washington, 1975—82; adj. faculty U. Md., College Park, Md., 1974—; mem. Bd. Equalization and Rev., Washington, 1981—82; sr. economist Occupl. Safety and Health Adminstrn., Washington, 1979—80; dir. Nat. Clearinghouse for Worker Safety and Health Tng., Bethesda, 1995—2000; co-chair instl. rev. bd. Ctr. Protect Workers Rights, Washington, 1996—, mem. constrn. econ. rsch. network, 2000—; peer rev. mem. US Dept. Energy, Washington, 1996, 97; mem. DOE adv. bd. Hazardous Materials Tng. Inst., 2004—, terrorism adv. bd., 2004—05, Newspaper Guild-Comms. Workers Am., 2001—; mem. tng. program rev. group NIOSH, 2005—. Author: Occupational Safety and Health in the Chemical Industry, 1981; mem. editl. rev. bd. Labor and Employment Rels. Assn., 2002—. Bd. dirs. Group Health Assn., Washington, 1982-88, 90-94; bd. dirs., Consumer Health Found., Washington, 1994—2009. Woodrow Wilson fellow, 1969-70; Bicentennial grantee Govt. Sweden, 1978. Democrat. Avocations: reading, kayaking, travel. Personal E-mail: rruttenberg@tds.net. Business E-Mail: rruttenberg@nlc.edu.

RUTTER, JEREMY BENTHAM, archaeologist, educator; b. Boston, June 23, 1946; s. Peter and Nancy Kendall (Comstock) Rutter; m. Sarah Robbins Herndon, Jan. 31, 1970; children: Benjamin Ryerson, Nicholas Kendall. BA in Classics with honors, Haverford Coll., 1967; PhD in Classical Archaeology, U. Pa., 1974; MA, Dartmouth Coll., 1993. Vis. asst. prof. dept. classics UCLA, 1975-76, from asst. prof. to prof. dept. classics, 1976—, prof. humanities, 2001—, chmn. dept. classics, 1992-98, 2003—06. Participant excavations, Germany, 1966, Italy, 1968—69, Greece, 1972—75, Greece, 1977—78, Greece, 1980—81, Greece, 1984—86, Greece, 1988—89, Greece, 1991—; mem. numerous coms. Am. Sch. Classical Studies, Athens. Author: Lerna III: The Pottery of Lerna IV, 1995; co-editor: Constructions of Childhood in Ancient Greece and Italy, 2007; mem. editl. adv. bd. Hesperia, Am. Jour. Archaeology; contbr. articles, revs. to profl. jours. With US Army, 1969—71, Vietnam. Woodrow Wilson fellow, 1967—68, NDEA fellow, U. Pa., 1968—69, 1971—73, NEH Rsch. grantee, 1979—81, Travel grantee, Am. Coun. Learned Socs., 1982, Sr. Faculty grantee, 1985—86, 1991—92, 2001—02, fellow, Inst. Advanced Studies, Hebrew U. Jerusalem, Isreal, 2008—09. Mem.: Classical Assn. New Eng., Archeol. Inst. Am. (mem. numerous coms., Olivia James Traveling fellow 1974—75), Am. Schs. Oriental Rsch., Phi Beta Kappa. Home: 47 Eagle Rdg Lebanon NH 03766-1900 Office: Dept Classics Dartmouth College Hanover NH 03755-3506 Office Phone: 603-646-2910. Business E-Mail: jeremy.rutter@dartmouth.edu.

RUTTER, MICHAEL LLEWELLYN, child psychology educator; b. Brummanna, Lebanon, Aug. 15, 1933; arrived in Eng., 1936; s. Llewellyn Charles and Winifred Olive (Barber) Rutter; m. Marjorie Heys, Dec. 27, 1958; children: Sheila Carol, Stephen Michael, Christine Anne. MB, BChir, U. Birmingham, Eng., 1955, MD with honors, 1963; diploma in psychol. medicine, U. London, 1961; degree (hon.), U. Leiden, 1985, Cath. U., 1990, U. Birmingham, 1990, U. Edinburgh, 1990, U. Chgo., 1993, U. Minn., 1993, U. Ghent, 1994; degree, U. Warwick, 1999, U. East Anglia, 2000, U. North London, 2000, U. York, 2005, U. Oxford, 2005; EdD (hon.), U. Dublin, 2007. Various tchg. positions in pediat., neurology, internal, 1955-58; registrar then sr. registrar Maudsley Hosp., London, 1958-62; mem. sci. staff MRC Social Psychiatry Rsch. Unit, London, 1962-65; sr. lectr. then reader U. London Inst. Psychiatry, 1966-73, prof. child psychiatry, 1973-98, hon. dir. MRC Child Psychiatry unit, 1984-98, with Social Genetic and Devel. Psychiatry Rsch. Ctr., 1994—98; prof. devel. psychopathology Inst. Psychiatry, 1998—. Nuffield med. traveling fellow Albert Einstein Coll. Medicine, N.Y.C., 1961-62; fellow Ctr. for Advanced Study in Behavioral Scis., Stanford, Calif., 1979-80; hon. prof. U. Amsterdam, 2001. Author: Helping Troubled Children, 1975, Maternal Deprivation Reassessed, 2nd edit., 1981, (with H. Giller) Juvenile Delinquency: Trends & Perspectives, 1983, (with M. Rutter) Developing Minds: Challenge and Continuity Accross the Lifespan, 1993, (with H. Giller, A. Hagell) Antisocial Behavior by Young People, 1998, (with T. Moffitt, A. Caspi and P. Silva) Sex Differences in Antisocial Behavior: Conduct Disorder, Delinquency and Violence in the Dunedin Longitudinal Study, 2001, (with M. Tienda) Ethnicity and Casual Mechanisms, 2005, Genes & Behavior: Nature-Nurture Interplay Explained, 2006; co-editor: Autism: A Reappraisal of Concepts and Treatment, 1978, Stress, Risk and Resilience In Children and Adolescents: Processes, Mechanisms and Interventions, 1994, Development Through Life: A Handbook For Clinicians, 1994, Psychosocial Disorders in Young People: Time Trends & Their Causes, 1995, Antisocial Behavior by Young People, 1998, Child and Adolescent Psychiatry, 4th edit., 2002, Ethnicity and Casual Mechanisims, 2005; editor: Scientific Foundations of Developmental Psychiatry, 1980, Developmental Neuropsychiatry, 1983. Recipient Goulstonian lectr. award, Royal Coll. Physicians, 1973, rsch. award, Am. Assn. Mental Deficiency, 1975, Salmon lectr. award, N.Y. Acad. Medicine, 1979, C. Anderson Aldrich award, Am. Acad. Pediat., 1981, Adolf Meyer ward lectr. award, APA, 1985, Disting. Sci. Contbn. award, 1995, Castilla del Pino prize for achievement in psychiatry, Spain, 1995, Lifetime Achievement award, IMFAR, 2002, G. Stanley Hall award, APA, 2003, Marmor award, 2003, Arnold Lucius Gesell prize, 2004, Bronfenbrenner award, 2005, Camille Cosby World of Children award, 2005; fellow, Royal Soc., 1987; Belding travelling scholar, 1963, Rock Carling fellow, 1979. Fellow Royal Soc. Medicine (London, hon.), Royal Coll. Pediat. and Child Health (hon. founding fellow 1996), Royal Coll. Psychiatrists (London, hon.), Kings Coll. London, Brit. Acad.; mem. AAAS (fgn. hon.), Internat. Soc. Rsch. in Child and Adolescent Psychiatry (pres. 1997-99), U.S. Nat. Acad. Edn. (fgn. assoc.), Brit. Pediat. Assn. (hon.), Assn. Child Psychology and Psychiatry (chmn. 1973-74), Brit. Psychol. Soc. (hon. fellow), Am. Acad. Child Psychiatry (hon. membership), NAS (fgn. assoc. Inst. Medicine, Sarnat Internat. prize in mental health 2001), Soc. Rsch. in Adolescence (John P. Hill award for excellence in theory devel. and rsch. 1992), Soc. Rsch. Child Devel. (pres. 1999-2001), Inst. Child Health (London, hon. fellow 1996), Internat. Acad. Rsch. in Learning Disabilities, Academia Europaea (founding mem.), Acad. Med. Scis. (founder, clin. v.p.). Home: 190 Court Ln London SE21 7ED England Office: SGDP Rsch Centre P080 Inst Psychiatry DeCrespigny Park London SE5 8AF England Office Phone: 44 2078480882. Business E-Mail: m.rutter@iop.kcl.ac.uk.

RUTTER, NATHANIEL WESTLUND, geologist, educator; b. Omaha, Nov. 22, 1932; s. John Elliot and Karleen (Ludden) R.; m. Mary Marie Munson, Sept. 11, 1961; children: Todd, Christopher. BS, Tufts U., 1955; MS, U. Alaska, 1962; PhD, U. Alta., 1965, DSc honoris causa, 2001, U. Córdoba, Argentina, 2006. Geologist Venezuelan Atlantic Refining Co., 1955-58; research scientist Geol. Survey Can., Calgary, Alta., 1965-74, head urban projects sect. Ottawa, Ont., 1974; environ. advisor Nat. Energy Bd., Ottawa, 1974-75; assoc. prof. dept. geology U. Alta., Edmonton, 1975-77, 77-80, prof., chmn. dept., 1980-89, 77-96, prof. dept. atmospheric scis., 1996-97, disting. univ. prof., 1997—, assoc. dean. faculty sci.; pres. Can. nat. com. Internat. Geol. Correlation Program, UNESCO, 1996-97. Pres. Internat. Union Quaternary Rsch. Congress, 1982-87; mem. Internat. Geosphere-Biosphere Program: A Study of Global Change, 1988-94; mem. rsch. com. Can. Global Change Program, 1992-94; chmn. global change com. INUQA, 1991-95; hon. prof. Chinese Acad. Sci., Beijing, 1994—; disting. lectr. Sigma Xi, 1995-97; mem. sci. bd. Internat. Union of Geol. Scis.-UNESCO, 1997—. Contbr. numerous articles to profl. jours.; assoc. editor Arctic, Geosci. Can. Quaternary Rsch.; mem. editl. bd. Quaternary Sci. Revs., Quaternary Rsch., Estonia Jour. Sci., Arctic; editor-in-chief Quaternary Internat. Named Officer Order of Can., 2001; recipient Queen's Golden Jubilee medal, 2003, Alberta Centennial medal, 2005, Disting. Alumni award U. Alberta, 2007; grantee Natural Scis. and Engring. Rsch. Coun. Can., grantee Energy, Mines and Resources. Fellow Royal Soc. Can.; mem. Assn. Profl. Engrs., Geologists and Geophysicists of Alta., Internat. Union Quaternary Rsch. (v.p. 1982-87, pres. 1987-91, hon. 1999), Can. Quaternary Assn. (v.p. 1981-82, Johnston medal 1997), Geol. Soc. Am. (mgmt. bd. dirs. quaternary geol. and geomorphology divsn. 1982-84, Disting. Career award 2003), Geol. Assn. of Can. (J. Willis Ambrose medal 1998), Internat. Union Quaternary Rsch. (hon.), Explorer's Club, Cosmos Club. Home: Rural Route 3 Stony Plain AB Canada T7Z 1X3 Office: U Alta Dept Earth & Atmospheric Scis Edmonton AB Canada T6G 2E3 Business E-Mail: nat.rutter@ualberta.ca.

RUTTINGER, GEORGE DAVID, lawyer; b. Detroit, Jan. 17, 1948; s. George Jacob and Margaret Mary (Smith) R.; m. Camille Ann Larson, Oct. 4, 1975; children: Jacob Charles, David Hayes, Philip George. AB with high distinction and honors, U. Mich., 1970, JD magna cum laude, 1973. Bar: Calif. 1975, D.C. 1975, U.S. Dist. Ct. D.C. 1975, U.S. Dist. Ct. Md. 1987, U.S. Ct. Appeals (D.C. and 4th cirs.) 1984, U.S. Ct. Appeals (1st cir.) 1988, U.S. Supreme Ct. 1984, U.S. Dist. Ct. (ea. dist.) Mich. 1995, U.S. Ct. Appeals (6th cir.) 1996, U.S. Ct. Appeals (3d cir.) 1999, U.S. Ct.Appeals (9th cir.) 2002. Law clk. to Hon. Malcolm R. Wilkey U.S. Ct. Appeals, Washington, 1973-74; assoc. Latham & Watkins, LA, 1974, Crowell & Moring LLP (formerly Jones, Day, Reavis & Pogue), Washington, 1975-79, ptnr., 1980—. Author: (with others) Containing Legal Costs: ADR Strategies for Corporations, Law Firms and Government, 1988; contbr. articles to profl. jours. Fellow Am. Bar Found. Office: Crowell & Moring LLP 1001 Pennsylvania Ave NW Fl 10 Washington DC 20004-2595 Business E-Mail: gruttinger@crowell.com.

RUTZKE, CORINNE JOHNSON, research scientist; b. Syracuse, NY, Mar. 26, 1960; d. Earl Allen and Patricia Wozneak Johnson; m. Michael Allen Rutzke, Sept. 22, 2001; children: Michael Bernard, Ella Jean. BS, Ohio State U., Columbus, 1983; MS, Cornell U., Ithaca, NY, 1998, PhD, 2000. Expt. coord., lab technician, dept. plant pathology Ohio State U., 1980—83; lab. technician, crew tng. specialist, gravitational plant physiology lab. U. Pa., Phila., 1983—92; project curriculum asst., rsch. assoc. Bionetics Corp., Kennedy Space Ctr., Fla., 1992—94; project sci. coord. Plant Space Biology Lab., Dynamic Corp., Kennedy Space Ctr., 1995—97; grad. rsch. assoc. Cornell U., Controlled Environment Agr. Program, 1997—2000, sr. rsch. assoc., 2000—03; exec. dir. Cornell U.'s NE Sun Grant Inst. Excellence, 2003—. Min. Roman Cath. Ch., Ithaca, 1979—2008. Grant, NASA, 1997—2000. Roman Catholic. Achievements include invention of a method for reduction of nitrate and oxalate in hydroponically-grown vegetables. Avocation: astronomy. Home: 88 East Miller Road Ithaca NY 14850 Office: Cornell University 330 Riley Robb Hall Ithaca NY 14853 Office Fax: 607-255-4080; Home Fax: 607-255-4080. E-mail: cfj4@cornell.edu.

RUUD, CLAYTON OLAF, engineering educator; b. Glassgow, Mont., July 31, 1934; s. Asle and Myrtle (Bleken) Ruud; m. Paula Kay Mannino, Feb. 24, 1990; children: Kelley Astrid, Kirsten Anne. BS in Metallurgy, Wash. State U., Pullman, 1957; MS in Materials Sci., San Jose State U., 1967; PhD in Materials Sci., U. Denver, 1970. Registered profl. engr., Calif., Colo. Asst. remelt metallurgist Kaiser Aluminum & Chem. Corp., Trentwood, Wash., 1957-58; devel. engr. Boeing Airplane Co., Seattle, 1958-60; mfg. rsch. engr. Lockheed Missiles & Space Corp., Sunnyvale, Calif., 1960-63; rsch. engr. FMC Corp., San Jose, 1963-67; sr. rsch. scientist U. Denver, 1967-79; prof. indsl. engring. Pa. State U., University Park, 1979—. Founder, developer, and co-director of quality and manufacturing management masters degree Pa. State U.; cons. in field; bd. dirs. Denver X-Ray Inst. Inc., Altoona, Pa. Editor series: Advances in X-Ray Analysis, Vol. 12-22, 1970-80, Nondestructive Character of Materials, Vol. 1-6, 1983-1996; editor X-Ray Spectometry, 1975-87; editl. com. Nondestructive Testing and Evaluation, 1991-1995; contbr. chpts. to books. Chmn. Nat. Acad. Sci. Safe Drinking Water Com., Washington, 1976-78. Recipient IR 100 award, 1983, Gov.'s New Product Award, Pa. Soc. Profl. Engrs., 1988. Fellow ASM Internat. (chmn. Resid. Stress Conf. 1989-91); mem. Internat. Ctr. for Diffraction Data, Soc. Mfg. Engrs., Metall. Soc. of AIME. Achievements include patents in x-ray analysis and residual stress measurement; invention of fiber optic based position sensitive scintillation X-ray detector, instrument for simultaneous stress and phase composition measurement; development of an X-ray diffraction instrument for manufacturing process quality control. Business E-Mail: cor1@psu.edu.

RUVIELLA-KNORR, JEANNE L., music educator, consultant; d. Jean and Marion Post Ruviella; m. H. Richard Knorr, May 26, 1962 (div. Dec. 24, 1993); children: Richard Post Knorr, Michelle Renee Mitchell. MusB, Boston U., 1962; MA, U. So. Calif., 1966; PhD, U. Md., 2004. Cert. advanced profl. cert. tchg. Md., Dalcroze cert. Longy Sch., Dalcroze-Orff-Kodaly cert. Manhattan Sch. Music. Music tchr. L.A. Pub. Schs., 1962—66, Burlington Pub. Schs., Vt.; prof. music edn. Shelton Coll., Cape Canaveral, Fla., 1968—74; music tchr., cons. Anne Arundel County Pub. Schs., Severna Park, Md., 1974—79; prof. music edn. Towson (Md.) U., 1979—97, prof. emerita, 1997—; prof. music edn. Frostburg State U., Md., 1999—2000; tchr. music Harford County Schs., Abingdon, Md., 2000—. Clinician Towson U., 1994—, developer Grad. Dalcroze-Orff-Kodaly Cert. program, co-dir. Dalcroze-Orff-Kodaly Cert. program, 1981—97, adj. faculty Dalcroze-Orff-Kodaly Cert. program, 1997—; cons. in field. Contbg. author: music series Share the Music, Grades 7-8, 1996—2005, Music and You, Grades 7-8, 1989—2005, co-compiler: keyboard proficiency packet for Towson U., rev. Leader women's support groups Chapelgate Ch., Marriottsville, Md., 2000—. Mem.: Md. Music Educators Assn., Music Educators Nat. Conf. (clinician 1983—87, 2000, 2005). Avocations: travel, music. Personal E-mail: ruviella@comcast.net.

RUVKUN, GARY B., molecular geneticist; b. Berkeley, Calif., Mar. 26, 1952; s. Sam and Dora R.; m. Natasha Staller. AB in Biophysics, U. Calif., Berkeley, 1973; PhD in Biophysics, Harvard U., 1982. Postdoctoral fellow MIT and Harvard U., Cambridge, Mass., 1982-85; jr. fellow Soc. Fellows Harvard U., Cambridge, 1982-85; asst. prof. to prof. genetics Harvard U., Cambridge, 1985. Mem. scientific adv. bd. Damon Runyon Walter Winchell Cancer Fund, 2001—05, Mass. Gen. Hosp. Cancer Ctr., 2003—07, Friedrich Meischer Rsch. Inst., Basel, Switzerland, 2005—06; mem. Harvard Microbial Sci. Initiative Organizing Com., 2003—, Harvard Origins of Life Initiative Organizing Com., 2004—; assoc. mem. Broad Inst. MIT/Harvard, 2003—; mem. NIH Nat. Adv. Coun. on Aging, 2004—07; mem. vis. com. Inst. Zoology, U. Zurich, 2005; invited presenter in the field. Contbr. several articles to jours.; editor: Developmental Biology, 1995—, Development, 1999—2005; bd. reviewing editors Science Mag., 2005—07. Recipient Faculty Rsch. award Am. Cancer Soc., 1989-, NIH Merit award, 2002-; co-recipient Lewis S. Rosenstiel award, Brandeis U., 2005, Warren Triennial prize, Mass. Gen. Hosp., 2007, Benjamin Franklin medal in Life Sci., Franklin Inst., 2008, Gairdner Found. Internat. award, 2008, Albert Lasker award for Basic Med. Rsch., Lasker Found., 2008 Mem.: Am. Acad. Arts & Sciences, Soc. Fellows, Harvard U. Achievements include findings regarding molecular basis of temporal pattern formation, molecular basis of cell lineage asymmetry, scores of homeobox genes in C. elegans; patents in the field; patents pending in the field. Office: Ctr for Computational and Integrative Biology Mass Gen Hosp Richard B Simches Rsch Ctr 185 Cambridge St 7th Fl Boston MA 02114 also: Mass Gen Hosp Wellman 8 50 Blossom St Boston MA 02114 Office Phone: 617-726-5959. Office Fax: 617-726-6893. Business E-Mail: ruvkun@molbio.mgh.harvard.edu.*

RUWE, BRADLEY N., lawyer; b. Fort Lee, Va., Nov. 18, 1970; BSBA, Xavier U., 1992; JD, Salmon P. Chase Coll. Law, 1996. Bar: Ohio 1997. Worked in Tax Dept. Peck, Shaffer & Williams LLP, Cin., ptnr. Named Cincy Leading Lawyer, Cincy Bus. Mag., 2006; named one of Ohio's Rising Stars, Super Lawyers, 2005, 2006. Mem.: Assn. Govtl. Leasing and Fin. (bd. mem.), Ohio Govt. Fin. Officers Assn., Ohio State Bar Assn., Cin. Bar Assn., Potter Stewart Inns of Ct., Moot Ct., Cin. Acad. Leadership for Lawyers. Office: Pack Shaffer & Williams LLP 201 E 5th St Ste 900 Cincinnati OH 45202 Office Phone: 513-621-3394. Office Fax: 513-621-3813.

RUWE, ROBERT PAUL, federal judge; b. Ohio, 1941; Grad., Xavier U., 1963; JD, Northern Ky. U., 1970. Spl. agent intelligence divsn. IRS, US Dept. Treasury, Washington, 1963—70, joined office chief counsel, 1970, trial atty. Indpls., dir. criminal tax divsn., dep. assoc. chief counsel, dir. tax litigation divsn.; judge US Tax Ct., Washington, 1987—2002, sr. judge, 2002—. Office: US Tax Ct 400 2nd St NW Washington DC 20217-0002*

RUXIN, PAUL THEODORE, lawyer; b. Cleve., Apr. 14, 1943; s. Charles and Olyn Judith (Koller) R.; m. Joanne Camy, May 25, 1965; children: Marc J., Sarah. BA, Amherst Coll., 1965; LLB, U. Va., 1968. Bar: Ill. 1968, U.S. Dist. Ct. (no. dist.) Ill. 1968, U.S. Ct. Appeals D.C. 1972. Assoc. Isham, Lincoln & Beale, Chgo., 1968—73, ptnr., 1974—77; ptnr., chmn. energy utilities sect. Jones Day, Cleve., 1977—2005, of counsel, 2006—. Mem. editl. com. Yale U. edit. Boswell Papers, 2003—. Mem. Hudson Archtl. and Hist. Bd. Rev., 1981-81; chmn. bd. govs. Folger Shakespeare Libr., 2007—; exec. bd. Greater Cleve. Boy Scouts Am., 1978-90; bd. dirs. Cleve. chpt. ARC, 1991-97; bd. trustees Newberry Libr., 2008-; vis. com. U. Chgo. Libr., 2008-Recipient Eminent Svc. medal, Amherst Coll., 2007. Mem. ABA, Chgo. Bar Assn., Internat. Assn. Bibliophiles, Rowfant Club, Chgo. Club, Caxton Club, Grolier Club, Chgo. Lit. Club. Office: Jones Day 77 W Wacker Dr Fl 35 Chicago IL 60601-1662 also: 901 Lakeside Ave Cleveland OH 44114-1116 Home Phone: 312-915-0533; Office Phone: 312-782-3939. E-mail: paultruxin@jonesday.com.

RUYLE-HULLINGER, ELIZABETH SMITH (BETH RUYLE), municipal financial advisor, consultant; b. Oct. 26, 1946; d. Daniel Lester and Mae (Coley) Smith; m. Craig Harlan Hullinger, Oct. 24, 1985; children: Leigh Ann Ruyle, Clint (dec.), Bret AA, St. Petersburg Jr. Coll., Fla., 1966; BA English, U. Fla., Gainesville, 1968; MPA, U. Ga., Athens, 1975. Rsch. asst. Emory U., Atlanta, 1969—70; health planner Met. Coun. for Health, Atlanta, 1960—72; coord. govtl. rels. Atlanta Regional Commn., 1972—76, coord. govtl. affairs, 1976—78; exec. dir. South Suburban Mayors' and Mgrs. Assn., East Hazel Crest, Ill., 1978—2000; pres. Chgo. Southland Econ. Devel. Alliance, 1999—2000; exec. v.p. Ehlers & Assocs., Lisle, Ill., 2000—. Exec. dir. South Towns Agy. Risk Mgmt., 1980-98, South Towns Area Benefits Coop., 1983-89, South Towns Bus. Growth Corp., 1983-90; cons. Planning Devel. Svc., Tinley Park, Ill., 1986— Contbr. articles to profl. and devel. mags Mem. World's Fair Adv. Com., Chgo., 1986, Met. Planning Coun., 1990-2000, Cook County Tax Reform adv. coun., South Suburban Arts Coun., 1987, Coun. Urban Econ. Devel., 1986; adv. coun. Urban Innovations, Chgo., 1995-2000, Chgo. Assembly Project, 1995-2000; mem. Regional Partnership, 1985-2000; bd. dirs. South Suburban Hosp., 1987-96, mem. governing coun., 1999-2006; bd. dirs. Fin. Cmty. Devel. Corp., 1998-2000. Mem. Internat. City Mgmt. Assn., Ill. City Mgmt. Assn., Met. City Mgrs. Assn., Ill. Govtl. Fin. Officers Assn., Ill. Tax Increment Assn., Lambda Alpha Methodist. Office: Ehlers & Assocs 550 Warrenville Rd Ste 220 Lisle IL 60532-5500 Office Phone: 630-271-3330, 630-271-3332. Business E-Mail: bruyle@ehlers-inc.com.

RUYTER, NANCY LEE CHALFA, dance educator; b. Phila., May 23, 1933; d. Andrew Benedict Chalfa and Lois Elizabeth (Strode) McClary; m. Ralph Markson (div.); m. Hans C. Ruyter, Dec. 7, 1968 (dec. Jan. 1998). BA in History, U. Calif., Riverside, 1964; PhD in History, Claremont Grad. Sch., 1970. Tchr. theater dept. Pomona Coll., 1965-72; instr. dance program U. Calif., Riverside, 1972-76, acting chair dance program, 1974-75; instr. dance dept. UCLA, 1976; instr. phys. edn. dept. Orange Coast Coll., 1976-77; asst. prof. dept. phys. edn. and dance Tufts U., 1977-78; asst. prof. phys. edn. dept. Calif. State U., Northridge, 1978-82; from asst. prof. to full prof. dance dept. U. Calif., Irvine, 1982—, assoc. dean Sch. Fine Arts, 1984-88, 95-96, chair dept. dance, 1989-91. Presenter in field. Appeared with Jasna Planina Folk Ensemble, 1972-77, 78-79, Di Falco and Co., 1955-57; choreographer, dir. numerous coll. dance prodns.; contbr. articles, revs. to profl. publs.; author: Reformers and Visionaries: The Americanization of the Art of Dance, 1979, The Cultivation of Body and Mind in Nineteenth-Century American Delsartism, 1999. Mem. Am. Soc. Theatre Rsch., Bulgarian Studies Assn., Congress on Rsch. in Dance (bd. dirs. 1977-80, 2003-08, pres. 1981-85), Folk Dance Fedn., Internat. Fedn. Theatre Rsch., Soc. Dance Rsch., Soc. Ethnomusicology, Soc. Dance History Scholars (steering com. 1980-81), Spanish Dance Soc., Theatre Libr. Assn. Office: U Calif Dept Dance Irvine CA 92697-2775 Office Phone: 949-824-7284. Business E-Mail: nlruyter@uci.edu.

RUZAL-SHAPIRO, CARRIE B., pediatric radiologist, educator; b. 1957; m. Peter Shapiro; children: Daniel, Billy. BS in Biochemistry, Princeton U., NJ; MD, Columbia U. Coll. Physicians & Surgeons, NY. Diplomate Am. Bd. Radiology. Intern Babies & Children's Hosp.-Columbia Presbyn. Med. Ctr.; resident radiology Columbia Presbyn. Med. Ctr., 1984—88, clin. fellowship pediat. radiology, 1988—89; assoc. prof. clin. radiology and pediat., dir. divsn. pediat. radiology Columbia U. Coll. Physicians & Surgeons, 1990—; attending dept. radiology NY Presbyn. Hosp.-Columbia U. Med. Ctr., 1990—. Vice-chair edn. dept. radiology Columbia U. Coll. Physicians & Surgeons. Contbr. articles to profl. jours. Recipient Am. Coll. Med. Physics award, 2006. Office: NY Presbyn Hosp Dept Radiology 622 W 168th St New York NY 10032 Office Phone: 212-305-9335. Office Fax: 212-305-5777.

RUZER, LEV SOLOMON, lab administrator, researcher; b. Odessa, Ukraine, June 24, 1922; s. Solomon Boris Ruzer and Genrietta Mark Rosenberg; children: Serge Lev, Genia Lev. D in Tech. Prof. Sci., U. Moscow, 1948. Cert. nuclear physicist Ministry Edn., USSR, 1977. Vis. rschr. Lawrence Berkeley Nat. Lab., Calif., 1961—79; chair lab. All

Union Inst. Physicotech. Measurement, Moscow. Recipient Gold & Silver medal, 1970. Independent. Achievements include patents for aerosol measurement methods. Home: 1909 Cedar St Berkeley CA 94709 Office: Lawrence Berkeley Nat Lab 1 Cyclotron Rd Berkeley CA 94720 Home Phone: 510-841-6932; Office Phone: 510-486-4641. Office Fax: 510-486-6658. Business E-Mail: lsruzer@lbl.gov.

RUZYLLO, EDWARD EMIL, medical educator; b. Kosciaszyn, Oct. 13, 1909; s. Michael and Julie (Wyspianska) R.; m. Alina Zawadzka, Sept. 26, 1936; children: Witold, Jerzy. MD, Warsaw U., 1935; PhD, Warsaw Med. Acad., 1949, DSc, 1954; MD (hon.), Albert Schweitzer Acad. Med., 2000, Poznan Acad. Medicine, 2003. Intern in medicine Warsaw Ujazdowski Hosp., 1935-37; instr., reader in medicine 1st dept. medicine Med. Acad. Warsaw, 1947-54, head dept. gastroenterology and metabolism, 1958-70, assoc. prof. medicine, 1970-80; prof. medicine 2d dept. medicine Postgrad. Med. Sch., Warsaw, 1958-69. Chmn. sci. council Min. Health and Social Welfare, 1974-79; dir., dean Postgrad. Med. Ctr., 1961-74. Author 5 books in field; editor-in-chief Materia Medica Polona, 1968-70; contbr. articles to profl. jours. Served with Polish Army, 1937-46. Recipient 1st degree award, Min. of Health, 1965, 1973, award, Albert Jurzykowski Found., 1980. Mem.: Polish Med. Alliance (Chgo.), Internat. Soc. for Progress in Internal Medicine, Polish Soc. Endocrinology, Polish Soc. Rheumatology, Polish Soc. Medicine, Polish Soc. Internal Medicine (pres. 1970—76, hon. pres. 2001—), Roman Acad. Med. Scis. (hon.), Bulgarian Soc. Gastroenterology (hon.), Czechoslovak Soc. Internat. Medicine (hon.), Argentinean Soc. Medicine (hon.), German Soc. Internal Medicine (hon.), Swedish Soc. Medicine (hon.), Internat. Soc. Internal Medicine (hon.). Home: UL Rudawska 3 m8 PL-02-069 Warsaw Poland Office: 1 Goszcynskiego PL-02-616 Warsaw Poland

RYAN, ALLAN ANDREW, JR., lawyer, director, educator, writer; s. Allan Andrew and Anne (Conway) Ryan; m. Nancy Foote, June 30, 1978; children: Elisabeth, Andrew. AB, Dartmouth Coll., 1966; JD magna cum laude, U. Minn., 1970. Bar: DC 1972, Mass. 1985. Law clk. to assoc. justice Byron R. White U.S. Supreme Ct., 1970-71; assoc. Williams, Connolly & Califano, Washington, 1974-77; asst. to Solicitor Gen. U.S., Washington, 1977-80; dir. office of spl. investigations, Dept. Justice, Washington, 1980-83, spl. asst. to atty. gen., 1983; pvt. practice law, 1983-85; with office of gen. counsel, Harvard U., 1985—2001, dir. intellectual property bus. sch., 2001—. Presenting counsel Internat. Commn. Inquiry on Kurt Waldheim, London, 1988; adj. prof. law sch. Boston Coll., 1990—; adj. prof. divsn. continuing edn. Harvard U., 1997—. Author: Quiet Neighbors: Prosecuting Nazi War Criminals in America, 1984; pres., editor-in-chief: Minn. Law Rev., 1969—70. Mem. exec. com. New Eng. region Anti-Defamation League, 1990—, mem. nat. commn., 2004—; chair Ctr. Civil Rights and Pub. Policy, 2003—; bd. dirs. Facing History and Ourselves Nat. Found., 1985—92; mem. adv. bd. Holocaust and human rights rsch. project Boston Coll. Law Sch., 1984—. Capt. USMC, 1971—74. Recipient Internat. Human Rights award, Anti-Defamation League, 1986, Leadership award, 1997, 2005. Mem.: ABA, Boston Bar Assn. Office: Harvard Bus Sch Publ 60 Harvard Way Boston MA 02163 Home Phone: 781-659-1342; Office Phone: 617-783-7849. Business E-Mail: allan_ryan@harvard.edu.

RYAN, AMY, actress; b. Queens, NY, Nov. 30, 1969; Actress (TV films) In the Deep Woods, 1992, Remembering Sex, 1998, Baseball Wives, 2002, (TV series) I'll Fly Away, 1992, The Naked Truth, 1995, The Wire, 2003—06, 100 Centre Street, 2001—02, (films) Roberta, 1999, A Pork Chop for Larry, 2000, You Can Count on Me, 2000, Keane, 2004, War of the Worlds, 2005, Capote, 2005, Looking for Comedy in the Muslim World, 2005, Marvelous, 2006, Shiner, 2006, Forward, 2007, Gone Baby Gone, 2007 (Best Supporting Actress, Wash., DC Area Film Critics Assn., 2007, Best Actress in a Supporting Role, Satellite Awards, 2007, Best Supporting Actress, San Francisco Film Critics Circle, 2007, Best Performance by an Actress in a Supporting Role, Phoenix Film Critics Soc. Awards, 2007, Best Supporting Actress, NY Film Critics Circle, 2007, Best Supporting Actress, Natinal Bd. Review, 2007, Best Supporting Actress, LA Film Critics Assn., 2007, Best Supporting Actress, Boston Soc. Film Critics, 2007, 2007 Best Supporting Actress, Critics Choice award, Broadcast Film Critics Assn., 2008), Before the Devil Knows You're Dead, 2007, Neal Cassady, 2007, Dan in Real Life, 2007, (TV miniseries) A Will of Their Own, 1998, (Broadway plays) Uncle Vanya, A Streetcar Named Desire. Office: Framework Entertainment Ste C 9057 Nemo St West Hollywood CA 90069

RYAN, AMY E., library director; Various positions including dir. cmty. partnerships and devel. Mpls. Pub. Libr.; dir. Hennepin County Libr. Sys., 2005—08; pres. Boston Pub. Libr., 2008—. Office: Boston Pub Libr Copley Sq 700 Boylston St Boston MA 02116

RYAN, ANTHONY WILLIAM, federal agency administrator; b. 1963; m. Ann Ryan; 4 children. Grad., U. Rochester, 1985; master's degree, London Sch. Econ. and Polit. Sci., 1986. Portfolio mgr. various firms including State Street Corp., The Boston Co.; ptnr. Grantham, Mayo, van Otterloo & Co., LLC; sr. adv. to sec. US Dept. Treasury, Washington, sr. mem. treas. fin. group, asst. sec. for fin. markets, 2006—08, acting sec. for domestic fin., 2008—. Office: US Dept Treasury 1500 Pennsylvania Ave NW Washington DC 20220*

RYAN, ARTHUR FREDERICK, retired diversified financial services company executive; b. Bklyn., Sept. 14, 1942; s. Arthur Vincent and Gertrude (Wingert) R.; m. Patricia Elizabeth Kelly; children: Arthur, Kelly Ann, Kevin, Kathleen. BA in Math., Providence Coll., 1963, D (hon.) of bus. adminstrn., 1994; student, Am. Coll., 1963—65; LHD (hon.), Dowling Coll.; DSc, NJ Inst. Tech., 2005. Area mgr. Control Data Corp., Washington, 1965-72; project mgr. data processing divsn. Chase Manhattan Corp., NYC, 1972-73, 2d v.p., 1973-74, v.p., 1974—77, sr. v.p., 1977—82, ops. exec., 1978-82, exec. v.p. corp. ops. and systems, 1982—84, exec. v.p. individual banking, 1984, head worldwide retail bank, 1984—90, vice chmn., 1985—90, pres., COO, 1990—94; chmn., pres., CEO Prudential Ins. Co. Am., Newark, 1994—99; (Prudential Ins. Co. Am. incorporated to become Prudential Fin., Inc., 1999); chmn., pres., CEO Prudential Fin., Inc., Newark, 2000—07, chmn., 2007—08. Bd. dirs. Prudential Fin., Inc., 1999—, Regeneron Pharmaceuticals, 2003—. Bd. trustees Providence Coll., 1992—, NY Presbyn. Hosp.; nat. bd. Local Initiatives Support Coalition; bd. dirs. New Am. Schools; co-chair Achieve, Inc., NJ United for Higher Sch. Standards, NJ Performing Arts Ctr. Lt. US Army, 1963—65. Recipient Nat. Alumni Personal Achievement Award, Providence Coll., 75th Anniversary Alumni Services Award, Diamond Anniversary Award, Keeper of the Dream award, Nat. Action Network, 2000, Patterson award, United Negro Coll. Fund/The Coll. Fund, 2000, Pub. Svc. award, NJ State CofC, 2001, Medal of Life award, PIUS XII Found., 2001, Cir. of Life Award, Million Dollar Round Table Found., 2002; co-recipient (with wife) Pelican award for Corp. and Cmty. Leadership, St. Vincent's Acad., 2001, (with wife) Inaugural Cmty. Leadership award, NJ Performing Arts Ctr. Women's Bd. Assn., 2002. Mem.: Am. Bankers Assn.

RYAN, BO (WILLIAM F. RYAN JR.), men's college basketball coach; b. Chester, Pa., Dec. 20, 1947; s. Butch Ryan; m. Kelly Ryan; children: Megan, Will, Matt, Brenna, Mairin. BBA, Wilkes U., Pa., 1969; grad. student, Villanova U. Asst. coach Coll. Racine, Wis.; head coach Sun Valley HS, Phila.; asst. coach U. Wis., Madison, 1976—84, head coach, 2001—; Platteville, 1984—99, Milw., 1999—2001. Mem. Divsn. I Men's Basketball Issues Com. NCAA. Author: Passing and Catching: A Lost Art, How to Run the Swing Offense, Applying and Attacking Pressure. Recipient Guardians of the Game award for Svc., Nat. Assn. Basketball Coaches, 2004; named Delaware County Coach of Yr., Coach of Yr. (6 times), Wis. Intercollegiate Athletic Conf., Divsn. III Coach of Yr. (4 times), Nat. Assn. Basketball Coaches, Big Ten Coach of Yr., 2002, 2003; named to Wilkes Athletic Hall of Fame, 2003. Office: U Wis Men's Basketball Kohl Ctr 601 W Dayton St Madison WI 53715 Office Phone: 608-262-4597. E-mail: bfr@athletics.wisc.edu.

RYAN, CAROL J., educational administrator; b. Niagara Falls, NY, June 13, 1939; d. Samuel Battaglia and Josephine Latona; m. John W. Ryan, Sept. 17, 1960; children: James, Kathleen, John Jr., Michael. BA, Niagara Univ., 1960; MEd, George Mason U., 1980. Cert. reading specialist emotional distbr., mental retardation K-12, specific lang. disabilities pre-K-12. Special edn. cons. Mass. Dept. of Youth Svcs., Worcester, Mass., 1982—84; edn. liaison Bureau of Instl. Sch., Westboro, Mass., 1986—87; edn. coord. Univ. Mass Med. Ctr., Westboro, Mass., 1987—98; edn. dir. Found. Sch., Alexandria, Va., 1998—2003, Largo, Md., 2003—. Mem.: Coun. of Exceptional Children. Office: The Found Sch 1330 McCormick Dr Largo MD 20774

RYAN, CHRISTINE BRETT, music educator; b. York, Pa., Mar. 27, 1965; d. James Joseph and Dorothy Regina (Wirtz) Brett; m. Donald Lee Ryan, Aug. 4, 1990; children: Cecily Anna, Michaela Brett. B of Music Edn., Westminster Choir Coll., 1987; M of Music Edn., Fla. State U., 1990; ABD, Boston U., 2008. Nat. bd. cert. tchr. 2004. Elem. music tchr. Hillsborough Pub. Schs., NJ, 1987—88; elem. and secondary music tchr. Ewing Twp. Pub. Schs., NJ, 1990—93; elem. music tchr. Hamburg Area Sch. Dist., Pa., 1993—95, secondary music tchr., 1996—. Mem. nat. devel. team and trainer Nat. Bd. Profl. Tchg. Stds., San Antonio, 2000—03; instr. music edn. Kutztown U., Pa., 2004—, instr. fine arts, 2004—. Condr.: Hamburg Cmty. Children's Chorus, 2000—05, St. Johns UCC/Kutztown Handbell Choir, 2003—, contbr.: Music! Its Role In Our Lives, 2004—05. Mem. Albany Twp. Hist. Soc., 2001—. Finalist Tchr. of Yr., Pa., 2007. Mem.: Music Educators Nat. Conf. Avocations: cooking, gardening. Personal E-mail: christineryan@entermail.net.

RYAN, DABERATH, chemistry professor; b. Sacramento, May 3, 1946; d. Clarence Arthur and Ernestine H. (Croy) Kouts; divorced. BS in Chemistry, So. Oreg. U., 1968; MS in Chemistry, Oreg. State U., 1971, MS in Food Sci. and Tech., 1987. Instr. So. Oreg. U., Ashland, 1971-72; prof., dept. chair Rogue CC, Grants Pass, Oreg., 1971—76; chemist State of Alaska, Juneau, 1978; chem. cons. Appleby Sailplanes, Albuquerque, 1978-79; prof. U. Alaska-S.E., Juneau, 1981—82, Mt. Hood CC, Gresham, Oreg., 1987, Coll. Siskiyous, Weed, Calif., 1987—2008. Mem. Am. Chem. Soc., Calif. CC, Two Yr. Coll. Chemistry Conf., Oreg. State U. Alumni Assn., So. Oreg. U. Alumni Assn. Avocations: outdoor recreation, fishing, camping, ATV riding. Home: PO Box 381 Montague CA 96064-0381 Business E-Mail: ryan@siskiyous.edu.

RYAN, DANIEL JOHN, university administrator; b. Buffalo, June 5, 1960; s. Michael E. and Joan F. R.; m. Sandra Suffoleto, Aug. 19, 1989. BA in Pol. Sci., Canisius Coll., Buffalo, 1982, MS in Edn., 1992; PhD in Edn., SUNY, Buffalo, 1997. Fin. cons. First Albany Corp., Buffalo, 1982-84; confidential investigator County of Erie, Buffalo, 1984-87; econ. mkt. analyst City of Buffalo, Buffalo, 1987-90; asst. dir. career planning Canisius Coll., Buffalo, 1990-97, asst. dean students svcs., 1997—; dir. career planning and placement SUNY, Buffalo. Lectr. Buffalo and Erie County Pub. Libr., Buffalo, 1990—; dir. career planning and placement SUNY Buffalo. Author: A Job Search Handbook for People with Disabilities, 2004. Pres. Univ. Dist. N. Buffalo Civic Assn., Buffalo, 1990-91; v.p. Kiwanis Club of N. Buffalo, 1987-88; vice chmn. City of Buffalo rep. Com., 1989-91, sec. 1993-95; chmn. Delaware Ward Rep. Com., 1985-91. Recipient Edward A. Parish award, Ea. Assn. Colls. and Employers. Mem. Nat. Assn. Student Personnel Admininstrn.(region II Outstanding New Profl.), N. Buffalo Community Devel. Corp., Assn. for Higher Edn. and Disabilities. Republican. Avocations: reading, raquetball. E-mail: dryan@buffalo.edu.

RYAN, DANIEL LEO, bishop emeritus; b. Mankato, Minn., Sept. 28, 1930; s. Leonard Bennett and Irene Ruth (Larson) Ryan. BA, Benedictine U., 1952; JCL, Pontificia Università Lateranense, Rome, 1960. Ordained priest Diocese of Joliet, Ill., 1956, parish priest, 1956—82, chancellor, 1965—78, vicar gen., 1977—79, aux. bishop, 1981—84; ordained bishop, 1981; bishop Diocese of Springfield, 1984—99, bishop emeritus, 1999—. Roman Catholic. Office: Diocese of Springfield PO Box 3187 1615 W Washington St Springfield IL 62708-3187 Office Phone: 217-698-8500. Office Fax: 217-698-0802. E-mail: dlryan@dio.org.

RYAN, DANIEL PATRICK, pediatrician; b. Mason City; MD, Johns Hopkins U. Sch. Medicine, Balt., 1979. Pediatric surgeon Mass. Gen. Hosp., Boston, 1987—. Office: Dept Pediatric Surgery Mass Gen Hosp 42 Fruit St Boston MA 02114 Office Phone: 617-726-8878. Business E-Mail: dryan@partners.org.

RYAN, DAVID ALAN, systems analyst; b. Cin., Nov. 13, 1961; s. James Patrick and Virginia Ann (Stewart) R. BS, Wright State U., 1983; MS, Tex. A&M U., 1988. Statistician U.S. Bur. of Census, Washington, 1988-92, computer specialist, 1992—. Vol. math. modeling Soil Conservation Svc., Washington, 1991-96; math. and. probability vol. Washington Opera, 1992—; data entry/programming vol. Opera Am., Washington, 1990-91; hist. rschr. Gasby's Tavern Mus., Alexandria, Va., 1991-94; mem. Bravo! for the Washington Opera, 1991-95. Recipient Vol. Svc. award Soil Conservation Svc., 1992, 93. Mem. Am. Statis. Assn., Capitol PC Users Group, Ballston-Va. Square Civic Assn. (exec. com. 1995—, sec. 1996—, NCAC rep. 1997-98), The Washington Opera Guild, The Washington Opera Camerata, The DC Wagner Soc., Opera Guild of No. Va. (bd. 2006-). Achievements include building a supercomputer at home in 2000. Avocations: classical music, ethnomusicology, history, geography, travel. Office: Bur of Census/CES Ste 208 Washington Plz II Washington DC 20233-6300

RYAN, DAVID THOMAS, lawyer; b. Torrington, Conn., Apr. 18, 1939; s. Edward John and Margaret (Murphy) R.; m. Dale Anderson, Aug. 21, 1965; children: Rachael Anderson, Conor Anne. BS, U. Md., 1961; LLB, Georgetown U., 1965. Bar: Conn. 1966, U.S. Dist. Ct. Conn. 1967, U.S. Ct. Appeals (2d cir.) 1969, U.S. Ct. Appeals (fed. cir.) 1982, U.S. Claims Ct. 1983, U.S. Supreme Ct. 1992. Ptnr. Cooney, Scully & Dowling, Hartford, Conn., 1966-77, Robinson & Cole, Hartford, 1977—. Fellow Am. Coll. Trial Lawyers; mem. Am. Bd. Trial Advs., Conn. Trial Lawyers Assn. (bd. dirs., mem. Gov.'s commn. on jud. reform, para jud. officer hon. Alfred V. Covell, sr. US dist. judge). Home: 126 Westerly Ter Hartford CT 06105-1117 Office: Robinson & Cole 280 Trumbull St Ste 26 Hartford CT 06103-3509 Office Phone: 203-275-8200. E-mail: dryan@rc.com.

RYAN, DEBBIE (DEBORAH A. RYAN), women's college basketball coach; BPE, Ursinus Coll., Collegeville, Pa., 1975; MPE, U. Va., Charlottesville, 1977. Asst. basketball and field hockey coach U. Va., 1975-77, head women's basketball coach, 1977—. Lectr. in field; adv. coach Nike; head coach US Jr. Nat. Team, 1988, Jr. World Championship Team, 1989, USA Basketball Sr. Nat. Women's Team, 2001, 03; mem. USA Basketball Women's Games Com. for 1989-92 quadrennium; dir. West team US Olympic festival, Chapel Hill, NC, 1987 (gold medal). Author: Virginia Defense, Virginia Summer Development Program, Women's Basketball Drills-Conditioning. Named Va. Assn. Intercollegiate Athletics for Women Coach of Yr., 1981, Converse Dist. III Coach of Yr., 1986, 87, Nat. Coach of Yr., Shreveport Jour., 1986, Outstanding Woman of Yr. Va. Women's Forum, 1991, Naismith Coach of Yr., Atlanta Tipoff club, 1991, Devel. Coach of Yr., USA Basketball, 2001; recipient Atlantic Coast Conf. Coach of Yr. award, 1984, 86, 87, 91, 93, 95, 2000, Women's Basketball Coaches Assn. Victory Club award, 2005; named to Women's Basketball Hall of Fame, 2007. Avocations: fishing, golf. Office: Univ Va University Hall PO Box 400827 Charlottesville VA 22904-4827 Office Phone: 434-982-5800. Office Fax: 434-982-5822. E-mail: dar2h@d.mail.virginia.edu.*

RYAN, DEBORAH LORRAINE, music educator; b. Pk Ridge, Ill., Jan. 23, 1978; d. Edward Patrick and Shelley Lorraine Ryan; m. Daniel Vincent Hennel, Sept. 22, 2007. MusM in Piano Performance, Roosevelt U., Chgo., 2003. Tchg. assoc. piano Consol. Music, Barrington, Ill., 1996—2000, Music Rm., Palatine, Ill., 2000—04, Elmhurst Coll., Ill., 2001—. Co-dir. Chamber Orch. Elmhurst Coll., Ill., 2006—, piano accompanist, 2001—, tchg. assoc. functional class piano, 2001—. Philanthropist-patroness Sigma Alpha Iota, Elmhurst, Ill., 2003. Achievements include creation of the Young Pianist's Camp.

RYAN, EDWARD A., lawyer, hotel executive; b. Newark, Oct. 24, 1953; AB summa cum laude, Univ. Pa., 1975, JD cum laude, 1978. Bar: DC 1978, Md. 1985. Atty. Crowell & Moring, Washington, 1978—84, Hogan & Hartson, 1984—89, ptnr., 1989—96; corp. atty. Marriott Internat., Washington, 1996—2006, exec. v.p., gen. counsel, 2006—. Editor (assoc.): Univ. Pa. Law Review. Mem.: ABA, Md. State Bar Assn., D.C. Bar, Phi Beta Kappa. Office: Marriott Internat 1 Marriott Dr Washington DC 20058-0001

RYAN, GEORGE WILLIAM, manufacturing executive; b. Sinking Springs, Ohio, Oct. 13, 1939; s. Winson Mark and Mary Edith (Smalley) R.; 1 child: Gina Kristin. Student, Wilmington Coll., Ohio, 1962. Process engr. B.F. Goodrich Co., Marietta, Ohio, 1962-66; product dev. mgr. Chrysler Corp., Sandusky, Ohio, 1966-70; asst. tech. mgr. Inmont Corp., Toledo, 1970-72; tech. mgr. Occidental Petroleum, Burlington, NJ, 1973; owner Ryan Devel. Corp., Peebles, 1973-88; prin. Ironwood Valley Ranch, Ohio, 1986—. Substitute tchr. Adams County Sch. Dist.; cons. Hooker Chem. Corp., Burlington, NJ, 1973; expert Internat. Exec. Svc. Core. Bd. dirs., Adams County C. of C., 2007-08, Missionary Evang. Ch. of Christ, pres.; active Adams County Workforce Commn.; mem. Rep. Inner Cir. Mem. Soc. Plastic Engrs., Peebles Ind. Inc. (sec., treas., bd. dirs., 1984-88), Lions Club. Republican. Office Phone: 937-587-2266. Personal E-mail: rydevryan@aol.com.

RYAN, GRETCHEN MARGARETE FRIEDA, art educator; b. Niederschona, Saxony, Germany, Nov. 2, 1929; arrived in U.S., 1952; d. Paul Robert Lutzner and Frieda Gertrud Lutzner-Kupsch; m. Raymond Andrew Ryan, May 12, 1952; children: Michael D., Ralph T., Robert P., Ronald J., Rex W., Renee G. Student, Berlin Art Acad., 1970; AA, Am. River Coll., Sacramento, 1975. Instr. art McClellan AFB, Sacramento, 1967—68, Am. Women's Club, Berlin, 1969—72, Edwards AFB, Calif., 1972—74, Am. River Coll., Sacramento, 1975—2005, Gretchen's Studio, Carmichael, Calif., 1986—. Tchr. art San Juan Sch. Dist., Sacramento, 1975—95; instr. art City of Sacramento, 1980—2006. California's Gold, 2000, Ancient Book of Future, 2002, Decorating 2 Life size Elk, Elk Grove, Calif., 2002, Decorating 1 Life size Lion, Sacramento, 2004. Recipient Restoring Meml. Auditorium resolution, Sacramento City Coun., Recognition award, Shriners Children's Hosp. Sacramento, Purchase award, USAF, 1976, award, Berlin Air Force, 1971, Cmty. Svc. award, Comdr. Air Force Berlin, 1972. Mem.: Sacramento Fine Arts Ctr., Valley Sculpture Artists (bd. dirs., v.p. 1998—), No. Calif. Arts Assn. (bd. dirs.). Avocations: crafts, exercise. Home and Studio: 6225 Luna Ln Carmichael CA 95608

RYAN, IONE JEAN ALOHILANI RATHBURN, retired education educator, counselor; b. Honolulu, Oct. 18, 1926; d. William Alexander and Lilia (Nainoa) Rathburn; m. Edward Parsons Ryan, June 23, 1962 (dec.); children: Ralph M., Lilia K. BEd, U. Hawaii, 1948; MS in Pub. Health, U. Minn., 1950; EdD, Stanford U., 1960. Lic. marital and family therapist, N.C. Tchr. W.R. Farrington High Sch., Honolulu, 1948; instr. to asst. prof. U. Hawaii, Honolulu, 1950-66; assoc. prof. to prof. East Carolina U., Greenville, 1966-90, prof. emerita, 1990—. Contbr. articles to profl. publs. Recipient first scholarship Honolulu C. of C., 1948-50.

RYAN, JACK, physician, retired hospital corporation executive; b. Benton Harbor, Mich., Aug. 26, 1925; s. Leonard Joseph and Beulah (Southworth) R.; m. Lois Patricia Patterson; children: Michele, Kevin, Timothy, Daniel. AB, Western Mich. U., 1948; postgrad., U. Mich. Law Sch., 1949-50, Emory U., 1950-51; MD, Wayne State U., 1955. Intern St. Luke's Hosp., Saginaw, Mich., 1955-56; pres. Meml. Med. Ctr., Warren, Mich., 1956-77; v.p. med. affairs Detroit-Macomb Hosps. Corp., 1976-77, pres. and chief exec. officer, 1977-96; ret., 1996. Assoc. prof. medicine Wayne State U., Detroit, 1974—; bd. chmn. Mich. Hosp. Ins. Co., 1990—. Recipient Disting. Alumnus award Wayne State U. Med. Sch., 1974, Wayne State U., 1979, Western Mich. U., 1989, Disting. Key award Mich. Hosp. Assn., 1986, Tree of Life award Jewish Nat. Fund, 1996. Fellow Am. Coll. Family Physicians, Am. Coll. Physician Execs., Detroit Acad. Medicine; mem. Internat. Health Econs. and Mgmt. Inst. (charter), Econ. Club Detroit, Detroit Athletic Club, Renaissance Club, Red Run Club. Avocations: civil war, history, golf, tennis. Home: 175 Hendrie Blvd Royal Oak MI 48067-2412

RYAN, JAMES, insurance company executive; b. Pitts., Jan. 21, 1937; s. Martin Charles and Lucy Elizabeth (Misklow) r.; m. Marlene Sullivan Ryan, Jan. 27, 1973. BA, U. Pitts., U. Louisville. Cert. ins. wholesaler. Chmn. Market Finders Ins. Corp., Louisville, 1972—. Com. chmn. Am. Assn. Mng. Gen. Agts., 1988-89; pres. Ky. Lloyd's Agts. Assn., 1985—; bd. dirs. Nat. Assn. Profl. Surplus Lines Office, Inc., 1983-86; pres. Ky. Surplus Lines Assn., Louisville, 1988-89; mem. adv. coun. Essex Ins. Co., 1991-93, Am. Equity Ins. Co., Scottsdale, Ariz., 1999. Pub. in Best Rev., 1995. Mem. Ky. Thoroughbred Owners & Breeders, Inc., Hon. Order of Blue Goose Internat., Kosair Shrine Temple, Hon. Order of Ky. Col. Named Adv. Coun. Colony Ins. Co., Glen Allen, Va., 1991-93, Hamilton Ins. Co., 1993, Cardinal Ins. Co., 1991-93. Mem. Profl. Ins.

Agts., Ind. Ins. Agts. Assn., Am. Assn. Mng. Gen. Agts. (cert., chmn. adv. com. 1991-92, bd. dirs. 1994-96, v.p. zone 2 1995-96, pres.-elect 1996-97, pres. 1997-98), Nat. Assn. Profl. Surplus Lines Offices (chmn. legis. com. 1988-89, Published Best Rev. 1995), Am. Assn. of Gen. Agts. Republican. Roman Catholic. Avocations: breeding and racing thoroughbred horses, golf. Office Phone: 502-423-1800. Business E-Mail: jryan@mfic.com.

RYAN, JAMES (JIMMY), lobbyist, diversified financial services company executive; BA, Loyola Coll., Balt.; JD, Cath. U. of America Columbus Ach. Law, Washington, 1993. Former aide to majority leader Harry Reid US Senate, Washington; sr. v.p. fed. govt. affairs Citigroup Inc., 2003—. Office: Citigroup 1101 Pennsylvania Ave NW #1000 Washington DC 20004 Office Phone: 202-393-0829.*

RYAN, JAMES LEO, federal judge; b. Detroit, Nov. 19, 1932; s. Leo Francis and Irene Agnes Ryan; m. Mary Elizabeth Rogers, Oct. 12, 1957; children: Daniel P., James R., Colleen M. Hansen, Kathleen A. LLB, U. Detroit, 1956, LLD (hon.), 1986, BA, 1992; LLD (hon.), Madonna Coll., 1976, Detroit Coll., 1978, Thomas M. Cooley Law Sch., Lansing, Mich., 1986. Atty. Waldron, Brennan & Maher, 1960—62; pvt. practice Redford Twp., Mich., 1962—66; Justice of peace, 1963—66; judge 3d Cir. Ct. of Mich., 1966—75; justice Mich. Supreme Ct., 1975—86; judge US Ct. Appeals (6th cir.), 1985—2000, sr. judge, 2000—. Faculty Nat. Jud. Coll., Reno; adj. faculty, bd. dirs. Ave Maria Sch. Law; adj. prof. Thomas M. Cooley Law Sch., 1979—85, U. Detroit, 1974—. Contbr. articles to profl. jours. Capt. JAGC USNR, 1957—92, ret. mil. judge USNR. Mem.: USNR Lawyers Assn., Detroit Bar Assn., Fed. Bar Assn., State Bar Mich., Fed. Judges Assn., K.M., K.C. Office: US Ct Appeals Theodore Levin Courthouse 231 W Lafayette Blvd Detroit MI 48226-2700*

RYAN, JAMES T., wholesale distribution executive; b. Aug. 4, 1958; BS, Miami U., Ohio, 1980; MBA, DePaul U., 1987. Mgmt. positions W.W. Grainger, Inc., Lake Forest, Ill., 1980—94, pres. parts divsn., 1994—96, v.p. info. services, 1996—2000, pres. grainger.com, 2000—01, exec. v.p. mktg. & sales, 2001—02, exec. v.p. mktg., sales & svc., 2002—04, group pres., 2004—06, pres., 2006—07, pres., COO, 2007—08, pres., CEO, 2008—09, chmn., pres., CEO, 2009—. Bd. dirs. W.W. Grainger, Inc., 2007—. Trustee Mus. Sci. & Industry, Chgo., DePaul U. Mem.: Econ. Club Chgo. Office: WW Grainger Inc 100 Grainger Pkwy Lake Forest IL 60045-5201 E-mail: james.ryan@grainger.com.*

RYAN, JAMES WALTER, physician, researcher; s. Lee W. and Emma E. (Haddox) R.; children: James P.A., Alexandra L.E., Amy J.S. AB in Polit. Sci., Dartmouth Coll., 1957; MD, Cornell U., 1961; D.Phil., Oxford U., Eng., 1967. Diplomate Nat. Bd. Med. Examiners. Intern, Montreal (Que.) Gen. Hosp., McGill U., Can., 1961-62, asst. resident in medicine, 1962-63; USPHS research asso. NIMH, NIH, 1963-65; guest investigator Rockefeller U., NYC, 1967-68, asst. prof. biochemistry, 1968; investigator Howard Hughes Med. Inst., 1968—71; assoc. prof. medicine U. Miami (Fla.) Sch. Medicine, 1968-79, prof. medicine, 1979-95, mem. vasc. biology ctr., 1995-00; prof. anesthesiology, pharmacology and toxicology Med. Coll. Ga., Augusta, 1995-00; sr. cons. ntGen, 2000—; chief scientist Ryogen, LLC, 2005—. Sr. scientist Papanicolaou Cancer Rsch. Inst., Miami, 1972-77; hon. med. officer to Regius prof. medicine Oxford U., 1965-67; vis. prof. Clin. Rsch. Inst. Montreal, 1974; mem. vis. faculty thoracic disease divsn., dept. internal medicine Mayo Clinic, 1974; vis. prof. Montreal Gen. Hosp./McGill U., 1985. Contbr. numerous articles on biochem. rsch. and pathology to sci. jours.; patentee in field. Rockefeller Found. travel awardee, 1962; William Waldorf Astor traveling fellow, 1966; USPHS spl. fellow, 1967-68; Pfizer travelling fellow, 1972; recipient USPHS Rsch. Career Devel. award NIH, 1968, Louis and Artur Luciano award for research of circulatory diseases McGill U., 1984-85. Fellow Am. Heart Assn. (mem. coun. cardiopulmonary diseases 1972—, coun. for high blood pressure rsch. 1976—); mem. AAAS, Am. Physiol. Soc., Am. Chem. Soc., Biochem. Soc., Am. Soc. Biochemist and Molecular Biology, Oxford and Cambridge Club (London), Sigma Xi. Baptist. Home: 3047 Lake Forest Dr Augusta GA 30909-3027 Office: ntGen Ryogen LLC 3047 Lake Forest Dr Augusta GA 30909

RYAN, JASON K., finance educator; b. Paris, Nov. 10, 1971; s. John William Ryan; m. Sari Susanna Silvanto, July 1, 2005. BA in History, Swarthmore Coll., Pa., 1995; MS in Bus. Adminstrn., Wash. U., St. Louis, 2000, MS in Internat. Affairs, 2002; PhD, U. Coll. Dublin, 2008. Asst. prof. St. Louis U., Madrid, 2005—07, U. Redlands, Calif., 2007—. Mem.: Acad. Mgmt. Office: Univ Redlands 1200 East Colton Ave Redlands CA 92374 Business E-Mail: jason_ryan@redlands.edu.

RYAN, JASON MICHAEL, lawyer; b. Wharton, Tex., Oct. 30, 1975; m. Megan A. Ryan, Dec. 30, 2000. BBA with honors, U. Tex., 1998, JD with honors, 2001. Bar: Tex. 2001, US Dist. Ct. (So. Dist.) Tex., US Ct. Appeals (5th cir.), US Ct. Appeals (11th cir.), US Ct. Appeals (Armed Forces), US Tax Ct. With Baker Botts LLP, Houston, 2001—08, Ryan Glover LLP, Houston, 2008—; reserve officer USN, 2005—. Editor-in-chief Am. Jour. Criminal Law; contbr. articles to law jours. Decorated Nat. Def. Svc. medal, Global War on Terror Svc. medal; recipient Pro Bono award, Nat. Law Jour., 2005; named Outstanding Young Houstonian, Houston Jaycees, 2007, Outstanding Young Texan, Tex. Jaycees, 2007. Mem.: ABA, Houston World Affairs Coun. (coun. cabinet), Houston Vol. Lawyers Program, Pro Bono Coll. of State Bar Tex., Houston Young Lawyers Assn. (bd. dirs.), Houston Bar Found., Houston Bar Assn., Energy Bar Assn., Alpha Phi Omega. Address: 6922 Van Etten Houston TX 77021 Office: Ryan Glover LLP 600 Travis Ste 6750 Houston TX 77002 Office Phone: 713-229-0202. Office Fax: 832-550-2063. Business E-Mail: jason.ryan@ryangloverllp.com. E-mail: jason.m.ryan@navy.mil.

RYAN, JOANNE WINONA, art administrator, artist, consultant, educator; b. Jersey City, May 24, 1932; d. James Joseph and Josephine Veronica (Di Blasi) R. BA, Caldwell Coll., 1963; MA, U. Notre Dame, 1969; PhD, NYU, 1981. Elem. tchr. Archdiocese of Newark, Newark and West Orange, NJ, 1951-60; secondary tchr., chmn. art dept. Mount St. Dominic Acad., Caldwell, NJ, 1960-70; instr., dir. art edn. Caldwell Coll., NJ, 1972-75, acad. dean, 1975-78, assoc. prof., 1975-81; dean acad. affairs, prof. Phila. Colls. Arts, 1982—87, v.p. dean acad. affairs, 1984—86, acting pres., 1983; pres. Creative Enterprises, 1987—2003. Exec. dir. Internat. Soc. for Advancement of Living Traditions in Arts, Mid. Atlantic region, N.Y.C., 1981-1990; adj. prof., Caldwell Coll., N.J., 2003—. Author: The Aesthetic Dimension of Process Philosophy, 1982; one-woman shows include Caldwell Coll., 1972, Muhlenberg Coll., Pa., 1973, 80 Washington Square East Galleries, NYC, 1980-81; exhibited in group shows at U. Notre Dame, 1969, Nutley Art Festival, NJ, 1972, Cath. Fine Arts Soc., 1972, Miniature Art Soc., 1972 (1st prize), Art Ctr. of Oranges, NJ, 1972, Caldwell Coll. Faculty Show, 2003, 09; artist, writer in residence W.S. Davis Estate, Orient, NY, 1972-73. Active Pa. Humanities Coun., Phila., 1984-1988; bd. advisors Art and Cmty. Inst., New Sch., NYC, 1975-83. Rsch. grantee NYU/John D. Rockefeller III Fund, NYC, 1972, Visceglia Found., Raritan, NJ, 1982. Mem. Coll. Art Assn., Cath. Fine Arts Soc. (sec.-treas. 1970-72). Office: Caldwell Coll Caldwell NJ 07006 Home Phone: 732-882-8660; Office Phone: 973-618-3254. Business E-Mail: jryan@caldwell.edu.

RYAN, JOHN DUNCAN, lawyer; b. Portland, Oreg., Dec. 20, 1920; s. Thomas Gough and Virginia Abigail (Hadley) R.; m. Florence A. Ryan, Jan. 30, 1970 (dec. 1987); m. Virginia Kane Wilson, June 15, 1996 BS, Fordham U., Bronx, NY, 1943; JD, Lewis & Clark Coll., Portland, 1950. Bar: Oreg. 1950. Pvt. practice, Portland, 1950—. Adj. instr. Northwestern Sch. Law Lewis & Clark Coll., 1953-70 Author: (poems) Expressions, 1993, Expressions II, 1995, No Road without a Turning, 2005, (book) Expressions, 1988, 1999, Cooking with John Ryan, 2002, More Cooking with John Ryan, 2008 Sgt. Air Corps, U.S. Army, 1942-46, ETO Recipient St. Thomas More award Catholic Lawyers for Social Justice, 1993 Mem. ABA (Oreg. del. 1985-93, chmn. spl. com. on law & literacy 1991-93), ATLA, Am. Coll. Trial Lawyers, Oreg. State Bar (bd. govs. 1963-67), Oreg. Trial Lawyers Assn. (Trial Lawyer of Yr. 1993), Multnomah County Bar Assn. (Professionalism award 1997), Washington County Bar Assn, Londer Learning Ctr. Multnomah County, Oregon (co-founder) Home and Office: 503 SW Colony Dr Portland OR 97219-7763 Office Phone: 503-293-2207. Personal E-mail: v.ryan@comcast.net.

RYAN, JOHN JOSEPH, physician; b. Columbus, Ga., Sept. 5, 1957; s. Joseph Vincent and Annie Elizabeth R.; m. Sonia Francisca Ryan, Nov. 17, 1984; children: Annie, Joseph, Catherine. BS in Med. Tech., Columbus U., Ga., 1978; MD, Nuevo Leon U., Mex., 1990. Diplomate Am. Bd. Family Practice. Intern Anderson Family Practice, Anderson, SC, 1991—92, resident, 1991—94; physician Lowry's Family Medicine, Chester, SC, 1994—98; pvt. practice Chester, 1998—2003; physician Thomas Moore Health Clinic, Fort Hood, Tex., 2005—06, McAllen Primary Care Clinic, 2005—06, Mediplex Health Clinic, 2006—. Bass Brownsville Diocese Choir, Holy Spirit Parish Choir. Fellow: Am. Acad. Family Practice; mem.: AMA, Tex. Acad. Family Practice, Rotary, KC (Grand Knight). Roman Catholic. Avocations: fishing, golf, gardening.

RYAN, JOHN MICHAEL, landscape architect; b. Chgo., Sept. 27, 1946; s. Terrance Joseph and Norma (Morris) R.; m. Victoria Jean Wheetley, June 26, 1986; children: Micheline Giannasi-Mennecke, Tony Giannasi, Nick Giannasi, Andrew Morris Jennings, Melissa Contance Victoria, Cameron Michael Montgomery. B in Landscape Architecture, U. Ill., 1969. Registered landscape architect, Ill., Mich., Ariz., Ind., Wis., Tenn., cert. CLARB. Assoc. landscape architect Carl Garnder & Assocs., Inc., Chgo., 1969-71; sr. landscape architect Collaborative Rsch. & Planning, Chgo., 1971-73; v.p. Michael L. Ives & Assocs., Inc., Downers Grove, Ill., 1973-84; pres. Ives/Ryan Group, Inc., Naperville, 1984—. Prin. works include renovation of Old Orchard Shopping Ctr., Skokie, Ill., Lake Katherine Nature Preserve, Palos Heights, Ill., Crystal Tree Residential Golf Course Cmty., Orland Park, Ill., Renaissance Schaumburg Hotel Conv. Ctr., Maravilla Sr. Living Rainforest Atrium, Vernon Hills, Ill. Trustee Wheaton Evangelical Free Ch., 2000-, Youth Lacrosse Coach, 2007-. Recipient Nat. Landscape award Am. Assn. Nurserymen, 1988, 92, Key award in landscape arch. Home Bldrs. Assn. Greater Chgo., 1981, 84, 90, Best Project Grand award Interiorscape mag., 2001. Mem. Am. Soc. Landscape Archs. (Merit award 1991, 94, 96), Assoc. Landscape Contractors Am. (Environ. Improvement Grand award 1997, 2000, Environ. Improvement honor award 2000), Ill. Landscape Contractors Assn. (Gold award 1991, 96, 2001, Silver award 1986, 90, 93, 2001, Merit award 1988, 91), Chgo. Hort. Soc., Perennial Plant Assn. (Nat. Honor award 1993), Morton Arboretum. Avocations: gardening, travel. Business E-Mail: jryan@ivesryangroup.com. *My life is committed to raising my dear children to the best of my ability in a loving christian atmosphere, which I believe to be my true purpose for being here. As a professional landscape architect, if I can enhance or imporve the environment for my children and their children, I have made a worthwhile professional contribution to my perceived purpose in life.*

RYAN, JOHN MORGAN, lawyer; b. Glen Ridge, NJ, May 18, 1936; AB, Dartmouth Coll., 1958; LLB, U. Va., 1963. Bar: Va. 1964. Lectr. at law Marshall-Wythe Sch. Law Coll. William and Mary, 1976-86; ptnr. Vandeventer Black LLP, Norfolk, Va.; gen. counsel Va. Internat. Terminals, Inc. Past chair Arts and Humanities Commn., Va. Beach, Va.; bd. dirs. Greater Norfolk Corp. Fellow: Va. Law Found., Am. Bar Found., Am. Coll. Trial Lawyers; mem.: ABA (labor rels., litigation sect.), So. Conf. Bar Pres., Nat. Conf. Bar Pres., Va. State Bar, Norfolk-Portsmouth Bar Assn., Maritime Law Assn. US (bd. dirs. 2005—08), Va. Bar Assn. (pres. 1988), S.E. Admiralty Law Inst., James Kent Am. Inn of Ct. (past pres.), 4th Cir. Jud. Conf., Hampton Rds. Maritime Assn. (legis. com.). Office: Vandeventer Black LLP 500 World Trade Ctr Norfolk VA 23510-1679 Office Phone: 757-446-8605, 757-446-8600. Business E-Mail: jryan@vanblk.com.

RYAN, JOHN R., educational association administrator, former academic administrator, career military officer; m. Diane L. Ackerman; children: Tricia, Kelly, Julie. Graduate, USN Acad., 1967; MSc in Adminstrn., George Washington U., 1975. Enlisted USN, 1968, advanced through grades to vice adm.; naval aviator Patrol Squadron 8, 1969-72; various assignments Naval Acad., 1972-75; served on USS Nimitz, 1975-77; adminstrv. officer Commander Patrol Wing Five, 1977-80; ops. officer Patrol Squadron Twenty-Six, 1980-81; various assignments Patrol Squadron Eleven, 1981-83, Office of Chief of Naval Ops., 1983-85; military asst. to exec. sec. Immediate Office of Sec. Defense, 1985-86; comdr. Patrol Squadron Thirty-One, Moffett Field, 1986-87; exec. asst. to dep. chief naval ops. Office of Chief of Naval Ops., 1987-88; comdr. Patrol Wing Ten, Moffett Field, 1988-90; various assignments U.S. Pacific Command, 1990-93; commdr., patrol wings US Pacific Fleet/Commdr., Anti-Submarine Warfare Forces, U.S. Pacific Fleet, 1993-95; commdr., maritime surveilance and reconnaissance force, us sicth fleet commdr., fleet air mediterranean/commdr. Maritime Air Forces, 1995-98; supt. USN Acad., 1998—2002; pres. SUNY Maritime Coll., 2002—04; interim pres. SUNY, Albany, 2004; acting chancellor SUNY Sys., 2005, chancellor, 2005—07; pres., chief exec. Ctr. for Creative Leadership, Greensboro, NC, 2007—. Decorated D.S.M., Legion of Merit with two gold stars, Meritorious Svc. medal with two gold stars. Office: Ctr For Creative Leadership 1 Leadership Pl Greensboro NC 27410

RYAN, JOHN WILLIAM, academic administrator; b. Chgo., Aug. 12, 1929; s. Leonard John and Maxine (Mitchell) R.; m. D. Patricia Goodday, June 20, 1949; children: Kathleen Elynne Ryan Acker, Kevin Dennis Mitchell, Kerrick Charles Casey. BA, U. Utah, 1951; MA, Ind. U., 1958, PhD, 1959; D Pub. Adminstrn., Nat. Inst. Devel. Adminstrn., Thailand, 1991; DLitt (hon.), U. St. Thomas, 1977; LLD (hon.), Ind. U., 1988, U. Notre Dame, 1978, Oakland City Coll., 1981, St. Joseph Coll., 1981, Hanover Coll., 1982, DePauw U., 1983, Manchester Coll., 1983, U. Evansville, 1985, Wabash Coll., 1986, U. Md., 1994, SD State U., 2005, S.Dakota State U., 2004. Rsch. analyst Ky. Dept. Revenue, Frankfort, 1954-55; vis. rsch. prof. U. Thammasat, Bangkok, 1955-57; asst. dir. Inst. Tng. for Pub. Svc. Ind. U., 1957-58; successively asst. prof., assoc. prof. polit. sci., assoc. dir., Bur. Govt. U. Wis., 1958-62; exec. asst. to pres., sec. of univ. U. Mass., Amherst, 1962-63, chancellor Boston, 1965-68; v.p. acad. affairs Ariz. State U., 1963-65; v.p., chancellor regional campuses Ind. U., Bloomington, 1968-71, pres., 1971-87, pres. emeritus, 1987—, prof. polit. sci., 1968-95, prof. pub. and environ. affairs, 1981-95, prof. emeritus, 1995—; cons. AID, 1991-92; chancellor SUNY, Albany, 1996—2000, chancellor emeritus, 2000—; hon. prof. Moscow State U., 1999. Interim pres. Fla. Atlantic U., 1989, U. Md., Balt., 1994; bd. dirs. Ind. U. Found., chmn. 1972-87; chmn. Nat. Adv. Bd. on Internat. Edn. Programs, 1985-89. Contbr. articles to profl. jours. Bd. govs. Pub. Broadcasting Svc., 1973-82; bd. visitors Air U., 1974-81; chmn. Air Force Inst. Tech Subcom., 1976-81; mem. univ. adv. com. Am. Coun. Life Ins.; bd. dirs. Corp. Community Coun., 1976; mem. nat. adv. coun. Pan Am. Games, 1985; mem. adv. bd. Assocs. for Religious and Intellectual Life, 1984—; active United Way Ind. Centennial Commn. Mem. Am. Soc. Pub. Adminstrn. (pres. Ind. chpt. 1969-70, nat. chpt. 1972-73, nat. coun. from 1970, Ind. Soc. Chgo. (non-resident v.p. from 1976, Am. Polit. Sci. Assn., Assn. Asian Studies, Am. Coun. Edn., Assn. Am. Univs. (chmn. 1981-82), Nat. Acad. Public Adminstrn., Ind. Acad., Explorers Club, Adelphia (hon.), Columbia Club (Indpls.), Skyline Club, Cosmos Club (Washington), Athenaeum (London), KC, Equestrian Order of Holy Sepulchre, Elks, Phi Kappa Phi, Phi Alpha Theta, Pi Sigma Alpha, Beta Gamma Sigma, Kappa Sigma (worthy grand master 1985-87). Office: Ind U SPEA 415 1315 E 10th St Bloomington IN 47405-1701 Home Phone: 812-824-9071; Office Phone: 812-855-5780. Personal E-mail: chancem123@aol.com. Business E-Mail: ryan@indiana.edu.

RYAN, JOHN WILLIAM, educational association administrator; b. Manchester, NH, Sept. 16, 1937; s. William Charles and Mary Ann (Marcoux) R.; m. Carol Jean Battaglia, Sept. 17, 1960; children: James, Kathleen, John, Michael. AB, St. Anselm Coll., 1959; MA, Niagara U., 1960; PhD, St. John's U., 1965. Asst. prof. history Gannon U., Erie, Pa., 1965-66; edn. specialist, div. grad. programs U.S. Office Edn., Washington, 1966-68, regional coordinator, grad. acad. programs, 1968-70; dir. univ. programs Univ. Assos., Inc., Washington, 1970-72; asst. to pres., sec. Council of Grad. Schs. in U.S., Washington, 1972-80; exec. v.p. Renewables Research Inst., Annandale, Va., 1980-81; exec. dir. Worcester (Mass.) Consortium Higher Edn., 1981-89, N.H. Coll. and Univ. Coun., Manchester, 1989-93; cons.; exec. dir. Mass. Vet. Med. Assn., Marlborough, Mass., 1995-98; cons., 1998—. Contbr. articles to profl. jours. Bd. dirs. Northern Va. CC, 1999—2007, Loudoun Healthcare, Inc., 2000—, Loudoun County Econ. Devel. Commn., 2000.

RYAN, JUDITH ANN, dean; d. Thomas Patrick and Ann Patricia Ryan. BA, Queens Coll., Flushing, NY, 1993; MS, Coll. Mt. St. Vincent, Riverdale, 1998. Cert. English 7-12 NY, Sch. Dist. Adminstr. NY. Coom. art tchr. IS204 NYC Bd. Edn., Long Island, NY, 1993—96, title I reading specialist, 1996—2000, title I dept. coord. Jackson Heights, 2000—03, dean of students, 2003—. Advisor liaison IS230, Jackson Heights, NY, 2004—06, fin. officer, 2006. Mem. NYC 2012 Campaign, NYC, 2003—05. Mem.: Nat. Coun. Tchrs. English, Assn. for Supr. and Cirrculum Devel. Office: IS230 73-10 34th Ave Jackson Heights NY 11372

RYAN, JUDITH W., geriatrics nurse, educator; b. Waterbury, Conn., Dec. 8, 1943; d. James Patrick Ryan and Edna (Swanson) Billings. BS, U. Conn., 1965; MS, Boston U., 1967; PhD, U. Md., 1984. RN, Md., Conn.; cert. adult nurse practitioner ANCC. Instr. U. Conn., Storrs, 1967-69; asst. prof. Ind. U., Purdue U., Indpls., 1969-73, U. Md., Balt., 1973-82, dir. primary care adult nurse pracitioner cert. program, dept. medicine, supportive care project, 1985-87, asst. prof. sch. nursing, 1987-95, asst. prof., 1976-82; clin. dir. EverCare, Balt., 1995-99; pres. Nurse Practitioners and Cons., P.C. of Prime Health Group, 2000—. Arbitrator Health Claims Arbitration Program, Md., 1976—; bd. mem. Md. Bd. Nursing, Balt., 1991-98, pres., 1993-96; trustee Md. Nurses Assn. Polit. Action Com., Balt., treas., 1989-91. Contbr. articles to profl. jours. Named Distinguished Practitioner Nursing, Nat. Acad. Practice, 1984-99. Mem. Am. Coll. Nurse Practitioners, Md. Nurses Assn. (2d v.p. 1986-88), Nurse Practitioner Assn. Md., Sigma Theta Tau, Phi Kappa Phi. Home: 1514 Woodside Ave Baltimore MD 21227 Office: 10989 Red Run Blvd Ste 208 Owings Mills MD 21117-3248 Office Phone: 410-654-8602 Ext. 103. Personal E-mail: jwryan128@comcast.net.

RYAN, JUDY, literature and language professor; b. Oakland, Calif., Oct. 7, 1947; d. Hal and Jeanette Leber; m. Tim Ryan, Apr. 4, 1968; children: Timothy Charles, Kelly Elane Bastian, Scott Taylor, Kasey Eileen Boone, Kathryn Elizabeth Poduska, Travis Wilson. M, CSU, Fresno, 1986. Music tchr. San Juan Unified Sch. Dist. & Clovis Unified Sch. Dist., Clovis, Calif., 1976—86; instr. English State Ctr. CC Dist., Fresno, Calif., 1986—. Pres. Ctr. Stage Prodns., Clovis, Calif., 2000—02. Mem.: Phi Theta Kappa (regional coord. 1991—, Robert Giles disting. advisor 1995, disting. regional coord. 1999). Avocations: writing, art, music. Office: Fresno City Coll 1101 E University Ave Fresno CA 93741 Office Phone: 559-442-4600 ext. 8107. Business E-Mail: judy.ryan@fresnocitycollege.edu.

RYAN, KATHY ANN, special education educator; b. Harrisburg, Pa., Mar. 5, 1963; d. Lee and Jean Bretz; m. Robert Ryan, June 21, 1986; children: Randy, Samantha. BS, Millersville U. Pa., 1981—85; MS, Va. Tech, Blacksburg, 2002—04; Student, Va. Commonwealth U., Richmond, 2009—. Cert. learning disability tchr. Va. Dept. Edn., 1985, emotional disturbance tchr. Va. Dept. Edn., 1985, mental retardation tchr. Va. Dept. Edn., 1985, spl. edn. tchr. Pa. Dept. Edn., 1985, vocational spl. needs tchr. Va. Dept. Edn., 2004. Tchr., dept. chair spl. edn. Stafford County Pub. Schs., Va., 1985—92; tchr., dept. chair, transition coord. Fredericksburg City Pub. Schs., Va., 1992. Recipient Tchr. of Yr. award, Fredericksburg City Schs., CEC; nominee Disney Tchr. of Yr. program. Mem.: ASCD, Learning Disability Assn., Coun. Exceptional Children, Omegacron, Phi Kappa Phi. Avocations: reading, crafts, music. Home: 5112 Signal Corps Dr Fredericksburg VA 22408 Office: James Monroe HS 2300 Washington Ave Fredericksburg VA 22401 Office Fax: 540-373-8643. Personal E-mail: karyan1@juno.com. Business E-Mail: kryan@cityschools.com.

RYAN, KATHY L., physiologist, researcher; b. Lampasas, Tex., Feb. 8, 1960; d. Timothy L. and Mary Beth Ryan. PhD, UT Health Sci. Ctr., San Antonio, 1989. Postdoc. fellow UT Health Sci. Ctr., 1990—92; rsch. assoc. Trinity U., San Antonio, 1992—99; rsch. physiologist US Army Inst. Surg. Rsch., Fort Sam Houston, Tex., 1999—. Lectr. St. Mary's U., San Antonio, 1997—2001. Contbr. scientific papers to profl. publ. Mem. Bulverde United Meth. Ch., Tex., 2002—08. Mem.: Am. Physiol. Soc. (com. appointment 2009—), Phi Beta Kappa, (Epsilon Chpt. Tex.). Office: US Army Inst Surg Rsch 3400 Rawley E Chambers Ave Fort Sam Houston TX 78234-6315

RYAN, KAY PEDERSEN, poet; b. San Jose, Calif., Sept. 21, 1945; d. Kay Richard and Bessie Margaret (Barrett) Pedersen; life ptnr. Carol Adair. BA, UCLA, 1967, MA, 1968. Chancellor Acad. Am. Poets, 2006—. Author: (poetry) Dragon Acts to Dragon Ends, 1983, Strangely Marked Metal, 1985, Flamingo Watching, 1994, Elephant Rocks, 1996, Say Uncle, 2000, Believe It or Not!, 2002, The Niagara River, 2005.

Recipient Ingram Merrill Found. award, 1995, Poetry award, Ingram Merrill Found., 1995, Maurice English award, 2001, Ruth Lilly Poetry prize, Poetry Found., 2004, Gold medal for Poetry, San Francisco Commonwealth Club, 2005, Union League Poetry prize, 2000; named US Poet Laureate, Libr. Congress, 2008; grantee, Nat. Endowment for Arts, 2001; fellow, Guggenheim Found., 2004.

RYAN, KELLI LORRAINE, ballerina, educator; b. Merced, Calif., June 26, 1957; d. Howard Fredrick Burley Adcock and Lorraine Cervantes-Adcock; m. Riley Ray Ryan III, May 1, 1999; 1 child, Victoria Alyn Bommarito Salda. M. in Psychology, San Jose State U., 1988. Ballerina Vaganova Choreographic/Kirov Ballet, USSR, 1977, Paris Opera Ballet, France, 1977, Diplomat of Elem., Intermediate and Advanced Cecchetti Syllabus Cecchetti Coun. Am., Calif., 1970, cert. hypnotherapist A.C.H.E., Calif., 1988. Instructress ballet/jazz for the deaf Berkley Sch. for Deaf, 1972—74; corps de ballet San Francisco Ballet, 1975—82; soloist Ballet Lausanne, Brussels, 1976—77; artistic dir. Alameda Dance Repertory Theater, Calif., 1978—82; soloist Ballet de Toscano, Florence, Italy, 1998—99; vol. instructress, ballet/movement for the developmentally disabled Calif., 1982—. Regional del. Nat. Dance Week, Calif., 2003—; mem. Nat. Dance Assn., Reston, Va., 2004—, Am. AAHPERD, Reston, 2004—. Solo performer (TV spl. - ballet) Isadora by Bejart; oil painting series for Vatican Coll., As It Is In Heaven (In the Vatican's permanent collection, 1998), watercolor series (aquarelli), Garden in the Rain (In the Vatican's permanent collection, 1999), The Rain, 1999; ballerina (performance L.A. Times Book Fest) Celebrate Nat. Dance Week. Mem. Gold Beach C. of C.; chmn. bd. Am. Ballet Conservatory, Atwater, Calif., 2003—05; bd. dirs. Curry Arts. Recipient Commendation of Pub. Svc., U.S. Congress, 18th Dist., 2004, cert. of recognition, Merced County Bd. Suprs., 2004. Mem.: Internat. Dance Coun., C.I.D. UNESCO, Paris. Conservative. Catholic. Achievements include founding American Ballet Conservatory; creation of tax-exempt ballet/music/art conservatory which provides scholarships to Central Calif.'s dance, art, music, photography, writing students; creating a ballet school which provides a comprehensive ballet conservatory education regardless of students ability to pay; development of method of instructing toddlers in ballet and foreign languages; a no fail smoking cessation method. Avocations: teaching piano, painting, sculpting to underprivilaged children, volunteer teaching art/dance to the developmentally disabled, photography. Office Phone: 541-247-6901. Personal E-mail: klryan@charter.net.

RYAN, KEVIN VINCENT, lawyer, former prosecutor; b. 1957; m. Anne Ryan; 2 children. BA in History, Dartmouth Coll.; JD, U. San Francisco. Prosecutor Alameda County Dist. Atty.'s Office; judge San Francisco Mcpl. Ct., 1996—98; mem. San Francisco Superior Ct., 1999, presiding judge criminal divsn.; US atty. (no. dist.) Calif. US Dept. Justice, San Francisco, 2002—07; ptnr. Allen Matkins Leck Gamble Mallory & Natsis LLP, San Francisco, 2007—. Bd. dirs. No. Calif. High Intensity Drug Trafficking Area Working Group; mem. Pres. Bush's Corp. Fraud Task Force; apptd. mem. subcom. Controlled Substances and Terrorism and Nat. Security, appointed to Jud. Coun.'s Exec. Legis. Action Network, Chief Justice of Calif. Supreme Ct.; appointed to Criminal Law Planning Com. of Calif. Continuing Jud. Studies Program, Governing Com. of Calif. Ctr. for Jud. Edn. and Rsch.; appointed to Adult Probation Dept.'s Oversight Com., Presiding Judge for Cts.; mem. exec. com. San Francisco Superior Ct.; mem. exec. com. Am. Inn of Cts., U. San Francisco Sch. Law; bd. govs. U. San Francisco Law Soc.; bd. trustees Schs. of Sacred Heart, San Francisco; mem. faculty Intensive Trial Advocacy Program, U. San Francisco Sch. Law; lectr. in field. Recipient Mcpl. Ct. Trial Judge of Yr., San Francisco Trial Lawyers' Assn., 1998. Office: Allen Matkins 3 Embarcadero Ctr 12th Fl San Francisco CA 94111-4074

RYAN, KEVIN WILLIAM, virologist, clinical research administrator; s. Joseph Michael Ryan and Etoile Evelyn Werth; m. Mary Ellen Lyman, June 1, 1974; children: Matthew Lyman, Mark Joseph. BS, U. Iowa, 1978; PhD, U. Mich., 1984. Staff fellow Nat. Inst. Allergy and Infectious Diseases, NIH, Bethesda, Md., 1984-86; rsch. asst. dept. virology and molecular biology St. Jude Children's Rsch. Hosp., Memphis, 1986-89, asst. mem., 1989-98; asst. prof. pathology U. Tenn. Coll. Medicine, Memphis, 1994-98; sci. rev. adminstr. Nat. Inst. Allergy and Infectious Diseases, NIH, Rockville, Md., 1998-2000; program officer virology vaccine and prevention rsch. prog. divsn. AIDS, Nat. Inst. Allergy and Infectious Diseases, NIH, Bethesda, Md., 2000—05; deputy chief Prevention Scis. Br., 2001—02, chief, 2002—05, lead program officer grant-supported internat. clin. rsch. in HIV/AIDS prevention, 2001—05; mem. working group NIAID, Comprehensive Internat. Program for Rsch. in AIDS (CIPRA), 2001—05; dep. dir. pediatrics, adolescent and maternal AIDS, Ctr. for Rsch. for Mothers and Children, Nat. Inst. Child Health and Human Devel., NIH, Rockville, Md., 2005—. Prin. investigator Nat. Inst. Allergy and Infectious Diseases, 1992—98; lead program officer HIV prevention trials network HPTN, 2002—05; govt. project officer HIV Network Prevention Trials (HIVNET) Internat. Master Contract for AIDS Rsch. NIAID, 2002—04; NIAID program officer Clin. Trials of Male Circumcision for HIV Prevention, 2002—05, Topical Microbicides Clin. Trials, 2002—05; NIAID Rep. HPTN Prevention Leadership Group, 2002—05; dep. chief Pediat., Adolescent and Maternal AIDS br. Ctr. for Rsch. Mothers and Children, Nat. Inst. of Child Health and Human Devel., NIH, 2005—; lead NICHD program officer Adolescent Medicine Trials Network, 2005—, Women and Infants HIV Transmission Study, 2005—; program officer Pediatric HIV-AIDS Cohort Study, 2005—; NICHD program officer Microbicide Trials Network, 2006—, Clin. Trials Optimize Pediat. HN Therapy, Naiadi, Kenya, 2006—, Clin. Trial Relevance Transion Nevirapinc Resistance, Johansburg, South Africa, 2006—, Lopinavir Rionavir Zidovudinc Prevent Perinatal HIV, Thailand, 2007—, Clin. Trails HIV & Malaria, Tororo, Uganda, 2008—; NICHD rep. on Internat. Working Group on Microbicides, 2007—. Contbr. articles to profl. jours., chpts. to tech. manuals. Recipient Merit award, NIH, 2000, Dir. award, 2002; fellow postdoctoral Mich. Cancer Rsch. Inst., U. Mich., 1982. Mem.: Am. Soc. for Microbiology. Roman Catholic. Avocations: woodworking, golf. Office: Nat Inst Child Health and Human Devel PAMA 6100 Executive Blvd Rockville MD 20852-0001 Business E-Mail: kr90p@nih.gov.

RYAN, L. TIMOTHY, chef, educator, academic administrator; b. Pitts. m. Lynne Ryan; 2 children. BS, U. New Haven; MBA, U. New Haven Sch. Bus. Adminstrn.; graduated, Culinary Inst. Am., 1977; EdD, U. Pa., Pa. Graduate Sch. Edu., Phila. Cert. Master Chef 1985. Asst. chef Ben Gross' Restaurant, Irwin, Pa.; exec. chef La Normande, Pitts.; joined Culinary Institute Am., Hyde Park, NY, 1982, exec. v.p., v.p. edu., dir., culinary edu., dept. head, culinary edu., chef-instructor, pres., 2001—. Developer Am. Bounty Restaurant. Author: The Culinary Olympics Cookbook, 1984, 1988, New Professional Chef, Techniques of Healthy Cooking, An American Bounty; editl. adv. com. mem.: Cheers, Seafood Bus., Take Out Bus. magazines, former chmn. editl. coun.: Nat. Culinary Review; contbr. to videos and television shows. Recipient Gold medals, Pitts. Culinary Arts Salon, 1981, Eastern Regional Olympic Tryouts, 1982, Gourmet Fair, Japan, 1983, Honor Roll Am. Chefs, Food & Wine magazine, 1983, Chef Yr. award, Am. Culinary Fedn., 1998, Presdl. medal, World Assn. Cooks Societies, 1998, Hon. Doctorate Foodservice medallion, N.Am. Assn. Food Equipment Manufacturers, Grand prize of show, Internat. Feinschmecker Parade, Austria; named Entrepreneur of Yr., Internat. Assn. Culinary Professionals, 2007; named to Am. Acad. Chefs, 1990. Mem.: Am. Culinary Fedn. (Pitts. chpt. bd. dirs. 1981—82, pub. rels. chair 1982—83, apprenticeship chair, Mid-Hudson chpt. 1982—84, culinary com. 1983—, team capt., US culinary team 1984, master chef com. 1985—, team capt., US Team, Culinary World Cup Competition 1986, team mgr., US team, Salon Culinaire Mondial 1987, team capt., US culinary team 1988, N.E. v.p. 1991—93, nat. pres. 1995—96, chmn. bd. 1996—97, team mgr., US team, Internat. World Culinary Arts Festival, four Gold Medals and World Championship (Hot Food Competition), Internat. Culinary Competition, Germany 1988, two team Gold medals, Salon Culinaire Mondial, Basel, Switzerland 1987, Team grand prize, Culinary World Cup Competition, Luxembourg 1986, Team medal for culinary excellence, Salon Culinary Art, NY 1985, Two gold medals and silver cup, Internat. Culinary Competition, Germany 1984). Achievements include launching the world's first bachelor's degree program in Culinary Arts Management and Baking and Pastry Arts Management; developing a highly successful publishing program; expanding the continuing education programs. Office: Culinary Inst Am 1946 Campus Dr Hyde Park NY 12538-1499

RYAN, LEO VINCENT, business educator; b. Waukon, Iowa, Apr. 6, 1927; s. John Joseph and Mary Irene (O'Brien) Ryan. BS, Marquette U., 1949; MBA, DePaul U., 1954; PhD, St. Louis U., 1958; postgrad., Catholic U. Am., 1951-52, Bradley U., 1952-54, Northwestern U., 1950; LLD, Seton Hall U., 1988; DHL, Ill. Benedictine U., 1997. Joined Order Clerics of St. Viator Roman Cath. Ch., 1950. Faculty Marquette U., Milw., 1957-65, dir. continuing edn. summer sessions, coord. evening divsns., 1959-65, prof. indsl. mgmt., 1964; prof., chmn. dept. mgmt. Loyola U., Chgo., 1965-66; dep. dir. Peace Corps, Lagos, Nigeria, 1966-67, dir. Western Nigeria Ibadan, 1967-68; asst. superior gen. and treas. gen. Clerics of St. Viator, Rome, 1968-69, dir. edn. Am. province Arlington Heights, Ill., 1969-74; pres. St. Viator H.S., 1972-74; dean, prof. mgmt. U. Notre Dame Coll. Bus. Adminstrn., Ind., 1975-80; dean DePaul U. Coll. Commerce, 1980-88, prof. mgmt., 1980-99; Wicklander prof. ethics DePaul U., 1993-94; prof. emeritus, 1999. Chmn. trust audit com. First Bank-Milw., 1980—85, chmn. audit and exam. com., 1985—90; nat. adv. coun. SBA, 1982—85, vice-chmn. minority bus., 1982—85, exec. com. Chgo. chpt., 1982—84; adv. coun. First Bank-Milw., 1991—93; bd. dirs. Henricksen & Co., Inc., 1987—; mem. adv. bd. Sch. Bus. U. Kiev, Ukraine, 2001; vis. adv. bd. DePaul U. Gallery and Mus., 2005—, Internat. Querbs Commn., 2000—; chmn. Querbs Commn. USA, 2001—; adj. prof. human devel. St. Mary's Coll., Winona, Minn., 1972—74; scholar-in-residence Mgmt. Sch. Imperial Coll. Sci. and Tech. U. London, 1988, Am. Grad. Sch. Internat. Mgmt., 1995; vis. scholar U. Calif., Berkeley, 1989, U. St. Thomas, Houston, 2006; vis. rsch. fellow Von Hugel Inst., 1992—93; guest scholar Kellogg Inst. Internat. Studies U. Notre Dame, 1997; vis. prof. U. Ife, Ibadan, India, 1967—68, Notre Dame, 2000, Helsinki Sch. Econs., 2000, Fulbright vis. prof., 1992—2002, Polish-Am. Ctr., U. Lodz, 1998, Poznan Acad. Econs., 1991, 1999—. Author: Human Action in Business, 1996, Etyka Biznesu, 1997, 4th edit., 2000, From Autarcy to Market: Polish Economics and Politics, 1945-1995, 1998, 2d edit., 1999, Students Focus on Business Ethics, 2000, Praxiology and Pragmatism, 2002, Poland: A Transformational Appraisal, 2003, Enterprenuership: Values and Responsibilities, 2009; mem. editl. bd. Internat. Jour. Value Based Mgmt., 1983-2003, Bus. Ethics Quar., 1983-2004, European Bus. Jour., 1990-2002, Mid Atlantic Jour. of Bus., 1990-2002, European Jour. Econs. Fin. and Adminstrv. Studies, 2006, Clerics of St. Viator Quar. Mem. Pres.'s Com. on Employment Handicapped, 1959—65; dir. Peace Corps tng. programs Marquette U., 1962—65; mem. Wis. Gov.'s Com. on Employment Handicapped, 1959—65, Wis. Gov.'s Com. on UN, 1961—64, Burnham Park Planning Commn., 1982—88; trustee St. Viator H.S., 2000—01, gov., 2001—03; mem. Iowa Gov. Heartland Leadership Coun., 2000—06; regent Seton Hall U., 1981—87, mem. acad. affairs com., 1981—87, chmn., 1983—87; trustee Lake Forest Grad. Sch. Mgmt., 1989—91, St. Mary of Woods Coll., 1978—81, Cath. Theol. Union, U. Chgo., 1992—95, Divine Word Coll., 1997—2006; nat. edn. com. US Cath. Conf., 1971—75, exec. com., 1973—75; nat. adv. bd. Benedictine Sisters Nauvoo, 1973—83; mem. Cath. Commn. Intellectual and Cultural Affairs, 1992—, Cath. Campaign for Am., 1994—98; sch. bd. Archdiocese of Chgo., 1972—75, vice-chmn., 1973—75, co-chair bus. and profl. com. Sesquetennial Com. Out Reach Divsn. Ctrl. Planning Group, 1993—94; in commn. Clerics of St. Viator, 1978—, provincial chpt., 1985—97, 2001—03, 2005—09, devel. adv. bd., 1996—2001, new foundations com., 1996—98, alt. mem., 1997—2001, provincial coun., 2001—03, coord. coun., US, Belize, Columbia, 2001—03, comprehensive devel. coun., 2004; mem. Joliet Diocesan Fin. Coun., 2007—, chmn., 2008—; bd. dirs. Internat. Bus. Ethics Inst., Am. Grad. Sch. Internat. Mgmt., 1995—97, Ctr. Pastoral Liturgy U. Notre Dame, 1976—79; dir. Ctr. for Enterprise Devel., 1992—95; mem. adv. com. Mgmt. Edn. in Poland U. Md., College Park, 1995—2000. Recipient Freedom award, Berlin Commn., 1961, Brother Leo V. Ryan award named in his honor, Cath. Bus. Edn. Assn., 1962, B'nai B'rith Interfaith award, Milw., 1963, chieftancy title, Asoju Atoaja of Oshogbo Oba Adenle I, Yorubaland, Nigeria, 1967, Disting. Alumnus award, Marquette U., 1974, DePaul U., 1976, Tchr. of Yr. award, Beta Alpha Psi, 1980, Centennial Alumni Achievement award, Marquette U., 1981, Boland Meml. Disting. Alumni award, St. Louis, 1989, Ryan Scholars in Mgmt. established in his honor, DePaul U., 1989, Outstanding Svc. award, 1991—93, Commerce Alumni award of merit, 1997, Disting. Alumni and Bicentennial awards, Jesuit Bus. Schs., 1989, Ryan Scholarship named in his honor, St. Viator H.S., 1992, Pres.' award, 1992, Lion award, 1997, Medal of Merit, Adam Mickiewicz U., 1995, Republic of Poland, 2007, Excellence in Tchg. award, Adam Mickiewicz U., 1997, DePaul Creativity Ctr. named in his honor, 1997, Ill. Ernst and Young Entrepreneur Supporter award, 1999, Creative Cutting Edge award, 1999, Vincentian U. Ethics Scholar award, 2000, Centennial award, Dominican U. Sch. Bus., 2002, Trustee award, Divine Coll., 2006, Disting. Svc. award, Poznan U. Economics, 2006, Civic award, City of Poznan, 2007, City of Pozan, Poland, 2007; named named Man of Yr., Jr. C. of C., Milw., 1959, Bus. Adminstrn. Alumni Man of Yr., Marquette U., 1974, hon. life chmn., Nat. Adv. Com., Ryan Creativity Ctr., Disting. Vis. Term Prof. Seton Hall U., 2001, Alumnus of Yr., St. Patrick Grade and HS, Waukon, Iowa, 2006; grantee USIA Acad. Specialists grantee, Poland, 1991—93; fellow, German Am. Acad. Exch. Coun., 1983, Kosciuszko Found. Adam Mickiewicz U., 1990,;, St. Edmund's Coll. Cambridge U., 1992; Nat. Assn. Purchasing Agts. faculty fellow, 1958, Milw. Bd. Realtors traveling fellow, 1964, Presdl. fellow, Am. Grad. Sch. Internat. Mgmt., 1989, Malone fellow in Islamic studies, Bahrain and Saudi Arabia, 1990, Fulbright fellow, Poland, 1993—95. Mem. KC (life), Cath. Bus. Edn. Assn. (nat. pres. 1960-62, nat. exec. bd. 1960-64), Assn. Sch. Bus. Ofcls. (nat. com. chmn. 1965-67), Am. Assembly Collegiate Schs. Bus. (com. internat. affairs 1977-84, chmn. 1981-84, bd. dirs. 1981-87, program chmn. 1979-80, exec. com., chmn. projects/svc. mgmt. com. 1984-86), Am. Fgn. Svc. Assn., Am. Assn. Profl. Ethics (bd. dir. 1996-98), Am. Philat. Soc., Allamakee County Hist. Soc. (charter life), Ancient Order of Hibernians, Atomic Vets. Assn., August Derleth Soc., Econ. Club Chgo., Coun. Fgn. Rels. (diplomat cir. 1980-2000), European Bus. Ethics Network Poland (hon. 1998), Soc. Bus. Ethics, (mem. exec. com. 1991—, pres. 1993-94, adv. bd. 1995-97), Assn. Social Econs. (life), Iowa Hist. Soc. (life), Iowa Postal History Soc., Iowa Geneological Soc., Iowa Heartland Leadership Coun., 2000-2006, Fulbright Assn. (life), Internat. Assn. for Bus. and Soc. (founder), Internat. Soc. for Bus., Econs. and Ethics (charter), Internat. Trade and Fin. Assn. (founder, bd. dir. 1989-92, 96-98, v.p. membership 1991-92, 96-97), Internat. Learned Soc. Praxiology, (hon. life, internat. adv. bd. praxiology ann.), Polish Inst. Arts and Scis. in Am., Postal History Soc., Polish Am. Historical Assn., New Salem Hist. Soc. (life), DePaul Inst. Bus. and Profl. Ethics (founder 1984, adv. bd. 1984-94, mus. adv. com., 2005—), Founders award 1999), USS Mt. McKinley Reunion Assn. (life, hon. chaplain AGC-7 1989-96, Disting. Svc. award 1991, 96), Friends of Nigeria (charter mem.), Alpha Sigma Nu, Alpha Kappa Psi (bd. dir. found. 1985-91, vice-chmn. 1987-91, chmn. scholarship com. 1987-91, chmn. devel. com. 1987, exec. com. 1990-91, Bronze Disting. Svc. award 1949, Silver Disting. Svc. award 1958, Recognition medal, 2001), Beta Alpha Psi, Beta Gamma Sigma (co-chair 75th Anniversary com. Ill., faculty advisor DePaul chpt. 1986-92), Century Travel Club (Silver award, Medal opf Merit Republic of Poland, 2007, Civic award City of Poznan, Poland, 2007), Delta Mu Delta, Pi Gamma Mu, Tau Kappa Epsilon. Office Phone: 847-870-4903. Business E-Mail: leovryan@viatorians.com.

RYAN, LEONARD EAMES, judge; b. Albion, NY, July 8, 1930; s. Bernard and Harriet Earle (Fitts) R.; m. Ann Allen, June 18, 1973; 1 child, Thomas Eames Allen-Ryan. Grad., Kent Sch., 1948; AB, U. Pa., 1954; JD, NYU, 1962. Bar: D.C. 1963, N.Y. 1963, U.S. Ct. Appeals (D.C. cir.) 1963, U.S. Dist. Ct. (so. and ea. dists.) N.Y. 1965, U.S. Ct. Appeals (2nd cir.) 1966, U.S. Supreme Ct. 1967. Field engr. constrn. U.S. Steel Fairless Works, Morrisville, Pa., 1951-52; reporter Upper Darby (Pa.) News, 1954; newsman AP, Pitts., Phila., Harrisburg, NYC, 1955-62; reporter, spl. writer on law N.Y. Times, 1962-63; info. adviser corp. hdqrs. IBM, NYC, 1963; trial atty. firm Perrell, Nielsen & Stephens, NYC, 1964-66; trial atty. civil rights div. Dept. Justice, Washington, 1966-68; asst. to dir. bus. affairs CBS News, NYC, 1968; program officer Office Govt. and Law, Ford Found., NYC, 1968-74; pvt. practice law, cons. pub. affairs, NYC, 1974-91; v.p., sec. W. P. Carey & Co., Inc., NYC, 1977—82; impartial hearing officer Edn. for all Handicapped Children Act of 1975, 1976-91; per diem adminstrv. law judge N.Y. State Agys., 1976-91; hearing examiner N.Y. State Family Ct., 1980-81; apptd. U.S. adminstv. law judge, 1991; adminstv. law judge Office Hearings and Appeals, San Rafael, Calif., 1991—93, Phila., 1993-94, NYC, 1994—. Arbitrator Small Claims Ct., N.Y.C., 1974-84; bd. dirs. Community Action for Legal Svcs. Inc., N.Y.C., 1971-77, vice-chmn., 1975-77; co-chmn. Citizens Com. to Save Legal Svcs., N.Y.C., 1975-76; bd. dirs. Lower East Side Svc. Ctr., N.Y.C., 1977-89. Author: (with Bernard Ryan Jr.) So You Want to Go Into Journalism, 1963; contbr. articles to profl. jours. Served with USAR, 1950-57. Mem. Am. Judicature Soc., N.Y. State Bar Assn., St. Elmo Club (Phila.), Heights Casino (Bklyn.). Home: 32 Orange St Brooklyn NY 11201-1634 Office: 111 Livingston St Brooklyn NY 11201-5078

RYAN, LISA, lawyer; b. Mineola, NY, May 16, 1969; m. Ian Robert Barnes, May 22, 2004. BA, Cornell U., Ithaca, NY, 1991; JD, Tulane U. Sch. Law, New Orleans, 1994. Bar: N.Y 1995, Ill. 1995. Intern Supreme Ct. N.Y., White Plains, 1994; assoc. Fragomen Del Rey, Bernsen & Loewy, LLP, Chgo., 1994—96, NYC, 1996—2003, ptnr., 2004—. Founder and editor-in-chief Tulane Jour. Internat. and Comparative Law, 1992—94; spkr. in field. Vol. Animal Haven, Queens, NY, 2003—04; mem. Friends of West River Trail, Londonderry, Vt., 2006. Mem.: ABA, Am. Immigration Lawyers Assn., Exec. Women's Golf Assn., Brit. Am. C. of C., Met. Mus. Art. Avocations: skiing, golf, tennis, hiking, reading. Office: Fragomen Del Rey 7 Hanover Sq Ste 800 New York NY 10004-2673 Office Phone: 212-891-7549.

RYAN, LISA KATHLEEN, environmental and medical science educator; b. Morgantown, W.Va., July 9, 1958; d. Richard Stoetzer and Ellen Stewart Wagner; m. Gill Diamond, Aug. 31, 1997; m. Niall Patrick Ryan, Oct. 3, 1981 (dec. Oct. 1, 1993); children: Allison Kathleen, Michael Richard Diamond, Sara Elana Diamond. BS in microbiology, Penn State U. Coll. of Sci., University Pk., 1980; MS in med. microbiology, W.Va. U. Med. Sch., Morgantown, 1983; PhD in toxicology, U. Pitts. Grad. Sch. Pub. Health, 1992. Rsch. biologist, immunotoxicology br. U.S. EPA, Rsch. Triangle Pk., NC, 1995—2000; asst. prof., dept. of pathology UMDNJ-New Jersey Med. Sch., Newark, 2000—03; asst. prof. dept. oral biology UMDNJ-N.J. Dental Sch., Newark, 2003—08; asst. prof. pulmonary divsn. Dept. Medicine, UMDNJ Med. Sch., 2008—; vis. sci. Pub. Health Rsch. Inst. NJ Med. Sch. Devel. Enzyme-Linked ImmunoSorbent Assay endotoxin detection Hyclone Diagnostics/Travenol Labs., 1981—82; rsch. fellow in medicine Mass. Gen. Hosp./Harvard Med. Sch., Boston, 1992—95; ORD regional sci. advisor EPA region 2 US EPA Office Sci. Policy, Washington, 1998—2000. Contbr. articles to profl. jours. Recipient Individual Nat. Rsch. Svc. award, NIH Nat. Heart, Lung and Blood Inst., 1994—97; grantee, Allegheny-Erie Regional chpt. Soc. Toxicology, 1991, NIH Nat. Inst. Allergies and Infectious Diseases, 2000—03, 2007—, NIH Nat. Heart, Lung and Blood Inst., 2003—07, NIH Inst. Environ. Health Scis., 2009—, Nat. Inst. Environ. Health Scis., 2009—. Mem.: AAAS, Sigma Xi, Am. Conf. of Govtl. Indsl. Hygenists, Am. Thoracic Soc., Am. Soc. for Microbiology, Soc. for Leukocyte Biology, Am. Assn. Immunologists, Soc. Toxicology. Achievements include patents for polymyxin agarose-lipopolysaccharide antigen and associated method. Avocations: swimming, ice skating, piano, clarinet, skiing. Office: Pub Health Rsch Inst UMDNJ NJ Med Sch Medicine Internat Ctr Pub Health 225 Warren St Newark NJ 07103 Office Phone: 973-854-3322. Personal E-mail: lkryan@aol.com. Business E-Mail: ryanlk@umdnj.edu.

RYAN, LOUISE, statistician, educator; b. Australia; BA in stats. and math., Macquarie U., Sydney, Australia, 1978; PhD in stats., Harvard U., 1983. From asst. prof. to Henry Pickering Walcott prof. biostatistics Harvard Sch. Pub. Health, Boston, 1985—2009, chair dept. biostatistics, 2006—09, adj. prof. biostatistics, 2009—; chief of math. and info. sciences Commonwealth Sci. and Rsch. Orgn., Australia, 2009—. Recipient Spiegelman award, Am. Pub. Health Assn., Mentors award, Harvard Sch. Pub. Health, Role Models award, Minority, Inc. Fellow: Internat. Stats. Inst., Am. Statis. Assn. (Disting. Achievement award, Environmetrics Sect., Elizabeth Scott award); mem.: Inst. Medicine. Office: CSIRO Math and Info Sciences Locked Bag 17 Bldg E6B Macquarie U Campus North Ryde NSW 1670 Australia Office Phone: 61 2 9325 3100. E-mail: louise.ryan@csiro.au.*

RYAN, MARGARET A., federal judge; b. May 23, 1964; BA cum laude, Knox Coll., 1985; JD summa cum laude, U. Notre Dame. Bar: Va. 1995, Colo. 2003, DC 2005, US Supreme Ct., US Dist. Ct. Appeals (4th circuit), US Dist. Ct. Colo., US Ct. Fed. Claims, US Supreme Ct. Va., US Supreme Ct. Colo. Comm. officer, co. comdr., platoon comdr. USMC, II and II Marine Expeditionary Forces, 1988—92; chief trial counsel USMC, Quantico, Va., 1995—97, Okinawa, Japan, 1995—97, aide de Camp to 31st comdt., 1997—99; with Cooper Carvin & Rosenthal, 1999—2000; law clk. to Honorable J. Michael Luttig US Ct.

Appeals (4th Circuit), 2000—01; law clk. to Justice Clarence Thomas US Supreme Ct., 2001—02; with Bartlit Beck Herman Palenchar & Scott, 2002—04; ptnr. Wiley, Rein & Fielding LLP, 2004—06; judge US Ct. Appeals for the Armed Forces, 2006—. Office: US Ct Appeals for the Armed Forces 450 E St NW Washington DC 20442*

RYAN, MARGARET AMY, chemist, researcher; b. San Diego, July 13, 1950; d. Ralph Russel Ryan and Margaret Emily Stender; life ptnr. Judith V. Branzburg, Oct. 1, 1982. AB, U. Chgo., 1972; BS, Met. State Coll., Denver, 1981; PhD, U. Mass., Amherst, 1987. Instr. Iran Novin Inst. Polit. Sci., Teheran, 1972—74, ELS, Denver, 1975—81; rschr. Ctr. Nat. Rsch. Sci., Meudon, France, 1987—88; prin. mem. engring. staff Jet Propulsion Lab., Pasadena, 1989—. Mem. bd. dir. ONE Nat. Gay and Lesbian Archives, LA, 2000—04; mem. bd. dir., mem. fin. com. AIDS Svc. Ctr., Pasadena, Calif., 1998—2002; co-founder, v.p., pres. Inst. Gay and Lesbian Edn., West Hollywood, Calif., 1992—96. Recipient Cert. of Recognition, NASA, 1991—2008, Space Act award, 1994, 1997, 2002, 2007, Spaceflight Awareness award, 2001, Exceptional Achievement medal, Achievement awards, Jet Propulsion Lab., 1996—2008. Mem.: Electrochem. Soc. (chair 1998—2000, mem., energy tech. divsn.). Achievements include patents for alkali metal thermal to electric converter; micro-scale thermoelectric elements; JPL electronic nose; photo electrochemical conversion of solar energy to electricity; development of polymer-carbon composite chemical sensors; electronic nose, air quality monitor for space habitat. Office: Jet Propulsion Lab 4800 Oak Grove Dr Pasadena CA 91109

RYAN, MARIANNE ELIZABETH, lawyer; b. Ft. Knox, Ky., Nov. 15, 1964; d. John L. and Frances J. (McIntosh) R. BA, Trinity Coll., Hartford, Conn., 1986; JD, Yale U., New Haven, Conn., 1991; MS in Info., U. Mich., Ann Arbor, 2003, grad. cert. in Sci., Tech. and Soc., 2006. Bar: Ill. 1991, US Dist. Ct. (no. dist.) Ill. 1991. Assoc. Pattishall, McAuliffe, Newbury, Hilliard & Geraldson, Chgo., 1991—93; internet editor Law Jour. EXTRA! The N.Y. Law Pub. Co., NYC, 1994—95; rsch. scholar Nat. Ctr. for Philanthropy and Law NYU Sch. Law, 1996—99; coord. tech. Americorps/Project F.I.R.S.T., NYC, 1999—2000; VISTA svc. leader Americorps/Ohio Campus Compact, Yellow Springs, 2000—01; resident fellow Lloyd Hall Scholars Program, U. Mich., Ann Arbor, 2002—03, Cmty. Info. fellow Alliance for Cmty. Tech., 2002—06, mem. behavioral sci. instl. rev. bd., 2006—08. Adj. prof. trademark and copyright law John Marshall Law Sch., Chgo., 1993. Exec. editor Yale Jour. on Regulation. Recipient Margaret Mann award, Sch. of Info., U. Mich., 2003; Olin fellow, U. Mich. Law Sch., 2004—05, Rackham Regents' fellow, U. Mich., 2004—07, 2009—, Jacob Javits fellow, U.S. Dept. Edn., 2005—09, Margaret Dow Towsley scholar, U. Mich., 2001—02, USA Funds Access to Edn. scholar, 2005—09, Microsoft summer fellow, U Mich., 2002. Mem.: ABA, Woodhull Inst. Ethical Leadership, Assn. Internet Rschrs., Assn. Practical and Profl. Ethics, Phi Beta Kappa. Home: 1150 Paddock Pl Apt 107 Ann Arbor MI 48108 Business E-Mail: meryan@umich.edu.

RYAN, MARK A., museum staff member; BS in Biology, U. Wyo., 1996, BA in History, 1996; MA in Mus. Sci., Texas Tech. U., 1999. Prog. mgr. McWane Ctr., Birmingham, Ala., 1999—2000; curatorial facility certification prog. coord. Tex. Hist. Commn., Austin, Tex., 2005—06; registrar/collections mgr. Plains Art Mus., Fargo, ND, 2000—05, v.p. collections & registration, 2006—. Exhbn. & collections advisor Children's Mus. at Yonkers Farm, ND State U. Mem.: Registrar's Com. of Mountain Plains Mus. Assn. (chmn. 2006—08, ND state rep. 2001—05, vice chmn. 2003—05, interim chmn. 2004), Registrar's Com. of Am. Assn. Musems (nominating com. 2003—04, profl. mentor 2003—, Kay Paris Meml. award 2002, Crozier Fine Arts award 2005), Am. Assn. Museums (Mary Korenic Fund for SPC Leadership & Profl. Devel. award 2004, Nancy Hanks Meml. award for Profl. Excellence 2007, Young Profl. award 2001), Mid-Am. Arts Alliance (adv. panelist for Exhbns. Focus Group 2007), Midwest Art Conservation Ctr. (bd. trustees 2006—), Lake Regions Arts Coun. (bd. dirs. 2006—, pres. bd. dirs. 2007—), Mountain-Plains Mus. Assn. (profl. mentor 2004—, prog. com. 2007, Colo./Wyo. Assn. Museums/Mountain Plains Mus. Assn. purchasing coop.). Office: Plains Art Mus 704 1st Ave N Fargo ND 58102 Office Phone: 701-232-3821 ext. 104. Office Fax: 701-293-1082. E-mail: mryan@plainsart.org.

RYAN, MARLEIGH GRAYER, language educator; b. NYC, May 1, 1930; d. Harry and Betty (Hurwick) Grayer; m. Edward Ryan, June 4, 1950; 1 child, David Patrick. BA, NYU, 1951; MA, Columbia U., 1956; postgrad., Kyoto U., 1958-59; PhD, Columbia U., 1965, cert. in Japanese Lit., 1968. Research assoc. Columbia U., NYC, 1960-61, lectr. Japanese, 1961-65, asst. prof., 1965-70, assoc. prof., 1970-72; vis. asst. prof. Yale U., New Haven, 1966-67; assoc. prof. U. Iowa, Iowa City, 1972-75, prof., 1975-81, chmn. dept., 1972-81; prof. Japanese SUNY, New Paltz, 1981-98, dean liberal arts and scis., 1981-90, prof. emeritus, 1999—; assoc. in rsch. Reischauer Inst. for Japanese Studies Harvard U., Cambridge, Mass., 1999—, chair study group on Asian Am. Lit., 2000—02; study group leader Harvard Inst., 2003—. Vice chmn. seminar on modern Japan, Columbia U., 1984-85, chmn., 1985-86; co-chmn. N.Y. State Conf. on Asian Studies, 1986, editor, 1993-99, mem. exec. com., 1993-96, sec., 1993-99, co-chmn., 1998. Co-author: (with Herschel Webb) Research in Japanese Sources, 1965; author: Japan's First Modern Novel, 1967, The Development of Realism in the Fiction of Tsubouchi Shoyo, 1975; assoc. editor: Jour. Assn. Tchrs. Japanese, 1962-71, editor, 1971-75. East Asian Inst. fellow Columbia U., 1955; Ford Found. fellow, 1958-60; Japan Found. fellow, 1973, Woodrow Wilson Ctr. Internat. Scholars fellow, 1988-89; recipient Van. Am. Disting. Book award Columbia, 1968 Mem. MLA (sec. com. on teaching Japanese Lang. 1962-68, mem. del. assembly 1979-87, mem. exec. com. div. Asian lit. 1981-86), Assn. Tchrs. Japanese (exec. com. 1969-72, 74-77), Assn. Asian Studies (bd. dirs. 1975-78, N.E. asian coun. 1975-78, coun. of confs., 1993-96), Midwest Conf. Asian Studies (pres. 1980-81) Business E-Mail: marleighryan@comcast.net. *Studying the most difficult language in the world has taught me patience and tact. One learns what it is to sit completely still at the Japanese No theatre and absorb wondrous sights and sounds in an atmosphere of absolute peace. Discovering the stillness in movement is perhaps the most important lesson we in the West can derive from our Asian experience.*

RYAN, MATT (MATTHEW THOMAS RYAN), professional football player; b. Exton, Pa., May 17, 1985; s. Michael and Bernice Ryan. BS in Mgmt., Boston Coll., 2007. Quaterback Atlanta Falcons, 2008—. Recipient Johnny Unitas Golden Arm award, 2007, Manning award, Sugar Bowl Com., 2007; named MVP, MPC Computers Bowl, 2005, Player of Yr., Atlantic Coast Conf., 2007, NFL Offensive Rookie of the Yr., AP, 2008. Achievements include being the third overall pick by the Atlanta Falcons in the NFL Draft, 2008. Office: Atlanta Falcons 4400 Falcon Pky Flowery Branch GA 30542*

RYAN, MEG (MARGARET MARY EMILY ANN HYRA), actress, film producer; b. Fairfield, Conn., Nov. 19, 1961; m. Dennis Quaid, Feb. 14, 1991 (div. July 16, 2001); 1 child, Jack Henry; 1 adopted child, Daisy True. Student, NYU. Established Fandango Films (then called Prufrock Pictures), 1994—2000. Mem. of jury Festival Internat. de Cannes, 2003. Appearences include (TV) One of the Boys, 1982, As The World Turns, 1982-84, Wild Side, 1985, (films) Rich and Famous, 1981, Amityville 3-D, 1983, Top Gun, 1986, Armed and Dangerous, 1986, Innerspace, 1987, Promised Land, 1987, D.O.A., 1988, The Presidio, 1988, When Harry Met Sally, 1989, Joe Versus the Volcano, 1990, The Doors, 1991, Prelude to a Kiss, 1992, Sleepless in Seattle, 1993, Flesh and Bone, 1993, When a Man Loves a Woman, 1994, Restoration, 1994, I.Q., 1994, French Kiss, 1995 (also prodr.), Two for the Road, 1996 (also prodr.), Courage Under Fire, 1996, Addicted to Love, 1997, Anastasia (voice), 1997, City of Angels, 1998, Hurlyburly, 1998, You've Got Mail, 1998, Hanging Up, 2000, Proof of Life, 2000, Kate & Leopold, 2001, In the Cut, 2003, Against the Ropes, 2004, In the Land of Women, 2007, The Deal, 2008, My Mom's New Boyfriend, 2008, The Women, 2008; prodr. Lost Souls, 2000, Desert Saints, 2002; exec. prodr. Northern Lights, 1997, The Wedding Planner, 2001. Vol. CARE humanitarian orgn. Recipient Golden Apple award Hollywood Women's Press Club, 1989, Woman of Yr. award Hasty Pudding Theatricals, 1994, ShoWest Conv. Actress of Yr. award, 1999, Am. Comedy Award, 1990, 1994, Women in Film Crystal Award, 1995, Bambi Lifetime Achievement award, 2008; named one of the Top 100 Movie Stars of All Time, Empire (UK) Magazine, 1997, The Most Powerful People in Hollywood, Premiere (USA) Magazine, 1999, Most Powerful People in Hollywood, Entertainment Weekly's, 1998. Office: Creative Artists Agency 2000 Avenue Of The Stars Los Angeles CA 90067-4700

RYAN, MELBAGENE T., retired food service and nutrition director; b. Arkadelphia, Ark., Jan. 6, 1927; d. Horace Samuel and Eunice Bridges (Moorman) Tull; m. Wayne Stuart Ryan, Dec. 26, 1954. BS in Edn., Henderson U., 1948; M in Edn., Tex. Women's U., 1951. Tchr. Eudora Pub. Schs., Ark., 1948-52; dir. food services Tex. Christian U., Ft. Worth, 1952-53, Tex. Women's U., 1953-58; dir. food and nutriton service Irving Ind. Sch. Dist., Tex., 1958-85. Project dir. to develop stds. excellence with a self study and evaluation Tex. Sch. Food Svc. Assn., 1985-88; cons. in field. Co-author and project dir.: (with others) Youth Advisory Council Resource Manual, 1978-79, Effective Food Service Management Using Computers, 1982. With child nutrition Tex. Sch. Food Svc. Assn., Washington, 1974-79; with legis. Am. Sch. Food Svc. Assn., Irving, 1980-85; mem. Denton Co. Hist. Commn., 1997—, Denton Co. Courthouse-on-the Square Mus., chmn. 1998—; mem. adv. bd. Lake Forest Good Samaritan Village, 1998—, Tex. Woman's U. Centennial Celebration, 2001, planning com., 1998-99, Denton Good Samaritan Village, 2003; chmn. Bayless Selby House Mus., 2002—. Recipient Food Facilities Design award Instns. Volume Feeding Awards Program, New Orleans, 1977, Trend Setter award, North Tex. Brokers Assn., Dallas, 1978; Melbagene Ryan Scholarship named in her honor by Dallas Profl. Friends, 1985. Mem. Denton Dietetic Assn. (pres. 1977-78), Tex. Dietetic Assn., Am. Dietetic Assn. (chmn. joint com. 1979-82), Tex. Sch. Food Svc. Assn. (pres. 1975-76, nutrition edn. 1975), Am. Sch. Food Svc. Assn. (conf. com. 1977-78, 1982-83), Tex. Women's U. Alumni Assn. Methodist.

RYAN, MICHAEL D., state supreme court justice; BA, St. John's U., Collegeville, Minn., 1967; JD, Ariz. State U., 1977. Dep. county atty. Maricopa County Atty.'s Office, 1977—85; judge pro tempore Superior Ct. State of Ariz., Maricopa County, 1985—86, judge Maricopa County, 1986—96, assoc. criminal presiding judge Maricopa County, 1993—96; judge Ariz. Ct. Appeals, Divsn. 1, 1996—2002, vice chief judge, 2001—02; justice Ariz. Supreme Ct., 2002—. Chair Scottsdale Jud. Appts. Adv. Bd., 1999—2002; vice chair Ariz. State Bar Task Force on Persons with Disabilities, 2002—; mem. Maricopa County Resource Site Team for Ctr. for Sex Offender Mgmt., 1996—2000, Ariz. Atty. Gen.'s Capital Case Commn., 2000—02; mem. adv. com. Nat. Ctr. for State Cts., Ctr. for Effective Pub. Policy, also State Justice Inst.'s Nat. Solutions Project, 2003—; chair Ariz. Supreme Ct. Com. on Keeping Record, 2004—. Infantry platoon comdr. USMC, 1968, Vietnam. Recipient Semper Fi award, First Marine Divsn. Assn., Phoenix chpt., 2001, Outstanding Alumnus award, Ariz. State Univ. Coll. Law, 2003, Disting. Achievement award, 2003, James A. Walsh Outstanding Jurist award, State Bar Ariz., 2005. Mem.: State Bar of Arizona (Judicial award of Excellence 2001), Maricopa County Bar Assn. (bd. dirs. 1987—91, 1997—2002, chair task force recruitment and retention of women and minorities 1997—2004, Henry S. Stevens Judge of the Yr. award 2001). Office: Ariz Supreme Ct 1501 W Washington Phoenix AZ 85007-3231*

RYAN, NOLAN, professional baseball team executive, former professional baseball player; b. Refugio, Tex., Jan. 31, 1947; s. Lynn Nolan and Martha (Hancock) Ryan; m. Ruth Elsie Holdruff, June 26, 1967; children: Reid, Reese, Wendy. Student, Alvin Jr. Coll., Tex., 1966—69. Pitcher NY Mets, NYC, 1966, 1968—71, Calif. Angels, 1972—79, Houston Astros, 1980—88, Tex. Rangers, 1989—93, pres., 2008—. Cattle rancher, China Grove, Ray and Gonzalvez, Tex.; owner Bass Inn, Waterfront Steakhouse and Grill, Round Rock Express (Pacific Coast League AAA team), Tex., Corpus Christi Hooks (Houston Astros AA team), 2004—; investor, ptnr. Express Bank Tex., 2003—. Co-author (with Steve Jacobson): Nolan Ryan: Strike-Out King, 1975; co-author: (with Bill Libby) Nolan Ryan: The Other Game, 1977; co-author: (with Joe Torre) Pitching and Hitting, 1977; co-author: (with Harvey Frommer) Throwing Heat: The Autobiography of Nolan Ryan, 1988; co-author: (with Tom House) Nolan Ryan's Pitcher's Bible, 1991; co-author: (with Jerry Jenkins) Miracle Man: Nolan Ryan, The Autobiography, 1992; co-author: (with others) Kings of Hill, 1992. Founder, bd. dirs. Nolan Ryan Found.; commr. Tex. Pks. and Wildlife Commn., 1995—2001, vice chmn., 1995—97; bd. dirs. Justin Cowboy Crisis Fund, Tex. Water Found., Natural Resources Found., Tex. With AUS, 1967. Named Am. League Pitcher of Yr., Sporting News, 1977; named to Am. League All-Star Team, 1972—73, 1975, 1977, 1979, Nat. League All-Star Team, 1981, 1985, 1989, Baseball Hall of Fame, 1999. Achievements include holding over 53 Major League records including most seasons pitched (27), most strikeouts (5,714) and most no-hit games (7); being the only Major League Baseball player to have his uniform retired by three different teams, the Angels, Astros and Rangers; holding Guinness Book of World Records for throwing the fastest baseball pitched (100.9 miles per hour). Office: Tex Rangers Rangers Ballpark Arlington 1000 Ballpark Way Arlington TX 76011

RYAN, PAUL, United States Representative from Wisconsin; b. Janesville, Wis., Jan. 29, 1970; s. Paul and Betty Ryan; m. Janna Ryan; 3 children. BS in Econs. and Polit. Sci., Miami U., Ohio, 1992. Aide Staff of US Senator Bob Kasten of Wis., Washington; econ. adv., speechwriter Empower Am., Jack Kemp, Bill Bennett, Washington; legis. dir. US Senate, Washington; mktg. cons. Ryan Inc., Ctrl., Janesville; mem. US Congress from 1st Wis. dist., 1999—, mem. ways and means com., mem. joint econ. com., mem. budget com. Mem.: Janesville YMCA, Janesville Bowmen Inc. Republican. Roman Catholic. Office: US House Reps 1113 Longworth House Office Bldg Washington DC 20515 Office Phone: 202-225-3031.*

RYAN, PETER, computer systems network executive; Sys. engr. IBM, dir. engring. tech. solutions Europe, Middle East and Africa (EMEA) divsn. v.p. Europe Parametric Tech.; pres. European ops. Aspect Devel., Zurich, 1999—2000; chmn. privately owned tech. co., 2000—06; sr. v.p. global sales & services (GSS) Europe, Middle East & Africa (EMEA) Sun Microsystems, Inc., 2006—07, sr. v.p. global sales Americas Region, 2007—08, exec. v.p. global sales & services, 2008—. Chmn. bd. eLateral Ltd., Wesupply Ltd., CopperEye, San Francisco, 2004. Office: Sun Microsystems Inc 4150 Network Cir Santa Clara CA 95054 Office Phone: 950-960-1300. Office Fax: 650-786-4557.

RYAN, RAY DARL, JR., academic administrator; b. Joliet, Ill., Dec. 2, 1945; s. Ray D. and Oral Ada (Smiley) R.; m. Marianne Rossetto, Aug. 28, 1965; children: Kimberley, Kristin, Matthew. BS, U. Wis., Menomonie, 1970; MEd, U. Mo., 1973, EdD, 1975; Doctorate (hon.), Tomsk Poly. Inst., Russia, 1992. Cert. vocat./tech. tchr., adminstr., chief sch. officer. Dep. supt. pub. instrn. Nev. Dept. Edn., Carson City; dep. supt. spl. programs Ariz. Dept. Edn., Phoenix, state dir., vocat. educator; exec. dir. Ctr. Edn. and Tng. for Employment Ohio State U., Columbus, assoc. dean rsch., internat. affairs. Bd. dirs., vice-chair Coun. Ednl. Devel. and Rsch.; pres., CEO Nat. Occup. Testing Inst., 1999. Mem. OTT, ASTD, Phi Delta Kappa, Epsilon Pi Tau, Omicron Tau Theta. Office: NOCTI 500 N Bronson Ave Big Rapids MI 49307 Home: 999 Tahoe Blvd Incline Village NV 89451-9500

RYAN, RAYMOND D., retired steel and insurance company executive; b. Big Timber, Mont., Feb. 7, 1922; s. Robert Allen and Elsie (Beery) R.; m. Dale Burnett, Jan. 17, 1943; children: Raymond Brant, Brenda Ruth, Ronald Dale. BA, U. Mont., Missoula, 1948, JD (hon.), 1970; LLM, NYU, 1949. Bar: Mont. 1948. Various fin. officer positions U.S. Steel and subsidiaries in U.S. and Venezuela, 1949-75; v.p., treas. U.S. Steel, 1975-83; pres. The Evergreen Group Inc., Stamford, Conn., 1984-94, chmn., 1995-96, Evergreen Benefits Inc., 1996-99, The Money Suite Co., Missoula, Mont., 1999—. With mil. police AUS, 1943-45, ETO. Mem. ABA, Met. Club (N.Y.C.), Phi Sigma Kappa, Phi Delta Phi. Home: PO Box 160601 Big Sky MT 59716-0601 Office Phone: 406-995-3397. Personal E-mail: raydryan@gmail.com. *Although luck and ambition are the basis of many apparently successful careers, true success comes from hard work, ethical relationships, dedication, and a willingness to accept responsibility.*

RYAN, REGINA CLAIRE (MRS. PAUL DEUTSCHMAN), editor, literary agent; b. NYC, June 19, 1938; d. Edward F.X. and Kathryn Regina (Gallagher) R.; m. Paul Deutschman, Apr. 11, 1970 (widowed, 2002). BA, Trinity Coll., 1960; postgrad., New Sch. for Social Research, 1960-61, N.Y. U. Film Sch., 1961, N.Y. U. Grad. Sch. English, 1962-63. Copywriter trainee, sec. J. Walter Thompson Co., NYC, 1960-64; asst. to mng. editor Alfred A. Knopf, Inc., NYC, 1964-67, editor, 1967-75; editor-in-chief, v.p. Gen. Books div. Macmillan Pub. Co., NYC, 1975-76; pres. Regina Ryan Pub. Enterprises, Inc., NYC, 1976—. Co-author: Janice LaRouche's Strategies for Women at Work, 1984, 1987. Active Larchmont-Mamaroneck Young Reps., 1960-64; campaign worker, speech writer mayoralty campaign, Larchmont, 1962, 64; mem. Manhattan Women's Polit. Caucus, 1972-74; mem. com. Jimmy Carter Presdl. Campaign; mem., chmn. Sherman Dem. Town Com., Conn., 1985-86; mem. Jewish Cmty. Ctr. for Sherman, 1998-2001; Justice of the Peace, Sherman, 1986-96. Mem. AARP, PEN Am. Ctr., Women's Media Group, Agts. Roundtable, Assn. Authors Reps., Internat. Women's Com. on Human Rights, Linnaean Soc. NY, NY Audubon Soc., NY Mycological Soc., Vet. Feminists Am. Democrat. Home and Office: 251 Central Park W New York NY 10024-4134 Office Phone: 212-787-5589.

RYAN, REX, professional football coach; b. Ardmore, Okla., Dec. 13, 1962; s. Buddy and Doris (Ward) Ryan; m. Michelle Ryan; children: Payton, Seth. Attended, Southwestern Okla. State U., Weatherford; BS in Phys. Edn., Ea. Ky. U., Richmond, MS in Phys. Edn., 1988. Defensive end coach Ea. Ky. U. Colonels, 1987—88; asst. head coach, defensive coord. N.Mex. Highlands U. Cowboys, 1989; defensive coord. Morehead State U. Eagles, 1990—93; defensive line coach Ariz. Cardinals, 1994, linebackers coach, 1995; defensive coord. U. Cin. Bearcats, 1996—97, U. Okla. Sooners, 1998; defensive asst. coach Balt. Ravens, 1999—2004, defensive coord., 2005—09, asst. head coach, 2008—09; head football coach NY Jets, 2009—. Hon. bd. mem. Md. Spl. Olympics. Named NFL Asst. Coach of Yr., Pro Football Weekly, Pro Football Writers Assn., 2006. Achievements include member of Super Bowl XXXV Championship winning Baltimore Ravens, 2001. Office: NY Jets 1000 Fulton Ave Hempstead NY 11550*

RYAN, ROBERT DAVIS, lawyer; b. Lynbrook, NY, Aug. 14, 1941; s. Thomas Francis and Agnes Frances (Davis) R.; children: John, Daniel, Carolyn. BBA, St. John's U., 1962; JD, Fordham U., 1972. Bar: N.Y. 1973, U.S. Dist. Ct. (so. and ea. dists.) N.Y. 1973, U.S. Ct. Appeals (2d cir.) 1975, U.S. Supreme Ct. 1984. Asst. dist. atty. Westchester County, White Plains, N.Y., 1972-77; assoc. Clark, Gagliardi & Miller, White Plains, 1977-82; ptnr. Rende, Ryan & Downes, White Plains, 1982—. Adj. prof. law St. John's U., 1992-95, 99—. Chmn. Cable TV Adv. Com., Lewisboro, N.Y., 1983-99. Mem. Assn. Trial Lawyers Am., N.Y. State Trial Lawyers Assn., Westchester County Bar Assn., N.Y. State Bar Assn. (continuing legal edn. com. trial lawyers sect.), No. Westchester Bar Assn. (bd, govs. 1987-92, pres. 1986-87), White Plains Bar Assn. Republican. Roman Catholic. Home: 1039 Rt 35 Cross River NY 10518 Office: Rende Ryan & Downes 202 Mamaroneck Ave Ste 600 White Plains NY 10601-5312 Business E-Mail: rryan@rrd-law.com.

RYAN, ROBERT KEVIN, legislative staff member; Chief of staff to Rep. Joe Moakley US House of Reps., Washington, 1997—2000, profl. staff, rules com., chief of staff to Rep. Stephen Lynch, 2001—. Fellow, Stennis Ctr. Pub. Svc. Leadership. Democrat. Office: 221 Cannon House Office Bldg Washington DC 20515 Office Phone: 202-225-8273. Office Fax: 202-225-3984.*

RYAN, SHELLI ANN, public relations executive; b. Blair, Nebr., Dec. 8, 1968; d. Gorlyn Lew and Ruthie Ann Hagerbaumer; m. Mark Anthony Ryan, Sept. 26, 1992. BS, Bellevue U., 1992; MPA, U. Okla., 1997. Accredited Pub. Rels., Pub. Rels. Soc. Am. Mgr. mktg. svcs. Electronic Display Sys., Grand Island, Nebr., 1988-90; mktg. rep. Keeler/Raynor/Hinz, Bellevue, Nebr., 1990-92; mktg. coord. Accent Svc. Co., Omaha, 1992-95; corp. comm. specialist Applied Comm., Inc., Omaha, 1995-96; prin. Ryan Designs, Omaha, 1996-98; pres. Ad Hoc Comm. Resources, Omaha, 1999—. Media spokesperson Am. Heart Assn., Omaha, 1990-95; pub. rels. judge Jr. Achievement, Omaha, 1990, 96. Recipient 40 under 40 award Midlands Bus. Jour., 2002; named Woman Yr. Am. Women's Bus. Assn., Omaha, 1996, Gold Citation of Excellence, Am. Mktg. Assn., 2004, Best of Show and Pinnacle award Am. Mktg. Assn., 2002, Profl. Achievement award Am. Women's Assn., 2005, Bronze award Vision awards League Am. Comms. Profls., 2005. Mem. Pub. Rels. Soc. Am. (sec. 1998, treas. 1997, pres. 2001, dir. 1996—), Am. Bus. Women's Assn. (pres. 1995-96, Profl. Achievement award 2005). Avocations: weightlifting, bicycling. Home: 6 Benevolo Dr Henderson NV 89011-3134

RYAN, STEPHEN M., lawyer; s. Alex L. Ryan and Lynda A. Turner; m. Christine M. Ryan, Dec. 31, 1988; children: Travis A., Caroline A., Taylor R. BA, U. Tex., 1988; JD with honors, U. Mich., 1997. Bar: Tex. 1997. B-52 navigator/electronic warfare officer USAF, 1988—94, active duty law student Ann Arbor, Mich., 1994—97, asst. staff judge adv. Barksdale AFB, La., 1997—2002; atty. Nathan Sommers Jacobs & Gorman, Houston, 2002—05, LeBoeuf, Lamb, Greene & MacRae LLP, Houston, 2005—07, Dewey & LeBoeuf LLP, Houston, 2007—; staff judge adv. 147th Fighter Wing, Tex. Air N.G., Houston, 2002—08, HQ Tex. Air Nat. Guard, 2008—. With Boys Scout America, Eagle Scout, 1982. Maj. USAF, 1988—2002, lt. col. Tex. ANG, USAFR, 2004—08, col., 2009—. Decorated Achievement medal USAF, Commendation medal, Meritorious Svc. medal, Air medal US Ctrl. Command, Humanitarian Svc. medal; recipient Corpus Juris Secundum award, Torts, 1995. Mem.: Res. Officers Assn., VFW, Delta Sigma Phi. Roman Catholic. Avocations: scouting, world travel, aviation. Office: Dewey & LeBoeuf LLP 1000 Main St Ste 2550 Houston TX 77002 Office Fax: 713-287-2100. Business E-Mail: sryan@dL.com.

RYAN, SYLVESTER DONOVAN, bishop emeritus; b. Catalina Island, Calif., Sept. 3, 1930; Grad., St. John's Sem., Camarillo, Calif. Ordained priest Archdiocese of LA, Calif., 1957, aux. bishop, 1990—92; ordained bishop, 1990; bishop Diocese of Monterey, Calif., 1992—2006, bishop emeritus, 2006—. Roman Catholic. Office: Chancery Office PO Box 2048 631 Abrego St Monterey CA 93940-3203 Office Phone: 831-373-4345. Office Fax: 831-373-1175.

RYAN, T. TIMOTHY (THOMAS TIMOTHY RYAN JR.), securities industry association executive; b. Washington, June 13, 1945; s. Thomas Timothy and Elizabeth (Ockershausen) R.; m. Judith Rush, June 13, 1970; children: Kathryn, Michael. AB, Villanova U., Pa., 1967; JD, Am. U., 1973. Bar: D.C. 1973. Atty. NLRB, Washington, 1973-74, Balt. and Washington, 1974-75, 76-80; dep. gen. counsel Pres. Ford Com., 1975-76; solicitor US Dept. Labor, 1981-83; assoc. Reed, Smith, Shaw & McClay LLP (formerly Pierson, Ball & Dowd), Washington, 1978—81, ptnr., 1983—90; dir. Office Thrift Supervision US Dept. Treasury, Washington, 1990-93; mng. dir. Global Govt. Institutions Group then vice chmn. investment banking for fin. institutions & govt. JP Morgan Chase & Co., NYC, 1993—2008; pres., CEO Securities Industry & Fin. Markets Assn., NYC, 2008—. Adj. prof. Georgetown U. Law Sch., 1979-83; mem. bd. overseas Pvt. Investment Corp., 1981-83; mem. bd. Program for Advancement of Tech. in India, 1985-90; bd. dirs. FDIC, Resolution Trust Corp., Neighborhood Re-investment Corp., 1990-93. 1st lt. USAR, 1967-70. 1st lt. USAR, 1967-70. Mem. ABA, D.C. Bar Assn., Am. Coun. Young Polit. Leaders (bd. dirs. 1983-89, pres. 1985-88), Congl. Country Club, Army and Navy, Deepdale. Republican. Roman Catholic. Office: Securities Industry & Fin Markets Assn 120 Broadway 35th Fl New York NY 10271 Office Phone: 212-313-1053. Business E-Mail: tryan@sifma.org.

RYAN, TERRY, professional sports team executive; b. Janesville, Wis., Oct. 26, 1953; m. Karilyn Ryan; children: Tim, Kathleen. Diploma in Phys. Edn., U. Wis., 1979. Profl. baseball player Minn. Twins, 1972-76, scouting dir., 1986-91, v.p. player pers., asst. gen. mgr., 1991-94, v.p., baseball pers., asst. gen. mgr., 1994, v.p., gen. mgr., 1994—2007, sr. adv. to gen. mgr., 2007—; profl. scout NY Mets, 1980-86. Named MLB Exec. of Yr., The Sporting News, 2002, 2006. Office: Minnesota Twins 34 Kirby Puckett Pl Minneapolis MN 55415-1596 Office Phone: 612-375-1366.

RYAN, THOMAS F., lawyer; b. Detroit, Nov. 4, 1943; BS, Ferris State U., 1965; JD magna cum laude, Wayne State U., 1971. Bar: Ill. 1972, US Ct. of Appeals (7th cir.) 1972, US Dist. Ct. (no. dist.) Ill. 1972, U.S. Supreme Ct. 1978. Joined Sidley & Austin (now Sidley Austin, LLP), Chgo., 1972—; ptnr. antitrust and bus. counseling Sidley Austin, LLP, Chgo., 1978—. Exec. com. Sidley Austin, LLP; adv. com. on cir. rules 7th Fed. Ct. Appeals. 1st lt. U.S. Army, 1966-68. Decorated Bronze star. Fellow Am. Coll. Trial Lawyers; mem. Chgo. Bar Assn. (mem. jud. evaluation com.), 7th Cir. Bar Assn. (bd. govs. 1986-89, 2nd v.p. 1990-91, pres. 1991-92). Office: Sidley Austin LLP 1 S Dearborn St Chicago IL 60603 Office Phone: 312-853-7497. Office Fax: 312-853-7036. Business E-Mail: tryan@sidley.com.

RYAN, THOMAS L., funeral company executive; BBA, U. Tex. CPA PricewaterhouseCoopers, 1988—96; fin. mgmt. positions Service Corp. Internat., Houston, 1996—2000, CEO European ops., 2000—02, pres. & COO, 2002—05, pres. & CEO, 2005—. Mem.: Young Presidents Org. Office: Service Corporation Internat 1929 Allen Pkwy Houston TX 77019

RYAN, THOMAS MICHAEL (TOM RYAN), pharmaceutical company executive; b. Patterson, NJ, Aug. 15, 1952; m. Cathy H. Ryan; 4 children. BS in Pharmacy, U. RI, 1975. Joined CVS Corp., Woonsocket, RI, from 1975, numerous managerial positions v.p. pharmacy ops., sr. v.p. pharmacy, 1988—90, exec. v.p. stores, 1990—96; pres., CEO CVS Pharmacy, Inc. (then part of Melville Corp.), Woonsocket, RI, 1993—96; vice chmn., COO CVS Corp., Woonsocket, RI, 1996—98, pres., CEO, 1998—2007, chmn., 1999—2007; pres., CEO CVS Caremark Corp., Woonsocket, RI, 2007, chmn., pres., CEO, 2007—. Bd. dirs. CVS Caremark Corp., 1996-, FleetBoston Financial Corp., 1997-2004, Bank of America Corp., 2004-, Yum Brands!, Inc., 2002- Office: CVS Caremark Corp One CVS Dr Woonsocket RI 02895*

RYAN, TIMOTHY ANDREW, literature and language professor; b. Bath, Avon, Eng., Jan. 3, 1971; s. Thomas and Susan Mary Ryan; m. Dee Anna Phares, Jan. 13, 2007. BA in Am. Studies, U. Reading, Eng., 1993; MA in English, U. Nev., 2000, PhD in English, 2004. Lectr., Am. studies King's Coll. London, 2004—06; lectr., english U. Nev., Reno, 2006—07; asst. prof., english Northern Ill. U., Dekalb, 2007—. Author: (book) Calls and Responses: The American Novel of Slavery since Gone with the Wind (Jules and Frances Landry award, 2008); contbr. articles to profl. jours. Office: Northern Ill Univ Dept English Reavis Hall Dekalb IL 60115 Office Phone: 815-753-3236. Business E-Mail: tryan@niu.edu.

RYAN, TIMOTHY E., publishing executive; b. Rochester, NY, 1959; m. Trish Ryan; children: Tim, Kelly. B. in Polit. Sci., U. Notre Dame; MBA, Northwestern U. Kellogg Sch. Mgmt. Circulation mgr. Chgo. Tribune, 1982—93, v.p. circulation & consumer mktg., 2005—07; v.p. circulation Phila. Inquirer, Phila. Daily News, 1993—2000; v.p. ops. & circulation Balt. Sun, 2000—05, pub. & CEO, 2007—. Recipient Tribune Co. Mgmt. award, 1992. Office: Baltimore Sun Co 501 N Calvert St PO Box 1377 Baltimore MD 21278 Office Phone: 410-332-6000.*

RYAN, TIMOTHY J., United States Representative from Ohio; b. Niles, Ohio, July 16, 1973; s. Rochelle Ryan. Student, Youngstown State U.; BA in Polit. Sci., Bowling Green State U., 1995; JD, Franklin Pierce Law Ctr., Concord, NH, 2000. Congl. aide Staff of US Rep. James A. Traficant of Ohio, 1995—97; intern Trumbull County Prosecutor's Office; mem. Ohio State Senate from 32nd dist., Columbus, 2001—02, US Congress from 17th Ohio dist., 2003—, mem. appropriations com., co-chair Mfg. Caucus, mem. Dem. steering and policy com. Recipient Legis. Leadership award for domestic mfg., US Bus. and Industry Coun., 2004, Friend of Nat. Pks. award, Nat. Pks. Conservation Assn., 2005. Mem.: Internat. Narcotic Enforcement Officers Assn., Ancient Order Hibernians, Sons of Italy, Elks. Democrat. Office: 197 W Market St Warren OH 44481 Office Phone: 202-225-5261, 330-373-0074. Office Fax: 330-373-0098.*

RYAN, UNA SCULLY, health science association administrator, medical educator; b. Kuala Lumpur, Malaysia, Dec. 18, 1941; d. Henry and Amy (Yee) Scully; m. Allan Dana Callow, May 26, 1989; children: Tamsin Randlett, Amy Jean Susan Ryan. BSc in Zoology, Chemistry & Microbiology, Bristol U., Eng., 1963; PhD in Cell Biology, Cambridge U., Eng., 1968. Fellow dept. biology U. Va., Charlottesville, 1964-66; fellow dept. medicine U. Miami, Fla., 1966-67, adj. asst. prof. biology Fla., 1968-71; dir. lab. for ultrastructure studies Howard Hughes Med. Inst., Miami, 1967-71; from instr. to assoc. prof. medicine U. Miami Sch. Medicine, 1967-80, prof. medicine, 1980-89; sr. scientist Papanicolaou Cancer Rsch. Inst., Miami, 1972-77; rsch. prof. surgery Washington U. Sch. Medicine, St. Louis, 1990—; dir. health scis. Monsanto Co., St. Louis, 1990-93; pres., CEO T Cell Scis., Needham, Mass., 1993-98; rsch. prof. medicine Boston U. Sch. Medicine, 1993—; pres., CEO AVANT Immunotherapeutics, Needham, Mass., 1998—. Dir. course W. Alton Jones Cell Sci. Ctr., 1979-81; dir. Hybridoma Facility, U. Miami, 1986-89; chair local organizing com. Internat. Coun. on Thrombosis and Hemostasis, 1984; chair Rev. Com. for Extracellular Matrix Interactions in Lung, 1983; chair various revs. NHLBI; chair Mass. Biotech. Coun., 2004-06; mem. various rev. and adv. coms.; bd. dirs. Albany Molecular Rsch. Inc., 2006- Author: J. Tissue Culture Methods, 1987, Pulmonary Endothelium in Health Disease, 1987, Endothelial Cells, 1988, Vascular Endothelium: Receptors and Transduction Mechanisms, 1989; editor: Tissue & Cell, 1981-87; rev. editor: In Vitro, 1986; reviewer profl. jours.; contbr. articles to profl. jours. UK state scholar, 1960, Country Major scholar, 1960; D.S.I.R. rsch. fellow, 1964, 65, Ethel Sargant Rsch. fellow, 1964-65, Sci. Rsch. Coun. fellow, 1966; recipient Louis and Artur Lucian award for rsch. in circulatory diseases, 1984, Merit award Nat. Heart, Lung and Blood Inst., 1986, Lillie award Woods Hole, Marine Bill, Lab., 1989, Order of Brit. Empire, 2002. Mem. Am. Soc. Cell Biology, Soc. Neurosci., Tissue Culture Assn., Internat. Soc. Heart Rsch., Am. Heart Assn. (coun. on basic rsch., coun. on circulation, cardiopulmonary coun.), Am. Physiol. Soc., Am. Microcirculatory Soc., European Soc. Microcirculation, Am. Thoracic Soc. (dir. course on culture of pulmonary endothelial cells), Internat. Soc. Applied Cardiovascular Biology, N.Y. Acad. Scis., Fla. Soc. Electron Microscopy, Sigma Xi. Office: AVANT Immunotherapeutics 119 4th Ave Needham MA 02494-2725

RYAN, VINCE, lawyer; b. Houston, Aug. 12, 1947; m. Teresa Pamela Rodriguez; 3 children. BA in English, U. Houston, 1969, JD, 1974; MA in History, Rice U., 1979. Bar: Tex. 1974. Assoc. James Patrick Smith, 1974—75, Thomas P. Duncan, Houston, 1975—76, Smith and Conner, Houston, 1976—79, Watrous, Joyce and Ryan, Houston, 1980—81; divsn. chief commrs. ct. divsn. Office of Harris County Atty., Houston, 1981—83, first asst., 1984—88, 2009—; of counsel Sinex & Stephenson, Houston, 1988—95; regional mng. atty. Calame Linebarger, Houston, 1996—98; of counsel Linebarger Goggan, Houston, 1998—2004, Travis Law Firm, Houston, 2004—06; atty. Harris County, 2009—. Dir. legal rsch. svc. U. Houston; adj. faculty U.S. Army Command and Gen. Staff Coll., 1988—. Mem. Dist. C Houston City Coun., 1988—94; alt. City of Houston rep. Houston-Galveston Area Coun., 1989—94; pres. Region 14, Tex. Mcpl. League, 1993—94; bd. dirs. Panama Canal Commn., 1995—99. With US Army, 1969—72, Vietnam, with US Army, 1990, ret. lt. col. USAR. Grad. fellow, 1977—78, Rsch. fellow, 1978—79. Mailing: 3720 Blue Bonnet Houston TX 77025 Office: Office of Harris County Atty 1019 Congress 15th Fl Houston TX 77002 Home Phone: 713-661-1941; Office Phone: 713-755-5101. Office Fax: 713-755-1553. Personal E-mail: vinceryanlaw@aol.com. Business E-Mail: vince.ryan@cao.hctx.net.

RYAN, WILLIAM ARTHUR, mechanical engineer; b. Milw., Nov. 19, 1954; s. Jerome Malachi and Dorothy (Phelps) R. MSME, U. Wis., 1980, MBA, 1981; PhD in Mech. Engring., Ill. Inst. Tech., 1995. Registered profl. engr., Wis. Engr. Philips Physics Lab. (Holland), The Netherlands, 1979, Affiliated Engrs., Madison, Wis., 1981-85, Lockwood Greene, Spartanburg, S.C., 1985-86; program team leader Gas Rsch. Inst., Chgo., 1986—. Lectr. in field. Contbr. over 16 articles to profl. jours.; holder 4 patents. Mem. ASHRAE (program subcom. chmn. 1988-90, sec. 1990-92, vice chmn. absorption com. 1992-94), Tau Beta Pi. Home: 400 N Walnut Ave Wood Dale IL 60191-1549 Office: Gas Rsch Inst 8600 W Bryn Mawr Ave Ste 1100S Chicago IL 60631-3562

RYAN, WILLIAM FRANCIS, priest; b. Renfrew, Ont., Can., Apr. 4, 1925; s. William Patrick Ryan and Helen Mary Doneg BA, Montreal U., 1951; MA in Labor Rels., St. Louis U., 1953; postgrad., Heythrop Coll., Oxon, Eng.; STL, St. Albert Coll., Louvain, 1958; PhD in Econs., Harvard U., 1964. Ordained priest Roman Catholic Ch., 1957. Asst. prof. econs. Loyola Coll., Montreal, Que., Canada, 1963-65; nat. dir. Social Justice Office Can. Conf. Cath. Bishops, Ottawa, Ont., 1964-70, gen. sec., 1984-90; founding dir. Ctr. of Concern, Washington, 1970-78; nat. supr. Jesuit Order, Toronto, Ont., Canada, 1978-84; chancellor Sch. Theology Regis Coll., Toronto, 1978-84; vis. sr. rsch. fellow Can. Inst. for Internat. Peace and Security, Ottawa, 1990-91; chair on Cath. social thought St. Paul U., Ottawa, 1991-92; 2001dir. Jesuit Project on Ethics in Politics, Ottawa, 1992. Exec. sec. Inter-religious Peace Colloquium, Washington, 1975-78; bd. dirs. Roncalli Internat. Found., Montreal, 1979-83, North/South Inst., Ottawa, 1979-91; spl. advisor to Internat. Devel. Rsch. Ctr., Ottawa, 1993-2000; coord. Jesuit Ctr. for Social Faith and Justice, 1997-2007, acting dir. Jesuit Forum Soc. Faith and Justice, 1997-2007; Jolectr. in field. Author: The Clergy and Economic Growth in Quebec, 1966, Culture, Spirituality and Economic Development—Opening a Dialogue, 1995, Our Way of Proceeding, in the Lab, The Temple and The Market: Reflections at the Intersection of Science, Religion and Development, 2000; co-author: Religious as Contemplatives in the 80's, 1984, The Lab, The Temple and The Market: Expanding the Conversation, 2001; translator: The Primacy of Charity in Moral Theology, 1961; co-editor: Globalization and Catholic Social Thought--Present Crisis, Future Hope, 2005; subject of biography Faith and Freedom—The Life and Times of Bill Ryan sj, by Jamie Swift and Bob Chodos, 2002; contbr. articles to profl. jours. Mem. Am. Econs. Assn. Roman Catholic. Avocations: hiking, skiing. Office: 70 Saint Mary St Toronto ON Canada M5S 1J3 Office Phone: 613-730-4569, 416-927-7887. E-mail: wfxrsj@web.ca.

RYANS, JOHN KELLEY, JR., marketing educator; s. John Kelley and Alta Mae Ryans; m. Cynthia Collins, Jan. 5, 1957. AB in Journalism, U. Ky., 1954; MS in Bus. Adminstrn., U. Tenn., 1958; DBA, Ind. U., 1965. Asst. prof. mktg. U. Md., College Park, 1964—68; assoc. prof. mktg. U. Ky., Lexington, 1968—69; prof. mktg. Kent State U., Ohio, 1970—94, Bridgestone prof., 1994—2003, emeritus Bridgestone prof., 2003—; Good chair global strategy Bowling Green State U., Ohio, 2003—04. Vis. prof. internat. bus. Columbia U., NYC, 1977; cons. in field. Co-author (with D. Peebles): The Management of International Advertising, 1983; co-author: (with W. Shanklin) Marketing High Technology, 1984, Thinking Strategically, 1985, Essentials for Marketing High Technology, 1987; co-author: (with J. Baker and D. Howard) International Business Classics, 1988; co-author: Marketing Strategy for New Europe, 1990; co-author: (with S. Paliwoda) International Marketing Reader, 1995; co-author: India Business, 2002, author 11 other books. 1st lt. USAF, 1955—57. Recipient 12-yr, award, No. Ohio US Dist. Export Coun., 2002; named Disting. Scholar, Kent State U., 1999, Ohio Commodore, Gov. of Ohio, 2000. Fellow: Acad. Internat. Bus.; mem.: Am. Mktg. Assn. Found., Cleve. World Trade Assn. (bd. dirs. 1972—2006). Avocations: sports, writing, travel, cruises. Office: Kent State U Coll Bus Dept Mktg Kent OH 44240 Personal E-mail: jkryans@juno.com.

RYBAK, JAMES PATRICK, retired engineering educator; b. Cleve., Mar. 16, 1941; s. John Anthony and Irene Marcella (Kovar) R.; m. Linda Louise Watkins, Oct. 12, 1968. BSEE, Case Western Res. U., 1963; MS, U. N.Mex., 1965; PhD, Colo. State U., 1970. Registered profl. engr., Colo. Mem. tech. staff Sandia Nat. Labs., Albuquerque, 1963-66; rsch. asst., NDEA fellow Colo. State U., Ft. Collins, 1966-70, postdoctoral fellow, 1970-72; prof. engring. and math. Mesa State Coll., Grand Junction, Colo., 1972—2005, asst. v.p. acad. affairs, 1986-88, v.p. acad. affairs, 1988-98, prof. emeritus, 2005—. Contbr. articles to profl. publs. including IEEE Transactions, Engring. Edn., Popular Electronics, Elektrosvyaz (Russia), Radio (Russia). Mem. adv. bd. Grand Mesa Youth Svcs., Grand Junction, 1986-88; bd. dirs. Hilltop Rehab. Hosp., Grand Junction, 1989-93, Salvation Army, Grand Junction, 1993—. NEDA fellow, 1968-70, THEMIS fellow, 1970-72. Mem. IEEE, Am. Soc. Engring. Edn. (vice chmn. Rocky Mountain sect. 1974-75, chmn. 1975-76). Avocation: amateur radio. Home: 314 Quail Dr Grand Junction CO 81507-2527 Business E-Mail: jrybak@bresman.net.

RYBAK, R.T., Mayor, Minneapolis; m. Megan O'Hara; 2 children. BA in Polit. Sci. and Comm., Boston Coll., 1978. Gen. mgr. WCCO TV & WCCO Radio; v.p. Internet Broadcast Sys.; pub., mgr., bus. ops. Twin Cities Reader; mayor City of Minneapolis, Minn., 2001—. Founder, mem. bd. Save the Water in Mpls.; served Minn. Soc. Architects, Night of the Penguin, Hennepin Ave. Adv. Com., Adv. Fedn. Minn., Eiji Oue Inaugural Com.; coach Little League Baseball, Youth Soccer; vol. reader Minn. Pub. Sch.; co-coord. Bill Bradley for Pres., 2000; co-chair Tony Bouza for Gov., 1994; bd. dir. Residents Opposed to Airport Racket. Democrat. Office: City Hall Rm 331 350 S Fifth S Minneapolis MN 55415 Office Phone: 612-673-2700. Office Fax: 612-673-2305.*

RYBCZYK, JOSEPH ANTHONY, physicist, researcher, writer, inventor; b. Phila., Oct. 19, 1935; s. Frank Rybczyk and Isabella Slivak; life ptnr. Dolores Brannan; m. Ruth Diane Menendez, Dec. 30, 1955 (div.); children: Brian Keith, Deborah Gale, Karen Marie. Tech. diploma, DeVry Inst. Tech., Chgo., 1976. Tech. cert. USAF, Air Training Command, Francis E. Warren Air Force Base, Cheyenne, Wyo., 1956, NASA cert. instr./examiner George C. Marshall Space Flight Ctr., Huntsville, Ala., 1965. Various positions Lockheed Martin Tactical Def. Systems, Horsham, Pa., 1959—96; ind. rschr. in theoretical physics, 1996—. Author: Millennium Theory of Relativity. With USAF, 1955—59. Achievements include research in theory of natural motion; millennium theory of relativity; time and energy; the laws of acceleration; time and energy, inertia and gravity; millennium relativity velocity composition; relativistic motion perspective; millenium relativity acceleration composition; integrated relativisitc velocity and acceleration compostion; millenium theory of inertia and gravity; the four principal kinetic states of material bodies; patents for encoding printing device, 1978; man-powered propulsion device, 1986; research in relativistic transverse doppler effect; the true nature of light propagaflin; the nature of super luminal speeds in velocity composition; relationship between E=Mc2 & F=ma; light speed effect. Home Fax: 215-918-0218. Personal E-mail: jarybczyk@verizon.net.

RYBCZYNSKI, WITOLD MARIAN, architect, educator, writer; b. Edinburgh, Mar. 1, 1943; arrived in Can., 1953; s. Witold Kasimir and Anna Jadwiga (Hofman) Rybczynski; m. Shirley Hallam, Nov. 15, 1974. Diploma, Loyola Coll., Montreal, 1960; B.Arch., McGill U., 1966, M.Arch., 1972, DSc (hon.), 2002; LLD (hon.), U. Western Ont., 2006. Pvt. practice architecture, Montreal, 1970-82; research assoc. McGill U., Montreal, 1972-75, asst. prof. architecture, 1975-80, assoc. prof., 1980-86, prof., 1986-93; Meyerson prof. of Urbanism U. Pa., 1994—. Cons. UN, Manila, 1976, Internat. Devel. Rsch. Ctr., Ottawa, 1977, Banco de Mex., 1979—80; sr. fellow Design Futures Inst., 2003; mem. Meml. and Mus. Cons. Group. Author: Paper Heroes: A Review of Appropriate Technology, 1980, Taming the Tiger: The Struggle to Control Technology, 1983, Home: A Short History of an Idea, 1986, The Most Beautiful House in the World, 1989, Waiting in the Weekend, 1991, Looking Around: A Journey Through Architecture, 1992, A Place for Art, 1993, City Life: Urban Expectation in a New World, 1995, A Clearing in the Distance, 1999 (J. Anthony Lukas Book Prize, Christopher award), One Good Turn, 2000, The Look of Architecture, 2001, The Perfect House, 2002; co-author: (with Laurie Olin) Vizcaya, 2005, Last Harvest, 2007, My Two Polish Grandfathers, 2008; contbg. editor: Saturday Night, 1990—2001; contbg. author Booknotes: Stories from American History, mem. adv. bd. Ency. Americana; founding editor: Wharton Real Estate Rev., 1996—; Slate, 2005—. Mem. adv. coun. Inst. Classical Arch., 2003—; mem. adv. bd. Chgo. Humanities Festival, 2003—; advisor Libr. Am. Landscape History, 2002—, mem. U.S. Commn. Fin. Arts, 2004—. Recipient QSPELL Lit. prize for nonfiction, 1988, 1989, Prix Paul-Henri Lapointe, 1988, Progressive Arch. Design award, 1991, Jurzykowski Found. award, 1993, Athaneum Lit. prize, 1997, 2001, Christopher award, 2000, J. Anthony Lukas prize, 2000, Vincent Scully prize, 2007, Seaside prize, 2007, Inst. honors, AIA, 2007; Ballard Real Estate scholar, 1994—95. Fellow: AIA (hon.); mem.: Am. Soc. Landscape Archs. (hon.). Office: Sch Design Meyerson Hall Philadelphia PA 19104 Office Phone: 215-573-0985. Business E-Mail: rybczyns@design.upenn.edu.

RYBERG, SUSAN GRIBBLE, librarian; b. Brownsville, Pa., Aug. 9, 1949; d. Robert M. and Virginia F. Gribble; m. Allen E. Ryberg, June 17, 1989. MLS, U. Pitts., 1972. Tech. svcs. libr. Point Pk. Coll., Pitts., 1971—97; reference libr. Mt. Olive Coll., Moye Libr., NC, 1997—. Reader Spoken Word Ministries, Mt. Olive, 2004. Mem.: NC Libr. Assn. Avocations: swimming, travel. Office: Mt Olive Coll Moye Libr 634 Henderson St Mount Olive NC 28365 Business E-Mail: sryberg@moc.edu.

RYBICKI, STEPHEN (STEVE RYBICKI), librarian; b. Hamtramck, Mich., June 23, 1941; s. Steven and Mary Rybicki; m. Clarice Larkins; children: James, Christina Rybicki-Kler. AMLS, U. Mich., Ann Arbor, 1969; MEd, Marygrove Coll., Detroit, 1973. Cert. in instrnl. tech. State of Mich., 1973. Reference libr. Detroit Pub. Libr., 1967—69, Macomb CC, Clinton Twp., Mich., 1970—; head libr. U. Detroit HS, 1969—70. Author: (poetry book) Pocket Poems. Home: 64549 Limerick Ln

Washington MI 48095 Office: Macomb CC 44575 Garfield Clinton Township MI 48038 Personal E-mail: captaincaddie@yahoo.com. Business E-Mail: rybickis@macomb.edu.

RYCE, DONALD THEODORE, JR., lawyer; b. New Orleans, Dec. 15, 1943; s. Donald Theodore Sr. and Martha (Herndon) R.; m. Claudine Dianne Walker, July 8, 1984 (dec.); children: Ted, Martha, Jimmy (dec.). BA, U. Fla., Gainesville, 1966, JD, 1968. Bar: Fla. 1968, U.S. Dist. Ct. (so. dist.) Fla. 1972, U.S. Ct. Appeals (5th and 11th cirs.) 1973. Jud. law clk. Fla. Dist. Ct. Appeals (4th cir.), West Palm Beach, 1968—70; ptnr. Hogg, Allen, Ryce, Norton & Blue, Miami, Fla., 1970—89, Donald T. Ryce, P.A., Miami, 1989—. Co-chmn. liaison com. labor and employment sect. NLRB, Fla., 1990-92, mem. publs. com., 1990-91, exec. coun. labor and employment sect., 1994-98, 2003—; apptd. chmn. missing children adv. bd. Fla. Dept. Law Enforcement, 1996—; hearing examiner Miami Dade County. Dir. Jimmy Ryce Ctr. for Victims of Predatory Abduction. Recipient Leadership award, Fla. Police Chiefs Edn. Rsch. Found., 1993, Pres. award, Fla. Network for Victim Witness Svcs., Inc., 1996, Laurie Wander Spirit of Life award, 1998, John and Reve Walsh award, 2005; named a Fla. Super Lawyer, 2008; named to Policeman Hall of Fame, 1996, Grand Knight of Order of Michael the Archangel. Mem. AAA (arbitrator employment law 2003—, labor law 2003—, comml. law 2003—, consumer law 2007-), Fla. Bar Assn., Fin. Industry Regulatory Authority (arbitrator), Nat. Arbitration Forum (arbitrator 2007-), Winter Haven C. of C. (Cmty. Leadership award 1994), Miami Rotary. Episcopalian. Avocations: gourmet cooking, bicycling, travel. Office: 900 Bay Dr #201 Miami Beach FL 33141 Office Phone: 772-492-0200. Office Fax: 772-492-0210. Business E-Mail: employerlawyer@yahoo.com.

RYCHLAK, JOSEPH FRANK, psychologist, educator; b. Cudahy, Wis., Dec. 17, 1928; s. Joseph Walter and Helen Mary (Bieniek) R.; m. Lenora Pearl Smith, June 16, 1956; children: Ronald, Stephanie. BS, U. Wis., 1953; MA, Ohio State U., 1954, PhD, 1957. Diplomate Am. Bd. Examiners in Profl. Psychology. Asst. prof. psychology Fla. State U., Tallahassee, 1957-58, Washington State U., Pullman, 1958-61; assoc. prof., then prof. psychology St. Louis U., 1961-69; prof. psychology Purdue U., West Lafayette, Ind., 1969-83, interim dept. head, 1979-80; prof. Loyola U. Chgo., 1983-99, Maude C. Clarke prof. humanistic psychology, 1983—, prof. emeritus, 1999—. Dir. Human Relations Ctr., Pullman, Wash., 1958-61; research cons. AT&T, 1957-82. Author: The Psychology of Rigorous Humanism, 1977, 2d edit., 1988, Discovering Free Will and Personal Responsibility, 1979, A Philosophy of Science for Personality Theory, 2d edit., 1981, Personality and Life Style of Young Male Managers, 1982, (with N. Cameron) Personality Development and Psychopathology, 2d edit., 1985, Artificial Intelligence and Human Reason: A Teleological Critique, 1991, Logical Learning Theory: A Human Teleology and Its Empirical Support, 1994, In Defense of Human Consciousness, 1997, The Human Image in Postmodern America, 2003; assoc. editor Psychotherapy: Theory, Rsch. and Practice, 1965-76, Jour. Mind and Behavior, 1985-94. With USAF, 1946-49. Named Outstanding Contbr. to Human Understanding, Internat. Assn. Social Psychiatry, 1971. Fellow Am. Psychol. Assn. (div. 24 pres. 1977-78, 86-87), Am. Psychol. Soc.; mem. Soc. Personality Assessment, Phi Beta Kappa. Roman Catholic. Home: 12974 Abraham Run Carmel IN 46033 Office Phone: 317-816-0073. E-mail: jrychlak@sbcglobal.net. *From my father I learned to have a sense of purpose, work hard, and assume responsibility. From my mother I learned not to take myself too seriously, and to realize that my achievements are never entirely up to me.*

RYCKMAN, ERIC MICHAEL, research scientist, educator; b. Gainesville, Fla., Aug. 30, 1980; s. Frederick Charles and Cathy Ann Ryckman; m. Michelle Lynn Cummings, Sept. 26, 2009. BS in Math. & Stats., U. Mich., Ann Arbor, 2002; MA in Math., UCLA, 2003, PhD in Math., 2007. Instr. UCLA, 2007; postdoc. scholar math. Calif. Inst. Tech., Pasadena, 2007—08, Harry Bateman rsch. instr., 2008—. Mem.: Math. Assn. America, Am. Math. Soc.

RYDALCH, ANN, federal agency administrator, former state senator; b. 1935; m. Vernal Rydalch. BS in Bus. Edn., Idaho State U. Mem. Idaho Senate, 1983—90; chmn. Feb. Lab. Consortium Tech. Transfer, 2001—; state rep. Idaho, 2004—. Past mem. Idaho Bicentennial Commn.; former vice chmn. Idaho Rep. Com. Republican. Office: ID Natl Energy & Envrn Lab PO Box 1625 MS 3810 2525 N Fremont Ave Idaho Falls ID 83415-3810

RYDBERG, MARSHA GRIFFIN, lawyer; b. Tampa, Fla., Dec. 11, 1946; d. Jack and Nibia (Santana) Griffin; m. Thomas Henry Rydberg; children: Kristen Elizabeth, Nancy Marshall. BA, Emory U., Atlanta, 1968; JD cum laude, Stetson U., DeLand, Fla., 1976. Bar: Fla. 1976, US Dist. Ct. (mid. dist.) Fla. 1977, US Dist. Ct. (so. dist.) Fla. 1984, US Ct. Appeals (11th cir.) 1977, US Supreme Ct. 1983. Christian youth worker Young Life Campaign, 1968-70; youth dir. First Presbyn. Ch., Tampa, 1970—72; assoc. Gibbons, Tucker, McEwen, Smith Cofer & Taub, Tampa, 1976-79, Taub & Williams, Tampa, 1979-83, ptnr., 1983-89, Rydberg & Goldstein, P.A., 1989-97, Foley & Lardner, 1997-2000; pvt. practice, 2000—. Bd. fellows U. Tampa; adj. prof. banking law and real property finance Stetson U. Coll. Law, 2000—. Contbr. articles to profl. jours. Bd. dirs. YMCA, 1977-79, Jr. League Tampa (atty. 1983-85), 1979-80, Leadership Tampa, 1993, 97, U. Club Tampa, 2000, 05, 06; pres. Tampa-Hillsborough County Drug Abuse Comprehensive Coord. Office, Inc., 1988-90, chmn. Tampa Downtown Partnership, 1995-96, bd. dirs. 1992-2005; elder Temple Terrace Presbyn. Ch., Fla., 1982-85; mem. local rules adv. com. US Mid. Dist. Ct., 1995-97; bd. dirs. Fed. Res. Bd. of Atlanta, Jacksonville, 1997-2002, chmn. 1999, 2002; commr. Tampa Housing Authority Bd., 1994-99, Prison Crusade Bd., 2000-05; mem. Tampa Young Life Com., 1992-2000, chmn., 1994-96; mem. Fla. Commn. on the Status Women, 1993-2001, chmn., 1996-98; bd. trustees The Spring, 1996-98, Eckerd Coll., 2000-06; chmn. NFL-Youth Edn. Town Ctr. Tampa Bay, Inc., 2000—; trustee Tampa Bay History Ctr., 2001—, vice chmn., 2007, Stetson U., 2004-06. Recipient Bob Sikes Incentive award, Judge Joe Morris award; named Woman of Distinction Girl Scouts US, Women in Bus., Tampa Bay Bus. Jour., 2002, Am. Jurisprudence awards for Excellence in evidence and constl. law. Fellow Am. Bar Found., Fla. Bar Found; mem. ABA (com. commendation zoning & property use 1985-88, chair bus. law sect. fin. instn. litig. com. 1992-2003), Am. Bankruptcy Inst., US Supreme Ct. Hist. Soc., Fla. Supreme Ct. Hist. Soc., Fla. Bar (bd. govs. 1993-99, exec. com. 1994-95, 97-98, coun. sects. chmn. 2004-05, exec. com. bus. law sect. 2001—, exec. com. real property, probate and trust law sect. 2002—, sec. 2002-03, v.p. 2003-04, chmn. 2004-05, Tradition of Excellence award 2000), Fla. Assn. Women Lawyers, Ferguson White Inn of Ct., Tampa Bay Bankruptcy Bar Assn., Hillsborough Assn. Women Lawyers, Hillsborough County Bar Assn. (pres. 1991-92, James M. Red McEwen award 1984-85, 87-88, 96-97), Athena Soc., Stetson U. Coll. Law Alumni Assn. (pres. 1993, bd. overseers 1994, chmn. 2003-05), Greater Tampa C. of C. (bd. dirs. 1995-2000, chair com. of 100 1998), Am. and Fla. Land Title Assn., Exch. Club of Tampa (pres. 1998), Phi Alpha Delta (Outstanding Scholastic Achievement award). Democrat. Home: 2606 W Prospect Rd Tampa FL 33629-5358 Office: 201 N Franklin St 1625 Tampa FL 33602 Office Phone: 813-221-2800. Business E-Mail: mrydberg@rydberglaw.com.

RYDÉN, BENGT GUNNAR, retired stock exchange executive; b. Stockholm, Oct. 30, 1936; s. Gunnar H. and Ragnhild L. (Soederbaum) Rydén; m. Monica I.H. Tillberg, May 18, 1961. MBA, Stockholm Sch. Econs., 1960, PhD, 1972. Dep. chief economist Fedn. Swedish Industries, Stockholm, 1965-66; editor-in chief Swedish "Veckans Affärer", Stockholm, 1971-73; chief exec. Ctr. Bus. and Policy Studies, Stockholm, 1974-84, Stockholm Stock Exch., 1985-98, exec. chmn., 1998-99; vice chmn. Swedish Acctg. Stds. Coun., 1989—2002; ret., 2002. Chmn. Internat. Fedn. Stock Exchs., 1995—97, Mus. Nat. Antiquities, Sweden, 1998—2005, Hallvarsson & Halvarsson AB, Sweden, 1999—2007, Seventh Swedish Nat. Pension Fund, 1999—2008, Pantor Engring. AB, 2000—; bd. dirs. Found. Fin. Rsch., Sweden, Svenskt Rekonstruktionskapital AB, Sweden, 2003—, Autobalance Svenska AB, 2004—, Nordic Investor Svcs. AB, 2006—; mem. Com. of Wise Men on the Regulation of European Securities Mkts., 2000—01, Govt. Commn. on Restoration Pub. Trust in Bus., 2002—04. Fellow, Indsl. Inst. Econ. and Social Rsch., 1966—70. Fellow: Swedish Acad. Auditing, Royal Swedish Acad. Engring. Scis. Business E-Mail: bengt.ryden@halvarsson.se.

RYDER, EDWARD FRANCIS, secondary school educator; b. Lynn, Mass., Mar. 25, 1931; s. Edward W. and Theresa (Callahan) R. BSBA, Salem State U., Winston-Salem, NC, 1954, EdM in Edn., 1973; EdM in Bus. Edn., Boston U., 1956. Cert. tchr., Mass. Bus. tchr. North Quincy (Mass.) H.S., 1968—98. Owner, pub. Sunnyside Pub. Co., 1975—. Author: The Art of Playing Bingo and Winning Consistently, 1980, The Art of Entering Sweepstakes and Winning Consistently, 1981, How To Save a Fortune Using Refunds and Coupons, 1983, How to Unlock the Secrets of Winning and Good Luck, 1983, How You Can Achieve Total Success Through Self-Hypnosis, 1984, Where to Buy Everything Wholesale--A Book of Lifetime Savings, 1984, A Guide to Over 1,000 Things You Can Get--For Free!, 1984, The Art of Betting Horses and Winning Consistently, 1985, Blackjack: How to Play and Win Like an Expert, 1985, Hot Dice! How to Leave the Table a Winner, 1986, Winning Secrets of a Poker Master, 1986, Picking Winners at the Harness Races, 1987, Winning Consistently at the Greyhound Races, 1987, Lucky Slots!! How to Beat the Casino Bandits, 1988, Secrets of Winning at Casino Roulette, 1988, Keno: The Art of Playing and Winning, 1989, How to Play and Win at Casino Baccarat, 1989, Secrets of Winning at Video Poker, 1990, Winning Secrets of a Master Sports Bettor--Football, 1991, Winning Secrets of a Master Sports Bettor--Basketball, 1992, Winning Secrets of a Master Sports Bettor--Baseball, 1992; all publs. updated, 1997. Roman Catholic. Home: 28 Sunnyside Rd Lynn MA 01905-1105 Office: Sunnyside Pubs 51 Willow St # 165 Lynn MA 01901-1108 Business E-Mail: gambleandwin@verizon.net.

RYDER, EDWARD JONAS, geneticist; b. NYC, Oct. 6, 1929; s. Wilfred Oliver and Tillie (Brown) R.; m. Elouise Jones Viales, Mar. 10, 1962; 1 child, Deborah Lynn; stepchildren: Robert Glenn Viales, Lawrence Dale Viales. BS, Cornell U., 1951; PhD, U. Calif., Davis, 1954. Geneticist Agrl. Rsch. Svc. USDA, Salinas, Calif., 1957—2003, rsch. leader, 1972—94, location leader, 1982-89. Author: Leafy Salad Vegetables, 1979, Lettuce, Endive and Chicory, 1999, (novel) The Departments, 2009; contbr. articles to profl. jours. Served as pvt. U.S. Army, 1954-56. Recipient award Grower mag. 1982, Superior Svc. award US Dept. Agr., 1997, named Scientists of Yr. Pacific West USDA Agrl. Rsch. Svc., 1994. Fellow Am. Soc. Hort. Sci. (Outstanding Rschr. award, 1995); mem. AAAS, Internat. Soc. Hort. Sci., Am. Genetics Soc. Democrat. Achievements include development of Salinas iceberg lettuce, use of flower time genes to reduce backcross breeding times by half, and identification of 30 genes, one third of those known in lettuce. Home: 77 Paseo Hermoso Salinas CA 93908-9171

RYDER, HENRY CLAY, lawyer; b. Lafayette, Ind., Feb. 18, 1928; s. Raymond Robert and Mina Elizabeth (Arnold) R.; m. Ann Sater Clay, Nov. 29, 1952 (dec.); children: David C., Sarah Paige Hugon, Anne Ryder O'Keefe; m. Velma Iris Dean, Aug. 27, 1976 (dec.). BS, Purdue U., 1948; LLB, U. Mich., 1951; LLD, Hanover Coll., 1998. Bar: Mich. 1951, Ind. 1952, U.S. Dist. Ct. (so. dist.) Ind. 1953, U.S. Ct. Appeals (7th cir.) 1957, U.S. Supreme Ct. 1981. Assoc. Buschmann, Krieg, DeVault & Alexander, Indpls., 1953-57, ptnr., 1957-60, Roberts & Ryder and successor firms, Indpls., 1960-86, Barnes & Thornburg (merger), Indpls., 1987-95, of counsel, 1996—. Pres. Ind. State Symphony Soc. Inc., 1979-82, bd. dirs., 1972-91, trustee, 1991—; chmn. United Way of Greater Indpls., 1984; vice chmn. Greater Indpls. Progress Com., 1979-86, chmn., 1987-89, mem. exec. com., 1979-2000; trustee Purdue U., 1983-89; trustee Hanover Coll., 1979-2003, chmn., 1988-98; bd. dirs. Hist. Landmarks Found. of Ind., 1985-96, chmn., 1992-95; bd. dirs. Purdue Rsch. Found., 1990-2006; trustee, Athenaeum Found., 2007-; hon. v.p. Ind. Soc. Chgo.; mem. cmty. bd. IUPUI U. Libr., 1998—2008, chmn. 2003-04; bd. govs. Heartland Film Festival, 2000—04, Athenaeum Found., 2007-, Lt. U.S. Army, 1951-53. Recipient Jefferson award Indpls. Star, 1983, Whistler award Greater Indpls. Progress Com., 1989; Sagamore of the Wabash, 1984; named Man of Yr., B'nai B'rith Soc., 1984, Ind. Acad., 1992, Lifetime Achievement award Nat. Soc. Fund Raising Execs., 1999, Spirit of Philanthropy award IUPUI., 2005. Fellow: Ind. Bar Found., Am. Bar Found.; mem.: ABA, Indpls. Bar Assn., Ind. Bar Assn., Ind. C. of C. (bd. dirs. 1991—94), Purdue U. Alumni Assn. (pres. 1975—77, Alumni Svc. award 1982, Citizenship award 1989), Columbia Club Found. (trustee 1990—2007, life trustee 2007—), Indpls. Lit. Club (pres. 2004—05), Kiwanis (Downtown Indpls. pres. 1983, Civic award 1981), Columbia Club (bd. dirs. 1987—90, sec. 1988, Benjamin Harrison award 1983, Columbian of Yr. award 2002), USAC Benevolent Found. (bd. dirs., pres. 1999—), USAC Properties (sec., bd. dirs. 1986—), US Auto Club (bd. dirs. 1982—2009, Pres.'s award 1989, Eddie Edenburn award 2000), Lawyers Club of Indpls. (pres. 1966). Republican. Presbyterian. Office: Barnes & Thornburg 11 S Meridian St Indianapolis IN 46204-3535

RYDER, ROBERT T., geologist, researcher; b. Bowling Green, Ohio, Sept. 23, 1941; s. Joseph T. and Helen Strong Ryder; m. Marlene M. Myers, Mar. 23, 1968; children: Robert M., Renee M. Baker. BS, Mich. State U., East Lansing, 1963; PhD, Pa. State U., State Coll., 1968. Petroleum geologist Shell Oil Co., 1969—73; rsch. geologist US Geol. Survey, Reston, Va., 1974—. Mem.: Yellowstone-Bighorn Rsch. Assn., Am. Assn. Petroleum Geologists (George V. Cohee award 2004), Geol. Soc. America. Home: 1326 Deep Run Ln Reston VA 20190 Office: US Geol Survey 12201 Sunrise Valley Dr MS 956 Herndon VA 20192 Business E-Mail: rryder@usgs.gov.

RYDER, ROBERT WINSOR, medical epidemiologist; b. NYC, Aug. 6, 1946; s. James F. and Nancy N. (Nickerson) R.; children: Hilary, Abby. BSc, Middlebury Coll., 1968; MD, Columbia U., 1972; MSc, London U., 1981. Diplomate Am. Bd. Internal Medicine. Intern Boston City Hosp., 1972-73, resident in medicine, 1973-74; staff mem. epidemic intelligence svc. Ctrs. for Disease Control, Atlanta, 1974-77; fellow in infectious diseases Harvard U. Med. Sch., Boston, 1977-78; dir. div. infectious disease Dept. Epidemiology and Pub. Health, Sch. Medicine Yale U., New Haven, 1993—; asst. prof. Sch. Medicine Johns Hopkins U., Balt., 1978-80, Tufts U., Boston, 1980-85; assoc. prof. Sch. Medicine Boston U., 1985-86; dir. AIDS project Ctrs. for Disease Control, Kinshasa, Zaire, 1986-90; prof. epidemiology Mt. Sinai Sch. Medicine, NYC, 1991-93; John Rodman Paul prof. of epidemiology Sch. Medicine Yale U., 1993—. Cons. WHO, Geneva, 1975-90. Contbr. articles on HIV transmission to profl. publs. Lt. comdr. USPHS, 1974-77. Milbank clin. scholar Milbank Found., Sch. Medicine Tufts U., 1980-85. Achievements include design and set up of world's largest cancer vaccine trial using hepatitis B virus vaccine to prevent liver cancer in West Africa; dir. of largest HIV/AIDS research project in Africa. Office: Dept Edpidem and Pub Health Yale U Sch Medicine 60 College St New Haven CT 06510-3210

RYDER, SUSAN R., elementary school educator; b. Ala. m. David Ryder. Lang. arts tchr. Estes Park (Colo.) Middle Sch., 2001—. Named Colo. Tchr. of Yr., 2007; grantee Nat. Writing Project Fellow, Dept. Edn., 2006. Office: Estes Park Middle Sch 1500 Manford Ave Estes Park CO 80517 Office Phone: 970-586-4439 ext 3278. Business E-Mail: susan_ryder@psdr3.k12.co.us.

RYDER, WINONA (WINONA LAURA HOROWITZ), actress; b. Winona, Minn., Oct. 29, 1971; d. Michael and Cynthia (Istas) Horowitz. Founder Roustabout Studios, 1999. Films include: Lucas, 1986, Square Dance, 1987, Beetlejuice, 1988, Great Balls of Fire, 1989, Heathers, 1989, Edward Scissorhands, 1990, Mermaids, 1990, Welcome Home, Roxy Carmichael, 1990, Night On Earth, 1992, Bram Stoker's Dracula, 1992, Age of Innocence, 1993 (Golden Globe for Best Supporting Actress, 1994, Academy award nominee, Best Supporting Actress, 1993), The House of the Spirits, 1994, Reality Bites, 1994, Little Women, 1994 (Acad. Awd. nom., Best Actress), How to Make An American Quilt, 1995, Looking for Richard, 1995, The Crucible, 1996, Boys, 1996, Alien Resurrection, 1997, Celebrity, 1998, Girl, Interrupted, 1999, Autumn in New York, 1999, Lost Souls, 2000, Mr. Deeds, 2002, S1mOne, 2002, The Day My God Died (narrator), 2003, The Heart Is Deceitful Above All Things, 2004, The Darwin Awards, 2006, A Scanner Darkly, 2006, The Ten, 2007, The Informers, 2009, Star Trek, 2009. Named one of Top Players Under 35, People mag., 1996; named to Hollywood Walk of Fame, 2000. Office: c/o William Morris Agy One William Morris Pl Beverly Hills CA 90212

RYDHOLM, RALPH WILLIAMS, advertising executive; b. Chgo., June 1, 1937; s. Thor Gabriel and Vivian Constance (Williams) R.; m. Jo Anne Beechler, Oct. 5, 1963; children: Kristin, Erik, Julia. BA, Northwestern U., Evanston, Ill., 1958, postgrad. in bus. adminstrn, 1958-59; postgrad. Advanced Mgmt. Program, Harvard U., Cambridge, Mass., 1982. Acct. trainee, copywriter Young & Rubicam Advt., Chgo., 1960-63; copywriter Post-Keyes-Gardner Advt., Chgo., 1963, E. H. Weiss Advt., Chgo., 1963-65; copy group head BBDO Advt., Chgo., 1965-66; with J. Walter Thompson Advt., Chgo., 1966-86, creative dir., v.p., 1969-76, exec. creative dir., 1976-86, sr. v.p., 1972-80, exec. v.p., dir., 1980-86; exec. v.p., chief creative officer, dir. Ted Bates Worldwide, NYC, 1986-87; mng. ptnr., chmn. mgmt. com., chief creative officer, chmn., CEO, EURO RSCG Tatham Advt., Chgo., 1987-98; bd. dirs. Euro RSCG, USA; pres. R2 Cons., 1999—; spl. counsel J. Walter Thompson, 1999-2000. Bd. dirs., ops. com., chmn. creative com., vice chmn., 1996, chmn., 1997-98; Am. Assn. Advt. Agys. guest spkr. Ad Age Workshop, 1969, 77, 86, Adweek Seminar, 1993, CLIO awards, 1995; keynote spkr. Stephen B. Kelly Awards, 1993, CEBA Awards, 1997, chmn. CEBA Awards, 1997. Friends com. Northwestern U.; Prin. for a Day, Chgo. Pub. Schs., 1998—; bd. dirs. Acad. for Urban Sch. Leadership, Chgo. Arts HS; bd. dirs Chi Pub. HS Arts; bd. advisors Context Media; mem. assoc. bd. Newberry Libr. Assn.; bd. dirs., adv. coun. leadership coun. Chgo. Pub. Edn. Fund; bd. dirs. PRO AD PAC, 1998—; former chmn. bd. dirs. Am. Scandinavian Coun.; dir. Am. Assn. Advt. Agys. Found., 1997—99; cons., bd. dirs. Exec. Svc. Corp., 2003—; mem. ABA common. on the Am. Jury; bd. advisors Context Media. Staff sgt. USAFR, 1959—65. Recipient Clio awards, Internat. Broadcast award, Lion awards, Cannes Film Festival, Addy awards; named one of Top 100 Creative Ad People Ad Daily, 1972, Advt. Exec. of Yr. Adweek, 1991, Best Man in Advt. McCalls and Adweek, 1992; named to Creative Leader Hall of Fame, Wall St. Jour., 1994. Mem.: ASCAP, Chgo. Advt. Fedn., Am. Advt. Fedn. (Silver medal lifetime svc. 1997), Lincoln Park Zoo, Friends of Chgo. River, Art Inst. Chgo., Fernwood, Friends of the Pks., Hon. Order Ky. Cols., Chgo. Com. Coun. on Global Affairs, Openlands, Internat. Club, Dunes Club (Mich.), Carlton Club, Tavern Club, Harvard Club NYC, Northwestern Club Chgo., Saddle and Cycle Club, Econ. Club Chgo. (bd. dirs. 1996—98), Harvard Club Chgo., Execs. Club Chgo., Club Internat., Chikaming Country Club (Mich.), Lost Dunes Club (Mich.), Phi Delta Theta. Office Phone: 312-280-7726. Personal E-mail: rydholm@aol.com.

RYERSON, DENNIS R., editor; b. Ames, Iowa, Apr. 20, 1948; children: Carey, Kirsten. Student, Iowa State U., U. No. Iowa. Announcer, news dir. Sta. KWBG, Boone, Iowa; reporter, then city editor Cedar Falls Record, 1969—73; news editor Scottsbluff Star-Herald, Nebr., 1973—74; editl. page editor Vancouver Columbian, Wash., 1974—83; chief editl. writer, then editl. dir. Cleve. Plain Dealer, 1983—88; mng. editor news Denver Post, 1988—89; editor editl. pages Des Moines Register, 1989-94; exec. editor Great Falls Tribune, Mont., 1994-95; v.p., editor Des Moines Register, 1995—2001; editl. page editor San Jose Mercury News, 2001—03; v.p., editor The Indianapolis Star, 2003—. Appeared on TV shows including Good Morning America, MacNeil/Lehrer News Hour, CBS Morning News, NPR's All Things Considered. Mem. Nat. Conf. Editl. Writers (past pres.), Am. Soc. Newspaper Editors, Rotary Club Ind. Office: Indianapolis Star PO Box 145 Indianapolis IN 46206-0145 Office Phone: 317-444-6169. E-mail: dennis.ryerson@indystar.com.*

RYERSON, MARJORIE GILMOUR, journalist, poet, photographer, educator; b. Germantown, Pa., Mar. 28, 1943; d. William Newton and Jean (Hamilton) R.; children: Nicholas, Emily. BA, Beloit Coll., Wis., 1965; MFA, U. Iowa, Iowa City, 1976. Assoc. editor, reporter, photographer White River Valley Herald, Randolph, Vt., 1981-85; dir. pub. rels. and fund devel. Gifford Meml. Hosp., Randolph, 1986; editor Country Courier mag., Barre, Vt., 1986-90; features editor Burlington Free Press, Vt., 1990; asst. prof. English dept. Johnson State Coll., Vt., 1990-91; prof. comm. dept. Castleton State Coll., Vt., 1991—2005, chair comm. dept. Vt., 1996-98; exec. dir. Water Music, Inc., 2003—; prof. external degree program Johnson State Coll., Vt., 2007—; editl. dir. Safer Soc. Press, Brandon, Vt., 2008—. Mem. faculty New Eng. Young Writers Conf., Middlebury Coll., 1991—; dir. Vt. Network Cmty. Newspapers, 1996—; journalism tchr. Dorothy Canfield Fisher Writing Conf., Burlington, 1993; mem. faculty Vt. Coun. Arts, 1992, lit. advisor; mem. state poet adv. com. for Vt.; vis. scholar Green Mountain Coll., Poultney, Vt., 2006—07; writing tchr. Young Vermonters Writing Conf. Champlain Coll., 2007—. Author: Water Music, 2003, Companions for the Passage: Stories of the Intimate Privilege of Accompanying the Dying, 2005; co-author: Not A Bad Seat in the House, 2007. Selectman, Town of Randolph, 1995; mem. Randolph Cmty. Devel. Corp. Bd., 1992-95;

corporator Gifford Meml. Hosp.; justice of the peace County of Orange; bd. dirs. Vt. Mozart Festival; vol. Big Bros./Big Sisters Program. Recipient Paul Keough Leadership award, 2003, Harry E. Schlenz Pub. Edn. medal, 2005; Vt. State Colls. faculty fellow, 2000—01. Mem.: Physicians for Social Responsibility, Authors' Guild, Am. Med. Writers Assn., Vt. League of Writers (hon.). Avocations: saxophone, piano, hiking, sailing, kayaking. Home: 36 Randolph Ave Randolph VT 05060 Office: PO Box 44 Randolph VT 05060 Business E-Mail: water05060@gmail.com.

RYERSON, PAUL SOMMER, lawyer; b. Newark, Oct. 2, 1946; s. Robert Paul and Audrey Mae (Sommer) R.; m. Susan Jean Duckrow, Aug. 7, 1971 (div. Apr. 1995); children: James Sommer, Jill Carin; m. Kenswynn Black, Jan. 26, 2002. BA, Wesleyan U., 1968; JD, Columbia U., 1971. Bar: N.Y. 1972, D.C. 1972, U.S. Ct. Appeals (D.C. cir.) 1973, U.S. Dist. Ct. D.C. 1973, U.S. Supreme Ct. 1976, U.S. Ct. Appeals (5th cir.) 1979, U.S. Ct. Appeals (4th cir.) 1980. Law clk. to judge Jack B. Weinstein U.S. Dist. Ct. ea. dist. N.Y., 1971-72; assoc. Arnold & Porter, Washington, 1972-79, ptnr., 1980-89, Jones Day, Washington, 1989—. Contbr. articles to profl. publs. Mem. ABA, D.C. Bar Assn. Home: 5809 Nicholson Ln North Bethesda MD 20852-5719 Office: Jones Day 51 Louisiana Ave NW Washington DC 20001-2113 Home Phone: 301-230-0278; Office Phone: 202-879-3939. E-mail: psryerson@jonesday.com.

RYGG, GLENN, retired music educator; b. Mayville, ND, Aug. 8, 1944; s. Conrad Ingemann Rygg and Helen Marie Vinje; m. Susan Gay Meidinger (div.); children: Jonathan, Jason. BSc in Instrnl. Music, Mayville State U., ND, 1966. Band, choir tchr., Fessenden, ND, 1966—76; band tchr. Rugby, ND, 1976—81; band, choir, English tchr. Rolla, ND, 1984—88; band tchr. Devils Lake, ND, 1988—2007; ret., 2007. Dir. Devils Lake Elks Cmty. Band, 1988—. Mem. Jaycees, Fessenden, 1968—76. Recipient 25 Yr. Svc. award, ND Music Educators Assn., 2000, Meritorious and Disting. Svc. award, VFW, Devils Lake, 2003. Mem.: Music Educators Nat. Conf., Elks Club. Lutheran. Avocations: painting, music. Home: 1113 4th Ave NE Devils Lake ND 58301-1822

RYIM, WON-GIL, mechanical engineer, engineering executive; b. Seoul, Republic of Korea, Aug. 11, 1968; s. Seung-hu Ryim and Hong-yeop Park; m. Hye-suk Lee, Sept. 20, 1998; children: Jiyu, Juho. BS in Mech. Design and Prodn. Engring., Seoul Nat. U., 1992, MS in Mech. Design and Prodn. Engring., 1994. Sr. engr. LG Prodn. Engring. Rsch. Ctr., Pyeongtaek, Republic of Korea, 1994—2001; chief engr. Larson Sys., Seoul, 2001—02; CEO Moldion, Bundang, Republic of Korea, 2002—. Auditor Harbees, Incheon, Republic of Korea, 2007—. Pvt. Repubic of Korea Mil., 1994—99. Mem.: Soc. Plastics Engrs. (assoc.). Achievements include development of computer-aided analysis software for injection molding process including automatic gate location determination; research in design optimization with applications in industry; applications of computer-aided engineering technology in injection molding in field. Office: Moldion Intellige II C-2106 Bundang-gu Jeongja-dong 24 Seongnam Kyunggi 463-841 Republic of Korea

RYLANCE, MARK (MARK WATERS), actor, performing company executive; b. Ashford, Kent, England, Jan. 18, 1960; s. David and Anne Waters; m. Claire van Kampen, 1989. Student, Royal Acad. Dramatic Arts, London, 1978—80. Assoc. mem. Royal Shakespeare Co.; artistic dir. Shakespeare's Globe Theatre, 1995—2005. Artistic dir., actor (plays) The Two Gentlemen of Verona, 1996, A Chaste Maid in Cheapside, 1997, Henry V, 1997, The Merchant of Venice, 1998, The Honest Whore, 1998, Antony and Cleopatra, 1999, Hamlet, 2000, Cymbeline, 2001, The Golden Ass, 2002, Twelfth Night, 2002, Richard II, 2003, Measure for Measure, 2004, The Tempest, 2005, The Storm, 2005; actor: (plays) Desperado Corner, 1981, Hamlet, 1988, Much Ado About Nothing, 1993 (Olivier award, Best Actor), Henry V, 1993, As You Like It, 1994, True West, 1994, Macbeth, 1995, Life x 3, 2000, Boeing Boeing, 2007 (Tony award for Best Performance by a Leading Actor in a Play, 2008), I Am Shakespeare, 2007, Peer Gynt, 2008; (Broadway plays) Boeing-Boeing, 2008 (Tony award for Best Performance by a Leading Actor in a Play, 2008); (TV films) Wallenberg: A Hero's Story, 1985, Incident in Judea, 1991, Love Lies Bleeding, 1993, Loving, 1995, Leonardo, 2003, Richard II, 2003, The Government Inspector, 2005 (BAFTA TV award, Best Actor, 2006); (films) The McGuffin, 1986, Hearts of Fire, 1987, The Grass Arena, 1991 (BBC Radio Times award, Best Newcomer), Prospero's Books, 1991, Institute Benjamenta, 1995, Angels and Insects, 1995, Intimacy, 2001, The Other Boleyn Girl, 2008 (Drama Desk award, Outstanding Actor in a Play, 2008).

RYLANDER, HENRY GRADY, JR., mechanical engineering educator; b. Pearsall, Tex., Aug. 23, 1921; married; 4 children. BS, U. Tex., 1943, MS, 1952; PhD in Mech. Engring., Ga. Inst. Tech., 1965. Design engr. Steam Div., Aviation Gas Turbine Div., Westinghouse Elec. Corp., 1943-47; from asst. to assoc. prof. mech. engring. U. Tex., Austin, 1947-68, research scientist, 1950, prof. mech. engring., 1968—, Joe J. King prof. engring., 1980—. Cons. engr. TRACOR, Inc., 1964-69; founding dir. Ctr. for Electromechanics, U. Tex., 1977-85, chmn., mech. engring. dept., 1976-86. Named Disting. Grad. Coll. Engring., U. Tex., Austin, 1989. Fellow ASME (Leonardo da Vinci award 1985); mem. ASME. Office: U Tex Coll Engring C2200 Austin TX 78712 Home Phone: 512-452-3740; Office Phone: 512-471-3044. Business E-Mail: hgr@mail.utexas.edu.

RYLES, GERALD FAY, investor, finance company executive; b. Walla Walla, Wash., Apr. 3, 1936; s. L. F. and Janie Geraldine (Bassett) R.; m. Ann Jane Birkenmeyer, June 12, 1959; children— Grant, Mark, Kelly. BA, U. Wash., 1958; MBA, Harvard U., 1962. With Gen. Foods Corp., White Plains, NY, 1962—66, Purex Corp., Ltd., Lakewood, Calif., 1966-68; cons. McKinsey & Co., Inc., Los Angeles, 1968-71; with Fibreboard Corp., San Francisco, 1971-79, v.p., 1973-75, group v.p., 1975-79; with Consol. Fibres, Inc., San Francisco, 1979-88, exec. v.p., 1979-81, pres., dir., 1981-86, chief exec. officer, 1986-88; cons. Orinda, Calif., 1988-90; with Interchecks Inc., 1990-92, pres., CEO, 1990-92; bus. exec., pvt. investor, 1992-94; chmn. bd., CEO Microserv, Inc., Kirkland, Wash., 1994—2001, chmn. bd., 2001—03. Bd. dirs. Giant Campus, Inc., Zumiez, Inc., Wash. State Bd. Accountancy. Capt. U.S. Army, 1958-66. Mem.: Harvard Bus. Sch. Assn., U. Wash. Alumni Assn. Republican. Episcopalian. Home: 127 3rd Ave Apt 301 Kirkland WA 98033-6177 Home Phone: 425-827-3519. Personal E-mail: g.ryles@verizon.net.

RYMAR, JULIAN W., manufacturing executive, director; b. Grand Rapids, Mich., June 29, 1919; m. Margaret Macon Van Brunt, Dec. 11, 1954; children: Margaret Gibson, Gracen Macon, Ann Mackall. Student, Grand Rapids Jr. Coll., 1937—39, U. Mich., 1940—41, Wayne State U., 1948—52, Rockhurst Coll., 1952—53, Naval War Coll., 1954—58. Entered as aviation cadet USN, 1942; comdg. officer Naval Air Res. Squadron, 1957—60, staff air comdr., 1960—64; advanced through grades to capt. USN, 1964; chmn. bd., CEO, dir. Grace Co., Belton, Mo., 1955—90; chmn. bd. dirs. Shock & Vibration Rsch. Inc., 1956—66; chmn. bd., CEO Bedtime Story Fashions. Bd. dirs. Am. Bank & Trust. Mem. Kans. City Hist. Soc.; trustee Missouri Valley Coll., 1969—74; pres. Rymar Found.; active Sch. Am. Rsch., Inst. Am. Arts, Mus. N.Mex. Found., Spanish Colonial Art Soc.; active various positions Episcopal Ch.; bd. dirs. Bros. of Mercy, St. Luke's Hosp. Mem.: Soc. Profl. Journalists, Friends of Art (exec. bd. 1971—74, pres., chmn. bd. govs.), Spanish Colonial Arts Soc., Mus. Indian Arts and Culture, Mus. Internat. Folk Art, Mus. Fine Arts, Mus. N.Mex. Found., Santa Fe Symphony, Soc. Fellows of Nelson Gallery Found. (exec. bd. 1972—77), Mil. Order World Wars, Navy League U.S. (pres. 1959—60, dir. 1960—70), Rockhill Homes Assn. (v.p.), Sch. Am. Rsch., Inst. Am. Indian Art, Quiet Birdman Club, Arts Club of Washington, Press Club, Univ. Mich. Club, Sigma Delta Chi. Episcopalian. Personal E-mail: rymarvb@nets.com.

RYMER, PAMELA ANN, federal judge; b. Knoxville, Tenn., Jan. 6, 1941; AB, Vassar Coll., 1961; LLB, Stanford U., 1964; LLD (hon.), Pepperdine U., 1988. Bar: Calif. 1966, US Ct. Appeals (9th cir.) 1966, US Ct. Appeals (10th cir.), US Supreme Ct. Dir., polit. rsch. and analysis Goldwater for President Com., 1964; v.p. Rus Walton & Assoc., Los Altos, Calif., 1965—66; assoc. Lillick McHose & Charles, LA, 1966—75, ptnr., 1973—75, Toy and Rymer, LA, 1975—83; judge US Dist. Ct. (ctrl. dist.) Calif., LA, 1983—89, US Ct. Appeals (9th cir.), LA, 1989—. Faculty The Nat. Jud. Coll., 1986-88; mem. com. summer ednl. programs Fed. Jud. Ctr., 1987-88, mem. com. appellate judge edn., 1996-99; chair exec. com. 9th Cir. Jud. Conf., 1990; mem. com. criminal law Jud. Conf. US, 1988-93, Ad Hoc com. gender-based violence, 1991-94, fed.-state jurisdiction com., 1993-96; mem. commn. on structural alternatives Fed. Cts. Appeals, 1997-98. Mem. editorial bd. The Judges' jour., 1989-91; contbr. articles to profl. jours. and newsletters. Mem. Calif. Postsecondary Edn. Commn., 1974-84, chmn., 1980-84; mem. LA Olympic Citizens Adv. Commn.; bd. visitors Stanford U. Law Sch., 1986-99, trustee, 1991-2001, chair, 1993-96, exec. com., chmn. bd. trustees com. acad. policy, planning and mgmt. and its ad. hoc. com. athletics., chmn. bd. visitors Sch. Law, 1987—; bd. visitors Pepperdine U. Law Sch., 1987—; mem. Edn. Commn. of States Task Force on State Policy and Ind. Higher Edn., 1987-89, Carnegie Commn. Task Force Sci. and Tech. Jud. and Regulatory Decisionmaking, 1990-93, Commn. Substance Abuse Coll. and Univ. Campuses, 1992-94, commn. substance abuse high schs. Ctr. Addiction and Substance Abube Columbia U.; bd. dirs. Constnl. Rights Found., 1985-97, Pacific Coun. Internat. Policy, 1995—, Calif. Higher Edn. Policy Ctr., 1992-97; Jud. Conf. US Com. Fed.-State Jurisdiction, 1993, Com. Criminal Law, 1988-93, ad hoc com. gender based violence, 1991-94; chair exec. com. 9th cir. jud. conf., 1990-94. Recipient Outstanding Trial Jurist award LA County Bar Assn., 1988; named David T. Lewis Disting. Jurist-in-Residence U. Utah, 1992. Mem. ABA (task force on civil justice reform 1991-93, mem. coord. com. agenda civil justice reform in Am. 1991), State Bar Calif. (antitrust and trade regulation sect., exec. com. 1990-92), LA County Bar Assn. (chmn. antitrust sect. 1981-82, mem. editl. bd. The Judges Jour. 1989-91, mem. com. professionalism 1988—, numerous other coms.), Assn. of Bus. Trial Lawyers (bd. govs. 1990-92), Stanford Alumni Assn., Stanford Law Soc. Calif., Vassar Club So. Calif. (past pres.). Office: US Ct Appeals 9th Cir US Court of Appeals Bldg 125 S Grand Ave Rm 600 Pasadena CA 91105-1621*

RYN, CLAES GÖSTA, political science professor; b. Norrköping, Sweden, June 12, 1943; permanent resident of U.S., 1979, naturalized, 2002; s. Gösta Karl and Cecilia Edit (Blom) R.; m. Marianne Carin Tedhagen, Aug. 30, 1969; children: Charlotte, Viveka, Elisabet. MA, Uppsala U., Sweden, 1967, postgrad., 1969—71, Syracuse U., 1968—69; PhD, La. State U., 1974. Asst. prof. politics Cath. U. Am., Washington, 1974-78, assoc. prof. politics, 1978-82, prof. politics, 1982—, asst. dean Sch. Arts and Scis., 1977-79, chmn. dept. politics, 1979-85. Adj. prof. govt. Georgetown U., 2002-05; vis. assoc. prof. U. Va., Charlottesville, 1981; co-founder, chmn. Nat. Humanities Inst., Washington, 1984—; referee, evaluator NEH, Dept. Edn., USIA, others; dir. confs. and lecture series; Richard M. Weaver fellowship selection com., 1980—; faculty sponsor Earhart Found., 1989-2008; awards com. Ingersoll Prizes, 1990; Salvatori doctoral fellowship selection com., 1990—; lectr. in US, Europe and China. Author: (with Bertil Häggman) Nykonservatismen i USA, 1971, Democracy and the Ethical Life, 1978, 2d rev. edit., 1990, Will, Imagination and Reason, 1986, 2d rev. edit., 1997, Individualism och gemenskap, 1986, The New Jacobinism, 1991, Unity Through Diversity (in Chinese), 2001, A Common Human Ground, 2003, America the Virtuous, 2003, Peter Viereck and Conservatism, 2005; editor: Humanitas, 1992—; co-editor (with George Panichas), joint-author: Irving Babbitt in Our Time, 1986; editor, author introduction for other volumes; contbr. articles to profl. jours.; mem. editl. bd. Modern Age, 1981—, Marknadsekonomisk Tidskrift, Sweden, 1986-92, This World, 1992—; editl. columnist Svenska Dagbladet, Sweden, 1996—. Mem. vestry St. Francis Episcopal Ch., Potomac, Md., 1986-88. Served with Swedish Army, Royal Life Company I 4 Regt., 1963, Signal Corps, 1967-68. Rsch. fellow Earhart Found., 1980-81, 87-88, Wilbur Found., 1980-81, 90, 93-94, others; Disting. Fgn. Scholar Lectures Peking U., 2000; recipient award King of Sweden, 1983, Will Herberg award Disting. Faculty Svc. Intercollegiate Studies Inst., 2003; named Outstanding Grad. Prof., Cath. U. Am., 1992, Hon. mem. Heimdal Uppsala U., 2007-. Mem. Phila. Soc. (trustee 1999, 2d v.p. 2000-01, pres. 2001-02), Acad. Philosophy and Letters (co-founder, mem., bd. dirs. 2006—, pres., 2007—). Episcopalian. Home: 10008 Crestleigh Ln Potomac MD 20854-1820 Office: Cath Univ Am Dept Politics Washington DC 20064-0001

RYNEARSON, ARTHUR JOHN, lawyer; b. Caracas, Venezuela, Apr. 18, 1949; s. Arthur Preston and Kathryn Loraine Rynearson; m. Mary Linda Patteson, Oct. 26, 1996. BA, Hamilton Coll., 1971; cert. in internat. and comparative law, U. San Diego, 1975; JD, Cornell U., 1976. Bar: D.C. 1976. Fgn. affairs analyst Congl. Rsch. Svc. Libr. of Congress, Washington, 1971—73; asst. counsel Legis. Counsel's Office US Senate, Washington, 1976—91, sr. counsel, 1991—99, dep. legis. counsel, 1999—2003. Lectr. Legis. Studies Inst., Washington, 1990—93, Meridian Internat. Ctr., Washington, 1999—2002, Internat. Law Inst., Washington, 1999—; adj. faculty mem. Am. Univ. Wash. Coll. of Law, 2004—. Bd. trustees Met. Meml., Washington. Mem.: D.C. Bar (internat. law sect., co-chair nat. security subcom. 1990—91), Am. Soc. Internat. Law, Phi Beta Kappa. Avocations: Native American cultures, tennis.

RYNKIEWICZ, STEPHEN MICHAEL, journalist; b. Sheboygan, Wis., Oct. 20, 1955; s. Walter Paul and Ruth Catherine (Van Hercke) R.; m. Brenda Gail Russell, Sept. 27, 1986. BA, U. Wis., 1976. Various staff assignments Chgo. Sun-Times, 1979-97, real estate editor, 1990-97; Internet prodr. Chgo. Tribune, 1997—. Pres. Ill. Freedom of Info. Coun., 1991-93; mem. profl. faculty Columbia Coll., Chgo., 1998. Pres. Chgo. Headline Club, 1991-92, treas., 2001-02; chmn. Peter Lisagor Awards for Exemplary Journalism, 2002-06; sec. Headline Club Found., 2004—. Recipient Web Site award, Nat. Assn. Real Estate Editors, 1997—2000, Editor and Pub. Best Newspaper Classified Site award, 2000, award for pub. svc., Online Journalism Assn., 2002, Pub. award, Chgo. Tribune, 2006. Mem. Soc. Profl. Journalists (regional dir. 1992-95, sec.-treas. 1995-96, membership chair 1997-98, diversity chair 1996-97, Peter Lisagor award 2003, 08), Nat. Soc. Real Estate Editors (bd. dirs. 1999-2000), Toastmasters Internat. (asst. div. gov. 2007-08), Sigma Delta Chi Found. (bd. dirs. 1995-96), East Village Assn. (bd. mem. 2007-). Office: Ste 400 435 N Michigan Ave Chicago IL 60611-4001

RYNN, NATHAN, physics professor, consultant; b. NYC, Dec. 2, 1923; s. Meyer and Rose (Wolkerwiczer) Rynkowsky; m. Glenda Brown, June 24, 1989; children by previous marriage: Jonathan, Margaret, David. BSEE, CCNY, 1944; MS, U. Ill., 1947; PhD, Stanford U., 1956. Rsch. engr. RCA Labs., Princeton, NJ, 1947-52; rsch. asst. Stanford U., Palo Alto, Calif., 1952-56, rsch. assoc., 1958; mem. tech. staff Ramo-Woolridge, LA, 1956-57; supr. Huggins Labs., Menlo Park, Calif., 1957-58; rsch. staff physicist Princeton U., 1958-65; prof. physics U. Calif.-Irvine, 1965-94, prof. physics emeritus, rsch. prof. physics, 1994—. Vis. prof. Ecole Polytechnique Fed. of Lausanne, Switzerland, 1984-90, Ecole Polytechnique, Paris, and other European univs. and labs., 1973-80; indsl. sci. advisor/cons., 1964—; com. mem. Plasma Sci. Com. Nat. Rsch. Coun.; founder and leader plasma physics rsch. facility (the Q-Machine). Contbr. articles and revs. to profl. jours. With USN, 1944-46. Grantee NSF, U.S. Dept. Energy, Air Force Geophys. Lab.; Fulbright sr. fellow, 1978. Fellow Am. Phys. Soc., IEEE, AAAS; mem. Sigma Xi. Avocation: woodworking. Office: U Calif Dept Physics & Astronomy Irvine CA 92697-4575 Office Phone: 949-824-5944. Business E-Mail: nrynn@uci.edu.

RYPINA, IRINA I., oceanographer; b. Nizhny Novgorod, Russia, Apr. 27, 1980; d. Iosif M. Rypin and Larisa E. Rypina; m. Ilya A. Udovydchenkov, Aug. 17, 2007. BS in Plasma Physics (hon.), Nizhny Novgorod State U., 2002; MS in Physics, U. La., Lafayette, 2003; PhD in Applied Marine Physics, RSMAS U. Miami, Fla., 2007. Tchg. asst. U. La., 2002—03; rsch. asst. RSMAS,AMP, U. Miami, 2003—07; postdoc. investigator PO dept. Woods Hole Oceanog. Inst., Mass., 2008—. Mem.: Acoustical Soc. Am., Am. Geophys. Union (Donald L. Turcotte award 2008), Sigma Pi Sigma Physics Honor Soc. Office: Woods Hole Oceanog Inst MS#21 360 Woods Hole Rd Woods Hole MA 02543 Office Fax: 508-457-2181. Business E-Mail: irypina@whoi.edu.

RYSKAMP, CHARLES ANDREW, museum director, educator; b. East Grand Rapids, Mich., Oct. 21, 1928; s. Henry Jacob and Flora (DeGraaf) R. AB, Calvin Coll., 1950; MA, Yale U., 1951, PhD, 1956; MA, Pembroke Coll., Cambridge U., 1954; Litt.D., Trinity Coll., Hartford, 1975; L.H.D., Union Coll., 1977. Nathan Hale fellow Yale U., 1954-55; instr. English Princeton U., 1955-59, asst. prof., 1959-63, assoc. prof., 1963-69; curator English and Am. lit. U. Library, 1967-69, prof., 1969—2005; emeritus prof. U. Libr. Procter & Gamble faculty fellow, 1958-59; jr. fellow Coun. of Humanities, 1960-61, John E. Annan preceptor, 1961-64; dir. Pierpont Morgan Libr., N.Y.C., 1969-87, dir. emeritus, fellow (hon.), 1997—; dir. Frick Collection, N.Y.C., 1987-97, dir. emeritus, fellow (hon.), 1997—; dir. vis. Inst. Advanced Study, Princeton, 1997-99; exhbn. of collection of drawings, Pierpont Morgan Libr., 2001; adv. bd. Skowhegan Sch. Painting and Sculpture, Pvt. Papers of James Boswell, Yale U.; vis. com. dept. drawings and printed books and med. and ren. Pierpont Morgan Libr. Coun. and Libr. Com., Frick Collection; bd. adv. Princeton U. Art Mus. Author: William Cowper of the Inner Temple, Esq, 1959, William Blake, Engraver, 1969; editor: (with F.A. Pottle) Boswell: The Ominous Years, 1963, The Cast-Away, 1963, Wilde and the Nineties, 1966, William Blake: The Pickering Manuscript, 1972, (with J. King) The Letters and Prose Writings of William Cowper, vol. I, 1979, vol. II, 1981, vol. III, 1982, Vol. IV, 1984, Vol. V, 1986, (with R. Wendorf) The Works of William Collins, 1979, (with J. Baird) The Poetical Works of William Cowper, vol. I, 1980, vols. II-III, 1995, (with J. King) William Cowper: Selected Letters, 1989, Report to the Fellows of the Pierpont Morgan Library, vols. 16-21, 1969-89, Charles Ryskamp and Friends, 1999, (with Scott Westrem) The Works of John Chalkhill, 1999, Of Cabbages and Kings, 2004, The Ladies, God Bless Them. Trustee, exec. com. Mus. Broadcasting, 1977-87; trustee John Simon Guggenheim Meml. Found., Libr. of Am.; trustee emeritus Corning Mus. Glass, Amon Carter Mus.; past vis. com. dept. paintings conservation Met. Mus. Art; patron William Blake Trust; bd. mgrs. Lewis Walpole Libr., Yale U.; bd. dirs., v.p. Gerard B. Lambert Found.; past v.p. Frederick R. Koch Found.; trustee Venetian Heritage. Decorated Order St. John of Jerusalem, comdr. Order Orange Nassau, The Netherlands, officer Order Leopold II, Belgium, comdr. Order of Falcon, Iceland; recipient Peter Stuyvesant award Dutch Am. West-India Co., 1987, Gold medal Holland Soc., 1991; Charles Ryskamp Rsch. fellowship, Am. Coun. Learned Socs. Mem. Am. Philos. Soc., Museums Coun. N.Y.C. (past v.p.), Keats-Shelley Assn. Am. (past v.p.), Master Drawings Assn. (past pres.), Met. Opera Assn. (bd. adv., chmn. art and archives com.), Drawing Soc. (nat. com.), Am. Assocs. Royal Nat. Theatre, Bibliog. Soc. Am., Acad. Am. Poets, Am. Antiquarian Soc., Assn. Art Mus. Dirs. (past pres.), NY Geneal. and Biog. Soc. (spl. corr.), Neuropathy Assn. (nat. adv. coun.), Cowper Soc., Assn. Internat. Bibliophilie (com. of Honor), Found. French Mus. (adv. bd.), Wordsworth Rydal Mount Trust, Grolier Club, Century Assn., Lotos Club, Knickerbocker Club, Elizabethan Club (New Haven), Roxburghe Club (London)

RYTKONEN, KATIE, psychologist; b. Marquette, Mich., Dec. 30, 1979; d. Ronald Rytkonen and MaryLynn Juidici, Peter Juidici (Stepfather). BA, Northern Mich. U., Marquette, 2002; Degree in Sch. Psychology, Western Ill. U., Macomb, 2005. Sch. psychologist Kendall County Spl. Edn. Coop, Yorkville, Ill., 2005—. Office: Kendall County Special Education Coop 201 Garden St Yorkville IL 60560 Business E-Mail: krytkonen@kcsec.org.

RYU, KISANG, educator; b. Gwangju, Republic of Korea, Dec. 1, 1972; m. Eunjung Yang. Degree in Hotel, Restaurant and Tourism Mgmt., Kans. State U., Manhattan, 2005. Asst. prof. U. New Orleans, 2006—. Contbr. conf. (Best Conf. Paper award, 2005). Mem.: Asian Pacific Tourism Assn., Internat. Coun. Hotel, Restaurant, Instl. Edn. Home: 62200 W End Blvd Apt 8308 Slidell LA 70461 Office: Univ New Orleans 449 Kirschman Hall 2000 Lakeshore Drive New Orleans LA 70148 Office Fax: 504-280-3189. Business E-Mail: kryu@uno.edu.

RYU, MANHO, application developer; b. Sochungdo, Kyungido, Korea, Mar. 23, 1957; arrived in U.S., 1983; s. Bongoh Ryu and Youngah No; m. Michelle M. Ryu, May 28, 1960; children: Angie L., Jason C. BS in Computer Sci., Abilene Christian U., Tex., 1986; BS in Applied Math., U. Tex. at Dallas, Richardson, 1988; MS in Applied Math., U. Tex. at Dallas, 1993; MS in Computer Sci., Kennedy-Western U., Boise, Idaho, 1992; PhD in Computer Sci., Kennedy-Western U., 1996. ASQ CSQE, CQA, RABQSA QMSPA. Programmer Korea Inst. Sci. and Tech., Seoul, 1976—82; computer operator Electrospace Sys., Richardson, 1988; lead programmer Info. Mgmt. Group, Plano, Tex., 1989—90; analyst, sys. supr. Epsilon Data Mgmt., Inc., Dallas, 1990—92; mgr. MIS dept. MB Direct, Inc., Dallas, 1992—93; dir. IS dept. Skyking Freight Sys., Dallas, 1993—94; sr. software engr. Spectra Vision Inc., Richardson, 1994—97, Estech Sys., Plano, 1997—98; sr. software devel. engr. Alcatel-Lucent NA, Plano, 1998—. Author: (software) Clean Man TXU, Cash Man TXU. Mem.: IEEE, Assn. Computing Machinery, Math. Assn. Am. Home: 7902 Bow Ct Frisco TX 75035

Office: Alcatel Lucent NA 3400 W Plano Pkwy Plano TX 75075 Office Phone: 972-477-9660. Personal E-mail: mmryu@yahoo.com. Business E-Mail: man.ryu@alcatel-lucent.com.

RYU, SAMUEL, surgeon; MD, Kyungpook U., Taegu, 1982. Diplomate Am. Coll. Radiology, 1996. Dir. radiosurgery Henry Ford Hosp., Detroit, 1999—. Achievements include first to spine and body radiosurgery. Office: Henry Ford Hosp 2799 W Grand Blvd Detroit MI 48202

RYUN, JIM (JAMES RONALD RYUN), former congressman; b. Wichita, Kans., Apr. 29, 1947; m. Anne Carol Snider, 1969; children: Ned, Drew, Catharine, Heather. BA, U. Kans., 1970. Founder, pres. Jim Ryun Sports, Inc.; mem. US Congressman from 2nd Kans. dist., 1996—2007; mem. armed svcs. com., budget com., fin. svcs. com. US Congress from 2nd Kans. dist. Participant Olympic Games, 1964, 68, 72; Founder Jim Ryun Running Camps. Recipient James E. Sullivan award, 1966, Silver medal 1500 meter run Olympic Games, 1968; Named Sportsman of Yr., SI mag., 1966, Athlete of Yr., ABC Wide World of Sports, 1966; Named to the US Tack & Field Hall of Fame, 2003, Nat. Distance Running Hall of Fame. Republican. Office: PO Box 826 Topeka Lawrence KS 66047 Office Phone: 785-273-8901. E-mail: info@jimryun.com.

RZEPKOWSKI, JAMES EDWARD, energy executive; b. Annapolis, Md., Mar. 8, 1971; s. Walter Jerome and Veronica Catherine (Gnacyk) R.; m. Laura E. Green, Aug. 23, 1997; children: Brian Myer. BA, U. Md., 1993. Computer aide Nat. Security Agy. U.S. Dept. Defense, 1988-89; office mgr. Md. Dept. Housing and Cmty. Devel., 1990; legis. intern to Sen. John A Cade Md. State Senate, 1992; state del. dist. 32 State of Md., 1995—2003; ins. office rep. State Farm Ins. Agy., 1993—; assoc. dep. sec. Md. Dept. Bus. and Econ. Devel., 2003—07; dir. workforce devel. Constellation Energy, 2007—. Adminstrv. asst. Crofton Convalescent Ctr., 1991; cashier Latelas Discount Liquors, 1992-93. State mem. Md. State Rep. Ctrl. Com., Annapolis, 1992; ofcl., player intramural sports U. Md.; pastoral coun. Cath. Student Ctr., 1992-93. Recipient Legis. Leadership award, The ARC of Md., 2000, Legislator of Yr. award, Anne Arundel County C. of C., 1996. Mem. K.C., Md. Medallion Soc. (charter), Eta Epsilon Alumni Assn. (pres. 1994—), Phi Beta Kappa, Omicron Delta Kappa, Alpha Lambda Delta, Golden Key, Pi Kappa Phi. Home: 8109 Huntmaster CT Glen Burnie MD 21061-6343 Office: 111 Market Pl Ste 200 Baltimore MD 21202

RZEPNICKI, TINA L., social sciences educator; b. South Bend, Ind., Sept. 19, 1950; d. Edmund and Erma Rzepnicki; m. Barry Rapoport, July 7, 1985; children: Erin Rapoport, Andrew Rapoport. BA, DePauw U., Greencastle, Ind., 1973; AM, U. Chgo., Sch. Social Svc. Adminstrn., Ill., 1978; PhD, 1982. Social worker House of Good Shepherd, Chgo., 1973—76; asst. prof. Fordham U., Grad. Sch. Social Svc., NYC, 1983—87; David and Mary Winton Green prof. U. Chgo., Sch. Social Svc. Adminstrn., 1987—, dep. dean faculty and acad. affairs, 2006—08. Cons. Hedge Funds Care, NYC, 2005—. Contbr. articles to profl. jours.;, author books. Malpas scholar, DePauw U., 1969—73. Mem.: NASW, Soc. Social Work and Rsch., Coun. Social Work Edn. Independent. Office: Univ Chicago SSA 969 E 60th St Chicago IL 60637 Business E-Mail: t-rzepnicki@uchicago.edu.

RZEWSKI, FREDERIC, composer; b. Westfield, Mass., 1938; Student, Harvard Coll., 1954—58, Princeton U., 1958—60. Co-founder, performer Musica Elettronica Viva, Rome, 1966—71; prof. composition Conservatoire Royal de Musique, Liege, Belgium, 1977—. Composer: The People United Will Never Be Defeated!, 1975, The Triumph of Death, 1988, Cadenza con o senza Beethoven, 2003, Nanosonatas, 2007; author: Nonsequiturs: Writings and Lectures on Improvisation, Composition, and Interpretation, 2007. Mem.: AAAL. Office: c/o Esther Freifeld EGF EPRC Rue de l'Aqueduc Bte 0 B-1050 Brussels Belgium*

RZONZEF, MICHEL, manufacturing executive; b. Liege, Belgium, July 13, 1963; Degree in Electro-Mech. Engring., U. Liege. Engring. test mgmt. positions & European region mktg. mgmt. positions through sales mgr. Goodyear Dunlop So. Ea. Europe The Goodyear Tire & Rubber Co., 1988—2001, dir., sales & mktg., 2002—07, v.p., sales & mktg., 2007—08, pres., Ea. Europe, Mid. East & Africa, 2008—. Office: The Goodyear Tire & Rubber Co 1144 E Market St Akron OH 44316 Office Phone: 330-796-2121. Office Fax: 330-796-2222.

SA, TONGMIN, education educator; b. Seoul, Republic of Korea, Mar. 21, 1960; s. Byungkwon and Kiwon Sa; m. Eunkyung Bae, Nov. 26, 1990; children: Seungyeon, Seungwhan. BS, Seoul Nat. U., 1984, MS, 1986; PhD, NC State U., 1990. Rschr. Agrl. Biotechnology Inst., Suwon, Republic of Korea, 1992—94; prof. Sun Moon U., Asan, Republic of Korea, 1994—99, Chungbuk Nat. U., Cheongju, Republic of Korea, 1999—. Achievements include characterizing plant microbe interaction and biofertilizer development. Home: Jangbok Villa-201 Secho-3-Dong SeochoKu Seoul Republic of Korea Office: Chungbuk Nat Univ Gaeshin-Dong Heungduck-Ku Chungbuk Cheongju 361-763 Republic of Korea Office Fax: 82-43-271-5921. Business E-Mail: tomsa@chungbuk.ac.kr.

SAAB, DEANNE KELTUM, real estate broker, appraiser; b. Allentown, Pa., Jan. 27, 1945; d. James A. and Agnes G. (Hanzlik) S. BA, Cedar Crest Coll., 1966; MS, U. Calif., Santa Barbara, 1973; realtors cert., Pa. State U., 1978. Cert. appraiser Assoc. Appraisal Inst., Pa., 1991; cert. sales profl. Nat. Assn. Home Builders, 1994. Tchr. Ojai (Calif.) Unified Sch. Dist., 1966-74; pvt. practice Allentown, 1978—; owner Heritage Gardens, Allentown, 1981—; pres., treas. DeAnne & Assoc., Inc., Allentown, 1987—. Co-founder, treas. performance group Lehigh Valley Folk Music Soc., 1996. Mem. AAUW (various offices, Best State Newsletter award 1987), Nat. Assn. Realtors, Pa. Assn. Realtors, Allentown Lehigh Valley Assn. Realtors, Cedar Crest Coll. Alumnae Assn. (class rep., various offices), Lehigh Valley Guild Craftsmen (various offices). Avocations: gourd, herbal crafting, painting, folk music performance. Home and Office: 1360 Dorney Ave Allentown PA 18103-9731 Personal E-mail: dksaab@ptd.net.

SAACKE, RICHARD GEORGE, retired biology professor; b. Newark, Oct. 31, 1931; s. George Edward Saacke and Minnie Techlar Keil; m. Ann Laird Litzelman, June 4, 1954; children: Wendy Jean Azzara, Kristen Lynn Blunk, Ronald James, David Wayne, Richard Scott. BSc, Rutgers U., NB, NJ, 1953; MS, Pa. State U., State Coll., 1955, PhD, 1962. Asst. prof. Pa. State U., 1962—65; asst. prof. to prof. Va. Poly. Inst, Blacksburg, 1965—2001, prof. emeritus, 2001—. Free lance cons. & lectr., 2001—. Past pres. Lions Internat., Blacksburg. 1st lt. Signal Corp US Army, 1955—58, Germany. Recipient Rsch. award, Nat. Assoc. Animal Breeders, 1985, Am. Dairy Sci. Assoc., 1985, Soc. Theriogenology, 1995, Casida award, Am. Soc. Animal Sci., 2006. Non-Partisan. Avocation: fishing. Office: Va Poly Inst Dept Dairy Sci Blacksburg VA 24061 Business E-Mail: saacke@vt.edu.

SAAD, GERMAINE H., business management professor, researcher; b. Bany-Suef, Egypt, Nov. 26, 1944; d. Hozayen and Helpis Saad; m. Ayoub Barsoum Ayoub, Feb. 5, 1972; 1 child, Mariane Ayoub; 1 child, Sameh Ragheb. B in Comm., Cairo U., Guiza, Egypt, 1964, MBA, 1970; MA, U. Pa., 1978, PhD, 1980. Demonstrator and educator Cairo U., Egypt, 1964—74; instr. U. Pa., Phila., 1975—78, 1978—80; prof. Ain-Shams U., Cairo, 1980—86, CUNY, NYC, 1982—84, Widener U., Chester, Pa., 1986—. Cons. Ctrl. Agy. for Orgns. and Adminstrns., Cairo, 1984—86; mem. editl. bd. Jour. Mgmt. Systems, Arlington, Va., 1989—95, Bus. Jour., New Haven, 1991—. Contbr. articles to profl. jours. Vol. Abington Meml. Hosp., Pa., 1999; bd. dirs. St. George Orthodox Ch., Norristown, Pa., 1997—2002. Christian-Orthodox. Avocations: painting, travel, artwork. Home: 1847 Watson Road Abington PA 19001 Office: Widener U One University Place Chester PA 19013 Business E-Mail: ghsaad@widener.edu.

SAAD, MICHAEL D., lawyer; b. Zanesville, Ohio, 1941; BS, Ohio State U., 1963, JD summa cum laude, 1966. Bar: Ohio 1966. Law clk. to Chief Justice Ohio State Supreme Ct., 1966—67; ptnr. Squire, Sanders & Dempsey LLP, Columbus, Ohio. Chmn. real estate & hospitality practice group Squire, Sanders & Dempsey LLP. Bd. dir. Ohio Housing Coun. Recipient Founder's Award, Ohio Capital Corp., 2002. Mem.: Order of Coif, Columbus Bar Assn. (fin. institutes com., real estate com., bankruptcy com.), Ohio State Bar Assn., Devel. Com. Ctrl. Ohio, ABA. Office: Squire Sanders & Dempsey LLP 1300 Huntington Ctr 41 South High St Columbus OH 43215-6197 Office Phone: 614-365-2735. Office Fax: 614-365-2499. Business E-Mail: msaad@ssd.com.

SAAD, THEODORE SHAFICK, retired microwave company executive; b. Boston, Sept. 13, 1920; s. Wadie Assad and Mary (Shalhoub) S.; m. Afeefi Abdelnour, May 5, 1943; children: Karen Jeanne, Janet Elaine. BSEE, MIT, 1941. Engr. Sylvania Electric Products, Danvers, Mass., 1941-42; rsch. assoc. radiation lab. Radiation Lab. MIT, Cambridge, 1942-45; sr. engr. Submarine Signal Co., Boston, 1945-49; v.p., chief engr. Microwave Devel. Labs., Waltham, Mass., 1949-53; engring. specialist Sylvania Electric Products, Woburn, Mass., 1953-55; pres., chmn. Sage Labs. Inc., Natick, Mass., 1955-93; ret., 1993. Cons. Horizon House Microwave, Norwood, Mass., 1958—. Editor: Microwave Engineers Handbook, 1971, Historical Perspectives of Microwave Technology, 1984; patentee in microwavetech. and passive components fields. Chmn. Concert Opera, Boston, 1997—. Fellow IEEE (life; Richard M. Emberson award 1996), AAAS; mem. Microwave Soc. of IEEE (hon. life; nat. lectr. 1972, Disting. Svc. award 1983, Centennial medal 1984, Career award 1992). Avocations: photography, reading, travel, music. Home: 52 Doublet Hill Rd Weston MA 02493-2331

SAADA, ADEL SELIM, civil engineer, educator; b. Heliopolis, Egypt, Oct. 24, 1934; came to U.S., 1959, naturalized, 1965; s. Selim N. and Marie (Chahyne) S.; m. Nancy Helen Hernan, June 5, 1960; children: Christiane Mona, Richard Adel. Ingénieur des Arts et Manufactures, École Centrale, Paris, 1958; MS, U. Grenoble, France, 1959; PhD in Civil Engring, Princeton U., 1961. Registered profl. engr., Ohio. Engr. Société Dumez, Paris, 1959; research assoc. dept. civil engring. Princeton (N.J.) U., 1961-62; asst. prof. civil engring. Case Western Reserve U., Cleve., 1962-67, asso. prof., 1967-72, prof., 1973—, chmn. dept. civil engring., 1978-98, Frank H. Neff prof. civil engring., 1987. R.J. Carroll Meml. lectr. Johns Hopkins U., 1990; cons., lectr. soil testing and properties Waterways Expt. Sta. (C.E.), Vicksburg, Miss., 1974-79; cons. to various firms, 1962—. Author: Elasticity Theory and Applications, 1974, 2d edit., 2009; contbr. numerous articles on soil mechanics and foundation engring. to profl. jours. Recipient Telford Prize Instn. of Civil Engrs., U.K., 1995, Disting. Leadership award Cleve. Tech. Socs., 2001. Fellow ASCE (named Outstanding Civil Engr. of Yr. Cleve. sect. 1992, G.Brooks Earnest award 2006); mem. Internat. Soc. Soil Mechanics, One Two One Athletic Club. Achievements include invention of pneumatic analog computer and loading frame. Home: 3342 Braemar Rd Shaker Heights OH 44120-3332 Office: Case Western Res U Dept Civil Engring Case Sch Engring Cleveland OH 44106 Office Phone: 216-368-2427. Business E-Mail: axs31@case.edu.

SAADEGHVAZIRI, MOHAMAD ALA, civil engineering educator; b. Sanandadj, Kurdistan, Iran, July 3, 1958; came to U.S., 1978; s. Abolgasem and Sanieh (Moatamadvaziri) S.; m. Mandana Ahsani, Aug. 7, 1987; children: Armin, Hanna, Azad BS, U. Ill., Urbana, 1982, MS, 1983, PhD, 1988. Registered profl. engr., N.J. Prof. dept., civil engring. NJ Inst. Tech., Newark, 1988—. Cons. various orgns., N.J., Ill. Contbr. articles to profl. jours. Fellow ASCE, ASTM, Am. Concrete Inst., Earthquake Engring. Rsch. Inst. Avocations: racquetball, tennis, soccer, reading. Office: NJ Inst Tech Dept Civil Engring University Heights Newark NJ 07102 Office Phone: 973-596-5813. Business E-Mail: ale@njit.edu.

SAADEH, CONSTANTINE KHALIL, internist, educator, health facility administrator; b. Beirut, Sept. 6, 1957; came to U.S., 1982; s. Khalil Constantine and Angel Janet (Iskendarian) S.; m. M. Celeste Gaylor; 2 children: Charles, McKenzie. BS in Biology-Chemistry, Am. U. Beirut, 1978, MD, 1982. Diplomate Nat. Bd. Med. Examiners, Am. Bd. Internal Medicine, Am. Bd. Allergy and Immunology, Am. Bd. Internal Medicine, Am. Bd. Rheumatology, Am. Bd. Geriatrics, Am. Acad. Pain Mgmt. Intern U. Miami, Jackson Meml. Hosp., Fla., 1982-83, resident in medicine Fla., 1983-85; fellow in clin. immunology Baylor Coll. of Medicine, Houston, 1985-87; fellow in rheumatology U. Colo. Health Sci. Ctr., Denver, 1987-88, instr. dept. internal medicine, 1988-89; acting chief med. svc. VA Med. Ctr., Amarillo, Tex., 1989, med. svc. staff physician, 1989—; asst. prof. dept. internal medicine Tex. Tech U. Health Scis. Ctr., Amarillo, 1989-91, assoc. prof. internal medicine and pediatrics, dir., 1991—, regional chair internal medicine, dir. residency program, 1992-98, assoc. prof. dept. microbiology and immunology, 1992—, clin. prof. dept. microbiol./immun., internal med., pediats., 1998—; pvt. practice Allergy ARTS, Amarillo, Tex.; pres. Amarillo Ctr. for Clin. Rsch., 2000—. Chief medicine N.W. Tex. Hosp., Amarillo, 1999-2001; lectr. in field. Contbr. articles to profl. jours. Fellow ACP, Am. Acad. Allergy and Immunology, Am. Coll. Rheumatology; mem. AMA, So. Med. Assn. (chmn. rheumatology sect. 1996-97, sec. internal medicine sect. 1997-99, assoc. councilor 1998-99). Home: 3000 S Hughes St Amarillo TX 79109-3515 Office: 6842 Plum Creek Dr Amarillo TX 79124 Home Phone: 806-374-8055; Office Phone: 806-353-7000. Business E-Mail: aarts@allergyarts.com.

SAADEH, SHERIF NABIL, gastroenterologist, hepatologist, researcher; b. Amman, Jordan, Nov. 29, 1969; s. Nabil Ibrahim Saadeh and Helen Aziz Ibrahim; m. Claudia-Aghareed Jamal Haddad; children: Omar, Kareem, Celina. MBBS, U. Jordan Faculty Medicine, MD, 1993. Cert. internal medicine Am. Bd. Internal Medicine, 1999, gastroenterology Am. Bd. Internal Medicine, 2003, hon. diplomate Am. Bd. Hosp. Physicians, Am. Coll. Ethical Physicians. Staff gastroenterologist/hepatologist Baylor U. Med. Ctr., Dallas, 2003—. Contbr. Recipient Rsch. award, North Am. Conf. Gastroenterology Fellows, 2002, fellowship, Am. Bd. Hosp. Physicians, 2002, America's Top Physician award, Consumer's Rsch. Coun. Am., 2003; grantee medical rsch. grant-subinvestigator, Nat. Insts. Health, 2001, medical rsch. grant, Cleve. Clinic Hepatology Inst., 2001. Fellow: Am. Coll. Hosp. Physicians; mem.: ACP, Jordan Med. Assn., European Assn. for Study of Liver, Tex. Soc. Gastroenterology and Endoscopy, Am. Coll. Gastroenterology, Crohn's & Colitis Found. Am., Am. Liver Found., AMA (Physician's recognition award 2004—07), Am. Soc. Gastrointestinal Endoscopy, Am. Gastroenterol. Assn., Am. Ass. Study Liver Diseases. Roman Catholic. Office: Al-Khalidi Medical Plz PO BOX 5321 11183 Amman Jordan Personal E-mail: saadeh@lycos.com.

SAAL, ILKA, literature and language professor; PhD, Duke U., Durham, NC. Assoc. prof. English U. Richmond, Va., 2002—; guest prof. Ghent U., Belgium, 2008—. Contbr. articles to profl. jours. (SAMLA Studies Book award, 2008). Recipient Sahla Studies Book award, 2008. Home: Kasteclstreat16 Antwerp 2000 Belgium

SAALFELD, FRED ERICH, science educator, researcher; s. Eric Arthur and Milla (Kessler) S.; m. Elizabeth Renner, Nov. 22, 1958; 1 child, Fred E. Jr. (dec.). BS cum laude, So. East Mo. State U., 1957; MS in Phys. Chemistry, Iowa State U., 1959, PhD in Phys. Chemistry, 1961. Instr. Iowa State U., Ames, 1961—62; chemist Naval Rsch. Lab, Washington, 1962—63, head mass spectrometry sect., 1963—74, head phys. chem. br., 1974—76, supt. chem. divsn., 1976—82; chief scientist Office Naval Rsch., London, 1979—80, dir. rsch. Arlington, Va., 1982—87, dir., 1987—93, dep. chief naval rsch., tech. dir., 1993—98, exec. dir., tech. dir., 1998—2002; disting. rsch. prof. Ctr. for Tech. and Nat. Security Policy Nat. Def. U., 2003—04; sr. fellow Potomac Inst. for Policy Studies, 2002—, bd. regents, 2007—. Author more than 500 publications, reports, presentations on applications of mass spectrometry to fields of combustion, laser, environ. analysis. Recipient Disting. Rank awards U.S. Pres., Washington, 1989, 96, Meritorious Rank award U.S. Pres., Washington, 1986, Robert Conrad award Sec. USN, Washington, 1988, Disting. Civilian Svc. award Sec. of Def./Dept. Def., 1999; named Fed. Exec. of Yr., Fed. Exec. Inst., Washington, 1991, named Fred E. Saalfed award for lifetime achievement in sci., Chief Naval Rsch., 2001. Fellow AAAS, Potomac Inst. Policy Studies (sr.); mem. Am. Chem. Soc. (councilor 1973-89), Am. Soc. Mass Spectrometry (sec. 1970-74), Combustion Inst., Chem. Soc. Washington (pres. 1972). Achievements include provision for science base for life support systems used in enclosed environments; development of educational programs used by USN for scientist training. Office Phone: 703-887-2197. Personal E-mail: fsaalfeld@verizon.net.

SAARI, DAVID JOHN, retired law educator; b. Va., Minn., Jan. 12, 1934; s. William Willard Saari and Amelia Haapala, Helmi Pesola (Stepmother); m. Madeleine Belanger (div.); children: Glenna, Lenore, Peter, Gail; m. Martha Elizabeth Sullivan, July 16, 1987. BA, U. Minn., Mpls., 1955, JD, 1959. Bar: Oreg. 1962, D.C. 2007. Legal rschr. League Oreg. Cities, U. Oreg., Eugene, 1959—64; ct. adminstr. Circuit Ct. Portland Oreg., 1964—67; rsch. assoc. Am. Bar Found., Chgo., 1967—68; dir. Ct. Mgmt. Study, Washington, 1968—70; mgr. LEX Computer Sys., Bethesda, Md., 1970—72; dir. sch. justice Am. U., Washington, 1972—75, faculty, prof. emeritus, 1972—99. Pres. Western Trial Ct. Adminstr., Portland, 1967, Nat. Assn. Trial Ct. Adminstr., Portland, 1968. Author: (books) American Court Management, Theories and Practices, 1982, Management of Court Reporters, 1985, Too Much Liberty, Perspectives on Freedom and the American Dream, 1995, Global Corporations and Sovereign Nations, Collision or Cooperation, 1999; contbr. articles various profl. jours.; author: A California Pioneer From New York(1802-1874), 2009, (book) Francis Ziba Branch. Mem. Eugene City Club, 1963—64, Nat. Assn. Ct. Mgrs., Williamsburg, Va., 1980—90. With USAR. Grantee monetary, Am. U., 1972—85. Independent. Unitarian. Avocations: sailing, skiing, travel, hiking. Home and Office: Dave's Art Farm 1451 Branch Mill Rd Arroyo Grande CA 93420

SAARI, DONALD GENE, mathematician, department chairman, economist; b. Ironwood, Mich., Mar. 9, 1940; s. Gene August and Martha Mary (Jackson) S.; m. Lillian Joy Kalinen, June 11, 1966; children: Katri, Anneli. BS, Mich. Technol. U., 1962; PhD, Purdue U., 1967, DSc (hon.), 1989, U. Caen, France, 1998, Mich. Tech. U., 1999. Research astronomer Yale U., New Haven, 1967-68; prof. dept. math. Northwestern U., Evanston, Ill., 1968-2000, prof. econs., 1988-2000, Pancoe prof. math., 1995-2000, chmn. dept., 1981-84; prof. U. Nanjing (China), 1995; disting. prof. econ., math U. Calif., Irvine, 2000—, dir. Ctr. for Decision Analysis, 2002—05, dir. Inst. Math. Behavioral Sci., 2003—. Cons. Nat. Bur. Standards, Gaithersburg, Md., 1979-86, Commn. 9, Internat. Astron. Union, 1985-91; nat. com. math. Nat. Rsch. Coun., 1997-2003, chair 2001-03, math./sci. edn. bd., 2001-07, Bd. Internat. Sci. Orgns., 2001-03, NRC com. on Internat. Inst. Applied Sys. Analysis, 2004-; chair trustees Math. Sci. Rsch. Inst., 2004-07. Assoc. editor Jour. Econ. Behavior and Orgn., 1988-94, Celestial Mechanics and Dynamical Astronomy. 1989-97, Econ. Theory, 1990-2007, Social Choice and Welfare, 1997—, Qualitative Theory of Dynamical Sys., 1999—, Positivity, 2000—. Recipient Duncan Black award, Pub. Choice Soc., 1991, Chauvenet prize Math. Assn. Am., 1995, Ford prize Math. Assn. Am., 1985, Allendorfer award Math. Assn. Am., 1999; Guggenheim fellow, 1988-89. Fellow AAAS, Am. Acad. Arts and Scis.; mem. NAS, Am. Math. Soc. (chief editor bull. 1999-2005, mem. coun. 1999-2005), Am. Astron. Soc., Soc. Indsl. and Applied Math. (editor jour. 1981-88), Econometric Soc. Office: U Calif Inst Math Behavorial Scis SSPA 2119 Irvine CA 92697-5100 Office Phone: 949-824-5894. Business E-Mail: dsaari@uci.edu.

SAAVEDRA, ABELARDO, former school system administrator; b. Feb. 18, 1951; m. Myrna Saavedra; children: Lisa, Elizabeth. BS, Texas A&I U., Kingsville, 1972, MS, 1974; PhD in Sch. Adminstrn., U. Mich., 1976. Teacher Corpus Christi Pub. Schools, asst. prin., prin.; supt. Corpus Christi Ind. Sch. Dist., 1993—2000; supt. SE dist. Houston Ind. Sch. Dist., 2001—02, exec. dep. supt. Sch. Support Svcs., 2002—04, supt., 2004—09. Adj. prof. U. Houston, Texas A&M U.; mem. Gov. Task Force Juvenile Justice. Chmn. bd. Greater Houston Chpt. Red Cross, March of Dimes; with WorkSource Bd. Dir. Recipient state and national recognition for development and adoption of "real-world academic standards" in all grade levels; named Supt. of Yr., Region 4 Edn. Svc. Ctr., 2008. Mem.: Tex. Bus. Edn. Coalition (co-chmn.), South Tex. Edn. R & D Ctr.*

SAAVEDRA, CHARLES JAMES, banker; b. Denver, Nov. 2, 1941; s. Charles James and Evangeline Cecilia (Aragon) S.; m. Ann Helen Taylor, 1967; children: Michael, Kevin, Sarah. BSBA, Regis U., Denver, 1963; postgrad., U. Calif., San Francisco, 1964-66. V.p. Western States Bankcard Assn., San Francisco, 1969-77; dir. info. systems World Airways, Inc., Oakland, Calif., 1977-79; v.p. computer svcs. First Nationwide Bank, San Francisco, 1979-83; sr. v.p. Wells Fargo Bank, San Francisco, 1983-92, Union Bank Calif., San Francisco, 1992—. Instr. Programming & Systems Inst., San Francisco, 1968-69; lectr. Am. Mgmt. Assn., 1984-2005, bd. dir. One Calif. Bank Oakland, 2006- Pres. Richt Direction Project Contra Costa County; bd. dirs. No. Calif. Family Ctr. With USNR, 1963-64. Mem. Data Processing Mgrs. Assn. (bd. dirs., chmn. program com. 1981), Am. Nat. Stds. Inst., Am. Bankers Assn.,

San Francisco Jaycees, Commonwealth Club Calif., Lake Lakewood Assn., Alpha Delta Gamma. Home: 210 Lakewood Rd Walnut Creek CA 94598-4826 Office Phone: 925-980-0911. Personal E-mail: jim_saa@yahoo.com.

SAAVEDRA-ARIAS, JOSÉ JAVIER, physics professor; b. Heredia, Costa Rica, Sept. 20, 1973; s. José Antonio Saavedra-Reyes and María Virginia Arias-Bustamante; m. Fanny Saravia-Arguedas; children: Javier Antonio Saavedra-Saravia, Fernando Alberto Saavedra-Saravia. BSc in Physics, U. Costa Rica, 2004; attending, U. PR, San Jose, Costa Rica, 2009. Asst. prof. U. Costa Rica, San Pedro, San José, 1994—2004; physics lab. technician U. Nat., Heredia, 2002—04, physics prof., 2005, U. Ciencias Médicas, San José, 2005. Grad. student rep. U. PR, San Juan, 2007—08. Inst. Funtional Nanomaterial fellowship, U. PR, 2008. Mem.: Am. Phys. Soc., Electrochem. Soc. Avocations: soccer, listen music, read, watch movies, travel. Home: 1162 Calle Tavarez Urb Garcia-Ubarri San Juan PR 00925 Office: Univ Puerto Rico Ponce De Leon Ave San Juan PR 00931 Business E-Mail: jsaavedr@gmail.com.

SABA, HUSSAIN ISMAIL, hematologist, researcher; m. Sabiha Rahman; children: Shereen Siddique, Rashid. MD, Bihar U., India, 1962; PhD, U. NC, Chapel Hill, 1970. Med. lic. Fla., NC. Chief med. oncology/hematology James A. Haley Veterans Hosp., Tampa, Fla., 1999—; prof. medicine U. South Fla. Coll. Medicine. Dir. hemophilia and thrombosis ctr. U. South Fla. Coll. Medicine, Tampa, Fla., dir. clin. rsch. malignant hematology program H. Lee Moffitt Cancer Ctr. and Rsch. Inst, co-dir. lymphoma and leukemia multidisciplinary ctr., 1989—96, dir. divsn. hematology, 1979—93, dir. divsn. hematology H. Lee Moffitt Cancer Ctr. and Rsch. Inst. Contbr. articles to profl. pubs., chapters to books. Mem.: Ea. Coop. Oncology Group (leukemia com.), Internat. Myelodysplastic Syndrome Found. (exec. bd. dirs.), Assn. Am. Physicians from South Asia (life; usf endowed scholarship com. mem.). Achievements include research in hematological and oncological malignancies and their treatment. Office: JAHVA Hosp USF Med Ctr and HLM VAR#111R 13000 Bruce B Downs Blvd Tampa FL 33612

SABAGH, DENYSE, lawyer; b. Washington, Sept. 27, 1948; JD, George Mason U., 1977. Bar: Va., DC, US Dist. Ct. (Ea. Dist.) Va., US Dist. Ct. Dist. DC, US Ct. Appeals DC Cir., US Dist. Ct. Dist. Md., Supreme Ct. Md., Supreme Ct. Va. Ptnr. Metzger, Hollis, Gordon & Alprin, Washington, 1977—97, Duane Morris LLP, 1997—. Co-chair nat. com. on legislation Enforcement Liaison Com., Immigration and Naturalization Svc., 1986, chair ann. cap. conf., 86, 87, 90, mem. bd. governors, 1988—, nat. sec., 1991—92, second v.p., 1993—94, first v.p., 1994—95, pres., 1996—97, chair, 1999; mem. Middle East Asylum Project, 1994—, FBI Arab American Adv. Com. Mem. bd. dirs. ACLU, 2000; mem. Nat. Multicultural Inst., 1990—, pres., 2004—; bd. mem. DC Rape Crisis Ctr., 1978—81, pres., 1979—81; mem. adv. counsel Washington Peace Ctr., 1992—95; mem. Potomac Massage Tng. Inst., 1990—2001, pres., 1991—94. Recipient Edith Lowenstein Meml. award for Excellence in Advancing the Practice of Immigration Law, 2003, Rose Bouziane Nader award, American-Arab Anti-Discrimination Com., 2006; named one of Top Immigration Lawyers in Washington DC, The Washingtonian, 2004, The Most Highly Regarded Individuals in Washington DC, 2005; named to Best Lawyers in America, 1997—, Global Leading Lawyers for Bus., Chambers Global, 2006—08, America's Leading Bus. Lawyers, Chambers USA, 2006—09, Washington DC Super Lawyers for Immigration, 2008. Mem.: American Immigration Lawyers Assn. (mem. bd. governors 1988—, chair legis. advocacy com. 2001—, gen. counsel 2003—05), Fairfax County Bar Assn., Arlington County Bar Assn., Va. State Bar, DC Bar, ABA. Office: Duane Morris LLP Ste 1000 505 9th St NW Washington DC 20004 Office Phone: 202-776-7817. Office Fax: 202-379-9867. Business E-Mail: DSabagh@duanemorris.com.*

SABAN, HAIM, investment company executive, television producer; b. Alexandria, Egypt, 1944; arrived in Israel, 1952, arrived in France, 1975, arrived in USA, 1983; m. Cheryl Saban, 1987; children: Ness, Tanya. TV series composer, 1975—95; chmn., CEO Saban Entertainment, LA, 1988—97, Fox Family Worldwide, LA, 1997—2001, Saban Capital Group, Inc., LA, 2001—; founder Saban Music Group, LA, 2002—. Bd. dirs. DirectTV Group, Inc., El Segundo, Calif., Societe TV Francaise 1, France, Univision, 2007—; bd. regents U. Calif., 2002—; founder Saban Ctr. Middle East Policy Brookings Inst., Washington, 2002, chair internat. adv. coun., trustee; chmn. supervisory bd. ProSiebenSat.1, Germany, 2003—07. Composer: (TV series) Heathcliff, He-Man & the Masters of the Universe, The Littles, Inspector Gadget, Mister T, Punky Brewster, Kissyfur, Rainbow Brite, She-Ra: Princess of Power, MASK, Popples, The Real Ghost Busters, Zoobilee Zoo, Dennis the Menace, Maxie's World, Beverly Hills Teens, C.O.P.S., Dragon Quest, The Super Mario Bros. Super Show!, Samurai Pizza Cats; exec. prodr.: (TV series) Kidd Video, 1984—87, Rambo, 1986, Mighty Morphin' Power Rangers, 1993—96, V.R. Troopers, 1994, Sweet Valley High, 1994—98, Power Rangers Zeo, 1996—97, Big Bad Beetleborgs, 1997, Breaker High, 1997—98, Power Rangers Turbo, 1997, Beetleborgs Metallix, 1997, Diabolik, 1997, Power Rangers in Space, 1998, Mystic Knights of Tir Na Nog, 1998, Power Rangers Lost Galaxy, 1999, Power Rangers Lightspeed Rescue, 2000, Power Rangers Time Force, 2001; (films) Mighty Morphin' Power Rangers: The Movie, 1995, Turbo: A Power Rangers Movie, 1997, Rusty: A Dog's Tale, 1998, Addams Family Reunion, 1998; (TV films) The Phantom of the Opera, 1990, Casper: A Spirited Beginning, 1997, Casper Meets Wendy, 1998; writer (TV series) Around the World in 80 Dreams, 1992. Advisor Pres.'s Export Coun. The White House; founder Saban Family Found., 1999—; active in Israeli Cancer Rsch. Fund, John Wayne Cancer Inst., U. Tel Aviv, Nat. Park Found., United Friends of the Children, William Jefferson Clinton Found., Motion Picture and Television Fund, Soroka Children's Hosp., Israel, Children's Hosp. LA, Milken Cmty. High Sch. Served in Israeli Def. Force. Named one of Forbes' Richest Americans, 2006, 50 Most Generous Philanthropists in the US, BusinessWeek. Democrat. Office: Saban Capital Group Ste 1050 10100 Santa Monica Blvd Los Angeles CA 90067 Office Phone: 310-557-5100.

SABAN, NICK (NICHOLAS LOU SABAN), college football coach, former professional football coach; b. Fairmont, W. Va., Oct. 31, 1951; m. Terry Constable, Dec. 18, 1971; children: Nicholas, Kristen. BS in Bus., Kent State U., 1973, MA in Sports Adminstrn., 1975. Grad. asst. Kent State U. Golden Flashes, 1973—74, linebackers coach, 1975—76; outside linebackers coach Syracuse U. Orangemen, 1977; secondary coach W. Va. U. Mountaineers, Morgantown, 1978—79, Ohio State U. Buckeyes, Columbus, 1980—81, US Naval Acad. Midshipmen, Annapolis, 1981; secondary coach & defensive coord. Mich. State U. Spartans, East Lansing, 1983—87, head coach, 1995—2000; secondary coach Houston Oilers, 1988—89; head coach Toledo U. Rockets, 1990; defensive coord. Cleve. Browns, 1991—94; head coach La. State U. Fighting Tigers, Baton Rouge, 2000—05, Miami Dolphins, 2005—07, U. Ala. Crimson Tide, Tuscaloosa, 2007—. Co-author (with Sam King): Tiger Turnaround: LSU's Return to Football Glory, 2001; co-author: How Good Do You Want to Be, 2005. Founder Nick's Kids; active Children's Miracle Network. Recipient Paul "Bear" Bryant award, Nat. Sportscasters & Sportswriters Assn., 2003, Eddie Robinson award, 2003; named Nat. Coach of Yr., AP, 2003, 2008, SEC Coach of Yr., 2003, 2008, Sporting News, 2008, Nat. Coach of Yr., 2008, Home Depot Coach of Yr., 2008. Achievements include coaching the Louisiana State University Fighting Tigers to the BCS National Championship, 2003. Avocation: golf. Office: U Ala Athletics Box 870393 Tuscaloosa AL 35487-0393*

SABANEGH, EDMUND SAMI, JR., urologist; b. Boston, Oct. 30, 1958; s. Edmund S. and Marlowe (Farnum) S.; m. Amy Wilburn, June 1, 1985; 1 child, Emily Wilburn. BSChemE summa cum laude, Princeton U., NJ, 1981; MD, U. Va., 1985. Diplomate Am. Bd. Urology. Urology resident Wilford Hall Med. Ctr., San Antonio, 1986-92, staff urologist, 1992-93, 1994-95, chmn. dept. urology, 1995—; male infertility/microsurgery fellowship Cleve. Clinic, 1993-94. Author: (with others) Atlas, Male Infertility, 1995; contbr. articles to profl. jours. Lt. col. USAF, 1985—. Mem. Soc. of Air Force Clin. Surgeons, Soc. of Govt. Svc. Urologists, Am. Urol. Assn., Am. Fertility Soc. Avocations: hiking, water-skiing, sailing, public speaking. Office: Wilford Hall Med Ctr Dept Urology 2200 Bergquist Dr Ste 1 Lackland AFB TX 78236-5300

SABAT, HEMANT KUMAR, communications and information technology industry leader; married. BSc in Tech., Indian Inst. Tech., Chennai, Madras, India, 1991, MSc, 1993; MBA, Ind. U., Bloomington, 2000. Bus. leader Fannie Mae Inc., Washington, 1999; product leader Sabre Inc., Dallas, 2000, Nortel Networks Corp., Richardson, Tex., 2000—03; gen. mgr. Perot Sys. Corp., Dallas, 2004—06; chmn., pres. & ceo Coscend Comm. Solutions, Dallas, 2007—. Invited keynote spkr. IEEE U. Tex., Dallas, 2003, Eighth Ann. Tex. Logistics Exec. Forum Conf., U. Newcastle, 2005, Indo-Am. C. of C., IEEE, 2006, 09, Tex. Woman's U. IEEE, 2005, IIT Alumni Assn. North Tex., 2008; CEO Netweavers, 2008. Contbg. editor sci. papers and articles; contbr. articles to profl. jours. Recipient Over 60 awards, Boy Scouts & Guides, 1978—92, Dr. Dhandapani prize, Indian Inst. Tech., 1991, Sudarshan Bhat Meml. prize, 1993, Vidya Bharti prize, Indian Inst. Metals, 1992, Appreciation award, 2003—08, Extraordinary Ability Recognition, Telecom & Info. Tech. Industries, US Govt., 2004. Office: Coscend Comm Solutions 19019 Preston Rd Ste 409 Dallas TX 75252 Office Fax: 314-248-7974. Business E-Mail: hemant.sabat@coscendcommunications.com.

SABAT, MICHAL, structural chemist; b. Jankowa, Lower Silesia, Poland, Sept. 9, 1947; s. Stanislaw and Jadwiga Sabat; m. Urszula Krzynowek, Jan. 7, 1977; 1 child, Agnes Elisabeth. MS, U. Wroclaw, Poland, 1970, PhD, 1976. Dir., molecular structure lab U. Va., Charlottesville, 1990—. Office: Univ Va Dept Chemistry Charlottesville VA 22904 Office Phone: 434-924-7862. Business E-Mail: ms5c@virginia.edu.

SABATHIA, C.C. (CARSTEN CHARLES SABATHIA), professional baseball player; b. Vallejo, Calif., July 21, 1980; m. Amber Sabathia; children: Carsten Charles III, Jaeden Arie. Pitcher Cleve. Indians, 2001—08, Milw. Brewers, 2008, NY Yankees, 2008—. Recipient Am. League Cy Young award, Maj. League Baseball, 2007, Bullet Rogan Legacy award, Negro Leagues Baseball Mus., 2008; named to Am. League All-Star Team, Maj. League Baseball, 2003—04, 2007. Achievements include leading the American League in: hits allowed per 9 innings pitched, 2001; shutouts 2006, 2008; complete games, 2006, innings, 2007, starts, 2007; leading the National League in: complete games, 2008; shutouts, 2008; becoming the youngest pitcher (27 years, 69 days old) to record 100 career wins on September 28, 2007. Office: NY Yankees Yankee Stadium One E 161st St Bronx NY 10451*

SABATINI, LAWRENCE, bishop emeritus; b. Chgo., May 15, 1930; s. Dominic and Ada (Piloi) Sabatini. PhL, Gregorian U., Rome, 1953, STL, 1957, JCD, 1960; MS in Edn., Iona Coll., 1968. Ordained priest Congregation of Missionaries of St. Charles, 1957; prof. canon law St. Charles Sem., SI, NY, 1960-71; pastor St. Stephen's Parish, North Vancouver, BC, Canada, 1970-78; provincial superior Missionaries of St. Charles, Oak Park, Ill., 1978; ordained bishop, 1978; aux. bishop Archdiocese Vancouver, BC, Canada, 1978-82; bishop Diocese Kamloops, BC, Canada, 1982-99, bishop emeritus, 1999—. Procurator, adviser Matrimonial Tribunal, NYC, 1964-71; founder, dir. RAP Youth Counseling Service, S.I., NY., 1969-71; vice ofcl. Regional Matrimonial tribunal of Diocese Kamloops, 1978-82; chmn. Kamloops Cath. Pub. Schs., 1982 Named Man of Yr. Confratellanza Italo-Canadese, 1979 Mem. Can. Canon Law Soc., Canon Law Soc. Am., Can. Conf. Cath. Bishops Roman Catholic. Office: Diocese Kamloops 612 N Western Ave Chicago IL 60612

SABATINI, NELSON JOHN, healthcare executive; b. Rochester, NY, Jan. 20, 1940; s. John R. and Ida M. (Ceconi) S.; m. Marilyn Jean Gromala, Jan. 19, 1963; children— John Nelson, Michael Christopher Student, Lewis Coll., Lockport, Ill., 1958-62; BA in Psychology, George Washington U., 1971, postgrad. Claims rep. Social Security Adminstrn., Chgo., 1962-65, various positions Balt., 1965-79, dep. dir. disability programs, 1979-81, exec. asst. to commr., 1981-82, assoc. commr., 1982—, dep. commr., 1983-88; dep. sec. health and mental hygiene State of Md., 1988, sec. health and mental hygiene, 1991—95, 2003—05; v.p. Univ. Md. Med. Systems, 1995, exec. v.p., 1995—2003; CEO Sabatini Cons. Group, 2005—; pres. Md. Care Improvement Plus, 2005—. Named Disting. Marylander of Yr. 1993; recipient Sec.'s cert. HHS, 1975; Commr.'s citation Social Security Adminstrn., 1977, 81; Presdl. Merit Rank award Pres. of U.S., 1984 Roman Catholic. Avocations: sailing, tennis. Office Phone: 443-827-3332. Business E-Mail: sconsultinggroup@comcast.net.

SABATINI, SANDRA, physician; b. NYC, Dec. 1, 1940; BS in Chemistry, Millsaps Coll., 1962; MS in Pharmacology, Marquette U., 1966; PhD in Pharmacology, U. Miss., 1968; MD in Internal Medicine, Tex. Med. Sch., 1974. Lic. physician, Ill., Tex. Intern in medicine U. Ill. Hosp., Chgo., 1974-75; asst. prof. U. Tex. Med. Sch., San Antonio, 1968-70; assoc. dir. U. Ill. Hosp., Chgo., 1977-78; asst. prof. U. Ill. Coll. of Medicine, Chgo., 1977-83, assoc. prof. medicine and physiology, 1983-84; attending physician in nephrology VA, Chgo., 1977-84; med. dir. Dialysis Unit U. Ill., Chgo., 1978-84; prof. internal medicine and physiology Tex. Tech. U. Health Sci. Ctr., Lubbock, 1985—, chmn. dept. physiology, 1993-96; attending physician in nephrology U. Med. Ctr., Lubbock, 1985—. Lab. instr. Millsaps Coll., Jackson, Miss., 1961-62; instr. pharmacology Bapt. Hosp. Sch. Nursing, Jackson, 1966-68; merit rev. mem. NSF, 1987, 91, 92; rev. mem. several orgns. including Chgo. Heart Assn., 1984, NIH, 1983, 86, 89-93, 96, Nat. Kidney Found., 1987, 89—, Am. Heart Assn., 1981-84, others; cons. U.S. Med. Licensing Exam/Nat. Bd. Med. Examiners, Step 1 Physiology Test Com., 1996-99. Editl. referee Am. Jour. Kidney Disease, Am. Jour. Physiology, Am. Jour. Nephrology, Annals of Internal Medicine, others; mem. editl. bd. Am. Jour. Nephrology, 1989-93, Seminars in Nephrology, 1984—; co-editor Am. Jour. Kidney Diseases, 1997—; author numerous publs. and abstracts in field; contbr. articles to profl. jours. Bd. dirs. YWCA of Lubbock, 1994-99; mem. Leadership Tex., 1994. Predoctoral fellowship grantee Marquette U., 1963-66; pub. health predoctoral fellow U. Miss. Med. Sch., 1967-69, gen. medicine sci. rsch. grantee U. Tex. Med. Sch., 1968-70, post-grad. fellow Karolinska Inst., Swedish Med. Coun., 1971, 73, NIH grantee, 1979-82, 84-99, Chgo. Heart Assn. grantee-in-aid, 1979-85, 99; grantee Nat. Eye Inst., 1979-80; recipient Banes Charitable trust award U. Ill., 1984-85, U.S. Olympic com. Rsch. Foudn., 1986-87; recipient Outstanding Alumnus award Tex. Med. Sch., 1994, numerous other awards in field. Fellow: ACP; mem.: AAUP, AAAS, ADA (hon.), Lubbock Arts Alliance, Leadership Tex. Alumnae Assn., Nat. Kidney Found. West Tex. (bd. dirs. 1993—99, Outstanding Vol. 1995, 2001, Disting. Svc. award 1996), Nat. Kidney Found. (numerous offices including chmn. several coms.), Italian-Am. Nephrologists, Inc., Internat. Soc. Nephrology, Ill. Kidney Found., Ctrl. Soc. Clin. Rsch., So. Soc. Clin. Rsch. (councillor 1997—99, pres.-elect 1999, pres. 2000), Assn. Chairs Dept. Physiology (councillor 1995—97), Am. Soc. Renal Biochemistry and Metabolism (pres.-elect 1994), Am. Soc. Pharmacology and Exptl. Therapeutics, Am. Soc. Nephrology, Am. Physiol. Soc., Am. Heart Assn., Am. Fedn. Med. Rsch., Lubbock Women's Club, Rotary Internat. Office: Tex Tech U Health Sci Ctr 3601 4th St Lubbock TX 79430-0001

SABATINO, THOMAS JOSEPH, JR., lawyer, pharmaceutical executive; b. Norwich, Conn., Dec. 3, 1958; s. Thomas J. and Germaine (Clement) S.; m. Joan Kathryn Turnbull, June 4, 1983. BS cum laude, Wesleyan U., Middletown, Conn., 1980; JD, U. Pa., 1983. Bar: Mass. 1983, Ill. 1985, Calif. 1989. Assoc. Testa, Hurwitz & Thibeault, Boston, 1983-85, Coffield Ungaretti Harris & Slavin, Chgo., 1985-86; corp. counsel Baxter Healthcare Corp., Deerfield, Ill., 1986-90; pres., CEO Secure Med. Inc., Mundelein, Ill., 1990-92; assoc. gen. counsel Am. Med. Internat., Dallas, 1992-93, v.p., gen. counsel, 1993-95; v.p., assoc. gen. counsel Tenet Healthcare Corp., Dallas, 1995—97; v.p., assoc. gen. counsel, asst. sec. Baxter Healthcare Corp., Deerfield, Ill., 1997—2004, sr. v.p., 1997—2004; exec. v.p., gen. counsel Schering-Plough Corp., Kenilworth, NJ, 2004—. Home: 1 Hildebrandt Rd Lebanon NJ 08833-4444*

SABATO, LARRY JOSEPH, political science professor, director; b. Norfolk, Va., Aug. 7, 1952; s. N.J. and Margaret F. (Simmons) S. BA, U. Va., 1974; postgrad., Princeton U., 1974-75; DPhil, Oxford U., 1977. Lectr. politics New Coll. Oxford U., 1977-78; Robert Kent Gooch prof. politics U. Va., Charlottesville, 1978—; founder, dir. U. Va. Ctr. for Politics, 1998—, Larry J. Sabato's Crystal Ball. Guest scholar Brookings Instn., 1980; Thomas Jefferson vis. prof. Downing Coll., Cambridge U., 1982. Author: The Rise of Political Consultants: New Ways of Winning Elections, 1981, Goodbye to Goodtime Charlie: The American Governorship Transformed, 1983, PAC Power: Inside the World of Political Action Committees, 1984, The Party's Just Begun: Shaping Political Parties for America's Future, 1988, Feeding Frenzy: How Attack Journalism Has Transformed American Politics, 1991, American Government: Roots and Reform, 1992, Dirty Little Secrets: The Persistence of Corruption in American Politics, 1996, Midterm Madness: The Elections of 2002, 2002, Toward the Millennium: The Elections of 1996, 1997, Overtime!, 2001, The Election 2002, Thriller, 2001, Get In The Booth: A Citizen's Guide to the 2004 Election, 2004, Divided States of America: The Slash and Burn Politics of the 2004 Presidential Election, 2005, Get in the Booth! A Citizen's Guide to the 2006 Election, 2006, The Sixth Year Itch: The Rise and Fall of the George W. Bush Presidency, 2007, A More Perfect Constitution, 2007. Danforth fellow, 1975; Kellog fellow, 1983; Rhodes scholar; recipient Thomas Jefferson award U. Va., 2001. Mem. Am. Polit. Sci. Assn., Phi Beta Kappa. Office: U Va Dept Politics 240 Cabell Charlottesville VA 22904*

SABATUCCI, JOSEPH P., chemist; b. Phila., July 11, 1955; s. Connie Sabatucci; m. Claire E. Canonico, Oct. 20, 2007. PhD, U. Rochester, NY, 1984. Discovery medicinal chemist Wyeth, Collgeville, Pa., 1985—. Mem.: ACS. Conservative. Achievements include patents for women's health. Avocations: boxing, guitar, music. Office: Wyeth 500 Arcola Rd Collegeville PA 19426

SABAU, CARMEN SYBILE, retired chemist; b. Cluj, Romania, Apr. 24, 1933; naturalized U.S. citizen; d. George and Antoinette Marie (Chiriac) Grigorescu; m. Mircea Nicolae Sabau, July 11, 1956; 1 child, Isabelle Carmen. MS in Inorganic and Analytical Chemistry, U. C.I. Parhon, Bucharest, Romania, 1955; PhD in Radiochemistry, U. Fridericiana, Karlsruhe, Fed. Republic of Germany, 1972. Chemist Inst. Atomic Physics, Bucharest, Romania, 1956—74; kernforschungszentrum Karlsruhe, Germany, 1975—76; chemist Joint Inst. of Nuclear Rsch., Dubna-Moscow, 1974—75, Argonne (Ill.) Nat. Lab., 1976-98; ret., 1998. Author: Ion-exchange Theory and Applications in Analytical Chemistry, 1967; contbr. articles to profl. jours. Active Romanian World Coun. Internat. Atomic Energy Agy. fellow, 1967-68, Humboldt fellow, 1970-72. Mem. Am. Romanian Acad. Arts and Sci., Internat. Soc. Intercomm. of New Ideas, Alexander von Humboldt Assn. Am., Alpha Friends of Antiquity, Rocky Mountain MLA. Home: 689 Banbury Way Bolingbrook IL 60440-1057 Personal E-mail: carmen_sabau@hotmail.com.

SABB, ANNMARIE LOUISE, retired chemist; b. New Brunswick, NJ, Sept. 21, 1942; d. Frank John and Marianne Previte; m. Frederick Joseph Sabb, Aug. 1, 1965; children: Frederick William, Jacqueline Marie. BA, Douglass Coll., New Brunswick, NJ, 1964; MS, Rutgers U., 1974; PhD, Princeton U., 1986. Sci. info. chemist FMC Corp., Balt., 1965—68; rsch. chemist Am. Cyanamid, Princeton, NJ, 1969—74; sr. scientist Ayerst Rsch., Princeton, 1986—88; sr. rsch. scientist Wyeth-Ayerst Rsch., Princeton, 1989—90, prin. scientist, 1991—2001; prin. rsch. scientist Wyeth Rsch., Princeton, 2002—06; ret., 2006. Grad. coll. faculty fellow Princeton U., 1992—93; conf. chair, co-organizer Strategic Rsch. Inst., NYC, 1997—99; grant reviewer NIH, Washington, 1999—2001; sci. adv. bd. Inst. for the Study of Aging, NYC, 1999—2005; editl. adv. bd. Bentham Sci. Publishers, Hilversum, Netherlands, 2002—05; panelist careers in sci. and lab. rsch. Princeton U., 2005; cons., reviewer, spkr. in field. Editor: Current Topics in Medicinal Chemistry; contbr. articles to profl. jours. Recipient Patent award, Wyeth-Ayerst Rsch., 1997—2005. Mem.: Soc. for Neuroscience, Am. Chem. Soc. (pres. of Princeton sect. 1990—91, Phoenix award 1991), Sigma Xi, Iota Sigma Pi, Phi Beta Kappa. Achievements include patents for antidementia agents, drugs for neurological illness, antipsychotic agents, others; discovery of heterocyclic ring system with activity at the human 5-HT2C receptor drugs for schizophrenia; patents for 1,4 diazocino, 7,8,1-hi indole derivatives as antipsychotic and anti obesity agents for treatment of depression US patent 7, 297, 704 (Nov. 20, 2007); research in treatment of psychiatric disorders using 5-HT2C agonist. Personal E-mail: annmarie_sabb@yahoo.com.

SABBAGH, MARWAN NOEL, physician, researcher; b. NYC, Dec. 18, 1965; s. Adib Habib and Entisar (Al Banna) S.; m. Ida Panyota Crocker, July 7, 1990; children: Habib E., Elias A. BA, U. Calif., Berkeley, 1987; MD, U. Ariz., 1991. Diplomate Am. Bd. Psychiatry and Neurology. Intern Good Samaritan Hosp., Phoenix, 1991-92; resident Baylor Coll. Medicine, Houston, 1992-95; fellow U. Calif., San Diego, 1995-97, asst. prof., 1997—; dir. clin. rsch., cons. Sun Health Rsch. Inst., Sun City, Ariz., 1999—. Assoc. dir. neurosci. Alvarado Hosp., San

Diego, 1997—; staff physician U. Calif. San Diego, 1995—, attending physician, 1995—. Contbr. articles to profl. jours. including Archives of Neurology, Jour. Neural Transmission, Am. Family Physician. Vol. physician St. Vincent de Paul, San Diego, 1996—. Grantee Stein Inst. Rsch. on Aging, 1996-97, NIH, 1999—; travel fellow Am. Neurol. Assn., 1996. Mem. AMA, Am. Acad. Neurology, Soc. Neurosci., Am. Fedn. for Clin. Rsch. Avocations: bicycling, martial arts, triathlons. Office: Neurosci Ctr 6645 Alvarado Rd # Set209 San Diego CA 92120-5208

SABBATH, JOSEPH WATERS, academic administrator; b. Paterson, NJ, May 24, 1969; s. George E. and Therese G. Sabbath; m. Laurie Anne Sabbath, Apr. 20, 1970; children: Samantha, Joseph. BA, St. Bonaventure U., NYC, 1991; MA in Edn., St. Peter's Coll., Jersey City, NJ, 2004; JD, Quinnipiac U., Hamden, Conn., 1995. Cert.: N.J. Adminstrv. Office of the Cts. (mediation and conciliation skills), bar: N.J. 1996; cert. prin., supr. N.J., tchr. social studies N.J., tchr. elem. edn. N.J., tchr. law enforcement N.J. Tchr. Paterson (N.J.) Pub. Schs., 2000—04; edn. adminstr. Passaic County Tech. Inst., Wayne, NJ, 2004—. Atty. Joseph W. Sabbath, Atty. at Law, Clifton, NJ, 1996—. Mem. planning bd. East Rutherford (N.J.) Planning Bd., 1998—2000; mem. Mayor's Youth Outreach Task Force, Paterson, NJ, 2000—03; pro bono atty. N.J. Admin Office of the Cts., Paterson, 1996—2006. Recipient Corpus Juris Secundum award, West Pub. Corp, 1994—95, Am. Jurisprudence award, Lawyers Coop. Pub., 1994, Robert L. Clifford Am. Inn of Ct. del. scholarship, Robert L. Clifford Am. Inn of Ct., 1997—99. Mem.: NRA, ASCD, NJ Legal Bar, N.J. Coun. for the Social Studies (corr.), N.J. Bar Assn. (corr.), N.J. Social Studies Supr.'s Assn. (corr.), N.J. Prins. and Suprs. Assn. (corr.), Kappa Delta Pi. Independent. Roman Catholic. Avocations: golf, skiing, hiking, exercise, hunting.

SABBATINI, MARCELLO, journalist, motor sports weekly director; b. Teramo, Abruzzo, Italy, Oct. 20, 1926; s. Ezio and Norina (Guerrieri) S.; m. Maria Pia Fiore, Jan. 23, 1956. Student Faculty of Law, U. Rome, 1945-49. Head sports Il Paese, Rome, 1949-54, Paese e Paese/Sera, Rome, 1954-58; dir. Autorama, Rome, 1959-60; head sports Telesera, Rome, 1960-61, chief staff, 1961-62; asst. editor Corriere dello Sport, Rome, 1963-65; dir. Automondo, Milan, 1965; direttore zesponsabile Autosprint, Bologna, Italy, 1966—81, gen. mgr., 1969-81, Motosprint, Bologna, 1976-81, Rombo, Rombo TV, Bologna, 1981-90; anchorman weekly motormagazine TV Cuore Rosso di TLRC, Modena, 2003—04; anchor Processo F.1 weekly TV show ODEON-TV, 2005. Editor news articles in field. Recipient numerous awards. Roman Catholic.

SABBERT, ANNE WARD, vision therapist, consultant; b. St. Louis, May 28, 1940; d. William Morgan Sr. and Annie Meroe (Burnet) Ward; m. Donald Silas Sabbert, June 29, 1963; children: Jeanne Welling Sabbert Smith, Kimberly Anne Sabbert Fleming, Amy Burnet Sabbert O'Brien, D. Scott Sabbert. AB, Washington U., St. Louis, 1961; MRE, Eden Theol. Seminary, Webster Groves, Mo., 1963; postgrad., Belleville Area Coll., 1979-81. Mem. staff Caroline Mission Inner City Neighborhood House, St. Louis, 1961-62, Meth. Childrens' Home of Mo., St. Louis, 1962-63; tchr. Washington (Mo.) Pub. Sch. Dist., 1963-68; ednl. tour dir. Wholesale Tours Internat., Inc., NYC, 1973, 79, 83; tour dir. D&A Custom Tours, Eng., Scotland and Wales, 1990, 96; ednl. tour dir. Adventure Tours, Costa Rica, 1994; vision therapist Drs. Gary Meier and Charles Friedman, Collinsville, Ill., 1979—. Curriculum author Optometric Extension Program Found., Inc., Santa Anna, 1985, cons., 1988—; presenter Mid-Am. Vision Conf., St. Louis, 1979-94, sec.-treas., 1987—; participant binocular and vision perception sect. Am. Acad. Optometry.; tour dir. NAWAS Internat. Travel Australia/New Zealand, 1997, Millennial Celebration of Oberammevgau Passion Play, Germany, 2000. Contbr. articles to profl. jour. Bd. dirs. Collinsville Ch. Women United, 1968—, del. Nat. conv.; bd. dirs. Chgo. United and Eden Sem. Fund Raising Com., Webster Groves, Mo., 1977-79; St. John's Health Care Bd., Collinsville, 1987—; founding mem., bd. dirs. Eden Village Care Ctr., Edwardsville, 1977-79; active LWV, 1970—, del. State Conv., 1971; mem. P.E.O. Lady Clairol scholar, 1980. Mem. Pi Beta Phi (treas. 1961, alumnae club 1962—), U. Ill. Mothers' Club. Mem. United Ch. of Christ. Avocations: foreign and domestic travel, writing, child advocacy activities. Home: 9237 Tea Rose LN Saint Louis MO 63126-2509

SABEK, OMAIMA M., biology professor, director; b. Cairo, Jan. 7, 1962; d. Mostafa H. Sabek and Ragaa Abdel Al Rahim; m. Mostafa Waleed Gaber, July 13, 1984; children: Yassin W. Gaber, Isis W. Gaber. PhD, U. Coll. London, Eng., 1989. Quality ctrl. analyst Bristol Meyers Squibb, Cairo, 1991—93; postdoc. trainee U. Tenn., Memphis, 1993—99. Named Outstanding Sci. Abstract, Tranplantation Soc., 2004—07; fellow, Harvard Med. Sch., 2005. Mem.: Am. Transplant soc., IPITA (Travel Award 2005). Independent. Avocations: travel, reading, music. Office: Methodist Rsch Hosp 6550 Fannin St Houston TX 77030

SABEL, BRADLEY KENT, lawyer; b. Charleston, Ill., Oct. 6, 1948; s. Walter Bernard and Charlotte (Ahlstrom) Sabel; m. Nancy Jean Parker, Apr. 4, 1984. BA, Vanderbilt U., 1970; JD, Cornell U., 1975; MS in Bus. Policy, Columbia U., 1983. Bar: NY 1976. Atty. Fed. Reserve Bank NY, NYC, 1975-80, asst. counsel, 1980, sec., asst. counsel, 1981-85, assoc. counsel, 1985-87, counsel, 1988-93, counsel, v.p., 1993-94; counsel Shearman & Sterling, NYC, 1994-97, ptnr., 1997—. Contbr. articles to profl. jours. Bd. dirs., treas. NY Chamber Orch., NYC, 1985—87. With US Army, 1970—72. Mem.: N.Y.C. Bar Assn. (former chmn. banking law com.). Home: 2 Midland Gdns Apt 4E Bronxville NY 10708-4727 Office: 599 Lexington Ave Fl C2 New York NY 10022-6030 Office Phone: 212-848-8410. E-mail: bsabel@shearman.com.

SABELLI, HECTOR CARLOS, psychiatrist, neuropharmacologist, educator; b. Buenos Aires, Argentina, July 25, 1937; came to U.S., 1966; s. Antonio and Elena (DiBenedetto) S.; m. Nora Hojvat, Dec. 22, 1960 (div.); children: Martin, Guido; m. Linnea Carlson, Jan. 18, 1980. BS, Colegio Mariano Moreno, Argentina, 1953; MD, U. Buenos Aires, 1959, PhD, 1961. Diplomate Am. Bd. Psychiatry and Neurology. Intern P.V. de Cordero Hosp., Argentina; rsch. fellow dept. pharmacology Argentine Coun. for Rsch., Chgo. Med. Sch., 1960-61; asst. prof. dept. pharmacology Chgo. Med. Sch. 1962-64, vis. prof., 1966-67, prof., 1967-79, chmn. dept. pharmacology, 1970-75; prof., chmn. inst. pharmacology U. Litoral, Rosario, Argentina, 1965-66; resident in psychiatry Rush-Presbyn.-St. Luke's Med. Ctr., Mt. Sinai Hosp. Med. Ctr., Chgo., 1976-79; asst. prof. dept. psychiatry Rush-Presbyn.-St. Luke's Med. Ctr., 1979-84, prof. dept. pharmacology, assoc. prof. dept. psychiatry, 1984—, adj. attending, 1979-81, asst. attending, 1981—, dir. psychobiology lab., 1979—; psychiatrist, Neuropsychiat. Hosp., career investigator Argentine Coun. for Rsch., Buenos Aires, 1964-65; founder, dir. McCormick Forum Clin. Philosophy. Author: Union of Opposites, 1989, Personalization. A New Vision for the Millenium, 1991, Caos Argentino, 1991: Diagnostico Y Enfogue Clinico, (bilingual play) Maria/Mary, 1992; editor: Chemical Modulation of Brain Function, 1973; contbr. articles to profl jours. Recipient Bennett award Soc. Biol. Psychiatry, 1963, Sci. Rsch. award Interstate Postgrad. Med. Assn. N.Am., 1970; Best Tchr. Yr. award Chgo. Med. Sch., 1975; runner-up 1984 Clin. Rsch. award Am. Acad. Clin. Psychiatrists, Community award Manic Depressive and Depressive Assn., Z. Moreno award Am. Soc. Group Psychotherapy and Psychodrama, 1993. Office: Midwest Neuropsychiat Assocs Ltd 1725 W Harrison St Ste 744 Chicago IL 60612-3863

SABER, AHEDA ARAFAT, chemistry professor; d. Amin and Widad Arafat; married; children: Suha M., Rana M., Maha M., Hysam M., Muna M. BSc, U. Jordan, Amman; MS in chemistry, AUB, Beirut, Lebanon; PhD in Chemistry, Ind. U., Bloomington, Ind., 1984. U. lectr. Govs. state U., U. Pk., 2006—, Birzeit U., Ramallah, Palestine, 1975—78; asst. prof. King Faisal U., Alkhobar, Saudi Arabia, 1987—91; adj. faculty Richard Daley coll., Chgo., 2003—, Prairie State Coll., Chgo. Heights, 2003—07, North Ctrl. Coll., Naperville, Ill., 2004, Elmhurst Coll., Ill., 2003—05, Benedictine U., Lisle, Ill., 2006—, Roosevelt U., Chgo., 2007, UIC, Chgo., 2007. Recipient, King Hussein Jordan, 1973. Mem.: Am. Chem. soc. Office: Govs State Univ 1 Univ Pk University Park IL 60466 Personal E-mail: ahedasaber@yahoo.com. Business E-Mail: a-saber@govst.edu.

SABER, AZIZ, engineering educator; m. Patricia Saber, Dec. 11, 1988; 1 child, Victor. BS in Engring., Am. U. of Beirut, 1984; MS in Civil Engring., U. Mich., Ann Arbor, 1985; PhD, Ga. Inst. Tech., Atlanta, 1998. Cert. profl. engr., Tex. Bd. Profl. Engrs., 1990. Prof. La. Tech U., Ruston, 1998—. Recipient Transp. Innovation Rsch. and Exploration, La. Transp. Rsch. Ctr., 1999, F.J. Taylor Undergrad. Tchg. award, La. Tech U. Found., 2007, Excellence in Edn., ASCE, 2000; named Prof. of Yr., 2007. Fellow: ASCE; mem.: Am. Concrete Inst., Am. Soc. Engring. Edn., Transp. Rsch. Bd. Achievements include research in infrastructures. Office: Louisiana Tech Univ 600 W Arizona Ave Ruston LA 71272 Office Fax: 318-257-2306. Business E-Mail: saber@latech.edu.

SABERSKY, ROLF HEINRICH, mechanical engineer; b. Berlin, Oct. 20, 1920; came to U.S., 1938, naturalized, 1944; s. Fritz and Berta (Eisner) S.; m. Bettina Sofie Schuster, June 16, 1946; children— Carol, Sandra. BS, Calif. Inst. Tech., 1942, MS, 1943, PhD, 1949. Devel. engr. Aerojet Gen. Co., 1943-46, regular cons., 1949-70; asst. prof. Calif. Inst. Tech., Pasadena, 1949-55, asso. prof., 1955-61, prof. mech. engring., 1961-88, prof. emeritus, 1988—. Cons. various indsl. orgns. Author: Engineering Thermodynamics, 1957, Fluid Flow, 4th edit., 1999; contbr. articles to profl. jours. Fellow ASME (Heat Transfer Meml. award 1977, 50th anniversary award Heat Transfer Div 1988); mem. Sigma Xi, Tau Beta Pi. Home: 1135 Calle De Los Amigos Santa Barbara CA 93105-5467 Office: Calif Inst Tech Divsn Engring & Applied Sci Pasadena CA 91125-0001 E-mail: sabersky@cox.net.

SABETI, MIKE A., endodontist, periodontist, educator; s. Hass and Mas Sabeti; m. Parvin Sabeti; children: Sara, Ali Sabet. MA, DDS, U. Tex., Houston, 2003. Cert. Periodontolist Tufts Sch. Dental Medicine, Mass., 1995, endodontics U. So. Calif., 2002. Asst. clin. prof. U. Tex. Dental Sch., Houston, 1995—2000; asst. prof. U. So. Calif., LA, 2002—. Reviewer Jour. Endodontics. Author: (clinical reseach) Role of herpesviruses in apical pathosis. Grantee, Am. Acad. Endodontics, 2001. Office Fax: 281-359-3680. Personal E-mail: sabeti2001@yahoo.com. Business E-Mail: sabeti@usc.edu.

SABHARWAL, SUNIL, emergency physician; b. New Delhi; s. Satish and Santosh Sabharwal. With, dept. vets. affairs SCI, West Roxbury, Mass., 2003—. With, dept. PM&R Harvard Med. Sch.

SABIA, NOREEN PATRICIA, psychologist; b. Manhattan, NY, Aug. 23, 1967; d. Harry William McMaster and Ellen Mary O'Sullivan; m. Sean Sabia, May 8, 1992; children: Dylan Michael, Danielle Patricia. MS, Coll. New Rochelle, NY. Cert. sch. psychologist NY State Dept. Edn., 2001. Sch. psychologist Fred S. Keller Sch., Yonkers, NY, 2002—06, Briarcliff Manor Sch. Dist., NY, 2006—. Office: Briarcliff Manor Sch Dist 45 Ingham Rd Briarcliff Manor NY 10510 Business E-Mail: nsabia@briarcliffschools.org.

SABIN, JOHN ROGERS, physics professor; b. Springfield, Mass., Apr. 29, 1940; s. Henry Bowman and Elizabeth (Rogers) S.; m. Claudia Ball, 1963 (div. 1978); children: Peter Bowman, Amanda Ball; m. Birgit Horn, Aug. 8, 1987; children: Lene Elizabeth Horn, Niels Kristian Horn. AB, Williams Coll., 1962; PhD, U. N.H., 1966. Asst. prof. chemistry U. Mo., Columbia, 1968—71; assoc. prof. physics U. Fla., Gainesville, 1971—77, prof., 1977—, dir. info. tech., Coll. Liberal Arts and Scis., 1998—2008, interim chmn. dept. physics, 2002; adjungeret prof. U. So. Denmark, 1992—; assoc. dean Coll. Liberal Arts and Scis., 2006—08. Guest prof. Odense (Denmark) U., 1980-92, Nordita prof., Odense, 1982-83, Fulbright prof., 1986, 91. Editor Advances in Quantum Chemistry; editor Internat. Jour. Quantum Chemistry; mem. editl. bd. Croatia Chemica Acta, 2000—, The Open Chemical Physics Jour. 2007-. Fellow Am. Phys. Soc., Am. Inst. Chemists; mem. Am. Chem. Soc., Danish Phys. Soc., Danish Chem. Soc. Home: 415 NW 23rd St Gainesville FL 32607-2618 Office: U Florida Dept Physics PO Box 118435 Gainesville FL 32611-8435 Home Phone: 352-336-8635; Office Phone: 352-392-1597. Business E-Mail: sabin@qtp.ufl.edu.

SABIO, DOROTHY, elementary school educator; b. Paterson, NJ, Aug. 18, 1963; d. Vincent Anthony and Loretta Grace Sabio. BA in Comm., William Paterson U., Wayne, NJ, 1986, M in Elem. Edn., 1991. Cert. elem. edn. N.J., 1991. Tchr. visual and performing arts Belmont Runyon Sch., Newark, 1992—, Maple Ave. Sch., Newark, 2007—. Cooperating tchr. Kean U., Union, NJ, 1996—97; sch. liaison N.J. Performing Arts Ctr., Newark, 1998—; mentor tchr. Belmont Runyon Sch., Newark, 2006—; judge N.J. state forensics tournament N.J. Speech and Theatre Assn.; presenter in field. Recipient Dr. Martin Luther King, Jr. award, Gov. Christine Todd Whitman and the N.J. Dept. State, 1998; named Newark Pub. Schools Tchr. of Yr., State Supt. Beverly Hall, 1999; VH-1 Music In Our Schools grantee, Pres. Bill Clinton, 2001. Mem.: Newark Tchrs. Union (assoc.). Avocations: ballet, piano, theater, travel. Home: 1408 Magnolia Ln Branchburg NJ 08876-6100 Office: Maple Ave Sch 33 Maple Ave Newark NJ 07112 Personal E-mail: dnsabio@gmail.com. Business E-Mail: dorothys@nps.epals.com.

SABLAN, GREGORIO CAMACHO (GREGORIO KILILI CAMACHO SABLAN), Delegate from the Northern Mariana Islands; b. Saipan, No. Mariana Islands, Jan. 19, 1955; m. Andrea Sablan; 6 children. Attended, U. Hawaii, Manoa, 1989—90. Mem. No. Mariana Islands Commonwealth Legis., 1982—86; aide US Senator Daniel Inouye; del., No. Mariana Islands US House of Reps., Washington, 2009—. Served with US Army, 1981—86. Independent. Roman Catholic. Office: US House Reps 423 Cannon HOB Washington DC 20515 Office Phone: 202-225-2646.*

SABLAN, RITA ALDAN, state official, school system administrator; b. Saipan, No. Mariana Islands, Oct. 24, 1956; d. Ignacio C. and Merced A. Deleon (Guerrero) Aldan; m. Francisco C. Sablan, June 2, 1979; children: Sonnie, Lela. BS, Coll. St. Mary, Omaha, 1978; MA, San Jose State U., 1983. Classroom tchr. Mt. Carmel Sch., Chalan Kanoa, Saipan; classroom tchr. Garapan Elem. Sch., Saipan, prin.; vice prin. Commonwealth No. Mariana Pub. Sch. Sys., asst. dep. commr. for instrn., 1991, commr. edn., 2006—. Chair exec. com. Edn. Week, Commonwealth No. Mariana Islands, 1992, chair ORA com. sch. restructuring, 1992; chair pacific region Healthy Children Ready to Learn Conf., 1993. Rsch. A Study on Pre-Sch. Edn. on Saipan. Vol. Hotline/ Crisis 1989—; Exec. Mem. Spl. Sports Championship, 1990; leader Boy Scouts Am. Grantee Prin.'s Inst. Peabody Coll. Vanderbilt U. Mem. ASCD, Nat. Coun. Social Studies, Leaders Ednl. Adminstrn. Devel. (adv. com.). Home: PO Box 1548 Saipan MP 96950-1548 Office: Commonwealth No Mariana Pub Sch Sys PO Box 501370 Saipan MP 96950*

SABLE, BARBARA KINSEY, retired music educator; b. Astoria, NY, Oct. 6, 1927; d. Albert and Verna (Rowe) Kinsey; m. Arthur J. Sable, Nov. 3, 1973. BA, Coll. Wooster, 1949; MA, Tchrs. Coll. Columbia U., NYC, 1950; DMus, U. Ind., 1966. Office mgr., music dir. Sta. WCAX, Burlington, Vt., 1954; instr. Cottey Coll., 1959-60; asst. prof. N.E. Mo. State U., Kirksville, 1962-64, U. Calif., Santa Barbara, 1964-69; prof. music U. Colo., Boulder, 1969—, prof. emeritus, 1992—. Author: (novels) The Vocal Sound, 1982; contbr. poetry and short stories to lit. jours. Mem.: Colo. Music Tchrs. Assn., AAUP, Nat. Assn. Tchrs. Singing (past state gov., assoc. editor bull.). Democrat. Avocation: poetry. Home: 3430 Ash Ave Boulder CO 80305-3432 Business E-Mail: bks@sable-boulder.com.

SABLE, MARJORIE R., social worker, educator; married. AB, Wash. U., St. Louis, 1971, MSW, 1975; MPH, U. NC, Chapel Hill, 1987, PhD. Lic. clin. social worker Mo. Social worker, Hosp. & Clinics U. Mo., Columbia, 1981—83, asst. to assoc. prof., Sch. Social Work, 1993—2008, assoc. dean, human environ. scis., 2003—08, dir. & prof., Sch. Social Work, 2008—. Rsch. analyst Mo. Dept. Health, 1986—88, bur. chief, 1988—92. Mem. Mo. Women's Health Coun., Jefferson City, 1999—2007. Recipient Chipman Outstanding Alumni award, UNC Sch. Pub. Health, 1995. Mem.: APHA (governing & sect. coun., com. chair 1993—), Coun. Social Work Edn., Soc. Social Work Rsch. Office: Univ Mo 730 Clark Hall Columbia MO 65211-4470 Office Fax: 573-882-8926. Business E-Mail: sablem@missouri.edu.

SABLE, ROBERT ALLEN, gastroenterologist; b. Bklyn., June 21, 1948; s. Benjamin and Sara S.; m. Valerie P. Kubie Kopelman, July 1, 1969 (div. Mar. 1982); 1 child, Jesse; m. Ellen Sue Finer, May 29, 1982; children: Scott, Eric. BS, MIT, 1969; MD, Albert Einstein U., 1973. Bd. cert. in internal medicine, gastroenterology and geriatrics Am. Bd. Internal Medicine. Staff physician N.Y. Telephone Co. Mid Manhattan Med. Dept., NYC, 1978-81; physician Riverdale Gastroenterology Cons., Bronx, 1981—; med. dir. Advanced Endoscopy Ctr., Bronx, 2007—09. Chief gastroenterology St. Barnabas Hosp., Bronx, 1982-2003, pres. med. bd., 1985-90; pres. divsn. coun. Montefiore Med. Ctr., 2001-03, pres. med. staff, 2005-08. Contbr. articles, reports, revs. to profl. jours. Fellow ACP, Am. Coll. Gastroenterology, Am. Gastroenterol. Assn.; mem. AMA, Am. Soc. for Gastrointestinal Endoscopy. Avocations: stamp collecting/philately, coin collecting/numismatics. Office: 3765 Riverdale Ave Ste 7 Bronx NY 10463 Home Phone: 914-591-6147; Office Phone: 718-549-4267. Personal E-mail: ra.sable@verizon.net.

SABLESKI, THOMAS LEE, secondary school educator; b. Dayton, Ohio, Mar. 9, 1946; s. Leon Thomas and Helen Catherine Sableski; m. Patty Lee Gibbs, May 3, 1969; children: Amy Marie Wittman, Matthew Thomas. BS, Wright State U., Dayton, 1968. Cert. in tchg. Ohio, 2005. Tchr. Carroll HS, Dayton, 1973—, yearbook advisor, 1984—, sports program pub., 1995—; tchr. Sinclair Coll., Dayton, 1976—. Sgt. USAF, 1968—74. Conservative. Roman Catholic. Avocations: cooking, reading. Office: Carroll HS 4524 Linden Ave Dayton OH 45432

SABLIK, MARTIN JOHN, research physicist; b. Bklyn., Oct. 21, 1939; s. Martin C. and Elsie M. (Fuzia) S.; m. Beverly Ann Shively, Nov. 26,1965; children: Jeanne, Karen, Marjorie, Larry. BA in Physics, Cornell U., 1960; MS in Physics, U. Ky., 1965; PhD, Fordham U., 1972. Jr. engr. The Martin Co., Orlando, Fla., 1962-63; instr. half-time U. Ky., Lexington, 1963-65; rsch. assoc. Fairleigh Dickinson U., Teaneck, NJ, 1965-67, instr. physics, 1967-72, asst. prof., 1972-76, assoc. prof., 1976-80; sr. rsch. scientist Southwest Rsch. Inst., San Antonio, 1980-87, staff scientist, 1987—2005; ret., 2005; tech. advisor, 2005—09; CEO Applied Magnetic and Phys. Modeling, LLC, 2007—. Local chmn. Intermag. Conf., San Antonio, 1995; mem. adv. bd. Conf. on Properties and Applications of Magnetic Materials, 1990-2003, Workshop on advances in Measurement Techniques and Instrumentation for Magnetic Properties Determination, 1994, Magnetic Materials, Measurements and Modeling Symposium, 1996, Magnetic Materials, Measurements and Microstructure Symposium, 1998, Symposium Magnetic Materials for Magnetoelectronic Devices, 2000; mem. exec. bd. Topical Group on Magnetism and Its Applications, 1996-97; mem. program com., assoc. editor Intermag 2000, Toronto; mem. Universal Network Magnetic Nondestructive Evaluation, 2005-. Mem. editl. bd.: Nondestructive Testing and Evaluation, 1989—; contbr. articles to profl. jours.; mem. editl. bd.: IEEE Transactions on Magnetics, 2002—, assoc. editor:, 2003—. Recipient Imagineer award Mind Sci. Found., 1989. Fellow Am. Soc. Nondestructive Testing (So. Tex. sect. chmn. 1983-84, 2001-02, treas. 2006-); mem. IEEE (sr.), Am. Phys. Soc., Applied Magnetic and Phys. Modelling, LLC (CEO,2007-) Roman Catholic. Avocation: photography. Office Phone: 210-522-3342, 210-684-6362. Personal E-mail: msablik@sctx.rr.com. Business E-Mail: msablikampm@sctx.rr.com.

SABLOFF, JEREMY ARAC, archaeologist; b. NYC, Apr. 16, 1944; s. Louis and Helen (Arac) S.; m. Paula Lynne Weinberg, May 26, 1968; children: Joshua, Saralinda. AB, U. Pa., 1964; MA, PhD, Harvard U., 1969. From asst. prof. to assoc. prof. Harvard U., Cambridge, Mass., 1969—76; assoc. prof. anthropology U. Utah, Salt Lake City, 1976-77; curator anthropology Utah Mus. Natural History, Salt Lake City, 1976-77; prof. anthropology U. N.Mex., Albuquerque, 1978-86, chmn. dept., 1980-83; Univ. prof. anthropology and the history and philosphy of sci. U. Pitts., 1986-94, chmn. dept. anthropology, 1990-92; Charles K. Williams II dir. U. Mus., U. Mus. Term prof. anthropology U. Pa., Phila., 1994—2004, prof. anthropology, curator Mesoamerican archaeology, 1994—2004, Edmund J. and Louise W. Kahn endowed term prof. social scis., curator Mesoamerican archaeology, 2004—05, Christopher H. Browne disting. prof. anthropology, curator Mesoam. archaeology, 2006—09; pres. Santa Fe Inst., 2009—. Sr. fellow for Pre-Columbian Studies, Dumbarton Oaks, 1986-92, chmn. 1989-92. Author: (with G.R. Willey) A History of American Archaeology, 1974, 2d edit., 1980, 3d edit., 1993, Excavations at Seibal: Ceramics, 1975, (with C.C. Lamberg-Karlovsky) Ancient Civilizations: The Near East and Mesoamerica, 1979, 2d edit., 1995, (with D. A. Freidel) Cozumel: Late Maya Settlement Patterns, 1984, The Cities of Ancient Mexico, 1989, rev. edit., 1997, The New Archaeology and the Ancient Maya, 1990, (with G. Tourtellot) The Ancient Maya City of Sayil: The Mapping of a Puuc Region Center, 1991, Archeology Matters, 2008; editor(with C.C. Lamberg-Karlovsky) The Rise and Fall of Civilizations, 1974, (with C.C. Lamberg-Karlovsky) Ancient Civilization and Trade, 1975, (with W.L. Rathje) A Study of Changing Pre-Columbian Commercial Systems, 1975, American Antiquity, 1977-81, (with G.R. Willey) Scientific

American Readings in Pre-Columbian Archaeology, 1980, Simulations in Archaeology, 1981, Supplement to the Handbook of Middle American Indians: Archaeology, 1981, Archaeology: Myth and Reality: A Scientific American Reader, 1982, Analyses of Fine Paste Ceramics, 1982, (with D. Meltzer and D. Fowler) American Archaeology: Past and Future, 1986, (with E.W. Andrews V) Late Lowland Maya Civilization: Classic to Postclassic, 1986, (with J.S. Henderson) Lowland Maya Civilization in the Eighth Century A.D., 1993, Tikal: Dynasties, Foreigners, and Affairs of State, 2003, (with W. Fash) Gordon R. Willey and American Archaeology, 2007, (with J. Marcus) The Ancient City, 2008. Pres. Kolb Found., 1995-2004; chair Smithsonian Coun., 1999-2001, chair sci. adv. commn., 2001-03; nat. ad. bd. Nat. Mus. Natural History. Grantee Nat. Geog. Soc., 1972-74, NSF, 1983-88, 2004-07, NEH, 1990-91. Fellow AAAS (sec. H. chair 1994-95), Am. Anthrop. Assn., Soc. Antiquaries London; mem. NAS, Am. Philos. Soc., Soc. Am. Archaeology (pres. 1989-91), Am. Acad. Arts and Sci., Internat. Soc., Comparative Study of Civilizations, Sigma Xi Office: Santa Fe Inst 1399 Hyde Pk Rd Santa Fe NM 87501-8943

SABO, MARTIN OLAV, former congressman; b. Crosby, ND, Feb. 28, 1938; s. Bjorn O. and Klara (Haga) S.; m. Sylvia Ann Lee, June 30, 1963; children: Karin, Julie. BA cum laude, Augsburg Coll., Mpls., 1959; postgrad., U. Minn., 1961-62. Mem. Minn. Ho. Reps. from 57B Dist., 1960-78, minority leader Dem.-Farmer-Labor party, 1969—73, speaker, 1973-78; mem. US Congress from 5th Minn. Dist., 1979—2006; chmn. Dem. Study Group; dep. majority whip 96th to 103rd Congresses; mem. permanent select com. on intelligence 102d Congress; chmn. Ho. Budget Com. 103d Congress; ranking minority mem. house budget com. 104th-106th Congress, mem. standards of official conduct com., appropriations com., ranking minority mem. subcom. on homeland security. Former mem. Nat. Adv. Commn. on Intergovtl. Rels.; past pres. Nat. Legis. Conf.; bd. regents Augsburg Coll. Mgr., player Dem. Congl. Baseball Team, 1987—. Recipient Disting. Alumni citation Augsburg Coll., Arms Control Leadership award Employees Union, Local 113, SEIU, AFL-CIO; named One of 200 Rising Young Leaders in Am. Time mag., 1974; Man of Yr. Mpls. Jr. C.of C., 1973-74, One of Ten Outstanding Young Men of Yr. Minn. Jr. C. of C., 1974; inducted Scandinavian Am. Hall of Fame, 1994. Mem. Nat. Conf. State Legis. Leaders (past pres.). Democrat. Office Phone: 202-225-4755.

SABODASH, VLADLENA, economics professor, researcher; b. Yakutsk, Russia, Dec. 10, 1982; BS, South Ural State U., Chelyabinsk, Russia, 2005; attending, Northeastern U., Boston, 2005—. Acct. asst. Zaryad Ltd., Chelyabinsk, Russia, 2002—04; taxation auditor Yural-bankaudit Co. Ltd., Chelyabinsk, 2004—05; rsch. asst. Northeastern U., Boston, 2005—, undergrad. instr., 2007—. Grantee, Fund Vladimir Potanin, 2004—05. Personal E-mail: sabodash.v@gmail.com.

SABSAY, DAVID, retired library director; b. Waltham, Mass., Sept. 12, 1931; s. Wiegard Isaac and Ruth (Weinstein) S.; m. Helen Glenna Tolliver, Sept. 24,1 966. AB, Harvard U., 1953; BLS, U. Calif., Berkeley, 1955. Circulation dept. supr. Richmond (Calif.) Pub. Library, 1955-56; city libr. Santa Rosa (Calif.) Pub. Library, 1956-65; dir. Sonoma County Library, Santa Rosa, 1965-92; libr. cons., 1992—. Coordinator North Bay Coop. Library System, Santa Rosa, 1960-64; cons. in field, Sebastopol, Calif., 1968—. Contbr. articles to profl. jours. Commendation, Calif. Assn. Library Trustees and Commrs., 1984. Mem. Calif. Library Assn. (pres. 1971, cert. appreciation 1971, 80), ALA. Clubs: Harvard (San Francisco). Home: 667 Montgomery Rd Sebastopol CA 95472-3020 E-mail: dsabsay@sonic.net.

SACCHETTA, PASQUALE JOSEPH, financial services executive; b. Bristol, Conn., July 11, 1964; s. Gaetano and Angela (DiMatteo) S.; m. Jodi Lynne Edelman, Feb. 9, 2002; children: Nicholas Alexander, Ethan Michael 1 stepchild, Alison Mackenzie Bertan. BS magna cum laude, Cen. Conn. State U., New Britain, 1999; MBA, Fordham U., NYC, 2002. Chartered life underwriter designation Am. Coll. Bryn Mawr, Pa., cert. fin. planner practitioner 2007, accredited estate planner designee 2008. Svc. mgr. First Nat. Supermarkets, Bristol, Conn., 1980-84; account exec. First Investors Corp., Glastonbury, Conn., 1984-86; CEO, pres. Cambridge-Newport Co., Wethersfield, 1986—92; pres. Continental Five Ins. Group Inc., Westport, 1991—, pres. wealth mgmt., 2006—. Consulting mem. Gerson Lehrman Group Fin. Svcs. Coun., 2006—. Supporting mem. Smithsonian Instn.; mem. ins. com. Town of Weston, 2003—; appointed mem. mucpl. law, liability and ins. com. Conn. Conf. Mcpls., 2005—; bd mem. World Wise Network Leadership coun. Fordham U. Grad. Sch.Bus., NY, 2007—; mem. Dem. Town Com., Weston, 2000—, vice chmn., 2003—04; chmn. St. Anthony's Ch. Altar Soc., Bristol, 1978. Mem. USTA (life), CCSU Alumni Assn., Fordham U. Alumni Assn., Pres.'s Assn., Nat. Assn. Ins. and Fin. Svc. Profls., Soc. Fin. Svc. Profl. (chpt. officer, 2001-03 2007-), Nat. Assn. Estate Planners & Couns., Estate Planning Coun. Lower Fairfield County, US Golf Assn., Westport C. of C., KC. Democrat. Roman Catholic. Avocations: tennis, golf, travel, reading, art collecting. Office: CFIG Wealth Mgmt PO Box 352 Westport CT 06881-0352 also: One Gorham Island Ste 303 Westport CT 06880

SACCO, JOE, professional hockey coach, retired professional hockey player; b. Medford, Mass., Feb. 4, 1969; Attended, Boston U., 1987—90. Right wing Toronto Maple Leafs, 1990—93, Anaheim Mighty Ducks, 1993—98, NY Islanders, 1997—99, Washington Capitals, 1999—2002, Phila. Flyers, 2002—03; asst. coach Lowell Lock Monsters, 2005—06, Albany River Rats, 2006—07; head coach Lake Erie Monsters, 2007—09, Colo. Avalanche, 2009—. Mem. Team USA, Olympic Games, Albertville, France, 1992; asst. coach Team USA, IIHF Men's World Championship, Switzerland, 2009. Office: Colo Avalanche Hockey Club Pepsi Ctr 1000 Chopper Circle Denver CO 80204*

SACCO, JOHN MICHAEL, accountant; b. NYC, Oct. 17, 1952; s. Anthony Carmine and Angelina (Pellegrino) Sacco. BS, St. John's U., 1974. CPA. Staff acct. Price Waterhouse & Co., NYC, 1974-75; semi-sr. acct. Seidman & Seidman, CPAs, White Plains, NY, 1976-77; sr. acct. Diamond Internat. Corp., NYC, 1977-79, Burns Internat. Security Svcs., Inc., Briarcliff Manor, NY, 1979-81; acctg. mgr. Burns Integrated Sys., Inc., Briarcliff Manor, NY, 1981-83; pvt. practice White Plains, NY, 1978—. Com. svc. mem. Acctg. Review Svc. Com., Audit Stads. Com., Employee Benefits Com. Mem.: NY State Soc. CPA. Republican. Roman Catholic. Home: 197 Upper Shad Rd Pound Ridge NY 10576-2237 Office: 108 Corporate Park Dr White Plains NY 10604 Office Phone: 914-253-8757. Business E-Mail: jmsaccocpa@verizon.net.

SACCO, LOUIS JOHN, software design architect; s. Louis John and Carol Ann Sacco; m. Arnez Marie Sacco, Sept. 28, 1997; 1 child, Anthony. BSc, Mich. State U., East Lansing, 1993; MS in Computer & Info. Sci., U. Mich., Dearborn, 1999. Cert. enterprise developer IBM, 2004. Software engr. Electronic Data Sys., Southfield, Mich., 1994—97; software specialist Daimler Chrysler, Auburn Hills, 1997—2001; prin. software engr. TechFlow, Inc., San Diego, 2001—04; sr. software engr. Mitchell Internat., 2004—05; sr. staff programmer analyst Qualcomm, 2005—. Writer and advisor: The Sphere, 1999—; contbr. articles to profl. pubs. Recipient Achievement award, TechFlow, 2003. Mem.: San Diego Java User Group (assoc.). Achievements include research in how to leverage message and CORBA in a distributed fashion. Avocations: mountain biking, golf, finance. Personal E-mail: lou@loutilities.com.

SACCO, RALPH LEWIS, neurologist; b. Atlantic City, Aug. 27, 1957; BS with distinction, Cornell U., 1979; MD cum laude, Boston U., 1983; MS in Epidemiology, Columbia U., 1989. Diplomate Am. Bd. Neurology, Nat. Bd. Med. Examiners. Resident med. svc. St. Luke's Hosp., NYC, 1983-84; resident neurology svc. Presbyn. Hosp. City N.Y., 1984-87; vis. clin. fellow, postdoctoral fellow in neurology Columbia U. Coll. Physicians and Surgeons, NYC, 1984-87, postdoctoral clin. fellow neurology and neuroepidemiology, 1987-89, asst. clin. neurology, 1987-89, asst. prof. neurology, 1989-91, asst. prof. neurolgy and pub. health (epidemiology), 1991-92, asst. prof. neurology and pub. health Sergievsky Ctr., 1993—; clin. asst. neurologist Presbyn. Hosp. City N.Y., 1987-89, asst. attending neurologist, 1989—. Ad hoc reviewer U.S.-Israel Binat. Sci. Found., 1991; spl. and ad hoc reviewer epidemiology and disease control NIH Study Sect., 1991—; cons. Tech. Evaluation Group NINDS, 1992, Ticlid Adv. Panel, Syntex, 1993. Mem. editorial bd. Neuroepidemiology, 1992, Neurology Chronicle, 1993, Headlines,1993; ad hoc reviewer Stroke, Neurology, Annals of Internal Medicine, Am. Jour. Medicine, Jour. Clin. Epidemiology, N.Y. State Jour. Medicine; contbr. articles and revs. to profl. jours., chpts. to books. Fellow Am. Heart Assn. (stroke coun., epidemiology coun.); mem. AMA, Am. Acad. Neurology (sec. neuroepidemiology sect. 1993—, co-chmn. neuroepidemiology session 1990, 92, quality stds. subcom. stroke task force 1993—), Alpha Omega Alpha, Tau Beta Pi, Eta Kappa Nu. Office: Neurol Inst 710 W 168th St New York NY 10032-2603

SACHA, ROBERT FRANK, osteopath, educator; b. East Chicago, Ind., Dec. 29, 1946; s. S. Frank John and Ann Theresa S.; m. Linda T. LePage, 1988; children: Joshua Jude, Josiah Gerard, Anastasia Levon, Jonah Bradley. BS, Purdue U., 1969; DO, Chgo. Coll. Osteo. Medicine, 1975; PharmD, Creighton U., 2004. Diplomate Am. Bd. Pediatrics, Am. Bd. Allery and Immunology. Pharmacist, asst. mgr. Walgreens Drug Store, East Chicago, Ind., 1969-75; intern David Grant Med. Ctr., San Francisco, 1975-76, resident in pediatrics, 1976-78; fellow in allergy and immunology Wilford Hall Med. Ctr., 1978-80; staff pediatrician, allergist Scott AFB (Ill.), 1980-83; practice medicine specializing in allergy and immunology Cape Girardeau, Mo., 1983—. Assoc. clin. instr. St. Louis U., 1980—; clin. instr. Purdue U., 1971-72, Pepperdine U., 1975-76, U. Tex.-San Antonio, 1978-80, assoc. clin. instr. So. Ill. U. Pres., Parent Tchrs. League; bd. gov. Chgo. Coll. Osteopathic Medicine. Maj. M.C. USAF, 1975-83, comdr. USNR. Named one of Top Pediatricians 2002-2003, Pediatric Allergy, Immunology. Fellow Am. Coll. Allergy, Am. Coll. Chest Physicians, Am. Acad. Pediatrics, Am. Acad. Allergy-Immunology, Am. Assn. Cert. Allergists; mem. ACP, AMA, Am. Acad. Allergy, Assn. Mil. Allergists, Am. Coll. Emergency Physicians, Mil. Surgeons and Physicians. Republican. Lutheran. Office: 351 Kelley Ct Cape Girardeau MO 63701 Office Phone: 573-651-4155. E-mail: bsacha@charter.net.

SACHAR, DAVID BERNARD, gastroenterologist, educator; b. Urbana, Ill., Mar. 2, 1940; s. Abram Leon and Thelma (Horwitz) Sachar; m. Joanna Maud Belford Silver, Aug. 29, 1961; children: Mark Benson, Kenneth Hulbert Belford(dec.). BA magna cum laude, Harvard Univ., 1959, MD cum laude, 1963. Cert. Am. Bd. Internal Medicine, diplomate Am. Bd. Gastroenterology. Intern Beth Israel Hosp., Boston, 1963-65, resident in internal medicine, 1967-68; asst. chief clin. rsch. Pakistan SEATO Cholera Rsch. Lab., Dhaka, Bangladesh, 1965-67; resident in gastroenterology Mt. Sinai Hosp., NYC, 1968-70, dir. divsn. gastroenterology, 1983-99, vice chmn. dept. medicine, 1992-99, dir. emeritus, 1999—, Arnold P. Gold Found. prof. medicine, 2005—08; instr. to prof. medicine Mt. Sinai Sch. Medicine, NYC, 1970-92, first Burrill B. Crohn prof. medicine, 1992-99; Dr. Hyman J. Zimmerman Meml. lectr. Georgetown U. Med. Sch., 2009. Co-chmn. work group on inflammatory bowel disease NIH, 1973—75; expert adv. panel gastroenterology and nutrition U.S. Pharmacopeial Conv., 1980—85; co-founder, sec., treas. Burrill B. Crohn Rsch. Found., NYC, 1984—; chmn. rsch. devel. com. Nat. Found. Ileitis and Colitis, 1984—89; K. H. Koster meml. lectr. Danish Soc. Gastroenterology, 1992; mem. Gastroenterology Leadership Coun. Task Force Fellowship Curriculum, 1994; guest lectr. Swedish Soc. Gastroenterology, 1995; internat. state art lectr. Falk Symposia, Germany, 1996; twentieth ann. Norman Tanner meml. lectr. St. George's Hosp. Med. Sch., London, 1997; internat. state art lectr., Belgium, 98, Brit. Soc. Gastroenterology, 1998, World Congresses Gastroenterology, Austria, 1998, Turkish Soc. Gastroenterology, 1998, World Congresses Gastroenterology, Italy, 1999, Hungarian Soc. Gastroenterology, 1999, Hellenic Soc. Gastroenterology, 1999; chmn. GI adv. bd. Solvay Pharm., Inc., 2000—02; internat. state art lectr. Falk Symposia, Germany, 2000—02; 25th ann. Nana Svartz meml. lectr., Örebro, Sweden, 2000; co chmn. 40th ann. post grad. course Portuguese Soc. Gastroenterology, 2000, internat. state art lectr., 03, Italy, 01, Spanish Soc. Gastroenterology, 2007, State Sci. Ctr. Coloproctology, Moscow, 2007, Romanian Soc. Gastroenterology & Hepatology, 2008; mem. GI adv. com. FDA, 2004—08, chmn., 2005—08; Dr. Albert M. Yunich Memorial Lectr. Albany Med Coll., 2007; Keynote lectr. 3rd Internat. Symp. Molecular Tech. Shahid Beheshti U. Med. Sci., Tehran, 2009. Editor: seven books and monographs on gastroenterology; contbr. chapters to books, articles to profl. jours. Trustee Bangladesh Coun. Asia Soc., NYC, 1972—75, Englewood Cliffs Bd. Edn., 1973—75; campaign com. Shulman for Congress, NJ, 2007—08. Capt. USPHS. Recipient Jacobi Medallion for Disting. Achievement, Mt. Sinai Alumni Assn., 1994, Alexander Richman Commemorative award for Humanism in Medicine, 1996, Norman Tanner medal, St. George's Hosp. Med. Sch., 1997, Gold Headed Cane award, 1997. Master: Am. Coll. Gastroenterology (program dir. com. 1991, Henry Baker Presdl. Lectr. 1989, Berk/Fise clin. achievement award 2005); fellow: ACP, Am. Gastroent. Assn. (first chmn. clin. tchg. project 1984—90, nominating com. 1993—94, chmn. immuno inflammatory disorders sectional nominating com. 1995, Disting. Educator award 1996, Found. Mentors Rsch. Scholar award honoree 2007); mem.: Gold Humanism Honor Soc., Internat. Orgn. Study of Inflammatory Bowel Disease (first Am. elected chmn. 1989—92, chmn. task force clin. phenomics 1992—2007), Crohn's and Colitis Found. Am. (grant rev. com. and coun. 1990—94, Disting. Svc. award 1991, NY Gov. medal 1992, 2007), Brazilian Soc. Gastroenterology (patron 2003), Internat. Guild Miniature Artisans (trustee 2004—07), Alpha Omega Alpha, Phi Beta Kappa. Achievements include co developer of oral rehydration therapy for diarrhea; development of resources and standards for clin. tchg. in gastroenterology; established Joanna and David B. Sachar International Award and Visiting Professorship in Inflammatory Bowel Disease. Avocation: piano. Office: Mt Sinai Med Ctr One Gustave L Levy Pl New York NY 10029 Business E-Mail: david.sachar@mountsinai.org.

SACHAR, LOUIS, writer; b. East Meadow, NY, Mar. 20, 1954; married, 1985; 1 child. Student, Antioch Coll.; BA, U. Calif., Berkeley, 1976; JD, Hastings Coll. Law, San Francisco, 1980. Part-time atty. Author: (children's books) Sideways Stories From Wayside School, 1978 (1979 Children's Choice Book), Johnny's in the Basement, 1981, Someday Angeline, 1983, Sixth Grade Secrets, 1987, There's A Boy in the Girls' Bathroom, 1987, The Boy Who Lost His Face, 1989, Wayside School is Falling Down, 1989, Dogs Don't Tell Jokes, 1991, Marvin Redpost: Kidnapped at Birth?, 1992, Marvin Redpost: Is He a Girl?, 1993, Marvine Redpost: Why Pick on Me?, 1993, Alone in His Teachers' House, 1994, Wayside School Gets a Little Stranger, 1995, Holes, 1998 (Newbery award, finalist Nat. Book Award), Class President, 1999, Stanley Yelnat's Survival Guide to Camp Green Lake, 2003, Small Steps, 2006 (Schneider Family Book award, 2007). Mem. Soc. Children's Book Writers and Illustrators, Authors Guild. Mailing: c/o Ellen Levine Trident Media Group Fl 36 41 Madison Ave New York NY 10010 Office: c/o Farrar Straus & Giroux 18 W 18th St New York NY 10011-4607

SACHDEO, AMIT, dentist, researcher; b. Allahabad, India, Feb. 07; s. Jogesh and Kiran Sachdeo. B in Dental Sci., Magadh U., 1997; MS, U. Bristol, 2000; postgrad., Harvard U., 2002—. CAD-CAM Training, Nobel Biocare, 2005; Esthetic Dentistry NY U., 2002, Human Participant Protections for Research Teams Nat. Cancer Inst., 2005, Cpr Am. Heart Assn., 2004, Public Oral Health Glasgow University-UK, 2001. Chief dental resident Sir Ganga Ram Hosp., India, 1997—98; resident Bristol Dental Sch., Bristol, England, 1998—2000; rsch. fellow-public oral health Glasgow U., Scotland, 2000—01; resident NYU, NYC, 2001—02; fellow Harvard U., Boston, 2002—. Contbr. articles to profl. jours. Grantee, ACP/P&G, 2004; fellow, Acad. Prosthodontics, 2005; scholar, Straumman, 2003. Mem.: ARC (life), Internat. Acad. Dental Rsch., Am. Acad. Dental Rsch., Am. Acad. Cosmetic Dentistry (life), Acad. Osseointigration (life), Am. Coll. Prosthodontists (life). Achievements include research in Biofilm formation in the Edentulous. Avocations: swimming, skiing, reading, rollerblading, writing, horseback riding. Office: Harvard U Dental Sch 188 Longwood Ave Boston MA 02115 Home: 464 Commonwealth Ave Ste 15 Boston MA 02215-2734 Home Fax: 617-432-0901. Personal E-mail: amit_sachdeo@hsdm.harvard.edu.

SACHDEVA, ASHUTOSH, pulmonologist, director; s. Subhash Chander and Vijay Kumari Sachdeva; m. Shipra Kalra; children: Neelay, Pritul. MBBS, Maulana Azad Med. Coll., New Delhi, 1996—96. Diplomate in internal medicine Am. Bd. Internal Medicine, 2002. Internist MedPoint Family Care Ctr., Milw., 2003—06; asst. clin. prof. internal medicine Med. Coll. Wis., Milw., 2006—; asst. prof. internal medicine St. Louis U., 2008—. Dir., pulmonary hypertension program St. Louis U., 2008—, assoc. dir., adult cystic fibrosis program, 2008—. Author: (poster presentation of original research) Society of Critical Care Medicine; contbr. moderator of fellow's session. Fund raiser Helpage India, Gugaon, Haryana, India, 1983—83. Mem.: Pulmonary Hypertension Assn., Am. Assn. Bronchology Interventional Pulmonology, Soc. Critical Care Medicine (Travel award 2004), World Assn. Bronchology, Am. Coll. Chest Physician (Recognition leadership devel. program award 2008), Am. Thoracic Soc. Achievements include research in Reported Vitamin D (25 OH) deficiency in Kidney failure patients & use of alternate immunospressive agent use in heart transplant patients; first to electromagnetic navigation bronchoscopy for placement of gold seeds in a minimally invasive way to help patients. Avocation: travel. Office: Saint Louis Univ 1402 S Grand Blvd 7th FDT Saint Louis MO 63104 Office Phone: 314-577-8856. Personal E-mail: sachashu@hotmail.com. Business E-Mail: asachde2@slu.edu.

SACHER, STEVEN JAY, lawyer; b. Cleve., Jan. 28, 1942; s. Albert N. and Cecil P. (Chessin) S.; m. Colleen Marie Gibbons, Nov. 28, 1970; children— Alexander Jerome, Barry Elizabeth, William Paul. BS, U. Wis., 1964; JD, U. Chgo., 1967. Bar: D.C. 1968. Assoc. solicitor Employee Retirement Income Security Act U.S. Dept. Labor, Washington, 1974-77; spl. counsel com. on labor and human resources U.S. Senate, Washington, 1977-79, gen. counsel, 1980-81; ptnr. Pepper Hamilton, Washington, 1982-88; shareholder Johnson & Gibbs, Washington, 1988-94; ptnr. Kilpatrick Stockton LLP, Washington, 1994—2007, Jones Day, Washington, 2007—. Adj. prof. law Georgetown U. Law Ctr., 1977; co-chair sr. editors Employee Benefits Law and Annual Supplements, Bur. Nat. Affairs, Washington, 1991-2000. Mem. adv. bd. BNA Pension and Benefits Reporter; mem. editorial bd. Benefits Law Jour., Jour. Pension Planning and Compliance. Founding mem. ERISA Roundtable, Washington. Recipient AV ranking, Martindale-Hubbell, 1984—, top-ranking, Chambers USA, 2005—; named Lawdragon's 100 Most Powerful Employment Attys. in America, Human Resource Exec. Mag., 2009; named one of Washington Super Lawyers, 2007—, Top 100 Washington Super Lawyers, 2009; named to Best Lawyers in Am., 1987—. Fellow Coll. Labor and Employment Lawyers, Am. Coll. Employee Benefits Counsel (charter); mem. ABA (mgmt. co-chmn. com. on employee benefits, sect. on labor and employment law 1988-91, chmn. prohibited trans. subcom., com. on employee benefits, sect. on taxation 1986-91), D.C. Bar Assn. Office: Jones Day 51 Louisiana Ave NW Washington DC 20001-2113 Office Phone: 202-879-5402. Business E-Mail: sjsacher@jonesday.com.

SACHS, ALAN ARTHUR, lawyer; b. Bklyn., Feb. 7, 1947; s. Herman and Clara Sachs; m. Marilyn Mushlin, May 19, 1974; children: David Henry, Stephen Edward. BA, Columbia U., 1967; JD, Harvard U., 1970. Bar: NY 1971, Wis. 1983, Mo. 1989. Law clk. to judge U.S. Dist. Ct. (ea. dist.) N.Y., 1970-71; assoc. Cleary, Gottlieb, Steen & Hamilton, NYC, 1971-79, Paskus, Gordon & Hyman, NYC, 1979-81; sec., gen. counsel The Trane Co., LaCrosse, Wis., 1981-85; sr. v.p., gen. counsel, sec. Edison Bros. Stores Inc., St. Louis, 1985—2001; ptnr. Haar & Woods, LLP, St. Louis, 2001—. Mem.: ABA, Bar Assn. Met. St. Louis. Office: Haar & Woods LLP 1010 Market St Saint Louis MO 63101 Office Phone: 314-241-2224. Business E-Mail: alansachs@haar-woods.com.

SACHS, DAVID HOWARD, surgeon, immunologist, educator; b. NYC, Jan. 10, 1942; s. Elliot and Elsie (Hurvitz) S.; m. Kristina Olsson, Mar. 15, 1969; children: Michelle, Jessica, Karin, Teviah. AB, Harvard U., 1963; DES, U. Paris, 1964; MD, Harvard U., Boston, 1968. Intern in surgery Mass. Gen. Hosp., Boston, 1968-69, resident in surgery, 1969-70, dir. transplantation biology rsch. ctr. surgery dept., 1991—; chief immunology br. Nat. Cancer Inst., Bethesda, Md., 1982-90; prof. surgery and immunology Harvard U. Med. Sch., 1991—. Capt. PHS, 1970-91. Recipient Roche Ernest Hodge Meml. award, Am. Soc. Transplantation, 2005. Avocations: gardening, fishing, windsurfing, skiing. Office: Mass Gen Hosp East Bldg 149-9019 13th St Boston MA 02129

SACHS, GEORGE, biology professor, physician; b. Austria; BSc, U. Edinburgh, 1957, MB, ChB, 1960, DSc, 1980; MD, U. Gothenburg, 1987. Instr. Albert Einstein Coll., 1961—62; rsch. assoc. Columbia U., 1962—63; asst. prof. medicine and physiology U. Ala., Birmingham, 1963—65, assoc. prof., 1965—70, prof., 1970—82, dir. membrane biology, 1974—82; prof. medicine and physiology, Wilshire chair in medicine UCLA, 1982—, co-dir. ctr. ulcer rsch. and edn., 1987—2002, dir. membrane biology lab., 1987—; sr. med. investigator VAGLAHS, LA, 1984—99, staff physician, 1999—. Contbr. articles to profl. jours. Recipient Beaumont Prize in Gatroenterology, Am. Gastroenterological

Assn., 1985, Hoffman LaRoche award, 1982, Gairdner Found. Internat. award, 2004, Ismar Boas Vorlesung Medal, German Gastroenterological Assn., 1992, others; named Dr. Norman Frankel Scholar, U. Chgo., 2005, Evans Scholor, Boston U., 2005. Office: UCLA 405 Hilgard Ave Los Angeles CA 90095 Office Phone: 310-268-3923. E-mail: gsachs@ucla.edu.*

SACHS, GREG ALAN, preventive medicine physician; BA in Biology, U. Chgo., 1981; MD, Yale U. Sch. Medicine, 1985. Diplomate Am. Bd. Internal Medicine, 1988, cert. in Geriatrics Am. Bd. Internal Medicine, 1990. Resident, internal medicine U. Chgo. Hosps. & Clinics, 1985—87; fellow, geriatric medicine U. Chgo., 1987—90, fellow, clin. med. ethics, 1988—90, asst. prof., medicine, 1990—97, dir., ethics consultation svc., 1992—95, asst. dir., MacLean Ctr. for Clin. Med. Ethics, 1993—99, dir., required ambulatory geriatrics rotation for medicine residents, 1993—97, assoc. prof., medicine, 1997—, found co-dir., The Memory Ctr., 1999—, dir., Hartford Found. Ctr. of Excellence in Geriatrics, 2000—, founding sect. chief, geriatrics, 2000—; scientist Ind. U. Ctr. for Aging Rsch.; investigator Regenstrief Inst. Inc.; dir. divsn. gen. internal medicine & geriatrics Ind. U., prof. medicine. Mem. editl. bd. Alzheimer's Disease and Assoc. Disorders, An Internat. Jour., 1995—, Second Opinion, 1999—2002, Jour. of Am. Geriatrics Soc., 2000—, reviewer for various jours. Mem. Cook County State's Atty.'s Task Force on Removal of Life-Sustaining Treatment, 1989—90; mem., cmty. ethics com. Chgo. Coun. for Jewish Elderly, 1990—94; reviewer, grant proposals on end-of-life care Retirement Rsch. Found., 1995—; mem., social sci., humanities, and policy adv. bd. The Brookdale Found., 1998—2000. Mem.: ACP, Nat. Alzheimer's Assn. (mem., ethics adv. panel 1995—, bd. dirs., Chgo. chpt. 1998—2000, chair, ethics adv. panel 2000—), Gerontological Soc. Am., Am. Geriatrics Soc. (mem., ethics com. 1992—, rep., coalition for quality end-of-life care 1996—99, chair, ethics com. 1998—2001, mem., pub. policy adv. group 2001—, New Investigator award 1994), Phi Beta Kappa, Alpha Omega Alpha. Office: Wishard Memorial Hospital 1001 W 10th St Indianapolis IN 46202-2879 Office Phone: 317-630-2564. E-mail: sachsg@iupui.edu.*

SACHS, JEFFREY DAVID, economist, educator; b. Detroit, Nov. 5, 1954; s. Theodore and Joan Sachs; m. Sonia Ehrlich Sachs; children: Lisa, Adam, Hannah. BA summa cum laude, Harvard U., 1976, MA in Econs., 1978, PhD in Econs., 1980; degree (hon.), St. Gallen U., Switzerland, 1990, Lingnan Coll. Hong Kong, 1998, Varba Econs. U., Bulgaria, 2000, Iona Coll. N.Y., 2000. Prof. internat. trade Harvard U., Cambridge, Mass., 1984—2002; prof. sustainable devel. Columbia U., NYC, 2002—, dir. Earth Inst., 2002—. Dir. Harvard Inst. Internat. Devel. Harvard U., 1995—99; chmn. commn. on macroecons. and health WHO, 2000—01; dir. Ctr. for Internat. Devel. Harvard U., 1998—2002; spl. advisor to Sec. Gen. Kofi Annan UN, NYC, 2002—06; cons. in field. Co-author: Macroeconomics in the Global Economy, 1992; author: Poland's Jump to the Market Economy, 1993, Development Economics, 1997, Macroeconomics in the Global Economy, 2003, The End of Poverty: Economic Possibilities of Our Times, 2005, Common Wealth: Economics from a Crowded Planet, 2008. Named one of The World's Most Influential People, TIME mag., 2005, New York's Influentials, New York mag., 2006, America's Best Leaders, US News & World Report, 2008. Mem.: Inst. Medicine. Office: The Earth Inst at Columbia Univ 314 Low Libr MC 4327 535 West 116th St New York NY 10027 Office Phone: 212-854-8704.*

SACHS, KATHERINE STEIN, art historian; m. Keith L. Sachs. Grad., Univ. Pa., 1969. Rsch. coord. Phila. Mus. Art. Mem. contemporary collector's com. Harvard Univ. Art Museums; council mem. Tate Internat.; chmn. bd. gov. Ferkauf Grad. Sch. Psychology, Yeshiva Univ.; mem. Trustees Council Penn Women, 2000—; chmn. bd. overseers Inst. Contemporary Art, Univ. Pa., 1998—. Named one of Top 200 Collectors, ARTnews Mag., 2004—08. Avocation: Collector of Contemporary Art. Mailing: Philadelphia Museum of Art Benjamin Franklin Pkwy Philadelphia PA 19130

SACHS, KEITH L., manufacturing executive; m. Katherine Stein. Grad., Univ. Pa., 1967; PhD (hon.), Hebrew Univ., Jerusalem, 2003. Chmn. Saxco Internat. Inc., Horsham, Pa. Trustee Phila. Mus. Art; chmn. bd. Am. Friends of Hebrew Univ. Named one of Top 200 Collectors, ARTnews Mag., 2004—08. Avocation: Collector of Contemporary Art. Office: Saxco International Inc 200 Gibraltar Rd Ste 101 Horsham PA 19044-2333

SACHS, LEO, geneticist, educator; b. Leipzig, Germany, Oct. 14, 1924; s. Elijah and Louise (Lichtblau) Sachs; m. Pnina Salkind; 4 children. BSc, U. Wales, Bangor, 1948; PhD, Trinity Coll., Cambridge U., 1951; DHC (hon.), Bordeaux U., 1985; MD (hon.), Lund U., 1997. Rsch. scientist John Innes Inst., 1951-52; mem. sci. staff Weizmann Inst. Sci., Rehovot, Israel, 1952—, prof., chmn. genetics dept., 1962—, Otto Meyerhof prof. molecular biology, 1968—. Contbr. articles to profl. jours. Recipient Israel prize for natural sci., 1972, Rothschild prize in biol. scis., 1977, Wolf Found. prize in medicine, Israel, 1980, Sloan prize, GM Cancer Rsch. Found., 1989, Warren Alpert prize, Harvard Med. Sch., 1997, Emet prize in life scis., 2002. Fellow: Royal Soc.; mem.: NAS (fgn. assoc.), Israeli Acad. Sci. & Humanities, Internat. Cytokine Soc. (hon. life). Office: Weizmann Inst Sci Dept Molecular Genetics Rm 226 Arthur & Rochelle Belfer Bldg Biomed Rsch Rehovot 76100 Israel Office Phone: 972 8 934 4068. Business E-Mail: leo.sachs@weizmann.ac.il.

SACHS, MARILYN STICKLE, writer, editor, educator; b. NYC, Dec. 18, 1927; d. Samuel and Anna (Smith) Stickle; m. Morris Sachs, Jan. 26, 1947; children: Anne, Paul. BA, Hunter Coll., 1949; MSLS, Columbia U., 1953. Children's libr. Bklyn. Pub. Libr., 1949-60, San Francisco Pub. Libr., 1961-67. Author: Amy Moves In, 1964, Laura's Luck, 1965, Amy and Laura, 1966, Veronica Ganz, 1968, Peter and Veronica, 1969, Marv, 1970, The Bears' House, 1971 (Austrian Children's Book prize 1977, Recognition of Merit award George C. Stone Ctr. for Children's Books 1989, nominee Nat. Book award, 1971), The Truth About Mary Rose, 1973 (Silver Slate Pencil award 1974), A Pocket Full of Seeds, 1973 (Jane Addams Children's Book Honor award 1974), Matt's Mitt, 1975, Dorrie's Book, 1975 (Silver State Pencil award 1977, Garden State Children's Book award 1978), A December Tale, 1976, A Secret Friends, 1978, A Summer's Lease, 1979, Bus Ride, 1980, Class Pictures, 1980, Fleet Footed Florence, 1981, Hello...Wrong Number, 1981, Call Me Ruth, 1982 (Assn. Jewish Librs. award 1983), Beach Towels, 1982, Fourteen, 1983, The Fat Girl, 1984, Thunderbird, 1985, Underdog, 1985 (Christopher 1986), Baby Sister 1986, Almost Fifteen, 1987, Fran Ellen's House, 1987 (award Bay Area Book Reviewers Assn. 1988, Recognition of Merit award George C. Stone Ctr. for Children's Books 1989), Just Like A Friend, 1989, At the Sound of the Beep, 1990, Circles, 1991, What My Sister Remembered, 1992, Thirteen, 1993, Ghosts in the Family, 1995, Another Day, 1997, Suprise Party, 1998, Jo Jo & Winnie, 1999, Jo Jo & Winnie Again, 2000, The Four Ugly Cats in Apartment 3D, 2002, Lost in America, 2005, First Impressions, 2006; co-editor: (with Ann Durell) Big Book for Peace, 1990 (Calif. Children's Book award 1991, Jane Addams Children's Book prize 1991); reviewer San Francisco Chronicle, 1970—. Mem. ACLU, Sierra Club, Authors' Guild. Democrat. Jewish. Avocations: reading, walking, baseball. Home: 733 31st Ave San Francisco CA 94121-3523 Home Phone: 415-752-2847.

SACHS, MURRAY, French language and literature educator, researcher; b. Toronto, Ont., Can., Apr. 10, 1924; came to U.S., 1946, naturalized, 1955; s. Thomas and Sarah (Roth) S.; m. Miriam Blank, Sept. 14, 1961; children: Deborah Ruth Sachs Gabor, Aaron Jacob. BA with 1st class honours, U. Toronto, 1946; AM in French and Romance Philology, Columbia U., 1947, PhD in French, 1953. Lectr. Sch. Gen. Studies Columbia U., NYC, 1946-48; lectr. U. Calif., Berkeley, 1948-50, U. Detroit, 1951-52, Williams Coll., Williamstown, Mass., 1954-57, asst. prof., 1957-60; asst. prof. French and comparative lit. Brandeis U., Waltham, Mass., 1960-61, assoc. prof., 1961-66, prof., 1966-96; emeritus Brandeis Univ., 1996—; chmn. dept. Brandeis U., Waltham, Mass., 1963-64, 67-71, 81-84, 90-91. Presenter, lectr. in field; mem. editl. adv. bd. 19th century French studies, 1974—, Purdue U. Monographs in Romance Langs., 1980-90, Cin. Romance Rev., 1988-2, Romance Quar., 1989—; mem. Nat. Humanities Faculty, Concord, Mass., Atlanta, cons., 1978-81; cons. humanities projects NEH, 1982-84, 92, rev. panelist, 1983, 89, 91; manuscript referee various jours. and univ. presses, others; cons. NEH Summer Inst. on Francophonie, 1993, 94, 97. Author: (with E.M. and R.B. Grant) French Stories, Plays and Poetry: A First-Year Reader, 1959; The Career of Alphonse Daudet: A Critical Study, 1965, The French Short Story in the Nineteenth Century: A Critical Anthology, 1969, Anatole France: The Short Stories, 1974; also articles and revs. to profl. jours. and reference works. Recipient Palmes Académiques, Govt. of France, 1971; Reuben Wells Leonard and Edward Blake scholar U. Toronto, 1942; Henry Alfred Todd fellow Columbia U., 1946-48; rsch. and travel grantee Williams Colls., summers 1955, 59. Mem. MLA (del. assembly 1971, 72, 76-78, exec. com. French 6 group 1970-73, 19th Century French lit. sect. 1975-76), Assn. Depts. Fgn. Langs. of MLA (rep. PhD granting depts. to exec. com. 1983-85, pres. 1985), Greater Boston Fgn. Langs. Collaborative (co-chmn. 1992-93, 93-94), Phi Beta Kappa (hon.). Jewish. Home: 280 Highland Ave West Newton MA 02465-2514 Office: Brandeis U Dept Romance and Comparative Lit 415 South St Waltham MA 02454-9110 Home Phone: 617-969-8039; Office Phone: 781-736-3225. Personal E-mail: mmsachs@verizon.net. Business E-Mail: sachs@brandeis.edu.

SACHS, STEPHEN WARREN, music educator, director; b. Gettysburg, Pa., Aug. 9, 1955; s. Luther Irvin and Joan Mcnew Sachs; m. Carolyn Robertson Reed, Aug. 23, 1975; children: Gregory Gardner, Martha Mcnew, Sarah Spangler, Roberta Reed. MusB, Lebanon Valley Coll., Annville, Pa., 1976; MusM, Ohio U., Athens, 1978; MusD, Cath. U. America, Washington, 1989. Prof. music Eastern Mennonite U., Harrisonburg, Va., 1978—2004, founder and co-chair piano tchrs. forum, 1996—2004; organist First Presbyn. Ch., Harrisonburg, 1996—99; dir. music ministries Otterbein United Meth. Ch., Harrisonburg, 1999—2004; prof. music and music chair Belhaven Coll., Jackson, Miss., 2004—; dir. music ministries Covenant Presbyn. Ch., EPC, Jackson, 2005—. Judge Nat. Guild Piano Tchrs., Ft. Worth, 1990—2000; bd. mem. Miss. Symphony Orch., Jackson, 2007—, mem. artistic adv. com., 2007—08. Musician: (piano) Rhapsody in Blue, Rhapsody on a Theme by Paganini. Mem.: Internat. Assn. Jazz Educators, Music Tchrs. Nat. Assn. (Nationally Cert. Tchr. of Music 1980—), Am. Liszt Soc., Am. Chess Fedn. Avocations: chess, reading, travel, sports, music. Home: 902 Euclid Ave Jackson MS 39202 Office: Belhaven Coll Music Dept 1500 Peachtree St Box 320 Jackson MS 39202 Home Phone: 601-353-6790; Office Phone: 601-974-6471. Office Fax: 601-974-6499. Personal E-mail: sachsswcr@juno.com. Business E-Mail: ssachs@belhaven.edu.

SACHSE, PETER, retail executive; b. Sheboygan, Wis. m. Jini Sachse; 2 children. B in Fin., U. Wis. Joined Macy's, Inc., Kansas City, Mo., 1980, mdse. mgr. Bullock's divsn., 1987—92, sr. v.p., gen. mdse. mgr. Bon Marche divsn. (now part of Macy's West), 1992—97, exec. v.p., gen. mdse. mgr. Macy's East NYC, 1997—99, vice chair, dir. of stores, 1999, pres., COO Bon Marche divsn., chief mktg. officer, 2003—07, 2009—, chmn., CEO macys.com, 2006—, pres. corp. mktg., 2007—09. Named a Power Player, Advt. Age, 2008. Office: Macys Inc Hdqs 7 W 7th St Cincinnati OH 45202 also: Macys Herald Square 151 W 34th St New York NY 10001 Office Phone: 513-579-7000. Business E-Mail: peter.sachse@macys.com.*

SACK, BRIAN P., bank executive, economist; b. 1970; married; 2 children. BA in Math., U. Vt., 1992; PhD in Econs., MIT, 1997. Staff mem. bd. governors FRS, Washington, 1997—2003, head monetary/fin. markets analysis sect., 2003—04; v.p., dir. monetary policy insights svc. Macroeconomic Advisers LLC, 2004—09; exec. v.p., head markets group Fed. Res. Bank NY, 2009—. Contbr. numerous artcles and rsch. papers to Quarterly Jour. Econs., Jour. Monetary Econs., Jour. Money Credit & Banking, Jour. Fixed Income, Jour. Futures Markets, Wall St. Jour., Fin. Times, BusinessWeek. Office: Fed Res Bank NY Head Office 33 Liberty St New York NY 10045 Office Phone: 212-720-5000.*

SACK, EDGAR ALBERT, electronics company executive; b. Pitts., Jan. 31, 1930; s. Edgar Albert and Margaret Valentine (Engelmohr) S.; m. Eugenia Ferris, June 7, 1952; children: Elaine Kimberley, Richard Warren. BS, Carnegie-Mellon U., 1951, MS, 1952, PhD, 1954. Dept. mgr. Westinghouse Rsch. Lab., Pitts., 1960-63; engrng. mgr. Westinghouse Microelectronics, Balt., 1963-65, ops. mgr., 1965-67, divsn. mgr., 1967-69; div. v.p. Gen. Instrument Corp., Hicksville, NY, 1969-73, group v.p., 1973-77, sr. v.p., 1977-84; pres., CEO Zilog Inc., Campbell, Calif., 1984-98, also chmn. bd. dirs.; pres. Productivity Assocs., Coronado, Calif.; founder, chmn. CDT, Inc., San Jose, Calif., 1998-99. Bd. dirs. Enfo-Web, Inc., Mountainview, Calif., LXi, Inc., Mountainview; vis. com. elec. engrng. dept. Carnegie-Mellon U., 1969-74; mem. indsl. adv. coun. SUNY, Stony Brook, 1979-83; mem. adv. com. on solid state electronics Poly. Inst. Tech., 1981-83. Author: Forward Controllership Business Management System, 1989, 2nd edit., 1993, Development of the Coronado Shores-A History, 2005; patentee in field. Mem. Action Com. L.I, 1982-84; bd. dir. Coronado Shores Assn. # 7, 2000-, landscaping and recreational com., 2000-, chair, 2002-03, treas., 2004-09; mem. Sharp Coronado Hosp. Aux., Satern and Cero Emergency Svcs. Orgns., 2008-; sec. San Diego Imperial Coun. of Vols., 2002; bd. dirs. Coronado Hosp. Found., 2003-04, chair projects and allocations com., 2004. Recipient 2nd Ann. Hammerschlag Disting. Lectr. award Carnegie Mellon U., 1995. Fellow IEEE, Poly. Inst. Tech.; mem. Semicondr. Industry Assn. (dir. 1982-85), Carnegie Mellon Alumni Assn. (Merit award 1981), Eta Kappa Nu (Outstanding Young Elec. Engr. 1959), Huntington Yacht Club (vice comdr. 1977), Tau Beta Pi (finalist San Francisco Entrepreneur of Yr. award 1991), Phi Kappa Phi, Satern & Cero Emergency Svcs. Orgns. Home and Office: 1780 Avenida Del Mundo Unit 404 Coronado CA 92118-4011 Personal E-mail: esack@pacbell.net.

SACK, GEORGE HENRY, JR., molecular geneticist, internist; b. Balt., Apr. 17, 1943; s. George Henry and Sophia Ann (Philippi) S. BA, Johns Hopkins U., 1965, MD, 1968, PhD, 1974. Diplomate Bd. Med. Genetics, Bd. Med. Examiners. Intern Johns Hopkins Hosp., Balt., 1968-69, asst. resident, 1969-70, fellow genetics, 1975-76; rsch. fellow Johns Hopkins Sch. Medicine, Balt., 1970-73; asst. prof. dept. medicine Johns Hopkins U., Balt., 1976-84, assoc. prof. dept. medicine and biol. chemistry, 1984—; molecular biologist Kennedy Inst., Balt., 1982-93, dir. exec. health program, 1996—2006; med dir. Hopkins USA, 2007—. Contbr. articles to profl. jours. Maj. USAR, 1973-75. Andrew W. Mellon scholar Johns Hopkins U., 1976, Kennedy Found. scholar, 1982-85. Fellow Am. Coll. Med. Genetics; mem. AMA, AAAS, Am. Soc. Human Genetics, Phi Beta Kappa. Office: Johns Hopkins Sch Medicine Dept Biol Chemistry P-615 Baltimore MD 21205 Office Phone: 410-955-4621, 410-735-6605. Business E-Mail: gsack@jhmi.edu.

SACK, ROBERT DAVID, federal judge, educator; b. Phila., Oct. 4, 1939; s. Eugene J. and Sylvia I. (Rivlin) Sack; BA, U. Rochester, 1960; LLB, Columbia U., 1963. Bar: NY 1963. Law clk. to judge Fed. Dist. Ct. of NJ, 1963—64; assoc. Patterson, Belknap & Webb, NYC, 1964—70; ptnr. Patterson, Belknap, Webb & Tyler, NYC, 1970—86, Gibson, Dunn & Crutcher, NYC, 1986-98; sr. assoc. spl. counsel US Ho. of Reps. Impeachment Inquiry, 1974; judge US Ct. Appeals (2d cir.), 1998—. Lectr. Practising Law Inst., 1973—97, Columbia U. Law Sch., 2001—, mem. bd. visitors, 2000—; adv. bd. Media Law Reporter. Author: Libel, Slander, and Related Problems, 1980, 2d edit., 1994, CD-ROM edit., 1995, Sack on Defamation-Libel, Slander, and Related Problems, 3d edit., 1999; co-author: Advertising and Commercial Speech, a First Amendment Guide, 1999; contbr. articles to profl. jours. Chmn. bd. dirs. Nat. Council on Crime and Delinquency, 1982—83; trustee seminars on media and society Columbia U. Sch. Journalism, 1985—92, NYC Commn. on Pub. Info. and Comm., 1995—98; v.p., bd. dirs. William F. Kerby and Robert S. Potter Fund. Recipient Learned Hand medal, Fed. Bar Coun., 2008. Fellow: Am. Bar Found.; mem.: ABA (bd. govs. forum com. on comm. law 1980—88), Fed. Bar Counsel, Assn. Bar City NY (chmn. comm. law com. 1986—89). Office: US Circuit Ct for 2d Circuit 40 Foley Sq New York NY 10007-1502*

SACKETT, BARNARD (BARNEY), actor, film producer, director, scriptwriter; Personal mgr. Bret Morrison "The Shadow" of Mutual Network Blue Coal Radio, jazz artist Sylvia Syms, 1950; press agt. summer stock co. Quarterdeck Theatre, Atlantic City, N.J., 1952—55; drama critic, celebrity interviewer Sta. WDAS and Metromedia WIP, Phila., 1953—68; owner/operator Wayne Ave. Playhouse, Phila., 1957—69, Aarde Cinema and Sackett's Screening Room, Phila., 1970—73, Onstage Theatre, Phila., 1986—89; liaison/coord. pvt. fin. placements West Hollywood, Calif. Opened TV prodn. agy. Empire State Bldg., NYC, Knickerbock Hotel, Hollywood, Banker's Securities Bldg., Phila., 1947; writer, prodr., dir. first TV live action film prodn. The Closed Affair Dumont TV Closed Circuit, NYC, 1948; writer, prodr., dir. comedy series The Penn Family WFIL-TV, 1949; concert impresario, 49; dir., prodr. all-star mil. prodn. Death of a Salesman, Earle Theatre, Phila., 1952; originator/operator Silent Movie Nickelodeon Theater, NYC; film actor Eroticon, Bad Girls Go To Hell; personal rep. Erlanger Theater, New Locust Theatre; entertainment dir. Carlos 'n Charlies Night Club, Hollywood. Author: (memoirs) Rough in the E.T., 2007, Bette, Hedy, Mae, Marlene and Me, 2007; writer, prodr., dir.: (weekly musical comedy) What a Show; Playtime; (weekly satirical soap opera) Rough in the E.T.; writer, prodr. (weekly satirical soap opera) Bette, Hedy, Mae & Who?; writer, prodr., dir.: (weekly TV series) The Gypsy Markoff Show; Bret Morrison and Lucille Manner Musical Review; Rehearsal with Maggie Teyte; writer, prodr.: (films) Eroticon; All Men Are Apes; Nickelodeon Days; Sweet Smell of Sex; talent coord.: United Nations Musical Review; presenter: concerts Acad. of Music, Witherspoon Concert Hall; presenter: (concerts) Town Hall. Mem. Hollywood C. of C., Beverly Hills C. of C., West. Hollywood C. of C. Served with US Army, 1943—45, WWII. Achievements include designing world's only three-stage musical theatre, Music-Go-Round Playhouse; interviewed hundreds of famous people from world of sports, theater, film and politics including Debbie Reynolds, Joan Crawford, Sugar Ray Robinson, Bette Davis, Charlton Heston, Otto Preminger, Alfred Hitchcock, Gary Cooper, John Wayne, Sammy Davis, Jr., Henry Fonda, and Hedy Lamarr; exclusive on-stage celebrity interviewer for Stanley Warner Motion Picture Theatres, Phila.; writer, prodr., dir. 71st Annual Easter Sunrise Svc. Office: 1311 N Fairfax Ave Ste 15 West Hollywood CA 90046 Office Phone: 323-851-8842. E-mail: promethean@sbcglobal.net.

SACKETT, CHARLES ACKLEY, physicist, educator; b. Eugene, Oreg., July 26, 1969; s. David Henry and Gail Shippy Sackett; m. Deana Roy Roy; children: Evangeline Frances, Henry Nashua. PhD, Rice U., Houstin, Tex., 1998. Assoc. prof. U. Va., Charlottesville, 2001—. Rsch. fellowship, Alfred P. Sloan Found., 2002. Mem.: Am. Phys. Soc. Achievements include research in bose-einstein condensation, atom interferometry. Office: Univ Va 382 McCormick Rd Charlottesville VA 22904

SACKETT, SUSAN DEANNA, writer; b. NYC, Dec. 18, 1943; adopted d. Maxwell and Gertrude Selma (Kugel) S. BA in Edn., U. Fla., 1964, MEd, 1965. Tchr. Dade County Schs., Miami, Fla., 1966-68, L.A. City Schs., 1968-69; asst. publicist, comml. coord. NBC-TV, Burbank, Calif., 1970-73; asst. to Gene Roddenberry, creator Star Trek, 1974-91; prodn. assoc. TV series Star Trek: The Next Generation, 1987-91, writer, 1990-91. Lectr. and guest spkr. Star Trek convs. in U.S., Eng., Australia, 1974-. Author, editor: Letters to Star Trek, 1977; co-author: Star Trek Speaks, The Making of Star Trek--The Motion Picture, 1979, You Can Be a Game Show Contestant and Win, 1982, Say Goodnight Gracie, 1986; author: The Hollywood Reporter Book of Box Office Hits, 1990, 2d edit., 1996, Prime Time Hits, 1993, Hollywood Sings, 1995, Inside Trek: My Secret Life with Star Trek Creator Gene Roddenberry, 2002. Mem. ACLU, Writers Guild Am., Am. Humanist Assn., Humanist Soc. Greater Phoenix (pres. 2000—), Mensa, Sierra Club, Am. Humanist Assn. (bd. dir., 2005—). Democrat.

SACKHEIM, ROBERT LEWIS, aerospace engineer, educator; b. NYC, May 16, 1937; s. A. Frederick and Lillian L. (Emmer) S.; m. Babette Freund, Jan. 12, 1964; children: Karen Holly, Andrew Frederick. BSChemE, U. Va., 1959; MSChemE, Columbia U., 1961; postgrad., UCLA, 1966—72. Project engr. Comsat Corp., El Segundo, Calif., 1969-72; project mgr. TRW, Redondo Beach, Calif., 1964-69, sect. head, 1972-76, dept. mgr., 1976-81, mgr. new bus., 1981-86, lab. mgr., 1986-90, dep. ctr. dir., 1990-93, ctr. dir., 1993-99; asst. dir, chief engr. for space propulsion systems Marshall Space Flight Ctr, NASA, Huntsville, Ala., 1999—2006; adj. prof. mech. and aerospace engrng. U. Ala., Huntsville, 2006—; ind. cons. in space and launch vehicles and propulsion sys. and tech. Instr. UCLA engrng. ext., 1986, Continuing Engrng. Edn., U. Ala., Huntsville, 2001; mem. adv. bds. NASA, Washington, 1989—; mem. peer rev. bd. various univs. and govtl. agys., 1990—; mem. Nat. Rsch. Coun./Aeronautics and Space Engrng. Bd., 1994—; mem. NRC com. propulsion evaluation, 2003; mem. various NASA investigation teams; guest lectr. various univs. and AIAA short courses. Author: Space Mission Analysis and Design, 1991, Space Propulsion Analysis and Design, 1994, Space Launch and Transportation Systems, 2004; contbr. chpt. to book, more than 250 articles to profl.

jours., confs. Mem. adv. bd. L.A. Bd. Edn., 1990-92; fund raiser March of Dimes, L.A., 1970-90, YMCA, San Pedro, Calif., 1974-86. Capt. USAF Reserve, 1960-63. Recipient 16 Group Achievement awards NASA, 1970, 78, 86, 2000, 2001, 2003, 2005, Sustained Svc. award AIAA, 2000, medal for outstanding tech. leadership NASA, Propulsion Outstanding Contbns. award French Acad. Aero/Astro., 2002, NASA/Dir.'s commendation, 2003, Presdl. Rank award for disting. fed. civil svc., 3 ann. TRW Chmn. awards, TRW PAtent of Yr. award, 1992, Govs. award for disting. svc. state Ala., 2004. Fellow AIAA (chmn. com. 1980-83, chmn. L.A. sect. 1997, chmn. Ala./Miss. sect. 2000, 2001, J.H. Wyld Propulsion award 1992, Shuttle Flag award 1984, Martin Schilling award 2001, Hermann Oberth award 2002, Holgar Toftoy award 2003), Internat. Acad. Astronautics, Nat. Acad. Engring., Sigma Xi. Achievements include 9 patents in field. Office: U Alabama Rm N249 Huntsville AL 35812 Office Phone: 256-824-5121. Business E-Mail: sackheir@uah.edu.

SACKMANN, INGE-JULIANA, astrophysicist; b. Schoenau, Prussia, Feb. 8, 1942; arrived in Can., 1955, arrived in Germany, 1968, arrived in US, 1971; m. Robert Fredrick Christy, Aug. 4, 1973. BA in Physics, U. Toronto, 1963, MA in Astronomy, 1965; PhD in Astrophysics, U. Toronto, Ontario, Canada, 1968. Postdoctoral fellow U. Gottingen, Germany, 1968—69, Max-Planck Inst. Physics and Astrophysics, Munich, 1969—71; rsch. fellow Calif. Inst. Tech., Pasadena, 1971—74, sr. rsch. fellow, 1976—81, faculty assoc., 1981—; rsch. assoc. Jet Propulsion Lab., Pasadena, 1974—76, U. Hamburg Observatory, Germany, 1971. Contbr. articles to numerous jour. publs. Recipient Alexander von-Humbolt award, Germany, 1970—71; named Personalities of America, Outstanding Scientists of 20th Century, 2000; Postdoc. fellowship, Nat. Rsch. Coun. Can., 1968—70. Avocations: children, flower arranging, growing organic garden, horseback riding, hiking. Office: Calif Inst Tech 157 West Bridge Lab 103-33 1201 East Calif Blvd Pasadena CA Business E-Mail: ijs@caltech.edu.

SACKNER, MARVIN ARTHUR, physician; b. Phila., Feb. 16, 1932; s. Albert B. and Goldie Mildred (Haber) S.; m. Ruth Karsch, June 24, 1956; children: Sara, Deborah, Jonathan. BS, Temple U., 1953; MD, Jefferson Med. Coll., 1957. Diplomate Am. Bd. Internal Medicine. Intern Phila. Gen. Hosp., 1957-58, med. resident, 1958-61; ACP rsch. fellow U. Pa., Phila., 1961-64; chief pulmonary disease Mt. Sinai Hosp., Miami Beach, Fla., 1964-74, dir. med. svcs., 1974-91, dir. med. svcs. emeritus Fla., 1992—; prof. medicine U. Miami, Fla., 1973—. Gov., chmn. pulmonary disease exam. bd. Am. Bd. Internal Medicine, 1977-80; chief exec. officer Non-Invasive Monitoring Systems, Inc., Miami Beach, Fla., 1986—. Author: Scleroderma, 1966; editor: Diagnostic Techniques in Pulmonary Disease, Parts I and II, 1980; mem. editorial bd. Fla. Med. Assn., 1974, Am. Rev. Respiratory Physiology, 1976-80, Jour. Applied Physiology, 1976-80, Annals Internal Medicine, 1979; patentee in field; contbr. articles to profl. jours. Pres. Art in Pub. Places, Inc., 1975-78; co-dir. Ruth and Marvin Sackner Archive of Concrete and Visual Poetry, 1979—; bd. dirs. Ctr. for Book Art, N.Y.C., 1987-93; mem. libr. com. Mus. Modern Art, N.Y.C., 1990-94. NEA grantee, 1977-78, Nat. Heart, Lung and Blood Inst. grantee, 1966—, others. Fellow ACP, Am. Coll. Chest Physicians; mem. Am. Thoracic Soc. (pres.1980), Am. Physiol. Soc., Grolier Club N.Y.C. Jewish. Office: Nims Inc 1666 79th St CSWY #400 Miami Beach FL 33141-4133

SACKS, DAVID O., Internet company executive, film production company executive; m. Jacqueline Tortorice, 2007. Grad., Stanford U., 1990—94; JD, U. Chgo., 1995—98. Mgmt. cons. McKinsey, 1999; COO PayPal, 1999—2002; founder, CEO Room 9 Entertainment LLC, 2002—; co-founder, CEO Geni, Inc., LA, 2006—. Named one of 10 Producers to Watch, Variety, 2005. Office: Geni Inc 9255 Sunset Blvd Ste 727 West Hollywood CA 90069

SACKS, HERBERT SIMEON, psychiatrist, educator, consultant; b. NYC, Nov. 29, 1926; s. Maxwell Lawrence and Anne (Edelstein) S.; m. Helen Margery Levin, Dec. 26, 1948; children: Eric Livingston, Katharine Bird, Douglas Lowell, Russell Avery AB magna cum laude, Dickinson Coll., 1948; MD, Cornell U., 1952. Diplomate Am. Bd. Psychiatry and Neurology and subspecialty Child and Adolescent Psychiatry. Clin. assoc. Western New Eng. Psychoanalytic Inst., New Haven, 1955-63; intern in pediatrics Yale-New Haven Med. Ctr., 1952-53; jr. asst. resident in psychiatry Yale Psychiat. Inst., 1953-54; sr. asst. resident in psychiatry, USPHS fellow Yale-New Haven Med. Ctr., psychiat. out patient dept., 1954-55; USPHS fellow in child psychiatry Yale U. Child Study Ctr., 1955-57; clin. dir. Mid-Fairfield Child Guidance Ctr., Norwalk, Conn., 1957-59; cons. Expt. in Internat. Living, Putney, Vt., 1962-69; sr. cons. U.S. Peace Corps, Washington, 1962-69; cons. AID, U.S. Dept. State, Office of Sahel, West Africa, 1974-84, Neurosci. Consultation Group, Grosse Point Farms, Mich., 1984-94; clin. prof. child and adolescent psychiatry Child Study Ctr., Yale U. Sch. Medicine, New Haven. Co-investigator, co-dir. Senegal River pilot health research program, New Haven and West Africa, 1976-78, co-investigator, co-dir. health sector, design team Senegal River integrated devel. project, 1981-83; vis. lectr. Yale Coll., 1969-71; mem. com. reviewers Dept. Commerce Nat. Bur. Standards, Inst. for Computer Scis. and Tech., Washington, 1975-77; mem. exec. com. Nat. Commn. on Confidentiality of Health Records, 1975-80 Author: Hurdles: The Admissions Dilemma in American Higher Education, 1978; contbg. author chpts. in books, articles on confidentiality, juvenile justice, higher edn., issues of youth in transition, other topics; author monographs Mem. Conn. Juvenile Justice Commn., Hartford, 1975-80; bd. advisors Dickinson Coll., Carlisle, Pa., 1980-85. Served to lt. (j.g.) U.S. Navy, 1944-46; PTO Fellow AMA, ACPO, Am. Psychiat. Assn. (trustee 1988-94, v.p. 1994-96, pres. 1997-98), Am. Acad. Child and Adolescent Psychiatry, Am. Orthopsychiat. Assn., Am. Coll. Psychiatrists; mem. Conn. Psychiat. Soc. (pres. 1976-77), Conn. Coun. Child and Adolescent Psychiatrists (pres. 1972-73), World Fedn. for Mental Health, Phi Beta Kappa. Avocations: farming, photography, fishing, lawn bowling. Home: 110 Laurel Rd New Haven CT 06515-2426 Office: 260 Riverside Ave Westport CT 06880-4804 also: Yale U Child Study Ctr PO Box 207900 New Haven CT 06520-7900 Office Phone: 203-227-0996.

SACKS, JOEL GERALD, ophthalmologist, educator; b. Chgo., Sept. 14, 1939; s. Louis and Rose S.; m. Cynthia Ann Dana, June 10, 1967; children: Charles, David, Martha. BA, Northwestern U., 1960, MS, 1962, MD, 1963; MBA, U. Cin., 1986. Diplomate, Am. Bd. Ophthalmology. NIH spl. fellow Md. Med. Legal Found., Balt., 1967-68; rsch. fellow Johns Hopkins Sch. Medicine, Balt., 1968-69; asst. prof. to assoc. prof. Northwestern U., Chgo., 1969-77; prof., dir. dept. ophthalmology U. Cin., 1977-94, prof. emeritus ophthalmology, 2005—; pres. Ophthalmic Cons., Inc., Cin., 1977-94; clin. prof. surgery Mich. State U., 1994-97; v.p. med. affairs, dir. med. edn. Butterworth Hosp., Grand Rapids, Mich., 1994-97; v.p., chief med. officer Touro Infirmary, New Orleans, 1998-99; clin. prof. ophthalmology Tulane U., New Orleans, 2000—06, prof. emeritus, 2006—. Pres. Med. Ctr. Fund Cin., 1985-88, Univ. Health Plan, Inc., Cin., 1987-89. Co-author: Neuropathology of Vision: an Atlas, 1973; contbr. articles to sci. jours. Founding mem. Beth Adam: The Cin. Congregation Humanistic Judaism, 1980. Capt. U.S. Army, 1967-74. Fellow Am. Acad. Ophthalmology (Honor award 1982); mem. Phi Beta Kappa, Alpha Omega Alpha. Home: 47 Fairway Oaks Dr New Orleans LA 70131-3339 Office Phone: 504-842-3995. Business E-Mail: jsacks@ochsner.edu.

SACKS, OLIVER WOLF, neurologist, writer; b. London, July 9, 1933; Came to U.S., 1960; s. Samuel and Muriel Elsie (Landau) S. BA, U. Oxford, 1954; MA, BM, BCh, Middlesex Hosp., London, 1958; DHL (hon.), Georgetown U., 1990, Coll. Staten Island, CUNY, 1991; DS (hon.), Tufts U., 1991, N.Y. Med. Coll., 1991; DS (hon.), Med. Coll. Pa., 1992, Bard Coll., 1992, U. Turin, 2003. Intern in medicine, surgery and neurology Middlesex Hosp., 1958-60; rotating intern Mt. Zion Hosp., San Francisco, 1961-62; resident in neurology UCLA, 1962-65; I.D. fellow in neuropathology and neurochemistry Albert Einstein Coll. Medicine, NYC, 1965-66, instr. neurology, 1966-75, asst. prof., 1975-78, assoc. prof., 1978-85, clin. prof. neurology, 1985—2007; prof. clin. neurology and clin. psychiatry Columbia U. Med. Ctr., NYC, 2007—; Columbia Artist Columbia U., NYC, 2007—. Adj. prof. psychiatry NYU, 1992-; sci. advisor Inst. Music and Neurologic Function, Beth Abraham Hosp., 1995-; cons. neurologist Comprehensive Epilepsy Ctr., Mt. Sinai Med. Ctr., 1999-; cons., speaker, lectr. in field; hon. lectureships in field. Author: Migraine, 1970, Awakenings, 1973, (Hawthornden prize 1975), A Leg To Stand On, 1984, The Man Who Mistook His Wife for a Hat, 1985, Seeing Voices: A Journey into the World of the Deaf, 1989 (Mainichi Pub. Culture award 1996), An Anthropologist on Mars, 1995 (George S. Polk award for mag. reporting 1994, Nat. Assn. Sci. Writers award 1994, Esquire Apple Waterstone's Book of Yr. 1995), The Island of the Color Blind, 1996, Uncle Tungsten: Memories of a Chemical Boyhood, 2001, Oaxaca Journal, 2002, Musicophilia: Tales of Music and the Brain, 2007. Bd. mem. N.Y. Bot. Garden. Recipient Oskar Pfister award APA, 1988, Harold D. Vursell Meml. award Am. Acad. and Inst. Arts and Letters, 1989, Communicator of Yr. Royal Nat. Inst. Deaf, 1991, Lewis Thomas prize Rockefeller U., 2002, Sloan Found. award, 2002, Pub. Comm. award NSF, 2004; Guggenheim fellow, 1989, others. Fellow Am. Acad. Arts and Scis., Am. Acad. Arts and Letters, NY Acad. Scis. (hon.); mem. Am. Acad. Neurology (presdl. citation 1991), Am. Fern Soc., Am. Neurological Assn. (hon.), Assn. Brit. Neurologists (hon.), Brit. Pteridological Soc., NY Mineralogical Club, NY Stereoscopic Soc., Soc. Neurosci., NY Inst. Humanities, Alpha Omega Alpha. Office: 2 Horatio St Apt 3G New York NY 10014-1638 also: Columbia U Med Ctr Neurological Inst of NY 710 W 168th St New York NY 10032 Office Phone: 212-633-8373. E-mail: mail@oliversacks.com, os2177@columbia.edu.

SACKS, PATRICIA ANN, librarian, consultant; b. Allentown, Pa., Nov. 6, 1939; d. Lloyd Alva and Dorothy Estelle (Stoneback) Stahl; m. Kenneth LeRoy Sacks, June 27, 1959. AB, Cedar Crest Coll., 1959; MS in Libr. Sci., Drexel U., 1965. News reporter Call-Chronicle, Allentown, 1956-59, 61-63; reference libr. Cedar Crest Coll., Allentown, 1964-66, head libr., 1966-73; dir. librs. Muhlenberg and Cedar Crest Colls., Allentown, 1973-94; dir. libr. svcs. Cedar Crest Coll., 1994; sr. fellow Lehigh Valley Assn. Ind. Colls., 1994-97, Ctr. Agile Ptnrs. in Edn., 1997-98; info. svcs. cons., 1998—. Del. On Line Computer Library Ctr. Users Council, Columbus, Ohio, 1977-84; cons. colls./health care orgns., libr. orgns. 1981—. Author: (with Whildin Sara Lou) Preparing for Accreditation: A Handbook for Academic Librarians, 1993; mem. editl. bd. Jour. Acad. Librarianship, 1982-84. Mem. United Way Lehigh Valley Coms., 1993—97; trustee Cedar Crest Coll., 1985—89; bd. dirs. John and Dorothy Morgan Cancer Ctr., 1994—96; mem. bd. Allentown Cmty. Concert, Pa., 2003—06. Named Outstanding Acad. Woman, Lehigh Valley Assn. Acad. Women, 1984, Muhlenberg Coll. Outstanding Adminstr., 1987, Alumni Tricorn award Muhlenberg Coll., 1989, Alumnae Achievement award Cedar Crest Coll., 1994. Mem. ALA (chmn. copyright com. 1985-87), Assn. Coll. and Rsch. Librs. (chmn. stds. and accreditation com. 1976-78, 81-84), Lehigh Valley Assn. Ind. Colls. (chmn. librs. sect. 1967-81, 88-92), AAUW, LWV, Wildlands Conservancy, Appalachian Mountain Club (Echo Lake naturalist 1997—), Phi Alpha Theta, Phi Kappa Phi, Beta Phi Mu. Democrat. Home: 2997 Fairfield Dr Allentown PA 18103-5413 Personal E-mail: sackspa@ptd.net.

SACKS, TEMI J., public relations executive; b. Phila. d. Jule and Adeline (Levin) S. BA, Temple U. Pubs. editor Del. Valley Regional Planning Commn., Phila.; comms. assoc. Fedn. Jewish Agys., Phila.; exec. v.p., mng. dir. consumer and healthcare divsns. Lobsenz-Stevens Inc., NYC; exec. v.p., dir. nat. healthcare practice Shandwick, NYC; pres. T.J. Sacks & Assocs. Inc., NYC. Mem. Healthcare Businesswomen's Assn., Healtcare Mktg. Assn., Women Execs. in Pub. Rels. Avocations: painting, skiing, jewelry design, antiques. Office Phone: 212-787-0787. Personal E-mail: tjsacks@tjsacks.com.

SACRIPANTI, PETER JOHN, lawyer; b. 1955; BA summa cum laude, Fordham U., 1982; JD, Pace U., 1984. Fed. prosecutor U.S. Dept. Justice; ptnr., mem. firm exec. mgmt. com. McDermott Will & Emery LLP. Recipient Ellis Island Medal Hon., 2001. Mem.: N.J. Bar Assn., D.C. Bar Assn., N.Y. Bar Assn. Office Phone: 212-547-5583. Office Fax: 212-547-5444. Business E-Mail: psacripanti@mwe.com.

SADAK, DIANE MARIE, director, performing arts educator; d. John Charles and Dolores Hope (Salvi) Sadak; m. Barry Kendall Smith, Oct. 18, 1999; children: Noel Kendall Smith-Sadak, Sage Noelle Smith-Sadak. MFA in Directing, Fla. State U., 1989; BA in Polit. sci. and Econs., Union Coll., 1985; studied with R. Armstrong, 2000—; student in Advanced Voice Intensives, Banff Ctr. Arts, 2001, student in Advanced Voice Intensives, 2003—04; student, Roy Hart Internat. Voice Intensive, Malerargues, France, 2005, student, 2008, Roy Hart Internat. Voice, Body Intensive, Arezzo, Italy, 2006. Staff artist Calif. Young Playwrights Project, San Diego, 1989—93; vis. prof. voice and acting Korean Nat. U. Arts, Seoul, Republic of Korea, 1997—98; guest artist Union Coll. and Schenectady County C.C., Schenectady, NY, 1998—99; asst. prof. acting and directing Towson U., Md., 1999—2005, assoc. prof., 2005—, head Acting Program Dept. Theatre Arts, 2000—04, program dir. MFA in theatre, dept. theatre arts, 2004—06; vis. artist-in-residence Accademia Dell' Arte Conservatory Phys. Theatre, 2006; tchr. Internat. Fedn. Makers Theatre, Athens, Greece, 2007. Cons. in field; presenter in field; guest artist Union Coll., Schenectady, NY, 1998—99, Schenectady County C.C., 1998—99; artist-in-residence Laurel Elem. Sch., San Diego, 1990—92; artist-in-residence Comprehensive Adolescent Treatment Ctr. Ensemble Arts Theatre, San Diego, 1991; adj. faculty Grossmont Coll., Calif., 1992; mem. Ctr. Internat. Voice, Ray Host Theatre, France, 2008—. Actor(Janis Joplin): (theatre) Legends,: Step On a Crack: Universe Unbound, 2008; author (performer): It's Not Funny, I'm Only Laughing; contbr. mgmt., prodr. Actors Alliance of San Diego; singer: (cabaret show) You're Gonna Hear From Me; actor(Lula): (theatre) Dutchman; dir.: The Cultural Hyphen; actor: A Cave In The Sky; dir.: Cabaret, Evita, Three Sisters, Hot 'N Throbbing, (theatre production) How To Succeed In Business Without Really Trying, (theatrical prodn.) Our Country's Good, The House of Bernarda Alba, Songs For A New World; actor: (indsl. video series) ACT Training Series; prodr.(dir. pub. rels.): San Diego Actors Festival; contbr. chapter to book; author: Ethnicity and Identity: Global Performance; dir.: Eleemosynary Hair, Adding Machine. Grantee Artist-In-Residence Funding, Calif. Arts Coun., 1990—92; Faculty Devel. and Rsch. grant, 2007—08. Mem.: Internat. Alliance Tchrs. and Scholars, Actors Equity Assn., Internat. Fedn. Theatre Rsch. (convener of working group 2002—). D-Liberal. Buddhist. Avocations: cooking, gardening, travel, yoga, reading, ceramics. Office: Towson U Dept Theatre Arts 8000 York Rd Rm 3027 Baltimore MD 21252 Business E-Mail: dsadak@towson.edu.

SADAN, MARK, photographer, film producer, artist; AA, Am. Acad. Dramatic Arts, NYC, 1963; MFA, NYU, 1969; MEd, U. Mass., Amherst, 1974. Pres., dir. Kiva Film, NY and Mass., 1969—75; prodr., dir. short films Sesame St., 1969—72; dir., photo film unit Anti Poverty Program, NYC, 1966—67. Vis. artist, prof., exhibitor Helena Kaushik Women's Coll., Malsisar, Rajasthan, India, 2009; vis. artist Abhinaya Inst. Dance, Mumbai, 2009. Cineprobes, 1969—73, The Mus. of Modern Art, N.Y.C., 1970—72, artist (films) Rosebud, Laughing Bear, Ann Arbor Film Festival, 1965—68, prodr., dir. Ecology Probe Planet Earth 74, The New Norway 81, photographer (books) Meditations of the Blessed Beauty, Tablet of Carmel, 1990—93; one-man shows include Nat. Photo Gallery, Riga, Latvia, 1989—90, Golden Lands, Golden Dreams, 2004, Nat. Mus. of Dance and Hall of Fame, 2004—, Mus. New Art, Parnu, Estonia, 2005, 2007, one-man shows include video installation, 2008, exhibitions include Am. Mus. Dance, 2000—02, Luminous Moments, Julia Margaret Cameron Mus., Isle of Wight, Great Britain, 2000; contbr. photographs pub. to profl. jour.; Combodia dance exhbn., NY Pub. Libr., Lincoln Ctr. Performing Arts, 2008; prodr. (dir.): (films) (on traumatic brain injury) The Other Breakfast Club, PBS, 2009; one-man shows include Juha margaret Canerow Mus., Isle Of Weight., exhibitions include Mus. New Art Estonia, 2005, Represented in permanent collections Lincoln Ctr., NY Pub. Lib.; dir.: (films) The Other Breakfast Club. Recipient Medal of Excellence for Photographic Art, Latvian Nat. Photographic Soc., 1990, Cine Golden Eagle, Cine Film Awards, 2003. Mem.: Sunday Photo Group (dir., lectr. 1982—2004), Film Video Workshop (founder, dir. 1969—74). Avocations: dance, photography, swimming, travel, movies. Home: PO Box 207 Ossining NY 10562 Office Phone: 914-762-8855. Personal E-mail: marksadan13@hotmail.com.

SADANA, AJIT, chemical engineer, educator; b. Rawalpindi, India, Feb. 14, 1947; arrived in US, 1980; s. Jai Chand and Jinder Sadana; m. Lopa Mudra Sadana, Jan. 16, 1953; children: Neeti, Richa. B, Indian Inst. Tech., 1969; M of Chem. Engring., U. Del., 1972, PhD, 1975. Project engr. Environengineering, Inc., Somerville, NJ, 1974—75; sr. scientific officer Nat. chem. Lab., Pune, India, 1975—80; assoc. prof. chem. engring. U. Miss., University, 1981—90, prof., 1990—. Vis. assoc. prof. Auburn U., Ala., 1980—81; engr. duPont, Inc., Newark, 1989; sr. fellow Naval Rsch. Lab., Washington, 1990, disting. fellow, 91; cons. in field. Author: Biocatalysis: Fundamentals of Enzyme Deactivation Kinetics, 1991, Bioseparations, 1997, Biosensors, 2002, 5th edit., 2007. Avocations: gardening, tennis. Home: 229 St Andrews Cir Oxford MS 38655 Office: U Miss Chem Engring Dept University MS 38677-1848 Home Phone: 662-513-6266; Office Phone: 662-915-5349. Business E-Mail: cmsadana@olemiss.edu.

SADDLEMYER, ANN (ELEANOR SADDLEMYER), humanities educator, critic, theater historian; b. Prince Albert, Sask., Can., Nov. 28, 1932; d. Orrin Angus and Elsie Sarah (Ellis) S. BA, U. Sask., 1953, DLitt, 1991; MA, Queen's U., 1956, LLD (hon.), 1977; PhD, U. London, 1961; DLitt (hon.), U. Victoria, 1989, McGill U., 1989, Windsor U., 1990, U. Toronto, 1999, Concordia U., 2000. Lectr. Victoria Coll., BC, 1956-57, instr. BC, 1960-62, asst. prof. BC, 1962-65; assoc. prof. U. Victoria, 1965-68, prof. English, 1968-71, Victoria Coll. U. Toronto, 1971-95; prof., dir. Grad. Ctr. for Study of Drama, U. Toronto, 1972-77, 85-86, prof. emerita dept. English, comparative lit., drama, 1995—; sr. fellow Massey Coll., 1975-88, master, 1988-95, master emerita, 1995—; Berg prof. NYU, 1975. Vis. prof. U. Victoria; dir. Hedgerow Press; mem. heritage adv. commn. North Saanich, 2004—06. Dir. Theatre Plus, 1972-84; dir. Colin Smythe Pubs.; author: (with Robin Skelton) The World of W.B. Yeats, 1965, In Defence of Lady Gregory, Playwright, 1966, Synge and Modern Comedy, 1968, J.M. Synge Plays Books One and Two, 1968, Lady Gregory Plays, 4 vols., 1970, Letters to Molly: Synge to Maire O'Neill, 1971, Letters from Synge to W.B. Yeats and Lady Gregory, 1971, Collected Letters of John Millington Synge, Vol. 1, 1983, vol. II, 1984, Theatre Business, The Correspondence of the First Abbey Theatre Directors, 1982, (with Colin Smythe) Lady Gregory Fifty Years After, 1987, Early Stages: Theatre in Ontario, 1980-1914, 1990, J.M. Synge: The Playboy of the Western World and Other Plays, 1995; (with Richard Plant) Later Stages: Theatre in Ontario, 1914-1970s, 1997, Becoming George--The Life of Mrs. W.B. Yeats, 2002; co-editor Theatre History in Canada, 1980-86, Selected Irish Drama; co-gen. editor Cornell Yeats series; editorial bds. Modern Drama, 1972-82, English Studies in Can., 1973-83, Themes in Drama, 1974-93, Shaw Ann., 1977—, Research in the Humanities, 1976-90; Irish Univ. Rev., 1970—, Yeats Ann., 1982-86; Studies in Contemporary Irish Lit., 1986—, Irish Studies Rev., 1997—, Studi Irlandesi; contbr. articles to profl. jours. Recipient Brit. Acad. Rose Mary Crawshay award, 1986, Disting. Svc. award Province of Ont., 1985, U. Toronto Alumni award of excellence, 1991, award yeats Soc. NY 2001; named Disting. Dau. of Pa., 1992, Woman of Distinction in Letters, Toronto, YWCA, 1994; Officer of Order of Can., 1995; Can. Coun. scholar, 1958-59, fellow, 1968, Guggenheim fellow, 1968, 77, sr. rsch. fellow Connaught, 1985. Fellow Royal Soc. Can., Royal Soc. Arts; mem. Internat. Assn. Study Irish Lit. (chmn. 1973-76), Internat. Shaw Soc., Assn. Can. Theatre Rsch. (pres. 1976-77), Can. Assn. Irish Studies, Assn. Can. Coll. and Univ. Tchrs. English. Home: 10876 Madrona Dr North Saanich BC Canada V8L 5N9 Personal E-mail: saddlemy@uvic.ca.

SADE, DONALD STONE, anthropology educator; b. Charleston, W.Va., July 17, 1937; s. Samuel and Charlotte Tracy (Stone) S.; m. Bonita Diane Chepko, Dec. 24, 1971 (div. Feb. 1994); children: Irony Cuervo del Norte, Omen Ondatra; m. Kerry L. Knox, Nov. 24, 1994. Grad., N.Y. State Ranger Sch., 1957; student, Hamilton Coll., 1957-60; AB, U. Calif., Berkeley, 1963, PhD, 1966. Instr. anthropology Northwestern U., Evanston, Ill., 1965-66, asst. prof., 1966-70, assoc. prof., 1970-75, prof., 1975-95, sr. lectr., 1995—97; scientist-in-charge Cayo Santiago, U. P.R., 1970-77; prof. emeritus Northwestern U., 1997—. Founder, pres. North Country Inst. for Natural Philosophy, Inc., Mexico, N.Y., 1980—. Sr. author: Basic Demographic Observations on Free-Ranging Rhesus Monkeys, 3 vols., 1985; editor: The North Country Naturalist, Vol. 1, 1987. Recipient Merit cert., Eastman Sch. Music., 2002, 2005, 2006, 2007, 2008, 2009; grantee, NSF, 1967—. Mem. Animal Behavior Soc., Guild Am. Luthiers, Nature Conservancy, Adirondack Mountain Club, Adirondack Coun., Guitar Found. America. *...and all I've done for want of wit, to memory now I can't recall. (Irish ballad).*

SADÉE, WOLFGANG, pharmacy educator; b. Bad Harzburg, Fed. Republic Germany, Mar. 25, 1942; came to U.S., 1971; PhD, Free U. Pharmacy, Berlin, 1968. Asst. prof. U. So. Calif., Los Angeles, 1971-73;

asst. prof. U. Calif.-San Francisco, 1973-75, assoc. prof., 1975-81, prof., 1981—. Author: Drug Level Monitoring, vol. 1, 1981 and vol. 2, 1986; editor Pharm. Research, 1984-95; contbr. articles to profl. jours. Mem. AAAS, Am. Assn. Pharm. Scientists. Office: Sch Pharmacy Univ Calif San Francisco CA 94143-0001

SADEGH, ALI M., mechanical engineering educator, researcher, consultant; b. Tehran, Iran, Sept. 1, 1950; came to U.S., 1974; s. Saleh S. Mir-Mohamad-Sadegh and Asam Lotfi; m. Guita Miremadi, July 10, 1980; children: Mietra, Cameron, Mona, Jasmin, David. BSME, Arya-Mehr U. Tech., Tehran, 1972; MSME, Mich. State U., 1975, PhD in Mechanics, 1978; postgrad., U. Mich., 1979. Registered profl. engr., Mich.; cert. mfg. engr. Design engr. Nat. Radio engrng. sect., Tehran, 1972-74; rsch. and teaching asst. Mich. State U., East Lansing, 1975-78; asst. prof. Arya-Mehr U. Tech., 1979-81; vis. asst. prof. Mich. State U., 1981-82; asst. prof. CUNY, NYC, 1982-87, assoc. prof., 1987-91, prof., 1991—, chmn. dept. mech. engrng., 1992-96, tchr. courses in solid mechanics, design and CAD/CAM, 1996—. Cons. Devel. Iranian Heavy Industries, Tehran, 1979-81; tech. cons. AC Rochester Gen. Motors Co., 1986-92; forensic engr., 1990—; cons. and presenter in field. Contbr. over 142 articles to profl. jours.; 11 patents in field. U. Mich. scholar, Ann Arbor, 1978-79; recipient 46 Rsch. awards NSF, AT&T Found., PSC-CUNY, others. Fellow ASME (Best Paper award 1992, Melville medal 1993), Soc. Mfg. Engrs. (chmn. chpt. 320); mem. Am. Acad. Mechanics, Biomed. Engrs. Soc., Sigma Xi. Achievements include patents in field. Home: 787 Oneida Trl Franklin Lakes NJ 07417-2216 Office: CUNY Dept Mech Engring 140th St and Convent Ave New York NY 10031 Business E-Mail: sadegh@ccny.cuny.edu.

SADEGHI, FARSHID, engineering educator; MS, U. Tenn., 1981; PhD, N.C. State U., 1985. Rsch. asst. U. Tenn., Chattanooga, 1979-81; teachng asst. N.C. State U., Raleigh, 1981-83, rsch. asst., 1983-85; asst. prof. Purdue U., West Lafayette, Ind., 1986-91, assoc. prof., 1991-96, prof., 1996—. Mem. ASME (Burt L. Newkirk award 1991), ATLE, SAE (Ralph Teeter award 1992), SME, ASEE, Tau Beta Pi. Achievements include discovery that temperature effects in lubricated contacts are significant and cannot be neglected. Office: Purdue U Sch Mechanical Engring West Lafayette IN 47907

SADEGHI-NEJAD, ABDOLLAH, pediatrician, educator; b. Meshed, Iran, Apr. 29, 1938; s. Abdolhossein and Azizeh (Jabbari) S.-N.; m. Marion M. Marquardt, Jan. 26, 1974; children: Nathan R., Adrienne R. BA, Beloit Coll., 1960; MS in Pathology, U. Chgo., 1964, MD, 1964. Diplomate Am. Bd. Pediatrics. Intern then resident U. Chgo., 1964-67; fellow pediatric endocrinology U. Calif., San Francisco, 1969-70; from asst. prof. to prof. pediatrics Tufts U., Boston, 1970—; chief pediat. endocrinology and metabolism divsn. Tufts Med. Ctr., 1989—. Author and co-author books and articles. Mem. town meeting Town of Brookline, Mass., 1987-2001, 2005—, mem. adv. com., 1993-99; founding mem. Friends of Lost Pond. Fellow Am. Acad. Pediatrics; mem. Am. Pediatric Soc., Am. Diabetes Assn., Endocrine Soc., European Soc. Pediatric Rsch., Lawson Wilkins Pediat. Endocrine Soc., Soc. Pediat. Rsch. Office: Tufts Med Ctr 800 Washington St Boston MA 02111-1526 Office Phone: 617-636-5335.

SADEK, SANAA MOUNIR, literature and language professor; d. Mounir Sadek Gad Allah and Samirah Azer Gerguis. PhD, Cairo U.; PhD in History, Zagazeeg U. Mng. editor Gen. Egyptian Book Orgn., Cairo, 1989—2001; asst. prof. arabic lang. & lit. US Naval Acad., Annapolis, Md., 2006—. Vis. asst. prof. arabic Bard Coll., Kingston, NY, 2003—06. With US Naval Acad., Annapolis, Md., 2006—09. Fullbright Scholarship, Minority Women Playwrits Am., 2000. Mem.: Md. Hall Creative Arts (Annapolis). Office Phone: 410-293-6342.

SADER, CAROL HOPE, former state legislator; b. Bklyn., July 19, 1935; d. Nathan and Mollie (Farkas) Shimkin; m. Harold M. Sader, June 9, 1957; children: Neil, Randi Sader Friedlander, Elisa Sader Waldman. BA, Barnard Coll., Columbia U., 1957. Sch. tchr. Bd. Edn., Morris, Conn., 1957-58; legal editor W. H. Anderson Co., Cin., 1974-78; freelance legal editor Shawnee Mission, Kans., 1978-87; mem. Kans. Ho. of Reps., 1987-94. Chair Ho. Pub. Health and Welfare Com., 1991-92; chair Joint Ho. and Senate Com. on Health Care Decisions for the 90's, 1992; vice chair Ho. Econ. Devel. Com., 1991-92; policy chair Ho. Dem. Caucus, 1993-94; appointee Kans. jud. qualifications commn. Kans. Supreme Ct., 1995-2004; apptd. Kans. Racing and Gaming Commn., 2003-, chmn., 2005—, Kans. State Bd. Healing Arts, 2003-08. Pres. LWV, Johnson County, 1983—85; mem. State of Kans. LWV Bd., 1986—87; pres. Johnson County Found. Aging, 2002—04, bd.mem., 2000—08; mem. Johnson County Charter Commn., 1999; mem. exec. bd. Johnson County C.C. Found., 2000—03; bd. mem., 1995—; mem. adv. group Kans. Gov.'s B.E.S.T. Team, 2002; cmty. adv. com. Kans. REACH Found., 2003—07; Dem. candidate for Kans. Lt. Gov., 1994; mem. Jewish Cmty. Rels. Bd., 1999—2006; adv. bd. Jewish Cmty. Rels. Adv. Bd., 2007—; mem. Jewish Heritage Found. Bd., 2007—; chmn. bd. trustees Johnson County C.C., Overland Park, Kans., 1984—86, trustee, 1981—86; bd. dirs. United Cmty. Svcs. of Johnson County, Shawnee Mission, 1984—92, Jewish Vocat. Svc. Bd., 1983—92, House of Menuha, 1998—99, Appleseed Found. Kans., 1999—2001, Midwest Ctr. Holocaust Edn., 1999—2004, 2006—, exec. bd., 1999—2004, 2006—; v.p. cmty. rels. Midwest Ctr. Holocaust Edn. Bd., 2007—09; pres. adv. bd. chair Johnson County C.C. Found., 2009—; chmn. Kans. State Holocaust Commn., 1991—94; pres. MAINstream Coalition, 1995—97, vice chair, 1998—2003, main pac bd. mem., 2008—; v.p. Kans. Advocates for Better Care, 1998—2001. Recipient Trustee award Assn. of Women in Jr. and C.C., 1985, awards Kans. Pub. Transit Assn., 1990, AARP, 1992, Assn. Kans. Theater, 1992, Nat. Coun. Jewish Women, 1992, Kans. Assn. Osteo. Medicine, 1992, Kans. Chiropractic Assn., 1992, United Com. Svcs. Johnson County, 1992, Disting. Pub. Svcs. award Johnson County, 1993, Hallpac Kans. Pub. Svc. award Hallmark Cards, Inc., 1993, Eddie Jacobsen award B'nai B'rith, 1994, Cmty. Svc. award House of Menuha, 1998, The Pillar award Greater K.C. Women's Political Caucus, 2003, Stand-Up, Speak-Out award Mainstream Coalition, 2003, Making Democracy Work award Johnson County League Women Voters, Kans., 2008. Democrat. Avocations: theater, travel. Home: 8612 Linden Dr Shawnee Mission KS 66207-1807

SADICK, NEIL SCOTT, dermatologist; b. Bronx, NY, June 1, 1951; s. Harry and Shirley (Tompkins) Sadick; 1 child, Sydney Kamin. BA, SUNY, Binghamton, 1973; MD, SUNY, Syracuse, 1977. Diplomate Am. Bd. Internal Medicine, 1980, Am. Bd. Dermatology, 1983, Am. Acad. Cosmetic Surgery, 2000, Am. Bd. Hair Restoration Surgery, 2001. Pvt. practice, NYC, 1983—; mem. adv. bd. Dermatologic Soc. Greater NY, 1994—; clin. prof. dermatology Cornell U, Monroe Coll. Surg. advisor Archives Dermatology; global med. advisor Christian Dior Beauty; guest lectr. at med. seminar classes and workshops worldwide. Author: (book) Your Hair, Helping to Keep It, 1994; asst. editor (jour.) Jour. Am. Acad. Dermatology, 1994—; author: (book) Sclerotherapy of Varicose Veins, 1996; asst. editor (jour.) Jour. Aesthetic and Cosmetic Surgery, —; contbr. several articles in peer-reviewed scientific jours., chapters to books. Mem.: Internat. Soc. Hair Restoration Surgery (bd. examiner), Cosmetic Surgery Found. (pres.), Am. Soc. Dermatological Surgery (bd. dirs.), Am. Cancer Soc. (summer fellow 1977), Manhattan Met. Dermatology Soc. (pres. 1995—96), NY Acad. Medicine, Dermatology Found. (vice chmn. 1993—), Am. Soc. Cosmetic Surgery (bd. dirs.,), Am. Acad. Dermatology (adv. bd. 1995—), Dermatologic Soc. Greater NY (adv. bd. 1994, pres. 1995—96), Am. Coll. Phlebology. (pres. 2002—04, bd. dir., Jobst award 1990), LI Dermatology Soc. Avocations: tennis, travel, antique pens. Office: Sadick Dermatology 911 Park Ave Ste 1A New York NY 10075 Home Phone: 212-288-8502; Office Phone: 212-772-7242. Business E-Mail: nssderm@sadickdermatology.com.

SADIK, MARVIN SHERWOOD, art historian, consultant, retired museum director; b. Springfield, Mass., June 27, 1932; s. Harry Benjamin and Florence (Askinas) S. AB magna cum laude, Harvard U., 1954, A.M., 1960; D.F.A. (hon.), Bowdoin Coll., Brunswick, Maine, 1978. Curatorial asst. Worcester (Mass.) Art Mus., 1955-57; curator Mus. Art Bowdoin Coll., 1961-64, dir., 1964-67, Mus. Art U. Conn. at Storrs, 1967-69, Nat. Portrait Gallery, Washington, 1969-81. Author: Colonial and Federal Portraits at Bowdoin College, 1966, The Drawings of Hyman Bloom, 1968, The Paintings of Charles Hawthorne, 1968, Edith Halpert and the Downtown Gallery, 1968, The Life Portraits of John Quincy Adams, 1970, Christian Gullager: Portrait Painter to Federal America, 1976, Portraits of George Bellows, 1981; co-author: American Portrait Drawings, 1980. Decorated knight Order Dannebrog Denmark; recipient Detur prize Harvard Coll., 1952, Maine State Art award, 1975, gold medal for exceptional svc. Smithsonian Instn., 1981; Harris fellow, 1957-61; Barr fellow, 1957-61; fellow Belgian Art Seminar, 1956. Fellow Pierpont Morgan Library; mem. Am. Antiquarian Soc., Colonial Soc. Mass. (corr.) Clubs: Century Assn, Grolier. Home: PO Box 6360 Scarborough ME 04070-6360 Office Phone: 207-885-9644.

SADIK-KHAN, JANETTE I., city manager, former federal agency administrator; b. San Francisco, Apr. 28, 1960; d. Orhan and Jane (McCarthy) Sadik-Khan; m. Mark Geistfeld, July 14, 1990. BA, Occidental Coll., 1982; JD, Columbia U., 1987. Bar: N.Y. Dep. dir. govtl. affairs Children's Def. Fund, Washington, 1982-83; co-dir. Found. for Youth Involvement, NYC, 1983-84; litigation assoc. Kaye, Scholer, Fierman, Hays & Handler, NYC, 1987-88; spl. counsel to the commr. NYC Dept. Transp., 1990-92; assoc. adminstr. budget & policy Fed. Transit Adminstrn., US Dept. Transp., dep. adminstr.; sr. v.p., pres., CEO, Company 39 Parsons Brinckerhoff, 2000—07; commr. NYC Dept. Transp., 2007—. Presenter in field. Contbr. articles to profl. jours. Recipient Harry S. Truman scholarship Occidental Coll., L.A., 1980; named Woman of Yr., Women Transp. Seminar, 2005 Office: City Hall 52 Chambers St Rm 203 New York NY 10007-1222*

SADIKOT, RUXANA T., internist, educator; MD, Grant Med. Coll., Mumbai, 1988. Cert. Am. Bd. Internal Medicine, 1998, in pulmonary medicine 2000, in critical care medicine 2002. Asst. prof. medicine Vanderbilt U., Nashville, 2001—05; assoc. prof. medicine U. Ill., Chgo., 2005—, attending physician, 2007—. Dir. micu Jesse Brown VA Hosp., Chgo., 2007—. Recipient Career Devel. award, Dept. Vets. Affairs, 2002—05, Advanced Career Devel. award, 2005—08, Merit Rev. award, 2008—. Master: RCP (UK); fellow: ACCP (hon.); mem.: Chgo. Respiratory Soc. (exec. mem. 2008), Am. Thoracic Soc. Office: Univ Ill 840 S Wood St MC 719 Chicago IL 60612 Office Fax: 312-996-4665. Business E-Mail: sadikot@uic.edu.

SADINENI, SURESH BABU, research scientist; b. Ongole, Andhra Pradesh, India, Aug. 22, 1975; s. RamaRao and Ramanamma Sadineni; m. Padmaja Chilukuri, May 22, 2003; 1 child, Saanvi. PhD, U. Nev., Las Vegas, 2005. Grad. tchg. asst. dept. mech. engring. U. Nev., Las Vegas, 2001—02, grad. rsch. asst. dept. mech. engring., 2002—05, rsch. faculty dept. mech. engring., 2005. Mem.: Am. Nuclear Soc. Achievements include development of Code to Predict Transient Behavior of a Nuclear Reactor Coupled to an Accelerator. Office: Univ Nev Dept Mech Engring 4505 Maryland Pkwy Las Vegas NV 89154 Home: 284 Sea Rim Ave Las Vegas NV 89148-2759 Personal E-mail: sbsadineni@yahoo.com.

SADJADI, FIROOZ AHMADI, electrical engineer, consultant, researcher, lecturer; b. Tehran, Iran, Mar. 18, 1949; came to U.S., 1968; s. Akbar Ahmadi and Fakhri (Mohsen) S. BSEE, Purdue U., 1972, MSEE, 1974; degree of Engr. in Electrical Engring., U. So. Calif., 1976; postgrad. U. Tenn., Knoxville, 1983. Rsch. asst. Image Processing Inst., U. So. Calif., L.A., 1974-76; cons. Oak Ridge Lab., Knoxville, 1980; researcher dept. elec. engring. U. Tenn., 1977-83; prin. rsch. scientist Honeywell Sys. and Rsch. Ctr., 1983-93; pres. Machine Intelligence Co., 1993—; sr. staff rsch. scientist Lockheed Martin Corp., 1993—. Mem. IEEE (sr.), Fellow: Soc. Photo-Optical Instrumentation Engrs., Sigma Xi. Contbg. author numerous profl. publs.; patentee in field. Business E-Mail: firooz.sadjadi@ieee.org.

SADJADI, MASOUD, science educator; PhD, Mich. State U., East Lansing, 2004. Asst. prof. Fla. Internat. U., Miami, 2004—. Office: Fla Internat Univ 11200 SW 8th St Miami FL 33199

SADLER, DAVID G(ARY), manufacturing executive; b. Iowa City, Mar. 14, 1939; s. Edward Anthony and Elsie June (Sherman) S.; m. Karen Sadler; children: Michael Robert, Katherine Louise. Student, St. Ambrose Coll., 1957—59; BS in Indsl. Adminstrn. and Prodn., Kent State U., 1961. Various mgmt. positions Ford Motor Co., Lorain, Ohio, 1962—67, Sperry-New Holland, Lebanon, Ohio, 1967—71; mgr. mfg. Allis Chalmer, Springfield, Ill., 1971—72; dir. mfg. Purolator, Inc., Fayetteville, NC, 1972—73; v.p. mfg. farm equipment and ops. truck divsn. White Motor Co., Eastlake, Ohio and Chgo., 1973—78; corp. v.p. mfg. Massey Ferguson Ltd., Toronto, Ont., Canada, 1978—80, Internat. Harvester, Chgo., 1980—81, sr. v.p. ops. staff, 1981—82, v.p. bus. devel., 1982, pres. diversified group, 1982—83, pres. internat. group, 1983—85; pres. AMI, Inc., Chgo., 1985—86; vice chmn., CEO Savin Corp., Stamford, Conn., 1986, chmn., CEO, 1986—89, also bd. dirs.; pres. Asset Mgmt. Internat., Westport, Conn., 1989—95; chmn., CEO Rowe Internat., Grand Rapids, Mich., 1995—2000, also bd. dirs., 2000—01; CEO Merisel, Inc., El Segundo, Calif., also bd. dirs.; chmn., CEO, bd. dirs. Global Motorsport Group, Inc., Morgan Hill, Calif., 2002—04. Bd. dirs. greater Chgo. Safety Coun., 1981-84,Hellmold Assocs. Opportunity Fund II. Roman Catholic. Home: 751 Bradford Farms Ln NE Grand Rapids MI 49525-3348 Personal E-mail: davidsadler@comcast.net.

SADLER, IRENE CONSTANCE, retired language educator; b. Sacramento; d. Harold J. and Ida E. Harrington; m. Jerry M. Sadler, June 1972; children: Marc A., Merissa N. MA, Sorbonne U., Paris, 1971. Prof., French Sierra Coll., Rocklin, Calif., 1990—2008, chair, world langs. dept., 2005—08, French prof., study abroad, 2005. Mem.: Alliance Francaise Sacramento, Calif. CC Fgn. Lang. Coun. (exec. bd. mem. 1998—99). Avocations: travel, reading, history, cooking.

SADLER, JUDITH K., retired special education educator, school system administrator; d. Joseph and Clare Kennedy Kaufman; m. Charles Gill Sadler, Dec. 22, 1962 (dec. Jan. 25, 1985); children: Laura Lea Cripe, Thomas Robert. BA, Northwestern U., Evanston, Ill., 1962; MS in Edn., Western Ill. U., Macomb, 1972, EdS, 1976. Cert. in K-12 & gen. adminstrv. State Ill., 1975, supt. 1978, in std. elem., secondary & spl. tchg. 2002. Spl. edn. elem. tchr. Chgo. Pub. Schs., 1962—69; elem. tchr., lab. sch. Western Ill. U., 1970—71, clin. supr. & faculty, spl. edn., 1994—2006; spl. edn. tchr. & head Macomb Cmty. Schs., 1971—75, prin., 1975—94. Youth exch. officer Macomb Rotary Club, 1999—2003; mem. McDonough County Humane Soc., Macomb, 2002—09; founder Survivors Book Club, Macomb, 2008—09; mem. Wesley United Meth. Ch., Macomb, 1974—2009, trustee, 2001—03; charter mem. Centennial Morning Rotary Club, Macomb, 2003—06; mem. Western Ill. Audubon Soc., Macomb, 2007—08. Avocations: reading, walking.

SADOCK, GEOFFREY JOHNSTON, English professor; b. NYC, Sept. 30, 1942; s. Jules Bertero and Rosabelle Johnston Sadock; m. Karen Nauta, Sept. 4, 1971; 1 child, Katharine Cordelia Johnston Sadock. BA with honors, Bklyn. Coll., NYC, 1964; MA, Tufts U., Medford, Mass., 1966; PhD, Brown U., Providence, 1973. Instr. Fairleigh-Dickinson U., Madison, NJ, 1971—72; prof. Bergen CC, Paramus, NJ, 1972—. Dir. honors program Bergen C.C., Paramus, NJ, 1996—2001. Contbr. articles to profl. jours. Recipient Presdl. Recognition award, SGC, 2004; fellow CCNY Grad. Ctr., NYC, 1991; Mid-Career fellow, Princeton U., 1994. Mem.: ALSC, NAS, NJCEA, NEA, KC (4th degree), Clan Johnston/e America, Am. Coun. Trustees and Alumni, Internat. Walter Pater Soc., Victorian Soc. Am. Avocations: Victorian architecture and restoration, antique lighting. Office Phone: 201-447-7168, 201-447-9284. Personal E-mail: geoffreyjsadock@optonline.net. Business E-Mail: gsadock@bergen.edu.

SADOFF, ROBERT LESLIE, psychiatrist, educator; b. Mpls., Feb. 8, 1936; s. Max and Rose C. (Karroll) S.; m. Joan A Handleman, June 21, 1959; children: Debra, David, Julie, Sherry. BA, U. Minn., 1956, BS, 1957, MD, 1959; MS, UCLA, 1963. Intern L.A. VA Hosp., 1959—60; resident in psychiatry UCLA, 1960—63; asst. prof. psychiatry Temple U., Phila., 1966—72; clin. prof. U. Pa., Phila., 1972—; pvt. practice Jenkintown, Pa., 1965—. Lectr. law Villanova U., 1972-85. Author: (with Marvin Lewis) Psychic Injuries, 1975, Forensic Psychiatry, 1975, 2d edit., 1988, Legal Issues in the Care of Psychiatric Patients, 1982, Violence and Responsibility, 1988, (with Robert I. Simon) Psychiatric Malpractice, 1992; editor: Psychiatric Clinics of North America, 1984. Bd. dirs. Joseph T. Peters Inst., Phila., 1980-92. Capt. M.C., U.S. Army, 1963-65. Recipient Earl Bond award U. Pa., 1979, VII ann. Nathaniel Winkelman award Phila. Psychiat. Ctr., 1988, Manfred Guttmacher award, 2993, Isaac Ray award, 2006. Fellow: Am. Coll. Legal Medicine, Am. Psychiat. Assn. (Manfred Guttmacher award 1993); mem.: Internat. Acad. Law and Mental Health (Philippe Pinel award 1995), Internat. Soc. for Philos. Enquiry (mentor 1987—), Am. Acad. Psychiatry and Law (pres. 1971—73), Am. Coll. Psychiatrists, Am. Red Magen David for Israel (nat. pres. 1986—2001). Avocation: collecting antique books in law and medicine. Office: The Pavilion Ste 326 261 Old York Rd Jenkintown PA 19046 Office Phone: 215-887-6144. Personal E-mail: sadoffbobsadoff@aol.com.

SADOH, GODWIN SIMEON, music educator; b. Lagos, Nigeria, Mar. 28, 1965; arrived in US, 1994; s. Anthony Sadoh and Taiwo Akinsanya. BA in Piano Performance and Composition, Obafemi Awolowo U., Ile-Ife, Nigeria, 1988; MA in Ethnomusicology, U. Pitts., 1998; MusM in Organ Performance, U. Nebr., 2000; MusD in Organ Performance and Composition, La. State U., 2004. Lectr. dept. music Obafemi Awolowo U., Ile-Ife, 1988—94; tchg. asst. U. Pitts., 1994—96; part-time faculty Sch. Music U. Nebr., Lincoln, Nebr., 1998—2000; music faculty Baton Rouge Coll., 2003—06; asst. prof. music LeMoyne-Owen Coll., Memphis, 2005—07, dir. Sacred Music Program, 2006—07, dir. concert choir, 2006—07; prof. music Talladega Coll., Ala., 2007—. Organist, choir dir. Eko Boys HS, Lagos, Nigeria, 1980—82, St. Stephen's Episc. Ch., Wilkinsburg, Pa., 1996—98; assoc. dir. music ministries First United Meth. Ch., Lincoln, Nebr., 1999—2000; founder and dir. Ile-Ife Choral Soc., Nigeria, 1990—94; asst. organist Cathedral Ch. Christ, Lagos, Nigeria, 1980—90. Author: (book) Joshua Uzoigwe: Memoirs of a Nigerian Composer-ethnomusicologist, 2007, Intercultural Dimensions in AYO Bankole's Music, 2007, Samuel Akpabot: The Odyssey of a Nigerian Composer- Ethnomusic Cologist, 2008, Thomas Ekundayo Phillips: The Doyen of Nigerian Church Music, 2009, The Organ Works of Fela Sowande: Cultural Perspectives, 2007; composer: Nigerian Suite No. 1 for Organ Solo (ASCAP PLUS Award, 2004), Impressions from an African Moonlight, The Misfortune of a Wise Tortoise for Organ and Narrator, 2005, Nigerian Suite No. 2 for Organ Solo, 2005, Five African Dances for Solo Ogran, 2007, Kabiyesi Hosana, 2005, Ise Oluwa, 2005, Ose Baba, 2005, Gbo Ohun Awon Angeli, 2005, Akoi Wata Geri, 2005, Keresimesi Odun de, 2005, Five African Marches for Organ Solo, 2006, (songs) Lord Send Your Power, 2006, Ose Jesu, 2006, A Bi Jesu, 2006, Open Your Mouth, 2006, Ope Lo Ye O, 2006, Nigerian Organ Symphony, 2008, Badagry for Woodwin Quartet, 2008, Summer Evening at Ile-Ife for Woodwind Quintet, 2009, 25 preludes on Yoruba Ch. Hymns for Organ, (hymn book) E Korin S'Oluwa (Sing Unto The Lord): Fifty Indigenous Church Hymns from Nigeria, 2005; contbr. articles to profl. jours. Organist, choirmaster Eko Boys HS, Lagos, 1980—82; preacher St. Stephen's Episc. Ch., Wilkinsburg, Pa., 1996—98, Christ Luth. Ch., Lincoln, 1999—2000; vis. preacher Redeeming The Time Ministries Internat., Baton Rouge. Recipient ASCAPlus award, Am. Soc. Composers, Authors and Publishers, 2008; scholar, La. State U., 2000—03, U. Pitts., 1997; Dora Dean Emerson Meml. Music fellowship, Sch. Music, U. Nebr., Lincoln, 1998, Alvin Hatton Organ scholarship, 2000—03. Mem.: ASCAP (See Honor's awards 2004, Plus award 2005, 2006), Musicological Soc. Nigeria, Soc. Ethnomusicology, Am. Guild Organists (scholarship 1998—2000), Organ Hist. Soc., The Hymn Soc., Nat. Assn. Composers, USA, The Coll. Music Soc., Pi Kappa Lambda. Evang. Achievements include first African to earn a doctorate degree in organ performance from any institution in the world. Avocations: cooking, movies, travel. Business E-Mail: godwin@godwinsadoh.com.

SADOSKI, MARK CHRISTIAN, education educator; b. Bristol, Conn., June 2, 1945; s. Waldmyr John Sadoski and Ruth Elaine Kantorski; m. Carol Ann Bove, June 28, 1969; 1 child, Thomas Christian. BS, So. Conn. State U., 1968, MS, 1973; PhD, U. Conn., 1981. Cert. reading, English, social studies tchr. Tchr., reading cons. Milford (Conn.) Pub. Schs., 1968-81; assoc. faculty So. Conn. State U., New Haven, 1978-81; prof. edn. Tex. A&M Univ., College Station, 1981—, Tex A&M U. Health Sci. Ctr., 2004—. Author: Conceptual Foundations of Teaching Reading, 2004, (with Allan Paivio) Imagery and Text: A Dual Coding Theory of Reading and Writing, 2001; mem. editl. bd. Reading Rsch. Quar., 1989—2007, Jour. Reading Behavior, 1990-95, Reading Psychology, 1990—, Jour. Literacy Rsch., 1995-2005, Info. Design Jour./Document Design, 1998—, Reading and Writing, 2001—; contbr. over 90 articles to profl. jours. and books. Accident prevention counselor S.W. region FAA, 1989-91. Recipient Disting. Alumnus award So. Conn. State U., 1994. Mem. Internat. Reading Assn. (outstanding dissertation award com. 1983-85, finalist Outstanding

Dissertation award 1982), Nat. Reading Conf. (Outstanding Book award com. 1994-99), Am. Ednl. Rsch. Assn. (outstanding book award com. 1994-2000), Soc. for Sci. Study of Reading (chair pubs. com. 1996-97), Phi Kappa Phi. Avocations: reading, photography. Office: Tex A&M Univ Dept Tchg Learning and Culture 4232 TAMU College Station TX 77843-4232 Business E-Mail: msadoski@tamu.edu.

SADOSKY, CORA SUSANA, mathematics educator; b. Buenos Aires, Argentina, May 23, 1940; d. Manuel and Cora (Ratto) S.; m. Daniel J. Goldstein, Apr. 23, 1965; 1 child, Cora Sol. Lic. in math., U. Buenos Aires, Argentina, 1960; Ph.D., U. Chgo., 1965. Prof. U. Central Venezuela, Caracas, 1974-80; assoc. prof. Howard U., Washington, 1980-85, prof. math., 1985—; mem. Inst. Advanced Study, Princeton, N.J., 1978-79, 83-84; vis. prof. U. Buenos Aires, 1984-85, Math. Scis. Research Inst., Berkeley, Calif., 1988—. Author: Interpolation of Operators and Singular Integrals, 1979; also articles. NSF vis. professorship for Women in Sci., 1983-84. Mem. Am. Math. Soc., Assn. for Women in Math (pres.-elect), Unión Matemática Argentina, Asociación Matemática Española. Office: Howard Univ Dept Math Washington DC 20059-0001

SADOULET, ELISABETH, economics professor; d. Louis and Colette Chaine; children: Loïc, Hélène Puccio, Samuel. Degree, U. Geneva, Switzerland, 1982. Prof. U. Calif., Berkeley, 1995—. Office: Univ Calif 207 Giannini Hall Berkeley CA 94720

SADOVE, ALAN MICHAEL, plastic surgeon; b. Chgo., Oct. 8, 1948; s. Max Samuel and Ethel (Segall) S.; m. Armin Altshuler, June 1, 1974; children: Scott Lawrence, Julia Claire. AB, Washington U., 1970; MD, Loyola U., Maywood, Ill., 1974; MS, U. Ill., Chgo., 1977. Intern Presbyn.-St. Luke's Hosp., Chgo., 1974—75, resident in gen. surgery, 1975—79; resident in plastic surgery U. Va., Charlottesville, 1979—81; fellow in plastic surgery NYU-Inst. Reconstructive Plastic Surgery, NYC, 1981—82; assoc. prof. surgery Ind. U. Sch. Medicine, 1982—; chief plastic surgery service, James Whitcomb Riley Hosp. for Children Ind. U. Med. Ctr., 1982—, med. dir. Burn Ctr., 1982—, dir. Oral-Facial Clinic, 1983—, med. dir. Craniofacial Anomalies team, 1982—; cons. VA Med. Ctr., Indpls.; mem. attending staff Wishard Meml. Hosp., Indpls. Mem. American Bd. Plastic Surgery (bd. dirs. 2003-10, chair), Chgo. Med. Soc., Ill. Med. Soc., AMA, ACS, Am. Soc. Plastic and Reconstructive Surgeons, Am. Cleft Palate Assn., Am. Burn Assn., Assn. Acad. Surgery, Am. Soc. Maxillofacial Surgeons, Marion County Med. Soc., Ind. State Med. Soc., Ohio Valley Soc. Plastic and Reconstructive Surgery, Sigma Xi. Office: Riley Towers Rm 1172 702 Barnhill Dr Indianapolis IN 46202-5128 also: Meridian Plastic Surgery Ctr 170 W 106th St Indianapolis IN 46290*

SADOVE, STEPHEN IRVING, retail executive; b. Washington, July 25, 1951; s. A. Robert and Harriet (Tenenbaum) S.; m. Karin Sadove; children: Stacy, David, Laurie. BA, Hamilton Coll., 1973; MBA, Harvard U., 1975. Asst. product mgr. desserts divsn. Gen. Foods Corp., White Plains, N.Y., 1975-76, assoc. product mgr., 1976-77, product mgr., 1977-80, group product mgr., 1980-82, category mgr., 1982-84, mktg. mgr., 1984-86, bus. unit mgr. meals divsn., 1986-88, v.p., gen. mgr., 1988-89, exec. v.p., gen. mgr. desserts divsn., 1989-91; pres. Clairol, Inc., Stamford, Conn., 1991-96, Bristol-Myers Squibb Beauty Care, Stamford, 1996-97, Bristol-Myers Squibb Beauty Care and Nutritionals, Stamford, 1998—2001; vice-chmn. Saks Inc., NYC, 2002—06, CEO, 2006—07, chmn., CEO, 2007—. Bd. dirs. Saks Inc., Ruby Tuesday Inc., 2002-. Trustee Hamilton Coll., Hazelden, A Better Chance. Avocations: tennis, golf, reading, arts. Office: Saks Inc 12 E 49th St New York NY 10017 Home: 7 Hickory Pine Ct Purchase NY 10577 Office Phone: 212-940-5305.

SADOW, HARVEY S., healthcare company executive; b. NYC, Oct. 6, 1922; s. Nat. and Frances Donna (Saveth) S.; m. Sylvia June Riber, Dec. 22, 1944 (div. 1966); children: Harvey Jr., Suzanne Gail, Todd Forrest, Gay Summer; m. Jacqueline Lucille Clavel, Jan. 24, 1969 (div. 1993); 1 adopted child, Daniel Jean Marie; m. Mary Morrissey McSwiggan, July 13, 1995. BS, Va. Mil. Inst., Lexington, 1947; MS, U. Kans., 1949; PhD, U. Conn., 1953, DSc (hon.), 2000. Intelligence officer CIA, Washington, 1951-53; assoc. dir. rsch. Lakeside Labs., Inc., Milw., 1953-56; med. rsch. cons. Milw., 1956; dir. clin. rsch. U.S. Vitamin & Pharm. Corp., NYC, 1957-64, v.p. R & D, 1964-68; sr. v.p. scientific affairs USV Pharm./Revlon Corp., NYC, 1969-71; pres., CEO Boehringer Ingelheim, Ltd. (named changed to Boehringer Ingelheim Pharms., Inc. 1984), Ridgefield, Conn., 1971-88, Boehringer Ingelheim Corp., Ridgefield, 1984-88, chmn. bd., 1988-90. Chmn. bd. Roxane Labs., Inc., Columbus, Ohio, 1981-88, Boehringer Ingelheim Animal Health, Inc., St. Joseph, Mo., 1981-88, Henley Co., N.Y.C., 1986-88, U. Conn. Rsch. and Devel. Corp., Storrs, 1984-87; bd. dirs. Anika Therapeutics, Inc., Trega Bioscis., Inc., chmn. 2000-01, Cortex Pharms., Inc., Irvine, Calif., chmn. bd., 1991-99; bd. dirs. Cholestech Corp., Hayward, Calif., chmn. bd. 1992-2000; adv. bd. Salk Inst. Biotechnology-Indsl. Assocs., Inc., La Jolla, 1988-90; chmn. bd. dirs. Acacia Bioscis. Inc., 1996-99, Rosetta Inpharmatics, Inc., 1999-2001. Co-author: Oral Treatment of Diabetes, 1967; contbr. articles to profl. jours. Bd. dirs. Pharm. Mfrs. Assn., 1983-90; chmn. Pharm. Mfrs. Assn. Found., 1988-90; bd. dirs. Conn. Bd. Higher Edn., Hartford, 1977-83, Govs. Tech. Adv. Bd., Hartford, 1984-87; mem. Conn. Commn. on Bus. Opportunity, Def. Diversification and Indsl. Policy, 1991-93; mem. bd. visitors Va. Mil. Inst., Lexington, 1987—, pres. bd., 1991-95; chmn. bd. Conn. Law Enforcement Found., Hartford, 1981-86, 92-97, U. Conn. Found., Storrs, 1984-87; chmn., pres.' coun. Am. Lung Assn., N.Y.C., 1986-87, York Sch., Monterey, Calif., 1988-89; trustee Conn. Coll., Groton, 1991-96, Aldrich Mus. Contemporary Art, Ridgefield, Conn., 1991-98. Capt. US Army, 1943—46. Decorated Disting. Svc. Cross, Fed. Republic of Germany, 1987; recipient Univ. medal U. Conn., 1987, Citizen of Yr. Conn. Chief of Police Assn., 1988, Recognition award Nat. Hypertension Assn., 1990, Humanitarian award Am. Lung Assn. Conn., 1993, Disting. Svc. award Conn. Innovations, Inc., 1996, Va. Mil. Inst. Found., 1998. Mem. Am. Soc. for Clin. Pharmacology and Therapeutics, Am. Fedn. for Clin. Rsch, Am. Diabetes Assn., Nat. Acad. Scis.(Pres.'s Circle), Danbury C. of C. (Abraham Ribicoff Community Svc. award City of Danbury 1987, bd. dirs. 1978-81), Union League (N.Y.C.), Masons, Sigma Xi, Sigma Pi Sigma, Phi Lambda Upsilon. Avocations: art collecting, photography, music, writing. Personal E-mail: hssadow@aol.com.

SADOWSKI, PETER T., lawyer; b. Warsaw, Oct. 30, 1954; came to U.S., 1968; s. Fryderyk and Maria (Jaklinska) S.; m. Denise A. Decker, Oct. 13, 1979; children: Katherine, Rachel. BA, St. Louis U., 1976; JD, St. Louis U. Law Sch., 1979. Asst. atty. gen. Mo. Atty. Gen.'s Office, Jefferson City, 1979-81; ptnr. The Stolar Partnership, St. Louis, 1981-96; shareholder Goldberg, Katz, Sadowski & Croft, St. Louis, 1996—99; exec. v.p., chief legal officer Fidelity Nat. Fin. Inc., Jacksonville, Fla., 1999—. Chmn. bd. dirs., greater needs com. YMCA, St. Louis, 1995—. Office: Fidelity National Financial 601 Riverside Ave Jacksonville FL 32204 Office Phone: 888-934-3354.

SADOWSKI, RAYMOND, electronics executive; married. BS in Acctg., Hunter Coll., NY, 1976. Acct. F. Schumacher; corp. acctg. supr. Avnet, Inc., 1978, acctg. mgr., asst. contr., contr., 1986, v.p., 1987—92, sr. v.p., 1992—, CFO, 1993—, asst. sec. Office: Avnet Inc 2211 S 47th St Phoenix AZ 85034-6403 Office Phone: 480-643-2000. Office Fax: 480-643-7370.

SADOWSKY, MICHAEL J., microbiologist, educator; married; 2 children. BS, U. Wis., Madison, 1977; MS in Biology/Microbiology, U. Wis., Oshkosh; PhD in Microbiology, U. Hawaii, 1983. Rschr. McGill U., 1983—85; molecular biologist Allied Corp.; biologist Nitrogen Fixation and Soybean Genetics Lab. USDA-ARS, Beltsville, Md.; asst. prof. Dept. Soil Sci. and Microbiology U. Minn., St. Paul, 1989, prof. Dept. Soil, Water, and Climate and Biotechnology Inst., dir. grad. studies Microbial Engring. Program, U. McKnight Disting. prof., 2005—. Co-creator Agricultural Microbe Genomes Confs. Editor: (jour.) Applied and Environ. Microbiology; assoc. editor Symbiosis and Microbes and the Environment; contbr. articles to profl. jours. NSF Grant, 2003. Fellow: Am. Acad. Microbiology; mem.: Am. Soc. Microbiology (Region V Coord. and Branch Archivist). Avocations: woodworking, amateur radio electronics. Office: U Minn 439 Borlaug Hall 1991 Upper Buford Cir Saint Paul MN 55108 Office Phone: 612-625-1244. Office Fax: 612-625-2208. E-mail: sadowsky@soils.umn.edu.

SADRAIE, HAMID REZA, civil engineer, researcher; b. Tehran, Iran, Jan. 28, 1975; arrived in US, 2000; s. Abbas Sadraie and Seddigheh Ghassemieh. BS, U. Tehran, Iran, 1996, MS, 1998; PhD, U. Minn., Mpls., 2006. Rsch. asst. U. Minn., Mpls., 2002—06; transp. engr. Caltrans, LA, 2006—. Contbr. articles to profl. jours. Mem.: Sigma Xi. Office: Caltrans 100 South Main St MS-16 Los Angeles CA 90012 Home: 425 13th Ave SE Apt 1301 Minneapolis MN 55414-2047 Business E-Mail: sadra002@umn.edu.

SADRUDIN, MOE, humanitarian organization executive; b. Hyderabad, India, Mar. 3, 1943; arrived in U.S., 1964; m. Azmath Qureshi, 1964; 3 children. BSME, Osmania U., Hyderabad, 1964; MS in Indsl. Engring., NYU, 1966; IE, MBA, Columbia U., 1970. Cons. project engr. Ford, Bacon & Davis, NYC, 1966; staff indsl. engr. J.C. Penney, NYC, 1966; sr. cons. Drake, Sheahan, Stewart & Dougall, NYC, 1968—70, Beech-Nut Inc. subs. Squibb Corp., NYC, 1970—72; founder, pres. Azmath Constrn. Co., Englewood, NJ, 1972—77; crude oil cons., fgn. govt. rep., 1977—88; pres. A-One Petroleum Co., Fullerton, Calif., 1985—95; chmn., CEO, Universal Humanitarian Found., Fullerton, 1989—. Govt. advisor Puerto Rico, 1980-82, Dominica, 1983-84, St. Vincent, 1981-82, Kenya, 1983-84, Belize 1984-85, Costa Rica 1983-86, Paraguay 1984-87. Chmn. Universal Humanitarian Found., 1989—; active LA World Affairs Coun. Mem.: Internat. Platform Assn. Achievements include planned to build several charitable hospitals in India. Address: Universal Humanitarian Found 2656 Camino Del Sol Fullerton CA 92833-4806 Office Phone: 714-526-0633. Personal E-mail: unihumfound@aol.com. *Personal philosophy: I learned from a young age that acquisition of knowledge, developing honesty and integrity and service to humanity in the form of charity, love and struggle to help the poor and needy, are the main foundation stones of a successful life. I believe that acquisition of wealth is only a means to an end and not an end in itself. With accumulation of wealth, one has to care for the underprivileged and try to improve their lot.*

SADUN, ALFREDO ARRIGO, neuro-ophthalmologist, scientist, educator; b. New Orleans, Oct. 23, 1950; s. Elvio H. and Lina (Ottoleghi) S.; m. Debra Leigh Rice, Mar. 18, 1978; children: Rebecca Eli, Elvio Aaron, Benjamin Maxwell. BS, MIT, 1972; PhD, Albert Einstein Med. Sch., Bronx, NY, 1976, MD, 1978. Intern Huntington Meml. Hosp. U. So. Calif., Pasadena, 1978—79; resident Harvard U. Med. Sch., Boston, 1979—82, HEED Found. fellow in neuro-ophthalmology Mass. Eye and Ear Inst., 1982—83, instr. ophthalmology, 1983, asst. prof. ophthalmology, 1984; dir. residential tng. U. So. Calif. Dept. Ophthalmology, LA, 1984-85, 90—; asst. prof. ophthalmology and neurosurgery U. So. Calif., LA, 1984—87, assoc. prof., 1987—90, full prof., 1990—, mem. internal review bd., F. Thornton endowed chair, prof. vision rsch., 2000—. Prin. investigator Howe Lab. Harvard U., Boston, 1981-84, E. Doheny Eye Inst., L.A., 1984—; examiner Am. Bd. Ophthalmology; mem. Nat. Residency Rev. Com. for Accreditations, 1993—, chmn., 1998—; mem. internal rev. bd. U. So. Calif.; mem. sci. exec. bd. K. Rasmussen Found.; mem. sci. adv. bd. Internat. Found. for Optic Nerve Diseases. Author: Optics for Ophthalmologists, 1988, New Methods of Sensory Visual Testing, 1989, 4 books; editor: Ophthalmology, 2000, Neuroprotection: Implications for Eye Disease, 2001; contbr. 230 articles to profl. jours., 70 chpts. to books. Recipient Pecan D. award, 1988—92, Rsch. to Prevent Blindness Sr. Investigator award, 1996—97, 1996, Lighthouse Internat. Pizart award, 1999, James Adams scholar, 1990—91, sr. investigator award, 1999—2000, Decade medal, Cuban Nat. Acad. Scis., Bradley Straatsma award, Am. Acad. Ophthalmology, 2003, Silver Fellow award, Assn. Rsch. Vision & Ophthalmogy, 2009. Fellow Am. Acad. Ophthalmology Neuro-Ophthalmologists, Assn. Rsch. in Vision and Ophthalmology; mem. NIH (Med. Scientists Tng. award 1972-78), Am. Assn. Anatomists, Assn. Univ. Prof. Ophthalmology (assoc.), Am. Bd. Ophthalmology (rep. to residency rev. com. 1994-2001), Soc. to Prevent Blindness, Nat. Eye Inst. (New Investigator Rsch. award 1983-86, rsch. grants 1988-91, 93-2002), Soc. Neuroscis., N.Am. Neuro-Ophthal. Soc. (chmn. membership com. 1990—, v.p. 1994—). Avocation: writing. Home: 2478 Adair St San Marino CA 91108-2610

SAEED, FAIZA J., lawyer; BA with highest distinction, U. Calif., Berkeley, 1987; JD magna cum laude, Harvard Law Sch., 1991. Bar: NY 1992, Calif. 1993, DC 1993. Assoc. Cravath, Swaine & Moore LLP, 1991—98, ptnr., corp., 1999—. Named a Young Global Leader, World Econ. Forum, 2006; named one of 45 Under Forty-Five, Am. Lawyer, 2003, Top 40 Lawyers Under 40, Nat. Law. Jour., 2005, The 100 Most Influential Women in NYC Bus., Crain's NY Bus., 2007. Mem.: Harvard Law Sch. Vis. Com., Calif. State Bar Assn., Internat. Bar Assn., ABA, NY State Bar Assn., Assn. Bar City of NY, Phi Beta Kappa. Office: Cravath Swaine & Moore LLP Worldwide Plaza 825 Eighth Ave New York NY 10019-7475 Office Phone: 212-474-1454. Office Fax: 212-474-3700. Business E-Mail: fsaeed@cravath.com.

SAEED, SHEHZAD, pediatrician, educator; MBBS, Dow Med. Coll., U. Karachi, Katachi, Sindh, MD, 1991. Diplomate Am. Bd. Pediat., 2001. Dir., pediat. subspecialty program U. Ala., Birimingham, 2004—, assoc. prof. & divsn. dir., pediatric gastroenterology, 2006—. Co dir. med. affairs com. local chpt. Crohn's & Colitis Found. America, Birmingham, Ala., 2004—. Mem.: NASPGHAN (internat. com. mem. 2007—). Office Phone: 205-939-9918.

SAEGER, JAMES SCHOFIELD, history professor, writer; b. Columbus, Ohio, Aug. 19, 1938; s. James Louttit and Elizabeth (Schofield) Saeger; divorced; children: James P., Edwin S. BA, Ohio State U., 1960, MA, 1963, PhD, 1969. V.p., dealer Jim Saeger Rambler Co., Columbus, Ohio, 1960—62; instr. history NC State U., Raleigh, 1965—67; from instr. to assoc. prof. history Lehigh U., Bethlehem, Pa., 1967—85, prof. history, 1985—. Co-dir. Gipson Inst. for 18th Century Studies, Bethlehem, 1979—91. Author: The Chaco Mission Frontier, 2000, Francisco Solano Lopez and the Ruination of Paraguay, 2007. Fellow, Orgn. Am. States, Paraguay, 1973—74, Fulbright Commn., 1981, NEH, 1988. Mem.: Conf. on Latin Am. History (com. mem. 0991—2005), Soc. Mil. History, Am. Hist. Assn. Avocations: golf, fishing, hiking, bicycling. Home: 239 Uncas St Bethlehem PA 18018 Office: Dept History Maginnes Hall 9 W Packer Ave Bethlehem PA 18015 Office Phone: 610-758-3366.

SAEGER, REBECCA, advertising executive; B in Psychology and Polit. Sci., Muhlenberg Coll., 1976; MBA, U. Pa., 1980. Various positions including sr. v.p., group dir. for Lever Bros. and Am. Express Ogilvy & Mather, NY, 1980—91; sr. v.p., group mgmt. supr., dir. account mgmt. Foote, Cone & Belding, San Francisco, 1991—97; exec. v.p. advt. and brand mktg. svcs. Visa USA, 1997—2001; exec. v.p. brand mgmt. and mktg. comm. Charles Schwab Corp., San Francisco, 2004—06, exec. v.p., chief mktg. officer, 2006—. Mem. exec. mgmt. com. Visa USA. Mem. mktg. com. San Francisco Symphony; mem. adv. bd. World Congress Sports. Mem.: Assn. Nat. Advertisers (bd. dirs.). Office: The Charles Schwab Corp 101 Montgomery St San Francisco CA 94104

SAEKS, ALLEN IRVING, lawyer; b. Bemidji, Minn., July 14, 1932; m. Linda J. Levin; 1 child, Adam Charles. BS in Law, U. Minn., 1954, JD, 1956. Bar: Minn. 1956, U.S. Dist. Ct. Minn. 1956, U.S. Ct. Appeals (8th cir.) 1957, U.S. Ct. Appeals (fed. cir.) 1959, U.S. Supreme Ct. 1959, U.S. Ct. Appeals (11th cir.) 1997; cert. civil trial specialist. Asst. U.S. atty. Dept. Justice, St. Paul, 1956-57; assoc. Leonard St. and Deinard, Mpls., 1960-63, ptnr., 1964—. Adj. prof. law U. Minn. Law Sch., 1960-65; chmn. lawyer trust acct. bd., Interest on Lawyers Trust Accounts, 1984-87; nat. bd. dirs. Equal Justice Works, Washington, 2002-05; chmn. adv. com. to evalute lawyer disciplinary sys. Minn. Supreme Ct., 2007-08. Pres. Jewish Cmty. Rels. Coun of Minn. and the Dakotas, 1994—96; bd. dirs. Citizens League, Mpls., 1984—87, chmn. property tax com., 1986—87. 1st lt. JAGC US Army, 1957—60. Recipient City of Mpls. award, 1996, Lifetime Commitment award, Cardozo Soc., 2001; named MN Lawyer Attorney of Yr., 2008, 2009; named one of Best Lawyers America, 2006—09. Fellow Am. Bar Found. (life); mem. ABA (commn. on interest on lawyers trust accts. 1990-93), Minn. State Bar Assn. (ethics task force, 2003, Pres. award 2003), Fund for the Legal Aid Soc. (chmn. 1997-98, Law Day Testimonial award 1996), Hennepin County Bar Assn. (pres. 1983-84, Professionalism award 2009), Order of Coif, Phi Delta Phi. Office: Leonard St and Deinard 150 S 5th St Ste 2300 Minneapolis MN 55402-4238 Office Phone: 612-335-1548. Business E-Mail: ais1548@leonard.com.

SAEKS, RICHARD EPHRAIM, engineering executive; b. Chgo., Nov. 30, 1941; s. Morris G. and Elsie E. S. BS, Northwestern U., 1964; MS, Colo. State U., 1965; PhD, Cornell U., 1967. Registered profl. engr., Tex. Elec. engr. Warwick Mfg. Co., Niles, Ill., 1961-63; asst. prof. dept. elec. engring. U. Notre Dame, 1967-71, assoc. prof., 1971-73; assoc. prof. depts. elec. engring., math. Tex. Tech U., Lubbock, 1973-77, prof., 1977-79, Paul Whitfield Horn prof. elec. engring., math. computer sci, 1979-83; prof., chmn. elec. engring. Ariz. State U., 1983-88; dean Armour Coll. Engring. Ill. Inst. Tech., 1988-91, Motorola prof., 1991-92; v.p. engring. Accurate Automation Corp., 1992-2000, chief tech. officer, 2000—. Cons. Research Triangle Inst., 1978-80, Marcel Dekker Inc., 1978-80. Author: Generalized Networks, 1972, Resolution Space Operators and Systems, 1973, Interconnected Dynamical Systems, 1981, System Theory: A Hilbert Space Approach, 1982, Shock Structure Analysis and Aerodynamics in a Weakly Ionized Gas, 2006; Editor: Large-Scale Dynamical Systems, 1976, Rational Fault Analysis, 1977, The World of Large Scale Systems, 1982; contbr. 200 articles to profl. jours. Recipient Disting. Faculty Research award Tex. Tech U., 1978, INC 500 award, 1994, SBA Rolnd Tibbets award, 1996, Joeseph G. Wohl Outstanding Career award, IEEE Systems, Man, and Cybernetics Society, 2004 Fellow: AIAA, IEEE (life), IEEE Systems Men and Cybernetics Soc. (pres. 1998—99). Achievements include patents in field. Business E-Mail: richard@saeks.org.

SAENGER, BRUCE WALTER, consulting firm executive; b. Hanover, NH, July 16, 1943; s. Werner Hugo and Natalie Bertha (Brown) S.; m. Cheryl Jeanne Bouchard, Nov. 6, 1976. BA, Pa. State U., 1969; postgrad., Am. Coll., Bryn Mawr, Pa., 1979, Coll. Fin. Planning, Denver, 1980. CPCU; ChFC; CLU; CFP; RHU; REBC; CIC. Agt. Nationwide Ins., Lansdale, Pa., 1969-73, dist. sales mgr. Springfield, Mass., 1973-75, Am. Mut., Braintree, Mass., 1975-77; dir. mktg. Bankers LIfe & Casualty, Chgo., 1977-78; pres., founder Sales Tng. Techniques, Southboro, Mass., 1979-81, The Saenger Orgn., Medway, Mass., 1981—2004; owner, pres. Saenger Consulting Group, Waterville Vallet, NH, 2004—. Mem. faculty Notre Dame U., South Bend, Ind., 1977-78, Northeastern U., Boston, 1984-92; mem. RHU Commn., Washington, 1979-81; dir. Northeastern U. Inst. Inst., Boston, 1985-93; mem. Mass. Ins. Dept. Continuing Edn. Rev. Com., 1985—; program dir. U. Del. Ins. Program, 1989-91; acad. cons. Mass. Soc. Lic. Ins. Advisers, 1995—; cons. in field. Author: Series 6 Study Book, 1983, Series 22 Study Book, 1984, Tax Shelter Market Guide, 1985, Marketing Mutual Funds, 1985, also articles. Bd. dirs. Lansdale Gen. Hosp., 1971-73, New Directions Theater Co., 1988-91, Penn State U. Alumni Assn., 2005-, Waterville Valley Resort Assn., 2006-; mem. Medway Bus. Coun., 1989-94, pres., 1990-92; chmn. Penn State U. Friends of Abington/Ogontz ROTC, 2004-; town moderator Waterville Valley, NH, 2006-. With U.S. Army, 1960-66. Recipient Ednl. Achievement award Profl. Ins. Agts. Assn., 1983, Alumni Achievement award Pa. State Alumni Assn., 2005; named Outstanding Fin. Exec. of Yr., Fin. Mgmt. Assn., 1993. Fellow Soc. CLUs (ednl. adv., bd. dirs. 1987-91), Soc. CPCUs (ednl. adv.), Life Mgmt. Inst. (Outstanding Lectr. award 1984); mem. Internat. Assn. Fin. Planners (ednl. adv., bd. dirs. 1986-92, pres. 1989-91), Internat. Assn. for Fin. Planning (chmn. bd. dirs. 1990-92), Soc. Cert. Ins. Counselors, Life Underwriters Assn., Inst. CFP (v.p. edn., bd. dirs. 1990-91), Mass. Assn. Health Underwriters (pres. 1992-93, Boston Bus. Ethics award 2001), Pa. State U. Alumni Soc. (bd. dirs. 2005-07). Republican. Roman Catholic. Avocations: skiing, golf. Home: 7 Drake's Brook Rd PO Box 304 Waterville Valley NH 03215-1018 Office: Saenger Consulting Group 31 Village Rd PO Box 350 Waterville Valley NH 03215 Office Phone: 603-236-3300. Business E-Mail: bsaenger@saengerconsulting.com.

SÁENZ, ALBERT WILLIAM, theoretical physicist, researcher, consultant; b. Medellín, Colombia, Aug. 27, 1923; arrived in US, 1941; s. Alberto Sáenz Moreno and Agnes (Williams) Sáenz; m. Pilar González García-Suelto, Sept. 7, 1957. BS, U. Mich., Ann Arbor, 1944, MA, 1945, PhD, 1949. From rsch. physicist to br. head Naval Rsch. Lab., Washington, 1950-66, br. head, 1966-76, divsn. cons., 1976-89, ret., 1989; rsch. prof. Cath. U., Washington, 1981—. Vis. fellow Ind. U., Bloomington, 1951-52; vis. prof. Johns Hopkins U., Balt., 1964; vis. sr. scientist Princeton U., NJ, 1976-77, Max Planck Inst., Stuttgart, Germany, 1990-91, Budker Inst. Nuc. Physics, Novosibirsk, Russia, 1996; cons. Naval Rsch. Lab., Washington, 1990—. Author: (with others) Long Distance Neutrino Detection, 1979, Mathematical Methods and

Applications of Scattering Theory, 1980, Coherent Radiation Sources, 1985, Relativistic Channeling, 1987, Synergetics, Order and Chaos, 1988, Essays in Classical and Quantum Dynamics, 1991, Asymptotics Beyond All Orders, 1991, others; editor numerous books; contbr. 56 articles to profl. jours. Fellow Am. Phys. Soc., Washington Acad. Scis.; mem. Am. Math. Soc., NY Acad. Scis., Cosmos Club. Democrat. Roman Catholic. Achievements include determination of stresses by their stress trajectories in plane elasticity, symmetry and degeneracy in quantum mechanics, general relativity, spin-wave theory of complex magnetic structures and spin-wave scattering of polarized neutrons, coherent bremsstrahlung and coherent pair production in crystals and quasicrystals, rigorous classical and quantum mechanical scattering theory, long-distance neutrino communication, averaging theory of periodic and nonperiodic classical dynamical systems and its quantum analogues, channeling stability studies, axial-to-planar channeling transition in crystals and quasicrystals, nonintegrability and chaos. Home: 6338 Old Town Ct Alexandria VA 22307-1227 Office: Naval Rsch Lab 4555 Overlook Ave SW Washington DC 20375-0001 Office Phone: 202-767-2968. Business E-Mail: saenz@dave.nrl.navy.mil.

SAENZ, MICHAEL, college president; b. Laredo, Tex., Oct. 25, 1925; s. C.A. and Pola R. Saenz; m. Nancy Elizabeth King; children: Michael King, Cynthia Elizabeth. BS in Acctg. with honors, Tex. Christian U., 1949, MEd, 1952; PhD in Econs., U. Pa., 1961. Dep. collector IRS, Ft. Worth, Dallas, 1949-52; adminstr. United Christian Missionary Soc., Bayamon, PR, 1954-57, 59-65, exec. sec. Indpls., 1965-71; acad. dean Laredo (Tex.) Jr. Coll., 1971-74; pres. N.W. campus Tarrant County Coll., Fort Worth, Tex., 1975—. Founder Nat. Comm. Coll. Hispanic Coun., 1985, bd. dirs., 1985—, pres., 1989-91; founder, co-dir. Nat. Hispanic Leadership Inst., 1989—; trustee Tex. Christian U., Brite Div. Sch., 1973-2001. Bd. dirs. Civic Ballet of Laredo, Ft. Worth chpt. NCCJ, Juliette Fowler Homes, Dallas; chmn. Aztec dist., dir. Gulf Coast coun. Boy Scouts Am., 1971-75; gov. Career Devel. Ctr., Arlington, Tex.; chmn. Laredo's Bicentennial Com., 1973-76; trustee, bd. dirs. United Way Ft. Worth, 1979-88; mem., vice moderator gen. bd. Christian Ch. (Disciples of Christ), 1991-93. Mem. Am. Assn. Cmty. Colls. (bd. dirs. 1991-94), Commn. Internat. Edn. Am. Coun. Edn., Tex. Jr. Coll. Tchrs. Assn., Tex. Assn. Jr. Coll. Instructional Adminstrs., Am. Acad. Polit. and Social Scis., Urban Ministries in Higher Edn., Civic Music Assn. Laredo, Rotary. Home: 4427 Tamworth Rd Fort Worth TX 76116-8127 Office: Tarrant County Coll NW Capmus 4801 Marine Pkwy Fort Worth TX 76179 E-mail: michael.saenz@teed.edu.

SAFAI, BIJAN, physician, investigator; b. Ardestan, Iran, Mar. 26, 1940; came to U.S., 1968; s. Abdol-Khalegh Safai and Kanom-Sadat Sadjaddi; m. Vera Plaskon, Sept. 16, 1978; 1 child: Matthew. MD, Tehran U., Iran, 1965; DSc, U. Gutenburg, Sweden, 1981. Diplomate Am. Bd. Dermatology, Am. Bd. Internal Medicine. Intern Nassau County Med. Ctr., East Meadow, NY, 1968-69; resident N.Y.U. Med. Coll. VA Hosp., NYC, 1969-70; resident in dermatology N.Y.U. Med. Coll., NYC, 1971-73; fellow in immunology Sloan-Kettering Inst. for Cancer & Allied Diseases, NYC, 1973-74; from asst. attending physician to chief dermatology svc. Meml. Hosp., NYC, 1974-93; from assoc. to attending physician in dermatology N.Y. Hosp., NYC, 1980-93; dir. dermatology Westchester County Med. Ctr., Valhalla, NY, 1993—; from asst. prof. to prof. in medicine/dermatology Cornell U. Med. Coll., NYC, 1974-93; prof., chmn. dept. dermatology N.Y. Med. Coll., NYC, 1993—, prof. dept. microbiology and immunology, 1994—. Teaching clin. asst. in dermatology NYU Med. Coll, N.Y.C., 1973-74; adj. mem. Rockefeller U., N.Y.C., 1982-84; rsch. assoc. Sloan-Kettering Inst. for Cancer and Allied Diseases, N.Y.C., 1977-79, asst. mem., 1979-83, assoc. mem., 1983-88; assoc. mem. Memorial Sloan-Kettering Cancer Ctr., N.Y.C., 1983-88, mem. 1988-93; mem. grad. sch. med. scis. N.Y. Med. Coll., Valhalla, 1994—; mem. adv. bd. Skin Cancer Found., 1982—; sec. dermatology sect. N.Y. Acad Medicine, 1988-89, chmn. 1989-90; mem. med. adv. bd. Cancer Rsch Instn., 1997—. Mem. editl. bd. Cancer Investigation, 1984-88, AIDS Rsch. and Human Retroviruses, 1986-90, Jour. of Acquired Immune Deficiency Syndromes, 1988—; contbr. numerous articles on immunodermatology to profl. jours. Mem. AIDS adv. task force, NCI/NIH, 1982-85; mem. AIDS Etiology task force, NCI, 1982-85; mem. ad hoc study sect. for AIDS, NIH, 1982-88; mem. spl. dermatology rev. group, GM2 study sect., NIH, 1990-96; mem. spl. rev. team NCI Intramural Rev., Lab. of Tumor cell Biology, 1987, 92, Medicine br., NCI, 1996; mem. study sect. on HIV, NCI, 1996; mem. spl. rev. group FDA Intramural Rev., 1995. Mem. AMA, Internat. Soc. Tropical Dermatology, Am. Fedn. for Clin. Rsch., Am. Acad. Dermatology (mem. AIDS com. 1989-91, task force on cutaneous oncology 1988-9, mem. adv. coun. 1988-91), Am. Dermatol. Soc. for Allery and Immunology, Soc. for Investigative Dermatology, Med. Soc. of State of N.Y., Med. Soc. of County of N.Y., N.Y. State Soc. Dermatology, Dermatol. Soc. of Greater N.Y., N.Y. County Health Svs. Rev. Orgn., N.Y. Acad. Scis., N.Y. Dermatol. Soc. (pres 1990-91, sec., treas. 1989-90), Dermatology Found., Z & E Fisher Med. Found. (pres. 1993—). Home: 340 E 64th St New York NY 10021-7503 Office: NY Med Coll Dept Dermatology Valhalla NY 10595 also: 625 Park Ave New York NY 10021-6545 Office Phone: 212-988-8918. Personal E-mail: safai@aol.com.

SAFAI, NICK M., chemical engineer, director; BSEE, Mich. State U., East Lansing, Oakland U., Rochester, Mich., 1972; MSEE in Aerospace Engring., Princeton U., NJ, 1974, MS in Mech. Engring., 1974, MS in Civil Engring., 1975, MA in Water Resources & Ops. Rsch., 1976, PhD, 1979. Coord. SLCC, 1986—95, chair engring. depts., 1995—. Coach County Recreational, Salt Lake City, 2002. Recipient Best Paper award, 2002, Tchg. Excellance award, 2004, Best Svc. award, 2004, Best Paper award, 2004—06, Educator Yr. award, 2004, Internat. Educator Contbn. award, 2005; grant, NSF, 1972—79, Dept. Energy, 1983—84, Dept. Def., 1984—86. Master: ASCE (faculty advisor local chair 2001, Educator Yr. and Chpt. Pres. 2004), ASME (assoc.; chair ann. programs 1997, Svc. award 2004—05); mem.: Am. Soc. Engring. Edn. (Chair ann. conf. tech program 1997—).

SAFARS, BERTA See FISZER-SZAFARZ, BERTA

SAFAVIAN, S. RASOUL, telecommunications industry executive; BSEE with highest honors, U. Kans., Lawrence, 1982; MSEE with honors, U. Kansas, Lawrence, 1984; PhD in Elec. Engring., Purdue U., West Lafayette, Ind., 1991. Sr. tech. mgr. LCC, MacLean, Va., 1995—2003; v.p. WFI, Reston, Va., 2003—05; v.p. CTO Bechtel, Frederick, Md., 2005—. Vis. faculty elec. engring. Purdue U., 1991—95, bd. mem., sch. engring.; adj. prof. George Wash. U.; affiliated faculty Pa. State U.; spkr. in field. Mem.: IEEE, Tau Beta Pi, Eta Kappa Nu. Achievements include design of the first commercial CDMA network. Avocations: tennis, skiing, horseback riding, painting, music. Office: Bechtel 5295 Wetview Dr Frederick MD 21703 Personal E-mail: srsafavian@yahoo.com. Business E-Mail: srsafavi@bechtel.com.

SAFDAR, AMAR, medical educator, researcher; s. Mohammad and Taj Safdar. MBBS, Dow Med. Coll., Karachi, MD, 1989. Diplomate Am. Bd. Medicine, Pa., 1994. Fellow infectious diseases Meml. Sloan-Kettering Cancer Ctr., NYC, 1996—99; assoc. prof. medicine M. D. Anderson Cancer Ctr., Houston, 2001—, dir. mycobacterial rsch., 2001—. Com. chair Internat. Immunocompromised Host Soc., Ga., 2002—08. Recipient Young Investigator's award, Internat. Immunocompromised Host Soc., 2000. Fellow: ACP. Achievements include research in cord blood stem cell derived influenza vaccine. Office: M D Anderson Cancer Ctr 1515 Holcombe Blvd Houston TX 77030 Office Fax: 713-745-6839. Business E-Mail: asafdar@mdanderson.org.

SAFDI, ALAN V., gastroenterologist, director; s. Stuart and Ann Safdi; m. Anne Safdi. BA, Northwestern U., Evanston, Ill., 1974; MD, U. Cin., 1978. Resident U. Calif., San Diego, 1978—81; pres. Ohio Gastroenterology & Liver Inst., Cin., 1987—, Cons. Clin. Rsch., Cin., 1998—. Chmn. sect. gastroenterology Deaconess Hosp., Cin., 1985—; med. dir. Tri-State Endoscopy Ctr., Cin., 2006—. Fellow, U. Cin., 1981—83, Am. Coll. Gastroenterology, 1991. Mem.: Phi Beta Kappa, Alpha Omega Alpha. Achievements include development of voice recognition software for electronic medical records. Home and Office: Ohio Gastroenterology & Liver Inst 2925 Vernon Pl Cincinnati OH 45219 Office Phone: 513-751-6667. Home Fax: 513-872-4553. Personal E-mail: asafdi@ohiogi.com.

SAFER, ALAN, statistician, educator; MS in Mktg. Rsch., Southern Ill. U., Edwardsville, 1995; PhD, U. Wyo., Laramie, 2000. Prof. stats. Calif. State U., Long Beach, Calif., 2000—. Named one of Campus-Wide Advisor of Yr., CSU Long Beach, 2008. Mem.: Southern Calif. Am. Statis. Assn.

SAFER, JOHN, sculptor; b. Washington, Sept. 6, 1922; s. John M. and Rebecca (Herzmark) S.; m. Joy Scott; children: Janine Whitney, Thomas. AB, George Washington U., 1947; DPhil (hon.), George Washinton U.; DFA (hon.), George Washington U., 2009; LLB, Harvard U., 1949. Chmn. NationsBank/DC, 1980-92; chmn. exec. com. Fin. Gen. Bankshares, 1977-80; bd. dirs. Nat. Air and Space Mus., The Shakespeare Guild, Materia. Represented in permanent collections at Smithsonian Am. Art Mus., Balt. Mus. Art, Corocoran Gallery Art, Dayton Art Inst., Frederik Meijer Sculpture Gardens, Folger Shakespeare Libr., Johns Hopkins U., Nat. Air and Space Mus., Washington Tennis Ctr., High Mus. Art, Atlanta, Milw. Mus. Art, Harvard Law Sch., Harvard Bus. Sch., Hofstra U., Mayo Clinic, Kimmel Cancer Ctr. Phila., Mayo Jacksonville, Fla., Phila. Mus. Art, San Francisco Mus. Art, Duke U. Med. Ctr., Embry-Riddle Aero. U., Georgetown U., George Washington U., Williams Coll., Wilmer Eye Dust, Scripps Rsch. Inst., Daniel Webster Coll., Am. Hosp., Paris, Embassy of U.S., London, Nassau, Beijing, New Delhi, Fayetteville (NC) Mus. Art, Nat. Jewish Mus., Nat. Peace Inst., Ponce (PR) Mus. of Art, UN, N.Y.C., corporate collections. including General Dynamics Celanese Corp., NY, Crown Equipment Corp., New Bremen, Ohio, First Union Bank of Md., Bank of Am. Ctr., Norfolk, Va., Gen. Mills Corp., Mpls, West Chase Corp., Houston, Nat. Air Traffic Controller, numerous others. 1st lt. USAAF, 1942-46. Mem.: Cosmos, Burning Tree, Harvard, Woodmont (Washington), Lyford Cay (Nassau), Linville Ridge (N.C.). Office: PO Box 6720 Mc Lean VA 22106-6720 Office Phone: 703-276-7766. Personal E-mail: johnsafer@mac.com.

SAFF, EDWARD BARRY, mathematics professor, dean; b. NYC, Jan. 2, 1944; s. Irving H. and Rose (Koslow) Saff; m. Loretta Singer, July 3, 1966; children: Lisa Jill, Tracy Karen, Alison Michelle. BS with highest honors, Ga. Inst. Tech., 1964; PhD, U. Md., 1968. Asst. prof. U. Md., 1968; post-doctoral rschr. Imperial Coll., London, 1968-69; from asst. prof. to assoc. prof. math. U. S. Fla., 1969—76, prof., 1976-86, disting. rsch. prof., 1986—2001, dir. Ctr. Math. Svcs., 1978-83, dir. Inst. Constructive Math., 1985—2001, dir. Ctr. Constructive Approximation, 2001—04; exec. dean Coll. Arts and Sci. Vanderbilt U., Nashville, 2004—07. Sr. vis. fellow Oxford U., 1978; hon. prof. Zhejiang Normal U. Author (with A. D. Snider): Fundamentals of Complex Analysis, 1976, 3d edit., 2003; author: (with A. W. Goodman) Calculus, Concepts and Calculations, 1981; author: (with A. Edrei and R. S. Varga) Zeros of Sections of Power Series; author: (with V. Totik) Logarithmic Potentials with External Fields, 1997; author: (with R. K. Nagle) Fundamentals of Differential Equations, 1993, Fundamentals of Differential Equations and Boundary Value Problems, 1993; author: (with D. S. Lubinsky) Strong Asymptotics for External Polynomials Associated with Weights on R, 1988; editor: Jour. Approximation Theory, 1990—; editor: (with R. S. Varga) Pade and Rational Approximation: Theory and Applications, 1977; editor: Cambridge U. Press, 1995—2001, Founds. Comp. Math., 1999—2004; editor-in-chief: Constructive Approximation Jour., 1983—, Computational Methods and Function Theory Jour., 2001—. Recipient Chancellor's Rsch. award, Vanderbilt U., 2005; grantee, NSF, 1970—72, 1980—; fellow, Fulbright Found., 1968—69, Guggenheim Found., 1978. Mem.: Math. Assn. Am., Am. Math. Soc., Sigma Xi. Office: Ctr Constructive Approximation Vanderbilt U Dept Math Nashville TN 37240 Office Phone: 615-322-7360. Business E-Mail: ed.saff@vanderbilt.edu.

SAFFACHE, PASCAL MARIE, dean, educator; b. Fort-de-France, Martinica, France, Aug. 5, 1971; s. Passionis Andre Saffache and Denise Cyr-Athis. M in Geography, U. Antilles Guyane, Schoelcher, France, 1995, PhD in Geography, 1998; PhD (hon.), Ricardo Palma U., Lima, Peru, 2009. Asst. U. Antilles Guyane, Schoelcher, 1997—2000, sr. lectr., 2001—, dir. dept. geography and phys. planning, 2002—05, dean faculty, 2005—09, pres., 2009—. Cons. Inst. Rsch. for Devel., Paris, 2002—04, Conservatoire Littoral, Caen, France, 2004—. Author: West Indian Coastlines at Stake: From Land Settlement to Stable Development, 2005, Glossary of Subjects Related to Land Settlement and Local Development, 2005. Recipient Local Devel. prize, Caisse des Dépôts et Consignations, 1998, Schoelcher Town prize, Ville de Schoelcher, 2000, Nat. Toyp prize, Jeune Chambre Internat., New Delhi, 2005, 2008, World Toyp prize, 2008, Blue Ribbon Ecology Trophy, Parc Naturel Regional de la Martinique, 2006. Mem.: Geog. Soc., European Interdisciplinary Acad. Scis. Office: U Antilles Guyane Campus Schoelcher-BP 7207 97275 Schoelcher Martinica West Indies Office Phone: 0696-240411. Business E-Mail: pascal.saffache@martinique.univ-ag.fr.

SAFFELS, ANNA WAYNE BROTHERS, retired mathematician, educator; b. Gallant, Ala., Nov. 6, 1928; d. Homer Ervin and Bertie Galloway Brothers; m. George Aaron Saffels (dec.); children: Michael Aaron, Elisabeth Anne. BS in Secondary Edn., Jacksonville State U., 1949; MA in Secondary Edn., U. Ala., Birmingham, 1973. Cert. tchr. Ala., 1949. Tchr. Ivalee Sch., Attalla, Ala., 1949—53, 1956—61, 1964—66; tchr. math. Etowah H.S., Attalla, Ala., 1966—86, ret., 1986. Pres. Etowah County Classroom Tchrs. Assn., 1967—68. Pianist Ivalee Bapt. Ch., 1950—2009, Sunday sch. tchr., 1950—97, dir. sr. activities, 2000—08. Nominee Jacksonville State Tchr. Hall of Fame, 1972, Presdl. award for excellence in math. tchg. Mem.: NEA, Ala. Edn. Assn., Alpha Delta Kappa (past pres. Ala. Alpha Xi chpt.), Kappa Delta Pi. Avocations: genealogy, stamp collecting/philately, photography, music, flower gardening. Home: 3194 Hwy 77 Attalla AL 35954-7140 Personal E-mail: awbsaffels@aol.com.

SAFFIOTTI, UMBERTO, pathologist; b. Milan, Jan. 22, 1928; came to U.S., 1960, naturalized, 1966; s. Francesco Umberto and Maddalena (Valenzano) S.; m. Paola Amman, June 21, 1958; children: Luisa M., Maria Francesca. MD cum laude, U. Milan, 1951, splty. diploma occupational medicine cum laude, 1957. Intern Inst. Pathol. Anatomy U. Milan, 1951-52, asst. to chmn. occupational medicine, chief lab. pathology, Inst. Occupational Medicine, 1956-60, fellow Inst. Gen. Pathology, 1957-60; rsch. asst. oncology, rsch. assoc. Chgo. Med. Sch., 1952-55, from asst. prof. to prof. oncology, 1960-68; mem. staff Nat. Cancer Inst., NIH, Bethesda, Md., 1968—, assoc. dir. carcinogenesis, 1968-76, chief lab. exptl. pathology, 1974-98, acting head Registry of Exptl. Cancers, 1988-98; scientist emeritus, 1998—; adj. prof., Environ. & Occ. Hlth. The George Washington U., Washington, 2000—07. Mem. pathology B study sect., NIH, 1964-68; former mem. various adv. coms. govt. agys.; mem. cancer prevention com. Internat. Union Against Cancer, 1959-66, panel on carcinogenicity, 1963-66; chmn. ad hoc com. evaluation low levels environ. carcinogens HEW, 1969-70. Co-editor books; contbr. articles to profl. jours. Bd. dirs. Rachel Carson Trust, 1976-79. Recipient Career Devel. award NIH, 1965-68, Superior Svc. Honor award HEW, 1971, Pub. Interest Sci. award Environ. Def. Fund, 1977, Spl. Recognition award USPHS, 1980 Fellow NYAS; mem. AAAS, Am. Assn. Cancer Rsch. (pres. Chgo. chpt. 1966-67), Am. Soc. Investigative Pathology, Soc. Toxicology, Sigma Xi. Democrat. Home: 5114 Wissioming Rd Bethesda MD 20816-2259 Office: NIH Nat Cancer Inst 6116 Executive Blvd Rm 7212 Bethesda MD 20892-2259 Business E-Mail: saffiotti@nih.gov.

SAFFIR, LEONARD, public relations executive; b. NYC, Apr. 19, 1930; s. Abraham and Getrude Saffir; m. Patricia Roemer (div. 1980); children: Andrew, Michelle; m. Wendy McConaughy (div. 1992); 1 child, Samantha; m. Eleanor Unger, 1997. Student, Syracuse U., 1948-51. Editor, bur. chief Internat. News Service, Dallas, Tokyo, 1953-58; producer Eng., Australia, Asia, 1958-60; ptnr. Haft, Saffir, Siegel Pub. Relations & Advt., NYC, 1960-62; asst. pub. N.Y. Standard, 1962-63; cons. Ferdinand Marcos, 1964; pub. Latin Am. Times, NYC, 1965; exec. v.p. Franchises Internat., NYC, 1965-69; press sec., chief of staff to Senator James Buckley U.S. Senate, Washington, 1970-76; pub., editor The Trib, NYC, 1977-78, The Sun, Bridgehampton, NY, 1978-84; exec. v.p. Porter/Novelli, NYC, 1984-90; pres. Jay DeBow & Ptnrs., NYC, Fla., 1989-90, Leonard Saffir & Assocs. Pub. Rels., 2000—; investigative reporter, columnist Lake Worth Herald, 2001—03. CEO Adventures One, 1998—2000, Celebrity Stores.com, 1998—2000. Author: Power Public Relations, 1992, Power Public Relations: How to Master the New PR, 2000, PR on a Budget, 2007. Campaign mgr. Marchi for Mayor, NYC, 1973, Buckely for Senator, NY, 1976. Sgt. USMC, 1951—53. Recipient Silver Anvil award, Pub. Rels. Soc. Am., Big Apple award, Mayor's award, City of NY, others. Mem.: Overseas Press Club (pres. 1988—89). Home: 6137 Rainbow Circle Lake Worth FL 33463 Office Phone: 561-289-3100. Personal E-mail: lenpr@bellsouth.net.

SAFIR, KEN, linguist, educator; b. NYC, Aug. 27, 1950; s. Marshall and Gladys Safir; m. Susan Sidlauskas, July 3, 1983; children: Emma, Miranda. PhD, MIT, Cambridge, 1982. Prof. linguistics Rutgers U., New Brunswick, NY, 1984—. Web site dir. Afranaph Project, Rutgers U., New Brunswick, 2005—. Grant, NSF, 2003—. Achievements include research in exploration of how linguistic ability is encoded in the brain. Office: Dept Linguistics Rutgers U 18 Seminary Pl Highland Park NJ 08904

SAFIR, PETER OLIVER, lawyer; b. NYC, Apr. 1, 1945; s. Marshall Philip and Gladys (Weissberger) S.; m. Ellen Beskind, Jan. 2, 1983; children: Jesse Oliver, Roland Smart, Archie Smart. AB in History, Princeton U., 1967; JD, Yale U., 1972. Bar: N.Y. 1973, D.C. 1975. Assoc. Breed, Abbott & Morgan, NYC, 1972—75, Kleinfeld Kaplan & Becker, Washington, 1975—78, ptnr., 1979—2002, Covington & Burling, Washington, 2002—, co-chmn., Food & Drug Regulatory Practice Group. Prof. lectr. food and drug law George Washington U. Law Sch., 1991—. Contbr. articles to profl., trade, and law jours. With US Army, 1968—71. Mem.: ABA (food and drug law sect.), Democrat. Office: Covington & Burling 1201 Pennsylvania Ave Washington DC 20004-2401 Office Phone: 202-662-5162. Office Fax: 202-662-6291. Business E-Mail: psafir@cov.com.

SAFIRA, BARABARA, science educator; b. Kaprzewnica, Poland, Feb. 18, 1959; d. Regina and Jon Pielecha; m. Hertzel Safira, Jan. 11, 1990; children: Arthur Dov, Ariela. Masters, Acad. Of Mining & Metallurgy, Kracov, Poland, 1986. Cert. phys. sci. tchr. N.J., 2001. Chem. engr. Cement Plant, Ozarow, Poland, 1986—87; rsch. chemist Sika, Lyndhurst, NJ, 1989—98; tchr. phys. sci. Wallington H.S., NJ, 2001—. Head instr. of engring. club Wallington H.S., NJ, 2002—09; asst. math. team Bergen County Acad., Hackensack, NJ, 2004—09. Office: Wallington HS 234 Main Ave Wallington NJ 07057 E-mail: safira@wboe.org.

SAFIRE, WILLIAM, journalist, foundation administrator; b. NYC, Dec. 17, 1929; s. Oliver C. and Ida (Panish) S.; m. Helene Belmar Julius, Dec. 16, 1962; children: Mark Lindsey, Annabel Victoria. Student, Syracuse U., 1947—49. Reporter NY Herald Tribune Syndicate, 1949-51; corr. WNBC-WNBT, Europe and Mid. East, 1951; radio-TV prodr. WNBC, NYC, 1954-55; v.p. pub. rels. Tex McCrary, Inc., 1955-60; pres. Safire Pub. Rels., Inc., 1960-68; sr. White House speechwriter Pres. Richard Nixon, Washington, 1969-73; polit. columnist NY Times, Washington, 1973—2005; columnist On Language, NY Times Mag., 1979—2008. Trustee Syracuse U., 2008-; chmn. Dana Found. Author: The Relations Explosion, 1963, Plunging into Politics, 1964, Safire's Political Dictionary, 1968, rev. edit., 1972—78, Before the Fall, 1975, Full Disclosure, 1977, Safire's Washington, 1980, On Language, 1980, What's the Good Word?, 1982, I Stand Corrected, 1984, Take My Word for It, 1986, Freedom, 1987, You Could Look It Up, 1988, Language Maven Strikes Again, 1990, Fumblerules, 1990, Coming to Terms, 1991, The First Dissident, 1992, Lend Me Your Ears, 1992, 1998, 2004, Good Advice on Writing, 1992, Quoth the Maven, 1993, In Love with Norma Loquendi, 1994, Sleeper Spy, 1995, Watching My Language, 1997, Spread the Word, 1999, Scandalmonger, 2000, Let a Simile Be Your Umbrella, 2001, No Uncertain Terms, 2003, The Right Word, 2004; co-author (with Leonard Safir): Good Advice on Writing, 1982, Words of Wisdom, 1989, Leadership, 1990; author: Safire's Political Dictionary, 5th edit., 2008. Mem. Pulitzer Bd., 1995-2004. With AUS, 1952-54. Recipient Pulitzer prize for Disting. Commentary, 1978, Presdl. Medal of Freedom, 2006. Republican. Office: The Dana Foundation 900 15th St NW Washington DC 20005 Business E-Mail: wsafire@dana.org.*

SAFKA, JIM, information technology executive, investment services company executive; m. Mandy Safka; 2 children. BS in Acctg., U. So. Ca.; MBA, J.L. Kellogg School of Management, Northwestern U. Brand and product mgmt. positions Alberto-Culver, Inc., Warner Bros., Paramount Pictures; product mgr., Quicken Financial Planner and Quicken-.com Intuit; positions up to v.p., mktg. E*Trade Fin. Corp., 1997—2002; v.p., gen. mgr. e-commerce AT&T Wireless, 2002—04; CEO Match-

.com, 2004—07, Primal Ventures, San Francisco, 2007—, IAC/InterActive Corp. (Ask.com), 2008—. Office: IAC Search & Media 555 12th St Ste 500 Oakland CA 94607

SAFLEY, HOLLI EWOLDT, music educator; d. Roy William and Marilyn Hedin Ewoldt; m. William Duane Safley, Aug. 4, 1979; children: Matthew William-Ewoldt, Erin Lynn-Ewoldt. MusB in Edn., Drake U., Des Moines, Iowa, 1974. Instr. vocal and instrumental music edn. Ackely-Geneva (Iowa) Schs., 1974—79; instr. instrumental music edn. Aurelia (Iowa) Cmty. Schs., 1979—88; instr. instrumental music Clay Ctrl. Cmty. Sch., Royal, Iowa, 1989—90, South O'Brien Cmty. Schs., Paulina, Iowa, 1990—96, Storm Lake (Iowa) Cmty. Schs., 1996—. Coach basketball, softball, track Ackley- Geneva (Iowa) Cmty. Schs., 1974—79; head coach volleyball, basketball Aurelia (Iowa) Cmty. Sch. Dist., 1979—84. Musician: Cherokee Symphony Orchestra; dir.: Aurelia (Iowa) H.S. Jazz Band (3rd Pl. award Iowa Jazz Championships, 1987), Jazz Festivals (1st Pl. awards). Recipient Tchr. Tenure award, Iowa Bandmasters, 2007. Mem.: Am. Sch. Band Dirs. Assn., Mu Phi Epsilon (pres. 1973—74), Am. Sch. Band Dirs. Assn. (state chair Iowa chpt. 2005—), N.W. Iowa Bandmasters Assn. (dist. pres. 1990—91), Iowa Bandmasters Assn. (dist. rep. All Iowa 8th Grade Honor Band 2004—), Iowa Music Educators Assn., Music Educators Nat. Conf., Iowa Edn. Assn., Mortar Bd. (treas. 1973—74). Avocations: golf, travel, gardening. Office: Storm Lake Middle School PO Box 638 Storm Lake IA 50588-0638 Office Fax: 712-732-8084. Personal E-mail: safmusic@iowatelecom.net. E-mail: hsafley@storm-lake.k12.ia.us.

SAFLEY, JAMES ROBERT, lawyer; b. Cedar Rapids, Iowa, Sept. 19, 1943; s. Robert Starr and Jean (Engelman) S.; m. Dianne Lee McInnis; children: Anne Michele, Jamie Leigh. BA, U. Iowa, 1965; JD, Duke U., 1968. Bar: Minn. 1968, U.S. Ct. Appeals (4th, 5th, 6th, 7th, 8th, 9th and 11th cirs.), U.S. Supreme Ct. Law clk. U.S. Dist. Ct. Minn., Mpls., 1968-69; assoc. Robins, Kaplan, Miller & Ciresi, Mpls., 1969-74, ptnr., 1974—. Mem. adv. coun. Women's Intercollegiate Athletics, U. Minn., 1988-94; mem bd. visitors Duke Law Sch, 2004—. Mem. ABA, Minn. State Bar Assn. (antitrust sect. chmn. 1985-87), Hennepin County Bar Assn., Duke Law Alumni Assn. (bd. dirs. 2001-03), Phi Beta Kappa. Office: Robins Kaplan Miller & Ciresi 2800 LaSalle Pla 800 Lasalle Ave Ste 2800 Minneapolis MN 55402-2015 Office Phone: 612-349-8274.

SAFONOV, MICHAEL GEORGE, electrical engineering educator, consultant; b. Pasadena, Calif., Nov. 1, 1948; s. George Michael and Ruth Garnet (Ware) S.; m. Nancy Kelshaw Schorn, Aug. 31, 1968 (div. Oct. 1983); 1 child, Alexander; m. Janet Sunderland, Feb. 25, 1985; 1 child, Peter. BSEE, MSEE, MIT, 1971, EE, 1976, PhDEE, 1977. Electronic engr. Air Force Cambridge Rsch. Lab., Hanscom AFB, Mass., 1968-71; rsch. asst. MIT, Cambridge, 1975-77; prof. elec. engring. U. So. Calif., LA, 1977—, assoc. chmn. dept., 1989-93, vice chmn. engring. faculty coun., 2001—02, chmn. engring. faculty coun., 2003—04. Vis. scholar Cambridge (Eng.) U., 1983-84, Imperial Coll., London, 1987, Calif. Inst. Tech., Pasadena, 1990-91; cons. Honeywell Systems and Rsch. Ctr., Mpls., 1978-83, Space Systems div. TRW, Redondo Beach, Calif., 1984, Northrop Aircraft, Hawthorne, Calif., 1985-91, also numerous others. Author: Stability and Robustness of Multivariable Feedback Systems (hon. mention Phi Beta Kappa 1981); co-author: (book and software) Robust-Control Toolbox, 1988; assoc. editor IEEE Trans. on Automatic Control, 1985-87, Internat. Jour. Robust and Nonlinear Control, 1989-93, Sys. and Control Letters, 1995—. Awards com. chair Am. Automatic Control Coun., 1993-95. Lt. (j.g.) USNR, 1972-75. Rsch. grantee Air Force Office Sci. Rsch., 1978—, NSF, 1982-84. Fellow IEEE, IFAC; mem. AIAA (sr.), Common Cause. Republican. Office: U So Calif Dept EE Sys MC 2563 3740 McClintock Ave # 310 Los Angeles CA 90089-2563 Home Phone: 310-551-0517; Office Phone: 213-740-4455. Business E-Mail: msafonov@usc.edu. *Consider first only the very simplest problem--but strive for a representation of the simplest problem that generalizes.*

SAFRA, JOSEPH, bank executive; s. Joseph Safra; married; 4 children. Co-owner, chmn. Safra Group; chmn., CEO Banco Safra S.A., Sao Paulo, Brazil; chmn. Safra Nat. Bank NY. Mem. adv. bd. Wharton U. Pa.; chmn. bd. dirs. Banque Jacob Safra (Suisse) S.A. Contbr. New Ctr. Brazilian Studies Oxford U., Hazon Yeshaya Soup Kitchens. Named one of World's Richest People, Forbes Mag., 2000—. Bank holdings span the Caribbean, New York and Europe and include Safra Bank NY, Banque Safra Luxembourg and First Internat. Bank Israel. Office: Safra Nat Bank NY 546 5th Ave New York NY 10036

SAFRAN, STEPHEN PHILIP, educational program coordinator; b. NYC, Oct. 30, 1950; s. William and Lillian F. Safran; m. Joan M. Schulman, Feb. 13, 1974; children: Adam, Elisa. BA, SUNY, Binghamton, 1972; MEd, Rutgers U., 1975; PhD, U. Va., 1980. Social worker Jewish Assn. Svcs., Bklyn., 1973-74; tchr. Glen Kirk Sch., Morristown, N.J., 1975-76, Matawan (N.J.) Regional High Sch., 1976-77; project dir. James Madison U., Harrisonburg, Va., 1979-80; asst. prof. Ohio U., Athens, 1980-86; vis. scholar Schonell Spl. Edn. Rsch. Ctr., Queensland U., 1987-88; assoc. prof. Ohio U., Athens, 1986-90, prof., 1990—, coord. spl. edn. programs, 1985-86, 90-92. Cons. Acad. for Ednl. Devel., Wash., 1979-80. Mem. editl. bd. Jour. Ednl. and Psychol. Consultation, 1988-2004, Internat. Jour. Disability, Devel. and Edn., 1994—, Remedial and Spl. Edn., 2002—, Jour. Positive Behavior Interventions, 2006—; contbr. articles to profl. jours. Bd. dirs. Tri-County Mental Health and Counseling Svcs., Athens, 1984-86, Southeastern Ohio Spl. Edn. Regional Resource Ctr., 1990-92; rep. Ohio Higher Edn. Consortium Spl. Edn., 2000-05. Mem. Coun. Exceptional Children, Coun. for Children with Behavioral Disorders, Coun. Learning Disabilities. Office: Ohio U Coll Edn McCracken Hall Athens OH 45701

SAFREN, CHERYL, artist, educator; d. Abraham Rothberg and Marilyn Pearl Finchler; m. Martin Safren, Jan. 19, 1975; children: Aviva Einhorn, Nathaniel Isaac. BFA, Pratt Inst., 1973; MSc, Hofstra U., 1996. Cert. tchr. N.Y. Edn. Dept., 1997. Tchr. art Manhasset (N.Y.) Union Free Sch. Dist., 2005—09, North Shore Hebrew Acad., Great Neck, NY, 1996—2005, Great Neck Pub. Sch. Dist., NY, 2009—. Instr. Hofstra U., Hempstead, NY, 1998. One-woman shows include AAAS, Washington, Discovery Mus., Bridgeport, Conn., U. Ctr. Gallery, Adelphi U., Garden City, NY, Inst. Tech., Lawrence Inst. Tech., Southfield, Mich., Great Neck Art Ctr., NY, Represented in permanent collections City of Aurora, Colo., City of Balatonfored, Hungary, Teleflex Internat., Thyssen Industries, Germany, U. Ga., Athens, U. Maine, Orono, Wyeth Pharms., Fla. State U., Talahassee, U. Montana, Missoula, Williamsburg Art & Hist. Ctr., Brooklyn. Mem.: Am. Chem. Soc., LI Arts Coun. Freeport (assoc.), NY State Art Tchrs. Assn. (assoc.), Art and Sci. Collaborations, Inc. (assoc.), NY Artists Equity (assoc.). Achievements include development of chemistry on metals art techniques and processes.

SAFRENO, CASEY, investment banker; b. 1959; m. Lisa Vinella. Mng. dir., investment banking group, co-head, healthcare investment banking Merrill Lynch & Co. Inc., San Francisco; mng. dir., global head, healthcare Lehman Brothers, San Francisco, 2003—. Recipient Rainmaker Prize, Dealmaker mag., 2006; named Personality of Yr., Corp. Fin. Week, 2004. Office: Lehman Brothers--30th fl 555 California St San Francisco CA 94104 Office Phone: 415-263-3300.

SAFT, STUART MARK, lawyer; b. NYC, Feb. 17, 1947; s. Stanley and Dorothy (Ligerman) S.; m. Stephanie C. Optekman, June 6, 1970; children: Bradley S., Gordon D. BA, Hofstra U., 1968; JD, Columbia U., 1971. Bar: N.Y. 1972, Fla. 1975, U.S. Dist. Ct. (so. dist.) N.Y. 1975, U.S. Supreme Ct. 1990. Ptnr. Dewey & LeBoeuf LLP, NYC. Chmn. bd. dirs. Coun. of NY Coops., NYC, 1981-; vice chmn. Nat. Coop. Bank; chmn. NYC Workforce Investment Bd.; chmn. bd. dirs., CEO Pvt. Industry Coun. NYC, 1994-2000. Author: Commercial Real Estate Forms, 3 vols., 1987, Commercial Real Estate Transactions, 1989, Commercial Real Estate Workouts, 1991, Real Estate Development: Strategies for a Changing Market, 1990, Commercial Real Estate Leasing, 1992, Real Estate Investor's Survival Guide, 1992, Commercial Real Estate Financing, 1993, Commercial Real Estate Forms, 3d edit., 11 vols., 2001, Commercial Real Estate Transactions, 2d edit., 1995, 3d edit., 2004, Commercial Real Estate Workouts, 2d edit., 1996, 2 vols., 2004, 3d edit. 2 vols., 2008; contbg. editor: The Real Estate Finance Jour., 1989—; contbr. articles to profl. jours. Capt USAR, 1968—76. Mem. ABA, Am. Coll. Real Estate Lawyers, N.Y. Bar Assn., Fla. Bar Assn. Office: Dewey LeBoeuf LLP 125 W 55th St New York NY 10019 Office Phone: 212-424-4285. Business E-Mail: ssaft@dl.com.

SAFYER, STEVEN MICHAEL, hospital administrator; b. NYC, Feb. 16, 1949; m. Pamela Marcus; 2 children. MD, Albert Einstein Coll. of Med., 1982. Cert. internal medicine. Intern Montefiore Med. Ctr., Bronx, NY, 1978—82, resident, 1983—85, v.p. med. affairs, 1997, sr. v.p., chief med. officer, 1998—2008, pres., CEO, 2008—; assoc. prof., dept. medicine Albert Einstein Coll. Medicine, 1987—, assoc. prof., dept. epidemiology & population health, 1987—. Office: Montefiore Med Ctr MMC Centennial Bldg 111 E 210 St 4th Fl Bronx NY 10467*

SAG, IVAN A., linguist, educator; PhD, MIT, 1976; prof Honoris Causa (hon.), Univ. Bucharest, 2001. V.p. Red White and Blues Prodns., Inc, Rochester, NY, 1969—71; spl. cons., Linguistic Inst. Univ. Mass., 1974; asst. prof., linguistics Univ. Pa., 1977—79, Stanford Univ., 1979—84, assoc. prof., 1984—88, prof., linguistics, symbolic sys., 1986—; affiliated faculty Stanford Symbolic Sys. Program, 1986—. Recipient Victoria Fromkin Prize, for disting. contributions to the field of linguistics, Linguistic Soc. Am., 2005; grantee Andrew Mellon Found. Fellowship, 1978—79. Fellow: Am. Acad. Arts & Scis. Office: Dept Linguistics Stanford Univ Stanford CA 94305 Home Phone: 650-854-6453. Business E-Mail: sag@csli.stanford.edu.

SAGAFI-NEJAD, TAGI, business educator; b. Bainabaj, Khorasan, Iran, Dec. 19, 1941; arrived in U.S., 1968; m. Nancy Gail Black Nov. 22, 1967; children: Jahan C. R., David J. H. MA, U. Pa., 1971, PhD, 1979. Lectr. U. Pa., Phila., 1974—76; asst. prof. U. Wash., Seattle, 1976—80, U. Tex., Austin, 1980—84; assoc. prof. Loyola Coll., Balt., 1984—93, prof., 1993—2002, dept. chair, 1995—96, prof. emeritus, 2002—; Keating-Crawford chair in internat. bus. Stillman Sch. Bus., Seton Hall U., 2002—03; Killam Disting. prof., dir. PhD program in internat. bus. Tex. A&M Internat. U., 2003—08, dir., Tex. Ctr., Border Entreprise & Econ. Devel., 2008—09, dir., Ctr. Study Western Hemisphere Trade, 2009—, dir., East Trade Inst., 2009—. Cons. UN Indsl. Devel. Orgn., 1982—84, U.S. Congress, 1983—84, UN Ctr. on Transnat. Corp., 1993—; lectr., spkr. in field; editor Internat. Trade Jour., 2007—. Author: Technology Transfer Trilogy, 1980, 1981; editl. bd. Transnational Corp., 1993— Recipient Best Paper award Acad. of Mgmt., 1994, Pacific Asia Mgmt. Inst., U. Hawaii, 1988. Mem. Acad. of Internat. Bus. (chair N.E. chpt. 1988-93), Acad. Mgmt., Acad. Mgmt. Iranian Scholars Assn. (founder, v.p. 1989-90), Mid. East Studies Assn., Mid. East Inst. Democrat. Avocations: gardening, golf, painting, walking. Office: Tex A&M Internat U 5201 University Blvd Laredo TX 78041-1900 Office Phone: 956-326-2547. Office Fax: 956-326-2544. Business E-Mail: tagi.sagafi@tamiv.edu.

SAGALOWSKY, ARTHUR I., urologist, educator; b. Indpls., Aug. 19, 1948; s. Meyer and Goldie Sagalowsky; m. Hanne Albaek, June 11, 1972; children: Julie, Jordan. BA, Ind. U., 1970; MD, Ind. U. Med. Ctr., 1973. Intern, resident Ind. U. Med. Ctr., Indpls., 1973—75, resident, 1975—78; clin. asst. prof. surgery and urology U. Tex. Southwestern Med. Ctr., Dallas, 1978—80, asst. prof. urology, 1980—84, assoc. prof. urology and surgery, 1984—89, prof. urology and surgery, 1989—. Surg. dir. renal transplantation U. Tex. Southwestern Med. Ctr., 1983—95, chief urologic oncology, dept. urology, 1995—, co-investigator NIH O'Brien Ctr. Urologic Rsch., 1993—2000, prin. investigator urology, 2000—, prin. investigator urology NIH Cancer Inst. Urologic Cancer Outreach Program, 1989—98. Fellow, Ind. U. Med. Ctr., Krannert Inst. Cardiology, 1967—69, U. Tex. Southwestern Med. Ctr., 1978—80. Avocations: piano, golf, fly fishing. Home: 4450 Cedarbrush Dallas TX 75346 Office: U Tex Southwestern Med Ctr Dept Urology 5323 Harry Hines Blvd Dallas TX 75390-9110 Office Phone: 214-648-3976. Business E-Mail: arthur.sagalowsky@utsouthwestern.edu.

SAGAN, M. J., architectural firm executive; m. Craig L. Haft; children: Nicholas, Claire, Owen. BA in Architecture, Pa. State U., 1982. Lic. NY, NJ, Conn., cert. NCARB. Assoc., staff designer George F. Henschel, Jr., AIA, 1982—83; assoc./project arch. Becker, Becker & Lamont, Inc., New Canaan, Conn., 1983—84; assoc. Shope Reno Wharton Assoc., Greenwich, Conn., 1984—88; sr. assoc. Anderson/Schwartz Arch., NYC, 1988—96; v.p. Anderson Architecture, NYC, 1996—2006; pres. MJ Sagan Architecture, 2006—. Exhibitions include Negotiating Domesticity/ The Greenwich Arts Coun., 2003, Princeton Pub. Libr., 2003. Recipient EDRA/Places Design award, 2003, Bldg. Team Project of the Yr.- Grand award, 2003, Good Design is Good Bus. award, 2002, Project award, Hudson River Pk., 2002, Gold award, 1994, Wallpaper Mag. Design award, 2004, AIA NJ, 2005, numerous other awards, AIA and others, Honor award, NJ AIA, 2008, Merit award, Columbus AIA, 2008. Several selected publications from 1986-2002 in mag. such as: Arch. Record, House & Garden, The New York Times, Interior Design, Vogue, Diseno Interior 70, House Beautiful, Abitare, and Record Interiors. Business E-Mail: info@mjsaganarchitecture.com.

SAGAN, PAUL, information technology executive; b. 1959; Grad., Medill Sch. Journalism, Northwestern U. News writer WCBS-TV, NYC, 1981—87, news dir., 1987—91; sr. v.p. Time Warner Cable, NYC, 1991—93; mng. editor News on Demand Time Inc., NYC, 1993—95, pres. and editor new media, 1995—97; sr. advisor World Econ. Forum, Geneva, 1997—98; with Akamai Technologies, Inc., Cambridge, Mass., 1998—, pres., 1999—, CEO, 2005—. Bd. dirs. EMC Corp., Mass. Trustee Northwestern U., co-chmn. Medill Sch. Journalism bd. advisors; mem. dean's coun. Kennedy Sch. Govt., Harvard U.; mem. presdl. adv. coun. Berklee Coll. Music, Boston; advisor MATCH charter pub. HS, Boston. Named Pub. Co. CEO of Yr., Mass. Networks Comm. Coun., 2007; named a Global Leader of Tomorrow, World Econ. Forum, 1996. Fellow: Am. Acad. Arts and Sciences. Achievements include designing and launching NY 1 News; co-founder Roadrunner and Pathfinder. Office: Akamai Technologies Inc 8 Cambridge Ctr Cambridge MA 02142

SAGAN, SCOTT, political science professor; b. Dearborn, Mich., Mar. 5, 1955; m. Sujitpan Bao Lamsam; children: Benjamin, Charlotte, Samuel. BA with high honors, Oberlin Coll., 1977; PhD, Harvard U., 1983. Spl. asst. to dir. and staff officer, nuclear/chem. divsn. Nuclear and Chem. Divsn., Orgn. Joint Chiefs of Staff, 1984—85, cons., strategic nuclear policy br., 1985—86; lectr., dept. govt. Harvard U., 1986—87; asst. prof. polit. sci. Stanford U., 1987—95, assoc. prof. polit. sci., 1995—2001, chmn. internat. rels. prog., 1995—97, vice-chmn., dept. polit. sci., 1996—99, prof. polit. sci., 2001—, co-dir. Ctr. Internat. Security and Cooperation; sr. fellow Freeman Spogli Inst. Internat. Studies, Stanford U. Cons. RAND Corp., 1987—91, Office of the Sec. of Def., 1987—91, Nat. Intelligence Coun., 2006—; adv. group to the Joint Chiefs of Staff on the Future of US-Soviet Military Rels., 1989—90; cons. Los Alamos Nat. Lab., 1989—95; adv. bd., Nuclear Weapons History proj. Nat. Security Archives, Washington, 1995—2000; steering com., Eliminating Weapons of Mass Destruction proj. Henry L. Stimson Ctr., Washington, 1994—97; disting. adv. panel for non-proliferation and arms control Sandia Nat. Lab., 2000—; steering com. Am. Assembly, 2006—; expert advisor Congl. Commn. on the Strategic Posture of the US, 2008—. Co-author: Living with Nuclear Weapons, 1983; co-author: (with Kenneth N. Waltz) The Spread of Nuclear Weapons: A Debate, 1995, The Spread of Nuclear Weapons: A Debate Renewed, 2002; author: Moving Targets: Nuclear Strategy and National Security, 1989, The Limits of Safety: Organizations, Accidents and Nuclear Weapons, 1993 (Best Book award, Am. Polit. Sci. Assn., 1994); editor: Civil Military Relations and Nuclear Weapons, 1994; co-editor: Planning the Unthinkable: How New Powers Will Use Nuclear, Chemical and Biological Weapons, 2000. Recipient Laurance and Naomi Hoagland prize, Stanford U., 1996, Dean's award, 1998—99, Deborah Misty Gerner Innovative Tchg. award, Internat. Studies Assn., 2008. Fellow: Am. Acad. Arts and Sciences; mem.: AAAS (com. sci. and internat. security 1995—96, com. internat. security studies 2007—, co-chair, initiative on the nuclear future 2007—), Am. Polit. Sci. Assn., Coun. Fgn. Rels. (CAC subcommittee on analysis and policy formulation 2003—05), Mayo Smith Soc., Internat. Inst. Strategic Studies, Pacific Coun. Internat. Policy. Office: Ctr Internat Security and Cooperation Encina Hall Stanford U Stanford CA 94305-6165 Office Phone: 650-725-2715. E-mail: ssagan@stanford.edu.

SAGARDÍA, ANTONIO (ANTONIO MIGUEL SAGARDÍA DE JESUS), attorney general; Grad., U. PR. Pub. prosecutor Regions of San Juan, Carolina and Caguas, PR, 1982—90; criminal trial atty. PR; atty. gen. PR, San Juan, 2009—. Mem. New Progressive Party of PR. Office: Office of Atty Gen GPO Box 902192 San Juan PR 00902-0192 Office Phone: 787-721-2900.*

SAGAWA, YONEO, horticulturist, educator; b. Olaa, Hawaii, Oct. 11, 1926; s. Chikatada and Mume (Kuno) S.; m. Masayo Yamamoto, May 24, 1962 (dec. Apr. 1988); children: Penelope Toshiko, Irene Teruko. AB, Washington U., St. Louis, 1950, MA, 1952; PhD, U. Conn., Storrs, 1956. Postdoctoral rsch. assoc. biology Brookhaven Nat. Lab., Upton, NY, 1955—57, guest in biology, 1958; asst. prof., then assoc. prof. U. Fla., 1957—64; dir. undergrad. sci. ednl. rsch. participation program NSF, 1964; cons. biosatellite project NASA, 1966—67; prof. horticulture U. Hawaii, 1964—; dir. Lyon Arboretum, 1967—91; assoc. dir. Hawaiian Sci. Fair, 1966—67, dir., 1967—68; rsch. assoc. in biology U. Calif., Berkeley, 1970—71; rsch. assoc. Bot. Rsch. Inst. of Tex., 1993—, Hawaii Tropical Bot. Garden, 1995—; external assessor U. Pertanian, Malaysia, 1994—; rsch. affiliate Bishop Mus., Honolulu, 2007—. Mem. Internat. Orchid Commn. on Classification, Nomenclature and Registration; fellow Inst. voor Toepassing van Atoomenergie in de Landbouw, U. Agr., Wageningen, The Netherlands, 1979-80; mem. sci. adv. bd. Nat. Tropical Bot. Garden, Kauai, Hawaii; councilor Las Cruces Bot. Garden, Costa Rica; cons. FAO, Singapore, 1971, USAID-Agribus. Assistance Program, Vols. in Overseas Coop. Assistance, UN Devel. Program-UN Internat. Short Term Adv. Resources; dir. Hawaii Tropical Bot. Garden; hon. scientist Rural Devel. Adminstrn., Republic of Korea, 1998—; cons. Fiji-N.Z. Bus. Coun., 1996, 97, 98, 99, 2000; cons. IRETA, Samoa, 1997, 98, 2003, 06, 08; cons. Nat. Hort. Rsch. Inst., Suwon, Republic of Korea, 1998, 2000, UN FAO, 2007-09. Editor: Hawaii Orchid Jour., 1972-99, Pacific Orchid Soc. Bull., 1966-71; mem. editl. bd. Allertonia, 1976; mem. editl. adv. bd. Jour. Orchid Soc. India, 2002—; contbr. numerous articles to profl. jours. Trustee Friends of Honolulu Bot. Gardens, 1973-99. Recipient Disting. Svc. award South Fla. Orchid Soc., 1968, Grand prize for Poster, 1st Nagoya Internat. Orchid Show, 1990, Cert. of Achievement Garden Club Am., 1995, Digest Doer's Profile, 2000, Gold award Hawaii Orchid Growers Assn., 1996; grantee Am. Orchid Soc., Atomic Energy Commn., NIH, HEW, Inst. Mus. Svcs., Stanley Smith Hort. Trust, Honolulu Orchid Soc. Fellow Am. Orchid Soc. (hon. life, Achievement Gold medal 1999); mem. AAAS, Internat. Assn. Hort. Sci., Am. Assn. Hort. Sci., Am. Inst. for Biol. Scis., Bot. Soc. Am., Hawn Bot. Soc. (past v.p.), Internat. Assn. Plant Tissue Culture, Internat. Palm Soc., Am. Anthurium Soc. (hon. life), Pacific Orchid Soc. (trustee 1994), Kaimuki Orchid Soc. (hon. life), Orchid Growers Hawaii (hon. life), Honolulu Orchid Soc. (hon., life), Lyon Arboretum Assn. (trustee 1974-91), Garden Club Honolulu (hon., life), Aloha Bonsai Club, Sigma Xi, Gamma Sigma Delta, Phi Kappa Phi (past pres., v.p., councillor U. Hawaii chpt.). Democrat. Office: U Hawaii TPSS St John Rm 102 3190 Maile Way Honolulu HI 96822-2279 Fax: 808-956-3894. Business E-Mail: yoneo@hawaii.edu.

SAGE, ANDREW PATRICK, systems engineering and management educator; b. Charleston, SC, Aug. 27, 1933; s. Andrew Patrick and Pearl Louise (Britt) S.; m. LaVerne Galhouse, Mar. 3, 1962; children: Theresa Annette, Karen Margaret, Philip Andrew. BS in Elec. Engring, The Citadel, Charleston, SC, 1955; SM, MIT, Cambridge, Mass., 1956; PhD, Purdue U., Lafayette, 1960; DEng (hon.), U. Waterloo, Can., 1987, Dalhousie U., Halifax, Nova Scotia, Can., 1997. Registered profl. engr., Tex. Instr. elec. engring. Purdue U., 1956-60; assoc. prof. U. Ariz., 1960-63; mem. tech. staff Aerospace Corp., Los Angeles, 1963-64; prof. elec. engring. and nuclear engring. scis. U. Fla., 1964-67; prof., dir. Info. and Control Scis. Center, So. Methodist U., Dallas, 1967-74; head elec. engring. dept. So. Meth. U., 1973-74; Quarles prof. engring. sci. and systems U. Va., Charlottesville, 1974-84, chmn. dept. chem. engring., 1974-75, chmn. dept. engring. sci. and systems, 1977-84, assoc. dean, 1974-80; First Am. Bank prof. info. tech. George Mason U., Fairfax, Va., 1984—, assoc. v.p. for acad. affairs, 1984-85, dean Sch. Info. Tech. and Engring., 1985-96, univ. prof., founding dean emeritus, 1996—. Cons. Martin Marietta, Collins Radio, Atlantic Richfield, Tex. Instruments, LTV Aerospace, Battelle Meml. Inst., TRW Sys., NSF, Inst. Def. Analyses, Planning Rsch. Corp., MITRE, Engring. Rsch. Assocs., Software Productivity Consortium; gen. chmn. Internat. Conf. on Sys., Man and Cybernetics, 1974, 87; mem. spl. program panel on sys. sci. NATO, 1981-82; trustee, cons. Ctr. Naval Analysis, 1990-94. Author: Optimum Systems Control, 1968, 2d edit., 1977, Estimation Theory with Applications to Communications and Control, 1971, System Identification, 1971, An Introduction to Probability and Stochastic Processes, 1973, Methodology for Large Scale Systems, 1977, Systems Engineering: Methodology and Applications, 1977, Linear Systems Control, 1978, Economic Systems Analysis, 1983, System Design for Human Interaction, 1987, Information Processing in Systems and Organizations, 1990, Introduction to Computer Systems Analysis, Design, and Applications, 1989, Software Systems Engineering, 1990, Decision Support Systems Engineering, 1991, Systems Engineering, 1992, Systems Management for Information Technology and Software Engineering, 1995, Handbook of Systems Engineering and Management, 1999, 2nd edit., 2009, Introduction to Systems Engineering, 2000; assoc. editor IEEE Transactions on Systems Sci. and Cybernetics, 1968-72; editor: IEEE Transactions on Systems, Man and Cybernetics, 1972-98; assoc. editor: Automatica, 1968-81; editor, 1981-96; mem. editl. bd. Systems Engrng, 1968-72, IEEE Spectrum, 1972-73, Computers and Elec. Engrng., 1972, Jour. Interdisciplinary Modeling and Simulation, 1976-80, Internat. Jour. Intelligent Sys., 1986—, Orgn. Sci., 1994-2002; editor Elsevier North Holland textbook series in sys. sci. and engring., 1970-88, John Wiley textbook series on sys. engrng. and mgmt., 1989—; co-editor-in-chief Jour. Large Scale Sys.: Theory and Applications, 1978-88, Info. and Decision Technologies, 1988-94, Info. and Sys. Engrng., 1995-96; editor in chief Sys. Engrng., 1998—; co-editor in chief Info., Knowledge and Sys. Mgmt., 1999—; contbr. articles to profl. jours. Recipient Norbert Wiener award, 1980, Joseph G. Wohl career award, 1991, Superior Pub. Svc. award Sec. of the Navy, 1994; Case Centennial scholar, 1980, Award Washington Soc. of Engrs., 1996. Fellow: AAAS (chmn. sect. M 1990), IEEE (life M. Barry Carlton award 1970, Centennial medal 1984, Outstanding Contbn. award 1986, Donald G. Fink prize 1994, Simon Ramo medal 2000), Internat. Coun. on Sys. Engrng. (Pioneer award 2002); mem.: NAE, Inst. for Ops. Rsch. and Mgmt. Sci., Washington Soc. Engrs. (award 1996), Am. Soc. Engrng. Edn. (Frederick Emmonds Terman award 1970, Centennial cert. for exceptional contbn. 1993), Internat. Fedn. Automatic Control (Outstanding Svc. award), IEEE Sys./Man and Cybernetics Soc. (pres. 1984—85), Tau Beta Pi, Eta Kappa Nu (eminent mem. award 2002), Sigma Xi. Home: 8011 Woodland Hills Ln Fairfax VA 22039-2433 Office: George Mason U Sch Info Tech Fairfax VA 22030-4444 Office Phone: 703-993-1506. Business E-Mail: asage@gmu.edu.

SAGE-GAVIN, EVA MARIE, retail executive; b. Boston, Sept. 26, 1958; d. Ross Francis and Theresa Veronica (Bufalo) S.; m. Dennis Gavin. BS in Indsl. and Labor Rels., Cornell U., Ithaca, NY, 1980. Affirmative action pers. specialist Xerox Corp., Washington, 1980-81, compensation analyst Rochester, NY, 1981-82, sales recruiter Boston, 1982, employment mgr., 1983, systems mktg. rep., 1983-85, pers. mgr. LA, 1985—86, human resources mgr. Irvine, Calif., 1986; dir. human resources PepsiCo, 1991, v.p. corp. human resources Taco Bell; sr. v.p. human resources Disney Consumer Products, 1997—2000, Sun Microsystems, Inc., 2000—03; exec. v.p. human resources and corp. comm. Gap Inc., 2003—. Mem. career adv. bd. Emmanuel Coll., Boston, 1983-85. Named one of Top 25 Most Powerful Women in HR, HR Exec. mag., 2005. Mem. Am. Soc. Pers. Adminstrn., Women in Mgmt., Xerox Women's Network (edn. com. 1988), Kappa Kappa Gamma. Democrat. Roman Catholic. Avocations: skiing, travel, boating, sailing, aerobics. Office: Gap Inc 2 Folsom St San Francisco CA 94105 Office Phone: 650-952-4400. Office Fax: 415-427-2553.

SAGEHORN, DAVID M., transportation company executive; BS in Accounting, U. Wis., Platterville; MBA, Marquette U. CPA. Corp. fin. CNH Global (formerly Case Corp.); sr. mgr. mergers and acquisitions Oshkosh Corp., Wis., 2000, dir. bus. devel. Wis., 2001—02, v.p. fin. Wis., 2002, v.p., treas. Wis., 2005—07, exec. v.p., CFO Wis., 2007—. Office: Oshkosh Corp PO Box 2566 Oshkosh WI 54903-2566 Office Phone: 920-235-9150.

SAGELY, MATT (CHRISTOPHER MATTHEW SAGELY), legislative staff member; b. June 17, 1971; m. Anna Sample, Feb. 19, 2000; 1 child. BA in Pub. Adminstrn., Henderson State U., 1995; MBA, Marymount U., 2000. Comm. specialist Am. Trucking Assn.; with Booz Allen Hamilton; sr. legis. asst. for Rep. Saxby Chambliss, US House of Reps.; legis. dir. for Rep. John Boozman, 2002, dep. chief of staff, 2002—07, chief of staff, 2007—. Office: Office of Congressman John Boozman 1519 Longworth House Office Bldg Washington DC 20515 Office Phone: 202-225-4301. Office Fax: 202-225-5713. E-mail: matt.sagely@mail.house.gov.*

SAGER, DONALD JACK, librarian, consultant, retired publishing executive; b. Milw., Mar. 3, 1938; s. Alfred Herman and Sophia (Sagan) Sager; m. Sarah Ann Long, May 23, 1987; children: Geoffrey, Andrew. BS, U. Wis., Milw., 1963; MSLS, U. Wis., 1964. Sr. documentalist AC Electronics divsn. GM, Milw., 1958-63; teaching asst. U. Wis., Madison, 1963-64; dir. Kingston (N.Y.) Pub. Libr., 1964-66, Elyria (Ohio) Pub. Libr., 1966-71, Mobile Pub. Libr., 1971-75, Pub. Libr. Columbus and Franklin County, Ohio, 1975-78; commr. Chgo. Pub. Libr., 1978-81; dir. Elmhurst Pub. Libr., Ill., 1982-83, Milw. Pub. Libr., 1983-91; pub. Highsmith Press, Ft. Atkinson, Wis., 1991-2000; pres. Gossage Sager Assocs. LLC, NYC, 2000—, CEO, 2008. Secy Online Computer Library Ctr, 1977—78, disting vis scholar, 1982; chmn investment comt PLA Pub Library, 1985—89, chmn mus comt, 1989—91, mem hist comt, 1993—95, chmn PLA nat conf comt, 1986—88; bd dirs Coun Wis Libraries, 1982—91, Urban Libraries Coun, 1985—93, secy, 1991—93; adj faculty Univ Wis, Milwaukee, 1984—91; consult in field. Author: Reference: A Programmed Instruction, 1970, Binders, Books and Budgets, 1971, Participatory Management, 1981, The American Public Library, 1982, Public Library Administrators Planning Guide to Automation, 1983, Managing the Public Library, 1984, Small Libraries, 1992, 3d rev. edit., 2000; co-editor: Urban Library Management Trends, 1989; contbg. editor: Public Libraries, 1990—2000; contbr. articles to profl. jours. Pres Milwaukee Civic Alliance, 1990—91; chmn Milwaukee United Way Campaign, 1984; pres Milwaukee Westown Asn, 1987—90; treas. Congl. Ch. Deerfield, Ill., 2002—05, bd. dirs., 2005—08; bd dirs Goethe House, 1985—91. With AUS, 1956—58. Mem.: ALA (councilor-at-large 1995—2003, policy monitoring comt, awards comt, chmn core values task force, Joseph Lippincott award 2005), Library Admin Asn Wis (chmn 1987—88), Wis Library Asn Found (chmn 1986—88), Wis Library Asn, Chicago Book Clin, Ill Library Asn, Pub Library Asn (pres 1982—83, bd dirs, vpres, pres-elect), Exchange Club Milwaukee (pres 1988—89). Office Phone: 312-961-5536. Business E-Mail: sagerdon@gmail.com.

SAGER, KELLI L., lawyer; b. 1960; Attended, U. Southern Calif., 1977—81; BA in Polit. Sci. and Journalism, West Ga. Coll., 1981; JD, U. Utah Sch. Law, 1985. Bar: Calf. 1985. Adj. prof. U. Southern Calif. Law Sch., 2002; ptnr. Davis Wright Tremaine LLP, LA. Mem. adv. com. Donald W. Reynolds Nat. Ctr. for Courts and Media, Nat. Jud. Coll., 2000—; mem. internat. adv. bd. Nat. Inst. Entertainment and Media Law, Southwestern U. Law, 2001—; mem. bd. dirs. Pub. Counsel, 2001—; mem. atty. com. Nat. Ctr. for State Courts, 2002—; bd. mem. LA Copyright Soc., 2002—, treas., 2005—. Bd. dirs. LA Youth News, 1995—2001. Recipient ACLU First Amendment award, 1996, adv. award, Calif. First Amendment Coalition, 1996, Freedom of Info. award, Soc. Prof. Journalists, 1996, First Amendment award, LA Youth/LA Times, 1998; named one of 45 Lawyers Under 45, Am. Lawyer mag., 1995, 40 Professionals Under 40, LA Bus. Jour., 1996, 50 Top Lawyers in LA, 1997, Lawyers of Yr., Calif. Lawyer mag., 1997, The 100 Most Influential Lawyers in Calif., LA Daily Jour., 1998—99, 2001—04, Top 50 Women Litigators in Country, Nat. Law Jour., 2001, 500 Leading Lawyers in Am., Lawdragon, 2005, 500 Leading Litigators in Am., 2006, America's Leading Bus. Lawyers, Chambers USA, 2005—06, Top 75 Women Litigators in Calif., Daily Jour., 2005—07, Southern Calif. Super Lawyers, 2007, The 50 Most Influential Women Lawyers in Am., Nat. Law Jour., 2007, 100 Power Lawyers, Hollywood Reporter, 2007; named to Best Lawyers in Am., 1997—99, 2000, 2003, 2005—07. Mem.: ABA (western divsn. chair Forum on Comm. Law 2002—, co-chair litig. sect., 1st amendment com. 2005—), Order of the Coif. Office: Davis Wright Tremaine LLP Ste 2400 865 S Figueroa St Los Angeles CA 90017-2566 Office Phone: 213-633-6800. Office Fax: 213-633-6899. Business E-Mail: kellisager@dwt.com.*

SAGER, LAWRENCE GENE, dean, law educator; b. 1941; AB, Pomona Coll., 1963; LLB magna cum laude, Columbia Coll., 1966. Bar: Calif. 1967. Asst. prof. U. Calif., LA, 1966—68, acting prof., 1968—71; assoc. prof NYU, NY, 1972—74, prof., 1974—95; Robert B. McKay prof. law, 1995—2002; Alice Jane Drysdale Sheffield Regents Chair in Law U. Tex., Austin, 2002—, dean, 2006—; John Jeffers rsch. chair law U. Texas, Austin. Vis. prof. law and social planning Woodrow Wilson Sch., Princeton, 1974-76; vis. prof. U. Mich., Harvard U., spring 1981, Boston U., 1986-89. Recipient Disting. Alumni Award, Pomona Coll. Mem. N.Y. CLU. Office: University of Texas School of Law 727 E Dean Keeton Street Austin TX 78705 Business E-Mail: lsager@law.utexas.edu.*

SAGER, MARGARET E.W., lawyer; b. Nashville, Nov. 16, 1960; BA summa cum laude, U. Richmond, 1982; JD, U. Va., 1985. Bar: Pa. 1985. Assoc. trust and estate dept. Duane, Morris & Heckscher, 1985—94; shareholder Heckscher, Teillon, Terrill & Sager, P.C., West Conshohocken, Pa. Named one of Top 100 Attys., Worth mag., 2005, 2006, 2009. Fellow: Am. Coll. Trust and Estate Counsel; mem.: ABA, Pa. Bar Assn., Montgomery County Bar Assn., Phila. Bar Assn. (chair probate and trust law sect. 2000, chair rules and practice com. 1992—96), Phi Beta Kappa. Office: Heckscher Teillon Terrill & Sager Ste 300 100 Four Falls West Conshohocken PA 19428-2900 also: Centre Sq E 12th Fl 1500 Market St Philadelphia PA 19102 Office Phone: 610-940-4171. Office Fax: 610-940-6042. E-mail: mewsager@htts.com.

SAGER, PHILIP TRAVIS, pharmaceutical executive, cardiologist, researcher; b. NYC, Jan. 23, 1956; s. Clifford Julius and Ruth (Levy) Sager; m. Linda Sager. BS in Chemistry and Biology, MIT, 1977; MD, Yale U., 1982. Diplomate Am. Bd. Internal Medicine, Am. Bd. Cardiology, Am. Bd. Cardiac Electrophysiology. Resident, fellow in cardiology and cardiac electrophysiology Yale U., New Haven, 1982—88; asst. prof. medicine Sch. Medicine, U. So. Calif., LA, 1988-90, asst. dir. electrophysiology, 1988-90, dir. Pacemaker Ctr., 1988-90; asst. prof. medicine Sch. Medicine, UCLA, 1990-96, assoc. tenured prof. medicine, 1996—2001; dir. cardiac electrophysiology UCLA/West LA VA Med. Ctr., 1990—2001; dir. cardiac rsch. Schering-Plough Rsch. Inst., 2001—04; clin. prof. medicine UMDNJ Med. Sch., 2002—07; sr. dir., U.S. lead physician Astrazeneca Inc., Wilmington, Del., 2004—, med. sci. sr. dir., 2006—08, exec. dir., CV rsch., 2006—08, global QT strategy leader, 2006—08; chief med. officer CardioDX, 2008—. Mem. cardiology adv. com. VA, Washington, 1990-94; cons. electrophysiology ACGME, Chgo., 1995-01; vis. prof. Kern Med. Ctr., Bakersfield, Calif., 1991, 94, U. Iowa Sch. Medicine, 1994, Northwestern U. Sch. Medicine, 1994, Yale U. Sch. Medicine, 1995, U. Calif., San Francisco, 1996; PhRMA topic leader, ICH E14 Expert Working Group 2002-05; PhRMA lead ICH E14 Implementation Group, 2005-; co-chair sci. com., mem. exec. com. FDA CV Safety Rsch. Consortium, 2005-06; chair Internat. DIA-FDA-HRS QT/CV Safety Conf., 2006-08, FDA PhRMA Evidentiary Standards Biomarkers, 2007—; cons. pharm. cos.; lectr. in field. Contbr. chpts. to books, numerous articles to profl. jours.; reviewer sci. jours. and sci. mags. Recipient many rsch. grants, including Am. Heart Assn., 1996. Fellow ACP, Am. Heart Assn., Am. Coll. Cardiology, Heart Rhythm Soc.; mem. Am. Fedn. Clin. Rsch., Nat. Assn. Pacing and Electrophysiology (program dirs. com. 1992-01, govt. com. 1994-01, co-chair program dirs. com. 1997-01), Phi Beta Kappa, Alpha Omega Alpha. Avocations: travel, bicycling, scuba diving, reading, movies. Office: CardioDX Inc 2500 Faber Pl Palo Alto CA 94303 Office Phone: 650-475-2744. Personal E-mail: psager@alum.mit.edu. Business E-Mail: psager@cardiodx.com.

SAGER, THOMAS LAUCK, chemical company executive, lawyer; b. Winchester, Mass., May 25, 1950; JD, Wake Forest U., 1976. Atty. labor and securities group DuPont Co., Wilmington, Del., 1976—94, assoc. gen. counsel, 1994—98, chief litig. counsel, 1998—99, v.p., asst. gen. counsel, 1999—2008, sr. v.p., gen. counsel, 2008—. Bd. mem. CPR Internat. Inst. for Conflict Prevention and Resolution, Del. Law Related Edn. Ctr., Atlantic Legal Found.; disting. lectr. Corp. Counsel Tech. Inst., 2005. Editor-in-chief The DuPont Legal Model...A New Era, 1996, The DuPont Legal Model...A New Era, 1997, Leaps and Bounds: Moving Ahead with the DuPont Legal Model; contbr. articles to profl. jours. Bd. overseers Widener U. Sch. Law; mem. law bd. visitors Wake Forest U. Sch. Law; bd. trustees NALP Found. Law Career Rsch. and Edn. Recipient Brundage Award, Wallace Law Registry, 1998, Recognition of Excellence, Am. Corp. Counsel Assn. Mem.: Minority Corp. Counsel Assn. (chmn.). Office: DuPont Co 1007 Market St Wilmington DE 19898*

SAGERHOLM, JAMES ALVIN, retired naval officer; b. Uniontown, Pa., Dec. 23, 1927; s. Frithiof Norris and Margaret Blocher S.; m. Margaret Ann Herrlich, June 7, 1952; children: Lisa Marie, Ann Denise, Jeannine Louise, Mark Christian BS, US Naval Acad., 2008; MA, Norwich U., 2009. Commd. ensign U.S. Navy, 1952, advanced through grades to vice admiral, 1983, exec. officer USS Sproston, 1961—63, navigator USS Seadragon, 1965, exec. officer blue crew USS Mariano G. Vallejo, 1966-67, comdg. officer gold crew USS Kamehameha, 1968-71, head gen. purpose warfare forces group Office of Chief Naval Ops., 1971, dep. exec. dir. Chief Naval Ops. Exec. Panel, 1972, exec. sec. Chief Naval Ops. Exec. Bd., 1973, comdr. Naval Intelligence Support Ctr. Washington, 1974-75, dep. dir. naval intelligence Chief Naval Ops., 1975-76, comdr. South Atlantic Force, U.S. Atlantic Fleet, 1976-78, dir. Office of Program Appraisal, Office of Sec. Navy, 1978-81, chief naval edn. and tng. Pensacola, Fla., 1983-85; exec. dir. Pres. Fgn. Intelligence Adv. Bd. White House, Washington, 1981-82; ret., 1985. Chmn. bd. dirs. Piedmont Environ. Coun., 1987-89; v.p. for nat. affairs Gen. George C. Marshall Home Found., 1990-91. Trustee Balt. Polytech. Inst. Found., 2000-03, U.S. Naval Acad. Found., 2005—. Commr. 2nd lt. Artillery, USMC, 2008. Decorated D.S.M., Legion of Merit, Def. Meritorious Svc. medal, Navy; named Disting. Alumnus, Balt. Poly. Inst., named to Hall of Fame. Mem. Naval Submarine League, U.S. Naval Inst., K.C. Roman Catholic. Avocations: golf, civil war history. Home: 414 Rockfleet Rd Unit 102 Timonium MD 21093-7582

SAGHAIAN, SAYED, economics professor; s. Hasan Saghaian and Ozra Nabati; m. Carolyn M. Costello, Jan. 10, 1989; children: Zacharia, Zane, Davoud. PhD, U. Ky., Lexington, 1992. Asst. prof. U. Ky., assoc. prof., 2008—. Office: Univ Kentucky 314 Barnhart Bldg Lexington KY 40546-0276 Office Fax: 859-257-7290. Business E-Mail: shsagh2@uky.edu.

SAGHER, OREN, neurosurgeon; b. Tel-Aviv, Oct. 18, 1963; s. Yoram and Daphna Sagher; m. Susan Dana Karp, May 28, 1989; children: Ethan Abraham, Abigail Karp, Daniel Reuben. BA, Boston U., 1983; MD, U. Chgo. Pritzker Sch. Medicine, 1987. Cert. in neurological surgery Am. Bd. Neurol. Surgery, 1997. Neurosurgery resident U. Va., Charlottesville, 1987—93; asst. prof. neurol. surgery U. Mich., Ann Arbor, 1993—2001, assoc. prof. neurol. surgery, 2001—, residency program dir., 2007—. Mem.: Am. Assn. Neurol. Surgeons. Office: Univ Michigan 1500 E Med Ctr Dr Ann Arbor MI 48104 Office Fax: 734-936-9294.

SAGMAN, ARTHUR M., radiologist; b. NYC; BS, U. Ariz., 1979, MS, 1980, MD, 1985. Transitional intern Good Samaritan Regional Med. Ctr., Phoenix, 1985—86; resident in diagnostic radiology Dartmouth-Hitchcock Med. Ctr., NH, 1986—90; fellow Health Sci. Ctr. U. Va., Charlottesville, 1990—91; radiologist Clin. Diagnostic Radiology, Phoenix, 1991—2004; med. dir. radiology Ariz. Physician's Ctr., Phoenix, 1991—95, Samaritan-Ahwatukee Foothills, Ariz., 1993; med. dir. dept. radiology Vencor Hosp., Phoenix, 1992—95; med. dir. ultrasound Good Samaritan Regional Med. Ctr., Phoenix, 1996—98, St. Joseph's Hosp. and Med. Ctr., Phoenix, 1998—2004, chmn. divsn. radiology, 2000—01, chmn. diagnostic and treatment svcs. dept., 2000—01, chmn. gen. radiology, 1998—2000, 2003—04; chmn. dept. radiology Paradise Valley Hosp., Phoenix, 2001—02; radiologist MedWise, Prescott, Ariz., 2004—. Mem.: Radiol. Soc. N.Am. Office: Medwise 790 Gail Gardner Prescott AZ 86305

SAGRAVES, ROSALIE, pharmacy practice educator, former dean; b. Portsmouth, Ohio, Nov. 5, 1945; d. Estil and Bernice Ione (Newman) Sagraves; m. Arthur Kameshka, Mar. 30, 1985. Student, Miami U., Oxford, Ohio; BS in Pharmacy, Ohio State U., 1969; PharmD, Phila. Coll. Pharmacy & Sci., 1978. Clin. pharmacist Ohio State U. Hosp., Columbus, 1969-72, clin. pharmacy coord., 1973-75, clin. pharmacist, 1975-76; clin. instr. Ohio State U. Coll. Pharmacy, Columbus, 1972-76; asst. prof. U. Tex. Coll. Pharmacy, Austin, 1978-84, assoc. prof., 1984-85, U. Okla. Coll. Pharmacy, Oklahoma City, 1985-92, prof., 1992-95, U. Ill. Chgo. Coll. Pharmacy, 1995—, dean, 1995—2006, co-dir. Ctr. Excellence in Women's Health, 1998—2006. Clin. pharmacy specialist Brackenridge Hosp., Austin, 1978—85; adj. assoc. prof. U. Okla. Coll. Medicine, 1985—95; clin. specialist Children's Hosp. Okla., 1985—95; bd. dirs. Advanced Life Scis. Holdings, Inc., Woodridge, Ill., 2001. Co-author: Clinical Pharmacology and Therapeutics in Nursing, 1985, Handbook of Applied Therapeutics, 1989, Pediatric Pharmacotherapy, 1990, Applied Therapeutics: The Clinical Use of Drugs, 2005; assoc. editor Pharmacy Today, 1994—98, reviewer Am. Jour. Pharm. Edn., sect. editor Jour. Pediatric Health Care; contbr. articles to profl. jours. Recipient Outstanding Tchg. award, U. Okla. Coll. Pharmacy, 1990, KE/Merck Vanguard award, 1994, Outstanding Alumnus award, Ohio State U. Coll. Pharmacy, 1995, Career Achievement award, Profl. Fraternaties Assn., 1996. Fellow: Am. Coll. Clin. Pharmacy; mem.: Ill. Pharmacy Found., Am. Soc. Parenteral & Enteral Nutrition, Am. Soc. Health-Sys. Pharmacists, Am. Assn. Colleges of Pharmacy, Am. Pharm. Assn., Phi Kappa Phi, Rho Chi, Kappa Epsilon (treas. 1987—91, pres. 1991—93, nat. adv. 1993—95, Alpha Iota Tchg. award 1987, 1993, 1994). Avocations: travel, reading, writing. Office: Coll of Pharmacy U Ill 833 S Wood St M/C 874 Chicago IL 60612-7229 E-mail: sartros@aol.com.*

SAGRIPANTI, JOSE-LUIS, biomedical scientist; BSChemE, U. Rosario, Santa Fe, Argentina, 1971, degree in Biochemistry with honors, 1977; DSc, U. Buenos Aires, 1984. Cert. in level III acquisition profl., Acquisition Corps. US Dept. Army, 2004; sr. exec. in nat. and internat. security John F. Kennedy Sch. Govt., Harvard U., 2005. Tchg. asst. physics U. Rosario, 1975—80, 1982—84, rschr., tchr. immunologist, 1980—82; Fogerty rsch. fellow NIH, Bethesda, Md., 1984—2000; rsch. scientist FDA, Rockville, Md., 1994—98; sci. advisor dept. commerce Gaithersburg, Md., 1994—98; sr. sci. advisor biochemistry Edgewood Chem. Biolo. Ctr., US Army Rsch., Devel. & Engring. Command, Aberdeen Proving Ground, 2000—. Sci. advisor Dept. Commerce, Gaithersburg, Md., 1994—98; advisor, dept. def. Joint Svcs. ChemBio Def., 2000; sr. tech. evaluation bd. Dept. Army, Alexandria, Va., 2005; nat. security studies program flag officers, DOD exec. Elliot Sch. Internat. Affairs. George Wash. U., 2007; dir., sci. leader Nat. Stds. Microbial Decontamination. Contbr. scientific papers to profl. publs. (Recognition of Outstanding Leadership, Divsn. Life Scis., Molecular Biology Br., 1986, Pub. Health Svc. Unit Commendation award, 1988, Quality award, 2000, Disting. Svc. award, Com. Homeland Security Applications, 2006). Recipient Merit medal, Poly. Inst., 2001. Mem.: Am. Assn. Aerosol Rsch., US Sr. Exec. Assn., Am. Soc. Virology. Achievements include patents pending for simultaneous detection of biological agents by solid-state hybridization and naked eye visualization; amino acid sites in flavivirus useful for development of diagnostics and vaccines; artificial chimeras engineered to simulate multiple biological threat agents; a disposable for multiplex field device to detect and identify a variety of microbial agents. Office: Edgewood Chem Biol Ctr Amsrd-Ecb-Rt Aberdeen Proving Ground MD 21010-5424 Business E-Mail: joseluis.sagripanti@usarmy.mil.

SAH, CHIH-TANG, electrical and computer engineering educator; b. Beijing, Nov. 10, 1932; s. Adam Peng-tung and Shu-shen Huang; m. Linda Chang, Nov. 29, 1959; children: Dinah W.Y., Robert L.Y. BS Physics, U. Ill., 1953, BSEE, 1953; MSEE, Stanford U., 1954, PhD, 1956; D honoris causa, U. Leuven, Belgium, 1975; Doctorate (hon.), Nat. Chao-Tung U., Taiwan, 2004. Research assoc. Stanford Electronics Lab., Palo Alto, Calif., 1956; sr. mem. tech. staff Shockley Transistor Corp., Palo Alto, 1956—59; head, mgr. physics dept. Fairchild Semiconductor Lab., Palo Alto, 1959-64; prof. physics and elec. engring. U. Ill., Urbana, 1962-88, dir. Ill. Solid State Electronics Lab.; Pittman Eminent Scholar chair, grad. research prof., chief scientist Coll. Engrng. U. Fla., Gainesville, 1988—. Program dir. 1st generation Si VLSI tech. Fairchild Corp., 1959-64; cons. Jet Propulsion Lab., Dept. Energy, Pasadena, Calif., 1976-85, Harry Diamond Lab., Washington, 1974-75, IBM Corp., NY, numerous other electronics firms 1964-88; advisor Intel Corp., Oreg., Calif., other semicondr. mfrs., 1988—; hon. prof. Peking U., 2003, Tsnghua U., 2003, Xiamen U., 2004. Author: Fundamentals of Solid-State Electronics, 1991, Transistor Reliability in Fundamentals of Solid-State Electronics—Solution Manual, 1996; founding editor Internat. Series Advances in Solid-State Electronics and Tech., 1991—; contbr. 300 articles to profl. jours. Recipient first high tech. award Asian Am. Mfg. Assn., 1982, Pioneer Recognition award Com. of the 100, 2002, Disting. Lifetime Achievement award Chinese Inst. Engrs. USA, 2003. Fellow IEEE (life, IRE Browder J. Thompson prize 1963, J.J. Ebers award 1980, Jack Morton award 1989), AAAS, Am. Phys. Soc., Franklin Inst. (life, Cert. of Merit award 1975); mem. US Semicondrs.

Industry Assn. (U. Rsch. award, 1998), Nat. Acad. Engring., Academia Sinica Taiwan (academician), Chinese Acad. Scis. (academician). Achievements include development of complementary metal-oxide semiconductor circuit; Si P-N junction diode phenomena Sah-Noyce-Shockley Theory; MOS transistor compact models, Sah, Pao, Jie; invention of deep-level transient spectroscopy Sah, Tasch, Yau; DCIV diagnosis for deep-submicron transistor design and reliability Sah, Cai, Wang, Jie. Office: 2716 NW 20th St Gainesville FL 32605-2999 Personal E-mail: tom_sah@msn.com.

SAHA, ABHIJIT, astronomer; s. Arun Kumar and Arundhati Saha; married. BSc in Physics with honors, U. Delhi, 1976, MSc in Physics, 1978; PhD, Calif. Inst. Tech., Pasadena, 1983. Rsch. assoc. Kitt Peak Nat. Obs., Tucson, 1983—85; Carnegie fellow Mt. Wilson & Las Campanas Obs., Pasadena, 1985—88; asst. scientist, asst. astronomer, assoc. astronomer Space Telescope Sci. Inst., Balt., 1988—97; assoc. astronomer, astronomer Nat. Optical Astronomy Obs., Tucson, 1997—. Mem.: Am. Astron. Soc.

SAHA, MITUL, engineer; b. Allahabad, Uttar Pradesh, Sept. 9, 1979; BS in Mech. Engring., Indian Inst. Tech., Kanpur, India, 2001; MS in Artificial Intelligence, Stanford U., 2005; PhD in Robotics, Stanford U., Calif., 2006. Rsch. scholar French Nat. Inst. Rsch. Computer Sci. & Control, Sophia Antipolis, France, 2000, Artificial Intelligence Lab., Stanford U., 2001—06; rsch. asst. Ctr. Robotics & Mechatronics, Indian Inst. Tech., Kanpur, India, 2005—06; postdoctoral scholar NIH Ctr. Biomed. Computation, Stanford U., 2006—. Contbr. scientific papers in field. Recipient Creative Design award, Indian Inst. Tech., 2000, Dept. Energy Travel award, Pacific Symposium Bio-Computatio, 2003; NIH Fellowship for Biomed. Rsch., Stanford U., 2006. Mem.: Sigma Xi. Achievements include development of motion planning kit, software for computing robot locomation; collision detection software for computer graphics; first to demonstrate autonomous robotic knot typing in 3-D. Office: Stanford Univ 318 Campus Dr Stanford CA 94305 Home: 37 Angell Ct Apt 412 Stanford CA 94305-7116 Business E-Mail: mitul@stanford.edu.

SAHA, SANDEEP AJOY, medical educator, researcher; m. Swagata Saha; 1 child, Satchit. MD, U. Mumbai, Seth GS Med. Coll. and King Edward VII Meml. Hosp., 2002. Cert. in internal medicine Am. Bd. Internal Medicine, 2007. Faculty hosp. physician Sacred Heart Med. Ctr., Spokane, Wash., 2007—; clin. instr. internal medicine U. Wash. Sch. Medicine, Seattle, 2007—; clin. rsch. assoc. Providence Med. Rsch. Ctr., Spokane, 2007—. Invited peer reviewer Southern Med. Jour., Birmingham, Ala., 2007—, Diabetes Obesity and Metabolism, Nottingham, 2007—, Anns. Internal Medicine, Phila., 2008—, European Heart Jour., Oxford, 2008—, Internat. Jour. Cardiology, Amsterdam, 2008—, Jour. Cardiovasc. Pharmacology and Therapeutics, LA, 2008—. Contbr. scientific papers. Mem.: ACP, Am. Heart Assn. Office: Sacred Heart Med Ctr 105 W 5th Ave Spokane WA 99220-2555 Home Fax: 509-474-5316. E-mail: sahas1@intmedspokane.org.

SAHA, SANTOSH CHANDRA, history educator; b. Oct. 23, 1937; BA in History with honors, Calcutta U., India, 1955, LLB, 1959, MA in History, 1960; Assoc. of Preceptors, Coll. of Preceptors, London, 1972; BA in History with honors, U. London, 1976; postgrad., U. Toledo, 1985-87; PhD, Kent State U., 1993. Asst. prof. history Bagula Degree Coll., West Bengal, India, 1960-62, Itachuna Coll., Burdwan U. India, 1962-65; head of dept., instr. history Miaza 27 Comprehensive Inst., Jimma, Ethiopia, 1965-68, Monze (Zambia) Secondary Sch., 1968-80; prin., instr. Adult Edn. Ctr., Monze, 1974-80; instr. history St. Paul's Cath. Sem., Gbarnga, Liberia, 1982-83; head of dept., asst. prof. history Cuttington U., Liberia, 1981-85; tchr. survey courses in European and U.S. history U. Toledo, 1985-88, instr. comty. and tech. coll., 1986-87; teaching fellow in history Kent (Ohio) State U., 1989-93; instr. African history Mt. Union Coll., Alliance, Ohio, 1994—. Prin., coord. Adult Edn. Ctr., Monze, 1970-79; dep. headmaster Monze Secondary Sch., 1978-79; regional chief examiner Zambian Sch. Sys. Exam., South Region, 1970-79; mem. faculty rsch. forum Cuttington U., 1983-85, student debates chmn., 1981-85, editor-in-chief, bd. historians The History of Cuttington University, 1983-85, acting head dept. history, 1984-85, editor Cutting Rsch. Jour., 1981-85; conf. presenter Gt. Lakes History Conf., Alendale, Mich., 1993, Ohio Valley History Cnf., Murray, Ky., 1986, 87, 88, 89, U.S. Ednl. and Agrl. Found., Monrovia, Liberia, 1983, 84. Author: Indo-U.S. Relations, 1947-1989: A Guide to Information Sources, 1990, A History of Agriculture in West Africa: A Guide to Information Sources, 1990, A History of Agriculture in Liberia, 1822-1970: Transference of American Values, 1990, History of the Tonga Chiefs and Their People in the Monze District of Zambia, 1994; contbr. articles to profl. jours. including Can. Jour. African Studies, Jour. of Negro History, Internat. Jour. African Hist. Studies, Jour. of Pakistan Hist. Soc., Leaders of the World, Women in World History, Indian Jour. of Social Work; contbr. book revs. and conf. papers in field. Mem. African Studies Assn. (conf. presenter 1993), Am. Hist. Assn., Third World Studies Assn., Assn. for Bibliography of History, Indian Polit. Sci. Assn. (Univ. Madras, India), World History Assn.

SAHAI, HARDEO, medical statistics educator; b. Bahraich, India, Jan. 10, 1942; m. Lillian Sahai, Dec. 28, 1973; 3 children. BS in Math., Stats. and Physics, Lucknow U., India, 1962; MS in Math., Banaras U., Varanasi, India, 1964; MS in Math. Stats., U. Chgo., 1968; PhD in Stats., U. Ky., Lexington, 1971. Lectr. math. and stats. Banaras U., Varanasi, India, 1964—65; asst. stats. officer Durgapur Steel Plant, West Bengal, India, 1965; statistician Rsch. and Planning divsn. Blue Cross Assn., Chgo., 1966; statis. programmer Cleft Palate Ctr. U. Ill., 1967; statis. programmer Chgo. Health Rsch. Found., 1968; mgmt. scientist Mgmt. Sys. Devel. Dept. Burroughs Corp., Detroit, 1971—72; from asst. prof. to prof. dept. math. U. PR, Mayaguez, 1972—82; vis. rsch. prof. Dept. Stats. and Applied Math. U. Ceara, Brazil, 1978—79; sr. rsch. statistician Travenol Labs., Inc., Round Lake, Ill., 1982—83; chief statistician US Army Hqrs., Ft. Sheridan, Ill., 1983—84; sr. math. statistician U.S. Bur. Census Dept. Commerce, Washington, 1984—85; sr. ops. rsch. analyst Def. Logistics Agy. Dept. Def., Chgo., 1985—86; prof. Dept. Biostats. and Epidemiology U. PR Med. Scis., San Juan, 1986—. Cons. PR Univ Cons., PR Driving Safety Evaluation Project, Water Resources Rsch. Inst., Travenol Labs., Campo Rico, PR, US Bur. Census, Washington, Lawrence Livermore Nat. Lab., Calif., others; vis. prof. U. Granada, Spain, U. Veracruzana, Mex., patrimonial prof. stats., 1997—; vis. prof. U. Nacional de Colombia, U. Nacional de Trujillo, Peru, 1993-94, hon. prof. stats., 1994—; adj. prof. dept. math. U. P.R. Natural Scis. Faculty, 1995—; Patrimonial prof. stafs U. Veracruzana, 1997—. Author: Statistics and Probability: Learning Module, 1984; author: (with Jose Berrios) A Dictionary of Statistical Scientific and Technical Terms: English-Spanish and Spanish-English, 1981, (with Wilfredo Martinez) Statistical Tables and Formulas for the Biological Social and Physical Sciences, 1996, (with Anwer Khurshid) Statistics in Epidemiology: Methods, Techniques and Applications, 1996, (with Satish C. Misra and Amwer Khurshid) Quotations on Probability and Statistics with Illustrations, 2004, (with Anwer Khurshid) A Pocket Dictionary of Statistics, 2000, (with Mohammad I. Ageel) The Analysis of Variance: Fixed, Random and Mixed Models, 2000, (with Mario M. Ojeda) A Glossary of Statistical, Sciebtfic and Technical Terms: English-Spanish, 2004, (with Lucas López Segovia and Hector W. Colón-Rosa) A Glossary of Medical Epidemiologic and Demographic Statistics: English-Spanish, 2003, (with Mario M. Ojeda) Un Manual de Distribuciones t, x2y F Centrales Y No Centrales, 2000, (with Mario M. Ojeda) A Glossary of Computer and Management Terms: English/Spanish, 2004, (with Mario M. Ojeda) Comparisons of Approximations to the Percentiles of Noncentral t, x2 and F Distributions, 2001, (with A. Khurshid) Pocket Dictionary of Statistics, 2001, (with Mario M. Ojeda) Analysis of Variance for Random Models, Vol. 1: Balanced Data and Vol. 2: Unbalanced Data, 2004; mem. editl. bd. Sociedad Colombiana de Matematicas, P.R. Health Scis. Jour.; contbr. editor Current Index to Stats.; reviewer Collegiate Microcomputer, Comm. in Statistics, Indian Jour. Stats., Jour. Royal Statis. Soc. (series D, The Statistician), New Zealand Statistician, Biometrics, Can. Jour. Stats., Technometrics, Problems, Resources and Issues in Math. Undergrad. Studies; contbr. more than 150 articles and papers to profl. and sci. jours., numerous articles to tech. mags. Active Dept. Consumer Affairs Svcs. Commonwealth of PR, San Juan, Dept. Anti-Addiction Svcs., Commonwealth of P.R., San Juan., Inst. of AIDS, Municipality of San Juan, VA Med. Ctr. of San Juan, Caribbean Primate Rsch. Ctr., Ctr. Addiction Studies Caribbean Ctrl. U. Recipient Dept. Army Cert. Achievement award, 1984, U. Ky. Outstanding Alumnus award, 1993, medal of honor U. Granada, 1994, plaque of honor U. Nacional de Trujillo, 1994; fellow Coun. Sci. and Indsl. Rsch., 1964-65, U. Chgo., 1965-68, Harvard U., 1979, Fulbright Found., 1982; U.P. Bd. Merit scholar, 1957-59, Govt. India Merit scholar, 1959-64; grantee NSF, 1974-77, NIMH, 1987-90, 91—, NIDA, 1991—. Fellow AAAS, Am. Coll. Epidemiology, Inst. Statisticians (charter statistician), Inst. Math. and Its Applications (charter mathematician), N.Y. Acad. Scis., Royal Statis. Soc.; mem. Internat. Statis. Inst., Internat. Assn. Tchg. Stats., Soc. Epidemiol. Rsch., Inst. Math. Stats., Bernouilli Soc. for Math. Stats. and Probability, Internat. Biometric Soc., Am. Soc. for Quality Control, Am. Stats. Assn., Japan Statis. Soc., Can. Statis. Soc., Inter-Am. Statis. Inst., Internat. Assn. Statis. Computing, Sch. Sci. and Math. Assn., Sigma Xi. Avocations: religious studies, philosophy, reading, gardening. Home: Urb Mayaguez Ter 7083 Calle B Gaudier Texidor Mayaguez PR 00682-6617 Personal E-mail: hardeosahat@yahoo.com.

SAHAI, TUHIN, research scientist; married. PhD, Cornell U., Ithaca, 2007. Rsch. scientist United Techs., East Hartford, Conn., 2007—. Contbr. articles to sci. jours. Recipient H. D. Block Tchg. award, Cornell U., 2007, Gt. Job award, United Techs., 2008; Mc Mullen fellowship, Cornell U., 2002. Mem.: Sigma Xi.

SAHAI SRIVASTAVA, SOMA, neurologist, educator; arrived in US, 1995; d. Sachidanand and Sudha Sahai; m. Krishna Srivastava; 1 child, Diya. Degree, Patna Med. Sch., India, 1968—91. Diplomate Am. Acad. Neurology, 2001, Am. Bd. Internal Med., 2001. Internship Patna Med. Coll., 1991—92, U. Southern Calif., Los Angeles, 1996—97, residency, 2001, asst. prof., 2001—; dir., neurology ambulatory care svcs. LAC USC Med. Ctr., Los Angeles, 2001—. Recipient Faculty Tchg. award, U. Southern Calif., 2000—01; named Best Intern of Yr., 1997. Fellow: Am. Acad. Neuromuscular Electrodiagnostic Medicine; mem.: Am. Acad. Nerology, Internat. Headache Soc. Hindu. Office: LAC USC Med Ctr 1100 N State St Los Angeles CA 90033 Home: 506 N Chapel Ave # D Alhambra CA 91801 Office Phone: 323-409-8686.

SAHAKIAN, LILLIAN ZAROUHI, artist, designer; d. Archak Agapov Sahakian and Mariam Zarouhi Zahrbhanelian-Sahakian. Secretarial pool First Nat. City Bank, NYC, 1954—55; sec., sales & mktg. Walker Mktg. Corp., Racine, Wis., 1958—59; typist, purchasing Kollsman Instrument Corp., Elmhurst, NY, 1963—70; supv. stenographer City Hosp. Ctr., 1974—78; exec. sec. Racine/Kenosha Cmty. Action Agy., 1979—80, Butter Buds Corp., Racine, 1989—91; mktg. specialist Johnson Internat., Inc., Racine, 1994—2003. Oil portrait - copy, Victor Choque (2nd Prize, 1955), exhibition, Early Oil Paintings-American Artist, Smithsonian, 1957, altar piece, Madonna & Child, St. Sarkis Ch., 1960, graphite rendering, Viet Nam Refugees - Grandmother & Grandson, 1964, watercolor painting, After Matisse, 1990, graphics logo, Lili Archak Studios, 2004, lifestyle interior designs, Interior Designs LLC. Choir mem. St. Hagop Ch., Wis., 1958—59. Scholar Entrepreneurial Incentive award, State of Wis., 2004. Mem.: NAMI Racine (bd. dirs. 1985—2006), Soc. for Tech. Comm., Kenosha Art Assn., Am. Inst. Graphic Artists. Independent. Avocations: reading, do it yourself home repairs, research on the internet & other, computer generated art, cooking. Office: Lili Archak Studios LLC 1117 Saxony Dr Racine WI 53402

SAHID, JOSEPH ROBERT, lawyer; b. Paterson, NJ, Feb. 14, 1944; s. Joseph James and Helen (Vitale) Sahid; m. Serra Yavuz; children: Annunziata, Joseph, Olivia. BS, Rutgers U., 1965; LLB, U. Va., 1968. Bar: NY 1973, US Dist. Ct. NY, US Ct. Appeals (2d and 3d cirs.), US Supreme Ct. Staff mem. Nat. Commn. Causes Prevention Violence, Washington, 1968-69; cons. Pres.'s Commn. Campus Unrest, Washington, 1970; assoc. Cravath, Swaine & Moore, NYC, 1972-77, ptnr., 1977-93, cons., 1994-97; ptnr. Barrack, Rodos & Bacine, NYC, 1995—96; pvt. practice NYC, 1996—. Mediator US Dist. Ct. (so. dist.) NY, NY Civil Ct.; arbitrator NY cts., FINRA. Author: (book) Rights in Concord, 1969; co-author: Law and Order Reconsidered, 1969; contbr. articles to profl. jours. Lt. USCG, 1968—72. Mem.: ABA, NY State Bar Assn. (profl. discipline com.), Bar Assn. City NY (profl. discipline com. mem. 2001—03, profl. responsibility com. mem. 2003—06, profl. discipline com. mem. 2006—09, 2008—09, profl. responsibility com. 2009—, mem. coop. condo mediation project, coun. children com., legal referral svc.). Office Phone: 646-657-0486. Personal E-mail: sahid@nysbar.com.

SAHIMI, MUHAMMAD, engineering educator; b. Tehran, Iran, Jan. 22, 1954; s. Habibollah Sahimi and Fatemeh Fakour Rashid; m. Mahnoush Babaei; children: Ali, Niloofar. BS, U. Tehran, 1977; PhD, U. Minn., Mpls., 1984. Asst. prof. U. So. Calif., LA, 1984—89, assoc. prof., 1989—94, prof., 1994—, chmn. chem. engring., 1999—2005, NOIC chair in petroleum engring., 2005—, prof. chem. engring. & materials sci., 2005—. Cons. Nat. Iranian Oil Co., Tehran, 1989—97, Avery Dennison Corp., Pasadena, Calif., 1997—. Contbr. columns in newspapers, articles to profl. jours. Commentator Inst. Pub. Accuracy, San Francisco, 2005—08, Kirn 670-Am, LA, 1997—2008. Recipient Humboldt Rsch. Fellowship award, Alexander von Humboldt Found., 1992, Kapitza Gold Medal award, Russian Acad. Natural Scis., 1999, Khwarizmi award, Govt. Iran, UNESCO, 2003. Mem.: Union Concerned Scientists, Soc. Petroleum Engrs., Materials Rsch. Soc., AIChE, Am. Phys. Soc. Independent. Muslim. Avocations: reading, writing. Office: Univ So Calif 925 Bloomwalk Los Angeles CA 90089-1211 Office Fax: 213-740-8053; Home Fax: 213-740-8053. Personal E-mail: moe@iran.usc.edu. Business E-Mail: moe@usc.edu.

SAHIN, MUSTAFA, neurologist, educator; s. Mehmet Sevki and Sumru Sahin; married. BS Magna cum Laude, Brown U., Providence, 1988; MD, PhD, Yale U. Sch. Medicine, New Haven, 1995. Cert. Mass. Bd. Registration Medicine, 2000, diplomate Am. Bd. Psychiatry and Neurology, 2001. Asst., neurology Children's Hosp., Boston, 2000—; instr., neurology Harvard Med. Sch., Boston, 2001—06, asst. prof., neurology, 2006—; dir. Multidisciplinary Tuberous Sclerosis Program, Boston, 2002—. Contbr. articles to profl. jours. Recipient Jr. Investigator award, Tuberous Sclerosis Alliance, 2005—08; R01 grant, Nat. Inst. Health, 2007—, grant, Nat. Orgn. Rare Disorders, 2007—08, SMN in miRNA processing grant, Whitehall Found., 2007—08. Mem.: Am. Acad. Neurology (SMA Found. Young Investigator award 2005), Mass. Med. Soc., Soc. Neurosci., Child Neurology Soc. (mem., sci. program com. 2007, Young Investigator award 2005), Alpha Omega Alpha Honor Med. Soc., Sigma Xi Honor Soc. Office: Children's Hosp 300 Longwood Ave CLSB 13074 Boston MA 02115 Business E-Mail: mustafa.sahin@childrens.harvard.edu.

SAHINER, BERKMAN, science administrator, educator; b. Turkey; PhD, U. Mich., Ann Arbor, 1993. Conf. chair Internat. Soc. Optical Engring., 2006—. Contbr. articles to numerous med. jours. Grantee, NIH, 2006—; Breast Cancer Rsch. grant, US Army Med. Rsch. and Materiel Command, 1996—2006. Achievements include research in computer-aided diagnosis. Office: Univ Mich MIB C480A 1500 E Medical Center Dr Ann Arbor MI 48109-5842

SAHIN SARIISIK, ASLI, engineer; d. Celal and Selma Sahin; m. Walter Volkan Sariisik. BS in Chemistry, Bogazici U., Turkey; MS in Chemistry, U. Mass. Amherst; PhD in Indsl. and Sys. Engring., Va. Tech, Blacksburg, 2007. Rsch. asst. U. Mass., Amherst, 1999—2004, Va. Tech., 2004—07; sr. devel. engr. Goodyear, Akron, Ohio, 2007—. Contbr. articles to profl. jours. Recipient 2d Pl. award, Ann. Indsl. Engring. Doctoral Colloqium and Poster Session, 2006. Mem.: Am. Soc. Mech. Engring., Indsl. Engring. Soc., Indsl. Engring. Honor Soc. Personal E-mail: sahinasli@yahoo.com.

SAHLEM, JAMES ROBERT, law librarian; b. Buffalo, Feb. 21, 1948; s. Lee M. and Mildred A. (Hibschweiler) S.; m. Susan Mary Schifferli, Aug. 9, 1969; children: Steven, Andrea, Gregory. BS in Mgmt., Canisius Coll., Buffalo, NY, 1970, MS in Edn., 1995; MLS, SUNY, Buffalo, 1971, ASC, 1985. Cert. pub. libr. profl., NY State Edn. Dept. Libr. trainee Bus. Labor Dept. Buffalo-Erie County Pub. Libr., Buffalo, 1970-71; libr. I Mobile Librs. Buffalo-Erie County Pub. Libr., Buffalo, 1971-74; libr. II Amherst Pub. Librs., Williamsville, NY, 1974-78; libr. III, dir. North Park Crane Brs., Buffalo, 1978-81; prin. law libr. NY State Supreme Ct. Libr. Buffalo, 1981—. Cons. Lippes, Silverstein et al, Buffalo, 1985—06. Co-author: (with Jo Ann M. Wahl and Kevin Bauer) Powers of the New York Court of Appeals 1952-1993 Supplement, 1994. Sec., We. NY Libr. Resources Coun. Mem. Am. Assn. Law Librs. (bd. dirs. Upstate NY), NY State Unified Cts. Law Librs. (pres.). Avocations: history, gardening. Office: NY State Supreme Ct Libr Buffalo 77 W Eagle St Buffalo NY 14202-3408 Office Phone: 716-845-9389. Business E-Mail: jsahlem@courts.state.ny.us.

SAHN, STEVEN ALAN, internist, educator; b. Bklyn., Jan. 25, 1943; s. Irwin H. and Mildred P. Sahn; m. Margaret Hoefer Sahn, June 8, 2002; children: Karen, Stacey, James, Michael, Rachel. BA, Duke U., 1964; MD, U. Louisville, 1968. Diplomate Am. Bd. Internal Medicine, Am. Bd. Pulmonary Medicine, Am. Bd. Critical Care Medicine. Intern in internal medicine U. Iowa Hosp., Iowa City, 1968-69, resident in internal medicine, 1969-71; fellow in pulmonary disease U. Colo. Health Sci. Ctr., Denver, 1971-73, instr. medicine, 1973-74, asst. prof. medicine, 1974-78, assoc. prof. medicine, 1978-83; prof. medicine, dir. divsn. pulmonary and critical care, allergy and sleep medicine Med. Univ. S.C., Charleston, 1983—, dir. allergy clin. immunology, 1983—. Vis. prof. U. Calif., San Francisco, 1980, Kans. U. Med. Ctr., Kansas City, 1981, U. Louisville Sch. Medicine, 1982, Wright State U. Med. Sch., Wright-Patterson AFB Hosp., Dayton, Ohio, 1982, Oreg. Health Scis. U., 1982, Vanderbilt U., Nashville, 1984, U. S.C. Sch. Medicine, 1985, U. Ariz. Health Sci. Ctr., Tucson, 1985, 92, 93, Yale U., New Haven, Conn., 1986, Hershey (Pa.) Med. Ctr., 1986, SUNY, Stonybrook, 1987, Dartmouth-Hitchcock Med. Ctr., Hanover, N.H., 1988, Maine Med. Ctr. U. Vt., Portland, Maine, 1988, Fitzsimmons Army Med. Ctr., Denver, 1989, Seton Hall U. Grad. Med. Edn., 1989, Newark, 1989, Loyola U. Med. Ctr., Chgo., 1989, Andrews AFB, Washington, 1990, Keesler AFB, Biloxi, Miss., 1990, U. Rochester, N.Y., U. Ala., Birmingham, 1990, N.Y. Med. Coll., 1990, Temple U. Sch. Medicine, Phila., 1990, U. Milan, Italy, 1990, Georgetown U. Med. Ctr., Washington, 1991, Albert Einstein Sch. Medicine, 1991, Johns Hopkins U. Sch. Medicine, Balt., 1991, Ind. U. Med. Ctr., 1994, Ohio State U. Sch. Medicine, 1994, 33 others; cons. Fitzsimons Army Med. Ctr., 1980-83, 88-90, DHEC of S.C., 1982—, USAF, 1989—93, FDA Office of Orphan Product Devel., 1993—95; presenter numerous seminars; keynote speaker numerous meetings. Author: (with J.E. Heffner) Pulmonary Pearls, 1988, vol. II, 1994, Critical Care Pearls, 1989; editor: (with L.B. Reller and R.W. Schrier) Clinical Internal Medicine, 1979, Pulmonary Emergencies, 1982, Diseases of the Pleura: Seminars in Respiratory Medicine, 1987, Infections of the Pleural Space: Seminars in Respiratory Infections, Vol. III, 1988, (with J.E. Heffner) Internal Medicine Pearls, 1993, (with J.E. Heffner) Cardiology Pearls, 1993, Tuberculosis Pearls, 1996, Critical Care Pearls, II, 1997, Respieratory Care Pearls, 1997; mem. editorial bd. Chest, 1987—, Pulmonary and Critical Care Update, 1988—, editor 2007-; dept. editor Pulmonary and Critical Care Pearls Chest, 1992—, Pulmonary Pearls Jour. Respiratory Disease, 1990—, Critical Care Pearls Jour. Critical Illness, 1990—; cons. to 53 editorial bd. Am. Jour. Diseases of Children, Am. Jour. Medicine, Am. Jour. Respiratory Critical Care Medicine, Cancer, Cancer Rsch., Annals of Internal Medicine, Chest, Critical Care Medicine, Jour. Am. Acad. Dermatoloty, Jour. Am. Med. Assn., European Respiratory Jour., Jour. Applied Physiology, Jour. Intensive Care Medicine, Jour. Laboratory and Clin. Medicine, Jour. Respiratory Diseases, Lung, Mayo Clinic Proceedings, Med. Toxicology, N.Y. State Jour. Medicine, Tubercle and Lung Diseases, Western Jour. Medicine; contbr. articles, reviews and abstracts to profl. jours., chpts. to books. Recipient Young Investigator Pulmonary Rsch. award NHLBI, 1975-77, grantee 1975-77; named one of Outstanding Med. Specialists in the U.S. Town and Country Mag., 1990, one of Best Med. Specialists in N.Am., 1995, one of 400 Best Doctors in Am., Good Housekeeping Mag., 1991, one of Best Drs. in Am., Am. Health Mag., 1995; grantee Milheim, 1977-78, Beecham, 1977-78, 82-83, Warner-Chilcott, 1978-79, Squibb, 1978, 79-80, Lilly, 1979-80, 81-82, Boehringer-Ingelheim, 1980, 89-90, Med. Coll. S.C., 1985-86, ALASC, 1985-86, 86-87, 87-88, 88-89, Lederle, 1988-92, Hoescht-Roussel, 1988-90, Support Systems Internat., 1990-92, 92-93, Cutter Biological, Miles, Inc., Glaxo, 1991-92, Schering-Plough, 1992-93, Tap Pharmaceuticals, 1993. Fellow Am. Coll. Chest Physicians (annual meeting com. 1986, gov. S.C. 1988-91, 91-94, organizing com. nat. pulmonary bd. review course 1990, 92, 94, membership com. 1992-93, annual internat. sci. program com. 1993-95, reviewer MKSAP 1994), Am. Coll. Physicians, Am. Coll. Critical Care Medicine; mem. Am. Fedn. Clin. Rsch. (so. sect.), Am. Thoracic Soc. (respiratory care com. 1978-80, rsch. coord. com. 1985-87, annual meeting com. 1985-89, chmn. sci. assembly on clin. problems 1986-87, coun. chpt. reps. 1987-90), Am. Lung Assn. (adv. bd. S.C. coastal br. 1985-87, 89-91, 92-94, med. review com. 1985-89), We. Soc. Clin. Investigation, S.C. Thoracic Soc. (sci.

planning com. 1985-86), Charleston County Med. Soc. Office: Med U SC Divsn Pulmonary & Crit Care Allergy & Sleep Medicine 171 Ashley Ave Charleston SC 29425-0001 Office Phone: 803-792-3167. Business E-Mail: sahnsa@musc.edu.

SAHOO, BISHWABHUSAN, chemist; married. PhD, Delhi U., India, 2001. Sr. rsch. scientist Obiter Rsch., Champaign, Ill., 2005—08; process rsch. scientist PCI Synthesis, Newburyport, Mass., 2008—. Contbr. articles to profl. jours. (Outstanding Invention award, 2002). Postdoc. fellowship, NSF, 2001. Fellow: Am. Inst. Chemist; mem.: Internat. Union Pure & Applied Chemistry, Am. Chem. Soc.

SAHOTA, AMRIK, medical researcher, educator, lab administrator; s. Sadhu Milkhy and Rao Kaur; m. Nirmala Thapar; children: Aneil, Jessica. BS in Biochemistry, Bath U., 1974; MS in Medicinal Chemistry, Loughborough U., 1976; PhD in Med. Genetics, Guy's Hosp. Med. Sch., London U., 1980. Diplomate in clin. molecular genetics Am. Bd. Med. Genetics, cert. Am. Bd. Med. Genetics, 1993, in molecular diagnostics Am. Bd. Clin. Chemistry, 2008; chartered biologist U.K. Postdoctoral fellow dept. molecular scis. Aston U., Birmingham, England, 1980—83; biochemist dept. hematology Gen. Hosp., Birmingham, England, 1983—85; rsch. assoc. dept. biology Ind. U., Bloomington, Ind., 1985—87; lab. dir. dept. med. and molecular genetics Ind. U. Med. Sch., Indpls., 1988—98; prof. genetics Rutgers U., Piscataway, NJ, 1998—; lab. dir. dept. pathology Robert Wood Johnson U. Hosp., New Brunswick, NJ, 2001—. Cons. Indpls.-Marion County Forensic Sci. Lab., 1991—98; adj. prof. dept. pathology Robert Wood Johnson Med. Sch., U. Medicine and Dentistry, NJ, 2001—05, clin. prof., 2005—. Contbr. articles to sci. jours.; editor conf. procs. Fellow: Royal Coll. Pathologists UK, Inst. Biology UK, Am. Coll. Med. Genetics; mem.: AAAS, NY Acad. Scis., Internat. Soc. for Nephrology, Assn. Molecular Pathology, Soc. for Study of Inborn Errors of Metabolism, Brit. Soc. Human Genetics, Am. Soc. Human Genetics, Am. Assn. Clin. Chemistry. Achievements include research in Genetic basis of kidney stone disease. Avocations: travel, reading, health and fitness. Office: Rutgers U Dept Genetics Life Scis Bldg 145 Bevier Rd Piscataway NJ 08854-8082 Business E-Mail: sahota@biology.rutgers.edu.

SAHOTA, PUNEET, medical researcher; Degree in Am. Studies Summa cum laude, Northwestern U., 2001, B in Am. Studies, 2002; PhD in Anthropology, Washington U., St. Louis, 2009—, attending, 2003—. Postdoc. fellow Nat. Congress Am. Indians, Policy Rsch. Ctr., Washington, 2009—. Mem., bd. trustees Telluride Assn., Ithaca, NY, 2001—08. Recipient Daniel Bonbright award, Northwestern U., 2001; fellow Med. Scientist Tng. Program fellowship, Wash. U. St. Louis, 2003—09, Postbaccalaureate Intramural Rsch. Tng. award, NIH, 2002—03; Mr. and Mrs. Spencer T. Olin fellowship, Wash. U., 2003—09. Mem.: Soc. Applied Anthropology, Soc. Med. Anthropology, Am. Anthrop. Assn., Phi Beta Kappa. Achievements include research in depression and diabetes among Native Americans; ethical, cultural, and political issues related to medical-genetics research in Native American communities.

SAHR, MORRIS GALLUP, financial planner; b. Schenectady, Nov. 28, 1928; s. Nathan and Esther (Gallup) S.; m. Sarah Diane Eisenberg, Dec. 23, 1956; children: Evelyn, David, Janet. AB, U. Oreg., 1951, MA, 1953; PhD, Calif. Open U., Sacremento, 1978. Cert. fin. planner, registered fin. cons. Pres. Deposit Mgmt. Svc., Inc., Charlottesville, Va., 1978—. Author: Nine Ways to Beat the High Cost of College, 1999, Annuity Owners' Mistakes, 2002; co-author: Your Book of Financial Planning, 1983, Encyclopedia of Financial Planning, 1984, The Financial Planner, 1986, Financial Planning Can Make You Rich, 1987; producer & dir., (TV series) Nova-Entitled: Washington Form Financial Planning, 1975-78. Chmn. Fairfax County Planning Commn., Va., 1964-68; del. White House Conf. on Aging, 1980, U.S. Congl. Adv. Bd., 1984-87; bd. dirs. Fairfax Indsl. Devel. Authority, 1985-95; adjudicator Am. Arbitration Assn., 1988-99; del to China, Eisenhower, People to People Amb. Program, 2000. With USN, 1953—55, Korean War. Recipient award Danforth Found.; named 1 of Top 200 Planners in U.S., Money Mag.; hon. fellow Kennedy Libr., 1985; Paul Harris fellow, 1989. Mem. Internat. Assn. Fin. Planning (founder, 1st pres. Metro Washington chpt.), Inst. Cert. Fin. Planners (nat. govt. affairs com.), Am. Assn. Practicing Fin. Planners (past pres.), Internat. Assn. of Registered Fin. Cons., Rotary (pres. Fairfax 1984-85, Rotary Srs. Project Internat. award). Home and Office: 1289 Courtyard Dr Charlottesville VA 22903 Office Phone: 434-978-2277, 434-970-2277. Personal E-mail: sahrdms@embarqmail.com.

SAHRAKORPI, SEPPO, senior research engineer; s. Matti L.S. and Sirpa Sahrakorpi; m. Renate Harrison; children: Zachary, Sahrakorpi. MSc, Tampere U. of Tech., 1996, PhD with commendation, 2001. Rsch. asst. Tampere U. Tech., 1996—2001; rsch. assoc. Northeastern U., Boston, 2002—07; ptnr. tech. engr. Totalview Technologies, 2007—08; sr. rsch. engr. Harvard U., 2008—. Sci. computing cons. Advanced Sci. Computation Ctr., Northeastern U., Boston, 2002—07, adj. prof., 2007; docent Tampere U. Tech., 2007. 2d lt. Finnish mil., 1991—92. Recipient Docent award, Tampere U. Tech., 2007, Adj. Prof. award, Northeastern U., 2007; grantee, Vilho, Yrjo and Kalle Found., Finland, 2002, The Acad. of Finland, 2001—02; fellow, Vilho, Yrjo and Kalle Found., Finland, 1999—2000, Tampere U. of Tech. Found., 2000; scholar, Found. for Advancement of Tech., Finland, 1997—98, Vilho, Yrjo and Kalle Found., Finland, 1998, Jenny and Antti Wihuri Found., Finland, 2000. Mem.: Am. Phys. Soc., European Phys. Soc., Finnish Phys. Soc. Achievements include research in fermiology and angle-resolved photoemission of high-temperature superconductors.

SAHU, GAUTAM K., medical educator; b. India; PhD, Calcutta U., India, 1996. Asst. prof. UTMB, Galveston, Tex., 2006—. Achievements include development of a primary cell model of HIV latency. Office: Univ Tex Med Br 301 University Blvd Rt #1070 Galveston TX 77555 Business E-Mail: gsahu2002@yahoo.com.

SAIA, ROBERT ANGELO, retired science educator; s. James and Helen Saia; m. Frances Altomare, Feb. 2, 1957; children: Roberta Ann Hommel, Elizabeth Barricelli, Suzanne Pombar, Gabrielle Story. BS, U. Maine, Orono, 1958; MS, NYU, 1966. Cert. secondary sch. earth sci. tchr. NY State Edn. Sys., 1959. Prof. Oceanside Sch. Sys., NY, 1959—89; pres. & founder Sci. by Saia, Deer Park, NY, 1975—; assoc. adj. prof. geology, astronomy, climatology Suffolk CC, Brentwood, NY, 1992—. Vol. Life Ctr., Deer Park, 2003—06; treas. v.p. Sci. Mus. LI, Plandome, NY, 1984—2005, bd. pres., 2000—04. Cpl. US Army, 1953—54, Ft Churchill, Manitoba, Can. Grantee, NSF, 1965—66. Mem.: Nat. Assn. Geology Tchrs., Am. Fedn. Tchrs. (organizer, charter mem. local HS bldg rep. 1965—89), Am. Legion, Sigma Phi Epsilon Frat. Roman Catholic. Achievements include development of sedimentation experiment the Squeezebox; landsat remote sensing science sets; research in geology of the Wurtsboro NY, Quadrangle, the effects of Sonic Booms on the seismic record. Avocations: fishing, travel. Home: 13 Dartmouth Dr Deer Park NY 11729 Business E-Mail: saiar@sunysuffolk.edu.

SAIBLE, STEPHANIE IRENE, editor-in-chief; b. Mobile, Ala., Sept. 11, 1954; d. Lewis J. Slaff and Phoebe-Jane (Berse) Meiss. Student, Va. Commonwealth U. Editorial asst. Woman's World mag. Bauer Pub. USA, Englewood, NJ, 1980—81, copywriter, 1981—83, assoc. articles editor, 1983—84, articles editor, 1984—85, sr. editor features dept., 1985—86, sr. editor services dept., 1986, editor-in-chief, 1994—. Contbr. articles to Woman's World, Modern Bride, New Body, Celebrity Beauty, Trim and Fit, Ladies Home Jour. Named Wonder Woman of Yr., Bus. Jour., NJ, 1986. Mem.: Women in Comms. Office: Woman's World Mag 270 Sylvan Ave Englewood Cliffs NJ 07632-2521*

SAID, M. SHERIF A., pathologist, consultant; s. Ali Said and Khairat Khatab; m. Susan Holly Sullivan, Mar. 6, 2003; 1 child, Seif Al-Dean. MBBCh, Ain Shams Med. Sch., Abbasia, Cairo, 1977; PhD, Med. Coll. Va., Richmond, 1993. Diplomate Am. Bd. Anatomic Pathology, 2002, Am. Bd. Cytopathology, 2006. Assoc. prof. pathology U. Colo., Denver, 2001—, dir. head and neck pathology, cons. head & neck and thyroid pathology, 2001—. Contbr. articles to profl. jours. Mem.: Am. Soc. Clin. Pathology. Achievements include research in head Nd neck cancers. Office: Univ Colo Denver PO Box 6510 12605 E 16th Ave Aurora CO 80045 Business E-Mail: sherif.said@uchsc.edu.

SAIDI, REZA, engineering educator; b. Abadan, Khozestan, Iran, Apr. 30, 1951; s. Ali and Bigom Saidi; m. Linda J. Linda Cropp, Dec. 21, 1986; children: Sara E., Azita, David A., Sam M.; m. Shahrfar Kasrai (div.). BA, Abadan Inst. Tech., Iran, 1974; MBA, U. Dallas, Irving, Texas, 1980; MS, U. Ky., Lexington, 1982; PhD, U. Ky., Kentuck, 1987. Acct. Tehran Refinery, Iran, 1976—77; asst. prof. Clarkson U., Potsdam, NY, 1988—91, Cath. U. Am., Washington, 1991—93, assoc. prof., 2008. Office: Cath Univ Am 620 Mich Ave Washington DC 20064 Office Fax: 202-319-4426. Business E-Mail: saidi@cua.edu.

SAIFER, MARK GARY PIERCE, pharmaceutical executive; b. Phila., Sept. 16, 1938; s. Albert and Sylvia (Jolles) S.; m. Phyllis Lynne Trommer, Jan. 28, 1961 (dec.); children: Scott David, Alandria Gail; m. Merry R. Sherman, June 26, 1994. AB, U. Pa., 1960; PhD, U. Calif., Berkeley, 1966. Acting asst. prof. zoology U. Calif., Berkeley, 1966, fellow, 1967-68; sr. cancer rsch. scientist Roswell Park Meml. Inst., Buffalo, 1968-70; lab. dir. Diagnostic Data Inc., Palo Alto, Calif., 1970-78; v.p. DDI Pharms., Inc., Mountain View, Calif., 1978-94, Oxis Internat., Inc., 1994-95; v.p., sci. dir. Mountain View Pharms., Inc., Menlo Park, Calif., 1996—, also bd. dirs. Lectr., expert witness in field. Author, patentee in field:, mem. editl. bd.: Current Pharm. Biotechnology Jour. Mem. AAAS (life), Am. Assn. Pharm. Scientists, Parenteral Drug Assn. Office: Mountain View Pharms Inc 3475 Edison Way Ste S Menlo Park CA 94025-1821 E-mail: saifer@mvpharm.com.

SAIGO, ROY HIROFUMI, academic administrator, botanist; b. Aug. 6, 1940; BA, U. Calif., Davis, 1962; PhD, Oreg. State U., Corvallis, 1969. Mem. faculty U. Wis., Eau Claire, 1967-84; intern acad. affairs U. Wis. Sys., Madison, 1976-77, dir. rsch. projects, summer 1976; asst. to dean Coll. Arts and Scis. U. Wis., Eau Claire, 1976-80; asst. dean, 1981-84; dean Coll. Natural Scis. U. No. Iowa, Cedar Falls, 1984-90; provost, v.p. acad. and student affairs Southeastern La. U., Hammond, 1990-94; chancellor Auburn U., Montgomery, Ala., 1994—2000; pres. St. Cloud State U., Minn., 2000—07, disting. acad. fellow, 2007—08; cons. Higher Edn. Leadership Diversity, 2008—. Bd. dirs. Bremer Bank. Bd. dirs. Children's Trust Fund, Ala. Shakespeare Festival, Montgomery Mus. Fine Arts, United Way; mem. alumni bd. Auburn U., Montgomery; mem. bd. dirs. Columbia East Med. Ctr., mem. Com. of 100. Recipient Charles E. Bessey award Bot. Soc. Am., svc. and contbn. award Am. Inst. Biol. Scis., Disting. Alumni award U. Calif., Davis, 1994; named Disting. Alumni fellow Oreg. State U, 2005; named to Alpha Gamma Rho Hall of Fame, Phi chpt., 1996. Fellow AAAS (life); mem. Am. Assn. Higher Edn., Am. Assn. State Colls. and Univs., Montgomery C. of C. (bd. dirs.), Phi Delta Kappa, Pi Kappa Phi, Omicron Delta Kappa, Sigma Xi Soc. Personal E-mail: rhsaigo@gmail.com.

SAIKI, PATRICIA, federal agency administrator, congressman; b. Hilo, Hawaii, May 28, 1930; d. Kazuo and Shizue (Inoue) Fukuda; m. Stanley Mitsuo Saiki, June 19, 1954; children: Stanley Mitsuo, Sandra Saiki Williams, Margaret C., Stuart K., Laura H. BA, U. Hawaii, 1952. Tchr. U.S. history Punahou Sch., Kaimuki Intermediate Sch., Kalani High Sch., Honolulu, 1952-64; sec. Rep. Party Hawaii, Honolulu, 1964-66, vice chmn., 1966-68, 82-83, chmn., 1983-85; rsch. asst. Hawaii State Senate, 1966-68; mem. Hawaii Ho. of Reps., 1968-74, Hawaii State Senate, 1974-82, 100th-101st Congresses from 1st Hawaii dist., Washington, 1987-91; adminstr. SBA, Washington, 1991-93. Mem. Pres.'s Adv. Coun. on Status of Women, 1969-76; mem. Nat. Commn. Internat. Women's Yr., 1969-70; commr. We. Interstate Commn. on Higher Edn.; fellow Eagleton Inst., Rutgers U., 1970; fellow Inst. of Politics, Kennedy Sch. Govt., Harvard U., 1993; bd. dirs. Bank of Am.-Hawaii, Landmark Systems Corp., Internat. Asset Recovery Corp.; mem. nat. selection com. Innovations in Am. Govt., Ford Found., Harvard U., 1999-2002. Mem. Kapiolano Hosp. Aux.; sec. Hawaii Rep. Com., 1964-66, vice chmn., 1966-68, chmn., 1983-85; del. Hawaii Constl. Conv., 1968; alt. del. Rep. Nat. Conv., 1968, del., 1984, Rep. nominee lt. gov. Hawaii, 1982, for U.S. Senate, 1990; Rep. nominee gov. Hawaii, 1994; mem. Fedn. Rep. Women; trustee Hawaii Pacific Coll.; past bd. govs. Boys and Girls Clubs Hawaii; mem. adv. coun. ARC; bd. dirs. Nat. Fund Improvement of Post-Secondary Edn., 1982-85, East West Ctr., 2003—, Nat. Pacific Ctr. on Aging, 2004-; past bd. dirs. Straub Med. Rsch. Found., Honolulu, Hawaii's Visitors Bur., Honolulu, Edn. Commn. of States, Honolulu, Hawaii Visitors Bur., 1983-85; trustee U. Hawaii Found., 1984-86, Hawaii Pacific Coll., Honolulu. Republican. Episcopalian. Avocation: golf. Home: 784 Elepaio St Honolulu HI 96816-4710 E-mail: pfsaiki@cs.com.

SAILE, DAVID GEORGE, architecture educator, researcher; b. Kettering, Eng., Feb. 3, 1943; s. George Claypoole Alec and Chambers Ethel, adopted s. Tom Saile; m. Kirsten Felicia Nigro, June 9, 1977; 1 child, Megan Alexandra. Dip. in Arch., Leicester Coll. Art & Design, Eng., 1966; MArch., U. Ill., Urbana, Champaign, 1969; PhD, U. Newcastle, Tyne, Eng., 1981. Cert. Arcuk, Archs. Registration Coun. UK, 1968. Founder, mem. and prin. investigator, housing rsch. and develo. program U. Ill., Urbana Champaign, 1969—71, asst. prof. architecture, 1970—71; lectr. architecture U. Newcastle, 1972—78; vis. lectr. architecture U. Ariz., Tucson, 1978—80; assoc. prof. architecture U. Kans., Lawrence, 1980—87, organizer & dir., grad. program, 1980—87; vis. assoc. prof. Ariz. State U., Tempe, 1987—89; prof. architecture & interior design U. Cin., 1990—, dir., ctr. study practice, 1990—94, dir., ms.arch. degree program, 2004—. Author (editor): (45 minute documentary video) Voices of Practice, life histories of architects in the Ohio Valley region, (with P. Akins, A. Harfmann, D. Friedman and J. Wentz); contbr. articles to profl. jours., chapters to books. Coordinating com. mem., search shelter workshop AIA and Cmty. Housing Partnership, Phoenix, 1987. Recipient James White Meml. prize, U. Ill., 1969; Rsch. grant, Am. Philos. Soc., 1977, Exxon Edn. Found., 1984. Mem.: Royal Inst. Brit. Archs. (Rsch. award 1976—77), Jour. Archtl. and Planning Rsch. (editl. bd. mem. 1992—2002), Environ. Design Rsch. Assn. (bd. dir. 1991—94). Achievements include director and co-director of six international and interdisciplinary conferences on built form & culture research; director of north american symposia on emerging forms of architectural practice and crossing boundaries in practice; chair of the organizing committee of power by design, 24th annual meeting of the environmental design research association, Chicago.

SAINI, SIMARJEET SINGH, electronics engineer; b. Mandi, India, Apr. 12, 1975; s. Balbir Singh Saini and Satish Kaur; m. Manpreet Kaur, Dec. 2, 2001; 1 child, Hardit Singh. PhD, U. Md., College Park, 2001. Lead rschr. Covega, Jessup, Md., 2000—04, lead app engr., 2005—; dir. optoelectronics Altanet Comm., Greenbelt, Md., 2004—05. Cons. BSNL, Jallandhar, Punjab, India, 1994—96; cons. r&d Potomac Optronics, Seoul, 2005—. Vol. Janhith, Patiala, Punjab, India, 2004—06. Recipient Disting. Rschr., ECE, U. Md., 2000; Army Rsch. Lab fellow, U.S. Army Rsch. Lab, 1996—97, Ednl. scholar, SPIE, 2000. Mem.: IEEE. Achievements include patents for resonant coupling for tapered waveguides; design of broadband gain chips for tunablelasers; patents for resonant coupling between waevguides over tapers; highly efficient semiconductor optical devices; patents pending for non-uniform current distribution for increased performance of SOA; method for parametric discrimination in fiber bragg grating sensors; design of highest performing semiconductor optical amplifiers in the world; research in highest sensitivity fiber bragg sensors for chemical and biological sensors; discovery of PARC, a new platform for monolithic integration of photonic devices; design of highest power super-luminiscent diode; first to rural area network for Punjab using TDMA system and frequency hopping. Home: 708 Zurich Dr Waterloo ON Canada Personal E-mail: simarjeet.saini@gmail.com.

SAINI, UMA ARYA, educational association administrator; b. Agra, India, July 24; d. Kedar Nath and Sita Arya. Adv. prof. lectr., Hindi Am. U., Wash., 1973—2000, asst. dean undergraduate programs kogod bus. sch., 2000—02; dir., language tchg. ctr. Johns Hopkins U., Balt., 2002. Pub. spkr. Vedic philosophy & Literature. Radio broadcasting, (First prize, 1962); author: (book) Aarati -Vaidika Mantras Key To Spiritual Knowledge, Written and Spoken Hindi. Pres. Arya Samaj Found. North America, Rockville, Md., 1985—2004. Recipient Award, Am. U., 1985, 1987, 1992. Mem.: AAUP, TESOL, AAUW, ACTFL. Office: Lsanguage Tchg Ctr Johns Hopkins 3400 N Charles St Baltimore MD 21201 Office Fax: 410-516-8808. Business E-Mail: usaini@jhu.edu.

SAINI, VINEY, research scientist; s. Harish Chander and Neelam Saini. MS, Kurukshetra U., 2005. Rsch. trainee Semiconductor Complex Ltd., Chandigarh, India, 2004; grad. rsch. asst. UALR Nanoechnology Ctr., Little Rock, 2006—. Contbr. articles to profl. jours., scientific papers. Grant, TEAMS, 2007—08. Business E-Mail: vxsaini@ualr.edu.

SAINT, EVA MARIE, actress; b. Newark, July 4, 1924; d. John Merle and Eva Marie (Rice) Saint; m. Jeffrey Hayden, Oct. 28, 1951; children: Darrell Hayden, Laurette Hayden. BA, DFA, Bowling Green State U., 1946; student, Actors Studio, 1950. Actor: various radio and TV dramatic shows, 1947—; (plays) The Trip to Bountiful, 1953 (Outer Cir. Critics award, NY Drama Critics award, 1953), The Rainmaker, 1953, Winesburg, Ohio, 1970, The Lincoln Mask, 1972, Summer and Smoke, 1973, Desire Under the Elms, 1974, The Fatal Weakness, 1976, Candida, 1977, Mr. Roberts, First Monday in October, 1979, Duet for One, 1982—83, The Country Girl, 1986, Death of a Salesman, 1994, Lover Letters, 1994—2005, 2009, On the Divide, 1994—2007, 2009, Touch the Names, 2005; (films) On the Waterfront, 1954 (Acad. Award for Best Suporting Actress, 1955), That Certain Feeling, 1956, Raintree Country, 1957, A Hatful of Rain, 1957, North by Northwest, 1959, Exodus, 1961, All Fall Down, 1962, 36 Hours, 1963, The Sandpiper, 1964, The Russians are Coming, The Russians are Coming!, 1965, Grand Prix, 1966, The Stalking Moon, 1969, Loving, 1970, Cance My Reservation, 1972, Nothing in Common, 1986, Marітté in Ecstacy, 1995, I Dreamed of Africa, 2000, Because of Winn-Dixie, 2005, Don't Come Knocking, 2005, Superman Returns, 2006; (TV films) The Macahans, 1976 (Emmy nominee), The Fatal Weakness, 1976, Taxill, 1978 (Emmy nominee), A Christmas to Remember, 1978, When Hell Was in Season, 1980, The Curse of King Tut's Tomb, The Best Little Girl in the World, 1981, Splendor in the Grass, 1981, Love Leads the Way, 1983, Jane Doe, 1983, Fatal Vision, 1984, The Last Days of Patton, 1876, A Year in the Life, 1876, Breaking Home Times, 1987, I'll Be Home for Christmas, 1988, Voyage of Terror: The Achille Lauro Affair, 1980, People Like Us, 1990 (Emmy award, 1990), Palomino, 1991, Kiss of the Killer, 1992, My Antonia, 1994, After Jimmy, 1996, Time to Say Goodbye, 1997, Titanic, 1997; (documentaries) Primary Colors: The Story of Corita, 1991, (with Bill Moyers) Children in America's Schools, 1997, Papa's Angels, 2000, Open House, 2003; co-prodr.: (theater) Fences, 2006, Desire Under the Elms, 2007.*

SAINT-AMAND, PIERRE NEMOURS, humanities educator; b. Port-Au-Prince, Haiti, Feb. 22, 1957; came to U.S., 1978; s. Nemours and Carmen (Clerveaux) Saint-A. BA, U. Montreal, 1978; MA, Johns Hopkins U., 1980, PhD, 1981. Asst. prof. Yale U., New Haven, 1981-82, Stanford U., Calif., 1982-86; assoc. prof. Brown U., Providence, 1986-90, prof., 1990—, Francis Wayland prof., 1996—. Vis. prof. Harvard U., Cambridge, Mass., 1991-2006, U. Iowa, Iowa City, 2001. Author: Diderot, Le Labyrinthe de La Relation, 1984, Séduire Ou La Passion des Lumières, 1986, Les Lois de L'Hostilité, 1992, The Libertine's Progress, 1994, The Laws of Hostility, 1996; editor: Diderot, 1984, Le Roman au Dix-huitième siècle, 1987, Autonomy in the Age of the Enlightenment, 1993, Thérèse philosophe, 2000, Confession d'une jeune fille, 2005. Fellow Stanford Humanities Ctr., 1985-86, John Simon Guggenheim Meml. Found., 1989; decorated chevalier dans l'Ordre des Palmes académiques, 2001. Office: Brown U PO Box 1961 Providence RI 02912-1961

ST. AMANT, KIRK, communications educator; m. Dori St. Amant; children: Lily Amant, Isabelle Amant. BA, Bowdoin Coll., Brunswick, Maine, 1993; MA, James Madison U., Harrisonburg, Va., 1998; PhD, U. Minn., St. Paul, 2002. Assoc. prof. tech. and profl. communication East Carolina U., Greenville, NC, 2008—. Contbr. articles to profl. jours. Mem. large, exec. com. Coun. Programs Tech. and Sci. Communication, 2006—08. Recipient Innovative Tchg. award, Tex. Tech U., 2006, Excellence Tech. award, Austin Soc. Tech. Communication, 2006, Lone Star Dallas Soc. Tech. Communication, 2007. Mem.: IEEE, Profl. Communication Soc. (mem., adminstrv. exec. com. 2004), Coun. Programs Tech. and Sci. Communication, Soc. Tech. Communication.

ST. ANTOINE, THEODORE JOSEPH, retired law educator, arbitrator; b. St. Albans, Vt., May 29, 1929; s. Arthur Joseph and Mary Beatrice (Callery) S.; m. Elizabeth Lloyd Frier, Jan. 2, 1960; children: Arthur, Claire, Paul, Sara. AB, Fordham Coll., 1951; JD, U. Mich., 1954; postgrad., U. London, 1957—58. Bar: Mich. 1954, Ohio 1954, DC 1959. Assoc. Squire, Sanders & Dempsey, Cleve., 1954; assoc., ptnr. Woll, Mayer & St. Antoine, Washington, 1958-65; assoc. prof. law U. Mich. Law Sch., Ann Arbor, 1965-69, prof., 1969—81, Degan prof., 1981-98, Degan prof. emeritus, 1998—, dean, 1971-78. Pres. Nat. Resource Ctr. for Consumers of Legal Svcs., 1974—78; mem. pub. rev. bd. UAW,

1973—2008, chmn., 2000—08; spl. counselor on workers' compensation Gov. of Mich., 1983—85; chmn. UAW-GM legal svcs. plan, 1983—95; reporter Uniform Law Commrs., 1987—92; mem. discipline bd. Mich. Atty., 1999—2005, vice chmn. discipline bd., 2000—02, chmn. discipline bd., 2002—05; life mem. Clare Hall, Cambridge (Eng.) U. Co-author: (with R. Smith, L. Merrifield, C. Craver and M. Crain) Labor Relations Law: Cases and Materials, 4th edit., 1968, 11th edit., 2005; editor: The Common Law of the Workplace: The Views of Arbitrators, 2d. edit., 2005; contbr. articles to profl. jours. 1st lt. JAGC US Army, 1955—57. Fulbright grantee, U. London, 1957—58. Mem. ABA (past sec. labor law sect., coun. 1984-92), Am. Bar Found., State Bar Mich. (chmn. labor rels. law sect. 1979-80), Nat. Acad. Arbitrators (bd. govs. 1985-88, v.p. 1994-96, pres. 1999-2000), Internat. Soc. Labor and Social Security Law (U.S. br. exec. bd. 1983-2009, vice chmn. 1989-95), Am. Arbitration Assn. (bd. dirs. 2000—, exec. com. 2008-), Nat. Workrights Inst. (bd. dirs. 2005-), Labor and Employment Rels. Assn., Coll. Labor and Employment Lawyers, Order of Coif (life). Democrat. Roman Catholic. Home: 1421 Roxbury Rd Ann Arbor MI 48104-4047 Office: U Mich Law Sch 625 S State St Ann Arbor MI 48109-1215 Office Phone: 734-764-9348. Business E-Mail: tstanton@umich.edu.

ST. AUBIN, KENDRA JANE, Librarian; b. Mpls., Mar. 8, 1946; d. Philip Maynard Peterson and Beth Marie (Johnson) Peterson; m. David K. St. Aubin, Apr. 12, 1980. BA, Macalester Coll., St. Paul, Minn., 1968; MA, U. Denver, Colo., 1969, Fairleigh Dickinson U., Teaneck, NJ, 1979. Sr. reference libr. NY Pub. Libr., NYC, 1973—76, reference libr., 1970—73; head reference & govt. docs Fairleigh Dickinson U., Teaneck, NJ, 1976—80; reference libr. Wheaton Coll., Norton, Mass., 1980—84; head tech. libr. Sippican, Inc., Marion, Mass., 1984—88; info. services libr. Codex Corp., Mansfield, Mass., 1988—91; chief cataloguer and coord. RI Hist. Soc. Libr., Providence, 1991—93; bibliographic svc. coord. Southern New Eng. Sch. Law, Dartmouth, Mass., 1993—2000; head collection devel. Bridgewater State Coll., Mass., 2000—. Contbr. articles to profl. jours. Trustee Elizabeth Tabor Libr., Marion, 1988—92; planning & budget comm. Southeastern Mass Libr. Sys., Lakeville, Mass., 2006—. Recipient Academic Excellence award, Bridgewater State Coll., 2005. Mem.: ALA, Spl. Librs. Assn. (R.I.chpt. pres. 1990—92, sec. 2001—05), Law Librs. New Eng. (program comm. coord. 1998), Assn. Coll. Rsch. Libr. (coll. lib sec. mem. chair 2002—06, New England chpt.sec. 2004—06, mem. chair 2006—), Assn. Lib Coll & Tech. Serv., Phi Beta Kappa, Phi Alpha Theta, Beta Phi Mu. Office: Bridgewater State Coll Maxwell Library Bridgewater MA 02325

ST. CLAIR, DONALD DAVID, lawyer; b. Hammond, Ind., Dec. 30, 1932; s. Victor Peter and Wanda Small; m. Sergine Anne Oliver, June 6, 1970 (dec. June 1974); m. Beverly Joyce Tipton, Dec. 28, 1987. BS, Ind. U., Bloomington, 1955, MS, 1963, EdD, 1967; JD, U. Toledo, Ohio, 1992. Bar: Ohio 1992, US Dist. Ct. (no. dist.) Ohio 1993, US Supreme Ct., 1996. Assoc. prof. Western Ky. U. Coll. Edn., Bowling Green, 1967-68, U. Toledo, 1968-77, prof., 1977-92; atty., ptnr. Garand, Bollinger, & St. Clair, Oregon, Ohio, 1992-97; pvt. practice Toledo, 1997—2006. Mem. Ohio Coun. Mental Health Ctrs., Columbus, 1978-79; dir. honors programs U. Toledo. Author: (poetry) Daymarks and Beacons, 1983, Impressions from an Afternoon in a Paris Courtroom, 1998; contbr. articles to profl. jours. Organizer Students Toledo Organized for Peace, 1970-71; mem. Lucas County Dem. Party, 1990—. With US Army, 1955-57. Mem. ABA, AAU (nat. bd. dirs. 1973-74), Am. Inns of Ct., Ohio Bar Assn., Toledo Bar Assn., Ohio Acad. Trial Lawyers, Toledo Power Squadron (comdg. officer 1981), Bay View Yacht Club, Ohio Criminal Def. Lawyers Assn., Lucas County Bar Assn., Maumee Valley Criminal Def. Lawyers Assn., Ottawa County Bar Assn., Masons (32 degree), Shriners, Ancient Order Friars, Phi Alpha Delta.

ST. CLAIR, GLORIANA STRANGE, librarian, dean; b. Tonkawa, Okla., Dec. 13, 1939; d. Glen Leroy and Doris Mildred (Furber) Strange. BA in English, U. Okla., 1962, PhD in Literature, 1970; MLS, U. Calif., Berkeley, 1963; MBA in Mgmt., U. Tex., San Antonio, 1980. Rsch. asst. U. Calif., Berkeley, 1962-63, asst. libr., 1963-65; cataloguer U. Okla., Norman, 1965-68; supervising libr. San Antonio Pub. Libr., 1980-84; head acquisitions divsn. Tex. A&M U. Librs., College Station, 1984-87, humanities bibliographer, 1985, head pers. ops., 1986; asst. dir. tech. automation and adminstrv. svc. Kerr Libr., Oreg. State U., Corvallis, 1987-90; assoc. dean, head info. access svcs. Pa. State U. Librs., University Park, 1990-98; dean univ. libr. Carnegie Mellon U., Pitts., 1998—. Editor Coll. & Rsch. Librs., 1990-96, Jour. Academic Librarianship, 1996—. Bd. dirs. U. Libr.,1998-; mem. vestry, mem. book discussion group Ch. Redeemer; examiner Pa. Quality Leadership, 1994. Sr. fellow UCLA, 1991. Mem. Assn. Coll. and Rsch. Librs. (chair editl. adv. bd. 1990-96). Home: 154 N Bellefield Ave Apt 80 Pittsburgh PA 15213-2640 Office: Univ Librs Carnegie Mellon U 4909 Frew St Pittsburgh PA 15213-3890 Home Phone: 412-683-4920; Office Phone: 412-268-2447. Office Fax: 412-268-2793.

ST. CLAIR, JESSE WALTON, JR., retired savings and loan association executive; b. Phila., Jan. 15, 1930; s. Jesse Walton and Susan Elizabeth (Leath) St. C.; m. Elizabeth Anne Bartlett, Oct. 6, 1951; children: Jesse Walton III, Susan Elizabeth, Bruce Bartlett, Anne Leath. BA, Coll. of William and Mary, 1951; MBA, U. Pa., 1958; postgrad., Harvard U., 1968. Trainee Fed. Res. Bank, Phila., 1955-57; with Girard Trust Bank, Phila., 1957-78, asst. treas., 1960-64, asst. v.p., 1964-67, v.p., 1967-70, sr. v.p., 1970-75, exec. v.p., 1976-78; pres., chief exec. officer First Nat. Bank of Allentown (Pa.), 1978-82; chmn., chief exec. officer Wilmington Savs. Fund Soc., 1982-90, ret., 1990. Trustee emeritus endowment fund Coll. William and Mary; former mem. exec. bd. Delmarva coun. Boy Scouts Am.; past trustee Wesley Coll. With USN, 1951-55. Mem. Wilmington Country Club, Theta Delta Chi. Republican. Methodist. Home: 726 Loveville Rd Rm 1032A Hockessin DE 19707-1532

ST. CLAIR, THOMAS MCBRYAR, mining and manufacturing company executive; b. Wilkinsburg, Pa., Sept. 26, 1935; s. Fred C. and Dorothy St. C.; m. Sarah K. Stewart, Aug. 1, 1959; children: Janet, Susan, Carol. AB, Allegheny Coll., 1957; MS, MIT, 1958; grad. advanced mgmt. program, Harvard U. With Koppers Co., Inc., Pitts., 1958-88, asst. to gen. mgr. engring. and constrn. div., 1966-69, comptroller, asst. treas., 1969-78, pres. Engineered Metal Products Group, 1978-83, v.p., asst. to chmn., 1983-84, v.p., treas., chief fin. officer, 1984-88; sr. v.p., chief fin. officer Phelps Dodge Corp., Phoenix, 1989-99; retired, 1999. Bd. dirs. Pitts. Theol. Sem.; trustee emeritus Allegheny Coll., Meadville, Pa. Mem. Fin. Execs. Inst., Duquesne Club (Pitts.). Presbyterian.

ST. CYR, MARGARET ANN (PEGGY ST. CYR), writer; b. Phila., May 1, 1932; d. Thomas Russell Reiling and Margaret Mary Cannon; m. Raymond Paul St. Cyr, May 14, 1952; children: Mary Louise, Sharon Ann, Margot Elizabeth, Daniel Paul, Mark Dennis. AA, Mesa CC, Ariz., 1977. Sec. to asst. contr. U. Pa. Hosp., Phila., 1965—67; sec. to chmn. dept. pathology Woman's Med. Coll., Phila., 1967—68; exec. sec. to asst. supt. Mesa Pub. Schs., 1969—81; advt. coord. Latter-day Sentinel, Phoenix, 1981—82; profl. writer, 1982—. Spkr. Family History Soc. Ariz. Author: From Conversion to Commitment, 1996, One Fold, One Shepherd, 1999; contbr. poetry to lit. publs. Sec. MARC Bd., Mesa, 1969—70, Mesa Constn. Week Com., 1972—74; co-founder East Falls Human Rels. Com., Phila., 1966; pres. PTA, 1965, 1966; sec. Dist. 29 Reps., Mesa, 1996, 4th vice chmn., 1997, 2d vice chmn., 1998, 1st vice chmn., 1999; precinct committeeman Dist. 18 Reps., 1994—. Served with Women's Army Corps US Army, 1950—51. Recipient, Chapel of 4 Chaplains, Phila., 1967, cert. appreciation, Maricopa County Reps., 1996, Lincoln Day award, 1999, Best Makeup award, Tempe Little Theatre, 1976, Best Actress, 1976, Best Makeup, 1977, Best Dir., 1977, Most Contbn. Mem., 1977, Best Actress, 1978, Internat. Poetry award, 2008; named Vol. of Yr., Maricopa County Reps., 1997. Mem. Lds Ch. Avocations: acting, singing, choir directing. Home: 724 S Kachina Mesa AZ 85204 Personal E-mail: pete724x@aol.com.

SAINT-CYR, MICHEL, plastic surgeon; b. Ottawa, Ontario, Canada, Aug. 9, 1968; s. Michelyne Rachel and Ian Hamilton; m. Rachel Lynne Merkord, May 25, 2007. BS, U. Ottawa, Can., 1997. MD U. Montreal, 1997, Fellow Royal Coll. Surgeons, 2002, cert. plastic surgery Royal Coll. Can., 2002. Asst. prof. plastic surgery U. Tex. Southwestern Med. Ctr., Dallas, 2005—. Dir. hand surgery clinic Parkland Meml. Hosp., Dallas, 2005—. Recipient Best Basic Sci. Study Presentation, Can. Soc. Plastic Surgeons, 2002, F.M. Woolhouse prize, Can. Soc. of Plastic Surgeons, 2002. Achievements include research in in vascular supply of the skin and flaps. Avocation: marathon running. Office: UT Southwestern Med Ctr 1801 Inwood Rd Dallas TX 75390-9132 Personal E-mail: michelsaintcyr@yahoo.ca. Business E-Mail: michel.saint-cyr@utsouthwestern.edu.

ST. FLORIAN, FRIEDRICH GARTLER, architect, educator; b. Graz, Austria, Dec. 21, 1932; came to US, 1967, naturalized, 1973; s. Friedrich and Anna Maria (Prassl) G.; m. Livia Campanella, Jan. 12, 1967; children: Alisia, Ilaria. M in Architecture, U. Graz, 1958; MS in Architecture, Columbia U., NYC, 1962; DFA honoris causa (hon.), RI Coll., Kingston, 2005, Brown U., Providence, 2006. Instr. architecture Columbia U., NYC, 1962-63; asst. prof. R.I. Sch. Design, Providence, 1963-70, assoc. prof., 1974-77; principal architect Friedrich St.Florian Architect, Providence, 1978—; prof. architecture R.I. Sch. Design, 1980—2004, prof. emeritus, 2004—, chmn. div. archtl. studies, 1977-78, dean of architecture, 1978-88, chief critic European Honors Program, 1991-93. Vis. asso. prof. MIT, Cambridge, 1970-71, 74-75 Works exhibited Nat. Inst. Architects, Rome, 1967, 14th Triennale, Milan, 1968, Moderna Museet, Stockholm, 1969, Hayden Gallery, MIT, 1973, Mus. Modern Art, NYC, 1975, 96, 2002, Drawing Ctr., NYC, 1979, Walker Art Ctr., Mpls., 1980, Georges Pompidou Ctr., Paris, 1994, Centre de Cultura Contemporania, Barcelona, 1994, Biennale di Venezia, 1996, Inst. d' Art Contemporain, Villeurfranne, 2000, Kunsthalle Frankfurt, 2003. Recipient Nat. Endowment for Arts award, 1972-73, 76-77, 79, 26th ann. Progressive Architecture Mag. award, 1979; Ctr. for Advanced Visual Studies fellow MIT, 1970-77, Rome Prize fellow, fellow Am. Acad. in Rome, 1985, Fulbright fellow, Henry Hering medal Nat. Sculpture Soc., 2007; named to RI Coll. Hall Fame, 2005. Mem. AIA (elevated coll. fellows, 2008). Design architect for the National World War II Memorial, Washington, D.C. Office: Friedrich St Florian FAIA 146 Westminster St Providence RI 02903 Home Phone: 401-272-3030; Office Phone: 401-831-8400. Business E-Mail: friedrich@fstflorian.com.

ST. GEORGE, ELAINE, art educator; b. Wilkes Barre, Pa., Mar. 11, 1948; d. John and Hilda St. George; m. Jeffrey Michael Roblyer (div.); children: Ginevra Gwen Wilson, Julia Gia Roblyer. BFA, U. Miami, 1970, MEd, 1972; MFA, U. NC, 1972. Prof. Broward CC, Davie, Fla., 1979—99; art tchr. Broward County Sch. Bd., Ft. Lauderdale, Fla., 1988—92; Prof. Palm Beach CC, Lakworth, Fla., 1999—. Restoration appraiser fine art, Delray Beach, Fla., 2004—. Paintings, original printmaking, pastel drawings, one-woman shows include Bailey Hall Broward CC, 1966. Mem.: Broward Ctr. Performing Arts, NYC Mus. Modern Art, Boca Raton Mus. Art, Ft. Lauderdale Mus. Art. Republican. Avocations: deep sea diving, tennis, horseback riding. Home and Office: 5095 Van Buren Rd Delray Beach FL 33484 Office Phone: 561-716-7959.

SAINT GEORGES CHAUMET, ERIC, electronics engineer; b. Paris, Sept. 1, 1956; s. Bertrand St. Georges Chaumet; m. Christine St. Georges Chaumet; children: Maureen St. Georges Chaumet, Laure St. Georges Chaumet, Anne-Claire St. Georges Chaumet. MS, Ecole Superieure d'Electricite, Gif-sur-Yvette, France, 1978. Hardware engr. ELA Med., Montrouge, France, 1980—81, IBM France, La Gaude, France, 1982—94; rschr. IBM T.J. Watson Rsch. Ctr., Hawthorne, NY, 1994—97; sr. rsch. engr. Tellabs Ops. Inc., Hawthorne, NY, 1997—2002; sr. prin. scientist NovaSol, Honolulu, 2003—. Mem.: IEEE, SPIE. Avocations: guitar, art, rock climbing, chess. Office: Nova Sol Ste 2800 Makai Tower 733 Bishop St Honolulu HI 96813 Business E-Mail: eric.saintgeorges@nova-sol.com. E-mail: eric.saintgeorges@ieee.org.

ST. GERMAIN, FERNAND JOSEPH, Former United States Representative, Rhode Island; b. Blackstone, Mass. s. Andrew Joseph and Pearl (Talaby) St. Germain; m. Rachel O'Neill, Aug. 20, 1953 (dec.); children: Laurene, Lisette. PhB in Social Sci, Providence Coll., 1948, LLD, 1965; LLB, Boston U., 1955; JSD (hon.), Suffolk U., 1976; DCL (hon.), Our Lady of Providence Sem., 1968; DBA (hon.), Bryant Coll., 1981; D in Pub. Svc. (hon.), Roger Williams Coll., 1981; LLB, Brown U., 1985. Bar: R.I. 1956, Fed. 1957, U.S. Supreme Ct. 1983. Mem. R.I. Ho. of Reps., 1952-60, 87th to 100th Congresses from 1st R.I. Dist., 1961-1989, chmn. house com. on banking fin. and urban affairs, 1980-88; ret., 1988. Served with AUS, 1949-52. Recipient Silver Shingle award for disting. public service Boston U. Sch. Law Alumni Assn., 1981, Alumni award disting. pub. service Boston U. Sch. Law, 1982 Mem. ABA, R.I., Bar Assn. Fed. Bar Assn., alumni assns. Our Lady of Providence Sem., Providence Coll., Boston U. Law Sch., Am. Legion. Democrat.

ST. GERMAIN, JEAN MARY, medical physicist; BS, Marymount Manhattan Coll., NYC; MS, Rutgers U. Cert. Am. Bd. Health Physics; lic. med. physicist, N.Y.; cert. Am. Bd. Med. Physics. USPHS fellow radiol. health Rutgers U., New Brunswick, NJ; fellow dept. med. physics Meml. Hosp., NYC; asst. physicist Cornell U. Med. Coll., NYC, 1968—71, instr. radiology (physics), 1971—78, clin. asst. prof., 1979—94; assoc. attending physicist Meml. Sloan-Kettering Cancer Ctr., 1993—2006, attending physicist, 2006—; acting chair dept. med. physics Meml. Hosp., 2007—. Vice chair Am. Bd. Med. Physics, 2004—, chair panel med. health physics, 1993—2000; cons. in field. Author: The Nurse and Radiotherapy, 1978; contbr. articles, chpts. to med. jours Fellow: Health Physics Soc. (Failla Meml. lectr. 1999, pres. NY chpt., pres. med. health physics sect.), Am. Assn. Physicists in Medicine (sec., bd. dirs., Disting. Svc. award 2005); mem.: Nat. Soc. Arts and Letters (regional dir., pres. N.Y. chpt., nat. career awards chair, nat. music chair), Radiol. and Med. Physics Soc. NY (past pres.), Am. Acad. Health Physics (treas. 1996—99), Am. Inst. Physics (govs. bd.), Iota Sigma Pi (treas., pres. V chpt.). Office: 1275 York Ave New York NY 10021-6007 Business E-Mail: stgermaj@mskcc.org.

SAINT-GIRARD, CHRISTIAN, theater director, actor, educator, choreographer, theater producer; b. NYC, May 29, 1954; s. Victoria J. Walter. Student, U. Oslo, 1972, Fordham U., 1972-74, Stella Adler Conservatory, NYC; studied with Uta Hagen and H. Berghof, HB Studios, NYC; studied dance, Joffrey Ballet; student dance, Am. Ballet Theatre; also others. Dir. Merry-Go-Round Playhouse, Auburn, NY, 1990-92; dir. edn. Polka Dot Playhouse, Bridgeport, Conn., 2002; artistic dir. Playhouse-on-the-Green, Bridgeport, Conn., 2002; dir. Theatre For Young Audiences, intern coord.; casting dir. Gretna Theater, 2007—. Mem. bd. advisors Actor's Outlet Theatre Ctr., N.Y.C., 1981-85, chmn. steering com., 1982-83; pres., producing artistic dir. Prodrs.' Assn. Real Theatre for Youth, Darien, Ct., 1986-87; tchr. workshops and classes; guest instr. acting and auditioning for mus. theatre and dance at profl. studios, including Actor's Outlet Theatre, Manhattan Theatre Workshop, N.Y.C., Studio at Once Upon a Time Prodns., Inc., N.Y.C., Phil Black's Dance Studio, N.Y.C., Darien Dance Ctr., Darien Arts Coun., Conn. Conservatory for Performing Arts, Workshop Prodns., Inc., Stratford (Conn.) Acad. Dance, Conn. Dance, Newtown (Conn.) Ctr. for Performing Arts, Showbiz Kids, Conn.; performer on Broadway in A Chorus Line, Grease, Shenandoah; on nat. tours in Camelot, A Little Night Music, Oliver!, title role in Pippin; performer in stock and dinner theatre in Funny Girl, Hello Dolly!, The King & I, Cabaret; and many others also appeared in TV pilots, feature films, commls. and operas. Author: (with Viveca Lindfors) (play) Three Boards and A Passion, 1981; librettist (mus. play) Alice in Wonderland, 1985, (ballet) The Red Shoes, 1987; librettist (mus. play) Small World, The Doctrine Is In, The Green Show, Rainy Day Stories, 2007; dir., choreographer Singin' in the Rain, She Loves Me, 42d Street, Cabaret, Mame, Into the Woods, Camelot, Applause, My Fair Lady, Unsinkable Molly Brown, Hello, Dolly!, Shenandoah, Music Man, Gypsy, Forty Carats, Chicago, On the Town, Twelfth Night, Cinderella, A Touch of Spring, West Side Story, Annie, Snow White, Pinocchio, Hansel and Gretel, Sleeping Beauty, The Magic Flute, Arsenic and Old Lace, Babes in Toyland, also others; choreographer Paint Your Wagon, Oklahoma, South Pacific, Fame Mem. SAG, AFTRA, Actors Equity Assn., Cath. Actors Guild. Roman Catholic. Avocations: painting, sketching, tennis.

SAINT-JACQUES, BERNARD, linguistics educator; b. Montreal, Que., Can., Apr. 26, 1928; s. Albert and Germaine (Lefebvre) Saint-J.; m. Marguerite Fauquenoy. MA, Sophia U., Tokyo, 1962; MS, Georgetown U., 1964; Doctorat es Lettres and Scis. Humaines, Paris U., 1975. Asst. prof. linguistics U. B.C., Vancouver, Canada, 1967—69, assoc. prof., 1969-78, prof., 1978-90, prof. emeritus, 1991—; prof. Aichi U., Japan, 1990—2003. Mem. U.S. Citizen Amb. Program, Order of the Rising Sun Author: Structural Analysis of Modern Japanese, 1971, Aspects sociolinguistiques du bilinguisme canadien, 1976, Language and Ethnic Relations, 1979, Japanese Studies in Canada, 1985, Studies in Language and Culture, 1995; editor: Intercultural Communication Studies, 1998; co-editor: Contrasting Political Institutions, 1997, (with M. Iwasaki) Democratic Viability in Politics, 2000. Leave fellow Can. Council, 1974; profl. fellow Japan Found., 1981; research fellow French Govt., 1982, Ohira Programme, Japan, 1983 Fellow Royal Soc. Can. Acad., Internat. Acad. Intercultural Rsch.; mem. Linguistic Soc. Am., Can. Soc. Asian Studies, Can. Linguistics Assn., Sietar Japan. Personal E-mail: bsaintj@telus.net.

ST. JOHN, ANTHONY PAUL, retired manufacturing executive; b. Washington, Jan. 13, 1937; s. Sterling St. John and Beulah Marston; m. Myra Grace Cornfeld, Oct. 30, 1959; children: James Sterling, Ivy Kemp Hurley, Mary Marston. JD, U. Va., Charlottesville, 1960; postgrad., Harvard U., Boston, 1979. Bar: Md. 1961. Atty. Amco Steel Corp., Balt., 1960—61, Nat. Labor Rels. Bd., Balt., 1961—65; asst. G.C., asst. v.p. law, v.p. union rels. Bethlehem Steel Corp., 1965—84; v.p. employee rels. Chrysler Corp., Auburn Hills, Mich., 1985—93. Adj. prof. Lehigh U., Bethlehem, 1993, 95; bd. dirs. Qualitech Steel Corp., 1999—2000. Bd. dirs. Moravian Acad., Bethlehem, 1978—85; chmn. Greater Detroit Alliance Bus., 1989—90; chmn. indsl. rels. com. Motor Vehicles Mfrs., 1990—92; bd. dirs. Henry Ford Hosp. NE, Bloomfield Hills, Mich., 1991—92, Red Cross of So. Mich., Detroit, 1989—92, Kids Peace Hosp., Bethlehem, 1993—95, Detroit C. of C., 1989—90, Muhlenberg Evening Coll., 1997—98. 1st lt. US Army, 1961—68. Mem.: Sanctuary Golf Club (sec. chmn. legal com.), Saucon Valley Country Club. Republican. Avocation: golf. Home: 1556 Saucon Valley Rd Bethlehem PA 18015 Address: 2957 Wulfert Rd Sanibel FL 33957 Personal E-mail: saintmyty@embarqmail.com.

ST. JOHN, HENRY SEWELL, JR., utility company executive; b. Birmingham, Ala., Aug. 18, 1938; s. H. Sewell and Carrie M. (Bond) St. John; m. J. Ann Morris, Mar. 7, 1959; children: Sherri Ann, Brian Lee, Teresa Lynn, Cynthia Faye. Student, David Lipscomb Coll., 1956—58, U. Tenn., 1958—59, U. Ala., 1962—64. Engring. aide Ala. Power Co., Enterprise, 1960—62, Birmingham, 1962—66; asst. chief engr. Riviera Utilities, Foley, Ala., 1966—71, sec.-treas., gen. mgr., 1972—2001. Chmn. Baldwin County unit Am. Cancer Soc., 1977; treas. Christian Care Ctr. Inc., 1981—; Deacon Foley Ch. of Christ, 1975—82, elder, 1983—; bd. dirs. AGAPE of Mobile, 1977—80; bd. dirs., pres. South Baldwin Civic Chorus, 1979—82; bd. dirs. Baldwin County Econ. Devel. Alliance, 1997—2001, exec. com., 1999—2001, sec., 1998—99, treas., 1999—2000, chmn., 2000—01. Mem.: IEEE (life), Chevrolet Nomad Assn. (bd. dirs. 1991—2002, v.p. 1993—2002), South Baldwin C. of C. (dir. 1972—75, pres. 1974, dir. 1981—90, 1992—95, amb. 2002—), Pub. Gas Assn. Ala. (bd. dirs. 1987—88), Am. Pub. Power Assn. (com. legis. and resolutions 1972—2001, chmn. State of Ala. mem. com. 1982—2001, com. on coms. 1997—2000, bd. dirs. 1997—2001, exec. com. 1999—2000, chmn. nat. membership com. 1999—2000, chmn. bylaws com. 2000—01, Kramer-Preston Pub. Svc. award 2002), United Mcpl. Distbrs. Group (bd. dirs. 1972—2001), Electric Cities Ala. (bd. dirs. 1983—2001, exec. com. 1989—2001, vice chmn. 2000—01, chmn. 2001, Heritage award 2005), Ala. Mcpl. Electric Authority (vice chmn. 1981—83, bd. dirs. 1981—2001, chmn. 1984—2001), Mcpl. Electric Utility Assn. Ala. (exec. com., dir. 1971—85), Ala. Consumer-Owned Power Distbrs. Assn. (chmn. 1974—75, sec.-treas. 1980, vice chmn. 1981, chmn. 1982—83), S.E. Electric Reliability Coun. (assoc.), South Ala. Power Distbrs. Assn. (life; chmn. 1973—74), Nat. Corvette Mus., Nat. Corvette Owners Assn., Azalea City Classic Chevy (bd. dirs., exec. com. 1989—99, v.p. 1991—92, 1996—99), Gulf Shores Golf (dir. 1974—75), Foley Quarterback (sec.-treas. 1984—85), Classic Chevy, Internat. (life). Home: PO Box 1817 Foley AL 36536-1817 Personal E-mail: stjohn@gulftel.com.

ST. JOHN, KRISTOFF, actor; b. NYC, July 15, 1966; s. Christopher Kristoff and Maria St. John; m. Mia St. John, 1991 (div. 1995); children: Julian, Paris; m. Allana Nadal, Nov. 24, 2001; 1 child, Lola. Studied, Actor's Studio, LA. Owner Moonboy Inc. prodn. com. Actor: (TV series) The Young and the Restless, 1991— (Outstanding Younger Actor in Drama Series, Daytime Emmys, 1992, Outstanding Actor in Daytime Drama Series, NAACP Image Awards, 1994, 1995, 1996, 1997, 2003,

2004, Outstanding Actor in Daytime Drama Series, NAACP Image award, 2007, 2008); guest appearances (TV series) Happy Days, 1976, The Cosby Show, 1984, A Different World, 1988, Jake and the Fatman, Diagnosis Murder, 1994, Hanging with Mr. Cooper, 1994—95, Martin, 1996, Suddenly Susan, 1998, Family Matters, 1998, For Your Love, 1999, Get Real, 1999; actor: (TV films) Roots II: The Next Generation, 1979, Beulah Land, 1980, Atlanta Child Murders, 1985, Finish Line, 1989; (films) The Champ, 1979, Avatar; dir.: (TV series) CBS Soap Break; host (fitness video) Kick Butt, 1999, host, prodr. (video) Backstage Pass. Avocations: movies, guitar.

ST. JOHN, TERRI, secondary school educator; b. Battle Creek, Mich., July 17, 1953; d. Donald George and Virginia Beth Kelley. AA, Kellogg CC, 1975; BA, U. Central Fla., 1981; MA in Edn., U. Sarasota, 1995, EdD, 2001. Cert. tchr. Fla. Tchr., debate coach Forest Hill HS, West Palm Beach, Fla., 1983—85; tchr., theatre dir. Lake Weir HS, Ocala, Fla., 1985—89; tchr., debate coach Lake Highland Prep Sch., Orlando, Fla., 1991—97, Sarasota (Fla.) HS, 1997—. Presenter in field. Supporter St. Labre Indian Sch., Ariz., 2001—, Mayo Clinic Rsch., Minn., 2002—. Recipient Outstanding Speech, Debate and Theatre Educator, NFHS, Fla., 2007; named Diamond Coach, Nat. Forensic League, 2005, Regional Coach of Yr., Fla. Forensic League Region III, 2005, 2006. Mem.: ASCD, Fla. Forensic League (v.p. ops. 2004—, 2d v.p. 2000—, mem. com. 2003—, named Region III Coach of Yr. 2005, 2006, named State Coach of Yr. 2006), Cath. Forensic League, Fla. Comm. Assn., Nat. Comm. Assn., Nat. Coun. Tchrs. English. Avocations: movies, golf, reading, theater. Office: Sarasota HS 1000 S Sch Ave Sarasota FL 34237 Business E-Mail: terri_st_john@sarasota.k12.fl.us.

ST. JULIEN, THAIS MARY, soprano, musician; d. George W. St. Julien Jr. and Rosemary Gloria Bourda. Pvt. vocal studies, Charles Paddock, New Orleans, 1973—81, Virginia Mac Watters, Bloomington, Ind., 1978—81, Norma Newton, Houston, 1981—88, Andrea von Ramm, New Orleans, 1986; pvt. recorder studies, Milton G. Scheuermann, Jr., 1975—80; apprentice, Des Moines Metro Opera Festival, Indianola, Iowa, 1987; Opera Workshop, Loyola U., New Orleans, 1977—78; Baroque performance practice, Skip Sempe, 1995. Asst. season ticket sales mgr. New Orleans Opera Guild, 1974—77; ensemble singer New Orleans Musica da Camera, 1974—78, principle vocal soloist, 1978—, asst. music dir., 1980—91, asst. instrument builder, 1981—, co-artistic dir., 1991—, founder/dir. Vox Feminae (women's vocal ensemble), 1994—, chief adminstr., 1999—; mgr. single ticket sales New Orleans Philharm. Orch., 1977—79; founder, soloist Banquette Opera, New Orleans, 1979—84; founding mem., calligrapher Scriptease Calligraphy, New Orleans, 1980—92; founding mem., soloist Ezcudantza (voice/guitar duo), New Orleans, 1982—85; part- time libr. technician Tulane U., Maxwell Music Libr., New Orleans, 1989—2005. Musical advisor Hermann Grima Ho. Mus., New Orleans, 1980—84; sec., adv. bd. Entergy Arts Bus. Ctr., New Orleans, 1997—2002; adv. bd. New Orleans Internat. Music Colloquium, 1998—2001; musical advisor Musica Antiqua, Albany, Oreg., 1998—2005; founding dir. music series Belle Alliance Hist. Plantation, Donaldsonville, La., 2002—; bd. pres. New Orleans Musica da Camera, New Orleans; instr. vocal masterclass S.W. Mo. State U.; presenter in field; founding artistic dir. Thursdays at Twilight Concert Series New Orleans Bot. Garden, 2003—. Musician (co-dir.): (albums) Satires, Desires and Excesses: Songs from the Carmina Burana, Natus Est: A Christmas Celebration, The Cross of Red: Music of Love and War from the Time of the Crusades, Maiden, Mother, Muse: The Women of the Cantigas of Alfonso X, Les Motets d'Arras: Songs and Dances of Medieval Arras, The Play of Robin and Marion, A Christmas Offering (Early Music Am./Millenium of Music Nat. Radio Competition, 1996), Natus Est, 1994, 1995, Now Make We Mirthe; musician: (co-dir., host) Alone of All Her Sex; musician: A Voice Still Heard, Early Jewish Music, (radio spl.) Praises from the Heart, Tristan et Iseult, on Cathedral, Court and Countryside Series, 1981; musician: (dir.) (albums) Medee; musician: Moonrise, Circles, Tristan et Iseult, on Cathedral, Court and Countryside Series, 1982, The Garden of Love; hist. music adv. (films) Interview with the Vampire; musician: Creole Cameos: Music of New Orleans Creoles of Color, Performances throughout the U.S.; prodr.(co-host): Continuum-WWNO2, Continuum; editor, contbr.: newsletter The Cypher (Am. Guild Organists, New Orleans); contbr. articles to profl. jours. Founding mem., pres. bd. dirs. St. Charles Ave. Com., New Orleans, 1972—75. Recipient Lifetime Achievement award, Gambit Newspaper, Tribute to the Classical Arts, 1997, Pioneer in Preservation Honor award, Hist. Dist. Landmarks Commn., 1997, Cert. of Appreciation in Thankfulness for Contributions to the City, City of New Orleans, 2001; named Vis. Artist in Residence with Musica da Camera, The Hist. Nat. Shrine of Our Lady of Prompt Succor, New Orleans, 1989—. Mem.: Soc. Am. Magicians (v.p. local assembly), La. Partnership for the Arts, Southeastern Medieval Assn., Entergy Arts Bus. Ctr., Am. Musicological Soc., Knights of Slights, Internat. Brotherhood Magicians (pres. local ring), Mensa. Avocations: magic, reading, drawing, photography. Office: New Orleans Musica da Camera 1035 Eleonore St New Orleans LA 70115 Business E-Mail: mdc@nomdc.org.

ST. LOUIS, MARTIN, professional hockey player; b. Laval, Que., Can., June 18, 1975; m. Heather St. Louis; 1 child. Grad., U. Vt., 1997. Profl. hockey player Cleve. Lumberjacks (IHL), 1997—98, Calgary Flames, 1998—2000, Tampa Bay Lightning, 2000—. Mem. Team Can., World Cup of Hockey, 2004. Recipient Lester B. Peterson award, 2004, Hart Meml. Trophy, 2004, Art Ross Trophy, 2004, First All-Star Team, NHL, 2004; co-recipient Bud Light Plus/Minus Award, 2004; named NHL Player of Yr., Sporting News, 2004; named to, NCAA East First All-Am. Team, 1995—97, NHL All-Star Game, 2003, 2004, 2007, 2008, 2009, Second All-Star Team, NHL, 2007. Achievements include being a member of Stanley Cup Champion Tampa Bay Lightning, 2004; being a member of World Cup Champion Team Canada, 2004. Office: c/o Tampa Bay Lightning 401 Channelside Dr Tampa FL 33602*

ST. MARTIN, CHARLOTTE, trade association administrator; b. 1945; BS, U. North Tex., 1967. Office mgr. to rep. James M. Collins U.S. Ho. of Reps., 1970; mgr. sales and catering The Fairmount Dallas, 1971—77; dir. sales and mktg. Loews Anatole Hotel, Loews Corp., 1977—82, pres., CEO, 1989—95; regional v.p. sales and mktg. Loews Hotels, Loews Corp., 1982—87, exec. v.p. sales and mktg., 1996—2005; pres. Dallas Convention and Visitors Bur., 1987—89; pres., CEO Charlotte St. Martin Enterprises, 2005—06; exec. dir. League of Am. Theatres and Producers, Inc., 2006—. Office: League Am Theatres and Producers Inc 226 W 47th St New York NY 10036-1487 Office Phone: 212-703-0222. Office Fax: 212-398-2409. E-mail: cstmartin@broadway.org.

ST. PIERRE, AMADA, psychologist, educator; d. Maureen St. Pierre; m. Lucas Ciardullo, Nov. 3, 2007. CAGS in Sch. Psychology, Rivier Coll., Nashua, 2008. Cert. mental health counselor NH bd. mental health, 2006. Chronic disease mgmt. Health First Family Care Ctr., Franklin, NH, 2001—04, clin. mental health counselor, 2004—07; prof. Hesser Coll., Manchester, 2007—08; sch. psychologist Goffstown Sch. Dist., NH, 2007—. Mem., crisis team response Dept. Mental Health, Concord, NH, 2004—. Mem.: NASP. Office: Goffstown Sch Dist 11 Sch St Goffstown NH 03045 Personal E-mail: st_pierre_amanda@hotmail.com. Business E-Mail: astpierre@goffstown.k12.nh.us.

ST. PIERRE, GEORGE ROLAND, JR., materials scientist, engineering executive, educator; b. Cambridge, Mass., June 2, 1930; s. George Rol and Rose Ann (Levesque) St. P.; m. Roberta Ann Hansen, July 20, 1956; children: Anne Renee, Jeanne Louise, John David, Thomas George; m. Mary Elizabeth Adams, Dec. 11, 1976; m. Gretchen Ann Butrick, June 29, 2001; 1 dau., Victoria Harris. BS, MIT, 1951, ScD, 1954; DSc (hon.), Ohio State U., 1998. Rsch. metallurgist Inland Steel Co., 1954-56; faculty Ohio State U., 1956—, prof. metall. engring., 1957-88, assoc. dean Grad. Sch., 1964-66, chmn. metall. engring., 1983-88, chmn. mining engring., 1985-92; dir. Ohio Mineral Rsch. Inst., 1984-92, prof., chmn. material sci. and engring., 1988-92, Presdl. prof., 1988-92, chmn., disting. u. prof. emeritus, 1992—; chief scientist Materials Directorate, Wright-Patterson AFB, 1995-96. Cons. in field; vis. prof. U. Newcastle, NSW, Australia, 1975; adv. com. materials sci. MIT, 1990-97; adv. bd. Argonne Nat. Lab., 1994-99. Editor: Physical Chemistry of Process Metallurgy, Vols. 7 and 8, 1961, Advances in Transport Processes in Metallurgical Systems, 1992, Transactions Iron and Steel Soc., 1994-2003; contbr. articles to profl. jours. Bd. dirs. Edward Orton Jr. Ceramic Found., 1989-92. With USAF, 1956-57. Recipient Milton (Mass.) Clarence Boylston Sci. prize, 1947; MacQuigg award, 1971; Alumni Disting. Tchr. award, 1978; named Disting. scholar Ohio State U., 1988, Presdl. prof. Ohio State U., 1988. Fellow Minerals, Metals & Materials Soc., AIME (bd. dirs. 1988-91, 93-96, Educator award 1996), Am. Soc. Materials Internat. (Bradley Stoughton Outstanding Tchr. award 1961, Gold medal 1987, Albert E. White award 1997); mem. Am. Inst. Mining Metall. and Petroleum Engrs. (Mineral Industry Edn. award 1987), Legion of honor 2003, Iron and Steel Soc. (Elliott lectr. 1994), Am. Contract Bridge League (diamond life master), Faculty Club (pres. 1990-92), Sigma Xi. Home: 4906 Stonehaven Dr Columbus OH 43220 Office: Ohio State U Dept Materials Sci/Engring 2041 N College Rd Columbus OH 43210-1124 Home Phone: 614-457-6168; Office Phone: 614-893-5287. Personal E-mail: gstpierr@columbus.rr.com.

SAINT-PIERRE, GUY, engineering executive; b. Windsor Mills, Que., Can., Aug. 3, 1934; s. Armand and Alice (Perra) Saint-P.; m. Francine Garneau, May 4, 1957; children: Marc, Guylaine, Nathalie. B in Applied Sci. in Civil Enging, Laval U., 1957; diploma, Imperial Coll., London, 1958; MSc, U. London, 1959; LLD (hon.), Concordia U., 1992; degree (hon.), Coll. Militaire Royal de Saint-Jean, 1993; DSc (hon.), Laval U., 1992; degree in Applied Sci. (hon.), Sherbrooke, 1994; DSe (hon.), Montreal U.; degree (hon.), Ottawa U., 2002. Registrar, Corp. Engrs. Que., 1964-66. V.p. Acres Que., 1967-70; minister of edn. Govt. Que., 1970-72, of industry and commerce, 1972-76; asst. to pres. John Labatt Ltd., Montreal, 1977—88, sr. v.p., 1977—88; pres., COO Ogilvie Mills Ltd., Montreal, 1977—88; pres., CEO, bd. dirs. The SNC-Lavalin Group Inc., 1989-96; chmn. bd. The SNC-Lavalin Group, Inc., 1996—2002; dir. Royal Bank of Can., 1990—2004, chmn. bd., 2001—04. Chmn. Bus. Coun. Nat. Issues, 1995—97; dir. Alcan Inc., 1995—2007, GM of Can., 1995—2004, Inst. Rsch. Public. Policy, 2003—, BCE, Bell Ban., 1994—2003. Gov. Conseil du Patronat de Que. Served as officer C.E. Can. Army, 1959—64. Decorated companion Order of Can.; named Canada's CEO of Yr., 1994, Canada's Internat. Exec. of Yr., 1996; recipient Sir John Kennedy Medal, 1993, Can. Engrs. Gold Medal award Can. Coun. Profl. Engrs., 1996; Engring. Inst. of Can.; inducted into Can. Bus. Hall of Fame, 2001. Mem.: Order Engrs. Que., Can. Mfrs. Assn. (chmn. bd., pres. 1987), Engring. Inst. Can., Montreal C. of C., Coun. Can. Unity (v.p.), Forest & Stream Club, Hermitage Club, Mt. Bruno Club, Mt. Royal Club, Can. Club Montreal (adv. com.). Liberal. Roman Catholic.

ST. PIERRE, RONALD LESLIE, public health and medical educator, academic administrator; b. Dayton, Ohio, Feb. 2, 1938; s. Leslie Frank and Ruth Eleanor (Rhoten) St.P.; m. Joyce A. Guilford, Apr. 1, 1961; children: Michele Christine, David Bryan. BS, Ohio U., 1961; M.Sc., Ohio State U., 1962, PhD, 1965. Instr. anatomy Ohio State U., Columbus, 1965-67, asst. prof., 1967-69, assoc. prof., 1969-72, prof., 1972—2002, chmn. dept. anatomy, 1972-81, assoc. v.p. health scis., 1981-83, sr. assoc. v.p. health scis. and acad. affairs, 1983—2002, assoc. dean Coll. Medicine and Pub. Health, 1987-96, vice dean Coll. of Medicine and Pub. Health, 1996-2000, exec. vice dean, 2000—02, interim dean pub. health, 1999—2002, assoc. v.p., prof. emeritus, 2002—06, spl. asst. to sr. v.p. health scis., 2002—06; assoc. dir. Cancer Rsch. Ctr., 1974-78; interim provost, v.p. for acad. affairs Capital U., Columbus, 2006—09. Vis. research asso. Duke U., 1966-67; cons. Battelle Meml. Inst., Columbus. Contbr. articles to profl. jours. Chmn. Ohio Gov.'s Com. on Employment of Handicapped, 1970-78; mem. state exec. com. Presdl. Commn. Employment of Handicapped, 1970-78, chmn., 1971-72; mem. planning and adv. council White House Conf. on Handicapped Individuals, 1975-78; mem. Columbus Mayor's Com. on Internat. Yr. of Disabled. Recipient Lederle Med. Faculty award, 1968-71, prize for basic research South Atlantic Assn. Obstetricians and Gynecologists, 1968, Outstanding Individual award Ohio Rehab. Assn., 1969, Gov.'s award for community service, 1973, Coll. Medicine Alumni Faculty Tchg. award, Ohio State U. Coll. Medicine, 2002, Univ. Disting. Svc. award, 2005. Mem. Am. Assn. Anatomists, Am. Assn. Immunologists, Soc. Exptl. Biology and Medicine, Sigma Xi (pres. Ohio State chpt. 1979-80) Republican. Presbyterian. Home: 8586 Button Bush Ln Westerville OH 43082-8675 Home Phone: 614-895-8123; Office Phone: 614-236-6108. Personal E-mail: rstpierre@insight.rr.com. Business E-Mail: rstpierr@capital.edu.

SAISSELIN, REMY GILBERT, fine arts educator; b. Moutier, Bern, Switzerland, Aug. 17, 1925; came to U.S., 1938, naturalized, 1944; s. Paul A. and Jeanne (Nydegger) S.; m. Nicole M. Fischer, May 31, 1955; children: Anne, Juliet, Peter. BA, Queens Coll., 1951; MA, U. Wis., Madison, 1952, MA in French, 1953, PhD, 1957. Asst. prof. French Western Res. U., Cleve., 1956-59; asst. curator publs. Cleve. Mus. Art, 1959-65; prof. French lit. U. Rochester, N.Y., 1965-70, prof. fine arts N.Y., 1970-87; prof. humanities Hobart & William Smith Coll., 1987-90. Asst. editor: Jour. Aesthetics and Art Criticism, 1959-62; author: Taste in Eighteenth Centruy France, 1965, Rule of Reason and Ruses of the Heart, 1970, Literary Enterprise in XVIII Century France, 1979, The Bourgeois and the Bibelot, 1984, The Enlightenment Against the Baroque, 1992; exhbns. landscapes, still lifes, and abstractions in France, 1997. Served with U.S. Army, 1944-46. Guggenheim fellow, 1972-73 Mem. Phi Beta Kappa. Home: Route de Sancerre 18220 Saint Ceols France Home Phone: 001 33 248 64 33 36.

SAITO, FRANK KIYOJI, import and export firm executive; b. Tokyo, Feb. 28, 1945; s. Kaoru and Chiyoko S.; m. Elaine Tamami Karasawa, Feb. 22, 1975; children: Roderic Kouki, Lorine Erika. LLB, Kokugakuin U., 1967. With import dept. Trois Co. Ltd., Tokyo, 1967-68; founder import/export dept. Three Bond Co., Ltd., Tokyo, 1968-71; sales mgr. Kobe Mercantile, Inc., San Diego, 1971-76; pres. K&S Internat. Corp., San Diego, 1976-97, K&S Techs., Inc., San Diego, 1997—. Office: 9710 Scranton Rd Ste 150 San Diego CA 92121-1771

SAITO, MAK, environmental scientist; BA, Oberlin Coll., Ohio, 1994; PhD, MIT-Woods Hole Oceanog., 2001. Assoc. scientist Woods Hole Oceanog. Instn., Mass., 2001—. Office: Woods Hole Oceanographic Inst 360 Woods Hole Rd Woods Hole MA 02543

SAITO, MAKOTO, economics professor; b. Japan, Aug. 30, 1940; s. Yoshie Saito and Shige Yamada. BA Commerce, Waseda U., Tokyo, 1967, MA Econs., 1972; ABD, Keio U., 1976. Lectr. Daito Bunka U., Tokyo, 1977-81, assoc. prof., 1981-90, prof. econs., 1990—. Vis. scholar U. Mich., Ann Arbor, 1982—83; vis. fellow Harvard U., Cambridge, Mass., 1983—84; short-term vis. scholar U. Cambridge, England, 1994; fin. advisor to the dir. gen. Internat. Biog. Ctr., England, 2008—. Mem.: Am. Econ. Assn., Mem. Am. Assn. for the Advancement Sci., Nat. Geog. Soc. Avocations: tennis, jogging, travel, arts, music. Home: Itabashi-ku 3-27-A-1202 Nakadai Tokyo 174-0064 Japan Office: Daito Bunka U 1-9-1 Takashimadaira Itabashi-ku Tokyo Japan Personal E-mail: vet06770@nifty.com.

SAITO, ROBERT SHUNICHI, writer, poet; b. Alameda, Calif., Sept. 9, 1933; s. Sam Shunji Saito and Yayeko Umegawa; m. Naida Cervantes, Dec. 7, 1966. Cert., Coronado Sch. Fine Arts, 1980. Enlisted USN, 1955, advanced through grades to chief petty officer, 1971, pers. officer USS Camden, 1972-75, ret., 1975. Pres. Mega Travel Inc., La Mesa, Calif., 1983-84. Author of poetry, short stories. Recipient 1st Pl. award for Batik, Coronado Art Assn., 1977. Roman Catholic. Avocations: batik art, photography, fishing, walking, tai-chi.

SAITOU, KAZUHIRO, engineering educator; b. Tokyo, Dec. 12, 1966; PhD, MIT, 1996. Asst. prof. U. Mich., Ann Arbor, 1997—2003, assoc. prof., 2003—. Recipient Career award, NSF, 1999. Mem.: IEEE, ASME, Soc. Mfg. Engrs., Sigma Xi. Office: U Mich Mech Engring Dept 2350 Hayward St Ann Arbor MI 48109-2125 Business E-Mail: kazu@umich.edu.

SAITTA, NANCY M., state supreme court justice; b. Detroit; married; 4 children. BS magna cum laude, Wayne State U., 1983, JD, 1986. Criminal def. atty., Detroit; atty. Pearson & Patton, Las Vegas; assoc. Gentile & Porter, Las Vegas; sr. dep. atty. gen., Children's Adv. State of Nev.; judge Las Vegas Mcpl. Ct., 1996—98, 8th Jud. Dist. Ct., 1998—2006; assoc. justice Nev. Supreme Ct., 2007—. Mem. Nev. State Juvenile Justice Commn.; founder Clark County Missing & Exploited Children Comprehensive Action Program (M/CAP), So. Nev. Fatality Rev. Team, Complex Litig. Divsn.; instr. Wayne State U., Criminal Justice Dept.; litig. instr. Am. Inst. Paralegal Studies; instr. U. Phoenix, Criminal Justice Dept. Mem. Clark County Pub. Edn. Found. Recipient For the Children award, Nev. Dist. Atty.'s Office, Dist. Atty. Outstanding Svc. award, Angels in Adoption award, US Congress, 2000, Child Advocate of Yr. award, 2001; named one of Top 500 Judges in Am., Law Dragon, 2005. Mem.: Clark County Bar Assn. (exec. com.), Ct. Apptd. Spl. Advocate (CASA) Found. Office: Nev Supreme Ct 201 S Carson St Ste 300 Carson City NV 89701-4702*

SAIZAN, PAULA THERESA, business consultant; b. New Orleans, Sept. 12, 1947; d. Paul Morine and Hattie Hayes Saizan; m. Paul R. Valteau Jr., Aug. 11, 2007. BS in Acctg. summa cum laude, Xavier U., 1969. CPA Tex. Sys. engr. IBM, New Orleans, 1969—71; acct., then sr. acct. Shell Oil Co., Houston, 1971—76, sr. fin. analyst, 1976—77, fin. rep., 1977—79, corp. auditor, 1979—81, treasury rep., 1981—82, sr. treasury rep., 1982—86; asst. treas. Shell Credit Inc., Shell Leasing Co., Shell Fin. Co., Houston, 1986—88, sr. pub. affairs rep., 1988—89, sr. staff pub. affairs rep., 1990—91, program mgr., 1991—96, sr. program mgr., 1996—97, mgr. constituent rels. and edn. support, 1997—2000, mgr. nat. and cmty. outreach, 2000—03, mgr. stakeholder mgmt., 2003—04, sr. advisor corp. affairs, 2005—. Pres. PTBS, Inc., Houston. Bd. dirs., Xavier U.; exec. coun. The Links, Incorporate; bd. dir., exec. com. mem. Nat. Coun. Negro Women, Inc.; del. White House Conf. on Small Bus., 1995; prior bd. svc., treas., sec. Greater Houston Convention & Visitors Bur., Houston Downtown Mgmt. Dist., NAACP Special Contbn. Fund, St. Joseph Hosp. Found., Cath. Charities Houston, UNCF Coll. Fund. SW. Mem. AICPA, NAACP (life mem., prior bd. dirs., trustee spl. contbn. fund), Tex. Soc. CPA, Assn. Governing Bds. of Univs. and Colls., Leadership Houston, LWV Houston, Xavier U. Alumni Assn., Nat. Coun. Garden Clubs (life), Nat. Congress Black Women, Alpha Kappa Alpha, Phi Gamma Nu, Kappa Gamma Phi. Roman Catholic. Home: 7601 Oak Fern Houston TX 77040-4407 Office: PTBS Inc 9211 West Rd Ste 143-146 Houston TX 77064 Business E-Mail: ptbs3@aol.com.

SAJERY, ALGENE T., legislative staff member; Scheduler, legis. asst., Rep. John Conyers US House of Reps., Washington, 2003—05, dep. chief of staff to Rep. Yvette Clarke, 2008—; pub. policy asst. Wash. Coun. of Agencies; lobbyist Lyondell Chem. Co. Democrat. Office: 1029 Longworth House Office Bldg Washington DC 20515 Office Phone: 202-225-6231. Office Fax: 202-226-0112.*

SAJJADI, HAMED, otolaryngologist; b. Tehran, Iran, 1956; came to U.S., 1974; BS in Chemistry, Creighton U., 1977, MD, 1981. Diplomate Am. Bd. Otolaryngology. Intern Martin Luther King/Drew Med. Ctr., 1981-82, resident in otolaryngology-head and neck surgery, 1982-86; fellow in neurol. otolaryngology Minn. Ear-Head-Neck Clinic, Mpls., 1986-87; pvt. practice Mpls.; assoc. prof. otolaryngology King Drew Med. Ctr./UCLA, 1987-91; assoc. prof. neurotology Minn. Ear Clinic, 1991—. Mem. staff Fairview Riverside Hosp., Mpls., 1991—, Mercy Health One; dir. neurology fellowship program Minn. Ear Clinic. Office: San Jose Ear & Sinus Med Ctr 2577 Samaritan Dr #845 San Jose CA 95124

SAJJALA, SESHADRI REDDY, agronomist; s. Venkata Krishna and Bharathi Sajjala; m. Geetha S. Chittem; 1 child, Sahithi. PhD in Agronomy, U. Agrl. Scis., Bangalore, 2003. Rsch. assoc. Agrl. Rsch. Sta., Anantapur, India, 2004—05; rsch. scientist Ala. A&M U., Normal, 2005—. Editl. bd. mem. Crop Rsch. Jour., Hissar, India, 2006—08. Contbr. articles to profl. jours. Recipient 3 Gold medals, U. Agrl. Scis., 2003, Crop Rsch. award, Agriculture Rsch. Info. Ctr., Hisar, 2004; Jr. Rsch. fellowship, Indian Counsel Agrl. Rsch., 1998—2000. Mem.: Am. Soc. Agronomy, Sigma Xi, Gamma Sigma Delta. Office: Ala A&M Univ 4800 Meridian St PO Box 1208 Normal AL 35762

SAK, GILBERT, music educator; b. Hong Kong, Oct. 17, 1967; MusB, Manhattan Sch. Music, NYC, 1991; MusM, Ball State U., Ind., 1992; PhD in Musical Arts, U. SC, Columbia, 2000; MEd, Open U. Hong Kong, 2006. 2d violin prin. SC Philharm. Orch., Columbia, 1994—95, Kalamazoo Symphony Orch., 1995—98; 1st violin tutti Malaysian Philharm. Orch., Kuala Lumpur, Selangor, Malaysia, 1998—2000; asst. prodr. Radio 4, Radio TV Hong Kong, Hong Kong, 2000—01; music instr. St. Stephen's Coll., Hong Kong, 2001—04; part-time lectr. Hong

Kong Acad. Performing Arts, 2003—; music dir. Potential Violin Inst., Hong Kong, 2005—, The Hong Kong Civic Youth Orch., 2005—; adj. faculty Hong Kong Bapt. U., 2006—; tutor Hong Kong Inst. Edn., 2009—. Advisor Scout Assn. Hong Kong, 2004. Mem.: Chamber Music Am. (assoc.), Phi Kappa Lambda, Mensa. Personal E-mail: gsgeiger67@hotmail.com.

SAKAGUCHI, TAKAO, physicist; b. Chiyoda, Tokyo, Oct. 21, 1971; s. Mitsuo and Kimie Sakaguchi; m. Kimiko Sekiguchi, Apr. 10, 2003. BS, Waseda U., Tokyo, 1994, MS, 1996, DSc, 1998. Asst. physicist Brookhaven Nat. Lab., Upton, NY, 2004—06, assoc. physicist, 2006—08, physicist, 2008—. Recipient Nuc. Physics, Young Scientist awards, Elsevier Sci., 2007. Office: Brookhaven Nat Lab Bldg 510 Upton NY 11973 Office Fax: 631-344-3253. Business E-Mail: takao@bnl.gov.

SAKAI, JAMES K., legislative staff member; b. Honolulu, July 28, 1927; m. Florence K. Tokairin, Feb. 14, 1953; 2 children. BA, U. Hawaii, 1951. Budget analyst State of Hawaii Dept. Budget and Fin., 1961—65; adminstrv. officer U. Hawaii Cmty. Colleges, 1966—68; dir., Budget and Fin. Depts. City and County of Honolulu, 1969—80; adminstrv. asst. to Senator Daniel K. Akaka US Senate, Washington, 1981—. Served with US Army, 1945—47. Mem.: Lions Club. Democrat. Office: 141 SHOB Washington DC 20510-1103 Office Phone: 202-224-6361. Business E-Mail: james_sakai@akaka.senate.gov.*

SAKAI, TAKEHIRO, surgeon; b. Hirosaki, Aomori, Japan, Feb. 3, 1972; s. Yu and Noriko Sakai. MD, Hirosaki U. Sch. Medicine, Japan, 1997, PhD, 2001. Lic. Ministry of Health, Labour, and Welfare, Japan, 1997, bd. cert. surgeon Japan Surg. Soc., 2003, bd. cert. surgeon in gastroenterology Japan Soc. Gastroenterology Surgery, 2005. Surgeon, head surgeon Aomori Rosai Hosp., Hachinohe, Japan, 2001—03, head surgeon, 2007—08, Kuroishi City Hosp., Aomori, Japan, 2003—05; surgeon Hirosaki City Hosp., 2005—07; asst prof., dept. thoracic and cardiovascular surgery Hirosaki U. Sch. Medicine, 2008—. Contbr. articles to profl. jours. Mem.: Japan Soc. Coloprotology, Japan Lung Cancer Soc., Japanese Assn. Acute Medicine, Japan Surg. Assn., Japanese Breast Cancer Soc., Japanese Soc. Gastroenterology (cert.), Japanese Gastric Cancer Assn., Japanese Assn. Thoracic Surgery, Japanese Soc. Abdominal Emergency Medicine, Japanese Soc. Gastroent. Surgery (cert.), Japan Surg. Soc. (cert.). Office: Hirosaki Univ Sch Medicine Dept Thoracic and Cardiovas Surgery 5 Zaifu-cho Hirosaki 036-8562 Japan

SAKAI, TOSHIHIKO, engineer; b. Nagoya, Aichi, Japan, July 17, 1943; s. Saichi and Yoshie (Taguchi) S.; m. Junko Fukuoka, Oct. 7, 1971; children: Eiji, Kenji; m. Natsuko Kamei, Nov. 25, 1989; children: Rei, Rui. B.Sc., Nagoya Inst. Tech., Japan, 1967; M.Sc., Ga. Inst. Tech., 1970; PhD, U.M.I.S.T., UK, 1974. Assoc. engr. Toyota Ctrl. R. & D. Labs., Inc., Aichi, Japan, 1967-75, rschr., 1975-84, sr. rschr., 1984-95. Mgr. tech. secretariat Toyota Ctrl. R & D Labs., Inc., Aichi, 1982—89, CEO staff, 1991—95, gen. mgr., 1989—95; councilor Tsuchiya Co., Ltd., Nagaya, Japan, 1995; dir., bd. dirs. Overseas Ops., 1995—2000; sr. mng. dir. NIC Corp. (Venture Capital), Nagoya, Japan, 2001—; exec. v.p., COO Techno Search, Inc., Nagoya, 2004—09, counselor, 2009—. Contbr. articles to profl. jours.; inventor and patentee in field. Submit referee Textile Machinery Soc. Japan. Fellow Textile Inst. (UK); mem. Soc. Fiber Sci. and Tech. Japan, Soc. Automotive Engr., The NPO Rsch. Assn. New Industry Creation (sr. mn. dir. 2001—), Nagoya Jr. Chamber (exec. v.p. 1982). Avocations: travel, driving, golf. Home: City Corp B1003 Ueda 3-1501 Tempaku Nagoya 468-0051 Japan Office: Techno Search Inc Nagoya C of C I Bldg 10-F Sakae 2-10-19 Naka Nagoya 460-0008 Japan Home Phone: 81-52-805-9090; Office Phone: 81-52-205-3021. Business E-Mail: sakait@techno-search.com.

SAKAI, YU, pathologist; b. Osaka, Japan, July 10, 1966; s. Kunisuke and Kazuko Sakai; m. Asako Kondo, June 10, 2000. MD, Nat. Def. Med. Coll., Tokorozawa, Japan, 1991; PhD, Juntendo U., Bunkyo-ku, Japan, 2002. Jr. resident Nat. Def. Med. Coll., Tokorozawa, 1991—93, sr. resident, 1995—97; physician Japan Self Def. Force Fukuoka Hosp., Kasuga, Fukuoka, Japan, 1993—94; pathologist Japan Self Def. Forces Ctrl. Hosp., Setagaya-ku, Tokyo, 1994—95, 1997—2005, Japan Self Def. Forces Sapporo Gen. Hosp., Japan, 2005—07; chief, test and evaluation sect. Mil. Medicine Rsch. Unit, Tokyo, 2007—09; chief, dept. pathology Kainan Hosp. Aichi Prefectural Welfare Fedn. Agrl. Coops., 2009—. Fellow: Japanese Soc. Pathology; mem.: Japanese Soc. Lab. Medicine, Japanese Soc. Clin. Cytology. Avocation: fishing. Office: Kainan Hosp Dept Pathology 396 Minami Honda Maegasu Yatomi Aichi 498-8502 Japan Personal E-mail: zwq04043@nifty.ne.jp.

SAKAMOTO, KATSUYUKI, retired academic administrator, psychologist, educator; b. LA, Oct. 24, 1938; m. Edna Christine Sakamoto; children: David Katsu, Bryce Yoshio. BA in Psychology, Calif. State U., Fresno, 1961, MA in Psychology, 1968; PhD in Exptl. Social Psychology, So. Ill. U., Carbondale, 1971; postgrad., Carnegie Mellon U., 1984. Acting dir. Army Edn. Ctr., Munich, 1962-63; dir. social svcs. Salvation Army, Fresno, Calif., 1964-66; assoc. prof. psychology Keuka Coll., Keyka Park, N.Y., 1971-78; prof. social psychology Ea. Oreg. State Coll., La Grande, 1978-85, assoc. dean, then acting dean, 1980-82, 84, assoc. dean acad. affairs, 1982-85; prof. psychology Ind. U. East, Richmond, 1985-91, vice chancellor for acad. affairs, 1985-90, spl. asst. to chancellor, 1990-91; prof., chancellor Calif. Sch. Profl. Psychology, Alameda, 1991-98, ret., 1998. Lectr. So. Ill. U., 1970-71; vis. prof. SUNY, Binghamton, 1973; adj. prof. Alfred (N.Y.) U., 1972-76, Nazareth Coll. Rochester, N.Y., 1975-78, Eisenhower Coll., Seneca Falls, N.Y., 1975-77; evaluator Western Assn. Schs. and Colls., 1991—; commr.-at-large North Ctrl. Assn. Colls. and Schs., 1989-91, educator, cons., 1986-91; mem. exec. bd. for study ctrs. in Japan, China and Korea, campus dir. Oreg. Sys. Higher Edn., 1980-85; bd. visitors Newark (N.Y.) Devel. Ctr., 1975-77; presenter in field. Contbr. articles to profl. jours. Bd. dirs. troop 119 Boy Scouts Am., Richmond, 1986-91, Project 100001, Townsend Cmty. Ctr., Richmond, 1987-89, Alameda Girls Club, Inc., 1992—, Asian Cmty. Mental Health Svcs., 1991—, Found. for Ednl. Excellence, Alameda, 1993—; pres., bd. dirs. Whitewater Opera Co., Richmond, 1987-91, Leadership Wayne County, Richmond, 1988-91; cons. teaching mini-grant program Richmond Cmty. Schs., 1988-91; mem. citizens adv. bd. Wayne County Sheriff's Dept., 1989-91. Mem. APA, Am. Assn. for Higher Edn., Am. Assn. State Colls. and Univs., Am. Assn. Univ. Adminstrs. (nat. v.p. 1990-92, bd. dirs. Found. 1991—), Am. Assn. for Higher Edn. (founding mem. Asian Am. caucus), Asian Am. Psychol. Assn. (treas., membership officer 1983-91, pres. 1988-91), Calif. Psychol. Assn., Nat. Assn. Acad. Affairs Adminstrs., Nat. Coun. Schs. Profl. Psychology, Rotary (bd. dirs. Alameda 1993—). Office: Calif School Of Prof Psychology 1 Beach St Ste 100 San Francisco CA 94133-1221 Home: 1650 Polo Park DR Reno NV 89523-7169

SAKAMOTO, NORMAN LLOYD, state legislator, civil engineer; b. Honolulu, May 22, 1947; s. Shuichi and Fusa (Hayashi) S.; m. Penelope A. Hayasaka, July 12, 1970; children: David H., Gregory F., Katherine E. BSCE, U. Hawaii, 1969; MSCE, U. Ill., 1970. Registered profl. engr., Calif., Hawaii; lic. spl. inspector, Hawaii; lic. contractor, Hawaii. Pres. Sundance Cir., Inc., Hwn Emporium, Inc.; engr. storm drain City of L.A., 1970-71, engr. streets and frwys., 1972-73; engr. hydrology C.E., 1971-72; v.p. S & M Sakamoto, Inc., Honolulu, 1973-85; pres. SC Pacific Corp., Honolulu, 1985—; mem. Dist. 15 Hawaii State Senate, Honolulu, 1996—. Bd. dirs. Bldg. Industry Assn., Honolulu, spl. appointee, 1991-92, pres.-elect, 1993, pres., 1994; bd. dirs. City Contractors Assn., Honolulu; trustee Home Builders Inst., 1993-96; del. White House Conf. on Small Bus., 1995; co-chair Hawaii Congress on Small Bus. Scoutmaster Honolulu area Boy Scouts America, 1989-92, asst. scoutmaster, 1993; mem. Aliamanu Clubhouse adv. bd. Boys and Girls Club; exec. com. Edn. Commn. of the States, 2006—. Named Remodeler of Month Bldg. Industry Assn., 1990, 91, 96, Remodeler of Yr., 1991, Legislator of Yr., Bldg. Industry Assn., 2003, Legislator of Yr., Friends of the Libr., 2004; recipient Excellence award U. Hawaii, 2005, Charles Dick Medal of Merit, Nat. Guard Assn. US, 2005, State Dirs. award, Career and Tech. Edn. U. Hawaii, 2006, Legis. Yr. award, Am. Sch. Health Assn., 2007. Mem. ASCE, Nat. Assn. Home Builders, Internat. Fellowship Christian Businessmen, Nat. Fedn. Ind. Bus. (Guardian of Small Bus. award 1999), Constrn. Industry Legis. Assn., C. of C., Nat. Fedn. Ind. Bus. (leadership coun., 2007, Leadership Coun. Emeritus award, 2007). Democrat. Evangelical. Office: SC Pacific Corp 3210-A Koapaka St Honolulu HI 96819 also: Hawaii State Capitol 415 South Beretania St Rm 230 Honolulu HI 96813 Office Phone: 808-586-8585. Business E-Mail: sensakamoto@Capitol.hawaii.gov.*

SAKAMOTO, RONALD RIKIO, lawyer, construction executive; b. Honolulu, Oct. 2, 1951; s. Richard Tadashi and Hideko Sakamoto; m. Marie Kanno, Jan. 14, 2006; 1 child, Aaron Naoyuki. B in Econs. with distinction, Whitman Coll., 1973; JD, U. Hawaii, 1979. Bar: Hawaii 1979. Atty. Damon Key Char & Bocken, Honolulu, 1979—89, Char Sakamoto Ishii Lum and Ching, Honolulu, 1989—, pres., 2004—; v.p. Tileco Inc., Kapolei, Hawaii, 1983—, also bd. dirs. Dir. officiating AYSO Nat. Games, 2008. Bus. and prodn. mgr. U. Hawaii Law Rev., 1978—79. Chair Friends William S. Richardson Sch. Law, Honolulu, 1982—87; bd. dirs. Hawaii Lupus Found., Inc., Honolulu, 1988—93, Hawaii Health Found., Honolulu, 1996—; sect. referee adminstr. sect. 7 (Hawaii) Am. Youth Soccer Orgn., 2005—; mem. law rev. adv. com. U. Hawaii Sch. Law, Honolulu, 1980—93; nat. referee commn. Am. Youth Soccer Orgn., Hawthorne, Calif., 2005—07, regional referee adminstr. region 178 Honolulu, 2003—05; pres. Assn. Apt. Owners 855 Olokele, Honolulu, 1980—81. Recipient Nat. Referee Spirit award, Am. Youth Soccer Orgn., 2009; named Referee of the Yr. Region 178, Honolulu, 2002, Referee Instr. of the Yr. Sect. 7, Hawaii, 2005, Referee of Yr., 2007, Outstanding Farringtonian, Farrington H.S., 1969; M.M. Scott scholar, Hawaiian Trust, 1969—73. Mem.: ABA, Hawaii State Bar Assn. (chmn. bus. law sect. 1985, chmn. tax sect. 1994—95), William S. Richardson Sch. Law Alumni Assn. (bd. dirs. 1979—85). Office: Char Sakamoto Ishii Lum and Ching 841 Bishop St # 850 Honolulu HI 96813

SAKIC, JOE (JOSEPH STEVEN SAKIC), retired professional hockey player; b. Burnaby, BC, Canada, July 7, 1969; m. Debbie Sakic; children: Mitchell, Chase, Kamryn. Center Colo. Avalanche (formerly Que. Nordiques), 1991—2009, capt., 1992—2009. Mem. Team Can., World Cup of Hockey, 1996, 2004, Team Can., Olympic Games, Nagano, Japan, 1998, Salt Lake City, 2002. Recipient Conn Smythe Trophy, 1996, Hart Trophy, 2001, Lester B. Pearson Award, 2001, Lady Byng Trophy, 2001, MVP Award, NHL All-Star game, 2004, NHL Found. Player Award, 2007; named NHL Player of Yr., Sporting News, 2001; named to NHL All-Star game, 1990—94, 1996, 1998, 2000—02, 2004, 2007. Achievements include being a member of Stanley Cup Champion Colorado Avalanche, 1996, 2001; being a member of gold medal winning Canadian Hockey Team, Salt Lake City Olympic Games, 2002; being a member of World Cup Champion Team Canada, 2004; becoming the 11th player in NHL history to record 1000 career assists, 2008.*

SAKIDJA, RIDWAN, research scientist; s. Heriyetti Sakidja; m. Upik Yunengsih, Jan. 13, 1996; children: Anisa Putri Yudawanti, Ardian Yudawan, Rezky Ichsan. PhD, U. Wis.-Madison, 2003. Rsch. assoc. U. Wis.-Madison, 2003—06, asst. scientist, 2006—. Contbr. 30 sci. papers. Mem.: TMS. Achievements include patents for oxidation resistant coatings for ultra high temperature transition metals and transition metal alloys; research in high temperature alloys; ultra-high temperature corrosion resistance coatings; patents pending for low temperature synthesis of integrated aluminide coatings for corrosion & wear resistance. Office: Univ Wis-Madison 1500 Engineering Dr Madison WI 53706 Business E-Mail: rsakidja@facstaff.wisc.edu.

SAKOWITZ, PHILIP E., federal agency administrator; BS, Long Island Univ., 1975. Youth activities dir., Fort Monmouth, NJ, 1975—78, Fitsimmons Army Med. Ctr., Colo., 1978—98; sports dir. NY Area Command, Fort Hamilton, 1981; chief cmty. morale services US Army Materiel Command, Alexandria, Va., 1981—88; dir. program anal. & evaluation US Army Cmty. & Family Support Ctr., Alexandria, Va., 1988—89; chief morale welfare & recreation Directorate of Personnel US Army Forces Command, Fort McPherson, Ga., 1989—96; asst. dep. chief of staff personnel & installation mgmt. US Army Forces Command, Fort McPherson, Ga., 1996—98; dep. chief of staff base ops. support US Army Training & Doctrine Command, Fort Monroe, Va., 1998—2002; dir. Installation Mgmt. Transformation Task Force, Arlington, Va., 2002; exec. dir. US Army Installation Mgmt. Command, Arlington, Va., 2002—08; dir., CEO Def. Commissary Agy., Fort Lee, Va., 2008—. Recipient Decoration for Exceptional Civilian Svc., US Army, Recognition for Svc. & Contributions to our Country, NAACP; named to Meritorious Presdl. Rank (2). Office: Def Commissary Agy 1300 E Ave Fort Lee VA 23801-1800 Office Phone: 804-734-8000.*

SAKS, JUDITH-ANN, artist; b. Anniston, Ala., Dec. 20, 1943; d. Julien David and Lucy-Jane (Watson) S.; m. Haskell Irvin Rosenthal, Dec. 22, 1974; 1 child, Brian Julien. Student, Tex. Acad. Art, 1957-58, Mus. Fine Arts, Houston, 1962, Rice U., 1962; BFA, Tulane U., 1966; postgrad., U. Houston, 1967. Curator student art collection U. Houston, 1968-72; artist Am. Revolution Bicentennial project Port of Houston Authority, 1975-76. One-woman shows include Alley Gallery, Houston, 1969, 2131 Gallery, Houston, 1969; group shows include Birmingham (Ala.) Mus., 1967, Meinhard Galleries, Houston, 1977, Galeire Barbizon, Houston, 1980, Park Crest Gallery, Austin, 1981, Margolis Gallery, 2005-06; represented in permanent collections at L.B. Johnson Manned Space Mus., Clear Lake City, Tex., Harris County Heritage Mus., Windsor Castle, Smithsonian Instn.; commns. include Pin Oak Charity Horse Show Assn., Roberts S.S. Agy., New Orleans, Cruiser Houston Meml. Rm., U. Houston; contbr. popular mags. Recipient art awards including 1st prize for water color Art League Houston, 1969, 1st prize for graphics, 1969, 1st prize for sculpture, 1968, Nat. 1st place award for original print DAR/Am. Heritage Com., 1987, Nat. 1st place award for acrylic painting, DAR, 2000, Nat. Hon. Mention for Acrylics, 2006, Tex. award for Acrylic, 2003, 06, Nat. 3rd place award for painting, 2003, Nat. 3rd prize for acrylic, 2005, Nat. 1st prize for acrylic, 2007, Tex. State 1st prize for drawing DAR, 2002, Shofar award, 2003, Outstanding Svc. award Boy Scout Troop 806, 2002, Tex. award for art, 2005, Artist Martha Washington Pin, 2008, Nat. 1st prize for Collage, 2009, Tex. 2nd Pl., Pressbook, 2009. Mem. Art League Houston, Houston Mus. Fine Arts, DAR (chpt. curator 1983-85, 93-95, 2007-09, rec. sec. 2001-03, libr. 2003-2005, counselor, 2005-07, chaplain, 2009-, Tex. Best Chpt. Chmn. award 2003, 06, Tex. award for art 2003, Tex. State 1st prize acrylic 2004, 2005, Tex. Cert. award for acrylic 2006), Daus. Republic of Tex., Magna Charta Dames, Colonial Dames America, Jamestowne Soc.

SAKS, STEPHEN HOWARD, accountant, health organization executive; b. Phila., May 16, 1941; s. Samuel and Edythe (Edelman) S.; m. Ruth Workman, Dec. 22, 1963; children: Amy Meryl, Brian Eric, Joshua Marc. BS in Econs., U. Pa., 1962. CPA, Pa. Staff acct. to ptnr. Peat, Marwick, Mitchell & Co., Phila., 1962-78; ptnr. Laventhol & Horwath, Phila., 1978-91; CFO Northeastern Health Sys., Phila., 1991—2001, Neumann Med. Ctr., Phila., 1992-98, Elkins Park Hosp., Pa., 2002—03; exec. dir. John F. Kennedy Meml. Hosp., Phila., 1998-99; v.p. fin. Cooper Health Sys., Camden, NJ, 1999—2001; interim CFO Whitman-Walker Clinic, Washington, 2004; dir. Shechtman Marks Devor PC, Phila., 2005—. Bd. dirs. Jewish Family and Children's Agy, Phila,. 1979-88; treas. Jewish Employment and Vocat. Svc., Phila., 1984-88; chmn. bd. overseers Gratz Coll., Melrose Pk., Pa., 1987-90; pres. Beth Sholom Men's Club, Elkins Pk., Pa., 1987-90. Mem. AICPA, Pa. Inst. CPAs, Healthcare Fin. Mgmt. Assn. (advanced). Democrat. Avocations: community activities, travel. Home Phone: 610-584-8353; Office Phone: 215-496-9339. Personal E-mail: shsaks@verizon.net. E-mail: ssaks@smd-pc.com.

SAKURADA, YUTAKA, retired chemist; b. Kyoto, Jan. 1, 1933; s. Ichiro and Chiyoko (Okumura) Sakurada; m. Keiko Sugimoto, May 10, 1960; children: Kazuhiro, Akihiro. BS, Kyoto U., 1956, MS, 1958, PhD, 1966. Rsch. fellow Cen. Rsch. Lab. Kuraray Co. Ltd., Kurashiki, Japan, 1958-62, 64-66; internat. fellow Stanford Rsch. Inst., Menlo Pk., Calif., 1962-64; tech. rep. N.Y. Office Kuraray Co. Ltd., NYC, 1968-71; mgr. Med. Bus. Devel. Div. Kuraray, Osaka, Japan, 1974-77, gen. mgr. Med. Products Div., 1977-88, gen. mgr. Corp. Rand D Div., 1988-89; mng. dir. Kuraray Plastics Co. Ltd., Osaka, 1989-91. Vice chmn. Japanese Soc. Biomaterials, Tokyo, 1987—96; pres. Haemonetics, Japan, 1991—2001, chmn. and CEO, Japan, 2001—05; pres. Haemonetics Japan/Asia, 2003—05, chmn., 2005—06; ret. Recipient Technology award The Soc. Polymers, 1984, Japanese Chem. Soc., 1985. Achievements include development of ethylene vinyl alcohol copolymer hollow fiber for hemo-dialyzer; development of dental adhesives. Home: GM Ebisunomori 1304 4-23-6 Ebisu Shibuya-ku Tokyo 150-0013 Japan Home Phone: 03 3444 5015. Personal E-mail: ysakurada@star.ocn.ne.jp.

SALA, MARZIO GIUSEPPE, research and development company executive; b. Rho, Milano, Italy, Dec. 27, 1974; s. Carlo Sala and Enrica Amboldi; life ptnr. Silvia Anicic; 1 child, Matteo Paul Aleksandar. PhD, Ecole Polytechnique Fédérale de Lausanne, Vaud, Switzerland, 2003. Rsch. asst. PhD Ecole Polytechnique Fédérale de Lausanne, 1999—2003; employee Sandia Nat. Laboratories, Albuquerque, 2003—05; rsch. asst. ETH Zürich, Switzerland, 2005—06; R&D engr. BMW-Sauber F1 Team, Hinwil, Zurich, Switzerland, 2006—. Recipient award, R&D Mag., 2004; fellow, MIT, 2003. Achievements include development of innovative solvers for high-performance computer models to model osteoporosis; research in modern techniques for scientific software development. Office: BMW-Sauber F1 Team Wildbachstrasse 9 Hinwil CH-8340 Switzerland Office Phone: 41-78-831-1316. Personal E-mail: marzio.sala@gmail.com.

SALACUSE, JESWALD WILLIAM, lawyer, educator; b. Niagara Falls, NY, Jan. 28, 1938; s. William L. and Bessie B. (Buzzelli) S.; m. Donna Booth, Oct. 1, 1966; children: William, Maria. Diploma, U. Paris, 1959; AB, Hamilton Coll., 1960; JD, Harvard U., 1963. Bar: NY 1965, Tex. 1980. Lectr. law Ahmadu Bello U., Nigeria, 1963-65; assoc. Conboy, Hewitt, O'Brien & Boardman, NYC, 1965-67; assoc. dir. African Law Ctr., Columbia U., NYC, 1967-68; prof., dir. Rsch. Ctr., Nat. Sch. Adminstrn., Zaire, 1968-71; Mid. East regional advisor on law and devel. Ford Found., Beirut, 1971-74, rep. in Sudan, 1974-77; vis. prof. U. Khartoum, Sudan, 1974-77; vis. scholar Harvard Law Sch., 1977-78; prof. law So. Meth. U., Dallas, 1978-86, dean, 1980-86; dean, prof. internat. law Fletcher Sch. Law and Diplomacy, Tufts U., Medford, Mass., 1986-94, Henry J. Braker prof. comml. law, 1994—. Fellow Inst. Advanced Legal Studies, U. London, 1995; vis. prof. Ecole Nat. Ponts et Chaussées, Paris, 1990-95, Inst. Empressa, Madrid, 1995, U. Bristol, U. London Sch. Oriental and African Studies, 1995—2003; cons. Ford Found., 1978-82, 93, US Dept. State, 1978-80, UN Ctr. on Transnat. Corps., 1988—, Harvard Inst. Internat. Devel., 1990—, Asia Found., 1992, Harvard Law Sch./World Bank Laos Project, 1991-93; with Sri Lanka fin. sector project ISTI/US AID, 1993-94; lectr. Georgetown U. Internat. Law Inst., 1978-94, Panam. U., Mexico City, 1981; chmn. com. on Mid. Ea. law Social Sci. Rsch. Coun., 1978-84; chmn. Asia Tigers Fund Inc., 2005—, Coun. Internat. Exch. Scholars, 1987-91, India Fund Inc., 2005—; bd. dirs. Emerging Markets Income Funds. I & II Inc., Global Ptnrs. Income Fund, Inc., Salomon Bros. Worldwide Income Fund, Inc., Emerging Markets Floating Rate Fund, Inc., Mcpl. Ptnrs. Funds I & II, Salomon Bros. High Income Funds I & II, Salomon Bros. 2008 Worldwide Dollar Govt. Term Trust, Mcpl. Ptnrs. Funds I & II; trustee Southwestern Legal Found., 1992-2004, Am. U. Paris, 1993-97; pres. Internat. Third World Legal Studies Assn., 1987-91; chmn. Inst. Transnat. Arbitration, 1991-93; pres. Assn. Profl. Schs. Internat. Affairs, 1988-89; Fulbright disting. chair in comparative law, Italy, 2000; pres. Internat. Ctr. for Settlement Investment Disputes Arbitration Tribunal, 2004—. Author: (with Kasunmu) Nigerian Family Law, 1966, An Introduction to Law in French-Speaking Africa, Vol. I, 1969, Vol. II, 1976, (with Steng) International Business Planning, 1982, Making Global Deals-Negotiating in the International Marketplace, 1991, The Art of Advice, 1994, (video course) Negotiating in Today's World, 1995, The Wise Advisor, 2000, The Global Negotiator, 2003, Leading Leaders, 2005, Seven Secrets for Negotiating With Government, 2008; contbr. articles to profl. jours. Mem. ABA, Dallas Bar Found. (trustee 1983-86), Coun. on Fgn. Rels., Am. Law Inst., Am. Soc. Internat. Law, Cosmos Club (Washington). Office: Tufts U Fletcher Sch Law-Diplomacy Medford MA 02155 Office Phone: 617-627-3633. Business E-Mail: jeswald.salacuse@tufts.edu.

SALAFSKY, SUSAN REBECCA, ecologist; MS, Colo. State U., Fort Collins, PhD, 2009. Tchg. asst. Colo. State U., 2005; ecologist USDA Forest Svc., Fort Collins, 1995—. Contbr. articles to profl. jours. Environ. fellowship, Anheuser-Busch & Colo. State U., 2007. Mem.: Am. Ornithologists' Union, Wildlife Soc., Ecol. Soc. Am. Office: USDA Forest Svc 3200 SW Jefferson Way Corvallis OR 97331 Business E-Mail: salafsky@lamar.colostate.edu.

SALAH, GREG, marketing executive; b. 1963; Grad., U. Mich., 1984. With USG Corp., Chgo., 1985—, sr. v.p. sales and mktg., USG Building Sys., 2007—. Named one of Best Marketers, BtoB Mag., 2007, 2008. Office: USG Corp 550 W Adams St Chicago IL 60661-3676 Office Phone: 312-436-3960.*

SALAHUDDIN, PARVEEN, information scientist, researcher; d. Talat Salahuddin; m. Ziaul Islam. BS, Aligarh Muslim U., India, 1981, MS, 1984, MPhil, 1986, PhD, 1989. Sr. bioinformatics officer Aligarh (India) Muslim U., 1991—. Presenter in field. Contbr. articles to profl. jours. Mem.: AAAS, Protein Soc. Avocations: reading, gardening, travel, music, cooking. Personal E-mail: parveen_salahuddin@yahoo.com.

SALAKHUTDINOV, ILDAR, physics professor, researcher; b. Kazan, Tatarstan, Russia, Aug. 4, 1963; s. Fan Salakhutdinov and Zemarrya Salakhutdinova; m. Alsu Valiullina, Nov. 15, 2003. MSc in Physics, Kazan State U., Tatarstan, 1985; PhD, A.M. Prokhorov Inst. Gen. Physics, Moscow, 1996. Rsch. engr. State Inst. Applied Optics, Kazan, Russia, 1985—89, jr. rsch. fellow, 1989—92; grad. rsch. asst. Vavilov State Optical Inst., St. Petersburg, Russia, 1992—95; rsch. fellow A.M. Prokhorov General Physics Inst., Moscow, 1995—99, sr. rsch. fellow, 1999—2001; rsch. scientist Micro Managed Photons A/S, Roskilde, Denmark, 2001—03; postdoctoral rsch. fellow Wayne State U., Detroit, 2004—07, asst. prof. rsch., 2007—. Invited prof. Unioversite Jean Monnet, St. Etienne, Loire, France, 1998. Mem. Coordination Coun. Dem. Movement of Tatarstan, 1990—92. Grantee Rsch. grant, Russian Found. Basic Rsch., 1999—2001. Mem.: IEEE, Opitcal Soc. Am. Achievements include patents for thermo active long range surface plasmon polariton guiding devices. Office: Wayne State Univ 5050 Anthony Wayne Dr Detroit MI 48202 Home: 722 Colonial Ct Birmingham MI 48009-3870 Office Fax: 313-577-1101. Personal E-mail: ildarsalakhutdinov@yahoo.com. Business E-Mail: ildar@eng.wayne.edu.

SALAM, A. F., economics professor; s. K. and S. Rahman; m. Jakia Salam. BS in Mech. Engring., Bangladesh U. Engring. and Tech., Dhaka, 1989; MBA, SUNY, Buffalo, 1995, PhD, 1998. Asst. prof. U. Louisville, 1997—2000; assoc. prof. U. NC Greensboro, 2000—. Rsch. grant, APICS, 2000—02, EPDIP grant, UNCG, 2003—04, Summer Rsch. Excellence grant, 2007—08, Dean's Rsch. Scholar Program grant, 2008. Office: Univ NC Greensbo 479 Bryan Sch Bus and Economics Greensboro NC 27402 Business E-Mail: amsalam@uncg.edu.

SALAM, ADIL, pulmonary critical care physician; arrived in US, 1997; s. Abdul Shakur ul and Mariam Salam; m. Nadia A. Malik, Aug. 16, 1996; 1 child, Minahil. Fellow of Sci., Govt. Coll., Pakistan, 1989; MBBS, Punjab U., Pakistan, 1995. Intern Atlantic City Med. Ctr., resident, ho. officer, 1997—2000; cardiac rehab. fellow Brigham and Women's Hosp., Boston, 2000—01; pulmonary fellow Bridgeport (Conn.) Hosp., 2001—. Mem.: ACP. Office: Bridgeport Hosp/ Yale U 267 Grant St Bridgeport CT 06610 Personal E-mail: adilsalam@optonline.net.

SALAM, GOHAR AZAM, physician, director; s. Muhammad Abdul and Zafar Salam; m. Asifa Gohar Bari, May 15, 1995; children: Sameed Ahmed, Mazeez Ahmed. MD, Dow Med. Coll., Karachi, Pakistan, 1992; DO, NY Coll. Of Osteo. Medicine, Old Westbury, 2000. Diplomate Am. Bd. Of Family Medicine, 1995. Attending physician emergency rm. Standish Cmty. Hosp., Standish, Mich., 1994—96, dir. rural health clinic, emergency rm., 1997; attending physician emergency rm. Greenville Hosp., Jersey City, 1997—99; asst. dir., family practice residency program Saginaw Coop. Hospitals Inc., Saginaw, Mich., 2000—01; capt. USAR, Atlanta, 2001—; physician and founder Vitreoretinal Cons. Ft. Wayne, Ind., 2005—; staff physician Parkview Hosp., Luth. Hosp., Ft. Wayne, 2005—. Surg. retina fellow, vis. lectr. Ind. U. Sch. of Medicine, 2004—05, clin. lectr., dept. of ophthalmology, 2005—; chief resident, dept. of ophthalmology North Shore U. Hosp., NYU Sch. of Medicine, Manhasset, 2003—04, resident, dept. of ophthalmology, 2001—03; faculty devel. fellow Faculty Devel. Inst., U. Mich., Ann Arbor, 2000—01; asst. prof., dept. of family medicine Mich. State U., Sch. of Human Medicine, Saginaw, Mich., 2000—01; chief resident, clin. instr., dept. of family medicine Saginaw Coop. Hosp., Mich. State U. Sch. of Human Medicine, 1994—95; resident, clin. instr., dept. of family medicine Mich. State U. Sch. of Human Medicine, 1992—94. Author: (review book) Ophthalmology Board Review; contbr. articles to profl. jours. Recipient Excellence in Rsch. Resident award, Am. Soc. of Cataract and Refractive Surgeons- Storm Eye Inst., 2004, Who's Who in Executives and Professionals, 2004—05, Thomas J. Zuber award for Excellence in Tchg., Saginaw Coop. Hospitals, Mich. State U. Coll. of Human Medicine, 2001, Louise E. Zeile award for Outstanding Jr. Resident, 1994; Merrill Grayson fellowship, Dept. of Ophthalmology, Ind. U. Sch. of Medicine, 2004. Mem.: AMA, Assn. of Rsch. in Vision and Ophthalmology, Am. Acad. of Ophthalmology. Home: 615 Tawny Ct Huntertown IN 46748 Office: Vitreoretinal Cons of Ft Wayne 3978 New Vision Dr Fort Wayne IN 46845 Personal E-mail: goharsalam@yahoo.com.

SALAMA, AMAN, language educator; children: Samah, Omar. PhD in Arabic Lit. Art and Humanities, Autonomos U., Madrid, 2004. Tchr. Richland Coll., Dallas, 2004—; arabic instuctor U. Tex., Dallas, 2004—.

SALAMA, C. ANDRE TEWFIK, electrical engineering educator; b. Heliopolis, Egypt, Sept. 27, 1938; arrived in Can., 1957; s. Tewfik and Sarine (Bigio) S.; m. Rhoda R. Kurtz, Dec. 19, 1974. BASc with honours, U. B.C., Vancouver, Can., 1961, MASc, 1963, PhD, 1966. Registered profl. engr., Ont. Mem. sci. staff Bell No. Rsch., Ottawa, Ont., Canada, 1966-67; asst. prof. elec. engring. U. Toronto, Ont., 1967-70, assoc. prof. Ont., 1970-77, prof. Ont., 1977-92, univ. prof. Ont., 1992—. Chmn., bd. dirs. Can. Microelectronics Corp., Kingston, Ont., 1984-98; program leader, bd. dirs. Micronet, Toronto, 1990—. Mem. editorial bd. Solid State Electronics, 1982-2000; contbr. over 300 articles to sci. jours. Recipient Izaak Walton Killam Meml. prize, 1994, Outstanding Lifetime Achievement award, Can. Semiconductor Tech. Conf., 2003, NSERC Lifetime Achievement award, 2004, Recognition award Rsch. Excellence and Outstanding Leadership Network Cures of Excellence, 2004; Info. Tech. Assn. Can. and Natural Scis. and Engring. Rsch. Coun. fellow U. Toronto, 1989-90. Fellow IEEE (assoc. editor Trans. on Cirs. and Systems 1987-89, Millenium medal 2000), Royal Soc. Can., Can. Acad. Engring.; mem. Electrochem. Soc., Assn. Profl. Engrs. Ont., Engring. Inst. Can. Avocations: swimming, sailing, scuba diving, horseback riding, reading. Office: U Toronto Dept Elec Engring Toronto ON Canada M5S 1A4 Home Phone: 416-482-4225; Office Phone: 416-978-8658.

SALAMA, MOHAMMAD, literature and language professor; married. PhD, U. Wis. Madison, 2005. Prof. San Francisco State U., 2005—, arabic program coord., 2005—.

SALAMANCA-RIBA, SUSANA ALICIA, mathematics professor; BA, U. Autonoma Metropolitana, Mexico City; PhD, MIT. Assoc. prof. math NM State Univ., Las Cruces. Achievements include being one of 18 top mathematicians and computer scientists (Atlas of Lie Groups Project) from the US to successfully map E8, one of the largest and most complicated structures in mathematics. Office: Dept Math SH260 NMSU PO Box 30001 Las Cruces NM 88003-8001 Office Phone: 505-646-2305. Business E-Mail: ssalaman@nmsu.edu.

SALAMON, LESTER MILTON, political science professor; b. Pitts., Jan. 11, 1943; s. Victor William Salamon and Helen (Sanders) Weiss; m. Lynda Anne Brown, June 27, 1965; children: Noah, Matthew. BA in Econs. and Pub. Policy, Princeton U., 1964; PhD in Govt., Harvard U., 1971. Instr. dept. polit. sci. Tougaloo Coll., Miss., 1966-67; asst. prof. Vanderbilt U., Nashville, 1970-73; assoc. prof. policy scis. and polit. sci. Duke U., Durham, NC, 1973-80, dir. Ctr. for Urban and Regional Devel., 1973—77; dep. assoc. dir. U.S. Office Mgmt. and Budget, Washington, 1977-79; dir. Ctr. for Governance and Mgmt. Rsch., Urban Inst., Washington, 1980-86; prof., dir. Inst. for Policy Studies, Johns Hopkins U., Balt., 1987-97, dir. Ctr. Civil Soc. Studies, 1997—. Author: America's Nonprofit Sector: A Primer, 1992, The Emerging Sector: Nonprofit Organizations in Comparative Perspective, 1994, Partners in Public Service: Government Nonprofit Relations in the Modern Welfare State, 1995, Defining the Nonprofit Sector: A Cross-National Analysis, 1996, International Guide to Nonprofit Law, 1997, The Resilient Sector, 2003; editor: Beyond Privatization, 1989, Human Capital and America's Future, 1991, Global Civil Society, 1998, The Tools of Government, A Guide to The New Governance, 2002, The State of Non-Profit America, 2002, Global Civil Society, 2004; mem. editl. bd. Adminstrn. and Soc., 1985—, Voluntas, 1988—, Nonprofit and Voluntary Sector Quar., 1990—, Pub. Adminstrn. Rev., 2000—. Mem. experts com. to ind. sector panel on nonprofit sector Nat. Acad. Pub. Adminstrn. Panel, EPA; mem. Balt. City Planning Commn., 1987—95; mem. adv. com on voluntary fgn. aid USAID; chmn. bd. dirs. Cmty. Found. of Chesapeake. Recipient Laverne Burchfield award Am. Soc. Pub. Adminstrn., 1977, Disting. Book award Assn. of Rschrs. on Nonprofit Orgns. and Vol. Action, Disting. Book award Ind. Sector, 2002, Disting. Achievement award Assn. Rschrs. on Nonprofit Orgns. and Vol. Action, 2004. Mem. Internat. Soc. Third Sector Rsch. (vice chmn. 1991-95), Nat. Acad. Pub. Adminstrn., Social Sci. Rsch. Coun. (nonprofit field com.). Avocations: tennis, swimming, carpentry, sailing. Home: 903 Lynch Dr Arnold MD 21012-1504 Office: Johns Hopkins U Inst Policy Studies 3400 N Charles St Baltimore MD 21218-2680 Business E-Mail: lsalamon@jhu.edu.

SALAMON, LINDA BRADLEY, retired English literature scholar; b. Elmira, NY, Nov. 20, 1941; d. Grant Ellsworth and Evelyn E. (Ward) Bradley; divorced; children: Michael Lawrence, Timothy Martin. BA, Radcliffe Coll., 1963; MA, Bryn Mawr Coll., 1964, PhD, 1971; Advanced Mgmt. Cert., Harvard U. Bus. Sch., 1978; D.H.L., St. Louis Coll. Pharmacy, 1993. Lectr., adj. asst. prof. Eng., Dartmouth Coll., Hanover, NH, 1967-72; mem. faculty lit. Bennington Coll., Vt., 1974-75; dean students Wells Coll., Aurora, NY, 1975-77; exec. asst. to pres. U. Pa., Phila., 1977-79; assoc. prof. English Washington U., St. Louis, 1979—88, prof., 1988-92, dean Coll. Arts and Scis., 1979-92; prof. English George Washington U., Washington, 1992—2007. Mem. faculty Bryn Mawr Summer Inst. Women, 1979—99; dean Columbian Coll. Arts and Scis., 1992—96. Author, co-editor: Nicholas Hilliard's Art of Limning, 1983; co-author: Integrity in the College Curriculum, 1985; contbr. numerous articles to literary and ednl. jours. Bd. dir. Assn. Am. Colls., vice chmn., 1985, chmn., 1986; bd. dir. Greater St. Louis council Girl Scouts U.S.A.; trustee Coll. Bd., St. Louis Coll. Pharmacy. Fellow Radcliffe Inst., 1973-74, Folger Shakespeare Libr., 1986, NEH Montaigne Inst., 1988, Fulbright fellow, Taiwan, 2003, Ringler fellow Huntington Libr, 2004; Am. Philos. Soc. Penrose grantee, 1974. Mem.: MLA, Cosmos Club, Phi Beta Kappa. Office: George Washington U Dept of Eng Rome Hall 760 801 22D St NW Washington DC 20052-0001 Business E-Mail: lbs@gwu.edu.

SALAMON, RENAY, real estate broker; b. NYC, May 13, 1948; d. Solomon and Mollie (Friedman) Langman; m. Maier Salamon, Aug. 10, 1968; children: Mollie, Jean, Leah, Sharon, Eugene. BA, Hunter Coll., 1969. Licensed real estate borker, N.J. Mgr. office Customode Designs Inc., NYC, 1966-68; co-owner Salamon Dairy Farms, Three Bridges, NJ, 1968-86; assoc. realtor Max. D. Shuman Realty Inc., Flemington, NJ, 1983-85; pres., chief exec. officer Liberty Hill Realty Inc., Flemington, NJ, 1985—. Cons. Illva Saronna Inc. (Illva Group), Edison, N.J. 1985—; real estate devel. joint venture with M.R.F.S. Realty Inc. (Illva Group), 1986—; bd. dirs. Anderson House. Mem. Readington twp. Environ. Commn., Whitehouse Sta., N.J., 1978-87, N.J. Assn. Environ. Commrs., Trenton, 1978—; fundraiser Rutgers Prep. Sch., Somerset, N.J., 1984-95; bd. dirs. Hunterdon County YMCA, 1987-95, Anderson House, 2000-04; mem. N.J.-Israel Commn., 1998—; bd. trustees Rutgers Prep. Sch., 2000-06; chair Hunterdon County Bd. Social Svc., 2002, 2004; chair Hunterdon County Health and Human Svcs. Commn., 2004-06. Named N.J. Broker Record, Forbes Inc., N.Y.C. 1987. Mem.: Realtors Land Inst. Republican. Jewish. Office: Liberty Hill Realty Inc 415 US Highway 202 Flemington NJ 08822-6021 Office Phone: 908-782-1919.

SALAMONE, FRANK ANTHONY, anthropology educator; b. Rochester, NY, Mar. 26, 1939; s. Angelo and Frances Phyllis (Polvino) S.; m. Virginia Ann O'Sullivan, Oct. 8, 1977; children: Frank Charles, Catherine Ann-Frances, Ako Mark, Stephen D., and Patrick Robert. BA, St. John Fisher Coll., 1961; MA, U. Rochester, 1966; PhD, SUNY, Buffalo, 1973. Vis. assoc. prof. So. Ill. U., Carbondale, 1977-78; chmn. and assoc. prof. Seton Sch., Iona Coll., Yonkers, N.Y., 1981-93; assoc. prof. Iona Coll., New Rochelle, N.Y., 1989—, prof. anthropology & chair. Author: Gods and Goods in Africa, 1985, The Culture of Jazz, 2009, Viewing an Ethnic Community and numerous others, 2009; editor: Art and Culture in Nigeria, 1992; editor of several books; contbr. over 100 articles to numerous publs. Pres. N.Y. Fullbright Assn., 1991-92; mem. Columbus Day Com. mem., Harrison, N.Y., 1992. Grantee NEH, 1976, 83, 89, 94, USIA, 1989-90; Fulbright fellow Nigeria. Fellow Anthrop. Assn., African Studies Assn., Am. Ethnol. Assn. Democrat. Roman Catholic. Avocations: jazz, literature, theater, opera. Office: Iona Coll North Ave New Rochelle NY 10801 Office Phone: 914-637-2746. Business E-Mail: fsalamone@iona.edu.

SALAMONE, JOSEPH CHARLES, polymer chemistry professor; b. Bklyn., Dec. 27, 1939; s. Joseph John and Angela (Barbagallo) S.; children: Robert, Alicia, Christopher. BS in Chemistry, Hofstra U., 1961; PhD in Chemistry, Poly. Inst. N.Y., 1967. NIH postdoctoral fellow U. Liverpool, England, 1966-67; rsch. assoc., Horace H. Rackham postdoctoral fellow U. Mich., Ann Arbor, 1967-70, adminstrv. sec., 1968-70; asst. prof., then assoc. prof. chemistry U. Mass., Lowell, 1970-76, prof., 1976-90, prof. emeritus, 1990—, dean Coll Sci., 1978-84, Disting. Rsch. fellow, 1984-90, chmn. dept. chemistry, 1975-78. Pres. Optimers Inc., Lowell, 1985-99; bd. dirs. Rochal Industries, Inc., Boca Raton, Fla.; chief sci. official, Rochal Industries, LLP; cons. editor CRC Press, Inc., Boca Raton, 1992-97; v.p. chem. rsch. Bausch and Lomb, 1997-2000, v.p. rsch., 2000-2005, v.p. and spl. adv., 2006. Author 2 books, 2 encys.; mem. editl. bd. Polymer, 1976-94, Jour. Macromolecular Sci.-Chemistry, 1985-2003, Progress of Polymer Sci., 1987-2002, ChemTech, 1995-99; adv. bd. Jour. Polymer Sci., 1974—; editor-in-chief Polymeric Materials Ency., 1993-97; contbr. over 170 articles to profl. jours.; holder 190 U.S. and internat. patents. Recipient Disting. Alumnus award Poly. Inst. N.Y., 1984, Herman F. Mark award for Recognition of Work in Applied Tech., Poly. U., 2005. Fellow Am. Inst. Med. and Biol. Engring. (chmn. industry coun. 2006-09); mem. Am. Chem. Soc. (chmn. divsn. polymer chemistry 1982, Indsl. Chemistry award 2004), Polymer Sci., Am. Acad. Ophthalmology (assoc.), Pacific Polymer Fedn. (sec., treas. 1988-90, dep. v.p. 1991-92, v.p., 1993, pres. 1994-95), Soc. Biomaterials (Clemson award for applied rsch.). Office Phone: 561-703-4007. Personal E-mail: jcsalamone@yahoo.com.

SALAMONE-KOCHOWICZ, JEAN GLORIA, retired bank executive; b. White Deer, Pa., Dec. 28, 1929; d. Dewey and Pearl Viola (Bastian) Smith; m. Daniel W. Salamone, Nov. 2, 1946 (div. 1977); children: Daryl Joseph, John Daniel; m. John T. Kochowicz, Feb. 10, 1990 (dec. 1993). Student, Bloomsburg State Coll., 1946, Am. Inst. Banking, 1974-85. Sec. Chef Boy-ar-Dee Foods, Milton, Pa., 1946-48, Arthur Andersen & Co., Washington, 1948-58; exec. sec. Citizens Bank and Trust Co., Riverdale, Md., 1970-74, asst. treas., 1974-77, asst. v.p., 1977-84; v.p. Citizens Bank, Laurel, Md., 1984-97; corp. sec. Citizens Bancorp (holding corp. for Citizens Bank), Laurel, 1982-96; ret., 1997. Trustee Prince George's Arts Coun., Riverdale, 1983-98, treas., 1983-89, pres. 1990-91. Mem. Fin. Women Internat. (pres. met. Md. group 1977-78), Chesapeake Cancer Alliance. Roman Catholic. Avocations: travel, photography, art collecting, volunteering.

SALANS, CARL FREDRIC, lawyer; b. Chicago Heights, Ill., Mar. 13, 1933; arrived in France, 1972; s. Leon and Jean (Rudnick) Salans; m. Edith Motel, Sept. 26, 1956; children: Eric Lee, Marc Robert, Christopher John. AB, Harvard U., 1954; BA, Cambridge U., Eng., 1956, MA, 1958, LLB, 1958; JD, U. Chgo., 1957. Bar: Ill. 1958, D.C. 1973, U.S. Supreme Ct. 1972, (admitted in France as conseil juridique) 1972, (admitted in France as avocat) 1992. With State Dept., 1959-72, dep. legal adviser, 1966-72; practice law Paris, 1972—; ret. ptnr. Salans & Assocs., Paris, 1978—. Legal adviser Geneva Conference on Laos, 1962, U.S. del. Vietnam Peace Talks, Paris, 1968—71; US rep. Draft The World Heritage Convention, 1972; vice-chmn. ICC Internat. Ct. Arbitration, 2002—08, 2009—, chmn., 2008; arbitrator internat. cases; arbitrator U.S.-Iran Claims Tribunal, The Hague; mem. editl. bd. ICC Arbitration Bulletin. Mem.: ABA (chmn. com. East-West trade and investment 1975—82), French Arbitration Assn., London (Eng.) Ct. Internat. Arbitration, Swiss Arbitration Assn., Am. Arbitration Assn. (panel arbitrators), Am. Soc. Internat. Law, Am. C. of C. in France (bd. dirs. 1977—87, chmn. laws and pub. affairs com. 1980—85). Home: 18 Ave Raphael 75016 Paris France Office: 5 Blvd Malesherbes Paris 75008 France Home Phone: 01 45 03 08 44; Office Phone: 33 1 42 68 48 00. E-mail: csalans@salans.com.

SALANT, RICHARD FRANK, mechanical engineer, educator; b. NYC, Sept. 4, 1941; s. Joseph and Augusta (Dick) S.; m. Barbel Lang, Sept. 9, 1962; children: Scott M., Stephanie. BS, MS, MIT, 1963, DSc, 1967. Registered profl. engr., Ga. Asst. prof. U. Calif. Berkeley, 1966-68; asst. prof., assoc. prof. MIT, Cambridge, 1968-72; mgr. fluid mech. and heat transfer Borg-Warner Rsch. Ctr., Des Plaines, Ill., 1972-87; prof., chair tribology rsch. group Ga. Inst. Tech., Atlanta, 1987—, Ga. Power Disting. prof., 2001—. Cons. fluid sealing tech., Atlanta, 1987—. Assoc. editor Jour. Tribology, 1993-99, Jour. Fluids Engring., 1984-87; mem. editl. bd. Jour. Engring. Tribology, 2006—, Mechanika, 2006—; contbr. articles to profl. jours. Fellow ASME (Henry R. Worthington medal 1996, Machine Design award 2003, Mayo D. Hersey award, 2009), Soc. Tribologists and Lubrication Engrs. (Edmond E. Bisson award 2000, Frank P. Bussick award 2002, 05, 07, 08). Achievements include patents in field. Home: 1138 Manning Farms Ct Dunwoody GA 30338-2648 Office: Ga Inst Tech Sch Mech Engring Atlanta GA 30332-0405 Business E-Mail: richard.salant@me.gatech.edu.

SALANT, STEPHEN WALTER, economics professor, researcher; b. Washington, Sept. 16, 1945; s. Walter S. and Edna G. Salant; m. Katherine D. Blair, July 26, 1980; children: Daisy-Marie, Shelley Anne, Claire Elizabeth. BA, Columbia U., NYC, 1967; PhD, U. Pa., Phila., 1973. Economist Fed. Res. Bd. Governors, Washington, 1972—78; sr. economist Fed. Trade Commn., Washington, 1979—81, Rand Corp., Santa Monica, Calif., 1981—85; prof. economics U. Mich., Ann Arbor, 1986—. Co-editor Rand Jour., Santa Monica, Calif., 1984—86; sci. com. Environ. Resource Econ., Toulouse, France, 1994—2004. Contbr. articles to profl. jours. Home: 1509 Sheridan Dr Ann Arbor MI 48104 Office: Univ Mich 611 Tappan St Ann Arbor MI 48109 Office Fax: 734-764-2769. Business E-Mail: ssalant@umich.edu.

SALANT, TALYA, medical researcher; b. Johannesburg, Feb. 2, 1974; d. David John and Anne Salant; m. Seth Nicholas DeAvila, Sept. 16, 2006; 1 child, Lila Salant DeAvila. PhD, U. Chgo., 2007. Rschr. U. Chgo., 1998—. Dancer (solo) Ballet Theatre, Boston, 1991—97. Recipient Award, Am. Coll. Preventive Medicine and Frank Family Found., 2004. Mem.: Phi Beta Kappa. Home: 1213 E 53rd St #3W Chicago IL 60615

SALAPATEK, JOHN (JOHN FRANKLIN), literature and language educator, writer; s. Frank and Sophie Salapatek; life ptnr. David White, Aug. 4, 1996. BFA, U. Ill., Urbana, 1981; diploma, Calif. State U., Northridge, 2004, Nat. U., Sherman Oaks, Calif., 2005. English tchr. Sylmar HS, Calif., 2002—05, Golden Valley HS, Santa Clarita, Calif., 2005—. Writer Connie Steven's Shane Prodns., LA, 1991—98. Co-author: (films) Children of the Corn 666: Isaac's Return; actor: (films) Children of the Corn, The Addam's Family, Addam's Family Values; (TV films) Tower of Terror, The Christmas Secret. Recipient Best Feature Screenplay: Horror, Shriekfest Film Festival, 2004; named Tchr. of Yr., Golden Valley HS, 2007—08, Educator of Yr., Calif. League HS, 2007—08. Mem.: NEA, SAG, Hart Dist. Tchrs. Assn., Calif. Tchrs. Assn.

SALAPURA, VALENTINA, computer science educator; b. Bos. Petrovac, Bosnia-Herzegovina, June 17, 1964; arrived in Austria, 1991; parents Milan Ostoje and Mira (Jeličić) S.; m. Michael Karl Gschwind, 1998. MSEE summa cum laude, U. Zagreb, Croatia, 1988, MS in Computer Sci. summa cum laude, 1991; PhD in Computer Sci., Tech. U., Vienna, 1996. Lic. engr. Rsch. asst. U. Zagreb, 1988-91; asst. prof. Tech. U. Vienna, 1992—. Cons. U. Zagreb, 1993-97, Wirtschafts U., Vienna, 1993-94; rschr. European Union Esprit, Brussels and Vienna, 1992—, IBM T.J. Watson Rsch. Ctr., Yorktown Heights, 2000-; reviewer IEEE Neural Networks Coun., Balt. and Vienna, 1994—. Reviewer IEEE Trans. on Fuzzy Sys.; contbr. articles to profl. jours. Mem. Assn. Computing Machinery. Avocations: travel, scuba diving, tennis. Office: IBM TJ Watson Research Ctr 1101 Kitchawan Rd Yorktown Heights NY 10598

SALAS, MAX, pediatrician, educator; MD, Nat. U. Mex., Mexico City, 1964. Diplomate Am. Bd. Pediats., 1969, Am. Bd. Pediatric Endocrinology, 1986. Rotating intern St. Luke's Hosp., St. Paul, 1963—64; resident in pediat. Children's Hosp., Boston, 1965—67, Sheffield, England, 1967—68; fellow in pediatric endocrinology Pitts. Children's Hosp., 1977—79, North Shore Univ. Hosp., Manhasset, NY, 1979—80; assoc. prof. pediat. Drexel U. Sch. Medicine, 2007. Office: St Peters Univ Hosp 254 Easton Ave New Brunswick NJ 08901-1977 Home Phone: 732-297-8562; Office Phone: 732-745-8574.

SALATHE, JOHN, JR., retired manufacturing executive; b. Montreal, Sept. 25, 1928; s. John and Ida (Schenk) S.; m. Harriet Edith Styles; children: Linda Paul, Craig. BSME, San Jose State U., 1950. Gen. mgr. Indsl. Steel Tank & Body Co., Berkeley, Calif., 1958-62; project mgr. Pacific Foundry div. PACCAR Inc., Renton, Wash., 1962-66, prodn. mgr., 1966-70, asst. gen. mgr., 1970-71, gen. mgr., 1971-79; asst. v.p. PACCAR Inc., Bellevue, Wash., 1979-81, v.p., 1981-90; ret., 1991. Bd. dirs. Jr. Achievement, Seattle, 1979-85; mem. adv. bd. Seattle Pacific U., 1985-95. Sloan fellow Stanford U., 1970. Mem. Soc. Mfg. Engrs. (sr.), Am. Soc. Quality Control (sr.). Avocations: gardening, boating, reading.

SALAVA, JENNIFER ANNE, psychologist; d. Robert Joseph and Janis Kay Salava. BA, U. Minn., Duluth, 1999; degree, U. Wis. Stout, Menomonie, 2003. Cert. sch. psychologist NASP, 2004. Sch. psychologist Ind. Sch. Dist. #196, Eagan, 2002—; adj. faculty mem. U. Wis. Stout, 2004—. Recipient Exemplary Svc. award, U. Wis. Stout, 2008. Mem.: NASP, Minn. Sch. Psychologist Assn. Business E-Mail: jennifer.salava@district196.org.

SALAZAR, ALEXANDER, bishop; b. San Jose, Costa Rica, Nov. 28, 1949; AA, East LA Coll., 1969; BA, Immaculate Heart Coll., LA, 1980; M. Div., St. John's Sem., 1984. Ordained priest Archdiocese of LA, Calif., 1984; assoc. pastor St. Gregory the Great parish, Whittier, Calif., Assumption of the Blessed Virgin Mary parish, Pasadena, Calif., St. Vibiana Cathedral; pastor St. Teresa of Avila parish, Silverlake, Calif.; vice-chancellor Archdiocese of LA, 2003—04; ordained bishop, 2004; aux. bishop Archdiocese of LA, 2004—. Roman Catholic. Office: Archdiocese of LA 3424 Wilshire Blvd Los Angeles CA 90010-2202

SALAZAR, JOHN PAUL, lawyer; b. Albuquerque, Feb. 6, 1943; s. Henry Houghton and Anita Salazar; m. Terri J. Bestgen, June 12, 1967; children: Monique Michelle, John Paul, Stephen Houghton. BA, U. N.Mex., 1965; JD, Stanford U., 1968. Bar: N.Mex. 1968, U.S. Dist. Ct. N.Mex. 1968, U.S. Ct. Appeals (10th cir.) 1968, U.S. Supreme Ct. 1979. Dir. Rodey, Dickason, Sloan, Akin & Robb, P.A., Albuquerque, 1968—, mem. exec. com., 1984—86, mng. dir., west side office, 1985—88, chmn., environ. law sect., 1989—92, mem. exec. com., 1992—93, chair, environ. and natural resources dept., 1992—95, mem. exec. com., 1999—2007, chair, bus. dept., 2000—. Bd. visitors Stanford U. Law Sch., Calif., 1973—76; state campaign chmn. Jeff Bingaman for Atty. Gen., 1978, Jeff Bingaman for U.S. Sen., 1982, 88, 94, 2000; mem. presdl. search com. U. N.Mex., 1989—90; co-chmn. Governor's Task Force on Responsible Use of Eminent Domain, 2006; mem. Albuquerque Econ. Forum, past chmn., gov. affairs com., 1990—96, past mem. bd. dirs., 1991—94, past vice chair, 1992—93; past hon. cmdr. Field Command Def. Nuc. Agy., Kirtland AFB. Sr. editor N.Mex. Environ. Law Handbook, 1990, 2d edit., 1991, 3d edit., 1993. Former bd. dirs. N.Mex. Symphony Orch.; vice chmn. City of Albuquerque Charter Revision com., 1970—71; active Albuquerque Unity, 1971—73; chmn. N.Mex. Disting. Pub. Svc. Awards Coun., 1986, 1987; chmn. city affairs com. Greater Albuquerque C. of C., 1972, v.p. govtl. affairs, 1973, pres.-elect, 1974, pres., 1975; active Presbyn. Hosp. Ctr. Assocs.; bd. dirs. Albuquerque Hispano C. of C., 2000—, vice-chair, 2001—04, chair, 2005; bd. dirs. Inter-Am. Found., 2007—. Mem.: ABA (environ. aspects of real estate transactions com., land use regulation com., real property, probate & trust law sect., land use planning & zoning com., state & local govt. sect., chair 2009), Albuquerque Armed Forces Adv. Assn., U. N.Mex. Alumni Assn. (bd. dirs. 1979—85, exec. com. 1982—85, pres. 1983—84), Nat. Assn. Indsl. and Office Parks (govs. bus. adv. coun. 1991—94, past mem. N.Mex. border commn., past chair com. border devel. and internat. trade, mem. exec. com.), N.Mex. State Bar Assn. (former mem. jud. selection com., mem. Real Property, Probate and Trust sect., mem. Pub. Law sect., mem. Natural Resources, Energy and Environ. Law sect., former sec., treas. Young Lawyers sect.), Albuquerque Bar Assn. (former mem. jud. selection com., former dir.). Roman Catholic. Office: Rodey Dickason Sloan Akin & Robb PA PO Box 1888 Albuquerque NM 87103-1888 Office Phone: 505-768-7220. Office Fax: 505-768-7395. Business E-Mail: jsalazar@rodey.com.

SALAZAR, JOHN TONY, United States Representative from Colorado; b. Alamosa, Colo., July 21, 1953; s. Henry and Emma Salazar; m. Mary Lou Salazar; children: Jesus, Esteban, Miguel. Attended, Colo. State U., 1971—72; BS in Bus. Adminstrn., Adams State Coll., Colo., 1981; grad., Colo. Agrl. Leadership Prog., 1993, Rapport Leadership Prog., 1997. Owner & operator El Rancho Salazar; chmn., CEO Spudseed.com; state rep. dist. 62 Colo. Ho. of Reps., Denver, 2002—04, mem. agrl., livestock & natural resources com., info. & tech. com.; mem. US Congress from 3d Colo. dist., 2004—, mem. agrl. com., transp. & infrastructure com., vets. affairs com. Bd. dirs. Rio Grande Water Conservation Dist., 1990—94, Gov.'s Econ. Devel. Adv. Bd.; mem. Colo. State Agrl Commn. Youth group co-coord. Dr. Michael P. Espinoza Challenge for Success; chair seed export com. Colo Cert. Seed Growers; youth leadership athletic dir. Manasa Elem. Sch., St. Joseph's Parish. Served with Criminal Investigations Divsn. US Army, 1973—76. Named Colo. Seed Grower of Yr., 1995—96; named an Outstanding Colo. Legislator, Colo. Bd. Veterans Affairs, 2006. Democrat. Roman Catholic. Office: US House Reps 326 Cannon House Office Bldg Washington DC 20515-0603 also: Dist Office Ste 702 225 N 5th St Grand Junction CO 81501 Office Phone: 202-225-4761. Office Fax: 202-226-9669. E-mail: john.salazar.house@state.co.us.*

SALAZAR, KEN (KENNETH LEE SALAZAR), Secretary of the Interior; b. Alamosa, Colo., Mar. 2, 1955; s. Henry and Emma Salazar; m. Hope Hernandez; children: Melinda, Andrea. BA in Polit. Sci., Colo. Coll., 1977; JD, U. Mich., 1981; LLD (hon.), Colo. Coll., 1993, U. Denver, 1999. Bar: Colo. 1981, U.S. Dist. Ct. Colo. 1981, U.S. Ct. Appeals (10th cir.) 1981, U.S. Supreme Ct. 1999. Farmer, rancher, Conejos County, Colo.; law clk. to atty. gen. State of Colo., Denver, 1979, chief legal counsel to gov., 1986—90, exec. dir. Dept. Natural Resources, 1990—94, atty. gen., 1999—2005; assoc. Sherman & Howard, Denver, 1981—86; dir. Parcel, Mauro, Hultin & Spaanstra, Denver, 1994—98; US Senator from Colo., 2005—09; sec. US Dept. Interior, Washington, 2009—. Gov.'s rep. State Bd. Equalization, Denver, 1990; mem. com. agr., nutrition, and forestry US Senate, com. energy and natural resources, com. veterans affairs, spl. com. ethics, spl. com. aging. Mem. Israel Friendship League, 1986—89; chair Great Outdoors Colo., Denver, 1993—94, Rio Grande Compact Commn., 1995—97, Sangre de Cristo Land Grant Commn., 1993—95; mem. Colo. Water Conservation Bd., Denver, 1990—, City and County of Denver Ethics Panel, 1993; gov.'s rep. State Bd. on Property Tax Equalization, 1987—91; del. Soviet-Am. Young Leadership Dialogue, 1984; mem. adv. com. Colo. U. Sch. Law Natural Resources Law Ctr., 1989—92; mem. Western Water Policy Rev. Adv. Commn., 1995—97; bd. dirs. Denver Cmty. Leadership Forum, 1988, Servicios de la Raza HUD 202 Project, 1985—89, chair, 1986. Recipient Friend of the First award, Colo. Press Assn., Profiles in Courage award, Conf. West Atty. Generals, Judge Learned Hand Human Relations award, Am. Jewish Com. Colo. Chapter, 2001; scholar Juan Tienda. Mem.: ABA, Am. Judicature Soc., Hispanic Bar Assn. (ABA task force on opportunities for minorities in legal profession, bd. dirs. 1986—87), Denver Bar Assn. (2d v.p. 1989, chair policy-cmty. rels. subcoms. 1982—84), Colo. Bar Assn. (bd. govs. 1989—90, task force to assess the legal profession 1986). Democrat. Roman Catholic. Avocations: basketball, outdoor activities, politics. Office: US Dept Interior 1849 C St NW Mail Stop 7229 Washington DC 20240 Office Phone: 202-208-3100.*

SALAZAR, OMAR MAURICIO, radiation oncologist, educator; b. Havana, Cuba, Sept. 22, 1942; came to U.S., 1959; naturalized, 1970; s. Aramis Victor and Nelida Raquel (Acosta) S.; m. Margarita Cristina Pedraza, July 7, 1979; children: Omar M.II, Sofia M. BS in Biology, Georgetown U., 1965; MD, U. P.R., 1969; MS, U. Rochester, 1974. Diplomate Am. Bd. Radiology. Intern U. Hosp. U. PR, Rio Piedras, 1969—70, radiotherapy resident, 1970—73, chief resident, 1972-73; instr., fellow U. Rochester, NY, 1973-74, asst. prof. NY, 1974-78, assoc. prof. NY, 1978-81; prof., chmn. dept. radiation oncology U. Md., Balt., 1981-95; prof., dir. radiation oncology La. State U. Med. Ctr., New Orleans, 1995—99; dir. dept. radiation oncology, dir. Ctr. Cancer Care Oakwood Health Sys., Dearborn, Mich., 1999—; pres. Assoc. in Radiation Oncology, PC, 2000—. Mem. CCIRC Nat. Cancer Inst., Bethesda, Md., 1980-84; prof. clin. oncology Am. Cancer Soc., 1989-1993; coord. USA, Circulo Radioterapeutas Ibero-Latino-Americanos-L.Am. Assn. Radiation Therapy, 1981-98, v.p., 1998-2000, pres. elect, 2000-2002, pres. 2002-2005, chmn., 2005— (Gold medal); expert cons. internat. Atomic Energy Agy., Vienna, Austria, 1996—; examiner Am. Bd. Radiology, Phila., 1983-93; chmn. site cancer visit Nat. Cancer Inst., Bethesda, 1983, site visitor, 1982; co-investigator Whitaker Found., 1983; prof. clin. oncology Am. Cancer Soc., 1989-94, motivational spkr. in field. Author: Moments of Decision/Primary Brain Tumors, 1979, Bronchogenic Carcinoma, 1981, Unveiling Mysteries to Create Miracles, 2002; contbr. articles to profl. jours. Arthur A. Ward Trust grantee, 1981; Am. Cancer Clin. Fellowship award, 1984-86. Fellow: Am. Coll. Radiation Oncology (past pres., past chmn. bd. dirs., chancellor, Gold medal), Am. Coll. Radiology; mem.: AMA, Am. Assn. Cancer Edn., Am. Radiol. Soc., Radiol. Soc. Am., Md. Radiol. Soc., Med. Chirurgical Soc., Tex. Radiol. Soc., Ea. Coop. Oncology Group (chmn. brain and lung com. 1979—80), Radiation Therapy Oncology Group, Mask and Bauble Dramatic Soc., Big Five Club. Roman Catholic. Avocations: baseball, basketball, writing, painting. Home Phone: 248-855-6677; Office Phone: 313-593-7335. Business E-Mail: salazaro@oakwood.org.

SALAZAR, STEVE, Councilman; b. Dallas, Aug. 3, 1965; s. Pedro and Catherine Salazar; m. Glenda Avila; 1 child, Esteban Glen. BA in Hist., U. Tex., Arlington, 1986; JD, U. Houston, 1988. Law clerk Law Offices Roberto Alonzo & Domingo Garcia; assoc. Garcia, Alonzo & Garcia, Dallas, 1988—90; former dep. mayor pro tem. Dallas City Coun., councilman, Dist. 6, 1995—2001, 2003—. Mem. Econ. Devel. com., Quality Life & Govt. Svcs. com., Trinity River Corridor Project com.; chmn. Housing com., Pub. Safety com. Steering com. Nat. Pub. Safety and Crime Prevention Nat. League Cities, steering com. Immigration Task Force; bd. trustees Dallas County Cmty. Coll. Dist., 1992—95. Avocation: marathons. Office: City Hall 1500 Marilla St Rm 5FS Dallas TX 75201 Office Phone: 214-670-4199. Office Fax: 214-670-5115.*

SALBERG, ANNE SCHOLBERG, retired librarian; b. Haddonfield, NJ, Jan. 2, 1940; d. Harold M. and Yarmila Scholberg; m. Richard L. Salberg, June 4, 1960; children: Suzanne Salberg Engrav, Katherine S. Mommer. Student, U. Colo., 1958—60. Libr. G.A. Jones Meml. Libr., Johnstown, Colo., 1966—98; ret., 1998. Contbr. columns in newspapers. Vol. Meals on Wheels, 1978—88; adv. bd. mem. Hover Home, 1998—2005. Named Outstanding Woman of Yr., 1988. Mem.: CJPEO, Sunshine Club, Chapeau Rouge Red Hat Club. Home: 435 Karsh Dr Longmont CO 80501-5217

SALBU, STEVE, dean, business educator; BA in Psychology, Hofstra U.; MA in Liberal Studies, Dartmouth Coll.; JD, Coll. William and Mary; MA, U. Pa., PhD in Orgn. and Strategy. Joined McCombs Sch. Bus., U. Tex., 1990, Bobbie and Coulter R. Sublett centennial endowed prof., 2000, dir. Ethics Program, assoc. dean grad. programs; dean, Stephen P. Zelnak chairholder Ga. Tech. Coll. Mgmt., Atlanta, 2006—. Vis. prof. Wharton Sch., U. Pa., U. Mich., Ind. U.; tchr. London Bus. Sch., Rotterdam Sch. Mgmt., IMADEC U., Vienna, U. Edinburgh, Helsinki Sch. Econs.; hon. sr. fellow Melbourne Law Sch.; Gourlay vis. endowed prof. bus. ethics Melbourne Bus. Sch. Former editl. bd. mem. Business Ethics Quarter; contbr. articles to profl. jours. Office: Ga Tech Coll Mgmt Ste 325 800 W Peachtree St NW Atlanta GA 30308 Office Phone: 404-894-2600. E-mail: steve.salbu@mgt.gatech.edu.*

SALCEDO, CLAUDIA S., language educator, lab administrator; b. La. d. Doris L. and Claude B. Smith; married; children: Sharon, Samuel, Rebeca. PhD, La. State U., Baton Rouge, 2002. Spanish prof., lab dir. Southeastern La. U., Hammond, 2003—. Comm. leader Hispanic Seventh-day Adventist Ch., Baton Rouge, 2007—08. Travel grant, U. Hawaii, 1992, Large and Small Tech. grants, SLU, 2006, CITI grant, Ctr. Faculty Excellence, SLU, 2003—04, 2007. Mem.: Southern Conf. Assn. Lang. Learning Tech. Mem. Seventh-Day Adventist Ch. Achievements include design of online technology resources for teachers; development of centro comercial software. Avocation: study abroad. Office Phone: 985-549-3746. Office Fax: 985-549-3088.

SALCEDO-DOVI, HECTOR EDUARDO, anatomist, educator, surgeon; b. Cordoba, Argentina, Nov. 9, 1958; s. Domingo and Rosa (Dovi) Salcedo; m. Adriana Gomez, Apr. 3, 1993; children: Camila, Marianna Luis. MD, U. Nat. Cordoba, 1984; DO, N.Y. Coll. Osteopathic Medicine, 1995. Lic. Tex., Conn., Fla., Calif. Asst. prof. anatomy, histology NY Coll. Osteo. Medicine, Old Westbury, 1990—93, prof. anatomy, physiology, 1993; chief intern Good Samaritan Hosp., 1996—, chief resident surgery, 2000. Fellow critical care/trauma, 2001—03. Mem.: ACS (bd. cert. gen. surgeon), Soc. CCM, Am. Coll. Chest Physicians, Am. Osteopathic Assn., Am. Med. Student Assn. Roman Catholic. Avocations: soccer, bicycling, tennis. Home: 1619 Sam Houston Dr Harlingen TX 78550

SALCETTI, MARIANNE, newswriter, educator; d. Robert Anthony Salcetti and Mary Jane Lusher; m. Michael Mrkvicka, May 21, 1977 (div. Mar. 1985); 1 child, Jacob Gene Mrkvicka; m. Dale Rhines, Mar. 18, 1989 (div. June 1995); 1 child, Amalia Margaret Rhines. BA in Polit. Sci., Ohio State U., 1972, MA in Journalism, 1975; PhD in Mass. Comm., U. Iowa, 1992. Editor Franklinton News, Columbus, Ohio, 1974—76; beat reporter Chillicothe (Ohio) Gazette, 1976—77; investigative and health reporter Colorado Springs Gazette Telegraph, 1977—78; editor, co-owner The Weekly News, Johnson County, Iowa, 1980—82; instr. U. Iowa Sch. Journalism and Mass Comm., Iowa City, 1982—87; adj. faculty John Carroll U. and Ursuline Coll., Cleve., 1988—89; asst. prof. dept. comm. John Carroll U., Cleve., 1990—2000; contbg. writer The Cleve. Free Times, 1995—98; spl. projects editor The Garden City (Kans.) Telegram, 2000—02; comm. cons. Water Preservation Com., Finney County, Kans., 2002; investigator-rschr. Rebein & Bangerter, Attys. at Law, Dodge City, 2002—. Editl. radio commentator KSUI/WSUI, 1984—87; Presdl. election commentator WHK, Cleve., 1992; legis. prodr.-reporter State Capitol Update High Plains Pub. Radio, 2003; asst. prof. journalism Keene (N.H.) State Coll., 2003—; lectr. and presenter in field. Contbr. articles to profl. jours. V.p. Greater Cleve. Labor History Soc., 1997—99. Recipient Investigative Reporting award, Inland Daily Press Assn., 1977, Best News Story of the Yr. award, Iowa Press Assn., 1980, Silver Gavel award, ABA, 1981, Nat. Scholar award, Gannett Found., 1986, 1st pl. consumer reporting, Ohio Soc. Profl. Journalists, 1998, 2nd pl. best explanatory journalism, 1998, two honorable mentions, Enterprise News, 2001, honorable mention, Spot News, 2001, Bus. Reporting, 2002; Grauel Faculty fellow, John Carroll, 1995, John F. Murray Dissertation Rsch. grantee, George Meany Meml. Archives, AFL-CIO, 1987. Mem.: Soc. Environ. Journalists, Kappa Tau Alpha. Avocations: reading, kayaking, gardening. Office: Keene State Coll 229 Main St Keene NH 03435 Home: PO Box 967 Troy NH 03465-0967 Office Phone: 603-358-2724. Business E-Mail: msalcetti@keene.edu.

SALCH, STEVEN CHARLES, lawyer, mediator, arbitrator; b. Palm Beach, Fla., Oct. 25, 1943; s. Charles Henry and Helen Louise (Alverson) S.; m. Mary Ann Prim, Oct. 7, 1967; children: Susan Elizabeth, Stuart Trenton. BBA, So. Meth. U., 1965, JD, 1968. Bar: Tex. 1968, US Tax Ct. 1969, US Dist. Ct. (so. dist.) Tex. 1969, US Dist. Ct. (ea. dist.) Tex. 1972, US Ct. Appeals (5th cir.) 1969, US Ct. Appeals (fed. cir.) 1982, US Ct. Fed. Claims, 1982. Assoc. Fulbright & Jaworski, Houston, 1968-71, participating assoc., 1971-75, ptnr., 1975—2008; sr. dir. taxation Grobstein Horwath & Co. LLC, Sherman Oaks, Calif., 2008. Mem. panel of disting. neutrals CPR Inst. Co-author: Tax Practice Before the IRS, 1994; contbr. articles to legal jours. Pres. Tealwood Owners Assn., 1982—83, Meml. H.S. PTA, 1985—86; hon. life mem. Tex. PTA, 1986—; mem. devel. bd. U. Tex. Med. Br., Galveston, 2002—, mem. health system adv. bd., 2008—; adv. dir. 1894 Grand Opera House Soc., 2002—, co-chmn. adv. bd., 2004—05. Mem.: ABA (coun. dir. 1985—88, vice chair tax sect. 1988—91, chair tax sect. 1996—97), Houston Bar Found., Am. Bar Found., Am. Coll. Tax Counsel (regent 5th cir. 1999—2006, sec.-treas. 2006—08, vice. chmn. 2008—), Am. Law Inst., Fed. Bar Assn., Houston Bar Assn., State Bar Tex. (Outstanding Tex. Tax Lawyer 2008), Theodore Tannenwald Foundation (trustee 2000—), Menard Soc., Colonial Williamsburg Found., Galveston Artillery Club, Pelican Club Galveston, Galveston Country Club, Order of Coif, Phi Delta Phi, Phi Eta Sigma, Beta Alpha Psi. Presbyterian. Home: 4600 Caduceus Pl Galveston TX 77551-5719 Office: 2228 Ships Mechanic Row Ste 200 Galveston TX 77550 Home Phone: 409-457-6994; Office Phone: 409-763-5551. Personal E-mail: scs@dellmail.com. *Set goals for yourself. Unless you know where you are and where you want to be in life, you will not be able to map a plan to accomplish your goals.*

SALCUDEAN, MARTHA EVA, mechanical engineer, educator; b. Cluj, Romania, Feb. 26, 1934; arrived in Can., 1976, naturalized, 1979; d. Edmund and Sarolta (Hirsch) Abel; m. George Salcudean, May 28, 1955; 1 child, Septimiu E. BEng, U. Cluj, 1956, postgrad., 1962; PhD, U. Brasov, Romania, 1969; DSc (hon.), U. Ottawa, Ont., Can., 1992, U. B.C., Can., 2001. Mech. engr. Armatura, Cluj, 1956-63; sr. rsch. officer Nat. Rsch. Inst. Metallurgy, Bucharest, 1963-75; part-time lectr. Inst. Poly., Bucharest, 1967-75; sessional lectr. U. Ottawa, 1976-77, from asst. prof. to assoc. prof. to prof., 1977-85; prof., head dept. mech. engring. U. B.C., Vancouver, 1985-93, assoc. v.p. rsch., 1993-96, acting v.p. rsch. pro-tem, 1995, Weyerhausen Indsl. Rsch. chair computational fluid dynamics, 1996—2002, prof., Weyerhausen indsl. chair emerita dept. mech. engring., 2002—. Mem. grant selection com. for mech. engring. Natural Scis. and Engring. Rsch. Coun. Can.; mem. Nat. Adv. Panel to Min. Sci. and Tech. on advanced indsl. materials, Can., 1990; mem. governing coun. NRC; mem. def. sci.e adv. bd. Dept. Nat. Def.; chair Sci. Coun. B.C. Contbr. numerous articles to profl. jours. Decorated Order of BC, 1998; recipient Gold medal BC Sci. Coun., Killam Rsch. prize U. BC; Rsch. Coun. Can. grantee, 1978—, Commemorative medal 125th anniversary Can. Confederation, 1993, Julian C. Smith medal Engring. Inst. Can., 1994-95, Meritorious Achievement award Assn. Profl. Engrs. & Geoscientists BC, 1996, Killam Meml. prize engring., 1998, Innovation award NSERC Synergy, 2007. Fellow CSME, Can. Acad. Engring., Royal Soc. Can.; mem. ASME, Assn. Profl. Engrs. Ont., Order of Can. (apptd. officer 2004). Home: 1938 Western Pkwy Vancouver BC Canada V6T 1W5 Office Phone: 604-822-2732. Business E-Mail: msal@interchange.ubc.ca.

SALDANA, ALFONSO MANUEL, lawyer; b. Lima, Peru, Sept. 4, 1960; came to U.S. 1969. s. Mario J. and Nelly (Davalos) S. BA, U. Miami, 1983; JD, Thomas M. Cooley Law Sch., 1986. Bar: Fla. 1987, US Dist. Ct. (so. dist.) Fla. 1987, US Dist. Ct. (mid. dist.) Fla. 1993, US Ct. Appeals (11th cir.) 1988, US Ct. Appeals (DC cir.) 1989, US Supreme Ct. 1996. Asst. atty. gen. Office Atty. Gen. Fla., West Palm Beach, 1987—93; pvt. practice Miami, Fla., 1993—. Author: Voluntary Disclosure of Attorney Work Product to A Third Party. When is the Privilege Waived?, 1993, Beyond the Appellate Brief: A Guide to Preparing and Delivering The Oral Argument, 1995, How to Write an Effective Appellate Brief, 2006. Office: 7845 Camino Real Str O-113 Miami FL 33143 Office Phone: 786-390-3588. Business E-Mail: appellatelawyer@bellsouth.net.

SALDIVAR, ENRIQUE, bioengineer, researcher; b. Mexico City, May 10, 1960; s. Pedro Saldivar Cadena and Alicia Salazar Flores; m. Adrienne Jane Sardella, Nov. 7, 1992; children: Cassandra Lane, Evan Valentine. MD, Universidad La Salle, 1983; MS, Universidad Autonoma Metropolitana, 1987; PhD, U. Calif., San Diego, 1992. Asst. prof. The Scripps Rsch. Inst., La Jolla, Calif., 1998—2003, sr. rsch. assoc., 1995—98, rsch. assoc., 1993—95, adj. faculty, 2003—; assoc. prof. La Jolla Bioengring. Inst., 2003—. Mem. Whitaker Inst. Biomed. Engring., La Jolla, 1997—; vis. scholar U. Calif., San Diego, 2001—; founder Rainmaker Tech., Santee, Calif., 2001—. Contbr. articles to profl. jours. Recipient Nat. Instrumentation prize, Mexican Soc. Physiol. Scis., 1987, U. Merit medal, Universidad Autonoma Metropolitana, Mex., 1987; scholar, CONACYT, 1985—87, 1988—91, UCSD, 1991—92, Fogarty-Japan Soc. Promotion of Sci. fellow, 1998, grantee, NIH, 1998—2003. Achievements include description and analysis of platelet interaction with surface bound proteins under flow; development of currently worldwide used technique to measure forming thrombus volume based on confocal microscopy.

SALE, MERRITT, classicist, educator, comparatist; b. New Haven, Nov. 27, 1929; s. William Merritt and Helen (Stearns) S.; m. Marilyn Mills, June 13, 1953 (div. Oct. 1967); children: Elizabeth, David; m. Anne Perkins, May 18, 1991. BA, Cornell U., 1951, MA, 1954, PhD, 1958. Engr. U.S. Metals Co., Carteret, NJ, 1951-52; instr. in classics Yale U., New Haven, 1957-58; asst. prof., assoc. prof. Washington U., St. Louis, 1958-75, chmn. classics dept., 1961-69, prof. classics and comparative lit., 1975—, chmn. comparative lit. dept., 1981-90. Author: Sophocles' Electra: Commentary with Introduction and Translation, 1970, Existentialism and Euripides, 1977, Homer and the Roland, 1993, The Government of Troy, 1995, The Oral-Formulaic Theory Today, 2006. Recipient Founder's Day award for Excellence in Teaching Washington U., 1978 Mem. Am. Philol. Assn., London Inst. for Classical Studies Home: 2342 Albion Pl Saint Louis MO 63104-2524 Personal E-mail: aperkins@midwest.net.

SALE, TOM S., III, financial economist; b. Haynesville, La., July 27, 1942; s. Thomas and Mary Belle (Fagg) S.; divorced; children: Jennifer Elizabeth, Sarah Elaine. BA, Tulane U., 1964; MA, Duke U., 1965; PhD, La. State U., 1972. CFA. Faculty mem. La. Tech. U., Ruston, 1965—75, prof. econs., 1975—98, ret., 1998. Head dept. econs. and fin. La. Tech. U., 1974-86, 90-95, dir. grad. studies Coll. Adminstrn and Bus., 1988-89; fin. cons. Contbr. articles to profl. jours. Mem. Southwestern Fin. Assn. (pres. 1985-86), CFA Inst. (exam. com. 1983-92, curriculum com. 1993-2004), Fedn. Bus. Disciplines (v.p. 1988-89, pres. 1989-90), CFA Soc. Dallas Fort Worth, Omicron Delta Kappa, Omicron Delta Epsilon. Episcopalian. Home: PO Box 1365 Ruston LA 71273-1365 Personal E-mail: tomsale3@yahoo.com.

SALEEBEY, DENNIS, humanities educator; b. San Diego, Aug. 29, 1936; s. Teddy Saleebey and June Hoff; m. Ann Weick, July 8, 1989; children: Jennifer Glass, David, John, Meghan. BA in Social Sci., U. Calif., Santa Barbara, 1958; PhD in Social Sci., U. Calif., Berkeley, 1967; M in Social Work, UCLA, Los Angeles, 1958—60. Prof. U. Kans., Sch. Social Welfare, Lawrence, 1987—2006, prof. emeritus, 2006—, dir., cmty. outreach program pub. housing Minn., 1987—97. Author: (textbook) The Strengths Perspective in Social Work Practice, Human Behavior and Social Environments: A Biopsychosocial Approach; contbr. articles. Faculty advisor & project dir. Teen Investment Project, Kansas City, 1998—2006; project advisor Kans. U. Outreach Pub. Housing, Kansas City, 1987—97; bd. mem. & cons. Cath. Cmty. Svcs., Lawrence, 1996—2002; faculty advisor & cons. Rosedale Devel. Ctr., Kansas City; advisor, cons. Van Go Mobile Arts, Lawrence, 2000—06; adv. bd. mem. Ecumenical Christian Ministries, Lawrence, 2007—09. With USAF, 1961—64, San Antonio. Recipient Chancellor's award Tchg. Excellence, U. Kans., 1992, award, Adelphi U., 1994; named Social Work Educator of Yr., U. Kans. Alumni Assn., 1991, Moses Disting. Prof., Hunter Coll., NY, 2002—03; named one of Lydia Rappoport Disting. Prof., Smith Coll., 1994. Mem.: Advances Social Work (editl. bd. mem. 2000—06), Jour. Primary Prevention (editl. bd. mem. 1999—2004), Social Work Jour. (mem. editl. bd. 1999—2001), Coun. Social Work Edn., Media & Publications Com. (bd. mem. 2000—03), Coun. Social Work Edn. (bd. dirs. mem. 1997—2000). Avocations: running, travel, creative writing, crossword puzzles. Home and Office: 1804 St Andrews Dr Lawrence KS 66047 Business E-Mail: denniss@ku.edu.

SALEH, ANIS NOUHAD, lawyer; BA in Polit. Sci., Emory U., Atlanta, 1989; JD, Fla. State U., Tallahassee, Fla., 1992. Bar: Fla. 1992, Ga. 1994, U.S. Dist. Ct. (so. dist.) Fla., U.S. Ct. Appeals (11th cir.), cert.: Fla. (in immigration and nationality law). Pres. Saleh & Assocs., P.A., Miami, Fla., 2000—, shareholder, 2000—. Mem.: ABA, State Bar Ga., Fla. Bar (mem. immigration certification com. 2001—04, vice-chair, immigration certification com. 2002—03, chair, immigration certification com. 2003—04), Am. Immigration Lawyers Assn. (pres. 2005—06, bd. dirs., South Fla. chpt. 2000—, pres.-elect 2004—05, first v.p. 2003—04, second v.p. 2002—03). Avocation: languages. Office: Saleh & Assocs PA 147 Sevilla Ave Coral Gables FL 33134 Office Phone: 305-448-0077. Business E-Mail: asaleh@salehlaw.com.

SALEH, BRIAN BEHROOZ, aerospace transportation executive; b. Tehran, Iran, Apr. 25, 1939; came to U.S., 1959; m. Farideh Navidi, May 12, 1983. BSEE, Northrop U., Ingelwood, Calif., 1967; MBA, Golden Gate U., San Francisco, 1973; instr. credential, Calif. Design engr. radio frequency cirs. Space Systems/Loral, Palo Alto, Calif., 1970—, mgr. GOES Comm. Subsys., 1974-76, program engr. NATO-III Satellite, 1976-79, mgr. Insat Program Engring., 1979-85, mgr. GOES Spacecraft Engring., 1985-91, mgr. GOES Spacecraft, 1991-92, dir. GOES Prodn. Program, 1992-95, dir. Telstar Program, 1995-97, sr. dir. Fixed Svc. Satellite Programs, 1997-98, sr. dir. common products and planning, 1998, sr. exec. dir. CD Radio Program, 1998-99, v.p. program mgmt., 1999—2002; pres. Aerospace Tech., San Jose, Calif., 2002—. Recipient Telstar 5 Program Mgmt. award, Loral Skynet, GOES I-M Project Group Achievement award, NASA, 2002. Personal E-mail: brian@saleh.com.

SALEH, FARIDA YOUSRY, chemistry professor; b. Cairo, June 17, 1939; came to U.S., 1968; d. Michael Yousry and Fakiha Yousef (Badawy) Wassif; m. Hosny Gabra Saleh, Oct. 8, 1959; children: Magda, Nagwa. BS, Ain Shams U., 1959; MS, Alexandria U., Egypt, 1967; PhD, U. Tex., Dallas, 1976. Postdoctoral rsch. assoc. Tex. A&M U., College Station, 1977-78; rsch. scientist II U. North Tex., Denton, 1978-83, asst. prof. chemistry, 1980-83, assoc. prof., 1985-94, prof., 1994—2005; ret., 2005. Cons. Stanford Rsch. Inst., Menlo Park, Calif., 1983-84, Allied Chems. Co., Hackettstown, N.J., 1985-86, Am. Chrome Chems., Corpus Christi, Tex., 1988-89, USEPA Rev. Panel, Washington, 1986—. Contbg. author book chpts. in field; contbr. more than 60 articles to profl. jours. Recipient Svc. award U.S. EPA, Washington, 1993; recipient numerous grants in field. Mem. Am. Chem. Soc., Internat. Union of Pure and Applied Chemistry, Internat. Humic Substances Soc., Assn. Women in Sci. Avocations: music, swimming, tennis. Home: 9521 Rivercrest Dr Denton TX 76207 Home Phone: 940-262-3277. Personal E-mail: alex4y@aol.com.

SALEH, JAIME, former Netherlands Antilles government official; b. Bonaire, Netherlands Antilles, Apr. 20, 1941; m. Marguerite Marie Saleh; 4 children. D, Utrecht U., 1966. Dep. prosecutor, Willemstad, Curacao, 1967-71; atty. Curacao, Netherlands Antilles, 1971-74; judge Netherlands Antilles High Ct. of Justice, 1974-79; chief justice High Ct. of Justice, 1979-90; gov. Netherlands Antilles, Willemstad, Curacao, Netherlands, 1990—2002, min. of state, 2004. Vis. prof. U. Utrecht, 2005. Address: Villapark Zuurzak B7 Willemstad Curacao Netherlands Antilles E-mail: marlex@cura.net.

SALEH, JOHN, lawyer; b. O'Donnell, Tex., June 29, 1928; s. Nahum and Arslie S. BBA, U. Tex., 1950, JD with honors, 1952; cert. U.S. Army Judge Advocate Sch., U. Va., 1953. Bar: Tex. 1952, U.S. Ct. Mil. Appeals, 1953, U.S. Tax Ct. 1954, U.S. Dist. Ct. (no. dist.) Tex. 1956, U.S. Ct. Appeals (5th cir.) 1960, U.S. Supreme Ct. 1961, D.C. 1982. Pvt. practice, Lamesa, Tex., 1954—. Tchg. instr. legal rsch. writing U. Tex. Sch. Law, 1950-52 Mem. editl. bd. Tex. Law Rev., 1951-52. Mem. ABA, ATLA, Tex. Law Rev. Assn. (life), Tex. Bar Assn. (spl. com. to study rev. code criminal procedure 1969-71), D.C. Bar Assn., Tex. Trial Lawyers Assn., Tex. Bar Found., Order of the Coif, The Million Dollar Advocates Forum, Phi Delta Phi. Home: 605 Doak Odonnell TX 79351 Office: PO Box 308 Odonnell TX 79351 Office Phone: 806-759-7147.

SALEH, PAUL N., former telecommunications executive; b. 1956; BSEE, MSEE, U. Mich., MBA in Fin. with distinction, 1985. Various leadership positions to treas. Honeywell Inc., 1985—96; sr. v.p., treas. The Walt Disney Co., 1997—99; sr. v.p., CFO Walt Disney Internat., 1999—2001; exec. v.p., CFO Nextel Communications, Inc. (merged with Sprint Corp.), 2001—05; CFO Sprint Nextel Corp., Reston, Va., 2005—08, acting CEO, 2007. Bd. dir. Wolf Trap Found. Named best CFO in telecom svcs./wireless sector, Institutional Investor mag., 2004, 2005; named one of 100 Most Influential People in Fin., Treasury & Risk Mgmt. mag., 2005.

SALEHI, AHMAD, research scientist; s. H. Salehi and E. Rustaee; m. Saghi Salehi, July 28, 1991; children: Persia, Aryana. MD, SBMU, Tehran, 1991; PhD, U. Amsterdam, 1996. Sr. scientist Stanford U., Calif., 1999—. Recipient Best Jr. Scientist, U. Leiden, 1996. Achievements include research in neurobiology of down syndrome and Alzheimer's disease. Office: Stanford Univ 1201 Welch Rd Stanford CA 94305 Office Fax: 650-498-6262. Business E-Mail: asalehi@stanford.edu.

SALEM, ENRIQUE T., information technology executive; b. 1965; BA in Computer Sci., Dartmouth Coll., 1987. V.p. Security Pacific Merchant Bank; head security bus. unit Symantec Corp., Cupertino, Calif., 1990—99; v.p. tech. & ops. Ask Jeeves Inc., 1999—2001; sr. v.p. products & tech. Oblix Inc., 2001—02; pres., CEO Brightmail Inc., 2002—04; sr. v.p. network and gateway security solutions Symantec Corp., Cupertino, Calif., 2004—06, sr. v.p. security products and solutions, 2006, sr. v.p. consumer products and solutions, 2006, group pres. consumer products, 2006—08, group v.p. worldwide sales and mktg., 2007—08, COO, 2008—09, pres., CEO, 2009—. Office: Symantec Corp 20330 Stevens Creek Blvd Cupertino CA 95014 Office Phone: 408-517-8000.*

SALEM, GEORGE RICHARD, lawyer; b. Jacksonville, Fla., Dec. 24, 1953; s. Kamel Abraham and Margaret Virginia (Bateh) S.; m. Rhonda M. Ziadeh, June 28, 1980; children: James George, Jihan Camille, Laila Suad, Sarah Rose. BA, Emory U., 1975, JD, 1977; LLM, Georgetown U., 1984. Bar: Ga. 1978, Fla. 1979, DC 1981. Ptnr. Thompson, Mann & Hutson, Washington, 1977-85; dep. solicitor US Dept. Labor, Washington, 1985-86, solicitor, 1986-89; ptnr., head of Middle East and US Dept. of Labor practices group Akin, Gump, Strauss, Hauer & Feld, Washington, 1990—2004; prin. AG Solutions, Law Offices of George R. Salem PLLC, 2005—; strategic advisor DLA Piper US LLP, 2005—. Bd. dirs. Overseas Pvt. Investment Corp. Contbr. articles to profl. jours. Nat. exec. dir. ethnic voters div. Reagan Bush '84; bd. dirs. United Palestinian Appeal, Inc., 1981-85, 86—; co-founder, mem. Arab Am. Inst., Jan.-Mar., 1985, Dec. 1986—, chmn. bd. dirs., 1999—; chmn. Arab-Ams. for Bush-Cheney, 2000; mem. Am. Arab Anti-Discrimination Com. 2000-03; chmn. Arab-Ams. for Bush-Quayle '88, '92; adv. bd. Search for Common Ground in the Mid. East, 2001—; exec. adv. bd. Mid. East Inst., 2002—; bd. dirs. Am. Com. on Jerusalem, 1995—, Emory Law Sch. Coun., 2000-2002, Emory Bd. Govs., 1997-2001. Recipient Ellis Island Medal of Honor, 1992. Fellow College of Labor and Employment Lawyers; mem. ABA (labor and employment law sect.), Ga. Bar Assn. (labor rels. div.), Fla. Bar Assn. (labor rels. div.), DC Bar Assn. (labor rels. div.), Nat. Assn. Arab Ams. (bd. dirs. 1987, pres. 1992-94), Am. Ramallah Club (pres. DC chpt. 1984, Wash. rep. 1982-84), Am. Ramallah Fedn. (chmn. human rights com., Washington rep. 1982-84), Arab Am. Rep. Fedn. (chmn. 1985), Century Club Nat. Rep. Heritage Groups Coun., Delta Theta Phi, Omicron Delta Kappa. Mem. Eastern Orthodox Christian Ch. Office: 500 Eighth St NW Washington DC 20004 Office Phone: 202-887-1140. Office Fax: 202-887-5550. Business E-Mail: gsalem@georgesalem.com.

SALEM, KAREN E., information technology executive; BS in Indsl. Engring., Pa. State U.; MBA, U. Cin. Sr. cons. Anderson Consulting; dir. bus. solutions Burger King; v.p. info. tech. Rexall Sundown; IT head AFC Enterprises; sr. v.p. and CIO Corning Cable Sys.; former sr. v.p. and CIO Winn-Dixie Stores, Inc., Jacksonville, Fla., 2002; sr. v.p. and CIO Ingram Micro, Santa Ana, Calif., 2005—. Office: Ingram Micro PO Box 25125 1600 E St Andrew Pl Santa Ana CA 92799-5125

SALEM, PHILIP ADEEB, medical educator; b. Bterram, El-koura, Lebanon, July 13, 1941; s. Adeeb and Lamia Salem; m. Wadad Jabboury Salem, Aug. 24, 1973; children: Dara, Rayya, Khaled. BS, Am. U. Beirut, Lebanon, 1961, MD, 1965. Lic. ECFMG, 1965, registered DEA,Tex., 1977. Intern (rotating internship) Am. U. Beirut, 1964—65; jr. asst. resident, dept. internal medicine Am. U. Hosp., Beirut, 1965—66, sr. asst. resident, dept. medicine, 1966—67, resident, dept. internal medicine, 1967—68; rsch. fellow med. oncology Meml. Sloan-Kettering Cancer Ctr., NYC, 1968—70, M.D. Anderson Hosp. and Tumor Inst., Houston, 1970—71, asst. prof. medicine, dept. devel. therapeutics, 1976, asst. internist, 1976—77; asst. prof. medicine Am. U. Med. Ctr., Beirut, 1971, asst. Internist, 1971—76, dir., cancer program, 1972, asst. prof. medicine,dir., Cancer Program, 1977, assoc. internist, 1977—87, asst. prof. medicine and ontology, 1978; Chairman Lebanese Nat. Unit Cancer Rsch., Beirut, 1983; assoc. prof. medicine, dept. med. ontology M. D. Anderson Cancer Ctr., Houston, 1987—90, asst. internist, dept. med. ontology, 1987—90, prof. medicine, 1990—91, internist, dept. med. oncology, 1990—91, cons., dept. med. oncology, 1991—2000, adjunct prof. medicine, dept. med. ontology, 1991—2000; dir. Cancer Rsch. Program St. Luke's Episcopal Hosp., Tex. Med. Ctr., 1991—; clin. prof. medicine U. Tex. Med. Sch. Houston, 1992—. Cons. Methodist Hosp., Houston, 2001—03; dir. cancer rsch. program St. Luke's Episcopal Hosp., Houston, 1991—. Recipient medal Achievement, Italian Assn. Pathologists, 1981, Distinguished Leadership award, Am. Biog. Inst., Inc., 1994, Al-Amal award, Ana Al-Arabi Festival, Washington, 1998, Numerous award; named Man of Yr. Medicine, ALMAJALLA, 1994. Office: Salem Oncology Ctr 6626Fannin St Ste 1630 Houston TX 77030 Business E-Mail: salem@pasalem.com.

SALEM, RHONDA ZIADEH, language and special education educator; d. Farhat and Suad Ziadeh; m. George Richard Salem, June 28, 1980; children: James, Jihan, Laila, Sarah. BA, U. Wash., Seattle, 1975; MA, U. NC, Chapel Hill, 1981. Cert. in spl. edn./learning disabilities U. Va., 2004. Tchr. spl. edn. and Russian lang. Langley HS, McLean, Va., 2003—. Mem.: Am. Coun. Tchrs. of Russian, Children with Attention Deficit Disorder, Coun. Exceptional Children. Home: 879 Centrillion Dr Mc Lean VA 22102

SALEM, THOMAS ERIC, electrical engineer, educator; s. William Fredrick and Marjorie Marie Salem; m. Karen B. Tymann, May 14, 1994; children: Madelyn Grace, Eric Timothy, Benjamin Thomas. BS in Engring., Grove City Coll., Pa., 1988; MSEE, U. Ala., 1993, PhD, 1996. Registered profl. engr., Pa., 1997. Project engr. E.I. Dupont DeNemours & Co., Aiken, SC, 1988—89, Westinghouse Savannah River Co., Aiken, 1989—95; asst. prof. engring. Pa. State U., Mont Alto, Pa., 1996—98, Elizabethtown (Pa.) Coll., 1998—2002; asst. prof. elec. engring. U.S. Naval Acad., Annapolis, Md., 2002—. Rsch. engr. U.S. Army Rsch. Lab., Adelphi, Md., 2004—, U.S. Naval Rsch. Lab., Washington, 2002—03; adj. lectr. Pa. State U., Harrisburg, Pa., 2000—01; sr. staff engr. ATC Diversified Electronics, Lancaster, Pa., 1999—2000; prin. electronics engr. TB Wood's Inc., Chambersburg, Pa., 1997—98. Recipient George Westinghouse Signature Excellence award, Westinghouse Savannah River Co., 1989, Westinghouse Total Quality Achievement award, 1991. Mem.: IEEE. Office: United States Naval Academy Maury Hall Mail Stop 14B 105 Maryland Av Annapolis MD 21402 Business E-Mail: salem@usna.edu.

SALEMBIER, VALERIE BIRNBAUM, publishing executive; b. Teaneck, NJ; d. Jack and Sara (Gordon) Birnbaum; m. Paul J. Block, Dec. 9, 1990. BA, Coll. New Rochelle, 1973. Advt. dir. Ms. Mag., NYC, 1976-79, assoc. pub., 1979-81; pub. Inside Sports Mag., NYC, 1982; sr. v.p. advt. USA Today, 1983-88; pub. TV Guide, Radnor, Pa., 1988; pres. N.Y. Post, NYC, 1988—90; pub. Family Circle Mag., NYC, 1991-93; sr. v.p. advt. N.Y. Times, 1993-95; v.p., pub. Esquire Mag., 1996—2003; sr. v.p., pub. Harper's Bazaar, NYC, 2003—. Lectr. in field. Author: (book) Rotissereie League Baseball, 1982; freelance mag. writer:. Chmn. N.Y.C. Police Found.; bd. dirs., past pres. Nat. Alliance Breast Cancer Orgns., former bd. dirs.; bd. dirs., past pres. Beneficial Orgn. Aid Ex-Fighters; former trustee Ctrl. Synagogue, Coll. New Rochelle; trustee N.Y.C. Sports Devel. Corp. Mem.: Women in Comm., Com. 200, Womens Forum. Office: Harpers Bazaar 300 W 57 St New York NY 10019

SALENTINE, THOMAS JAMES, pharmaceutical executive; b. Milw., Aug. 8, 1939; s. James Edward and Loretta Marie S.; m. Susan Anne Sisk, Apr. 16, 1966; children: Anne Elizabeth, Thomas James Jr. BS in Acctg., Marquette U., Milw., 1961. CPA, Ind., Wis. Sr. audit mgr. Price Waterhouse, Milw., 1961-74; dir. corp. acctg. Ward Foods Inc., Wilmette, Ill., 1974-78; corp. contr. Johnson Controls Inc., Milw., 1984-85; v.p., contr. Stokely Van Camp Inc., Indpls., 1978-87; exec. v.p., CFO Bindley Western Industries Inc., Indpls., 1987—2001, also bd. dirs.; ptnr. Bindley Capital Ptnrs., LLC, 2001—. Bd. dirs. Priority Healthcare Corp., Nat. Refrigeration Svcs. Inc. Chmn. com. United Way, Indpls., 1989-90. Lt. USN, 1962-65. Mem. AICPA, Fin. Execs. Inst. Republican. Roman Catholic. Home: 3991 Gulf Shore Blvd Naples FL 34103 Office Phone: 317-704-4154.

SALERNO, F. ROBERT, travel company executive; b. Springfield, Mass. married; 2 children. D., Marquette U., 1972. Vice pres. eastern region Avis, 1982—87, v.p. field ops., 1987—90, sr. v.p., gen. mgr., 1990—95, exec. v.p. ops., 1995—96, pres., COO, 1996—2002; CEO Cendant Car Rental Group, 2003—06; pres., COO Avis Budget Group, Parsippany, NJ, 2006—. Office: Avis Budget Group 6 Sylvan Way Parsippany NJ 07054

SALERNO, JOHN C., biochemist; m. Susan Me Smith. BSc in Physics, MIT, Cambridge; PhD in Biophysics, U. Pa. Med. Sch., Phila., 1977. Prof. biology Rensselaer Poly. Inst., Troy, 1980—2006; adj. prof. biology SUNY, Albany, NY; vis. prof. Yale U. Sch. Medicine; adj. prof. Emory U. Sch. Medicine, Atlanta; neel disting. prof. biotechnology Kennesaw State U., Ga., 2006—; NIH fellow Duke U. Sch. Medicine. Dir. bioinformatics Rensselaer Poly., 1997—2004, chair biology; ptnr. Aeneas Biotechnology. Contbr. scientific papers. Recipient Rensselaer Early Career award, RPI. Mem.: AAAS, Nitric Oxide Soc., ASBMB. Achievements include patents for biotechnology, control of NO synthesis; research in bioenergetics, membrane protein structure, enzymology; discovery of pulsed activity of signaling enzymes; identified control elements in nitric oxide synthase; devised magnetic resonance lineshape models; discovered heme copper active site. Office: Kennesaw State Univ 1000 Chastain Rd Acworth GA 30102 Business E-Mail: jsalern3@kennesaw.edu.

SALERNO, SISTER MARIA, advanced practice nurse, educator; b. Syracuse, NY; d. Joseph and Josephine (Ostrowski) S. Diploma in nursing, St. Joseph's Hosp., Syracuse, 1962; BSN summa cum laude, Cath. U. Am., Washington, 1974, MS in Nursing, 1976, PhD in Nursing, 1981; cert. nurse practitioner, U. Rochester, 1984. RN, N.Y., Md., Washington; cert. adult, geriatric nurse practitioner ANCC; joined Sisters of Third Franciscan Order, Roman Cath. Ch., 1963. Staff nurse St. Joseph Hosp. Health Ctr., Syracuse, 1962-63; sr. charge nurse ICU, gen. med. and surg. units St. Elizabeth Hosp., Utica, NY, 1965-66, head nurse pediat. unit, 1966-69; head nurse ECF Loretto Geriatric Ctr., Syracuse, 1969-72; lectr. Cath. U. Am., Washington, 1977—78, 1980—81, asst. prof. nursing, 1978-79, 81-92, assoc. prof., 1992—2009, dir. primary care adult/geriatric nurse practitioner programs, 1984—2009, co-dir. FNP program, 1994-97; dir. Adult CNS Nurse Educator Program, 2004—09; gen. councilor Sister St. Francis, 2008—. Contbr. chpts. to books; contbr. articles to profl. jours. Vol. nurse practitioner Cmty. of Hope, Washington; instl. animal care and use com. George Washington U., 1996-2009, Cath. U. Am. 2000-09, Veteran's Adminstrn. Med. Ctr., 2004-09; scholarship com. Franciscan Found. for the Holy Land, 1996-. Grantee NIH, 1984-89, Cath. U. Am., 1989-90. Mem.: AAUP, ANA, D.C. League for Nursing (bd. dirs. 1995—97, 1999—2009), D.C. Nurse Practitioners Assn. (nom. com. 2006—07), N.Y. Acad. Scis., Nat. League for Nursing, Nat. Orgn. Nurse Practitioner Facilities, Nat. Gerontol. Nurses Assn., Am. Coll. Nurse Practitioners, Am. Acad. Nurse Practitioners, Cath. U. Am. Nursing Alumni Assn. (pres. 1986—87, chpt. exec. bd. 1992—2003, treas. 1998—2003), Nat. Italian Am. Found. (assoc.), Sigma Theta Tau (grad. counselor Kappa chpt. 1985—87, awards com. 1987—89, grad. counselor Kappa chpt. 1991—97, eligibility com. 1991—97, 2002—03, grad. counselor Kappa chpt. 2006—09). Roman Catholic. Office: Sisters of St Francis Corp Office 2500 Grant Blvd Ste 3 Syracuse NY 13208 Business E-Mail: salerno@cua.edu, msalerno@sosf.org.

SALERNO, PATRICIA J., elementary school educator; married. BS in Edn., Ohio State Univ.; MA in Edn., Univ. Ariz. Tchr. Izmir Elem. Sch., Turkey, Fort Campbell (Ky.) Schs., Vicenza Elem. Sch., Italy. Named Dept. Def. Dependents Schs. Tchr. of Yr., 2006. Office: Vicenza Elem Sch Unit 31401 Box 11 APO AE 09630 Business E-Mail: Patricia.Salerno@eu.dodea.edu.

SALERNO, SALVATORE, medical educator; b. LA; s. Ben and Lebra Salerno. PdD, Brandeis U., Waltham, Mass., 1986; MSc in Oriental Medicine, Am. Acad. Acupuncture and Oriental Medicine, Roseville, Minn., 2007. Cert. L.Ac. Minn. Bd. Med. Practice, 2007. Author: (book) Red November Black November Culture and Community in the Industrial Workers of the World. Office: Mpls Cmty and Tech Coll 1501 Hennepin Ave Minneapolis MN 55403 Business E-Mail: salvatore.salerno@minneapolis.edu.

SALES, EUGENIO CARDINAL DE ARAUJO, cardinal, archbishop emeritus; b. Acari, Brazil, Nov. 8, 1920; s. Celso Dantas and Josefa de A. Sales Student, Sem. Fortaleza City. Ordained priest Archdiocese of Natal, Brazil, 1943, aux. bishop, 1954—62, apostolic adminstr., 1962—68; prof., spiritual dir. Archdiocese of Natal Seminary; ordained bishop, 1954; apostolic adminstr. Archdiocese of São Salvador da Bahia, Brazil, 1964—68, archbishop, 1968—71; elevated to cardinal, 1969; cardinal-priest S. Gregorio VII, 1969—; archbishop Archdiocese of São Sebastião do Rio de Janeiro, Brazil, 1971—2001, archbishop emeritus, 2001—; bishop Brazil, Oriental Rites, 1972—2001. Editor: The Pastors Voice. Roman Catholic. Avocation: reading. Office: Archdiocese of São Sebastião do Rio de Janeiro Rua Benjamin Constant 23/502 Gloria CP 1362 20241-150 Rio de Janeiro Brazil

SALES, JAMES BOHUS, lawyer; b. Weimar, Tex., Aug. 24, 1934; s. Henry B. and Agnes Mary (Pesek) Sales; m. Beuna M. Vornsand, June 3, 1956; children: Mark Keith, Debra Lynn, Travis James. BS, U. Tex., 1956, LLB with honors, 1960. Bar: Tex. 1960. Practiced in, Houston, 1960—; head litig. dept. Fulbright & Jaworski, 1979—99, sr. ptnr.,

1960—2000, of counsel, 2000—. Author: Products Liability in Texas, 1985; co-author: Texas Torts and Remedies, 6 vols., 1986; assoc. editor: Tex. Law Rev., 1960; contbr. articles to profl. jours. Trustee South Tex. Coll. Law, 1982—88, 1990—2005, A.A. White Dispute Resolution Ctr., 1991—94; cir. chair membership Supreme Ct. Hist. Soc., 1998—2001; trustee Tex. Supreme Ct. Hist. Soc., 2003—; chair commrs. Tex. Access Justice Commn., 2004—; bd. dirs. Tex. Resource Ctr., 1990—97, Tex. Bar Hist. Found., 1990—2001. Recipient Lifetime Achievement award, U. Tex. Law Sch. Alumni, 2005; named among Best Lawyers in Am., 1989—. Fellow: Nat. Conf. Bar Pres. (coun. 1989—92, Outstanding Svc. award 2007), Houston Bar Found. (chmn. bd. 1982—83, sustaining life), Am. Bar Found. (state chmn. 1993—98, sustaining life, Outstanding Svc. award 2009), Tex. Bar Found. (trustee 1991—95, vice-chmn. 1992—93, chmn. 1993—94, chair adv. bd. planned giving 1994—2004, sustaining life mem.), Internat. Acad. Trial Lawyers, Am. Coll. Trial Lawyers (state chmn. 1993—96), Am. Bd. Trial Advocates; mem.: FBA, ABA (ho. of dels. 1984—2003, mem. Commn. on IOLTA 1995—97), Bar Assn. 5th Fed. Cir., Gulf Coast Legal Found. (bd. dirs. 1982—85), Houston Bar Assn. (bd. dirs. 1970—79, pres.-elect 1979—80, pres. 1980—81), Tex. Law Rev. Assn. (bd. dirs. 1996—2002, pres. 1999—2000), Tex. Assn. Def. Counsel (v.p. 1977—79), State Bar Tex. (bd. dirs. 1983—88, chmn. bd. 1985—86, pres. 1988—89, Pres.'s award 2006), So. Tex. Coll. Trial Advocacy (dir. 1983—87), So. Conf. Bar, Internat. Assn. Def. Counsel, The Forum, Order of Coif, Inns of Ct. (bd. dirs. 1981—84), Westlake Club (bd. govs. 1980—85). Roman Catholic. Home: 10803 Oak Creek St Houston TX 77024-3016 Office: Fulbright & Jaworski 1301 McKinney St Houston TX 77010-3095 E-mail: jsales@fulbright.com.

SALES, MITZI S., science educator; b. Toronto, Ontario, Canada, Feb. 1, 1978; d. Argeo Cadiz and Milagros Albano Sales. BA in Sci., Brown U., 2000, MA in Secondary Biology, 2003. Tchr., sci. dept. E. W. Thurston Mid. Sch., Westwood, Mass., 2003—06, Rye Country Day Sch., Rye, NY, 2006—; upper sch. scis. tchr. Rye County Day Sch. Choreographer, musical E. W. Thurston Mid. Sch., 2005—06, dir., honoring our voices, 2005—06. Mem.: Nat. Sci. Tchrs. Assoc. Achievements include development of honoring our voices curriculum. Office: Rye Country Day Sch 1 Cedar St Rye NY 10580 Personal E-mail: mitzi1000@hotmail.com.

SALETTA, MARY ELIZABETH (BETTY SALETTA), sculptor; b. Miami, Fla., Sept. 30, 1941; d. Earl Robert and Alta Florence Cotner; m. Albert Michael Saletta, July 1, 1959; children: Tia Suzanne, Kamber Ann. Graphic artist Moore Bus. Forms Inc., Modesto, Calif., 1960-67, Live Oak Pub. Co., Oakdale, Calif., 1977-80; freelance artist U.S. Forest Svc., Modesto Irrigation Dist., Stanislaus Schs., New Don Pedro Dam Project, Calif., 1967-77; sculptor Saletta Sculpture, Oakdale, 1980—. Mem. adv. bd. Calif. State U. Coll. Arts, Letters and Sci., Turlock, 1999-2002; charter mem., dir. Downtown Arts Project, Modesto, 1992-96. One-woman shows City of Oakdale Redevel. Agy., 1990, Modesto C. of C., 1996; group shows include Calif. State U. Stanislaus, Turlock, 1986, Cowboy Artist Am. Mus., Kerrville, Tex., 1988, Benson Park Sculpture Garden, Loveland, Colo., 1989, 90, 93, Danada Sculpture Garden, Chgo., 1991, 93, Tucson Mus. Art, 1995; represented in permanent collections Tucson Mus. Art, Buckaroo Hall of Fame, cities of Modesto, Oakdale, Ripon, Calif., Stockton, Los Banos, Montery, San Leandro, Calif.; sculptures include life-size pub. sculptures Yesterday Is Tomorrow, 1991, Paperboy, 1995, Am. Graffiti, 1997, Stockton Firefighters Meml., 1998, World War II Meml., 1999, Nursing, the Finest Art, 2001, Chief Estanislao, 2001, Firefighter Sculpture produced at Laguna Beach Pageant of the Masters, 2002, Henry Miller Meml., 2005, Story Time, 2006. Recipient Excellence in Fine Art award Bank Am., Stockton, Calif., 1959, Best of Show award Western Art Roundup, Winnamucca, Nev., 1987, 88, Excellence in Visual Arts award Stanislaus Arts Coun., Modesto, 1999. Mem. Nat. League Am. Pen Women, Ctrl. Calif. Art League (advisor 1991, Best of Show award 1987), Rotary (bd. dirs. Oakdale 1997-99, pres. 2007-). Democrat. Avocations: horses, skiing, mountain climbing, fishing. Home: 4255 Wellsford Rd Oakdale CA 95361-7930 Fax: 209-572-4089. E-mail: salettasculpture@aol.com.

SALGO, PETER LLOYD, internist, writer, anesthesiologist, journalist, commentator; b. NYC, Nov. 9, 1949; s. Michael Nicholas and Ruth F. Salgo. BA, Columbia U., 1971, MD, 1975. Diplomate Am. Bd. Internal Medicine, Am. Bd. Anesthesiology; lic. physician, N.Y., Calif., Mass.; instrument rated comml. pilot. Internal medicine intern Columbia Presbyn. Med. Ctr., NYC, 1975-76, resident in internal medicine, 1976-78; vis. faculty fellow intensive care medicine and anesthesiology, dept. anesthesiology Columbia U., NYC, 1979-81; lectr. Harvard Med. Sch., Boston; clin. prof. medicine and anesthesiology Columbia P&S; mem. staff in anesthesia and medicine Mass. Gen. Hosp., Boston; attending in anesthesia and internal medicine Presbyn. Hosp., NYC, assoc. vice chmn. dept. anesthesiology, chmn. inter-I.C.U. com., assoc. dir. surg. ICU. Host syndicated TV broadcast Healthcare 2000; aviation med. examiner FAA; comml. pilot. instrument Rated; host nat. radio med. program Sta. PRN, 1979—81; writer, producer, host med. info. broadcast Sta. WCBS-TV, NYC, 1980—81; med. corr. Sta. WCBS News, 1981—2000; corr. CBS Network Radio News, 1982—92; host. Healthtalk, 1982—88; med. corr. Sta. CNBC, 1989—, CNBC TV Network, 1989—93; host The Doctor Is In, Eyada.com, 2000—01; cons. to networks on med. content of TV programs; corr. Patient Info. Network, 1989—; anchor Americas Vital Signs, CNBC TV Network, Med. Crossfire, 2001—; host Second Opinion PBS, 2003—; lectr. in field.; expert guest on John F. Kennedy, Jr., crash NTSB Report Discovery Network, 2002; expert guest, med. cons. Fox News, 2001—02. Author: The Heart of the Matter, 2004. Recipient Leonard Pullman award Columbia U., 1971, Blakesley award Am. Heart Assn., Journalism award Medic-alert Found., Honorable Mention in Journalism, UPI, Alumni Assn. medal Columbia U. P&S, 1975, Emmy award for excellence in broadcast journalism, Journalism award Lions Eye Found. Fellow ACP; mem. AAAS, AMA, AFTRA, N.Y. State Med. Soc., N.Y. County Med. Soc., Am. Soc. Anesthesiologists. Office: Presbyn Hosp Dept Anesthesiology New York NY 10032 Home Phone: 212-327-0133; Office Phone: 212-305-6494. E-mail: pls1@columbia.edu.

SALHANY, LUCILLE S. (LUCY SALHANY), broadcast executive; b. 1946; married; 2 children. LHD (hon.), Emerson Coll., 1992. Program dir. WKBF-TV, Cleve., 1967; program mgr. WLVI-TV, Boston, 1975—79; v.p. television & cable programming Taft Broadcasting Co., 1979—85; pres. Paramount Domestic TV, 1985—91; chmn. 20th Century Television, 1991—93, Fox Broadcasting Co., 1993—94; pres. United Paramount Network (UPN), 1994-97; pres., CEO JH Media, Boston, 1998—2004, HJ Media, LifeFX Networks Inc., 2002—04; co-founder, mng. ptnr. Echo Bridge Entertainment, Needham, Mass., 2004—. Bd. dirs. Hewlett-Packard Co., Am. Media Co., Inc., ION Media Networks, Inc., 2006—. Bd. trustees Emerson Coll.; profl. adv. bd. ALSAC/St. Jude Children's Rsch. Hosp. Recipient Sherrill C. Corwin Human Rels award, Am. Jewish Com., 1995, Silver Satellite award, Am. Women in Radio and TV, 1995, HELP Humanitarian award, 1997, Avatar award, Cable Fin. Mgmt. Orgn., Silver Circle award, Nat. Acad TV Arts and Sci.; named Exec. of Yr., Caucus for Prodrs., Writers & Dirs. Achievements include becoming the first woman to manage an American broadcast television network, 1993. Office: Echo Bridge Entertainment Ste 500 75 Second Ave Needham Heights MA 02494 Office Phone: 781-444-9680.

SALI, BILL (WILLIAM THOMAS SALI), former United States Representative from Idaho; b. Portsmouth, Ohio, Feb. 17, 1954; s. Gregory and Dorothy Hazel (Wilkinson) Sali; m. Terry Sue Petersen, Aug. 20, 1976; children: Jennifer, Levi, Micah, Anna, Rachel, Christina. BBA, Boise State U., 1981; JD, U. Idaho, 1984. Bar: Idaho, US Ct. Appeals (9th cir.). Pvt. law practice, Meridian, Idaho, 1984—2006; mem. Idaho House Reps. from Dist. 21A, Boise, 1990—2006, vice chmn. health & welfare com., 1993—2006; mem. US Congress from 1st Idaho dist., 2007—09, mem. oversight & govt. reform, nat. resources com. Named Champion of Family, Idaho Family Forum, 1992. Mem.: Idaho Bar Assn. Republican. Avocation: country music.*

SALICKI, ROMAN, commercial photographer; Photographer Vogue mag., London; has worked with Helmut Newton, David Bailey and Richard Avedon; freelance photographer L.A. Achievements include photos appearing in publications in more than 140 countries in fashion, celebrity and news magazines including Vogue, Vanity Fair, OK, House & Garden, Entertainment Weekly and Glamour and almost every major newspaper. Office: 1310 N Stanley Ave Los Angeles CA 90046 Office Phone: 323-876-0304. Business E-Mail: romansalicki@sbcglobal.net.

SALIGMAN, HARVEY, retired consumer products and services company executive; b. Phila., July 18, 1938; s. Martin and Lillian (Zitin) S.; m. Linda Powell, Nov. 25, 1979; children: Martin, Lilli Ann, Todd Michael, Adam Andrew, Brian Matthew BS, Phila. Coll. Textiles and Sci., 1960. With Queen Casuals, Inc., Phila., 1960-88, v.p., 1966-68, pres., chief exec. officer, 1968-81, chmn., 1981-88; pres., chief operating officer Interco Inc., St. Louis, 1981-83, chief exec. officer, 1983-85, 1985-89, chmn., 1989-90; ret. Bd. dirs. Ameren Corp. (formerly Union Electric). Trustee Washington U., St. Louis, Nantucket Hist. Assn. Mem. St. Louis Club, Masons.

SALIMATH, MANJULA S., management educator; d. V. S. and Premadevi V. Malimath; m. Shanmukh S. Salimath; 1 child, Varada S. MS, Bangalore U., India; PhD, Wash. State U., Pullman. Cert. Calif. Tax Edn. Coun. Asst. prof. U. North Tex., Denton, 2006—. Editor Advances Mgmt., 2009—; faculty advisor Students Free Enterprise. Contbr. articles to profl. jours. Recipient State award, Directorate Youth Svcs. & Sports, Govt. of Karnataka, 1987, 1989, award, Jawaharlal Nehru Meml. Fund, New Delhi, 1988, Gold medal, Bangalore U., 1989, Outstanding Rsch. award, So. Mgmt. Assn., San Antonio, 2004, Tchg. Asst. Excellence award, Grad. & Profl. Student's Assn., Wash. State U., 2004—05; Nat. Merit scholarship, Ministry of Human Resource Devel., Govt. of India, 1987—89, Jr. Rsch. fellowship, U. Grants Commn., New Delhi, 1990—93, Publ. grant, Indian Coun. for Social Sci. Rsch., Govt. of India, New Delhi, 1999, Jr. Faculty Summer Rsch. fellowship, U. North Tex., 2006—07. Mem.: Women Acad. Internat. Bus., Western Acad. Mgmt., So. Mgmt. Assn., Acad. Internat. Bus., Acad. Mgmt., Beta Gamma Sigma. Office: Univ N Tex 1155 Union Cir # 305429 Denton TX 76203-5017

SALINAS, CARLOS DOMINIC, literature and language professor, consultant; s. Horacio and Martenia Salinas; m. Jayme Evans Weede, June 7, 1997; children: Matthew Patrick, Alexander Christopher. PhD, Purdue U., West Lafayette, Ind., 2000. Asst. prof. communication U. Tex., San Antonio, 2000—06, asst. prof. English El Paso, 2006—. Pvt. practise, El Paso, 2006—. Vis. scholar, The Ednl. Testing Svc., 2007. Office: Univ Tex El Paso 500 W Univ Dr El Paso TX 79968 Business E-Mail: cdsalinas@utep.edu.

SALINAS, MARTIN, energy executive; Sr. audit mgr. KPMG, San Antonio, 2002—04; joined Energy Transfer Ptnrs., LP, Dallas, 2004, controller, treas., 2004—08, CFO, 2008—. Office: Energy Transfer Company 3738 Oak Lawn Ave Dallas TX 75219-4333 Office Phone: 214-981-0700. Office Fax: 214-981-0703.

SALINAS, RAUL G., Mayor, Laredo, Texas; BA in Law Enforcement & Criminology, U. Md. Former police officer US Capitol, Wash., DC; ret. agent FBI; former aide to Hon. Eligio (Kika) De La Garza; asst. legal attache US Embassy, Mexico City; mayor City of Laredo, Tex., 2006—. Office: City Hall 1110 Houston St Laredo TX 78040 Office Phone: 956-791-7389. Fax: 956-791-7314. E-mail: rgsalinas@ci.laredo.tx.us.*

SALINGER, FRANK MAX, lawyer; b. Landau, Isar, Germany, Dec. 4, 1951; s. Karl and Ingeborg F. (Herold) S.; m. Susan Ann Wagner, May 20, 1978. Student, Columbia Union Coll., Takoma Park, Md., 1969-72; JD, U. Balt., 1975. Bar: Md. 1975, U.S. Dist. Ct. Md. 1975, U.S. Ct. Appeals (4h cir.) 1978, U.S. Tax Ct. 1978, U.S. Ct. Mil. Appeals 1978, U.S. Ct. Appeals (5th cir.) 1982, U.S. Supreme Ct. 1983, U.S. Ct. Appeals (11th cir.) 1984, U.S. Ct. Appeals (9th cir.) 1986, D.C. 1986, U.S. Ct. Appeals (3d cir.) 1989. Pvt. practice, Balt., 1975-77; counsel Md. State Senate, Annapolis, 1975-76; assoc. counsel Am. Fin. Corp., Silver Spring, Md., 1977-78; govt. rels. counsel Truck Trailer Mfrs. Assn., Washington, 1978-80; v.p., gen. counsel, dir. govt. affairs Am. Fin. Svcs. Assocs., Washington, 1980-92; v.p. govt. rels. Advanta Corp., Wilmington, Del., 1992—. Co-author: (with Alvin O. Wiese and Robert E. McKew) A Guide to the Consumer Bankruptcy Code, 1989; (with Robert W. Green) State Regulations and Statutes on Consumer Credit, 1989, Federal Consumer Credit Regulations and Statutes, 1989. City councilman, Laurel, Md., 1976-78, zoning commr., 1976-78; chmn. Md. State Young Reps., 1977-78; bd. dirs. Am. Bankruptcy Inst., Washington, 1986-88. Mem. ABA (mem. com. on consumer fin. svcs., subcoms. on interest rate regulation and state regulation), Am. League Lobbyists (chair fin. svcs. sect. 1995-97), Federalist Soc. Law and Pub. Policy, Capitol Hill Club, 1st State Cmty. Loan Fund (Wilmington, Del.) (dir.). Republican. Office: Advanta Corp One Righter Pkwy Wilmington DE 19803 Business E-Mail: fsalinger@advanta.com.

SALINGER, J.D. (JEROME DAVID SALINGER), author; b. NYC, Jan. 1, 1919; s. Sol and Miriam (Jillich) S.; m. Claire Douglas, 1953 (div. 1967); children: Margaret Ann, Matthew; m. Colleen. Student, Valley Forge Mil. Acad., Columbia U., Ursinus Coll. Author: Catcher in the Rye, 1951, Nine Stories, 1953, Franny and Zooey, 1961, Raise High the Roof Beam, Carpenters; and Seymour: An Introduction, 1963; contbr. stories to New Yorker mag. Sgt. AUS, 1942-46. Address: care Harold Ober Assocs 425 Madison Ave New York NY 10017-1110

SALINS, PETER D., political science professor, academic administrator; b. Berlin, June 15, 1938; came to U.S., 1939; s. Irwin and Ilse Daisy (Lessler) S.; m. Rochelle Chensky, Apr. 4, 1971; children: Jessica Elizabeth, Jonathan Andrew. BArch, Syracuse U., 1961, M in Regional Planning, 1968, PhD, 1969. Registered architect, Mass. Chmn. dept. urban affairs and planning Hunter Coll., CUNY, 1973-93, 96-97, prof. dept. urban affairs and planning, 1980-97, dir. grad. program in urban planning, 1993-95, dir. urban rsch. ctr., 1995-97; provost, vice chancellor acad. affairs SUNY Sys. Adminstrn., Albany, 1997—2006; prof. dept. polit. sci. Stony Brook U., 1996—, Univ. prof. dept. polit. sci., 2006—. Sr. fellow Manhattan Inst. Policy Rsch., NYC, 1985—; mem. Planning Accreditation Bd., Chgo., 1990—; Catherine Bauer Wurster lectr. U. Calif., Berkeley, 1993; dir. SUNY Rsch. Found., 1997—2006. Author: The Ecology of Housing Destruction, 1980, Assimilation, American Style, 1997; co-author: Scarcity by Design, 1992; editor: Housing America's Poor, 1987, New York Unbound, 1988; co-editor Jour. of Am. Planning Assn., 1988-93 (Excellence award 1992, Journalism award 1994). Mem. planning com. Am. Acad. Sci., Washington, 1971-72; mem. adv. panel White House Domestic Policy Unit, Washington, 1977; dir. Citizens Housing and Planning Coun., NYC, 1988—; trustee Lavanburg Found., NYC, 1987—, chmn., Landmarks Preservation Com., Village of Baxter Estates, Nassau County, NY, 1992-99; mem. mayor's adv. commn. NYC Health and Hosps. Corp., 1995-96. Fellow: Am. Inst. Cert. Planners; mem.: ASPA (v.p. 1982—84, Luther Gulick award for outstanding acad. 1994), Am. Econ. Assn., Am. Planning Assn. (v.p. 1986—88, policy bd. mem. 1986—, N.Y. met. chpt.), Lambda Alpha. Avocations: golf, reading, hiking. Office Phone: 631-632-7672. Business E-Mail: peter.salins@stonybrook.edu.

SALISBURY, ALAN BLANCHARD, information technology officer; b. Newark, Jan. 21, 1937; s. Lloyd Wade and Elizabeth Barry (Blanchard) S.; m. Florence Dorothy Conrad, May 21, 1971; children: Katherine Anne, Barbara Lynn. BS with distinction, U.S. Mil. Acad., 1958; MSEE, Stanford U., 1964, PhD, 1973; postgrad., Indsl. Coll. of Armed Forces, Washington, 1978. Commd. 2d lt. Signal Corps U.S. Army, 1958, advanced through grades to Maj. Gen., ret., 1987; asst. prof. U.S. Mil. Acad.. West Point, N.Y., 1964-67; chief of data communications lst Signal Brigade, Republic of Vietnam, 1968-69; tech. adv. Directorate of Mgmt. Info., Washington, 1970-71; dir. U.S. Army Ctr. for Tactical Computer Sci., Ft. Monmouth, N.J., 1975-77; project mgr. Operations Tactical Data Systems, Ft. Monmouth, N.J., 1978-82; program mgr. Joint Tactical Fusion Program, Washington, 1982-84; comdr. U.S. Army Info. Systems Engring., Ft. Belvoir, Va., 1984-87; pres. Contel Technology Ctr., Fairfax, Va., 1987-91; exec. v.p. Microelectronics & Computer Tech. Corp., Austin, Tex., 1991-93; pres. Learning Tree Internat. USA, Inc., Reston, Va., 1993-99; ind. cons., 1999—. Bd. dirs. Sybase, Dublin, Calif., Challenger Ctr. for Space Sci. Edn., Alexandria, Va., 1990-2008; dir. Noblis, Inc., Fairfax, Va., Assn. Grads. U.S. Mil. Acad.; chmn. Ctr. for Nat. Software Studies, 1996-2009; bd. visitors Software Engring. Inst. Carnegie Mellon U., 1988-2002, Coll. of Engring. U. Md., 1993-2001. Author: Microprogrammable Computer Architectures 1976, numerous articles in profl. jours.; founding editor Journal of Systems & Software, 1979-85. Decorated Bronze Star (2), 1969, D.S.M., 1987. Mem. Inst. for Elec. & Electronic Engrs. (sr.), Assn. for Computing Machinery, Armed Forces Communications & Electronics Assn. (chpt. pres. 1981-82), Phi Kappa Phi, Soc. of the Sigma Xi. Office Phone: 703-821-2215. Personal E-mail: abslsbry@aol.com.

SALISBURY, DALLAS L., researcher, director; b. Everett, Wash. BA, U. Wash., 1970; MPA in Pub. Policy and Adminstrn., Syracuse U., 1973. With Employee Benefit Security Adminstrn. US Dept. Labor, 1975—76, Pension Guaranty Corp. US Dept. Labor, 1977—78, U.S. Dept. Justice, 1974, Wash. State Legislature, 1971-72, Employee Benefit Rsch. Inst., Washington, 1978—, pres., CEO, mem. bd. trustees. Bd. dir. FINRA Investor Edn. Group; lectr. in field; cons. in field. Mem. editl. adv. bd. Benefits Quar., Employee Benefits Jour.; contbr. articles to profl. jours. Mem. Employee Retirement Income Security Act of 1974 adv. coun. US Sec. Labor; pres.'s adv. coun. Pension Benefit Guaranty Corp. Fellow Nat. Acad. Human Resources. Office: Employee Benefit Research Inst 1100 13th St NW Washington DC 20005

SALISBURY, FRANK BOYER, botanist, educator, writer; b. Provo, Utah, Aug. 3, 1926; s. Frank M. and Catherine (Boyer) S.; m. Lois Marilyn Olson, Sept. 1, 1949; children: Frank Clark, Steven Scott, Michael James, Cynthia Kay, Phillip Boyer (dec.), Rebecca Lynn, Blake Charles; m. Mary Thorpe Robinson, June 28, 1991. BS, U. Utah, Salt Lake City, 1951, MA, 1952; PhD, Calif. Inst. Tech., Pasadena, 1955. Asst. prof. botany Pomona Coll., Claremont, Calif., 1954-55; faculty Colo. State U., Ft. Collins, 1955-66, prof. plant physiology, 1961-66; plant physiologist Expt. Sta., 1961-66; prof. plant physiology Utah State U., Logan, 1966-97, disting. prof. Agr., 1987-97, prof. emeritus, 1997—, head dept. plant sci., 1966-70; tech. rep. plant physiology AEC, Germantown, Md., 1973-74. Vis. prof. U. Innsbruck, Austria; Lady Davis fellow Hebrew U. Jerusalem, 1983; mem. aerospace medicine adv. com. NASA, 1988-93, life scis. adv. com., 1986-88, chmn. NASA Controlled Ecol. Life Support System Discipline Working Group, 1989-94; leader of project to grow wheat through a life cycle in Russian space station, Mir, 1990-97. Author: The Flowering Process, 1963, Truth by Reason and by Revelation, 1965, The Biology of Flowering, 1971, The Utah UFO Display, 1974, The Creation, 1976, The Case for Divine Design, 2006; co-author: (with R.V. Parke) Vascular Plants, Form and Function, 2d edit., 1970, (with C. Ross) Plant Physiology, 1969, 4th edit., 1992; (with W. Jensen) Botany: An Ecological Approach, 1972, Botany, 2d edit., 1984, (with others) Biology, 1977; editor Jour. Plant Physiology, Ams. and the Pacific Rim, 1989-96; editor, contbr.: Units, Symbols, and Terminology for Plant Physiology, 1996; editor: Geochemistry and The Biosphere, 2006. Trustee Colo. State U. Rsch. Found., 1959-62; leader People to People bot. del. to South Africa, 1984, to China, 1988, Soviet Union, 1990; fin. sec. Ohio Columbus Mission LDS Ch., 1997-99. NSF sr. postdoctoral fellow Germany and Austria, 1962-63. Fellow AAAS; mem. Am. Soc. for Gravitational and Space Biology (Founders award 1994), Am. Soc. Plant Physiologists (editorial bd. 1967-92), Am. Inst. Biol. Scis. (governing bd. 1976-79), Bot. Soc. Am. (merit award 1982), Sigma Xi, Phi Kappa Phi. Mem. Lds Ch. Home: 2250 Bryan Cir Salt Lake City UT 84108-2711 Home Phone: 801-583-6569; Office Phone: 801-281-1575. *This is an extremely exciting time to live! Science has provided marvelous insight into the cosmos, the earth, and the nature of life. The fact that mankind exists and can contemplate it all cries out that it has purpose and direction. My life is full to overflowing because God's revelation of Himself adds the final capstone to this beautiful structure.*

SALISBURY, FRANKLIN C., JR., foundation administrator; s. Franklin and Tamara Salisbury. BA in Econs., Yale U., New Haven, 1978; MA, U. Chgo.; MDiv, Yale Divinity Sch.; JD, U. Ga., 1992. Chmn. Consumer Utilities Bd., Washington; joined Nat. Found. Cancer Rsch., Bethesda, Md., 1993, pres., CEO, 1997—. Chmn. bd. dirs. Asian Fund Cancer Rsch., Hong Kong. Office: Nat Found Cancer Rsch 4600 E West Hwy Ste 525 Bethesda MD 20814*

SALISBURY, JOHN, chemist, researcher; s. James and Judith Salisbury; m. Rosanne De Maio, June 26, 2004. BA, Coll. Holy Cross, Worcester, MA; MS, U. RI, Kingston. Scientist Pfizer Inc, Groton, Conn., 2001—.

SALISBURY, ROBERT HOLT, political science professor; b. Elmhurst, Ill., Apr. 29, 1930; s. Robert Holt and Beulah (Hammer) S.; m. Rose Marie Cipriani, June 19, 1953; children: Susan Marie (dec.),

Robert Holt, Matthew Gary. AB, Washington and Lee U., 1951; MA, U. Ill., 1952, PhD, 1955. Mem. faculty Washington U., St. Louis, 1955-65, prof., 1965-97, prof. emeritus, 1997—, chmn. dept. polit. sci., 1966-73, 86-92, dir. Center for Study Pub. Affairs, 1974-77, Sidney W. Souers prof. govt., 1982-97. Vis. prof. SUNY, Buffalo, 1965, So. Ill. U., Edwardsville, 1975; affiliated scholar Am. Bar Found., 1981-95; cons. U.S. Conf. Mayors, 1965, Hartford (Conn.) C. of C., 1964, NSF, 1973. Author: Interest Groups Politics in America, 1970, Governing America, 1973, Citizen Participation in the Public Schools, 1980, Interests and Institutions, 1992, The Hollow Core, 1993; contbr. articles to profl. jours. Mem. St. Louis County Charter Commn., 1967, Gov.'s Commn. on Local Govt., 1968-69. Guggenheim fellow, 1990; Rockefeller Ctr. scholar, 1990. Mem. Mo. Polit. Sci. Assn. (pres. 1964-65), Am. Polit. Sci. Assn. (exec. council 1969-71, v.p. 1980-81), Midwest Polit. Sci. Assn. (pres. 1977-78), Pi Sigma Alpha. Democrat. Methodist. Home: 709 S Skinker Blvd Saint Louis MO 63105-3225 Office: Washington U Dept Polit Sci Saint Louis MO 63130

SALITERMAN, RICHARD ARLEN, lawyer; b. Aug. 3, 1946; s. Leonard Slitz and Dorothy (Sloan) S.; m. Laura Shrager, June 15, 1975; 1 child, Robert Warren. BA summa cum laude, U. Minn., 1968; JD, Columbia U., 1971; LLM, NYU, 1974; grad., FBI Citizens Acad., Mpls. and Washington, 2006. Bar: Minn. 1972, DC 1974. Legal staff subcom. on antitrust and monopoly U.S. Senate, Washington, 1971-72; acting dir., dep. dir. compliance and enforcement divsn. Fed. Energy Office, NYC, 1974; mil. atty. Presdl. Clemency Bd., White House, Washington, 1975; pres. Saliterman & Siefferman, PC, Mpls., 1975—. Adj. prof. law Hamline U., 1976-81. Author: Advising Minnesota Corporations and Other Business Organizations, 4 vols., 1975; chmn. Hennepin County Bar Jour., 1985-87. Trustee, sec. Hopkins Edn. Found.; trustee W. Harry Davis Found., 1990-96; pres. Twin Cities Coun.; nat. bd. dirs. Navy League U.S., Washington, 1997—, nat. judge adv., 2001-02; bd. dirs., sec. The Pavek Mus., 1992—; bd. dirs. Mpls. Urban League, 1983-87. Lt. USN, 1972-75, res., 1975—. Home Phone: 952-545-6424; Office Phone: 612-339-1400. Business E-Mail: rsaliterman@saliterman-law.com.

SALITERMAN, STEVEN S., internist, educator; b. Mpls., June 6, 1951; s. Leonard S. and Dorothy Saliterman; m. Peg E. Maloney, Aug. 24, 1986; children: David Edward, Paul Wesley. BA in Physiology summa cum laude, U. Minn., 1972; MD, Mayo Med. Sch., Rochester, Minn., 1977; grad., Mayo Grad. Sch. Medicine, 1980. Diplomate Am. Bd. Internal Medicine 1983. Pvt. practice, St. Louis Park, Minn., 1981—; sr. aviation med. examiner FAA, Washington, 1981—. Rsch. com. Pk. Nicollet's Meth. Hosp., St. Louis Park, Minn., 1996—2003, chmn. dept. medicine, 2001—05; dept. biomed. engring. U. Minn., Mpls., 2002—, adj. assoc. prof., 2008—, faculty nano & microsystems applications ctr., 2006—; exec. com. Meth. Hosp., St. Louis Park, 2004—05, quality assurance com., 2004—05. Author: (textbook) Fundamentals of BioMEMS and Medical Microdevices, 2006; contbr. articles to profl. jours. Recipient Achievement award, US Army, 1969, Acheivement award, Profl. Engrs. Soc. Minn., 1969, Physician's Recognition award, AMA, 2006; fellow, NASA Johnson Space Ctr., 1973—74, NASA Ames Rsch. Ctr., 1976; Nat. Youth Sci. Camp scholar, Minn. State Sci. Fair, 1969. Fellow: ACP; mem.: Mayo Alumni Assn., Internat. Soc. for Optical Engring., Mayo Plummer Soc., Phi Beta Kappa. Achievements include patents for computerized simulator for critical care training & catheterization; design of 7027 computer system; laser activated amphibian monitor system. Avocations: swimming, hiking, photography, amateur radio. Office: 6490 Excelsior Blvd Ste W-110 Saint Louis Park MN 55426 Office Phone: 952-920-8771. Personal E-mail: stevensaliterman@comcast.net.

SALK, JANE ELLEN, educator; b. Evansville, Ind., May 1, 1957; d. Roland and Joan (Wolfson) Salk. AB in Bus., U. Chgo., 1978; MA in Sociology, U. N.C., 1984; PhD in Mgmt., MIT, 1992. Lectr./instr. Northeastern U., Boston, 1985-86; case rsch. staff Harvard Bus. Sch., Boston, 1985-86; teaching and rsch. asst. MIT, Cambridge, 1986-89, 90-91; asst. prof. orgnl. behavior and internat. bus. Fuqua Sch. Bus., Duke U., Durham, N.C., 1991-95; assoc. prof. ESSEC, 1995-98; prof., 1999—. Cons. to internatl. companies, joint venture orgns. in Europe. Author: Contbr. over 25 articles to profl. jours., chpts. to books. Fulbright scholar, 1989-90; Kenan fellow, U. N.C., 1982-83. Mem. Acad. Internat. Bus., Acad. Mgmt. Office: Univ of Texas at Dallas Sch of Mgmt 4 408 Richardson TX 75083

SALKIN, BARBARA RUTH, social worker; b. Washington, Sept. 16, 1938; d. David and Bess Marguerite (Satkin) S. BA, UCLA, 1960; MSW, U. Calif., Berkeley, 1962. Lic. clin. social worker, Calif. Clin. social worker Neuropsychiat. Inst. UCLA, 1962-79, Kaiser-Permanente, Woodland Hills, Calif., 1979—2004; pvt. practice San Fernando, Calif., 2004—. Contbr. articles to profl. jours. Mem. Nat. Assn. Social Work (cert.), Soc. Clin. Social Work, LA Blues Soc. Democrat. Jewish. Avocations: travel, music, dance. Office: Nagar Psychology Ctr 11273 Laurel Canyon Blvd San Fernando CA 91340-4300 Office Phone: 626-590-5086. Personal E-mail: barbarasalkin@att.net.

SALKIND, MICHAEL JAY, science administrator, metallurgical engineer; s. Milton and Esther (Jaffe) S.; m. Miriam E. Schwartz, Aug. 16, 1959 (div. 1979); children: Michael Jay, Elizabeth Jane, Jonathan Hillson, Joshua Isaac; m. Carol T. Gill, Dec. 23, 1990. B in Metall. Engring., Rensselaer Polytech. Inst., Troy, NY, 1959, PhD, 1962. Chief advanced metallurgy United Techs. Rsch. Labs., East Hartford, 1964-68; chief structures and materials Sikorsky Aircraft div. United Techs. Corp., 1968-75; dir. product devel. Avco Systems div., 1975-76; mgr. structures NASA, 1976-80; dir. aerospace scis. Air Force Office of Sci. Rsch., 1980-89; pres. Ohio Aerospace Inst., 1990—2003, Bus.Tech. Network, 2003—; prin. Indus Internat., 2003—. Adj. faculty metallurgy Trinity Coll., Hartford; adj. faculty aerospace U. Md., College Park, 1982-85; adj. faculty materials Johns Hopkins U., Balt., 1985-89; chair Ohio Math. and Sci. Coalition; adj. faculty Kent State U., Ohio, 2007- Cons. editor Internat. Jour. Fibre Sci. and Tech.; editor Applications Composite Materials, 1973; contbr. to profl. jours. and textbooks. Evaluator Accreditation Bd. Engring. and Tech., 1989—1995; mem. Daniel Guggenheim Medal Bd. Awards, 1984-90; mem. Spirit of St. Louis Medal Bd., 1984-89; bd. dirs. Citizens' Acad. Charter Sch., Cleve. Internat. Program, NCCJ, Cleve. Coun. World Affairs, Diversity Ctr. Corp. Sustainability Network; co-chair Buckeye F.I.R.S.T. Robotics Competition; chair industry adv. bd. Kent State U., Coll. Tech. Capt. ord. US Army, 1962-64. Recipient Disting. Leadership award, Cleve. Tech. Socs. Coun., 2002. Fellow AAAS, AIAA (assoc.), ASM Internat.; mem. ASME (Disting. lectr. 1989-93), ASTM (chmn. com. D-30 on high modulous fibers and their composites 1968-74), Am. Helicopter Soc., AIME, Brit. Inst. Metals, Rsch. Soc. Am., Plansee Soc., India Ohio C. of C., Cosmos Club, Union Club, 50 Club, Leadership Cleve., Sigma Xi, Alpha Sigma Mu. Personal E-mail: michaelsalkind@roadrunner.com. Business E-Mail: michael.salkind@indusin.com.

SALKY, BARRY A., surgeon; b. Memphis, Nov. 10, 1944; s. Jake and Mary Salky; m. Alma Halski; children: Jonathan, Adam. MD, U. Tenn., Memphis, 1970. Diplomate Am. Bd. Surgery. Intern Mt. Sinai Hosp., NYC, 1971—73, resident in internal medicine, 1975—78, clin. prof. surgery, 1996—2004, prof. surgery, 2004—, chief divsn. laparoscopic surgery, 1992—96, 2004—. Author: Laparscopy for Surgeons, 1990, Advanced Laparoscopy for Surgeons, 1994. Maj. US Army, 1973—75. Recipient Ambassador's award, Am. Friends of Rambom Med. Ctr., 1995. Fellow: ACS, Am. Coll. of Gastroenterology; mem.: Soc. Surgery Alimentary Tract, Soc. Am. Gastrointestinal Endoscopic Surgeons (v.p. 1997—98). Jewish. Avocations: golf, travel. Office: Mt Sinai Hosp 5 E 98th St 14th Fl New York NY 10029 Office Phone: 212-241-6156. Business E-Mail: barry.salky@mountsinai.org.

SALL, LARRY DAVID, library director; b. Portland, Oreg., July 10, 1941; s. David Elmer and Lillian Elisabeth Sall; m. Louise Kuhn, Dec. 13, 1967 (div. Aug. 6, 1978); m. Judy Claire McQuade, Nov. 24, 1978; 1 child, Karl Fredrick. BA, U. Idaho, 1964; exch. fellow, U. Munich, Germany, 1967—68; PhD, Wayne State U., 1971. Assoc. dir. spl. collections U. Tex. -Dallas, Richardson, 1982—99, dir. librs., 1999—2004, dean of librs., 2004—. Translator: (memoir) Pioneer Aviator in China, 1998; contbr.: (biography of Lamar Muse) Encyclopedia of American Business History: The Airline Industry. Friends adv. bd. Dallas Pub. Libr., 2004; libr. adv. bd. So. Meth. U., Dallas, 2003; bd. dirs. Frontiers of Flight Mus., Dallas, 1999. Mem.: Audubon Tex. (bd. dirs. 2004, bd. dirs. Dallas chpt. 2001), Am. Birding Assn. (assoc.), Dallas Com. Fgn. Rels. (assoc.), Tex. Philatelic Assn. (assoc.; pres. 1991—95), Richardson Ctrl. Rotary Club (assoc.; pres. 1989—90), Richardson Rotary Club (assoc.). Achievements include development of History of Aviation collection and others, U. Tex.-Dallas. Avocations: bird watching, mountain hiking, scuba diving, travel, reading. Office: Univ Texas at Dallas PO Box 830643 Richardson TX 75083-0643 Office Fax: 972-883-2473. Business E-Mail: sall@utdallas.edu.

SALLAH, MAJEED (JIM), retired real estate developer; b. Boston, Aug. 5, 1920; s. Herbert K. and Rose (Karem) Sallah; m. Aline C. Powers, Apr. 10, 1970; children: Christopher M., Melissa Rose. Pres., dir. Glo-Bit Fish Co., Gloucester, Mass., 1947—48, Live-Pak of Ohio, Inc., 1947—51, Cape Ann Glass Co., Gloucester, 1950—72, Marias Restaurant, 1960—, Cape Ann Realty Co., 1961—. Pres., treas., dir. Gloucester Hot-Top Constrn. Co., Goucester, 1967—75; pres., bd. dir. SGF Corp., 1983—85, SALFAD, Inc., Rossford, Ohio; pres., treas. Points East, Inc.; trustee Christopher Investment Trust; bd. dir. Lustal, Inc.; bd. dir., ptnr. Barsal, Inc., Toledo, Hamsal, Inc. Pres. Lebanese-Am. Bus. Men's Club; treas. Lebanese-Maronite Soc. With US Army, 1942—45. Decorated Bronze Star. Mem.: Gloucester Assoc., Cape Ann Investment Corp., Gloucester Fraternity Assn., Lions, Am. Legion, Amvets, Loyal Order of Moose, Elks, Ky. Cols. (hon.). Roman Catholic. Home and Office: 56 Hilltop Rd Gloucester MA 01931-0078

SALLEE, WANDA JEAN, music educator; b. Seminole, Okla., Nov. 30, 1929; d. John Mordecai Cooper and Mary Blanche Jenkins-Cooper; m. William J. Sallee, Jan. 6, 1951; children: Susan Dwan, Martha Jean. MusB in Piano Theory, Okla. State U., 1950; student in Edn. and Pedagogy, Levine Sch. Music, 1990. Cert. tchr. music Am. Coll. Musicians. Tchr. music Hobart (Okla.) Elem. Schs., 1950—51, Mangum (Okla.) Elem. Schs., 1951—52; dir. ch. music First Bapt. Ch., Mangum, 1952—57, Westover Bapt. Ch., Arlington, Va., 1959—72; pvt. piano tchr. Mangum, 1952—58; tchr. Sallee Music Studio, Arlington, Va., 1959—94, Dallas, 1994—. Dir. music Bapt. Ch., Arlington, 1959—72; bd. trustees Oak Hill Acad., Va., 1965—68; presenter in field. Vol. Reagan-Bush Campaign, Arlington, 1980. Mem.: Music Tchrs. Nat. Assn., Am. Coll. Musicians (adjudicator, nat. guild judge), Richardson (Tex.) Music Tchrs. Assn. (pres., v.p., corr.sec.), Tex. State Music Tchrs. Assn. (chmn. practice student affiliate 2003—, named Piano Tchr. of Yr. 2002), Sigma Alpha Iota (life). Avocations: poetry, writing, reading, painting, eggery. Home and Office: 13639 Mansfield Point Ln Houston TX 77070-3472 Personal E-mail: wjs6214@airmail.net.

SALLER, DEVEREUX NATHANIEL, medical educator, director; b. Bryn Mawr, Pa., Feb. 25, 1956; s. Devereux Nathaniel and Marjorie Dobbs Saller; m. Carol Kathleen Kelley; children: Christopher Devereux, Brendan Peter. BS, Pa. State U., Univ. Pk., 1978; MD, Jefferson Med. Coll., Phila., 1982; MS, U. Md., Balt., 1989. Cert. in ob-gyn. ABOG, Dallas, 1989, in maternal fetal medicine 1990, in clin. genetics ABMG, Bethesda, 1993. Asst. prof. Brown U., Providence, 1989—92; assoc. prof. U. Rochester, NY, 1992—2001; prof., dir. maternal fetal medicine W.Va. U., Morgantown, 2001—03, U. Va., Charlottesville, 2003—, med. dir., Prenetal Diagnosis and Treatment Ctr., 2003—, med. dir. labor and delivery, 2005—. Office: Univ Va 1215 Lee St Charlottesville VA 22908 Office Fax: 434-982-0058. Business E-Mail: dns3f@virginia.edu.

SALLEY, C. DEWITT, JR., education educator, director; b. Dermott, Ark., Jan. 2, 1985; s. Carleton DeWitt Salley and Kathrin Ann Cikanek, Harry Richard Cikanek (Stepfather); m. Leslie Ann Richardson, Oct. 15, 2005. BS in Profl. Writing, Mo. State U., Springfield, 2003; MS in Online Tchg. and Learning, Calif. State U., East Bay, Hayward, 2005; EdD in E-Learning and Tchg. Online, Northcentral U., Prescott Valley, Ariz., 2006—. Cert. online instr. Learning Resources Network, 2004. Adj. instr. tchr. edn. Ozarks Tech. CC, Springfield, 2004—, dir. online tchg. & learning, 2005—; adj. grad. faculty online tchg. & learning Calif. State U., East Bay, 2008—. Bd. dir. mem. Mo. Distance Learning Assn., Columbia, 2008—; external reviewer online MSN program Samuel Merritt U., Oakland, Calif., 2009—. Recipient Award, Two-Year Coll. English Assn., 2004, Excellence Edn. award, Ozarks Tech. CC, 2008. Mem.: Mo. CC Assn. Home: 1615 West Winchester St Springfield MO 65807 Office: Ozarks Tech CC 1001 E Chestnut Expressway Springfield MO 65802 Office Fax: 417-447-7509. Business E-Mail: salleyc@otc.edu.

SALLEY, JOHN JONES, retired academic administrator, oral pathologist; b. Richmond, Va., Oct. 29, 1926; s. Thomas Raysor and Kathryn (Josey) S.; m. Jean Gordon Cunningham, Dec. 21, 1950; children: Katharine Gordon, John Jones, Martha Cunningham. Degree, Va. Mil. Inst., 1945, US Army Air Force, 1946; DDS, Med. Coll. Va., 1951; PhD, U. Rochester, 1954; DSc, Boston U., 1975. Research fellow U. Rochester, 1951-54; from instr. to prof., chmn. dept. oral pathology Med. Coll. Va., 1954-63, prof. emeritus, 1991—; prof. pathology, dean Sch. Dentistry U. Md., 1963-74, dean emeritus Sch. Dentistry, 1977—, ret., 1991; v.p. research and grad. affairs Va. Commonwealth U., Richmond, 1974-85; acting pres. Va. Ctr. for Innovative Tech., 1985, v.p., 1985-87. Cons. divsn. rsch. grants NIH, 1962—66; cons. US Naval Hosp., Portsmouth, Va., USPHS Hosp., Balt., 1963—74, VA Hosp., Balt., 1964—74, US Naval Dental Sch., Bethesda, Md., 1966—75, WHO, 1969—75; cons. Sch. Dentistry, San Marcos U., Lima, Peru, 1965—69; spl. cons. Nat. Inst. Dental Rsch., NIH, 1957—64; dental health divsn. USPHS; mem. Md. Adv. Coun. Comprehensive Health Planning, 1968—74, Nat. Health Coun., 1970—71; pres. Am. Assn. Dental Schs., 1971—72, Conf. So. Grad. Schs., 1983—84; sr. program cons. Robert Wood Johnson Found., 1978—84; mem. career devel. rev. com. VA, 1974—78; mem. com. health care resources in VA, NRC, 1974—77; mem. Va. Gov.'s Task Force Sci. and Tech., 1982—83; sci. advisor to Gov. of Va., 1984—86; mem. rsch. com. Va. State Coun. Higher Edn., 1974—84; chmn. task force Coun. Grad. Schs. in US, 1979—82. Conbtr. articles in field; editorial rev. bd.: Jour. Dental Edn, 1974-78. Bd. dirs. Md. divsn. Am. Cancer Soc., 1963-70, Am. Fund Dental Health, Rappahannock C.C. Found., 1999—; bd. dirs. Nat. Found. Dentistry for the Handicapped, 1986, pres., 1992-94; mem. adv. bd. Va. Inst. for Devel. Disabilities, 1987-91; bd. trustees Middlesex County Pub. Libr., 1994-98, pres., 1995-97. With USAAF, 1944-46. Recipient Outstanding Civilian Service medal Dept. Army, 1961, Disting. Citizenship award State Md., 1974. Fellow AAAS, Am. Coll. Dentists; mem. ADA, Nat. Conf. Univ. Research Adminstrs., Am. Acad. Oral Pathology, Internat. Assn. Dental Research (Novice award 1953), Internat. Med. Informatics Assn. (chmn. working group 1989-92), Sigma Xi, Sigma Zeta, Omicron Kappa Upsilon. Episcopalian (vestryman). Home and Office: 1500 Westbrook Ct Apt 2140 Richmond VA 23227

SALLIS, JAMES, writer; b. Helena, Ark., Dec. 21, 1944; s. Chappelle Horace and Mildred Clodine (Liming) S. Student, Tulane U., 1961-63, U. Tex., 1985-87. Tchr. intensive writing workshops Clarion (Pa.) Coll., U. Wash., Tulane U., Loyola U., Phoenix Coll., Otis Coll., L.A.; guest lectr. modern poetry, European lit., art; writer short stories, essays, poetry and trans. Editor New Worlds 1966-68; editor: (anthologies) The War Book, 1972, The Shores Beneath, 1973; features writer, reviewer, columnist Tex. Jazz, 1980-83, lead book reviewer Dallas Morning News, 1981-83; book reviewer Washington Post Book World, L.A. Times, 1993—; columnist Mag. of Fantasy and Sci. Fiction, Web Del Sol, Boston Globe, 2000–; author: A Few Last Words, 1972, The Guitar Players, 1982, 94, Jazz Guitars, 1984, The Long-Legged Fly, 1992, Saint Glinglin (translator), 1993, Difficult Lives, 1993, Moth, 1993, Black Hornet, 1994, Limits of the Sensible World, 1994, Renderings, 1995, The Guitar in Jazz, 1996, Ash of Stars: On the Writings of Samuel R. Delany, 1996, Death Will Have Your Eyes, 1997, Eye of the Cricket, 1997, Bluebottle, 1999, Gently into the Land of the Meateaters, 2000, Chester Himes: A Life, 2000, Time's Hammers, 2000, Sorrow's Kitchen, 2000, Ghost of a Flea, 2001, Cypress Grove, 2002, A City Equal To My Desire, 2004, A James Sallis Reader, 2005, Drive, 2005, Cripple Creek, 2006, Potato Tree and Other Stories, 2007, Salt River, 2007.

SALLQUIST, GARY ARDIN, retired minister, non-profit executive; b. Sioux City, Iowa, July 7, 1938; s. Hal Thurston and Rosemary (Daggett) S.; m. Joyce Darleen Casey, June 10, 1960; children: Susan L. Rail, Steven P. BA, U. Nebr., Omaha, 1960; MDiv, Princeton Theol. Sem., 1993; D of Ministry, La. Bapt. U., 1997; D, Am. Coll. ChFC, CLU. Pres. Planned Giving Sys., Cin., 1987—90; min. adult edn. Coll. Hill Presbyn. Ch., Cin., 1993—95; dir. planned giving Promise Keepers, Denver, 1995—98; v.p., divsn. higher edn. PhilanthroCorp, Woodland Park, Colo., 1998—2000; headmaster Miami Valley Christian Acad., Cin., 2001—06, headmaster emeritus, 2007—; dir. equipping and adminstrn. North Cinn. Cmty. Ch., 2008—09. Author: A Seminary Journey, 1995, The Counsel of Many, 1999, God's Messages/Dr. Gardner Taylor, 2003, For the Love of God/Dr. David Willis, 2004, The Making of a Miracle, 2007. Pres. Omaha Jaycees, 1966-67; dirs. Creighton-St. Joseph Hosp., Omaha, 1975-81, Leadership Cin. Alumni Assn., 1987-89, dir equipping and administrn. North Cin. Cmty. Ch, 2008-. Mem. U. Nebr. Omaha Alumni Assn. (pres. 1968-70, Outstanding Alumnus award 1977), Pi Kappa Alpha (nat. pres. 1970-72). Avocations: basketball, running, tennis, reading, public speaking. Home: 5300 Barony Pl Cincinnati OH 45241

SALM, STEVEN J., history professor; PhD, U. Tex., Austin, 2003. Instr. U. Tex., Austin, 2002—03; assoc. prof. Xavier U., New Orleans, 2003—. Author: (book) Culture and Customs of Ghana; editor: Globalization and Urbanization in Africa, 2004, Nigerian Cities, 2004, Urbanization and African Cultures, 2005, African Urban Spaces in Historical Perspective, 2005. Oral History grant, NEH, 2006—. Mem.: West African Rsch. Assn., Ghana Studies Coun., African Studies Assn. Office: Xavier Univ Dept History 1 Drexel Dr New Orleans LA 70119 Home Fax: 504-309-7610. Personal E-mail: sjsalm@hotmail.com. Business E-Mail: sjsalm@xula.edu.

SALMAN, ABDULJABBAR A., agronomist; b. Baghdad, Iraq, Aug. 30, 1951; came to U.S., 1982; s. Hashimia A. Hussan Salman; m. Raida A. Hashim; 1 child, Nore A. BSc, U. Mosul, Iraq, 1974, MSc, 1977; PhD, U. Wis., 1988. Faculty U. Basrah, Iraq, 1979-91; postdoctoral staff U. Fla., Gainesville, 1993; vis. scientist Colo. State U., Ft. Collins, 1997—. Vice chmn. soil sci. dept. U. Basrah, 1990-91. Mem. editl. bd. Basrah Jour. Agrl. Sci., 1990-91; contbr. articles to profl. jours. U. Basrah scholar, 1982-85. Mem. Am. Soc. Agronomy, Internat. Soil Sci. Soc. Avocations: reading, travel, camping. E-mail: jsalman432@yahoo.com.

SALMAN, ROBERT RONALD, lawyer; b. NYC, Dec. 26, 1939; s. Samuel L. and Lillian Gertrude (Sincoff) S.; m. Reva Carol Rappaport, June 16, 1963; children: Elyse D. Spiewak, Suzanne A. Werther. BA magna cum laude, Columbia U., 1961, LLB cum laude, 1964. Bar: NY 1965, US Supreme Ct. 1974, US Ct. Appeals (2nd cir.) 1967, US Ct. Appeals (3rd cir.) 1993, US Ct. Appeals (11th cir.) 1985, US Ct. Appeals (9th cir.) 1979, US Dist. Ct. so. dist., ea. dist.) NY 1969. Assoc. Proskauer, Rose, Goetz & Mendelsohn, NYC, 1964-67; asst. corp. counsel Law Dept. NY, NYC, 1967-69; assoc. Phillips, Nizer, NYC, 1969-73; ptnr. Phillips, Nizer, Benjamin, Krim & Ballon, NYC, 1973-87, Reavis & McGrath, NYC, 1987-88, Carter, Ledyard & Milburn, NYC, 1988-94, Phillips & Salman, NYC, 1994-97, Phillips Salman & Stein, NYC, 1997-2000, Duane Morris LLP, NYC, 2001—02; inspector gen. NJ Dept. of Transp., 2002—. Adj. prof. Seton Hall Law Sch., Newark, NJ, 1995-98. Contbr. articles to profl. jours. Mem. N.J. Dem. State Com., 2001—; pres. Marlboro Jewish Ctr., 1982—84. Recipient NEGEV Builder award Israel Bonds, 1980, Award of Honor UJA Fedn., 1981. Mem.: Assn. Bar City of N.Y. Avocations: charitable and communal work, baseball, reading, writing. Personal E-mail: rrsalman@aol.com.

SALMANS, CHARLES GARDINER, banker; b. Washington, Apr. 23, 1945; s. Marion K. and Agnes A. (Gardiner) S.; m. Robin Elizabeth Wakeman, June 8, 1986; children: Jonathan, Peter, Charles II. BS, Northwestern U., 1967; MBA in Fin., Columbia U., 1970. Account supr. Burson-Marsteller, NYC, 1970-74; v.p. Bankers Trust Co., NYC, 1974-84; sr. v.p., divsn. head Chem. Bank, NYC, 1984-96; global bank mng. dir. Chase Manhattan Bank (merger with Chem. Bank 1996), NYC, 1996; sr. v.p., head of corp. comm. and investor rels. Quick & Reilly/Fleet Securities Inc., NYC, 1996—98; sr. v.p. corp. comms. FleetBoston Fin. (merger), NYC, 1998—2004; sr. v.p. corp. comm. Bank of Am. (merger), NYC, 2004—; dir. global pub. rels. Mercer, Inc., NYC, 2005—. Mem. editl. adv. bd. Grad. Sch. of Bus., Columbia U., NYC, 1984—; chmn. bus. adv. com. Guggenheim Mus., NYC, 1994—. Home: 6 Red Rose Cir Darien CT 06820-4928 Office: Mercer Inc 1166 Avenue of the Americas New York NY 10036-2708 Home Phone: 203-656-0296; Office Phone: 212-345-4512. Business E-Mail: charles.salmans@mercer.com.

SALMASSI, SADEGH, physician; b. Baghdad, Iraq, Aug. 14, 1946; s. Jafar and Kobra (Alavi) S.; m. Tahereh Ali Nazari, Jan. 17, 1970; children: Ali (dec.), Nahal. BS, Pahlavi U., 1966, MD, 1973. Diplomate Am. Bd. Pathology, Am. Bd. Gen. Practice in Medicine and Surgery. Instr. pathology U. Ill. Sch. Medicine, Chgo., 1975-80; asst. prof. pathology, assoc. chmn. dept., dir. blood bank U. Mo., Kansas City, 1980-84; chmn. family practice Delano (Calif.) Regional Med. Ctr., 1984-86, 2007—08; pres. Delano Regional Med. Group, 1989-96. Chief of staff Delano Regional Med. Ctr., 1989. Fellow Am. Coll. Internat. Physicians, Coll. Am. Pathologists, Am. Acad. Family Physicians, Am. Acad. Cosmetic Surgery, Am. Acad. Cosmetic Surgeons; mem. AMA, Am. Acad. Gen. Physicians, Calif. Med. Assn. Office: Sadegh Salmassi MD & Assocs Urgent Care Ctr 719 Main St Delano CA 93215-2935 also: Salmassi Cosmetic and Med Inst 719 Main St Delano CA 93215-2935 Office Phone: 661-725-5877, 661-725-7060, 661-339-0292. Personal E-mail: mdfcap@aol.com. Business E-Mail: salmassi@salmassimd.com.

SALMELA, DAVID DANIEL, architect; b. Wadena, Minn., Mar. 28, 1945; s. Laurie Fredrick and Lempi Christine (Matti) S.; m. Gladys Elaine Hanka, June 23, 1967; children: Cory, Chad, Tia, Kai, Brit. Grad. high sch., Sebeka, Minn.; LHD (hon.), U. Minn., 2007, PhD (hon.). Registered profl. architect, Minn., Wis. Draftsman McKenzie Hague & Gilles, Mpls., 1965-66, A.G. McKee, Hibbing, Minn., 1966, ABI Contracting, Virginia, Minn., 1966-69, Archtl. Resources, Hibbing, 1969-70; designer, arch. Damberg Scott Peck & Booker, Virginia, 1970-89; arch. Mulfinger Susanka, Duluth, Minn., 1989-90; prin. Salmela Fospick Ltd., Duluth, 1990-94, Salmela, Arch., Duluth, 1994—. Author: (monograph) Salmela Architect. Recipient Design award, N.Am. Wood, 1994, 1998, 2 Design awards, 2002, Design award, 2003. Fellow: AIA (Minn. Honor awards 1985—2005, Nat. Honor award 1998, 2 Nat. Honor awards 2005, Am. Architecture awards, Northern America Design awards, Archtl. Record House, Phaidon Atlas Contemporary World Architecture Louise Bethune award, Minn. Gold medal 2008). Home and Office: Salmelaarchitect 630 W 4th St Duluth MN 55806 Home Phone: 218-724-3553; Office Phone: 218-724-7517. E-mail: ddsalmela@charter.net.

SALMINEN, SEPPO OSSIAN, plant biochemist; s. Oswald Salminen and Hulda Kaarina Savolainen; m. Joanne Katherine Bednarski, Aug. 31, 1966. PhD, U. Calif. at Riverside, 1973. Postdoc. fellow U. Man., Winnipeg, Canada, 1973—77, Ohio Agrl. Devel. Ctr., Wooster, 1984—86, rsch. assoc., 1986—2007, NRC Can., Saskatoon, Saskatchewan, 1977—82; sessional lectr. U. Alta., Edmonton, Canada, 1982—83. Contbr. scientific papers to profl. jours. Office Phone: 702-463-0367. Business E-Mail: josep@cox.net.

SALMOIRAGHI, GIAN CARLO, physiologist, educator; b. Gorla Minore, Italy, Sept. 19, 1924; came to U.S., 1952, naturalized, 1958; s. Giuseppe Carlo and Dina (Rinetti) S.; m. Eva Tchoukourlieva, Dec. 5, 1970; 1 child, George Charles MD, U. Rome, 1948; PhD, McGill U., 1959; DSc (hon.), Hahnemann U., 1995. Sr. med. officer Internat. Refugee Orgn., Naples, Italy, 1949-52; research fellow Cleve. Clinic Found., 1952-55; lectr. dept. physiology McGill U., Montreal, Que., Canada, 1956-58; from neurophysiologist to dir., div. spl. mental health research NIMH, Washington, 1959-73; assoc. commr. research N.Y. State Dept. Mental Hygiene, Albany, 1973-77; assoc. dir. for research Nat. Inst. Alcohol Abuse, HHS, Bethesda, Md., 1977-84; prof. neurology and physiology Hahnemann U., Phila., 1984—94, vice provost for research affairs, 1984-85, chmn. dept. physiology, asst. v.p sci. affairs, 1986-94; clin. prof. psychiatry George Washington U., 1966-73. Contbr. articles to profl. jours. Recipient Superior Service award HEW, 1970 Fellow Am. Coll. Neuropsychopharmacology; mem. AAAS, Am. Physiol. Soc., Am. Soc. Pharmacology and Exptl. Therapeutics, Internat. Brain Research Orgn., Internat. Soc. Psychoneuroendocrinology, Am. Psychiat. Assn., Soc. Neurosci., Royal Soc. Medicine, Soc. Biol. Psychiat., Assn. Research Neurol. and Mental Disease, Research Soc. Alcoholism, Assn. Chmn. Dept. Physiology, Sci. Research Soc., Sigma Xi. Clubs: Cosmos (Washington). Home: 8216 Hamilton Spring Ct Bethesda MD 20817-2714 Personal E-mail: gsalmoiraghi@pol.net.

SALMON, DANIEL ARYEH, public health policy fellow; b. Columbus, Ohio, Jan. 7, 1968; s. Raphael Jack Salmon and Ruth Helen (Wexberg) Poh; m. Shannon Kellner Keeffe, Sept. 10, 1993; children: Jordan Kellner Keeffe Salmon, Kyle Sarah Keeffe Salmon. BA, Rutgers U., 1991; MPH, Emory U., 1997. HIV prevention cmty. coord. Health Visions, Inc., Pennsauken, N.J., 1993-95; contractor Ctr. Disease Control and Prevention, Atlanta, 1995-97, pub. health policy analyst, 1997—. Mem. APHA, Am. Coll. Health Care Execs. Avocations: watersports, amateur radio, gardening. Office: Ctrs Disease Control and Prevention MSA-11 1600 Clifton Rd Atlanta GA 30333 Fax: 404-639-3036. E-mail: dqs2@cdc.gov.

SALMON, MARLA E., dean, nursing educator; b. Vermillion, SD, May 2, 1949; d. Everett Lloyd and Marceline Louise (Adamson) Salmon; m. Jerry Steven Anderson, Aug. 1, 1984; children: Jessica Louise White, Matthew Lawrence White. BA cum laude, U. Portland, 1971, BSN cum laude, 1972; MSN, 1999; ScD, Johns Hopkins U., 1977; DSc (hon.), UNMC, 2003. Dir. patient advocacy program Johns Hopkins U., Balt., 1974-75, instr., 1975-78; asst. prof. U. Minn., Mpls., 1978-82, asst. dir. PRONA, 1978-79, acting dir. PRONA, 1978-80, dir. pub. health nursing programs, 1980-85, assoc. prof., 1982-86; prof. pub. health nursing, chmn. dept. U. N.C., Chapel Hill, 1986-92; dir. nursing div., Bureau Health Professions HHS, Rockville, 1991-97; prof., dean Grad. Sch. Nursing U. Pa., Phila., 1997-99, dir. grad. studies; dean, prof. Nell Hodgson Woodruff Sch. Nursing Emory U., Atlanta, 1999—2008, founding dir., Lillian Carter Ctr. Internat. Nursing; Robert G. and Jean A. Reid endowed dean in nursing U. Wash., Seattle, 2008—, prof. psychosocial and cmty. health, prof. global health, 2008—. Bd. dirs. Nat. Adv. Coun. Nursing Rsch., NIH Inst. the Internat. Edn. Students, Joint Commn. on Accreditation Healthcare Orgn. Nursing Adv. Coun.; cons. in field. Co-editor: News Outlook, 1989—91; author: Nurse: A World of Care, 2008 (Am. Jour. Nursing Book of Yr. award, 2008); contbr. articles to profl. jours. Trustee Robert Wood Johnson Found., 2002—; mem. Presdl. Task Force Health Care Reform, Washington, 1993; US del. WHO, Geneva, 1995. Recipient Recognition award, Assn. State Territorial Dirs. Nursing, 1993, Achievement award, Nat. Black Nurses Found., 1994, Presdl. award for Meritorious Exec., The White House, 1995; Fulbright scholar, 1972—73, W. K. Kellogg fellow, 1984—87, Reflective Leadership fellow, 1985—86, Rsch. grantee, 1975—78. Fellow: Am. Acad. Nursing; mem.: APHA, ANA (v.p. coun. cmty. health nursing 1988—, mem. task froce credentialing 1989), Women's Health Leadership Trust, Assn. Cmty. Health Nurses Educators, N.C. Nurses Assn., N.C. Pub. Health Assn., N.C. League Nursing, Nat. League Nursing, Am. Tae Kwon Do Assn., Sigma Xi, Delta Omega, Sigma Theta Tau. Avocations: athletics, gardening. Office: Univ Wash Sch Nursing Box 357260 Seattle WA 98195 Business E-Mail: msalmon@u.washington.edu.*

SALMON, MATT, Former United States Representative, Arizona, communications executive; b. Salt Lake City, Jan. 21, 1958; s. Robert James and Gloria (Aagard) S.; m. Nancy Huish, June, 1979; children: Lara, Jacob, Katie, Matthew. BA in English Lit., Ariz. State U., 1981; MA in Pub. Adminstrn., Brigham Young U., 1986. Mgr. pub. affairs U.S. West, Phoenix, 1988-94; mem. Ariz. State Senate, Mesa, 1990-94, U.S. Congress from 1st Ariz. dist., Washington, 1995-2001; mem. internat. rels. and sci. coms., asst. major whip; exec. v.p. APCO Worldwide, Scottsdale, Ariz., 2001—; chmn. Ariz. State Republican Party, 2006—. Bd. dirs. Mesa United Way, 1990—, Ariz. Sci. Mus., 1992—. Recipient Outstanding Svc. award Ariz. Citizens with Disabilities, 1991, Excellence in Govt. award Tempe Ctr. for Handicapped, 1992; named Outstanding Young Phoenician, Phelps Dodge/Phoenix Jaycees, 1990, Outstanding Legislator, Mesa United Way, 1991. Republican. Mem. Lds Ch. Avocations: tennis, racquetball, bicycling. Office: 3501 N 24th St Phoenix AZ 85016

SALMON, ROBIN ROBERTSON, museum curator, editor; b. Columbia, SC, Mar. 18, 1952; d. Homer Hoyt and Elsie Rose (Garvin) Robertson; m. Timothy Dane Salmon, Dec. 1, 1979 (div. 1990); 1 child, Alexander Robertson; m. J. Grover Shuler, Mar. 8, 1997. BA, MA, U. SC, 1973; postgrad., U. SC, Conway, 1981-82; grad. Mus. Mgmt. Inst., U. Calif., Berkeley, 1992. Cert. Am. Soc. Appraisers, 1999. Historian & archivist Brookgreen Gardens, Murrells Inlet, SC, 1975—97, editor publ., 1978—96, v.p. academic affairs, cur. collections, 1990—95, v.p. collections, curator of sculpture, 1995—. Sculpture cons. SC State Mus., Columbia, 1984; mem. founding com. Georgetown (SC) County Arts Coun., 1987-88; regional advisor SC Arts Commn., Columbia, 1987; developer mus. edn. programs, 1981; advisor US Mint, State Quarters Project & medallic art projects, 2002-; advisor SC ETV Art Website for Schools, 2002-; bd. dirs. SC Arts Alliance, 2006-. Contbr.: Paul Manship: Changing Taste in America, 1985, A Century of American Sculpture Treasures from Brookgreen Gardens, 1981, rev., 1988, Spirit of the Wild Things: The Art of Sandy Scott, 1998, The Sculpture of Grainger McKoy, 1999, Marshall M. Fredericks: Sculptor, 2003, Language of Art: Rosie Sandifer, 2007; author: Brookgreen Gardens Sculpture, Vol. II, 1993, American Masters: Sculpture from Brookgreen Gardens, 1996, Images of America: Brookgreen Gardens, 2006; co-author: Masterworks of American Sculpture, 1999; contbr. articles to manuscripts, booklets, guide and scripts. Mem. SC Abandoned Cultural Property Bd., 1992, SC Save Outdoor Sculpture Project adv. bd., 1993. Named Young Career Woman Bus. & Profl. Women, 1977-78, Career Woman of Yr., 1989-90; recipient Inaugural Brookgreen Culture award, Brookgreen Gardens, 2005; rsch. fellow Waccamaw Ctr. Hist. & Cultural Studies, Coastal Carolina U., 1993-. Mem. Am. Assn. Mus. (S.E. mus. conf., edn. com., chair SEMC curators com. 1993-), Nat. Sculpture Soc. (bd. dirs. 1996-2006, editl. bd. Sculpture Rev. mag., 1996-, mem. exhbns. com., 1997-, chair exhbns. com., 1997-2004, 2006-, adv. bd. dirs., 2006-, Allied Profl. mem., 1991, Sculpture House Ann. award, 2007), SC Fedn. Mus. Republican. Office: Brookgreen Gardens PO Box 3368 Pawleys Island SC 29585 Office Phone: 843-235-6012. E-mail: rsalmon@brookgreen.org.

SALMON, WILLIAM COOPER, mechanical engineer, company executive; b. NYC, Sept. 3, 1935; s. Chenery and Mary (Cooper) S.; m. Josephine Stone, Sept. 16, 1967; children: William Cooper Jr., Mary Bradford, Pauline Alexandra. SB in Mech. Engring., MIT, 1957, SM in Mech. Engring., 1958, Mech. Engr., 1959, SM in Mgmt. Sci., 1969. Registered profl. engr., Mass. Sr. engr. Microtech, Cambridge, 1959—60; 1st lt. US Army Ord. C., Aberdeen, Md., 1960; asst. sci. adv. US Dept. State, Washington, 1961—74, sr. adv. sci. and tech., 1978—86; counselor sci. and tech. Am. Embassy, Paris, 1974—78; exec. officer NAE, Washington, 1986—99, exec. officer emeritus, adv. to pres., 1999—2001; sec., treas. Internat. Coun. Academies Engring. and Technol. Scis., Inc., 2000—. Interim exec. dir. Am. Assn. Engring. Soc., 2005—. Recipient Superior Honor award Dept. State, 1984, Meritorious Svc. award Pres. US, 1968, Kenneth A. Roe award Am. Assn. Engring. Socs., 1996, Chair's award, 2006; Sloan fellow MIT, 1969. Fellow: ASME; mem.: NSPE, Nat. Soc. Sons Colonial New Eng., Jr. Engring. Tech. Soc. (pres. 1998—2001), Mil. Order Loyal Legion of US, Soc. Colonial Wars, Cosmos Club, Masons. Episcopalian. Home and Office: 3601 N Peary St Arlington VA 22207-5345 Office Phone: 703-527-5782. Office Fax: 703-526-0570. E-mail: wsalmon@nae.edu, caets@nae.edu.

SALOMON, DALAL MARIA, financial consultant; b. Tela, Honduras, Sept. 22, 1955; came to the US, 1956; d. John and Widad (Isaac) S. BS in Bus., Mich. State U., 1977; grad., Fin. Planning Inst., Richmond, Va., 1994. V.p. sales and mktg. New Dawn, Inc., Lansing, Mich., 1977-81; pvt. practice bus. cons. Washington, 1981-82; fin. planner Wallace Fin. Group, Bethesda, Md., 1982-84; fin. advisor Wachovia Securities (formerly Wheat First Securities), 1984, founder, mng. dir., investment officer Salomon & Ludwin Fin. Consulting. Mem. premier advisor program Wachovia Securities, mem. dirs. adv. coun., mem. sr. leadership coun., mem. pres.'s club, mem. chmn.'s cir. excellence. Mem. bd. dirs. Va. Birth-Related Neurological Injury Compensation Program, 2006—. Named one of The 30 Top Fin. Advisors for Va., R.J. Shook, 2005—08, The Top 100 Women Fin. Advisors, Barron's, 2006, 2007, 2008. Avocations: sports, travel. Office: Salomon & Ludwin Group Wachovia Securities 901 E Byrd St Richmond VA 23219-4047

SALOMON, MARILYN, artist; b. Ann Arbor, Mich., Jan. 30, 1943; d. William Iane and Sarah Sheon; m. Charles Sam. Salomon, Dec. 22, 1962; children: Teri(dec.), Alicia, Cliff. BA, UCLA, 1965; postgrad., Calif. State U., Northridge, 1969-70, 88, Miriam Ariav, Israel, 1970. Elem. edn. tchr., Simi Valley, Calif., 1966-69; artist, 1970—; lectr. Prescott Fine Arts Docents, Ariz., 2008—. Guest lectr. Internat. Batik Conf., Ghent, Belgium, 1999, Scottsdale Art League, 2003, Payson Art League, 2005, Rodriquez HS, Fairfield, Calif., 2002-08; asst. art curator mus. show, Lancaster, Calif., 1993; leader workshop Surface Designer Nat. Conf., Calif. State U., Northridge, 1988; represented by Judith Hale Gallery, Los Olivos, Calif., Galleries West, Jackson Hole, Wy., Pepper Tree Show, Santa Ynez, Calif., 2003, 04, 05, 06, 07, 08; participant Internat. Batik Exhibit, Hanover, Germany, 2002, Internat. Batik Exhibit, Cologne, Germany, 2002, Internat. Batik Exhibit, Dortmund, Germany, 2002, Ryman Found. show, 2000-05, 06, 07, World Batik Exbhn., Boston, 2005, Stone Ave. Gallery, Tucson, 2006, Phippen Art Mus., Prescott, Ariz., 2007; lectr. in field; subject of TV interview Process of Batik, 2001. One-woman shows include Ranch House, Ojai, Calif., 1975-78, Gallerie 507, Carlsbad, Calif., 1984, Sun West Gallery, Prescott, Ariz., 1986, Art Beat Gallery, Agoura, Calif., 1987, Jewish Cmty. Ctr., Long Beach, Calif., 1985; exhibited in group shows at Cygnet Gallery, Santa Rosa, Calif., 1981, Jewish Fedn. Bldg., Olympic Exhbn., LA, 1984, La Quinta Arts Found., 1985-91, Thousand Oaks Mus., 1988-89 (1st pl. 1988, Purchase award 1989), Calif. Luth. U., 1989, Nat. Mus. History, Santa Barbara, Calif., 1990, City of La Quinta, 1991 (Purchase award), Lancaster Mus., 1992-93, 98, Conejo Valley Mus., 1992 (2d pl. award), Riverside Mus. Art, 1998, Walt Disney Ryman Found., Burbank, Calif., featured artist, 1997-99, Horizen Fine Arts, Jackson, 2002, Phippen Art Mus., 2006 (1st pl. mixed media, 2nd pl. 2008, 3rd pl. 2009), Galleries West, Jackson, Wy., 2008; featured artist represented in permanent collections City of Tempe, City of Thousand Oaks, City of La Quinta, Taft Entertainment, Cancer Inst. Ariz.; featured in TV interview KTVK, Ariz., 2000-07, Taught Batik to Children with Special Needs at Whispering Hope Ranch, Payson, Ariz., 2007; works appear in Batik for Artists & Quilters, 2000, Led Workshop, 2007. Workshop leader Surface Designer's Nat. Conf., Calif. State U., Northridge, 1988; studio home tour Westlake Art Guild, Calif., 1989, Pan Hellenic Home Tour Riverside featured Salomon's Art, 1986; home studio tour Payson Art League, 2004, 05, 06, 07, 08, 09. Mem. (elected charter mem.) Women's Nat. Mus., Phoenix Art Mus, Am. Indian Mus., Wash. Avocations: hiking, yoga, reading, music, gardening. Home: HC 2 Box 261D Payson AZ 85541-9418 Personal E-mail: marilyn@batiksbymarilyn.com.

SALOMON, MARK, chemist; s. Meyer and Rose Salomon; m. Carol L. Linden; children: Debra L. Bowler, Karen Benjamin. PhD in Chemistry, U. Ottawa, Ont., Can. With USMC, 1960—68; chief scientist MaxPower, Inc., Harleysville, Pa., 1995—. Contbr. articles to profl. jours. Mem.: Internat. Union Pure and Applied Chemistry (editor 1990—2008). Home: 2 Eastborne Dr Little Silver NJ 07739 Office: MaxPower Ind 141 Christopher Ln Harleysville PA 19438 Business E-Mail: mark.salomon@maxpowerinc.com.

SALOMON, ROGER BLAINE, retired language educator; b. Providence, Feb. 26, 1928; s. Henry and Lucia Angell (Capwell) S.; m. Elizabeth Helen Lowenstein, June 14, 1950; children: Pamela, Wendy. BA, Harvard, 1950; MA, U. Calif., Berkeley, 1951, PhD, 1957. Instr. Mills Coll., Oakland, Calif., 1955-57; instr., then asst. prof. Yale U., New Haven, 1957-66; mem. faculty Case Western Res. U., Cleve., 1966—, prof. English, 1969—, Oviatt prof. English, 1990, chmn. dept., 1974-80, part-time prof. English, 1994-99; Oviatt prof. English emeritus, 1999—. Mem. adv. screening com. Am. lit. Sr. Fulbright-Hayes Program, 1973-76, chmn., 1975; mem. grants-in-aid selection com. Am. Council Learned Socs., 1976-78 Author: Twain and the Image of History, 1961, Desperate Storytelling: Post-Romantic Elaborations of the Mock-Heroic Mode, 1987, Mazes of the Serpent: An Anatomy of Horror Narrative, 2002. Served to 1st lt. USAF, 1952-53. Morse fellow, 1960-61; Guggenheim fellow, 1972-73 Mem. AAUP, MLA. Home: 2830 Coventry Rd Cleveland OH 44120-2231 Office Phone: 216-368-2340.

SALOMONSON, VINCENT VICTOR, meteorologist, educator; b. Longmont, Colo., July 19, 1937; s. Victor Philip and Eunice Cole Salomonson; m. Peggy Lucille Swanner, Feb. 11, 1944; children: Scott Houston, Aaron Phillip, Sarah McBride, Karla Canning, Carol Marie. BS in Agrl. Engring., Colo. State U., Ft. Collins, Colo., 1959; BS in Meteorology, U. Utah, Salt Lake City, Utah, 1960; MS in Agrl. Engring., Cornell U., Ithaca, NY, 1964; PhD, Colo. State U., Ft. Collins, Colo., 1968. Weather officer USAF, Washington, 1959—62; from rsch. meteorologist Goddard Space Flight Ctr. to sr. scientist NASA, Greenbelt, Md., 1962—2001, sr. scientist earth scis. directorate Goddard Space Flight Ctr., 2001—05; rsch. prof. U. Utah, Salt Lake City, 2005—. Contbr. over 130 articles to profl. jours. Bishop LDS Ch., Bowie, Md. 1st lt. USAF, 1959—62. Recipient Exceptional Sci. Achievement medal, NASA, 1976, 1983, William T. Pecora award, NASA and U.S. Geol. Survey, 1987, Honor Alumnus award, Colo. State U., 1987, William Nordberg award, NASA Goddard Space Flight Ctr., 2002; named Meritorious Exec., Sr. Exec. Svc., U.S. Govt., 1993, Disting. Exec. Sr. Exec. Svc., 1998; Goddard Sr. fellow, NASA Goddard Space Flight Ctr., 2002. Fellow: IEEE (mem. com. 1980—87, Disting. Achievement award 1998), Am. Soc. Photogrammetry and Remote Sensing (pres. 1991—92). Mem. Lds Ch. Office: University of Utah 135 S 1460 E Rm 809 Salt Lake City UT 84112-0110 Office Fax: 801-585-3681. Personal E-mail: vincesalomonson@msn.com. Business E-Mail: vincent.v.salomonson@nasa.gov.

SALONEN, ESA-PEKKA, conductor, music director; b. Helsinki, Finland, June 30, 1958; married; 3 children. Student, Sibelius Acad., Helsinki, D (hon.), 2003; studied composition with Einojuhani Rautavaara, studied conducting with Jorma Panula; D (hon.), Hong Kong Acad. Performing Arts, 2009. Prin. guest condr. Oslo Philharm. Orch., 1985—90, Philharmonia Orch., London, 1985—94, prin. condr., artistic adv., 2008—; prin. condr. Swedish Radio Symphony Orch., 1985—95; artistic adv. Stockholm Chamber Orch.; music dir. LA Philharm. Orch., 1992—2009, condr. laureate, 2009—, Walt & Lilly Disney chair, 1992—2009. Artistic dir. Helsinki Festival, 1995—96, Baltic Sea Festival, Stockholm, 2003—; condr. Vienna Philharm., Salzburg Festival, Austria, 2009. Guest condr. London Orch., Berlin Orch., Paris Orch., LA Orch., Phila. Orch. Recipient Siena prize, Chigiana Musical Acad., 1993, Opera award, Royal Philharm. Soc., 1995, Conductor award, 1997, Litteris et Artibus medal, Sweden, 1996, Officier Ordre des Arts et des Lettres, France; named Musician of Yr., Musical America Worldwide, 2006. also: LA Philharm Orch 151 S Grand Ave Los Angeles CA 90012-3013 Office: Columbia Artists Mgmt Llc 1790 Broadway # 6 New York NY 10019-1412*

SALONEN, PEKKA OLAVI, electrical engineer; b. Helsinki, Aug. 18, 1973; s. Antti and Raija Salonen; m. Sanna Starkman; children: Arttu Santeri, Eetu Oskari. MSEE, Tampere U. Tech., Finland, 1997, D in Tech., 2001. Electronics designer Mitron Oy, Forssa, Finland, 1996—97; rschr. Tampere U. Tech., 1997—2001, rsch. dr., 2001—03; vis. postdoctoral rschr. UCLA, 2003—04; rf-team mgr. Patria Aviation Oy, Tampere, 2005—06, R&D mgr., 2007—. Vis. scholar Nokia Oyj, 2003. Grantee, IEEE Antennas and Propagation Soc., 2004; scholar scholarship, Nokia Oyj, 2001. Mem.: IEEE. Office: Patria Aviation Oy / Sys Naulakatu 3 Tampere 33100 Finland Home: Ratakistonkatu 23 B 16 33300 Tampere Finland Business E-Mail: pekka.salonen@patria.fi.

SALOPEK, PAUL F., reporter, foreign correspondent; b. Barstow, Calif., Feb. 9, 1962; m. Linda Lynch. BS in Environ. Biology, U. Calif., Santa Barbara, 1984. Local newspaper reporter, Roswell, N.Mex., 1985—90; bur. chief Gannett News Svc., Mexico City, 1990; reporter El Paso Times, Tex.; writer Nat. Geographic mag., 1992—95; fgn. corr. Chgo. Tribune, 1996—. Recipient Pulitzer Prize for Explanatory Reporting, 1998, Pulitzer Prize for Internat. Reporting, 2001, Bob Considine award, Overseas Press Club America, 2007, George Polk award for Internat. Reporting, 2008. Office: Chgo Tribune 435 N Michigan Ave Chicago IL 60611*

SALOVEY, PETER, academic administrator, psychology professor; b. Cambridge, Mass., Feb. 21, 1958; s. Ronald and Elaine Y. (Gross) S.; m. Marta Elisa Moret, June 15, 1986. BA in Psychology, Stanford U., Calif., 1980, MA in Sociology, 1980; PhD in Psychology, Yale U., New Haven, Conn., 1986, MS in Psychology, 1983, MPhil in Psychology, 1984; DEd (hon.), U. Pretoria, South Africa, 2009. Lic. psychologist, Conn. Asst. prof. Yale U., New Haven, 1986-90, assoc. prof., 1990-95, prof. psychology, epidemiology and pub. health, 1995—, chmn. dept. psychology, 2000—03, Chris Argyris prof. psychology, prof. mgmt. and epidemiology and pub. health, 2001—, dean Grad. Sch. Arts and Scis., 2003—04; dean Yale Coll., New Haven, 2004—08; provost Yale U., New Haven, 2008—. Cons. psychologist West Haven (Conn.) VA Med. Ctr., 1986—; dep. dir. Ctr. for Interdisciplinary Rsch. on AIDS, 1997-2006; mem. NSF Social Psychology Adv. Com., 1994-97; mem.

NIMH Nat. Adv. Mental Health Coun., 2003-07, NIMH Behavioral Sci. Task Force, 2000, Author: Peer Counseling, 1983, The Remembered Self, 1993, Psychology, 1993, The Emotionally Intelligent Manager, 2004; editor: Reasoning Inference & Judgement in Clin. Psychology, 1988, The Psychology of Jealousy and Envy, 1991, Emotional Development and Emotional Intelligence, 1997, At Play in the Fields of Consciousness, 1999, The Wisdom in Feeling: Psychological Processes in Emotional Intelligence, 2002, Social Psychology of Wealth, 2003, Key Readings in Emotional Intelligence, 2004; editor: Rev. of Gen. Psychology, 1996-2002; assoc. editor Psychol. Bull., 1991-96, Emotion, 2000-2002; contbr. articles to profl. jours. Named Presidential Young Investigator, NSF, Washington, 1990, Mensa Edn. & Rsch. Found. award 2001, Nat. Cancer Soc. CIS Ptnr. rsch. award, 2001, SAMHSA Excellence award, 2005 Fellow APA, Am. Psychol. Soc., Internat. Soc. for Rsch. on Emotion (treas. 1992-96), Soc. for Gen. Psychology (pres. 2004), Phi Beta Kappa, Sigma Xi, Ct. Acad. Sci. & Engring., 2009 Democrat. Jewish. Achievements include rsch. on psychological consequences of the arousal of mood and emotion, emotional intelligence, and motivators of health-protective behaviors, especially those relevant to the prevention of cancer and HIV/AIDS. Office: Yale U Provost PO Box 208365 New Haven CT 06520-8365 Office Phone: 203-432-4444, 203-432-4546. Business E-Mail: peter.salovey@yale.edu.

SALOY, MONA LISA, literature and language professor; d. Louis Saloy and Olga Fitch. MA, San Francisco State U., Calif., 1982; MFA, La. State U., Baton Rouge, 1988, PhD, 2005. Vis. assoc. prof. U. Wash., Seattle, 2005—07; assoc. prof. Dillard U., New Orleans, 1991—. Poet in residence African Am. Hist. & Cultural Soc., San Francisco, 1983—85; spkr., guest writer Nat. Black Jewish Conf., New Orleans, 1996—, Tenn. Williams,New Orleans Lit. Festival, 1997; spkr. New Orleans Jazz & Heritage Festival, 2001—03; moderator Soc. Study So. Lit., Lafayette, La., 2002; spkr., presenter Tom Dent Lit. Festival, New Orleans, 2003; spkr. Jack Kerouac Conf. on Beat Lit., U. Mass., Lowell, Mass., 2003; spkr., guest writer Assn. Writers & Writing Programs, Balt., 2003, Savannah State U., Ga., 2003; spkr., presenter Am. Folklore Soc. Ann. Conf., Milw., 2006; spkr., guest writer Santa Barbara C.C., 2006; guest writer Lakeside Sch., Seattle, 2008; keynote spkr. La. Coun. Tchrs. English, Baton Rouge; spkr. La. Creole Rsch. Assn., New Orleasna; fellow, guest writer DeBose Fine Arts Fesival; spkr., presenter Purdue African Am. Cultural Ctr., New Orleans, 2008. Contbr. articles to profl.jours. (Truman State U. award, 2005). Scholar La. Endowment Humanities, New Orleans, 2008—. Recipient Commd. Poem medal, Nat. Constn. Ctr., Am., 2006, Creative Writing award, La. Bd. Regents, Dillard U., 2003, Artie, Arts Excellence award, Delta Sigma Theta Sorority, 1989, 1996; Dissertation fellowship, NEH, 1994—95, Rsch. Travel grant, United Negro Coll., Andrew W. Mellon Found., 2004. Mem.: MLA, La. Folklore Soc., Am. Folklore Soc., La. Creole Rsch. Assn. (conf. co chair 2008). Roman Catholic. Avocations: swimming, gardening, interior decorating, sewing, languages. Office: Author Folklorist 2601 Gentilly Boulevard New Orleans LA 70122 Office Fax: 504-816-4381. Business E-Mail: msaloy@dillard.edu.

SALSBERG, ARTHUR PHILIP, publishing executive; b. Bklyn., Aug. 28, 1929; s. Solomon William and Rae (Miller) S.; m. Rhoda Gelb, Sept. 11, 1960; children: Charles Martin, Solomon William. BBA, CCNY, 1951. Mng. editor Ojibway Press, NYC, 1957-64; advt. and promotion mgr. RCA Corp., Harrison, NJ, 1965-67; editor N.Am. Pub. Co., Phila., 1967-70; v.p., gen. mgr. Lawyers World, Inc., Phila., 1970-72; editorial dir. Ziff-Davis Pub. Co., NYC, 1973-83; editor, assoc. pub. CQ Communications, Inc., Hicksville, NY, 1984—. Mag. and newspaper pub. cons.; electronics instr.; local campaign publicist, speech writer for town mayor, town coun., libr. bd., sch. bd. Author: Complete Book of Video Games, 1977, Collier's Ency. Yearbook, 1977, 78, 79, 80, 81, 82, First Book of Modern Electronics Fun Projects, 1986, Second Book of Modern Electronics Fun Projects, 1986; editor: Audio Mag, 1967-70, Lawyers World, 1970-72, Popular Electronics, 1973-83, Comm. Handbook, 1973-83, Stereo Directory, 1973-83, Tape Recorder Directory, 1973-83, Citizens Band Handbook, 1976-83, Invitation to Electronics, 1972-83, Modern Electronics, 1984-91, Computer Craft, 1992-93, MicroComputer Jour., 1994-96; assoc. pub.: Amateur Radio Equipment Buyers Guide, 1988, 89, 90, 91, 92, Amateur Radio Antenna Buyers Guide, 1989, 90, 91-92. Publicity chmn. Nassau coun. Boy Scouts Am., 1975; mem. adv. com. Bramson OR Tech. Inst., 1975. With AUS, 1951-53, Korea. Recipient Indsl. Mktg. Mag. award, 1959 Home: 7844 Lexington Club Blvd Apt A Delray Beach FL 33446-3426

SALSBERY, MEREDITH A., legislative staff member; Intern, Senator Mark Dayton US Senate, Washington, 2003; comm. dir. Tim Walz's Congl. Campaign, Minn., 2006; comm. dir. to Rep. Tim Walz US House of Reps., Washington, 2007—, dist. dir., Rep. Tim Walz Mankato, Minn., 2007—, econ. recovery coord., Rep. Tim Walz, 2009—. Democrat. Office: Dist Office 227 E Main St #220 Mankato MN 56001 Office Phone: 507-388-2149.*

SALT, ALFRED LEWIS, priest; b. Hackensack, NJ, Apr. 30, 1927; s. Alfred John and Lily (Tittle) S.; m. Elizabeth May Loveland, June 18, 1949; children: Richard John, Michael Rob, Christopher William, Katharine Anne. BA with honors, Bishop's U., Lennoxville, Can., 1949, MA in History, 1951, BD, 1960; grad. advanced mgmt. program, Harvard U., 1970; D Ministry, Grad. Theol. Found., 1988. Ordained to ministry Episcopal Ch. as deacon, 1951, as priest, 1952. Incumbent St. Philip's, Sawyerville, Que., Canada, 1951—52, St. John the Evangelist, Portneuf, Que., 1952—54; rector Christ Ch., Stanstead, Que., 1954—62, St. Michael's Ch., Sillery, Que., 1962—72, All Saints Ch., Millington, NJ, 1972—93; hon. asst. Grace Ch., Port Huron, Mich., 1993—98, Trinity Ch., Lexington, Mich., 1998—2001, St. Monica's Ch., Naples, Fla., 2002—03, St. John's Ch., Naples, 2004—06, St. Mary's, Bonita Springs, Fla., 2007—. Bishop's chaplain Diocese of Que., 1962, hon. canon, 1970; pres. Morris Convocation. Morris County, N.J., 1974-78, retreat condr., 1979—; with Victorious Ministry Through Christ, Orlando, Fla., 1981-92, dir., 1986-92, v.p., 1989-92; dir. VMTC Can., 1995-2002. Author: Compass Book on Healing, 1996; contbr. articles to religious jour. Mem. Superior Coun. Edn., Que., 1964-70; commr. Que. Protestant Sch. Bd., 1970-72; trustee Heath Village, Hackettstown, N.J., 1974-76; mem. Passaic Twp. Welfare Bd., Millington, 1977-78, 82. With USAAC Res., 1944-45; with USN, 1945-46. Mem. Naples Deanery Clericus, Order St. Luke (chaplain), Harvard Club of Naples, Worker Sisters of Holy Spirit/Worker Brothers of Holy Spirit. Home (Summer): 190 Chemin Du Lac North Hatley QE J0B 2C0 Canada Personal E-mail: alemsalt@comcast.net. *The more I come to know Jesus, the more I come to know myself. The more I submit myself to Him, the less I depend upon myself.*

SALTARELLI, MICHAEL ANGELO, bishop; b. Jersey City, Jan. 17, 1933; BA, Seton Hall U., 1956; MA in Religious Studies, Manhattan U., 1975. Ordained priest Archdiocese of Newark, NJ, 1960; ordained bishop, 1990; aux. bishop Archdiocese of Newark, 1990—95; bishop Diocese of Wilmington, Del., 1995—2008, bishop emeritus, 2008—. Roman Catholic. Office: Diocese of Wilmington 1925 Delaware Ave Wilmington DE 19899-2030 Office Phone: 302-573-3100. Office Fax: 302-573-3128. Business E-Mail: pbossi@cdow.org.

SALTER, EDWIN CARROLL, retired pediatrician; b. Oklahoma City, Jan. 19, 1927; s. Leslie Ernest and Maud (Carroll) S.; m. Ellen Gertrude Malone, June 30, 1962; children: Mary Susanna, David Patrick BA, DePauw U., 1947; MD, Northwestern U., 1951. Intern Cook County Hosp., Chgo., 1951-53; resident in pediatrics Children's Meml. Hosp., Chgo., 1956-58, Cook County Hosp., Chgo., 1956-58; practice medicine specializing in pediatrics Lake Forest, Ill., 1958-97; attending physician Lake Forest Hosp., 1958—97, pres. med. staff, 1981-82. Attending physician Children's Meml. Hosp., Chgo.; clin. faculty mem. dept. pediatrics Northwestern U. Med. Sch. Served to capt. M.C., U.S. Army, 1954-56 Mem. AMA, Ill. State Med. Soc., Lake County Med. Soc. (pres. 1984), Phi Beta Kappa Republican. Methodist. Home: 19 N Maywood Rd Lake Forest IL 60045-3233

SALTER, ELIZABETH MARY, academic administrator; d. Robert William Salter; m. John Carl Kolar, June 14, 1980; children: Victoria, Ian. BA, U. Toronto, Ont., 1971, M of Mus. Studies, 1972; MA, U. Calgary, Alta., Can., 1974; PhD, U. Toronto, Ont., 1984. Asst. prof. U. Toronto, 1985—87; asst. to dean U. Tex., Dallas, 1994—95, coll. master, 1995—2000, assoc. dean, 2000—. Co-author: Craniofacial Anthropometry, 1996. Recipient Praxis award, Wash. Assn. Profl. Anthropologists, 1997; named Best Tchr. Social Scis., U. Toronto, 1987. Avocation: reading. Office: U Tex-Dallas Interdisciplinary Studies GR26 800 W Campbell Rd Richardson TX 75080-3021 Office Phone: 972-883-2484. Business E-Mail: emsalter@utdallas.edu.

SALTER, JAMES, writer; b. Passaic, NJ, June 10, 1925; m. Ann Altemus, June 6, 1951 (div. 1976); children: Allan Conard, Nina Tobe, Claude Cray, James Owen; m. Kay Eldredge; 1 child, Theo Shaw. BS, USMA, 1945; M in Internat. Affairs, Georgetown U., 1950. Author: The Hunters, 1957, The Arm of Flesh, 1961, A Sport and a Pastime, 1967, Light Years, 1976, Solo Faces, 1981, Dusk and Other Stories, 1989 (Pen, Faulkner prize 1989), Burning the Days, 1997, Cassada, 2001, Gods of Tin: The Flying Years, 2004, Last Night, 2005, There and Then: The Travel Writing of James Salter, 2006; Co-Author (with Kay Salter) Life is Meals, 2006. Lt. Col. USAF, 1960. Recipient, Edith Wharton Prize, NY State Author, 1998—, English Speaking Union Prize, Pen/West Prize, John Steinbeck Prize. Office: ICM Literary 825 8th Avn New York NY 10019

SALTER, MARK, speechwriter; b. Davenport, Iowa, 1955; s. Pete Salter; m. Diane M. Salter; 2 children. Grad., Georgetown U., Washington, DC. Speechwriter UN Amb. Jeane Kirkpatrick; chief speechwriter Senator John McCain, 1989—, former chief of staff; sr. advisor Senator John McCain's Presdl. Campaign. Co-author (with John McCain): Faith of My Fathers: A Family Memoir, 2000, Worth the Fighting For: A Memoir, 2002, Why Courage Matters: The Way to a Braver Life, 2004, Character is Destiny: Inspiring Stories Every Young Person Should Know and Every Adult Should Remember, 2005, Hard Call: Great Decisions and the Extraordinary People Who Made Them, 2007. Named one of 25 Most Influential Republicans, Newsmax Mag., 2008. Republican. Office: John McCain 2008 PO Box 16118 Arlington VA 22215 Office Phone: 703-418-2008.*

SALTER, MARY JO, poet; b. Grand Rapids, Mich., Aug. 15, 1954; d. Albert Gregory and Lormina (Paradise) S.; m. Brad Leithauser, 1980; children: Emily Salter, Hilary Garner. BA cum laude, Harvard U., 1976; MA, Cambridge U., 1978. Instr. Harvard U., 1978-79; instr. English conversation Japan, 1980-83; lectr. English Mt. Holyoke Coll., South Hadley, Mass., 1984—, Emily Dickinson sr. lectr. in humanities, 1995—2007; prof. writing seminars Johns Hopkins U., Balt., 2007—, Andrew W Mellon prof. humanities, 2009—. Staff editor Atlantic Monthly, 1978-80; poet-in-residence Robert Frost Place, 1981; poetry editor The New Republic, 1992-95. Author: Henry Purcell in Japan, 1985, Unfinished Painting, 1989 (Lamont prize in poetry 1988), The Moon Comes Home, 1989, Sunday Skaters: Poems, 1994 (Nat. Book Critics Circle award nomination 1994), A Kiss in Space: Poems, 1999, Open Shutters: Poems, 2003, A Phone Call to the Future, 2008; co-editor: Norton Anthology of Poetry, 5th edit., 2005; contbr. to periodicals including New Yorker, New Republic, Kenyon Rev. Amy Lowell scholar, 1995; recipient Discovery prize Nation, 1983; Nat. Endowment for Arts fellow, 1983-84, Guggenheim fellow, 1993. Mem. Internat. P.E.N. Office: care Alfred A Knopf Inc 1745 Broadway New York NY 10019

SALTER, ROBIN S., immunologist, educator; d. Robert N. and Vivian K. Stong; m. Richard M. Salter, Nov. 3, 2004. BA, Macalester Coll., St. Paul, Minn., 1972; MS, U. Wis. Madison, 1978, PhD, 1981. NRSA predoc. fellow, Lab. Genetics U. Wis., Madison, 1975—75, rsch. asst., Wis. Regional Primate Rsch. Ctr., 1975—78; postdoc. assoc. U. Minn. Med. Sch., Mpls., 1982—84, SW Found. Biomed. Rsch., San Antonio, 1985—86; rsch. scientist, hematology, oncology Children's Hosp. Orange County, Calif., 1986—87; assoc. prof. biology Oberlin Coll., Ohio, 1987—; vis. scientist Lovelace Med. Ctr., Albuquerque, 1994, Lab. Genetics, NIAID, NIH, Bethesda, Md., 1999—2001; engr. MITRE Corp., McLean, Va., 2003—04. Sec. Ohio Acad. Sci., Columbus, 1994—96; mem., firca study sect. NIH, Washington, 1994—97, mem., grip study sect., 2002; chair, biology dept. Oberlin Coll., 2002—05; cons. NSF, Grad. rsch. Fellowship Program, Washington, 2002—07. Contbr. articles to profl. jours. Recipient Presdl. scholarship, US Govt., 1968; grantee, Am. Cancer Soc., 1992—94, NIH, 1993—98, NSF, 2007—. Mem.: AAAS, Am. Assn. Immunologists, Sigma Xi, Phi Beta Kappa (pres., zeta chpt. of ohio 1996—97). Avocations: travel, yoga. Office: Oberlin Coll 119 Woodland St Oberlin OH 44074 Office Fax: 440-775-8960. Business E-Mail: robin.salter@oberlin.edu.

SALTER, RUSSELL DAVID, medical educator, researcher; b. Oakland, Calif., July 21, 1958; s. Albert Lockwood and Mary Joy Salter; m. Beate Kohler, Sept. 19, 1982; 1 child, Kathryn Rachel. PhD, Duke U., Durham, NC, 1985. Postdoc. fellow Stanford U., Calif., 1986—89; prof. U. Pitts., 1990—. Multiple Rsch. grants, NIH, Am. Cancer Soc., 1992—2008. Mem.: Am. Assn. Immunologists. Achievements include discovery of a role for tunneling nanotubules in communication between dendritic cells of the immune system. Office: Univ Pitts 200 Lothrop St Pittsburgh PA 15213

SALTI, RAMZI, literature and language professor; b. Beirut, 1966; s. Munir Salti and Vera Hakeem. BA (hon.), Santa Clara U., Calif., 1988; MA, U. Calif., Riverside, 1991, PhD, 1997. Cert. in oral proficiency tester Arabic Am. Coun. Tchg. Fgn. Languages, 2007. Instr. French U.C. Riverside, Calif., 1989—93; lectr. Arabic lang. & lit. Stanford U., Calif., 1997—; lectr. Arabic lit. Santa Clara U., Calif., 2003—05. Reviewer Arabic lit. World Lit. Today, Norman, Okla., 1989—; entertainment writer West Hollywood Weekly, Calif., 1994—95. Contbr. to essays; author: (book) The Native Information and Other Stories. Mem. Human Rights Campaign, Washington, 2006—08. Recipient Stanford Dean's award, 2004—05. Mem.: ACTFL (Oral Proficiency Tester cert. 2007). Liberal. Mem. Christian Ch. Avocations: reading, music, languages, writing. Office: Stanford Univ African & Middle Eastern Langs & Lits Stanford CA 94305 Personal E-mail: ramzisalti@aol.com. Business E-Mail: rsalti@stanford.edu.

SALTIEL, ALAN ROBERT, biochemist; b. New Brunswick, NJ, Nov. 29, 1953; s. Samuel Albert and Betty (Berg) S.; m. Swanna Elizabeth Cameron, May 30, 1981; children: Jason Ariel, Aren David, Jared Robert. AB (magna cum laude) in Zoology, Duke U., 1975; PhD in Biochemistry, U. NC, 1980. Postdoctoral rsch. scientist, Dept. Molecular Biology Wellcome Rsch. Lab., Rsch. Triangle Pk., NY, 1981—84; asst. prof. Rockefeller U., NYC, 1984-90; sr. dir. dept. signal transduction. Parke-Davis Pharm. Rsch. Divsn., Warner Lambert Co., Ann Arbor, 1990—96, sr. rsch. fellow, dept. signal transduction, 1992—95, disting. rsch. fellow, dept. signal transduction, 1995—2000, sr. dir., dept. cell biology, 1996—2000; adj. assoc. prof., dept. physiology U. Mich. Sch. Medicine, Ann Arbor, 1990—94, adj. prof., dept. physiology, 1994—2001, prof., dept. internal medicine and molecular and integrative physiology, 2001—; John Jacob Abel collegiate prof. life sciences U. Mich., Ann Arbor, 2002—; sr. rsch. scientist Life Sciences Inst., U. Mich., Ann Arbor, 2001—, assoc. dir., 2002, dir., 2002—. Mem. NY State Health Rsch. Coun., Diabetes Rsch. Sect., 1985-89; mem. sci. rev. com., Juvenile Diabetes Found., NYC, 1988-91; adj. asst. prof., dept. cell biology, Cornell U. Sch. Medicine, 1988-91; mem. com. on rsch. Am. Diabetes Assn., Alexandria, Va., 1990-93; mem. physiological chemistry study sect., NIH, 1993-97; cons. Sankyo Pharma Rsch. Inst; Kinase adv. bd., Vertex Pharm., Inc.; external adv. bd. U. Pa. Diabetes Ctr.; scientific adv. bd. Quatrx Pharm., Invitrogen, Phenomix; invited presenter in field. Editorial bd. mem. Am. Jour. Physiology 1995-2001, Diabetes, 1997-99, Jour. Biological Chemistry, 1997-2002, Current Opinion in Oncologic, Endocrine and Metabolic Drugs, 1998-, Molecular Endocrinology, 2000-01, Cell Metabolism, 2004-; assoc. editor, Jour. Cellular Biochemistry, 1989-, Jour. Clin. Investigation, 1997-2002, bd. consulting editors 2002-; dep. editor, Molecular Medicine 2002-; contbr. several articles to profl. jours. Recipient New Investigator award NIH, 1984; named Irma T. Hirschl scholar, 1986, Established Investigator, Am. Heart Assn., 1989, Disting. Scientist in Basic Rsch., Clin. Ligand Assay Soc., 2006. Mem. AAAS, Am. Soc. Biochem. & Molecular Biology, Am. Soc. Pharm. & Exptl. Therapeutics (mem. exec. com., molecular pharmacology divsn., 1994-99, John Jacob Abel award, 1990), Endocrine Soc., Harvey Soc., Am. Soc. Clin. Investigation (hon.), Am. Diabetes Assn.(Rosalyn S. Yalow R&D award, 1984), NY Acad. Sciences, Inst. Medicine., Biochemical Soc., N.Am. Soc. for the Study Obesity, Pluto Soc., Am. Assn. Pathologists, Sigma Xi Achievements include discovery of the structure of the second messenger of insulin action; rsch. in role of protein phosphorylation in Nerve Growth Factor action; biology of protein-lipid interactions; biology of lipoproteins; patents in field. Office: Life Sciences Inst U Mich 210 Washtenaw Ave 3rd Fl Ann Arbor MI 48109-2216 Office Phone: 734-615-9787. Office Fax: 734-763-6492. E-mail: saltiel@umich.edu.

SALTSGAVER, CAROL MADELEINE, mathematics professor; d. Marcher Latimore and Anne Marie Rose Madeleine Wilson; m. Michael Ray Saltsgaver, Aug. 14, 1996; children: Cheyenne Marie, Savannah Rose. MS in Math., U. Okla., Norman, 1997. Math. instr. Okla. Sch. Sci. and Math., Muskogee, 2002—05; clin. instr. math. U. Ill. at Springfield, 2005—. Troop leader Girl Scouts, Springfield, 2006—. Mem.: AAUP. Home: 1801 S State St Springfield IL 62704 Office: Univ Illinois at Springfield One University Plz Springfield IL 62703 Business E-Mail: csalt2@uis.edu.

SALTSMAN, JOHN B., JR., (CHIP SALTSMAN), political organization administrator; b. Nashville, Mar. 24, 1968; BS, Christian Brothers U., 1990, MBA. V.p. strategic planning McKenzie Mgmt. Co., Cleveland, Tenn.; West Tenn. field rep. Pres. Bush Re-election Campaign, 1992; with Office of Congressman Don Sundquist; campaign field dir. Don Sundquist Gubernatorial Campaign, 1994; adminstrv. asst. to Gov. State of Tenn., commr. transp. Tenn., 1995; exec. dir. Tenn. Rep. Caucus, 1996; chmn. Tenn. Rep. Party, Nashville, 1999—2001; devel. dir. for Senator Bill Frist Nat. Rep. Senatorial Com., 2002; sr. political advisor VOLPAC; nat. campaign mgr. for Gov. Mike Huckabee's Presdl. Campaign, 2007. Mem. state fin. com. Gov. Sundquist's Re-election Campaign, 1998. Republican. Office: 21 GOP 4717 Centennial Blvd Nashville TN 37209 Office Fax: 615-386-0026. E-mail: inbox@chipsaltsman.com.*

SALTZ, AMY, theater educator, director; b. Bklyn. d. Jerome Lawrence and Florence Zunser Saltz. BA, Univ. Wis. Staff repertory dir. The Acting Co., NYC, 1976—79; adj. assoc. prof. theater arts Columbia U., NYC, 1986—87; adj. prof. directing Rutgers U., New Brunswick, NJ, 1987—2000; adj. assoc. prof. drama Yale U., New Haven, 1991—. Assoc. artistic dir. Napa Valley Theater Co., St. Helena, Calif., 1970—73; theater auditor NY State Coun. Arts, NYC, 1970—79; dir. Eugene O'Neill Nat. Playwright's Conf., Waterford, Conn., 1981—99; Tony Award voter Am. Theater Wing Soc. Stage Dirs. & Choreographers, NYC, 1985—93; final selection com. O'Neill Nat. Playwrights' Conf., Waterford, 1990—99; adv. bd. 7 Devils Playwright's Conf., McCall, Idaho, 2001—; individual artist, new works panelist Mass. Cultural Coun., Boston, 2001, 2005—; dirs. project panelist The Drama League, NYC, 2005—; directing fellowship panelist Nat. Endowment Arts, Theater Comm. Group, NYC; plays in process selection com. panelist Theatre Comm. Group, NYC; playwright, dirs. panel Theater Comm. Group, NYC; artistic dir. InHouse Theater Co., NYC; award panelist Edith Oliver award; award panelist Eric Kocher award; award panelist Herbert Brokin award; award panelist Charles MacArthur award; theatre panelist, on-site evaluator Mass. Cultural Coun., Boston; guest dir. NYU, Tisch Sch. of the Arts, NYC, The Juilliard Sch., NYC; dir. program Rutgers U., 2000—. Dir.: (plays) Brave New World: A Response To 9/11, The Buriel Society, Connecticut Critics Circle, Something Unspoken: One Act Plays by Tennessee Williams, A Midsummer Night's Dream, Fishing, Final Placement; dir., dir.: (plays) A Delicate Balance, Man and Superman, A Case of You, Arms and the Man, Hedda Gabler (Time Out Best Area Play of Season, 1994), Heidi Chronicles (Handy award, Best dir. & best prodn., 1991), Funeral March for a One-Man Band (Joseph Jefferson award for Best Dir. & Best Prodn., 1980), A Voice of My Own (NY Times Top 10 Off Broadway Shows, 1980), Tiny Mommy; (TV series) Search for Tomorrow, Another World; author: (plays) Touch (Grammy Award Nominee, 1970); dir.: (theater) To Kill A Mockingbird; (plays) Diary of Anne Frank, Cloud 9. Mem.: Am. Dirs. Inst. (adv. bd. mem.), Am. Assn. Theatre in Higher Edn. (panelist), Dirs. Guild Am., League Profl. Women Theater, Soc. Stage Dirs. & Choreographers (exec. bd. mem. 1984—93). Achievements include aided in the development of new work by numerous prestigious writers including Neal Bell, Lee Blessing, Adam Rapp, John Patrick Shanley and August Wilson; directed at major theatres across the country including The Public Theatre, NYC, Playwrights Horizons, NYC, The Second Stage, NYC and Theatre for a New Audience, NYC; Yale Repertory Theatre, Seattle Rep, Actor's Theater of Louisville, Ivanhoe Theatre, Chicago, St. Nicholas, Chicago, Syracuse Stage, Great Lakes Theatre Festival, Cincinatti Playhouse. Office: Rutgers U Theatre Arts Dept 2 Chapel Dr New Brunswick NJ 08901 Home: 305 E 24th St Apt 9d New York NY 10010-4025 Office Fax: 732-932-1409; Home Fax: 212-924-5009. Personal E-mail: ascl594@aol.com. Business E-Mail: asaltz@rci.rutgers.edu.

SALTZ, HOWARD JOEL, newspaper editor; b. Bronx, NY, Apr. 11, 1960; s. Fred Raymond and Sheila Lois (Goldberg) S. BA in Liberal Arts, SUNY, Stony Brook, 1983. Reporter Greenwich Time, So. Conn. Newspapers divsn. Times Mirror, 1983-85; with MediaNews Group, 1985—, N.J. Advance, Dover, 1985-87, editor, 1987-88, Hamilton (Ohio) Jour.-News, 1988-89, Fremont (Calif.) Argus, 1989-91, Johnstown Tribune-Democrat, 1991; dep. bus. editor Denver Post, 1996-98, dep. mng. editor features, 1998-2000, multimedia editor, 2000—02, assoc. editor/new media & strategic devel., 2002—06; v.p. content develop. Media News Group Interactive, 2006—. Adv. com. dept. journalism Ohlone Coll., Fremont, Calif., 1990-91. Bd. dirs. YMCA, Fremont-Newark, Calif., 1990-91, Johnstown Area Heritage Assn., 1991-93. Mem. Greater Johnstown C. of C. (bd. dirs. 1991-96), Soc. Profl. Journalists (bd. dirs. Northern Calif. chpt. 1990-91). Avocations: skiing, travel, scuba. Address: 535 Garfield St Denver CO 80206-4513 Office: Media News Group Interactive 101 W Colfax Ave Ste 950 Denver CO 80202 Business E-Mail: hsaltz@medianewsgroup.com.

SALTZ, LEONARD BRUCE, oncologist; b. NYC, Apr. 25, 1957; s. Jack and Anita (Belfer) S.; m. Gail Michele Riess, June 17, 1989; children: Emily Nicole, Kimberly Julia, Victoria Paige. BSc, Stanford U., 1979; MD, Yale U., 1983. Diplomate Am. Bd. Internal Medicine, 1986, Diplomate Subspeciality of Hematology, Am. Bd. Internal Medicine, 1988, Diplomate Subspeciality of Med. Oncology, Am. Bd. Internal Medicine, 1989. Intern internal medicine The NY Hosp., NYC, 1983-84, resident internal medicine, 1984-86; postdoctoral assoc. Lab. of Immunology, Rockefeller U., NYC, 1986-87; fellow hematology-oncology The NY Hosp., Cornell U. Med. Ctr., NYC, 1986-89, asst. attending physician, 1988-89; clin. asst. attending physician Meml. Sloan-Kettering Cancer Ctr., NYC, 1989-93, asst. attending physician, asst. mem., 1993—98, assoc. attending physician, 1998—2005, mem. patient care com. dept. medicine, 1989—, mem. inpatient care com. of the clin. coun., 1990-93, coord. solid tumor svc. conf. dept. medicine, 1991-93; prof. medicine Cornell U., 2006—. Pres. NY Hosp. Housestaff Assn., NYC, 1985-86; instr. in medicine Cornell U. Sch. Medicine, NYC, 1992-93, asst. prof. medicine, 1993-98, assoc. prof. medicine, 1998—, prof. medicine, 2005-. Recipient Career Devel. award Am. Cancer Soc., 1993. Mem. ACP, Am. Soc. Clin. Oncology, Am. Assn. for Cancer Rsch.

SALTZ, RENATO, plastic surgeon; b. Uruguaiana, Brazil, Aug. 29, 1956; came to US, 1982; s. Jayme and Berta Saltz; m. Marcia Bartczak, Mar. 6, 1982; children: Bianca, Felipe. MD, U. Fed. Rio, Grande do Sul, Porto Alegre, 1980; postgrad., U. Ala., 1987-89, Med. Coll. Ga., 1990-92. Diplomate Am. Bd. Surgery, Am. Bd. Plastic Surgery. Mem. med. staff U. Fed. Rio, 1975-80; intern in gen. surgery Jackson Meml. Hosp., Miami, Fla., 1982-83, resident in gen. surgery, 1983-86, chief resident in gen. surgery, 1986-87; resident in plastic surgery U. Ala., Birmingham, Ala., 1987-88, chief resident in plastic surgery, 1989, fellow in hand, aesthetic and microsurgery, 1989-90; plastic surgeon Med. Coll. Ga., Augusta, 1990-94, asst. prof. sect. plastic surgery dept. surgery, 1990—94, dir. microsurgery and rsch. lab. sect. plastic surgery, 1990—94; assoc. prof. plastic reconstruct surgery U. Utah, 1994—2002, dir. Summit Plastic Surgery Ctr., 1994—2002; plastic surgeon Saltz Plastic Surgery & Spa Vitória, Salt Lake City, 2002—, Saltz Plastic Surgery & Skin Care Ctr., Park City, 2002—. Lectr., presenter in field; vis. prof. divsn. plastic surgery W.Va. U., Morgantown, 1989, vis. prof. divsn. plastic surgery, U. Ala., Birmingham, 1991; vis. prof. divsn. plastic surgery Fundaçã0o Faculdade Fed. Ciêcias Médicas de Porto Alegre, Brazil, 1993; founder Image Reborn Found. Utah Contbr. articles to profl. publs., chpts. to books; author videotapes. Recipient 3rd prize in resident competition Southeastern Soc. Plastic and Reconstructive Surgeons, 1988, 2nd prize in resident competition Southeastern Soc. Plastic and Reconstructive Surgeons, 1989. Fellow ACS, Internat. Coll. Surgeons; mem. AMA, Am. Burn Assn., Am. Soc. Reconstructive Microsurgery, Plastic Surgery Rsch. Coun., Am. Soc. Plastic and Reconstructive Surgery, Inc., Jackson Med. Soc., Brazilian Plastic Surgery Soc., Southeastern Surg. Congress, Richmond County Med. Soc., Rocky Mountain Assn. Plastic and Reconstructive Surgeons (past pres.), Am. Soc. Aesthetic Plastic Surgery (v.p.), Am. Soc. Plastic Surgery (v.p.), Salt Lake Surgical Soc., Salt Lake Plastic Surgery Soc., Internat. Soc. Aesthetic Surgery (chmn. edn. coun.), Utah plastic Surgery Soc. Office: Saltz Plastic Surgery and Spa Vitoria 5445 S Highland Dr Salt Lake City UT 84117 also: Saltz Plastic Surgery 5445 Highland Dr Salt Lake City UT 84117-7629 Office Phone: 801-274-9501, 435-655-6612. Business E-Mail: info@saltzplasticsurgery.com.

SALTZBURG, STEPHEN ALLAN, law educator, consultant; b. Phila., Sept. 10, 1945; s. Jack Leonard and Mildred (Osgood) Adelman; m. Susan Lee, March 10, 1990; children: Mark Winston, Lisa Marie, Diane Elizabeth, David Lee Musselh. AB, Dickinson Coll., 1967; JD, U. Pa., 1970. Bar: Calif. 1971, D.C. 1972, Va. 1976. Law clk. U.S. Dist. Ct. (no. dist.) Calif., San Francisco, 1970-71, U.S. Supreme Ct., 1971-72; asst. prof. law sch. U. Va., Charlottesville, 1972-74, assoc. prof., 1974-77, prof., 1977-87, Class of 1962 prof., 1987-90; Howrey prof. trial advocacy, litigation and profl. responsibility George Washington U. Law Sch., Washington, 1990—2004, Wallace and Beverley Woodbury univ. prof., 2004—. Reporter Alaska Rules of Evidence, 1976-77, Alaska Civil Jury Instrns., 1979-81, Adv. Com. on Rules of Criminal Procedure, 1984-89, Va. Rules on Evidence, 1984-85, Civil Justice Act Adv. Group, U.S. Dist. Ct. D.C., 1992-93, chmn., 1994-99, assoc. independant councel, 1987-88; dep. asst. atty. gen. criminal divsn. U.S. Dept. Justice, 1988-89; ex officio mem. U.S. Sentencing Commn., 1989-90; mem. adv. com. on Fed. Rules of Criminal Procedure, 1989-95, on Fed. Rules of Evidence, 1992-95; mediator dispute resolution program U.S. Ct. Appeals, 1993—. Author: Evidence in America, 1987, American Criminal Procedure, 7th edit., 2004, Criminal Law: Cases and Materials, 1994, 2d edit., 2000, Evidence: The Objection Method, 1997, 2d edit., 2000, Federal Rules of Evidence Manual, 1975, 9th edit., 2006, Federal Rules of Evidence Trial Book, 1998, A Modern Approach to Evidence, 2d edit., 1982, Military Rules of Evidence Manual, 5th edit., 2004, Basic Criminal Procedure, 1994, 4th edit., 2005, Military Evidentiary Foundations, 1994, 2d edit., 2000, Trying Cases to Win: Anatomy of a Trial, 1999, Trying Cases to Win: Evidence: Weapons for Winning, Vol. 1, 2000, Vol. 2, 2002, Vol. 3, 2004, California Federal Evidence Trial Book, 1999, Ohio Rules of Evidence Trial Book, 1999, Washington Evidence Trial Book, 1999. Mem.: ABA (chmn. com. on trial advocacy criminal justice sect. 1992—96, co-chmn. task force on civil trial stds. litig. sect. 1996—97, task force on Ind. Counsel Act litig. sect. 1997—99, mem. criminal justice sect. coun. 2000—, task force on terrorism and the law 2001—02, litigation sect. coun. 2001—04, ho. of dels. 2001—05, task force on gatekeeper regulation and the profession 2002—, task force on enemy combatants 2002—, chair ABA Justice Kennedy Commn. 2003—04, co-chair commns. effective criminal sanctions 2005—), Am. Law Inst. Office: George Washington U Law Sch 2000 H St NW Washington DC 20052 Home Phone: 204-797-9028; Office Phone: 202-994-7089. Business E-Mail: ssaltz@law.gwu.edu.

SALTZER, JEROME HOWARD, computer science educator; b. Nampa, Idaho, Oct. 9, 1939; s. Joseph and Helene (Scheuermann) S.; m. Marlys Anne Hughes, June 16, 1961; children— Rebecca, Sarah, Mark. BS, MIT, 1961, MS, 1963, Sc.D., 1966. Faculty dept. elec. engring. and computer sci. MIT, Cambridge, Mass., 1966—, now prof. emeritus and sr. lectr.; tech. dir. Project Athena, Cambridge, Mass., 1984-88. Cons. Chem. Abstracts Svc., 1968-88, IBM Corp., 1970-84. Mem. Mayor's Telecomms. Adv. Bd., Newton, Mass., 1984—2006. Fellow AAAS, IEEE (life); mem. NRC (computer sci. and telecom. bd. 1991-93), NAE, Assn. for Computing Machinery (mem. com. on computers and pub. policy 1984—), Eta Kappa Nu, Tau Beta Pi. Home: 2635 E Plateau Dr Boise ID 83712 Office Phone: 617-253-6016. E-mail: saltzer@mit.edu.

SALTZMAN, BRIAN, physician, surgeon, educator; b. July 24, 1953; BA, Tufts U., Medford, Mass., 1974; MD, Cornell U., Ithaca, NY, 1979. Fellow in endourology N.Y. Hosp., Cornell Med. Ctr., NYC, 1985-86; asst. prof. urology Mt. Sinai Med. Ctr., NYC, 1986-89; asst. prof. surgery Harvard Med. Sch., Boston, 1989-99, assoc. prof. surgery, 1999—. Office Phone: 617-332-0116. Business E-Mail: bsaltzma@caregroup.harvard.edu.

SALTZMAN, IRENE CAMERON, consumer products company executive; b. Cocoa, Fla., Mar. 23, 1927; d. Argyle Bruce and Marie T. (Neel) Cameron; m. Herman Saltzman, Mar. 23, 1946 (dec. May 1986); children: Martin Howard (dec.), Arlene Norma Hanly. Owner Irene Perfume and Cosmetics Lab., Jacksonville, Fla., 1972—. Mem. Cummer Mus. Art, Jacksonville, 1972-, Convention Visitors Bur., Jacksonville. Mem. NAFE, Nat. Assn. Profl. and Exec. Women, Ret. Judge Advocates Assn. of USAF (hon.), Mil. Officers Assn. Am., Trade, Cosmetic, Toiletry and Fragrance Assn., Ret. Officers Assn., Soc. Cosmetic Chemists (affiliate), Jacksonville Sister Cities Assn., Conventional Visitors Bur. CVB Jacksonville, Ponte Vedra Club. Democrat. Episcopalian. Avocations: aviation, painting, travel, swimming, golf. Home: 2701 Ocean Dr S Jacksonville Beach FL 32250 Office Phone: 904-641-5171. Business E-Mail: irene@ireneparfums.com.

SALTZMAN, JARED, performing arts educator, lighting designer; b. NYC, Apr. 14, 1950; s. Perle and David Saltzman; m. Marjorie Harris, May 28, 1972; children: Aimee Perle, Arielle Jessica. MA, NYU, 1976. Cert. entertainment electrician Entertainment Tech. Cert. Program Coun. Prof. Bergen CC, Paramus, NJ, 1973—; head electrician IATSE Local 632, NJ, 1978—. Mem.: NEA, Internat. Alliance of Theatrical Stage Employees, US Inst. for Theatre Tech. Office: Bergen Cmty Coll 400 Paramus Rd Paramus NJ 07652

SALTZMAN, JOSEPH, journalist, educator, television producer; b. LA, Oct. 28, 1939; s. Morris and Ruth (Weiss) S.; m. Barbara Dale Epstein, July 1, 1962; children: Michael Stephen Ulysses, David Charles Laertes. BA, U. So. Calif., 1961, 1990; MS, Columbia U., 1962. Freelance writer, reporter, prodr., 1960—; reporter Valley Times Today, LA, 1962-64; editor Pacific Palisades Palisadian Post, 1964; sr. writer, prodr. CBS-TV, LA, 1964-74; freelance broadcast cons. LA, 1974—; prof. journalism U. So. Calif., LA, 1974—, acting dir. Sch. Journalism, 1999; assoc. dir. Sch. Journalism U. So. Calif. Annenberg, 1996-99; assoc. dean Annenberg Sch. Comm., 1999—2003; sr. prodr. investigative unit Entertainment Tonight, 1983; dir. Image of the Journalist in Popular Culture project Norman Lear Ctr., Annenberg Sch. Comm., U. So. Calif., 2001—. CFO The Jester & Pharley Phund. Author: Frank Capra and the Image of the Journalist in American Film, 2002; prodr.(writer): (documentaries) Black on Black, 1968, The Unhappy Hunting Ground, 1971, The Junior High School, 1971, The Very Personal: Death of Elizabeth Schell-Holt-Hartford, 1972, Rape, 1972, Why Me?, 1974, Entertainment Tonight, 1983; editor (columnist): USA Today Mag., 1983—; King Features Syndicate, 1983—92; contbg. editor: Emmy Mag., 1986—90, Roberts Reviewing Svc., 1964—95, others. Recipient AP cert. of excellence and merit, 1968, 72, 73, 74, 75, Edward R. Murrow awards for disting. achievements in broadcast journalism, 1969, 72, Alfred I. duPont-Columbia U. award in broadcast journalism, 1973-74, Silver Gavel award ABA, 1973, Ohio State award Am. Exhbn. Ednl. Radio-TV Programs and Inst. for Edn. by Radio-TV Telecom. Ctr., 1974, Broadcast Media awards San Francisco State U., 1974, 75, Media award for excellence in comm. Am. Cancer Soc., 1976, Disting. Alumni award U. So. Calif., 1992, Alumni award Columbia U. Grad. Sch. Journalism, 2005; Seymour Berkson fellow, 1961; Robert E. Sherwood fellow, 1962; alt. Pulitzer traveling fellow, 1962-63. Mem. NATAS (regional Emmy awards 1965, 68, 74, 75), Radio-TV News Assn. (Golden Mike awards 1969, 71, 73, 75), Writers Guild Am., Greater LA Press Club (awards 1968, 74, 75), Columbia U. Alumni Assn., U. So. Calif. Alumni Assn., Skull and Dagger, Blue Key, Phi Beta Kappa, Sigma Delta Chi, Pi Sigma Alpha, Alpha Epsilon Rho. Home: 2116 Via Estudillo Palos Verdes Peninsula CA 90274-1931 Office: U So Calif Annenberg Sch Journalism Univ Park Los Angeles CA 90089-0001 Office Phone: 310-377-8883. Business E-Mail: saltzman@usc.edu.

SALTZMAN, PHILIP, television producer, writer; b. Sonora, Mexico, Sept. 19, 1928; came to US, 1929, naturalized, 1948; s. Louis and Vanya (Liberman) S.; m. Caroline Veiller, Jan. 24, 1960; children: Jennifer, Daniel, Tony. BA, UCLA, 1951, MA, 1953. Free lance writer, 1958-68. Pres. Woodruff Prodns., Inc. Writer: (TV shows) Alcoa Goodyear Theater, 1959, Richard Diamond, 1959, Rifleman, 1961, Perry Mason, 1964, Dr. Kildare, 1964, Fugitive, 1964, Twelve O'Clock High, 1966; prodr., writer: (TV shows) Felony Squad, 1966-69, F.B.I, 1969-73, Barnaby Jones, 1973-77; prodr., writer, creator Intertect, 1973; prodr.: (TV movie) The FBI vs. Alvin Karpis, 1974, Attack on Terror: The FBI vs. the KKK in Mississippi, 1975, Brinks: The Great Robbery, 1976; co-writer: (feature film) The Swiss Conspiracy, 1975; creator, writer, prodr.: (TV movie) Crossfire, 1975; exec. prodr.: (TV series) Barnaby Jones, 1978-80, Escapade, 1978, Colorado C-I, 1978, A Man Called Sloane, 1979, The Aliens Are Coming, 1979, Freebie and the Bean, 1980; prodr.: (TV shows) Bare Essence, 1982; supervising prodr.-writer Partners in Crime, 1984; prodr., writer Crazy Like a Fox, 1985; prodr., co-writer (TV movie) That Secret Sunday, 1986; exec. supervising prodr. The New Perry Mason movies, 1987-88; exec. supervising prodr., writer Jake and The Fatman, 1987-88; supervising prodr. Columbo, 1989-90; creator, writer The Caller, 1991. Mem. dean's coun. Coll. Letters and Sci., UCLA, Friends of English, UCLA. Mem. Writers Guild Am., West, Caucus for Writers, Producers, Dirs., Acad. TV Arts and Scis., PEN Ctr. USA West.

SALUSKY, ISIDRO B., pediatric nephrologist, educator; b. Buenos Aires, Sept. 3, 1948; MD, U. Buenos Aires, 1971. Diplomate Am. Bd. Pediat., cert. in Pediat. Nephrology. Intern pediat. Pedro de Elizalde Hosp., Buenos Aires, 1972—73, resident pediat., 1973—75; fellowship pediat. nephrology Hosp. Enfants Malades, Paris, 1976—79; advanced rsch. fellow nutritional metabolism V.A. Wadsworth Med. Ctr., LA, 1979—81; fellowship pediat. nephrology UCLA Med. Ctr., 1981—82, prof. pediat. nephrology, 1982—; attending physician Mattel Children's Hosp./UCLA Med. Ctr. Dir. pediat. dialysis prog. UCLA Med. Ctr., 1984—, assoc. dir. dialysis prog., 1989—, prog. dir. gen. clin. rsch. ctr., 1991—. Contbr. articles to profl. jours. Dir. summer urban health rsch. prog. UCLA/Drew U. Ctr. of Excellence for Minorities, 1995—98; chair edn. com. USA Olympic Transplant Games, LA, 1992. Mem.: Nat. Kidney Found. (pres. elect medical adv. bd. 1991—92, pres. medical adv. bd. 1992—94), Am. Soc. Pediat. Nephrology, Internat. Pediat. Nephrology Assn., Internat. Soc. Peritoneal Dialysis, Soc. Bone and Mineral Rsch. Office: UCLA Med Ctr Dept Pediat Nephrology 10833 Le Conte Ave Los Angeles CA 90095 Office Phone: 310-206-6987. Business E-Mail: isalusky@pediatrics.medsch.ucla.edu.

SALVADOR, MARI LYN C., museum director; Chief curator Maxwell Mus. Anthropology, U. N.Mex; prof. anthropology U. N.Mex; dir. San Diego Mus. of Man, 2004—. Author: The Art of Being Kuna: Layers of Meaning Among the Kuna of Panama, 1997. Mem.: Calif. Assn. Museums (bd. mem.). Office: Mus of Man 1350 El Prado Balboa Park San Diego CA 92101 Business E-Mail: msalvador@museumofman.org.

SALVADOR, MELCHOR NEPOMUCENO, engineering educator; b. Marikina, Metro Manila, The Philippines, Jan. 6, 1915; s. Justo Guevarra and Maxima (Nepomuceno) S.; m. Leonora Josef, Jan. 19, 1946; children: Jaime, Ricardo, Dante. BS in Electrical Engring., U. of The Philippines, 1939, BS in Mech. Engring., 1939; MA in Engring. Edn., Adamson U., The Philippines, 1976; EdD in Gen. Edn., Quezon U., The Philippines, 1990. Registered engr. The Philippines. Power supr. engr. Manila Elec. Co., 1939-69; prof. physics, electrical and mech. engring. Adamson U., Manila, 1949—, supr. physics and electronics lab., 1978-79, head elec. engring., 1979-85, officer in charge Coll. Engring., 1985-85; prof. electrical engring. Quezon U., Manila, 1978—. Counseling, tutoring in the field 1978-85; lectr. Outreach Program 1986-90. Adviser Helping and Sharing Ozanam Sch. of Charity, Manila, 1985-90; organizer-adviser Young Rizalists Adamson U., Manila, 1974, Knights of Rizal Marikina, Manila, 1986, Jose Rizal Sun Yat-Sen Soc. Quezon U. Manila, 1992. Recipient Citizens Coun. for Mass. Media plaque, 1971, U.P. Alumni Assn. plaque, 1989, Golden Father award The Philippines, 1994. Fellow Philippine Assn. for Advancement Sci.; mem. Inst. Integrated Elec. Engrs. (Most Outstanding Prof. award 1980), KC (Grand Knight 1970-71, plaque of distinction 1988), Knights of Rizal (knight comdr., chmn. 1977-85, Disting. Svc. Cross award 1991). Roman Catholic. Achievements include construction of robot at Adamson U. The Philippines; building a miniature power plant panel board with Motor-Generator Set. Home: 107 A Mabini St San Rogue Marikina City 1801 Philippines

SALVANESCHI, LUIGI, real estate developer, management consultant, educator; b. Casale, Italy, 1929; came to U.S., 1959; s. Ernesto and Carolina (Bassignana) S.; m. Lenore M. Rickels, Aug. 20, 1958; 1 child, Margherita Lina. Classical Maturity, Valsalice, Torino, Italy, 1950; PhD, Vatican U., Rome, 1958; cert. in real estate, UCLA, 1965. Restaurant mgr. McDonalds Co., Chgo., 1959-61, restaurant mgr. and supr. Los Angeles, 1961-63, real estate mgr., 1964-68, v.p. real estate Oakbrook, Ill., 1969-83; sr. v.p. real estate and constrn. Kentucky Fried Chicken, Louisville, 1983-88; pres., COO, dir. Blockbuster Entertainment, Ft. Lauderdale, Fla., 1988-91; disting. adj. prof. Barry Univ., 1991—. Adj. prof. Sch. Bus. U. Louisville, 1987; dir. Fla. Fun-Train subs. First Am. Rwys., Hollywood, Fla. Author: Location, Location, Location, 1997, Renaissance 2000: Liberal Arts Essentials for Tomorrow's Leaders, 1998. Dir. Ft. Lauderdale Internat. Movie Festival. Served as 2d lt. in Italian Infantry, 1945-46. Recipient Outstanding Italo-Am. award Italian Am. Fedn., 1991; named Colonel of the Commonwealth of Ky., 1984. Mem. Nat. Assn. Real Estate Execs. (co-founder, bd. dirs.). Roman Catholic. Avocations: mountain hiking, reading. Office: Barry Univ Sch of Bus 11300 NE 2nd Ave Miami FL 33161-6695

SALVATI, EDWARDO A., surgeon; b. Buenos Aires, Nov. 11, 1939; arrived in U.S., 1969; BS, Jose Manuel Estrada, Buenos Aires, 1957; MD, La Platta Med. Sch., Buenos Aires, 1963. Diplomate Am. Bd. Orthopedic Surgery. Intern Hosp. de Quilmes, Buenos Aires, 1962—63; resident U. Florence, Italy, 1963—65; fellow Hosp. Spl. Surgery, NYC, 1969—72, asst. attending orthop. surgeon, 1972—75, chief hip svc., 1975—91, attending orthop. surgeon, 1983—, dir. hip and knee svc., 1991—, assoc. scientist rsch. divsn., 1993—; from instr. to assoc. prof. clin. orthop. surgery Weil Med. Coll. Cornell U., NYC, 1969—83, prof., 1983—. Asst. attending orthop. surgeon N.Y. Hosp., 1972—75, assoc. attending orthop. surgeon, 1976—83, attending orthop. surgeon, 1983—, Presbyn. Hosp., 1983—; lectr. in field. Guest editor: Hip Internat., 1992; cons. reviewer Hip Internat., mem. editl. bd., cons. reviewer Jour. Bone and Joint Surgery, Clin. Orthop. and Related Rsch., Jour. Arthoplasty, mem. editl. bd. Advances Orthop., Jour. Orthop. Techniques, Internat. Orthop., La Chirurgia degli Organi di Movimenti, Long-Term Effects Med. Implants; contbr. articles to profl. jours. Grantee, Hip Soc., 2003, Orthop. Rsch. and Edn. Found., 1998, 2004—05; Rhone-Poulenc Rhorer Rsch. grantee, Hip Soc., 1998, Zimmer grantee, 2002—05. Mem.: AMA, Sociedad Medica Hispanoamericana, Venezuelan Soc. Orthop. Surgery and Traumatology, Columbian Soc. Orthop. Surgery and Traumatology, Argentine Med. Soc., Argentine Soc. Orthop. and Traumatology, N.Y. State Soc. Orthop. Surgeons, N.Y. Acad. Medicine, New York County Med. Soc., Med. Soc. State of N.Y., Latinoamerican Soc. Orthop. and Traumatology, Internat. Hip Soc., Am. Assn. Hip and Knee Surgeons, Am. Hip Soc., Am. Orthop. Assn., Am. Acad. Orthop. Surgery, Assn. Medica Argentina (hon.). Office: Hosp Spl Surgery 535 E 70th St New York NY 10021

SALVATIERRA, OSCAR, JR., transplant surgeon, urologist, educator; b. Phoenix, Apr. 15, 1935; s. Oscar and Josefine S.; m. Pamela Moss; children: Mark, Lisa Marie. BS, Georgetown U., 1957; MD, U. So. Calif., 1961. Intern, resident in surgery and urology U. So. Calif.-Los Angeles County Med. Ctr., 1961-66; practice medicine Pomona, Calif., 1968-72; chief staff Casa Colina Hosp., 1972; post doctoral fellow in transplantation U. Calif.-San Francisco, 1972-73, asst. prof. surgery and urology, 1973-75, assoc. prof., 1975-81, prof., 1981-91, chmn. transplant service, 1974-91; attending surgeon and urologist Moffitt Hosp., 1973—; exec. dir. Pacific Transplant Inst., 1991-94; prof. surgery/pediatrics, dir. pediat. renal transplantation Stanford U. Med. Ctr., 1994—2006, attending surgeon, urologist and pediat.; advising dean Sch. Medicine Stanford U., 2005—; prof. surgery & pediat. Standford U., Emeritus Sch. Medicine, 2006—. Chair faculty senate Stanford U. Sch. Medicine, 2002—04; study sect. NIH, 1981-85, nat. adv. bd., 1986-92, chmn. nat. adv. bd. 1990-92, chmn. spl. study sect., 1997, 99 Mem. editl. bd. Transplantation and Immunology, 1984—, Transplantation, 1987—, Transplantation Procs., 1990—, Pediat. Transplantation, 1998—; assoc. editor Am. Jour. Kidney Diseases, 1987-89; contbr. over 290 articles and chpts. to med. lit. Nat. bd. advisors Agent Orange Class Assistance Program, 1988-96. With M.C., U.S. Army, Vietnam, 1966-68. Decorated Army Commendation medal, Grande Ufficiale of Italian Rep. Knighthood with title His Excellency; recipient Chancellor's award for pub. svc., U. Calif., 1986, Commendation resolution, Calif. State Legislature, 1990, Presdl. medal and Diploma of Honor, Argentina, 1999, Rambar-Mark award, Stanford U., 1999, Franklin Ebaugh award, 2003, Albion Walter Hewlett award, 2007, Stanford, 2007; named Oscar Salvatierra Symposium in his honor, 2001; grantee, NIH, 1974—76, 1980—83, 1988—90, 2003—, USPHS, 1986—89; Oscar Salvatierra Ann. Lectureship in Transplantation, in his honor, Stanford U., 2005—. Fellow ACS (bd. govs. 1986-92); mem. Am.

Surg. Assn., Am. Soc. Transplant Surgeons (bd. dirs. 1977-85, pres. 1983-84, chmn. adv. com. on issues 1984-87), Soc. Univ. Surgeons, Soc. Univ. Urologists, N.Y. Acad. Scis., Am. Soc. Nephrology, Internat. Transplantation Soc. (bd. dirs. 1984—, pres.-elect 1996-98, pres., 1998-2000, Contbns. to Soc. medallion 2006), Soc. Pediatric Urology, Am. Urol. Assn., Nat. Kidney Found. (Pioneer award 2004, Nat. Kidney Found. Lifetime Champion of Hope award, 2009), Renal Physicians Assn. (bd. dirs. 1984-87), Pacific Coast Surg. Assn., San Francisco Surg. Soc., United Network Organ Sharing (bd. dirs. 1984-88, pres. 1985-86), Internat. Soc. for Organ Sharing (bd. dirs. 1991—, pres. 1993-95), Am. Soc. for Multicultural Health and Transplant Profls. (pres. 1992-94, Lifetime Achievement award, 2005), Nafziger Surg. Soc. Achievements include being the principle lay figure in passage and enactment of National Organ Transplant Act, 1984; introduction of Pope John Paul II to the 18th International Transplantation Congress for Encyclical on Organ Transplantation, 2000; Dr. Oscar Salvatierra award is named after him from Center of Excellence, Stanford University, 2009-. Office: Stanford U Med Ctr 703 Welch Rd Ste H2 Palo Alto CA 94304-1708

SALVATORE, DIANE J., publishing executive; BA in Journalism, Pa. State U.; MA in English/Creative Writing, NYU. Rschr., reporter The Soho News, NYC; editl. asst. Met. Home, NYC, Cosmopolitan, NYC; sr. assoc. editor Ladies' Home Jour., NYC, 1985—88; articles assoc. editor Glamour, NYC, 1988—89; sr. editor Redbook, NYC, 1989—94; dep. editor Good Housekeeping, NYC, exec. editor, 1994—99; editor in chief YM, NYC, 1998—2002; exec. dir. Marie Claire, 2001; dir. editl. ops. Hearst Mag., 2002; editor in chief Ladies Home Jour., NYC, 2002—08; v.p., publisher Broadway Books, NYC, 2009—. Contbr. articles and short stories in various nat. periodicals. Mem.: Am. Soc. Mag. Editors. Office: Broadway Books 1745 Broadway New York NY 10019 Office Phone: 212-455-1025. Office Fax: 212-455-1313. E-mail: diane.salvatore@meredith.com.

SALVATORE, LOUIS R., manufacturing executive; Dir. Ford Motor Co.; v.p. procurement MTD Products, Inc.; v.p. global purchasing Lear Corp., Southfield, Mich., 1996—98, v.p., pres. DaimlerChrysler divsn., 1998, pres. Ford and elec. systems divsns., pres. Ford, elec. systems and interior systems divsns., 2004, sr. v.p., pres. Asian Customer Group, 2005—08, sr. v.p., pres. global seating systems, 2008—. Mem. adv. bd. William P. Reuther Libr. Office: Lear Corp 21557 Telegraph Rd PO Box 5008 Southfield MI 48086 Office Phone: 248-447-1500. Office Fax: 248-447-1722.

SALVENDY, GAVRIEL, industrial engineer, educator; b. Budapest, Hungary, Sept. 30, 1938; came to US, 1968; s. Paul and Katarina (Brown) S.; m. Catherine Vivien Dees, Apr. 1, 1966; children: Laura Dorit, Kevin David. MSc in Indsl. Psychology, U. Birmingham, Eng., 1966, PhD in Indsl. Psychology, 1968; D (hon.), Academia Sinica, 1995, Chinese Acad. Scis., 1995. Asst. prof. indsl. engring. SUNY, Buffalo, 1968-71; assoc. prof. indsl. engring. Purdue U., 1971—77, prof., 1977—84, 1999—, NEC prof. indsl. engring., 1984-99; chair prof., head dept. indsl. engring. Tsinghua U., Beijing, 2001—. Fulbright disting. prof. mech. engring. U. Belgrade, Yugoslavia, 1979-81; chmn. Internat. Commn. Human Aspects in Computing, Switzerland, 1986-91. Co-author: Prediction and Development of Industrial Work Performance, 1973, Human Aspects of Computer Aided Design, 1987; sr. editor: Machine-Pacing and Occupational Stress, 1981, Social, Ergonomic and Stress Aspects of Work with Computers, 1987, Designing and Using Human-Computer Interfaces and Knowledge Based Systems, 1989; editor: Handbook of Industrial Engineering, 1982, 3d edit., 2001, Human Computer Interaction, 1984, Handbook of Human Factors, 1987, 3d edit., 2006, Cognitive Engineering in the Design of Human Computer Interaction and Expert Systems, 1987; founding editor: Internat. Jour. on Human-Computer Interaction, Internat. Jour. Human Factors in Mfg., Human-Computer Interaction, 1st and 2d edits., 2002, 07; co-editor: Work with Computers: Organizational Management, Stress and Health Aspects, 1989, Human Computer Interaction: Software and Hardware Interfaces, 1993, Human-Computer Interaction: Applications and Case Studies, 1993, Design of Work and Development of Personnel in Advanced Manufacturing, 1994, Organization and Management of Advanced Manufacturing, 1994, Advanceds in Applied Ergonomics, 1996, Handbook of Human Factors and Ergonomics, 3rd edit. 2006, Design of Computing Systems (2 vols.), 1997, Ergonomics in Manufacturing, 1998, Handbook of Industrial Engineering, 3d edit., 2001; contbr. articles to profl. jours., chpts. to books. Pres. Lafayette Jewish Sunday Sch., 1980-81. Recipient Friendship award Sci. and Engring., Govt. China, 2006, John Fritz medal, Am. Assn. Engring. Socs., 2007. Fellow APA, Inst. Indsl. Engrs. (sr., Phil Carroll award 1973), Human Factors and Ergonomics Soc. (past officer), Ergonomics Soc. (hon., life mem.), Internat. Ergonomics Assn.; mem. NAE. Office: Sch Indsl Engring Purdue U 315 N Grant St West Lafayette IN 47907-2023 Office Phone: 765-463-2628, 765-494-5426. Office Fax: 765-494-0874. E-mail: salvendy@purdue.edu.

SALVESON, MELVIN ERWIN, management sciences corporation chief executive, educator; b. Brea, Calif., Jan. 16, 1919; s. John T. and Elizabeth (Green) S.; m. Joan Y. Stipek, Aug. 22, 1944; children: Eric C., Kent Erwin BS in Engring., U. Calif. Berkeley, 1941; MS, MIT, Cambridge, 1947; PhD, U. Chgo., 1952. Cons. McKinsey & Co., NYC, 1947—48; asst. prof., dir. Mgmt. Sci. Rsch. Project UCLA, 1948—54; mgr. advanced data sys., cons. strategic planning GE, Louisville and NYC, 1954—57; pres. Mgmt. Scis. Corp., LA, 1957—67; group v.p. Control Data/CEIR, Inc., 1967—68; pres. Electronic Currency Corp., 1964—; chmn. OneCard Internat., Inc., 1983—92, UniCard Sys. Inc., 1992—. Bd. dirs. Diversified Earth Scis., Inc., Eco Rx Inc., Excel Enterprise Inc., Veritas et Justus Inc., Algeran, Inc., Electronic Currency Corp., So. Calif. Econ. Alliance, founder, pres., 1992-96; bd. dirs. Am. Soc. for Edn. and Econ. Devel., founding chair, 1996-98; exec. dir. Am. Found. for Edn. and Econ. Devel.; founder MasterCard Sys., LA, 1966; chmn. Corp. Strategies Internat.; prof. bus. Pepperdine U. 1972-85; adj. prof. U. So. Calif., Webster U., U. Phoenix, 1972-2008; adviser data processing City of LA, 1962-64; futures forecasting IBM, 1957-61; adviser strategic sys. planning USAF, 1961-67; info. sys. Calif. Dept. Human Resources, 1972-73, City of LA Automated Urban Data Base, 1962-67; tech. transfer NASA, 1965-70; mem. bd. trustees, Long Beach City Coll., 1990-95 Contbr. 45 articles to profl. sci. jours. Served to lt. comdr. submarine engring. USN, 1941—46. Named to Long Beach City Coll. Hall of Fame; recipient Dist. Alumnus award Calif. Coll. Sys., 1992 Fellow: AAAS, Inst. Mgmt. Sci. (founder, past pres.), Inst. for Ops. Rsch. and Mgmt. Scis. (founder, fellow, pres. 1956—57); mem.: CSSP Alumnus, Calif. Yacht Club, Founders Club (LA Philharm. Orch.). Republican. Office: 515 Ocean Ave # 405 S Santa Monica CA 90402-2623 Office Phone: 310-917-1911. Personal E-mail: mesalveson@aol.com.

SALVI, RICHARD, psychologist, otolaryngologist, educator; BS in Psychology, ND State U., 1968; PhD in Experimental Psychology, Syracuse U., 1975. Asst. prof. U. Tex., 1980—84, assoc prof., 1984—87; prof. dept. communicative disorders & sciences SUNY U. Buffalo; dir. Ctr. for Hearing & Deafness, 2003—. Editorial bd. Hearing Rsch., 1993—, Audiology & Neuro-Otology, 1995—, Internat. Tinnitus Jour., 1997—, Noise & Health, 1998—, Am. Acad. Audiology, 1999—, Jour. Audiological Medicine & Sciences Related to Communicative Disorders, 2005—; med. adv. bd. Martha Entenmann Tinnitus Rsch. Ctr.; internat. adv. bd. U. Coll. London Ctr. for Auditory Rsch. Mem.: Am. Tinnitus Assn. (Scientific Adv. com. 2001—). Office: Center for Hearing & Deafness 137Q Cary Hall Buffalo NY 14214 Office Phone: 716-829-5310. Office Fax: 716-829-2980. E-mail: salvi@buffalo.edu.*

SALVINI, EMIL ROBERT, publishing executive, writer, historian; b. Jersey City, June 8, 1949; s. Armando and Marie Salvini; m. Nancy Ann Levenstein, Dec. 12, 1971; children: Amy Cara, Beth Lauren. BA, William Paterson U., 1971; degree, Harvard Bus. Sch., 2001. Pres. Wheal-Grace Corp., Belleville, NJ, 1975—. Author: The Summer City by the Sea, 1995, Boardwalk Memories, Tales of the Jersey Shore, 2005, Hobey Baker American Legend, 2005, Jersey Memories, Vintage Images of the Jersey Shore, 2006. Commr. Cape May Hist. Preservation Commn., Cape May, NJ, 2004—06. Mem.: North Jersey Country Club, Harvard Bus. Sch. NY, Harvard Club Boston, Harvard Club NY. Achievements include invention of GreenPrint program. Avocations: writing, golf, travel. Office: Wheal-Grace Corp 300 Ralph St Belleville NJ 07109 Office Phone: 973-450-5950; Home Fax: 973-839-1403. E-mail: esalvini@wheal-grace.com.

SALVINI, GIORGIO, physicist, researcher; b. Milan, Apr. 24, 1920; s. Ascanio and Maria (Sardella) S.; m. Costanza Catenacci, Apr. 24, 1951; children: Paola, Francesco, Stefano, Giovanna, Pietro. Physics degree summa cum laude, U. Milan, 1942; engring. degree (hon.), U. L'Aquila, 1991. Assoc. prof. Superior Physics, Milan, 1945-48; vis. researcher U. Princeton, NJ, 1949; instr. U. Cagliari, Italy, 1951-52; project dir. U. Pisa, Italy, 1953-55; faculty gen. physics Physics Inst., Rome, 1955-65; researcher Nat. Labs., Frascati, Italy, 1966-74, Centro Europeo de Ricerche Nucleari, Rome, 1975-89; instr., researcher physics dept. U. Rome, 1990—. Min. Univ. and Sci. Rsch., 1995-96; instr. physics U. La Sapienze, 1959-89; dir. nat. labs. Frascati, Italy, 1953-60. Collaborator, coord. various scientific encys.; collaborator Dictionary of Phys. Scis.; contbr. articles to profl. jours. Pres. del Comitato Sci. esatte e Naturali, UNESCO, Rome, 1989—; pres. com. Internat. Security and Arms Control, Rome, 1990—, Def. of Human Rights, Rome, 1990—. Mem. INFN (pres. 1966-69), ECFA (pres. 1971-73), Accademia Nazionale dei Lincei (pres. 1990-94, v.p. 1994-97, hon. pres. 1998—), Accademia Nazionale delle Sci. Achievements include research in properties of the eta mesons; discovery of W.Z heavy bosuns. Avocation: painting. Home: Via Senafe 19 00199 Rome Italy Office: Acad Nat dei Lincei Via della Lungara 10 00165 Rome Italy E-mail: siorgio.salvini@zoma1.infn.it.

SALVO, J. C., lawyer; b. Council Bluffs, Iowa, Dec. 10, 1947; JD, Creighton U. Sch. of Law, Omaha, Neb., 1972. Bar: Iowa 1972, Nebr. 1972, US Dist. Ct. (Dist. Nebr.) 1972, US Dist. Ct. (So. Dist. Iowa) 1972, US Supreme Ct. 1980, US Dist. Ct. (No. Dist. Iowa) 1983, US Ct. Appeals (8th Cir.) 1984. County atty., Shelby County, Iowa, 1977—82; ptnr. Salvo, Deren, Schenck & Lauterbach, PC, Harlan, Iowa, 1972—. Shelby County atty., 1977—82. Fellow: Iowa Acad. of Trial Lawyers (pres. 1998); mem.: Iowa Supreme Ct. Nominating Commn., Iowa Supreme Ct. Grievance Commn., Assn. of Trial Lawyers of Am., Am. Bar Assn., Neb. State Bar Assn., Iowa State Bar Assn. (bd. gov. 1999—2003, v.p. 2003, pres.-elect 2004, pres. 2005), Phi Alpha Delta. Office: Salvo Deren Schenck & Lauterbach PC 711 Court St Harlan IA 51537-0509 Office Phone: 712-755-3141. Office Fax: 712-755-3144. Business E-Mail: jasalvo@sdsllaw.com.

SALVODON-STALLINGS, CYNTHIA JUDY, psychologist; b. Bklyn., July 2, 1974; d. Ginette Sam; m. Damon Victor Stallings, July 11, 2008. MEd, U. Mass., Boston, 2001. Cert. in advance grad. study U. Mass., Boston, 2002. Case worker Heart Share Human Svc., Bklyn., 1997—99; psychologist Cambridge Rindge and Latin HS, Mass., 2002—03; counselor Graham & Parks Sch., Cambridge, 2003—04, Found. Acad. HS, Bklyn., 2006—07; psychologist NYC Sch. (George Washington Carver, Ron Brown Acad., The Wortman Sch., Automotive HS, The Van Aresdale Campus Sch., EL Puente HS), Bklyn., 2004—. Mem. CCC Dance Ministry Club, 2007—08. Step dance trainer. Missionary Atlantic Bridge, Netherlands, 2000; mem. CCC Youth Missions, Guatemala, 2007; youth leader & dancer Christian Cultural Ctr., Bklyn., 2006—. Recipient Gospel Chior award, SUNY Stony Brook. Avocations: travel, dance, singing, cooking, drawing. Office: Dept Edn 131 Livingston St Brooklyn NY 11201-5105 Personal E-mail: csalvodon@hotmail.com. Business E-Mail: csalvodon@schools.nyc.gov.

SALVUCCI, LINDA, history professor; b. Pittston, Pa., Mar. 28, 1951; d. Joseph A. and Helen Shegelski Kerrigan; m. Richard Salvucci, Aug. 25, 1973; children: Martin J., Rosemary C. AB in History, Villanova U., 1973; AM in History, Princeton U., 1979, PhD in History, 1985. Asst. prof. history Trinity U., San Antonio, 1985—91, assoc. prof. history, 1991—. Chmn., mem. coms. various confs. in field. Co-author: (textbook) Call to Freedom, various edits., 2000—05; contbr. articles to profl. publs. Trustee St. Luke's Episc. Sch., 1998—2005, vice chmn., 2002—04; bd. editors The Americas, 2002—06; bd. dirs. Youth Orchs. San Antonio, 2005—06. Recipient Hubert Herring award for best article, Pacific Coast Coun. on L.Am. Studies, 1985, Coll. Tchrs. award, NEH, 1988—89, prize, Conf. on L.Am. History, 2001. Mem.: Hist. Soc. (bd. govs. 2006—), Nat. Coun. History Edn. (trustee 2005—, vice chair 2009—), Omohundro Inst. Early Am. History and Culture, Am. Hist. Assn. Office: Trinity U Dept History 1 Trinity Pl San Antonio TX 78212 Office Phone: 210-999-7628.

SALYER, KENNETH E., surgeon; b. Kansas City, Kans., Aug. 18, 1936; s. Everett A. and Laurene S.; m. Luci Lara-Salyer; children: Kenneth E. Jr., Leigh Green-Salyer. BS, U. Mo., 1958; MD, U. Kans., 1962. Intern Parkland Meml. Hosp., Dallas, 1962-63, resident in gen. surgery, 1963-67; fellow in surgery U. Tex. SW Sch. Med., Dallas, 1965-67, founder, dir. residency tng. program, 1969-78; prof. surgery, chair plastic surgery, 1969-78; resident in plastic surgery U. Kans. Sch. Med., Kansas City, 1967-69; founder, dir. Internat. Craniofacial Inst., Dallas, 1986—. Editl. bd. mem. Annals of Plastic Surgery, 1977-79, Jour. of Speech and Hearing Disorders (editl. cons.) 1982, Tex. Medicine (editl. cons.) 1981-85, Jour. of Craniofacial Surgery, 1990—, Italian Jour. Craniomaxillofacial Surgery, 1990—, Argentinian Jour. Plastic Surgery (internat. consultative coun. 1995—). Author: Techniques in Aesthetic Craniofacial Surgery, 1989, Cleft Lip and Palate Treatment Center: A Booklet for Parents, 1994, (with J. Bardach) Surgical Techniques in Cleft Lip and Palate, 1987, 2d edit. 1991, (with others) The Atlas of Craniomaxillofacial Surgery, 1982; editor: Symposium on Plastic Surgery in the Orbital Region, 1976; author various book chpts. Recipient Nat. Inst. Health award public health svc., sr. clin. traineeship Cancer Control Program 1967-69, Plastic Surgery Resident Program Participation award 2nd place 1967-69, scholar. competition (hon. mention) Edn. Found. Am. Soc. Plastic and Reconstructive Surgeons, 1972, Rsch. Grant award Ednl. Found. Am. Soc. Plastic and Reconstructive Surgeons 1975-76, Hektoen Gold medal for original investigation "Spectrum of Rsch. and Clin. Mgmt. of Craniofacial Anomalies" exhibit at AMA, San Francisco 1977, selected hon. mem. Japanese Soc. Craniofacial Surgery 1993, selected chmn. med. adv. bd. Children's Craniofacial Assn. 1993; grantee Internat. NIH Microvascular Surg. Rsch. 1969, Vets. Admin. Hosp. Maxillofacial Rsch. 1972-78, Sid Richardson Found. med. rsch. 1975-76, Gen. Electric Found. for Craniofacial Deformities 1985-87; recipient various awards for videos. Mem. AMA (mem. various coms.), Am. Acad. Pediat. (exec. com. section on plastic surgery, founding mem., sec.-treas. 1987-90, chmn. 1991—), Am. Assn. of Pediat. Plastic Surgery (founding mem., chmn. 1991—), Am. Assn. Plastic Surgery (mem. various coms.), Am. Burn Assn., Am. Cleft Palate Assn. (mem. various coms.), Am. Coll. Surgeons, Am. Soc. for Aesthetic Plastic Surgery, Am. Soc. Maxiofacial Surgery (pres. 2003-04), Am. Soc. Plastic and Reconstructive Surgery (mem. various coms.), Am. Soc. for Reconstructive Microsurgery, Argentine Soc. of Plastic Surgery, Children's Craniofacial Assn. (chmn. med. adv. bd.), Chirugio Soc., Craniofacial Biology Group, Dallas County Med. Soc., Dallas Soc. Plastic Surgery, Euro. Assn. for Craniomaxillofacial Surgery, Internat. Coll. Surgeons, Internat. Confederation for Plastic Reconstructive Surgery (founding mem.), Internat. Craniofacial Club, Internat. Craniofacial Travel Club, Internat. Soc. Clin. Plastic Surgery, Internat. Soc. Cranofacial Surgery (pres. 2001-03), Lipoplasty Soc. of N.A., Inc., Plastic Surgery Rsch. Coun. (chmn. 1978), Soc. for Biomaterials, Soc. Craniofacial Genetics, Soc. Head and Neck Surgery, So. Med. Assn., Southwestern Med. Found., Tex. Soc. Plastic Surgery (mem. various coms., pres.-elect 1982-83, pres. 1983-84), Tex. State Med. Assn., Wound Healing Soc, Craniofacial Surgery Fellowship (founder and dir. 1979-2006), Japanese Soc. Craniofacial Surgery, World craniofacial Found. (founder and chmn. 1990-), Am. Soc. Craniofacial Surgery (pres. 1996-99). Avocations: skiing, running, travel. Office Phone: 972-566-6669.

SALYER, STEPHEN LEE, educational program administrator; b. Lexington, Ky., July 20, 1950; s. Ralph Conley and Margaret Green C C Salyer; m. Susan D. Moeller; children: Samuel, Duncan, Clara stepchildren: Walden, Sethly. BA, Davidson Coll., 1972; MPA, Harvard U., 1975. Pres. Citizens' Com. on Population and the Am. Future, Washington, 1972-73; cons. Rockefeller Family Assocs., NYC, 1973-75; assoc. pub. issues program Population Coun., NYC, 1977-79; asst. to the pres. Ednl. Broadcasting Corp., Sta. WNET TV, NYC, 1975-76, v.p. corp. affairs, 1979-80, v.p. program devel. and mktg., 1981-82, sr. v.p. edn. divsn., 1982-86, sr. v.p. mktg. and comm., 1986-88; pres., CEO Pub. Radio Internat., Mpls., 1988—2005, Salzurb Global Sem., Washington, 2005—; also bd. dirs. Salzurb Sem., 2005—, think tank pres. Chmn. bd. dirs. Pub. Interactive, LLC, 1999—2005. Co-author: (with James J. Bausch) Toward Safe, Convenient and Effective Contraceptives, 1978. Mem. Nat. Commn. on Population Growth and the Am. Future, Washington, 1970—72; bd. dirs. Guidestar, Inc., 2001—, Davidson Coll., 2004—; fellow Japan Soc. US-Japan Leadership, 1996. Root-Tilden scholar, NYU Sch. Law, 1976—79, Salzburg Seminar fellow, 1974, Brit.-Am. Program fellow, 1990. Mem. Harvard Club (N.Y.C.). Home: 9510 Midwood Rd Silver Spring MD 20910 Office: 1828 L St NW Washington DC 20036

SALZ, JAMES JOSEPH, medical association administrator; m. Judith Salz; children: James, Mark. MD, Duke U., SC, 1965. Diplomate Am. Bd. Ophthalmology, Calif., 1972. Pres. Laser Vision Med. Assocs., Beverly Hills, Calif., 1972—. Recipient Lifetime Achievement award, Am. Acad. Ophthalmology, 2008. Office: Laser Vision Med Assocs 240 Southern La Cienega Blvd 250 Beverly Hills CA 90211 E-mail: drsalz@drsalz.com.

SALZBERG, BARRY F., accounting firm executive; b. Oct. 21, 1953; m. Evelyn Salzberg. BS in Acctg., Bklyn. Coll., 1974; JD, Bklyn. Law Sch., 1977; LLM in Taxation, NYU. Joined Deloitte & Touche USA LLP, 1977—, ptnr., 1985—96, tri-state group mng. ptnr., 1996—99, nat. tax dep. mng. ptnr., 1999—2000, nat. tax mng. ptnr., 2000—03, US mng. ptnr., 2003—07, CEO, 2007—. Chmn. bd. YMCA Greater NY, 2004—07; bd. mem. Jackie Robinson Found. Recipient CEO Diversity Leadership award, Bus. Women's Network, 2004. Mem.: AICPA, NY County Lawyers Assn., NY State Soc. CPAs, NY State Bar Assn. Office: Deloitte & Touche USA LLP 1633 Broadway New York NY 10019-6754 Office Phone: 212-492-3688.*

SALZBURG, BRUCE A., state attorney general; b. Mass., 1947; m. Phyllis Salzburg; 2 children. AB in Econs., U. Miami, 1972, JD, 1975. Bar: Wyo. 1978, Wyo. Supreme Ct., US Supreme Ct., US Ct. Appeals (10th cir.), US Ct. Appeals, DC, US Ct. Fed. Claims, US Dist. Ct. Wyo., US Dist. Ct., Colo. With US Army Security Agency, West Berlin, Germany, 1965—69; sr. asst. atty. gen. State of Wyo., 1979—83, atty. gen., 2007—; pvt. practice Wyo., 1983—2007. Mem.: Wyo. Trial Lawyers Assn., Defense Rsch. Inst., Am. Inns of Ct. Democrat. Office: Office of Atty Gen 123 Capitol Bldg 200 W 24th St Cheyenne WY 82002 Office Phone: 307-777-7841. Office Fax: 307-777-6869.*

SALZER, JAMES, biology professor; s. Peter and Doris Salzer; m. Barbara Hempstead, Sept. 9, 1982; children: Rebecca, Abigail. BSc, Stanford U., Palo Alto, Calif., 1973; MD, Wash. U., St. Louis, PhD, 1980. Diplomate Am. Bd. Neurology and Psychiatry, 1986. MS COE co-dir. NY U. Sch. Medicine, NYC, MSTP dir., 1997—2004, prof., cell biology and neurology, 1999—. Recipient Stephen C. Reingold award, Nat. Multiple Sclerosis Soc., 2007; Irma T. Hirschl grant, 1994. Office: NY Univ Sch Medicine 522 1st Ave New York NY 10016

SALZMAN, ARTHUR GEORGE, retired architect; b. Chgo., June 20, 1929; s. Russell Harvey Salzman and Mildred Olive (Olsen) Erickson; m. Joan Marie Larson, Aug. 16, 1952; children: Lisa Jo Salzman Braucher, David Ralph. BS in Archtl. Engring., U. Ill., 1952; MArch, Ill. Inst. Tech., 1960. Nat. Coun. Archtl. Registration Bds. Architect Skidmore, Owings & Merrill, Chgo., 1960, Mies van der Rohe, Arch., Chgo., 1960-69; assoc. The Office of Mies Van Der Rohe, Chgo., 1969-81; v.p. FCL Assocs., Chgo., 1981-86; exec. v.p. Lohan Assocs., Chgo., 1986-91; pvt. practice Evanston, Ill., 1992—2007; cons., 2007. Bldg. code restructuring com. City of Chgo., 1994-96, bldg. code electronic version com., 1997, bldg. code rev. com., 1998-2004; adj. prof. arch. Ill. Inst. Tech., Chgo., 2005-06. V.p. Chgo. area Unitarian-Universalist Coun., Chgo., 1974—76; bd. dirs. Savoy-aires, Evanston, Ill., 1985—88, 1990—93, pres., 1992—93; active Chgo. Com. on High Rise Bldgs. Emeritus cpl. US Army, 1952—54. Mem. AIA (bd. dirs. Chgo. chpt. 1992-96, sec. 1994-96, Ill. region bd., alt. del. 1997-98, del. 1999-2000, emeritis 2007—, Disting. Svc. award for profl. excellence 2003), Am. Soc. Testing and Materials Internat., Constrn. Specifications Inst. (emeritus 2007—), Internat. Code Coun. (profl.), Precast-Prestressed Concrete Inst., North Shore Musicians Club. Avocations: acting, singing, writing. Personal E-mail: salzmanagev@sbcglobal.net.

SALZMAN, DAVID ELLIOT, entertainment industry executive; b. Bklyn., Dec. 1, 1943; s. Benjamin and Rose Harriet (Touby) S.; m. Sonia Camelia Gonsalves, Oct. 19, 1968; children: Daniel Mark, Andrea Jessica, Adam Gabriel. BA, Bklyn. Coll., 1965; MA, Wayne State U., 1967. Dir. TV ops. Wayne State U., 1966-67; producer Lou Gordon Program, 1967-70; program mgr. Sta. WKBD-TV, Detroit, 1970-71, Sta. KDKA-TV, Pitts., 1971-72, gen. mgr., 1973-75; program mgr. Sta.

KYW-TV, Phila., 1972-73; chmn. bd. Group W Prodns., NYC and Los Angeles, 1975—; founder, pres. United Software Assocs., 1980-81; creator News Info. Weekly Service, 1981; exec. v.p. Telepictures Corp., 1980-84, vice chmn., 1984; pres. Lorimar Telepictures Corp. (merger Telepictures and Lorimar, Inc.), 1985-90, Lorimar TV, 1986-90; creator Newscope: Nat. TV News Cooperative, 1983; pres., CEO David Salzman Entertainment, Burbank, Calif., 1990-93; co-CEO Quincy Jones-David Salzman Entertainment (QDE), 1993—; exec. prodr. Jenny Jones Show, 1991—2003; CEO Epi Ctr. Ventures LLC, 2000. Exec. prodr. Mad-TV, 1995—2009, The Rerun Show, Jumble, In the House, 68th Ann. Acad. awards, Concert of the Americas, 1995, Vibe-TV, 1997-98, Steel, 1997, Their Eyes Were Watching God, 2005; CEO David Salzman Enterprises, 1998—; co-owner Vibe Mag., 1995-2006, Spin Mag., 1995-2006, Sta. WNOL-TV, 1995, Sta. WATL-TV, 1995, Sta. KCWE-TV, 1995-2006, Sta. WGRB-TV, 1998, Franklin Mint & Morgan Mint, 2006-; guest lectr. at schs.; bd. govs. Films of Coll. and Univ. Students; co-prodr. (Broadway shows) Urinetown, The Dinner Party, 2001, Into the Woods, 2002. Contbr. articles to profl. jours. Bd. dirs. Pitts. Civic Light Opera, Am. Blood Bank, Pitts., Hebrew Inst., Jewish Community Ctr., Harrison, NY, Temple Etz Chaim, USC Sch. Cinema-TV, Emory U. Ctr. Leadership, Emory Bus. Sch., Bklyn. Coll. Found., HELP group; co-founding bd. mem. AMGEN Tour Calif., Tour Calif. Cycling Race, 2006, 07, 08, 09. Recipient award Detroit chpt. Am. Women in Radio and TV, 1969, award Golden Quill, 1971, award Golden Gavel, 1971, local Emmy award, 1972, award AP, 1974, Gold medal Broadcast Promotion Assn., 1983, Lifetime Achievement award Bklyn. Coll., 1990, Disting. Alumnus award, Golden Plate award Am. Acad. Achievement, 1995, Ovation award, Wayne State U.; BPME Gold medal San Francisco Film Festival, 1984, N.Y., 1985, Chgo., 1986, Tree of Life award Jewish Nat. Fund, 1988. Mem. Acad. TV Arts and Scis., Nat. Assn. TV Program Execs., Radio-TV News Dirs. Assn., Am. Mgmt. Assn., Am. Film Inst., Brooklyn Coll. Found. Office: Sunset Bronson Studio 5800 sunset Blvd Bldg 10 2nd Fl Hollywood CA 90028 Office Phone: 323-762-8116. Business E-Mail: davids@madtv.com. *"Be prepared."*

SALZMAN, MICHELE RENEE, historian, educator; b. Bklyn., Aug. 2, 1952; d. Aron and Sylvia Salzman; m. Steven Gregory Brint, 1985; children: Juliana, Benjamin. BA, Bklyn. Coll. CUNY, 1973; MA, Bryn Mawr Coll., 1975, PhD, 1981. Classics lectr. Swarthmore (Pa.) Coll., 1980; vis. asst. prof. classics Columbia U., NYC, 1980-82; asst. prof. classics Boston U., 1982-90, assoc. prof. classics, 1990-95; assoc. prof. history U. Calif., Riverside, 1995—2000, prof., 2000—, chair history dept., 1999—2000, mem. steering com. multi-campus rsch. group, 1999—. Project dir. Inst. for Antiquity and Christianity, Claremont Grad. U., 1999—. prof. in charge of Intercollegiate Ctr. for Classified Studies in Rome, 2003-04. Author: (book) On Roman Time: The Codex-Calendar of 354 and the Rhythms of Urban Life in Late Antiquity, 1990, The Making of a Christian Aristocracy: Social and Religious Change in the Western Roman Empire, 2002; mem. editl. bd.: Am. Jour. Archaeology; contbr. articles to profl. jours. Grantee Am. Philol. Soc., 1983; fellow Ctr. for Ideas and Soc., U. Calif., Riverside, 1996, Am. Coun. Learned Socs., 1983; Mellon Fellow in Classical Studies Am. Acad. Rome, 1986-87, Lucy Shoe Merritt Residence scholar, Am. Acad. Rome, 2008; recipient APA Outreach award, 2008 Mem. Am. Philol. Assn. (chair Colloquium on Late Antiquity 1993-97), Classical Assn. So. Calif., N.Am. Patristics Soc., Assn. for Ancient History, Phi Beta Kappa, U. Calif. (steering com.) Avocations: running, tennis, reading. Office: U Calif-Riverside Dept History Riverside CA 92521-0001 Home Phone: 909-625-2745; Office Phone: 951-827-1991. Business E-Mail: michele.salzman@ucr.edu.

SALZWEDEL, JACK C., insurance company executive; b. DeForest, Wis. m. Sarah Salzwedel; 4 children. BS, Wartburg Coll., 1982. Ins. sales positions through v.p. Am. Family Mut. Ins. Co., Madison, Wis., 1983—2000, v.p. personal lines div., 2000—03, v.p. life & health ins. ops., 2003—05, exec. v.p., 2005—06, pres., COO, 2007—. Office: Am Family Mut Ins Co 6000 American Pkwy Madison WI 53783

SAM, DAVID, federal judge; b. Hobart, Ind., Aug. 12, 1933; s. Andrew and Flora (Toma) S.; m. Betty Jean Brennan, Feb. 1, 1957 (dec. Aug. 2000); children: Betty Jean, David Dwight, Daniel Scott, Tamara Lynn, Pamela Rae, Daryl Paul, Angie, Sheyla; m. Bennie Lynn Malnar, Jan. 5, 2005. BS, Brigham Young U., 1957; JD, Utah U., 1960. Bar: Utah 1960, U.S. Dist. Ct. Utah 1966. Sole practice and ptnr., Duchesne, Utah, 1963-76; dist. judge State of Utah, 1976-85; judge U.S. Dist. Ct. Utah, Salt Lake City, 1985-97; chief judge U.S. Dist. Ct., Salt Lake City, 1997—99, sr. judge, 1999—. Atty. City of Duchesne, 1963-72; Duchesne County atty., 1966-72; commr. Duchesne, 1972-74; adv. com. Codes of Conduct of Jud. Conf. US, 1987-91, Jud. Coun. of 10th Cir., 1991-93; mem. US Del. to Romania, Aug. 1991. Chmn. Jud. Nomination Com. for Cir. Ct. Judge, Provo, Utah, 1983; bd. dirs. Water Resources, Salt Lake City, 1973-76. Served to capt. JAGC, USAF, 1961-63. Named Judge of Yr., Utah State Bar, 1999. Avocations: beekeeping, reading, sports. Office: US Dist Ct US Courthouse 350 S Main St Ste 441 Salt Lake City UT 84101-2180 Office Phone: 801-524-6190. Business E-Mail: david_sam@utd.uscourts.gov.

SAM, JOSEPH, retired university dean; b. Gary, Ind., Aug. 15, 1923; s. Andrew and Flora (Toma) S.; m. Frances Adickes, Sept. 11, 1945; children: Sherrie, Joseph A., Suzanne F. Student, Drake U., 1942-43; BS, U. SC, 1948; PhD, Kans. U., 1951. Sr. research chemist McNeil Labs., Phila., 1951-54; research group leader Bristol Labs., Syracuse, NY, 1955-57; sr. scientist E.I. duPont de Nemours & Co., Inc., 1957-59; faculty U. Miss., 1959-86, prof. pharm. chemistry, 1961-68, chmn. dept., 1963-68, dir. univ. research, 1968-81, asso. vice chancellor research, 1981-86; dean U. Miss. (Grad. Sch.), 1968-86. Fulbright lectr. Cairo U., 1965-66 Mem. Am. Pharm. Assn. (found. research achievement award in pharm. and medicinal chemistry 1968), Rho Chi, Phi Lambda Upsilon, Phi Kappa Phi. Home: PO Box 351 University MS 38677-0351 E-mail: jsam@olemiss.edu.

SAMANTA, BISWANATH, engineering educator; BTech with Honors, Indian Inst. Tech., Kharagpur, 1981, PhD, 1987. Asst. prof. Indian Inst. Tech., 1987—91; lectr. Sultan Qaboos U., Muscat, Oman, 1991—96, asst. prof., 1997—2001, acting head, dept. mech. engring., 1998—99, assoc. prof., 2001—07; vis. assoc. prof. U. NSW, Sydney, 2004; internat. vis. prof. Robert Morris U., Moon Township, Pa., 2005; vis. assoc. prof Villanova U., Pa., 2006, postdoc. rsch. faculty, 2007—09, adj. assoc. prof., 2008—, rsch. assoc. prof., 2009—. Contbr. scientific papers to profl. jours. (Best paper award, 1998). Numerous grants. Mem.: IEEE, ASME, ASNE, Engring. Medicine and Biology Soc., IEEE Computational Intelligence Soc. Office: Villanova Univ Mech Engring 800 Lancaster Ave Villanova PA 19085 Business E-Mail: biswanath.samanta@villanova.edu.

SAMAR, VINCENT JOSEPH, lawyer, philosophy lecturer; b. Syracuse, N.Y., Feb. 12, 1953; s. George Edward and Harriett Helen (Bejnarowicz) S. A.B. in Polit. Sci., Syracuse U., 1975, M.P.A., J.D., 1978; postgrad. in philosophy U. Chgo., 1979—. Bar: N.Y. 1980, U.S. Dist. Ct. (no. dist.) N.Y. 1980, Ill. 1983, U.S. Dist. Ct. (no. dist.) Ill. 1983, U.S. Ct. Appeals (7th cir.) 1983. Law clk. Libit, Lindaurv & Henry, Chgo., 1980-81; philosophy lectr. Roosevelt U., Chgo., 1981-82, St. Xavier Coll., Chgo., 1982-84, Loyola U., Chgo., 1984—; assoc. Foss, Schuman, Drake & Barnard, Chgo., 1983-85; research asst. Cottfield, Ungaretti, Harris & Slavin, Chgo., 1985—. Research asst. Transportation Negligence, 1984. Mem. ACLU, Chgo. Bar Assn., Ill. State Bar Assn., Beta Theta Pi. Office: Rochester Inst of Tech 96 Lomb Memorial Dr Rochester NY 14623 Home: 99 Idlewood Rd Rochester NY 14618

SAMARANAYAKE, V. A., science educator, director; s. Vanniarachchige William and Dona Chandrawathi Samaranayake; m. Yolanda Juico Juico, Dec. 20, 1984; children: Suraj Vindana, Chamal Ranjana. PhD, Kans. State U., Manhattan, 1983. Programmer Dept. Census and Stats., Colombo, 1973—77; vis. asst. prof. U. Cin., 1989—90; vis. scientist Internat. Rice Rsch. Inst., Los Banos, Philippines, 1990—91; assoc. prof. Mo. U. Sci. & Tech., Rolla, 1989—98, dir. grad. studies, 1998—, prof., 2003—. Mem. Optimist Club Rolla, 1996—2009; treas. Rolla Knights Soccer Club, 2006—09; pres. Rolla Area Youth Soccer League, 2007—09; alt. commr. southern dist. Mo. Youth Soccer Assn., St. Louis, 2008—09. Recipient Outstanding Student Advisor award, U. Mo., Rolla, 1998; grantee grant, Mo. Dept. Higher Edn., 2005—09; Rsch. grant, HHS, 1991, 1995, grant, Inst. Rsch. Poverty, 1994—95, Mo. Dept. Higher Edn., 1996—2003, Alcohol Beverage Med. Rsch. Found., 1997. Mem.: Mid-Mo. (ASA Chpt.) (pres. 1997—98), Am. Statis. Assn. (chpt. rep. coun. 1998—2002, dist. 4 vice chair 2004—06, chair elect 2009—, coun. chpts. 2009—). Office: Mo S & T 400 W 12th St Rolla MO 65409-0020 Office Phone: 573-341-4658. Business E-Mail: vsam@mst.edu.

SAMARANCH, JUAN ANTONIO (MARQUÉS DE SAMARANCH), former international sports organization executive; b. Barcelona, July 17, 1920; s. Francisco and Juana (Torelló) S.; widowed; children: Maria Teresa, Juan Antonio. Doctor honoris causa, several Internat. univs. With Spanish Olympic Com., from 1956, pres., 1967-70; hon. life pres. Internat. Olympic Com. Mem. internat. Olympic com., Lausanne, Switzerland, 1966-2001, v.p., 1974-78, pres., 1980-2001; pres. Caja de Pensiones para la Vejez y de Ahorros de Cataluña y Baleares, Spain, 1987; Spanish Ambassador to USSR and People's Republic of Mongolia, 1977-80; mcpl. councillor, Barcelona; nat. fel. for phys. edn. and sports, 1967-71; pres. Diputacion, Barcelona, 1973-77. Decorated Grand Croix.

SAMARDJIEV, IVAN JORDANOV, medical researcher; s. Jordan Michailov Samardjiev and Stefka Ilieva Boeva. MS in Vet. Biophysics, Moscow Vet. Acad., 1990. X-ray crystallography Pfizer Inc., Groton, Conn., 1997—, sr. rsch. assoc., 1998—. Achievements include research in X-ray crystallography, powder analysis and single crystal small molecules.

SAMARDZIC, VELJKO, engineering company executive, researcher; s. Radoje and Ljeposava Samardzic. BS in Mech. Engring., NJ. Inst. Tech., Newark, 2001, PhD in Mech. Engring., 2008. Tchg. and rsch. asst. NJ. Inst. Tech., 2001—08, faculty substitute, 2005—06; rsch. engr. Frontier Performance Polymers Corp., Dover, NJ, 2008—. Dir. Metro NY- NJ. ASM Internat., 2006—. Contbr. scientific papers. Mem. running programs:emerging profls. and advising student chpts. Metro NY-NJ ASM Internat., 2006—; pres. Metro NY -NJ ASM Internat. Student Chpt., Newark, 2001—02, Material Advantage Student Program NY-NJ Metro Area, Newark, 2002—07, Grad. Assn. Mech. Engring. Students, Newark, 2005—06. Recipient Excellence Tchg. award, 2004; fellowship, NJ. Sci. and Tech. Com., 2008—. Mem.: ASME, ASM Internat. NY-NJ Metro Chpt. (pres. local chpt. and serving bd. dirs. NY-NJ 2001—), Pi Tau SIgma Nat. Honor Soc. Mech. Engrs. (sec. local chpt. 2000—01), Tau Beta Pi Nat. Engring., Sigma Xi Sci. Rsch. Soc. (Cert. of Recognition 2007). Home: 292 Lawton Ave Apt 24 Cliffside Park NJ 07010

SAMARDZICH, BARB, automotive executive; BS in Mech. Engring., U. Fla.; MS in Mech. Engring., Carnegie Mellon U., Pitts.; MS in Engring. Mgmt., Wayne State U., Detroit. Various positions comml. nuclear fuel divsn. Westinghouse Electric Corp., 1981—90; various positions powertrain divsn. Ford Motor Co., 1990—98, chief prog. engr. F650/F750 Ford trucks, 1998—99, gulity dir. European ops. small/medium vehicle ctr., 1999—2000, chief engr. automatic transmision ops., 2000—02, exec. dir. small FWD & RWD vehicles, 2002—05, v.p. Ford Motor Co., 2005—, v.p. powertrain ops., 2005—08, v.p. global powertrain engring., 2008—. Recipient Women in Engring. Top Achievement award, Design News, 2004; named a Leading Woman in N.Am. Automotive Industry, Automotive News, 2005; named one of Most Influential Women in Bus., Crain's Detroit Bus. mag., 2007. Office: Ford Motor Co N Am Hdqs 1 American Rd Dearborn MI 48126 Business E-Mail: bsamardzich@ford.com.*

SAMAREL, ALLEN MARK, physician, biochemistry and cell biology educator; b. NYC, June 4, 1951; s. Victor and Dulcy (Saltiel) S.; m. Joan Werber, June 19, 1979; children: Michael, Darla. BS, Queens Coll., 1972; MD, Harvard U., 1976. Resident Mt. Sinai Hosp., NYC, 1976-79; fellow Northwestern U. Med. Sch., Chgo., 1979-82, asst. prof., 1982-85, assoc. prof., 1985-88; prof. Loyola U., Chgo., 1988—, dir. rsch. Cardiovasc. Inst., 1994—. Chmn. clin. scis. study sect. NIH, Washington, 1991-94. Recipient Rsch. Ctr. Devel. award NHLBI/NIH, 1985-90. Fellow Am. Heart Assn. (basic sci. coun.), Internat. Soc. for Heart Rsch.; mem. Am. Soc. for Cell Biology. Office: Loyola U Med Ctr 2160 S 1st Ave Maywood IL 60153-3304 Office Phone: 708-327-2821.

SAMARTINI, JAMES ROGERS, retired appliance company executive; b. Cleve., Apr. 13, 1935; s. Leonard Henry and Grace Rogers (Tully) S.; m. Irene Ann Kurnava, Sept. 16, 1961 (dec. June 1994); m. Julia S. Rubin, Sept. 8, 1996; children: David L., James F., Patrick R. AB, Dartmouth Coll., 1957; MBA, Harvard U., 1961. Fin. supr. Ford Motor Co., Dearborn, Mich., 1966-72; v.p. fin. and adminstrn. Thonet Industries Inc., York, Pa., 1972-74; from asst. controller to v.p., CFO Mead Corp., Dayton, 1974-86; CFO Whirlpool Corp., 1986-91, exec. v.p., chief adminstrv. officer Benton Harbor, Mich., 1991-95; ret., 1995. Bd. dirs. Peoples State Bank, St. Joseph, Mich., 1987-95. Trustee, treas. Marvelwood Sch., 2004—; mem. adv. bd. Salvation Army; chmn. bd. trustees Whirlpool Found., 1993—95; trustee Dayton Opera Assn., 1977—86, pres., 1985—86; bd. dirs. Epilepsy Assn. We. Ohio, 1986, S.W. Mich. Symphony Orch., 1991—93; mem. bd. fin. Town of Kent (Conn.), 1999—2005, mem. zoning bd. appeals, 2001—. Mem.: Kent. Libr. Assn. (bd. dirs., treas. 2002—05), Fin. Execs. Inst. (bd. dirs. 1983—86). Home: PO Box 129 South Kent CT 06785-0129

SAMBERG, ANDY, actor; b. Berkeley, Calif., Aug. 18, 1978; Grad., U. Calif., Santa Cruz, NYU Film School. Co-founder, mem. The Lonely Island, NYC, 2001—. Writer G-Phoria, 2004, MTV Movie Awards, 2004, 2005; actor: (TV special) Comedy Central Laughs for Life Telethon, 2004; (TV series) Saturday Night Live, 2005—; (films) Hot Rod, 2007, (voice) Space Chimps, 2008, I Love You, Man, 2009; guest appearances (TV series) 40 Most Awesomely Bad Dirrty Songs...Ever, 2004, Arrested Development, 2005, Premium Blend, 2005, The Late Show with David Letterman, 2006, Conan O'Brien, 2006. Recipient WIRED Rave Award - TV, 2006. Office: United Talent Agency Inc 9560 Wilshire Blvd Ste 500 Beverly Hills CA 90212 Office Phone: 310-273-6700. Office Fax: 310-247-1111.

SAMBI, PIETRO, archbishop; b. Sogliano al Rubicone, Italy, June 27, 1938; DST, PhD in Sacred Theology, Canon Law. Ordained priest, 1964; with Diplomatic Corps of Holy See, Cameroon, 1969, Apostolic Nunciature, Jerusalem, 1971, Cuba, 1974, Algeria, 1975, Nicaragua, 1979, Belgium, 1981, counselor India, 1984; ordained bishop, 1985; archbishop, Apostolic Pro-Nuncio to Burundi, 1985—91; archbishop, Apostolic Pro-Nuncio to Indonesia, 1991—98; archbishop, Apostolic Nuncio to Cyprus, 1998—2005; archbishop, Apostolic Nuncio to Israel, 1998—2005; archbishop, Apostolic Nuncio to Jerusalem and Palestine, 1998—2005; archbishop, Apostolic Nuncio to USA, 2005—. Apostolic delegation Jesusalem & Palestine, Algeria, 1978. Roman Catholic. Office: Nunciature to USA 3339 Mass Ave NW Washington DC 20008

SAMBORA, RICHIE (RICHARD STEPHEN SAMBORA), musician, singer, songwriter; b. Perth Amboy, NJ, July 11, 1959; s. Adam and Joan Sambora; m. Heather Locklear, Dec. 17, 1994 (div. Apr. 11, 2007); 1 child, Ava Elizabeth. LHD, Kean U., 2004. Musician of various bands including Screaming Mimis, Mercy, The Next, Message, and Duke Williams & The Extremes; guitarist, vocalist, songwriter Bon Jovi, 1983—. Musician: (solo albums) Stranger In This Town, 1991, Undiscovered Soul, 1994; musician, vocalist (albums) Bon Jovi, 1984, 7800 Fahrenheit, 1985, Slippery When Wet, 1986, Bon Jovi Live, 1987, New Jersey, 1988, Keep the Faith, 1992, Crossroad, 1994, These Days, 1995, Bon Jovi, 1999, Crush, 2000, Bounce, 2002, Distance, 2003, This Left Feels Right, 2003, 100,000,000 Bon Jovi Fans Can't Be Wrong, 2004, Have a Nice Day, 2005, cameo appearances (films) Staying Alive, 1983, On The Line, 2001, guest appearances American Dreams, 2003. Avocations: watching sporting events, including football, basketball, and boxing, jet-skiing, fishing, golf.

SAMEC, DIANE PATRICIA, retired elementary school educator; b. Oak Pk., Ill., Mar. 17, 1942; d. Albert Vincent Samec and Helen Hrubec. BA, Hope Coll., Holland, Mich., 1964; MSc in edn., No. Ill. U., DeKalb, 1988. Tchr. Interboro Schools, Glenolden, Pa., 1964—65, Sch. Dist. u-46, Elgin, Ill., 1966—2004; ret., 2004. Vol. and mem. Willow Creek Cmty. Ch., South Barrington, 1986—, Sherman Hosp. Aux. Ch., Elgin, 2004—. Mem.: Nat. Audubon Soc., Elgin Ret. Teachers Assn., Elgin Edn. Assn., Ill. Edn. Assn., Nat. Edn. Assn., Willow Creek Comm. Ch., Nat. Wildlife Assn., Environ. Def., Sierra Club, Fox Valley Beaux Arts Women's Club. Avocations: travel, reading, photography.

SAMELSON, LAWRENCE ELLIOT, medical researcher; b. Chgo., Apr. 18, 1951; s. Charles F. and Natalie (Rudeis) S.; m. Elizabeth Trosman, June 8, 1980; children: Seth Aaron, Rebecca Ellen. BA, U. Rochester, 1972; MD, Yale U., 1977. Resident in internal medicine U. Chgo. Hospitals, 1977-80; rsch. assoc. Lab. Immunology Nat. Inst. Allergy and Infectious Diseases, NIH, Bethesda, Md., 1980-85; sr. staff fellow Cell Biology and Metabolism Br., Nat. Inst. Child Health and Human Devel., NIH, Bethesda, 1985-87, named sr. investigator, 1988, chief Sect. Lymphocyte Signaling, 1995, dep. branch chief, 1995; chief Lab. Cellular and Molecular Biology Ctr. Cancer Rsch., Nat. Cancer Inst. NIH, Bethesda, 1999—, dep. dir. Ctr. Cancer Rsch., Nat. Cancer Inst., 2006—. Contbr. articles to profl. publs. Achievements include research in T cell structure and function, T cell activation, and biochemistry of signal transduction. Office: Ctr Cancer Rsch Lab Cellular and Molecular Biology 37 Convent Dr Bldg 37 Rm 2066 Bethesda MD 20892-4256 Office Phone: 301-496-9683. Office Fax: 301-496-8479. E-mail: samelson@helix.nih.gov.

SAMET, DEE-DEE, lawyer; BA, U. Ariz., 1962, JD, 1963. Bar: Ariz. 1964. Pvt. practice, Tucson, 1974—. Arbitrator U.S. Dist. Ct. Ariz., Gender Equality Task Force, 1993; judge pro tem Pima County Superior Ct., 1985—; Ninth Cir. Lawyer rep., 1990-93; mem. Jud. Performance Rev. Commn., 1996-99; pres. Casa de los Ninos, 2003-05. Mem. Fed. Bar Assn. (pres. Tucson chpt. 2004—), State Bar Ariz. (family law sect., workers compensation sect., trial law sect., co-chair workers compensation sect. 1988-89, gender bias task force, bd. govs. 1994-97, pres. 1999-2000, chair workers compensation sect. 2004, chair alternative dispute resolution sect. 2005-06), Am. Arbitration Assn. (nat. panel arbitrators, com. on exams., supreme ct. state Ariz. 1984-91), Pima County Bar Assn. (bd. dirs. 1994—, pres. 2007-), Nat. Assn. Counsel for Children, Ariz. Assn. Counsel for Children, So. Ariz. Women Lawyers Assn. (bd. dirs. 1990, pres. 1994-95, treas. alt. dispute resolution sect. 2003-04), Nat. Orgn. Social Security Claimants' Reps., Inn of Cts. Office: Dee-Dee Samet PC 717 N 6th Ave Tucson AZ 85705-8304 Office Phone: 520-624-8595. Business E-Mail: dee-dee@samet.psemoil.com.

SAMET, JACK I., lawyer; b. NYC, Aug. 6, 1940; s. William and Tillie (Katz) Samet; m. Helen Ray, Feb. 12, 1967; 1 child, Peter Lawrence. BA, Columbia U., 1961; JD, Harvard U., 1964. Bar: N.Y. 1964, Calif. 1973. Assoc. Whitman & Ransom, NYC, 1966-69, Hall, Casey, Dickler & Howley, NYC, 1969-73; ptnr. Ball, Hunt, Hart, Brown & Baerwitz, LA, 1973-81, Buchalter, Nemer, Fields & Younger, LA, 1981-94, Baker & Hostetler, LA, 1994—2006, active ret. ptnr., 2007—, mem. policy com., 1997-98, ptnr.-in-charge, 1997-98. Arbitrator Nat. Assn. Securities Dealers, LA, 1976—2003; spkr., panelist Calif. Continuing Edn. Bar, 1988. Actor: Playhouse W., 2005—07, Beverly Hills Playhouse, 2007—, Good Time Max, Amour, It's Another Beautiful Day, Empty Apartment, Welcome Home Soldier, A Midsummer Night's Dream, 2009, Cinema Solutions. Named a So. Calif. Superlawyer, 2004—09. Mem.: ABA, NY Bar Assn., Calif. Bar Assn., Screen Actor's Guild, Am. Bd. Trial Advs., Million Dollar Advs. Forum, Sport Club/LA. Avocations: exercise, reading, acting. Home: 2741 Aqua Verde Cir Los Angeles CA 90077-1502 Office: Baker Hostetler 600 Anton Blvd Ste 900 Costa Mesa CA 92626 Personal E-mail: jsamet@belairmail.com. Business E-Mail: jsamet@bakerlaw.com.

SAMET, JONATHAN MICHAEL, epidemiologist, educator; b. Va., Mar. 26, 1946; BA in Chemistry and Physics, Harvard Coll., 1966; MD, U. Rochester, 1970; MS in Epidemiology, Harvard Sch. Pub Health, 1977. Diplomate Am. Bd. Internal Medicine, Nat. Bd. Med. Examiners. Intern in medicine U. Ky. Med. Ctr., Lexington, 1970-71; asst. resident in medicine U. N.Mex. Affiliated Hosps., Albuquerque, 1973-74, sr. resident, 1974-75; rsch. fellow in clin. epidemiology Channing lab. Harvard Med. Sch., Boston, 1975-78, rsch. assoc. in medicine, 1978-83; epidemiologist Cancer Rsch. and Treatment Ctr. U. N.Mex., Albuquerque, 1980-87, asst. prof. medicine, 1978-82, assoc. prof. medicine, 1982-88, assoc. prof. family, cmty., and emergency medicine, 1985-88, prof. family, cmty., and emergency medicine, 1986-94, prof. medicine, 1988-94, clin. prof. medicine, 1994—; prof., chmn. dept. epidemiology The Johns Hopkins U., Balt., 1994—, co-dir. risk scis. and pub. policy inst., 1995—; dept. preventive medicine, dir. U. Southern Calif., Inst. Global Health. Chief pulmonary divsn. U. N.Mex Hosp., Albuquerque, 1985—94, chief pulmonary and critical care divsn. dept. medicine,

1985—94; mem. indoor air quality and total human exposure com., sci. adv. bd. US EPA, 1987—95, 2007—, clean air sci. adv. com. chmn., 2008—; chmn. biol. effects ionizing radiation VI com. NRC, 1994—98, mem. bd. environ. studies and toxicology, 2002, chmn., 2003—09, chmn. com. rsch. priorities airborne particulate matter, 1998—2004; chmn. Inst. Medicine, 1997, chmn. com. asbestos, 2004—06, chmn. com. evaluation presumptive disability decision making process for vets., 2006—; co-dir. Inst. Global Tobacco Control, 1998—; chmn. epidemiology and disease control study sect. 2 NIH, 2002. Editor pro tem Am. Jour. of Epidemiology, 1991—92; editor: Am. Jour. of Epidemiology, 1992—98; assoc. editor Tobacco Control: An Internat. Jour., 1991—; editor: Epidemiologic Revs., 1994—2002, Epidemiology, 2002—07; co-editor-in-chief: Air Quality, Atmosphere and Health, 2007—. With US Army, 1971—73. Recipient Clinton P. Anderson award, Am. Lung Assn., N.Mex, 1988, Excellence in Environ. Health Rsch. award, Rochester Sch. Medicine and Dentistry, 2006, Distinguished Alumni award, U. Rochester, 2006, Tobacco Day award, WHO, 2007. Fellow: AAAS, Am. Coll. Epidemiology (pres. 2000—01, Surgeon Gen.'s medallion 2006); mem.: Am. Cancer Soc. (co-chair com. cancer and environment 2008—), US EPA (clean air sci. adv. com., sci. adv. bd. 2007—), Md. Thoracic Soc., Internat. Soc. Indoor Air Quality and Climate, Internat. Epidemiol. Assn., N.Mex. Thoracic Soc. (sec.-treas. 1982—83, v.p. 1983—84, pres. 1984—85), Am. Thoracic Soc. (long range planning com. environ. and occupational health assembly 1992—, program com. behavioral scis. sect. 1994—95, Pub. Svc. award 2006), Soc. for Epidemiol. Rsch. (pres.-elect 1988—89, exec. com. 1988—91, pres. 1989—90), Delta Omega Alpha, Alpha Omega Alpha. Office: Keck Sch Medicine Univ Southern Calif 1441 Eastlake Ave NIT 4436 Los Angeles CA 90008-9175 Office Phone: 323-865-0803. Personal E-mail: jsamet@aol.com. Business E-Mail: jsamet@usc.edu.

SAMET, NACHUM, retired dental educator; b. Haifa, Israel, Mar. 11, 1959; m. Naama Rubinstein, Aug. 20, 1985; children: Dor, Omer, Yuval. DMD, Hebrew U., Jerusalem, 1987. Cert. prosthodontist Israel, 1992. Dir., removable partial dentures Hebrew U., Hadassah Sch. Dental Medicine, 1991—94, dir., fixed partial denture and occlusion, 1992—94, co-dir., removable dentures, 2000—02, dir., removable partial dentures, 2000—02; dir., multidisciplinary dental clinic Maccabi Healthcare Orgn., Ramat Hasharon, Israel, 1994—2001, Raanana, Israel, 2001—02; dir., doctoral prosthodontics Harvard U., Sch. Dental Medicine, Boston, 2003—, instr. restorative dentistry and biomaterials scis., 2002—06, asst. prof. restorative dentistry & biomaterials scis., 2006—. Recipient Rector's award for Best Tchg., Hebrew U., 1991—92, Dean's award, 1991—93, 2001—02, Best Lectr. prize, Israel Soc. Prosthetic Dentistry, 1992, Best Tchr. award, Harvard U., 2004, 2006, 2007—08, Disting. Faculty award, 2006; named one of Best Tchrs. of Yr., 2007. Mem.: Internat. Assn. Dental Rsch., Am. Dental Edn. Assn., Am. Acad. Periodontology, Acad. Osseointegration, Israel Soc. Prosthetic Dentistry, Israel Dental Assn., Omicorn Kappa Upsilon. Office: Harvard Univ 188 Longwood Ave Boston MA 02115 Business E-Mail: nachum_samet@hsdm.harvard.edu.

SAMFILIPPO, CHRIS MARTIN, finance educator, consultant; b. Wyandotte, Mich., July 14, 1956; s. Charles and Youly Samfilippo; m. Kim Lou Unger, Sept. 1, 1979; 1 child, Allyson Rae. MBA, Wayne State U., Detroit, 1996. Lectr. III U. Mich., Dearborn, 1998—; v.p. mktg., cons. Hybra-Drive Sys., LLC, Deerfield, 2006—. Cons. CS, LLC, Allen Pk., Mich., 2003—. Mem.: Am. Mktg. Assn. (faculty advisor collegiate chpt. 2006—08). Conservative. Office: Univ Mich Dearborn 19000 Hubbard Dr FCS 12A Dearborn MI 48126 Home Fax: 313-271-9836. Business E-Mail: cmsam@umd.umich.edu.

SAMFORD, YETTA GLENN, JR., lawyer, director; b. Opelika, Ala., June 8, 1923; s. Yetta Glenn and Mary Elizabeth (Denson) S.; m. Mary Austill, Sept. 6, 1949; children: Mary Austill Lott, Katherine Park Alford, Yetta Glenn III (dec.). BS, Auburn U., Ala., 1947; LLB, U. Ala., Tuscaloosa, 1949, LLD (hon.), 1995; DHL (hon.), U. Mobile, Ala., 2001. Bar: Ala. 1949, U.S. Dist. Ct. (mid. dist.) Ala. 1950, U.S. Ct. Appeals (5th cir.) 1961, U.S. Ct. Appeals (11th cir.) 1981. Pvt. practice, Opelika, Ala.; ptnr. Samford & Denson LLP and Predessors, 1949—. Mem. Ala. Senate from Lee and Russell counties, 1958-62; mem. bd. edn.Opelika City, 1963-75, pres. 1966-74; mem. State of Ala. Bd. of Corrections, 1969-75; mem. adv. bd. State Docks, 1987-2000. Trustee U. Mobile, 1963-92, life trustee, 1992—, trustee U. Ala., 1972-93, trustee emeritus, 1993— Mem. Ala. Law Inst. (exec. com.), Ala. Acad. of Honor, Masons, Phi Delta Phi, Omicron Delta Kappa, Alpha Tau Omega. Republican. Baptist. Home: 615 Terracewood Dr Opelika AL 36801-3850 Office: Samford & Denson LLP PO Box 2345 Opelika AL 36803-2345 Office Phone: 334-745-3504. Personal E-mail: sdhpb@mindspring.com.

SAMI, SEDAT, civil engineering, educator; b. Istanbul, Turkey, Oct. 23, 1928; came to U.S., 1956; s. Huseyin and Neyire S.; m. Dagmar Elisabeth Ellwanger, June 9, 1958; children: Iskender, Elisabeth. Diplom Ingenieur, Tech. U. Istanbul, Turkey, 1951; MS in Mech. and Hydraulics, U. Iowa, 1957, PhD in Fluid Mechanics, 1966. Registered profl. engr., Ill. Design engr. Chas. T. Main, Inc., Turkey, 1951-52, asst. chief engr., 1952-55; chief desing engr. Eti Yapi Constrn. Co., Ltd., Ankara, Turkey, 1958-60, v.p. engring., 1960-61; asst. prof. civil engring. Mid. East Tech. U., Ankara, Turkey, 1961-63; asst. prof. engring. So. Ill. U., Carbondale, 1966-69, assoc. prof. engring. mechancis, 1969-72, prof. engring. mechanics, 1972—99, chmn. dept. civil engring. and mechanics, 1992—99, acting dean engring., 1998—99, prof. emeritus, 1999—. Co-author: Engineering Mechanics; Statics, 1994, Engineering Mechancis: Dynamics, 1994, Kavaklarda mikrofon var (in Turkish), 2002, Silent Capitulations, 2006, Sessiz Kapitulasyonlar, 2008; contbr. over 40 articles to profl. jours. including Jour. Fluid Mechancis, Jour. Hydraulic Engring. Adv. Ill. Gov.'s Sci. Adv. Com., Chgo., 1990-98. Lt. C.E., Turkish Army, 1955-56. Fellow ASCE. E-mail: sesami1@verizon.net.

SAMILJAN, KATRIANA, lawyer; b. Sacramento, Oct. 11, 1969; BA magna cum laude, Harvard Coll., Cambridge, Mass., 1991; JD, Harvard Law Sch., 1998. Former bankruptcy atty., Seattle; pvt. practice atty. Bush Strout & Kornfield, Seattle. Named Wash. Rising Star, SuperLawyer Mag., 2001—08. Mem.: ABA, Turnaround Mgmt. Assn., Am. Bankruptcy Inst., King Co. Bar Assn., Wash. State Bar Assn., Fed. Bar Assn. Office: Bush Strout and Kornfield 5000 Two Union Sq 601 Union St Seattle WA 98101-2373 Office Phone: 206-521-3857. Business E-Mail: ksamiljan@bskd.com.

SAMKOFF, LAWRENCE MARK, neurologist, educator; s. Max David and Francine June Samkoff; m. Sharon Hillary Stall, May 21, 1995; 1 child, Jordan Ted. BA, Amherst Coll., Mass., 1980; MD, NYU, Valhalla, 1984. Cert. in food allergy & anaphylaxis network Am. Acad. Neurology, Minn., 1999. Fellow Albert Einstein Coll. Medicine, Bronx, NY, 1989—92, asst. prof. neurology, 1989—92, NYU Med. Coll., Valhalla, 1992—2001; assoc. prof. neurology U. Rochester, NY, 2001—.

SAMMARCO, PAUL WILLIAM, ecologist, researcher; b. Hackensack, NJ, Oct. 18, 1948; s. Giacomo and Esther (Galanti) S.; m. Jean Sogioka, May 29, 1971 (div. 1996); children: Mimi Cecile, Dustin Paul, Jack Isao; m. Donna M. Melancon, Aug. 12, 1998; stepchildren: Lindsay Claire, Ben Charles. BA, Syracuse U., 1970, postgrad., 1970—71; cert., Marine Biology Lab., Woods Hole, Mass., 1971, Fairleigh Dickinson U., 1972; PhD, SUNY Stony Brook, 1977. Tchg. asst. Syracuse U., NY, 1970—71; tchg. asst. Discovery Bay Marine Lab. SUNY-Stony Brook Overseas Acad. Program, Jamaica, 1974; tchg. asst. SUNY, Stony Brook, 1971—77; asst. prof. Clarkson U., Potsdam, NY, 1977—79; vis. asst. prof. tropical ecology SUNY Potsdam, St. Croix, V.I., 1979; sr. rsch. scientist Australian Inst. Marine Sci., Townsville, Queensland, 1979—89; coord. Shelf Seas Rsch. Program, 1985—86; dir. environ. rsch. Resource Assessment Commn. Prime Minister's commn. on natural resources, Canberra, Australia, 1989—91; exec. dir. La. Univs. Marine Consortium, Chauvin, 1991—95, prof., 1995—. Adj. prof. La. State U., U. La. at Lafayette, 1992-2008, U. New Orleans, Nicholls State U., 1992-, U. Campinas-Brazil, 1997-99, Ctrl. Queensland U., Australia, 1997-2002, U. Maine at Orono, 2001—03; pres. Endless Shores Music Pubs.; pres. P&J Records, LLC. Composer, arranger, prodr. popular and sacred music; former mem. Australian Chamber Choir, Wesley Choir, Canberra; co-author: (with S. Kolian) Mariculture and Other Uses for Offshore Oil and Gas Platforms: Rationale for Retaining Infrastructure, 2005; editor: (with M.L. Heron) The Bio-Physics of Marine Larval Dispersal, 1994, Marine Biology (Berlin), 2000—, Aquatic Biology, 2007—; contbr. numerous articles to profl. jours.; editl. advisor Marine Ecology Progress Series, 1985-93; co-editor: Procs. 6th Internat. Coral Reef Symposium, 1988, Procs. 8th Internat. Coral Reef Symposium, Procs. Internat. BioIndicators Conf., Jour. Environ. Bioindicators, 2007. Mem. La. State Gov.'s Platform for Mariculture Task Force, 2004-05; mem. chancel choir First United Meth. Ch., Houma, La. Recipient Internat. Sci. Exch. award, 1988-89. Mem. ASCAP, Assn. Marine Labs. Caribbean (exec. dir.-elect), Australian Marine Scis. Assn. (keynote spkr. 1981, counselor 1984-89, chmn., organizer nat. conf. 1987, chmn. Australia Acad. Sci. Boden Conf. 1990), Internat. Soc. Reef Studies (counselor 1997-2000), Australian Coral Reef Soc., Sigma Xi. Office: La Univs Marine Consortium 8124 Highway 56 Chauvin LA 70344-2110 Office Phone: 985-851-2876. Business E-Mail: psammarco@lumcon.edu.

SAMMARTINO, JANIS LYNN, federal judge; b. Phila., 1950; AB, Occidental Coll., 1972; JD, U. Notre Dame, 1975. Bar: Calif. 1975. Law clk. to Hon. Douglas Seely Superior Ct., Joseph County, Ind., 1975—76; dep. city atty. San Diego City Atty.'s Office, 1976—94; judge Mcpl. Ct. of City of San Diego, 1994—95, Superior Ct. of San Diego County, 1995—2007, US Dist. Ct. (so. dist.) Calif., 2007—. Office: US Dist Ct 940 Front St San Diego CA 92101

SAMMET, JEAN E., computer scientist; b. NYC; d. Harry and Ruth S. BA, Mt. Holyoke Coll., Sc.D. (hon.), 1978; MA, U. Ill. Group leader programming Sperry Gyroscope, Great Neck, NY, 1955-58; sect. head, staff cons. programming Sylvania Electric Products, Needham, Mass., 1958-61; with IBM, 1961-88; adv. program mgr. Boston, 1961-65; program lang. tech. mgr. IBM, 1965-68; programming tech. planning mgr. Fed. Systems div., 1968-74, programming lang. tech. mgr., 1974-79, software tech. mgr., 1979-81, div. software tech. mgr., 1981-82, programming lang. tech. mgr., 1983-88; programming lang. cons. Bethesda, Md., 1989—. Chmn. history of computing com. Am. Fedn, Info. Processing Socs., 1977-79; mem. exec. com. Software Patent Inst., 1991—, edn. com., 1992—, chair edn. com., 1992-93; bd. dirs. Computer Mus., 1983-93. Author: Programming Languages: History and Fundamentals, 1969; editor-in-chief: Assn. Computing Machinery Computing Revs, 1979-87; contbr. articles to profl. jours. Recipient Fellow award, Computer History Mus., 2001. Fellow Assn. for Computing Machinery, 1994, (charter; pres. 1974-76, Disting. Svc. award 1985), Computer History Mus.; mem. NAE, Upsilon Pi Epsilon. Home and Office: 3124 Gracefield Rd Apt 311 Silver Spring MD 20904-5818

SAMMLER, ANNE MICHELLE, healthcare educator; b. Binghampton, NY, Oct. 1968; d. Robert (Stepfather) and Carol Anne Roach, Fredrick Thaddeus Mastine; m. Sean Edward Sammler, May 2, 1992; children: Aleni, Alexis. BS in Health Edn. summa cum laude, SUNY, Brockport, 2003. Aquinas CERT coord. Rochester City Fire Dept., cert. instr. ARC, tchr. NY. Co-chmn. Reading is Fundamental, Rochester, NY, 1998—2002; religious edn. instr. Sacred Heart Cathedral, Rochester, 1999—2002; health educator Aquinas Inst, Rochester, 2003—, red ribbon week coord., 2006, prom promise coord., 2007, AQ cert. points of distbn. mass ER vaccination coord., 2007. Team leader breast cancer walks Am. Cancer Soc., Rochester, 2004; team leader, vol. Spl. Olympics, Rochester, 2000; team leader, fund raiser Am. Heart Assn., Rochester, 2005, heart walk leader, 2007; mem. Operation Offence Section Team, 2007—; AQ unity Health Coord. Substance Edn. Program. Scholar, Health Sci. Dept., Brockport State U., 2003. Mem.: AAHPERD (corr.), Eta Sigma Gamma (corr.), Alpha Chi (life). Avocations: running, reading, canoeing. Office: Aquinas Inst 1127 Dewey Ave Rochester NY 14613 Business E-Mail: asammler@aquinasinstitute.com.

SAMMONS, JEFFREY LEONARD, foreign language educator; b. Cleve., Nov. 9, 1936; s. Harold Leonard and Therese (Herrmann) S.; m. Kathryn Josephine Stella, July 1958 (div. 1962); 1 child, Rebecca Kathryn Serabrini; m. Christa Ann Smith, Oct. 20, 1967; children: Charles Leonard, Harold Hawthorne, Benjamin Gardner. BA, Yale U., 1958, PhD, 1962. Instr., asst. prof. Brown U., Providence, 1961-64; asst. prof. German, Yale U., 1964-67, assoc. prof., 1967-69, prof., 1969—2001, prof. emeritus, 2002—, Leavenworth prof. German, 1979—2001; Craig vis. prof. German, Rutgers U.2003. Author: Heinrich Heine: The Elusive Poet, 1969, Six Essays on the Young German Novel, 1972, Literary Sociology and Practical Criticism, 1977, Heinrich Heine: A Modern Biography, 1979, Wilhelm Raabe: The Fiction of the Alternative Community, 1987, The Shifting Fortunes of Wilhelm Raabe, 1992, Ideology, Mimesis, Fantasy: Charles Sealsfield, Friedrich Gerstäcker, Karl May and Other German Novelists of America, 1998, Friedrich Spielhagen: Novelist of Germany's False Dawn, 2004, Heinrich Heine: Alternative Perspectives, 1985-2005, 2006, Kuno Franck's Edition of the Classics: A Critical & Historical Overview, 2009; translator: Heinrich Heine, Ludwig Borne, a Memorial, 2006. Guggenheim fellow, 1972-73, Am. Coun. Learned Socs. fellow, 1977-78, Travel grantee, 1983; Duke August Libr., Wolfenbuttel Ger. adoptive stipend, 1983. Mem. MLA, Am. Assn. Tchrs. German, Goethe Soc. N.Am., Conn. Acad. Arts and Scis., N.Am. Heine Soc. Home: 211 Highland St New Haven CT 06511-2001 Business E-Mail: jeffrey.sammons@yale.edu.

SAMMONS, MARY FRANCES, retail executive; b. Portland, Oreg., Oct. 12, 1946; d. Lee W. and Ann (Cherry) Jackson; m. Nickolas F. Sammons, Sept. 12, 1967; 1 child, Peter. BA, Marylhurst Coll., Oreg., 1970. Buyer Fred Meyer Inc., Portland, 1975-80, v.p., merchandiser, 1980-85, sr. v.p. apparel & home electronics group, 1996, exec. v.p., apparel, home & home electronics group, 1997—98; pres. Fred Meyer Stores, Portland, 1998, pres., CEO, 1999; pres., COO Rite Aid Corp., Camp Hill, Pa., 1999—2003, pres., CEO, 2003—07, chmn., pres., CEO, 2007—08, chmn., CEO, 2008—. Pres. Rite Aid Found.; bd. dirs. Rite Aid Corp., 1999—, StanCorp Financial Group, Inc., 2008—, First Horizon Nat. Corp.; chmn. Nat. Assn. Chain Drug Stores. Recipient Woman of Achievement award, YWCA, Portland, 1987; named one of The 100 Most Powerful Women, Forbes mag., 2005—09, 50 Most Powerful Women in Bus., Fortune mag., 2006, 2007, 50 Women to Watch, Wall St. Jour., 2006. Mem. Am. Mgmt. Assn. Office: Rite Aid Corp 30 Hunter Ln Camp Hill PA 17011 Office Phone: 717-761-2633. Business E-Mail: msammons@riteaid.com.*

SAMMONS, MORGAN TAYLOR, psychologist; b. Waldport, Oreg., Feb. 17, 1954; s. William Marland and Peggy Ann Sammons. BS in fgn. svc., Georgetown U., 1975; M in counseling, Ariz. State U., 1983, PhD, 1989. Bd. dir. Nat. Register of Health Svc. Providers in Psychology, Washington; psychopharmacology curriculum cons. Nova Southeastern U., Ft Lauderdale, Fla., 2001—, Fairleigh Dickinson U., Teaneck, NJ, 2000—, Alliant Internat. U., San Francisco, 1999—; adj. asst. prof. Uniformed Svcs. U. Health Sci., 2002; assoc. editor Psychol. Svcs. Editor: (book) Combined Treatments for Mental Disorders: A Guide to Psychological and Pharmacological Interventions, 2001, Prescriptive Authority for Psychologists: A History and Guide, 2003; contbr. articles to profl. jours. Capt. USN. Fellow: APA (rep. to APA coun. divsn. 55 2002—, mem. divsns. 19, 31, 42, 55, presdl. citation 1994, 1996, 2000, Karl Heiser award 2004, disting. contrbn.in pub. sector award 2005), Md. Psychol. Assn. (pres. 2001—02, Tchr. of Yr. 1998), Nat. Acads. Practice. Avocations: conservation, skiing, backpacking. Personal E-mail: msammons@mindspring.com.

SAMOCHA, TZACHI MATZLIACH, research and development company executive, director; married. PhD, Tel Aviv U., 1980. Dir. R & D AgriLife Rsch., Corpus Christi, Tex., 1988—. Regents fellow, Tex. A & M Sys., 2006. Office: AgriLife Rsch Mariculture Lab 4301 Waldron Rd Corpus Christi TX 78418 Business E-Mail: t-samocha@tamu.edu.

SAMOJLIK, EUGENIUSZ, medical educator, health facility administrator; b. Kuchmy-Bialystok, Poland, Aug. 20, 1933; s. Michael and Anastazia S.; m. Anna Morozewicz, Apr. 10, 1965; children: Dorothy, Michael. BS in Biomedicine, U. Warsaw, 1958, PhD in Reproductive Endocrinology, 1964. Rsch. asst. Maternity Inst. Dept. Pharmacology, Warsaw, 1958-62, sr. asst., 1962-66; asst. prof., chief reproductive pharmacology & toxicology Inst. Pharmacy Dept. Pharmacology, Warsaw, 1966-70; assoc. prof., chief hormone rsch. lab. Med. Acad. Dept. Clin. Endocrinology, Warsaw, 1970-73; staff rschr. II Syntex, Inc. Rsch. Divsn., Palo Alto, Calif., 1974-75; asst. prof. physiology, dir. radioimmunoassay lab. Milton S. Hershey (Pa.) Med. Ctr., Divsn. Endocrinology, 1975-80; staff endocrinologist VA Med. Ctr. Dept. Medicine, Sect. Endocrinology, East Orange, NJ, 1980-82; dir. endocrine lab. Newark Beth Israel Med. Ctr., Dept. Medicine, 1982-92; assoc. prof. medicine divsn. endocrinology U. Medicine & Dentistry-N.J. Med. Sch., Newark, 1982—; chief endocrine lab. dept. Labs. NBIMC, 1994-96. Vis. researcher UCLA Sch. Medicine, Torrance, Calif., 1973; vis. scientist Nat. Inst. Child Health Human Devel., Reproductive Br., Bethesda, Md., 1973-74; lectr. in field. Mem. internat. adv. bd. Jour. Assisted Reproductive Tech. and Andrology, mem. editorial bd., 1996; contbr. articles to profl. jours. Grantee WHO, 1973-74, Ciba-Geigy, 1982-83, Nat. Cancer Inst., 1983-86, 85-88; tng. program fellow Worcester Found. Experimental Biology, Shrewsbury, Mass., 1967-69. Mem. AAAS, Am. Soc. Andrology, Am. Assn. Clin. Chemistry, Nat. Acad. Clin. Biochemistry, Acad. Medicine NJ, Endocrine Soc. Home: 73 Sykes Ave Livingston NJ 07039-1318 Fax: 973-972-5185. E-mail: samojleu@yahoo.com.

SAMOLE, MYRON MICHAEL, lawyer, management consultant; b. Nov. 29, 1943; s. Harry Lionel and Bess Miriam (Siegel) Samole; m. Sandra Rita Port, Feb. 2, 1967; children: Stacey Ann, Karen Lynn, Rena Marie, David Aaron. Student, U. Ill., 1962—65; JD, DePaul U., 1967. Bar: Ill. 1967, U.S. Dist. Ct. (no. dist.) 1968, U.S. Ct. Appeals (7th cir.) 1968, Fla. 1981, U.S. Dist. Ct. (so. dist.) 1989, U.S. Ct. Appeals (11th cir.) 2001. Sole practice, Chgo., 1967—79, Miami, 1981—. Bd. dirs. The Sports Collection, Inc., pres. Samole Enterprises, Inc. 1986-, Carcand, Inc. 1986-. Pres. Young Israel Kendall. Mem.: Trial Lawyers Assn., Fla. Bar Assn., Ill. State Bar Assn., Chgo. Bar Assn., ABA, Phi Alpha Delta. Office: Samole & Berger PA 9700 S Dixie Hwy Ste 1030 Miami FL 33156-2865 Office Phone: 305-670-5070. Business E-Mail: msamole@samoleberger.com.

SAMOLLOW, PAUL B., medical educator, researcher; b. San Francisco, Mar. 20, 1948; m. Catherine M. Battaglia, Dec. 14, 1968; children: David Dunham, Matthew Patrick. BA, U. Calif., San Diego, 1971; PhD, Oreg. State U., Corvallis, 1978. Instr. Oreg. State U., 1978; assit. prof. Dept. Biology, Humboldt State U., Arcata, Calif., 1978, U. Mont., Missoula, 1979, Dept. Biology, Lehigh U., Bethlehem, Pa., 1987—91; postdoc. rsch. assoc. Hawaii Inst. Marine Biology, Kaneohe, 1979—81; postdoc. scientist Dept. Genetics, SW Found. Biomed. Rsch., San Antonio, 1981—84, asst. scientist, 1984—87, assoc. scientist, 1991—2005; prof. Dept. Vet. Integrative Bioscis., Tex. A&M U., Coll. Sta., 2005—. Contbr. articles to numerous profl. jours. Nat. Svc. Rsch. award, NIH, 1983—85, Rsch. grant, 1983—85, 1989—, The Ellwood Found., 1994—95, Samuel Roberts Noble Found., Inc., 1994—96, NSF, 1982—89. Mem.: AAAS, Genetics Soc. Am., Tex. Genetics Soc. (pres. 2000—01, Disting. Svc. award 2005). Achievements include research in proposal to sequence the first marsupial genome natural selection and genetic structure in natural populations, X-chromosomes inactivation in mammals. Avocations: hiking, scuba diving, backpacking. Office: TX A&M Univ MS 4458 College Station TX 77843-4458 Business E-Mail: psamollow@cvm.tamu.edu.

SAMOLYK, KEITH ANDREW, cardiovascular perfusionist, director; s. Edward and Margret Samolyk; 1 child, Tyler Andrew. BS, Northeastern U., Boston MA, 1989. Cert. perfusion tech. Northeastern U., Boston, 1989, lic. Cardiovascular Perfusionist Commonwealth of Mass., 2001. Cardiovasc. perfusionist Johns Hopkins Hosp., Balt., 1990—95; pediatric specialist perfusion Hartford (Conn.) Hosp., 1996; supr. QA, staff perfusionist Winthrop U. Hosp., Mineola, NY, 1997—2000; staff perfusionist Boston Med. Ctr., 2001—, St Elizabeths Med. Ctr., Boston, 2001—; staff perfusionist (per diem) Maine Med. Ctr., Portland, 2003—. Pres., CEO Global Blood Resources LLC, Somers, Conn., 2001—. Author journal papers. Recipient Alumni award profl. promise, Northeastern U., 1989, Gold award co. global blood resources, Conn. Quality Innovation award, 2006. Mem.: Windsor Marksmen Assn., Soc. for Advancement of Blood Mgmt. (assoc.), Windsor Club. Achievements include invention of Hemobag Whole Blood Salvaging device for Surgery; 3 patents. Avocations: golf, skiing, hunting, fishing. Personal E-mail: ksamolyk@comcast.net.

SAMONS, LOREN J., II, classicist; b. Little Rock, Ark., Aug. 18, 1964; s. Loren Jerome and Yvonne Varnell Samons; m. Jamie K. Rea, Jan. 9, 1988. BA, Baylor U., Waco, Tex., 1986; AM, Brown U., Providence, 1987; PhD, 1991. Vis. asst. prof. humanities Reed Coll., Portland, Oreg., 1992—93; assoc. dean Boston U., 2002—05, prof. & chmn. classical studies, 2006—. Author: Empire of the Owl, What's

Wrong with Democracy? From Athenian Practice to American Worship. Recipient Metcalf award, Boston U., 1998, Gitner award, 1997. Mem.: Assn. Ancient Historians. Office: Boston Univ 745 Commonwealth Ave Boston MA 02215

SAMOSHIN, VYACHESLAV VLADIMIROVICH, chemistry professor, science educator, researcher; PhD in Organic Chem., Moscow State U., 1982, D of Chem. Scis., 1991. Prof., head dept. organic chemistry Moscow State Acad. Fine Chem. Tech., 1992—97; prof. U. of the Pacific, Stockton, Calif., 1997—. Contbr. articles to chem. jours. and books. Mem.: Russian Mendeleev Chem. Soc., Am. Chem. Soc. Achievements include research in organic synthesis and stereochemistry. Office: U of the Pacific 3601 Pacific Ave Stockton CA 95211 Office Fax: 209-946-2607. Business E-Mail: vsamoshin@pacific.edu.

SAMPAS, DOROTHY MYERS, retired government official; b. Washington, Aug. 24, 1933; d. Lawrence and Anna Cornelia (Henkel) Myers; m. James George Sampas, Dec. 8, 1962; children: George, Lawrence James. AB, U. Mich., 1955; postgrad., U. Paris, 1955-56; PhD, Georgetown U., 1970; cert., Nat. War Coll., Washington, 1987, Naval Post Grad. Sch., 1993. Cert. Def. Resource Mgmt. Inst. Registered lobbyist State Legis. Mich., 1954—55; with Bur. Pub. Affairs Dept. State, Washington, 1958-60, analyst Bur. of Adminstrn., 1973-75, div. chief, dep. chief Office of Position and Pay Mgmt., 1979-83, div. chief Office of Mgmt., 1983-84, dir. Office of Mgmt., 1984-86; vice consul Am. Consulate Gen., Hamburg, Fed. Republic Germany, 1960-62; cons. Trans Century Corp., Washington, 1972; gen. svcs. officer Am. Embassy, Brussels, 1975-79, embassy minister-counselor Beijing, 1987-90; minister-counselor U.S. Mission to UN, NYC, 1991-94; Am. ambassador to Islamic Republic of Mauritania, 1994-97; ret., 1998. Vol. Sibley Meml. Hosp., 1999—. Mem.: Cosmos Club. Presbyterian. Home: 4301 Massachusetts Ave NW Apt 3008 Washington DC 20016-5564

SAMPATH, RAMANATHAN, chemical engineer, educator; s. Annapoorani Ramanathan; m. Malaiarasi Annamalai, Feb. 12, 1986; 1 child, Devi Sampat. PhD, W.Va. U., Morgantown, 1994. Exec. engr. Oil & Natural Gas Commn., Agartala, Tripura, India, 1984—87; summar faculty NASA, Hattiesburg, Miss., 1988; adj. prof. Morehouse Coll., Atlanta, 1988—; postgrad. rsch. fellow US DoE, Morgantown, W.Va., 1989—93; environ. mgr. US EPA, Atlanta, 1989—; asst. prof. Clark Atlanta U., 1995—99, adj. prof., 2007—. Mem.: AIChE, Combustion Inst. Home: 1415 Grovehurst Dr Marietta GA 30062

SAMPER, CRISTIÁN, museum director; b. San José, Costa Rica, Sept. 25, 1965; B., Univ. de Los Andes, Bogotá, Colombia, 1987; M., Harvard Univ., 1989, PhD in Biology, 1992. Rsch. dir. La Planada Nature Reserve, Colombia, 1989—91; adj. prof. biology Univ. del Valle, Cali, Colombia; dir. environment divsn. Found. Higher Edn., Colombia, 1992—95; chief science advisor Govt. of Colombia, 1995—2001; founder, dir. Alexander von Humboldt Inst., Colombia, 1995—2001; chmn. subs. body of sci., tech., and technol. advice UN Conv. on Biol. Diversity, 1999—2001; dep. dir. & staff scientist Smithsonian Tropical Rsch. Inst., Panama, 2001—03; dir. Smithsonian Nat. Mus. Natural History, Washington, 2003—07, 2008—; acting sec. Smithsonian Inst., 2007—08. Bd. dirs. Am. Assn. Museums, Ctr. Internat. Forest Rsch. Recipient Derek Bok prize, Harvard Univ., Nat. Medal of the Environment, Colombia, 2001. Mem.: Am. Assn. Museums. Office: Nat Mus of Natural History Smithsonian Inst MRC 106, PO Box 37012 Washington DC 20013-7012

SAMPLE, ALEXANDER KING, bishop; b. Kalispell, Mont., Nov. 7, 1960; s. Alexander K. and Joyce Sample. BS, Mich. Tech. Univ., 1982, MS, 1984; JCL, Angelicum Acad., Rome, 1996. Ordained priest Diocese of Marquette, Mich., 1990; ordained bishop, 2006; bishop Diocese of Marquette, 2006—. Mem.: KC. Roman Catholic. Office: Diocese of Marquette PO Box 550 444 S Fourth St Marquette MI 49855 Office Phone: 906-227-9115. Office Fax: 906-225-0437.

SAMPLE, ALTHEA MERRITT, retired secondary education educator, conductor; b. Miami, Fla., Apr. 6, 1937; d. Otis and Alma (Carter) S. BS in Music Edn., Fla. A&M U., Tallahassee, 1960; Master in Music Edn., U. Miami, 1971. Tchr. elem. music edn. Dade County, Miami, 1960-65, dir. jr. hs orch., 1965-84, dir. orch. sr. hs, 1984—; dir. orch. Miami Northwestern Performing Arts Ctr., 1984—. Clin. tchr. internship program U. Miami, 1988-90; clinician Broward County Orch. Evaluation, 1986, 87; participant workshops in field, 1965—. Coord. North Area Festival, 1988; conducted Supt.'s Honors Orch., 1988, 92, South Area Festival Orch., 1989, tribute Dr. George Bornoff Concert, 1994, Gov. Fla. Inaugural Concert, 1991; performed Nat. Educator Reception, 1993; sponsor Miami Herald Silver Knight Award winners, 1988, 90, 92. Recipient Black Music Achievement award, 1992, Outstanding Educator award US Rep. Dante Fussell, 1992, Disting. Alumnus award Fla. A&M U., 1997; named Area III Tchr. of Yr., Dade County, 1992; named to Dade County Schs. Music Educators Hall of Fame, 2006. Mem. United Tchrs. Dade, Fla. Orch. Assn., Fla. Music Educators, Dade Music Educators, Nat. Alliance Educators, Eta Phi Beta. Democrat. Episcopalian. Avocations: reading, playing flute, violin, organ, tennis. Home: 15720 E Bunche Park Dr Opa Locka FL 33054-2020

SAMPLE, FREDERICK PALMER, former college president; b. Columbia, Pa., May 22, 1930; s. William Walter and Erna Rebecca (Roye) S.; m. Mary Jane Drager, Aug. 19, 1951; children: Jeffrey Lynn, Roger Lee. AB, Lebanon Valley Coll., 1952; LHD, Lebanon Valley Coll., 2006; MEd, Western Md. Coll., 1956; DEd, Pa. State U., 1968; D in Pedagogy, Albright Coll., 1968. Tchr. Annville (Pa.) High Sch., 1952-53; tchr. Red Lion Area (Pa.) High Sch., 1953-57, prin., 1957-59, supervising prin., 1959-64; supt. Manheim Twp. Sch. Dist., Neffsville, Pa., 1964-68; pres. Lebanon Valley Coll., Annville, Pa., 1968-83; supt. Bellefonte (Pa.) Area Sch. Dist., 1987-92. Ednl. cons.; adminstr. Bucknell U., 1985-87. Mem. Phi Delta Kappa. Republican. Home: 401 Ford Dr Elizabethtown PA 17022-3194 E-mail: fps0522@dejazzd.com. *Despite failures, difficulties, and disappointments I have tried to find the honorable, responsible, productive, true, and humane solutions to problems and make decisions for progress.*

SAMPLE, JOSEPH SCANLON, foundation executive; b. Chgo., Mar. 15, 1923; s. John Glen and Helen (Scanlon) S.; m. Patricia M. Law, Dec. 22, 1942 (div.); children: Michael Scanlon, David Forrest, Patrick Glen; m. Miriam Tyler Willing, Nov. 19, 1965 (dec.). BA, Yale U., 1947. Trainee, media analyst, media dir. Dancer-Fitzgerald-Sample, Inc., advt. agy., Chgo., 1947-50, v.p., media dir., 1952-53; pres. Mont. Television Network KTVQ, Billings, KXLF-AM-TV, Butte, Mont., KRTV, Great Falls, Mont., KPAX-TV, Missoula, Mont., 1955-84; dir., prodr. Yellowstone Pub. Radio KEMC, Billings, 1993—. Chmn. Wheeler Ctr. Mont State U., 1988—. Served with AUS, 1943-46. With U.S. Army, 1950-52. Mem. Rotary, Yellowstone Country Club, Port Royal Club, Hole in The Wall Golf Club, Hilands Golf Club, Naples Yacht Club. Home: 606 Highland Park Dr Billings MT 59102-1909 Office: 14 N 24th St Billings MT 59101-2422 Office Phone: 406-256-5667. Personal E-mail: scatman01@msn.com.

SAMPLE, STEVEN BROWNING, academic administrator; b. St. Louis, Nov. 29, 1940; s. Howard and Dorothy (Cunningham) Sample; m. Kathryn Brunkow, Jan. 28, 1961; children: Michelle Sample Smith, Elizabeth Ann. BS, U. Ill., 1962, MS, 1963, PhD, 1965; DHL (hon.), Canisius Coll., 1989, Hebrew Union Coll., 1994, Northeasetern U., 2004; LLD (hon.), U. Sheffield, Eng., 1991; EdD (hon.), Purdue U., 1994; EdD, Northwestern U., 2004; DL (hon.), U. Nebr., 1995; DSc, U. Notre Dame, 2005; DSc (hon.), SUNY, 2006. Sr. scientist Melpar Inc., Falls Ch., Va., 1965—66; assoc. prof. elec. engring. Purdue U., Lafayette, Ind., 1966—73; dep. dir. Ill. Bd. Higher Edn., Springfield, 1971—74; exec. v.p. acad. affairs, dean Grad. Coll., prof. elec. engring. U. Nebr., Lincoln, 1974—82; prof. elec. and computer engring. SUNY, Buffalo, 1982—91; pres. U. So. Calif., LA, 1991—, prof. elec. engring., 1991—, Robert C. Packard pres.'s chair, 1995—. Bd. dirs. Santa Catalina Id. Co., Intermec, William Wrigley Jr. Co., 1997—2008, Advanced Bionics, AMCAP/Am. Mut. Fund, Inc., Keck Sch. Medicine; vice-chmn. Western NY Tech. Devel. Ctr., Buffalo, 1982—91; chmn. bd. dirs. Calspan-UB Rsch. Ctr., Inc., Buffalo, 1983—91; mem. Calif. Coun. Sci. and Tech., Irvine, Calif., 1998—2003, L.A. Bus. Advisors, Nat. Acad. of Engring., 1998—; cons. in field; chmn. Pacific-10 Conf., 1997—99. Author: Contrarian's Guide to Leadership, 2001, (ref. book) New Dictionary of the History of Ideas, 2004; contbr. articles to profl. jour. Timpanist St. Louis Philharm. Orch., 1955—58; chmn. Western NY Regional Econ. Devel. Coun., 1984—91; trustee U. at Buffalo Found., 1982—91, Studio Arena Theatre, Buffalo, 1983—91, Western NY Pub. Broadcasting Assn., 1985—91; chmn. Gov.'s Conf. on Sci. and Engring. Edn., Rsch. and Devel, 1989—91; sr. warden Ch. of Our Savior, 1996—98; mem. Calif. Bus.-Higher Edn. Forum (CBHEF), 1995—97; trustee LEARN, 1991—96; mem. bd. dir. 1st Interstate Bancorp, 1991—96, Galaxy Inst. Edn., 1991—94, Niagara Mohawk Power Corp., 1988—91; vestry Ch. of Our Savior, 1996—2001; mem. bd. gov. LA Annenberg Met. Project (LAAMP), 1994—2000; mem. bd. dir. Western Atlas, Inc., 1994—97, The Presley Co., 1991—96; bd. dir. Buffalo Philharm. Orch., 1982—91, Regenstrief Med. Found., Indpls., 1982—, Rsch. Found. SUNY, 1987—91; bd. dir. LA chpt. World Affairs Coun.; bd. dir. Rebuild LA Com., Coalition of 100 Club, LA; mem. bd. dir. Dunlop Tire Corp., 1987—91, Greater Buffalo C. of C., 1985—91, United Way Buffalo and Erie County, 1985—91; bd. dir. U. So. Calif. Keck Sch. Medicine; bd. trustees J. Paul Getty Trust, 2004—06; mem. leadership coun. Literacy Network of Greater L.A., 2004—; mem. Calif. Commn. for Jobs and Econ. Growth, 2004—. Recipient Disting. Alumnus award, U. Ill., 1980, Alumni Honor award, U. Ill. Coll. Engring., 1985, citation award, Buffalo Coun. on World Affairs, 1986, Outstanding Elec. Engr. award, Purdue U., 1993, Humanitarian award, Nat. Conf. Christians and Jews, 1994, Hollzer Meml. award, Jewish Fedn. Coun. Greater L.A, 1994, Eddy award, LA County Econ. Devel. Corp., 2000, Norton medal, SUNY, 2004, Humanitarian award, Alfred Mann Found., 2004, Heart of City award, Ctrl. City Assn. LA, 2005, KCET Visionary award, 2005, Disting. Bus. Leader award, LA Area C. of C., 2006; named Engr. of Yr., NY State Soc. Profl. Engrs., 1985; fellow, Sloan Found., 1962—63, Grad. fellow, NSF, 1963—65, Am. Coun. Edn. fellow, Purdue U., 1970—71. Mem.: NAE, IEEE (Outstanding Paper award 1976, Founders medal 2008, fellow 2008), Am. Acad. Arts and Sci., Assn. Pacific Rim Univ. (co-founder, chmn. 1997—2002), Coun. on Fgn. Rels., Nat. Assn. State Univ. and Land-Grant Coll. (ednl. telecomms. com. 1982—83, chmn. coun. of pres. 1985—86, edn. and tech. com. 1986—87, exec. com. 1987—89), Assn. Am. Univ. (exec. com. 1995—2000, vice-chmn. 1997—98, tenure com. 1997—2001, chmn. 1998—99, assessing quality of univ. edn. and rsch. com. 2000—05, co-chair task force on rsch. accountability 2001—02, internationalization com. 2002—). Episcopalian. Achievements include patents in field. Office: U So Calif Office of Pres University Park Adm 110 Los Angeles CA 90089-0012 Office Phone: 213-740-2111.

SAMPRAM, ELLIS SENANU KOJO, physician; s. Francis Yao Sampram and Amelia Akosua Agbo; m. Lene Birgitte Pedersen, June 23, 1990; children: Daniella Sefa, Patrick Sena. MD, Lund U., Sweden, 1994, PhD student, 2008—. Cert. gen. surgeon Sweden, 2001, Norway, 2002. Rsch. asst., inst. exptl. rsch. Aarhus U. Hosp., Denmark, 1994, housemanship, 1994—96; surg. resident Sweden, 1996—2001; postdoc. rsch. fellow Cleve. Clinic Found., 2001—04; house staff physician Case Western Rsch. Sys., Forum Health, Youngstown, Ohio, 2004—06, North Shore LI Jewish Health Sys., Manhasset, NY, 2006—. Contbr. articles to profl. jours. Bd. chmn. Project Sub-Sahara, a non-govtl. orgn. NGO, Vancouvar, Wash., 2002. Recipient award, Sweden-America Rsch. Found., 2001, Swedish Heart Lung Found. Rsch., 2001. Mem.: AMA.

SAMPRAS, PETE, retired professional tennis player; b. Washington, Aug. 12, 1971; s. Sam and Georgia Sampras; m. Bridgette Wilson, Sept. 30, 2000, 2 children, Christian Charles, Ryan Nikolaos. Mem. U.S. Davis Cup team., named to Olympic Team Atlanta, 1996 Co-author (with Pete Bodo): A Champion's Mind: Lessons from a Life in Tennis, 2008. Chmn. ATP Tour Charities program, 1992. Winner tournaments including Phila., 1990, Manchester, 1990, US Open, 1990, 1993, Grand Slam Cup, 1990, L.A., 1991, Indpls., 1991, Lyon, 1991, IBM/ATP Tour World.Championship-Frankfurt, 1991, 94, US Pro Indoor, 1992, Lipton Internat., 1993, Wimbledon, 1993, 94, 95, 97, 98, 99, 2000; Australian Open, 1994, 97, Italian Open, 1994, US Open, 1990, 93, 95, 96, 2002, San Jose Open, 1996, Memphis Open, 1996, ATP Tour World Championship/Hannover, Germany, 1996, Australian Open Wimbledon, 1997, Advanta Championships, 1998, Champions Cup, 2007; ranked # 1 during 1993, 94 season, finalist Australian Open, 1995; ret., 2003; named to Internat. Tennis Hall of Fame, 2007. Achievements include 1st male to win the US Open, Wimbledon, and Australian Open in succession, mem. US Davis Cup Team, 1991, became only the fourth player to finish as No. 1 three (or more) consecutive years, 1st player to surpass $5 million in a season, all-time leader in career earnings, named ATP Tour Player of the Year, 1993-94, Jim Thorpe Tennis Player, 1993. Office: ATP Tour 420 W 45th St New York NY 10036-3503

SAMPSON, DAVID ALLAN, insurance association executive, former federal agency administrator; b. Washington, Ind., July 2, 1957; s. Beryl Harrel and Laura Evelyn (King) S.; m. Karen Ann Nichols, Dec. 10, 1978. BA, David Lipscomb Coll., Nashville, 1978; MDiv, New Orleans Bapt. Theol. Sem., 1982; D in Ministry, Abilene Christian, 1990. Min. Westchurch Ch. of Christ, Hammond, Ind., 1978-82; sr. min. Park Row Ch. of Christ, Arlington, Tex., 1982—; pres., CEO Arlington (Tex.) C. of C.; chmn. Tex. Coun. on Workforce and Econ. Competitiveness; asst. sec. for econ. devel. US Dept. Commerce, Washington, 2001—05, acting dep. sec., 2005, dep. sec., 2005—07; pres., CEO Property Casualty Insurers Assn. Am., Des Plaines, Ill., 2007—. Bd. dirs. emergency chaplain program Arlington Community Hosp., 1985—, Overseas Private Investment Corp., 2005-; adv. bd. Arlington Meml. Hosp., 1985—; bd. dirs. Neo-natal Bioethics Review Bd., 1986—Contbr. articles to profl. jours. Mem. United Way; bd. dirs. Arlington Ind. Sch. Dists, Communications Bd., 1985—. Named Arlington's Minister of Yr., Kiwanis, 1985. Mem. Arlington C. of C. (bd. dirs. 1985—, chmn. emergency preparedness com. 1985—), Arlington Ministerial Assn. (pres. 1985-86), Soc. Biblical Lit., Internat. Ch. Soc. (chmn. North Tex. chpt.), Phi Alpha Theta. Lodges: Rotary. Republican. Avocations: travel, tennis. Office: Property Casualty Insurers Assn Am 2600 S River Rd Des Plaines IL 60018

SAMPSON, DAVID ARTHUR, research scientist; b. Detroit, July 3, 1956; PhD, Colo. State U., Fort Collins, 1992. Vis. prof. U. Antwerp, Wilrijk, Belgium, 1997—99; rsch. assoc. NC State U., Raleigh; rsch. scientist Va. Poly. Inst. and State U., Blacksburg, 2001—05; academic profl. Ariz. State U., Tempe, 2008—. Recipient Academic Performance award, Northern Ariz. U., 1988. Mem.: Am. Geophys. Union, Ecol. Soc. Am. Avocation: rock climbing. Home: 1831 East Apache Blvd Tempe AZ 85281 Office: Ariz State Univ PO Box 878209 Tempe AZ 85287 Business E-Mail: david.a.sampson@asu.edu.

SAMPSON, DONNA RENE, mathematics educator; b. Columbia, SC, Mar. 26, 1957; d. James Bradford and Celia Meetze Sampson; children: Shoshone Sampson Willis, Shuyon Sampson Willis. BA in Math., Lehman Col., Bronx, NY, 1979; MA in Edn., U.S. Internat. U., San Diego, Calif., 1991. Math. tchr. John Philip Sousa Jr. HS, Bronx, 1979—81, Luther Burbank Jr. HS, Burbank, Calif., 1981—95, Carver Mid. Sch., Sanford, Fla., 1995—96, Croons Acad., Sanford, 1996—98, Southern HS, Guam, 1998—99, North HS, Phoenix, 1999—. Mem.: NEA, Tchr. Assn. Avocations: dance, kickboxing, weightlifting, reading, skating.

SAMPSON, EARLDINE ROBISON, education educator; b. Russell, Iowa, June 18, 1923; d. Lawrence Earl and Mildred Mona (Judy) Robison; m. Wesley Claude Sampson, Nov. 25, 1953; children: Ann Elizabeth, Lisa Ellen. Diploma, Iowa State Tchrs. Coll., 1943, BA, 1950; MS in Edn., Drake U., 1954; postgrad., No. Ill. U., Iowa State U., 1965-66, 74. Cert. tchr. Iowa, guidance counselor Iowa. Tchr. elem. sch. various pub. sch. sys., 1943-48; cons. speech and hearing Iowa Dept. Pub. Instrn., Des Moines, 1950-52; speech therapist Des Moines Pub. Schs., 1952-54, 55; lectr. spl. edn. No. Ill. U., DeKalb, 1964-65; tchr. of homebound Cedar Falls (Iowa) Pub. Schs., 1967-68; asst. prof. edn. U. No. Iowa, Cedar Falls, 1968; asst. prof., counselor Wartburg Coll., Waverly, Iowa, 1968-70; instr. elem. edn., then head of advising elem. edn. Iowa State U., Ames, 1972-82; field supr. elem. edn. U. Toledo, 1988, 89; ind. cons. Sylvania, Ohio, 1989—. Cons. Des Moines Speech and Hearing Ctr., 1958-59; cons. Sartori Hosp., Cedar Falls, 1967-69; spkr. in field. Fellow, NDEA, 1965. Methodist. Avocations: poetry, reading, music, photography. Home: 4047 Newcastle Dr Sylvania OH 43560-3450 *My creed is based on the words of Edwin Markham: "There is a destiny that makes us brothers; none goes his way alone. All that we send into the lives of others comes back into our own." Just reward came from a former student who stated "I have never known you to compromise your principles".*

SAMPSON, HUGH ALBERT, JR., medical educator; b. Winnipeg, Man., Nov. 1, 1948; naturalized; BA, Hamilton Coll., 1971; MD, SUNY, Buffalo, 1975. Diplomate Am. Bd. Pediats., Am. Bd. Allergy and Immunology. Resident Children's Meml. Hosp.-Northwestern U., Chgo., 1975—78; fellow in allergy and immunology-pulmonary medicine Duke U. Med. Ctr., Durham, NC, 1978—80, mem. staff, 1980—86; prof. pediat. Johns Hopkins U., Balt., 1986—97; prof., pediat. Mt. Sinai Sch. of Medicine, NYC, 1997—. Co-author: Intestinal immunology and Food Allergy, 1995, Food Allergy: Adverse Reactions to Foods and Food Additives, 2003, Pediatric Allergy: Principles and Practice, 2008. Fellow Am. Acad. Allergy and Immunology; mem. Am. Pediat. Soc., Am. Acad. Pediats. (Brett Ratner award 2004), Am. Assn. Immunologists, Soc. Pediat. Rsch., Inst. Medicine, Henry Kunkel Soc., Sigma Xi, Alpha Omega Alpha. Mem. Soc. Of Friends. Avocations: jogging, sailing, skiing. Office: Mt Sinai Sch Medicine One Gustave L Levy Pl Box 1198 New York NY 10029 Office Phone: 212-241-5548. Business E-Mail: hugh.sampson@mssm.edu.

SAMPSON, JOHN EUGENE, food products executive, consultant; b. Feb. 25, 1941; s. Delbert John and Mary Etta (Dodrill) S.; m. Mary Margaret Treanor, Aug. 14, 1965; children: J. Mark, Sharon. AB with distinction, Nebr. Wesleyan U., 1963; MBA, Ind. U., 1964. Mgmt. asst., exec. trainee Office Sec. Def., Washington, 1963—64; mem. staff Com. Econ. Devel., Washington, 1964—69; coord. environ. planning Gen. Mills Inc., Mpls., 1969—72, mgr. devel. planning, 1972—74; dir. corp. planning Cen. Soya Co. Inc., Ft. Wayne, Ind., 1974—76, v.p. corp. planning, 1976—80, v.p. corp. planning and devel., 1980—82, v.p. corp. devel., corp. sec., 1982—84; v.p. corp. planning and devel. Internat. Multifoods, Inc., 1984—96; pres. Sampson Assocs., Edina, Minn., 1996—. Author: How to Sell Your Business and Get the Best Price For It, 2003. Mem. bd. govs. Nebr. Wesleyan U., 1974-80; chmn. bd. trustees St. Joseph United Meth. Ch., Ft. Wayne, 1984; bd. dirs., treas. North Ind. United Meth. Found., 1981-84; lay mem. North Ind. Ann. Conf. United Meth. Ch., 1980-84; bd. dirs. Anthony Wayne coun. Boy Scouts Am., 1984; lay mem. Minn. Ann. Conf. United Meth. Ch., 1985-91, 97-00; chmn. conf. bd. devel. Minn. United Meth. Conf., 1986-91; chmn. bd. trustees Hennepin Ave. United Meth. Ch., Mpls., 1990-92, chair adminstrv. coun., 1993-95, lay leader, 1995-98; chair exec. com. North Naples (Fla.) United Meth. Ch., 2002-05, co-chmn. bldg. com., 2002-05, chair bd. trustees, 2005-2008. Mem. Ind. U. Sch. Bus. Alumni Assn. (pres. 1984-85), Interlachen Country Club, Country Club of Naples (bd. dirs. 2004-, pres. 2008-). Home: Unit 1701 4451 Gulf Shore Blvd N Naples FL 34103 also: 6612 Gleason Ter Edina MN 55439-1131 Home Phone: 239-435-0805, 952-941-6309; Office Phone: 952-928-0800.

SAMPSON, JOHN HOWARD, neurosurgeon, educator; b. Ottawa, Ont., Can., Nov. 15, 1966; Student, St. John's Coll., 1986; BS, U. Manitoba, 1990; MD, U. Monitoba, 1990; PhD with honors, Duke U., 1996. Investigator U. Manitoba, Winnipeg, Manitoba, 1987—89; intern in surgery Duke U. Med. Ctr., Durham, NC, 1990—91, resident in neurosurgery, 1991—98, asst. prof. in surgery and pathology, 1998—. Patentee of anti-siphon valve, vaccination with antigen-specific, genetically modified allogeneic cells, modified peptide vaccinations against the EGFR mutants, naked MAbs that recognize the EGFR mutation as therapeutic agents, soluble microcrystalline formulation of temozolomide for intrathecal use; contbr. articles and abstracts to profl. jours.; author: (book chpt.) Conn's Current Therapy, 1992, Neurological Surgery: A Comprehensive Reference Guide to the Diagnosis and Management of Neurosurgical Problems, 1996, Neurosurgery, 2d edit., 1996, The DREZ Operation, 1996, Gene Transfer and Therapy for Neurological Diseas, 1998, Russell and Rubinstein's Pathology of Tumors of the Nervous System, 6th edit., 1998, Neurosurgery, The Scientific Basis of Clinical Practice, 2001, Operative Neurosurgery, 2001, Brain Tumor Immunotherapy, 2001, Basic References in Neurosurgery, 1992. Recipient Natalie Riedle award, 1988, Gerald B. Grindley, Am. Assn. Cancer Rsch., 1996, Continuing Med. Edn. award, 1996; grantee, Kimmel Found., Demingen Corp., IVAX Pharm.; fellow, Duke U. Grad Sch., 1994—96, Am. Brain Tumor, 1994—95, Terry Seelinger, Duke U., 1996, Pediat. Brain Tumor Found., 1996—97; scholar Allan Bronfman Family, 1988. Mem.: AMA, ACs, AAAS, Soc. Neurosci., Soc. Neuro-Oncology, Mensa, N.Y. Acad. Scis., Congress Neurol., Am. Soc. Clin. Oncology, Am. Assn. Neurol. Surgeons (joint sect. tumors, joint sect. neurotrauma and critical care, Rsch. Fellow 1996, 1995, Young

Clin. Investigator award 1999), Am. Assn. Cancer Rsch., Duke Comprehensive Cancer Ctr. (assoc.), Phi Delta Theta. Office: Duke Univ Med Ctr 4505 Busse Bldg Trent Dr Durham NC 27701 Home: 2007 Windgate Dr Durham NC 27705-2434

SAMPSON, KELVIN DALE, professional basketball coach, former college basketball coach; b. Laurinburg, NC, Oct. 5, 1955; s. John W. and Eva (Brewington) S.; m. Karen Sue Lowry, June 16, 1979; children: Lauren Elizabeth, Kellen Matthew. BS, Pembroke State U., 1978; MS, Mich. State U., 1980. Asst. coach Mont. Tech. U., 1979—80, head coach, 1981—85; asst. coach Wash. State U. Cougars, 1985—87, head coach, 1987—94, U. Okla. Sooners, Norman, Okla., 1994—2006, Ind. U. Hoosiers, Bloomington, 2006—08; asst. coach Milw. Bucks, 2008—. Contbr. articles to profl. jours. Named Big Eight Coach of Yr., 1995, Nat. Coach of Yr., AP, 1995. Mem. Nat. Assn. Basketball Coaches (Dist. Coach of Yr. 1991, PAC 10 Coach of Yr. 1991, Nat. Coach of Yr., 2002) Avocations: golf, reading, exercise. Office: Milw Bucks 1001 N Fourth St Milwaukee WI 53203*

SAMPSON, ROBERT NEIL, professional society administrator, consultant; b. Spokane, Wash., Nov. 29, 1938; s. Robert Jay and Juanita Cleone (Hickman) S.; m. Jeanne Louise Stokes, June 7, 1960; children—Robert W., Eric S., Christopher B., Heidi L. BS in Agr, U. Idaho, 1960; M.Public Adminstrn., Harvard U., 1974. Soil conservationist Soil Conservation Service, Burley, Idaho, 1960-61, work unit conservationist Orofino, Idaho, 1962-65, agronomist Idaho Falls, Idaho, 1967-68, info. specialist Boise, 1968-70, area conservationist, 1970-72, land use specialist Washington, 1974-77, dir. environ. services div., 1977; land use program mgr. Idaho Planning and Community Affairs Agy., Boise, 1972-73; exec. v.p. Nat. Assn. Conservation Dists., Washington, 1978-84, Am. Forestry Assn., Washington, 1984-95; sr. fellow Am. Forests, Washington, 1995-2000; affiliate prof. Dept. Forest Resources U. Idaho, 1997—. Instr. soils and land use Boise State U., 1972; F.K. Weyerhaeuser vis. fellow in comml. forestry Yale Sch. Forestry and Environ. Studies, 2001; pres., The Sampson Group, Inc., 1996—, Vision Forestry LLC, 2000—; rsch. scientist, Yale Sch. Forestry and Environ. Studies, 2001—; land use and forestry cons. Author: Farmland or Wasteland: A Time To Choose, 1981, For Love of the Land, 1985, With One Voice; contbr. articles to profl. and popular publs. Pres. Orofino Golf Assn., 1966, Clearwater County Search and Rescue Unit, 1966-67; chmn. Nat. Commn. on Wildfire Disasters, 1992-94. Recipient President's citation Soil Conservation Soc. Am., 1978; named Boise Fed. Civil Servant of Year Boise Fed. Bus. Assn., 1972 Fellow Soil and Water Conservation Soc. (Hugh Hammond Bennett award 1992); mem. Soc. Am. Foresters. Presbyterian. Office Phone: 703-924-0773. Personal E-mail: neil@visionforestry.com.

SAMPSON, SARA ANN, law librarian, educator; BS, Ohio State U., Columbus, 1993; JD, Ohio State U., 1997; MLIS, Kent State U., Ohio, 2004. Bar admission: Ohio 1997. Jud. law clk. Ohio Fourth Dist. Ct. Appeals, Circleville, 1997—2003; weekend reference libr. Capital U. Law Libr., Columbus, 1999—2003; reference libr. & adj. prof. Ohio State U. Coll. Law, 2003—06; head reference Georgetown Law Libr., Wash., 2006—. Author: (book) Ohio Legal Research. Sec.-treas. Am. Assn. Law Libraries, Academic Law Libraries Spl. Interest Sect., 2008—; treas. U. Luth. Chapel Ohio State U., Columbsu, 2000—06. Mem.: Beta Phi Mu. Office: Georgetown Law Library 111 G St NW Washington DC 20001 Business E-Mail: sas235@law.georgetown.edu.

SAMPSON, WILLIAM ROTH, lawyer; b. Teaneck, NJ, Dec. 11, 1946; s. James and Amelia (Roth) S.; 1 child, Lara; m. Drucilla Jean Mort, Apr. 23, 1988; stepchildren: Andy, Seth. BA in History with honors, U. Kans., 1968, JD, 1971. Bar: Kans. 1971, Mo. 2004, U.S. Dist. Ct. Kans. 1971, U.S. Dist. Ct. (we. dist.) Mo. 2004, U.S. Ct. Appeals (10th cir.) 1982, U.S. Ct. Claims 1985, U.S. Ct. Appeals (8th cir.) 1992; US Ct. Appeals (7th cir.) 2009. Assoc. Turner & Balloun, Great Bend, Kans., 1971; ptnr. Foulston & Siefkin, Wichita, Kans., 1975-86, Shook, Hardy & Bacon LLP, Kans. City, 1987. Adj. prof. advanced litig. U. Kans., 1994; mem. faculty trial tactics inst. Emory U. Sch. Law, 1994-97; mem. merit selection panel US Dist. Ct. Kans., 1999; lectr., presenter in field. Author: Kansas Trial Handbook, 1997, 2d edit., 2006; mem. Kans. Law Rev., 1969—71, editor, 1970—71; contbr. articles to profl. jours. Chmn. stewardship com. Univ. Friends Ch., Wichita, 1984-86; bd. dir. Friends U. Retirement Corp., Wichita, 1985-87, Lied Ctr. Kans., 1994-97, Nat. Found. Jud. Excellence, 2004—, program chmn., 2005, 06, pres., 2008-09; chmn. capital fund drives Trinity Luth. Ch., Lawrence, Kans., 1990-93, mem. ch. coun., 1990-92, stewardship com. Trinity Episcopal Ch., 2002—. Lt., Judge Advocate General's Corps, USNR, 1971-75. Named one of Best Lawyers in Am., 1995—, Mo. Kans. Super Lawyers, 2005—. Fellow: Kans. Bar Found., Am. Bar Found.; mem.: ABA, Lawyers for Civil Justice (bd. dirs. 2003—05), Am. Inn Ct. (Judge Hugh Means chpt. Master of Bench), Kans. U. Law Soc. (bd. govs. 1993—96, disting. alumnus 2008), Kans. Assn. Def. Counsel (pres. 1989—90, legis. coun. 1991, 1993, William H. Kahrs Disting. Achievement award 1994), Def. Rsch. Inst. (Kans. state rep. 1990—98, nat. bd. dirs. 1998—2000, nat. pres. 2003—04, chmn. strategic planning com. 2006—08, chair commercial litigation program 2007), Internat. Assn. Def. Coun. (faculty mem. trial acad. 1994), Am. Bd. Trial Advs. (pres. Kans. chpt. 1990—91, nat. bd. dir. 1990—91), Wichita Bar Assn. (bd. dirs. 1985—86), Johnson County Bar Assn. (bench-bar com. 1989—, Boss of Yr. award 1990), Douglas County Bar Assn., Kans. Bar Assn. (chmn. Kans. coll. advocacy 1986, CLE com. 1987—88, long-range planning), Assn. Def. Trial Attys., Club at Porto Cima, Order of the Coif, Omicron Delta Kappa, Phi Alpha Theta, Delta Sigma Rho. Republican. Episcopalian. Avocations: jogging, golf, travel, reading. Office: Shook Hardy & Bacon LLP 2555 Grand Ave Kansas City MO 64108-2613 Home Phone: 785-749-5358; Office Phone: 816-474-6550. Office Fax: 816-421-5547. Business E-Mail: wsampson@shb.com.

SAMRA, NICHOLAS JAMES, bishop emeritus; b. Paterson, NJ, Aug. 15, 1944; s. George H. and Elizabeth L. (Balady) Samra. BA, St. Anselm Coll., 1966; BD, St. John Sem., Brighton, Mass., 1970. Ordained priest Eparchy of Newton, Mass., 1970; assoc. pastor St. Anne Ch., North Hollywood, Calif., 1970—78; pastor Holy Cross Ch., Anaheim, Calif., 1973—78, St. John The Bapt. Ch., Northlake, Ill., 1978—81, St. Michael Ch., Hammond, Ind., 1978—81, St. Anne Ch., West Paterson, NJ, 1981—89; ordained bishop, 1989; aux. bishop Eparchy of Newton, Mass., 1989—2005, aux. bishop emeritus Mass., 2005—. Transl.: articles on Melkite subjects. Chaplain Police Athletic League Supporters, North Hollywood, 1970; vicar gen., corp. v.p., and regional bishop of Midwest region Diocese of Newton; mem. Ecumenical Commn., LA, 1974—78. Mem.: US Conf. Catholic Bishops, Christian Churches Together in the USA, Cath. Archives Assn. Roman Catholic. Office: 32406 Barclay Sq Warren MI 48093-6101 Office Phone: 586-756-1971. Office Fax: 586-756-1976. E-mail: nsamra@prodigy.net.

SAMS, JEREMY, theater director, composer; b. London, Jan. 12, 1957; s. Eric Sams; m. Maria Friedman; 2 children. Lyricist: (Broadway plays) Ghetto, 1989; composer: (Broadway plays) Some Americans Abroad, 1990, Arcadia, 1995; translator Indiscretions, 1995, The Rehearsal, 1996; author, adaptation: (Broadway plays) Waiting in the Wings, 1999; Amour, 2002; Chitty Chitty Bang, 2005; dir.: Noises Off, 2001, 13, 2008; musical dir.: (London/West End plays) Sunday in the Park with George, 1990; Assassins, 1992; lyricist The Threepenny Opera, 1994; dir.: Passion, 1996, The Sound of Music, 2006; composer: (TV films) Old Times, 1991, Uncle Vanya, 1991, Persuasion, 1995, (TV miniseries) Have Your Cake and Eat It, 1997, (films) The Mother, 2003, Enduring Love, 2004. Office: c/o Bernard B Jacobs Theater 242 W 45th St New York NY 10036*

SAMS, LOUISE S., broadcast executive, lawyer; b. Atlanta, 1957; BA magna cum laude, Princeton U., 1979; JD, U. Va. Sch. Law, 1985. Bar: NY 1986, Ga. 1995. Corp. assoc. White & Case, NYC, 1986—93; with Turner Broadcasting Sys., Inc., Atlanta, 1993—, exec. v.p., gen. counsel, 2000—; pres. Turner Broadcasting Sys. Internat., Atlanta, 2003—. Mem. editl. bd. U. Va. Jour. Internat. Law, 1983—84, exec. editor, 1984—85. Mem. bd. dirs. Princeton U. Named one of The 50 Most Influential Women Lawyers in America, Nat. Law Jour., 2007. Mem.: ABA, State Bar Ga., NY State Bar Assn. Office: Turner Broadcasting System Inc 1 CNN Ctr 100 Internat Blvd Atlanta GA 30303 Office Phone: 404-827-1700. Office Fax: 404-827-2437. E-mail: louise.sams@turner.com.*

SAMS, RONALD F., career military officer; BA, Mich. State U., 1972; grad., Squadron Officer Sch., 1977; MA in Ednl. Systems Mgmt., Chapman U., 1978; student, Air Command and Staff Coll., Maxwell AFB, Ala., 1984, Air War Coll., 1993. Commd. 2d lt. USAF, 1972, advanced through grades to lt. gen., 2006; squadron co-pilot, aircraft comdr., instr. pilot 9th Air Refueling Squadron USAF, Beale AFB, Calif., 1974-79; from instr. pilot to faculty instr. pilot 93d Air Refueling Squadron, SAC Ctrl. Flight Instr. Course, Castle AFB, Calif., 1979-83; faculty instr. Air Command and Staff Coll. USAF, Maxwell AFB, Ala., 1984-86; chief tanker crew tng. br., Directorate of Tng. Hdqs. Strategic Air Command, Offut AFB, Nebr., 1986-89; comdr. 70th air refueling squadron USAF, Grissom AFB, Ind., 1989-90; asst. dep. comdr. ops. 305th Air Refueling Wing USAF and chief air refueling ops. 1703rd Wing, Grissom AFB, Ind. King, Khalid, Airport, Riyadh, Saudi Arabia, 1990-91; dep. comdr. 305th ops. group USAF, Grissom AFB, Ind., 1991-92; dir. ops. mgmt. Tanker Airlift Control Ctr., USAF, Scott AFB, Ill., 1993-94; comdr. 4409th ops. group (provisional) USAF, Ridyah AFB, Saudi Arabia, 1994-95; mil. asst. to dir. Defense Tech. Security Adminstrn. Defense Threat Reduction Agy. The Pentagon, Washington, 1995-98; comdr. 55th Wing USAF, Offutt AFB, Nebr., 1998—2000; inspector gen. Air Combat Command, Langley AFB, Va., 2000—02; dir. intelligence, surveillance & reconnaissance, dep. chief of staff, Air & Space Ops. USAF, Washington, 2002—06; inspect. gen. Dept Air Force US Dept Def., Washington, 2006—. Decorated Bronze Star medal, Defense Superior Svc. medal, Air medal, Aerial Achievement medal with 2 oak leaf clusters, Meritorious Svc. medal with 6 oak leaf clusters, Air Force Organizational Excellence award, Combat Readiness medal, Nat. Defense Svc. medal, Armed Fores Expeditionary medal, S.W. Asia Svc. medal with 2 service stars, Kuwait Liberation medal Kingdom of Kuwait, Kuwait Liberation medal Kingdom of Saudi Arabia. Office: USAF 1140 Air Force Pentagon Rm 4E1076 Washington DC 20330

SAMSON, ALLEN LAWRENCE, investor, retired bank executive; b. Milw., Nov. 16, 1939; s. Harry E. and Rose (Landau) S.; m. Vicki Faye Boxer, July 3, 1977; children: Daniel, Rachel; children from previous marriage: Nancy, David. BS, U. Wis., 1962, LLB, 1965. Bar: Wis. 1965. Asst. dist. atty. Milw. County Dist. Attys. Office, 1965-67, dep. dist. atty., 1968-70; assoc. Samson & Nash, Milw., 1967-68; ptnr. Samson, Friebert, Sutton and Finerty, Milw., 1970-73; v.p., sec. Am. Med. Svcs., Inc., Milw., 1973-83, exec. v.p., chief exec. officer, 1983-86, chmn., chief exec. officer, 1986-90; cons. nursing homes Samson Med. Mgmt. Co., Milw., 1990-93; pres. Liberty Bank, Milw., 1994—2001; vice chmn. State Fin. Bank, 2001—03; trustee State of Wis. Investment Bd., 2003—. Pub. mem. State of Wis. Investment Bd., 2003—; pub. mem. nursing home study Wis. Legis. Bur., 1988-89; mem. bd. visitors U. Wis. Law Sch., 1992—; mem. health policy adv. coun. Med. Coll. Wis., 1992-96. Bd. dirs. Nat. Found. Jewish Culture, 1996—98; trustee Milw. Ballet, 1982—89, Milw. Art Mus., 2001—, pres. bd. trustees, 1992—95; bd. dirs. Milw. Symphony Orch., 1995—2002, treas., 1996—2000; bd. dirs. Wis. Womens Bus. Initiative, War Meml. Corp., 1993—95, Jewish Fedn., 1985—, pres., 2000—02; bd. dirs. Milw. Jewish Home, 1992—96, Jewish Cmty. Ctr., 1985—96; pres. Milw. Parks Found., 1998—; gen. chmn. Wis. Israel Bond Campaign, 1993—94, chmn., 1996—98, bd. dirs., exec. com., 1986—; gen. chmn. ann. camp Milw. Jewish Fedn., 1990—91; pres. Jewish Vocat. Svc., 1976—78; Alexis de Tocqueville's leadership chmn. United Way campaign, 1995; First Tee of Milw. County Adv. Bd. Recipient Kaplan prize for econ. devel. Govt. of Israel, 1986, United Way Fleur de Lys award, 1996, Israel Bonds Star of David award, 1999. Avocations: tennis, skiing, golf. Home: 42108 N 101st Way Scottsdale AZ 85262

SAMSON, C. MICHAEL A., ophthalmologist; s. Cesar Rimando and Emerita Arenas Samson; m. Rose Ly, Nov. 13, 1999; children: James Michael, Caitlin Iris, Elise Lea. MD, SUNY HSC, Bklyn., 1994; MBA, NYU Stern Sch. Bus., NYC, 2008. Diplomate Am. Bd. Ophthalmology, 2000. Co-dir., uveitis svc. NY Eye & Ear Infirmary, NYC, 2000—. Pres., CEO CLS Pharms., NYC, 2006—. Recipient Resident's award, NY Eye & Ear Infirmary, 2003, 2008; named Outstanding Profls., Cambridge, 2008; named one of Best Drs. in America, 2005—08, Top Ophthalmologists in America, 2007; Ocular Inflammation grant, Morton P. Hyman Found., 2006—. Mem.: Am. Acad. Ophthalmology. Office: NY Eye & Ear Infirmary 310 E 14th St New York NY 10003 Office Fax: 212-979-4512. Business E-Mail: csamson@nyee.edu.

SAMSON, CHARLES HAROLD, JR., (CAR), retired engineering educator, consultant; b. Portsmouth, Ohio, July 12, 1924; s. Charles Harold and Gertrude (Morris) S.; m. Ruth Aileen Baumbach, Sept. 12, 1947; children: Peggy Aileen, Charles Harold III. BS, U. Notre Dame, 1947, MS, 1948; PhD, U. Mo., 1953. Registered profl. engr., Tex., Ind. Asst. field rep. Loebl, Schlossman and Bennett (archs. and engrs.), Chgo., 1948-49; structures engr. Convair Aircraft, Ft. Worth, 1951-52, sr. structures engr., 1952-53, project aerodynamics engr., 1956-58, project structures engr., 1958-60; asst. prof. civil engring. U. Notre Dame, 1953-56; office engr. Wilbur H. Gartner & Assocs., South Bend, Ind., 1954; grad. lectr. civil engring. So. Meth. U., Dallas, 1952-53, 56-60; prof. structural engring. and mechanics, depts. aerospace and civil engring. Tex. A&M U., College Station, 1960-64, prof. civil engring., 1964-94, prof. emeritus, 1994—, head dept., 1964-79, assoc. head dept., 1989-92, constrn. area engring. leader, dir. ctr. constrn. edn., 1992-93; rsch. engr. Tex. Transp. Inst., Tex. A&M U., 1960-62, head structural rsch. dept., 1962-65, acting pres., 1980-81, v.p. planning, 1981-82. Varsity tennis coach U. Notre Dame, 1953-56; pres. S.W. Athletic Conf., 1979-81; v.p. NCAA, 1981-83, mem. coun., 1983-85; cons. sys. engring. and quality mgmt.; Tex. Quality Award examiner, 1998-99, sr. examiner, 2000. Contbr. articles to profl. jours. Pres. Brazos Valley Symphony Soc., 2000—02. With USNR, 1943—46, asst. to pub. works officer civil engr. corps USNR, 1946, active USNR, 1955—56, resigned lt. j.g. USNR, 1958. Recipient Gen. Dynamics-Ft. Worth Excellence in Tchg. award, 1962, Engring. hon. award U. Notre Dame, 1982, Outstanding Contbns. to Engring. and Scientific Profession award Calif. Soc. Profl. Engrs., 1987, Mo. Honor award for Disting. Svc. in Engring., 2006, Disting. Alumni award U. Mo. Civil Engring. Acad., 2006; co-recipient Vol. Excellence award Tex. Assn. Symphony Orchestras, 2005. Fellow ASCE (life), Nat. Inst. Engring. Mgmt. and Sys. (pres. 1989-90), NSPE (past v.p., chmn. profl. engrs. in edn., pres. 1987-88, award 2000); mem. Am. Soc. Engring. Mgmt., Am. Soc. Engring. Edn., Tex. Soc. Profl. Engrs. (past nat. dir., pres. 1973-74, Tex. Engring. Dream Team 2000), Nat. Assn. Parliamentarians, Internat. Soc. Sys. Sci., Order of Engr. (chmn., bd. govs. 1989-91), Am. Soc. Quality, Internat. Coun. Sys. Engring., Nat. Eagle Scout Assn., Sigma Xi, Sigma Gamma Tau, Tau Beta Pi, Phi Kappa Phi, Chi Epsilon. Home: 810 Dogwood Ln Bryan TX 77802-1144 Office Phone: 979-779-0333. Personal E-mail: charleshsamson@msn.com.

SAMSON, DAVID, lawyer; BA, Rutgers U., 1961; LLB, U. Pa. Law Sch., 1965. Law sec. Hon. Nathan L. Jacobs, NJ Supreme Court, 1965—66; founding prin. Wolff & Samson, 1972; gen. counsel NJ Turnpike Authority, 1982—90; atty. gen. State of NJ, 2002—03; sr. ptnr. Wolff & Samson, 2003—. Mem. Gov. Commn., 1990—91; chmn. Gov. Task Force, 1987—89; legal cons. Ethics Com., 1981—85, N.J. Supreme Court Com., 1973—77; legal cons. to atty. gen. Adv. com. on Governmental Immunity, 1967—68. Mem.: U.S. Supreme Court, N.Y. Bar Assn., Am. Bar Found., Am. Bar Assn., N.J. State Bar Assn., Essex County Bar Assn. Office: Wolff & Samson One Boland Dr West Orange NJ 07052

SAMSON, DAVID P., professional baseball team executive; b. Milw., 1968; m. Cindi Samson; 3 children. B in Econs., U. Wis., Madison, 1990; JD, Benjamin N. Cardozo Sch. Law, 1993. With, Criminal Appeals Clinic Benjamin N. Cardozo Sch. of Law; founder, pres. News Travels Fast; with Morgan Stanley, 1996—99; exec. v.p. Montreal Expos, 1999—2002; pres. Fla. Marlins, 2002—. Spkr. in field. Active Challenged Athletes Found.; pres. Fla. Marlins Cmty. Found. Named Book of Hope honoree, Crohn's and Colitis Found., 2007; named one of Forty Under 40, Sports Bus. Jour., 2003—04. Mem.: NY State Bar, Miami Film Soc. Achievements include completing the Ford Ironman World Championship Triathlon, 2006. Avocation: movies. Office: Florida Marlins Dolphin Stadium 2269 Dan Marino Blvd Miami FL 33056

SAMSON, LEONA D., biological engineering educator, research center director; BSc in Biochemistry, Aberdeen U., Scotland, 1974; PhD, London U., 1978; MA (hon.), Harvard U., Cambridge, Mass., 1992. Postdoctoral rschr. U. Calif., San Francisco, 1978—80, Berkeley, 1980—83; from asst. prof. to full prof. dept. molecular and cellular toxicology Harvard Sch. Pub. Health, 1983—2001; prof. biol. engring. and toxicology MIT, 2001—, dir. MIT Ctr. for Environ. Health Scis., MIT Toxicogenomics Rsch. Program, 2001—, mem. Cancer Ctr., 2001—, prof. biology, 2004—, affiliate mem. Broad Inst., 2004—. Mem. Computational and Systems Biology Initiative; mem. bd. sci. counselors NIEHS, NCI; mem. coun. extramural grants ACS. Recipient Burroughs Wellcome Toxicology Scholar award, 1993, Charlotte Friend Women in Cancer Rsch. award, 2000; named Am. Cancer Soc. Rsch. Prof., 2001. Fellow: AAAS; mem.: Internat. Assn. Environ. Mutagen Socs. (v.p. 2005—), Environ. Mutagen Soc. (pres. 2004, Rsch. Excellence award 2001), Inst. Medicine. Office: Ctr for Environ Health Scis MIT Bldg 56-235 Cambridge MA 02139 Business E-Mail: lsamson@mit.edu.

SAMSON, RICHARD MAX, theater director, investment company executive; b. Milw., June 13, 1946; s. Harry E. and Rose (Landau) Samson; m. Nancy K. Pinter; children: Gina Shoshana, Alayna Tamar 1 stepchild, Christopher P. BA, U. Wis., 1968. Dir., owner Puppet Co., Jerusalem, 1972-73; pres. Century Hall, Inc., Milw., 1974-75; dir. purchasing Am. Med. Svcs., Inc., Milw., 1973-74, v.p., 1974-82, exec. v.p., 1982-86, pres., 1986-90, Samson Investments, Milw., 1990—2002. Bd. dirs. Liberty Bank, Milw., 1999—2004; sec. Super Sitters, Mequon, Wis., 1987—2004. Dir.(co-prodr.): (puppet plays) Loss of Breath: The Unfinished Life and Death of Edgar Allan Poe, 1999, (co-creator): (plays) Einstein: Hero of the Mind, 2002, Stones of Wisdom, 2003, The Apollo of Bellac, 2004, The Trial - Adapted from Franz Kafka, 2005, Smoldering Fires, 2006; designer: (mask and puppet design), 2006; The Ballad of Josef K., 2008; co-dir.: Milwaukee's All-City People's Parade and Pageant, 2009. Pres. bd. dirs. Theatre X, Milw., 1982, Holton Youth Ctr., Milw., 1994, Children's Outing Assn., 1996, Jewish Found. Econ. Opportunity, 1996—2004; v.p. bd. dirs. ArtReach, Milw., 1987; mem. funding bd. Wis. Cmty. Fund, 1989—93; dir. Mask and Puppet Co. Milw., 1992—; treas. nat. bd. dirs. Am. for Peace Now, 2002—04; bd. dirs. Bnai Or Religious Fellowship, 1988—93, Milw. Jewish Coun., 1992—94, The Shalom Ctr., 2006—. Recipient Humanitarian Peace award, Ecumenical Refugee Coun., 1989, Social Justice award, Wis. Cmty. Fund, 1997, Human Rels. award, Wis. region NCCJ, 1998, Cmty. Svc. Human Rels. award, Wis. chpt. Am. Jewish Com., 2000. Avocations: chess, comic book collecting, puppetry. Office: Milwaukee Mask & Puppet Theatre 100A E Pleasant St Milwaukee WI 53212-3975

SAMUEL, ASANTE T., professional football player; b. Ft. Lauderdale, Fla., Jan. 6, 1981; s. Jasper and Christine Samuel; children: A.J., Ashante, Amaya, Aleesa. B in Bus., U. Ctrl. Fla., Orlando, 2003. Defensive back New Eng. Patriots, 2003—07, Phila. Eagles, 2008—. Named 1st Team All-Pro, AP, 2007; named to Am. Football Conf. Pro Bowl Team, NFL, 2007, Nat. Football Conf. Pro Bowl Team, 2008. Achievements include member of the Super Bowl Championship winning New England Patriots, 2004, 2005; leading the National Football League in: interceptions (10), 2006. Office: Phila Eagles NovaCare Complex One NovaCare Way Philadelphia PA 19145*

SAMUEL, CHARLES E., virologist, biochemist, educator; b. Portland, Oreg., 1945; married; 2 sons. BS in Chemistry, Mont. State U., 1968; PhD in Biochemistry, U. Calif., Berkeley, 1972. USPHS trainee U. Calif., Berkeley, 1968-72; postdoctoral tng. in virology Duke Med. Sch., Durham, N.C., 1974; asst. prof. U. Calif., Santa Barbara, 1974-79, assoc. prof., 1979-83, prof., 1983—, chmn. interdept. program biochem. and molecular biology, 1987-95; mem. Materials Rsch. Lab., 1992—2006; chmn. dept. molecular, cellular, and devel. biology U. Calif., Santa Barbara, 1995-98, 2001—04, C.A. Storke prof. molecular biology, 2002—. Guest prof. U. Zurich, 1986-87, U. Freiberg, 2005; prin. investigator NIAID, NIH, 1975—. Mem. editl. bd. Virology, 1980—, Jour. Virology, 1984-95, 2006—, Jour. Biol. Chemistry, 1989-93, 96-2000, Jour. Interferon and Cytokine Rsch., 1980—; assoc. editor Jour. Biol. Chemistry, 2000—; contbr. over 150 articles to profl. jours. Recipient Damon Runyon award, 1972, Career Devel. award NIH, 1979, Merit award NIH, 1989, Wellcome award, 1994, Humboldt award, 2001. Fellow AAAS, Am. Acad. Microbiology; mem. Am. Soc. Biochemistry-Molecular Biology, Am. Soc. for Virology, Internat. Soc. for Interferon Rsch. Avocations: fishing, music. Office: Univ Calif Dept Molecular Cellular and Devel Biology Santa Barbara CA 93106

SAMUEL, MAY LINDA, environmental scientist; d. Joe and Elvira Dixon; m. Earl Samuel; children: Annette Heyward, April Heyward. BS in Biology and Chemistry magna cum laude, Benedict Coll., 1977; MPH in Environ. Health Sci., U. SC, 1982; DD, Inst. Christian Works Coll. and Sem., 1996, PhD, ThD, 1999. Broadcaster Radio Sta. WGCV, Columbia, SC, 1984—86; asst. dir. environ. health scis. Benedict Coll., Columbia, 1990—; exec. dir. SC Environ Econ. Justice Network, Columbia, 2003—. Prof. biology Allen U., Columbia, 1984—86; cons. Inst. for Energy and Environ. Rsch., Tacoma Park, Md., 1999—2004. Contbr. articles to profl. jours. Founder, pastor Light of the World Ch., Winnsboro, SC, 1995—. Recipient SC Dept. Health and Environ. Control award, 1990, SC Dept. Corrections award, 1990; grantee, Dept. of Energy, 1995—97, EPA, 1996—99, Assn. Environ. Health, 2002—03, Sierra Club, 2003. Avocations: travel, reading. Office: Benedict Coll 1600 Harden St Columbia SC 29204-1058 Office Phone: 803-788-0370. Personal E-mail: samuelame@hotmail.com. Business E-Mail: samuelm@benedict.edu.

SAMUEL, PAUL, retired cardiologist; b. Janoshaza, Hungary, Feb. 17, 1927; arrived in U.S., 1954, naturalized, 1960; s. Adolf and Magda (Zollner) Samuel; m. Gabriella R. Zeichner, Mar. 27, 1954; children: Robert Mark, Adrianne Jill. Baccalaureat, Kemeny Zsigmond Gymnasium, Budapest, Hungary, 1945; MD, U. Paris, 1953. Intern Queens Hosp. Ctr., NYC, 1954-55; resident LI Jewish Med. Ctr., New Hyde Park, NY, 1959-61; pvt. practice Forest Hills, NY, 1961—2000; adj. prof. Rockefeller U., NYC, 1971-81; adj. prof. medicine Cornell U., NYC, 1979—; ret., 2000. Dir. Arteriosclerosis Rsch. Lab. LI Jewish-Hillside Med. Ctr., New Hyde Park, 1961—2001; chmn. NY Lipid Rsch. Club Rockefeller U., 1977—78; clin. prof. medicine Albert Einstein Coll. Medicine, Bronx, NY, 1981—. Contbr. articles to profl. jours. Fellow: Am. Coll. Cardiology; mem.: ACP, Am. Fedn. Clin. Rsch., Am. Heart Assn. (fellow coun. arteriosclerosis, Disting. Achievement award), Harvey Soc. Home: 25 Nassau Dr Great Neck NY 11021-2163

SAMUEL, RALPH DAVID, lawyer; b. Augusta, Ga., May 8, 1945; s. Ralph and Louise Elizabeth (Wurreschke) S.; m. Lynn Christel Malmgren, June 12, 1971; children: Lynn Britt, Ralph Erik. AB, Dartmouth Coll., 1967; JD, Dickinson Sch. of Law, 1972. Bar: Pa. 1972, U.S. Dist. Ct. (ea. dist.) Pa. 1972, U.S. Ct. Appeals (3d cir.) 1973, U.S. Supreme Ct. 1976. Law clk. to hon. judge John P. Fullam U.S. Dist. Ct. (ea. dist.) Pa., Phila., 1972-74; assoc. MacCoy, Evans & Lewis., Phila., 1974-76; ptnr. Samuel and Ballard, P.C., Phila., 1976-98; pres., CEO Ralph D. Samuel & Co., P.C., Phila., 1998—. Established Samuel Poetry Fellow Dartmouth Coll., Hanover, N.H., 1994. Contbr. articles to profl. jours., poetry to publs. Pres. Cedar Park Neighbors, Phila., 1975-78, West Mt. Airy Neighbors, Phila., 1981-82.; Trustee George Sch., Newtown, Pa., 1983-90; chmn. bd. dirs. Stapeley in Germantown, 1985-90, bd. dirs., mem. fin. com., 2007-09, treas., 2008-09; chmn. budget com. Phila. Yearly Meeting of Friends, 1991-93; bd. dirs., mem. fin. com. Phila. Ranger Corps., 1992-94; mem. Chase Fund Com., 2000; mem. ethics com. Friends Hosp., 2007-. Mem. Pa. Soc., Athenaeum of Phila., Sunday Breakfast Club. Mem. Soc. Of Friends. Avocations: music, writing, squash, tennis. Office: PO Box 35185 Philadelphia PA 19128-0185 Office Phone: 215-893-9992. Office Fax: 215-701-1085. Business E-Mail: RalphSamuel@RalphSamuel.com.

SAMUEL, ROBERT THOMPSON, optometrist; b. Kansas City, Mo., June 27, 1944; s. Manlius Thompson and Helen Evelyn (Syverson) S. BA, William Jewell Coll., 1966; postgrad., U. Mo., Kansas City, 1967; MS, U. Mo., 1968; DOptometry, U. Tenn., Memphis, 1971; postgrad., U. Mo., St. Louis, 1995, Northeastern State U., 1998. Cert. optometrist Mo. Buyer Recco, Inc., Kansas City, Mo., 1963-67; histology lab. instr. William Jewell Coll., Liberty, Mo., 1965-66; pvt. practice optometry Gladstone, Mo., 1972—; staff doctor O.H. Gerry Optical Clinics, 1996—. Panel doctor Ford Motor Co., Claycomo, Mo., 1985—, Union Pacific R.R., Kansas City, 1985—, TWA Airlines, 1990, Union Carbide, 1990. Publicity coord. Rep. Party, Kansas City, Mo., 1975-76; chmn. Save Your Vision Week, Kansas City, 1977; mem. Theatre League of Kansas City, 1976—, Kansas City Mus., 1986—, Friends of Art, 1985, Friends of Mo. Town 1955, 1980—. Recipient Outstanding Young Men of Am. award Jaycees, 1978, Good Citizens award DAR, 1962. Mem. Am. Optometric Assn., Mo. Optometric Assn., Optometric Soc. Greater Kansas City, Heart of Am. Contact Lens Congress, Am. Acad. Sports Vision, Vol. Optometric Svcs. for Humanity, Smithsonian Assocs., Lions (exec. bd. dir. Lions Eye Clinic 1974-84, bd. dirs. 1982—, Outstanding Svc. award 1973, 74, editor Lions Optometric Ctr. Quar. 1974-84), Kappa Alpha Order (treas. 1966). Republican. Lutheran. Avocations: photography, music, piano, swimming, travel. Home: 6325 N Monroe Ave Kansas City MO 64119-1923 Office: 1170 W 152 Hwy Liberty MO 64068-2035 also: 5601 NE Antioch Rd Kansas City MO 64119-2302 Office Phone: 816-453-7290.

SAMUEL, SELESNICK H., otolaryngologist, educator; MD, NY U. Sch. Medicine, NJ. Diplomate neurotology subspecialist Am. Bd. Otolaryngology. Prof. & vice chmn. Dept. Otorhinolaryngology, Weill Cornell Med. Coll., NYC, 1991—. Mem.: Am. Neurotology Soc. (pres. 2009—). Office: Weill Cornell Med Coll 1305 York Ave 5th Fl New York NY 10021

SAMUELI, HENRY, electrical engineer, educator, professional sports team executive; b. Buffalo, Sept. 20, 1954; s. Aron and Sala (Traubman) S.; m. Susan Faye Eisenberg, Aug. 22, 1982; children: Leslie Pamela, Jillian Meryl, Erin Sydney. BSEE, UCLA, 1975, MSEE, 1976, PhD in Elec. Engring., 1980. Staff engr. TRW Inc., Redondo Beach, Calif., 1980-83, section mgr., 1983-85, cons., 1985—89; co-founder, chief scientist PairGain Techs., Inc., Tustin, Calif., 1988—94; co-founder, chief tech. officer Broadcom Corp., Irvine, Calif., 1991—, v.p. rsch. & devel. & co-chmn., 1991—2003, chmn., 2003—08; asst. prof. UCLA, 1985-90, assoc. prof., 1990-94, prof., 1994—95, disting. adj. prof., elec. engring. and computer sci., 2003—. Co-owner Anaheim Ducks (formerly Mighty Ducks of Anaheim, 2005—. Named one of Top 20 Entrepreneurs of 1997, The Red Herring Mag., 1997, one of Top 50 Cyber Elite, Time Digital Mag., 1997; Schs. Engring. at both U. Calif. Irvine and UCLA named in honor of; recipient Presdl. award, U. Calif., 2000, Irvine medal, 2000, Alumnus of Yr. award, UCLA Sch. of Engring. and Applied Sci., 2000, Golden Plate award, Acad. Achievement, 2006. Fellow: IEEE (Circuits and Systems Soc. Indsl. Pioneer award 2000), Am. Acad. Arts & Sci.; mem.: NAE. Republican. Jewish. Holder of 22 US patents. Address: U Calif Irvine Henry Samueli Sch Engring Elec Engring and Computer Sci 325 Engineering Tower Irvine CA 92697-2625 Office: Broadcom Corporation 5300 California Ave Irvine CA 92617-3038

SAMUELS, DONALD L., lawyer; b. Washington, May 8, 1961; s. Jack Donald Samuels and Francis Diane (Katcher) Yeoman; m. Sherri Tobin Samuels. AB, Brown U., 1983; JD, Columbia U., 1986. Bar: Calif. 1986, Colo. 1996, Tex. 1998, U.S. Dist. Ct. (cen., no., ea. and so. dists.), U.S. Dist. Ct. Colo. 1997, U.S. Ct. Appeals (9th cir.) 1989, Colo. 1996, U.S. Ct. Appeals (7th cir.) 1996, U.S. Ct. Appeals (10th cir.) 1997, U.S. Supreme Ct. 2004. Law clk. Hon. William D. Keller, LA, 1986-87; assoc. Sidley & Austin, LA, 1987-94, ptnr., 1994-95, Samuels & Samuels, LA, 1995-97; officer, dir., shareholder Ireland & Stapleton, Denver, 1997—2002; ptnr. Holme, Roberts & Owen, LLP, Denver, 2002—. Mem. ABA, Calif. Bar Assn., Colo. Bar Assn., Tex. Bar Assn., Phi Beta Kappa. Home: 5692 S Florence St Greenwood Village CO 80111-3713 Office: Holme Roberts & Owen LLP Ste 4100 1700 Lincoln St Denver CO 80203-4541 Home Phone: 303-770-9119; Office Phone: 303-866-0548. Business E-Mail: donald.samuels@hro.com.

SAMUELS, DOROTHY J., journalist, writer; b. NYC, May 15, 1951; d. Herman and Roz Silver; m. Peter G. Samuels, Dec. 26, 1971; children: Laurah, Tom, Jenny. AB, Bryn Mawr Coll., 1972; JD, Northeastern U., 1975. Bar: NY. Atty. Brown & Wood, NYC, 1975—76; exec. dir. Com. for Pub. Justice, NYC, 1976—79, N.Y. Civil Liberties Union, NYC, 1979—81; cons. Ford Found., NYC, 1981—83. Mem. editl. bd. NY Times, NYC, 1985—. Author: (novels) Filthy Rich, 2001; contbr. book Then and Now, 2000, articles to mags. Office: NY Times 620 Eighth Ave New York NY 10018-1405 Business E-Mail: dosamu@nytimes.com.

SAMUELS, FERN JACQUELINE, artist, educator; b. Chgo., Feb. 16, 1931; d. Noah S. and Ann (Zager) Andrews; m. Howard Stanley Samuels, Sept. 17, 1950 (dec.); children: Mitchell, Paul, David. BFA, Loyola U., Chgo., 1973; MFA, Sch. Art Inst. Chgo., 1983. Instr.-coord. Mundelein Coll., Chgo., 1976-83; faculty Columbia Coll., 1978-2000. Instr. workshops Field Mus., Chgo., 1976, Lake Forest Coll., Chgo., 1976, Lincoln Park Cultural Ctr., Chgo., 1973, Ill. Inst. Tech., Chgo., 1980—, Latin Sch., Chgo., 1976; juror St. Louis Arts Guild, 1998; chmn. Nat. Assn. Women Artists, 2007. One-woman shows include Northwestern U., 1988, Ea. Ill. U., Chgo., 1989, Countryside Gallery, 1988, Upstart Gallery, 1990, Soho 20, N.Y.C., 1993, Loyola U., 1995, Morraine Valley Coll., 1995, McDonough Mus. Art, 1997, Fyr Place Gallery, 2000, Gallery on Azeele, 2000, Mos Art Gallery, Lake Park, Fla., 2004, Cornell Mus., Del Ray, Fla., 2004 (1st award), City Hall, Palm Beach Gardens, 2007, Amsterdam Whitney Gallery, NY, 2008, South Palm Beach Town Hall, 2009; exhibited in group shows including Smithsonian Air and Space Mus., 1983, Freeport Mus., 1995, Rockford Mus., 1996, Butler Inst. Am. Art, 1998, Lafayette Mus., 1999, Columbus Mus. Art, 2000, So. Ohio Mus., 2000, South Bend Regional Mus., 2000, Univ. Mus. S.D., 2001, Gallery 228, N.Y.C., 2003, Galleria Prinarde, 2007, Northwind U., West Palm Beach, 2007, Amsterdam Whitney Gallery, NYC, 2007, Amory Art Ctr., Fla., 2007, Arts Club Chgo., 2007, 15th Woman Made Gallery, 2007, Artists Palm Beach, 2009, Leepa Ptnr. Mus., 2009. Mem. LWV, Chgo., 1969—; founding mem. Alternative Fibers, Chgo., 1982; chairperson, coord. Seven Ethnic Museums, Chgo., 1986; membership chmn. ARC Gallery, Chgo., 1983-86, pres. 1988-90; bd. dirs. Artist Book Works, Chgo., 1992-93. Recipient Best of Show award Women in the Visual Arts, Boca Raton, Fla., 2001, Judges Recognition award, Boca Raton, 2001, 2nd award Boca Mus. Artists Guild, 2001, 1st award, 2002, 1st prize Women in Visual Arts, Del Ray, Fla., 2002, Mus. Exhibits, 2002, Jewish Mus., Miami, Norton Mus., West Palm Beach, Fla., 2002, 2004, Cornell Mus. of Art and Sci., Del Ray, 2002, Art Club Chgo., 2003, Permanent Collection, Rutgers U., 2003, 1st award Northwood U., West Palm Beach, Fla., 2003, 1st award Boca Mus. Artist Guild, 2003; grantee Columbia Coll., 1981; Fern Samuels Scholarship Fund est. Columbia Coll., Chgo., 1st award Milagro Art Ctr., Del Ray Fla., 2003, 1st award Boca Mus. Artist Guild, 2003, Artist Guild Inc 1st award, 2005, Women in the Visual Arts 1st award, 2005, Fla. Artist's Group, 2nd award, 2005. Mem. Nat. Assn. Women Artists, Internat. Soc. Exptl. Artists, Arts Club Chgo., Chgo. Soc. Artists, City of Hope (Bobby Blechman chpt. founding mem.), Sch. Art Inst. Chgo. Alumni (2d prize 2002), ARC Gallery (Chgo.) (founding mem., pres. 1983-95). Democrat. Avocations: reading, music, theater, exercise. Home: 114A Palm Bay Dr S Palm Beach Gardens FL 33418 E-mail: ucars1@aol.com.

SAMUELS, JANET LEE, lawyer; b. Pitts., July 18, 1953; d. Emerson and Jeanne (Kalish) S.; m. David Arthur Kalow, June 18, 1978; children; Margaret Emily Samuels-Kalow, Jacob Richard Samuels-Kalow, Benjamin Charles Samuels-Kalow. BA with honors, Beloit Coll., 1974; JD, NYU, 1977. Bar: N.Y. 1978, D.C. 1980. Staff atty. SCM Corp., NYC, 1977-80, corp. atty., 1980-83, sr. corp. atty., 1983-85, assoc. gen. counsel Allied Paper div., 1983-86, corp. counsel, 1986, Holtzmann, Wise & Shepard, 1986-88. Mem. N.Y. State Bar Assn., Mortar Board, Phi Beta Kappa. Personal E-mail: janet.samuels@gmail.com. E-mail: JanetLSamuels@yahoo.com, JLS@creativity-law.com.

SAMUELS, JOHN, lawyer; Grad., Vanderbilt U.; JD, U. Chgo.; LLM in Taxation, NYU. Adj. prof. taxation NYU Law Sch., 1975—86; dep. tax legis. counsel US Dept. Treasury, Washington, 1976, tax legis. counsel; ptnr. Dewey Ballantine, Washington, NYC; joined GE, 1988, v.p., sr. counsel tax policy and planning, mem. corp. exec. coun., mem. Cap. Corp. bd. dirs., mem. pension bd.; vis. lectr. Yale Law Sch., 1997—. Chmn. Internat. Tax Policy Forum; mem. Bus. Roundtable Tax Coordinating Com. Mem. vis. com. U. Chgo. Law Sch. Fellow: Am. Tax Policy Inst. Office: GE 3135 Easton Tpke Fairfield CT 06828-0001*

SAMUELS, JOHN STOCKWELL, III, mining company executive, financier; b. Galveston, Tex., Sept. 15, 1933; s. John Stockwell and Helen Yvonne (Poole) S.; children: Evelyn Kathleen, John Stockwell, Ainlay Leontine, Peter Ashton Hayes. AB, SM, Tex. A&M U., 1954; JD, Harvard U., 1960. Bar: N.Y. 1961. With Chadbourne, Parke, Whiteside & Wolff, NYC, 1960-73; pres. Internat. Carbon & Minerals, NYC, 1973-78, Carbomin Group, Inc., NYC, 1978—, U.S. Reduction Inc., 1996—, Translux Group, Inc., 2004. Chmn. bd. J.S. Samuels & Co. Bd. dirs. City Center Music and Drama, Inc., N.Y.C.; chmn. bd. dirs. N.Y.C. Ballet, N.Y.C. Opera, 1976-81, Lincoln Ctr. Theatre, N.Y.C., 1979-81, Lincoln Ctr., N.Y.C. With U.S. Army, 1954-57. Mem. Century Assn. Democrat. Episcopalian. Personal E-mail: jss@txdubai.com.

SAMUELS, LESLIE B., lawyer; b. St. Louis, Nov. 10, 1942; s. Joseph E. and Dorothy J. (Bernstein) S.; m. Judith B. Thorn, June 19, 1966 (div. Aug. 1976); children: Colin T., Polly B.; m. Augusta H. Gross, Nov. 8, 1980. BS in Econs., U. Pa., 1963; LLB magna cum laude, Harvard U., 1966; postgrad., London Sch. Econs., 1966-67. Bar: N.Y., 1969, U.S. Dist. Ct. (so. dist.) N.Y. 1973, U.S. Tax Ct., 1980, U.S. Supreme Ct. 1994; CPA. Tax analyst Gulf Oil Co., London, 1967-68; assoc. Cleary Gottlieb Steen & Hamilton LLP, NYC, 1968-75, ptnr., 1975-93, 96—; asst. sec. for tax policy U.S. Dept. Treasury, Washington, 1993-96; vice-chair com. fiscal affairs OECD, 1994-96. Mem. Pres.'s Com. on the Arts and the Humanities, Washington, 1994-96. Editor Law Rev.; contbr. articles to profl. jours. Dir. Lower Manhattan Cultural Coun., N.Y.C., 1981-93, Roy Lichtenstein Found., N.Y.C., 1999—; active Carter-Mondale Transition Planning Group, Washington, 1976-77. Fulbright fellow London Sch. Econs., 1966-67. Mem. N.Y. State Bar Assn., Assn. of Bar of City of N.Y., Harvard Club (N.Y.C.). Democrat. Office: Cleary Gottlieb Steen & Hamilton LLP One Liberty Plaza New York NY 10006 Home Phone: 212-535-4209; Office Phone: 212-225-2250. Business E-Mail: lsamuels@cgsh.com.

SAMUELS, MARTIN ALLEN, neurologist; b. Cleve., June 24, 1945; BA, Williams Coll., 1967; MD, U. Cin., 1971. Diplomate Am. Bd. Internal Medicine, Am. Bd. Psychiatry and Neurology (examiner 1983-90). Intern in internal medicine Boston City Hosp., 1971-72, jr. resident in internal medicine, 1972-73, chief resident in internal medicine, 1974-75; jr. resident in neurology Mass. Gen. Hosp., Boston, 1973-74, clin. fellow in neuropathology, 1975-76, sr. resident in neurology, 1976-77, clin. assoc. neurology, 1988-95, sr. cons., 1995—; staff physician Mass. Rehab. Hosp., Boston, 1975-76; jr. assoc. medicine Brigham and Women's Hosp., Boston, 1977-81, assoc. medicine, 1981-82, physician, 1982-88, neurologist-in-chief, 1988—; assoc. neurology Beth Israel-Deaconess Hosp., Boston, 1987—. Clin. fellow in neurology Harvard Med. Sch., Boston, 1973-74, 76-77, clin. fellow neuropathology, 1975-76, from instr. to assoc. prof. neurology, 1977-93, prof., 1993-; tchg. assoc. medicine Boston U. Sch. Medicine, 1974-75; chief neurology sect. VA Med. Ctr., West Roxbury, Mass., 1977-81, chief rehab. medicine svc., 1978-80; chief neurology svc. Brockton-W. Roxbury VA Med. Ctr., 1981-88; founding editor, JournalWatch Neurology, 1999, editor-in-chief, 1999- Ad hoc reviewer Neurology, Annals Neurology, Annals Internal Medicine, New Eng. Jour. Medicine; mem. sci. adv. bd. Clin. Brain Imaging; mem. editl. bd. Neurologist; contbr. articles to profl. jours. Recipient Disting. Alumni award, U. Cin. Coll. Medicine, 1996, Daniel Drake medal, 2005, Harvard Med. Sch. Faculty prize for Excellence in Teaching, AB Baker award for Lifetime Achievement in Neurologic Edn., 2006, H. Houston Merritt award, Am. Acad. Neurology, 2007. Mem. AAAS, ACP, Am. Acad. Neurology, Royal Soc. Medicine (London), Pan Am. Med. Assn., Boston Soc. Neurology and Psychiatry, Am. Neurol. Assn. Office: Brigham and Women's Hosp 75 Francis St BB 204 Boston MA 02115-6106 Office Phone: 617-732-5355. E-mail: msamuels@partners.org.

SAMUELS, SANDOR ELI, lawyer, diversified financial services company executive; b. LA, Aug. 22, 1952; m. Claudia Wallack; 3 children. AB summa cum laude, Princeton U., NJ, 1974; JD, UCLA, 1977. Bar: Calif. 1977, US Dist. Ct. (ctrl. dist. Calif.) 1977. Law clk. to Hon. Irving Hill US Dist. Ct. (ctrl. dist. Calif.), 1977—79; atty. Munger, Tolles & Olson, 1979—83, First Interstate Bancorp, 1984—88, sr. v.p., asst. gen. counsel, 1988; sr. v.p., gen. counsel Fox Inc., 1989—90; sr. v.p., gen. counsel, sec. Countrywide Fin. Corp., Calabasas, Calif., 1990—91, mng. dir., legal, gen. counsel. sec., 1991—2000, sr. mng. dir., legal, gen. counsel, sec., 2001—03, sr. mng. dir., chief legal adv., sec., 2003, exec. mng. dir., chief legal adv., asst. sec. Bd. dirs. U. Judaism, Ziegler Sch. Rabbinic Studies, Shalhevet Sch., Bet Tzedek Legal Svcs., Adat Ari El Synagogue. Mem.: Mortgage Bankers Assn. Am. (chmn. legal services com. 1995—96), State Bar Calif., LA County Bar Assn., ABA, Order of the Coif. Office: Countrywide Fin Corp 4500 Park Granada Calabasas CA 91302-1613

SAMUELS, WARREN JOSEPH, retired economics professor; b. NYC, Sept. 14, 1933; s. Emanuel Abraham and Lillian Naomi (Glazer) S.; m. Sylvia Joan Strake, June 27, 1954; children: Kathy Joan Samuels Nagy, Susan Jill. BBA, U. Miami, Coral Gables, Fla., 1954; MS, U. Wis., 1955, PhD, 1957. Asst. prof. econs. U. Mo., Columbia, 1957-58, Ga. State U., Atlanta, 1958-59; from asst. prof. to assoc. prof. U. Miami, Coral Gables, 1959-68; prof. econs. Mich. State U., East Lansing, 1968—98. Cons. in field. Author: Classical Theory of Economic Policy, 1966, Pareto on Policy, 1974; editor: Fundamentals of the Economic Role of Government, 1989, Economics as Discourse, 1990, Economics, Government and Law, 2002, A Companion to The History of Economic Thought, 2003, Essays in the History of Economics, 2004, The Legal-Economic Nexus, 2007. Pres. History of Econs. Soc., 1981-82, Assn. for Social Econs., 1988. Mem. Am. Econ. Assn., So. Econ. Assn., Assn. for Evolutionary Econs., Law and Soc. Assn., History of Sci. Soc., History of Econs. Soc. (pres. 1981-82), Assn. for Social Econs. (pres. 1988), Nat. Tax Assn. Avocations: cooking, mystery stories. Home: 8476 SW 10th Rd Gainesville FL 32607 Home Phone: 352-331-7126. Personal E-mail: wjsamuels@bellsouth.net. Business E-Mail: samuels@msu.edu.

SAMUELS, WILLIAM MASON, physiology association executive; b. Dover, Ohio, Jan. 17, 1929; s. William Mason and Anne Frieda (Fankhauser) S.; m. Joanne Gorenflo, Oct. 2, 1971; children: Robert Lee, Ann Frances. AB, U. Ky., 1951; postgrad., Georgetown U., 1952. Mng. editor for Ind., Courier-Jour. & Times, Louisville, 1955-65; dir. office of v.p. U. Ky. Med. Center, Lexington, 1965-70; exec. dir. Am. Soc. Allied Health Professions, Washington, 1973—78; assoc. Schs. Allied Health Professions, 1970—73; exec. dir. Am. Assn. Blood Banks, Washington, 1978-80, Nat. Soc. Med. Research Washington, 1980-84, Am. Physiol. Soc., Bethesda, Md., 1984-92; retired, 1992—. Contbr. articles to profl. jours. Mem. secretarist Nat. Commn. Health Certifying Agys.; v.p. Coalition Health Funding; cons. to fed. agys.; vol. Habitat for Humanity, Boca Raton; elder Presbyn. Ch., corp. dir. With USAF, 1951-53, USAFR, 1954-76, lt. col. ret. Named Ky. Man of Yr. Sigma Phi Epsilon, 1968 Mem.: AMA (coun. on allied health edn. accreditation), Washington Soc. Assn. Execs., Health Staff Soc., Am. Hosp. Assn. (coun. on edn.), Am. Optometric Assn. (coun. on edn., coun. on optimetric clin. care, nat. commn. on paraoptometric cert.), Am. Soc. Assn. Execs., Pinehurst (NC) Country Club, Lions. Presbyterian. Home: 6055 S Verde Trail H-120 Boca Raton FL 33433-4406

SAMUELSON, CECIL O., JR., academic administrator; b. 1942; m. Sharon Giauque; 5 children. BS, MS, MD, U. Utah. V.p. health scis. U. Utah, Salt Lake City, 1970-90; sr. v.p. Intermountain Health Care, Inc., Salt Lake City, 1990—94; dean IHC Hosps. Inc., Salt Lake City, 1990—; pres. Brigham Young U., Provo, Utah, 2003—. Pres. LDS Ch. No. Area, Utah; Pres. LDS Ch. Europe No. Area; mem. First Quorum of the Seventy, Ch. of LDS, 1994—2003. Office: Office of the Pres Brigham Young U Provo UT 84602 Office Phone: 801-422-2521.*

SAMUELSON, DREY, legislative staff member; b. Lincoln, Nebr., Dec. 5, 1952; s. Ronald Kent and Patricia Ann (Raun) S. BA, U. Nebr., 1970-75; attended, U. Ariz., Tucson, 1984—85. Field rep. Congressman Tom Daschle, Sioux Falls, SD, 1979-81; adminstrv. asst. Nebr. Farmers Union, Lincoln, 1981-83; writer Tucson, 1984-86; chief of staff to Tim Johnson US House Representatives, Washington, 1987—96, US Senate, Washington, 1997—. Contbr. article to mags. V.p. Lancaster County Dem., Lincoln, Nebr., 1983; campaign mgr. Tim Johnson for Congress, Sioux Falls, SD, 1986. Democrat. Unitarian. Office: Office of Senator Tim Johnson 136 Senate Hart Office Bldg Washington DC 20510-4104 Office Phone: 202-224-5842. E-mail: drey_samuelson@johnson.senate.gov.*

SAMUELSON, KENNETH LEE, lawyer; b. Natrona Heights, Pa., Aug. 22, 1946; s. Sam and Frances Bernice (Robbins) Samuelson; m. Marlene Ina Rabinowitz, Jan. 1, 1980; children: Heather, Cheryl. BA magna cum laude, U. Pitts., 1968; JD, U. Mich., 1971. Bar: Md. 1972, DC 1980, U.S. Dist. Ct. (trial bar) Md. 1984. Assoc. Weinberg & Green, Balt., 1971-73, Dickerson, Nice, Sokol & Horn, Balt., 1973; asst. atty. gen. State of Md., 1973-77; pvt. practice Balt., 1978; ptnr. Linowes and Blocher, Silver Spring, Md., 1979-93, Semmes, Bowen & Semmes, Balt. and Washington, 1993—95, Wilkes Artis, Chartered, Washington, 1995—2001, Deckelbaum Ogens & Raftery, Bethesda, Md., 2001—08; founder Samuelson Law Offices, LLC, Washington, 2008—. Spkr. in field. Bd. govs. Washington Bldg. Congress, 1998—2001; spkr. CoreNet Global, 2006, Harvard Bus. Club Washington, 2006; bd. dirs. DC Assn. Retarded Citizens, Inc., 1986—2001. Mem.: ABA (moderator various real estate and bankruptcy programs 1986—2008, co-chair tech. com. 1999—2006, coun. mem. sect. real property, probate and trust law

2000—06), Am. Coll. Real Estate Lawyers (moderator, spkr. at various bankruptcy, leasing and telecom. programs 1998—2008), Internat. Assn. Attys. and Exec. in Corp. Real Estate (spkr. in field 2006, CLE spkr. 2006—07, spkr. in field 2007), Am. Inns of Ct. (spkr. on various transactional issues in bankruptcy cases 2006—08, law seminars internat. spkr. & moderator programs comml. leases 2008—09, Nat. Underwriters Stewart Title 2008), Montgomery County Bar Assn. (mem. jud. selections com. 1988—90), Internat. Coun. Shopping Ctrs. (organized co-faculty program "univ." 1988, NAFTA 1992, condemnations 1994, leasing 1997, high tech. effects 1998, pub./pvt. partnerships 1999), E. Coast Builders Conf., Apt. and Office Bldg. Assn. Met. Washington, Civil Code Drafting Com. Russian Legis., Nat. Assn. Corp. Real Estate Execs., Washington Assn. Realtors, Inc., DC Bldg. Industry Assn., Am. Arbitration Assn. (arbitrator, mediator 1995—2003), Md. Inst. Continuing Profl. Edn. Lawyers, Md. Bar Assn. (litig. sect. 1982—84, real property, planning and zoning sect., chmn. comml. trans. com.), DC Bar (mem. comml. real estate com., chmn. legal opinions project), Lambda Alpha, Phi Beta Kappa. Office: Samuelson Law Offices LLC 2020 Pa Ave NW 417 Washington DC 20006 Office Phone: 202-494-0848. Business E-Mail: cyberlegal@comcast.net.

SAMUELSON, PAUL ANTHONY, economist, educator; b. Gary, Ind., May 15, 1915; s. Frank and Ella (Lipton) Samuelson; m. Marion E. Crawford, July 2, 1938 (dec.); children: Jane Kendall, Margaret Wray, William Frank, Robert James, John Crawford, Paul Reid; m. Risha Eckaus, 1981; 1 stepchild, Susan Miller. BA, U. Chgo., 1935; MA, Harvard U., 1936, PhD (David A. Wells prize 1941), 1941; LLD (hon.), U. Chgo., Oberlin Coll., 1961, Boston Coll., 1964, Ind. U., 1966, U. Mich., 1967, Claremont Grad. Sch., 1967, Seton Hall U., 1971, U. N.H., 1971, Keio U., 1971, Widener Coll., 1982, Cath. U. at Riva Aguero U., Lima, Peru, 1980, Harvard, 1972, Gustavus Adolphus Coll., 1974, U. So. Calif., 1975, U. Pa., 1976, U. Rochester, 1976, Emmanuel Coll., 1977, Stonehill Coll., 1978, Indiana U. of Pa., 1993; DLitt (hon.), Ripon Coll., 1962, No. Mich. U., 1973, Valparaiso U., 1987, Columbia U, 1988; LHD (hon.), Williams Coll., 1971; DSc (hon.), U. Mass., 1972, U. R.I., 1972, Tufts U., 1988, East Anglia U., Norwich, Eng., 1966, Rennselaer Poly. Inst., 1998; D (hon.), U. Catholique de Louvain, Belgium, 1976, City U., London, 1980, New U. Lisbon, 1985, Univ. Nat. de Educacion a Distancia, Madrid, 1989, Univ. Politecnica de Valencia, Spain, 1991; D in Social Scis. (hon.), Yale U., 2005. Prof. econs. MIT, 1940—65, inst. prof., 1966, prof. emeritus, 1986; mem. staff Radiation Lab., 1944—45; prof. internat. econ. relations Fletcher Sch. Law & Diplomacy, Tufts U., 1945; cons. Nat. Resources Planning Bd., 1941—43, WPB, 1945, US Dept. Treasury, 1945—52, 1961—74, Bur. Budget, 1952, RAND Corp., 1948—75, Fed. Res. Bd., 1965—; mem. Council Econ. Advisers, Exec. Office of the Pres., 1960—68; econ. adviser to Pres. Kennedy The White House; sr. adviser Brookings Panel on Econ. Activity; mem. spl. commn. on social scis. NSF, 1967—68; cons. Congl. Budget Office, Federal Reserve Bd., 1965—; Gordon Y Billard Fellow MIT, Boston, 1986—; vis. prof of polit. econ. Ctr. Japan-U.S. Bus. and Econ. Studies, NYU, 1987—2005. Mem. nat. adv. com. Inst. for Rsch. on Poverty; lectr. in field. Author: Foundations of Economic Analysis, 1947, enlarged edit., 1983, Readings in Economics, 1955; author: (with R. Dorfman and R.M. Solow) Linear Programming and Economic Analysis, 1958; author: Collected Scientific Papers, 5 vols., 1966, 1972, 1978, 1986, Economics 1948-1980; co-author (with William Nordhaus): Economics, 1985—; author: numerous other books; columnist Newsweek, 1966—81; assoc. editor: Jour. Pub. Econs., Jour. Internat. Econs., Jour. Fin. Econs., Jour. Nonlinear Analysis, adv. bd.: Challenge Mag.; contbr. articles to profl. jours. Chmn. Pres.'s Task Force Maintaining Am. Prosperity, 1964; mem. Nat. Task Force on Econ. Edn., 1960—61; econ. adviser to Pres. John F. Kennedy, 1959—63; mem. adv. bd. Nat. Commn. Money and Credit, 1958—60. Recipient David A. Wells prize, Harvard U., 1941, John Bates Clark medal, Am. Econ. Assn., 1947, Alfred Nobel Meml. prize, 1970, medal of Honor, U. Evansville, Ill., 1970, Albert Einstein Commemorative award, 1971, Alumni medal, U. Chgo., 1983, Britannica award, 1989, Gold Scanno prize, Naples, Italy, 1990, Paul A. Samuelson Professorship established in his name, MIT, 1991, Nat. Medal of Sci., Washington, 1996; fellow hon. fellow, London Sch. Econs. and Polit. Sci., Guggenheim, 1948—49, rsch. fellow, Ford Found., 1958—59. Fellow: Econometric Soc. (v.p. 1950, pres. 1951), Am. Philos. Soc., Am. Econ. Assn. (hon.; pres. 1961), Brit. Acad. (corr.); mem.: NAS, AAAS, Nat. Assn. Investment Clubs (Disting. Svc. award in Investment Edn. 1974), Leibniz-Akademie der Wissenschaften und der Literatur (corr.), Internat. Econ. Assn. (pres. 1966—68, hon. pres.), Com. Econ. Devel. (commn. on nat. goals, rsch. adv. bd. 1959—60), Club of Econ. and Mgmt. (medal, hon. Valencia, Spain 1990), Omicron Delta Epsilon (trustee), Phi Beta Kappa. Office: MIT E52 # 383C Dept Econs 50 Memorial Dr Cambridge MA 02142 Office Phone: 617-253-3368.

SAMUELSON, PETER A., management consultant; b. Taipei, Taiwan, Feb. 14, 1968; s. David Morris and Millie Marie (Nelson) Samuelson; married; 1 child. BA, Greenville Coll., Ill., 1990; JD, Yale U., 1993. Legal rschr. Lovell White Durrant, Hong Kong, 1993-94; assoc. Hughes Hubbard Reed, NYC, 1994-96, McKinsey & Co., Inc., NYC, 1996; dir. strategic planning Byran Cave, St. Louis; pres. Americans United for Life, Chgo., 2004—. Bd. dirs. Americans United for Life, St. Louis, 2000—; trustee Ctr. Bioethics and Culture. Summer rsch. grantee Ford Found., 1993. Methodist. Office: Americans United for Life 310 S Peoria Ste 500 Chicago IL 60607 E-mail: peter.samuelson@usa.net.

SAMUELSON, ROBERT JACOB, journalist; b. NYC, Dec. 23, 1945; s. Abraham and Joan (Kahn) Samuelson; m. Judith Herr, July 10, 1983; children: Ruth, Michael, John. AB in Govt., Harvard U., 1967. Reporter Washington Post, 1969-73, contbg. editor, columnist, 1977—; free-lance writer Washington, 1973-76; reporter, columnist National Jour. mag., Washington, 1976-84; contbg. editor, columnist Newsweek, Washington, 1984—. Author: The Good Life and Its Discontents: The American Dream in the Age of Entitlement, 1995, Untruth: Why the Conventional Wisdom Is (Almost Always) Wrong, 2001, The Great Inflation and Its Aftermath: The Past and Future of American Affluence, 2008. Recipient Nat. Mag. award, 1981, Gerald Loeb award for Commentary, 1983, 1986, 1993, Nat. Headliner award for Best Spl. Interest Column, 1987, Nat. Headliner award for Feature Column on a Single Subject, 1992, 1993, John Hancock award for Best Bus./Fin. Columnist, 1993. Office: Newsweek Ste 1220 1750 Pennsylvania Ave NW Washington DC 20006-4578

SAMUELSSON, MARCUS (KASSHUN TSEGIE), food service executive; b. Ethiopia; Degree, Culinary Inst. Göteborg, Switzerland. Chef Aquavit, NYC, 1991, worked under Jan Sendel, exec. chef & co-owner, 1995—, opened Mpls.; chef Georges Blanc, Lyon, France; exec. chef & co-owner AQ Café at Scandinavia House, NYC; exec. chef, owner Merkato 55, NYC. Chosen to cook for Sweden's royal family; chosen to cook at gala dinner honoring the late Patrick Clark at Tavern on the Green; launched new line of traditional Swedish prepared foods; chef's coun. Chefs for Humanity. Featured Gourmet, USA Today, Food and Wine, NY Times, Australian Vogue Entertaining, appeared CNN, Discovery Channel, ABC's Good Morning Am., (numerous local N.Y. TV programs); author: Aquavit: And the New Scandinavian Cuisine, 2003, The Soul of a New Cuisine: A Discovery of the Foods & Flavors of Africa, 2006 (Libr. Jour. Fall Editor's Pick, 2006). Recipient three-star restaurant rev. for Aquavit, NY Times, four-star rating, Forbes, three and a half-star rating, Crain's; named Best Rising Star Chef, James Beard Found., 1999; named one of Great Chefs Am., Culinary Inst. Am.; named to Power 150, Ebony mag., 2008. Avocations: museums, art galleries. Office: Aquavit Inc 424 Madison Ave Rm 1410 New York NY 10017-1160

SAMUELSSON, MIKAEL, professional hockey player; b. Mariefred, Sweden, Dec. 23, 1976; Right wing San Jose Sharks, 2001, NY Rangers, 2001—03, Pitts. Penguins, 2003, Fla. Panthers, 2003—04, Detroit Red Wings, 2005—. Achievements include being a member of gold medal winning Swedish Hockey Team, Torino Olympics, Italy, 2006; being a member of Stanley Cup Champion Detroit Red Wings, 2008. Office: Detroit Red Wings Joe Louis Arena 600 Civic Center Dr Detroit MI 48226

SAMY, RAVI, otolaryngologist; b. Chennai, India, June 26, 1969; m. Cgrrle Samy; children: Emma, Gabeield. BS in Zoology magna cum laude, Duke U., Durham, NC, 1991, MD, 1995. Diplomate Am. Bd. Otolaryngology, 2001, cert. in nuerologgy ABO, 2004. Resident gen. surgery Stanford U. Med. Ctr., Calif., 1995—96, resident otolaryngology, 1996—99, chief resident otolaryngology, 1999—2000; asst. prof. Southwestern Med. Ctr., Dallas, 2002—05, U. Cin., 2005—; fellow Otology, neurology, skull base surgery U. Iowa Hosps. and Clinics, Iowa City, 2000—02. Contbr. articles to jours. publs., chapters to books. Recipient Cin. Creates Co. award, Svc. Action award, Stanford U. Med. Ctr., 1996; named to Deans List, Duke U., 1988—90. Fellow: ACS, Am. Neurotology Soc.; mem.: Acoustic Neuroma Assn., Tex. Med. Assn., Dallas County Med. Soc., Assn. Rsch. Otolaryngology, Pediat. Soc. Greater Dallas, North Am. Skull Base Soc., Cin. Soc. Otolaryngology, The Politzer Soc., Phi Eta Sigma, Am. Acad. Otolarygology, Duke U. Cornerstone Soc., Duke Club (North Tex.), Golden Key, Phi Beta Kappa. Office: Univ Cin 231 Albert Sabin Way Cincinnati OH 45269 Office Fax: 513-558-5203. Business E-Mail: ravi.samy@uc.edu.

SANABRIA, SERGIO LUIS, architecture educator; b. La Habana, Cuba, Oct. 14, 1944; m. Linda Alice Holubar, Feb. 1, 1969. Prof. Miami U., Oxford, Ohio, 1980—. Office: Miami Univ Dept Architecture & Interior Design Oxford OH 45056 Business E-Mail: sanabrsl@muohio.edu.

SAN AGUSTIN, JOE TAITANO, political organization worker, educator; b. Agana, Guam, Oct. 15, 1930; s. Candido S. and Maria P. (Taitano) San A.; m. Carmen Santos Shimizu, June 18, 1955; children: Mary, Ann, Joe, John. BA, George Washington U., 1954, MA, 1956. Chief budget and mgmt. Office of Govt. Guam, Agana, 1966-68; dir. dept. adminstrn. Govt. Guam, Agana, 1968-74; senator Guam Legislature, Agana, 1977—95; asst. v.p. Bank of Guam. Minority leader 16th Guam Legislature, 1981-82, vice-speaker 17th and 18th Guam Legislature, 1983-86, chmn. com. on ways and means 17th and 18th Guam Legislatures, 1983-86, chmn. com. on health, edn. and welfare 19th Guam Legislature, 1987, chmn. com. on edn., 1991, econ. com.; speaker 20th, 21st, 22nd Guam Legislature, 1989-95, chmn. econ. com. Guam Legis., 1975. bd. dirs. Bank of Guam, Agana; chmn. bd. dirs. Guam Greyhound, Inc., Guam Aqua Rsch. Inc.; chmn. Guam Dem. Party, Gov. Co. Employee Retirement Bd.; adj. instr. U. Guam. Democrat. Roman Catholic. Business E-Mail: jtsa@kyentus.guam.net.

SANAK, FRANCENE ELIZABETH, librarian; d. Valencia Sanak. MusB, Western Mich. U., Kalamazoo, 1974; MILS, U. Mich., Ann Arbor, 1975. Dir. Lincoln Pk. Libr., Mich., 1987—99, Trenton Vets. Meml. Libr., Mass., 1999—. Youth svcs. libr. Redford Twp. Libr., Mich., 1983—87. Violist Dearborn Symphony Orch., Mich., 2008. Mem.: Trenton Vets. Meml. Libr., Mich. Libr. Assn. Roman Catholic. Avocations: reading, music, travel. Office: Trenton Vets Meml Libr 2790 Westfield Rd Trenton MI 48183 Business E-Mail: tren@trenton.lib.mi.us.

SANANMAN, MICHAEL LAWRENCE, neurologist; b. Bklyn., Oct. 11, 1939; s. Jack and Sarey (Bykofsky) S.; m. Elisa Joan Freeman, Apr. 12, 1964; children: Amy, Peter. AB, Swarthmore Coll., 1960; MD, Columbia U., 1964. Diplomate Am. Bd. Psychiatry and Neurology. Intern U. Hosp., San Francisco, 1964-65; resident in neurology N.Y. Neurol. Inst., NYC, 1966-69; practice medicine specializing in neurology Elizabeth, N.J., 1972—. Cons. neurologist Rahway (N.J.) Hosp., Trinitas Hosp., N.J., Union Hosp., N.J.; instr. neurology Columbia U., N.Y.C., 1971-75; assoc. clin. prof. neurology U. Medicine and Dentistry N.J., Newark, 1975—. Lt. comdr. M.C., USNR, 1969-71. Mem. AMA, Am. Acad. Neurology, Am. Epilepsy Soc., N.J. Acad. Medicine, Am. Eastern EEG Socs., Am. Assn. EMG and Electrodiagnosis. Office: 700 N Broad St Elizabeth NJ 07208-2310 Office Phone: 908-354-3994. Personal E-mail: Mikesan48@aol.com.

SANBERG, PAUL RONALD, medical educator; b. Coral Gables, Fla., Jan. 4, 1955; s. Bernard and Molly (Spector) Sanberg BS with honors, York U., 1976; MS, U. B.C., 1979; PhD, Australian Nat. U., 1981, DSc, 1998; grad. diploma sci. edn., West Australia Inst. Tech., 1986. Post-doctoral fellow Johns Hopkins Med. Sch., Balt., 1981—83; asst. prof. Ohio U., Athens, 1983—86; assoc. prof. U. Cin., 1986—89; prof. Brown U., Providence, 1990—92, U. South Fla., Tampa, 1992—2003, assoc. v.p., 2003—, disting. prof., 2003—, assoc. dean, 2003—06, chair neurosci., 1997—2005, dir. Ctr. of Excellence for Aging and Brain Repair, 2000—. Co-founder Saneron Therapeutics, Inc., 2000—. Recipient award Am. Coll. Neuropsychopharmacology, Tourette Syndrome Assn., Sir. J.G. Crawford medal, Ove Ferno prize Coll. Internat. Neuropsychopharmacology; grantee NIH, Am. Heart Assn., Childrens Med. Rsch. Found., Hereditary Disease Found., Huntington's Disease Found., Outstanding Rschr. award Sigma Xi; named Healthcare Hero, Tampa Bay Bus. Jour., 2006. Mem. APA, Soc. for Neurosci., Psychonomic Soc., Internat. Brain Rsch. Orgn., Internat. Behavioral Neurosci. Soc. (pres. 1994, Outstanding Rschr. award 2004), Am. Soc. for Neural Transplant (pres. 1995), Cell Transplant Soc. (pres. 1996, editor). Home: 11751 Pilot Country Dr Spring Hill FL 34610-7912 Office: U South Fla Coll Medicine Dept NeuroSurgery & Brain Surgery MDC 78 12901 Bruce B Downs Blvd Tampa FL 33612-4742 Business E-Mail: psanberg@health.usf.edu.

SANBORN, GEORGE FREEMAN, JR., genealogist; b. Laconia, NH, Jan. 18, 1944; s. George Freeman and Charlotte (Dearborn) S.; m. Melinde Laura Lutz, Mar. 30, 1984 (div.); children: Ruth Alice, Lowell Freeman. AB, Boston U., 1967; AM, U. Ill., 1968; MEd, U. N.H., 1981. French tchr. Souris (P.E.I., Can.) Regional H.S., 1968-69; French and occupational studies tchr. Massey-Vanier H.S., Cowansville, Que., Canada, 1969-70; French and English tchr. Kings Coll. Sch., Windsor, N.S., Canada, 1970-71; translator, revisor Province of N.B., Fredericton, 1971-73; sr. govt. revisor Province of Ont., Toronto, 1973-75; French and Spanish tchr. Tilton (N.H.) Sch., 1978-80; living unit coord. Laconia (N.H.) State Sch., 1982-83; ref. libr. New Eng. Hist. Geneal. Soc., Boston, 1983-85, acquisitions libr., dir. libr. ops., 1985-95, publs. asst., 1996-2000, ref. libr., 2000—05. Editor The N.H. Geneal. Record, 1990-93; co-compiler Vital Records of Hampton, N.H., 1992, 98; compiler: Deaths of Prince Edward Islanders in Massachusetts, 1889-1900, 6 vols., 2006; contbr. articles to profl. jours. Fellow Am. Soc. Genealogists; mem. Soc. Cin., Soc. Mayflower Descs., New Eng. Hist. Geneal. Soc., P.E.I. Geneal. Soc., N.H. Soc. Genealogists (pres. 1988-95), Geneal. Soc. Vt. (chair publs. com. 1992-96), N.B. Geneal. Soc., Cape Breton Genealogy and Hist. Assn. Democrat. Presbyterian. Avocations: gardening, bantam raising, Scottish Gaelic language, antique glass and china. Home: 15 Leslie Crescent 9 Charlottetown PE C1C 1P7 Canada

SANBORN, KATHY, musician, recording artist and author; BA in Psychology, Calif. State U., Sacramento, 1989. Author: The Seasons of Your Career, 2003; singer (composer): (CD) Peaceful Sounds, 2008; columnist (to various web sites). Mem.: Golden Key Honor Soc. (life). Business E-Mail: kathy@kathysanborn.com.

SANBORNE, ERIKA L., psychology professor; b. Lowell, Mass., Oct. 1, 1974; d. Eleanor Schonbom Morgan. MA, U. Mass., Lowell, 2002; attending, Andover Newton Theol. Sch., Mass., 2009. Lic. educator Mass., 2005. Math support program developer Middlesex CC, Lowell, 2003—; psychology educator U. Mass., Lowell, 2004—. Contbr. articles to profl. jour. Seminarian. Non-commd. officer USCG, 1994—97, San Juan, Puerto Rico. Decorated Comdt.'s Letter Commendation US, Meritorious Unit Commendation, Transp. Gold medal award, Humanitarian Svc. award. Mem.: APA, Soc. Cmty. Rsch. and Action. Office: Univ Mass Mahoney Hall 870 Broadway St Lowell MA 01854 Business E-Mail: erika_sanborne@uml.edu.

SANCHEZ, ALITA CASSANDRA, physical education educator, personal trainer; d. John Phillip and Florinda Lou Sanchez; m. Christopher Brendan McManus, July 31, 2006; 1 child, Sarah. BA in English Lit., U. Calif., Santa Cruz, 1991; tchg. credential, San Francisco State U., 1997. Adapted phys. edn. specialist Hayward Unified Sch. Dist., Calif., 1997—98, Oakland Unified Sch. Dist., Calif., 1998—. Vol. adult leader Family Resource Network, Oakland, 2001—05; vol. coach/capt. Students Run Oakland, 2002—05. Mem.: Calif. Assn. Health, Phys. Fitness, Recreation and Dance, Am. Coll. Sports Medicine (cert. health and fitness instr.).

SANCHEZ, ANGEL, apparel designer; b. Venezuela; Degree in Architecture, Simon Bolivar U., Caracas, Venezuela, 1984. Architect; launched first clothing label Venezuela, 1991; head designer Angel Sanchez evening collection, NYC, 1997—; debuted bridal collection, 1999. Costume designer Danzaho, Venezuela, Teatro Nacional, Venezuela, off-Broadway show Orphans, NYC. Recipient Golden Coast Fashion award, Buyers and Retailers of North America, 1998, MODA award, Washington, DC, 1999, New Star award, Miami, 2000, Casita Maria New Designer award, NYC, 1999. Mem.: Coun. Fashion Designers of America. Achievements include designing evening dresses and wedding gowns to various Hollywood stars. Office: Angel Sanchez Inc 148 W 37th St 7th Fl New York NY 10018*

SANCHEZ, CINDI ASBURY, physical education educator; d. Edgar Allen and Idabell Rogers Asbury; m. Sonny Anthony Sanchez, July 12, 1980; children: Erin, Sonny. BS, North Tex. State U., Denton, 1976. Tchr. phys. edn. Poteet (Tex.) Ind. Sch. Dist., 1976—78; tchr. phys. edn., coach Schertz (Tex.), Cibilo, and Universal City Ind. Sch. Dist., 1978—81; tchr. phys. edn. St. Mary's Episcopal Sch., Edmond, Okla., 2000—, pres. phys. edn., 2004, Fitness Challenge Active Lifestyle Model Sch., 2000—08, Trinity Sch., 2007—09. Bd. dirs. Parents Helping Parents, Edmond, 2002—. Recipient Small Sch. State Champion, Pres.' Phys. Fitness Challenge, 2006, 2007; named Mathews Elem. Vol. of Yr., Plano Ind. Sch. Dist., 1993, Small Sch. State Champion, Pres.' Phys. Fitness Challenge, 2004, 2005. Mem.: AAHPERD, Okla. Alliance for Health, Phys. Edn., Recreation, and Dance. Avocations: softball, soccer, woodworking, landscaping. Office: Trinity Sch 1120 E Hefnei Rd Oklahoma City OK 73131 Office Phone: 405-341-9541.

SANCHEZ, DANMARY, research scientist; b. Havana, Cuba, Dec. 23, 1977; arrived in US, 1991; d. Daniel Sanchez and Mara Haydee Ramirez; m. Roberto Perez Albertini, May 31, 2003. BS in Computer Engring., Fla. Internat. U., Miami, 1999, MS in Computer Engring., 2001, PhD in Elec. Engring., 2006. Software engr. IBM, Research Triangle Park, NC, 1998, Motorola, Plantation, Fla., 1999—; rsch. sci. Fla. Internat. U., Miami Children's Hosp., Miami, 2003—. Catequist St. Cecilia Cath. Ch., Miami, 1999—. Recipient Grad. Rsch. fellowship, NSF, 1999—2004, Motorola scholarship, 1999, IBM scholarship, 1998—99, Fla. Acad. scholarship, State of Fla., 1995—99, Fla.-Ga. Alliance for Minority Participation scholarship, 1997—99, Noel Betancourt scholarship, Assn. of Cuban Am. Engrs., 2006. Mem.: IEEE, Assn. of Cuban Am. Engrs. (sec. 1998—99), Eta Kappa Nu (pres. 1997—98), Tau Beta Pi (pres. 1998—99). Republican. Roman Catholic. Achievements include research in Three Dimensional Brain Fiber Tracking Modeling in Diffusion Tensor Imaging; EEG Analysis for Automatic Detection of Interictal Spikes in Epilepsy. Avocations: travel, photography, dancing. Office: Florida Internat U EAS 2220 10555 W Flagler St Miami FL 33175 Home: 3547 SW 180th Way Hollywood FL 33029-1689

SANCHEZ, EDUARDO J., academic administrator, former state agency administrator, physician; m. Katherine Sanchez; 4 children. BS in Biomed. Engring. & Chemistry, Boston Univ.; MS in Biomed. Engring., Duke Univ., Durham, NC; MPH, Univ. Tex.; MD, Univ. Tex. Southwestern Med. Sch., 1988. Cert. family practice. Private family practice, Austin, Tex., 1992—2001; chief med. officer Austin-Travis County Dept. Health & Human Svc., 1994—98; commr. Tex. Dept. Health, Austin, 2001—04, Tex. Dept. State Health Svcs., Austin, 2004—06; dir., Inst. Health and Policy U. Tex. Recipient Louis B. Russell award, Am. Heart Assn., 2004, Public Health award, Am. Acad. Family Physicians, 2005. Office: Inst Health and Policy Univ Tex LBJ Sch Pub Affairs Rm SRH 3 312 Austin TX 78712-1536 Office Phone: 512-471-8970. Business E-Mail: Eduardo.J.Sanchez@uth.tmc.edu.*

SANCHEZ, FABIAN, dancer; m. Jacqueline Sanchez. Profl. & competitive dancer, 1992—; three-time finalist US Open Am. Rhythm Championship; four-time winner Fred Astaire Nat. Championship; winner US Rising Star Championship, Am. Rhythm divsn., 1999, World Mambo Championship, 2006—; profl. dancer Dancing with the Stars, ABC, 2008—. Co-owner Fred Astaire Dance Studio, Birmingham, Ala.; nat. dance bd. Fred Astaire Dance Studios. Office: Fred Astaire Dance Studio Ste J 1941 Hoover Ct Birmingham AL 35226 Office Phone: 205-979-4777. E-mail: fadshoover@bellsouth.net.

SANCHEZ, FREDDY (FREDERICK PHILLIP SANCHEZ), professional baseball player; b. Hollywood, Calif., Dec. 21, 1977; Attended, Glendale CC, Calif., Dallas Baptist U., Okla. City U. Infielder Boston Red Sox, 2002—03, Pitts. Pirates, 2004—09, San Francisco Giants,

2009—. Recipient Tony Conigliaro award, 2006; named to Nat. League All-Star Team, Maj. League Baseball, 2006, 2007, 2009. Achievements include leading the National League in: doubles (53), batting average (.344), 2006. Office: San Francisco Giants 24 Willie Mays Plz San Francisco CA 94107*

SANCHEZ, ISAAC CORNELIUS, chemical engineer, educator; b. San Antonio, Aug. 11, 1941; s. Isaac Jr. and Marce (Aguilar) S.; m. Patty Praytor; children: Matthew, Timothy, Treb, Kamron. BS with honors, St. Mary's U., 1963; PhD, U. Del., 1969. Postdoctoral Nat. Bureau Standards, Gaithersburg, Md., 1969-71; assoc. scientist Xerox Corp., Webster, NY, 1971-72; asst. prof. U. Mass., Amherst, 1972-77; rsch. chemist Nat. Bureau Standards, Gaithersburg, 1977-86; fellow Alcoa, Pitts., 1986-88; prof. U. Tex., Austin, 1988—. H.A. disting vis. prof. U. Akron (Ohio), 1995. Mem. editorial bd. Jour. Polymer Sci., 1986-92, Polymer, 1987—; contbr. over 100 articles to profl. jours. Lt. USN, 1963-67. Recipient William J. Murray Endowed Chair in engring U. Tex., 1997, Bronze medal U.S. Dept. Commerce, 1980, Silver medal, 1983, E.U. Condon award Nat. Bur. Standards, 1983. Fellow Am. Phys. Soc.; mem. AAAS, AIChE, Am. Chem. Soc., Nat. Acad. Engring., Materials Rsch. Soc., Soc. Plastics Engrs. (Internat. Rsch. award 1996) Avocations: golf, lay ministry, birdwatching. Office: Univ Tex Chem Engring Dept Austin TX 78712 Office Phone: 512-471-1020. E-mail: sanchez@che.utexas.edu.

SANCHEZ, JOANNA MARIE, communications educator; b. Bklyn., Apr. 17, 1957; d. Joseph Vincent Maffei and Marie Grace Maffei-Hill; 1 child, Antonio Amador. BS in Anthropology, U. Calif., Riverside, 1998; MA in Anthropology, SUNY, Albany, 2001, ArtsD in Anthropology, 2008, ArtsD in Communication, 2008. Lectr. SUNY, Albany, 2001—06, ann. guest lectr., 2006—, asst. prof. communication Cobleskill, 2006—, instr., english and spanish, 2003—06, chair, 2007, faculty governance exec., 2008—. Book reviewer Multicultural Rev.; editor United U. Professions, Cobleskill, 2007—; cio adv. bd. Albany U., 2008—. Contbr. scientific papers. Sponsor Christian Found. Children Aging, Kansas City, Okla. Recipient Phi Beta Kappa, Iota Chpt., U. of Calif. at Riverside, 1998, Positive Difference award, Office Student Svcs., U. at Albany, 2006, Exemplary Performance award, NOCCCD Bd. Trustees, 1996. Mem.: Latin Am. Studies Assn. (assoc.), Am. Anthrop. Assn. (assoc.), NE Mesoamerican Epigraphers Assn. (assoc.). Achievements include research in analysis of Nahua Ritual Day Name Sequence as Textual Artifact; approach to understanding the Nahua ritual pictographic code system; describe cyclical narrative structures in Nahuatl Historia Tolteca-Chichimeca; development of comprehensive restructuring of University Academic Advisement System; seminar on challenges of academic integrity and 21st century transformation of literacy; Phi Beta Kappa, Iota Chapter 1998. Avocations: sewing, cooking. Office: State Univ NY Ryder Hall 102 Cobleskill NY 12043 Business E-Mail: sanchejm@cobleskill.edu.

SANCHEZ, JOSE TOMAS CARDINAL, cardinal, archbishop; b. Pandan, The Philippines, Mar. 17, 1920; ThD, UST Manila. Ordained priest Diocese of Sorsogon, Philippines, 1946; vicar gen. Diocese of Sorsogon & Legazpi, Philippines; prof. Holy Rosary Sem.; ordained bishop, 1968; aux. bishop Diocese of Nueva Caceres, Philippines, 1968—71; coadjutor bishop Diocese of Lucena, Philippines, 1971—76, bishop, 1976-82; archbishop Archdiocese of Nueva Segovia, Philippines, 1982—86; sec. Congregation for Evangelization of Peoples, Rome, 1985-91; elevated to cardinal, 1991; cardinal-deacon S. Pio V a Villa Carpegna, 1991—2002, cardinal-priest, 2002—; pres. Adminstrn. of the Patrimony of the Holy See, Rome, 1991—93; prefect Congregation for the Clergy, Rome, 1991—96, prefect emeritus, 1996—. Pres. Pontifical Sanctuary of Pompei, Loreto, and Bari, Commn. Preservation Artistic and Historic Patrimony Holy See, 1991-93. Roman Catholic. Office: Piazza Pio XII 3 Palazzo delle Congregazioni 00193 Rome Italy

SANCHEZ, KARLA ANN, language educator; m. Steven Alfred Sanchez, Aug. 17, 1991; 1 child, Lydia. AA, Colo. Mountain Coll., 1984—86; BS in environ. sci., Prescott Coll., 1986—89. Colorado State Professional Teacher License State of Colo., 2002. Field instr. Keystone Sci. Sch., Dillon, Colo., 1989—90; outdoor edn. instr./counselor Farm and Wilderness, Plymouth, Vt., 1989; seasonal naturalist Pueblo State Recreation Area, Colo., 1991; summer sci. instr. Marine Sci. Ctr., Poulsbo, Wash., 1992; after sch. sci. acad. instr. Pueblo Sch. Dist. 60, Colo., 1995; student tchr. Minnequa Elem., Pueblo, Colo., 1998; mid. and h.s. lang. arts tchr. Mountain Valley Sch., RE-1, Saguache, Colo., 1999—. Chair Cadre, Bully Proofing Your Sch., Saguache, Colo., 2001—, SPOT Intervention Team, Saguache, Colo., 2001—. Author: (anthology of poetry) Celebrate! Poets Speak Out (Poet of High Merit, 2002). Docent Prescott Animal Pk., Ariz., 1988—99, N.Mex Mus. of Natural History, Albuquerque, 1991—92; vol. Beyond Fishing, Saguache, Colo., 1992—2005, Pueblo, Colo., 1992—2005; svc. mem. AmeriCorps, Saguache, Colo., 2004—05; religious educator Cmty. of Christ, Pueblo, Colo., 1996—98. Recipient Outstanding Vol., Pueblo Greenway and Nature Ctr., 1998, Outstanding Educator in Youth Services, Concerned Parents of Pueblo and Pueblo Youth Naturally, 1991; named Outstanding Tchr. of Yr., Mountain Valley Sch. Dist., 2004—05. Mem.: Tchrs. Edn. Assn. (Outstanding mem. 1997, 1998), Mountain Valley Edn. Assn., Colo. Edn. Assn., Nat. Coun. of Teachers of English, ASCD, So. Poverty Law Ctr., Friends of the Ctr. D-Liberal. Cmty. Of Christ. Avocations: fishing, camping, walking, reading. Office: Mountain Valley Sch RE-1 PO Box 127 403 Pitkin Ave Saguache CO 81149-0127 Office Fax: 719-655-0269. E-mail: sanchezk@valley.k12.co.us.

SANCHEZ, LAURA ANN, music educator; b. Jamaica, NY, Sept. 26, 1959; d. Arthur F. and Audrey M. Crowe; m. David T. Sanchez, Aug. 4, 1990. AAS, Nassau C.C., 1979; BA, Molloy Coll., 1981; MS, LI U. C.W. Post Coll., 1984. Music tchr. Uniondale Pub. Schools, NY, 1985—. Dir.: (performance) Calif. Ave. School Ensemble (First Pl., Dr. Martin Luther King Nassau County award, 2000). Corr. sec. Uniondale Cmty. Coun., NY. Mem.: Nassau Music Educators Assn., Music Educators Nat. Conf., Tech. in Music Edn., N.Y. State Sch. Music Assn. Office: Calif Ave Sch 236 California Ave Uniondale NY 11553 E-mail: lsanchez@uniondaleschools.org.

SANCHEZ, LEONEDES MONARRIZE WORTHINGTON (HIS ROYAL HIGHNESS DUKE DE LEONEDES OF SPAIN SICILY GREECE), fashion designer; b. Flagstaff, Ariz., Mar. 15, 1951; s. Rafael Leonedes and Margaret (Monarrize) S. BS, No. Ariz. U., 1974; studied, Fashion Inst. Tech., NYC, 1974-75; AA, Fashion Inst. D&M, LA, 1975; lic., La Ecole de la Chambre Syndical de la Couture Parisian, Paris, 1976-78; certificate, La Mason de Couture, Paris, 2000. Lic. in designing. Contract designer/asst. to head designer House of Bonnet, Paris, 1976—; dress designer-in-residence Flagstaff, 1978—; mem. faculty No. Ariz. U., Flagstaff, 1978-80; designer Ambiance, Inc., LA, 1985—; designer Interiors by Leonedes subs. Studio of Leonedes Couturier, Ariz., 1977, Calif., 1978, London, Paris, 1978, Rome, 1987, Milan, Spain, 1989, Palazzo de Leonedes, 1998, designer Liturgical Vesture subs.; CEO Leonedes Internat., Design Consortium, Leonedes Internat. Ltd., 1999—; designer El Castillo de Nuevo Espana, Santa Fe, La Maison de Couture, Paris, 2000, La Maison de Couture DeLeonedes Internat., Paris, 2001, His Royal Highness Duke DeLeonedes Leonedes XIV Global Subs., His Royal Highness Duke DeLeonedes Leonedes XIV Royal Consortium Cartel, London, Mobiliare Europa, 2002, Mobiliare Pan Americano Atlantico, South Am., Caribbean, 2005, Mobiliare Asia Pacifico, Taipei, Hong Kong, Beijing, China, 2005, Mobiliare England, Ireland, Scotland, 2006, Empresa de El Estudio De Leonedes, Empresa Mobiliare Latino, Empresa De H.R.H. Duke De Leonedes, 2007; chamber syndicate De Mobiliare Estidio De Leonedes Internat. South Am., El Caribe, Spain, Studio Leonedes, 2005, Studio of Leonedes Consortium Cartel, 2006, Mobiliare Consortium Cartel, 2007, Isla De Leonedes, Imperial Consortium Cartel, 2006, Mobiliare America, 2007, Cartel de la Nouvelle, France, 2007, Mobiliare Nouvelle, France, 2007, Mobiliare, Basel, Switzerland, 2008, Mobiliare Basil Switzerland Zheng He Leonedes XFin. Svcs. H.R.H. Duke De Leonedes XIV Fin. Svcs., H.R.H. Duke De Leonedes XIV Global Conglomerate, H.R.H. Duke De Leonedes XIV Asian Conglomerate, H.R.H. Duke De Leonedes XIV Studio Leonedes Conglomerate, H.R.H. Duke De Leonedes XIV Conglomeraten Mobiliare, H.R.H. Duke De Leonedes XIV Consortium Cartel Basil Switzerland, H.R.H. Duke De Leonedes XIV Global Subs. Basil Switzerland, H.R.H. Duke De Leonedes XIV Fin. Svc. Basil Switzerland. Owner, CEO, designer Leonedes Internat., Ltd., London, Milan, Paris, Spain, Ambian Ariz, Calif., Appolonian Costuming, Ariz., London, Milan, Paris, El Castillo de Leonedes, Sevilla, Spain, Villa Apollonian de Leonedes, Mykonos, Greece, Palazzo de Leonedes Internat., Sicily; cons. House of Bonnet, Paris, 1976—, Bob Mackie, Studio City, Calif., 1974-75; CEO, designer artistical dir., Leonedes internat.; appointee commn. on religious antiquities Congregation on the Arts, The Vatican, Italy, 1998. Bd. dirs. Roman Cath. Social Svcs., 1985-86, Northland Crisis Nursery, 1985—; bd. dirs., chmn. Pine Country Transit, 1986-88; pres. Chicanos for Edn.; active master's swim program ARC, Ariz., 1979—; eucharistic min., mem. art and environ. com., designer liturgical vesture St. Pius X Cath. Ch.; vol. art tchr., instr. St. Mary's Regional Sch., Flagstaff, 1987-90, vol. art dir.; mem. Flagstaff Parks and Recreation Commn., 1994-96, citizens' adv. com. master plan, 1994-96; mem. cmty. bd. adv. com. Flagstaff Unified Sch. Dist., 1995; active Duke de Leonedes Found. de Nuevo Espana, Santa Fe, Duke de Leonedes Found. de Neuvo Espana, Santa Fe; prin. chair Duke de Leonedes Found., The Netherlands, 1995; de neuvo espana Duke de Leuedes Found., Santa Fe, N.Mex., 1996. Decorated Duke de Leonedes (Spain), 1994, His Royal Highness (Spain, Greece, Sicily), 1998; recipient Camellian Design award 1988, Atlanta, De Nuevo award Duke DeLeonedes Found., Santa Fe, Barcelona, Ireland, 2004, Spain, Greece, Sicily; named His Imperial Magedy LeonedesX, 1979-2009,Leonedes HRH Duke De Leonedes Basil Switzerland, HRH Duke De Leonedes Nouvella, France, Que., Can., Mem. AAU (life, chairperson swimming Ariz. 1995, vice chairperson physique, mem. citizen adv. bd. parks and recreation, chairperson state of Ariz. physique, swimming, adv. to Olympic inquiry com., advisor to internat. Olympic com. on physique), Am. Film Inst., Am. Assn. Hist. Preservation, Costume Soc., Am. Nat. Physique Com., Internat. Consortium Fashion Designers, Nat. Cath. Ednl. Assn., La Legion de Honour de la Mode Parisienne, Social Register Assn., Phi Alpha Theta (historian 1972-73, pres. 1973-74), Pi Kappa Delta (pres. 1972-73, historian 1973-74). Republican. Avocations: bodybuilding, swimming. Office: El Castillo de Leonedes Seville Spain also: El Castillo de Nuevo Espana Santa Fe NM 87501 also: Villa de Apollonian de Leonedes Mykonos Greece Mailing: PO Box 61623 Phoenix AZ 85082-1623

SÁNCHEZ, LINDA T., United States Representative from California; b. Orange, Calif., Jan. 28, 1969; m. Jim Sullivan, Apr. 13, 2009; 1 child, Joaquin Sanchez. BA in Spanish Lit., U. Calif., Berkeley, 1991; JD, UCLA, 1995. Bar: Calif. 1995. Clk. to hon. Chief Justice Terry Hatter, Jr. Ctrl. Dist. Ct., Calif.; compliance officer Internat. Brotherhood Elec. Workers Nat. Elec. Contractors Assn., 1998—2002; mem. US Congress from 39th Calif. dist., 2003—, US House Judiciary Com., US House Ways & Means Com. Campaign aide Loretta Sanchez for US Congress, 1996, 1998; mem. Congl. Hispanic Caucus; co-founder Congl. Labor & Working Families Caucus; exec. sec.-treas. Orange County ctrl. labor coun. AFL-CIO; lectr. Nat. Assn. Elected & Apptd. Ofcls., 1998—. Co-author (with Loretta Sanchez): Dream in Color: How the Sanchez Sisters Are Making History in Congress, 2008. Mem.: Internat. Brotherhood Elec. Workers (Local 441). Democrat. Roman Catholic. Office: US Congress 1007 Longworth Office Bldg Washington DC 20515-0539 also: Dist Office Ste 106 4007 Paramount Lakewood CA 90712 Office Phone: 562-429-8499, 202-225-6676. Office Fax: 562-938-1948, 202-226-1012.*

SÁNCHEZ, LORETTA, United States Representative from California; b. Lynnwood, Calif., Jan. 7, 1960; BA in Economics, Chapman U., Orange, Calif., 1982; MBA in Fin., Am. U., 1984. Fin. mgr. Orange County Transp. Authority, 1984-87; asst. v.p. Fieldman Rolapp & Assocs., 1987-90; strategic mgmt. cons. Booz, Allen & Hamilton Inc., 1990—93; owner, operator AMIGA Advisors Inc., 1993—96; mem. US Congress from 47th Calif. dist., 1997—, US House Armed Services Com., US House Homeland Security Com. Mem. Blue Dog Dems., New Dem. Coalition, Older Americans Caucus, Women's Congl. Caucus, Law Enforcement Caucus, Hispanic Caucus, Congl. Sportsman's Caucus, Congl. Human Rights Caucus. Co-author (with Linda Sanchez): Dream in Color: How the Sanchez Sisters Are Making History in Congress, 2008. Mem. Hispanic adv. coun. Pepperdine U., Malibu, Calif.; pres. Nat. Soc. Hispanic MBAs, 1993; mem. Anaheim Assistance League, 1995—; bd. dirs. Providence Speech & Hearing Ctr., Orange, 1985—; trustee Chapman U., 2001—. Mem.: Am. Assn. Univ. Women, Anaheim Rotary Club, Los Amigos Orange County. Democrat. Roman Catholic. Office: US Congress 1230 Longworth Ho Office Bldg Washington DC 20515-0547 also: Dist Office Ste 101 12397 Lewis St Garden Grove CA 92840 Office Phone: 202-225-2965. Office Fax: 714-621-0401. E-mail: loretta@mail.house.gov.*

SANCHEZ, MANUEL, retired social services administrator, writer; b. Los Palacios, Cuba, June 6, 1932; s. Emilio and Elena (Lopez) Sanchez. JD, Havana U., Cuba, 1959. Bar: N.J. 1975. Supr. Dept. Social Svcs., NYC, 1964—90; ret., 1990. Author: The Daring Mysteries, 1991, Stories for a Rainy Afternoon, 2005. Avocation: reading. Home: 2530 SW 21 Ter Miami FL 33145

SÁNCHEZ, MARGARITA MARÍA, science educator; b. Medellín, Colombia, Sept. 15, 1964; d. Alberto and Margarita Sánchez; m. Francis B. Jacob, July 1; 1 child, Pauline Jacob. PhD, Rutgers U., NJ, 1999. Asst. prof. Wagner Coll., Staten Island, NY, 2001—. Home: 9 Turner Pl Brooklyn NY 11218 Office: Wagner Coll 1 Campus Rd Staten Island NY 10301 Business E-Mail: msanchez@wagner.edu.

SANCHEZ, MARK, professional football player; b. Long Beach, Calif., Nov. 11, 1986; s. Nick Sanchez and Olga Macias. Student in comm., U. So. Calif., LA, 2005—09. Quarterback NY Jets, 2009—. Named Offensive MVP, Rose Bowl, 2009. Office: NY Jets Football Club Inc 1000 Fulton Ave Hempstead NY 11550*

SANCHEZ, MARY ANNE, retired secondary school educator; b. Galesburg, Ill., Aug. 4, 1939; d. Stephen Mingare and M. Margaret Kennedy; m. J. Manuel Sanchez, Dec. 26, 1980. BS in Edn., Western Ill. U., 1961; MA, Ill. State U., 1970. Tchr., Stanford, Ill., 1962-64, Titusville, Fla., 1964-66, Montgomery County Bd. Edn., Chevy Chase, Md., 1969-72, Hillsborough County Bd. Edn., Tampa, Fla., 1972-96; ret., 1996. Mary Anne Sanchez Young Woman scholarship named in her honor by Social Studies Dept. Leto Comprehensive H.S., 1999. Mem. Nat. Coun. for Social Studies, Fla. Coun. for Social Studies, Adult Edn. Assn. Home: 2715 W Ivy St Tampa FL 33607-1922

SANCHEZ, PEDRO ANTONIO, soil scientist, administrator; b. Havana, Cuba, Oct. 7, 1940; s. Pedro Antonio Sr. and Georgina (San Martin) S.; m. Cheryl Palm, 1990; children: Jennifer, Evan, Juliana. BS in Agronomy, Cornell U., 1962, MS in Soil Sci., 1964, PhD in Soil Sci., 1968; DSc (hon.), U. Guelph, 2004. Grad. asst. U. Philippines/Cornell Grad. Edn. Program, Los Baños, Philippines, 1965-68; asst. prof. soil sci. N.C. State U., Raleigh, 1968-73, leader tropic soils program dept. soil sci., 1971-76, assoc. prof. soil sci., 1973-79, prof. soil sci., 1979-91, coord. tropic soils program, 1979-82, 84-91, prof. emeritus soil sci. and forestry, 1991—; co-leader Nat. Rice Program Peru N.C. State U. Agrl. Mission to Peru, Lambayeque, Peru, 1968-71, chief Lima, Peru, 1982-83; coord. beef-tropical pastures program Ctr. Internat. Agrl. Tropical, Cali, Colombia, 1977-79; tech. chief Inst. Nat. Investigation and Promotion Agropercuaria, 1982-83; dir. Ctr. for World Environment and Sustainable Devel. Duke U./N.C. State U./U. N.C. Chapel Hill, 1990-91; dir. gen. Internat. Ctr. for Rsch. in Agroforestry, Nairobi, Kenya, 1991—2001; vis. prof. of tropical resources Coll. of Natural Resources, U. Calif., Berkeley, 2002; prof. Earth Inst., Columbia U., 2003—. Adj. prof. tropical conservation Duke U., 1990; chmn. exec. com. Univ. Consortium on Soils of Tropics; lead analyst land and water sect. World Food and Nutrition Study, NAS, Washington, com. on selected biological problems of humid tropics, chmn. com. on sustainable and environment in humid tropics; conselho assessor do Centro de Pesquisa Agropecuarias dos Cerrados, EMBRAPA, Brasilis, Brazil; consejo directivo del Centro Nacional de Investigationes Agropecuarias de Carimagua, ICA-CIAT, Colombia; mem. tech. adv. bd. Commissao do Plano da Lavoura Cacauiera, Itabuna, Bahia, Brazil; coord. Soil Mgmt. Collaborative Rsch. Support Program Planning Grant, USAID/BIFAD, Washington; vice-chmn. internat. steering com. Red de Investigacion Agroecologica para la Amazonia-REDINAA, Amazon Rsch. Network, leader soil project; mem. steering com. Formation Internat. Bd. on Soils Rsch. and Mgmt., chmn. acid tropical soils network coord. com.; mem. tech. com. Soil Mgmt. CRSP; mem. com. on tropical deforestation Office of Tech. Assessment, U.S. Congress; mem. Internat. Com. on Land Clearing and Devel.; mem. coord. com. Tropical Soil Biology and Fertility Program; chmn. bd. mgmt. Tropical Soil Biology and Fertility Program; cons. Ford Found., USAID, Inst. Interamericano Scis. Agrl., Rockefeller Found., NAS, TVA, Venezuelan Soc. Soil Sci., World Bank, New Zealand Soc. Soil Sci., Consultative Group on Internat. Agrl. Rsch., Empresa Brasileira de Pesquisa Agropecuaria, FAO, Royal Swedish Acad. Scis., Ecosystems Ctr. Woods Hole Oceanographic Inst., IB-SRAM, Consejo Nat. Sci. and Tech. Peru, UNESCO-Main in Biosphere Program, U.S. EPA, CIAT, WWF, Rainforest Alliance, U.S. Congress. Author: Properties and Management of Soils in the Tropics, 1981; co-author: Suelos Acidos: Estrategia para su Manejo con Bajos Insumos en America Tropical, 1983; editor: A Review of Soils Research in Tropical Latin America, 1973; co-editor: Curso de Capacitacion sobre el Cultivo del Arroz, 1969, Multiple Cropping, 1976, Pasture Production in Acid Soils of the Tropics, 1979, Amazonia: Agriculture and Land Use Research, 1982, Land Clearing and Development in the Tropics, 1986, Management of Acid Tropical Soil for Sustainable Agriculture, 1987, Myths and Science of Soils of the Tropics, 1992; mem. editl. adv. bd. Field Crops Rsch., Tropical Agriculture, Agroforestry Systems, Geoderma; contbr. articles to sci. and profl. jours. Recipient Agronomy Achievement award Nat. Plant Food Inst., 1960, Diploma Merit Peru Min. Agriculture, 1971, Diploma Honor, Colombian Inst. Agropecuario, 1979, INIPA, 1985, Order Agrl. Merit, Govt. Peru, 1984; named hon. prof. U. Nat. Amazonia Peruana, 1987, fellow, MacArthur Found., 2003, World Food prize, 2002 Fellow Am. Acad. Arts and Scis., Am. Soc. Agronomy (bd. dirs., chmn. divsn. internat. agronomy, Internat. Svc. in Agronomy award 1993), Soil Sci. Soc. Am. (Internat. Soil Sci. award 1993); mem. AAAS, Internat. Soil Sci. (vice chmn. commn. VI 1986, chmn. 1994-98), Latin Am. Assn., Agrl. Scis., Latin Am. Assn. Pecuarias Peru, Latin Am. Soc. Sci. Suelo, Assn. Investigators Agrl. and Pecuarias Peru, Soc. Colombia Sci. Suelo (hon., bd. dirs.), Soc. Peru Sci. Suelo (hon.) Soil Sci. Soc. N.C., Sigma Xi, Sigma Iota Rho. Office: Earth Inst at Columbia U P O Box 1000 Palisades NY 10964

SANCHEZ, RICARDO S., retired military officer; b. Rio Grande City, Tex., 1953; B in Math. and History, Tex. A&I U.; M in Ops. Rsch. and Sys. Analysis Engring., Naval Postgrad. Sch. Commd. officer U.S. Army, 1973, advanced through ranks to lt. gen., 2003, ret., 2006, platoon leader 4th Bn., 68th Armor, 82nd Airborne Divsn., aide-de-camp to the asst. divsn. comdr. 82nd Airborne Divsn., action control officer Office of the Sec. of the Joint Staff, U.S. Forces Korea/Eighth U.S. Army, ops. officer and exec. officer 3rd Bn., 8th Cavalry, 3rd Armored Divsn. Gelnhausen, Germany, dep. ops. officer 3rd Armored Divsn. Frankfurt, Germany, comdr. 2nd Bn., 69th Armor, 197th (Separate) Inf. Brigade Ft. Benning, Ga., investigator Office U.S. Army Insp. Gen. Agy. Washington, comdr. 2nd Brigade, 1st Inf. Divsn. Ft. Riley, Kans., dep. chief staff U.S. So. Command Miami, Fla., dir. ops. U.S. So. Command, asst. divsn. comdr. for support 1st Inf. Divsn., dep. chief staff ops. U.S. Army Europe Heidelburg, Germany, commdg. gen. V Corps 1st Armored Divsn., 2001—03, commdg. gen. Coalition Ground Forces (Combined Joint Task Force 7) Iraq, 2003—04, commdg. gen. V Corps, 2003—04, 2004—06, commdr. Multi-Nat. Force Iraq, 2004. Co-author (with Donald T. Phillips): Wiser in Battle: A Soldier's Story, 2008. Decorated Def. Superior Svc. medal, Legion of Merit, Bronze Star with V device and oak leaf cluster, Joint Svc. Commendation medal, Army Commendation medal, Meritorious Svc. medal with four oak leaf clusters, Army Achievement medal with oak leaf cluster, Liberation of Kuwait medals, S.W. Asia Campaign medal.

SANCHEZ, ROBERT E., corporate financial executive; BS in Elec. Engring., U. Miami; MBA, Wharton Sch. U. Pa. Former controls engr. Pratt & Whitney Aircraft; former applications engr. Fla. Power & Light; regional finance dir., group dir. fin. analysis, mgr. strategic planning, v.p. asset mgmt., sr. v.p. global transp. mgmt. Ryder System Inc., 1993—2003, sr. v.p. & CIO, 2003—05, exec. v.p. ops. US Fleet Mgmt., 2005—07, exec. v.p. & CFO, 2007—. Chmn. Ryder United Way Campaign. Recipient Engr. of Yr. award, ACE, 2001, Young Hispanic Leadership award, 2002. Mem.: Assn. Cuban Engrs. (bd. mem.), Miami-Dade Beacon Coun. (bd. mem.), United Way Leadership Circle, Wharton Alumni Assn. Office: 11690 NW 105th St Miami FL 33178 Office Phone: 305-500-3726.*

SANCHEZ, ROBERT FORTUNE, archbishop emeritus; b. Socorro, N.Mex., Mar. 20, 1934; s. Julius C. and Priscilla (Fortune) Sanchez. Student, Immaculate Heart Sem., Santa Fe, 1954, Gregorian U., Rome, 1960. Ordained priest Archdiocese of Santa Fe, N.Mex., 1959, dir.

extension lay volunteers, 1965—68, chmn. priest pers. bd., 1968—72, vicar gen., 1974, archbishop, 1974—93, archbishop emeritus N.Mex., 1993—; prof. St. Pius X HS, Albuquerque, 1960—68; ordained bishop, 1974. Rep. instl. ministry pastoral care N.Mex. Council Chs., 1968; pres. Archdiocesan Priests Senate, 1973—74; rep. region X Nat. Fedn. Priests Councils, 1972—73; chmn. ad hoc com. Spanish speaking U.S. Cath. Conf. Roman Catholic. Office: Archdiocese of Santa Fe The Cath Ctr 4000 St Josephs Pl NW Albuquerque NM 87120-1714

SANCHEZ, ROBERT FRANCIS, journalist; b. Bradenton, Fla., Jan. 1, 1938; s. Robert and Frances Alice (Thompson) S. BS in English Edn., Fla. State U., 1959, MS, 1962, postgrad., 1971-74. Mem. faculty Fla. State U., Tallahassee, 1962-67; mem. faculty Fla. A&M U., Tallahassee, 1968-71; writer, editor Tallahassee Democrat, 1965-74; editl. writer Miami Herald, 1974-2000; dir. pub. policy James Madison Inst., Tallahassee. Co-recipient Pulitzer Prize, 1983 Republican. Methodist. Home: 2324 Williams Rd Tallahassee FL 32311 Office: James Madison Inst 2017 Delta Blvd Tallahassee FL 32315

SANCHEZ, STEVEN M., financial executive; m. Marie Vigil, Sept. 11, 1992; children: Nate, Erica, Emily. Diploma in Acctg., San Joaquin Valley U., 1990. Advisor John Hancock Fin., Fresno, Calif., 1991—93; pres., wealth advisor Sanchez and Associates, Phoenix, 1993—. Contbr. fin. articles to profl. jours. Leader marriage ministry U. of the Family, Phoenix, 2004—06. Recipient Ethics and Excellence award, Nat. Ethics Bur., 2002. Mem.: Nat. Assn. Ins. and Fin. Advisors (assoc.). Conservative. Nazarene. Avocations: travel, music. Home and Office: Sanchez & Associates Fin Group 4802 E Ray Rd Ste23 Phoenix AZ 85044 Personal E-mail: smnee1061@aol.com.

SANCHEZ, TERESA, medical educator; b. Barcelona, Oct. 7, 1973; d. Santiago Sanchez and Teresa Garcia Vao; m. Michael Joseph Kluk, Sept. 15, 2007. PhD cum laude distinction, U. Barcelona, Sch. Pharmacy, 2001. Asst. prof. cell biology U. Conn. Sch. Medicine, Farmington, 2005—08; asst. prof. surgery Beth Israel Deaconess Med. Ctr., Harvard Med. Sch., Boston, 2008—. Recipient Presentation award, N.Am. Vascular Biology Orgn., 2004. Mem.: Am. Heart Assn. (Tex.) (reviewer 2006—, Nat. Scientist Devel. grant 2006—). Achievements include patents for regulation of vascular permeability and endothelial cell apoptosis by FTY720. Office: Beth Israel Deaconess Med Ctr 99 Brookline Ave RN-227A Boston MA 02215

SANCHEZ, TOMAS DAVID, history professor; b. Oxnard, Calif., May 11, 1949; s. Fidel Victor and Guadalupe Sanchez; m. Maria Ernestina Sanchez; children: Lisa Marie, Monica Isabel, Graciela Sanchez-Bautista, David F. Topiltzin, Miguel E. Teohua. BA in History, Chicano Studies, Calif. State U., Northridge, 1972; MA in History, U. Calif., Santa Barbara, 1975. Prof. history Oxnard Coll., Calif., 1975—83, head dept. behavioral social sci., 1983—87, divsn. dir. arts letters and sci., 1987—91, interim dean continuing edn., 1990—91, interim v.p. instrn., 1996—97, interim pres., 1997; prof. history Moorpark Coll., Calif., 1991—2004, Ventura Coll., Calif., 2004—. Certificated mgmt. assn. Ventura C.C. Dist., Calif., 1987—91; accrediting commn. cmty. jr. coll. Western Assn. Sch. Coll., Aptos, Calif., 1993—; adv. bd. mem. Mexihcayotl Soc. Arts Humanities, Oxnard, 1997—2000; fundraising bd. Carnegie Art Mus., Oxnard, 1998—. Democrat. Roman Catholic. Avocations: history, art, travel, politics. Office: Ventura Coll 4667 Telegraph Rd Ventura CA 93003 Office Fax: 805-654-6466.

SANCHEZ, VICTORIA WAGNER, science educator; b. Milw., Apr. 11, 1934; d. Arthur William and Lorraine Marguerite (Kocovsky) Wagner; m. Rozier Edmond Sanchez, June 23, 1956; children: Mary Elizabeth, Carol Anne, Robert Edmond, Catherine Marie, Linda Therese. BS cum laude, Mt. Mary Coll., 1955; MS, Marquette U., 1957; postgrad., U. N.Mex., 1979-86, U. Del., 1990. Cert. secondary tchr., N.Mex. Chemist Nat. Bur. Standards, Washington, 1958-60; tchr., chmn. sci. dept. Albuquerque Pub. Schs., 1979-94. Chmn. pub. info. area conv. Nat. Sci. Tchrs. Assn., 1984, mem. sci. rev. com. Albuquerque Pub. Schs., 1985-86, 92-93, dedication of N.W. Regional Sci. Fair, 1994, Gov.'s Summit on Edn., 1991, 92, Gov.'s Steering Com. Systemic Change in Math. and Sci. Edn.; panel mem. NSF, 1991-93. Bd. dirs. Encino House, Albuquerque, 1976-92, treas., 1977-79; leader Albuquerque troop Girl Scouts U.S., 1966-77; cmty. interpreter Environ. Open Space Divsn. City Albuquerque, N.Mex., 2000—. Named Outstanding Sci. Tchr., NW Regional Sci. Fair, Albuquerque, 1983, 88, 90, N.Mex. Parents of Yr., 2001; recipient St. George's award N.Mex. Cath. Scouting Com., 1978, Focus on Excellence award ASCD, Albuquerque, 1985, 89, Presdl. awards for excellence in sci. and math., 1989; Rozier and Victoria Sanchez Family, Outstanding Family in Philanthropy, 2007. Mem. AAUW (officer Albuquerque br. 1976-77, N.Mex. divsn. 1977-78), NSTA, N.Mex. Sci. Tchrs. Assn. (treas. 1988-90), Albuquerque Sci. Tchrs. Assn. (treas. 1984-85, v.p., pres.-elect 1986-87, pres. 1987-88, Svc. to Sci. award 1994), N.Mex. Acad. Sci., Am. Coun. on Edn. (math. and sci. edn. nat. com. 1990-92), DuPont Honors Workshop for Tchrs., Albuquerque Rose Soc. (sec. 1962-63). Democrat. Roman Catholic. Avocations: reading, fishing, hiking, needlecraft, camping. Home: 7612 Palo Duro Ave NE Albuquerque NM 87110-2315

SANCHEZ-KENNEDY, MARIA, museum director; b. Pueblo, Colo. BA in Anthropology, U. N.Mex.; MA in Mus. Sci., Texas Tech U. Curator edn. Nev. State Railroad Mus., Carson City, Nev.; exec. dir. Bessemer Hist. Soc., Pueblo, Colo., 2001—08, Steelworks Mus. Industry & Culture, 2001—08, Colo. Fuel & Iron Corp. Archives, 2001—08; mgr. Robert Hoag Rawlings Pub. Libr. Infozone News Mus., Pueblo, Colo., 2008—. Mem.: Colo.-Wyo. Assn. Museums (chair 2006—07, 2007—08). E-mail: maria.sanchez@cfisteel.org.

SANCHEZ-RAMOS, ROBERTO J., former attorney general; b. 1968; BS in Computer Sci. and Engring., MIT, 1989; JD summa cum laude, U. PR, 1998; LLM, Yale U., 1993. Admitted to practice: PR, Washington, DC, Supreme Ct. US, US Ct. Appeals for the First Cir. Law clk. to Hon. Federico Hernandez Denton Supreme Ct. PR, 1993—94; assoc. Arnold & Porter LLP, Washington, 1994—96; law clk. to Hon. A. Wallace Tashima US Ct. Appeals (9th cir.), Pasadena, Calif., 1996—97; trial atty., civil divsn., fed. programs br. US Dept. Justice, Washington, 1999—2000; solicitor gen. PR, San Juan, 2001—04, atty. gen., 2004—08. Recipient West Publishing award for Excellence in the Study of Anglo-Am. Law, Acad. Excellence award, PR Atty. Bar Assn. Mem.: Eta Kappa Nu Assn., Sigma Xi.

SANCHEZ-SILKMAN, JENNIFER CHRISTINE, elementary school educator; b. Bronx, NY, Sept. 11, 1974; d. George Peter Sanchez and Lucille Ann Ramirez; m. Jeffrey Howard Silkman, Dec. 22, 2000; 1 child, Julian Michael Silkman. BS in Elem. Edn., Iona Coll., New Rochelle, NY, 1996; MS in Early Childhood Edn., Coll. New Rochelle, 2000; post grad. in curriculum and tchg., Tchrs. Coll. Columbia U., NYC, 2002—04. Lic. (permanent) tchr. K-6 N.Y. State and N.Y.C., spl. edn. K-12 N.Y. State and N.Y.C. Tchr. grade 3 St. Francis de Chantal Sch., Bronx, NY, 1998—2002; tchr. grade 4 Pub. Sch. 182, 2002—. Tchr. rep. St. Francis de Chantal Sch. PTA, 2000—01. Mem.: ASCD. Roman Catholic. Avocations: walking, exercise, dance, music. Office: PS 182 601 Stickball Blvd Bronx NY 10473

SANCHEZ-SOTELO, JOAQUIN, surgery consultant; b. Madrid, Mar. 12, 1968; s. Joaquin Sanchez Cota and Adoracion Sotelo Laredo; children: Pablo Sanchez, Marta Sanchez. MD, Univ. Autonoma de Madrid, Spain, 1989, PhD, 1992. Cons. orthop. surgery Hosp. La Paz, Madrid, 2001—04, Dept. Orthop. Surgery Mayo Clinic, Rochester, Minn., 2004—. Spl. fellow adult reconstruction Mayo Clinic, Rochester, Minn., 2001, asst. prof., 2004—. Author scientific papers. Recipient Jesus Galan award, Spanish Bd. Medicine, 1992, Coventry Rsch. award, Mayo Clinic, 2001; named Tchr. of Yr. in Orthopedics, 2005. Mem.: Madrid Orthop. Assn., Spanish Assn. Shoulder and Elbow Surgeons, Am. Acad. Orthop. Surgeons, Spanish Orthop. Assn., Mayo Fellows Assn. Achievements include research in orthopedic surgery. Office: Dept Orthop Surgery Mayo Clinic 200 First St SW Rochester MN 55905 Office Fax: 507-284-5539.

SANCHEZ-WAY, RUTH DOLORES, public health administrator; b. NYC, Aug. 8, 1940; d. Manuel and Cruz Maria Sanchez; m. Harley Milton Dirks, Feb. 9, 1974 (dec. Aug. 1986); stepchildren: Timothy, Darcy Kimmel, Marcine Thomas, James, David, Dale; m. David Vincent Way, Apr. 16, 1988. BS in Chemistry, St. John's U., Bklyn., 1962; MSW in Social Work, Fordham U., 1965; PhD in Pub. Adminstrn., NYU, 1978; diploma in Mgmt. Devel., Emory U., Atlanta, 1981; diploma, Inst. Fed. Health Care Execs., Geroge Washington U., 1993; LHD (hon.), Fordham U., NYC, 2006. Cert. social worker, Md.; cert. prevention profl. Spl. asst. to dir. Nat. Inst. Alcohol Abuse and Alcoholism HEW, Rockville, Md., 1971-79, assoc. dep. adminstr. Equal Employment Opportunity, 1979-83, office asst. Sec. Health, 1979—83; dep. dir. Adolescent Pregnancy Programs Health and Human Svcs., Washington, 1983-91; assoc. adminstr. minority health concerns Substance Abuse & Mental Health Svcs. Adminstrn., Health and Human Svcs., Rockville, 1993-96, divsn. dir. Ctr. for Substance Abuse Prevention, 1991-96, acting dep. dir. Ctr. for Substance Abuse Prevention, 1997, acting dir., 1997—2000, dir., 2000—02; assoc. dir. Ctr. for Faith-Based and Cmty. Initiatives, HHS, 2002—03; v.p. tng. and cmty. devel. Mgmt. Scis. for Devel., 2003—. Bd. dirs. Nat. Health Coun., Washington, 1987-94, Nat. Coun. on Alcoholism and Drug Dependence, N.Y.C., 1979-91, Nat. Orgn. Adolescent Pregnancy Parenting and Prevention, Washington, 1991-93. Nat. operational vol. Girl Scouts US, NYC, 1996-; mem. com. lions quest Lions Clubs Internat. Found., 2003-, friends of Pax Lodge World Found. for Girl Guides and Scouts, 2006-; disaster vol. Am. Red Cross, Ctrl. Md., 2005-; mem. pastoral coun., women's guild Our Lady Sorrows Ch., 2003-. Recipient Excellence in Govt. Svc. award Mex.-Am. Legal Def. and Ednl. Fund, 2000, Presdl. Meritorious Exec. Rank award SES, 1998, Sec.'s award for disting. svc. HHS, 2001; primary care policy fellow USPHS. Mem. NASW, APHA, Chesapeake Multihull Assn. (past commodore, Kilmon award 1996). Roman Catholic. Avocations: sailing, skiing, jazzercise. Office: Mgmt Scis for Devel 4301 Connecticut Ave NW Ste 140 Washington DC 20008 Office Phone: 202-537-7410. Business E-Mail: rsanchez@msdglobal.com.

SAND, DUANE, think-tank associate; b. May 8, 1965; m. Holly Sand, Apr. 9, 1994; children: Allen, Hannah. BSc in Computer Sci., US Naval Acad., Annapolis, Md., MS in Indsl. Engring. Cert. nuc. engr., US Dept. Energy. Rep. candidate, ND US Senate, 2000; Rep. at-large candidate, ND US House of Representatives, 2004; state dir. Americans for Prosperity North and South Dakota. Lt. comdr. USN, navigation and ops. officer USS Florida USN, Persian Gulf. Republican. Mailing: PO Box 7214 Bismarck ND 58507 Office Phone: 701-751-2531.

SANDAGE, ALLAN REX, astronomer; b. Iowa City, June 18, 1926; s. Charles Harold and Dorothy (Briggs) S.; m. Mary Lois Connelley, June 8, 1959; children: David Allan, John Howard. AB, U. Ill., 1948, DSc (hon.), 1967; PhD, Calif. Inst. Tech., Pasadena, 1953; DSc (hon.), Yale U., New Haven, Conn., 1966, U. Chgo., 1967, Miami U., Oxford, Ohio, 1974, Graceland Coll., Iowa, 1985; LLD (hon.), U. So. Calif., 1971; D (hon.), U. Chile, 1992. Astronomer Mt. Wilson Obs., Palomar Obs., Carnegie Instn., Washington, 1952—; Peyton fellow Princeton U., 1952; asst. astronomer Hale Obs., Pasadena, Calif., 1952-56; astronomer Obs. Carnegie Instn., Pasadena, Calif., 1956—; sr. rsch. astronomer Space Telescope Sci. Inst. NASA, Balt., 1986—; Homewood Prof. of physics Johns Hopkins U., Balt., 1987-89. Vis. lectr. Harvard U., 1957; mem. astron. expdn. to South Africa, 58; cons. NSF, 1961—64; Sigma Xi nat. astronomer U. Basel, 1985, 92, lectr., vis. prof., 94; vis. rsch. astronomer U. Calif., San Diego, 1985—86; vis. astronomer U. Hawaii, 1986; Lindsey lectr. NASA Goddard Space, Durham, England, 1992; Grubb-Parsons lectr. U. Durham, England, 1992. Assoc. editor: Ann. Rev. Astronomy and Astrophysics, 1990—2005. Served USN, 1945—46. Recipient Helen Warner prize, Am. Astron. Soc., 1960, Pope Pius XI Gold medal, Pontifical Acad. Sci., 1966, Rittenhouse medal, 1968, US Pres. medal of Sci., 1971, Russell prize, 1973, Adon medal, Obs. Nice, 1988, Crafoord prize, Swedish Royal Acad. Scis., 1991, Tomalla Gravity prize, Swiss Phys. Soc., 1993, Peter Gruber Found. prize for cosmology, 2000; Fulbright-Hays scholar, Australia, 1972. Mem.: Astron. Soc. Pacific (Gold medal 1975), Royal Soc. London (fgn.), Franklin Inst. (Elliott Cresson medal 1973, Gruber Cosmology prize 2000), Royal Astron. Soc. Can., Royal Astron. Soc. (Eddington medal 1963, Gold medal 1967), Lincei Nat. Acad. (Rome), Phi Beta Kappa. Home: 8319 Josard Rd San Gabriel CA 91775-1003 Office: 813 Santa Barbara St Pasadena CA 91101-1232 Office Phone: 626-304-0246.

SANDAGE, BOBBY, JR., pharmaceutical executive; b. Arkadelphia, Ark., Aug. 22, 1953; s. Bobby Winston and Joan (Fisher) S.; m. Denise McAhren, Feb. 14, 1981; children: B. Winston, Brittany J. BS in Pharmacy, U. Ark. Coll. Pharmacy, Little Rock, 1975; PhD, Purdue U. Sch. Pharmacy and Pharmacal Sci., West Lafayette, IN, 1981. Registered pharmacist. Evp, R & D Indevus Pharmaceuticals, Inc., Lexington, Mass., 1991—. Adj. prof. pharmacology Mass. Coll. Pharmacy, Boston, 1991—. Contbr. articles to profl. jours. Recipient Upjohn award Upjohn, 1975, Merck award Merck Pharm., Arkansas, 1975. Mem. Am. Soc. Clin. Pharmacology and Therapeutics (membership com. 1985-88), Am. Coll. Clin. Pharmacology, Soc. Neurosci. Mem. Christian Ch. Avocation: golf. Office: Indevus Pharm Inc 33 Hayden Ave Lexington MA 02421

SANDAHL, BONNIE BEARDSLEY, nursing administrator; b. Washington, Jan. 17, 1939; d. Erwin Leonard and Carol Myrtle (Collis) Beardsley; m. Glen Emil Sandahl, Aug. 17, 1963; children: Cara Lynne, Cory Glen. BSN, U. Wash., 1962, MN, 1974; cert. pediat. nurse practitioner, 1972. Dir. Wash. State Joint Practice Commn., Seattle, 1974-76; instr. pediatric nurse practitioner program U. Wash., Seattle, 1976, course coord. quality assurance, 1977-78; pediatric nurse practitioner/health coord. Snohomish County Head Start, Everett, Wash., 1975-77; clin. nurse educator (specialist), nurse mgr. Harborview Med. Ctr., Seattle, 1978-97, dir. child abuse prevention project, 1986-97; mgr. Children's Ctr., Providence Health Sys. Northwest, 1997-2000; v.p. clin. svcs. and ops., COO Seattle Children's Home, 2000—03, exec. dir., 2003—05; sch. nurse Seattle Pub. Schs., 2006—. Spkr. legis. focus on children, 1987; clin. assoc. dept. pediatrics U. Wash. Sch. Medicine, 1987—; clin. faculty U. Wash. Sch. Nursing, 1987—97; mgr. Providence Gen. Children's Ctr., Everett, 1997—2000; gov. appointee State Interagy. Coord. Coun., 1998—, gov. appointee chair, 2003—. Interim chair nat. coun. health planning and devel. HHS, 1980—87; mem. task force pharmacotherapeutic courses Puget Sound Health Sys. Agy., 1975—88, pres., 1980—82; mem. task force pharmacotherapeutic courses Wash. State Bd. Nursing, 1985—86; mem. child devel. project adv. bd. Mukiteo Sch. Dist., 1984—85; mem. parenting adv. com. Edmonds Sch. Dist.; chmn. hospice-hom health task force Snohomis County Hospice Program, Everett, 1984—85, bd. dirs. hospice, 1985—87, mem. adv. com., 1986—88; mem. Wash. State Health Coordinating Coun., 1977—82, chmn. nursing home bed projection methodology task force, 1986—87; mem. adv. com. uncompensated care Wash. State Legislature, 1983—84; mem. joint select com. Tech. Adv. Com. Managed Health Care Sys., 1984—85; pres. Alderwood Manor Cmty. Coun., 1983—85; treas. Wash. St. Women's Polit. Caucus, 1983—84; mem. com. examine changes in Wash. State Criminal Sex Law, 1987; appointee county needs assessment com. Snohomish County Govt. United Way, 1989, 1994; chair human svcs. adv. coun. Snohomish County Human Svcs. Dept., chmn. adv. com., 1998—; gubernatorial appointee state interagency coordinating coun. Health Svcs. Adv. Com. Wash. State, 1995—97. Recipient Golden Acorn award, Seattle-King County PTA, 1973, Katherine Rickey Vol. Participation award, 1987. Mem.: ANA (chair com. examiners maternal-child nursing practice 1988—90), King County Nurses Assn. (1st v.p. 1992—96, pres. 1996—97, Nurse of the Yr. 1985), Wash. State Nurses Assn. (chair healthcare reform task force 1992—96, Hon. Leadership award 1981), Sigma Theta Tau. Home: 1814 201st Pl SW Lynnwood WA 98036-7060

SANDALOW, DAVID BLAKE, federal agency administrator; b. 1957; BA in Philosophy, Yale Coll., 1978; JD, U. Mich. Law Sch., 1982. Assoc. dir. for global environment White House Coun. Environ. Quality; sr. dir. environ. affairs NSC; asst. sec. of state for oceans, environment & sci. US Dept. State; sr. fellow World Resources Inst., Washington; exec. v.p. World Wildlife Fund (WWF), Washington, 2001—03; energy & environment scholar, sr. fellow Fgn. Policy Studies prog. Brookings Instn., Washington, 2004—09; asst. sec. for domestic policy & internat. affairs US Dept. Energy, 2009—. Author: Freedom From Oil: How the Next President Can End the United States' Oil Addiction, 2007. Democrat. Office: US Dept Energy 1000 Independence Ave SW Washington DC 20585 Office Fax: 202-586-4403.*

SANDALOW, TERRANCE, law educator; b. Chgo., Sept. 8, 1934; s. Nathan and Evelyn (Hoffing) Sandalow; m. Ina Davis, Sept. 4, 1955; children: David Blake, Marc Alan, Judith Ann. AB, U. Chgo., 1954, JD, 1957. Bar: Ill. 1958, Mich. 1978. Law clk. to judge Sterry R. Waterman U.S. Ct. Appeals (2d cir.), 1957-58; law clk. to justice Potter Stewart U.S. Supreme Ct., Washington, 1958-59; assoc. Ross, McGowan & O'Keefe, Chgo., 1959-61; assoc. prof. law U. Minn., Mpls., 1961-64, prof., 1964-66; prof. law U. Mich., Ann Arbor, 1966-2000, dean Law Sch., 1978-87, Edson R. Sunderland prof. law, 1987-2000, dean emeritus and Edson R. Sunderland prof. law emeritus, 2000—. Author (with F. I. Michelman): (book) Government in Urban Areas, 1970; author: (with E. Stein) Courts and Free Markets, 1982; contbr. articles to legal jours. and periodicals. Mem. Mpls. Commn. Human Rels., 1965—66. Recipient Profl. Achievement award, U. Chgo. Alumni; fellow, Ctr. Advanced Study in Behavioral Scis., 1972—73. Fellow: Am. Acad. Arts Scis.; mem.: Order of Coif (nat. pres. 2001—04), Phi Beta Kappa (hon.). Office: U Mich Law Sch Hutchins Hall Ann Arbor MI 48109-1215 Home Phone: 734-994-4289. Personal E-mail: terrysan@comcast.net. Business E-Mail: sandalow@umich.edu.

SANDBERG, ARLENE, elementary school educator; BS in Elem. Edn., Kans. State Univ.; MS in Spl. Edn., Fitchburg State Univ., Mass. Tchr. Mass., Va., NY, Hawaii, Pa., 1979—98; ESL tchr. Mountain View Elem. Sch., Anchorage, 1998—. Named Alaska Tchr. of Yr., 2006. Office: Mountain View Elem Sch 4005 McPhee Ave Anchorage AK 99508 Office Phone: 907-742-3926 ext. 3013. Business E-Mail: sandberg_arlene@asdk12.org.

SANDBERG, IRWIN WALTER, retired electrical and computer engineering educator; b. NYC, Jan. 23, 1934; s. Ben and Estelle S.; m. Barbara A. Zimmerman, June 15, 1958; 1 dau. Heidi L. B.E.E., Poly. Inst. Bklyn., 1955, M.E.E., 1956, D.E.E., 1958. Tech. aid Bell Telephone Labs., Inc., Murray Hill, NJ, summer 1954, mem. tech. staff, 1958-67, head systems theory research dept., 1967-72, mem. math. and statis. research ctr., 1972-86; prof. elec. and computer engring. U. Tex., Austin, 1986—, Cockrell Family Regents chair in engring. emeritus; engr. Wheeler Labs., Great Neck, NY, summer 1955. Vis. prof. U. Calif.-Berkeley, 1965; U.S. del. Union Radio Scientifique Internationale, Munich, Germany, 1966; U.S. nat. inst. rep. Advanced Study Inst. on Network and Signal Theory, NATO, Bournemouth, Eng., 1972; lectr. study inst. NATO (Knokke), Belgium, 1966, Copenhagen, 1970; disting. invited spkr. Asilomar Conf., 1973-74; main lectr. European Conf. on Circuit Theory and Design, The Hague, 1981; advisor Inst. Electronics, Info. and Comm. Engrs., Tokyo; advisor Am. Men and Women of Sci., 1993. Patentee (in field). Recipient Best Paper award Asilomar Conf., 1970, Achievement award IEEE Circuits and Systems Soc., 1986, Classic Paper citation ISI press, 1984, Outstanding Alumnus award Poly. U., 1993. Fellow IEEE (life, adminstrv. com. group circuit theory 1969-70, vice chmn. group circuit theory 1971-72, Centennial medal, Millennial medal, Cirs. and Sys. Soc. Golden Jubilee medal, Cirs. and Sys. Soc. disting. lectr.), AAAS; mem. NAE, Soc. for Indsl. and Applied Math., Acad. Medicine, Engring. and Sci. Tex., Eta Kappa Nu, Sigma Xi, Tau Beta Pi Home: 8505 Hickory Creek Dr Austin TX 78735-1527 Office: Univ Tex Dept Elec Comp Engr Austin TX 78712 Home Phone: 512-328-1004; Office Phone: 512-471-6899. E-mail: sandberg@ece.utexas.edu.

SANDBERG, RYNE DEE, baseball coach, retired professional baseball player; b. Spokane, Wash., Sept. 19, 1959; s. Derwent and Elizabeth S. Sandberg; m. Cindy White; children: Lindsey, Justin. Infielder Phila. Phillies, 1981, Chgo. Cubs, 1982—94, ret., 1994; baseball analyst ESPN Radio, 2004; mgr. Class-A Peoria Chiefs, 2007—08, Double-A Tenn. Smokies, 2009—. Recipient Golden Glove award, Maj. League Baseball, 1983—91, Silver Slugger award, 1984, 1985, 1988—92; named Nat. League MVP, Maj. League Baseball, 1984, Player of Yr., Sporting News, 1984; named to Nat. League All-Star Team, Maj. League Baseball, 1984—93, Baseball Hall of Fame, 2005. Achievements include leading the National League in: triples (19), 1984; runs (114), 1984, (104), 1989, (116), 1990; home runs (40), 1990. Office: Tenn Smokies 3540 Line Dr Kodak TN 37764*

SANDBERG, SHERYL KARA, Internet company executive; b. 1969; d. Adele and Joel Sandberg; m. David Bruce Goldberg, Apr. 17, 2004; 2 children. BA in Economics, summa cum laude, Harvard U., 1991, MBA, 1995. Economist The World Bank; mgmt cons. McKinsey & Co.; chief of staff to sec. US Dept. Treasury, Washington, 1999—2001; v.p. global online sales & ops. Google Inc., Mountain View, Calif., 2001—07; COO Facebook, Inc., Palo Alto, Calif., 2008—. Bd. dirs. eHealthInsurance

Services, Inc., 2006—. Recipient John H. Williams prize, Harvard U.; named a Woman to Watch, Advt. Age, 2009; named one of 50 Most Powerful Women in Bus., Fortune mag., 2007, 2008, 50 Women to Watch, Wall St. Jour., 2008, Most Influential Women in Tech., Fast Co., 2009. Office: Facebook Inc 1601 S California Ave Palo Alto CA 94304 Office Phone: 650-543-4800. Office Fax: 650-543-1801.*

SANDBURG, HELGA, author; b. Maywood, Ill., Nov. 24, 1918; d. Carl and Lilian (Steichen) S.; m. George Crile, Jr., Nov. 9, 1963; children by previous marriage: John Carl Steichen, Paula Steichen Polega. Student, Mich. State Coll., 1939-40, U. Chgo., 1940. Dairy goat breeder, also personal sec. to father, 1944-51; sec. manuscripts div., also for keeper of collections Library of Congress, 1952-56; adminstrv. asst. for papers of Woodrow Wilson, 1958-59; writer, lectr., 1957—. Author: (novels) The Wheel of Earth, 1958, Measure My Love, 1959, The Owl's Roost, 1962, The Wizard's Child, 1967; (non-fiction) Sweet Music, A Book of Family Reminiscence and Song, 1963; (with George Crile, Jr.) Above and Below, 1969; (poetry) The Unicorns, 1965; To A New Husband, 1970, The Age of the Flower, 1994; (young adult novels) Blueberry, 1963; Gingerbread, 1964; (juveniles) Joel and the Wild Goose, 1963; Bo and the Old Donkey, 1965, Anna and the Baby Buzzard, 1970; Children and Lovers: 15 Stories by Helga Sandburg, 1976; (biography) A Great and Glorious Romance: The Story of Carl Sandburg and Lilian Steichen, 1978; "...Where Love Begins", 1989, (recorded poems) From in the Dream: Helga Sandburg Reads her Poems, 2001; also numerous short stories; rep. in collections.; contbr. short stories, poems, articles to popular mags. including Seventeen. Recipient Va. Quar. Rev. prize for best short story, 1959, Borestone Mountain poetry award, 1962, Poetry award Chgo. Tribune, 1970; 2d prize 7th Ann. Kans. Poetry Contest, Florence Roberts Head Ohioana Book award, 1990; grantee Finnish Am. Soc. and Svenska Inst., 1961 Mem. Authors Guild, Poetry Soc., Am. Milk Goat Record Assn., Am.-Scandinavian Found., Nat. Nubian Club, Coun. Save the Dunes, Am. Luxembourg Soc., Acad. Am. Poets. Address: 2060 Kent Rd Cleveland Heights OH 44106-3339 E-mail: helgacrile@steichen.ws.

SANDE, THEODORE ANTON, architect, educator, foundation executive; b. New London, Conn., Nov. 21, 1933; s. Lars Anton and Viola (Edgcomb) S.; m. Solveig Inga-Maj Imselius, Aug. 6, 1960; children: Susanne Ingrid, Lars Michael. BSc in Architecture, RI Sch. Design, 1956; MArch, Yale U., 1961; PhD, U. Pa., 1972; grad. Cultural Instns. Mgmt. Program, Mus. Collaborative, 1983; postgrad., Attingham (Eng.) Summer Sch., 1980. Vis. prof. history of architecture Rensselaer Poly. Inst., fall 1973-74, U. Pa., 1976-77; adj. prof. Am. studies and history Case-Western Res. U., 1981—92. Vis. lectr. in historic preservation Cleve. State U., summer 1994, spring 1998; lectr. art Williams Coll., 1972-75; attended teleconfs. non-profit orgn. mgmt. Drucker Found., 1992. Designer, Arkitekt, Hakon Ahlberg, SAR, Arkitekt, Stockholm, 1960, designer, Washburn, Luther & Rowley, Architects, Attleboro, Mass., 1961-62, Barker & Turoff, Architects, Providence, 1962-63, jr. partner, Turoff Assocs., Architects, 1964-67, partner, Turoff & Sande, Architects, Providence, 1968-70, prin. Ted Sande, Architect, Cranston, R.I., 1970, Cleve., 1993—, emeritus architect, R.I., 2004— author: Industrial Archaeology: A New Look at the American Heritage, 2d edit, 1978; contbg. author: Guidebook to Philadelphia Architecture, 1974; editor: New England Textile Mill Survey, 1971; co-editor: Historic Preservation of Engineering Works, 1981; contbr. articles to profl. jours.; two-man show drawings, Providence Art Club, 1970. Dir. profl. svcs. office hist. properties Nat. Trust Hist. Preservation, Washington, 1975—77, dir. planning and devel., 1977—78, acting v.p. office hist. properties, 1978—79, v.p., 1979—80; mem. Old Georgetown Bd. Nat. Commn. Fine Arts, 1979—81; co-chmn. Conf. Indsl. Archeology Smithsonian Instn., 1971; active Shaker Heights Landmark Commn., 1982—84, Cleve. Landmarks Commn., 1985—2004; mem. archtl. bd. rev. Village of Hunting Valley, Ohio, 2000—; mem. Leadership Cleve. Class 86/87, Ohio Gov.'s Commn. on Bicentennials the NW Ordinance and U.S. Const., 1986—89, Cleve. Bicentennial Commn., 1992—94, Stan Hywet Hall and Gardens, Akron, Ohio, trustee, 1997—2005; chmn. Schweinfurth Trust, 1999—2006; hist. preservation cons. Village of Chagrin Falls, Ohio, 2007—; mem. vis. com. Mandel Sch. Scis., Case We. Res. U., 1993—2003; trustee U. Circl Inc., 1981—93, Nat. Rock and Roll Mus. and Hall of Fame, mem. exec. bdlg. com., 1993—95; instnl. rep. Cleve. Arts Consortium, 1987—93. Fellow: We. Res. Hist. Soc. (life; exec. dir. 1981—93, exec. dir. emeritus 1993—); mem.: SAR, AIA (com. hist. resources 1972—74), Cleve. Restoration Soc. (pres. 1994—97, trustee, hon., life trustee), Ohio Mus. Assn. (trustee 1982—87), Am. Assn. Mus., Internat. Com. for Conservation of Indsl. Heritage (chmn. bd. dirs. 1978—81), Soc. Archtl. Historians (preservation com. 1972—74), Soc. Indsl. Archeology (co-founder, 1st pres. 1971—72, dir. 1973—76, project supr. handbook on adaptive use of indsl. bldgs., gen. chmn. 15th ann. conf.), Philos. Club Cleve. (past pres.), Rowfant Club (past pres. 2002—03, coun. of fellows). Episcopalian. Home: 13415 Shaker Blvd Ste 11-H-4 Cleveland OH 44120-1586

SANDER, CLARENCE ELLIS, JR., retired protective services official; b. Delray, Fla., Dec. 15, 1946; s. Clarence Ellis and Daisy Bell Sanders; m. Theresa Ann Sander (dec.); children: Sharlene Michelle Sanders, Lawrence Ellis Sanders(dec.); m. Susan Virgina Lee. Cert. in drafting, Washinton Drafting, 1975. Security guard Smithsonian Inst., Washington; police officer US Treasury Dept., Washington; ret. Author poems. Lance corp. USMC, 1966—69. Recipient Martin Luther King award, 2005, Albert Galitan award, 2007, Law Enforcement Honor award, Svc. award, US Treasury Dept., 2007. Mem.: Fraternal Order of Police (congl. liason 2003), Am. Fedn. Govt. Employees (shop steward). Avocations: poetry, singing, dance, fishing, hunting. Home: 7304 Pacella Ct Clinton MD 20735

SANDER, ELLIOT GENE (LEE SANDER), former transportation executive; b. May 3, 1956; m. Lisa Ellen Lempel, Oct. 14, 1990. BS in Fgn. Svc., Georgetown U. Dir. transit NY Dept. Transp.; dep. dir. Office Mgmt. & Productivity NYC; dep. commr. & state rent adminstr. NY Divsn. Housing & Community Renewal; asst. gen. mgr. for surface transit & gen. mgr., Manhattan bus divsn. NYC, exec. dir. operational svc., Bur. Traffic Ops., dep. dir. divsn. parking, spl. asst. to city coun. pres., budget analyst Office Mgmt. & Budget, commr. Dept. Transp., 1994—96; with Frederic R. Harris Inc., 1996—2000; commr. NYC Taxi & Limousine Commn., 1997—2000; sr. v.p., dir. corp. strategic develop. DMJM Harris, 2000—06; exec. dir., CEO Met. Transit Authority (MTA), 2006—09. Dir. Rudin Cr. for Trans. Policy and Mgmt Robert F. Wagner Sch. of Pub. Svc. at NYU, 1996—; publisher NY Trans. Jour.; former chmn. com. one large U.S. cities Transportation Rsch. Bd.; sr. adv. Nat. Assn. of City Trans. Officials; mem. citizen adv. bd. Lower Manhattan Devel. Corp., 2002—; founder, co-chmn. Empire State Trans. Alliance.*

SANDER, FRANK ERNEST ARNOLD, law educator; b. Stuttgart, Germany, July 22, 1927; came to U.S., 1940, naturalized, 1946; s. Rudolf and Alice (Epstein) S.; m. Emily Bishop Jones, Apr. 26, 1958; children: Alison Bishop, Thomas Harvey, Ernest Ridgway Sander. AB in Math. magna cum laude, Harvard U., 1949, LLB magna cum laude, 1952. Bar: Mass. 1952, US Supreme Ct. 1952. Law clk. to Chief Judge Magruder U.S. Ct. Appeals, 1st Cir., 1952-53; law clk. to Justice Frankfurter, U.S. Supreme Ct., 1953-54; atty. tax divsn. Dept. Justice, 1954-56; with firm Hill & Barlow, Boston, 1956-59; mem. faculty Harvard Law Sch., 1959—, prof. law, 1962—, Bussey prof., 1981—, assoc. dean, 1987-2000, emeritus, 2006—. Spl. fields fed. taxation, family law, welfare law, dispute resolution; chmn. Coun. on Role of Cts.; mem. panels Am. Arbitration Assn., Fed. Mediation and Conciliation Svc.; chmn. Coun. on Legal Edn. Opportunity, 1968—70; cons. Dept. Treasury, 1968; treas. Harvard Law Rev., 1951—52; mem. dispute resolution standing com. Mass. Supreme Jud. Ct., 1994—2004; drafting com. Uniform Mediation Act, 1998—2001. Author: (with Westfall and McIntyre) Readings in Federal Taxation, 2d edit., 1983, (with Foote and Levy) Cases and Materials on Family Law, 3d edit., 1985, (with Gutman) Tax Aspects of Divorce and Separation, 4th edit., 1985, (with Goldberg, Rogers and Cole) Dispute Resolution, 5th edit., 2007. Mem. tax mission Internat. Program Taxation to Republic of Colombia, 1959; mem. com. on civil and polit. rights President's Commn. on Status of Women, 1962-63; trustee Buckingham Browne and Nichols Sch., 1969-75; chmn. Mass. Welfare Adv. Bd., 1975-79. With AUS, 1946-47. Recipient Whitney North Seymour medal Am. Arbitration Assn., 1988, spl. award for disting. svc. to dispute resolution Internat. Inst. Conflict Prevention and Resolution, 1990, Lifetime Achievement award Internat. Acad. Mediators, 2006, Am. Coll. Civil Trial Mediators, 2008. Mem. ABA (chmn. standing com. dispute resolution 1986-89, Kutak medal 1993, D'Alemberte-Raven award 1999), Boston Bar Assn., Phi Beta Kappa. Office: Harvard U Sch of Law Cambridge MA 02138 Home: 100 Newbury Ct Apt 113 Concord MA 01742 Office Phone: 617-495-3184.

SANDER, JOHN L., broadcast executive; Grad., U. Cin., 1964. With WLWC-TV, Columbus, Ohio, 1965—66, WTOL-TV, Toledo, 1966—78, gen. mgr., 1980—82; sta. mgr. WDSU, New Orleans, 1978—80; pres. & gen. mgr. KTSP-TV, Phoenix, 1982—85; pres. TV divsn. Taft Broadcasting, Cin., 1985—88; gen. mgr. WAGA-TV, Atlanta, 1988—97; exec. v.p. TV group Belo Corp., Dallas, 1997—2001, exec. v.p. media ops., 2001—04, pres. media ops., 2004—06, vice-chmn., 2006, sr. advisor, 2006—. Vice chmn. bd. FOX, 1995, 96; chmn. NBC Affiliate Bd., 2000—02; bd. dirs. Broadcast Music, Inc., 2002—06, vice chmn., 2006—07, chmn., 2007—. Chmn. bd. dirs. United Way of Met. Atlanta, 1995. Mem.: TV Assn. Broadcasters (former chmn.), Nat. Assn. Broadcasters (joint chmn. 2007—). Office: BMI Ste 570 3340 Peachtree Rd NE Atlanta GA 30326 Office Phone: 404-261-5151.

SANDER, LEE See SANDER, ELLIOT

SANDERCOX, ROBERT ALLEN, academic administrator, minister; b. Akron, Ohio, May 20, 1932; s. Monroe J. and Elverda (Arnold) S.; m. Nancy Lee Wertz, Sept. 13, 1958; children— Alison Grace, Megan Louise, Robert Philip BA, Bethany Coll., W. Va., 1954; M.Div., Yale U., 1957; postgrad., U. Buffalo, W.Va. U.; LittD, Bethany Coll., 1989. Ordained to ministry Christian Ch. (Disciples of Christ). Asst. minister Park Ave Christian Ch., NYC, 1954-57; asst. provost Bethany Coll., 1957-60, v.p., dean students, 1960-75, v.p., dir. devel., 1975-79, interim pres., 1979-80, v.p., provost for coll. advancement, 1980-89, sr. v.p., 1989-95, cons. to the pres., 1995-97, sr. v.p. emeritus, 1997—. Chmn. Brooke County Mus. Bd., 1995—98; trustee Christian Ch. Disciples of Christ in W.Va., Parkersburg, 1984—88; chmn. Brooke County Landmarks Commn., 1988—98; trustee Bethany Coll., 2004—07, Lititz Moravian Congregation, Pa., 2009—. Recipient Alumni Disting. Service award Bethany Coll., 1982 Mem. Coun. Advancement and Support Edn., Duquesne Club (Pitts.), Univ. Club Jacksonville, Order of Symposiarch, Rotary, Kiwanis (pres. 1967), Alpha Sigma Phi (nat. treas. 1982-84, v.p. 1984-86, grad. sr. pres. 1986-88, bd. dir., trustee Ednl. Found. 1982-95, chmn. Ednl. Found. 1994-95, Delta Beta Xi svc. award 1960). Home: 715 Buckwood Ln Lititz PA 17543 Personal E-mail: rsandercox@dejazzd.com.

SANDERLIN, JAMES L., energy executive, lawyer; s. Linwood and Elsie R. Sanderlin; m. Ginger Sanderlin; children: Meredith, Elaine, Barry. B, Randolph-Macon Coll., Ashland, Va.; law degree, U. Va., 1966. With McGuireWoods, Richmond, Va.; from various positions to sr. v.p. law Dominion, Richmond, 2000—. Bd. dirs. Tredegar Nat. Civil War Ctr. Found., Richmond, Richmond Pub. Libr.; co-chair VCU/MCV Heart Ctr. Fund. Office: Dominion PO Box 26532 Richmond VA 23261-6532 Office Phone: 804-819-2103. Office Fax: 804-273-4271.

SANDERS, ADRIAN LIONEL, retired educational consultant; b. Paragould, Ark., Aug. 3, 1938; s. Herbert Charles and Florence Theresa (Becherer) S.; m. Molly Jean Zecher, Dec. 20, 1961. AA, Bakersfield Coll., 1959; BA, San Francisco State U., 1961; MA, San Jose State U., 1967. 7th grade tchr. Sharp Park Sch., Pacifica, Calif., 1961-62; 5th grade tchr. Mowry Sch., Fremont, Calif., 1962-64; sci. tchr. Blacow Sch., Fremont, Calif., 1964-76; 5th grade tchr. Warm Springs Sch., Fremont, 1977-87, 5th grade gifted and talented edn. tchr., 1987-94; ret., 2006; edn. cons., 1994—2006. Mem. San Diego Hist. Soc., 1999, Mingei Internat. Mus., Balboa Park-San Diego; vol. 7 km. Race for Alzheimer's Disease Willow Glen Founders Day, San Jose, 1988-92. Named Outstanding Young Educator, Jr. C. of C., Fremont, Calif., 1965. Mem. Zoolog. Soc. San Diego, Calif. Ctr. for the Arts (Escondido), Calif. Retired Tchrs. Assn., 1994-, San Jose State U. Alumni Assn., 2006-. Avocations: photography, travel, collecting license plates. Home and Office: 1437 Stoneridge Cir Escondido CA 92029-5514

SANDERS, ALEXANDER MULLINGS, JR., judge; b. Columbia, SC, Sept. 29, 1938; s. Alexander Mullings Sr. and Henrietta Courtrier (Thomas) S.; m. Zoe Caroline Dutrow; 1 child, Zoe Caroline. BS, U. S.C., 1960, LLB, 1962; LLM, U. Va., 1990. Bar: S.C. 1962, U.S. Dist. Ct. S.C. 1962, U.S. Supreme Ct. 1975, U.S. Ct. Appeals (4th cir.) 1976. Sr. ptnr. Sanders & Quackenbush, Columbia, 1974-83, Sanders & Nettles, 2002—; of counsel Adams & Quackenbush, Columbia, 1983; chief judge S.C. Ct. Appeals, Columbia, 1983-92; pres. Coll. Charleston, SC, 1992—2001. Adj. faculty U. S.C., Columbia, 1965-92, Harvard U. Law Sch., Cambridge, Mass., 1983-2009; bd. dirs. Nat. Bank of S.C. Mem. S.C. Ho. Reps., Columbia, 1966-74, S.C. Senate, Columbia, 1976-83; chair bd. trustees Nat. Jud. Coll., chair bd. chzrloston Sch. Law, 2002-; Served with USAR, 1956-64. Mem. ABA, S.C. Bar Assn. Office: Coll of Charleston Off of Pres Charleston SC 29424 Home Phone: 843-577-6572; Office Phone: 873-953-5755. Business E-Mail: goffp@cofc.edu.

SANDERS, BARRY, retired professional football player; b. Wichita, July 16, 1968; s. William and Shirley Sanders. Student, Okla. State U., 1986—89. Running back Detroit Lions, 1989—99. Co-author (with Mark E. McCormick): Now You See Him: The Barry Sanders Story, 2003. Recipient Heisman Trophy award, 1988; named NFL Rookie of Yr., 1990, NFL Offensive Player of the Yr., 1997, 1994, NFL Player of the Yr., 1991, 1997; named to Sporting News Coll. All-Am. team, 1987, 1988, Pro Bowl, 1989—98. Achievements include holds NCAA single season record in rushing yards (2,628); led NFL in rushing, 1990, 94, 96, 97; #3 all-time on NFL rushing list (15,269); inducted into the pro and college NFL Hall of Fame, 2004. Office Phone: 305-674-7221, 213-291-1847. Business E-Mail: jb@barry.sanders.com.

SANDERS, BARRY R., lawyer; b. Oak Park, Ill., July 21, 1957; s. Eugene Haze and Muriel Efty Sanders; m. Diane Gaffney Sanders, Dec. 28, 1985; 1 child, Mattie Maria Murielle. BA, U. Va., 1979, Cambridge U., 1981; LLM, U. Tex., 1983; MA, Cambridge U., 1986. Bar: Calif. 1984, Ariz. 1985, U.S. Dist. Ct. (no. dist.) Calif. 1984, U.S. Dist. Ct. (ea. dist.) Calif. 1985, U.S. Dist. Ct. Ariz. 1987, U.S. Ct. Appeals (9th cir.) 1989, U.S. Supreme Ct. 1996, U.S. Ct. Appeals (8th cir.) 2001. Shareholder Pohlman & Sanders, PA, Phoenix, 1989—91, Ryley, Carlock & Applewhite, PA, Phoenix, 1991—99, Allen, Price, Padden & Sanders PC, Phoenix, 1999—2005, Mariscal Weeks McIntyre & Friedlander, P.A., 2005—. Recipient Henry prize in Moral Philosophy, U. of Aberdeen, Scotland, 1978. Mem.: State Bar Ariz. (chair antitrust sect. 1998—99, 2002—03). Avocation: golf. Office: Mariscal Weeks McIntyre & Friedlander P A 2901 N Ctrl Ave Ste 200 Phoenix AZ 85012 Business E-Mail: barry.sanders@mwmf.com.

SANDERS, BERNARD (BERNIE SANDERS), United States Senator from Vermont, former congressman; b. Bklyn., Sept. 8, 1941; s. Eli and Dorothy (Glassberg) Sanders; m. Jane O'Meara, 1988; children: Levi, Heather, Carina, David. Student, Bklyn. Coll.; BA, U. Chgo., 1964. Freelance writer, carpenter, youth counselor, 1964-76; dir. Am. People's Hist. Soc., Burlington, Vt., 1976-81; mayor City of Burlington, Vt., 1981-89; mem. faculty Harvard U., Cambridge, Mass., 1989, Hamilton Coll., Clinton, NY, 1990; mem.-at large US Congress from Vt., 1991—2007; US Senator from Vt., 2007—. Mem. Progressive Caucus, US Congress, mem. fin. svcs. com., ranking minority mem. fin. instns. and consumer credit subsommittee, mem. govt. reform com. Co-author: Outsider in the House, 1997. Chmn. Vt. Liberty Union Party, 1975-76, candidate for Vt. gov., 1972, 76, 86, US Senate, 1971, 74. Independent. Jewish. Office: US Senate 2233 Rayburn House Office Bldg Washington DC 20515 Office Phone: 202-224-5141. Office Fax: 202-228-0776.*

SANDERS, BOB (DEMOND SANDERS), professional football player; b. Erie, Pa., Feb. 24, 1981; s. Marion and Jean Sanders. Student in African Am. world studies, U. Iowa, Iowa City. Defensive back Indpls. Colts, 2004—. Active Colts Cmty. Tuesdays Program, 2004. Named First Team All-Am. Football Conf., Pro Football Weekly/Pro Football Writers of Am., 2005, First Team All-Pro, AP, 2005, 2007, NFL Defensive Player of Yr., 2007; named to Am. Football Conf. Pro Bowl Team, 2005, 2007. Achievements include being the first defensive back since the Colts moved to Indianapolis to make the Pro Bowl, 2005; being the first player in Colts franchise history to be named the Associated Press' Defensive Player of the Year, 2007; being the highest paid safety in the history of the NFL as of 2007. Mailing: c/o Indpls Colts RCA Dome 100 S Capitol Ave Indianapolis IN 46225

SANDERS, BRYAN HOWARD, law educator, consultant; b. Cleve., Sept. 2, 1960; s. Howard William and Marian Sanders; m. Virginia Sanders, July 31, 1982. BS in Govt., Evangel U., 1982; JD, Oral Roberts U., 1985; JD (hon.), Regent U., 1991. Atty. W. Owen Fields and Assocs., Tulsa, Okla., 1985—87; v.p. and gen. counsel Logos Devel. Corp., Elyria, Ohio, 1987—90; pres. Reconciliation Ministries, Elyria, Ohio, 1987—90; prof. legal studies Evangel U., Springfield, Mo., 1990—; prin. Hollingsworth, Sanders & Tow, LLC, Springfield, 2006—08; assoc. Hollingsworth Towe; 2nd assoc. LLC, Springfield, 2008—. V.p. Conflict Mgmt. Cons., Louisville, 1991—2005; instr. Springfield Police Acad., 1998—; bd. dirs. legal affairs Assn. Christian Tchrs. and Schs., Springfield. Co-author: A Legal Primer for Church Discipline, 1992; contbr. articles to mags. Mem.: Christian Prelaw Soc. (founding pres. 2003—), Christian Legal Soc., Fellowship of Cos. for Christ Internat. (area coord. 1997—2002), Assn. for Conflict Resolution. Mem. Assemblies Of God. Avocations: golf, reading. Office: Evangel Univ 1111 N Glenstone Ave Springfield MO 65802 Business E-Mail: sandersb@evangel.edu.

SANDERS, CARL E., lawyer, former Governor of Georgia; b. Augusta, Ga., May 15, 1925; s. Carl T. and Roberta (Ailey) S.; m. Betty Bird Foy, 1947; children: Betty Foy, Carl E. Jr. LLB, Univ. Ga., 1947. Bar: Ga. 1947. Mem. Hammond, Kennedy & Sanders, Augusta, Ga., 1948—52; sr. mem. Sanders, Thurmond, Hester & Jolles, Augusta, Ga., Sanders, Hester, Holley, Ashmore & Boozer; chmn., mem. exec. com. Troutman Sanders LLP (formerly Troutman, Sanders, Lockerman & Ashmore), Atlanta, 1967—2006, chmn. emeritus, 2006—; mem. Ga. House Reps., 1954—56, Ga. State Senate, 1957—62, pres. pro tem, 1960—62; gov. State of Ga., 1963—67. Chmn., rules com. Dem. Nat. Conv., 1964; mem., exec. com. Nat. Gov. Conf., 1964—65; chmn. Appalachian Gov. Conf., 1964—65; vice chmn. Southern Gov. Conf., 1965—66; mem. Nat. Commn. on Urban Affairs, 1967; bd. dir. Pub. Broadcasting Corp., 1968—70; chmn., fin. com. Dem. Party, Ga., 1974—83; bd. dir. Healthdyne, 1986—96, Matria Healthcare, 1996—, Wachovia Atlanta Adv. Bank Bd.; mem. Atlanta Com., Olympic Games, 1996. Served to 1st lt. (first pilot of B-17 heavy bomber) USAF, WWII. Recipient Order of Sacred Treasure Gold and Silver award, Emperor and Govt. of Japan, 1989; named a Super Lawyer, Atlanta Mag., 2004. Mem.: ABA, Lawyers Club of Atlanta, Atlanta Bar Assn., Phi Delta Phi. Democrat. Achievements include being inducted into Athletic Hall of Fame, 1968, Aviation Hall of Fame, 1997. Office: Troutman Sanders LLP Ste 5200 600 Peachtree St NE Atlanta GA 30308-2216 Office Phone: 404-885-3100. Office Fax: 404-962-6674. Business E-Mail: carl.sanders@troutmansanders.com.

SANDERS, CHARLOTTA ELISABETH, nuclear engineer, educator; b. Vastervik, Sweden, Feb. 14, 1971; d. Hans J. Nilsson and margareta Gunilla Carlsson; m. Mark Callis Sanders, Aug. 24, 1996. BS in Mech. Engring., Brigham Young U., Provo, Utah, 1994; MS in Nuc. Engring., Tex. A&M U., College Station, 1995; PhD in Engring. in Nuc. & Reactor Physics, Royal Inst. Tech., Stockholm, 1999. Cert. profl. nuclear engr., Bd. Profl. Engrs. & Land Surveyors, Nev., 2003. Reactor physicist Studsvik Nuc., Nykoping, Sweden, 1998—2000; rsch. assoc. Oak Ridge Nat. Lab., Tenn., 2000—02; sr. nuc. engring. specialist Bechtel SAIC Co., LLC, Las Vegas, Nev., 2002—. Adj. prof. U. Nev., Las Vegas, 2006—. Contbr. articles to profl. jours. Recipient Riley Bechtel Merit award, Bechtel Nat., Inc., 2004—05. Mem.: Nev. Local Am. Nuc. Soc. Sect. (vice-chmn. 2005), Environmentalists Nuc. Power (vice-chmn. 1998—2000), Women In Nuc. (Las Vegas valley women in nuc. chpt. exec. coun. mem. 2004), Am. Nuc. Soc. (profl. women in ans com. mem. 1999, exec. com. mem. radiation protection & shielding divsn. 2005). Avocations: golf, travel, skiing. Home: 1930 Village Ctr Cir 3-256 Las Vegas NV 89134 Office: Bechtel SAIC Co LLC 1180 Town Center Dr Las Vegas NV 89144

SANDERS, DALE R., lawyer; b. NYC, Feb. 1, 1946; 1 child. Bar: Fla. 1970, Wyo. 1991, U.S. Dist. Ct. (so. dist.) Fla. 1971, U.S. Tax Ct. 1972. Atty. Kirsch & Druck, P.A., Ft. Lauderdale, Fla., 1970-71, Kirsch, Digiulian, Druck et al, Ft. Lauderdale, Fla., 1971-72, Digiulian, Spellacy, Lyons, Ft. Lauderdale, Fla., 1972-77, Lyons & Sanders, Chartered, Ft. Lauderdale, Fla., 1977—. With USAR, 1969-75. Mem.:

Broward County Trial Lawyers Assn. (pres. 1980), Broward County Bar Assn. (pres. 1990), Fla. Bar (bd. govs. 1991—95, mem. 17th cir. jud. nominating commn. 1992—96, vice chair 1996—2002, mem. State of Fla. jud. qualifications commn.). Office: Lyons and Sanders Chartered 1301 E Broward Blvd Ste 220 Fort Lauderdale FL 33301

SANDERS, DONALD BENJAMIN, neurologist, educator; b. Sumter, SC, Aug. 3, 1938; s. Colclough E. and Frances Ann Sanders; m. Lynda Louise Frank, July 19, 1976; children: Colclough Allison, Kathleen Chatterton. BS, Univ. of the South, 1959; MD, Harvard Med. Sch., 1964. Diplomate Am. Bd. Neurology, Am. Bd. Electrodiagnostic Medicine. Asst. prof. neurology U. Va. Med. Sch., Charlottesville, 1973-77, assoc. prof. neurology, 1978-80; prof. medicine Duke U. Med. Sch., Durham, N.C., 1980—. Contbr. articles to profl. jours. Maj. USAF, 1969-72. Fellow Am. Acad. Neurology; mem. Am. Neurol. Assn., Am. Assn. Electrodiagnostic Medicine (bd. dirs. 1993-95, pres. 1996-97). Office: Duke U Med Ctr PO Box 3403 Durham NC 27710

SANDERS, ELIZABETH ANNE WEAVER (BETSY SANDERS), management consultant, coach, writer; b. Gettysburg, Pa., July 25, 1945; Student, Gettysburg Coll., 1963—65; BA in German Lang. and Linguistics, Wayne State U., 1967; MEd, Boston U., 1970; postgrad., U. Wash., 1976—78. With Nordstrom, 1971—90, v.p., gen. mgr., 1978—90; prin. The Sanders Partnership, Sutter Creek, Calif., 1971-90, prin., owner, 1990—; founder, dir. Nat. Bank So. Calif., 1971-90. Bd. dirs. Wal Mart Stores, Inc., Washington Mut., Wellpoint Health Sys., Inc., Wolverine Worldwide, Inc., Denny's Inc., H.F. Ahmanson Co., Carl Karcher Enterprises, Sport Chalet, St. Joseph Health Sys., spkr. in field, mgmt. cons., exec. coach, life coach, mentor, facilitator in leadership, svc., creating cultures. Author: Fabled Service, 1995. Trustee Gettysburg Coll.; regent U. Pacific; adv. bd. mem. Bimbo Bakeries USA. Recipient Woman of Achievement in Bus. award YWCA South Orange County, Director's Choice award, 1997; named Woman of Yr. Bus. and Industry YWCA North Orange County, Humanitarian of Yr. NCCJ, Author of Yr., 1996, Dir. of Yr., Corp. Gov. Forum for Corp. Dirs., 2002. Mem. Internat. Women's Forum. Home: 12835 Sutter Creek Rd Sutter Creek CA 95685-9733 Office: The Sanders Partnership PO Box 14 Sutter Creek CA 95685-0014 Office Phone: 209-267-5400. E-mail: betsanders@aol.com.

SANDERS, FRANKLIN D., retired insurance company executive; b. Newton, Mass., Apr. 24, 1935; s. Franklin and Ethel Shriner (Dulaney) S.; m. Jane Gray Collier, June 18, 1960; children— Cynthia, Franklin D., Nancy, Carolyn. AB, Amherst Coll., 1957; MBA, Harvard U., 1959. With 1st Boston Corp., NYC, 1960-86, mng. dir., 1976-86; pres. Aegis Ins. Services Inc., Jersey City; ret. Treas., bd. dirs. Assoc. Electric & Gas Ins. Services, Ltd., Hamilton, Bermuda, 1986-97. Chmn. Republican Exec. Com., Bernardsville, N.J., 1965-72, Bernardsville Zoning Bd. of Adjustment, 1966-99; trustee Episcopal Diocese of Vt., 2005—, Wally Byam Caravan Club Internat., 2008-. Mem. Harvard Club (N.Y.C.). Avocations: sailing, skiing, golf.

SANDERS, GERALD HOLLIE, communications educator; b. Mt. Vernon, Tex., Dec. 10, 1924; s. Elmer Hugh and Velma Mae (Hollowell) S.; m. Mary Dean Crew, July 18, 1947; children: Michael Dwaine, Rose Ann, Susan Kathleen, Randall Wayne. BA, Southeastern Okla. U., 1947; MA, Tex. Tech U., 1969; PhD, U. Minn., 1974. Program dir. Sta. WEWO, Laurenburg, NC, 1947—49; sports dir. Sta. KFYO, Lubbock, Tex., 1949—50; gen. mgr. Sta. KLVT, Levelland, Tex., 1950—51, 1953—54; sports dir. Sta. KCUL, Ft. Worth, 1954—55; asst. mgr. Sta. KDAV, Lubbock, 1955—57; mgr. Sta. KCBD, Lubbock, 1957—58; owner Sta. KSEL, Lubbock, 1958—67, Sta. KBUY, Amarillo, Tex., Sta. KERB, Kermit, Tex., Sta. KBEK, Elk City, Okla., Sta. KZZN, Littlefield, Tex.; lectr. comm. Coll. of Wooster, 1967—68, asst. prof, 1968—75, assoc. prof., 1975—91, chmn. dept. comm., 1974—81, Miami U., Oxford, Ohio, 1981—92, prof. emeritus comm., 1992—. Disting. lectr. Jinan U., Zhong Shan U., Fudan U., Nanjing U., Beijing U., China, 1989; cons. in field, Oxford, 1982—; polit. and trial cons., 1996—. Author: Introduction to Contemporary Academic Debate, 1983; contbr. articles. to profl. jours. Active Political Campaigns. Served to col. USMC, 1943-46, PTO, 1951-53, Korea. Recipient Disting. Svc. award Delta Sigma Rho-Tau Kappa Alpha, 1991, Am. Forensic Assn., 1991. Mem. Am. Forensic Assn. (pres. 1978-82), Speech Comm. Assn., Speech Comm. Assn. of Ohio (pres. 1976-77), Disting. Svc. award 1978), Am. Inst. Parliamentarians, Soc. Trial Cons. Presbyterian. Avocations: sports, political campaigns. Home: 200 Country Club Dr Oxford OH 45056-9050 Office: Advocacy Unltd PO Box 457 Oxford OH 45056-0457 Home Phone: 513-523-6948; Office Phone: 513-523-0227. E-mail: gsanders@one.net.

SANDERS, GINA SUSAN, publishing executive; b. 1960; d. Arnold R. and Joyce Sanders; m. Steven Oliver Newhouse, Feb. 28, 1993; 2 children. BA magna cum laude, Tufts U., 1982. Account mgr. House & Garden Condé Nast Publs., 1988, advt. dir. Details mag., 1993—94, pub., 1994—97, pub. Gourmet mag., 1997—2002, v.p., 2000—02, founding pub., v.p. Teen Vogue, 2002—08, v.p., pub. Lucky mag., 2008—. Named Pub. of Yr., Condé Nast, 2005; named to The 10 Under 50 List, Adweek mag., 2005, A-List, Advt. Age, 2005. Office: Lucky 4 Times Sq New York NY 10036

SANDERS, HARVEY GIBERT, JR., lawyer; s. Harvey Gibert and Sue Lee Sanders; m. Barbara Langley, June 10, 1956 (dec.); children: Suzanne Sanders Putnam, Harvey G. Sanders, III, Barry L.; m. Nancy Anne Sanders, Dec. 2, 2002. BS, U. SC, Columbia, 1957, LLB, 1960. Bar: SC, US Dist. Ct. SC 1960, US Ct. Appeals (4th cir.) 1960. Mem. plaintiff's exec. com. Am. Honda MDL Dealerships Litig., Baltimore, 1995—2000; co-class counsel Borman v. Am. Honda MDL Litig., Baltimore, 2000—02; assoc. Leatherwood Walker Todd & Mann, P.C., Greenville, SC, 1960—64, shareholder, 1974—. Instr. accounting Palmer Bus. Coll., Columbia, 1960—62; bd. dirs. Greenville Symphony Orch., 2000—08. Editor (assoc.): U. SC Law Rev., 1958—59. Aide SC State Senate, Columbia, 1955—59; mem., exec. com. Miss SC Pageant, Columbia, 1965—95, legal counsel, All Am. City Com., Greenville, SC, 1965; pres. Greenville Jaycees, 1966—67, Greenville Literacy Assn., 1969—70, Greenville County Commn. on Alcoholism, 1970—73; v.p. USC Alumni Assn., Carolina Scholars Scholarship Selection Com., Columbia, SC; bd. dirs. Greenville C. of C., 1967, v.p. govt. affairs, 1972, gen. counsel, 1976—78, Cmty. Found. of Greater Greenville, 1987; bd. dir. Greenville Art Mus., 1968, Greenville Symphony Orch. Named to Hall of Fame, Greenville-Jaycee. Mem.: ABA (assoc.), SC. Bar (assoc.; mem. exec. com. Young Lawyers Sect.), Greenville County Bar (assoc.; exec. com. mem. 1986—88, pres. 1987), Order of Wig and Robe, Greenville Touchdown Club, J.L. Mann Booster Club (pres. 1982—83), Greenville Country Club (pres. 1979), DeBordieu Club, The Res. Club, Colonial Club (pres. 1974), Greenville Young Lawyers Club (v.p. 1976), Greenville-Pickens Gamecock Club (v.p. 1965, pres. 1966), The Commerce Club, Kiwanis Club of Greenville (bd. dir. 1976—77), Phi Alpha Delta (Chief Justice 1959). Baptist. Avocations: golf, boating, travel, reading. Office: Leatherwood Walker Todd & Mann PC 300 E McBee Ave Ste 500 Greenville SC 29601 Office Fax: 864-240-2498. Business E-Mail: hsanders@lwtm.com.

SANDERS, HEYWOOD T., finance educator; b. Washington, Nov. 28, 1948; married. PhD, Harvard U., Cambridge, Mass., 1975. Asst. prof. U. Ill., Champaign, 1976—81; assoc. prof. Trinity U., San Antonio, 1982—2001. Prof. U. Tex., San Antonio, 2001—. Contbr. articles to profl. jours. Bd. mem. Monte Vista Hist. Assn., San Antonio, 1990—96. Fellowship, Woodrow Wilson Nat. Fellowship, 1970. Mem.: Urban Affairs Assn. Business E-Mail: heywood.sanders@utsa.edu.

SANDERS, J. TED, academic administrator, former educational association administrator; Tchr. Mountain Home, Idaho, Bur. Indian Affairs pub. sch. sys.; supt. of edn. State of N Mex., 1979—85, State of Ill., 1985—89; dep. sec. US Dept. Edn., 1989—91, acting sec., 1990—91; supt. pub. instrn. State of Ohio, 1991—95; pres. So. Ill. U., 1995—2000, Edn. Commn. of the States, 2000—05; exec. chmn. Cardean Learning Group, 2005—08; chmn. Ellis U., Chgo., 2008—. Bd. dirs. PLATO Learning Inc., 2004—09. Office: Ellis U 111 N Canal St Ste 380 Chicago IL 60606*

SANDERS, JACK THOMAS, religious studies educator; b. Grand Prairie, Tex., Feb. 28, 1935; s. Eula Thomas and Mildred Madge (Parish) S.; m. M. Patricia Chism, Aug. 9, 1959 (dec. Oct. 1973); 1 son, Collin Thomas; m. Susan Elizabeth Plass, Mar. 3, 1979. BA, Tex. Wesleyan Coll., 1956; M.Div., Emory U., 1960; PhD, Claremont Grad. Sch., 1963; postgrad., Eberhard-Karls U., Tuebingen, Germany, 1963-64. Asst. prof. Emory U., Atlanta, 1964-67, Garrett Theol Sem., Evanston, Ill., 1967-68, McCormick Theol. Sem., Chgo., 1968-69; assoc. prof. U. Oreg., Eugene, 1969-75, prof., 1975-97, head dept. religious studies, 1973-80, 85-90, prof. emeritus, 1997—. Author: The New Testament Christological Hymns, 1971, Ethics in the New Testament, 1975, 2d edit., 1986, Ben Sira and Demotic Wisdom, 1983, The Jews in Luke-Acts, 1987, Schismatics, Sectarians, Dissidents, Deviants: The First One Hundred Years of Jewish-Christian Relations, 1993, Charisma, Converts, Competitors: Societal and Sociological Factors in the Success of Early Christianity, 2000; editor: Gospel Origins and Christian Beginnings, 1990, Gnosticism and the Early Christian World, 1990; mem. edit. bd. Jour. Bibl. Lit., 1977-83. Mem. policy bd. Dept. Higher Edn. Nat. Council Chs., N.Y.C., 1971-73. NDEA grad. study fellow, 1960-63; Fulbright Commn. fellow, 1963-64; Am. Coun. Learned Socs. travel grantee, 1981; NEH fellow, 1983-84. Mem. Assn. for Jewish Studies, Soc. Bibl. Lit. (regional sec. 1969-76, sabbatical rsch. award 1976-77). Democrat. Home: 704 NW 3d Dr Pendleton OR 97801-1411 Office: U Oregon Dept Religious Studies Eugene OR 97403 E-mail: jsands@oregontrail.net.

SANDERS, JACQUELYN SEEVAK, psychologist, educator; b. Boston, Apr. 26, 1931; d. Edward Ezral and Dora (Zoken) Seevak; 1 child, Seth. BA, Radcliffe Coll., 1952; MA, U. Chgo., 1964; PhD, UCLA, 1972. Counselor, asst. prin. Orthogenic Sch., Chgo., 1952—65; rsch. assoc. UCLA, 1965—68; asst. prof. Ctr. for Early Edn., LA, 1969—72; assoc. dir. Sonia Shankman Orthogenic Sch., U. Chgo., 1972—73, dir., 1973—93, dir. emeritus, 1993—; curriculum cons. day care ctrs. LA Dept. Social Welfare, 1970—72; instr. Calif. State Coll., LA, 1972; lectr. dept. edn. U. Chgo., 1972—80, sr. lectr., 1980—93, clin. assoc. prof. dept. psychiatry, 1990—93, emeritus, 1993—; instr. edn. program Inst. Psychoanalysis, Chgo., 1979—82. Cons. Osawatomie State Hosp., Kans., 1965—68; reading cons. Foreman HS, Chgo.; treas. Chgo. Inst. Psychoanalysis, 2003—. Author: Greenhouse for the Mind, 1989; editor (with Barry L. Childress): Psychoanalytic Approaches to the Very Troubled Child: Therapeutic Practice Innovations in Residential & Educational Settings, 1989; editor: Severely Disturbed Children and the Parental Alliance, 1992; editor: (with Jerome M. Goldsmith) Milieu Therapy: Significant Issues and Innovative Applications, 1993; editor: The Seevak Family, The Zoken Family; contbr. articles to profl. jours. Mem. vis. com. univ. sch. rels. U. Chgo.; bd. dirs. KAM Isaiah Israel Congregation, 1997—2001; bd. dirs., treas. Chgo. Inst. for Psychoanalysis. Recipient Alumna award, Girls' Latin Sch., Boston, Bettelheim award, Am. Assn. Children's Residential Ctrs., Disting. Svc. award, Radcliffe Assn., 2002; scholar Radcliffe Coll. scholar, 1948—52; Univ. fellow, UCLA, 1966—68. Mem.: Chgo. Inst. for Psychoanalysis, Assn. Children's Residential Ctrs. (past pres.), Harvard Club (bd. dirs. 1986—2001, Chgo.), Radcliffe Club (sec.-treas. 1986—87, pres. 1987—89, Chgo.). Home: 5842 S Stony Island Ave Apt 2G Chicago IL 60637-2033

SANDERS, JAMES, JR., city councilman; b. Queens, NY; BA, CUNY, 1984. Asst. dist. mgr. for US Rep. Floyd Flake; city councilman Dist. 31 NY City Coun., 2002—. Served as infantryman USMC. Democrat. Mailing: Dist Off 226-18 Merrick Blvd Queens NY 11413 Office Phone: 718-527-4356, 212-788-7216. Office Fax: 718-527-4402. Business E-Mail: sanders@council.nyc.ny.us.*

SANDERS, JAMES ALVIN, retired minister, retired religious studies educator; b. Memphis, Nov. 28, 1927; s. Robert E. and Sue (Black) S.; m. Dora Cargille, June 30, 1951; 1 son, Robin David. BA magna cum laude, Vanderbilt U., 1948, BD with honors, 1951; student, U. Paris, 1950-51; PhD, Hebrew Union Coll., 1955; DLitt, Acadia U., 1973; STD, U. Glasgow, 1975; DHL, Coe Coll., 1988, Hebrew Union Coll., 1988, Hastings Coll., 1996, Calif. Luth. U., 2000. Ordained teacher Presbyn. Ch., 1955; instr. French Vanderbilt U., 1948-49; faculty Colgate Rochester Div. Sch., 1954-65, assoc. prof., 1957-60, Joseph B. Hoyt prof. O.T. interpretation, 1960-65; prof. O.T. Union Theol. Sem., NYC, 1965-70, Auburn prof. Bibl. studies, 1970-77; adj. prof. Columbia, NYC, 1966-77; prof. Bibl. studies Sch. Theology and Grad. Sch., Claremont, Calif., 1977-97, ret., 1997; vis. prof. Union Theol. Seminary and Columbia U., 1997-98. Ann. prof. Jerusalem Sch. of Am. Schs. Oriental Rsch., 1961-62; fellow Ecumenical Isnt., Jerusalem, 1972-73, 85; vis. prof. U. N.Mex., 1992, Southwestern U., 1992, Calif. Luth. U., 1992, 94, Willamette U., 1993, U. So. Ariz., 1993, Jewish Theol. Sem., 2001—; session chair, Internat. Congress for Fiftieth Anniversary of Dead Sea Scrolls, Jerusalem, 1997; mem. internat. O.T. text critical com. United Bible Socs., 1969—; mem. nat. adv. acad. bd. Hebrew Union Coll., 1997—; co-founder, exec. officer Ancient Bibl. Manuscript Ctr. for Preservation and Rsch., 1977-80, pres., 1980-2003, pres. emeritus, 2003—; chmn. bd. Shepherd U., L.A., 2002—, bd. mem. Early Manuscripts Electronic Literacy, 2005-, bd. adv. Mus. of Archeology and the Bible, 2006-,; vis. prof. Yale Divinity Sch., 1998, Jewish Theol. Seminary, 2001; lectr. in field Author: Suffering as Divine Discipline in the Old Testament and Post-Biblical Judaism, 1955, The Old Testament in the Cross, 1961, The Psalms Scroll of Qumran Cave 11, 1965, The Dead Sea Psalms Scroll, 1967, Near Eastern Archaeology in the Twentieth Century, 1970, Torah and Canon, 1972, 1974, 2d edit., 2005, Identité de la Bible, 1975, God Has a Story Too, 1979, Canon and Community, 1984, From Sacred Story to Sacred Text, 1987, Luke and Scripture, 1993; editor: Paul and the Scriptures of Israel, 1993, Early Christian Interpretation of the Scriptures of Israel, 1993, The Function of Scripture in Early Jewish and Christian Tradition, 1998, The Canon Debate, 2002; contbr. over 280 articles to profl. jours.; mem. editl. bd. Jour. Bibl. Lit., 1970—76, Jour. for Study Judaism, Bibl. Theology Bull., Interpretation, 1973—78, New Rev. Std. Version Bible Com., A Gift of God in Due Season, 1996, The Quest for Context and Meaning, 1997. Trustee Am. Schs. Oriental Research. Fulbright grantee, 1950-51, Lilly Endowment grantee, 1981, NEH grantee, 1980, 91-92; Lefkowitz and Rabinowitz interfaith fellow, 1951-53, Rockefeller fellow, 1953-54, 85, Guggenheim fellow, 1961-62, 72-73, Human Scis. Rsch. fellow, 1989. Mem. Soc. Bibl. Lit. and Exegesis (pres. 1977-78), Phi Beta Kappa, Phi Sigma Iota, Theta Chi Beta. Home: PO Box 593 Claremont CA 91711-0593 Home Phone: 909-624-2651. Personal E-mail: sandersja@aol.com.

SANDERS, JAMES GRADY, biogeochemist; b. Norfolk, Va., June 10, 1951; s. Allen Buford and Maple Seretha (Myers) S.; m. Dorothea L. Palmer, 2001. BS in Zoology, Duke U., 1973; MS in Marine Scis., U. N.C., 1975, PhD in Marine Scis., 1978. Postdoctoral investigator Woods Hole (Mass.) Oceanog. Instn., 1978-80; vis. scientist Chesapeake Biol. Lab. U. Md., Solomons, 1980-81; asst. curator Estuarine Rsch. Ctr., Md. Acad. Natural Scis., 1981-85, assoc. curator, 1985-89, curator, 1989-99, dir., 1983-99, v.p., 1999; chair dept. ocean, earth and atmospheric scis. Old Dominion U., Norfolk, 1999-2001; dir. Skidaway Inst. Oceanography, Savannah, Ga., 2001—. Cons. EPA Sweden, Stockholm, 1985-90; mem. Md. Sea Grant Adv. Com., College Park, 1983-90, Environ. Commn., Calvert County, Md., 1981-88; mem. environ. biology panel Office R&D EPA, Washington, 1986-95, sci. adv. bd., ecol. processes and effects com., 2003—; EPA Sci. Adv. Bd., 2007-09; bd. dirs., SE Coastal Ocean Observing Regional Assn., 2007-, bd. dirs. Am. Chestnut Land Trust, 1997-1999; mem. bd. govs. Consortium for Oceanog. Rsch. and Edn., 1999-2007, exec. com., 2003-07; mem. adv. bd. SC Sea Grant Program, 2005—; mem. bd. trustees Consortium for Ocean Leadership, 2008-, exec. com. mem., 2009-. Assoc. editor Estuaries, 1996-99; mem. editl. bd. Environ. Toxicology and Chemistry, 2000-03; contbr. more than 70 articles to sci. jours. Grantee NOAA, EPA, NSF. Mem. AAAS, Am. Geophys. Union, Am. Soc. Limnology and Oceanography, Estuarine Rsch. Fedn. (treas. 1993-97), So. Assn. Marine Labs. (pres. 2004-05), Nat. Assn. Marine Labs. (pres., 2008-09), Oceanography Soc. Achievements include first identification of relationships between algal growth and chemical transformations of arsenic in aquatic systems. Office: Skidaway Inst Oceanography 10 Ocean Science Cir Savannah GA 31411 Home: 11 Wesley Crossing Savannah GA 31411 Office Phone: 912-598-2400. Business E-Mail: jim.sanders@skio.usg.edu.

SANDERS, JERRY, Mayor, San Diego, former social services executive; b. San Pedro, Calif., July 14, 1950; m. Rana Sampson; children: Jamie, Lisa. AA, Long Beach City Coll., 1970; BA in Pub. Adminstrn., Nat. U., 1988; student, San Diego State U. Cert. P.O.S.T mgmt. Police officer San Diego Police Dept., 1973-93, chief of police, 1993-99; CEO United Way San Diego, 1999—2005; mayor City of San Diego, 2005—. Bd. dirs. The Nat. Conf., San Diego State U. Cmty. Adv. Bd., Children's Initiative, Youth Econ. Enterprise Zones, Am. Red Cross San Diego; mem. cmty. leaders adv. bd. ElderHelp of San Diego. Recipient Headliner of Yr. award San Diego Press Club, 1984, 93, Exceptional Performance citation for SWAT leadership, 1986. Office: Office of Mayor 202 C St 11th Fl San Diego CA 92101 Office Phone: 619-236-6330. Office Fax: 619-236-7228. Business E-Mail: JerrySanders@sandiego.gov.*

SANDERS, JOANNE, councilwoman; b. Gary, Ind. 1 child. B in Indsl. Mgmt., Purdue U. Krannert Sch. Bus.; MPA, Ind. U. Sch. Pub. and Environ. Affairs. Dir. Ind. State AFL-CIO Labor Inst. for Tng.; councillor-at-large Indpls.-Marion County City-County Coun., 1999—, minority leader; internat. rep. Internat. Alliance Theatrical Stage Employees. Del., state and nat. Dem. conventions Dem. Party, vice precinct com. person, precinct com. person, vice ward chair, 1994—; mem. adv. bd. Ind. Commn. for Women; mem. exec. bd. Ctrl. Ind. Labor Coun.; mem. JWJ Workers' Rights Bd.; bd. mem. Bethlehem House. Mem.: Coalition Labor Union Women (former Ind. v.p., Ind. rep. to nat. exec. bd.). Democrat. Office: 5144 N Carrollton Ave Indianapolis IN 46205 also: Indpls Marion County City County Coun 241 City County Bldg 200 E Washington St Indianapolis IN 46204 Office Phone: 317-283-6040, 317-327-4242. Business E-Mail: jmsanders@msn.com.*

SANDERS, JOE MAXWELL, JR., pediatrician; b. Hartsville, SC, July 5, 1940; m. Dorothy Garvin, June 6, 1963; children Joe M. III, Eric T. BS, The Citadel, 1962; MD, Med. U. S.C., 1967. Diplomate Am. Bd. Pediatrics. Rotating intern, resident in pediatrics Letterman Army Med. Ctr., San Francisco, 1967-70; fellow in adolescent medicine San Francisco Children's Hosp., 1970-71; chief adolescent medicine svc. Fitzsimmons Army Med. Ctr., 1971-86; dir. adolescent medicine svc. Med. Coll. Ga., 1986-88; assoc. exec. dir. Am. Acad. Pediatrics, Elk Grove Village, Ill., 1988-93, exec. dir., 1993—2004; ret., 2004. Asst. clin. prof. pediatrics U. Colo. Health Scis. Ctr., 1971-76, assoc. clin. prof., 1976-83, clin. prof. 1983-86; assoc. prof. pediatrics Med. Coll. Ga., 1986-88; clin. prof. pediatrics, U. Chgo., 1991—; cons. for adolescent medicine Surgeon Gen. Army, 1976-86; mem. med. com. Rocky Mt. Planned Parenthood, 1981-86; vis. prof. dept. pediatrics U. Kansas (Wichita), 1984, 87, dept. pediatrics and family practice, E. Tenn. State U., Johnson City, 1985, U. Fla., Gainesville, 1987, Fitzsimmons Army Med. Ctr., Denver, 1989, U. Chgo., 1991, Baylor Coll., Houston, 1994, others. Contbr. numerous articles and abstracts to profl. jours., chpts. to books; mem. editl. bd. Jour. Current Adolescent Medicine, 1979-81, Substance Abuse: A Guide for Profls., 1985-88; reviewer Pediatrics, 1984—, Jour. Pediatrics, 1986—, Jour. Adolescent Health, 1986—, Am. Jour. Diseases of Children, 1987—, Jour. Am. Med. Assn., 1987—; guest lectr., speaker at many sci. confs. and med. soc. meetings. Mem. teenage coord. coun. Richmond County Health Dept., 1986-88, head start health adv. com. CSRA Econ. Opportunity Authority, Inc., 1986-88; med. cons. Alexian Bros. Med. Rels. Com. Decorated Legion of Merit, U.S. Army, 1987; recipient Adele Hoffman award, Sect. on Adolescent Health, 1988. Fellow Am. Acad. Pediatrics (com. on adolescence 1980-87, chmn. 1983-87, chmn. uniformed svcs chpt. 1981, 84, mem. exec. com. mil. pediatrics sect. 1976-79, sec.-treas. 1976-77, chmn. 1977-79, mem. steering com. to establish non-geographic mil. dist. chpt., mem sect. on adolescent health 1979—, program com. 1981-83, task force on substance abuse, chmn. 1984-85, cons. 85-87, task force on sch. based clinics, 1987—), Soc. Adolescent Medicine (edn. com., ambulatory care com., 1975-80, chmn. nominating com. 1978, exec. coun. 1980-83, chmn. awards com. 1990-93, pres. 1987-88, past pres's. coun. 1988—, Outstanding Achievement award 1994); mem. AMA (mem. planning com. nat. coalition on adolescent health, rep. Am. Acad. Pediatrics, Soc. Adolescent Medicine to Coalition 1987—, chmn. working group on rsch. agenda 1987-88, adv. com. on unintentional injuries 1987), Ambulatory Pediatric Assn., So. Soc. for Pediatric Rsch., Soc. Med. Cons. to Armed Forces, Order Mil. Med. Merit, Sigma Xi.

SANDERS, JOEL STEVEN, lawyer; b. Mpls., Mar. 25, 1955; s. David M. and Miriam (Gelfand) S.; m. Carol G. Bieri, May 25, 1984; children: Daniel, Elizabeth. BA, Antioch Coll., 1976; JD, U. Calif., Berkeley, 1982. Bar: Calif. 1982, US Dist. Ct. (no. dist.) Calif. 1982, US Dist. Ct. (cen. dist.) Calif. 1984, US Ct. Appeals (9th cir.) 1983. Law clk. to Hon. Procter R. Hug Jr. US Ct. Appeals (9th cir.), 1982-83; atty. antitrust div. US Dept. Justice, San Francisco, 1983-87; assoc. Gibson, Dunn & Crutcher, San Francisco, 1987-91; ptnr. Gibson, Dunn & Crutcher LLP, San Francisco, 1992—, ptnr.-in-charge, Bay Area offices, 1995—2000.

Former adj. asst. prof. law Univ. Calif. Hastings Coll. of Law. Assoc. editor Calif. Law Rev., 1980-82. Mem. ABA, State Bar of Calif., Bar Assn. of San Francisco, Order of Coif. Office: Gibson Dunn & Crutcher Ste 3000 555 Mission St San Francisco CA 94105-2933 Office Phone: 415-393-8200. Office Fax: 415-374-8439. Business E-Mail: jsanders@gibsondunn.com.

SANDERS, JOHN LASSITER, retired academic administrator; b. Four Oaks, NC, June 30, 1927; s. David Hardy and Louie Jane (Lassiter) S.; m. Ann Beal, Aug. 14, 1954; children— Tracy Elizabeth Sanders Justus, Jane Nesbit, William Hardy. AB, U. N.C., 1950, JD, 1954. Bar: NC 1955. Law clk. to judge U.S. Ct. Appeals, 1954-55; pvt. practice Raleigh, NC, 1955-56; mem. faculty Inst. Govt., UNC, Chapel Hill, 1956-94, dir., 1962-73, 79-92, v.p. planning at Univ., 1973-78. Served with USNR, 1945-46. Recipient NC award State of NC, 1996. Democrat. Baptist. Home: 750 Weaver Dairy Rd Apt 102 Chapel Hill NC 27514 Office: U NC CB 3330 Knapp Sanders Bldg Chapel Hill NC 27599-3330 Home Phone: 919-918-3666; Office Phone: 919-843-3287. E-mail: sandersj@email.unc.edu.

SANDERS, JOSEPH, law educator; b. St. Louis, July 23, 1944; s. Robert Dewey and Helen Sanders; m. Mary Sanders, Aug. 20, 1966; children: Robert, Thomas, Elizabeth Gillespie. BA, Northwestern U., Evanston, Ill., 1966, PhD, 1974; JD, Northwestern U., Chgo., 1969. Bar: Ill. 1969. Asst. prof. U. Mich., Ann Arbor, 1972—80; prof. U. Houston, 1983—. Author: (book) Bendectin on Trial, Invitation to Law and Social Science, Everyday Justice, Social Science In Court. Mem.: Am. Law Inst., Law & Soc. Assn (editor, law & soc. rev. 2001—03). Methodist. Office: Univ Houston Law Ctr 100 Law Ctr Houston TX 77204 Business E-Mail: sanders@uh.edu.

SANDERS, JULIUS RAY, music company executive; b. Williamston, Md., Jan. 5, 1956; s. Sanders and Wright. AA, Martin CC, 1980, MS in Bus., 1999. Engineering Of Computer WILLIAMSTON, 1999. Prin., owner Musical And Lyric. Co., Balt., 2000—; promoter sale rep. Ind. Contractor Joint Venture, Balt., 2001—. Gen. ptnr. Am. Majority Trustees Ltd, Balt., 1995—. Singer (producer): (songs) Song Lyric. Home and Office: Musical And Lyric CO 610 Homestead St Baltimore MD 21218-3556 Personal E-mail: jrsanders2002@hotmail.com. Business E-Mail: musicalandlyric@netscape.net.

SANDERS, KEITH PAGE, journalism educator; b. Ashland, Ohio, Sept. 25, 1938; s. Merwin Morse and Phyllis Pearl (Snyder) S.; m. Jane Carmel Adams, June 11, 1966; children: Paige Ann, Kevin Scott. BS in Journalism, Bowling Green State U., 1960; MS in Journalism, Ohio U., 1964; PhD in Mass. Comm., U. Iowa, 1967. Sports editor Ashland (Ohio) Times Gazette, 1960-61, Dover (Ohio) Daily Reporter, 1961-62; instr. journalism Bowling Green (Ohio) State U., 1963-64, U. Iowa, Iowa City, 1965-67; prof. journalism U. Mo., Columbia, 1967—2001, assoc. dean grad. studies Sch. Journalism, 1986-87, 90-91, O.O. McIntyre disting. prof., 1993, prof. emeritus, 2002—. Cons. in field. Contbr. articles to profl. jours. including Journalism Quar., Mass Media Rev., Jour. Broadcasting, Electronic Jour. of Comm.; assoc. editor Mass Comm. Rev., 1981-92, mem. editl. bd., 1972-98; mem. editl. bd. Journalism Monographs, 1973-80, Mass Comm. and Soc., 1998-2006. Recipient Award for Outstanding Achievement U. Mo. Alumni Assn., 1986; Joyce Swan Disting. Faculty award U. Mo., 1973; inducted into Columbia Bowling Hall of Fame, 1999, Presdl. award, Assoc. Edn. Journalism & Mass Communication, 2008. Mem.: Soc. Profl. Journalists, Assn. for Edn. in Journalism/Mass Comm. (Trayes Prof. of Yr. 1987), Internat. Soc. for Sci. Study of Subjectivity (treas. 1990—95), Mo. State-US Bowling Congress (2d v.p. 2006—), Mo. State Bowling Assn. (bd. dirs. 2000—06, Dir. of Yr. 2005), Omicron Delta Kappa, Kappa Tau Alpha (exec. dir. 1991—). Avocations: bowling, golf, fishing. Home: 6551 N Creasy Springs Rd Columbia MO 65202-8093 Office: Univ of Missouri Sch Journalism Columbia MO 65211-1200

SANDERS, KENTON MORRIS, medical educator; b. June 16, 1950; m. Sherryl Lynn Abbott; children: Ryan, Geoffrey, Kendra. BA in Chemistry, U. Calif., Santa Cruz, 1972; PhD in Physiology, UCLA, 1976. NIH postdoctoral fellow UCLA Med. Sch., 1976-78; postdoctoral research fellow Mayo Med. Sch., Rochester, Minn., 1978-79, asst. prof. physiology, 1979-82; assoc. prof. U. Nev., Reno, 1982-85, prof., 1986—, chmn., 1987—. Recipient Research Career Devel. award NIH, 1983-88; fellow Am. Heart Assn., 1978-79, U. Coll., London, 1984; NIH grantee, 1980—. Mem. Am. Physiol. Soc., Biophys. Soc., Am. Motility Soc., Am. Gastroenterology Soc. Office: U Nev Sch Medicine Dept Physiology & Cell Biology Reno NV 89557-0001 Business E-Mail: ksanders@medicine.neveda.edu.

SANDERS, LEE MICHAEL, medical association administrator, educator; s. Howard and Dale Sanders; m. Andrea Piperakis, Aug. 30, 1997; children: Jenna, Zoe. BA, Harvard U., 1990; MD, Stanford U., Calif., 1994; MPH, U. Calif., Berkeley, 2000. Diplomate Am. Bd. Pediat., 1998. Instr. Stanford U., Calif., 1998—2000; asst. prof. U. Miami, Fla., 2000—06, assoc. prof., 2006—; med. dir. Reach Out and Read Fla., Boynton Beach, 2001—; regional med. dir. Children's Med. Svc. Miami North, Fla., 2007—; curriculum dir. Jay Weiss Ctr. Soc. Medicine and Health Equity, Miami, Fla., 2007—. Mem. Health Literacy PAC (AAP), Elk Grove, Ill., 2006—08; nominating com. Acad. Pediat. Assn., McLean, Va., 2008—. Physician bd. mem. Reach Out and Read Nat., Somerville, Mass., 2007—. Presdl. scholar, US Dept. Edn., 1986, Gen. Pediat. Rsch. grant, Maternal and Child Health Bur., USDHHS, 1998—2000, Generalist Physician scholar, Robert Wood Johnson Found., 2003—07, grant, Nat. Inst. Child Health and Devel., 2008—. Fellow: Am. Acad. Pediat. (state exec. bd. mem. 2007—08). Office: Univ Miami Miller Sch Med 1601 NW 12th Ave Miami FL 33136 Office Fax: 305-243-2918.

SANDERS, LUCINDA (LUCY SANDERS), information technology organization executive; BS in Computer Sci. summa cum laude, La. State U., 1975; MS in Computer Sci., U. Colo., 1978. Mem. technical staff AT&T Bell Labs, 1977—82, R&D develop. mgr., 1982—95; R&D dir. Lucent Bell Labs, 1995—96; chief tech. officer Lucent Customer Care Solutions: Bell Labs, 1996—99; v.p. R&D, chief tech. officer Avaya, Inc. CRM Solutions: Avaya Labs, 1999—2001; exec. in residence, Alliance for Tech., Learning, and Soc. (ATLAS) U. Colo., Boulder, 2001—, co-founder, CEO, Nat. Ctr. for Women & Info. Tech. (NCWIT), 2004—. Bd. dir. Gold Systems and Solidware Technologies; bd. trustee, Math. Scis. Rsch. Inst. U. Calif., Berkeley; mem., Info. Tech. Rsch. and Develop. Ecosystem Comm. Nat. Academies; mem. adv. bd. U. Col., ATLAS, 1999—2001, U. Denver Women's Coll. Applied Computing Program, 2001—, Denver Pub. Sch. Sys. Computer Magnet, 2002—; mem. sci. adv. bd., Dept. Computer Sci. U. Colo., 2002—; mem. Colo. Inst. Tech. Telecommunications Study, 2002, NSF Planning Grant for the Nat. Ctr. for Women and Info. Tech., 2003, Colo. Inst. Tech. Planning Grant for the Nat. Ctr. for Women and Info. Tech., 2003, Colo. Inst. Tech. Digital Currents Summer Camp, 2004, NSF Extension Svcs. Grant for Implementing effective practices across the country, 2005; CIO panelist, VoIP, Silicon Flatirons Telecommunications Program, 05; mem. adv. coun. U. Colo. Engring., 2005—; program chair Grace Hopper Celebration of Women in Computing, 2006, conf. chair, 07; panelist Google Faculty Summit, 2006, Dept. Edn. Summit on Math and Sci., 2006; plenary panelist Microsoft Faculty Summit, 2006; panelist Google Faculty Summit, 2006; independent cons. for customer svc. (call ctr.) industry, 2001—; invited spkr. in field. Contbr. articles to profl. jours.; guest expert Voice Over IP (VoIP), mem. queue editl. bd. Assn. for Computing Machinery, 2004, guest Nat. Pub. Radio, The Best of Our Knowledge Show, 2004, IT conversations interview VoIP & Women in Innovation, 2004, VoIP Panelist Haas Bus. Sch., U. Calif., Berkeley, 2004, guest Nat. Pub. Radio, Market Place, 2005. Bell Labs program leader, NSF/Colo. Sch. Mines Native Am. Math Camp, 1989—2000; mem. Crest View Habitat Wetlands Environ, Restoration Project, 1990—. Recipient Silicon Valley Tribute to Women in Industry award, 2000, U. Colo. at Boulder Disting. Engring. Alumni award for Industry and Commerce, 2004, Soroptimist Internat. LA Women of Vision award, 2006; named to Women in Tech. Internat. Hall of Fame, 2007; Bell Labs Fellow award, 1996, Aspen Inst. Exec. Seminar Academic Scholarship, 2005. Achievements include patents in field. Mailing: U Colo Campus Box 322 Boulder CO 80309-0322 Office: Nat Ctr for Women & Info Tech 231 ATLAS Bldg U Colo 1125 18th St Boulder CO 80309 Office Phone: 303-735-5108, 303-735-6671. Office Fax: 303-735-6606. E-mail: Lucinda.Sanders@colorado.edu.

SANDERS, MARION YVONNE, retired geriatrics nurse; b. St. Petersburg, Fla., Dec. 4, 1936; d. Ira Sumpter and Maude Mae (Cherry) Sanders; children: Dwayne Irwin, Princess Charrie. BS, Fla. A&M U., 1959; MS, Nova U., Ft. Lauderdale, Fla., 1992. RN Fla. Staff nurse Lantana (Fla.) TB Hosp., 1960-61, Mercy Hosp., St. Petersburg, 1961; gen. duty nurse VA, Tuskegee, Ala., 1961-62; staff nurse John Andrews Hosp., Tuskegee, 1962-63; gen. duty staff nurse Brewster Meth. Hosp., Jacksonville, Fla., 1963-65, Duval Med. Ctr., Jacksonville, 1965-66; pvt. duty nurse Dist. 2 Registry, Jacksonville, 1966-70; supr. Eartha White Nursing Home, Jacksonville, 1970; staff nurse Bapt. Hosp., Jacksonville, 1971-73, City-County Methadone Clinic, Jacksonville, 1976-78; pvt. duty nurse Home Nursing, Jacksonville, Fla., 1982-86, pvt. duty geriatric nursing and gerontology specialist, 1995—2001, Sr. Companion Svc. Corp., 1997-98; ret., 2001. Mem. Ideas for Am.'s Future, 1997, 1998, NAACP, 1997—2009; vol. shelter mgr. ARC, Miami, Fla., 1992—94; vol. cmty. activist, 1994; respite and relief sr. companion vol. Urban Jacksonville Cathedral Found., 1996—2009; vol. Jacksonville Cmty. Rels. Bd., 1996—2009, Jacksonville Inc. Cathedral Found., 1997—2006, respite, 2007; sr. companion Svc. Corp., 1997—98, 1999, 2005—09; mem. Brewseter's and Cmty. Nurses Alumni, 1998—2000, 2001—02; vol. cmty. svcs., elem. grades tutor, polit. campaigns, tchr. health edn.; mem. NAACP, 1998—2009; vol. Rep. Nat. Com., 1997—2000, 2001—02, 2005, Rep. Senatorial Com., 1999, Rep. Com. Fla., 1997—98, Northside Rep. Club, 1997, 1998, 1999; active St. Stephen AME Ch., Jacksonville, tch. Bible studies for youth, advocate for poor, homeless and prisoners; mem. Prison Fellowship Ministries, 2007. Recipient cert. of Recognition, Rep. Party, Fla. and Washington, 1990, Rep. Congl. Orgn., 1988, 1990, 1999, Nurses Hall of Fame, Ams. Biographic Inst., 2009. Mem.: ANA (mem. polit. actions com.), Nova Southeastern U. Alumni Assn., Fla. A&M U. Alumni Assn., Fla. Sheriff's Assn., Fla. Nurses Assn., Women's Missionary Soc. (life). Republican. Methodist. Avocation: reading.

SANDERS, MARLENE, news correspondent, journalism educator; b. Cleve., Jan. 10, 1931; d. Mac and Evelyn (Menitoff) Sanders; m. Jerome Toobin, May 27, 1958 (dec. Jan. 1984); children: Jeff, Mark. Student, Ohio State U., 1948—49. Writer, prodr. Sta. WNEW-TV, NYC, 1955-60, P.M. program Westinghouse Broadcasting Co., NYC, 1961-62; asst. dir. news and pub. affairs Sta. WNEW, NYC, 1962-64; anchor, news program ABC News, NYC, 1964-68, corr., 1968-72, documentary prodr., writer, anchor, 1972-76, v.p., dir. TV documentaries, 1976-78; corr. CBS News, NYC, 1978-87; host Currents Sta. WNET-TV, NYC, 1987-88; host Met. Week in Rev., 1988-90; host Thirteen Live Sta. WNET-TV, 1990-91; prof. dept. journalism NYU, NYC, 1991-93, adj. prof. journalism, 1996—; adj. prof. journalism, adminstr. Columbia U. Grad. Sch. Journalism, NYC, 1994-95. Profl.-in-residence Freedom Forum Media Studies Ctr., 1997-2000; freelance broadcaster, narrator; bd. dirs. womensenews.org.; chair RSVP, Inc., 1997-. Co-author: Waiting for Prime Time: The Women of Television News, 1988. Mem. NYC Commn. on Women's Issues, 2003—05. Recipient award NY State Broadcasters Assn., 1976, award Nat. Press Club, 1976, Emmy awards, 1980, 81, others. Mem. Am. Women in Radio and TV (Woman of Yr. award 1975, Silver Satellite award 1977), Women in Comm. (past pres.), Coun. Fgn. Rels. Office Phone: 212-877-1250. Personal E-mail: sanders110@aol.com.

SANDERS, PATRICIA SMITH, language educator, consultant; b. St. Louis, Nov. 28, 1944; d. Maudeva (Williams) and John Bert Smith; m. Melvin Leon Sanders, Jan. 20, 1967; children: Darren Anthony, Marlon Chadley. BA Edn., Harris Tchrs. Coll., St. Louis, 1966. Tchr. elem. St. Louis Pub. Schs., 1966—67; tchr. lang. arts, soc. studies Knob Noster Sch. Dist., Mo., 1968—70; tchr. lang. arts Parkway Sch. Dist., St. Louis, 1970—72, Ladue Sch. Dist., St. Louis, 1973—2005; ednl. cons. St. Louis, 2005—. Coach h.s. dance squad Ladue Sch. Dist., St. Louis, 1976—2000; chair English dept. Ladue H.S., St. Louis, 2000—05; tchr. Mo. Scholar Acad., Columbia, 1988—91; ednl. cons. Cooperating Sch. Dists. St. Louis, 1999—2005. Pres. Archway chpt. The Links, Inc., St. Louis, 2004—; fin. sec. St. Louis chpt. The MOLES, Inc., 2006—; mem. St. Louis Alumnae chpt. Delta Sigma Theta Sorority, Inc., 1964—; bd. dirs. Harris Stowe State U. Alumni Assn., St. Louis, 2006—, Pres. Coun. Hopewell Ctr., 2002; rec. sec. exec. bd. Mo. Dance Team Assn., St. Louis, 1990—. Recipient Spirit of Inclusion Scholarship named in my honor, Ladue H.S., 2005; named Tchr. of Yr., 2001—02. Fellow: Ednl. Policy Fellowship Program; mem.: Greater St. Louis English Tchrs. Assn. (pres. 1995—98). Avocations: travel, reading, dance, writing, exercise.

SANDERS, PHYLLIS MAY, musician; b. Cleve., Aug. 7, 1922; d. Charles Lester and Marjorie (Roof) Flick; m. Roger Fred Sanders, Aug. 3, 1946 (div. 1986); children: William Paul, Richard Allen, Bruce Edward, Patricia Ann. MusB in Edn., Drake U., Des Moines, 1944. Music tchr. Jefferson (Iowa) jr. high schs., 1944-45, Des Moines jr. high schs., 1945-46; organist, choir dir. Columbia U. Meth. Ch., Columbia Station, Ohio, 1963-83; organist Magyar United Ch. of Christ, Elyria, Ohio, 1984—. Dir. Lorain County Community Messiah Chorus, Elyria, 1981, 88-91; dir., founder Choraliers, Columbia Station, 1975-80, Olmsted Singers, Olmsted Falls, Ohio, 1975-80. Mem. Southwest Chorus, Berea, Ohio, 1988-90, Berea Sr. Ctr. Chorus, 1978—; pres. Columbia Rep. Women, Columbia Station; mem. Columbia Mothersingers, Cleve. Messiah Chorus, 1991—. Mem. Sigma Alpha Iota, Beta Gamma Kappa. Republican. Mem. Christian Ch. (Disciples Of Christ). Avocations: ceramics, needlecrafts. Home: 6119 West River Rd S Elyria OH 44035-5431

SANDERS, RICHARD BROWNING, state supreme court justice; b. Tacoma; 1 child: Laura. BA, U. Wash., 1966, JD, 1969. Assoc. Murray, Scott, McGavick & Graves, Tacoma, Wash., 1969, Caplinger & Munn, Seattle, 1971; hearing examiner State Wash., Olympia, 1970; pvt. practice Wash., 1971-95; justice Wash. Supreme Ct., Olympia, 1995—. Adj. prof. U. Wash. Sch. Law; lectr. in field. Contbr. articles to profl. jours. Office: Supreme Court of Washington Temple of Justice PO Box 40929 Olympia WA 98504-0929 Fax: (360) 357-2092. E-mail: j_r.sanders@courts.wa.gov.*

SANDERS, RICHARD HENRY, lawyer; b. Chgo., Apr. 10, 1944; s. Walter J. and Marian (Snyder) Sikorski; m. Sharon A. Marciniak, July 8, 1967 (dec.); child, Douglas Bennett, Kathvyn G. Haynes; m. Susan Gerhardt Nalepa, Feb. 19, 2005; child Kathryn Haynes BS, Loyola U., Chgo., 1967; JD, Northwestern U., 1969. Bar: Ill. 1969, Ind. 1990, DC 1990, US Dist. Ct. (no. dist.) Ill. 1970, US Dist. Ct. (no. and so. dists.) Ind. 1990, US Ct. Appeals (7th cir.) 1990, US Supreme Ct. 1990. Assoc. Vedder, Price, Kaufman & Kammholz, Chgo., 1969-76, ptnr., 1976—2003, mem. exec. com., 1991-93, health law area leader, 1989—95, 2001—04, 2006—, shareholder, 2003—, chmn. tech. com., 2003—. Adj. prof. Sch. of Law Northwestern U., 1994—; mem. svc. dispute resolver panel Am. Health Lawyers Assn. Alt. Dispute Resolution, 2000—. Bd. trustees Chgo. Acad. for the Arts, 2006—; bd. dirs. Smart Love Parenting Ctr., 2004—, Breath of Life Found., 2007—. Fellow Am. Bar Found.; mem. ABA, Ill. Bar Assn. (chmn. health sect. 1989-90), Chgo. Bar Assn., Ind. Bar Assn., DC Bar Assn., Am. Health Lawyers Assn., Ill. Assn. Health Attys., Univ. Club, Evanston Golf Club (Skokie). Avocations: skiing, diving, photography, golf. Office: Vedder Price Kaufman & Kammholz 222 N La Salle St Ste 2600 Chicago IL 60601-1100 Home Phone: 312-787-5784; Office Phone: 312-609-7644. Personal E-mail: nhs449@earthlink.net. Business E-Mail: rsanders@vedderprice.com.

SANDERS, RICHARD KINARD, actor; b. Harrisburg, Pa., Aug. 23, 1940; s. Henry Irvine and Thelma S. BFA, Carnegie Inst. Tech., 1962; postgrad. (Fulbright scholar), London Acad. Music and Dramatic Art, 1962-63. Pres. Blood Star, Inc. Mem. various acting cos., Front St., Memphis, Champlain Shakespeare Festival, Vt., Center Stage, Balt., N.Y. Shakespeare Festival, N.Y.C., Chelsea Theater Center, N.Y.C., Mark Taper Forum, Los Angeles, Arena Stage, Washington; appeared on: (Broadway) Raisin; (TV series) Les Nessman on WKRP in Cincinnati and The New WKRP in Cincinnati, Paul Sycamore in You Can't Take It With You, Mr. Beanley in Spenser; writer of many episodes of WKRP and other situation comedies; writer NBC movie Max and Sam; numerous TV and film appearances. Vol. Peace Corps, Northeastern Brazil, 1966-69. Recipient Buckeye Newshawk award, 1974-79, Silver Sow award, 1979 Mem. Writers Guild Am., Screen Actors Guild, AFTRA, Actors Equity Assn. Office: PO Box 1644 Woodinville WA 98072-1644

SANDERS, ROBIN RENEE, United States Ambassador to Nigeria; b. Hampton, Va., July 05; d. Robert M. and Geneva (Machoney) Sanders. BA, Hampton Inst.; MA, MS, Ohio U., 1979. Broadcast lic. FCC 3d Class. Editl. asst. Essence mag., NYC, 1974—76, Fgn. Broadcast Info. Svc., Washington, 1976—77; intern account exec. Burson-Marsteller Co., NYC, 1977—78; pub. rels. assoc. Seventeen mag., 1979—80; polit. and counselor officer Am. Embassy, Dominican Republic, 1980—83; consular officer Am. Consulate, Oporto, Portugal, 1983—86; dep. polit. sect. chief Am. Embassy Khartoum, Sudan, 1986—88; spl. asst. AF Bur., 1989; dir. for pub. diplomacy for Africa US Dept. State; dir. for Africa NSC, 1988—89, 1997—99; spl. asst. for L.Am., Africa and internat. crime for the under sec. for polit. affairs US Dept. State, Washington; chief of staff, sr. fgn. policy US Ho. Reps. Internat. Rels. Com.; US amb. to Republic of Congo US Dept. State, Brazzaville, 2002—05; internat. adv., dep. comdt. Indsl. Coll. the Armed Forces, Washington, 2005—07; US amb. to Nigeria US Dept. State, Abuja, 2007—. Rschr. dept. internat. rels. Ohio U., 1978; TV prodr. dept. gerontology Hampton Inst., 1976—77; joint chief of staff commdr., 2007; Merit Congo, 05. Dir. Nat. Security Coun., 1989; polit. econ. officer Namibia, 1989. Recipient 1st place award for painting Two Faces, Scholastic Art Bd., 1981, Dept of State Meritorious award, 1989, three State Dept. Superior Honor awards, three State Dept. Meritorious Honor awards; Journalism scholar, Syracuse U., 1970. Mem.: Coun. on Fgn. Rels., Am. Fgn. Service Assn., Mus. African Art, Thursday Luncheon Group, Alpha Kappa Mu, Alpha Kappa Alpha. Office: DOS Amb 8320 Abuja Pl Washington DC 20521

SANDERS, WALLACE WOLFRED, JR., civil engineer; b. Louisville, June 24, 1933; s. Wallace Wolfred and Mary Jane (Brownfield) S.; m. Julia B. Howard, June 9, 1956; children— Linda, David. B.C.E., U. Louisville, 1955; MS, U. Ill., Urbana, 1957, PhD, 1960; M.Engring., U. Louisville, 1973. Research asst., then research assoc. U. Ill., 1955-60, asst. prof., 1960-64; mem. faculty Iowa State U., Ames, 1964-98, prof. civil engring., 1970-98, assoc. dir. engring. research, 1980-91, assoc. dean research, 1988-91, interim asst. vice provost for research and advanced studies, 1991-92. Cons. to govt. and industry. Contbr. numerous papers to profl. jours. Bd. dirs. Northcrest Cmty., Ames, 1976-82, 92-98, pres., 1987-91, 96-2003; bd. dirs. Am. Bapt. Homes of the Midwest, Mpls., 1998—. Mem. ASCE (R.C. Reese research prize 1978), Am. Welding Soc. (Adams Meml. membership award 1971), Am. Ry. Engring. Assn., Am. Soc. Engring. Edn. Baptist. Home and Office: 1924 Northcrest Cir Ames IA 50010-5113 Home Phone: 515-232-7184. Business E-Mail: wsanders@iastate.edu.

SANDERS, WALTER JEREMIAH, III, (JERRY SANDERS), retired computer company executive; b. Chgo., Sept. 12, 1936; m. Tawny Sanders; 4 children. BSEE, U. Ill., Champaign-Urbana, 1958. Design engr. Douglas Aircraft Co., 1958—59; sales engr. Motorola Semiconductor, 1959—61; sales mgr. to group dir. mktg. Semiconductor divsn. Fairchild Camera and Instrument Corp., 1961—69; co-founder Advanced Micro Devices, Inc., Sunnyvale, Calif., 1969, CEO, 1969—2002, chmn., 1969—2004. Recipient Robert N. Noyce award, Semiconductor Industry Assn., 1991, Medal of Achievement, Am. Electronics Assn., 2001. Mem.: NAE.

SANDERS, WILLIAM EUGENE, marketing executive; b. Asheboro, NC, Nov. 16, 1933; s. Arthur Ira and Picola (Loftin) S.; m. Velna Elizabeth Sumner, June 8, 1957; children: William Eugene Jr., George Herbert Sumner. AB in Polit. Sci., U. N.C., 1956, postgrad. in Law, 1956-57. Marketing rep. Encyclopaedia Britannica, Greensboro, NC, 1957-60, Am. Pubs., Chgo., 1960-66; pres. S&W Distbrs., Inc., Asheboro, NC, 1966—. Little league coach Civitans, Greensboro, 1967—68. With USAR, 1957—63. Named Hon. Amb. Dept. of Labor, Ky., 1976, Ky. Col., 1976, Hon. Mem. La. Lt. Gov. Staff, 1984; recipient Cert. Appreciation Jefferson Davis Parish Libr., Jennings, La., 1986, Top Sales award Am. Media. Corp., 1996, Marshall Cavendish Top Prodn. award, 1990-91, Mktg. award Am. Media, 1995, Gold Cir. award Penworthy Books, 1999, 2000, 01, Marshall Cavendish quota Prodn. award, 1999, 2000, Rosen Prodn. award, 2002. Mem.: Gen. Alumni Assn. (co-chmn. Greensboro chpt. 1979—80, Rosen Prodn. award 2001—02, 2006), State Libr. Assn. S.C., State Libr. Assn. N.C., State Libr. Assn. La., State Libr. Assn. W.Va., State Libr. Assn. Va. Democrat. Methodist. Office: S&W Distbrs Inc 312 Sunset Ave Ste 4 Asheboro NC 27203 Office Phone: 336-633-3900.

SANDERS, W(ILLIAM) EUGENE, JR., retired internist; b. Frederick, Md., June 25, 1934; s. W(illiam) Eugene and E. Gertrude (Wilburn) Sanders; m. Christine Culp, Feb. 22, 1974. AB, Cornell U., 1956, MD, 1960. Diplomate Am. Bd. Internal Medicine. Intern Johns Hopkins Hosp., Balt., 1960-61, resident, 1961-62; instr. medicine Emory U. Sch. Medicine, Atlanta, 1962-64; chief med. resident, instr. U. Fla. Coll. Medicine, Gainesville, 1964-65, asst. prof. medicine and microbiology, 1965-69, assoc. prof., 1969-72; prof., chmn. dept. med. microbiology, prof. medicine Creighton U. Sch. Medicine, Omaha, 1972-95, prof. emeritus, 1995—. Cons.-in-rsch. Fla. Dept. Health and Rehab. Svcs., 1966—. Editor: Am. Jour. Epidemiology, 1974—95; contbr. scientific papers to profl. jours. Med. officer USPHS, 1962—64. Recipient Rsch. Career Devel. award, NIH, 1968—72; John and Mary R. Markle scholar in acad. medicine, 1968—73. Mem.: N.Y. Acad. Scis., Thoracic Soc., Am. Lung Assn., Soc. Epidemiol. Rsch., Infectious Diseases Soc. Am., Am. Soc. Microbiology, Sigma Xi, Phi Beta Kappa, Phi Kappa Phi. Achievements include patents for enocin antibiotic and RBE limonene and perrilyl alcohol. Home: 1901 Pennsylvania Ave Englewood FL 34224-5530 E-mail: ecsanders@gls3c.com. *Each day provides more challenges and more opportunities than the preceding. No individual can possibly cope with each of these in any given day. Success depends upon establishing priorities and maintaining them. Fight only those battles and pursue with fervor only those opportunities that improve both one's self and one's fellow man.*

SANDERS, WILLIAM JOHN, research scientist; b. Detroit, July 10, 1940; s. John William and Charlotte Barbara (Linsday) Steele; m. Gary Roberts, Sept. 12, 1961; children: Scott David, Susan Deborah. BS, U. Mich., 1962; MSEE, U. Calif., Berkeley, 1964. Sr. rsch. scientist Stanford (Calif.) U., 1967-97; pres. Sanders Data Systems, 1991—. Pres. Computers in Cardiology, 1990-93, dir., 2000—, dir. info. svcs., 2001—. Inventor cardiac probe; contbr. articles to profl. jours. Mem. IEEE Computer Soc. Avocation: bicycling. Office: Sanders Data Sys 3980 Bibbits Dr Palo Alto CA 94303-4531 Business E-Mail: bill@sandersdata.com.

SANDERSON, ARTHUR CLARK, engineering educator; b. Providence, Oct. 23, 1946; s. Robert Leroy and Julia Ayer (Oldham) S.; m. Susan Rita Walsh, Aug. 14, 1971; children: Angeline Mirada, Andrew McWain. BS, Brown U., 1968; MS, Carnegie-Mellon U., 1970, PhD, 1972. Rsch. engr. Westinghouse Electric Corp., Pitts., 1968-70; vis. rsch. scientist Delft (The Netherlands) U. Tech., 1972-73; prof. Carnegie-Mellon U., Pitts., 1973-87, co-dir. robotics inst., 1981-87; rsch. dir. Philips Rsch. Labs., Briarcliff Manor, NY, 1985-87; prof., dept. chmn. Rensselaer Poly. Inst., Troy, NY, 1987—; divsn. dir. elec. & comm. systems NSF, Arlington, Va., 1998-2000; v.p. rsch. Rensselaer Poly. Inst., 2000—. Vis. prof. Univ. Iberoamericana, Mexico City, 1975-77, Inst. Info. Sci. & Elecs., U. Tsukuba, Japan, 1996-97. Contbr. 3 books, over 250 articles to profl. jours. Fellow AAAS, IEEE (pres. robotics and automation soc. 1989, 90); mem. AIAA (mem. space automation and robotics tech. com.), Am. Assn. Artificial Intelligence, Soc. Mfg. Engrs. Office: Rensselaer Poly Inst 110 8th St Troy NY 12180-3522 Home: 18 Barberry Coast Rd Newmarket NH 03857 E-mail: sandea@rpi.edu.

SANDERSON, CHRISTINE GRAVES, literature and language educator; b. Bad Cannstadt, Germany, Sept. 8, 1955; d. James Clarence and Emma Schneider Graves; children: James Edward, Gregory Lawrence, Sean William, Thomas Patrick. BA in English, Spring Hill Coll., 1977; MA in English, La. State, 1980. Cert. Tchr. La., 1983. Tchr., tech. coord. Archbishop Chapelle HS, Metairie, La., 1980—. Cons. Coll. Bd., Atlanta, 2001—. Reviewer: magazine VOYA, 2001—; contbr. articles in field. Mem.: Nat.Cath. Edn. Assn. Roman Catholic. Avocations: reading, computers. Office: Archbishop Chapelle HS 8800 Veterans Blvd Metairie LA 70003 Office Fax: 504-466-3191. Business E-Mail: csanderson@archbishopchapelle.org.

SANDERSON, DAVID R., physician; b. South Bend, Ind., Dec. 26, 1933; s. Robert Burns and Alpha (Rodenberger) S.; divorced, 1978; children: David, Kathryn, Robert, Lisa; m. Evelyn Louise Klunder, Sept. 20, 1980. BA, Northwestern U., 1955, MD, 1958. Cons. in medicine Mayo Clinic, Rochester, Minn., 1965—87, chmn. dept. thoracic disease, 1977—87, cons. in medicine Scottsdale, Ariz., 1987—2000, chmn. dept. internal medicine, 1988—96, vice chmn. bd. govs., 1987—94. Assoc. dir. Mayo Lung Project, Nat. Cancer Inst., Rochester. Contbr. articles to profl. jours. Recipient Noble award Mayo Found., Rochester, Chevalier Jackson award Am. Bronchoesophagologic Assn., 1990. Fellow ACP, Am. Coll. Chest Physicians (gov. for Minn. 1981-87); mem. Am. Bronchoesophagologic Assn. (pres. 1986-87), World Assn. for Bronchology, Internat. Bronchoesophagologic Soc., Internat. Assn. Study of Lung Cancer, AMA, Sigma Xi, Sigma Chi (Significant Sig award 1989). Presbyterian. Home: 10676 E Bella Vista Dr Scottsdale AZ 85258-6086 Office: Mayo Clinic Arizona 13400 E Shea Blvd Scottsdale AZ 85259-5499 Home Phone: 480-860-6782; Office Phone: 480-301-8000. Personal E-mail: dsanderson958@cox.net.

SANDERSON, DEVON LEE, elementary school educator; b. St Elizabeth, Jamaica; s. George Sanderson and Josephine M. Scarlett-Vaccianna; m. Pauline Vinette Harvey. Cert., Bethlehem Moravian Coll. Cert. nursing asst., 2005. Tchr. Goshen and Belle Plain Basic Schools, Clarendon, Jamaica, 1988—91, Ashton All Age Sch., Westmoreland, Jamaica, 1994—2000, Eber Preparatory and Kindergarten Sch., Jamaica, 2001—03; tchr. Caribbean exam. coun. Bethel Town All Age Evening Inst., 2002—04. Freelance writer-elect Inst. Children's Lit., Conn. Author: (poetry) It is Spria 9 (Editor's Choice award), A Classical Masterpiece. Former mem. Montego Bay Writer's Club; former writer, contr. Western Mirror Newspaper; student elect Long Ridge Writers Group, West Redding, Conn. Recipient 1st Place Esteem award, Poetry Jamaica, 2003, Merit award cert. for poetry writing, World of Poetry, 1990. Avocations: reading, gardening, writing, singing. Home: 105 Memorial Dr New Castle DE 19720

SANDERSON, DOUGLAS JAY, lawyer; b. Boston, Apr. 21, 1953; s. Warren and Edith S. Sanderson; m. Audrey S. Goldstein, June 6, 1982; children: Scott M.G., Phoebe H.G. BA, Trinity Coll., Hartford, Conn., 1974; JD, George Washington U., 1977. Bar: Va. 1977, D.C. 1978, U.S. Dist. Ct. (ea. dist.) Va. 1978, U.S. Ct. Appeals (4th cir.) 1978. Assoc. Bettius, Rosenberger & Carter, P.C., Fairfax, Va., 1977-82; ptnr. Bettius & Sanderson, P.C. and predecessor firms, Fairfax, 1982-86; prin. Miles & Stockbridge P.C., Fairfax, 1986-95; br. head Miles & Stockbridge, Fairfax, 1989-91; co-owner McCandlish & Lillard, P.C., Fairfax, 1995—. Trustee Cambridge Ctr. Behavioral Studies, Cambridge, 1981-90. Editor: Consumer Protection Reporting Svc., 1976-77. Bd. dirs. Legal Svcs. No. Va., Inc., 1991-97, pres., 1993-95; vol. counsel Arts Coun. of Fairfax County, Inc., 1991--. Mem. ABA, Va. Bar Assn., Fairfax Bar Assn., London County Bar Assn., Ctrl. Fairfax C. of C. (bd. dirs. 1988-93). Avocations: sports, reading. Office: McCandlish & Lillard 11350 Random Hills Rd Ste 500 Fairfax VA 22030-6044 Office Phone: 703-273-2288.

SANDERSON, JAMES RICHARD, retired naval officer, financial consultant; b. Selma, Calif., Dec. 27, 1925; s. Charles Maxwell and Edith (Wente) S.; m. Betty Lee Bradley, Sept. 19, 1947. Student, U. Calif.-Berkeley, 1943-44, U. Wash., 1944, U. Willamette, 1944-45; grad., USNR Midshipman Sch. at Columbia U., 1945, Nat. War Coll., 1966; student, Gen. Line Sch., Monterey, Calif., 1953, Sr. Officers Ship Material Mgmt. Course, Idaho Falls, Idaho, 1979; BA in Internat. Affairs, George Washington U., 1968. Served as enlisted man U.S. Naval Res., 1943-45; commd. ensign USN, 1946, advanced through grades to vice adm., 1980; gunnery officer U.S.S. Mansfield, 1946-47, U.S.S. Bausell, 1947-48; flight trainee Naval Air Sta., Pensacola, Fla., 1949, Corpus Christi, Tex., 1950; served in Attack Squadron 195, Alameda, Calif., 1950-52; flight instr. Naval Air Sta., Pensacola, 1953-55; served in Attack Squadron 16, 1955-57; air ops. officer on staff Comdr. Carrier Div. Four, U.S.S. Forrestal, 1957-60; ops. officer Attack Squadron 43, Naval Air Sta., Oceana, Va., 1960-62; comdg. officer Attack Squadron 76, 1962-63; comdr. Attack Carrier Air Wing Three in U.S.S. Saratoga, 1963-65; spl. support plans officer, Pacific Area Strategic Plans and Policy Div., Office of Chief of Naval Ops., Washington, 1966-67; exec. asst. and sr. aide to dep. chief. naval ops., 1967-69; comdg. officer U.S.S. Ranier, 1969-70; dep. chief of staff for ops. and plans U.S. Sixth Fleet, 1970-71; comdg. officer U.S.S. Saratoga, 1971-73; dep. comdr. Naval Striking and Support Forces, So. Europe, Naples, Italy, 1973-76; vice dir. ops. Joint Chiefs of Staff, Washington, 1976-77; asst. dep. chief naval ops. for plans, policy and ops., 1977-79; comdr. Task Force Sixty, U.S. 6th Fleet, 1979-80, Carrier Group Two, 1979-80, Battle Force Sixth Fleet, 1979-80, Carrier Striking Force So. Region, 1979-80; dep. and chief staff, comdr. in chief Atlantic/U.S. Atlantic Fleet, Norfolk, Va., 1980-83; ret., 1983; exec. cons. Exec. Planning & Investment Co., Inc., Virginia Beach, Va., 1983-85; sr. v.p. for corp. ops. Computer Dynamics, Inc., 1984-86; asst. to pres. Eastern Computers, Inc., 1986—94; cons., prin. Exec. Planning and Investment Co., Inc., 1986-94; sr. fellow joint and combined warfare course Jt. Forces Staff Coll., 1994—. Comdr. engr. USNR, 1945, comdr. engr. vice administrn USN, 1945. Decorated 21 campaign medals, including D.S.M., Legion of Merit with 3 gold stars, D.F.C., Meritorious Service medal, Air medal with 4 gold stars, Navy Commendation medal with combat distinguishing device. Master: KT, Scottish Rite 33; mem.: NRA, U. Calif. Alumni Assn., Assn. Naval Aviation, Naval Acad. Athletic Assn., Nat. War Coll. Alumni Assn, George Washington U. Alumni Assn., Tailhook Assn., Order of Daedalians, Nat. Wildlife Assn., Nat. Assn. Individual Investors, KT Eye Found., Nat. Eagle Scout Assn. (regent, Disting. Eagle Scout award 1994), Smithsonian Assn., The Golden Eagles, Nat. Skeet Shooting Assn., Army Navy Country Club (Arlington, Va.), Mystic Shrine, Royal Order of Scotland, Royal Arch, Shriners, Knights Templar, Sojourners.

SANDERSON, JANET ANN, United States Ambassador to Haiti; b. Tucson, Ariz., Apr. 1955; BA in Govt., Coll. William & Mary, 1977; MA in Nat. Security Studies, Naval War Coll., 1993. Vice consul/econ. officer US Embassy, Dhaka, Bangladesh, 1978—80; liaison officer in charge of assistance programs in the West Bank & Gaza Strip US Agy. for Internat. Devel. (USAID), Tel Aviv, 1980—82; petroleum attache US Embassy, Kuwait City, Kuwait, 1982—84; desk officer for Kuwait & United Arab Emirates US Dept. State, Washington, 1984—86, desk officer US Mission to Orgn. for Econ. Coop. (OECD), 1986—88; econ. min. counselor US Embassy, Cairo, 1993—97, econ. counselor Amman, Jordan, 1989—92, dep. chief of mission, 1997—2000; US amb. to Algeria US Dept. State, Algiers, 2000—03; US Dept. State diplomat-in-residence U. Calif., Berkeley, 2003—05; US amb. to Haiti US Dept. State, Port-au-Prince, 2006—. Recipient Herbert A. Salzman award for Internat. Econ. Performance, US Dept. State, 1996, Superior Honor award, Meritorious Honor award. Mailing: US Embassy 3400 Port Au Prince Pl Washington DC 20521-3400*

SANDERSON, JIHONG W., finance educator, consultant; d. Guangqing Wu and Hueilong Ru; m. Jon Sanderson. BA in Economics (hon.), GueiZhu Fin. & Economy Coll., China, 1985; MBA in Tech. Mgmt., Haas Sch. Bus., U. Calif., Berkeley, 2002. Pres. BCA Consulting, Bay Area, Calif.; lectr. and dir. mgmt. tech. China fellow program, Haas Sch. Bus. U. Calif., 2003—, founder and exec. dir. Ctr. Rsch. on Chinese & Am. Strategic Coop., 2005—07; dir. and vis. prof. Inst. Mgmt. Innovation & Orgn. at Chinese Acad. Sci. & Tech. Mgmt., Shanghai, 2008—. Chairwam Reward Capital Mgmt., JiangShu, China, 2007—. Mem. APAPA, Bay Area, 2005—08. Business E-Mail: jihong@haas.berkeley.edu.

SANDERSON, JOHN LEWIS, financial advisor; b. Roslyn, NY, Mar. 4, 1952; s. Edward and Mildred Meyer Satenstein; m. Leslie Ford, Mar. 24, 1979; children: Kent Edward, Clayton Ford, Claire Joan, John Lewis. BSc, Ohio U., Athens, 1974. Sr. v.p. Kidder Peabody, NYC, 1983—94; v.p. DLJ, NYC, 1996—2000; exec. v.p. Jefferies & Co., NYC, 2000—02; v.p. Morgan Stanley, Prescott, Ariz., 2002—. Scoutmaster Boy Scouts Am., Bronxville, NY, 1992—2002. Master: Masons; mem.: Hassa Yampa Country Club, Siwanoy Country Club. Conservative. Protestant. Avocations: golf, hunting, history. Home: 1994 Hidden Canyon Way Prescott AZ 86305

SANDERSON, MARY LOUISE, medical association administrator; b. Fairmont, W.Va., Oct. 29, 1942; d. Lawrence Oliver and Frances Evelyn (Shuttleworth) Shingleton; m. William W. Olmstead III, Dec. 1966 (div. June 1974); children: William W. IV, Happy; m. Lester F. Davis, III, Oct. 1979 (div. Dec. 1986); m. David S. Sanderson, Sept. 1992. Student, Vassar Coll., 1960-62, Carnegie Mellon, 1962-63. Real estate broker, N.C. Exec. sec. Creative Dining, Raleigh, NC, 1980-83, Sea Pines Plantation Co., Hilton Head, SC, 1973-79; adminstr. Am. Bd. Neurological Surgery, Houston, 1983—. Vol. Interact, Raleigh, 1984-86, M.D. Anderson Cancer Ctr./Camp Star Trails, 1994-96; docent Mordecai House Hist. Preservation, Raleigh, 1981-83; mem./vol. Reach to Recovery, 1995-2001, Houston Symphony, 2002-, Mus. of Fine Arts, Houston, 1999-. Recipient Vol. award N.C. State Gov., 1986. Mem. Am. Soc. Assn. Execs. Democrat. Episcopalian. Office: Am Bd Neurol Surgery 6550 Fannin St Ste 2139 Houston TX 77030-2718

SANDERSON, RALPH, medical educator; BS, U. Ala., Tuscaloosa, 1975; PhD, U. Ala., Birmingham, 1986. Postdoc. fellow Stanford U., Calif., 1986—89; prof. pathology U. Ark. Med. Scis., Little Rock, 1989—2006, drs. Mae and Anderson Nettleship chair, oncologic pathology, 2002—06; prof. pathology U. Ala., 2006—. Dir. basic rsch. Ark. Cancer Rsch. Ctr., Little Rock, 1999—2006. Recipient DOD Breast Cancer award, Dept. Def., 1999—2002; grantee, NIH, 1992—; fellowship, Arthritis Found., 1987—89. Mem.: AAAS, Am. Soc. Matrix Biology, Metastasis Rsch. Soc., Am. Assn. Cancer Rsch., Am. Soc. Cell Biology. Office: Univ Ala Birmingham 1530 3rd Ave S Rm 814 Birmingham AL 35294

SANDFORD, JOHN (JOHN ROSWELL CAMP), writer, journalist; b. Cedar Rapids, Iowa, Feb. 23, 1944; m. Susan Lee Jones, 1966 (dec. May 2007); children: Roswell, Emily. BA in Am. Studies, U. Iowa, 1966, MA in Journalism, 1971. Reporter Cape Girardeau SE Missourian, 1968—70, Miami Herald, 1971—78, St. Paul Pioneer Press, 1978—90; freelance book reviewer Ft. Worth Star Telegram. Author: (nonfiction) The Eye of the Heart, 1988, Plastic Surgery, 1989, (novels) The Night Crew, 1997, Dead Watch, 2006, Murder in the Rough, 2006, (Kidd series) The Fool's Run, 1989, The Empress File, 1991, The Devil's Code, 2000, The Hanged Man's Song, 2003, (Virgil Flower series) Dark of the Moon, 2007 (Publishers Weekly bestseller), Heat Lightning, 2008 (Publishers Weekly bestseller), Rough Country, 2009, (Prey series) Rules of Prey, 1989, Shadow Prey, 1990, Eyes of Prey, 1991, Silent Prey, 1992, Winter Prey, 1993, Night Prey, 1994, Mind Prey, 1995, Sudden Prey, 1996, Secret Prey, 1998, Certain Prey, 1999, Easy Prey, 2000, Chosen Prey, 2001, Mortal Prey, 2002, Naked Prey, 2003, Hidden Prey, 2004, Broken Prey, 2005, Invisible Prey, 2007, Phantom Prey, 2008 (Publishers Weekly bestseller), Wicked Prey, 2009 (#1 Publishers Weekly bestseller). Prin. financier archeol. project, Jordan Valley, Israel. With US Army, 1966—68. Recipient Pulitzer prize for feature writing, 1986. Avocations: archaeology, painting, photography, hunting, fishing. Office: c/o Putnam Books 375 Hudson St New York NY 10014*

SANDFORD, VIRGINIA ADELE, retired motivational speaker, writer; b. Tacoma, Nov. 29, 1926; d. Fred John and Lucille Lillian (Skok) Wepfer; m. Calvert H. Sandford, Sept. 16, 1949 (div. 1970); children: Susan L., Kaye E., James C. Student, U. Wash., 1946-49. Tchr. stringed instruments dept. music Puyallup (Wash.) Sch. Dist., 1944-46; sec. Fife (Wash.) Sch. Dist., 1969-72; exec. sec. Tacoma (Wash.) Sch. Dist., 1972-75; tchr. ednl. sec. program Clover Park Vocat. Tech. Inst., Tacoma, 1975-82; profl. spkr., seminar prodr. Virginia Sandford & Assocs., Tacoma, 1982—. Author: You Can't Smell the Roses When You're Pushing Up Daisies, 2001. Violinist, Tacoma Symphony, 1972-75. Mem. Am. Vocat. Assn., Wash. Vocat. Assn., Ednl. Office Personnel, Nat. Spkrs. Assn., Pacific N.W. Spkrs. Assn., Alpha Chi Omega. Office Phone: 253-927-1830. E-mail: vsandford@nventure.com.

SANDHOFER, CATHERINE, psychology professor; d. Michael and Jo Ann Momeni; m. Robert Sandhofer, May 20, 1995; children: Simon, Maya. PhD, Ind. U., Bloomington, 2002. Prof. UCLA, 2004—. Office: UCLA Franz Hall Los Angeles CA 90095 Business E-Mail: sandhof@psych.ucla.edu.

SAN DIEGO, ARMANDO G., retired military officer, pathologist, consultant; b. Manila, Philippines, June 17, 1934; arrived in U.S., 1959; s. Amado Robles San Diego and Vicenta Sanvectores Gonda; m. Lolita Aves Tan, Apr. 20, 1959; children: Eric, Eileen, Jerry. AA, U. Santo Tomas, 1954, MD, 1959. Diplomate Am. Bd. Pathology, Forensic Examiners, and Forensic Medicine, cert. in anatomical and clinical pathology Am. Bd. Pathology, 1969, lic. physician Philippine Republic, 1959, Ill., 1969, NY, 1969, Calif., 1975, cert. forensic examiner Am. Bd. Forensic Examiners, 1995, in forensic medicine Am. Bd. Forensic Medicine, 1996. Intern Du Page County Hosp., Elmhurst, Ill., 1960; pathology resident Ravenswood Med. Ctr., Chgo., 1961, Columbus-Cuneo Med. Ctr., Chgo., 1962—65; pathologist Keesler USAF Med. Ctr., Biloxi, Miss., 1967—70; capt. USAF, 1967—74, advanced through grades to col., 1974—96, ret., 1996; chmn. Dept. Pathology USAF Regional Hosp., Clark AFB, Philippines, 1970—74, USAF Regional Hosp., March AFB, Riverside, Calif., 1974—79, David Grant USAF Med. Ctr., Fairfield, Calif., 1979—85; chief pathology and lab. medicine Sheppard AF, Wichita Falls, Tex., 1985—87; assoc. chief hosp. svcs. Sheppard Hosp., Wichita Falls, 1987—88, comdr. and chief med. staff, 1993—96; ret., 1996. Adv. Solano County Regional Occupl. Program, Calif., 1984—85; assoc. med. examiner U.S. Med. Examiner Sys. Armed Forces Inst. Pathology; med. dir. med. lab. tng. program Sch. Healthcare Scis. USAF; flight surgeon augmentee Aerospace Medicine Dept. Sheppard AFB; cons. in forensic pathology. Contbr. articles to profl. jours. Dir. med. mission Wichita County Med. Alliance, Wichita Falls, 2001, Filipino Am. Club North Tex., Wichita Falls, 2005; vol. physician Annual Hotter "N" Hell Bike Race, Wichita Falls, 1988—2005; mem. appraisal rev. bd. Wichita County, 2000—05. Decorated Nat. Def. Svc. medal USAF, Meritorious Svc. medal, Legion of Merit medal. Fellow: Coll. Am. Pathologists (life; del. 1987—90, inspector lab. accreditation program), Am. Coll. Forensic Examiners (life), Am. Soc. Clin. Pathology (life; adv. coun. 1987—90); mem.: Soc. Med. Cons. to Armed Forces, Soc. Armed Forces Med. Lab. Scientists, Ret. Officers Assn. (life), Assn. Mil. Surgeons U.S. (life), Filipino-Am. Club (pres. 1999—). Avocations: car collecting, painting, bicycling, hunting.

SANDITZ, LISA, painter; b. St. Louis, 1973; Student, Studio Art Ctr. Internat., Florence, Italy, 1994; BA, MacAlester Coll., Minn., 1995; MFA, Pratt Inst., Bklyn., 2001. One-woman shows include The Rite Spot, San Francisco, 1998, Pratt Inst., Bklyn., 2001, Onefront Gallery, NYC, 2001, P.S. 122, NYC, 2003, CRG Gallery, NYC, 2003, 2005, Rodolphe Jansen Gallery, Brussels, 2004, Kemper Mus. Contemporary Art, Kansas City, 2006, ACME, LA, 2006, exhibited in group shows at Filler, Three Blue Lights, San Francisco, 1998, Pier Show, Bklyn. Working Artist Coalition, 2000, No Comment, Blake-Sherlock Gallery, NYC, 2000, Six Artists Drawings, im n il Gallery, Bklyn., 2000, Hello Franklin, 2003, Need to Know Basis, Geoff Young Gallery, Great Barrington, Mass., 2002, Sugarfree, The Puffin Room, NYC, 2002, Singing My Song, ACME, LA, 2004, Tugboat, 2007, Galerie Tanit, Munich, 2004, No Man's Land, Shoshana Wayne Gallery, LA, 2005, Landscape Confection, Wexner Ctr. Arts, Ohio, 2005, Orange County Mus. Art, Newport Beach, Calif., 2006, New Prints, Internat. Print Ctr., NYC, 2005, Ridykeulous, Participant Inc., NYC, 2006, Grounds for Progress, Ctr. Curatorial Studies, Bard Coll., NY, 2008, Beware of the Wolf II, Am. Acad. Rome, 2008. Fellow Guggenheim Found., 2008. Office: ACME Spaces 1&2 6150 Wilshire Blvd Los Angeles CA 90048*

SANDLER, ADAM, actor; b. Bklyn., Sept. 9, 1966; m. Jackie Titone, June 22, 2003; children: Sadie Madison, Sunny Madeline. Grad., NYU. Actor: (films) Remote Control (also writer), 1987, Shakes the Clown, 1992, Coneheads, 1993, Airheads, 1994, Bullet Proof, 1996, Punch Drunk Love, 2002, Spanglish, 2004, Reign Over Me, 2007; actor, writer: Billy Madison, 1995 (also composer), Happy Gilmore, 1996, Bulletproof, 1996; actor, exec. prodr.: The Animal, 2001, Mr. Deeds, 2002, Anger Management, 2003, The Longest Yard, 2005, Bedtime Stories, 2008, Funny People, 2009; actor, exec. prodr., writer: The Waterboy, 1998, Big Daddy, 1999, Little Nicky, 2000; actor (voice), prodr., writer, also writer (songs) soundtrack: Eight Crazy Nights, 2002; actor, soundtrack song(s) Going Overboard, 1989, Mixed Nuts, 1994, The Wedding Singer, 1998, 50 First Dates, 2004; actor, prodr., Click, 2006, I Now Pronounce You Chuck and Larry, 2007; writer, actor, prodr.: Deuce Bigalow: European Gigolo, 2005, You Don't Mess with the Zohan, 2008; prodr.: Benchwarmers, 2006; exec. prodr. (films) Deuce Bigalow: Male Gigolo, 1999, Joe Dirt, 2001, The Master of Disguise, 2002, Hot Chick, 2002, Dickie Roberts: Former Child Star, 2003, Grandma's Boy, 2006, Strange Wilderness, 2007; exec. prodr. (TV) The Mayor, 2003, The Dana & Julia Show, 2004, Gay Robot, 2006; TV appearances include Saturday Night Live: The Best of Chris Farley, 1998, Saturday Night Live: The Best of Mike Myers, 1998, Saturday Night Live: The Best of Phil Hartman, 1998, The Cosby Show, 1987-1988, Couch, 2003; actor, writer Saturday Night Live (Emmy award nomination for writing 1991, 92), 1990-95; appeared on TV programs ABC Afterschool Special, Testing Dirty, 1990, Saturday Night

Live Mother's Day Special, 1992, MTV Music Video Awards, 1994, Saturday Night Live Presents President Bill Clinton's All-Time Favorites, 1994, The 37th Annual Grammy Awards, 1995, The ESPY Awards, 1996; rec. artist (albums) They're All Gonna Laugh at You!, 1993, What the Hell Happened to Me?, 1996 (also exec. prodr.), What's Your Name, 1997, Stan and Judy's Kid, 1999 (set record for most comedy albums sold in first week released), Shhh...Don't Tell, 2004; exec. prodr. (TV series) Rules of Engagement, 2007-. Named Funny Male Star, People's Choice Awards, 2000, 2006, 2009, Choice Comedian, Teen Choice Awards, 2006, 2008; recipient Generation award, MTV Movie Awards, 2008; named one of 50 Most Powerful People in Hollywood, 2004-06, 100 Most Powerful Celebrities, Forbes.com, 2007. Office: c/o Baker-Winouker-Ryder 9100 Wilshire Blvd 6th Fl Beverly Hills CA 90212*

SANDLER, ALAN BART, oncologist; b. Cleve., June 30, 1956; s. David and Lillian Sandler; m. Kathy Jean Wright, May 16, 1987; children: Grant Elliott, Matthew Benjamin, David Nicholas. MD, Rush Med. Sch., Chigo., 1987. Diplomate in med. oncology Am. Bd. Internal Medicine, 2006. Assoc. prof. medicine Ind. U. Med. Sch., Indpls., 1992—2000, Vanderbilt U. Med. Sch., Nashville, 2000—09; prof. medicine divsn. chair heamatology oncology Oreg. Health Sci. U., 2009—. Mem.: Am. Soc. Clin. Oncology, Alpha Omega Alpha Med. Soc. Office: Oreg Health Sci Univ 3181 SW SAm JAckson Pk Rd Portland OR 97239 Office Phone: 503-494-8634. Business E-Mail: alan.sandler@vanderbilt.edu.

SANDLER, BETTY MOORE, lawyer; b. Martin, Ky., Dec. 10, 1947; BA, U. Ky., 1969; JD, U. Ky. Coll. Law, 1981. Bar: Ky. 1981, US Supreme Ct. 1985, Commonwealth of Va. 1986, US Bankruptcy Ct., E Dist. of Va. 1990. Lobbyist & fed. legislative analyst US Congress; Commr. in Chancery, 31st Judicial Circuit, Va.; prin. Nichols Zauzig Sandler P.C. Founding pres. Prince William County Bar Found. Contbr. articles to profl. law guides, books, publ. Named one of Top 20 Divorce Attys., Washingtonian; named to Top Lawyers, Best Lawyers in America, 2005, 2006, Va. Super Lawyers, 2006, 2007, DC Super Lawyers, 2007. Fellow: Am. Acad. of Matrimonial Lawyers (AAML), Internat. Acad. of Matrimonial Lawyers (IAML); mem.: No. Va. Bankruptcy Bar Assn. Office: Nichols Zauzig Sandler PC 12660 Lake Ridge Dr Woodbridge VA 22192-2335 Office Phone: 703-492-4200. Office Fax: 703-492-4201.

SANDLER, GERALD HOWARD, computer scientist, information technology executive, educator; b. NYC, Sept. 17, 1934; s. Irving and Sally S.; m. Ann Sandler; children: Eric, Steven. BS, CUNY, 1956, MS, 1957. With Grumman Aerospace, 1963-83; past pres. Grumman Data Systems & Svcs., Bethpage, NY, 1983-95; pres. GHS Enterprises, 1995—; prof. computer sci. Poly. U., Farmingdale, NY, 1995—. Author: System Engineering, 1963. Home: 46 Bonnie Dr Westbury NY 11590-2804

SANDLER, IRVING HARRY, art critic, art historian; b. NYC, July 22, 1925; s. Harry and Anna (Robin) S.; m. Lucy Freeman, Sept. 4, 1958; 1 child, Catherine Harriet. BA, Temple U., 1948; MA, U. Pa., 1950; PhD, NYU, 1976. Instr. in art history NYU, 1960-71; prof. emeritus art history SUNY, Purchase; art critic N.Y. Post, NYC, 1960-65. Author: The Triumph of American Painting: A History of Abstract Expressionism, 1970, The New York School: Painters and Sculptors of the Fifties, 1978, Alex Katz, 1979, Al Held, 1984, American Art of the 1960s, 1988; editor (with Amy Newman) Defining Modern Art: Selected Writings of Alfred H. Barr Jr., 1986, Mark di Suvero at Storm King Art Ctr., 1996, Art of Postmodern Era: From Late 1960s to Early 1990s, 1996, Natvar Bhavsar, 1998, Stephen Antonakos, 1999, A Sweeper-Up After Artists: A Memoir, 2003, From Avant-Garde to Pluralism: An On-The-Spot History, 2006, Esteben Vicente: The Aristocratic Eye, 2007, Abstract Expressionism and the American Experience, 2009. Recipient Lifetime Achievement award, Internat. Assn. Art Critics, 2008; John Simon Guggenheim fellow, 1965; Nat. Endowment for Arts fellow, 1977. Mem. Coll. Art Assn., Internat. Assn. Art Critics. Home: 60 E 8th St Apt 19E New York NY 10003 Office Phone: 212-533-7447.

SANDLER, LUCY FREEMAN, art history educator; b. NYC, June 7, 1930; d. Otto and Frances (Glass) Freeman; m. Irving Sandler, Sept. 4, 1958; 1 child, Catherine Harriet. BA, Queens Coll., 1951; MA, Columbia U., 1957; PhD, NYU, 1964. Asst. prof. NYU, 1964-70, assoc. prof., 1970-75, prof. fine arts, 1975-86, Helen Gould Sheppard prof. art history, 1986—2003, chmn. dept., 1975-89; editorial cons. Viator, UCLA, 1983-97; Helen Gould Sheppard prof. emerita, 2003—. Author: The Peterborough Psalter in Brussels, 1974, The Psalter of Robert De Lisle in the British Library, 1983, new edit., 1999, Gothic Manuscripts 1285-1385, 1986, 'Omne Bonum': A Fourteenth-Century Encyclopedia of Universal Knowledge, 1996, The Ramsey Psalter, 1999, Der Ramsey-Psalter (Glanzlichter der Buchkunst 12), 2003, Der Bestiarium aus Peterburgh/The Peterborough Bestiary, 2003, The Lichtenthal Psalter and the Patronage of the Bohun Family, 2004, (with Jonathan J.G. Alexander and James H. Marrow) The Splendor of the Word, Medieval and Renaissance Illuminated Manuscripts, NY Pub. Libr., 2005, Studies in Manuscript Illumination 1200-1400, 2008; editor: Essays in Memory of Karl Lehmann, 1964, Art the Ape of Nature: Studies in Honor of H.W. Janson, 1981, Coll. Art Assn. Monograph Series, 1970-75, 86-89, Gesta, 1991-94; asst. editor Art Bull., 1964-67, mem. editl. bd., 1994; mem. editl. bd. Jour. Jewish Art, 1978, Speculum, 1994. Trustee Godwin-Ternbach Mus., Queens Coll., 1982-94; chair dels. exec. com. Am. Coun. Learned Socs., 2002-04. NEH fellow, 1967-68, 77; fellow Pierpont Morgan Library; Guggenheim fellow, 1988-89. Fellow: Medieval Acad. Am. (councillor 2002—05), Soc. Antiquaries (London); mem.: AAUP, Coll. Art Assn. (pres. 1981—84), Internat. Ctr. Medieval Art (adv. bd., bd. dirs. 1976—80, 1984—87, 1989—92, 1995—2001). Home: 60 E 8th St Apt 19E New York NY 10012 Office: NYU Dept Art History New York NY 10003 Office Phone: 212-998-8181.

SANDLER, RICHARD H., pediatric gastroenterologist; MD, Mich. State U. Coll. Human Medicine. Resident, pediatrics Mich. State U., Lansing; fellow, pediatric gastroenterology, hepatology, and nutrition Harvard Med. Sch., Boston Children's Hosp.; fellow, human metabolism and nutrition Mass. Gen. Hosp., Boston; asst. in medicine, instr., divsn. of gastroenterology and nutrition The Children's Hosp., Harvard Med. Sch., Boston, 1989—90; dir. Biomed. Acoustics Rsch. Group, Evanston, Ill., 1990—, pres., CEO, 1997—; assoc. prof., pediatrics Rush Med. Coll., Chgo., 1990—; adj. assoc. prof., biomed. engring. U. Ill., Chgo., 2002—. Office: Rush Univ Med Ctr 1725 W Harrison St Chicago IL 60612 Address: 1725 W Harrison St Ste 946 Chicago IL 60612 Office Phone: 312-942-2889.

SANDLER, STANLEY IRVING, chemical engineering educator; b. NYC, June 10, 1940; s. Murray C. and Celia M. (Kamenetsky) S.; m. Judith Katherine Ungar, June 17, 1962; children: Catherine Julietta, Joel Abraham, Michael Howard. BChemE, CCNY, 1962; PhD, U. Minn., 1966. Chartered engr., European Union. NSF postdoctoral fellow Inst. Molecular Physics U. Md., College Park, 1966—67; successively asst. prof., assoc. prof., prof. dept. chem. engring. U. Del., Newark, 1967-82, H.B. du Pont prof., 1982—2000, chmn. dept., 1982—86, dir. Ctr. Molecular and Engring. Thermodynamics, 1992—, interim dean Coll. Engring., 1992, H.B. duPont chair, 2000—; hon. professorial fellow U. Melbourne, Australia, 2004—; Exxon Mobil prof. Nat. U. Singapore, 2006—09. Vis. prof. Imperial Coll., London, 1973—74, U. Nat. del Sur, Bahia Blanca, Argentina, 1985, Tech. U., Berlin, 1981, Berlin, 1988—89, U. Queensland, Brisbane, Australia, 1989, Brisbane, 96, U. Calif., Berkeley, 1995, U. Melbourne, Australia, 2003, hon. professorial fellow dept. chem. and biomolecular engring., 2004—; cons. maj. oil and chem. cos. Author: Chemical and Engineering Thermodynamics, 1977, 3d edit., 1998, 4th edit., 2006, Modeling Vapor-Liquid Equilibrium, 1998, Chemical, Biochemical and Engineering Thermodynamics, 2006; editor: Fluid Properties and Phase Equilibria, 1977, Chemical Engineering Education in a Changing Environment, 1989, Kinetic and Thermodynamic Lumping of Multicomponent Mixtures, 1991, Models for Thermodynamic and Phase Equilibria Calculations, 1993, AI Chem E. Jour., 2000—; mem. adv. bd. Jour. Chem. Engring. Data, Chem. Engring. Edn., Indsl. Engring. Chem. Rsch., Indian Chem. Engr., Engring. Sci. and Tech. (Malaysia); also numerous articles. Mem. adv. bd. chem. engring. La. State U., Carnegie-Mellon U., Princeton U. Recipient U.S. Sr. Scientist award Alexander von Humboldt Found., 1988, Francis Alison award U. Del., 1993, Ashton Cary award Ga. Tech. U., 1994, Phillips Lecture award Okla. State U., 1993, Rossini Lectureship award Internat. Union Pure Applied Chemistry, 1998; Miegunyah fellow U. Melbourne, Australia, 2003, hon. professorial fellow, 2004—; Hikal Chemcon Dist. Spkr. award, Indian Inst. Chem. Engrs., 2004. Fellow Inst. Chem. Engrs. (Britain), AIChE (jour. adv. bd., editor 2000—, Profl. Progress award 1984, Warren K. Lewis award 1996, Del. Soc. award 1998, Founders award, 2004), U.S. Nat. Acad. Engring., Am. Chem. Soc. (award Del. sect. 1989, E.V. Murphree award 1997), Am. Soc. Engring. Edn. (lectr. chem. engring. div. 1988), Cosmos Club (Washington). Jewish. Avocations: jogging, stamp collecting/philately. Home: 202 Sypherd Dr Newark DE 19711-3627 Office: U Del Dept Chem Engring Newark DE 19716 Office Phone: 302-831-2945. Business E-Mail: sandler@udel.edu.

SANDLER, TODD MICHAEL, economist, political scientist, educator; b. Mt. Kisco, NY, Dec. 16, 1946; s. Louis and Susie Sandler; m. Jean Marie Murdock, June 28, 1985; 1 child, Tristan Jon. BA, SUNY, Binghamton, 1968, MA, 1969, PhD, 1971. Asst. prof. Ariz. State U., Tempe, 1971-76; assoc. prof. U. Wyo., Laramie, 1976-79, prof., 1979-85, U. S.C., Columbia, 1985-86; prof. econs. and polit. sci. Iowa State U., Ames, 1986-2000, Disting. prof., 1995—2001; Dockson prof. U. So. Calif., LA, 2000—07; Shukla prof. U. Tex., Dallas, 2006—. Author: Collective Action: Theory and Applications, 1992, Global Challenges, 1997, Economic Concepts for the Social Sciences, 2001, Global Collective Action, 2004; co-author: The Theory of Externalities, Public Goods and Club Goods, 1986, The Economics of Defense, 1995, (book) The Theory of Externalities, Public Goods and Club Goods, 2d edit., 1996, International Terrorism in 1980s, 1989, The Political Economy of NATO, 1999, The Future of Development Assistance: Common Pools and International Public Goods, 1999, Regional Public Goods: Typologies, Provision, Financing, and Development Assistance, 2002, The Political Economy of Terrorism, 2006; co-editor: Defense Economics, 1989—94, Handbook of Defense Economics, 1995;: Handbook of Defense Economics, 2007, Economics of Defense, 2001, Economics of Conflict, 2003; assoc. editor: Jour. Environ. Econs. and Mgmt., 1988—89, Jour. Pub. Econ. Theory, 1999—2005; assoc. editor Rev. Internat. Organizations; mem. editl. bd.: Pub. Fin. Rev., Fiscal Studies, Bull. Econ. Rsch., Internat. Studies Quar., Terrorism and Political Violence; mem. editl. bd. Am. Jour. Polit. Sci., Internat. Studies Perspective, Rev. of Internat. Orgns., chmn. editl. bd. Jour. Conflict Resolution, 2004—; spl. adv. editor: Def. and Peace Econs., 2000—, reviewer: numerous internat. orgns. Recipient Duncan Black award, Pub. Choice Soc., 2005; co-recipient Rsch. Related to Prevention of Nuc. War award, Nat. Acad. of Scis., 2003; grantee NSF, 1989, 1993; fellow NATO postdoctoral, 1977, 1998—2000, Australian Nat. U., 1981, 1994, Sr., Inst. Policy Reform, 1990—91, 1992—94, Hon., U. Wis.-Madison, 1990. Mem.: Pub. Choice Soc., So. Econ. Assn., Assn. Environ. and Resource Econs., Royal Econ. Soc., Am. Econ. Assn., Internat. Def. Econs. Assn. (exec. bd.). Office: U Tex Dallas Sch Econ Polit and Policy Scis 800 W Campbell Rd Richardson TX 75080 Business E-Mail: tsandler@utdallas.edu.

SANDLIN, STEPHANIE HERSETH, United States Representative from South Dakota, lawyer; b. Aberdeen, SD, Dec. 3, 1970; d. Ralph Lars and Joyce Herseth. BA summa cum laude in Polit. Sci. and Govt., Georgetown U., 1993, MA in Polit. Sci., 1996; JD, Georgetown U. Law Ctr., 1996. Bar: SD. Law clerk Staff of US Dist. Ct. Judge Charles Kornmann, Pierre, 1998—99, Staff of US 4th Cir. Ct. Appeals Judge Diana Gribbon Motz, Balt., 1999—2000; atty. Skadden, Arps, Slate, Meagher & Flom LLP, Washington, 2001; exec. dir. SD Farmers Union Found., 2003—04; mem. US Congress from SD at-large, 2004—, mem. Blue Dog Coalition, mem. agr. com., mem. resources com., mem. vets. affairs com., ranking minority mem. econ. opportunity subcommittee. Prof. Georgetown U. Law Ctr., 1997, Augustana Coll., 2003, SD State U., 2003; tchr. Fund for Am. Studies; counsel on energy and telecom. issues SD Pub. Utilities Commn., Pierre; bd. dir. First Nat. Bank, Brookings, SD. Sr. editor Georgetown U. Law Rev. Mem. Rotary Internat., Brookings, SD; co-chair Rural Working Grp.; legal counsel for the elderly. Recipient Small Bus. Adv., Small Bus. Survival Com., 2004. Mem.: SD Bar Assn., Phi Beta Kappa. Democrat. Lutheran. Office: US House of Reps 331 Cannon House Office Bldg Washington DC 20515-4101 Office Phone: 202-225-2801.

SANDLOW, JAY IRA, urologist, researcher; b. Chgo., Aug. 27, 1961; s. Leslie Jordan and JoAnne (Fleischer) S.; m. Bridget Ann Bruggeman Sandlow, May 28, 1989; 1 child, Samantha Leigh Sandlow. BS, U. Ill., Champaign, 1983; MD, Rush U., Chgo., 1987. Resident Dept. Urology U. Iowa Hosp., 1987-93; fellow dept. urology, 1993-95; assoc. dept. urology, 1994-95; asst. prof. dept. urology, 1995—. Contbr. articles and book chpts. to profl. jours. Chpt. advisor Sigma Alpha Mu, Iowa City, 1987-92. Recipient Rsch. scholarship Am. Found. Urologic, 1993-95, Rockefeller Found., 1994-96. Mem. AMA, Am. Urology Assn., Am. Fertility Soc., Am. Coll. Surgeons. Avocations: golf, music, bicycling, reading. Office: Univ Iowa Hosps and Clinics Dept Urology 200 Hawkins Dr Iowa City IA 52242-1009 Home: 3711 Tremont Ct Mequon WI 53092-6306

SANDMAN, BRADFORD AARON, coach, educator; b. Omaha, Dec. 11, 1957; s. Darrel Alfred and Alice Sandman; m. Beth Marie Bokorney; children: Keegan Gregary, Colton Bradford. BS, Stephen F. Austin State U., Tex., 1980; Med, Prairie View A&M U. of Tex., 2004. Tchr., coach Sealy HS, Tex., 1985—90, Langham Creek HS, Houston, 1990—. Master: Sr. Men (sponsor), Fellowship of Christian Athletes (sponsor), Unity Club (sponsor); mem.: Honor Soc. Com., Gang Task Com. Home: 303 Briar Ridge Bellville TX 77418 Office: Langham Creek HS 17610 Fm 529 Houston TX 77095 Personal E-mail: bradford.sandman@cfisd.net.

SANDMAN, JAMES JOSEPH, lawyer; b. Albany, NY, June 16, 1951; s. Edgar A. and Margaret M. (Dugan) S.; m. Elizabeth D. Mullin, June 2, 1985; children: Joseph M., Elizabeth D. AB summa cum laude, Boston Coll., 1973; JD cum laude, U. Pa., 1976. Bar: Pa. 1976, D.C. 1977, U.S. Supreme Ct. 1980, Colo. 1982. Law clk. to judge U.S. Ct. Appeals (3d cir.), Wilkes-Barre, Pa., 1976-77; assoc. Arnold & Porter, 1977—83, ptnr., 1984—2007, mng. ptnr., 1995—2005, sr. pro bono ptnr., 2007; gen. counsel DC Pub. Schools, Washington, 2007—. Exec. editor U. Pa. Law Rev., 1975-76. Mem. bd. overseers U. Pa. Law Sch., 1998—2007; trustee Wilkes U., 2002—08, NALP Found., 2005—08; bd. dirs. Washington Performing Arts Soc., Internat. Sr. Lawyers Project, Meyer Found. Mem. ABA (house of dels., 2006-07, standing com. on pro bono and public svc., 2007—08), DC Bar., (bd. gov. 2003-08, pres. 2006-07, pro bono com. 2008-), DC Cir. Jud. Conf. Com. (pro bono legal svcs. 2007-, DC state adv. com. to US civil rights com. 2008-), Order of Coif, Phi Beta Kappa. Democrat. Office: DC Pub Schools 825 N Capitol St NE Washington DC 20002 Home Phone: 202-363-1320; Office Phone: 202-442-5158. Office Fax: 202-442-5098. Business E-Mail: james.sandman@dc.gov.

SANDMAN, PETER M., risk management consultant; b. NYC, Apr. 18, 1945; s. Howard Edwin and Gertrude Leah (Orgel) S.; m. Susan Marie Goertzel, June 18, 1967 (div. 1975); m. Jody Sue Lanard, June 10, 1990; children: Alison, Jennifer; 1 stepchild, James Sachs. BA in Psychology, Princeton U., 1967; MA in Comm., Stanford U., 1968, PhD, 1971. Reporter Toronto (Ont.) Star, Canada, 1966; stringer Time, 1966-67; instr. comm. Stanford (Calif.) U., 1968-70; instr. journalism Calif. State Coll., Hayward, 1970; sr. editor The Magazine, 1970; asst. prof. Ohio State U., Columbus, 1971-72; asst. prof. natural resources, journalism U. Mich., Ann Arbor, 1972-75, assoc. prof. natural resources, 1975-77; assoc. prof. comm., coord. Cook Coll. comm. program Rutgers U., New Brunswick, NJ, 1977-83, prof. journalism, 1983-94, prof. dept. human ecology, 1992-94; adj. prof., 1994—. Adj. prof. TV, radio Ithaca (NY) Coll., 1976, grad. program in pub. health Rutgers U., 1986—, dept. environ. and cmty. medicine Robert Wood Johnson Med. Sch., Rutgers U., 1987—; adv. com. environ./occupl. health info. program 1984-89; founder, dir. environ. comm. rsch. program NJ Agrl. Exptl. Sta., Rutgers U., 1986-92; vis. scholar urban and environ. policy Tufts U., Medford, Mass., 1990-91; rsch. prof. George Perkins Marsh Inst., Clark U.; comm. coun. Environ. Def. Fund, 1985—; bd. advisors grad. program in tech. and sci. comm. Drexel U., Phila., 1988—; cons. on comm. ACP, 1976-79, Cousteau Soc., 1977-79, Pres. Com. on the Accident at Three Mile Island; specialist in comm. coop. ext. svc. U.S. Dept. Agr., 1977-86; cons. risk commn. office policy analysis EPA, 1986-88; exec. com. Sci. Writing Educators Group, 1978-81; cons. ARCO Chem., Boise Cascade, Chevron, Ciba-Geigy, Consumers Power, Dow, Du Pont, Johnson and Johnson, Johnson Wax, Procter and Gamble, Union Carbide, others. Cons. editor Random House, 1982-89, McGraw-Hill, 1989-94, Holt, Rinehart and Winston, 1978-81; contbg. editor Apt. Life, 1971-75; freelance writer, 1966—; editl. bd. Pub. Rels. Rsch. Ann., 1981-91, Jour. Pub. Rels. Rsch., 1991-94; editl. adv. bd. Environ. and Behavior, 1976-86; contbr. articles to profl. jours. Bd. dirs. N.J. Environ. Lobby, 1984-90, Nuclear Dialogue Project, 1985-90, pres. 1986-90; pub. info. com. N.J. chpt., Am. Cancer Soc., 1981-86, vice-chmn., 1983-86; comm. coord. N.J. Campaign for a Nuclear Weapons Freeze, 1982-85; socioeconomic subcom., com. on biotechnology agr. divsn. Nat. Assn. State Univs. and Land Grant Colls., 1988-90; bd. advisors Environ. Scientists for Global Survival, 1988-91; sci. review panel, radium/radon adv. bd. N.J. Dept. Environ. Protection, 1987-88; com. to survey the health effects mustard gas and lewisite Inst. Medicine, NAS, 1992. Mem. AAUP, ACLU (bd. dirs. N.J. chpt. 1984-87), Environ. Def. Fund, Nat. Assn. Profl. Environ. Communicators, Sci. Writing Educators Group, Soc. for Risk Analysis, Soc. Environ. Journalists, Internat. Assn. Pub. Participation Practitioners, Sigma Delta Chi. Home: 59 Ridgeview Rd Princeton NJ 08540-7601 Office Phone: 609-683-4073. Personal E-mail: peter@psandman.com.

SANDMIRE, DAVID A., biology professor; BS in Biochemistry, U. Wis., Madison, 1985, MD, 1989, MA in History Sci. and Medicine, 1994. Prof. U. New Eng., Biddeford, Maine, 1994—. Author: (book) Medical Tests That Can Save Your Life. Recipient Outstanding Adj. Faculty award, Southern Maine Tech. Coll., 1991—92, Debra J. Summers Meml. award, U. New Eng., 1996—97, 2001—02, Disting. Academic Svc. award, 1995—96, 2004—05. Mem.: Internat. Alliance Tchr. Scholars. Office: Univ New Eng 11 Hills Beach Rd Biddeford ME 04005

SANDNESS, PAUL K., lawyer, energy executive; b. 1954; BA, Valley City State U.; JD, U. ND. Bar: 1979. Various positions including sr. atty. MDU Resources Group, Inc., 1980—2004, gen. counsel, sec., 2004—. Office: MDU Resources Group Inc 1200 W Century Ave PO Box 5650 Bismarck ND 58506-5650*

SANDOK, SCOTT, economics educator, healthcare educator; b. Warminster, Pa., Aug. 12, 1976; s. Len and Ellen Sandok; m. Angela Guimont, Sept. 2, 2007; children: Maria Brandel, Joseph Brandel, Anthony Brandel. BS, U. Wis., Eau Claire, 1998; MS in Economics, Iowa State U., Ames, 2002. Sr. healthcare analyst BlueCross BlueShield, Eagan, Minn., 2002—; instr. economics Normandale CC, Bloomington, Minn., 2008—. Mem. supervisory com. BlueStone Fed. Credit Union, Eagan, 2005—07. Recipient Excellence in Tchg. award, Iowa State U., 2002. Office: Normandale CC 9700 France Ave S Bloomington MN 55431

SANDOVAL, ARTURO, jazz musician; b. Havana, Cuba, Nov. 6, 1949; arrived in US, 1990, naturalized, 1999; s. Arturo and Cira (Arocha) S.; m. Carmen Marianela, Oct. 17, 1975; 1 child, Arturo Jr. Prof. Fla. Internat. U., 1990—. Lectr. in field; bd. dirs., ednl. com. Chgo. Symphony Orch., 1994; featured artist Dizzy Gillespie UN Orch., Live at Royal Festival Hall album (Grammy 1991). Performed with Cuban Orch. Modern Music; guest artist BBC Symphony, London, Leningrad Symphony; founding mem. Irakere mus. group; albums include Irakere I, 1978, (Grammy award, Best Latin Album), Irakere II, 1980, To a Finland Station, 1982, Breaking the Sound Barrier, 1983, Tumbaito, 1986, No Problem, 1986, Straight Ahead, 1988, Flight to Freedom, 1991, I Remember Clifford, 1992 (2 Grammy nominations), Dream Come True, 1993, Danzon (Dance On), 1993 (Grammy award, Best Latin Jazz Peformance, 1995, Billboard award for Best Latin Jazz Album, 1995), Cubano, 1994, Arturo Sandoval & The Latin Train, 1995 (Billboard award for Best Latin Jazz Album, 1996), Latin Train, 1995, Tren Latino, 1995, Concerto, 1995, Swingin, 1996, Just Music, 1996, Hot House, 1998 (Grammy award, Best Latin Jazz Performance, 1998, Billboard award, Best Latin Jazz Album, 1998), Americana, 1999, Ronnie Scott's Jazz House, 2000, For Love or Country, 2001, LA Meetings, 2001, My Passion for the Piano, 2001, From Havana with Love, 2003, Trumpet Evolution, 2003 (Lattin Billboard award, 2004), Live at the Blue Note, 2005, Arturo Sandoval & the Latin Jazz Orch., 2007, Arturo Sandoval & His Group, 2007, Rumba Palace, 2007 (Latin Grammy award, Best Latin Jazz Album, 2007), (TV films) The Perez Family, 1995, Sacred Waters, 2006, (TV films) For Love or Country: The Arturo Sandoval Story, 2000 (Emmy award for Outstnading Music Composition, 2001). Named Cuba's Best Instrumentalist,

1982-1990; named to Walt Disney World Jazz Hall of Fame, 1994; recipient Gold Tucan award, Brazil, 1988, Golden Feather award for Artist of Yr., LA Times, 1991, Internat. Jazz award, Clearwater Jazz Holliday, 1993, Hispanic Achievement award, 1994, Nat. Assn. Rec. Arts & Sciences Found. award for Excellence in Music Edn., 1994, Am. Jazz award, 1997, ASCAP Founder's award, 2001, Heroes award, Nat. Assn. Rec. Arts & Sciences, 2002. Roman Catholic. Home: 4706 Granada Blvd Coral Gables FL 33146-1250

SANDOVAL, ARTURO ALONZO, artist, educator; b. Espanola/Cordova, N.Mex., Feb. 1, 1942; s. Lorenzo Sandoval and Cecilia Eulalia (Archuleta) Harrison; (div. Sept. 1982); 1 child, Avalon Valentine Galaglorial. Student, U. Portland, 1959; BA, Calif. State Coll., LA, 1964, MA, 1969; MFA, Cranbrook Acad. Art, Bloomfield Hills, Mich., 1971. Designer, illustrator Western Lighting Corp., LA, 1964-66; advt. designer, adult edn. instr. spl. svcs. USN, Yokosuka, Japan, 1966; interior design asst. Walter B. Broderick & Assocs., La Mesa, Calif., 1967; asst. prof. art dept. U. Ky., Lexington, 1974—76, assoc. prof., 1976—86, prof., 1986—, dir. art dept. Barnhart Gallery, 1976—, curator, 1979—. Teaching asst. Calif. State Coll., L.A., 1969, Cranbrook Acad. Art, Bloomfield Hills, 1969-71; fiber art demonstrator Mus. Art, Grand Rapids, Mich., 1970; batik and tie-dye demonstrator Gwynn's Fabric Shop, Birmingham, Mich., 1970; instr. Calif. State Coll., L.A., 1970, So. Ill. U., Carbondale, 1971, Edwardsville, 1971, 72, 73, asst. prof., 1971-73; presenter various lectures and workshops throughout the U.S., 1973—; juror Mo. Women Festival Arts, St. Louis, So. Ill. U., East St. Louis, 1974, Paramount Arts Assn., Ashland, Ky., 1975, Ind. Weavers Guild, Indpls., 1979, Fed. Corrections Inst., Lexington, 1979, Hawaii Craftsman Hui and Art Dept. U. Hawaii, Manoa, Honolulu, 1982, art dept. Va. Intermont Coll., Bristol, 1982, Arrowmont Sch. Arts and Crafts, Gatlinburg, Tenn., 1984, Ctr. Contemporary Art, U. Ky., Lexington, 1984, Guild Greater Cin., Carnegie Art Ctr., Covington, Ky., 1989, S.C. Arts Commn., Charleston, 1990, Adams Art Gallery, Dunkirk, N.Y., 1994; visual arts cons. Ky. Arts Commn., Frankfort, 1977; curator Visual Arts Ctr. Alaska, Anchorage, 1982, Ky. Art and Crafts Found., Inc., Louisville, 1985; mem. artist adv. panel Ky. Art and Crafts Found., Louisville, 1986, 87, 92-2000; visual arts cons. Arts Midwest, 1987; artistic advisor Ky. Guild Mktg. Bd., Berea, 1988, 91, 92, 93; bd. trustees Ky. Guild 1995-98, Am. Craft Coun., N.Y.C., 1996—; vis. artist/critic Allen R. Hite Inst., U. Louisville, 1992; vis. artist Coll. Human Environ. Scis., U. Ky., Lexington, 1993; vis. artist/ lectr. fiber dept. Cranbrook Acad. Art, Bloomfield Hills, Mich., 1994, Art. Dept. St. Louis Comm. Coll.-Florissant Valley, 2001, U. Ariz., 2001; curator Art Quilts 2001, River Oaks Square Art Ctr., Louisiana, 2001; alumni-endowed rsch. prof. U. Ky., 2007-. Exhibited in group shows at Yeiser Art Ctr., Paducah/Paramount Arts Ctr., Ashland/S.E. Cmty. Coll., Cumberland, 1994, Textile Arts Centre, Chgo., 1994, Winnipeg (Man., Can.) Art Gallery, 1994, Riffe Gallery, Ohio Arts Coun., Columbus, 1994, Royal Hiberian Acad., Gallagher Gallery, Dublin, Ireland, Cooper Gallery, Barnsley, South Yorks, Gt. Britain, Shipley Art Gallery, Gateshead, Gt. Britain, 1994, Grand Rapids (Mich.) Art Mus., 1994, Whatcom Mus. History and Art, Bellingham, Wash., The Rockwell Mus., Corning, N.Y., Mus. Art, Washington State U., Pullman, The Hyde Collection, Glen Falls, N.Y., 1994, U. Art Galleries, U. S.D., Vermillion, 1994, Barnhart Gallery, U. Ky., Lexington, 1994, Sawtooth Ctr. Visual Art, 1994, Santa Fe Gallery, Santa Fe Cmty. Coll., Gainesville, Fla., 1994, Liberty Gallery, Louisville, 1994, Asahi Shimbun Gallery, Tokyo, Takashimaya Gallery, Osaka, 1994, Minn. Mus. Art, Landmark Ctr., St. Paul, 1994, S.C. State Mus., Columbia, 1994, Galbreath Gallery, Lexington, 1994, U.K. Art Mus., 1998, Giles Gallery, Richmond, Ky., 2004, Ky. Mus. of Art and Design, 2004, Ronald Barr Gallery, New Albany, Ind., 2004, City Gallery, S.C., 2004, Tuska Gallery, Ky., 2004, Pres. Room. Ky., 2004, numerous others; represented in permanent collections at Wabash Coll., Crawfordsville, Ind., Greenville County Mus. Art, Greenville, S.C., Mus. Modern Art, N.Y.C., St. Mary's Coll., Notre Dame, Ind., Coll. St. Rose, Albany, N.Y., Bowling Green (Ohio) StateU., U. Notre Dame, Transylvania U., Lexington, U. Ky. Mus. Art, Lexington, Mid-Am. Rare Coin Auction Galleries, Lexington, Henry Luce Found., N.Y.C., Lexington Ctrl. Libr., UK Art Mus., Nat. Mus. Am. Art, Renwick Gallery, J.B. Speed Art Mus., Louisville, Linda Schwartz Gallery, Tuska Gallery, Pres.'s Room, KY, Shands Gallery, Friedman Gallery, KGAG Offices, Actor's Theater, Ronald Barr Gallery, Opera House Gallery, Waltron Ltd., Whitehouse, N.J., Nat. Hispanic Cultural Arts Ctr., Albuquerque, N.Mex., Rocky Mt. Quilt Mus., Golden, Colo., Mus. Art and Design, N.Y. Recipient Alexandra Korsakoff Galston Meml. prize St. Louis Artist's Guild, 1971, Mus. Merit award Mus. Arts and Scis., Evansville, 1972, Creative Rsch. Grant So. Ill. U.-Edwardsville Rsch. Found., 1972, Craftsman fellowship Nat. Endowment Arts, Washington, 1973, Friend of Mus. award Mus. Arts and Scis., Evansville, 1973, Clay Eugene Jordan ann. bequest prize crafts St. Louis Artist's Guild, 1973, Teaching Improvement grant U. Ky. Rsch. Found., 1974, Travel grant U. Ky. Rsch. Found., 1977, Judges Choice award Berea (Ky.) Coll., 1978, Handweaver's Guild Am. award, 1978, Fiber award LeMoyne Art Found., Tallahassee, 1981, Elise Strout Merit award Mus. Arts and Scis., Evansville, 1981, Handweavers Guild Am. award, 1983, Martha Ryan Merit award Mus. Arts and Scis., Evansville, 1984, Best of Show award Gayle Willson Galleries, Southampton, 1984, Juror's merit award Brenau Coll., Gainesville, Ga., 1985, Installation Grant Ind. Arts Commn., Ft. Wayne, 1985, All Smith fellowship Ky. Arts Coun., Frankfort, 1987, 2006, Merit award Spotlight '88 Am. Craft Coun., fellow, 2008, Southeast Conf., Tuscaloosa, Ala., 1988, Merit award Mus. Arts and Scis., Evansville, 1989, Design Grant, Arts and Cultural Coun. for O.A. Singletary Ctr. Arts, Lexington, 1990, Visual Arts fellowship Nat. Endowment for Arts, Washington, 1992, Hon. award Ky. Crafts Mktg. Bd., Frankfort, 1994, Rude Osolnik Craftsman award Ky. Crafts Mktg. & KAC Fund, 1998, 1st pl. Lexington Art League, Reverse Raffle, Lexington, 1999, Art-in-Arch. Program commn. Gen. Svcs. Adminstrn., London, Ky., 2002; Artist award Ky. Gov.'s award in the arts, 2003, Merit award ACCSE, 2006, Kirwan Meml. prize U. Ky., 2007; grantee NEA, Pyramid Atlantic Press, Riverdale, Md., 1996; Gen. Svcs. Adminstrn.; Kirwan prize, U. Ky, 2007, Alumni professorship, 2007—. Mem. Lexington Fiber Guild Inc., Louisville Visual Arts Assn., Ky. Art and Craft Found., Inc., Ky. Guild Artists and Craftsmen, Am. Craft Coun., Friends of U. Ky. Mus. Art, Friends of Fiber Art, Surface Design Assn. Home: PO Box 25153 Lexington KY 40524-5153 Office: Univ Ky Dept Art Coll Fine Arts 207 Fine Arts Bldg Lexington KY 40506-0022 Home Phone: 859-273-8898; Office Phone: 859-230-9635.

SANDOVAL, BRIAN EDWARD, federal judge, former state attorney general; b. Redding, Calif., Aug. 5, 1963; s. Ronald L. and Gloria Sandoval; m. Kathleen T. Sandoval; children: James, Madeline, Marisa. B in English & Econ., U. Nev., 1986; JD, Ohio State U., 1989. Bar: Nev., Calif., DC. Mem. Nev. State Assembly, 1995—97; atty. McDonald, Carano, Wilson, McCune Bergin, Frankovich & Hicks, Reno, 1989—91, Robinson, Belaustegui, Robb & Sharp, Reno, 1991—95, Gamboa, Sandoval & Stovall, Reno, 1995—99, Sandoval Law Office, Reno, 1999—2003; atty. gen. State of Nev., Carson City, 2003—05; judge US Dist. Ct. Dist. Nev., Reno, 2005—. Mem. Nev. Gaming Commn., 1998—2001, chmn., 1999—2001; mem. State and Local Officials' Adv. Com. US Dept. Homeland Security. Bd. trustees Children's Cabinet, Reno, St. Jude's Ranch for Children, Washoe County Law Libr., Nev. Recipient Torch of Liberty, Anti-Defamation League, 2003; named Public Lawyer of the Yr., Nevada St. Bar Assoc., 2004. Republican. Office: US Dist Ct 400 S Virginia St Reno NV 89501

SANDOVAL, RIK (CHARLES SANDOVAL), broadcast executive; b. Chgo., May 20, 1952; s. Placido Jr. and Ophelia (Lugo) S. BA in Communications, Columbia Coll., 1974. With prodn. dept. Sta. WSNS-TV, Chgo., 1971-72; dir., producer Sta. WCAE-TV, St. John, Ind., 1972-73; producer Sta. WBBM-FM, Chgo., 1973-74; prodn. mgr. Sta. WLS-TV, Chgo., 1972-76, on-air mgr., 1976-77; sr. publicist, producer Sta. KABC-TV, Hollywood, Calif., 1977-79; dir. creative svcs. Sullivan & Assocs, LA, 1979-81; producer ABC, Hollywood, 1981-82; pres. Sandoval Prodns., Studio City, Calif., 1982-87; sr. v.p. The Agy., Studio City, 1987-88; pres. Tri-Mark Group, Inc., Studio City, 1988-92; dir. world wide ops. publicity MGM Studios, Culver City, Calif., 1992; dir. mktg. and pub. rels. Entergamement, Inc., LA, 1993—94; dir. ops. GTE Interactive Media, Carlsbad, Calif., 1994-97, dir. corp. comm., 1994-97; v.p. pub. rels. and mktg. comm. Neale-May & Ptnrs., Palo Alto, Calif., 1998—; v.p. tech., sr. exec. on iMac launch Edelman Pub. Rels. World Wide, Mountain View, Calif., 1998—; v.p. publ. rels. Access Comms. Sega Dreamcast Launch and Online Strategic Svcs., 1999—; sr. dir. corp. comm. Silicon Motion, Inc., San Jose, Calif., 2000—. Judge The Clio Awards; prodr., writer Miss Hawaiian Tropic Beauty Pageant, 1992; head writer Mad Scientist Toon Club, 1993; exec. dir. Computer Game Developers Assocs., Los Altos, Calif., 1997. Producer, writer: (broadcast promotions) A.K.A. Pablo, 1984 (Silver award), Entertainment Tonight, 1984 (Silver award), Hunter, 1985, People, 1985 (Telly award, 1985, Gold Statuette award); head writer Mad Scientist Toon Club, 1993. Mem. NOSOTROS, L.A., 1987. Recipient 8 Clio nominations, 1977, 79-81, 2 Gold medals Internat. Radio Festival N.Y., 1985, 4 Bronze Telly awards, 1983-88, Silver Telly award, 1988, 2 ITVA awards, 1988, 3 Silver Telly awards, 1991, 4 Silver Telly awards, 1992, 2 Bronze Telly awards, 1992. Mem. Broadcast Promotion Mktg. Execs. (Gold medal, Silver medal 1985, 2 Bronze Telly award statuettes 1989, Silver Telly award statuette 1989. ITVA award), Nat. Assn. Broadcasters (cert. merit 1974), The Publicist Guild, Acad. TV Arts and Scis., Pub. Rels. Soc. Am. Roman Catholic. Avocations: art deco antiques, fine wine collector, Karate, pre-columbian artifacts, modern art collector.

SANDOZ, GEORGE ELLIS, JR., political science educator; b. New Orleans, Feb. 10, 1931; s. George Ellis and Ruby (Odom) S.; m. Therese Alverne Hubley, May 31, 1957; children: Ellis III, Lisa, Erica, Jonathan. BA in History, La. State U., 1951, MA in Polit. Sci., 1953; D in Polit. Sci., U. Munich, Germany, 1965; PhD (hon.), Palacky U., Olomouc, 1995; DSc (hon.), U. Francisco Marroquín, 2002. Capitol Hill policeman U.S. Ho. of Reps., Washington, 1952-53; instr. to prof. La. Poly. Inst., Ruston, 1959-68; prof., head dept. polit. sci. East Tex. State U., Commerce, 1968-78; prof. polit. sci., chmn. La. State U., Baton Rouge, 1978—, dir. Eric Voegelin Inst., 1987—, Hermann Moyse Jr. disting. prof. polit. sci., 2006—. Mem. Nat. Coun. on the Humanities, Washington, 1982-88; lectr. in field. Author: Political Apocalypse, 1971, 2d edit., 2000, Conceived in Liberty, 1978, The Voegelinian Revolution, 1981, 2nd edit., 2000, A Government of Laws, 1990, 2d edit., 2000; editor: The Collected Works of Eric Voegelin, 1986-2009; author introduction, editor: Political Sermons of the American Founding Era, 1730-1805, 1991, 2nd edit., 2nd vols., 1998, Roots of Liberty, 1993, Annagi Edn., 2008, Politics of Truth, 1999, Republicanism, Religion and the Soul of America, 2006. Nat. co-chair Reagan-Bush Presidency, Washington, 1984. Pvt. 1st lt. USMC, 1953-56. Fulbright scholar Bd. Fgn. Scholarships, Washington, 1964-65, Fulbright 40th Anniversary Disting. Am. scholar USIA, Italy, 1987. Mem. Am. Polit. Sci. Assn., So. Polit. Sci. Assn. (coun. 1982-85), Southwestern Polit. and Social Sci. Assn. (pres. 1987-88). Republican. Baptist. Avocations: hunting, fishing, tennis. Home: 2843 Valcour Aime Ave Baton Rouge LA 70820-4424 Office: La State U Eric Voegelin Inst 240 Stubbs Hall Baton Rouge LA 70803-0001 Office Phone: 225-578-2552. Business E-Mail: esandoz@lsu.edu.

SANDQUIST, GARY MARLIN, engineering educator, researcher, consultant, writer, military officer; b. Salt Lake City, Apr. 19, 1936; s. Donald August Sandquist and Lillian (Evaline) Dunn; m. Kristine Powell, Jan. 17, 1992; children from previous marriage: Titia, Julia, Taunia, Cynthia, Carl; stepchildren: David, Michael, Scott, Diane, Jeff. BSME in Mech. Engring., U. Utah, 1956—60; MS in Engring. Sci., U. Calif., Berkeley, 1960—61; PhD in Mech. Nuclear Engring., U. Utah, 1961—64, MBA Exec. MS, 1993—95. Cert. quality auditor; registered profl. engr., Utah, NY, Minn., Calif.; cert health physicist; diplomate Am. Acad. Environ. Engring. Staff mem. Los Alamos (N.Mex.) Sci. Lab., 1966; postdoctoral fellow MIT, 1969-70; rsch. prof. surgery Med. Sch., U. Utah, Salt Lake City, 1974—85, prof., dir. nuc. engring. dept. mech. engring., 1975—2007, acting chmn. dept., 1984-85, adj. prof. civil engring., 1996—2007; expert in nuc. sci. Internat. Atomic Energy Agy., UN, 1980—; chief scientist Rogers and Assocs. Engring. Corp., Salt Lake City, 1980—90, sr. nuclear engr., 1998—; sr. health physicist URS Corp., 1990—; mgr., owner Applied Sci. Profls., LLC, Salt Lake City, 1998—. Vis. scientist MIT, Cambridge, Mass., 1969-70; advisor rocket design Hercules, Inc., Bachus, Utah, 1962; sr. nuc. engr. Idaho Nat. Engring. Lab., Idaho Falls, 1963-65; cons. nuc. sci. State of Utah, 1982—; vis. prof. Ben Gurion U., Beer Sheva, Israel, 1985, disting. vis. prof. U.S. Mil. Acad., West Point, N.Y., 2003-05; affiliate faculty Idaho State U., 1998-; cons. various cos.; spkr. Nuc. Energy Inst., 1990—; mem. radiation adv com., EPA. Author: Geothermal Energy, 1973, Introduction to System Science, 1985, over 700 pub. presentations, reports in sci. and tech. Comdr. USNR, 1954-56, Korea; ret. Comdr. USNR, 1954—56, Intel officer USNR. Recipient Glen Murphy award in nuc. engring. Am. Soc. Engring. Edn., 1984. Fellow ASME, Am. Nuc. Soc.; mem. Am. Soc. Quality (sr.), Am. Health Physics Soc., Am. Soc. Engring. Edn., Alpha Nu Sigma, Sigma Xi, Tau Beta Pi, Pi Tau Sigma. Republican. Mem. Lds Ch. Achievements include development of 17 major computer codes; participated in 200 technical meetings, conferences, Government hearings. Home: 2564 E Neffs Cir Salt Lake City UT 84109 Office: U Utah 2232 Merrill Engring Bldg Salt Lake City UT 84112 Home Phone: 801-273-0200; Office Phone: 801-904-4125.

SANDRA, G. KOENIG, school librarian; d. Gary and Maria G. Sutton; m. Darvin Sutton, June 12, 1993; children: Andrew Stephen Koenig, Christopher Allan Koenig. Degree in Elem. Edn., Toccoa Falls Coll., Ga., 1991. Cert. in libr. sci. Tex., 2001. Libr. La Joya ISD, Penitas, Tex., 1992—. Bible fellowship asst. coord. Calvary Bapt. Ch., Mcallen, Tex., 2004—08. Recipient Tex. Educator Excellence award, Tex. Edn. Agy., Best Buy. Office: La Joya ISD 1801 Diamond Ave Penitas TX 78576

SANDRIDGE, DONALD OTIS, music educator; b. Waynesboro, Va., Aug. 31, 1950; s. Otis Chester and Lucille Spitler Sandridge. Mus EdB, James Madison U., Harrisonburg, Va., 1973; MS in Edn., Old Dominion U., Norfolk, Va., 1983; Advanced Cert., Westminster Choir Coll., Princeton, NJ, 1986. Cert. Nat. Registered Music Educator 1985. Min. of music Bethany United Meth. Ch., Gloucester Point, Va., 1975—82, Orcutt Bapt. Ch., Newport News, Va., 1983—85, First Presbyn. Ch., Newport News, Va., 1988—94; dir. of choral activities Gloucester County Pub. Schs., Va., 1973—2004; ret. Chmn. fine arts dept. Gloucester H.S., Va., 1973—2004; chairperson Gloucester County Parks and Recreation Commn., 1999—; bd. dir. Hampton Rds. Educators Credit Union, v.p., 2007, treas., 08. Concert chmn. Mid. Peninsula Cmty. Concert Assn., Gloucester, Va., 1975—2001; state sponsor Nat. Beta Club (Va. chpt.); bd. dirs. Gloucester C. of C., 2005—06, v.p., 2007. Recipient Freedom Goode award, Gloucester County, Youth Adv. award, 30 Yr. Sponsor award, Nat. Beta Club. Mem.: Abingdon Ruritan Club (bd. dir. 2001—, v.p. 2007, pres. 2008). Presbyn. Home: PO Box 1271 7736 Points Pl Gloucester Point VA 23062 Personal E-mail: dotissinger@aol.com.

SANDRIDGE, WILLIAM PENDLETON, JR., lawyer; b. Winston-Salem, NC, Jan. 27, 1934; m. Jane Carolyn Yeager, Dec. 10, 1966; children: Jane, William. AB, U. N.C., 1956; LLB, U. Va., 1961. Bar: N.C. 1961. Mem. Womble Carlyle Sandridge & Rice, PLLC, Winston-Salem, 1962—. Chmn., bd. dirs. Horizons Residential Care Ctr., 1980, Food Bank N.W. N.C., Inc., 1988-89, Data Max Corp., 1996. Office: Womble Carlyle Et Al One W Fourth St Winston Salem NC 27101

SANDROK, RICHARD WILLIAM, lawyer; b. Evergreen Park, Ill., July 8, 1943; s. Edward George and Gertrude Jeanette (Van Stright) Sandrok; m. Rebecca Fittz, June 19, 1973; children: Richard William, Jr., Alexander Edward, Philip Robert, Erika Joy. BA, Wheaton Coll., Ill., 1965; JD, U. Ill., 1968. Bar: Ill. 1968, U.S. Dist. Ct. (no. dist.) Ill. 1971, ct. apptd. arbitrator: Cook, DuPage, Kane and Will counties. Assoc. Hinshaw Culbertson Moelmann Hoban & Fuller, Chgo. and Wheaton, 1971-75, ptnr. Wheaton, 1976-89, Lisle, Ill., 1989—2001; sole practice Glen Ellyn, Ill., 2001—. Arbitrator Ill. State Mandatory Arbitration. Reviewer: Legal Checklists. Capt. US Army, 1969—71. Mem.: Ill. Ct. Sys. Arbitrator, Assn. Def. Trial Attys., DuPage County Bar Assn. (chmn. med./legal com. 1978—79), Am. Arbitration Assn. (arbitrator). Home: 818 Revere Rd Glen Ellyn IL 60137-5537 Office: Richard W Sandrok Atty at Law 818 Revere Rd Glen Ellyn IL 60137 Office Phone: 630-790-1583. E-mail: RWS283@yahoo.com.

SANDS, ARTHUR T., biopharmaceutical executive, medical geneticist; BA in Econ. & Polit. Sci., Yale U.; MA, Baylor Coll. of Medicine, PhD, 1992. Former Am. Cancer Soc. postdoctoral fellow, dept. of human and molecular genetics Baylor Coll. of Medicine, 1992—95; co-founder (with Allan Bradley), pres., CEO Lexicon Pharms. (formerly Lexicon Genetics), The Woodlands, Tex., 1995—. Bd. mem. Tex. Inst. for Genomic Medicine. Recipient BioHouston Life Sci. award, 2004. Achievements include developing large-scale gene knockout technology for use in drug discovery. Office: Lexicon Pharms 8800 Technology Forest Pl The Woodlands TX 77381-1160 Office Phone: 281-863-3000. Office Fax: 281-863-8088.*

SANDS, HAROLD WINTHROP, banker, financial planner; b. NYC, Aug. 25, 1926; s. Harold Aymar and Muriel Winthrop Sands; m. Joan Hodges Baker, Sept. 6, 1961; children: Harold, Serena. Grad., St. George's Sch., 1946; student, CBS-NBS Tellers' Acad., 1950—52, Am. Inst. Banking, 1967—69; postgrad., Miami Dade U., 1968—71. V.p., devel. officer, regional mgr. S.E. Banks, Miami, London, Europe, Caribbean, 1967-79; v.p. Marine Midland Bank N.V., London, 1979-85; sr. cons., fin. adviser Sun Life Assurance Soc., London, 1985-87; U.K. rep. Wright Investment Svc., London, 1987-92; v.p. Kreditbank Global Mgmt., Miami, 1993-94; dir., trustee Kapok Bermuda Ltd., London, 1994-96; gen. ptnr. The Winthrop Group L.P., Newport, RI, 1996-2001; gen. mgr. Peace Mgmt. Group LLC, Newport, RI, 2002—. Founder Lorimex Internat., N.Y.C., 1952-60; CEO acctg., sales Paramount Pictures Corp., N.Y.C., 1950-52; founder, CEO Distbrs. for Mexico Rex Chain Belt, Ampudia A.S. Mex., 1960-67. Chair N.Am. com. London C. of C., 1985-88, chmn. Caribbean com., 1988-91; hon. treas. European Atlantic Group, 1980—; mem. Rep. Com.; mem. Woolnoth Soc. Coun., City of London, 1980-93; trustee La Farge Restoration Fund of Newport, 1996—; trustee Preservation Soc. Newport, mem. fin. and edn. coms., 1994-2000; com. mem. Tall Ships Salute, 1995; bd. dirs. Newport Hist. Soc., 2001-07. Master sgt. U.S. Army, 101st Armed Cav., 1949-54. Decorated Imperial House of David, 1995, Comdr. of Most Revered Order of the Star of Ethiopia, Freeman of the City of London. Mem.: SAR (Newport chpt.), Order of Founders and Patriots R.I. (gov.), The Worshipable Co. Internat. Bankers London (liveryman), Order of 1st Families of R.I. (gov.), Soc. Colonial Wars (Providence and Boston chpts., lt. gov.), RAC Club London, Ida Lewis Club (Newport, R.I.), Clambake Club, Reading Rm. Club (gov.), Ends of the Earth Club London, Broad St. Ward Club London, Rotary Internat., Pilgrim's London. Avocations: sailing, tennis, skiing, boating, chess. Home: 10 Cherry Creek Rd Newport RI 02840 Fax: 401-846-1066. Personal E-mail: hss6518@aol.com.

SANDS, JEFF MICHAEL, medical educator; s. Joseph and Jean Lillian Sands; m. Abbe Maureen Zorn, Nov. 23, 1986; children: Jared Samuel, Jenna Shari. BA summa cum laude, Harvard Coll., Cambridge, 1977; MD, Boston U., Mass., 1981. Diplomate internal medicine Am. Bd. Internal Medicine, 1984, nephrology Am. Bd. Internal Medicine, 1992. Asst. prof. medicine Emory U., Atlanta, 1989—93, assoc. prof. medicine, 1993—98, prof. medicine and physiology, 1998—, assoc. dean clinical and translational rsch., 2006—. Renal divsn. dir. Emory U., 2002—; exec. vice chair dept. medicine emory, 2009—. Editor-in-chief Am. Jour. Physiology, Bethesda, 2001—07. Rsch. grants, NIH, 1989—. Mem.: Am. Physiol. Soc. (councillor 2003—06), Am. Soc. Nephrology (program com. chmn. 2003—04), Am. Soc. Clin. Investigation, Am. Assn. Physicians. Achievements include research in renal physiology. Office: Emory U Renal Divsn WMB Rm 338 1639 Pierce Drive Atlanta GA 30322 Business E-Mail: jeff.sands@emory.edu.

SANDS, KEVIN B., cosmetic dentist; Grad., U. Southern Calif. Sch. Dentistry; grad. Advanced Anterior Aesthetic Dentistry, Las Vegas Institute for Advanced Dental Studies. Pvt. practice, Beverly Hills. Featured in Life & Style, InTouch, US, In Style Weddings, Item and others, featured on E! and TLC. Mem. Beverly Hills C. of C., Calif. Mem.: ADA, Acad. Cosmetic Dentistry, Calif. State Dental Assn. Office: 414 N Camden Dr Ste 940 Beverly Hills CA 90210 Office Phone: 310-273-0111. Office Fax: 310-271-0584.

SANDS, MATTHEW LINZEE, physicist, researcher; b. Oxford, Mass., Oct. 20, 1919; m. Freya Kidner, 1978; children: Michael, Richard, Michelle. BA, Clark U., 1940; MA, Rice U., 1941; PhD, MIT, 1948. Physicist U.S. Naval Ordnance Lab., 1941-43, Los Alamos Sci. Lab., 1943-46; research asso., then asst. prof. physics Mass. Inst. Tech., 1946-50; sr. research fellow, asso. prof., prof. physics Calif. Inst. Tech., 1950-63; prof., dep. dir. Linear Accelerator Center, Stanford, 1963-69; prof. physics U. Calif.-Santa Cruz, 1969-85, prof. emeritus, 1985—, fellow Kresge Coll.; vice chancellor for sci., 1969-72; pres. Sands-Kidner Assocs., Inc., 1986-90. Vis. prof. U. Paris-Sud, spring 1976; mem. Commn. Coll. Physics, 1960-66, chmn., 1964-66; cons. Office Sci. and Tech., ACDA, Inst. Def. Analyses, 1962-67; mem. Pugwash Conf. Sci. and World Affairs, 1960-63; cons. on accelerator physics, 1975-93. Author: (with W.C. Elmore) Electronics-Experimental Techniques, 1948, (with R.P. Feynman and R.B. Leighton) The Feynman Lectures on Physics, 3 vols, 1965, (with others) Physical Science Today, 1973; mem. editl. bd.: Il Nuovo Cimento, 1972-85; contbr. articles to profl. jours.

Fulbright scholar Italy, 1952-53. Fellow Am. Phys. Soc. (Robert R. Wilson prize 1998); mem. Am. Assn. Physics Tchrs. (Disting. Service award 1972), Fedn. Am. Scientists, AAAS. Achievements include research in electronic instrumentation for nuclear physics; electron storage rings; science and public affairs; science education; high-energy physics; accelerators; cosmic rays. Home: 160 Michael Ln Santa Cruz CA 95060-1704 Personal E-mail: mattsands@sbcglobal.net.

SANDS, MICHAEL LEE, infectious diseases physician; b. Newark, Jan. 6, 1947; married; 3 children. BA, Rutgers U., 1968; MD, Georgetown U., 1972; MPH, Tulane U., 1975. Diplomate Am. Bd. Internal Medicine, Am. Bd. Infectious Diseases, Am. Bd. Clin. Pathology/Microbiology; Cert. of Knowledge in Clin. Tropical Medicine. Med. intern St. Mary's Hosp. and Med. Ctr., San Francisco, 1972-73, resident in internal medicine, 1973-74; fellow in infectious diseases La. State U., New Orleans, 1975-77; internal medicine staff, infectious disease cons. Kaiser Found. Hosp., Honolulu, 1977-78; chief venereal disease control San Francisco Dept. Health, 1979-80; fellow in clin. microbiology Northwestern Meml. Hosp., Chgo., 1980-81; chief clin. microbiology VA Lakeside Med. Ctr., Chgo., 1981-83; dir. clin. microbiology Baystate Med. Ctr., Springfield, Mass., 1983-96; dir. communicable disease divsn. Duval County Health Dept., Jacksonville, Fla., 1996—. Venereologist City of New Orleans, 1975-77; dir. sexually transmitted diseases clinic Northwestern Med. Faculty Found., Chgo., 1981-83; cons. clin. mycology, clin. microbiology lab., Northwestern Meml. Hosp., 1981-83, attending infectious disease svc., 1981-83; attending infectious disease svc. VA Lakeside Med. Ctr., 1981-83; mem. infectious disease svc. dept. medicine Baystate Med. Ctr., 1983-96, dir. travelers vaccination and immunization svc., 1985-96, dir., prin. investigator NIH AIDS Clin. Trials group subunit, 1989-94; asst. vis. physician Charity Hosp., New Orleans, 1975-77, clin. instr. medicine U. Hawaii Sch. Medicine, Honolulu, 1978-79, attending physician infectious disease svc. dept. medicine San Francisco Gen. Hosp., 1979-80; asst. prof. pathology and medicine Northwesten U. Med. Sch., Chgo., 1981-83; asst. prof. medicine Tufts U. Sch. Medicine, 1983-96; clin. assoc. prof. medicine U. Fla., 1996—; head hosp. infection control Kaiser Found. Hosp., Honolulu, 1977-78; chief. venerial disease control San Francisco Dept. Health, 1979-80; chief clin. microbiolgy la. VA Lakeside Med. Ctr., Chgo., 1981-83; dir. sexually transmitted disease clinic Northwestern Med. Faculty Found., Chgo., 1981-83; dir. clin. microbiology lab., dir. outpatient infectious disease svcs., dir. Baystate Med. Ctr., Springfield., Mass, 1983-96; dir. com. dis. divsn. Duvan County Pub. Health, Jacksonville, 1996—; mem. internal medicine staff, infectious disease cons. Kaiser Found. Hosp., 1977-78, St. Mary's Hosp. and Med. Ctr., San Francisco, 1978-80; mem. attending staff internal medicine San Francisco Gen. Hosp., 1978-80; mem. infectious diseases and clin. microbiology staffs Northwestern Meml. Hosp., Chgo., 1981-83; mem. pathology staff VA Lakeside Med. Ctr., 1981-83; mem. continuing edn. com. San Francisco City Clinic, 1981-83; me. adv. com. on communicable diseases Adovcates for Pub. Health, Sacremento, Calif., 1981-83; mem. rsch. adv. bd. Howard Brown Meml. Clinic., Chgo., 1981-83; mem. infection control com., outpatient care com. Va Lakeside Med. Ctr., 1982-83; ad hoc grant reviewer Nat. Inst. Child and Human Devel., 1983, 92; mem. med. quality assurance com. Baystate Med. Ctr., internal medicine residency com., pathology coun., rsch. investigatos com., medicine rsch. com., AIDS multidusciplinary group com., chmn. AIDS clin. task force, AIDS partnership com., instl. rev. bd. Mem. Am. Soc. Microbiology, Am. Soc. Tropical Medicine and Hygiene, Wilderness Medicine Soc., Infectious Diseases Soc. Am., Internat. Soc. Travel Medicine. Avocations: scuba diving, underwater photography, Aikido, furniture refinishing, iaido. Office: Duval County Health Dept 515 W 69th St Jacksonville FL 32206

SANDS, RICHARD E., food products executive; b. Canandaigua, NY, Mar. 3, 1951; s. Marvin Sands and Marilyn Alpert; m. Sharon Gillick, Apr. 1991. BA, Univ. Vt., 1974; MA, Univ. NC, 1978, PhD, 1979. Teaching rsch. asst. psychology dept. U. N.C., Chapel Hill, 1974-79; exec. trainee Canandaigua Wine Co. Inc., 1979; exec. v.p. Constellation Brands, Inc., Fairport, NY, 1982-86, pres., COO, 1986—93, pres., CEO, 1993—2002, chmn., CEO, 2002—07, chmn., 2007—. Office: Constellation Brands Inc 207 High Point Dr # 100 Victor NY 14564-1061

SANDS, RICK (RICHARD SANDS), former film company executive; BA with honors in Economics and Film, Syracuse U. Regional sales mem. Columbia Pictures, v.p. domestic distbn. divsn., 1978; exec. v.p., CFO Miramax Films, 1990—93, RHI Entertainment (sold to Hallmark Entertainment), 1993—95; pres. internat. Miramax Films, 1995—97, chmn. worldwide distbn., 1997—2002, COO, 2002—04; pres., COO DreamWorks SKG, 2005—06; COO Metro-Goldwyn-Mayer Inc., LA, 2006—08. Trustee Will Rogers Motion Pictures Pioneers Found. Recipient Humanitarian award, Variety Boys and Girls Club of Queens, 2003.

SANDS, ROBERT, food products executive; b. Canandaigua, NY, June 10, 1958; B., Skidmore Coll., 1981; JD, Pace U. Sch. Law, 1984. CEO NY Wine and Culinary Ctr., Inc., NY; assoc. Harter, Secrest & Emery; v.p. Constellation Brands, Inc., Fairport, NY, 1990—93, gen. counsel, 1986—2000, exec. v.p., 1993—2000, CEO, internat., 1998—2000, group pres., 2000—02, COO, 2002—07, pres. Fairport, NY, 2002—, CEO, 2007—. Bd. dirs. NY Wine and Culinary Ctr., Inc., NY, Constellation Brands, Inc., 1990—. Pres. bd. trustees Harley Sch.; bd. trustees F.F. Thompson Health Sys.; chmn. bd. trustees ViaHealth Sys. Office: Constellation Brands Inc Bldg 100 207 High Point Dr Victor NY 14564-1061 Office Phone: 585-678-7100.*

SANDS, SHARON LOUISE, graphics designer, artist; b. Jacksonville, Fla., July 4, 1944; d. Clifford Harding Sands and Ruby May MacDonald; m. Jonathan Michael Langford, Feb. 14, 1988. BFA, Ctrl. Washington U., 1968; postgrad, UCLA, 1968. Art dir. East West Network, Inc., LA, 1973-78, Daisy Pub., LA, 1978; prodn. dir. L.A. mag., 1979-80; owner, creative dir. Carmel Graphic Design, Carmel Valley, Calif., 1981-85; creative dir., v.p. The Video Sch. House, Monterey, Calif., 1985-88; graphic designer ConAgra, Omaha, 1988; owner, creative dir. Esprit de Fleurs, Ltd., Carmel, Calif., 1988-99; owner Sweden by the Sea, Carmel, 1999—2001; owner, dir. Sands Art Studios, Penn Valley, Calif., 1999—. Lectr. Pub. Expo, LA, 1979; panelist Women in Mgmt., LA, 1979; designer corp. ID Carmel Valley CC, 1981, 90; redesign of local newspaper, Carmel, Calif., 82. One-woman shows include Ananda Retreat Ctr., Nevada City, Calif., 2004, Nevada City Winery, 2004, Lake Wildwood, 2006—09; contbr. articles to profl. mags. Recipient 7 design awards, Soc. Pub. Designers, 1977, 1978, Maggie award, LA, 1977, 5 Design awards, Ad Club Monterey Peninsula, 1983, 1985, 1987, Design awards, Print Mag. N.Y., 1986, Desi awards, N.Y., 1986, 1988, Oil Painting awards, Monterey Jazz Festival, 1999. Mem.: Sierra Club. Democrat. Avocations: oil painting, interior decorating, hiking. Home and Studio: Lake Wildwood 18807 Chaparral Dr Penn Valley CA 95946-9688

SANDS, VELMA AHDA, lawyer; d. John T. and Thelma Jane (Davis) Carlisle BS, Calif. State U., Dominguez Hills, 1976; JD, Southwestern U., 1985. CPA. Cons. KPMG Peat Marwick Main, LA, 1980—81; v.p. Security Pacific Bank, LA, 1981—86; contr. L.A. Investors, 1986; mgr. IRC divsn. FN Realty Svcs., Pasadena, Calif., 1986—88; mgr. fin. reporting Luz Internat. Ltd., LA, 1988—89; pvt. practice law LA, 1990—2004; staff counsel State Calif., 1992—; temp. judge L.A. Superior Ct., 1996—2004. Instr. Fame Entrepreneurial Tng. Program; co-pres. Multicultural Bar Alliance, 2001-02 Participant career day programs for local high schs.; mem. United We Stand Scholar Black Woman Lawyers Assn., 1982; recipient Commendation City of L.A., 2001, Cert. of Commendation, Gov. Calif. 2001, U.S. Senate 2001, Cert. of Recognition, Calif. State Assembly, 2001, Cert. Spl. Recognition, U.S. Rep. 2001, Cert. Congratulations Black Woman Lawyers Assn., 2002; Cert. Appreciation, Superior Ct. Calif., RBD Comm., Inc. award - 1st Ann., Samuel L. Williams Spirit of Law award for outstanding contbn. in field of law, 2001 Mem. ABA, NAFE, Nat. Assn. Bank Women (chair ways and means com. of scholarship fund 1986, scholar 1984), So. Calif. Chinese Lawyers Assn., L.A. County Bar Assn., John M. Langston Bar Assn. (pres. 2000, Pres.' Spl. Recognition award 1997, Appreciation award 2000), L.A. Bench and Bar Affiliates (scholarship com., meeting host, scholar 1983), Am. Bridge Assn., Phi Alpha Delta Office: 300 E Esplanade Dr 9th Fl Oxnard CA 93036 Home: 11130 Pine Ave Lynwood CA 90262-2960 Home Phone: 805-612-0891; Office Phone: 800-281-1622.

SANDSTEAD, HAROLD HILTON, physician, researcher, educator, director; b. Omaha, May 25, 1932; s. Harold Russel and Lula Florence (Hilton) S.; m. Kathryn Gordon Brownlee, June 6, 1959 (dec. May 13, 1989); m. Victoria Regan Liddle, Feb. 14, 1990 (div. Oct. 1993); m. Wilma Helen Carter Streaker, Sept. 25, 2004 (div. July 2008); children: Eleanor McDonald, James Brownlee, William Harold. BA in Pre-Medicine, Ohio Wesleyan U., 1954; MD, Vanderbilt U., 1958. Cert. Am. Bd. Internal Medicine, 1967, Am. Bd. Nutrition, 1967, Am. Bd. Physician Nutrition Specialists, 2001; lic. physician Tex. Intern, internal medicine Barnes Hosp. Washington U., St. Louis, 1958—59, asst. resident, internal medicine, 1959—60; asst. resident, pathology Vanderbilt U. Hosp., Nashville, 1960-61; asst. surgeon USPHS U.S. NAMRU 3, Cairo, 1961-63; rsch. resident, internal medicine Thayer VA Hosp., Vanderbilt U., Nashville, 1963-64; chief med. resident, internal medicine Vanderbilt U. Hosp., Nashville, 1964-65; instr. internal medicine, asst. prof. biochemistry Med. Sch. Vanderbilt U., Nashville, 1965-70, asst. prof. internal medicine, assoc. prof. biochemistry in nutrition, 1970-71; dir. USDA-ARS Human Nutrition Rsch. Ctr., Grand Forks, ND, 1971-84; adj. prof. biochemistry and internal medicine Sch. Medicine U. ND, Grand Forks, 1971-84; dir. USDA-ARS Human Nutrition Rsch. Ctr. on Aging at Tufts U., Boston, 1984-85; prof. nutrition Tufts U., Medford, Mass., 1984-85; prof. preventive medicine and community health U. Tex. Med. Br., Galveston, 1985—2006; chmn. preventive medicine and community health Med. Br. U. Tex., Galveston, 1985-90, prof. internal medicine, biochem. and molecular biology, 1986—2006, prof. emeritus preventative medicine and cmty. health and internal medicine, 2006—. Cons. IAEA, FAO, WHO, Internat. Programme on Chem. Safety, UN Environment Programme, Agency Internat. Devel., Nat. Cancer Inst., Nat. Inst. Child Health and Human Devel., Nat. Eye Inst., Nat. Heart, Lung, and Blood Inst., Officer Internat. Rsch., NIH, FDA, EPA, USDA, Food Nutrition Bd., NRC, Inst. Medicine, NAS. Life Sciences Rsch. Office, Fedn. Am. Societies Exptl. Biology, US Pharmacopeia, Am.Acad.Pediat., ACS, Am. Soc. Parenteral and Enteral Nutrition, Am. Health Found., Mead Johnson Co., Internat. Lead Zinc Rsch. Org., Nat. Cattlemen's Beef Assn., NeuroBioTex; clinician, Nutrition Survey Panama, Interdepartmental Com. Nutrition & Nat. Devel., NIH, 1967; field team dir., Texas Nutrition Survey, 10 State Nutrition Survey, US Nutrition Program, NIH, 1968; clinician, Kentucky Nutrition Survey, 10 State Nutrition Survey, US Nutrition Program, NIH, 1969; panel mem., White House Conf. on Food, Nutrition & Health, 1969, Am. Bd. Nutrition, 1975-81, USDA, ARS, human studies rev. com. (chmn., 83-85), 1976-85; rsch. adv. com., NSLS X-Ray Microprobe, Brookhaven Nat. Lab., 1984-90; advisor, Am. Coun. on Sci. & Health, 1988-; FASEB Wellcome vis. prof. in Basic Med. Sci., Pa. State U., 1988; zinc information nutrition ctr. adv. bd. Am. Zinc Assn., 1999-, Permanent Commn. on Occupl. Health, 2004-07. Mem. editl. bd. Jour. Nutrition, 1972-76, 81-85, Am. Jour. Clin. Nutrition, 1975-78, Annual Rev. Nutritional Rsch., 1975-1991, Jour. Lab. Clin. Medicine, 1978-1983, Biol. Trace Element Rsch., 1979—, Nutrition Rsch., 1981-85, Nutritional Reports Internat., 1981-88, Trace Elements Medicine Biology, 1983-98, Jour. Trace Elements Exptl. Medicine, 1982-2004, Jour. Am. Coll. Nutrition, 1987-88, Nutrition Rsch. Newsletter, 1989-98, Cancer Prevention, 1990-1994; contbr. over 300 articles to profl. jours., chapters to books. 4 ISI Citation Classics, asst. surgeon USPHS, 1961—63. Recipient Future Leader award, Nutrition Found., 1968—71, Hull Gold medal, with HC Meng, AMA, 1970, Special Recognition award, Vanderbilt U. Sch. Medicine, 1971, Mead Johnson award, Am. Inst. Nutrition, 1971, WO Atwater award medal and lecture, US Dept. Agr., 1984, Ellen Swallow Richard Meml. Lecture, U. NC Inst. Nutrition, 1985, Sam & Mary Roberts Nutrition medal and Lecture, U. Kans. Sch. Medicine, 1985, Raymond Ewell Meml. lecture, U. Buffalo, SUNY Sch. Medicine, 1985, Special Recognition award, USDA Agrl. Rsch. Svc., 2004. Fellow ACP, Am. Soc. Nutrition (Mead Johson award 1972, fellow 1998); mem. Am. Soc. Clin. Nutrition (pres. 1982-83), Internat. Soc. for Trace Element Rsch. in Humans (pres. 2002-04, Raulin award 2007), Cosmos Club, Sigma Xi, Alpha Omega Alpha. Achievements include description of adverse effects of lead poisoning on renin-aldoserone function, pituitary-adrenal function, and pituitary-thyroid function; description of zinc deficiency in Egyptian adolescents, endocrine functions, and effects of zinc treatment; confirmation in rat of essentiality of zinc for nucleic acid and protein synthesis; confirmation in rats of the essentiality of zinc for wound healing; demonstration of some effects of zinc deficiency on development and function of rat on brain and on function later in life; demonstration of essentiality of zinc for neuropsychological functions of children and premenopausal women; demonstration of inhibition of zinc absorption by folic acid, demonstration by zinc kinetics of associations between iron status by serum ferritin and zinc status and associations between zinc status by zinc kinetics and plasma zinc concentration in premenopausal women; demonstration of zinc deficiency among low-income pregnant black teenagers Mexican-American children and premenopausal US women. Office: U Tex Med Br Ewing Bldg Galveston TX 77555-1109 Home: 77005 Seawall Blud 407 Galveston TX 77551 Office Phone: 409-772-4661. Business E-Mail: hsandste@utmb.edu.

SANDSTROM, DALE VERNON, state supreme court justice; b. Grand Forks, ND, Mar. 9, 1950; s. Ellis Vernon and Hilde Geneva (Williams) Sandstrom; m. Gail Hagerty, Mar. 27, 1993; children: Jack, Carrie, Anne. BA, ND State U., 1972; JD, U. ND, 1975. Bar: ND 1975, US Dist. Ct. ND 1975, US Ct. Appeals (8th cir.) 1976. Asst. atty. gen., chief consumer fraud & antitrust divsn. State of ND, Bismarck, 1975-81, securities commr., 1981-83, pub. svc. commr., 1983-92, pres. pub. svc. commn., 1987-91; justice ND Supreme Ct., Bismarck, 1992—. Chair ND Commn. on Cameras in the Courtroom, 1993—, Joint Procedure Com., 1996—, mem. adminstrv. coun., 2005-; mem. exec. com. ND Jud. Conf., 1995—, chair-elect, 1997-99, chair, 1999-2001; mem. Gov.'s Com. on Security and Privacy, Bismarck, 1975-76, Gov.'s Com. on Refugees, Bismarck, 1976; chmn. Gov's Com. on Comml. Air Transp., Bismarck, 1983-84. Mem. platform com. ND Reps., 1972, 76, exec. com., 1972-73, 85-88, dist. chmn., 1981-82; former chmn. bd. deacons Luth. Ch.; mem. ch. coun., exec. com., chmn. legal and constl. rev. com. Evang. Luth Ch. Am., 1993—; mem. exec. bd. dirs., No. Lights Coun., dist. chair Boy Scouts America, 1998-2000. Named Disting. Eagle Scout, Boy Scouts America, 1997, Master of Coll. Arts, Humanities, & Social Scis., ND State U., 2002; recipient Cmty. Svc. award, ND State Bar Assn., 2002. Mem. ABA, ND Bar Assn., Big Muddy Bar Assn., Nat. Assn. Regulatory Utility Commrs. (electricity com.), N.A. Assn. Securities Adminstrs., Order of De Molay (grand master 1994-95, mem. Internat. Supreme coun., Legion of Honor award), Nat. Eagle Scouts Assn. (regent for life), Shriners, Elks, Eagles, Masons (33d degree, chmn. grand youth com. 1979-87, Youth Leadership award 1986), Bruce M. VanSickle Am. Inn of Court (pres. 1999-2001), ND Judges Assn. (v.p. 2005-). Office: State ND Supreme Ct Judicial Wing 1st Fl 600 E Boulevard Ave Bismarck ND 58505 Office Phone: 701-328-2221. Business E-Mail: DSandstrom@ndcourts.com.*

SANDSTRÖM, SIGRID, painter; b. Stockholm, 1970; Student, Cooper Union for the Advancement Sci. and Art, 1995; BFA, Acad. Minerva, Groningen, Netherlands, 1997; student, Skowhegan Sch. Painting and Sculpture, Maine, 2000; MFA Alice Kimball English traveling fellowship, Yale U., 2001. Asst. prof. studio arts Bard Coll., Annandale-on-Hudson, NY, 2005—. One-man shows include I Know Where I'm Going, Inman Gallery, Houston, 2002, Ginnungagap, 2004, Action, 2006, New Paintings, 2008, Tillflykter, Galleri Gunnar Olsson, Stockholm, 2003, Hrönir, 2004, Märkt, 2007, Sighting, Brant Gallery, Mass. Coll. Art, Boston, 2004, Her Black Flags, Mills Coll. Art Mus., Oakland, Calif., 2005, Ginnungagap, Frye Mus., Seattle, 2006, Recent Paintings, Edward Thorp Gallery, NYC, 2007, exhibited in group shows at Pertaining to Painting, Contemporary Art Mus., Houston, 2003, Edge of Darkness, LeRoy Neiman Gallery, Columbia U., 2005, Aqua, Inman Gallery, Miami, 2006, Probably, Inman Gallery, Houston, 2008, Gallery Artists, Edward Thorp Gallery, NYC, 2007, Learning by Doing, Mus. Fine Arts, Houston, 2008. Recipient Culture award, Am.'s Soc., NYC, 1997, Eliza Randall prize, 2002, 2003, Artadia award, 2003; grantee De Groote Brugmans Fond, Groningen, 1995, Anna Whitlocks Minnesfond, Stockholm, 2000; fellow Glassell Sch. Art, Mus. Fine Arts, Houston, 2001—03, Stiftelsen Längmanska Kulturfonden, Stockholm, 2003, Barbro Osher Found., 2004, John Simon Guggenheim Meml. Found., 2008. Office: Dept Studio Arts Bard Coll Annandale On Hudson NY 12504 Office Phone: 845-758-7679. E-mail: sandstrom@bard.edu, sigridsandstrom@yahoo.com.*

SANDUM, ALLAN IRA, retired biology educator; b. Mpls., Apr. 22, 1939; s. Carl A. and Stella E. Sandum; m. Vondal Juliene Howell, June 20, 1975; children: Erica Nicole, Jessica Dawn, Randall L., Tina C. Thompson. BS, BA, U. Minn., Mpls., MS, 1966. Cert. secondary tchr. Ariz. State, 1964. Jr. high sci. tchr. Twin Falls, Idaho, 1664—1966; biology tchr. Tucson Unified Sch. Dist., 1966—94, Prima Jr. Coll., Tucson, 1994—2004. Democrat. Avocations: bicycling, hiking. Home: 895 Saturn Dr Chino Valley AZ 86323 Office: Yavapai Coll 1100 E Sheldon St Prescott AZ 86301 Personal E-mail: avsandum@cableone.net.

SANDVICK, JANET ROSE, history educator; b. Cleve., Oct. 30, 1959; d. Thomas John and Judith Diane Leonti; m. Scott Joseph Sandvick, June 13, 1984; children: Maureen, Stephanie, Scott M. BE, Baldwin Wallace Coll., Berea, Ohio, 1993, MEd, 1997. Cert. tchr. 1-8, elem. adminstrn. Ohio, mid. adminstrn. Ohio. 6th grade tchr. Applewood Elem., Brunswick, Ohio, 1993—97; 7th grade history tchr. Willetts Mid. Sch., Brunswick, 1997—99, at risk 8th grade tchr., 2000—01, 8th grade history tchr., 2001—; adminstrv. intern Brunswick City Schs., 1999—2000, subject area coord., 2003—06. Mem.: Ohio Mid. Sch. Assn., Ctrl. Ohio Saddle Club Assn., Appaloosa Horse Club. Home: 6751 Spring Glen Dr Valley City OH 44280 Office: Willetts Mid Sch 1045 Hadcock Rd Brunswick OH 44212

SANDWELL, DAVID, geophysicist, educator; BS in Physics, U. Conn., 1975; MS in Geophysics, UCLA, 1978, PhD in Geophysics and Space Physics, 1981. Rsch. geophysicist Nat. Geodetic Survey, 1982—85; rsch. scientist U. Tex., Austin, 1985—89; assoc. prof. geophysics Scripps Inst. Oceanography, La Jolla, Calif., 1989—93, prof. geophysics, 1993—. Fellow: Am. Acad. Arts and Sciences, Geol. Soc. America (George P. Woollard award 2004), Am. Geophys. Union (pres. elect geodesy sect. 2008, Bowie lecture 1995); mem.: Soc. Exploration Geophysics, Internat. Assn. Geodesy. Office: Scripps Inst Oceanography UC San Diego 9500 Gilman Dr La Jolla CA 92093-0225 Office Phone: 858-534-7109. E-mail: dsandwell@ucsd.edu.

SANDWELL, KRISTIN ANN, special education educator; b. Topeka, Jan. 13, 1955; d. Edwin C. and E. Maxine (Nelson) Henry; m. Steve Sandwell, Dec. 27, 1997; children: Dustin Grimm, Chris Creek, Brandon Grimm, Sarah Sandwell, Paul Sandwell. AA, Hutchinson CC, Kans., 1986; BS, McPherson Coll., Kans., 1989; MEd, Wichita State U., 1992. Cert. tchr. elem., gifted. Math/parenting tchr. Flint Hills Job Corps Ctr., Manhattan, Kans., 1992; gifted facilitator Unified Sch. Dist. 353, Wellington, Kans., 1993-94, Unified Sch. Dist. 260, Derby, Kans., 1995-97; tchr. City of Wichita Summer Youth Employment Program-Edn., 1997—98; gifted facilitator Unified Sch. Dist. 259, 1998—. Head injury counselor, life skills trainer Three Rivers Ind. Living Ctr., Wamego, Kans., 1992; facilitator Summer Youth Employment Edn. Program, 1997-98. Epiphany Festival prodr. Trinity Luth. Ch., McPherson, 1991, 93; CASA organizer McPherson Coll., 1988-89; vol. Coun. on Violence Against Persons, McPherson, 1990-92. Mem. ASCD. Avocations: reading, travel, working with disability issues. Office Phone: 316-973-6450. Personal E-mail: ksandwell@yahoo.com.

SANDY, JOHN A., legislative staff member; b. Twin Falls, Idaho, June 8, 1948; m. Robin Sandy; 1 child, Alex McConnell. BS in Agr., U. Idaho. Farmer; senator, dist. 22 Idaho State Senate, Boise, 1995—2002, asst. majority leader; chair Idaho Bond Bank, Boise; chief of staff Gov. James Risch, Idaho, 2006—08; chief of staff to Senator James Risch US Senate, Washington, 2009—. Mem. agrl. affairs, state affairs, edn., transp. coms. Idaho State Senate; mem. exec. bd. Nat. Coun. State Governments; Idaho rep., vice chair We. States Coun. State Govt., 1992—98. Former chmn. Idaho Rep. Party. Republican. Methodist. Office: Office US Senator James E Risch Russell Senate Office Bldg Washington DC 20510 Office Phone: 202-224-2752. Business E-Mail: john_sandy@risch.senate.gov.*

SANDY, LEWIS GORDON, physician, healthcare executive; b. Detroit, July 18, 1958; s. William Haskell and Marjorie Mindel (Mazor) S.; m. Kathleen Anne Morgan, June 17, 1984; children: Matthew, Natalie, Jonah. BS, U. Mich., 1979, MD, 1982; MBA, Stanford U., 1988. Diplomate Am. Bd. Internal Medicine, Nat. Bd. Med. Examiners. Intern Beth Israel Hosp., Boston, 1982-83, resident, 1983-85; Robert Wood Johnson clin. scholar U. Calif., San Francisco, 1985-86, clin. fellow in medicine, 1986-88; instr. Harvard Med. Sch., 1988-91; assoc. chief internal medicine Harvard Community Health Plan, Boston, 1988-89, dir. Health Ctr., 1989-91; v.p. Robert Wood Johnson Found., Princeton, NJ, 1991—96, exec. v.p., 1997—2003, UnitedHealthcare, Edina, Minn.,

2003—07; sr. v.p. UnitedHealth Group, Minnetonka, Minn., 2007—; sr. fellow U. Minn. Sch. Pub. Health, 2004—; bd. dirs. America Health Ins. Plans, 2007—09. Cons. Kaiser Found. Health Plan, Oakland, Calif., 1987-88. Fellow ACP; mem. AMA, Soc. Gen. Internal Medicine, Acad. Health, Alpha Omega Alpha. Home: 4800 Sunnyslope Rd E Edina MN 55424 Office: 9900 Bren Rd E Minnetonka MN 55343

SANDY, WILLIAM HASKELL, training and communication systems executive; b. NYC, Apr. 28, 1929; s. Fred and Rose S.; m. Marjorie Mazor, June 15, 1952; children: Alan, Lewis, Barbara. AB, U. Md., 1950, JD, 1953; postgrad. Advanced Mgmt. program, Harvard Bus. Sch., 1970—71. Bar: Md. 1953. From planner-writer to acct. supr. Jam-Handy Orgn., Detroit, 1953—64, v.p., 1964—69, sr. v.p., 1969—71; pres. Sandy Corp., Troy, Mich., 1971—88, chmn., 1988—96; pres. Rudgate Corp., Bloomfield Hills, Mich., 1996—. Bd. dirs. U. Mich. Press, Asolo Repertory Theatre. Author: Forging the Productivity Partnership, 1990. Bd. govs. Northwood Inst., 1976-80; bd. dirs. Cranbrook Sci. Inst., Met. Ctr. High Tech., 1993, Birmingham (Mich.) Cmty. House, 1997-2003, Mich. Opera Theatre; pres. Graphic Arts Coun., 1992-93; trustee Detroit Inst. Arts, 1992-93; v.p. nat. exec. coun. Harvard Bus. Sch., 1985-89; mem. Bloomfield Hills Zoning Bd., Walsh Coll. Leader in Residence, Pres.'s Adv. Coun.; mayor City of Bloomfield Hills, 1996-97; mem. Troy Downtown Devel. Authority, 1996-99; Inst. for Humanities trustee U. Mich. Mem. Am. Mktg. Assn. (pres. Detroit chpt. 1975), Nat. Found. Am. Mktg. Assn (bd. dirs. 1998), S.E. Mich. BBB (bd. dirs. 1999), Adcraft Club, Harvard Bus. Sch. Club (pres. Detroit chpt. 1983-85). Home (Summer): 596 Rudgete Rd Bloomfield Hills MI 48304 Home Phone: 941-383-6837, 248-540-2001. Personal E-mail: sandyfamily@aol.com.

SANES, JOSHUA RICHARD, neurobiologist, researcher, educator; b. Buffalo, Sept. 5, 1949; s. Irving and Carlyn (Mildred) S.; m. Susan Corcoran, Dec. 27, 1982; children: Jesse, Amelia. BA, Yale U., 1970; MA, PhD, Harvard U., 1976. With US Congress, Office of Tech. Assessment, 1976—77, U. Calif., San Francisco; asst. prof., dept. physiology Washington U. Med. Sch., St. Louis, 1980-85, assoc. prof., 1985-89, alumni endowed prof. neurobiology, dept. anatomy and neurobiology, 1989; prof. molecular and cellular biology Harvard U., Cambridge, Mass., Paul J. Finnegan Family dir., Ctr. for Brain Neuroscience, Dept. Molecular and Cellular Biology, 2005—. Mem. neurology study sect. NIH, Washington, 1988; mem. nat. adv. coun., Nat. Inst. Neurological Disorders and Stroke, NIH, 1999-2003; mem. adv. com., human embryonic stem cell rsch., NRC and Inst. Medicine, 2006-; mem. scientific adv. bd. Stowers Inst. for Med. Rsch., 2006-, Searle Scholar program, Max-Planck Inst. for Neurobiology in Munich, Howard Hughes Med. Inst. Contbr. articles to profl. jours.; mem. editl. bd. Cell, Journal of Cell Biology, Neuron Fellow AAAS, Am. Acad. Arts & Scis.; mem. NIH (bd. sci. counselor 1993—), Soc. for Neurosci. (councilor 1990—), Muscular Dystrophy Assn. (scientific adv. bd. 1991—), NAS. Office: Harvard U Sherman Fairchild Bldg 7 Divinity Ave Rm 143 Cambridge MA 02138 Office Phone: 617-496-8683. Office Fax: 617-496-9590. Business E-Mail: sanesj@mcb.harvard.edu.

SANETO, RUSSELL PATRICK, pediatric neurologist, epileptologist, neurobiologist; b. Burbank, Calif., Oct. 10, 1950; s. Arthur and Mitzi (Seddon) S.; m. Kathleen D. Saneto. BS with honors, San Diego State U., 1972, MS, 1975; PhD, U. Tex. Med. Br., 1981; DO, U. Osteo. Medicine and Surgery, 1994. Tchg. asst. San Diego State U., 1969-75; substitute tchr. Salt Lake City Sch. Dist., 1975; tchg. and rsch. asst. U. Tex. Med. Br., 1976-77, NIH predoctoral fellow, 1977-81, postdoctoral fellow, 1981; Jeanne B. Kempner postdoctoral fellow UCLA, 1981-82, NIH postdoctoral fellow, 1982-87; asst. prof. divsn. neurosci. Oreg. Regional Primate Rsch. Ctr., Beaverton, 1987-89; asst. prof. dept. cell biology and anatomy Oreg. Health Scis. U., Portland, 1988-90, U. Osteo. Medicine and Surgery, 1991-94, Cleve. Clinic, 1994-2001; assoc. prof. neurology and pediat. U. Wash. Seattle Children's Hosp., 2001—. Lectr. rsch. methods Grad. Sch., 1982; vis. scholar in ethics So. Bapt. Theol. Sem., Louisville, 1981; sci. advisor United Mitochondrial Disease Found. Mem. editl. bd. Epilepsy.com, Pediat. Neurology; contbr. articles to profl. jours. Mem. scientific adv. bd. United Mitochondrial Disease Found., Northwest Epilepsy Found., Hemispherectomy Found.; Herrisg sec. found. Mitochondrial Medicine Soc., 2007—08. Recipient Merit award Nat. March of Dimes, 1978; named one of Outstanding Young Men in Am., 1979, 81, one of Men of Significance, 1985. Mem. AAAS, Am. Acad. Pediats., Am. Acad. Neurology, Am. Epilepsy Soc., Bread for World, Winter Cofs. Brain Rsch., Neuroscis. Study Program, N.Y. Acad. Scis., Am. Soc. Neurochemistry, Soc. Neurosci., Sigma Sigma Phi. Democrat. Mem. Evangelical Free Ch. Office: Univ Wash Seattle Children's Neurology B-5552 4800 Sand Point Way NE Seattle WA 98105

SANETTI, STEPHEN LOUIS, lawyer; b. Flushing, NY, June 25, 1949; s. Alfred Julius Sanetti and Yolanda Marie (DiGioia) Boyes; m. Carole Leighton Koller, Sept. 21, 1974; children: Christopher Edward, Dana Harrison. BA in History with honors, Va. Mil. Inst., 1971; JD, Washington and Lee U., 1974. Bar: Conn. 1975, U.S. Ct. Mil. Appeals 1975, U.S. Dist. Ct. Conn. 1978, U.S. Ct. Appeals (2d cir.) 1979, U. S. Supreme Ct. 1980. Litigation atty. Marsh, Day & Calhoun, Bridgeport, Conn., 1978-80; gen. counsel Sturm, Ruger & Co., Southport, Conn., 1980—2008, v.p., 1993-2000, bd. dirs., 1998—2008, sr. exec. v.p., 2000—03, vice chmn., 2000—03, pres., COO, 2003—08. Dir. Product Liability Adv. Coun., 1988-2002; tech. advisor Assn. Firearm and Toolmark Examiners; chmn. Legis. and Legal Affairs com. Sporting Arms and Ammunition Mfrs. Inst., 1993-2001, pres., CEO, 2008-; bd. govs. Nat. Shooting Sports Found., Newtown, Conn., 2002-08, pres., CEO 2008-. Served to capt., chief criminal law 1st Cavalry Div. Staff Judge Advocate, U.S. Army, 1975-78. Mem. Am. Acad. Forensic Sci., Def. Rsch. Inst. Republican. Roman Catholic. Office: Nat Shooting Sports Found 11 Mile Hill Rd Newtown CT 06470

SANFELICI, ARTHUR H(UGO), editor, writer; b. Haledon, NJ, May 23, 1934; s. Hugo and Anna (Schilder) S.; m. Betty Louise Van Riper, Aug. 10, 1957; children: Brian Arthur, Amy Elizabeth, Gary Hugh, Bruce Richard. Attended, Lehigh U., 1952-55. Assoc. editor Flying Mag., NYC, 1961-64; mng. editor Am. Aviation Mag., Washington, 1964-68; dist. sales mgr. Gates Learjet Co., NYC, 1969-71; exec. editor Airport World Mag., Westport, Conn., 1971-74; spl. project editor Aircraft Owners & Pilots Assn., Washington, 1974-75, mng. editor Pilot mag., 1975-79, editor AOPA Newsletter, AOPAirport Report, Gen. Aviation Nat. Report, 1979-88; pub. cons., 1989-90; sr. editor Flight Safety Found., Washington, 1989-92; editor S-Cubed divsn. Maxwell Labs., Alexandria, Va., 1992-95; comms. dir. Helicopter Assn. Internat., Alexandria, 1996-97; editor Shooting Sports USA, 1997-98. Editor, compiler: Yesterday's Wings; editor emeritus Aviation History Mag., Leesburg, Va., 1990—; author: 135 Ways to Get Even With Your Kids, 2003. Pilot USAF, 1955—60. Mem. Aeronautic Assn., Aero Club of Washington, Soc. Aerospace Comms. Home: 44476 Oakmont Manor Sq Ashburn VA 20147

SANFILIPPO, ANTONIO, chief scientist; b. Partanna, Italy, Aug. 26, 1956; s. Angelo Sanfilippo and Cecilia Ternini; m. Charlotte Boynton, May 6, 1983. Laurea, U. Palermo, Italy, 1979; MA, Columbia U., NYC, 1982, MPhil, 1986; PhD, U. Edinburgh, Eng., 1989. Dir., rsch. strategy & planning Textology Ltd., Herzelia, Israel, 2002—03; chief scientist Pacific NW Nat. Lab., Richland, Wash., 2003—. Rsch. assoc. U. Edinburgh, 1989—90, U. Cambridge, England, 1990—92; rsch. supr., mgr. SHARP Lab. Europe, Oxford, England, 1992—98; sr. cons. European Commn., Luxembourg, 1998—2000; dir., advanced devel. LingoMotors Inc., Cambridge, Mass., 2000—01; dir., text mining SRA Internat., Fairfax, Va., 2001—02. Recipient Lab. Director's award, Pacific NW Nat. Lab., 2008. Achievements include patents pending for method and system for disambiguating syntactic word multiples; methods and apparatuses for cross-ontological analytics; research in leading five year project on pathway prediction in stroke pathobiology funded by the National Health Institutes; led a consortium of national laboratories that established the motivation and intent thrust research area at the department of homeland security, science and technology directorate. Office: Pacific NW Nat Lab 902 Battelle Blvd PO Box 999 Richland WA 99352 Office Phone: 509-375-2677. Office Fax: 509-375-2443. Business E-Mail: antonio.sanfilippo@pnl.gov.

SANFILIPPO, FRED PAUL, academic administrator, medical educator, pathologist; b. Racine, Wis., Aug. 30, 1949; s. Paul Joseph and Therese (Rhode) Sanfilippo; m. Janet Lee Thompson, 1973; children: Lisa, Joseph. Student, Max Planck Inst. Exptl. Medicine, Gottingen, Germany, 1966—68; BA in Physics, MS in Physics, U. Pa., 1970; PhD in immunology, Duke U., 1975, MD, 1976. Diplomate Am. Bd. Pathology, lic. physician NC, Md. Intern in anatomic pathology Duke U. Hosp., 1976—77, resident in anatomic and clin. pathology, 1977—79, postdoctoral rschr. divsn. tumor virology dept. surgery, 1976—79; asst. prof. pathology and exptl. surgery, lectr. immunology Duke U., 1979—84, from assoc. prof. to prof. pathology, 1984—93, from assoc. prof. to prof. exptl. surgery, 1985—93, prof. immunology, 1990—93; attending pathologist Duke U. and Durham VA Hosps., 1979—93; staff mem. Duke Surg. Pvt. Diagnostic Clinic, 1979—93; dir. Transplantation Lab Durham VA Hosp., 1979—93; dir. immunopathology Duke U. Med. Ctr., 1982—93, exec. com. dept. pathology, 1989—91; Baxley Prof. and chair pathology dept. John's Hopkins U., Balt., 1993—2000; pathologist-in-chief Johns Hopkins Hosp., Balt., 1993—2000; sr. v.p. health scis. Ohio State U., Columbus, 2000—, exec. dean health scis., 2004—, dean. coll. medicine; CEO Ohio State U. Med. Ctr.; exec. v.p. health affairs, CEO Woodruff Health Scis. Ctr., chmn. Emory Healthcare Emory U., 2007—. Mem. Duke Comprehensive Cancer Ctr., 1979—93; dir. rsch. Johns Hopkins Comprehensive Transplant Ctr.; mem. Third Frontier Commn. Adv. Bd., Ohio, 2004—; cons. Battelle Human Affairs Rsch. Ctrs., Seattle, 1985—93, NSF of Switzerland, 1992—93, numerous US govt. adv. coms.; mem. editl. bd. Transplantation, 1985—, Pathobiology, 1989—, Transplantation Now, Japan, 1989—, Pathology, Rsch. and Practice, 1990—, Human Immunology, 1992—, Lab. Investigation, 1993—, Xeno, 1994—, Virchows Archiv, 1998—, Transplant Immunology; reviewer Am. Jour. Kidney Diseases, Am. Jour. Ophthalmology, Am. Jour. Pathology, New Eng. Jour. Medicine, Jour. of AMA, Jour. Am. Soc. Nephrology, Jour. Clin. Investigation, Jour. Leukocyte Biology, Kidney Internat., others; contbr. numerous articles to prof. jours.; speaker and presenter in field. Bd. trustees Omeris, Columbus, Ohio, 2004—. Recipient Kermit G. Osserman Award, Myasthenia Gravis Found., 1976, Wiley D. Forbus Award, NC Soc. Pathologists, 1979, Reach for Sight Physician Investigator Award, 1990; grantee numerous, NIH. Fellow: Am. Soc. Clin. Pathologists (coun. on edn. and rsch. 1994—96); mem.: Southeastern Organ Procurement Found. (exec. com 1992—97, sec. 1992—93, treas. 1993—94, v.p. 1994—95, pres. 1995—96), Assn. for Rsch. in Vision and Ophthalmology, Am. Soc. Nephrology, Am. Soc. Transplant Physicians (pres. 1985—86), Am. Soc. Histocompatibility and Immunogenetics, Transplantation Soc., US-Can. Acad. Pathology, Am. Assn. Med. Colls., Am. Assn. Immunologists, AMA, Am. Soc. Investigative Pathology (pres. 2002—03), Intersociety Pathology Coun., Assn. Pathology Chairs (sr. fellow), Am. Soc. Transplantation (past pres.), Alpha Omega Alpha. Office: Emory U Woodruff Health Scis Ctr 1440 Clifton Rd Atlanta GA 30322 Office Phone: 404-778-0234. Office Fax: 404-778-3100. E-mail: fred.sanfilippo@emory.edu.*

SANFORD, BEVERLY SHAW, museum director; m. Don Sanford; 3 children. BS in Health and Phys. Edn., Wake Forest U., Winston-Salem, NC, 1970; MH in Human Devel. and Learning, U. NC, Charlotte, 1980; PhD in Edn., Pacific Western U., LA, 1997. Tchr. Charlotte-Mecklenburg Schs., 1970—81; life ctr. coord., 1981—84; dir., programs and edn. Sci. Mus. of Charlotte, Inc., 1984—91; v.p., programs and edn. Discovery Pl., Inc., 1991—95; exec. dir. SciWorks, 1996—. Adj. instr. Gardner-Webb Coll., 1988, U. NC, Charlotte, 1995. Bd. dirs. YMCA of Northwest NC; mem. bd. advisors Wake Forest U. Sch. Medicine Ctr. Excellence Rsch., Tchg. and Learning; bd. dirs. Forsyth County Tourism Devel. Authority. Mem.: NC Grassroots Sci. Mus. (pres. 1999—2001, bd. dirs.), Assn. Sci. Tech. Ctrs. (bd. dirs.), NC Mus. Coun. (pres. 1996—98, bd. dirs.), Southeastern Mus. Coun. (bd. dirs.), Winston-Salem Rotary Club. Office: SciWorks Sci Ctr and Environ Pk 400 W Hanes Mill Rd Winston Salem NC 27105 Office Phone: 336-767-6730. Office Fax: 336-661-1777. Business E-Mail: bssanford@sciworks.org.

SANFORD, DAVID BOYER, journalist, editor; b. Denver, Mar. 4, 1943; s. Filmore Bowyer and Alice Irene (Peterson) S. BA with honors, U. Denver, 1964; MS in Journalism with honors, Columbia U., 1965. With New Republic mag., Washington, 1965-76, mng. editor, 1970-76, Politics Today (formerly Skeptic), Santa Barbara, Calif., 1976-78, contbg. editor, 1978-79; editorial writer Los Angeles Herald Examiner, 1978-79; mng. editor Harper's mag., NYC, 1979-80; editor Wall St. Jour. mag., 1980-81; sr. spl. writer Wall Street Jour., 1981—. Syndicated columnist, 1970-71; commentator Can. Broadcasting Corp., 1967-76; judge Heywood Broun award Newspaper Guild, 1971; mem. print screening com. Champion-Tuck awards, 1985, 86, Judge Wuxtry award, 1990. Author: Who Put the Con in Consumer?, 1972, Me and Ralph, 1976; editor, co-author: Hot War on the Consumer, 1970. Recipient Sackett Law prize, Columbia, 1965, Eckenberg prize, 1965, Gold award, NY Art Dirs. Club, 1977, Wuxtry award for disting. achievement in headline writing, Internat. Soc. for Gen. Semantics, 1989, Pulitzer prize, 1997, Sci.-in-Soc. award, Nat. Assn. Sci. Writers, 1997, disting. headline writing award, NY Newspaper Publisher award, 2007, Needline Writing award, 2008; Centennial scholar, 1960—64, NY Newspaper Guild fellow, 1964—65. Mem. Phi Beta Kappa, Omicron Delta Kappa, Am. Assn. Sunday & Feature Editors. Democrat. Home: 118 Prospect Park W Brooklyn NY 11215-4270 Office Phone: 212-416-2597. Personal E-mail: david.sanford@wsj.com.

SANFORD, DOUGLAS WALKER, archaeologist, educator; b. Alexandria, Va., Mar. 23, 1952; s. Harry Walker and Virginia Roberta Sanford; m. Juliet Dickinson Womack; 1 child, Sarah Dickinson. BA in Anthropology, Coll. William and Mary, Williamsburg, Va., 1974; MA in Am. Civilization, U. Pa., Phila., 1979; PhD in Anthropology, U. Va., Charlottesville, 1995. Asst. archaeologist Monticello, Thomas Jefferson Meml. Found., Charlottesville, 1979—84; dir. Ctr. Hist. Preservation U. Mary Washington, Fredericksburg, Va., 1997—2005, assoc. prof., 2001—; asst. prof. Mary Washington Coll., Fredericksburg, 1994—2001. Grant, NEH, 2007—09. Mem.: Mid. Atlantic Archeol. Conf. (rec. sec. 1995—2004), Soc. Hist. Archaeology. Achievements include research in African American archaeology. Office: Univ Mary Washington 1301 College Ave Fredericksburg VA 22401 Business E-Mail: dsanford@umw.edu.

SANFORD, KIMBERLY LYNN, social sciences educator; d. Harold and Lynda Joyce Sanford. MA in Social Sci., Miss. Coll., Clinton, 1991. Social sci. instr. Miss. Delta CC, Moorhead, Miss., 2000—. Office: Mississippi Delta CC Po Box 668 Moorhead MS 38761

SANFORD, LINDA S., information technology executive; b. Jan. 21, 1953; d. William J. and Catherine A. Sanford; 2 children. BA, St. John's U., NY; MS in Ops. Rsch., Rensselaer Poly. Inst., Troy, NY. From mem. staff to gen. mgr. IBM, Westchester, NY, 1975—98, gen. mgr., global industries, 1998—2000, sr. v.p., group exec., storage systems group, 2000—03, sr. v.p. enterprise on demand transformation and info. tech. Somers, 2003—. Mem. bd. dirs. ITT Industries, 1998—. Bd. dirs. St. John's U., Rensselaer Poly. Inst., Bus. Coun. of NY State. Named one of 50 Most Influential Women in Bus., Fortune Mag., Top 10 Innovators in Tech. Industry, Info. Week Mag., 10 Most Influential Women in Tech., Working Woman Mag., Most Influential Women in Technology, Fast Company, 2009; named to Women in Tech. Internat. Hall of Fame. Mem.: NAE. Office: IBM Corp Rte 100 Somers NY 10589*

SANFORD, MARK (MARSHALL CLEMENT SANFORD JR.), Governor of South Carolina, former United States Representative from South Carolina; b. Ft. Lauderdale, Fla., May 28, 1960; s. Marshall Clement and Peggy Sanford; m. Jenny Sullivan, 1989; children: Marshall, Landon, Bolton, Blake. BBA, Furman U., 1983; MBA, U. Va., 1988. With Goldman Sachs, 1988, CRC Realty, 1988-89; prin. Southeastern Ptnrs., 1989—93, Norton & Sanford, 1993—95, 2001—02; mem. US Congress from 1st S.C. Dist., 1995-2001; gov. State of SC, Columbia, 2003—. Chmn. Republican Governors Assn., 2008—09. Mem. USAFR. Mem.: Preservation Soc. Charleston. Republican. Episcopalian. Avocations: windsurfing, running. Office: Office of the Governor PO Box 12267 Columbia SC 29211 Office Phone: 803-734-2100. Office Fax: 803-734-5167.*

SANFORD, T(HOMAS) DENNY, bank executive; b. Dec. 23, 1935; s. William B. and Edith C. Sanford; m. Colleen Anderson Sanford, 1995 (div. 2003); children: Scott, William. BA in Psychology, U. Minn., 1958. CEO First Premier Bank, 1986—, Premier Bankcard; CEO, chmn. United Nat. Corp. Named one of 50 Most Generous Philanthropists, Business Week, 2006. Donated several million dollars to Sioux Valley Hospitals & Health Systems to transform the facility into a major research institution for children's health. The hospital has promised to rename the institution in his honor Sanford Health. Other recent donations include several millions to convert an abandoned mine into a science laboratory, for the children's hospital, and to the health system to expand projects involving the University of South Dakota's School of Medicine. Office: United National Corp 601 South Minnesota Ave Sioux Falls SD 57104

SANGER, DAVID E., news correspondent; b. White Plains, NY, July 5, 1960; Grad. magna cum laude, Harvard Coll., 1982. With NY Times, 1981—, corr., bur. chief Tokyo, then chief Washington econ. corr. and sr. writer, 1994—99, chief White House corr., 1999—. Mem. Aspen Strategy Group. Author: The Inheritance: The World Obama Confronts and the Challenges to American Power, 2009; TV appearances include Washington Week, Charlie Rose Show, The Daily Show, This Week with George Stephanopoulos. Co-recipient Pulitzer Prize for Nat. Reporting, 1987, 1999, Weintzal prize for Diplomatic Reporting, Georgetown Inst. Study of Democracy, 2004, Deadline News Reporting award, Am. Soc. Newspaper Editors, 2004. Mem.: Coun. Fgn. Rels., White House Corrs. Assn. (Aldo Beckman award 2003, Merriman Smith Meml. award 2003, 2007). Office: NY Times Washington Bur 1627 I St NW Ste 700 Washington DC 20006 Office Phone: 202-862-0300.*

SANGER, FREDERICK, retired molecular biologist; b. Rendcomb, Gloucestershire, Eng., Aug. 13, 1918; s. Frederick and Cicely Sanger; m. Margaret Joan Howe, 1940; children: Robin, Peter Frederick, Sally Joan. BA, St. John's Coll., Cambridge U., 1940, PhD, 1943; D.Sc. (hon.), Leicester U., 1968, Oxford U., 1970, Strasbourg U., 1970, Cambridge U. Beit Meml. Med. Research fellow U. Cambridge, 1944-51, rsch. scientist dept. biochemistry, 1944-61, rsch. scientist, div. head Med. Rsch. Coun. Lab. of Molecular Biology, 1962-83. Contbr. articles in field to sci. jours. Fellow King's Coll., Cambridge U., 1954; recipient Corday-Morgan Medal and Prize, Chem. Soc., 1951, Nobel prize for chemistry, 1958, 80; Gairdner Found. ann. award, 1971, 79, William Bate Hardy prize Cambridge Philos. Soc., 1976, Copley medal Royal Soc., 1977, Hon. Fellow, Royal Coll. Pathologists, 1993, Commander, Order Brit. Empire, 1963, Order of Merit, 1971, Companion of Honour, 1981, Millenium Fellow, Royal Soc. Chemistry, 2000. Mem. Am. Acad. Arts and Scis. (hon. fgn. mem.), Am. Soc. Biol. Chemists (hon.), Fgn. Assn., Acad. Sci. Argentina, Acad. Sci. Brazil, Japanese Biochemical Soc. (hon.) Assn. Química Argentina (corr.), NAS. Two time Nobel Prize winner in chemistry for work on amino acids and gene sequencing.

SANGER, JOSEPH WILLIAM, cell biologist; s. Joseph James and Mary Jackson S.; m. Jean McGilvray, Sept. 12, 1964; children: John McGilvray, Matthew Kernan. BS, Manhattan Coll., 1962; PhD, Dartmouth Coll., 1968; MA (hon.), U. Pa., 1976. Assoc. in anatomy U. Pa. Sch. Medicine, Phila., 1971-72, asst. prof., 1972-76, assoc. prof., 1976-85, prof., 1985—2005; chair, cell biology grad. program U. Pa., Phila., 1990-95, interim chmn. Dept. Cell and Devel. Biology, 2003—05; prof., chair dept. cell & devel. biology SUNY Upstate Med. U., Syracuse, NY, 2006—, interim vp rsch., 2007—08. Exec. trustee Marine Biol. Lab., Woods Hole, Mass., 1991-93, trustee, 1990-93, Bermuda biol. St., Saint George's Bermuda, 1977-79; vis. scientist EMBL, Heidelberg, Germany, 1979-1980. Editor: (video) Cell Motility and the Cytoskeleton, 1991-98; editl. bd. cell motility and cytoskeleton Wily-Liss, N.Y.C., 1986—, assoc. editor, 2006-, editl. bd. Chinese Jour. of Geriatric Cardiology, 2004-06; contbr. articles to profl. jours. Humboldt fellow Humboldt Found., 1979-80. Fellow AAAS (nominating com. 2000-2003), AAA (elected mem. bd. dir. 2008-). Home: 404 Bradford Pkwy Syracuse NY 13224 Office: SUNY Upstate Med Univ 1137 Weiskotten Hall Syracuse NY 13210 Office Phone: 315-464-8538. Business E-Mail: sangerjo@upstate.edu.

SANGER, STEPHEN W., retired consumer products company executive; b. Cin., Apr. 10, 1946; m. Karen Sanger; 2 children. BA in History, DePauw U., 1986; MBA, U. Mich., 1970. Marketing & sales positions Procter & Gamble, 1970—73; with Gen. Mills, Inc., Mpls., 1974—83, v.p., gen. mgr. Northstar Divsn., 1983—86, v.p., gen. mgr. new bus. devel., 1986, pres. Yoplait USA, 1986—88, pres. Big G Divsn., 1988, sr. v.p., 1989—92, vice chmn., 1992-96, pres., 1993-95, chmn., CEO, 1995—2007, chmn., 2007—08. Bd. dirs. Gen. Mills, Inc., 1992-2008,

Target Corp., 2000-, Wells Fargo & Co., 2003-, Grocery Manufacturers of America; mem. Bus. Coun., Bus. Roundtable; bd. adv. Retail Food Industry Ctr. Treas. Guthrie Theatre Found., Mpls.; bd. mem. Catalyst, Minnesota Bus. Partnership.

SANGESLAND, ODD EINAR, mechanical engineer, consultant; b. Bklyn., Aug. 7, 1929; s. Erling and Olga S. (Sorensen) Sangesland; m. Ellen Marie Piene, June 27, 1953; children: David William, Marianne Louise, Steven Michael, Laura Ellen Wardwell. BS summa cum laude in Mech. Engring., Poly. U., Bklyn., 1956, MME, 1960, student, 1962. Registered profl. engr., NY, 1962. Clk. indsl. sales Gen. Electric, NY, 1952—55; engr. Grumman Aerospace Corp., Bethpage, NY, 1955—90; pvt. practice cons. Plainview, NY, 1991—. Presenter in field. Scoutmaster Boy Scouts Am., Plainview, 1965—75. Sgt US Army, 1950—52, Korea. Mem.: Profl. Engring. Soc., Am. Soc. Heating, Refrigeration and Air Conditioning Engrs. (life), Greater LI Running Club, Sons Norway (trustee 1982—2006). Independent. Lutheran. Achievements include patents for solar energy collector; heat pipes to use heat from light fixtures; first to thermal control of orbiting astronomical observatory the 1st space telescope; configuration & thermal control of Pegasus the 1st satellite to measure size, direction, quantity of micrometeorites. Home: 17 Felice Ln Plainview NY 11803-6413 Personal E-mail: eosang@aol.com.

SANGHERA, DHARAMBIR K., biology professor; d. Kulwant S. and Swaran K. Sandhu; m. Jagtar S. Sanghera, June 14, 1993; children: Sara K., Gursumeet S. PhD, Guru Nanak Dev U., Punjab, 1992; FAHA (hon.), 2007. Adj. assoc. prof. U. Okla., Coll. Pharmacy; assoc. prof. U. Okla., Health Sci. Ctr., Coll. Med., 2007—. Hon. vis. cons. human geneticist Dyanand Med. Coll. and Hosp., Ludhiana, Punjab. Health related cmty. outreach Sukhmani Sahib Soc., Patiala, Lions Club, Ludhiana, Rotary Internat., Jalandhar, 2003—08. Recipient Internat. Rsch. Scientist Devel. award, Fogarty Internat. Ctr., NIH, 2002—05, 2005—; Indian Coun. Sci. and Indsl. Rsch. fellow, CSIR, 1988—91. Fellow: Am. Heart Assn.; mem.: Okla. Ctr. Neurosci., Internat. Genetic Epidemiology Soc., Am. Diabetes Assn., Am. Soc. Human Genetics. Achievements include patents for identification of the apolipoprotein H mutations and their diagnostic uses. Home: 917 WB Meyer Pky Edmond OK 73025 Office: Univ Okla Health Sci Ctr 975 NorthEast 10th St 254A-BRC Oklahoma City OK 73104

SANGI-HAGHPEYKAR, HALEH, educator; b. Tehran, Iran, Dec. 13, 1963; parent Nahid Abrarpour, Zia Sangi; m. Kayvon Haghpeykar; children: Shyon Haghpeykar, Ahria Haghpeykar. PhD, U. Tex., 1992. Asst. prof. Baylor Coll. Medicine, Houston, 1992—. Office: Baylor College Of Medicine 1 Baylor Plz Houston TX 77030-3411 Office Phone: 713-798-8057. Office Fax: 713-798-7564. Business E-Mail: halehs@bcm.tmc.edu.

SANGIOVANNI, JOHN PAUL, ophthalmic epidemiologist, eye and vision researcher; s. John Paul and Marie SanGiovanni; m. Brigitte SanGiovanni. BA, Boston Coll., 1988; MA, Brandeis U., 1993; MS, Harvard U., 1994, DSc, 1999. Neuroanatomy rsch. asst. Harvard Med. Sch./McLean Hosp., Belmont, Mass., 1988—91; study coord. Children's Hosp./Harvard Med. Sch., Boston, 1993—95; rsch. cons. Harvard Med. Sch./Children's Hosp., Boston, 1996—2000; rsch. asst. UN U., Boston, 1996—97; rsch. assoc. Internat. Nutrition Found., Boston, 1999—2000; rsch. cons. Harvard Sch. Pub. Health/Coll. Alcohol Study, Boston, 1999—2000; rsch. fellow Nat. Eye Inst., NIH, Bethesda, Md., 2000—04, staff scientist, 2004—; project officer Age-Related Eye Disease Study, 2004—08, Age-Related Eye Disease Study 2, 2004—; chairp MIT Comm. Assn. Rsch. in Vision and Ophthalmology, Rockville, 2006—08; DSMB mem. Found. Fighting Blindness, 2008—. Chairp disting. clin. tchr.'s award com. NIH, Bethesda, 2001—02. Contbr. manuscripts to sci. publs. Recipient NIH Dir.'s award, 2008, Early Career award, ISSFAL, 2009; Albert Schweitzer Urban fellow, 1996—97, Teagle Found. scholar, 1994—99, NAS/Sigma Xi grantee in aid of rsch., NAS, 1997. Mem.: Internat. Soc. Study Fatty Acids and Lipids, Assn. for Rsch. in Vision and Ophthalmology, Sigma Xi. Achievements include research in role of dietary long-chain polyunsaturated fatty acids in pathogenesis of retinal disease; nutritional factors associated with age-related eye disease; novel method of measuring visual acuity in infants; risk factors for pediatric cataract; genomic research on complex disease. Office: Nat Eye Inst NIH Clin Trial Br 10 Center Dr MSC 1204 Bldg 10 CRC Rm 3-2521 Bethesda MD 20892-1204

SANGIULIANO, BARBARA ANN, tax director; b. Bronx, NY, Dec. 28, 1959; d. Patrick John and Mildred (Soell) Gallo; m. John Warren Sangiuliano, Aug. 28, 1982. BA, Muhlenberg Coll., Allentown, Pa., 1982; MST, Seton Hall U., South Orange, NJ, 1989, JD, 1997; LLM in Tax (hon.), NY Law Sch., 2008. Bar: NJ 1997, NY 2006; CPA, NJ, 1987, CPA, Fla., 2007; CMA. Sr. tax cons. Ernst & Young LLP, Iselin, NJ, 1998—2003, Deloitte Tax LLP, Parsippany, NJ, 2003—06; tax cons. Smolin, Lupin & Co. PA, Fairfield, NJ, 2006—07, RSM McGladrey, NYC, 2007—08; tax dir. IPC Inc., 2008—. Mem. AICPA, ABA, NJ Soc. CPAs (past pres. Union County chpt.), NJ Bar Assn., Inst. Mgmt. Accts., Mensa, Omicron Delta Epsilon, Phi Sigma Iota. Republican. Roman Catholic. Avocations: reading, bicycling, fencing. Home: 340 William St Scotch Plains NJ 07076-1430 Office: IPC Inc 3 2nd St Jersey City NJ 07311 Office Phone: 201-253-2341.

SANGREE, WALTER HINCHMAN, social anthropologist, educator; b. NYC, June 15, 1926; s. Carl Michael and Constance (LaBoiteaux) S.; m. Mary Lucinda Shaw, June 14, 1952 (div. Jan. 1986); children: Margaretta Elizabeth, Mary Cora; m. Ilse Michaelis, Dec. 31, 1988. AB, Haverford Coll., 1950; MA, Wesleyan U., 1952; PhD, U. Chgo., 1959. Asst. prof. anthropology U. Rochester, NY, 1957-64, assoc. prof., 1964-73, prof., 1973-95, prof. emeritus, 1995—, chmn. dept. anthropology, 1974-77, acting chmn. dept., 1990; vis. scholar dept. anthropology Harvard U., 1979-80. Vis. scholar Ctr. for Population Studies, Harvard U., 1986-87; rsch. fellow African Studies Ctr., Boston U., 1998—. Author: Age, Prayer & Politics in Tiriki, Kenya, 1966; contbr. articles to profl. jours. Co-clk. Rochester Friends Meeting, 1977-79. Fulbright scholar U.K. and Kenya, 1954-56; NSF research fellow Nigeria, 1963-65 Mem. Am. Anthrop. Assn., African Studies Assn., Sigma Xi. Democrat. Mem. Soc. Of Friends. Home and Office: 11 Hilltop Rd Wellesley MA 02482 Office Phone: 781-237-1962. E-mail: wsangree@mac.com.

SANG-SIK, YEO, civil engineer, consultant; PhD, Drexel U., Phila., 2007. Geosynthetic inst. fellow Drexel U., Phila., 2003—07; sr. staff profl. Geosyntec Cons., San Diego, 2007—. Mem.: Am. Soc. Civil Engring. Achievements include research in geomaterials for geotechnical and geoenvironmental applications. Personal E-mail: geosynthetic@gmail.com.

SANGSTER, PAUL EDWARD, retired radiologist; b. Washington, June 14, 1939; s. George Edward and Leona Jacqueline (Yoder) Sangster; m. Sandra Lucille Shaum, June 1, 1980; 4 children. BS, U. Mich., Ann Arbor, 1962; MS, U. Ariz., Tucson, 1968, MD, 1974. Diplomate Am. Bd. Radiology. Surg. internship U. Calif., San Diego, 1974—75; radiol. residency U. Ariz., 1975—78; radiologist Northern Ariz. Radiology, 1978—2006; priviledges Winslow Meml. Hosp., PHS Hosp., Hopi Health Care. Pres. Coconino County Med. Soc., Flagstaff, Ariz., 1988—89; lectr. physiology dept. No. Ariz. U., Flagstaff, 1992—98. Mem.: Am. Roentgen Ray Soc., Am. Coll. Radiology. Achievements include research in metapyrochatechase study of an oxygenase. Avocations: hiking, golf, reading, racquetball.

SANI, ROBERT LEROY, chemical engineering professor; b. Antioch, Calif., Apr. 20, 1935; m. Martha Jo Marr, May 28, 1966; children: Cynthia Kay, Elizabeth Ann, Jeffrey Paul. BS, U. Calif.-Berkeley, 1958, MS, 1960; PhD, U. Minn., 1963. Postdoctoral researcher dept. math Rensselaer Poly. Inst., Troy, NY, 1963-64; asst. prof. U. Ill., Urbana, 1964-70, assoc. prof., 1970-76; prof. chem. engring. U. Colo., Boulder, 1976—, assoc. dept. chair, 2007—; co-dir. Ctr. for Low-g Fluid Mechanics and Transport Phenomena, U. Colo., Boulder, 1986-89, dir., 1989—. Assoc. prof. French Ministry Edn., 1982, 84, 86, 92, 94, 95, 96, 97; cons. Lawrence Livermore Nat. Lab., Calif., 1974-84. Contbr. numerous chpts. to profl. publs.; co-author three books; mem. editorial bd. Internat. Jour. Numerical Methods in Fluids, 1981—, Revue Européenne des Éléments Finis, 1990—, Internat. Jour. Computational Engring. Sci., 1998—, Internat. Jour. Computational & Numerical Analysis & Applications, 2000-. Guggenheim fellow, 1970 Mem. AICE, Soc. for Applied and Indsl. Math., World User Assn. in Applied Computational Fluid Dynamics (bd. dirs.). Democrat. Office: U Colo Dept Chem & Biol Engring UCB 424 Boulder CO 80309-0424 Office Phone: 303-492-5517. Business E-Mail: robert.sani@colorado.edu.

SANIGA, ERWIN MARTIN, educator, painter; b. Charleroi, Pa., June 16, 1946; s. Erwin and Gloria Lee Saniga; m. Karen Lee Geary, May 15, 1971 BS, Pa. State U., 1969, MBA, 1970, PhD, 1975. Asst. prof. U. Del., Newark, 1977-79, assoc. prof., 1979-82, prof., 1982—, Dana Johnson prof., 2000. Cons. multiple orgns., 1975-2000. Contbr. articles to profl. jours. Supr. Little Britain Twp., Nottingham, Pa., 1996-2008. Capt. U.S. Army, 1971-72. Mem. Am. Soc. Quality, Phi Kappa Phi, Beta Gamma Sigma, Alpha Pi Mu. Business E-Mail: sanigae@lerner.udel.edu.

SANISLO, PAUL STEVE, lawyer; b. Cleve., Feb. 8, 1927; s. Paul and Bertha (Kasa) S.; m. Mary Ellen P. Conroy, May 7, 1949; 1 child, Susan J. BA, Baldwin-Wallace Coll., 1948; JD, Cleve. State U., 1961. Bar: Ohio 1961, U.S. Dist. Ct. (N.E. dist.) Ohio 1964. Order clk. Am. Agrl. Chem. Co., Cleve., 1948-52; safety engr. Park Drop Forge Co., Cleve., 1952-62, personnel mgr., 1954-62; assoc. then ptnr. Spohn & Sanislo, L.P.A., Cleve., 1962-81; pres., 1981-86; ptnr., pres. Sanislo, Bacevice & Assocs. LPA, Cleve., 1987-98; pres. Sanislo & Assocs. Co. LPA, 1998-2000; of counsel Stewart & Dechant, Cleve., 2000—. Spl. counsel Atty. Gen. Ohio, 1971; arbitrator Am. Arbitration Assn., 1972-78. Mem. Cleve. City Coun., 1964-67; trustee Cleve.-Marshall Law Sch., 1962-63; trustee Cleve.-Marshall Ednl. Found., 1963-68, pres., 1980-83; mem. Solon city Bd. Edn., Ohio, 1972-83, pres., 1974-83; chmn. Solon Charter Rev. Commn., 1971, mem., 2000—; past mem., organizer, legal adv. Solon Drug Abuse Ctr.; mem. Cuyahoga County Dem. Exec. Com.; ward leader 29th Ward Dem. Club, 1965-71, also past pres.; trustee Solon Dem. Ward Club, 1972-75. Recipient Disting. Svc. award City of Solon, 1984, Solon Bd. Edn., 1984, Solon Edn. Assn., 1984. Mem. Bar Assn. Greater Cleve. (Merit Svc. award 1978-79, chmn. workers compensation sect. 1975-96), Ohio Bar Assn., Cuyahoga County Bar Assn., Assn. Trial Lawyers Am., Cleve.-Marshall Law Sch. Alumni Assn. (pres. 1967-68), Hungarian Bus. and Tradesmen's Club (pres. 1967-68), Cleve. Assn. Compensation Attys. (pres. 1973-86). Democrat. Roman Catholic. Avocations: golf, travel. Office: Stewart & DeChant 1440 Standard Bldg Cleveland OH 44113 Office Phone: 216-781-2258.

SANJIAN, ARA, history professor; s. Garabed Krikor Sanjian and Mayda Artine Jekjenian. PhD in Modern History, SOAS, U. London, 1994; MA in History Armenian People, Yerevan State U., Armenia, 1991. Asst. prof. Haigazian U., Beirut, 1995—2005; assoc. prof. U. Mich.-Dearborn, 2006—, dir., armenian rsch. ctr., 2006—. Office Fax: 313-593-5219. Business E-Mail: arasan@umd.umich.edu.

SANKAR, CHETAN SUBRAMANIAN, management information systems educator; b. Chittor, India, Nov. 19, 1950; came to U.S., 1977; s. Cedarampattu and Padmavathi (Venkatraman) Subramanian; m. Lakshmi Jayaraman, Mar. 6, 1977; children: Akila, Shivram. BS, Regional Engring. Coll., Trichy, India, 1971; MBA, Indian Inst. Mgmt., Calcutta, 1973; PhD, U. Pa., 1981. Stores mgr. Balmer Lawrie & Co., Calcutta, 1973-74; rsch. assoc. Indian Inst. Mgmt., 1974-77; asst. prof. Temple U., Phila., 1981-85; mem. tech. staff AT&T Bell Labs., Holmdel, N.J., 1985-89; asst. prof. MIS, Auburn (Ala.) U., 1989—. Contbr. articles to profl. jours. Chmn. AT&T Asian Am. Week, 1989; sec. India Cultural Assn., Auburn, 1990. Grantee Office Naval Rsch., 1979, Office Mgmt. and Budget, 1980. Mem. IEEE, Decision Scis. Inst., Inst. Mgmt. Sci., Info. Resource Mgmt. Assn. Avocations: swimming, jogging, reading. Office: Auburn U 322 E Thach Ave Auburn AL 36830-5415

SANKAR, PAMELA LEE, social sciences educator; m. Gregg Gorton, Aug. 16, 1986; children: Jedd Sankar-Gorton, Eliza Sankar-Gorton. PhD, U. Pa., Phila., 1992. Prof. U. Pa., 1996—. Achievements include research in social construction of race in genetics. Office: Ctr Bioethics 3401 Market St Ste 320 Philadelphia PA 19104 Business E-Mail: sankarp@mail.med.upenn.edu.

SANKAR, RAMAN, pediatric neurologist; b. India, Mar. 04; PhD, U. Wash., Seattle, 1974; MD, Tulane U. Sch. Medicine, New Orleans, 1986. Diplomate Am. Bd. Psychiatry & Neurology, special qualifications in child neurology. Postdoc. rsch. assoc. U. Wash., 1974—75; asst. then assoc. prof. medicinal chemistry Xavier U., New Orleans, 1975—82; intern pediat. Children's Hosp. LA, 1986—87, resident pediat., 1987—88; resident neurology UCLA Sch. Medicine, 1988—89; fellowship pediat. neurology, 1989—91; prof. pediat. neurology Mattel Children's Hosp. at UCLA, 1991—; staff UCLA Med. Ctr. Mem. profl. adv. bd. Epilepsy Found., 2000—. Contbr. articles to profl. jours. Fellow: Am. Acad. Neurology; mem.: Child Neurology Soc. (mem. rsch. com. 2000—), Soc. Neurosci., Am. Epilepsy Soc. Office: UCLA Med Ctr Dept Pediat Neurology 10833 Le Conte Ave 22 474MDCC Los Angeles CA 90095-1752 Office Phone: 310-825-9169. Business E-Mail: RSankar@ucla.edu.

SANKARANARAYANAN, JAYASHRI, medical educator, researcher; d. Sankaranarayanan Sivaramakrishnan and Chandra Sankaranarayanan. BPharm, Prin. K.M. Kundnani Coll. Pharmacy, Mumbai, India, 1989; MPharm, Prin. K.M. Kundnani Coll. Pharmacy, 1992; PhD, Purdue U., W. Lafayette, Ind., 2004. Med. svcs. mgmt. trainee Burroughs Wellcome India, Ltd., Mumbai, 1992—93, med. svcs. exec., 1993—96; med. svs. sr. exec. Glaxo India, Ltd., Mumbai, 1996—97; med. svcs. mgr. RPG, Mumbai, 1997—2000; asst. prof., coll. pharmacy U. Nebr. Med. Ctr., Omaha, 2004—. Faculty mentor, designer State-wide Cmty. Svc. Medicare Part D, Omaha. Grantee Cancer and Smoking Disease Rsch. grant, Nebr. State HHS, 2006—07, Colorectal Cancer Screening Assessment Rsch. grant, Cancer Awareness, Rsch., Edn. & Svc., 2006—07. Mem.: Acad. Health, Am. Assn. Colls. Pharmacy, Am. Pharmacists Assn., Internat. Soc. Pharmacoeconomics and Outcomes Rsch. (Best Podium Presentation award 2006), Omicron Delta Kappa (hon.), Sigma Xi (assoc.), Alpha Zeta chpt. Rho Chi (life). Home: 5102 Grover St #6 Omaha NE 68106 Office: Univ Nebr Med Ctr 986045 Nebraska Medical Center Omaha NE 68198-6045

SANKARANARAYANAN, SUBRAMANIAN KRS, chemical engineer, researcher; b. Trichy, Tamil Nadu, India, Dec. 15, 1978; s. Sankaranarayanan K.R. Subbarayulu and Janaki Sankaranarayanan; m. Reetu Singh, Feb. 21, 2003. PhD, U. South Fla., Tampa, 2007. Rsch. asst. U. South Fla., 2003—07; postdoc. rschr. Harvard U., Cambridge, Mass., 2007—. Assoc. developer Invensys Corp., Lake City, Calif., 2002—03. Contbr. scientific papers (Outstanding Rschr. award, 2007). Recipient Gold medal, Nagpur U., 2000. Mem.: AIChE, IEEE Sensors, Electrochem. Soc., Sigma Xi. Achievements include design of surface acoustic wave sensor; development of focused surface acoustic wave device; discovery of biofouling elimination mechanism; research in corrosion mechanisms; invention of ovarian cancer sensor. Office: Harvard Univ 9 Oxford St Cambridge MA 02138 Personal E-mail: skrssank@gmail.com. Business E-Mail: krss@deas.harvard.edu.

SANKS, ROBERT LELAND, environmental engineer, retired educator; b. Pomona, Calif., Feb. 19, 1916; s. John B. and Nellie G. (Church) Sanks; m. Mary Louise Clement, May 16, 1946 (dec. Oct. 1994); children: Margaret Russell, John Clement; m. Edith Millen Harrington, Dec. 2, 1999. AA, Fullerton Jr. Coll., Calif., 1936; BS, U. Calif., Berkeley, 1940; MS, Iowa State Coll., Ames, 1949; PhD, U. Calif., Berkeley, 1965. Registered profl. engr., Mont. Draftsman City of La Habra Calif., 1940; asst. engr. Alex Morrison cons. engr., Fullerton, Calif., 1941; jr. engr. US Army Engrs., LA, 1941-42; asst. rsch. engr. dept. civil engring. U. Calif.-Berkeley, 1942-45; structural engr. The Austin Co., Oakland, Calif., 1945-46; instr. dept. civil engring. U. Utah, Salt Lake City, 1946-49, asst. prof., 1949-55, assoc. prof., 1955-58; structural engr. The Lang Co., Salt Lake City, 1950; instrument man Patti McDonald Co., Anchorage, 1951; checker Western Steel Co., Salt Lake City, 1952; structural engr. Moran, Proctor, Meuser and Rutledge, NYC, 1953, F.C. Torkelson Co., Salt Lake City, 1955; soils engr. R.L. Sloane & Assocs., Salt Lake City, 1956; prof., chmn. dept. civil engring. Gonzaga U., Spokane, Wash., 1958-61; prof. dept. civil engring. Mont. State U., Bozeman, 1966-82, prof. emeritus, 1982—; vis. prof. U. Tex.-Austin, 1974-75; part-time sr. engr. Christian, Spring, Sielbach & Assoc., Billings, Mont., 1974-82. Cons. engr., 1945—; lectr. at pumping sta. design workshops, 1988—; assoc. specialist San. Engring. Research Lab., 1963-65, research engr., 1966. Author: Statically Indeterminate Structural Analysis, 1961; co-author: (with Takashi Asano) Land Treatment and Disposal of Municipal and Industrial Wastewaters, 1976, Water Treatment Plant Design for the Practicing Engineer, 1978; editor-in-chief: Pumping Station Design, 1989 (award Excellence profl. & scholarly pub. div. Assn. Am. Pubs. 1989), 2d edit., 1998, co-editor 3d edit., 2006; contbr. articles on civil engring. to profl. pubs. Mem. Wall of Fame, Fullerton H.S., 1987, Hall of Fame, Mont. Profl. Engrs., 2005; NSF fellow, 1961-63 Mem. ASCE (life, chmn. local qualifications com. intermountain sect. 1950-56, pres. intermountain sect. 1957-58), Am. Water Works Assn. (pres. Mont. sect. 1981-82, George Warren Fuller award), Mont. Water Environ. Fedn., Assn. Environ. Engring. Profs., Rotary, Sigma Xi, Chi Epsilon. Home: 1201 Highland Blvd Apt D309 Bozeman MT 59715 Home Phone: 406-587-8220; Office Phone: 406-599-6156. Personal E-mail: bsanks@mcn.net.

SAN MIGUEL, MANUEL, painter, historian, composer, poet; b. Guayama, P.R., Sept. 29, 1930; s. Manuel and Luisa (Griffo) San M.; m. Sandra Bonilla, July 12, 1969; children: Manuel, Ana. Student, U. P.R., 1947-51, U. Pa., 1966-68, Arts Students League, NYC, 1968-69. Historian San Juan Nat. Historic Site, Nat. Park Svc., 1953-63; exec. sec. Acad. Arts and Scis., San Juan, 1963-64. Founder mus. and study collection El Morro Castle San Juan Nat. Hist. Site; co-founder Caribbean Art Gallery, San Juan, PR, Galeria Campeche, NYC; cons. in field. Exhibited in U. P.R., 1958, 62, Ateneo de P.R., 1962, Pan-Am. Union, Washington, 1963, Bienal Mex., 1972, Bienal Rio de Janeiro, 1976, Orange County Schs. Mus. Art, Orlando, Fla., 1992, Mus. Modern Art, Paris, 1994, Expo of the Americas, Orlando, 1996, 98, Galeriá Santiago, San Juan, P.R., 2000, Galeria Campeche, San Juan, P.R., 2001, Simon Bolivar Gallery, Caracas, 2001, Galerie Santiago, 2003, Galeriá Colibri, Santo Domingo, numerous other nat. and internat. exhbns.; contbr. monographs on historical work in San Juan Nat. Historic Site to U.S. Nat. Archives, Washington; contbr. poetry to anthologies including Anthology of Latin American Poets, vol. II, 1987; rec. artist popular music of P.R.; soloist U. P.R. choir, Carnegie Hall, N.Y.C., 1949. Capt. U.S. Army, 1951-53, Korea. Decorated Bronze Star with valor clasp and oak leaf cluster, Purple Heart, Combat Infantryman Badge, others; named One of Ten Outstanding Hispanic Men, Orlando, Fla., 1991; recipient Recognition award for contbns. to Hispanic Am. Culture, Govt. P.R., 1996, Hispanic Heritage Found., medal Painters & Designers 20th Century, Cambridge, Eng., 2000; Coqui de Oro award for contbns. to Puerto Rican arts Casa de P.R., Inc., 1999. Mem. AAAS, VFW (life), Disabled Am. Vets. (life), Am. Legion, Ateneo de P.R. (bd. govs. 1959-60), Am. Biog. Inst. (bd. advisors, life mem. bd. govs.), Am. Philatelic Soc. (postal commemorative soc.), Inst. P.R. Culture (cons.), P.R. Philatelic Assn. (charter), Internat. Platform Assn., Lions (Lion of Yr. 1962-63). Achievements include documentary research in the restoration of Castillo San Marcos, St. Augustine, Fla., Castillo San Felipe de Barajas, Colombia, South Am., and restoration of San Juan fortifications and city walls.

SAN MIGUEL, SANDRA BONILLA, social worker; b. Santurce, PR, May 23, 1944; d. Isidoro and Flora (Carrero) Bonilla; m. Manuel San Miguel, July 12, 1969. BA, St. Joseph's Coll., 1966; MS in Social Work, Columbia U., 1970. Cert. social work mgr., sch. social work specialist. Case worker Dept. Labor, Migration Divsn., NYC, 1966—68; clin. social worker N.Y.C. Housing Authority, NYC, 1968—69, Children's Aid Soc., NYC, 1969—71; sr. social worker Traveler's Aid Soc., San Juan, 1971—74; coord., supr. Dept. Addiction Control Svcs., San Juan, 1974—77; substance abuse div. dir. Seminole County Mental Health Ctr., Altamonte Springs, Fla., 1978—81; cons. pvt. practice Hispanic Cons. Svcs., Winter Springs, Fla., 1982—2004; adj. prof. Seminole C.C., Lake Mary, Fla., 1986—90; sch. social worker Seminole County Pub. Schs., Sanford, Fla., 1986—91, lead sch. social worker, 1991—. Pres.'s minority adv. coun. U. Ctrl. Fla., 1982-2008, vice-chair, 1982-86, chair, 1986-90; bd. regents EEO adv. com. State U. Sys. Fla., 1985-89; bd. dirs. Seminole Cmty. Mental Health Ctr., 1986-94, 95-2001, v.p., 1988-90, pres., 1990-91; adv. bd. Nat. Devereux Found. Ctrl. Fla., 1993-98, women's adv. bd. South Seminole Hosp., Fla., 1994-96; mem. multicultural cmty. adv. com. Seminole County Pub. Schs., 1993-2004; mem. Fla. Consortium on Tchr. Edn. for Am. Minorities, 1990-96; mem. local com. Hispanic Info. and Telecomms. Network, 1990; mem. Seminole County (Fla.) Juvenile Justice Coun., 1993-96; mem. statewide student svcs. adv. com. Dept. Edn. Fla., 1993-96, student svcs. adv. group, 1996-97; cmty. adv. com. sch. social work U. Ctrl. Fla.,

2000—06. Recipient Pres.'s Outstanding Svc. award, UCF, 1991, Ponce de Leon Hispanic Cmty. award, 1992, Bd. Svc. Recognition Plaque, Seminole Cmty. Mental Health Ctr., 1991, Outstanding Contribution to Student Svcs. cert., Fla. Dept. Edn., 1995, Manuel Martinez award for Outstanding Contbns. to Puerto Rican Cmty. in Ctrl. Fla., La Casa de Puerto Rico, 1999; named Ednl. Support Ctr. Tchr. of Yr., Seminole County Pub. Schs., 2000. Mem.: NASW (appt. nat. sch. social work credential com. 1996—99), Nat. Network Social Work Mgrs., Collegiate Social Workers P.R., Fla. Assn. Student Svcs. Adminstrs. (pres-elect 2006—07, pres. 2007—08), Sch. Social Work Assn. Am. (founding mem.), Fla. Assn. Sch. Social Workers (co-founder minority caucus 1988, columnist quar. newsletter article Minority Corner 1988—92, bd. dirs. 1989—, sec. 1990—92, v.p. 1992—93, pres. 1993—94, chmn. legis. com. 1994—, website article From the Gallery 2001—, Leadership Plaque 1994, Adminstr. of Yr. 1999, pres.'s award 2007), St. Joseph's Coll. Alumni Assn., Columbia U. Alumni Assn. (nat. bd. dirs. 1997—2001). Mailing: PO Box 195933 Winter Springs FL 32719 Personal E-mail: sanmiguel1969@earthlink.net.

SANNER, GEORGE BRADLEY, bank executive; b. Balt., Sept. 20, 1953; s. George E. and Marjorie (Hohman) S.; m. Ann Margaret Tehan, Aug. 31, 1991 (div.); children: Anne, Meredith, Kimberly. BA, U. Va., 1974; MBA, Loyola Coll., Balt., 1978. Asst. v.p. Union Trust Co., Balt., 1974-82; v.p. Am. Security Bank, Washington, 1982-86; sr. v.p. Bank of Md., Towson, 1986-87; mng. dir. Provident Bank of Md., Balt., 1987-94; sr. v.p. FCNB Bank, Frederick, Md., 1994-95; pres./CEO Regal Bancorp, Owings Mills, Md., 1995—; also bd. dirs. Bd. dirs. Md. Bank Svcs., Inc.; bd. dirs., chmn. Atlantic Ctrl. Bankers Bank; pres., CEO, bd. dir. Regal Bank and Trust. Airman USAF, 1973-75. Mem. Md. Bankers Assn., Alpha Sigma Nu. Republican. Presbyterian. Avocations: golf, tennis, amateur radio. Office: Regal Bancorp 11436 Cronhill Dr Owings Mills MD 21117-3814 E-mail: bsanner@regalbank.com.

SANNER, GEORGE ELWOOD, electrical engineer; b. Rockwood, Pa., Aug. 30, 1929; s. Dennis Charles and Alverda (Growall) S.; m. Marjorie Mary Hohman, July 1, 1951; children: George Bradley, Marjorie Rosalie, Cathy Ann. BS, U. Pitts., 1951; postgrad., Johns Hopkins U., 1957—58; cert. network engr., Mercer U., 1999. Registered profl. engr., Md.; cert. cost acctg. mgmt.; Microsoft profl. network cert. MCP, MCP+I, MCSE; cert A+ Computer Tech. Industry Assn. Supervisory engr. Westinghouse Electric Corp., Balt., 1952—58, chief scientist, cons. engr. def. and space ctr., 1964—72; chief engr., program mgr. radio divsn. Bendix Corp., Balt., 1958—64, engring. mgr. Calif. inst. tech. jet propulsion labs. Pasadena, Calif., 1980—81; pres., gen. mgr. Santron Corp., Balt., 1972—79; v.p. engring. M-Tron Industries divsn. Curtiss Wright Corp., Yankton, SD, 1979—80; sr. engring. specialist engring. ctr. Litton Data Sys., New Orleans, 1981—83; cons. engring. mgmt. AIL divsn. Eaton Corp., Deer Park, NY, 1983—87; sr. prin. engr. Am. Electronics Labs, Inc., Lansdale, Pa., 1987—92; cons. Atlanta, 1992—; electronic sys. & telemktg. dir. Regal Bank & Trust, Owings Mills, Md., 2007—. Eisenhower european People to People Tour Countries, 1978. Patentee in field. Vestryman Immanuel Ch., Sparks-Glencoe, Md., 1969-70; trustee St. Paul's Sch. for Boys, Balt., 1965-67; mem. bishop's secretariat Diocese of LI, Garden City, NY, 1985-87; mem. exec. com. Scriptural Coalition, Diocese of Phila., 1990-92; mem. Rep. Nat. Com.(life) Eisenhower Comm., 2009, Rep. Presdl. Trust, Nat. Rep. Senatorial Com., Nat Rep. Congressional Com.; lic. lay reader Anglican Cath. Ch. A.K. Mellon Found. scholar, 1947-50, Carnegie Inst. Tech. scholar, 1947-51 Mem. IEEE, IEEE Computer Soc., Quarter Century Wireless Assn., Judicial Watch, Heritage Found. Anglican. Address: 2501 Hidden Hills Dr Marietta GA 30066-5241 Office Phone: 770-419-7268.

SANNER, JOHN HARPER, retired pharmacologist; b. Anamosa, Iowa, Apr. 29, 1931; s. Lee Michael and Helen (Grace) S.; m. Marilyn Joan Eichorst, Dec. 28, 1958; children: Linda Leigh, Steven Bradley. BS, U. Iowa, 1954, MS, 1961, PhD, 1964. Rsch. investigator G.D. Searle & Co., Skokie, Ill., 1963-69, sr. rsch. investigator, 1969-75, rsch. fellow, 1975-86, ret., 1986—. Contbr. articles to profl. jours. Mem. Deerfield (Ill.) Cable and Telecomm. Commn. 1st lt. USAFR, 1955-57. Mem.: Ill. Videographers Assn. Democrat. Achievements include pioneering research in prostaglandin antagonists. Avocation: video photography and production. Office: Sanner Video Svc PO Box 199 Deerfield IL 60015-0199 Personal E-mail: johnsanner@comcast.net.

SANOCKI, EDWARD JOHN, JR., lawyer; b. Detroit, Nov. 8, 1950; s. Edward John and Josephine (Gosk) Sanocki; m. Sheila Gail Behar, Aug. 5, 1978 (dec. 1997); children: Michael David, Kenneth John; m. Deborah Fairbanks, May 25, 2002. BA, U. Mich., 1972; MA, U. Tenn., 1974; JD, N.Y. Law Sch., 1977. Bar: N.Y. 1978, U.S. Dist. Ct. (so. dist.) N.Y. 1978, U.S. Dist. Ct. (ea. dist.) N.Y. 1993, U.S. Ct. Appeals (2d cir.) 1993. Assoc. Julien & Schlesinger, P.C., NYC, 1978-84, ptnr., 1984-90, Sanocki, Newman & Turret, LLP, 1997—; pvt. practice NYC, 1990—97. Speaker Miss. Trial Lawyers Assn., Jackson, 1988, So. Trial Lawyers Assn., New Orleans, 1989. Co-writer Products Liability column N.Y. Law Jour., 1989-90. Mem. Assn. Trial Lawyers Am. (sustaining), N.Y. State Trial Lawyers Assn. (chmn. products liability com. 1987-88, bd. dirs. 1990-92, speaker 1990-93). Roman Catholic. Home: 17 Azalea Trl Westfield NJ 07090-1684 Office: 225 Broadway 8th Fl New York NY 10007 Office Phone: 212-962-1190.

SANQUIST, NANCY JOHNSON, real estate technology consultant, educator; b. Muncie, Ind., Aug. 31, 1947; d. Charles Elof and Pauline Lydia (Murphy) S.; m. James M. Johnson, Dec. 1988. BA, UCLA, 1970; MA, Bryn Mawr Coll., 1973; MS, Columbia U., 1978. Cert. facilities mgr. Instr. Lafayette Coll., Easton, Pa., 1973—74, Muhlenberg Coll., Bethlehem, Pa., 1974—75, Northampton Area CC, Bethlehem, 1974—75; dir. Preservation Office City of Easton, 1977—78; cons. El Pueblo de Los Angeles State Hist. Pk., 1978—79; dir. restoration Bixby Ranch Co., Long Beach, Calif., 1979—82; mgr. computer applications Cannel-Heumann & Assoc., LA, 1982—84; dir. Computer-Aided Design Group, Marina del Rey, Calif., 1984—93; v.p. PAE Facility Mgmt. Svcs., LA, 1993—97, Vanderweil Facility Advisors, Boston, 1997—99; dir. strategic initiatives Peregrine Sys., San Diego, 1999—2002; strategic asset mgmt. adv. Autodesk, San Rafael, Calif., 2003; v.p. Manhattan Software, 2004—; adj. prof. U. San Diego Grad. Sch. Bus., 2004—05. Adj. instr. UCLA, 1979-86, Grad Sch. Calif. State U., Dominguez Hills, 1981. Author numerous tech. articles and manuals. Bd. dir. Historic Easton, Inc., 1977-78, Simon Rodia's Towers in Watts, LA 1979-81, LA Conservancy, 1982-86, Friends of Schindler House, West Hollywood, Calif., 1978-98, pres., 1982-85; mem. Del Mar Libr. Bd., 2005—; v.p. Del Mar Village Assn., 2005—. Recipient Outstanding Contbn. award Nat. Computer Graphics Assn., 1987. Fellow Internat. Facility Mgmt. Assn. (seminar leader, lectr. N.Am., Asia, Australia, Europe and Mid. East 1987—); mem. Del Mar Village Assoc.(v.p. design), DEl Mar Forum Based Code Com.(vice cahir, 2009-) Avocations: travel, art, photography, architecture. Office Phone: 858-699-0827. E-mail: nsanquist@manhattansoftware.com.

SANSALONE, MARY JANE, dean, structural engineer, educator; b. Cin., Sept. 9, 1958; d. John Richard and Jane Claire (Beck) Sansalone; m. Bill Streett. BS summa cum laude in Civil Engring., U. Cin., 1982; MS in Structural Engring., Cornell U., Ithaca, NY, 1984; PhD in Structural Engring., Cornell U., 1986; MPA, Harvard U., Cambridge, Mass., 1999. Rsch. structural engr. Nat. Bur. Stds., 1986-87; vis. asst. prof. engring. Cornell U., 1987-88, asst. prof. structural engring., 1988-91, assoc. prof., 1992-97, assoc. dir. Sch. Civil and Environ. Engring., 1993—94, 1996—97, prof. structural engring., 1997—2006, vice provost acad. programs, 1998—99; v.p. planning NYU, 2002—03; dean Sch. Engring. and Applied Sci. Washington U., St. Louis, 2006—. Co-founder, v.p. Impact-Echo Cons., Inc., 1994-98; co-founder Impact-Echo Instruments, LLC, Ithaca, 1997. Author: (with W.B. Streett) Impact-Echo--Nondestructive Evaluation of Concrete and Masonry, 1997; patentee in field; contbr. articles to profl. jours. Recipient Nat. Prof. of the Yr. award Coun. Advancement & Support Edn., 1993. Fellow AAAS, Am. Concrete Inst. (Wason medal for materials rsch. 1991); mem. ASCE (Engr. Yr. award Upstate NY region 1991), Am. Soc. Testing and Materials (Allen Yorkdale award 1997), Soc. Profl. Engrs. (Engr. Yr. award NY/Pa. region 1991), Sigma Xi. Office: Sch Engring Washington U One Brookings Dr Box 1163 Saint Louis MO 63130 Business E-Mail: mjs39@cornell.edu.

SANSALONE, WILLIAM ROBERT, biochemist, educator, biomedical researcher; b. Vineland, NJ, Feb. 16, 1931; s. Fortunato and Rosa (Pelle) Sansalone; m. Alice E. Koury, June 25, 1960; 1 child, Catherine. BS, Rutgers U., 1953, PhD, 1961; MS, U. NH, Durham, 1955. Biochemistry rsch. asst. U. Conn., Storrs, 1955-56; instr. biochemistry SUNY Downstate Med. Ctr., Bklyn., 1961-64, asst. prof. biochemistry, 1964-70, assoc. prof., 1970-71; project scientist NIH, Bethesda, Md., 1971-72, sr. project scientist, 1972-73, exec. sec. biochemistry study sect., 1973-74, program dir. rev., 1974-83, assoc. dir. sci. program ops., 1983-87, dir. office of program planning and evaluation, 1987-96; sr. fellow Georgetown U., Washington DC, 1999—2002, adj. prof. biochemistry, 2002—. Vis. assoc. prof. physiology and biophysics Med. Coll. Pa., Phila., 1970. Contbr. articles to profl. jours. Served to 1st lt. USAF, 1956—58. Mem.: AAAS, Soc. Exptl. Biology and Medicine, Am. Soc. Nutritional Scis., Biophys. Soc., Harvey Soc., Sigma Xi, Alpha Gamma Rho (chpt. treas. 1968—70). Roman Catholic. Home: 6835 Old Stage Rd Rockville MD 20852-4359 Personal E-mail: ws31@verizon.net.

SANSARICQ, GUY A., bishop; b. Jeremie, Haiti, Oct. 6, 1934; Attended, Minor Sem. of Les Cayes, Haiti; PhL, St. Paul Pontifical Sem., Ottawa, Ont., Canada, 1956, STL, 1960; M in Social Scis., Pontifical Gregorian U., Rome, 1971. Ordained priest Diocese of Les Cayes, Haiti, 1960, parochial vicar, 1960—61; chaplain for Haitian immigrants The Bahamas, 1961—68; parochial vicar Sacred Heart parish, Bklyn., 1971—93; pastor St. Jerome parish, Bklyn., 1993—; ordained bishop, 2006; aux. bishop Diocese of Bklyn., 2006—. Co-founder Haitian-Americans United for Progress. Roman Catholic. Office: Diocese of Bklyn PO Box C 75 Greene Ave Brooklyn NY 11202

SANSEVERINO, RAYMOND ANTHONY, lawyer; b. Bklyn., Feb. 16, 1947; s. Raphael and Alice Ann (Camerano) S.; m. Karen Marie Mooney, Aug. 24, 1968 (dec. 1980); children: Deirdre Ann, Stacy Lee; m. Victoria Vent, June 6, 1982 (div. 1995); m. Kimberley Frank, May 11, 2002; 1 child: Sophia Josephine. AB in English Lit., Franklin & Marshall Coll., Lancaster, Pa., 1968; JD cum laude, Fordham Law Sch., Manhattan, NY, 1972. Bar: NY 1973, US Dist. Ct. (so. and ea. dists.) NY 1973, US Ct. Appeals (2d cir.) 1974, US Supreme Ct. 1986. Assoc. Rogers & Wells, NYC, 1972—75, Corbin & Gordon, NYC, 1975—77; ptnr. Corbin Silverman & Sanseverino LLP, NYC, 1978—2001, mng. ptnr., 1985—2001; ptnr. Brown Raysman Millstein Felder & Steiner LLP, NYC, 2001—06, chair comml. real estate leasing group, 2001—06, mem. exec. com., 2003—06; ptnr. Loeb & Loeb LLP, NYC, 2006—, chair comml. real estate leasing group, 2006—, chmn. NY real estate dept., 2007—08, chmn. real estate dept., 2008—. Contbr. articles to profl. jours.; articles editor Fordham Law Rev., 1971-72. Bd. trustees Franklin & Marshal Coll., 2006—. Recipient West Pub. Co. prize, 1972. Mem. ABA, Assn. Bar City NY, NY State Bar Assn., Twin Oaks Swim and Tennis Club (bd. dirs. 1981-2002, pres. 1993-2001), Alumni Assn. Franklin & Marshall Coll. (bd. dirs., 2001-08, chair devel. and philanthopy com. 2003-04, treas. 2004-05, exec. com. 2004-08, v.p. 2005-06, pres. 2006-07, past pres., 2007—08). Republican. Roman Catholic. Office: Loeb & Loeb LLP 345 Park Ave New York NY 10154 Office Phone: 212-407-4008.

SANSOM, DENNIS LEE, philosopher, educator; b. Austin, Tex., July 31, 1951; s. Hugh Alvin and Bettye Jo Sansom; m. Beverly Burnside, May 31, 1980; children: Stephen, Jonathan. Prof., chair dept. philosophy Samford U., Birmingham, Ala., 1988—. Author: (text book) Christian Ethics: How Distinctive Aspects of Christianity Shape Ethics; contbr. articles to profl. jours. Mem.: Am. Philos. Assn. & Soc. Christian Philosophers (regional officer 1998—2000). Avocations: golf, birdwatching, bicycling. Office: Samford Univ 800 Lakeshore Dr Birmingham AL 35229 Business E-Mail: dlsansom@samford.edu.

SANSOM, WILLIAM B., consumer products executive; BS in Civil Engring., The Citadel. Commr. transp., commr. fin. and adminstrn. Tenn. State Govt., 1979—83; CEO H.T. Hackney Co., Knoxville, Tenn., 1983—, chmn. bd. dirs. Mem. bd. dir. Martin Marietta Materials, NC, 1994—, First Tenn. Nat. Corp.; chair Tenn. Valley Authority. Address: HT Hackney Co PO Box 238 Knoxville TN 37901-0238 Fax: 423-456-1291.*

SANSONE, GUY, restructuring company executive; BA, SUNY, Albany. CPA. Accounting and auditing mgr. Deloitte & Touche, LLP; CFO Telegroup, Inc.; pres., co-CEO, bd. dirs. Rotech Healthcare, Inc.; sr. v.p. Integrated Health Svcs., Inc.; interim CFO, mem. leadership team HealthSouth Corp.; mng. dir., head Healthcare Industry Group Alvarez & Marsal LLC, NYC; pres., CEO, chief restructuring officer Saint Vincent Cath. Med. Ctr., NYC, 2005—09. Office: Alvarez & Marsal LLC 600 Lexington Ave New York NY 10022 Office Phone: 212-759-4433. Office Fax: 212-759-5532.*

SANSONETTI, THOMAS L., lawyer, former federal agency administrator; b. Hinsdale, IL, May 18, 1949; BA in Fgn. Affairs, with distinction, U. Va., 1971, MBA, 1973; JD, Washington and Lee U., 1976. Chief of staff, legis. dir. to Congressman Craig Thomas US Ho. Reps; assoc. solicitor on energy and natural resources US Dept. Interior, 1987—89, solicitor, 1990—93; ptnr. Holland & Hart LLP, Cheyenne, Wyo., 1993—2001, 2005—; asst. atty. gen. for environment & natural resources US Dept. Justice, Washington, 2001—05. Founder Wyo. Tennis Assn., 1978; mem. Wyo. Rep. Nat. Com., 1996—2002; chmn. Wyo. Rep. Party, 1983—87; gen. counsel Rep. Nat. Com., 2001; leader Bush-Cheney transition team Interior Dept., 2001. Republican. Office: Holland & Hart LLP 2515 Warren Ave Cheyenne WY 82001-3162 Office Phone: 307-778-4200. Office Fax: 307-778-8175. E-mail: tlsansonetti@hollandhart.com.

SANSTEAD, WAYNE GODFREY, state official, school system administrator; b. Hot Springs, Ark., Apr. 16, 1935; s. Godfrey A. and Clara (Buen) S.; m. Mary Jane Bober, June 16, 1957; children: Timothy, Jonathan. BA in Speech and Polit. Sci, St. Olaf Coll., 1957; MA in Pub. Address and Group Comm., Northwestern U., 1966; EdD in Secondary Edn., U. ND, 1974. Tchr., Luverne, Minn., 1959-60; dir. forensics Minot High Sch., ND, 1960-71, tchr. social sci. ND, 1960-78; mem. ND Ho. of Reps., 1965-70, 83-85, ND Senate, 1971-73; lt. gov. State of ND, Bismarck, 1973-81, supt. pub. instrn., 1985—. Served with AUS, 1957-59. Recipient Disting. Alumnus award St. Olaf Coll., 1991, Literacy award, Internat. Reading Assn., 1993, Nat. Fedn. Outstanding Speech Educator award, 1995; named Outstanding Freshman Senator A.P., 1971, Outstanding Young Educator, N.D. Jr. C. of C., 1967, Outstanding Young Man, Minot Jr. C. of C., 1964, Communicator of the Yr., Nat. Forensic League, 1992, Advocate of Yr., Am. Sch. Counselor Assn., 1994; James J. Hill Found. scholar, Coe Family Found. scholar, 1963, Eagleton scholar Rutgers U., 1969. Mem. ND Edn. Assn., NEA (legis. com. 1969—), Central States Speech Assn., Am. Forensic Assn., Jr. C. of C., Sons of Norway, Elks, Toastmasters. Democrat. Lutheran. Home: 1120 Columbia Dr Bismarck ND 58504-6514 Office: State Supt ND Dept Pub Instrn 600 E Boulevard Ave Dept 201 Fl 9-10-11 Bismarck ND 58505-0440 Office Phone: 701-328-4570. Business E-Mail: wsanstead@nd.gov.*

SANSWEET, STEPHEN JAY, journalist, writer, marketing executive; b. Phila., June 14, 1945; s. Jack Morris and Fannie (Axelrod) S. BS, Temple U., Phila., 1966. Reporter Phila. Inquirer, 1966-69; reporter Wall Street Jour., Phila., 1969-71, Montreal, Que., Canada, 1971-73, LA, 1973-84, dep. bur. chief, 1984-87, bur. chief, 1987-96; dir. specialty mktg. Lucasfilm Ltd., San Francisco, 1996—97, dir. content mgmt. and fan rels., 1997—; sr. editor Star Wars Galaxy Mag., 1996-2000; columnist Star Wars Insider, 1994—. Lectr. bus. journalism U. So. Calif., LA, 1984-87. Author: The Punishment Cure, 1976, Science Fiction Toys and Models, 1981, Star Wars: From Concept to Screen to Collectible, 1992, Tomart's Price Guide to Worldwide Star Wars Collectibles, 1994, 2d edit., 1997, The Quotable Star Wars, 1996, Star Wars Scrapbook: The Essential Collection, 1998, Star Wars Encyclopedia, 1998, Star Wars Collectibles: A Pocket Manual, 1998, Anakin Skywalker: The Story of Darth Vader, 1998, Star Wars: The Action Figure Archive, 1999, The Star Wars Vault, 2007, The Complete Star Wars Encyclopedia, 2008, Star Wars: 1000 Collectibles, 2009; co-author: The Star Wars Poster Book, 2005, Star Wars Chronicles: The Prequels, 2005; cons. editor: Star Wars Galaxy card sets, 1993, 2d series, 1994, 3d series, 1995; editor: Star Wars Trilogy Spl. Edn. card sets, 1997. Recipient award for best fire story Phila. Fire Dept., 1968, Pub. Svc.-Team Mem. award Sigma Delta Chi, 1977; finalist Loeb award, 1990. Mem. Soc. Profl. Journalists. Avocation: collecting toys and movie memorabilia. Office: Lucasfilm Ltd PO Box 29901 San Francisco CA 94129

SANT, ROGER W., retired energy executive; M, Harvard U. Instr. corp. fin. Stanford U. Grad. Sch. Bus.; founder several businesses; asst. adminstr. energy conservation & environ. U.S. Fed. Energy Adminstrn., Washington; dir. Mellon Inst.'s Energy Productivity Ctr.; co-founder AES Corp., Washington, 1981, CEO, 1981—93, chmn. bd., 1981—2003, chmn. emeritus, 2003—06. Bd. dir. Marriott Internat. Inc. Author: The Least-Cost Energy Strategy; co-author: Creating Abundance-America's Least-Cost Energy Strategy; contbr. articles to profl. jours. Chmn. Summit Found., Summit Fund, Washington; bd. dir. World Wildlife Fund, chmn., 1994—2000; regent, chmn. exec. com. Smithsonian Institution; bd. dir. Anacostia Waterfront Corp., Nat. Symphony Orch., DC Coll. Access Prog., Tudor Place. Mailing: Summit Foundation Ste 525 2100 Pennsylvania Ave NW Washington DC 20037

SANTANA, CARLOS, musician; b. Autlan de Navarro, Mexico, July 20, 1947; m. Deborah Santana, Apr. 21, 1973 (separated 2007); children: Salvador, Stella, Angelica. Guitarist Santana Mgmt., San Rafael, Calif., 1987—; co-founder Milagro Found. Prin. Guts and Grace Records, 1993. Founder, guitarist Santana, 1966—, albums include, 1968, Abraxas, 1970, Santana III, Caravanserai, 1972, Welcome, 1973, Greatest Hits, 1974, Barboletta, 1974, Lotus, 1975, Amigos, 1976, Festival, Moonflower, 1977, Inner Secrets, 1979, Marathon, 1979, Swing of Delight, 1980, Zebop, 1981, Shango, 1982, Havana Moon, 1983, Beyond Appearances, 1985, Freedom, 1987, Viva Santana!, 1988, Doin' It, 1990, Spirits Dancing In the Flesh, 1990, Milagro, 1992, Brothers, 1994, Sacred Fire: Live in South America, 1995, Dance of the Rainbow Serpent, 1995, Supernatural, 1999 (Grammy award for Song of Yr., 2000, Grammy award for Record of Yr., 2000, Grammy award for Album of Yr., 2000), Shaman, 2002, All That I Am, 2005, Multi-Dimensional Warrior, 2008, solo albums include Devadip Carlos-Oneness: Silver Dreams, Golden Reality, 1979, Blues for Salvador, 1987 (Grammy award for Best Instrumental Rock Performance, 1989), appeared in film Soul to Soul, 1971, Love and Music, 1971, Fillmore, 1972, Dominoes: An Uncensored Journey Through the 60s, The All-Star Reggae Session, 1988, Santana: Viva Santana (A Conversation with Carlos), 1989, Carlos Santana: Sacred Fire: Live in Mexico, 1993, History of Rock 'N' Roll, Vol. 6, History of Rock 'N' Roll, Vol. 7, 1995, Blue Note-A Story of Modern Jazz, 1996, Ricky Martin: One Night Only, 1999, 1999, world-wide concert tours with Santana Band, performed and recorded with Buddy Miles, Herbie Hancock, McCoy Tyner, John McLaughlin, Jose Feliciano, Wayne Shorter and Alice Coltrane, Aretha Franklin, Olatunji; rec. artist: Arista Records. Recipient Gold Medal award, 1977, Century award Billboard Mag., 1996, Spl. Achievement award ALMA, 1999, Legend Award, World Music Awards, 2005; named to Hall of Fame, NAACP Image award, 2006, Rock and Roll Hall of Fame, 1998. Office: Santana Mgmt PO Box 10348 San Rafael CA 94912-0348 *Keep an open heart, focus on the positive, be true to your innermost feelings, but most of all make time to visit the Lord within.*

SANTANA, JOHAN (JOHAN ALEXANDER SANTANA ARAQUE), professional baseball player; b. Tovar, Merida, Venezuela, Mar. 13, 1979; m. Yasmile Santana; children: Jasmily, Jasmine. Pitcher Minn. Twins, 2000—07, NY Mets, 2008—. Recipient Am. League Cy Young award, 2004, 2006, Player's Choice award, Am. League's most outstanding pitcher, 2004, 2006, Am. League Triple Crown, 2006, Gold Glove award, 2007; named Am. League Pitcher of Yr., Sporting News, 2004, 2006, Player of Yr., Baseball America, 2006; named to Am. League All-Star Team, Maj. League Baseball, 2005—07, Nat. League All-Star Team, 2009. Achievements include becoming the first pitcher since 1961 to give up four or fewer hits in ten straight starts; setting a new Minnesota Twins franchise season record for strikeouts (265), 2004; leading the American League in: ERA, 2004, 2006; strikeouts, 2004, 2005, 2006; wins, starts, innings, 2006; leading the National League in: ERA, starts, innings, 2008. Office: NY Mets Citi Field 126th St & Roosevelt Ave Flushing NY 11368*

SANTANA, LYMARI JEANETTE, lawyer; b. Augusta, Ga., 1968; married. BA with honors in Polit. Sci., U. PR, Rio Piedras, 1991; JD with honors, Mich. State U. Detroit Coll. Law, 1994. Bar: Mich. 1994, Minn. 2000. With James M. Hacker, P.C., Mt. Clemens, Mich.; asst. prosecutor Village of New Haven, Mich.; asst. US atty. No. Dist. Ala.;

founding shareholder Mack & Santana Law Offices, P.C.; of counsel Mansfield, Tanick & Cohen, P.A., Mpls. With Judge Adv. Gen. Corps US Army, 1995—2000, criminal trial def. counselor 82nd Airborne Divsn. US Army, 1998. Decorated Meritorious Svc. medal; recipient Rising Star, Minn. Super Lawyers Mag., 2008; named a, 2005, 2006, 2007. Mem.: Nat. Hispanic Bar Assn., Minn. Hispanic Bar Assn. (pres. 2004—05, sec. 2001—03), Hennepin County Bar Assn. Avocations: reading, sports, movies. Office: Mack & Santana Law Offices PC 1700 US Bank Plz South 220 S 6th St Minneapolis MN 55402 Office Phone: 612-605-0967. Business E-Mail: lymari@macksantanalaw.com.

SANTANA, SUZETTE M., language educator; arrived in US, 1990; d. Silvia Malinoski. BA in Spanish Edn., Siena Coll., Loudonville, NY, 1998; MA in Spanish-Linguistics, State U. Albany, NY, 1999. Cert. tchr. in Spanish (7-12) NY. Spanish tchr. Cambridge Ctrl. Sch., NY, 2000—01, Albany Acad. Arts, 2001—02; adj. prof. Hudson Valley CC, Troy, NY, 2002, Empire State Coll., Saratoga Springs, NY, 2002—03; asst. prof. Spanish Adirondack CC, Queensbury, NY, 2003—08, academic advisor humanities, 2005—. Presenter conf. NY Assn. Fgn. Lang. Tchrs., Saratoga Springs, 2006; program dir., edn., cmty. confs. local area, 2007—08. Modern dancer Dance Co., 2007. Mem.: Am. Coun. Tchg. Fgn. Langs. Avocations: dance, music, travel, poetry, pottery. Personal E-mail: santanas@sunyacc.edu.

SANTANGELO, GASPARE CHARLES, education educator, retired principal; b. NYC, June 1, 1937; s. Joseph and Rose Santangelo; m. Josephine A. Gaulli, June 29, 1980; children: Christina, Robert De Lia Jr. children: Steven, Robert, Joseph, Philip. BS, St. Francis Coll., NYC, 1958; MS, SUNY, New Paltz, 1966; PhD, Pacific Western U., LA, 1990. Cert. tchr. N.Y., supt. schs. Calif., sch. dist. adminstr. N.Y. Tchr. and asst. prin. South Huntington (N.Y.) Schs., 1959—68; adminstrv. asst. to the supt. of schs. San Diego City Schs., 1968—71; tchr. and prin. South Country Schools, Bellport, NY, 1971—92; assoc. prof. edn. Dowling Coll., Oakdale, NY, 1992—2003. Dir. Ctr. for Human Interaction, East Patchogue, NY, 1982—99. Author: (training manual) A Rational Approach to Stress Management, 1984, (instructional manual) A Nation in Crisis AIDS: Identifying the Risks, 1988. Achievement in Sci. fellow, Nat. Inst. Sci., 1966. Personal E-mail: gcsant@aol.com.

SANTANGELO, MARIO VINCENT, retired dentist; b. Youngstown, Ohio, Oct. 5, 1931; s. Anthony and Maria (Zarlenga) S. Student, U. Pitts., 1949-51; DDS, Loyola U., Chgo., 1955, MS, 1960. Instr. Loyola U., 1957—70, asst. prof., 1960-66, assoc. prof., 1966-70, chmn. dept. radiology, 1962-70, dir. dental aux. utilization program, 1963-70, chmn. dept. oral diagnosis, 1967-70, asst. dean, 1969-70; pvt. practice Chgo., 1960-70; ret., 1970. Cons. Cert. Bd. Am. Dental Assts. Assn., 1967-75, VA Rsch. Hosp., 1969-75; counselor Chgo. Dental Assts. Assn., 1966-69; mem. dental student tng. adv. com. divsn. dental health USPHS, HEW, 1969-71; cons. dental edn. rev. com. NIH, 1971-72; cons. region IV, USPHS, HEW, Atlanta, 1973-76, region V, Chgo., 1973-77; mem. Commn. on Dental Edn. and Practice, Fedn. Dentaire Internat., 1984-92; mem. bd. visitors Washington U. Sch. Dental Medicine, St. Louis, 1974-76; mem. project staff Dental Edn. in the US, 1976. Contbr. articles to dental jours. 1st Lt. USAF, 1955—56, Capt. USAF, 1956—57. Recipient Dr. Harry Strusser Meml. award NYU Coll. Dentistry, 1985. Fellow Am. Coll. Dentists (life); mem. ADA (life, asst. sec. coun. dental edn. 1971-81, acting sec. 1981-82, sec. 1982-90, dir. 1990-92, asst. sec. commn. on dental accreditation 1975-81, acting sec. 1981-82, sec. 1982-90, dir. 1990-92, acting sec. commn. continuing dental edn. 1981-82, sec. 1982-90, dir. 1990-92), Ill. State Dental Assn. (life), Chgo. Dental Assn. (life), AMA (edn. work group 1982-86), Assembly Specialized Accrediting Bodies (coun. on postsecondary accreditation 1981-92, award of merit 1992), Am. Assn. Dental Schs., Odontographic Soc. Chgo. (life), Am. Acad. Oral Pathology, Am. Acad. Dental Radiology, Can. Dental Assn. (commn. on dental accrediation award of merit 1992), Am. Acad. Oral Medicine, Am. Assn. Dental Examiners (hon.), Blue Key Honor Soc., Omicron Kappa Upsilon, Xi Psi Phi. Home: 1440 N Lake Shore Dr Chicago IL 60610-1626

SANTANGELO, SUSAN L., psychiatry professor; d. John Lawrence and Beverly Ann (Conant) Santangelo. ScD, Harvard Sch. Pub. Health, Boston, 1992. Assoc. prof. epidemiology Harvard Sch. Pub. Health, 1994—; assoc. prof. psychiatry Harvard Med. Sch., Boston, 2002—. Master: Phenotype Working Group, Autism Consortium (chairperson 2006—09); fellow: Nat. Inst. Mental Health (prin. investigator 2004—), Nat. Rsch. Svc. (Rsch. Fellowship 1987—92), Dept. Def. (prin. investigator 2008—); mem.: Behavioral Genetics & Epidemiology Study Sect., NIH, Molecular Autism (editl. bd. mem. 2009), Am. Jour. Med. Genetics Part B, Neuropsychiatric Genetics (editl. bd. mem. 2007—09), Internat. Soc. Psychiat. Genetics (Jr. Investigator award 1993), Internat. Genetic Epidemiology Soc., Am. Soc. Human Genetics. Buddhist. Avocations: travel, kayaking, reading, walking. Office: Harvard Med Sch Mass Gen Hosp 185 Cambridge St CPZN 6-256 Boston MA 02114 Office Fax: 617-726-7876. Business E-Mail: ssantangelo@parteners.org.

SANTAOLALLA, GUSTAVO, musician, composer, record producer; b. Buenos Aires; Founder Surco Records, LA, 1997. Recordings: Santaolla, 1982, GAS, 1995, Roncoco, 1998; composer of movie soundtracks of Amores perros, 2000, 21 Grams, 2003, Diarios de motociclata (Motorcycle Diaries), 2004, Brokeback Mountain, 2005 (Oscar award for best original score, Acad. Motion Pictures Arts & Sciences, 2006), North Country, 2005, Babel, 2006 (Anthony Asquith award for Achievement in Film Music, British Acad. Film and TV Arts, 2007, Oscar award for best original score, 2007); producer for Carnabailito (Gary Kerpel), Nuevo (Kronos Quartet). Named one of 25 Most Influential Hispanics, Time Mag., 2005, 50 Smartest People in Hollywood, Entertainment Weekly, 2007. Mailing: Surco Records 1501 Baxter St Los Angeles CA 90026

SANTARPIA, SUSAN MARIE, psychologist; d. Walter L. and Jane F. Sawicki; children: Tessa M., Nina F. BA, SUNY, Buffalo, 2002, MA, 2005; PhD in Clin. Psychology, Walden U., Minn., 2008. Cert. sch.psychologist NY State Edn. Dept., 2005. Sch. psychologist New Directions Youth & Family Svc., Lockport, NY, 2005—; neuropsych technician Veteran's Hosp., Buffalo, 2008—. Author: (book) Student's Beliefs about Writing and Communication with Text, Sounds, and Images; contbr. scientific papers. Mem.: APA, Internat. Soc. Neurofeedback Rsch., Am. Psychol. Assn., Golden Key Internat. Honour Soc. Home: 9 Edna Pl Buffalo NY 14218-1311 Office: Dent Neurologic Inst 200 Sterling Dr Orchard Park NY 14127 Personal E-mail: smsantarpia@yahoo.com.

SANTEL, PATRICK FRANCIS X., lawyer; b. New Orleans, Apr. 2, 1967; s. Joseph and Honora Santel; m. Julie Santel, May 27, 1995; children: Connor, Maura, Delia. BA, Boston Coll., Chestnut Hill, Mass., 1985—89; JD, Seattle U., 1997—2000. Bar: Wash. 2001. Legal internship RealNetworks, Inc., Seattle, 1999—2000; corp. atty. Click2learn, Inc., Bellevue, Wash., 2001—04, SumTotal Systems, Inc., Bellevue, 2004—05; corp. counsel LexisNexis CourtLink, Inc., Bellevue, 2005—. Mng. editor Seattle U. Law Rev., 1999—2000; contbr. articles to profl. jours. Local mem. LexisNexis Cares Program. Mem.: ABA, Wash. Bar Assn., Wash. Lawyers for Arts. D-Liberal. Roman Cath. Avocations: travel, cooking. Office: LexisNexis CourtLink Inc 13427 NE 16th St Bellevue WA 98005 Office Fax: 425-467-4893. Business E-Mail: patrick.santel@lexisnexis.com.

SANTELLI, RICK, news correspondent, former financial executive; b. 1956; BS, U. Ill., Champaign/Urbana. Stock trader Chgo. Mercantile Exchange, 1979; v.p. interest rate futures and ops. at Chgo. Bd. Trade for Drexel, Burnham, Lambert; v.p instl. futures and ops. Rand Fin. Svcs., Inc.; v.p instl. trading and hedge accts. Sanwa Futures, L.L.C.; on-air editor CNBC Bus. News, Chgo., 1999—. Mem. Chgo. Mercantile Exch., Chgo. Bd. of Trade. Office: CBS Corp Hdqs 51 W 52nd St New York NY 10019 Office Phone: 212-975-4321. Office Fax: 212-975-4516.*

SANTELLI, ROBERT, museum director, historian; married; 3 children. BA in Am. History, Monmouth U.; MA in Am. Studies, U. So. Calif.; PhD in Am. Studies, NYU. Freelance music journalist, NJ; asst. prof. music dept. Monmouth U., West Long Branch, NJ, 1988—94, created Popular Music Studies program; adj. prof., guest lectr., Am. studies dept. Rutgers U., 1993—94; asst. curator Rock & Roll Hall of Fame Mus., Cleve., 1994—95, v.p. edn. & pub. programs, 1995—2000, developed Hall of Fame Series, developed Am. Music Masters Series; CEO, artistic dir. Experience Music Project, Seattle, 2000—06; exec. dir. GRAMMY Mus., LA, 2008—. Contbr. articles to Rolling Stone, CD Review, Downbeat, Backstreets, NJ Monthly, NY Times, Asbury Park Press, Cleve. Plain Dealer, and many others; author: The Big Book of Blues, 1994, Greetings from E Street: The Story of Bruce Springsteen & the E Street Band, 2006; co-author: American Roots Music, 2002, Martin Scorsese Presents the Blues: A Musical Journey, 2004; co-editor: Hard Travelin': The Life & Legacy of Woody Guthrie, 1999. Mem.: Nat. Music Mus. Alliance (founder, exec. dir.), Recording Acad. (v.p. Northwest ch. 2001—06). Office: GRAMMY Mus Ste 200 714 W Olympic Blvd Los Angeles CA 90015 Office Phone: 213-765-6800. E-mail: grammyinfo@grammymuseum.org.

SANTER, BENJAMIN DAVID, atmospheric scientist; b. Washington, June 3, 1955; BS Environ. Scis. with 1st class honors, U. East Anglia, Norwich, Eng., 1976; NATO Rsch. Studentship, U. East Anglia, 1977, PhD in Climatology, 1987. Jr. rsch. assoc. Sch. Environ. Scis. U. East Anglia, Norwich, Eng., 1978-79, rsch. assoc. climatic rsch. unit, 1983-87; project engr. dept. new techs., air pollution and Dornier Sys. GmbH, Friedrichshafen, Germany, 1980-83; postdoct., rsch. scientist Max-Planck Inst. Meteorologie, Hamburg, Germany, 1987-92; physicist earth and environ. scis. directorate Lawrence Livermore Nat. Lab., Livermore, Calif., 1992—. Expert witness German Bundestag Enquete Commn. Hearings on Greenhouse-Gas-Induced Climate Change, Bonn, Germany, 1992; cons. Battelle Pacific Northwest Lab., 1992-93, mem. sci. adv. panel climate change, data and detection program NOAA, 1995—; mem. Climate Variability and Predictability Numerical Experimentation Group, 1995—; participant numerous confs., workshops; lectr. in field. Co-author: Proceedings of NATO Advanced Study Institute on Physically-Based Modelling and Simulation of Climate and Climatic Change, 1988, Science and Engineering on Supercomputers, 1990, Supercomputer '90, Greenhouse-Gas-Induced Climate Change: A Critical Appraisal of Simulations and Observations, 1991, Global Warming: Concern for Tomorrow, 1993, Agricultural Dimensions of Global Climate Change, 1993, Dahlem Workshop on Global Changes in the Perspective of the Past, 1993, Climate Change int the Intra-American Sea, 1993, Communicating About Climate: the Story of the Model Evaluation Consortium for Climate Assessment, 1997; mem. editl. bd. Climatic Change, 1996—; contbr. numerous articles to profl. jours., chpts. to books. MacArthur fellow John D. and Catherine T. MacArthur Found., 1998; Ford Travel scholar, 1974; recipient Outstanding Scientific Paper award U.S. Dept. Commerce Environ. Rsch. Lab. Nat. Oceanic and Atmospheric Adminstrn., 1997, Norbert Gerbier-MUMM Internat. award World Meteorol. Orgn., 1998, E.O. Lawrence award U.S. Dept. Energy, 2002. Mem. Am. Geophys. Union. Achievements include research in climate modeling and greenhouse-gas effects supporting the hypothesis that human activity contributes to global warming. Office: Lawrence Livermore Nat Lab PCMDI PO Box 808 L-264 Livermore CA 94551-0808 Home: 2160 Goldenrod Ln San Ramon CA 94583-5555 Fax: (925) 422-7675. E-mail: santer1@llnl.gov.

SANTHANAM, KALATHUR S. V., chemist, researcher; b. Tirupati, Andhra, India, Sept. 11, 1938; s. Kalathur and Kalathur (Vijayalaxmi) Duraiswamy; m. Santhanam Chari Komalavalli; children: Rohini, Shalini. BSc with honors, Sri Venkateswara U., Tirupati, India, 1958, PhD, 1964; postdoctoral, Tex. U., Austin, 1964-68. Sr. prof. Tata Inst. Fund. Rsch., Mumbai, India, 1968—98; dir., prof. Rochester Inst. Tech., NY, 2001—. Vis. scientist U. Mich., Ann Arbor, 1971-73, Brookhaven Nat. Lab., Upton, NY, 1986, CNRS, Hevdon, France, 1989, 1990, 1994, 1996, PSI Switzerland, 1991, 1992; rsch. assoc. U. Tex., Austin, 1976, 80-81; vis. prof. U. Guelph, Can., 1979, U. Victoria, Can., 1982-90, Rochester Inst. Tech., NY, 1999; cons. Ctrl. Electrochem. Rsch. Inst., Karikudi, India, 1975-76, Nehru Sci. Centre, Mumbai, India, 1983-86, Chemapol, Mumbai, 1993-96. Author: Photoelectrochemical Solar Cells, 1988, Ion-sensing Electrodes and Electrochemical Instrumentation, 1990, Introduction to Hydrogen Technology, 2008; contbr. articles to profl. jours., papers in field, chpts. to books. Chmn. Bombay Assn. Sci. Edn., Mumbai, 1982, Bioelectrochem. Soc. India, Mumbai, 1990-96. With Indian mil., 1951-53. Univ. Grants Commn. scholar, New Delhi, 1961-63, Nat. Inst. Sci. India Acad., New Delhi, 1964. Fellow SAEST India (chmn. 1983-89); mem. ACS, Mat. Res. Soc., Saxon Acad. (corr.), Sigma Xi. Office: Rochester Inst Tech Ctr Materials Sci Engring Rochester NY 14623 Office Phone: 585-472-2920. Personal E-mail: santhanam@localnet.com. Business E-Mail: ksssch@rit.edu.

SANTHANARAMAN, GOPALAKRISHNAN, computer scientist; s. Narayana and Shanthi Santhanaraman; m. Harini Ramaprasad, Aug. 28, 2006. B in Tech., Inst. Tech., Banaras Hindu U., India; M in Computer Sci., U. SC., Columbia; PhD, Ohio State U., Columbia. Grad. rsch. assoc. Ohio State U., 2002—. Summer fellow, Indian Acad. Sci., 1997, Pacific NW Nat. Lab., 2005. Mem.: IEEE. Hindu. Avocations: badminton, yoga, reading, tennis, travel. Personal E-mail: gopalsan@gmail.com. Business E-Mail: santhana@cse.ohio-state.edu.

SANTI, E. SCOTT, engineering executive; BS in Acctg., U. Ill., 1983; M in Mgmt., Northwestern U., 1992. Sales rep. Buildex divsn. Ill. Tool Works (ITW), 1983, various sales and mktg. mgmt. positions Buildex and Paslode divsn., 1985—94, gen. mgr. Vortec divsn., 1995—97, v.p., gen. mgr. Hobart Ground Power bus., 1997—98, v.p., gen. mgr. Hobart Bros. businesses, 1998, group v.p. Welding Products, 2002—03, pres. Welding Products Focus Markets Group, 2003—04, exec. v.p., 2004—08, vice chmn., 2008—. Office: Ill Tool Works 3600 W Lake Ave Glenview IL 60026-1215 Office Phone: 847-724-7500. Office Fax: 847-657-4572.*

SANTÍ, ENRICO MARIO, humanities educator; s. Mario Jose Santí García and Olga Gertrudis Pera Hernandez; m. Nivia Montenegro, Feb. 2, 1990; children: Alexis Enrico, Venissa Teresita, Camila Margarita. BA, Vanderbilt U., Nashville, Tenn., 1972; PH.D., MPhil, MA, Yale U., New Haven, Conn., 1976. Prof. Spanish Georgetown U., Wash., 1987—2000; william t. bryan endowed chair U. Ky., Lexington, 2000—. Prof. romance studies and comparative lit. Cornell U., Ithaca, NY, 1977—87. Author: (essay) Pablo Neruda: The Poetics Of Prophecy. Academic adv. bd. mem. Ctr. A Free Cuba, Wash., 2000—08. Fellow Sr. Fellowship, Nat. Endowment Humanities, 2002—03. Avocation: art collecting. Office: Dept Of Hispanic Studies Univ Of Kentucky Lexington KY 40509 Office Fax: 859-323-9077. Business E-Mail: esant2@uky.edu.

SANTIAGO, CLAUDI, manufacturing executive; b. Spain; m. Nuria Santiago; 2 children. Studied, INSEAD, Fontainebleau, France, Georgetown U.; M in Computer Sci., Universidad Autonoma of Barcelona. Project mgr. info. svcs. GE, 1980, worldwide mktg. leader info. svcs. Rockville, Md., 1991, Paris, joined Nuovo Pignone bus., 1997—99, pres., CEO oil & gas, 1999—, sr. v.p., 2006—. Recipient Chmn. Leadership award, GE, 2006. Avocations: tennis, art. Office: Oil and Gas GE Via Felice Matteucci 2 50127 Firenze Italy Office Phone: 39 055 423 211. Office Fax: 39 055 423 2800.

SANTIAGO, DIANA, music educator; d. Noel Eduardo Rodriguez and Fausta Jorge-Lopez; m. Lino Santiago, Dec. 20, 1986; children: Mariana, Natalia, Lino Emmanuel. BA in Secondary Edn. Chemistry, Cath. U., PR; MA in Curriculum and Instrn., Kean Coll., Union; MA in Ednl. Leadership, William Paterson U., Wayne, NJ. Quality control chemist asst. Biocraft, Fairfield, NJ; tchr. compensatory edn. high sch. math. Irvington Bd. Edn., NJ; tchr. bilingual/bicultural mid. sch. Newark Pub. Schs., sch. treas., coord. sch. test, facilitator whole sch. reform, developer, coord. dist. and sch. leadership team iv math., 2004—. Cons. Newark Pub. Schs., sch. peer rev. com., sch.-cmty. liason, mem. NJ state CAPA; presenter in field. Mem.: Nat. Coun. Tchrs. Math., Nat. Staff Devel. Coun., William Paterson U. Alumni Assn., Kean Alumni Assn. Home: 122 Cherryville Hollow Road Flemington NJ 08822 Office: Newark Public Schools 2 Cedar St Newark NJ 07102 Personal E-mail: lsantiago@patmedia.net.

SANTIAGO, FRANCISCO JOSÉ HERNANDO, judge; b. June 4, 1936; LLB. Judge Mil. Supreme Ct., Spain, 1986—89, Adminstrv. Ct., Spain, 1989—97; magistrate Supreme Ct. of Spain, Madrid, 1994—97, pres., 2001—. Office: Tribunal Supremo de Espana Pza de la Villa de Paris s/n 28071 Madrid Spain

SANTIAGO, RAYMOND, library director, educator; b. NYC, July 13, 1949; s. Raymond and Livia Santiago; m. Crystal C. Capelis, May 15, 1979; 1 child, Jason Esrael. BFA, Rochester Inst. Tech., NY, 1974; MLS, SUNY, Buffalo, 1975. Co-chair, head non-print svcs. World U., San Juan, 1978—84; libr. Tampa-Hillsborough Pub. Libr. Sys., Fla., 1984—88, sect. mgr. Fla., 1988—90; supr. libr. svcs. Miami-Dade Pub. Libr. Sys., Fla., 1990—91, asst. dir. Fla., 1991—98, dir. Fla., 1998—. Adj. faculty Sch. Libr. and Info. Sci., U. South Fla., 1994—. Named Libr. of Yr., Libr. Jour., 2003. Mem. ALA, Pub. Libr. Assn., Fla. Libr. Assn. Office: Miami-Dade Pub Libr Sys 101 W Flagler St Miami FL 33130-1504 Office Phone: 305-375-5184. Business E-Mail: santiagor@miamidade.gov.

SANTINA, DALIA, nutritionist, writer, skin care specialist; b. Amman, Jordan, Sept. 24, 1954; d. Mahmoud Daoud Abbasi, Widad Abbasi; m. Mohammed Shafiq Santina. BA in English Lit., U. Riyadh, Saudi Arabia, 1977; diploma in computer programming, Western Bus. Coll., 1980; diploma in Skin Aesthetics, Career Acad. Beauty, 1989; PhD in Holistic Nutrition, Clayton Coll. Natural Health, 1994. Cert. paramedical acne 1990, glycolic acid services 1991, mgmt. aging and sundamaged skin 1992, natural pharmacology 1992, aesthetic peeling 1992, oxygenation of the skin 1993, lymphatic drainage massage techniques 1994, homeopathic esthetiocology 1994, iridology diploma 1995, cert. chem. peels 1996, hydrotherapy 1997, glycolic treatments 1998, diploma in iridology 2003, cert. in herbology 2003. Exec. asst. to v.p. Am. Health Ctr., Newport Beach, Calif., 1988—89; skin care co. Skinclub, Huntington Beach, Calif., 1991—96; lectr. holistic nutrition/skin health issues, 1999—. Translator computer sys. tng. manuals, Dallas, 1983—84; tech. translator England and No. Ireland, 1984. Author: Holistic Skin Is...In, 2001, Super Supplements for Skin, Body & Mind, 2004; contbr. articles to profl. jours. Recipient Gold medal in Table Tennis, Sports Bd., Kuwait, 1972. Avocations: horseback riding, reading, antiques. Home Phone: 949-786-0672. Personal E-mail: dalia4skin@msn.com.

SANTINI, DANILO JOHN, energy economist, urban systems engineer; b. Louisville, Mar. 10, 1945; s. Danilo Gene Santini and Mary Margaret (Dink) Brown; m. Tomma Jean Trent, Dec. 28, 1969; children: Laura Trent, Danilo Thomas. BArch, MIT, 1968; MS in Bus. and Econs., Ill. Inst. Tech., 1972; PhD Urban Systems/Pub. Policy Analysis, Northwestern U., 1976. High sch. tchr. math. and sci. George Washington High Sch., Charleston, W.Va., 1968-70; asst. scientist Argonne (Ill.) Nat. Lab., 1974-79, scientist, 1980-92, sect. mgr., 1993—, sr. economist, 2003. Archtl. draftsman Bowman & Assocs., Vecellio and Kreps, Charleston, Va., 1963-70, Teng & Assocs., Chgo., 1971-72; lectr. in econs. U. Ill. at Chgo., 1983, Lewis U., Romeoville, Ill., 1984; mem. alternative fuels com. Transp. Rsch. Bd., Washington, 1989—96, chmn., 1996-2002. Contbr. chpts. to books, articles to profl. jours. Trustee, mem. bldg. com. Friendship United Meth. Ch., Bolingbrook, Ill., 1991—96; asst. coach Pony-Colt Baseball, Bolingbrook, 1984-86; active Am. Field Svcs., 1989-90. Northwestern U. fellow, 1972-74, Ill. Inst. Tech. fellow, 1970. Mem. Am. Econs. Assn., Internat. Assn. Energy Economists (chpt. pres. 1985-86), Internat. Inst. Forecasters, Regional Sci. Assn., Sigma Iota Epsilon. Avocations: bowling, walking. Office: 364 Julianna Cir Franklin TN 37064

SANTINI, GINO, pharmaceutical executive; b. Cesena, Italy; Grad. in Mech. Engring., U. Bologna, Italy, 1981; MBA, U. Rochester, NY, 1983. Pres. SERM and skeletal products; fin. planning assoc. Eli Lilly and Co., Italy, 1983, pharm. dir. Belgium, 1990—91, gen.mgr. Eli Lilly Compania de Mex. Mexico City, 1991, area dir. L.Am., 1994—95, v.p. corp. stategy and bus. devel., 1996—97, pres. women's health bus. unit, 1997—99, pres. US ops., 1999—2004, sr. v.p. corp. strategy and policy, 2004—, mem. policy and strategy com., 2004—, mem. sr. mgmt. coun., 2004—. Bd. trustees Healthcare Leadership Coun.; assoc. mem. bd. Nat. Assn. Chain Drug Stores. Chmn. Nobel of Ind.; mem. exec. com. Indpls. C. of C. Office: Eli Lilly and Co Lilly Corp Ctr Indianapolis IN 46285 Office Phone: 317-276-2000.

SANTINI, JORGE A., Mayor, San Juan, Puerto Rico; b. San Juan, 1960; BA, U. P.R.; law degree cum laude, Interam. U. Ptnr. Miranda Cardenas & Córdova, 1986—93; legal advisor Gov. of P.R., 1994—96; mem. Sen. of P.R., 1996—99; mayor City of San Juan, 2001—. Chmn. Sen. Jud. Com.; vice-chmn. Govt. and Fed. Affairs Com., Banking, Consumer Affairs, and Pub. Corps. Com. Lt. col. Puerto Rico Nat. Guard. New Progressive Party. Office: PO Box 70179 San Juan PR 00902-4100 Office Phone: 787-724-7171.*

SANTISI, TERRI M. (THERESA M. SANTISI), multimedia company executive; b. Mar. 5, 1954; BS magna cum laude, Boston Coll., 1976. With Ernst & Young; CFO EMI Music Publishing Worldwide; exec. v.p., gen. mgr. EMI Music N.Am.; mng. ptnr. KPMG; CFO Interpublic Group of Cos.; exec. v.p., chief fin. & adminstrv. officer IMG, 2006—. Mem. adv. bd. She Made It program Mus. TV and Radio; bd. dirs., mem. exec. com. NYC Outward Bound.

SANTMAN, LEON DUANE, lawyer, former federal government executive; b. Phila., July 29, 1930; s. Elmer William and Anna Mary (Moffitt) S.; m. Juliet Gloria Peacock, June 16, 1952; 1 dau., Lorri Leigh Santman Myers. BS, U. S. COAST Guard Acad., 1952; LLB, U. Houston, 1953; LLM, George Washington U., 1968. Bar: Tex. 1963, Md. 1974. Commd. ensign U.S. Coast Guard, 1952, advanced through grades to comdr., 1967, ret., 1972; assoc. gen. counsel Cost of Living Council, Washington, 1972-74; asst. gen. counsel U.S. Dept. Transp., Washington, 1974-77, dir. Materials Transp. Bur., 1977-85; dir. ship ops. Maritime Adminstrn., 1985-88. Episcopalian.

SANTOMERO, ANTHONY M., financial consultant, former bank executive, public policymaker; b. NYC, Sept. 29, 1946; s. Camillo and Jean (Oddo) Santomero; m. Marlena Belviso, Aug. 21, 1971; children: Jill Renee, Marc Anthony. AB, Fordham U., 1968; PhD, Brown U., 1971; EDhe (hon.), Stockholm Sch. Econs., 1992; LHC, U. Rome, 2003. Cert. risk profl., Bank Adminstrn. Inst., 2001. Asst. prof., then assoc. prof., then prof. fin. Wharton Sch., U. Pa., Phila., 1972-84, R.K. Mellon prof. fin., 1984—2002, R.K. Mellon prof. fin. emeritus, 2002—, vice dean, dir. grad. div., 1984-87, dep. dean, 1990-94; dir. Wharton Fin. Instns. Ctr., 1995-2000; pres. Fed. Res. Bank Phila., 2000—06; sr. advisor McKinsey & Co., 2006—. Asst. prof. economics Baruch Coll., CUNY, 1971—72; vis. prof. European Inst. Advanced Studies Mgmt., Brussels, 1977—78, Stockholm Sch. Econs., 1989—90, U. Rome, Tor Vergata, 1994—97, Ecole Superieure des Scis. Economiques and Commerciales, France, 1977—78; bd. dirs. Renaissance Reinsurance Co., Ltd., 2008—, Penn Mutual Life Insurance Co., 2008—, Columbia Funds, 2008—, Citigroup Inc., 2009—, Citibank, N.A., 2009—. Author: Financial Markets, Instruments and Institutions, 1997, 2001, Challenges for Modern Central Banking, 2001; contbr. articles to profl. jours. Mem. Fin. Economists Roundtable; bd. mem. Mann Ctr. Performing Arts Union League Phila., 2005—08; bd. trustees Drexel U.; chmn. Econ. Adv. Bd., Swedish Inst. Fin. Rsch., Mayor's Coun. Econ. Advisors, 2000—03. Decorated hon. knighthood Republic of Italy; recipient Global Citizen award, Global Interdependence Ctr., 2005. Mem.: Am. Econs. Assn., Am. Fin. Assn. Roman Catholic. Personal E-mail: asantomero@comcast.net.

SANTONA, GLORIA, lawyer, food products executive; b. Gary, Ind., June 10, 1950; d. Ray and Elvira (Cambeses) S.; m. Douglas Lee Frazier, Apr. 12, 1980; 1 child, Daniel BS in Biochemistry, Mich. State U., 1971; JD cum laude, U. Mich., 1977. Bar: Ill. 1977. Atty. McDonald's Corp., Oak Brook, Ill., 1977-82, dir., 1982-86, assoc. gen. counsel, 1986-92, asst. v.p., 1989-93, v.p., sec., dep. gen. counsel, 1996-99, v.p., gen. counsel, sec., 1999-2001, sr. v.p., gen. counsel, sec., 2001—03, exec. v.p., gen. counsel, sec., 2003—. Bd. dirs. Aon Corp. Bd. trustees Rush U. Med. Ctr. Named a Women of Achievement, The Anti-Defamation League, 2008. Mem. ABA, Chgo. Bar Assn., Am. Corp. Counsel Assn., Am. Soc. Corp. Secs., Constl. Rights Found. Chgo. Office: McDonalds Corp 1 McDonalds Plz Oak Brook IL 60523-1911*

SANTONI, BRANDON GERAD, engineering educator, researcher; b. Casper, Wyo., July 2, 1976; s. Gary Leon and Terry Ann Santoni; m. Amy Sue Lyons, Aug. 24, 2008. BS, Tex. Tech U., Lubbock, 1998; MS, Colo. State U., Ft. Collins, 2003, PhD, 2006. Undergrad. rsch. asst. Tex. Tech. U. Health Scis. Ctr., 1997—98, U. Wyo., Laramie, 1999—2000; grad. rsch. asst. Colo. State U., 2001—06, musculoskeletal oncology rsch. fellow, 2006—08, postdoc. rsch. fellow, 2007—08, rsch. scientist, 2008—, assoc. instr., 2008—; rsch. assoc. Clemson U., SC, 2006—07. Contbr. articles to profl. jours. Recipient Mark S. Boomberg award, Vet. Orthop. Soc., 2008; Rsch. grant, Musculoskeltal Transplant Found., 2004—06. Mem.: Colo. State U. Instl. Rev. Bd. (alt. mem. 2008—), Am. Soc. Bone and Mineral Rsch., Internat. Bone and Mineral Soc., Orthop. Rsch. Soc., Tau Beta Pi Engring. Honor Soc. Office: Colo State Univ 300 W Drake Rd Campus Delivery 1678 Fort Collins CO 80523 Business E-Mail: bgsant@holly.colostate.edu, bgsant@engr.colostate.edu.

SANTONI, RONALD ERNEST, philosophy educator; b. Arvida, Que., Can., Dec. 19, 1931; s. Fred Albert and Phyllis (Tremaine) S.; m. Marguerite Ada Kiene, June 25, 1955; children: Christina, Marcia, Andrea, Juanita, Jonathan, Sondra. BA, Bishop's U., Lennoxville, Que., 1952; MA, Brown U., 1954; PhD, Boston U., 1961; postgrad., U. Paris-Sorbonne, 1956-57. Asst. prof. philosophy U. Pacific, Stockton, Calif., 1958-61; postdoctoral rsch. fellow Yale U., New Haven, 1961-62; asst. prof. philosophy Wabash Coll., Crawfordsville, Ind., 1962-64; faculty Denison U., Granville, Ohio, 1964—, prof. philosophy, 1968—2002, chmn. dept., 1971-73, 82-84, 92, Maria Theresa Barney chair in philosophy, 1978—, prof. emeritus, 2002—. Peace lectr. Bethel Coll., Spring, 1985; vis. scholar in philosophy Cambridge U., Eng., 1986, 90, 94, 97, 99, 2001, vis. lectr. in philosophy, 1990; vis. fellow Clare Hall, Cambridge U., 1986, elected life mem.,1986, life mem., vis. scholar, 1990, 94, 97, 99, 2001, 03, 04, 06, 08; vis. fellow in philosophy Yale U., 1975, 81, 93-94, 97; keynote spkr. 2d Internat. Conf. on Nuclear Free Zones, Cordoba, Spain, 1985; Internat. Studies Assn., London, 1989, spkr. and U.S.A. co-chair Internat. conf. Internat. Philosophers for Prevention of Nuclear Omnicide, Moscow, 1990; del. and raporteur UN meeting of Peace Messenger Orgns., Dagomys, Sochi, USSR, 1991; invited participant Colloquium on Technological Risks to Environment, Montreal, 1993; invited spkr. U. Paris (Sorbonne), 2004, Internat. Conf. Honoring Centenary of J.P. Sartre, U. Amiens, France, 2005; spkr. in field. Contbg. author: Current Philosophical Issues: Essays in Honor of C.J. Ducasse, 1966, Towards the Understanding and Prevention of Genocide, 1984, Nuclear War: Philosophical Perspectives, 1985, Genocide: A Critical Bibliographic Review, 1988, Just War, Nonviolence and Nuclear Deterrence: Philosophers on War and Peace, 1992, The Institution of War, 1991, Violence and Human Co-Existence, 1994, Hiroshima's Shadows, 1998, The Encyclopedia of Genocide, 1999, Human Coexistence and Sustainable Development, 2001, Das Sein und das Nichts, 2003, Global Studies Encyclopedia, 2003, Dictionnaire Sartre, 2004, Sartre Today: A Centenary Celebration, 2005-06, Pourquoi Sartre? 2006, German, 2009, Uber Sartre: Perspektiven und Kritiken, 2005, Sartre: le philosophe, l'intellectuel, et la politique, 2007; author: Bad Faith, Good Faith and Authenticity in Sartre's Early Philosophy, 1995, Sartre on Violence: Curiously Ambivalent, 2003; editor, contbr. Religious Language and the Problem of Religious Knowledge, 1968; co-editor Social and Political Philosophy, 1963; contbg. editor Internet on the Holocaust and Genocide; mem. editl. bd. Jour. Peace and Justice Studies; contbr. over 164 publ. in profl. jours. and nat. mags. V.p. NAACP, Licking County, 1967; co-organizer Crawfordsville (Ind.) Human Rights Coun., 1962-64; nat. exec. com. Episcopal Peace Fellowship, 1968-78; internat. coun. Internat. Inst. on the Holocaust and Genocide, 1985—; nat. coun. Fellowship of Reconciliation, 1988-89; trustee Margaret Hall Sch., Versailles, Ky., 1972-74; nat. bd. dirs. Promoting Enduring Peace, 1982-2002, 06—. Canadian Govt. Overseas fellow Royal Soc. Can., 1956-57; Church Soc. for Coll. Work faculty fellow, 1961-62; Yale postdoctoral rsch. fellow, 1961-62; Danforth assoc., 1963-64; Soc. for Religion in Higher Edn. postdoctoral fellow, 1972—; Yale rsch. fellow, 1975; guest fellow Berkeley Coll., Yale U., 1975, 81, 93-94, 97, elected assoc. fellow, 1994—; vis. fellow in philosophy Yale U., 1981, 93-94, 97; Robert C. Good faculty fellow Denison U., 1985-86, 2000-01, Robert C. Good faculty fellow, 1993-94; elected life mem. Clare Hall, Cambridge (Eng.) U., 1986; elected mem. High Table, King's Coll., Cambridge U.,spring summer 1999; recipient Mellon award for disting. faculty Denison U., 1972, Crossed Keys Faculty of Yr. award Denison U., 1986-87; Philosophy, Freedom and Action Conf. held in his honor, 2002. Mem. Am. Philos. Assn., Ch. Soc. for Coll. Work, Soc. for Phenomenology and Existential Philosophy, Internat. Philosophers for Peace (v.p. 1983-85, v.p. cen. div. 1990-91, internat. pres. 1991-96, internat. exec. com. 1996—), Sartre Soc. of N.Am. (exec. com. 1994—), Sartre Circle (coord. 1997—), le groupe d'Etudes Sartriennes, Gandhi-King Soc., Union of Bi-Nat. Profls. Against Omnicide (v.p. 1978—), Institut für Axiologische Forschungen (exec. com.), Concerned Philosophers for Peace (founding 1980—, pres. 1996-97), Fellowship of Reconciliation, Radical Philosophers Assn., Amnesty Internat., OxFam Am., ACLU. Episcopalian. Home: 500 Burg St Granville OH 43023-1005 Office Phone: 740-587-6318. Business E-Mail: santoni@denison.edu. *Gratitude for what one has been given, commitment to personal growth and integrity, some "gracious gall", listening to the world's humiliated, and a recognition that any genuine success is always a gift of grace, never fully earned or deserved.*

SANTOPIETRO, ALBERT ROBERT, lawyer; b. Providence, Oct. 18, 1948; s. Alfred and Marie (Epifanio) Santopietro; m. Linda Santopietro; children: Hope, Spencer, Anna. BA, Brown U., 1969; JD, U. Va., 1972. Bar: R.I. 1973, Conn. 1983, Mass. 1997, U.S. Dist. Ct. R.I. 1973, Ill. 1974, U.S. Dist. Ct. Mass. 1997. Atty. Met. Life Ins. Co., Oak Brook, Ill., 1974—75, Seligman Group, NYC, 1975—76, Mut. Benefit Life Ins. Co., Newark, 1976—78, asst. counsel, 1978—81; counsel Aetna Ins. Co., Newark, 1982—91; assoc. counsel Conn. Mutual Life Ins. Co., Hartford, 1991—95; 2d v.p. and assoc. gen. counsel Mass. Mutual, 1995—; spl counsel Babson Capital Mgmt. LLC, 2006—. Home: 142 Pond Brook Rd Huntington MA 01050-9620 Office: PO Box 22 Northampton MA 01061-0022 Home Phone: 413-210-2741; Office Phone: 413-667-3290. Personal E-mail: asantopietrolaw@aol.com.

SANTORUM, RICK (RICHARD JOHN SANTORUM), lawyer, former United States Senator from Pennsylvania; b. Winchester, Va., May 10, 1958; s. Aldo and Catherine (Dughi) S.; m. Karen Garver, June 2, 1990; children: Elizabeth Anne, Richard John Jr., Daniel James, Sarah Maria, Peter Kenneth. BA in Polit. Sci., Pa. State U., 1980; MBA, U. Pitts., 1981; JD, Dickinson Sch. Law, 1986. Bar: Pa. 1986. Adminstrv. asst. to Sen. Doyle Corman Pa. State Senate, Harrisburg, 1981-86, exec. dir. local govt. com., 1981-84, exec. dir. transp. com., 1984-86; assoc. Kirkpatrick & Lockhart LLP, Pitts., 1986-90; mem. US Congress from 18th Pa. dist., Washington, 1991-95; US Senator from Pa., 1995—2007; mem. agr., nutrition, & forestry com., fin. com., rules & adminstrn., banking, housing, & urban affairs, spl. com. on aging; chmn. Senate Republican Conf., 2001—07; cons. Eckert Seamans Cherin & Mellott, LLC, Pitts., 2007—. Sr. fellow The Ethics & Pub. Policy Ctr., 2007—; polit. contr. Fox News Channel, 2007—; bd. dirs. Universal Health Services, Inc., 2007—. Author: Rick Santorum: A Senator Speaks Out on Life, Freedom and Responsibility, 2005, It Takes A Family: Conservatism and the Common Good, 2005. Bd. dirs. Mt. Lebanon Extended Day Program, 1987-91; mem. Child Advocacy Project, 1987-91. Recipient Award for Legis. Excellence, Am. Soc. Consultant Pharmacists, 1997, Award for Mfg. Legis. Excellence, Nat. Assn. Mfrs., 1999, Disting. Svc. award, Brent Soc. of Arlington, Va. Diocese, 1999, Med. Miracle award, Healthcare Leadership Coun., 2000, John Paul II award, Inst. Psychol. Sciences, 2003, Legis. of the Yr., Nat. Multiple Sclerosis Soc., 2003, Friend of Seniors award, Bucks County, Pa. Area Agy. on Aging, 2004, Higher Edn. Leadership award, Washington Ctr. Internships and Academic Studies, 2005. Mem. KC, Italian Sons and Daus. Assn., Allegheny County Bar Assn. Child Advocacy Program. Republican. Roman Catholic. Avocations: golf, racquetball. Office: Eckert Seamans Cherin & Mellott LLC 1747 Pennsylvania Ave NW Ste 1200 Washington DC 20006 also: Ethics & Pub Policy Ctr 1015 15th St Ste 900 Washington DC 20005 E-mail: rsantorum@eckertseamans.com.

SANTOS, BENJAMIN GUZMAN, physician, anesthesiologist; b. Manila, Feb. 24, 1923; arrived in USA, 1953; s. Fidel and Felomena Santos; m. Karen Renee Lindsey, Dec. 5, 1998; children: Ben Jr., Marlene Gaviria, Kristy Greene, Steven. Student, U. Philippines, U. Santo Tomas, Manila, San Beda Coll.; MD, Manila Ctrl. U. Sch. of Medicine, 1952. Cert. degree in anesthesia Baroness Erlanser Hosp. Sch. Anesthesia, Chatanooga, 1962, diploma in hypnosis New Orleans, 1968. Intern Mt Sinai Hosp., Miami Beach, 1953—54; house doctor Tampa Mcpl. Hosp., Fla., 1955; intern Piedmont Hosp., Atlanta, 1958—60; anesthesia intern, cert. in anesthesia Baroness Erlanger Hosp., Chattanooga, 1960—62; anesthesiologist Anesthesiologist Associated, Chattanooga, 1962—93; freelance anesthesiologist Chattanooga, 1993—95; ret., 1995. Active mem. Fil-Am., Tenn. Mem.: AMA, Profl. Assn. Divsn. Am. Inst. Hypnosis, Chattanooga-Hamilton County Med. Soc. (50 Yrs. of Leadership and Svc. award 2003), Tenn. Med. Soc., Am. Assn. Anesthesiologists. Roman Catholic. Avocations: reading, travel, dance. Office: PO Box 5254 Chattanooga TN 37406-0254 Home: 6760 Hickory Brook Rd Chattanooga TN 37421 Home Phone: 423-954-9986; Office Phone: 423-227-6760. Personal E-mail: bsantos007@comcast.net.

SANTOS, HERBERT JOSEPH, JR., lawyer; b. Reno, Feb. 17, 1963; s. Herbert Joseph Sr. and Jeanette Dorothy (Olivera) S.; m. Kimberly Ellen Saylors, Mar. 8, 1986; children: Herbert Joseph III, Jarred Adam, Hannah McKenzie. BA in Sociology, U. Nev., Las Vegas, 1985; JD, U. of the Pacific, 1991. Bar: Nev. 1991, Calif. 1992, U.S. Dist. Ct. Nev. 1992, U.S. Supreme Ct. 1999. Head social worker Cmty. Welfare, Inc., Reno, 1986-87; inspector Nev. Athletic Commn., Reno, 1986-87; sr. legal rsch. asst. County Sacramento, Calif., 1987-91; assoc. Law Offices of Terry A. Friedman, Ltd., Reno, 1991-98; owner The Law Firm of Herb Santos Jr., 1999—. Mem. State Bar Law Office Mgmt. and Procedures Com., 1996-98; chair election canvassing com. Nev. Bd. Govs, access to justice com., 1998, temp. apptd. jud. selection com. Author (instrn. manual) ORR, County of Sacramento Bankruptcy Forms and Procedures Manual with Practice Pointers, 1990; editor: The Writ, 1997-98; appeared in: (films) Kingpin, Father's Day, (TV miniseries) The Last Don, The Cheater's Partner in Mafia!, Body and Soul, Diamonds. Mem. Cmty. Coalition, Reno, 1986-87; mentor U. Nev., Reno, 1993—. Recipient Am. Jurisprudence award, 1991, Mem. ABA (young lawyers divsn., del. for State of Nev. 1996, 97, 98, 99), ATLA, Nev. Trial Lawyers Assn., State Bar Nev. (exec. coun. mem. young lawyers sect. 1993—, pres. young lawyers sect. 1996-97, com. chair Ask-a-Lawyer young lawyers sect. 1994—. chair pub. com. 1996-97, Pro-Bono award 1997, apptd. alternate dispute resolution sect.-long range planning 1998), Washoe County Bar Assn. (exec. coun., sgt.-at-arms 1997-98, treas. 1998-99, sec. 1999—, Bar Leader award 1998), Am. Inns of Ct. (Hon. Bruce Thompson chpt. 1995-97). Republican. Roman Catholic. Avocations: boxing, basketball, golf. Office: The Law Firm of Herb Santos Jr Liberty Ctr 350 S Center St Ste 350 Reno NV 89501-2113 Home: 14205 Prairie Flower Ct Reno NV 89511-6710

SANTOS, ISABEL RODRIGUEZ, marketing educator; Mktg. tchr. Lorenzo Coballes Gandia HS, Hatillo, PR. Named PR Tchr. of Yr., 2007. Office: Lorenzo Coballes Gandia HS PO Box 1357 Hatillo PR 00659 E-mail: isaymario99@yahoo.com.

SANTOS, LEONARD ERNEST, lawyer; b. Caracas, Venezuela, Aug. 5, 1946; s. Paul Joseph and Frieda (Epstein) S.; m. Jeannie Bernadette Niedermeyer, Oct. 28, 1978; children: Jonathan, Matthew, Andrew. BA cum laude, Tufts U., 1967; JD, NYU, 1971. Bar: Ariz. 1972, D.C. 1972, U.S. Dist. Ct. D.C. 1972, U.S. Ct. Appeals (9th and 5th cirs.) 1972, U.S. Supreme Ct. 1972. Law clk. to cir. judge US Ct. Appeals (9th cir.), San Francisco, 1971-72; assoc. Hogan & Hartson, Washington, 1972-76; sr. atty. internat. affairs US Dept. Treasury, Washington, 1976-83; internat. trade counsel US Senate Fin. Com., Washington, 1983-87; ptnr. Verner, Liipfert, Bernhard, McPherson & Hand, Washington, 1987-89, Perkins Coie, Washington, 1989-98; ptnr., exec. dir. Santos Family Found., Washington, 2000—; pres. Martin Santos Properties, LLC, 2001—, JMA Properties, LLC, 2003—. Note and comment editor NYU Law Jour., 1970; contbr. legal publs.; editor ABA Compendium of Foreign Trade Remedy Laws, 1998. Exec. dir. Dole for Pres. campaign, Washington, 1988, 96. Mem. NAFTA (chpt. 19 dispute settlement panels) Independent. Roman Catholic. Avocations: architecture, economics. Office: Martin Santos Prop LLC 5185 MacArthur Blvd NW Ste 705 Washington DC 20016 Office Phone: 202-236-0174. Personal E-mail: santlen@aol.com.

SANTOS, ROLANDO AGUILAR, economics professor; b. Manila, May 22, 1962; s. Roque Santos and Esperanza Aguilar; life ptnr. Steven Howard Emery, Sept. 21, 1997. BA in Economics, De La Salle U., Manila, 1982; MA in Economics and Internat. Affairs, Ohio U., Athens, 1987; PhD in Economics, Northeastern U., Boston, 1992. Instr. economics De La Salle U., 1982—85; instr. Bowling Green State U., Huron, Ohio, 1991—94; prof. economics Lakeland CC, Kirtland, Ohio, 1994—, dir. ctr. internat. edn., 1998—2007. Cons. US Dept. Edn., Bus. and Internat. Edn. Grant, Washington. Pres. Asians and Friends Cleve., 1995—2008. Recipient Cultural Diversity award, Lakeland CC, 2001. Mem.: Midwest Econ. Assn., Philippine C. of C. (pres. 2007—08), Am. Econ. Assn., Ohio Asian Am. C. of C. (pres. 2005—07). Democrat. Home: 2811 Fairmount Blvd Cleveland Heights OH 44118 Office: Lakeland CC 7700 Clocktower Dr Kirtland OH 44094 Office Fax: 440-525-7602. Business E-Mail: rsantos@lakelandcc.edu.

SANTOS, SANTOS V., literature and language professor, researcher; d. Olympio dos Santos and Alda do Valle Santos; m. Enrique Mayer, Sept. 2, 2001; 1 child, Manuela dos Santos Leal. PhD in L.Am. Lit., U. São Paulo, Brazil, 1992. Cert. in tchg. Brazilian Edn. Ministry. Asst. prof. Fed. Fluminense U., Niteroi, Rio de Janeiro, Brazil, 1985—93, assoc. prof., 1993—95, coord. L.Am. and Caribbean interdisciplinary group prial, 1994—95; lectr. Yale U., New Haven, 1995—96, asst. prof., 1996—2001, dir. grad. studies, 1999, assoc. prof., 2002—06; prof. Grad. Ctr., NYC, 2006—; exec. organizer Americas Soc., Grad. Ctr., CUNY, Film Soc. Linclon Ctr., Ctr. Cultural Brazil, 2008. Author: (short stories) Flauta e Cavaquinho (Interior Ministry of Brazil award), (book) Tropical Kitsch, 2004 (Academic award, L.Am. Studies Assn., 2006). Mem. exec. com. Brazilian Comparative Lit. Assn., Rio de Janeiro, 1994—96; mem. nat. screening com. grad. program Fulbrigh Program, NYC. Recipient award, Morse Fund, Yale U., 1996—2000; grantee Griswold Funds, Whitney Humanities Ctr., Yale U., 1998—2006, Frederick W. Hilles Publ. Fund, 2000—01; fellow, Sorbonne and U. Paris X, 1999—2000; fellowship, Morse Fund, Yale U., 1999—2000, Faculty Travel grant, Coun. L.Am. Studies, Yale U., 1998, Sr. fellowship, Yale U., 2003—04, Faculty Rsch. grant, Yale Ctr. Internat. and Area Studies, 2004—06, CUNY IDS grant, IDS Cuny, 2008.

SANTOS, SHARON LEE, parochial school educator; b. Perth Amboy, NJ, June 23, 1955; d. John Anthony Santos and Dolores Estelle Barrett. BA in History, Kean U., 1978, MA in Guidance and Counseling, 1985; MA in Systematic Theology, Seton Hall U., 1998. Religious sr. Franciscan of Our Lady of Guadalupe; cert. tchr. K-12, guidance counelor N.J., religion tchr. Diocese of Metuchen, N.J. Tchr. Archdiocese of Newark, Diocese of Metuchen, Perth Amboy, Fords, NJ, Woodbridge, NJ; dir. religious edn. Vicariate of Perth Amboy, St. Mary Parish, New Monmouth, NJ. Adv. bd. on evangelization Diocese of Metuchen, 1999; spkr. in field. Mem.: Cath. United Faith, Fellowship of Cath. Scholars, St. Edith Stein Guild (life), Kappa Delta Phi. Avocations: astronomy, gardening. Office: St Mary Cath Ch 26 Leonardville Rd New Monmouth NJ 07748 Home: 17 Cherry Tree Farm Rd Middletown NJ 07748 Office Phone: 732-671-8550.

SANTOS PICO, JOSE V., neurosurgeon; s. Jose Santos Grillo and Catina Pico; m. Carol Ilene Spahn, Mar. 25, 2006; children: Jose Santos Martinez, Maria Cecilia Santos Martinez. B, U. PR, Mayaguez, 1976; MD, Caribbean U., San Juan, 1980. Diplomate Am. Bd. Neurol. Surgery, 2003. Intern Detroit Memorial Hosp., 1980—81; resident U. PR, San Juan, 1981—86; neurosurgeon Pavia Hosp., San Juan, 1986—, Hima San Pablo Med. Ctr., PR. Mem.: Cyberknife Soc., Congress Neurol. Surgeons. Office: 712 Ponce de Leon Ave San Juan PR 00918 Business E-Mail: jvsantosmd@aim.com.

SANTOSUOSSO, PATRICK See SMITH, PATRICK

SANTO TOMAS, LINUS HIPOLITO, pulmonologist; b. Quezon City, Philippines; MD, U. Philippines, Manila, 1991; MS in Epidermiology, Med. Coll. Wis., Milwaukee, 1999. Cert. Am. Bd. Internal Medicine, 1996, in pulmonary disease 1998, in critical care 1999. Assoc. chief Pulmonary and Critical Care, Med. Coll. Wis., 2006—08. Recipient Young Investigator award, Chest Found., 2003, award, Best Drs., 2005—08, United Health Care, 2005—07. Fellow: Am. Coll. Chest Physician; mem.: Am. Thoracic Soc. Office: Med Coll Wis 9200 W Wisconsin Ave Milwaukee WI 53226

SANTRY, BARBARA LEA, venture capitalist; b. Key West, Fla., Jan. 20, 1948; d. Jere Joseph and Frances Victoria (Appel) S. BS in Nursing, Georgetown U., 1969; MBA, Stanford U., 1978. Program analyst, br. chief U.S. Dept. HEW, Washington, 1973-76; mgr. cons. div. Arthur Andersen and Co., San Francisco, 1978-80; asst. v.p. Am. Med. Internat., Washington, 1980-83; v.p. Alex Brown and Sons, Inc., Balt., 1983-86; ptnr. Wessels, Arnold and Henderson, Mpls., 1986-88; v.p. Dain Bosworth Inc., Mpls., 1988-90, sr. v.p., 1990-91; ptnr. Pathfinder Venture Capital Funds, Menlo Park, Calif., 1991—2005, Capstone Ventures, Menlo Park, Calif., 1996—. Sr. cons. Quorum Consulting, San Francisco. Trustee Stanford Bus. Sch. Trust, 1996-2002. Served to lt. USNR, 1967-72.

SANUA, MARIANNE RACHEL, historian, educator; b. Boston, Mar. 1, 1960; d. Victor D. and Stella (Sardell) S. BA, Princeton U., 1982; postgrad., Hebrew Univ. Jerusalem, 1982-84, Jewish Theol. Seminary, 1985-87; MA, Columbia U., 1988, PhD, 1994. Editorial asst. Congress Monthly mag. Am. Jewish Congress, 1984-86; tchr. high sch. history program Jewish Theol. Seminary, 1986-91; intern dept. Jewish life Jewish Home and Hosp. Aged, 1987-95; instr. U. Wash., Seattle, 1993-94; rschr. Mus. Jewish Heritage, NYC, 1996—. Lectr. Sephardic Ho. Speaker's Bur., 1991-92; adj. asst. prof. Queens Coll., 1991-92, 94, Touro Coll., 1995. Contbr. articles to profl. jours. Recipient Leo Wasserman prize Am. Jewish Hist. Soc., 1987, award Lucius N. Littauer Found., Meml. Found. Jewish Culture, Nat. Found. Jewish Culture; Presdl. fellow Columbia U., 1987-90; Rabbi Theodore S. Levy Tribute fellow Am. Jewish Archives, 1989-90; scholar German Acad. Student Exchange, 1990; Hazel D. Cole fellow in Jewish Studies U. Wash., 1993-94. Avocations: music, opera, jewish song. Home: 2416 Quentin Rd Brooklyn NY 11229-2416

SAN VICENTE PORTES, LUIS, finance educator; PhD, Georgetown U., Washington, 2005. Advisor, gen. direction revenue and pricing policies Mex. Ministry Fin., Mexico City, 1990—2000; advisor, natural gas bus. devel. unit Petroleos Mexicanos, Mexico City, 1998—99; asst. prof. Montclair State U., Upper Montclair, NJ, 2005—. Cons. Inter Am. Devel. Bank, Washington, 2002—03. Contbr. articles to profl. jours. Mem.: Internat. Banking Economics and Fin. Assn., Western Econ. Assn., Am. Econ. Assn. Office: Montclair State Univ 1 Normal Ave Partridge Hall 438 Upper Montclair NJ 07043 Office Fax: 973-655-4456. Business E-Mail: portesl@mail.montclair.edu.

SANYOUR, MICHAEL LOUIS, JR., diversified financial services company executive; b. Richmond, Va., Aug. 24, 1930; s. Michael Louis, Sr. and Betty (Toobert) Sanyour; m. Therese Marie McCarthy, June 1, 1951 (dec. Sept. 25, 2002); children: Jeffrey, Mark, Jennifer, Florence, Norman, Ned. AA, Union Coll., 1952; SB, Rutgers U., 1954, postgrad., 1978-82; MBA, Harvard U., 1956; postgrad., Am. Coll., 1987-92. CLU; ChFC. V.p. Harbridge Ho., Inc., Boston, 1956-63, also dir.; corp. v.p. mktg. Volkswagen Am., Inc., Englewood Cliffs, NJ, 1963-70; pres., CEO Subaru Am., Pennsauken, NJ, 1970-75, also dir., Wofac Co., Bridgewater, NJ, 1975-82; exec. v.p., dir. Sci. Mgmt. Corp., 1975-82; pres., CEO, dir. Metrologic Instruments Inc., Blackwood, NJ, 1982-85; pres., COO, dir. Avant-Garde Computing, Inc., Mt. Laurel, NJ, 1985-86; prin., dir. CMS Cos., Phila., 1986—. Bd. dirs. Phila. Film Soc., 2005—, Phila. Shakespeare Festival, 1995—2006. Co-author: (book) Chief Executive's Handbook, 1975, Am. Mgmt. Assn.'s Publs., 1990. Trustee West Jersey Chamber Music Soc., 1983—, pres., 1987—88; councilman Moorestown, NJ, 1988—98; dep. mayor, 1999—2002; mayor, 2003—04; bd. dirs. Meml. Health Alliance, 1992—97, ARC Burlington County, 1989—94, Coriell Inst. Med. Rsch., 1992—, v.p., 2002—; bd. dirs. World Affairs Coun., Phila., 1992—98, Moorestown Cmty. House, 2000—06, Phila. Pres.'s Orgn., 1994—97, vice chmn., 1992—93, chmn., 1993—94; class sec. HBS Class of '56, 1986—96. With USNG, 1948—56. Decorated knight of St. John's of Jerusalem; recipient Alumni award, Rutgers U., 1954, award, Am. Cancer Soc., 1978—79. Mem.: L3, World Affairs Coun. Phila., Automotive Orgn. Team, World Pres.'s Orgn., South Jersey C. of C. (v.p., dir.), Am. Mensa Ltd., Harvard Club (N.Y.C.), Union League (Phila.) (bd. dirs. 1993—97), Harvard Bus. Sch. Club (Phila.) (pres. 1980—81, chmn. 1983—84, dir. 1984—), Rotary (pres. Moorestown 1987—88, bd. dirs.), Legatus, Delta Sigma Pi, Beta Gamma Sigma. Home: 201 E Maple Ave Moorestown NJ 08057-2011 Office: 308 E Lancaster Ave Ste 300 Wynnewood PA 19096-2145 Home Phone: 856-234-2063, 267-514-2221; Office Phone: 610-896-3009, 610-896-3000. Business E-Mail: mls@cmsco.com.

SANZ, ALEJANDRO (ALEJANDRO SÁNCHEZ PIZARRO), singer; b. Madrid, Dec. 18, 1968; s. María Pizarro and Jesús Sánchez; m. Jaydy Michel, Dec. 1998 (div. Nov. 2005); children: Manuela, Alexander. Singer: (albums) Viviendo de Prisa, 1991, Basico, 1993, Si Tú Me Miras, 1993, 3, 1995, Más, 1997, El Alma al Aire, 2000 (Record of Yr., Album of Yr., Song of Yr., Best Male Pop Vocal, 2001), MTV Unplugged, 2001, Discografia Completa, 2003, No Es lo Mismo, 2003 (Record of Yr., Album of Yr., Song of Yr., Best Male Pop Vocal, Best Engineered Album, Latin Grammy Awards, 2004, Best Latin Pop Album, Grammy Awards, 2004), El Tren de los Momentos, 2006 (Best Latin Pop Album, Grammy Awards, 2008), (songs) (with Shakira) La Tortura, 2005 (Song of Yr., Record of Yr., Latin Grammy Awards, 2006). Office: Warner Music Latina 3400 W Olive Ave Burbank CA 91505

SANZ, LUIS E., gynecologist, educator; b. Camaguey, Cuba; m. Miriam D. Sanz; 1 child, Monica G. MD, Georgetown U., 1976. Uro-gynecology and vaginal reconstruction surgery dept. ob-gyn. Va. Hosp. Ctr., Washington, 1980. Author: Gynecologic Surgery, 1995; contbr. over 40 articles to profl. jours., chapters to books. With US Army, 1966—68, Vietnam. Decorated Vietnam Campaign medal U.S. Army. Fellow: ACOG (assoc.; memberr). Roman Catholic. Avocations: biking, reading, travel, weightlifting. Office: 1625 N George Mason Dr #475 Arlington VA 22101 E-mail: lsanz@virginiahospitalcenter.com.

SANZENBACHER, RICHARD, humanities educator; b. Toledo, Jan. 26, 1945; PhD, Bowling Green State U., Ohio, 1979. Tchg. fellow Bowling Green State U., 1974—79; prof. Embry Riddle U., Daytona Beach, Fla., 1985—. Home: 125 A Blue Heron Daytona Beach FL 32119 Office: Embry Riddle Univ 800 S Clyde Morris Daytona Beach FL 32114 Business E-Mail: sanzenbr@erau.edu.

SANZONE, THOMAS J., diversified financial services company executive; b. 1960; BS in Computer Sci., Hofstra U., 1982. Prog. analyst Salomon Bros., 1984—91, sr. op. officer fixed income & equity trading, 1991—96, mng. dir., head glob. application develop., 1996; chief info. officer corp. & investment bank Citigroup Inc., 1999—2005; chief info. officer Credit Suisse, 2005—08; exec. v.p., chief adminstrv. officer Merrill Lynch & Co., Inc, 2008—. Office: Merrill Lynch & Co Inc 4 World Fin Ctr 250 Vesey St New York NY 10080

SAOUAF, SANDRA J., immunologist, consultant; d. William R. and Mary Jane Jerrold Jones; m. Anthony Saouaf. PhD, U. Pa., Phila., 1992. Postdoc. fellow Bristol Myers Squibb Pharm. Rsch. Inst., Princeton, NJ, 1992—96; sr. scientist Glaxo SmithKline Dept. Protein Biochemistry, King of Prussia, Pa., 1996—97; rsch. specialist U. Pa. Dept. Pathology and Lab. Medicine, Phila., 2002—07; CEO Sci. Answers, LLC, Moorestown, NJ, 2007—. Mem.: Assn. Women Sci. (exec. bd. mem. 2002—03), Am. Assn. Cancer Rsch., Girl Scouts America (troop leader 2006—), Phi Beta Kappa. Achievements include patents pending for use of histone deacetylase inhibitors to treat autoimmune disease; research in CD147 signal transduction; kinetic activation of tyrosine protein kinases in B lymphocytes. Office: Sci Answers LLC 41 Brooks Rd Moorestown NJ 08057 Office Fax: 856-273-6395. Business E-Mail: science001@verizon.net.

SAPAN, JOSHUA WARD, cable television executive; b. NYC, Nov. 28, 1950; s. Maxwell and Tessa (Kaner) S. BA, U. Wis., 1976. Adv. mgr. Teleprompter Manhattan Cable TV, NYC, 1977-78; sr. v.p. mktg. Showtime Networks, NYC, 1979-87; pres., CEO Rainbow Media Holdings, Inc., NYC. Dir. Seventh Day, N.Y.C. Author: Cable TV, 1986. Bd. dirs. Am. Mus. of Moving Image, 1987—, Hebrew Home for Aged, 1987—; chair Cable TV Adminstrn. for Marketers Ednl. Found., 1999—. Mem. NCable TV Adminstrn. and Mktg. Soc. (com. chmn. 1980-88). Democrat. Jewish. Office: Rainbow Media Holdings Inc 200 Jericho Quadrangle Jericho NY 11753-2704 Office Fax: 516-803-1199.

SAPER, JOEL R., neurologist, educator; b. Joliet, Ill., Feb. 6, 1943; s. Leonard and Jeanette (Kristal) S.; children: Lisa, Justin, Lauren. BS in History, U. Wis., 1965; MD, U. Ill., Chgo., 1969. Diplomate Am. Bd. Psychiatry and Neurology, Am. Bd. Pain Medicine, diplomate headache bd. United Coun. Neucological Subspecialists, 2006. Intern Michael Reese Hosp., Chgo., 1969-70; resident U. Mich. Med. Ctr., Ann Arbor, 1970-73; instr. U. Mich. Med. Sch., Ann Arbor, 1973-75, asst. prof., 1975-78; founder, dir. Mich. Head Pain and Neurol. Inst., Ann Arbor, 1978—; dir. Head Pain Treatment Program, Chelsea, Mich., 1978—; clin. prof. neurology Mich. State U., Lansing, 1989—. Author: Freedom from Headaches, 1978, Soft Back Edition, 1981, Consumer Report Edition, 1981, Clinical and Basic Neurology for Health Professionals, 1981;: Help for Headaches, 1983, Headache Disorders, 1983, Controversies and Clinical Variants of Migraine, 1987, Handbook of Headache Management, 1992, 2nd edition, Handbook of Headache Management, 1999; Topics in Pain Mgmt., 1985—2001; contbr. chapter to book. Chair physicians' subcom. State of Mich. House Health Care Task Force, 1993-94; chair Mich. Coun. on Pain, 1995-96; nat. chmn. Pain Care Coalition, 1995-. Recipient John Graham Sr. Clinician award, Am. Headache Soc., 1995, Phillip M. Lippe MD award, 1996. Fellow: ACP; mem.: Am. Coun. on Headache Edn. (chmn. 1994—95), Am. Pain Soc. (cons. to bd. 1992—), Am. Headache Soc. (pres. 1992—94, bd. mem.), Am. Acad. Neurology (edn. com. 1992—), Am. Acad. Pain Medicine (bd. mem. 1992, 1998—). Office: Mich Head Pain and Neurol Inst 3120 Professional Dr Ann Arbor MI 48104-5131

SAPERS, CARL MARTIN, lawyer, educator; b. Boston, July 16, 1932; s. Abraham E. and Anne (Herwitz) Sapers; m. Judith H. Thompson, Nov. 29, 1959; children: Jonathan Simonds, Rachel Elizabeth, Benjamin Lovell. AB, Harvard U., 1953, JD, 1958. Bar: Mass. 1958. Assoc. Hill, Barlow, Goodale & Adams, Boston, 1958—65; ptnr. Hill & Barlow, 1965—96, of counsel, 1997—2002. Spl. asst. atty. gen. criminal divsn. Commonwealth of Mass., 1963—65; spl. cons. Mass. Ethics Commn., 1978—79; adj. prof. Harvard Grad. Sch. Design, 1983—; mem. Mass. Bd. Registration Medicine, 1995—98, vice chair, 1997—98; mem. JAMS, Global Engring. & Constrn. Panel, 2009—. Moderator Town of Brookline, 1982—91. With US Army, 1953—55. Mem.: AIA (hon. Allied Professions medal 1975), Am. Coll. Constrn. Lawyers (bd. dirs. 1989—, pres. 1993), Am. Arbitration Assn. (bd. dirs. 1987—2000, Whitney North Seymour medal 1991), Boston Bar Assn. (coun. 1970—73, 1991—94). Home: 26C Bradbury St Cambridge MA 02138 E-mail: csapers@gsd.harvard.edu.

SAPERSTEIN, DAVID, writer, film director, television personality; b. Bklyn. s. Louis and Celia S.; m. Ellen Mae Bernard; children: Ivan, Ilena. Student, CCNY Film Inst., CCNY. With CBS-TV Ed Murrow Show-Person To Person; writer, prodr., dir. Skyline Films, Inc., 1963-83. Asst. prof. film NYU Grad. Sch., Tisch Sch. Arts, 1992-93; instr. screenwriting Manhattan Marymount Coll., 1996-99, N.Y. Film Acad., 1997. Lyricist 90 pub. songs; theatrical prodns. include musicals Blue Planet Blue, Clowntown; author: Cocoon, 1985 (bestseller), Fatal Reunion, 1987 (Book of the Month selection), Metamorphosis: The Cocoon Story Continues, 1988, Red Devil: The Book of Satan, 1989, Funerama, 1994, Dark Again, 1999, Retribution, 2003, A Christmas Visitor, 2004-08, Butterfly Tomorrow's Children, Manolo's Journey, The Enemies of Awe, A Christmas Passage, 2008, A Christmas Gift, 2009; movies include Cocoon (Best Original Story for Screen 1985, 2 Acad. awards); writer, dir. My Sister's Keeper, Personal Choice (Beyond the Stars), Hearts & Diamonds; writer Torch, Sara Deri, Queen of America, Italian Ices, Joshua's Golden Band, Roamers, Vets, Do Not Disturb, Snatched, Jack in the Box, (with Joe Cacaci) SchoolHouse, Point of Honor, Roberto!, The John Gill Story: In Defense of Ivan the Terrible, Joshua's Golden Band, Fighting Back, Babs' Labs, Silyan, (nonfiction) Woman in the Year 2000, 1975; writer, prodr. Hallmark channel (with George Samerjan) A Christmas Visitor, 2002; co-author (with James Rush) A Christmas Gift, 2009, (with George Samerjan) Christmas Passage, 2006; writer, dir. music videos Dr. Bill, Teenage Mutant Ninja Turtles, Fallow Angel, Wowii; segment prodr. for Northstar Ent./PBS Reppies; dir. over 300 TV commls.; writer dir. over 200 documentaries, corp. and indsl. films, videos including Dance of the Athletes (Emmy nomination), Explorers in Aqua-Space, Rodeo: A Matter of Style; creator first interactive internet publishing at www-.darkagain.com. Recipient Cine Golden Eagle award, N.Y. Film Festival award, San Francisco Film Festival award, Venice Film Festival award, Melbourne Film Festival award, N.Y. Art Dirs. award, Chgo. Film Festival award, Townsend Harris medal CCNY, 1998, Daniel Perle award, Pocono Film Festival, 2007. Mem. Writer Guild Am., Dir. Guild of Am., BMI, Nat. Honor Soc. Office: Ebbets Field Prodns Ltd Wykagyl Station PO Box 42 New Rochelle NY 10804-0042

SAPERSTEIN, LEE WALDO, mining engineering educator; b. NYC, July 14, 1943; s. Charles Levy and Freda Phyllis (Dornbush) S.; m. Priscilla Frances Hickson, Sept. 16, 1967; children: Adam Geoffrey, Clare Freda. BS in Mining Engring., Mont. Sch. Mines, 1964; DPhil in Engring. Sci., Oxford U., 1967. Registered profl. engr., Ky., Mo., Pa. Laborer, miner, engr. The Anaconda Co., Butte, Mont., and N.Y.C., 1963-64; asst. prof. mining engring. Pa. State U., University Park, 1967-71, assoc. prof., 1971-78, prof., 1978-87, sect. chmn., 1974-87; prof., chmn. dept. mine engring. U. Ky., Lexington, 1987-93; dean Sch. Mines and Metallurgy U. Mo., Rolla, 1993—2004, prof. mining engring., 1993—2006, prof. emeritus, 2007—, cons., dean emeritus Sch. Mines and Metallurgy, 2004—. Chmn. engring. accreditation commn., 1989-90, bd. dirs. Accreditation Bd. for Engring. and Tech., 1992-2001, sec. of bd., 1995-98, pres.-elect, 1998-99, pres. 1999-2000, ABET fellow. Contbr. articles to refereed jours. Rhodes scholar Oxford U., 1964-67; recipient Linton E. Grinter Disting. Svc. award, 2004. Mem. ASEE, Soc. Mining, metallurgy and Exploration, Inc. (disting. mem. AIME-Soc. Mining Engrs.), Am. Assn. Rhodes Scholars. Home: PO Box 1408 Nantucket MA 02554-1408 Office: 20 New St Nantucket MA 02554 Office Phone: 573-578-7750. Personal E-mail: leesaperstein@comcast.net.

SAPHIR, RICHARD LOUIS, pediatrician; b. NYC, May 1, 1933; s. Samuel and Grace (Greenberg) Saphir; m. Judith Schwartz, Dec. 6, 1958; 1 child, Steven. BA, NYU, 1954; MD, SUNY, NYC, 1958. Diplomate Nat. Bd. Med. Examiners, Am. Bd. Pediat. Asst. attending pediatrician Mt. Sinai Hosp., NYC, 1965—71, asst dir., pediat. acute care clinic, 1970—78, 1971—82, assoc. clin. prof. pediat., 1982—88, attending pediatrician, 1982—; chief, pediatric svcs. U.S. Naval Hosp., Newport, RI, 1967—69; clin. prof. pediat. Mt. Sinai Sch. Medicine, NYC, 1988—. Bd. dirs. Mt. Sinai Children's Ctr. Found., NYC, 1987—. Contbr. articles to profl. jours. Chmn. cmty. and adv. com. N.Y.C. Info. and Counseling Program for Sudden Infant Death Syndrome, 1979—81; med. bd. YMHA, NYC, 1982—86. Comdr. USNR, 1967—69. Fellow: NY County Med. Soc. (vice chmn. com. child welfare 1974—85), NY Pediat. Soc. (pres. 1978—79), Am. Acad. Pediats. (com. sci. meetings 1985—97, chmn. prep course 1991—96, editl. adv. bd. Continuing Med. Edn. audiotapes 1991—2001, ednl. program rep. ambulatory care quality improvement program 1992—2002, ednl. advisor proficiency testing program 1996—99, editl. bd. Pediat. in Rev. 1997—2003, ednl. adv. Uniformed Svcs. pediat. seminar 1997—, mem. super cont. med. edn. planning com. 2000—06, chmn. super cont. med. edn. planning com. 2002—06, com. on continuing med. edn. 2002—06, editl. bd. Pediat. 2009—), NY Acad. Medicine (treas. 1987—89). Office: BSM Pediatrics PC 55 E 87th St New York NY 10128-1043 Home Phone: 212-362-8486; Office Phone: 212-722-4950.

SAPIENZA, JOHN THOMAS, retired lawyer, director; b. South Orange, NJ, Feb. 26, 1913; s. James C. and Rosalie (Giaimo) S.; m. Virginia H. Gignoux, Feb. 12, 1972; children by previous marriage: John Thomas, James K. AB summa cum laude, Harvard U., 1934, LL.B. magna cum laude, 1937. Bar: N.Y. 1938, D.C. 1943. Law clk. Judge A.N. Hand, NYC, 1937-38, Justice Stanley Reed, Washington, 1938-39; assoc. firm Wright, Gordon, Zachry & Parlin, NYC, 1939-41, Covington & Burling LLP, Washington, 1941-48, ptnr., 1949-87, ret. ptnr., 1987. Dir. Hiram Walker-Gooderham & Worts Ltd., 1971-86, Hiram Walker & Sons, Inc., 1971-86, Hiram Walker Resources Ltd., 1981-86, Wyman Gordon Co., 1973-83; dir. Am. Security Bank, N.A., 1975-83, dir. emeritus, 1983-88. Pres.: Harvard Law Rev, 1936-37. Trustee George Washington U., 1978-88, emeritus trustee, 1988—. Served to lt. comdr. USNR, 1943-46. Mem. ABA, D.C. Bar Assn., Am. Law Inst., Confrerie des Chevaliers du Tastevin, Burning Tree Club (Washington), Met. Club (Washington), Leisure World Country Club (Silver Spring, Md.), Phi Beta Kappa. Home: Apt 104 15107 Interlachen Dr Silver Spring MD 20906-5626 Home Phone: 301-598-4953; Office Phone: 202-662-5319.

SAPIENZA, MADELINE, historian, researcher; b. Washington, Jan. 27, 1950; d. Angelo Frank and Elaine Madeline (Cipriano) Sapienza. BS in French Lang., Georgetown U., Washington, 1972, MA, 1975; PhD in Am. History, Cath. U. Am., 1990. History, French HS tchr., Washington, 1976—80; adult ESL tchr. Lado Internat. Coll., Washington, 1979—80, 1994; legis. sec. US House Reps., Washington, 1980—83; part-time adminstrv. asst. and rschr. CBS News, Washington, 1983—92; adminstrv. coord. Wash. law dept. CBS, Inc., Washington, 1988—94; historian, rschr. US Army Ctr. Mil. History, Washington, 1986—88; docent Stephen Decatur Mus. House Nat. Trust for Hist. Preservation, Washington, 1997—99. Contbr. articles to profl. jours. and reference books. Bd. dirs. Rep. Women Capitol Hill, Washington, 1982—83, mem. various coms., 1982—83. Recipient Letter of Commendation, US Army, 1986, Dept. of Army Commendation award, US Army Ctr Mil. History, 1987. Mem.: Catholic League: For Religious and Civil Rights (life), John Carroll Soc. Washington, Assn. US Army (life), Phi Beta Kappa. Roman Catholic.

SAPIN, BURTON MALCOLM, political science professor; b. NYC, Dec. 14, 1926; s. Julius Sidney and Selma (Greifer) S.; m. Barbara Miller Piane, Dec. 11, 1960 (div. Aug. 1984); children: Julia Elizabeth, David Ralph; m. Judith Leitner, Sept. 12, 2001. AB, Columbia U., 1945, AM, 1947; PhD, Princeton U., 1953. Rschr. Brookings Instn., Washington, 1958-60; asst. prof. MIT, Cambridge, Mass., 1960-61; policy ofcl. U.S. Dept. State, Washington, 1961-65; prof. polit. sci. U. Minn., Mpls., 1965-69; dean Sch. Internat. Affairs George Washington U., Washington, 1969-83, prof. polit. sci. and internat. affairs, 1969-94, prof. emeritus, 1994—. Cons. Rand, Washington, 1994-97; vis. prof. Kansai U., Osaka, Japan, summer, 1991, Internat. U. Japan, Niigata, Japan, 1985, Hopkins-Nanjing Program, Nanjing, China, 1987-88. Author: Foreign Policy Decision Making, 1954, 2002, Making of U.S. Foreign Policy, 1966; contbr. articles to profl. jours. With USN, 1945-46. Democrat. Jewish. Home: 4515 Willard Ave Apt 1009S Chevy Chase MD 20815

SAPIRIE, STEPHEN ALAN, international public health consultant; b. Milw., June 17, 1938; s. Samuel Ralph and Florence Katheryn (Canatsey) Sapirie; m. Manana Gagua; children: Mark, Nicholas. BSc, U. Tenn., 1960; MBA, Am. U., Washington, 1968; D in Pub. Health, U. N.C., 1980. Chief mgmt. sys. Naval Command Sys., Washington, 1966—68; computer sys. analyst WHO, Geneva, 1968—70, health sys. analyst, 1970—74, health planner Burma, Thailand, 1974—75, program mgmt. officer New Delhi, 1978—85, scientist family health divsn. Geneva, 1985—90, chief strengthen county health info., 1990—98. Dir. INFORM Mgmt. Scis. for Health, Boston, 1999—. Co-author: Health Project Management, 1974. Lt. USN, 1960—66. Avocations: tennis, skiing. Office: Mgmt Scis Health 784 Memorial Dr Cambridge MA 02139 Business E-Mail: ssapirie@msh.org.

SAPOFF, MEYER, retired electronics executive; b. NYC, June 2, 1927; s. Benjamin and Mary (Charney) Sapoff; m. Lynn Joy Sapoff; children: Robert J., Judy B. Schiffman. Student, Mohawk Coll., 1946—48; BSEE magna cum laude, Poly. Inst. Bklyn., 1950, postgrad., 1952—53, MIT, 1951, U. Pa., 1951—52; MSEE, Drexel Inst. Tech., 1952. Rsch. engr. Franklin Inst. Labs., Phila., 1950-52; rsch. fellow sr. grade Poly. Inst. Bklyn., 1952-53; dir. rsch. Victory Engring. Corp., Springfield, NJ, 1953-57, dir. engring., 1957-63, v.p., 1963-69; cons., sr. staff scientist Keystone Carbon Co., St. Mary's, Pa., 1969-70; pres. Thermometrics, Inc., Edison, NJ, 1970-86, chmn. bd. dirs., 1986-93, sr. staff cons., 1993-96; pres. MS Cons., Princeton, NJ, 1993—96; ret., 1996. Chmn. E20 temperature com. 6th Symposium Temperature, Measurement and Control in Sci. and Industry; U.S. del. to tech. com. 65th Internat. Electrotech. Commn.; cons. in field. Contbr. articles to profl. jours.; patentee in field. Active West Orange (NJ) PTA, 1960—76, Citizens League West Orange, 1962—75; trustee George St. Playhouse, New Brunswick, NJ, 1993—2001; bd. dirs. Jewish Ctr., Princeton, 1995—98, fin. chmn., 1995—96, v.p. fin., 1996—98; bd. dirs. United Jewish Fedn. Princeton Mercer Bucks, 1998—2008, treas., 2001—03. Recipient Indsl. Rsch. IR-100 award, 1974; fellow, Poly. Inst. Bklyn., 1953; scholar, NYU, 1948—50. Mem.: AAAS, ASTM (1st vice-chmn. E20 com. temperature measurement 2000—05, award of merit 1998), IEEE, Am. Ceramic Soc., Poly. Inst. Bklyn. Alumni Assn., Tau Beta Pi, Eta Kappa Nu.

SAPOLSKY, HARVEY MORTON, political scientist, educator; b. Haverhill, Mass., Feb. 21, 1939; s. Abraham and Anne Betty (Selig) S.; m. Karen P. Stenbo, Aug. 27, 1966. BA, Boston U., 1961; MPA, Harvard U., 1963, PhD, 1967. Mem. faculty MIT, 1966—2006, prof. polit. sci., 1977—2006, dir. comm. forum, 1987-95, dir. security studies program, 1989—2006; dep. dir. Univ. Health Policy Consortium, 1978-83, assoc. chmn. faculty, 1981-83. Vis. prof. U. Mich., 1971—72; cons. Artificial Heart Assessment Panel Nat. Heart and Lung Inst., Washington, 1972—73; mem. Ethics and Health Policy Panel Hastings (N.Y.) Ctr., 1979—80; mem. com. on Fed. Rsch. on Effect of Ionizing Radiation NRC, Washington, 1980—81, mem. com. on Risk Perception and Comm., 1987—88; mem. com. on tech. alternatives to anti-pers. mines,

1999—2001; mem. Sec. of Energy's Task Force on Alternative Futures for Dept. of Energy Labs, 1994—95; mem. adv. com. U.S. Army Command and Gen. Staff Coll., 2005—; mem. ednl. adv. com. US Army, 2007—. Author: The Polaris System Development, 1972, (with D. Altman and Richard Greene) Health Planning and Regulation, 1981, (with A. Drake, S. Finkelstein) The American Blood Supply, 1982, Science and the Navy, 1990, (with E. Gholz and C. Talmadge) US Defense Politics: The Origins of Security Policy, 2008; editor: Consuming Fears: The Politics of Product Risks, 1986; co-editor: Federal Health Programs, 1981, (with S. Altman), 1981, (with R. Crane, W.R. Newman and E. Noam) The Telecommunications Revolution, 1992; contbr. articles to profl. jours. Mem. AAAS (sec. sect. social and econ. scis. 1968-73), Am. Polit. Sci. Assn., Nat. Acad. Social Ins., Coun. on Fgn. Rels. Home: 37 Edgemoor Rd Belmont MA 02478-3916 Office: MIT Security Studies Program E38-600 Cambridge MA 02139 Home Phone: 617-489-2449; Office Phone: 617-253-5265. Business E-Mail: sapolsky@mit.edu.

SAPON-WHITE, RICHARD E., librarian; s. Herbert M. and Judith P. White; m. Sarah Sapon-White; children: Ari, Rena. BSc, U. Toronto, Ont., 1977; MPH, UCLA, 1979; MLS, So. Conn. State U., New Haven, 1989. Sci. cataloger Va. Tech., Blacksburg, 1990—96; catalog libr. Oreg. State U., Corvallis, 1996—2008, head cataloging, 2008—. Numerous com. appointments ALCTS and ACRL, 1991—. Contbr. articles to numerous profl. jours. Named a Fulbright awardee, Czech Republic, 2005; grant, Engring. Info. Found., 2007. Mem.: Czechoslovak Soc. Arts and Scis., Fulbright Assn., Oreg. Libr. Assn. (chair, internat. rels. round table 2000—01, 2008—09), Assn. Coll. and Rsch. Librs. (chair, profl. edn. 1994—96), Assn. Libr. Collections and Tech. Svcs. (libr. resources and tech. svcs. editl. bd. 2001—03), Beta Phi Mu (Inductee 1993). Liberal. Jewish. Avocation: genealogy. Office: Oregon State Univ 121 The Valley Library Corvallis OR 97331-4501 Business E-Mail: richard.sapon-white@oregonstate.edu.

SAPORITO-HINES, LUCILLE ANN, special education educator; b. Rockford, Ill., July 27, 1950; d. John Raymond and Margarent Ann Saporito; children: Matthew Joseph Hines, Christine Ann Hines. MS, Aurora U., Ill., 2004. Cert. in edn. Western Ill., 1972. Spl. edn. tchr. Harlem Dist. 122, Loves Park, Ill., 1972—; adj. prof. Nat. Louis U., Chgo., 2006—. Adj. prof. St. Xavier U., Chgo., 2005—. Recipient, Golden Apple Found., 2002, Harlem Sch. Dist. 122, 2002, Disting. Tchr. award, 1996. Mem.: Phi Delta Kappa. Democrat. Roman Catholic. Avocation: reading. Office: Loves Pk Elementary Sch 344 Grand Ave Loves Park IL 61111 Business E-Mail: lhines@harlem122.org.

SAPP, GENA JOHNSON, secondary school educator; b. Dublin, Jan. 7, 1967; d. Margaret and Don Johnson; m. Richard Thomas Sapp, July 14, 1990; children: Lauren Rachael, Richard Thomas. B in Home Economics, Ga. Southern U., Statesboro, 1990, M in Early Childhood Edn., 2003. Cert. blackboard State Ga., DTAE, 2003; CPR, first aid instr., Am. Heart Assn., 2003; fire safety instr. State Ga., 2004. Tchr. Burke County HS, Waynesboro, Ga., 1990—2000; coll. instr. Swainsboro Tech. Coll., Ga., 2001—08. Dir. Swainsboro Tech Child Devel. Ctr., 2005—08. Recipient Lighthouse Candidate award, Swainsboro Tech. Coll., 2004, Rick Perkins award, 2005, award, Bright From The Start, Dept. Early Care and Learning, 2008. Mem.: NAEYC. Office: Swainsboro Tech Coll 346 Kite Rd Swainsboro GA 30401 Business E-Mail: gsapp@swainsborotech.edu.

SAPP, JOHN RAYMOND, lawyer; b. Lawrence, Kans., June 18, 1944; s. Raymond Olen and Amy (Kerr) S.; m. Linda Lee Tebbe, July 3, 1965; children: Jeffrey, Jennifer, John. BA, U. Kans., 1966; JD, Duke U., 1969. Bar: Wis. 1969, U.S. Dist. Ct. (ea. dist.) Wis. 1969, U.S. Ct. Appeals (7th cir.) 1974, U.S. Ct. Appeals (4th cir.) 1984, U.S. Supreme Ct. 1974. Assoc. Michael, Best & Friedrich, Milw., 1969-76, ptnr., 1976-90, mng. ptnr., 1990—2004, sr. ptnr., 2004—. Dir. Roadrunner Freight Sys., Milw., 1992-2004, J.J. Keller Co., 2003-. Author: (book) Making Partner, A Guide for Law Firm Associates, 2005. Bd. dirs. Milw. Symphony, 1981-95, mem. exec. com., 1993-95; bd. dirs. Boy Scouts Am., Milw., 1986—95, pres. 1990-92; mem. Milw. Arts Bd., 1990, Greater Milw. Com.; bd. dirs. Zool. Soc., 1995-, v.p., 2000-05, chmn., 2005-07; bd. dirs. Lex Mundi, 1997-2000, mem. exec. com., 1997-2001; bd. dirs. Jr. Achievement Greater Milw., 2001—04. Avocations: golf, curling, print collecting. Office Phone: 414-271-6560. Business E-Mail: jrsapp@michaelbest.com.

SAPP, PEGGY G., pastor, editor, writer, speech professional; d. Arthur Charles and Mae Belle (Graves) Gibby; m. Roger W. Sapp, Sr., Sept. 4, 1965 (dec.); children: Roger Warren II, LaDonna Hope Sapp Ranke, Jonathan T., Angela Faith Sapp Little. Degree in Bus. Adminstrn., Marsh Bus. Coll., Atlanta, 1963; degree in Theology/Missions, Pentecostal Bible Inst., Jackson, Miss., 1966; degree in Bus. Adminstrn., Mid. Ga. Coll., Cochran, 1968; degree in Theology, Moody Bible Inst., Chgo., 1985. Dean students Inst. Biblical Studies, Dublin, Ga., 1978—83; radio bible tchr. Voice of Truth Ministries, Dublin, 1985—, Bible instr.-tchr., 1985—; adminstr. Ch. Jesus Christ Christian Sch., Dublin, 1986—94; editor Ch. Jesus Christ Orgn., Kingsport, Tenn., 1991—, ordained minister, 1971—, motivational spkr., 1991—; sr. pastor Ch. Jesus Christ Full Gospel, Dublin, 1994—; cert. correctional assoc. Johnson State Prison, Wrightsville, Ga., 2000—, spkr., counselor, 2000—. Author: (books) Anointed Leadership Series, 1985, Institute of Biblical Studies, 1994, (periodical) The Broken Vessel, 2001; editor: (mag. periodicals) The Messenger, 1991. Mem.: Assn. Christian Counselors. Achievements include assisted in providing curriculum for founding of Inst. Biblical Studies, Cebu, Philippines. Office: Ch Jesus Christ Full Gospel 759 Vernon Woodard Rd Dublin GA 31027

SAPPÉ, See MOOSA, AHMED

SAPPENFIELD, CHARLES MADISON, architect, educator; b. Columbia, SC, Mar. 17, 1930; s. Charles Madison and Elizabeth Olive (Moss) S.; m. Mary Frances McGowan Dec. 14, 1963 (div. June 1990); children— Charles Ross, Sarah Kathleen B.Arch., N.C. State U., 1956; Cert., Denmark's Royal Acad., Copenhagen, 1961. Asst. prof. N.C. State U., Raleigh, 1956-57, asst. prof., 1961-63; head archtl. firm C.M. Sappenfield, Asheville, N.C. and Muncie, Ind., 1961—; assoc. prof. Clemson U., SC, 1963-65; prof. architecture Ball State U., Muncie, Ind., 1965-94, prof. emeritus, 1994—, dean, 1965-81, dean emeritus, 1994—, dir. Design Indiana, 1983-88. Awards juror Interfaith Forum on Religious Art and Architecture, 1981, Am. Cons. Engrs. Council, 1982; mem. accreditation teams Nat. Archtl. Accrediting Bd., 1967-82. Archtl. works include: Dormitories, U. N.C., Gumpert residence, Dave residence. Pres. Asheville Art Mus., N.C., 1964-65; chmn. Ind. Commn. on Aging, Indpls., 1983-85; pres. Alpha Day Care Ctr. for Elderly, Muncie, 1985; mem. State Planning Adv. Commn., Indpls., 1974-82. Served with U.S. Army. Recipient Gold medal for svc. Ball State U., 1983; named Sagamore of the Wabash, Gov. of Ind., 1982 Fellow AIA (dir. nat. bd. dirs. 1989-92); mem. Ind. Soc. Archs. (pres. 1976), Ind. Archtl. Found. (chmn. 1975), Am. Soc. Landscape Archs. (awards juror 1983), Danish Fedn. Archs. (hon., Aeresmedallion 1987), Fulbright Alumni Assn., Alpha Rho Chi. Lodges: Rotary, Civitan. Democrat. Episcopalian. Avocations: bicycling, photography. Home and Office: 11607 Oakmont Ct Fort Myers FL 33908

SAPPINGTON, SHARON ANNE, retired school librarian; b. West Palm Beach, Fla., Sept. 15, 1944; d. A.D. and Laura G. (Jackson) Chambless; m. Andrew Arnold Sappington III, June 11, 1966; children: Andrew Arnold IV, Kevin Sean. Student, Fla. So. Coll., 1962—64; BA in Edn., U. Fla., 1966; postgrad., U. Ala., 1980. Tchr. 5th grade Tates Creek Elem., Lexington, Ky., 1966—68; tchr. 4th grade Sadieville Elem., Ky., 1968—69; libr. media specialist A.H. Watwood Elem., Childersburg, Ala., 1980—98, ret., 1998. Guest storyteller Young Author's Conf., Winterboro, Lincoln, Sylacauga, and Fayetteville, Ala., 1982-94; vis. com. Southeastern Accreditation Assn.; program presenter Internat. Reading Assn., Birmingham, Ala., 1983; guest spkr. rare children's books By the Way TV talk show, 1983; pres. Tale Tellers of St. Augustine, 2003—05; chmn. RSVP Read Aloud Program, 2002-04. Creator, presenter: (slide presentation) Tellers of Tales and Sketchers of Dreams, 1983, (multimedia programs) Dinosaurs, Teddy Bears, and Wild Things, 1990, Shanghaied in the Beijing Airport, 1994. Circle chmn., Sunday tchr. Grace United Meth. Ch., Birmingham, 1973, 92-95; delivery mem. Meals on Wheels, Birmingham, 1975-76; radio reader for the blind WBHM Pub. Broadcasting, Birmingham, 1980; guest spkr., program presenter Jaycees, Kiwanis, and C. of C., Childersburg, 1993-94. Grantee Title I grantee, 1991, Stutz Bearcat grantee, 1992. Mem. AAUW (lit. chmn. St. Augustine chpt., 2005-07), ALA, Internat. Platform Assn., Am. Assn. Sch. Librs., Ala. Libr. Assn. (children's and sch. divsn. publicity chmn. 1991-93, chmn. Nat. Libr. Week in Ala. 1993-94, Outstanding Youth Svcs. award 1989), People to People Internat. (libr. del. to China 1993), Kappa Delta Pi. Democrat. Methodist. Avocation: book collecting. Home: 5131 Shore Dr Saint Augustine FL 32086-6473

SAPRA, PUJA, research scientist; d. Yudhishter Lal and Usha Sapra; m. Brijesh Gulati; children: Ria Gulati, Rishab Gulati. BSc, All India Inst. Med. Scis., New Delhi, 1998; MS, U. Strathclyde, Glasgow, 1999; PhD, U. Alta., Edmonton, AB, Canada, 2003. Sr. scientist Immunomedics Inc., Morris Plains, NJ, 2003—05; scientist Enzon Pharms., Piscataway, NJ, 2005—. Brit. Chevening Scholarship, Brit. Coun. India, 1998—99, Rsch. grant, AHFMR, Can., 1999—2003, NIH, 2005. Mem.: Am. assn. pharm. scientists, European Hematology Assn., Am. Soc. Hematology, Am. Assn. Cancer Rsch. Achievements include research in antibodies, drug delivery, cancer chemotherapy & oncology; development of formulations of anticancer drugs that are undergoing clinical evaluation. Home: 19 Monmouth Ave Edison NJ 08820 Personal E-mail: psapra@hotmail.com.

SAPS, MIGUEL, pediatrician, gastroenterologist; b. Montevideo, Uruguay, June 11, 1960; m. Gilda Schaffer. MD, U. de la Republica, Montevideo, 1985. Asst. prof. pediat. Northwestern U., Feinberg Sch. Medicine, Chgo., 2004—; attending physician Children's Meml. Hosp., Chgo., 2004—, dir. gastrointestinal motility and functional bowel disorders program, 2004—. Recipient Rsch. award, Am. Coll. Gastroenterology, 2003—07; Seed grant, Northwestern U., 2008. Mem.: Nat. Com. Prevention of Child Abuse, N.Am. Soc. Pediat. Gastroenterology, Heptology & Nutrition, Liver Transplant Com., Montevideo Children's Hosp., Uruguayan Gastroent. Soc., Soc. Prevention of Child Abuse. Office: Children's Meml Hosp 2300 Children's Plaza Box 65 Chicago IL 60614-3394 Office Fax: 773-880-4036. Business E-Mail: msaps@childrensmemorial.org.

SAPSOWITZ, SIDNEY H., entertainment and media company executive; b. NYC, June 29, 1936; s. Max and Annette (Rothstein) Sapsowitz; m. Phyllis Skopp, Nov. 27, 1957; children: Donna Dawn Chazen, Gloria Lynn Aaron, Marsha Helene Gleit. BBA summa cum laude, Paterson State U., NJ, 1980. Various fin. and oper. systems positions Metro Goldwyn Mayer, Inc., NYC, 1957-68; exec. v.p., dir. Penta Computer Assoc. Inc., NYC, 1968-70, Cons. Actuaries Inc., Clifton, NJ, 1970-73; exec. v.p., CFO Am. Film. Theatre, NYC, 1973-76, Cinema Shares Internat Dristb. Corp., NYC, 1976-79; sr. cons. Solomon, Finger & Newman, NYC, 1979-80; exec. v.p., CFO Metro Goldwyn Mayer, LA, 1980-82; various positions leading to sr. exec. v.p. fin. and adminstrn., chief fin. operating and adminstrv. officer MGM/UA Entertainment Co., Culver City, Calif., 1982-86, mem. bd. dirs., exec. com., 1982—89; fin. v.p.; chief adminstrv. and ops. officer, Office of Pres., dir. United Artists Corp., Beverly Hills, Calif., 1986-87; chmn. bd., CEO MGA/UA Telecommunications Corp., Beverly Hills, 1986-89; sr. exec. v.p., bd. dirs., mem. exec. com. MGA/UA Communications Co., 1986-89; chmn., CEO Sid Sapsowitz & Assocs., Inc., 1989—. Pres., Wayne Conservative Congregation, N.J., 1970-77; mem. bd. govs. exec. com. City of Hope, 1990-. Mem. Am. Mgmt. Assn., Am. Film Inst., Acad. Motion Picture Arts and Scis., Fin. Exec. Inst., TV Acad. Arts and Scis., KP (chancellor comdr.).

SARACEVIC, TEFKO, information science educator; married; 2 children. MS in Libr. Sci., Case Western Reserve U., 1962, PhD in Info. Sci., 1970. Prof. comm., info. and libr. studies Rutgers U., New Brunswick, NJ. Editor-in-chief: Info. Processing and Mgmt., 1985—. Avocations: reading, skiing. Office: Rutgers U Sch Comm Info & Libr Studies 4 Huntington St New Brunswick NJ 08901-1071 Office Phone: 732-932-7500 Ext. 8222. E-mail: tefko@scils.rutgers.edu.

SARACHIK, MYRIAM PAULA MORGENSTEIN, condensed matter physicist, educator; b. Antwerp, Belgium, Aug. 8, 1933; arrived in US, 1947; d. Solomon and Sarah (Segal) Morgenstein; m. Philip Sarachik, Sept. 6, 1954; 1 child, Karen Beth. AB, Barnard Coll., 1954; MS, Columbia U., 1957, PhD, 1960; DSc (hon.), Amherst Coll., 2006. Rsch. assoc. IBM Watson Labs., Columbia U., NYC, 1960-61; mem. tech. staff Bell Telephone Labs., Murray Hill, NJ, 1962-64; asst. prof. physics CCNY (CUNY), 1964-67, assoc. prof., 1967-70, prof., 1971—, Disting. prof. physics, 1995—. Advisor NSF, NRC, DOE Contbr. articles to profl. jours. Recipient NYC Mayor's award for excellence in sci. and tech., 1995, Sloan Pub. Svc. award, 2004, Oliver E. Buckley prize in Condensed Matter Physics, 2005, L'Oreal/UNESCO for Women in Sci. (N.Am.) Laureate, 2005. Fellow AAAS, Am. Phys. Soc. (pres. 2003), N.Y. Acad. Scis.; mem. NAS, Am. Acad. Arts and Scis. Office: CCNY (CUNY) Divsn Sci MR429 Physics Dept Convent Ave and 138 St New York NY 10031 Office Phone: 212-650-5618. Business E-Mail: sarachik@sci.ccny.cuny.edu.

SARALEGUI, CRISTINA MARIA, Spanish language television personality, journalist; b. Havana, Cuba, Jan. 29, 1948; came to U.S., 1960; d. Francisco and Cristina (Santamarina) Saralegui; m. Marcos Avila, June 19, 1984; 3 children. Student mass comm., U. Miami. Features editor Vanidades Continental, Miami, Fla., 1970-73; editor Cosmopolitan Spanish, Miami, 1973-76, editor-in-chief, 1979-89; dir. enterntainment Miami Herald, 1976-77; editor-in-chief Intimidades mag., Miami, 1977-79, TV y Novelas mag., 1986-89; hostess The Cristina Show Univision Network, 1989—; publisher Cristina the Magazine; hostess Cristina Opina, ABC radio program. Keynote spkr. Union Am. Women, P.R., 1981, Legendary Women of Miami. Featured in bestseller Latin Beauty, 1982; author autobiography My Life as a Blonde, 1998. Mem. internat. jury Miss Venezueala Pagent, 1982, Miss Columbia Pagent, 1987; bd. dir. Nat. Council of La Raza, Mus. TV & Radio; mem Nat. Council, AmFar. Recipient 10 Emmy awards; Keys to City Cartagena, Colombia, 1987; award of Distinction for Leadership, AmFar, 1995; Outstanding Communicator of the Year award, Nat. Org. for Women in Comm., 1996; Star on the Walk of Fame, 1999; Cmty. Svc. award, Nat. Council La Raza, 2000; Corp. Leader award, Nat. Network of Hispanic Women; VIP Honoree of the Year, Am. Cancer Soc., 2000; Gracie Allen Tribute award, Found. of Am. Women in radio & TV, 2001; Lifetime Achievement award, Imagen Found., 2002. Named one of the 25 Most Influential Hispanics, Time Mag., 2005. Mem. NAFE, Women in Comm. (key note spkr. 1986), Am. Soc. Profl. and Exec. Women, Am. Mgmt. Assn., Nat. Network Hispanic Women (Corp. Leader award), Latin Bus. and Profl. Women's Club. Republican. Roman Catholic. Office: The Christina Show 9405 NW 41st St Miami FL 33178-2301*

SARAN, SHAILEE, dietician; b. New Delhi, Nov. 12, 1975; permanent resident, 2007; d. Suresh and Reeta Saran; m. Sundar Venkat Kalyan Varanasi, Mar. 10, 2003. BSc in Home Economics, Delhi U., 1996, MSc in Food and Nutrition, 1998; MS in Nutrition, Barnes Jewish Coll., St. Louis, 2007. Registered dietitian Am. Dietetic Assn., 2006, lic. Fontbonne U., St Louis, 2006. Sr. sci. officer in nutrition Nutrition Found. India, New Delhi, 1998—2003; sr. sci. officer Ctr. Rsch. Nutrition Support Sys., New Delhi, 1999—2003; dietetic internship Barnes Jewish Coll., Wash. Med. Ctr., St. Louis, 2005—06; clin. dietitian SSM St. Joseph Health Ctr., Wentzville, Mo., 2006—, BJC Progress West Healthcare Ctr., St. Louis, 2007—. Mem. exec. organizing com. IX Asian Congress of Nutrition, Delhi, 2000—03; mem. exec. organizing com. practical pediatric nutrition course Ctr. Rsch. Nutrition Support Sys. and Apollo Ctr. Advanced Pediat., Delhi, 2001—03. Asst. editor: nutrition in disease management-update series quar. jour.; contbr. articles to profl. jours. Recipient Ninth John M. Kinney Internat. Nestle award for Pediat. Nutrition, 2004; Jeanette Spector Nursing Edn. Fund- Instl. scholarship, Barnes Jewish Coll., 2006—07. Mem.: Am. Dietetic Assn., Internat. Union Health Edn., Parenteral and Enteral Nutrition Soc. Asia, Indian Dietetic Assn., Nutrition Soc. India (Young Scientist award 2000), Indian Soc. Parenteral and Enteral Nutrition (life; exec. bd. mem. 2002—04, treas. 1999—2004), Delhi Dietetic Assn. (life). Achievements include research in the use of fermented foods to combat stunting and failure to thrive. Office: SSM St Joseph Health Ctr-Wentzville 500 Medical Dr Wentzville MO 63385 also: Progress West Healthcare Ctr 2 Progress Point Pkwy Mail Stop 88 O'Fallon MO 63368 Personal E-mail: s_shailee@hotmail.com.

SARANDON, SUSAN, actress; b. NYC, Oct. 4, 1946; d. Phillip Leslie and Lenora Marie (Criscione) Tomalin; m. Chris Sarandon, Sept. 16, 1967 (div. 1979); children: Eva Maria Livia Amurri, Jack Henry Robbins, Miles Guthrie Robbins. BA in Drama and English, Cath. U. Am., 1968. Actress: (plays) include An Evening with Richard Nixon, 1972, A Coupla White Chicks Sittin' Around Talkin', 1980-81, A Stroll in the Air, Albert's Bridge, Private Ear, Public Eye, Extremities, 1982, Exit the King, 2009; (films) Joe, 1970, Lady Liberty, 1972, The Rocky Horror Picture Show, 1975, Lovin' Molly, 1974, The Front Page, 1974, The Great Waldo Pepper, 1975, Dragon Fly, 1976, Crash, 1976, The Other Side of Midnight, 1977, The Last of the Cowboys, 1978, Checkered Flag or Crash, 1978, Pretty Baby, 1978, King of the Gypsies, 1978, Something Short of Paradise, 1979, Loving Couples, 1980, Atlantic City, 1980 (Prix Genie Best Fgn. Actress award 1981, Acad. award nominee 1981), Tempest, 1982 (Best Actress award Venice Film Festival 1982), The Hunger, 1983, The Buddy System, 1984, Compromising Positions, 1985, The Witches of Eastwick, 1987, Bull Durham, 1988, Sweet Hearts Dance, 1988, A Dry White Season, 1989, The January Man, 1989, White Palace, 1990, Thelma and Louise, 1991 (Acad. award nominee for best actress 1992, Golden Globe award nominee 1992), The Player, 1992, Light Sleeper, 1992, Bob Roberts, 1992, Lorenzo's Oil, 1992 (Acad. award nominee 1993), The Client, 1994 (Acad. award nominee for best actress), Little Women, 1994, Safe Passage, 1994, Dead Man Walking, 1995 (Golden Globe award nominee for best actress 1996, Acad. award for Best Actress 1996), James and the Giant Peach (voice), 1996, 187 (voice), 1997, Illuminata, 1998, Twilight, 1998, Stepmom (also producer), 1998, Joe Gould's Secret, 1999, Baby's in Black, 1999, Cradle Will Rock, 1999, Anywhere But Here, 1999, (voice) Rugrats in Paris: The Movie - Rugrats II, 2000, Moonlight Mile, 2002 (also exec. prodr.), The Banger Sisters, 2002, Igby Goes Down, 2002, Noel, 2004, Shall We Dance?, 2004, Alfie, 2004, Jiminy Glick in La La Wood, 2004, Elizabethtown, 2005, In the Valley of Elah, 2007, Mr. Woodcock, 2007, Emotional Arithmetic, 2007, Enchanted, 2007, Bernard and Doris, 2008, Speed Racer, 2008; (TV appearances) The Haunting of Rosalind, 1973, F. Scott Fitzgerald and The Last of the Belles, 1974, Who Am I This Time, 1982, A.D., 1985. Mussolini: The Decline and Fall of Il Duce, 1985, Earthly Possessions, 1999, Friends, 2001 (Emmy nominee), Malcolm in the Middle, 2002 (Emmy nominee), Ice Bound, 2003., The Exonerated, 2005; (TV series) A World Apart, 1970-71, Search for Tomorrow, 1972-73; TV miniseries: Children of Dune, 2003; narrator (films) The Shape of Water, 2008. Recipient Bette Davis Lifetime Achievement award, Boston U., 2008. Mem. AFTRA, Screen Actors Guild, Actors Equity, Acad. Motion Picture Arts and Scis., NOW, MADRE, Amnesty Internat., ACLU Office: Internat Creative Mgmt care Samuel Cohen 40 W 57th St New York NY 10019-4001*

SARANI, SIAMAK, aerospace engineer; s. Mahmoud Sarani and Yakhchi Asgarzadeh; m. Maryam Momeni Sarani, Mar. 12, 1997; children: Alireza, Iman. Degree in Engring., U. Southern Calif., LA, 2002. Spacecraft control & autonomy Boeing Space & Comm., El Segundo, Calif., 1995—2000; sr. guidance & control sys. engr. Jet Propulsion Lab., Pasadena, Calif., 2000—. Recipient Space Act award, NASA, 2007. Mem.: Am. Inst. Aeronautics & Astronautics. Muslim. Achievements include patents for titan density reconstruction using spacecraft guidance, navigation, and control data. Home: 23519 Friar St Woodland Hills CA 91367 Office: Jet Propulsion Lab 4800 Oak Grove Dr Pasadena CA 91109-8099 Office Phone: 818-393-9082. Business E-Mail: siamak.sarani@jpl.nasa.gov, ssarani@socal.rr.com.

SARAPH, PRASAD VAMAN, research scientist, industrial engineer; arrived in U., 1998; BSME, Govt. Engring. Coll., Aurangabad, India, 1992; MS, Indian Inst. Tech., 1995; MS Engring., U. Calif., Berkeley, 1999. Prodn. supr. Universal Luggage Mfg. Co., Aurangabad, Maharashtra, India, 1992—93; rsch. assoc. Inst. Devel. Studies U. Sussex, Brighton, England, 1995—96; cons. A.F. Ferguson & Co, Mumbai, Maharashtra, India, 1996—97; grad. rsch. asst. U. Calif., Berkeley, 1998—99; sr. engr. Bayer Corp., Berkeley, 2000—01, project mgr., 2001—02; head Dept. Long Term Planning Bayer Biol. Products, Berkeley, 2003—05, supply chain excellence lead, 2006—; global sales & ops. planning vendor managed inventory & supply parameter agreements roll-out lead Bayer Health Care, 2009—. Track coord. healthcare and biotechnology Winter Simulation Conf., 2004—05. Author: Corporate Restructuring: Crompton Greaves and the Challenge of Globalization, 1998; contbr. articles to profl. jours. Recipient First Pl. award, Indian Inst. Tech., 1993, Inst. Indsl. Engrs., 1999. Mem.: YWCA,

Capoeira Narahari (capoeirista 2000—). Achievements include first to implement mixed integer programming based supply chain planning in biopharma industry; introduce and successfully implement of discrete event simulation techniques in the biopharmaceuticals industry; analysis methodology for impact of regulatory strategy on biopharmaceutical product and process life cycle management; successfully introduce optimization tools in supply chain planning for biopharmaceuticals; implement mixed integer program in biotech for production planning; research in use of dynamic simulation for risk analysis in biopharmaceuticals industry; development of hierarchical strategic capacity analysis methodology for biopharmaceutical manufacturing; and implementation of organizational decision support structure for biopharmaceutical industry; and implementation of world's largest mixed integer program and the first MIP for supply chanin planning in biopharmaceuticals industry. Avocations: martial arts, classical music, stamp collecting/philately, reading. Office: Bayer HealthCare LLC Biological Products 800 Dwight Way Berkeley CA 94710 Personal E-mail: psaraph@yahoo.com. Business E-Mail: prasad.saraph.b@bayer.com.

SARASON, IRWIN G., psychology professor; b. Newark, Sept. 15, 1929; s. Max and Anna Sarason; m. Barbara June Ryrholm, Sept. 19, 1953; children: Suzanne, Jane, Donald. BA, Rutgers U., Newark, 1951; MS, U. Iowa, 1953; PhD, Ind. U., 1955. Intern clin. psychology VA Hosp., West Haven, Conn., 1955-56; from asst. prof. psychology to prof. emeritus U. Wash., Seattle, 1956—2003, prof. emeritus, 2003—. Co-author: Abnormal Psychology, 1972, 11th edit., 2005; editor: Jour. Personality and Social Psychology, 1985-91; author over 300 articles. The Netherlands Inst. for Advanced Study fellow, Wassenaar, 1975, 85. Fellow APA, Japan Soc. for Promotion of Sci., AAAS, Western Psychol. Assn. (pres. 1978-79), Wash. State Psychol. Assn. (pres. 1965). Avocations: travel, music, reading. Home: 13516 42nd Ave NE Seattle WA 98125-3826 Office: U Wash Dept Psychology Box 351525 Seattle WA 98195-0001 Business E-Mail: isarason@u.washington.edu.

SARAVANABHAVAN, SHEILA, education educator; b. Tuticorin, India, Sept. 10, 1948; came to U.S., 1988; d. Nazareth and Ruby (Motha) Corera; m. R. C. Saravanabhavan, Sept. 10, 1975; 1 child, Yamini Saravanan. MA in English, Madurai U., India, 1974; MA in Spl. Edn., No. Ariz. U., 1989, MA in Bilingual Edn., 1990, EdD in Leadership, 1994. Cert. in learning disabled, gifted, and ESL, spl. edn. Assoc. lectr. PSG Poly., India, 1978-80; lectr. Coll. of Commerce, Addis Ababa, Ethiopia, 1980-88; asst. prof. Mo. Western State Coll., St. Joseph, 1994—. Presenter ATE, AACTE, WCCI. Contbr. book revs. to profl. publs. Mem. CEC (presenter 1996), Phi Kappa Phi, Kappa Delta Pi, Delta Kappa Gamma. Roman Catholic. Home: 2939 Van Ness St NW Apt 1207 Washington DC 20008-4611 Office: Mo Western State Coll 4525 Downs Dr Saint Joseph MO 64507-2246

SARAVO, ANNE COBBLE, clinical psychologist, mental health consultant; b. Atlanta, Feb. 23, 1938; d. William Edwin and Iris Benny (Norman) Cobble; m. James Vincent Saravo, Sept. 27, 1958; children: Stacy Anne Nathan, Lisa Ames Furmanek. BA, Tex. Tech. U., 1959; MS, U. Mass., 1964, PhD, 1965; postgrad., Regional Health Authority, London, 1978-79, U. So. Calif., 1980-81. Lic. psychologist, Calif., Ga., SC. Assoc. prof. psychology Antioch Coll., Yellow Springs, Ohio, 1966-69; cons. Winchester (Eng.) Day Treatment Nursery Sch., 1971-73; sch. psychologist Muroc Unified Sch. Dist., Edwards AFB, Calif., 1974-75; clinical psychologist Antelope Valley Hosp., Lancaster, Calif., 1975-76, Farnborough Hosp., Kent, Eng., 1978-80, Orange County Mental Health Svc., Calif., 1981—97, chief adult out-patient svc., 1984-87, chief adult inpatient svcs., 1987-95; pvt. practice clin. psychology Seal Beach, Calif., 1981, Atlanta, 2004—, Beaufort, SC, 2007—; program mgr. Medi-Cal Inpatient Managed Care, 1995-97; med. advisor Medicare, Calif. Nat. Heritage Ins. Corp., 1995—. Bd. dirs. High Hopes Neurol. Recover Group, Costa Mesa, Calif., chair profl. adv. bd., 1988-2001; oral examination commr. Calif. Bd. Psychology, 1989-1999; geriatric coord. Orange County Mental Health Svcs., 1985-87; profl. adv. bd. Orange County Caregiver Resource Ctr., 1989-1999; mem. Alzheimers Disease rev. panel Calif. Dept. Mental Health, 1990-91; expert reviewer Calif. Bd. Psychology, Med. Bd. Calif., 2000—; invited spkr. in field. Contbr. articles to profl. jours. Chairperson Conf. Geriatric Mental Health, Asilomar, Calif., 1986, So. Calif. Geriatric Mental Health Coordinators, 1985-87; vol. disaster mental health team Red Cross, 2001-; pianist Beaufort Orch., 2004-05; performer TCU, Van Cliburn Inst., 2004-05; piano recital Beaufort Orch. League Benefit, 2009. U.S. Pub. Health fellow Fels Research Inst., 1966-67. Mem. APA, Calif. Psychol. Assn. (chair medicare/pub. sector subcom. 1990-96, co-chair reimbursement and managed care com. 1996-97, bd. dirs. divsn. pvt. practice 1998), Ga. Psychol. Assn. (mem. legislative com. 2003-), SC Psychol. Assn., Nat. Acad. Neuropsychology (grad.), Brit. Psychol. Soc., Gerontol. Soc. Am. Avocation: piano. Office: 219 Scotts St #351 Beaufort SC 29902 Home Phone: 843-838-9998; Office Phone: 770-597-3261. Personal E-mail: chateaucobble@yahoo.com.

SARAVOLATZ, LOUIS DONALD, epidemiologist, medical educator; b. Detroit, Feb. 15, 1950; s. Samuel and Saya Betty (Chonich) S.; m. Yvette Susanne Braymer, Oct. 6, 1990; children: Samuel Francis, Louis Donald II, Stephanie Nicole. BS, U. Mich., Ann Arbor, 1972, MD, 1974. Fellow Am. Coll. Epidemiology. Intern Henry Ford Hosp., Detroit, 1974-75, 1975-77, fellow, 1977-79, dir. hosp. epidemiology, 1979-82, divsn. head infectious diseases, 1982-96, dir. infectious diseases rsch. lab., 1982-96; prof. medicine Case-Western Res. U., 1993-96, Wayne State U. Sch. Medicine, Detroit, 1996—. Clin. prof. medicine U. Mich. Med. Sch., Ann Arbor, 1986-96; mem. AIDS clin. drug devel. com. NIH, 1990-95; chmn. dept. internal medicine St. John Hosp. and Med. Ctr., 1996—. Contbr. over 170 articles to profl. publs. Active Blue Ribbon Com. on AIDS State of Mich., Detroit, 1990; chmn. physician com. on AIDS Greater Detroit Health Coun., 1989. Master: ACP, Am. Coll. Physicians; fellow: Royal Soc. Medicine (London), Infectious Diseases Soc. Am. (chmn. antimicrobial use and clin. trials com. 2000—03). Office Phone: 313-343-3362. Business E-Mail: louis.saravolatz@stjohn.org.

SARAZIN, CRAIG LEIGH, astronomer; b. Milw., Aug. 11, 1950; s. Valley V. and Martha V. (Gustafson) Sarazin; children: Stephen N., Andrew T. BS in Physics, Calif. Inst. Tech., 1972; MA in Physics, Princeton U., 1973, PhD in Physics, 1975. Millikan fellow Calif. Inst. Tech., Pasadena, 1975; mem. Inst. Advanced Study, Princeton, NJ, 1975-77; asst. prof. U. Va., Charlottesville, 1977-79, assoc. prof. dept. astronomy, 1979-86, prof., 1986-96, W.H. Vanderbilt prof. astronomy, 1996—, chmn. dept., 1992-95. Vis. asst. prof. U. Calif., Berkeley, 1979; vis. scientist Nat. Radio Astronomy Obs., Charlottesville, 1977-82; vis. prof. physics Inst. Advanced Study, 1981-82, Joint Inst. Lab. Astrophysics vis. fellow U. Colo., Boulder, 1985-86; mem. com. on Space Astronomy Astrophysics, Washington, 1984-86, mem. x-ray astronomy working group, 1989-99, mem. Heineman prize com., 1995-98; chmn. Chandra users com., 1993-01, Advanced Satellite for Cosmology and Astrophysics users com., 1995-2000; mem. High Energy Astrophysics from Space Panel, 1999-2000; chmn. USRA Sci. Coun., 2000-06; mem. program assessment com. Beyond Einstein, 2006-07; chmn. NASA X MUI Newton Users Com. 2009-. Author: X-ray Emission from Clusters of Galaxies; contbr. numerous articles to profl. jours. NSF grantee, 1981-86, NASA grantee, 1979-82, 86—; recipient Haren Fischer Physics prize Calif. Inst. Tech., 1971. Mem. Am. Astron. Soc., Internat. Astron. Union. Home: 664 Courtyard Ct Charlottesville VA 22903-7876 Office: U Va Dept Astronomy PO Box 400325 Charlottesville VA 22904-4325 Home Phone: 434-293-3270; Office Phone: 434-924-4903. Business E-Mail: sarazin@virginia.edu.

SARBACKER, DONALD LEROY, economics professor; b. Madison, Wis., Dec. 22, 1935; s. Lloyd August Sarbacker and Kathryn Sartbacker Barbara; m. Jeanette Lettie Sayne, July 29, 1989; children: Mark Gordon, Ann Marie Simmons. MBA in Mgmt. with honors, Mich. State U. Advanced Mgmt. Program, Lansing, 1979. Fin. planing specialist, Fla., 2004. 1st v.p. Smith Barney, St. Petersburg, Fla., 1992—2006; economics prof. Hillsborough CC, Tampa, Fla., 1992—; prof. bus. Southeastern U., Lakeland, Fla., 2006—08. Cons. Price Waterhouse, Tampa, 1988—92. Contbr. articles to profl. publs. Spkr., fundraiser Somebody Cares Tampa Bay, Tampa, 1999—2002. Recipient Disting. Toastmaster award, Internat. Toastmasters, 1996, Excellence Client Svcs. award, Smith Barney, 2002; named Businessman of Yr., Somebody Cares Tampa Bay, 2001; named one of Top 50 Prodr., Smith Barney, 2000; named to Hall of Fame, Internat. Toastmasters. Mem.: Beta Gamma Sigma Honors Soc. Conservative. Baptist. Home: 10502 Castleford Way Tampa FL 33626-1708 Home Fax: 813-926-9431. Personal E-mail: donjnett1@verizon.net.

SARBANES, JOHN PETER SPYROS, United States Representative from Maryland, lawyer; b. Balt., May 22, 1962; s. Paul S. and Christine (Dunbar) Sarbanes; m. Dina Eve Caplin, 1988; 3 children. AB cum laude, Woodrow Wilson Sch. Public & Internat. Affairs, Princeton U., 1984; JD, Harvard U., 1988. Bar: Md. 1988, DC. Law clk. to Hon. J. Frederick Motz, US Dist. Ct. Md., 1988—89; assoc. through ptnr. Venable LLP, Balt., 1989—2006, mem. hiring com., 1992—96, chmn. health care practice, 2000—06; mem. US Congress from 3nd Md. dist., 2007—, mem. edn. & workforce com., resources com., govt. oversight com. Pres. Pub. Justice Ctr., Balt., 1994—97; spl. asst. to supt. schools State of Md. Spl. asst. State Supt. Schools, Md.; bd. mem. Inst. for Christian & Jewish Studies. Fulbright Scholar, 1985. Mem.: ABA, Md. Bar Assn., DC Bar. Democrat. Greek Orthodox. Office: 426 Cannon House Office Bldg Washington DC 20515 also: 600 Baltimore Ave Ste 303 Towson MD 21204 also: Arundel Ctr Ste 349 44 Calvert St Annapolis MD 21401*

SARBANES, PAUL SPYROS, former United States Senator from Maryland; b. Salisbury, Md., Feb. 3, 1933; s. Spyros P. and Matina (Tsigounis) S.; m. Christine Dunbar, June 11, 1960; children: John Peter, Michael Anthony, Janet Matina. AB in Public and Internat. Affairs, magna cum laude, Princeton, 1954; BA in Philosophy, Politics and Economics, Rhodes Scholar, Oxford U., Eng., 1957; LLB, Harvard, 1960. Bar: Md. 1960. Law clk. to Hon. Morris A. Soper US Ct. Appeals (4th Cir.), 1960-61; assoc. Piper & Marbury LLP, Balt., 1961-62; adminstrv. asst. to chmn. Walter W. Heller Coun. Econ. Advisors, Exec. Office of the Pres., Washington, 1962—63; exec. dir. Charter Revision Commn., Balt., 1963-64; assoc. Venable, Baetjer & Howard LLP, Balt., 1965-70; mem. Md. House Delegates, 1967-71, US Congress from 3rd Md. Dist., 1971—77; US Senator from Md., 1977—2007; mem. US Senate Banking Housing & Urban Affairs Com., 1977—2007, chmn., 2001—03; mem. Joint Econ. Com., 1979—2007, US Senate Budget Com., 1993—2007. Co-author (with David R. Obey): The Changing American Economy: Papers from the Fortieth Anniversary Symposium of the Joint Economic Committee of the US Congress, 1986. Recipient Nat. Disting. Svc. award, Am. Pub. Transit Assn., 1999, Paul H. Douglas Ethics in Govt. award, Inst. Govt. & Pub. Affairs, U. Ill., 2003, Restore Am. Hero award, Nat. Trust for Historic Preservation and HGTV, 2005. Fellow: Am. Acad. Arts & Sci. Democrat. Greek Orthodox.

SAREMBOCK, IAN JOSEPH, internist, cardiologist; b. Cape Town, South Africa, June 9, 1951; arrived in US, 1982, naturalized, 1986; m. Ghita Marueen Sarembock; children: Craig Murray, Kerri Lauren. MD, U. Cape Town, 1975, PhD, 1988. Diplomate Am. Bd. Internal Medicine, Am. Bd. Cardiovasc. Medicine, Am. Bd. Interventional Cardiology. Sr. house officer dept. internal medicine U. Cape Town and Groote Schuur Hosp., Cape Town, 1979-80, resident in internal medicine, 1980-83, sr. registrar Cardiac Clinic, 1985-86; Velva Schrire meml. rsch. fellow Cardiac Clinic Groote Schur Hosp., 1983-85; postdoctoral rsch. assoc. divsn. cardiology Yale U., New Haven, 1986-88; attending cardiologist divsn. cardiology VA Ctr., West Haven, Conn., 1987-88; asst. prof. internal medicine cardiovasc. divsn. U. Va. Health Scis. Ctr., Charlottesville, 1988-93, assoc. prof. internal medicine cardiovasc. divsn., 1993-99, dir. coronary care unit, 1988—2007, prof. internal medicine cardiovasc. divsn., 1999—2007; interventional cardiologist, 1988—2007; cardiology cons. Salem VA Med. Ctr., Va., 1988—2000; dir. Ctr. Interventional Cardiology, U. Va. Health System, 2005—07, Ohio Heart & Vascular Ctr., Cin., 2007—. Lectr., presenter in field; invited prof. Heart-Lung Inst., Utrecht, Netherlands, 1992; mem. faculty restenosis summits, Cleve. Clinic, 1992, 93, 97. Contbr. articles to profl. publs. Mem. policy working com., house staff supervision Commonwealth of Va., 1990-2007. With South African Def. Force, Med. Corps, 1977—78. Grantee U. Va. Sch. Medicine, 1989, Beecham Labs., 1989-90, Am. Heart Assn., 1989-91, 91-92, 95-98, NIH, 1991-94, 2000-05; named Harrison DFisting. Tchg. Prof. Internal Medicine, 2006-07. Fellow ACP, Coll. Physicians South Africa, Am. Coll. Cardiology (allied health profls. com. 1993—), Coun. Thrombosis Atherosclerosis and Vascular Biology; mem. AAAS, Am. Heart Assn. (bd. dirs. Charlottesville/Albermarle divsn. 1991—, mem. Va. affiliate rsch. peer rev. subcom. 1992—, thrombosis coun. 1987, fellow coun. on clin. cardiology 1989), South African Med. and Dental Coun. Jewish. Office: Ohio Heart Vascular Ctr 4750 E Galbraith Rd Ste 103 Cincinnati OH 45236 Office Phone: 513-985-0022. E-mail: sarembock@ohioheart.org.

SAREMI, FARHOOD, radiologist; s. Fattolah Saremi and Fatemah Najafi; children: Shervin, Arvin. MD, U. Tehran, Iran, 1983. Cert. med. dr. Med. Bd. Calif., 1998. Chief cardiothoracic imaging U. Calif., Irvine, Orange, 2002—. Mem.: RSNA (award 2000, 2006). Office: Univ Calif Irvine 101 City Dr S Orange CA 92868 Business E-Mail: fsaremi@uci.edu.

SAREYAN, ANDY, publishing executive; m. Nancy Marshall; children: Alex, Eliza. BA in Econs., summa cum laude, Middlebury Coll.; MBA, Stanford U. Various consumer mktg. positions Time Inc., 1987—91; consumer mktg. dir., Can. and Latin Am. Time Internat., 1991—93; v.p., consumer mktg. and develop. Entertainment Weekly Time Inc., 1993—97, v.p., assoc. pub. In Style, 1997—99, founding pub. Real Simple, 1999; pres. Parenting Group, 2001—02, Entertainment Weekly, NY, 2002—05; exec. v.p., pub. Better Homes & Gardens mag. Meredith Corp., NYC, 2006—, chief brand officer nat. media group, 2009—. Office: Better Homes & Gardens 125 Park Ave New York NY 10017*

SARGENT, CHARLES LEE, manufacturing executive; b. Flint, Mich., Mar. 22, 1937; s. Frank T. and Evelyn M. (Martinson) S.; m. Nancy Cook, June 9, 1962; children: Wendy L., Joy A., Candace L. B ME, GM Inst., 1960; MBA, Harvard U., 1962; D in Engring. (hon.), Kettering U., 2004. Reliability engr. AC Spark Plug div. GM, Flint, 1962-63; with Thetford Corp., Ann Arbor, Mich., 1962-95, pres., chmn. bd. dirs., 1974-95, Thermassan Corp., 1969-72; pres., owner Quality Boat Lifts, Inc., Fort Myers, Fla., 1996—2007. Trustee Lincoln Cons. Schs., 1973-77, Ketterine U., 1989-2004, chmn. 1995-97. Sch. bd. Lincoln Consolidated Schs., Ypsilanti, Mich.; elder Presbyn. Ch. Recipient Entrepreneurial Achievement award GMI, 1989; named Entrepreneur of the Yr., Harvard Bus. Sch. Club of Detroit, 1981, Engring. Achievement award Kettering U., 1999. Mem. Barton Hills Country Club (bd. dirs. 1985-87, pres. 1987), Harvard Bus. Sch. Club of Detroit (bd. dirs. 1983-93). Achievements include patents in field. Avocations: travel, golf. Home: 4931 Bonita Bay Blvd 602 Bonita Springs FL 34134

SARGENT, DAVID JASPER, academic administrator; b. Manchester, NH, Aug. 5, 1931; s. Merton Jasper and Marguerite (Riley) S.; m. Shirley Woodbury Swift, Dec. 21, 1951. Student, U. NH, 1949-51; JD magna cum laude, Suffolk U., Boston, 1954; LLD (hon.), Suffolk U., 1978. Bar: NH 1954, Mass. 1954, US Supreme Ct. 1978. Assoc. Kowal and Sargent, Boston, 1954-57; asst. prof. Suffolk U. Law Sch., Boston, 1955—58, assoc. prof., 1958—62, prof., 1962—, dean, 1972—89; pres. Suffolk U., Boston, 1989—. Chmn. Mass. Supreme Ct. Commn. on the Future of the Cts., 1989-; cons. Am. Trial Lawyers Assn., 1957-81; mem. Mass. Jud. Selection Com., 1974-77, Nat. Bd. Trial Advocacy, 1978—. Contbr. articles to legal publications. Bd. trustees Anatolia Coll., Thessaloniki, Greece. Recipient Nat. Svc. award Am. Trial Lawyers Assn., 1968, Outstanding Alumnus award Suffolk U. Law Sch., 1978; hon. mem. Minn. Bar. Mem. ABA, Am. Law Inst., Mass. Bar Assn., NH Bar Assn., Masons. Episcopalian. Office: Suffolk U President's Office 25th Fl 8 Ashburton Pl Boston MA 02108-2770

SARGENT, JOHN, psychiatrist; b. Mar. 27, 1947; MD, U. Rochester, 1973. Diplomate in psychiatry, child and adolescent psychiatry Am. Bd. Psychiatry and Neurology; diplomate Am. Bd. Pediats.; approved clin. supr. Am. Assn. Marriage and Family Therapy. Intern and resident pediat. U. Wis., Madison, 1973—77; resident child and adolescent psychiatry Phila. Child Guidance Ctr., 1978—80; resident gen. psychiatry Hosp. U. Pa., Phila., 1984—87; dir. child and adolescent psychiatry U. Pa. Med. Sch., 1989—97, dir. adult residency program, 1989—97; mem. staff Children's Hosp. Phila., Phila. Child Guidance Ctr., 1980—97; dir. edn. and rsch., dean Karl Menninger Sch. Psychiatry & Mental Health Svcs., Topeka, 1997—2001; prof. psychiatry Baylor Coll. Medicine, Houston, 2001—08; dir., divsn. child and adolescent psychiatry Ben Taub Hosp., Houston, 2001—, Tufts Med. Ctr., 2008—; prodr., psychiatry and pediats. Tufts U. Sch. Medicine, 2009—. Assoc. prof. psychiatry and pediat. U. Pa. Med. Sch., 1987-97; Pfeiffer/Adams prof. psychiatry Karl Menninger Sch. Psychiatry. Mem. editl. bd. Jour. Am. Acad. Child and Adolescent Psychiatry, Family Process, Bull. of Menninger Clinic; co-author: Madness, Chaos and Violence: Therapy with Families at the Brink; co-editor: Primary Care Pediatrics; contbr. over 60 articles to profl. jours. Dep. dir. Ea. European Child Abuse and Child Mental Health Program, Soros Found. and Children's Mental Health Alliance, 1997-2003. Office: Tufts Medical Center Dept of Psychiatry 800 Washington St Box 1007 Boston MA 02111 Home Phone: 781-259-0667; Office Phone: 617-636-8768. Business E-Mail: jsargent@tuftsmedicalcenter.org.

SARGENT, JOSEPH DENNY, insurance executive; b. West Hartford, Conn., Sept. 11, 1929; s. Thomas Denny and Elizabeth (Owen) S.; m. Mary A. Tennant, June 25, 1955; children: Robert Tennant, Thomas Denny II, Mary Diane, Suzanne Davis. BA, Yale U., 1952. Ptnr. Conning & Co., Inc., Hartford, Conn., 1957-86, mng. ptnr., 1986-92; chmn., CEO Conning & Co., Hartford, Conn., 1986-91, chmn., 1992, vice-chmn., 1993-95; chmn. Conning Internat., London, 1986-92; vice chmn. Conning & Co., 1993-95; chmn. Bradley, Foster & Sargent, 1995—. Bd. dirs. Bristol, Conn., Tenwick Reins., Stamford, Conn.; past trustee MMI Co., Chgo., Mut. Risk, Bermuda, Policy Mgmt. Sys., Columbia, S.C.; chmn. Conn. Surety Corp., Hartford, 1993-97, Bradley, Foster & Sargent, Hartford, Beazley Furlonge Holdings, Ltd., London; trustee McLean Fund; chmn., treas. SKI Ltd, 1956-96. Past trustee Wadsworth Atheneum, Children's Svcs. of Conn.; trustee Hartford Hosp. Mem.: Yale Club (Hartford), Hartford Club, Hartford Golf Club. Home: 25 Colony Rd West Hartford CT 06117-2215 Office: City Place II 185 Asylum St Hartford CT 06103-3408

SARGENT, MARGARET HOLLAND, portrait artist, actress, writer; b. Hollywood, Calif., Dec. 30, 1927; d. Cecil Claude and Norma Mary Holland; m. Howard L. Sargent, June 22, 1947; children: Christopher Lee, Kenneth Dean. Student, UCLA, 1945—47, student, 1954—55; studies with Herbert Abrams, NY, 1958—61. Owner Sargent Portraits, LA, 1977—; actress, writer Camelot Prodns., LA, 1983—85. Lectr. Met. Mus. Art. Prin. portraits include, Gerald Ford, Margaret Thatcher, for Time, Inc., Tennesee Williams, Gen. and Mrs. Alexander Haig, Supt. L.G. Dave R. Palmer, Lt. Gen. Daniel W. Christman, Kristin Baker, Andrea Hollen for U.S. Mil. Acad. Mus., L.G. Kenneth L. Tallman, Hawaii Gov. George R. Ariyoshi, Army Chief Staff Gen. John Wickham, William Gates Sr. and Mary Maxwell Gates, Kent Kresa, CEO of Northrop Grumman Corp., Gilbert Maurer, pres. Hearst Mags., and family, Frank Holland, Jules S. Stein and Lew Wasserman for Music Corp. Am., Prince Turki Saud, Princess Areeg Saud, Dorothy Bullitt, King Broadcasting, Elmer Nordstrom for Swedish Hosp, Jonathan D. Varat dean of UCLA Sch. Law, William Matthew Byrne, Jr., Fed. Ct. Judge, LA mayor James K. Hahn, Vice Adm. James B. Stockdale, Rear Adm. James E. Service, Rear Adm. Ronald J. Kurth, Rear Adm. James R. Stark, Vice Adm. Arthur K. Cebrowski, Rear Adm. Jacob L. Shuford for US Naval War Coll., exhibited in group shows at NY, 1974. Recipient Painting Yr. award, 1974, 1st pl. for profl. oils, AFL-CIO, 1979. Mem.: SAG, AFTRA, Coun. Leading Am. Portrait Painters (mem. coun.), Am. Portrait Soc. (bd. cert. 1983, credentials com. 1983—84), Actors Equity Assn., Salmagundi Art Club (Navy Art Cooperation and Liaison Com. award for oil painting 1976). Home and Office: Sargent Portraits 2750 Glendower Ave Los Angeles CA 90027-1139 Office Phone: 323-660-2214, 323-660-6549. Personal E-mail: megsarg@pacbell.net.

SARGENT, MILDRED CROW, retired history educator, writer; b. Nashville, Feb. 4, 1922; d. Edward Martin and Alpha Eunice Black; m. Arnold Dale Crow, Dec. 10, 1938 (dec. Aug. 18, 1988); children: Larry Wayne Crow, David Hardin Crow, Gerald Dale Crow(dec.), Richard Clayton Crow(dec.); m. John Wesley Sargent, Oct. 25, 1993. BS in Social Studies and English, Mid. Tenn. State Coll., Murfreesboro, 1965; MA in History and Libr. Sci., Mid. Tenn. State U., Murfreesboro, 1967, postgrad., 1971—82. Cert. tchr. Tenn. Bd. Edn., geneal. cert. State of NC Archives. Dist. mgr. World Book Ency., Nashville, 1959; English tchr. Antioch HS, Tenn., 1965—66; history tchr. Two Rivers HS, Nashville, 1967—70; libr. Gladeville Elem., Wilson County Bd. Edn., Lebanon, Tenn., 1982—83, libr. West Elem., 1983—86. Author: William Few: A Founding Father, 2 vols., 2006, Andrew and Eliga Johnson Biography; editor Cmty. News, Donelon, Tenn., 1966—68; contbr. V.p. PTA Mc Garoch Elem. Sch., 1966—68; floor mgr., conv. del. NEA, 1969. Mem.: AAUW, Am. Legion Aux., Phi Alpha Theta, Kappa Delta Pi, Pi Gamma

Mu. Democrat. Achievements include unveiling the Women Support the War stamp in Washington, DC. Avocations: bridge, ballroom dancing, golf, symphony performances, travel. Home: 2309 Dundee Ln Nashville TN 37214 Home Fax: 615-882-9275. Personal E-mail: johnsrsargent@bellsouth.com.

SARGENT, PAMELA, writer; b. Ithaca, NY, Mar. 20, 1948; BA, SUNY, Binghamton, 1968, MA, 1970. Mng. editor, Binghamton, 1970-73; asst. editor, 1973-75; Am. editor Bull. Sci. Fiction Writers Am., Johnson City, NY, 1983-91. Author: Cloned Lives, 1976, Starshadows, 1977, The Sudden Star, 1979, Watchstar, 1980, The Golden Space, 1982, The Alien Upstairs, 1983, Earthseed, 1983, Eye of the Comet, 1984, Homesmind, 1984, Venus of Dreams, 1986, The Shore of Women, 1986, The Best of Pamela Sargent, 1987, Alien Child, 1988, Venus of Shadows, 1988, Ruler of the Sky, 1993 (Nebula best novelette award 1992, Locus best novelette award 1993, Electric Sci. Fiction award 1993), Climb the Wind: A Novel of Another America, 1999, (with Ron Miller) Firebrands: The Heroines of Science Fiction and Fantasy, 1998, Child of Venus, 2001, Behind the Eyes of Dreamers and Other Short Novels, 2002, The Mountain Cage and Other Stories, 2002, Eye of Flame: Fantasies, 2003, Thumbprints, 2004, Farseed, 2007; editor: (anthology) Women of Wonder, 1975, Bio-Futures, 1976, More Women of Wonder, 1976, The New Women of Wonder, 1978, (with Ian Watson) Afterlives, 1986, Women of Wonder, The Classic Years, 1996, Women of Wonder, The Contemporary Years, 1995, Nebula Awards 29, 1995, Nebula Awards 30, 1996, Nebula Awards 31, 1997, Conqueror Fantastic, 2004. Office: care Richard Curtis Assocs Inc 171 E 74th St New York NY 10021-3221 Personal E-mail: pamsargent@gmail.com.

SARGENT, ROBERT GEORGE, engineering educator; b. Port Huron, Mich., June 14, 1937; s. George O. and Marie L. (Roome) S.; m. Dorothy Baum, 1970; 1 dau., Tiffany. BSE, U. Mich., 1959, MS, 1963, PhD, 1966. Elec. engr. Hughes Aircraft Co., Culver City, Calif., 1959-61; faculty mem. Syracuse U., 1966—, asst. prof., 1966-70, assoc. prof., 1970-81, prof. indsl. engring. and ops. research, 1982-96, chmn. dept., 1982-85, prof. elec. and computer engring., 1994-96, prof. elec. engring. and computer sci., 1996—. Vis. faculty Cornell U., 1981-82, Ctr. Econ. Rsch. Tilburg U., 1996; bd. dirs. Winter Simulation Conf., 1974-84, chmn. bd., 1979-81, gen. chmn., 1977, TIMS Coll. on Simulation and Gaming, 1978-80; pres. WSC Found., 2003-. Dept. editor Comms. of Assn. Computing Machinery, 1980-85; mem. editl. adv. bd. ACM Transactions on Modeling and Simulations, 1989-98; mem. adv. bd. Jour. of Simulation, 2005—; contbr. articles to profl. jours. Recipient Svc. award Winter Simulation Conf., 1984, 40th Anniversary Landmark award 2007. Fellow Inst. Ops. Rsch. and Mgmt. Scis. (Disting. Svc. award for Simulation 1988, Lifetime Profl. Achievement award 2002); mem. Assn. Computing Machinery (nat. lectr 1985-89, Svc. award 1985), Inst. Indsl. Engrs. (Svc. award 1985), Soc. Computer Simulation (bd. dirs. 1984-87), Computer Soc. IEEE (mem. exec. com. simulation 1985-99). Office: Syracuse U Dept Elec Engring and Computer Sci Syracuse NY 13244-0001

SARGENT, RONALD L., retail office and business products executive; b. 1955; m. Jill Sargent; 2 children. BS in Economics, Harvard U., 1977, MBA, 1979. Various mgmt. and planning positions The Kroger Co., 1974-89; regional v.p. ops. Staples Inc., 1989—92, v.p. Staples Direct, 1992—94, pres. Staples Contract & Comml., 1994—98, COO, 1998—2002, pres., 1998—2005, CEO, 2002—, chmn., 2005—. Bd. dirs. Staples Inc., 1999—, Aramark Corp., 2002—, Mattel Inc., 2004—, The Kroger Co., 2006—. Office: Staples Inc PO Box 9265 Framingham MA 01701-9265*

SARGENT, THOMAS ANDREW, retired political science professor; b. Indpls., Apr. 24, 1933; s. Thomas Edward and Inez (Secrest) S.; m. Cecily Constance Fox-Williams, 1965 (dec.); children: Sarah Beatrice, Andrew Fox; m. 2d Frances Petty, 1987. BA, DePauw U., Greencastle, Ind., 1955; MA, Fletcher Sch. Law and Diplomacy, Tufts U., 1959, MA in Law and Diplomacy, 1968, PhD, 1969. With First Nat. City Bank, NYC, 1959-64, asst. accountant, 1963-64; asst. sec. Irving Trust Co., NYC, 1964-66; mem. faculty Ball State U., Muncie, Ind., 1969-89, dir. London Ctr., 1973-74, chmn. polit. sci. dept., 1977-80, prof. polit. sci., 1979-89, prof. emeritus, 1989—, acting asst. to dean Coll. Scis. and Humanities, 1981-82, assoc. dean Coll. Scis. and Humanities, 1982-85, dir. spl. programs Minnetrista Ctr., 1985-87; dir. E.B. Ball Ctr., Muncie, 1987-89, dir. emeritus, 1989—. Contbg. editor Ripon Forum, 1973-78. Bd. dirs., exec. v.p. Ea. Ind. Cmty. TV, Muncie, 1974-76, pres., 1976-77; mem. nat. bd. govs. Ripon Soc., Washington, 1976-84; mem. Indpls. Com. Fgn. Rels., 1977-2004, com. fgn. rels. Ctrl. Ind., 2004—, bd. dirs., 2005—; bd. dirs. Hist. Muncie, Inc., 1979-85, pres., 1980; bd. dirs. Muncie Civic Theatre Assn., 1978-81, 90-96, 1st v.p., 1992-96; exec. dir. Ind. Consortium for Internat. Programs, 1982-88; mem. Ind. Real Estate Commn., 1983-91; trustee DePauw U., 1983—; bd. dirs. Muncie Symphony Orch., 1985-95, pres., 1991-93; mem. bd. govs. Minnetrista Cultural Ctr., Muncie, 1989-94, chmn., 1992-94; trustee Malpas Trust, 1990—, pres., 1997—; bd. dirs. Arts Ind., Inc., 1992-99, Muncie Children's Mus., 1994-2000, v.p., 1996-97, pres. 1997; trustee Ind. Colls. Ind., 1996—, United Meth. Meml. Home, Warren, Ind., 1997-2006; mem. strategy coun. North Ind. Conf. United Meth. Ch., 2000-08. 1st lt. USAF, 1955-58. Named Sagamore of Wabash, 1988. Mem. Am. Polit. Sci. Assn., Delaware County Hist. Alliance (bd. dirs. 1980-86, 87-95, pres., 1987-91), Soc. Profl. Journalists, Delaware Country Club, Maxinkuckee Yacht Club (Culver, Ind.), Rotary, Phi Delta Theta. Republican. United Methodist. E-mail: tsarg123@aol.com.

SARGENT, WALLACE LESLIE WILLIAM, astronomer, educator; b. Elsham, Eng., Feb. 15, 1935; naturalized, 2004; s. Leslie William and Eleanor (Denniss) S.; m. Anneila Isabel Cassells, Aug. 5, 1964; children: Lindsay Eleanor, Alison Clare. B.Sc., Manchester U., 1956, M.Sc., 1957, PhD, 1959. Research fellow Calif. Inst. Tech., Pasadena, 1959-62; sr. research fellow Royal Greenwich Obs., 1962-64; asst. prof. physics U. Calif., San Diego, 1964-66; mem. faculty dept. astronomy Calif. Inst. Tech., 1966—, prof., 1971-81, Ira S. Bowen prof. astronomy, 1981—, dir. Palomar Obs., 1997-2000. Miller prof. U. Calif., Berkeley, 1993; Thomas Gold lectr. Cornell U., Ithaca, NY, 1995; Sackler lectr. Harvard U., Cambridge, Mass., 1995, U. Calif., Berkeley, 1996; Icko Iben lectr. U. Ill., 2002. Contbr. articles to profl. jours. Alfred P. Sloan fellow, 1968-70. Fellow Am. Acad. Arts and Scis., NAS, Royal Soc. (London); mem Am. Astron. Soc. (v.p. 2004-07, Helen B. Warner prize 1969, Dannie Heineman prize 1991, Henry Norris Russell Lectureship, 2001), Royal Astron. Soc. (George Darwin lectr. 1987, assoc. 1998), Astron. Soc. Pacific (Bruce Gold medal 1994), Internat. Astron. Union. Clubs: Athenaeum (Pasadena). Home: 400 S Berkeley Ave Pasadena CA 91107-5062 Office: Calif Inst Tech Astronomy Dept 105-24 Pasadena CA 91125-0001 Office Phone: 626-395-4055.

SARGENT, WALTER HARRIMAN, II, lawyer; b. Norfolk, Va., Aug. 26, 1958; s. Richard E. and Martha F. (Bassett) S. BS in Philosophy, MIT, 1980, BS in Computer Sci. and Engring., 1980; JD, Harvard U., 1987. Bar: Colo. 1987, U.S. Dist. Ct. Colo. 1988, U.S. Ct. Appeals (3d, 6th, 9th and 10 cirs.), U.S. Supreme Ct. 1992. Assoc. Holme Roberts & Owen, Colorado Springs, 1987-95; pvt. practice Colorado Springs, 1995—; bd. trustees Colorado Legal Aid Found., 1998—2004. Bd. dirs. ARC of the Pikes Peak Region, 1991-97, Coalition for Adult Literacy, Colorado Springs, 1989-93. Recipient John M. Olin prize in law and econs. Harvard Law Sch., 1987, John M. Olin fellow, 1987, fellow Am. Acad. Appellate Lawyers, 2004—. Mem. ABA (appellate practice com.), Colo. Bar Assn. (appellate practice subcom.), Am. Acad. Appellate Lawyers. Avocation: distance running. Home: 1632 N Cascade Ave Colorado Springs CO 80907-7409 Office: Walter H Sargent A Profl Corp 1632 N Cascade Ave Colorado Springs CO 80907-7409 Home Phone: 719-632-2319; Office Phone: 719-577-4510. Personal E-mail: wsargent@wsargent.com.

SARGENT, WILLIAM WINSTON, retired anesthesiologist; b. Oshkosh, Wis., Feb. 28, 1933; s. Sprague Spencer and Lila Jane (Gjermundson) S. BS in Medicine, U. Ill., Chicago, 1955, MD, 1957; MS in Anesthesiology, U. Minn., 1967. Diplomate Am. Bd. Anesthesiology. Staff anesthesiologist St. Anthony Hosp., Rockford, Ill., 1960-61, Swedish Am. Hosp., Rockford, 1960-61; instr. anesthesiology U. Minn., Mpls., 1967-74, asst. prof. anesthesiology, 1974-80; staff anesthesiologist St. Luke's Hosp., Duluth, Minn., 1980-95, ret., 1995. Contbr. articles to profl. jours. Capt. USAF, 1961-64, France. Fellow Am. Coll. Anesthesiologists; mem. AMA, Am. Soc. Anesthesiologists, Minn. Soc. Anesthesiologists, Minn. State Med. Assn., St. Louis County Med. Soc. Presbyterian.

SARGON, SIMON A., composer, professor of composition; b. Mumbai, Apr. 6, 1938; s. Benjamin Isaac Sargon and Esther Cottin; m. Bonnie Glasgow, Nov. 17, 1961; 1 child Olivia Sargon Glasgow BA in Music, Brandeis U., 1959; MS in Composition, Juilliard Sch. Music, NY, 1962. Instr. Julliard Sch., NYC, 1967—68, Sarah Lawrence Coll., Bronxville, NY, 1968—71; chmn. dept. voice Rubin Acad. Music, Jerusalem, 1970—74; dir. music Temple Emanu-El, Dallas, 1974—2001, condr. choir; prof. music Southwestern U., Dallas, 1983—. Assisting artist South Meth. U., Dallas, 1983—, Cin. Cll. Music, Ohio, 2003—05, U. Ill., 2003—05, U. Nevada, Las Vegas, 2003—05, U. Ohio, 2003—05; composer in residence Bradley U., Peoria, Ill., 1998, Susquehanna U., Pa., 2000, U. Mo., Columbia, 2001. Composer: El Nora, 2004, Questings (horn concerto), 2005; composer and pianist: Shema, Gasparo, 1998, A Clear Midnight, 2001, Flame of the Lord, 2004, Homage to Hafiz, 2007, numerous others; pianist: Songs of Alma Mahler, 2002; narrator: Town Music of Bremen; Performance at Music in the Mountains, 2006. Condr. Festival Jewish Choirs, Indpls., 2002—04, Washington, 2007. Recipient Sigma Iota award, 1988, Honors Commd. Composer Tex. Music Assn., 1993, 2003, finalist Nat. Opera Assn. Composition Competition, 1997, Honors Adjudicator Guild Temple Musician's Young Composer, 1998, 2001, 03, 04, Music Tchr.'s Nat. Assn., 2007; grantee Meadows Found., 1986, Meadows Wind Ensemble, 2003, Voices Change Coomn., 1988, 2007. Mem. Phi Beta Kappa, Phi Kappa Lambda, Dallas Symphony Assn. (bd. dirs. 1978-79), Am. Soc. Composers Authors Pubs. (award) Office: South Methodist Univ Dallas TX 75223

SARGSYAN, DAVIT, library director; b. Yerevan, Armenia, Oct. 6, 1957; s. Mkrtich Sargsian and Elena Davtyan; m. Valentina Alaverdian, Apr. 19, 1956. Diploma, Yerevan State U., 1979; D in Social Scis. (hon.), Internat. Acad., 2006. Philologist, jr. editor Sovetakan Grogh pub. House, 1980-82, sr. editor, 1982-90; officer CC of CP of Armenia, 1990-91; dir. Hayastan Pub. House, 1991-98; head of apparatus Min. of Culture, Republic of Armenia, 1998; dir. Nat. Libr. of Armenia, 1998—. Founder newspaper Spiritual Fatherland; co-pres. sci. and creative intelligentsia forum CIS, rep. RA. Recipient F. Nansen Golden medal, 2005, Golden medal, Min. Culture, 2007, Hakob Meghapart Golden Apricot medal, Nat. Libr. Armenia, 2007, Mesrop Mashtots medal, Hai Dprutiun Social Orgn., 2007, Golden medal, Am. Agrl. Acad., 2007, A Pushkir Social award, United Nationas Com., 2007. Mem. Union Armenian Writers, Union Armenian Journalists, Libr. Assn. Armenia (pres. 2005), European Acad. Nat. Sci., Hanoven. Mem. Armenian Rev. Con. Party. Mem. Apostolic Ch. Avocations: reading, hunting. Office: Nat Libr Armenia Terian 72 Yerevan 375009 Armenia Office Phone: 584259. Personal E-mail: nla@arm.r.am, dsargsyan@mail.ru, sargsyar.davit@gmail.com.

SARI, ROBERT B., lawyer, retail executive; b. 1956; BA, U. Mich.; JD, Cleve.-Marshall Coll. Law. Bar: Calif. 1981. V.p. legal affairs Thrifty PayLess, Inc., 1994—97; assoc. counsel Rite Aid Corp., Camp Hill, Pa., 1997—2000, v.p. legal affairs, 2000, sr. v.p., dep. gen. counsel, sec., 2000—02, sr. v.p., gen. counsel, sec., 2002—05, exec. v.p., gen. counsel, sec., 2005—09, Nordstrom Inc., 2009—. Office: Nordstrom, Inc 1617 Sixth Ave 6th Fl Seattle WA 98101 Office Phone: 717-975-5833. E-mail: rsari@riteaid.com.*

SARIC, WILLIAM SAMUEL, aerospace engineering educator; b. Chgo., Sept. 28, 1940; s. Sam and Antonia (Cerovac) S.; m. Carol Powlick, Aug. 25, 1962 (div. Aug. 1987); 1 child, William George; m. Helen L. Reed, Mar. 17, 1990. BSME, Ill. Inst. Tech., 1963, PhD in Mechanics, 1968; MSME, U. N.Mex., 1965. Registered profl. engr., Va. Instr. Ill. Inst. Tech., Chgo., 1966-68; assoc. prof. Va. Poly. Inst. and State U., Blacksburg, 1975-79, prof., 1979-84, Tohoku U., Sendai, Japan, 1991-92; prof. mech. engring. Ariz. State U., Tempe, 1984—2005, prof. emeritus, 2005—; prof. aerospace engring. Tex. A&M U., College Station, 2005—. Mem. fluid dynamics panel AGARD/NATO, 1989-95. Contbr. over 100 articles to profl. jours., chpts. to books. Recipient Sci. Achievement award AGARD/NATO, 1996, G.I. Taylor medal Soc. Engring. Sci., 1993, Alumni award for rsch. excellence Va. Poly. Inst. and State U., 1984. Fellow AIAA (assoc., mem. tech. com. fluid dynamics 1975-78), AMSE (chmn. applied mech. divsn. 1991-92), Am. Phys. Soc. (exec. com. divsn. fluid dynamics 1985-86); mem. NAE. Office: Tex A&M U Engring 3126 TAMU College Station TX 77843 Office Phone: 979-862-1749. E-mail: saric@tamu.edu.

SARIPALLI, LALITHA DEVI, biologist, educator; d. Kalyana Sundaram and Lakshmi Kanthamma Saripalli. PhD in Zoology, Andhra U., 1979. Scientist Ctrl. Marine Fisheries Inst., Cochin, Kerala, India, 1977—89; postdoc. fellow Dept. Pharmacology, Biology, U. Rochester, NY, 1989—93, Kans. state U., Manhattan, 1993—94; rsch. asst. prof. dept. biology U. Ala., Birmingham, 1995—96; faculty Savannah State U., Ga., 1997—2000, South U., Savannah, 2000—03; instr. Savannahtech. Coll., 2003—. Scientist & cons. State Fisheries Insts., Kakinada, Andhra Pradesh, 1979—87. Contbr. articles to numerous publs. Postdoc. scholarship, Govt. India, 1989—93. Mem.: World Aquaculture Soc., Soc. Neurosci. (network tropical fisheries scientists 1984), Sigma Xi. Achievements include research in isolated & classified neurons from invertebrates; opioid binding sites on murine lymphocytes; population dynamics of penaeid shrimps; bopyrid parasites of shrimps or taxonomy. Avocations: reading, gardening, travel. Home: 3202 Cedar St Thunderbolt Savannah GA 31404 Office: Savannahtech Coll 5717 White Bluff Rd Savannah GA 31405-5521 Office Phone: 912-443-5830. Personal E-mail: lalipalli@netzero.com. Business E-Mail: lsaripalli@savannahtech.edu.

SARKAR, JAYANTA, economist, educator; s. Baidyanath and Sandhya Sarkar; m. Dipanwita Datta, Aug. 4, 2000; 1 child, Aritro Datta. MA in Economics, Jawaharlal Nehru U., New Delhi. India, 1995; MPhil in Economics, Jawaharlal Nehru U., New Delhi, India, 1997; MA in Economics, Southern Meth. U., Dallas, 2002, PhD, 2006. Lectr. Kirori Mal Coll., U. Delhi, New Delhi, 1998—99; economics assoc. Deepak Talwar & Assocs., New Delhi, 1999—2000; tchg. asst. economics Southern Meth. U., 2000—04, adj. lectr. economics, 2004—06; asst. prof. economics La. Tech U., Ruston, 2006—. Rsch. cons. Fed. Res. Bank Dallas, 2003. Contbr. scientific papers. Mem.: Southern Econ. Assn., Am. Econ. Assn., Omicron Delta Epsilon (Life memership 2002). Avocations: travel, photography, reading, sports. Office: La Tech Univ College Business Ruston LA 71272

SARKAR, JOY, engineer, educator; s. Tapan Kumar and Bharati Sarkar. BS in Physics, Indian Inst. Tech., Kharagpur, 2001; MS in Applied Physics, Rice U., Houston, 2004; PhD in Elec. & Computer Engring., U. Tex., Austin, 2007. Grad. rsch. asst. Rice U., Houston, 2002—04, U. Tex., Austin, Calif., 2004—07; product devel. engr. Intel Corp., Folsom, Calif., 2005, 2005, reliability engr. Santa Clara, Calif., 2006—07, sr. reliability engr., 2007—08; sr. R & D engr. Numonyx, 2008—. Tech. reviewer Addison Wesley Profl. Pub., 2000—01; invited panelist, cons. Panel Intelligence, LLC, Boston, 2007; reviewer IEEE Electron Devices Soc., 2007—. Contbr. articles to profl. jours. V.p. ISAR Rice U., Houston, 2002—03. Recipient Rajiv Gandhi Sci. Talent scholarship, Dept. of Sci. and Tech., Govt. of India, 2001, Ben Streetman Prize for Outstanding Rsch., U. of Tex., 2007; grantee Debesh Kamal scholarship, R. K. Mission Inst. Culture, 2001, B. D. Bangur Endowment Trust, 2001; fellow, Jawaharlal Nehru Ctr. for Advanced Sci. Rsch., 1999, 2000, Rice Quantum Inst., Rice U., 2001-2002. Mem.: IEEE. Achievements include development of progresses in non-volatile technology. Avocations: golf, music. Personal E-mail: jsarkar@gmail.com. Business E-Mail: joy.sarkar@numonyx.com.

SARKER, MAHFUZUR RAHMAN, microbiologist; b. Dhaka, Bangladesh; arrived in U.S., 1997; BSc, U. Dhaka, Bangladesh, 1982, MSc, 1985, MPhil, 1990; PhD, U. Tokushima, Japan, 1995. Rsch. assoc. U. Pitts., 1997—2000; asst. prof. Oreg. State U., Corvallis, Oreg., 2000—. Recipient Presdl. Early Career award, U.S. Govt., 2004. Office: Oregon State University Campus Way 220 Nash Hall Corvallis OR 97331

SARKIS, ZIAD JOSEPH, private equity executive; b. Beirut, July 8, 1968; arrived in France, 1975; s. Nicolas and Claude (Moussalli) Sarkis; m. Elisabeth Kalman, June 21, 1997; 4 children. BAS in Anthropology, Econs. and Math. with distinction and honors, Stanford U., 1990, MS in Engring. and Mgmt., 1990; PhD in Econs., Oxford U., Eng., 1998. Cons. McKinsey & Co., San Francisco, 1990, NYC, 1991—92, Paris, 1992; ptnr. AT Kearney, NYC, London, Paris, 1992—94; co-founder, sr. ptnr., bd. dirs. Mitchell Madison Group, NYC, London, Paris, 1992—2000; ptnr. PAI Ptnrs. (formerly Paribas Affaires Industrielles), London, Paris, 2001—. Bd. dirs. Yoplait. Greek Catholic. Office: PAI Ptnrs 28 Old Brompton Rd Ste 320 London SW73SS England Business E-Mail: ziad.sarkis@paipartners.co.uk.

SARKISIAN, CHERILYN See **CHER**

SARKOZY, OLIVIER (PIERRE OLIVIER SARKOZY), investment banker; b. May 26, 1969; Mng. dir. Credit Suisse First Boston, NYC; global head, banks, fin. inst. group UBS Warburg, NYC, 2002—. Recipient Rainmaker prize, Dealmaker mag., 2006. Office: UBS Warburg 1285 Ave of Americas New York NY 10019 Office Phone: 800-221-3260.

SARLE, CHARLES RICHARD, health facility executive; b. Saratoga Springs, NY, Sept. 21, 1944; s. John Robert and Marjorie Elizabeth (Swick) S.; m. Marion D. Wallace, June 21, 1968; children: Richard Charles, Robert Edmond. BBA cum laude, Northea. U., 1968; MBA, Babson Coll., 1973. CPA, Mass., Vt. Staff acct. Price Waterhouse & Co., Boston, 1968-70, George Kanavich, CPA, Wellesley, Mass., 1970-72; controller Human Resource Inst., Boston, 1972-73, adminstr., 1973-77; controller Brattleboro (Vt.) Retreat, 1977-78, dir. adminstrn., 1978-85, v.p., 1985-88, chief exec. officer, 1988-97; pres., CEO Carrier Clinic, Belle Mead, NJ, 1997—. Speaker in field. Mem. commn. Vt. Health Bldg. Fin. Agy., 1978—90; trustee Austine Sch. for Deaf and Hard of Hearing, 1990—97, pres., 1994—97; trustee Winston Prouty Ctr. for Child Devel., 1982—97, treas., 1983—90, sec., 1991—97; trustee Health Rsch. and Edn. Trust NJ, 1998—99, NJ Hosp. Assn., 2000—06, policy devel. com., 1998—2001, fin. com., 2000—, investment com. mem., 2001—, audit compliance commn. mem., 2006—; bd. govs. NCCJ, 1998—2003, exec. com., 1999—2003. Recipient recognition award Brattleboro C. of C., 1985. Fellow AICPA, Mass. Soc. CPA, Am. Coll. Healthcare Execs. (regent Va. br. 1991-95); mem. Am. Hosp. Assn. (del.-at-large 1988-92, del.-at-large to regional policy bd.), Nat. Assn. Pvt. Psychiat. Hosps. (bd. dirs. polit. action com. 1983-93, trustee 1998-2000, 2007-), Nat. Psychiat. Alliance (trustee 1989-96, pres. 1994-96), Vt. Soc. CPA (Cmty. Svc. award 1984), Hosp. Fin. Mgmt. Assn. (hosp. cost com. 1985-96), Rescue, Inc. (trustee 1982-83), New Eng. Healthcare Assembly (trustee 1995-97). Avocations: skiing, fishing, tennis, photography. Home: PO Box 840 Belle Mead NJ 08502-0840 Office: Carrier Clinic Rt 601 Belle Mead NJ 08502 E-mail: rsarle@carrierclinic.com.

SARMA, DANDAPANTULA NANDAKUMARA, senior scientist; s. Dandapantula Nalini and Dandapantula Venkateshwara Sarma; m. Polasani Vandana; 1 child, Dandapantula Prahlad. PhD, Banaras Hindu U., Varanasi, India, 1994. CRTA fellow Nat. Cancer Inst., Bethesda, Md., 2004—05; pharmacist, 2004—; sr. scientist US Pharmacopeia, Rockville, Md., 2006—; adj. prof. Thomas J. Long Sch. Pharmacy U. Pacific, Stockton, Calif. Spkr. Adverse Event Assessment and Reporting of Dietary Supplements: A US Perspective. Drug Info. Assn. Annual Meeting, San Diego, 2009; contbr. articles to profl. jours. Achievements include patents for method of suppressing allogenic immune response or prevention and treatment of graft versus host disease or graft rejection; a novel process for isolation of berberine from berberine containing plant material. Office: 12601 Twinbrook Pky Rockville MD 20852 Office Phone: 301-816-8354, Business E-Mail: dns@usp.org.

SARMA, RADHA J., cardiologist, educator; arrived in U.S., 1968; m. Jonnalagedda S.M Sarma; 1 child, Srinivas J. MBBS, Andhra Med. Coll., Visakhapatnam, India, 1966. Diplomate Am. Bd. of Internal Medicine, 1977, Am. Bd. of Internal Medicine, 1977, Cardiovascular Diseases Am. Bd. of Internal Medicine, 1979. Asst. prof. of medicine USC Sch. of Medicine, Los Angeles, Calif., 1975—77; dir., noninvasive cardiology Rancho Los Amigos Med. Ctr., Downey, Calif., 1978—81; dir. noninvasive cardiology King-Drew Med. Center-UCLA, Los Angeles, Calif., 1981—87; chief of cardiology USC Rancho Los Amigos Med. Ctr., Downey, Calif., 1987—96; med. dir. of cardiology & critical care Northridge Hosp. Med. Ctr., Northridge, Calif., 1996—98; assoc. prof. of medicine USC Keck Sch. of Medicine, Los Angeles, Calif., 1998—; dir. cardiac exercise lab. LACUSC Med. Ctr; assoc. dir.

echocardiography lab. LACUSC Med. Ctr. Contbr. articles to profl. jour. V.p. Fedn. of Indo-American Assn., LA, Calif., 1996—97; v.p., planning Fedn. of IndoAmerican Assn. (F.I.A.), LA, Calif., 1996—97; vice-chair Vedic Edn. and Social Cultural Orgn. (VESCO), LA, Calif., 2000; coord. 11th tana conf. Telugu Assn. of N.Am. (TANA), Anaheim, Calif., 1995—96; web master Calif. Chpt. of Am. Coll. of Cardiology, Anaheim, Calif., 2001; mem. & regional faculty Am. Heart Assn., LA, Calif., 1998; pres. Telugu Assn. of So. Calif., LA, Calif., 1994—95; regional faculty, task force mem. Am. Heart Assn., LA, Calif., 1998. Grantee Grant in Aid, Am. Heart Assn., 1980-1982. Fellow: ACP, Am. Heart Assn., Am. Coll. of Cardiology. Avocations: computers and electronics, music, dance. Office: USC Keck Sch of Medicine LACUSC Medc 1200 N State St Rm 7440 Los Angeles CA 90033 E-mail: sarma@usc.edu.

SARNAT, BERNARD GEORGE, plastic surgeon, educator, researcher; b. Chgo., Sept. 1, 1912; s. Isadore M. and Fanny (Silverman) S.; m. Rhoda Elaine Gerard, Dec. 25, 1941; children: Gerard, Joan. SB, U. Chgo., 1933, MD, 1937; MS, DDS, U. Ill., 1940. Diplomate Am. Bd. Plastic Surgery, 1947. Intern Los Angeles County Gen. Hosp., 1936-37; resident oral and plastic surgery Cook County Hosp., Chgo., 1940-41; asst. to Dr. Marshall Davison (gen. surgery) Univ. Hosp., Chgo., 1942-43; asst. to Drs. Vilray P. Blair and Louis T. Byars (plastic and reconstructive surgery), St. Louis, 1943-46; practice medicine specializing in plastic surgery Chgo., 1946-56, Beverly Hills, Calif., 1956-91; asst. histology U. Ill. Coll. Dentistry, 1937-40, prof., head dept. oral and maxillofacial surgery, 1946-56; asst. dept. surgery, divsn. plastic surgery Washington U. Sch. Medicine, St. Louis, 1944-46; prof., dir. dept. oral and plastic surgery St. Louis U. Coll. Dentistry, 1945-46; clin. asst. prof. surgery (plastic surgery) U. Ill. Coll. Medicine, 1949-56; adj. prof. oral biology Sch Dentistry UCLA, 1969—, mem. Dental Rsch. Inst., 1974-95, adj. prof. plastic surgery Sch. Medicine, 1974—; attending staff Cedars-Sinai Med. Ctr., LA, 1956-91, emeritus, 1991—, mem. staff, sr. rsch. scientist, chief plastic surgery, 1961-81. Cons. in gen., plastic and maxillofacial surgery VA Regional Office, Chgo., 1956; lectr. in field. Sr. author: (with Isaac Schour) Oral and Facial Cancer, 2d edit., 1957, (with Daniel Laskin) Surgery of the Temporomandibular Joint, 1964; editor: (with Daniel Laskin) The Temporomandibular Joint A Biological Basis for Clinical Practice, 4th edit., 1991, (with Andrew D. Dixon) Factors and Mechanisms Affecting Growth of Bone, 1982, Normal and Abnormal Bone Growth: Basic and Clinical Research, 1985, Fundamentals of Bone Growth: Methodology and Applications, 1991; contbr. chpts. to books, articles to profl. jours. Co-winner Joseph A. Capps prize for med. rsch. Inst. Medicine, Chgo., 1940, Frederick B. Noyes prize, 1940; recipient Kerbs award for rsch. plastic and reconstructive surgery, 1950, 1st prize, sr. award Found. Am. Soc. Plastic and Reconstructive surgeons, 1957, Beverly Hills Acad. of Medicine award, 1959, Nat. Achievement award medicine Phi Epsilon Pi, 1964, 1st prize Am. Rhinologic Soc., 1980, medal Hebrew U., Jerusalem, 1985, medal Tel Aviv U., 1985, Disting. Svc. Alumni award U. Chgo. Pritzker Sch. Medicine, 1987, hon. award Am. Soc. Maxillofiacial Surgeons, 1990, Dallas B. Phemister Profl. Achievement award Dept. Surgery U. Chgo., 1993, Disting. Alumnus award U. Ill. Coll. Dentistry, 1994, Craniofacial Biology Rsch. award Internat. Assn. for Dental Rsch., 1995, Disting. Scientist award, Pioneer in Medicine award Cedars-Sinai Med. Ctr., L.A., 1999, Profl. Achievement citation U. Chgo. Alumni Assn., 2003, citatioon of excellence in rsch. Plastic Surgery Ednl. Found., 2003, Profl. Achievement award U. Ill. Alumni Assn., 2004. Fellow ACS, AAAS, Am. Assn. Plastic Surgeons (hon. award 1993); mem. Calif. Med. Soc., L.A. Med. Soc., Am. Soc. Plastic and Reconstructive Surgeons, Plastic Surgery Rsch. Coun. (founding mem., chmn. 1957), Am. Soc. Maxillofacial Surgeons (hon.), Calif. Soc. Plastic Surgeons, Beverly Hills Acad. Medicine (pres. 1962-63), Internat. Assn. Craniofacial Biology, Am. Assn. Pediat. Plastic Surgeons (hon.), Am. Assn. Phys. Anthropologists, Internat. Assn. Study Dento-Facial Abnormalities (hon.), Sigma Xi, Omicron Kappa Upsilon, Zeta Beta Tau, Phi Delta Epsilon, Alpha Omega (Internat. Achievement medal 1988). Home: 1875 Kelton Ave Apt 301 Los Angeles CA 90025-8505

SARNELLE, JOSEPH R., publishing executive; b. Bklyn., Aug. 24, 1951; s. Alphonse Louis and Julie Lena (Mingarelli) S.; m. Ruth Patricia Cullen, Aug. 5, 1982 (dec.); children: Cullen Joseph, D'Arcy Emilie. BA, Cornell U., 1973; postgrad., Sch. Visual Arts, NYC, 1976—77, The New Sch., 1979—80. Graphic artist Lewahl KC Graphics, NYC, 1974-76; editor United Bus. Publs., NYC, 1976-79; mng. editor Lebhar-Friedman Inc., NYC, 1979-88; assoc. mng. editor HomeOwner Mag., NYC, 1988-90; mgr. online sys. devel. Info. Builders Inc., NYC, 1990—. Cons. video Markham-Novelle Pub. Rels., NYC, 1988—89; cons. Best info. Family Media, NYC, 1990—91. Author, dir. (videos) J. Roland Pepe's Guide to New York City, 1980, Underground Roundup, 1981. McMullen scholar, Cornell U., Regents scholar, State of N.Y., 1969; recipient Best Headline of Yr. award Lebhar-Friedman Inc., 1982. Office: Info Builders Inc 2 Penn Plz New York NY 10121 E-mail: joe_sarnelle@ibi.com.

SARNOFF, ANN M., publishing executive, former sports association executive; b. Nov. 2, 1961; m. Richard I. Sarnoff; 2 children. BS in Mktg., Georgetown Univ., 1983; MBA, Harvard Bus. Sch., 1987. Strategic consul. Marakon Assoc., Stamford, Conn., 1987—93; v.p. bus. develop. Nickelodeon, 1994, exec. v.p. consumer products, bus. develop.; dir. corp. devel. Viacom, 1993—94, COO, VH1, Country Music Television, 2001—04; COO WNBA, 2004—05; pres. Dow Jones Ventures, NYC, 2006—. Mem. bd. trustees Georgetown Univ. McDonough Sch. Bus. Office: Dow Jones & Co 1 World Fin Ctr 200 Liberty St New York NY 10281

SARNOFF, DEBORAH SUSAN, dermatologist, educator; b. Bklyn., Jan. 8, 1954; d. Norman and Ruth Sarnoff; m. Robert H. Gotkin, May 28, 1983. BA summa cum laude, Cornell U., 1975; MD, George Wash. U., 1980. Diplomate Am. Bd. Dermatology, 1984. Internship Wash. Hosp. Ctr., 1980-81; resident in dermatology NYU Med. Ctr., NYC, 1981-83, chief resident, 1983-84, fellow in Mohs skin cancer surgery, 1985-86; dermatologic surgeon Cosmetique Dermatology, Laser & Plastic Surgery, LLP, Greenvale, NY, 1985—; clin. asst. prof. NYU Med. Ctr., 1989—2001, clin. assoc. prof., 2001—08, clin. prof., 2009; pvt. practice Cosmetique Dermatology Laser & Plastic Surgery LLP NYC, 1988—; active med. staff North Shore CIJ, Glen Cove. Clin. rsch. dermatology br. NIH, Bethesda, Md., 1987-88; v.p. Skin Cancer Found. NYC 2007-. Author: (books) Beauty and the Beam, 1998, Instant Beauty, 2002. Fellow: Am. Soc. Laser Medicine & Surgery, Nat. Council Medical Soc., Am. Acad. Dermatology, Am. Coll. Physicians. Office: 625 Park Ave New York NY 10065 also: 31 Northern Blvd Greenvale NY 11548

SARNOFF, LILI-CHARLOTTE (LOLO SARNOFF), artist; b. Frankfurt, Germany (as Swiss citizen), Jan. 9, 1916; arrived in U.S., 1940; d. Willy and Martha (Koch von Hirsch) Dreyfus; m. Stanley Jay Sarnoff, 1948; children: Daniela Martha Bargezi, Robert L. Grad., Reimann Art Sch., Germany, 1936, U. Berlin, 1938; student, U. Florence, Italy, 1936—38; DFA (hon.), Corcoran Coll. Art & Design, 2003. With Red Cross Swiss Motor Corps, 1939—40; Red Cross nurse Bellevue Hosp., NYC, 1942—47; rsch. asst. Harvard Sch. Pub. Health, 1950—54; rsch. assoc. cardiac physiology Nat. Heart Inst., Bethesda, Md., 1954—59; pres. Rodana Rsch. Corp., Bethesda, 1959—61; v.p. Catrix Corp., Bethesda, 1959—61; prin., owner Dara's Sr. Pets for Srs., 2003. Inventor Flolite light sculptures under name Lolo Sarnoff, 1968—; one-woman shows include Agra Gallery, Washington, 1969, Corning (N.Y.) Glass Ctr. Mus., 1970, Gallery Two, Woodstock, Vt., 1970, Gallery Marc, Washington, 1971, 1972, Franz Bader Gallery, 1976, Gallery K, 1978, 1981, 1985, 1987, 1991, Retrospective Show, 1995, Alwin Gallery, London, 1981, Galerie von Bartha, Basel, Switzerland, 1982, La Galerie L'Hotel de Ville, Geneva, 1982, Pfalzgalerie, Kaiserslautern, Germany, 1985, Galerie Les Hirondelles, Geneva, 1988, Represented in permanent collections. Founder, chmn. bd. Arts for Aging, Inc., Bethesda, 1988—; chmn. bd. Dara's Canine Found., Inc., 1999—. Recipient Golda Meir award, 1995, Life Commitment to Arts award, Swiss Am. Cultural Exch., 1999, Path of Achievement award for Arts and Humanities, Montgomery County, Md., 2000, Outstanding Citizen award, Iona Sr. Citizen Svcs., Washington, 2002, Chevalier de L'Ordre des Arts et Des Lettres, République Française, 2006. Home: 7507 Hampden Ln Bethesda MD 20814-1331 Personal E-mail: lolos@erols.com.

SARNOFF, RICHARD, digital publishing executive; m. Ann Misiaszek; 2 children. BA summa cum laude, Princeton U., NJ; MBA, Harvard Bus. Sch., 1987. Joined Bantam Doubleday Dell, Inc., 1987, various positions including dir. mktg. Bantam pub. divsn., v.p. strategic planning, sr. v.p. and gen. mgr. diversified pub. group, then sr. v.p. corp. devel., 1995—98, exec. v.p., CFO, 1996—98, Random House, Inc., 1998—2000, pres., new media, corp. develop. group, 2000—06, pres. Random House Ventures, LLC, pres. Bertelsmann Digital Media Investments, 2006—. Bd. dirs. Princeton Review, Inc., 1998—, Audible, Inc., 2001—, Activision Blizzard, Inc., 2005—, Oak Hill Capital Fund II; supervisory bd. Bertelsmann AG, 2002—; co-chmn. Bertelsmann, Inc., 2008—. Bd. dirs. Bronx Lab Sch., Children's Mus. Manhattan, Ctr. for Comm. Mem.: Assn. Am. Pub. (chmn. bd. dirs.). Office: BDMI 1745 Broadway New York NY 10019*

SARNOFF, THOMAS WARREN, television executive; b. NYC, Feb. 23, 1927; s. David and Lizette (Hermant) S.; m. Janyce Lundon, May 21, 1955; children: Daniel, Timothy, Cynthia. Grad., Phillips Acad., 1939-43; student, Princeton, 1943-45; BS in Elec. Engring., Stanford U., 1948, postgrad. Sch. Bus. Adminstrn., 1948-49; D.H.L., Columbia Coll. Engaged in prodn. and sales with ABC, Inc., 1949-51; prodn. Metro-Goldwyn-Mayer, 1951-52; with NBC, 1952-77; v.p. prodn. and bus. affairs NBC (Pacific div.), 1956-60, v.p. adminstrn. West Coast, 1960-62, v.p. charge West Coast, 1962-65, staff exec. v.p. West Coast, 1965-77; pres. NBC Entertainment Corp., 1972-77, Sarnoff Internat. Enterprises, 1977-81, Sarnoff Entertainment Corp., 1981—; exec. v.p. Venturetainment Corp., 1981-87, pres., 1987—96. Bd. dirs. Multimedia Games, Inc., 1998-2006, chmn. bd., 2004-06, cons., 2006-08. Exec. producer Bonanza: The Next Generation, 1987, Bonanza: The Return, 1993, Back to Bonanza Retrospective, 1993, Bonanza: Under Attack, 1995. Mem. Calif. Commn. for Reform Intermediate and Secondary Edn. Pres., Research Found., St. Joseph Hosp., Burbank, 1965-73, Permanant Charities Com. of Entertainment Industries, 1971-72; nat. trustee Nat. Conf. Christians and Jews. Served with Signal Corps AUS, World War II. Mem. Acad. TV Arts and Scis. (chmn. bd. trustees 1972-74, chmn. past pres.'s coun. 1989-92), Acad. TV Arts and Scis. Found. (pres. 1990-99, chmn., CEO 1999—2005, chmn. emeritus 2005-), The Caucus for Prodrs., Writers and Dirs. Office: 2451 Century Hl Los Angeles CA 90067-3510 Office Phone: 310-203-9234. Personal E-mail: tsarnoff@aol.com.

SAROFIM, FAYEZ SHALABY, finance company executive; b. Nov. 19, 1928; m. Louisa Stude (div. 1990); m. Linda Hicks (div. 1996); 5 children. BS in Food Technology, U. Calif., Berkley, 1949; MBA, Harvard, 1951. Founder, chmn., pres. Fayez Sarofim & Co., 1958—. Bd. mgr. Meml. Sloan-Kettering Cancer Ctr.; coun. mem. Rockefeller Univ.; bd. dir. Alley Theatre, Houston Ballet Found., Mus. Fine Arts, Houston; dir. Tex. Heart Inst. Named one of Top 200 Collectors, ARTnews, 2004—08, 400 Richest Americans, Forbes, 2006. Mem.: Houston Symphony Soc. (former vice chmn. bd. dirs.). Avocation: collector of Coptic sculpture, Old Masters, 19th century art, Am. Impressionism, modern & contemporary art. Office: Fayez Sarofim & Co Ste 2907 Two Houston Ctr Houston TX 77010

SARPONG, KWABENA DUA, biology professor; s. Kwame Frimpong and Felicia Bernadette Sarpong. BS, Ga. State U., Atlanta, 1999, MS, 2002. Tutor Ga. Perimeter Coll., Decatur, 2004—, instr. biology, 2005—, advisor, 2005—. Vol. Children's Healthcare Atlanta, 1997—. Home: 7827 Kiverton Pl Atlanta GA 30350 Personal E-mail: a1kwabena@hotmail.com.

SARRAMON, JEAN-PIERRE FERNAND LOUIS, urologist, educator; b. Toulouse, France, Jan. 18, 1938; s. Henri and Jacqueline (Pellegrin) S.; m. Marie-France Lhez, Mar. 19, 1964; children: Christine, Benedicte. Baccalaureate in Lit. and Philosophy, St. Joseph Coll., Toulouse, 1956; MD, Med. Faculty Toulouse, 1970. Intern in medicine U. Hosp., Toulouse, 1964; prosector in anatomy Med. Sch., Toulouse, 1970, chief of clinic in surgery, 1970-71, asst. prof. urology, 1972-77, assoc. prof., 1978-90, prof., 1990—2006, prof. emeritus, 2006—; chief of svc., chmn. urology, renal transplantation/ANDrdo U. Hosp., 1982—; dir. exptl. surgery dept. C.H.U. Purpan, Toulouse, 1985—. Mem. U. Nat. Counsel, 1987; mem. faculty, lectr. European Sch. Urology; pres. 96th French Congress Urology, 2002; expert Supreme Ct. Appel, 2003. Mem. editl. bd. Le Progres en Urologie, 1990, Internat. Jour. Impotence Rsch., 1990, Les Annales d'Urologie, Archivio Italiano di Urologia, Nephrologia Andrologia, 2001; contbr. chpts. to books. Hon. officer French Armed Forces, 1975—. Decorated chevalier Legion of Honor (France); recipient clin. rsch. prize Languedoc Acad., 2005; named Prof. Exceptional Class Univ., 2000, Prof. Emeritus U., 2007. Mem. French Transplantation Soc., French Soc. Urology (pres. 2002-03), French Coll. Urologists (mem. adminstrv. coun.), European Urol. Assn., Am. Urol. Assn. (corr.), Soc. Internat. d'Urologie, Belgium Urol. Assn., European Orgn. for Rsch. and Treatment of Cancer, European Soc. Male Genital Surgery (v.p.), Adminstrv. French Urol. Counsel, Internat. Microsurgery Soc., European Soc. Organ Transplantation, Internat. Soc. Impotence Rsch., Conseil Nat. des Univs., Nat. French Surgery Acad. (titular mem. 2009), Expert Supreme Nat. Court Appeal, Languedoc Acad. Roman Catholic. Avocations: horseback riding, mountain climbing, sailing, golf, skiing, racing cycles. Home: 9 Rue Espinasse 31000 Toulouse France Office: Urological Dept CHU Rangueil-Chemin Du Vallon 31000 Toulouse France Office Phone: 0561323229, 0561323201. Business E-Mail: sarramon.jp@chu-toulouse.fr.

SARRATORE, STEVEN T., academic administrator; BA, Mich. State U., East Lansing, 1975; MFA, Wayne State U., Detroit, 1977. Assoc. vice chancellor academic programs IPFW, Fort Wayne, Ind., 2001—08; vice chancellor academic affairs Ind. U. Kokomo, Ind., 2008—. Scenic and lighting designer various. Recipient ACTF Gold medal, Kenndy Ctr., 1999. Office: Ind Univ Kokomo 2300 S Washington Kokomo IN 46904 Business E-Mail: ssarrato@iuk.edu.

SARRAZIN, NATALIE ROSE, music educator, researcher; m. Anand K. Dwivedi; 1 child, Arjun M. Dwivedi. MusB, Hartt Sch. Music, Hartford, Conn., 1986; MusM, Peabody Conservatory, Johns Hopkins U., Balt., 1993; PhD in Ethnomusicology, U. Md., Coll. Pk., 2003. Cert. in k-12 edn. Mass., 1989. Asst. prof. Coll. Brockport, SUNY, 2006—. Vis. asst. prof. U. Va., Charlottesvile, 2000—05. Contbr. monographs and articles to profl. publs. Bd. mem. Hunter Inst. Young Children, Brockport, 2007—. Office: Coll Brockport SUNY 350 New Campus Dr Brockport NY 14420 Business E-Mail: nsarrazi@brockport.edu.

SARREALS, SONIA, data processing executive, consultant; b. NYC, Sept. 17, 1938; d. Espriela and Sadie Beatrice (Scales) Sarreals; m. Waldro Lynch, Sept. 18, 1981 (div. Oct. 1983). BA in Langs. summa cum laude, CCNY, 1960; cert. in French, Sorbonne, Paris, 1961. Systems engr. IBM, NYC, 1963-69; cons. Babbage Systems, NYC, 1969-70; project leader Touche Ross, NYC, 1970-73; sr. programmer McGraw-Hill, Inc., Hightstown, NJ, 1973-78; staff data processing cons. Cin. Bell Info. Systems, 1978-89; sr. analyst AT&T, 1989-92; lead tech. analyst Automated Concepts Inc., Arlington, Va., 1992—96; tech. cons. Tecsys., Reston, Va., 1996—2008. Elder St. Andrew Luth. Ch., Silver Spring, 1992-96. Downer scholar CUNY, 1960; Dickman Inst. fellow Columbia U., 1960-61. Mem.: Assn. for Computing Machinery, Phi Beta Kappa. Democrat. Avocations: needlecrafts, sewing. Home: 13705 Beret Pl Silver Spring MD 20906-3030 Office: Teksystems 12343 Sunrise Valley Dr Reston VA 20191

SARRIS, ANDREW GEORGE, film critic; b. Bklyn., Oct. 31, 1928; s. George Andrew and Themis (Katavolos) S.; m. Molly Clark Haskell, May 31, 1969. AB, Columbia, 1951. Film critic Village Voice, NYC, 1960-89, N.Y. Observer, 1989—. Editor-in-chief Cahiers du Cinema in English; instr. Sch. Visual Arts, 1965-67; asst. prof. N.Y. U., 1967-69; assoc. prof. films Columbia Sch. Arts, N.Y.C., 1969-81, prof., 1981—. Author: The Films of Josef Von Sternberg, 1966, Interviews with Film Directors, 1967, The Film, 1968 The American Cinema, 1968, Confessions of a Cultist, 1970, The Primal Screen, 1973, The John Ford Movie Mystery, 1976, Politics and Cinema, 1978. Served with Signal Corps AUS, 1952-54. Guggenheim fellow, 1969; recipient William K. Everson award for Film History, Nat. Bd. Review, 2008. Mem. Am. Film Inst. (dir.), Soc. Cinema Studies, Nat. Soc. Film Critics, N.Y. Film Critics. *I keep on working toward that last deadline.*

SARRO, THOMAS JOHN, biology professor; b. Far Rockaway, NY, May 24, 1951; s. Michael John and Florence Rose Sarro; m. Katherine Baker Sarro, Oct. 23, 1980; 1 child, Rebecca. PhD, NY U. Prof. Mt. St. Mary Coll., Newburgh, NY, 1975—. Rsch. assoc. Mohonk Preserve, New Paltz, NY, 1995—. Home: 1 Flamingo Dr Newburgh NY 12550 Office: Mt St Mary Coll 330 Powell Ave Newburgh NY 12550 Business E-Mail: sarro@msmc.edu.

SARROS, P. PETER, diplomat, consultant; b. Greece, Aug. 20, 1935; (parents Am. citizens); s. Basil and Helen Sarros BA summa cum laude, Hobart Coll., 1957; M Pub. and Internat. Affairs, Princeton U., 1959, PhD, 1964. US fgn. svc. officer Dept. of State, Washington, 1960—92, sr. cons. fgn. affairs, 1993—2008. Spl. amb. to the Vatican, 1978; charge U.S. Mission to The Vatican, 1975—80; acting dep. asst. sec. for Human Rights, 1980—82; dir. Regional Polit. Affairs for Latin Am., 1985—92; adj. prof. diplomacy George Mason U., 1992—93; diplomatic assignments in Venezuela, Dominican Republic and Iceland, 1961—67; diplomat in residence Sch. Advanced Internat. Studies Johns Hopkins U., 1972—73. W. Wilson fellow Princeton U., 1957-60; recipient Superior Honor award Dept. State. Mem. Am. Fgn. Svc. Assn., Ft. Myer Officers Club, Phi Beta Kappa Avocation: bibliophile. Home: 1200 N Nash St Apt 249 Arlington VA 22209-3616 Office: Dept of State IRM/OPS Washington DC 20520 Office Phone: 202-736-7237.

SARRY, CHRISTINE, ballerina; b. Long Beach, Calif., May 25, 1946; d. John and Beatrice (Thomas) S.; 1 child, Maximilian Sarry Varriale. With Joffrey Ballet, 1963—64, Am. Ballet Theatre, 1964—68, prin. dancer, 1971—74; leading dancer Am. Ballet Co., 1969—71; ballerina Eliot Feld Ballet, 1974—81. Dir. faculty Ballet Tech., NYC; also freelance guest tchr. Performed ballets choreographed by Agnes Demille, Antony Tudor, Jerome Robbins, Twyla Tharp, Eliot Feld; appeared at White House, 1963, 67; U.S. Dept. State tours include, Russia, 1963, 66, S.Am., 1964, 76, various tours of N.Am., Orient, Europe, various appearances U.S. nat. TV; partnered by Mikhail Baryshnikov. Office Phone: 212-777-7710 x 307. E-mail: csarry@balletech.org.

SARSGAARD, PETER, actor; b. Scott AFB, IL, Mar. 7, 1971; m. Maggie Gyllenhaal, May 2, 2009; 1 child, Ramona. BA in History, Washington U., 1994. Actor: (off-Broadway plays) Kingdom of Earth, Laura Dennis; (Broadway plays) The Seagull, 2008; (films) Dead Man Walking, 1995, Minor Details, 1998, The Man in the Iron Mask, 1998, Desert Blue, 1998, Another Day in Paradise, 1998, Boys Don't Cry, 1999, The Cell, 2000, Housebound, 2000, The Center of the World, 2001, Bacon Wagon: The Movie, 2001, Empire, 2002, The Salton Sea, 2002, K-19: The Widowmaker, 2002, Unconditional Love, 2002, Death of a Dynasty, 2003, Shattered Glass, 2003, Garden State, 2004, Kinsey, 2004, The Dying Gaul, 2005, The Skeleton Key, 2005, Flightplan, 2005, Jarhead, 2005, Rendition, 2007, The Mysteries of Pittsburgh, 2008, Elegy, 2008, An Education, 2009, In the Electric Mist, 2009; (TV films) Freak City, 1999.*

SARSON, EVELYN PATRICIA See KAYE, EVELYN

SARSYNSKI, ELAINE A., insurance company executive; Grad. in Econs., Smith Coll., Northampton, Mass.; MBA in Fin. and Acctg., Columbia U., NYC. With Aetna Life and Casualty, 1981—98, head real estate investments and mortgage fin. ops.; CEO Suffield Twp., Conn.; mng. dir., head portfolio mgmt. group Babson Capital Mgmt., 2005; sr. v.p. Mass. Mut. Life Ins. Co., Springfield, 2005—06, chief adminstrv. officer, 2005—, exec. v.p., 2006—; pres., CEO MassMutual Internat. LLC. Mem. Mass. Econ. Devel. Coun.; bd. trustees Baystate Health Inc., Springfield. Office: MassMutual Fin Group 1295 State St Springfield MA 01111-0001 Office Phone: 800-767-1000.

SARTAIN, JAMES EDWARD, lawyer; b. Ft. Worth, Feb. 9, 1941; s. James F. and May Belle (Boaz) S.; m. Barbara Hardy, Aug. 17, 1962; 1 child, Bethany Sartain Hughes. BA, Tex. A&M U., 1963; LLB, Baylor U., 1966. Bar: Tex. 1966, U.S. Ct. Mil. Appeals, 1971, U.S. Dist. Ct. (no. dist.) Tex. 1974. Staff atty. Dept. Justice, Washington, 1970-72; staff atty. to U.S. Sen. William L. Scott Fairfax, Va., 1972; pvt. practice Ft. Worth, 1973—2001, Abilene, Tex., 2001—. Bd. dirs. Ft. Worth Boys Club, 1980-89, Oakwood Cemetery, Ft. Worth, 1979-84; adv. dir. Grady McWhinney Rsch. Found., Abilene, Tex., 12th Armored Divsn. Meml. Mus., Abilene. Capt. arty. U.S. Army, Vietnam. Fellow Coll. State Bar Tex.; mem. ABA, NRA, VFW, Abilene Bar Assn., Baylor Law Alumni Assn., Masons, Phi Delta Phi. Republican. Presbyterian. Home: PO Box 450 Abilene TX 79604-0450 Home Phone: 325-690-1129.

SARTAIN, JAMES PETER, bishop; b. Memphis, June 6, 1952; Attended, St. Meinrad Coll., Ind.; STL, Pontifical Athenaeum San Anselmo, 1979. Ordained priest Diocese of Memphis, 1978; mem. adminstrv. coun. Inst. for Priestly Formation; ordained bishop, 2000; bishop Diocese of Little Rock, 2000—06, Diocese of Joliet, Ill., 2006—. Mem.: US Conf. Cath. Bishops (mem. adminstrv. com., chair com. on home missions). Roman Catholic. Office: Diocese of Joliet 425 Summit St Joliet IL 60435 Office Phone: 815-722-2110. Office Fax: 815-722-6602.

SARTAIN, LIBBY, Internet company executive; married; 1 child. BA, So. Methodist U.; MBA, U. North Tex. Various positions Southwest Airlines, 1988—98, v.p. people, 1998—2001; sr. v.p. human resources, chief people Yahoo Yahoo!, Inc., Sunnyvale, Calif., 2001—. Bd. dirs. Peet's Coffee & Tea Inc., 2007—. Fellow: Nat. Acad. Human Resources; mem.: Soc. Human Resource Mgmt. (former chmn.). Office: Yahoo Inc 701 1st Ave Sunnyvale CA 94089 Office Phone: 408-349-3300. Office Fax: 408-349-3301.

SARTOR, DANIEL RYAN, JR., lawyer; b. Vicksburg, Miss., June 2, 1932; s. Daniel Ryan and Lucy Leigh (Hubbs) S.; m. Olive Guthrie Moss, Oct. 12, 1957; children— Clara M., Daniel Ryan, Walter M. BA, Tulane U., 1952, LL.B., 1955. Bar: La. 1955. Instr. Tulane U., New Orleans, 1955-56, asst. prof., 1956-57; ptnr. Snellings, Breard, Sartor, Inabnett & Trascher, Monroe, La., 1957—2001, of coun., 2002—. Contbr. articles to profl. jours. Fellow Am. Coll. Trust and Estate Counsel, Am. Bar Found., La. Bar Found.; mem. La. State Law Inst. (mem. coun. 1969—, sec. civil law sect. 1969-97, sr. officer 1997—), La. State Bar Assn. (chmn. sect. on trust estate, probate and immovable property 1973-74, bd. govs. 1974-75), Lotus Club, Bayou DeSiard Country Club. Democrat. Methodist. Home: 2405 Pargoud Blvd Monroe LA 71201-2326 Office: Snellings Breard Sartor 1503 N 19th St Monroe LA 71201-4960 Office Phone: 318-387-8000. Business E-Mail: rsartor@snellingslawfirm.com.

SARTOR, DAVID P., composer; b. Nashville, May 25, 1956; s. Grayl Bruce and Kathleen Lipscomb Sartor; m. Nancy White Sartor, Oct. 6, 1984; children: John Russell Laws, Sharon Rebecca Farrell. BMus with highest honors, U. Tenn., 1978. Composer: Veni Emmanuel-Fantasy of Abstractions for Concert Band, 1976, Medieval Manifesto for Unaccompanied Contrabass, 1977, Affectations for Brass Quintet, 1977, Variants For Solo Trombone, 1977, Open Door for Organ, 1977, Thrice Told Tales of the Pomegranate Forest for Trumpet, Violin and Bass Clarinet, 1978 (winner U Tenn.Chamber Music Composition, 1978, Contest award New Music For Young Ensembles, 1978), Illusions for Percussion Ensemble, 1981, O Worship the King for Orchestra, 1982, Synergistic Parable for Concert Band, 1985 (Ostwald award Am. Bandmasters Assn., 1987, Composition Contest award Appalachian State U., 87), Polygon for Brass Quintet, 1987 (Nat. Fine Arts award Ill., 1993), We Will be Glad for Chorus, Brass, Timpani and Organ, 1994, Prelude on William Billings' "When Jesus Wept" for Organ, 1996, Postlude on William Billings' "Paris" for Organ, 1996, Thy Light Is Come for Chorus, Brass, Timpani and Organ, 1997, Psalm 67 for Chorus, Organ and Trumpet, 1998, Metamorphic Fanfare for Orchestra, 2000 (Masterworks award), Concerto For Orchestra, 2001 (Masterworks award, Finalist, Columbia Symphony Orch's Am. Composer Competition), Simple Blessing for Organ, 2002, Welcome, Christmas Day! for Chorus and Instruments, 2002, Diplomatic Solution for 4 Violoncellos, 2003, Cat's Eye for Brass Ensemble, 2003, Black Ball Counts Double for Strings, 2003 (Masterworks award), Commendation, Oare Internat. Composing Contest, 2003, Fanfare A4 for Brass Quartet, 2003, Crown Him! for Chorus, Orchestra and Organ, 2004, Ascension for Brass and Timpani, 2005, Search Your Heart for Christmas for Chorus and Violoncello, 2005, Parabola for Brass and Timpani, 2006, Amid the Cruel Winter's Snow for Chorus and Celesta, 2007, Reveries for String Orchestra, 2007 (award, Burlington Chamber Orch. Composer Competition, 2009), Dies Irae for Brass and Timpani, 2007, Passages for String Orch., 2009. Mem. Woodmont Christian Ch., Nashville, Tenn. Recipient award, Thor Johnson Meml. Commn., 2007, various nat. and internat. commns., performances and residencies; Meet The Composer grantee, Creative Connections, NY, 2004. Mem.: ASCAP (20 consecutive panel awards 1989—2008), World Assn. Symphonic Bands and Ensembles, Am. Composers Forum, Ctr. for Promotion of Contemporary Composers, Nat. Assn. Composers USA, Am. Fedn. Musicians, Am. Music Ctr., Soc. Composers, Inc., Pi Kappa Lambda, Phi Kappa Phi. Office: PO Box 190308 Nashville TN 37219-0308 Office Fax: 908-673-1179. Business E-Mail: mail@davidsartor.com.

SARTORELLI, ALAN CLAYTON, pharmacologist, educator; b. Chelsea, Mass., Dec. 18, 1931; m. Alice C. Anderson, July 7, 1969. BS, New Eng. Coll. Pharmacy Northeastern U., 1953; MS, Middlebury Coll., Vt., 1955; PhD, U. Wis., 1958; MA (hon.), Yale U., 1967. Rsch. chemist Samuel Roberts Noble Found., Ardmore, Okla., 1958—60, sr. rsch. chemist, 1960—61; mem. faculty dept. pharmacology Yale Sch. Medicine, New Haven, 1961—, prof., 1967—, head devel. therapeutics program Comprehensive Cancer Ctr., 1974—90, chmn. dept. pharmacology, 1977—84, 1998—2000, dir. Comprehensive Cancer Ctr., 1984—93, Alfred Gilman prof. pharmacology, 1987—, prof. epidemiology, 1991—97. Head devel. therapeutics program Comprehensive Cancer Ctr., 1974—90, chmn. dept. pharmacology, 1977—84, 1998—2000, dep. dir., 1982—84, dir., 1984—93, Alfred Gilman prof. pharmacology, 1987—; Charles B. Smith vis. rsch. prof. Meml. Sloan-Kettering Ctr., 1979; William N. Creasy vis. prof. clin. pharmacology Wayne State U., 1983; Mayo Found. vis. prof. oncology Mayo Clinic, 1983; Walter Hubert lectr. Brit. Assn. Cancer Rsch., 1985; Pfizer lectr. in clin. pharmacology U. Conn. Health Ctr., 1985; William N. Creasy vis. prof. clin. pharmacology Bowman Gray Sch. Medicine, 1987; Wellcome vis. prof. basic sci. U. Pitts. Sch. Medicine, 1990; sci. adv. bd. ImmunoGen, Inc., 1981—90, U. Ind. Cancer Ctr., 1992, Cancer Inst. NJ, 1993—2000, Cell Pathways, Inc., 1993—2003; chmn. cancer sci. adv. bd. ViraChem., Inc., 1986—93, The Liposome Co., 1986—2001, Vion Pharms., 1993—, bd. dirs., chmn. sci. adv. bd.; chmn. vis. sci. adv. com. Columbia U. Comprehensive Cancer Ctr., 1986—99; chmn. pres.'s cancer adv. bd. Fox Chase Cancer Ctr., 1992—2007; clin. investigation rev. com. Nat. Cancer Inst., 1968—72, mgmt. cons. to dir. divsn. cancer treatment, 1975—77, bd. sci. counselors, divsn. cancer treatment, 1978—81, chmn. com. to establish nat. coop. drug discovery groups, 1982—83, chmn. spl. rev. com. Outstanding Investigator grant applications, 1992, chmn. ad hoc contracts tech. rev. group, 93; instnl. rsch. grants com. Am. Cancer Soc., 1971—76, coun. analysis and projection, 1978—79; cons. in biochemistry U. Tex. M.D. Anderson Hosp. and Tumor Clinic, Houston, 1970—76; cons. Sandoz Forschungs-Institut, Vienna, 1977—80; mem. exptl. therapeutics study sect. NIH, 1973—77, working cadre nat. large bowel cancer project, 1973—76; adv. com. Cancer Rsch. Ctr., Washington U. Sch. Medicine, 1971—75, SLSB Ptnrs., L.P., 1992—96; sci. adv. com. U. Iowa Cancer Ctr., 1979—83; external adv. com. Wis. Clin. Cancer Ctr., 1978—79, Duke Comprehensive Cancer Ctr., 1983—94; external adv. bd. U. Ariz. Cancer Ctr., 1982—92, U. So. Calif. Cancer Ctr., 1983—93, Clin. Cancer Rsch. Ctr., Brown U., 1980—86; nat. program com. 13th Internat. Cancer Congress, 1979—81; cons. Bristol-Myers Co., 1982—93, selection com. prize in cancer rsch., 1977—85, chmn., 1979—81, chmn. selection com. award for disting. achievement in cancer rsch., 1989—92; bd. advisors Drug and Vaccine Devel. Corp. (Ctr. for Pub. Resources), 1980—81, Specialized Cancer Ctr., Mt. Sinai Med. Ctr., 1981—90, Grace Cancer Drug Ctr., Roswell Park Meml. Inst., 1986—89; med. and sci. adv. com. grants rev. subcom. Leukemia Soc. Am., 1983—88; program planning com. Mary Lasker-Am. Cancer Soc. Conf., 1986; external sci. rev. com. Massey Cancer Ctr., 1989—94; bd. visitors Moffit Cancer Ctr. U. South Fla., 1989—92; dep. dir. Cancer Prevention Rsch. Unit for Conn., 1989—93, acting dir., 1991—93; nat. bd. Look Good...Feel Better program Cosmetic Toiletry and Fragrance Assn., 1989—91; organizing com. Conf. on Bioreductive Drug Activation, 1993—94; chmn. bd. spl. cons. Inst. for Cancer Therapeutics, 1993; sci. adv. bd. U. Ill. Cancer Ctr., 2001; chmn. sci. adv. bd. Celator Pharms. Inc., 2002—. Regional editor Am. Continent Biochem. Pharmacology, 1968—2003, exec. editor, 1993—2003, editor-in-chief Cancer Comm., 1969—93, Oncology Rsch., 1993—; editor: Handbuch der experimentellen Pharmakologie vols. on antineoplastic and immunosuppressive agts., series on cancer chemotherapy Am. Chem. Soc. Symposium, 1976; founder, exec. editor Pharmacology and Therapeutics, 1975—2003, editl. bd. Internat. Ency. Pharmacology and Therapeutics, 1972—94, Seminars in Oncology, 1973—83, Chemico-Biol. Interactions, 1975—78, Jour. Medicinal Chemistry, 1977—82, Cancer Drug Delivery, 1982—85, Jour. Enzyme Inhibition, 1984—2002, Jour. Liposome Rsch., 1986—92, In Vivo, 1990—2002, Cancer Biotherapy, 1992—97, Cancer Rsch., Therapy and Control, 1993—97, Oncology Reports, 1995—, Molecular and Cellular Differentiation, 1996—, mem. adv. bd. Advances in Chemistry Series, ACS Symposium Series, 1977—80, editl. adv. bd. Cancer Rsch., 1970—71, assoc. editor, 1971—78, Current Awareness in Biol. Scis., Current Advances in Pharmacology and Toxicology, 1983—88, Cancer Cells, 1989—91, Jour. Exptl. Therapeutics and Oncology, 1995—, exec. adv. bd. Ency. of Human Biology, 1987—90, Dictionary of Sci. and Tech., 1989—91, editl. cons. Biol. Abstracts, 1984—88; contbr. articles to profl. jours. Bd. dirs. Schubert Performing Arts Ctr., 1992—2001, Schubert Opera Bd., 1991—2000, chmn., 1993—. Recipient Outstanding Alumni award, Northeastern U., 1987, Mike Hogg award, M.D. Anderson Cancer Ctr., U. Tex., 1989, Alumni Achievement award, Middlebury Coll., 1990, AACR-Bruce F. Cain Meml. award, 2001, Drug Discovery and Devel. award, Glaxo SmithKline, 2002. Fellow: AAAS, N.Y. Acad. Scis.; mem.: Coun. Biology Editors, Conn. Acad. Sci. and Engring., Inst. Medicine NAS (com. on govt. industry collaboration in biomed. rsch. and edn. 1989, mem. Forum on Drug Devel. and Regulation 1989—93), Assn. Am. Cancer Insts. (v.p. 1986, liaison rep. to Nat. Cancer Inst. 1986, bd. dirs. 1986—89, pres. 1987—88, chmn. bd. dirs. 1989), Am. Soc. Pharmacology and Exptl. Therapeutics (award com. 1988, chmn. 1992, award in exptl. therapeutics 1986, Otto Krayer award 2002), Am. Soc. Cell Biology, Am. Soc. Biochemistry and Molecular Biology, Am. Soc. Microbiology, Am. Chem. Soc., Am. Assn. Cancer Rsch. (dir. 1975—78, chmn. publs. com. 1981—88, dir. 1984—87, v.p. 1985—86, fin. com. 1985—88, exec. com. 1985—89, pres. 1986—87, chmn. exec. com. 1987, chmn. awards com. 1987, chmn. nominating com. 1993—95, mem. devel. com. 1995—97). Home: 4 Perkins Rd Woodbridge CT 06525-1616 Office: Yale U Dept Pharmacology 333 Cedar St New Haven CT 06520-8066 Home Phone: 203-387-8925; Office Phone: 203-785-4533. E-mail: alan.sartorelli@yale.edu.

SARTORI, MICHAEL A., lawyer; b. St. Louis; BSEE, Univ. Notre Dame, 1987, MSEE, 1989, PhD, 1991; JD cum laude, Georgetown Univ., 1998. Bar: Va. 1998, DC 1999, US Patent & Trademark Office, US Ct. Appeals (4th, Fed. cir.). Sr. project mgr. USN Naval Surface Warfare Ctr., 1991—94; patent examiner US Patent & Trademark Office, 1994—96; ptnr., Patent Prosecution, Intellectual Property Litigation Venable LLP, Washington, 2003—, chmn. Patent Prosecution group, 2005—. Lectr. Catholic Univ. Am, 1991. Contbr. articles to profl. jours. Mem.: ABA, Am. Intellectual Property Law Assn. Achievements include patents in field of underwater acoustics. Office: Venable LLP 575 7th St NW Washington DC 20004 Office Phone: 202-344-4004. Office Fax: 202-344-8300. Business E-Mail: masartori@venable.com.

SARTORIS, JOSEPH MARTIN, bishop emeritus; b. LA, July 1, 1927; Ordained priest Archdiocese of LA, 1953, aux. bishop, 1994—2002, aux.bishop emeritus, 2002—; ordained bishop, 1994. Roman Catholic. Home: 1988 Rolling Vista Dr Unit 21 Lomita CA 90717-3761

SARTORI-VALINOTTI, JULIO, medical educator; s. Julio C. Sartori and Maria M. Valinotti; m. Marcia R. Venegas-Pont, Apr. 4, 2009. MD summa cum laude, U. Nacional Asuncion, Paraguay, 2000. Cert. Ednl. Commn. Fgn. Med. Grad., 2008. Intern, Hosp. de Clinicas, Facultad de Ciencias Medicas U. Nacional Asuncion, 2001—02, internal medicine resident, Hosp. Clinicas, Facultad Ciencias Medicas, 2002—05; post-doc. fellow U. Miss. Med. Ctr., Jackson, 2005—07, instr. physiology, 2007—. Contbr. articles to profl. jours., chapters to books. Recipient Best Intern, Rotary Internship Program Sch. Medicine U. Nacional de Asuncion, 2002. Mem.: Soc. Free Radical Biology & Medicine, Am. Physiol. Soc. (Rsch. Recognition award 2007), Am. Heart Assn. Roman Catholic. Avocations: travelling, reading. Office: Mayo Clinic Rochester MN

SARUK, MICHAEL, dermatologist, educator; b. Chgo., Nov. 1, 1951; s. Marvin Saruk and Geraldine Ruth Freeman; m. Louise Link, 1991; m. Anne Faulkner, 1977; children: Benjamin Dov, Jonathan Simon, Evan Samuel. BS, U. Ill., 1973; MD, Rush U., 1977. Diplomate Am. Bd. Dermatology, 1983, Am. Bd. Pathology, 1981, Am. Bds. Pathology and Dermatology, 1981. Asst. prof. pathology and dermatology U. Pitts. Sch. Medicine, 1982—83; instr. dermatology U. Pa. Sch. Medicine, Phila., 1984—86; clin. instr. dermatology Mt. Sinai Sch. Medicine, NYC, 1987—92; clin. asst. prof. dermatology U. Pa. Sch. Medicine, 1993—99, clin. assoc. prof., dermatology, 1999—. Cons., advisor Novartis Pharms., 2002—; cons., clin. investigator Aventis Pharms., 2002—04, Astellas Pharms., 2004—, Allergan Pharms., 2002—05, Galderma Pharms., 2004—05, Centocor - subs. of Johnson and Johnson, 2005—; asst. med. examiner Office of Med. Examiner, New Haven County, Conn., 1978—82, Celgene, 2008—. Co-author: (medical text) Soft Tissue Tumors; contbr. articles to profl. jours. Founding sponsor Magnolia Speech Sch. Demonstration Program, Berwyn, Pa., 2002. Fellow: Am. Soc. Dermatologic Surgery, Am. Soc. Mohs Surgery, US & Can. Acad. Pathology, Am. Acad. Dermatology, Am. Soc. Dermatopathology; mem.: Dermatology Found. (vice-chair Ea. Pa. 1997—2000), Del. Acad. Dermatology (pres. 1997—98), Pa. Acad. Dermatology, Soc. Investigative Dermatology, Phi Beta Kappa. Achievements include Start of the pigmented lesion clinic for the diagnosis and treatment of pigmented disorders of the skin, including moles and melanoma, in the department of dermatology, University of Pittsburgh, 1982; Start of What Is Now One Of The Largest Private Group Dermatology And Plastic Surgery Practices In The Delaware Valley, Employing A Multidisciplinary Approach To The Treatment Of Cutaneous Diseases. Office: Atlantic Skin & Cosmetic Surgery Group Silver Side Rd Ste 107 Webstar Bldg 3411 Wilmington DE 19810 Office Fax: 610-296-3963.

SARUKHAN, ARTURO, ambassador; BA, Coll. Mex.; MA, Johns Hopkins U., 1991. Chief of staff Embassy of Mex., 1993—95, dir. counternarcotics and law enforcement, 1995—98; sr. adv. to sec. Min. Fgn. Affairs United Mexican States, 1998—2000, chief of staff policy planning, 2000—03; consul gen. Consulate Gen. of Mex., NYC, 2003—06; amb. to US Govt. of Mex., Washington, 2007—. Office: 1911 Pennsylvania Ave NW Washington DC 20006 Office Phone: 202-728-1600. Office Fax: 202-728-1698.

SARUNDAJANG, SINYO HARRY, government official; b. Kawangkoan, North Sulawesi, Indonesia, Jan. 16, 1945; s. Jost Albert Sarundajang and Juliana Liow; m. Deetje Adelien Tambuwun; children: Ivan, Vanda, Fabian, Eva, Shinta. Bachelor, Sam Ratulangi U., Manado, 1968; Sarjana, Untag U., Jakarta, 1970; adminstrn., L'Adminstrn. Territorial U., De Nice, France, 1976; cert. in devel. adminstrn. group sch. pub. policy, Birmingham U., Eng., 1994; cert., Inst. for Housing and Urban Devel. Studies, Rotterdam, The Netherlands, 1994; cert. exec. mgmt. program, U. Pitts., 1995; cert. exec. program and health fin. managed care, U. Calif., 1996; cert. nat. resilience inst., Dept. Def., Jakarta, 2000. Chief govt. adminstrn. bur. Gov. Office North Sulawesi Province, Manado, Indonesia, 1974—78; sec. Minahasa Regency Tondano, 1978—86; mayor Bitung Municipality, Bitung, 1986—2000; acting chmn. Manado-Bitung Integrated Econ. Devel., Manado, 1999—2000; expert assts. Min. Home Affair, Jakarta, 2000—01; gen. inspector Dept. Home Affairs, Jakarta, 2001—05; acting gov. North Maluku, Indonesia, 2002—03, Maluku, 2003—04; gov. North Sulawesi, 2004—. Recipient Satya Lencana Wira Karya medal, Pres. Republic Indonesia, Jakarta, 1995—97, 2001, Anugerah Aksara medal, Pres. Rep. Indonesia, Jakarta, 1996, Cooperative Relation Treaty award, Govt. Philippines, 1999; grantee Health Edn. grant, WHO, 1995. Avocations: chess, tennis. Office: Govs Office JL 17 Agustus Manado Indonesia Home: Govt Residential Bumi Beringin Manado Indonesia Office Phone: 62 431 844 885. Business E-Mail: togap2002@yahoo.com.au.

SARVER, ROBERT G., professional sports team owner; s. Jack Sarver; m. Penny Sanders, Nov. 2, 1996; 3 children. BBA, U. Ariz., 1982. CPA 1983. Founder, pres. Nat. Bank Ariz., 1984—94; lead investor, CEO GB Bancorporation, 1995—97; chmn., CEO Calif. Bank and Trust (formerly Grossmont Bank), San Diego, 1995—2002; dir., mem. credit com. Zions Bancorporation, 1995—2001, exec. v.p., 1998—2001; pres., chmn., CEO Western Alliance Bancorporation, 2002—; chmn., CEO Torrey Pines Bank, 2003—; co-founder S.W. Value Ptnrs.; mng. ptnr. Phoenix Suns, Ariz., 2004—. Bd. dirs. SkyWest Airlines, Meritage Corp., Phoenix. Mem. adv. bd. U. Ariz. Sarver Heart Ctr.; bd. trustees Japanese Am. Nat. Mus., LA. Avocations: golf, tennis, volleyball. Office: Alliance Bank Ariz 2701 E Camelback Rd Ste 110 Phoenix AZ 85016*

SARWARK, JOHN FRANCIS, orthopaedic surgeon, educator; b. Aurora, Ill., Jan. 24, 1954; m. Maria Panico Sarwark; children: John, Robert, Annie. BS, U. Ill., Champaign, 1975; MD, Northwestern U., 1979. Resident in orthop. surgery Northwestern U., 1979—84; attending pediat. orthop. surgeon Childrens Mercy Hosp., Kansas City, Mo., 1985—88, Childrens Meml. Hops., Chgo, 1988, divsn. head pediat. orthop. surgery Chgo., 2003—; asst. prof. orthop. surgery Northwestern U. Med. Sch., Chgo, 1988—94, assoc. prof. orthop. surgery, 1994—2001; med. dir. ctr. childhood safety Childrens Meml. Hosp., Chgo., 1997—; prof. orthop. surgery Northwestern U. Med. Sch., Chgo., 2001—. Faculty Med. Ethics and Humanities Program, Northwestern U. Med. Sch., Chgol, 1996-99. Contbr. articles to profl. jours. Mem. Pathways Awareness Found., Glenview, 1993—. Recipient Berkheiser award, Inst. Medicine, Chgo., 1990. Fellow: Pediat. Orthop. Soc. N.Am. (mem.-at-latge 1992—93, mem.-at-large 2002—04, bd. dirs.), Scoliosis Rsch. Soc. (edn. com. 1996—2000, fellow com. 2000—), Am. Acad. Pediat. (exec. com. orthopedic sect. 1997—, chair 2002—04), Am. Acad. Orthop. Surgeons (faculty chmn. com. on pub. edn. 1998—2001, assoc. editor Orthopedic Knowledge Online 2003—), Am. Orthop. Assn., Alpha Omega Alpha. Avocations: fine arts, travel. Office: Divsn Pediat Orthopaedic Surgery Childrens Meml Hosp 2300 N Childrens Plz Box #69 Chicago IL 60614-3363 Office Phone: 773-327-1270. Business E-Mail: jsarwark@childrensmemorial.org.

SAS, ROBERT JOSEPH, JR., geologist, researcher; MS in Applied Geosci., San Francisco State U., 2008. Geologist Geol. Soc. America. and Yosemite Nat. Pk., El Portal, Calif., 2008—. Contbr. articles to profl. jours. Coll. Sci. and Engring. Adv. Bd. scholarship, San Francisco State U., 2007. Mem.: Am. Geophys. Union, Geol. Soc. Am.

SASAHARA, ARTHUR ASAO, cardiologist, educator, researcher; b. Del Rey, Calif., May 11, 1927; s. Harold Hango and Blanche (Takayama) S.; m. Alice Ann Guenther, Apr. 2, 1955; children: Ann Mariko, Claire Michiko, Ellen Reiko, Karen Hideko, Mark Tadao. AB, Oberlin Coll., 1951; MD, Case Western Res. U., 1955; AM (hon.), Harvard U., 1987. Diplomate Am. Bd. Internal Medicine. Intern Boston City Hosp., 1955-56; jr. asst. med. resident Mass. Gen. Hosp., Boston, 1956-57; fellow in cardiology West Roxbury VA Med. Ctr., Mass., 1957-58, Children's Hosp. Med. Ctr., Boston, 1958-59; sr. resident in medicine Yale-New Haven Med. Ctr., 1959-60; asst. chief med. svc., dir. cardiopulmonary lab., dep. chmn. rsch. and edn. com. VA Hosp. West Roxbury, 1960-70, chief cardiopulmonary sect., 1971-74, assoc. chief staff for rsch. and edn., 1970-76, chief med. svc., 1974-82, West Roxbury-Brockton VA Hosp., 1982-87; prof. medicine Harvard Med. Sch., Boston, 1974-93, prof. emeritus, 1993—; cons. cardiovascular-pulmonary diseases Boston, 1965-87; cons. pediatric cardiology Children's Hosp. Med. Ctr., Boston, 1976-86; physician Brigham and Women's Hosp., Boston, 1979-82, sr. physician, 1982—. Dir. thrombolytics rsch. pharm. products divsn. Abbott Labs., Abbott Park, Ill., 1987—95, sr. med. dir., 1995—97; sr. physician cardiovascular divsn. Brigham and Women's Hosp., 1998—. Author-editor: Pulmonary Embolic Disease, 1965, Pulmonary Emboli, 1975, New Therapeutic Agents in Thrombosis and Thrombolysis, 1997, 2d edit., 2002; contbr. articles to profl. jours.; designer constant infusion med. pump, Harvard Apparatus Co., 1973; mem. editl. bd. New Eng. Jour. Medicine, 1971-73, Jour. Nuclear Medicine, 1981-83, Am. Jour. Medicine, 1971-72, Circulation, 1973-78, VASA, 1978-85, Jour. Cardiovasc. Medicine, 1980-86, Primary Cardiology, 1986-89. With U.S. Army, 1945-47. NIH grantee, 1963-82; VA grantee, 1961-87. Fellow ACP, Am. Coll. Chest Physicians, Am. Coll. Cardiology; mem. AAAS, Internat. Soc. Fibrinolysis and Thrombolysis, Am. Fedn. Clin. Rsch., Internat. Soc. Thrombosis and Hemostasis, Am. Heart Assn., N.Am. Thrombosis Forum (founding dir. 2007-), Alpha Omega Alpha. Democrat. Episcopalian. Home: 1115 Beacon St # 12 Newton MA 02461-1154 Personal E-mail: aasasahara@comcast.net.

SASAKI, AKIHIKO, cardiologist; s. Kozo and Yukiko Sasaki; m. Yoko Sano, Sept. 12, 1992; children: Hiroki, Miki. MD, Tokyo Med. U., 1988, PhD, 1996. Diplomate Japan, 1988. Instr. Tokyo Med. U., Shinjuku-ku, 1995—2000; dir. Sasaki Med. Clinic, Nakano-ku, Tokyo, 2000—. Vis. lectr. Tokyo Med. U., Shinjuku-ku, 2001—. Contbr. articles to profl. jours. Recipient Jos Willems Young Investigators award, Internat. Soc. for Computerized Electrocardiology, 1997, award, Japanese Soc. of

Electrocardiology, 1997, Jos Willems Young Investigators award, Internat. Soc. for Computerized Electrocardiology, 1998, 1999, Sasa Meml. award, Tokyo Med. U., 2000; grantee Rsch. grant, 1995. Fellow: Japanese Soc. Internal Medicine; mem.: Japanese Soc. Electrocardiology, The Japanese Coll. Cardiology, Internat. Soc. Electrocardiology, The Japanese Circulation Soc. (bd. cert. 1997—), The Japan Med. Assn. Achievements include research in symmetrical T waves using a first derivative electrocardiogram. Office: Sasaki Med Clinic 3-36-12 Yayoicho Nakano-ku Tokyo 164-0013 Japan Office Fax: 81-3-3372-0548. Personal E-mail: a-sasaki@fa2.so-net.ne.jp. Business E-Mail: a-sasaki@sasaki-medical-clinic.jp.

SASAKI, CLARENCE TAKASHI, surgeon, educator; b. Honolulu, Jan. 24, 1941; s. Tsutomu and Carla Harumi (Mirikitani) S.; m. Carolyn Elizabeth Lindahl, June 26, 1967; children: Peter Gordon, John Eric. BA, Pomona Coll., 1962; MD, Yale U., 1966. Diplomate: Am. Bd. Otolaryngology. Intern San Francisco Hosp., U. Calif., 1966-67; resident in surgery Dartmouth Med. Sch., 1967-68; resident in otolaryngology Yale U. Med. Sch. Hosps., New Haven, 1970-73, faculty mem., 1973—, assoc. prof., 1977-82, prof. surgery, 1982—, chief sect. otolaryngology, 1981—, Charles Ohse prof. surgery, 1988—, vice chmn. dept. surgery, 1996. Author: Surgery of the Skull Base, Head and Neck Surgery, Vol. 1 Atlas Otolarynogology, Vocal Fold Physiology, Laryngeal Function in Phonation and Respiration, Neurological Diseases of the Larynx, Laryngeal Physiology for the Surgeon, 2008; mem. editl. bd. profl. jours. Served to maj. M.C. U.S. Army, 1968-70. Recipient award Fowler Triological Soc., 1979. Mem. Am. Acad. Otolaryngology (1st prize clin. rsch.), Am. Soc. Head and Neck Surgery (coun.), Assn. Rsch. Otolaryngology, Am. Laryngol. Rhinol. and Otol. Soc. (coun., sec. ea. sect. 1990, v.p. 1998), New Eng. Otolaryngology Soc. (pres. 1987, coun.), Assn. Acad. Depts. Otolaryngology (coun.), Am. Laryngol. Assn. (coun. 2008, Casselberry award 1999), Pan Pacific Surg. Assn., Soc. for Neurosci., Soc. Neurovascular Surgery, Soc. for Head and Neck Surgeons, Am. Neurotolog. Soc., Pan Am. Assn. Oto-rhino-laryngology and Bronchoesophagology, Conn. Med. Soc., N.Y. Acad. Scis., Soc. Univ. Otolaryngologists, Collegium ORLAS, Cartesian Soc. (co-dir.), Am. Bronchoesophagological Assn. (mem. coun., treas. 2003, pres. 2007, Broyles-Maloney award 2004), N.Am. Skull Base Soc., Laryngeal. Cancer Assn. (Padua), Am. Otol. Soc., Dysphagia Rsch. Soc. (treas., pres.), Lawn Club, Mory's Assoc., Yale Club, Phi Beta Kappa, Sigma Xi. Office: Yale U Med Sch Dept Surgery PO Box 208041 333 Cedar St New Haven CT 06520-8041 Office Phone: 203-785-2592.

SASAKI, MIKIO, trading company executive; b. Oct. 8, 1937; BS, Waseda U., 1960. Various positions Mitsubishi Corp., 1960—93; pres. Mitsubishi Internat. Corp., NYC, 1993—94; mng. dir. Mitsubishi Corp., Tokyo, 1994—98, pres., 1998—2004, chmn., 2004—. Vice-chmn. bd. councillors Japan Bus. Fedn.; mem. exec. com. Japan-U.S. Bus. Council. Mem.: Japan Fgn. Trade Coun. (chmn. 2004). Office: Mitsubishi Corp 6-3 Marunouchi 2-chome Chiyoda-ku Tokyo 100-8086 Japan Office Phone: +81-3-3210-2121.

SASAKI, ROBERT J., financial services executive; b. Oakland, Calif., May 7, 1962; s. Joseph and Kimiko (Sakanashi) S.; m. Momoe Shimabukuro; children: Lisa, Lynn. BA, U. Calif., Berkeley, 1984; MA, Harvard U., 1988. Arbitrageur L.F. Rothschild, Unterberg, Towbin, Inc., NYC, 1986-88, Merrill Lynch & Co., Inc., NYC, 1988-89, JP Morgan, Tokyo, 1989-2001, Bear Stearns Co., Inc., Tokyo, 2001—04; mng. mem. Pacific Property Capital, LLC, San Francisco, 2004—; chmn., CEO K and S Co., Inc., 2005—. Co-founder Free Merchant.Com, Inc., Emeryville, Calif.; founder Robert J. Sasaki Fund for Rsch. in Vision Neurosci., U. Calif., Berkeley, 2004—. Mem. Nat. Eagle Scout Assn. (life), Harvard Club of NYC, Young Pres. Orgn., Tokyo Am. Club, Faculty Club Berkeley, Peninsula Golf and Country Club, U. Calif. Berkeley Found. (mem. real estate com.). Republican. Buddhist. Avocations: skiing, tennis, japanese art. Home: 881 Vista Rd Hillsborough CA 94010 Office: 50 California St Ste 1500 San Francisco CA 94111

SASAKI, YOSHI KAZU, meteorology educator, researcher; b. Akitacity, Akita-ken, Japan, Jan. 2, 1927; s. Kosuke and Itsu Sasaki; m. Koko Anna Sasaki, Feb. 26, 1931; children: Yoshihikko, Sachihiko Larry, Sachiko Anna, Kazuhiko James. BS, Tokyo U., 1951, DSc, 1955. Rsch. scientist, project dir. Tex. A&M Coll., College Station, 1956—60, U. Okla., Norman, 1960—63, adj. assoc. prof., 1963—67, prof., 1967—74, George Lynn Cross rsch. prof., 1974—94, George Lynn Cross rsch. prof. emeritus, 1994—. Rsch. dir. Naval Environ. Prediction Rsch. Facility, Monterey, Calif., 1974—75; dir. Coop. Inst. Mesoscale Meteorol. Studies, Norman, 1980—86. Contbr. articles to profl. jours. Governor's coun. Asian Am. Affairs State Okla., Oklahoma City, 1995—2008. Recipient Regents award, U. Okla., 1991, award for Outstanding Contbn. on Internat. Collaboration and Friendship Promotion, Fgn. Min. Japan, 1992, Fujiwara award, Meteorol. Soc. Japan, 2000, medal, Emperor Japan, 2004, Inducted into Hall of Fame, Okla. Higher Edn. Heritage Soc., 2004; Fellow, Am. Meteorol. Soc., 1974. Achievements include the day Mar. 8, 2001 proclaimed as Dr. Yoshi K. Sasaki Day. Home: 906 Timberdell Norman OK 73072 Office: Univ Oklahoma 120 David L Boren Blvd NWC 5321 Norman OK 73072 Home Fax: 405-321-5800. Business E-Mail: yks@ou.edu.

SASANI, MEHRDAD, engineering educator; m. Faezeh Rashid; children: Puya, Ava. PhD, U. Calif., Berkeley, 2001. Cert. profl. engr., Calif., 2003. Assoc. prof. Northeastern U., Boston, 2001—. Prin. investigator, rsch. & edn. How Bldgs. Resist Structural Collapse. Recipient Career award, NSF, 2006—. Mem.: Structural Engring. Inst. Achievements include research in progressive collapse resistance of structures. Office: Northeastern Univ 400 Snell Engring Ctr Boston MA 02115 Business E-Mail: sasani@neu.edu.

SASE, JOHN FRANCIS, economist; b. Detroit, Nov. 11, 1950; s. James Edward and Mabel (Carlson) S.; m. Julie Gale Sase; children: Elizabeth Anne, Rebecca Marie. MBA, U. Detroit, 1978, MA in Econs., 1982; PhD in Econs., Wayne State U., 1992. Instr. Oakland U., Rochester Hills, Mich., 1990—; pres. S.A.S.E. Assocs., Southfield, Mich., 1992—; head rsch. Focus: Hope-MTI, Detroit, 1992—. Outside dir. asset funds Comerica Bank, Detroit, 1992—. Mem. Am. Econ. Assn., Nat. Assn. Bus. Econs. Avocation: music. Office: Focus Hope 1200 Oakman Blvd Detroit MI 48238-2998

SASEK, GLORIA BURNS, English language and literature educator; b. Springfield, Mass., Jan. 20, 1926; d. Frederick Charles and Minnie Delia (White) Burns; m. Lawrence Anton Sasek, Sept. 5, 1960. BA, Mary Washington Coll. of U. Va., 1947; student, U. Paris, 1953, U. per Stranieri, Perugia, Italy, 1955; MA, Radcliffe Coll., 1954; EdM, Springfield Coll., 1955. Tchr., head dept. jr. and sr. hs English, Pub. Schs., Somers, Conn., 1947—59; tchr. English, Winchester (Mass.) Pub. Schs., 1959—60; mem. faculty La. State U., Baton Rouge, 1961—2007, asst. prof. English, 1971-96, part time tchr., 1996—2007, chmn. freshman English, 1969-70. Recipient George H. Deer Disting. Tchg. award, La. State U., 1977, Disting. Undergrad. Tchg. award, Amoco Found., 1994, commendation, La. Ho. of Reps., 1996; named La. State U. Yearbook Favorite Prof., 1978. Mem. MLA, AAUP (chpt. v.p. 1981-84), South Ctrl. MLA, South Ctrl. Renaissance Soc., South Ctrl. Conf. on Christianity and Lit. Office: 1458 Kenilworth Pkwy Baton Rouge LA 70808 Personal E-mail: gsasek1@lsu.edu.

SASENICK, JOSEPH ANTHONY, health care company executive; b. Chgo., May 18, 1940; s. Anthony E. and Caroline E. (Smicklas) S.; m. Betty Cheung, Dec. 22, 2007; children: Richard Allen, Susan Marie, Michael Joseph. BA, DePaul U., 1962; MA, U. Okla., 1966. With Miles Labs., Inc., Elkhart, Ind., 1963-70; product mgr. Alka-Seltzer, 1966-68, dir. mktg. grocery products divsn., 1968-70; with Gillette Corp., Boston, 1970-79, dir. new products/new ventures, personal care divsn., 1977; v.p. diversified cos. and pres. Jafra Cosmetics Worldwide, 1977-79; mktg. dir. Braun AG, Kronberg, W. Ger., 1970-73; chmn. mng. dir. Braun U.K. Ltd., 1973-77; with Abbott Labs., North Chicago, 1979-84, corp. v.p., pres. consumer products divsn., 1979-84; pres., CEO, Moxie Industries, 1984-87; pres., CEO Personal Monitoring Technologies, Rochester, NY, 1987; pres. Bioline Labs., Ft. Lauderdale, Fla., 1988; mng. dir., ptnr. Vista Resource Group, Newport Beach, Calif., 1988-90; pres., CEO, Alcide Corp., Redmond, Wash., 1991-92, chmn., CEO, 1992—2004; founder Board Romm Ltd., 2004; life sci. commercialization cons. Washington Biotech. & Biomed. Assn., Seattle. Mem. Columbia Tower Club, Wash. Athletic Club. Home and Office: Board Room Ltd 1301 Spring St # 24J Seattle WA 98104 Office Phone: 206-732-6703. Personal E-mail: jasasenick@msn.com.

SASHIN, DONALD, physicist, educator; b. NYC, Dec. 11, 1937; s. David and Pearl (Taub) S.; m. Kathleen Flaherty, July 24, 1967; children: Deirdre Moira, Courtenay Aileen. BS in Physics, MIT, 1960; MS in Physics, Carnegie Inst. Tech., 1962; PhD in Physics, Carnegie Mellon U., 1968. Instr. radiology and radiation health U. Pitts., 1967-70, asst. prof. radiology, 1970-74, asst. prof. indsl and environ. health, 1970-77; asst. prof. radiation health, 1977-87; assoc. prof. radiology U. Pitts., 1974—, assoc. prof. radiation health, 1987-89, assoc. prof. environ. and occupl. health, 1989-2000. Contbr. articles to profl. jours., patentee in field. Recipient Cum Laude award sci. exhibit Radiol. Soc. N.Am., 1977, cert. of merit sci. exhibit, 1979. Mem. IEEE, AAAS, Am. Phys. Soc., Am. Assn. Physicists in Medicine, Soc. Nuclear Medicine, Health Physics Soc., Sigma Xi. Democrat. Roman Catholic. Avocations: golf, fishing, swimming, sailing. Home: 4360 Centre Ave Pittsburgh PA 15213-1403 Office: PET Facility B938 PUH/UPMC 200 Lothrop St Pittsburgh PA 15213-2546 Home Phone: 412-683-1468; Office Phone: 412-647-0713.

SASLOW, DEBBIE L., cancer control specialist, director; d. H. Arnold and Ann E. Weinstat; children: Kayla M., Rianna N. BS, Brown U., 1983—87; PhD, Yale U., 1987—92. Coord., president's nat. action plan on breast cancer PHS Office on Women's Health, Washington, 1995—97; dir., breast and gynecologic cancers Am. Cancer Soc., Atlanta, 1997—. Spkr. in field. Office: 250 Williams St 6th Floor Atlanta GA 30303

SASMAN, IRENE DEAK HANDBERG, publishing executive; b. Jamaica, NY; d. Paul and Irene (Dyroff) Deak; children: Roger B. Handberg III, Ryan Paul Handberg; m. Timothy Carl Sasman. BS, Fla. State U.; MEd, U. N.C., 1970. Cert. tchr. in reading and math., N.C. Lead tchr., reading specialist Chapel Hill (N.C.) City Schs., 1966-69; dir. learning lab. Seminole Community Coll., Sanford, Fla., 1974-78; basic skills cons. EDL/McGraw-Hill Book Co., Orlando, Fla., 1978-82; regional dir. EDL/Arista Pub., Orlando, 1982-84; mktg. mgr., product mgr. Arista/Regents/EDL-Hachette, NYC, 1984-85; v.p. mktg. and sales Raintree Pubs., Milw., 1985, gen. mgr., pub., 1985-87; dir. spl. projects Simon & Schuster, Englewood Cliffs, NJ, 1987-88, v.p. corp. devel. NYC, 1988-90, sr. v.p., 1990-91; chmn. Irene Handberg Internat., NYC, 1991—; pres. The Learning Connection, New York, NY, 1991—. Co-author: EDL/McGraw-Hill Teacher's Guide. Elected precinct woman com. Dem. County Com., Fla.; capt. Nat. Cancer So., Fla., chmn. Sch. Adv. Com., Fla. NSF fellow U. N.C., 1969; recipient Svc. award Jr. Achievement. Mem. Chief Exec. Officers Group (coun. small bus. execs.), Sales and Mktg. Execs., Profl. Dimensions, Chief Exec. Officers Club. Lutheran. Avocations: spectator sports, art, music, skiing. Office: The Learning Connection 300 E 93rd St Apt 29C New York NY 10128-6109

SASMOR, JAMES CECIL, publishing representative, educator; b. NYC, July 29, 1920; s. Louis and Cecilia (Mockler) S.; 1 child from previous marriage, Elizabeth Lynn; m. Jeannette L. Fuchs, May 30, 1965. BS, Columbia U., NYC, 1942; MBA, Calif. Western U., 1977, PhD, 1979. Fellow, Diplomate Am. Bd. Med. Psychotherapists, Am. Assn. Sex Educators, Counselors and Therapists; lic. healthcare risk mgr., Am. Inst. Med. Law; diplomate Am. Bd. Sexology, Am. Bd. Disability Analysts (sr. analyst); cert. tchr. health scis. Registered rep. Nat. Assn. Security Dealers, 1956—57; founder, owner J.C. Sasmor Assocs., Pub.'s Reps., NYC, 1959—89; co-founder, pres., dir. adminstrn. Continuing Edn. Cons., Inc., 1976—. Pub. cons., 1959—; clin. assoc. U. So. Fla. Coll. Medicine, 1987-89, mem. adj. faculty Coll. Nursing, 1980-89; dir. Ednl. Counseling Comprehensive Breast Cancer Ctr., U. So. Fla. Med. Ctr., 1984-89, client libr. mental health inst., 1979-89; lectr. divsn. allied health nursing and pub. svc. Yavapai Coll.; co-leader study tours to fgn. countries. Author: Economics of Structured Continuing Education in Selected Professional Journals, Perception May Be Reality Vols. I, II and III; contbr. (chpts. to Childbirth Education: A Nursing Perspective); contbr. articles to profl. jours. Team tchr. childbirth edn. Am. Soc. Childbirth Educators; pres. Sedona unit Am. Cancer Soc., Ariz., 1995—2000, co-chmn. adult edn. com., founder Am. Cancer Soc. edn. dept. Sedona Med. Ctr., 1995—2005; county nursing ednl. cons. ARC, chmn. instrnl. com. on nursing and health, 1979—85; founding mem. coun. trustees Ariz. Nurses Found., 1998; co-leader study tours Russia Profl. Seminar Cons., 1986, ICOWHI, New Zealand and Australia, 1990, China People to People Citizen Amb. Program, 1996, Spain, Morocco Yavapai Coll. Health Inst., 1999, France and Eng. U. Tours Comparative Nursing, 2001; bd. dirs. Tampa chpt. ARC; bd. dirs. Ariz. divsn., mem. pub. edn. com. Gunnery/CIC officer USN, 1942—58, PTO, lt. USNR, ret. Recipient cert. of appreciation ARC, 1979, Am. Fgn. Svc. Assn., 1988, Dept. Health and Rehab. Svcs. award for Fla. Mental Health Inst. Svc., 1980; Internat. Coun. Sex Edn. and Parenthood fellow Am. U., 1981, Accomplished Elder award Ariz. Coun. of Govts. Mem. NAACOG (bd. dirs. Tampa chpt.), Nat. Assn. Pubs. Reps. (pres. 1965-66), Am. Soc. Psychoprophylaxis in Obstetrics (dir. 1970-71), Am. Soc. Childbirth Educators (co-founder, dir. 1972—), Internat. Coun. Women's Health Issues (chmn. resources com.), Health Edn. Media Assn., Nursing Educators Assn. Tampa, Lions (bd. dirs. Found. Ariz. 1991-2000, past pres. Sedona club, bd. dirs., chair sight, hearing, and scholarship coms., Melvin Jones fellow), Phi Theta Kappa (Honors scholar 2000-04, hon., advisor chpt. 1996-2002, granted visionary status). Home: 235 Arrowhead Dr Sedona AZ 86351-8900 Office: PO Box 2282 Sedona AZ 86339-2282 Office Phone: 928-284-9897. Personal E-mail: drjcsasmor@msn.com.

SASNETT, KATHLEEN BETH, theater educator, director; d. Leonard Maurice Moore and Elizabeth Ellen Hanson; m. Roger Harris Sasnett, June 9, 1978; children: Joseph Roger, Nicole Elizabeth Sasnett-Hudson, Benjamin Harris. MusB in Vocal Performance, U. Wash., Seattle, 1987; MusM, Ctrl. Wash. U., Ellensburg, 2001; MusD, Ohio State U., Columbus, 2006. Cert. tchr. Wash. State. Vocal music specialist Wash. State Pub. Sch., Kenmore, Wash., 1993—2002, Kingston, Wash., 1993—2002, Redmond, Wash., 1993—2002; opera studio dir. Sunderman Conservatory Music, Gettysburg Coll., Pa., asst. prof. voice and opera, 2006—, coord. vocal activities, 2006—, vocal dir. musical prodns. theatre arts, 2006—. Adv. bd. mem. Adams Country Sch. Musical Theatre, Gettysburg, 2008—. Contbr. articles; singer: Soprano Soloist. Dir. musical theatre opera Cmty. Outreach, Redmond, 1995—99; performer Benefit and Cmty. Free Concerts, 2004—06, dir., 2004—06, ALS Lou Gehrig's Disease Hope Found., King Prussia, Pa., 2006—08; performer benefit prodns. ALS (Lou Gehrig's Disease) Hope Found., 2006—08; dir. Visitor's Ctr. Ch. Jesus Christ Latter-day Saints, Washington, 2006—08, performer cmty. goodwill concerts, 2006—08. Recipient Grad. Outstanding Achievement award, Ohio State U., 2006; fellowship, 2004—05. Mem.: Nat. Assn. Tchrs. Singing, Coll. Music Soc., Phi Kappa Phi. Mem. Reorganized Lds Ch. Home: 237 North Stratton St #1 Gettysburg PA 17325 Office: Sunderman Conservatory Music 300 North Washington #403 Gettysburg PA 17325 Office Fax: 717-337-8558. Personal E-mail: kathleen@sasnett.com. Business E-Mail: ksasnett@gettysburg.edu.

SASS, ARTHUR HAROLD, educational training administrator; b. NYC, Nov. 22, 1928; s. Maxwell Sigmund and Alice May (McGillick) S.; m. Eleanore G. Schmidt, Dec. 31, 1949; children: Nancy, Arlene, Susan, Eric. BS, SUNY Oswego, 1949; EdM, Rutgers U., 1959, postgrad., 1960—68. Cert. chief sch. adminstr. Tchr. Millsboro Pub. Sch. Sys., Del., 1949—51, Eatontown (N.J.) Pub. Sch. System, NJ, 1955—66; coord. coop. indsl. edn. Monmouth Regional H.S., Tinton Falls, NJ, 1966—68; prin. Mt. Holly Pub. Sch. Sys., NJ, 1968—71; supt. Lumberton Twp. Pub. Sch. Sys., NJ, 1971—72, Lacey Twp. Pub. Sch. Sys., NJ, 1973—74; analyst mil. pers. Naval Sea Sys. Command, Washington, 1975—79; head employee devel. Naval Rsch. Lab., Washington, 1979—83, 1985—90; acad. dir. Naval Res. Engring. Duty Officer Sch., Leesburg, Va., 1983—85. Pres. DEVPRO, Inc., Warrenton, Va., 1985—; prin. founder Dept. Def. Sci. and Engring. Apprentice Program; established nation's first fed. svc. high sch. coop. indsl. edn. program, 1967. Author: Guide to the Naval Ammunition Depot, 1967; editor: (brochure) Commodore John Barry-Father of the U.S. Navy, 1976. Chmn. Shade Tree Commn., Little Silver, NJ, 1968—75, Rapidan/Rappahannock (Va.) Cmty. Mental Health Ctrs., 1980—81; mem. Va. Gov.'s Adv. Bd. for Emergency Med. Svcs., 1994—96, Shade Tree Commn., Monmouth County, NJ, 1969—75; dir. Peninsula Agy. on Aging, Williamsburg, Va., 2004; deacon Warrenton Ch. of Christ, 1985, elder, 1995—99; deacon Williamsburg Ch. of Christ, 2005. Recipient Tng. Officers' Conf. Disting. Svc. award, 1988, Outstanding Contbn. to Engring. Edn. and Rsch award George Washington U., 1991. Mem. ASTD, SAR, Res. Officers Assn. (v.p. Va. chpt. 1982-83), Naval Res. Assn. (Plimsoll Mark award 1975), Am. Soc. Naval Engrs., Navy League, Wash. Acad. Scis., Tng. Dirs. Forum. Republican. Avocation: outdoor activities. Home and Office: 604 Dam Lake Ct Williamsburg VA 23185-2796

SASS, CYNTHIA N., lawyer; BA in Econs. and Theater, Smith Coll., Northampton, Mass., 1984; JD, U. Richmond, Va., 1987. Bar: Fla. 1987, US Dist. Ct. (mid. and so. dists.), Fla., US Ct. Appeals (11th cir.), US Supreme Ct., cert.: Fla. (cir. ct. mediator). Asst. state atty. State Atty. of 13th Judicial Cir., Tampa, 1987—90; assoc. Alley & Alley, Tampa, 1990—93; sole practitioner Law Offices of Cynthia N. Sass, Tampa, 1993—94; ptnr. Bole & Sass, Tampa, 1997—99; atty. Law Offices of Cynthia N. Sass, PA, Tampa, 1999—. Contbr. articles to profl. jours. Mem.: Hillsborough County Bar Assn., Nat. Employment Lawyers Assn. (pres.-elect Fla. chpt. 1998—99, pres. Fla. chpt. 1999—2000), Fla. Bar (exec. coun. mem. 1998—2004, co-chair individual rights com. 1999, co-chair judicial edn. com. 2002—03, CLE chair 2003—04, legal edn. chair 2004—05, chair-elect 2005—06, chair 2006—, labor and employment law sects. 2007—). Business E-Mail: csasss@sasslawfirm.com.

SASS, DAWN MARIE, state treasurer; b. Milw., 1959; d. Richard and Patricia S. BA in Hist. & Polit. Sci., Univ. Wis., 1994. Probation officer to custody placement specialist Milw. Juvenile Detention Ctr.; child welfare worker Milw. County; office asst. III Wis. Parks Dept.; sales assoc. Boston Store, 2001—07; pharmacy tech. St. Luke's Hosp., 2004—07; former treas. Wis. Electrical Contractors' Corp.; state treas. State of Wis., 2007—. Mem.: Am. Fedn. State, County, Mcpl. Employees, The Nature Conservancy, World Wildlife Fund, Milw. County Zoological Soc. Democrat. Cath. Office: State Treas One S Pinckney St Ste 550 PO Box 7871 Madison WI 53707-7871 Office Phone: 608-266-1714. Office Fax: 608-266-2647. Business E-Mail: treasury@ost.state.wi.us.*

SASS, MARY MARTHA, freelance writer, artist; b. Chgo. d. George James and Arbutus Laraine (Schwartz) Harles; m. Roger Edward Sass, June 29, 1968. BS in Edn., U. Ill., 1965; MA in Guidance and Counseling, Northeastern Ill. U., 1977. Cert. secondary educator, guidance counselor, Ill. Tchr. English Kelvyn Park High Sch., Chgo., 1965-83; freelance writer, Skokie, Ill., 1983—. Lectr. North Suburban Libr. Sys., Chgo., 1992; author radio scripts Chgo. Pub. Libr. Broadcasting Sys.; author short stories, essays and articles; newsletter columnist; illustrator short stories and essays. Author (and illustrator): The Katy Ornament, 2002; editor: Odd Couple of the Constitution, 2005; illustrator One Smart Chipmunk!, 2007; exhibitions include Oakton C.C., 1993, All Chgo. Juried Art Show Skokie Pub. Libr., 1993, 1994, 1995, 1996, 1997 (hon. mention), 1998, 1999, 2000, 2001, Skokie Art Guild Show, 2002—08, Woman's Club Evanston Ann. Art Exhibit, 1994, 1995, 1996, 1997, 1998, 1999, 2000, Skokie Hist. Soc., 1993, 1994 (hon. mention), 1995, 1996, 1997, 1998, 1999, 2000 (First prize, 2000), 2001, 2002, 2003 (First prize), Allstate Ins., 1995, 1996, 1997, Blue Moon Art Gallery, 1999, Devonshire Cultural Ctr., 2002, Morton Grove Pub. Libr., 2002, 2004, Lincolnwood Village Hall Gallery, 2005, Emily Oaks Nature Ctr, 2006, 2007, 2008—09, South Shore Cultural Ctr., 2006, Shore Early Intervention Ctr., 2006—07, Chgo. Cultural Ctr., 2007, Represented in permanent collections Artists Archives, Chgo. Pub. Libr. Vol. Emily Oaks Nature Ctr. Skokie Park Dist., Ill.; mem. Art Guild Bd.; mem charity auctions Children's Meml. Hosp., Pediatric AIDS Unit, Chgo., 2000, Toylend, Chgo., 2004. Recipient Radio Script hon. mention award Take One Nat. Radio Theatre Competition, 1994, Women in Cable award for cable TV documentary, Memoir 2d pl. award Nat. League Am. Pen Women, 2006, Creative Non-fiction 2d pl. award Nat. League Am. Pen Women, 2006, Ill. Assn. Pk. Dist. Cmty. Svc. award, 2007, Art Guild Svc. award, 2007; Nat. Pub. Radio scholar, 1984. Mem. Chgo. Artist's Coalition, Nat. Pks. and Conservation Assn., Greenpeace, Nature Conservancy, Pk. Activist Network, Sr. Artists' Network, Ocean Conservancy, World Wildlife Fund. Avocations: classical guitar, sculpting, cable television writing and production, gardening. Office Phone: 847-674-7118. Personal E-mail: maryhsass@aol.com.

SASS, NEIL LESLIE, toxicologist; b. Balt., Oct. 24, 1944; s. Samuel and Blanche (Radoon) S.; m. Anita Paige Hoswell, June 29, 1984. BS, Wake Forest Coll., 1966; MS, W.Va. U., 1969, PhD, 1971; MS, Johns Hopkins U., 1984. Commd. officer USPHS, 1966, advanced through grades to capt., 1988, comdr. Preventive Medicine unit, 1989; served as rsch. toxicologist med. labs. U.S. Army, Edgewood Arsenal, Md., 1971-74; chief clin. investigations William Beaumont Army Med. Ctr., El Paso, Tex., 1974-77; toxicologist Bur. of Foods FDA, Washington, 1977-82; spl. asst. to dir. Ctr. for Food Safety and Applied Nutrition, FDA, Washington, 1982-99; dir. divsn. toxicological rsch. Ctr. for Food Safety and Applied Nutrition, Washington, 1996-99; chief toxicologist, state counterterrorism coord., chem. lab. dir. Ala. Dept. Pub. Health, Montgomery, 1999—. Jewish. Office: Ala Dept Pub Health The RSA Tower 201 Monroe St Ste 1450 Montgomery AL 36104-3735 Home: 2160 Woodley Rd Montgomery AL 36111-1013 Home Phone: 334-832-2322; Office Phone: 334-206-5973. Business E-Mail: nsass@adph.state.al.us.

SASS, RIVKAH K., library director; d. Richard and Betty Henricksen; m. Abe J. Sass; children: Ilana E., Gabriel S.(dec.). BA in Polit. Sci., Sonoma State Coll., Rohnert Park, Calif., 1974; MLS, U. Wash., Seattle, 1978. Pub. svcs. libr. Spokane County and Spokane Pub. Librs., 1978—83; cmty. libr. coord. Chehalis br. Timberland Regional Libr., Tumwater, Wash., 1983—89; continuing edn. cons. Wash. State Libr., 1989—93; dep. state libr. Md. State Libr., 1994—96; sr. product mgr. Thomson Corp., 1996—99; info. svcs. coord. Multnomah County Libr., Portland, Oreg., 1999—2003; exec. dir. Omaha Pub. Libr., 2003—. Recipient Spirit of Literacy award, Literacy Ctr. of Midlands, 2006; named Libr. of Yr., Libr. Jour., 2006; named one of Movers and Shakers, 2002. Mem.: ALA, Nebr. Libr. Assn., Mountain Plains Libr. Assn., Jane Austen Soc. N.Am., Rotary Internat. Office: Omaha Pub Libr PO Box 241125 Omaha NE 68124 Office Phone: 402-444-4844. E-mail: rsass@omahapubliclibrary.org.

SASSAROLI, ANGELO, science educator, researcher; married; 1 child, Donatello. DSc, U. Electro-Comm., Tokyo, 2002. Rsch. assoc. Tufts U., Medford, Mass., 2002—06, rsch. asst. prof., 2007—. Office: Tufts Univ 4 Colby St Medford MA 02155 Business E-Mail: angelo.sassaroli@tufts.edu.

SASSE, BENJAMIN ERIC, public policy educator, former federal agency administrator; b. Nebr., Feb. 22, 1972; s. Gary and Jean Sasse; m. Melissa McLeod; children: Elizabeth, Katherine. AB, Harvard U., Cambridge, Mass., 1994; MA in Liberal Arts, St. John's Coll.; PhD in Am. History, Yale U., New Haven. Chief staff Office Legal Policy US Dept. Justice, 2003—05; chief staff to Rep. Jeff Fortenberry US Congress; asst. prof. pub. affairs Lyndon B. Johnson Sch. Pub. Affairs, U. Tex., Austin; counselor to sec. US Dept. Health & Human Svcs., asst. sec. for planning & evaluation, 2007—09. Co-editor: Here We Stand!: A Call From Confessing Evangelicals For A Modern Reformation, 1996. Recipient Theron Rockwell Field Prize, George Washington Egleston Prize. Republican. Office: LBJ School Public Affairs U Texas PO Box Y Austin TX 78713 Office Phone: 202-690-7858, 512-471-3033. E-mail: sasse@mail.utexas.edu.*

SASSE, MARY HAWLEY, retired language educator, editor; b. Argyle, Wis., July 9, 1932; d. Homer Garth and Grace Rose Hawley; m. Edward Benjamin Sasse, Dec. 29, 1951 (dec. Feb. 1994); children: Wendy Jo, Julie Rae, Sara Lee, Cindy Lu. BS, U. Wis., 1965, MS, 1967; PhD, So. Ill. U., 1979. Tchr. McFarland (Wis.) Cmty. Schs., 1965-66, Carbondale (Ill.) Cmty. H.S., 1967-92; chair English dept., 1980-85; instr. John A. Logan Coll., Carterville, Ill., 1995; prof. So. Ill. U., Carbondale, 1996-99; ret., 1999. Cons. Scott Foresman Pub. Co., Glenview, Ill., 1992-94, Ill. State Bd. Edn., Springfield, 1976, 83, 91; leader workshops, presenter Nat. Coun. Tchrs. Eng., Ill. Assn. Tchrs. English confs., 1975—; invited spkr. in field. Author: Novel Guide for House Made of Dawn, 1996; editor, author Ill. English Bull., 1981—; co-author: Reader, Text and Context: Literature in the Classroom, 1988; editor: Therefore: Mayme Kratz, 2002, Postmodern Messenger: Jaune-Quick-to-See, 2004, Dan Collins: Return to the Garden, 2003, Terence LaNoue: Layers Concealed and Revealed, 2003, Paint on Metal: Modern and Contemporary Explorations and Discoveries, 2005; editl. asst. Trouble in Paradise: Examining Discord between Nature and Society, 2009. Mem. NCTE (exec. coun. 1990-92), Assn. for Study of Am. Indian lits., Soc. for Study of Multi-Ethnic Lits. of the U.S., So. Ill. Assn. Tchrs. of English (pres. 1974-75), Ill. Assn. Tchrs. English (life, pres. 1980-81, publs. com., minority affairs com.). Avocations: reading, writing, travel. Home: 2004 W Meadow Ln Carbondale IL 62901-2007 Office Phone: 618-457-7249. E-mail: marysasse@aol.com.

SASSER, JAMES RALPH, former United States Senator from Tennessee; b. Memphis, Sept. 30, 1936; s. Joseph Ralph and Mary Nell (Gray) S.; m. Mary Gorman, Aug. 18, 1962; children: Gray, Elizabeth. Student, U. Tenn., 1954-55; BA, Vanderbilt U., 1958, LLB, 1961. Bar: Tenn. 1961. Ptnr. Goodpasture, Carpenter, Woods & Sasser, Nashville, 1961-76; US Senator from Tenn., 1977-1994; fellow, Inst. of Politics Harvard U., 1995; US amb. to China US Dept. State, Beijing, 1996-99; J.B. & Maurice Shapiro vis. prof. Elliot Sch. Internat. Rels., George Washington Univ., 2000; foreign policy advisor to vice-pres. Gore Gore 2000, Washington, 2000; sr adv. FedEx Corp.; sr. counselor APCO Worldwide. Trustee Nat. Geographic Soc. Chmn. Tenn. State Dem. Exec. Com., 1973-76; so. vice chmn. Assn. Dem. State Chmn., 1975-76. Served with USMCR, 1958-65. Mem. Council on Fgn. Rels., Com. on US-China Rels. (vice-chmn.), ABA, NCCJ (dir. Nashville chpt.), UN Assn.(past pres.), Nashville Com. Fgn. Relations, Am. Judicature Soc. Democrat. Methodist.

SASSER, ROBERT, retail executive; Various positions to sr. v.p. Roses Stores, Inc., sr. v.p. merchandise and mktg., 1997—99; v.p., gen. merchandise mgr. Michaels Stores, Inc., 1994—96; sr. v.p., COO Dollar Tree Stores, Inc., Chesapeake, Va., 1999—2004, pres., COO, 2001—04, pres., CEO, 2004—. Office: Dollar Tree Stores Inc 500 Volvo Pkwy Chesapeake VA 23320

SASSI, BRIAN A., health insurance company executive; BA, Calif. State U., LA. Mgmt. Transamerica Occidental Life Insurance Co., Provident Life and Accident Insurance Co.; v.p. ops. Blue Cross of Wash./Alaska; joined Blue Cross of Calif., 1989, gen. mgr. key large group accounts, v.p. ops. and strategic initiatives, gen. mgr. small group accounts west region, pres., CEO BC Life & Health affiliate; pres., CEO Consumer Bus. Unit, exec. v.p. WellPoint, Inc., Indpls., 2008—. Bd. dirs. Calif. C. of C.; mem. Calif. Bus. Roundtable, Calif. Assn. Health Plans. Fellow: Life Mgmt. Inst. Office: WellPoint, Inc 120 Monument Cir Indianapolis IN 46204*

SASSO, JOHN, advertising and public strategies executive; BA, Boston U., 1970. Chief of staff Gov. Michael Dukakis, Mass., 1983—87; sr. v.p. Hill, Holliday, Connors, Cosmopulos, Inc., Advt., Boston, 1988—90; pres. Advanced Strategies, 1990—. Mgr. Geraldine Ferarro v.p. campaign, 1984; advisor Dukakis pres. campaign, 1988; bd. dirs. Fannie Mae Found., 1993—; gen. election mgr. of the DNC then sr. advisor Kerry-Edwards pres. campaign, 2004—. Bd. dirs. Heller Sch. Social Policy at Brandeis U.*

SASSO, RUTH MARYANN, retired educator; b. Bridgeport, Conn., Dec. 9, 1928; d. Angelo Nicholas and Mildred Rita (Hayes) Sasso BS in Edn., St. Joseph Coll., 1957, MA, 1968. Tchr. Catholic Schs. of Conn., 1950-68; founder, dir. Berkeley Primary Sch., Waterbury, Conn., 1969-71; from assoc. prof. to prof. early childhood edn., coord. child care program Naugatuck Valley CC, Waterbury, 1971—99, dir. early childhood edn., coord. child care program, 1971—99, founder, dir. early childhood child devel. ctr., 1976—99. Mem. adv. council on early childhood edn. Conn. Dept. Edn.; cons. in field; adv. council Waterbury YMCA Day Care Ctr., 1980—; mem. adv. com. to Magnet Sch., Waterbury, Infant/Toddler Day Care, Wilson Sch., Waterbury; mem. adv. com. home cons. high sch. curriculum Conn. State Dept. Edn. Author: Field Placement Manual for Student Teachers, 1971, rev., 1980; Observation Manual in Early Childhood Edn., 1979. Vol. Maple Hill Sch. Naugatuck, Ct., 2001-; bd. dirs. Child Care Ctr. Abused Children, Waterbury, 1971—; pres. St. Francis Sch. Bd., Naugatuck, 1989; chair Prek com. Office of Cath. Schs., Archdiocese of Hartford, Conn., 1990-91, mem. Office of Cath. Schs., 1992—. Recipient Service award Head Start Policy Com., Danbury, Conn., 1973, YWCA Women in Leadership award, 1992, Twenty Yr. Appreciation award Naugatuck C.C., 1992. Mem. Nat. Assn. Edn. Young Children (validator), Soc. Nutrition Edn., Action Children's TV, Nat. Council Campus Child Care Centers. Democrat. Roman Catholic. Home and Office: 93 Barn Finch Cir Naugatuck CT 06770-4879 E-mail: ruth.sasso@comcast.net.

SASSON, COMILLA, medical researcher; b. Abu Dhabi, United Arab Emirates, Jan. 26, 1979; d. Satwant Kaur and Jagmohan Singh Sasson. MD, U. Ill., Chgo., 2003; MS, U. Mich., Ann Arbor, 2009. Diplomate Am. Bd. Emergency Medicine, 2007. Pres. Emergency Medicine Residents' Assn., Dallas, 2003—06; Robert Wood Johnson clin. scholar U. Mich., 2007—. Mem.: Am. Coll. Emergency Physicians. Achievements include research in cardiac arrest & effective utilization of resources. Office: Univ Mich 1150 W Med Ctr Dr Ann Arbor MI 48109

SASSOON, CATHERINE, pulmonologist, educator; d. Tan and Sie; m. Harry Sassoon; 1 child, Rosette. MD, Gadjah Mada Faculty Medicine, Yogyakarta, Indonesia. Diplomate critical care medicine Am. Bd. Internal Medicine, pulmonary medicine Am. Bd. Internal Medicine, sleep medicine Am. Bd. Internal Medicine. Prof. medicine U. Calif., Irvine, 2000—; chief pulmonary & critical care medicine VA Long Beach Healthcare Sys., Calif., 2009—. Editl. bd. mem. Am. Jour. Respiratory and Critical Care Medicine. Contbr. articles to profl. jours. Recipient VA Merit Rev. award, Med. Rsch., Dept. Veterans Affairs. Mem.: Am. Physiol. Soc., Am. Acad. Sleep Medicine, Soc. Critical Care Medicine, Am. Coll. Chest Physicians, Am. Thoracic Soc. Achievements include research in mechanisms of diaphragmatic dysfunction in critical-illness myopathy. Office: VA Long Beach Healthcare Sys-UC Irvine 5901 E 7th St Long Beach CA 90822

SASTRY, SOSALE SHANKARA, electrical engineer, computer scientist, dean, educator; B, Indian Inst. Tech., Bombay, 1977; MS, U. Calif., Berkeley, 1979, MA in Math., 1980, PhD, 1981; MA (hon.), Harvard U., 1994. Asst. prof. MIT, 1980—82, U. Calif., Berkeley, 1983—84, assoc. prof., 1984—88, prof., 1988—, dir. Electronics Rsch. Lab., 1996—99, chmn. dept. elec. engring. and computer scis., 2001—04, dir. Ctr. Info. Tech. Rsch. in Interest of Soc., 2005—, dean, Coll. Engring., 2007—; dir. info. tech. office DARPA, 1999—2001. Vis. fellow Australian Nat. U., 1985; prof. U. Rome, 1990, 91, U. Pisa, 1995, 98; vis. Vinton Hayes prof. MIT, 1992; Gordon McKay prof. Harvard U., 1994; mem. Air Force Sci. Adv. Bd., 2002—; bd. mem. Fedn. Am. Scientists, 2002—; mem. bd. trustees Internat. Computer Sci. Inst., Berkeley, 2003—, bd. chmn., 2004—. Co-author: (books) A Mathematical Introduction to Robotic Manipulation, 1994, An Invitation to 3-D Vision From Images to Models; co-editor: Hybrid Systems II: Lecture Notes in Computer Science, 1995, Hybrid Systems IV: Lecture Notes in Computer Science, 1997, Hybrid Systems: Computation and Control, 1998, Essays in Mathematical Robotics, 1998; author: Nonlinear Systems: Analysis, Stability, and Control, 1999; co-author: over 250 technical papers. Recipient Gold medal, Pres. India, 1977, Presdl. Young Investigator award, NSF, 1985, David Marr prize, Internat. Conf. in Computer Vision, 1999, Disting. Alumnus award, Indian Inst. Tech., 1999, Ragazzini award, Am. Control Coun., 2005; Faculty Devel. grant, IBM, 1983. Fellow: IEEE, Am. Acad. Arts & Sciences; mem.: NAE. Office: U Calif Deans Office 320 McLaughlin Hall # 1700 Berkeley CA 94720

SATAN, MIROSLAV, professional hockey player; b. Topolcany, Slovakia, Oct. 22, 1974; m. Ingrid Satan. Left wing Edmonton Oilers, 1995—97, Buffalo Sabres, 1997—2005, NY Islanders, 2005—08, Pitts. Penguins, 2008—. Mem. Slovakian Nat. Team, Olympic Games, Lillehammer, Norway, 1994, Slovakian Nat. Team, World Championships, 1996; player NHL All-Star Game, 2000, 03. Achievements include being a member of Stanley Cup Champion Pittsburgh Penguins, 2009. Office: Pittsburgh Penguins 66 Mario Lemieux Pl Pittsburgh PA 15219*

SATCHER, DARAKA E. (DOK), legislative staff member; b. LA, Sept. 13, 1974; BA, Morehouse Coll, Atlanta, 1996; JD, Emory U., Decatur, Ga., 1999. Legis. asst. for Rep. John Spratt, US House of Reps., Washington, 2000—01; legis. asst. to Senator Debbie Stabenow, US Senate, 2002—03; legis. dir. for Rep. Harold Ford, US House of Reps., 2005—07; chief of staff Rep. Hank Johnson, US House of Reps., 2007—. Office: Office of Congressman Hank Johnson 1133 Longworth House Office Bldg Washington DC 20515 Office Phone: 202-225-1605. Business E-Mail: daraka.satcher@mail.house.gov.*

SATCHER, DAVID, public health service officer, former Surgeon General of the United States; b. Anniston, Ala., Mar. 2, 1941; s. Wilmer and Anna Satcher; m. Nola Satcher; children: Gretchen, David, Daraka, Daryl. BS, Morehouse Coll., 1963; MD, PhD, Case Western Reserve U., 1970; recipient of many honorary degrees and numerous disting. honors. Resident and fellow Strong Mem. Hosp., U. Rochester, UCLA, and King Drew; former faculty UCLA Sch. Medicine and Pub. Health; faculty, chair dept. family medicine King-Drew Med. Ctr., LA, interim dean, 1977—79; dir. King-Drew Sickle Cell Rsch. Ctr.; prof., chmn. dept. cmty. and family medicine Morehouse Sch. Medicine, Atlanta, 1979—82; pres. Meharry Med. Coll., Nashville, 1982—93; dir. Ctrs. for Disease Control and Prevention, Atlanta, 1993—98; adminstr. Agy. for Toxic Substances and Disease Registry, 1993—98; surgeon gen. US Dept. Health & Human Services, Washington, 1998—2002, asst. sec. health, 1998—2001; sr. vis. fellow Kaiser Family Found., Washington, 2002—; dir. Nat. Ctr. for Primary Care at Morehouse Sch. Medicine, Atlanta, 2002—, also interim pres., 2005—. Apptd. mem. Coun. of Grad. Med. Edn., 1986, chmn.; former Robert Wood Johnson Clin. Scholar; former Macy Faculty Fellow; bd. dir. MetLife Inc., 2007—, Jonhson & Jonhson, 2002. Recipient Watts Grassroots award for cmty. leadership, 1979, Nat. Conf. Christians and Jews awards, 1985, Black Achievment award, Ebony Mag., 1994, Brewslow award in pub. health, 1995, Dr. Nathan B. Davis award, AMA, 1996, Lifetime Achievement award, NY Acad. Medicine, 1997, Bennie Mays Trailblazer award, Nat. Found. for Infectious Diseases, Jimmy and Roslyn Carter award, Discovery Health Channel Med. Honors, 2004; named Nashvillian of Yr., 1992. Fellow: Am. Acad. of Family Physicians; mem.: Inst. Medicine NAS, Alpha Omega Alpha, Phi Beta Kappa. Focuses on promoting healthly lifestyles and ending disparities in health; as director of the CDC, he raised childhood immunization rates to 78% in 1996 from 55% in 1992. Office: Nat Ctr for Primary Care at Morehouse Sch Medicine 720 Westview Dr SW Atlanta GA 30310 Office Fax: 404-756-5767.*

SATEIA, MICHAEL JOHN, psychiatrist, educator; MD, Duke U. Med. Sch., Durham, NC, 1974. Diplomate in psychiatry Am. Bd. of Psychiatry and Neurology, 1980, in sleep medicine 2008. Chief, sect. sleep medicine Dartmouth Med. Sch., Lebanon, NH, 1986—2008, prof. psychiatry, 2002—. Pres. Am. Acad. Sleep Medicine, Westchester, Ill., 2004—05. Editor: (textbook) Sleep Medicine. Fellow: Am. Acad. Sleep Medicine. Office: Sleep Disorders Ctr One Med Ctr Dr Lebanon NH 03756

SATHER, GLEN CAMERON, professional sports team executive, former professional hockey coach and player; b. High River, Alta., Can., Sept. 2, 1943; m. Ann Sather; children: Justin, Shanon. Left wing Boston Bruins, 1967—69, Pitts. Penguins, 1969—71, NY Rangers, 1971—73, St. Louis Blues, 1973—74, Montreal Canadiens, 1974—75, Minn. North Stars, 1975—76; head coach Edmonton Oilers, 1977—89, gen. mgr., 1981—2000, pres., 1982—2000, alt. gov., 1990—2000; pres., gen. mgr. NY Rangers, 2000—, head coach, 2003—04. Gen. mgr., head coach Team Canada, World Cup of Hockey, 1996. Recipient Jack Adams Award, NHL, 1986. Achievements include being the head coach of Stanley Cup Champion Edmonton Oilers, 1984, 1985, 1987, 1988; being inducted into the Hockey Hall of Fame, 1997. Office: NY Rangers 2 Pennsylvania Plaza New York NY 10121

SATHER, JOHN HENRY, biologist, educator, dean; b. Presho, SD, July 12, 1921; s. Anton and Anna (Imster) S.; m. Shirley M. Johnson, Aug. 21, 1948; children: Kristi, Signe, Ingrid. BS, U. Nebr., 1943, PhD, 1952; MA, U. Mo., 1948. Research biologist Nebr. Game, Forestation and Parks Commn., Lincoln, 1948-55; prof. biol. scis. Western Ill. U., Macomb, 1955—; dean Western Ill. U. (Grad. Sch.), 1964-79, emeritus grad. dean, 1979—. Tech. advisor on nat. wetland inventory, 1975-87, mem. Nat. Wetlands Tech. Coun., 1976—; mem. environ. adv. bd. U.S. Army Chief Engrs., 1978-82; pres. Central States Univs. Inc., 1978-79; leader U.S. team to establish hydrobiol. research sta., India, 1981; mem. N.Am. Riparian Coun., 1984—; wetlands cons. U.S. EPA, 1988—, Bombay Nat. History Soc., 1988—, USSR, 1991. Edward K. Love fellow, 1946-48; recipient Wildlife Soc. Spl. Recognition award, 1987, Gaylord Donnelley-Nature of Ill. Found. award, 1994. Mem. AAAS, Ecol. Soc. Am., Explorers Club, Sigma Xi. Achievements include coordinating Fed. effort to develop a wetland value assessment methodology. Avocation: research on life history and ecology of Great Plains muskrat in Nebr., wetland ecosystems, life history and ecology studies of ring-necked pheasant in Nebr., radio-telemetry studies of movements of white-tailed deer and muskrats, survey of effects of water level fluctuations of Great Lakes upon wildlife populations, wetland values. Home: 747 E Park Center Blvd Apt 104 Boise ID 83706-6508 Home Phone: 208-859-1754.

SATHY, ANUP, lawyer; BS with highest honors, U. Ill., 1992; JD cum laude, Northwestern U., 1995. Bar: Ill. 1995, US Dist. Ct. (no. dist. Ill.), US Bankruptcy Ct. (no. Ill., Del., so. NY, ea. La., Md., so. Ohio, so. Tex.). Ptnr. Kirkland & Ellis, Chgo. Contbg. editor: ABI Jour.; asst. editor: Norton Bankruptcy Law & Practice; contbr. articles in law jours. Office: Kirkland & Ellis 200 E Randolph Dr Chicago IL 60601 Office Phone: 312-861-2046. Office Fax: 312-861-2200. E-mail: asathy@kirkland.com.

SATHYAMOORTHY, MUTHUKRISHNAN, engineering educator, associate provost; b. Sathanur, Tamil Nadu, India, Feb. 21, 1946; s. Kuppusamy and Visalakshi Muthukrishnan; m. Chitra Subbiah, May 26, 1971; children: Mohanakrishnan, Kumaran. B in Civil Engring., U. Madras, India, 1967; M in Engring. Mechanics, Indian Inst. of Tech., Madras, India, 1969, PhD in Aero. Engring., 1973. Lectr. Indian Inst. of Tech., Madras, India, 1969-74; rsch. fellow U. Birmingham, Eng., 1974-76; asst. prof. Clarkson U., Potsdam, NY, 1979-82, assoc. prof., 1982-92, assoc. prof., exec. officer, 1992-94, prof., exec. officer, 1994-97, prof., chair, 1997-2001; dean engring. W.Va. U. Inst. Tech., 2001—06; assoc. provost U. Tex., Tyler, 2006—. Vis. rsch. faculty U. Calgary, Can., 1977-79. Contbn. author: Handbook of Civil Engineering Practice, 1988; editor: Material Nonlinearity in Vibrations, 1985; author: Nonlinear Analysis of Structures, 1998. Recipient Appreciation cert. U.S. Army, 1990, Outstanding Advisor award Clarkson U., 1993, Tau Beta Pi Faculty award, 1997, Disting. Tchg. award Clarkson Univ., 2001. Fellow ASME (mem. nat. student sect. com. 1992-94, mem. gen. awards com. 1994-99, Nat. Faculty Advisor award 1993, Dedicated Svc. award 1999); AIAA (assoc.), Aero. Soc. India. Avocations: overseas travel, camping, photography, fishing. Office: Office Assoc Provost U Tex at Tyler 3900 University Blvd Tyler TX 75799 Home: 13325 White Tail Dr Tyler TX 75707 Office Phone: 903-565-5939. Business E-Mail: msathy@uttyler.edu.

SATHYANARAYANA, SHEELA, pediatrician, educator; BA, Duke U., 1997; MD, U. Southern Calif. Sch. Medicine, 2002; MPH, U. Wash. Sch. Pub. Health, 2007. Resident U. Wash. CHRMC, 2002—05; asst. prof. divsn. gen. pediatrics U. Wash. Office: University of Washington Dept of Pediatrics 1100 Olive Way Ste 500 M/S 8-1 Box 35930 Seattle WA 98101 Office Phone: 206-884-1037. E-mail: sheela.sathyanarayana@seattlechildrens.org.*

SATHYAVAGISWARAN, LAKSHMANAN, pathologist, county official; b. Madras, India, Mar. 17, 1949; MD, Stanley Med. Coll., Madras U., 1971. Intern,anatomical clin. pathology Jewish Hosp. Med. Ctr., Bklyn., 1972—73; resident, forensic pathology Columbia U., St. Luke's Hosp., NY, 1973—77; resident, internal medicine County of LA, 1977—78, dep. med. examiner, 1978—92, chief med. examiner-coroner, 1992—; resident, infectious diseases Bklyn. Cumberland Med. Ctr., NY, 1980—81; fellow, infectious disease Columbia U. Harlem Hosp., NY, 1981—82; fellow UCLA King Drew Med. Ctr., 1982—83; staff mem. LA County, U. Southern Calif. Med. Ctr. Clin. prof., pathology U. Southern Calif. Keck Sch. Medicine, UCLA Geffen Sch. Medicine. Achievements include being the medical examiner during the O.J. Simpson murder trial and testified during the criminal and civil trials; testified in the trials of Dean Carter and Phil Spector; performed the autopsy of the body of Micheal Jackson on June 26, 2009. Office: 623 W Duarte Rd Ste 2 Arcadia CA 91007 Office Phone: 626-574-7587.*

SATIN, JOSEPH, language educator, retired dean; b. Phila., Dec. 16, 1920; s. Reuben Philip and Harriet (Price) Satin; m. Selma Rosen (dec. 1978); children: Mark, Diane; m. Barbara Jeanne Dodson (dec. 1987); m. Terrye Sagan, 1992. BA, Temple U., 1946; AM, Columbia U., 1948, PhD, 1952. Instr. integrated studies W.Va. U., Morgantown, 1952-54; prof. English and Comparative Lit. Moorhead (Minn.) State U., 1954-63; chmn. dept. English and Journalism Midwestern U., Wichita Falls, Tex., 1963-73; dean Sch. Arts and Humanities Calif. State U., Fresno, 1973-89. Mgr.concert series Moorhead State U., 1956—61; mem. nat. bd. con. NEH, Washington, 1979—; dir. London semester Calif. State U., Fresno, 1982—92; dir. Frank Lloyd Wright Auditorium Project. Author: (book) Ideas in Context, 1958, The 1950's: America's "Placid" Decade, 1960, Reading Non-Fiction Prose, 1964, Reading Prose Fiction, 1964, Shakespeare and His Sources, 1966, Reading Literature, 1968, The Humanities Handbook (2 vols), 1969, (poems) The Journey Upward, 1999, Poems on the Internet (www.Poetry.com), 2000; editor: (book) Frank Lloyd Wright-Letters to Apprentices, 1982, Letters to Architects, 1984, Letters to Clients, 1986, Treasures of Taliesin, 1985, The Guggenheim Correspondence, 1986, Frank Lloyd Wright: His Living Voice, 1987, Frank Lloyd Wright, The Crowning Decade, 1989; translator: Federico Fellini, Comments on Film, 1987; contbr. Encyclopedia Int Educ, 1978; dir: Univ Press, Calif State Univ, 1982—92. With US Army, 1943—46, ETO. Named Nat Grand Prize Winner, Nat Library Poetry N Am Ann Poetry Contest, 1998. Jewish. Avocations: creative writing, music. Home: 65 Maywood Dr San Francisco CA 94127-2007 E-mail: tewilder@juno.com.

SATINE, BARRY ROY, lawyer; b. NYC, July 25, 1951; s. Norman S. and Fay (Mekles) S.; m. Janice Bea Halfond, Aug. 4, 1974; children: David, Leah. BA, CCNY, 1972; JD, George Washington U., 1975. Bar: N.Y. 1976, D.C. 1977, U.S. Dist. Ct. (so. dist.) N.Y. 1978, U.S. Supreme Ct. 1979, U.S. Dist. Ct. (ea. dist.) N.Y. 1982, U.S. Ct. Appeals (2d cir.) 1989. Trial atty. U.S. Civil Svc. Commn., Washington, 1975—78; atty. AT&T, NYC, 1978—81, N.Y. Tel. Co., NYC, 1981—82; mem. assoc. Surrey & Morse, NYC, 1982—84, ptnr., 1985, Jones Day, 1986—. Mem.: Assn. of Bar of City of N.Y. Office: Jones Day 222 East 41st St New York NY 10017 Office Phone: 212-326-3904. Business E-Mail: barryrsatine@jonesday.com.

SATINSKY, BARNETT, lawyer; b. Phila., June 17, 1947; s. Alex and Florence (Talsky) S.; m. Fredda Andrea Wagner, June 17, 1973; children: Meagen, Sara Beth, Jonathan. AB, Brown U., 1969; JD, Villanova U., 1972. Bar: Pa. 1972, U.S. Dist. Ct. (ea. dist) Pa. 1975, U.S. Dist. Ct. (mid. dist.) Pa. 1975, U.S. Ct. Appeals (3d cir.) 1981. Law clk. Phila. Ct. Common Pleas, 1972-73; dep. atty. gen. Pa. Dept. Justice, Harrisburg, 1973-75; 1st asst. counsel Pa. Pub. Utility Commn., Harrisburg, 1975-77, chief counsel, 1977; assoc. Fox, Rothschild, O'Brien & Frankel, LLP, Phila., 1978-81; ptnr. Fox Rothschild LLP, Phila., 1981—. Children Svcs. Rev. com., United Way Southeast Pa., 1984-86; bd. dirs. ACLU, Harrisburg, 1973-74, Voyage House, Inc., 1994-96. Mem. ABA (pub. utility, labor and employment law sects., employee benefits com. 1984—), Pa. Bar Assn. (labor rels., pub. utility law sects. 1980—, pub. utility law com., governing coun. 1991-93), Phila. Bar Assn. (labor law com. 1980—, chmn. pub. utility law com. 1988-91), Nat. Assn. Coll. and Univ. Attys., Nat. Assn. Regulatory Commrs. (staff subcom. law 1977), Soc. for Human Resource Mgmt., Louis D. Brandeis Law Soc. Democrat. Jewish. Office: Fox Rothschild LLP 2000 Market St Philadelphia PA 19103-3291 Office Phone: 215-299-2088. Business E-Mail: bsatinsky@foxrothschild.com.

SATLIN, LISA M., pediatrician, educator; BA, Mt. Holyoke Coll., South Hadley, Mass., 1975; MD, Columbia U., NYC, 1979. Intern and resident Babies Hosp. Columbia U., NYC, 1979—82; prof. pediat. and medicine, chief divsn. pediatric nephrology Mt. Sinai Sch. Medicine, NYC, 1997—. Fellow in pediat. nephrology Albert Einstein Coll. Medicine, 1982—86. Grantee, NIH, 1986—. Mem.: Am. Pediatric Soc., Soc. Pediatric Rsch., Am. Soc. Pediatric Nephrology (councilor 2003—07), Am. Soc. Nephrology (pres. 2008—), AAP. Achievements include research in ontogeny and mechanoregulation of epithelial ion transport in the distal nephron. Office: Mt Sinai Sch Medicine One Gustave L Levy Pl New York NY 10029

SATO, EUNICE NODA, former mayor, consultant; b. Livingston, Calif., June 8, 1921; d. Bunsaku and Sawa (Maeda) Noda; m. Thomas Takashi Sato, Dec. 9, 1950; children: Charlotte Patricia, Daniel Ryuichi and Douglas Ryuji (twins). AA, Modesto Jr. Coll., 1941; BA, U. No. Colo., 1944; MA, Columbia U., 1948. Pub. sch. tchr. Mastodon Twp. Schs., Alpha, Mich., 1944-47; ednl. missionary Reformed Ch. Am., Yokohama, Japan, 1948-51; coun. mem. City of Long Beach, Calif., 1975-86; mayor, 1980-82. Sec. corp. bd. LA County Health Sys. Agy., 1978-79. Monthly contbr. articles to 2 neighborhood papers, 1975-86. Bd. dirs. Long Beach chpt. ARC, 1975-00; mem. exec. com. ARC, 1978-91, 93-99, past pres. and v.p., mem. Calif. state svc. coun., 1995-01; bd. dirs. Goodwill Industries, 1978-82; trustee St. Mary's Bauer Med. Ctr., 1977—; pres. Industry Edn. Coun., Long Beach, 1984-86, mem. exec. bd., 1984-2007; bd. dirs. Industry Edn. Coun. of Calif.; treas. So. Calif. Consortium of I.E.C., 1984-86, pres., 1988-89; mem. State Adv. Group on Juvenile Justice and Delinquency Prevention, 1983-91, Calif. Coun. Criminal Justice, 1983-92; legis. com. Girl Scout coun. Calif., 1986-92, chair, 1991-92; bd. dirs. Long Beach coun. Girl Scouts U.S., 1981-92; with Region III United Way, 1974-88; mem. Asian Pacific adv. com. Calif. Dept. Rehab., 1985-87, recreation commn. City of Long Beach, 1985-86, pub. safety policy com. League Calif. Cities, 1981-86; cmty. econ. and housing devel. com. So. Calif. Assn. Govts., 1976-86; Calif. Task Force to Promote Self-Esteem and Personal and Social Responsibility, 1987-90; Long Beach chpt. pres. NCCJ, 1987-88; pres. Internat. Cmty. Coun., 1986-87, bd. dirs. 1986-01; pres. Japanese Am. Reps., 1987, 88, exec. bd. mem. 1987-03, 04-07; presdl. appointee Nat. Adv. Coun. Ednl. Rsch. and Improvement, 1991-94; pres. Aux. to Sch. Theology, Claremont, 1990-91, exec. bd. 1989-91; nat. selective svc. sys. local bd. 138, 1990-01; SCA Edison Co. Equal Opportunity adv. coun., 1990-94; chair selection com. Leadership Long Beach, 1990-91, sec. exec. bd., 1991-92, bd. govs. 2003—; chair adv. bd. AIESEC, 1990-92; chmn. Long Beach Area Rep. Party, 1990-92; asst. sec. cen. com., L.A, 1990-92; sec.-gen. coun. on fin. and adminstrn. United Meth. Ch., 1992-00; appointed by Gov. to commn. on tchr. credentialing State Calif., 1994; LA coun. svc. coun. ARC, 1995-99; chair adminstrv. bd. Leisure World Cmty. Ch., 1996-02; rep. to South Coast Ecumenical Coun., 1993-02, chair pastor parish rels. com., 2000; chair Parents Day Festival com. Greater LA County, 1996-00; with Blue Ribbon com. Effective Parenting in Long Beach, 1997-99; mem. adult and elder care adv. com. Long Beach City Coll., Calif., 2004-07; caregiver Grace First Presbyn. Ch., 2005—, vol., Ch. Jesus Christ of Latter Day Saints, Long Beach State. Recipient Outstanding Svc. award Long Beach Coord. Coun., 1969, Mother of Yr. award Silverado United Meth. Ch., 1973, Hon. Svc. award Calif. PTA, 1963, Continuing Svc. award, 1974, Hon. Life Membership award Nat. PTA, 1974, Outstanding Laywoman of Yr. award Long Beach Area Coun. Chs., 1976, Woman of Yr. award State Women's Coun.-C. of C., 1979, Long Beach Internat. Bus. and Profl. Women's Club, Nat. Merit award DAR, 1982, Citizen of Yr. award Los Altos YMCA, 1982, Calif. Cmty. Pool Handicapped award, 1982, Outstanding Citizen award Torch Club of Long Beach, 1983, W. Odie Wright award Industry Edn. Coun., 1990, Humanitarian award NCCJ, 1992, Vol. of Yr. award ARC, 1995, 1st Life Membership award Long Beach chpt. UN Assn., Kunsho award Order of Sacred Treasure, Gold Rays with rosette from Japanese Govt., 1996, Sr. Vol. of Yr. Long Beach C.C., 1999, Al Taucher Rep. of Yr. award, 2001, Excellence in Leadership award Leadership Long Beach, 2004; Ann. Hall of Fame honoree Long Beach Century Club, 2006. Mem. Industry Edn. Coun. Long Beach (hon. life), Long Beach C. of C. (Dewey Smith cmty. svc. award), Lions Club (hon. life, Internat. Found. Melvin Jones fellow 2004, Outstanding Contrbn. award 2000), Boys Club of Long Beach Found.(life), Soroptimist Internat. (Woman of Distinction in Econ. and Social Devel. 2001), Alpha Iota. Republican. Presbyterian. Home: Bixby Village 551 Pittsfield Ct Unit 101 Long Beach CA 90803-6355

SATO, GLENN KENJI, lawyer; b. Honolulu, Jan. 6, 1952; s. Nihei and Katherine (Miwa) S.; m. Donna Mae Shiroma, Apr. 4, 1980 (dec. Aug. 1985); m. Nan Sun Oh, Mar. 27, 1987 (dec. Nov. 1997); children: Gavan, Allison, Garrett; m. Sandra K. Kumagai, Nov. 21, 1999. BBA, U. Hawaii, 1975; JD, U. Calif., San Francisco, 1977. Bar: Hawaii 1978, U.S. Dist. Ct. Hawaii, 1978, U.S. Ct. Claims 1990. Assoc. Fujiyama, Duffy & Fujiyama, Honolulu, 1978-80, 83-87, ptnr., 1987-95; stockholder Law Offices of Glenn K. Sato, Honolulu, 1980-82; pres. ISL Svcs., Inc., Honolulu, 1983; ptnr. Sato & Thomas, Honolulu, 1995-98; pvt. practice Honolulu, 1998—. Vice chmn. Pattern Jury Instrn. Com., State of Hawaii, Honolulu, 1993. Treas. Polit. Action Com., Honolulu, 1993. Mem. Platform Assn., Beta Gamma Sigma. Avocations: golf, hunting, target shooting, surfing. Office: 888 Mililiant St PH 1 Honolulu HI 96813-2918

SATO, HIROYUKI, materials engineer, researcher; s. T. and M. Sato. PhD, MB in Engring., Tohoku U., Sendai, Japan, 1990. Rsch. assoc. Tohoku U., Sendai, Miyagi, Japan, 1990—97, lectr., 1997—99; assoc. prof. Hirosaki U., Hirosaki, Aomori, Japan, 1999—. Vis rschr. Tech. U. Hamburg, Germany, 1997—98; vis. prof. U. Erlangen, Germany, 2005, U. Tenn., 2005—06. Mem.: Japan Soc. Mech. Engrs., Iron and Steel Inst. Japan, Japan Inst. Light Metals, Minerals, Metals & Materials Soc., Japan Inst. of Metal. Avocations: radio, travel. Office: Hirosaki University Sci and Tech Intell Mech Bunkyo-3 Aomori Hirosaki 0368561 Japan

SATPATHY, RUBY, cardiologist, researcher; married. MD in Internal Medicine, Creighton U., Omaha, Nebr., 2006. Cert. in medicine Nebr., cardiologist Iowa. Fellow, cardiology Creighton U., 2003—06, 2007—. Contbr. articles to profl. jours. Cmty. activities and health fairs. Personal E-mail: rubydrruby@rediffmail.com.

SATRE, DEREK DAVIES, psychologist, researcher; s. Neal and Jeanne Satre. BA, U. Calif., Berkeley, 1989; MPhil, U. Cambridge, 1990; PhD, U. So. Calif., LA, 2001. Lic. clin. psychologist Calif., 2001. Rschr. Kaiser Permanente Divsn. Rsch., Oakland, 2001—; asst. adj. prof. psychiatry U. Calif., San Francisco, 2004—. Clin. psychologist U. Calif., 2003—. Contbr. scientific papers, chapters to books. Grantee, NIH, 2005; fellow, Nat. Inst. Aging, 1997—2001, Nat. Inst. Drug Abuse, 2001—04, U. Calif., San Francisco, 2001—04. Mem.: APA, Gerontol. Soc. Am. Episcopalian. Avocations: travel, rowing, tennis. Office: U Calif 401 Parnassus Ave Box 0984 San Francisco CA 94143 E-mail: dereks@lppi.ucsf.edu.

SATRE, PHILIP GLEN, casino entertainment executive, lawyer; b. Palo Alto, Calif., Apr. 30, 1949; s. Selmer Kenneth and Georgia June (Sterling) S.; m. Jennifer Patricia Arnold, June 30, 1973; children: Malena Anne, Allison Neal, Jessica Lilly, Peter Sterling. BA, Stanford U., 1971; JD, U. Calif.-Davis, 1975; postgrad. sr. exec. program, MIT, 1982. Bar: Nev. 1975, Calif. 1976. Assoc. Vargas & Bartlett, Reno, 1975-79; v.p., gen. counsel, sec. Harrah's, Reno, 1980-83, sr. v.p., 1983-84; pres. Harrah's East, Atlantic City, 1984; pres., CEO Harrah's Hotels and Casinos, Reno, 1984-91; dir., sr. v.p. Gaming Group The Promus Cos., Inc., Memphis, 1988-91, dir., pres., COO, 1991-94, dir., pres. CEO, 1994-95; pres., CEO Harrah's Entertainment, Inc., Memphis, 1995—97, chmn., pres., CEO, 1997—2005; dir. JDN Realty Co., Memphis, 1999—; chmn. NV Energy Inc., Reno, 2008—. Bd. dirs. Rite Aid Corp., 2005—, Nordstrom, Inc., 2006—. Active The Stanford Athletic Bd., 1996—; dir., treas. Nat. Jud. Coll., Reno; bd. dirs. Nat. Ctr. for Responsible Gaming, Nat. WWII Mus., Nev. Cancer Inst., and Sierra Pacific Resources; trustee Stanford U. Mem. ABA, Nev. Bar Assn., Calif. Bar Assn., Order of Coif, Phi Kappa Phi, Stanford Alumni Assn. (pres. Reno chpt. 1976-77), Young Pres. Orgn., The Bus. Roundtable. Office: PO Box 29526 Las Vegas NV 89126-9526*

SATTEL, DANIEL, geophysicist; b. Bad Durkheim, Germany, June 8, 1965; Vordiplom, U. Karlsruhe, Germany, 1986; MS, Oreg. State U., 1990; Diploma, U. Tubingen, Germany, 1992; PhD, Macquarie U., Australia, 1996. Mgr. EM interpretation Fugro Airborne Surveys, Perth, Australia, 1996—2004; cons. geophysicist, 2004—. Mem. Am. Geophys. Union, Soc. Exploration Geophysicists, European Assn. Geoscientists and Engrs., Australian Soc. Exploration Geophysicists. Home: 1119 12th St Golden CO 80401 Personal E-mail: dsattel@earthlink.net. E-mail: daniel_sattel@yahoo.com.

SATTER, DAVID ARNOLD, author, journalist; b. Chgo., Aug. 1, 1947; s. Clarice (Stone) and Mark Jerome Satter; m. Marie-Helen Gugenheim, Jan. 9, 1982 (div. Nov. 20, 1991); children: Raphael, Claire Anne; m. Olga Yuzefona Printseva, June 30, 1994 (div. Nov. 24, 2004); 1 child, Mark Daniel. BA, U. Chgo., 1968; BLitt, Oxford U., Eng., 1971. Reporter Los Angeles Times, 1972, Chgo. Tribune, 1972-76; corr. Fin. Times London, Moscow, 1976-82, Wall Street Jour., 1982—88; author Alfred A. Knopf, Inc., Chgo., 1982-84, NY and Paris, 1984—. Spl. corr. Wall St. Jour., Chgo., 1982-84, N.Y. and Paris, 1984-88; expert testimony fgn. affairs com. U.S. Ho. of Reps., 1982, 99, 2007, Ho. com. on Fin. Svc., 2007 Contbr. articles to profl. jours.; author: Age of Delirium: the Decline and Fall of the Soviet Union, 1996, Darkness at Dawn: the Rise of the Russian Criminal State, 2003. Speaker policy planning staff U.S. State Dept., Washington, 1982, speaker open forum, 1982; speaker U.S. Del. Start Talks, Washington, 1983, Internat. Sakharon Hearings, London, 1985. Rhodes scholar, 1968; Guggenheim fellow, 1984-85; U.S. Inst. Peace grantee, 1987-88, Lynde and Harry Bradley Found., grantee 1987-88, Bradley Found., 1986, Smith Richardson Found. 1986, U.S. Inst. Peace. 1986, Earhart Found., 1988, William H. Donner Found. 1998-2004, Thornton D. Hooper fellowship, Foreign Policy Rsch. Inst., Phila., 1990,Rsch Fellowship, Hoover Inst. Stanford U. 2003-2008, Vis. Professorship Fellowship. U. of Illinois, Urbana-Champaign, 2008, John Simon Gugenheim Fellowship., Guggenheim Foundation, 1984 Judaism. Home and Office: 5331 Nevada Ave NW Washington DC 20015 E-mail: satter.david@gmail.com.

SATTERFIELD, DAVID MICHAEL, federal official; b. Balt., Dec. 18, 1954; m. Martha Satterfield; 2 children. BA, U. Md., 1976; JD, Georgetown U. Law Ctr., 1978. With US Fgn. Svc., 1980—, dir. Exec. Secretariat staff, 1990—93; dir. Bur. Near East and South Asian Affairs NSC, 1993-96; dir. Office of Israel & Arab-Israeli Affairs US Dept. State, 1996—98, US amb. to Lebanon Beirut, 1998—2001, prin. dep. asst. sec., Bur. Near Ea. Affairs, 2001—04, dep. asst. sec., 2004—05; dep. chief of mission Am. Embassy, Baghdad, 2005—06; sr. adv. for sec., sr. coord. for Iraq US Dept. State, 2006—. Recipient Presdl. Meritorious Exec. Rank award, Disting. Honor award, US Dept. State, Sr. Performance award, Superior Honor award (6).*

SATTERLEE, SCOTT A., trucking executive; BA, U. St. Thomas. Mgmt. positions through Salt Lake City branch mgr. & dir. ops. C.H. Robinson Inc., Eden Prairie, Minn., 1991—2002, v.p., transp., 2002—07, sr. v.p., 2007—. Bd. dir. Fastenal Co., 2009—. Office: CH Robinson Inc 14701 Charlson Rd Eden Prairie MN 55344 Office Phone: 952-937-8500. Office Fax: 952-937-6714.*

SATTERLEE, THOM, literature educator, director; b. Batavia, NY, Mar. 7, 1967; s. Douglas William and Virginia Helen Satterlee; m. Kathleen Joy Faust, Sept. 2, 1989. BA, Houghton Coll., NY, 1989; MA, SUNY Brockport, NY, 1994; MFA, U. Ark., Fayetteville, 1998. Assoc. prof. English Taylor U., Upland, Ind., 2000—, program dir., 2006—. Author: (poetry to anthology) Burning Wyclif (ALA Notable Books award, 2007); translator: (poetry) The Hangman's Lament: Poems of Henrik Nordbrandt (Transl. prize, Am.-Scandinavian Found., 1998). Recipient LA Times Book prize finalist, LA Times, 2007; Nat. Endowment Arts Fellowship in poetry, 2008—. Mem.: Assn. Writers & Writing Programs. Office: Taylor Univ Dept English Upland IN 46989 Business E-Mail: thsatterlee@taylor.edu.

SATTERTHWAITE, CAMERON B., physics professor; b. Salem, Ohio, July 26, 1920; s. William David and Mabel (Cameron) S.; m. Helen Elizabeth Foster, Dec. 23, 1950 (div. July 1979); children: Mark Cameron, Tod Foster, Tracy Lynn, Keith Alan, Craig Evan (dec.). BA, Coll. Wooster, 1942; postgrad., Ohio State U., 1942-44; PhD, U. Pitts., 1951. Chemist Manhattan dist. project Monsanto Chem. Co., Dayton, Ohio, 1944-47; research chemist DuPont, Wilmington, Del., 1950-53; researcher, adv. physicist Westinghouse, Pitts., 1953-61; asso. prof. physics U. Ill., Urbana, 1961-63, prof., 1963-79, prof. emeritus, 1979—; prof. physics Va. Commonwealth U., Richmond, 1979-85, prof. emeritus, 1985—, chmn. dept. physics, 1979-82. Program dir. NSF, 1975-76; field sec. Friends Com. on Nat. Legis., 1988-90. Contbr. articles to profl. jours.; patentee in field. Sch. dir., Monroeville, Pa., 1959-61; trustee, mem. fin. com. Southeastern Univs. Research Assn., 1980-85; Democratic nominee for U.S. Congress, 1966; del. to Dem. Nat. Conv., 1968, 72, 2000; sec. Urbana Free Libr. Found., 1998-2002. Fellow Am. Phys. Soc.; mem. Fedn. Am. Scientists (chmn. 1968), Exch. Club Urbana. Home: 101 W Windsor Rd #1114 Urbana IL 61802-6663 Home Phone: 217-344-6642. Business E-Mail: csattert@uiuc.edu.

SATTERTHWAITE, GEORGE, II, security firm executive; b. San Jose, Costa Rica, Apr. 18, 1935; s. Livingston Lord andAdelaide (Bristol) S.; m. Helen Marie McCann, June 28, 1958 (div. July 1982); children: Patricia Ann, Livingston Lord, Frank Lord; m. Deanna Marie Kelliher, Apr. 30, 1983; 1 child, Kelley Elizabeth. BA in Internat. Rels., U. Pa., 1957; MA in History, Johns Hopkins U., 1965. Commd. 2d lt. U.S. Army, 1957, advanced through grades to col., 1979, retired, 1987; chief indsl. security Planning Rsch. Corp., McLean, Va., 1987-89; corp. dir. security PRC Inc., McLean, 1989-96; cons., 1996-98; cons., contracts officer SSI Inc., McLean, Va., 1998—2000, photography and security cons., 2000—. Mem. County Bd. Elections, Prince George County, 2003—; mem. admissions coun. U. Pa., 2002—. Mem.: SAR (chpt. sec. 2007—), Mil. Officers Assn. Am. (life), Piscataway Citizens Assn. (bd. dirs. 2003—). Republican. Roman Cath. Avocations: photography, music, volks marching, travel. Home and Office: 513 Holly Rd Fort Washington MD 20744-6606 Home Phone: 301-292-2312. Personal E-mail: GS2nd@aol.com.

SATTERTHWAITE, TONY, manufacturing executive; BCE, Cornell U., Ithaca, NY; MBA, Stanford U., Calif. Gen. field engr. Schlumberger Ltd.; head, southeast Asia region Cummins, Inc., head, Asia-Pacific bus., mng. dir., ops. Ramsgate, England, 1999—2001, v.p., ops., 2001—03, v.p., generator set bus., 2003—08, pres., Cummins Power Generation, 2008—. Office: Cummins Inc PO Box 3005 Columbus IN 47202-3005 Office Phone: 812-337-5000.

SATTLER, BRUCE WEIMER, lawyer; b. South Gate, Calif., July 30, 1944; s. LeRoy Edward and Mary Beth (Weimer) S.; m. Earle Martha Ross, July 22, 1972. BA, Stanford U., 1966, JD, 1969. Bar: Colo. 1969, U.S. Dist. Ct. Colo. 1969, U.S. Dist. Ct. Mont. 1982, U.S. Dist. Ct. (no. dist.) Tex. 1989, U.S. Ct. Appeals (10th cir.) 1969, U.S. Ct. Appeals (9th cir.) 1984. Assoc. Holland & Hart, Denver, 1969-75, ptnr., 1975-87; supervising trial atty. Equal Employment Opportunity Commn., Denver, 1973; ptnr. Morris, Lower & Sattler, Denver, 1987-90, Faegre & Benson, Denver, 1990—2004. Bd. dirs. ACLU of Colo., Denver, 1975-80, 88-94, 2003-, Colo. Legal Svcs., Legal Aid Soc. of Metro Denver, 1976—, Colo. Lawyers Com., Denver, 1990-94, Children's Legal Clinic, Denver, 1989-91, Colo. Women's Employment and Edn., Denver, 1986-89. Fellow Coll. Labor and Employment Lawyers; mem. Denver Bar Assn., Colo. Bar Assn., Am. Col. Trial Lawyers. Office Phone: 303-321-5837. Business E-Mail: bruce@mesattler.com.

SATTLER, ROLF, retired plant morphologist, educator; b. Göppingen, Germany, Mar. 8, 1936; arrived in Can., 1962; s. Otto and Emma Sattler; m. Liv Hamann, May 1, 1963 (div. 1985). PhD, U. Munich, 1961; DSc (hon.), Colombo U. Asst. prof. McGill U., Montreal, Que., Canada, 1964-69, assoc. prof., 1969-77, prof., 1977-97, emeritus prof., 1997—. Author: Organogenesis of Flowers, 1973 (Lawson medal 1974), Biophilosophy, 1986, Wilber's AQAL Map and Beyond, 2008; editor: Theoretical Plant Morphology, 1978, Axioms and Principles of Plant Construction, 1981; contbr. articles to profl. jours. NATO fellow, 1962-64. Fellow Royal Soc. Can., Linnean Soc. London; mem. Can. Bot. Assn., Sci. and Med. Network. Home Phone: 613-547-8916. Personal E-mail: rolf.sattler@sympatico.ca, sattler.rolf@gmail.com.

SATTLEY, WILLIAM MATTHEW, biology professor, researcher; b. Centralia, Ill., June 20, 1975; s. Steven Max Sattley and Patrice Ann Fry; m. Ann Renee Sauber, July 21, 2001. PhD, So. Ill. U., Carbondale, 2006. Postdoc. rsch. assoc. Wash. U., St. Louis, 2006—08; asst. prof. biology MidAmerica Nazarene U., Olathe, Kans., 2008—. Contbr. articles to numerous publs. Internal Rsch. grant, MidAmerica Nazarene U., 2008. Mem.: Am. Soc. Microbiology. Conservative. Office: MidAmerica Nazarene Univ 2030 E College Way Olathe KS 66062 Office Phone: 913-971-3675. Office Fax: 913-971-3403. Business E-Mail: wmsattley@mnu.edu.

SATYA, LAXMAN D., history professor; s. Veera Raju Satyawada and Manikyam Devi. PhD, Tufts U., Boston, 1994. Prof. history Lock Haven U. Pa., 1994—. Author: (books) Ecology, Colonialism, and Cattle;

Cotton and Famine in Berar, Medicine, Disease and Ecology in Colonial India. Named Disting. Scholar of Yr., Lock Haven U. Pa., 2002—03. Mem.: Assn. Asian Studies. Office: Lock Haven Univ Pa 207A Raub Hall Lock Haven PA 17745

SATYAN, SHYAMA, ophthalmologist; m. Satyan Kalkunte, Feb. 5, 1999; 1 child, Prithvi Kalkunte. MD, Banaras Hindu U., Varanasi, 1997. Cert. ECFMG, 2006. Rsch. asst. Pediat. Women & Infant Hosp. Warren Alpert Med. Sch. Brown U., Providence, 2008; resident, dept. internal medicine Queens Hosp. Ctr. Mt. Sinai Sch. Medicine, Jamica, NY, 2008—. Cons. ophthalmologist Aditya Jyot Eye Hosp., Mumbai, Maharashtra, India, 1999—2000, retina fellowship, 2000; cons. ophthalmologist Nethradhama Eye Clinic & Surg. Ctr., Bangalore, Karnataka, India, 2000—02, Narayana Nethralaya Superspeciality Eye Hosp. & Postgrad. Inst. Ophthalmology, Bangalore, 2002—05; inpatient clin. externship, internal med. & critical care Kent Hosp., 2007. Author: (book) Angiography Newer Diagnostic Imaging in Ophthalmology, 2005; contbr. chapters to books & articles to publs. Mem.: Karnataka Ophthal. Assn., Bombay Ophthalmologists Assn., Am. Acad. Ophthalomology, Delhi Ophthal. Soc., All India Ophthal. Soc. Home: 312 Waseca Ave Barrington RI 02806 Office: Queens Hosp Mt Sinnai Sch Medicine Jamaica NY 11432 Personal E-mail: prithvishyama@hotmail.com.

SATZ, LOUIS K., publishing executive; b. Chgo., Ill., Apr. 28, 1927; s. Harry Addison and Faye Satz; m. Janet Maas, Jan. 2, 1952 children: Jay, Jonathan BS in Mktg, U. Ill., 1949. Circulation dir. Pubs. Devel. Corp., Chgo., 1953, Guns mag., Jr. Arts and Activities, 1961; wholesaler sales mgr., then v.p., dir. sales Bantam Books, Inc., NYC, 1962-80, sr. v.p., dir. diversified markets, 1980-84; pub. Passport Books, Lincolnwood, Ill., 1985-88; pres. Louis K. Satz Assocs., Pub. Cons., NYC, 1988-91; ptnr. Scott/Satz Group, Pub. Cons., Walnut Creek, Calif., 1991—. Guest lectr. Sarah Lawrence Coll.Pub. Sch., Pace U.; faculty Hofstra U., Denver Pub. Inst.; cons. World Book Encyclopedia; bd. dirs. NY is Book Country, Brandeis U. Pub. Scholarship Fund, Oscar Dystel Fellowship NYU. Served with AUS, World War II, ETO. Mem. Am. Assn. Pubs. (chmn. small books mktg. div. 1975) Personal E-mail: louksatz@comcast.net.

SAUCERMAN, ALVERA ADELINE, elementary school educator; b. Colorado Springs, Nov. 29, 1932; d. Alva Arthur and Delpha Adeline (Cole) Gieck; m. James Ray Saucerman; 1 child, James Randall. Student, Stephens Bus. Sch., Denver, 1950—51; AA, Scottsbluff Coll., 1961; BEd, NW Mo. State U., 1965, MEd, 1971. Cert. French, reading specialization and learning disabilities tchr. Tchr. Lake Alice Sch., Nebr., 1961-62, West Nodaway Sch., Clearmont, Mo., 1965-67; remedial reading tchr. Maryville R II, Mo., 1968-74, dir. learning lab., 1975-88, tchr. learning disabilities, 1974-97; ret. Lectr. spl. edn. N.W. Mo. State U., Maryville, 1978—97. Mem. Maryville State Tchrs. Assn. (sec. 1978-79), AAUW (life, pres. 1981-83 Maryville Br.), Mo. State Tchrs. Assn. (life), Delta Kappa Gamma, Kappa Delta Pi (life). Avocations: travel, photography, reading, dance. Home: 1331 NW 107th Ter Gainesville FL 32606-5489

SAUCIER, GENE DUANE, state legislator, import/export company executive; b. Dallas, Sept. 25, 1931; s. Albert L. and Myrtle Irene (West) S.; m. Marilyn Emmy Cox, Dec. 27, 1952 (div. Sept. 1980); children: Alan, Steve, Renee; m. Giulia Riga LaCagnina, Nov. 28, 1981. BS in Agronomy Soils, Miss. State U., 1953; MS in Counseling, U. So. Miss., 1970, EdD in Adult Edn., 1978. Builder, developer Saucier Co., Hattiesburg, Miss., 1957-70; dir. admissions U. So. Miss., Hattiesburg, 1970-74, dean spl. acad. svcs., 1974-84, asst. v.p. bus. and fin., 1984-93; mem. Miss. Ho. of Reps., Jackson, 1993-99; ret., 1999. Mem. Fed. Land Coun., 1997—2003; scoutmaster Boy Scouts Am., 1960—70, chmn. camping and activities Pine Burr area, 1970; bd. dirs., founder Hub Coun., 2000; bd. dirs. Miss. Wild Turkey Fedn., Pine Burr chpt., 2000. 1st lt. pilot USAF, 1953—56. Named Forrest County Tree Farmer of Yr., 1996, Miss. Tree Farmer Yr., 1996; recipient Forestry award Miss. Wildlife Fedn., 1997, Legislator of Yr. Coastal Conservation Assn., 1997. Mem. So. Assn. Collegiate Registrars and Admissions Officers (bd. dirs. 1981, local arrangements chmn. 1981, v.p. admissions and fin. aid 1982-83, pres. 1985-86), Miss. Assn. Collegiate Registrars and Admissions Officers, Miss. Forestry Assn. (exec. bd. dirs. 1992-94, bd. dirs. 1992-94), Soc. Am. Foresters (cert. rev. bd. 2003-05), Am. Legion (life), Miss. Nature Conservancy, Forrest/Lamar Forestry Assn. (pres. 1989-92, 2007—08), Resource Conservation & Devel.(co-chair, 2008-, mem. 2009), Audubon (v.p. Forest County chpt. 2004), Sigma Chi (life), Phi Delta Kappa, Omicron Delta Kappa. Home Phone: 601-268-2388. Personal E-mail: treefarm43@hotmail.com.

SAUCIER, GUYLAINE, corporate financial executive; b. Noranda, Que., Can., June 10, 1946; d. Gérard and Yvette (Thiffault) S. Chartered acct., École Hautes Etudes Commls., Montreal, Can., 1971. Formerly chair Joint Com. on Corp. Governance. Bd. dirs. Axa Assurances Inc., Bank Montreal, Areva Group, Danone. Fellow Inst. Chartered Accts., Inst. Corp. Dirs.; mem. Order Can. Avocation: tennis. Office Phone: 514-397-5494. Business E-Mail: gsaucier@gsaucier.com.

SAUER, DAVID ANDREW, librarian, writer; b. Urbana, Ill., Feb. 25, 1948; s. Elmer Louis and Frances (Hill) S. BA, Northwestern U., 1970; MS, Simmons Coll., 1975. Reference libr. Boston U., 1976-78, bibliographer, 1978-84, sci. bibliographer, 1984-88, founder and head libr. Stone Sci. Libr., 1988-94; v.p. info. svcs. CyberHelp, Inc., 1995-98; sr. tech. editor Qualcomm, Inc., 1997-2000, 2003—04, sr. tech. writer, 2004—06, staff tech. writer, 2006—; tech. pubs. supr. QCP Inc., 2000—01, staff tech. writer/libr., 2001—02; librarian San Diego Maritime Mus., 2002—03. Co-author of 12 books including: Access for Windows 95: The Visual Learning Guide, 1995, Windows NT 4.0 Visual Desk Reference, 1997, Discover Netscape Communicator, 1997. Mem. S.W. Corridor Project, Boston, 1977-87, Forest Hills Neighborhood Improvement Assn., Boston, 1977-90, Forest Hills/Woodbourne Neighorhood Group, 1991-94. Mem. ALA, IEEE, Spl. Librs. Assn., Soc. Tech. Comm. Democrat. Home: 2340 29th St San Diego CA 92104

SAUER, JEFF, university hockey coach; b. St. Paul; m. Jamie Sauer Adler; children: Chip, Beth. BA in Sociology, Colo. Coll., 1965. Asst. hockey, baseball coach Colo. Coll., Colo. Springs, 1966-68, head coach hockey, 1971-82; asst.coach hockey U. Wis., Madison, 1968-71, head coach hockey, 1980—. Mem. U.S. Olympic Hockey Com., 1984; coach Olympic Festival, 1987, USA Select Team, Pravda Cup, Leningrad, Russia, 1989, Team USA, Goodwill Games, 1990, U.S. Nat. Team World Championships, 1995, U.S. Select Team, Tampere Cup, Finland, 1997, coach, organizer youth hockey camps in summer; asst. coach USA World Jr. Team, 2003—; head coach USA Team TUI Cup, Manheim, Germany, Gold medal-winning hockey team Deaf Olympics, Salt Lake City, 2007. Counselor Stan Mikita's Hockey Camp for Hearing Impaired, Chgo. Named We. Coll. Hockey Assn. Coach of Yr. 1972-73, 74-75 (Colo. Coll.); NCAA championship (Wis.) 1983, 90, WCHA championship 1987-88, 97-98, WCHA Playoff Championship, 1982-83, 87-88, 94-95. Office: Western Collegiate Hockey Assn 559 D'onofrio Dr Ste 103 Madison WI 53719 Personal E-mail: coachjsauer@juno.com.

SAUER, LEONARD AUSTIN, retired medical researcher; b. Schenectady, NY, Aug. 20, 1929; s. George and Blanche Sauer; m. Marlene Morack, June 25, 1955; children: Beneth, David, George. BS, Cornell U., Ithaca, NY, 1956; MD, U. Rochester, NY, 1960; PhD, Rockefeller U., NY, 1967. Assoc. prof. medicine & biochemistry Yale U. Sch. Medicine, New Haven, 1967—74; sr. rsch. physician emeritus Bassett Rsch. Inst., Cooperstown, NY, 1974—. Mem.: Endocrine Soc., Soc. Exptl. Biology, Am. Assn. Biol. Chemists. Liberal. Home: PO Box 3 Stevensville MT 59870 Office: Bassett Rsch Inst 1 Atwell Rd Cooperstown NY 13326

SAUER, MARY JULIA, special education educator; b. Pitts., Oct. 10, 1949; d. Edward Henry and Julia Ann (Polkabla) Sauer; 1 child, Jason Michael Sauer; m. John Harold Moore, Oct. 27, 1990 (div.); 1 adopted child, Jocelyn Quan. BS in Art Edn., Edinboro State Coll., 1971; MS in Spl. Edn., Clarion State Coll., 1980; postgrad, U. Pitts., 1988—. Cert. art tchr., spl. edn. tchr. for mentally retarded. Tchr. Polk (Pa.) State Sch. & Hosp., 1971-72; vol. VISTA, Bath, NY, 1972-73; tchr. Polk Ctr., 1973-80, program specialist, 1980-92, residential svc. supr., qualified mental retardation profl., 1992—. Lectr., speaker, video on local TV on history of Polk Ctr., 1987. Patentee beer bottle shaped cake pan; cakes displayed in TV videos and in various mags.; author, co prodrs. Pride in Their Work, creator history video Polk Ctr., Some Leaky Boot Statues, Polk Center--100 Years; creator video A Century of Care-The History of the Evolution of Institional Care of the Devlopment Disabled. Past vol. Big Bros./Big Sisters. Democrat. Roman Catholic. Avocations: cake decorating, reading. Home: PO Box 97 Franklin PA 16323

SAUER, MATTHEW JAMES, history professor; b. Pontiac, Ill., Nov. 7, 1958; s. George Edward and Mary Lorain Sauer; m. Judith Lynn Lambes, Aug. 22, 1982; children: Megan Marie Kramer, Randolph Edward. PhD, U. Cin., 1995. Adj. prof. history U. Cin., 1999—2008, accommodation coord., 2001—. Cons. Imaging History, Cin., 1985—2008. Ch. leadership Calvary Episcopal ch., Cin., 2007—08. Recipient Suma Cum Laude, Wright State U., 1980. Mem.: Am. assn. state & local historians. Democrat. Episcopal. Avocation: farming. Home: 2165 Elysian Place Cincinnati OH 45219 Office: Univ Cincinnati 2600 Clifton Ave Cincinnati OH 45221-0213

SAUER, RAYMOND D., JR., economics professor; b. Lubbock, Tex., Feb. 15, 1956; s. Raymond D. and Gay Luvonne Sauer; m. Mary Carol Matheson; children: Matthew W., Gregory C., Kathryn Marie. PhD, U. Wash., Seattle, 1985. Prof. economics Clemson U., SC, 1988—. Contbr. economics rsch. articles. Office: Clemson Univ John E Walker Dept Economics Clemson SC 29634-1309

SAUERMAN, NANCY, psychology professor; m. Bruce Bachmann; children: Rachel Bachmann, David Bachmann. Prof. psychology and human sexuality Kirkwood CC, Cedar Rapids, Iowa, 1979—. Co-chair, bd. mem. Adolescent Pregnancy Prevention Coalition, Cedar Rapids, 2000—03; faculty advisor Kirkwood Democrats, Cedar Rapids, 1999—2008; bd. mem. Iowa Med. Aid Fund, Cedar Rapids, 2008—. Office: Kirkwood CC 6301 Kirkwood Blvd SW Cedar Rapids IA 52406 Business E-Mail: nancy.sauerman@kirkwood.edu.

SAUFLEY, LEIGH INGALLS, state supreme court chief justice; b. Portland, Maine, June 21, 1954; m. William Saufley; 2 children. BA, U. Maine, Orono, 1976; JD, U. Maine Sch. of Law, 1980. Pvt. practice, Ellsworth; asst. counsel U.S. VA; asst., then dep. atty. gen. Maine, 1981-90; judge Maine Dist. Ct., 1990—93; justice Maine Superior Ct, 1993—97; assoc. justice Maine Supreme Judicial Ct., 1997—2001, chief justice, 2001—. Mem.: ABA. Maine's first female chief justice. Office: Cumberland County Courthouse PO Box 368 142 Federal St Portland ME 04112-0368 E-mail: amanda.j.martin@maine.gov.*

SAUK, JOHN JOSEPH, dean, educator; b. Detroit, Sept. 23, 1942; s. John Joseph and Alexandria Lennor Sauk; m. Elaine Carol DiMatteo, Aug. 24, 1965; children: Christine Marie Strauss, Joseph Andrew. BS, U. Detroit, Mich., 1963, DDS, 1967; MS, U. Minn., Mpls., 1969; PhD (hon.), U. Athens, Greece. Cert. Am. Bd. Oral and Maxillofacial Pathology, 1973. Asst. prof., pathology U. Detroit, 1971—73; prof., pathology and human genetics U. Minn., Mpls., 1973—85; prof., diagnostic sciences pathology U. Md., 1985—2007; assoc. dean U. Md., Dental Sch., Balt., 1985—2007; dean Sch. Dentistry, U. Louisville, 2007—; prof. James G Brown Cancer Ctr., Louisville, 2007—. Ptnr. Bus. 1st, 2008. With US Navy, 1969—71, Great lakes, Ill. Fellow: Ky. Inst. Medicine, Piere Fauchard Acad., Internat. Acad. Oral Oncology, AAAS, Am. Head and Neck Soc., Am. Coll. Dentists, Am. Acad. Oral Pathology; mem.: Am. Soc. Bone and Mineral Rsch., Am. Assn. Dental Schs., Internat. Assn. Oral Pathologists, Am. Soc. Human Genetics, Internat. Am. Assn. Dental Rsch., ADA. Achievements include patents for composition and method for osseous repair; physically stable composition; surface localized colligin in carcinoma cells; carcinoma cells. Office: Univ Louisville 501 S Preston Louisville KY 40202 Office Fax: 502-852-3364. Business E-Mail: john.sauk@louisville.edu.

SAUL, ANDREW M., investment company executive; b. NYC, 1946; m. Denise Saul; 2 children. BS, Wharton Sch. Fin., U. Pa., 1968. Exec. v.p. Brooks Fashion Stores, 1968—80, pres., 1980—85, BR Investors, 1985—86; gen. ptnr. Saul Partners, 1986—; dir. Caché Inc., 1986—, chmn., 1993—2000. Chmn. Fed. Retirement Thrift Investment Bd.; trustee Fedn. of Jewish Philanthropies, United Jewish Appeal; commr. Met. Transp. Authority, NY, 1996—; mem. exec. com. Mt. Sinai Med. Ctr., chmn. audit com.; trustee Sarah Neuman Nursing Home, Wharton Sch., Univ. Pa.; bd. mem. Manhattan Inst.; trustee & mem. Chmn. Council Met. Mus. Art, NYC. Named one of Top 200 Collectors, ARTnews Mag., 2004—08. Avocation: Collector of Chinese Bronzes, Modern & Contemporary Art, especially Postwar American. Office: Caché Inc 1440 Broadway New York NY 10018*

SAUL, B. FRANCIS, II, bank executive, director; b. Washington, Apr. 15, 1932; s. Andrew Maguire and Ruth Clark (Sheehan) S.; m. Elizabeth Patricia English, Apr. 30, 1960; children: Sharon Elizabeth, B. Francis III, Elizabeth Willoughby, Andrew Maguire II, Patricia English Grad., Georgetown Prep. Sch., 1950; BS, Villanova U., 1954, DCS (hon.), 1989; LLB, U. Va., 1957; LLD (hon.), Nat. U. Ireland, 1998. Bar: D.C. 1959. Chmn., pres. B.F. Saul Co., Chevy Chase, Md., 1957—; chmn., trustee B.F. Saul Real Estate Investment Trust Co., Chevy Chase, 1964—; with Chevy Chase Bank, F.S.B., 1969—, chmn., CEO, founder; chmn. Fin. Gen. Bankshares, Inc., 1978-82; chmn., CEO, trustee Saul Ctrs., Inc., 1993—. Chmn. bd. dirs. 1st Am. Bankshares, Inc., Washington, 1978—85; dir. Colonial Williamsburg Hotel Properties, Inc., 1983—96. Honors com. John F. Kennedy Ctr. Performing Arts, 1995—; trustees coun. Nat. Gallery of Arts, 1995—; dir. bd. visitors and govs. Washington Coll., 1995—; hon. trustee Brookings Inst., 1993—; dir. Nat. Sporting Libr., 1998—; trustee Fed. City Coun., Nat. Geog. Soc., 1985—, Suburban Hosp., 1972—76, Johns Hopkins Med. Bd., 2000—01, Corcoran Gallery Art, Washington, 1972—90; bd. dirs. Wadsworth Preservation Trust, 1983—91; vis. com. Sch. Arch. U. Va., Greenway, 1985—90, Portsmouth (RI) Abbey Sch., 1979—84, United World Coll. of Am. West, Montezuma, N.Mex., 1982—85, D.C. Fund for Creative Space, 1980—82, D.C. chpt. ARC, 1964—86, Cork U. Found., 1997—; mem. Ea. Shore Land Conservancy, 2002—, Md. Agrl. Soc. Eastern Shore, James Madison Coun., 1997—; trust fund bd. Libr. of Congress, 2003; archdiocese fin. coun. for Archbishop of Washington, 1990—. Mem. Mortgage Bankers Assn. Met. Washington (pres. 1968), Nat. Assn. Real Estate Investment Truste (pres. 1973-74), Internat. Coll. Auditors Prefecture Econ. Affairs Holy See, Alfalfa Club, Alibi Club, Met. Club, Knights of Malta, Chevy Chase Club, Burning Tree Club, Friendly Sons of St. Patrick (pres. 1992), Wianno Club, The Brook Club, Bohemian Club, Md. Club, White's Club (London) Roman Catholic. Office: BF Saul Co 7501 Wisconsin Ave Bethesda MD 20814

SAUL, IRVING ISAAC, lawyer; b. July 9, 1929; s. Israel Jacob and Jennie (Green) S.; m. Lita Brown, Dec. 29, 1950; children: Joanne Ilene, Sandra Lynn. BA, Washington and Jefferson Coll., 1949; postgrad., Georgetown U., 1949, Ohio State U., 1951; LLB, U. Pitts., 1952. Bar: Ohio 1952, U.S. Dist. Ct. (so. dist.) Ohio 1954, U.S. Supreme Ct. 1961, U.S. Ct. Appeals (6th cir.) 1966, U.S. Dist. Ct. (no. dist.) Ohio 1967, U.S. Dist. Ct. (ea. dist.) Wis. 1973, U.S. Ct. Appeals (7th cir.) 1978, U.S. Ct. Appeals (4th cir.) 1978, U.S. Ct. Appeals (fed. cir.) 1991. Pvt. practice, Dayton, Ohio, 1952—. Cons. in antitrust litigation; bd. advs. Fed. Civil Practice Abstracts, 1986-88, Ohio Dist. Ct. Rev., 1988-2002; adj. prof. complex litigation Sch. of Law U. Dayton, 1996-98; lectr. in field. Contbr. articles to profl. jours. James Gillespie Blaine scholar, 1948. Mem. Ohio Bar Assn. (chmn. fed. cts. and practice com. 1977-79, chmn. pvt. enforcement com. 1979-92, bd. govs. antitrust sect. 1982-94), Dayton Bar Assn. (chmn. fed. ct. practice com. 1976-77, 78-80, chmn. com. on judiciary 1987-88), Am. Judicature Soc., Masons (Shriner), Phi Beta Kappa. Jewish. Office: 113 Bethpolamy Ct Dayton OH 45415-2512 Office Phone: 937-278-4858.

SAUL, NORMAN EUGENE, historian, educator; b. LaFontaine, Ind., Nov. 26, 1932; s. Ralph Odis and Jessie (Neff) S.; m. Mary Ann Culwell, June 27, 1959; children: Alyssa, Kevin, Julia. BA, Ind. U.- Bloomington, 1954; MA, Columbia U., 1959, PhD, 1965; postgrad., Leningrad State U., 1960-61. Asst. prof. Brown U., 1965-68; vis. assoc. prof. Northwestern U., 1969-70; assoc. prof. U. Kans., Lawrence, 1970-75, prof. history, 1975—, chmn. dept. history, 1981-89. Inst. Advanced Study, Princeton, 2000. Author: Russia and the Mediterranean 1797-1807, 1970, Sailors in Revolt, 1917, 1978, Distant Friends: The United States and Russia, 1763-1867, 1991, Concord and Conflict: The United States and Russia, 1867-1914, 1996, War and Revolution: The United States and Russia, 1914-1921, 2001, Friends or Foes?: The United States and Soviet Russia, 1921-1941, 2006, Historical Dictionary of United States-Russian/Soviet Relations, 2009; editor: Russian-American Dialogue on Cultural Relations, 1776-1914, 1997. Fulbright scholar, London, 1954-55, Helsinki, 1968-69, Soviet Am. Exch. scholar Internat. Rsch. and Exch. Bd., Moscow, 1973-74, 91-92; fellow Ford Found., 1957-59, Hall Ctr. for Humanities, 1989, 95; recipient Byron Caldwell Smith Book award for Distant Friends, 1993, Robert H. Ferrell book award for Concert and Conflict, Soc. Historians Am. Fgn. Rels., 1997, Pub. Scholar award Kans. Humanities Coun., 1997, Higuchi Rsch. award U. Kans., 1997, Steeples award for Svc. to Kans., 2000, Herbert Hoover Libr. Assn. award, 2001, Franklin and Eleanor Roosevelt Inst. award, 2002. Mem. Am. Assn. Advancement of Slavic Studies, Kans. State Hist. Soc., Kans. Assn. Historians, Phi Alpha Theta. Home: 1002 Crestline Dr Lawrence KS 66049-2607 Business E-Mail: nsaul@ku.edu.

SAUL, PETER A., artist, educator; b. San Francisco, Aug. 16, 1934; s. Arthur Charles and Mabel Clare (Kelso) S.; m. Vicki Goorman, Jan. 1960 (div. Aug. 1975); children: Rufin, Leif; m. Sarah Patricia Lutz; 1 child, Gwendolyn. BFA, Washington U., St. Louis, 1956; student, Stanford U., Calif. Sch. Fine Arts. Prof. art U. Tex., Austin. Solo exhbns. include Allan Frumkin Gallery, NYC and Chgo., Galerie Breteau, Paris, La Tartaruga Gallery, Rome, Reed Coll., Portland, Oreg., Youngstown (Ohio) State U., Frumkin Struve Gallery, Chgo., Tex. Gallery, Houston, Frumkin/Adams Gallery, NYC, Galerie Bonnier, Geneva, Galerie du Centre, Paris, Herbert Palmer Gallery, LA, Ynglingagatan I, Stockholm; exhibited in group shows at Art Inst. Chgo., U. Mich., Ann Arbor, San Francisco Mus. Modern Art, Rose Art Mus./Brandeis U., Mcpl. Mus., The Hague, Mus. Modern Art, NYC, Mus. Modern Art, Paris, Whitney Mus. Am. Art, Taft Mus., Cin., Chrysler Mus., Norfolk, Va., Mus. Art, Ft. Lauderdale, Fla., Inst. Contemporary Arts, London, RI Sch. Design, Providence, U. NC at Greensboro, Phyllis Kind Gallery, NYC and Chgo., Mus. Contemporary Art, LA, Frumkin/Adams Gallery, Nolan/Eckman, NYC, numerous others; represented in collections at Art Inst. Chgo., Carnegie Inst., Pitts., Centre Pompidou, Paris, Kansas City Art Inst., Met. Mus. Art, NYC, Mus. of Art, Honolulu, Mus. Modern Art, NYC, San Franciso Mus. Modern Art, Stedelijk Mus., Ostende, Belgium, Whitney Mus. Am. Art, others. Recipient New Talent award, Art in America mag., 1962, AAAL award, Am. Acad. Arts and Letters, 2001, Artist's Legacy Found. award, 2008; grantee William and Norma Copley Found., 1962, Nat. Endowment Arts, 1980, 1985; fellow Guggenheim Found., 1993. Office: c/o George Adams Gallery 7th Fl 41 W 57th St New York NY 10019 Mailing: PO Box 571 Germantown NY 12526-0571 Office: c/o David Nolan Gallery 560 Broadway New York NY 10012*

SAUL, RALPH SOUTHEY, diversified financial services company executive; b. Bklyn., May 21, 1922; s. Walter Emerson and Helen Douglas (Coutts) S.; m. Bette Jane Bertschinger, June 16, 1956; children: Robert Southey, Jane Adams. BA, U. Chgo., 1947; LL.B., Yale U., 1951. Bar: D.C. 1951, N.Y. 1952. With Am. Embassy, Prague, Czechoslovakia, 1947-48; assoc. Lyeth & Voorhees, NYC, 1951-52; asst. counsel to gov. State of N.Y., 1952-54; staff atty. RCA, 1954-58; with SEC, 1958-65, dir. divsn. trading and markets, 1963-65; v.p. corporate devel. Investors Diversified Services, Inc., Mpls., 1965-66; pres. Am. Stock Exch., NYC, 1966-71; co-chief exec., chmn. mgmt. com. 1st Boston Corp., 1971-74; chmn., CEO. INA Corp., Phila., 1975-82, CIGNA Corp., Phila., 1982-84. Trustee Com. for Econ. Devel., Brookings Inst.; mem. adv. coun. Pub. Co. Acctg. Oversight Bd. With USNR, 1943-46, PTO. Mem. ABA, Union League, Merion Golf Club, Links Club. Office: Cigna Corp One Tower Bridge 100 Front St Ste 1445 West Conshohocken PA 19428 Office Phone: 610-260-1260. Personal E-mail: yobigdad@aol.com.

SAUL, WILLIAM EDWARD, engineering educator; b. NYC, May 15, 1934; s. George James and Fanny Ruth (Murokh) S.; m. J. Muriel Held Eagleburger, May 11, 1976. BSCE, Mich. Tech. U., 1955, MSCE, 1961; PhD in Civil Engring., Northwestern U., 1964. Registerd profl. engr., Wis., Idaho, Mich., profl. structural engr., Idaho. Mech. engr. Shell Oil Co., New Orleans, 1955-59; instr. engring. mechanics Mich. Tech. U., Houghton, 1960-62; asst. prof. civil engring. U. Wis., Madison, 1964-67, assoc. prof., 1967-72, prof., 1972-84; dean, prof. civil engring. U. Idaho Coll. Engring., Moscow, 1984-90; prof. civil engring. Mich. State U., East Lansing, 1990—2000, chmn. dept. civil and environ. engring., 1990-95, chmn. emeritus, prof. emeritus, 2000. Cons. engr., 1961—; vis. prof. U. Stuttgart, Germany, 1970-71. Co-editor Conf. of Methods of Structural Analysis, 1976. Bd. dirs. Idaho Rsch. Found., 1984-90. Fulbright fellow 1970-71; von Humboldt scholar, 1970-71. Fellow

ASCE (pres. Wis. sect. 1983-84), NSPE (bd. dirs., 2005-06), Mich. Soc. Profl. Engrs. (Steinman award 2003); mem. Internat. Assn. Bridge and Structural Engrs., Am. Concrete Inst., Am. Soc. Engring. Edn., Sigma Xi, Phi Kappa Phi, Tau Beta Pi, Chi Epsilon Avocations: hiking, reading, travel, gadgets. Home: 1971 Cimarron Dr Okemos MI 48864-3905 Office: Mich State U 3546 Engring Bldg E East Lansing MI 48824 Business E-Mail: saul@egr.msu.edu.

SAULSBURY, FRANK T., pediatric immunologist and rheumatologist; b. Lexington, Nebr., Aug. 27, 1947; MD, U. Nebr. Coll. Medicine, 1972. Diplomate Am. Bd. Pediat. Intern pediat. Johns Hopkins U. Hosp., Balt., 1972—73, resident pediat., 1973—75, fellowship pediat. immunology, 1977—79; med. alumni. prof. pediat. U. Va. Sch. Medicine, 2002—; head divsn. pediat. immunology and rheumatology U. Va. Health Sys. Contbr. articles to profl. jours. Mem.: Am. Pediat. Soc. Office: U Va Sch Medicine Dept Pediat PO Box 800386 Charlottesville VA 22908 Office Phone: 434-924-1906. Office Fax: 434-982-4246. Business E-Mail: fts@virginia.edu.

SAUM, ELIZABETH PAPE, community volunteer; b. Evanston, Ill., Aug. 7, 1930; d. Karl James and Catherine (Schwall) Pape; m. William Joseph Saum, Dec. 31, 1960; children: JeanMarie, Katherine Anne, Mary Elizabeth. BA in English cum laude, Fontbonne Coll., 1952; MA in English, Northwestern U., 1958. Cert. tchr., Ill. Tchr. Our Lady of Perpetual Help, Glenview, Ill., 1952-55, Wilmette (Ill.) Jr. High Sch., 1955-61; dir. religion edn. St. Paul's Ch., Valparaiso, Ind., 1972-76; activities dir. Heritage Manor Nursing Home, Plano, Tex., 1982-84; exec. dir. Jessamine County Assn. Exceptional Citizens, Nicholasville, Ky., 1985-89; ret., 1989. Radio reader WNIN, Evansville, Ind., 2007—; sec. Goodwill Aux., Evansville, Ind., 2008—. Pres. bd. dirs. Women's Neighborly Orgn., Lexington, 1977-81; mem. Bluegrass Long-Term Care Ombudsman, Lexington, 1984-89; bd. dirs. Women's History Coalition Ky., Midway, 1985-90, Sr. Citizens East, Louisville, 1991-93, treas., 1992-93; creator, pres. Ky. Women's Heritage Mus., Lexington, 1986-90; adminstrn. coord. Transfiguration Ch., Goshen, Ky., 1991-93; liturgy coord. St. Stephen's Ch., Cadiz, Ky., 1996—2004; pres. Friends of the Libr., Trigg County, Ky., 1997-2000; vol. quilt tchr., 1997-; lectr. St. Mary Ch., 2005, mem. liturgy com. Mem. AAUW (bd. dirs. Ky. br. 1977-81, 85-96, named gift honoree 1988, v.p. Ednl. Found. 1988-94, 95-96, co-pres. Ky. br. 1994-96, named gift honoree Lexington br. 1987, pres. 1984-86, 88-90, Louisville br. editor newsletter 1990-93, treas. 1991-93, v.p. Ednl. Found. 1991-93, mem. br.-state adv. bd. Ednl. Found. 1996-98), Lexington Newcomers (editor newsletter 1976-78), Trigg County Quilter's Guild (pres. 1995-97). Democrat. Roman Catholic. Home: 7709 Paige Dr Newburgh IN 47630 Personal E-mail: bills31@sbcglobal.net.

SAUMELL, EILEEN MARY, psychologist; b. West Islip, NY, May 8, 1968; MEd in Psychology, Queens Coll., NY, 2004. Psychologist Amityville Sch. Dist., NY, 2004—06, West Babylon Sch. Dist., NY, 2006—. Mem.: NASP. Personal E-mail: eileensaumell@aol.com.

SAUNDERS, ALAN KEITH, professional football coach; b. London, Feb. 1, 1947; naturalized, USA, 1960; m. Karen Saunders: children: Korrin Elizabeth, William Joseph, Robert Charles. Grad., San Jose State U., 1969; MA, Stanford U., 1970; postgrad., U. So. Calif., 1983-85. Grad. asst. U. Southern Calif., 1970—71; wide receivers coach U. Mo. Tigers, 1972; offensive backfield coach Utah State U. Aggies, 1973-75; asst. head coach U. Calif. Golden Bears, 1976-81; offensive coordinator, quarterback coach U. Tenn. Volunteers, 1982; wide receivers coach San Diego Chargers, 1983—86, head coach, 1986-88; asst. head coach, wide receivers coach Kans. City Chiefs, 1989—98, offensive coord., 2001—06; asst. head coach, wide receivers coach St. Louis Rams, 1999—2000, offensive coord., 2008—, Wash. Redskins, 2006—08. Mem. ad-hoc com. state lic. and designated sports Calif. State Legis.; hon. chmn. S.D. chpt. Arthritis Found.; bd. dirs. Easter Seal Soc., San Diego; bd. govs. Athletes for a Stronger America; mem. S.D. Chem. Dependency Adv. Bd. Recipient Grad. Fellowship Acad. Excellence, State of Calif., Golden State award, 1989; named Master's 5K Nat. Champion, Rd. Runners Club Am.; named to Hall of Fame, San Jose State U. Achievements include being one of four foreign-born head coaches in NFL history; member 1967 Academic All-American football team. Office: St Louis Rams One Rams Way Saint Louis MO 63045 Office Phone: 314-516-8834.

SAUNDERS, ANDREW, real estate company executive, real estate developer; Lic. Real Estate Broker. Developer in the Hamptons, 1996; broker Sotheby's Internat. Realty, 2001—07; founder, pres. Saunders & Associates Realty, NY, 2007—. Named Hamptons Mem., Who's Who in Luxury Real Estate; named one of Top 50 Real Estate Agents in the Country (ranked #43), Wall Street Journal, 2007. Office: Saunders & Associates Realty 2287 Montauk Highway PO Box 603 Bridgehampton NY 11932 Office Phone: 631-537-5454. Office Fax: 631-537-9484. Business E-Mail: AS@SaundersRE.com. E-mail: info@saunderRE.com.*

SAUNDERS, CHARLES ALBERT, lawyer; b. Boulder, Colo., Jan. 18, 1922; s. Charles and Anna (Crouse) S.; m. Betti Friedel, Oct. 18, 1946; children— Melanie, Stephen, Cynthia, Shelley. BA, U. Houston, 1942; LLB, U. Tex., 1945. Bar: Tex. 1945. Ptnr. firm Fulbright & Jaworski, L.L.P., 1959—. Editor: How To Live-and Die-With Texas Probate, 8 vols., 1968, Texas Estate Administration, 1975. Bd. dirs. Houston Symphony Soc., 1964—; bd. dirs. Am. Lung Assn., San Jacinto, 1965—, pres., 1972-73; past mem. bd. govs. U. Houston. Recipient Leon Jaworski award for cmty. svc., Houston Bar Assn., 1997, U. Tex. Law Sch. Disting. Alumnus award in Cmty. Svc., 1999. Mem. ABA, State Bar Assn., Houston Bar Assn., Am. Coll. Trust and Estate Coun. (regent 1972-80, pres. 1978-79), Internat. Acad. of Estate and Trust Law, Assn. Cmty. TV (bd. dirs. 1970—). Republican. Presbyterian. Home: 19 Willowron Dr Houston TX 77024-7618 Office: Fulbright & Jaworski 1301 Mckinney St Ste 5100 Houston TX 77010-3031 Office Phone: 713-651-5374. Business E-Mail: csaunders@fulbright.com.

SAUNDERS, CHARLES BASKERVILLE, JR., retired association executive; b. Boston, Dec. 26, 1928; s. Charles Baskerville and Lucy (Carmichael) S.; m. Margaret MacIntire Shafer, Sept. 9, 1950; children— Charles Baskerville III, George Carlton, Margaret Keyser, Lucy C., John R. Grad., St. Mark's Sch., 1946; AB, Princeton, 1950. News reporter, polit. columnist Ogdensburg (N.Y.) Jour., 1950-51; edn. reporter Hartford (Conn.) Times, 1951-53; asst. dir. pub. relations Trinity Coll., Hartford, 1953-55; asst. dir. pub. info. Princeton, 1955-57; legis. asst. Sen. H. Alexander Smith, 85th Congress, 1957-58; asst. to asst. sec. for legislation HEW, 1958-59; asst. to sec. Arthur S. Flemming, 1959-61, dep. asst. sec. for legislation, 1969-71; asst. to pres. Brookings Instn., 1961-69; dep. commr. of edn. for external affairs U.S. Office Edn., 1971-72; dep. asst. sec. for edn. HEW, 1973-74; dir. govt. relations Am. Council on Edn., 1975-78, v.p. for govt. relations, 1978-87, sr. v.p., 1987-92. Author: Brookings Institution: A Fifty-Year History, 1966, Upgrading the American Police, 1970, Four Centuries in America, 2000, rev. edit., 2006. Mem. Montgomery County Bd. Edn., 1966-70, Md. Higher Edn. Commn., 1989-2002 (chmn. 1994-95, vice chmn. 1995-2002); chmn. bd. dirs. Md. Higher Edn. Loan Corp., 1994-95. Mem. Jamestowne Soc. Democrat. Presbyterian. Home: 7622 Winterberry Pl Bethesda MD 20817-4848 Personal E-mail: saunders3@earthlink.net.

SAUNDERS, DONALD LESLIE, hotel executive, real estate developer; b. Brookline, Mass., Jan. 28, 1935; s. Irving M. Saunders and Shirley Brown; m. Liv Ullmann, 1985; children: Lisa M., Pamela R. AB in Econs., Brown U., Providence, RI, 1957; grad., Inst. Real Estate Mgmt., 1963; LLB, Pine Manor Coll., Brookline, Mass., 1989. Cert. property mgr. Inst. Real Estate Mgmt., Ill., lic. real estate broker Mass. Chmn., pres., CEO The D.L. Saunders Real Estate Corp., Boston, 1957—; CEO, chmn. The D.L. Saunders Cos., The Boston Pk. Plz. Hotel, LLC, 1976—; ptnr. SaunStar Land Co., 20 & 50 Park Plaza Complex, LLC. Bd. dirs. Park Sch. Corp., Brookline, Mass., Brown U. Sports Found., 2002—; with Brown U. Comml. Real Estate Devel. Co.; mem. real estate subcom. Brown U.; pres. Farview Inc., 1976—; trustee emeritus Brown U., 1972—, gov. emeritus, 1996—, John Carter Brown Libr.; mem. Better Bus. Bur. of Mass., Inc.; prime ministers coun. Combined Jewish Philanthropies, 2007—. Mem. Nat. Assn. Realtors, Ea. Point Residents Assn. (Gloucester, Mass.), Ocean Reef Club, Ocean Reef Yacht Club, Brown U. Club (Boston), Lotos Club, The Players, Union League Club (NYC), Hope Club (Providence), Boston Tennis and Racquet Club, Ea. Point Yacht Club, Belmont Country Club, Union Club, Charles River Yacht Club, Confrerie Chaine des Rotisseurs, N.Y.C. Office: DL Saunders Cos 20 Park Plz Boston MA 02116-4399 Business E-Mail: lmcnulty@dlsaunders.com.

SAUNDERS, FLIP (PHILIP D. SAUNDERS), professional basketball coach; b. Cleve., Feb. 23, 1955; m. Deborah K. Saunders; children: Ryan, Mindy, Rachel, Kimberly Attended, U. Minn. Asst. coach U. Minn. Golden Gophers, 1981—86, U. Tulsa Golden Hurricane, 1986-88; head coach Rapid City Thrillers, Continental Basketball Assn., SD, 1988-89, La Crosse Catbirds, Continental Basketball Assn., Wis., 1989-94, gen. mgr., 1991-93, team pres., 1991-94; head coach Sioux Falls Skyforce, Continental Basketball Assn., SD; gen. mgr., head coach Minn. Timberwolves, 1995—2005; head coach Detroit Pistons, 2005—08, Washington Wizards, 2009—. Head coach US Men's Basketball Team Goodwill Games (gold medal), Brisbane, Australia, 2001. Named Continental Basketball Assn. Coach of Yr., 1990, 92. Achievements include head coach of the Continental Basketball Association championship winning La Crosse Catbirds, 1990, 1992. Office: Washington Wizards 601 F St NW Washington DC 20004*

SAUNDERS, GEORGE LAWTON, JR., lawyer; b. Mulga, Ala., Nov. 8, 1931; s. George Lawton and Ethel Estell (York) S.; children: Kenneth, Ralph, Victoria; m. Terry M. Rose. BA, U. Ala., 1956; JD, U. Chgo., 1959. Bar: Ill. 1960. Law clk. to chief judge U.S. Ct. Appeals (5th cir.), Montgomery, Ala., 1959-60; law clk to Justice Hugo L. Black U.S. Supreme Ct., Washington, 1960-62; assoc. Sidley & Austin, Chgo., 1962-67, ptnr., 1967-90; founding ptnr. Saunders & Monroe, Chgo., 1990—. With USAF, 1951-54. Fellow: Am. Coll. Trial Lawyers; mem.: Law Club, Quadrangle Club, Point-O-Woods Club, Chgo. Club, Order of the Coif, Phi Beta Kappa. Democrat. Baptist. Home: 179 E Lake Shore Dr Chicago IL 60611-1306 Office: Saunders Monroe Law Offices 20 S Clark St Ste 1720 Chicago IL 60603-1847 Personal E-mail: glsaunders@sbcglobal.net.

SAUNDERS, HAROLD HENRY, foundation administrator; b. Phila., Dec. 27, 1930; s. Harold Manuel Saunders and Marian Elizabeth Weihenmayer; m. Barbara Mc Garrigle, May 4, 1963 (dec. Oct. 1973); children: Catherine Elizabeth, Mark Harril; m. Carol Eleanor Jones Cruse, June 2, 1990. AB, Princeton U., 1952; PhD, Yale U., 1956; LittD, New Eng. Coll., 1999; D of Internat. Rels., Dickinson Coll., 2004. With CIA, Washington, 1959—61; sr. staff Nat. Security Coun., Washington, 1961—74; dir. intelligence and rsch., asst. sec. Near East and South Asian affairs Dept. of State, Washington, 1974—81; fellow Am. Enterprise Inst. Brookings Inst., Washington, 1981—91; profl. lectr. Johns Hopkins U., SAIS, George Mason U., 1984—91; dir. internat. affairs Kettering Found., Washington, 1991—; pres. Internat. Inst. Sustained Dialogue, 2002—. Author: The Other Walls: Arab-Israeli Peace Process in Global Perspective, 1985, 91, A Public Peace Process: Sustained Dialogue to Transform Racial and Ethnic Conflicts, 1999, Politics Is About Relationship: Blueprint for the Citizens' Century, 2005. Trustee Princeton U., 1996—2000; pres. Class of '52, 2002—07; bd. dirs. Hollings Ctr., 2007—; ruling elder Lewinsville Presbyn. Ch., McLean, Va., 1971—; bd. dirs. East-West Inst., NYC, 1981—89, Ptnrs. Dem. Change, San Francisco, 1995—2005, InterNews, Arcata, Calif., 1999—2001. Lt. USAF, 1957—59. Recipient Disting. Fed. Civilian Svc. award Pres. U.S., 1978, Disting. Honor award Dept. of State, 1981, First Disting. Achievement award Germantown Acad., Phila., Lifetime Achievement award Search for Common Ground, 2004. Mem. Internat. Soc. Polit. Psychology (gov. coun. 1991-94), Coun. Fgn. Rels., Princeton Club N.Y., Nassan Club Princeton (NJ), Phi Beta Kappa. Avocation: writing. Home: 2101 Lorraine Ave Mc Lean VA 22101 Office: Kettering Found 444 N Capitol St NW Washington DC 20001

SAUNDERS, JOHN WARREN, JR., biology professor, consultant; b. Muskogee, Okla., Nov. 12, 1919; s. John Warren and Amanda Mary (Schlattweiler) S.; m. Lilyan Clayton, Feb. 27, 1942; children: Sarah Elizabeth Reeder, John Warren, Margaret Ann Geist, Mary Katherine Brown. BS, U. Okla., 1940, MS, 1941; PhD, Johns Hopkins U., 1948. Jr. instr. in biology Johns Hopkins U., Balt., 1941-43, 46-48; instr. zoology U. Chgo., 1948-49; from assoc. prof. to prof. Marquette U., Milw., 1949-66; prof. anatomy U. Pa., Phila., 1966-67; prof. biology SUNY, Albany, 1967-85; author and cons. in pvt. practice Falmouth, Mass., 1985—. Adv. panel devel. biology NSF, Washington, 1961-66; trustee Marine Biol. Lab., Woods Hole, Mass., 1969-72; emeritus prof. biol. scis. SUNY, Albany. Author: Animal Morphogenesis, 1968, Principles of Animal Development, 1970, Developmental Biology, 1982; contbr. numerous articles to profl. jours. Bd. dirs. Milw. divsn. Am. Cancer Soc., 1960-65; elected mem. Town Meeting, Falmouth, Mass., 1988-95. Lt. (s.g.) USN, 1943-46, PTO. Recipient Joseph Rigge Disting. Svc. award Marquette U., 1988, Edwin Grant Conklin medal, 1996, Disting. Alumnus award U. Okla. Coll. Arts and Scis., 2007. Fellow AAAS; mem. NAS, Assn. Am. Anatomists, Soc. for Devel. Biology (pres. 1968-69), Am. Soc. Zoologists (sec. 1964-66), NAS. Democrat. Roman Catholic. Home and Office: 110 Dillingham Ave Apt 209 Falmouth MA 02540 Personal E-mail: saundred@comcast.net.

SAUNDERS, JOSEPH W., finance company executive; BS, U. Denver, 1967, MBA, 1968. V.p., credit card ops. Bank of Am., 1984—85; with Household Fin. Corp., 1985—97; chmn., CEO Fleet Credit Card Services L.P., 1997—2001; chmn. bd, CEO & pres. Providian Fin. Corp., 2001—05; pres. card services divsn. Washington Mutual, Inc., Seattle, 2005—07; exec. chmn., CEO Visa Inc., 2007—. Office: PO Box 8999 San Francisco CA 94128-8999

SAUNDERS, LONNA JEANNE, lawyer, broadcast journalist, talk host, writer; b. Cleve. d. Jack Glenn and Lillian Frances (Newman) Slaby. Student, Dartmouth Coll.; AB in Polit. Sci. with honors, Vassar Coll.; JD, Northwestern U., 1981; cert., Mass Media Inst., Stanford, Calif., 1992. Bar: Ill. 1981. News dir., morning news anchor Sta. WKBK-AM, Keene, NH, 1974-75; reporter Sta. KDKA-AM, Pitts., 1975; pub. affairs dir., news anchor Sta. WJW-AM, Cleve., 1975-76; helicopter traffic reporter WERE-AM Radio, Cleve., 1976-77; morning news anchor Sta. WBBG-AM, Cleve., 1978; talk host, news anchor Sta. WIND-AM, Chgo., 1978-82; atty. Arvey, Hodes, Costello & Burman, Chgo., 1981-82; host, "The Stock Market Observer", news anchor WCIU-TV, Chgo., 1982-85; staff atty. Better Govt. Assn., Chgo., 1983-84; news anchor, reporter Sta. WBMX-FM, Chgo., 1984-86; pvt. practice law Chgo., 1985—; news anchor Sta. WKQX-FM, Chgo., 1987; arbitrator Cir. Ct. 17th Jud. Dist., Ill., 2005—; tchr. Ill. Pub. Schs., 2006—, Ohio Pub. Schs., 2006—. Instr. Columbia Coll., Chgo., 1987-90; guest talk host Sta. WMCA, NYC, 1983, Sta. WMAQ, Chgo., 1988, Sta. WLS, Chgo., 1989, Sta. WWWE, Cleve., 1989, Sta. KVI, Seattle, 1994, WCBM-AM, Balt., 1996, WRC-AM, Wash., DC, 1997; host, prodr. The Lively Arts, Cablevision Chgo., 1986; talk show host The Lonna Saunders Show, Sta. KIRO-AM, Seattle, 1995-96; news anchor, WTOP-AM Radio, Washington, DC, 1996-97; talk host, "Today and Tomorrow show", WMAL-AM radio, Washington, DC, 1997, freelance reporter, CBS Radio Network, NYC, 1975—; atty. Lawyers for Creative Arts, Chgo., 1985-91; guardian Ad litem and child rep., 2005—; mem. tv production com. Chgo. Bar Assn., 2005-. Mem. editl. bd. Jour. Criminal Law and Criminology, 1979-81; creator pub. affairs program WBBM-AM, Chgo., 1985; law columnist Chgo. Life Mag., 1986-99; sports columnist Indians Ink mag., Cleve., 1998-2000; writer Rock River Times newspaper, 2004; guest columnist Gainesville Sun, Fla., 1998-99, Rockford Register Star Newspaper, 1998-; performer (film) The Color of Money, Chgo., 1986; contbr. articles to profl. jours., columns to mags. and newspapers. Atty., county counsel voter protection project Kerry-Edwards 2004, Inc.; mem. women's action coun. Amnesty Internat., 2000—. Recipient Akron Press Club award for best pub. affairs presentation, 1978; grantee Scripps Howard Found., 1978-81; AFTRA George Heller Meml. scholar, 1980-81. Fellow Am. Bar Found.; mem. ABA (mem. exec. coms. Lawyers and the Arts, Law and Media 1986-92, chmn. exec. com. Law and Media 1990-91, 91-92, Young Lawyers divsn. liaison to Forum Com. on Comm. Law 1991-93, Commn. for Partnership Programs 1993-94, regional divsn. chair Forum on Comm. Law 1995-96). Roman Catholic. Avocations: theater, piano, baseball, films.

SAUNDERS, MARTIN, chemistry educator, researcher; b. 1931; BS, CCNY; PhD, Harvard U., 1956. Prof. chemistry Yale U., New Haven, 1955—; Kharasch prof. U. Chgo., 1983. Contbr. articles to profl. jours. including Science, Nature, J. Am. Chem. Soc. Recipient Sr. U.S. Scientist award Alexander von Humboldt Found. 1977-78, 85, Arthur C. Cope Scholar award Am. Chem. Soc., 1998-99, James Flack Norris award in Physical Organic Chemistry, 2005. Fellow: Japanese Soc. Promotion of Natural Sci.; mem.: NAS, Am. Acad. Arts and Scis. Achievements include creation of new methods for studying carbocations, one of the three main species of reactive intermediates in organic reactions; discovery of detailed mechanisms and rates of very rapid rearrangement reactions of cation intermediates. Office: Yale U Dept Chemistry 225 Prospect St New Haven CT 06520-8107 Office Phone: 203-432-3974. Business E-Mail: ms@gaus90.chem.yale.edu.

SAUNDERS, PATRICIA GENE KNIGHT, freelance writer, editor; b. Tulsa, Nov. 29, 1946; d. Eugene Merritt and Patricia May (Hough) Knight; m. Joseph Eugene Saunders, June 24, 1989. BA, Baylor U., 1969. Nat. advt. sec. Sta. KTVT-TV, Ft. Worth, 1969-71; tchr. Arlington Ind. Sch. Dist., Tex., 1971-77, Garland Ind. Sch. Dist., Tex., 1977-79; payroll, spl. projects assoc. Electronic Data Systems, Dallas, 1979-81; adminstrv. asst. Diversifield Innovators, Dallas, 1981-82; system ops. mgr. Span Instruments, Plano, Tex., 1982-86; data processing mgr. Claire Mfg., Addison, Ill., 1986-87, Everpure, Inc., Westmont, Ill., 1987-88; software cons. Software Alternatives, Inc., Downers Grove, Ill., 1988-89; sys. ops. asst., cons. J&J Maintenance, Inc., Austin, Tex., 1989-90; pres., computer cons. Cardinal Software Solutions, Inc., Austin, 1990-93; editor Holt, Rinehart & Winston, Austin, 1993-99. Mem.: U. Tex.-Blanton Mus. Art, Writers' League Tex., Soc. Children's Book Writers and Illustrators, Nat. Mus. Women in Arts, Nat. Arbor Day Found., Nat. Wildlife Fedn., NY Met. Mus. Fine Art, Smithsonian Instn. Republican. Baptist. Avocations: cats, gardening, travel, movies, reading, photography. Home: 410 Teal Ln Kyle TX 78640-8888 Office Phone: 512-262-2062. Office Fax: 512-268-1625. E-mail: pgs2508@austin.rr.com.

SAUNDERS, PATRICK REED, history professor; b. Portsmouth, Ohio, May 21, 1948; s. Merritt Reed and Patricia Ann Saunders; m. Antoinette Mary Schaffer, Oct. 21, 1972; children: Patrick Reed II, Katherine Antoinette Saunders-Fox, Corrie Elizabeth Saunders-Horn. BA in Liberal Studies, Bowling Green State U., Ohio, 2002; MA in Am. Culture Studies, Bowling Green State U., 2003. Cert. social studies and earth scis. tchr. Ohio State Bd. Edn., 2003. Adj. prof. BGSU Firelands, Huron, Ohio, 2003—; working class studies instr. Ctr. Working Class Studies, Youngstown, Ohio, 2006. Prodr.: (TV series) Vantage Point, EndNotes; contbr. newspaper; pub. (online social commentary) www.runningforthecountyline. Labor mem. Firelands Labor-Mgmt.-Citizens Com., Norwalk, 1979—85; pres. Firelands Area Chpt. Vietnam Veterans Am., Norwalk, 1985—89; bd. mem. Huron County Bd. Elections, Norwalk, 1992—2003; founder book scholarship BGSU Fireland; chair Huron County Dem. Party, Norwalk, 1994—2001; chair, commr. Huron County Pk. Commn., Norwalk, 1979—83. Petty officer Seabees USN, 1968—72, Western Pacific, Indian Ocean. Recipient John Hogsett Meml. award, Huron County Dem. Party, 1990, Soc. of Flame award, BGSU Firelands, 2002; named Vietnam Vet. of Yr., Chpt. 322, Vietnam Vets. Am., 1987. Mem.: Working Class Studies Assn. (assoc.). Progressive. Avocations: reading, motorcycling, poetry. Office: BGSU Firelands One University Dr Huron OH 44839 Business E-Mail: prsaund@bgsu.edu.

SAUNDERS, PAUL CHRISTOPHER, lawyer; b. NYC, May 21, 1941; s. John Richard and Agnes Grace (Kelly) Saunders; m. Patricia Newman, Sept. 14, 1968; children: Dr. Paul Christopher, Michael Eagan. AB, Fordham Coll., 1963; JD, Georgetown U., 1966; Certificat, Institut d'Études Politiques, Paris, 1962. Bar: NY 1966, DC 1967, US Supreme Ct 1969. Assoc. Cravath, Swaine & Moore LLP, NYC, 1971-77, ptnr., litig., 1977—; disting. visitor from practice Georgetown U. Law Ctr., 2003—. Mem ed bd: Georgetown Law Jour, 1965—66; founder, editor-in-chief The Advocate, 1969—70. Trustee Fordham U., 1991—96, 2004—; bd. regents Georgetown U., 1991—96, bd. visitors Law Ctr., 1996—; trustee, vice-chmn Fordham Prep. Sch., 1986—94; v.p., bd. dirs. Legal Aid Soc., 1983—88; bd. dirs., trustee Lawyers Com. Civil Rights Under Law, 1985—, co-chair, 1995—97; dir. Vols. Legal Svc., Inc., 1999—2007; bd. dirs. Office of the Appellate Defender, 1999—2009; mem. NY State Judicial Inst. on Professionalism in the Law, 2000—, chair, 2007—; chmn. bd. dirs. Constitution Project, 2000—07, bd. dirs., 2000—. Capt JAGC US Army, 1967—71. Decorated Meritorious Svc. medal; recipient John Carroll medal, Georgetown U., 1995, Whitney N. Seymour award, Lawyers Com. Civil Rights Under Law, 2000, Paul R. Dean award, Georgetown U. Law Ctr., 2006. Fellow: Am. Bar Found., Am. Coll. Trial Lawyers; mem.: JIBA, Inst.

Transnational Arbitration, London Ct. Internat. Arbitration, Assn. Bar City N.Y., NY State Bar Assn., Westchester Country Club (Rye, NY), Apawamis Club (Rye, NY), Phi Beta Kappa, Pi Sigma Alpha. Democrat. Roman Catholic. Office: Cravath Swaine & Moore LLP Worldwide Plz 825 8th Ave Fl 39 New York NY 10019-7475 Home: 1220 Park Ave New York NY 10128 Office Phone: 212-474-1404. Office Fax: 212-474-3700. Business E-Mail: psaunders@cravath.com.

SAUNDERS, SALLY LOVE, poet, educator; b. Bryn Mawr, Pa., Jan. 15, 1940; d. Lawrence and Dorothy (Love) S. Student, Sophia U., Tokyo, Japan, 1963, U. Pa., Columbia; BS, George Williams Coll., 1965. Tchr. Shipley Sch., Bryn Mawr, 1962-65, Agnes Irwin Sch., Wynnewood, Pa., 1964-65, Montgomery County Day Sch., Wynnewood, 1962, Miquon (Pa.) Sch., Waldron Acad., Merion, Pa., 1965-66, Phelps Sch., Malvern, Pa., 1965-70, Frankford Friends Sch. Phila., 1965-66, Haverford (Pa.) Sch., 1965-66, Friends Sem. Sch., NYC, 1966-68, Ballard Sch., NYC, 1966-67, Lower Merion Sch., Ardmore, Pa., nights 1967-71, Univ. Settlement House, Phila., 1961-63, Navajo Indian Reservation, Fort Defiance, Ariz., 1963, Young Men's Jewish Youth Center, Chgo., 1964-65, Margaret Fuller Settlement House, Cambridge, Mass., 1958-61; poetry therapist Pa. Hosp. Inst., 1969-74, also drug rehab. house Phila.; poet in residence Tyrone Guthrie Ctr., Newbliss, Ireland, Aug. 1988; poetry workshop leader Pendle Hill Quaker Ctr., Wallingford, Pa., Apr. 1988; poetry week leader Ferry Beach, Saco, Maine, summer 1988. Pioneer in poetry therapy. Poet, 1946—; poems pub. in periodicals including others; author: Past the Near Meadows, 1961, Pauses, 1978, Fresh Bread, 1982, Random Thoughts, 1992, Patchwork Quilt, 1993, Quiet Thoughts and Gentle Feelings, 1996, Word Pictures, 1998, Bits of Thought, 2006; contbr. poems to newspapers. Mem. Acad. Am. Poets, Nat. Fedn. State Poetry Socs., Am. Poetry League, Nat. League Am. Pen Women, Poetry Therapy Assn. (v.p.), Avalon Orgn., Authors Guild, Nat. Writers Club, Pen and Brush Club, N.H.Poetry Soc., Pa. Poetry Soc., Cath. Poetry Soc. (asso.), Fla. State Poetry Soc. (asso.) Episcopalian. Home: 2030 Vallejo St Apt 501 San Francisco CA 94123-4854 also: 639 Timber Haven Devon PA 19333 E-mail: slovesndrs@aol.com. *So often during my life I have found great comfort and strength in writing and reading poetry. With my poetry I want to help others to get in touch with their own powers. Poetry, to me, is a rare and beautiful freedom and this is what I want to share with others.*

SAUNDERS, STEVEN R., international public policy specialist; s. Lawrence J. and Sara (Leinoff) Saunders; m. Maureen Collins, May 28, 1977; children: Keira, Erin, Burke. BA, Washington & Lee U., 1968. Dep. mayor Town of Oyster Bay, NY, 1970—74; staff asst. NY State Legis., Albany, 1974—75; legis. dir. US Rep. Norman F. Lent, Washington, 1975—77; comm. dir. Nat. Rep. Senatorial Com., Washington, 1977—79; staff dir. Rep. Conf. of the US Senate, Washington, 1979—81; asst. US trade rep. Exec. Office of the Pres., Washington, 1981—82; pres. Saunders & Co., Alexandria, Va., 1982—. Pres. N.Am.-Mongolia Bus. Coun., Alexandria, 1998—. Editor: Japan Hands: Who's Who in US-Japan Relations in the US Government, 1990. Pres. Zorig Found. USA, Alexandria, 2000—05, bd. trustees, 2000—; co-chmn. Am. Coun. Young Polit. Leaders, 1982—89. Recipient Businessman for Liberty award, Liberty Ctr., 2001, Investment Envoy of the Yr. award, Govt. Mongolia-Ulaanbaatar, 2002, Order of Polar Star medal, Pres. of Mongolia, 2007. Mem.: Am. Mgmt. Assn. (internat. coun. 1995—), Theodore Roosevelt Assn. (trustee 1970—2009). Republican. Avocation: Buddhist art. Office: Saunders & Co 1015 Duke St Alexandria VA 22314 Office Phone: 703-549-1555.

SAUNDERS, TERRY ROSE, lawyer; b. Phila., July 13, 1942; d. Morton M. and Esther (Hauptman) Rose; m. George Lawton Saunders Jr., Sept. 21, 1975. BA, Barnard Coll., 1964; JD, NYU, 1973. Bar: D.C. 1973, Ill. 1976, U.S. Dist. Ct. (no. dist.) Ill. 1976, U.S. Ct. Appeals (7th cir.) 1976, U.S. Supreme Ct. 1983. Assoc. Williams & Connolly, Washington, 1973-75, Jenner & Block, Chgo., 1975-80, ptnr., 1981-86, Susman, Saunders & Buehler, Chgo., 1987-94; pvt. practice Law Offices of Terry Rose Saunders, Chgo., 1995—2002; ptnr. Saunders & Doyle, Chgo., 2002—. Author: (with others) Securities Fraud: Litigating Under Rule 10b-5, 1989. Recipient Robert B. McKay award NYU Sch. Law. Mem. ABA (co-chair class actions and derivative suits com. sect. litig. 1992-95, task force on merit selection of judges, co-chair consumer and personal rights litig. com. sect. litigation 2000-02), Chgo. Bar Assn., Order of Coif, Union League Club. Office Phone: 312-551-0051. Business E-Mail: trsaunders@saundersdoyle.com.

SAUNDERS, W(ARREN) PHILLIP, JR., economics professor, consultant, writer; b. Morgantown, W.Va., Sept. 3, 1934; s. Warren Phillip and Thelma Marie (Dotson) S.; m. Nancy Lee Trainor, June 16, 1956; children: Kathleen M., Kevin W., Keith A., Kent T., Kristine A. BA, Pa. State U., 1956; MA, U. Ill., 1957; PhD, MIT, 1964. Instr. econs. Bowdoin Coll., Brunswick, Maine, 1961-62; rsch. assoc., from asst. to assoc. prof. econs. Carnegie-Mellon U., Pitts., 1962-70; prof. to prof. emeritus in Econ. Ind. U., Bloomington, 1970—; assoc. dean Coll. of Arts and Scis. Ind. U., Bloomington, 1974-78, chmn. dept. econs., 1988-92. Cons. Agy. for Instructional Tech., Bloomington, 1976-78, 81-84, 92-93. Author: (books) Political Dimension of Labor-Management Relations, 1986; author, editor: Framework for Teaching Basic Economic Concepts, 1995; (Workbooks) Introduction to Macroeconomics (18th edit.), 1998, Introduction to Microeconomics (18th edit.), 1998; contbr. articles to Am. Econ. Rev., 1964—. Chmn. staff-parish rels. com. First United Meth. Ch., Bloomington, 1982-94. Recipient Vilard award for disting. rsch., Nat. Assn. Econ. Educators, N.Y.C., 1986, Leavey award for edn. Freedoms Found., Valley Forge, Pa., 1986, Disting. Svc. award. Nat. Coun. Econ. Edn., 1995. Mem. Am. Econ. Assn., Midwest Econ. Assn. (1st v.p. 1988-89), Soc. Econs. Educators (pres. 1992-93). Home: 3725 E Brownridge Rd Bloomington IN 47401-4209 Office: Ind Univ Dept Econs Bloomington IN 47405 E-mail: saunders@indiana.edu.

SAUNDERS, WILLIAM HUNDLEY, JR., retired chemist, educator; b. Pulaski, Va., Jan. 12, 1926; s. William Hundley and Vivian (Watts) S.; m. Nina Velta Plesums, June 25, 1960 (dec. June 1982); children: Anne Michele, Claude William; m. Barbara Andrews, Apr. 27, 2002 (dec. May 2005) BS in Chemistry, Coll. William and Mary, 1948; PhD in Organic Chemistry, Northwestern U., 1952. Rsch. assoc. MIT, 1951-53; instr. U. Rochester, 1953-56, from. asst. prof. to assoc. prof., 1956-64, prof. chemistry, 1964-91, faculty sr. assoc., 1991-95, chmn. dept., 1966-70, prof. emeritus, 1996—. Author: Ionic Aliphatic Reactions, 1965; (with A.F. Cockerill) Mechanisms of Elimination Reactions, 1973; (with L. Melander) Reaction Rates of Isotopic Molecules, 1980; contbr. numerous articles to profl. jours. With US Army, 1944—45, ETO. Guggenheim fellow, 1960—61, Sloan Found. fellow, 1961—64, NSF sr. postdoctoral fellow, 1970—71. Mem. Am. Chem. Soc., Royal Soc. Chemistry, Phi Beta Kappa, Sigma Xi, Phi Lambda Upsilon. Democrat. Unitarian Universalist. Avocations: bicycling, cross country skiing, travel. Home: 15 Parkwood Ave Rochester NY 14620-3401 Office: U Rochester Dept Chemistry River Sta Rochester NY 14627 Office Phone: 585-275-4235. Business E-Mail: saunders@chem.rochester.edu.

SAURET, MARTINE, French educator; b. Paris, Aug. 1, 1955; came to U.S., 1982; d. George Henri and Andrée Lucie (Vallet) S.; m. John Joseph Stronczer, Aug. 10, 1984; 1 child, Roxanne Andree. MA in French, U. Minn., 1984, PhD, 1991; cert. commerce internat., U. Paris III, 1982. Asst. coord. U. Minn., Mpls., 1989-90; French instr. St. Johns U., Collegeville, 1990-91, asst. prof. French, 1991-92, Western Mich. U., Kalamazoo, 1992-97, assoc. prof. French, 1997—. Author: Gargantua et les, 1997; translator The Graphic Unconsious in Early modern French Writing, 2000; contbr. articles to profl. jours. FRACASF grantee Western Mich. U., 1995, 2000, faculty rsch. support grant, 1992, 2000. Office: Western Mich U Fgn Langs Kalamazoo MI 49008 E-mail: mourtinesauret@umich.edu.

SAUSMAN, KAREN, zoological park administrator; b. Chgo., Nov. 26, 1945; d. William and Annabell (Lofaso) S. BS, Loyola U., 1966; student, Redlands U., 1968. Keeper Lincoln Park Zoo, Chgo., 1964-66; tchr. Palm Springs (Calif.) Unified Sch., 1968-70; ranger Nat. Park Svc., Joshua Tree, Calif., 1968-70; zoo dir. The Living Desert, Palm Desert, Calif., 1970—. Natural history study tour leader internat., 1974—; part-time instr. Coll. Desert Natural History Calif. Desert, 1975-78; field reviewer conservation grants Inst. Mus. Svcs., 1987—, MAP cons., 1987—, panelist, 1992—; internat. studbook keeper for Sand Cats, 1988-2001, for Cuvier's Gazelle, Mhorr Gazelle, 1990-2000; co-chair Arabian Oryx species survival plan propogation group, 1986-95; spkr. in field. Author Survival Captive Bighorn Sheep, 1982, Small Facilities-Opportunities and Obligations, 1983; wildlife illustrator books, mags, 1970—; editor Fox Paws newsletter Living Desert, 1970—, ann. reports, 1976—; natural sci. editor Desert Mag., 1979-82; compiler Conservation and Management Plan for Antelope, 1992; contbr. articles to profl. jours. Past bd. dirs., sec. Desert Protective Coun.; adv. coun. Desert Bighorn Rsch. Inst., 1981-85; bd. dirs. Palm Springs Desert Resorts Convention and Visitors Bur., 1988-94; bd. dirs., treas. Coachella Valley Mountain Trust, 1989-92. Named Woman Making a Difference Soroptomist Internat., 1989, 93, 97, Woman of Distinction, Riverside Bus. Press, 2000. Fellow Am. Assn. Zool. Parks and Aquariums (bd. dirs., accredation field reviewer, desert antelope taxon adv. group, caprid taxon adv. group, felid taxon adv. group, small population mgmt. adv. group, wildlife conservation and mgmt. com., chmn. ethics com. 1987, mem. com., internat. rels. com., ethics task force, pres'. award 1972-77, outstanding svc. award 1983, 88, editor newsletter, Zool. Parks and Aquarium Fundamentals 1982); mem. Internat. Species Inventory System (mgmt. com., policy adv. group 1980-96, trustee 1997-2004), Calif. Assn. Mus. (v.p. 1992-96), Calif. Assn. Zoos and Aquariums, World Assn. Zoos and Aquariums (coun. 2002-, governing coun. 2000-, pres. 2005-07), Western Interpretive Assn. (so. Calif. chpt.), Am. Assn. Mus., Arboreta and Bot. Gardens So. Calif. (coun. dirs.), Soc. Conservation Biology, Nat. Audubon. Soc., Jersey Wildlife Preservation Trust Internat., Nature Conservancy, East African Wildlife Soc., African Wildlife Found., Kennel Club Palm Springs (past bd. dirs., treas. 1978-80), Scottish Deerhound Club Am. (editor Scottish Deerhounds in N.A., 1983, life mem. U.K. chpt.), Internat. Bengal Cat Soc. (pres. 1994-96). Avocations: pure bred dogs, cats, dressage, painting, photography. Office: The Living Desert 47 900 Portola Ave Palm Desert CA 92260 E-mail: kastld@aol.com.

SAUVAGNAT, HENRY GABRIEL, entrepreneur, sales executive; b. Aurillac, France, June 1, 1954; s. Marcel Sauvagnat and Simone Abeil; m. Laurence Madeleine Brun-Sauvagnat, June 2, 1978; children: Claire, Marie. Baccalaureat, Stanislas, Paris, France, 1972; BS, Univ. Wyo., Laramie, Wyo., 1975; B of Comm., Univ. McGill, Montreal, Can., 1983; MBA, Univ. Syracuse, 1985. Pres. Chempap Inc., Montgomery, Vt., 1985—98; dir. sales & corp affairs Greenfield Cascades, Courbevoie, France, 1998—. Dir. Chempap, Montgomery, Vt., 1985—98, Greenfield, France, 1998—. Coaching dir. Jay Peak Ski Club, Vt., 1990—93; assn. pres. Alpine Haven, Vt., 1993—95. Home: PO Box 465 Montgomery Center VT 05471-0465

SAUZIER, MARIA CONSUELA, psychiatrist, educator; b. Bucarest, Romania, Mar. 18, 1947; m. Peter Joseph Musliner; 1 child, Alexandra Musliner. MD, U. Vienna, 1971. Cert. med. dr. Mass. Bd. Registration, 1975. Rschr. Tufts-NEMC, Boston, dir., family crisis program, 1980—85; cons. Cambridge Health Alliance, 1985—; tchr. Harvard Med. Sch., Cambridge, 1985—. Trauma cons. Various Orgns., 1980—. Tchr. & supr. Various Orgns., Mass., 1980—2009. Recipient Outstanding Psychiatrist award, Mass Psychiat. Soc., 1995, Harvard Consol. Psychiatry, 2001, Am. Psychiat. Assn., 2003, Cambridge Health Alliance Divsn. Psychiatry, 2006. Achievements include research in sexual abuse trauma in children. Home and Office: 42 Antrim St Cambridge MA 02139

SAVAGE, CHARLES, reporter, news correspondent; b. Ft. Wayne, Ind., 1975; m. Luiza Savage; 1 child, Will. BA in English and Am. Lit., Harvard Coll., 1998; M., Yale Law Sch., 2003. Staff The Jour. Gazette, Ft. Wayne; govt. & politics reporter Miami Herald, 1998—2002; Washington corr. Boston Globe, Washington, 2003—08; reporter NY Times, 2008—. Author: Takeover: The Return of the Imperial Presidency and the Subversion of American Democracy, 2007 (Constitution Project award for Constl. Commentary, 2007). Recipient Pulitzer Prize for Nat. Reporting, The Pulitzer Board, 2007; Knight Found. journalism fellow, Yale Law Sch., 2002—03. Office: NY Times 620 Eighth Ave New York NY 10018*

SAVAGE, ELDON PAUL, retired environmental health educator; b. Bedford, Iowa, Apr. 4, 1926; s. Paul and Nora (Arthur) S.; m. Ella May, June 5, 1948; children: Steven P., Michael D. BS, U. Kans., 1950; MPH, Tulane U., 1958; PhD, Okla. U., 1968. Coord. environ. sanitation demonstration projects USPHS, Kans., Iowa and Pa., 1950-64; chief state aids sect. pesticide ctr. Ctr. for Disease Control, Atlanta, 1964-70; chief chem. epidemiology sect. Inst. Rural Environ. Health, Colo. State U., Ft. Collins, 1970-84, prof., dir. environ. health divsn., 1984-85, head dept. environ. health, 1985-90, dir. environ. health svcs., 1987-93, prof. emeritus, 1993—. Contbr. articles to profl. jours. Mem. Am. Acad. Sanitarians (sec., treas., diplomate), Nat. Environ. Health Assn., Sigma Xi, Gamma Sigma Delta. Home: Savage EE Arabian Horses 5220 Apple Dr Fort Collins CO 80526-4302 Office: Colo State U Inst Rural Envrion Health Fort Collins CO 80523-0001

SAVAGE, JAMES FRANCIS, retired editor; b. Boston, July 23, 1939; s. James and Hanora (Enright) S.; m. Sharon Kaye Base, May 29, 1965; 1 son, Sean. AA, Boston U., 1959, BS, 1961. Reporter Quincy (Mass.) Patriot Ledger, 1961-63; reporter Miami (Fla.) Herald, 1963-67, investigative reporter, 1967-78, investigations editor, 1978-84, assoc. editor investigations, 1984—2003. Investigative reporter Boston Herald Traveler, 1967 Served with AUS, 1962. Recipient Nat. Headliners award, 1969, Fla. Press Assn. award, 1972, George Polk Meml. award for investigative reporting, 1973, 80, Pub. Service award Nat. A.P. Mng. Editors, 1974, 80, award Fla. Soc. Newspaper Editors, 1974, 75, Nat. Disting. Service award Sigma Delta Chi, 1979, 87, Pulitzer Prize Staff award for Nat. Reporting, 1987, Outstanding Investigative Reporting award Investigative Reporters and Editors, 1988, Disting. Alumni award Boston U. Coll. Communications, 1990, Pulitzer Prize Staff Pub. Svc. award, 1993; Profl. Journalism fellow Stanford, 1974-75 Home: 1004 Orange Is Fort Lauderdale FL 33315-1651 Office: 1 Herald Plz Miami FL 33132-1609

SAVAGE, JOHN EDMUND, computer science educator, researcher; b. Lynn, Mass., Sept. 19, 1939; s. Edmund J. and Eldora A. (Guay) S.; m. Patricia Joan Landers, Jan. 29, 1966; children: Elizabeth, Kevin, Christopher, Timothy ScB, ScM, MIT, 1962, PhD, 1965. Mem. tech. staff Bell Telephone Labs., Holmdel, NJ, 1965-67; prof. computer sci. Brown U., Providence, 1967—, chmn. dept. computer sci., 1985-91. Vis. prof. Tech. U. Eindhoven, 1973—74, U. Paris, 1980—81, Warwick U., 1991—92, Ecole Polytechique, 2004—05; vis. Inst. Nat. Rsch. Info. Automatic, Rocquencourt, France; cons. in field. Author: The Complexity of Computing, 1977; author: (with others) The Mystical Machine, 1986; author: Models of Computation: Exploring the Power of Computing, 1996; editor (with Thomas Knight): Advanced Research in VLSI and Parallel Systems, 1992; chmn. editl. bd. Computing Rsch. News, 1990—96, mem. editl. bd. Jour. Computer and Sys. Scis., 1993—, patentee data scrambler, 1970, means and methods for generating permutation of a square, 1976, stochastic assembly of sublithographic interfaces, 2005, sublithographic nanoscale memory architecture, 2005. Mem. MIT Corp. vis. com. dept. elec. engring. and computer sci., 1991-2002. Fulbright-Hays grantee, 1973; NSF fellow, 1961, Guggenheim fellow, 1973 Fellow AAAS, IEEE (life), Assn. Computing Machinery; mem. Computing Rsch. Assn. (bd. dirs. 1990-96), Sigma Xi, Tau Beta Pi. Avocations: reading, bicycling, walking. Office: Brown U Dept Computer Sci 115 Waterman St Providence RI 02912-9016 Office Phone: 401-863-7642. Business E-Mail: john_savage@brown.edu.

SAVAGE, JOSEPH GEORGE, academic administrator; b. Bklyn. s. Joseph George Jr. and Eileen (Schnell) S.; m. Lynn Ann Campbell; children: Kimberly, Patricia, Joseph IV. BA, Oswego Coll., 1977; postgrad., Seton Hall U., 1985. With Nat. Multiple Sclerosis Soc., NYC, 1977—80; dir. devel., mktg. Clara Mass Meml. Med. Ctr., Belleville, N.J., 1980-81; exec. dir. Found. of St. Joseph's Hosp. Med. Ctr., Paterson, N.J., 1981-89; sr. v.p. St. Francis Hosp. Heart Ctr., Roslyn, N.Y., 1989-92; v.p. St. Vincents Hosp. and Med. Ctr., NYC, 1992-98; exec. v.p. Cathedral Health Care Sys., Newark, 1998—2001; v.p. exec. adminstrn. Caldwell Coll., NJ, 2001—. Commr. health City of Clifton, 1990-94; bd. dirs. N.Y. Heart Coun., 1989-93, Cath. Family and Cmty. Svcs., 1992-2006, Osweo Coll. Alumni, 1992—, St. Mary's Hosp., Passiac, N.J., 1993-99, 2000—; bd. trustees Caldwell Coll. Fellow Nat. Assn. Hosp. Devel. (communication chair 1982-85, edn. chair 1985-86, bd. dirs., regional dir. 1988-89), Friendly Sons of St. Patrick NY, Ancient Order of Hibernians, Rotary (past pres. Clifton Club, Paul Harris fellow, Walter Head fellow), Caldwell Club(chmn. project Iraci Freedom), Roman Catholic. Avocations: swimming, golf. Office: Caldwell Coll 9 Ryerson Ave Caldwell NJ 07006-1558 Home: 300 Alexandria Dr Hackettstown NJ 07840-3804 Home Phone: 973-885-6715; Office Phone: 973-618-3242. E-mail: jsavage@caldwell.edu.

SAVAGE, KIM I., academic administrator; d. William T. and Sylvia V. Savage; 1 child, Nicholas. BA, North Ctrl. Coll., 1977; MEd, Oreg. State U., 1980. Asst. dir., Hermann Hall Ill. Inst. Tech., Chgo., 1977—78; program advisor Oreg. State U., Corvallis, 1978—80; asst. program dir. Ohio State U., Columbus, 1980—81; various positions in student centers adminstrn. U. Ill., Chgo., 1981—2001, campus aux. svcs., 2001—05, asst. to vice chancellor student affairs, 2005—06, assessment coord. for student affairs, 2006—. Contbr. articles to profl. jours. Chmn. Downers Grove Twp. Dem. Orgn., Ill., 2006—, precinct committeeman, 2000—06; mem. Ill. Dem. Women, Springfield; dir. Alford Am. Family Assn., Florissant, Mo., 2001—04. Recipient Staff Leadership award, Assn. Coll. Unions Internat. Region, 2006. Mem.: AAUW, LWV, Assn. Coll. Unions Internat. (various regional and nat. leadership positions 1980—2003, pub. policy liaison 2005—), Woodridge Toastmasters (v.p. 2005—). Avocations: gardening, genealogy.

SAVAGE, MARK RANDALL, lawyer; b. Chicopee, Mass., Mar. 10, 1959; m. Lucia Clara Savage; children: David, Ryan. BA, U. Calif., Berkeley, 1982; JD, Stanford U., 1988. Bar: Calif. Jud. law clk. to Judge James Holden, North Bennington, Vt., 1988-89; mng. atty. Pub. Advs., Inc., San Francisco, 1989—2003; sr. atty. Consumers Union of U.S., Inc., San Francisco, 2003—. Gen. counsel Cmty. Tech. Found. Calif., San Francisco, 1998—2008; bd. dirs. Family Bridges, Inc., Oakland, Calif., 2003-08 Contbr. articles to profl. jours. Bd. dirs. Unitarian Ch., Oakland, Calif., 2006—09, Inst. for Civic Arts and Pub. Spaces, Inc., Albuquerque, 1996—2001. Recipient Drum Maj. award So. Christian Leadership Conf., 1998, Diversity, Innovation and Reform in Edn. award, 1995, El Fuego Nuevo award Assn. Mex. Am. Educators, 1999, Leadership Recognition award Calif. Primary Care Assn., 1999, Screaming Eagle award Calif. Reinvestment Coalition, 2004, Calif. Lawyer Attys. of Yr. award, 2007. Office: Consumers Union 1535 Mission St San Francisco CA 94103-2566 Home Phone: 510-261-8263; Office Phone: 415-431-6747. Business E-Mail: Mark.Savage@pacbell.net.

SAVAGE, MAUREEN WALLS, retired history professor; b. Paterson, NJ, Nov. 16, 1930; d. George A. and Mary Duffy Walls; m. Harry Michael Savage, Nov. 27, 1948; children: Terry, Aileen, Kathleen, Timothy, Russell. BA, Rutgers U., Newark, 1963; MA, Rutgers U., New Brunswick, NJ, 1974. Tchr. social studies, English grades 7-8 pub. schs., Orange, NJ, 1963—66, tchr. social studies, English, world history grades 7-12 Cranford, NJ, 1966—88; prof. polit. sci. Coll. St. Elizabeth, Convent Station, NJ, 1998; prof. Irish history and culture Stockton Coll., Pomona, NJ, 1993—2003. Historian Ctr. for Cmty. Arts, Cape May, NJ, 1996—2006; curator Historic Colonial Ho., Cape May, 2003, African Am. history exhibits, 1996—; pres., v.p., moderator LWV, Cape May County, 1990—, nominating com. state bd., 2002—; leader NJ del. 75th anniversary women's suffrage re-enactment, Washington, 1995. Grantee NJ Hist. Soc., Historic Commn. Cape May County. Mem.: Greater Cape May Hist. Soc. (v.p. 2001—), Irish Am. Cultural Soc. Roman Catholic. Avocations: piano, history, Irish dancing, travel, theater. Home: 916 Columbia Ave Cape May NJ 08204 Home Fax: 609-898-8107. Personal E-mail: hmsavage@verizon.net.

SAVAGE, MICHAEL (MICHAEL ALAN WEINER), radio personality, commentator; b. Bronx, NY, Mar. 31, 1942; m. Janet A. Savage (div.); children: Russell, Rebecca; m. Sheila Weiner-Rozzo, 1964 (div. 1967). BA in Sociology and Edn., CUNY Queens Coll., 1963; MS in Ethnobotany, U. Hawaii, 1970, MA in Medical Anthropology, 1972; PhD in Nutritional Ethnomedicine, U. Calif., Berkeley, 1978. HS tchr., NYC; fill-in talk show host Sta.KGO, San Francisco, 1994—95; talk radio host Sta.KSFO, San Francisco, 1995—2003; host (nationally-syndicated) The Savage Nation, Talk Radio Network, 1999—; host (TV) The Savage Nation MSNBC, 2003. Author: (books) The Death of the White Male, 1991, The Savage Nation: Saving America from the Liberal Assault on Our Borders, Language, and Culture, 2003 (#1 NY Times bestseller), The Enemy Within: Saving America from the Liberal Assault on Our Schools, Faith, and Military, 2004, Liberalism is a Mental Disorder, 2005, The Political Zoo, 2006, Psychological Nudity, 2008; author: (as Michael A. Weiner, Ph.D.) Plant a Tree, 1975, Bugs in Peanut

Butter, 1976, Man's Useful Plants, 1976, The Taster's Guide to Beer: Brews and Breweries of the World, 1977, Earth Medicine, Earth Food, 1980, The Way of the Skeptical Nutritionist, 1981, The Art of Feeding Children Well, 1982, Nutrition Against Aging, 1983, Secrets of Fijian Medicine, 1983, Vital Signs, 1983, Getting Off Cocaine, 1984, Dr. Weiner's High Fiber Counter, 1984, Maximum Immunity, 1986, Reducing the Risk of Alzheimer's, 1987, The Complete Book of Homeopathy, 1989, The Herbal Bible, 1992, Healing Children Naturally, 1993, Herbs That Heal: Prescription for Herbal Healing, 1994, The Antioxidant Cookbook, 1995. Recipient Freedom of Speech award, Talkers Mag., 2007. Mem.: Paul Revere Soc. (founding mem.). Jewish. Address: Talk 910 KNEW 340 Townsend St San Francisco CA 94107 Office: c/o Talk Radio Network PO Box 3775 Central Point OR 97502 Office Phone: 800-449-8255. E-mail: michaelsavage@paulreveresociety.com.*

SAVAGE, MICHAEL JOHN KIRKNESS, oil industry, performing arts company executive and winegrower; b. Birmingham, Eng., Oct. 28, 1934; arrived in U.S., 1962, naturalized, 1981; s. Leonard W. H. and Hilda C. (Fletcher) Savage; m. Elisabeth Karl, June 21, 1965 (div.); m. Virginia Hooper, Aug. 31, 1978; 1 child, Matthew Nicholas. MA in Econs. and Law with honors, Cambridge U., 1958; postgrad., Manchester Bus. Sch., Eng., 1965; Diploma in Arabic, Middle E. Ctr. for Arab Studies, Shemlan, Lebanon, 1967. Various positions Brit. Petroleum Co. Ltd., 1958-82, internat. dir. London, 1982; pres. BP Alaska Inc., San Francisco, 1977, Sohio Petroleum Co., San Francisco, 1978-82; founder/pres. Merlin Petroleum Co., San Francisco, 1983-88, Savage Petroleum Co., Sausalito, Calif., 1992—95; bd. dirs., mng. dir. San Francisco Opera, 1994-99; exec. dir. bd. dirs. Napa Valley Opera House, Napa, Calif., 2000—04, Lincoln Theater, Napa Valley, Calif., 2004—07, bd. dirs., 2004—. Trustee San Francisco Conservatory Music, 1983—, chmn., 1990—94, lifetime trustee, 2008—; owner Sarafornia Cellars LLC, 1997—; trustee Alaska Pacific U., 1982—86; dir. Napa Valley Mustard Festival, 2005—08. Avocations: music, tennis, skiing, mountain walking, winegrowing. Office: 3060 Lake County Hwy Calistoga CA 94515

SAVAGE, RANDALL ERNEST, journalist; b. Commerce, Ga., Mar. 3, 1939; s. Ernest Kyle and Sara Beatrice (Collins) S.; m. Joyce Carol Martin, Nov. 26, 1964 (div. May 1984); children: Kimberly Dawn, Bradley Kyle; m. Mary Elizabeth Hallmark, Aug. 4, 1984; children: Brock Morgan, Laura Marie, Shaw Hamilton. Student, U. Md.-European Div., RAF Bentwaters, Eng., 1967-69; BA in Journalism, U. Ga., 1972. Service sta. worker Collins Service Sta., Commerce, Ga., 1958; billing clk. Benton Rapid Express, Atlanta, 1958-61; truck driver So. Oil Co., High Point, NC, 1964-65; reporter Commerce News, Ga., 1972; sr. spl. projects reporter Macon Telegraph and News, Ga., 1972—, polit. and investing reporter Ga. Served with U.S. Army, 1961-64; with USAF, 1966-69. Recipient 3rd place in news AP, Atlanta, 1976, 2nd place in news AP, Atlanta, 1976, 1st place in sports AP, Atlanta, 1984; 2d place in news Green Eyeshades award, 1976; Pulitzer prize, 1985, Outstanding Alumnus award Henry W. Grady Coll. of Journalism and Mass Communication, U. Ga., 1989. Baptist. Avocations: jogging, softball, fishing, free-lance writing. Home: 985 Chads Ford Ct Macon GA 31210-1572 Office: WMAZTV 1314 Gray Hwy 31211 Macon GA 31201

SAVAGE, SHERELYN SUE, secondary school educator; d. Robert Louis and Catherine Marie Cook; m. Michael Gerard Savage; children: Kelly Marie Clemons, Kristen Marie Brinton. BS in Secondary Edn., Ohio State U., Columbus, 1973; MEd in Reading Edn., U. Ctrl. Fla., Orlando, 2005. Cert. profl. tchg. Fla., 1990, tchr. Nat. Bd. Profl. Tchg. Stds., 2000. Tchr. Alliance City Schs., 1974—75, North Canton City Schs., 1975—76, Barberton City Schs., Ohio, 1987—90, Marion County Pub. Schs., Ocala, Fla., 1990—; tchr., youth svcs. Indian River Sch., Massillon, Ohio, 1985—87. Mem. Fla. Assn. Theatre Edn., 1997—, Internat. Reading Assn., 2005—. Named Tchr. of Yr., Dunnellon HS, 1993. Home: 4511 Se 47th Pl Ocala FL 34480-8876 Office: Belleview HS 10400 Se 36th Ave Belleview FL 34420

SAVAGE, SUSAN M., Secretary of State, Oklahoma, former mayor; b. Tulsa, Okla., 1936; married; 2 children. Student, U. Aix-Marseilles, Aix-en-Provence, France, 1969, City of London Poly., Eng., 1972; BA in Sociology with honors, Beaver Coll., 1974. Pre-trial rep. Phila. Ct. Common Pleas, 1974-75; criminal justice planner Montgomery County Criminal Justice Unit, 1975-77; exec. dir. Met. Tulsa Citizens Crime Com., 1977-87; vol. coord. Vote Yes For Tulsa, 1987; chief of staff to mayor City of Tulsa, 1988-92, mayor, 1992—2002; sec. state State of Okla., Oklahoma City, 2003—. Active Lee Elementary Sch. PTA; bd. dirs., treas. Okla. Crime Prevention Assn.; bd. dirs. Youth Svcs. of Tulsa County, 1984-88, pres., 1986-87; co-chair Safe Streets/Enhanced 911 Steering Com., 1987; mem. C. of C. Task Force/Community Edn. Network, 1983. Mem. U.S. Conf. Mayors (chmn. com. energy and environment). Democrat. Office: Office Sec of State State Capitol Rm 101 Oklahoma City OK 73105 Home: 224 NW 33rd St Oklahoma City OK 73118-8614 Office Phone: 405-521-3911. Office Fax: 405-521-3771. Business E-Mail: susan.savage@sos.state.ok.us.

SAVAGE, TERRY, television personality, journalist, stockbroker; Grad., U. Mich. Registered investment advisor stocks and commodity futures. Founding mem., 1st woman trader Chgo. Bd. Options Exch.; mem. Internat. Monetary Market; columnist Chgo. Sun Times, Chgo.; personal fin. columnist Barron's Online; featured columnist MSN Money web site; owner, columnist pvt. web site www.TerrySavage.com. Bd. dirs. Devon Energy, Broadway Stores, Chicago Mercantile Exchange; former bd. mem. McDonald's Corp., Pennzoil-Quaker State Corp.; former co-editor Options Trading Strategies newsletter; spkr. in field. Host Money Talks; author: Terry Savage's New Money Strategies for the 90s, 1993, Terry Savage Talks Money: The Common-Sense Guide to Money Matters, 1999, The Savage Truth on Money, 1999; columnist Chgo. Sun-Times. Dir. Chgo. Mus. Sci. and Industry, Northwestern Meml. Hosp. Found., Econ. Club Chgo., Execs. Club Chgo., Jr. Achievement Ill., Ill. Coun. on Econ. Edn., Women's Bus. Devel. Ctr. Recipient Outstanding Consumer Journalism award Nat. Press Club, 1987, Dir.'s Choice award, 1994, 2 Emmy awards, Outstanding Personal Finance Columnist award, Northwestern U.; Woodrow Wilson fellow in Am. history and econs. Mem. Phi Beta Kappa. Office: Chicago Sun Times 350 N Orleans St Ste 1270 Chicago IL 60654-2148 also: Terry Savage Productions Ltd 350 N Orleans St Chicago IL 60654-1975 Office Phone: 312-266-1717. Office Fax: 312-266-3334. Business E-Mail: terry@terrysavage.com. E-mail: savage@suntimes.com.*

SAVAGE, THOMAS RYAN, lawyer; b. Milw., Dec. 1, 1947; s. John F. and Dorothy R. (Ryan) S.; m. Patricia C. Savage: children: Ryan, Patrick, Molly. BA, Quincy Coll., 1969; JD, Marquette U., 1973. Bar: Wis. 1973, U.S. Dist. Ct. (ea. and we. dists.) Wis. Sr. atty. Clark Oil & Refining Corp., Milw., 1973-82; assoc. Mulcahy & Wherry, Milw., 1982-84; v.p., sec., gen. counsel Sta-Rite Industries, Milw., 1984-92; v.p. adminstrn., gen. counsel Briggs & Stratton Corp., Wauwatosa, Wis., 1992—97, sr. v.p. adminstrn., 1992—. Mem. Dist. Export Coun., Milw., 1983-88, Gov.'s Adv. Coun. on Internat. Trade, Madison, Wis., 1982-85; solicitor United Way, Milw., 1990; bd. dirs. Goodwill Industries Wis., 1995—. Mem. Am. Counsel Assn. (bd. govs. Wis. chpt. 1988-94, pres. 1993-94), Engine Mfrs. Assn. (pres. 2001-02). Office: Briggs & Stratton Corp 12301 W Wirth St Wauwatosa WI 53222-2110 Office Phone: 414-259-5333.

SAVAGE, WILLIAM WOODROW, JR., historian, consultant, social sciences educator; b. Richmond, Va., Oct. 13, 1943; s. William Woodrow and Margaret Savage; m. Sheila Bobalik, July 30, 1983; 1 child, William Woodrow III. BA in Journalism, U. S.C., 1964, MA in History, 1966; PhD in History, U. Okla., 1972. Instr. Coll. Gen. Studies U. S.C., Columbia, 1966; vis. lectr. history Iowa State U., Ames, 1970; asst. editor U. Okla. Press, Norman, 1972-75; from asst. prof. to assoc. prof. history U. Okla., Norman, 1974—89, prof., 1989—. Tech. adviser Korine-Dunlap Prodns., Nashville, 1982—83; adviser Am. Frontier Project, NYC, 1982—85; bd. cons. editors Popular Culture Librs., Binghamton, NY, 1991—99; mem. editorial advisory bd. Jour. Scholarly Publishing, 2009—. Author: The Cherokee Strip Live Stock Association, 1973, The Cowboy Hero, 1979, Singing Cowboys and All That Jazz, 1983, Comic Books and America, 1945-54, 1990; editor: Indian Life, 1977, Cowboy Life, 1993; co-editor: The Frontier, 1979; editor (newsletter): Comparative Frontier Studies, 1975—86, Norman and Cleve. County Hist. Mus., 1975; co-prodr., host (TV series) Norman Cable TV, 1986—88; columnist: Okla. Gazette, 1993—95, Jour. Scholarly Publ., 2004—; contbr. articles to profl. jours. Recipient Spl. Recognition award, Okla. Jazz Hall of Fame, 1993. Mem.: So. Hist. Assn., Okla. Hist. Soc., Phi Alpha Theta, Omicron Delta Kappa, Sigma Delta Chi. Avocations: panelology, mixed media and collage. Office: Univ Okla Dept History 455 W Lindsey Rm 424 Norman OK 73019-2004 Office Phone: 405-325-6001.

SAVAGEAU, JUDITH A., epidemiologist, researcher; MPH, Yale U. Sch. Medicine, New Haven, 1980. Supr. vols. Mass. Assn. Blind, Brookline, 1976—78; rsch. assoc. Yale U. Sch. Medicine, New Haven, 1978—80; epidemiologist Boston U. Med. Sch., 1980—84; planning analyst Rochester Area Hosps. Corp., NY, 1984—87; sr. project dir. U. Rochester Med. Ctr., 1987—90; epidemiologist, biostatistician U. Mass. Med. Sch., Worcester, 1990—, dir., Epi-biostats. course, 1995—, dir., sr. scholars program, 2007—. Contbr. articles to med. jours. (Sarah Stone Excellence Tchg. award, 2008). Mem., sec. exec. com. Mass. Commn. Blind, Rehab. Coun., Boston, 1996—2008; mem. Mass. Assn. Blind Cmty. Svcs., Inc., 2008. Named Midred Hilliard Vol. of Yr., Mass. Commn. Blind. Mem.: APHA, Mass. Pub. Health Assn., Acad. Health, Soc. Epidemiologic Rsch. Office: Univ Mass Med Sch 55 Lake Ave N Rm A3-203 Worcester MA 01655 Business E-Mail: judith.savageau@umassmed.edu.

SAVALL, BRAD M., pharmaceutical executive, researcher; s. Robert R. and Suzanne J. Savall; m. Savall L. Saldamando, Jan. 11, 2003; children: Collin R., Ryan A. PhD, U. Mich., Ann Arbor, 2002. Sr. assoc. Amylin Pharms., San Diego, 1994—97; sr. scientist Johnson & Johnson, San Diego, 2002—. Bd. mem. Serra Mesa Planning Group, San Diego, 2007—. Fellowship, Abbott Pharms., 2000—02. Mem.: Am. Chem. Soc. Achievements include design of novel immune system modulators. Office: Johnson & Johnson Merryfield Row San Diego CA 92121

SAVARD, DENIS JOSEPH, former professional hockey coach; b. Pointe Gatineau, Que., Can., Feb. 4, 1961; m. Mona Savard; 1 child, Tanya. Center Chgo. Blackhawks, 1980—90, 1995—97, Montreal Canadiens, 1990—93, Tampa Bay Lightning, 1993—95; devel. coach Chgo. Blackhawks, 1997, asst. coach, 1997—2006, head coach, 2006—08. Player NHL All-Star Game, 1982—84, 1986, 88, 91. Recipient Michel Briere trophy, 1979—80. Achievements include being a member of Stanley Cup Champion Montreal Canadiens, 1993; being inducted into the Hockey Hall of Fame, 2000.

SAVARD, MARC, professional hockey player; b. Ottawa, Ont., Can., July 17, 1977; Center NY Rangers, 1997—99, Calgary Flames, 1999—2002, Atlanta Thrashers, 2002—06, Boston Bruins, 2006—. Named to NHL All-Star Game, 2008, 2009. Avocation: golf. Home: Boston Bruins TD Banknorth Garden 100 Legends Way Boston MA 02114*

SAVARI, SERAP AYSE, engineering educator, researcher; b. Astoria, NY, Nov. 4, 1968; d. Aykut and Sirin Savari. MS, MIT, Boston, 1991, PhD, 1996. Mem. tech. staff Bell Labs., Lucent Techs., Murray Hill, 1996—2003; acad. guest faculty computer sci. and comm. sys. Swiss Fed. Inst. Tech., 2003; assoc. prof. dept. elec. engring. and computer sci. U. Mich., Ann Arbor, 2004—07, Tex. A&M U., College Station, 2008—. Adj. prof. dept. elec. engring. and computer sci. U. Mich., Ann Arbor, 2003. Contbr. articles to profl. jours. Team leader info. processing Internat. Symposium on Info. Theory, 2005; mem program. com. Info. Theory Workshop, 2004, 2006—07, mem. program com., 2007, Internat. Symposium in Info. Theory, 2001, 2002, 2004, 2008—09; mem. tech. program com. Data Compression Conf., 2000—09; bell labs rep. Ctr. Discrete Math. and Theor. Computer Sci., 2001—03. Mem.: IEEE (program com. data compression conf. 2000—09, program com. symposium 2001, 2002, assoc. editor Source Coding IEEE Transactions on Info. Theory 2002—05, program com. symposium 2004, team leader program com. info. processing 2005, program com. symposium 2009), Toastmasters, Tau Beta Pi, Phi Beta Kappa. Office: 235E wisenbeker Bldg 3128 TAMU College Station TX 77843-3128 Home: 4050 Pendleton Dr Apt 1324 Bryan TX 77802 Business E-Mail: savari@ece.tamu.edu.

SAVARIN, CECILE GERALDINE, science administrator; d. Guy Savarin and Michele Lonjaret; life ptnr. Jerry Murry; 1 child, Emilie Michele Murry. B, Lycee Boivin, Dijon, France, 1993; diploma in Engring., CPE Lyon, France, 1997; PhD, Emory U., Atlanta, 2001. Sr. scientist Amgen, Thousand Oaks, 2006—07, Merck & Co, New Jersey, Rahway, 2001—06; regulatory affairs sr. mgr. Amgen, Thousand Oaks, Calif., 2007—. Recipient award, Rhone Alpes, France, 1997, Boerhinger Ingelheim, 1999; fellowship, Emory U., 1997—2001. Mem.: Am. Chem. Soc. Home: 1016 Via Anita Newbury Park CA 91320 Office: One Amgen Ctr Dr Mail Stop 17-1-A Thousand Oaks CA 91362 Personal E-mail: cecilesavarin@gmail.com. Business E-Mail: csavarin@amgen.com.

SAVAS, EMANUEL S., management educator, public official; b. NYC, June 8, 1931; s. John and Olga (Limbos) S.; m. Helen Andrew, Dec. 25, 1955; children: Jonathan, Stephen. BA, U. Chgo., 1951, BS, 1953; MA, Columbia U., 1956, PhD, 1960; PhD (hon.), U. Piraeus, Greece, 2000. Control systems cons. IBM, Yorktown Heights and White Plains, NY, 1959-65; urban systems mgr. NYC, 1966-67; 1st dep. city adminstr. Office of Mayor of N.Y.C., 1967-72; chmn. Mayor's Urban Action Task Force, 1969-72; prof. pub. mgmt. Columbia U., NYC, 1972-83, dir. Center for Govt. Studies, 1973-83, assoc. dir. Center for Policy Rsch., 1973-81; asst. sec. for policy devel. and rsch. HUD, Washington, 1981-83; prof. mgmt. Baruch Coll., CUNY, 1981-94, prof. public affairs, 1994—, dir. public policy program, 1994-97, chm. dept. mgmt., 1986-93; dir. Privatization Rsch. Orgn., 1986—. Cons. NSF, HUD, Dept. Transp., Dept. Energy, World Bank, AID, U.S. Dept. State, Pres.'s Commn. on Privatization, UN, UN Devel. Program, ILO, UNIDO, USIA, also others; mem. voting bd. Blue Cross and Blue Shield Greater N.Y., 1976-79, bd. dirs., 1979-81; mem. Pres.-Elect's Urban Affairs Task Force, 1980, N.Y. State Senate Adv. Commn. on Privatization, 1990-95; mem. Gov. Pataki privatization coun., N.Y., 1995-2000; dir. U.S.-USSR Joint Project on Mgmt. of Large Cities, 1973-81; advisor on privatization Govt. Poland, 1990-92, Govt. Lesotho, 1992, Govt. Ukraine, 1993, N.Y.C. Mayor Giuliani, 1994-98, Govt. South Africa, 1996, Govt. Botswana, 1996, Govt. Philippines, 1997, others. Author: Computer Control of Industrial Processes, 1965, Organization and Efficiency of Solid Waste Collection, 1977, Privatizing the Public Sector, 1982, Moscow's City Government, 1985, Privatization, 1987, Privatization and Public-Private Partnerships, 2000, 22 fgn. edits., Privatization in the City, 2005, others; editor: Alternatives for Delivering Public Services, 1977, Privatization for New York, 1992, Managing Welfare Reform in New York City, 2005; co-editor The New Public Management, 2002; mem. editl. bd. Urban Affairs Quar., Privatization Report, Privatization Watch, State and Local Govt. Rev.; contbr. 115 articles to profl. jours. Mem. NYC Mayor-elect Giuliani transition team, 1993, NY Gov.-elect Pataki transition team, 1994; mem. Tenafly (NJ) Borough Coun., 1996. With US Army, 1953-55, Korea. Recipient Systems Sci. and Cybernetics award IEEE, 1968, Louis Brownlow award Am. Soc. Public Adminstrn., 1970, Honor award Templeton Found., 1989, Leadership award Nat. Coun. Pub.-Private Partnerships, 1993, Outstanding Acad. award Am. Soc. Pub. Adminstrn., 1996, Presidential Excellence award for Disting. Scholarship, 2006, named Presidential Prof., 2007. Mem. Sigma Xi, Psi Upsilon. Clubs: City of N.Y. (trustee 1974-77, Richard Childs award 1979). Greek Orthodox. Office: CUNY Baruch Coll Box D 901 17 Lexington Ave New York NY 10010-5518 Office Phone: 646-660-6780. Personal E-mail: prisect@aol.com.

SAVELL, CATHERINE, humanities educator; d. Jacobus Spijkerman and Paulette Chazal; m. Geoffrey Carter Savell, June 28, 1975 (div. Mar. 3, 1994); children: Stephanie Anne, Nathalie Elisabeth, Christine Laura. MA, Middlebury Coll., Vermont, 1982. Instr. Loyola Coll. in Md., Baltimore, 1987—. Office: Loyola Coll in Md 4501 NCharles St Baltimore MD 21210 Business E-Mail: csavell@loyola.edu.

SAVELSKI, MARIANO J., chemical engineer, educator; BE in Chem. Engring., U. Buenos Aires, 1990; ME in Chem. Engring., U. Tulsa, Okla., 1994; PhD in Chem. Engring., U. Okla., Norman, 1999. Assoc. prof. Rowan U., Glassboro, NJ, 1999—2008; quality engr. Kellogg Argentina, Buenos Aires, 1995—96. Process engr. Sade Skanska, Buenos Aires, 1987—91. Mem.: Am. Soc. Engring. Edn., AIChE. Office: Rowan Univ 201 Mullica Hill Rd Glassboro NJ 08028

SAVENOR, BETTY CARMELL, painter, printmaker; b. Boston, Sept. 2, 1927; d. Harry Hyman and Sally Carmell; m. Jack Savenor, June 1, 1948; children: Alan, Barry, Ronald. Student, Jackson Van Ladau Sch. Fashion, Brandeis U., DeCordova Mus.; BFA, Mass. Coll. Art, 1993. Represented by Gallery 333, Falmouth, Mass., So.Watercolor Soc. Exhibited in group shows at Guild of Boston Artists, Salmagundi Club, N.Y., Boston Printmakers, U. Mass., Harvard U., Okla. U., Brandeis U., Purdue U., Ind., Attleboro (Mass.) Mus., Western N.Mex. U., Montclair Art Mus., N.J., Duxbury Art Complex, Mass., Morris Mus. Arts & Scis., N.J., George Walker Vincent Smith Mus., Mass., Nat. Gallery, N.Y., Fairleigh Dickinson U., N.J., Fitchburg Art Mus., Mass., Boston C. of C., Fed. Res. Bank of Boston, Adelphi U., N.Y., Stonehill Coll., Cahoon Mus. Am. Art, Midwest Mus. Art, Ind., Allied Artists Am., N.Y., Bentley Coll., Mass.; represented in permanent collections Fairfield Med. Assn., Vackerville, Calif., Bank of Boston, Data Products, NEC Info. Sys., Inc., Skowhegan Bank, Maine, Sheraton Corp., Hollywood, Calif., Tex. A&M U., and New Orleans, Meadows Country Club, Fla., U. Tampa, First Bank of Concord, N.H., Indian Head Bank, N.H., New Eng. Life Ins. Co., Conn. Mut. Ins. Co., Liberty Mut. Ins. Co., Velcro Mgmt., Jo-Ann Fabrics, Tampa Energy Corp., Fla., Weisner Assocs., Fla.; pubs. include Collograph Printmaking, Best of Watercolor, Painting Textures, Best of Watercolor, The Collected Best of Watercolor. 2002, Internat. Soc. Exptl. Artists, Solo Show Fla. West Symphony Gallery, 2007, Sarasota Fine Arts Soc. Artists Collectors Tour, 2008, Fine Arts Soc. Sarasota, Creators & Collectors Tour 2008-09; one man shows include Unitarian U. Gallery, Sarasota, Fla. 2009. Juror for numerous art shows, Mass.; demonstrator for many art socs. Recipient Nicholas Reale Meml. award for graphics Allied Artists Am., First Frontier Collage Soc., Guiller Gall. Awd., TX, 1999, Sarasota Visual Art Ctr., First Prize, 1999-00, Fla., Art League of Manatee, Fla., Printmaker Awd., 2000. Mem. Nat. League of Am. Pen Women (award of excellence 1998), New Eng. Watercolor Soc. (sec. 1983-93, Best Contemporary Watercolor prize 1990, Pelikan Disting. award 1997, Bronze medal 1998), New Eng. Watercolor Soc. (Excellence in Abstraction 2002), Nat. Assn. Women Artists (prize 1982, 87, 89, 1st prize 2002), Northwest Watercolor Soc. (signature mem.), Cape Cod Art Assn. (Jurors Merit award 1992-94, 1st prize in graphics 1993-95, 97, 2002), Nat. League Am. PEN Women (Best in State award 1983-95, 39th Nat. Exhbn. award of excellence 1998), Fine Arts Soc. Satasota Fl., Creators Collectors Tour, Concord Art Assn. (Gold medal 1985, 1st prize 1991, Yarmouth Art award 1998), Falmouth Art Guild (best in show 1997, best contemporary, 2008), Catamet Art Ctr. (1st prize 2002), Teco Co. (Hon. Mention 2003), Tampa, Women's Contemporary Artists, Art Ctr., Long Boat Key Art Ctr., N.W. Watercolor Soc., So. Watercolor Soc., New Eng. Watercolor Soc., Internat. Soc. Experimental Artists, Southern Watercolor Soc., Northwestern Watercolor Soc., New England Watercolor Soc., Internat. Soc. Contemporary Artists (1st prize 2008). Democrat. Jewish. Avocations: tennis, swimming, decorating.

SAVEROT, PIERRE-MICHEL, nuclear waste management company executive; b. Charnay les Macon, France, Aug. 30, 1952; m. Francoise Solamito; children: Cyprien, Luc, Scott-Eugene. MS, Northwestern U., 1977. Formerly with SGN, Sybelpro, Cogema Inc., Numatec, West Valley Nuclear Svcs., NUSYS; sr. cons., asst. to pres. JAI Corp., Fairfax, Va., 1994—. Mem. Inst. Nuclear Waste Mgmt. (chmn. 1996—). Home: 3112 White Daisy Pl Fairfax VA 22031-1463 Office: JAI Corp 2750 Property Ave Fairfax VA 22031-4312 Office Phone: 703-645-0440. Office Fax: 703-645-0445.

SAVIC, JELENA, mathematics educator; d. Johanna Gertrude and Vid Spacoje Savic. BS (hon.), N.E. Ill. U., 1973, M in Math. Edn., 1989; MS in Ednl. Leadership, Concordia U., 2007. Edn. K-9 Ill., 1973, edn. 9-12 Ill., 1979, bilingual edn. Ill., 1993, ESL edn. Ill., 1993. H.s. math tchr. Ctrl. Jr. H.S., Evergreen Park, Ill., 1973—79, Proviso East H.S., Maywood, Ill., 1979—99; instrnl. technologist Proviso West H.S., Hillside, Ill., 1999—2007. Workshop presenter - tchr. topics Proviso Twp. 209, Maywood, Ill., 1999—2007; writer ednl. curriculum Proviso Twp. H.S., Hillside, Ill., 1999—; sch. photographer Proviso West H.S., Hillside, Ill., 2000—; home schooling instr. U. Nebr.-Lincoln, 2002—. Filmmaker (animated short film) The Insect Reaction (Best Film, 1992). Walk animals mem. Humane Farming Assn., Chicago, 2003; humanitarian Serbia orphanages and refugee camps, 2006. Recipient Larry Stilgebauer Tech. award, West 40 Ednl. Ctr., 1988, 2001; named 1 of Top 10 Tchrs. in US nat. TV documentary, Arnold Shapiro Prodns., 1984, featured spkr. Channel 5 More You Know Edn., Channel 5 Nat. TV, 1984. Mem.: Ill. Fedn. Tchrs. Avocations: photography, filmmaking, dance, designing costumes. Home: 3228 N Newland Chicago IL 60634 Office: Proviso W HS 4701 W Harrison St Hillside IL 60162 Office Phone: 773-503-7337. Home Fax: 773-777-7383. Personal E-mail: jxm73@hotmail.com.

SAVICKAS, MARK LEE, psychology professor; b. Cleve., Apr. 28, 1947; s. John Michael and May Savickas; m. Mary Ann Kuhar, Aug. 2, 1975; 1 child, Suzanne. BA, John Carroll U., Cleve., 1968, MA, 1971; PhD, Kent State U., Ohio, 1975. Lic. psychologist Ohio, 1977. Career counselor John Carroll U., 1969—75, asst. prof. psychology, 1975—77; adj. prof. counseling Kent State U., 1975—; prof. and chair, behavioral scis. NE Ohio U. Coll. Medicine, Rootstown, 1977—. Vis. prof., psychology faculty Vrije U., Brussels, 2005—08; vis. prof. bus. sch. Loughborough U., 2007—; rsch. fellow, Ctr. Multicultural Rsch. Mich. State U., 2008—. Contbr. articles to profl. jours., chapters to books. Bd. dirs. Internat. Assn. Ednl. and Vocat. Guidance, Ottawa, 2000—; pres. elect, counseling psychology divsn. Internat. Assn. Applied Psychology, Australia, 2008—. Recipient Disting. Achievement award, Soc. Vocat. Psychology, 2006, Eminent Career award, Nat. Career Devel. Assn., 1996. Fellow: ACA, APA (Internat. Lifetime Achievement award 2007), Nat. Career Devel. Assn., Am. Psychol. Soc. Roman Catholic. Avocations: travel, music, reading. Office: NE Ohio Univs Coll Medicine 4209 State Rt 44 Rootstown OH 44272-0095 Office Fax: 330-325-5901. Business E-Mail: ms@neoucom.edu.

SAVIDGE, TOR, medical educator; b. London, Dec. 22, 1964; s. Geoffrey and Paula Savidge; m. Jennifer Galbraith, Mar. 5, 1994; children: Robyn, Kerrie, Josie, Tamsin. PhD, U. Cambridge, Eng., 1991. Asst. prof. Harvard Med. Sch., Boston, 1999—2004; assoc. prof. UTMB, Galveston, Tex., 2005—. Dir. SciTor Ltd., 1998—2009. Editor: (med. textbook) Microbial Imaging. Recipient Rsch. award, NIDDK, Bd. Found., Crohn's & Colitis Found. Office: Univ Tex Med Br University Boulevard Galveston TX 77555 Business E-Mail: tcsavidg@utmb.edu.

SAVILLE, DERRIC JAMES, lawyer; b. Ft. Madison, Iowa, Oct. 2, 1964; s. Jacob Abraham and Brenda K. (Lawrence) S.; m. Jeannene Irene Abbott, Mar. 21, 1987. BS, U. Iowa, 1987; M of Studies in Law, JD cum laude, Vt. Law Sch., 1991. Bar: Minn. 1991, U.S. Dist. Ct. Minn. 1995, Upper Sioux Cmty. Tribal Ct. 1996. Atty. Saville Law Office, Mpls., 1991—98; with Saville Title Svcs., Inc., Plymouth, Minn. Chair subcom. Dist. Planning Adv. Commn. #279, Maple Grove, Minn., 1994-96. Articles editor Ferae Naturae, 1991, Author Collapsing Fear, 2003, New Years, Epicurus, 2005 and numerous others. State del. Reform Party, Maple Grove, 1996; chair mental health adv. bd. Hennepin County Commitment Def. Project, 1998-2002. Mem.: Brain Injury Assn. Minn. (bd. dirs. 1996—2000, chair 1998—99), Minn. Head Injury Assn. (bd. dirs. 1995—96). Avocations: fishing, hiking, golf. Office: Saville Title Svcs Inc 505 Hwy 169 N Ste 230 Plymouth MN 55441 Home Phone: 763-427-2031; Office Phone: 763-398-0377. E-mail: dsaville@savilletitleservices.com.

SAVILLE, PAUL C., construction executive; BBA, Coll. William & Mary, Williamsburg, Va., 1977; MBA, U. Pitts. With automotive ops. Rockwell Internat.; with Ryan Homes, 1981, v.p. bus. planning to CFO; sr. v.p. fin., CFO, treas. NVR Inc., McLean, Va., 1993—2002, exec. v.p., CFO, treas., 2002—05, pres., CEO, 2005—. Named to The Va. 100, Va. Bus. mag., 2005. Office: NVR Inc Plaza America Tower 1 11700 Plaza America Dr Ste 500 Reston VA 20190-4792 Office Phone: 703-956-4000. Office Fax: 703-956-4750.

SAVILLE, THORNDIKE, JR., coastal engineer; b. Balt., 1925; AB, Harvard U., Cambridge, Mass., 1947; MS, U. Calif., Berkeley, 1949. Registered profl. engr., D.C. Rsch. asst. U. Calif., Berkeley, 1947-49; hydraulic engr. Beach Erosion Bd. and Coastal Engring. Rsch. Ctr., Washington, DC and Ft. Belvoir, Va., 1949-81, chief rsch. divsn., 1964-71, tech. dir., 1971-81; cons., 1981—. Contbr. more than 85 articles to engring. and sci. publs. With US Army, 1943—46. Recipient Meritorious Civilian Svc. award, Dept. Army, 1981, Comdr.'s award, 1998, Annual Nat. Cap. award, DC Coun. Engrs. and Archs., 1964, Annual Sci. Achievement in Engring. Scis. award, 1964. Fellow: ASCE (Huber award 1963, Moffatt-Nichol award 1979, Internat. Coastal Engring. award 1991), AAAS, Wash. Acad. Scis. (bd. mgrs. 1962—69); mem.: Am. Shore and Beach Preservation Assn. (bd. dirs. 1976—97, v.p. 1988—95, M. P. O'Brien award 1997), Permanent Internat. Assn., Navigation Congresses (hon.; U.S. commr. 1971—78, U.S. commr. emeritus 1987—, U.S. rep. PTC II 1991—98), Nat. Acad. Engring., Am. Geophys. Union, Cosmos Club (Washington). Home and Office: 5601 Albia Rd Bethesda MD 20816-3304

SAVITRIPRIYA, SWAMI, Hindu religious leader, author; b. Apr. 1, 1930; Ordained Hindu nun, Holy Order of Sannyas, 1975. Founder Shiva-Shakti Ashram, 1975. Author (translator): A Garland of Jewels, 2009, The Bhagavad Gita: How To Journey Through Life To Enlightenment, The Narada Bhakti Sutras: The Blissful Path of Divine Love, The Guru Gita: The Devine Guru's Message to The World, Shiva Stotravali: Utpaladeva's Love Songs To Shiva, The Katha Upanishad, The Kena Upanishad & The Prasna Upanishad. E-mail: savitripriya_sw@hotmail.com.

SAVITS, BARRY SORREL, surgeon; b. Phila., Feb. 14, 1934; s. Frank and Sophia (Cohen) S.; children: George, Frank, Alexander. BA, Princeton U., 1955; MD, U. Pa., 1959; cert. surg. residency, Mt. Sinai Hosp., NYC, 1965. Prof. surgery Project Hope, Ecuador, 1965-66; instr. surgery Albert Einstein Med. Coll., Bronx, NY, 1966-67; surgeon LaGuardia Med. Group, Queens, NY, 1970-72; dir. surgery St. Mary's Hosp., Bklyn., 1973-91, Kingsbrook Jewish Med. Ctr., Bklyn., 1991-2000; attending N.Y. Meth. Hosp., 2000—, SUNY-Univ. Hosp. of Bklyn., 1995—; clin. asst. prof. surgery SUNY Health Scis. Ctr., Bklyn., 1975—. Vis. surgeon Hope-Ecuador, 1965-66, Care-Medico, Afghanistan, 1976. Comdr. USN, 1967-69. Fellow ACS (gov. 1991-97); mem. Soc. Am. Gastrointestinal Endoscopic Surgeons, Assn. Acad. Surgery, Assn. Surg. Program Dirs., Bklyn. Surg. Soc. (pres. 1992-93). Jewish. Avocation: reading. Office: 263 7th Ave Ste 4E Brooklyn NY 11215 Home Phone: 212-675-2327; Office Phone: 718-832-4992. Office Fax: 718-832-4692. Personal E-mail: bsavits@aol.com.

SAVITSKY, DANIEL, retired structural engineer, educator; b. NYC, Sept. 26, 1921; s. Maxim and Anna (Oleksiw) S.; m. Mary Wysocki; children: Jean, James, Anne. BCE, CCNY, 1942; MSc, Stevens Inst. Tech., 1952; PhD, NYU, 1971. Registered profl. engr., NY. Structural engr. EDO Corp., College Point, NY, 1942-44; aero. rsch. scientist Nat. Adv. Com. for Aero., Langley Field, Va., 1944-47; prof. emeritus Stevens Inst. Tech., Hoboken, NJ, 1947—. Chmn. high speed vehicle com. Internat. Towing Tank Conf., 1978-88; cons. Naval Studies Bd., Nat. Rsch. Coun. Author: (with others) Yearbook of Science and Technology, 1987; patentee hydrofoil controls. Fellow Soc. Naval Architects and Marine Engrs. (hon. mem., Adm. Cochrane award 1967, 2007, Davidson medal 1996), Royal Inst. Naval Architects (medal, 2008), Niantic Bay Yacht Club (Conn.), Sigma Xi. Roman Catholic. Avocations: sailing, skiing, tennis. Home: 597 Delcina Dr Westwood NJ 07675-6111 Office: Davidson Lab 711 Hudson St Hoboken NJ 07030-5953 Office Phone: 201-216-5307. Business E-Mail: dsavitsk@stevens.edu.

SAVITT, SUSAN SCHENKEL, lawyer, mediator; b. Bklyn., Aug. 21, 1943; d. Edward Charles and Sylvia (Dlugatch) S.; m. Harvey Savitt, July 2, 1969 (div. 1980); children: Andrew Todd, Daniel Cory. BA magna cum laude, Pa. State U., 1964; JD, Columbia U., 1968. Bar: N.Y. 1968, U.S. Dist. Ct. (so. and ea. dists.) N.Y. 1973, U.S. Tax Ct. 1973, U.S. Ct. Appeals (2d cir.) 1981, U.S. Supreme Ct. 1980, U.S. Dist. Ct. (we. dist.) N.Y. 1996. Atty. Nassau County Legal Svcs., Freeport, N.Y., 1973-74; asst. corp. counsel City Yonkers, 1977-78; from assoc. to ptnr. Epstein, Becker & Green, P.C., NYC, 1978-94; ptnr. Winston & Strawn, NYC, 1994—2004, Schenkel-Savitt Firm, Hastings on Hudson, NY, 2005—. Adj. prof. Elizabeth Seton Coll., Yonkers, 1982-83; mediator Vol. Mediation Panel, US Dist. Ct. (so. dist.) NY, 1997—, US Dist. Ct. (ea. dist.) NY, 1999—. Mem. Hastings-on-Hudson Sch. Bd., 1984-93, v.p., 1986, 87-88, pres., 1989-90, 92-93; mem NYU exec. coun. Met. Ctr. for Ednl. Rsch. Devel. and Tng., 1987-90; bd. dirs. Associated Blind, 1993-95, Nat. Child Labor Com., 2001-04, Liberal Arts Alumni Coun., Pa. State U., 2001-07, bd. dirs., 2003-05, Search for Change, 1996—2002, sec., 1998-2002; bd. dirs. Pa. State Profl. Women's Network of NY, 1996-2003, pres., 1998-2000. Mem. ABA (Bus. law sect., litigation, dispute resolution and labor law sect.), ACRGNY, NY State Bar Assn. (labor law sect.), NY Women's Bar Assn., Westchester Women's Bar Assn., Fed. Bar Coun., Pa. State Alumni Club (v.p. Westchester County 1985-87), Phi Beta Kappa, Alpha Kappa Delta, Pi Gamma Mu.

SAVITZ, DAVID A., epidemiologist; BA, Brandeis U.; MS, Ohio State U., 1978; PhD, U. Pitts., 1982. Rschr. Battelle-Columbus Labs., Columbus, Ohio, 1977—79; pub. health svc. trainee in epidemiology U. Pitts., 1979—81; asst. prof. preventive medicine and biometrics U. Colo. Sch. Medicine, Denver, 1981—85; asst. prof. epidemiology U. NC Sch. Pub. Health, Chapel Hill, 1985—89, assoc. prof. epidemiology, 1989—92, prof. epidemiology, 1993—2005, chair epidemiology, 1996—2005, Cary C. Boshamer disting. prof., 2003—05; Charles W. Bludhorn prof. cmty. and preventive medicine Mt. Sinai Sch. Medicine, NYC, 2005—, prof. obstetrics, gynecology and reproductive sci., 2005—, dir. Ctr. Excellence in Epidemiology, Biostatistics and Disease Prevention, 2005—. Author: Interpreting Epidemiologic Evidence. Fellow: Am. Coll. Epidemiology; mem.: Inst. Medicine, Am. Epidemiological Soc., Soc. Pediatric and Perinatal Epidemiologic Rsch., Internat. Soc. Environ. Epidemiology, Internat. Epidemiological Assn., Soc. Epidemiologic Rsch. (sec.-treas. 1987—91, exec. com. 1994—97, pres. 2000—01), Am. Pub. Health Assn., Delta Omega (Theta chapt.). Office: 17 E 102 St New York NY 10029 Office Phone: 212-241-7025. Office Fax: 212-996-0407. E-mail: david.savitz@mssm.edu.*

SAVITZ, MAXINE LAZARUS, retired aerospace transportation executive; b. Balt., Feb. 13, 1937; d. Samuel and Harriette (Miller) Lazarus; m. Sumner Alan Savitz, Jan. 1, 1961; children: Adam Jonathan, Alison Carrie. BA in Chemistry magna cum laude, Bryn Mawr Coll., 1958; PhD in Organic Chemistry, MIT, 1961. Instr. chemistry Hunter Coll., NYC, 1962-63; sr. electrochemist Mobility Equipment Rsch. and Devel. Ctr., Ft. Belvoir, Va., 1963-68; prof. chemistry Federal City Coll., Washington, 1968-72; program mgr. NSF, Washington, 1972-74; dir. FEA Office Bldgs. Policy Rshc. U.S. Dept. Energy, Washington, 1974-75, dir. div. indsl. conservation, 1975-76, from dir. div. bldgs. and community systems to dep asst sec., 1975-83; pres. Lighting Rsch. Inst., 1983-85; asst. to v.p. engring. Ceramic Components div. The Garrett Corp., 1985-87; gen. mgr. ceramic components divsn. AlliedSignal Inc., Torrance, Calif., 1987-99; gen. mgr. tech. partnerships Honeywell, Torrance, Calif., 1999—2001, ret., 2001; prin. Washington Adv. Group. Bd. dirs. Am. Coun. Energy Efficient Economy, Draper Corp., Fedn. Am. Scientists, Energetics, Inc.; cons. State Mich. Dept. Commerce, 1983, NC Alternative Energy Corp., 1983, Garrett Corp., 1983, Energy Engring. Bd., Nat. Rsch. Bd., 1986—93, Office Tech. Assessment, U.S. Congress Energy Demand Panel, 1987—91; nat. materials adv. bd. NRC, 1989—94, mem. bd. energy and environ. sys., 2002—, bd. dirs. divsn. engring. and phys. sci., 2003—06; chmn. US Advanced Ceramic Assn., 1992; adv. com. divsn. ceramics/materials ORNL, 1989—92, adv. com. dir., 1992—96; mem. lab. adv. com. Pacific NW Nat. Lab., 2000—07; adv. bd. Sec. Energy, 1992—2002; mem. Def. Sci. Bd., 1993—96; vis. com. adv. tech. Nat. Inst. Stds. and Tech., 1993—98, Nat. Sci. Bd., 1999—2004; mem. adv. bd. Sandia Sci., 2006—. Contbr. articles to profl. jours. Mem. policy com. NAE, 1994—98. NSF postdoctoral fellow, 1961, 62, NIH predoctoral fellow, 1960, 61. Mem. NAE (v.p. 2006-), AAAS, PCAST.

SAVITZ, SAMUEL J., actuarial consulting firm executive; s. Paul and Ann (Gechman) S.; m. Selma Goldberg, June 15, 1958; children: Jacqueline Beverly, Steven Leslie, Michelle Lynn. BS in Fin., Temple U., Phila., 1958; postgrad., 1965, U. Pa., 1960-62. Pension analyst provident Mut. Life Ins. Co., Phila., 1958-61; v.p. The Wirkman Co., Phila., 1961-64; pres. Samuel J. Savitz & Assoc., Inc., Phila., 1964-86; sr. prin. Laventhol & Horwath, Phila., 1986-90; chmn. Savitz Orgn., Inc., Phila., 1990—. Vis. lectr. U. Pa., Phila., 1960, La. State U., 1972-74; faculty Villanova U., 1971-75; cons. in field. Contbr. articles to profl. jours. Bd. dirs. Phila. All-Star Forum, 1987-95; vice chmn. Mann Music Ctr., 1992—2005, Phila. Orch., 2005—; vice chmn., trustee Fgn. Policy Rsch. Inst., 1996—, Pa. Acad. Fine Arts, 1998—2006, Nat. Liberty Mus. and Edn. Ctr., 1999—; chmn. Encore Series, Inc., 1999—, Philly Pops, 1999—, Florentine Festivals USA, Inc., 2000-02, Regional Performing Arts Ctr., 2002—, Kimmel Ctr. for Performing Arts, 2002—, Nat. Mus. Am. Jewish History, 2002—, Abraham Lincoln Found., 2006-. With USAR, 1954—62. Mem. Am. soc. Pension Actuaries (dir. 1969-75), Union League Phila. Jewish. Home: 470 Conshohocken State Rd Bala Cynwyd PA 19004-2639 Office: 1845 Walnut St Philadelphia PA 19103-4708 Business E-Mail: samsavitz@savitz.com.

SAVNER, DAVID A., lawyer; b. Chgo., Mar. 15, 1944; m. Libby Savner; children: Jennifer, Michael. BA, Northwestern U., 1965, JD magna cum laude, 1968. Bar: Ill. 1968. Ptnr. Jenner & Block, Chgo., 1987—98; sr. v.p., gen. counsel, sec. Gen. Dynamics Corp., Falls Church, Va., 1998—. Editor Northwestern U. Law Rev., 1967-68. Mem. ABA, Chgo. Bar Assn., Chgo. Coun. Lawyers, Order of Coif. Office: General Dynamics Corp 2941 Fairview Park Dr Ste 100 Falls Church VA 22042-4513*

SAVOIE, BRIETTA DOLORES GIGER, retired librarian; b. Milw., Aug. 28, 1933; d. Walter and Vera Margaret (Rueger) Giger; m. Edmond Albert Savoie, Oct. 11, 1959; children: Philip Edmond, Raymond Walter, Anne-Marie Margaret. BA, Ohio State U., 1955; MSLS, Columbia U., NYC, 1957. Profl. librarian's cert. NY, NJ. Libr. Bklyn. Pub. Libr., 1957—59; cataloger, reference libr. New Sch. Social Rsch., NYC, 1959—60; children's libr. Teaneck Pub. Libr., NJ, 1981—86; asst. reference and circulation libr. River Edge Pub. Libr., NJ, 1986—92, libr. adult svcs., 1992—2002; ret., 2002. Substitute reference libr. Glen Rock Pub. Libr., NJ, 2005—. V.p. United Way of Ridgewood, Glen Rock, Hohokus and Midland Park, NJ, 1980—81; pres. Ridgewood chpt. UN Assn., 1981—85; mem. Fair Housing Coun. Northern NJ. Mem.: ALA, LWV (chmn. voter registration Glen Rock chpt. 1978—81, chmn. membership Glen Rock chpt. 2004—, co-pres. Glen Rock chpt. 2005—09), Nat. Arbor Day Soc., UN Assn., Native Am. Rights Fund, So. Poverty Law Ctr. Klanwatch Project, Sierra Club. Democrat. Unitarian. Avocations: international relations, social justice, environmental protection, bicycling, gardening. Home: 654 Doremus Ave Glen Rock NJ 07452-2033

SAVOIE, FELIX HENRY, III, orthopaedic surgeon; b. Paincourtville, La., Oct. 11, 1956; s. Felix Henry J. and Coralie Lucille (Dolese) S.; children: Christopher, Robert, John Reagan. BS in biochem., La. State Univ., 1978, MD, 1982. Orthopaedic resident U. Miss. Medical Ctr., Jackson, 1982-87; fellow in hand surgery Medical Coll Wis., Milw., 1987-88; fellow in arthroscopy & sports medicine Orthopaedic Rsch. of Va., Richmond, 1988; asst. prof. orthopaedics U. Miss. Medical Ctr., Jackson, 1989-90; dir. upper extremity svc. Miss. Sports Medicine, Jackson, 1990—. Editorial bd. Arthoscopy, Wake Forest, N.C., 1993—. Author, editor: Arthroscopy of the Elbow, 1995; chpts. in book: Arthroscopic Reconstruction of the Shoulder, 1995, McGinty et al: Arthroscropy, 1995, Orthopaedic Clinics N. Am. Recipient Charles Nee award Am. Shoulder & Elbow Soc., 1992. Fellow Am. Acad. Orthopaedic Surgeons; mem. Arthroscopy Assn. N.Am. (mem. edn.com. 1995—), Am. Shoulder & Elbow Soc. (CPT coding com. 1994—). Roman Catholic. Office: Miss Sports Medicine 1325 E Fortification St Jackson MS 39202-2442

SAVOIE, SEAN MICHAEL, lighting designer, educator; MFA, U. Cin., Ohio., 2005. Lighting designer Wash. U., St. Louis, 2007—; prodn. mgr. The Muny, St. Louis, 2008—. Free lance stage design Various Profl. Theatres, 1996—. Designer (lighting) See What I Wanna See (Outstanding Lighting Design award, 2007). Tech. advisor Muddy Waters Theatre, St. Louis, 2008. Mem.: USITT, ESTA. Office: WA Univ St Louis 1 Brookings Dr- Box 1108 Saint Louis MO 63130

SAVOY, SUZANNE MARIE, nursing educator; b. NYC, Oct. 18, 1946; d. William Joseph and Mary Patricia (Moclair) Savoy. BS, Columbia U., 1970; M in Nursing, UCLA, 1978; PhD in Nursing, Loyola U., 2004—. RN, cert. clin. nurse specialist, clin. nurse leader. Staff nurse MICU, transplant Jackson Meml. Hosp., Miami, 1970-72; staff nurse MICU Boston U. Hosp., 1972-74, VA Hosp., Long Beach, Calif., 1974-75; staff nurse MIRU Cedars-Sinai Med. Ctr., LA, 1975-77; critical care clin. nurse specialist Anaheim (Calif.) Meml. Hosp., 1978-81; practitioner, instr. Rush-Presbyn.-St. Luke's Med. Ctr. Coll. Nursing, Chgo., 1982-88; rsch. assoc. dept. neurosurgery Rush U., 1984-88; clin. rsch. assoc. Medtronic, Inc. Drug Adminstrn. Sys., Mpls., 1988-91; staff nurse critical care Harper Hosp., Detroit, 1992-93; clin. nurse specialist, surg./trauma crit. care Detroit Receiving Hosp., 1993-95; clin. instr. Wayne State U. Coll. of Nursing, Detroit, 1991-96; adult crit. care clin. nurse specialist Saginaw (Mich.) Gen. Hosp., 1996—98; cardiac clin. nurse specialist Covenant Healthcare Sys., Saginaw, 1998—2005; asst. prof. Saginaw Valley State U. Coll. Nursing, 2005—. Adj. faculty Wayne State U. Coll. Nursing, 1996—98, program coord. Crit. Care ACNP-CC MSN, 1993—96; neurosci. clinician acute stroke unit Harper Hosp., Detroit, 1989; edn. cons. Critical Care Svcs., Inc., Orange, Calif., 1979—81; mem. staff Convenant Healthcare, 2005—08. Contbr. articles to profl. jours. Mem.: RN Aim (treas. 2008—), Am. Assn. Spinal Cord Injury Nursing (mem. rsch. com. 1993—95), Assn. Health Care Quality (treas. 2002—04), Am. Assn. Crit. Care Nurses (bd. dirs. Long Beach chpt. 1981—82, treas. NEMC chpt. 1999—2001), Am. Assn. Neurosci. Nurses (treas. Ill. chpt. 1983—85, pres. 1986—87, SE Mich. chpt. 1992—96, bd. dirs., treas., program chair), Theta Chi (nominating com. chair 2008—), Sigma Theta Tau, Lambda Gamma Phi (bd. dirs. 1994—96). Roman Catholic. Office Phone: 989-964-7026. Personal E-mail: cardioapn@aol.com. Business E-Mail: smsavoy@svsu.edu.

SAVOYE, MARY, dietician, researcher; b. New Haven, June 13, 1961; d. Anthony DeLucia and Thomasina Consiglio; m. Joseph DeSanti, Sept. 23, 1997; children: Michael Aj DeSanti, Cameron Anthony DeSanti, Kaye Thomasina DeSanti. BS in Dietetics, St. Joseph U., West Hartford, Conn., 1993; AS in Bus. Adminstrn., Quinnipiac U., Hamden, Conn., 1987. Cert. diabetes eductor Am. Assoc Diabetes Educators, 1996, dietitian-nutritionist State Conn., 1994. Rsch. dietitian Yale U. Sch. Medicine, New Haven, 1994—, dir. bright bodies program, 1997—. Pres. Smart Moves, LLC, Hamden, 1993—. Mem.: N.Am. Assn. Study of Obesity, Am. Assn. Diabetes Educators, Am. Diabetes Assn. (vol. spkr.), Am. Dietetic Assn. Office: Yale Univ Sch Medicine 2 Church St S Ste 201 New Haven CT 06520 Office Fax: 203-785-5675. Business E-Mail: mary.savoye@yale.edu.

SAVRAN, DAVID, theater educator; b. Providence, Jan. 13, 1950; BA, Harvard Coll., Cambridge, Mass., 1971; MFA, Carnegie-Mellon U., Pitts., 1974; PhD, Cornell U., Ithaca, NY, 1978. Assoc. prof. drama U. Regina, Sask., Canada, 1978—88; prof. English Brown U., Providence, 1988—2001; disting. prof. Vera Mowry Roberts chair Am. theatre Grad. Ctr., CUNY, NYC, 2001—. Co-editor: (books) The Masculinity Studies Reader, 2002; author: A Queer Sort of Materialism: Recontextualizing American Theater, 2003. Mem.: Am. Soc. Theatre Rsch. (v.p. 2003—06). Office: Grad Ctr CUNY 365 Fifth Ave New York NY 10016 Business E-Mail: dsavran@gc.cuny.edu.

SAVRANN, RICHARD ALLEN, lawyer; b. Boston, July 29, 1935; s. Abraham B. and Doris (Curhan) S.; m. Diane Barbara Kleven, Dec. 22, 1957; children: Stephen Keith, Russell Clark. BA, Harvard U., 1956, JD, 1959. Bar: Mass. 1959, U.S. Dist. Ct. Mass. 1963, U.S. Ct. Appeals (1st cir.) 1965. Exec. Klev Bro. Mfg., Derry, NH, 1959-63; assoc. Law Office of Jerome Rappaport, Boston, 1963-68; asst. atty. gen. Commonwealth of Mass., Boston, 1968-70; ptnr. Newell, Savrann & Miller, Boston, 1970-75; sr. ptnr. Kunian, Savrann & Miller, Boston, 1976-81, Singer, Stoneman, Kunian & Kurland, P.C., Boston, 1981-88, Singer, Kunian & Kurland, P.C., Boston, 1988-90; sr. ptnr, Curhan, Kunian, Goshko, Berwick and Savrann, P.C., Boston, 1990-92; ptnr. Burns and Levinson, LLP, Boston, 1993—2001, Gargill, Sassoon & Rudolph LLP, Boston, 2001—02, Rudolph Friedmann LLP, Boston, 2002—05, Law Office of Richard A. Savrann, West Palmbeach, 2005—. Active Andover (Mass.) Housing Authority, 1972—90, chmn., 1984—90; pres. Hospice of Greater Lawrence, North Andover, 1984; bd. dirs. Boston Latin Sch. Found., 1987, clk., 1992—98; bd. dirs. Comite Internat. de Sci. pour La Santè et l'Environ., Paris, 1993—2000. Mem. Fed. Bar Assn., Fla. Bar, Mass. Bar Assn., Palm Beach County Bar Assn., Eastpointe Country Club (v.p., Palm Beach Gardens, Fla.), Harvard Club (Andover) (pres. 1985-98), Harvard Club (Palm Beach). Avocations: golf, opera. Home: 13866 Greensview Dr Palm Beach Gardens FL 33418 Home Phone: 561-627-3493; Office Phone: 561-964-6404. Business E-Mail: rsavrann@havedebt.com.

SAVRANSKY, VLADIMIR M., research scientist; b. Zaporizhzhia, Ukraine, Apr. 11, 1967; s. Mikhail Abramovich Savransky and Elizaveta Solomonovna Savranskaya; m. Tatyana M. Ginzburg, Oct. 13, 1990; 1 child, Sofya V. MD, St. Petersburg's State I. Pavlov Med. U., Russia, 1991, PhD, 1994. Surgeon, dept. gen. surgery St. Petersburg's State I. Pavlov Med. U., 1993—94, asst. prof. surgery, dept. gen. surgery, 1994—2001; rsch. assoc., divsn. pulmonary and critical care medicine Johns Hopkins U. Sch. Medicine, Balt., 2005—08; adj. faculty Natural Scis. Dept. Montgomery Coll., Germantown, Md., 2006—; prin. scientist Emergent Biosolutions Inc., Gaithersburg, Md., 2008—. Home: 5705 Brewer House Cir 201 Rockville MD 20852 Office: Emergent Biosolutions Inc 300 Profl Dr Gaithersburg MD 20879 Personal E-mail: vsavransky@yahoo.com. Business E-Mail: savranskyv@ebsi.com.

SAVRIN, LOUIS, lawyer; b. Phila., Jan. 20, 1927; s. William Philip and Anna (Sass) S.; m. Barbara J. Schwimmer, Jan. 16, 1954; children: Jonathan Eric, Philip Wade, Daniel Scott. BS, NYU, 1948; JD, U. Pa., 1951. Bar: N.Y. 1952. Atty. tax dept. Arthur Young & Co., NYC, 1951-55; pvt. practice NYC, 1955—2005. Gen. counsel, sec. Pickwick Internat., Inc., N.Y.C., 1965-77 Assoc. editor: U. Pa. Law Rev, 1949-51. Mem. sch. bd. Dist. 21, Bklyn., 1962-68; docent Whitney Mus. Am. Art. With US Army, 1945—46. Mem. B'nai B'rith (pres. lodge 1957-59, named to lodge Hall of Fame 1967, Torch of Freedom award Anti-Defamation League 1982). Home: 50 Park Ave Apt 17H New York NY 10016-3082 Home Phone: 212-683-3860.

SAWAI, DAHLEEN EMI, language educator; b. Honolulu, Mar. 13, 1954; d. Kiyoto and Aiko Sawai. BA, U. Hawaii, Manoa, 1975, diploma in elem. edn., 1977, diploma in secondary edn., 1981, MEd, 1984. Cert. tchr. Hawaii. English tchr. Tokyo Family Court, 1977—78; Japanese tchr. Kailua H.S., Honolulu, 1978—80; English tchr. Family Ct. Probation Officer Tng. Sch., Tokyo, 1983—84; Japanese tchr. W. R. Farrington H.S., Honolulu, 1985—; educator Consortium for Tchg. Asia and the Pacific in the Schs., Honolulu, 1989—95; mentor tchr., 1995—. Instr. Sch. Cmty. Based Mgmt., Honolulu, 2000—04; interpreter Star Tanjo, 1976; chmn. dept. world langs. W.R. Farrington HS, Honolulu, 2001—, lead instr. Internat. Studies Acad., 2008—. Dir. Moanalua Gardens Cmty. Assn., Honolulu, 1976—77, sec., 1978—80; ad hoc com. mem. Sch. Cmty. Coun., 2005. Scholar, Keio Gijuku Daigaku, 1982—84. Mem.: Hawaii State Tchrs. Assn., Hawaii Assn. Lang. Tchrs., Nat. Coun. Japanese Lang. Tchrs., Farrington Alumni and Cmty. Found., Japanese Cultural Ctr. Hawaii, Temari Ctr. Asian and Pacific Arts, Alliance Drama Edn., Pi Lambda Theta.

SAWALHA, AMR, medical educator; b. Munster, Germany, Dec. 1, 1974; MD, Jordan U. Sci. and Tech., 1998. Cert. Am. Bd. Internal Medicine, 2003, Am. Bd. Rheumatology, 2005. Fellow, rheumatology U. Mich., Ann Arbor, 2003—05; asst. prof. medicine U. Okla., Oklahoma City, 2005—, adj. asst. prof. pathology, 2008—; asst. mem. Okla. Med. Rsch. Found., Oklahoma City, 2005—. Contbr. scientific papers to profl. publs. (Arthritis Nat. Rsch. Found. scholarship, award, Japan Coll. Rheumatology). Recipient numerous awards from Chinese Med. Assn., Fedn. Clin. Immunology Socs., ACP, U. Mich., 2002—08. Mem.: Am. Fedn. Med. Rsch., Ctrl. Soc. Clin. Rsch., Am. Assn. Advancement of Scis., Am. Assn. Immunologists, Am. Coll. Rheumatology (fellow 2005). Achievements include patents pending for discovery of a genetic association between lupus and a gene on chromosome X. Office: Univ Okla 825 NE 13th St MS#24 Oklahoma City OK 73104 Office Fax: 405-271-4110. Business E-Mail: amr-sawalha@omrf.ouhsc.edu.

SAWALLISCH, WOLFGANG, conductor; b. Munich, Aug. 26, 1923; s. Wilhelm and Maria (Obermeier) Sawallisch; m. Mechthild Sawallisch, 1952 (dec. 1998); 1 child, Jörg. Student, Wittelsbacher Gymnasium, Munich, Musikalische Ausbildung; D (hon.), Curtis Inst. Music, Phila., Westminister Choir Coll., Rider U., Lawrenceville, NJ, Villanova U., Pa. Condr., Augsburg, Germany, 1947-53; music dir. Cologne Opera, 1960-63; prin. condr. Vienna Symphony, 1960—70; condr. Hamburg Philharm. Orch., 1960-73, hon. mem., 1973—; music dir. Bavarian State Opera, Munich, 1971—92, Phila. Orch., 1993—2003, condr. laureate, 2003—. Prof. Staatliche Hochschule fur Musik, Cologne, 1960—63; artistic dir. Suisse Romande Orch., Geneva, 1973—80; founded music sch. Wolfgang Sawallisch Stiftung, Bavaria, Germany, 2002; permanent condr. Teatro alla Scala, Milan; hon. condr. laureate NHK Symphony Orch., Tokyo. Rec. artist US, Britain. Decorated Order of Rising Sun Japan, Chevalier Legion d'Honneur, France; recipient Bruckner Ring, Vienna Symphony Orch., 1980, Toscanini Gold Baton, Italy, 1993, Suntory Music award, Japan, 1993, Gov.'s Disting. Artist award, State of Pa., Avatar award for artistic excellence, Arts & Bus. Coun. Phila. Mem.: Bavarian Acad. Fine Arts, Robert Schumann Soc. Munich (hon.). Office: Phila Orch 260 S Broad St Fl 16 Philadelphia PA 19102-5002*

SAWAYA, GEORGE F., obstetrician, gynecologist, educator; BS in Organic Chemistry, Hendrix Coll., 1985; MD, Vanderbilt U. Sch. Medicine, 1990. Resident UCSF, 1990—94, fellow, 1994—96, asst. adj. prof. dept. obstetrics, gynecology & reproductive sciences, 1996—97, asst. prof. dept. obstetrics, gynecology & reproductive sciences, 1997—2003, assoc. prof. dept. obstetrics, gynecology & reproductive sciences, 2003—. Recipient Rhoda Goldman Rsch. award, Mt. Zion Health Sys., 1997, Tchg. award, UCSF Med. Sch., 1998, Edn. Contributions award, 2003. Mem.: APGO (Tchg. award 2000), Alpha Omega Alpha. Office: UCSF Box 0856 San Francisco CA 94143-0856 Office Phone: 415-502-4090. Office Fax: 415-502-4065. E-mail: sawayag@obgyn.ucsf.edu.*

SAWAYA, RAYMOND, neurosurgeon; b. Latakia, Syria, May 5, 1949; s. Emile and Josephine (Boulos) S.; m. Kristin Tveit; children: Marc-Emile, Corinne Marguerite. MD, St. Joseph U., Beirut, 1974. Diplomate Am. Bd. Neurol. Surgery. Intern Beeckman-Downtown Hosp., NYC, 1974-75; resident in surgery SUNY, Syracuse, 1975-76; resident in neurosurgery U. Cin., 1976-80, Johns Hopkins Hosp., Balt., 1981; vis. scientist NIH, Bethesda, Md., 1981-82; assoc. prof. U. Cin., 1983-90, dir. div. neuro-oncology, 1983-90; neurosurgeon Mayfield Neurol. Inst., Cin., 1983-90; prof., chmn. dept. neurosurgery U. Tex. M.D. Anderson Cancer Ctr., Houston, 1990—; prof., chmn. Baylor Coll. Medicine, 2005—. Contbr. numerous articles on neurosurgery to profl. jours. Research Adv. Group grantee VA Med. Ctr., 1984. Mem. Am. Radium Soc., Tex. Med. Assn., Am. Assn. Neurol. Surgeons, Congress of Neurosurgeons, Soc. Surg. Oncology, Houston Neurol. Soc. (pres.), Johns Hopkins Alumni Assn. Roman Catholic. Avocations: music, bridge, swimming. Office: 1515 Holcombe Blvd # 442 Houston TX 77030-4009 E-mail: rsawaya@mdanderson.org.*

SAWCZUK, IHOR S., urologist; b. NYC, Oct. 5, 1952; s. Stefan and Stefania (Mruczkewycz) S. BA, NYU, 1974; MD, Med. Coll. of Pa., 1979. Diplomate Am. Bd. Urology. Chief Allen Pavilion Urology Columbia-Presbyn. Med. Ctr., NYC, 1988—99; prof. urology Columbia U., NYC, 1993—, vice chmn. Dept. of Urology, 1994—2001; chmn. urology Hackensack (NJ) U. Med. Ctr., 2001—, chief urologic oncology Cancer Ctr.; prof. surgery U. Medicine and Dentistry NJ, Newark, 2003—07; prof. urology Touro U. Coll. Medicine, 2007—, chmn. urology, 2007—, assoc. dean academic affairs. Adv. bd. Kidney Cancer Assn., 1994—, Kidney and Urology Found., 2002—; dep. dir. Internat. Coop. Urological Edn. Project, 1994-96. Co-editor: (book) Urologic Clinics of North America, 1993. Bd. dirs. Children of Chernobyl, Short Hills, N.J., 1992-98. Recipient Young Investigator award Nat. Kidney Found., 1987, Alpha Omega Alpha Vol. Clin. Faculty award N.J. Med. Sch., 2003. Mem. ACS, Am. Urol. Assn. (scholar 1986), N.Y. Acad. Scis., Soc. Internat. de Urologie, Soc. Urologic Oncology, Minimally Invasive Robotics Assn. Office Phone: 201-336-8090.

SAWERS, SIR JOHN, ambassador; b. July 26, 1955; s. Colin Simon Hawkesley and Daphne Anne Sawers; m. Avril Helen Shelley Lamb, 1981; 3 children. BS in Physics and Philosophy, U. Nottingham, Eng., 1977; student, U. St. Andrews, U. Witwatersrand, Johannesburg. Prin. pvt. sec. to Fgn. Sec. Douglas Hurd Govt. UK, London, 1993—95, head embassy's fgn. and def. policy issues team Washington, 1996—98, fgn. affairs advisor to Prime Min. Tony Blair London, 1999—2001, amb. to Egypt Cairo, 2001—03, polit. dir. Fgn. & Commonwealth Office London, 2003—07, spl. rep. Baghdad, Iraq, permanent rep. to UN NYC, 2007—; internat. fellow Harvard U., Cambridge, Mass., 1995—96. Named Knight Comdr. of St. Michael and St. George, UK. Avocations: theater, hiking, tennis, bicycling. Office: UK Mission to UN One Dag Hammarskjold Plz 885 Second Ave New York NY 10017 Office Phone: 212-745-9200. Office Fax: 212-745-9316.

SAWICKI, GERALDINE, social studies educator; b. Phila., Jan. 4, 1951; m. John Sawicki, Feb. 20, 1971; children: Christian, Mara Metzgar. BA, NY U., 1996, MA in Equivalency, 1999. Campaign mgmt. mem. Rep. Party, Allentown, Pa., 1982—89; with pub. rels. Morning Call, Allentown, Pa., 1988—89; mgr. field ops. US Bur. Census, Allentown, Pa., 1989—90, with field ops. Phila., 1991—92; lectr. Lehigh Carbon CC, Schnecksville, Pa., 2000—04, academic advisor, 2000—04; lectr. Modesto Jr. Coll., Calif., 2004—. Recipient Founders Day award, NY U., 1996. Mem.: Alpha Kappa Delta, Phi Theta Kappa, Phi Beta Kappa. Avocations: travel, hiking, bicycling. Office: Modesto Jr Coll 435 College Ave Modesto CA 95350 Business E-Mail: sawickig@mjc.edu.

SAWICKI, GREGORY, pulmonologist; s. Janusz and Elzbieta Sawicki. MD, Harvard Med. Sch., Boston, 2001. Diplomate Am. Bd. Pediat., 2004. Pediat. pulmonologist Children's Hosp. Boston, 2007—. Office: Children's Hosp Boston 300 Longwood Avenue Boston MA 02115

SAWICKI, ZBIGNIEW PETER, lawyer; b. Hohenfels, Germany, Apr. 13, 1949; came to U.S., 1951; s. Witold and Marianna (Tukiendorf) S.; m. Katheryn Marie Loman, Aug. 19, 1972; children: James, Jeffrey, Jessica, Jason. BSChemE, Purdue U., 1972; MBA, Coll. St. Thomas, St. Paul, 1977; JD, Hamline U., 1980. Bar: Minn. 1980, U.S. Dist. Ct. Minn. 1981, U.S. Ct. Appeals (8th cir.) 1981, U.S. Patent and Trademark Office 1981, U.S. Ct. Appeals (fed. cir.) 1982, Can. Patent Office 1994, Can. Trademark Office 1995. Process engr. 3-M Co., St. Paul, 1973-75; process engrng. supr. Conwed Corp., St. Paul, 1975-77; shareholder, bd. dirs. Kinney & Lange, Mpls., 1980—2003, Westman, Champlin & Kelly, 2003—. Bd. dirs. Orono (Minn.) Hockey Boosters, 1992—2000. With USAF, 1970-76. Mem. Am. Intellectual Property Assn., Internat. Trademark Assn., Minn. Intellectual Property Assn. (past treas.), Licensing Exec. Soc., The Federalist Soc., Am. Legion. Home: 4510 N Shore Dr Orono MN 55364-9602 Office: Westman Champlin & Kelly 900 2d Ave S Ste 1400 Minneapolis MN 55402-1624 Office Phone: 612-330-0581. Business E-Mail: psawicki@wck.com.

SAWMA, GABRIEL M., law educator; b. Beirut, Dec. 15, 1945; s. Mourad S. and Rachel A. Sawma; m. Arlette J. Loutfi; children: Christine Rachel, Lillian. Degree in Law, Lebanese U. Law Sch., Beirut, 1970. Bar: Lebanese Bar Assn. 1970, Am. Bar Assn. Lawyer Rizkallah & Farah Law Firm, Beirut, 1970—75; Mid. East export cons. Stylist Internat., Ridgefield, NJ, 1976—80. Ceo Am. Wire Hangers, Robinsville, NJ, 1981—84. Author: (quranic book) The Qur'an: Misinterpreted, Mistranslated, and Misread. The Aramaic Language of the Qur'an. Home: PO Box 112 Plainsboro NJ 08536 Office: Fairleigh Dickinson Univ 285 Madison Ave Madison NJ 07940-1099 Business E-Mail: gabriels@fdu.edu.

SAWTELLE, CARL S., psychiatric social worker; b. Boston, July 14, 1927; s. Carl Salvador and Martha (Bellamacina) S.; BA, Suffolk U., Boston, 1951; MSW, Simmons Sch. Social Work, 1953; m. Thelma Florence Ramsay, Aug. 20, 1950; children: Tracy Lynn, Lisa June. Social worker Tewksburry (Mass.) State Hosp., 1952; psychiat. social worker, head psychiat. social worker, dir. clin. social work Taunton (Mass.) State Hosp., 1953-74; 1st dir. clin. social work, Plymouth, Mass., 1974-78; co-founder, v.p. 1st legally established War On Poverty program Triumph, Inc., Taunton; co-founder 1st Greater Taunton Coun. on Alcoholism, 1972. With USCG, 1944-46. 1st lic. social worker in Mass., 1980. Mem. Nat. Assn. Social Workers (co-founder Southeast Mass. chpt. 1957, pres. 1957, Spl. Mass. Chpt. award 1978), Acad. Cert. Social Workers (chmn. 1962-72), Am. Legion, Mass. Mental Health Social Workers Assn. (co-founder, pres. 1972-74, other offices). Created innovated programs, resources, opportunities, svcs. to state mental hosp. patients and their families; mentor to young social workers; contbr. advancement of knowledge, practice quality and standards of psychiat. social work; father of licensing and registration of Social Workers in Mass. Home: 9 Tracywood Rd Canton MA 02021-3501

SAWYER, CHARLES F., lawyer; b. 1956; Student, Northwestern U. Sch. Music, 1974—76; AB in Econ. with honors and high distinction, U. Mich., 1978; JD, U. Chgo., 1981. Bar: Minn. 1982. Law clerk, Hon. Charles L. Levin, 1981—82; assoc. Dorsey & Whitney LLP, Mpls., 1982—88, ptnr., corp. dept., 1989—, and co-chair, securitization group. Exec. editor Univ. Chgo. Law Rev., 1980—81. Office: Dorsey & Whitney LLP Ste 1500 50 S Sixth St Minneapolis MN 55402-1498 Office Phone: 612-343-7986. Office Fax: 612-340-8738. Business E-Mail: sawyer.charles@dorsey.com.

SAWYER, CHERYL LYNNE, educational association administrator, consultant; b. Balt., Mar. 8, 1954; d. Carolyn (Brooks) Bulcken; m. Gary W. Sawyer, July 16, 1976; children: Jesse, Stacy. BA in English, Sam Houston State U., 1976; MA in Behavioral Scis., U. Houston, Clear Lake, 1984; EdD in Adminstrn. and Supervision, U. Houston, University Park, 1993. Lic. psychol. assoc. Tex., specialist sch. psychology., cert. trauma cons., tchr. English, history, psychology, learning disabilities Tex., diagnostician, counselor, spl. edn. counselor, assoc. sch. psychologist, crisis prevention intervention instr. Tex., elem. tchr. Tchr. Alvin (Tex.) Ind. Sch. Dist., 1976-84, LaMarque (Tex.) Ind. Sch. Dist., 1985-90; ednl. cons. Dickinson, Tex., 1992—; dir. acute children's programs Devereux Found., League City, Tex., 1994-97; counselor LaMarque (Tex.) Ind. Sch. Dist., 1997-98; tchr. Dickinson Ind. Sch. Dist., 1998—2000; assoc. prof. counselor edn. U. Houston, Clear Lake, 2000—, coord. counselor edn., 2000—. Mem. adv. bd. spl. edn. Santa Fe Sch. Dist., 1993, 94, 95; mem. adv. bd. drug and alcohol prevention LaMarque Sch. Dist., 1989, 90, 91, 92; spkr. child-related psychol. issues; presenter in field. Contbr. articles to profl. jours. Mem. Am. Counseling Assn., Tex. Counseling Assn., Nat. Assn. for Gifted, Coun. for Exceptional Children, Dickinson Civic Assn. (bd. dirs. 1996-99, 2002-4), Beta Sigma Phi, Phi Delta Kappa, Chi Sigma Iota. Home: 12308 Marion Ln Dickinson TX 77539-9224 Office Phone: 281-283-3559. Business E-Mail: sawyer@uhcl.edu.

SAWYER, DANA WAIDE, religious studies educator; b. Jonesport, Maine, July 4, 1951; s. Waide Fairfield Sawyer and Joanne Elizabeth Gray; m. Stephani Marie Briggs, Aug. 8, 2003; children: Sophie Louise, Emma Holt. BA, Western Conn. State U., Danbury, Conn., 1973; MA, U. Hawaii, Honolulu, 1978, U. Iowa, Iowa City, 1988. Prof. religion and philosophy Maine Coll. Art, Portland, 1989—; adj. prof. Asian religions Bangor Theol. Sem., Maine, 1989—. Author: (biography) Aldous Huxley. V.p., bd. trustees Siddhartha Sch. Project, Freeport, Maine, 1996—2008. Mem.: Internat. Aldous Huxley Soc., Soc. Asian and Comparative Philosophy. Avocation: mountain climbing. Office: Maine College Of Art 522 Congress St Ste 4 Portland ME 04101-3494

SAWYER, DIANE, newscaster, journalist; b. Glasgow, Ky., Dec. 22, 1945; d. E. P. and Jean W. (Dunagan) Sawyer; m. Mike Nichols, Apr. 29, 1988. BA, Wellesley Coll., 1967. Reporter Sta. WLKY-TV, Louisville, 1967—70; adminstr. press office White House, 1970—74; rschr. Richard Nixon's memoirs, 1974—78; gen. assignment reporter, then Dept. State corr. CBS News, 1978—81; co-anchor Morning News CBS, 1981—, co-anchor Early Morning News, 1982—84; corr., co-editor 60 Minutes CBS-TV, 1984—89; co-anchor PrimeTime Live (now known as Prime-Time Thursday) ABC News, 1989—; co-anchor Day One, 1995, Turning Point, 1996, Good Morning Am. ABC News, NYC, 1999—. Recipient 2 Peabody awards for pub. svc., 1988, Robert F. Kennedy award, 13 Emmy awards, 2 Dupont awards (one Spl.), IRTS Lifetime Achievement award, Robert F. Kennedy Journalism award, 2007; co-recipient George B. Polk award for TV reporting, 2005; named one of 100 Most Powerful Women, Forbes mag., 2005, 2007, 2008, The 50 Most Powerful Women in NYC, NY Post, 2007; named to TV Hall of Fame, 1997. Office: Good Morning America Fl 10 147 Columbus Ave New York NY 10023-5900

SAWYER, DOLORES, motel chain executive; b. Shreveport, La., Oct. 16, 1938; d. Orlan B. Greer and Doris Lucile (Sanders) Eckman; m. Raymond Lee Sawyer Jr., June 11, 1960 (dec. Mar. 2007); children: Lisa Kay, Linda Faye. BSN, Northwestern State Coll., 1960; MSN, Tex. Woman's U., 1975. Supr. obstetrics dept. Highland Hosp., Shreveport, La., 1962-64; head nurse (3-11 shift) Scott and White Meml. Hosp., Temple, Tex., 1966-71, dir. of nursing edn., 1975-76; sch. nurse Temple Ind. Sch. Dist., 1971-72; instr. Mary-Hardin Baylor Coll., Belton, Tex., 1972-74; asst. prof., clin. specialist U. Tex. Arlington, 1976-86; v.p. Budget Host Internat., Arlington, Tex., 1986-96, sr. v.p., 1996—, also bd. dirs., chmn. bd., owner. Recipient Amoco Outstanding Tchg. award, 1981. Mem. Sigma Theta Tau. Republican. Methodist. Avocations: reading, scrapbooks, gardening, crafts, piano. Office: Budget Host Internat Ste B 2307 Roosevelt Dr Arlington TX 76016-5865 Home Phone: 817-496-4449; Office Phone: 817-861-6088. Personal E-mail: rsawyerl@airmail.net. Business E-Mail: dsawyer@budgethost.com.

SAWYER, ERIC WARREN, composer, music educator; b. E. Patchogue, NY, June 2, 1962; s. Raymond Francis and Curry Sawyer; m. Cheryl Cydney Zoll, Dec. 16, 1990; 1 child, Lydia Jasmine. PhD, U. Calif., Davis, 1994. Chair, composition and theory Longy Sch. Music, Cambridge, Mass., 1998—; assoc. prof. chair, music Amherst Coll., Mass., 2002—. Composer: (opera) Our American Cousin, (piano trio) Lincoln's Two Americas (Ravinia Festival Composition prize, 2008), Three For Trio, violin concerto, (vocal) The Mountain Echo, string quartet, (orch.) Three Pieces for Orchestra (Joseph Bearns prize, 1988). Pres. Live in Concert, Inc., Amherst, 2006—08. Recipient C. D. Jackson award, Tanglewood Music Ctr., 1985; fellow, Harvard U., 1988—91. Mem.: Am. Composer Forum. Home: 104 Northampton Rd Amherst MA 01002 Office: Amherst Coll Arms Music Ctr Amherst MA 01002 Business E-Mail: ewsawyer@amherst.edu.

SAWYER, ERROL, photographer; b. Miami, Fla., Aug. 8, 1943; s. Robert Earl Sawyer and Mamie Lucille (Williams) Donaldson; m. Rochelle Tia Relyea (div.); m. Mathilde Yvonne Fisher Sawyer; 1 child, Victor Leonard. Degree, NY U., 1966. Photographer Errol Sawyer Photography Inc., Paris, 1971—78, 1984—85, NYC, 1978—84, Amsterdam, 1999—. Guest prof. photography Tech. U., Delft, Netherlands, 2006—. Photographer (exhibitions) Children in East End, 1989, Paris, 1993, Graffiti, 1993, City Mosaic, 2000. Home: 1 ER Wetering dwars St 39 Amsterdam North Holland 1017TL Netherlands

SAWYER, JAMES S., chemicals executive; BS in Geology, Wesleyan U.; MBA, MIT. Asst. treas. Praxair, Inc., Danbury, Conn., 1985—86, mgr. capital markets planning, 1986—89, area treas. Europe, 1989—92, asst. treas., 1992—94, v.p., treasurer, 1994—2000, v.p., CFO, 2000—03, sr. v.p., CFO, 2003—06, exec. v.p., CFO, 2006—. Mem.: Conf. Bd. Sr. Fin. Officers Council, Fin. Executives Inst. Office: Praxair 39 Old Ridgebury Rd Danbury CT 06810-5113

SAWYER, JOHN EDWARD, management educator; b. Florence, Ariz., July 26, 1954; s. Almus Wilmore and Betty (Mossman) S.; m. Dana Lee Strandberg, Aug. 5, 1989; children: Adrian John, Alexander Lyn, Jordan Estelle. BA in Psychology, Calif. State U., Long Beach, 1977; MA in Counseling Edn., Calif. State U., Fresno, 1979; AM in Indsl./Orgnl. Psychology, U. Ill., 1985, PhD of Indsl./Orgnl. Psychology, 1987. Project dir. Youth Svc. Bur., Modesto, Calif., 1979-81; counselor Horizons Youth Svc. Bur., Livermore, Calif., 1981-82; lectr., tchg. asst. U. Ill., Urbana, 1982-87; asst. prof. Tex. A&M U., College Station, 1987-91; asst. prof. mgmt. U. Del., Newark, 1991-95, assoc. prof., 1995—2003, mgmt. area head, 1998—2001, chair dept. bus. adminstrn., 2001—06, prof., 2003—. Human resources rschr. Xerox Corp., Rochester, N.Y., 1985-86; orgnl. cons. Mercy Hosp., Urbana, 1983, Tex. Dept. Mental Health, San Antonio, 1989-90; trainer, cons. DuPont Merck Pharm. Co., Wilmington, 1994, Hercules, Wilmington, 1996. Mem. editl. bd. Jour. Mgmt., Jour. Behavioral Decision Making, Jour. Applied Behavioral Scis., Orgnl. Behavior & Human Decision Preserves; contbr. chpt. in book and articles to profl. jours. Grantee Tex. Engring. Experiment Sta., 1989, Tex. Higher Edn. Coordinating Bd., 1990, Gen. Univ. Rsch. Program, 1993, Ctr. for Info. Sys. Mgmt. Edn. and Rsch., 1994, NSF-IOC, 2004. Mem. APA, Acad. Mgmt. (invited guest editl. bd.), Judgment and Decision Making Soc., Soc. Indsl. and Orgnl. Psychology. Home: 214 Cullen Way Newark DE 19711-6112 Office: Univ Delaware Dept Bus Adm Newark DE 19716 Office Phone: 302-831-1787. Business E-Mail: sawyerj@lerner.udel.edu.

SAWYER, JOHN WESLEY, retired mathematics and computer science educator, consultant; b. Nov. 2, 1917; s. Joseph Edmond and Inez Avent Sawyer; m. Edna Matthews, Aug. 31, 1939 (dec. Jan. 31, 2002); 1 child, John Wesley Jr. BA, Wake Forest Coll., 1938, MA, 1941, U. Mo., 1948, PhD, 1951. Instr. math. U. Mo., Columbia, 1946—51; assoc. prof. math. Ga. State U., Atlanta, 1951—53, U. Richmond, Va., 1953—56; prof. computer sci. Wake Forest U., Winston-Salem, NC, 1956—88, emeritus prof. computer sci., 1988—. In-house cons. R. J.

Reynolds Tobacco Co., Winston-Salem, 1958—86. Contbr. (book) Operations Research Tools for Systems Engineering, articles to profl. jours. Music dir. Wake Forest Bapt. Ch., Winston-Salem, 1964—89; bd. dirs. Salemtowne Retirement Cmty., Winston-Salem, 1999—2004; pres. (4 terms) Atlantic Coast Conf., Greensboro, NC, 1964—86; v.p. NCAA, Kansas City, Mo., 1980—84. Named Tar Heel of Week, Raleigh (N.C.) News & Observer, 1977; grantee NSF, 1960. Fellow: AAAS (life); mem.: Math. Assn. Am., Ops. Rsch. Soc. Am. Achievements include development of computer simulations for business and manufacturing operations; creation and development of computer science department at Wake Forest University. Home: 6113 Salemtowne Dr Winston Salem NC 27106-3497

SAWYER, LINDA, advertising executive; b. NY; married; 2 children. BA magna cum laude, George Washington U. Various advt./mktg. positions Avrett, Free & Ginsberg, SSC& B, Ted Bates Worldwide, NYC, Goldberg Marchesano, Washington; v.p., account dir. Deutsch, Inc. (Interpublic Group), NYC, 1989—92, exec. v.p., dir. acct. mgmt., 1992—96, gen. mgr., 1996—2001, mng. ptnr., 1996—, COO, 2001—05, CEO, 2005—. Vice-chmn. Advt. Ednl. Found.; bd. dirs. Am. Assn. Advt. Agy.'s Inc., dir.-at-large, 2005—08. Apptd. bd. dirs. Jr. Achievement NY. Named a Woman to Watch, Advt. Age, 2002. Office: Deutsch Inc 111 Eighth Ave New York NY 10011 Office Phone: 212-981-7600. Business E-Mail: linda_sawyer@deutschinc.com.*

SAWYER, MALCOLM JAMES, JR., religious studies educator; b. Farmington, Maine, Oct. 31, 1951; s. Malcolm James and Bertha Brindley Sawyer; m. Kay Lynn Fuqua, Dec. 15, 1973; children: James Daniel, Jonathan David, Joel Nathaniel, Joshua William. BA, Biola U., 1973; ThM, Dallas Theol. Sem., 1978, PhD, 1987. Asst. prof. Simpson Coll., San Francisco, 1984—89; prof. Western Sem., Los Gatos, Calif., 1989—2007, Tozer Sem., Redding, Calif., 2007—. Bd. mem. Bay Cities Bible Inst., Oakland, Calif., 1995—97; mem. adv. bd. Christian Counseling Internat., Scott's Valley, Calif., 1999—2002. Author: Charles Augusts Briggs and Tensions in Late Nineteenth Century America Theology, 1994, The Survivor's Guide to Theology, 2006, Taxonomic Charts on Biblical and Theological Studies, 1999; co-author: Reinventing Jesus, 2006; co-editor Who's Afraid of the Holy Spirit?, 2005; contbr. articles to profl. jours. Fellow, Christus Nexus, 2005—. Mem.: Am. Acad. Religion, Soc. for Bibl. Lit., Evang. Theol. Soc. (far west pres. 2001—02). Home: 16485 Severn Rd San Leandro CA 94578

SAWYER, MICHAEL E., library director; b. Martinez, Calif., June 8, 1953; s. William and Shirley (Greenberg) Sawyer. BA in Hist. and Govt., Columbia Coll., Mo., 1974; MLS, U. Pitts., 1976, Cert. of advance study, 1978. Libr. Southern Ohio Correctional Facility, Lucasville, 1977-84; adminstrv. asst. Findlay-Hancock County Pub. Libr., Findlay, Ohio, 1984-85; libr. Chillicothe Correctional Inst., Ohio, 1985-89; dir. Auglaize County Pub. Dist. Libr., Wapakoneta, Ohio, 1989-92, Clinton Pub. Libr., Iowa, 1993-98, Northwestern Regional Libr., Elkin, NC, 1998—2003, Rangeview Libr. Dist., Thornton, Colo., 2003—07; dep. dir. Tulare County Libr., Visalia, Calif., 2007—08; dir. Calcasieu Parish Pub. Libr., Lake Charles, La., 2009—. Author: A Bibliographical Index of Five English Mystics, 1978; co-editor: Classics Jour., 1983—87; contbr. articles to prpfl. jours. Recipient Bill Butler Meml. award, 1987, Al Marish Meml. award, Correctional Edn. Assn., 1988, Exceptional Svc. award, Assn. Specialized & Coop. Libr. Agy.'s, 1989, Nat. Achievement Citation award, Pub. Libr. Assn., 1994, Future award, ALA Libr., 2002, Merit award, La. Libr. Assn., 2009—; named an Outstanding Ohioan, Ohio Jaycees, 1988. Mem.: US JCI Senate (Ohio state pres. 1988—89, historian 1997—), Rotary Club. Office: Calcasieu Parish Pub Libr 301 W Claude St Lake Charles LA 70605 Office Phone: 337-721-7147. Business E-Mail: msawyer@calcasieu.lib.la.us.

SAWYER, PHILIP NICHOLAS, surgeon, educator, health science facility administrator; b. Bangor, Maine, Oct. 25, 1925; s. Frank S. and Linda (Makanna) S.; m. Grace Makla, June 13, 1953; children: Margaret Ann, Elizabeth Lynn, Susan Jean, Philip Michael. BS, Harvard U., 1947; MD, U. Pa., 1949. Diplomate Am. Bd. Surgery, Am. Bd. Thoracic Surgery. Intern Hosp. of U. Pa., Phila., 1949-50, resident in surgery, fellow, 1953-56; chief resident in surgery, fellow in pathology St. Luke's Hosp., NYC, 1956-57; instr., asst. prof. surgery SUNY Downstate Med. Ctr., Bklyn., 1957-62, assoc. prof., 1962-66, prof., head vascular surgery svc., 1966-84, prof. emeritus, 1985—; pres. Interface Biomed. Labs. Corp.; prof. surgery N.Y. Med. Coll., 1991-96; vis. surgeon, head vascular surg. svcs. Kings County Hosp., Bklyn., 1972-85. Hon. cons. Meth. Hosp., Bklyn.; hon. assoc. attending, head vascular surg. svcs. St. John's Episcopal Hosp., Far Rockaway, N.Y.; hon. attending surgery VA Hosp., Bklyn.; hon. cons. cardiovascular and thoracic surgeon Norwalk (Conn.) Hosp.; hon. cons. vascular surgeon Caledonian Hosp., Bklyn.; prin. investigator Office Naval Rsch., NIH, Am. Heart Assn., 1953-84, NIH, 1957-86; disting. lectr. worldwide. Founding editor Jour. Investigative Surgery; assoc. editor: Am. Jour. Med. Electronics, Jour. Biomed. Rsch. Engring.; editor: Biophysical Mechanisms in Vascular Homeostasis & Intravascular Thrombosis, 1965, Vascular Grafts, 1976, Modern Vascular Grafts, 1987; co-editor: Surgical Resident's Manual, 1980, Vascular Diseases, Current Controversies, 1981; contbr. over 300 articles to med. jours.; numerous patents on heart valves, vascular grafts, hemostatic agts., vascular wall protective agts. Recipient Clemson award for basic biomaterials rsch. Soc. for Biomaterials, 1985; Markle scholar, 1959-64. Mem. Acad. Surg. Rsch. (Jacob Markowitz award 1986), AAAS, Am. Assn. for Thoracic Surgery, Am. Chem. Soc., Am. Coll. Cardiology, ACS, Am. Coll. Chest Physicians, AMA, Am. Heart Assn., Am. Nuclear Soc., Am. Soc. for Artificial Internal Organs, IEEE, Internat. Cardiovascular Soc., Soc. for Thoracic Surgeons, Soc. Univ. Surgeons, Soc. for Vascular Surgery, European Soc. for Microcirculation, Fedn. Am. Socs. for Exptl. Biology, Cardiovascular Soc. (pres.), Harvard Club (N.Y.C.), Sigma Xi, others. Avocation: collecting historical weapons. Office: 7324 Ridge Blvd Brooklyn NY 11209

SAWYER, RICHARD DEWIGHT, JR., psychologist; b. Pittsfield, Mass., May 14, 1957; s. Richard DeWight and Mary-Lou Gilman Sawyer; m. Denise Marie Skogen, Oct. 24, 2008; children: Carlson Mary, Kaylyn Louise. Cert. ednl. specialist James Madison U., Harrisonburg, Va., 1992; psychologist Nat. Cert. Sch., 2008. Cognitive retrainer Woodrow Wilson Rehab. Ctr., Fishersville, Va., 1985—89; psychologist Richmond Pub. Schs., Va., 1992—. Mem.: Va. Assn. Sch. Psychologists, Nat. Assn. Sch. Psychologists. Liberal. Avocations: travel, music, sports. Office: Richmond Pub Schs 301 North 9th St Richmond VA 23219 Personal E-mail: rdsjrsps75@yahoo.com.

SAWYER, ROBERT MCLARAN, historian, educator; b. St. Louis, Nov. 12, 1929; s. Lee McLaran and Harrie (Alcock) S.; m. Patricia Ann Covert, Nov. 23, 1955; children— Ann Marie, Lee McLaran, Gail Louise. BS, S.E. Mo. State Coll., 1952; MA, U. Ill., 1953; PhD, U. Mo., 1966. Tchr. Rolla Public Schs., Mo., 1955; asst. prof., then asso. prof. history U. Mo., Rolla, 1956-67; mem. faculty U. Nebr., Lincoln, 1967—, prof. history of edn., 1969—2006, chmn. dept. history and philosophy of edn., 1975-81, coun. mem. Coll. Arts and Scis., 1979—2006, emeritus prof., 2006—. Vis. prof. Ark. State U., Jonesboro, 1966; proposal reviewer Nat. Endowment Humanities, 1979 Author: The History of the University of Nebraska, 1929-1969, 1973, The Many Faces of Teaching, 1987, The Art and Politics of College Teaching, 1992, The Black Student's Guide to College Success, 1993, The Handbook of College Teaching, 1994; contbr. articles to profl. jours. With AUS, 1953—55. Mem. Orgn. Am. Historians, History Edn. Soc., Am. Ednl. Studies Assn., Soc. Profs. Edn., Phi Alpha Theta, Phi Delta Kappa. Home: 2640 S 35th St Lincoln NE 68506-6623 Office: Univ Nebr 29 Henzlik Hall Lincoln NE 68588

SAWYER, THOMAS EDGAR, management consultant; b. Homer, La., July 7, 1932; s. Sidney Edgar and Ruth (Bickham) S.; m. Joyce Mezzanatto, Aug. 22, 1954; children: Jeffrey T., Scott A., Robert J., Julie Anne. BS, UCLA, 1959; MA, Occidental Coll., 1969; PhD, Walden U., 1990. Project engr. Garrett Corp., LA, 1954-60; mgr. devel. ops. TRW Systems, Redondo Beach, Calif., 1960-66; spl. asst. to gov. State of Calif., Sacramento, 1967-69; prin., gen. mgr. Planning Rsch. Corp., McLean, Va., 1969-72; dep. dir. OEO, Washington, 1972-74; assoc. prof. bus. mgmt. Brigham Young U., 1974-78; pres., chmn. bd. Mesa Corp., Provo, Utah, 1978-82; pres., dir. Sage Inst. Internat., Inc., Provo, 1982-88; chmn. bd., CEO Pvt. Telecom. Networks, Inc. (name changed to Nat. Applied Computer Techs, Inc.), Orem, Utah, 1988-98; chief tech. officer GST Telecom. (formerly Greenstar Telecom., Inc.), San Francisco, 1993-98, also bd. dirs. Vancouver, Wash., 1995-98; chmn. bd. NeTrue Comm., Inc., Fullerton, Calif., 1998—2002; chmn. bd., CEO Telecom, Inc., Salt Lake City, 2002—06; sr. dir. Econ. Rsch. Inst., AIM Holdings (formerly MMG Holdings), Tokyo, 2003—; consul gen. for Republic of Liberia Monrovia, 2004—; dir. ops. First European Investment Found., Fruitland Park, Fla., 2004—. Bd. dirs. Intechna Corp., HighTech Corp., Indian Affiliates, Inc., Greenstar USA, Inc., San Francisco, 1994-98, GST Global Comm., Inc., Vancouver, Can., 1998-2002, Highpoint Telecom., Inc., Vancouver, 1998-01, World Wide Wireless Comm., Inc., Salt Lake City, 1998-2000, Columbia Hosp., Orem, 1998-05; sr. dir. Econ. Rsch. Inst., AIM Holdings, Ltd., Tokyo, 2003-; consul gen. for Republic of Liberia, Monrovia, 2004—. Author: Assimilation Versus Self-Identity: A Modern Native American Perspective, 1976, The Promise of Funding a New Educational Initiative Using the Microcomputer, 1988, Computer Assisted Instruction: An Inevitable Breakthrough, Current Challenges of Welfare: A Review of Public Assistance as Distributive Justice, 1989, New Software Models for Training and Education Delivery, 1989, New Organizations: How They Deviate from Classical Models, 1989, Increasing Productivity in Organizations: The Paradox, 1989, An Introduction and Assessment of Strategic Decision Making Paradigms in Complex Organizations, 1989, The Future of Technology in Education, 1989, Impact of Failure by Senior Executives to Receive Accurate Critical Feedback on Pervasive Change, 1990, The Influence of Critical Feedback and Organizational Climate on Managerial Decision Making, 1990. Chmn. Nat. Adv. Coun. Indian Affairs, Utah State Bd. Indian Affairs, So. Paiute Restoration Com., Utah Cmty. Mediation Ctrs., 2002-05; trustee Utah Valley State Coll., Orem, 2000-05, Coll. Ea. Utah, Price, 2001—; mem. Utah Dist. Export Coun., Utah dist. SBA Coun.; mem. adv. coun. Nat. Bus. Assn.; mem. Utah Job Tng. Coordinating Coun. Served with USMC, 1950-53. Mem. ASPA, Am. Mgmt. Assn., Utah Coun. Small Bus. (dir.), Utah State Hist. Soc. (bd. dirs. 1993-99), Masons. Republican. Mem. Lds Ch. Home: 548 W 630 S Orem UT 84058-6154 Home Phone: 801-860-9944; Office Phone: 801-944-4090. Business E-Mail: tesawyer@tesawyer.com.

SAWYER, WILLIAM C., lawyer; b. Bangor, Maine, Aug. 26, 1929; s. Frank S. and Linda M. (Makanna) S.; m. Mary A. Eaton (div.); m. Joan N. Gardner; children: William D., Constance, Faith. AB cum laude, Harvard Coll., 1951, JD, 1954. Bar: Mass., U.S. Dist. Ct. Mass., U.S. Ct. Mil. Appeals, U.S. Supreme Ct. Assoc. Palmer & Dodge, Boston, 1958-61; ptnr. Sawyer, Burlingham, Tucker & Salloway, Boston, 1961-85, Dicara, Selig, Sawyer & Holt, Boston, 1985-90, Clarkin, Sawyer & Phillips, P.C., Boston, 1990—. Contbr. articles to profl. jours. Bd. trustees Mass. Conv. Ctr. Authority, 1991-97; pres., treas., chmn. Metro. Area Planning Coun., 1975-87; pres. Mass. Assn. Regional Planning Agys., 1980, 87; bd. dirs. Nat. Assn. Regional Couns., 1980-86; mem. Mass. Selectman's Assn., 1975—; bd. selectman Town of Action, 1967-75, chmn., 1969, 75; Rep. candidate Mass. Atty. Gen., 1990; pres. New Eng. Rep. Coun.; Rep. candidate Congress, 5th Congl. Dist., Mass., 1980. 1st lt. U.S. Army, 1955. Recipient Regional Leadership award Planning Commns. and Couns. New Eng., 1987, and others. Mem. ABA, Mass. Bar Assn., Boston Bar Assn. Avocations: golf, painting, reading. Office: Clarkin Sawyer & Phillips PC 1 Center Plz Ste 240 Boston MA 02108-1801 Business E-Mail: wcs@csplaw.com.

SAWYER, WILLIAM DALE, internist, educator, dean, foundation administrator; b. Roodhouse, Ill., Dec. 28, 1929; s. Cloyd Howard and Eva Collier (Dale) S.; m. Jane Ann Stewart, Aug. 25, 1951; children: Dale Stewart, Carole Ann. Student, U. Ill., 1947-50; MD cum laude, Washington U., St. Louis, 1954; ScD (hon.), Mahidol U., Bangkok, 1988; DPH (hon.), Chiang Mai U., Thailand, 1993, Chulalongkorn U., 1998. Intern Washington U.-Barnes Hosp., 1954-55, resident, 1957-58, fellow, 1958-60; asst. prof. microbiology Johns Hopkins U., Balt., 1964-67; prof., chmn. dept. microbiology Rockefeller Found.-Mahidol U., Bangkok, 1967-73, Ind. U. Sch. Medicine, Indpls., 1973-80; prof. depts. medicine, microbiology and immunology Wright State U., Dayton, Ohio, 1981-87, dean Sch. Medicine, 1981-87; pres. China Med. Bd. N.Y., Inc., 1987-97. Adj. prof. biology Ball State U., Muncie, Ind., 1978-80; hon. prof. microbiology Sun Yat Sen U. Med. Sci., 1987; hon. prof. Peking Union Med. Coll., 1989; hon. advisor Beijing Med. U.; cons. U.S. Army Med. R & D Command, WHO Immunology Ctr., Singapore, 1969-73; mem. bd. sci. advisers Armed Forces Inst. Pathology, 1975-80, chmn., 1979-80; adj. prof. medicine and microbiology and immunology N.Y. Med. Coll., Valhalla, 1990-96; hon. prof. China Med. U., 1995, West China U. Med. Sci., 1995, Zhejiang Med. U., 1995, Jiujang Med. Coll., 1995, Hunan Med. U., 1996, Xian Med. U., 1996, Shanghai Med. U., 1996. Contbr. numerous articles to profl. jours. Mem. Lobund adv. bd. U. Notre Dame; dir. Georgetown Area Cmty. Found., 1998-2002, pres. 1999; mem. exec. com. Georgetown Cmty. Resource Ctr., 2000-03. Served to maj. M.C., USA, 1955-64. Recipient Gold medal of merit Airlangga U., Indonesia, 1992, Pub. Health Recognition award Asia-Pacific Acad. Consortium Pub. Health, 1993, China Health medal, 1996, White Magnolia award, 1996. Fellow ACP; mem. AAAS, Am. Soc. Microbiology (br. pres. 1976), Sci. Rsch. Soc. Am., Am. Fedn. Clin. Rsch., Ctrl. Soc. Clin. Rsch., Infectious Diseases Soc. Am., Soc. Exptl. Biology and Medicine, Am. Acad. Microbiology, Am. Assn. Pathologists, Assn. Am. Med. Colls. (coun. deans 1980-87), Phi Beta Kappa, Sigma Xi, Alpha Omega Alpha. Home: Temple Meridian # 14 4312 S 31st St Temple TX 76502 Personal E-mail: wllmsawyer@aol.com.

SAWYER-MORSE, MARY KAYE, nutritionist, educator; b. Ft. Stockton, Tex. BA in Psychology, S.W. Tex. State U., 1978; MS in Nutrition, Incarnate Word Coll., 1987; PhD, U. Tex., 1997. Lic. dietitian. Nutrition svcs. con. Christian Sr. Svcs., 1985-87, exec. dir., 1987-90; nutrition svcs. cons. Alternative Adult Day Care Ctr., 1989-90; pvt. cons. dietitian, 1990—; cmty. dietitian Health Enhancement Ctr. Humana Hosp. Met., 1990-91; assoc. prof., dietetic program dir. U. Incarnate Word, San Antonio, 1991—2004; dir. Heath Mgmt., UMR, 2004—. Presenter Innovative Nutrition Svc. Model S.W. Tex. Gerontol. Soc. Ann. Meeting, 1988, Diabetic Homebound Svcs. Nat. Conf. Meals-On-Wheels Am., 1989; spkr. in field. Contbr. articles to profl. jours. Recipient Disting. Rsch. award, 1977, 1978, Acad. Excellence award, 1978, Women's Leadership award, YWCA, 1988, Creative Tchg./Rsch. award, 1994; named Tex. Dietetic Educator, 2003; grantee, U.S. Dept. Edn., 1997—2000; Carnation Corp. scholar, 1995. Mem.: Nat. Spkrs. Assn. (devel. dir. 2000—01, Tex. Dietetic Educator of the Yr. 2003), San Antonio Dist. Dietetic Assn., Tex. Dietetic Assn., Am. Dietetic Assn. (sec. 1990—92, mem. nominating com. 1993—94, dietetic educators practice group). Office Phone: 830-997-1552. Personal E-mail: morsemk@msn.com.

SAWYERS, CHARLES L., oncologist, hematologist, educator; b. Nashville, Jan. 26, 1959; s. John L. and Julia Edwards Sawyers; m. Susan Gail Schneck, Oct. 21, 1990. BA in history of sci., Princeton U.; MD, Johns Hopkins U., 1985. Cert. Internal Medicine, 1988, Hematology, 1992, Medical Oncology, 1991. Intern in medicine U. Calif., San Francisco, 1985—86, resident in hematologic oncology, 1986—88; Howard Hughes fellow in hematologic oncology UCLA, 1988—91, prof. medicine, molecular pharmacology and urology; investigator Howard Hughes Med. Inst., 2003—06, 2008—; dir. human oncology and pathogenesis prog. Meml. Sloan-Kettering Cancer Ctr., NYC, 2006—. Sci. adv. bd. Agios Pharmaceuticals, Cambridge, Mass.; bd. sci. councilors Nat. Cancer Inst. Recipient Richard and Hinda Rosenthal Found. award, Am. Assn. Cancer Rsch., 2005, Dorothy P. Landon prize for Translational Cancer Rsch., 2009, David A. Karnofsky award, Am. Soc. Clin. Oncology, 2005. Mem.: Inst. Medicine. Achievements include development of imatinib (Gleevec), 2001; dasatinib (Sprycel), 2006. Office: Meml Sloan-Kettering Cancer Ctr 1275 York Ave New York NY 10065 Office Phone: 646-888-2594, 646-888-2163. Office Fax: 646-888-2595. E-mail: martinb@mskcc.org.*

SAWYERS, ELIZABETH JOAN, retired librarian, director; b. San Diego, Dec. 2, 1936; d. William Henry and Elizabeth Georgiana (Price) S. AA, Glendale Jr. Coll., 1957; BA in Bacteriology, UCLA, 1959, M.L.S., 1961. Asst. head acquisition sect. Nat. Library Medicine, Bethesda, Md., 1962-63, head acquisition sect., 1963-66, spl. asst. to chief tech. services div., 1966-69, spl. asst. to assoc. dir. for library ops., 1969-73; asst. dir. libraries for tech. services SUNY-Stony Brook, 1973-75; dir. Health Scis. Library Ohio State U., Columbus, 1975-90, spl. asst. to dir. Univ. librs., 1990—2007. Mem. Assn. Acad. Health Scis. Library Dirs. (sec./treas. 1981-83, pres. 1983-84), Med. Library Assn., Am. Soc. for Info. Sci., Spl. Libraries Assn., ALA

SAWYERS, NORMA ANN, elementary school educator, real estate agent, property manager; b. Detroit, Aug. 10, 1931; d. Austin Sipple and Viola (Anderson) Neeb; m. Thomas J. Stevenson Jr., June 20, 1953 (div. Feb. 1983); children: Mark Stevenson, Lori Ann Smith, Thomas J. Stevenson III; m. Gordon E. Sawyers, July 6, 2003. BS, Mich. State U., 1953; MA, Wayne State U., 1972. Tchr. Grosse Pointe Schs., Mich., 1969—87; real estate sales staff Schweitzer, Prudential, Grosse Pointe, 1979—2000; owner, pres., real estate developer Thompson Marlor Fin. Mgmt. Co., Grosse Pointe, 1980—. Bridge dir. Celebrity Cruise Line, 2001—, Norweigian Cruise Line, 2001—; developer condominium conversion Stevenson Condominium, Grosse Pointe, 1995; lectr., spkr. in field. Treas. PTA, Grosse Pointe, 1968; vol. Hospice, Grosse Pointe, 1990—94, Meals on Wheels, Grosse Pointe, 1999—2003; mem. St. James Luth. Ch., Grosse Pointe, 1940—2006; chair handchimes, dir. of bridge Spirit of Grace Luth. Ch., Surprise, Ariz. Mem.: PEO, Am. Contract Bridge League (dir.), Delta Kappa Gamma (Woman of Distinction 1980). Republican. Avocations: sailing, bridge, bicycling, travel, exercise. Home (Winter): 1617 Heathermore Colleyville TX 76034-6643

SAWYIER, MICHAEL TOD, lawyer, director; b. Boston, Mass., Jan. 6, 1948; s. Calvin Parker and Fay (Horton) Sawyier; m. Judith Puistonen Sawyier, June 6, 1968; children: Julianne Patricia, Justine Fay, Alexandra Lee, Sydney Anne Helena. BA, Harvard U., 1969; JD, U. Chgo., 1972; LLM, Yale U., 1973, John Marshall Law Sch., 2001. Atty. adviser Office of Legal Adviser U.S. Dept. State, Washington, 1974—75; assoc. Pillsbury, Madison and Sutro, San Francisco, 1975—77, Baker and McKenzie, Chgo., 1977—79, Foss, Schuman, Drake & Barnard, Chgo., 1979—87; ptnr. Mathewson, Hamblet & Casey, Chgo., 1987—89, Sawyier and Stewart, Chgo., 1989—93, Watt and Sawyier, Chgo., 1993—2002; prin. Law Offices Michael T. Sawyier, 2002—. Bd. dirs. Am. Inst. Sindhulogy, 2006. Recipient Paul Cornell prize, Hyde Park Hist. Soc., Chgo., 1982. Mem.: ABA, Am. Soc. Internat. Law., Tex. Bar Assn., Ind. Bar Assn., Chgo. Bar Assn., Ill. Bar Assn., Chgo. Club, Saddle and Cycle Club, Chgo. Rotary Club. Office: 150 N Michigan Ste 2700 Chicago IL 60601-3713 Home Phone: 773-472-9771; Office Phone: 312-856-9741. Business E-Mail: mtsawyier@estateplanningattorneychicago.com.

SAX, JOSEPH LAWRENCE, lawyer, educator; b. Chgo., Feb. 3, 1936; s. Benjamin Harry and Mary (Silverman) S.; m. Eleanor Charlotte Gettes, June 17, 1958; children: Katherine Elaine Dennett, Valerie Beth Sax, Amber Sax Rosen. AB, Harvard U., 1957; JD, U. Chgo., 1959; LLD (hon.), Ill. Inst. Tech., 1992; LLD (hon.), Columbia U., 2009. Bar: D.C. 1960, Mich., 1966, U.S. Supreme Ct. 1969, US Ct. Appeals (Fed. cir.), 2008. Atty. U.S. Dept. Justice, Washington, 1959-60; pvt. practice law Washington, 1960-62; prof. U. Colo., 1962-65, U. Mich., Ann Arbor, 1966-86; dep. asst. sec. and counselor U.S. Sec. Interior, Washington, 1994-96; prof. U. Calif. Law Sch., Berkeley, 1986—. Fellow Ctr. Advanced Study in Behavioral Scis., 1977-78, Order of the Coif Disting. Visitor, 2004. Author: Waters and Water Rights, 1967, Water Law, Planning and Policy, 1968, Defending the Environment, 1971, Mountains Without Handrails, 1980, Legal Control of Water Resources, 4th edit., 2006, Playing Darts with a Rembrandt, 1999. Recipient Blue Planet prize, 2007. Fellow; AAAS. Office Phone: 510-642-1831. Business E-Mail: saxj@law.berkeley.edu.

SAX, MARY RANDOLPH, speech and language pathologist; b. July 13, 1925; d. Bernard Angus and Ada Lucile (Thurman) TePoorten; m. William Martin Sax, Feb. 7, 1948. BA magna cum laude, Mich. State U., 1947; MA, U. Mich., 1949. Supr. speech correction dept. Waterford Twp. Schs., Pontiac, 1949—69; lectr. Marygrove Coll., Detroit, 1971-72; pvt. practice in speech and lang. pathology Wayne and Oakland Counties, Mich., 1973—. Co-investigator Support Pers. Profl. Practice of Speech-Lang. Pathology; counselor to divsn. stroke liaisons Am. Heart Assn. Mich.; liaison between Am. Heart Assn. of Mich. and Am. Heart Assn., Dallas, 1996—98; adj. speech pathologist, Southfield, Mich.; lectr. on stroke Mich. Spkrs. Bur., Am. Heart Assn., 1990—; pub. spkg. coach, 1989—; mem. adj. faculty SS Cyril and Methodius Sem., Orchard Lake, Mich., 1989—90; adj. St. Mary's Prep. Sch., Orchard Lake, 1990—; mem. Met. Detroit Operation Stroke com. Am. Stroke Assn., 1999—2004, mem. med. subcom. to move area hosps. to become primary stroke ctrs. with active stroke teams; founder, mem. Stroke Project Task Force for Detroit, 1993—98; com. mem. Charette, study Arch. and Design for phys. restructuring Franklin, Mich., 1993; invited speech pathology del. Internat. Health Programs People to People Citizen Amb. Program, 1996; mem. sci. coun. on stroke Am. Heart Assn., Dallas, 1980—2002; mem. quality improvement and med. edn. subcom. Am. Heart Assn. New Heart and Stroke Network Metro Detroit; mem. stroke adv. com./stroke advocacy com. States of Midwest affiliate Am. Heart Assn., 1995—2005; invited USA rep., speech & lang. pathology Med. People to People Amb. Program Neurol. Ctrs., Czech Republic, Hungary, Austria, 2001; mem. stroke advocacy and stroke advisory coms., Am. Heart Assn. Greater Midwest Affiliate, Mich., Ind., Ill., Wis., ND, SD, Minn. Contbr. articles to profl. jours. including Lang. and Lang. Behavior Abstracts, Lang. Speech and Hearing Svcs., Speech Lang. Hearing Jour. Active Franklinites for Responsible Govt.; mem. stroke com. Mich. Heart Assn., 1982—99; founder, pres. Lakeview Assn. Sylvan Lake, Mich., 2006—. Recipient Svc. Recognition award Coll. Edn. Mich. State U.; grantee Inst. Articulation and Learning, 1969, others; Christian svc. commn. St. Owen, Birmingham co-chmn. blood dr. Red Cross, Franklin, Mich., 1991—. Mem.: Trustee Southfield Township, Founders Soc. of Detroit Inst. Arts, Franklin Found. (mem. natural resources adv. coun. 1991—99, bd. dirs. 1994—98), Pvt. Practitioners Speech-Lang. Pathology (co-founder), Internat. Assn. Logopedics and Phoniatrics (Switzerland), Am. Heart Assn. Mich. (mem. stroke awareness seminars, continuing edn. for physicians and other profls., planning and operation edn.), Mich. Speech-Lang.-Hearing Assn. (cmty. & hosp. com., pvt. practitioner liason, developer structural parameters, State Clin. Svcs. award, Selection Com. State award), Am. Speech-Lang.-Hearing Assn., Mich. Humane Soc., Gamma Phi Beta, Kappa Delta Pi, Phi Kappa Phi, Theta Alpha Phi. Achievements include research in language and speech acquisition in children in reference to the development of and prediction of biological speech change; research interests in developmental phonatory voice disorders, and in adult acquisition of language and speech relative to central and autonomic nervous systems. Office: 31320 Woodside Dr Franklin MI 48025-2027

SAXBE, WILLIAM BART, lawyer, former United States Attorney General, former United States Senator from Ohio; b. Mechanicsburg, Ohio, June 24, 1916; s. Bart Rockwell and Faye Henry (Carey) S.; m. Ardath Louise Kleinhans, Sept. 14, 1940; children: William Bart, Juliet Louise Saxbe Blackburn, Charles Rockwell. AB, Ohio State U., 1940; LLB, 1948; degree (hon.), Central State U., Findlay Coll., Ohio Wesleyan U., Walsh Coll., Capital U., Wilmington Coll., Ohio State U., Bowling Green State U. Bar: Ohio 1948, DC. Practiced in, Mechanicsburg, Ohio, 1948-55; ptnr. Saxbe, Boyd & Prine, 1955-58; mem. Ohio Ho. Reps., 1947—54, majority leader, 1951-52, speaker, 1953-54; atty. gen. State of Ohio, 1957-58, 63-68; ptnr. Dargusch, Saxbe & Dargusch, 1960-63; US Senator from Ohio, 1969-74; atty. gen. US Dept. Justice, 1974—75; US amb. to India US Dept. State, New Delhi, 1975-77; ptnr. Chester, Saxbe, Hoffman & Wilcox, Columbus, Ohio, 1977-81; of counsel Jones, Day, Reavis & Pogue, Cleve., 1981-84, Pearson, Ball & Dowd (merger Pearson, Ball & Dowd and Reed, Smith & McClay), Washington, 1984-93, Chester Willcox & Saxbe, Columbus, Ohio, 1994—; ind. spl. counsel Central States Teamsters Pension Fund, 1982—. Served with 107th Cav. AUS, 1940-42, 107th Cav. USAAF, 1942-45; col. Res. Mem. ABA, Ohio Bar Assn., Am. Judicature Soc., Chi Phi, Phi Delta Phi. Clubs: Mason (Rufus Putnam Disting. Svc. Award), University, Columbus Athletic, Scioto Country, Urbana Country, Burning Tree Country, Bethesda, Md., Country of Fla., Boynton Beach. Republican. Episcopalian. Office: Chester Wilcox & Saxbe LLP 65 E State St Ste 1000 Columbus OH 43215*

SAXE, DEBORAH CRANDALL, lawyer; b. Lima, Ohio, July 23, 1949; d. Robert Gordon and Lois Barker (Taylor) Crandall; m. Robert Saxe, June 3, 1989; children: Elizabeth Sara, Emily Jane. BA, Pa. State U., 1971; MA, UCLA, 1973, JD, 1978. Bar: Calif. 1978, D.C. 1979, U.S. Dist. Ct. D.C. 1979, U.S. Dist. Ct. (ea. dist.) Calif. 1981, U.S. Dist. Ct. (ctrl. dist.) Calif. 1982, U.S. Dist. Ct. (no. and so. dists.) Calif. 1987, U.S. Ct. Appeals (4th and D.C. cirs.) 1979, U.S. Ct. Appeals (6th cir.) 1985, U.S. Ct. Appeals (8th and 9th cirs.) 1987, U.S. Ct. Appeals (2nd cir.) 1990, U.S. Supreme Ct. 1982, U.S. Dist. Ct. (no. dist.) Ill. 2001, U.S. Ct. Appeals (7th cir.) 2001. Assoc. Seyfarth, Shaw, Fairweather & Geraldson, Washington, 1978-83, Jones, Day, Reavis & Pogue, Washington, 1983-85, LA, 1985-87, ptnr., 1988-97; shareholder Heller Ehrman LLP, 1997—2005; ptnr. Jones Day, LA, 2006—. Judge pro tem, Small Claims Ct., L.A., 1985-88. Co-author: Advising California Employers, 1990, 3d edit., 2007; contbg. editor Employment Discrimination Law, 1989. Bd. dirs. Constitutional Rights Found., 1997—2002; chair Eisner Pediatric and Family Med. Ctr., LA, 1996—98, bd. dirs., 1990—2003, Los Angeles County Bar Found., 1997—99. Fellow: Coll. Labor and Employment Lawyers; mem.: ABA (labor law sect. 1978—, Chamber Ptnr. 2004—09, Best Lawyers Am. 2006, 2007, 2008, 2009), LA County Bar Assn. (labor and employment law sect. 1985—, mem. exec. com. 1988—, chair 2002—03, trustee 2005—08, sr. lawyers divsn. 2009—, mem. exec. com. 2009—), Calif. Bar Assn. (labor law sect. 1985—), Phi Beta Kappa, Pi Lambda Theta. Office: Jones Day 555 S Flower St 50th Fl Los Angeles CA 90071 Office Phone: 213-489-3939. Office Fax: 213-243-2539. Business E-Mail: dsaxe@jonesday.com.

SAXE, LEONARD, social psychologist, educator; b. NYC, June 12, 1947; s. Theodore and Majorie (Mayers) S.; m. Marion Gardner, Aug. 9, 1970; 1 child, Daniel. BS in Psychology, U. Pitts., 1969, MS in Psychology, 1972, PhD in Social Psychology, 1976. Asst. instr. U. Pitts., 1973-75; asst. then assoc. prof. psychology Boston U., 1976-88, assoc. dir. Ctr. Applied Social Sci., 1982-84, dir., 1984-87; rsch. prof. Heller Sch. Social Welfare Brandeis U., Waltham, Mass., 1988-90, adj. prof. psychology, adj. rsch. prof., 1990—; prof. psychology Grad. Ctr. CUNY, 1991—; head social-personality psychology, 1993-95; prof. social policy Brandeis U., dir. Cohen Ctr. Modern Jewish Studies; prof. Jewish Cmty. Rsch., 2006—. Fulbright sr. lectr. U. Haifa, Israel, 1981—82; mem. task force Children's Mental Health Rsch. Inst. of Medicine-NAS, 1988—89; mem. rev. coms. HHS-Healthcare Fin. Adminstrn. NIMH, Nat. Inst. Drug Abuse, Dept. Edn.; cons., contractor Office Tech. Assessment, U.S. Congress, 1980—88; bd. govs. U. Haifa, 1993—; bd. dirs. Steinhardt Social Rsch. Inst. Author: (with others) Children's Mental Health: Problems and Treatment, 1987,)with A. Sales) How Goodly Are Thy Tents, (with M. Fine) Social Experiments: Methods for Design and Evaluation, 1981, (with B. Chazan) Ten Days of Birthright Israel, 2008; editor: (with M.J. Saks) Advances in Applied Social Psychology, Vol. 3, 1986, (with D. Koretz) New Directions for Program Evaluation, 1982, (with D. Bar-Tal) The Social Psychology of Education: Theory and Research, 1978; contbr. chpts. to books, articles to profl. jours.; assoc. and mng. editor Personality and Social Psychology Bull., 1978-81; revieweer in field. Congl. fellow Office Tech. Assessment, 1979. Fellow APA (bd. dirs. sect. social and ethical responsibility 1985-88, Disting. Contbn. award 1989), AAAS, Soc. Psychol. Study Social Issues (coun. 1982-84, 87-89). Office: Cohen Ctr MS014 Brandeis U Waltham MA 02454 Office Phone: 781-736-3952. E-mail: saxe@brandeis.edu.

SAXENA, ARJUN NATH, physicist; b. Lucknow, India, Apr. 1, 1932; came to U.S., 1956, naturalized, 1976; s. Sheo and Mohan (Piyari) Shanker; m. Veera Saxena, Feb. 9, 1956; children: Rashmi, Amol, Varsha, Ashvin. BSc, Lucknow U., 1950, MSc, 1952, profl. cert. in German, 1954; post MS diploma, Inst. Nuc. Physics, Calcutta, India, 1955; PhD, Stanford U., 1963. Rsch. asst. Stanford U., 1956-60; mem. tech. staff Fairchild Semicondr. Co., Palo Alto, Calif., 1960-65; dept. head Sprague Electric Co., North Adams, Mass., 1965-69; mem. tech. staff RCA Labs., Princeton, NJ, 1969-71; pres., chmn. bd. Astro-Optics, Phila., 1972; pres. Internat. Sci. Co., Princeton Junction, NJ, 1973—. Disting. vis. scientist Centre de Récherches Nucléaires, Strasbourg, France, 1973, 77; sr. staff scientist, mgr. engring. Data Gen. Corp., Sunnyvale, Calif., 1975-80; mgr. process tech. Signetics Corp., Sunnyvale, 1980-81; Gould AMI scientist, dir. advanced process devel. Gould AMI Semicondrs., Santa Clara, Calif., 1981-87; dir. Ctr. for Integrated Electronics, prof. dept. elec. and computer system engring. Rensselaer Poly. Inst., Troy, N.Y., 1987-96, emeritus prof., 1996—; disting. vis. scientist Inst. Microelectronics, Stuttgart, Germany, 1993-94. Contbr. articles to semicondr. tech., optics, nuc. and high-energy physics to sci. jours.; patentee in field. Treas. pack 66 Boy Scouts Am., West Windsor, N.J., 1970-74. Recipient Disting. Citizen award State of N.J., 1975. Mem. IEEE (life, sr.), Stanford U. Alumni Assn. (life). Achievements include establishment of a fellowship in his and his wife's name at Rensselaer Polytechnic Institute. Home: 4217 Pomona Ave Palo Alto CA 94306-4312

SAXENA, BRIJ B., endocrinologist, biochemist, educator; PhD, India; DSc, U. Muenster, W.Ger.; PhD, U. Wis., 1961; DSc (hon.), Bundelkhand U., India, 2002. Asst. prof. biochemistry and endocrinology N.J. Coll. Medicine., 1966-74; assoc. prof. biochemistry Cornell U. Med. Coll., NYC, 1974—, prof. biochemistry, 1974—, prof. endocrinology, 1981—, dir. div. reproductive endocrinology, Harold and Percy Uris endowed prof. reproductive biology, 2000—. Contbr. articles to profl. jours. Recipient Career Scientist award N.Y.C. Health Research Council; Upjohn research award; Campoz da Paz award. Fellow Royal Soc. Medicine (London); mem. Am. Soc. Biol. Chemists, AAAS, Endocrine Soc., Harvey Soc., Am. Physiol. Soc., Am. Chem. Soc. Office: Cornell U Med Coll 515 E 71st St Ste 412 New York NY 10021-4805 Office Phone: 212-746-3067. Business E-Mail: brs2003@med.cornell.edu.

SAXENA, PARUL, special education educator, psychologist; b. Delhi, Mar. 1, 1976; arrived in US, 2006; d. Prakash Bahadur and Sarla Saxena. BA in Psychology with honors, U. Delhi, 1996, MA in Psychology, 1998, MPhil in Psychology, 2000; MS in Psychotherapy, Inst. Psychology and Mgmt. Scis., Mumbai, 2003; postgrad. in Psychology, Avinashlingam U. for Women, Coimbatore, India, 2008—. Cert. sch. psychologist State Dept. Edn., SC, highly qualified spl. educator State Dept. Edn., SC; in mgmt. and tng. for learning disabled Indian Nat. Portage Assn., 2006, rehab. psychologist RCI, India. Rehab. psychologist Jain Neuro Ctr., Delhi, 1998—99; psychologist mng. sec. Save the Children with Mental Retardation and Disability Found., Delhi, 1999—2006; dir. Ctr. Child Psychology, Delhi, 2006—; spl. edn. tchr. Williamsburg County Sch. Dist., Hemingway, SC, 2006—08; sch. psychologist Clarendon County Sch. Dist. #2, 2008—. Rehab. counsellor to in-charge crisis intervention unit All India Confederation for Blind, Delhi, 1998—99; guest lectr. Vivekanad Coll., U. Delhi, 2000—01; consulting psychologist TVS Motors, Bangalore, Karnataka, India, 2002—06, Delhi Psychiatry Ctr., 2004—05, Bharat Nat. Pub. Sch., Delhi, 2005—06. Subject of numerous interviews Indian, English and Hindi daily and weekly newspapers and mags., news channels in India including DD Metro and Channel 7; author, editor: Attention Deficit Hyperactivity Disorder: Collective Papers, 2002, Psychotherapy for Day to Day Life, 2005; contbr. chapters to books, articles to profl. jours. Mem.: Rehab. Coun. India (licentiate), Internat. Soc. Early Intervention (life). Achievements include work for the children with disabilities was recognized by the then President of India, Dr. A.P.J. Abdul Kalam in April 2006, in the President House, New Delhi, India; research in the intervention with children with ADHD. Avocations: reading literature, mythology, theology, parapsychology, working with disabled children. Personal E-mail: parulsaxena@indiatimes.com. Business E-Mail: psaxena@wcsd.k12.sc.us.

SAXENA, ROMIL, pathologist, educator; d. Rajendra Mohan and Rani Saxena; m. Sunil Badve. MBBS, MD, Grant Med. Coll., Mumbai, India. Diplomate Am. Bd. Pathology, 1998. Resident pathologist Sir JJ Group of Hosps., Bombay, 1985—87; sr. registrar, histopathology Tata Meml. Hosp. for Cancer, Bombay, 1987—88, sr. registrar, hematopathology, 1988—90; registrar, dept. pathology, S.E. Thames Regional rotation King's Coll. Hosp., Farnborough Hosp., 1990—91; lectr., dept. pathology King's Coll. Hosp., London, 1991—95; resident, dept. pathology Albert Einstein Sch. Medicine, Bronx, NY, 1995—96; fellow, gene therapy and liver pathology Mt. Sinai Med. Ctr., NYC, 1996—98; fellow, gastrointestinal pathology Yale U. Sch. Med., New Haven, 1998—2002; asst. prof., dept. pathology Mt. Sinai Sch. Medicine, NYC, 2002—08; asst. prof. depts. pathology and lab. med. Ind. U. Sch. Medicine, Indpls., 2002—08, assoc. prof. depts. pathology and lab. med., 2008—, assoc. prof. dept. medicine. Dir., anatomic pathology Richard L. Roudebush VA Med. Ctr., Indpls., 2002—04; lectr. in field in liver transplantation pathology. Contbr. articles to profl. jours., chapters to books. Fellow: Royal Coll. Pathologists (assoc.); mem.: Internat. Acad. Pathology (assoc.), Laennec Hepatopathology Soc. (assoc.), Hans Popper Hepatopathology Soc. (assoc.), US and Can. Acad.Pathology (assoc.). Achievements include expertise in liver hepatopathology and transplantation pathology. Avocation: writing. Office: Ind Univ Clarian Health 350 W 11th St Indianapolis IN 46202

SAXER, RICHARD KARL, metallurgical engineer, retired military officer; b. Toledo, Aug. 31, 1928; s. Alexander Albert and Gertrude Minnie (Kuebeler) S.; m. Marilyn Doris Mersereau, July 19, 1952; children: Jane Lynette, Robert Karl, Kris Renee, Ann Luette. Student, Bowling Green State U., 1946-48; BS, U. S. Naval Acad., 1952; MS in Aero. Mechanics Engring., Air Force Inst. Tech., 1957; PhD in Metall. Engring., Ohio State U., 1962; grad., Armed Forces Staff Coll., 1966, Indsl. Coll. Armed Forces, 1971; disting. grad., Air Force Inst. Tech., 2003. Commd. 2d lt. U.S. Air Force, 1952, advanced through grades to lt. gen., 1976; electronics officer, mech. officer (4th Tactical Support Sqadron, Tactical Air Command), Sandia Base, N.Mex., 1953-54; electronics and mech. officer, spl. weapons assembly sect. supr. (SAC 6th Aviation Depot Squadron), French Morocco, 1954-55; project engr. mech. equipment br. Air Force Spl. Weapon's Center, Kirtland AFB, N.Mex., 1957-59; project officer Nuclear Safety div., 1959-60; assoc. prof. dept. engring. mechanics Air Force Inst. Tech., 1962-66; asso. prof., dep. dept. head USAF Acad., 1966-70; comdr., dir. Air Force Materials Lab., Wright-Patterson AFB, Ohio, 1971-74; dep. for Reentry System Space and Missile Systems Orgn., 1974-77; dep. for aero equipment Aero. Systems Div., 1977-80, dep. for tactical systems, 1980, vice comdr., 1981-83; aero. systems div. dir. Def. Nuclear Agy., 1983-85, ret., 1985; pres. R.K. Saxer & Assocs., 1985-91; CEO Universal Tech. Corp., Dayton, Ohio, 1991—96. Research and tech. com. materials and structures NASA, 1973-74; chmn. planning group aerospace materials Interagy. Council Materials, 1973-74; mem. Nat. Mil. Adv. Bd., 1971-74, NATO adv. group for research and devel., 1973-74 Contbr. articles to profl. jours. Decorated Def. Disting. Svc. medal, Legion of Merit, Meritorious Service medal USAF, D.S.M., Joint Svc. Commendation medal, Air Force Commendation medal with 3 oak leaf clusters, Army Commendation medal U.S., Def. Superior Service medal, Cross of Gallantry with palm Vietnam, Def. Meritorious Service medal; recipient Disting. award for systems mgmt. Air Force Assn., 1979; Disting. Alumnus award Ohio State U., 1986, Disting. Alumni award Air Force Inst. Tech., 2003. Mem. Air Force Assn., Am. Def. Preparedness Assn. (pres. Dayton 1977-78), Sigma Xi, Phi Lambda Epsilon, Alpha Sigma Mu, Masons, Shriners. Home: 215 Dalfaber Ln Springboro OH 45066-1571

SAXILD, CHRISTINE ANN, science educator; d. Stanley Walter and Lillian Jean Gorski; m. James Nmi Saxild, May 27, 1983; 1 child, Victoria Jean Kiwazek. MS, U. Wis., Eau Claire, 1993. Divsn. chair, assoc. prof. Mt. Senario Coll., Ladysmith, Wis., 1989—2002, dean, Outreach, 1998—2000; instr. Wis. Indianhead Tech. Coll., Ashland, 2002—. Mem.: APA. Office: Wis Indianhead Tech Coll 2100 Beaser Ave Ashland WI 54806

SAXINGER, WILLIAM CARL, microbiologist; b. Chgo., Oct. 4, 1941; s. Otto and Mary Saxinger; m. Judith Ann Conroy, Aug. 17, 1967; children: Justin, Daniel, Anne. BS in Chemistry, U. Ill., Champaign, 1963, PhD in Microbiology, 1969. NAS, NRC, postdoc. rsch. assoc. NASA, AMES Rsch. Ctr., Exobiology Divsn., Moffett Field, Calif., 1969—71; rsch. assoc. lab. chem. evolution, dept. chemistry U. Md., Coll. Pk., 1971—72, asst. rsch. prof., lab. chem. evolution, 1972—76; sr. staff fellow, lab. tumor cell biology NIH, Nat. Cancer Inst., Bethesda, Md., 1972—75, sr. investigator, microbiologist, 1975—85, sr. investigator, supervisory microbiologist, office dir. Ctr. Cancer Rsch. Frederick, Md., 1976—, sr. investigator, supervisory microbiologist, lab. tumor cell biology, 1985—96. Cons. devel. of blood bank screening Ortho Diagnostics, Raritan, NJ, 1987; del. US Dept. State, Washington. Contbr. scientific papers. Computer support for spl. needs classes Ivymount Sch., Rockville, Md., 1998—2005. Recipient Tech. Transfer award, Dirs. Nat. Cancer Inst. and Divsn. Cancer Etiology, 1972. Independent. Lutheran. Achievements include patents for polypeptides comprising IL-6 ligand binding receptor domains; polypeptides that bind HIV gp120 and related nucleic acids, antibodies; discovery of markers for possible infection by human leukemia virus HTLV-I in US blood donors; HIV bind to cell receptors in a preliminary promiscuous fashion rendering the design of a multivalent vaccine more feasible; patents for competitive ELISA for the detection of antibodies. Avocations: computers, photography, music, Aikido. Home: 6814 Renita Ln Bethesda MD 20817 Office: Nat Cancer Inst NIH Bldg 37 1041A Bethesda MD 20892 Business E-Mail: csaxinger@verizon.net.

SAXMAN, ANNA ESTHER, lawyer; b. Latrobe, Pa., May 14, 1949; d. Harry Suydam and Eleanor Ruth S.; m. Robert Halpert, Feb. 18, 1989. BS magna cum laude, U. Vt., 1978, JD magna cum laude, 1985. Clk. to presiding justice Vt. Supreme Ct., Montpelier, 1985-86; assoc. Langrock, Sperry, Parker & Wool, Burlington, Vt., 1986—; atty. Vt. Defender Gen., dep. defender gen., 2000—. Mem. Task Force on Gender Bias in the Legal System, Montpelier, 1988—. Editor U. Vt. Law Rev. Pres., bd. trustees Vt. Assn. for Mental Health, Montpelier, 1989—. Mem. ABA, ATLA, Vt. Bar Assn. (chmn. women's sect. 1989—, chmn. com. on rights of the mentally and physically handicapped, 1988-89, pres. 2003-04). Office: Vermont Def Gen Office 120 State St Montpelier VT 05620-3301

SAXON, BURTON ROY, humanities educator; b. Aurora, Ill., June 22, 1947; s. Samuel and Jennie (Weisman) S.; m. Janet Hunter, June 21, 1969 (div. Dec. 1979); m. Myra Denise Hamburg, June 5, 1983; children: Jeffrey, Rebekah. BA, Carleton Coll., 1969; MAT, Wesleyan U., 1971; EdD, Columbia U., 1977; LHD (hon.), Quinnipiac U., 2006. Tchr. R.C. Lee High Sch., New Haven, 1970-75, 77-80; tchr., facilitator Hillhouse High Sch., New Haven, 1980—2006, New Haven-Yale Internat. Studies Ctr., 1989-93, New Haven-Yale Saturday Sem., 1989—. Vis. instr. edn. Yale U., 1976—. Co-author: Invitation to Psychology, 1980, 89; contbr. articles to profl. jours. Chmn. New Haven Bd. Edn. Family Life Edn. Com., 1979-83; co-founder Children's Coop Daycare, 1970-79. Named New Haven Tchr. of Yr., 2004—05, Conn. Tchr. of Yr., 2005; grantee, NSF, 1974—75. Democrat. Jewish. Avocations: baseball, bridge, movies, plays, tennis. E-mail: burtsaxon@sbcglobal.net.

SAXON, RANDALL LEE, pastor, author, educator; b. Waverly, NY, Oct. 28, 1947; s. Sherman Kenyon and Velma Marie (Dunning) S.; m. Diane Louise Kennedy, June 23, 1973 (div. Feb. 1985); children: Heather Marie, David Arthur; m. Anna Louise Clock, Mar. 15, 1986; children: Jennifer Elizabeth, Austin Todd. BA, Mansfield U., 1969; MDiv, Princeton Sem., 1973; certificate, Mansfield Coll., Oxford, Eng., 1980, Wadham Coll., Oxford, 2003; D of Ministry, Drew U., 1992. Ordained to ministry Presbyn. Ch. U.S.A., 1973. Asst. pastor United Meth. Ch., Flemington, 1970—71, Fewsmith Presbyn. Ch., Bellville, 1972—73; intern pastor Wattsburg (Pa.) Presbyn. Ch., 1971—72, East Greene Presbyn. Ch., Erie, Pa., 1971—72; asst. chaplain Bayberry State Hosp., Phila., 1973; assoc. pastor Presbyn. Ch., Gettysburg, Pa., 1973—78; sr. pastor 1st Presbyn. Ch., Southampton, 1978—86, Presbyn. Ch. of the Covenant, Port Arthur, Tex., 1986—91, 1st Presbyn. Ch., Wilmette, Ill., 1991—94, Peoria, Ill., 1994—2004; pastor United Presbyn. Ch., Peoria, 2004—; instr. parish nursing program OSF St. Francis Med. Ctr., Peoria, Ill., 1995—99; instr. Inst. Learning in Retirement Bradley U., Peoria, Ill., 1995—; instr. social scis. Ill. Ctrl. Coll., East Peoria, Ill., 1999—. Nat. chaplain Sigma Theta Epsilon, Mansfield, Pa., 1968-72; permanent clk. Presbytery of Carlisle, Camp Hill, Pa., 1975-77, Synod of the Trinity, Camp Hill, 1977-78; jour. clk. Presbytery of L.I., Commack, N.Y., 1980-84; mem. Presbytery of Great Rivers; guest lectr. in field. Author: Voices in the Wilderness, 1985, At the Ffeete of Christe and His Church, 1981, Developing A Ministry of Evangelism With Baby Boomers in A Suburban Setting, 1992, America's Debt to the Native American, 1999, Watch Your Mouth! A Brief History of Everyday Words and Phrases, 2003, Good Grief, Gravestones!, 2005; editor: Special Prayers and Prose for Special People of God, 1998; author articles, poetry, hymns. Program dir. Camp Brule, Boy Scouts Am., Forksville, Pa., 1972; dir. Youth in Govt. Seminar, Harrisburg, Pa., 1977; v.p. Internat. Seamen's Ctr., Houston, 1987-89; chairperson City Task Force on Edn. Summit, Port Arthur, 1990-91; active Presbyn. Hist. Soc.; camp commr. Boy Scouts Am., Forksville, Pa., 1971, dist. commr., Peoria, Ill., 1999 Recipient cert. Shinnecock Indian Tribe, 1981; named an Outstanding Young Man of Am., Jaycees, 1971; Susquehanna Collegiate Inst. grantee, 1972. Mem. Acad. Parish Clergy, Am. Soc. Ch. History, Presbyn. Hist. Soc., Presbyn. Writers Guild, Ctr. Theology and Natural Scis., Presbyn. Assn. Sci, Tech., and Christian Faith, Surrat Soc., Am. Forestry Assn., Presbyns. Renewal Creation, Scottish Soc. S.E. Tex. (pres. 1990-91), Ill. State Hist. Soc., The Co. of Pastors, The Lincoln Party, The Lincoln Project, Abraham Lincoln Assn., Nat. Eagle Scout Assn., Rotary (pres. 1977-78), Tri-county Lincoln Bicentennial Commn. Democrat. Avocations: coin collecting/numismatics, canoeing, whitewater rafting, skydiving, gardening. Home: 3628 N Breckenridge Ct Peoria IL 61614-8034 Office: United Presbyn Ch 2400 W Northmoor Rd Peoria IL 61614-3343 Home Phone: 309-681-9291; Office Phone: 309-693-2002. Business E-Mail: rls@unitedpc.org.

SAXON, WOLFGANG ERIK GEORG, journalist, writer; b. Leipzig, Germany, Sept. 5, 1930; arrived in US, 1952; s. Erich Otto and Klâre (Wochatz) Richter; m. Anna Forti, 1967. BS, Columbia U., 1954; postgrad., Russian Inst., 1960. Newspaper reporter, obituarist New York Times, NYC, 1956—2006; freelance writer, 2006—. Draftee to specialist US Army, 1954—56. Mem.: Phi Beta Kappa, The Silurians. Independent. Agnostic. Avocations: reading, walking, travel. Business E-Mail: saxon@nytimes.com.

SAXTON, CAROLYN VIRGINIA, museum director; b. Charleston, W.Va., June 24, 1948; d. Robert Everett and Jo Ann S.; children: Jon Hamilton Rickey Jr., Leigh Ann Rickey; m. Harlow William Gregory Jr., May 27, 1989. BA, W.Va. Wesleyan Coll., 1971; postgrad., Loma Linda U., 1989-91. Cert. Fund Raising Exec. Counselor Open Door, Annapolis, Md., 1971-73; social worker Salvation Army, Charleston, 1977-79; patient educator Womens Health Ctr., Charleston, 1979-83; community edn. specialist Shawnee Hills Mental Health, Charleston, 1983; exec. dir. W.Va. Nat. Abortion Rights Action League, Charleston, 1983-86; lobbyist Charleston, 1986; exec. dir. Community Hospice, Ashland, Ky., 1986-89; dir. home hospice Home Hospice VNA North, Evanston, Ill., 1989-90; exec. dir. Community Chest Oak Park/River Forest, Ill., 1990—2004, Oak Park/River Forest Cmty. Found., 1993—2005, Lubeznik Ctr. for the Arts, Mich. City, Ind., 2005—. Mem. Ky. Cancer Program Network, Ashland, 1986—89, Citizens Coun. Oak Park/River Forest H.S., 1991—93, W.Va. Task Force on Adolescent Residential Treatment Ctr./Drug Abuse, 1983, Jr. League Charleston, 1982—86; chmn., usher com. Paramount Women's Assn., Ashland, 1988—89; mem. Nat. Abortion Rights Task Force on Minor's Access, 1986—87; mem. com. on minor's access W.Va. Dept. Health, 1986—87; mem. choir 1st Presbyn. Ch., Ashland, 1986—89, Sunday sch. tchr., 1988—89; mem. choir Fair Oaks Presbyn. Ch., 1990—92, bd. deacons; mem. First United Meth. Ch., chair adminstrn. coun., 1997—99. Mem. Assn. Fundraising Profls. (programming com. 1991-93, internat. conf. com. 1994-95, scholarship com. 1994-95, bd. dirs. 1995-97, spl. interest group com. chair 1995, 96), Nat. Hospice Orgn. (award of excellence 1988), Ky. Assn. Hospice (bd. dirs., mem.-at-large 1989, chmn. nominating com. 1988-89), Coun. for Non-Profits (vol. action com. 1988-89, co-chmn. cmty. support com. 1989), Zonta (status of women com., program com.), Women in Mgmt. (treas. 1993-95), Rotary (program co-chair, bd. dirs. 1993-95, co-chair spl. events 1994-95, sec. 1996-98, sgt.-at-arms 1998-2002, v.p. 2002, pres. 2004, Paul Harris Fellow), Ogden Dune Hist. Soc. (bd. mem. 2007-), Northwest Ind. Planned Giving Group, 2006-, Acting chair 2008-09, Cmty. Founds. Advancement Network, Northwest Ind. AFP Chpt.(pres elect. 2009-), Ogden Dunes Cmty. Fund Com. Democrat. Avocations: travel, reading, collecting miniatures and antique valentines, duplicate bridge. Home: 11 Skyline Dr Portage IN 46368 Office: Lubezink Ctr for the Arts 101 W 2nd St Michigan City IN 46360

SAXTON, CELESTE DAWN, social studies educator, consultant; b. Balt., Feb. 27, 1958; d. Harvey Lewis and Angela Alice-Attardo Saxton; children: Sara Megan Sciarretta, Natalie Allison-Bianca Sciarretta. AA in Arts & Sci. Transfer, Villa Julie Coll., Stevenson, Md., 1978; BS in History & Secondary Edn., Hood Coll., Frederick, Md., 1980; MS in Sch. Adminstrn. & Supervision, The Johns Hopkins U., Balt., 1993; EdD in Ednl. Leadership & Adminstrn., Nova Southeastern U., Ft. Lauderdale, Fla., 2002. Tchr. social studies Balt. County Pub. Schs., Towson, 1980—86; mid. sch. interdisciplinary team leader Balt. County Pub. Sch., 1986—90, chair social studies dept., 1990—96, mentor tchr. county level, 1996—97, h.s. adminstr., 1997—2002, social studies supr. & educator, 2002—. Sat adminstrv. coord. Balt. County Pub. Schs., 1997—2002, sch.-based minority achievement coord., 1989—93. Advisor for 1st mid. sch. key club Kwanis, Reisterstown, Md., 1987—89; team leader-highway clean-up Md. State Dept. Transp., Westminster, 1998—2001; student govt. advisor Balt. County Pub. Schs., 1989—93. Scholar, Balt. County Pub. Schs., 1999—2001. Mem.: Md. Coun. Social Studies, Nat. Coun. Social Studies. Roman Catholic. Avocations: reading, gardening, swimming, boating, travel. Home: 548 Old Bachmans Valley Road Westminster MD 21157 Office: Carroll County Public Schools 125 N Court Street Westminster MD 21157 Office Fax: 410-751-3159; Home Fax: 410-751-3159. Business E-Mail: cdsaxto@k12.carr.org.

SAXTON, JIM (HUGH JAMES SAXTON), former United States Representative from New Jersey; b. Nicholson, Pa., Jan. 22, 1943; s. Hugh R. and Helen M. (Billings) Saxton; m. Helen Jean Gadomski, June 9, 1965; children: Jennifer, James Martin. BA in Edn., East Stroudsburg State U., Pa., 1965; student, Temple U. Tchr. Bordentown Pub. Schs., NJ, 1965-68; owner, realtor Jim Saxton Realty Co., Bordentown, NJ, 1968-85; mem. NJ Gen. Assembly from Dist. 8, 1976—81, asst. minority whip, 1981; mem. NJ State Senate, 1981-84, asst. minority whip, 1981—84; mem. US Congress from 3rd NJ dist., 1993—2009, US Congress from 13th NJ dist., 1984—93. Mem. armed svcs. com. US Congress, mem. natural resources com., ranking Rep. mem. joint econ. com. Chair Am. Cancer Com.; mem. Burlington Coun. Boy Scouts America; mem. Bordentown C. of C., NJ. Recipient Henry M. Jackson Disting. Svc. award, Jewish Inst. Nat. Security Affairs, 2003, Leadership award, Nat. Marine Sanctuary Found., 2003; named Outstanding Fed. Legislator of Yr., NJ Vets. of Fgn. Wars, 2000. Mem.: USAF Assn., Leadership Found. NJ, Rotary, Elks. Republican. Methodist.*

SAXTON, WILLIAM MARVIN, lawyer; b. Joplin, Mo., Feb. 14, 1927; s. Clyde Marvin and Lea Ann (Farnan) S.; m. Helen Grace Klinefelter, June 1, 1974; children: Sherry Lynn, Patricia Ann Painter, William Daniel, Michael Lawrence. AB, U. Mich., 1949, JD, 1952. Bar: Mich. Mem. firm Love, Snyder & Lewis, Detroit, 1952-53, Butzel, Long, Detroit, 1953—, dir., chmn., CEO, 1989-96, dir. emeritus, 1997—. Lectr. Inst. Continuing Legal Edn.; sec., bd. dirs. Fritz Broadcasting, Inc., 1983-97; mem. mediation tribunal hearing panel for 3d Jud. Dist. Mich., 1989—, 6th Jud. Dist., 1994—. Trustee Detroit Music Hall Ctr. Soc. for the Performing Arts, 1984-99; trustee Hist. Soc. US Dist. Ct. (ea. dist.) Mich., 1992-95, pres., 1993-95. Recipient Disting. award Mich. Road Builders Assn., 1987. Master of Bench Emeritus Am. Inn of Court; fellow Am. Coll. Trial Lawyers, Am. Bar Found., Am. Coll. Labor and Employment Lawyers, Mich. Bar Found.; mem. ABA, FBA, Detroit Bar Assn. (dir. 1974-79, Goodnow Pres.'s award 1996), Mich. Bar Assn. (atty. discipline panel, Disting. Svc. award 1998, Champion of Justice award, 2003), Detroit Indsl. Rels. Rsch. Assn. (treas. 1980—, v.p. 1982, pres. 1984-85), Mich. Young Lawyers (pres. 1954-55), Am. Law Inst., Indsl. Rels. Rsch. Assn. Am. Arbitration Assn., U.S. 6th Cir. Ct. Appeals (life, mem. jud. conf., mem. bicentennial com.), Am. Inn Ct., Cooley Club, Renaissance Club, Detroit Golf Club (dir. 1983-89), Detroit Athletic Club. Office: Butzel Long 150 W Jefferson Ave Ste 100 Detroit MI 48226-4416 Office Phone: 313-225-7001.

SAY, BURHAN, retired physician; b. Istanbul, Turkey, Feb. 26, 1923; came to U.S. 1951; s. Ethem Serif and Ayse Say; m. Elizabeth E. Jackson, Nov. 5, 1955; children: Tony, Daniel Demir. MD, U. Istanbul, 1946. Diplomate Am. Bd. Pediatrics, Am. Bd. Med. Genetics. Asst. prof. pediatrics Hacettepe U., Ankara, Turkey, 1960-64, prof. pediatrics, 1964-73; clin. prof. of pediatrics U. of Okla./Tulsa Med. Coll., 1975—; ret. Dir. H.A. Chapman Inst., Tulsa, 1982—; v.p. Children's Med. Ctr., Tulsa, 1988—. Contbr. articles to profl. jours. Pres. Am. Cancer Soc., Tulsa, 1980-90, Great Plains Genetics Soc., Tulsa, 1993. Lt. Turkish Army, 1946-48, Turkey., Fulbright scholar, Boston, 1966—68. Avocation: sports. Home: 6216 E 99th St Tulsa OK 74137-5503 Home Phone: 918-299-5891. Personal E-mail: mbsay@cox.net.

SAYER, RONALD J., composer, educator; b. Rochester, NY, Oct. 12, 1961; s. Barbara Sayer. B Music Edn., U. Mo., Kansas City, 1985; MEd, Tex. Wesleyan U., 2002. Instr. vocal music Lansing Unified Sch. Dist., Kans., 1985—97; artistic dir. Marshall (Mo.) Cmty. Chorus, 2000—; instr. vocal music Marshall (Mo.) H.S., 1997—, chmn. fine arts dept., 2000—, V.p. Mid-Mo. Fine Arts Coun., Marshall, 2002—. Mem. music com. St. Peter's Cath. Ch., Marshall, 1999—2003. Recipient Tchr. award, Mo. Fine Arts Acad., 2000, 2002—04, 2006, Sharon Murphy award, Kans. NEA, 1996, Tchr. of the Yr., Marshall HS, 2006;, U. Mo.-Kansas City scholar, 1994. Mem.: Nat. Assn. Tchrs. Singing, Mo. Choral Dirs. Assn. (chmn. cmty. choirs 2002—04), Music Educators Nat. Conf., Am. Choral Dirs. Assn. (chmn. cmty. choirs southwest divsn. 2004—), Pope John Paul II Cultural Ctr., Omicron Delta Kappa, Pi Kappa Lambda, Phi Mu Alpha Sinfonia. Home: 1017 S Ann Drive Marshall MO 65340 Office: Marshall Public Schs 805 S Miami Ave Marshall MO 65340

SAYERS, GALE, computer company executive, retired professional football player; b. Wichita, Kans., May 30, 1943; s. Roger Earl and Bernice (Ross) S.; m. Ardythe Elaine Bullard, Dec. 1, 1973; children: Gale Lynne, Scott Aaron, Timothy Gale, Gaylon, Guy, Gary. Student phys. edn., Kans. U., N.Y. Inst. Finance. Running back Chgo. Bears Profl. Football Team, 1965—72; then asst. to athletic dir. Kans. U.; athletic dir. So. Ill. U., to 1981; v.p. mktg. Computer Suppy by Sayers, Northfield, Ill., 1984—86; pres. Crest Computer Supply Co., Skokie, Ill., 1986—; pres., CEO Sayers Computer Source, Mt. Prospect, Ill., 1983—2006, chmn.; pres., CEO Sayers40, Inc., Mt. Prospect, Ill., 2006—. Columnist Chgo. Daily News; bd. dir. Global Healthcare Exchange, 2003. Author: (with Al Silverman) I Am Third, 1970, (with Fred Mitchell) Sayers: My Life and Times, 2007 Co-chmn. legal def. fund sports com. NAACP; co-ordinator Reach-Out program, Chgo.; hon. chmn. Am. Cancer Soc.; commr. Chgo. Park Dist. Named NFL Rookie of Yr., 1965; NFL Pro Bowl MVP, 1966, 1967, 1969; named to Pro Football Hall of Fame, 1977 Mem. Kappa Alpha Psi. Office: Sayers Computer Source 1150 Feehanville Dr Mount Prospect IL 60056-6007

SAYERS, MARTIN PETER, pediatric neurosurgeon; b. Big Stone Gap, Va., Jan. 2, 1922; s. Delbert Bancroft and Loula (Thompson) S.; m. Marjorie W. Garvin, May 8, 1943; children: Daniel Garvin Sayers, Stephen Putnam Sayers, Julia Hathaway Sayers Bolton, Elaine King Sayers Buck. BA, Ohio State U., 1943, MD, 1945; postgrad., U. Pa., 1948-51. Intern Phila. Gen. Hosp., 1945-46; resident in neurosurgery U. Pa. Hosps., Phila., 1948-51; practice medicine specializing in neurosurgery Columbus, Ohio, 1951—; mem. faculty Ohio State U., Columbus, 1951-87, clin. prof. neurosurgery, 1968-87, emeritus, chief dept. pediatric neurosurgery, 1960-87. Cons. Bur. Crippled Children Services Ohio.; Neurosurgeon Project Hope, Ecuador, 1964, Ceylon, 1968, Cracow, Poland, 1979. Served as lt. jr. grade M.C. USN, 1946—48. Mem. Am. Assn. Neurol. Surgeons (chmn. pediatric sect.), Congress Neurol. Surgeons (pres.), Neurosurg. Soc. Am. (pres.), Am. Soc. Pediatric Neurosurgery, Soc. Neurol. Surgeons. Office: 931 Chatham Ln Columbus OH 43221-2417

SAYERS BUTLER, PATRICIA ANN, secondary school educator; b. Lebanon, Oreg., May 28, 1952; d. Earl Harold and Geraldine Mae (McCabe) Sayers; m. Joseph K. Butler, June 18, 1977; children: Christopher John, Kadiatu Marie. Student, N.C. Wesleyan Coll., 1970-72; BS in Edn., U. Ark., 1974; MS in Math., Ball State U., 1981; postgrad., Purdue U., 1987, postgrad., 1994, Ind. U., 1990, Ind. Wesleyan U., 1998. Vol., tchr. math. Peace Corps, Pendembu, Sierra Leone, 1974-76; tchr. math. Stuttgart (Ark.) Jr. High Sch., 1976-77; tchr., coach Frankfort (Ind.) Jr. High Sch. and Mid. Sch., 1978—. Religion instr. St. Mary's Cath. Ch., Frankfort, 1986-2006; leader troop 336, Girl Scouts U.S.A., Frankfort, 1986-1995 Mem. NEA, Nat. Coun. Tchrs. Math., Ind. Tchrs. Math., Ind. Tchrs. Assn., Frankfort Edn. Assn., Ind. Coaches Girls Sports Assn., NRA. Avocations: reading, sewing, handicrafts, sports, camping. Home: 903 S Jackson St Frankfort IN 46041-3035 Office: Frankfort Mid Sch 329 N Maish Rd Frankfort IN 46041-2800 E-mail: butlerp@frankfort.k12.in.us.

SAYGILI, GOKHAN, civil engineer, researcher; b. Nevsehir, Turkey, Feb. 17, 1980; s. Necla and Fahrettin Saygili. PhD, U. Tex., Austin, 2008. Rsch. asst. U. Tex., Austin, 2005—08. Personal E-mail: gokhansaygili@gmail.com.

SAYLES, EVA, artist; b. NYC, June 10, 1928; BA, Bklyn. Coll., 1949; studied with Will Barnet, Art Students League. Mem. coop. Amos Eno Gallery, NYC, 1989—; pub. spkr. in field. One-woman shows include Pen and Brush Club, NYC, 1971 (1st prize in mems. oil exhibit), St. Bartholomew's Ch., NYC, 1970, Amos Eno Art Gallery, 1992, Port Chester Coun. for Arts, 1992; exhibited in group shows at Queens Mus., NYC, 1983, Knickerbocker Artists Exhibit, NYC, 1970, Pen and Brush Club, 1970, Marcolio Ltd., 1969, Vera Lazuk Galler, Cold Springs Harbor, 1966, Greenwich Art Soc., Conn., 1987, Nat. Assn. Women Artists; represented in private collections; appearances on TV and radio; contbr. articles (newspapers) Greenwich Time, Conn., Jour. News, Westchester, NY; contbr. poetry to anthologies. Bd. dirs. Port Chester Coun. Arts, NY, 1989—. Recipient prize, Art Students League; scholarship. Mem. Nat. Assn. Women Artists (publicity, advt., grantwriting chairwoman), Pen and Brush Club (publicity chairwoman, first prize for painting called Life), Greenwich Arts Coun., Greenwich Art Soc., Oratorio Soc. (choir mem.). Achievements include always painting scientific theories of cells and molecules, especially in the sixties. Avocations: music, singing, writing, dance, philosophy. Studio: PO Box 510 Port Chester NY 10573-0510

SAYLES, LEONARD ROBERT, management educator, consultant; b. Rochester, NY, Apr. 30, 1926; s. Robert and Rose (Sklof) S.; m. Kathy Ripin; children: Robert, Emily. BA with highest distinction, U. Rochester, 1946; PhD in Econs. and Social Sci., MIT, 1950. Asst. prof. Cornell U., 1950-53, U. Mich., 1953-56; prof. emeritus Grad. Sch. Bus. Adminstrn., Columbia U., 1956-91, prof. bus. adminstrn., 1962—, head div. indsl. relations and orgnl. behavior, 1960-72; adviser to adminstr. NASA, 1966-71. Disting. vis. lectr. McGill U., 1974 Author: (with G. Strauss) The Local Union, 1953, Managerial Behavior, 1964, Human Behavior in Organizations, 1966, (with E. Chapple) Measure of Management, 1961; Behavior of Industrial Work Groups, 1958, Individualism and Big Business, 1963, (with W. Dowling) How Managers Motivate, 1971, (with M. Chandler) Managing Large Systems; Organizations for the Future, 1971, 2d edit., 1993, (with G. Strauss) Personnel, 4th edit, 1980, Managing Human Resources, 2d edit, 1981, Leadership, 1979, (with R. Burgelman) Inside Corporate Innovation, 1985, Managing in Real Organizations, 1989, The Working Leader, 1993, (with K. Ripin) Insider Strategies for Outsourcing Information Systems, 1999, (with C. Smith) The Rise of the Rogue Executive, 2004; mem. editorial bd. Human Orgn., 1957-62 Trustee Seacrest Sch., 1996-97. Fellow Am. Anthropol. Assn.; mem. Phi Beta Kappa. Home Phone: 239-597-7840; Office Phone: 914-693-5158. Personal E-mail: lrsayles@gmail.com.

SAYLES, WAYNE GERALD, numismatist, writer, publisher; b. Waukesha, Wis., Mar. 8, 1943; s. Wayne F. Sayles and Betty Joy Harris; m. Sharon L. Greshay, 1962 (div. 1982); m. Janet M. Foth Olson, 1984 (div. 1993); m. Doris Jean Ivey, 1997; children from previous marriage: Scott Allen, Steven Andrew, Stephanie Anne Sayles Bloedorn. B of Gen. Studies, U. Nebr., 1972; MA, U. Wis., 1986. Enlisted USAF, 1961, advanced through grades to capt., 1976, comdr. 2081st comms. squadron Goodfellow AFB, Tex., 1973, comdr. detachment 15, 2140 comm. group Athens, Greece, 1975, AF advisor to air res. forces and Air Nat. Guard, 1976—80, comm. sys., mil. airlift comd. inspector, 1980—82, ret., 1982; pres. Celator, Inc., Lodi, Wis., 1986—; exec. dir. Ancient Coin Collectors Guild, Gainesville, Mo., 2004—. Pub. Clio's Cabinet, Lodi, Wis., 1986—. Editor: (jour.) The Celator, 1987—99; author: Ancient Coin Collecting, vol. I, 1996, 2d edit., 2003, Ancient Coin Collecting, vol. II, 1997, Ancient Coin Collecting, vol. III, 1997;: 2d edit., 2007, Ancient Coin Collecting, vol. IV, 1998, Ancient Coin Collecting, vol. V, 1998, Ancient Coin Collecting, vol. VI, 1999, Turkoman Figural Bronze Coins and Their Iconography, 2 vols., 1992—96, The Ned H. and Gloria A. Griner Greek and Roman Coin Collection, Ball State U. Mus. Art, 2002, monographs; contbr. articles to encys., to jour.; author (publisher): First To Fall: The William Edward Cramsie Story, 2008. Sec., exec. dir. Ancient Coin Collectors Guild, Gainesville, Mo., 2004—; author Ancient Coin Collecting Blog, Gainesville, Mo., 2006—; bd. edn. Am. Cmty. Schs., Athens, 1974—75; v.p. bd. edn. Lodi Sch. Dist., Wis., 1988—93. Decorated Meritorious Svc. medal with two oak leaf clusters USAF, Commendation medal, Nat. Def. Svc. medal, Armed Forces Expeditionary medal; recipient Air Force Good Conduct medal, Minute Man award, Air NG, 1980, Numismatic Ambassador award, Krause Publs., 2006, Exceptional Contbns. Ancient Numismatics award, Ancient Coin Collectors Guild, 2006. Fellow: Royal Numis. Soc. (London), Am. Numis. Soc. (life); mem.: Ninth Air Force Assn., Mil. Officers Assn. (life), Numis. Lit. Guild (Extraordinary Merit award 1988), Oriental Numis. Soc., Classical and Medieval Numis. Soc., Am. Israel Numis. Assn. (life), Hellenic Numis. Soc. (life). Achievements include founder of The Celator, numismatic journal; founder of the Ancient Coin Collectors Guild. Avocations: coin collecting/numismatics, travel, genealogy. Home and Office: Ancient Coin Collectors Guild PO Box 911 Gainesville MO 65655 Personal E-mail: wgs@wgs.cc. Business E-Mail: director@accg.us.

SAYLOR, MICHAEL J., computer software company executive; b. Lincoln, Nebr., Feb. 4, 1965; B in Aeronautics and Astronautics, MIT, 1987. Venture mgr. DuPont Chem. Corp.; co-founder, CEO MicroStrategy, Inc., Vienna, Va., 1989—, pres., 1989—2000, 2005—. Named KPMG High Tech Entrepreneur of Yr., 1996, Ernst & Young Software Entrepreneur of Yr., 1997, one of Top 10 Entrepreneurs, Red Herring Mag., 1998; USAF scholar. Avocations: reading, music, studying history and architecture. Office: MicroStrategy Inc 1861 International Dr Mc Lean VA 22102 Office Phone: 703-848-8600. Office Fax: 703-848-8610.*

SAYLOR, PETER M., architect; b. Phila., July 26, 1941; s. Harry T. and Dorothy (Johnson) S.; m. Caroline Metcalf, Apr. 4, 1970; children: Thomas S., Elizabeth B. BArch, U. Pa., 1963, MArch, 1965. Registered arch., Pa., N.J., N.Y., Ohio, Mich., Va., NC. Architect Mitchell-Giurgola, Phila., 1967-70; ptnr. SaylorGregg Architects, Phila., 1970—. Design critic, juror U. Pa., 1975—; bd. dirs. Found. for Architecture, Phila., 1980-90. Bd. dirs. Chestnut Hill Cmty. Assn., Phila., 1976—79, v.p., 1979; bd. dirs. All Saints Hosp., Wyndmoor, Pa., 1981—86, Cathedral Village Retirement Cmty., 1998—2001. Recipient various bldg. design award Fellow AIA (bd. dirs. Phila. chpt. 1973-82, chpt. pres. 1981-82); mem. Pa. Soc. Archs., Chestnut Hill Hist. Soc. (bd. dirs. 1988-95, pres. 1989-92), Phila. Soc. Preservation of Landmarks (bd. dirs. 1989-96, pres. 1993-94), Phila. Mus. Art (friends bd. dirs. 1990-93), Phila. Cricket Club (bd. dirs. 1985-91), Mask and Wig Club (pres. 1980-81, bd. dirs. 1970-84). Republican. Episcopalian. Office: SaylorGregg Archs 100 S Broad St Philadelphia PA 19110-1023 Office Phone: 215-972-0500. Business E-Mail: psaylor@saylorgregg.com.

SAYLOR, THOMAS G., state supreme court justice; b. Meyersdale, Pa., Dec. 14, 1946; BA in Govt., U. Va., 1969; JD, Columbia U., 1972; LLM, U. Va., 2004. Atty. pvt. practice, 1972—82; 1st asst. dist. atty. Somerset County, 1973-76; dir. Pa. Bur. Consumer Protection, 1982-83; 1st dep. atty. gen. Commonwealth of Pa., 1983-87; atty. pvt. practice, 1987—93; judge Pa. Superior Ct., 1993—97; justice Pa. Supreme Ct., 1997—. Contbr. articles to legal publications. Bd. overseers Widener U. Sch. Law. Mem. ABA, Am. Law Inst., Pa. Bar Assn., Cumberland County Bar Assn., Dauphin County Bar Assn., Appellate Judges Conf. Office: Fulton Bldg 16th Fl 200 N 3d St Harrisburg PA 17101*

SAYLOR-CASTELGRANT, ELIZABETH ANN, educational association administrator; d. Clement Joseph Saylor and Mary Patricia Kerrigan-Saylor; m. Daniel Peter Castelgrant, Apr. 20, 1991; 1 child, Daniel Peter Castelgrant. BS in Health and Phys. Edn., East Stroudsburg U., Pa., 1972. Registered provider NJ. Health and phys. edn. tchr. West Amwell Sch., West Amwell, NJ, 1972—85, Flemington Raritan Schs., NJ, 1985—2000; UniServ leadership trainer NJ Edn. Assn., Trenton, 2000—07, UniServ field rep., region 13 Flemington, 2007—. Part-time cons. NJ Edn. Assn., Trenton, 1991—2000, staff contact for the student, 2000—07, staff contact to the AID NJ Edn. Assn. program, 2002—. Pub. rels. chair Spl. Olympics, Hunterdon, NJ, 1975—80; mem. steering com. Juvenile Task Force, Flemington, 1980—83; mem. task force Sch. Health and Edn. Resource Ctr., Flemington, 1983—85; cons. North Hunterdon In-Svc. Day, Clinton, NJ, 1983; mem. EIC Tchr. Adv. Bd., Morristown, NJ, 1983—86; active Hunterdon County Dental Health Commn., 1989—2001, chair, 1995—2001; trustee Hunterdon/Somerset Bus. and Edn. Alliance, Branchburg, NJ, 1991—, pres., 2004—07; mem. paradigm pioneer com. Hunterdon County Staff Devel. Coop., 1993—2000, steering com., 1996—2000; decision making com. Flemington Raritan Participatory, 1996—2000; NJ Edn. Assn. coord. Angel's Wings, Trenton, 2001—. Mem.: AAHPERD, NEA, AAUW, Hunterdon-Somsert County Bus. and Edn. Partnership (adv. bd. steering com. 2001/SCANS project 1991—97), Flemington-Raritan Edn. Assn. (v.p.-at-large 1987—2000, shared decision making com. 1993—2000), Hunterdon County Edn. Assn. (pres. 1978—82, 1990—92, v.p. 1992—), NJ Edn. Assn. (mem. rights com. 1972—2000, chair 1975—2000, del. assembly 1978—83, chair Be Heard Campaign 1980, mem. fair play com. 1983—, del. assembly 1990—92, 1998—2000), NJ Retired Educators, Nat. Edn. Ret. Educators Assn., Delta Kappa Gamma (1st v.p. Rho chpt.), Nat. Quill and Scroll Soc., Alpha Omicron Pi (life). Office: NJ Edn Assn 27 Minneakoning Rd Macedo Pk Flemington NJ 08822 Office Phone: 908-782-2168. Personal E-mail: lcastelgrant@aol.com.

SAYRE, DONNA, elementary school educator; b. Goshen, NY; d. Wesley and Dorothea Sayre. BS summa cum laude in Edn., Bloomsburg U., 1995, MEd in Reading, 1997. Reading tchr. Port Jervis City Sch. Dist., NY, 1998—. Participant Relay for Life Am. Cancer Soc.; bd. mem. Amy Bull Crist Reading Coun., 2005—07; Sunday sch. tchr. Craigville Bible Ch., Chester, NY, 2005—07, nursery provider, 2005. Mem.: NY State Reading Assn., Internat. Reading Assn., Amy Bull Crist Reading Coun. (v.p. 2005—06).

SAYRE, JOHN MARSHALL, retired lawyer, former government official; b. Boulder, Colo., Nov. 9, 1921; s. Henry Marshall and Lulu M. (Cooper) S.; m. Jean Miller, Aug. 22, 1943; children: Henry M., Charles Franklin, John Marshall Jr., Ann Elizabeth Sayre Taggart (dec.). BA, U. Colo., 1943, JD, 1948. Bar: Colo. 1948, U.S. Dist. Ct. Colo. 1952, U.S. Ct. Appeals (10th cir.) 1964. Law clk. trust dept. Denver Nat. Bank, 1948-49; asst. cashier, trust officer Nat. State Bank of Boulder, 1949-50; ptnr. Ryan, Sayre, Martin, Brotzman, Boulder, 1950-66, Davis, Graham & Stubbs, Denver, 1966-89, of counsel, 1993—2007; asst. sec. of the Interior for Water and Sci., 1989-93. Bd. dirs. Boulder Sch. Dist. 3, 1951-57; city atty. City of Boulder, 1952-55; gen. counsel Colo. Mcpl. League, 1959-63; prin. counsel No. Colo. Water Conservancy Dist. and mcpl. subdist., 1964-87, spl. counsel, 1987, bd. dirs. dist., 1960-64; former legal counsel Colo. Assn. Commerce and Industry. Lt. (j.g.) USNR, 1943-46, ret. Decorated Purple Heart; recipient William Lee Knous award U. Colo. Law Sch., 1999. Fellow Am. Bar Found. (life), Colo. Bar Found. (life); mem. ABA, Colo. Bar Assn., Boulder County Bar Assn. (pres. 1959), Denver Bar Assn., Nat. Water Resources Assn. (Colo. dir. 1980-89, 93-95, pres. 1984-86), U. Colo. N&T Resources Law Ctr. (adv. bd., 1993-2007), Denver Country Club, Phi Beta Kappa, Phi Gamma Delta, Phi Delta Phi. Home Phone: 541-317-5646.

SAYRS, ELIZABETH, music educator; m. Gregory Sayrs; children: Nicolas Proctor, Katharine. BA in Music, Wellesley Coll., Mass., 1990; MA in Music Theory, Eastman Sch. Music, Rochester, NY, 1992; PhD in Music Theory, Ohio State U., Columbus, 1997. Assoc. prof. Ohio U., Athens, 2004—. Author: (textbook) MFun; contbr. chapters to books, articles to profl. jours. Recipient Disting. Tchg. award, Ohio U. Sch. Music, 2007; Rsch. grant, Ohio U. Rsch. Coun., 2006—08, 1804 Grant, Ohio U., 2006—08. Office: Ohio Univ 591A Glidden Hall Athens OH 45701 Business E-Mail: sayrs@ohio.edu.

SAZAMA, KATHLEEN, pathologist, lawyer; b. Sutherland, Nebr., May 8, 1941; d. Roger William and Esther Mary (Reitz) Paulman; m. Franklin Jed Sazama, Aug. 26, 1962; children: Clare Ann, Jill Patrice. BS, U. Nebr., 1962; MS, Am. U., 1969; MD, Georgetown U., 1976; JD, Cath. U. Am., 1990. Diplomate Am. Bd. Pathology; lic. pathologist Mich., Va., Md., D.C., Calif., Pa., Tex.; bar: Md. Intern and resident Georgetown U. Med. Ctr., Washington, 1976-78; resident NIH, Bethesda, Md., 1978-79; clin. asst. prof. pathology Uniformed Svcs. U. Health Scis., Bethesda, 1981-89; clin. affiliate Ferris State Coll., Big Rapids, 1985-86; chief lab. of blood bank practices FDA Ctr. for Biologics Evaluation and Rsch., Bethesda, 1986-89; cons. Ober, Kaler, Grimes & Shriver, Balt., 1989-90; assoc. med. dir. Sacramento (Calif.) Med. Found. Blood Ctr., 1990-92; asst. clin. prof. pathology U. Calif., Davis, 1990-92, assoc. prof., dir. clin. pathology, 1992-93; prof. pathology and lab. medicine Allegheny U. of the Health Scis., Phila., 1994—99; v.p. for faculty acad. affairs U. Tex./M.D. Anderson Cancer Ctr., Houston, 2000—02, prof. lab. medicine, 2000—. V.p. bd. Met. Washington Blood Banks, Inc., 1981-84; pres. bd. Am. Assn. Blood Banks, 2003-04; spkr. in field. Author: (with others) Stat: The Laboratory's Role, 1986; contbr. numerous articles to profl. jours. Comdr. USPHS, 1986-89. Fellow Coll. Am. Pathologists, Am. Soc. Clin. Pathologists; mem. ABA, Am. Health Lawyers Assn. (bd. dirs.), Health Lawyers Assn., Soc. Advancement Blood Mgmt. (bd. dirs., pres.-elect, 2007-), Phi Kappa Phi, Beta Beta Beta. Avocations: tennis, playing bridge. Address: Univ of Texas MD Anderson Cancer Center 1515 Holcombe Blvd # 800 Houston TX 77030-4009 Office Phone: 713-792-7791. Business E-Mail: ksazama@mdanderson.org.

SAZEGAR, MORTEZA, artist; b. Tehran, Iran, Nov. 11, 1933; s. Hassan Ali and Zahra (Frootan) S.; m. Patricia Jean Kaurich, July 13, 1959. BA, U. Tex., El Paso, 1955, BS, 1956; postgrad., Baylor U. Coll. Medicine, 1956-57, Cornell U., 1958-59. One man exhibitions include, Poindexter Gallery, N.Y.C., 1964, 67, 69, 71, 73, 75, 77, group exhibitions include, Detroit Inst. Arts, 1965, Chgo. Art Inst., 1965, Univ. Art Mus., U. Tex., Austin, 1965, 72, Whitney Mus. Am. Art, 1970, Cleve. Mus. Art, 1972, Corcoran Gallery Art, Washington, 1973, Tyler Sch. Art, Temple U., Phila., 1979; represented in permanent collections, Whitney Mus. Am. Art, N.Y.C., San Francisco Mus. Modern Art, Riverside Mus., N.Y.C., U. Mass., Amherst, Corcoran Gallery Art, Prudential Ins. Corp. Am., Mus. Contemporary Art, Tehran, Iran. Mem. Artists Equity Assn. Democrat. Address: 1223 Homeville Rd Cochranville PA 19330-1712

SAZONOV, EDWARD STANISLAVOVICH, computer engineer, researcher; b. Khabarovsk, Russia, Oct. 22, 1971; arrived in US, 1996; s. Stanislav Vasilevich Sazonova and Yulia Dmitrievna Sazonov; m. Nadezhda A Koreshkova, Nov. 22, 1996; children: Dmitriy children: Timothy. Degree in Sys. Engring., Khabarovsk State U. Tech., Russia, 1993; MSEE, W.Va. U., 1999, PhD in Computer Engring., 2002. Lectr., rsch. and tchg. asst. W.Va. U., Morgantown, W.Va., 1997—2003; asst. prof. Dept. Elec. and Computer Engring. Clarkson U., Potsdam, NY, 2003—. Contbr. scientific papers, articles to profl. jours. Grantee, N.Y. State Energy R&D Authority, 2004—05, Transp. Rsch. Bd. Nat. Academies, 2005—, NSF, NIH. Mem.: IEEE. Achievements include patents for method of duplex data transmission; patents pending for wireless system for structural health monitoring. Office: Clarkson University 8 Clarkson Ave Potsdam NY 13699 E-mail: esazonov@ieee.org.

SBRAMANIAM, CHITRA P., educational consultant; b. Chennai, Tamil Nadu, India, May 12, 1968; d. Pathiavadi and Lalitha Subramaniam; 1 child, Arvind Mallikarjunan. BS in Life Sci., U. Madras, 1988, MS in Clinical Biochemistry, 1990. Tchr. Carmel Convent HS, India, 1990—92; rsch. assoc. Nat. Dairy Rsch. Inst., Bangalore, India, 1992—94; program analyst TRW Group, Austin, Tex., 1994—96; program chair, lead faculty mem. Internat. Acad. Design and Tech., 2000—05; co-owner, cons. Ednl. Interactive Group Inc., 2004—. Office: Internat Acad Design and Tech 18229 Collridge Dr Tampa FL 33647

SCACCIA, FRANK JOHN, facial surgeon, otolaryngologist; b. Teaneck, NJ, June 21, 1959; s. Ralph John and Angelina Josephine Scaccia. BS magna cum laude, Duke U., Durham, NC, 1981; MD, Wake Forest U., Winston-Salem, NC, 1985. Diplomate Am. Bd. Facial Plastic and Reconstructive Surgery, Am. Bd. Otolaryngology and Head and Neck Surgery. Resident in gen. surgery Monmouth Med. Ctr., Long Branch, NJ, 1985—88; resident in otolaryngology Case Western Res. U., Cleve., 1988—92; surgeon Otolaryngology Assocs., Red Bank, NJ, 1992—98; surgeon, CEO Riverside Plastic Surgery and Sinus Ctr., Red Bank, 1998—. Mem. staff Riverview Med. Ctr., Red Bank, Bayshore Cmty. Hosp., Holmdel, NJ. Contbr. articles to med. jours. Vol. surgeon Face to Face, 1992—; vol. Parker Clinic, Red Bank. Recipient Jack Anderson prize for scholastic excellence, Am. Bd. Facial Plastic and Reconstructive Surgery, 1995; named Top Beauty Dr., NJ Savvy Living, 2005—09, Top NY Metro Dr., Castle Connolly, 2006, 2007, Am. Top Dr., 2006, 2007. Fellow: ACS, Internat. Coll. Surgeons, Am. Acad. Facial Plastic and Reconstructive Surgery, Am. Acad. Otolaryngology; mem.: NJ Med. Soc., Monmouth County Med. Soc., Phi Beta Kappa. Avocations: running, bicycling, classical guitar. Home: 700 Ocean Ave Unit # 1 Sea Bright NJ 07760 Office: 70 E Front St Ste 3 Red Bank NJ 07701 Home Phone: 732-747-0845; Office Phone: 732-747-5300. Personal E-mail: acce000007@yahoo.com.

SCADDEN, DAVID THOMAS, hematologist, oncologist, research scientist; b. 1953; BA in English Lit., Bucknell U., 1975; MD, Case Western Res. U., 1980. Diplomate Am. Bd. Internal Medicine. Intern Brigham-Women's Hosp., Boston, 1980-81, resident in internal medicine, 1981-83, fellow in hematology/oncology, 1983-86; with Dana Farber Inst. Brigham & Women's Hosp., Boston; Gerald & Darlene Jordan prof. medicine Harvard U.; co-dir. Harvard Stem Cell Inst., 2004—; dir. Center for Regenerative Medicine, Mass. Gen. Hosp.; chief of hematologic malignancies Mass. Gen. Hosp. Co-chmn. Dept. of Stem Cell and Regenerative Biology, Harvard U.; mem. bd. of scientific counselors Nat. Cancer Inst.; bd. of external experts Nat. Heart, Lung and Blood Inst.; assoc. mem. Broad Inst. Recipient Clin. Scientist award in Translational Rsch., 2002, award, Burroughs Wellcome Fund, Doris Dute Found. Mem.: Inst. of Medicine, Nat. Acad. Scis. Achievements include research in defining hematopoietic stem cell niche translating stem cell research to medical therapy; adult hematopoietic stem cells with emphasis on their interaction with the microenvironment and cell cycle control. Office: AIDS Rsch Ctr Mass Gen Hosp Fruit St Boston MA 02114 also: Ctr for Regenerative Medicine and Tech Mass Gen Hosp 13th St Bldg 149 Rm 5212D Boston MA 02129 Office Phone: 617-726-5615. Office Fax: 617-724-2662. Business E-Mail: scadden.david@mgh.harvard.edu.

SCADUTO, PROVVIDENZA, language educator; b. Chivasso, Torino, Italy, Apr. 5, 1966; d. Domenico and Adele D'Acquisto Scaduto. BA, U. San Diego, 1994; MA, Calif. State U, San Marcos, 1998. Instr. italian Palomar Coll., San Marcos, 2006—; instr. letters MiraCosta Coll., Oceanside, Calif., 2006—. Avocations: painting, writing, cooking. Home: 817 Avenida Codorniz San Marcos CA 92069

SCAIFE, RICHARD MELLON, publishing executive, philanthropist; b. Pitts., July 3, 1932; s. Alan and Sarah Mellon Scaife; m. Frances L. Gilmore (div.); children: Jennie, David; m. Margaret Battle, June 1, 1991 (separated 2005). BA in English, U. Pitts., 1957. Owner, pub. Tribune-Review Publishing Co. Trustee, The Heritage Found., 1985-; Chmn., trustee Sarah Scaife Found., Inc.; donor, chmn., trustee Carthage Found., Allegheny Found. Named one of Forbes' Richest Americans, 2006, 25 Most Influential Republicans, Newsmax Mag., 2008. Republican. Office: Pitts Tribune Review DL Clark Bldg 503 Martindale St 3rd Fl Pittsburgh PA 15212*

SCALA, JAMES, health facility administrator, consultant, writer; b. Ramsey, NJ, Sept. 16, 1934; s. Edvigi and Lorene (Hendricksen) Scala; m. Nancy Peters, June 15, 1957; children: James, Gregory, Nancy, Kimberly. BA, Columbia U., 1960; PhD, Cornell U., 1964; postgrad., Harvard U., 1968; LHD (hon.), Hofstra U., 1998. Cert. nutrition specialist. Staff scientist Miami Valley Labs., Procter and Gamble Co., 1964-66; head life scis., dir. fundamental rsch. Owens Ill. Corp., 1966-71; dir. nutrition T.J. Lipton Inc., 1971-75; dir. health scis. Gen. Foods Corp., 1975-78; v.p. sci. and tech. Shaklee Corp., San Francisco, 1978-85, sr. v.p. sci. affairs, 1986-87. Lectr. Georgetown U. Med. Sch.; instr. U. Calif., Berkeley; nutritionist U.S. Olympic Ski Team, 1981—87. Author: Making the Vitamin Connection, 1985, The Arthritis Relief Diet, 1987, 2d edit., 1989, Eating Right for a Bad Gut, 1990, 2d edit., 1992, Eating Right for a Bad Gut, new edit., 1999, The High Blood Pressure Relief Diet, 1988, 2d edit., 1990, Look 10 Years Younger, Feel 10 Years Better, 1991, 2d edit., 1993, Prescription for Longevity, 1992, 2d edit., 1994, If You Can't/Won't Stop Smoking, 1993, The New Arthritis Relief Diet, 1998, 25 Natural Ways to Manage Stress and Avoid Burnout, 2000, 25 Natural Ways to Relieve Irritable Bowel Syndrome, 2000, 20 Natural Ways to Reduce the Risk of Prostate Cancer, 2001, 25 Natural Ways to Lower Blood Pressure, 2002; editor: Nutritional Determinants in Athletic Performance, 1981, New Protective Roles for Selected Nutrients, 1989; columnist: Dance mag.; contbr. articles to profl. jours. With USAF, 1953—56. Disting. scholar, U. Miami, Fla., 1977, Atlantic U., 1977. Fellow: Am. Coll. Nutrition; mem.: AAAS, Am. Diabetic Assn., Mt. Diablo Astron. Soc., Eastbay Astron. Soc., Astron. Soc. Pacific (bd. dirs., chmn. devel. coun.), Inst. Food Technologists, Am. Soc. Cell Biology, Sports Medicine Coun., Brit. Nutrition Soc., Am. Inst. Nutrition, Oakland Yacht Club, Olympic Club (San Francisco), Sigma Xi. Libertarian. Avocations: astronomy, photography. Office Phone: 925-283-2753. Personal E-mail: jscala2@comcast.net. *I am in awe of the incredible resiliency of living things, but most of all the human spirit.*

SCALES, CHRISTINE, Councilwoman; m. Richard Scales; children: Andrew, William, Joseph. Substitute high sch. tchr. City of Indpls., 2001—; councillor, dist. 4 Indpls.-Marion County City-County Coun., 2007—. Ward chmn. Washington Twp., Ind.; rep. Washington Twp. Adv. Bd. Parent advisor Habitat for Humanity. Republican. Mailing: 5133 Plantation Dr Indianapolis IN 46250 Office: 241 City-County Bldg 200 E Washington St Indianapolis IN 46204 Office Phone: 317-578-8901, 317-327-4242. Office Fax: 317-327-4230. Business E-Mail: cscales_2000@yahoo.com.*

SCALES, JEAN NORRIS, retired English language educator; b. Frankfort, Ky., June 9, 1930; d. Ernest Mishael and Mallia Reto (Poole) Norris; m. Jay Hugh Scales, Apr. 4, 1969. BA in English, Prairie View U., 1951; MA in Journalism, State U. Iowa, 1953; MA in English, U. Mich., 1959; PhD in English, U. N.C., 1980. Asst. prof. lang. arts Jackson (Miss.) State U., 1953-56; tchr. English Prairie View (Tex.) U., 1957-59; assoc. prof. English N.C. Cen. U., Durham, 1959-90. Contbr. articles to profl. jours. Active UN Assn. USA, Durham, 1960—, Ctr. for Peace Edn., Chapel Hill, N.C., 1991. Danforth Summer Study grantee Danforth Found., U. Mich., 1962, 63, U. Bridgeport, 1967. Mem. United Nations Assoc., Alpha Kappa Mu, Theta Sigma Phi. Baha'I. Avocations: reading, cooking, travel. Home: 1903 Essex Rd Durham NC 27704-5055 Personal E-mail: jjscales@msn.com.

SCALES, JOHN ALAN, physics professor; b. Louisville, June 24, 1957; s. John Osbourn and Barbara Rose Scales; m. Pamela Lynn Hause, Aug. 4, 1979; children: William Laurence, Emma Rose. BS in Physics, U. Del., Newark, 1979; PhD in Physics, U. Colo., Boulder, 1984. Chartered physicist Inst. Physics, 1999. Assoc. prof. geophysics Colo. Sch. Mines, Golden, 1992—99, prof. geophysics, 1999—2005, prof. physics, 2005—. Vis. prof. IPGP, U. Paris, 1992, French Acad. Sci., Paris, 1999—2000. Author: (book) Theory of Seismic Imaging; contbr. scientific papers. Co-founder Samizdat Press, Free Book Site, Golden. Fellowship, Japanese 21st Century Ctr. Excellence, 2004. Fellow: Royal Astron. Soc., Inst. Physics; mem.: Am. Phys. Soc., Sigma Xi. Office: Colo Sch Mines 1500 Illinois Golden CO 80402 Business E-Mail: jscales@mines.edu.

SCALES, PAT R., retired library association executive, director; MLIS, George Peabody Coll. for Teachers of Vanderbilt U., 1970. Tchr. children's lit. Furman U., 1976; libr. mid. sch.; dir. libr. info. services SC Governor's Sch. of Arts and Humanities. Founder Communicating Through Lit. prog.; chair Newbery Award Com., 1992, Laura Ingalls Wilder Com., 2001, Caldecott Com., 2002—; mem. Intellectual Freedom Com., Freedom To Read Found. Author: Teaching Banned Books; contbr. Book Links mag. Named one of Five Most Influential Librarians in 20th Century in SC. Mem.: AASL (Intellectual Freedom award 1983, 2003), Assn. for Libr. Svc. to Children (mem. bd. dirs. 2005—, pres.-elect 2007—), ALA (Grolier award 1997).

SCALES, RICHARD LEWIS, retired sales executive; b. Indpls., Nov. 16, 1928; s. Ortho Lorton and Nina L. (Julian) S.; m. E. Jean Rankin, Dec. 21, 1951; children: Richard, Allan, Anne. BSME, Purdue U., 1952. Rsch. and devel. engr. Bell Labs./Western Electric, Chgo., also Whippany, N.J., 1955-58; sales engr. Bodine Electric Co., Chgo., 1958-61; dist. sales mgr. Wabash (Ind.) Magnetics, 1961-66; founder, chmn. bd. (emeritus) Richard Scales Assocs., Wabash, 1966—, RSA Inc., Wabash, 1985—. Contbr. articles to mag. Elder, Presbyn. Ch. Lt. USNR, 1952-55, Korea. Recipient Paul Harris award Rotary Internat. Republican. Avocations: computers, photography. Home: 550 Sommers Ave Wabash IN 46992-2021 Personal E-mail: rlscales@netusa.net.

SCALET, J. CHRIS (JAMES CHRISTOPHER SCALET), pharmaceutical executive; BS in Mgmt. Sci. and Computer Systems, Okla. State U.; student Exec. Development Prog. Kellogg Sch. Mgmt., Northwestern U. V.p., info. tech., CIO MAPCO Inc., 1993—97; sr. v.p., info. tech., CIO Internat. Paper, 1998—2003; sr. v.p., info. services., CIO Merck & Co., Inc., 2003—05, sr. v.p. global services, CIO, 2006—08, exec. v.p. global services, CIO, 2008—. Office: Merck PO Box 100 Whitehouse Station NJ 08889-0100

SCALETTA, HELEN MARGUERITE, volunteer; b. Sioux City, Iowa, Apr. 13, 1927; d. Ralph J. and Ruth Cora (Coyle) Beedle; m. Phillip Jasper Scaletta, May 21, 1946; children: Phillip Ralph, Cheryl Diane Kesler. AA in Bus., Edwards Coll. Bus., Sioux City, 1946. Acct. Towners Dept. Store, Iowa City, 1947—48; legal sec. Phillip Scaletta, Sioux City, 1950—74; svc. chmn. Easter Seal Soc., Lafayette, Ind., 1970—88; rec. sec. Home Hosp. Aux., Lafayette, 1989. Danced in Civic Theatre Follies, 1962. Orch. mem. June's All-Girl Ensemble, 1943-50. Pres. Newcomers club YWCA, Lafayette, 1967-68, mem. chmn., bd. dirs., 1979; leader Girl Scouts Am., Ft. Wayne, Ind., 1960-63; chmn. Mental Health Inc., Ft. Wayne, 1960-61, Cancer Crusade, West Lafayette, 1973-74; precinct worker Rep. Cen. Com., West Lafayette, 1974-76; Nat. Missions sec. 1st Presbyn. Ch., 1957. Recipient Citation Easter Seal Soc., 1981, Ernestine Duncan Collins Pearl Ct. award Sigma Kappa, 1997. Mem. Purdue U. Women's Club (pres. 1973-74), Lafayette Country Club (golf chmn. 1971, 90, bowling pres. 1992-93, golf co-chair Battleground 9-hole group 1996), Purdue Women's Bowling League (treas. 1978-79), Cosmopolitan Club, YWCA (Diamond award, 2005), Sigma Kappa (corp. bd., sec., treas. 1971-99), Kappa Kappa Sigma (pres. 1972), Sigma Kappa Lafayette Alumnae (pres. 1970, 1988-93, Ernestine Duncan Collins Pearl Court award 1997). Avocations: collecting dolls, bowling, golf, sports. Home: One Via Verde Lafayette IN 47906

SCALETTA, PHILLIP RALPH, III, lawyer; b. Iowa City, Dec. 18, 1949; s. Phillip Jasper and Helen M. (Beedle) S.; m. Karen Lynn Scaletta, May 13, 1973; children: Phillip, Anthony, Alexander. BSIM, MS, Purdue U., 1972; JD, Ind. U., 1975. Bar: Ind. 1975, U.S. Dist. Ct. Ind. 1975, Ill. 1993. Assoc. Ice Miller, Indpls., 1975-81, ptnr., 1981—, mng. ptnr., 2007—. Contbr. articles to profl. jours. Chmn. Ind. Continuing Legal Edn. Found., Indpls., 1989; mem. Environ. Quality Control Water Com., 1988-98. Mem. Ind. Bar Assn., Indpls. Bar Assn., Def. Rsch. Inst., Internat. Assn. Def. Counsel, Gyro Club Indpls. (v.p. 1992-93, pres. 1993-94, bd. dirs. 1990—). Avocations: golf, skiing, tennis. Home: 7256 Tuliptree Trl Indianapolis IN 46256-2136 Office: Ice Miller 1 American Sq Indianapolis IN 46282-0020 Office Phone: 317-236-2330. Business E-Mail: scaletta@icemiller.com.

SCALIA, ANTONIN GREGORY, United States supreme court justice; b. Trenton, NJ, Mar. 11, 1936; s. S. Eugene and Catherine Louise (Panaro) Scalia; m. Maureen McCarthy, Sept. 10, 1960; children: Ann Forrest, Eugene, John Francis, Catherine Elisabeth, Mary Clare, Paul David, Matthew, Christopher James, Margaret Jane. AB, Georgetown U., 1957; student, U. Fribourg, Switzerland, 1955—56; LLB, Harvard U., 1960. Bar: Ohio 1962, Va. 1970. Assoc. Jones Day Cockley & Reavis, Cleve., 1961—67; assoc. prof. U. Va. Law Sch., 1967—70, prof., 1970—74; gen. counsel Office Telecommunications Policy, Exec. Office of Pres., 1971—72; chmn. Adminstrv. Conf. US, Washington, 1972—74; asst. atty. gen. Office Legal Counsel US Dept. Justice, Washington, 1974—77; prof. law U. Chgo., 1977—82; judge US Ct. Appeals (DC circuit), 1982—86; assoc. justice US Supreme Ct., Washington, 1986—. Vis. prof. Georgetown Law Ctr., 1977, Stanford Law Sch., 1980—81; resident scholar American Enterprise Inst., 1977. Editor: Regulation mag., 1979—82; author: A Matter of Interpretation: Federal Courts and the Law, 1998; co-author (with Bryan A. Garner): Making Your Case: The Art of Persuading Judges, 2008. Sheldon fellow, Harvard U., 1960—61. Mem.: Va. Bar Assn., Ohio Bar Assn. Republican. Catholic. Office: US Supreme Ct One First St NE Washington DC 20543-0001*

SCALIA, EUGENE, lawyer; b. Cleve., Aug. 14, 1963; s. Antonin and Maureen (McCarthy) S.; m. Patricia Larsen, Oct. 16, 1993; children: Antonin, Megan McCarthy, John Christie, Bridget Ann, Luke Francis. BA, U. Va., 1985; JD, U. Chgo., 1990. Bar: Calif. 1990, Va. 1993, D.C. 1995. Asst. to chief of staff U.S. Dept. Edn., Washington, 1985-87; assoc. Gibson, Dunn & Crutcher, LA, 1990-92, assoc. ptnr. Washington, 1993—2001, ptnr., 2003—; asst. to atty. gen. U.S. Dept. Justice, Washington, 1992-93; solicitor U.S. Dept. Labor, 2002—03. Mem. vis. com. U. Chgo. Law Sch., 1998—2001. Editor-in-chief U. Chgo. Law Rev., 1989-90, mem. adv. bd., 1996—. Named Lawyer of Yr., Compliance Reporter mag., 2006, Top Washington, DC Lawyer in Employment Litig., Wash. Bus. Jour., 2006; named one of Litigation's Rising Stars, The Am. Lawyer, 2007. Roman Catholic. Office: Gibson Dunn & Crutcher Ste 900 1050 Connecticut Ave NW Washington DC 20036-5306 Office Phone: 202-955-8500. E-mail: escalia@gibsondunn.com.

SCALING, SAM T., obstetrician, gynecologist; b. Fort Monmouth, NJ, Aug. 16, 1945; s. Sam T. and Helen Louise Scaling; m. Lisa Janine Peck, Aug. 6, 1988; 1 child, Micah;children from previous marriage: Traci, Craig, Chad, Chris, Cory, Tiffany. BS, U. N.Mex., Albuquerque, 1967; MD, U. Tenn., Memphis, 1971. Diplomate Am. Bd. Ob/Gyn. Intern Confederate Meml. Med. Ctr., Shreveport, La., 1971—72; resident in ob-gyn. Baylor Coll. Medicine, Houston, 1975—78, chief resident ob/gyn., 1977—78; pvt. practice Obstetrics, Gynecology and Infertility Casper, Wyo., 1978—; founder, pres. Women's Health Assocs. Wyo., Casper, 2001—; med. staff Wyo. Med. Ctr., 1978—; chmn. dept. ob/gyn. Wyo. Med. Ctr., Meml. Hosp. Natrona County, 1981—83, 1986—88, 2001, 2002—05, sec. med. staff, 1989—91, vice chief of staff, 1991—93, chief of staff, 1993—95. Clin. asst. prof., instr. ob/gyn. Wyo. Family Practice Program, Casper, 1978—; v.p. Wyo. State Bd. Med. Examiners, 1984—92, 1989—90, pres., 1990—92; presenter in field; med. dir. Casper Family-Centered League Lamaze Prepared Childbirth, 1980—84, Christ-Centered Childbirth, 1984—87, Caring Ctr., Casper, 1986—90, Wyo. Med. Ctr. PMS Clinic, 1987—90. Author childrens books. Mem. Little Dilly Golf Tournament com. Casper Country Club, 1994—96; mem. adv. bd. Caring Ctr., 2001—; mem. Healing Pl. Counseling Ctr. adv. bd. Highland Park Cmty. Ch., 1994—95; v.p. bd. dirs. Casper Children's Chorale, 1981—82; bd. dirs. Wyo. Cmty. Health Care Alliance, 1997—, Christian Solidarity Worldwide-USA, 1997—2000. Maj. USAF, 1972—75. Named to Am.'s Top Obstetricians and Gynecologists, Consumers Rsch. Coun. Am., 2002—03, 2007; NSF summer scholar, N.Mex. Highlands U., 1962. Fellow: ACS, ACOG, Am. Fertility Soc.; mem.: Am. Soc. Reproductive Medicine (mem. nat. adv. coun. 1997), Natrona County Med. Soc., Am. Assn. Pro Life Obstetricians and Gynecologists, Am. Coll. Physician Execs., Soc. Reproductive Surgeons, Am. Assn. Gynecologic Laparoscopists, Wyo. State Med. Soc., Ctrl. Assn. Obstetricians and Gynecologists, Found. N.Am. Wild Sheep (life), Alaska Profl. Hunters Assn., Bass Anglers Sportsman Soc. (life), N.Am. Hunting Club (life), Boone and Crockett Club (life), Safari Club Internat. (life), Rocky Mountain Elk Found., Alpha Omega Alpha. Republican. Mem. Ch. Of God. Avocations: hunting, fishing, hiking, gun collecting, coin collecting/numismatics. Office: Women's Health Assocs Wyo 1125 E 2d Casper WY 82601 Office Phone: 307-577-4226.

SCALISE, STEVE (STEPHEN JOSEPH SCALISE), United States Representative from Louisiana, former state legislator; b. New Orleans, Oct. 6, 1965; m. Jennifer Letulle; 1 child, Madison Carol. BS in Computer Programming, La. State U. Software engr., computer programmer, La.; mem. La. Ho. of Reps. from Dist. 82, 1996—2007, mem. appropriations, house & govt. affairs, labor & indsl. rels. com. & joint com. on budget; mem. La. State Senate from Dist. 9, 2008, US Congress from 1st La. Dist., 2008—. Bd. mem. Teach For America, New Orleans, Am. Italian Renaissance Found., Jefferson Sr. Ctr. Recipient Letter of Commendation, US Naval Reserve, Disting. Svc. award, La. Restaurant Assn., Patrick F. Taylor Rep. Leadership award, Bus. Champion award, New Orleans Regional C. of C., Outstanding Legislator award, Victims and Citizens Against Crime; named Legislator of Yr., Alliance for Good Govt. Jefferson/New Orleans chap., Citizens Against Lawsuit Abuse, 1999, New Orleans Regional C. of C., 2001, Man of Yr., Associated Builders and Contractors, 2001; named a, Ctrl. Metairie Chap. AARP, 1998. Mem.: Young Leadership Coun. New Orleans, La. Young Rep. Republican. Roman Catholic. Office: US Congress 1205 Longworth Ho Office Bldg Washington DC 20215-1801 Office Phone: 202-225-3015. Office Fax: 202-226-0386.*

SCALLEN, THOMAS KAINE, broadcast executive; b. Mpls., Aug. 14, 1925; s. Raymond A. and Lenore (Kaine) S.; m. Bille Jo Brice; children by previous marriage: Thomas, Sheila, Patrick, Eileen, Timothy and Maureen (twins). BA, St. Thomas Coll., 1949; JD, U. Denver, 1950. Bar: Minn. Asst. atty. gen. State of Minn., Mpls., 1950-55; sole practice Mpls., 1955-57; pres. Med. Investment Corp., Mpls., 1957—, Internat. Broadcasting Corp., Mpls., 1977—; owner Harlem Globetrotters. Pres., exec. producer Ice Capades; chmn. bd. dirs. Century Park Pictures Corp., Los Angeles, chmn. bd. dirs. Blaine-Thompson Co., Inc., N.Y.C; chmn. Apache Plastics, Inc., Stockton, Calif. Served with AUS. Mem. World Pres. Orgn., Minn. Club, Calhoun Beach Club, L.A. Athletic Club. Clubs: University (St. Paul, Mpls.), Rochester (Minn.) Golf and Country, Edina (Minn.) Country, Athletic (Mpls.). Home: Heron Cove Windham NH 03087 Office: Internat Broadcasting Corp 80 S 8th St Ste 1601 Minneapolis MN 55402-2207 Office Phone: 612-333-5100.

SCALZO, CHRISTOPHER M., entrepreneurship and business educator; b. Rochester, NY, Sept. 24, 1965; s. Frank and Barbara Scalzo; m. Hanney Sarkis, May 2, 1992; children: Rachel, Thomas, Christina. BS, SUNY, Brockport, 1990; MBA, St. John Fisher Coll., Rochester, 1993; PhD in Bus. Adminstrn., U. Phoenix, Ariz., 2007; Degree in DBA, U. Phoenix, 2007. Asst. prof. Morrisville State Coll., NY, 2000—, assoc. prof. Adj. prof. Davenport U., Mich., 2007—08. SCORE Seminar grant, Kaufman Found., Syracuse U., 2008—. Mem.: USASBE. Home: 4975 Alexis Dr Liverpool NY 13090 Office: Morrisville State Coll 110-112 Charlton Hall Morrisville NY 13408 Business E-Mail: scalzocm@morrisville.edu.

SCALZO, JOSEPH, history professor; b. Decollatura, Calabria, Italy, Aug. 28, 1956; s. Riccardo and Lina Scalzo; m. Ellen Rose Imperato, Sept. 7, 1991; 1 child, Richard George. BA, St. John Fisher Coll., Rochester, NY, 1979; MA, Syracuse U., NY, 1988; PhD, U. Rochester, 1996. Cert. in secondary social studies edn. NY, 1989. Adj. instr. Genesee CC, Batavia, NY, 2004—07, SUNY Empire State Coll., Saratoga Springs, 2007—, SUNY Coll., Brockport, 2007—08, Geneseo, 2008—. Contbr. articles to profl. publs. Recipient Lina and A. William Salamone prize, U. Rochester, 1992; Fulbright fellowship, US and Italian Govts., 1991. Mem.: AAUP. Democrat. Roman Catholic. Home: 56 Lakeview Pk Rochester NY 14613 Office: SUNY Coll Geneseo 1 College Cir Geneseo NY 14454 Office Phone: 585-733-1482. Office Fax: 585-245-5161. Personal E-mail: jscalzo@frontiernet.net. Business E-Mail: scalzo@geneseo.edu.

SCANDURA, JOSEPH MICHAEL, neuroscientist, application developer; b. Bay Shore, NY, Apr. 29, 1932; s. Joseph and Lucy S.; m. Alice Baker, Aug. 13, 1960; children: Jeanne, Janette, Joseph, Julie. AB, U. Mich., 1953, MA, 1955; PhD, Syracuse U., 1962; postdoctoral, Stanford U., summer 1964, 68-69, U. Calif.-Berkeley, summer 1968, MIT, summer 1972; postgrad., U. Kiel, W.Ger., 1975, Inst. Ednl. Tech., Italy, summer 1978. Tchr. math., sci. White Plains, Bay Shore, 1953-56; instr. math., head wrestling coach Syracuse U., NY, 1956-63; asst. prof. edn., math. SUNY-Buffalo, 1963-64; research asst. prof. math. edn. Fla. State U., Tallahassee, 1964-66; dir. instructional systems, structural learning U. Pa., Phila., 1966-96; Fulbright prof. U. Koblenz & Dresden, 1998-99. Vis. rsch. prof. Drexel U., 2005; founder, chmn. Intelligent Micro Systems, Narberth, Pa., 1978-2002; chmn. bd. sci. advisors MERGE Rsch. Inst., 1973-2002; prin. investigator NIST Advanced Tech. Program Project on Automating Supply Chain; cons. U.S. Office Edn., NSF, NAS, Tex. Instruments, Borg-Warner, U.S. Army; organizer, lectr., participant profl. confs., 1963—; dir. NATO Advanced Study Inst. on Structural Process Theories of Complex Human Behavior, 1977; coach undefeated Ea. Intercollegiate Wrestling Championship Team, 1963. Author: Mathematics - Concrete Behavioral Foundations, 1971, (with others) An Algorithmic Approach to Mathematics - Concrete Behavioral Foundations, 1971, Structural Learning I - Theory and Research, 1973, Problem Solving - A Structural Process Approach with Instructural Implications, 1977, (with A.B. Scandura) Structural Learning and Concrete Operations - An Approach to Piagetian Conservation, 1980, Cognitive Approach to Software Development, 1988, Prodoc (comprehensive suite of software devel. and maintenance tools), 1989, Cognitive Approach to Software Engineering and Re-engineering, 1991, ongoing projects; Flexys-customizable reengineering automation, Autobuilder-automated specification and implementation component based software while guaranteeing correctness, intelligent tutor authoring of devel. sys. model IT and tutor IT, 1992—, NATO Advanced Study Inst., 1993, Automated Software Conversions and Re-engineering, 1993, NSF; contbr. 200 articles to profl. jours.; editor: Research in Mathematics Education, 1967, Structural Learning II - Issues and Approaches, 1976, (with C.J. Brainerd) Structural Process Models of Complex Human Behavior, 1978, Knowledge Representation in Standard Learning Theory & Relationship to Adaptive Learning and Tutoring Systems, 2007; developer, producer numerous computer-based instructional systems and software devel. systems; multiple software patents. Recipient Renssalaer award, 1949, Bausch and Lomb award, 1949, Nat. AAU Wrestling Champion and Outstanding Wrestler award, 1955; Fulbright scholar, 1975-76, 1998-99; U.S. Office Edn. fellow, 1978-79; NSF grant, Authority Adaptive & Configarable Tutoring Sys., 2008. Fellow: APA (chmn. E.L. Thorndike award com. 1974—79), Structural Learning Soc. (sr.; chmn. 1969—80, editor in chief Jour. Structural Learning 1976—90, chmn. 1985—88, Jour. Structural Learning and Intelligent Systems 1990—2001, chmn. 1995—, founder, sr. advisor Tech., Instr., Cognition & Learning 2002—); mem.: IEEE, AAUP, Univ. Profs. for Acad. Order, Psychonomic Soc., Math. Assn. Am., Nat. Coun. Tchrs. Math. (past fed. funds com. chmn.), Am. Ednl. Rsch. Assn. (chmn. tech., instrn., cognition and learning), Assn. Computing Machinery, Phi Delta Kappa, Phi Eta Sigma, Phi Kappa Phi. Home: 1249 Greentree Ln Narberth PA 19072-1219 Office: U Pa Instructional Systems Philadelphia PA 19104 *Accomodation to -- as well as leadership of -- groups, institutions and/or societies is an essential ingredient of success in most walks of life. There are circumstances, however, which require inner direction, whether developing a new scientific paradigm or standing firm against political pressures. Although vindication is rarely complete and often delayed, following one's best instincts yields its own rewards—perhaps the satisfaction of ultimately being proven right but more often simply knowing one did what had to be done.*

SCANIFFE, JOSEPH ALBERT, anesthesiologist, consultant; s. Angelo and Agnes Mary Scaniffe; m. Lidia Brigette Munteanu, Apr. 8, 2006; children: Richard Anthony, Christopher Michael, Brigette Annette Mocan. BS in Engring., US Mil. Acad., West Point, NY; MBA, U. So. Calif., LA; MD, Uniformed Svcs. U. Health Scis., Bethesda, Md., 1985. Diplomate Am. Bd. Anesthesiology, 1990. Commd. 2d lt. US Army, airborne ranger, pathfinder Air Assault, Aviation, advanced through grades to lt. col.; nuc. weapons assembly team chief 9th Inf. Divsn., Ft Lewis, Wash.; exec. officer D/1/84th FA, Ft Lewis, Wash.; attack helicopter platoon comdr. 101st Airborne Divsn., Ft Campbell, Ky.; task force logistics officer 101st Airborne Divsn. Task Force, Germany; comdr. A/3/319th FA 101st Airborne Divsn., Ft Campbell; instr. advanced ground/air tactics Armor Ctr., Ft Knox, Ky.; staff anesthesiologist Madigan Army Med. Ctr., Tacoma, 1989—90, chief clin. svcs./vascular anesthesia Ft Lewis, Wash., 1991—97; asst. chief anesthesia 82d Airborn Divsn. 5th Mobile Army Surg. Hosp., Iraq, Saudi Arabia, Kuwait, Persian Gulf War; ptnr. Swedish Med. Ctr., Seattle, 1998—2003; ptnr. Milford Anesthesia Assocs. Bristol Hosp., Conn., 2003—, chief dept. anesthesia, 2009—. Asst. prof. Uniformed Svcs. U. Sch. Medicine, Bethesda, 1991—97; faculty Acad. Health Scis., San Antonio, 1991—97; clin. instr. U. Wash., Seattle, 2000—03. Humanitarian Med. Aid Mission, Dominican Republic, 2007, Bolivia, 2009. Decorated Meritorious Svc. medal US Army, Army Commendation medal, Army Achievement medal, Nat. Def. Svc. medal, SW Asia Svc. medal, Armed Forces medal, Kuwait Liberation medal Kingdom of Saudi Arabia and Kingdom of Kuwait; recipient Expert Field Medicine award; named one of Am.'s Top Anesthesiologists, Consumers' Rsch. Coun. Am., 2006, 2007, 2008. Master: Am. Bd. Anesthesiology; mem.: Milford Anesthesia Assn. (bd. dir.), Assn. Mil. Surgeons (life, Outstanding Leadership and Acad. award 1985), Conn. State Soc. Anesthesiology, Soc. Cardiovasc. Anesthesiologists, Internat. Anesthesia Rsch. Soc., Am. Soc. Regional Anesthesia, Am. Soc. Anesthesiologists. Independent. Roman Catholic. Achievements include development of operational/combat anesthesia machine. Avocations: hiking, bicycling, racquetball, fishing, woodworking. Home: 11 Glenmore Dr Farmington CT 06032

SCANLAN, JAMES PATRICK, philosophy and Slavic studies educator; b. Chgo., Feb. 22, 1927; s. Gilbert Francis and Helen (Meyers) S.; m. Marilyn A. Morrison, June 12, 1948. BA, U. Chgo., 1948, MA, 1950, PhD, 1956. Research fellow Inst. Philos. Research, San Francisco, 1953-55; instr. Case Inst. Tech., Cleve., 1955-56; from instr. to assoc. prof. Goucher Coll., Balt., 1956-68; prof., dir. Slavic Ctr. U. Kans., Lawrence, 1968-70; prof. Ohio State U., Columbus, 1971-91, dir. Slavic Ctr., 1988-91, prof. emeritus, 1992—. Vis. rsch. scholar Moscow State U., 1964-65, 69, 98, Acad. Scis. USSR, Moscow, 1978, 93, Russian State U. for the Humanities, 1995; fgn. vis. fellow Slavic Rsch. Ctr., Hokkaido U., Sapporo, Japan, 1987-88. Author: Marxism in the USSR, 1985, Dostoevsky the Thinker, 2002, Russian trans., 2006; editor: Historical Letters by Peter Lavrov, 1967, Soviet Studies in Philosophy, 1987—92, Russian Studies in Philosophy, 1992—97, Technology, Culture and Development: The Experience of the Soviet Model, 1992, Russian Thought After Communism, 1994; co-editor: Russian Philosophy, 1965, Marxism and Religion in Eastern Europe, 1976. Served with USMC, 1945-46. Woodrow Wilson Internat. Ctr. fellow, 1982; recipient Translation award Nat. Translation Ctr., 1967, Faculty Rsch. award Fulbright-Hays, 1982-83. Mem. Am. Philos. Assn., Am. Assn. Advancement Slavic Studies, Phi Beta Kappa. Home: 1000 Urlin Ave Apt 206 Columbus OH 43212-3324 Personal E-mail: scanlan.1@osu.edu.

SCANLAN, ROBERT DENNIS, systems analyst; s. William E. and Elizabeth Jean Scanlan; life ptnr. Linda P. Chakales; children: Benjamin Oakley, Daniel Tyler. BS in Edn., U. Memphis, Tenn., 1979; BS in Computer Info. Sys., St. Leo U., Fla., 2004. Sr. logistics analyst BAE Sys., St. Inigoes, Md., 2008; navy marine corp intranet analyst Smartronix, Inc; sr. logistics engr. Wyle Labs.; aviation maintenance adminstrn. USN, 1980—2002. Adj. instr. Coll. Southern Md., La Plata; aviation maintenance adminstrn. US Navy, Norfolk, Va., 1980—2002. Home: 41473 Miss June Ct Leonardtown MD 20650 Office: ITT Company Exploration Dr Lexington Park MD 20636 Personal E-mail: rdscanlan@yahoo.com.

SCANLAN, THOMAS JOSEPH, former academic administrator; b. NYC, Mar. 5, 1945; s. Thomas Joseph and Anna Marie (Schmitt) S. BA in Physics, Cath. U. Am., 1967; MA in Math., NYU, 1972; PhD in Bus. Adminstrn., Columbia U., 1978; LLD (hon.), Coll. Mt. St. Vincent. Prin. Queen of Peace HS, North Arlington, NJ, 1972-75; dir. fin., edn. NY Province, Bros. of Christian Sch., Lincroft, NJ, 1978-81; vice chancellor Bethlehem U., Israel, 1981-87; pres. Manhattan Coll., Bronx, NY, 1987—2009. Bd. dirs. Am. Coun. on Edn. Trustee Commn. on Ind. Colls. and Univs., 2002, Assn. Cath. Colls. and Univs., 1994—. Recipient Pro Ecclesia et Pontifice medal, Pope John Paul II, Vatican City, 1986. Mem. Bros. of Christian Schs., Am. Coun. Edn., Assn. Cath. Colls. and Univs. (trustee 1994—), Assn. Am. Colls., Nat. Cath. Edn. Assn., Nat. Asns. Ind. Colls. and Univs., Nat. Collegiate Athletic Assn. (exec. com. and divsn. 1), Metro Atlantic Athletic Assn., Equestrian Order of the Holy Sepulchre of Jerusalem, Phi Beta Kappa, Beta Gamma Sigma, Phi Beta Kappa Fellows. Avocations: golf, reading, movies. Home Phone: 718-884-0503; Office Phone: 718-862-7301. Business E-Mail: thomas.scanlan@manhattan.edu.*

SCANLON, CHARLES FRANCIS, retired military officer, writer, publisher; b. Nashville, Jan. 31, 1935; s. Francis James Gordon and Dorothy Rose (Compton) S.; m. Barbara Coddington Wall Scanlon, June 18, 2005; children: Teri, Brett, Ashlyn, Kellie. BA in Polit. Sci., U. Fla., 1960; grad., Command and Gen. Staff Coll., Ft. Leavenworth, Kans., 1970, Naval War Coll., Newport, RI, 1977; MA in Am. Studies, U. Hawaii, 1974; postgrad., Pa. State U., 1982, Harvard U., 1984-92. Commd. 2d lt. U.S. Army, 1960, advanced through grades to maj. gen., 1988; chief collection U.S. Army Europe, Heidelberg, Germany, 1977-78; comdg. officer 66th Mil. Intelligence Brigade, Munich, 1978-80; chief ops. U.S. Army Intelligence and Security Command, Arlington, Va., 1980-82; exec. officer Dept. Army Asst. Chief Staff Intelligence, Washington, 1982-83; dep. commdr. gen. U.S. Army Intelligence and Security Command, Arlington, 1983-85; dir. estimates Def. Intelligence Agy., Washington, 1985-86, dir. attaches, 1986-90; comdg. gen. U.S. Army Intelligence and Security Command, Ft. Belvoir, Va., 1990-93; ret., 1993; pres. Internat. Security, Counterintelligence Cons. Svcs., Fairfax Station, Va., 1993—, Satellite Beach, Fla., 1993—99, Melbourne Beach, Fla., 1999—2004, Indian Harbour Beach, Fla., 2004—. Decorated Def. D.S.M., Army D.S.M., Nat. Intelligence D.S.M., Legion of Merit with 3 oak leaf clusters, Bronze Star with 2 oak leaf clusters; elected to U.S. Mil. Intelligence Hall of Fame, 1995. Mem. Assn. US Army, Nat. Mil. Intelligence Assn. (pres. 1974-76), 101st Airborne Divsn. Assn., Berlin US Military Vets. Assn., Def. Intelligence Alumni Assn., Sigma Nu, Wuesthoff Health System Found. (bd. mem.2007-09). Presbyterian. Avocations: boating, scuba diving, racquetball, soaring, reading. Home and Office: 16F Marina Isles Blvd Indian Harbor Beach FL 32937 Personal E-mail: chuckscanlon@aol.com.

SCANLON, DOROTHY THERESE, history professor; b. Bridgeport, Conn., Oct. 7, 1928; d. George F. and Mazie (Reardon) Scanlon. AB, U. Pa., 1948, MA, 1949, Boston Coll., 1953; PhD, Boston U., 1956; postdoctoral scholar, Harvard U., 1962—64, postdoctoral scholar, 1972. Tchr. history and Latin Marycliff Acad., Winchester, Mass., 1950—52; tchr. history Girls Latin Sch., Boston, 1952—57; prof. Boston State Coll., 1957—82, Mass. Coll. Art, Boston, 1982—95, prof. emerita, 1995—; lectr. Cape Mus. Fine Arts, Dennis, Mass., 1997—. Author: Instructor's Manual to Accompany Lewis Hanke, Latin America: A Historical REader, 1974; contbr. Biographical Dictionary of Social Welfare, 1986. Recipient Disting. Svc. award, Boston State Coll., 1979, Faculty award of excellence, Mass. Coll. Art, 1985, Faculty Disting. Svc. award, 1987. Mem.: AAUW, AAUP, History of Sci. Soc., Am. Assn. History of Medicine., Am. Studies Assn., Orgn. Am. Historians, Am. Hist. Assn., L.Am. Studies Assn., Delta Kappa Gamma, Phi Alpha Theta. Home: 23 Mooring Ln Dennis MA 02638-2321 Office: Mass Coll Art Dept History 621 Huntington Ave Boston MA 02115-5801

SCANLON, GEORGE PATRICK, transportation services executive, accountant; b. Chgo., Sept. 29, 1957; s. George Patrick and Ann Marie (McInerney) S. BBA, U. Notre Dame, 1979; MBA in Fin., U. Miami, 1984. CPA, Ill., Fla. Sr. acct. Price Waterhouse, Chgo., 1979-82, sr. analyst corp. audit dept., 1982-84, mgr. corp. audit dept., 1984-85, sr. mgr. control analysis dept., 1985-87; div. controller, aviation leasing and svcs. div. Aviation Sales Co., Inc., Miami, 1988-90; sr. mgr. acquisition control Ryder Sys., Inc., Miami, Fla., 1982, dir. corp. acctg., 1990-91, group dir. audit svcs., 1991-93, group dir. corp. planning, 1993-95, v.p. corp. planning, 1995-97, sr. v.p. corp. planning, contr., 1997-2000; CFO Seisint, Inc., Boca Raton, Fla., 2000—01, DataCore Software Corp., Ft. Lauderdale, Fla., 2001—04; exec. v.p., CFO, also prin. acctg. officer Levitt Corp. (formerly Woodbridge Holdings Corp.), Ft. Lauderdale, Fla., 2004—08; exec. v.p., CFO BFC Fin. Corp., Ft. Lauderdale, Fla., 2007; exec. v.p. fin., CFO Fidelity Nat. Info. Services, Jacksonville, Fla., 2008—. Mem. Am. Inst. CPA's, Fla. Inst. CPA's. Clubs: Notre Dame (Miami) (bd. dirs. 1986-95, treas.). Roman Catholic. Avocations: golf, baseball. Office: Fidelity Nat Info Services 601 Riverside Ave Jacksonville FL 32204 Business E-Mail: george.scanlon@fnis.com.

SCANLON, JANE CRONIN, mathematics professor; b. NYC, July 17, 1922; d. John Timothy and Janet Smiley (Murphy) Cronin; m. Joseph C. Scanlon, Mar. 5, 1953 (div.); children: Justin, Mary, Anne, Edmund. Student, Highland Park Jr. Coll., 1939-41; BS, Wayne State U., 1943; MA, U. Mich., 1945, PhD, 1949. Mathematician Air Force Cambridge Research Center, 1951-54; instr. Wheaton Coll., Norton, Mass., 1954-55; asst. prof. Poly. Inst. Bklyn., 1957-58, asso. prof., 1958-60, prof., 1960-65; prof. math. Rutgers U., New Brunswick, N.J., 1965-91, prof. emerita, 1991—. Cons. Singer-Kearfott Div., Naval Research Lab. Office Naval Research Fellow Princeton, 1948-49; Horace H. Rockham Postdoctoral fellow U. Mich., 1950-51, Rutgers Research Council fellow, 1968-69, 72-73; NSF vis. professorship for women Courant Inst., NYU, 1984-85. Author: Fixed Points and Topological Degree in Nonlinear Analysis, 1964, Advanced Calculus, 1967, Differential Equations: Introduction and Qualitative Theory, 1980, 2d edit., 1994, 3d. edit., 2008, Mathematics of Cell Electrophysiology, 1980, Mathematical Aspects of Hodgkin-Huxley Neural Theory, 1987; editor: Analyzing Multiscale Phenomena Using Singular Perturbation Methods, 1999. Mem. Am. Math. Soc. Home: 110 Valentine St Highland Park NJ 08904-2106 Office: Rutgers U Dept Math New Brunswick NJ 08903 Personal E-mail: croninscanlon@optonline.net, croninscanlon@verizon.net.

SCANLON, JANICE LYNN, retired gifted and talented educator; b. Goodland, Kans., July 28, 1940; d. Milton Parish Jr. and Bertha May Adams Parish. BS, Ft. Hays State U., 1962; MA, U. Denver, 1980. Tchr. kindergarten, music Brewster Pub. Schs., Kans., 1962—63; tchr. kindergarten Jefferson County Pub. Schs., Lakewood, Colo., 1963—81; tchr. gifted Washington Twp. Pub. Schs., Sewell, NJ, 1983—98; ret., 1998. Del. gifted tchrs. to visit China with People to People, 1990; sec. N.J. Tchrs. Gifted, 1990—92; pres. Jefferson County Kindergarten Tchrs. Assn., Lakewood, Colo., 1964—65. Author: Jefferson County Kindergarten Curriculum, 1974; actor: (films) Teaching Children in Remote Areas, 1968; contbg. author (lessons in book) Teaching Children in Remote Areas, 1968; author: Guides for Washington Twp. Schs., 1983—98; co-author: Ruleton and Its School, 2005, Adams and Parrish Family, 2005. Mem. Outstanding Vol. Group, NC, 2007, Palm Aire Nine Hole Women's Golf Assoc., 2000—, v.p., 2001—02, pres., 2002—03; active Clare's Sewing Angels, Dem. Party, S.E. Manatee County, Fla., 2003—; presenter Indian hist. Ch. of Incarnation Sch., 2001—, St. Martha's Sch. Recipient Presdl. award, Palm Aire Nine Hole Women's Golf Assoc., 2007; co-recipient Outstanding Vol. Group award, Haywood County, NC, 2007; scholar, Kiwanis Club, Goodland, Kans., 1958, Tuition grant, U.S. Edn. Office, U. Denver, 1978—80. Mem.: N.J. Ret. Tchrs. Assn., Clare's Angels, Palm Aire Women's Club (fundraiser 1999—), Alpha Delta Kappa (treas., devotions leader). Democrat.

Roman Catholic. Avocations: travel, painting, quilting, genealogy, golf. Home: 7222 Coachlight St Sarasota FL 34243 Personal E-mail: josescan@aol.com, josephscanlon@yahoo.com.

SCANLON, PAT H., lawyer; b. Houma, La., Aug. 4, 1936; s. Leo Joseph and Mary (Ezell) S.; m. Carlene Myers, June 10, 1961; children: Margaret, Pat, Jr., Cissy, John. BS in Geology, La. State U., 1957; LLB with distinction, U. Miss., 1960. Assoc. Satterfield, Shell, Williams & Buford, Jackson, Miss., 1960-62; ptnr. Young, Scanlon & Sessums, Jackson, 1962—95; mem. Scanlon, Sessums Parker & Dallas PLLC, 1995-2002; mem. Watkins & Eager PLLC, 2003—; chmn., commnr. Miss. Jud. Performance Commn., Jackson, 1980-83; instr. Jackson Sch. Law, 1963-66; chmn. Miss. Law Inst., Jackson, 1970. Mem. editorial bd. Miss. Law Jour., 1959-60; contbr. articles to profl. jours. Mem. vestry St. James Episcopal Ch., Jackson, 1972-75, 79-82). Served to capt. USAR. Fellow Am. Coll. Trial Lawyers, Internat. Soc. Barristers, Am. Bar Found., Miss. Bar Found. (pres. 1986-87, trustee 1980-83); mem. Miss. Bankruptcy Conf. (pres. 1984-85), Miss. Young Lawyers Assn. (pres. 1969-70), Miss. State Bar Assn. (2d v.p. 1970-71, pres. 1988-89), Hinds County Bar Assn. (pres. 1974-75), Fed. Bar Assn. (pres. Miss. chpt. 1972-73), Am. Arbitration Assn. (panel mem.), Nat. Arbitration Forum (panel mem.). Office: 1650 Mirror Lake Plaza 2829 Lakeland Dr Jackson MS 39232 Business E-Mail: pat@ms-adr.com.

SCANLON, TERRENCE MAURICE, think-tank executive; b. Milw., May 1, 1939; s. Maurice John and Anne (Hayes) S.; m. Judy Ball, June 14, 1969; children: Michael Mansfield, Justin Ball, Brendan Hayes. BS, Villanova U., 1961. Staff asst. The White House, Washington, 1963-67; with SBA, Washington, 1967-69, Dept. of Commerce, Washington, 1969-83, mem. office Minority Bus. Enterprise, 1969-80, with Internat. Trade Adminstrn., 1980-81, with Minority Bus. Devel. Agy., 1981-83; mem. Consumer Product Safety Commn., Washington, 1983-89, vice chmn., 1983-84, chmn., 1985, 86-89; v.p., treas. The Heritage Found., Washington, 1989-91, v.p. corp. rels., 1991-94; chmn., pres. Capital Rsch. Ctr., Washington, 1994—. Am. Polit. Sci. Assn. Congl. fellow, 1967-68 Mem. Sovereign Mil. Order of Malta, University Club. Office: Capital Rsch Ctr 1513 16th St NW Washington DC 20036-1401 Home: 2425 L St NW Apt 240 Washington DC 20037 Office Phone: 202-483-6900. Business E-Mail: tscanlon@capitalresearch.org.

SCANNELL, HERB, broadcast executive; m. Sarah Scannell; 1 child, Caroline. BA in English and History, Boston Coll. Dir. program promotion Showtime/The Movie Channel; dir. programming Nickelodeon, NYC, 1988—89, v.p. programming, 1989—90, sr. v.p. programming; exec. v.p. Nickelodeon Networks, pres., 1996—2006; group pres. MTV Networks, NYC, 2003—06.

SCANTLEBURY, VELMA PATRICIA, surgeon; b. Barbados, Oct. 6, 1955; came to U.S., 1970; d. Delacey Whitstanley and Kathleen (Jordan) S.; 2 children. BS, LI U., 1977; MD, Columbia U., 1981; DS (hon.), LI U., 1998, Seton Hall Coll. PA. Intern in surgery Harlem Hosp. Ctr., NYC, 1981-82, resident in surgery, 1982-86; fellow in transplantation U. Pitts., 1988, assoc. prof. surgery, 1998—2002; prof. surgery, dir. transplantation U. South Ala. Med. Ctr., Mobile, 2002—. Mem. med. advisory bd. Nat. Kidney Found. Vol. King County Hosp., Bklyn., 1972. Recipient Martin Luther King Sch. award, 1973-74, Am. Fedn. Tchrs. Sch. award, 1973-75, Nat. Med. Found. award 1977-78, Joseph Collins Found. Sch. award 1978, Gift of Life award Nat. Kidney Found., OMNI Life Models award, Women of Spirit award Carlow Coll.; named Outstanding Young Women of Am. 1988. Fellow, ACS; mem. AMA (listed by AMA as nation's first African-Am. female transplant surgeon), P&S Alumni Assn., Black and Latin Students Orgn. (treas. N.Y.C. 1979-80), Slpha Epsilon Delta, Phi Sigma Soc. (sec. Bklyn. chpt. 1976-77), Am. Soc. Transplantation, Am. Soc. Transplant Surgeons, Soc. Black Academic Surgeons, Am. Soc. Minority Health and Transplant Professionals (bd. dirs.), Internat. Women's Forum We. Pa., Nat. Assn. Negro Bus. and Profl. Women. Democrat. Office: Univ S Ala Med Ctr 2451 Fillingim St Mobile AL 36617-2293

SCARABELLI, TIZIANO MARIA, molecular biologist, cardiologist, educator; b. Vercelli, Italy, July 11, 1963; s. Mario Giuseppe Scarabelli and Aristea Dina Tagliaferro; m. Carol Andrea Chen, Sept. 30, 2000. MD, U. Turin, Italy, 1990, postgrad., 1993—95, U. Brescia, 1995—99; PhD, U. Coll. London, 2002. Ho. officer Columbus Ctr. of Cardiology, Milan, 1990—91; specialist registrar Sch. Clin. Pathology U. Turin, 1993—95; specialist registrar, chmn. cardiology U. Brescia, Italy, 1995—99; fellow in molecular biology Inst. of Child Health, Gt. Ormond St. Hosp., U. Coll. London, 1999—2002; assoc. prof. internal medicine Wayne State U., Detroit, 2002—. Med. officer Italian Air Force, 1991—92. European Cmty. scholar in clin. pathology, U. Turin, 1993—95, European Cmty. scholar in clin. cardiology, U. Brescia, Young Investigator Fellowship grantee, Italian Soc. of Cardiology, 1998, Europen Soc. of Cardiology, 1999, Grad. Sch. Rsch. scholar, U. Coll. London, 1999—2002. Mem.: Basic Cardiovasc. Coun. of the Am. Heart Assn. (New Investigator award 2001). Achievements include research in quantitative assessment of cardiac myocyte apoptosis in tissue sections using fluorescence-based tecniques enhanced with counterstains; apoptosis of endothelial cells which precedes and induces myocyte cell apoptosis in ischaemia/reperfusion injury; different signaling pathways inducing apoptosis in endothelial cells and cardiac myocytes during ischaemia/reperfusion; description of cardioprotection mediated by urocortin, which promotes hemodynamic and bioenergetic recovery and improves cell survival in the isolated rat heart exposed to ischemia/reperfusion; discovery of minocycline as a new cardioprotective agent and description of its molecular mechanism of action. Office: St John Hosp Divsn Cardiology PBII Ste 470 22201 Moross Rd Grosse Pointe MI 48236 Home: 41619 Steinbeck Gln Novi MI 48377-2869 Personal E-mail: tscarabelli@hotmail.com. Business E-Mail: tiziano.scarabelli@stjohn.org.

SCARBOROUGH, CHUCK (CHARLES BISHOP SCARBOROUGH III), newscaster; b. Pitts., Nov. 4, 1943; s. Charles Bishop and Esther Francis (Campbell) S.; m. Linda Anne Gross, Dec. 14, 1972; children: Charles Bishop IV, Elizabeth Anne; m. Anne Ford Uzielli, Oct. 2, 1982; m. Ellen Carol Ward, Sept. 25, 1994. BS, U. So. Miss., 1969, LittD (hon.). Prodn. mgr. Sta.-WLOX-TV, Biloxi, Miss., 1966-68; reporter, anchorman Sta.-WDAM-TV, Hattiesburg, Miss., 1968-69; reporter, anchorman, mng. editor Sta.-WAGA-TV, Atlanta, 1969-72; reporter, anchorman Sta.-WNAC-TV, Boston, 1972-74, NBC News, NYC, 1974—. Author: (novels) Stryker, 1978, The Myrmidon Project, 1981, Aftershock, 1991. Served with USAF, 1961-65. Recipient awards for journalism AP (9), 1969-72, 31 Emmy awards, 1974-2009, award Aviation/Space Writers Assn., 1977, 78, 88, UPI award for journalism NY Press Club award, 1988, 89, Sigma Delta Chi award, Deadline Club award, Terry Anderson Journalism award Working Press Assn. NJ, 1992, Best in Bus. award, Washington Rev. Journalsam, 1994, Humanitarian award, Juvenile Diabetes Found., 2005; named NYC's Best Anchor Team (with Sue Simmons), NY Daily News, 2003 Mem.: Phi Kappa Phi. Office: NBC News 30 Rockefeller Plz New York NY 10112-0036

SCARBOROUGH, JOE (CHARLES JOSEPH SCARBOROUGH), newscaster, former United States Representative from Florida; b. Atlanta, Apr. 9, 1963; s. George Francis and Mary Joanna (Clark) Scarborough; m. Melanie Ann Hinton, July 19, 1986 (div. Apr. 5, 1999); children: Joey, Andrew; m. Susan Waren, Oct. 20, 2001; 1 stepchild, Kate. BA, U. Ala., 1985; JD, U. Fla. Coll. Law, 1990. Bar: Fla. 1991. Atty., Pa., 1990; mem. US Congress from 1st Fla. Dist., Washington, 1995—2001, mem. govt. reform com., judiciary com., armed svc. com.; ptnr. Beggs & Lane, Fla.; host Scarborough Country MSNBC, 2003—07, co-host, Morning Joe, 2007—. Co-chmn. New Federalists; bd. dirs. Emerald Coast Pediat. Primary Care, Inc. Author: Rome Wasn't Burnt in a Day: The Real Deal on How Politicians, Bureaucrats, and Other Washington Barbarians are Bankrupting America, 2004, The Last Best Hope: Restoring Conservatism and America's Promise, 2009 (Publishers Weekly bestseller). Recipient Friend of Taxpayer award, Americans for Tax Reform, Guardian of Small Bus. award, Nat. Fedn. Ind. Bus., Spirit of Enterprise award, US C. of C., Taxpayer's Hero award, Coun. for Citizens Against Govt. Waste, Guardian of Sr. Rights, 60 Plus Assn. Republican. Baptist. Office: c/o NBC News 30 Rockefeller Plaza New York NY 10112*

SCARBOROUGH, MARION NICHOLS, nutritionist, recreational facility executive; b. Enosburg Falls, Vt., July 26, 1915; d. George Leonard and Clara May (Woodward) Nichols; m. Mat. Scarborough, Aug. 30, 1950 (dec. Mar., 1960); 1 child Mary Anne Scarborough O'Donnell Adams. ASS, Green Mountain Coll., Poultney, Vt., 1935; BS, Kans. State U., 1937; MPH, Harvard U., 1947. Chief dietitian Newton (Mass.) Wellesley Hosp., 1938-43, 182d Gen. Hosp., U.S. Army, 1943-45; nutritionist, author food exch. list U.S. Pub. Health Diabetes Sect., Boston, 1947-50; staff nutritionist Fla. Bd. Health, Jacksonville, 1950-52; owner Happy Acres Ranch, Inc., Jacksonville, 1953—. Sec. Fla. Assn. Children Under Six ECA, 1965, pres., 1966, 67. Commd. officer USPHS, 1948-50. Mem. APHA, Am. Dietetic Assn., Am. Camping Assn., Nat. Assn. Edn. of Young Children. Episcopalian. Avocations: childrens' day care, summer camp. Home and Office: Happy Acres Ranch Inc 7117 Crane Ave Jacksonville FL 32216-9012

SCARBOROUGH, ROBERT HENRY, JR., entrepreneur; b. Hawkinsville, Ga., Mar. 12, 1923; s. Robert Henry and Janet Augusta (Burton) S.; m. Walterene Brant, July 1, 1946; children— Robert Henry, James Burton BS, U.S. Mcht. Marine Acad., 1944; BBA, U. Hawaii, 1969, MBA, 1971; MS, George Washington U., 1971, Armed Forces Staff Coll., 1963, Nat. War Coll., 1971. Commd. lt. (j.g.) USCG, 1949; advanced through grades to vice adm., 1978; chief Office of Ops. USCG, 1974-75, chief of staff, 1975-77, comdr. 9th Coast Guard Dist., 1977-78, vice comdt. Washington, 1978-82, ret., 1982; exec. dir. Navy League U.S., 1982-84; pres. Polaris Potomac Corp., 1985-96. Entrepreneur, 1996—. With USNR, 1942-49 Decorated DSM, Legion of Merit. Mem. Beta Gamma Sigma Office: 5357 37th St N Arlington VA 22207-1312

SCARCHUK, LYNN NETTLETON, retired music educator; b. Hartford, Conn., July 25, 1950; d. Russell Chaffee Nettleton and Katharine Risley Chaffee; 1 child, James Paul. BS, Western Conn. State U., 1968—72; MS, Ctrl. Conn. State U., 1978. Tchr. Meriden Bd. Edn., Meriden, Conn., 1972—2007, Jefferson Mid. Sch., Meriden, 1972—84, Washington Mid. Sch., Meriden, 1984—87; choral dir., tchr. Maloney HS, Meriden, 1988—2007; ret., 2007. Dir.(and prodr.): (sch. prodn.) Oklahoma, 1990, My Fair Lady, 1992, Anything Goes, 1994, South Pacific, 1996, 42d St, 1998, Hello Dolly, 2000, Crazy for You, 2002, Footloose, 2004 (hon. mention for set building, Mag.), Seussical, 2006. Music dir. Kiwanis Club Kapers, Meriden, Conn., 2000—01. Mem.: Conn. Music Educators Assn. (25 Yrs. Svc. award). Avocations: travel, bicycling.

SCARDAMALIA, MARLENE, education educator, researcher; PhD, U. Toronto, 1973. K-12 theme leader TeleLearning Network of Centres of Excellence, 1996—2002; pres.' chair in edn. & knowledge technologies Ontario Inst. for Studies in Edn., U. Toronto, 2002—; dir. Inst. for Knowledge Innovation and Tech. Contbr. articles to profl. jours. Recipient Jose Vasconcelos World Award of Edn., 2006; named Rschr. of Yr., Telelearning Network of Centres of Excellence, 1997; fellow Ctr for Advanced Study in the Behavioral Scis., 1992—93. Fellow: Can. Psychological Assn.; mem.: Can. Inst. for Advanced Rsch., Human Devel. Program, US Nat. Acad. Edn. Office: Ontario Inst for Studies in Edn 252 Bloor St W Toronto ON Canada M5S 1V6 Office Phone: 416-923-6641 2264. E-mail: mscardamalia@kf.oise.utoronto.ca.

SCARDINO, DAME MARJORIE MORRIS, publishing executive; b. Flagstaff, Ariz., Jan. 25, 1947; d. Robert Weldon and Beth (Lamb) Morris; m. Albert James Scardino, Apr. 19, 1974; children: Adelaide Katherine Morris, William Brown, Albert Henry Hugh. BA, Baylor U.; JD, U. San Francisco. Ptnr. Brannen Wessels & Searcy, Savannah, Ga., 1976-85; pub. Ga. Gazette Pub. Co., Savannah, 1978-85; pres. The Economist Newspaper Grp., Inc., NYC, 1985-93; chief exec. The Economist Grp., London, 1993-97, Pearson P.L.C., London, 1997—. Non-exec. dir. Nokia Corp. Trustee Carter Ctr.; bd. dir. MacArthur Found., Atlantic Council of U.S.; trustee Victoria and Albert Mus. Named Dame Comdr. British Empire, 2002; named one of 50 Most Powerful Internat. Women in Bus., Fortune Mag., 2008. Office: Pearson PLC 80 Strand London WC2R ORL England*

SCARIA, ABRAHAM, molecular biologist, director; b. India; PhD, Ind. U. Sch. Medicine, Indpls., 1986. Postdoc. fellow molecular virology St. Louis U. Sch. Medicine, 1987—93; sr. fellow med. genetics U. Wash. Sch. Medicine, Seattle, 1993—94; rsch. scientist Genzyme Corp., Framingham, Mass., 1994—2004, sci. dir., 2004—. Contbr. articles to profl. jours. Mem.: Assn. Rsch. Vision & Opthalmology, Am. Soc. Gene Therapy. Achievements include patents in field. Office: Genzyme Corp 49 NY Ave Framingham MA 01701 Office Fax: 508-661-8842. Business E-Mail: abraham.scaria@genzyme.com.

SCARLATA, PAUL ANTHONY, oral surgeon; b. McKeesport, Pa., Apr. 3, 1935; s. Joseph Mario and Josephine Gloria (Battaglia) S.; m. Mary Jane Parks, June 15, 1963 (dec. 1982); children: Stephanie, Anthony, Christopher, Matthew, Sarah; m. Darla K. Hosler, May 27, 1988 (div. 1994); m. Helen Walterick Meyers, Jan. 3, 2006. BS, U. Pitts., 1957, DDS, DMD, U. Pitts., 1961. Resident in oral surgery Western Pa. Hosp., Pitts., 1962-63, St. Luke's Hosp., NYC, 1963-64; practice gen. dentistry and oral surgery Chambersburg, Pa., 1967—; chief dental svc. Chambersburg Hosp., 1974-76, 82-84. Treas. Franklin County (Pa.) Heritage, 1971—, pres., 1977-78; fgn. student exch. host Youth for Understanding, appointed regional field dir. Capt., oral surgeon AUS, 1964—67, Mannheim, Germany. Recipient Buhl Planetarium Sci. award 1st prize Astronomy 6″ Newtonian Reflector, 1952. Mem. ADA (life), Pa. Dental Assn., We. Pa. Assn. Oral Surgeons, Gt. Lakes Soc. Oral Surgeons, N.Y. Soc. Clin. Oral Pathologists, Am. Dental Soc. of Anesthetists, Cumberland Valley Dental Soc. (pres. 1982-83), Am. Legion (life), Chambersburg Club, Antique Studebakers Club, Antique Auto Assn. (life), K.C., Pitts. Athletic Club. Home: 6703 Congressional Terr Fayetteville PA 17222-9403 also: 6703 Congressional Ter Fayetteville PA 17222-9403 Personal E-mail: poppars@comcast.net.

SCARLATA, RONALD ALAN, theater educator, director; b. Rochester, Ny, Mar. 25, 1946; s. Anthony and Josephine Scarlata; m. Cynthia Ann Owens; children: Jennifer, Amy. MA, UCLA. Standard secondary tchng. cert. UCLA. Drama dir. West Torrance HS, Calif., 1972—92; prof. theatre El Camino Coll., Torrance, 1992—. Mem.: Theatre Comm. Group, Southern Calif. Ednl. Assoc., Am. Assn. Higher Edn. Office: El Camino Coll 16007 Crenshaw Blvd Torrance CA 90506 Business E-Mail: rscarlat@elcamino.edu.

SCARLETT, ELIZABETH ANN, foreign language educator; b. Bklyn., Apr. 11, 1961; d. Thomas Peter and Mary Elizabeth (Hogan) S.; m. David Edward Wagner, Apr. 23, 1995. BA in Comparative Lit. cum laude, Washington U., 1983; MA in Romance Langs. and Lits., Harvard U., 1986, PhD in Romance Langs. and Lits., 1991. Arts editor Washington U. campus newspaper Student Life, St. Louis, 1979-80; Spanish drill instr. Washington U., St. Louis, 1982-83; English lang. asst. Lycée Polyvalent Paul-Sabatier, Carcassonne, France, 1983-84; Spanish tchg. fellow Harvard U., Cambridge, Mass., 1985-88, 89-91; rschr., writer Harvard Student Agys., Cambridge, 1986, travel guide editor, 1987; vis. asst. prof. dept. English lang. U. Seville, Spain, 1988-89; asst. prof. Spanish dept. Spanish, Italian and Portuguese U. Va., Charlottesville, 1991—. Author: Under Construction: The Body in Spanish Novels, 1994 (Choice award 1995); editor: Let's Go: Spain, Portugal & Morocco, 1988, Let's Go: Mexico, 1988; contbr. chpt. to book. Fulbright French Tchg. Assistantship, Fulbright-Hays Program and French Govt., Carcassonne, France, 1983-84; grantee Harvard U., 1984-91, 85; Sesquicentennial fellow U. Va., 1995. Mem. MLA, Am. Assn. Tchrs. Spanish and Portuguese, Assn. Internat. de Hispanistas, New Novel Assn.

SCARLETT, LYNN (PATRICIA LYNN SCARLETT), former federal agency administrator; b. Pitts., Dec. 8, 1949; d. James Miles and Virginia (Young) S.; m. James R. Trotter, May 6, 1978; 1 child, Rachel Scarlett Trotter. BA, U. Calif., Santa Barbara, 1970, MA, 1972. Vis. lectr. U. Calif., Santa Barbara, 1980-81; book rev. editor Reason Mag., Santa Barbara, 1982-85; dir. rsch. Reason Found., Santa Monica, Calif., 1985-89, v.p. rsch., 1990—2001, pres., CEO, 2001; asst. sec. policy, mgmt. & budget US Dept. Interior, Washington, 2001—05, dep. sec., 2005—09, acting sec., 2006. Mem. task force Calif. Joint Legis. Com. on Surrogate Parenting, Calif., 1989-90; panel reviewer Project 88 Phase II, 1990; chmn. issues com. Citizens for Balanced Community, Santa Barbara, 1989—; chmn. "How Clean Is Clean" Working Group, Nat. Environmental Policy Inst., 1993-98; bd. dirs. Laguna Blanca Sch., Santa Barbara. Author: (chpt.) Food Politics, 1982; contbr. articles to profl. jours. Chmn. Jim Trotter for City Coun., Carpinteria, Calif., 1990—; mem. parents aux. Laguna Blanca, 1986-88. Geneva Inst. of Internat. Studies fellow, 1974-75. Mem. Friends of Girls Club Corp. (2d v.p. 1986-87). Republican. Avocations: birdwatching, drawing, swimming.*

SCARNATI, JOSEPH B., III, Lieutenant Governor of Pennsylvania, state legislator; b. Brockway, Pa., Jan. 2, 1962; s. Joseph II and Yvonne Scarnati; m. Sheryl Hetrick, Dec. 1, 1990; 3 children. BA in Bus. Admin., Pa. State U., DuBois, 1982. Bus. owner; mem. Brockway Borough Coun., Pa., 1986—96; mem. Dist. 25 Pa. State Senate, Harrisburg, 2001—, vice chmn. environ. resources and energy, 2001—, mem. ex-officio, all standing committees, pres. pro tempore, 2007—, pres.; lt. gov. State of Pa., Harrisburg, 2008—. Chmn. Jefferson County Rep. Party; pres. Jefferson County Devel. Coun. Mem.: NRA, Gunowners America. Republican. Roman Catholic. Office: 292 Capitol Bldg Senate Box 203025 Harrisburg PA 17120-3025 also: Dist Office 315 Second Ave Ste 203 Warren PA 16365 Office Phone: 717-787-7084, 814-726-7201. Office Fax: 717-772-2755, 814-726-7012. Business E-Mail: jscarnati@pasen.gov.*

SCARNECCHIA, SUELLYN, academic administrator, lawyer; BA, Northwestern U., 1978; JD, U. Mich., 1981. Bar: Mich. Ptnr. McCroskey, Feldman, Cochrane & Brock, Battle Creek, Mich.; clin asst. prof. U. Mich. Sch Law, 1987, clin. prof. law, 1993, clin. coord., 1994—96, assoc. dean clin. affairs, 1996—2002, assoc. dean adminstrn., 1999—2001, asst. provost academic and faculty affairs, 2002; dean, prof. law U. N.Mex Sch. Law, Albuquerque, 2003—08; v.p., gen. counsel U. Mich., Ann Arbor, 2008—. Atty. U. Mich. Child Advocacy Law Clinic, 1987; bd. dirs. Clin. Legal Edn. Assn.; panelist Mich. Atty. Disciplinary Bd.; tech. adv. Mich. Supreme Ct. Task Force on Gender and Race Bias. Chair jud. nominating comm. State of N.Mex. Mem.: Women Lawyers Assn. Mich. (past pres.), Battle Creek Area Orgn. Against Domestic Violence (past bd. pres.). Office: Ctrl Campus Legal Office 5010 Fleming Bldg 503 Thompson St Ann Arbor MI 48109-1340 Office Phone: 734-764-0305. Business E-Mail: suellyns@umich.edu.*

SCARNECCHIA, TIMOTHY, history professor; b. Warren, Ohio; PhD, U. Mich., Ann Arbor, 1994. Vis. prof. UNC, Charlotte, NC, 1995—96; rsch. affiliate Makerere Inst. Social Rsch., Kampala, Uganda, 1996—97; vis. prof. U. Mich., 1997—99; vis. prof. and profl. lectr. Georgetown U., Washington, 2002—06; asst. prof. Kent State U., Ohio, 2007—. Author: The Urban Roots of Democracy and Political Violence in Zimbabwe: Harare and Highfield; contbr. articles to profl. jours. Mem.: Am. Hist. Assn., African Studies Assn. Office: Dept History 305 Bowman Hall PO Box 5190 Kent OH 44242-0001 Business E-Mail: tscarnec@kent.edu.

SCARPA, ANTONIO, federal agency administrator, physiologist, medical educator; b. Padua, Italy, July 3, 1942; s. Angelo and Elena (DeRossi) Scarpa. MD cum laude, U. Padua, 1966, PhD in Pathology, 1970; student, Weizmann Inst. Sci., Israel, U. Utrecht, Netherlands, U. Bristol, Eng.; MA (hon.), U. Pa., 1978. Asst. prof. biochemistry/biophysics U. Pa., Phila., 1973-76, assoc. prof., 1976-80, prof., 1980-86, dir. biomed. instrumentation group, 1983-86; prof. medicine Case Western Res. U., Cleve., 1986—98, David & Inez Myers prof., 1998—2005, chmn. dept. physiology & biophysics, 1986—2005; dir. Ctr. Sci. Rev., NIH, Bethesda, Md., 2005—. Permanent mem. peer review com.'s NIH, 1983—2003. Mem. editl. bd. Circulation Rsch., 1978—81, Biophys. Jour., 1979—82, Jour. Muscle Rsch., 1979—85, Physiol. Rev., 1982—90, Magnesium, 1982—95, FASEB Jour., 1987—92, Molecular Cellular Biochemistry, 1988—2005;, editor (numerous med. text. and journs.); contbr. articles to profl. jours. Grantee Nat. Heart, Lung & Blood Inst., Nat. Inst. Alcohol Abuse & Alcoholism, Nat. Inst. Diabetes & Digestive & Kidney Diseases, Am. Heart Assn. Mem.: Fedn. Am. Societies Exptl. Biology, Assn. Am. Med. Colleges, Biophys. Soc. (exec. coun. 1980—83, 1985—89, 1994—97, treas. 1998—2003), Am. Soc. Biol. Chemistry, Am. Soc. Physiologists. Avocations: farming, sailing, painting. Office: NIH CSR 6701 Rockledge Dr MSC 7768 Bethesda MD 20892-7776 Office Phone: 301-435-1109. Business E-Mail: scarpat@csr.nih.gov.*

SCARPA, MICHAEL, former apparel executive; b. 1956; Budget mgr. Liz Claiborne, Inc., NYC, 1983, v.p., divisional controller, 1991—95, v.p., fin. planning and ops., 1995—2000, v.p., CFO, 2000—02, sr. v.p.,

CFO, 2002—05, sr. v.p., fin. & distbn., CFO, 2005—07, COO, 2007—08, The Talbots, Inc., Hingham, Mass., 2008—. Office: The Talbots Inc 175 Beal St Hingham MA 02043 Office Phone: 212-354-4900. Office Fax: 212-626-3416.*

SCARPELLI, BOB (ROBERT), advertising executive; b. Mar. 4, 1957; m. Julie Scarpelli. Copywriter Needham Harper, Chgo., 1977—80, creative dir., 1980—86, DDB Needham Worldwide, 1986—94; chief creative officer DDB Chgo., 1994—95, vice chmn., 1995—2001, chmn., 2001; US chief creative officer DDB Worldwide, 2000—05, worldwide chief creative officer, 2005—, chmn., 2006—. Bd. dirs. DDB Worldwide Comm. Group, Inc., 1998—, Chgo. Internat. Film Festival, Va. Commonwealth U. AdCenter, Chgo. Creative Club; chmn. Internat. ANDY Awards, 2000, Radio Mercury Awards, 2001, Irish Internat. Advt. Festival, 2001, Clio Festival, 2003. Bd. dirs. Partnership for Drug-Free America. Office: DDB Worldwide 437 Madison Ave 5th Fl New York NY 10022 Office Phone: 212-415-2000. Business E-Mail: bob.scarpelli@ny.ddb.com.*

SCARPONE CAPORALE, GERALD D. JOSEPH, bishop emeritus; b. Watertown, Mass., Oct. 1, 1928; s. Alfonso Scarpone and Virginia Caporale. Degree, Franciscan Sch. Philosophy, 1950-52, Franciscan Sch. Theology, 1953-56; DD, 1979. Ordained priest Order of Friars Minor, 1956; pastor Franciscan Missionary, Jutiapa, Guatemala, 1956-62; ordained bishop, 1979; coadjutor bishop Diocese of Comayaga, Honduras, 1979; bishop Diocese of Comayagua, 1979—2004, bishop emeritus, 2004—. Roman Catholic. Avocation: collecting religious stamps. Office: Diocese of Comayagua Obispado Apartado 41 Calle de la Catedral 12101 Comayaga Honduras

SCARR, SANDRA WOOD, retired psychology educator, researcher; b. Washington, Aug. 8, 1936; d. John Ruxton and Jane (Powell) Wood; m. Harry Alan Scarr, Dec. 26, 1961 (div. 1970); children: Phillip, Karen, Rebbecca, Stephanie; m. James Callan Walker, Aug. 9, 1982 (div. 1994). AB, Vassar Coll., 1958; AM, Harvard U., 1963, PhD, 1965. Asst. prof. psychology U. Md., College Park, 1964-67; assoc. prof. U. Pa., Phila., 1967-71; prof. U. Minn., Mpls., 1971-77, Yale U., New Haven, 1977-83; Commonwealth prof. U. Va., Charlottesville, 1983-95, chmn. dept. psychology, 1984-90; CEO, chmn. bd. dirs. KinderCare Learning Ctr., Inc., 1995-97; ret., 1997. Mem. nat. adv. bd. Robert Wood Johnson Found., Princeton, N.J., 1985-91; coord. coun. psychology SUNY Bd. Regents, N.Y.C., 1984-92; prof. Kerstin Hesselgren, Sweden, 1993-94. Author: Race, Social Class and Individual Differences in IQ, 1981, Mother Care/Other Care, 1984 (Nat. Book award APA 1985), Caring for Children, 1989; editor Jour. Devel. Psychology, 1980-86, Current Directions in Psychol. Sci., 1991-95. Fellow Ctr. for Advanced Studies, Stanford U., Calif., 1976-77; grantee NIH, NSF, others, 1967-95. Fellow AAAS, APA (chmn. com. on human rsch. 1980-83, coun. of reps. 1984-89, bd. dirs. 1988-90, Award for Disting. Contbn. to Rsch. on Pub. Policy 1988), Am. Psychol. Soc. (bd. dirs. 1992—, pres. 1996-97, James McKeen Cattell award 1993); mem. Am. Acad. Arts and Scis. (coun. mem. 1995-2000), Behavior Genetics Assn. (pres. 1985-86, exec. coun. 1976-79, 84-87, Dobzhansky award 2004), Soc. for Rsch. in Child Devel. (governing coun. 1974-76, 87-93, chmn. fin. com. 1987-89, pres. 1989-91), Internat. Soc. for Study of Behavioral Devel. (exec. bd. 1987-94). Avocations: gardening, growing Kona coffee, breeding labrador retrievers. Home: 78-6915 Palekana Rd Holualoa HI 96725-8708 Office Phone: 808-322-9445. Personal E-mail: sandrascar@aol.com.

SCARRITT, THOMAS VARNON, newspaper editor; b. Tuscaloosa, Ala., Jan. 28, 1953; s. Charles Wesley and Valerie (Varnon) S.; m. Kathryn Rush Hubbard, Dec. 28, 1973; children: Sara Kathryn, Thomas Varnon Jr. BA in Journalism, U. N.C., 1974; MBA, Samford U., 1995. Reporter The Birmingham (Ala.) News, 1975-79, Washington corr., 1979-83, news editor, 1983-85, editl. page editor, 1986-89, exec. editor, 1989-97, editor, 1997—. Bd. dirs. Workshops Inc. Mem. Am. Soc. Newspaper Editors, Soc. Profl. Journalists, Kiwanis (Birmingham), Phi Beta Kappa. Episcopal. Home: 4240 Clairmont Ave S Birmingham AL 35222-3724 Office: The Birmingham News 2201 4th Ave N Birmingham AL 35203-3840 Home Phone: 205-591-4109; Office Phone: 205-325-2205. E-mail: tscarritt@bhamnews.com.

SCARSE, OLIVIA MARIE, cardiologist, consultant; b. Chgo., Nov. 10, 1950; d. Oliver Marcus and Marjorie Ardis (Olsen) S. BS, North Park Coll., 1970; MD, Loyola U., Maywood, Ill., 1973. Diplomate Am. Bd. Internal Medicine, Am. Bd. Cardiovascular Diseases. Surg. intern Resurrection Hosp., Chgo., 1974; resident in internal medicine Northwestern U., Chgo., 1974-77; cardiovascular disease fellow U. Ill., Chgo., 1977-80; dir. cardiac catherization lab. Cook County Hosp., Chgo., 1981; dir. heart sta. MacNeal Hosp., Berwyn, Ill., 1983; dir. electrophysiology Hines VA Hosp., Maywood, Ill., 1984-85; dir. progressive care Columbus Hosp., Chgo., 1985-88, pvt. practice, 1984—, Ill. Masonic Hosp., Chgo., 1989-96. Founder Physician Cons. for Evaluation of Clin. Pathways, Practice Parameters and Patient Care Outcomes, 1991—. Dir. continuous quality improvement Improvement Columbus, 1990-95; mem. presdl. ad hoc com. on prevention and treatment of domestic violence Chgo. Med. Soc., 1997—. Pillsbury fellow Pillsbury Fund, 1980. Fellow Am. Coll. Cardiology; mem. AMA, ACP, Chgo. Med. Assn., Ill. State Med. Assn., Am. Heart Assn. (coun. on clin. cardiology), Crescent Countries Found. for Med. Care, Physicians Health Network, Cen. Ill. Med. Rev. Orgn. Avocations: dance, acting, modeling, singing. Home and Office: 2650 N Lakeview Ave Apt 4109 Chicago IL 60614-1833

SCATENA, LORRAINE BORBA, retired rancher, women's rights advocate, researcher; b. San Rafael, Calif., Feb. 18, 1924; d. Joseph and Eugenia (Simas) de Borba; m. Louis G. Scatena, Feb. 14, 1960, dec. Nov. 1995; children: Louis Vincent, Eugenia Gayle. BA, Dominican Coll., San Rafael, 1945; postgrad., Calif. Sch. Fine Arts, 1948, U. Calif., Berkeley, 1956—57. Cert. elem. tchr. Calif. Tchr. Dominican Coll., 1946; tchr. of mentally handicapped San Anselmo (Calif.) Sch. Dist., 1946; tchr. Fairfax (Calif.) Pub. Elem. Sch., 1946—53; asst. to mayor Fairfax (Calif.) City Recreation, 1948—53; tchr., libr. U.S. Dependent Schs., Mainz am Rhine, Germany, 1953—56; translator Portugal Travel Tours, Lisbon, 1954; bonding sec. Am. Fore Ins. Group, San Francisco, 1958—60; rancher, farmer Yerington, Nev., 1960—98. Hostess com. Caldecott and Newbury Authors' Awards, San Francisco, 1959; mem. Nev. State Legis. Commn., 1975; coord. Nevadans for Equal Rights Amendment, 1975-78, rural areas rep., 1976-78; testifier Nev. State Senate and Assembly, 1975, 77; mem. adv. com. Fleischmann Coll. Agr. U. Nev., 1977-80, 81-84; speaker Grants and Rsch. Projects, Bishop, Calif., 1977, Choices for Tomorrow's Women, Fallon, Nev., 1989. Poetry presenter World Congress on Arts and Comm., Lisbon, Portugal, 1999, Washington, 2000, St. John's Coll.-Cambridge U., 2001, Vancouver, B.C., Can., 2002; contbr. articles to profl. jours. Trustee Wassuk Coll., Hawthorne, Nev., 1984-87; mem. Lyon County Friends of Libr., Yerington, 1971—, Lyon County Mus. Soc., 1978—; sec., pub. info. chmn. Lyon County Rep. Women, 1968-73, program v.p., 1973-75; mem. Lyon County Rep. Ctrl. Com, 1973-74, Marin County Soc. Artists, San Anselmo, Calif., 1948-53; charter mem. Eleanor Roosevelt Edn. Fund for Women and Girls, 1990, sustaining mem., 1992—; Nev. rep. 1st White House Conf. Rural Am. Women, Washington, 1980; participant internat. reception, Washington, 1980; mem. pub. panel individual presentation Shakespeare's Treatment of Women Characters, Nev. Theatre for the Arts, Ashland, Oreg., Shakespearean Actors local performance, 1977; mem. Nev. Women's History Project, U. Nev., 1996—; mem. pres.'s circle Dominican U. Calif., 1997-; mem. Bancroft Libr.'s coun. U. Calif., Berkeley, 2002-. Recipient Outstanding Conservation Farmer award Mason Valley Conservation Dist., 1992, Soroptimist Internat. Women Helping women award 1983, invitation to first all-women delegation to U.S.A. from People's Republic China, U.S. House Reps., 1979; Public Forum Travel grantee Edn. Title IX, Oakland, Calif., 1977; Internat. Biog. Ctr. (Cambridge) fellow World Lit. Acad., 1993. Mem. AAUW (life mem. nat. br. 1975—, Leaders Circle 1998-), Lyon County Ret. Tchrs. Assn. (unit pres. 1979-80, 84-86, v.p. 1986-88, Nev. State Outstanding Svc. award 1981, state conv. gen. chmn. 1985), Rural Am. Women Inc., AAUW (br. pres. 1972-74, 74-76, chair edn. found. programs 1983—, state conv. gen. chmn. 1976, 87, state sec. 1970-72, state legis. program chmn. 1976-77, state chmn. internat. rels. 1979-81, state pres. 1981-83, br. travelship, discovering women in U.S. history Radcliffe Coll. 1981, State Humanities award 1975, Future Fund Nat. award 1983, Lorraine Scatena endowment gift named in her honor for significant contbns. to AAUW Ednl. Found. 1997), Mason Valley Country Club, Italian Cath. Fedn. (pres. 1986-88), Uniao Portuguesa Estado da Calif., Nat. Mus. of Women in the Arts (charter mem., 1987, assoc., mem. mus. coun. 2000—). Roman Catholic. Avocations: writing, photography, travel, Azores history. Home: PO Box 247 Yerington NV 89447-0247

SCAVARDA, DONALD ROBERT, composer, artist; b. Iron Mountain, Mich., June 18, 1928; m. Barbara Janet Regner, Nov. 13, 1965. MMus, U. Mich., 1953. Co-founder, organizer Once Festival Musical Premieres, Ann Arbor, Mich., 1960-65. Composer: Groups For Piano, 1959, Sounds for Eleven, 1961, (Haiku song cycle) In the Autumn Mountains, 1961, Matrix for Clarinetist (widely recognized as the pioneering work in discovery and development of clarinet multiphonics), 1962, (piano, clarinet, 8mm film) Landscape Journey, 1963, (film score for electronic realization) Greys, 1963, (multiple film projection and tape) Caterpillar, 1965; paintings include Chamber Music, 1997, Portrait of Helen P., 1998; video films: Cinamatrix, 2002, Colorscapes, 2007, Matrix for Piano, 2008; composed recs. named to Top 10 List, Art Forum Mag., 2003; boxed CD-set, Music From the Once Festival-1961-1966, 2003. Fulbright scholar, 1953; recipient 1st prize for Fantasy For Violin And Orchestra BMI Inc., 1954. Mem.: World Wildlife Fund, Humane Soc. U.S. Home: PO Box 1908 Ann Arbor MI 48106-1908 Personal E-mail: scavardadr@att.net.

SCELSA, JOSEPH VINCENT, sociologist, educator, dean; b. NYC, Dec. 7, 1945; s. Albert John and Katherine Mary S.; m. Joyce Ann Tisi, Nov. 13, 1981; 1 child, Jonathan. AA, LIU, 1966, BA, 1968; MA, CUNY, 1973, MSEd, 1978; MA, Columbia U., 1983, EdD, 1984. Lic. mental health counselor, NY, 2006; cert. sch. counselor, NY. Counselor, tchr. NYC Bd. Edn., 1970-78, coord. career and occupational edn., 1979; coord. specialized counseling CUNY, 1979-81; pvt. practice counseling, NYC, 1975—; lectr. grad. faculty Herbert H. Lehman Coll., CUNY, 1980—; dean Calandra Inst., CUNY, 1994—; prof. student pers. Queens Coll., CUNY, 1999, v.p., prof. emeritus, 2008. Consul gen. of Italy in NY; pres. Italian Am. Mus., 2001—. Active Coun. of 1000 nat. Italian-Am. Found.; past cive chair multi cultural adv. bd. NYC Bd. Edn., 1990-91; NY State Mentoring Program Adv. Bd., 1990—; bd. dirs. Nat. Ethnic Coalition Orgns., 1990—, Coalition Italo-Am. Assn., 2000—; Italian Apostalate, NY, 1993. Decorated cavaliere Order of Merit Republic of Italy; recipient Disting. Alumni award LIU, 1985, Organizational Leadership award Coalition Italo-Am. Assns., Inc., 1988, Americus award Bronx Community Coll., 1989, Role Model award Club DaVinci, 1990, Inte I-A Student Assn. award, CUNY, 1991, Intergroup Rels. Chancellor's award, 1994, FIERI Leadership award, 1993, Philip Mazzei award, 1993, Ellis Island medal of honor, 1997, N.Y. State Govs. award for Excellence, 1999, Medal for 3d Millennium, 2000, Good Shapers Award, Woman & Work Program, 2005; named House of Savoy, 1997; Italian fellow John Jay Coll., 1993; inductee St. Lucy's Hall of Fame, 1996. Mem. Am. Counseling Assn., Am. Mental Health Counselors Assn. (cert. of recognition 1979, counselor of yr. 1983-84), Nat. Acad. Cert. Clin. Mental Health Counselors, Nat. Bd. for Cert. Counselors, Am.-Italian Hist. Assn., NY State Mental Health Counselors Assn. (past pres., Outstanding Work award 1980), Ill. Club. Home: 41 Carwall Ave Mount Vernon NY 10552-1211

SCERNO, JOSEPH BENEDICT, management consultant executive, arbitrator; b. Bklyn., Dec. 25, 1936; s. Benedict and Mary (DeMartini) S.; m. Patricia Ann, June 11, 1960 (div. 1997); children: Joseph, George. BS, NYU, 1962; MA in Counseling, Marywood U., Scranton, Pa., 1977. Cert. sr. practitioner human resource mgmt. Human Resource Accreditation Inst., Washington, 1975. V.p., gen. mgr. Express Haulage Corp., NYC, 1959—62; asst. v.p. indsl. rels. Tech. Materials Corp., Mamaroneck, NY, 1962—66; v.p. indsl. rels. Occidental Petroleum Corp., LA, 1966—72; v.p. pers. Hosp. Joint Diseases ad Med. Ctr., NYC, 1972—74; v.p., dir. employee cmty. rels. Intext, Inc., Scranton, 1974—79; v.p. human resources GBP Industries, Buffalo, 1979—84; v.p., pres. human resources Coastal Corp., Bklyn., 1984—88; commr. Fed. Mediation and Consiliation Svcs., Washington, 1988—97; pres. SJM Holdings, Ltd., Clarks Summit, Pa., 2002—; mng. dir. Jospeh B. Scerno Assocs., Internat. Mgmt. Consultancy, Clarks Summit, 1997—. Arbitrator NY State Panel Arbitrators, NYC, 1966—88; cons. City Scranton, Pa., 1976—79; arbitrator Joseph B. Scerno Arbitrators, Clarks Summit, 1997—. Author: Managing from the 21st Century and Beyond: Human Centered Facilitative Management, 1997. With USAF, 1954—57, Korea. Hon. Ky. Col. Mem.: VFW, Elks, Lehigh Country Club, Soc. Human Resource Mgmt., MENSA, Pa. Soc., NY Acad. Scis., Air Force Assn., Acad. Am. Poets, Acad. Polit. Scis., Tenn. Squires, Acad. Am. Writers, Am. Legion, Zeta Beta Tau (charter pres. 1960—), Mu Gamma Tau (hon.), Pi Sigma Epsilon (hon.). Avocations: golf, travel, sailing.

SCEUSA, NICHOLAS A., pharmacologist; b. Bklyn., July 22, 1948; s. Nicolo Sceusa and Maria Rita Anastasi; m. Donna Lynn Klein, Feb. 23, 1973; children: Amanda, Nicholas. BS in Biology, Syracuse U., 1971; BS in Pharmacy, L.I. U., 1977; PharmD, U. Ill., Chgo., 1996. Registered pharmacist, N.Y. Sr. staff pharmacist King Khalid Univ. Hosp., Riyadh, Saudi Arabia, 1984-86, Tawam Hosp., Al Ain, United Arab Emirates, 1986-87; staff pharmacist II St. Luke's - Roosevelt Hosp., NYC, 1987—90; staff pharmacist St. Clare's Hosp., 1990—95; pres., CEO Gelsus Rsch. and Consulting, Inc., 1997—. Author (with others): The Secret History of Italian-American Evacuation and Internment during World War II; contbr. articles to profl. jours. Advisor to Sch. Bd. Dist. 3, N.Y.C., 1996-98. Mem.: Am. Assn. Pharm. Scientists, Masons (treas.). Episcopalian. Achievements include patents for biofiltration and (Teorell-Meyer) dosage forms; invention of RAPID drug delivery system; rechargeable cardiac stent; new forms of surgical bandages and novel nutraceutical products. Avocations: hunting, fishing, outdoors, science, invention. Home and Office: 145 W 96th St Ste 1A New York NY 10025-6449 Office Phone: 212-663-7905. Office Fax: 212-280-1255. Personal E-mail: gelsus@verizon.net.

SCHAAB, ARNOLD J., lawyer; b. Newark, 1939; s. Robert George and Pauline Schaab; m. Marcia Stecker, 1964 (div. 1978); children: Emily Diana, Genevieve, Robert George II; m. Patricia Caesar, 1981 (div. 1996); m. Susan McGlamery, 2000. BA, New Sch. U., 1962; LLB, Harvard U., 1965. Bar: NY 1967, US Dist. Ct. (so. and ea. dists.) NY 1967. Assoc. Chadbourne & Parke, NYC, 1966-69; ptnr. Anderson, Kill & Olick, NYC, 1969-78; sr. ptnr. Pryor Cashman LLP, NYC, 1978—. Chmn. Literacy Ptnrs., Inc. Fulbright scholar Law Faculty U. Paris. Fellow NY Bar Found., Am. Bar Found.; mem. ABA (vice chair internat. fin. transactions com., sections bus. law, dispute resolution internat. law practice), NY State Bar Assn. (chmn. internat. law practice sect., chmn. spl. com. free trade Ams., mem. com. alternative dispute resolution, house dels., fin. com., long range planning com., by-laws com.), Assn. Bar City NY (com. pvt. investment funds, com. internat. trade, com. fgn. comparative law), Univ. Club (treas., chmn. fin. com., chmn. audit com., mem. coun.), Archaeol. Inst. Am., Bibl. Archaeology Soc., Army and Navy Club. Office: Pryor Cashman LLP 410 Park Ave New York NY 10022-4441

SCHAAD, DEE EDWIN, art educator; b. Hastings, Nebr., Sept. 6, 1943; s. Edwin August and Virginia Ellen (Holly) S.; m. Kathryn Jeanne Albro, June 21, 1967; children: Amy L., Marcus A. B Arts Edn., U. Nebr., Kearney, 1966, MS in Edn., 1971; MFA, U. Nebr., Lincoln, 1973. Tchr. art Northwest H.S., Grand Island, Nebr., 1966-67, Robin Mickle Jr. H.S., Lincoln, 1967-71; grad. asst. U. Nebr., Lincoln, 1971-73; tchr. art Lincoln East H.S., 1973-75; tchr. ceramics Southeast Nebr. C.C., Lincoln, 1973-75; prof. art U. Indpls., 1975—, chmn. dept. art and design, 1994—. Cons. Ind. Hist. Bur., 1989; bd. dir. Ctrl. Ind. Scholastic Art Awards. One-man shows include Walker Art Ctr. Gallery, 1994; group exhbns. include Smithsonian Instn. Nat. Air and Space Mus., Washington, 1986-87, Univ. Art Galleries, Memphis State U., 1987, Millersville (Pa.) U., 1989, Univ. Mus., So. Ill. U., Carbondale, 1990, San Angelo Mus. Fine Art, 1990. 33d Ann. Mid-State Craft Exhbn., 1993, Concordia Coll., 1994, Grossmont Coll., 1995, Muskingum Coll., New Concord, Ohio, 1996, McMurray U., Abilene, Tex., 1996, U. Evansville, Ind., 1997, Ronald Barr Gallery, Ind. U. S.E., New Albany, 1998, Louisville Virual Arts Assn., 1999, Baldheaded Potters of Am., Denver, 2000, Arthur Butcher Gallery, Concord Coll., Athens, W.Va., 2000, Sheldon Swope Art Mus., Terre Haute, 2004, Ind. U.-Purdue U., Ft. Wayne, Ind., 2004, Richmond (Ind.) Mus. Art, 2004, Nat. Invitational, Indpls., 2004, Rosewood Gallery, Kettering, Ohio, 2004, Armory Art Ctr., Palm Beach, Fla., 2005, Tex. Tech. U., Lubbock, 2005, Thaddeus Gallery, Laporte, Ind., 2005, Francis, Marion U., Florence, SC, 2006, Leageads of Myth History and Current Events Center for Contemporary Ceramics, 2009, Collections Mus. Nebr. Art, Kearney, Nebr., U. Evansville, Ind., Sheldon Swope Mus. Art, Terre Haute, Ind. and other public and private collections. Recipient John Gormley award of excellence Clayfest VIII Herron Gallery Indpls. Ctr. Contemporary Art, 1992; Best of Show, Clayfest 2004, 2008, Ctr. Contemporary Art, Indpls., Artist fellowship, Art Council Indpls., 2007-08. Mem. Nat. Coun. Edn. Ceramic Arts (bd. dir.), Midwest Coll. Art Assn., Ind. Artist Craftsmen (hon. life; bd. dir. 1989—), Potters Guild Ind. (v.p. 1979, pres. 1980, 92-93), Coalition Indpls. Artists. Avocations: running, spectator sports. Home: 3582 Byrd Dr Indianapolis IN 46237-1521 Office: U Indpls 1400 E Hanna Ave Indianapolis IN 46227-3630 Office Phone: 317-788-3253, 317-788-3387. E-mail: dschaad@uindy.edu.

SCHAAF, DOUGLAS ALLAN, lawyer; b. Green Bay, Wis., Nov. 18, 1955; s. Carlton Otto and Fern (Brunette) S.; m. Kathlyn T. Bielke, Feb. 23, 1988. BBA magna cum laude in Internat. Bus., St. Norbert Coll., DePere, Wis., 1978; JD, U. Notre Dame, 1981. Bar: Ill. 1981, Calif. 1987. Assoc. McDermott, Will & Emery, Chgo., 1981-84, Skadden, Arps, Slate, Meagher & Flom, 1984-89; ptnr. Paul Hastings, Janofsky & Walker, LA, 1989—, chair tax dept., 2006—. Adj. faculty mem. John Marshall Law Sch., 1984-87. Atty. Chgo. Vol. Legal Services, 1984-87; bd. dirs. Orange County Alzheimer's Assn., 1993-2008. Mem. Orange County Bar Assn. (chair tax sect. 1994-96). Office: Paul Hastings Janofsky & Walker 695 Town Center Dr Ste 1700 Costa Mesa CA 92626-7191 Office Phone: 714-668-6221. Office Fax: 714-668-6441. Business E-Mail: dougschaaf@paulhastings.com.

SCHAAF, LINDA ANN, nurse, educator; b. Balt., Feb. 15, 1944; d. Wilbert Frederick and Rosina Catherine (Lutz) S. Diploma, St. Agnes Hosp. Sch. Nursing, 1967; BSN, U. Md., 1971; MSN, Cath. U. Am., 1973. RN; adult nurse practitioner, post masters cert., 1999. Staff nurse, charge nurse St. Agnes Hosp., Balt., 1967-71; staff nurse Provident Hosp., Washington, 1972-73; pvt. duty nurse Med. Personnel Pool, Washington, 1973; practitioner, tchr. Rush-Presbyn. St. Luke's Med. Ctr., Chgo., 1973-80; staff nurse Critical Care Services, Inc., Chgo., 1980-82; assoc. prof. Ill. Benedictine Coll., Lisle, 1980—90, St. Xavier U., Chgo., 1990—99, Chgo. State U., 2000—. Clin. educator, cons. Glendale Heights (Ill.) Community Hosp., 1983—; cons. curriculum Trinity Coll., Washington Hosp. Ctr., Washington, 1976. Bd. dirs. Woodridge (Ill.) Unit Am Cancer Soc., 1984—; mem. Chgo. Heart Assn., 1973—. Mem. Am. Nurses Assn. (cert.), Ill. Nurses Assn., Am. Assn. Critical Care Nurses (cert. critical care RN), Nat. League for Nursing, Ill. League for Nursing (program developer 1976), Am. Heart Assn. (council on cardiovascular nursing 1970—), Sigma Theta Tau, Internat. Honor Soc. Nursing. Democrat. Roman Catholic. Avocations: handicrafts, travel, cultural events, ch. activities. Office: Chicago State U 9501 South King Drive Chicago IL 60628 Home: 133 Thomas Road Bolingbrook IL 60440-1352 Personal E-mail: lindaschaaf49@hotmail.com. Business E-Mail: lschaaf@csu.edu.

SCHAAL, BARBARA ANNA, evolutionary biologist, educator; BS in Biology with honors, U. Ill., Chgo., 1969; MPhil in Population Biology, Yale U., 1971, PhD in Population Biology, 1974. spkr. in field. Faculty mem. U. Houston, 1974—76, Ohio State U., 1976—80; assoc. prof. biology Washington U., St. Louis, 1980-86, prof., 1986—; prof. genetics Wash. U. Sch. Medicine, Spencer T. Olin prof. biology in arts and scis., 2000, chair dept. biology, 1993-97, mem. various coms. Assoc. editor Molecular Biology and Evolution, Am. Jour. Botany, Molecular Ecology, Conservation Genetics. Trustee St. Louis Acad. Scis. Fellow AAAS, Am. Acad. Arts & Sciences; mem. NAS (v.p. 2005-), Bot. Soc. Am. (pres. 1995-96, Merit award 1999), Nature Conservancy (trustee Mo. chpt.). Achievements include research on the evolutionary process within plant populations; first woman to be elected vice president of the NAS. Office: Washington U Dept Biology Campus Box 1229 304 McDonnell Hall 1 Brookings Dr Saint Louis MO 63130-4899 Office Phone: 314-935-6822. Business E-Mail: schaal@biology.wustl.edu.*

SCHAAP, JAMES IKE, finance educator; s. James Ike and Marilyn Therese Schaap; m. Marilyn Therese Root; 1 child, Joshua Lawrence. PhD, Fielding Grad. U., Santa Barbara, California, 2006. Adj. prof. U. Nev., Reno, 1990—, Norwich U., Northfield, Vt., 2007—. Contbr.

articles to profl. jours. Therapist Paws For Love, Reno, 2008. Cpl. USMC, 1964—67, Camp Pendleton. Decorated numerous awards USMC. Mem.: Acad. Mgmt. Business E-Mail: jjschaap@charter.net.

SCHAB, DANIEL J., mathematics educator; B in Math., Grand Valley State Univ., 1981; M in Ednl. Adminstrn., Mich. State Univ., 1991. Math. tchr. Lansing (Mich.) Cath. Ctrl. H.S., 1981—94, Williamston (Mich.) H.S., 1994—. Recipient Outstanding Alumni K-12 Tchr. award, Coll. Edn., Mich. State Univ., 2006, Lansing Regional C. of C. Excellence in Edn. award, 1987, 1994; named Mich. Tchr. of Yr., 2006; grantee Einstein Fellowship, Wash., 2003—04; Toyota Internat. Tchr. Program participant, 2000. Mem.: Mich. Assn. Mid. Sch. Educators, Mich. Coun. Tchrs. Math., Nat. Coun. Tchrs. Math. Office: Williamston High Sch 3939 Vanneter Rd Williamston MI 48895 Business E-Mail: schabd@michigan.gov.

SCHABERG, PAUL G., plant physiologist; s. Frank and Helen Schaberg; m. Patricia J. O'Brien, Feb. 14, 1985; children: Kurt, Emma O'Brien. PhD in Botany, U. Vt., Burlington, 1996. Rsch. plant physiologist USDA Forest Svc., South Burlington, 1989—. Recipient Exemplary Achievement awards, USDA Forest Svc., 2001, 2003, 2005—08. Mem.: Soc. Am. Foresters, Soc. Conservation Biology, Internat. Assn. Ecology, Ecol. Soc. Am., Am. Inst. Biol. Scis. Achievements include research in impacts of anthropogenic factors (e.g., acid rain, nutrient relations and climate change) on tree health and productivity; important to biologists, ecologists, policy makers and forest managers in North America and around the World. Office: USDA Forest Svc 705 Spear St South Burlington VT 05403

SCHACHT, CATHERINE ANN, musician, mezzo soprano; b. Racine, Wis., Feb. 3, 1950; d. Wallis August and Doris (Carlson) S. MusB cum laude, U. N.Mex., 1983. Instr. music N.Mex. Acad. for Scis. and Math., Santa Fe, 1999—2000. Chamber music coach Elder Hostel, Jemez Springs, N.Mex., 1991-99; owner, pres. Desert Song Music. Composer: (art song) Once in a Song, 1991, (choral) Prayer for Choristers, 1991, (chant) Eagle Poem, 1992, Katy's Song, 1993, Song for a Women's Gathering, 1995, (song cycle) Passages, includes Baptismal Song, Wedding Vows, Song of Wholeness, In Memoriam, 1999, House Blessing Song for Habitat for Humanity, 2002, It Is Good to Give Thanks to the Lord, 2005; violinist with N.Mex. Symphony, Albuquerque, 1978-89, Opera Southwest, Albuquerque, 1982-89, San Juan Symphony, Durango, Colo., 1987—, Santa Fe (N.Mex.) Symphony, 1990—, New S.W. Symphony, Albuquerque, 1992, Ariz. Opera, 1996, Albuquerque Civic Light Opera, 1992—, concertmaster, 1996, others; singer with N.Mex. Symphony Chorus, 1990-91, Santa Fe Symphony Chorus, 1991-92, others; alto soloist Charpentier Midnight Mass Santa Fe Symphony, 1992; trumpet and piano recital Duo Classico Corrales Cultural Arts Coun., 1994; singer, guitarist (CD)Tonal Tapestry. Organist, pianist Rio Rancho Presbyn. Ch., 1991-99; violinist Terzetto String Trio; singer, guitarist Desert Song; min. music Messiah Luth. Ch., 1999-2003; organist Holy Cross Luth. Ch., 2003-; keyboard accompanist Albuquerque Civic Chorus. Mem. Am. Fedn. Musicians (sec. 1988-90), Chamber Music Am. Democrat. Avocations: weaving, art history, interior decorating. Home: 3939 Rio Grande Blvd NW Albuquerque NM 87107-3147 E-mail: desertsong@mindspring.com.

SCHACHT, HENRY MEVIS, writer, consultant; b. Pasadena, Calif., Feb. 28, 1916; s. Henry and Amelia (Claussen) S.; m. Mary Joan Turnbull, Dec. 30, 1937; children: Henry John, Linda Joan. BA, U. Calif., Berkeley, 1936. Info. specialist U. Calif., Berkeley, 1936-42; dir. agr. NBC, San Francisco, 1942-59, ABC, San Francisco, 1959-60; agrl. columnist San Francisco Chronicle, 1959-93. Dir. agrl. info. U. Calif., 1961-65; v.p. corp. relations, corp. sec. Calif. Canners & Growers, San Francisco, 1965-81; freelance writer, 1936—; cons. radio-TV to FAO of UN, Cairo, 1963, Mexico City, 1965, Tokyo, 1966; dir. Calif. Co. for Internat. Trade; dir. Agrl. Issues Ctr., U. Calif. Author: (books) To the 21st Century - Study of Agribusiness to theYear 2000, 1983, History of the San Francisco Engineers Club, 1987, The Long and Winding Trail (History of the California Cattlemen's Association), 1991, Vision Solo - California Agriculture Report to State Dept. of Food and Agriculture, 1999, The California Cowboy, 2000. Pres. U.S. Fruit Export Coun., 1972-75; exec. sec. Commn. Calif. Agr. and Higher Edn., 1993-95; adv. bd. Agrl. Issues Ctr. U. Calif., 1990—2002. Mem. Pub. Rels. Soc. Am., Pub. Rels. Roundtable San Francisco, Nat. Assn. Farm Broadcasters, Agrl. Rels. Coun., Nat. Canners Assn. (dir. 1966-81) Home: 60 Hiller Dr Oakland CA 94618-2351

SCHACHT, JOCHEN HEINRICH, biochemistry educator; b. Königsberg, Fed. Republic Germany, July 2, 1939; arrived in U.S., 1969; s. Heinz and Else (Sprenger) S.; m. Helga Hildegard Seidel, Jan.27, 1967; children: Miriam Helga, Daniel Jochen. BS, U. Bonn, Fed. Republic Germany, 1962; MS in Chemistry, U. Heidelberg, Fed. Republic Germany, 1965, PhD in Biochemistry, 1968. Asst. research chemist, Mental Health Research Inst. U. Mich., Ann Arbor, 1969-72, from asst. prof. to assoc. prof. biochemistry, Dept. Biol. Chemistry & Otolaryngology, 1973-84, prof., 1984—, chmn. grad. program in physiol. acoustics, 1981—; hon. prof. Med. Acad. of the Chinese PLA, Beijing, 1998. Vis. prof. Karolinska Inst., Stockholm, 1979-80; acting dir. Kresge Hearing Rsch. Inst., U. Mich., 1983-84, assoc. dir., 1989-99, dir., 2000—; mem. hearing rsch. study sect. USPHS, NIH, Nat. Inst. Neurol. and Communicative Disorders and Stroke, 1986-89, Task Force Nat. Strategic Rsch. Plan, Nat. Insts. Deafness and Communication Disorders, USPHS, NIH; hon. prof. Hunan Med. U., Changsha, China, 1999—, Tonghi Med. U., Wuhan, China, 1999—; guest prof. Fourth Mil. Med. U., Xian, China, 1999—. Mem. edit. bd. Hearing Rsch., 1990-2008; assoc. editor Audiology & Neuro-Otol., 1995—; contbr. more than 200 articles to profl. jours., book chpts., revs.; co-editor Neurochemistry of Cholinergic Receptors, 1974, Auditory Trauma, Protection and Repair, 2008, Sketches of Otohistory, 2008. Fogarty Sr. Internat. fellow NIH, 1979, Sen. J. Javitz Neurosci. investigator, 1984; recipient Chercheur Etranger rsch. award INSERM, Paris, 1986, 94, Animal Welfare award Erna-Graff Found., Berlin, 1987, Disting. Faculty Achievement award U. Mich., 1989, Employer of Yr. award Nat. Capital Assoc. Coop. Edn. and Gallaudet U., Washington. Fellow Am. Assn. Advancement Sci.; mem. Am. Soc. Neurochemistry, Internat. Soc. Neurochemistry, Soc. for Neurosci., Assn. for Rsch. in Otolaryngology, Am. Soc. Biol. Chemists, Assn. Espanola de Audiologia Exptl. Avocations: photography, travel, birding. Office: Univ Mich Kresge Hearing Rsch Inst Ann Arbor MI 48109-5616 Home Phone: 734-665-7101; Office Phone: 734-763-3572. Business E-Mail: schacht@umich.edu.

SCHACHTEL-GREEN, BARBARA HARRIET LEVIN, retired epidemiologist; b. May 27, 1921; d. Lester and Ethel (Neiman) Levin; m. Hyman Judah Schachtel, Oct. 15, 1941 (dec. Jan. 1990); m. Louis H. Green, Feb. 26, 1995; children: Bernard, Ann Molly. Student, Wellesley Coll., 1939—41; BS, U. Houston, 1951, MA in Psychology, 1967; PhD, U. Tex., Houston, 1979. Psychol. examiner Meyer Ctr. for Devel. Pediat., Tex. Children's Hosp., Houston, 1967-81; instr. dept. pediat. Baylor Coll. Medicine, Houston, 1967-81, asst. prof. dept. medicine, 1982—2005; ret., 2005. Asst. dir. biometry and epidemiology Sid W. Richardson Inst. for Preventive Medicine, Meth. Hosp., Houston, 1981-88, dir. quality assurance, 1988-93; instl. rev. bd. for human rsch. Baylor Coll. Medicine, Houston, 1981-87, 97—; devel. bd. U. Tex. Health Sci. Ctr., Houston, 1987-97; dean's adv. bd. Sch. Arch., U. Houston, 1987-89. Contbr. articles to profl. jours. V.p., bd. dirs. Houston-Harris County Mental Health Assn., 1966—67; vice-chmn. bd. mgrs. Harris County Hosp. Dist., Houston, 1974—90, chmn., 1990—92, bd. dirs., 1970—93; trustee Inst. Religion in Tex. Med. Ctr., 1990—, vice chmn., 2000—; sec. Bo Harris County Hosp. Dist. Found. Bd., 1993—; bd. dirs. Congregation Beth Israel, 1993—95, Planned Parenthood of Houston, Inc., 1994—2000, Houston Ind. Sch. Dist. Found., 1993—2001, Crisis Intervention, 1994—96. Named Great Texan of Yr., Nat. Found. for Ilietis and Colitis, Houston, 1982, Outstanding Citizen, Houston-Harris County Mental Health Assn., 1985, Robert Eckles County Judge, 2006; recipient Good Heart award B'nai Brith Women, 1984, Women of Prominence award Am. Jewish Com., 1991, Mayor's award for outstanding vol. svc., 1994. Mem. APA, APHA, Wellesley Club of Houston (pres. 1968-70). Avocations: golf, tennis, books. Home: 2527 Glen Haven Blvd Houston TX 77030-3511 Home Phone: 713-668-3600. Personal E-mail: barabara.louis@gmail.com.

SCHACHTER, EDWIN NEIL, pulmonologist, educator; b. NY, May 10, 1943; BA, Columbia U.; MD, NYU, 1968. Cert. internal medicine, pulmonary medicine, critical care medicine. Intern, medicine Bellevue Hosp. Ctr., NY, 1968—69, resident NY, 1969—70, NY, 1972—73; fellow Yale U. Sch. Medicine, Lung Rsch. Ctr., 1973—74; asst. prof. to assoc. prof. medicine Yale U., 1975—84; chief pulmonary divsn. St. Albans Naval Hosp.; med. dir. respiratory care dept. Yale New Haven Hosp.; prof. cmty. medicine Mt. Sinai Med. Ctr., dir. Respiratory Care Dept.; chmn. pulmonary medicine Mt. Sinai Med. Sch. Lt. comdr. USN. Mem.: Nat. Assn. Med. Dirs. Respiratory Care (former pres.), Ct. Thoracic Soc. (former pres.), Am. Lung Assn. (former pres.). Office: Pulmonary Associates 5 E 98th St 8th Fl New York NY 10029 Office Phone: 212-241-5656. E-mail: Neil@thegooddoctor1.com.*

SCHACHTER, JAMES ROBERT, editor; b. Glendale, Calif., July 20, 1959; s. Stanley Herman and Margot (Lipiner) S.; m. Pamela Haag, May 19, 1985; children: Ariela Shira, Miriam Rachel, Naomi Tikvah, Benjamin Lev. BA, Columbia U., 1980. Cert. fellow punch sulzberger news media exec. leadership program Columbia U. Journalism Sch., 2008. Reporter Jacksonville Jour., Fla., 1980-82, Kansas City Star, Mo., 1982-84, labor writer, 1984-85; reporter LA Times, San Diego, 1985-87, bus. writer LA, 1987-90, asst. bus. editor, 1990-93, Sunday bus. editor, 1993-94, sr. asst. bus. editor, 1994-95; enterprise editor Bus. Day New York Times, NYC, 1995—97, editor Sunday Money and Bus., 1997—2000, dep. editor Bus. Day, 2000—04, dep. culture editor, 2004—06; dep. editor New York Times Mag., 2006—08; editor Digital Initiatives, 2008. Recipient award of Distinction, Soc. Newspaper Design, 1992, Cert. of Merit, Greater L.A. Press Club, 1989, 90, Bus. and Fin. Journalism award John Hancock Ins. Co., 1988, Best News Article award San Diego Press Club, 1987, Best Local News Reporting award Inland Daily Press Assn., Chgo., 1984, winner, NY Times Co. Punch Sulzberger, 2008. Mem. Investigative Reporters and Editors. Office Phone: 212-556-1144. Business E-Mail: jims@nytimes.com.

SCHACTER, BERNICE ZELDIN, biotechnology consultant, researcher; b. Phila., June 20, 1943; d. Aaron and Jean (Beckman) Zeldin; m. Lee Phillip Schacter, Aug. 23; children: Elizabeth, Sara. AB, Bryn Mawr Coll., Pa., 1965; PhD, Brandeis U., Waltham, Mass., 1970. Instr. U. Miami (Fla.), 1971-72, Johns Hopkins U., Balt., 1974-76; mem. staff Cleve. Clinic, 1976-77; asst. prof. pathology Case Western Res. U., 1977-82, assoc. prof. pathology, 1982-84; sr. scientist Bristol-Myers, Wallingford, Conn., 1984-86; assoc. dir. Bristol-Myers Squibb Pharm. Rsch. Inst., Wallingford, 1986-91; v.p. rsch. Bio Transplant Inc., 1991-93, biotechnology cons. Vis. prof. Wesleyan U., Middletown, Conn., 1988—; mem. Nat. Inst. Allergy and Infectious Disease Transplantation Biol. Adv. Com., Bethesda, Md., 1977-82; mem. U. Conn. Environ. Health Adv. Com., Storrs, 1986-91. Contbr. articles to profl. jours. Mem. Am. Assn. Immunologists, Am. Soc. Histocompatibility and Immunogenetics (v.p. 1983-84). Home: 1003 Oriente Ave Wilmington DE 19807-2260 Office: 1003 Oriente Ave Wilmington DE 19807-2260

SCHADER, CHARLES R., insurance company executive; Grad., Dartmouth Coll., Hanover, NH; LLM in Corp. Law, NYU, JD. Joined Am. Internat. Group, Inc. (AIG), NYC, 1984, sr. v.p.-claims, 2000—08, chief claims officer gen. insurance, 2008—; sr. v.p., chief claims Chartis Inc., 2009—. Bd. mem. RAND Inst. Civil Justice. Office: Chart Industries Inc Ste 300 One Infinity Corp Ctr Cleveland OH 44125 Office Phone: 440-753-1490. Office Fax: 440-946-6166.*

SCHADOW, KAREN E., public speaking trainer, educator; b. Mar. 1949; 1 child, Kelby. BA in comm. and humanities magna cum laude, Fla. State U., 1971, MA in theatre magna cum laude, 1973. Previous cameraperson numerous programs, ABC TV, previous prodn. staff mem.; pres. The Voice of Success!, NYC. Adj. asst. prof. NYU, 1990—; instr. Bergen Cmty. Coll., NJ; creator, presenter various lectures and seminars for sch. and orgn. including Nat. Acad. TV Arts & Scis., NY Coalition Women in Arts and Media, Ctr. Arts Edn., The Learning Annex, nationwide; prodr. student career conf. NY Women in Comm., 2002—05; nominating judge Drama League. Mem.: Nat. Acad. TV Arts & Scis. (past mem. bd. govs., Emmy award 1984), Fla. State U. Theatre Project, New England Soc., Univ. Film & Video Assn., Screen Actors Guild, Actors' Equity, NY Women in Comm. (v.p. student affairs). Office Phone: 212-563-2615. Business E-Mail: karen@thevoiceofsuccess.com.

SCHADY, KATHLEEN, pharmaceutical executive; d. Mildred Schady; m. Paul Gaynor; children: Pryce Gaynor, Pierce Gaynor. BA in Biology, Adelphi U., Garden City, NY, 1974; MS in Cell Biology, C.W. Post Coll., Greenvale, NY, 1975; PhD in Microbiology and Biochemistry, Rutgers U., New Brunswick, NJ, 1978. Cert. med. technologist Am. Soc. Clin. Pathology. Scientist, microbiology dept. Ethicon, Inc., Somerville, NJ, 1978—80, mgr., 1980—86; project mgr. Johnson & Johnson Sterilization Sci. Grp., Somerville, 1986—89; dir. pharmceutical quality assurance Ortho Pharm. Corp., Raritan, NJ, 1989—91; exec. dir., quality assurance Ortho Pharm., Raritan, 1991—93, Ortho-McNeil Pharm., Raritan, 1993—93; v.p. quality Ortho Biotech, Raritan, 1993—2000; v.p. qa biologics & parenterals Pharm. Sourcing Group Americas Bd., Raritan, 2000—02; v.p. bulk quality ops. Centocor, Malvern, Pa., 2002—03; v.p. Purdue Pharma, West Paterson, NJ, 2004—. Contbr. articles to profl. jours. Mem.: Quality Exec. Bd., Internat. Soc. Pharm. Engring. Achievements include development of a tech transfer process that was part of a continuous improvement initiative; supporting the optimization of a clinical supplies program to ensure availability of supplier for critical clinical studies. Office: Purdue Pharma 700 Union Blvd Totowa NJ 07512-2210 Office Fax: 973-247-9902. Business E-Mail: kathleen.schady@pharma.com.

SCHAECHTER, MOSELIO, microbiology educator; b. Apr. 26, 1928; children: Judy, John. Student, Cen. U., Ecuador, 1947-49; MA, U. Kans., 1952; PhD, U. Pa., 1954. Postdoctoral fellow State Serum Inst., Copenhagen, 1956-58; from instr. to asst. prof. to assoc. prof. U. Fla., Gainesville, 1958-62; from assoc. prof. to disting. prof. dept. microbiology Tufts U., Boston, 1962-95, prof. emeritus, 1995—. Adj. prof. San Diego State U., 1995—, U. Calif., San Diego, 2004—. Editor: Molecular Biology Bacterial Growth, 1985, Escherichia coli and Salmonella Typhimurium, 1987, 95, Mechanisms of Microbiol. Disease, 1989, 92; author: In the Company of Mushrooms, 1997, Microbe, 2005. Mem. Am. Soc. Microbiology (pres. 1985-86, chmn. internat. activities), Am. Soc. Med. Sch. Microbiology Chmn. (pres. 1984-85), Soc. Gen. Microbiology, Boston Mycol. Club, Sigma Xi. Avocation: field mycology. Home: 8515 Costa Verde Blvd Apt 554 San Diego CA 92122 Business E-Mail: mschaech@sunstroke.sdsu.edu.

SCHAEFER, BARBARA W., rail transportation executive; B, U. Nebr., Lincoln; JD, U. Nebr. Coll. Law; grad. in Mgmt. Devel. Program, Harvard U. Pvt. practice atty., Omaha; sr. v.p. human resources Union Pacific Corp., 1997—, corp. sec., 2004—. Bd. trustees Weitz Funds. Bd. mem. Children's Hosp., Lauritzen Bot. Gardens, U. Nebr. Found. Recipient Welcome T. Bryant Bd. Mem. of Yr. award, Urban League, 2000, 2001, Light of Wellness Leadership award, Wellness Coun. Midland, 2004; named a Woman of Vision, YWCA Omaha, 2001. Fellow: Nebr. State Bar Assn. Found. Office: Union Pacific Corp 1400 Douglas St Omaha NE 68179 Office Phone: 402-544-5000.

SCHAEFER, BONNIE (E. BONNIE SCHAEFER), retail executive; b. Chgo., Mar. 16, 1963; d. Rowland Schaefer. From sales assoc. to store mgr. Claire's Stores, Inc., 1987—90, v.p. real estate, 1994—2002, co-vice chmn., 1999—2002, co-chmn., 2002—, co-CEO, 2002—. Bd. dirs. Claire's Stores, Inc., 1998—, Claire's Nippon. Office: Claires Stores Inc 3 SW 129th Ave Pembroke Pines FL 33027 Office Phone: 954-433-3900. Office Fax: 954-433-3999.

SCHAEFER, CHARLES JAMES, III, advertising executive, consultant; b. Orange, NJ, Dec. 17, 1926; m. Eleanor Anne Montville, Apr. 8, 1961; 1 child, Charles James IV. AB, Dartmouth Coll., 1948, M in Comml. Sci., 1949. Mgr. foods promotion Beech-Nut, 1949—52; v.p. Dickie-Raymond, 1952-67; sr. v.p. Metromedia, 1968-69; exec. v.p., treas. The DR Group, Boston and NYC, 1969-76, pres., 1976-87; exec. v.p., dir. Needham Harper Worldwide Inc., NYC, 1984-87; chmn. bd. Marcoa DR Group, Inc., NYC, 1987-88; cons. Rapp Collins Marcoa, NYC, 1989-92; advt. cons., 1992—. Pres. Dartmouth Coll. Class of 1948, 1998-2000; trustee, mem. exec. com. Direct Mktg. Ednl. Found., 1983-89; campaign chairperson United Way Millburn-Short Hills, 1994, 95, trustee, 1991-98, 2000—, v.p., 2004—; mem. alumni coun. Dartmouth Coll., 2008-. With USN, 1945—46. Mem. Direct Mktg. Assn. (chmn. awards com. 1971-76, Hall of Fame com. 1978-81, ethics com. 1981-86), Assn. Direct Mktg. Agys. (pres. 1980-82, gen. chmn. Caples awards 1985, chmn. Direct Mktg. Days NY 1988, NY Direct Marketer of Yr. award 1987, Silver Apple award 1989, contbr. to jour.), Dartmouth Club of NY (pres. 1968-70), Lotos Club (bd. dirs. 1985-88, treas. 1987-88), Canoe Brook Country Club (Summit, NJ). Home and Office: 307 Hobart Ave Short Hills NJ 07078-2207

SCHAEFER, CHERYL PLASTER, physics professor; d. Robert Wayne and Mary Jean Plaster; children: Sarah Jo Carney, Douglas Alan, Samantha Jane, Rex Austin. BS, U. Mo., Columbia, 1979; MA, Mo. State U., 2001; PhD, U. Mo., 2004. Dir. dietary Lebanon Care Ctr., Mo., 1980—82; cons. dietitian Foster Health Care Group, Springfield, 1982—92; asst. prof. physics Mo. State U., 2003—. Contbr. to profl. journs. Pres. Lebanon Heart Assn., Mo., 1982—84; bd. mem. Laclede Early Edn. Program, Lebanon, 1986—88, Lebanon Habitat of Humanity, 1995—97. Mem.: Am. Assn. Physics Teachers. Conservative. Avocations: quilting, painting, reading, sewing. Office: Mo State Univ 901 S National Ave Springfield MO 65807 Home Fax: 417-836-6226. Business E-Mail: cherylschaefer@missouristate.edu.

SCHAEFER, DAVID A., dentist; b. Louisville, Ky. m. Suzanne Schaefer; 3 children. DMD, U. Louisville, 1991; grad., Dawson Ctr. for Advanced Dental Study, 2002. Pvt. practice, Louisville, 1992—. Consulting dentist Forum at Brookside; spkr. in field. Bd. mem. Kentuckiana Chap. Juvenile Diabetes Rsch. Found. Mem.: Am. Acad. Cosmetic Dentistry, Ky. Acad. Cosmetic Dentistry, Ky. Dental Assn., Louisville Dental Soc., Acad. Gen. Dentistry (Fellowship Award 1991), Ky. Acad. Gen. Dentistry (acting pres. 1999—2001, bd. dirs., participant Give-Back-A-Smile program). Office: Foxwood Bldg - Suite 203 7807 Shelbyville Rd Louisville KY 40222 Office Phone: 502-423-9555. Office Fax: 502-423-7701. E-mail: care@smilesoflouisville.com.

SCHAEFER, ELEANOR MONTVILLE, retired publishing executive; b. Worcester, Mass., June 27, 1926; d. Joseph Samuel and Monica Savage Montville; m. Charles James Schaefer; 1 child, Charles James IV. AB, Trinity U., 1949. Radio/tv dept. Sullivan Staufer Colwell & Bayles, Inc., NYC, 1949—50; promotion dept. staff Life Mag., NYC, 1951—52; asst. promotion mgr. Sports Illustrated, NYC, 1953—59; promotion mgr. Glamour mag., NYC, 1960. V.p. League Women Voters, 1971—77; found. dir. Summit Coll. Club; vol. auxilliary mem. Assn. U. Women, Summit, NJ, 1998—99. Mem.: Trinity U. Alumni Assn. (past pres. 1959—60), Summit Coll. Club, Canoe Brook Country Club. Achievements include being first woman staffer on "Project X" which eventually became Sports Illustrated. Avocations: golf, interior decorating. Home: 307 Hobart Ave Short Hills NJ 07078 E-mail: montvilles@aol.com.

SCHAEFER, FRANK WILLIAM, III, microbiologist, researcher; b. Dayton, Ohio, Sept. 1, 1942; s. Frank William Jr. and Irene Josephine (Krouse) S. BA, Miami U., Oxford, Ohio, 1964; MS, U. Cin., 1970, PhD, 1973. Rsch. assoc. parasitologist U. Notre Dame, South Bend, Ind., 1973-78; U.S. EPA EPA, Cin., 1978—. Mem. ASTM, AAAS, Am. Soc. Parasitology, Am. Soc. Microbiology, Am. Water Works Assn., Soc. Protozoologists, Sigma Xi. Home: 9948 McCauley Woods Dr Sharonville OH 45241-1489 Office: US EPA 26 Martin Luther King Dr Cincinnati OH 45268 Office Phone: 513-569-7222. Personal E-mail: fschaefer@zommtown.com. Business E-Mail: schaefer.frank@epa.gov.

SCHAEFER, GORDON EMORY, food products executive; b. 1932; married. BS, Marquette U., 1956. CPA Wis. With Peat, Marwick, Mitchell & Co., 1955-59; contr., sec. Wells Badger, Badger Carton Co., 1960—64; treas. Pabst Brewing Co., Milw., 1965-72, v.p. adminstrn., 1972-75, v.p. ops., 1975—80, exec. v.p. ops, 1980—85, dir.; pres., dir. Krier Foods Inc., Belgium, Wis., 1981-85, Corrs Beverages, Chgo., 1985-86; dir. bus. devel. Lakeside Packing Co., Manitowoc, Wis., 1989-92; mng. dir. Robertson Assocs., Mfg. Europe Ltd., Cardiff, Wales, 1993-94. Bd. dirs. Fox Fin. Co., Berg Industries, Inc.; fin. and ops. cons.; owner, operator Schaefer's Orchards. Home: 1626 Vivian Ct West Bend WI 53090-8961

SCHAEFER, HENRY FREDERICK, III, chemistry professor; b. Grand Rapids, Mich., June 8, 1944; s. Henry Frederick Jr. and Janice Christine (Trost) S.; m. Karen Regine Rasmussen, Sept. 2, 1966; children: Charlotte, Pierre, Theodore, Rebecca, Caleb. BS in Chem. Physics, MIT, 1966; PhD in Chem. Physics, Stanford U., 1969; D (hon.), U. Plovdiv, 1998, U. Sofia, 1999, Beijing Inst. Tech., 1999, Huntington

U., 2002, North-Eastern Hill U., Shillong, India, 2008, Babes-Bolyai U., Cluj-Napoca, Romania, 2009. From asst. prof. to prof. chemistry U. Calif., Berkeley, 1969—87; Graham Perdue prof., dir. Ctr. for Computational Chemistry U. Ga., Athens, 1987—. Apptd. Professeur d'Echange U. Paris, 1977, Gastprofessor Eidgenössische Technische Hochshule, Zürich, 1994, 95, 97, 2000, 02, 04, 06, 08; Wilfred T. Doherty prof., dir. Inst. Theoretical Chemistry, U. Tex., Austin, 1979-80, chemistry prof. emeritus U. Calif., Berkeley, 2004-; lectr. in field. Author: Science and Christianity: Conflict or Coherence? 2008; contbr. articles to profl. jours. including Electronic Structure of Atoms and Molecules: A Survey of Rigorous Quantum Mechanical Results, 1972, Modern Theoretical Chemistry, 1977, Quantum Chemistry, 1983, A New Dimension to Quantum Chemistry, 1994; editor Molecular Physics, 1991-94, editor in chief, 1995-2005. Recipient Pure Chemistry award Am. Chem. Soc., 1979, Leo Hendrik Baekeland award, 1983, Schrödinger Medal, 1990, Centenary medal Royal Soc. Chemistry, London, 1992, Gold medal Comenius U., Bratislava, Slovakia, 2000, Biennial Gold medal U. Sofia, 2009; Sloan fellow, 1972, Guggenheim fellow, 1976-77; named one of 100 Outstanding Young Scientists in Am., Sci. Digest, 1984, named 3d Most Highly cited chemist in world Science Watch, 1992. Fellow AAAS, Am. Phys. Soc., Am. Sci. Affiliation, Am. Acad. Arts and Scis., Royal Soc. Chemistry (London); mem. Internat. Acad. Quantum Molecular Sci., Am. Chem. Soc. (chmn. divsn. phys. chemistry 1992, award in theoretical chemistry 2003, Ira M. Remsen award 2003), World Assn. Theoretical and Computational Chemists (pres. 1996-2005, Joseph O. Hirschfelder prize, 2005, Biennial Grand award Sofia U., 2008). Presbyterian. Office: U Ga Ctr Computational Quantum Chemistry Athens GA 30602 Office Phone: 706-542-2067. Business E-Mail: sch@uga.edu.

SCHAEFER, JAME, religious studies educator; d. William J. Ehegartner and Norma I. Eppler; m. Wendelin W. Schaefer, Dec. 22, 1962; children: Joseph W., Peter F., Laura E. Momcilovic, Gretchen C. BA in Polit. Sci., Marquette U., 1961, PhD in Religious Studies, 1994; MA in History, U. West Fla., 1974. Cons. pub. participation in energy and environment issues, Sheboygan, Wis., 1986—2002; prof. religion and sci. Marquette U., Milw., 1995—; dir. interdisciplinary minor in environ. ethics Coll. Arts and Sci., Marquette U., Milw., 2001—03, 2005—. Numerous appts. to local, state and fed. govtl. positions, 1980—2002. Author: Theological Foundations for Environmental Ethics, 2009; contbr. articles to profl. jours. Mem. Energy Task Force State Wis., 1980—81; chair Radioactive Waste Rev. Bd. State Wis., 1982—83, vice-chair, 1983—85, chair edn. com., 1985—89; mem. Spl. Com. Low-Level Radioactive Waste Mgmt., State Legislature, State Wis., 1983—84; chair Local Emergency Response Planning Com. Sheboygan County, Wis., 1987—94; mem. Low-Level Radioactive Waste Coun., State Wis., 1988—2000, Citizens Adv. Com., Sheboygan River and Harbor Remedial Action Plan, Wis., 1990—96. Recipient Quality and Excellence in Tchg. Sci. and Religion award, Ctr. Theology and Natural Sci., 1998, Religion and Sci. Course award, John Templeton Found., 1996; Rosamund Gifford scholar. Mem.: Cath. Theology and Global Warming Interest Group (coord. 2008), Internat. Soc. Study Religion, Nature and Culture, Coll. Theology Soc., Soc. Christian Ethics, Internat. Soc. Environ. Ethics, Cath. Theol. Soc. Am. (convenor Theology and Ecology Group 2001—07), Am. Acad. Religion. Roman Catholic. Office: Marquette Univ Dept Theology 115 Coughlin Hall Milwaukee WI 53201-1881 Office Phone: 414-288-3742. Business E-Mail: schaeferj@marquette.edu. E-mail: jamesphd@wi.rr.com.

SCHAEFER, JAMES THEODORE, writer, editor, educator; s. Walter Charles and Louise Petersen Schaefer; m. Karen Elaine Moon, Sept. 16, 1972; children: Patrick Charles, Theodore Glen, Daniel John, Marie Louise. AA, Grand Rapids Jr. Coll., Mich., 1963—65; BA in English & Writing, Mich. State U., E.Lansing, 1965—69; MA in Tchg. Writing, summa cum laude, Ea. Mich. U., Ypsilanti, 2003—05, MA in Comm., summa cum laude, 2007. Cert. tchr.cons. Nat. Writing Project, 2004. Regional editor Muskegon Chronicle, Mich., 1969—70; freelance writer, editor & rschr. Ann Arbor, Mich., 1970—74; publisher/editor Shining Waters Press, 1974—88; sr. editor Comparative Studies Soc. & History, Ann Arbor, 1988—99; prof. Washtenaw CC, Ann Arbor, 1999—, Wayne County CC, Detroit, 2003—. Founder, exec. prodr. & host Riprap: The Academic Book TV Program, Ann Arbor, 1997—; co-founder Orchard Internet Radio, Ann Arbor, Mich., 1999, coord., 2000—02; cons. Wayne County CC, 2003—04. Editor: (book) The Magical State: Nature, Money, and Modernity, by Fernando Coronil; author: Breathe/Exhale; editor: (manuscript) Food in Global History, The Construction of Minorities, States of Violence; prodr.: (video) Falling Leaves; cons. (book) Two Dreams in One Bed: Empire, Social Life, and the Origins of the North Korean Revolution in Manchuria. Co-chair peace project task force Ea. Mich. U., 2006; jr. warden, vestry mem. St. Andrew's Episcopal Ch., Ann Arbor, 2000—03. Mem.: Acad. Am. Poets, Am. Ednl. Rsch. Assn., Nat. Comm. Assn., Nat. Coun. Tchrs. English (assoc.), Phi Kappa Phi. Avocations: reading, writing, music. Office: Wayne CC 9555 Haggerty Rd Belleville MI 48111 also: Washtenaw CC LA 178 4800 E Huron River Dr PO Box 1610 Ann Arbor MI 48106-1610

SCHAEFER, JOANN, public health service officer; MD, Creighton Univ., 1995. Cert. family medicine. Private practice, Omaha, 1995—2002; instr. Creighton Univ. Sch. Med., Omaha, 1997—2003, assoc prof., 2003; dep. chief med. officer Nebr. Dept. Health & Human Svc., Lincoln, 2002—05, chief med. officer, dir. regulation & licensure, 2005—. Named a Local Legend, Am. Med. Women's Assn. Mem.: Am. Acad. Family Physicians, AMA, Nebr. Acad. Family Physicians, Metro Omaha Med. Soc., Nebr. Med. Assn. (Physician of the Yr. 2004). Office: Nebr Dept Health & Human Svc 301 Centennial Mall S Lincoln NE 68509*

SCHAEFER, KIM, music educator; married; 2 children. Student, Utah State Univ., Colo. State Univ., SD State Univ. Cert. Nat. Bd. Tchg. Standards. Music tchr. Whitehorse HS, Navajo Reservation, Montezuma Creek, Utah, 1998—. Dist. arts coord., 2004—. Named Utah Tchr. of Yr., 2007. Mem.: Music Educator's Nat. Conf., Utah Music Educator's Assn. (Superior Accomplishment award 2004), Tri-M Honor Soc. (chair). Achievements include being fluent in Navajo. Office: Whitehorse High Sch PO Box 660 Montezuma Creek UT 84534 Home Phone: 801-633-6755; Office Phone: 435-678-1887.

SCHAEFER, M. ELAINE, music educator, conductor; b. Frederick, Okla., Apr. 13, 1945; d. Arthur Lloyd and Mary Ellen Bush; m. Edward T. Vrable, July 28, 2001; children: Joel, Anne Marie, Scott Patrick Gillespie. Student, Diablo Valley Coll., Pleasant Hill, Calif., 1961—63, Chico State Coll., Calif., 1963—64; BA, Calif. State U. Hayward, 1967; MusM, U. Regina, Sask., Can., 1988. Tchrs. cert. Calif., 1967. Instrumental music tchr. Kenilworth Jr. HS, Petaluma, Calif., 1967—72; music tchr. Incline Village HS, Nev., 1972—78; instrumental and choral tchr. Humboldt HS, Sask., Canada, 1978—86; music tchr. Balgonie HS, Sask., Canada, 1988—96; music instr., condr. Coll. Siskiyous, Weed, Calif., 1996—. Adjudicator Sask. Music Festivals, 1985—96; condr. Holy Rosary Cathedral Choir, Regina, Sask., 1987—96, Royal Can. Mounted Police Choir, 1987—89; pres. Sask. Choral Dirs., 1989—90. Bd. mem. Sask. Coun. Cultural Orgns., 1990—96. Sgt. US Army, 1974—78. Recipient award of Appreciation, Sask. Music Educators, 1982; named Tchr. of Yr., Coll. of Siskiyous, 2006, Faculty Mem. of Yr., 2006. Fellow: Nat. Assn. Jazz Educators, Calif. Music Educators Assn., Am. Choral Dirs.; mem.: Internat. Fedn. Choral Music, Assn. Can. Choral Dirs. (bd. mem.), Nat. Assn. Jazz Educators, Calif. Music Educators Assn., Am. Choral Dirs. Roman Catholic. Home: 5925 Mule Deer Ct Weed CA 96094 Office: College Siskiyous 800 College Ave Weed CA 96094 Office Phone: 530-938-5315. Business E-Mail: schaefer@siskiyous.edu.

SCHAEFER, MARILYN LOUISE, artist, writer, educator; b. Cedar Rapids, Iowa, Apr. 22, 1933; d. Henry Richard and Maria Augusta (Dickel) S. AA, Monticello Coll. for Women, 1953; BFA, Cranbrook Acad. Art, 1956, MFA, 1960; MA cum laude, U. Chgo., 1958; MA, St. John's Coll., Santa Fe, 1979. Rsch. asst. editor Encyclopaedia Britannica, Chgo., 1960-63; humanities editor Encyclopedia Americana, NY, 1964-68; acquisitions editor Litton Ednl. Pub., NY, 1968-70; from instr. to prof. emeritus art and advt. design dept. N.Y.C. Tech. Coll. CUNY, 1970—. Contbg. editor Encyclopedia Americana, 1979—, Coll. Teaching jour., 1979. Contbr. articles to profl. jours. including Art and Auction mag., Art and Antiques mag., Am. Artist mag., Encyclopedia Americana, 1970—. Luce Found. postgrad. study fellow St. John's Coll., 1976-79; Ingram Merrill Found. grantee, 1983-84. Mem. AAUW, CUNY Acad. Arts and Scis. Home: 306 W 76th St New York NY 10023-8065 Office: NYC Tech Coll CUNY 300 Jay St Brooklyn NY 11201-1909

SCHAEFER, MARY ANN, health facility administrator, consultant; b. Chgo., May 18, 1942; d. Joseph and Mary A. (Kozyra) Strosnik; m. Robert Earl Schaefer, May 18, 1963; children: Debra Ann, Robert Joseph, James Edward (dec.). Diploma in nursing, St. Francis Hosp. Sch. Nursing, Evanston, Ill., 1962; BA, Nat. Coll. Edn., Evanston, 1980; MBA in Health Svc. Mgmt., Webster U., 1990; MJ in Health Law, Loyola U., Chgo., 1993. Med. and surg. nurse Resurrection Med. Ctr., Chgo., 1962-79, charge nurse labor and delivery, 1978-79; coord. maternal child care Humana, Hoffman Estates, Ill., 1979-81; nurse mgr. labor and delivery Resurrection Med. Ctr., Chgo., 1981-91; mgr. Family Birthplace Resurrection Med. Ctr., Chgo., 1991-98; cons., prin. M/B Assocs.-Consultants Perinatal Healthcare and Edn., Barrington, 1994-98; mgr. Maternal-Child Health Sherman Hosp., Elgin, Ill., 1998-00, dir. women's svcs., 2000—06; dir. bd. Elgin Well Child Ctr., 2002—06; cons. Good Shepherd Hosp., Barrington, Ill., 2006—; nurse Valley Plastic Surgery, West Dundee, 2006—. Seminar leader on childbirth edn., legal issues in nursing; adj. faculty law & ethics Harper Coll. Palatine, Ill. Contbr. to Motor Facilitation Handbook; editorial bd. Essentials publ., Resurrection Med. Ctr. Mem. Assn. Women's Health, Obstetric and Neonatal Nurses (cert. in inpatient obstetric nursing, instr. principles and practice electronic fetal monitoring), Assn. Healthcare Accrediation Profls., Chgo. Health Care Risk Mgmt. Soc. Home: 5806 Prairie Ridge Rd Crystal Lake IL 60014-4601 Personal E-mail: maryannschaefer@aol.com.

SCHAEFER, MARY K., school system administrator; b. Waukesha, Wis., Sept. 1, 1969; d. Richard R. and Jayne Marie Schaefer. BS, U. Wis., LaCrosse, 1992; MA in Tchg., Sacred Heart U., Stamford, Conn., 2004. Cert. tchr. elem. edn. Conn., 2000, responsive classroom I trainer N.E. Found. Children, 2005, intermediate adminstr. Sacred Heart U. Stamford, Conn., 2008. Tchr. St. Mary's, Elm Grove, Wis., 1993—99, Hart Magnet Sch., Stamford, 1999—2006, curriculum assoc. staff devel., 2006—08; curriculum assoc. literacy Stamford Pub. Schs., 2008—. Scorer Conn. Mastery Test, Stamford, 2001—04; mem. grant com. GE Coll. Bound, Stamford, 2004—06. Mentor BEST Prog., Stamford, 2004—. Urban Sch. Leaders fellowship, 2008—09. Mem.: NEA, Nat. Staff Devel. Coun., Nat. Coun. Tchrs. Math., Pi Lamda Theta. Personal E-mail: magerk5@aol.com.

SCHAEFER, PATRICIA, retired librarian; b. Ft. Wayne, Ind., Apr. 23, 1930; d. Edward John and Hildegarde Hartman (Hormel) S. MusB, Northwestern U., 1951; MusM, U. Ill., 1958; AMLS, U. Mich., 1963; DLS (hon.), Ind. Inst. of Tech., 2003. With U.S. Rubber co., Ft. Wayne, 1951-52; sec. to promotion mgr. Sta. WOWO, Ft. Wayne, Ind., 1952, sec. to program mgr., 1953-55; coord. publicity and promotion Home Telephone Co., Ft. Wayne, 1955-56; sec. Fine Arts Found., Ft. Wayne, 1956-57; libr. asst. Columbus (Ohio) Pub. Libr., 1958-59; audio-visual libr. Muncie (Ind.) Pub. Libr., 1959-86, asst. libr. dir., 1981-86, libr. dir., 1986-95; ret. Chmn. Ind. Libr. Film Cir., 1962-63; treas. Ind. Libr. Film Svc., 1969-70, 83-85; mem. libr. adv. coun. Milton S. Eisenhower Libr., Johns Hopkins U.; mem. presdl. counsellors Johns Hopkins U., 1994—; bd. dirs., Franklin Electric Co., 1982-2004, cons., 2004—. Weekly columnist Libr. Lines, Muncie Evening Press, 1981-83; program annotator Muncie Symphony Orch., 1963-2003, Masterworks Chorale, 1982-2003; contbr. articles to profl. jours. Bd. dirs. Muncie Symphony Assn., 1964-74, 85-91, Ctrl. City Bus. Assn., 1986-92; bd. trustees, Ind. Inst. Tech., 1992-, Ind. Humanities Coun., 1996-2002, 05—, Sta. WIPB-TV, 1996-2002, Muncie Ctr. for the Arts, 1999-2001, Nature Conservancy Ind., 2007—; mem. adv. coun. Coll. Fine Arts, Ball State U.; adv. com., bookshop dir. Midwest Writers Workshop, 1976-77; sec. Del. County Coun. for the Arts, 1978-79, pres., 1979-81, bd. dirs., 1985-86; pres.'s coun. Berea Coll., 1990-2001; bd. dirs. Muncie YWCA, 1977-82, 85-89, 95-2001, treas. 1981-82, 88-89; adv. com., Minnetrista Cultural Ctr., 1998-2001; gen. chmn. Ind. Renaissance Fair, 1978-79; pres. Muncie Matinee Musicale, 1965-67; bd. dirs., Cornerstone Ctr. for the Arts, 2006-; past pres. Ind. Film and Video Coun.; adv. bd. Cmty. Found. Muncie and Delaware County; bd. dirs. Wapehani coun. Girl Scouts US, 1989-96, Hoosier Heartland chpt. ARC, 1997-2003, Ball State U. Found., 2006—; bd. dirs. Cardinal Fund, Ball State U., 2007-. Named Woman Achievement Pub. Svc., 1986, Ind. Woman of Yr. Arts, Ball State U., 2008; recipient Sagamore of the Wabash award Gov. State of Ind., Outstanding Libr. award Ind. Libr. Fedn., 1995, Cert. of Congrl. Recognition, 1995, Cert. of Achievement, Women's Coalition, 1996, Cert. of Appreciation, Masterworks Chorale, 1998. Mem. ALA, Ind. Libr. Assn. (pres. 1987-88), Nat. League Am. Pen Women (pres. Muncie br. 1974-78), Altrusa (pres. 1986-87, cmty. svc. award 2000), Art Students League, Del. Country Club, Delta Zeta, Mu Phi Epsilon. Republican. Roman Catholic. Home: 5400 W Deer Run Ct Muncie IN 47304-5775

SCHAEFER, ROBERT WAYNE, banker; b. Balt., Feb. 28, 1934; s. Roland Elmer and Lillian (Reid) S.; m. Elaine Lennon, May 18, 1963; children: Linda, Karen. Student, Balt. City Coll., 1949-51; BS in Acctg., U. Balt., 1955; MBA in Fin., Loyola Coll., 1971. C.P.A., Md. With First Nat. Bank of Md., Balt., 1951-55, 59—, comptroller, 1961—, v.p., 1965-69, sr. v.p., 1969-73, exec. v.p., 1973-96; exec. dir. France-Merrick Founds., Balt., 1996—. Instr. accounting N.C. State Coll., 1956-58; instr. accounting, econs., taxes, credit Balt. chpt. Am. Inst. Banking, 1960-66, chair investment com. State of Md. Retirement System, Baltimore Fire, Police Retirement System, 2000-07. Mem. Balt. City Sch. Bd., 1973-75, Balt. City Bd. Fin.; bd. dirs., treas. Balt. Area United Fund, 1964-79; past bd. dirs. Balt. coun. Boy Scouts Am., Balt. chpt. ARC, Boys Latin Sch.; trustee, pres. Wesley Home for Aged; bd. dirs. Balt. City Aquarium, Roland Park Country Sch., Md. Gen. Hosp., Western Md. Coll., 1981-92, Lyric Theatre, 1985-96, Enoch Pratt Libr., 1986-93, Ind. Coll. Fund Md., 1990—, Coun. on Econ. Edn., YMCA Ctrl. Md., 1992, U. Balt. 1st lt. USMCR, 1956-58. Mem.: Fin. Execs. Inst., Md. CPA Assn., Bank Adminstrn. Inst. (past pres., bd. dirs. Balt. chpt.), U. Balt. Found., U. Balt. Alumni Assn. (bd. dirs. 1972—), Ctr. Club, Johns Hopkins Club, L'Hirondelle Club, Valley Country Club. Republican. Methodist (bd. dirs., mem. finance com.). Home: 5903 Meadowood Rd Baltimore MD 21212-2436 Office: Village of Cross Keys Quadrangle E Ste 302 2 Hamill Rd Baltimore MD 21210-1813 Office Phone: 410-464-2004. Personal E-mail: rwsels@aol.com. Business E-Mail: rschaefer@france-merrickfdn.org.

SCHAEFER, RONALD DEAN, secondary school educator; s. Russell Earl and Jewell Dean Schaefer; m. Jeanette Rozanne Bradshaw, Sept. 1, 1962; children: Ronald David, Christina Ann. BA, So. Ill. U., Edwardsville, 1963; MS, So. Ill. U., Carbondale, 1965, PhD, 1969. Analytic chemist Dow Chemical Co., Midland, Mich., 1969—72; mgr. quality control Dow Diagnostics, Indpls., 1972—77; dir. quality assurance/quality control HYCEL Corp., Houston, 1977—79; rsch. scientist Boehringer-Hennheim Corp., Tustin, Calif., 1979—81; dir. quality assurance/quality control Ciba Corning Diagnostics, Irvine, Calif., 1981—99; educator Santa Ana HS, 1999—. Home: 5 Fulton Irvine CA 92620 Office: 520 W Walnut St Santa Ana CA 92701 Personal E-mail: ronjeanette@hotmail.com, ronald_schaefer@yahoo.com.

SCHAEFFER, CHARLES PERRY, writer, editor; b. Cumberland, Md., Mar. 20, 1926; s. Charles Perry and Dorothy Frances Schaeffer; m. Eliza Ann Riggins, June 16, 1950; children: Sally Ann Canepa, John, Jennifer Bartell. BA, U. Md., 1950. Writer U.S. Info. Agy., Washington, 1950—53; news picture writer UPI, NYC, 1953—54; reporter Balt. Evening Sun, 1954—55, Am. Aviation Publs., Md., 1955—61; sci. writer Newhouse Newspapers, Washington, 1961—65; writer, exec. editor Kiplinger Personal Fin. Mag. (formerly Changing Times) Kiplinger Washington Editors, Inc, 1966—89. Mem. profit sharing bd. Kiplinger Washington Editors. Contbg. author: anthology Esquire's World of Humor, 1964, Saturday Review's Phoenix Nest, 1965; author: short mystery fiction, 2002—; contbr. articles to mags. Chmn. scout troop Walter Reed Army Med. Ctr., Silver Spring, Md., 1971—72; pres Neighborhood Civic Assn., Silver Spring, 1963—64; bd. dirs. Woodlin Elem. Sch., Silver Spring, 1963—64. EM 3/C USN, 1943—46, PTO. Decorated Phillippine Liberation Ribbon, 2 Stars USN, Pacific Theater Ribbon, Six Stars, Victory medal, Am. Theater ribbon; recipient Blakeslee Nat. Sci. Writing award, Am. Heart Assn., 1965. Mem.: Soc. Profl. Journalists, Nat. Assn. Sci. Writers (life), Nat. Press Club (1st pl. consumer journalism 1987). Home: 6036 Chatsworth Ln Bethesda MD 20814

SCHAEFFER, ERIC D., theater director, performing company executive; b. 1964; BFA, Kutztown U.; continued studies, Crew and Alsager Coll. Visual Arts, Eng. Co-founder, artistic dir. Signature Theatre, Arlington, Va., 1990—; artistic dir. Sondheim Celebration Kennedy Ctr., Washington, 2002, founder Overtures musical theatre inst., 2003. Dir.: (plays) Sweeney Todd, 1991 (Helen Hayes award for Outstanding Musical and Dir., 1992), 2002, Assasins, 1992 (Helen Hayes award for Outstanding Musical and Dir., 1993), Into the Woods, 1994 (Helen Hayes award for Outstanding Musical, 1995), Cabaret, 1995, Passion, 1996 (Helen Hayes award for Outstanding Musical and Dir., 1997), 2002, Sunday in the Park with George, 1997, 2002, Sweet Adeline, 1997, A Little Night Music, 1997, The Rhythm Club, 1998, 2000, Putting It Together, 1998, Witches of Eastwick, 2000, The Gospel According to Fishman, 2002, 110 in the Shade, 2003, Follies, 2003, The Christmas Carol Rag, 2003, Twentieth Century, 2003, Allegro, 2004 (Helen Hayes award for Outstanding Musical and Dir., 2005), One Red Flower, 2004, The Highest Yellow, 2004, Pacific Overtures, 2005; (Broadway plays) Putting It Together, 1999, Glory Days, 2008. Recipient Elizabeth Campbell award for Arts in Arlington, Honored Citizen award, Arlington Sch. Bd., Jonathan Larson Performing Arts Found. award, Profl. Mentor prize, Duke Ellington Sch. Arts; named a Washingtonian of Yr., 2002. Office: Signature Theatre 4200 Campbell Ave Arlington VA 22206 Office Phone: 571-527-1860. Office Fax: 703-845-0236.

SCHAEFFER, LEONARD DAVID, health insurance company executive; b. Chgo., July 28, 1945; s. David and Sarah (Levin) Schaeffer; m. Pamela Lee Sidford, Aug. 11, 1968; children: David, Jacqueline. BA, Princeton U., 1969. Mgmt. cons. Arthur Andersen & Co., 1969—73; dep. dir. mgmt. Ill. Mental Health/Devel. Disability, Springfield, 1973—75; dir. Ill. Bur. of Budget, Springfield, 1975—76; v.p. Citibank, N.A., NYC, 1976—78; asst. sec. mgmt. and budget HHS, Washington, 1978, adminstr. HCFA, 1978—80; exec. v.p., COO Student Loan Mktg. Assn., Washington, 1980—82; pres., CEO Group Health, Inc., Mpls., 1983—86; chmn., CEO Blue Cross of Calif., Woodland Hills, 1986—96, WellPoint Health Networks Inc., Thousand Oaks, Calif., 1992—2004; chmn. WellPoint Inc., 2004—05; sr. advisor Tex. Pacific Group, 2006—. Bd. dirs. Allergan, Inc., Irvine, Calif., 1993—, AMGEN Inc., Thousand Oaks, 2004—, Quintiles Transnational Corp., 2008—; bd. councilors U. So. Calif. Sch. Policy, Planning & Devel., 1988—; bd. dirs., exec. com. Blue Cross-Blue Shield Assn., Chgo., 1986—2004; mem. Congl. Prospective Payment Assessment Commn., 1987—93, Pew Health Professions Com., Phila., 1990—93; chmn. bd. trustees Nat. Health Found., LA, 1992—2001; chmn. bd. dirs. Nat. Inst. Health Care Mgmt., 1993—2006; co-chair adv. coun. dept. health care policy Harvard Med. Sch., 1998—2003, bd. fellows, 2003—; founding chmn. Coalition for Affordable and Quality Healthcare, 2000; regents lectr. U. Calif., Berkeley, Calif., 2005—06; sr. advisor Tex. Pacific Group, 2006—; chmn. Surg. Care Affiliates, Birmingham, Ala., 2007—; Judge Robert Maclay Widney chair and prof. U. Southern Calif., 2008. Bd. govs. Town Hall, LA, 1989—2006; trustee The Brookings Inst., Nat. Health Mus., 2000—; adv. coun. Dept. Econs. Princeton U., NJ; adv. group Coun. on Health Care Econs. and Policy. Recipient Citation for Outstanding Svc., Am. Acad. Pediat., 1981, Disting. Pub. Svc. award, HEW, Washington, 1980; fellow, Kellogg Found., 1981—89; Internat. fellow, King's Fund Coll., London, 1990—. Mem.: Am. Assn. Health Plans (bd. dirs. 2001—04), Health Ins. Assn. Am. (chmn. 1999), Inst. Medicine NAS, Regency Club, Princeton Club, Cosmos Club. Office: 1733 Ocean Ave Ste 325 Santa Monica CA 90404 E-mail: lds@northbp.com.

SCHAEFFER, PETER (PETER VIKTOR SCHAEFFER), urban and regional planning educator; b. Zurich, Switzerland, Aug. 26, 1949; s. Victor and Catharina M. (Sciuchetti) S.; m. Patricia Marie Dresler, June 1, 1976; 1 child, Joseph Victor. Licenciate in Econ., U. Zurich, 1975; MA in Econs., U. So. Calif., 1979, PhD in Econs., 1981. Asst. prof. urban and regional planning U. Ill., Urbana, 1981-88; assoc. prof. U. Colo., Denver, 1987-93, dir. urban and regional planning, 1988-93; prof., dir. divsn. resource mgmt. W.Va. U., Morgantown, 1993—2006, dir., divsn. family consumer scis., 2004—06. Vis. prof. Swiss Federal Inst. of Technology, Zurich, 1999-2000. Mem. editl. bd. Jour. Planning Edn. and Rsch., 1989-2006, Internat. Regional Sci. Rev., Jour. Planning Lit., 1996-, The Open Urban Studies Jour., 2007-, Inst. Info. Sys. and Social Change, 2009-; contbr. chpts. to books, articles to profl. jours. and books. Plan commr. City of Urbana, 1984-87; bd. dirs. Internat. Ctr. for Tourism Planning and Design, Denver, 1993-96; bd. dirs. Lightstone Found., Moyers, W.Va., 1995—2004, pres., 1997—2004. Mem. Am. Econ. Assn., Regional Sci. Assn. (treas. 1987-97), Southern Regional Sci. Assn. (pres. 2008-09). Avocations: literature, history, hiking. Office: W Va U Div Resource Mgmt PO Box 6108 Morgantown WV 26506-6108 E-mail: Peter.Schaeffer@mail.wvu.edu.

SCHAEFFLER, GEORG, lawyer, manufacturing executive; b. Oct. 19, 1964; s. Maria-Elisabeth Schaeffler. Lic. oec. HSG, U. of St. Gallen, Switzerland, 1990; JD cum laude, Duke U., LL.M. in International and Comparative Law, 1999. Bar: Texas 2000. With INA Schaeffler Group, Herzogenaurach, Germany, 1990—96, owner, 1996—; assoc. fin. and internat. groups Haynes and Boone LLP, Dallas, 2000—. 1st Lt. German Air Force reserves, 1984—86. Named one of World's Richest People, Forbes Mag., 2003—. Mem.: ABA. Office: Haynes and Boone LLP Ste 3100 901 Main St Dallas TX 75202-3789

SCHAEFFLER, MARIA-ELISABETH, manufacturing executive, small business owner; b. Prague, Czech Republic; m. Georg Schaeffler (dec. 1996); 1 child, Georg. Student, Vienna U. Med. Sch. Owner INA-Holding Schaeffler KG, 1996—, ptnr., chmn. adv. bd., 2005—. Chair advisory bd. Dresdner Bank. Mng. bd. Nuremberg Society of Opera Friends; honorary mem. of the university coun. Friedrich Alexander U., Erlangen-Nuremberg, 2002—; curator Region Nuremberg e.V.; mem. university coun. U. Hanover, 2004—06; adminstrv. bd. Germanisches Nationalmuseum; exec. com. Opernfreunde Nuremberg e.V. Recipient Steckkreuz award, 1996, German Cross of Merit with Ribbon, 2001, Bavarian Order of Merit, 2003, Family Entrepreneur of Yr., Impulse Mag. & Intes Akademie für Familienunternehmen, 2004; named hon. citizen of Hochstadt an der Aisch, Germany, 2002, hon. citizen Herzogenaurach, 2006; named one of World's Richest People, Forbes Mag., 2003—; named to Golden Book of dist. Erlangen-Höchstadt, Germany, 2006. Mem.: Nuremberg C. of C. (steering com. 2001—, Medal of Honor 2001). Transylvania Univ. of Brasov (hon.; apptd. by rector, Prof. Ion Visa 2005—). Achievements include being the first woman elected to Nuremberg C. of C. steering com. Avocation: opera. Office: INA-Holding Schaeffler KG Industriestraße 1-3 91074 Herzogenaurach Germany

SCHAELICKE, LAMBERT, computer engineer; s. Dieter and Iris Schaelicke; m. Rita Penza; children: Indri L., Matti L. PhD, U. Utah, Salt Lake City, 2001. Asst. prof., dept. computer sci. and engring. U. Notre Dame, Ind., 2001—05; staff engr. Intel Corp., Ft. Collins, Colo., 2005—. Recipient Tchg. award, U. Notre Dame, Dept. Computer Sci. and Engring., 2002; SPANIDS grant, NSF, 2002—05. Mem.: IEEE. Achievements include design of high-speed network intrusion detection system.

SCHAFER, ANDREW I., hematologist, department chairman; b. Budapest, Hungary; married; 3 children. MD, U. Pa., Phila. Cert. in hematology, internal medicine, oncology. Resident U. Chgo.; fellow in hematology Brigham and Women's Hosp.; asst. prof. medicine Harvard U. Med. Sch., 1981—87, assoc. prof. medicine, 1987—89; chief hematology and oncology West Roxbury VA Hosp., Brockton VA Hosp., Mass., 1984—89; prof. medicine, assoc. dean Baylor U. Sch. Medicine, Houston, 1989—98; chmn. dept. medicine, chief internal medicine svc. The Meth. Hosp., Houston, 1998—2002; chmn. dept. medicine U. Pa. Sch. Medicine, 2002—07, Weill Cornell Med. Coll., NYC, 2007—, E. Hugh Luckey Disting. prof. medicine, 2007—; physician-in-chief NY-Presbyn. Hosp. Weill Cornell Med. Ctr., 2007—. Adj. prof. biomed. engring. Rice U., Tex.; prin. investigator NIH; bd. extramural advisors Nat. Heart, Lung and Blood Inst.; bd. dirs. Assn. Professors of Medicine; pres. Am. Soc. Hematology, 2007; pres. elect Assoc. Profs. Medicine, 2009—. Founding editor-in-chief: The Hematologist, mem. editl. bd.: Platelets, Circulation, Jour. Cardiovascular Risk, Am. Jour. the Med. Scis., Am. Jour. Medicine, Annual Rev. Medicine, Current Medicinal Chemistry; contbr. articles to profl. jours., chapters to books. Recipient Milton Fund award, Harvard U. Med. Sch., 1984; named Established Investigator, Am. Heart Assn. Fellow: Am. Heart Assn. Coun. on Arteriosclerosis, Thrombosis and Vascular Biology; mem.: Assn. Am. Physicians, Am. Soc. Clin. Investigation. Office: Office of the Chmn NY Presbyn Hosp Weill Cornell Med Coll 530 E 70th St M 522 New York NY 10021 Office Phone: 212-746-4720. Office Fax: 212-746-8793.

SCHAFER, BETTE JANE, education educator; m. John Charles Schafer, Aug. 17, 1973; children: J'Lynne Mundle, J'Nelle Lee. PhD in Curriculum and Instrn., U. Mo., Columbia, 2004. Prof. edn. Hannibal-LaGrange Coll., Mo., 1989—. Chair edn. divsn., dir. tchr. edn., dir. grad. studies Hannibal-LaGrange Coll., 1993—. Mem.: Delta Kappa Gamma Soc. Internat. Office: Hannibal-LaGrange Coll 2800 Palmyra Rd Hannibal MO 63401 Office Phone: 573-629-3108. Business E-Mail: bscha@hlg.edu.

SCHAFER, CHARLES J., communications systems company executive; Various sr. fin. mgmt. positions Hazeltine Corp., 1969—84; various positions Loral Corp., 1984—96; pres. Tactical Def. Systems Divsn. Lockheed Martin; v.p. bus. ops. L-3 Comm. Holdings, Inc., NYC, 1998, COO, pres. Products Group, 1999—, sr. v.p., 2002—. Office: L-3 Comm Holdings Inc 600 Third Ave New York NY 10016 Office Phone: 212-697-1111. Office Fax: 212-805-5477.

SCHAFER, ED (EDWARD THOMAS SCHAFER), former United States Secretary of Agriculture, former Governor of North Dakota; b. Bismarck, ND, Aug. 8, 1946; s. Harold and Marian (Nelsen) Schafer; m. Nancy Kegel Jones, 1992; children: Edward Thomas Jr., Ellie Sue; stepchildren: Eric Jones, Kari Jones. BSBA, U. N.D., 1969; MBA, Denver U., 1970. Quality control inspector Gold Seal, 1971-73, v.p., 1974, chmn. mgmt. com., 1975-78, pres., 1978-85; owner/dir. H&S Distbn., 1976—97; pres. Dakota Classics, 1986—, TRIESCO Properties, 1986—, Fish 'N Dakota, 1990-94; gov. State of N.D., Bismarck, 1992—2000; co-founder, CEO Extend America, Bismarck, 2002—08; sec. USDA, Washington, 2008—09. Chair Midwest Governors Assn., 1995, Interstate Oil & Gas Compact Commn., 1995, We. Governors Assn., 1997, Econ. Devel. Com., Nat. Governors Assn., 1999, Rep. Governors Assn., 2000; co-founder, co-chair Governors Biotechnology Partnership, 2000. Chmn. N.D. Micro Bus. Mktg. Alliance; pres. N.D. Heritage Group; adv. coun. Distributive Edn. Clubs of Am.; lectr. Hugh O'Brien Leadership Found.; counselor Junior Achievement; dir. Bismarck Recreation Coun.; trustee Missouri Valley Family YMCA; plankowner USS Theodore Roosevelt; ann. support com. Medcenter One Found.; mem. Bismarck State Coll. Found., bd. mem. U. ND Alumni Found., 2005-08. Mem. NRA, Theodore Roosevelt Assn. (Theodore Roosevelt Medora Found., United Sportsman of N.D., U. N.D. Pres. Club, U. Mary Pres. Club, Bismarck-Mandan Rotary. Republican. Lutheran.

SCHAFER, ELIZABETH DIANE, historian, writer; b. Opelika, Ala., Sept. 26, 1965; d. Robert Louis and Carolyn Louise (Henn) S. BA in History cum laude, Auburn U., 1986, MA in History of Sci., 1988, PhD in History of Tech. magna cum laude, 1993; MA summa cum laude, Hollins Coll., 2003; MFA summa cum laude, Hollins U. Archivist Lee County Hist. Soc. Mus., 1988—. Ind. scholar, 1993—; presenter in field. Author: Exploring Harry Potter, 2000, Lake Martin: Alabama's Crown Jewel, 2002, Auburn: Plainsmen, Tigers and War Eagles, 2003, Auburn Football, 2004; co-author: Women Who Made A Difference in Alabama, 1995, (hist. overview) Alabama Veterinary Medical Assocation Celebrating 100 Years 1907-2007, 2007; cons. editor Ency. of Sci., 1998; freelance editor various tech. docs.; editl. asst. Proceedings of the We. Soc. for French History, 1988-91, Nat. Forum: The Phi Kappa Phi Jour., 1990-91; contbr. History News Svc.; reviewer Children's Lit. database; contbr. articles to profl. jours., encys., mags., chpts. to books. Recipient hon. mention poetry Writer's Digest, 1994 hon. mention children's non-fiction, 1997, children's non-fiction and fiction, 1998, Writer's Digest, Shirley Henn Meml. award Critical scholar, Hollins Coll., 1998. Mem. AAAS, AAUW, Am. Hist. Assn., Orgn. Am. Historians, Soc. History Tech., History Sci. Soc., Women's History Network, N.Y. Acad. Scis., So. Hist. Assn., Soc. Children's Book Writers and Illustrators, Children's Lit. Network, Ala. Poetry Soc., Children's Lit. Assn., Ala. Writer's Forum, Authors Guild, Mystery Writers Am., Lancaster Mennonite Hist. Soc., Lee County Hist. Soc. (life mem.), Auburn U. Alumni Assn. (life), Descs. Mex. War Vets., DAR (chpt. historian), Mystery writers of America, Phi Alpha Theta. Home and Office: PO Box 57 Loachapoka AL 36865-0057 Personal E-mail: Elizabeth_D_Schafer@yahoo.com.

SCHAFER, GERALD LEWIS (JAY SCHAFER), library director; b. El Paso, Tex., Apr. 20, 1949; s. Norman Oscar and Clarice Schafer. BA, U. Tex., El Paso, 1971; MLS, U. Denver, 1973. Info. specialist Denver Rsch. Inst., 1973-75; area mgr. Denver Pub. Libr., 1975-80; dir. profl. communications Skidmore, Owings & Merrill, Denver, 1981-84; coord. collection devel. svcs. to asst. dir. for rsch. svcs. Auraria Libr., Denver, 1984—97; dir. libr. and info. svcs. Hatch Library, Bay Path Coll., Longmeadow, 1997—2000; coord. collection devel. U. Mass., Amherst, 2000—04, interim dir. librs., 2004—05, dir. librs., 2005—. Chair collections task force Colo. State Libr., Denver, 1993—94; v.p., pres. elect Mgmt. Coun. Boston Libr. Consortium, 2006—. Mem.: ALA, Colo. Libr. Assn. Avocation: architecture. Office: Dir Librs U Mass Amherst Amherst MA 01003-9275 Office Phone: 413-545-0284. E-mail: jschafer@library.umass.edu.

SCHAFER, JACQUELINE ELLEN, federal agency administrator; b. Greenport, NY; AB, Middlebury Coll., 1967. Analyst, rsch. asst. Fed. Reserve Bank NY, 1967—70; legis. asst. to Sen. James L. Buckley U.S. Senate, 1971—76; asst. sec. installations and environ. U.S. Navy; regional adminstr. region 2 U.S. Environ. Protection Agy., 1982—93; dir. Calif. Dept. Fish and Game, 1993—99, Ariz. Dept. Environ. Quality, 1999—2002; dep. asst. adminstr. bur. econ. growth US Agy. Internat. Devel. (USAID), 2002—05, asst. adminstr. for econ. growth agrl. & trade, 2005—. Office: US Agy Internat Devel (USAID) 1300 Pennsylvania Ave NW Washington DC 20523*

SCHAFER, JAMES ARTHUR, physiologist; b. Buffalo, Oct. 10, 1941; s. Joseph James and Gladys Lita (Lighty) S.; m. Margaret Anne Schiefer, Aug. 16, 1964; children: James Arthur Jr., Kirsten Ann. BS, U. Mich., 1963, PhD, 1968. Postdoctoral fellow Gustav-Embden Ctr., Frankfurt, Germany, 1968-69, Duke U., Durham, NC, 1969-70; asst. prof. U. Ala., Birmingham, 1970-72, assoc. prof., 1972-76, prof., 1976—2004, prof. emeritus, 2004—, sr. scientist Nephrology Rsch. and Tng. Ctr. Birmingham, 1980—. Author: (with H. Valtin) Renal Function. Mechanisms Preserving Fluid and Solute Balance in Health, 3d edit., 1994; editor Am. Jour. Physiology: Renal, 1983-89, mem. editl. bd., 2001-07; assoc. editor News in Physiol. Scis., 1997-03; cons. editor Jour. Clin. Investigation, 1998-03; mem. editl bd. Jour. Gen. Physiology, 1979-97, adv. editor, 1998-2007; mem. editl. bd. Kidney Internat., 1990-95; author textbooks on physiology; editor sci. monographs in Membrane Transport in Biology, 1992, Methods in Membrane and Transporter Research, 1994; contbr. articles to profl. jours. Chmn. rsch. com. Nat. Kidney and Urol. Diseases Adv. Bd. U.S. Dept. HHS, 1987-90. Fellow Jane Coffin Childs Meml., 1968-69; recipient Robert F. Pitts. Meml. award Internat. Union Physiol. Scis., Sydney, Australia, 1983, Homer W. Smith award Am. Soc. Nephrology and NY Heart Assn., 1993, Max Planck-Von Humboldt Rsch. award, Govt. of Germany, 1994. Mem. Am. Physiol. Soc. (councilor 1992-95, pres.-elect 1995-96, pres. 1996-97, past pres. 1997-98, Carl W. Gottschalk award 2001, Robert W. Berliner award 2004), Am. Soc. Nephrology (sec.-treas. 1989-92, councilor 1992-95), Am. Soc. Clin. Investigation (hon.), Fedn. Am. Socs. Exptl. Biology (bd. dirs. 1995-99, exec. com. 1996-97, pub. affairs exec. com. 1997-99), Am. Heart Assn. (Established Investigator award, 1971-76), Biophys. Soc., Int. Soc. Nephrol., Soc. Gen. Physiol. Avocations: classical music, mountain hiking, skiing. Office: U Ala Dept Phys & Biophysics 834 MCLM Bldg 1918 University Blvd Birmingham AL 35294-0005 Office Phone: 205-934-7106.

SCHAFER, JOHN STEPHEN, poet; b. NYC, Sept. 5, 1934; s. Stephen James and Siiri (Halmi) S.; m. Gertrud Rosa Fleischmann, June 14, 1958; children: Sylvia F., John Stephen, Karen D., Kristen H. BA, Rutgers U., 1956, MBA, 1963. Advt. research mgr. Union Carbide Corp., NYC, 1959—65; rsch. mgr. Bus. Week, NYC, 1965—66; v.p. Opinion Rsch. Corp., Princeton, NJ, 1966—80; pres. Am. Econ. Found., Cleve., 1981—2002, trustee, 1975—2002; v.p., dir. Ams. for Competitive Enterprise System, Phila., 1970-82. Editor: Linde Electric Welding Progress, 1959-62, ORC Pub. Opinion Index, 1968-72, AEF Straight Talk, 1981-82, Bellcore Exch., 1993-94; works pub. in Famous Poems of the Twentieth Century, 1996, Perceptions in Harmony, 1998, The Communicator, 2000-08, Best Poems and Poets of 2003, 2004, others. Polit. pollster Ed Clark for U.S. Pres., 1980; chmn. N.J. Libertarian party, 1983; nat. dir. U.S. Jaycees, 1965-66, v.p. N.J., 1964-65. Served to 1st lt. U.S. Army, 1957-59. Mem. Jr. Chamber Internat. (hon. life), Philosophean Soc., Scabbard and Blade, Delta Phi Alpha Presbyterian. Home: 114 Walton Palm Rd Panama City FL 32413-7311 Home Phone: 850-231-3108.

SCHAFER, MARIE, nurse, educator; d. Eric Martelly and Jacqueline Gabriel; m. Raymond Schafer, July 19, 1997. BA, Fla. Internat. U., Miami, 1994; BSN, Barry U., Miami Shores, Fla., 1997, MSN, 2003. Acting nurse mgr. Miami VA Healthcare Sys., 1998—2001, staff nurse, 2001—03, 2003—04, nurse educator, 2003—. Cons. William Sterns & Assoc., Miami, 2003—04; case mgr. Home Health Agy., Miami, 2003—04. Editor (editor-in-chief): (newsletter) Nightingale News; contbr. articles to profl. jours. Named Excellence Award in Tchg. finalist, Nursing Spectrum, 2006. Mem.: Am. Soc. Parenteral Enteral Nutrition, Am. Holistic Nurses' Assn., Fla. Nurses Assn., Sierra Club. Office: Miami VA Healthcare Sys 1201 NW 16th St Miami FL 33125 Home Fax: 18772160328. Personal E-mail: mariem@gate.net. E-mail: marie.schafer@med.va.gov.

SCHAFER, ROBERT LOUIS, agricultural engineer, researcher; b. Burlington, Iowa, Aug. 1, 1937; s. Marion Louis and Pansy (Head) S.; m. Carolyn Louise Henn, Aug. 1, 1959; 1 child, Elizabeth Diane. BS, Iowa State U., 1959, MS, 1961, PhD, 1965. Agrl. engr. Agrl. Rsch. Svc., USDA, Ames, Iowa, 1959-64, Auburn, Ala., 1964-95. Co-author: Advances in Soil Dynamics, 1994; contbr. articles to profl. jours. Fellow Am. Soc. Agrl. Engrs. (McCormick Case Gold medal 1997). Home: PO Box 189 Loachapoka AL 36865-0189 E-mail: rls1955@gmail.com.

SCHAFER, RONALD WILLIAM, electrical engineering educator; b. Tecumseh, Nebr., Feb. 17, 1938; s. William Henry and Esther Sophia Schafer; m. Dorothy Margaret Hall, June 2, 1960; children: William R., John C. (dec.), Katherine L., Barbara Anne. Student, Doane Coll., Crete, Nebr., 1956-59; BEE, U. Nebr., 1961, MEE, 1962; PhD in Elec. Engring., MIT, 1968. Tech. staff Bell Labs., Murray Hill, NJ, 1968-74; John and Marilu McCarty prof. elec. engring. Ga. Inst. Tech., Atlanta, 1974—2004, Inst. prof., 1991—2004, emeritus prof., 2004—; HP fellow Hewlett-Packard Labs., Palo Alto, Calif., 2004—. Chmn. bd. Atlanta Signal Processors Inc., 1983-2001. Co-author: Digital Signal Processing, 1974, Digital Processing of Speech Signals, 1979, Speech Analysis, 1979, Discrete-Time Signal Processing, 1989, 2d edit., 1999, Computer-Based Exercises for Signal Processing Using Matlab, 1995, DSP First: A Multimedia Approach, 1998, Signal Processing First, 2003. Recipient Class of 34 Disting. Prof. award Ga. Inst. Tech., 1985. Fellow IEEE (Emanuel R. Piore award 1980, Edn. medal 1992, 3d millennium award 2000), Acoustical Soc. Am.; mem. IEEE Processing Soc. (soc. award 1982, edn. award 2000), Nat. Acad. Engring. Democrat. Office: Hewlett-Packard Labs 1501 Page Mill Rd Palo Alto CA 94304 Office Phone: 650-857-4142.

SCHAFER, SHARON MARIE, anesthesiologist; b. Detroit, Mar. 23, 1948; d. Charles Anthony and Dorothy Emma (Schweitzer) Pokriefka; m. Timothy John Schafer, Nov. 12, 1977; children: Patrick Christopher, Steven Michael. BS in Biology, Wayne State U., 1971, MD, 1975; MBA in Practice Mgmt., Madonna U., 2000. Diplomate Am. Bd. Anesthesiology. Intern, resident Sinai Hosp. Detroit, 1975-78; pvt. practice anesthesiology Troy, Mich., 1988—. Mem. AMA, Am. Soc. Anesthesiologists. Roman Catholic. Home and Office: 5741 Folkstone Dr Troy MI 48085-3154 Office Phone: 248-879-6246. E-mail: sharschafer@att.net.

SCHAFERMEYER, ROBERT WILLIAM, emergency physician, educator, health policy consultant; b. St. Louis, Jan. 9, 1948; s. William Jacob and Virginia Rose S.; m. An-ping Yuan, May 12, 1973; children: Christina, David, Matthew, Joseph. Student, St. Louis U., 1966-69; MD, U. Mo., 1973. Diplomate Am. Bd. Emergency Medicine, Am. Bd. Pediats., sub-bd. pediat. emergency medicine. With. dept. emergency medicine East Tenn. Children's Hosp., Knoxville, 1979—81; mem. dept. emergency medicine Carolinas Med. Ctr., Charlotte, NC, 1981—; clin. assoc. prof. pediats. U. N.C. Sch. Medicine, Chapel Hill, 1981-85, clin. prof. emergency medicine and pediats., 1994—; assoc. chair dept. emergency medicine Carolinas Med. Ctr., Charlotte, 1982—, chief dept., 2007—. Dir. E.D. Cons. and Lectrs., Charlotte, 90—. Assoc. editor: Pediatric Emergency Medicine Concepts and Clinical Practice, 1992; editor: Pediatric Emergency Medicine: A Comprehensive Study Guide, 1995, 2002, 3rd edit., 2009; contbr. articles and revs. to profl. jours. including Annals Emergency Medicine Jour.; reviewer Pediat. Emergency Medicine, Acad. Emergency Medicine; past mem. editl. bd. Pediat. Emergency Med. Jour. Com. mem. MEMAC Adv., Mecklenberg County, 1991-93; mem. task force Drug Abuse for County Commrs., Mecklenberg, 1989-90. Lt. commdr. USPHS, 1974—76. EMS-C grantee Maternal and Child Health, 1992-94. Fellow Am. Coll. Emergency Physicians (bd. dirs. 1994-2002, pres.-elect 1999-2000, pres. 2000-01, past pres. 2001-02, Weigenstein Outstanding Leadership award 2004); mem. Am. Acad. Pediats., NC chpt. Am. Coll. Emergency Physicians (councillor 1984-94, bd. dirs. 1983-89, pres. 1986-88, Leadership/Svc. award 1988, George Podgorny Emergency Medicine Svc. award 1996), Soc. Acad. Emergency Medicine (bd. dirs. 2004-07), Mecklenburg County Med. Soc. (bd. dirs. 2009-). Roman Catholic. Avocations: tae kwon do, photography, skiing. Office: Carolinas Med Ctr 1000 Blythe Blvd Charlotte NC 28203-5812 Office Phone: 704-355-3181.

SCHAFF, HARTZELL VERNON, cardiac surgeon; b. Holdenville, Okla., Feb. 24, 1948; s. Hartzell Vernon and Ruth N. (Stuckey) S.; m. Voni Faith Schafer, Mar. 3, 1973; children: Brynn, Leslie, Sarah, Matthew. Student U. Okla., 1966-69, MD, 1973. Diplomate Am. Bd. Surgery, Am. Bd. Thoracic Surgery. Intern dept. surgery Johns Hopkins Hosp., Balt., 1973-74, asst. resident, 1974-75, fellow cardiovascular surg. rsch. lab., 1975-76, sr. asst. resident, 1976-78, resident cardiac and thoracic surgery, 1978-80; cons. thoracic and cardiovascular surgery, Mayo Med. Sch., Rochester, Minn., 1980—, asst. prof. surgery, 1980-85, assoc. prof., 1985-92, co-dir. cardiovascular surg. rsch. lab., 1985—, prof. surgery, 1992-94, Stuart W. Harrington prof. surgery, 1994—, chair divsn. cardiovascular surgery. Mem. editl. bd. Jour. Thoracic and Cardiovascular Surgery; contbr. articles to profl. jours., chpts. to books. Recipient L.G. Moorman award, 1973; George D. Zuidema Resident Rsch. award, 1980; Fulbright Vis. Prof. Cardiac Surgery, 1986, 87. Fellow ACS, Am. Coll. Cardiology, Assn. for Acad. Surgery, Am. Heart Assn., Soc. Univ. Surgeons, Soc. Thoracic Surg. Edn.; mem. AMA, Am. Assn. Clin. Anatomists, Internat. Assn. Cardia Biol. Implants, Priestley Soc., Johns Hopkins Med. And Surg. Assn., Sigma Xi, Phi Eta Sigma, Alpha Omega Alpha. Republican. Episcopalian. Home: 433 19th Ave SW Rochester MN 55902-2923 Office: Mayo Clinic 200 1st St SW Rochester MN 55905-0002 Office Phone: 507-284-2511. Office Fax: 507-284-0161.

SCHAFF, MANYA, foundation administrator; b. Chgo., Mar. 12, 1931; d. Louis Lipkin and Allene Ewing; m. Jay Barash Schaff, Mar. 25, 1951 (div. Jan. 20, 1971); children: Pamela Beth, William Franz Kim, Elizabeth Aline; m. Dimitri Polonsky, PhD, June 27, 1971 (div. Dec. 14, 2000). MusB, Northwestern U., 1953. Tchr. Carnegie-Mellon U., Pitts., 1961—65, Chatham Coll., Pitts., 1964—71, Immaculate Heart Coll., LA, 1972—79; instr. UCLA, 1973—79; program dir. Performing Tree, Inc., LA, 1982—88; program officer The Ahmanson Found., Beverly Hills, Calif., 1988—; tchr., performer Shady Side Acad., Pitts., 1968—71. Panelist L.A. Cultural Affairs Dept., 1983—85, L.A. Ednl. Partnership, Small Grants to Teachers, 1988—98; sr. facilitator Inst. for the Arts, Pitts. Pub. Schs., Pitts., 1985; bd. dir. Vista Del Mar Child Care, LA, 1979—82. Editor: Piano for Two Directory. Bd. dirs. Chamber Music Soc. of L.A., 1990—95. Recipient Drawing prize, Assoc. Artists Pitts., 1963, Pennational Artists Annual, 1964, Fiber Art prize, Annual Ehrman Mansion Show, 1977. Mem.: Pi Kappa Lambda (life), Sigma Alpha Iota (life). Democrat. Home: 2139 Roscomare Rd Los Angeles CA 90077 Office: The Ahmanson Found 9215 Wilshire Blvd Beverly Hills CA 90210 Personal E-mail: mschaff@mindspring.com.

SCHAFFER, DAVID EDWIN, retired systems administrator; b. Nov. 3, 1929; s. Karl and Jeanette (Gotthelf) S.; m. Ariel Williams Sullivan, May 3, 1951 (dec. Dec. 2004) stepchildren: Adrienne Sullivan Smith, James W. Sullivan; m. Patricia Owen, Feb. 25, 2006; stepchildren: Christopher Owen, Patricia Taylor. Student, Wharton Sch. of U. Pa., 1948-49; BA, New Sch. for Social Rsch., 1959. Spl. edn. tchr. of emotionally disturbed children various schs. and hosps., 1954-65; br. mgr. 1st Westchester Nat. Bank, New Rochelle, NY, 1965-66; v.p. Longines-Symphonette Inc.; spl. asst. to chmn. bd. Longines Wittnauer Inc., Larchmont, NY, 1966-72; pvt. practice mgmt. cons. Franconia, NH,

1973-77; v.p., dir. ops. Carroll Reed Ski Shops, Inc., 1978-80; ret. Instr. econs. Am. Inst. Banking, 1965-66. Moderator, Town of Franconia, 1973-2005; founding trustee emeritus Frost Pl., 1975—; bd. dirs. White Mountain Community Svcs., 1973-77; bd. dirs., past pres. No. N.H. Mental Health Services, 1975-77. Prodr.: numerous record albums. Vol., bd. dirs. Hospice of the Littleton Area, Jansen Hospice; mem. com. St. Mathews Chapel, Sugar Hill, N.H. With Signal Corps, AUS, 1951-53. Mem. Direct Mail Credit Assn. Am. (founding mem.), Asso. Retail Credit Men of N.Y.C., Direct Mail Assn. Am. (past chmn. subcom. on consumer affairs and regulatory agys.), Profile Club (pres., dir.). Democrat. Episcopalian. Home: 21 River Rd Franconia NH 03580

SCHAFFER, DAVID IRVING, lawyer; b. NYC, Oct. 17, 1935; s. Frank and Edith (Montlack) S.; m. Lois Ann Warshauer, June 16, 1957; children: Susan Edith (dec.), Eric Michael. BA, U. Pa., 1956; LL.B., Harvard U., 1959. Bar: N.Y. 1960. Assoc. Shearman & Sterling, NYC, 1960-65; sec., counsel Yale Express System, Inc., NYC, 1965-66; sr. v.p., gen. counsel, sec. Avis, Inc., Garden City, NY, 1966-83; v.p., gen. counsel U.S. Surgical Corp., Norwalk, Conn., 1983-86; of counsel Meltzer, Lippe, Goldstein & Schlissel, LLP, Mineola, NY, 1986-89; ptnr. Meltzer, Lippe, Goldstein & Breitstone, LLP, Mineola, 1989—. Past pres. Nassau County Legal Aid Soc., 1984-86. Bd. dirs. United Cmty. Fund, Great Neck, N.Y., 1980, Great Neck Estates Civic Assn., 1998—, L.I. Venture Group, 1998-2003. With USAR, 1960. Mem. ABA, N.Y. State Bar Assn., Nassau County Bar Assn., L.I. Software Network, Harvard Club. Democrat. Home: 31 Amherst Rd Great Neck NY 11021-2910 Office: Meltzer Lippe Et Al 190 Willis Ave Mineola NY 11501-2693 Office Phone: 516-747-0300. Personal E-mail: dlefty35@optonline.net. Business E-Mail: dschaffer@meltzerlippe.com.

SCHAFFER, DEBORAH BETH, English language educator; b. Syracuse, NY, May 12, 1955; d. Elliott Jacob and Bernice Esther (Samuels) S. BA, U. Rochester, 1976; MA, Ohio State U., 1978, PhD, 1982. Teaching and research assoc. linguistics Ohio State U., Columbus, 1977-82, lectr. ESL, 1983; asst. prof. English, Ea. Mont. Coll., Billings, 1983-87, assoc. prof., 1987-92; prof. Mont. State U. Billings, 1992—, dir. writing lab., 1995—2001. Co-editor: Language Files, 1979; contbr. articles to profl. jours. Mem. Linguistic Soc. Am., Nat. Coun. Tchrs. English, Popular Culture Assn. (sect. chmn. 1991—2005), Mont. Assn. Tchrs. English and Lang. Arts, Phi Beta Kappa, Phi Kappa Phi. Democrat. Jewish. Avocations: film, science and contemporary fiction. Office: Mont State Univ Billings Dept English 1500 University Dr Billings MT 59101-0245 Office Phone: 406-657-2950. Business E-Mail: dschaffer@msubillings.edu.

SCHAFFER, JULIE V., pediatric dermatologist, researcher; MD, Yale U. Sch. Medicine, New Haven, 2000. Diplomate Am. Bd. Pediat., Am. Bd. Dermatology. Resident dermatology Yale U. Sch. Medicine, 2001—04; clin. fellowship pediat. dermatology NYU Med. Ctr., 2004—05, asst. prof. dermatology and pediat.; dir. pediat dermatology NYU Dermatol. Assoc. Contbr. articles to profl. jours. Mem.: Women's Dermatol. Soc., Am. Acad. Dermatology (Young Investigator award 2007), Dermatology Found. (Med. Career Devel. award 2007, 2008). Achievements include research in clinical and molecular investigation of genetic and congenital skin diseases. Office: NYU Dept Dermatology Faculty Practice Tower 530 1st Ave New York NY 10016 Office Phone: 212-263-5889.

SCHAFFER, ROBERT W. (BOB SCHAFFER), former congressman; b. Cin., July 24, 1962; s. Robert James and Florence Ann (Bednar) Schaffer; m. Maureen Elizabeth Menke, Feb. 8, 1986; children: Jenniffer, Emily, Justin, Sarah, Mary. BA in Polit. Sci., U. Dayton, 1984; doctorate (hon.), Colo. Tech. U. Rep. caucus speechwriter Ohio Gen. Assembly, 1984-85; legis. asst. State of Ohio, Columbus, 1985; majority adminstrv. asst. Colo. State Senate, Denver, 1985-87, mem., 1987-96, US Congress from 4th Colo. dist., Washington, 1997—2003, mem. agr. com., edn. & workforce com., resources com. Owner No. Front Range Mktg. & Distbn. Inc., 1990—94; mem. Rep. Policy Com., GOP Theme Team, Ukraine Caucus, Nat. Rep. Hispanic Assembly; human svcs. com. mem. Nat. Conf. State Legislatures; chmn. Jud. Confirmation Network, State Vets. & Mil. Affairs Com., Senate Fin. Com.; vice-chmn. Senate Edn. Com., Colo. State Bd. Edn.; commr. Eighth Jud. Dist. Nominating Commn., Colo. Advanced Tech. Inst. Mem. Mental Health Bd. Larimer County, 1986—87; chmn. Leadership Prog. of Rockies. Recipient Spirit of Enterprise award, US C. of C.; named Nat. Legislator of Yr., Rep. Nat. Legislators Assn., 1995, Bus. Legislator of Yr., Colo. Assn. Commerce & Industry; named a Taxpayer Champion, Colo. Union Taxpayers, 1995. Mem.: Air Force Assn., Nat. Fedn. Ind. Bus., KC, Jaycees (Mover and Shaker award 1989). Republican. Roman Catholic. Avocations: backpacking, skiing, baseball, painting, reading. Home: 5027 Alder Ct Fort Collins CO 80525-5588*

SCHAFFER, SANDRA SUE, artist, educator; b. Kansas City, Mo., Jan. 12, 1947; d. Robert William and Marian Frances Effertz; m. Larry Alan Schaffer, Nov. 10, 1972; children: Kristen Noelle, Scott David. BA in Psychology, U. Mo., Columbia, 1969; MEd in Learning Disabilities, Ctrl. Mo. State U., Warrensburg, 1974. Diagnostician and learning disabilities specialist Cenl. Mo. State U. Artist, Kansas City, Mo., 1997—. Diagnostician, spl. edn. coord. The Plaza Acad., Mercier, Mo., 2003—. One-woman shows include Corridor Gallery, 2005, Park Ctrl. Gallery, 2006, two-peson exhbn., Irene B. French Meml. Gallery, 2007, exhibitions include Finding the Extraordinary in the Ordinary: Works from Peru, Nepal and other Travels, Nepali Matron (MKEC Engring. award Kans. Watercolor Soc. Regional Show, 2004), Ledgemates (Excellence award Red River Watercolor Soc. Nat. Show, 2004), Rooftop Perspective (Past Pres.'s award N.W. Watercolor Soc. Nat. Show, 2001), Village Life (Friends Cash award Miss. Watercolor Soc. Nat. Show, 2001), Mo. State U., 2009; contbr. articles to publs. Newsletter editor Watercolor Honor Soc., Springfield, Mo., 2004—06; bd. dirs. Mattie Rhodes Arts Ctr., Kansas City, Mo., 1994—95. Recipient First Pl. award, Wyo. Watercolor Soc. Nat. Exhbn., 2001, New Orleans Sch. of Fine Art and Daler-Rowney award, La. Watercolor Soc. Internat. Show, 2002, Nielsen-Bainbridge award, Western Colo. Watercolor Soc. Nat. Show, 2001, Colvin Cash award, Baker Arts Ctr. Nat. Show, 2003, Pacific Gallery Artists' award, Pensicola Art League Nat. Show, 2004, Catherine M. Mulkare Cash award, RI Watercolor Soc., 2005, Merit award, Watercolor Art Soc. Houston, 2005, Juror's Art award, Ctr. Nat. Show, 2005, Merit award, Red River Watercolor Soc., 2005, Distinction award, Mo. Watercolor Soc. Nat. Show, 2007, Cash award, Watercolor USA, 2007, Brown Forman Patron Purchase award, Jack Richeson and Daniel Smith awards, Ky. Watercolor Soc. Nat. Show, 2007, Purcahse award, Watercolor USA Exhbn., 2008, Cover Art award, Kans. City Voices, 2008, Daniel Smith Artist Materials & Catalog, 2009. Mem.: Calif. Watercolor Soc. (signature mem. 2009), Transparent Watercolor Soc., Mo. Watercolor Soc. (bd. dirs. 2007—, George Latta Cash award 2005), Watercolor West Watercolor Soc., N.W. Watercolor Soc. (signature mem.), Tex. Watercolor Soc. (Purple Sage award, signature mem.), Watercolor Honor Soc. (assoc.; bd. dirs. 2004—06, 2008—, elected pres. 2008—, Winsor-Newton award 2004, signature mem.). Democrat. Unitarian Universalist. Avocations: travel, bicycling, reading. Home: 12700 E 64th Ct Kansas City MO 64133 Office: The Plaza Acad 4232 Mercier Kansas City MO 64111 Home Fax: 816-373-2112. Personal E-mail: lschaffer@kc.rr.com.

SCHAFFER, SETH ANDREW, lawyer; b. Bklyn., Jan. 7, 1942; m. Karen (Kiki) Cohn, Dec. 1, 1968; children: Amanda, Julia, James. BA in Econs. magna cum laude, Harvard U., 1963, LLB cum laude, 1967; postgrad., Cambridge U., Eng., 1964. Bar: N.Y. 1970, U.S. Dist. Ct. (so. dist.) N.Y. 1973, U.S. Ct. Appeals (2nd cir.) 1973, U.S. Supreme Ct. 1980. Tchr. math. and econs. York (Pa.) Country Day Sch., 1967-68; assoc. dir. Vera Inst. Justice, 1969-72; asst. U.S. atty. U.S. Dist. Ct. (so. dist.) N.Y., 1972-75; chief counsel Moreland Act Commn. on Nursing Homes, NYC, 1975-76; of counsel Stanley S. Arkin, P.C., Attys. at Law, 1976-77; v.p., gen. counsel, sec. of univ. NYU, NYC, 1977-93, sr. v.p., gen. counsel, sec., 1993—2005; deputy commnr. for legal matters NYPD, 2005—. Adj. prof. law NYU Sch. Law. Dir. Nat. Ctr. Philanthropy and the Law, N.Y.C. Henry fellow Cambridge U., 1964. Mem. Nat. Assn. Coll. and Univ. Attys. (past pres.), Assn. of Bar of City of N.Y., Phi Beta Kappa. Home: 3 Washington Mews New York NY 10003-6608 Office: Deputy Commnr for Legal Matters NYPD One Police Plaza New York NY 10038 Home Phone: 212-677-8350; Office Phone: 646-610-8423. Business E-Mail: andrew.schaffer@nyu.edu.

SCHAFFNER, ADAM DAVID, plastic surgeon; b. Chgo., Sept. 26, 1971; s. Dorann Cohn, Robert Marc and Marjorie Schaffner (Stepmother); m. Marcie Suzanne Rubin, June 10, 2007. BS in Biology with highest honors, summa cum laude, Emory U., Atlanta, 1993; MD, Rush U., Chgo., 1998. Diplomate Am. Bd. Otolaryngology, 2004, Am. Bd. Facial Plastic and Reconstructive Surgery, 2007, lic. NY, 2000, Calif., 2003, Conn., 2004, Mich., 2007, DC, 2009, Va., 2009. Clin. asst. inst. SUNY at Stony Brook, 1998—2003, internship surgery, 1998—99, residency otolaryngology-head and neck surgery, 1999—2003; fellowship facial plastic and reconstructive surgery Mittelman Facial Plastic Surgery Ctr., 2003—04; mem. med. staff Stanford Hosp., 2003—04, Sound Shore Med. Ctr. of Westchester, New Rochelle, NY, 2004—07, Greenwich Hosp., Conn., 2004—07, Georgetown Univ. Hosp., 2009—; clin. asst. prof. Weill Med. Coll., Cornell U., 2005—08; residency plastic and reconstructive surgery Detroit Med. Ctr., Wayne State U., 2007—09; asst. prof. clin. plastic and reconstructive surgery Georgetown U. Sch. Medicine, 2009—. Rsch. assoc. CDC, Atlanta, 1992—93; summer rsch. fellow NCI, Bethesda, Md., 1994; vol. cons. in field ABC News, 2004—; trainer, cons., mem. spkrs. bur. Sanofi-Aventis, 2005—06; cons. Pfizer Upper Respiratory New Products N.Am. Market Coun., 2005, BioForm Med., 2005, Gerson Lehrman Healthcare Coun., 2006—, Kythera Pharm., 2007—08; mem. med. com. US Open Championship Golf Tournament, 2006. Contbr. articles to profl. jours. Participant FACE to FACE Domestic, 2004—, FACE to FACE Internat., 2006—; mem. exec. com. Rush Cmty. Svc. Initiatives Program, Chgo., 1996—98; steering com. co-chmn. St. Basil's Free People's Clinic, Chgo., 1996—98; vol. Egleston Children's Hosp. at Emory U., Atlanta, 1991—93; mem., bd. dirs. Elec. Pear Prodns., 2006—. Recipient The Jack Boozer, PhD award for Social and Religious Ethics, Emory U., 1992, CibaGeneva award for outstanding cmty. svc., 1996, Guide to Am.'s Top Surgeons, Consumers' Rsch. Coun. Am., 2009; named to, 2007, 2008, America's Cosmetic Doctors and Dentists, Castle Connolly Med.; Messing Meml. Merit scholar, Zeta Beta Tau Found., 1993, Humanitarian Efforts Travel grantee, Am. Acad. Otolaryngology-Head and Neck Surgery Found., 2002. Fellow: ACS, Am. Acad. Otolaryngology-Head and Neck Surgery, Am. Acad. Facial Plastic and Reconstructive Surgery (mem. Found. Continuing Med. Edn. com. 2004—, mem. Emerging Trends and Technologies com. 2004—, mem. Ad Hoc com. on Patient Advocacy 2008—, mem. FACE to FACE com. 2008—); mem.: AMA. Avocations: piano, swimming, theater, travel, skiing. Office Fax: 914-819-0488. Personal E-mail: aschaffner@gmail.com.

SCHAFFNER, BERTRAM HENRY, psychiatrist; b. Erie, Pa., Nov. 12, 1912; s. Milton and Gerta (Herzog) S. Student, Harvard U., 1928-29, 32-33; AB, Swarthmore Coll., 1932; MD, Johns Hopkins U., 1937; diploma, William Alanson White Inst., 1953. Diplomate Am. Bd. Psychiatry, Am. Bd. Neurology. Intern Johns Hopkins Hosp., Balt., 1937-38; resident in neurology Mt. Sinai Hosp., NYC, 1938-39; resident in psychiatry Bellevue Hosp., NYC, 1939-40, N.Y. State Psychiat. Inst., NYC, 1946-47; pvt. practice psychiatry and psychoanalysis NYC, 1947—. Lectr. Sch. Nursing Cornell U., N.Y.C., 1950-60; mem. faculty, clin. supr. in psychotherapy William Alanson White Inst. Psychoanalysis, 1960—, med. dir. HIV svc., clin. supr. psychoanalysis, 1993—; cons., editor confs. Josiah Macy Jr. Found., 1949, 50, 51; cons. U.S. Children's Bur., 1946-47, Bur. Mental Health, V.I., 1954-60, World Fedn. Mental Health, 1958-68, others; mem. N.Y. County dist. bd. Com. on Gay and Lesbian Issues; cons. WHO, 1960-67; founder, exec. dir. U.S.-Caribbean Aid to Mental Health, Inc., 1960-68; organizer Biennial Caribbean Confs. for Mental Health, 1959-65; organizer, cons. Caribbean Fedn. for Mental Health, 1959-65; mem. rsch. study Pre-Soviet Russian Family in the Research in Contemporary Cultures, Columbia U., 1949-51. Mem. editl. bd. Jour. of Gay and Lesbian Psychotherapy, 1987—; author: Father Land: A Study of Authoritarianism in the German Family, 1948; contbr. numerous articles to profl. publs. Mem. acquisitions com. The Bklyn. Mus. of Art, 1995—; trustee Bklyn. Mus. of Art. Recipient Adolf Meyer award for Disting. Svc. on Behalf of Improved Care and Treatment of the Mentally Ill in the Caribbean, 1961. Fellow AMA (life), Am. Psychiat. Assn. (chmn. 1983-86, mem. com. on AIDS N.Y. County dist. br. 1989-99, life), Am. Acad. Psychoanalysis (life), Caribbean Psychiat. Assn.; mem. Group for Advancement of Psychiatry (chair internat. rels. com. 1960-65, chair com. on human sexuality 1987-98), Internat. Acad. Sex Rsch. Avocation: collecting asian and indian art. Home and Office: 220 Central Park S New York NY 10019-1417 Home Phone: 212-265-5539; Office Phone: 212-265-5539. Personal E-mail: bertschmd@aol.com.

SCHAFFNER, HOWARD SHELDON, lawyer; b. Chgo., Nov. 2, 1943; s. Irving and Frieda Schaffner; m. Gail Schaffner, July 14, 1970; children: Paula, Stacy. JD, John Marshall Law Sch., 1970. Bar: Ill. 1970. Asst. state's atty. Cook County States Atty.'s Office, Chgo., 1970-78; ptnr. Hofeld & Schaffner, Chgo., 1978—. Mem. ABA, Ill. State Bar Assn., Ill. Trial Lawyers Assn. (bd. mgrs. 1980—; author Cont. Legal Edn. 1980—, Ill. Inst. Cont. Legal Edn. 1980, 83, 86), Ill. State Bar Assn., Internat. Soc. Barristers Office: Hofeld & Schaffner 30 N Lasalle St Ste 3120 Chicago IL 60602-2576 Office Phone: 312-372-4250.

SCHAFFNER, KAREN ANN (KAREN FIELD), real estate broker; d. Abraham Terry and Ida (Smith) Rogovin; m. Barry S. Crown, 1954 (div. 1969); children: Laurie Jayne, Donna Lynn, Bruce Alan, Bradley David; m. Michael Lehmann Field, 1969 (div. 1977); m. Ronald E. Schaffner, Apr., 1998. Student, Vassar Coll., 1953-54, Harrington Inst. Interior Design, 1973-74, Roosevelt U., 2008—. Cert. real estate residential specialist. Owner Karen Field Interiors, Chgo., 1970-86, Karen Field & Assocs. Realtors, Chgo., 1980-81; pres., ptnr. Field-Pels & Assocs. Realtors, Chgo., 1981-86; with top sales volume Sudler-Marling, Inc., Chgo., 1989; sales broker Koenig & Strey GMAC, Chgo., 1992—. Mem. Women's Coun. Camp Henry Horner, Chgo., 1960; bd. dirs., treas. Winnetka Pub. Sch. Nursery (Ill.), 1961-63; pres. Jr. Aux. U. Chgo. Cancer Rsch. Found., 1960-66, mem. exec. com. women's bd., 1965-66, first co-chair Grand Auction U. Chgo. Cancer Rsch. Found.; bd. dirs., sec. United Charities, Chgo., 1966-68, Victory Gardens Theatre, Chgo., 1979; co-founder, pres. Re-Entry Ctr., Wilmette, Ill., 1978-80; mem. br. Child Abuse Svcs., Chgo., 1981-89, Stop AIDS Real Estate Divsn., 1988, AIDS Walkathon Com., 1990; bd. dirs. The Chgo. Ctr. for Self-Taught Art, 1993-96. Recipient Servian award Jr. Aux. of U. Chgo. Cancer Rsch. Found., 1966, Margarite Wolf award Women's Bd., U. Chgo. Cancer Rsch. Found., 1967, Founder's award, 1997, WAIT Woman of Day. Mem. Chgo. Real Estate Bd., Chgo. Assn. Realtors, English Speaking Union (jr. bd. 1958-59), Art Inst. Chgo., Field Mus., Arts Club Chgo., Confrerie de la Chaine des Rotisseurs (Dame de la Chaine), Fulton River Dist. Assn., Koenig and Strey GMAC Pres.'s Club. Office: Koenig & Strey GMAC 900 N Michigan Ave Ste 1700 Chicago IL 60611-1514 Office Phone: 312-893-3556. Business E-Mail: kfield@ksgmac.com.

SCHAFFNER, WILLIAM, medical educator; BA, Yale U., New Haven, Conn.; MD, Cornell U., Med. Coll., NY. Prof. of Medicine, Divsn. of Infectious Diseases Vanderbilt U. Sch. Medicine, Nashville, prof., chmn. Dept. of Preventive Medicine. Mem. steering com. Nat. Network for Immunization Info.; mem. bd. dirs. Nat. Found. for Infectious Diseases; pub. health policy and communicable disease control cons. Centers for Disease Control and Prevention, World Health Org., Tennessee Dept. of Health, Am. Coll. of Physicians. Contbr. scientific papers, chapters to books; co-editor: (scientific journals) Hospital Infection Control, European Journal of Clinical Microbiology, Patient Care. Recipient Epidemiology Lecturer Award, Soc. of Healthcare, 1996; named a Fulbright Scholar, Albert Ludwigs U., Freiburg, Germany. Office: Vanderbilt University Medical Ctr Suite 2600 Village at Vanderbilt Nashville TN 37212 Office Phone: 615-322-2037. Business E-Mail: william.schaffner@vanderbilt.edu.

SCHAFRIK, ROBERT EDWARD, materials engineer, technology manager, information technologist; b. Cleve., Feb. 6, 1946; s. Edward E. and Sylvia E. (Farina) S.; m. Mary L. Schuhmann, Sept. 21, 1968; children: Robert E., Catherine M. Spage, Franki S., Steven J. Aerospace Engr., Air Force Inst. Tech., Dayton, Ohio, 1974; Metall. Engr., Ohio State U., 1979; degree in Info. Sys., George Mason U., 1996; Degree in Metallurgy, Case Western Reserve U., 1967. Registered profl. engr., Ohio. Commd. 2d lt. U.S. Air Force, 1968, advanced through grades to lt. col., 1984; div. chief air superiority Hdqrs. Air Force Systems Command, Andrews AFB, Md., 1984-87; div. chief Strategic Def. Initiative Office, Washington, 1987-88; ret. U.S. Air Force, 1988; v.p. R&D Technology Assessment and Transfer, Inc., Annapolis, Md., 1988-91; dir. Nat. Materials Adv. Bd., Washington, 1991-97, Bd Mfg. and Engring. Design, 1994-97; dept. staff engr. GE Aircraft Engines, Cin., 1997-98, gen. mgr. materials and process engring dept., 1999—. Contbr. articles to profl. jours. Chair Bicentennial Commn., Huber Heights, Ohio, 1975-77. Fellow ASM Internat. (chair Fed. Affairs com. 1997-2000, co-chair Gordon Rsch. Conf., theoretical founds. for product design and mfg.), Am. Inst. Aeronautics and Astronautics (assoc. fellow, mem. technical com.-mgmt.); mem. IEEE, TMS. Achievements include exploratory development research on titanium aluminides; program management for Air Force industrial modernization programs; program management F-16 engine projects; program management for Air Force integrated computer-aided manufacturing program; directing accomplishment of 33 major reports while at NRC providing policy advice on materials and manufacturing related issues to Federal Government, Industry and Academia; directing development add qualification of new materials, and the introduction of all materials into GE aero-engines and their derivatives. Office: GE Aviation 1 Neumann Way PO Box 156301 Cincinnati OH 45215-6301

SCHAIE, K(LAUS) WARNER, human development and psychology educator; b. Stettin, Germany (now Poland), Feb. 1, 1928; came to U.S., 1947, naturalized, 1953; s. Sally and Lottie Luise (Gabriel) S.; m. Coloma J. Harrison, Aug. 9, 1953 (div. 1973); 1 child, Stephan; m. Sherry L. Willis, Nov. 20, 1981. AA, City Coll., San Francisco, 1951; BA, U. Calif., Berkeley, 1952; MS, U. Wash., 1953, PhD, 1956; DPhil (hon.), Friedrich-Schiller U., Jena, Germany, 1997; ScD (hon.), W.Va. U., 2002. Lic. psychologist, Calif., Pa. Fellow Washington U., St. Louis, 1956-57; asst. prof. psychology U. Nebr., Lincoln, Nebr., 1957-64, assoc. prof., 1964—67; prof. chmn. dept. psychology W.Va. U., Morgantown, W.Va., 1968—73; prof. psychology, dir. Gerontology Rsch. Inst., U. So. Calif., 1973-81; Evan Pugh prof. human devel. and psychology Pa. State U., University Park, 1981—2008, Evan Pugh prof. emeritus, 2008—, dir. Gerontology Ctr., 1985—2003; affiliate prof. psychiatry and behavioral scis. U. Wash., 1991—. Devel. behavior study sect. NIH, Bethesda, Md., 1970-72, chmn., 1972-74, chmn. human devel. and aging study sect., 1979-84, expert panel in comml. airline pilot retirement, 1981, data and safety bd. shep project, 1984-91. Author: Developmental Psychology; A Life Span Approach, 1981, Adult Development and Aging, 1982, 5th rev. edit., 2002, Japanese, Chinese and Spanish edits., 2003, Intellectual Development in Adulthood: The Seattle Longitudinal Study, 1996, Developmental Influences on Adult Intelligence, 2005; editor: Handbook of Psychology of Aging, 1977, 6th rev. edit., 2006, Longitudinal Studies of Adult Development, 1983, Cognitive Functioning and Social Structure over the Life Course, 1987, Methodological Issues in Research on Aging, 1988, Social Structure and Aging: Psychological Processes, 1989, Age Structuring in Comparative Perspective, 1989, The Course of Later Life, 1989, Self-Directedness: Cause and Effects Throughout the Life Course, 1990, Aging, Health Behaviors and Health Outcomes, 1992, Caregiving Systems: Formal and Informal Helpers, 1993, Societal Impact on Aging: Historical Perspectives, 1993, Adult Intergenerational Relations: Effects of Societal Change, 1995, Older Adults Decision Making and the Law, 1996, Impact of Social Structures on Decision Making in the Elderly, 1997, Impact of the Workplace on Older Persons, 1998, Handbook of Theories of Aging, 1999, Mobility and Aging, 2000, Evolution of the Aging Self, 2000, Effective Health Behavior in the Elderly, 2002, Mastery and Control in the Elderly, 2003, Influence of Technology on Successful Aging, 2003; Independent Aging: Living Arrangements and Mobility, 2003, Religious Influences on Health and Wellbeing in the Elderly, 2004, Historical Influences on Lives and Aging, 2005, Social Structures, Self-Regulation and Aging, 2006, Demographic Influences on Health and Wellbeing in the Elderly, 2007, Social Structures and Aging Individuals, 2008; editor Ann. Rev. Gerontology and Geriat., vol. 7, 1987, vol. 11, 1991, vol. 17, 1997, series editor, 1996—; contbr. articles to profl. jours. Fellow APA (coun. reps. 1976-79, 83-86, Disting. Contbn. award, 1992), Am. Psychol. Soc., Gerontol. Soc. (Kleemeier award, 1987, Disting. Mentorship award, 1996, Lifetime Achievement award, 2008); mem. Psychometric Soc., Internat. Soc. Study Behavioral Devel., Mensa (Lifetime Achievement award, 2000). Unitarian Universalist. Avocations: hiking, stamps. Home: 2500 6th Ave North Apt 1 Seattle WA 98109 Office Phone: 206-281-4050. Business E-Mail: schaie@u.washington.edu.

SCHAKE, LOWELL MARTIN, zoology educator, writer; b. Marthasville, Mo., June 6, 1938; s. Martin Charles and Flora Olinda (Rocklage) S.; m. Wendy Anne Walkinshaw, Sept. 11, 1959; children: Sheryl Anne, Lowell Scott. BS, U. Mo., 1960, MS, 1962; PhD, Tex. A&M U., 1967. Asst. prof. Tex. A&M U., College Station, 1965-67, assoc. prof., 1969-72, prof., 1972-84, asst. prof., area livestock specialist Lubbock, 1967-69; prof., head animal sci. dept. U. Conn., Storrs, 1984-92; prof., chmn. animal sci. dept. Tex. Tech. U., Lubbock, 1992—95. Developer applied animal ethology program Tex. A&M U., 1970, New Eng. Biotech Conf. series, 1990, S.W. Beef Forum, 1993; chmn. Am. Registry of Profl. Animal Scientist Com. on Profl. Stds., 1988; chmn. Nat. Com. Exec. Officers of Animal Vet., Dairy and Poultry Sci. Depts., 1992; cons. Alpart, Kingston, Jamaica, 1975, U.S. Feeds Grain Coun., 1970-73, A.O. Smith Products Inc., 1968-92, Humphrey Land & Cattle Co., Dallas, 1980-86; lectr. in field. Author: Growth and Finishing of Beef Cattle, A Class Handbook, 1982, La Charrette: Village Gateway to the American West, 2003, 2005, On The Wings Of Cranes: Larry Walkinshaw Lifestory, 2008; contbr. articles to profl. jours. Recipient Innovative Teaching award Tex. A&M U., 1978. Mem. Am. Soc. Animal Sci., Plains Nutrition Coun. (adv. bd. 1967-80, sec.-treas. 1994-95, founder), Nat. Assn. Colls. and Tchrs. Agr., Am. Registry Profl. Animal Scientists (dir. for Northeast 1987-89), Coun. for Agr. Sci. and Tech. World Conf. on Animal Prodn., Am. Soc. Dairy Sci., Tiger Club (College Station) (pres.), Gamma Sigma Delta. Republican. Avocations: genealogy, fishing, gardening, birdwatching. Home: 142 Five Dove Cir Port Aransas TX 78373 Office Phone: 361-749-2315. Personal E-mail: wschake1@centurytel.net.

SCHAKOWSKY, JANICE, United States Representative from Illinois; b. Chgo., May 26, 1944; d. Irwin and (Cosnow) Danoff; m. Harvey E. Schakowsky, Feb. 17, 1965 (div. 1980); children: Ian, Mary; m. Robert B. Creamer, Dec. 6, 1980; 1 stepchild, Lauren. BS, U. Ill., 1965. Cert. elem. tchr. Ill. Tchr. Chgo. Bd. Edn., 1965-67; organizer Ill. Pub. Action Coun., Chgo., 1976-85; exec. dir. Ill. State Coun. Sr. Citizens, Chgo., 1985-90; mem. Ill. Ho. Reps., 1990-98, US Congress from 9th Ill. dist., 1999—; mem. banking and fin. svcs. com., 1999—2000; mem. govt. reform com., 1999—2000; Ho. Dem. leadership team-deputy whip; mem. energy and commerce Com. Del. Nat. Dem. Conv., 1988; bd. dirs. Ill. Pub. Action, 4 C's Day Care Coun., Evanston; mem. steering com. Cook County Dem. Women, 1986—90; mem. governing coun. Am. Jewish Congress, 1990—. Named Rookie of Yr., Ill. Environ. Coun., 1991, Legislator of Yr., Cmty. Action Assn., 1991, Champaign County Health Care Assn., 1992, Ill. Nurses Assn., 1992, Coalition Citizens with Disabilities/Ill. Coun. Sr. Citizens, 1993, Ill. Assn. Cmty. Mental Health Agys., 1994; named an Outstanding Legislator, Interfaith Coun. for Homeless, 1993. Mem.: NOW, ACLU, Rogers Park Hist. Soc., Evanston Friends of Libr., Evanston Hist. Soc., Evanston Mental Health Assn., Ill. Pro-Choice Alliance, Nat. Coun. Jewish Women. Democrat. Jewish. Avocations: travel, horsebackriding, reading. Office: US Ho Reps 1027 Longworth Ho Office Bldg Washington DC 20515-1309 also: Dist Office 5533 Broadway St Chicago IL 60640 Office Phone: 202-225-2111. Office Fax: 202-226-6890.*

SCHALL, ALVIN ANTHONY, federal judge; b. NYC, 1944; s. Gordon William and Helen Schall; m. Sharon Frances LeBlanc, Apr. 25, 1970; children: Amanda Lanford, Anthony Davis. BA, Princeton U., 1966; JD, Tulane U., 1969. Bar: NY 1970, US Dist. Ct. (so. and ea. dists.) NY 1973, US Ct. Appeals (2d cir.) 1974, DC 1980, US Ct. Fed. Claims 1982, US Ct. Appeals (fed. cir.) 1987, US Supreme Ct. 1989, US Ct. Appeals (DC cir.) 1991, US Dist. Ct. DC 1991. Assoc. Shearman & Sterling, NYC, 1969—73; asst. US atty. ea. dist. NY Borough of Bklyn., 1973—78, chief appeals divsn., 1977—78; trial atty. civil divsn. US Dept. Justice, Washington DC, 1978—87, sr. trial counsel, 1986—87, asst. to atty. gen., 1988—92; ptnr. Perlman & Ptnrs., Washington DC, 1987—88; judge US Ct. Appeals (Fed. cir.), Washington DC, 1992—. Office: 717 Madison Pl NW Washington DC 20439-0002*

SCHALL, ELLEN, dean, political science professor; BA, Swarthmore Coll.; JD cum laude, NYU. Commr. NYC Dept. Juvenile Justice, 1983; Martin Cherkasky prof. health policy and mgmt. Robert F. Wagner Grad. Sch. Pub. Svc., 1992—, co-founder Rsch. Ctr. for Leadership in Action, dean, 2002—. Selection com. Innovations in Am. Govt. Awards, 1999—2004, 2006—. Mem.: NY State Juvenile Justice Task Force, Women's Forum, Inc. Office: NYU Wagner 295 Lafayette St, Rm 2100-A New York NY 10012-9604 Office Phone: 212-998-7438. E-mail: ellen.schall@nyu.edu.*

SCHALLER, GEORGE BEALS, zoologist; b. Berlin, May 26, 1933; s. Georg Ludwig S. and Bettina (Byrd) Iwersen; m. Kay Suzanne Morgan, Aug. 26, 1957; children: Eric, Mark. BS in Zoology, U. Alaska, 1955, BA in Anthropology, 1955; PhD in Zoology, U. Wis., 1962. Rsch. assoc. Johns Hopkins U., Balt., 1963—66; rsch. zoologist Wildlife Conservation Soc., Bronx, NY, 1966—. Rsch. assoc. Am. Mus. Natural History. Author: The Mountain Gorilla, 1963 (Wildlife Soc. award 1965), The Year of the Gorilla, 1964, The Deer and the Tiger, 1967, The Serengeti Lion, 1972 (Nat. Book award 1973), Golden Shadows, Flying Hooves, 1973, Mountain Monarchs, 1977, Stones of Silence, 1980, The Giant Pandas of Wolong, 1985, The Last Panda, 1993, Tibet's Hidden Wilderness, 1997, Wildlife of the Tibetan Steppe, 1998; co-editor (with E.Vrba) Antelopes, Deer and Relatives, 2000, A Naturalist and Other Beasts, 2007. Decorated Order of Golden Ark, Netherlands, 1978; recipient Gold medal World Wildlife Fund, 1980, Explorers medal Explorers Club, 1990, Cosmos prize Japan, 1996, Tyler Environ. prize, 1997; Ctr. Advanced Study in Behavorial Scis. fellow Stanford U., 1962, fellow Guggenheim Found., 1971. Office: Wildlife Conservation Soc Bronx Park Bronx NY 10460 also: Panthera Found 8 W 40th St New York NY 10018 Business E-Mail: asiaprogram@wcs.org, gschaller@parthera.org.

SCHALLER, JANE GREEN, pediatrician; b. Cleve., June 26, 1934; d. George and May Alice (Wing) Green; children: Robert Thomas, George Charles, Margaret May. AB, Hiram Coll., Ohio, 1956; MD cum laude, Harvard U., 1960. Diplomate Am. Bd. Pediat., Am. Bd. Med. Examiners. Resident in pediat. Children's Hosp.-U. Wash., Seattle, 1960-63; fellow immunology Children's Hosp. U. Wash., 1963-65; faculty U. Wash. Med. Sch., 1965-83, prof. pediat., 1975-83; head divsn. rheumatic diseases Children's Hosp., Seattle, 1968-83; prof., chmn. dept. pediat., pediatrician-in-chief Tufts U. Sch. Medicine/New Eng. Med. Ctr., 1983-98; Karp prof. pediat. Tufts U. Sch. Medicine, Boston, 1983—, disting. prof., 1995—. Vis. physician Med. Rsch. Coun., Taplow, Eng., 1971-72; adj. prof. diplomacy The Fletcher Sch. Law and Diplomacy, Tufts U., 1998-2000. Contbr. articles to profl. jours. Bd. dirs. Seattle Chamber Music Festival, 1982-85; trustee Boston Chamber Music Soc., 1985—; mem. Boston adv. coun. UNICEF, tech. advisor UN Study on the Impact of Armed Conflict on Children, 1995-97; chmn., adv. com. children's rights divsn. Human Rights Watch, 1995—; mem. adv. com. Middle East divsn., 1998—; exec. com. Women's Commn. for Refugee Women and Children Internat. Rescue com., 1989-94, adv. coun. 1994—. Mem.: AAAS, Royal Coll. Pediats. U.K., Internat. Women's Forum, Mass. Women's Forum, Harvard U. Med. Sch. Alumni Coun. (v.p. 1977—80, pres. 1982—83), Physicians for Human Rights (founding pres. 1986—89, exec. com. 1986—), Com. Health in So. Africa (exec. com. 1986—92), Assn. Med. Sch. Pediat. Chmn. (exec. com. 1986—89, rep. to coun. on govt. affairs and coun. acad. socs.), New Eng. Pediat. Soc. (pres. 1991—93), Am. Coll. Rheumatology, Internat. Pediat. Assn. (pres.-elect 1998—2001, pres. 2001—04, exec. dir. 2004—), Am. Acad. Pediat. (exec. com. sect. on internat. child health, head children's rights program, rep. to UNICEF), Am. Pediat. Soc., Soc. Pediat. Rsch., Inst. Medicine of NAS, Saturday Club, Tavern Club, Aesculapian Club (pres. 1988—89). Office: International Pediatric Association Executive Director 4480 Oak Street, Room 2D 14 Vancouver BC V6H 3V4 Canada Business E-Mail: jschaller@tufts-nemc.org.

SCHALLER, JEAN, geneticist; MS, U. SC., Columbia, 2006. Diplomate genetic counselor Am. Bd. Genetic Counseling, 2007. Genetic counselor Myriad Genetic Labs., Salt Lake City, 2006—. Achievements include research in adrenoleukodystrophy.

SCHALLERT, EDWIN GLENN, lawyer; b. LA, Aug. 7, 1952; s. William Joseph and Rosemarie Diane (Waggner) S. AB, Stanford U., 1974; JD, MPP, Harvard U., 1981. Bar: N.Y. 1974, U.S. Ct. Appeals (7th cir.) 1986, U.S. Ct. Appeals (2d cir.) 1989, U.S. Dist. Ct. (so. dist.) N.Y. 1975. Legis. aid to U.S. rep. Les Aspin, Washington, 1975-78; law clk. to Hon. J. Skelly Wright, 1981-82; law clk. to Hon. Thurgood Marshall, 1982-83; assoc. Debevoise & Plimpton LLP, NYC, 1983-89, ptnr., 1989—, mem. litig. dept., 1983—90. Mem. Internat. Inst. for Strategic Studies, Coun. Fgn. Rels. (term mem. 1983-88), Phi Beta Kappa. Democrat. Avocation: tennis. Office: Debevoise & Plimpton LLP 919 Third Ave New York NY 10022 Office Phone: 212-909-6295. Office Fax: 212-909-6836. E-mail: egschallert@debevoise.com.

SCHALLERT, WILLIAM JOSEPH, actor; b. LA, July 6, 1922; s. Edwin Francis and Elza Emily (Baumgarten) S.; m. Rosemarie Diann Waggner, Feb. 26, 1949; children: William Joseph, Edwin G., Mark M., Brendan C. BA, UCLA, 1946. Co-founder, owner Circle Theatre, Hollywood, Calif., 1947-50. Appeared in motion pictures, TV, stage, radio, 1947—; movies include Lonely Are the Brave, Heat of the Night, Charley Varrick, Red Badge of Courage, Teachers; starred in TV series Patty Duke Show, 1963-66, Nancy Drew Mysteries, 1977-78, Little Women, 1979, The New Gidget, 1986-88, The Torkelson's, 1991-92, Recount Justice Stevens, 2008; starred as judge in stage play and film The Trial of the Catonsville Nine, N.Y.C., Los Angeles, 1971 (Obie award 1971); starred as Dr. Pangloss in Candide, L.A., 1995; recorded voice of Abraham Lincoln for permanent installation at Lincoln Mus., Springfield, Ill., 2004. Trustee Motion Picture and TV Fund, 1977—. With AUS, 1942-44; with USAAC, 1944-45. Fulbright fellow Brit. Repertory Theatre, 1952-53. Mem. ASCAP, SAG (pres. 1979-81, trustee pension and health plan 1983—, founder Com. for Performers with Disabilities 1981—, Ralph Morgan award 1993). Office: Gursey Schneider 1888 Century Pk E # 900 Los Angeles CA 90067-1735 Personal E-mail: schlrt80@yahoo.com.

SCHALLHORN, STEVEN, ophthalmologist; Former dir. cornea & refractive surgery Naval Med. Ctr.; former mgr. refractive surgery program US Navy; ophthalmologist Clearview Eye & Laser Med. Ctr. Visiting prof. Harvard, USC, Baylor Coll. Medicine; cons. NASA, NATO, FAA. Ret. capt. USN. Decorated Legion of Merit USN; recipient Joint Chiefs of Staff award, Lans Refractive Surgery award. Fellow: Am. Acad. Ophthalmology; mem.: ASCRS, AMA, Am. Bd. Ophthalmology. Office: Clearview Eye & Laser Medical Care 6255 Lusk Blvd Ste 100 San Diego CA 92121*

SCHALLY, ANDREW VICTOR, endocrine oncologist, researcher; b. Poland, Nov. 30, 1926; arrived in USA, 1957, naturalized, 1962; s. Casimir Peter and Maria (Lacka) Schally; m. Ana Maria Comaru, Aug. 1976 (dec. Sept. 2004). BSc, McGill U., Can., 1955, PhD in Biochemistry, 1957; 29 hon. doctorates. Research asst. biochemistry Nat. Inst. Med. Research, London, 1949—52; dept. psychiatry McGill U., Montreal, Que., 1952—57; rsch. assoc., asst. prof. physiology and biochemistry Coll. Medicine, Baylor U., Houston, 1957—62; assoc. prof. Tulane U. Sch. Medicine, New Orleans, 1962—67, prof., 1967—2006; chief Endocrine Polypeptide and Cancer Inst. VA Med. Ctr., New Orleans, 1962—2006, with Miami, Fla., 2006—; Disting. Leonard Miller Prof. Pathology U. Miami Sch. Medicine, 2006—. Sr. med. investigator VA, 1973—99, disting. med. rsch. scientist, 1999—. Author: The Hypothalamus and Pituitary in Health and Disease, 1972; contbr. articles to profl. jours. Recipient Van Meter prize, Am. Thyroid Assn., 1969, Ayerst-Squibb award, Endocrine Soc., 1970, William S. Middletown award, VA, 1970, Ch. Mickle award, U. Toronto, 1974, Gairdner Internat. award, 1974, Borden award, Assn. Am. Med. Colls. and Borden Co. Found., 1975, Albert Lasker Basic Rsch. award, 1975, Legion d'Honneur, Chevalier Grade, France, 2004; co-recipient Nobel prize for medicine, 1977; fellow sr. rsch. fellow, USPHS, 1961—62. Mem.: AAAS, NAS, Am. Assn. Cancer Rsch., Royal Acad. Medicine Spain, Acad. Sci. Mex., Acad. Sci. Russia, Acad. Sci. Hungary, Acad. Medicine Poland, Acad. Medicine Venezuela, Nat. Acad. Medicine Brazil, Mex. Acad. Medicine, Soc. Internat. Brain Rsch. Orgn., Soc. Exptl. Biol. Medicine, Soc. Biol. Chemists, Am. Physiol. Soc., Endocrine Soc. Achievements include research in TRH, the releasing factor of the thyroid stimulating hormone; hypothalamic luteinizing hormone releasing factor, LH-RH, the brain's master key to the body's control reproductive function; the application of hypothalamic hormones for cancer therapy. Avocations: swimming, soccer. Home: 3801 Collins Ave Apt 1506 Miami Beach FL 33140 Office: VA Hosp Research 151 1201 NW 16 St Miami FL 33125 Office Phone: 305-575-3477. Office Fax: 305-575-3126. Business E-Mail: andrew.schally@va.gov.

SCHALOW, FRANK HICKEY, philosopher, educator; b. Denver, Feb. 23, 1956; s. Berthold Erich and Frances Schalow. BA summa cum laude, U. Denver, 1978; MA, Tulane U., 1980, PhD, 1984. Vis. asst. prof. Loyola U., New Orleans, 1984-86, asst. prof., 1986-90, assoc. prof., 1990-92; lectr. Dillard U., New Orleans, 1993—; vis. assoc. prof. Xavier U., New Orleans, 1994-97, U. New Orleans, 1995—. Mem. editl. adv. bd. Auslegung U. Kans., Lawrence, 1983-97, Heidegger Studies U. Wis., LaCrosse, 2000—; mem. dissertation adv. bd. Union Inst., Cin., 1999—. Author: Imagination and Existence, 1986, Renewal of the Heidegger-Kant Dialogue, 1992, Language and Deed, 1998, Heidegger and the Quest for the Sacred, 2001, Incarnality of Being, 2006; co-author: Traces of Understanding, 1990. Mem. Am. Philos. Assn., N.Am. Heidegger Conf. (sec. convenor 1992), S.W. Philosophy Soc. (exec. com. 1993), Phi Beta Kappa. Avocation: golf. Home: 7310 Freret St New Orleans LA 70118 Office: U New Orleans Lakefront Campus New Orleans LA 70148 Business E-Mail: fschalow@uno.edu.

SCHAMUS, JAMES ALLAN, film producer and company executive, screenwriter; b. Detroit, Sept. 7, 1959; s. Julian John Schamus and Clarita (Gershowitz) Karlin; m. Nancy Jean Kricorian; children: Nona Esther, Djuna Mariam. AB, U. Calif., Berkeley, 1982, MA, 1984. Asst. prof. Columbia U., NYC, 1991-97, assoc. prof., 1997—; co-pres., co-chmn. GOOD Machine (bought by Universal Pictures and merged into new studio, Focus), NYC, 1991—2002; co-pres. Focus Features, NYC, 2002—06, pres., 2006; CEO specialty film divsn. NBC Universal, Inc., 2006—. Assisted in the finding of Independent TV Series, 1988; involved with Aparatus. Actor Keep It for Yourself, 1991; prodr: (films) The Golden Boat, 1991, Chicken Delight, 1991, Roy Cohn/Jack Smith, 1994, Walking and Talking, 1996, She's the One, 1996, Assault on Precinct 13, 2005; assoc. prodr., co-writer (films): Eat Drink Man Woman, 1994; assoc. prodr. In the Soup, 1992; exec. prodr.: (films) Warrior: Poison, 1991, The Life of Leonard Peltier, 1992, Swoon, 1992, What Happened Was..., 1994, Safe, 1995, The Brothers McMullen, 1995, Greetings From Africa, 1996, Arresting Gena, 1997, Office Killer, 1997, The Myth of Fingerprints, 1997, Wonderland, 1997, Happiness, 1998, Lola and Billy the Kid, 1999, Love God, 1999, The Lifestyle: Group Sex in the Suburbs, 2000, Crouching Tiger Hidden Dragon, 2000 (also writer), Buffalo Soldiers, 2001, Auto Focus, 2002; co-prodr. Thank You and Good Night, 1991, Sense and Sensibility, 1995; writer (films) Tortilla Soup, 2001; writer, prodr.: (films) The Wedding Banquet, 1993, Pushing Hands, 1995, The Ice Storm, 1997 (Best Screenplay, Cannes Film Festival 1997), Ride with the Devil, 1999, Hulk, 2003, Brokeback Mountain, 2005 (Best Theatrical Motion Picture, Producer Guild Am., 2006, Best Feature, Spirit Independent award, 2006, Outstanding Film, British Acad. Film and TV Arts, 2006) Recipient Brian Greenbaum award, 1994, NBC Screenwriter's Tribute, Natucket Film Festival, 2002; named one of 50 Most Powerful People in Hollywood, 2006. Mem. Assn. for Ind. Video and Film (bd. dirs.). Office: NBC Universal Inc 30 Rockefeller Plz New York NY 10112

SCHANBACHER, DAVID CHARLES, lawyer; s. Leonard George and Eva Louise Schanbacher; m. Michele M Medrow, Apr. 26, 1997 (div.); children: Danae Blake, Taggert Hunter. BA, Shippensburg State Coll., Pa., 1983; JD, Duquesne U., Pitts., 1986. Bar: Pa. Supreme Ct. 1986. Assoc. atty. Mark, Weigle & Perkins, Shippensburg, Pa., 1991—97; atty./ptnr. Hoffmeyer & Semmelman, LLP, York, 1997—. Law clk. Patrick Narcisi, Esquire & Harry Kennedy, Esquire, Pitts., 1985—86; spl. agt. FBI, Kingston, NY, 1986—91; lectr. & author Pa. Bar Assn., Pa. Bar Inst. Contbr. articles to profl. pubs. Com. mem. Buildings & Facilities Com. of YMCA, York, Pa., 1998—2000; pres. York Hosp. Aux., York, Pa., 2006—08, co-chair of nominating com. and governance com., 2003—08; mem. Sept. Ho. Sr. Ctr., York, Pa., 2000—03; non-voting mem. York Hosp. Aux., York, Pa., 2007—08. Recipient Academic All-American Football Player, Coll. Sports Info. Directors of Am., 1982. Mem.: York County Bar Assn., Family Law Coun. of Pa. Bar Assn., Family Law Sect. of York County Bar Assn., Criminal Law Sect. of York County Bar Assn., Family Law Sect. Coun. of the Pa. Bar Assn. (co-chair rules ct. com. 2008). Avocations: cycling, sports, traveling. Office: Hoffmeyer & Semmelman LLP 30 North George Street York PA 17401 Office Fax: 717-852-8780. Business E-Mail: dschanbacher@hoffsemm.com.

SCHANDLER, JON B., hospital administrator; b. Paterson, NJ, Apr. 19, 1950; s. Jack Morris and Deborah Londner Schandler; m. Amy Miller, Mar. 23, 1975; children: Matthew, Karen. BS, Villanova U., 1972; MBA, Fordham U., 1979. CPA NY. Sr. acct. Price Waterhouse & Co., NYC, 1973—76; contr. White Plains Hosp. Ctr. (WPHC), White Plains, NY, 1976—80, COO, 1980—81, pres., CEO, 1981—. Mem.: No. Met. Hosp. Assn., NY Soc. C.P.A.'s, Am. Inst. C.P.A.'s, Gamma Phi. Office: White Plains Hosp Med Center 41 E Post Rd White Plains NY 10601*

SCHANFIELD, FANNIE SCHWARTZ, community volunteer; b. Mpls., Dec. 25, 1916; d. Simon Zouberman and Mary (Schmilovitz) Schwartz; m. Melvin M. Stock, Oct. 27, 1943 (dec. Apr. 1944); 1 child, Moses Samuel Schanfield; m. Abraham Schanfield, Aug. 28, 1947; children: David Colman, Miriam Schanfield Kieffer. Student, U. Minn., 1962-75. Author: My Thoughts, 1996, Son, I Have Something to Tell You, 1997, Ma, I Wrote It Down, 1997, 20 April 44 WWII, 2001, The Other Family's Kids, 2004, The Duplex: Fran and Dan Lived Upstairs, 2004, I Was There. Bd. dirs. Jewish Cmty. Ctr., Mpls., 1975-96, chairperson older adult needs, 1982-88; past pres. Bnai Emet Women's League, Mpls., 1988-90; rschr., advocate Hunger Hennepin County, Mpls., 1969-75; sec. Joint Religious Legis. Coalition; v.p., bd. dirs. Cmty. Housing Svc., Mpls., 1971-85. Recipient Citation of Honor, Hennepin County Commn., 1989, Lifetime Achievement award Jewish Cmty. Ctr. Greater Mpls., 1995, Mpls. Jewish Fedn. citation, 2006. Mem. Lupus Found. Minn., Internat. Soc. Poets, Hadassah (pres. 1967-69, Citation 1969, Nat. Leadership award 2006). Jewish. Avocations: needlepoint, rug hooking, writing.

SCHANK, JEFFREY CHARLES, science educator, researcher; b. Omaha, Mar. 6, 1955; s. Charles E. and Lois A. Schank; m. Brenda D. Brinton; 1 child, Jeff. PhD, U Chgo., 1991. Postdoc. fellow U. Chgo., 1991—94, Ind. U., Bloomington, 1994—98; prof. U. Calif., Davis, 1998—. Postdoc. fellow, NSF, 1991—93, NIH, 1991—94, 1996—98, Ctr. Integrative Study of Animal Behavior, 1994—96. Office: Univ Calif One Shields Ave Davis CA 95616 Business E-Mail: jcschank@ucdavis.edu.

SCHANWALD, STEVE, professional sports team executive; Grad., U. Md., 1977. Dir. sports mktg. USAF Acad., 1978; dir. promotions Pitts. Pirates, 1979—80; asst. v.p. mktg. Chgo. White Sox, 1981—86; exec. v.p. bus. ops. Chgo. Bulls, 1987—; sr. v.p. mktg. United Ctr., Chgo. Guest lectr. U. Chgo. Bus. Sch., Northwestern Kellogg Grad. Sch. Bus., U. Notre Dame Bus. Sch., Am. Mktg. Assn. Founder, pres. CharitaBulls; bd. mem. James Jordan Boys and Girls Club. Recipient local Emmy award. Mem.: Chgo. Econ. Club. Office: Chgo Bulls United Ctr 1901 W Madison St Chicago IL 60612-2459*

SCHAPER, HERBERT WALTER AUGUST, retired chemist, researcher; b. Celle, Germany, Oct. 22, 1930; s. Hermann and Marie (Koch) Schaper; m. Karla Helene Koebernick, June 24, 1960; 1 child, Lars-Arne. Abitur, Gymnasium Celle, 1950; Diplom Chemiker, Tech. U. Hannover, 1958; Dr.rer.nat, Kautschuk-Inst. Hannover, 1962. Chemist rsch. devel. rubber and polyurethanes Phoenix AG, Hamburg, Germany, 1962—78, dir. polyurethanes rsch. and devel., 1978—93; ret., 1993. Dir. polyurethane rsch. cons. prod. plants Phoenix AG, 1978—93. Contbr. articles various profl. jours. Mem.: ADAC - German Automotive Club, SAE Internat., Deutsche Kautschukgesellschaft. Lutheran. Avocations: skiing, football, tennis. Home: Hagedornstr 22 Hamburg D20149 Germany Home Phone: 0049-40-442362. Home Fax: 0049-40-45035367.

SCHAPER, LEONARD W., retired engineering educator; BSEE, Newark Coll. Engring., 1967; SMEE, MIT, Cambridge, Mass., 1968; Dr. Engr. Sc., NJ Inst. Tech., Newark, 1973. Instr., elec. engring. NJ Inst. Tech., 1968—71, asst. prof, civil engring., 1973—78; mem. tech. staff AT&T Bell Labs., Whippany, NJ, 1978—81, supr., tech. planning, 1981—86, head, tech. program analysis, 1986—90; dir., thin film Alcoa Electronic Packaging, Rancho Bernardo, Calif., 1990—92; dir., HiDEC U. Ark., Fayetteville, 1992—2002, prof., elec. engring., 1992—. Cons., electronic packaging, 2003—. Editor: (book) Integrated Passive Component Technology; contbr. numerous articles to engring. jours., chapters to books, numerous sci. papers to conf. Founding mem. Friends Fayetteville, 1994—2000; alderman City Coun., Fayetteville, 1995—98.

Fellow: IEEE (mem. bd. govs., Components, Packaging and Mfg. Tech. Soc. 2007—, Outstanding Sustained Tech. Contbns. award 1996), Internat. Microelectronics and Packaging Soc. (pres. 1995—96, William D. Ashman award 2002). Achievements include patents for electronic packaging; invention of interconnected mesh power system.

SCHAPIRO, DONALD, lawyer; b. NYC, Aug. 8, 1925; s. John Max and Lydia (Chaitkin) S.; m. Ruth Ellen Goldman, June 29, 1952 (dec. Aug. 1991); m. Linda N. Solomon, Oct. 10, 1993; children: Jane G., Robert A. AB, Yale U., 1944, LL.B., 1949. Bar: N.Y. 1949. Assoc. Paul, Weiss, Rifkind, Wharton & Garrison, NYC, 1949-51; asst. chief counsel subcom. ways and means com. on adminstrn. revenue laws U.S. Ho. of Reps., Washington, 1951-52; assoc. Barrett, Smith, Schapiro, Simon & Armstrong, NYC, 1952-55, partner, 1955-88; ptnr. Chadbourne & Parke, 1988—. Vis. lectr. law Yale U. Law Sch., 1949-78, 94-95, instr. law and econs., 1945-49. Mem. Order of Coif, Phi Beta Kappa, Phi Delta Phi. Home: 1035 5th Ave New York NY 10028-0135 Office: Chadbourne & Parke 30 Rockefeller Plz Fl 32 New York NY 10112-0129 E-mail: dschapiro@chadbourne.com.

SCHAPIRO, MARY L., federal agency administrator; b. NYC, June 19, 1955; d. Robert D. and Susan (Hall) S.; m. Charles A. Cadwell, Dec. 13, 1980, 2 children BA, Franklin and Marshall Coll., 1977; JD, George Washington U., 1980. Bar: DC 1980. Trial atty., 1980-81; counsel to chmn. Commodity Futures Trading Commn. (CFTC), 1981-84; sr. v.p. Futures Industry Assn., 1984, gen. counsel, 1984-88; commr. US Securities & Exchange Commn. (SEC), Washington, 1988-94, acting chmn., 1993—94; chmn. Commodity Futures Trading Commn. (CFTC), Washington, 1994-96; pres. Nat. Assn. Securities Regulation, Inc., Washington, 1996—2002; vice chmn., pres., regulatory policy oversight divsn. Nat. Assn. Securities Dealers (NASD), Washington, 2002—06, chmn., CEO, 2006—07; CEO Fin. Industry Regulatory Authority, Inc. (FINRA), Washington, 2007—09; chmn. US Securities & Exchange Commn. (SEC), Washington, 2009—. Bd. dirs. Duke Energy Corp., 1999—2009, Kraft Foods Inc., 2001—09; chmn IOSCO SRO Consultative Com., 2002—06; mem. Tech. Com. and the Develop. Markets Com. of the Internat. Org. of Securities (IOSCO), President George W. Bush's Advisory Coun. on Financial Literacy, 2008. Bd. trustees, vice chmn. audit com. Franklin and Marshall Coll.; mem. advisory bd. RAND Corp. LRN-RAND Ctr. Corp. Ethics, Law & Governance. Recipient Visionary award, Nat. Coun. Econ. Edn. (NCEE), 2008; named Fin. Women's Assn. Pub. Sector Woman of the Yr., 2000; named one of 50 Women to Watch, The Wall St. Jour., 2006, 100 Most Powerful Women, Forbes mag., 2009. Office: SEC 100 F St NE Washington DC 20549*

SCHAPIRO, MIRIAM, artist; b. Toronto, Ont., Can., Nov. 15, 1923; d. Theodore and Fannie (Cohen) S. BA, State U. Iowa, 1945, MA, 1946, MFA, 1949; doctorate (hon.), Wooster Coll., 1983, Calif. Coll. Arts Crafts, 1989, Mpls. Coll. Art Design, 1994, Miami U., 1995, Moore Coll. Art, Phila., 1995. Co-orginator Womanhouse, Los Angeles, 1972, Heresies mag., N.Y.C., 1975; co-originator feminist art program Calif. Inst. Arts, Valencia, 1971; founding mem. Feminist Art Inst., N.Y.C.; mem. adv. bd. Women's Caucus for Art; assoc. mem. Heresies Collective; lectr. dept. art history U. Mich., 1987. Works in numerous books and catalogues; numerous one-woman shows including, Galerie Liatowitsch, Basel, Switzerland, 1979, Lerner Heller Gallery, N.Y.C., 1979, Barbara Gladstone Gallery, N.Y.C., 1980, Spencer Mus. Art, Lawrence, Kans., 1981, Everson Mus., Syracuse, N.Y., 1981, Galerie Rudolf Zwirner, Cologne, Fed. Republic Germany, 1981, Staatagalerie, Stuttgart, Fed. Republic Germany, 1983, Dart Gallery, Chgo, 1984, Bernice Steinbaum Gallery/Steinbaum Krauss Gallery, N.Y.C., 1986, 88, 90, 91, 94, 97, Brevard Art Ctr. and Mus., Melbourne, Fla., 1991, Guild Hall Mus., East Hampton, N.Y., 1992, ARC Gallery, Chgo., 1993, James Madison U., Harrisburg, Va., 1996, Nat. Mus. Am. Art Smithsonian Inst., Washington, 1997. others; retrospective exhbn., Wooster (Ohio) Coll. Art Mus., 1980; exhibited in numerous group shows, including, Palais de Beaux Arts, Brussels, 1979, Inst. Contemporary Art, Phila., 1979, Delahunty Gallery, Dallas, 1980, Indpls. Mus., 1980, Va. Mus., Richmond, 1980, Laguna Gloria Mus., Austin, Tex., 1980, R.O.S.C., Dublin, Ireland, 1980, Biennale of Sydney, Australia, 1982, Zurich, Switzerland, 1983, Sidney Janis Gallery, N.Y.C., 1984, Am. Acad. Arts and Letters, N.Y.C., 1985, Mus. Modern Art, N.Y.C., 1988, Whyte Mus. Can. Rockies, Banff, Alta., 1991, Nat. Mus. Women in Arts., Wash., 1993, Jane Voorhees Zimmerli art mus. Rutger's U., New Brunswick, N.J., 1994, Mus. of F.A. Boston, 1994, Santa Barbara Mus. of Art, 1994, Hudson River Mus. of Westchester, Yonkers, N.Y., 1995, Mus. of Contemporary Arts, Los Angeles, Calif. Bronx Mus. of the Arts, N.Y., 1995, Columbus (Ga.) Mus., 1996, Parrish Mus., Southampton, N.Y., 1997, Austin (Tex.) Mus., 1997, Whitney Mus., 2000; represented in permanent collections, Hirshhorn Mus., Washington, Bklyn. Mus., Met. Mus. Art, N.Y.C., Mus. Contemporary Art, San Diego, Mpls. Inst. Art, Mulvane Art Center, Topeka, Nat. Gallery Art, Washington, N.Y.U., Peter Ludwig Collection, Aachen, Germany, Stanford U., Palo Alto, Calif., Univ. Art Mus., Berkeley, Calif., Whitney Mus., N.Y.C., Worcester (Mass.) Art Mus., Santa Barbara (Calif.) Mus. Art, Nat. Mus. Am. Art Smithsonian Inst., Washington, also others; author: (books) Women and the Creative Process, 1974, Rondo: An Artists Book, 1988; sculpture Anna and David, Rosslyn, Va., 1987. Guggenheim fellow, 1987, Nat. Endowment for Arts fellow; grantee Ford Found.; recipient numerous other grants and fellowships. Mem. Coll. Art Assn. (past dir.). Office: Elly Flomenhaft Gallery 547 W 27th St Ste 308 New York NY 10001 Office Phone: 631-329-8951. *Process and ideology in an opulent, multilayered, eccentric and hopeful abstract art: 1. The need for order and stability. 2. The need to destroy order and stability in order to find something else. 3. Finding something else. Pattern, itself an architectural species, reflects order and stability. Then a need to create chaos as though life itself were taking place. Finally the bonding layer by layer, the interpenetration of paint, fabric, photograph, tea towel, ribbon, lace, and glue. A collage: a simultaneity; a visual dazzlement, a multi-layering, a final message for the senses. And the ideology which inspires the work itself? That is feminism, the wish to have the art speak as a woman speaks. To be sensitive to the material used as though there were a responsibility to history to repair the sense of omission and to have each substance in the collage be a reminder of a woman's dreams. All of my works are auto-biographical. They are about the yearnings of a woman who decided a long time ago to become a painter.*

SCHAPIRO, MORTON OWEN, academic administrator; m. Mimi Schapiro; children: Matt, Alissa, Rachel. BA in economics, Hofstra U., 1975; PhD, U. Pa., 1979. Prof. economics, asst. provost Williams Coll., 1980—91; chair, dept. economics U. So. Calif., 1991—94, dean, Coll. Letters, Arts and Sciences, 1994—2000, v.p. planning, 1998—2000; prof. economics Williams Coll., 2000—09, pres., 2000—09, Northwestern U., 2009—. Commentator Pub. Radio Internat; expert witness on econ. issues in higher edn. U.S. Congress; bd. dirs. Marsh & McLennan Cos. Inc., 2002—. Co-author (with Michael S. McPherson): Keeping College Affordable, 1991, Paying the Piper, 1993, The Student Aid Game, 1998; contbr. articles to profl. jours. Office: Northwestern U Office of Pres 633 Clark St Evanston IL 60208-1100 Office Phone: 847-491-8413. E-mail: nu-president@northwestern.edu.*

SCHAPP, REBECCA MARIA, museum director; b. Stuttgart, Fed. Republic Germany, Dec. 12, 1956; came to U.S., 1957; d. Randall Todd and Elfriede Carolina (Scheppan) Spradlin; m. Thomas James Schapp, May 29, 1979. AA, DeAnza Coll., 1977; BA in Art, San Jose State U., 1979, MA in Art Adminstrn., 1985. Adminstrv. dir. Union Gallery, San Jose, Calif., 1979-82; from mus. coordinator to dep. dir. de Saisset Mus. Santa Clara (Calif.) U., 1982-92, dir., 1993—. Mem. San Francisco Mus. Modern Art; bd. dirs. Works of San Jose, v.p. 1983-85. Mem. Non-Profit Gallery Assn. (bd. dirs.). Democrat. Avocations: racquetball, walking, bicycling, camping. Office: De Saisset Mus Santa Clara U 500 El Camino Real Santa Clara CA 95050-4345

SCHAPPERT, JOHN CONRAD, computer software company executive; b. North Miami, Fla., July 14, 1970; s. John and Barbara Ann (Nash) S.; m. Kelly Elizabeth Johnson, May 4, 1996. AA with honors, Miami Dade C.C., Fla., 1990. Programmer Visual Concepts, San Mateo, Calif., 1991-94; pres. Tiburon Entertainment, Maitland, Fla., 1994—98; with Electronic Arts, Inc., Redwood City, Calif., 1998—2007, gen. mgr. Electronic Arts Tiburon, 1998—2002, gen. mgr. Electronic Arts Can., 2002, group gen. mgr., COO worldwide studios, sr. v.p., COO worldwide studios, COO, 2009—; corp. v.p. LIVE software & services, interactive entertainment bus. divsn. Microsoft Corp., Redmond, Wash., 2007—09. Programmer (video games) Desert Strike, 1992, John Madden Football 94, 1993-94; programmer, project leader Bill Walsh College Football, 1993; developer, dir. John Madden Football 97, 1996, others. Named Programmer of the Yr. Electronic Arts, 1994; named one of 40 Under 40, Bus. in Vancouver, 2005. Office: Electronic Arts Inc 209 Redwood Shores Pky Redwood City CA 94065

SCHAR, DWIGHT C., construction executive; b. 1942; With Ryan Homes, Washington, 1986-77, NVLand, 1977—, NVR Inc., 1980-86, pres., CEO, 1986—2005, chmn., 2005—. Bd. dirs. NVCompanies Inc. Office: Dwight Schar 11700 Plaza America Dr Ste 500 Reston VA 20190-4792

SCHARF, CHARLES W., diversified financial services company executive; b. 1965; m. Amy E. Scharf; 2 children. BA, Johns Hopkins U., 1987; MBA, N.Y. U. With Comml. Credit Corp., 1987-95; various sr. positions to CFO Salomon Smith Barney, 1995-98; CFO global corp. & investment bank Citigroup Inc., 1998-2000; exec. v.p., CFO Bank One Corp., Chgo., 2000—02, head retail banking, 2002—04; CEO retail fin. services J.P. Morgan Chase & Co., NYC, 2004—. Bd. dirs. Travelers Property Casualty Corp., 2002—05, Visa U.S.A., 2003—07, Visa Inc., 2007—. Office: JP Morgan Chase & Co 270 Park Ave New York NY 10017*

SCHARF, ERIC, lawyer, educator; b. San José, Costa Rica, Mar. 10, 1970; s. Salomón Scharf and Masha Taitelbaum; m. Galit Flasterstein, June 10, 1995. B. Law with honors, U. Costa Rica, San José, 1992, JD with honors, 1994; LLM with honors, Columbia U., NY, 1999; student, Coll. Insurance, 1999, Practicing Law Inst., 2000. Bar: Costa Rica; lic. notary pub., Costa Rica. Legal asst. Facio & Cañas Law Firm, San José, 1989-94, assoc., 1994—2000; fgn. assoc. Brown & Wood LLP, NY, 1999—2000; ptnr./mem. Feinzaig Scharf & van der Putten, San José, 2000—. Prof.'s asst. U. Costa Rica, San José 1992-93, prof. Roman Law 1995-1997, Civil Law and Obligations U. Costa Rica 1997-1998, 2001-2002. Contbr. articles to profl. jours. Exec. sec. Law Students Assn., U. Costa Rica, 1989-90. OAS Scholar 1998-1999, Columbia Law Sch. Rubin Fellow 1998-1999, Columbia Law Sch. Harlan Fiske Stone Scholar 1999. Mem. Costa Rican Bar, Internat. Insurance Soc., Costa Rica Assn. Internat. Law (treas. 1994-96), Costa Rica Assn. Ins. Law (treas. 2008-), Assn. Legal Study Free Trade Agreement (tres. 2005-06). Jewish. Avocations: bicycling, swimming. Office: Feinzaig Scharf & Van der Putten Paseo Colón Torre Mercedes Bldg 8th Fl PO Box 11957-1000 San José Costa Rica Home Phone: 506-2228-7878; Office Phone: 506-2295-6699. Office Fax: 506-2295-6644. Business E-Mail: escharf@fsvlaw.com.

SCHARF, MICHAEL PAUL, law educator; b. Pitts., Apr. 25, 1963; s. Harry and Joan (Seder) S.; m. Trina Elizabeth Smith, May 9, 1988; 1 child, Garrett Michael. AB, Duke U., 1985, JD, 1988. Bar: D.C. 1989. Jud. clk. U.S. Ct. Appeals (11th cir.), Jacksonville, Fla., 1988-89; atty.-adviser Office Legal Adviser, U.S. Dept. State, Washington, 1989-93; asst. prof. law New England Sch. of Law, Boston, 1993—96, assoc. prof. law, 1996—98; prof. law New England Sch. Law, Boston, 1998—2002, Case Western U., 2002—; founder, ptnr. Publ. Internat. Law Policy Group, 1995—. Mem. U.S. Del. to 46th and 47th Sessions of UN Gen. Assembly, U.S. Del. to 49th Session of UN Human Rights Commn.; adj. prof. Georgetown U. Law Ctr., Washington, 1992; chmn. bd. dirs. Internat. Model UN Assn. Inc. N.Y.C., 1984-88; dir. New Eng. Ctr. for Internat. Law and Policy, 1996—02; expert commentator Ct. TV, 1996; dir. Frederick K. Cox Internat. Law Ctr., 2003—. Author: An Insider's Guide to the International Criminal Tribunal for the Former Yugoslavia, 1995, International Criminal Law: Cases and Materials, 1996, Balkan Justice: The Story Behind the First International War Crimes Trial Since Nuremberg, 1997, The Internat. Criminal Tribunal For Rwanda (with Morris), 1998, The Law of International Organizations, 2001, Peace with Justice? 2002, Slobodan Milosevic on Trial, 2002, Saddam on Trial, 2006. Nominee Nobel Peace Prize, 2005. Mem. ABA (U.S. Govt. rep. blue ribbon task force on internat. criminal ct. 1991-93), D.C. Bar (chmn. steering com. internat. law sect. 1991-93), Internat. Law Assn. (exec. com. Am. br. 1996—), Internat. Assn. Penal Law (dep. sec. gen.), Order of Coif, U.N. Assn. Greater Boston (bd. dirs. 1993—); Pub. Internat. Law Group (bd. dir., 1996-); Internat. Law Students Assn. (bd. dirs. 1999—). Avocations: skiing, sailing, tennis, softball, guitar. Office Phone: 216-368-3299. E-mail: michael.scharf@case.edu.

SCHARF, STEPHANIE A., lawyer; m. Jeffry Mandell; children: Meredith, Jonathan. BA, Rutgers U.; MA, Stanford U.; PhD, U. Chgo., 1978, JD, 1985. Bar: Ill. 1985, US Dist. Ct. (no., ctrl. and so. dists.) Ill., US Dist. Ct. (no. dist.) Ind., US Dist. Ct. (we. dist.) Mich., US Ct. Appeals (first cir.), NY 2008. Sr. study dir. Nat. Opinion Rsch. Ctr., Chgo.; ptnr. Schoeman Updike Kaufman & Scharf, Chgo. Author: Consumer Fraud Litigation: Law and Defenses in Illinois, 2004, The Business of Drug Development, 2004, Direct-to-Consumer Advertising of Prescription Pharmaceuticals and Medical Devices, 2004, Through the Glass Ceiling: Best Practices for Women Lawyers and Their Firms, 2004, Benchmarking for Success: Introducing NAWL Assessment Questionnaire, 2004, A Business Approach to Minimizing Product Liability Litigation, 2005, New Rulings In Drug Cases Highlight Debate Over Pre-emption, 2006, Punitive Damages in Supreme Court: How Much is Too Much?, 2007, Foreign Plaintiff's Battle to Keep Class Claims in U.S. Courts, 2007, FDA Proposes Revised CBE Rules and Reiterates Preemptive Authority, 2008; co-author: The Media and Products Litigation, 1996, Communications Specialists Help With Damage Control, 1997, Marketing Pharmaceutical Products on the Internet: Managing Risks and Limiting Liabilities in the World of E-Commerce, 2001, Post-Sale Duties to Warn, Recall, and Retrofit Defective Products in Illinois, 2003, The Evidentiary Impact of Regulatory Action on Product Litigation in the United States, 2004, Immigration Reform and the Federal Law of Employment Discrimination, FDA's Comments Herald New Strength for Preemption Defense in Drug Product Litigation, 2006; editor: The Use of Epidemiology in Tort Litigation: A Survey of Federal and State Jurisdictions, 2003; co-editor: The Use of Toxicology in Tort Litigation, 2005, Current Law, Strategies and Practices in Product Liability Litigation, 2009; contbr. articles to profl. jours. Bd. mem. The Youth Campus, Chgo.; chair, Best Interest of the Child Subcommittee Cir. Ct. Cook County, mem. Chief judge's Pub. Guardian Com. Harper Fellow, Univ. Chgo. Mem.: ABA (co-editor Product Liability newsletter 1997—2000, editor Mass Torts newsletter 2001, co-chair sect. litig. products liability com. 2005—07, mem. mass torts com., bd. dirs., mem. spl. com. bioethics), NAWL Found. (pres. 2008—), Internat. Assn. Def. Counsel, Spl. Com. Bioethics, Pub. Guardian Com., Best Interest of Child Subcom. of Child Protection Adv. Com. (chair 1995—96), Circuit Ct. Cook County, Def. Rsch. Inst., Ill. Bar Found. (bd. mem. 2005—), Univ. Chgo. Women's Bus. Group, Products Liability Adv. Coun. (mem. case selection com.), Nat. Assn. Women Lawyers (bd. dirs. 2000—08, chair, Survey of Retention and Promotion of Women in Law Firms 2006, chair, com. for evaluation of Supreme Ct. nominees), U. Chgo. Women's Bus. Group. Office: Schoeman Updike Kaufman Scharf 333 W Wacker Dr Ste 300 Chicago IL 60606 Office Phone: 312-726-6000. Business E-Mail: sscharf@schoeman.com.

SCHARF, THOMAS W., engineering educator; b. Allentown, Pa., July 6, 1971; s. William and Rosemary Scharf; m. Nikki Breedlove, Nov. 6, 2004; 1 child, Max. BS, Pa. State U., Univ. Pk., 1994; degree in Metall. and Materials Engring., U. Ala., Tuscaloosa, 1997, degree in Metall. and Materials Engring., 2000. Postdoc. rsch. assoc. Naval Rsch. Labs., Washington, 2000—03; mem. tech. staff Sandia Nat. Labs., Albuquerque, 2003—05; prof. dept. materials sci. and engring. U. North Tex., Denton, 2005—. Author: (book) Baltimore's Boxing Legacy 1894-2004; contbr. chapters to books. Recipient Young Investigator award, Am. Chem. Soc.; grant, NSF, 2007—, Am. Chem. Soc., 2007—08. Mem.: Soc. Tribologists and Lubrication Engrs. (pres. solid lubricants tech. com. 2007—08). Office: Univ N Tex 1155 Union Cir #305310 Denton TX 76203-5017 Business E-Mail: scharf@unt.edu.

SCHARF, WILLIAM, artist; b. Media, Pa., Feb. 22, 1927; s. Lester William and Ebba (Anderson) S.; m. Diana Denny, Mar. 11, 1947 (div. 1951); 1 child, William Denny; m. Sally Kravitch, Mar. 25, 1956; 1 child, Aaron Anderson. Student, Barnes Found., 1946-47; cert. in painting, Pa. Acad. of Fine Arts, 1947. Instr. Mus. Modern Art, NYC, 1964, Sch. Visual Arts, NYC, 1965-73, San Francisco Inst. Fine Arts, 1963, 66, 69, 74, 89. One-man shows include David Herbert Gallery, NYC, 1960, 62, San Francisco Inst. Fine Arts, 1969, Neuberger Mus., Purchase, NY, 1976, High Mus., Atlanta, 1978, Armstrong Gallery, NYC, 1987, U. Mich. Mus. Art, Ann Arbor, 1993, Phillips Collection, Washington, 2000-01, Frederick R. Weisman Mus., Malibu, Calif., 2001, 07, P.S.1, MOMA, Queens, 2002, Richard York Gallery, NYC, 2004, Meredith Ward Fine Art, NYC, 2005, 2009; Mercury Gallery, Boston, 2007-08; exhibited in group shows at Guggenheim Mus., NYC, 1982, Hirschl-Adler Gallery, NYC, 1980, Smith-Anderson Gallery, Palo Alto, Calif., Nat. Mus. Am. Art, Washington, 1987, 91-92, Am. Acad. and Inst. Arts and Letters, NYC, 1989, 91, Richard York Gallery, NYC, 2002, Nat. Acad. Design Mus., NYC, 2003, 05, 09, Nat. Head Design Mus., 2007; represented in permanent collections Ark. Arts, Little Rock, Phila. Mus., Boston Inst. Contemporary Art, Bklyn. Mus., Carnegie Museum Art, Pitts., Pa., Solomon R. Guggenheim Mus., NYC, Newark Mus., Nat. Mus. Am. Art, Smith Coll. Mus., Northampton, Mass., Zimmerli Mus., Rutgers U., New Brunswick, NJ, U. Mich. Mus. art., Phillips Collection, Washington, The Neuroscience Inst., San Diego, The High Mus., Atlanta, Colgate U., Telfair Mus. of Art, Savannah, Ga., Rose Art Mus., Brandeis U., Montgomery (Ala.) Mus. Art, Cath. U., Washington, Fogg Art Mus. Harvard U., Cambridge, Mass., Yale U. Mus., New Haven, Colo. Springs Fine Arts Ctr., Colo. Trustee Rothko Found., NYC, 1979—87; instr. Art Students League, NY, 1987—. With USAF, 1945—46. Emmlen Cresson fellow Pa. Acad. Fine Arts, 1948. Mem.: Nat. Acad. Design, Soc. of Illustrators, Artist Equity Assn.

SCHARFF, JOSEPH LAURENT, lawyer; b. New Orleans, Oct. 2, 1935; s. Joseph Roy and Celia Ray S.; m. Mary Susan Greulach, June 29, 1963; children: Catherine Elizabeth, Robert Laurent, Anne Victoria. BS in Journalism, Northwestern U., 1957; JD, Harvard U., 1964. Bar: D.C. 1965, U.S. Supreme Ct. 1970, U.S. Ct. Appeals (D.C. cir.) 1965, U.S. Ct. Appeals (2nd cir.) 1980, U.S. Ct. Appeals (5th cir.) 1973, U.S. Ct. Appeals (10th cir.); U.S. Ct. Claims 1965. From assoc. to ptnr. Pierson, Ball & Dowd, Washington, 1964-89; ptnr. Reed Smith Shaw & McClay, Washington, 1989-95, counsel, 1996. Mem. ABA (fair trial-free press com. 1973-76, com. reps. media 1985-95, co-chmn. 1989-92), Fed. Comm. Bar Assn., Soc. Profl. Journalists, Radio-TV News Dirs. Assn. (counsel 1965-95, Disting. Svc. award 1987, J. Laurent Scharff Legal Internship established 1996), Media Inst. (First Amendment Adv. Coun. 1993-2003). Home and Office: 12000 Turf Ln Reston VA 20191-2123

SCHARLEMANN, ROBERT PAUL, theology studies educator, minister; b. Lake City, Minn., Apr. 4, 1929; s. Ernst Karl and Johanna Meta (Harre) Scharlemann. Student, Northwestern Coll., Watertown, Wis., 1946-49; BA, Concordia Coll. and Sem., St. Louis, 1952; BD, MDiv, Concordia Coll. and Sem., 1955; Dr. theol., U. Heidelberg, Germany, 1957. Ordained to ministry Luth. Ch., 1960. Tchr. Luth. parochial sch., Mobridge, SD, 1949—50; instr. philosophy Valparaiso U., 1957-59; postdoctoral fellow Yale U., 1959-60; pastor Bethlehem Luth. Ch., Carlyle, Ill., 1960-62, Grace Luth. Ch., Durham, NC, 1962-63; asst. prof. religion U. So. Calif., 1963-64, assoc. prof., 1964-66; assoc. prof. religion U. Iowa, Iowa City, 1966-68, prof., 1968-81; Commonwealth prof. religious studies U. Va., Charlottesville, 1981-97, prof. emeritus, 1997—. Fulbright-Hays prof. U. Heidelberg, 1975—76. Author: Thomas Aquinas and John Gerhard, 1964, Reflection and Doubt in the Thought of Paul Tillich, 1969, The Being of God, 1981, Inscriptions and Reflections, 1989, The Reason of Following, 1991, L'intemporel et l'éternel, 1993, Can Religion be Understood Philosophically?, 1995, The Mystical Correlate of Symbolic Appearing, 2001, Religion and Reflection, 2004; editor: Jour. Am. Acad. Religion, 1980—85; contbr. articles to profl. jours. Fulbright scholar, U. Heidelberg, 1955—57. Mem.: Soc. Philosophy Religion, Deutsche Paul-Tillich Gesellschaft, Am. Theol. Soc., Am. Acad. Religion, European Soc. Culture. Lutheran.

SCHAROLD, MARY LOUISE, psychoanalyst, psychiatrist, educator; b. Wichita Falls, Tex., Mar. 3, 1943; d. Walter John and Louise Helen (Hartmann) Baumgartner; m. William Ballew McCollum, Aug. 23, 1964 (div. 1981); m. Harry Karl Scharold, June 19, 1982; children: Margaret Louise, Walter Ballew. BA with highest distinction, U. Kans., 1964; attended, U. Kans. Sch. Medicine, 1964—66; MD, Baylor Coll. Medicine, 1968; attended, Houston-Galveston Psychoanalytic Inst., 1974—76; postgrad., Topeka Inst. Psychoanalysis, 1981. Diplomate Am. Bd. Psychiatry and Neurology, 1975, cert. adult psychoanalysis Am. Psychoanalytic Assn., 1982. Intern Meml. Bapt. Hosp., Houston, 1968-69; resident in psychiatry Baylor Coll. Medicine, Houston, 1969—72, chief resident, 1971-72; psychiatrist Houston, 1972—; psychoanalyst, 1981—. Asst. prof. Baylor Coll. Medicine, Houston, 1973-76, asst. clin. prof., 1981-84, assoc. clin. prof., 1984—; dir. Baylor Psychiat. Clinic,

Houston, 1973-76; co-dir. Rice U. Psychiat. Svc., Houston, 1981-82; asst. clin. prof. U. Kans. Sch. Medicine, Kansas City, 1977-81; tchg. assoc. Topeka Psychoanalytic Inst., 1984-86; tchg. analyst, Houston-Galveston Psychoanalytic Inst., 1986-90, tng. and supervising analyst, 1990—, v.p., 1994-96, pres., 1996-01, bd. dirs., 2001-04; acting pres. bd. trustees Child Devel. Ctr., 2005, sec. bd. trustees, 2005-. Contbr. articles to profl. pubs. Adv. bd. Leavenworth (Kans.) Mental Health Assn., 1977-81; sec. bd. trustees, Child Devel. Ctr., 2005-. Watkins scholar U. Kans., 1961-64; Grad. Fellowship award, Pi Beta Phi, 1965; recipient Hilltopper, Ten Outstanding Sr. Women, U. Kans., 1963, Greater U. Fund award, 1964, U. Kans., Eugen Kahn award, Outstanding Baylor Psychiatry Resident, 1972, 1st Disting. Svc. award, Houston-Galveston Psychoanalytic Soc., 2004; named Outstanding Woman Med. Student, AMWA, Houston Branch, 1968; named to Best Doctors in Am., 1998, 2007. Mem. Am. Psychiat. Assn. (disting. life fellow, mem. com. quality assurance 1986-87, chair Tex. peer rev. 1984-88), Am. Coll. Psychoanalysts, Am. Psychoanalytic Assn. (cert. 1982, peer rev. com. 1985-90, prof. ins. commn. 1986-93, bd. profl. stds. 1994-2001, CME com. 1994-96, exec. coun. 1994-96, cert. com. 1995-98, preparedness and progress com. 1998-2006, chair preparedness and progress com. 2000-06, coordinating com. bd. profl. stds. 2000-06, bylaws com. 2001—, fin. com. 2003—, councilor-at-large 2005—, chair councillors-at-large, 2007—, hon. membership.com, 2005-, election oversight com., 2005—, compliance task force, 2006-07, com. on coun., 2006—2008, annual meeting task force 2008, audit com. 2008—), Am. Group Psychotherapy Assn., Ctr. Advanced Psychoanalytic Studies, Houston Psychiat. Soc. (v.p. 1984-85, pres.-elect 1985-86, pres. 1986-87), Houston-Galveston Psychoanalytic Soc. (sec.-treas. 1984-86, pres.-elect 1986-88, pres. 1988-90, alt. councillor 1994-96), Houston Group Psychotherapy Soc. (adv. bd. 1984-85), Mortar Bd., Phi Beta Kappa, Delta Phi Alpha, Alpha Omega Alpha, Pi Beta Phi Alumni Assn. Republican. Lutheran. Office: 2301 Westheimer Rd Houston TX 77098-1317 Home Phone: 713-590-2301; Office Phone: 713-590-2302. Personal E-mail: mlscharold@mindspring.com.

SCHAROUN, SUSAN L., psychologist, educator; b. Syracuse, NY, Sept. 3, 1955; d. Elizabeth Hilliker and Rupert Merrill Scharoun; 1 child, Elizabeth Hynds. BS, SUNY Coll. Environ. Sci. and Forestry, Syracuse, 1978; BS in Biology, Syracuse U., 1978, BA in German, 1978, PhD, 1983. Postdoc. fellow U. Rochester Med. Sch., 1983—84; assoc. psychologist NYS-Office Mental Retardation and Devel. Disabilities, Syracuse, 1983—; prof. Le Moyne Coll., Dept. Psychology, Syracuse, 1988—, chair, 2001—. Contbr. articles to profl. jours. Mem.: AAMR. Liberal. Office: Le Moyne Coll 1419 Salt Springs Rd Syracuse NY 13215 Office Phone: 315-445-4788. Business E-Mail: scharoun@lemoyne.edu.

SCHARSCHMIDT, BRUCE FREDERICK, physician; b. Cleve., Mar. 6, 1946; s. Lewis Wilson and Roselyn Elizabeth (Klein) Scharschmidt; m. Peggy Sue Crawford Scharschmidt, June 4, 1977; children: Tiffany, Brent. BS, Northwestern U., 1966, MD, 1970. Diplomate Am. Bd. Internal Medicine. Intern U. Calif., San Francisco, 1970—71, resident medicine, 1971—72, fellow, 1975—77, asst. prof. medicine, 1977—81, assoc. prof. medicine, 1981—85, prof., 1985—96; assoc. dir. Liver Ctr., 1983—96; cons. liver transplantation US, Calif. govts., 1983—; v.p. Chiron Corp., 1996—2006, Novartis, 2006—08; sr. v.p. Hyperion Therapeutics Inc., 2008—. Editl. bd. Hepatology Jour., 1981—86; assoc. editor Gastroenterology, 1981—86; editor Jour. Clin. Ivestigation, 1987—92. Contbr. articles to profl. jours. Lt. comdr. USPHS, 1972—75. Recipient Rsch Career Devel. award, 1977—82; grantee, NIH, 1980—2000. Mem.: Assn. Am. Physicians, Western Assn. Physicians, Western Soc. Clin. Investigation, Soc. Exptl. Biology & Medicine, Am. Liver Found. (bd. dir.), Internat. Assn. Study Liver, Am. Gastroenterol. Assn., Am. Assn. Study Liver Disease, Am. Soc. Clin. Investigation (pres. 1992—93), Am. Fedn. Clin. Rsch., Nathan Smith Davis Club (alumni bd. & pres.), Western Gut Club, Phi Eta Sigma, Alpha Omega Alpha. Republican. Office Phone: 650-745-7851. Personal E-mail: bruce.scharschmidt@gmail.com.

SCHATKIN, ANDREW JAMES, lawyer; b. NYC, Aug. 19, 1948; s. Sidney Bernhard and Amy Wheeler (White) S. AB in Classical Langs. cum laude, CUNY, 1969; MDiv, Princeton Theol. Sem., 1973; JD, Villanova U., 1976; Diploma, U. Strasbourg, France, 1984; Cert. in Internat. Law, Acad. Internat. Law, The Hague, The Netherlands, 1985. Bar: NY 1977, US Dist. Ct. (so. and ea. dists.) NY 1978, US Dist. Ct. (no. dist.) NY 1998, US Ct. Claims 1991, US Ct. Mil. Appeals 1991, US Ct. Appeals (2d cir.) 1979, US Ct. Appeals (fed. cir.) 1991, US Supreme Ct. 1991. Dep. county atty. Nassau County Atty., Mineola, NY, 1977-81; Assoc. Rivkin, Leff, Sherman and Radler, Garden City, NY, 1981-82; pvt. practice Bayside, NY, 1982-86; Atty. Office of Hearings and Appeals, Social Security Adminstrn., New Haven, 1986-87; staff atty. Criminal Def. Divsn. Legal Aid Soc., NYC, 1987-94; pvt. practice Jericho, NY, 1994—. Adj. prof. in paralegal studies Borough of Manhatten CC, 2002; adj. prof. in criminal law St. Francis Coll., 2005; adj. instr. in matrimonial and criminal law CW Post Coll., 2005; adj. prof. paralegal studies Queens Borough CC, 2006; adj. prof. paralegal studies, legal rsch. & writing Hofstra U., 2009. Author 5 books and chpts. to books; contbr. over 150 articles to profl. jours. Named one of Outstanding Young Men of Am., 1979. Mem. ABA (criminal justice sect., family law sect., internat. law and practice sect., labor and employment law sect.), Nat. Assn. Criminal Def. Lawyers (scholarship 1994, 95), NY State Assn. Criminal Def. Lawyers, NY State Defenders Assn., NY State Bar Assn., Suffolk County Bar Assn., Queens County Bar Assn., Nassau County Bar Assn. Republican. Lutheran. Avocations: reading, writing, classical music, travel, languages. Home: 21050 41st Ave Bayside NY 11361-1965 Office: 350 Jericho Tpke Jericho NY 11753-1317 Home Phone: 718-229-2761; Office Phone: 516-932-8120. Personal E-mail: schatkin@yahoo.com.

SCHATTEN, GERALD PHILLIP, stem cell biologist, reproductive biologist, educator; b. NYC, Nov. 1, 1949; s. Frank and Sylvia Schatten; children, Daniel, Madeline, Samantha. BS, U. Calif., Berkeley, 1971, PhD, 1975. Instr. U. Calif., Berkeley, 1975; postdoctoral fellow Rockefeller Found., 1976-77; from asst. prof. to prof. Fla. State U., Tallahassee, 1979-86; prof. molecular biology, zoology and obstetrics gynecology U. Wis., Madison, 1986-97, rsch. dir. women's health rsch., 1997—, dir. integrated microscopy resource for biomed. rsch., 1986-92, dir. gamete and embryo biol. tng. program, 1989-97; program dir. Mellon Ctr. of Excellence in Reproductive Biology, 1996-97, 99—; prof. ob-gyn. and cell-devel. biology, sr. scientist Oreg. Regional Primate Rsch. Ctr. Oreg. Health Scis. U., Portland, 1997-2001; dir. Pitts. Devel. Ctr., dep. dir. Magee-Women's Rsch. Inst., Pitts., 2001—, vice chair, prof. dept. ob/gyn./reproductive scis., prof. cell biology and physiology, 2001—. Dir. gamete and embryo biol. tng. program U. Wis., Madison, 1989-97; exec. bd. UNESCO Internat. Cell Rsch. Orgn., 1995—; co-dir. frontiers in reprodn. course Marine Biol. Lab., Woods Hole, Mass., 1998-2001. Editor Current Topics in Devel. Biology, 1996-2007 Recipient Rsch. Career Devel. award NIH, 1981-86, Merit award, 1997-, Sadler award, 1998; Purkinge medal of sci. Czech Acad. Scis., 2000, Patrick Steptoe medal, brit. Fertility Socs., 2005, Stem Cell Sci. and Policy award, Genetics Policy Inst., 2005, Pioneer Human Embryonic Stem Cell award, Stanfor U., 2005. Mem.: Nat. Inst. Aging Coun. Office: Univ PItts Pitts Devel Ctr 204 Craft Ave Pittsburgh PA 15213

SCHATTSCHNEIDER, DORIS JEAN, retired mathematics professor; b. NYC, Oct. 19, 1939; d. Robert W. Jr. and Charlotte Lucile (Ingalls) Wood; m. David A. Schattschneider, June 2, 1962; 1 child, Laura E. AB, U. Rochester, NY, 1961; MA, Yale U., New Haven, Conn., 1963, PhD, 1966. Instr. in math. Northwestern U., Evanston, Ill., 1964—65; asst. prof. U. Ill., Chgo., 1965—68; prof. Moravian Coll., Bethlehem, Pa., 1968—2002, prof. emerita, 2003—. Project dir. Fund for Improvement of Post-Secondary Edn. US Dept. Edn., 1991—93, project dir. Fund for the Improvement of Post-Secondary Edn., 1995—97; vis. scholar U. VI., 2004. Co-author (with W. Walker): (books and models) M.C. Escher Kaleidocycles, 1977, 1987; co-author: (videos and activities) Visual Geometry Project, 1986—91, A Companion to Calculus, 1995, 2nd edit., 2005; author: M.C. Escher: Visions of Symmetry, 1990, 2nd edit., 2004; editor: Geometry Turned On, 1997, M.C. Escher's Legacy, 2003. Exhbn. curator Allentown Art Mus., 1979, Payne Gallery, 1987. Grantee NEH rsch. grantee, 1988—90. Mem.: Assn. for Women in Math., Am. Math. Soc., Math. Assn. Am. (editor 1980—85, gov. 1980—89, 1st v.p. 1994—96, Allendoerfer award 1979, Meritorious Svc. award 1991, Dist. Math. Tchg. award 1993), Pi Mu Epsilon (councillor 1990—96). Mem. Moravian Ch. Office: Moravian Coll Math Dept PPHAC 1200 Main St Bethlehem PA 18018-6650 E-mail: schattdo@moravian.edu.

SCHATZ, BRIAN E., political organization administrator, environmentalist, former state legislator; b. Oct. 20, 1972; m. Linda Kwok Kai Yun; 1 child, Tyler. BA in Philosophy, Pomona Coll. Tchr. Punahou Sch.; mem. Dist. 25 Hawaii House of Reps., 1999—2006; CEO Helping Hands Hawaii; chmn. Dem. Party of Hawaii, 2008—. Dir. Makiki Cmty. Libr., Ctr. for a Sustainable Future. Recipient Pres.'s Award, Hawaii Audubon Soc., Bank of Hawaii Cmty. Leader of the Yr., 2004, NOAA's Environ. Hero Award. Democrat. Office: Dem Party of Hawaii 1050 Ala Moana Blvd, #26 Honolulu HI 96814 Office Phone: 808-596-2980.*

SCHATZ, GARY STEWART, marketing professional; b. NYC, 1951; s. Irving and Esther Schatz; m. Rita Schatz. BA, Syracuse U., NY, 1973; MBA, Canadian Sch. Mgmt., 1994. Lic. debt collector. With Century 21, Inc., Montvale, NJ, 1975—82; mktg. rep. Centrac Rsch., Bergenfield, NJ, 1982—84; regional field rep. Certified Mktg., Inc., Kinderhock, NY, 1994—99; pvt. practice NYC, 1999—. Mem. consumer panel NPD Group, Fort Washington, NY, 1990—93. Vol. U.S. Army Corps. Engrs., 1996—98. Mem.: Am. Inst. Computer Scis. Home: 353 W 57th St New York NY 10019 Office Phone: 888-240-6089.

SCHATZ, GOTTFRIED, biochemistry educator; b. Strem, Austria, Aug. 18, 1936; arrived in Switzerland, 1974; s. Andreas and Anna (Lantos) S.; m. Merete Petersen, Aug. 11, 1962; children: Isabella, Peer, Kamilla. PhD in Chemistry and Biochemistry (summa cum laude), U. Graz, Austria, 1961; Doctorate (hon.), Comenius U., Bratislava, 1996, U. Stockholm, 2000. Asst. prof., dept. biochemistry U. Vienna, Austria, 1961-68; postdoctoral fellow Pub. Health Rsch. Inst., NYC, 1964-66; assoc. prof. biochemistry and molecular biology Cornell U., Ithaca, NY, 1968-73, prof. biochemistry and molecular biology, 1973-74; prof. biochemistry Biozentrum, U. Basel, Switzerland, 1974—2000, chmn., 1983-85, prof. emeritus, 2000—. Adv. panel, biochemistry and biophysics, US Sci. Found., 1973-74; mem. fellowship com., European Molecular Biology Orgn., 1978-82; mem. scientific adv. com., European Molecular Biology Lab., Heidelberg, 1986-89; adv. bd. Max-Planck Inst. Biochemistry, Martinsried/Munich, 1984-86; mem. Swiss adv. bd., Basel Inst. Immunology, 1985-88; mem. adv. bd. Maurice E. Müller Inst. für hochauflosende Elektronenmikroskopie am Biozentrum, Basel, 1983-85; sec.-gen. European Molecular Biology Orgn., Heidelberg, Fed. Republic Germany, 1984-89; mem. adv. bd., Max-Planck Inst. Cell Biology, Ladenburg/Heidelberg, 1983-; chmn. adv. bd., Inst. for Molecular Pathology, Vienna, 1987-99; scientific adv. bd., biology dept., Princeton U., NJ, 1988-91; mem. adv. bd. Swiss Cancer Rsch. Inst., Lausanne, 1990-92; mem. Swiss Nat. Rsch. Coun., Berne, 1990-2000; chmn. adv. bd., Ctr. for Molecular Biology, Heidelberg, 1990-92; adv. bd., Inst. for Molecular Biology and Biotechnology, Iraklion, Crete, 1990-92; chmn. evaluation com., Max Delbrück Centrum, Berlin, 1996, Nat. Coun. Scientific Rsch. (CNRS), divsn. Inst. Curie, Paris, 1998-; strategic adv. com., Inst. Pasteur, Paris, 2000-. Contbr. numerous papers to sci. jours. Recipient Innitzer prize, 1967, Emil Christian Hansen Gold medal Carlsberg Found., Copenhagen, 1983, Sir Hans Krebs medal Fedn. European Biochem. Socs., Berlin, 1986, Otto Warburg medal German Biochem. Soc., 1988, Schleiden medal Germany Acad. Scis., 1993, Marcel Benoist prize Benoist Found., Berne, 1993, Gairdner Found. Internat. award, 1998, Order of Merit, Republic of Austria, 2000, Wilson medal, Am. Soc. Cell Biology, 2000, Antonio Feltrinelli Internat. prize, 2004; co-recepient Louis Jeantet prize for medicine Jeantet Found., Geneva, 1990, Order for Arts and Scis. Republic of Austria, 1992, Lynen medal, U. Miami (U.S.A.), 1997. Mem. AAAS (fgn.), NAS (U.S.-fgn. mem.), German Acad. Leopoldina, Japanese Biochem. Soc.(hon. mem.), Austrian Acad. Scis., Royal Swedish Acad.(fgn. mem.), Protein Soc. (coun. 1993-99), Austrian Acad. Sciences (mem. adv. bd., Molecular Biology Inst., Salburg, 1994-96), Royal Netherlands Acad. Scis., Rheinland-Westphalian Acad. Scis., Swiss Sci. and Tech. Coun. (pres. 2000-03). E-mail: gottfried.schatz@unibas.ch.*

SCHATZ, IRWIN JACOB, cardiologist, educator; b. St. Boniface, Man., Can., Oct. 16, 1931; came to US, 1956, naturalized, 1966; s. Jacob and Reva S.; m. Barbara Jane Binder, Nov. 12, 1967; children: Jacob, Edward, Stephen and Brian (twins). Student, U. Man., Winnipeg, 1951, MD with honors, 1956. Diplomate: Am. Bd. Internal Medicine. Intern Vancouver (B.C.) Gen. Hosp., 1955-56; resident Hammersmith Hosp., U. London, 1957, Mayo Clinic, Rochester, Minn., 1958-61; head sec. peripheral vascular disease Henry Ford Hosp., Detroit, 1961-68; asso. prof. medicine Wayne State U., 1968-71, chief sect. cardiovascular disease, 1969-71; assoc. prof., asso. dir. sect. cardiology U. Mich., 1972-73, prof. internal medicine, 1973-75; prof. medicine John A. Burns Sch. Medicine, U. Hawaii, 1975—, chmn. dept. medicine, 1975-90, interim chmn. dept. medicine, 2003—05. Author: Orthostatic Hypotension, 1986; contbr. numerous articles to med. jour. Mem. jud. coun. State of Hawaii Supreme Ct., 2000—. Rockefeller Found. scholar, 1991. Master ACP (bd. gov. 1984-89, Laureate award Hawaii chpt. 1992, Mayo Clinic Disting Alumni award, 2009); fellow Am. Coll. Cardiology (bd. gov. 1980-84); mem. Am. Heart Assn. (fellow coun. cardiology), Am. Fedn. Clin. Rsch., Asian-Pacific Soc. Cardiology (v.p. 1987-91), Accreditation Coun. for Grad. Med. Edn. (chmn. residence rev. com. internal medicine 1989-95), Hawaii Heart Assn. (pres.), Western Assn. Physicians, Am. Autonomic Soc. (chmn. bd. gov., pres. 1996-98), Pacific Interurban Club. Jewish. Office: 1356 Lusitana St Honolulu HI 96813-2421

SCHATZ, MONA CLAIRE STRUHSAKER, social worker, educator, consultant, researcher; b. Phila., Jan. 4, 1950; d. Milton and Josephine (Kivo) S.; m. James Fredrick Struhsaker, Dec. 31, 1979 (div.); 1 child, Thain Mackenzie. BA, Metro State Coll., 1976; postgrad., U. Minn., 1976; MSW, U. Denver, 1979; D Social Work/Social Welfare, U. Pa., 1986. Tchg. fellow U. Pa., 1981—82; asst. prof. S.W. Mo. State U., Springfield, 1982—85; prof. Colo. State U., Ft. Collins, 1985—2006; dir. social work divsn. Wyo. Edn. and Rsch. Inst., 2006—. Cons. Mgmt. and Behavioral Sci. Ctr., Wharton Sch. U. Pa., 1981-82; field coord. Colo. State U., 1986-88, dir. non-profit agy. adminstrn. program, 1995-97, dir. project Edn. and Rsch. Inst. Fostering Families, 1987—, dir. youth agy. adminstrn. program Am. Humanics, 1988-90; mem. coun. foster care cert. program We. Gov.'s U., 1998—; resource specialist South N.J. Health Sys. Agy., 1982; adj. faculty mem. U. Mo., Springfield, 1994; med. social worker Rehab. and Vis. Nurse Assn., 1985-90; mem. Colo. Child Welfare Adv. Com., Family Conservation Initiative; internat. cons. and trainer Inst. for Internat. Connections, Azerbaijan, Russia, Latvia, Albania, U.S., Hungary, Ukraine, Romania, Australia, Republic of Korea, Australia, China, New Zealand, 1992—; vis. prof. U. Canberra, Australia, 2006; scholar vis. prof. Mokwon U. Korea. Contbr. articles to profl. jours. including Jour. Social Work Edn., Jour. Baccalaureate Social Work, Internat. Jour. Social Work, New Social Worker, Chosen Child: Internat. Adoption Mag., others. Cons., field rep. Big Bros./Big Sisters Am., Phila., 1979-83; acting dir., asst. dir. Big Sisters Colo., 1971-78; owner Polit. Cons. Colo., Denver, 1978-79; active Food Co-op, Ft. Collins, Foster Parent, Denver, Capital Hill United Neighbors, Adams County (Denver) Social Planning Coun., Colo. Justice Coun., Denver, Regional Girls Shelter, Springfield; bd. dirs. Crisis Helpline and Info. Svc Scholar Lilly Endowment, Inc., 1976, Piton Found., 1978; recipient Spl. Recognition award Big Bros./Big Sisters Am., 1983, Recognition award Am. Humanics Mgmt. Inst., 1990, Innovative Tchg. award, Ctr. for Tchg. and Learning/Colo. State U., Jack Cermak Adv. award, 2003. Mem. Inst. Internat. Connections (bd. dirs., adv. bd.), Coun. Social Work Edn., Nat. Assn. Deans and Dirs. (bd. dirs), SWE Commn. Profl. Devel., Group for Study of Generalist Social Work, Social Welfare History Group, NASW (nominating com. Springfield chpt., state bd. dirs., No. Colo. rep.), Student Social Work Assn. Colo. State U. (adv. 1986-89), Permanency Planning Coun. for Children and Youth, NOW (treas. Springfield chpt. 1984-85), Student Nuc. Awareness Group (advisor), Har Shalom (tchr. youth edn. program), Alpha Delta Mu. Democrat. Avocations: cooking, travel, reading, bicycling, sewing. Office: Univ Wyoming Divsn Social Work 1000 E Univ Ave Dept 3632 Laramie WY 82071 Office Phone: 307-766-4933. Business E-Mail: mschatz@uwyo.edu.

SCHATZ, PHILIP, psychology professor; s. Nathan and Lorraine Schatz; m. Ellen Fenigstein, Sept. 6, 1997. PhD, Drexel U., Phila., 1995. Assoc. prof. psychology St. Joseph's U., Phila., 1998—. Office: Saint Joseph's Univ 5600 City Ave 222 Post Hall Philadelphia PA 19131 Business E-Mail: pschatz@sju.edu.

SCHATZ, RICHARD A., cardiologist; b. Glen Oaks, NY; m. Jinda Schatz; 2 children. Degree in Biology, SUNY, Buffalo, 1973; MD, Duke U., Durham, NC, 1976. Cert. internal medicine, cardiology. Cardiac rschr. Duke U., Thoraxcentre, Rotterdam, Netherlands; rschr. Oxford U. Radcliffe Infirmary, England; intern and resident US Army Med. Ctr., San Francisco, San Antonio; asst. chief cardiology Brooke Army Med. Ctr., San Antonio, acting chief cardiology, 1986; clin. assoc. prof. U. Tex. Health Sci. Ctr.; dir. rsch. and edn. Ariz. Heart Inst., Phoenix; rsch. dir. cardiovascular interventions Scripps Clinic Heart, Lung and Vascular Ctr., La Jolla, Calif., 1990—. Head, cardiovasc. tech. sch., cardiology clin., coronary angioplasty divsn., and cardiac catheterization labs. Brook Army Med. Ctr.; co-chmn. divsn. cardiology Scripps Clinic, Calif. Contbr. articles to profl. jours. Recipient Davidson Scholarship award, Duke U., 1976, Lange Med. Publs. award, 1977, Disting. Alumnus award, 2003, Barton Hayes Soc. Lifetime Scholar award, 2005; Rsch. grant, Johnson & Johnson, 1988. Fellow: Am. Coll. Cardiology; mem.: Phi Beta Kappa. Achievements include co-inventor (with Julio C. Palmaz) of the Palmaz-Schatz intracoronary stent; research in stem cell and gene transfer for patients with atherosclerosis. Avocations: golf, skiing, tennis, hiking, fishing. Office: Scripps Clinic Torrey Pines 10666 N Torrey Pines Rd S1-056 La Jolla CA 92037 Office Phone: 858-554-5248.

SCHATZBERG, ALAN FREDERIC, psychiatrist, researcher; b. NYC, Oct. 17, 1944; s. Emanuel and Cila (Diamand) S.; m. Nancy R. Silverman, Aug. 27, 1972; children: Melissa Ann, Lindsey Diamand. BS, NYU, 1965, MD, 1968; MA (hon.), Harvard U., 1989. Diplomate Nat. Bd. Med. Examiners, Am. Bd. Psychiatry and Neurology. Intern Lenox Hill Hosp., NYC, 1968-69; resident in psychiatry Mass. Mental Health Ctr., Boston, 1969-72; clin. fellow in psychiatry Harvard Med. Sch., Boston, 1969-72, asst. prof. psychiatry, 1977-82, assoc. prof., 1982-88, prof., 1988-91; interim psychiatrist-in-chief McLean Hosp., Belmont, Mass., 1984-86, dir. depression rsch. facility, 1985—, svc. chief, 1982-84, 86-88; psychiatrist adv. panel Eli Lilly & Co., Indpls., 1986-93; clin. dir. Mass. Mental Health Ctr., Boston, 1988-91; Kenneth T. Norris, Jr. prof. psychiatry and behavioral scis. Stanford (Calif.) U., 1991—, chmn. dept. psychiatry and behavioral scis. Sch. Medicine, 1991—. Cons. AMA Videoclinics, Chgo., 1979-83; mem. AMA/FAA panel on health regulations, Chgo., 1984-86; mem. NIH Biol. Psychopathology and Clin. Neuroscis. Intitial Rev. Group, 1991-95, chmn., 1993-94, ITMA Rev. Group, 2007-09. Co-author: Manual of Clinical Psychopharmacology, 1986, 6th edit., 2007; co-editor: Depression: Biology, Psychodynamics and Treatment, 1978, Hypothalamic-Pituitary-Adrenal Axis, 1988, Textbook of Psychopharmacology, 1996, 4th edit., 2007; mem. editl. bd. McLean Hosp. Jour., 1975—88, Jour. Psychiat. Rsch., 1988—, co-editor-in-chief, 2000—, mem. editl. bd. Harvard Rev. Psychiatry, 1992—, Anxiety, 1993, Jour. Clin. Psychopharmacology, 1993—, Archives of Gen. Psychiatry, 1995—, Psychoneuroendocrinology, 1995—, Am. Jour. Psychiatry, 2002—05, assoc. editor-in-chief Depression and Anxiety, 1992—2007, translational field editor Neuropsychopharmacology, 2002—07; contbr. more than 400 articles to profl. publs., chapters to books. Maj. USAF, 1972-74. Rsch. grantee NIMH, 1984-87, 94—, Poitras Charitable Found., 1985-93, Pritzker Found., 1997—; recipient Mood Disorders Rsch. award Am. Coll. Psychiatrists, 2002, Klerman Lifetime Rsch. award Nat. Depressive and Manic Depressive Assn., 1998, Strecker award U. Pa., 2002, Falcone award Nat. Alliance Rsch. in Schizophrenia and Affective Diseases, 2005. Fellow: APA (Rsch. award 2002), Soc. Biol. Psychiatry (pres. 2005—06), Am. Coll. Psychiatrists (Disting. Svc. award in psychiatry 2005), Am. Coll. Neuropsychopharmacology (coun. 1994—97, pres. 2000—01), Am. Psychopathol. Assn.; mem.: NAS, Am. Psychiat. Assn. (pres. 2009—), Inst. Medicine, No. Calif. Psychiat. Soc. (v.p. 1997—99), Mass. Psychiat. Soc. (coun. 1987—90). Avocations: travel, swimming, fine arts, theater. Office: Stanford U Sch Medicine 401 Quarry Rd Rm 300 Stanford CA 94305-5717 Office Phone: 650-723-6811. Business E-Mail: afschatz@stanford.edu.

SCHATZKAMER, LAURA, biology professor; d. William Max Schatzkamer and Mary Virginia Bray; 1 child, Benjamin Schatzkamer Scott. MS, NY U., 1987. Adj. instr. biology CC Allegheny County, Pitts., 1991—; asst. prof. biology Carlow U., Pitts., 2006—. Home: 5301 Riverfront Dr Pittsburgh PA 15238 Office: Carlow Univ 3333 Fifth Ave Pittsburgh PA 15213 Business E-Mail: schatzkamerll@carlow.edu.

SCHAU, HARVEY CHARLES, physicist; b. Kalamazoo, Dec. 19, 1949; s. Harvey Charles and Evelyn Opal (Wheeler) S.; m. Sharron Rhonda Solomon Goldstein, Aug. 23, 1973 (div. Sept. 1984); 1 child, Jennifer Blake. BS, Fla. Atlantic U., Boca Raton, 1972, MS, 1973; PhD, U. Fla., Gainesville, 1975. Physicist Gen. Dynamics Corp., Pomona, Calif., 1976-78; engr. Martin Marietta Corp., Orlando, Fla., 1978-80; physicist Exxon Corp., Orlando, 1980-82, Naval Rsch. Lab., Orlando, 1983-89, Hughes Missile Sys. Co., Tucson, 1990—2006. Pres. Meridian Sys., Orlando, 1980—. Contbr. articles to profl. jours. Mem. IEEE, Internat. Soc. Optical Engrs. Avocations: skin diving, blues guitar. Home and Office: 2564 CHESTERFIELD CT Titusville FL 32780-5911

SCHAUB, MARILYN MCNAMARA, theology studies educator; b. Chgo., Mar. 24, 1928; d. Bernard Francis and Helen Katherine (Skehan) McNamara; m. Thomas Schaub, Oct. 25, 1969; 1 child, Helen Ann. BA, Rosary Coll., 1953; PhD, U. Fribourg, Switzerland, 1957; diploma, Ecole Biblique, Jerusalem, 1967. Asst. prof. classics and Bibl. studies Rosary Coll., River Forest, Ill., 1957-69; prof. Bibl. studies Duquesne U., Pitts., 1969-70, 73-01. Participant 8 archeological excavations, Middle East; hon assoc Am Schs Oriental Research, 1966—67, trustee, 1986—89; Danforth assoc, 1972—80; admin dir expedition to the Southeast Dead Sea Plains, Jordan, 1989—. Author: (book) Friends and Friendship for St. Augustine, 1964; translator (with H Richter): Agape in the New Testament, 3 vols, 1963—65. Mem.: Am Acad Religion, Cath Biblical Asn, Soc Biblical Literature. Democrat. Home: 25 Mckelvey Ave Pittsburgh PA 15218-1452

SCHAUB, MATT (MATTHEW RUTLEDGE SCHAUB), professional football player; b. West Chester, Pa., June 25, 1981; m. Laurie Schaub. Grad., U. Va., Charlottesville, 2004. Quarterback Atlanta Falcons, 2004—06, Houston Texans, 2007—. Participant Atlanta Falcons Coaches Acad., 2004. Named Player of Yr., Atlantic Coast Conf., 2002, Offensive Player of Yr., 2002, First Team All-Conf., 2002. Office: The Houston Texans Two Reliant Pk Houston TX 77054*

SCHAUB, ROBERT GEORGE, pharmaceutical executive; b. Bellevue, Pa., Dec. 16, 1947; s. Edward Clarence Schaub and Barbara Marie Zuratovitch; m. Kathy Ann Gates, Apr. 3, 1983; 1 child, Caitlin Elizabeth. BS, U. Nev., Las Vegas, 1970; PhD, Wash. State U., 1973. Postdoctoral fellow Wash. Heart Assn., Pullman, Wash., 1973—75, Temple U. Med. Sch., Philadelphia, 1975—77; asst. to assoc. prof. U.Tenn., Knoxville, 1977—81; rsch. scientist Upjohn Co., Kalamazoo, 1981—90; sr lab. head to dir. Genetics Inst., Cambridge, Mass., 1990—97; sr. dir. to asst. v.p. Wyeth Pharmaceuticals, Cambridge, 1997—2006; v.p. Archemix Corp., Cambridge, 2006—. Adj. prof. Boston U. Sch. Medicine, 2006—. Recipient Outstanding Educator of Yr., U. Tenn., 1978. Mem.: AAAS, Internat. Soc. Thrombosis and Haemostasis, Am. Soc. Hematology, Soc. Leukocyte Biology, Am. Soc. Investigative Pathology, Am. Physiol. Soc., Sigma Xi. Achievements include patents in field. Office: Archemix Corp 300 Third St Cambridge MA 02142 Office Fax: 617-621-9300. Business E-Mail: bschaub@archemix.com.

SCHAUENBERG, TREVOR A., corporate financial executive; B in Fin., U.Iowa, 1991. Joined fin. mgmt. program GE Co., 1991, mem., corp. audit staff, officer, v.p., corp. investor comm., 2008—; exec. audit mgr. GE Capital, 1997; CFO, insurance holdings GE Comml. Fin., London, 1999—2001; CFO GE Capital Solutions, 2006—07, v.p., 2006—07; CFO GE Ins. Solutions Global Property Casualty Reinsurance, Germany, GE Infrastructure Transp. Office: General Electric Co 3135 Easton Turnpike Fairfield CT 06828*

SCHAUER, FREDERICK FRANKLIN, law educator; b. Newark, Jan. 15, 1946; s. John Adolph and Clara (Balayti) S.; m. Margery Clare Stone, Aug. 25, 1968 (div. June, 1982); m. Virginia Jo Wise, May 25, 1985 (div. Jan., 2009). AB, Dartmouth Coll., 1967, MBA, 1968; JD, Harvard U., 1972. Bar: Mass. 1972, U.S. Supreme Ct. 1976. Assoc. Fine & Ambrogne, Boston, 1972-74; asst. prof. law W.Va. U., Morgantown, 1974-76, assoc. prof., 1976-78, Coll. William and Mary, Williamsburg, Va., 1978-80, Cutler prof., 1980-83; prof. of law U. Mich., Ann Arbor, 1983-90; Frank Stanton prof. of 1st Amendment Kennedy Sch. of Govt., Harvard U., Cambridge, Mass., 1990—2008, acad. dean, 1997—2002, acting dean, 2001; David and Mary Harrison disting. prof. law U. Va., 2008—. Vis. scholar, mem. faculty law Wolfson Coll. Cambridge (Eng.) U., 1977-78; vis. prof. Law Sch., U. Chgo., 1990, 05; vis. fellow Australian Nat. U., 1993, 98; William Morton Disting. sr. fellow in humanities Dartmouth Coll., 1991; vis. prof. law Harvard Law Sch., 1996, 97, 00, 04, 05, 06, 08; Ewald Disting. vis. prof. law U. Va., 1996, vis. prof. govt. Dartmouth Coll., 1997; disting. vis. prof. law U. Toronto, 2000; Fischel-Neil Disting. vis. prof. law, 2005; George Eastman vis. prof. Oxford U., 2007-08, fellow Balliol Coll., 2007-08. Author: The Law of Obscenity, 1976, Free Speech: A Philosophical Enquiry, 1982 (ABA cert. merit 1983), Supplements to Gunther Constitutional Law, 1983-96, Playing by the Rules: A Philosophical Examination of Rule Based Decision-Making in Law and Life, 1991, The First Amendment: A Reader, 1992, 2d edit., 1995, The Philosophy of Law, 1995, Profiles, Probabilities and Sterotypes, 2003, thinking Like a Lawyer, 2009; editor: Legal Theory, 1995-2000; contbr. articles to profl. jours. Mem. Atty. Gen.'s Commn. on Pornography, 1985-86. Served with Mass. Army N.G., 1970-71. NEH fellow, summer 1980, Guggenheim fellow, 2001-02. Fellow Am. Acad. Arts and Scis., Radcliffe Inst. Adv. Studies; mem. Am. Philos. Assn. (chair com. philosophy and law 2006-2007), Am. Soc. Polit. and Legal Philosophy (v.p. 1996-99), Assn. Am. Law Schs. (chmn. sect. constl. law 1984-86). Office: Univ Va Sch Law 580 Massie Rd Charlottesville VA 22903 Office Phone: 434-924-6777. Business E-Mail: schauer@virginia.edu.

SCHAUER, MARK HAMILTON, United States Representative from Michigan; b. Howell, Mich., Oct. 2, 1961; s. Robert Charles and Myra (Trafton) Schauer; m. Christine Schauer; 3 children. BA in Sociology and Spanish, Albion Coll., Mich., 1984; MPA, Western Mich. U., Kalamazoo, 1986, Mich. State U., East Lansing, 1996. Assoc. planner Calhoun County Planning Dept., Marshall, Mich., 1984-85, sr. planner, 1985-86; planning dir. Community Action Agy. Southctrl. Mich., Battle Creek, 1987, exec. dir., 1987—92; coord. Calhoun County Human Svcs. Coordinator Coun., 1992—96; mem., dist. 62 Mich. House Reps., 1996—2002, mem. energy & tech. com., health policy com.; mem., dist. 19 Mich. State Senate, 2003—09, minority fl. leader; mem. US Congress from 7th Mich. Dist., 2009—. Active Big Brother Big Bros./Big Sisters South Ctrl. Mich., 1985-86; vol. coach Marshall Recreation Dept., Marshall, 1986. Mem.: Optimist Internat. Democrat. Methodist. Office: US Congress 1408 Longworth House Office Bldg Washington DC 20515-2207 also: Dist Office 800 W Ganson Jackson MI 49202 Office Phone: 202-225-6276, 517-780-9075. Office Fax: 202-225-6281, 517-780-9081.*

SCHAUER, PHILIP R., surgeon; b. Jan. 31, 1961; BS, Tex. A&M U., Coll. Station; MD, Baylor Coll. Medicine, Houston, 1986. Intern, surgery U. Tex. Health Sci. Ctr., San Antonio, resident, surgery, 1993, chief resident, gen. surgery; fellow, laparoscopic surgery Duke U. Med. Ctr., Durham, NC, 1995; dir., endoscopic surgery, dir. bariatric surgery, dir. Mark Ravitch/Leon Hirsh Ctr. for Minimally Invasive Surgery U. Pitts. Med. Ctr.; dir., Bariatric and Metabolic Inst. Cleve. Clinic, Ohio, 2004—, chief, minimally invasive gen. surgery, 2004—; prof. surgery Cleve. Clinic Lerner Coll. Medicine of Case Western Reserve U. Mem. adv. coun. Am. Bd. Surgery; bd. gov. Fellowship Coun.; fiduciary role MISS Surgery Symposium, Physician Reviews of Surgery, LLC, RemedyMD, Inc., Surgical Excellence; invited spkr. in field; cons. in field. Assoc. editor Surgery for Obesity and Related Diseases, mem. several editl. bds. Named one of Best Doctors in America. Fellow: ACS; mem.: Obesity Soc., Soc. Clin. Surgery, Ctrl. Surgical Soc., Soc. Surgery Alimentary Tract, Soc. U. Surgeons, Am. Surgical Assn., N.Am. Soc. for the Study of Obesity, Internat. Fedn. Surgery for Obesity, Am. Soc. for Bariatric Surgery (past. chmn. rsch., tng. and credentialing com.), Soc. Am. Gastrointestinal and Endoscopic Surgeons (bd. govs.), Am. Soc. for Metabolic and Bariatric Surgery (immediate past pres.). Achievements include being the innovator in the development of numerous minimally invasive gastrointestinal procedures and also bariatric surgical techniques and devices for weight loss and diabetes control. Office: Cleve Clinic Main Campus Mail Code M61 9500 Euclid Ave Cleveland OH 44195 Office Phone: 216-444-4794.

SCHAUER, SHELIA I., bank executive; married; 2 children. Attended, U. Okla., U. N.Mex., Albuquerque, San Juan Coll., Farmington, N.Mex., Am. Inst. Banking. Teller Sunwest Bank, mgr. credit. dept., asst. cashier, br. mgr., asst. v.p.; organizer, dir., pres., CEO Four Corners Cmty. Bank, 2000—. Past pres. Fin. Women Internat., Am. Inst. Banking, state rep. Active United Way; mem. banking edn. com. San Juan Coll. Recipient Sunbest award, 1996; named one of 25 Most Powerful Women in Banking, US Banker, 2008. Office: Four Corners Cmty Bank 500 W Main St Ste 101 Farmington NM 87401 Office Phone: 505-565-2779. Business E-Mail: schauer@thebankforme.com.*

SCHAUER, THOMAS ALFRED, insurance company executive; b. Canton, Ohio, Dec. 24, 1927; s. Alfred T. and Marie A. (Luthi) S.; m. Joanne Alice Fay, Oct. 30, 1954; children: Alan, John, David, Susan, William. BSc, Ohio State U., 1950. With Ind. Ins. Svc. Corp., 1964—, Ind. Benefit Svc. Corp., 1984—2003. Dir. Bank One, Akron, N.A., Ohio, 1991-97, mem. adv. bd., 1997-2000. Chmn. Joint Hosp. Blood Com., 1974; bd. dirs. McKinley Life Ins. Co., 1991-95; bd. dirs. Better Bus. Bur., Canton, 1970-81, chmn., 1979-80; bd. dirs. area YMCA, 1974-92, v.p., 1975-82, pres., 1982-84; trustee Canton Cemetery Assn., 1988-91, Stark County Blue Coats, 1987-, Plain Local Schs. Found., 2004-, pres., 2008; bd. dirs. Hosp. Bur. Ctrl. Stark County, 1972-78; vice chmn. bd. Aultman Hosp., 1981-84, chmn., 1984-87; chmn. Aultman Health Svcs. Assn., 1990-93; pres. Aultman Hosp. Found., 1987-90, trustee, 1971-98, trustee emeritus, 1998—; pres. Schauer Family Fund, Inc., 1968—; bd. dirs. United Way, 1974-84, pres., 1976-78; mem. distbn. com. Stark County Found., 1977-87, chmn. distbn. com., 1984-87, dir. Dime Bank, Canton, 1965-72, First Nat. Bank of Canton/Ctrl. Trust Co. NE Ohio, N.A., 1972-91; adv. bd. Malone Coll., 1979-92; trustee Kent State U., 1980-88, trustee emeritus, 1988—, N.E. Ohio Univs. Coll. Medicine, 1983-88; past trustee Canton Urban League, Boys Village, Smithville, Ohio, Canton Art Inst., Buckeye Coun. Boy Scouts Am. With USN, 1946-48. Recipient gold key award United Way Ctrl. Stark County, 1981, award of merit Canton C. of C., 1984, red triangle award Canton Area YMCA, 1985. Mem. Chartered Ins. Inst. London, Nat. Assn. Mfg., Am. Soc. CPCUs, Am. Soc. CLUs, Assn., Advanced Life Underwriters, Am. Risk and Ins. Assn., Am. Soc. Pension Actuaries, Stark County Accident and Health Underwriters (past pres.), Canton Club (past pres.), Brookside Country Club, Atwood Yacht Club. Home: 1756 Dunbarton Ave NW Canton OH 44708-1807 Personal E-mail: tomschauer@att.net.

SCHAUF, VICTORIA, pediatrician, educator; b. NYC, Feb. 17, 1943; d. Maurice J. and Ruth H. (Baker) Bisson; m. Michael Delaney; 2 children. BS in Microbiology with honors, U. Chgo., 1965, MD with honors, 1969. Intern in pediat. U. Chgo. Hosp., 1969—70; resident in pediat. Sinai Hosp. of Balt., 1970—71; chief resident pediat. Children's Hosp. Nat. Med. Ctr., Washington, 1971—72; rsch. trainee NIH, Bethesda, Md., 1972; adj. asst. prof. microbiology Rush Med. Coll., Chgo., 1972—74; prof. pediat., head pediatric infectious diseases U. Ill., Chgo., 1974—84; med. officer FDA, Rockville, Md., 1984—86; chmn. dept. pediat. Nassau County Med. Ctr., East Meadow, NY, 1986—90; prof. pediat. SUNY, Stony Brook, 1987—94; pvt. practice, 1995—; chief pediatric svcs. Ridgecrest Regional Hosp., 2005—. Vis. prof. Rockefeller U., 1990-92; mem. vis. faculty Chiang Mai (Thailand) U., 1978; mem. ad hoc com. study sects. NIH, Bethesda, 1981-82; bd. dirs. Pearl Stetler Rsch. Found., Chgo., 1982-84; cons. FDA, 1987-88, 93-95, Can. Bur. Human Prescription Drugs, Ottawa, 1990-2004, Biotech. Investors, 1993-95, Calif. Children's Svcs., 2005—; course dir. pediat. infectious diseases rev. course Cornell U. Med. Coll., N.Y.C., 1994, faculty, 1995. Co-author: Pediatric Infectious Diseases: A Comprehensive Guide to the Subspecialty, 1997; prodr. radio and TV programs in field; contbr. articles to profl. jours., chpts. to books. Vol. physician Cook County Hosp., Chgo., 1974-84; mem. adv. com. Nat. Hansen's Disease Ctr., La., 1986, Nassau County Day Care Coun., N.Y., 1988-90; mem. adv. bd. Surg. Aid to Children of World, N.Y., 1986-90; commr., sec. Kern County Children and Families Commn., 1999-2002; bd. dirs. Indian Wells Valley Cmty. Found., 2001-. Am. Lung Assn. grantee U. Ill., 1977; recipient contract NIH, U. Ill., 1978-81, grantee, 1979-84. Fellow Infectious Diseases Soc. Am.; mem. Pediatric Infectious Diseases Soc. (exec. bd.), Soc. Pediatric Rsch., Am. Pediatric Soc., AAAS, Am. Soc. Microbiology, Am. Acad. Pediat., Phi Beta Kappa, Alpha Omega Alpha. Avocation: walking. Home Phone: 760-384-2399; Office Phone: 760-371-2128. Business E-Mail: vschauf@pol.net.

SCHAUMBER, PETER CAREY, federal agency administrator; b. NYC, May 29, 1942; m. Kathleen Charbonnet; children: Kathleen, Drew, Alexandra. BA, Georgetown U., 1964; JD, Georgetown U. Law Ctr., 1968. Asst. corp. counsel Dist. of Columbia; asst. US atty. DC US Dept. Justice; sr. trial atty., assoc. dir. law dept. divsn., Office Comptr. of the Currency US Dept. Treasury; ptnr., dir. litigation dept. Colton & Boykin P.C., 1980—87; of counsel Wickwire Gavin, 1987—93; adj. prof. law Nat. Law Ctr George Washington U.; mem. NLRB, 2002—. Adj. prof. Georgetown U. Sch. Bus. Office: NLRB 1099 14th St NW Washington DC 20570-0001*

SCHAUMBURG, HERBERT HOWARD, neurology educator; b. Houston, Nov. 6, 1932; m. Joanna Jane Austin; children: Barnabas Paul, Kristin Elizabeth. AB cum laude, Harvard Coll., 1956; MD, Washington U., 1960. Instr. in neurology Albert Einstein Coll. of Medicine, NYC, 1964-67, asst. prof. neurology, 1967-69, assoc. prof. neurology, 1972-76, prof., 1976—, vice chmn., 1977-84, acting chmn., 1984-86, chmn., 1986—; instr. pathology Harvard Med. Sch., Boston, 1969-71. Mem. Am. Acad. Neurology, Am. Assn. Neuropathologists, Am. Neurol. Assn., Soc. Toxicology, Soc. Neurosci. Home: 616 King Ave City Island Bronx NY 10464 Office: Albert Einstein Coll Medicine 1300 Morris Park Ave Bronx NY 10461-1926 Home Phone: 718-885-1261; Office Phone: 718-430-2002. Business E-Mail: schaumb@aecom.yu.edu.

SCHAUPP, JOAN POMPROWITZ, trucking executive, writer; b. Green Bay, Wis., Sept. 29, 1932; d. Joseph and Helen Elizabeth (VanderLinden) Pomprowitz; m. Robert James Schaupp, Sept. 4, 1956; children: Margaret Schaupp Siebert, Frederick, John Robert, Elizabeth Schaupp Sidles. BS cum laude, U. Wis., 1954; cert. in theology, St. Norbert Coll. Theol. Inst., 1979; MA, U. Wis., Green Bay, 1982; DMin, Grad. Theol. Found., 1996. Woman's editor Green Bay Press-Gazette, 1955-56; freelance writer Green Bay, 1957-75; sec.-treas., dir. L.C.L. Transit Co., Green Bay, 1962-70; chmn., dir. P & S Investment Co., Green Bay, 1982—, mgmt. cons., 1984-89, dir. strategic planning, 1992, vice chmn., 1994—. Pres. The Manna Co., Green Bay, 1992—; adv. com. Women's Ctr. St. Norbert Coll., 1999—; chmn. P&S Investment Co., 2004. Author: Jesus Was a Teenager, 1972, Woman Image of Holy Spirit, 1975 (Thomas More Book award), Elohim: A Search for a Symbol for Human Fulfillment, 1995. Master gardener De Pere Beautification Com., Wis., 1991-92; design cons. Nat. Fedn. Grden Clubs, 2004; lector St. Francis Xavier Cathedral, Green Bay, 1991-92. Recipient Ambassador award, St. Norbert Coll., 1997, Disting. Svc. award, 2004, Disting. Citizenship award, St. Norbert Coll. Alumni Assn., 2004. Mem.: Nat. Press Club, Nat. Fedn. Press Women, Am. Acad. Religion, Franciscan Internat., Secular Franciscan Order (vice min. Assumption Province 1991—92), Equestrian Order of the Holy Sepulchre Jerusalem (lady grand cross), Soc. Bibl. Lit. Avocations: gardening, walking, swimming.

SCHECHNER, RICHARD, theater director, educator; b. Newark, Aug. 23, 1934; s. Sheridan and Selma Sophia (Schwarz) S.; m. Carol Martin; children: Samuel MacIntosh, Sophia Martin. BA, Cornell U., 1956; postgrad., Johns Hopkins U., 1957; MA, State U. Iowa, 1958; PhD, Tulane U., 1962. Asst. prof. theatre Tulane U., 1962-66, assoc. prof., 1966-67; prof. performance studies NYU; 1967-91, Univ. prof., 1991—; co-founder, co-dir. New Orleans Group, 1965-67; founder, dir. Performance Group, NYC, 1967-80; founder, artistic dir. East Coast Artists, 1991—; Andrew H. White prof.-at-large Cornell U., 1999—2005; sr. fellow Ctr. for Cultural Sociology, Yale U., 2004—. Hon. prof. Shanghai Theatre Acad., 1995—; prof. titular adj. Instituto Superior de Arte, Havana, Cuba; bd. dirs. Theatre Comms. Group, 1977-78; advisor Internat. Theatre Inst., 1975-77, Ctr. Performance Rsch., Aberwrystwich, Wales, 1993-97; pres. Bunch of Exptl. Theatres, 1975, 77, Fulbright Theatre Discipline Com., 1988-91. Author: Public Domain, 1968, Environmental Theater, 1973 (with others) Theatres, Spaces, Environments, 1975, Essays on Performance Theory, 1977, 2d edit. 1988, 3d edit., 2003, (with others) Makbeth, 1977, The End of Humanism, 1982, Performative Circumstances, 1983, Betweeen Theater and Anthropology, 1985, (with Samuel MacIntosh-Schechner) The Engleburt Stories: North to the Tropics, 1987, The Future of Ritual, 1993, Performance Studies-An Introduction, 2002, 2d edit., 2006, Over, Under and Around, 2004, (with others) Yokastas, 2003; editor: Dionysus in 69, 1970; adv. editor: Asian Theatre Jour., 1985-; co-editor: Free Southern Theater, 1968, Ritual, Play, and Performance, 1976, By Means of Performance, 1990; gen. editor: (series) Worlds of Performance, 1993-2007, (with Lisa Wolford) Grotowski Sourcebook, 1997, (with Carol Martin) Enactments, 2005-; editor: The Drama Rev., 1962-69, 85—, contbg. editor, 1971-85; adv. editor Jour. Ritual Studies, 1987—, Asian Theatre Jour., 1985-; dir. Dionysus in 69, 1968, Macbeth, 1969, Commune, 1970, The Tooth of Crime, 1972, Mother Courage, 1975, The Marilyn Project, 1975, Oedipus, 1977, Cops, 1978, The Balcony, 1979, The Red Snake, 1981, Richard's Lear, 1981, The Cherry Orchard, 1983, Prometheus Project, 1985, Don Juan, 1987, Tomorrow He'll Be Out of the Mountains, 1989, Ma Rainey's Black Bottom, 1992, Faust/Gastronome, 1993, The Oresteia, 1995, Three Sisters, 1997, Hamlet, 1999, Waiting for Godot, 2002, Yokastas, 2003, Yokastas Redux, 2005, Hamlet: That is The Question Shanghai, 2007. Served with AUS, 1958-60. Recipient Modello prize, 1985, Contbns. to Theatre Spl. award New England Theatre Conf., 1991, Work in Theatre award Towson State U., 1991, Lifetime Achievement award Performance Studies Internat., 2002, Assn for Theatre in Higher Edn. Career Ach. award, 2008, medal Zasluzony Ola Kultury Polskie, 2009; grantee John D. Rockefeller 3d Fund, 1971-72, 76, Asian Cultural Coun., 1988, 95; Guggenheim fellow, 1976, Fulbright fellow, 1976, 83, N.Y. Inst. Humanities fellow, 1987-94, NEH sr. rsch. fellow, 1988, Humanities fellow Princeton U., 1992, Am. Inst. Indian Studies fellow, 1997, Montgomery fellow Dartmouth Coll., 1998, Am. Coun. Learned Socs. fellow, 2005, Ctrl. Sch. Speech and Drama fellow, London, 2005. Office: NYU 721 Broadway 6th Fl Washington Sq New York NY 10003 Office Phone: 212-998-1638. Business E-Mail: rs4@nyu.edu.

SCHECHTER, ALAN NEIL, medical researcher; b. NYC, June 28, 1939; s. Sidney S. and Mildred (Levy) S.; m. Geraldine Poppa, Feb. 6, 1965; children: Daniele, Andrew. AB, Cornell U., 1959; MD, Columbia U., 1963. Lic. MD, N.Y., Calif. Intern, resident Albert Einstein Coll. Medicine, NYC, 1963-65; from rsch. assoc. to med. officer Nat. Inst. Arthritis and Metabolic Diseases, NIH, Bethesda, Md., 1965-72; sect. chief Chem. Biology Lab Nat. Inst. Diabetes and Digestive and Kidney Diseases, NIH, Bethesda, 1972-81, lab. chief Chem. Biology Lab., 1981—. Bd. dirs. Found. for Advanced Edn. in Sci., Bethesda, Stetten Mus. Med. History, Bethesda. Patentee in field; editor 5 books; contbr. numerous articles to profl. jours. Capt. USPHS, 1983—2001. Home: 5405 Beech Ave Bethesda MD 20814-1733 Office: NIH Chem Biology Lab Nat Inst Diab Digest Kidney Dis 9000 Rockville Pike Bethesda MD 20892-0003

SCHECHTER, ARTHUR LOUIS, lawyer; b. Rosenberg, Tex., Dec. 6, 1939; s. Morris and Helen (Brilling) S.; m. Joyce Proler, Aug. 26, 1965; children: Leslie Schechter Karpas, Jennifer Schechter Rosen. BA, U. Tex., 1962, JD, 1964; postgrad., U. Houston, 1964-65. Bar: Tex. 1964, U.S. Dist. Ct. (ea. and so. dists.) Tex. 1966, U.S. Ct. Appeals (5th cir.), U.S. Supreme Ct. 1976; cert. Tex. Bd. Legal Specialization to Personal Injury Trial Law, 1964-. Pres. Arthur L. Schechter P.C., Houston, 1992-94, Schechter & Marshall, Houston, 1994-96; amb. U.S. to Commonwealth Bahamas, 1998-2000; atty. Schechter, McElwee & Shaffer, LLP, Houston, 2001—05; shareholder Greenberg Traurig, LLP, Houston, 2005—06; sr. counsel Schechter McElwee Shaffer & Harris LLP, Houston, 2006—. Mediator Arthur Schechter Group, 2006—; spkr. Marine Law Sem., 1983; spkr. in field. Contbr. articles to profl. jours. Bd. dirs. Theatre Under the Stars, Houston, 1972—78, Congregation Beth Israel, Houston, 1972—84, pres., 1982—84; bd. dirs. Inst. Internat. Edn., 1996—98, S.E.A.R.C.H., 1996—98; pres. Am. Jewish Com., Houston, 1982—84, chmn. fgn. rels. com., chmn. United Jewish Campaign exec. com., chmn., 1993—94; pres. Jewish Fedn. Ctr. Houston, 1994—96; mem. Deans Coun. U. Tex. Law Sch.; chmn. bd. Harris County Met. Transit Authority, 2002—04; chmn. internat. traveler task force Mayor of Houston, 2005; mng. trustee mem. fin. com. Dem. Nat. Com., 1992, fin. chmn. Tex. Clinton/Gore '96; vice chmn. Clinton/Gore Jewish Leadership Coun., 1996; v.p. exec. com. Nat. Jewish Dem. Coun., 1992, chmn., 2004—06; mem. Leadership Ctr. Dem. Senatorial Campaign Com.; trustee mem. Kerry/Edwards and Dem. Nat. Com.; fin. coun. Nat. Dem. Orgn., 1992—, 1979; chmn. bd. Met. Transit Authority of Harris County, 2002—04; bd. dirs. U. Tex. Med. Sch. Recipient Career and Recovery Resources Barrier Breaker award, United Way Agy., 2003, Search's Outstanding Leadership award, 2003,

Israel Bonds Nat. Leadership award, 2004, Lifetime Achievement award, NJDC, 2006, Nat. Jewish Dem. Coun., 2006, Starlight Leadership award, Coun. of Jewish Women, 2006; named a Tex. Super Lawyer, 2006; named one of Houston's Most Fascinating Mems. of the Med. Cmty., 2003. Home: 19A West Ln Houston TX 77019-1007 Home Phone: 713-961-5558; Office Phone: 713-757-7811. Personal E-mail: arthurschechter@gmail.com. Business E-Mail: aschechter@smslegal.com.

SCHECHTER, GERALDINE POPPA, hematologist; b. NYC, Jan. 16, 1938; d. Josif and Victoria (Nosi) P.; m. Alan Neil Schechter, Feb. 6, 1965; children: Daniele Malka, Andrew M.R. AB, Vassar Coll., Poughkeepsie, NY, 1959; MD, Columbia U., 1963. Diplomate Am. Bd. Internal Medicine (bd. dirs. 1990-95, mem. hematology com. 1985-91). Intern, then resident Presbyn. Hosp., NYC, 1963-65; resident, fellow, rsch. assoc. VA Med. Ctr., Washington, 1965-70, staff physician, 1970-74, chief hematology, 1974—; asst., assoc. prof. medicine George Washington U., Washington, 1971-81, prof. medicine, 1981—. Residency rev. com. internal medicine Am. Coun. for Grad. Med. Edn., 1996—. Mem. editl. bd. Blood, 1985-89; contbr. articles to hematologic jours. Office: VA Med Ctr Hematology Sect 50 Irving St NW Washington DC 20422-0001

SCHECHTER, NEIL LAWRENCE, pediatrician, educator; b. NYC, Sept. 12, 1947; s. Stanley and Sylvia Schechter; m. Carlota Patricia Geyer, Aug. 27, 1977; children: Benjamin Birch, Anna Carlota. BA, Northwestern U., Evanston, Ill., 1969; DO, Mich. State U., East Lansing, 1973; MD, U. Conn. Sch. Medicine, Farmintgon, 1982. Diplomate Am. Bd. Pediat., 1979. Dir. devel. pediat. St. Francis Hosp. Med. Ctr., Hartford, 1979—; prof. pediat. U. Conn. Sch. Medicine, Farmington, 1992—; dir. pain relief program Conn. Children's Med. Ctr., Hartford, 2000—. Editor: Pain in Infants, Children and Adolescents, 2000; contbr. articles to profl. jours. Recipient medal, Copernicus Med. Inst., Poland, 1989, Jeffrey Lawson award, Am. Pain Soc., 2000; scholar Bellagio Study Ctr., Rockefeller Found., 2004; Dozor Vis. Prof., Ben Gurion U., 2005. Fellow: Am. Acad. Pediat.; mem.: Soc. Devel. Behavioral Pediat., Academic Pediatric Assn., Internat. Assn. Study of Pain. Achievements include one of the first to report on the disparity in pain management between adults and children. Office: Conn Children's Med Ctr 282 Washington St Hartford CT 06106 Office Fax: 860-545-8661. Business E-Mail: nschech@ccmckids.org.

SCHECHTER, ROBERT SAMUEL, chemical engineer, educator; b. Houston, Feb. 26, 1929; s. Morris S. and Helen Ruth Schechter; m. Mary Ethel Rosenberg, Feb. 15, 1953; children: Richard Martin, Alan Lawrence (dec.), Geoffrey Louis. BS in Chem. Engring, Tex. A&M U., 1950; PhD in Chem. Engring, U. Minn., 1956. Registered profl. engr., Tex. Asst. prof. chem. engring. U. Tex. at Austin, 1956-60, assoc. prof., 1960-63, prof., 1963—; adminstrv. dir. Ctr. Statis. Mechs. and Thermodynamics, 1968-72, chmn. dept. chem. engring., 1970-73, chmn. petroleum engring., 1975-78, E.J. Cockrell, Jr. prof. chem. and petroleum engring., 1975-81, Dula and Ernie Cockrell prof. engring., 1981-83, Getty prof. engring., 1984-85, Getty Oil Centennial chair in Petroleum Engring., 1985-89, W.A. (Monty) Moncrief Centennial Endowed chair in Petroleum Engring., 1989-97; prof. emeritus U. Tex., 1997. Vis. prof. U. Edinburgh, Scotland, 1965-66; Disting. vis. prof. U. Kans., spring 1968; vis. prof. U. Brussels, 1969; Disting. Lindsay lectr. Tex. A&M U., 1993; cons. in field. Author: Variational Method in Engineering, 1967, (with G.S.G. Beveridge) Optimization: Theory and Practice, 1970, Adventures in Fortran Programming, 1975, (with B.B. Williams and J.L. Gidley) Acidizing Monograph, 1979, (with D.D. Shah) Enhanced Oil Recovery by Surfactants and Polymers, 1979; (with Maurice Bourrel) Microemulsions and Related Systems, 1988, Oil Well Stimulation, 1991; contbr. (with D.D. Shah) numerous articles to profl. jours. Served to 1st lt., Chem. Corps AUS, 1951-53. Decorated Chevalier Order Palmes Academique, 1978; recipient Outstanding Teaching award U. Tex., 1969, Outstanding Paper award, 1973, Gen. Dynamics award for Excellence in Engring. Teaching, Gen. Dynamics Corp., 1987, Sr. Rsch. award Engring. Rsch. Coun. of Am. Soc. Engring. Educators, 1991. Mem. AIME (Industry Edn. award 1998), AIChE (Founders award 1998), Am. Chem. Soc., Soc. Petroleum Engrs. (John Franklin Carll award 1994, Improved Oil Recovery Pioneer 1996), Nat. Acad. Engrs., Sigma Xi, Tau Beta Pi. Achievements include developing methods of measuring surface viscosity and ultra low inter-facial tensions; discovering instability of thermal diffusion. Home: 4700 Ridge Oak Dr Austin TX 78731-4724 Office: U Tex Dept Petroleum & Geosystems Austin TX 78712 Office Phone: 512-471-3245. Business E-Mail: rsschechter@mail.utexas.edu.

SCHECHTER, STEPHEN L., political scientist; b. Washington, Nov. 28, 1945; s. William J. and Blossom (Rapaport) S.; m. Stephanie A. Thompson, Feb. 16, 1993; 1 child, Sarah J.; 1 stepdaughter: Kelly Anne Thompson. BA, Syracuse U., 1967; PhD, U. Pitts., 1972. Acting dir. Ctr. for Study of Federalism/Temple U., 1973-76; asst. to full prof. polit. sci. Russell Sage Coll., Troy, N.Y., 1977—; exec. dir. N.Y. State Commn. on Bicentennial of U.S. Constitution, 1986-90. Dir. Coun. for Citizenship Edn. Russell Sage Coll., NY, 1990—, dir. MAT/social studies program; coord. We The People, 1992-2003; pres. NY State Coun. on Social Edn., 1992-93; co-dir. civic edn. exch. program Civitas of Russia, 1994—; sr. rsch. advisor NY State Commn. on the Capital Region, 1995-97; mem. Social Sci. Edn. Consortium, 1999; adv. com. for participation in govt. NY State Edn. Dept., 1999—; co-dir. NY State Consortium Civic Learning, 2004—; co-dir. Civitas-Eurasia, 2008-. Co-editor: World of the Founders: New York Communities in the Federal Period, 1990, Contexts of the Bill of Rights, 1990, New York and the Union, New York and the Bicentennial, 1990; editor: Roots of the Republic: American Founding Documents Interpreted, 1990, Social Sci. Record, 1993-96, others; contbr. articles to profl. jours., chpts. to books Chmn. Rensselaer County Bicentennial Commn., 1991; commr. Albany City Charter Revision Commn., 1997-98; dir. Troy-Sage Homeownership Partnership. Recipient Disting. Svc. award, N.Y. State Soc. Coun., 2005. Mem. Nat. Coun. Social Studies (state del. 1991), Internat. Assn. Ctrs. for Fed. Studies (co-founder 1976), Am. Polit. Sci. Assn., N.Y. State Acad. Pub. Adminstrn. Office: Russell Sage Coll 45 Ferry St Troy NY 12180-4115

SCHECHTERMAN, LAWRENCE, lawyer, chef, business consultant; b. Elizabeth, NJ, June 23, 1943; s. Josef and Sylvia (Berger) S.; children: Jill Laura, Danielle Sara, Gregory Jared. BA, U. Miami, Fla., 1966; JD, Suffolk U., 1969; LLM, NYU, 1973; AS in Culinary Arts, Art Inst. Ft. Lauderdale, 2001. Tax assoc. Coopers & Lybrand, NYC, 1969-70; assoc. Bendit, Weinstock & Sharbaugh, Newark, 1970-72; pvt. practice East Brunswick, NJ, 1972-81; gen. counsel Equinox Solar, Inc., Miami, 1981-83; mem. Lawrence Schechterman, P.A., Boca Raton, Fla., 1983—94; pres. Ocean Cons. Group divsn. Securities Arbitration Recovery, Inc., Boca Raton, 1993-97; pvt. chef Boca Raton, 2000—; bridgetender C&S Engring., Boca Raton, Fla., 2006—08; chef Publix Greenwise Market, Boca Raton, 2008—. Author: In the Mood with Food, A Bachelor's Guide to Wooing Her with Food, 1998, 2000, 01, 07; (poetry) New Dimensions: An Anthology of American Poetry, 1967, The Harmony of Silence, 2000, Touched by Grace, 1999, Touched by Love, 1999, Surrounded By Dreams, 1998, A Trusting Heart, 2000 (Best Poems and Poets award, 2007); contbr. articles to profl. jours. Mem. coun. Twp. of East Brunswick, NJ, 1976—80; pres. B'nai Torah Congregation of Boca Raton Inc., 1987—89, trustee, 1989—91. Mem.: B'nai B'rith Mens Lodge 2935, South Plainfield, NJ (charter pres., co-founder 1973—74). Office: 20937 St Andrews Blvd Apt 18 Boca Raton FL 33433-1716 Office Phone: 561-477-4998. Business E-Mail: lorenzo4@bellsouth.net.

SCHECHTMAN, SAUL, conductor; b. Winchester, Conn., Sept. 4, 1924; s. Isidore Schechtman and Clara Goodman; m. Carolyn Raney, July 31, 1952; children: Carol, Julia. BA, Bklyn. Coll., 1947; post grad., Juilliard Sch. of Music, NYC, 1949. Music dir. Bronx Symphony Orch., NYC, 1953—56; conductor, music dir. Omnibus Program (CBS), NYC, 1954—57; music dir. Bergen Philharmonic, Teaneck, NJ, 1956—60, Carnival (Broadway show), NYC, 1961—63, Hello Dolly, NYC, 1966—70, Orch. Piccola, Balt., 1976—80; kapellmeister Theatre Oberhausen, Oberhausen, Germany, 1981—84. Composer: Auntie Mame, 1956, Diaspora variations, 1989, German Radio Orchs., 1990—94; dir.: (plays) Kiss Me Kate, 1958, How To Succeed in Business, 1963—64, My Fair Lady, 1960. Pvt. 1st class US Army, 1943—46, Europe. Fellowship in orch. conducting, Juilliard Sch. of Music, 1949—51. Mem.: Am. Soc. Composers, Authors and Publishers. Avocation: tennis. Home: 134 Cathedral Ave Hempstead NY 11550

SCHECK, BARRY C., legal association administrator, educator; b. Queens, NY, Sept. 19, 1949; BS, Yale U., 1971; JD, U. Calif., Berkeley, 1974. Bar: N.Y. 1974. Staff atty. Legal Aid Soc. NYC, 1974—77; prof. Law, dir. Clin. Legal Edn., Trial Advocacy Programs Benjamin N. Cardozo Sch. Law, Yeshiva U., NYC, 1977—, dir. Jacob Burns Ctr. for Study of Law and Ethics, 1977—, lawyer, dir. Innocence Project, 1992—. Former faculty mem. Nat. Inst. Trial Advocacy and Def. Coun.; tchr., organizer trial advocacy programs numerous pub. defender offices, bas assns. and law firms; commn. mem. NY State Commn. on Forensic Sci.; lectr. in field; commr. Forensic Sci. Rev. Bd. NY. Co-author: Raising and Litigating Claims of Electronic Surveillance, Actual Innocence: Five Days to Execution and Other Dispatches from the Wrongly Convicted; contbr. articles to profl. jours. Commr. NY Forensic Sci. Rev. Bd.; co-founder, co-dir. Innocence Project, 1992—; bd. dir. Nat. Inst. of Justice's Commn. on the Future of DNA Evidence, 1999. Named one of 100 Most Influential Lawyers in America, Nat. Law Jour., 2006. Mem.: Assn. Bar NYC (com. on criminal cts.), Nat. Assn. of Criminal Defense Lawyers (life; pres., bd. dirs., co-chair, DNA Task Force, Most Outstanding Criminal Def. Lawyer in Am., Robert C. Heeney award 1996). Office: Nat Assn Criminal Defense Lawyers 1660 L St NW Washington DC 20036-5603 also: Benjamin N Cardozo Sch Law Innocence Project 100 5th Ave 3d Fl New York NY 10011 Fax: 202-872-8690. E-mail: barry@nacdl.org.*

SCHECTER, ARNOLD JOEL, public health physician, researcher; b. Chgo., Dec. 1, 1934; s. Benjamin and Leonore Natalie (Lyon) S.; m. Martha-Jean Berenson, Feb. 14, 1964; children: Benjamin, David, Anna. BA in Liberal Arts, U. Chgo., 1954, BS in Physiology-Neurophysiology, 1957; MD, Howard U., 1962; MPH, Columbia U., 1975. Diplomate Am. Coll. Preventive Medicine; med. lic., Ky., N.Y., N.J., N.C. Postdoc. dept. anatomy Harvard Med. Sch., Boston, 1962—64; instr. dept. medicine Mass. Gen. Hosp., Harvard Med. Sch., Boston, 1964-65; intern Beth Israel Hosp., Boston, 1966; gen. practitioner, sr. aviation med. examiner West Point, Ky., 1969-70; med. dir. inpatient rehab. ctr., drug and alcohol rehab. program Region Eight Mental Health and Mental Retardation Bd., Inc., Louisville, 1971-72; asst. prof. dept. psychiatry, divisional drug and alcohol abuse SUNY Downstate Med. Ctr., Bklyn., 1973-75; clin. assoc. prof. dept. preventive medicine N.J. Med. Sch., Newark, 1975-79; prof. dept. preventive medicine SUNY Upstate, Binghamton, 1979—98; prof. environ. & computational health scis. U. Tex. Sch. Pub. Health, Dallas, 1999—; pres. Zumwalt Inst. for Environ. Health Inc., 1996—. Spl. expert Nat. Inst. Environ. Health Scis. NIH, 1997—98; cons. U.S. EPA, Washington, 1985—86, Washington, 1999—2000, WHO, 1986—90; sci. peer reviewer dioxin U.S. EPA, 1995, 2000; peer reviewer A.T.S.D.R. of C.D.C., 1995—2005; dir. clin. rsch. in drug abuse, coord., faculty mem. Career Tchr. Tng. Ctr., SUNY Downstate, 1972—75; assoc. dir. office primary health care edn., office of the dean NJ Med. Sch., 1976—79; advisor Environ. Def. Fund, 1991—92, Nat. Vets. Legal Svcs. Project, 1991—92; co-founder assoc. editor Am. Jour. Drug and Alcohol Abuse, NYC, 1973—78, editl. bd., 1978—86; editl. adv. bd. Substance and Alcohol Actions/Misuse, Elmsford, NY, 1979—85; adj. prof. epidemiology U. N.C. Sch. Pub. Health, 1998—2004; adj. prof. occupl. medicine Duke Med. Ctr., 1998—99; editl. adv. bd. mem. Environ. Health Perspectives, 2008—. Editor: Rehabilitation Aspects of Drug Dependence, 1977, Treatment Aspects of Drug Dependence, 1978, Biomedical Issues in Drug Abuse, 1981, Sociological Issues in Drug Abuse, 1981, Dioxins and Health, 1994; sr. editor: 2d edit., 2003; environmental sect.editor Maxcy Rosenau Last Public Health and Preventive Medicine, 14th edit., 1998; editor: 15th edit., 2007; co-editor: Drug Abuse: Modern Trends, Issues and Perspectives, 1978; co-editor: (with H. Alksne, E. Kaufman) Critical Concerns in the Field of Drug Abuse, 1978; contbr. over 200 articles to profl. jours., books. Maj., physician MC US Army, 1967-69. Recipient Pacesetter award Commonwealth Mass., 1990. Fellow: ACP, Am. Coll. Occupl. and Environ. Medicine, Am. Coll. Preventive Medicine; mem.: AAAS, APHA (chair Vietnam caucus), Soc. Epidemiology Rsch., Tex. Pub. Health Assn., Soc. Epidemiologic Rsch., Am. Occupl. and Environ. Medicine Assn., Am. Coll. Epidemiology. Achievements include discovery of very low dioxin and PBDE levels, US food contaminated with dioxins, dibeuzeturans; PBDES which are found mainly in meat, fish & diary products; PBDE brominated flame retardant contamination in breast milk of all US mothers tested, and that these levels as well as blood and food are highest in the world; PBDES can be measure of in all total tissues studied; PCB transformer fires can lead to contamination of buildings by dioxins; Agent Orange elevated dioxin body burden exists decades after exposure in Vietnamese and in American Vietnam Veterans; dioxin contamination exist in body tissues of the general population of the US; dioxin hot spots in Vietnam with current contamination of Vietnamese by contaminated food; development of congener specific tissue dioxin analysis as biomarker for dioxin exposure; developed naltrexone, a narcotic antagonist in rehabilitation of opiate addicts; US food is contaminated with PBDE brominates flame retardants. Home: 16606 Loch Maree Ln Dallas TX 75248-1711 Office: U Tex Sch Pub Health 6011 Harry Hines Blvd Dallas TX 75248 Office Phone: 214-336-8519. Personal E-mail: ajschecter@aol.com. Business E-Mail: arnold.schecter@utsouthwestern.edu.

SCHECTER, WILLIAM H., bank executive; B in Fin., Ohio State U., Columbus; grad., Stonier Grad. Sch. Banking, 1975. Sr. v.p. corp. banking BancOhio, Nat. City Corp., Cleve., 1984, pres. Nat. Fin. Corp., bd. dirs., chmn. emeritus Nat. City Equity Ptnrs., Inc., sr. v.p., sr. advisor, 1989—. Bd. dirs. Boykin Lodging Co. Bd. dirs. Menorah Park. Office: Nat City Corp Nat City Ctr 1900 E 9th St Cleveland OH 44114-3484 Office Phone: 216-222-2000.

SCHEEDER, LOUIS, theater producer, director, educator; b. NYC, Dec. 26, 1946; s. Louis W. and Julia H. (Callery) S. BA in English Lit., Georgetown U., 1968; postgrad., Sch. of Arts, Columbia U., 1968-69; MA in Performance Studies, NYU, 1995, PhD in Performance Studies, 2004. Founder, dir. The Classical Studio Tisch Sch. of the Arts, NYU, 1991—, Master Tchr., 1995—2004, assoc. arts prof., 2004—06, arts prof., 2006—, assoc. dean faculty, 2006—. Dir. Shakespeare Ensemble, NYU Tisch Sch. of the Arts, 1989-90; mem. adv. council Nat. Com. on Arts and Edn., 1977-82; mem. D.C. Commn. on Arts and Humanities, 1976-80; bd. advs. New Playwrights' Theatre of Washington, 1975-82; asst. stage mgr. Arena Stage, Washington, 1969-70; assoc. artistic dir., dir., Folger Theatre Group, Washington, 1971-73, dir. producer, 1973-81; cons. Ctr. for Renaissance and Baroque Studies U. Md., 1984-91; asst. dir. Royal Shakespeare Co. Stratford-Upon-Avon, Eng., 1988. Dir., prodr. plays including Creeps (Am. premiere), 1973, The Farm (Am. premiere), 1974, The Collected Works of Billy the Kid (Am. premiere), 1975, Henry V, 1976, The Fool (Am. premiere), 1976, Mummer's End (world premiere), 1977, Teeth 'n' Smiles (Am. premiere), 1977, Two Gentlemen of Verona, 1977, Mackerel (world premiere), 1978, Black Elk Speaks (tour), 1978, Richard III, 1978, Whose Life Is It Anyway? (Am. premiere), 1978, Richard II, 1978, As You Like It, 1979, Custer (Kennedy Ctr.), 1979, Charlie and Algernon (Kennedy Ctr.), 1980, Crossing Niagara (Am. premiere), 1981, Love's Labour's Lost, 1981; also dir. Broadway, Off Broadway, regional prodns. including (Broadway) Charlie and Algernon, 1980, (Off Broadway) Creeps, 1973, Passover, 1986, (Off-Off-Broadway) The Gettysburg Sound Bite, 1989, Brunch at Trudy and Paul's, 1990, The Christmas Rules, 1991, The Monkey Business, 1992, Mankynde, N.Y Fringe Festival, 2005; dir. All's Well That Ends Well, 1990; dance: dir. Near Ruins, Ruby, 1996, Let's Go Thundering, 1997, Give Us a Kiss, Johnny, 1998, Keeper, 1999; prodr. How I Got That Story (Off Broadway), 1982, Diamonds (Off Broadway), 1984, Today, I Am a Fountain Pen (Off Broadway), 1986; dir. Man. Theatre Ctr., 1982, 83, 84, Nat. Arts Ctr., Ottawa, Ont., Can., 1984, Hedda Gabler, Ctr. Stage, Toronto, 1985, Reg: Life in the Trees, GeVa Theatre, 1991; asst. dir. Broadway prodn. Carrie, 1988, Pacific Rep. prodn. Merchant of Venice, 2002, Much About Nothing 2004, Santa Monica Shakespeare Project, 2004, All's Well that Ends Well, 2005, King Lear, 2006, Richard III Shakespeare Santa Monica, 2007; mem. The Factory London 2007, co-dir: Hamlet 2007, Cymbeline, NY Classical Theatre, 2008; author: (with Shane Ann Younts) All the Words on Stage: A Complete Pronunciation Dictionary for the Plays of William Shakespeare, 2002. Bd. advisors Women's Project, 2006—. Recipient Dixon award Georgetown U., 1968, Alumni Achievement award Georgetown U. Alumni Club Met. Washington, 1981, Mayor's Arts award, D.C., 1982, Acad. Excellence award NYU, 1995, Hall of Fame, Georgetown Theatre Alumni, 2005. Mem.: Soc. Stage Dirs. and Choreographers, Episc. Actors' Guild (life; coun. 1990—96, 2002—04, 2006—). Home: 7 Stuyvesant Oval New York NY 10009-1901 Business E-Mail: louis.scheeder@nyu.edu.

SCHEEL, NELS EARL, corporate financial executive, accountant; b. Spencer, Wis., Sept. 25, 1925; s. Roland Edward and Louise Ernestine Scheel; m. Elaine Marie Carlisle, Aug. 28, 1949; children: Thomas W., John E., Martha L., Mark A., Mary E. BA, Youngstown Coll., 1949; MBA, U. Pa., 1950. CPA, Ohio. Staff acct. Lybrand Ross Bros., Cleve., 1950-54; asst. controller Century Foods, Youngstown, Ohio, 1954-62; treas., controller The Bailey Co., Cleve., 1962-63, Golden Dawn Foods, Sharon, Pa., 1963-82; v.p., chief fin. officer Peter J. Schmitt Co., Sharon, 1982-89; cons. to industry Columbiana, 1989—. Part-time faculty Youngstown (Ohio) State U., 1954—94; bd. mem. Sovereign Cirs., Inc., North Jackson, Ohio, 1992—2001, bd. chmn., 1995—99, sec.-treas., 1999—2001. Pres. Crestview Bd. Edn., Columbiana, Ohio, 1970-81; trustee Columbiana Cmty. Found., 2002—. Staff sgt. AUS, 1943-46, PTO, hon. discharge. Mem. Am. Inst. CPA's, Ohio Soc. CPA's.

SCHEELER, CHARLES P., lawyer; b. 1956; BS, U. NC, Chapel Hill, 1978; JD cum laude, Harvard Law Sch., 1981. CPA; bar: Md. Asst. US atty. Dist. Md. US Dept. Justice, 1984—89; ptnr. DLA Piper, Balt., 1989—. Chmn. CollegeBound Found.; bd. dirs. Rosedale Fed. Savings Loan Assn., 1991—; bd. trustees Johns Hopkins Medicine. Named to Am.'s Leading Lawyers for Bus., Chambers USA. Mem.: Beta Alpha Psi, Phi Beta Kappa. Achievements include serving as lead counsel to Senator George J. Mitchell for his investigation into the use of performance enhancing substances in Major League Baseball. Office: DLA Piper 6225 Smith Ave Baltimore MD 21209-3600 Office Phone: 410-580-4250. Office Fax: 410-580-3001. Business E-Mail: charles.scheeler@dlapiper.com.

SCHEELER, JAMES ARTHUR, architect; b. Pontiac, Ill., Dec. 20, 1927; s. Aman B. and Jane (Steele) S.; m. Barbara Jean Lloyd, Sept. 2, 1950; children: James Erich, Carl Aman, Orissa Jane Elizabeth; m. Nancy S. Kneece, June 2, 2007. BS with highest honors, U. Ill., 1951, MS, 1952; postgrad., U. Liverpool, 1952-53. Grad. asst. U. Ill., Urbana, 1950-52; draftsman-designer Lundeen & Hilfinger, Bloomington, Ill., 1952-53; designer Skidmore, Owings & Merrill, Chgo., 1955-59; partner Richardson, Severns, Scheeler & Assos., Inc., Champaign, Ill., 1959-65, v.p., treas., 1965-71; vice chmn. bd., dir. Prodn. Systems for Architects and Engrs., Inc., 1973-81. Vis. critic U. Ill., 1959-60. Mem. Plan Commn., Champaign, 1966—71, chmn., 1969-71; mem. Champaign County Regional Planning Commn., 1967-71; bd. dirs. Nat. Center for a Barrier-Free Environment, 1978—81, pres., 1981. Served with USN, 1946-47. Recipient various archtl. awards.; Francis J. Plym fellow, 1953-54; Fulbright fellow, 1953. Fellow AIA (hon.; treas. Ctrl. Ill. chpt. 1967-68, sec. 1968-69, pres. 1970-71, nat. dep. exec. v.p. 1971-76, pres. corp. 1974-78, exec. v.p. 1977-78, program devel. group exec. 1976-85, sr. exec. 1985-88, v.p. design practice group 1989, resident fellow 1990—, Edward D. Kemper award 2000), Internat. Union Archs. Profl. Practice Commn. (sec., co-dir. 1994-2003, internat. union archs. coun. 2005—), Royal Australian Inst. Architects (hon.), Korean Inst. Archs. (hon.); mem. Ill. Arts Coun. (archtl. adv. bd. 1966-71), Montessori Soc. Champaign-Urbana (dir. 1964-66), Gargoyle, Scarab, Phi Kappa Phi, Lambda Chi Alpha, Lambda Alpha, Cosmos Club, Fedn. Colls. Archs. Republic Mex. (hon.), Japan Inst. Architect (hon.). Episcopalian. Address: 1411 Belcastle Ct Reston VA 20194-1245

SCHEER, BRENDA CASE, architect, educator; b. Ponca City, Ohio, Dec. 23, 1951; m. David Ross Scheer, Nov. 28, 1992. MArch, Rice U., 1977. Registered architect, Ohio. Assoc. prof. U. Cin., 1990—; pres. Scheer & Scheer, Inc., Cin., 1994—. Prin. works include City Centre Bldg., Terre Haute, Ind. Trustee Cin. Forum on Architecture and Urbanism, Cin., 1995—. Recipient Chgo. Inst. of Architecture and Urbanism award, 2000, Ohio Honor award AIA, 2000, Cin. Honor award, 2000. Mem. Am. Inst. Cert. Planners. Office: U Cin PO Box 210016 Cincinnati OH 45221-0016

SCHEER, JOSEPH H., artist, education educator; b. Heildeberg, Germany, Sept. 6, 1958; arrived in U.S., 1960; s. James H. and Kathleen M. Scheer. BFA, Alfred Univ., Alfred, NY, 1984; MA, Univ. New Mex., Albuqerque, New Mex., 1986, MFA, 1987. Artist ind., Los Nutrius, N.Mex., 1986—89; prof. print media Sch. Art Design Alfred Univ., Alfred, NY, 1989—; co-dir. Inst. Electronic Art Alfred Univ., Alfred,

NY, 1997—. Author: Night Visions: Secret Designs of Moths, 2003, Night Flyers, 2003; one-man shows include over 30; contbr. articles pub. in over 50 profl. jour. Recipient Silver award, 16th Gold Internat., Chgo., 2003, Stiftung Bockkunst Best Book Design award, Frankfurt, Germany, 2003; grantee Project grant, NYSCA, 2001. Mem.: Entomol. Soc. Am., Lepidoptersit Soc., Phi Kappa Phi. Office: Sch of Art & Design Alfred Univ 2 Pine St Alfred NY 14802

SCHEER, R. SCOTT, physician; b. NYC, Oct. 24, 1938; s. Leonard and Josephine (Holtschl) S.; m. Beverly Joan Henry Scheer, Dec. 27, 1940; children: Kirsten Leigh, Laura Lynn. AB, Cornell U., 1960; MD, SUNY, Buffalo, 1965. Diplomate Am. Bd. Radiology (cert.), Am. Bd. Nuc. Medicine (cert.), Nat. Bd. Med. Examiners (cert.). Intern Santa Barbara (Calif.) Cottage Hosp., 1965-66; resident Cornell Univ.-N.Y. Hosp., 1966, Phila. Gen. Hosp., 1968-71; staff radiologist Meth. Hosp., Phila., 1971-72; assoc. dir. radiology Coatesville (Pa.) Hosp., 1972-77; dir. dept. radiology Norristown (Pa.) State Hosp., 1973-93; dir., chief exec. officer Med. Imaging Svcs., Chester Springs, Pa., 1977—; dir. radiology Scranton (Pa.) Imaging Ctr., 1993-94; cons. radiologist Oxford Valley Imaging Ctr., 1992-95, mng. ptnr. Langhorne, Pa., 1995-97; dir. radiology Allied Med. Group, Phila., 1997—; dir. diagnostic imaging lab. Premier Rsch. Worldwide, Phila., 1998—; cons. radiologist Berwick (Pa.) Hosp., 2000—. Cons. radiol. expert, 1981—; attending radiologist Pottstown Meml. Med. Ctr., 1977-93; cons. in MRI, Fonar Corp., 1990-92; cons. radiologist U.S. Radiology Assocs., Bensalem, Pa., 1996-97; mem. med. bd. Foxexec. Health Exams. Internat., 2001—. Capt. U.S. Army Med. Corps, 1966-68. Recipient N.Y. State Regents Med. scholarship, 1961. Mem. AMA, Am. Coll. Radiology, Radiol. Soc. N.Am., Pa. Med. Soc., Pa. Radiol. Soc., Chester County Med. Soc., Am. Inst. of Ultrasound in Medicine, Pa. Coll. Nuclear Medicine, Union League of Phila., Valley Forge Mountain Racquet Assn. Republican. Presbyterian. Avocations: photography, gardening, tennis. Home: 711 Pondview Way Downingtown PA 19335-4573

SCHEETZ, ALLISON PAIGE, medical educator; b. Atlanta, Nov. 19, 1963; d. Bobby Reid Scheetz and Augusta Claire (Dunn) Sherrer; m. David Edwin Mathis, Feb. 13, 1993; children: Taylor Nicole Mathis, Morgan Lindsay Mathis. BA in Psychology, BS in Biology, Mercer U., 1986, MD, 1992. Diplomate Am. Bd. Internal Medicine, Adolescent Medicine. Intern Med. Ctr. Ctrl. Ga./Mercer U. Sch. Medicine, Macon, 1992-93, resident, chief resident in internal medicine, 1993-95, instr. medicine dept. internal medicine, 1995-96, asst. prof., 1996-2001, asst. program dir., 1996-00, dir. resident edn., 1996-00, instr. dept. pediats., 1996-99, asst. prof. dept. pediats., 1999—2005, clerkship dir., 2000—07, assoc. prof., 2001—, fourth yr. program dir., 2008—; med. dir. Health South Rehab. Hosp., 2002—. Consulting physician Health South Rehab. Hosp., Macon, 1997—. Mem. ACP, AMA, Soc. Gen. Internal Medicine, Mercer U. Sch. Medicine Alumni Assn. (bd. dirs. 1997-99), Alpha Omega Alpha. Republican. Baptist. Achievements include research on thiazolidinedione, community acquired pneumonia, and medical student attitudes. Office: Mercer Health Sys Dept Internal Medicine 707 Pine St Macon GA 31201-2106

SCHEETZ, ANITA A., library director; d. John and Audrey O. Valach; m. Thomas H. Scheetz, Aug. 17, 1974; children: Amanda S. Bishop, Penny A. Filler, Rachel E. Miotke. MLIS, U. Okla., Norman, 2001. Cert. K-12 libr. Mont. Office Pub. Instrn., 1989. Part-time sch. libr. Rau Elem. Sch., Sidney, Mont., 1982—85; libr. asst. Sidney Pub. Libr., 1985—91; libr. dir. Ft. Peck Tribal Libr., Poplar, Mont., 1991—. Leader Richland County 4-H, Sidney, 1974—2000; mem. Peoples Congl. Ch., Sidney, 1980. Mem.: Mont. Libr. Assn. (ASLD chair 2008—). Independent. Congregationalist. Office: Fort Peck Tribal Libr Box 398 Poplar MT 59255 Business E-Mail: ascheetz@fpcc.edu.

SCHEFDORE, RONALD L., dentist; BS in Biology with honors, Southern Ill. U., 1979, DMD, 1983; Implant Cert., Northwestern U., 1985. Pvt. practice, Westmont, Ill. Author & lectr. Dentist Worldwide, 2001—. Author: Better Service Better Dentistry, 2003. Mem.: ADA, Am. Acad. Cosmetic Dentistry, Ill. Dental Assn., Chgo. Dental Soc. Office: 345 West Ogden Ave Westmont IL 60559 Office Phone: 630-971-0682. Office Fax: 630-971-0072. Business E-Mail: celebritysmiles@aol.com.

SCHEFF, JONATHAN H., health and medical products executive; B, Amherst Coll., Mass.; MD, Tufts U., Boston; MBA, U. San Diego; grad. Advanced Mgmt. Program, Harvard Bus. Sch. Cert. internal medicine. Med. dir. Southbay NavCare Clinic; cons. Milliman & Robertson, San Diego; regional med. dir. CHAMPUS divsn. Aetna Health Plans, San Diego; various positions including v.p. govt. health affairs and sr. v.p. health care ops. Found. Health Corp.; pres., chmn. bd. dirs. Found. Health Med. Group, Inc., Sacramento; chmn. bd. dirs. Thomas Davis Med. Ctrs., Tucson; chief med. officer, sr. v.p. TRICARE Med. Mgmt. for Health Net Fed. Svcs., Inc. Health Net, Inc., sr. v.p., chief med. officer, 2003—07, 2008—. Office: Health Net Inc 21650 Oxnard St Woodland Hills CA 91367 Office Phone: 818-676-6000.*

SCHEFF, THOMAS JOEL, sociologist, educator; b. Wewoka, Okla., Aug. 1, 1929; s. Arthur C. and Sarah (Goldman) S.; children: Karl J., Robin A., Julie S. BS, U. Ariz., 1950; MA, U. Calif., Berkeley, 1953, PhD, 1960. Asst. prof. sociology U. Wis., Madison, 1960-64; prof. sociology U. Calif., Santa Barbara, 1965—. Author: Being Mentally Ill, 1966, 3rd edit., 1999, Catharsis in Healing, 1979, Microsociology, 1990; co-author: (with Suzanne Retzinger) Emotion and Violence, 1991, Bloody Revenge, 1994, Emotions and the Social Bond, 1997, Goffman Unbound: A New Paradigm in the Social Sciences, 2006; contbr. to numerous essays. With U.S. Army, 1953-55. Mem. Am. Sociol. Assn. (chmn. sect. on sociology of emotions 1988-91), Pacific Sociol. Assn. (pres. 1996). E-mail: scheff@soc.ucsb.edu.

SCHEFFEL, KENNETH PAUL, retired archivist; b. Cin., Aug. 18, 1937; s. Edwin Reuben and Ivy Catherine (Happel) Scheffel. AB, Columbia U., NYC, 1959; MS, U. Wis., 1963. Archivist U. Mich., Ann Arbor, 1967—2003, archivist emeritus, 2003—. Mem.: So. Hist. Assn., Orgn. of Am. Historians. Methodist. Home: 7857 Harrison Ave Apt 4 Mount Healthy OH 45231-3151 Personal E-mail: kenschef@umich.edu.

SCHEFFING, DIANNE ELIZABETH, special education educator; b. St. Louis, Mar. 17, 1963; d. Eugene Shibley Scheffing Jr. and Sarah Ann (Lukens) Scheffing. BS, Mo. Bapt. Univ., 1988; MA, Fontbonne U., St. Louis, 1999, A in Computer Edn., 2005; postgrad., Webster U., St. Louis, 2002. Cert. elem. edn. grades 1-8 Mo., mild/moderate cross-category grades K-12 Mo., severely developmentally delayed 2002. Kindergarten tchr. asst. Andrews Acad., St. Louis, 1989—91; sci. tchr. edn. dept. St. Louis Sci. Ctr., 1994—96; tchr. asst. multi-handicapped Kehrs Mill Elem./Rockwood Sch. Dist., St. Louis, 1996—2000; tchr. spl. edn. Gateway/Hubert Wheeler State Sch. for Severely Handicapped, St. Louis, 2000—. Mem., sec. St. Louis Young Reps. Club, 1988—94; majority mem. Bethel #44 Internat. Order of Job's Daughters, St. Louis, 1978—84; mem. Rose Hill Chpt. #20 Order Eastern Star. Named Woman of Yr., St. Louis Young Reps. Club, 1992, 1994. Mem.: Am. Cancer Soc. Methodist. Avocations: Olympic supporter, bowling, travel. Office: Gateway/Hubert Wheeler State Sch 100 S Garrison Saint Louis MO 63103 Personal E-mail: applecore@prodigy.net.

SCHEFFLER, IMMO ERICH, molecular biologist, educator; b. Dresden, Germany, Dec. 17, 1940; s. Erich and Brunhilde S.; m. Diana, Aug. 14, 1965; 1 child, Timothy. BSc, U. Manitoba, 1963, MSc, 1964; PhD, Stanford U., 1968. Assoc. prof. to prof. biology U. Calif., San Diego, 1976—. Author: Mitochondria, 1999; editl. bd. Jour. Biol. Chemistry, 1994—. Recipient award for sr. U.S. scientists Alexander von Humboldt Found., 1984-85; Helen Hay Whitney fellow, 1968-71. Mem. AAAS, Am. Soc. Biochemistry & Molecular Biology. Office: U Calif San Diego 9500 Dr La Jolla CA 92093-0322

SCHEFFLER, ISRAEL, philosopher, educator; b. NYC, Nov. 25, 1923; s. Leon and Ethel (Grünberg) S.; m. Rosalind Zuckerbrod, June 26, 1949; children: Samuel, Laurie. BA, Bklyn. Coll., 1945, MA, 1948; M.H.L., Jewish Theol. Sem., 1949; PhD (Ford fellow 1951), U. Pa., 1952; A.M. (hon.), Harvard U., 1959; D.H.L. (hon.), Jewish Theol. Sem., 1993. Mem. faculty Harvard U., 1952-92, prof. edn., 1961-62, prof. edn. and philosophy, 1962-64, Victor S. Thomas prof. edn. and philosophy, 1964-92, professor emeritus, 1992—, hon. research fellow in cognitive studies, 1965-66, co-dir. Philosophy Edn. Rsch. Ctr., 1983-98, dir. Philosophy Edn. Rsch. Ctr., 1998—2003; scholar-in-residence The Mandel Ctr., Brandeis U., 2003—. Fellow Center for Advanced Study in Behavioral Scis., 1972-73 Author: The Language of Education, 1960, The Anatomy of Inquiry, 1963, Conditions of Knowledge, 1965, Science and Subjectivity, 1967, Reason and Teaching, 1973, Four Pragmatists, 1974, Beyond the Letter, 1979, Of Human Potential, 1985, Inquiries, 1986, In Praise of the Cognitive Emotions, 1991, Teachers of My Youth, 1995, Symbolic Worlds, 1997, Gallery of Scholars, 2004, Worlds of Truth: A Philosophy of Knowledge, 2009; co-author: Work, Education and Leadership, 1995; editor: Philosophy and Education, 1958, 66; co-editor: Logic and Art, 1972, Visions of Jewish Education, 2003; contbr. articles to profl. jours. Recipient Alumni Award of Merit Bklyn. Coll., 1967, Disting. Svc. medal Tchrs. Coll., Columbia, 1980, Benjamin Shevach award Boston Hebrew Coll., 1995; Guggenheim fellow, 1958-59, 72-73; NSF grantee, 1962, 65. Mem. Am. Acad. Arts and Scis., Am. Philos. Assn., Philosophy Edn. Soc., Nat. Acad. Edn. (charter), Philosophy of Sci. Assn. (prs. 1973-75), Charles S. Peirce Soc. (pres. 1998). Address: Apt 328 125 B Seminary Ave Auburndale MA 02466

SCHEFFLER, LINDA WEINGARTEN, psychologist, educator; b. NYC, Feb. 15, 1936; d. Robert Lee and Helen (Sonnenstrahl) Weingarten; m. Philip B. Scheffler, July 1, 1966. BA, U. Mich., 1957, MA, 1958, PhD, 1963. From asst. prof. to assoc. prof. counseling CUNY, NYC, 1969-91. Pvt. practice psychology, N.Y.C., 1972—. Author: Help Thy Neighbor-How Counseling Works and When It Doesn't, 1984. Pres. Met. Coll. Mental Health Assn., N.Y.C., 1983-84. Avocations: gardening, studio art, water colour. Home Phone: 212-744-3014; Office Phone: 212-744-3321. Business E-Mail: lws3@mac.com.

SCHEFFMAN, DAVID THEODORE, economist, management educator, consultant; b. Milaca, Minn., Dec. 1, 1943; s. David Theodore and Fern Virginia (Maas) Scheffman; 1 child, Christopher. BA magna cum laude, U. Minn., 1967; PhD, MIT, 1971. Lectr. Boston Coll., 1970-71; from asst. prof. to assoc. prof. Univ. Western Ont., London, Canada, 1971-81; sr. economist FTC, Washington, 1979-82, dep. dir., 1983-86; prof., dir. Inst. Applied Econs. Concordia U., Montreal, Que., Canada, 1982-83; dir., bur. econs. FTC, Washington, 1985-88; Justin Potter prof., adj. prof. bus. strategy and mktg. Vanderbilt U., Nashville, 1989-99, prof. of bus. strategy and mktg., 1999—; dir. LECG, NYC, 1993-2001, 2003—, Bur. Econs., FTC, Washington, 2001—03; adj. prof., dir. bus. strategy Cornell U., 2001—02. Adj. prof. Georgetown U. Law Ctr., Washington, 1986; cons. Ont. Econ. Coun., Toronto, 1973-81, GM, 1977, Ctrl. Oil Inquiry, Ottawa, Ont., 1982-84, Ctrl. Govt., Ottawa, 1979-81, Can. Competition Tribunal, 1987-89, Can. Bur. Competition Policy, 1988-91, U.S. Sentencing Commn., 1988-89, PepsiCo, 1989-2000, Kraft Gen. Food, 1989-2001, PacifiCorp, 1989-93, NERA, 1991-93, Boeing, 1992-96, Berwind Industries, Inc., 1993-95, Comm. Ctrl., Inc., Applied Innovation, Inc., TEC, 1995-98, Nortel, 1995, Coca Cola, 1996-98. Author: Speculation and Monopoly in Urban Development: Analytical Foundations, 1977, An Economic Analysis of Provincial Land Use Policies in Ontario, 1980, Social Regulation in Markets for Consumer Goods and Services, 1982, An Economic Analysis of the Impact of Rising Oil Prices on Urban Structure, 1983, Strategy, Structure, and Antitrust in the Carbonated Soft Drink Industry, 1992. Dissertation fellow NSF, 1967-68; vis. scholar U. Minn., 1978. Office: LECG 1725 I St NW #800 Washington DC 20006 Office Phone: 202-466-4422. Business E-Mail: dscheffman@lecg.com.

SCHEGLOFF, EMANUEL ABRAHAM, social studies educator; b. NYC, July 24, 1937; s. Ber Mendelev and Helen Faller Schegloff; m. Myra Jill White, July 15, 1962; 1 child, Naomi Eve. BA magna cum laude, Harvard Coll., Cambridge, MA, 1958; MA, U. Calif., Berkeley, 1967; PhD, 1967. Asst. prof. sociology Columbia U., NYC, 1965—72; disting. prof. sociology, applied linguistics UCLA, 1972—. Recipient McGovern Lectr. award, U. Tex., 1985, Starr Lectr. award, Middlebury Coll., 1987; fellow, Netherlands Inst. Advanced Study, 1978—79, Palo Alto, 1998—99, John Simon Guggenheim Meml. Found., 1998—99. Business E-Mail: scheglof@soc.ucla.edu.

SCHEHR, KEVIN JOHN, art gallery owner; b. Tulsa, Mar. 23, 1966; s. Louis Valentine Schehr, Jr. and Bonnie Louise Sadle; m. Melissa Aileen Boeckl, Feb. 4, 1995; m. Melissa Diane Bell, June 1, 1985 (dec. Feb. 22, 1992); children: Kevin John Schehr, Jr., Alicia Katelyn. AS, Fla. C.C. at Jacksonville, 1990; B. of Vocat. Edn., So. Ill. U., 1990; MBA, U. of Phoenix, 1999. Ops. mgr. New Orleans Windustrial, New Orleans, 1992—95; v.p. Source Prodn. & Equipment Co, Inc., St. Rose, La., 1995; pres. Galerie Rouge, Inc, New Orleans, 2002—. Nat. alerting officer Am. Disaster Res., 2003—05; vol. USA Freedom Corps, Washington, 2003—. With USN, 1985—92, 1st lt. Miss. State Guard, 2005—. Recipient Pres.'s Vol. Svc. award Silver, USA Freedom Corps, 2004, Pres.'s Vol. Svc. award Gold, 2005. Mem.: Am. Soc. for Non-Destructive Testing (assoc.; New Orleans sect. chmn. 1996—2002), Naval Order of the U.S., State Guard Assn. of the U.S. (assoc.), Am. Legion, VFW (life). Roman Catholic. Home: 2658 Hudson Pl New Orleans LA 70131 Office: Galerie Rouge 509 Royal St New Orleans LA 70130-2113 Personal E-mail: kschehr826@aol.com.

SCHEIBE, KARL EDWARD, psychology professor; b. Belleville, Ill., Mar. 5, 1937; s. John Henry and Esther Julia (Friesen) S.; m. Elizabeth Wentworth Mixter, Sept. 10, 1961; children: David Sawyer, Robert Daniel. BS, Trinity Coll., 1959; PhD, U. Calif.-Berkeley, 1963; MA (hon.), Wesleyan U., 1973. Faculty mem. Wesleyan U., Middletown, Conn., 1963—73, prof. psychology, 1973—2005, prof. emeritus, 2005—. Vis. prof. U. So. Calif., 1974; dir. rev. panels NSF Sci. Profl. Devel. Program, 1975-81; cons. Am. Council Edn., 1975-81 Author: Beliefs and Values, 1970, Mirror, Masks, Lies and Secrets, 1979, Studies in Social Identity, 1983, Self Studies: The Psychology of Self and Identity, 1995, The Drama of Everyday Life, 2000. Trustee Trinity Coll., Hartford, Conn., 1977-83; moderator congregation First Ch. of Christ, Middletown, 1981-82. Woodrow Wilson fellow, 1959; NSF fellow, 1961; NIMH research grantee, 1964-68; Fulbright fellow Cath. U. Sao Paulo, Brazil, 1972-73, 84. Mem. Am. Psychol. Assn., Eastern Psychol. Assn., Conn. Acad. Arts and Scis., Phi Beta Kappa Congregationalist. Home: 11 Long Ln Middletown CT 06457-4046 Office: Wesleyan U Wasch Ctr for Ret Faculty Middletown CT 06459-0001 Office Phone: 860-685-2173. Business E-Mail: kscheibe@wesleyan.edu.

SCHEIBEL, ARNOLD BERNARD, psychiatrist, educator, research director; b. NYC, Jan. 18, 1923; s. William and Ethel (Greenberg) Scheibel; m. Madge Mila Ragland, Mar. 3, 1950 (dec. Jan. 1977); m. Marian Diamond, Sept. 1982. BA, Columbia U., NYC, 1944, MD, 1946; MS, U. Ill., 1952. Intern Mt. Sinai Hosp., NYC, 1946-47; resident in psychiatry Barnes and McMillan Hosp., St. Louis, 1947-48, Ill. Neuropsychiat. Inst., Chgo., 1950-52; asst. prof. psychiatry and anatomy U. Tenn. Med. Sch., 1952-53, assoc. prof., 1953-55, UCLA Med. Ctr., 1955-67, prof., 1967—, mem. Brain Rsch. Inst., 1960—, acting dir. Brain Rsch. Inst., 1987-90, dir., 1990-95. Cons. in field. Contbr. numerous articles to tech. jours, chpts. to books.; mem. editl. bd. Brain Rsch., 1967-77, Developmental Psychobiology, 1968—, Internat. Jour. Neurosci., 1969—, Jour. Biol. Psychiatry, 1968—, Jour. Theoretical Biology, 1980—; assoc. editor News Report, 1989—. Mem. Pres.'s Commn. on Aging, Nat. Inst. Aging, 1980—. Served with AUS, 1943-46; from lt. to capt. M.C. AUS, 1948-50. Guggenheim fellow (with wife), 1953-54, 59; recipient Disting. Svc. award Calif. Soc. Biomed. Rsch., 1998. Fellow Am. Acad. Arts and Scis., Norwegian Acad. Scis., Am. Psychiat. Assn. (life, Harriet and Charles Luckman Disting. Tchg. award 1997) AAAS; mem. Am. Neurol. Assn., Soc. Neuorosci., Pyschiat. Rsch. Assn., Soc. Biol. Psychiatry, So. Calif. Psychiat. Assn. Home: 16231 Morrison St Encino CA 91436-1331 Office: UCLA Dept Neurobiology Los Angeles CA 90024 Business E-Mail: scheibel@mednet.ucla.edu. *Intense personal tragedy can embitter life and choke off further personal creativity. It may also offer the opportunity to open new doors in the discovery of self. I am more aware than ever of my good fortune in having the opportunity to teach, to continue investigative work in the structure and function of the brain, and to give love and care to those who need it. I am more than ever convinced that loving and being loved is the greatest good that we can know, the state in which we most nearly fulfill our roles as human beings.*

SCHEIBEL, KENNETH MAYNARD, journalist; b. Campbell, Nebr., May 17, 1920; s. G. Alfred and Rachel Christine (Koch) S.; m. Helen Schmitt, May 14, 1955 (div. Sept. 1977); children: Victor Warren Schmitt, William Becker Schmitt, Kenneth Jr., Sally. Student, George Wash. U., Washington, DC, 1938—41; BA, U. Va., Charlottesville, 1947, MA, 1949. Mag. salesman Periodical Pubs. Svc. Bur., Inc., 1935-38; reporter Internat. News Svc., Washington, 1940-41, Wall St. Jour., Washington, 1949-51; Washington corr. Gannett Newspapers, 1951-63; syndicated columnist N.Am. Newspaper Alliance, 1963-64; chief Washington bur. Donrey Media Group, 1964-67; founder, bur. chief Washington Bur. News, 1967—; founder nat. syndicated column Washington Farm Beat, 1970-85. Washington corr. Wis. State Jour., 1963-66, LaCrosse Tribune, Wis., 1963-66, Billings Gazette, Mont., 1964-71, V.I. Network, 1966-67, Moline Daily Dispatch, Ill., 1967-68, Drovers' Jour., 1967-68, Newport News Daily Press & Times Herald, Va., 1969-71, Packer Pub. Co., 1964-74, Gasoline Retailer, 1966-67, Okla., Farmer Stockman; congl. corr. F-D-C Reports, 1975-77; Washington columnist Farm Jour., 1960-75; dir. Nat. Press Bldg. Corp., 1973, v.p. pres. club and bldg corp., 1974; covered nat. polit. convs., campaigns; v.p. Fraser Assocs. (pub. rels.), Washington, 1976-79; Congl. broadcast interviewer; founder Wash. Broadcast News, Ft. Smith, Ark., Miami, Las Vegas. Contbr. nat. mags., newspaper syndicates. Incorporator and Mem. War Meml. of Korea, Washington, 1981; editor Nat. Ctr. Fin. and Econ. Info., U.S.-Saudi Arabian Joint Econ. Commn., Riyadh, 1985-86; Capt. AUS, 1941-46, 755th Tank Bn., 1st armored divsn., 1942-45, Europe, N. Africa, Italy. Decorated Bronze star, US Army Occupation medal, Combat Infantryman badge; co-recipient Croix De Guerre (France), pre-WWII, Nat. Def. Svc. medal, Battle Stars 4 Italian Campaign 2 amphibious landings, US Army Reserve, 1946-51, Night Cable officer, Allied Force Hdqs. London, 1942, Victory medal, WWII, 1945, Thoth award for excellence in pub. rels., 1980. Mem. Izaak Walton League Am., White House Corrs. Assn., Overseas Press Club of Am., Am. Radio Relay League, Nat. Press Club (Washington; fin. sec., gov. 1969-73, vice chmn. bd. 1971, v.p., pres., 1974), Sigma Chi. Presbyterian. Avocation: amateur radio. Home: The Hermitage of Northern Virginia 5000 Fairbank Ave #514 Alexandria VA 22311 Office Phone: 703-797-3935. Personal E-mail: kenscheib@earthlink.com. *The greatest sins are timidity and self indulgence, the greatest virtue is to love. Live each day, don't fret about yesterday or tomorrow. Enjoy the senses, learn from others, and never forget that both love and hate are returned.*

SCHEIBER, HARRY N., law educator, historian; b. 1935; BA, Columbia U., 1955; MA, Cornell U., 1957, PhD, 1961; MA (hon.), Dartmouth Coll., 1965; D.Jur.Hon., Uppsala U., Sweden, 1998. Instr. to assoc. prof. history Dartmouth Coll., 1960-68, prof., 1968-71; prof. Am. history U. Calif., San Diego, 1971-80; prof. law Boalt Hall, U. Calif., Berkeley, 1980—. Chmn. jurisprudence and social policy program, 1982-84, 90-93, assoc. dean, 1990-93, 96-99; The Stefan Riesenfeld prof., 1991—; vice chair Univ. Academic Senate, 1993-94, chair 1994-95; acting dir. Ctr. for Study Law and Soc., 1999-2001; dir. Earl Warren Legal Inst., 2002-05, Inst. for Legal Rsch., 2005—, Sho Sato Program, 1993—; co-dir. Law of the Sea Inst., 2002-; Fulbright disting. sr. lectr., Australia, 1983, marine affairs coord. Calif. Sea Grant Coll. Program, 1989-2000; vis. rsch. prof. Law Inst. U. Uppsala, Sweden, 1995, hon. prof. DiTella U., Buenos Aires, 1999; cons. Calif. Jud. Coun., 1992-93; Cassel lectr., Stockholm U., 2003. Author: The Wilson Administration and Civil Liberties, 1960, Ohio Canal Era, 1970, Inter-Allied Conflicts and Ocean Law (1945-1953), 2001; co-author: American Law and the Constitutional Order, 1988, The State and Freedom of Contract, 1998, American Law and the Constitutional Order, 1978, Law of the Sea: The Common Heritage and Emerging Challenges, 2000, Bringing New Law to Ocean Waters, 2004, Earl Warren and the Warren Court, 2006, Emerging Concepts of Rights in Japanese Law, 2007, Frontier Issues in Ocean Law, 2009, Oceans in the Nuclear Age, 2009, Japanese Family Law in Comparative Perspective, 2009; editor: Yearbook of the California Supreme Court Historical Society, 1994—2006; contbr. articles to profl. jours. Chmn. Littleton Griswold Prize Legal History, 1985-88, 2006-07, pres. NH Civil Liberties Union, 1969-70; chmn. Project '87 Task Force on Pub. Programs, Washington, 1982-85; dir. Berkeley Seminar on Federalism, 1986-95; cons. judiciary study U.S. Adv. Commn. Intergovernmental Rels., 1985-88, Pew Oceans Commn., 2002-03, Nat. Rsch. Coun., 2002-03, Joint Ocean Commn. Initiative, sci. adv. bd. couns., 2007-, Joint oceans Commn. State Calif.; dir. NEH Inst. Constitutionalism, U. Calif., Berkeley, 1986-87, 88-91; cons. state Ocean Protection Coun., 2008-. Recipient Sea Grant Colls. award, 1981-83, 84-85, 86-2002; fellow Ctr. Advanced Study in Behavioral Scis., Stanford Calif., 1967, 71; Guggenheim fellow, 1971, 88; Rockefeller Found. humanities fellow, 1979, NEH fellow, 1985-86; NSF grantee 1979, 80, 88-89. Fellow AAAS, Am. Acad. Arts and Scis., U. Calif. Humanities Rsch. Inst., Am. Soc. for Legal History (hon.; pres. 2003—), Japan Soc. for Promotion of Sci. (invitational fellow); mem. Am. Hist. Assn., Orgn. Am. Historians, Agrl. History Soc. (pres. 1978), Econ. History Assn. (trustee 1978-80), Law and Soc. Assn. (trustee 1979-81, 96-99), Nat. Assessment History and Citizenship Edn. (chmn. nat. acad. bd. 1986-87), Marine Affairs and Policy Assn. (bd. dirs. 1991-96), Ocean Governance Study Group (steering com. 1991-2004), Internat. Coun. Environ. Law, Calif. Supreme Ct. Hist. Soc. (bd. dirs. 1993—, v.p. 1997-98). Office: U Calif Berkeley Law Sch Boalt Hall Berkeley CA 94720-7200 Office Phone: 510-643-9788. E-mail: scheiber@law.berkeley.edu.

SCHEIBER, LAURA LEE, archaeologist, educator; b. St. Paul, Dec. 18, 1968; d. Anthony Robert Scheiber and Marcia Lee Agee. BA, U. Wyo., Laramie, 1990, MA, 1993; PhD, U. Calif., Berkeley, 2001. Asst. prof. anthropology Ind. U., Bloomington, 2002—. Co-dir. Exploring Social and Hist. Landscape of Greater Yellowstone Ecosys., Cody, Wyo., 2005—. Editor: (non-fiction) Archaeological Landscapes on the High Plains. Rsch. grant, NSF, 2008—. Mem.: Plains Anthrop. Soc. (Lincoln, Nebr.) (v.p. 2004—05). Avocation: genealogy. Office: Ind Univ 701 E Kirkwood Ave Bloomington IN 47404

SCHEIBER, STEPHEN CARL, psychiatrist; b. NYC, May 2, 1938; s. Irving Martin and Frieda Olga (Schor) S.; m. Mary Ann McDonnell, Sept. 14, 1965; children: Lisa Susan, Martin Irving, Laura Ann. BA, Columbia Coll., 1960; MD, SUNY, Buffalo, 1964. Diplomate Am. Bd. Psychiatry and Neurology. Intern Mary Fletcher Hosp., Burlington, Vt., 1964-65; resident in psychiatry Strong Meml. Hosp., Rochester, NY, 1967-70; asst. prof. U. Ariz., Tucson, 1970-76, assoc. prof., 1976-81, prof., 1981-86; exec. sec. Am. Bd. Psychiatry and Neurology, Inc., Deerfield, Ill., 1986-89, exec. v.p., 1989—2006; pres., CEO Isaac Ray Ctr., Inc., Chgo., 2008—. Adj. prof. psychiatry Northwestern U., Chgo., 1986—, Med. Coll. Wis., Milw., 1986-2006, clin. prof. psychiatry, 2006—. Co-editor: The Impaired Physician, 1983, Certification, Recertification and Lifetime Learning in Psychiatry, 1994, Core Competencies for Psychiatric Practice, 2003, Core Competencies for Neurologists, 2003; contbr. articles to profl. jours. Mem. med. adv. com. Casas de los Ninos, Tucson, 1974-86; mem. mental health adv. com. Tucson Health Planning Coun., 1974-75; med. student interviewer Office of Med. Edn., 1975; mem. Glenbrook (Ill.) North H.S. Boosters Club, 1988-91; treas. Robert E. Jones Found., 1988-96. Surgeon USPHS, 1965-67. Recipient Outstanding Tchr. award, U. Ariz., 1986, Disting. Life and Career Achievement award, SUNY, Buffalo Med. Alumni Assn., 1998; grantee Group Therapy Outcome Studies on Inpatient Svc., 1980, Dialysis and Schizophrenia Pilot Project, NIH, 1978. Fellow: Am. Assn. Dirs. Psychiat. Residency Tng. (pres. 1981—82), Am. Coll. Psychiatrists (bd. regents 1992—2001, treas. 1995—2001, Disting. Svc. award 2007), Group for Advancement of Psychiatry (life; invited mem., chmn. mem. edn. com. 1987—91, bd. dirs., sec. 1993—97, pres.-elect 1997—99, pres. 1999—2001), Am. Psychiat. Assn. (life; chmn. impaired physician com. 1985—88, cons. 1988—92, 2008—, Disting. Life Fellow 2002, Vestermark award 2007), Assn. Acad. Psychiatry (life; parliamentary sec. 1979—84, treas. 1984—88, pres.-elect 1988—89, pres. 1989—90, Lifetime Educator award 2002, Disting. Life Fellow 2006); mem.: Am. Bd. Med. Specialties (Disting. Svc. award 2007), Benjamin Rush Soc. (sec. treas. 2004—06, v.p. 2006—08, pres. 2008—), Oracle Heights Club (pres. 1983—84). Democrat. Jewish. Office: Isaac Ray Ctr Inc 1725 W Harrison St #110 Chicago IL 60612 Office Phone: 312-563-2464.

SCHEIBLE, DAVID W., paper company executive; BS, MBA, Purdue Univ. V.p., gen. mgr. Avery Denison Corp., 1993—99; pres. flexible div. Graphic Packaging Internat., 1999, COO, 1999—2003; exec. v.p. comml. ops. Graphic Packaging Corp., Marietta, Ga., 2003—04, COO, 2004—06, pres., CEO, bd. dir., 2007—. Office: Graphic Packaging Corp 814 Livingston Ct Marietta GA 30067

SCHEICH, JOHN F., lawyer; b. Bklyn., Aug. 6, 1942; s. Frank A. and Dorothy (O'Hara) Scheich. BA, St. John's U., NYC, 1963, JD, 1966; postgrad., John Marshall Law Sch., Chgo., 1968. Bar: N.Y. 1967, U.S. Ct. Internat. Trade Admission 1969, U.S. Dist. Ct. (ea. and so. dists.) N.Y. 1971, U.S. Ct. Appeals (2d cir.) 1971, U.S. Supreme Ct. 1975, Pa. 1980. Spl. agt. FBI, U.S. Dept. Justice, Washington, 1966-69; asst. dist. atty. Queens County, Kew Gardens, N.Y., 1969-72; pvt. practice Richmond Hill, NY, 1970—76, 1979—91; ptnr. Raia & Scheich, P.C., Richmond Hill, 1976-79; sr. ptnr. Scheich & Goldsmith, PC, Richmond Hill, 1991—95, 2003—, Scheich, Goldsmith & Dreishpoon, PC, Richmond Hill, 1996—2003; mortgage settlement atty. GMAC, NY, 1996—2007. Mem. assigned counsel panel for indigent defendants in major felony and murder cases 9th and 11th jud. dists. N.Y. State Supreme Ct., Queens County, 1972—94; v.p. Ra-Li Brokerage Corp., 1975—, bd. dirs.; lectr. Lawyers in Classroom, 1979—91; chmn. arbitration panel Civil Ct. City of N.Y., 1981—90; trial judge St. John's U. Sch. Law Civil Trial Inst. Student Competition, 1992—; lectr. estate planning Nat. Bus. Inst., 1994; mem. adv. bd. 1st Am. Title Ins. Co. Am., 1995—2004; mortgage settlement atty. Gen. Motors Acceptance Corp. N.Y. State, 1996—. Editor: Conashaugh Courier, 1989-92; mem. editorial bd., 1988-92; contbg. columnist, 1981-89. Active Performing Arts Ctr. Pinellas County, St. Petersburg, 1995—2003; mem. Com. for Beautification of East Norwich, Nassau County, LI, NY, 1983—, bd. dirs., 1993—96, pres., 1996—; mem. Friends of the Arts, Locust Valley, LI, NY, 1985—; chmn. tri-centennial celebration com. Village of East Norwich, 1996—97; mem. St. Edward the Confessor Sch. Bd., Syosset, NY, 1986—90; nat. trust and estate assoc. Meml. Sloane Kettering Cancer Ctr., NYC, 1994—; active Internat. Wine Ctr., 1985—96; mem. Fransiscan Ctr. Guild, Tampa, Fla., 1996—, Tilles Ctr. Performing Arts, Inc., Long Island U., Brookville, NY, 1997—, Lincoln Ctr. Performing Arts, Inc., 1985—, Bravo Soc., 1994—, Concern for Dying, 1984—2002, Sea Cliff Chamber Players, 1992—99; active Pact, Inc. Ruth Eckerd Hall-Richard B. Baumgardner Ctr. for Performing Arts, Clearwater, Fla., 1995—2001, Rep. Nat. Senate Adv. Coun., 1997—2002, Rep. Nat. Com. Chmn.'s Honor Roll (cert. Achievement 1998), 1997; appointed to Bus. Advisory Coun. by Nat. Repub. Congressional Comm.; mem. East Norwich Rep. Club, 1982—, bd. dirs., 1984—87, 1993—, v.p., 1987—89, pres., 1989—93; mem. Nat. Rep. Senatorial Com., 1988—2004, Nassau County Rep. Com., Town of Oyster Bay, 1993—, Holy Name Soc. of Our Lady of Perpetual Help Ch., 1963—, sec., 1965—67, v.p., 1969—71, pres., 1971—73; parish coun. Our Lady of Perpetual Help Roman Cath. Ch., 1976—82, pres., 1978—80, fin. com., adv. to pastor, 1970—82, chmn. fin. com., 1979—82; active St. Edward the Confessor Ch., Syosset, 1982—90, St. Vincent Ch., Dingman Hills, Pa., 1977—2004, St. Dominic's Ch., Oyster Bay, NY, 1982—, apptd. pastor's adv. coun. on estate planning, 1998—2003, mem. St. Dominic's Legacy Soc., 1998—; mem. St. John Vianney Roman Cath. Ch., St. Petersburg Beach, Fla., 1994—, Internat. Platform Assn., 1977—97; bd. dirs. Northslope II Homeowners Assn., Shawnee-on-Delaware, Pa., 1988—90, Shawnee-on-Del., Pa., 1992—94, 2000—02, Conashaugh Lakes Cmty. Assn., Milford, Pa., 1981—90; mem. adv. coun. Our Lady Perpetual Help Sch. Bd., 2007—; organizing mem. Conashaugh Lakes Lot Owners interim com., 1977—81, sec., 1981—82, v.p., 1982—84, pres., 1984—86, past pres., 1986—88; Non-Resident Fellow, James Beard Found., NYC, 1995—. Recipient J. Edgar Hoover award, 1967, award of appreciation, Civil Trial Inst., St. John's U. Sch. of Law, 1991, 95, Disting. Svc. award, 1992, cert. of appreciaiton Conashaugh Lakes Cmty. Assn., 1990, Dist. Svc. award Kiwanis Club, 1992, Cert. of Merit for Disting. Svc. award Nassau County Exec. Hon. Thomas Gulotta, 1989, Presdl. Order of Merit award Pres. George Bush, 1991, Order of Merit award Nat. Rep. Senatorial Com., 1994, Cert. Achievement, Rep. Nat. Com., 1998; named one of Best Trial Lawyers in the U.S., Town and Country Mag., 1985; non-resident fellow James Beard Found., N.Y.C., 1995—, Blue Ribbon Survey Commn. cert. of recognition, 2002. Mem. ABA (cert. of appreciation Am. Bar Endowment 1992), ATLA, Pa. State Bar Assn., NY State Bar Assn., Queens County Bar Assn., Nassau County Bar Assn., NY State Trial Lawyers Assn., Ciminal Cts. Bar Assn., John Marshall Lawyers Assn. (bd. dirs. 1992—, pres. 1992-97, treas. 1997—), Soc. Former Spl. Agts. of FBI (nat. chpt., L.I. chpt., chmn. L.I. chpt. 2003-06, charter chmn. 2003-06), NY State Assn. Criminal Def. Lawyers, LeGaL Lawyers Assn. (bd. dirs. 2001—, bd. dirs. found. 1995-98, 2001—, sec. 2003-06, v.p., 2006, pres., 2007), St. John's Coll. Alumni Assn., Asst. Dist. Attys. Assn. Queens County, St. John's U. Sch. of Law Alumni Assn., St. John's Prep. Sch. Alumni Assn., Friends of the Arts of Nassau County, Inc., Cath. Lawyers Guild of Queens County, NY, KC, Brookhaven Wine Lovers Soc., East Norwich Civic Assn. (bd. dirs. 2002-04), Sun Island Assn. (bd. dirs. 2001-02, 2007-), Heritage Soc., St. John's U. McCallen Soc., Business Advisory Coun., Phi Alpha Delta. Avocation: fine wines. Home: 170 Sugar Toms Ln East Norwich NY 11732-1153 Office: Scheich & Goldsmith PC 103-42 Lefferts Blvd South Richmond Hill NY 11419-2012 also: 109 Newbridge Rd Hicksville NY 11801-3908 Office Phone: 718-843-7200, 516-433-3300.

SCHEICHER, RALPH HENDRIK, research scientist; b. Würzburg, Germany, June 11, 1975; s. Georg and Gabi Scheicher. PhD in physics, SUNY, Albany, 2000—04. Rschr. Uppsala U., Sweden, 2007—; vis. asst. prof. Mich. Technol. U., Houghton, 2005—07. Recipient C. L. Andrews Tchg. Asst. of Yr. award, Dept. Physics, SUNY Albany, 2002; German Academic Exch. Svc. scholarship, 1998—99, Postdoctoral grant, Wenner-Gren Found. Stockholm, 2008. Mem.: Am. Phys. Soc. Green Party. Achievements include several important discoveries in the fields of nano-biotechnology and hydrogen storage. Avocations: swimming, running, chess, travel. Office: Dept Physics & Mat Sci Uppsala Univ Box 530 Uppsala SE-751 21 Sweden Office Fax: 46 18 471-3524. Business E-Mail: ralph.scheicher@fysik.uu.se.

SCHEID, STEVEN L., investment company executive; 3 children. BS in acctg., Michigan St. U. CFO The Charles Schwab & Co. Inc., 1996—99, vice-chmn. San Francisco, 1999—2002; CEO Charles Schwab Investment Mgmt., 1999—2002; pres. Schwab Retail Group, 2000—02; chmn. Janus Capital Group, Denver, 2004—, CEO, 2004—06. Fed. Reserve Bank of San Francisco's representative Fed. Advisory Coun., 2001—02; bd. dirs. The PMI Group Inc., Auto Desk Inc. Avocations: piano, clarinet, running, wine collecting. Office: Janus Capital Group Inc 151 Detroit St Denver CO 80206-4923

SCHEIDEL, WALTER, historian; b. Vienna, July 9, 1966; s. Alfred and Ilse Scheidel. PhD, U. Vienna, 1993; degree in Habilitation, U. Graz, 1998. Vis. prof. U. Chgo., 2000—02; prof. classics Stanford U., Calif., 2003—, chair, dept. classics, 2008—. Author: (book) Death on the Nile: Disease and the Demography of Roman Egypt, Measuring Sex, Age and Death in the Roman Empire, Grundpacht und Lohnarbeit in der Landwirtschaft des roemischen Italien; editor: The Cambridge Economic History of the Greco-Roman World, Rome and China, The Dynamics of Ancient Empires, The Ancient Economy, Debating Roman Demography, The Oxford Handbook of Roman Studies. Erwin Schroedinger fellowship, Austrian Rsch. Coun., 1995, Moses and Mary Finley fellowship, Darwin Coll., Cambridge, Eng., 1996—99, New Directions fellowship, Mellon Found., 2005—06, Mellon-Sawyer grant, 2007—08. Achievements include research in ancient social and economic history; first to work on ancient population history.

SCHEIDT, BRIAN R., geologist, educator; s. A Scheidt Robert and Patricia K Scheidt. AS, Joliet Jr. Coll., Ill., 1996; BS in Geology, Ea. Ill. U., Charleston, 1998; MS in Geology, Southern Ill. U., Carbondale, 2001. Geoscience instr. Lincoln Land CC, Springfield, Ill., 2001—02; adj. instr. and lab. mgr. Austin Peay State U., Clarksville, Tenn., 2002—03; asst. prof. Mineral Area Coll., Pk. Hills, Mo., 2003—. Mem. East Ozarks Audubon, Farmington, Mo., 2003—08. Office: Mineral Area Coll 5270 Flat River Rd Park Hills MO 63601 Business E-Mail: bscheidt@mineralarea.edu.

SCHEIDT, W. ROBERT, chemistry educator, researcher; b. Richmond Heights, Mo., Nov. 13, 1942; s. Walter Martin and Martha (Videtich) S.; m. Kathryn Sue Barnes, Aug. 9, 1964; children: Karl Andrew, David Martin. BS, U. Mo., 1964; MS, U. Mich., 1965, PhD, 1968; postdoctoral studies, Cornell U., 1970. Asst. prof. U. Notre Dame, Ind., 1970-76, assoc. prof., 1976-80, prof., 1980—, William K. Warren prof., 1999—. Vis. prof. U. Wash., Seattle, 1980, U. Paris (Orsay), Paris, 1991, U. René Descartes, 2005, 06, U. Strasbourg, France, 1998; mem. rev. sec. Metallobiochemistry NIH, Bethesda, 1991—96. Contbr. articles to profl. jours. Fellow AAAS; mem. Am. Chem. Soc. (assoc. editor Chem. Revs. jour. 1980-85), Am. Crystallographic Assn., Biophys. Soc., Sigma X. Democrat. Office: U Notre Dame Dept Chemistry Notre Dame IN 46556 Business E-Mail: scheidt.1@nd.edu.

SCHEIMAN, EUGENE R., lawyer; b. Bklyn., July 15, 1943; BA, L.I. U., 1966; JD cum laude, Bklyn. Law Sch., 1969. Bar: NY 1970, US Dist. Ct. (so. and ea. dists.) NY 1971, US Ct. Appeals (1st cir.) 1972, US Ct. Appeals (5th cir.) 1973, US Ct. Appeals (4th cir.) 1974, US Supreme Ct. 1976, US Ct. Appeals (2nd cir.) 1977, US Ct. Appeals (fed. cir.), US Ct. Appeals (11th cir.) 1989, US Ct. Appeals (3rd cir.) 1990. Formerly shareholder Buchanan Ingersoll, NYC; with McCarter & English LLP, NYC. Editor-in-chief Bklyn. Law Rev., 1969. Named NY Super Lawyer, 2006—09. Fellow Am. Bar Found.; mem. ABA (sect. on individual rights and responsibilities, franchise forum constrn. forum), NY State Bar Assn., Assn. Bar. City of NY, Philonomic Honor Soc., County Bar Assn. (constrn. law forum). Office: Arent Fox LLP 1675 Broadway New York NY 10019 Office Phone: 212-484-3949. Business E-Mail: eugene.scheiman@arentfox.com.

SCHEIN, EDGAR HENRY, management educator; b. Zurich, Mar. 5, 1928; came to U.S., 1939, naturalized, 1944; s. Marcel and Hilde (Schoenbeck) S.; m. Mary Louise Lodmell, July 28, 1956; children: Louisa, Elizabeth, Peter. PhB, U. Chgo., 1946, BA, 1947, Stanford U., 1948, MA, 1949; PhD, Harvard U., 1953. Tchg. asst. stats. Stanford U., 1947-49; tchg. asst. social psychology Harvard U., 1949-52; rsch. psychologist, neuropsychiatry div. Walter Reed Army Inst. Rsch., also chief social psychology sect., 1952-56; mem. faculty MIT, 1956—, prof. orgnl. psychology and mgmt., 1964—, chmn. orgn. studies group Sloan Sch. Mgmt., 1972-81, Sloan Fellows prof. mgmt., 1978-97, prof. emeritus, 1995—; mem. bd., exec. com. Nat. Tng. Labs., 1962-64; cons. to govt. and industry, 1956—. Author books and articles in field. Capt. AUS, 1950-56. Recipient Aux. Rsch. award Social Sci. Rsch. Coun., 1958. Fellow APA; mem. Acad. Mgmt. Home Phone: 617-864-7540. Business E-Mail: scheine@comcast.net.

SCHEIN, RODNEY M., electronics engineer, educator; 2 children. BSEE with Honors, U. Wash., Seattle, 1965, MBA, 1968. Electronics tech. instr. Edmonds CC, Lynnwood, Wash., 1971—2005, robotics & electronics tech. instr., 2005—. Tech. tng. cons. & trainer Fluke Co., Everett, Wash., 1984—90; electronics technician trainer Intermec Corp., Everett, 1990—2001. Author: (instructional dvd's) DC, AC & Linear, Advanced Digital, Advanced Computers, and Advanced Linear Electronics. Fifth grade boys tchr. U. Presbyn. Ch., Seattle, 1984—; trustee Alongside Ministries Internat., Oakland, Calif., 1988—2006, chairperson. Recipient Exceptional Falcuty award, Edmonds CC Found., 2006. Mem.: Electronics Mfg. Assn., Beta Gamma Sigma. Mem. Christian Ch. Achievements include design of curriculum for training technicians how to use electronics principles in real-world electronics products; curriculum for training technicians how to test and troubleshoot real world electronic products; development of robotics training curriculum for technicians. Avocations: woodworking, sailing, travel. Office: Edmonds CC 20 000 68th Ave W Lynnwood WA 98036 Business E-Mail: rschein@edcc.edu.

SCHEIN, VIRGINIA ELLEN, psychologist; b. June 23, 1943; d. Jacob Charles and Anne Schein; m. Rupert F. Chisholm (dec. 2004); 1 child, Alexander Nikos. BA cum laude, Cornell U., 1965; PhD, NYU, 1969. Lic. psychologist, Pa. Sr. rsch. assoc. Am. Mgmt. Assn., NYC, 1969-70; mgr. personnel rsch. Life Office Mgmt. Assn., NYC, 1970-72; dir. personnel rsch. Met. Life Ins. Co., NYC, 1972-75; assoc. prof. Sch. Mgmt. Case Western Res. U., Cleve., 1975-76; vis. assoc. prof. Sch. Orgn. and Mgmt. Yale U., New Haven, 1977-80; mgmt. cons., 1975—; assoc. prof. psychology Bernard M. Baruch Coll. CUNY, 1982-85; prof. mgmt. and psychology Gettysburg Coll., Pa., 1986—2006, prof. emerita mgmt. and psychology, 2007—. Chair mgmt. dept. Gettysburg Coll., 1993—95. Author: Working from the Margins, 1995; co-author: Power and Organization Development, 1988; mem. editl. rev. bds. Acad. Mgmt. Review, 1979-82, Women Mgmt. Rev., 1991-, Acad. Mgmt. Execs., 1992-98; contbr. articles to profl. jours. Bd. dirs. Family Planning Ctr., 1988-91, Pvt. Industry Coun., 1990-93, Keystone Rsch. Ctr., 1996-98, Women Cmty. Svc., 1997-2003; bd. dirs. Survivors, Inc., pres. bd. dirs., 1991-92, Adams County Children and Youth Adv. Bd., 2003-04; UN/Non-govt. orgn. rep., Internat. Assn. Applied Psychology, 2007-08; bus. vol. Phila. Arts and Bus. Coun., 2007-09. Mem.: APA (coun.rep. 1978—80, com. women 1980—83), Internat. Assn. Applied Psychology (divsn. orgnl. psychology chair sci. program com. 1995—98, pres.-elect 1998—2002, pres. 2002—06), Acad. Mgmt. (rep. orgn.devel. divsn. 1979—81, exec. com. women mgmt. divsn. 1994—97), Met. Assn. Applied Psychology (pres. 1973—74), Psi Chi. Personal E-mail: vschein@gettysburg.edu.

SCHEINBERG, PHYLLIS F., federal agency administrator; BA, Simmons Coll.; MS, U. Calif. Sr. budget examiner trasp. and natural resources, office mgmt. and budget Exec. Office Pres., Washington, 1981—90; dir. transp. issues US Gen. Acctg. Office, Washington; acting asst. sec. budget and programs, CFO US Dept. Transp., Washington, dep. asst. sec. budget & programs, 2001—05, asst. sec. budget & programs, CFO, 2005—. Recipient 9/11 medal, Sec. Transp., 2002, James A. Blum award, Am. Assn. Budget & Program Analysis, 2003; named a Meritorious Exec., 2003. Fellow: Nat. Acad. Pub. Adminstrn. Office: US Dept Transp 1200 New Jersey Ave Washington DC 20590 Office Phone: 202-366-9191, 202-366-4000. Office Fax: 202-366-6031.*

SCHEINDLIN, RAYMOND PAUL, professor Hebrew literature; b. Phila., May 13, 1940; s. Irving and Betty (Bernstein) S.; m. Shira Ann Joffe, 1969 (div. 1981); children— Dov Baer, Dahlia Rachel; m. Janice C. Meyerson, 1986. BA, U. Pa., 1961; M.H.L., Jewish Theol. Sem., NYC, 1963; PhD, Columbia U., NYC, 1971. Ordained rabbi, 1965. Asst. prof. McGill U., Montreal, Que., Canada, 1969-72; asst. prof. Cornell U., Ithaca, NY, 1972-74; assoc. prof. Jewish Theol. Sem. of Am., NYC, 1974-85, prof. Hebrew lit., 1985—, provost, 1984-90; dir. Shalom Spiegel Inst. of Medieval Hebrew Lit., 1996—; rabbi Congregation Baith Israel Anshei Emes, Bklyn., 1979-82; fellow Cullman Ctr. Scholars and Writers, NY Pub. Libr., 2005—06. Mem. publ. com. Jewish Publ. Soc., Phila., 1985-90; mem. internat. adv. com. Ctr. for Judaic Studies U. Pa., 1995—; mem. bd. acad. advisors Catalan Mus. Jewish Culture, Gerona, Spain, 1993—; mem. editl. com. Jewish Quar. Rev., 1995—. Translator: (novella) Of Bygone Days by Mendele Mokher Seforim, 1973, Jewish Liturgy: A Comprehensive History by Ismar Elbogen, 1993; author: Form & Structure in the Poetry of Al-Mu'tamid Ibn 'Abbad, 1974, 201 Arabic Verbs, 1978, Wine, Women, and Death: Medieval Hebrew Poems on the Good Life, 1986, The Gazelle: Medieval Hebrew Poems on God, Israel and the Soul, 1991, Chronicles of the Jewish People, 1996, The Book of Job, 1998, A Short History of the Jewish People, 1998, (libretto) Miriam and the Angel of Death, 1984, The Song of the Distant Dove: Pilgrimage Poems by Judah Halevi, 2007, 501 Arabic Verbs, 2007; mem. editl. com. Prooftexts, 1988—2004, Edebiyat, 1992—, Studies in Muslim-Jewish Rels., 1992—; mem. editl. bd. Arabic and Mid. Ea. Lits., Medieval Iberia; co-editor The Literature of Al-Andalus, 2000. Fellow Cullman Ctr. Scholar and Writers, N.Y Publ. Libr., 2005—. Recipient Jewish Cultural Achievement award Nat. Found. for Jewish Culture, 2004; Guggenheim fellow, 1988, Annenberg Inst. fellow, 1993; sr. assoc. fellow Oxford Centre for Postgrad. Hebrew Studies. Fellow: Am. Acad. Jewish Rsch. (mem. exec. com. 2003—); mem.: PEN Am. Ctr., Jewish Publ. Soc. (bd. dirs. 1987—93), Assn. Jewish Studies, World Union Jewish Studies, Soc. Judeo-Arabic Studies. Home: 420 Riverside Dr New York NY 10025-7773 Office: Jewish Theol Sem Am 3080 Broadway New York NY 10027-4650 Home Phone: 212-866-3372. Personal E-mail: rscheindlin@aol.com.

SCHEINER, DAVID LAWRENCE, internist; b. Buffalo, Sept. 3, 1938; MD, Columbia U. Coll. Physicians and Surgeons, 1963. Cert. Am. Bd. Internal Medicine, 1970, lic. Ill. Med. intern U. Chgo. Hosp., 1963—64, resident, 1964—67, gen. internist, Minas Maooris Hosp., Hyde Pk. Assocs. Medicine Ltd.; advocate Hyde Pk. Med. Group. Primary care physician Barak Obama, 1987—. Office: Hyde Pk Med Group 1515 E 52nd Pl Chicago IL 60615 Office Phone: 773-493-8212. Office Fax: 773-955-2166.

SCHEINHOLTZ, LEONARD LOUIS, lawyer; b. Pitts., June 2, 1927; s. Bernard A. and Marie (Getzel) Scheinholtz; m. Joan R. Libenson, Aug. 16, 1953; children: Stuart, Nancy, Barry. BA, U. Pa., 1948, MA, 1949; LLB, Columbia U., 1953. Bar: Pa. 1954, US Ct. Appeals (3d cir.) 1959, US Ct. Appeals (6th cir.) 1968, US Supreme Ct. 1972, US Ct. Appeals (4th cir.) 1973, US Ct. Appeals (5th cir.) 1981, US Ct. Appeals (11th cir.) 1991, US Ct. Appeals (2d cir.) 1993. Assoc. Reed, Smith, LLP, Pitts., 1953—62, spl. ptnr., 1962—64, gen. ptnr., 1964—97, head labor dept., 1980—86, of counsel, 1997—. Dir. Am. Arbitration Assn., NYC, 1980—96. Author: Exemption Under the Anti-Trust Laws for Joint Employer Activity, 1982, The Arbitrator as Judge and Jury: Another

Look at Statutory Law in Arbitration, 1985. Vice-chmn. Pa. AAA Fedn., Harrisburg, 1982—85; chmn. AAA East Motor Club, 1979—82; trustee Jewish Healthcare Found., 2004—; bd. dirs. Nat. Aviary, 1999—, United Jewish Fedn., Pitts., 1997—2000; trustee Montefiore Hosp., Pitts., 1976—79. With USN, 1945—46. Mem.: ABA, Allegheny County Bar Assn., Pa. Bar Assn. Republican. Jewish. Home: 746 Pinoak Rd Pittsburgh PA 15243-1153 Office: Reed Smith LLP Mellon Sq 435 6th Ave Pittsburgh PA 15219-1886 Business E-Mail: lscheinholtz@reedsmith.com.

SCHEINMAN, NANCY JANE, psychologist; b. NYC, June 23, 1955; d. Norman Sinclair and Vivian Estelle (Goodwin) Tischenkel; m. Stephen Robert Scheinman, June 15, 1990; children: Cassie Leigh, William Mayer. BA, Vassar Coll., 1977; MS, U. Miami, 1986, PhD, 1988. Intern Duke Med. Ctr., Durham, N.C., 1988; pvt. practice Miami, Fla., 1991—. Founder, dir. Hosp. Based Alternative Medicine Ctr. Contbr. to books and articles to profl. jours. U. Miami fellow, 1988-90. Mem. Am. Psychol. Assn., Soc. Behavioral Medicine, Phi Beta Kappa. Independent. Jewish. Avocations: swimming, tennis. Personal E-mail: nancyscheinman@aol.com.

SCHEINMAN, STEVEN JAY, dean, medical educator; b. Monticello, NY, Oct. 22, 1951; 2 children. AB summa cum laude, Amherst Coll., 1973; MD cum laude, Yale U., 1977. Diplomate Am. Bd. Internal Medicine in Neprology, lic. physician N.Y., Conn. Resident internal medicine Yale-New Haven Hosp., 1977-80; chief resident internal medicine Upstate Med. Ctr., Syracuse, NY, 1980-81, fellow nephrology, 1981-83, Yale-New Haven Hosp., 1983-84; asst. prof. medicine SUNY Upstate Med. U., Syracuse, 1984-90, asst. prof. pharmacology, 1988-90, assoc. prof. medicine and pharmacology, 1990-94, prof. medicine and pharmacology, 1994—, chief nephrology divsn. dept. medicine, 1994—2004, exec. v.p., dean Coll. Medicine, 2004—, officer-in-charge, 2006. Vis. scientist MRC Molecular Medicine Group, Royal Postgrad. Med. Sch. Hammersmith Hosp., London, 1992, London, 95; vis. scholar dept. biochemistry U. Oxford, 1985; attending physician U. Hosp., Syracuse, Crouse-Irving Meml. Hosp., Syracuse, VA Med. Ctr., Syracuse; dir. Nephrology Fellowship Program, 1993—; spkr. seminars, confs., orgns. Assoc. editor: Neph SAP, 2002—04; mem. editl. bd. Yale Jour. Biology and Medicine, 1975—77, Jour. Am. Soc. Nephrology, 2000—02, mem. NIDDK Spl. Rev. Group, 1998—; contbr. Recipient Lange award, Yale U. Sch. Medicine, 1976, Resident Merit award, ACP (Conn. chpt.), 1980, Nat. Rsch. Svc. award, NIH, 1981—83, Clin. Investigator award, 1985—90, Charles R. Ross Rsch. award, SUNY-Health Sci. Ctr., 1992, Pres.'s award for Excellence and Leadership in Rsch., SUNY Upstate Med. U., 2001, Chancellor's Rsch. Recognition award, SUNY, 2002; grantee, Nat. Inst. Arthritis Diabetes Digestive and Kidney Diseases, 1981—83, 1985—90, 1995—2002, 2000—04, 2003—, Am. Heart Assn., 1985, 1988—90, 1990—91, 1992—95, 1995—97, NATO, 1995—98. Mem.: Rsch. Found. SUNY (bd. mem. 2007—), Assn. Am. Med. Colls. Coun. Deans, Assn. Subspecialty Profs., Nat. Kidney Found., Am. Heart Assn. Coun. on Kidney, Am. Soc. Bone and Mineral Rsch., Am. Physiol. Soc., Internat. Soc. Nephrology, Am. Soc. Nephrology (mem. editl. bd. Jour. 2000—02), Am. Fedn. Med. Rsch., Am. Soc. Clin. Investigation, Alpha Omega Alpha, Phi Beta Kappa. Office: Office of Dean SUNY Upstate Med Univ 1257 Weiskotten Hall Syracuse NY 13210 Office Phone: 315-464-9720. Business E-Mail: scheinms@upstate.edu.

SCHEIRING, MICHAEL JAMES, college official; b. Canton, Ohio, Oct. 11, 1949; s. Robert J. and Madonna L. (Geisigi) S.; m. Marcia L. Young, May 13, 1972; children: Kristy L., Lauren M. BA, Kent State U., 1971, MPA, 1972. Sect. supr. N.J. Dept. Treasury, Trenton, 1974-78; policy analyst to gov. Trenton, 1978-80; dir. adminstrn. N.J. Dept. Community Affairs, Trenton, 1980-82; dir. corp. budgeting N.J. Transit Corp., Newark, 1982-83; v.p. adminstrn. and fin. Thomas A. Edison Coll., Trenton, 1983—; exec. dir. Gov. Mgmt. Rev. Com., Gov.'s Office, Trenton, N.J., 1990-93. Trustee N.J. Ednl. Computer Corp., 1984-90; trustee, comptroller Edison Found., Trenton, 1984—; mem. adv. bd. National Ctr. Productivity; past pres. U.D. Dollars for Scholars Found.; pres. Cerebral Palsy of NJ; chmn. Trenton Audit Commn.; mem. citizen's delegation to China; trustee Robert Wood Johnson U. Hosp. Hamilton. Contbg. author: N.J. Zero-Based Budgeting, 1979. Named Vol. of Yr. N.J. United Cerebral Palsy; recipient Libr. Champion award. Mem. ASPA (nat. coun., v.p. programs 1984, v.p. membership 1985, pres. 1987-89), Old Barracks Assn. (trustee, past pres.), Rotary (pres.). Roman Catholic. Home: 2 Lotus Ln Trenton NJ 08648-3211 Office: Thomas Edison State Coll Trenton NJ 08625 Home Phone: 609-883-4651; Office Phone: 609-984-1110 x 2300. E-mail: mscheiring@tesl.edu.

SCHEJBAL, DAVID, dean; b. Prague, Czech Republic, Feb. 12, 1961; s. Jaroslav and Eva Schejbal; life ptnr. Judith Richardson. PhD, U. Conn., Storrs, 1990. Assoc. dean U. Coll., Northwestern U., Evanston, Ill., 1992—99; assoc. vice chancellor U. Ill., Urbana, 1999—2007; dean, continuing edn., outreach and e-learning U. Wis., Madison, 2007—. Mem.: U. Continuing Edn. Assn. (bd. mem. 2007—08). Democrat. Office: Univ Wis Ext 505 S Rosa Rd Ste 200 Madison WI 53719-1277 Business E-Mail: david.schejbal@conted.uwex.edu.

SCHEKMAN, RANDY W., molecular biology administrator, biochemist; b. St. Paul, Dec. 30, 1948; married, 1973; 1 child. BA, UCLA, 1970; PhD in Biochemistry, Stanford U., 1975; PhD (hon.), U. Geneva, 1997. Fellow U. Calif., San Diego, 1974-76, from asst. to assoc. prof. Berkeley, 1976-83, prof., 1983—, head divsn. biochemistry and molecular biology, 1990-97, co-chair dept. molecular and cellular biology, 1997—. Fellow Woodrow Wilson Found., 1970, Cystic Fibrosis Found., 1974, John S. Guggenheim Found., 1982-83; recipient Research award in microbiology & immunology, Eli Lilly, 1987, Lewis S. Rosenstiel award in basic biomedical sci., 1994, Gairdner Found. Internat. award, 1996, Albert Lasker award for basic med. rsch., Albert and Mary Lasker Found., 2002, Louisa Gross Horwtiz prize, Columbia U., 2002; named Amgen award lecturer, Protein Soc., 1999, Berkeley Faculty Rsch. lecturer, U. Calif., 1999. Mem. Am. Soc. Microbiology, Am. Soc. Biochemists & Molecular Biologists, Am. Acad. of Arts & Sciences (elected 2000), NAS (elected 1992); hon. mem. Japanese Biochemical Soc.; foreign assoc. EMBO. Achievements include research on molecular mechanism of secretion and membrane assembly in eucaryotic cells. Office: U Calif Dept Molecular Cell Bio 401 Barker Hall Spc 3202 Berkeley CA 94720-3202 Office Phone: 510-642-5686. E-mail: schekman@uclink4.berkeley.edu.*

SCHELBERT, HEINRICH RUEDIGER, nuclear medicine physician; b. Wuerzburg, Germany, Nov. 5, 1939; MD, U. Würzburg, Germany, 1964. Diplomate Am. Bd. Nuclear Medicine. Intern Mercy Med. Ctr., Phila., 1966-67, resident, 1967-68, 70-71; resident in cardiology U. Dusseldorf, Germany, 1971-72; fellow in cardiology, resident in nuclear medicine U. Calif., San Diego, 1968-69, asst. rsch. cardiologist, 1972-75, assoc. rsch. radiologist, 1975-76; hosp. assoc. UCLA Med. Ctr., 1977—; prof. radiol. scis. UCLA Sch. Medicine, 1980-90, prof. pharmacol. and radiol. scis., 1993—. Editor-in-chief: Jour. Nuc. Medicine, 2004. Recipient Georg von Hevesy prize 2d Internat. Congress World Fedn. Nuclear Medicine and Radiation Biology, 1978, 3d Internat. Congress World Fedn. Nuclear Medicine and Radiation Biology, 1982, Disting. Sci. award, Acad. Molecular Imaging, 2006. Fellow Am. Coll. Cardiology; mem. Am. Heart Assn. (disting. scientific achievement award 1989), Soc. Nuclear Medicine (Herrman L. Blumgart pioneer lectr. award 1989, George De Hevesy Nuclear Medicine Pioneer award 1998), German Soc. Nuc. Med. (hon.), Swiss Soc. Nuc. Medicine (hon.; editor-in-chief, nuc. medicine). Office: David Geffen Sch Medicine UCLA Dept Molecular Med B2 085J Box 956948 Los Angeles CA 90095-6948 Office Phone: 310-825-3076. Business E-Mail: hschelbert@mednet.ucla.edu.

SCHELD, WILLIAM MICHAEL, internist, educator; b. Middletown, Conn., Aug. 15, 1947; s. William Herman and Lucille Laverne (Houchens) S.; m. Susan Ella Vaughan, June 14, 1969; 1 child, Sarah Walker. BS, Cornell U., 1969, MD, 1973. Diplomate Am. Bd. Internal Medicine. Intern, then resident U. Va. Sch. Medicine, Charlottesville, 1973-76, fellow in infectious diseases, 1976-79, asst. prof., 1979-82, assoc. prof., 1982-88, prof., assoc. chair dept. infectious diseases, 1988—. Chair Inter-sci. Conf. on Antimicrobial Agents and Chemotherapy. Editor: Infections of the Central Nervous System, 1991, 97, 2004; contbr. sci. articles to profl. publs., chpts. to books. Fellow ACP, Infectious Diseases Soc. Am. (pres. 2002-2003); mem. Am. Soc. Clin. Investigation, Nat. Found. Infectious Diseases (pres.), Alpha Omega Alpha. Achievements include research on meningitis and other central nervous system infections, bacterial endocarditis, sepsis, anthrax, etc. Home: 2075 Earlysville Rd Earlysville VA 22936-9634 Office: U Va Health Systems Box 801342 Charlottesville VA 22908 Office Phone: 934-924-5991.

SCHELER, BRAD ERIC, lawyer; b. Bklyn., Oct. 11, 1953; s. Bernard and Rita Regina (Miller) S.; m. Amy Ruth Frolick, Mar. 30, 1980; children: Ali M., Maddie H., Zoey B. BA with high honors, Lehigh U., 1974; JD, Hofstra U., 1977. Bar: N.Y. 1978, U.S. Dist. Ct. (so. and ea. dists.) N.Y. 1978. Assoc. Weil, Gotshal & Manges, NYC, 1977-81; sr. ptnr., chmn. bankruptcy and restructuring practice Fried, Frank, Harris, Shriver & Jacobson, LLP, NYC, 1981—. Contbg. author: Collier on Bankruptcy, 15th edit. revised, Norton Annual Survey of Bankruptcy Law; rsch. editor Hofstra U. Law Rev., 1975-77. Treas., bus. mgr. Trustees of Gramercy Park, NYC, 1979-87; bd. trustees Lehigh U., bd. adv. leadership coun., Linderman Libr. Project, Wall St. Coun., Coll. Bus. and Econs., K&A Register of Restructuring Profls.; bd. dirs., inMotion Justice for All Women, chair. Fellow Am. Coll. Bankruptcy; mem. ABA (bus. bankruptcy com. corp. banking and bus. law sect., creditors' rights com. litig. sect.), N.Y. State Bar Assn., Assn. Bar City of N.Y. (com. on bankruptcy and corp. reorgn. 1991-94), Sigma Alpha Mu (v.p. 1973). Jewish. Home: 94 Larchmont Ave Larchmont NY 10538-3723 Office: Fried Frank Harris Shriver & Jacobson LLP 1 New York Plz Fl 23 New York NY 10004-1980 Office Phone: 212-859-8019. Business E-Mail: Schelbr@ffhsj.com.

SCHELL, ALLAN CARTER, retired electrical engineer; b. New Bedford, Mass., Apr. 14, 1934; s. Charles Carter and Elizabeth Schell; m. Shirley T. Sardineer; children: Alice Rosalind, Cynthia Anne. BS, MSE.E., MIT, Cambridge, 1956, Sc.D., 1961; student, Tech. U. Delft, Netherlands, 1956-57. Research physicist Air Force Cambridge Research Labs., Bedford, Mass., 1956-76, Guenter Loeser Meml. lectr., 1965; dir. electromagnetics directorate Rome Air Devel. Ctr., Bedford, 1976-87; chief scientist Hdqrs. USAF Systems Command, 1987-92; chief scientist, dep. dir. sci. and tech. Hdqrs. USAF Materiel Command, 1992-94. Dir. Electro; vis. assoc. prof. MIT, 1974; chair dept. of elec. engring. adv. coun. U. Pa., 1992-94. Contbr. articles to profl. jours. Pres. Aurora Highlands Civic Assn., Arlington, Va. Lt. USAF, 1958—60. Recipient Fulbright award, 1956-57, NSF fellow, 1955-56, 60-61, Presdl. Rank award, Meritorious Exec. award, 1989, two Air Force Meritorious Civilian Svc. awards. Fellow IEEE (John T. Bolljahn award 1966, Centennial Medal, 1984, Third Millennium Medal, 2000, bd. dirs. 1981-82, editor IEEE Press 1976-79, editor-in-chief Procs. of IEEE 1990-92); mem. IEEE Antennas and Propagation Soc. (pres. 1978, editor tran. 1969-71, chair awards and fellows com., 2000-05, APS Disting. Achievement award 2006), Internat. Sci. Radio Union, MIT Alumni Assn. (bd. dirs. 2003-05), Sigma Xi, Tau Beta Pi. Achievements include patents in field. Business E-Mail: a.schell@ieee.org.

SCHELL, FARREL LOY, transportation engineer; b. Amarillo, Tex., Dec. 14, 1931; s. Thomas Phillip and Lillian Agnes (McKee) S.; m. Shirley Anne Samuelson, Feb. 6, 1955; children: James Christopher, Maria Leslyn Schell Peter. BS, U. Kans., 1954; postgrad., Carnegie-Mellon U., 1974. Registered profl. engr., Calif., Colo. Resident engr. Sverdrup & Parcel, Denver, 1957-61; project engr. Bechtel Corp., San Francisco, 1961-62, Parsons, Brinckerhoff-Tudor-Bechtel, San Francisco, 1962-67; mgr. urban transp. dept. Kaiser Engrs., Oakland, Calif., 1967-78; program dir. San Francisco Mcpl. Rwy I.C., 1978-80; project mgr. Houston Transit Cons., 1980-83, Kaiser Transit Group, Miami, 1983-85; mgr. program devel. Kaiser Engrs., Oakland, 1985-87; project mgr. O'Brien-Kreitzberg & Assocs., San Francisco, 1987-89; sr. project mgr. Bay Area Rapid Transit Dist., Oakland, Calif., 1989—96. Dir./CEO Schelter Devel. Corp., Piedmont, Calif., 1982—. Contbr. articles to profl. jours. Chmn., bd. dirs. Achenbach Graphic Arts Coun., 1996-2002. Lt. (j.g.) USN, 1954-57, PTO. Mem. ASCE, ASME, Nat. Soc. Profl. Engrs., Nat. Coun. Engring. Examiners, Am. Planners Assn., Am. Pub. Transit Assn., Lakeview Club, Scarab Club, Pachacamac Club, Sigma Tau, Tau Beta Pi. Avocations: fly fishing, camping. Home: 100 Bay Pl #1517 Oakland CA 94610 Personal E-mail: fschell2@mac.com.

SCHELL, J. MICHAEL, metal products executive, lawyer; BA, Columbia Univ., 1969; JD, Boston Univ., 1976. Atty. Cadwalader, Wickersham & Taft, 1976—79, Skadden, Arps, Slate, Meagher & Flom LLP, NYC, 1979—84, ptnr., mergers & acquisitions practice, 1984—2005; vice-chmn. global banking Citigroup, NYC, 2005—08; exec. v.p. bus. develop. & law Alcoa, NYC, 2008—09, exec. v.p. bus. develop., 2009—. Trustee Lake Forest Acad., Ill., Am. Inst. for Contemporary German Studies; mem. bd. vis. Boston Univ. Sch. Law, Columbia Univ., Georgetown Univ.; bd. dir. Gordon A. Rich Meml. Found.; past trustee Boston Univ. Office: Alcoa 390 Park Ave New York NY 10022*

SCHELL, MELVIN FRANK, JR., real estate agent; b. Binghamton, NY, Feb. 3, 1938; s. Melvin Frank and Irene Schell; m. Dollie Sedot Knowles, May 31, 1958; children: Mark Stephen, Jeremy Joel. BA, Tenn. Temple U., 1971; MBA, Ga. State U., 1987. Ordained Minister of the Gospel Briarlake Bapt. Ch., Atlanta GA, 1976; lic. Real Estate Agent Ga. Real Estate Commn., 2002, Fla. Real Estate Commn., 2004. Mktg. rep. Internat. Bus. Machines, Inc., Chattanooga, 1960—73; asst. min. First Alliance Ch., Atlanta, 1973—74; exec. dir. Evangelism Explosion Atlanta, Atlanta, 1974—75; pres. Ch. Growth Ministries, Atlanta, 1976—81, Omega Info. Systems, Inc., Atlanta, 1981—2003; regional mgr., AT&T computers MicroAge, Tempe, Ariz., 1990—91; pres. Aarist Internat., Inc, Atlanta, 1993—2003; real estate agt. Prudential Ga. Realty, Gainesville, Ga., 2002—, Century 21 Prestige Realty, Key West, Fla., 2005—06; reverse mortgage adviser. Cons. to churches and non-profit organizations Fuller Evangelistic Assn., Pasadena, Calif., 1980—83. Author: (training materials) The Total Church Growth Model. Electronics technician second class USN, 1956—59, Key West, Fla. Decorated Good Conduct medal USN; recipient Class Pres., Internat. Bus. Machines, Inc., 1972. Dedicated Follower Of Jesus Christ.

SCHELL, NORMAN BARNETT, preventive medicine physician, consultant; b. NYC, May 25, 1925; s. Jack and Ada Sylvia (Rosen) S.; m. Lila Barbara Mendelsohn, Aug. 27, 1950; children: Martin, Judith, Steven. AB cum laude, NYU, 1946, MD, 1950; MPH, Harvard U., 1971. Diplomate Am. Bd. Pediats., Am. Bd. Preventive Medicine, Nat. Bd. Med. Examiners; lic. physician, N.Y. Rotating intern Beth Israel Hosp., NYC, 1950-51; asst. resident in pediats. Mt. Sinai Hosp., NYC, 1951—52; clin. fellow in pediats. N.Y.-Cornell Med. Ctr., NYC, 1952-53; pvt. practice Jericho and Hicksville, NY, 1956-69; pub. health physician Nassau County Health Dept., Mineola, NY, 1969-76, dep. commr., 1976-90. Asst. prof. preventive medicine SUNY, Stony Brook, 1974-90; pediat. cons. N.Y. State Health Dept., 1956-69, HEW Project Head Start, N.Y.C., 1968-75; emeritus pediat. staff Nassau County Med. Ctr. Author: Keys to Childhood Illnesses, 1992; contbr. articles to profl. jours. Lt. M.C., USN, 1953-55, capt. M.C., USNR, 1981-85. Recipient Physician Recognition award AMA, 1970, Grade 1A Health Officer N.Y. State Health Dept., 1973. Fellow Am. Acad. Pediats. (com. on sch. health 1971-77, citation com. on med. edn. 1977), Am. Coll. Preventive Medicine, N.Y. Acad. Medicine; mem. Am. Coll. Legal Medicine (assoc.), Nassau County Med. Soc. (chmn. sch. health com.), Harvard Club N.Y.C., West Point Club, Phi Beta Kappa. Avocations: photography, classical music, computer technology. Home and Office: 999 Hwd Rd NE Apt 130 Marietta GA 30068

SCHELL, WILLIAM JOSEPH, IV, industrial engineer; b. Arlington Heights, Ill., July 16, 1975; s. William Joseph and Barbara Ann Schell; m. Melanie Noel Bury; children: Ana India, Megan Mae. BS in Indsl. and Mgmt. Engring., Mont. State U., Bozeman, 1997, MS, 1999; PhD student in Engring. Mgmt., U. Ala., Huntsville, 2004—. Cert. in industry, Utah Bd. Profl. Engrs., 2002. Indsl. engr. U. Tech. Assistance Program, Bozeman, 1997—99, Am. Express Travelers Cheques, Salt Lake City, 1999—2000, mgr. strategic ops., 2000—02, project mgr. six sigma, 2000—00; six sigma master black belt Am. Express Fin. Advisors, Mpls., 2002—04, mgr. bus. transformation, 2002—04; dir. global bus. transformation Am. Express Global Comml. Card, NYC, 2004—07; v.p. ops. engring. Wells Fargo Bank NA, Shoreview, Minn., 2005—07; head strategy execution Printing Less Com, Livingston, Mont., 2007—08, v.p. startegy and devel., 2008—. Contbr. articles to profl. jours. Mem. Dog Handler, Salt Lake City, 1999—2002; bd. pres. Sigma Phi Epsilon Frat., Bozeman, 2007; bd. treas. Children's Pl., Bozeman, 2007—08. Recipient Chmn. award, Am. Express Co., 2000—02. Mem.: Am. Soc. Engring. Mgmt., Inst. Indsl. Engrs. (local chpt. dir. 2003—07, dir. twin cities chpt. 2003—07), USA Triathlon. Dfl. Avocations: skiing, motorcycling, running, scuba diving. Office: Printing Lesscom 100 PFL Way Livingston MT 59047 Personal E-mail: wjschell@hotmail.com. Business E-Mail: bschell@printingforless.com.

SCHELLBERG, THOMAS, economics professor; b. Rochester, NY, July 7, 1952; s. Robert E. and Bertha F. Schellberg; m. Michelle Schellberg, June 30, 2007. PhD in Economics, U. Minn., Mpls., 1986. Instr., economics SUNY Oswego, Casper Coll., Wyo., 1994—. Contbr. articles to publs. Bd. dirs. Casper Nordic. Doctoral fellowship, Sloan Found., 1984. Mem.: Am. Econ. Assn. Avocations: bicycling, canoeing, winemaking, cross country skiing, kayaking. Home: 1417 Bonnie Brae Casper WY 82601 Office: Casper Coll 125 College Dr Casper WY 82601 Business E-Mail: schellbe@caspercollege.edu.

SCHELLENBERGER, ROBERT EARL, retired management educator, department chairman; b. Janesville, Wis., July 25, 1932; s. Ervin William and Adelaide Louise (Keller) S.; m. Linda Eula Todd, Dec. 30, 1961; children: Brian T., Keith W., Heidi L. BSBA, U. Wis., 1958, MBA, 1959; PhD, U. N.C., 1963. Personnel supr. Libby McNeill and Libby, Janesville, Wis., 1957-58; from asst. prof. to assoc. prof. chmn. div. stats. dept. bus U. Md., College Park, 1963-68; chair dept. mgmt. So. Ill. U., Carbondale, Ill., 1968-70, dir. planning Sch. Human Resources Devel., 1970-71, prof. mgmt., 1968-71; vis. prof., dir. program evaluation Babcock Grad. Sch. Mgmt., Wake Forest U., Winston-Salem, NC, 1971-73; prof. dept. mgmt. Temple U., Phila., 1973-81, from chmn. dept. mgmt. to asst. to acad. vice chancellor, 1975-77; prof. decision scis. dept. East Carolina U., Greenville, NC, 1981-2000, chmn. decision scis. dept., 1989-95; ret., 2001. Pres. Md. Rsch. and Cons., Hyattsville, 1964-67; v.p. Ea. Acad. Mgmt., 1967; cons. Comml. Credit Corp., Balt., 1966. Author: Managerial Analysis, 1967, Policy Formulation, 1978, 2d edit., 1982; co-editor Jour. of Econs. and Bus., 1976; developer (software package) MANYSYM, 1965, 68, 78, 82, 86. Chmn. Utilities Com., Carbondale, 1970-72. Title IV NDEA fellow U. N.C., 1960-62, Earhart Jr. fellow U. Wis. Mem. Assn. for Bus. Simulation, SE Decision Scis. Inst., Decision Scis. Inst. (bd. dirs. 1974-77), Beta Gamma Sigma. Personal E-mail: dcschell@embarqmail.com.

SCHELLHORN, HENRY, mathematics professor; b. Lausanne, Switzerland, Apr. 18, 1966; s. Jean-Pierre Schellhorn and Nadine Dony; m. Malina Stefanovska, July 20, 1997; 1 child, Theodore Philip. Diploma in Elec. Engring., Ecole Poly. Féd. Lausanne, 1988; MS, Stanford U., 1992; PhD, UCLA, 1995. Sr. cons. Andersen Consulting, 1988—91; product mgr. Treasury Svcs. Corp., 1996—97; prin. rsch. engr. Oracle Corp., 1997—2002; asst. prof. fin. U. Lausanne, 2002—05; asst. prof. math. Claremont Grad. U., Calif., 2005—08. Contbr. articles to profl. jours. Recipient Best Paper award, World Congress on Engring. and Computer Sci., 2008, Internat. Bus. Economics Rsch. Meeting, Las Vegas, 2003. Achievements include patents in field. Home: 1512 Glendon Ave Los Angeles CA 90024 Office: Claremont Grad Univ 710 N College Claremont CA 91711 Personal E-mail: hschellhorn@yahoo.com. Business E-Mail: henry.schellhorn@cgu.edu.

SCHELLING, DONALD LAWRENCE, lawyer; b. Clearwater, Fla., June 5, 1959; s. Dorothy Ann Allen and Donald Anthony Schelling; m. Myrna Ytis Marca, Aug. 11, 1996. BSc, U. Manchester, England, 1985; PhD, Dundee U., Scotland, 1991; JD, No. Ill. U., 2001. USPTO Registration: US Patent Office 2002. Patent atty. Townsend and Townsend and Crew, San Francisco, 2001—04, Polsinelli Shalton Welte Seulthaus, Kans. City, Mo., 2004—, Bozicevic Field & Francis LLP, East Palo Alto, Calif., 2004—. Author: Regulation of Hepatic Phosphatases, Patent Law Primer. Mem.: ABA, Am. Intellectual Property Assn., Calif. Bar Assn., Brit. Biochemical Soc., San Francisco Intellectual Law Assn., Veterans Rugby Club, Carnoustie Golf Club, PAD. Achievements include research in regulation of phosphatases by ancillary proteins. Office: Bozicevic Field & Francis LLP 1900 University Ave East Palo Alto CA 94303 Business E-Mail: schelling@bozpat.com.

SCHELLING, THOMAS CROMBIE, economist; b. Oakland, Calif., Apr. 14, 1921; s. John M. and Zelda M. (Ayres) S.; m. Corinne T. Saposs, Sept. 13, 1947 (div. 1991); children: Andrew, Thomas, Daniel, Robert; m. Alice M. Coleman, Nov. 8, 1991. AB in Econ., U. Calif.,

Berkeley, 1944; PhD in Econ., Harvard U., 1951; Doctorate (hon.), The RAND Grad. Sch. of Policy Analysis; Doctorate Honoris Causa, Erasmus U. Rotterdam. Economist US Bur. of the Budget, Washington, 1945—46, The Marshall Plan, Copenhagen and Paris, 1948—50; economist, Exec. Office of Pres. The White House, Washington, 1951—53; assoc. prof. and prof. econs. Yale U., 1953-58; prof. economics Harvard U., Cambridge, Mass., 1958-90, mem., John F. Kennedy Sch. Govt., 1969—90, Lucius N. Littauer prof. polit. economy emeritus; prof. econs. and pub. affairs U. Md., College Park, 1990—2003, disting. prof., 1990—2003, disting. prof. emeritus. Sr. staff mem. RAND Corp., 1958-59; chmn. rsch. adv. bd. Com. Econ. Devel., 1978-81, 84-85; mem. sci. adv. bd. USAF, 1960-64, def. sci. bd., 1966-70; mem. mil. econ. adv. panel CIA, 1980-85; dir. Inst. for Study of Smoking Behavior and Policy, Harvard U., 1984-90; trustee Aerospace Corp., 1984-93; trustee Ctr. for Advancement of Health; co-faculty mem. New Eng. Complex Systems Inst. Co-author (with Morton H. Halperin): Strategy and Arms Control, 1961; author: Nat. Income Behavior, 1951, Internat. Economics, 1958, The Strategy of Conflict, 1960, Arms and Influence, 1966, Micromotives and Macrobehavior, 1978, Thinking Through the Energy Problem, 1979, Choice and Consequence, 1984, Strategies of Commitment, 2006. Recipient Frank E. Seidman Disting. award in polit. economy, 1977; Nobel Prize in Econ. Sci., 2005. Fellow AAAS, Assn. for Pub. Policy Analysis and Mgmt., Am. Econ. Assn. (pres. 1991, Disting. Fellow award); mem. NAS (Award Behavioral Rsch. Relevant to the Prevention of Nuclear War, 1993), Inst. Medicine, Ea. Econ. Assn. (pres. 1996). Office: Univ Md Sch Pub Policy College Park MD 20742-0001 Mailing: 4506 Wetherill Rd Bethesda MD 20816 Business E-Mail: tschelli@umd.edu.*

SCHELLMAN, JOHN A., chemistry professor; b. Phila., Oct. 24, 1924; s. John and Mary (Mason) S.; m. Charlotte Green, Feb. 10, 1954; children: Heidi M., Lise C. AB, Temple U., 1948; MS, Princeton U., 1949, PhD, 1951; PhD (hon.), Chalmers U., Sweden, 1983. USPHS postdoctoral fellow U. Utah, 1951-52, Carlsberg Lab., Copenhagen, 1953-55; DuPont fellow U. Minn., Mpls., 1955-56, asst. prof. chemistry, 1956-58; assoc. prof. chemistry Inst. Molecular Biology, U. Oreg., Eugene, 1958-63, prof. chemistry, rsch. assoc., 1963—. Vis. Lab. Chem. Physics, Nat. Inst. Arthritis and Metabolic Diseases, NIH, Bethesda, Md., 1980; vis. prof. Chalmers U., 1986, U. Padua, 1987. Contbr. articles to profl. jours. Served with U.S. Army, 1943-46. Fellow Rask-Oersted Found., 1954, Sloan Found., 1959-63, Guggenheim Found., 1969-70. Fellow Am. Phys. Soc., Biophys. Soc.; mem. NAS, Am. Chem. Soc., Am. Soc. Biochemistry and Molecular Biology, Am. Acad. Arts and Scis., Phi Beta Kappa, Sigma Xi. Democrat. Business E-Mail: john@molbio.uoregon.edu.

SCHELM, ROGER LEONARD, information systems specialist; b. Kingston, NY, July 29, 1936; s. Frederick G. and Elizabeth M. (Wojciehowski) S.; m. Gloria Mae Dutterer, June 13, 1958; children: Sandra Lee Kern, Theresa Jean Sollitto, Ginger Lisa Shah. BA in Polit. Sci., Western Md. Coll., 1958; MA in Pub. Adminstrn., Am. U., 1970; postgrad., U. Md., 1960-62. Analytic equipment programmer Nat. Security Agy., Ft. Meade, Md., 1958-60; computer cons. various cons. firms Balt., 1960-68, Washington, 1960—68; mgr. army plans and programs Informatics Inc., Bethesda, Md., 1968; mgr. def. programs Automation Tech. Inc., Wheaton, 1968-69; dir. advanced planning Genasys Corp., Washington, 1969-71; mgr. info. systems Ins. Co. North Am., Phila., 1971-72, sect. mgr. computing ops., 1972-74; mgr. tech. services INA Corp., 1974-75; mem. spl. tech. projects INA Corp. merger with Conn. Gen. Ins. Co. to form CIGNA Corp. 1982, 1975-76, asst. dir. tech. services, 1977, asst. dir. spl. tech. projects, 1977-78, asst. dir. adminstrn., 1978-79, asst. dir. resource mgmt., data ctr. design, contingency planning, 1979-80; dir. corp. info. tech. now CIGNA Corp., 1981-82, dir. planning and control ops. div., 1982-83, v.p. strategic planning, systems div., 1983-84, v.p. applied research/expert systems, systems div., 1984-92; co-founder, pres. Schelm Internat., Inc., Cherry Hill, NJ, 1992—2002. Mem. adj. faculty Camden Coll., N.J., 1978-82; mem. Camden County EDP Adv. Com., 1980-82; mem. faculty Drexel U., Phila., 1983-95. Author: Ednl. Computer mag., 1982; mem. editl. adv. bd., author Small Sys. World mag., 1982-84; mem. editl. adv. bd. Spang-Robinson Report, 1986-87, Machine Intelligence News, 1987-93, AI Expert mag., 1985-88; cons. editor Expert Sys. Jour., 1987-91. Tech. advisor various sch. bds., colls., univs. and non-profit orgns. Served to capt. U.S. Army, 1959. Mem. Am. Assn. Artificial Intelligence, Assn. Computing Machinery (founder Delaware Valley chpt. vice. chmn., program chmn. 1983-84, chmn. 1984-85, founder Del. Valley Spl. Interest Group in Artificial Intelligence, 1985, vice chmn. 1985-87), World Future Soc. Home and Office: 506 Balsam Rd Cherry Hill NJ 08003-3202

SCHELP, RICHARD HERBERT, retired mathematics professor; b. Kans. City, Mo., Apr. 21, 1936; s. Herbert and Ida Louise Schelp; m. Billie Marie Schelp, Dec. 20, 1958; children: Lisa Marie Martin, Richard John. BS in Math. and Physics, Ctrl. Mo. U., 1959; MS in Math., Kans. State U., Manhattan, 1961, PhD in Math., 1970. Assoc. mathematician applied physics lab. Johns Hopkins U., Balt., 1961—66; instr. math. Kans. State U., Manhattan, 1966—70; asst. prof. math. U. Memphis, 1970—74, assoc. prof. math., 1974—79, prof. math., 1979—2001, prof. emeritus, 2001—. Chair spl. session Fifth Hungarian Combinatorics Conf., Keszthely, Hungary, 1976, First Japan Conf. Graph Theory and Application, 1986, First China-USA Conf. on Graph and Applications, 1986, Seventh Hungarian Combinatorics, Eger, 1987; chair session Probabilistic Workshop, Budapest, Hungary, 1998; vis. rschr. Hungarian Acad. Scis.-Math. Inst., 1985, 90, Lab. Rsch. and Info., U. Paris-Sud, 1993, Hungarian Acad. Scis.-Computer and Automation Inst., 1994; presenter in field. Mem. editl. bd. Jour. Graph Theory, 1981—, co-mng. editor, 1981-86; reviewer Math. Revs.; contbr. more than 160 articles to profl. jours. Recipient Disting. Alumnus award, Kans. St. U, 1999—2000, Bd. Visitors Eminent Faculty award, U. Memphis, 2001; named Outstanding Educators Am., 1975; grantee Internat. Rsch. and Exch. (travel), 1985, 1990, NSF, 1986—87, 1992—95, Nat. Security Agy., 1988—91; fellow NSF, U. Mass., summer, 1968. Mem. Am. Math. Soc. (organizer spl. session 1997), Math. Assn. Am., Inst. for Combinatorics and its Applications, NY Acad. Sci., Renyi Math. Inst. Hungarian Acad. Scis. (Budapest), (sr. rschr., 2008), (European Union grant). Home: 355 Leonora Dr Memphis TN 38117-2102 Office: Dept Math Scis Univ Memphis Memphis TN 38152-0001 Home Phone: 901-767-3474; Office Phone: 901-678-2495. Business E-Mail: rschelp@memphis.edu.

SCHELSKE, CLAIRE L., limnologist, educator; s. Theodore J. and Ida S. S.; m. Betty Breukelman, June 2, 1957; children: Cynthia, John, Steven. AB, Kans. State Tchrs. Coll., Emporia, 1955, MS, 1956; PhD, U. Mich., 1961. Tchg. and rsch. asst. dept. biology Kans. State Tchrs. Coll., 1952-55, vis. instr., summer 1960; teaching fellow dept. zoology U. Mich., 1955-57; asst. prof. radiol. health dept. environ. health U. Mich. (Sch. Public Health); asst. research limnologist Gt. Lakes Research Div., Inst. Sci. and Tech., 1967-68, assoc. rsch. limnologist, 1969-71, rsch. limnologist, 1971-87; asst. dir. Gt. Lakes Research Div., Inst. Sci. and Tech. (Gt. Lakes Research Div.), 1970-72, acting dir., 1973-76, assoc. prof. limnology, dept. atmospheric and oceanic sci., 1976-87; assoc. prof. natural resources Sch. Natural Resources, 1976-86, prof., 1986-87; Carl S. Swisher prof. water resources U. Fla., Gainesville, 1987-2000, eminent scholar emeritus, 2001—. Research fellow Inst. Fisheries Research, Mich. Dept. Conservation, 1957-60; research assoc. U. Ga. Marine Inst., 1960-62; fishery biologist, supervisory fishery biologist, chief Estuarine Ecology Program, Bur. Comml. Fisheries, Radiobiol. Lab., Beaufort, N.C., 1962-66; adj. asst. prof. dept. zoology N.C. State U., Raleigh, 1964-66; tech. asst. Office Sci. and Tech., Exec. Office of Pres., Washington, 1966-67; cons. Ill. Atty. Gen., 1977-79; eminent scholar emer., 2001. Author: (with J.C. Roth) Limnological Survey of Lakes Michigan, Superior, Huron and Erie, 1973. Recipient Disting. Alumnus award Emporia State U. (formerly Kans. State Tchrs. Coll.), 1989, Edward S. Deevey Award for Outstanding Sci. Achievement, Fla. Lake Mgmt. Soc., 2000. Fellow: AAAS, Am. Inst. Fishery Rsch. Biologists (regional and dist. dir. South-Ctrl. Gt. Lakes chpt. 1977—80); mem.: Soc. Internat. Limnology (nat. rep. 1998), Internat. Assn. Gt. Lakes Rsch. (editl. bd. 1970—73, chmn. 20th Conf. 1977, assoc. editor 1984—93), Ecol. Soc. Am. (assoc. editor 1972—75), Am. Soc. Limnology and Oceanography (sec. 1976—85, v.p. 1987—88, pres. 1988—90, Ruth Patrick award for sci. problem solving 2003). Home: 2738 SW 9th Dr Gainesville FL 32601-9003 Office: Dept Geol Sci Land Use and Environ Change Inst PO Box 112120 Gainesville FL 32611 E-mail: schelsk@ufl.edu.

SCHEMAN, L. RONALD, lawyer, author, bank executive; b. Aug. 9, 1931; s. Mac and Eleanor (Minkowitz) Scheman; m. Lucy M. Duncan; children: Ann, Corinne, Jennifer, Daniel. BA with distinction cum laude, Dartmouth Coll., 1953; JD, Yale U., 1956. Bar: N.Y., 1956, D.C., 1979. Pvt. practice law, Hartford, Conn., 1957, NYC, 1958-59; fellow Inter-Am. Cultural Conv., Brazil, 1959-61; atty. dept. legal affairs OAS, Washington, 1961-64, planning officer, 1968-70, asst. sec. gen. for mgmt., 1975-84; exec. dir. Pan Am. Devel. Found., 1964-68; pres. Porter Internat. Co., Washington, 1970-75; ptnr. Coudert Bros., Washington, 1984-85; exec. dir. Ctr. Advanced Studies of the Americas, 1985-87; ptnr. Kaplan, Russin and Vecchi, 1987-90, Heller, Rosenblatt and Scheman, 1990-93; U.S. exec. dir. Inter-Am. Devel. Bank, Washington, 1993-98; chmn. Internat. Fin. Group, Greenberg, Traurig, 1998-2000; secretariat Inter-Am. Commn. on Human Rights, 1961-64; dir. gen. Inter-Am. Agy. for Cooperation and Devel., 2000—04; chmn. Kissinger McLarty Assocs., 2005—, sr. advisor, 2005—; CEO Imalls Global, 2006—. V.p. fin. Robert R. Nathan Assocs., 1974-75; pub. Soviet Bus. and Trade, 1973-75; dir. Vision mag., 1973-74; assoc. dir. Coun. of Ams., 1976—; adj. prof. internat. orgn. George Washington U., 1979-83. Author: (books) Foundations of Freedom, 1966, The Inter-Am. Dilemma, 1988, The Alliance for Progress, A Retrospective, 1989, Greater Am., 2003, (articles) on inter-Am. affairs to profl. jours.; bd. editors: Mng. Internat. Devel. quar. Trustee Inter-Am. Bar Found., 1967-74; trustee Pan Am. Devel. Found., 1987-94, pres., 1976-83; chmn. Mus. of Americas Found., 1998-2002, The Americas Endowment, 2003—; adv. bd. Coll. Charleston; pres. Uruguay—U.S. C. of C., 1999-2000; mem. exec. com. Am. Jewish Com. of Washington; bd. dirs. East-West Trade Coun., 1974-75, Ctr. for Advanced Studies of the Ams., 1984-87, Free Enterprise Found., Cmty. Access Found.; pres. The Ams. Endowment, 2004—. Decorated Order Bernardo O'Higgins (Chile), 1967, Russian Fedn., 1992. Mem. Washington Fgn. Law Soc. (bd. govs. 1965-67, pres. 1968), Am. Fgn. Law Assn. (v.p. 1971), Cosmos Club, Phi Beta Kappa. Home: 85 Tradd St Charleston SC 29401 Office: 3 Broad St Charleston SC 29401 Office Phone: 843-723-9480, 843-856-5116. Personal E-mail: ronald.scheman@yahoo.com.

SCHEMBRI, CHRIS, communications company executive, media specialist; b. 1971; BA in Comm., U. Windsor, Ont., Can., 1992, MBA, 2005. Regional planner to sr. ptnr., media dir. J. Walter Thompson Co., Detroit, 1997—2004; sr. v.p. media planning/partnerships Discovery Comm. Inc., 2004—08; v.p. media svcs. AT&T Inc., 2008—. Office: AT&T Inc Hdqs 175 E Houston San Antonio TX 78205 Office Phone: 210-821-4105. Office Fax: 210-351-2071.*

SCHEMNITZ, SANFORD DAVID, wildlife biology professor; b. Cleve., Mar. 10, 1930; s. David Arthur Schemnitz; m. Mary Margaret Newby, July 8, 1958; children: Ellen Kay, Steven, Stuart. Student, U. Wis., 1948-50; BS in Wildlife, U. Mich., 1952; MS in Wildlife, U. Fla., 1953; PhD in Wildlife, Okla. State U., 1958. Cert. wildlife biologist. Conservation aide State of Mich. Dept. Conservation, Ann Arbor, 1951-52; game research biologist State of Minn. Dept. Conservation, St. Paul, 1958-59; asst. prof. wildlife Pa. State U., University Park, 1960-61; prof. wildlife resources U. Maine, Orono, 1962-75; dept. head fish and wildlife sci. N.Mex. State U., Las Cruces, 1975-81, prof. wildlife scis., 1981—97. Mem. resource adv. coun. Bur. Land Mgmt., N.Mex., 1996-99. Editor: Wildlife Management Techniques Manual, 1980; contbr. over 100 articles to profl. jours. Fulbright Prof. Council for Internat. Exchange Scholars, Kathmandu, Nepal, 1983, Kenya, 1990. Mem. Am. Soc. Mammalogists, The Wildlife Soc. (life, S.W. regional rep. 1979-80), Ecol. Soc. Am., Wilson Ornithol. Soc., N.Mex. Wildlife Fedn. (bd. dirs. 1983-2006), Sigma Xi. Home: 8105 Dona Ana Rd Las Cruces NM 88007-6305

SCHENCK, JACK LEE, retired electric utility executive; b. Morgantown, W.Va., Aug. 2, 1938; s. Ernest Jacob and Virginia Belle (Kelley) S.; m. Rita Elizabeth Pietschmann, June 7, 1979; 1 son, Erik. BSE.E., BA in Social Sci., Mich. State U., 1961; MBA, NYU, 1975. Engr. AID, Tunis, Tunisia, 1961, Detroit Edison Co., 1962-63; engr., economist OECD, Paris, 1963-70; v.p. econ. policy analysis Edison Electric Inst., NYC and Washington, 1970-81; v.p., treas. Gulf States Utilities Co., Beaumont, Tex., 1981-92, sr. v.p., CFO, 1992-94. Cons. on electric utility restructuring and privatization in the former Soviet Union, 1994—. Mem. Internat. Assn. Energy Econs., Triangle Club, Eta Kappa Nu. Republican. Office Phone: 281-360-3960. E-mail: schenck1@aol.com.

SCHENCK, JOHN FREDERIC, physician; b. Decatur, Ind., June 7, 1939; s. John C. Schenck and Mildred Blosser; m. Jane Stark, Oct. 12, 1962 (div. 1982); children: Brooke, Kimberly, David; m. Susan J. Kalia, Oct. 8, 1994; 1 stepchild, Tania. BS in Physics, Rensselaer Poly. Inst., 1961, PhD in Physics, 1965; MD, Albany Med. Coll., NY, 1977. Staff scientist electronics lab. GE, Syracuse, NY, 1965-73; assoc. prof. elec. engring. Syracuse (NY) U., 1970-73; intern Albany Med. Ctr. Hosp., 1977-78; staff mem., sr. scientist GE Global Rsch., Schenectady, NY, 1973—; mem. med. staff Ellis Hosp., Schenectady, 1981—98. Adj. asst. prof. dept. radiology U. Pa., 1983-2000; adj. prof. neurology Albany Med. Coll., 2003-; chmn. Workshop on Advances in Magnetic Resonance Imaging Safety and Compatibility, McLean, Va., 1996; dir. Magnetic Resonance Imaging rsch. Neurosci. Rsch. Ctr., Albany Med. Ctr., 2001-. Contbr. articles pub. to profl. jours. Recipient S.S. Greenfield award Am. Assn. Physicists in Medicine, 1993; Nat. Merit scholar, 1957-61; NSF fellow, 1962-63, Coolidge fellow GE, 2003. Fellow: Am. Phys. Soc., Internat. Soc. Magnetic Resonance Medicine (Gold medal, 2009); mem. IEEE, AAAS, NY Acad. Scis., Sigma Xi. Achievements include 20 patents for magnetic resonance imaging. Home: 22 E Claremont Dr Voorheesville NY 12186-9104 Office: GE Global Rsch Bldg K1 NMR Schenectady NY 12309 Office Phone: 518-387-6543. Business E-Mail: schenck@research.ge.com.

SCHENCK, WILL, publishing executive; Various sales/advt. positions Vanity Fair mag. Condé Nast Publs., sr. acct. mgr. to exec. travel dir. Gourmet mag., 1998; assoc. pub. Men's Jour. Wenner Media LLC, 2003—05, pub., 2005—08, pub. Rolling Stone, 2008—. Office: Rolling Stone 1290 Ave Americas New York NY 10104 Office Phone: 212-484-1616.*

SCHENDEL, DAN ELDON, management consultant, finance educator; b. Norwalk, Wis., Mar. 29, 1934; s. Leonard A. and Marian T. (Koch) S.; m. Mary Lou Sigler, Sept. 1, 1956; children: Suzanne, Pamela, Sharon. BS in Metall. Engring., U. Wis., 1956; MBA, Ohio State U., 1959; PhD (Ford Found. fellow), Stanford U., 1963. With ALCOA, 1956, U.S. Civil Svc., 1959-60, SRI, 1963-65; prof. mgmt., dir. exec. edn. programs Purdue U., Lafayette, Ind., 1965-85, Blake Family endowed chair emeritus in strategic mgmt.; vis. prof. U. Mich., 1988-89, U. Chgo., 1990-91, 1999—2004. Former dean German Grad. Internat. Sch. Mgmt. and Adminstrn., Hannover, Germany, 1999-2005; pres. Strategic Mgmt. Assocs., Inc. Author: (with others) Strategy Formulation: Analytical Concepts, 1978, Divided Loyalties, 1980, Fundamental Issues in Strategy, 1994; editor: (with others) Strategic Management: A New View of Business Policy and Planning, 1979; founding and cons. editor Strategic Mgmt. Jour., 1980-2007; founding editor Strategic Entrepreneurship Jour., 2006—. With USAF, 1956—59. Fellow Acad. Mgmt., Strategic Mgmt. Soc. (founding pres., treas.); mem. Univ. Club Chgo. Home: 1327 N Grant St West Lafayette IN 47906-2463 Office: Krannert Grad Sch Mgmt Purdue U West Lafayette IN 47907 Office Phone: 765-494-4386. Business E-Mail: schendel@purdue.edu.

SCHENDEL, STEPHEN ALFRED, surgeon, educator; b. Mpls., Oct. 10, 1947; s. Alfred Reck and Jeanne Shirley (Hagquist) S.; children: Elliott, Mélisande. BA, St. Olaf Coll., Northfield, Minn., 1969; BS with high distinction, U. Minn., 1971, DDS, 1973; diplome asst. etranger with high honors, U. Nantes, France, 1980; MD, U. Hawaii, 1983. Diplomate Am. Bd. Plastic Surgery, Nat. Bd. Med. Examiners, Nat. Bd. Dental Examiners, Am. Bd. Oral and Maxillofacial Surgery (adv. com., bd. examiner 1991-95). Intern, then resident in oral and maxillofacial surgery Parkland Meml. Hosp., Dallas, 1975-79; resident in gen. surgery Baylor U. Med. Ctr., Dallas, 1983-84, Stanford (Calif.) U. Med. Ctr., 1984-86, resident in plastic surgery, 1986-89, acting assoc. prof. surgery, 1989-91, assoc. prof., 1991-95, head divsn. plastic and reconstructive surgery, 1992—2002, dir. residency tng., 1992-98, chmn. dept. functional restoration, 1994—2001, prof. surgery, 1995—2002, prof. emeritus surgery, 2007; head plastic surgery, dir. Craniofacial Ctr. Lucile Salter Packard Children's Hosp., Stanford, 1991—2007, chief pediat. surgery, 1997—2002. Asst. to Dr. Paul Tessier, Paris, 1987-88; asst. dept. stomatology and maxillofacial surgery Centre Hospitalier Regional Nantes, 1979-80; med. bd. Lucile Salter Packard Children's Hosp. at Stanford, 1991—. Assoc. editor Selected Readings in Oral and Maxillofacial Surgery, 1989—; mem. editl. bd. Jour. Cranio-Maxillofacial Surgery; contbr. articles to profl. jours., chpts. to books. Recipient Disting. Alumnus award St. Olaf Coll., 1993; Fulbright fellow, Nantes, 1979-80, Chateaubriand fellow Govt. of France, 1987-88. Fellow ACS, Am. Acad. Pediat.; mem. Internat. Soc. Craniofacial Surgeons, European Assn. Cranio-Maxillofacial Surgeons, Am. Soc. Pediat. Plastic Surgeons, Am. Assn. Plastic Surgery, Soc. Baylor Surgeons (founding), Am. Cleft Palate-Craniofacial Assn., Am. Soc. Plastic Surgeons (sec. 1996—), Am. Soc. Maxillofacial Surgeons (sec., pres. 2000-01), Assn. Acad. Chairmen Plastic Surgery, Zedplast (bd. dirs. 1993—), Omicron Kappa Upsilon. Avocations: fly fishing, painting and sculpture. Office: Stanford U Med Ctr Divsn Plastic Reconstr Surg 770 Welch Rd Ste 400 Palo Alto CA 94304 Home Phone: 650-261-1031; Office Phone: 650-723-5824, 650-328-0511. Business E-Mail: sschendel@stanford.edu.

SCHENK, DALE BERNARD, pharmaceutical executive, neuroscientist; m. Maria Torres, Sept. 9, 1978; children: Anais, Sara. BA cum laude, U. Calif., San Diego, 1979, PhD, 1984. Scientsit Scios/Nova, Mountain View, Calif., 1984-87; sr. scientist and project leader Athena Neuroscis., South San Francisco, 1987-90, sr. scientist, dir. immunochemsitry, 1990-93, project leader, mgr., 1993-94, dir. neurobiology, 1994—98; v.p. neurobiology Elan Corp., plc, South San Francisco, 1998—99, sr. v.p. discovery rsch., 1999—2003, sr. v.p., chief sci. officer, 2003—, exec. v.p., 2007—. Presenter in field. Ad Hoc reviewer jours.; contbr. numerous articles to profl. jours.; patentee in field. Grantee Am. Liver Found., 1983, NIH, 1986, 89, 90. Mem. AAAAS, Am. Soc. Hypertension (founder), US Chess Fedn. Office: Elan Corp plc 800 Gateway Blvd South San Francisco CA 94080 Office Phone: 650-877-0900. Office Fax: 650-877-7669.*

SCHENK, JOSEPH BERNARD, museum director; b. Glendale, Ariz., Mar. 28, 1953; m. Jacqueline Van Lierop; children: Brian, Stuart. BA in Mus. Staff Preparation, Huntingdon Coll., 1974; MA in Art Edn., Ball State U., 1979; postgrad., U. Calif., Berkeley, 1986. Exhibits asst. Hunter Mus. of Art, Chattanooga, 1974-75; asst. dir. Alford House/Anderson Fine Arts Ctr., Anderson, Ind., 1976, exec. dir., 1976-79, Okefenokee Heritage Ctr., Waycross, Ga., 1979-83; dir. So. Forest World, Waycross, 1979-83, Chattahoochee Valley Art Mus., LaGrange, Ga., 1983-88, Mobile (Ala.) Mus. of Art, 1988—. V.p. Ala. Mus. Assn., 1994-96, pres., 1996-98; adv. panelist Visual Arts Fellowships, Ala. State Coun. on the Arts, 1994-95, Profl. Touring Panel Ga. Coun. for Arts, 1983-84, PRACSO Panel Ga. Coun. for Arts, 1984-86, Arch. & Environ. Arts Ind. Arts Commn., 1978-79, Mus. Ind. Arts Commn., 1977-79; Ind. rep. Small Mus. Com. Midwest Mus. Conf., 1978-79. Pub. numerous art catalogs; editor newsletter Ga. Assembly of Community Arts Agys., 1987-88. Art juror at numerous pub. and pvt. art shows; bd. dirs. Ga. Alliance for Arts Edn., 1982-84, Assn. Ind. Mus., 1979, Mobile Arts Coun., 1989-90, Ga. Assembly Community Arts Agys., 1986-88; commr. Madison County Hist. Home, Anderson, 1977-79; mem. dedication com., cons. Krannert Fine Arts Ctr., Anderson Coll., 1979; mem. com. forest festival tourism and conventions Waycross/Ware County C. of C., 1979-83; bd. dirs. Southeastern Ga. Travel and Tourism Assn., 1981-83, sec., 1981-82, pres., 1982-83. Grantee Nat. Endowment for Arts, Ala. State Coun. on Arts, Mobile Arts Coun., Ga. Endowment for Humanities, Ga. Coun. Arts, Ala. Arts Found., Inst. Mus. and Libr. Svcs., Ga. Gov.'s Intern Program, others; recipient Spark Plug of Yr. award Waycross Jaycees, 1981; Mus. Mgmt. Inst. scholar, 1986. Mem. Am. Assn. Mus., Southeastern Mus. Conf., Ala. Mus. Assn., Rotary (Paul Harris fellowship 1997), Mobile United (Grad. Leadership Mobile 1998), Mobile Area Mus. Assn. (pres. 1993-95). Home: 4850 Museum Dr Mobile AL 36608-1917 also: 324 Bayshore Dr Corpus Christi TX 78412-2608

SCHENK, QUENTIN FREDERICK, retired social work educator, psychologist, mayor; b. Fort Madison, Iowa, Aug. 25, 1922; s. Fred Edward John and Ida (Sabrowsky) S.; m. Patricia J. Kelley, Aug. 6, 1946 (div. Apr. 1970); children: Fred W. (dec. 1972), Patricia, Karl, Martha;

m. Emmy Lou Willson, May 23, 1970 (dec. Dec. 7, 2007). BA, Willamette U., 1948; MS, U. Wis., 1950, MS in Social Work, 1953, PhD, 1953. Lic. ind. clin. social worker, Wis.; cert. longterm care, Ariz. Asst. prof. social work U. Wis.-Madison, 1953-55, prof., chmn. extension social work, 1961-63; prof., former dean Sch. Social Welfare, Milw., 1962-68, prof. emeritus, 1990—; assoc. prof. U. Mo., 1955-61; project specialist Ford Found., 1968-71. Spl. cons. on urban mission in Africa United Presbyn. Ch., 1971-, World Council Chs., 1971-; advisor to Haile Sellassie I U., Addis Ababa, Ethiopia, 1968-71; Alderman City of Cedarburg (Wis.), 1974-82, mayor, 1982-86. Author: (with Emmy Lou Schenk) Pulling Up Roots, 1978, Welfare Society and the Helping Professions, 1981; author sect. on Ethiopia, Welfare in Africa, 1987; contbr. articles, bulls., reports to profl. lit. Mem. Nat. Trust for Hist. Preservation, Wis. Hist. Preservation Negotiating Bd., 1975-76; chmn. bd. Guest House, Milw., 1987-89; mem. Sierra Club, Planned Parenthood, Unitarian Ch. S.E. Ariz. (v.p. 1999), ACLU, Dem. Party of Ariz. With USNR, 1942—46, carrier pilot WWII, ret. lt. Decorated Air medal with four gold stars, Disting. Flying Cross; recipient Presdl. citation Pres. Harry Truman, 1948; scholar Fulbright Found., 1959-60. Mem. DAV (life), Am. Assn. Ret. Persons, Aircraft Owners and Pilots Assn., Nat. Audubon Soc., Nature Conservancy. Democrat. Unitarian Universalist. Avocations: hiking, boating, travel. Home: 3443 E Wild Rabbit Rd Hereford AZ 85615-9653 Home Phone: 520-803-0670. Personal E-mail: qschenk@mac.ccm.

SCHENK, THOMAS, photographer; b. Ill. BFA, Phila. Coll. Art. Assoc. with Found. World Inc. creative prodn. agy., NYC. Contbr. photos to Dutch mag., Vogue, Surface, Interview, NY Times, Gloss, Purple, Arena, Allure, Details. Avocation: show horses. Mailing: c/o Jordan Shipenberg Art Dept 48 Greene St # 4 New York NY 10013 Office Phone: 212-925-4222 ext 105. E-mail: jordan@art-dept.com.

SCHENKER, GREGG L., real estate company executive; b. 1966; Grad. in Real Estate, NYU. Real estate broker/mgr. Helmsley-Spear; founding ptnr. ABS Ptnrs. Real Estate, 1999; co-mng. ptnr., real estate adv. svc. provider Wealthy Ptnrs. & Instl. Clients. Mem.: Young Men's and Women's Real Estate Assn. NY (past chmn.), Real Estate Bd. NY (mem. comml. bd. dirs., mem. sales brokers com., mem. loft and secondary market com., Young Real Estate Man of Yr. award 2008), Flatiron 23rd St. BID Assn. (bd. mem., chmn. 2008—09). Office: ABS Partners Real Estate 200 Park Ave S New York NY 10003 Office Phone: 212-400-6071. Office Fax: 212-400-9494. Business E-Mail: gschenker@absre.com.

SCHENKER, LEO, retired utilities executive; b. Vienna, Jan. 3, 1922; came to U.S., 1952, naturalized, 1959; s. Max and Selda Lea (Podhorcer) S.; m. Alda R. Tinson, Jan. 20, 1949; children: Michael Gregory, Deborah Anne. BS with first class honors, U. London, 1942; MA in Sci. (Can. Inst. Steel Constrn. fellow), U. Toronto, 1950; PhD, U. Mich., 1954. Mng. dir. METAG Ltd., London, 1945-48; asst. rsch. engr. Hydro-Electric Power Commn. of Ont. (Can.), Toronto, 1948-52; rsch. assoc. U. Mich., Ann Arbor, 1952-54; with Bell Telephone Labs., 1954-87, various positions, dir. mil. electronic tech., 1968-71; dir. Loop Maintenance Systems Lab., 1971-80, exec. dir. Central Office Ops. div., 1980-83, exec. dir. network system planning div., 1983-84, exec. dir. tech. info. div., 1984-87. Adj. prof. elec. engring. Cooper Union, N.Y.C., 1989-97. Served with RAF, 1942-45. Recipient Duggan medal Can. Inst. Steel Constrn., 1970 Fellow IEEE, Sigma Xi, Phi Kappa Phi. Home: 3228 Fellowship Rd Basking Ridge NJ 07920 Personal E-mail: leoschenker@fvonline.net.

SCHENKER, MARC BENET, preventive medicine physician, medical educator, department chairman; b. LA, Aug. 25, 1947; s. Steve and Dosella Schenker; m. Heath Massey; children: Yael, Phoebe, Hilary. BA, U. Calif., Berkeley, 1969; MD, U. Calif., San Francisco, 1973; MPH, Harvard U., Boston, 1980. Instr. medicine Harvard U., Boston, 1980-82; asst. prof. medicine U. Calif., Davis, 1982-86, assoc. prof., 1986-92, prof., 1992—, chmn. dept. pub. health scis., 1995—. Fellow ACP; mem. Am. Thoracic Soc., Am. Pub. Health Assn., Soc. Epidemiologic Rsch., Am. Coll. Epidemiology, Soc. Occupl. Environ. Health, Internat. Commn. Occupl. Health, Assn. Tchrs. Preventive Medicine, Phi Beta Kappa, Alpha Omega Alpha. Office Phone: 530-752-5676.

SCHENKER, STEVEN, internist, educator; b. Poland, Oct. 5, 1929; came to US, 1943, naturalized, 1946; s. Alfred and Ernestyna S.; m. Sally Ann Wood, May 11, 1956; children: Julie C. Schenker Burn, Steven A., David S., Andrew G., Jennifer E. Schenker Campeggi; m. Jo Ann Neumann, Nov. 24, 1985. BA, Cornell U., Ithaca, NY, 1951, MD, 1955. Intern Harvard Service-Boston City Hosp., 1955-56, resident in medicine, 1956-58; asst. prof. medicine U. Cin. Sch. Medicine, 1961-63; asst. prof. U. Tex., Southwestern Sch. Medicine, 1963-67, assoc. prof. medicine, 1967-70; prof. medicine, biochemistry, dir. div. gastroenterology Vanderbilt U. Sch. Medicine, Nashville VA Hosp., 1970-82; prof. medicine and pharmacology U. Tex. Sch. Medicine, San Antonio, 1982—, dir. divsn. gastroenterology, 1982—2001. Chmn. study sect. Nat. Inst. on Alcohol Abuse and Addiction, 1980-83; chmn. study sects. VA, 1985-88. Editor: Hepatology, 1985-90; contbr. numerous articles in field to profl. jours. Recipient Markle award, 1963; Career Devel. award NIH, 1968; Jurzykowski Found. for Research in Medicine award, 1979, Alcoholism Research Soc. award 1987. Mem. Am. Assn. for Study of Liver Diseases (pres. 1980, Disting. Svc. award 1997), Am. Soc. Clin. Investigation, Assn. Am. Physicians, Am. Gastroent. Soc., Am. Soc. Pharm. and Exptl. Therapeutics, Am. Soc. Clin. Nutrition, Internat. Soc. for Study of Liver Diseases, Alpha Omega Alpha. Home: 26025 Mesa Oak Dr San Antonio TX 78255-3533 Office: U Tex Med Sch San Antonio TX 78284

SCHENKKAN, DIRK MCKENZIE, lawyer; b. Durham, NC, Aug. 9, 1949; s. Robert Fredric and Jean (McKenzie) S.; m. Patricia Sinnott, Nov. 11, 1979; children: Jean, Penelope, Victoria. AB highest honors, U. Tex., 1971; JD, Yale U., 1975. Bar: Calif. 1976, U.S. Dist. Ct. (no. dist.) Calif. 1976, U.S. Ct. Appeals (9th cir.) 1978, U.S. Dist. Ct. (ea. dist.) Calif. 1987. Rsch. assoc., tutor Law Sch. Yale U., New Haven, 1975-76; arbitrator Fed. & State Cts. No. Dist., Calif., mediator San Francisco; prin. Howard, Rice, Nemerovski, Canady, Falk & Rabkin, San Francisco, 1976, dir. Contbr. articles to profl. jours. Bd. dirs. San Francisco Neighborhood Legal Assistance Found., 1984—, Assn. Bus. Trial Lawyers, 1994—, San Francisco Girls Chorus, 1994—, Pacific Primary Sch., San Francisco, 1985-88. Named No. Calif. Super Lawyer, by Law & Politics., 2004—06. Mem. ABA, Calif. Bar Assn., Bar Assn. San Francisco, Assn. Bus. Trial Lawyers, Rotary Internat. fellow U. Kent Canterbury, England 1972-1973, Phi Beta Kappa. Office: Howard Rice Nemerovski Canady Robertson & Falk 3 Embarcadero Ctr 7th Fl Ste 7 San Francisco CA 94111-4074 Office Phone: 415-434-1600, 415-399-3055. Office Fax: 415-217-5910. Business E-Mail: dschenkkan@hrice.com. E-mail: dschenkkan@howardrice.com.

SCHENKKAN, ROBERT FREDERIC, playwright, screenwriter; b. Chapel Hill, Mar. 19, 1953; s. Robert Frederic Sr. and Jean (McKenzie) Schenkkan; m. Maria Dahvana Headley; children: Sarah Victoria, Joshua McHenry. BA in Theatre Arts, U. Tex., 1975; MFA in Acting, Cornell U., 1977. Author: (plays) Final Passages, 1981, The Survivalist, 1982 (best of the fringe award Edinburgh Festival, 1984), Tachinoki, 1987, Tall Tales, 1988 (Playwrights Forum award, 1988, Best One Act Plays, 1993), Heaven on Earth, 1989 (Julie Harris Playwright award Beverly Hills Theatre Guild, 1989), The Kentucky Cycle, 1991 (Pulitzer prize for drama, 1992, L.A. Drama Critics Circle Best Play award, 1992, Penn Ctr. West award, 1993, Best Play Tony award nominee, 1993, Best Play Drama Desk award nominee, 1993), Conversations with the Spanish Lady and Other One-Act Plays, 1993, The Dream Thief, 1998, Handler, 1999, The Marriage of Miss Hollywood and King Neptune,The Devil and Daniel Webster, 2002, By the Waters of Babylon, 2004, Lewis and Clark Reach the Euphrates, 2005, (TV) Crazy Horse, (Miniseries) The Andromeda Strain, The Pacific, (Mous) Spartacus, (films) The Quiet American, 2002. Grantee Vogelstein Found., 1982, Arthur Found., 1988, Fund for New Am. Plays, 1990, Calif. Arts Coun., 1991. Mem.: SAG, Actors Equity, Writers Guild, Ensemble Studio Theatre, Dramatists Guild.

SCHEPIS, ANTHONY JOSEPH, artist, educator; b. Cleve., Mar. 6, 1927; s. Andrew Peter Schepis and Sarah Antonette Miraglia; children: Andrea, Pamela, Roman. Diploma, Cooper Sch. Art, Cleve., 1951; cert. painting, Cleve. Inst. Art, 1955; MA, Kent State U., Ohio, 1977. Instr. drawing and painting Cooper Sch. Art, Cleve., 1957—74; instr. drawing Cuyahoga C.C., Cleve., 1974—75, Lakeland C.C., Kirtland, Ohio, 1975—76; instr. drawing and painting Cleve. Inst. Art, 1976—78, prof. drawing and painting, 1979—96, prof. emeritus, 1999. Chair found. art dept. Cooper Sch. Art, Cleve., 1965—70. Represented in permanent collections Massillon Mus., Butler Inst. Am. Art, Canton Mus. Art, Richmond Art Mus. Recipient Individual Fellowship award, Ohio Arts Coun., 1980, Major Painting award, Cleve. Mus. Art, 1988, Thomas J. Ruddy Meml. award, Associated Artists Pitts.-Carnegie Mus. Art, 1999. Mem.: Cleve. Artists Found. Avocation: collecting recordings early 20th century Italian folk singers. Home: 125 Osprey Heights Dr N Winter Haven FL 33880 Personal E-mail: ajschepis@yahoo.com.

SCHEPKIN, VICTOR D., biophysicist; s. Dmitri V. and Evdokia I. Schepkin; m. Mary Hinton, Sept. 9, 2000; children: Elena V. Schepkina children: Svetlana V. Epifanova; m. Alexandra N. Kolesova, July 20, 1968 (div. June 6, 2000). MS in Radio Physics, Kazan State U., 1968, PhD in Physics, 1978. Cert. in bus. adminstrn. U. Ill., Urbana Champaign, 1999. MR physicist Kazan State U., 1970—81; vis. scientist Clarendon Lab., Oxford U., England, 1980; sr. scientist State Sci. Ctr. Applied Microbiology, Obolensk, Moscow Region, Russia, 1981—92; scientist U. Calif., Berkeley, 1992—94, Lawrence Berkeley Nat. Lab., Calif., 1994—97, Wake Forest U., Winston Salem, NC, 1997—98; sr. rsch. specialist U. Ill., 1998—2002, co lectr. with prof. Paul Lauterbur, 2000—01; faculty, rsch. investigator U. Mich., Ann Arbor, 2002—06; assoc. scholar scientist Nat. High Magnetic Field Lab. FSU, Tallahassee, 2006—. Lectr. physics Kazan Inst. Energy, Russia, 1980—81. Contbr. scientific papers to profl. jours. Mountaineering instr. All Union Mountaineering Assn., Moscow, 1980—92. Grantee, NIH, NCI, 2006—. Mem.: Magnetic Resonance Medicine. Achievements include first to double NMR in solids and its applications. Avocations: skiing, swimming, travel. Office: Natl High Magnetic Field Lab 1800 E Paul Dirac Dr Tallahassee FL 32310 Business E-Mail: schepkin@magnet.fsu.edu.

SCHEPP, RICHARD D., lawyer, retail executive; b. July 1960; m. Beth Schepp. BBA, U. Wis., Eau Claire; JD, U. Wis. Atty. Quarles & Brady, Milw.; dir. legal affairs, asst. corp. sec. Shopko Stores, Inc., 1992—96, v.p. legal affairs, corp. sec., 1996—98, sr. v.p., gen. counsel, 1998—2000; sr. v.p. Kohl's Corp., 2000—01, gen. counsel, sec., 2000—, exec. v.p., 2001—. Office: Kohls Corp N56 W17000 Ridgewood Dr Menomonee Falls WI 53051-5660 Office Phone: 262-703-7000.

SCHEPPACH, TRACEY L., communications media company executive; b. 1970; BS in Fin. and Acctg., U. Colo., Boulder, 1991; MBA, Northwestern U. Kellogg Sch. Mgmt., Ill., 1999. CPA 1992. Mktg. dir. Monsanto Co.; product devel. Wink, Inc.; v.p. programming OpenTV Liberty Media Corp.; sr. v.p., video innovation dir. Starcom USA Starcom MediaVest Grp., Chgo. Recipient SABRE award, Holmes Grp.; named a Woman to Watch, Advt. Age, 2008. Office: Starcom Worldwide Global Hdqs 35 W Wacker Dr Chicago IL 60601 Office Phone: 312-220-3535. Office Fax: 312-220-6530. Business E-Mail: tracey.scheppach@smvgroup.com.*

SCHEPPKE, JIM, library director; MLS, U. Tex., Austin. Ind. bookseller; with West Tex. Libr. Sys., Tex. State Libr.; adminstr. libr. devel. Oreg. State Libr., Portland, 1986—91, interim dir., 1991, state libr., 1991—. Bd. dirs. Bibliographical Ctr. Rsch., Colo. Mem.: Oreg. Libr. Assn. (pres. 1991, Libr. of Yr. award 1996). Office: Oreg State Libr 250 Winter St NE Salem OR 97301-3950 Office Phone: 503-378-4367. E-mail: jim.b.scheppke@state.or.us.

SCHER, HOWARD DENNIS, lawyer; b. Ft. Monmouth, NJ, Apr. 23, 1945; s. George Scher and Rita (Eitches) Zar; m. Linda J. Scher; children: Seth Micah, Eli David, Nicholas Earl, Sara Catherine. BA, Brandeis U., 1967; JD, Rutgers U., 1971. Bar: Pa. 1971, NY, 2008, U.S. Dist. Ct. (ea. dist.) Pa. 1971, U.S. Ct. Appeals (3rd cir.) 1971, U.S. Supreme Ct. 1975. Asst. city solicitor City of Phila., 1971-73; assoc. Goodis, Greenfield, Henry & Edelstein, Phila., 1973-77, Montgomery, McCracken, Walker & Rhoads, Phila., 1977-80, ptnr., 1980-2001; shareholder Buchanan Ingersoll & Rooney P.C., Phila., 2001—; dir. Buchanan Ingersoll P.C., Phila., 2006—; mng. shareholder Phila., NYC. Trustee Fedn. of Jewish Agys. of Greater Phila., 1994-2002; dir. Akiba Hebrew Acad., Merion, Pa., 1996-98; mem. pres.'s coun. Brandeis U.; chair Jewish Employment and Vocat. Svcs., 1998-02; chmn. Com. of Seventy, 2002. Fellow Am. Coll. Trial Lawyers, Internat. Acad. Trial Lawyers; mem. ABA, Pa. Bar Assn. (dir.), Phila. Bar Assn. (chmn. fed. cts. com. 2001-02), Brandeis U. Alumni Assn. (v.p. 1983-87). Home: 2222 Locust St Philadelphia PA 19103-5511 Office: Buchanan Ingersoll & RooneyPC 50 S 16th St 32nd Fl Philadelphia PA 19102 Home Phone: 215-985-0692; Office Phone: 215-665-3920. Office Fax: 215-665-8760. Business E-Mail: howard.scher@bipc.com.

SCHER, PETER LAWRENCE, diversified financial services company executive, lawyer; b. NY, Apr. 12, 1961; s. Stanley J. and Susan (Goldman) Scher; m. Kimberly Helen Tilley, Apr. 8, 1995; children: Jacob, Jonah. BA, Am. U., 1983, JD, 1987. Bar: NY 1988, DC 1989. Atty. Keck Mahin & Cate, Washington, 1989—91; chief of staff to Senator Max Baucus US Senate, 1991—93, staff dir. Senate Com. Environ. & Pub. Works, 1993—95; chief of staff Office US Trade Rep., Exec. Office of the Pres., 1995—96, US spl. trade negotiator for agrl., 1997—2000; chief of staff US Dept. Commerce, 1996—97; ptnr., internat. trade practice Mayer Brown Rowe & Maw LLP, Washington, 2000—07, ptnr. in-charge, 2007—08; exec. v.p. global govt. rels. pub. policy J.P. Morgan Chase & Co., NYC, 2008—. Contbr. articles to profl. jours. Mem. working group on US-E.U. trade & econ. issues Atlantic Council of the US, 2000—01. Mem.: DC Bar Assn., NY Bar Assn. Democrat. Jewish. Office: JP Morgan Chase & Co 270 Park Ave New York NY 10017*

SCHER, RITA ANN, librarian; b. NYC, Mar. 19, 1944; d. Henry and Beatrice Brand Samet; m. Murray Howard Scher, June 6, 1964; 1 child, Elena Colette. BA, CUNY, NYC, 1964; MLS, Columbia U., NYC, 1966. Libr. Binghamton U., NY, 1966—68, U. Tex., Austin, 1968—71; libr. dean East Tenn. State U., Johnson City, 1971—. Office: East Tenn State Univ Box 70665 Johnson City TN 37614 Office Fax: 423-439-5222. Business E-Mail: scherr@etsu.edu.

SCHERAGA, HAROLD ABRAHAM, retired physical chemistry professor; b. Bklyn., Oct. 18, 1921; s. Samuel and Etta (Goldberg) S.; m. Miriam Kurnow, June 20, 1943; children: Judith Anne, Deborah Ruth, Daniel Michael. BS, CCNY, 1941; A.M., Duke U., 1942, PhD, 1946, Sc.D. (hon.), 1961, U. Rochester, 1988, U. San Luis, 1992, Technion, 1993, U. Gdansk, 2005. Teaching, research asst. Duke U., 1941-46; fellow Harvard Med. Sch., 1946-47; instr. chemistry Cornell U., 1947-50, asst. prof., 1950-53, assoc. prof., 1953-58, prof., 1958-65, Todd prof. chemistry, 1965-92, Todd prof. chemistry emeritus, 1992—, chmn. dept., 1960-67. Vis. assoc. biochemist Brookhaven Nat. Lab., summers 1950, 51, cons. biology dept., 1950-56; vis. lectr. div. protein chemistry Wool Rsch. Labs., Melbourne, Australia, 1959; vis. prof. Weizmann Inst., Israel, 1970-80, Soc. for Promotion Sci., Japan, Aug. 1977; Ramachandran prof., India, 2002; mem. tech. adv. panel Xerox Corp., 1969-71, 74-79; mem. biochemistry tng. com. NIH, 1963-65, reviewers res., 1995-98; mem. rsch. career award com. NIGMS, 1967-71, NIH BBCA study sect. mem., 1998-2002; commn. molecular biophysics Internat. Union for Pure and Applied Biophysics, 1965-69, mem. commn. macromolecular biophysics, 1969-75, pres., 1972-75, mem. commn. subcellular and macromolecular biophysics, 1975-81; adv. panel molecular biology NSF, 1960-62; Welch Found. lectr., 1962, Harvey lectr., 1968, Gallagher lectr., 1968, Lemieux lectr., 1973, Hill lectr., 1976, Venable lectr., 1981; co-chmn. Gordon Conf. on Proteins, 1963; mem. coun. Gordon Rsch. Confs., 1969-71. Author: Protein Structure, 1961, Theory of Helix-Coil Transitions in Biopolymers, 1970; co-editor Molecular Biology, 1961-86; mem. editl. bd. Physiol. Chemistry and Physics, 1969-75, Mechanochemistry and Motility, 1970-71, Thrombosis Rsch., 1972-76, Biophys. Jour., 1973-75, Macromolecules, 1973-84, Computers and Chemistry, 1974-84, Internat. Jour. Peptide and Protein Chemistry, 1982-96, Jour. Peptide Rsch., 1997—; corr. PAABS Revista, 1971-73; mem. editl. adv. bd. Biopolymers, 1963—, Biochemistry, 1969-74, 85—, Structural Chemistry, 1989-93, Jour. Computational Polymer Sci., 1991-95, Jour. Biomolecular NMR, 1991—, Computational and Theoretical Polymer Sci., 1996-2000, Jour. Biomed. Sci., 1994—, Jour. Am. Chem. Soc., 1995-2000. Mem. Ithaca Bd. Edn., 1958-59; Bd. govs. Weizmann Inst., Israel, 1970-97; mem. staff Naval Research Lab. Project, Air Force OSRD Project, World War II. Fulbright, Guggenheim fellow Carlsberg Lab., Copenhagen, 1956-57, Weizmann Inst., Israel, 1963; NIH Spl. fellow Weizmann Inst., 1970; Fogarty scholar NIH, 1984, 86, 88-91; recipient Townsend Harris medal CCNY, 1970, Chemistry Alumni Sci. Achievements award, 1977, Kowalski medal Internat. Soc. Thrombosis and Haemostasis, 1983, Linderstrøm-Lang medal Carlsberg Lab., 1983, Internat. Soc. of Quantum Chemistry and Quantum Pharmacology award in Theoretical Biology, 1993, Stein & Moore award Protein Soc., 1995; named Hon. mem. Soc. Polymer Sci. Japan, 1995. Fellow AAAS, Biophys. Soc. (coun. 1967-70); mem. NAS, Am. Peptide Soc. (hon.), Am. Chem. Soc. (chmn. Cornell sect. 1955-56, mem. exec. com. div. biol. chemistry 1966-69, vice chmn. divsn. biol. chemistry 1970, chmn. divsn. biol. chemistry 1971, Eli Lilly award 1957, Nichols medal 1974, Kendall award 1978, Pauling award 1985, Mobil award 1990, Repligen award 1990, IBM award for computers in chem. and pharm. rsch. 1997, Hirschmann award in peptide chem., 1999, Goodman award, 2009), Am. Soc. Biol. Chemists, Am. Acad. Arts and Scis., N.Y. Acad. Scis. (hon. life), Hungarian Biophys. Soc. (hon.), Phi Beta Kappa, Sigma Xi, Phi Lambda Upsilon. Home: 212 Homestead Ter Ithaca NY 14850-6220 Business E-Mail: has5@cornell.edu.

SCHERB, RICHARD JOHN, science educator; s. John William and Joy Elaine Scherb; life ptnr. Irene Quinn; children: Stephanie, Marianne Laura. BS, Ashland U., Ohio, 1980. Cert. paramedic NY State DOH, 1985, NYC REMAC, 1985; instr. Coord. NY State DOH, 1987, regional faculty NY State DOH, 1989. Paramedic Luth. Med. Ctr., Bklyn., 1990—; adj. lectr. Coll. SI, 1991—. Instr. Shaolin Kung Fu, SI, 1998. R-Conservative. Avocations: Kung Fu, travel, dance. Office: Coll SI 2800 Victory Blvd Staten Island NY 10314 Home Phone: 732-388-6249. Office Fax: 718-982-3852. Personal E-mail: rscherb@aol.com. Business E-Mail: scherb@mail.csi.cuny.edu.

SCHERER, FREDERIC MICHAEL, economics professor; b. Ottawa, Ill., Aug. 1, 1932; s. Walter King and Margaret (Lucey) Scherer; m. Barbara A. Silbermann, Aug. 17, 1957; children: Thomas, Karen, Christina. AB with honors, U. Mich., 1954; MBA with high distinction, Harvard U., 1958, PhD, 1963; D (hon.), Univ. Hohenheim, 1996. Asst. prof. Princeton (N.J.) U., 1963-66; prof. econs. U. Mich., Ann Arbor, 1966-72; chief economist FTC, Washington, 1974-76; prof. econs. Northwestern U., Evanston, Ill., 1976-82; Joseph Wharton prof. polit. economy Swarthmore (Pa.) Coll., 1982-89; Aetna prof. pub. policy and mgmt. Harvard U., Cambridge, Mass., 1989-2000, emeritus prof., 2000—. Vis. prof. Ctrl. European U., Prague, 1993—94; Arthur Andersen disting. visitor U. Cambridge, 1997; lectr. Princeton U., 2000—05; Ludwig Erhard vis. prof. U. Bayreuth, 2000; vis. prof. Haverford Coll., 2004—06. Author: The Weapons Acquisition Process, 1964, Industrial Market Structure and Economic Performance, 1970, revised edit., 1980, 1990, The Economics of Multi-Plant Operation, 1975, Innovation and Growth, 1984, International High-Technology Competition, 1992, Competition Policies for an Integrated World Economy, 1994, Industry Structure, Strategy and Public Policy, 1996, New Perspectives on Economic Growth and Technological Innovation, 1999, Quarter Notes and Bank Notes, 2004; co-author: Mergers, Sell-Offs and Economic Efficiency, 1987. Mem. adv. panel NSF, Washington, 1980—83, U.S. Office Tech. Assessment, 1989—93, U.S. Bur. of Census, 1997—2000. Recipient Lifetime Achievement award, Am. Antitrust Inst., 2002; grantee, NSF, 1970, 1979, 1982, Sloan Found., 1996; sr. rsch. fellow, Internat. Inst. Mgmt., 1972—74, Census fellow, Am. Stats. Assn., 1989—90, Baker scholar, Harvard U., 1957, Centennial Rsch. grantee, O'Melveny & Myers, 1989. Mem.: Indsl. Orgn. Soc. (pres. 1992), Am. Econ. Assn. (v.p. 1988), European Assn. for Rsch. in Indsl. Econs. (co-founder 1974). Roman Catholic. Avocations: musicology, music. Home: 53 Standish St Cambridge MA 02138 Office: John F Kennedy Sch Govt Harvard U Cambridge MA 02138 Office Phone: 617-495-1154. Business E-Mail: mike_scherer@harvard.edu.

SCHERER, HAROLD NICHOLAS, JR., electric power industry executive; b. Plainfield, NJ, Apr. 5, 1929; s. Harold Nicholas and Nora (McDonough) S.; m. Jane Neely, Sept. 6, 1952 (div.); children: Anne Scherer McConnell, Peter; m. Patricia Condon, May 4, 1974; stepchildren: James, John, Joseph, Jeffery Ludwig, Jean Ludwig Ransdell. BE, Yale U., 1951; MBA, Rutgers U., 1955. Registered profl. engr., N.J., Mass. Various engring. positions Pub. Svc. Electric and Gas Co., Newark, 1951-63, Am. Electric Power Svc. Corp., NYC, 1963-68, asst. chief. elec. engr., 1968-69, chief elec. engr., 1969-73, v.p. elec. engr., 1973-82, sr. v.p. elec. engring. Columbus, Ohio, 1982-90, also dir., until

1990; pres. Commonwealth Electric Co., Wareham, Mass., 1990-93, Cambridge (Mass.) Electric Light Co., Canal Electric Co., Com/Steam Co., 1990-93. Bd. dirs. Commonwealth Electric Co., Cambridge Electric Light Co., Com/Steam Co., Commonwealth Svcs. Co., Canal Electric Co.; joint U.S.-USSR working group on power transmission, 1975-81, joint U.S.-Italy working group on power transmission, 1979-88; vice-chmn. Am. Nat. Stds., NYC, 1985-87; v.p. U.S. Nat. Com., 1985-93, pres., 1993-99, chmn. U.S. tech. com. Internat. Conf. on Large High Voltage Electric Sys., 1985-91, internat. adminstrv. coun., 1988-99, internat. exec. com., 1993-99; engring. rev. bd. Bonneville Power Adminstrn., 1984-94; chmn. elec. sys. and equipment com. Edison Electric Inst., 1989-90, pres. power engring. edn. found., 1992-96; chmn. blue-ribbon panel Pacific Coast Blackouts, Bonneville-Power Adminstrn., 1996-97; bd. dirs. NY State Ind. Sys. Operator, 1998-2008, chmn. audit and compliance com., 1998-2006; cons. in field Contbr. articles to profl. jours. Pres. N.J. Jr. C. of C., 1960-61; councilman City of Plainfield, 1963-65; majority leader Plainfield City Coun., 1964-65; mem. Watchung (N.J.) Hills Regional H.S. Bd. Edn., 1970-72; pres. Woods at Josephinum Civic Assn., Worthington, Ohio, 1983-84; trustee, treas. Beech Leaf Landing Trust, 2001-. Recipient Clayton Frost award U.S. Jaycees, 1961, Young Man of Yr. award Plainfield Jaycees, 1963, Lifetime Achievement award T&D Mag., 1990. Fellow IEEE (v.p. power engring. soc. 1988-89, pres. 1990-91, William Habirshaw award for transmission and distbn. engring. 1986, Disting. Mem. award Internat. Conf. on Large High Voltage Electric Systems 1996, Hon. Mem. award Internat. Conf. on Large High Voltage Electric Systems 2000, Philip Sporn award U.S. nat. com. Internat. Conf. on Large High Voltage Electric Systems 2002); mem. NAE, Yale Club N.Y.C., Tau Beta Pi, Beta Gamma Sigma. Home and Office: 467 Bay Ln Centerville MA 02632-3352 Home Phone: 508-775-6516. Personal E-mail: schererhn@aol.com.

SCHERER, JAMES R., research scientist; b. Kansas City, Dec. 31, 1931; s. Oscar Jacob and Anne Marie Scherer. BS, St. Mary's Coll., 1953; PhD, U. Minn., 1958. Rsch. chemist Dow Chem. Co., Midland, Mich., 1958—63, Western Regional Rsch. Lab., USDA, Albany, Calif., 1963—87; sr. staff scientist U. Calif., Berkeley, 1989—2008, part time scientist, 2009—. Contbr. articles to profl. jours. Fellow: Am. Inst. Chemists; mem.: Optical Soc. Am., Am. Chem. Soc. Avocation: fly fishing. Office Phone: 510-418-1776. Business E-Mail: jscherer@zinc.cchem.berkeley.edu.

SCHERER, MARCIA JOSLYN, psychologist, researcher, educator; b. Buffalo, June 9, 1948; d. Alfred John and Marjorie (Greene) J.; m. John Vincent Scherer Jr., Jan. 2, 1976. BS, Syracuse U., NY, 1970; MS, SUNY, Buffalo, 1977; MPH, PhD, U. Rochester, NY, 1986. Cert. rehab. counselor. Editor Mental Health Assn., Buffalo, 1973-80; psychotherapist Erie County Dept. Mental Health, Buffalo, 1980-82; asst. prof. Nat. Tech. Inst. for Deaf, Rochester, NY, 1986-95, assoc. prof., 1995-96; pres., dir. Inst. Matching Person and Tech., Inc., 1997—; dir. consumer evaluations, sr. rsch. assoc. Ctr. Assistive Tech., Occupl. Therapy U. at Buffalo, 1996-98; assoc. prof. phys. medicine and rehab. U. Rochester Med. Ctr., 1997—2008, prof. phys. medicine and rehab., 2008—. Asst. prof. psychology Eastman Sch. Music, Rochester, 1989-95; sr. rsch. assoc. Internat. Ctr. Hearing and Speech Rsch., Rochester, 1989—2007; prof. Rocky Mountain U. Health Professions, 2008-. Author: Communication in the Human Services: A Guide to Therapeutic Journalism, 1980, Living in the State of Stuck, 1993, 4th edit., 2005, Connecting to Learn: Educational and Assistive Technology for People with Disabilities, 2004, (assessment instruments) Assistive Technology Device Predisposition Assessment, 1989, (assessment instrument) Educational Technology Predisposition Assessment, 1990, (assessment instruments) Workplace Technology Predisposition Assessment, 1991, Health Care Technology Predisposition Assessment, 1992, Matching Assistive Technology and Child, 1997, Matching Assistive Technology and Child School Version, 2008, Hearing Tech. Predisposition Assessment, 2004, Cognitive Support Technology Predisposition Assessment, 2007, (CD) Improving The Match Of Person and Technology, 2005; co-author: Assistive Technology in the Workplace, 2006; editor: (book) Assistive Technology: Matching Device and Consumer for Successful Rehabilitation, 2002, (jour.) Disability and Rehabilitation: Assistive Technology, 2005—; co-editor: Psychological Assessment in Medical Rehabilitation, 1995, Evaluating, Selecting and Using Appropriate Assistive Technology, 1996; mem. editl. bd.: Tech. and Disability, 1990—98, Disability and Rehab., 1998—, Assistive Tech., 1996—2003, Spinal Cord Injury Psychosocial Process, 2004—, Rehabilitation Psychology, 2005—07; contbr. articles to profl. jours. Mem. adv. bd. Nat. Ctr. Med. Rehab. Rsch., NIH, 2006—. NIH grantee, 2000, 02, 06, Ctr. Disease Control, 2007; recipient Literary award Rho Chi Sigma, 1984, James Hanson Humanitarian award Grad Sch. Edn. U. Buffalo, 2005. Fellow: APA (treas. Divsn. 22 2001—04), Rehab. Engring. and Assistive Tech. Soc. N.Am. (bd. dirs. 1997—99, fellow 2008), Am. Congress Rehab. Medicine (fellow 2002, sec. 2002—07, Disting. Svc. award 2007); mem.: AAUW (life grantee 1983), Authors League Am. Inc., Authors Guild Inc., Assn. Spinal Cord Injury Psychologists and Social Workers, NY Acad. Scis., Assn. for Advancement of Assistive Tech. in Europe, Australian Rehab. and Assistive Tech. Assn., Am. Bd. Med. Psychotherapy and Psychodiagnosticians, Chi Sigma Iota (life). Methodist. Avocations: creative writing, fossils and minerals. Home and Office: 486 Lake Rd Webster NY 14580-1055 Personal E-mail: impt97@aol.com.

SCHERER, RONALD CALLAWAY, voice scientist, educator; b. Akron, Ohio, Sept. 11, 1945; s. Belden Davis and Lois Ramona (Callaway) S.; children: Christopher, Maria. BS, Kent State U., 1968; MA, Ind. U., 1972; PhD, U. Iowa, 1981. Research asst. U. Iowa, Iowa City, 1979-81, asst. research scientist, 1981-83, adj. asst. prof., 1983-88, adj. assoc. prof., 1988—; adj. asst. prof. U. Denver, 1984-86; asst. adj. prof. U. Colo., Boulder, 1984-93, adj. assoc. prof., 1993-96; rsch. scientist Denver Ctr. Performing Arts, 1983—88, sr. scientist, 1988—96; lectr. voice and speech sci. Nat. Theatre Conservatory, Denver, 1990-94; asst. clin. prof. Sch. Medicine U. Colo., Denver, 1988—96; assoc. prof. Bowling Green State U., Ohio, 1996—2001, prof., 2001—05, 2006—. Adj. assoc. prof. U. Okla., 1992-96; affiliate clin. prof. U. No. Colo., 1993-96; Oberlin Coll. affiliate scholar, 1996—; mem. exec. and legis. bd. Nat. Ctr. Voice and Speech, 1990-96; adj. prof. Drexel U., Phila., 2006-; G. Paul Moore lectr., The Voice Found., 2002; rsch. prof. U. Cin., 2005-06. Author: (with Dr. I. Titze) Vocal Fold Physiology: Biomechanics, Acoustics and Phonatory Control, 1983; contbr. articles to profl. jours. Nat. Inst. Dental Research fellow, 1972-76. Fellow: Internat. Soc. Phonetic Scis. (auditor 1988—91); mem.: Am. Assn. Phonetic Scis. (nominating com. 1985—87, counselor 2000—03, councelor 2000—03), Internat. Assn. Logopedics and Phoniatrics, Acoustical Soc. Am., Am. Speech-Lang.-Hearing Assn., Internat. Arts Medicine Assn., Collegium Medicorum Theatri, Sigma Xi, Pi Mu Epsilon (G. Paul Moore lectr.). Office Phone: 419-372-2515.

SCHERER, VICTOR RICHARD, physicist, computer scientist, musician, consultant; b. Poland, Feb. 7, 1940; came to U.S., 1941; s. Emanuel and Florence B. Scherer; m. Gail R. Dobrofsky, Aug. 11, 1963; children: Helena Cecile, Markus David. BS magna cum laude, CCNY, 1960; MA, Columbia U., 1962; PhD, U. Wis., 1974. Health physics asst. Columbia U., NYC, 1961-63; rsch asst. physics. dep. U. Wis., Madison, 1967-74; project assoc., project mgr. Inst. for Environ. Studies, World Climate-Food Rsch. Group, 1974-78; specialist computer sys. U. Wis. Acad. Computing Ctr., 1978—2008; coord., sr. cons. Divsn. Info. Tech. U. Wis., Madison; concert pianist; tchr.; promoter contemporary composers. Researcher in particle physics, agroclimatology, soil-yield relationships and computer graphics; cons. on computer sys., electronic mail, geographic analysis, help desk and supercomputing applications. Fellow AEC, 1960-61. Mem. AAAS, Am. Phys. Soc., Am. Meteorol. Soc., Am. Soc. Agronomy, Assn. Computing Machinery, Nat. Computer Graphics Assn., Phi Beta Kappa, Sigma Xi. Office: U Wis-Madison Divsn Info Tech 1210 W Dayton St Madison WI 53706-1613 Office Phone: 608-262-3570. Business E-Mail: scherer@doit.wisc.edu.

SCHERGER, JOSEPH EDWARD, family physician, educator; b. Delphos, Ohio, Aug. 29, 1950; m. Carol M. Scherger, Aug. 7, 1973; children: Adrian, Gabriel. BS summa cum laude, U. Dayton, 1971; MD, UCLA, 1975. Family practice residency U. Wash., Seattle, 1975-78; clin. instr. U. Calif. Sch. Medicine, Davis, 1978-80, asst. clin. prof., 1980-84, assoc. clin. prof., 1984-90, clin. prof., 1990—, dir. predoctoral program, 1991-92; med. dir. family practice and community medicine Sharp Healthcare, San Diego, 1992-96; assoc. dean primary care, chair dept. family medicine U. Calif., Irvine, 1996—2001, prof. dept. family medicine, 1996—2001, prof. family and preventive medicine San Diego, 2003—; dean Fla. State U., Coll. Medicine, Tallahassee, 2001—03; v.p. primary care Eisenhower Med. Ctr. Med. dir. AmeriChoice, 2006—09; consulting med. dir. Lumetra, 2007—. Editor (in chief): (med. jour.) Hippocrates. Recipeient Hippocratic Oath award UCLA, Calif. Physician of Yr. award Am. Acad. Family Physicians. Mem. NAS (mem. Inst. Medicine), Am. Acad. Family Physicians, Soc. Tchrs. Family Medicine. Office Fax: 760-674-3629. Business E-Mail: jscherger@emc.org.

SCHERICH, EDWARD BAPTISTE, retired diversified company executive; b. Inland, Nebr., Dec. 3, 1923; s. Clarence H. and Clara E. (Baptiste) S.; m. Hyacinth Rau, Aug. 11, 1945 (div. 1980); children: Carol, Eileen, John.; m. Antoinette Currera, 1981; 1 stepdau., Sylvia McNamara. BBA, Tulane U., 1948. Acct. Colo. Milling & Elevator Co., Denver, 1948-50; accountant, office mgr. Southdown, Inc., New Orleans, 1950-55, controller, 1955-69; v.p. finance, sec., treas. Southdown Sugars Inc., New Orleans, 1970-73; v.p., sec., treas. Southdown Land Co., New Orleans, 1971-75; sec.-treas. Southdown, Inc., Houston, 1975-78, v.p., sec., 1979-84, treas., 1980-83; ind. fin. cons., 1984—2008; pres. Valmax Inc., 1989—2008. Served in USNR, 1943-45. Mem. Beta Gamma Sigma. Home: 633 Brouilly Dr Kenner LA 70065-1101

SCHERLER, KATHY LOUISE, music educator, researcher; b. Oklahoma City, Aug. 17, 1958; d. Jimmie Mack Cosby and Avis Norvell Cosby (Bailey); m. David Kent Scherler, Jr., Aug. 5, 1978; children: David Kent III, Kale Cosby. BA, Cameron U., 1980; MusM, Tex. A & M, 1982; PhD in Music Edn., U. No. Tex., 2005. Mid. sch. choral dir. Hugo Jr. HS, Okla., 1980—81; choral dir. Valliant HS, Okla., 1981—83; music tchr. Wilson Elem. Sch., Bartlesville, Okla., 1988—90; choral dir. North Lamar HS, Paris, Tex., 1990—94; adj. prof. music Dallas Bapt. U., 1995—2000; tchg. fellow U. North Tex., Denton, 1996—98; music tchr. Walnut Hill Elem. Sch., Dallas, 1998—99; mid. sch. choral dir. Sam Houston Mid. Sch., Irving, Tex., 1999—2001; HS choral dir. Grapevine HS, Grapevine, Tex., 2001—02; asst. prof. music Midwestern State U., Wichita Falls, Tex., 2004—. Author: (jour. article) Southwestern Musician; dir.: (conducted chorus and orch.) Messiah by Handel; musician: (voice recital) Les Filles de Cadix by Leo Delibes, (soprano soloist) Gloria by Vivaldi, Merry Wives of Windsor by Otto Nicolai, Trial by Jury by Gilbert and Sullivan, Help, Help the Globolinks by Menotti, The Prodigal Son by Debussy; author: (paper presentation) 19th Ann. Conf. on Interdisciplinary Qualitative Studies; musician (and lectr.): (recital) Coll. Music Soc., So. Ctrl. chpt., Midwestern State U. Faculty Forum; dir.(co-dir.): (opera) Die Fledermaus; musician: (voice recital) U. North Tex., Dallas Bapt. U., Der Hirt auf dem Felsen, by Schumann. Accompanist Meml. Bapt. Ch., Grapevine, Tex., 2000—06. Recipient Okla. All State Choir, 1974—76, winner Sweepstakes Choral Competition, U. Interscholastic League, 1994, Superior Ratings: Grapevine High Choir, 2001—02, music scholarship, Cameron U., Lawton, Okla., 1976—79, Best Actress award, Okla. Theater Ctr., 1976, Best in Class for Superior Ratings, Blue Bonnet Choral Festival, 2002; finalist, Nat. Assn. Tchrs. of Singing, 1987; grantee, Midwestern State U. Fine Arts Dept., 2005. Mem.: Tex. Assn. Coll. Tchrs., Coll. Music Soc., Am. Choral Dirs. Assn., Phi Delta Kappa, Tex. Music Educators Assn., Nat. Assn. Tchrs. of Singing, Music Educators Nat. Conf. Office: Midwestern State U 3410 Taft Blvd Wichita Falls TX 76308-2099 Home: 121 Mustang Springs Sunset TX 76270 Business E-Mail: kathy.scherler@mwsu.edu.

SCHERR, BARRY PAUL, foreign language educator; b. Hartford, Conn., May 20, 1945; s. Joseph and Helen Lillian (Shapiro) S.; m. Sylvia Egelman, Sept. 8, 1974; children: Sonia, David. AB magna cum laude, Harvard U., 1966; AM, U. Chgo., 1967, PhD, 1973. From acting asst. prof. to asst. prof. U. Washington, Seattle, 1970-74; from asst. prof. to prof. Russian, Dartmouth Coll., Hanover, NH, 1974—, chmn. dept. Russian, 1981-90, 96-97, chmn. program linguistics and cognitive sci., 1989-96, assoc. dean for humanities, 1997—2001, assoc. provost, 2001, provost, 2001—. Co-organizer Internat. Conf. Russian Verse Theory, 1987, Internat. Conf. Anna Akhmatova and the Poets of Tsarskoe Selo, 1989, Internat. Conf. Eisenstein at 100: A Reconsideration, 1998. Author: Russian Poetry: Meter, Rhythm and Rhyme, 1986, Maxim Gorky, 1988; co-author The Shining World: Exploring Aleksandr Grin's Grinlandia, 2007; co-trans. The Seeker of Adventure, Alexander Grin, 1989; mem. editorial bd. Slavic and East European Jour., 1978-88; co-editor: Russian Verse Theory: Procs. of the 1987 Conference at UCLA, 1987, O RUS! Studia litteraria Slavica in honorem Hugh McLean, 1995, A Sense of Place: Tsarskoe Selo and Its Poets, 1993, Twentieth-Century Russian Literature, 2000, Eisenstein at 100: A Reconsideration, 2001; co-translator, co-editor Maksim Gorky: Selected Letters, 1997; contbr. articles to profl. jours. Scholar Harvard Coll., 1963-66; fellow NDEA, 1966-69; grantee Internat. Rsch. and Exch. Bd., 1969-70, NEH, 1987, 89, U.S. Dept. Edn., 1987-89, Dartmouth Coll. Sr. Faculty, 1988; summer rsch. grantee Grad. Sch., Inst. Comparative and Fgn. Area Studies U. Wash., 1973. Mem. MLA (mem. exec. com. assoc. dept. fgn. langs. 1983-85, del. assembly 1986-88, Scaglione Book prize, selection com., 2007-), Am. Assn. Advancement Slavic Studies, Am. Assn. Tchrs. Slavic and East European Langs. (pres. 1987-88, founder, past pres. No. New Eng. chpt., numerous coms.). Office: Dartmouth Coll Russian Dept Reed Hall Hanover NH 03755-3506 Office Phone: 603-646-2070. Business E-Mail: Barry.scherr@Dartmouth.edu.

SCHERR, BERNARD, music educator; m. Donna Scherr; 1 child, Scherr Jonathan. PhD, U. Oreg., Eugene. Assoc. prof. music Hardin Simmons U., Abilene, Tex., 2000—. Home: 282 Sanford Ln Abilene TX 79602 Office: Hardin Simmons Univ 2200 Hickory St Abilene TX 79698 Business E-Mail: bscherr@hsutx.edu.

SCHERR, LAWRENCE, internist, healthcare educator, historian; b. NYC, Nov. 6, 1928; s. Harry and Sophia (Schwartz) S.; m. Peggy L. Binenkorb, June 13, 1954; children: Cynthia E., Robert W. AB, Cornell U., 1950, MD, 1957; DSc (hon.), Long Island U., 1990, North Shore-LIJ Health Sys. Grad Sch., 2004. Diplomate Am. Bd. Internal Medicine (bd. dirs., sec.-treas. 1979-86). Intern Cornell Med. divsn. Bellevue Hosp. and Meml. Ctr., NY, 1957-58, asst. resident, 1958-59, rsch. fellow cardiorenal lab., 1959-60, chief resident, 1960-61, co-dir. cardiorenal lab., 1961-62, asst. vis. physician, 1961-63, assoc. vis. physician, 1963-65, dir. cardiology and renal unit, 1963-67, assoc. dir., 1964-67, vis. physician, 1966-68; physician to out-patients NY Hosp., 1961-63, asst. attending physician, 1963-66, assoc. attending physician, 1966-71, attending physician, 1971-2000; asst. attending physician, cons. Sloan-Kettering Cancer Ctr., 1962—2000. Chmn. dept. medicine North Shore Univ. Hosp., 1967-01, chmn. emeritus, 2001-, dir. acad. affairs, 1969-93, sr. v.p. med. affairs, 1993-00; exec v.p. med. and acad. affairs North Shore-LI Jewish Health Sys., 1998-00, trustee, 2000—, chief acad. officer, sr. v.p. acad. affairs, 2000-05, Betsey Cushing Whitney acad. dean emeritus, historian, 2005—; asst. in medicine Med. Coll. Cornell U., 1958-59; rsch. fellow NY Heart Assn., 1959-60; instr. medicine Cornell U. Med. Coll., 1960-63, asst. prof., 1963-66, assoc. prof., 1966-71, David J. Greene disting. prof. medicine Weill Cornell Coll. Medicine, 1971-96, assoc. dean, 1969-96, Betsey Cushing Whitney prof. emeritus medicine, 2006-; prof. medicine NYU Sch. Medicine, 1996-05; career scientist Health Rsch. Coun., NYC, 1962-66; tchg. scholar Am. Heart Assn., 1966-67; pres. NY State Bd. Medicine, 1974-75; chmn. Accreditation Coun. for Grad. Med. Edn., 1988, NY State Coun. on Grad. Edn., 1990-92, with Korean Warfare Amphibious Force US Navy, 1950-53. Contbr. articles to profl. jours. Mem. US White House Rev. Coun., Nat. Health Policy devel., 1993. Combat officer USN, 1950—53, Korea. Decorated NY State Conspicuous Svc. medal, Korean Pres. Unit Citation for Meritorious Svc. Fellow NY Acad. Medicine, Am. Heart Assn. (coun. on clin. cardiology); master ACP (chmn. and gov. Downstate NY region II 1975-80, regent 1980-86, chmn. bd. regents 1985-86, chmn. bd. regents emeritus, nat. pres. 1987-88, pres. emeritus, Alfred Stengel Meml. medal); mem. AMA, Am. Fedn. Clin. Rsch., Harvey Soc., NY Med. Soc., Nassau County Med. Soc., Assn. Am. Med. Colls., Am. Clin. and Climatologic Assn., Fed. Law Enforcement Found. (Cmty. Svc. award, 2008), Am. Coun. Grad. Med. Edn.(chmn. 1987), Am. Bd. Internat. Medicine(Sec. Treasured bd. 1984-86). Office: N Shore LIJ Health Sys 125 Community Dr Great Neck NY 11021-5502 Office Phone: 516-465-2536. Business E-Mail: scherr@nshs.edu.

SCHERRE, CLARE R., diversified financial services company executive; BA, Harvard Coll., Cambridge, Mass., 1992; MBA, Harvard U. Bus. Sch., 1996. Summer assoc. Goldman Sachs & Co., NYC, 1995, full-time assoc., 1996—99, bus. unit mgr., corp. fin. and high tech. depts., 1991—2001, mergers and strategic adv. group, 2001—02, sector captain gen. industrials, industrials & natural resources dept., 2002—03, mng. dir. industrials group, 2003—, ptnr., 2006—. Active Liberty Sci. Ctr., Jersey City. Named one of Top 25 Nonbank Women in Fin., US Banker, 2008. Office: Goldman Sachs & Co 85 Broad St New York NY 10004*

SCHERRER, DEBORAH KING, computer scientist, educational association administrator; b. LA, Apr. 28, 1946; d. Archie W. and Frances M. (Weibel) King; m. Philip H. Scherrer, June 24, 1967; children: Amanda Kathrine, Benjamin Douglas. BA, U. Calif. Berkeley, 1968, postgrad., 1968-70. Computer scientist, sci. programmer Lawrence Berkeley Lab., Calif., 1973-84; pres., software engr., project mgr. Mt. Xinu, Inc., Berkeley, 1984-94; EPO project mgr. Stanford U., Palo Alto, Calif., 1996—98; mgr. Software Automation Group, Transmeta, 1998—2002, dir. EPO Stanford, Calif., 2002—. Sci. programmer Crimean Astrophys. Observatory, Crimea, USSR, summer 1975; pres. Carousel MicroTools, El Cerrito, Calif., 1982-84; chair AM. Geophysical Union Space Physics and Aeronomy Edn. com., 2006—. Editl. adv. bd. Computing Sys. jour., 1988-96; editl. rev. bd. Unix Rev. mag., 1984-96; contbg. editor Unix, World mag., 1982-84; mem. editl. bd. Computer mag., 1995—; contbr. articles to profl. jours. Participant Project Astro Astron. Soc. of Pacific, Castro Valley, 1992—; project leader Astronomy 4-H, Castro Valley, 1990—; pres., bd. dirs. Palomares Canyon Homeowners Assn., Castro Valley, 1993—. Recipient Acad. Driver award Unix Sys. Lab., 1993. Mem. IEEE Computing Soc. (tech. adv. bd. 1992—, bd. govs. 1997—, v.p. 2000—, mem. ednl. activities bd.), Usenix Assn. (pres., bd. dirs. 1980-92, Lifetime Achievement award 1996), Assn. Computing Machinery, Tri-Valley Stargazers. Avocations: astronomy, conservation activities. Home: 30261 Palomares Rd Castro Valley CA 94552-9638

SCHERZER, ALFRED L., developmental pediatrician; s. Morris Scherzer and Elizabeth Levitch; children: Elizabeth S. Herbster, Andrea L., Martha E. MSPH, Columbia U. Sch. Pub. Health, NYC, 1950; EdD, Tchrs. Coll., Columbia U., 1954; MD, Columbia U. Coll. Physicians and Surgeons, 1963; MA in Med. Sociology, Yale U., New Haven, 1957. Diplomate Am. Bd. Pediat., 1969. Emeritus clin. prof. pediat. Weill-Cornell U. Med. Coll., NYC, 1963—94; clin. prof. pediat. and preventive medicine SUNY, Sch. Medicine, Stony Brook, 2005—. Med. dir. NYC Bd. Edn., Divsn. Spl. Edn., 1970—95; pres. Am. Acad. for Cerebral Palsy and Devel. Medicine, 1985—86. Contbr. articles to profl. jour. Achievements include research in early diagnosis of development and childhood disability in the developing world. Office: Stony Brook Children's Svc 15 W 2nd St Riverhead NY 11901

SCHETTLER, PAUL D., chemistry professor; b. Salt Lake City, Mar. 31, 1937; m. Karen Hegsted, Feb. 11, 1965. PhD, Yale U., Conn., 1963. Postdoc. fellow U. Utah, Salt Lake City, 1963—64, Antioch Coll., Yellow Springs, Ohio, 1966—67; prof., chemistry Juniata Coll., Huntingdon, Pa., 1967—. Home: 11274 Standing Stone RD Huntingdon PA 16652 Office: Juniata Coll 1700 Moore St Huntingdon PA 16652 Office Fax: 814-641-3685. Business E-Mail: schettler@juniata.edu.

SCHETZ, JOSEPH ALFRED, aerospace engineer, educator; b. Orange, NJ, Oct. 19, 1936; s. Alfred John and Teresa (Zappa) S.; m. Katherine Frances Giorgianni, Jan. 31, 1959; children: Holly, Joseph, Katherine, John. BS, Webb Inst. Naval Architecture, 1958; MS, MA, PhD, Princeton U. Sr. scientist Gen. Applied Sci. Lab., Westbury, NY, 1961-64; assoc. prof. aerospace engring. U. Md., 1964-69; Fred D. Durham chair aerospace and ocean engring. Va. Poly. Inst. and State U., Blacksburg, 1999—, chmn. dept., 1969-93. Cons. Applied Physics Lab., Johns Hopkins, 1964-96, Atlantic Rsch. Corp., Alexandria, Va., 1966-72, Du Pont Corp., Richmond, Va., 1980-85; guest prof. Inst. for Theoretical Gas Dynamics, Aachen, Germany, summer 1970; religious edn. tchr. St. John's Roman Cath. Ch., Colesville, Md., 1965-69; prin. H.S. religion St. Mary's Roman Cath. Ch., Blacksburg, 1970-71; vis. scholar Beijing Rsch. Lab., 1985; vis. scientist Wright Labs., Dayton, Ohio, 1993. Author books; contbr. chpts. to books; contbr. articles to profl. jours. Republican precinct chmn., Montgomery County, Md., 1965-69; mem. Rep. Exec. Com., 1973-86; faculty adviser Va. Poly. Inst. Rep. Club, 1973-76. Fellow AIAA (assoc. editor jour. 1975-77, editor-in-chief edn. book series, publs. com. 1978-84, edn. com. 1978-81, air breathing propulsion tech. com. 1994-97, Pendray Aerospace Lit. award 1997, Air

Breathing Propulsion Tech. award 1998, Aerospace Contbn. to Soc. award 1999, J. Leland Atwood award 2004), ASME (life); mem. Soc. Naval Architects and Marine Engrs., Sigma Gamma Tau, Tau Beta Pi, Sigma Xi. Home: 607 Rainbow Ridge Dr Blacksburg VA 24060-5535 Office Phone: 540-231-9056. E-mail: ptiger@vt.edu.

SCHEUERMAN, WILLIAM E., academic administrator, political science professor; m. Louise Scheuerman; 3 children. Grad., CUNY, PhD in Polit. Economy. Prof. polit. sci. SUNY, Oswego; pres. Nat. Labor Coll., Silver Spring, Md., 2008—. Chair NY State Pub. Higher Edn. Conf. Bd. Author: The Steel Crisis, 1986; co-author (with Sid Plotkin): Private Interests, Public Spending, 1994; contbr. articles to profl. jours. Mem.: United Univ. Professions (pres. 1993—2007, v.p. academics, chief negotiator 1988—91). Office: Nat Labor Coll George Meany Campus 10000 New Hampshire Ave Silver Spring MD 20903 Office Phone: 301-431-6400. Office Fax: 301-431-5411.

SCHEUNEMANN, RANDY (RANDALL J. SCHEUNEMANN), lobbyist; b. 1960; s. Paul and Gladys Scheunemann; m. Patricia Scheunemann. BA, U. Minn., 1982. Nat. security advisor Senator Bob Dole, Kans., 1993—96, sr. advisor Kans., 1996; mem. Rep. Platform Com., 1996; nat. security advisor Senator Trent Lott, Miss., 1997—99; dir. Project for the New Am. Century, 1997—; pres. Mercury Group, Inc., Alexandria, Va., 1998; founder, pres. Orion Strategies LLC, Washington, 2001—; def. and fgn. policy coord. John McCain Presdl. Campaign, 1999—2000, chief fgn. policy aide, 2007—08; cons. Office of the Secretary of Defense, 2001; founder, pres., exec. dir. Com. for the Liberation of Iraq, 2002—03. Office: Orion Strategies 918 Pennsylvania Ave SE Washington DC 20003-2140*

SCHEXNAYDER, CHARLOTTE TILLAR, state legislator; b. Tillar, Ark., Dec. 25, 1923; d. Jewell Stephen and Bertha (Terry) Tillar; m. Melvin John Schexnayder Sr., Aug. 18, 1946; children: M. John Jr., Sarah Holden, Stephen. BA, La. State U., Shreveport, 1944, postgrad., 1947—48. Asst. editor La. Agrl. Extension, Baton Rouge, 1944; editor The McGehee (Ark.) Times, 1945-46, 48-53; editor, co-publisher The Dumas (Ark.) Clarion, 1954-85, pub., 1985-99; mem. Ark. Ho. of Reps., Little Rock, 1985-99, asst. speaker pro tem, 1995—. Pres. Ark. Assn. Women, 1955, Nat. Newspaper Assn., Washington, 1991-92, Ark. Press Assn., Little Rock, 1982, Nat. Fedn. Press Women, Blue Springs, Mo., 1977-78, Litte Rock chpt. Soc. Profl. Journalists, 1973; mem. pres.'s coun. Winrock Internat., 1990—; chmn. Dumas Area Cmty. Found., 2000-02; pres. Main Street Dumas. Editor: Images of the Past, 1991. 1st woman mem. Ark. Bd. Pardons and Parole, 1975-80; mem. Ark. Legis. Coun., 1985-92; bd. dirs. Women's Found. Ark., sec. 1999—; bd. dirs. Chicot-Desha Port Indsl. Com.; v.p. Desha County Mus., 1989—; dir. Dumas Indsl. Found., 1986—; exec. com. Ark. Ctrl. Radiation Therapy Inst., 1991-92; mem. adv. bd. Ark. Profl. Women Achievement, 1992—; vice chair Ark. Rural Devel. Commn., 1991-96, chair 1996-97; mem. Winrock Internat. Adv. Coun., 1991—; founding incorporator Ark. Waterways Commn., 1996—, bd. dirs.; bd. visitors Manship Sch. Comm., La. State U., 1998—; bd. dirs. Main Street Ark., Hist. Preservation Alliance Ark.; active Ark. Transitional Employment Coun., 1999—, Ark. Transitional Employment Assistance Bd., 2000; sec. Dumas Area Cmty. Fund, 2000—; bd. dirs. Enterprise Corp. for the Delta, 1999-2002, Dumas Main St., v.p.; bd. dirs. Historic Preservation Alliance Ark, 2000—; outstanding bd. mem. Ark. Main St., 2002; outstanding bd. chair Ark. Cmty. Found., 2003. Named Disting. Alumnus Ark. A&M Coll., 1971, Woman of Achievement Nat. Fedn. Press Women, 1970, Outstanding Arkansan C. of C., 1986; recipient Ark. Profl. Women of Distinction award No. Bank, Little Rock, 1990, Emma McKinney award Nation's Top Cmty. Newspaper Woman, 1980, Journalist award Nat. Conf. of Christians and Jews, 1989, Lifetime Achievement award Nat. Fedn. Press Women, 1992, Outstanding Svc. award Ark. Assn. Elem. Prins., Disting. Svc. award Ark. Press Assn., 1993, Disting. Svc. award Internat. Soc. Weekly Newspaper Editors, 1996, Golden Svc. award Ark. Press Assn., 1996, State Leadership award Ark. Waterways Commn., 1996, Horizon award League Women Voters Ark., 1998 Ernie Deane award U. Ark., 2005, Chilcote award Ark. Cmty. Found., 2006; named to La. State U. Alumni Hall of Distinction, 1994, Journalism Hall of Fame La. State U., 1998; named one Top 100 Ark. Women, Ark. Bus., 1995-98; named Outstanding Bd. Mem. of Yr., Main Street Ark., 2002, Outstanding Bd. Mem., Ptnrs. of Ark. Cmty. Found., 2003, Extraordinary Svc. award Ark. Cmty. Found., 2006; honored Outstanding Svc. Women's Found. Ark., 2003. Mem.: Main St. Dumas (pres. 2005), Ark. Delta Coun. (chmn., pres. Dumas Main St., mem. Main St. Ark. adv. bd.), Pi Beta Phi (Crest award 1992). Democrat. Roman Catholic. Home Phone: 870-382-5255. Personal E-mail: cschexnayder@centurytel.net.

SCHEXNIDER, VIRGINIA REEVES, school psychologist; d. Curtis Reeves Sr. and Virginia Cundiff Reeves; m. Alvin James Schexnider, July 1, 1978; children: Alvin James, Elena Cundiff. BA, Fisk U., Nashville, 1975; MA, U. Va., Charlottesville, 1978. Dir. student assessment ctr. Va. State U., Petersburg, 1980—81; sch. psychologist Richmond City Pub. Schs., Richmond, 1993—96; lic. sch. psychologist Winston-Salem/Forsyth County Pub. Schs., NC, 1996—2002; cert. sch. psychologist Va. Beach City Pub. Schs., 2002—. Directorship The Richmond Symphony, 1989—94, Reynolda Ho. Mus. of Am. Art, Winston-Salem, NC, 1997—2003. Mem.: NASP (assoc.), Va. Acad. Sch. Psychologists (assoc.), Fisk U. Alumni Assn. (life), U. Va. Alumni Assn. (life), Phi Beta Kappa.

SCHEYER, DANIEL, lawyer; b. Bklyn., May 13, 1928; s. Emanuel and Clara (Cohen) S.; m. Audrey C. Deutsch, July 27, 1950; children: Lawrence, Richard. AB, NYU, 1947; JD, Columbia U., 1950. Bar: N.Y. 1950. Assoc. Carb, Luria, Glassner, Cook & Kufeld, NYC, 1957-66; ptnr., 1966—99, counsel, 1999—2005; pvt. practice Port Washington, NY, 2005—. Mem., chmn. Bd. Zoning and Appeals, Village of Sands Point, N.Y., 1987-94, trustee, 1994—. Lt. col. USAR. Fellow Am. Coll. Trust and Estate Counsel; mem. ABA, NY State Bar Assn., NY City Bar Assn., Manhasset Bay Yacht Club. Home Phone: 516-883-9029; Office Phone: 516-883-9029. Personal E-mail: dscheyer@verizon.net.

SCHEYER, ERIC TODD, dentist, periodontist, surgeon, educator; b. Exeter, NH, Nov. 2, 1970; s. Fredrick Dougal Scheyer and Lorna Marie Robinson; m. Stephanie Rae Nielsen, Aug. 31, 2001; 1 child, Ella Sophia. BS in Biology, Ariz. State U., Tempe, 1993; DDS magna cum laude, Med. Coll. Va., Richmond, 1998; cert. in periodontics, U. Tex. Health Sci. Ctr., San Antonio, 2001. Lic. in periodontics U. Tex. Health Sci. Ctr., 2001. Periodontics and implant dentist Perio Health Profls., Houston, 2001—; asst. clin. prof. U. Tex. Dental Br., Houston, 2002—. Rschr., lectr. Perio Health Clin. Rsch. Ctr., Houston, 2001—; guest. lectr. U. Tex. Health Sci. Ctr., San Antonio. Contbr. peer reviewed publs. to profl. jours. Active biking and triathlon events for cancer and MS. Grantee, Am. Cancer Soc. Mem.: ADA, Perio Health Implant Study Group, Soc. Contemporary and Progressive Periodontics, Greater Houston Dental Soc., Acad. Osseointegration, Houston Soc. Periodontist, Internat. Congress Oral Implantologists, Am. Acad. Periodontology, SW Soc. Periodontists (John F. Prichard award 2001). R-Conservative. Achievements include research in tissue engineering. Avocations: mountain and road biking, fishing, skiing. Office: Perio Health Profls 3400 So Gessner Rd Ste 102 Houston TX 77063 Office Phone: 713-783-5442. Office Fax: 713-952-0614. Business E-Mail: etsperio@swbell.net, info@periohealth.com.

SCHIANO, GREG, college football coach; b. Wyckoff, NJ, June 1, 1966; m. Christy Schiano; 4 children. Grad., Bucknell U. Grad. asst. Rutgers U., 1989—90; defensive backs coach Penn St. U., 1991—95; defensive asst. Chgo. Bears, 1996—97, defensive backfield coach, 1998; defensive coord. U. Miami, 1999—2000; head football coach Rutgers U., New Brunswick, NJ, 2000—, defensive coord., 2005—. Recipient Coach of Yr., Liberty Mutual, 2006; named Big East Coach of Yr., 2006, Nat. Coach of Yr., Home Depot, 2006, Coach of Yr., Walter Camp Football Found., 2006. Achievements include leading Rutgers football to first ever win against top 5 opponent, 2006. Office: Rutgers U Dept Athletics Louis Brown Athletic Ctr 83 Rockafeller Rd Piscataway NJ 08854

SCHIANO, THOMAS DOMINIC, hepatologist, director; s. Dominic Anthony and Elizabeth Marie Schiano. MD, Universidad Del Noreste, Tampico, Mexico, 1987. Cert. medicine NY, 1990, bd. cert. in internal medicine, gastroenteology, clin. nutrition, transplant hepatology. Med. dir. liver transplantation Mt Sinai Med. Ctr., NYC, 2003—. Home: 225 E 95th st apt 19G New York NY 10128 Office: The mount sinai med ctr 19 E 98th St New York NY 10029 Office Fax: 212-241-2138. Business E-Mail: thomas.schiano@msnyuhealth.org.

SCHIAPPA, DAVID S., legislative staff member; b. Washington, Nov. 3, 1962; married; 2 children. Grad., U. Md., 1984; student, Johns Hopkins U. Sch. Profl. Studies in Bus. & Edn. Began work in Rep. Cloakroom US Senate, Washington, 1984, Rep. fl. asst., 1994—96, asst. sec. for majority, 1996—2001, sec. for minority, 2001—03, 2007—, sec. for majority, 2003—07. Republican. Office: US Senate Capitol Bldg S 337 Washington DC 20510*

SCHICK, BARBARA JEAN, medical technician, educator; d. Earl Walter and Anna Mae Schick. BS in Med. Tech., Lycoming Coll., Williamsport, 1957. Cert. in MT ASCP, 1956. Generalist med. technologist Meml. Med. Ctr., Williamson, W.Va., 1957—60, Williamsport Hosp., 1961—63, Habersham County Med. Ctr., Demorest, 1994—; instr. med. lab North Ga. Tech. Vocat. Sch., Clarkesville, 1963—71; med lab mgr. Newnan Hosp., Ga., 1971—76, Habersham County Hosp., Demorest, Ga., 1976—80; chem. quality assurance technician Ethicon, Inc., Cornelia, Ga., 1981—94. Adj. instr. North Ga. Tech. Coll., Clarkesville, 2002—. Mem.: Cir. Hope Domestic Violence Shelter (past pres.). Episcopalian. Home: 464 Oakey Mountain Rd Clarkesville GA 30523-1219 Office: Habersham County Med Ctr Historic 441 N Demorest GA 30535 Business E-Mail: bschick@windstream.net.

SCHICK, EDGAR BREHOB, language educator; b. Phila., June 28, 1934; s. Claude Ernest and Martha Henrietta (Brehob) S.; m. Margaret Barbara Buehl, Feb. 12, 1938; children: Susanne, Christina. AB magna cum laude, Muhlenberg Coll., 1955; MA, Rutgers U., 1962, PhD, 1965. Asst. prof. German SUNY, Binghamton, 1963-68, asst. to pres. Albany, 1968-72, asst. prof., 1968-72; v.p. acad. affairs St. John Fisher Coll., Rochester, NY, 1972-78, exec. v.p., 1978-80, assoc. prof., 1972-80; pres. Nasson Coll., Springvale, Maine, 1980-83; provost, v.p. acad. affairs, prof. Eastern Ill. U., Charleston, 1984-87; exec. dir. Bd. Trustees, Md. State Univs. & Colls., Annapolis, 1987-88; vice chancellor for policy and planning U. Md. System, Adelphi, 1988-91; sr. fellow Am. Assn. State Colls. and Univs., 1991-94; cons. Assn. Governing Bds., 1993-95; interim v.p., dean St. Mary Coll., Lawrence, Kans., 1997-98; pres. Luther Inst., Washington, 1998—2003, pres. emeritus, 2003—; interim provost, v.p. Acad. Affairs Manhattanville Coll., Purchase, NY, 2008—. Chmn. visitation team Mid. States Assn. Colls. and Schs., Phila., 1975-79; cons. IBM, Yorkville, N.Y., 1968, Nat. Luth. Campus Ministry, 1968-85, USAID, 1992-95. Author: Metaphorical Organicism in the Early Herder, 1971, Shared Visions of Public Higher Education Governance: Structures and Leadership Styles That Work, 1992, The "Local Board" in Multi-Campus Public Universities, 1994; contbr. articles on German lit. and higher edn. to profl. jours. Bd. dirs. United Way, 1981-82, Maine Ind. Colls. Assn., 1981-93, Deaton Hosp., Balt.; v.p. Christ Luth. Ch. Found., Balt.; mem. Accreditation Bd. for Engring. Tech.; pres. Oakleigh Forest Civic Assn. Grantee, Carnegie Found.; fellow Univ. fellow, Rutgers U., New Brunswick, N.Y., 1962—63. Mem. Am. Assn. Higher Edn., Am. Assn. Univ. Adminstrs., Registry for Coll. and Univs. Presidents, Am. Assn. State Colls. and Univs., Am. Assn. Tchrs. German, Assn. for Instl. Rsch., Soc. for Coll. and Univ. Planning, Thomas Mann Soc., Nat. Soc. Fund-Raising Execs. Lutheran. Home: 106 Quinn Rd Severna Park MD 21146-3015 Personal E-mail: ebschick@verizon.net.

SCHICK, HARRY LEON, investment company executive; b. NYC, Oct. 24, 1927; s. Martin and Sadie (Spitz) S.; m. Eleanor Alter, Oct. 17, 1982; m. Inge Nussbaum, Oct. 12, 1964 (div. Nov. 1971); 1 child, Susan. AB magna cum laude, Bklyn. Coll., 1947; MS, Columbia U., NYC, 1948; postgrad., NYU, 1948-52. Securities analyst Sutro Bros., NYC, 1948-52; asst. to pres. Clairdale Enterprises, Inc., NYC, 1953-66; mgr. arbitrage dept. First Manhattan Co., NYC, 1966-69, gen. ptnr., 1969-91, mng. dir., 1992—. Lectr. Donaldson Sch. Orgn. and Mgmt., Yale U., New Haven, 1978-88, NYU Grad. Sch. Bus. Adminstrn., NYC, 1977; lectr. in field. Trustee Washington Inst. for Near East Rsch. Mem. Inst. Chartered Fin. Analysts, Am. Fin. Assn., Am. Econ. Assn., N.Y. Soc. Security Analysts (bd. dirs. 1975-76), Beta Gamma Sigma. Jewish. Home: 215 E 68th St Apt 15Y New York NY 10065 Office: First Manhattan Co 437 Madison Ave New York NY 10022-7001 Home Phone: 212-988-4573; Office Phone: 212-756-3350. Business E-Mail: hschick@firstmanhattan.com.

SCHICK, ROBERT MICHAEL, lawyer; b. Elizabeth, NJ, Oct. 3, 1954; s. Donald E. and Virginia (Dotterweich) S.; m. Shelley Woodward, May 26, 1979; children: Cameron, Catherine. AB, Princeton U., 1976; JD, U. Houston, 1981. Bar: Tex. 1981, U.S. Dist. Ct. (so. dist.) 1981, U.S. Dist. Ct. (ea. dist.) 1995, U.S. Dist. Ct. (no. dist.) 2005, U.S. Dist. Ct. (we. dist.) 2006, cert.: Tex. Bd. Legal Specialization (civil trial law), Tex. Bd. Legal Specialization (personal injury trial law). Assoc. Vinson & Elkins LLP, Houston, 1981-88, ptnr., 1989—, co-head Litig. Sect. Fellow: Am. Coll. Trial Lawyers, Tex. Bar Found.; mem.: Product Liability Adv. Coun. Office: Vinsons & Elkins LLP First City Tower 1001 Fannin St Ste 2500 Houston TX 77002-6706 Office Phone: 713-654-4582. Business E-Mail: rschick@velaw.com.

SCHICK, THOMAS, diversified financial services company executive; Sr. exec. v.p. Shearson Lehman Brothers, 1986—92; exec. v.p. pub. affairs and comms. Travel Related Svcs. sub. Am. Express, 1992—93, Am. Express Co., 1993—. Office: Am Express Co World Fin Ctr 200 Vesey St New York NY 10285*

SCHICKLI, JEANNE HLAVKA, virologist, researcher; BA in Biology, Carleton Coll., Northfield, Minn., 1975; MS in Chem. Engring., Yale U., New Haven, 1981; PhD in Microbiology, U. Colo., Denver, 2000. Sr. scientist Medimmune, Inc., Mountain View, Calif., 2002—. Contbr. articles to profl. jours. Achievements include patents pending for variant of human metapneumovirus. Office: Medimmune Inc 297 N Bernardo Ave Mountain View CA 94043

SCHICKMAN, MARK ISAAC, lawyer; b. Teaneck, NJ, Mar. 17, 1951; AB with honors, Columbia U., 1971, JD, 1974. Bar: Calif. 1974. Mem. Fox and Grove, San Francisco; ptnr. Freeland Cooper & Foreman LLP, San Francisco. Past chair Calif. Jud. Nominees Evaluation Commn. V.p. Am. Jewish Congress, 1977; bd. dirs. San Francisco Vol. Legal Svcs. Project, 1979-82; sec. Jewish Cmty. Rels. Coun., 1991, vice chair, 1993—, active, 1977—; chair Jewish Pub. Affairs Com. Calif., 1986-90. Mem. ABA (mem. exec. coun. young lawyers divsn. 1981-82, assembly clk. 1982-83, assembly spkr. 1983-84, house dels. 1984-87, mem. coun. sect. individual rights and responsibilities 1983-87, vice chair labor law com. gen. practice sect., hair labor law com. gen. practice sect. 1994—, vice chair TIPS employer-employee com. 1991—, bd. govs. 14th dist. 2009-), State Bar Calif. (mem. human rights com. 1980-82, bd. govs. 1963-64), Bar Assn. San Francisco (bd. dirs. 1978-79, 86-88, chair exec. com. 1991, pres.-elect 1995, pres.), Calif. Young Lawyers Assn. (bd. dirs. 1978-83, sec. 1981, pres. 1982), Barristers Club San Francisco (pres. 1978). Office: Freeland Cooper & Foreman LLP 150 Spear St Ste 1800 San Francisco CA 94105 Office Phone: 415-541-0200. Office Fax: 415-495-4332. E-mail: mis@freelandlaw.com.*

SCHIEBLER, GEROLD LUDWIG, pediatrician, educator; b. Hamburg, Pa., June 20, 1928; s. Alwin Robert and Charlotte Elizabeth (Schmoele) Schiebler; m. Audrey Jean Lincourt, Jan. 8, 1954; children: Mark, Marcella, Kristen, Bettina, Wanda, Michele. BS, Franklin and Marshall Coll., 1950; MD, Harvard U., 1954. Intern pediat. and internal medicine Mass. Gen. Hosp., Boston, 1954—55, resident, 1955—56; resident pediat. U. Minn. Hosp., Mpls., 1956—57, fellow pediatric cardiology, 1957—58, rsch. fellow, 1958—59; rsch. fellow sect. physiology Mayo Clinic and Mayo Found., 1959—60; from asst. prof. pediatric cardiology to prof. emeritus U. Fla., 1960—2001, prof. emeritus, 2001—. Dir. divsn. Children's Med. Svcs. State of Fla., 1973—74, area med. dir., 1974—2000, cons., 2001—. Author (with L.P. Elliott): The X-ray Diagnosis of Congenital Cardiac Disease in Infants, Children and Adults, 1968, 1979; author: (with L.J. Krovetz and I.H. Gessner) Pediatric Cardiology, 1979. Recipient Lifetime Achievement award, Coll. Medicine, 2004; named Children's Med. Svcs. Pediatrician of Decade, Gov. Jeb Bush, 1999. Mem.: AMA (Benjamin Rush award 1993), AAAS, Fedn. State Med. Bds. (Svc. award 2008), Fla. Med. Assn. (past v.p., bd. govs., pres. 1991—92, Cert. Of Merit 2008), Fla. Heart Assn. (past pres.), Fla. Pediat. Soc. (exec. com.), Soc. Pediatric Rsch. (emeritus), Am. Coll. Cardiology, Am. Acad. Pediat. (Abraham Jacobi award 1993), Inst. Medicine NAS, Alpha Omega Alpha, Phi Beta Kappa. Home: 408 Beachside Villas Amelia Island Plantation Amelia Island FL 32034-6551 Home Fax: 904-277-7211. Business E-Mail: gls@health.ufl.edu.

SCHIEFFER, BOB, newscaster; b. Austin, Tex., Feb. 25, 1937; m. Patricia Penrose; children: Susan, Sharon. BA in Journalism, Tex. Christian U., 1959. Reporter Ft. Worth Star-Telegram; news anchorman Sta. WBAP-TV, Dallas-Ft. Worth; joined CBS News, 1969, Pentagon corr., 1970-74, White House corr., 1974-79, chief Washington corr., 1982—2005; anchorman CBS Sunday Night News, 1972—77, CBS Evening News (Saturday edit.), 1977—96, CBS Morning News, 1979-80, 1985; anchor, Face the Nation CBS News, 1991—; interim anchor CBS Evening News, NYC, 2005—06, weekly commentator, polit. analyst, 2006—. Mem. Emmy award-winning team CBS Evening News with Walter Cronkite, 1971; participant CBS news spls. and spl. reports including, Peace and the Pentagon, 1974, Watergate-The White House Transcripts, 74, The Mysterious Alert, 74, 76, Ground Zero, 81, others; moderator Bush-Kerry presdl. debate, 2004, Obama-McCain presdl. debate, 2008. Author: This Just In: What I Couldn't Tell You On TV, 2003 (NY Times Bestseller), Face the Nation: My Favorite Stories from the First 50 Years of the Award-Winning News Broadcast, 2004, Bob Schieffer's America, 2008; co-author (with Gary Paul Gates): The Acting President, 1989. Served as capt. and info. officer USAF. Recipient Paul White award, Radio-TV News Directors Assn., 2003, Leonard Zeidenberg First Amendment award, 2008, Internat. Radio & TV Soc. Found. award, 2004, Helen Thomas award for excellence in journalism, Am. News Women's Club, 2004, 7 Emmy awards including one for Lifetime Achievement; named Broadcaster of Yr., Nat. Press Found., 2002; named a Living Legend, Libr. Congress; named to Broadcasting/Cable Hall of Fame, 2002. Office: Face the Nation with Bob Schieffer 2020 M St NW Washington DC 20036-3304*

SCHIEFFER, J(OHN) THOMAS (TOM), United States Ambassador to Japan, former professional baseball team executive; b. Ft. Worth, Oct. 4, 1947; s. John E. and Gladys (Payne) Schieffer; m. Susanne Silber, Sept. 22, 1979; 1 child, Paul Robert. BA in Govt., U. Tex., 1970, MA in Internat. Rels., 1972, JD. Bar: Tex. 1979. Mem. Tex. Ho. of Reps., 1973—79; pvt. law practice, 1979—89; ptnr.-in-charge of ballpark devel. Tex. Rangers Baseball Club, 1990—91, pres., 1991—99, gen. ptnr., 1994—99; pres. J. Thomas Schieffer Mgmt. Co. & Pablo Oper. Co., 1989—2001; US amb. to Australia US Dept. State, Canberra, 2001—05, US amb. to Japan Tokyo, 2005—. Office: DOS Amb 9800 Tokyo Pl Washington DC 20521*

SCHIESEL, SETH, reporter; Grad., Yale Univ., 1994, JD, 1997. Tech., gaming reporter NY Times, NYC, 1996—. Office: Bus Day Desk NY Times 229 W 43rd St New York NY 10036 Office Phone: 212-556-7135. Office Fax: 212-556-1448. Business E-Mail: thegamer@nytimes.com.

SCHIESER, HANS ALOIS, education educator; b. Ulm, Germany, July 15, 1931; arrived in U.S., 1965; s. Alois and Anna (Stegmann) S.; m. Margret H. Schröer, June 6, 1962; children: Peter, Elisabeth. BA, Kepler Gymnasium, Ulm, 1952; MA in Philosophy, U. Passau, Fed. Republic Germany, 1959; EdM, Pedagogic Acad., Weingarten, Fed. Republic Germany, 1962; PhD, Loyola U., Chgo., 1970. Head tchr. Pestalozzischule, Ulm, 1964-65; learning disabilities tchr. Jeanine Schultz Meml. Sch., Skokie, Ill., 1966-67; co-dir. Oak Therapeutic Sch., Evanston, Ill., 1967-70; from assoc. prof. to prof. edn. DePaul U., Chgo., 1969-91, prof. emeritus, 1991—. Cons. in field; program cons. Delphian Soc., L.A., 1977-90; rschr., tchr. in Germany, 1991—; active in tchrs. edn. Midwest Montessori Tchr. Tng. Ctr., Evanston, Ill.; guest prof. State U. Chelyabinsk, State Linguistic U., Irkutsk, Russia, 1998-2005; ord. prof., dean of studies Gustav-Siewerth-Akademie, Germany, 1995-2003. Author chpts. in books; contbr. articles to profl. jours.; adv. bd. Ann. Edits. Sociology, Dushkin Pub. Group, 1985-91. Pres. N.Am. Family Svc. Found., Oak Lawn, Ill., 1974-91; bd. dirs. S.O.S. Children's Villages USA, Washington, 1986-94; pres. emeritus S.O.S. Children's Village Ill., Inc., Chgo.; bd. govs. Invest-in-Am. Nat. Found., Phila., 1988-90. Rsch. grant DePaul U., 1985-86, Rsch. sabbatical, 1989. Mem. Am. Ednl. Studies Assn., Nat. Soc. for Study of Edn., Philosophy of Edn. Soc. U.S.A., Soc. Educators and Scholars (bd. dirs. 1984-90), Am.

Montessori Soc., Thomas More Gesellschaft/Amici Mori Europe, Phi Delta Kappa (pres. Zeta chpt., Chgo. 1973-75). Home: Veilchenweg 9 D-89134 Bermaringen Germany also: 400 E Main/6B/DJURI Evanston IL 60202 Office: DePaul U 2320 N Kenmore Ave Chicago IL 60614-3210 Personal E-mail: profschieser@aol.com, prof_schieser@hotmail.com.

SCHIESS, BETTY BONE, priest; b. Cin., Apr. 2, 1923; d. Evan Paul and Leah (Mitchell) Bone; m. William A. Schiess, Aug. 28, 1947; children: William A. (dec.), Richard Corwine, Sarah. BA, U. Cin., 1945; MA, Syracuse U., 1947; MDiv, Rochester Ctr. for Theol. Studies, 1972. Ordained priest Episcopal Ch., 1974. Priest assoc. Grace Episc. Ch., Syracuse, NY, 1975; mem. NY Task Force on Life and Law (apptd. by gov.), 1985—; chaplain Syracuse U., 1976-78, Cornell U., Ithaca, NY, 1978-79; rector Grace Episc. Ch., Mexico, NY, 1984-89. Cons. Women's Issues Network Episc. Ch. in US, 1987—; writer, lectr., cons. religion and feminism, 1979—. Author: Take Back the Church, Indeed The Witness, 1982, Creativity and Procreativity: Some Thoughts on Eve and the Opposition and How Episcopalians Make Ethical decisions, Plumline, 1988, Send in the Clowns, Chrysalis, Journal of the Swedenborg Foundation, 1994, Cassandra in the Temple, Chrysalis, Journal of the Swedenborg Foundation, 1998, Why Me, Lord: One Woman Ordination to the Priesthood with Commentary and Complaint, 2003; co-editor: (with Mary Alice Burke) The Little Yankee: from Riches to Rags letters of Many Ann Corliss: 1815-1830, 2008; contbr. forward to book, A Still Small Voice! Women Ordination and the Church, Frederick W. Schmidt Jr., 1996. Bd. dir. People for Pub. TV in NY, 1978, Religious Coalition for Abortion Rights; trustee Elizabeth Cady Stanton Found., 1979; mem. NY State Task Force Life and the Law, 1983-96. Recipient Gov. award Women of Merit in Religion, 1984, Ralph E. Kharas award ACLU Ctr., NY, 1986, Goodall disting. alumna award & Hills Sch., 1988, Human Rightes award Human Rights Commn. of Syracuse and Onondaga County, NY, 1989; inducted into Nat. Women's Hall of Fame, 1994. Mem. NOW (Syracuse), Internat. Assn. Women Ministers (dir. 1978 pres. 1984-87), Na'amat US (hon. life), Mortar Bd., Theta Chi Beta. Democrat. Home and Office: 6987 Van Antwerp Dr Cicero NY 13039-9739 Personal E-mail: bettyboneschiess@gmail.com. Business E-Mail: wschiess@twcny.rr.com.

SCHIESSER, HEATH, health products executive; Grad. cum laude, Trinity U.; MBA, Harvard U., Mass. Worked in devel. of new ventures; co-founder online pharmacy Express Scripts; mgmt. cons. McKinsey & Co.; sr. v.p. mktg. and sales WellCare Health Plans, Tampa, Fla., 2002—05, pres. prescription ins., 2005—06, sr. advisor, Medicare products, 2006—08, pres., CEO, 2008—. Bd. dirs. WellCare Health Plans, 2004—. Office: WellCare Health Plans 8725 Henderson Rd Tampa FL 33634*

SCHIFF, ADAM BENNETT, United States Representative from California, lawyer; b. Framingham, Mass., June 22, 1960; s. Edward Maurice and Sherrill Ann (Glovsky) Schiff; m. Eve Schiff; children: Alexa Marion, Elijah Harris. BA, Stanford U., 1982; JD cum laude, Harvard U., 1985. Bar: Calif. 1986. Assoc. Gibson, Dunn & Crutcher, LA, 1986; criminal prosecutor US Atty.'s Office, LA, 1987—93; mem. Calif. Senate, 1996—2000, chmn. judiciary com.; mem. US Congress from 29th Calif. dist., Washington, 2000—, mem. judiciary com., internat. rels. com., appropriations com. Spl. assignment to Czechoslovakia Justice Dept., Bratislava, 1992; mem. New Dem. Coalition, Dem. Homeland Security Task Force, Safe Neighborhoods Task Force, Ho. Edn. Caucus, Congl. Caucus Armenian Issues, Arts Caucus, Ho. Democracy Assistance Commn., 2005—; co-founder Freshman for Reform, Dem. Study Grp. Nat. Security, Congl. Internat. Anti-Piracy Caucus, 2003. Mock trial coach Burbank HS; nat. bd. mem. Big Brothers Big Sisters of America. Mem.: Glendale C. of C., Burbank C. of C. Democrat. Jewish. Avocation: creative writing. Office: US House of Reps 2447 Rayburn House Office Bldg Washington DC 20515-0529 Office Phone: 202-225-4176. Business E-Mail: congressman.schiff@mail.house.gov.*

SCHIFF, DAVID TEVELE, investment banker; b. NYC, Sept. 3, 1936; s. John Mortimer and Edith Brevoort (Baker) Schiff; m. Martha Elisabeth Lawler, May 11, 1963; children: Andrew Newman, David Baker, Ashley Reynolds. B.Engring., Yale U., 1958. Trainee Chem. Bank NY Trust, NYC, 1959-62; analyst Madison Fund, NYC, 1962; assoc., then partner Kuhn, Loeb & Co., NYC, 1963-77, vice chmn., 1977; mng. dir. Lehman Bros. Kuhn Loeb Inc., NYC, 1977-83, also bd. dirs.; mng. ptnr. Kuhn, Loeb & Co. (formerly KLS Enterprises), 1984—. Bd. dirs. Crown Life Ins. Co., Toronto, 1971—92; mem. lower Manhattan adv. bd. Chem. Bank, 1977—85; dir., vice chmn. Am. Crown Life Ins. Co., NYC, 1981—95; bd. advisors Venture Capital Fund Am., 1996—; mem. leadership coun. Yale Sch. Forestry and Environ. Studies, 2000—08; mem. adv. bd. Yale Ctr. Environ. Law and Policy, 2006—. Trustee Wildlife Conservation Soc., 1965—, chmn., 1996—2007, chmn. emeritus, 2007—; trustee Met. Mus. Art, 1971—, Citizens Budget Commn., NYC, 1973—, Greater NY coun. Boy Scouts Am., 1965—91, Beekman Downtown Hosp., 1966—82, chmn., 1975—79; trustee Brooks Sch., North Andover, Mass., 1972—90, treas., 1987—90; bd. govs. Yale U. Art Gallery, 1973—97, Fed. Hall Meml. Assn.; mem. adv. bd. dirs. Outward Bound, Inc., 1983—99; mem. Provident Loan Soc. NY; bd. dirs. Am. Hosp. Paris Found., NYC, 1987—2006. With US Army, 1959. Mem.: Century Assn., Yale Club (NYC), Mill Reef Club (Antigua), Maroon Creek Club (Aspen, Colo.), River Club, Brook Club, Econ. Club (NYC), Pilgrims of US (mem. exec. com.). Episcopalian. Home: 770 Park Ave New York NY 10021-4153 Office: 50 Rockefeller Plz 15th Fl New York NY 10020-1622 Office Phone: 212-655-7044. Personal E-mail: gorilla@kuhnloebco.com.

SCHIFF, ERIC ALLAN, physics professor; b. LA, Aug. 29, 1950; s. Gunther Hans and Katharine Shepard (MacMillan) S.; m. Nancy Ruth Mudrick, Aug. 12, 1973; children: Nathan, Evan. BS, Calif. Inst. Tech., 1971; PhD, Cornell U., 1979. Rsch. assoc. U. Chgo., 1978-81; asst. prof. Syracuse (N.Y.) U., 1981-87, assoc. prof., 1987-95, prof., 1995—, dept. chair, 1997—2003, assoc. dean sci. and math., 2003—08. Vis. Brown U., Providence, 1988-90, Xerox Palo Alto Rsch. Ctr., 1995. Contbr. articles to profl. jours. Rsch. grant NSF, 1983-86, 2002-06. Mem. Am. Phys. Soc. (exec. com. NY state chpt. 1991-94), Materials Rsch. Soc. (symposium organizing com. 1992-97, 2003-04), Internat. Conf. Amorphous and Nanocryst Semicondrs. (organizing com. 1999, 2007). Office: Syracuse U Dept Physics Syracuse NY 13244-1130 Office Phone: 315-443-3901.

SCHIFF, GARY STUART, academic administrator, educator, consultant; b. Bklyn., Mar. 27, 1947; s. Jacob and Lillian (Grumet) S.; children: Jeremy Jay, Rina Joy. BA, Bin Hebrew Lit., Yeshiva U., 1968; MA, Columbia U., 1970, Cert. in Middle East Studies, 1973, PhD, 1973; DHL (hon.), Gratz Coll., 1997. Asst. prof. Jewish studies and polit. sci. CUNY, 1973-76; dir. Mid. East affairs Nat. Jewish Cmty. Rels. Coun., NYC, 1976-78; exec. asst. to pres. Acad. for Ednl. Devel., NYC, 1978-83; pres., prof. Middle East studies Gratz Coll., Melrose Park, Pa., 1983-97. Vis. prof. Balt. Hebrew U., 1997, Washington Coll., Md., 1999-2000, 2000-2001; vis. asst. prof. polit. sci. Yeshiva U., 1973-77. Author: Tradition and Politics: The Religious Parties of Israel, 1977, The Energy Education Catalog, 1981; contbr. articles to profl. jours. Grantee NEH, Ford Found., Danforth Found., Woodrow Wilson Found., William Penn Found., Pew Charitable Trusts. Mem. Assn. of Colls. of Jewish Studies (bd. dirs.), Assn. for Israel Studies (v.p.), Coun. for Jewish Edn. (bd. dirs.), Assn. for Jewish Studies, World Jewish Congress (governing bd.), Am. Jewish Com. (N.Y. chpt. bd. dirs., Phila. chpt. communal affairs commn.). Avocations: cantorial music, boating, cats. Home: 29182 Ricks Landing Rd Kennedyville MD 21645-3306 E-mail: garygrant@aol.com.

SCHIFF, GUNTHER HANS, lawyer; b. Cologne, Germany, Aug. 19, 1927; came to U.S., 1936; s. Hans and Alice (Goldstein) S.; m. Katharine MacMillan, Jan. 27, 1950 (div. 1957); children: Eric Alan, Mary Alice; m. JoAnn R. Schiff; children: Jage, Hans. BSFS., Georgetown U., 1949, JD, 1952. Bar: D.C. 1952, Calif. 1953. Assoc., ptnr., of counsel various firms, Beverly Hills, Calif., 1954-94; pvt. practice Beverly Hills, Calif., 1994—. Sec. Los Angeles Copyright Soc., Beverly Hills, 1975-76 Contbr. articles to profl. jours. Pres. Beverly Hills Civil Svc. Commn., 1984-85, 88-89; pres. Free Arts for Abused Children, 1993-94, dir.; chmn. Rent Control Rev. Bd., Beverly Hills, 1980-84; trustee Young Musicians Found. With USNR, 1945-46. Mem. ABA, Beverly Hills Bar Assn. (chmn. Resolutions Com. 1977-78), Los Angeles County Bar Assn., Los Angeles Copyright Soc., USCG Aux., Calif. Yacht Club. Avocations: sailing, skiing, golf. Office: 9430 W Olympic Blvd Beverly Hills CA 90212-4552 Home Phone: 310-271-7770; Office Phone: 310-557-9081, 310-275-3754. Personal E-mail: hgschiff@pacbell.net.

SCHIFF, HOWARD IRWIN, urologist; b. Bklyn., May 15, 1948; s. Frank and Mildred Schiff; m. Debbie Mathews Schiff, Aug. 29, 1970; children: Jonathan, Richard, Robin, Meredith, Amanda. BA, Hofstra U., 1970; MS, W.Va. U., 1973, MD, 1975. Diplomate Am. Bd. Urology, lic. physician N.Y. Intern dept. surgery Montefiore Hosp., Bronx, 1975—77; intern dept. urology Mt. Sinai Med. Ctr. N.Y., 1977—80; asst. attending physician Mt. Sinai Med. Ctr., NYC, 1980—; consulting urologist City Hosp. Ctr., Elmhurst, NY, 1980—2004; attending urologist Beth Israel Med. Ctr., NYC, 1983—2003; asst. attending physician Weill-Cornell Med. Ctr., NYC, 2001—; asst. attending urologist North Shore U. Hosp., Manhasset, NY, 2005—; cons. urologist Hosp. Special Surgery, NYC, 2008—. Asst. clin. prof. urology Mt Sinai Sch. Medicine, NYC, 1982—; adj. asst. clin. prof. urology Weill-Cornell Sch. Medicine, NYC, 2001—. Contbr. articles to profl. jours. Recipient Ferdinand Valentine Residents Essay award, N.Y. Acad. Mag., 1979, Physicians Recognition award, AMA, 1980—; named one of Best Drs. in N.Y., N.Y. Mag., 1998, 2000, 2001, Best Drs. in NY Metro Region, Castle Connelly Guide, 1997—2009, NY Times Super Drs., 2009. Fellow: ACS; mem.: Am. Urol. Assn. Office: 1120 Park Ave New York NY 10128 Office Phone: 212-996-6660. Personal E-mail: hschiff@prodigy.net, hschiffmd@gmail.com.

SCHIFF, JAN PEDERSEN, conductor, voice educator; b. Chgo., Dec. 26, 1945; d. Charles Albert and Thelma Jane Pedersen; m. Tom Schiff, Oct. 1, 1988. BA in Music Edn./Voice, Augsburg Coll., Mpls., 1968; MusM in Conducting, U. Colo., 1974. Vocal music tchr. DuSable Upper Grade Ctr., Chgo., 1968—69; music tchr., choral dir. Kelvyn Pk. H.S., Chgo., 1969—70; choral cons. Oslo Barnasangerlag, 1970—71; music tchr. Broomfield Secondary Sch. for Boys, London-Woolwich, 1971—72; choral/vocal instr. Wilkes Coll., Wilkes-Barre, Pa., 1974—76; choral condr. Somerset County Coll., Northbranch, NJ, 1976—77; vocal instr. L.A. City Coll., 1977—86; choral condr., vocal instr. Long Beach City Coll., Calif., 1978—86; founder/condr. Hollywood Chorale, Calif., 1980—86; music dir. Cmty. Congl. Ch., Tiburon, Calif., 1987—91; voice class instr. Coll. Marin, Kentfield, Calif., 1988—93; founder, artistic dir. SingersMarin, Mill Valley, Calif., 1987—. Pvt. vocal instr., Mill Valley, Calif., 1976—; guest condr. Singer: (cd of original songs) Dreamer. Mktg. com. Marin Symphony, San Rafael, Calif., 1996—2001. Recipient Bronze Halo award, So. Calif. Motion Picture Coun., 1983, Susan B. Anthony award for cultural achievement in Hollywood, Hollywood Bus. Women, 1985, Vol. of Yr. award, Mill Valley C. of C., 2001, Cert. of Commendation, Marin County Women's Commn., 2002, Milley award for contbns. to music in Mill Valley, Milley Award Com., 2003; scholar Peggy Christiansen Benson Meml. scholarship, Music Dept., Augsburg Coll., 1967. Mem.: Internat. Fedn. of Choral Music, Music Tchrs.s Assn. Calif., Conductors Guild, Chorus Am., Nat. Assn. Tchrs. of Singing (L.A. chpt. pres. 1983—84, San Francisco chpt. treas. 1989—91), Am. Choral Dirs. Assn. (life), Beta Chi Epsilon, Pi Kappa Lambda. Avocations: gardening, gourmet cooking. Home: 308 Shoreline Hwy Mill Valley CA 94941 Office: SingersMarin 1038 Redwood Hwy Bldg A Mill Valley CA 94941 Office Fax: 415-383-7289. Business E-Mail: sing@singersmarin.org.

SCHIFF, JEFFREY ALLEN, environmental sculptor, educator; b. Rolla, ND, Aug. 23, 1952; s. Donald Wilfred and Rosalie (Pergament) S.; m. Blair Tate, Dec. 30, 1978; children: Walker and Clayton. BA, Brown U., 1974; MFA, U. Mass., 1976. Prof. Wesleyan U., Middletown, Conn., 1987—. Instr. Boston Coll, 1980-81, Clark U., RI Sch. Design. Exhbns. include Boston Inst. Contemporary Art, 1979, Rose Art Mus., 1986, San Diego Mus. Contemporary Art, 1987, Williams Coll. Mus., 1988, Sculpture Ctr., NYC, 1993, Katonah Art Mus., 1996, Real Art Ways, Hartford, Conn., 1998, San Jose Mus. Art, 2000, Cathedral St. John the Divine, NY, 2001, Olin Meml. Libr., Wesleyan U., 2003, Exit Art, NYC, 2005, 2006, Proteus Gowanus, Bklyn., 2006; pub. commissions include Lexington Mall, Balt., 1986, South Station R.R. Terminal, Boston, 1990-95, Thompson Sq., Charlestown, Mass., 1986-95. Recipient Rome prize, Am. Acad. Rome, 1977, award for Design Collaboration, Boston Soc. Architects, 1991; fellow Mass. artists Found., 1975, 1980, 1985, Nat. Endowment Arts, 1976, 1984, Rockefeller Found., 2002, NY Found. Arts (sculpture), 2003, Bogliasco Found., 2005, Guggenheim Found., 2008; Boston/Kyoto Sister City traveling grant, 1984, Fulbright Sr. Scholar Rsch. fellow, 1998 Democrat.

SCHIFF, JOHN JEFFERSON, JR., finance company executive; BS, Ohio State U., 1965. Chmn., CEO John J. & Thomas R. Schiff & Co., Inc., 1983-96; COO Cin. Fin. Corp., 1998—99, pres., CEO, 1999—2006, CEO, 2006—08, chmn. Trustee Am. Inst. Chartered Property Casualty Underwriters; dir. Cinergy Corp., Fifth Third Bancorp, Cin. Bengals Inc., John J. & Thomas R. Schiff & Co. Inc., Std. Register Co. Office: Cin Fin Group PO Box 145496 Cincinnati OH 45250-5496

SCHIFF, LAWRENCE ALAN, dentist; b. NYC, June 11, 1954; s. Leonard Julius and Mildred Ruth Schiff; m. Susan Lynn Zemmel, Aug. 17, 1986; children: Chelsea Ann, JonDavid. BA, Colgate U., Hamilton, NY, 1976; DMD, Fairleigh Dickinson U., Hackensack, NJ, 1980. Residency in gen. practice U. Pa., Phila., 1981; clin. assoc. instr., sch. dental medicine U Pa., 1981—86; pvt. practice Erdenheim, Pa., 1986—. Coach SE Pa. Youth Lacrosse Assn. Fellow: Acad. Gen. Dentistry; mem.: ADA, Phila. County Dental Assn., Montgomery Bucks Dental Assn., Am. Acad. Cosmetic Dentistry, Beta Beta Beta. Achievements include research in effects of estrogen on collagen crosslinking. Avocations: golf, skiing. Office: 813 Bethlehem Pike Erdenheim PA 19038 Business E-Mail: smilsvr@comcast.net.

SCHIFF, MARTIN, physician, surgeon; b. Phila., July 16, 1922; s. Isidore and Cecelia (Miller) S.; m. Mildred Tepley, Jan. 5, 1946; children: Denise Schiff Simon, Michael, David BS, Pa. State U., 1943; MD, U. Calif.-Irvine, 1951. Intern L.A. County Gen. Hosp., 1950-51; gen. practice medicine specializing in bariatrics LA, 1951—. Lectr. L.A. area community colls. Author: Eat & Stay Slim, 1972, Miracle Weight-Loss Guide, 1976, One-Day-At-A-Time Weight Loss Plan, 1980, (5 tapes) Weight Loss Plan for Health, Happiness & A Longer Life Span, 1982, The Thin Connection, 1986, Lose Unwanted Pounds Permanently Without Dieting/Trying/Playing Games, 1998, Weight Control-Fact or Fiction?, 1999, The Power of Your Will, 1999, Connections: Feelings and Emotions, 2000, YOU: A Guide to Yourself and a Mental Roadmap to Your Inner Being, 2002, Mental Conditions and Situations-Fact or Fiction?, 2006, An Overview and Understanding of Mental Activity and Action, Conditions and Situations, 2006, Weight Thinkers, 2006. Lt. USN, 1943-45, PTO Mem. AMA, Calif. Med. Assn., L.A. Med. Assn., Am. Soc. Weight Control Specialists. Office Phone: 310-454-6172.

SCHIFF, MOLLY JEANETTE, artist, researcher; b. Chgo., Oct. 19, 1927; d. David Nathan and Beatrice (Aisenberg) Rice; m. Haskell Schiff, June 12, 1946; children: Darryll Nat, Lesley Nan, Brad Scott, Rae Ellyce Student, U. Chgo., 1958—63, student, 1968—69; BFA, Art Inst., Chgo., 1962, MFA, 1963, MA Edn., 1969. Cert. Art tchr. Ill. Instr. art Chgo. Bd. Edn. and Park Dist., 1962—66, Jewish Cmty. Ctrs., Chgo., 1962—65; pvt. practice Chgo., 1962—; instr. art New Trier Extensions, Winnetka, Ill., 1965—78, Evanston Art Ctr., Ill., 1965, St. Tarsissus Sch., Chgo., 1968, Young Artists Studio Art Inst., Chgo., 1968—69, Ill. Visually Handicapped Inst., Chgo., 1968—73, Govs. State U., Monee, Ill., 1975—76. Cons. Markal Corp., Chgo., 1968-94; cons., presenter, regional rep. Shiva Corp., Chgo., 1984-87, exhbn. co-chair 1990-91, 2005-06. Prin. works include Facades, 1971 (Honors award 1971), Drawn Paintings, 1976 (Honors award 1976), Acapulco Balcony, 1978 (Honors award 1980), Mexican Scenics, 1980 (Honors award 1980), Figures on Paper, 1988-89 (Honors award 1989), Low Seam, 1988 (Honors award), Latest Impressions, 1989 (Honors award), Acapulco Nite View, 1989 (Honors award), Latest Impressions, Mannequin Cut Outs, 1990 (Honors award 1990), Mannequin Soiree 1992 (Honors award 2000), Union League, 1993 (Honors award), Jarvis Still Life, 1993 (Honors award), Blue Moon, 1997 (Honors award), Triplets, 1997 (Honors award 1998), Sunset at Pushkar, 1998 (Honors award 1999), Rain Forest, Brazil, 2003 (Honors award 2003), I'm Not Square, 2003 (Honors award 2003-04), I Forgot My Sketch Book, 2003 (Honors award 2004), V is For Vashti, 2003 (Honors award 2003-2004); exhibitions include Water Images, Chgo. Cultural Ctr., 1998, 99, I Remember Purim-A Visual Narrative, Chgo. Sinai Congregation, 2006, Biennale Internat., Florence, Italy, 2003, I Remember Purim, Loyola Univ. Art Mus. Chgo., 2007; wang artist, Saatchi Gallery; one womem show: Window Views In & Out, Cook County, Treass. Office, Chgo., 2008, Temple Israel Museum, Bloomfield, Mich., 2009 Pres. I.G.C. chpt. Am. Jewish Congress, Chgo., 1955 Recipient Cash award Foremost Corp., 1963, Ill. Dept. Energy and Natural Resources, 1988, Purchase award Rotarian Mag., 1978, Ill. State Mus., 1978, Nite View, 1989, Honors award U.S. State Dept., 1996-2000. Mem. Archives, Figurative Art League, Nat. Mus. Women in Arts, Chgo. Artists Coalition, Chgo. Soc. Artists, Am. Jewish Artists Assn. (program dir. 1970-74, 89-93, pres. 2004-2005, exhbn. com. 2006), Dutch Folk Art Assn. (cons., juror 1979), Alumni Assn. Art Inst. Chgo., Am. Jewish Artists Club, Scan Chgo. (bd. dir. 1988-91) Avocations: tour directing, travel. Office Phone: 312-274-0930. Personal E-mail: mollyjart@msn.com.

SCHIFF, NICHOLAS D., neurologist; b. June 30, 1965; BA with honors, Stanford U., Calif., 1987; MD with honors, Cornell U. Med. Coll., NY, 1992. Resident neurology NY Hosp.; assoc. prof. neurology, neurosci. tenure Weill Cornell Med. Coll. Dir. Lab. Cognitive Neuromodulation; assoc. attending neurologist NY-Presbyn./Weill Cornell Hosps.; inventor tech. Cornell U.; cons., adv. IntElect Med. Inc. Contbr. articles to profl. jours., chapters to books; co-author: (med. text) Diagnosis of Stupor and Coma, 2007. Recipient Rsch. award for Innovation, Soc. Neurosci., 2007; named one of The 100 Most Influential People in the World, TIME mag., 2008. Mem.: Am. Bd. Psychiatry, Neurology (diplomat), Am. Neurological Assn. Office: Weill Med Coll 1300 York Ave F610 New York NY 10065 Office Fax: 212-746-8532.

SCHIFF, PETER DAVID, investment advisor, economist; b. New Haven, 1964; s. Irwin Schiff; 1 child. BS in Fin. & Acctg., U. Calif., Berkeley, 1987. Lic. 4,7,24,27,53,55,63 FINRA Series. Fin. cons. Shearson Lehman Bros.; joined Euro Pacific Capital Inc., 1996, pres. Calif., 2000—05, pres., chief global strategist Darien, Conn., 2005—. Econ. adv presdl. campaign Ron Paul, 2008. Author: Crash Proof: How to Profit from the Coming Economic Collapse, 2007, The Little Book of Bull Moves in Bear Markets: How to Keep Your Portfolio Up When the Market is Down, 2008; contbr. articles to profl jours.; host (Internet/radio show) Wall St. Unspun, contbg. commentator Newsweek Internat., appearances include CNBC, CNN, CNN Internat., Fox News, Bloomberg TV, Fox Bus. Republican. Achievements include accreditation with accurate forecasts on the US stock market, economy, real estate, mortgage meltdown and credit crunch of 2008. Office: Euro Pacific Capital Inc 10 Corbin Dr Ste B Darien CT 06820 Office Phone: 203-662-9700. Office Fax: 203-662-9771. Business E-Mail: pschiff@europac.net.*

SCHIFF, RICHARD, actor; b. Bethesda, Md., May 27, 1955; s. Edward and Charlotte Schiff; m. Sheila Kelley, 1996; children: Gus, Ruby Christine. Grad., CCNY, 1983. With Actors Gang; founder, artistic dir. Manhattan Repertory Theatre. Dir.: (plays, off-Broadway) Antigone; actor: (films) Arena Brains, 1988, Medium Straight, 1989, Young Guns II, 1990, Stop! Or My Mom Will Shoot, 1992, Rapid Fire, 1992, The Public Eye, 1992, Malcolm X, 1992, The Bodyguard, 1992, Hoffa, 1992, My Life, 1993, Ghost in the Machine, 1993, The Hudsucker Proxy, 1993, Major League II, 1994, Speed, 1994, Tank Girl, 1995, Skinner, 1995, Rough Magic, 1995, Se7en, 1995, City Hall, 1996, The Arrival, 1996, The Trigger Effect, 1996, Grace of My Heart, 1996, Michael, 1996, Santa Fe, 1997, Touch, 1997, Volcano, 1997, Loved, 1997, The Lost World: Jurassic Park, 1997, Deep Impact, 1998, Doctor DoLittle, 1998, Heaven, 1998, Living Out Loud, 1998, Crazy in Alabama, 1999, Forces of Nature, 1999, Gun Shy, 2000, Whatever It Takes, 2000, Forever Lulu, 2000, Lucky Numbers, 2000, What's the Worst That Could Happen?, 2001, I Am Sam, 2001, People I Know, 2002, With It, 2004, Ray, 2004, Civic Duty, 2006, Waiting, 2007, Martian Child, 2007; (TV films) Trenchcoat in Paradise, 1989, Till Death Us Do Part, 1992, Cruel Doubt, 1992, The Positively True Adventures of the Alleged Texas Cheerleader-Murdering Mom, 1993, Amelia Earhart: The Final Flight, 1994, Saved by the Bell: Wedding in Las Vegas, 1994, Special Report: Journey to Mars, 1996, The Taking of Pelham One Two Three, 1998, The Pentagon Wars, 1998; (TV series) Relativity, 1996—97, The West Wing, 1999—2006 (Emmy award, best supporting actor in drama series,

2000); (plays) Goose and Tom Tom (Dramalogue award, best actor), Urban Folktales (Ovation award), Underneath the Lintel, 2006. Recipient Townsend Harris medal, CCNY, 2000. Home: 524 Lorraine Blvd Los Angeles CA 90020-4732

SCHIFF, ROBERT, healthcare consulting company executive; b. NYC, Jan. 7, 1942; s. Henry and Jeanette (Levine) S.; m. Adrianne Bendich, Aug. 16, 1964 (div. July 1979); children: Jorden, Debra; m. Joann McTaggart, Aug. 24, 1986. BS, CCNY, 1964; MS, Iowa State U., 1966; PhD, U. Calif., Davis, 1968. Asst. prof. anatomy Tufts U. Sch. Medicine, Boston, 1969-72; mgr. serology rsch. Hyland divsn. Baxter Labs., Costa Mesa, Calif., 1972-74; dir. R & D J.T. Baker Diagnostics, Bethlehem, Pa., 1974-77; dir. diagnostic R & D Hoffmann-LaRoche, Nutley, N.J., 1977-80; group v.p. Warner Lambert Co., Morris Plains, N.J., 1980-82; pres., CEO Schiff & Co., Inc., West Caldwell, N.J., 1982—. Del. Nat. Commn. for Clin. Lab. Stds., 1979-80; vice chmn. R & D Coun. N.J., 1980-82; bd. dirs. E.P.I. subs. E-Z-EM, Westbury, N.Y., 1991-98. Contbr. numerous articles to profl. jours.; patentee in field. Bd. dirs. Pharm. Tng. Inst., 2002. Post Doctoral fellow U. Calif., Davis, 1969; Aid to Cancer Rsch. grantee, Mass., 1970. Fellow Regulatory Affairs Profl. Soc.; mem. NY Acad. Sci., Regulatory Affairs Profl. Soc. (cert., bd. editors Focus 2006), Am. Soc. Quality Control (cert. quality auditor), Am. Assn. Clin. Chemistry, Brit. Inst. Regulatory Affairs, Parenteral Drug Assn., Sigma Xi. Avocation: flying. Office: Schiff & Co 1129 Bloomfield Ave West Caldwell NJ 07006-7123 Office Phone: 973-227-1830. Personal E-mail: rschiff13@aol.com.

SCHIFF BERMAN, PAUL, dean, law educator; AB in Anthropology summa cum laude, Princeton U., NJ, 1988; JD summa cum laude, NYU Sch. Law, NYC, 1995. Adminstrv. dir. The Wooster Group, NYC, 1988—92; founder, artistic dir. Spin Theatre, NYC, 1989—95; adminstrv. dir. Ontological Hysteric Theatre at St. Mark's Ch., NYC, 1992—95; claimant rep. Unemployment Action Ctr., NYC, 1992—95; intern Neighborhood Defender Svc. Harlem, NYC, 1992—93; summer intern Laufman, Rauh and Gerhardstein, Cin., 1993; summer assoc. Sullivan & Cromwell, NYC, 1994, pro-bono extern, 1996—97; summer assoc. Jenner & Block, Washington, 1995; law clk. Hon. Harry T. Edwards US Ct. Appeals (DC), 1995—96; law clk. Hon. Ruth Bader Ginsburg US Supreme Ct., 1997—98; assoc. prof. U. Conn. Sch. Law, Hartford, 1998—2002, prof. law, 2003—06, Jesse Root prof. law, 2006—08; dean, Found. prof. law Ariz. State U. Sandra Day O'Connor Coll. Law, Tempe, 2008—. Cons. Cummings & Lockwood, Hartford, 1998—2003, Day, Berry & Howard, Hartford, 1998—2005, Wiggan & Dana, New Haven, 2004—06, McKee Nelson, Washington, 2008; pro bono counsel US Ct. Appeals (DC), 2003; counsel US Ct. Appeals (2d cir.), 2006; vis. prof. Princeton U., 2006—07. Contbr. articles to profl. jours., chapters to books. Named one of Connecticut's New Leaders of the Law, Conn. Law Tribune, 2004. Mem.: Assn. Am. Law Schools, Am. Soc. Internat. Law, Assn. the Study of Law, Culture and the Humanities. Office: ASU Sandra Day O'Connor Coll Law Armstrong Hall McAllister & Orange St PO Box 877906 Tempe AZ 85287 Office Phone: 480-965-6188. Business E-Mail: paul.s.berman@asu.edu.*

SCHIFFER, CHARLES ALAN, oncologist, educator; b. Bklyn., Apr. 11, 1944; s. Mortimer and Esther (Ginsberg) S.; m. Judy T. Schiffer, June 14, 1970 (dec. Aug. 1992), Pamela Schiffer; 1 child, Joshua T. MD, Brandeis U., 1968, NYU, 1968. Diplomate Am. Bd. Internal Medicine, Am. Bd. Med. Oncology. Intern, resident, chief resident NYU Sch. Medicine, 1968-72; staff fellow, sr. investigator Nat. Cancer Inst., Balt., 1972-81; chief divsn. malignancies, hematology U. Md. Cancer Ctr., Balt., 1981—97; prof. medicine and oncology Barbara Ann Karmanos Cancer Inst., Wayne State U. Sch. Medicine, Detroit, 1997—; prin. investigator, clinical trials of Gleevec Wayne State U. Sch. Medicine, Detroit, 1999—. Prof. oncology and medicine U. Md. Sch. Medicine, Balt., 1983-1997; chair oncology drug adv. com. FDA, Rockville, Md., 1992-95; chair leukemia com. Cancer and Leukemia Group B, Chgo.; cons. various pharm. cos.; vis. prof. numerous univs. Editor: Neoplastic Diseases of Blood, Leukemia sect., Current Opinion in Oncology; mem. editl. bds. Blood, Jour. Clin. Oncology, Internat. Jour. Hematology, Transfusion Medicine Reviews and Transfusions; contbr. chpts. in books and articles to profl. jours. Lt. comdr. USPHS, 1972-81. Recipient Humanitarian award Arlene Wyman Guild, 1992, Dr. John J. Kenney award, Leukemia/Lymphoma Soc. Am., 2006, Celegene award for Career Acheivement in Hematology, 2006; named Best Doctor, Am. Health Mag., Best Cancer Specialist in the US, Good Housekeeping Mem. Am. Soc. Hematology (coms.), Am. Soc. Clin. Oncology (coms.). Avocations: skiing, biking, music, reading. Office: Hudson-Webber Cancer Rsch Ctr 4100 John R Detroit MI 48201 Address: Weisberg Cancer Treatment Ctr 31995 Northwestern Hwy Farmington MI 48334 Office Phone: 313-576-8737. Business E-Mail: schiffer@karmanos.org, schiffer@wayne.edu.

SCHIFFER, LOIS JANE, lawyer; b. Washington, Feb. 22, 1945; d. Benjamin and Clara (Goldberg) Schiffer. BA, Radcliffe Coll., Cambridge, Mass., 1966; JD, Harvard U., Cambridge, Mass., 1969. Bar: Mass. 1969, DC 1971, US Supreme Ct. 1973. Legal svcs. lawyer Boston Legal Assistance Project, 1969-70; ct. law clk. DC Circuit Ct., Washington, 1970-71; assoc. Leva, Hawes, Symington, Martin, Oppenheimer, Washington, 1971-74; lawyer Ctr. for Law and Social Policy, Washington, 1974-78; chief gen. litig. sect. Land and Natural Resources divsn. U.S. Dept. Justice, Washington, 1978-81, spl. litig. counsel, 1981-84; gen. counsel Nat. Pub. Radio, Washington, 1984-89; ptnr. Nussbaum & Wald, Washington, 1989-93; acting asst. atty. gen. environ. and natural resources divsn. US Dept. Justice, Washington, 1993-94, asst. atty. gen. environ. and natural resources divsn., 1994-2001; sr. v.p. for pub. policy Nat. Audubon Soc., 2001—02; ptnr. Baach Robinson & Lewis, Washington, 2002—05; gen. counsel Nat. Capital Planning Commn., Washington, 2005—. Adj. prof. environ. law Georgetown U. Law Ctr., Washington, 1986—; lectr. Harvard Law Sch., 2004; bd. dirs. DC Appleseed, Internat. Sr. Lawyers Project, Audubon, Naturalist Soc. Bd. dirs. Women's Legal Def. Fund, 1975—86, Am. Rivers, 1989—93, ACLU/NCA, 1982—93, pres., 1988—90. Fellow: Am. Bar Found.; mem.: ABA, Am. Law Inst., Phi Beta Kappa. Democrat. Jewish. Avocations: reading, movies, hiking. Home: 4640 Brandywine St NW Washington DC 20016-4449 Home Phone: 202-363-0841. Business E-Mail: lois.schiffer@ncpc.gov.

SCHIFFER, STEPHEN, philosopher, educator; BA in Philosophy, Univ. Pa., 1962; DPhil, Oxford Univ., 1970. Prof., philosophy, dept. chair NYU. Author: Meaning, 1972, Remnants of Meaning, 1987, The Things We Mean, 2003. Fellow: Am. Acad. Arts & Scis. Office: Dept Philosophy NYU 5 Washington Pl New York NY 10003 Office Phone: 212-998-8227. Office Fax: 212-995-4179. Business E-Mail: ss72@nyu.edu.

SCHIFFMAN, DANIEL, lawyer, arts advocate; b. NYC, Nov. 7, 1932; s. Jacob and Eva (Katzin) Schiffman; m. P.G. Galex, June 26, 1955 (div.); m. Nancy A. Ozelli, Apr. 7, 1990. BBA, CCNY, 1959; JD, NYU, 1962. Bar: NY 1962, US Dist. Ct. (so. dist.) NY 1966, US Ct. Appeals (3d cir.) 1966, US Dist. Ct. (ea. dist.) NY 1979, US Supreme Ct. 1975, US Ct. Appeals (2d cir.) 1980, US Ct. Appeals (1st cir.) 1988, US Ct. Appeals (4th cir.) 1998. Musician, 1950—55; pub. acct. Morris, Sherwood & May CPA, NYC, 1956—59, Meyerson and Levine, CPA, NYC, 1959—61; legal sec. to chief city magistrate City of NY, 1961—62; assoc. Maxwell and Diamond, NYC, 1962—66; mem. Schiffman and Ellenbogen, NYC, 1975—78, Schiffman and Frank, NYC, 1996—2004; pvt. practice, NYC, 1966—74, 1978—96, 2004—. Cons., lectr. Practising Law Inst., NYC, 1963—68, NYC, 1982; counsel, migration div. Commonwealth of PR Labor Dept., 1970—72; counsel to adminstr. Commonwealth of PR Econ. Devel. Adminstrn., 1971—73; advisor US GSA, 1979; lectr., moderator, panelist World Gaming Congress, 1987—99; panelist Global Gaming Expo., 2006; co-chair, moderator, planning com. mem. ALI-ABA CLE courses, 1998, 2000, 01; moderator and panelist ABA, 1988, 2001; referee, special master, mental hygiene evaluator, guardian ad litem, receiver Supreme and Surrogate's Cts., NY, 1991—; adv. com. Little Hoover Com., Calif., 1997. Mem. staff: NYU Law Rev., 1961—62, contbg. author: Casino Credit and Collection Law, 1989, Internat. Casino Law, 1991, 1993, 1999, 2007, columnist and contbg. author: The Gaming Lawyer, 1998—2007, Global Gaming Bus. Mag., 2003—, mem. ed. bd.: Gaming Law Rev., 1997—. Bd. dirs. Am. Symphony Orch., 1989—2005, treas., 1990—93, sec., 1997—2004; adv. bd. Swiss Global Artistic Found., 2008—; bd. dirs. MAESTRO Found., London, 1985—87; treas. Citizens for a Responsive Congress, 1978—80; co-founder, exec. prodr., founding pres. (hon.) Cala Records, Inc., 1991—. Recipient Nat. Arts Club Pres. Medal, 1989. Mem.: Am. Fedn. Musicians, NYC Jr. C. of C. (legal advisor 1980—90), Internat. Masters of Gaming Law (bd. dir. membership com., publications com.), Internat. Assn. Gaming Advs. (formerly Internat. Assn. Gaming Attys.), Assn. Bar City NY, Nat. Arts Club (bd. dirs. 1986—, chmn. music com. 1986—, Pres.'s medal 1989). Home: 903 Park Ave New York NY 10075-0362 Office Phone: 212-628-6433.

SCHIFFMAN, GERALD, microbiologist, educator; b. NYC, May 22, 1926; s. Samuel and Mollie (Brookner) S.; m. Lillian Ebert, July 12, 1951; children: Stewart, Howard. BA cum laude, NYU, 1948, PhD, 1954. Asst. prof. microbiology Coll. Physicians and Surgeons, Columbia U., NYC, 1960—63; asso. prof. dept. research medicine and microbiology U. Pa., Phila., 1963-70; prof. SUNY Health Sci. Ctr., Bklyn., 1970-97, disting. svc. prof., 1995-97, prof. emeritus, 1997. Cons. Contbr. articles to profl. jours. Served in U.S. Army, 1943-45, ETO. Decorated Bronze Star; recipient Nichols award, 1947; Atomic Energy fellow, 1948-52; NIH grantee, 1974-94. Mem. Am. Assn. Immunologists, Am. Chem. Soc., Am. Soc. Microbiology, AAAS, Harvey Soc., Soc. Complex Carbohydrates, Sigma Xi, Phi Beta Kappa, Mu Chi Sigma, Pi Mu Epsilon. Jewish. Office: 450 Clarkson Ave Brooklyn NY 11203-2056 Personal E-mail: gs1246@verizon.net.

SCHIFFMAN, HAROLD FOSDICK, Asian language educator; b. Buffalo, Feb. 19, 1938; s. Merl and Mathilda (Keller) S.; m. Marilyn Gail Hornberg, June 10, 1978; 1 son, Timothy Marc Rajendran. BA, Antioch Coll., 1960; MA, U. Chgo., 1966, PhD, 1969. Lectr. anthropology U. Calif.-Davis, 1966-67; asst. prof. U. Wash., Seattle, 1967-73, assoc. prof., 1973-78, prof., 1978-95, chmn. dept. Asian langs., 1982-87; prof. South Asian studies U. Pa., Phila., 1995—2002, acad. dir. Penn Lang. Ctr., Luce prof. lang. learning, 1995-2000, rsch. dir. Penn Lang. Ctr., 2000—, prof. emeritus, 2007—; dir. Consortium Lang. Policy and Planning, 2001—, Pedagogical Materials Project South Asia Lang. Resource Ctr., 2002—05. Trustee Am. Inst. Indian Studies, Chgo., 1979-82; lang. dir. Southeast Asian Summer Studies Inst., 1992-93, mem. lang. adv. com., 1993-94. Author: A Grammar of Spoken Tamil, 1979, A Reference Grammar of Spoken Kannada, 1983, Linguistic Culture and Language Policy, 1996, A Reference Grammar of Spoken Tamil, 1999; co-editor: Dravidian Phonological Systems, 1975; co-author: Language and Society in South Asia, 1981. Pres. bd. dirs. Seattle Pro Musica (choral group), 1976-78; mem. Pacific Northwest Chamber Chorus, Seattle, 1983-87. Sr. fellow Am. Inst. Indian Studies, 1976, 78; grantee U.S. Office Edn., 1971, 74, 78, NEH, 1984-87, Smithsonian Inst., 1984-87, Fulbright Rsch., 1993-94. Mem. Assn. Asian Studies (S. Asia council 1982-85), Am. Inst. Indian Studies (trustee 1979-82), Soc. S. Indian Studies (sec.-treas. 1973-75), Internat. Assn. Tamil Research (v.p. 1987-89). Mem. Soc. Of Friends. Office: U Pa Dept South Asia Studies 820 Williams Hall Philadelphia PA 19104-6305 Business E-Mail: haroldfs@gmail.com.

SCHIFFMAN, HOWARD SCOTT, law and environmental educator; b. Phila., May 17, 1964; s. Gerald and Lillian Schiffman. BA, Boston U., 1985; JD, Suffolk U., 1988; LLM, George Washington U., 1996; PhD, U. Wales (Cardiff), 2007. Bar: Mass. 88, NY 89, U.S. Dist. Ct. (ea. and so. dists.) NY 89, U.S. Supreme Ct. 00. Staff atty. Legal Aid Soc. NY, Bklyn., 1988—93, 1996—99; from adj. lectr. to clin. asst. prof., Sch. Continuing and Profl. Studies NYU, NYC, 1996—2005, dir. MS program in global affairs, Sch. Continuing and Profl. Studies, 2004—08, clin. assoc. prof., Sch. Continuing and Profl. Studies, 2005—09; adj. assoc. prof., environ. conservation edn. NYU Steinhardt Sch. Culture, Edn. and Human Devel., 2009—. Author: (book) Marine Conservation Agreements: The Law & Policy of Reservations And Vetoes, 2008; corr. editor: Jour. Internat. Wildlife Law and Policy, 1998—; contbr. articles to profl. jours. Bd. advisor Islands First, 2008—; advisor UN Mission Republic Palau, 2007—. Mem.: ABA, Internat. Law Assn., Am. Soc. Internat. Law. Jewish. Business E-Mail: howard.schiffman@nyu.edu.

SCHIFFMAN, LOUIS F., management consultant; b. Poland, July 15, 1927; s. Harry and Bertha (Fleder) S.; m. Mina R. Hankin, Dec. 28, 1963; children: Howard Laurence, Laura Lea. BChemE, NYU, 1948, MS, 1952, PhD, 1955. Rsch. engr. Pa. Grade Crude Oil Assn., Bradford, 1948-50; tchg. fellow dept. chemistry NYU, 1950-54; rsch. chemist E.I. DuPont de Nemours & Co., Wilmington, Del., 1954-56, Atlantic Refining Co., Phila., 1956-59; project leader, group leader, head corrosion sect. Amchem Products Inc., Ambler, Pa., 1959-70; pres. Techni Rsch. Assocs. Inc., Willow Grove, Pa., 1970—. Bd. dirs. Techno Ventures, Inc., Tecxchange.com; real estate developer: ptnr. Bay Properties Co., Bay Club Marina, Margate, N.J., Willow Grove (Pa.) Assocs.; pub., editor Patent Licensing Gazette, 1968—, World Tech., 1975—; panelist on forum patents and inventions Delaware Valley Industry, 1973; mem. adv. oversight com. NSF, 1975, moderator energy conf. ERDA, Washington, 1976, Las Vegas, 1977; mem. adv. group in small bus. R&D programs Dept. Def., 1980. Editor: (with others) Guide to Available Technologies, 1985; contbr. to Encyclopedia of Chemical Technology, 1967; contbr. articles to profl. jours.; patentee in field. Recipient Founders Day award NYU, 1956. Fellow Am. Inst. Chemists; mem. Am. Chem. Soc., N.Y. Acad. Scis., Lic. Exec.s Soc., Tech. Transfer Soc., Assn. Univ. Tech. Mgrs., Assn. Small Rsch. Cos. (editl. contbr. newsletter), Sigma Xi, Phi Lambda Upsilon. Home: 1001 Easton Rd 206M Willow Grove PA 19090 Office: Techni Rsch Assocs Inc PO Box 1036 Willow Grove PA 19090-0922 Personal E-mail: techniresearch@yahoo.com.

SCHIFFNER, ADRIENNE ANITA, art historian, educator; b. Jersey City, June 7, 1947; d. Thomas B. and Anita (Grosvenor) McAndrews; m. Richard Burchett (div.); children: Anita Claussen, Arianne Burchett; m. Charles Robert Schiffner, Jan. 22, 1983. BA in Art History, Ariz. State U., Tempe, 1989, MA in Art History, 2001. Cert. CC tchr. Ariz. Dir. Main Trail Galleries, Scottsdale, Ariz., 1972—73; archivist Frank Lloyd Wright Found., Scottsdale, 1977—83; v.p. Charles Schiffner Arch. Ltd., Phoenix, 1983—2000; program coord. pres. cmty. enrichment programs Ariz. State U., Tempe, 2000—03, instr. art history, 2003—04; tchr. art history Xavier Coll. Prep., Phoenix, 2002—. Lectr. in field; adj. faculty mem. Rio Salado CC, Phoenix, 2003—06. Chmn. living rm. restoration project Taliesin West, Scottsdale; mem. Phoenix Arts Commn.; mem. adv. bd. Ariz. State U. Art Mus., Tempe, 1998—2000; chmn. grants com. Phoenix Arts Commn., 1985—88; bd. dirs. Ariz. chpt. Nat. Soc. Arts and Letters, 1992—95; bd. dirs. Ballet Ariz., Phoenix, 1999—2001. Taliesin fellow, Frank Lloyd Wright Found., 1973—83. Mem.: Coll. Art Assn., Soc. Archtl. Historians, French Heritage Soc. (pres.), Ariz. State U. Coll. Fine Arts Alumni Assn. (co-pres. 2002—). Home: 5202 E Osborn Phoenix AZ 85018 Office: Xavier Coll Prep 4710 N 5th St Phoenix AZ 85012

SCHIFFNER, CHARLES ROBERT, architect; b. Reno, Sept. 2, 1948; Robert Charles and Evelyn (Keck) S.; m. Iovanna Lloyd Wright, Nov. 1971 (div. Sept. 1981); m. Adrienne Anita McAndrews, Jan. 22, 1983. Student, Sacramento Jr. Coll., 1967-68, Frank Lloyd Wright Sch. Architecture, 1968-77. Registered architect, Ariz., Nev., Wis. Architect Taliesin Associated Architects, Scottsdale, Ariz., 1977-83; pvt. practice architecture Phoenix, 1983—. Lectr. The Frank Lloyd Wright Sch. of Architecture, 1994, 95. Named one of 25 Most Promising Young Americans Under 35, U.S. mag., 1979; recipient AIA Honor award Western Mountain Region, 1993, Western Home awards Sunset Mag., 1989, 91, AIA Ariz. Merit award, 1993 and numerous others. Home: 5202 E Osborn Rd Phoenix AZ 85018-6137 Office: 2944 N 44th St Ste 101 Phoenix AZ 85018

SCHIFFRIN, MILTON JULIUS, physiologist; b. Rochester, NY, Mar. 23, 1914; s. William and Lillian (Harris) S.; m. Dorothy Euphemia Wharry, Oct. 10, 1942; children: David Wharry, Hilary Ann. AB, U. Rochester, 1937, MS, 1939; PhD cum laude, McGill U., 1941. Instr. physiology Northwestern U. Med. Sch., Chgo., 1941—45; lectr. pharmacology U. Ill. Med. Sch., 1947—57, clin. asst. prof. anesthesiology, 1957—61; with Hoffmann-La Roche, Inc., Nutley, NJ, 1946—79, dir. drug regulatory affairs, 1964—71, asst. v.p., 1971—79; pres. Wharry Rsch. Assn., Seattle, 1979—. Chmn. Everglades Health Edn. Ctr., 1986—87. Author: (with E.G. Gross) Clinical Analgesics, 1955; editor: Management of Pain in Cancer, 1957. Bd. dirs. Univ. Adult Day Ctr., 1993—; mem. adv. bd. Regional Ombudsman Program, 1998—, Residents Coun. Washington, 1998—. Capt. USAAF, 1942-46. Mem. Am. Med. Writers Assn. (bd. dirs. 1967-70, pres. N.Y. chpt. 1967-68, nat. pres. 1972-73), Am. Physiol. Soc., Internat. Coll. Surgeons, Am. Therapeutic Soc., Coll. Clin. Pharmacology and Therapeutics, Am. Chem. Soc. Home and Office: Unit 308 4400 Stone Way N Seattle WA 98103-7486 Office Phone: 206-284-8809. Personal E-mail: grampared@comcast.net.

SCHIFRIN, LALO, composer; b. Buenos Aires, June 21, 1932; Student, Juan Carlos Paz and Olivier Messiaen.; PhD (hon.), RISD, 1989. Tchr. composition UCLA, 1970-71; guest condr. Israel Philharm, L.A. Philharm, L.A. Chamber Orch., Indpls. Symphony, Atlanta Symphony. Argentinian rep., Internat. Jazz Festival, Paris, 1955, formed own jazz group; composer for stage, modern dance, TV; with Dizzy Gillespie's band, 1962; film and TV composer, Hollywood, Calif., 1964—; compositions: (for ballet) Jazz Faust, 1963, (for orch.) Piano Concerto # 1, 1986, Cantos Aztecas, 1989, Concerto for guitar and orch., 1986, Concerto for double bass and orch., 1987, Three tangos for flute, harp and strings, 1987, Dance concertantes for clarinet and orch., 1990, Impressions for trumpet and orch., 1990, La Nouvelle Orleans Woodwind Quintet, 1991, Concerto # 2, 1992, Cantares Argentinos, 1992, Symphony # 1 for orch., 1993, Symphonic Impressions of Oman (recorded by London Symphony), 2001, (opera) The Trial of Louis XVI, 1988; theme for TV series Mission: Impossible (2 Grammy awards); film scores include The Cincinnati Kid, 1965, Cool Hand Luke, 1967, The Fox, 1968; film scores include Kelly's Heroes, 1970, W.U.S.A., 1970, Bullit, 1970, Dirty Harry, 1971, THX-1138, 1971, The Beguiled, 1971, Magnum Force, 1973, Enter the Dragon, 1973, The Four Musketeers, 1975, The Eagle Has Landed, 1977, Voyage of the Damned, 1976, Rollercoaster, 1977, Telefon, 1977, Boulevard Nights, 1979, The Concorde-Airport '79, 1979, Competition, 1981, Sudden Impact, 1984, The Sting II, 1985, The Fourth Protocol, 1987, Tango, 1996, Rush Hour, 1998, Rush Hour 2, 2001; TV series The Young-Lawyers, Mannix, 'Mission Impossible', Starsky and Hutch; writer orchestration for Grand Finale medley for Carreras, Domingo and Pavarotti, Rome, 1990, Dodger Stadium, 1994, Eiffel Tower, 1998, Yokohama, Japan, 2002; commd. Steinway Found piano concerto The Americas, selected by Nat. Symphony Orch., 1992. Recipient 4 Grammy awards, 1967, 1969, 1986, 6 Acad. award nominations Acad. Motion Picture Arts and Scis., 1966, 67, 75, 77, 80, 82, Walk of Fame award Hollywood C. of C.; chevalier de l'Ordre des Arts et des Lettres French gov.

SCHIFTER, RICHARD, lawyer; b. Vienna, July 31, 1923; came to US, 1938; s. Paul and Balbina (Blass) S.; m. Lilo Krueger, July 3, 1948; children: Judith, Deborah, Richard P., Barbara, Karen BS in Social Sci. summa cum laude, CCNY, 1943; LLB, Yale U., 1951; DHL (hon.), Hebrew Union Coll., 1992. Bar: Conn. 1951, DC 1952, US Supreme Ct. 1954, Md., 1958. Assoc. Fried, Frank, Harris, Shriver & Jacobson, Washington, 1951-57, ptnr., 1957-84; dep. US rep. with rank of ambassador UN Security Coun., NYC, 1984-85; asst. sec. of state for human rights and humanitarian affairs Dept. State, Washington, 1985-92; US rep. UN Human Rights Commn., Geneva, 1983-86, 93; spl. asst. to pres., counselor Nat. Security Coun., Washington, 1993-97, spl. adviser to Sec. of State, 1997-2001. Head US del. Conf. on Security and Cooperation in Europe Experts Meeting on Human Rights, Ottawa, Ont., Can., 1985, Dem. Insts., Oslo, 1991; bd. dirs. US Inst. Peace, 1986-92; mem. Congl. Commn. on Security and Cooperation in Europe, 1986-92. V.p., pres. Md. Bd. Edn., Balt., 1959-79; chmn. Md. Gov.'s Commn. on Funding Edn. of Handicapped Children, 1975-77, Md. Values Edn. Commn., 1979-83, Montgomery County Dem. Cen. Com., Md., 1966-70; del. Dem. Nat. Conv., 1968; bd. govs. Am. Jewish Com., 1992-93, 01-04, mem. exec. com., 2001-04; chmn. Internat. Rels. Commn., 2001-04; chmn. bd. dirs. Ctr. for Democracy and Reconciliation in Southeastern Europe, 2002-06, Am. Jewish Internat. Rels. Inst., 2005-; bd. trustees Inst. Christian and Jewish Studies, 2000-. With US Army, 1943-46, ETO, office of mil. govt. for Germany, 1946-48. Decorated Austrian Gt. Golden Decoration with star, comdr. Order of the Romanian Star, Bulgarian Stara Planina Order 1st class; recipient Disting. Svc. award, Sec. of State, 1992. Mem. Phi Beta Kappa. Democrat. Jewish. Home: 6907 Crail Dr Bethesda MD 20817-4723 Personal E-mail: rschifter@aol.com.

SCHIFTER, STEPHAN CLAY, retired finance educator; b. Abington, Pa., Nov. 1, 1944; s. Erich Stephan and Margaret Weaver Schifter; m. Catherine Crutchfield, Aug. 17, 1974. BS, U. Pa., Phila., 1967, MBA, 1971. Pres. Secura Corp., Phila., 1987—94; ptnr. KPMG Peat Marwick, Phila.; instr., fin. & economics Thomas Jefferson U., Phila. Dir., treas. AH Coun., Phila., 2004—; dir., v.p. Del. Valley Stroke Coun., Phila., 2007—. Mem.: Del. Valley Venture Ptnrs., Wharton Alumni Club

(Phila.) (treas. 1978—82, dir.). Achievements include patents for vehicle status monitor & management system, satellite communications. Avocations: travel, history, golf, cooking. Home: 1420 Locust St Philadelphia PA 19102 Personal E-mail: stephan.schifter@comcast.net.

SCHILIRO, PHILIP M., federal official; b. Bklyn., Aug. 6, 1956; BS in Polit. Sci., Hofstra U., LI, 1978; JD, Lewis & Clark Law Sch., Portland, Oreg., 1981. Adminstrv. asst. to Rep. Henry D. Waxman US House of Reps., 1982—97; chief of staff US House Oversight & Govt. Reform Com., 1997—2004, 2005—08; policy dir. to Senator Tom Daschle US Senate, 2004; congressional liaison Barack Obama's Presdl. Campaign, 2008; dir. legis. affairs The White House, Washington, 2009—. Dem. staff dir. Ho. Com. Oversight & Govt. Reform, 1997—2003, Dem. chief of staff, 2005—08; staff dir. Dem. Leadership Com., 2004; dir congl. rels. presdl. transition team, Washington, 08. Democrat. Office: The White House Office Legis Affairs 1600 Pennsylvania Ave NW Washington DC 20500 Office Phone: 202-456-1414.*

SCHILL, MICHAEL H., dean, law educator; b. Schenectady, NY, 1958; AB, Princeton U., 1980; JD, Yale Law Sch., 1984. Law clerk Hon. Marvin Katz Ea. Dist. Pa., 1984—85; assoc. Fried, Frank, Harris, Shriver & Jacobson, 1985—87; vis. lectr. Yale Law Sch., 1987; asst. prof. law U. Pa. Law Sch., 1987—91, assoc. prof., 1991—92; prof. law and real estate U. Pa. Law Sch. and Wharton Sch., 1993—95; vis. prof. Harvard Law Sch., 1999; dir. Furman Ctr. for Real Estate and Urban Policy, NYU, 1994—2004; prof. law and urban planning NYU Sch. Law and Robert F. Wagner Grad. Sch. Pub. Svc., 1995—2003, Wilf Family Prof. in property law and prof. urban planning, 2003—04; dean, prof. law UCLA Sch. Law, 2004—. Asst. counsel N.Y. State Assembly, Com. Housing, 1979; dir. Study of Neighborhood Reinvestment Princeton Urban and Regional Rsch. Ctr., 1980—81; vis. faculty U. Miami Law Sch., Grad. Prog. in Real Estate, 1994. Co-author: Revitalizing America's Cities: Neighborhood Reinvestment and Displacement, 1983, Reducing the Cost of New Housing Construction in New York City, 1999, The State of New York City's Housing and Neighborhoods, 2001; author: Housing and Community Development in New York City: Facing the Future, 1999; contbr. articles to law jours. Office: UCLA Sch Law Box 951476 Los Angeles CA 90095-1476 E-mail: schill@law.ucla.edu.*

SCHILLER, BARBARA, retired special education educator; b. NYC, Jan. 1, 1943; d. Harry M. and Lee C. Browner; m. Charles Philip Schiller, July 16, 1967; children: Andrew Barry, Zachary Alan. BS in Edn., SUNY, Cortland, 1964; MS in Edn. of Visually Impaired, Hunter Coll., 1971. Tchr. children with limited vision NYC Bd. Edn., 1964—95. Sculpture exhbns., SUNY, Purchase, 1980—2005, sculpture in two-person show, Gallery at Marmara, N.Y.C., 2003, Cirque d'Art, N.Y., 2003, sculpture juried show, Katonah Mus., N.Y., 2003—09, sculpture in permanent collections, Amsterdam Whitney Gallery, N.Y.C., 2004—, Broome St. Gallery, NYC, Juried In Exhibition at Hammond Mus., NY. Mem. bd. gov. Temple Beth Shalom, Mahopac, NY, 1995—2004. Recipient NY award for sculpture, Knickerbocker Artists, multiple awards 8 first place, Quilts Along the Bay, Barnegat, NJ, 2003—04; named Woman of Yr., Temple Beth Shalom, Mahopac, NY, 2004. Mem.: ASCA, Am. Soc. Contemporary Artists (pres. 2009—, treas. 2008—, pres. 2009, Isobel Folb Sokolow Meml. 2007, ASCA award for sculpture 2007), Studio Art Quilt Assn., Pen and Brush, Katonah Mus. Artists Assn., No. N.Mex. Quilters Guild, State Quilter Guild NJ, No. Star Quilters Guild, Hadassah. Avocations: reading, interior decorating, music, doll making, jewelry making. Home: 3600 Curry St Yorktown Heights NY 10598 Personal E-mail: bobbybschiller@gmail.com.

SCHILLER, DONALD CHARLES, lawyer; b. Chgo., Dec. 8, 1942; s. Sidney S. and Edith (Lastick) S.; m. Eileen Fagin, June 14, 1964; children— Eric, Jonathan Student, Lake Forest Coll., 1960-63; JD, DePaul U., 1966. Bar: Ill. 1966, US Dist. Ct. (no. dist.) Ill. 1966, US Supreme Ct. 1972. Ptnr. Schiller, DuCanto & Fleck LLP, Chgo., 1966—; lectr. in law U. Chgo. Law Sch., 2001—. Chair domestic rels. adv. com. Cir. Ct. Cook County, 1993—2001, co-chmn. rules revision com., 2003—; spkr. profl. confs. Contbr. chpts. and articles to profl. publs. Mem. steering com. on juvenile ct. watching, LWV, 1980-81. Recipient Maurice Weigle award, Chgo. Bar Found., 1978, Disting. Alumni award, DePaul U., 1988, various certs. of appreciation from numerous profl. groups; named one of Am.'s Best Divorce Lawyers, Town and Country, 1986, 1998, Nat. Law Jour., 1987, Best Lawyers in Am., 1987—, Chgo.'s Best Divorce Lawyers, Crain's Chgo. Bus., 1981, Today Chgo. Woman, 1985, Inside Chgo. Mag., 1988, Chgo Sun Times, 2000, Worth Mag., 2002, Nat. Top 500 Lawyers, Law Dragon Mag., 2005, 2006, 2007, 10 Top Ill. Lawyers, Super Lawyers Mag., 2006, 2007, Leading Laws Mag., 2006, 2007. Fellow Am. Bar Found., Am. Acad. Matrimonial Lawyers (nat. chair continuing legal edn. 1993-94); mem. ABA (bd. govs. 1994-97, chmn. family law sect. 1985-86, Ill. State del. 1980-84, mem. Ho. of Dels. 1984-2003, editor-in-chief Family Law Newsletter 1977-79; mem. editorial bd., assoc. editor Family Adv. Mag. 1979-84, speaker at confs. and meetings), Am. Bar Retirement Funds (pres. 2005-06, adv. bd. mem. 2007—), Ill. Bar Assn. (pres. 1987-88, chmn. family law sect. 1976-77, editor Family Law Bull. 1976-77, bd. govs. 1977-83, treas. 1981-84, v.p. 1984-86, chmn. various coms., lectr., incorporator and pres. Ill. State Bar Assn. Mutual Ins. Co., Inc. 1988-89), Chgo. Bar Assn., Am. Coll. Family Law Trial Lawyers (diplomate). Office: Schiller DuCanto & Fleck LLP 200 N La Salle St 30th Fl Chicago IL 60601-1098 Office Phone: 312-609-5560. Business E-Mail: dschiller@sdflaw.com.

SCHILLER, LAWRENCE JULIAN, film producer, writer; b. NYC, Dec. 28, 1936; s. Isidore and Jean (Liebowitz) S.; children: Suzanne, Marc, Howard, Anthony, Cameron. BA, Pepperdine Coll., 1958. Photojournalist Life mag., 1959-69, Paris Match, 1960-69, London Sun. Times, 1960-69. Producer, dir.; (films) Hey, I'm Alive, The Winds of Kitty Hawk, Marilyn, Raid on Short Creek, An Act of Love, The Executioner's Song (Emmy award), Peter the Great (Emmy award), By Reason of Insanity, Margret Brourke-White Story, Plot to Kill Hitler, Double Jeopardy, Perfect Murder, Perfect Town, American Tragedy, Master Spy: The Robert Hanson Story, Henry Lee Series; author: Cape May Court House, Into the Mirror, American Tragedy, Perfect Murder, Perfect Town, Marilyn; collaborator: (with Albert Goldman) Lenny Bruce (with Eugene Smith) Minamata, (with Norman Mailer) The Executioner's Song (Pulitzer prize 1980), Oswald's Tale; (with O.J. Simpson) I Want To Tell You. Chmn. bd. dirs. Am.-Soviet Film Initiative, 1988; Am. del. Moscow Internat. Forum on Peace, 1987; mem. USSR-USA Bi-Lateral Talks, 1988. Recipient numerous awards in photojournalism Nat. Press Photographers Assn., Acad. award for The Man Who Skied Down Everest, 1975 Mem. Nat. Press Photographers Assn., Calif. Press Photographers Assn., Dirs. Guild of Am., Acad. of Motion Picture Arts and Scis. Democrat. Jewish. Personal E-mail: lschiller@klscomm.com.

SCHILLER, MARJORIE A., special education professor; b. Chgo., June 24, 1950; d. Donald A and Donna Schiller; children: Daniel Shapiro, Max Shapiro. PhD, U. Ariz., 1990. Asst. prof. Ohio State U., Columbus, 1991—95; behavior specialist Tucson Unified Sch. Dist., Tucson, 1995—2000; chair of tchr. edn. Ctrl. Ariz. Coll., Coolidge, 2000—. Adj. prof. Prescott Coll., Tucson, 1996—. Author (book chpt.): Access to Art Education, 1999; contbr. articles to profl. jours. Mem.: Coun. Exceptional Children. Avocations: making jewelry, painting. Office: Central Arizona College 8470 N Overfield Rd Coolidge AZ 85718 Home: 7340 N OPunta Tucson AZ 85704 Home Phone: 320-797-1811; Office Phone: 520-494-5035. Business E-Mail: mschiller@centralaz.edu.

SCHILLER, PETER HARKAI, biomedical engineering and physics educator; Dorothy W. Poitras prof. med. engring. and med. physics MIT, Cambridge, Mass. Contbr. articles to profl. jours. Fellow: Am. Acad. Arts & Scis.; mem.: NAS. Office: MIT E25-634 Bldg 46-6041 77 Massachusetts Ave Cambridge MA 02139 Office Phone: 617-253-9339. Office Fax: 617-253-8943. Business E-Mail: phschill@mit.edu.

SCHILLER, PHILIP W., computer company executive; b. 1960; BS in Biology, Boston Coll., 1982. Former programmer, sys. analyst Mass. Gen. Hosp.; former IT mgr. Nolan, Norton & Co., Lexington, Mass.; various mktg. positions Apple Computer Inc., 1986—93; dir. product mktg. FirePower Sys., Menlo Park, Calif., 1993—95; v.p. product mktg. Macromedia, Inc., San Francisco, 1995—97; sr. v.p. worldwide product mktg. Apple Inc. (formerly Apple Computer Inc.), Cupertino, Calif., 1997—, interim v.p. mktg., 2006. Delivered keynote address MacWorld Conf. & Expo, San Francisco, 2009. Achievements include having been instrumental in the development and marketing of iMac, iBook, PowerBook G4, iPod, Mac OS X, and subsequent products. Office: Apple Inc 1 Infinite Loop Cupertino CA 95014 Office Phone: 408-996-1010.*

SCHILLER, PIETER JON, retired venture capital executive; b. Orange, NJ, Jan. 14, 1938; s. John Fasel and Helen Roff (Roberts) S.; m. Elizabeth Ann Williams, Nov. 20, 1965; children— Cathryn Ann, Suzanne Elizabeth. BA in Econs. with honors, Middlebury Coll., 1960; MBA, NYU, 1966. Fin. analyst Merck & Co., Inc., NYC, 1960—61; fin. analyst, asst. divsn. contr., dir. auditing, then asst. contr. Allied Chem. Corp., NYC and Morristown, NJ, 1961—75, treas., 1975—79, v.p. planning and devel., 1979—83; exec. v.p. diagnostic ops. Allied Health & Sci. Products Co., 1983—86; pres. subs. Instrumentation Lab., Lexington, Mass., 1983—86; gen. ptnr. Advanced Tech. Ventures, Waltham, Mass., 1986—2005, ptnr. emeritus, 2006—. Bd. dirs. CytoLogix Corp., Waltham, Mass.; bd. advisors Fresh Tracks Capital, LLC, Shelburae, Vt. Chmn. bd. trustees Newark Boys Chorus Sch., 1976—78, pres. bd., 1974—76; trustee Colonial Symphony Soc., 1978—85, v.p., 1980—82, pres., 1982—83; active Morris Mus., Morristown, Concord Mus., Mass., 1994—96, v.p., 1996—2000, chmn. bd. trustees, 2002—06; pres. Middlebury Coll. Alumni Assn., 1994—96; chmn. allocations com. United Way of Morris County, 1974—79, v.p. bd. dirs., mem. exec. com., 1979—80; trustee Morris Mus. Arts and Scis., 1980—83; bd. dirs. New Eng. Coun., Boston, 1983—86; v.p. Middlebury Coll. Alumni Assn., 1992—94; bd. dirs. John Adams Innovation Inst., Westborough, Mass., 2005—, Chatham Marconi Maritime Ctr., Mass., 2007—. Mem. Fin. Execs. Inst. Republican. Episcopalian. Avocations: skiing, photography. Home: 18 S Meadow Rdg Concord MA 01742-3051 Office Phone: 781-290-0707.

SCHILLER, VIVIAN L., broadcast executive, former Internet company executive; b. 1961; BA in Russian and Soviet Studies, Cornell U., 1983; MA in Russian, Middlebury Coll., 1984. Russian interpreter, prodn. coord. Turner Broadcasting Systems, Inc., v.p., gen. mgr. Turner Original Productions, exec. v.p. CNN productions; sr. v.p., gen. mgr. Discovery Times Channel The NY Times Co., 2002—05, sr. v.p. TV and video, 2005—06, exec. v.p., gen. mgr. Discovery Times Channel, 2005—06; sr. v.p., gen. mgr. NYTimes.com, 2006—08; pres., CEO Nat. Pub. Radio (NPR), Washington, 2009—. Bd. govs. Banff TV Festival; mem. Coun. Fgn. Rels., Nat. TV Acad. Exec. Peer Group. Supervising prodr. (TV documentaries) A Century of Women, 1994, Moon Shot, 1994, sr. prodr. Hank Aaron: Chasing the Dream, 1995, Hollywood's Amazing Animal Actors, 1996, Biker Women, 1996, Survivors of the Holocaust, 1996 (Emmy award for Outstanding Informational Spl., 1996), Animal ER, 1996, Pirate Tales, 1997, Twin Stories, 1997, Warner Bros. 75th Anniversary: No Guts, No Glory, 1998, Dying to Tell the Story, 1998, prodn. mgr. Terror's Children, 2003, The New Face of Late Night TV, 2003, exec. prodr. (documentaries) Word Wars, 2004, Off to War, 2005. Recipient five Emmy awards, two Peabody awards, Alfred I. duPont-Columbia U. award, 2007. Office: Nat Pub Radio 635 Massachusetts Ave NW Washington DC 20001*

SCHILLER, WILLIAM RICHARD, surgeon; b. Bennett, Colo., Jan. 14, 1937; s. Francis T. and Frances M. (Finks) S.; m. Beverlee Schiller; children from previous marriage: Julie, Lisa. BS, Drury Coll., Springfield, Mo., 1958; MD, Northwestern U., 1962; MA in Liberal Arts, St. John's Coll., 2005. Diplomate Am. Bd. Surgery; cert. of added qualifications in surg. critical care, 1987, recertified in surg. critical care, 1994. Intern Passavant Meml. Hosp., Chgo., 1962-63; resident Northwestern U. Clin. Tng. Program, Chgo., 1963-68; assoc. prof. surgery Med. Coll Ohio, Toledo, 1970-78; prof. surgery U. N.Mex, Albuquerque, 1978-83; dir. Trauma Ctr. St. Joseph's Hosp., Phoenix, 1983-89; dir. burn and trauma ctr. Maricopa Med. Ctr., Phoenix, 1989-98; prof. surgery So. Ill. U., Springfield, 1998—2002; ret., 2002. Clin. prof. surgery U. Ariz. Health Sci. Ctr.; prof. surgery Mayo Grad. Sch. Medicine, Rochester, Minn. Contbr. chpts. to books, articles to profl. jours. Served as maj. M.C. U.S. Army, 1968-70, Vietnam. Recipient Disting. Alumnus award for career achievement, Drury Coll., 2004. Fellow ACS; mem. Am. Assn. Surgery of Trauma, Cen. Surg. Assn., Western Surg. Assn., Soc. Surgery of Alimentary Tract, Am. Burn Assn., Internat. Soc. of Surgery. Republican. Home: 784 Aspen Compound Santa Fe NM 87501 Personal E-mail: wrschiller@hughes.net.

SCHILLING, CURT (CURTIS MONTAGUE SCHILLING), retired professional baseball player; b. Anchorage, Nov. 14, 1966; m. Shonda Schilling; children: Gehrig, Grant, Gabriella, Garrison. Student, Yavapai CC, Prescott, Ariz. Pitcher Balt. Orioles, 1988—90, Houston Astros, 1991, Phila. Phillies, 1992—2000, Ariz. Diamondbacks, 2000—03, Boston Red Sox, 2004—09; ret., 2009. Founder Curt's Pitch for ALS; co-founder Curt and Shonda Schilling Melanoma Found. America. Recipient Lou Gehrig Meml. award, 1995, Roberto Clemente award, 2001, Hutch award, Fred Hutchinson Cancer Rsch. Ctr. Seattle, 2001, Branch Rickey award, Rotary Club Denver, 2001, Jim "Catfish" Hunter Humanitarian award, NC ALS Assn., 2001, #1 Good Guy of Yr. award, Sporting News, 2004; co-recipient Sportsmen of Yr. award, Sports Illustrated, 2001; named Nat. League Championship Series MVP, 1993, World Series MVP, 2001, Outstanding Pitcher, Nat. League Players Choice Awards, 2001, 2002; named to Nat. League All-Star Team, Maj. League Baseball, 1997, 1998, 1999, 2001, 2002, Am. League All-Star Team, 2004. Achievements include leading the National League in strikeouts (319), 1997, (300), 1998; wins (22), 2001; leading the in wins American League (21), 2004; member of World Series Champion: Arizona Diamondbacks, 2001; Boston Red Sox, 2004, 2007. Avocation: history. Office: c/o The SHADE Found N Valley Med Plz 3811 E Bell Rd Ste 106 Phoenix AZ 85032*

SCHILLING, EMILY GAENZLE, research scientist; d. Lawrence Wilson Gaenz;e and Wilhelmina Smith Gaenzle; m. Jonathan Scott Schilling, Oct. 6, 2001. BA in Biology and French, Colgate U., Hamilton, NY, 1997; MS in Ecology and Environ. Sci., U. Maine, Orono, 2002, PhD in Ecology and Environ. Sci., 2008. Internat. field program coord. Am. Mus. Natural History, NYC, 1998—99; biology tchr. Grace Ch. Sch., NYC, 1999—2000; grad. rsch. asst. U. Maine, 2002—. Contbr. articles to profl. publs. Fellowship, NSF, 2002—05. Mem.: North Am. Benthological Soc., Soc. Conservation Biology (sec. Minn. chpt. 2008—).

SCHILLING, FREDERICK AUGUSTUS, JR., geologist, consultant; b. Phila., Apr. 12, 1931; s. Frederick Augustus and Emma Hope (Christoffer) Schilling; m. Ardis Ione Dovre, June 12, 1957 (div. 1987); children: Frederick Christopher, Jennifer Dovre. BS in Geology, Wash. State U., 1953; PhD in Geology, Stanford U., 1962. Cert. engring. geologist, Calif.; registered geologist Calif., environ. assessor Calif. Computer geophysicist United Geophys. Corp., Pasadena, Calif., 1955-56; geologist various orgns., 1956-61, U.S. Geol. Survey, 1961-64; underground engr. Climax (Colo.) Molybdenum Co., 1966-68; geologist Keradamex Inc., Anaconda Co., M.P. Grace, Ranchers Exploration & Devel. Corp., Albuquerque and Grants, N.Mex., 1968-84, Hecla Mining Co., Coeur d'Alene, Idaho, 1984-86, various engring. and environ. firms, Calif., 1986-91; prin. F. Schilling Cons., Canyon Lake, Calif., 1991—. Author: Bibliography of Uranium, 1976. Del. citizen amb. program People to People Internat., USSR, 1990—91. With US Army, 1953—55. Fellow: Explorers Club; mem.: Internat. Platform Assn., Soc. Mining Engrs., Am. Assn. Petroleum Geologists, Geol. Soc. Am., Adventurer's Club LA, Kiwanis, Masons, Sigma Xi, Sigma Gamma Epsilon. Republican. Presbyterian. Avocation: track and field. Home and Office: F Schilling Cons 30037 Steel Head Dr Canyon Lake CA 92587-7460 Office: F Schilling Cons 14661 Myford Rd Ste C Tustin CA 92780-7205 Home Phone: 951-244-8999; Office Phone: 714-731-8438. Business E-Mail: faschill@pacbell.net.

SCHILLING, HEATHER ANNE, education educator; married. MEd, Ind. Purdue, Fort Wayne. Lic. tchr. Ind., 1990. English and history tchr. Whitko HS, South Whitley, Ind., 1990—2001; edn. prof. Manchester Coll., Ind., 2003—. Mem.: Tri Kappa (pres. 1996—2009). Office: Manchester Coll 604 E College Ave North Manchester IN 46962 Personal E-mail: haschilling@manchester.edu.

SCHILLING-NORDAL, GERALDINE ANN, retired secondary school educator; b. Springfield, Mass., Feb. 4, 1935; d. Robert Milton and Helen Veronica Schilling; m. Reidar Johannes Nordal. BS, Boston U., 1956, MEd, 1957; postgrad., Springfield Coll., Anna Maria Coll. Tchr. art Agawam Jr. HS, Mass., 1957-58, Agawam HS, 1958—2003, head art dept., 1970-95, K-12 art acad. coord., 1995-96. Instr. oil painting univ. ext. course Agawam Night Sch., 1957-58; instr. creative arts Agawam Evening Sch., 1973-80. Active Agawam Town Report Com., 1967-77, Agawam Hist. Commn., 1979-87, Agawam Arts and Humanities Com., 1979-85, Agawam Minerva Davis Libr. Study Com., 1987-88, Agawam Cultural Coun., 1994-97; sec. Agawam Town Beautification Com., 1974-87; mem. town tchrs. rep. Agawam Bicentennial Com., 1975-77; chmn. 40th anniversary St. John the Evangelist Ch., Agawam, 1986, co-chmn. 50th anniversary com., 1996, mem. renovation com., 1983; decoration chmn. town-wide Halloween Parties, 1971, 94; past recruiter Miss Agawam Pageant, 1972-76; appeal vol. Cath. Charity, 1995-02; mem. Agawam Cath. Womens Club, 1995—, banquet com., 1997, 99, co-chmn., 2002-04, 07-; Mr and Mrs Club Agawam Bapt. Ch., 2007-; Art Judge, Hampden County 4H, 1998-2002, chmn. various sch. reunions. Mem. NEA, AARP, Agawam Edn. Assn. (sec. 1970-74, 76-77, h.s. addition dedication com. 1998-99, scholarship com., 1997, Agawam Tchrs. Wall of Fame for 45 Yrs. Svc. 2002), Hampden County Tchrs. Assn., Mass. Tchrs. Assn., Mass. Art Edn. Assn., Nat. Art Edn. Assn., New Eng. Art Edn. Assn., Mass. Cath. Order Foresters, West Springfield Neighborhood House Alumni Assn. (pres. 1966, advisor 1968), West Springfield H.S. Alumni Assn. (3d v.p. 1968-70, 1st v.p. 1970-71, pres. 1972-74), Boston U. Alumni Club Springfield Area (organizer area giving campaigns 1957-62, class agt. 1985—; area scholarship com. 1995—), Retired Educators Assn. Mass.(sec. Hamfden West Chpt., 2009-), Ret. State, County and Mcpl. Employees Assn., Agawam Ret. Employees Assn., St. Anns Soc. (scholarship com., 2009), Springfield Mus., Ramapogue hist. Soc., Am. Legion (life), St. John's Over 60 Club (chmn. spring banquet, 2008-09), Zeta Chi Delta (pres. 1955-56), Delta Kappa Gamma (art chair, reservation chmn. art work and hist. archives, hospitality 50th and 60th ann. com.). Office: PO Box 291 Agawam MA 01001

SCHILLINGS, DENNY LYNN, retired history professor, educational and grants consultant; b. Mt. Carmel, Ill., June 28, 1947; s. Grady Lynn and Mary Lucille (Walters) S.; m. Karen Krek; children: Denise, Corinne. AA, Wabash Valley Coll., 1967; BEd, Ea. Ill. U., 1969, MA in History, 1972; MA in Adminstrn., Govs. State U., 1996; postgrad., Ill. State U., No. Ill. U. Grad. asst. dept. history Ea. Ill. U., Charleston, 1969; tchr. Edwards County High Sch., Albion, Ill., 1969-70, Sheldon (Ill.) High Sch., 1971-73, Homewood-Flossmoor (Ill.) High Sch., 1973—2003, tchr. history, grants and devel. mgr., 1994—2003; supr. history dept. Coll. Liberal Arts and Scis, No. Ill. U., Dekalb, 2003—; ret., 2003; adj. prof. Trinity Christian Coll., 2003—. Participant, con. Atlantic Coun. U.S. and NATO, Washington, 1986, Internat. Soviet-U.S. Textbook Project Conf., Racine, Wis., 1987; moderator Soviet-U.S. Textbook Study: Final Report, Dallas, 1987; chair history content adv. com. Ill. Tchr. Certification Requirements Com. 1986; mem. Ill. State Bd. Edn., Com. to Establish Learner Outcomes, 1984, Joint Task Force on Admission Requirements Ill. State Bd. on Higher Edn., 1986—; mem. adv. com. for Jefferson Found. Sch. Programs, 1987-90, Ill. State Bd. Edn.'s Goals Assessment Adv. Com., 1987-90; chair Ill. Learning Standards Project, 1996-97; pres. Corinne Jeannine Schillings Found., 2004—. Author: (with others) Economics, 1986, The Examination in Social Studies, 1989, Links Across Time and Place: A World History, 1990, Illinois Government Text, 1990, 99, 2003, Challenge of Freedom, 1990; author: The Living Constitution, 1991, 3d edit., 2002; co-editor: Teaching the Constition, 1987; reviewer, cons. for ednl. instns. and organizations; chair editorial bd. Social Edn., 1983; contbg. editor Social Studies Tchr., 1987-88. Mem. steering com. Homewood-Floosmoor High Sch. Found., 1983-84; elected bd. edn. Homewood Elem. Dist. 153, 1999—, found. pres., 2005—. Mem. NEA, Am. Hist. Assn. (James Harvey Robinson prize com. 1990-91), Ill. Coun. Social Studies (v.p. 1981, editor newsletter 1979-84, pres. 1983), Ill. Edn. Assn. (Gt. Lakes coord. com. 1982-83), Nat. Coun. Social Studies (publs. bd. 1983-86, bd. dirs. 1987-90, 94-96, exec. com. 1989-90, chair conf. com. 1989-90, pres. 1993-94, program planning com. 1989, 91), Phi Alpha Theta. Avocations: computers, reading. Home and Office: 18447 Aberdeen St Homewood IL 60430-3525 Home Phone: 708-957-3684.

SCHILLOW, NED WILLIAM, mathematics professor; b. Skippack, Pa., Aug. 3, 1950; s. William James and Doris Elizabeth (Shaffer) S. BS, Ursinus Coll., Collegeville, Pa., 1972; MS, Rutgers U., 1974; MEd, Temple U., Phila., 1976. Sec. tchr. Cherry Hill (N.J.) Sch. Dist., 1974-76; prof. math. Lehigh Carbon C.C., Schnecksville, Pa., 1976—.

Assoc. editor the UMAP Jour., 1986—2005; asst. newsletter editor Pa. State Math. Assn. Two Yr. Colls., 1982-90; columnist Mo. Coun. Tchrs. Math. newsletter, 1985-90; contbr. articles to profl. jours. and chpts. to books. Recipient Faculty Appreciation award Student Govt. of Lehigh Carbon C.C., 1987, George Elison Faculty Svc. award, 1988, Employee Recognition award, 1989, Pa. Outstanding Teaching award State Commn. for C.C., 1992, Faculty Excellence award, Lehigh Carbon C.C., 2003; NSF-MSP grantee, 2003—08, Outstanding Math. Tchg. award, Pa. State Math Assn., 2008 Mem. Math Assn. Am., Am. Math. Assn. of 2-Yr. Colls., Nat. Coun. Tchrs. Math. (rep. 1988—), Pa. State Math. Assn. of 2-Yr. Colls. (exec. bd. 1982—), Pa. Coun. Tchrs. Math (exec. bd. 1979-84, conv. publicity com. 1991-92, conu exhibits chair, 2006-07), Ea. Pa. Coun. Tchrs. Math. (exec. bd. 1979—2006, pres. 1980-82). Republican. United Ch. of Christ. Avocations: reading, travel, crystal. Home: PO Box 539 Skippack PA 19474 Office: Lehigh Carbon CC 4525 Education Park Dr Schnecksville PA 18078-2510 Home Phone: 610-584-6448; Office Phone: 610-799-1752. Business E-Mail: nschillow@lccc.edu.

SCHILSKY, RICHARD LEWIS, oncologist, researcher; b. NYC, June 6, 1950; s. Murray and Shirley (Cohen) S.; m. Cynthia Schum, Sept. 24, 1977; children: Allison, Meredith. BA cum laude, U. Pa., Phila., 1971; MD with honors, U. Chgo., 1975. Diplomate Nat. Bd. Med. Examiners, Am. Bd. Internal Medicine (subspecialty med. oncology); lic. physician, Mo., Ill. Intern, resident medicine Parkland Meml. Hosp., Southwestern Med. Sch., Dallas, 1975-77; clin. assoc. medicine br. and clin. pharmacology br. Divsn. Cancer Treatment, Nat. Cancer Inst., Bethesda, Md., 1977-80, cancer expert clin. pharmacology br., 1980-81; asst. prof. dept. internal medicine U. Mo. Sch. Medicine, Columbia, 1981-84; asst. prof. dept. medicine U. Chgo. Pritzker Sch. Medicine and Michael Reese Med. Ctrs., 1984-86, assoc. prof. dept. medicine, 1986-89; assoc. dir. joint sect. hematology and med. oncology U. Chgo. and Michael Reese Med. Ctrs., 1986-89; assoc. prof. dept. medicine, assoc. dir. sect. U. Chgo. Pritzker Sch. Medicine, 1989-91, prof. dept. medicine sect. hematology-oncology, 1991—; dir. U. Chgo. Cancer Rsch. Ctr., 1991-99; chmn. Cancer and Leukemia Group B, Chgo., 1995—; assoc. dean clin. rsch. biol. scis. divsn. U. Chgo., 1999—2007. Vivian Saykaly vis. prof. oncology McGill U., 1992; sci. com. Internat. Congress on Anti-Cancer Chemotherapy, 2002; adv. panel on hematologic and neoplastic disease U.S. Pharmacopeial Conv., 1991-95; cancer ctr. support grant rev. com. Nat. Cancer Inst., NIH, 1992-95; expert panel on advances in cancer treatment, 1992-93; mem. Cancer Ctrs. Working Group, 1996-97; oncologic drugs adv. com. FDA, 1996-2000, chmn., 1999-2000; mem. clin. trials implementation com. Nat. Cancer Inst., 1997-98, mem. bd. sci. advisors, 1999—, chmn., 2009-, mem. clin. trials working group, 2004-05, mem. translational rsch. working group, 2005-07, mem. clin. trials adv. com., 2007-. Mem. editl. bd. Investigational New Drugs, 1988-95, Jour. Clin. Oncology, 1990-93, Contemporary Oncology, 1991-95, Jour. Cancer Rsch. and Clin. Oncology, 1991—, Seminars in Oncology, 1997—; assoc. editor Clin. Cancer Rsch., 1994—, Cancer Therapeutics, 1997-99, Cancer, 2000—07; contbr. articles to profl. jours., chpts. to books. With USPHS, 1977-80. Recipient Spl. Advancement for Performance award VA, 1983, Fletcher Scholar award Cancer Rsch. Found., 1989; grantee VA, 1981-87, Am. Cancer Soc., 1983-86, 92-95, Ill. Cancer Coun., 1985-86, Michael Reese Inst. Coun., 1985-86, Nat. Cancer Inst., 1987, 88-90, Burroughs-Wellcome Co., 1987-88, NIH/Nat. Cancer Inst., 1988— Fellow ACP; mem. AAAS, Am. Soc. Clin. Oncology (bd. dirs. 2002-05, pres.-elect 2007, pres. 2008-2009, immediate past pres., 2009-), Am. Assn. Cancer Rsch. (chmn. Ill. state legis. com. 1992—), Am. Fedn. Clin. Rsch. (senator Midwest sect. 1983-84, councilor 1983-86, chmn. 1988-89), Am. Cancer Soc. (bd. dirs. Ill. divsn. 1997—), Am. Assn. Cancer Edn., Am. Soc. Clin. Pharmacology and Therapeutics, Ctrl. Soc. Clin. Rsch., N.Y. Acad. Scis., Assn. Am. Cancer Insts. (bd. dirs. 1995-99), Chgo. Soc. Internal Medicine, Am. Fedn. for Med. Rsch., Am. Soc. Clin. Oncology, Assn. Patient Orientated Rsch., Sigma Xi, Alpha Epsilon Delta, Alpha Omega Alpha. Office: U Chgo Biol Scis Divsn 5841 S Maryland Ave MC 1000 Chicago IL 60637-1463 Office Phone: 773-834-3914. Office Fax: 773-834-3915. Business E-Mail: rschilsk@medicine.bsd.uchicago.edu.

SCHILZ, JODYE LYNN DICKSON, history professor; b. Glen Rose, Tex., May 26, 1953; d. James L. and Mary Ruth Dickson; m. Thomas Frank Schilz, Aug. 22, 1981. AA, Weatherford Coll., Tex., 1978; BA in History, Tex. Christian U., Fort Worth, degree Summa Cum Laude, 1981, MA in History, 1982. Cert. CC instr. Calif., 1989. Adj. prof. MGSC Minn. State U., Mankato, 1986—89; adj. prof. San Diego Miramar Coll., 1990—. Editl. cons. Tex. State Hist. Assn., Austin, 1984—. Co-author: (history book) Buffalo Hump and the Penateka Comanches; contbr. articles to profl. jours. Bd. mem. CATV Bd., St. Peter, Minn., 1988—89; asst. dir. Altar Guild, St.Bartholomew's Episcopal Ch., San Diego, 1999—2002; state pres. Walter P. Webb Soc., Austin, 1980—81. Co-recipient Caldwell award, Walter P. Webb State Hist. Soc., 1977, 1979; scholarship, Daughters Tex. Republic, 1980, Grad. fellowship, Minority Groups Studies Ctr., Minn. State U., 1988. Mem.: Phi Alpha Theta, Pi Sigma Alpha, Phi Theta Kappa. Democrat. Episcopalian. Avocations: doll collecting, writing, quilting. Office: San Diego Miramar Coll 10440 Black Mountain Rd San Diego CA 92126 Business E-Mail: jschilz@sdccd.edu.

SCHIMBERG, A(RMAND) BRUCE, retired lawyer; b. Chgo., Aug. 26, 1927; s. Archie and Helen (Isay) S.; m. Barbara Zisook; children: Geoffrey, Kate. PhB, U. Chgo., 1949, JD, 1952. Bar: Ohio 1952, Ill. 1955, U.S. Supreme Ct. 1987. Assoc. Paxton & Seasongood, Cin., 1952-55; ptnr. Schimberg, Greenberger, Kraus & Jacobs, Chgo., 1955-65, Leibman, Williams, Bennett, Baird & Minow, Chgo., 1965-72, Sidley & Austin, Chgo., 1972-92, counsel, 1993-94; ret., 1994. Lectr. U. Chgo., 1953-54; gen. counsel Comml. Fin. Assn., 1978-94; past mem. editl. bd. Lender Liability News. Mng. and assoc. editor U. Chgo. Law Rev., 1951-52; contbr. articles to legal jours. Bd. dirs. U. Chgo. Law Sch. Alumni Assn., 1969-72; dir. vis. com. U. Chgo. Law Sch., 1980-83. Recipient Homer Kripke Lifetime Achievement award for contbns. to comml. fin. law, 1998. Mem. ABA (chmn. subcom. and charter mem. comml. fin. svcs. com.), Am. Coll. Comml. Fin. Lawyers (pres. 1994-95, bd. regents), Ill. Bar Assn. (chair comml. banking, bankruptcy sect. 1972-73), Chgo. Bar Assn. (chair ucc com., 1966, bd. mgrs. 1968-70, chair judiciary com. 1971-72), Law Club Chgo., Mid-Day Club, Lake Shore Country Club. Home: 132 E Delaware Pl Apt 5002 Chicago IL 60611-4944

SCHIMBERG, BARBARA, organizational development consultant; b. Chgo., Nov. 30, 1941; d. David and Tybe Zisook; children from previous marriage: Brian Hodes, Valery Lodato; m. A. Bruce Schimberg, Dec. 29, 1984. BS, Northwestern U., 1962. Ptnr. Just Causes, cons. not-for-profit orgns., Chgo., 1978-86. Cons. in philanthropy, community involvement, and organizational devel., 1987—; Chgo. cons. Population Resource Ctr., 1978-82. Former mem. women's bd. dirs. Mus. Contemporary Art; bd. dirs., vice chmn. Med. Rsch. Inst. Coun., Michael Reese Med. Ctr.; bd. dirs., chmn. Midwest Women's Ctr.; trustee Francis W. Parker Sch.; bd. dirs. Women's Issues Network Found., 1991-98, pres., 1993-94; mem. adv. bd. Med. Rsch. Inst. Coun., Children's Meml. Hosp. Mem. ACLU (adv. com.), Women's Bd. U. Chgo. Office: 7241 E Xentaua Canyon Dreer Tucson AZ 85750 Personal E-mail: bschimberg@gmail.com.

SCHIMEK, DIANNA RUTH REBMAN, state legislator; b. Holdrege, Nebr., Mar. 21, 1940; d. Ralph William and Elizabeth Julia (Wilmot) Rebman; m. Herbert Henry Schimek, 1963; children: Samuel Wolfgang, Saul William. AA, Colo. Women's Coll., 1960; student, U. Nebr., Lincoln, 1960-61; BA magna cum laude, U. Nebr., Kearney, 1963. Former tchr. and realtor; mem. Nebr. Legislature from 27th dist., Lincoln, 1989—2009; chmn. govt., mil. and vets. affairs com. Nebr. Legislature, Lincoln, 1993—94, 1999—2006, vice chair urban affairs com., 1995-98; chmn. Performance Audit Com., 2007—08. Dem. Nat. committeewoman, 1984-88; chmn. Nebr. Dem. Com., 1980-84; mem. exec. com. Dem. Nat. Com., 1987-88; past pres., sec. bd. dirs. Downtown Sr. Ctr. Found., 1990-96; mem. exec. bd. Midwestern Legis. Conf., 1995-2009, co-chair health and human svcs. com., 1995-96; exec. dir. Nebr. Civil Liberties Union, 1985; former bd. dirs. Nebr. Repertory Theater, Exon Found., 1997-2000; mem. adv. bd. Martin Luther Home, 1997-2003; chair Midwestern Legis. Conf. Coun. of State Govts., 2000-01, co-chair com. intergovtl. affairs; mem. Midwest Interstate passenger Rail Commn., 2001-05; mem. exec. bd. Coun. State Govts., 2000-09; chair NCSL Task Force on Initiative and Referendum, 2001-02; bd. dirs. Habitat Humanity, 2006—. Recipient Outstanding Alumni award, U. Nebr., 1989, Tribute award, YWCA, 1992, Friend of Psychology award, NE Psychol. Assn., 1998, Woman of Yr. award, Nova Chpt. Bus. & Profl. Women, 1999, Disting. Svc. award, Nat. Guard Assn., 2000, Woman of Distinction award, Soroptomists, 1999, Legis. of Yr. award, NE Dental Hygienists Assn., 2001, Disting. Svc. award, NE League of Municipalities, 2002, Lincoln Interfaith Leadership award, 2003, Harold Steck award, ARC of NE, 2004, Alice Paul award, Lancaster Status of Women Commn., 2006, Civil Libertarian of Yr. award, ACLU Nebr., 2006, Patty Steele Meml. award, Am. Cancer Soc., Ethics in Govt. award, Common Cause, others, Friend Edn. award, NSEA, 2007, Friend Medicine award, NMA, 2007, Patriots award, 2008, Lifetime Achievement award, Voices for Children, 2009, Cmty Leader award, Friendship Home, 2009; Toll fellow, 1999. Mem. Nat. Conf. State Legislators Women's Network (bd. dirs. 1993-96, 1st vice chmn.), PEO, Mayflower Soc., Delta Kappa Gamma (hon.), Mortar Bd. (cmty. advisor 1998, hon.), Rotary Internat., Ponca Tribe (hon., NE Applessed bd. mem. 2009, Bar. None Housing bd. mem. 2009, Heritage Nebr. bd. mem. 2009), Nat. Trust Hist. Presentation (adv. coun. mem. 2009). Democrat. Unitarian Universalist. Home: 6437 Lone Tree Dr Lincoln NE 68512 Home Phone: 402-423-0262.

SCHIMMEL, DAVID M., law educator; b. Balt., Mar. 30, 1934; s. Isidore William and Blanche (Sakols) S.; m. Barbara Barlin, June 18, 1961; children: Suzanne, Jonathan, Joanna. BA, Duke U., 1955; JD, Yale U., 1958; BHL, Hebrew Union Coll., 1962. Bar: Md. 1959, Mass. 1985, U.S. Supreme Ct. 1963. Assoc. Schimmel, Hettleman and Tatelbaum, Balt., 1959-60; ops. officer West African div. U.S. Peace Corps, Washington, 1962-63, exec. officer office of planning, evaluation and rsch., 1964-66; assoc. dir. Peace Corps Ethiopia, Addis Ababa, 1963-64; dir. Vols. to Am. U.S. Dept. State, Washington, 1966-67; dir. Peace Corps V.I. Tng. Ctr., 1967-68; assoc. prof. Sch. Edn. U. Mass., Amherst, 1968-72, prof., 1972—, dir. ednl. policy and adminstrn. program, 1989-93; dir. Svc. Learning Commonwealth Honors Coll., 1998-2000. Vis. scholar UCLA, 1975; lectr. Grad. Sch. Edn., Harvard U., Cambridge, Mass., 1984-85, vis. prof., 1998—. Co-author: The Rights of Students and Teachers, 1982, Parents, Schools and the Law, 1987 (Am. Sch. Bd. Jour. "Must" book of 1988), A Bicentennial Guide for Lawyers and Teachers, 1990, Teachers and the Law, 7th edit., 2007, School Law, 2008; mem. authors com. Edn. Law Reporter, St. Paul, 1984-97, mem. editl. adv. com., 1998—. Mem. Mass. Cmty. Svc. Commn., 1990-94; bd. dirs. Jewish Fund Justice, 1996—. 2d lt. U.S. Army, 1959. Grantee NEH, 1982; recipient Disting. Achievement award Ednl. Press Assn. Am., 1995; U. Mass. Disting. Acadamic Outreach award, 1999 Mem. Mass. Assn. Law-Related Edn. (bd. dirs., pres. 1975-81, 86-90, Disting. Svc. award 1981), Ednl. Law Assn., Phi Alpha Delta. Democrat. Avocation: tennis. Home: 200 W Pomeroy Ln Amherst MA 01002-3260 Office: U Mass 265 Hills S Amherst MA 01003

SCHIMMELBUSCH, WERNER HELMUT, psychiatrist; b. Vienna, Nov. 16, 1937; came to U.S., 1954; s. Hans Mowgli and Anneliese Martha (Koeppe) S.; m. Faye Karina Wrangel, Dec. 29, 1958 (div. Mar. 1967); m. Jeanette Ramona Dyal, Mar. 26, 1971; children: Andre Curt, Anne Ramona. PhD, U. Wash., Seattle, 1962; psychiatrist, Yale U., 1968; adult psychoanalyst, Seattle Inst. Psychoanalysis, 1977, child psychoanalyst, 1992. Dir. Seattle Psychiat. Soc. & Inst., Seattle, 2006—; pvt. practice Seattle, 1969—. Clin. prof. U. Wash., Seattle, 1984—; tng. and supervising psychoanalyst Seattle Inst. Psychoanalysis, 1990—. Capt. U.S. Army, 1963-65. Mem. Am. Psychiatric Assn., Am. Psychoanalytic Assn., Seattle Psychoanalytic Soc. and Inst. (pres. 1979-80, 94-96, dir. 2006), Ctr. Adv. Psychoanylytic Studies. Avocations: skiing, hiking, sailing. Office: 4033 E Madison St Seattle WA 98112-3104 Office Phone: 206-322-6219.

SCHIMMENTI, JOHN JOSEPH, lawyer; b. NYC, Mar. 21, 1938; s. John Marcus and Mae M. (Miranti) Schimmenti; m. Mary Elizabeth Sleep, Apr. 18, 1964. BA, Columbia Coll., 1959; JD, Georgetown U., Washington, 1962, LLM, 1964. Bar: DC 1962, NY 1964, Calif. 1965, US Dist. Ct. (ctrl. dist.) Calif. 1965, US Ct. Appeals (9th cir.) 1966, US Supreme Ct. 1961. Trial atty., Anti-Trust divsn. US Dept. Justice, Washington, 1962—64; trial atty., lands divsn. LA, 1965—67; trial atty. Santa Fe R.R., LA, 1968—72; ptnr. Schimmenti & Berberian, 1971—. Mem.: Columbia U. Alumni Southern Calif. (pres. 1978), LA Bar Assn. (condemnation com. mem. 1983), S.W. Dist. Bar Assn. (pres. 1983), El Segundo Rotary Club (pres. 1977). Republican. Roman Catholic. Office: Schimmenti Mullins & Berberian Unit 303 5630 Ravenspur Dr Rancho Palos Verdes CA 90275-3535 Home Phone: 310-541-4906; Office Phone: 310-874-4801.

SCHIMPF, DAVID MICHAEL, theology studies educator, department chairman; b. Sheboygan, Wis., May 28, 1958; s. Richard and Barbara Schimpf; m. Patricia Miller Schimpf. BA, Macalester Coll., St. Paul; PhD, Marquette U., Milw., 1988. Instr. Assumption Coll., Worcester, Mass., 1988—92; assoc. prof., theology Marian U., Fond Du Lac, Wis., 1992—, chair, dept. humanities, 2008—. Named Wis. Prof. of Yr., Carnegie Found., 1998. Mem.: Midwest Popular Culture Assn. (area chair, religion and popular culture 2003—). Independent. Roman Catholic. Avocations: gardening, hiking. Office: Marian Univ 45 S Nat Ave Fond Du Lac WI 54935 Personal E-mail: dschimpf@charter.net. Business E-Mail: dschimpf@marianuniversity.edu.

SCHINDEL, DONALD MARVIN, retired lawyer; b. Chgo., Jan. 5, 1932; s. Harry L. and Ann (Schiff) S.; m. Alice Martha Andrews, Apr. 24, 1960; children: Susan Yost, Judith Harris, Andrea Glickman. BS in Acctg., U. Ill., 1953; JD, U. Chgo., 1956. Ptnr. Sonnenschein, Nath & Rosenthal, Chgo., 1956-2000, ret., 2000. Author: Estate Administration and Tax Planning for Survivors, 1987, supplements, 1988-1996. Pres. United Way Highland Park-Highwood, Ill., 2000—03; v.p. campaign United Way of the North Shore, 2004—05; pres. Congregation Beth Or, Deerfield, Ill., 1983—85. Fellow Am. Coll. Trust and Estate Counsel; mem. ABA, Ill. Bar Assn., Chgo. Bar Assn. (chmn. probate practice com. 1981-82); Chgo. Estate Planning Coun. (Austin Fleming Disting. Svc. award 1999). Avocations: tennis, travel, bridge, golf, running. Home: 636 Rice St Highland Park IL 60035-5012

SCHINDERLE, ROBERT FRANK, retired hospital administrator; b. Mayville, Wis., Aug. 3, 1923; m. Elizabeth, June 23, 1949; children: David, Gary, Mary, Brian. BS, Marquette U., Milw., 1949; MS, Northwestern U., Evanston, Ill., 1959. Asst. office mgr. Western Leather Co., Milw., 1949-51; mgr. bus. office St. Francis Hosp., Peoria, Ill., 1951-55; credit mgr. Mercy Hosp., Chgo., 1955-59, asst. to adminstr., 1957-58, controller, 1958-59, asst. adminstr., 1959-65, St. Joseph Hosp., Joliet, Ill., 1965-70, assoc. adminstr., 1970-71, adminstr., 1971-76, exec. dir., 1976-86; adminitr., chief exec. officer St. Joseph Med. Ctr., 1976—86; dir. corp. legis. affairs and devel. Franciscan Sisters Health Care Corp., Mokena, Ill., 1986-89, ret.; dir. Current Affairs & Devel., 1986—89. Chmn. Areawide Hosp. Emergency Svcs. Coun. Bd. dirs. Region IX Health Systems Agy., Our Lady of Angels Retirement Home, Joliet, Joliet YMCA, St. Joseph Coll. Nursing, Joliet. Fellow Am. Coll. Health Care Execs. (life); mem. Am. Hosp. Assn., Ill. Hosp. Assn. (chmn. 1975-76), Ill. Hosp. Licensing Bd. (chmn. 1982-97, vice chmn. 1997-), Catholic Hosp. Assn. (dir.), Ill. Cath. Hosp. Assn. (chmn. 1972-73), Lodges: Rotary, Elks, KC, Delta Sigma Pi Bus. Frat., Beta Gamma Sigma. Roman Catholic. Home: 24017 W Newkirk Dr Plainfield IL 60544-1838

SCHINDLER, ALBERT ISADORE, physicist, researcher; b. Pitts., June 24, 1927; s. Jonas and Esther (Nass) S.; m. Phyllis Irene Liberman, June 17, 1951; children— Janet Mae, Jerald Scott, Ellen Susan. BS, Carnegie Inst. Tech., 1947, MS, 1948, DSc, 1950. Research asst. Carnegie Inst. Tech., Pitts., 1947-50, research physicist, 1950-51; supervisory rsch. physicist Naval Rsch. Lab., Washington, 1951-75; assoc. dir. research for material sci. and component tech. Naval Research Lab., 1975-85; prof. materials engring. and physics Purdue U., West Lafayette, Ind., 1985-92, cons., 1992-97, dir. Ind. Ctr. for Innovative Superconductor Tech., 1988-91, dir. Midwest Superconductivity Consortium, 1990-91; dir. div. materials rsch. NSF, Washington, 1988-90; chief scientist Office Naval Rsch., Arlington, Va., 1997-99; cons., 1999—. Cons. in field. Recipient E.O. Hulburt award Naval Research Lab., 1956, Nat. Capitol award for applied sci., 1962, Pure Sci. award Naval Research Lab.-Sci. Research Soc. Am., 1965, award Washington Acad. Scis., 1965, USN Disting. Achievement in Sci. award, 1975, Alumni Merit award Carnegie Mellon U., 1976, Sr. Exec. Service award Dept. Navy, 1983, Superior Pub. Svc. award Dept. Navy, 1999. Fellow Am. Phys. Soc., Washington Acad. Scis.; mem. Sigma Xi. (dir.) Home: 6615 Sulky Ln Rockville MD 20852-4344 Home Phone: 301-770-0232.

SCHINDLER, FRED H., professor; b. Berwyn, Ill., May 20, 1951; s. Henry D. and Melba M. Schindler; m. Evelyn Trogner, Aug. 27, 1972; children: Carlson E., Trogner J. BS, U. Ill., Urbana, 1972; MS, U. Iowa, 1974, PhD, 1995. Instr. Ctrl. CC, Hastings, Nebr., 1979—88; prof. biology Indian Hills CC, Ottumwa, Iowa, 1991—. Sec. Spoke Folk, Ottumwa. Mem.: Iowa Assn. CC Biology Tchrs., Iowa Acad. Scis. Achievements include research in development and validation of an ecology issue attitude instrument for college students. Avocation: bicycling. Home: 418 Bryan Rd Ottumwa IA 52501 Office: Indian Hills CC 525 Grandview Ottumwa IA 52501 Office Fax: 641-683-5206. E-mail: fschindl@indianhills.edu.

SCHINDLER, JO ANN, retired library director; BA, U. Hawaii, Manoa; MLS, U. Calif., Berkeley. With San Francisco Pub. Libr. Sys., LA County Libr. Sys.; head Bus., Sci., and Tech. Sect. Hawaii State Pub. Libr. Sys., dir., state libr.; ret., 2007. Named Hawaii State Pub. Libr. Sys. Employee of Yr., 1999, MCI Cybrarian of Yr. for State of Hawaii. Mem.: ALA, Hawaii Libr. Assn.

SCHINDLER, WILLIAM STANLEY, retired public relations executive; b. Detroit, Jan. 4, 1933; s. William Henry and Katherine (Schilling) S. Student, Wayne State U., 1950-53. Sr. v.p. Campbell-Ewald Co., Warren, Mich., 1968-85; v.p. pub. rels. Detroit Med. Ctr., 1985-92; interim v.p. Wayne State U., Detroit, 1993. Cons. to bus., univs., and founds.; v.p. Sandusky Pub. Co., Mich. Editor: Progress Report-New Detroit, Inc, 1969. Past mem. Detroit Hist. Commn., Detroit Fire Commn.; chmn. Detroit CSC; mem. Gov.'s Sesquicentennial Commn., Peoria, Ariz. Fire Pension Bd., Pers. Bd., Hist. Preservation Com.; mem. trans. needs assessment com.; mem. Bond Election Com.; pres. United Churchmen of Detroit; bd. dirs. Adult Well-Being Svcs., Sacred Heart Rehab. Ctr., Brush Park Devel. Authority, Harper Hosp. Aux.; mem. Citizens Bond Commn. With US Army, 1954—56. Decorated Commendation Medal with pendant. Mem. Pub. Rels. Soc. Am., Adcraft Club Detroit, Detroit Press Club, Sons Whiskey Rebellion, Recess Club, Univ. Club, Detroit Athletic Club, Prismatic Club, Box 12 Club, Heard Mus. Coun. Home: 8741 W Wescott Dr Peoria AZ 85382-8773

SCHINGOETHE, DAVID JOHN, dairy cattle nutritionist; b. Aurora, Ill., Feb. 15, 1942; s. John Ernest and Helen Dorothy (Tesch) A.; m. Darlene Kay Wennlund, June 6, 1964; children: Darcy Lynn (Schingoethe) Haber, Deanna Rae Gall. BS in Agrl. Sci.-Dairy Sci., U. Ill., 1964, MS in Dairy Sci., 1965; PhD in Dairy & Nutrition, Mich. State U., 1968. Asst. prof. dairy sci. S.D. State U., Brookings, 1969-73, assoc. prof. dairy sci., 1973-80, prof. dairy sci., 1980—. Cons. Nat. Sunflower Assn., Bismarck, N.D., 1985-86, Hubbard Milling Co., Mankato, Minn., 1985, Dairymen, Inc., Kingsport, Tenn., 1986-87, Land O' Lakes, Arden Hills, Minn., 1996. Mem. editl. bd. Jour. of Dairy Sci., Champaign, Ill., 1973-78, 91-96, editor, 1998-07, Inver Grove Heights, Minn., US BioEnergy, 2006-07. Recipient Gamma Sigma Delta Rsch. award S.D. State U., 1987, F.O. Butler Rsch. award S.D. State U., 1985. Mem. Am. Dairy Sci. Assn. (pres. 2000-01, dir. 1996-99, Am. Feed Industry Assn. award 1989, Nutrition Profl. award 1996, Land O'Lakes award, 2003, Award of Honor, 2006), Am. Soc. Animal Sci., Coun. Agrl. Sci. and Tech., Am. Soc. Nutrition, Am. Oil Chem. Soc., Brookings Lions Club (pres. 1985-86); fellow 2007. Lutheran. Achievements include author or co-authorship of 490 articles in refereed and popular press publs. Office: SD State Univ Dairy Sci Dept PO Box 2104 Brookings SD 57007-0647 Business E-Mail: david.schingoethe@sdstate.edu.

SCHINK, JAMES HARVEY, lawyer; b. Oak Park, Ill., Oct. 2, 1943; s. Norbert F. and Gwendolyn H. (Hummel) S.; m. Lisa Wilder Haskell, Jan. 1, 1972 (div. 1980); children: David, Caroline, Elizabeth; m. April Townley, Aug. 14, 1982. BA, Yale U., 1965, JD, 1968. Bar: Ill. 1968, Colo. 1982. Assoc. Sidley & Austin, Chgo., 1968; law clk. to judge U.S. Ct. Appeals, Chgo., 1968-69; assoc. Kirkland & Ellis LLP, Chgo., 1969—72, ptnr., 1972—. Sustaining fellow Art Inst. Chgo. Mem. ABA, Ill. Bar Assn., Chgo. Bar Assn., Chgo. Club, Saddle and Cycle Club, Mid-Am. Club, Econ. Club Chgo., Sonnenalp Golf Club, Vail Racquet Club, Vail Mountain Club, Yale Club Chgo., Racquet Club Chgo., Game Creek Club. Republican. Presbyterian. Home: 1530 N State Pkwy

Chicago IL 60610-1614 Office: Kirkland & Ellis LLP 300 N Lasalle Chicago IL 60654 Home Phone: 312-951-0036; Office Phone: 312-862-2258. Business E-Mail: jschink@kirkland.com.

SCHINK, JULIAN C., oncologist, director; s. David R. and Lee Burnette Schink; m. Sharon M. Savaiano, July 13, 1980; children: Maureen O'Neill, Matthew, Christopher, Peter. MD, U. Tex. Health Sci. Ctr., San Antonio, 1982. Diplomate gynecologic oncology Am. Bd. Ob-Gyn., 1990. Dir. divsn. gynecologic oncology Robert H. Lurie Comprehensive Cancer Ctr., Chgo., 2004—; v.p. Soc. Gynecologic Oncology, Chgo., 2008—. Office: Northwestern Univ Feinberg S O M 250 E Superior Chicago IL 60611

SCHIOLDAGER, AMY LEE, investment company executive; BSc in Bus. Adminstrn., Fin., Calif. State U., Hayward, 1989. Registered rep. series 7, 63, 24, 3 NASD, 2000. Fund acct. Barclays Global Investors, San Francisco, 1989—2001, mng. dir., global head index equity, 1991—. Mem. adv. bd. Russell Investment Grp., Tacoma, 2002—07, Std. & Poors Index, 2006—, Dow Jones Wilshire Index, 2006—. Author: Active Index Investing: The Unique Challenges of US Equity Index Management, Real Estate Investing: The REIT Way. Recipient award, Wall St. Jour., 1989. Mem.: Fin. Women's Assn. Office: Barclays Global Investors 400 Howard Str San Francisco CA 94105 Business E-Mail: amy.schioldager@barclaysglobal.com.

SCHIPPER, JAN D., language educator; m. Rick Schipper, June 28, 1980; 1 child, Caitlin. Assoc. prof. English Vol. State CC, Gallatin, Tenn., 1998—. Contbr. scientific papers. Mem.: Phi Kappa Phi. Office: Vol State CC 1480 Nashville Pike Gallatin TN 37066 Business E-Mail: jan.schipper@volstate.edu.

SCHIRAY, MICHEL, economist, research scientist, consultant; b. Vichy, 03 Allier, France, Nov. 24, 1942; s. Alexis and Xenia (Loukine) Schiray. BA in Humanities and Human Scis., U. Paris, Sorbonne, 1967; MS in Econs., U. Paris, 1968. Rsch. dir., rschr. Nat. Ctr. Sci. Rsch., Paris, 1977—2002, dir. rsch. group psychotropics, politics and soc., 1994—97, rsch. dir., 2003—; coord. internat. rsch. project United Nations Ednl., Sci. and Cultural Orgn.-Most Program, United Nations Office for Drugs and Crime, Paris, 1998—2002. Rschr. Internat. Rsch. Ctr. on Environment and Devel., 1974—2008, Ho. Scis. Humanities, 1975—2008, Rsch. Ctr. on Contemporary Brazil, 1989—2008; prof., rschr. Fed. & State U. Rio de Janeiro, 1989—93, 1998—2002. Author: (book) Third World and Industrialized World, 1978; coord. (scientific jour.) Brazilian Economy and Globalization, 2000, (scientific report) Globalization, Drugs and Criminalization, 2002. Achievements include research in globalization, environment, social development and poverty, employment and informal economy, information and communication technologies, Drugs and economic criminality. Home: 9 rue Saulnier Paris 75009 France Office: Maison des Scis de l'Homme 54 blvd Raspail Paris 75006 France Business E-Mail: schiray@msh-paris.fr.

SCHIRBER, ANNAMARIE RIDDERING, retired speech and language pathologist, educator; b. Somerset County, NJ, Dec. 18, 1941; d. Pieter C. and Marie Louise (Kerk) Riddering; m. Eric R. Schirber, Aug. 25, 1960; children: Stefan Rene, Ashley Brooke. BA in Speech and Hearing Therapy, Rutgers U., 1964; MA in Edn. of Deaf and Hard of Hearing, Smith Coll., 1968; postgrad., Rutgers U., 1987-93. Cert. tchr. of deaf, hard of hearing, spl. edn., speech correctionist, speech-lang pathologist, N.J. Speech therapist Manatee County Bd. Edn., Bradenton, Fla., 1968-69; speech-lang. specialist Lawrence Twp. Pub. Schs., Lawrenceville, NJ, 1969—2002, Montgomery Twp. Bd. Edn., Skillman, NJ, 2003, Rock Brook Sch., Skillman, 2003—07. Adj. instr. comm. dept. Trenton (N.J.) State Coll., 1983-87; vis. lectr. Rutgers U., New Brunswick, 1993. Author: Teaching Auditory Processing Skills to Children, 1994; co-author: (with Erica Winebrenner) Speech Activities for Children, 1994, Language Activities to Teach Children at Home, 1994. Mem. exec. com. Women's Coll. Symposium, Princeton, N.J., 1982-84; mem. nat. alumnae admissions com. Smith Coll., Northampton, Mass., 1984-86. Grantee Lawrence Twp. Bd. Edn., 1973, 89, 90, Lawrence Twp. Edn. Found., 1999, 2001. Mem. Ctrl. Jersey Speech-Lang. and Hearing Assn. (exec. com. 1996-2007, v.p. 1985, pres. 1986-87), Princeton Area Smith Coll. Club (exec. com. 1996-2007, pres. 1998-2000), Smith Coll. Club Sarasota, Fla. (exec. com. mem. 2008-), AAUW, Venice, Fla.(br. sec., 2009), Southbay Women's Club (sec., treas. 2008-09). Home: 1505 Danforth Ln Osprey FL 34229

SCHIRER-SUTER, MYRON, library director; s. Marion and Jeanne Schirer; m. Cordelia Schirer-Suter, Mar. 9, 2002; 1 child, Cedric Theophil Johannes. BA, David Lipscomb Coll., Nashville, Tenn.; MAR, David Lipscomb U.; MSLIS, U. Ill., Urbana Champaign; EdD, Pepperdine U., LA. Libr. Friends U., Wichita, Kans., 1995—2000, Pepperdine U., LA, 2000—04; dir. libr. svc. Gordon Coll., Wenham, Mass., 2004—. Office: Gordon Coll 255 Grapvinr Rd Wenham MA 01984

SCHIRMEISTER, CHARLES F., retired lawyer; b. Jersey City, June 18, 1929; s. Charles F. and Louise P. (Schneider) Schirmeister; m. Barbara Jean Fredericks, Feb. 9, 1952; children: Pamela, Charles Bradford. BA, U. Mich., 1951; LLB, Fordham U., 1956. Bar: N.Y. 1956, U.S. Dist. Ct. (so. dist.) N.Y. 1961, U.S. Ct. Appeals (2d cir.) 1961, U.S. Supreme Ct. 1961. Asst. dist. atty. New York County, NY, 1956-61; assoc. Thelen, Reid & Priest, NYC, 1961-71, ptnr., 1971-94; ret., 1994. Trustee Ocean Grove (N.J.) Camp Meeting Assn.; deacon Cmty. Congl. Ch., Short Hills, NJ. Capt. USMC, 1951—53. Mem.: Canoe Brook Country Club (Summit, NJ), Univ. Club (NYC), Sigma Alpha Epsilon. Republican. Avocations: tennis, oenology, golf. Home: 15 Beechcroft Rd Short Hills NJ 07078-1648

SCHIRMER, BARBARA ROSE, special education educator, academic administrator; b. NYC, Dec. 23, 1948; d. Jack and Bella (Schiller) Edberg; m. John M. Schirmer, Aug. 22, 1971; children: Alison, Todd. BS, U. Buffalo, 1970; MEd, U. Pitts., 1971; EdD, U. Buffalo, 1983. Cert. spl. edn. tchr., N.Y. Tchr. W.Va. Sch. for the Deaf, Romney, 1971-72; tchr. Boston Sch. for the Deaf, Mass., 1972-74; asst. prof. Univ. Wis., Milw., 1982-83; assoc. prof. Lewis and Clark Coll., Portland, Oreg., 1985—97, assoc. dean, 1993—97; chair and prof. Kent State U., 1997—2001; dean, prof. Miami U., Oxford, Ohio, 2001—04; v.p. acad. affairs, provost, prof. U. Detroit, 2004—; pres. Oakley Acad., 2009—. Author: Language and Literary Development in Children Who Are Deaf, 2000, Psychological, Social and Educational Dimensions of Deafness, 2001, What's Special about Special Education, 2006; mem. editl. adv. bd. Reading Rsch. and Instrn., Jour. Literacy Rsch., Tchg. Exceptional Children; contbr. articles to profl. jours.; author: Teaching The Struggling Reader, 2009. Mem.: Internat. Reading Assn., Am. Ednl. Rsch. Assn., Coun. Exceptional Children, Con. Am. Instn. Deaf. Office: U Detroit 4001 W McNichols Rd Detroit MI 48221 Home: PO Box 700350 Plymouth MI 48170-0946 Personal E-mail: brschirmer@aol.com. Business E-Mail: barbara.schirmer@udmercy.edu, barbara.schirmer@oakleyacademy.org.

SCHIRO, JAMES JOSEPH, insurance company executive; b. Bklyn. m. Tomasina Schiro; 2 children. BS, St. John's U., 1967, D of Comml. Sci. (hon.), 1995; grad., Amos Tuck Sch. Exec. Program, Dartmouth Coll. Exec. Program. CPA. With Pricewaterhouse Coopers, 1967—2001; CEO PricewaterhouseCoopers, NYC, 1998—2001; COO-Fin. Zurich Fin. Svcs. Group, 2002, CEO, 2002—. Bd. govs. World Econ. Forum; bd. dirs. PepsiCo, Royal Philips Electronics, Goldman Sachs; mem. found. bd. IMD, Lausanne. Vice chmn., mem. bd. trustees Am. Friends Lucerne Festival, Inst. Advanced Study, Princeton, St. John's U; mem. bd. advisors Tsinghua Sch. Economics, Beijing. Recipient Ellis Island Medal of Honor, 1994, St. John's U. Alumni Pietas medal, 1992, Avenue of the Americas Assn.'s Gold Key award, 1992. Office: Zurich Fin Svcs Mythenquai 2 8022 Zurich Switzerland Office Phone: 41-44-625-2040. Business E-Mail: james.schiro@zurich.com.

SCHIRO, STEVE, computer software company executive; Bachelors degree in Economics, Claremont McKenna Coll. With Procter & Gamble Co., Intuit Inc., Borland Internat. Inc., Ansa Software; corp. v.p. home & retail divsn. Microsoft Corp., 1995—2002, v.p. retail sales and mktg., 2002—. Bd. dirs. Software Publishers Assn., 1995—97; retail adv. bd. Gartner Groups. Mem. Seattle Sports & Events Coun. Mem.: Consumer Products Coun. Office: Microsoft Corp Home & Retail Divsn 1 Microsoft Way Redmond WA 98052-6399

SCHIROKAUER, CONRAD, history professor; b. Leipzig, Germany, Apr. 29, 1929; s. Arno and Erna Schirokauer; m. Lore Strich, Nov. 26, 1956; children: David Walter, Oliver Arno. BA, Yale U., New Haven, Conn., 1950; PhD, Stanford U., Calif., 1960. Prof. CUNY, NYC, 1962—91; sr. scholar, adj. prof. Columbia U., NYC, 1993—. Author: (textbooks) A Brief History of Chinese & Japanese Civilizations. With US Army, 1955—57. Fellow, ACLU, 1967—69. Mem.: Assn. Asian Studies. Home: 340 Lantana Ave Englewood NJ 07631 Office: Columbia U New York NY 10027 Office Fax: 212-662-7289. Business E-Mail: cs176@columbia.edu.

SCHISGAL, MURRAY, playwright; b. NYC, Nov. 25, 1926; s. Abraham and Irene (Sperling) S.; m. Reene Schapiro, June 29, 1958; children: Jane, Zachary. Student, Bklyn. Conservatory of Music, 1948, L.I. U., 1950; LLB, Bklyn. Law Sch., 1953; BA, New Sch. Social Research, 1959. Playwright, screenwriter and prodr. movies, TV and theatre. Author: The Typists and The Tiger, London, 1960, N.Y.C., 1963, Ducks and Lovers, London, 1961, Knit One, Purl Two, Boston, 1963, Luv (One of the Best Plays of 1964-65), London, 1963, N.Y.C., 1964, Fragments, Windows and other plays, 1965, Best Short Plays, 1981, 83, 85; contbr. to Best Short American Plays 1994-1995; original TV plays The Love Song of Barney Kempinski, 1966, Natasha Kovolina Pipishinski, 1976; off-Broadway Fragments, 1967, The Basement, 1967; Jimmy Shine, 1968, 69, Shooting Towards the Millinneum, 1997, Playtime, 1997; Broadway The Chinese, N.Y.C., 1970 (pub. in Best Short Plays of the World Theatre 1973), Dr. Fish, 1970, An American Millionaire, 1974, All Over Town, 1974 (pub. Best Plays 1974-75); screenplay The Tiger Makes Out, 1967, The Pushcart Peddlers, prod. off-off-Broadway, 1979 (pub. as The Pushcart Peddlers, The Flatulist and other plays); novel Days and Nights of a French Horn Player, 1980, Walter and the Flatulist; prod. off-Broadway The Downstairs Boys, 1980, The Songs of War, 1989; prod. regional theatre A Need for Brussels Sprouts, 1981, Play Time, Denver Ctr. Theatre, 1991, The Japanese Foreign Trade Minister, Cleve. Playhouse, 1992, 74 Georgia Ave., 1992, Circus Life, 1992; prod. Broadway Twice Around the Park, 1982; Other Plays, 1983, Closet Madness and Other Plays, 1984, Popkins, Paris, 1990, Play Time, 1991, The Songs of War, 1989; prod. Off Broadway The New Yorkers, 1984, Circus Life, 1995; prodr. Extensions, 1994; co-author: screenplay Tootsie (Winner Los Angeles Film Critics, N.Y. Film Critics, Nat. Soc. Film Critics, Writers Guild Am. award for best comedy); author Luv and Other Plays, 1983, The Rabbi and the Toyota Dealer, 1985, Jealousy, There are No Sacher Tortes in Our Society, 1985, Old Wine in a New Bottle, 1987, Road Show, 1987, Man Dangling, 1988, Oatmeal and Kisses, 1990, (with others) Best Short American Plays of 1991, 92-93, Sexaholics and Other Plays, 1995, Extensions, 1994, Circus Life, 1995, The Artist and The Model (Best Am. Short Play), 1994-95, Play Time (Published by Dramatists Play Svc., 1997), The Man Who Couldn't Stop Crying (Best Am. Short Plays, 1997-98), We Are Family, 2002, produced regional theaters and Berlin undertitle Warum Nicht and Prague, 2003; produced in Rome Regret Undertitle Tutti in Famiglia, 2004; produced in Paris under title La Regard, 2002; 74 Georgia Ave. produced in regional theater, 2002; First Love (Best Am. Short Plays 1991-2000); prodr. feature films A Walk on the Moon, 1999, (cable TV) The Devil's Arithmetic, 1999, Boys and Girls, 2000, Clubland, 2000 (also exec. prodr.); exec. prodr. (cable TV) A Separate Peace, 2003. Recipient Vernon Rice award otustanding achievement off-Broadway Theatre, 1963; Outer Circle award Outstanding Theatre, 1963; named Outstanding Playwright, 1963. Office: care Arthur B Greene 101 Park Ave 26th Fl New York NY 10178-0002

SCHIZER, DAVID MICHAEL, dean, law educator; b. Bklyn. s. Zevie Baruch and Hazel Gerber Schizer; m. Meredith Wolf; 2 children. BA in History, summa cum laude, Yale U., 1990, MA in History, 1990, JD, 1993. Law clerk for Judge Alex Kozinski US Ct. Appeals, 1993—94; for Justice Ruth Bader Ginsburg US Supreme Ct., 1994—95; tax law atty. Davis Polk & Wardwell, NYC, 1995—98; prof. Columbia U. Law Sch., NYC, 1998—, Wilbur H. Friedman prof. tax law, 1998—2004, chair Columbia appointment com., 2002—04, dean, Lucy G. Moses prof. law, 2004—. Chair Columbia U. Clerkship Com., 2000—02. Exec. editor Yale Law Jour.; contbr. articles to law jours. Recipient Willis L.M. Reese Prize for Excellence in Tchg., 2002; named one of Top 40 Lawyers Under 40, Nat. Law Jour., 2005, 40 Under 40, Crain's NY Bus., 2006. Mem.: Tax Forum, Tax Club, N.Y. State Bar Assn. Tax Sec. (exec. com., co-chair Com. on Fin. Insts.). Achievements include becoming youngest dean of Columbia Law School in history. Office: Columbia U Sch Law Dean's Office 8th Fl Jerome L Greene Hall 435 W 116th St New York NY 10027 Office Phone: 212-854-2675. Office Fax: 212-854-9740. E-mail: dschiz@law.columbia.edu.*

SCHIZER, ZEVIE BARUCH, lawyer; b. Bklyn., Dec. 19, 1928; s. David and Bertha (Rudavsky) S.; m. Hazel Gerber, Aug. 23, 1962; children: Deborah Gail, Miriam Anne, David Michael. BA magna cum laude, NYU, 1950; JD, Yale U., New Haven, 1953. Bar: N.Y. 1954, U.S. Dist. Ct. (so. and ea. dist.) N.Y. 1959, U.S. Ct. Appeals (2d cir.) 1959, U.S. Supreme Ct. 1959. Assoc. Guzik & Boukstein, NYC, 1953-54; teaching fellow NYU Sch. Law, 1954-55; assoc. Philips, Nizer, Benjamin & Krim, NYC, 1955-56, Aranow, Brodsky, Einhorn & Dann, NYC, 1956-57; asst. counsel jud. inquiry Appellate Divsn. 2nd Dept., Bklyn., 1957-62; assoc. Hays, Porter, Spanier & Curtis, NYC, 1963-68, ptnr., 1968-85; sec. United Aircraft Products, Inc., Dayton, Ohio, 1970-83; ptnr. Schizer & Schizer, NYC, 1985—. Trustee Bklyn. Pub. Libr., 1966—2003, pres., 1985—88, N.Y. Young Dem. Club, NYC, 1960—61; trustee East Midwood Jewish Ctr., Bklyn., 1991—, pres., 2003—06; dir. N.Y. met. region United Synagogue Conservative Judaism, NYC, 2004—. Mem. N.Y. County Lawyers Assn. (mem. profl. ethics com., mem. com. on profl. discipline), Phi Beta Kappa. Democrat. Jewish. Home: 505 W End Ave Apt 5D New York NY 10024-4320 Office: Schizer And Schizer 505 W End Ave Apt 5d New York NY 10024-4320 Office Phone: 212-943-3340.

SCHJERVEN, ROBERT E., retired manufacturing executive; With McQuay-Perfex Inc., Trane Co.; v.p. mktg. and engring. Heatcraft Inc. (subs. Lennox Internat. Inc.), 1986—88, v.p., gen. mgr., 1988—91; pres., COO Armstrong Air Conditioning Inc., 1991—95, Lennox Industries Inc. (subs. Lennox Internat. Inc.), 1995—2000; COO Lennox Internat. Inc., 2000—01, CEO, 2001—07; ret., 2007. Office: 2140 Lake Park Blvd Richardson TX 75080

SCHLAEPFER, ISABEL RUBIO, research scientist; d. Jose Maria Rubio and Isabel Reneses; m. Joseph William Schlaepfer, July 5, 1992; children: Nicolas William, Maria Isabel. BS in Genetics with honors, U. Navarra, Pamplona, Spain, 1991; MA, U. Colo., Denver, 1993; PhD in Integrative Physiology, U. Colo., Boulder, 2008. Cert. in behavioral genetics Inst. Behavioral Genetics, 2008. Profl. rsch. asst. U. Colo., Denver, 1992—2004, Boulder, 2004—05. Contbr. articles to sci. jours. Parent-tchr. coalition BVSD, Broomfield, Colo., 2006—08. Mem.: Am. Soc. Human Genetics. Achievements include discovery of mouse gene Munc18c(L) or Stxbp3b. Avocations: tennis, music. Business E-Mail: isabel.schlaepfer@ucdenver.edu.

SCHLAERTH, JOHN BURR, oncologist, gynecologist; b. Buffalo, Nov. 1, 1942; s. John Norbert and Margaret Henrietta (Heath) Schlaerth; m. Katherine Regina Dowling, Jan. 27, 1968; children: John Burr Jr., Alan Charles, William Joseph, Elizabeth Catherine, Michael Robin, Mary Christine, James Andrew. BS in Pure Sci. Biology, Lemoyne Coll., Syracuse, NY, 1964; MD, SUNY, Buffalo, 1968. Lic. Physician Calif., 1970. Intern rotating surgery LA County Med. Ctr., 1968—69; resident ob-gyn Womens Hosp. LA County-USC Med. Ctr., 1969—73; asst. prof. ob-gyn. U. So. Calif. Sch. Medicine, LA, 1977—82, assoc. prof., 1982—87, prof. clin. ob-gyn., 1987—94; gynecologic oncologist Womens Cancer Ctr., Palo Alto, Calif., 1994—97, Pasadena, Calif., 1997—2005, Pacific Gynecologic Specialists, Burbank, Calif., 2005—. Maj. US Army, 1973—75. Fellow, Gynecol. Oncology U. So. Calf. Sch. Medicine, 1975—77. Mem.: Pacific Coast Ob-Gyn. Soc., Internat. Soc. Genecologic Oncology, Soc. Gynecol. Oncologists. Republican. Roman Catholic. Office: Pacific Gynecol Specialists 501 S Buena Vista St Burbank CA 91505

SCHLAFF, BARBARA E., lawyer; b. Detroit, Mar. 21, 1950; BA, Brandeis U., 1971; attended, U. Mich. Law Sch.; JD, Boston Coll., 1974. Bar: D.C. 1979, Md. 1980. Ptnr., Employee Benefits, Taxation practices Venable LLP, Balt. Mem. adv. com. Univ. Balt. Law Sch. Officer Ctr. for Jewish Edn.; trustee, past v.p. Har Sinai Congregation. Mem. ABA, Md. State Bar Assn., D.C. Bar, Bar Assn. Balt. City. Office: Venable LLP 750 E Pratt St Baltimore MD 21202 Office Phone: 410-244-7494. Office Fax: 410-244-7742. Business E-Mail: beschlaff@venable.com.

SCHLAFLY, HUBERT JOSEPH, JR., communications executive; b. St. Louis, Aug. 14, 1919; s. Hubert J. and Mary Ross (Parker) S.; m. Leona Martin, June 12, 1944. BSEE, U. Notre Dame, 1941; postgrad., Syracuse U., 1946—47; DHL (hon.), Sacred Heart U., 2003; LHD (hon.). Electronics engr. Gen. Electric Co., Schenectady, 1941-44, Syracuse, 1946-47; project engr. radiation lab. MIT, 1944-45; dir. TV rsch. 20th Century-Fox Film Corp., NYC, 1947-51; founder, v.p. Teleprompter Corp., NYC, 1951-74, pres., 1971-72, exec. v.p. tech. devel., 1972-74; pres. Transponder Corp., Greenwich, 1977-86; chmn., CEO Portel Services Corp., 1984-86; chmn., pres. Portel Services Network, Inc., 1987-91, chmn. bd., 1991-97, ret., 1998. Cons. in field; industry coord., chmn. exec. com., cable tech. adv. com. FCC, 1972—75; adviser com. telecomm. Nat. Acad. Engring.; adviser Sloan Commn. Cable Comms.; mem. engring. adv. coun. U. Notre Dame, 1977, vice chmn., 83, chmn., 84; bd. dirs., sec. Milbrook Corp., 1994—2001; lectr. in field. Author: Computer in the Living Room, 1977. Bd. govs. Milbrook Club, 1993-98. Recipient Engring. Honor award, U. Notre Dame, 1976, Emmy award, NATAS, 1992, 1999, Sci. Initiative award, Sacred Heart U., 1997, Discovery award, 2001, David Sarnoff citation award, Radio Club Am., 2004. Fellow Soc. Motion Picture and TV Engrs.; mem. IEEE (life, Delmer Ports award 1979), Nat. Cable TV Assn. (chmn. standards com. 1965-69, chmn. domestic satellite com. 1971-73, chmn. future svcs. com. 1972, assns. com. 1981, Outstanding Tech. Achievements award 1974, named Cable TV Hall of Fame 2008), Electronic Industries Assn. (chmn. broadband cable sect. 1971-73, founding chmn. broadband comm. com.), Soc. Cable TV Engrs. (sr.), Fairfield Found. (hon.); named Notre Dame alumni Man of Yr., 1992, Rotary (pres. Greenwich club 1991-92), Knights of Malta, Knight St. Gregory the Great. Roman Catholic. Achievements include patents in field. Personal E-mail: hschlafly@aol.com.

SCHLAFLY, PHYLLIS STEWART, writer; b. St. Louis, Aug. 15, 1924; d. John Bruce and Odile (Dodge) Stewart; m. Fred Schlafly, Oct. 20, 1949; children: John F., Bruce S., Roger S., Phyllis Liza Forshaw, Andrew L., Anne V. BA, Washington U., St. Louis, 1944, JD, 1978, D in Humane Letters, 2008; MA, Harvard U., 1945; LLD, Niagara U., 1976. Bar: Ill. 1979, DC 1984, Mo. 1985, U.S. Supreme Ct. 1987. Syndicated columnist Copley News Svc., 1976—2008; with Creators Syndicate, 2008—. Broadcaster Spectrum, CBS Radio Network, 1973—78; commentator Matters of Opinion sta. WBBM-AM, Chgo., 1973—75, Cable TV News Network, 1980—83; pres. Eagle Forum, 1975—. Author, pub.: Phyllis Schlafly Report, 1967—; author: A Choice Not an Echo, 1964, The Gravediggers, 1964, Strike From Space, 1965, Safe Not Sorry, 1967, The Betrayers, 1968, Mindszenty The Man, 1972, Kissinger on the Couch, 1975, Ambush at Vladivostok, 1976, The Power of the Positive Woman, 1977, First Reader, 1994, Turbo Reader, 2001, Feminist Fantasies, 2003, The Supremacists: The Tyranny of Judges and How to Stop It, 2004; editor: (book) Child Abuse in the Classroom, 1984, Pornography's Victims, 1987, Equal Pay for Unequal Work, 1984, Who Will Rock the Cradle, 1989, Stronger Families or Bigger Government, 1990, Meddlesome Mandate: Rethinking Family Leave, 1991. Del. Rep. Nat. Conv., 1956, 1964, 1968, 1984, 1988, 1992, 1996, 2004, alt., 1960, 1980, 2000, 2008; 1st v.p. Nat. Fedn. Rep. Women, 1964—67; nat. chmn. Stop ERA, 1972—; mem. Ronald Reagan's Def. Policy Adv. Group, 1980, Commn. on Bicentennial of U.S. Constn., 1985—91, Adminstrv. Conf. U.S., 1983—86; pres. Ill. Fedn. Rep. Women, 1960—64; mem. Ill. Commn. on Status of Women, 1975—85. Recipient 10 Honor awards, Freedom Found., Brotherhood award, NCCJ, 1975; named Woman of Achievement in Pub. Affairs, St. Louis Globe-Democrat, 1963; named one of 10 Most Admired Women in World, Good Housekeeping poll, 1977—90, 100 Most Important Women of 20th Century, Ladies Home Jour., 1998. Mem.: DAR (nat. chmn. Am. history 1965—68, nat. chmn. bicentennial com. 1967—70, nat. chmn. nat. def. 1977—80, 1983—95), ABA, Ill. Bar Assn., Phi Beta Kappa, Pi Sigma Alpha. Office: Eagle Forum 7800 Bonhomme Ave Saint Louis MO 63105-1906 Office Phone: 314-721-1213. Business E-Mail: phyllis@eagleforum.org.

SCHLAGEL, RICHARD H., retired philosophy educator; b. Springfield, Mass., Nov. 22, 1925; m. Josephine W. Regar, 1962. BS in Pre-Med cum laude, Springfield Coll., 1949; MA in Philosophy, Boston U., 1952, PhD, 1955. Instr. philosophy Coll. of Wooster, 1954-55; instr. Clark U., 1955-56; asst. prof. George Washington U., 1956-62, assoc. prof., 1962-68, prof., 1968—, chmn. dept., 1965-69, 70-71, 77-83, named Elton prof. philosophy, 1986, Elton prof. emeritus, 2001—08. Sabbatical, Paris, with travel throughout Europe, 1962-63, 69-70, 76-77, 83-84, 90-91. Author: The Vanquished Gods: Science, Religion, and the Nature of Belief, 2001, From Myth to Modern Mind: A Study of the Origins and Growth of Scientific Thought, vol. 1, Theogony through Ptolemy, 1995, vol. 2, Copernicus through Quantum Mechanics, 1996; Contextual Realism: A Metaphysical Framework for Modern Science, 1986; contbr. articles and reviews to profl. jours. Borden Parker Browne fellow, 1953-54. Mem. AAUP, Am. Philos. Assn., Washington Philosophy Club (v.p. 1964-65, pres. 1965-66). Home Phone: 202-462-4554. Personal E-mail: richschlagel@aol.com.

SCHLAGETER, ROBERT WILLIAM, museum administrator; b. Streator, Ill., May 10, 1925; s. Herman Pete and Ida (Ladtkow) S.; divorced; children— David Michael, Robert William Diploma, Karl Ruprecht Univ., Heidelberg, Fed. Republic Germany, 1950; BA, U. Ill., Champaign-Urbana, 1950, MFA, 1957. Asst. prof. U. Tenn., Knoxville, 1952-58; dir. Mint Mus. Art, Charlotte, NC, 1958-66; assoc. dir. Downtown Gallery, NYC, 1966, Ackland Art Ctr., U. NC, Chapel Hill, 1967-76; dir. Cummer Gallery Art, Jacksonville, Fla., 1976-92, dir. emeritus, 1992—. Fine arts cons. corp. and pvt. collecting, 1993—. Author: (exhbn. catalogue) Winslow Homer's Florida, George Inness' Florida, Martin Johnson Heade Florida, Robert Henri-George Bellows. Served with U.S. Army, 1943-45, ETO

SCHLAM, MARK HOWARD, international marketing executive; s. Murray J. and Sophia S. BSEE (N.Y. State Regents scholar), Poly. Inst. Bklyn., 1972, MSEE, 1973. Sales assoc. F.W. Madigan Real Estate Co., Flushing, N.Y., 1973-74; sales engr. Dayton T. Brown, Inc., Bohemia, N.Y., 1975-77; sr. mktg. rep. advanced systems Sperry Marine Systems, Gt. Neck, N.Y., 1977-80; pres. Mark H. Schlam Co. Internat., Melville, N.Y., 1980—, MHSCO Internat. Corp., East Northport, N.Y., 1987—, Bina Internat. Corp., 2007—. Assoc. editor Poly. Press, Bklyn., 1969-76. Asst editor: Computer Processing in Communications, 1970, Submillimeter Waves, 1971; assoc. editor Computers and Automata, 1971, Computer-Communications Networks and Teletraffic, 1972, Optical and Acoustical Micro-Electronics, 1975, Computer Software Engineering, 1976. Mem. Audio Engring. Soc., Acoustical Soc. Am., AIAA, Am. Soc. Naval Engrs., Armed Forces Communications and Electronics Assn., IEEE, Soc. Tech. Communication, Soc. Automotive Engrs., AAAS, Nat. Pilots Assn., Assn. Old Crows, Nat. Soc. Profl. Engrs., Realtors Nat. Mktg. Inst., Poly. Inst. N.Y. Alumni Assn. (assoc. dir. 1973—), Masons, Tau Delta Phi. Office: PO Box 97 East Northport NY 11731-0097 Business E-Mail: mordechai@optonline.net.

SCHLAPBACH, DAVID, lawyer; BA summa cum laude, U. Va.; MA, Stanford U.; JD, Yale U. Atty. Blackwell Sanders Peper Martin LLP, St. Louis; joined First Data, 1996, dep. gen. counsel internat. Paris, 2000—04; gen. counsel, sec. Western Union Co., Englewood, Colo., 2004—06, exec. v.p., sec. gen. counsel, 2006—. Office: Western Union Co PO Box 6992 Greenwood Village CO 80155-6992 Office Phone: 866-405-5012.

SCHLARBAUM, SCOTT E., forester, educator; s. Donald E. Schlarbaum and Helen Louise Knedler; m. Julie Ellen Hubbard, Dec. 6, 1980. BS, Colo. State U., Ft. Collins, 1974, PhD, 1980; MS, U. Nebr., Lincoln, 1977. Postdoc. assoc. Kans. State U., Manhattan, 1981—83; prof. U. Tenn., Knoxville, 1984—2002, james r. cox prof., 2002—. Office: Univ Tenn Dept Forestry Wildl & Fish Knoxville TN 37996-4563

SCHLARMAN, JULIE JO, history professor, consultant; b. Dubuque, Iowa, May 26, 1958; d. Joseph Raymond and Madeline Mary Schlarman. BA in Gen. Art, Iowa State U., Ames, 1982; MA in Studio Art, U. Wis., Superior, 1985; MA in Country House Studies, U. Leeds, Eng., 1999; PhD, U. Southampton, Eng., 2003. Docent, site supr. Nat. Miss. River Mus., Dubuque, 1986—89, educator, site supr., 1994—98; adj. faculty Northeast Iowa CC, Peosta, 1992—98; gallery asst. Harewood House Trust, West Yorkshire, England, 1999; adj. lectr. Richmond, Am. Internat. U., London, 2000—03; sr. rsch. officer U. Essex, Dept. Art History, Colchester, England, 2003—05; external examiner U. London, Queen Mary Coll., 2004; asst. prof. Simpson Coll., Indianola, Iowa, 2005—08, U. SD, Vermillion, 2008—. Co-chair Dubuque County Hist. Soc., 1995—98; AP reader Coll. Bd., Princeton, NJ, 2007—. Author articles to profl. jours. Precinct capt. Iowans For Hillary, Des Moines, 2007. Recipient Faculty Devel. award, U. Essex, 2004; Travel and Rsch. grant, Harewood House Trust, West Yorkshire, 1999, Faculty Arts Tuition grant, U. Southampton, 1999—2002, Samuel J. Kress Travel fellowship, Soc. Archtl. Historians, 2003, Rsch. fellowship, Arts and Humanities Rsch. Bd., Gt. Britain, 2003—05, Travel grant, Coll. Art Assn., 2005, Course Devel. grant, Lilly Found., 2007. Mem.: State Hist. Soc. Iowa, Cmty. Design award Com.; Iowa Archtl. Found., Iowa Hist. Preservation Alliance, Soc. Archtl. Historians, Am. Soc. 18th-Century Studies, Coll. Art Assn. Liberal. Druid. Home: 1114 Cornell St Apt 102 Vermillion SD 57069

SCHLARMAN, STANLEY GIRARD, bishop emeritus; b. Belleville, Ill., July 27, 1933; Student, St. Henry Prep. Sem., Belleville, Gregorian U., Rome, St. Louis U. Ordained priest Diocese of Belleville, Ill., 1958, aux. bishop Ill., 1979—83; ordained bishop, 1979; bishop Diocese of Dodge City, Kans., 1983—98, bishop emeritus Kans., 1998—. Roman Catholic. Office: Hincke-Sense Residence 2620 Lebanon Ave Belleville IL 62221 Office Phone: 618-235-9601. Office Fax: 618-277-0387. E-mail: sschlarman@diobelle.org.

SCHLECHTE, JOHN WARREN, research scientist; BS, Tex. A&M U., MS, 1989; PhD in Quantitative Fisheries Mgmt, U. Wash., Seattle, 1996. Fisheries-statis. cons. Skalski Statis. Consulting, Seattle, 1995—97, Bio Analysts, Redmond, Wash., 1996—97; fisheries statistician NMFS, Silver Spring, Md., 1997—99; biometrician TPWD, Mt Home, Tex., 1999—. Coach AYSO, Little League, YMCA, 1999—2009. Recipient Best Presentation award, Tex. Chpt. Am. Fisheries Soc., 1999, John F. Dequine Best Paper award, Am. Fisheries Soc., 2001; Lechner fellowship, U. Wash. Mem.: Am. Fisheries Soc. Office: TPWD 5103 Junction Hwy Mountain Home TX 78058 Business E-Mail: warren.mmix@gmail.com.

SCHLECK, CHARLES ASA, archbishop emeritus; b. Milw., Wis., July 5, 1925; D (hon.), San Carlos U., 2001. Ordained priest Congregation of Holy Cross, 1951; ordained bishop, 1995; undersecretary Congregation for the Evangelization of Peoples, 1986—95, official, 1995—2000, official emeritus, 2000—. Roman Catholic. Office: Piazza di Spagna 48 00187 Vatican City Italy

SCHLEEDE, GLENN ROY, marketing professional, consultant; b. Lyons, NY, June 12, 1933; m. Sandra Christine Klafehn, Dec. 27, 1958; children: Kristen M., Kimberly J., Kendall E. BA, Gustavus Adolphus Coll., 1960; MA, U. Minn., 1968; advanced mgmt. program, Harvard U., 1987. Research asst. Indsl. Relations Ctr., U. Minn., Mpls., 1960-61; mgmt. intern, then contractor personnel specialist AEC, Argonne, Ill. and Germantown, Md., 1961-65; asst. chief div. natural resources U.S. Office Mgmt. and Budget, Exec. Office of Pres., Washington, 1965-72, exec. assoc. dir., 1981; dep. assoc. dir. Office of Policy Analysis, AEC, Germantown, 1972-73; assoc. dir. energy and sci. Domestic Council, The White House, Washington, 1973-77; sr. v.p. Nat. Coal Assn., Washington, 1977-81; pres. New Eng. Energy Inc., Westborough, Mass., 1982-92, also bd. dirs.; v.p. New Eng. Power Service Co., Westborough, 1982-92, also bd. dirs.; v.p. New Eng. Electric System, Westborough, 1986-92; pres., CEO, dir. Energy Market and Policy Analysis, Inc., Reston, Va., 1992—2003; freelance analyst, writer Round Hill, Va., 2003—. Author numerous speeches, papers and congl. testimony on various nat. energy policy issues. Recipient Disting. Alumni in Bus. award Gustavus Adolphus Coll. Alumni Assn., St. Peter, Minn., 1987. Republican. Lutheran. Avocations: reading, travel, carpentry. Home: 18220 Turnberry Dr Round Hill VA 20141-2574 Personal E-mail: empainc@aol.com.

SCHLEGEL, FRED EUGENE, lawyer; b. Indpls., July 24, 1941; s. Fred George and Dorothy (Bruce) S.; m. Jane Wessels, Aug. 14, 1965; children: Julia, Charles, Alexandra. BA, Northwestern U., 1963; JD with distinction, U. Mich., 1966. Bar: Ind. 1966. Assoc. lawyer Baker & Daniels, Indpls., 1966-72, ptnr., 1972—; vice chmn. Meridian St. Preservation Commn., Indpls., 1975-90. Contbr. articles to profl. jours. Chmn. Pub. Schs. Edn. Found., Indpls., 1988—90; pres. Festival Music Soc., 1974—75, 1979, 1986—87; bd. dirs. Indpls. Symphony Orch., chmn., 2002—04; bd. dir. Arts Coun., Indpls, 1996—2002. Mem. ABA, Ind. Bar Assn., Energy Bar Assn., Northwestern U. Alumni Club Indpls. (pres. 1992-94). Episcopalian. Office: Baker and Daniels 300 N Meridian St Ste 2700 Indianapolis IN 46204-1782 Office Phone: 317-237-1410. Business E-Mail: fred.schlegel@bakerd.com.

SCHLEGEL, HANS, astronaut; b. Uberlingen, Germany, Aug. 3, 1951; m. Heike Schlegel-Walport; 7 children. Diploma in physics, U. Aachen, Germany, 1979. Mem. acad. staff, solid state physicist Rheinisch Westfalische Technische Hochschule, U. Aachen, 1979—86; specialist in non-destructive testing methodology R&D dept. Institut Dr. Förster GmbH & Co. KG, Reutlingen, Germany, 1986—88; basic astronaut tng. German Aerospace Rsch. Ctr., 1988—90, prime payload specialist D-2 mission, 1990—93; payload tng. Cologne, Germany and Johnson Space Ctr., Houston, Tex., 1990—93; cosmonaut candidate. German-Russian Mir-'97 mission, served as crew interface coord. Y.A. Gagarin Tng. Ctr., Moscow, 1995—97, 2nd bd. engr. tng. and cert., 1997—98; astronaut European Astronaut Corps., 1998—; mission tng. specialist NASA, 1998; worked in ISS Branch on mechanisms & structures, on crew equipment and the ISS sys., 1999—2002; worked in the Robotics Branch and as ISS CAPCOM; lead ISS CAPCOM for Increment 10, 2004—05; lead astronaut Johnson Space Ctr., 2005—. Payload specialist STS-55 aboard Space Shuttle Columbia, 1993; crew mem. Atlantis STS-122 mission to deliver the European Space Agency's Columbus Lab. to the ISS, 2008. Contbr. publications and scientific reports in the field of semiconductor physics. Paratrooper, 2nd lt. Fed. Armed Forces. Recipient Fed. Svc. Cross 1st Class, Germany, Medal of Friendship, Russia. Mem.: Am. Field Svc. Germany, German Phys. Soc. Avocations: skiing, scuba diving, flying, reading. Office: NASA Johnson Space Ctr Astronaut Office/CB Houston TX 77058

SCHLEGEL, JOHN FREDERICK, management consultant, personal trainer; b. Ogden, Utah, Dec. 18, 1944; s. Max Joseph and Mary Georgia (Whittaker) S.; m. Priscilla Mary Hecht, Sept. 8, 1967. BS in Pharmacy, U. Pacific, 1967; D of Pharmacy, U. So. Calif., 1972, MS in Edn., 1980; ScD in Pharmacy (hon.), Mass. Coll. Pharmacy, 1984, L.I. U., 1985. Lic. pharmacist, Calif., Nev.; cert. assoc. exec. Chief pharmacist U. So. Calif. Sch. Pharmacy, LA, 1967-73, postdoctoral fellow, 1972—73, dir. pharmacy admissions, 1973-75; dir. office student affairs Am. Assn. Colls. Pharmacy, Alexandria, Va., 1975-77, asst. exec. dir., 1977-81, exec. dir., 1981-84; CEO Am. Pharm. Assn., Washington, 1984-89; exec. v.p., CEO Am. Acad. Facial Plastic and Reconstructive Surgery, Washington, 1989-92; pres. Schlegel & Assocs., 1992—. Cons. in field. Contbr. over 100 articles on pharmacy, health care and assn. mgmt.; presenter in field. Nat. del. White House Conf. on Aging, Washington, 1981. Disting. alumnus U. So. Calif. Sch. Pharmacy, 1985, U. the Pacific Sch. Pharmacy, 1987. Fellow Am. Soc. Assn. Execs.; mem. Fla. Soc. Assn. Execs., Phi Delta Chi (charter, bd. counsellors), Alpha Psi Ed Found. (pres.). Avocations: tennis, classical music, gardening, bridge. Office: 3390 Highlands Bridge Rd Sarasota FL 34235-6859 Office Phone: 941-341-0434. Business E-Mail: jschlegel@comcast.net.

SCHLEGEL, PETER NILES, urologist, educator; b. Malden, Mass., Feb. 17, 1958; s. Niles Matthew and Mary Patricia (McIntyre) S.; children: Andrew Peter, Lucy Filice, Nicholas Halloran. AB, Hamilton Coll., 1979; MD, U. Mass., 1983. Diplomate Am. Bd. Urology, Nat. Bd. Med. Examiners; lic. physician, N.Y. Intern in gen. surgery and resident Johns Hopkins Hosp., Balt., 1983-85, resident, chief resident in urology, 1985-89, instr. urology, 1989; fellow-in-residence The Population Coun., NYC, 1989-91, staff scientist, 1991—; asst. attending surgeon New York Hosp., NYC, 1991-96; assoc. attending surgeon N.Y. Hosp., NYC, 1996—; assoc. vis. physician Rockefeller U., NYC, 1991—; asst. prof. urology Cornell Med. Coll., NYC, 1991-96, assoc. prof. urology, 1996—2004, prof., 2004—, vice chmn. urology, 1999-2001, acting chmn., 2001—03, chmn., 2003—. Vis. prof. Austria, Israel, Indonesia, Japan, Saudi Arabia, Brazil, others; vis. fellow Royal Coll. Surgeons, 1993; co-dir. Ctr. for Male Reproduction and Microsurgery, Cornell Inst. for Reproductive Medicine, 2000—03; lectr. in field. Former co-editor Jour. Audiology; mem. numerous editl. bds.; contbr. numerous articles, abstracts to profl. jours., chpts. to books. Recipient Edwin Beer Program award N.Y. Acad. Medicine, 1996-98, New Investigator award Am. Found. for Urol. Disease, 1993-95, fellow, 1989-91; fellow Am. Cancer Soc., 1986-87, NIH, 1989-91; established Clinician award ESHRE, 1996; named one of Medical Marvels, New York Mag., 2006 Mem.: Am. Bd. Urology (trustee 2009—), Soc. for Male Reprodn. /Urology (pres.), Soc. for Study of Male Reprodn. (pres.), Am. Urol. Assn., Soc. for Basic Urol. Rsch., Soc. for Study of Reprodn., Am. Soc. Andrology, Am. Soc. Reproductive Medicine (bd. dirs.), Alpha Omega Alpha. Roman catholic. Avocation: sailing. Office: New York Hosp Dept Urology 525 E 68th St New York NY 10021-4885 Office Phone: 212-746-5491. E-mail: pnschleg@med.cornell.edu.

SCHLEI, THOMAS K, social sciences educator; s. Kenneth W. and Marjorie L. Schlei; m. Heidi A. Schlei, July 17, 1976; children: Andrew M., Rebecca L., Brian P. BS in Fire Sci. Mgmt., Southern Ill. U., Carbondale, 1992; MS in Vocat. Edn., U. Wis., Stout, 1996; PhD in Urban Edn., U. Wis., Milwaukee, 2007. Cert. exec.fire officer Nat. Fire Acad., 1998. Fire chief Sussex Fire Dept., Wis., 1979—2000, vol. firefighter, 1979—2000; fire svc. instr. Waukesha County Tech. Coll., Pewaukee, Wis., 1991—. Cons. Wis. Tech. Coll. Fire Svc. Curriculum Com., Madison, 1995—. Mem.: Wis. Soc. Fire Svc. Instrs. (bd. mem. 2006—08). Office: Waukesha County Tech Coll 800 Main St S-234 Pewaukee WI 53072 Business E-Mail: tschlei@wctc.edu.

SCHLEICHER, NORA ELIZABETH, bank executive, treasurer, accountant; b. Balt., Aug. 10, 1952; d. Irvin William and Eleanor Edna S.; m. Ray Leonard Settle Jr., July 27, 1985. AA cum laude, Anne Arundel Community Coll., 1972; BS summa cum laude, U. Balt., 1975. CPA, Md. Staff auditor Md. Nat. Bank, Balt., 1975-76, sr. staff auditor, 1976-77, supr. auditing dept., 1977-78; full charge acct. Wooden & Benson, CPA's, Balt., 1978-81; asst. to treas. First Fed. Savs. & Loan Assn., Annapolis, Md., 1981, asst. treas., 1982-83, v.p., 1984; v.p., treas. First Fed. Savs. & Loan Assn. (now First Annapolis Bank), 1984—. Bd. dirs., treas. Coll. Manor Community Assn. Mem. AICPA, Md. Assn. CPA's, Fin. Mgrs. Soc., Coll. Manor Community Assn. (bd. dirs., treas.). Methodist. Office: First Annapolis Savs Bank 1832 George Ave Annapolis MD 21401-4103

SCHLEIER-SMITH, JOHANN, Internet company executive; AB in Physics and Math., Harvard U. Co-founder Avivon Inc.; tech. dir. Limespot.com LLC; co-founder, chief tech. officer Jumpstart Technologies, 2000—05, Tagged.com, San Francisco, 2004—. Grantee NSF Grad. Rsch. Fellowship, Hertz Found. Fellowship Rsch. Grant. Office: Tagged Inc 110 Pacific Ave Mall Box #117 San Francisco CA 94111

SCHLEIFER, STEVEN J., psychiatrist, educator; b. NYC, Mar. 10, 1950; s. Jack and Caroline (Rapps) S.; m. Sarah L. Rosenberg, Dec. 1971; children: Jonathan, Jason, Justin, Tara. MD, Mt. Sinai Sch. of Medicine, 1975; BA, Columbia Coll., 1971. Diplomate Nat. Bd. Med. Examiners, Am. Bd. Psychiatry and Neurology. Asst. prof. of psychiatry Mt. Sinai Sch. of Medicine, New York, NY, 1982—87; assoc. prof. of psychiatry UMDNJ-New Jersey Med. Sch., Newark, 1987—92, prof. of psychiatry NJ, 1992—, chair, dept. of psychiatry NJ, 1992—2001. Cons. NIH, Bethesda, Md., 1984—, Hackensack U. Med. Ctr., NJ, 1988—, Veterans Adminstrn. Med. Ctr., East Orange, NJ, 1988—2002; chief of svc., dept of psychiatry UMDNJ-Univ. Hosp., Newark; chief of svc. UMDNJ-Univ. Behavioral Healthcare, Newark, 1992—2002. Contbr. articles to profl. jours. Grantee NIMH, 1982, Chernow Found., N.Y.C., 1983, Upjohn Co., Kalamazoo, 1989, NIAAA, 1990. Fellow Am. Psychiat. Assn. (disting.); mem. NJ Psychiat. Assn., Soc. Biol. Psychiatry, Am. Psychosomatic Soc., Psychoneuroimmunology Rsch. Soc., Acad. Psychosomatic Medicine, Brain, Behavior and Immunity (editl. bd. mem., annals of behavioral medicine) Avocations: opera, skiing. Office: UMDNJ-New Jersey Med Sch 183 South Orange Ave Newark NJ 07103 E-mail: schleife@umdnj.edu.

SCHLEIFER, THOMAS C., management consultant, author, lecturer; BS in Constrn. Mgmt., E. Carolina U., 1989, MS in Constrn. Mgmt., 1990; PhD, Herriot-Watt U., 1994. Owner Schleifer Bros., Inc., Hanover, NJ, 1964-75; owner, founder, pres., internat. cons. firm CMA Cons. Group, Morristown, NJ, 1976-86; dir. appropriate tech., vol. Habitat for Humanity, Americus, Ga., 1987-88; assoc. prof. Ariz. State U., Tempe, 1990-92; eminent scholar Del E. Webb Sch. Constrn., Ariz. State U., 1993-94; eminent scholar Del E. Webb Sch. Constrn. Ariz. State U., Tempe, 2001—. Vis. prof. East Carolina U., 1989-90; former chmn. continuing edn. com. Associated Gen. Contractors Am.; lectr. and presenter in field. Author: Construction Contractors' Survival Guide, 1990, Glossary of Suretyship and Related Terms, 1981; contbr. articles to profl. jours. Bd. advisors Habitat for Humanity Internat., 1989—. Mem. Am. Inst. Constructors (bd. dirs. 1990-93), Am. Arbitration Assn. (N.J. adv. coun. 1968-75), Am. Concrete Inst. (edn. com. 1972-76), Associated Gen. Contractors Am. (chmn. continuing edn. com. 1970-76), Assn. Advancement 3d World (internat. adv. coun. 1988-91). Home and Office: 5625 N 75th Pl Scottsdale AZ 85250-6471 Personal E-mail: tschleifer@aol.com.

SCHLENDER, WILLIAM ELMER, management sciences educator; b. Sawyer, Mich., Oct. 28, 1920; s. Gustav A. and Marie (Zindler) S.; m. Lela R. Pullen, June 9, 1956 (dec. June 1983); m. Margaret C. Krahn, Mar. 3, 1987. AB, Valparaiso U., 1941; MBA, U. Denver, 1947; PhD, Ohio State U., 1955. With U.S. Rubber Co., 1941-43, 46; asst. prof., assoc. prof. bus. adminstrn. Bowling Green State U., 1947-53; asst. prof. bus. orgn., prof. Ohio State U., 1954-65, asst. dean, 1959-62; assoc. dean Ohio State U. (Coll. Commerce and Adminstrn.), 1962-63; prof. mgmt. U. Tex., 1965-68, chmn. dept., 1966-68; dean Cleve. State U. Coll. Bus. Adminstrn., 1968-75, prof. mgmt., 1975-76; Internat. Luth. Laymen's League prof. bus. ethics Valparaiso (Ind.) U., 1976-79, Richard E. Meier prof. mgmt., 1983-86, Richard E. Meier prof. emeritus, 1986—. Vis. assoc. prof. mgmt. Columbia U., 1957-58; vis. prof. mgmt. U. Tex., Arlington, 1981-82; cons. in field; bd. govs. Internat. Ins. Soc., 1972-90. Author: (with M.J. Jucius) Elements of Managerial Action, 3d edit., 1973, (with others) Management in Perspective: Selected Readings, 1965; editor: (with others) Management in a Dynamic Society, 1965; mem. editl. bd. Jour. Acad. Mgmt., 1966-72; contbr. articles to profl. jours. Mem. Assn. Ohio Commodores. Served with AUS, 1943-45. Decorated Bronze Star; Exec. Order of Ohio Commodore in recognition of contbn. to econ. devel., Gov. Ohio, 1972. Fellow Acad. Mgmt.; mem. Indsl. Rels. Rsch. Assn. (pres. N.E. Ohio chpt. 1971-72), Am. Legion, Tau Kappa Epsilon, Rotary, Beta Gamma Sigma, Sigma Iota Epsilon, Pi Sigma Epsilon, Alpha Kappa Psi, Phi Kappa Phi. Home (Summer): PO Box 446 Sawyer MI 49125-0446 Office: Coll Bus Adminstrn Valparaiso U Valparaiso IN 46383 Home Phone: 269-426-3934. Personal E-mail: bschlend@aol.com. *I resolved long ago that where I worked and what I did would be guided not by prestige considerations, but by the answers to three questions: (1) Will my work allow me to grow by discovering and developing my capabilities? (2) Will it make a significant contribution to my profession and to the community? (3) Will I enjoy doing it? My career, and my personal philosophy, have these underlying guidelines.*

SCHLER, MICHAEL LAWRENCE, lawyer; b. NYC, May 6, 1949; m. Joan McClure, 1982. AB, Harvard U., 1970; JD, Yale U., 1973; LLM in Taxation, NYU, 1979. Bar: N.Y. 1974. Law clk. to Judge Max Rosenn U.S. Ct. Appeals (3d cir.), Wilkes Barre, Pa., 1973-74; assoc. Cravath Swaine & Moore, NYC, 1974-82, ptnr., tax dept., 1982—. Contbr. articles to profl. jours. Pres. Am. Tax Policy Inst., trustee. Fellow Am. Coll. Tax Counsel; mem. N.Y. State Bar Assn. (chair tax sect. 1994-95), NY Tax Forum (chair). Office: Cravath Swaine & Moore LLP 825 8th Ave New York NY 10019-7475 Office Phone: 212-474-1588. Office Fax: 212-474-3700. Business E-Mail: mschler@cravath.com.

SCHLESINGER, ADAM, musician; b. Oct. 31, 1967; Grad., Williams Coll. Bassist Ivy, 1994—, Fountains of Wayne, 1995—99, 2001—; prin. Scratchie Records, NYC, 1995—; co-owner Stratosphere Sound, NYC, 1999—. Musician & prodr. (Ivy albums) Lately, 1994, Realistic, 1995, Apartment Life, 1997, Long Distance, 2001, Guestroom, 2002, In the Clear, 2005, (Fountains of Wayne albums) Fountains of Wayne, 1996, I Want an Alien for Christmas, 1997, Utopia Parkway, 1999, Welcome Interstate Managers, 2003, Traffic and Weather, 2007; composer: (songs) Stacy's Mom, 2003 (ASCAP award, BMI Pop award); composer & prodr. (film soundtracks) That Thing You Do!, 1996 (Oscar nomination for Best Original Song, Golden Globe award nominee for Best Original Song, 1997), prodr. There's Something About Mary, 1998, Sweet and Lowdown, 1999, Me, Myself & Irene, 2000, Scary Movie, 2000, Josie & the Pussycats, 2001, Because of Winn-Dixie, 2005, Robots, 2005, composer Music & Lyrics, 2007; composer: (Broadway plays) Cry-Baby, 2008. Office: c/o MOB Agy 6404 Wilshire Blvd #505 Los Angeles CA 90048 also: Stratospheric Sound 239 11th Ave New York NY 10001

SCHLESINGER, B. FRANK, architect, educator; b. NYC, Sept. 17, 1925; s. Augustus and Ethel (Brower) S.; m. Draga A. Christy; children: Jeff, Nike, Katherine, Daniel, Christy Anna; 1 stepson, Frances L. Haley Jr. Student, Middlebury Coll., 1946—48; BS, U. Ill., 1950; MArch, Harvard U., 1954. Draftsman Hugh Stubbins Assocs., 1953-55, Marcel Breuer, 1955-56; pvt. practice architecture Princeton, NJ, 1956-59, Doylestown, Pa., 1959-69, Phila., 1969-71, Washington, 1971—. Instr. archtl. design U. Pa., 1957-60; vis. critic Columbia Sch. Architecture, 1962-63, U. Pa., 1965; prof. architecture Sch. Architecture, U. Md., 1971-2001, prof. emeritus, 2001—. With USNR, 1943-46. Wheelwright fellow Harvard U., 1963; AIA fellow, 1970; Disting. Designer fellow Nat. Endowment for the Arts, 1984; recipient Design awards Pa. Soc. Archs., 1960-65, 69, 84, Bronze medal, 1965, Silver medal, 1973; Design awards Progressive Arch., 1966-67, 69, 72, 74; Design awards Interfaith Forum on Religion, Art and Arch., 1987, 92; Design awards Philia. chpt. 1960-61, 1963-65, 1968-69; Design awards No. Va. chpt. 1975, 2001; Design awards Wash. chpt. 1990, 92, 95, 2002, 05; Centennial medal Wash. chpt. 2001. Mem.: Associated Harvard Alumni (dir. 1972), Harvard Grad. Sch. Design Alumni Assn. (pres. 1971—73). Address: 1015 33rd St NW Apt 806 Washington DC 20007-3538 Office Phone: 202-333-0344. E-mail: schlesingerfaia@msn.com.

SCHLESINGER, DEBORAH LEE, retired librarian; b. Cambridge, Mass., Sept. 13, 1937; d. Edward M. and Edith D. (Schneider) Hershoff; divorced; children: Suzanne, Richard. BA, U. Mass., 1961; MS, Simmons Coll., 1974; postgrad., U. Pitts., 1983. Reference librarian Bently Coll., Waltham, Mass., 1964-65; dir. Carnegie Library, Swissvale, Pa., 1973-77, South Park Twp. Library, Library, Pa., 1977-81, Monessen (Pa.) Library, 1981-82, Lewis & Clark Library, Helena, Mont., 1983—88, 1989—2004, ret., 2004; state librarian Mont. State Library, Helena, Mont., 1988-89. Vis. scholar Pitts. Regional Library Ctr., 1982-83. Editor Pa. Union List, 1982-83. Mem. exec. bd. Mont. Cultural Advocacy, 1983-2004. Mem. Mont. Libr. Assn. (chmn. legis. com. 1984-92, lobbyist 1992-2001), AAUW (exec. com. 1985-86). Clubs: Montana (Helena). Democrat. Avocations: flying, painting, reading, rafting, travel. Personal E-mail: dbooks@aol.com.

SCHLESINGER, HARVEY ERWIN, judge; b. June 4, 1940; BA, The Citadel, 1962; JD, U. Richmond, 1965. Bar: Va. 1965, Fla. 1965, U.S. Supreme Ct. 1968. Corp. counsel Seaboard Coast Line R.R. Co., Jacksonville, Fla., 1968-70; chief asst. U.S. atty. Mid. Dist. Fla., Jacksonville, 1970-75, U.S. magistrate judge, 1975-91, U.S. Dist. judge, 1991—. Adj. prof. U. North Fla., 1984-91; mem. adv. com. on Fed. Rules of Criminal Procedure, 1986-93; mem. Jud. Conf. Adv. Com. on Adminstrn. of Magistrate Judges Sys., 1996-2003, chmn., 1998-2003; chmn. U.S. Dist. Ct. Forms Working Group, Washington, 1983—, Jud. Conf. Ad hoc Com. on Long Range Planning, 1998-2003; Jud. Conf. Jud. Officers Resources Working Group, 1998-99; 11th Cir. Dist. Judges Assn., 1991—, sec., treas. 1996- 97, v.p. 1997-98, pres.-elect., 1999-2001, pres., 2001-02. Bd. dir. Pine Castle Ctr. for Mentally Retarded, Jacksonville, 1970-87, pres., 1972-74, chmn. bd. dirs., 1973-74; trustee Pine Castle Foundation, 1972-76, Congregation Ahavath Chesed, Jacksonville, 1970—, v.p., 1975-80, pres., 1980-82; v.p. S.E. Coun. Union Am. Hebrew Congregations, 1984-88; asst. commr. for exploring North Fla. Coun. Boy Scouts Am., 1983-86, exec. com., 1986-98, adv. bd., 1998—; active Boy Scouts Am. Nat. Jewish Com. on Scouting, Irving, Tex., 1986-93, Fla. Sesquicentennial Commn., 1995-96; trustee River Garden Home for Aged, 1982—, sec., 1985-1990; co-chmn. bd. gov. Jacksonville chpt. NCCJ, 1983-1993, presiding co-chmn. 1984-89; nat. bd. trustees, NYC, 1986-93; trustee Jacksonville Cmty. Found., 2000—, vice-chair, 2003-05, chmn. 2006-08. Capt. JAGC, U.S. Army, 1965-68. Recipient Silver Beaver award Boy Scouts Am., 1986; George Washington Medal of Honor, Freedoms Found., Valley Forge, Pa., 1987, Silver Medallion Humanitarian award NCCJ, 1992, Founders award, Fed. Magistrate Judges Assn., 1999, William Green award for profl. excellence U. Richmond Law Sch., 2000, Jurist of Yr. award Am. Bd. Trial Adv., 2001, 08. Mem. ABA (fed. rules of evidence and criminal procedure com. 1979-98, Nat. Conf. Spl. Ct. Judges, 1975-90, conf. newsletter editor, 1988-90, Nat. Conf. Fed. Trial Judges, 1990—2001, chmn. legis. com., 1996-97, Flascher award 1989), Va. Bar Assn., Fla. Bar Assn., Fed. Judges Assn., Jacksonville Bar Assn.; Fed. Bar Assn. (pres. Jacksonville chpt. 1974, 75, 81-82), Am. Judicature Soc., Chester Bedell Am. Inns of Ct. (pres. 1992-96), Rotary (Paul Harris fellow, pres. S. Jacksonville club), Masons (past master, past venerable master, knights comdr. of Ct. Honour, 33 degree Scottish Rite bodies), Shriners. Office: 300 N Hogan St Ste 11-150 Jacksonville FL 32202-4246 Office Phone: 904-549-1990.

SCHLESINGER, IRWIN D., neurologist; b. Bklyn., Sept. 13, 1935; s. Edward Schlesinger and Eva Parkoff; m. Marcia Rubinstein; 1 child, Lisa. BS, Bklyn. Coll., 1956; MD, SUNY, Med. U., Syracuse, 1961. Diplomate Am. Bd. Psychiatry and Neurology, Am. Bd. Clin. Neurophysiology. Intern then resident medicine Cornell med. divsn. Bellevue Hosp., NYC, 1961—63; resident neurology Albert Einstein Coll. Medicine Bronx Mcpl. Hosp., 1965—68; neurologist Neurol. Specialities L.I., Manhasset, NY, 1968—. Attending neurologist N. Shore Univ. Hosp., Manhasset, 1968—; staff neurologist L.I. Jewish Med. Ctr., Glen Oaks, NY, 1969—; cons. neurologist St. Francis Hosp., Roslyn, NY, 1975—; clin. assoc. prof. neurology Cornell U. Med. Coll., NYC, 1971—95, NYU Med. Sch., NYC, 1995—. Capt. USAF, 1963—65. Fellow: ACP, Am. Acad. Neurology; mem.: AMA, Am. Acad. Sleep Medicine, Am. Clin. Neurophysiology Soc., Am. Assn. Electrodiagnostic Medicine, Alpha Omega Alpha. Office: 3 Delaware Dr Lake Success NY 11042

SCHLESINGER, JAMES RODNEY, economist, former United States Secretary of Defense; b. NYC, Feb. 15, 1929; s. Julius and Rhea (Rogen) S.; m. Rachel Line Mellinger, June 19, 1954 (dec. Oct. 10, 1995); children: Cora K., Charles L., Ann R., William F., Emily, Thomas S., Clara, James Rodney. AB summa cum laude, Harvard U., 1950, AM, 1952, PhD, 1956; LLD (hon.), The Citadel, 1975, U. SC, 1976, Ind. U. Pa., 1976, NYU, 1976, Ohio State U., 1977; DHL (hon.), Wittenburg U., 1977, Occidental Coll., U. Toledo, U. NC, Asheville, Hampden-Sydney Coll., No. Va. CC. Asst. prof. economics U. Va., 1955—58, assoc. prof., 1958—63; sr. staff mem. RAND Corp., Santa Monica, Calif., 1963-67, dir. strategic studies, 1967-69; cons. Bur. of Budget, 1965—69, asst. dir., 1969—70, acting dep. dir., 1969—70; asst. dir. Office Mgmt. & Budget, Exec. Office of the Pres., 1970-71; chmn. Atomic Energy Commn., 1971-73; dir. CIA, 1973; sec. US Dept. Def., 1973-75; vis. scholar Johns Hopkins Sch. Advanced Internat. Studies, 1976-77; spl. adv. to Pres. on energy The White House, 1977; sec. US Dept. Energy, 1977-79; counselor Ctr. for Strategic and Internat. Studies, Georgetown U., 1979—; sr. adv. Lehman Brothers Holdings, Inc., 1979—. Acad. cons. Navel War Coll., 1957; cons. bd. govs. Fed. Reserve Bd., 1962—63; bd. trustees MITRE Corp., 1985; mem. US Commn. on Nat. Security/21st Century (Hart/Rudman Commn.), 1998—2001, Panel to Assess the Reliability, Safety, & Security of the U.S. Nuclear Stockpile, 1999—2003, Homeland Security Adv. Coun., 2002—, Arms Control & Nonproliferation Advisory Bd., 2006; chmn. Ind. Panel Investigation of Abuses at Abu Ghraib Prison, 2004; co-chmn. Def. Sci. Bd., 2006; chmn. Task Force on Nuclear Weapons Mgmt., US Dept. Def., 2008—09. Author: The Political Economy of National Security, 1960, America at Century's End, 1989; co-author: Issues in Defense Economics, 1967. Recipient Disting. Intelligence Svc. Medal, 1975, Disting. Svc. Medal, Dept. Army, 1976, Disting. Pub. Svc. Medal, Dept. Navy, 1976, Exceptional Civilian Svc. Medal, Dept. Air Force, 1976, Nat. Security Medal, 1979, Nat. Meritorious Citation, Navy League, Disting. Svc. Award, Mil. Order of World Wars, James Doolittle Award, William Oliver Baker Award; grantee Frederick Sheldon prize fellow, Harvard U., 1950—51. Fellow: Nat. Acad. Pub. Adminstrn.; mem.: Am. Acad. Diplomacy, Phi Beta Kappa. Republican. Presbyterian.

SCHLESINGER, LEONARD ARTHUR, academic administrator; b. NYC, July 31, 1952; s. Joe and Edith (Smukler) S.; m. Phyllis Barbara Fineman, Dec. 23, 1972; children: Rebecca, Emily, Katharine. BA, Brown U., 1972; MBA, Columbia U., 1973; DBA, Harvard U., 1979. Mgr. Procter & Gamble, Green Bay, Wis., 1973-75; asst. prof., assoc. prof. bus. sch. Harvard U., Boston, 1978-85; exec. v.p., COO Au Bon Pain, Inc., Boston, 1985-88; prof. bus. adminstrn. Harvard U., Boston, 1988-98; sr. v.p. Brown U., 1998-99; exec. v.p., COO Limited Brands, Columbus, Ohio, 1999—2003, vice chmn., COO, 2003—07; pres. Babson Coll., Wellesley, Mass., 2008—. Past bd. dir. Limited Brands, Columbus, Ohio Editor: Human Resources Mgmt. Jour., Jour. Mgmt. Inquiry; contbr. articles to profl. jours. Jewish. Avocations: travel, music, hiking. Home: 396 Washington St 324 Wellesley MA 02481 Office: Pres Office Babson Coll Babson Park MA 02457 Office Phone: 781-239-4624. Business E-Mail: lschlesinger@babson.edu.

SCHLESINGER, LISA, playwright, educator; d. Benjamin and Sandra Schlesinger; m. Benjamin Schmidt, May 5, 2004; children: Alexi, Sam, Sophia Lily. MFA, Writers Workshop, U. Iowa, 1990, MFA, 1995. Playwright residence Coe Coll., Cedar Rapids, Iowa, 2000—06; vis. prof. playwriting U. Iowa, 2002—06; prof. playwriting Columbia Coll. Chgo., 2006—08, playwriting program, coord., 2007—08. Author: (play) Harmonicus Mundi (Commn. EST and Sloan Found. award, 2004), Celestial Bodies (TCG and NEA Playwrights Residency award, 2005), Same Egg, Bones of Danny Winston (Tampa Performing Arts Playwriting award, 1996), (radio drama) Rock Ends Ahead (BBC Internat. Playwriting award, 1996). Recipient Artslink Internat. award, CEC Artslink Internat., 1996—2003, First prize Internat. Playwriting Competition, BBC, 1997; finalist Creativity Motion award, 2007, Sundance, 2007; grant, Ensemble Studio Theatre and Sloan Found., 2006—08. Mem.: TCG (Playwrights Residency award), Dramatists Guild.

SCHLESINGER, SANFORD JOEL, lawyer; b. NYC, Feb. 8, 1943; s. Irving and Ruth (Rubin) Schlesinger; m. Lianne Lazetera; children: Merideth, Jarrod, Alexandra. BS in Govt. with hons., Columbia U., 1963; JD, Fordham U., 1966. Bar: NY 1966, US Dist. Ct. (so. and ea. dists.) NY 1967, US Ct. Appeals (2d cir.) 1968, US Ct. Internat. Trade 1969, US Tax Ct. 1993, US Supreme Ct. 1978. Assoc. Frankenthaler & Kohn, NYC, 1966—67; asst. atty. gen. trusts and estates bur. charitable found. div. State of NY, NYC, 1967—69; ptnr. Rose & Schlesinger, NYC, 1969—81, Goldshmidt, Oshatz, Powsner & Saft, NYC, 1981—85; ptnr., head trusts and estates dept. Shea & Gould, NYC, 1985—93; ptnr., head wills and estates dept. Kaye Scholer LLP, NYC, 1993—2004, ptnr. co-chair family owned bus. practice group, 1993—2004; founding ptnr. Schlesinger Gannon & Lazetera LLP, NYC, 2004—. Adj. faculty Columbia U. Sch. Law, 1989-94; adj. prof. NY Law Sch., 1978-2003; adj. prof. estate planning grad. program U. Miami Grad. Sch. Law, 1995-2003, NY State Bar Jour., 1995-2005, emeritus, 2005-; dir. NY State Bar Found., 2004-; mem. estate planning adv. com. Practising Law Inst., 1990—; bd. advisors and contbrs. Jour. Corp. Taxation, 1989-96; lectr. in field; condr. workshops in field. Author: Estate Planning for the Elderly Client, 1984, Planning for the Elderly or Incapacitated Client, 1993; columnist, mem. editl. bd. Estate Planning mag., 1995—; contbr. articles to profl. jours. Mem. adv. bd. Inst. Fed. Taxation NYU, 1988-96, chmn., 1993-94; mem. legis adv. com. Scarsdale Sch. Bd., NY, 1981-83, mem. nominating com., 1979-82; pres. dist. 17 NYC Cmty. Sch. Bd., 1970-71; mem. fin. and estate planning adv. bd. Commerce Clearing House, 1988-; mem. adv. bd. Tax Hotline, 1997-; mem. profl. adv. coun. Rockefeller U., 1994-, The Metropolitan Mus. of Art, 2006-; mem. NY Presbyn. Hosp. Planned Giving Adv. Coun., 2004-, mem., profl. adv. coun. The Lighthouse, 2008-. Fellow Am. Coll. Trust and Estate Counsel (chmn. Downstate NY 2001-07), Nat. Assn. Estate Planners & Counsel Estate Planning Hall of Fame; mem. ABA (chmn. social security and other govt. entitlements com. 1990-91, chmn. probate and trust com.-estate planning, drafting charitable giving coms., 1992-94), Internat. Acad. Estate & Trust Law (Academician 1992—), Nat. Acad. Elder Law Attys., Bklyn. Bar Assn., Bar Assn. City of NY, NY State Bar Assn. (treas. trusts and estates sect. 1991-92, sec. trusts and estates sect. 1992-93, chmn. trusts and estates sect. 1994-95, chmn. exec. com. 1st jud. dist. 1987-91, jour. bd. editors 1995-). Avocations: baseball, writing. Office: Schlesinger Gannon & Lazetera LLP 535 Madison Ave New York NY 10022 Home Phone: 212-980-4632; Office Phone: 212-652-3777. Business E-Mail: sschlesinger@sglllp.com.

SCHLESINGER, SARAH JANE, medical educator, researcher; b. Chgo., Feb. 28, 1960; d. Edward S. and Renee C. Schlesinger; m. Terrace Room, June 20, 1982. Grad., Wellesley Coll., Mass.; MD, Rush Med Coll., Chgo., 1985. Cert. Anatomic Pathology. Intern otolaryngology Albert Einstein Coll. Medicine, Bronx, NY, 1985—86, resident anatomical pathology, 1986—87, NY Hosp., NYC, 1987—89, resident, 1989—90; asst. prof. pathology Cornell U., 1990, SUNY, Buffalo, 1991—94; asst. prof. Georgetown U. Med. Coll., Washington, 1994—2001; adj. faculty Rockefeller U., NYC, 2001—03, assoc. prof. clin. investigation, 2003—, rschr. Aaron Diamond AIDS Rsch. Ctr. Lab head Walter Reed Army Med. Ctr., Washington, 1990—2002; attending physician Buffalo Gen. Hosp., 1991—94; rschr. pathology Roswell Pk. Cancer Inst., NY, 1991—94; staff Armed Forces Inst. Pathology, Md., 1994; staff divsn. retrovirology Walter Reed Army Inst. Rsch., Rockville, Md., 1995. Contbr. articles to profl. jours. Office: Aaron Diamond AIDS Rsch Ctr Rockefeller U 455 First Ave 7th Flr New York NY 10016 Office Phone: 212-448-5056. Office Fax: 212-725-1126. Business E-Mail: schless@rockefeller.edu.*

SCHLESINGER, STEPHEN CANNON, foreign policy consultant; b. Boston, Aug. 17, 1942; s. Arthur Meier and Marian (Cannon) S.; m. Judith Barbara Elster, Mar. 18, 1984; 1 child, Sarah Elizabeth. BA in Am. History and Lit. cum laude, Harvard U., 1964, JD, 1968; cert. study in European History, Cambridge U., 1965. Legal asst. to pres. N.Y. State Urban Devel. Corp., 1968; founder, editor The New Dem., 1969-72; speechwriter Dem. Presdl. Candidate George McGovern, 1972; staff writer TIME Mag., 1974-78; editorial writer, chief polit. corr. N.Y. Post, 1978; spl. asst. to Gov. Mario Cuomo, 1983-90; dir. for internat. orgns. N.Y. State Dept. Econ. Devel., 1990—94; vis. scholar Taub Urban Rsch. Ctr. NYU, 1995-97; spl. advisor UN Ctr. for Human Settlements, 1995-97; dir. World Policy Inst. at New Sch. U., NYC, 1997—2006; adj. fellow Century Found., NYC, 2008—. With Gore Presdl. Campaign, 2000, Kerry Presdl. Campaign, 2004; mem. internat. election observer teams Nat. Dem. Inst., 1993, 90; tchg. fellow in English composition Harvard U., 1968; adj. prof. Am. politics New Sch. U., 1976-77; lectr. Royce Carlton Agy., 1984-88. Author: The New Reformers, 1975, Bitter Fruit: The Untold Story of the U.S. Coup in Guatemala, 1982, Act of Creation: The Founding of the United Nations, 2003 (Harry Truman Book award 2004); co-editor: Journals 1952-2000 Arthur Schlesinger Jr., 2007; contbr. articles to profl. jours., mags. and newspapers; columnist: Boston Globe, 1973-74. Mem. Coun. Fgn. Rels., Roosevelt Inst., PEN, Author's Guild, Overseas Press Club, UN Correspondents Assn. Unitarian Universalist. Avocations: bicycling, jogging, skiing, swimming, tennis. Home: 500 W 111th St Apt 4A New York NY 10025-1905 E-mail: scsje@aol.com.

SCHLESS, PHYLLIS ROSS, investment banker; d. Lewis H. and Doris G. Ross; m. Aaron Backer Schless, 1970; 1 son, Daniel Lewis Ross. Cert., Neighborhood Playhouse Sch. of Theatre, 1962, N.Y. Sch. Interior Design, 1964; BA in Econs., Wellesley Coll., 1964; MBA, Stanford U., 1966. Cert. theater prodns. Am. League Theater Owners and Prodrs. Assoc. internat. fin. Kuhn Loeb & Co., NYC, 1966—70; fin. cons., 1971—73; sr. fin. analyst Trans World Airlines, NYC, 1974—75; corp. fin., mergers and acquisitions Lazard Freres & Co., 1976—79; dir. mergers and acquisitions Am. Can Co., Greenwich, Conn., 1979—82; v.p. mergers and acquisitions Bear, Stearns & Co., NYC, 1982—84; sr. v.p. corp. acquisitions Integrated Resources, 1984—85; chmn., CEO Ross Fin. Svcs. Group Inc., 1986—; supervisory dir. Merrill Lynch HYTS Funds, 1991—96. Bd. dirs. Calvary Hosp. Fund Bd., 1990-2000, chair investment com., 1995-99, Nat. Found. Tchg. Entrepreneurship NY Metro Bd., 2000-05; trustee A.R. Tinker Fund, 1993-2004, hon. trustee, 2004—; trustee Nat. Child Labor Com., 1981-95, chmn., 1992-94; trustee New World Found., 1986-92, chair fin. com., treas. 1988-92; bd. dirs. Stanford Bus. Sch. Assn., N.Y., 1994-2004; adj. asst. prof. NYU, 1996—, Columbia U. Sch. Bus., 2001—; bd. dirs. Nat. Found. Tchg. Entrepreneurship, metro. N.Y. chair, 2000-05. Pres. Greater Bridgeport Nat. Coun. Jewish Women, 1971-73, bd. dirs., 1974-75; bd. dirs. Girls Clubs Am., 1975-89, mem. exec. com., 1982-89, pres., 1984-86; bd. dirs. Pauline Koner Dance Co., 1979-81, So. Conn. Child Guidance Clinic, 1981-83, New Canaan United Way, 1981-83; treas. Wellesley Class '64, 1984-89. Mem. Univ. Club. Office Phone: 212-223-1781.

SCHLESSINGER, JOEL, dermatologist, researcher, entrepreneur; b. Columbus, Ohio, Sept. 14, 1960; s. Bernard S. and June Hirsch Schlessinger; m. Nancy Beth Gordon, Oct. 29, 1989; children: Claire Elizabeth, Daniel Isaac. BA in Biology, U. RI, Kingston, 1977—81; degree in Basic Scis., Brown U., Providence, 1981—83; MD, Baylor Coll., Houston, 1983—85. Lic. MD Fedn. Licensing Exam., 1985, cert. pediatrician Am. Bd. Pediat., 1988, dermatologist Am. Bd. Dermatology, 1992, general cosmetic surgeon Am. Bd. Cosmetic Surgery, 1999. Residency in pediat. U. Ala., Birmingham, 1985—88; residency in dermatology Wash. U., St. Louis, 1989—92; CEO Skin Specialists, PC, Omaha, 1993—, LovelySkin.com, Omaha, 1997—, Advanced Skin Rsch. Ctr., Omaha, 2001—. Nat. dir. clin. rsch. ExCel Cosmeceuticals, Bloomfield Hills, Mich., 1998—; adv. bd. Medicis Corp., Scottsdale, Ariz., 2000—; mem. nat. edn. found. Allergan Corp., Irvine, Calif., 2000—; adv. bd. Stiefel Corp., Coral Gables, Fla., 2005—; presdl. adv. bd. Connetics Corp., Palo Alto, Calif., 2004—; adv. bd. Artes Med., San Diego, 2005—. Contbr. articles to profl. jours. including Cosmetic Dermatology, Jour. Drugs in Dermatology, Skin and Aging Mag., Archives Dermatology, others. Bd. mem. Beth El Synagogue, Omaha, 2000—06; bd. mem. alumni schools com. Brown U., 1997—; bd. trustees Millard Pub. Schs. Found., 1999—2005; curriculum com. mem. Millard Pub. Schs., Omaha, 2000—; gov. bd. Omaha Symphony, 2007—, filmstreams bd., 2007—. Recipient Svc. Honor, Millard Pub. Schs. Found., 1999—2005, Best Cosmetic Surgeon in Omaha, Omaha Mag., 2000—08, Best Dermatologist in Omaha, Reader Mag., 2002—07. Fellow: Am. Assn. Cosmetic Surgery (assoc.); mem.: Am. Soc. Cosmetic Dermatology & Aesthetic Surgery (co-founder 1999, pres. 2006—07, Disting. Svc. award 2003—06), Am. Soc. Dermatologic Surgery (assoc.; post grad. edn. com. 2005—06), Am. Numis. Assn. (assoc.), Am. Soc. Laser Surgery & Medicine (assoc.), Nebr. Med. Assn. (assoc.; bd. pres. 2005—06), Am. Acad. Dermatology (assoc.; polit. unpaid lobbyist 1998—, Model State Soc. award 2005—06), Nebr. Dermatology Soc. (assoc.; pres. 2003—06, Model State Soc. award for first time under my presidency 2005—06), Brown Nebr. Club (pres. 2006—), Classic Thunderbird Club Internat. (assoc.), Nebr. Thunderbird Club (assoc.), Phi Beta Kappa (assoc.). Jewish. Achievements include development of one of the largest skincare websites in the world, LovelySkin. Avocations: travel, photography, kickboxing, scuba diving. Office: Skin Specialists PC 2802 OakView Mall Dr Omaha NE 68144 Office Fax: 402-334-8627; Home Fax: 402-334-8627. Business E-Mail: skindoc@lovelyskin.com.

SCHLEY, WAYNE ARTHUR, political scientist, consultant; b. Hamilton, Mont., May 22; AA, Shasta Coll., 1960; BS, Sacramento State U., 1963; MS, Am. U., 1974; postgrad., U. Alaska, 1970, Harvard U. Cert. high sch. tchr. (lifetime), Calif. Dept. Edn. Tchr., admin. Placer H.S., Auburn, Calif., 1963-70; spl. asst. to Sen. Ted Stevens, Washington, 1971-77; staff dir. minority and majority subcom. civil svc. Post Office and Gen. Svcs., Washington, 1977-86; minority staff dir. Senate Com. on Rules and Adminstrn., Washington, 1987-92; commr. U.S. Postal Rate Commn., Washington, 1992-95; cons. on legis. and postal issues Washington, 1995—. Elected bd. dirs. Assn. Postal Commerce, 2003-06; chmn. Calif. Teenage Reps., 1963-64; regional v.p. Calif. Young Reps., 1964-66, state sgt. at arms, 1966-67; mem. Placer County Rep. Ctrl. Com., 1965-70. Recipient Cert. of Achievement, JFK Sch. Govt. Harvard U., 1982. Home and Office: 614 Massachusetts Ave NE Washington DC 20002-6006 Office Phone: 202-547-9476. Personal E-mail: was2nat@hotmail.com.

SCHLEY, WILLIAM SHAIN, otolaryngologist; b. Columbus, Ga., Sept. 21, 1940; s. Frances Brooking Schley and Susie (Smith) Mathews. BA, Emory U., 1962, MD, 1966. Intern mixed surg. The Roosevelt Hosp., NYC, 1966-67, resident in surgery, 1967-68; resident in otorhinolaryngology N.Y. Hosp.-Cornell Med. Ctr., NYC, 1970-73; clin. instr. otorhinolaryngology Cornell U. Med. Coll., 1972-75, clin. asst. prof., 1975-81, assoc. prof., 1982—, acting chmn. dept. otorhinolarygology, 1988-94, chmn. dept. otorhinolarygology, 1994—2005. Otorhinolaryngologist to outpatients with pvt. patient privileges N.Y. Hosp., 1973-75, asst. attending otorhinolaryngologist with pvt. patient privileges, 1975-81, assoc. attending, 1992—, acting otorhinolaryngologist-in-chief, 1988-94, otorhinolaryngologist-in-chief, 1994-2005; assoc. asst. surgeon otolaryngology Manhattan Eye, Ear, Nose and Throat Hosp., 1988-99; v.p. and sec. med. bd. N.Y. Hosp., 1994-97, pres., 1998-99; pres., v.p. med. bd. The N.Y. and Presbyn. Hosp., 1998, pres., 1998-99, mem. ex officio bd. trustees, 1998-99; mem. co-chmn. vis. day com. The N.Y.

Hosp.-Cornell Med. Ctr., 1995-98; pres. N.Y. Hosp.-Cornell Med. Coll. Alumni Coun., 1996-98; course dir. Salzburg Cornell Med. Seminars, 1996—2007, steering com., 1999—. Author: (with others) Pulmonary Diseases of the Fetus Newborn and Child, 1978; contbr. numerous articles to profl. publs. Vestry St. James Ch., N.Y.C., 1994-97; chmn. The Third Age Coun. St. James Ch., 2007-; mem. ad hoc bd. visitors Emory U., 1994-95; bd. dirs. Health Advs. for Older People, 1997—, v.p., 2000—; mem. adv. bd. Sch. Medicine Emory U., 2000—, chmn. adv. bd., 2002—; chmn. third age coun. St. James Ch., 2007—. Lt. comdr. USNR. Recipient The Emery medal, 2001; Homes fellowship, 1998. Fellow ACS (Manhattan dist. #2 com. on applicants 1991-97, Manhattan Credentials Com. 1991-99); mem. Am. Acad. Otolaryngology-Head and Neck Surgery, Med. Soc. State of N.Y., N.Y. State Soc. Otolaryngology-Head and Neck Surgery (exec. coun. 1974-80, dist. dir. 1980), County Med. Soc. N.Y., N.Y. Laryngol. Soc. (sec.-treas. 1981-84, v.p. 1984-85, pres. 1985-86), N.Y. Bronchoscopic Soc. (v.p. 1986-94, pres. 1994-97), N.Y. Clin. Soc. (v.p. 1998-99, pres. 1999-2000, sec.-treas, 2005-07), Assn. Emory Alumni (bd. govs. 1990-97, pres.-elect 1993-94, pres. 1994-95), Omicron Delta Kappa. Episcopalian. Avocations: astronomy, ornithology. Home: 430 E 63d St Apt 5E New York NY 10065-7927 Office: DS10 449 E 68th St New York NY 10021-6310 Office Phone: 212-746-2223. E-mail: schley@med.cornell.edu.

SCHLEYER, PAUL VON RAGUÉ, chemistry educator; b. Cleve., Feb. 27, 1930; s. Charles Ernest and Hulda Betty (Kamphausen) S.; m. Ingeborg Venema, Dec. 29, 1969; children by previous marriage: Betti, Laura, Karen. AB, Princeton U., 1951; MA, Harvard U., 1956, PhD, 1957; PhD Honoris Causa, U. Lyon, France, 1971. Instr., Princeton U., 1954-58, asst. prof., 1958-63, assoc. prof., 1963-65, prof., 1965-69, Eugene Higgins prof. chemistry, 1969-76; prof. U. Erlangen-Nuremberg, Germany, 1976; sr. fellow U. So. Calif., 1978; Graham Perdue prof. chemistry Univ. Ga., Athens. Vis. prof. U. Colo., 1963, U. Würzburg, Germany, 1967, U. Mich., 1969, U. Munich, 1969, Carnegie Mellon U., 1969, Kyoto (Japan) U., 1970, U. Münster, Germany, 1971, U. Geneva, 1972, U. Groningen, The Netherlands, 1972-73, 90; vis. U. Jerusalem, 1973, U. Paris, 1973, U. Louvain, Belgium, 1974, U. Regensburg, Germany, 1975, Case Western Res. U., 1976-77, U. Western Ont., 1978, Carnegie-Mellon U., 1977-78, U. Copenhagen, 1979-80, U. Utrecht, 1982, 85, U. Barcelona, 1983, Technion, Haifa, Israel, 1993; disting. vis. prof. U. Ga., 1990—; cons. to industry, 1955—. Co-author: The Nonclassical Ion Problem, 1977, AB INITIO Molecular Orbital Theory, 1986; mem. editl. bd. Chem. Revs., 1969-72, Jour. Am. Chem. Soc., 1970-79, Revs. Chem. Intermediates, 1982—, Jour. Phys. Organic Chemistry, 1987—, Heteroatom Chemistry, 1988, Tetrahedron Pubs., 1990—, Chem. Comms., 1990-96; co-editor series Carbonium Ions, vol. 1, 1968, vol. 2, 1970, vol. 3, 1972, vol. 4, 1973, vol. 5, 1977, Lithium Chemistry, 1995, Stable Carbocation Chemistry, 1997; editor Jour. Computational Chemistry, 1981—, Theoretical Structures of Molecules, 1993, 94; editor-in-chief Ency. Computational Chemistry, 1997; contbr. 850 rsch. articles to tech. jours. Mem. rev. com. NIH, 1967-70. Recipient von Humboldt sr. scientist award U. Munich, 1974-75; A.P. Sloan research fellow, 1962-66; Fulbright fellow, also; Guggenheim fellow U. Munich, 1965; von Baeyer prize German Chem. Soc. 1986, J.F. Norris award in Phys. Organic Chemistry Am. Chem. Soc., 1987, Heisenberg medal World Assn. Theoretical Chemists and Hungarian Chem. Soc., 1987, Ingold Medal Royal Soc. Chemistry, 1988; Cope scholar Am. Chem. Soc., 1990. Fellow AAAS, Am. Acad. Arts & Scis., Bavarian Acad. Scis., Merck-Schuchardt Chair (Belgium 1991), World Assn. Theoretical Organic Chemists (pres. 1990-96), Internat. Acad. Quantum Chem. Sci. Office: Univ Georgia Dept Chemistry Athens GA 30602-2525 Office Fax: 706-542-0406. Business E-Mail: schleyer@chem.uga.edu.

SCHLEYER, WILLIAM T., cable company executive; b. Phila. BS in Mech. Engring., Drexel U.; MBA, Harvard Bus. Sch. Mgr. IBM, Abbott Labs.; from sys. mgr. to pres., COO US West Media Group Continental Cablevision, 1977-97; pres., COO MediaOne, Boston, 1997—2000; prin. Pilot House Ventures, LLC, 2001; pres., CEO, broadband services unit AT&T Corp., 2001—03; chmn., CEO Adelphia Communications Corp., Greenwood Village, Colo., 2003—. Office: Tele Communications Inc 183 Inverness Dr W Englewood CO 80112-5203

SCHLICHER, RONALD LEWIS, former ambassador; With Fgn. Svc., 1982—; min.-counselor sr. fgn. svc.; vice-consul Dhahran, 1982—84; consul Damascus, Syria, 1984—86; staff asst. Bur. Near Ea. Affairs US Dept. State; dep. prin. officer Am. Embassy, Alexandria, Egypt, 1987—89, first sec. Cairo, 1989—91; chief civilian officer Multinational Force and Observers, Israel, 1991—92; dep. dir. regional affairs Office of Coord. Counter Terrorism, 1994—97; dep. chief of mission Am. Embassy, Beirut, 1994—97; dir. office Egyptian and N. African affairs, Bur. Near Eastern Affairs US Dept. State, Washington, 1997—2000; chief of mission, counsul-gen. Am. Embassy, Jerusalem, 2000—02; dir. Iraqi Task Force, 2003; dep. asst. sec. US Dept. State, Washington, US amb. to Cyprus Nicosia, 2005—08. Recipient Disting. Honor award, Superior Honor award (3), Meritorious Honor award (2), Nat. Human Intelligence Collector award, Christian A. Herter award.*

SCHLICHTING, CATHERINE FLETCHER NICHOLSON, librarian, educator; b. Huntsville, Ala., Nov. 18, 1923; d. William Parsons and Ethel Loise (Breitling) Nicholson; m. Harry Fredrick Schlichting, July 1, 1950 (dec. Aug. 1964); children: James Dean, Richard Dale, Barbara Lynn. BS, U. Ala., 1944; MLS, U. Chgo., 1950. Asst. libr. U. Ala. Edn. Libr., Tuscaloosa, summers 1944-45; libr. Sylacauga (Ala.) H.S., 1944-45, Hinsdale (Ill.) H.S., 1945-49; asst. libr. Centre for Children's Books, U. Chgo., 1950-52; instr. reference dept. libr. Ohio Wesleyan U., Delaware, 1965-69, asst. prof., 1969-79, assoc. prof., 1979-85, prof., 1985—, curator Ohio Wesleyan Hist. Collection, 1986—, student pers. libr., 1966-72. Author: Introduction to Bibliographic Research: Basic Sources, 4th edit., 1983, Checklist of Biographical Reference Sources, 1977, Audio-Visual Aids in Bibliographic Instruction, 1976, Introduction to Bibliographic Research: Slide Catalog and Script, 1980; info. cons. (documentary) Noble Achievements: The History of Ohio Wesleyan 1942-1992, 1992, 150 Years of Excellence: A Pictorial View of Ohio Wesleyan University, 1992. Mem. adminstrv. bd. Meth. Ch., 1973-81, chmn. adminstrv. bd., 1985—, mem. coun. on ministries, 1975-81, chmn., 1975-77, trustee, 1999—2003. Recipient Algernon Sidney Sullivan award U. Ala., 1944, Hon. Alumna award Ohio Wesleyan U., 1997; Ohio Wesleyan U.-Mellon Found. grantee, 1972-73, 84-85; GLCA Tchg. fellow, 1976-77. Mem. ALA, Ohio Libr. Assn., Midwest Acad. Libr. Conf., Acad. Librs. Assn. Ohio (dir. 1984-86), AAUP (chpt. sec. 1967-68), United Meth. Women (pres. Mt. Vernon dist. 1994-97, newsletter editor 1998-2002), Ohio Wesleyan Woman's Club (exec. bd. 1969-72, 77-79, 81-84, pres. 1969-70, sec. 1977-78), History Club (pres. 1971-72, v.p. 1978-79, 2003-04) Fortnightly Club (pres. 1975-76, 87-88, 2003-04), Am. Field Svc. (pres. Delaware chpt. 1975-76), Kappa Delta Pi, Alpha Lambda Delta. Democrat. Home: 116 Willow Brook Way S Delaware OH 43015 Office: Ohio Wesleyan U La Beeghly Library Delaware OH 43015

SCHLICHTING, NANCY MARGARET, hospital administrator; b. NYC, Nov. 21, 1954; BA, Duke U., 1976; MBA, Cornell U., 1979. Adminstrv. resident Meml. Hosp. Cancer, NYC, 1978; fellow Blue Cross-Blue Shield Assn., Chgo., 1979-80; asst. dirs. ops. Akron (Ohio) City Hosp., 1980-81, assoc. dir. planning, 1981-83, exec. v.p., 1983-88, Riverside Meth. Hosps., Columbus, Ohio, 1988-92, pres., COO, 1992-93, pres., CEO, 1993-96; pres. Ea. region Cath. Health Initiatives, Aston, Pa., 1996-97; exec. v.p., COO Summa Health Sys., Akron, Ohio, 1997—98; sr. v.p., chief adminstrv. officer Henry Ford Healthcare Sys., Detroit, 1998—99, exec. v.p., COO, 1999—2003, pres., CEO, 2003—, Henry Ford Hosp., 2001—03. Bd. dirs. Fifth Third Bank Corp., First Nat. Bank of Ohio, Mich. Health and Hosp. Assn., Greater Detroit Area Health Council, Walgreen Co., 2006—. Trustee Kresge Found. Office: Henry Ford Health Sys 1 Ford Pl Detroit MI 48202

SCHLICHTING, WILLIAM HENRY, lawyer, writer; b. Austin, Minn., Jan. 24, 1944; s. John Frederick and Frances Amelia (Garbisch) Schlichting. BA, St. Olaf Coll., 1966; MS, U. Chgo., 1970; JD, Columbia U., 1973; LLM in Taxation, NYU, 1979. Bar: NY 1974, Minn. 1981, US Tax Ct. 1982. Assoc. Shea & Gould, NYC, 1973—76; editor Law Jour. Pub. Co., NYC, 1976—79, Matthew Bender & Co., Inc., NYC, 1979—81; assoc. Peterson, Hanson, Schlichting & Davies, Albert Lea, Minn., 1981—83; gen. counsel, sec. Med. Venture, Inc., Mpls., 1983—89; writer Matthew Bender & Co., Inc., NYC, 1989—91; acquisitions editor, classifier West Group, Eagan, Minn., 1991—2002; bd. dirs. The Aliveness Project, Inc., 2004—, pres., chmn., 2005—08. Writer Butterworth Legal Pub., Mason divsn., St. Paul, 1983—84. Author, editor Banking Law, 1979—81, Clark's Digest-Annotator, 1976—79; contbr. articles to profl. jours. Mem. investments and fin. com. Philanthrofund Found., 2005—08. Fellow, NSF, 1966—70; Erik Hetle scholar, 1966—67. Mem.: Minn. Bar Assn., Phi Beta Kappa, Sigma Pi Sigma. Lutheran. Home: 5901 Laurel Ave #325 Golden Valley MN 55416-1075 Personal E-mail: wmhenrys@comcast.net.

SCHLICK, AUSTIN C., lawyer; b. NYC, 1963; BA in History, magna cum laude, Princeton U., 1985; JD, Yale Law Sch., 1990. Bar: Pa. 1994, DC 1996. Law clk. to Chief Judge Abner Mikva US Ct. Appeals (DC Cir.), 1990—91; law clk. to Justice Sandra Day O'Connor US Supreme Ct., 1991—92; assoc. Klein, Farr, Smith & Taranto, Washington, 1992—93; assoc. to ptnr. Kellogg, Huber, Hansen, Todd & Evans, Phila. & Washington DC, 1993—2000; ptnr. Kellogg, Huber, Hansen, Todd, Evans & Figel PLLC, Washington, 2006—; asst. solicitor gen. Office of Solicitor Gen., US Dept. Justice, Washington, 2000—04; dep. gen. counsel Fed. Communications Commn., Washington, 2004—05, acting gen. counsel, 2005. Office: Kellogg Huber Hansen Todd Evans & Figel Ste 400 1615 M St NW Washington DC 20036 Office Phone: 202-326-7907. Office Fax: 202-326-7999. E-mail: aschlick@khhte.com.

SCHLIEVE, HY C. J., school administrator; b. Mandan, ND, Apr. 4, 1952; s. Calvin L. and Loretta L. (Johnson) S.; m. Terri Ann Hansen, Dec. 30, 1977; children: Derek, Aaron, Jessica. BA, N.D. State U., 1974, MS, 1984; EdD, Calif. Coast U., 1994. Tchr., coach Halliday Pub. Sch., ND, 1974-75, Drake Pub. Sch., ND, 1975-76, Montpelier Pub. Sch., ND, 1976-81; prin. Unity Pub. Sch., Petersburg, ND, 1981-83, Page Pub. Sch., ND, 1983-85; supt. Wolford Pub. Sch., ND, 1985-87, Garrison Pub. Schs., ND, 1987-93; prin. Buhl Joint Sch. Dist. 412, Idaho, 1993-95, Oconto Falls Area Sch. Dist., Wis., 1995-99; supt. Ellendale Pub. Schs. #40, ND, 1999—. Com. mem. NDASA Rsch. and Evaluation, Garrison, 1988-93; fiscal agt. Mo. Hills Consortium, McLean County, N.D., 1989-93; cons. asbestos Garrison Pub. Sch. Dist., 1987-93. Sec. Govtl. Affairs Com., Garrison, 1987-93; mem. Tourism Com., Garrison, 1988-92, Econ. Devel. Com., 1988-89. Recipient Nat. Superintendent of the Yr. awd., North Dakota, Am. Assn. of School Administrators, 1992. Mem. Nat. Assn. Secondary Sch. Prins. (prin. assessor tng. 1990), NSBA Fed. Policy Coords. Network. Avocations: golf, hunting, fishing, bowling, outdoor activities. Office: Ellendale Pub Schs PO Box 400 321 N 1st St Ellendale ND 58436

SCHLINK, BERNHARD, law educator, writer; b. Grossdornberg, Bielefeld, Germany, July 6, 1944; JD, Ruprecht Karl U., Heidelberg, Germany, 1975; grad., Albert-Ludwigs-U., Freiburg, Germany, 1981. Prof. Rheinische Friedrich-Wilhelms-U., Bonn, Germany, 1982-91, J. W. Goethe U., Frankfurt, Germany, 1991-92; prof. constl./adminstrv. law & philosophy of law Humboldt-U., Berlin, 1992—. Judge Constnl. Ct. Nordrhein-Westfalen, Germany, 1988—2006; cons. on draft of Constn. for German Dem. Republic, 1990, Lithuanian Constn., 1992. Author: (titles in English) The Reader, 1997 (NY Times bestseller, Publishers Weekly bestseller, Hans Fallada prize, Italy, 1997, Prix Laure Bataillon, France, 1997), Flights of Love: Stories, 2001, Self's Punishment, 2005, Self's Deception, 2007, Homecoming, 2007, Guilt about the Past, 2009, numerous titles in German. Fellow NY Pub. Libr. Ctr. for Scholars & Writers, 2008. Achievements include writing the first German book to reach the number one position in the NY Times bestseller list. Office: Humboldt U Unter den Linden 6 D-10099 Berlin Germany also: Random House Inc 1745 Broadway New York NY 10019*

SCHLITZ, LAURA AMY, school librarian, writer; b. Balt. BA, Goucher Coll., Towson, Md., 1977. Libr., chief storyteller Park Sch. Balt., 1991—. Author: (books) The Hero Schliemann: The Dreamer Who Dug For Troy, 2006, A Drowned Maiden's Hair, 2006, Good Masters! Sweet Ladies!: Voices from a Medieval Village, 2007 (Newbery medal, 2008), The Bearskinner: A Tale of the Brothers Grimm, 2007. Mailing: Park Sch PO Box 8200 Brooklandville MD 21022*

SCHLODER, JOHN E., museum director; BS, Duquesne U., 1969; diplôme d'Ancien Elève, L'Ecole du Louvre, Paris, 1973; licence L'Institut d'Art et d'Archéologie, U. Paris-Sorbonne, 1973, doctorat L'Institut d'Art et d'Archéologie, 1988; MPhil, Columbia U., 1980. Chargé de Mission Musée du Louvre, Paris, 1979-82; asst. curator Cleve. Mus. Art Edn Dept., 1982-85, assoc. curator, 1985-86, adminstr. pub. programs, 1986-88, asst. dir. edn. and pub. programs, 1988-92; dir. Birmingham Mus. Art, Ala., 1992-96, Joslyn Mus. Art, Omaha, 1997—2000, Mus. Fine Arts, St. Petersburg, Fla., 2001—. Vis. prof. Colégio Andrews, Rio de Janeiro, Brazil, 1980-81, Vaculdade Candido Mendes, Rio de Janeiro, 1981-82; adj. prof. dept. art history Case Western Res. U., Cleve., 1984-92; lectr. in field. Mus. rep. Northeastern Ohio Inter-Mus. Coun., 1984-92; trustee Cleve. Sch. Arts, 1991-92; active Southeast Mus. Conf., 1992—; mem. Leadership Birmingham, 1994-95; bd. dirs. Op. New Birmingham, 1993—; mem. Birmingham Olympic programming com., mem. outreach com., 1994—. Lurcy Trust fellowship, 1975, Columbia U. Traveling fellowship, 1975, 76, U. Cambridge, Eng. Leverhulme fellowship, 1977, Kellogg Project fellowship Smithsonian Instn., 1987; scholarship J. Paul Getty Trust, 1989; vis. Scholar grantee The Japan Found., 1995; recipient French Govt. award, 1975, award of achievement for best cmty. event Northern Ohio Live Mag., 1991. Mem. Am. Assn. Mus., Assn. Art Mus. Dirs., Internat. Lab. for Visitor Studies, Visitor Studies Assn., Ala. Mus. Assn., Birmingham Area Mus. Assn., Soc. de l'Historie de l'Art Français, Rotary Club Birmingham. Office: Museum Fine Arts 255 Beach Drive NE Saint Petersburg FL 33701 Business E-Mail: jschloder@fine-arts.org.

SCHLOEGEL, SCOTT P., legislative staff member; b. Berwyn, Ill., Dec. 9, 1967; m. Kirsten L. Bondeson, May 22, 1993; 2 children. BS, No. Mich. U., 1990. Legis. aide to Rep. Bart Stupak Mich. House of Reps., Lansing, 1990, legis. aide to Rep. Ken DeBeausaert, 1991—92; dist. adminstr. to Rep. Bart Stupak, US House of Reps., Washington, 1993—97, chief of staff, 1997—2007, 2007—; profl. staff mem. US House Com. on Energy and Commerce, Washington, 2007. Avocations: sports, family. Office: Office of Congressman Bart Stupak 2268 Rayburn House Office Bldg Washington DC 20515-0001 Home: 6505 Lignum St Springfield VA 22150-1143 Office Phone: 202-225-4735. Office Fax: 202-225-4744. E-mail: scott.schloegel@mail.house.gov.*

SCHLOERB, PAUL RICHARD, surgeon, educator; b. Buffalo, Oct. 22, 1919; s. Herman George and Vera (Gross) S.; m. Louise M. Grimmer, Feb. 25, 1950; children: Ronald G., Patricia S. Johnson, Marilyn A. Hock, Dorothy S. Hoban, P. Richard. AB, Harvard U., 1941; MD, U. Rochester, 1944. Intern U. Rochester Med. Sch., 1944—45, asst. resident, 1947—48, instr. surgery, 1952; rsch. fellow, resident Peter Bent Brigham Hosp., Boston, 1948—52; faculty U. Kans. Med. Ctr., Kansas City, 1952—79, prof. surgery, 1964—79, 1988—2006, prof. surgery emeritus, 2006—, dean for rsch., 1972—79, dir. nutritional support svc., 1993—2002; prof. surgery U. Rochester (NY) Med Ctr., 1979—88, adj. prof. surgery, 1988—90; surgeon Strong Meml. Hosp., 1979—88, dir. Surg. ICU, 1979—85, dir. surg. nutritional support service. Contbr. over 100 articles to profl. jours. Lt. (j.g.), M.C. USNR, 1944-45; to lt. 1953-55. Mem. AMA, ACS, AAAS, Am. Surg. Assn., Soc. U. Surgeons, Am. Physiol. Soc., Internat. Soc. Surgery, Ctrl. Surg. Assn., Am. Assn. for Surgery of Trauma, Am. Assn. Cancer Rsch., Biomed. Engring. Soc., Am. Inst. Nutrition, Am. Soc. Clin. Nutrition, Surgery Biology Club 2, Sigma Xi. Achievements include first to measure total body water in humans J. Clin. Invest. Office: Dept Surgery U Kansas Med Ctr Kansas City KS 66160-0001 Home Phone: 913-451-8998; Office Phone: 913-588-7565. Business E-Mail: pschloer@kumc.edu.

SCHLOM, JEFFREY BERT, research scientist; b. NYC, June 22, 1942; s. David and Anna Schlom; m. Kathleen; children: Amy Melissa, Steven Michael. BS (Pres.'s scholar), Ohio State U., 1964; MS, Adelphi U., 1966; PhD, Rutgers U., 1969. Instr. Columbia Coll. Phys. and Surg., 1969-71, asst. prof., 1971-73; chmn. breast cancer virus segment Nat Cancer Inst., NIH, Bethesda, Md., 1973-76, chief Lab. Tumor Immunology and Biology, 1983—, head Exptl. Oncology Sect., 1976-83, head Immunotherapeutics Group; prof. George Washington U., Washington, 1975—. Disting. lectr. Can. Cancer Soc., 1985 Contbr. articles to profl. jours. Recipient Dir.'s award NIH, 1977, 89, Tech. Transfer award NIH, 1994, 95, 96, Disting. Scientist award Turin U., 1996, others. Mem. Am. Assn. Cancer Rsch. (Rosenthal award 1985), Am. Soc. Cytology (Basic Rsch. award 1987). Office: Nat Cancer Inst / Ctr Cancer Rsch 10 Center Dr, MSC 1750 Bldg 10, Rm 8B09 Bethesda MD 20892 Office Phone: 301-496-4343. Office Fax: 301-496-2756. Business E-Mail: js141c@nih.gov.

SCHLOSS, HADASSAH, auditor; b. Buenos Aires, Nov. 18, 1950; came to US, 1977; d. Moises Zysman and Sofia (Zack) Kuperwasser; m. Peter Gordon Schloss, Mar. 27, 1977; 1 child, Merav Karen (dec.). BBA in Acctg., U. Tex., Austin, 1993. Clk. State of Tex., Austin, 1990—93, adminstrv. tech. III, 1993, internal auditor I, 1993—94, internal auditor II, 1994—95, program adminstr. open records sect., 1995—2005, cost rules adminstr., 2005—. Co-chair Open Records Steering Com., Austin, 2005—; mem. Freedom of Info. Found. Tex. Recipient James Madison award Freedom Info. Found. Tex., 1996, Open Doors award, Soc. profl. Journalist, Ft. Worth Chapt., 2006. Jewish. Avocations: reading mystery, suspense, biographies, sewing, cooking. Home: 6704 Roseborough Dr Austin TX 78747-4023 Office: Office of Attorney General 209 W 14th St Austin TX 78701 Address: PO Box 12548 Austin TX 78711-2548 Office Phone: 512-475-2497.

SCHLOSS, HOWARD MONROE, financial regulatory service executive; b. Rochester, NY, Jan. 30, 1960; m. Deborah Tawney; children: Michael Austin, Lindsay Taylor, Gabriella Greer. BFA in Journalism, So. Meth. U., 1982. Copy editor Fort Worth Star-Telegram, asst. to the op-ed page editor, 1983-87; writer, editor UPI, Dallas, 1982; dep. comm. dir., comm. dir. Dem. Congl. Campaign Com., 1987-91; acct. supr. Powell Tate, 1991-93; dep. asst. sec. for pub. affairs US Dept. Treasury, Washington, 1993-95, asst. sec. for pub. affairs, 1995—99; v.p. pub. affairs NY Stock Exch., 1999—2000; sr. v.p. comm. & govt. rels. NASD, 2000—07, Fin. Industry Regulatory Authority, 2007—. Office: Financial Industry Regulatory Authority 1735 K St NW Washington DC 20006

SCHLOSS, JOHN VINTON, biochemist; b. St. Louis, May 11, 1951; s. John H. and Lois F. (Dawson) S.; children: John L., Carol M. BS, U. Tulsa, 1973; PhD, U. Tenn., Oak Ridge, 1978. Postdoctoral researcher biochemistry dept. U. Wis., Madison, 1978-81; prin. investigator cen. rsch. dept. Du Pont Co., Wilmington, Del., 1981-87, rsch. supr. cen. rsch. dept., 1987-91; prof. dept. medicinal chemistry U. Kans., 1991—. Editor: Biosynthesis of Branched Chain Amino Acids, 1990, Enzymatic and Model Carboxylation and Reactions for Carbon Dioxide Utilization, 1990; contbr. more than 50 articles to profl. jours. Office: Dept Medicinal Chemistry U Kans 4070 Malott Hall Lawrence KS 66045-7564

SCHLOSS, NATHAN, retired economist; b. Balt., Jan. 14, 1927; s. Howard L. and Louise (Levi) S.; m. Rosa Montalvo, Mar. 1, 1958; children: Nina L., Carolyn D. BS in Bus., Johns Hopkins U., 1950. Buyer Pacific Coast gen. merchandise office Sears Roebuck & Co., Los Angeles, 1955-60; staff asst. econ. rsch. dept. Chgo., 1960-63; sr. market analyst corp. rsch. dept. Montgomery Ward & Co., Chgo., 1963-65; rsch. mgr. real estate dept. Walgreen Co., Chgo., 1970-72; v.p. rsch. and planning Maron Properties Ltd., Montreal, Que., Can., 1972-74; corp. economist, fin. analyst Real Estate Rsch. Corp., Chgo., 1974-88, sr. v.p., 1986-88, treas., chief fin. analyst, 1982-88; economist Office of Ill. Atty. Gen., Chgo., 1988-97. Cons. in field, 1965-97. Contbr. articles on fin. and market analysis of real estate to profl. jours. Mem. Plan. Commn., village of Wilmette, Ill., 1975-77, tech. adv. com. on employment and tng. data Ill. employment and Tng. Coun., 1979-82, tech. adv. com. Ill. Job Tng. Coordinating Council, 1983-87; mem. com. on price indexes and productivity fgn. labor Bus. Rsch. Adv. Coun. of Bur. Labor Stats, Dept. Labor, 1979-88, chairperson, 1985-86, com. on employment and unemployment. Recipient Commendable Svc. Citation, Bur. Labor Stats., Dept. Labor, 1987. Mem. Am. Mktg. Assn., Nat. Assn. Bus. Economists, Ill. Econ. Assn., Lambda Alpha. Home and Office: 115 Hollywood Ct Wilmette IL 60091-3122 Office Phone: 847-251-9582.

SCHLOSS, NEIL M., automotive executive; B in Fin., San Diego State U.; MBA, Santa Clara U., Calif. Fin. analyst controller's office Ford Aerospace Ford Motor Co., 1982, with Ford Motor, 1990, various risk mgmt./internat. fin. positions treas.'s office Ford Credit, 1991—95, mgr. domestic fin. to mgr. internat. fin. Ford Motor, 1995—97, mgr. N.Am./European fin. Ford Credit, 1997, asst. treas. Ford Credit, 1998—99, dir. fin. strategy treas.'s office, 1999—2002, dir. global risk mgmt. treas.'s office, 2002, asst. treas., 2003—07, v.p., treas., 2007—. Office: Ford Motor Co N Am Hdqs 1 American Rd Dearborn MI 48126 Business E-Mail: nschloss@ford.com.*

SCHLOSSER, C. ADAM, hydrologist; m. Carolyn Welsch Schlosser, Aug. 7, 1999; children: Ethan, Nathaniel. BS, U. Mass., Amherst, 1989; MSc, U. Md., Coll. Pk., 1992, PhD, 1995. Rsch. scientist Geophys. Fluid Dynamics Lab., Princeton, NJ, 1995—97, Ctr. Ocean Land Atmosphere Studies, Beltsville, Md., 1997—2001; assoc. rsch. scientist NASA Goddard Space Flight Ctr., Greenbelt, Md., 2001—03; prin. rsch. scientist MIT, Cambridge, 2003—. Recipient Outstanding Postdoc. Support award, NASA, 2003; grantee Govt. Sponsored Clte Rsch. Projects, NOAA, NSF, DOE, UNDP, 1998—; Grad. Rsch. fellowship, U. Md., 1990—92. Mem.: Am. Meteorol. Soc. (Editors Choice award 2005), Am. Geophys. Union, AMS Com. Hydrology. Office: Jt Prog Sci and Pol Glbl Chg E40-413 1 Amherst St Cambridge MA 02139 Office Fax: 617-253-3983. Business E-Mail: casch@mit.edu.

SCHLOSSER, HERBERT S., broadcasting company executive; b. Atlantic City, Apr. 21, 1926; s. Abraham and Anna (Olesker) S.; m. Judith P. Gassner, July 8, 1951; children: Lynn C., Eric M. AB summa cum laude, Princeton, 1948; LL.B., Yale, 1951. Bar: N.Y. 1952. Assoc. firm Wickes, Riddell, Bloomer, Jacobi & McGuire, NYC, 1951-54, Phillips, Nizer, Benjamin, Krim & Ballon, NYC, 1954-57; with NBC, 1957-78; v.p., gen. mgr. Calif. Nat. Prodns., Inc. sub. NBC, 1960-61, dir. talent and program adminstrn., 1961-62, v.p. talent and program adminstrn., 1962-66; v.p. programs West Coast NBC, 1966-72; exec. v.p. NBC-TV Network, 1972-73, pres., 1973-74, mem. bd. dirs., 1973-78; pres. NBC, Inc., 1974-78, CEO, 1977-78; exec. v.p. RCA, 1978-85; sr. advisor broadcasting and entertainment Schroder & Co., Inc., NYC, 1986—2000; sr. advisor, ind. cons. comms. investment banking Citigroup Global Markets Inc., 2000—. Ptnr. Arts and Entertainment Cable Network, RCA/Columbia Home Video. Trustee Internat. Radio and TV Found., 1972-74; former mem. govs. Ford's Theatre Soc.; former trustee Nat. Urban League; chmn. bd. Am. Mus. of the Moving Image; bd. dirs. Chamber Music Soc. of Lincoln Ctr. With USNR, 1944-46. Recipient Humanitarian award NCCJ, 1974, Gold Brotherhood award 1978 Mem. ABA, Assn. Bar City N.Y., Coun. on Fgn. Rels., Acad. TV Arts and Scis., Advt. Coun. (past dir.), Yale Law Sch. Assn., Internat. Radio and TV Soc. (trustee 1973-74), Hollywood Radio and TV Soc. (trustee 1970-72), Century Assn., Princeton Club (N.Y.), Phi Beta Kappa (pres. alumni assn. So. Calif. 1970-72. Office: Citigroup Global Markets 388 Greenwich St New York NY 10013-2375

SCHLOSSER, LISA, chief information officer; BA in polit. sci., Ind. U., Pa.; Master's degree in adminstrn., Ctrl. Mich. U. Mil. intelligence officer US Army; dir. info. security services Troy Sys.; sr. mgr. eSecurity solutions Ernst & Young; v.p. bus. ops. and response svcs. Global Integrity; assoc. chief info. officer for info. tech. security US Dept. Transp., Washington, assoc. chief info. officer for investment mgmt.; chief info. officer US Dept. Housing and Urban Devel. (HUD), Washington, 2005—. Officer USAR. Office: US Dept Housing and Urban Devel 451 7th St SW Washington DC 20410 Office Phone: 202-708-0306.*

SCHLOSSMAN, JOHN ISAAC, architect; b. Chgo., Aug. 21, 1931; s. Norman Joseph and Carol (Rosenfeld) S.; m. Shirley Goulding Rhodes, Feb. 8, 1959; children: Marc N., Gail S. Mewhort, Peter C. Student, Grinnell Coll., 1949-50; BA, U. Minn., 1953, BArch, 1955; MArch, MIT, 1956. Registered architect, Ill. Archtl. designer The Architects Collaborative, Cambridge, Mass., 1956-57; architect Loebl Schlossman & Hackl and predecessors, Chgo., 1959-65, assoc., 1965-70, prin., 1970-98, cons. prin., 1998—. Bd. overseers Coll. Arch. Ill. Inst. Tech., Chgo.; adv. bd. Coll. of Arch. and Landscape Arch. U. Minn., 2003-06; founding bd. dirs. Chgo. Archtl. Assistance Ctr., 1974-79 Chmn. Glencoe Plan Commn., Ill., 1977-82; mem. Village of Glencoe Contextual Design Rev. Commn., 2005-0; trustee Com. for Green Bay Trail, Glencoe, 1970-77, Chgo. Arch. Found., 1971-75, Graham Found. for Advanced Studies in Fine Arts, 1995-99, pres. 1999-2001; adv. bd. dirs. Merit Sch. of Music, Chgo., 1983-93, pres., 1988-90, hon. trustee, 1996; governing mem. Chgo. Symphony Orch.; mem. founders coun. Field Mus., Chgo.; mem. zoning and planning com. Greater North Michigan Ave. Assn., Chgo., 2000-01; mem. Nat. Trust Coun., Nat. Trust for Hist. Preservation, Washington. Named dir. for life Young Men's Jewish Coun., Chgo., 1971; Rotch travelling scholar, 1957; sustaining fellow Art Inst. Chgo. Fellow AIA (trustee ins. trust 1971-76, chmn. ins. com. 1974-75, v.p. Chgo. chpt. 1975, chmn. architects liability com. 1976, 80-82, hon. found. trustee 1995—), Tavern Club (gov. 1986-88, v.p. 1990), The Club at Symphony Ctr., The Arts Club, Alpha Rho Chi. E-mail: jschloss5@sbcglobal.net.

SCHLOSSMAN, STUART FRANKLIN, physician, educator, researcher; b. NYC, Apr. 18, 1935; s. Abe and Pearl (Susser) Schlossman; m. Judith Seryl Rubin, May 25, 1958; children: Robert, Peter. BA magna cum laude, NYU, 1955, MD, 1958; MA, Harvard U., 1975; MD (hon.), U. Heidelberg, 2006. Intern in medicine med. divsn. III Bellevue Hosp., NYC, 1958—59, asst. resident in medicine med. divsn. III, 1959—60; Nat. Found. fellow dept. microbiology Coll. Physicians Columbia U., NYC, 1960—62; asst. physician med. svc. Vanderbilt Clinic, Coll. Physician USPHS, Washington, 1960—62; Ward hematology fellow dept. internal medicine Sch. Washington U., St. Louis, 1962—63; rsch. assoc. lab. biochemistry Nat. Cancer Inst. USPHS, Washington, 1963—65; clin. instr. in medicine Sch. of Medicine George Washington U., 1964—65; assoc. in medicine, dir. blood bank Beth Israel Hosp., Boston, 1965—66; instr. Med. Sch. Harvard U., Boston, 1966—68, asst. physician, 1967—68, chief clin. immunology, 1971—73; physician Beth Israel Hosp., Boston, 1968—; from asst. to assoc. prof. medicine Harvard Med. Sch., Boston, 1968—77, prof., 1977—, Baruj Benacerraf prof. medicine, 1990—, chief divsn. tumor immunology and immunotherapy, 1973—; sr. physician Brigham and Women's Hosp., Boston, 1976—. Mem. editl. bd. Jour. of Immunology, 1969—74, Cellular Immunology, 1970—, Human Immunology, 1979—84, Clin. Immunology and Immunopathology, 1979—, mem. editl. bd.Hybridoma Hybridoma, 1980—, Cancer Investigation, 1981—, Stem Cells, 1981—, Cancer Revs., 1984, Internat. Jour. of Cell Cloning, 1983—86, mem. adv. bd. Cancer Treatment Reports, 1976—80, assoc. editor Human Lymphocyte Differentation, 1980—82; contbr. articles to profl. jours. Recipient Solomon Berson Achievement award, 1984, Robert Koch prize and medal, 1984. Fellow: AAAS; mem.: NAS, Assn. Am. Physicians, Am. Soc. Clin. Investigation, Am. Soc. Immunologists, Am. Soc. Hematology, Inst. of Medicine of NAS, Alpha Omega Alpha. Office: Dana-Farber Cancer Inst Divsn Tumor Immunology 44 Binney St Mayer 557 Boston MA 02115-6084 Office Phone: 617-632-3325. Business E-Mail: stuart_schlossman@dfci.harvard.edu.

SCHLOSSTEIN, RALPH L., investment company executive; b. Feb. 17, 1951; BA, Dennison U., 1972; MA in Pub. Policy, U. Pitts. Economist Congressional Joint Econ. Com., Washington, 1974—77; dep. to asst. sec. US Dept. Treasury, Washington; assoc. dir. Domestic Policy Coun. The White House, Washington; assoc. investment banking divsn. Lehman Brothers Inc., 1981—84, mng. dir., 1984—88, co-head mortgage & savings institutions group, 1984—88; co-founder BlackRock, Inc., NYC, 1988, pres., 1988—2007, adv., 2007—08; CEO HighView Investment Group, LLC, NYC, 2008—09; pres., CEO Evercore Partners, Inc., NYC, 2009—. Vis. bd. overseers JFK Sch. Govt., Harvard U.; bd. fin. institutions ctr. The Wharton Sch., U. Pa.; trustee Am. Mus. Nat. History, Trinity Sch., James Beard Found., New Visions for Pub. Edn., The Pub. Theater; bd. advisors Marujupu LLC. Office: Evercore Partners Inc 55 E 52nd St New York NY 10055 Office Phone: 212-857-3100. Office Fax: 212-857-3101.*

SCHLOTER, PHILIPP, information technology executive; b. Munich; BA in Econ., Stanford U., Calif., 2003, BS in Computer Sci., 2003, MSEE, 2005; Mktg. Leadership, Kellogg Sch. Mgmt., Evanston, Ill., 2004. Product mgr. Microsoft, Redmond, Wash., 2003—04; cons. Deutsche Telecom. Consulting, San Mateo, Calif., 2006—07, head product & svc. innovation, 2006; CEO Pixto, Inc. (acquired by Nokia), San Francisco, 2006—07; gen. mgr. Nokia, San Francisco, 2007—. Bd. mem. Stanford Club Wash., Seattle, 2004, PIXTO Inc., 2005—07; co-founder New Co. (now Reactrix, Inc.), 2001. Author: Racism and the Internet: The Need for Global Consensus, Global Exchange: Reading and Writing in a World Context, 2005. Civil svc. worker, Rurtalwerkstaetten, Germany, 1999—2000. Recipient award, Cisco Systems, 2002, CEO Excellence award, Detcon Inc., Deutsche Telekom, 2005. Mem.: SDForum, Stanford Alumni Assn. Personal E-mail: pschloter@stanfordalumni.org.

SCHLOTMAN, J. MICHAEL, food products executive; Grad., U. Ky., Lexington. CPA. With The Kroger Co., Cin., 1985—, v.p. fin. svcs. & control, 1995—2000, CFO, 2000—, sr. v.p., 2003—. Office: Kroger 1014 Vine St Cincinnati OH 45202*

SCHLOTTERBECK, DAVID L., health products executive; BSEE, GM Inst.; MSEE, Purdue U.; grad., Stanford U. Exec. Inst., 1984. Exec. v.p., COO Nellcor, Inc., 1991—94; pres., CEO Vitalcom, Inc., 1995—97; pres., COO Pacific Sci. Co., 1997—98, ALARIS Med. Systems, 1999—2004; CEO clinical technologies & services Cardinal Health Inc., 2004—06, CEO clinical & medical products, 2006—09. Bd. dirs. Virtual Radiologic Corp., 2008—; vice chmn. Cardinal Health Inc., 2008—09. Office: Cardinal Health Inc 7000 Cardinal Pl Dublin OH 43017*

SCHLOTTERBECK, WALTER ALBERT, manufacturing executive, lawyer; b. NYC, Dec. 22, 1926; s. Albert Gottlob and Maria Louise (Fritz) S.; m. Pauline Elizabeth Hoerz, Sept. 2, 1951; children— Susan, Thomas, Paul. AB, Columbia U., 1949, LL.B., 1952. Bar: N.Y. 1953. Counsel Gen. Electric Co. (various locations), 1952-87; v.p., corp. counsel Gen. Electric Co., NYC, 1970-77, sec., 1975-76; gen. counsel Gen. Electric Co. (various locations), 1976-87, sr. v.p., 1977-87. Served with USNR, 1944-46. Home: 201 Overlake Dr E Medina WA 98039-5331

SCHLOTTMANN, PEDRO U. J., physics professor; m. Josefa L. Troya-Schlottmann; 1 child, Norbert. PhD, Tech. U. Munich, 1973; degree in Physics, U. Cuyo, Bariloche, Rio Negro, Argentina, 1970. Prof. physics Temple U., Phila., 1986—90, Fla. State U., Tallahassee, 1990—. Contbr. articles to numerous profl. sci. jours. Numerous grants, US Dept. of Energy and NSF. Mem.: Am. Phys. Soc. Office: Fla State Univ Dept Physics Tallahassee FL 32306

SCHLOW, MICHAEL, food service executive; b. Bklyn. Diploma, Acad. Culinary Arts N.J.; trained with Mark Straussman. Chef, owner Radius, Boston; chef Coco Pazzo, Le Madri; exec. chef Sapore di Mare, LI, 75 Main; owner Ariel & Michael; chef, owner Radius, Boston, 1999—. Author: (cookbooks) It's About Time: Great Recipes for Everyday Life, 2005. Recipient Culinary Award of Excellence, Robert Mondavi Winery, 2000, American Express Best Chef: Northeast award, James Beard Found., 2001; named Best Chef (twice), Boston Mag.; named one of America's Best New Chefs, Food & Wine mag., 1996. Office: Radius 8 High St Boston MA 02110

SCHLUETER, DAVID ARNOLD, law educator; b. Sioux City, Iowa, Apr. 29, 1946; s. Arnold E. and Helen A. (Dettmann) S.; m. Linda L. Boston, Apr. 22, 1972; children: Jennifer, Jonathan. BA, Tex. A&M U., 1969; JD, Baylor U., 1971; LLM, U. Va., 1981. Bar: Tex. 1971, DC 1973, US Ct. Mil. Appeals 1972, US Supreme Ct. 1976. Legal counsel US Supreme Ct., Washington, 1981—83; assoc. dean St. Mary's U., San Antonio, 1984—89, prof. law, 1986—, Hardy prof. trial advocacy, dir. advocacy programs, 2000—; reporter Fed. Adv. Com. on Criminal Rules, 1988—2005. Chmn. JAG adv. coun., 1974-75. Author: Military Criminal Justice: Practice and Procedure, 1982, 7th edit., 2008, Military Crimes and Defenses, 2007; (with others) Military Rules of Evidence Manual, 1981, 6th edit., 2006, Texas Rules of Evidence Manual, 1983, 8th edit., 2009, Texas Evidentiary Foundations, 1992, 3d edit., 2005, Military Evidentiary Foundations, 1994, 2d edit., 2000, 3d edit., 2007, Military Criminal Procedure Forms, 1997, 2d edit., 2003, Federal Evidence Tactics, 1997, Texas Rules of Evidence Trial Book, 2000; editor-in-chief: Emerging Problems Under the Federal Rules of Evidence, 3d edit., 1998; contbr. articles to legal publs. Maj. JAGC, US Army, 1972-81. Fellow Am. Law Inst., Tex. Bar Found. (life), Am. Bar Found. (life); mem. ABA (vice-chmn. criminal justice sect. coun. 1991-94, vice-chmn. com. on criminal justice and mil. 1983-84, chmn. standing com. on mil. law 1991-92, mem. standing com. on armed forces law, chmn. editl. adv. bd., Criminal Justice Mag., 1989-91, 2000-), Tex. Bar Assn. Republican. Lutheran. Office: St Marys U Sch Law 1 Camino Santa Maria St San Antonio TX 78228-8603

SCHLUETER, JUNE MAYER, literature educator, writer; b. Passaic, NJ, Nov. 4, 1942; m. Paul Schlueter. BA in English magna cum laude, Fairleigh Dickinson U., 1970; MA in English, Hunter Coll., CCNY, 1973; PhD in English and Comparative Lit., Columbia U., 1977. Asst. prof. Lafayette Coll., Easton, Pa., 1977-84, assoc. prof., 1984-91, prof., 1991-92, Charles A. Dana prof., 1992—2008, head English dept., 1992-93; asst. to provost, 1986-90; acting provost., 1993-94; provost Lafayette Coll., Easton, Pa., 1994—2006. Fulbright prof. Gesamthochschule Kassel Univ., Fed. Republic Germany, 1978-79; chmn. Shakespeare Seminar Columbia U., 1989-91, 2004-06, exec. bd., 1989—; active NEH summer seminar for coll. profs., 1981, lectr. Commonwealth Partnership Summer Lit. Inst., 1985-87, dir. summer seminar for sch. tchrs., 1988, selection panel, 1989, 91, evaluator Instl. Grant Program, 1990. Author: Metafictional Characters in Modern Drama, 1979, The Plays and Novels of Peter Handke, 1981, Dramatic Closure: Reading the End, 1995; (with James K. Flanagan) Arthur Miller, 1987; (with James P. Lusardi) Reading Shakespeare in Performance: King Lear, 1990; editor: Feminist Rereadings of Modern American Drama, 1989, Modern American Drama: The Female Canon, 1990, Critical Essays: The Two Gentlemen of Verona, 1995; (with Paul Schlueter) The English Novel: Twentieth Century Criticism, Vol. 2: Twentieth Century Novelists, 1982, Modern American Literature, Supplement II, 1985, An Encyclopedia of British Women Writers, 1988, Francis A. March: Selected Writings of the First Professor of English, 2005; (with Enoch Brater) Approaches to Teaching Beckett's Waiting for Godot, 1991; (with Paul Nelsen) Acts of Criticism: Performance Matters in Shakespeare and His Contemporaries, 2006; co-editor Shakespeare Bull., 1983-2003; assoc. editor Stages, 1984-90; editl. bd. Studies in Am. Drama, 1945-Present, 1989—2000; editl. cons. Modern Drama, Theatre Jour., PMLA, Studies in Twentieth Century Lit., Shakespeare Quar., others; contbr. revs., essays to profl. jours. Bd. govs. Fairleigh Dickinson U., Rutherford, N.J., 1985-90, bd. dirs., Madison, N.J., 1997-2005; mem. adv. com. Lehigh Valley Ednl. Coop., 1988-90; selection panel German Acad. Exch. Svc., Bonn, 1979; bd. dirs. Pa. Shakespeare Festival, 2007-. Rsch. grantee Lafayette Coll., 1977-93, NEH summer rsch. grantee, 1990, DAAD summer rsch. grantee, 1991. Mem. MLA, Shakespeare Assn. Am., Internat. Shakespeare Assn., Coll. English Assn., Samuel Beckett Soc., AAUP, Columbia Shakespeare Seminar. Home: 123 High St Easton PA 18042-1609 Office: Lafayette Coll Lafayette College Easton PA 18042

SCHLUP, PHILIP, research scientist; b. Sumiswald, Bern, Switzerland, Feb. 6, 1976; s. Martin and Kathrin Schlup. BSc with honors, U. Otago, Dunedin, New Zealand, 1997, PhD, 2003. Rsch. fellow ETH Zurich, Switzerland, 2003—05; postdoc. rschr. Colo. State U., Ft. Collins, 2006—08, rsch. scientist, 2008—. Internat. Presdl. fellow, Colo. State U., 2008—. Mem.: Deutsche Physikalische Gesellschaft, Optical Soc. America. Office: Colo State Univ 1320 Campus Delivery Fort Collins CO 80523 Business E-Mail: philip.schlup@colostate.edu.

SCHLUTER, PETER MUELLER, electronics executive; b. May 24, 1933; s. Fredric Edward and Charlotte (Mueller) S.; m. Jaquelin Ambler Lamond, Apr. 18, 1970 (div. June 1990); children: Jane Randolph Amitsis, Charlotte Mueller Bashforth, Anne Ambler; m. Christine Moon Van Ness, Feb. 7, 1998. BME, Cornell U., 1956; postgrad., Harvard U. Grad. Sch. Bus. Adm, 1982. Sr. engr. Thiokol Chem. Corp., Brigham City, Utah, 1958-59; assoc. Porter Internat. Co., Washington, 1960-65, v.p., pres., treas., dir., 1966-70; pres., treas., dir. Zito Co., Derry, NH, 1970-72; internat. bus. cons. Washington, 1972-74; v.p., dir. Buck Engrng. Co. Inc. (now Lab-Volt Sys., Inc.), Farmingdale, NJ, 1975, pres., CEO, dir., 1975—. Mem. Rep. Inaugural Book and Program Com., 1969; cmty. adv. bd. Monmouth coun. Girl Scouts US, NJ; adv. coun. Monmouth U. Sch. Bus. Adminstrn.; bd. dirs. United Way of Monmouth County; trustee Monmouth Med. Ctr.; N.Am. rep., mem. presidium WORLDDIDAC, Bern, Switzerland, v.p., 1996—. Recipient Golden Osprey award So. Monmouth County C. of C., 1995. Fellow City and Guilds of London Inst. (hon.); mem. World Assn. Mfrs. and Distbrs. of Ednl. Materials (N.Am. rep.), Met. Club Washington, Sanctuary Golf Club Sanibel, Pi Tau Sigma. Office: PO Box 686 Farmingdale NJ 07727-0686 Home: 4455 Gulf Pines Dr Sanibel FL 33957 Business E-Mail: pschluter@labvolt.com.

SCHLUTER, ROBERT ARVEL, physicist; b. Salt Lake City, Aug. 27, 1924; s. Arvel R. and Florence (Leach) S.; 1 child, Jonathan R. BS, U. Chgo., 1947, PhD, 1954. Rsch. assoc. U. Chgo. Inst. for Nuc. Studies, 1954; from instr. to asst. prof. MIT Lab. for Nuc. Studies, Cambridge, 1955-60; assoc. physicist Argonne (Ill.) Nat. Lab., 1961-72; prof. physics and astronomy Northwestern U., Evanston, Ill., 1961-92, prof. emeritus, 1992—. Guest scientist Brookhaven (NY) Nat. Lab., 1955-70, Lawrence Radiation Lab., U. Calif., Berkeley, 1958-60; guest appointee Aspen Inst. for Humanities, 1967; adv. Northwestern Rev., Northwestern Chronicle, 1985-92. Contbr. chapters to books. Served with Los Alamos, Manhattan Project, C.E., U.S. Army, 1943-46. Grantee, AEC NSF, Dept. Energy, NASA. Mem.: Nat. Assn. Scholars, Am. Phys. Soc., Am. Alpine Club. Achievements include first to observe K-Mesic X-rays, measure lambda hyperon magnetic moment, 2d and 3d excited states of the proton; research in experimental hydrodynamics. Avocations: mountain climbing and exploration, history of science. Home: 241 N Vine St Apt 902E Salt Lake City UT 84103-1971 Office: Northwestern U Dept Physics and Astronomy 2145 Sheridan Rd Evanston IL 60208-0834 Business E-Mail: schluter@northwestern.edu.

SCHMAEMAN, CYNTHIA, biology professor; married. MS, Auburn U. Montgomery, Ala., 2007. Lab coord. & instr. Auburn U., 2007—. Business E-Mail: schmacy@auburn.edu.

SCHMALE, NEAL E., utilities company executive; BS in Petroleum Engrng., Colo. Sch. Mines; LLD, Loyola U. With UNOCAL, sr. v.p., pres. petroleum products and chem. divsn., CFO; exec. v.p., CFO Sempra Energy, San Diego, 1997—2005, pres., COO, 2006—. Office: Sempra Energy 101 Ash St San Diego CA 92101-3017

SCHMALENSEE, RICHARD LEE, economics and management professor, former dean; b. Belleville, Ill., Feb. 16, 1944; s. Fred and Marjorie June (Veigel) S.; m. Edeth Diane Hawk, Aug. 19, 1967; children: Alexander Clayton, Nicholas Hawk. SB, MIT, 1965, PhD in econs., 1970. Asst. prof. econs. U. Calif., San Diego, 1970—74, assoc. prof. econs., 1974—77; instr. Sloan Sch. Mgmt., MIT, Cambridge, Mass., 1967—69, asst. prof., 1970, assoc. prof. applied econs., 1977-79, prof., 1979—, prof. dept. econs., 1986—, Gordon Y Billard Prof. of Econs. and Mgmt., 1988-99, dep. dean, 1996—98, interim dean, 1998, dean, 1998—2000, John C Head III Dean, 2001—07, dean emeritus, 2007—, Howard W. Johnson prof. applied econs., 2007—; dir. Ctr. for Energy and Environ. Policy Rsch. MIT, Cambridge, Mass., 1991-99, 2008—. Vis. prof. Harvard Bus. Sch., 1985—86, U. Louvain, Belgium, 1985, vis. assoc. prof., rsch. fellow, Belgium, 1973—74; vis. scholar dept. econs. Harvard U., 1980—81; editl. bd. Jour. of Econs. and Mgmt. Strategy, 1992—98; assoc. editor Internat. Jour. Indsl. Orgn., 1982—89, Jour. Econ. Perspectives, 1992—98; bd. editors Am. Econ. Review, 1982—86; assoc. editor Jour. Indsl. Econs., 1977—81, bd. editors, 1981—89; founding editor Regulation of Econ. Activity, 1978—89, co-editor, 1989—; mem. Pres.'s Coun. Econ. Advisers, 1989—91; bd. dirs. Am. Coun. for Capital Formation Ctr. for Policy Rsch., 1991—, environ. policy fellow, 1997—98; rsch. assoc. Nat. Bur. Econ. Rsch., 1992—; Internat. Rsch. Fellow Kiel Inst. World Econs., 2001—; spl. cons. NERA Econ. Cons., 1981—89, 1991—2004; bd. dirs. Internat. Securities Exch., 2000—09, Internat. Data Group, 2004—; dir. LECG, LLC, 2004—; editor chief Competition Policy Internat., 2005—08, chmn. editl. bd., 2009—. Author: The Economics of Advertising, 1972, Applied Microeconomics, 1973, The Control of Natural Monopolies, 1979; co-author: An Introduction to Applied Macroeconomics, 1973, Markets for Power, 1983, Economics, 1988, Paying with Plastic, 1999, Markets for Clean Air, 2000, Did Microsoft Harm Consumers? Two Opposing Views, 2000, Paying With Plastic, 2nd edit., 2005, Invisible Engines, 2005, Catalyst Code, 2007; co-editor: The Empirical Renaissance in Industrial Economics, 1987, Handbook of Industrial Organization, 1989, Management: Inventing and Delivering Its Future, 2003. NSF grant, 1975-77, 81-83; Co-recipient Edward A. Hewett Prize, Am. Assn. for the Advancement of Slavic Studies, 1995 Fellow: AAAS, Econometric Soc.; mem.: Internat. Acad. Mgmt., Am. Econ. Assn. (nominating com. 1987, exec. com. 1993—95, mem. Govt. rels commn. 2009—). Office: MIT Sloan Sch Mgmt 50 Memorial Dr Rm E52-410 Cambridge MA 02142-1347

SCHMALSTIEG, WILLIAM RIEGEL, retired Slavic languages educator; b. Sayre, Pa., Oct. 3, 1929; s. John William and Dorothy Augusta (Riegel) S.; m. Emily Lou Botdorf, Mar. 28, 1952; children: Linda, Roxanne. BA, U. Minn., 1950; postgrad., Columbia U., 1952; MA, U. Pa., 1951, PhD, 1956; PhD (hon.), Vilnius U., 1994. Instr. U. Ky., Lexington, 1956-59; asst. prof. Lafayette Coll., Easton, Pa., 1959-63; assoc. prof. U. Minn., Mpls., 1963-64; prof. Pa. State U., University Park, 1964—2002, head dept. Slavic langs., 1969-91. Appointed Edwin Erle Sparks prof. Slavic Lang., 1990. Author: (with L. Dambriunas and A. Klimas) An Introduction to Modern Lithuanian, 1966, 4th edit., 1990, 5th edit., 1993, reprinted as Beginner's Lithuanian, 1999, An Old Prussian Grammar, 1974, Studies in Old Prussian, 1976, Indo-European Linguistics, 1980, An Introduction to Old Church Slavic, 1976, 2d edit., 1983, A Lithuanian Historical Syntax, 1988; (with Warren Held and Janet Gertz) Beginning Hittite, 1988, A Student Guide to the Genitive of Agent in the Indo-European Languages, 1995, An Introduction to Old Russian, 1995, The Historical Morphology of the Baltic Verb, 2000; editor Gen. Linguistics, 1971-82; mem. editl. adv. bd. Jour. Indo-European Studies, Baltistica, Archivum Lithuanicum, Lietuviu Kalbotyros Klausimai, Baltu Filologija. Served to 1st lt. US Army, 1952—54. NEH grantee, 1978-79, Fulbright grantee and exch. scholar Acad. Scis., Vilnius, USSR, 1986; recipient Humanities medal Pa. State U., 1983, Friend of Lithuania award Knights of Lithuania, 1990, Lithuanian Govt. Mazvydas medal, 1997; named Disting. Alumnus Breck Sch., 1990. Mem.: Lingustic Soc. Am., Lithuanian Acad. Scis. (fgn.), Assn. Advancement Baltic Studies (pres. 1982—84). Episcopalian. Home: 814 Cornwall Rd State College PA 16803-1430 Personal E-mail: emily@leanonemily.com.

SCHMALZ, CARL NELSON, JR., artist, educator, art historian, printmaker; b. Ann Arbor, Dec. 26, 1926; s. Carl Nelson and Esther Dorothy (Fowler) S.; m. Dolores Irene Tourangeau, Dec. 2, 1950; children: Stephen Theodore (dec.), Mathew Nelson, Julia Irene. AB, Harvard U., 1948, MA, 1949, PhD, 1958; MA (hon.), Amherst Coll., 1969. Teaching fellow in fine arts Harvard U., Cambridge, Mass., 1950-52; asst. prof. Bowdoin Coll., Brunswick, Maine, 1953-62; curator, asst dir. Walker Art Mus., 1953—62; asst. prof. Harvard U., Cambridge, Mass., 1960; prof. Amherst Coll., 1962—95, prof. emeritus, 1995—; prof. Heartwood Coll. Art, Kennebunk, Maine, 2006—. Lectr. in field; workshop tchr. in field. Author: Watercolor Lessons from Eliot O'Hara, 1974, Watercolor Your Way, 1978, Finding and Improving Your Painting Style, 1986, paperback, 1992; co-suthor: Science Education in the United States: Issues, Crises and Priorities, 1990; author numerous essays and reviews; exhibited in one-man shows including Cambridge (Mass.) Art Assn., 1948, Laing Gallery, Portland, Maine, 1955, Amherst (Mass.) Coll., 1963, U. Mass., 1965, W.C. Rawls Mus., Va., 1972, Concord (Mass.) Art Assn., 1974, Govt. House, Hamilton, Bermuda, 1979, Jones Library, Amherst, Mass., 1979, The Arlington, Kennebunkport, Maine, 1980, Harmon-Meek Gallery, Naples, Fla., 1987, 91, 92, 98, Gallery at 6 Deering St., Portland, Maine, 1987, 91, Fretz Gallery, Portland, 1987-88, Marsh Gallery, Amherst Coll., 1995, Kennebunk Free Libr., 2005, Rolly-Michaux Gallery, Boston, 2007; exhibited in group shows including Jordan Marsh Co., 1947, 48, 50, 71-73, Colby Coll., 1958, Carnegie Inst., Pitts., 1963, FAR Gallery, N.Y.C., 1964-68, Am. Watercolor Soc., 1966, 68, 70, Bowdoin Coll. Mus., 1973, Balt. Watercolor Soc., 1976, Boston Atheneum, 1979, Watercolor U.S.A. Honor Soc., 1989, 91, Maine Art Gallery, 1991, Rolly-Michaux Gallery, Boston, 1995, 2007, Kennebunk Free Libr., 2004; represented in permanent collections: Signet Soc., Cambridge, Mass., Walker Art Mus., Brunswick, Maine, Jones & Laughlin Steel Corp., Diners Club Am., Kalamazoo Art Center, Hampshire Coll., Zanesville Art Inst., Blue Cross/Blue Shield, Philharmonic Ctr. for the Arts, Naples, Fla., Springfield (Mo.) Art Mus., Amherst Coll., Bowdoin Coll., Hampshire Coll., Kalamazoo Art Inst., Springfield (Mo.) Art Mus.; work published in various pubs. including The Artist's Guide for Using Color, 1992, The Artist's Mag., 1994, Splash 3: Ideas and Inspirations, 1994. Mem. exec. bd. Interfaith Housing Corp., Amherst, 1966-76; pres. bd. trustees Amherst Day Sch., 1966-69; mem. Pelham Arts Lottery Coun., 1984-90; mem., v.p. bd. dirs. Portland Mus. Art, 1957-62. Bacon fellow, 1951; recipient 1st prize watercolor Cambridge Art Assn. Ann., 1947, 1st prize for traditional watercolor Virginia Beach Boardwalk Show, 1965, South Mo. Trust purchase award Watercolor U.S.A., 1970, 1st prize watercolor 30th Ann. Kennebunk River Club Show, 1985, Purchase prize Watercolor U.S.A., 1997. Mem.: Coll. Art Assn., The Signet Soc., Watercolor U.S.A. Honor Soc. Democrat.

SCHMALZ, ROBERT FOWLER, geology educator; b. Ann Arbor, Mich., May 29, 1929; s. Carl Nelson and Esther Dorothy (Fowler) S.; m. Barbara Ann Leetch, July 18, 1964; children: Timothy F., Dorothy L. AB with honors, Havard Coll., 1951; AM, Harvard U., 1954, PhD, 1959. Cert. profl. geologist. Rsch. asst. Harvard/W.H.O.I., Cambridge, Mass., 1957-58; asst. prof. Pa. State U., University Park, 1958-63, assoc. prof., 1963-69, prof. of geology, 1969-91, chmn. geology, 1971-74, undergrad. coord., 1974-77, prof. of geology emeritus, 1992—. Trustee Bermuda Biol. Sta., 1967-79; mem. adv. com. Appalachian Compact Users Radio Isotopes, University Park. Editor: Science Education in the United States, 1991, Environmental Radon, 1990, Management of Hazardous Materials and Wastes, 1989, Natural and Technological Disasters, 1992; contbr. articles to profl. jours. Vice-chmn. then chmn. State College (Pa.) Borough Water Authority, 1978—98; mem., vice-chmn. then chmn. U. Area Joint Authority, 1998—; mem. adv. com. Ctr. County PAWS, 2005—; mem. State Coll. Borough Sewer Authority, 1998—2001; bd. dir. Friends Palmer Mus. Art, 2005—; bd. dir., treas. Friends Schlow Ctr. Region Libr., 2006—. With US Army, 1955—57. Recipient Wilson Teaching award Earth and Mineral Sci. Coll., 1969, Lindback Teaching award Pa. State U., 1970, XYZ award, StateColl. Borough, 1994. Fellow AAAS, Geol. Soc. Am. (sr.); mem. Am. Assn. Petroleum Geologists (disting. lectr. 1977-78), Soc. Econ. Mineralogists and Petrologists, Pa. Acad. Sci., Explorers Club, Cosmos Club, Sigma Xi., Am. Geophysical Union, Geochem. Soc., Palmer Mus. Art(Docent) Avocations: historical railroad operations, sailing. Home: 305 E Mitchell Ave State College PA 16803-3637 E-mail: rfs3@psu.edu.

SCHMALZRIED, MARVIN EUGENE, financial consultant; b. Dighton, Kans., Nov. 11, 1924; s. Carl D. and Marie M. (Bahm) S.; m. Jean Landino, Nov. 27, 1946 (dec.); children— Darlene, Candace, Cynthia, Derek, Valerie, Rebecca; m. Judith Reichardt Stuart, Oct. 23, 2004. BBA, Northwestern U., 1949; LL.B., U. Conn., 1955. Bar: Conn. bar 1955; C.P.A., Conn. Acct. Webster, Blanchard & Willard, CPA's (named changed to Price Waterhouse & Co.), Hartford, Conn., 1950-55; contr., asst. treas. J.B. Williams Co., Glastonbury, Conn., 1955-57; treas., sec. Curtis 1000, Inc. (name changed to Am Bus. Products, Inc.), Atlanta, 1957-61; asst. to pres. Wyeth Labs., NYC, 1961-63, comptroller, 1964-67, v.p., 1967-72, sr. v.p., 1972-84; pres. Venda Vid, Inc., NYC, 1986-90; sr. v.p. View-Master Ideal Group, Inc., NYC, 1987-90; exec. v.p. Strategics Inc., 1993-95. Recipient Gold medal Conn. Soc. C.P.A.'s, 1953 Mem. AICPA, ABA, Old Greenwich Friday Evening Reading Soc. (pres.) Clubs: Darien Country, Bent Tree Country. Home and Office: 4874 Cherry Laurel Cir Sarasota FL 34241-6442

SCHMANDT, JURGEN A., public affairs educator; b. Mar. 4, 1929; PhD, U. Bonn, Germany, 1956. Prin. adminstr. OECD, Paris, 1960-65; assoc. dir. program sci. and tech. Harvard U., Cambridge, Mass., 1965-71; prof. pub. affairs U. Tex., Austin, 1971—2001; dir. and disting. fellow Houston Advanced Rsch. Ctr., The Woodlands, Tex., 1985—. Author: Acid Rain and Friendly Neighbors, 1988, The Regions and Global Warming, 1992, Scarce Water, 1998, Navigating the Waters of the Paso del Norte, 1999, Sustainable Development, 2000. Home: 11 Hull Circle Dr Austin TX 78746-3709 Office Phone: 281-363-7913. E-mail: jas@harc.edu.

SCHMANDT-BESSERAT, DENISE, archaeologist, educator; b. Ay, France, Aug. 10, 1933; came to U.S., 1965, naturalized, 1970; d. Victor and Jeanne (Crabit) Besserat; m. Jurgen Schmandt, Dec. 27, 1956; children: Alexander, Christopher, Phillip. Ed., Ecole du Louvre, 1965; D (hon.), Kenyon Coll., 2008. Rsch. fellow in Near Eastern Archaeology Peabody Mus. Harvard U., Cambridge, Mass., 1969-71; fellow Radcliffe Inst., Cambridge, 1969-71; asst. prof. Middle Eastern studies U. Tex., Austin, 1972-81, assoc. prof., 1981-88, prof., 1988—2004; acting chief curator U. Tex. Art Mus., 1978—79. Vis. assoc. prof. U. Calif., Berkeley, 1987-88; curator Legacy of the Middle East exhbn. Jeddah (Saudi Arabia) Hist. Preservation Dept. Author: Before Writing, 1992, How Writing Came About, 1996, History of Counting, 1999, When Writing Met Art, 2007; adv. editor Tech. and Culture, 1978-92; editl. adv. bd. Archaeology Odyssey, 2003-06; mem. editl. bd. Written Communication, 1993-95, Visible Lang., 1985—, Explorations in Media Ecology, 2001-05, Ancient Adminstrn., 2001; mem. editl. bd. Near Eastern Archaology, 2005—, Scripta, 2008-; contbr. articles to profl. jours. Recipient Kayden Nat. U. Press Book award, 1992, Robert W. Hamilton Author award, 1998, 2008, Walter J. Ong award Media Ecology Assn., 2004; named in Am. Scientist, 1999; Wenner-Gren Found. grant, 1970-71, NEA grant, 1974-75, 77-78, ACLS grant, 1984, Deutscher Akademischer Austauschdienst grant, 1986, NEH grant, 1992; NEH fellow, 1979-80, U. Wis. Inst. for Rsch. in Humanities fellow, 1984-85, USIA, Am. Ctr. Oriental Rsch. fellow, 1994-95, 97, 2001, Malone fellow 1997, 99, 2005, Weeks fellow Humanities Rsch. Ctr. Stanford U., 2003—; ACOR-CAORC fellowship, Amman, Jordan, 2009. Mem. Am. Oriental Soc., Archeol. Inst. Am. (governing bd. 1983-89), Am. Anthropol. Assn., Am. Schs. of Oriental Rsch., Centro Internat. Rsch. Archeologiche e Anthropologiche e Storiche (Rome). Business E-Mail: dsb@mail.utexas.edu.

SCHMEITS, RONALD L., advocacy organization executive, bank executive; b. Nebr. m. Ann Schmeits. Student, U. Nebr.; MBA in Bank Mgmt., Rutgers U., NJ. Mayor City of Jordan, Minn., 1976—80; pres., CEO, dir. Internat. Bank, Raton, N.Mex., CEO, chmn. bd. Trinidad, Colo.; chmn. bd., dir. Farmers and Stockmens Bank, Clayton, N.Mex.; v.p., dir. Raton Capital Corp. Chmn. bd. trustees NRA Whittington Ctr., Raton, N.Mex. Mem. Philmont inspection team Boy Scouts of America; mem. Gov.'s Bus. Adv. Com., N.Mex.; dir. US-Can. River Compact Commn.; mem. Raton C. of C.; dir. U. N.Mex. Found. Fin. Com. Mem.: NRA (life; bd. dirs. 2000, benefactor mem. 2005—, pres. 2009—, first v.p., chmn. membership com., chmn. investment oversight com., vice chmn. fin. com., vice chmn. publs. policies com., mem. audit com., mem. meeting site selection com.), N.Mex. Bankers Assn., NRA Heritage Soc., Mo. Valley Arms Collectors Assn., Ducks Unlimited, Single Action Shooting Soc., Whittington Ctr. Gun Club, N.Mex. Wildlife Found., Amateur Trapshooting Assn., Rocky Mountain Elk Found., Rotary, Elks. Avocation: hunting. Office: Internat Bank 200 S Second St PO Box 1028 Raton NM 87740*

SCHMELTZER, EDWARD, lawyer; b. NYC, Aug. 22, 1923; s. Harry A. and Julia (Hoffman) S.; m. Elizabeth Ann Cooper, June 19, 1949; children: Henry Cooper, Elizabeth Sabine. BA, Hunter Coll., NYC, 1950; MA, Columbia U., NYC, 1951; JD, George Washington U., Washington, 1954. Bar: DC 1954, U.S. Supreme Ct 1958. Economist PHA, 1951-53; econ. cons., 1953-54; trial atty. Fed. Maritime Bd. Maritime Adminstrn., 1955-60; dir. bur. domestic regulation Fed. Maritime Commn., 1961-66, mng. dir., 1966-69; ptnr. Morgan, Lewis & Bockius, 1969-76, Schmeltzer, Aptaker & Shepard, 1976—99, of counsel, 2001; sr. v.p., gen. counsel Sea Star Line, Jacksonville, 1999—2001. US rep. 12th Diplomatic Conf. on Internat. Maritime Law, Brussels, 1967, 13th Diplomatic Conf., Brussels, 1968. Mem. bd. editors: Jour. Maritime Law and Commerce; Contbr. articles to profl. jours. Served with USAAF, 1943-46. Recipient Fed. Maritime Commn.; Distinguished Service award, 1969. Mem. Maritime Adminstrv. Bar Assn. (pres. 1971-73), Cosmos Club (Washington). Office: 10412 Buckboard Pl Potomac MD 20854-3805 Home Phone: 301-299-7441; Office Phone: 309-299-9030. Business E-Mail: eacs@comcast.net.

SCHMELZER, JANET L., history professor, researcher; b. Milw., Dec. 7, 1950; d. Robert Benjamin and Jessie Mae (Brady) Schmelzer; m. Charles H. Woods III, June 28, 1998. BA, Tex. Christian U., Ft. Worth, 1973, MA in History, 1975, PhD in Am. History, 1978. Instr. Temple (Tex.) Jr. Coll., Tex., 1978—79; asst. prof. Sam Houston State U., Huntsville, Tex., 1979—80; vis. asst. prof. Tex. Tech. U., Lubbock, 1980—82; asst. prof. U. Nebr., Lincoln, 1982—83; prof. Tarleton State U., Stephenville, 1983—. Author: Where the West Begins, 1985; co-author: Texas USA, 1996. Pres. Southwestern Hist. Assn., 1992—93, Erath County Women's Plit. Caucus, 1987—88. Fellow, Eleanor Roosevelt Inst., 1980; Moody fellow, Lyndon Baines Johnson Found., 1979. Mem.: Tex. Faculty Assn. (pres. 2004—), East Tex. Hist. Assn., So. Hist. Assn., Tex. State Tchrs. Assn. (bd. dirs.), Tex. State Hist. Assn. (Disting. Spkr. 2005, Coral H. Tullis award 1993), Southwestern Social Sci. Assn. (pres. 2001—02), Phi Alpha Theta (internat. adv. bd. 1995—99), Delta Zeta. Democrat. Methodist. Office: Tarleton State Univ Stephenville TX 76402

SCHMEMANN, SERGE, journalist; b. Paris, Apr. 12, 1945; arrived in U.S., 1951; s. Rev Alexander and Juliana (Ossorguine) Schmemann; m. Mary Schidlovsky, Sept. 13, 1970; children: Anne, Alexander, Nathalie. BA cum laude, Harvard U., 1967; MA, Columbia U., 1971; LittD (hon.), Middlebury Coll., 1995. Desk editor AP, NYC, 1972—75, UN corr., 1975—77, South Africa corr., 1977—79, Moscow corr., 1979—80; Moscow bur. chief New York Times, 1980—87, 1991—95, Bonn bur. chief, 1987—90, Jerusalem bur. chief, 1995—98, dep. fgn. editor, 1998—2001, UN bur. chief, 2001—02; editor, editl. page Internat. Herald Tribune, Paris, 2003—. Author: Echoes of a Native Land: Two Centuries of a Russian Village, 1997, When the Wall Came Down: The Berlin Wall and the Fall of Communism, 2006; contbr. articles to profl. publs. With US Army, 1968—70, Vietnam. Recipient Hal Boyle award, Overseas Press Club, 1986, Pulitzer Prize for coverage of German reunification, 1991, Emmy award for Outstanding Individual Achievement in a Craft, Nat. TV Acad., 2003. Mem.: Phi Beta Kappa. Avocations: carpentry, piano. Office: Internat Herald Tribune, 6 bis, rue des Graviers 92521 Paris France also: New York Times 620 8th Ave New York NY 10018-1405 Office Phone: 33 1 4143 91 80. E-mail: serge@nytimes.com.

SCHMENNER, ROGER WILLIAM, business educator; b. Balt., May 3, 1947; s. Charles H. and Gwendolyn (Jackson) S.; m. Barbara Nell Driscoll, Feb. 14, 1976; children: William, Andrew. AB, Princeton U., 1969; PhD, Yale U., 1973. Rsch. assoc., lectr. Yale U., New Haven, 1973-74; asst. prof. Harvard U. Bus. Sch., Cambridge, Mass., 1974-78; rsch. assoc. Harvard-MIT Joint Ctr. for Urban Studies, 1978-80; assoc. prof. Duke U. Fuqua Sch. Bus., Durham, N.C., 1980-86; prof. Sch. Bus. Ind. U., Indpls., 1987—, assoc. dean, 1998—2007, chief staff to the chancellor, 2007—. Vis. prof. IMD, Lausanne, Switzerland, 1986—87, 1992—93, 2002—03; cons. in field. Author: Production and Operations Management, 1981, 5th edit., 1993, Making Business Location Decisions, 1982, Service Operations Management, 1995. Office: Ind U Sch Bus 801 W Michigan St Indianapolis IN 46202-5199

SCHMERTZ, ERIC JOSEPH, lawyer, educator, commissioner; b. NYC, Dec. 24, 1925; married; 4 children. AB, Union Coll., 1948, LLD (hon.), 1978; cert., Alliance Francaise, Paris, 1948; JD, NYU, 1954; LLD (hon.), Hofstra U., 2008. Bar: NY 1955. Internat. rep. Am. Fedn. State, County and Mcpl. Employees, AFL-CIO, NYC, 1950-52; asst. v.p., dir. labor tribunals Am. Arbitration Assn., NYC, 1952-57, 59-60; indsl. relations dir. Metal Textile Corp. subs. Gen. Cable Corp., Roselle, NJ, 1957-59; exec. dir. NY State Bd. Mediation, 1960-62, corp. dir., 1962-68; labor-mgmt. arbitrator, NYC, 1962—; mem. faculty Hofstra U. Sch. Bus., 1962-70; prof. Hofstra U. Sch. Law, 1970—, Edward F. Carlough disting. prof. labor law, 1981-98, dean Sch. Law, 1982-89, disting. prof. emeritus of law, 1998—; of counsel The Dweck Law Firm, NYC, 1999—; commr. labor rels. City of NY, 1990-91. Scholar-in-residence Pace U. Sch. Law, 1998-2000, Disting. Practioner in residence, 2005—; 1st Beckley lectr. in bus. U. Vt., 1981; bd. dirs. Wilshire Oil Co.; mem. NY State Pub. Employment Rels. Bd., 1991-97; cons. and lectr. in field. Co-author: (with R.L. Greenman) Personnel Administration and the Law, 1978; contbr. chpts. to books, articles to profl. jours., to profl. law confs., seminars and workshops. Mem. numerous civic orgns. Served to lt. USN, 1943-46. Recipient Testimonial award Southeast Republican Club, 1969; Alexander Hamilton award Rep. Law Students Assn.; Eric J. Schmertz Disting. Professorship Pub. Law and Pub. Svc. established Hofstra Law Sch., 1993. Mem. Nat. Acad. Arbitrators, Am. Arbitration Assn. (law com., Whitney North Seymour Sr. medal 1984), Fed. Mediation and Conciliation Svc., NY Mediation Bd., NJ Mediation Bd., NJ Pub. Employment Rels. Bd., Hofstra U. Club, Princeton Club. Office: The Dweck Law Firm 75 Rockefeller Plz New York NY 10019 Office Phone: 212-687-8200. Business E-Mail: schmertz@dwecklaw.com.

SCHMERTZ, MILDRED FLOYD, editor-in-chief, writer; b. Pitts., Mar. 29, 1925; d. Robert Watson and Mildred Patricia (Floyd) S B.Arch., Carnegie Mellon U., 1947; M.F.A., Yale U., 1957. Archtl. designer John Schurko, Architect, Pitts., 1947-55; assoc. editor Archtl. Record, NYC, 1957-65, sr. editor, 1965-80, exec. editor, 1980-85, editor-in-chief, 1985-90. Vis. lectr. Yale Sch. Architecture, 1979— Editor, contbr.: New Life for Old Buildings, 1982; contbr. articles to profl. jours.; chpts. to books. Bd. mgrs. Jr. League, City of N.Y., 1964-65; commr. N.Y. Landmarks Preservation Commn., 1988-92 Fellow AIA; mem. Mcpl. Art Soc. N.Y., Century Assn. (N.Y.C.) Home and Office: 310 E 46th St Apt 15E New York NY 10017-3002

SCHMETT, KIM D., lawyer; b. Oakland City, Ind., Dec. 11, 1952; s. Charles Raymond and Ruth Laverne (Cromer) Schmett; m. Connie L. Russell; 2 children. BA, Eastern Ill. U., 1975; JD, Chgo. Kent Coll. Law, 1979. Bar: Iowa 1979, Ill. 1979, US Dist. Ct. (so. dist.) Iowa 1981, US Dist. Ct. (no. dist.) Iowa 1985. Former parliamentarian Iowa Senate; mem. Carmichael Gov. Campaign, Miss., 1975, Senator Charles Percy's Advisor Com., 1975—79; exec dir. Coll. Rep. Nat. Com., 1976—77; dir. Grassley Congl., Iowa, 1978, 1979—80; pres. West Congl., 1980, Young Congl., 1980; instr. Lewis U., 1982, Des Moines Area Cmty. Coll., 1991—2000; mem. Iowa Job Svc. Bd Appeals, 1984—86; chief adminstrn. law judge, Iowa dept. inspections & appeals, 1986—95; dir., 1996—2000; chmn. Polk County Rep. Party, 1989—90, 1993—95; legal counsel Iowa State Rep. Party, 1993—2000; chief staff, congressman Greg Ganske, 2000—03; ptnr. Koupal, Schmett & Bailey, 1979—80, Schmett Law Firm, 1979—84, Schmett & Assoc., 1980—; legal counsel William Penn. U., 2009—; exec. dir. Coalition Family & Children Svcs., Iowa, 2003—09. Faculty mem. Des Moines Area CC, 1992—99, Lewis U., 1983, Am. Inst. Bus., Des Moines, 1981; legal counsel to Rep. Party of Iowa, 1994—2000. Mem.: Nat. Pub. Policy Com., Child Welfare League America, Alliance Children and Families. Republican. Protestant. Office: Coalition for Family and Children's Svcs in Iowa 1111 9th St Ste 235 Des Moines IA 50314 also: Schmett & Assoc 10141 Lincoln Ave Clive IA 50325 Office Phone: 515-244-0074. E-mail: kim@iachild.org.

SCHMETTERER, ROBERT ALLEN, advertising executive; b. NYC, Nov. 23, 1943; s. Robert Mayer and Rosalie (Fernandez) S.; children: Adam, Tyler; m. Stacy Lynn Chiarello, Sept. 26, 1987. BS, Fairleigh Dickinson U., 1967, MBA, 1970. Sales promotion mgr. Brit. Motor Corp., Leonia, NJ, 1963-68; market research dir. Volvo, Rockleigh, NJ, 1968-71; v.p. market rsch. Scali, McCabe, Sloves Inc., NYC, 1971-73, sr. v.p. dir. account service, 1974-79, exec. v.p., chief oper. officer, mng. dir., 1979-84; pres., chief exec. officer/worldwide HCM, NYC and Paris, 1984-87; pres., ptnr. Messner Vetere Berger McNamee Schmetterer, NYC, 1987—97; chmn., CEO Euro RSCG Worldwide, NYC, 1997—2004; pres., COO Havas, 2002—04. Bd. dirs. N.Y.C. Partnership, 1987. Author: Leap: A Revolution in Creative Business Strategy, 2003. Bd. dirs. NYC Partnership, 1985—87, NYC Hist. House Trust, 1992—97, J Mandle Performance, Inc., chmn.; pres. Bob and Stacy Schmetterer Found. Inc. Mem.: Vineyard Haven Yacht Club, NY Yacht Club, Coral Beach and Tennis Club, Ocean Reef Club. Unitarian Universalist. Avocations: yachting, music, reading, tennis. Home (Summer): The Swindle 662 Chappaquonsett Rd Vineyard Haven MA 02568 Home (Winter): Ocean Reef Club 24 Dockside Ln PMB 398 Key Largo FL 33037

SCHMETZER, ALAN DAVID, psychiatrist; b. Louisville, Sept. 3, 1946; s. Clarence Frederick and Catherine Louise (Wootan) Schmetzer; m. Janet Lynn Royce, Aug. 25, 1968; children: Angela Beth, Jennifer Lorraine. BA, Ind. U., 1968, MD, 1972. Diplomate Am. Bd. Psychiatry and Neurology, subsplty. cert. in addiction psychiatry; diplomate Am. Psychotherapy Assn., Am. Bd. Forensic Med. Examiners, Assn. Convulsive Therapy. Intern Ind. U. Hosps., Indpls., 1972-73, resident, 1972-75; dir. clinics PCI, Inc., Anderson, Beech Grove, Kokomo, Ind., 1975-79; psychiat. cons. Cmty. Addiction Svcs. Agy., Indpls., 1975-80; instr. psychiatry in primary care Family Practice Residency Programs St. Francis Hosp., St. Vincent's Hosp. and Ind. U. Hosps., Indpls., 1975-91; med. dir. Child Guidance Clinic of Marion County, Indpls., 1980-81; chmn. psychiatry dept. St. Francis Hosp., Beech Grove, 1980-82; med. dir. Crisis Intervention Unit Midtown Mental Health Ctr., 1980-90, dir., 1990-96, med. dir., 1996-98; coord. emergency psychiat. svcs. Ind. U. Med. Ctr., Indpls., 1980-90, asst. prof. psychiatry, 1975-94, assoc. prof. psychiatry, 1994—2002, prof. psychiatry, 2002—, coord. psychiat. edn. of med. students, 1989-95, asst. chmn. dept. psychiatry, 1993-96, dir. psychiat. edn., 1995-97, vice chmn. edn. dept. psychiatry, 1997—, dir.

psychiatry residency tng., 1998—, dir. addiction psychiatry residency tng. Indpls., 1999—; chief psychiatry Wishard Meml. Hosp., 1990-98; chief rsch. unit, pres. med. staff Larue D. Carter Meml. Hosp., 2007—. Primary psychiat. cons. Ind. Dept. Mental Health and Addiciton, 1988-89; med. dir. Ind. Divsn. Mental Health, 2001-03; supt. Larue D. Carter Meml. Hosp., 2003-05; examiner Am. Bd. Psychiatry and Neurology; addiction psychiatrist Midtown Mental Health Ctr., 2006-07; med. dir. Ind. U. Psychiat. Mgmt., Inc., 2007—. Contbr. articles to profl. jours. Maj. Ind. N.G., 1972-79. Decorated Army Commendation medal, 1978; recipient Residents award for outstanding teaching, 1985, 90, 97, 2003, Roeske Excellence in Teaching award, 1992, Med. Student Psychiatry Clin. Tchg. award, 2000, Irma Bland Residency Tchg. award, 2005, Alumnus of the Yr., Silver Creek H.S., 2005, Eugene E. Levitt svc. award in psychology, 2003, Exemplary Psychiatrist award NAMI, 2004, named one of Best Doctor's in Am., 2003-04, 06-07, Am. Top Psychiatrists, 2006. Fellow Am. Psychiat. Assn., Am. Ortho-psychiat. Assn.; mem. AMA (Physicians Recognition award 1978-), Ind. Med. Assn., Indpls. Med. Soc., Ind. Psychiat. Soc. (pres. 1989-90, 97-98), Am. Acad. Clin. Psychiatry, Univ. Faculty Club Indpls. (v.p. 1999-2000, pres. 2000-01), Athenaeum Turnverein Club, Alpha Phi Omega, Phi Beta Pi, Psi Chi, Alpha Epsilon Delta. Presbyterian. Office: Dept Psychiatry 1111 W 10th St PB-A212 Indianapolis IN 46202-4800 Office Phone: 317-274-1224. Business E-Mail: aschmetz@iupui.edu.

SCHMID, ALFRED ALLAN, economist; b. Dawson, Nebr., Mar. 12, 1935; s. Alfred E. and Florence A. Schmid; m. Alice B. Todd, 1956 (dec.); children: Elizabeth, John; m. Kay A. McDevitt, 1985. BS, U. Nebr., 1956; MS, U. Wis., 1957, PhD, 1959. Asst. prof. Mich. State U., East Lansing, 1959-64, assoc. prof., 1964-68, prof., 1968-98, Univ. Disting. prof., 1998—2006, emeritus, 2006—. Vis. scholar Resources for the Future, Washington, 1964-65; mem. World Bank Mission to Romania, 1993. Author: Property, Power and Public Choice, 1978, 2d edit., 1987, (Chinese trans. 1999) Law and Economics, 1980, Benefit-Cost Analysis, 1989, Conflict and Cooperation, 2004; mem. edit. bd. Land Econs., 1969-71, Jour. Econ. Issues, 1972-75, Am. Jour. Agrl. Econs., 1978-80. Mem. East Lansing Planning Commn., 1973-75. Mem. Am. Agrl. Econs. Assn. (Quality of Comm. award 1992), Assn. for Evolutionary Econs. Avocations: travel, writing. Office: Mich State Univ Dept Agr Food Resource Econs East Lansing MI 48824 Home Phone: 517-337-1217. Business E-Mail: schmid@msu.edu.

SCHMID, CHARLES ERNEST, acoustical engineer, academic administrator; b. Jamaica, NY, Oct. 30, 1940; s. Edson Scofield Schmid and Agatha Sofia Zimmermann; m. Linda Dexter, June 18, 1966; children: Andrew, Jenny. BSEE, Cornell U., 1963; MSEE, U. Conn., 1968; PhD, U. Wash., 1977. Systems engr. Gen. Dynamics/Electric Boat, Groton, Conn., 1963-66; fellow Honeywell, Seattle, 1966-90; exec. dir. Acoustical Soc. Am., Melville, NY, 1990—. With physics vis. com. U. Wash., 1999—. Numerous citizen com., Bainbridge Island, Wash. Congl. Sci. Engrng. fellow AAAS, Washington, 1985-86. Fellow Acoustical Soc. Am. (Disting. Svc. award 2008); mem. Am. Inst. Physics (gov. bd. 1991—, exec. com. 1993-99, 2003-07), Internat. Commn. Acoustics. Office: Acoustical Soc of Am 2 Huntington Quadrangle Melville NY 11747-4502

SCHMID, JOHN A., musician, voice educator; b. Danville, Ill., Oct. 27, 1944; s. Herman A. and Marjorie E. Schmid; m. Kara Sue Schmid, Sept. 20, 1986; 1 child, Jordan Olivia. MusB, Butler U., 1968; MusM, Jordan Coll., 1969; student of pvt. voice, Indiana U., 1979. Accompanist Butler U., Indpls., 1968—70, voice instr., 1970—87; dir. music and studios Fairview Presbyn., Indpls., 1982—; chorus master Indpls. Opera, 1984—; dir. Indpls. Matinee Musicale Ensemble, 2003—. Voice tchr., coach Butler U., 1970—82; dir. Fairview Studies, 1982—. Mem.: Nat. Assn. Tchrs. of Singing, Nat. Assn. Tchrs. Music, Presbyn. Assn. of Musicians, Nat. Choral Dir. Assn. Presbyn. Avocations: cooking, opera. Office: Fairview Studios 4609 N Capitol Ave Indianapolis IN 46208 Office Phone: 317-253-5982. Business E-Mail: jschmid@fairviewpresbyterian.org.

SCHMID, PATTI A., library director; d. Harold and Anna May Schmid. BA, Drew U., Madison, NJ, 1971, M in Theol. Studies, 1975; MS in Libr. Sci., Cath. U. of Am., Washington, 1980. Libr. ops. cons., procurement analyst Bus. Mgmt. Rsch. Assocs., Arlington, Va., 1980—82, info. and systems mgr., 1983—89; bibliographic and quality assurance profl. Raven Systems and Rsch., Inc., Washington, 1982; dir. rsch. and info. mgmt. ODS Inc., Silver Spring, Md., 1984—92; cost and billings mgr. OAO Corp., Greenbelt, Md., 1989—91; tech. asst. III-libr. Cumberland County Coll. Libr., Vineland, NJ, 1992—97, head libr., 1997—. Adj. faculty Cumberland County Coll., Vineland, 1997—; presenter in field. Editor: (glossary) Federal Contracting Handbook. Mem.: NAFE, AAUW, Cumberland Librs. United Electronic Sys., Virtual Academic Libr. Environment, Coun. NJ Coll. and Univ. Libr. Dirs., NJ Edn. Assn., NJ Libr. Assn. Office: Cumberland County Coll Libr 3322 College Dr Vineland NJ 08360 Office Fax: 856-691-1969.

SCHMID, SIGI, professional soccer coach; b. Tübingen, West Germany, Mar. 20, 1953; arrived in US, 1962; children: Erik, Kurt, Kyle. BS in Econs., UCLA, 1976; MA in Bus. Adminstrn., U. So. Calif. CPA Calif. Asst. coach UCLA Bruins, 1977, 1979, head coach, 1980—99, LA Galaxy, 1999—2004, Ohio Columbus Crew, 2006—. Asst. coach US nat. team FIFA World Cup, 1994; US under-20 nat. team coach FIFA World Youth Championship, 1998—99, 2005. Named NSCAA Coach of Yr., 1997, MLS Coach of Yr., 2008. Office: Crew Training Ctr 4153 Alum Creek Dr Columbus OH 43207 Office Fax: 614-447-4130.*

SCHMIDER, MARY ELLEN HEIAN, American studies educator, academic administrator; b. Chippewa Falls, Wis., Apr. 17, 1938; d. A. Bernard and Ellen Dagmar (Gunderson) Heian; m. Michael Heaton Leonard, June 16, 1962 (div. Oct. 1969); 1 child, William Gunerius S. Leonard; m. Carl Ludwig Schmider, June 17, 1970; 1 child, Dagmar Heian (née Schmider) Meinders. BA in English Lit. magna cum laude, St. Olaf Coll., Northfield, Minn., 1960; MA in English Lit., U. So. Calif., 1962; PhD in Am. Studies, U. Minn., 1983. Mem. founding faculty in English, Calif. Luth. Coll., Thousand Oaks, Calif., 1961-64; instr. dept. English U. Vt., Burlington, Vt., 1964-70; instr. Univ. writing program U. RI, South Kingston, RI, 1973-77; grad. asst. dept. rhetoric U. Minn., Mpls., 1975-76; dir. continuing edn./cmty. svc. Moorhead State U., Minn., 1977-86, dean grad. studies and grad. faculty, 1983-95; US Fulbright lectr. Lanzhou U., Gansu, China, 1997. Mem. bd. pensions Luth. Ch. in Am., Mpls., 1982—87; mem. bd. higher edn. and schs. Evang. Luth. Ch. in Am., Chgo., 1987—95; cert. coll. mgmt. Carnegie Mellon U., Pitts., 1987; bd. dirs. Luth. Brotherhood, Mpls., 1988—2001; collegiate full prof. U. Md. U. Coll., Heidelberg, Germany, 2000—03; adj. prof. UMUC, Adelphi, Md., 2003—; mem. Am. Speakers Program, Cultural Sect., U.S. Embassy, Austria & Italy, 1988, Japan, 93, China, 2004, Romania, 06; U.S. Fulbright sr. lectr. Cyril and Methodius U., Skopje, Macedonia, 2005—06; resource faculty Gender Studies inst. Euro-Balkan Region, 2006. Contbr. chapters to books. Mem. exec. comm. Minn. Humanities Commn., St. Paul, 1983-89, chair, 1987-88. Bush Leadership fellow, 1987; Named Disting. Alumna, Chippewa Falls HS Wall of Fame, 2008. Mem. US Fulbright Assn. (nat. bd. mem., 2008-), Am. Studies Assn., Phi Beta Kappa, Phi Kappa Phi Lutheran. Avocations: swimming, design, music, travel, knitting. Personal E-mail: mehscls@yahoo.com.

SCHMIDHAUSER, JOHN RICHARD, retired political science professor, former congressman; b. NYC, Jan. 3, 1922; s. Richard J. and Gertrude (Grabinger) S.; m. Thelma Lorraine Ficker, June 9, 1952; children: Steven, Paul, Thomas, John C., Martha, Sara, Susan. BA with honors, U. Del., 1949; MA, U. Va., 1952, PhD, 1954. Instr. U. Va., 1952-54; asst. prof. polit. sci. U. Iowa, 1954-64, prof. polit. sci., 1967-73, U. So. Calif., 1973-92, prof. emeritus, 1993—2009. Mem. 89th Congress 1st dist. Iowa.; research fellow Research Inst. on Jud. Process, Social Sci. Research Council, 1958; sr. fellow law and behavorial scis. U. Chgo. Law Sch., 1959-60; Talbot vis. prof. govt. U. Va., 1982-83. Author: The Role of Supreme Court as Final Arbiter in Federal-State Relations, 1789-1957, 1958, The Supreme Court; Its Politics, Personalities and Procedures, 1960, Constitutional Law in the Political Process, 1963, (with Berg) The Supreme Court and Congress, 1972, (with Berg and Hahn) American Political Institutions and Corruption, 1976, (with Totten) Whaling in Japan-U.S. Relations, 1978, Judges and Justices, 1979, Constitutional Law in American Politics, 1984, Comparative Judicial Politics, 1987; contbr. chpt. to book; also numerous articles in jours. Chmn. Citizens Action Com. for Fair Representation in Iowa Legislature, 1961; dist. chmn. Operation Support Pres. Kennedy and Johnson, 1961—; chmn. Johnson County Dem. Ctrl. Com., 1961-64; del. Iowa Dem. Convs., 1956, 58, 60, 62; mem. Dem. Nat. Com. Alumni Coun., 1986—; chmn. Santa Barbara, Calif. Dem. Ctrl. Com., 1991-92; mem. exec. com. Los Padres chpt. of the Sierra Club, 1992-96; sec. Santa Barbara Dem. League, 1993-96. With USNR, 1941-45, PTO. Recipient Raubenheimer award U. So. Calif., 1991, Golden Key award for Comparative Rsch, 1991. Mem. Iowa City Mgr. Assn. (bd. reps. 1956-59, chmn. handbook revision 1958), Internat. Polit. Sci. Assn. (chmn. research com. for comparative jud. studies 1980-88), Am. Polit. Sci. Assn., Western Polit. Sci. Assn. (v.p., program chmn. 1980-81, pres.-elect 1981-82), AAUP (sec.-treas. State U. Iowa 1958-59, mem. com. on relationship fed. and state govt. to higher edn., mem. exec. com. U. So. Calif. chpt. 1983-92), Humanities Soc., Raven Soc., Phi Beta Kappa, Phi Kappa Phi. Unitarian (chmn. Iowa City Soc. Men's Club 1960-61). Avocations: French horn, public policy writing, gardening, classical music. Home: 726 Arbol Verde St Carpinteria CA 93013-2508 E-mail: jschmidhauser@verizon.net. *For the young today the opportunity for a good education puts them at the threshold of great opportunities. I encourage them to enjoy that with the same spirit that my generation experienced.*

SCHMIDLY, DAVID J., academic administrator, biology professor; b. Levelland, Tex., Dec. 20, 1943; m. Janet Elaine Knox, June 2, 1966; children: Katherine Elaine, Brian James. BS in Biology, Tex. Tech U., 1966, MS in Zoology, 1968; PhD in Zoology, U. Ill., 1971. From asst. prof. to prof. dept. wildlife fisheries scis. Tex. A&M U., College Station, 1971-82, prof., 1982-96, head dept. wildlife, 1986-92, CEO, campus dean Galveston, 1992-96; chief curator Tex. Coop. Wildlife Coll., College Station, 1983-86; v.p. Tex. Inst. Oceanography, 1992-96; v.p. rsch. and grad studies, dean grad. sch., tech. transfer Tex. Tech U., Lubbock, 1996—2002, prof. biol. scis., 1996—2002, pres., 2000—02; sys. CEO, pres. Okla. State U., Stillwater, 2002—07; pres. U. N.Mex., 2007—. Cons. Nat. Park Svc., Wildlife Assocs., Walton and Assocs., Continental Shelf Assn., LGL; lectr. in field; press adv. com. Tex. A&M U., 1983-96; charter mem. Tex. A&M U. Faculty Senate, 1983-85, chmn. Scholarship Com., 1978-82. Author: The Mammals of Trans-Pecos Texas including Big Bend National Park and Guadalupe Mountains National Park, 1977, Texas Mammals East of the Balcones Fault Zone, 1983, The Bats of Texas, 1991, The Mammals of Texas, 1994, Texas Natural History: A Century of Change, 2002; contbr. articles to profl. jours. Trustee Tex. Nature Conservancy, 1991—; mem. adv. bd. Ft. Worth Zoo, 2000. Recipient Dist. Prof. award Assn. Grad. Wildlife and Fisheries Scis., 1985, Donald W. Tinkle Rsch. Excellence award Southwestern Assn. Naturalists, 1988, Diploma Recognition La Universidad Autonoma de Guadalajara, 1989, La Universidad Autonoma de Tamaulipas, 1990. Fellow Tex. Soc. Sci. (bd. dirs. 1979-81); mem. AAAS, Am. Soc. Mammalogists (life, editor Jour. Mammalogy 1975-78), Am. Inst. Biol. Scis. (bd. dirs. 1993—, coun. affiliate socs. 1989—), Am. Naturalist, Soc. Marine Mammalogy (charter mem.), Soc. Systematic Zoology, The Wildlife Soc. Soc. Conservation Biology, Nat. Geog. Sci. Soc., S.W. Assn. Naturalists (life mem., bd. govs. 1980-86, 91—, pres. 1981, trustee 1986—), Tex. Mammal Soc. (pres. 1985-86), Assn. Systematic Collections (bd. dirs.), Chihuahuan Desert Rsch. Inst. (v.p. bd. scientists 1982—, bd. dirs. 1991), Mexican Soc. Mammalogists, Sigma Xi (v.p. 1986-87, pres. 1987-88), Disting. Scientist award 1991), Coun. Pub. Univ. Pres. and Chancellors (exec. com. 2000), Golden Key, Beta Beta Beta, Phi Sigma, Phi Kappa Phi. Office: U NMex Office of Pres MSC05 300 Scholes Hall Rm 144 Albuquerque NM 87131 Office Phone: 505-277-2626. Business E-Mail: unmpres@unm.edu.

SCHMID-SCHOENBEIN, GEERT WILFRIED, biomedical engineer, educator; b. Albstadt, Baden-Wurttemberg, Germany, Jan. 1, 1948; came to U.S., 1971; s. Ernst and Ursula Schmid; m. Renate Schmid-Schoenbein, July 3, 1976; children: Philip, Mark, Peter. Vordiplom, Liebig U., Giessen, Germany, 1971; PhD in Bioengring., U. Calif., San Diego, 1976. Staff assoc. dept. physiology Columbia U., NYC, 1976-77, sr. assoc., 1977-79; asst. prof. dept. applied mechs. & engring. scis. U. Calif., San Diego, 1979-84, assoc. prof., 1984-89, prof., 1989-94, prof. dept. bioengring., 1994—. Editor: Frontiers in Biomechanics, 1986, Physiology and Pathophysiology of Leukocyte Adhesion, 1994, Molecular Basis of Microcirculatory Disorders, 2002; author more than 280 rsch. reports. Recipient Melville medal ASME, 1990, Ratschow medal European Soc. Phlebology, 1999. Fellow Am. Inst. for Med. and Biol. Engring., Am. Heart Assn.; mem. NAE, Biomed. Engring. Soc. (pres. 1991-92), Am. Microcirculatory Soc. (pres. 2003-04), N.Am. Soc. Biorheology (pres. 1989-99), European Microciculatory Soc., Am. Physiol. Soc., Am. Mech. Engring. Soc. Achievements include bioengineering research on cardiovascular disease, microcirulation, bioengineering, and lymphology. Office: U Calif San Diego Dept Bioengineering Gilman Dr 9500 0412 La Jolla CA 92093-0412

SCHMIDT, BENNO CHARLES, JR., lawyer; b. Washington, Mar. 20, 1942; s. Benno Charles and Martha (Chastain) S.; children by previous marriage— Elizabeth, Benno III, Christina. BA, Yale U., 1963, JD, 1966; LLD (hon.), Princeton U., 1986; LittD (hon.), Johns Hopkins U., 1987; LLD (hon.), Harvard U., 1987. Bar: D.C. 1968. Law clk. Chief Justice Earl Warren, U.S. Supreme Ct, Washington, 1966-67; spl. asst., asst. atty. gen. Office Legal Counsel U.S. Dept. Justice, Washington, 1967-69; Harlan Fiske Stone prof. constl. law Columbia U., NYC, 1969-86, dean Law Sch., 1984-86; pres., prof. law Yale U., New Haven, 1986-92; chmn. Edison Schs., NYC, 1992—2007. Author: Freedom of the Press versus Public Access, 1976; (with A.M. Bickel) The Judiciary and Responsible Government 1910-1921, 1984. Chmn. bd. Coun. For Aid to Edn.; trustee Kauffm Found.; chmn. bd. trustees CUNY, 2000-. Office: Edison Schools 521 5th Ave Rm 1100 New York NY 10175-1599

SCHMIDT, BOB, psychologist; b. Springfield, Minn., Nov. 9, 1954; s. LeRoy and Janice Schmidt; m. Jan Beckenhauer, Aug. 17, 1975; children: Jonathan, Jared. PhD, U. Denver, 2002. NCSP NASP, 1989, cert. sch. psychologist CDE, 1992. Sch. psychologist Kern County Supt. Schs., Bakersfield, Calif., 1987—88, Tulare County Dept. Edn., Visalia, Calif., 1988—92, Colo. Springs Sch. Dist. II, Colo., 1992—97, 2004—, prin., 1997—2004, cons. and instr., 2006—08; psychologist Four Seasons Med. Ctr., Colo. Springs, 2004—06, Centennial Health, Colo. Springs, 2006—. Ch. planter Fellowship Bible Ch., Colo. Springs, 1985—87. Recipient Black belt Tae-Kwon-Do, ITF, 1996. Mem.: CSSP (licentiate), NASP (licentiate). Independent. Achievements include development of educational-based emotional disabilities determination processes. Home: 6660 Delmonico #200 Colorado Springs CO 80919 Office: Colo Springs Sch Dist II 1115 N El Paso St Colorado Springs CO 80903 Personal E-mail: doc.schmidt@yahoo.com. Business E-Mail: schmirl@d11.org.

SCHMIDT, BUFFIE, finance educator; b. Columbia, SC, Feb. 23, 1975; d. Melissa T Williams and Joe E Williams, Jr; m. Frank J. Schmidt, Jr; 1 child, Franklin III. BS in Computer Sci. and Math., Brenau U., Gainesville, Ga., 1997; MBA, Augusta State U., Ga., 1999, attending, 2006—. Fin. Walt Disney World, Orlando, Fla., 1994—98; compusa Instr., Augusta, 2000—01; bus. analyst Electrolux, Augusta, 2000—01, sr. fin. analyst, fin. mgr., 2001—02, IT project mgr., 2002—03, sr. ops. project mgr., 2003—04; prof. Augusta State U., 2007—. Adj. faculty Troy U., Ala., 2003—08. Accreditattion and program devel. So. Bible Inst. and Sem., Augusta, 2006—08. Mem.: Phi Lambda Theta, Phi Delta Kappa, Alpha Lambda Delta (v.p. 1995—96), Omicron Delta Kappa (v.p. 1996—97), Alpha Gamma Delta (v.p. 1996—97, Highest GPA 1994—96). Avocation: travel. Home: 6018 Sanibel Dr Augusta GA 30909 Office: ASU: Hull Coll Bus 2500 Walton Way Augusta GA 30904 Personal E-mail: buffie.schmidt@yahoo.com. Business E-Mail: bschmidt@aug.edu.

SCHMIDT, CHAUNCEY EVERETT, banker, director; b. Oxford, Iowa, June 7, 1931; s. Walter Frederick and Vilda (Saxton) S.; m. Anne Garrett McWilliams, Mar. 3, 1954; children: Carla, Julia, Chauncey Everett. BS, U.S. Naval Acad., 1953; MBA, Harvard U., 1959. With First Nat. Bank, Chgo., 1959-76, v.p., gen. mgr. br. London, Eng., 1965-68, v.p. for Europe, Middle East, Africa, 1968-69, sr. v.p. Chgo., 1969-72, exec. v.p., 1972, vice chmn. bd., 1973, pres., 1974-76; chmn. bd., chief exec. officer, dir. Bank of Calif. N.A., San Francisco, 1976—; chmn. bd., pres., chief exec. officer, dir. BanCal Tri-State Corp., 1976—. Dir. Amfac, Inc., Honolulu; mem. Adv. Council Japan-U.S. Econ. Relations; adv. bd. Pacific Rim Bankers Program. Exec. bd. and pres. San Francisco Bay Area council Boy Scouts Am.; council SRI Internat.; bd. dirs. Bay Area Council; bd. govs. San Francisco Symphony; trustee U.S. Naval War Coll. Fedn., Newport, R.I. Served with USAF, 1953-56. Mem. Assn. Res. City Bankers, Am. Bankers Assn., Internat. Monetary Conf., Calif. Bankers Clearing House Assn. (dir.), Calif. Roundtable (dir.), Japan-Calif. Assn. Clubs: Comml. (Chgo.); Bankers (San Francisco), Bohemian (San Francisco). Home: 40 Why Worry Farm Woodside CA 94062-3654 Office: Ste 140 525 Middlefield Rd Menlo Park CA 94025

SCHMIDT, CHRISTOPHER C., orthopedist; MD, U. Wis., Madison, 1989. Diplomate in orthop.surgery ABOS, 1998, in caq hand surgery ABOS, 1999. Dir. Mt. Carmel Orthop. Residency Program, Columbus, Ohio, 1997—2000; shoulder, elbow & hand surgeon AOA, Pitts.; intern, gen. surgery U. Pitts., 1989—90, orthop. resident, 1990—95; fellow Ind. Hand Ctr., Ind. U., 1995—96. Recipient O'Donoghue award, Am. Orthop. Soc. Sports Medicine, 1997. Mem.: Am. Acad. Orthop. Surgeons, Am. Soc. Surgery Hand (assoc.). Achievements include research in ligament and tendon healing. Avocations: tennis, golf, guitar, travel. Office: Aoa 1307 Federal St Pittsburgh PA 15212

SCHMIDT, CYRIL JAMES, librarian; b. Flint, Mich., June 27, 1939; s. Cyril August and Elizabeth Josephine S.; m. Martha Joe Meadows, May 22, 1965; children: Susan, Emily. BA, Cath. U. Am., 1962; MSLS, Columbia U., 1963; PhD, Fla. State U., 1974. Asst. bus. and industry dept. Flint Pub. Library, 1963-65; reference librarian Gen. Motors Inst., Flint, 1965; asso. librarian S.W. Tex. State U., San Marcos, 1965-67; head undergrad. libraries, asst. prof. Ohio State U., 1967-70; dir. libraries SUNY, Albany, 1972-79; also mem. faculty SUNY (Sch. Library and Info. Sci.); univ. librarian Brown U., Providence, 1979-81; exec. v.p. Rsch. Libraries Group, Stanford, Calif., 1981-89; prin. cons. Schmidt & Assocs., Palo Alto, Calif., 1989—; univ. prof. San Jose (Calif.) State U., 1992—. Author papers in field. Libr. Svcs. Act fellow, 1962-63, Higher Edn. Act fellow, 1970-72 Mem. ALA, ACLU, Pi Sigma Alpha, Beta Phi Mu. Home: 244 Forest Ave Palo Alto CA 94301-2510 Business E-Mail: jim_schmidt@sjsu.edu.

SCHMIDT, DANIEL EDWARD, IV, lawyer, arbitrator; b. NYC, Dec. 17, 1946; s. Daniel Edward III and Mary (Mannion) S.; m. Gail Kennedy, Sept. 5, 1980; children: Kathryn Kennedy, Michael Kennedy. BA, St. Lawrence U., 1971; postgrad., New Sch., 1972; JD, St. John's U., 1975. Bar: N.Y. 1976; cert. arbitrator. From asst. counsel to assoc. gen. counsel Prudential Property & Casualty, Holmdel, NJ, 1978—81, assoc. gen. counsel, divsn. head, 1981—82; v.p., assoc. gen. counsel, asst. sec. Prudential Reins Co., Newark, 1982—84; dir., v.p., gen. counsel, corp. sec. Scor U.S. Group, NYC, 1984—86, dir., sr. v.p., gen. counsel, corp. sec., 1986—89; dir., exec. com., sr. v.p., gen. counsel, corp. sec. Sorema N.A. Group, NYC, 1989—94, dir., exec. com., exec. v.p., group gen. counsel, 1995—99, dir. exec. com., group exec. v.p., chief legal officer, 1999—2000; dep. gen. mgr., gen. counsel, corp. sec. Sorema Internat. Holding, N.V., Netherlands, 1993—96; U.S. counsel Groupama, France, 1996—2000; cons. Sorema NA Group, 2000—03. Pvt. practice comml. arbitrator, umpire, Little Silver, N.J. and Scottsdale, Ariz., 1987—; reins. lectr., 1986—; founding dir., 1994-2003; pres., 1999-2002, chmn. 2002-2003, bd. dirs. ARIAS (U.S.), N.Y.C. Assoc. editor Arias-U.S. Quar. Presiding judge Ecclesiastical Trial Ct., 1999—2000, Episcopal Diocese of N.J., 1997—2000; bd. dirs. Marine Corps Scholarship Found., NJ, 2007—; bd. dirs., exec. com. ARC, Monmouth County, Shrewsbury, NJ, 1981—84. With US Army, 1967—70. Mem. ABA, Am. Arbitration Assn. (panel comml. arbitrators, roster of umpires, panel internat. arbitrators), N.Y. Bar Assn., Assn. Internat. Droit des Assureurs (U.S. chpt.), Bamm Hollow Country Club, Desert Mountain Club, Sands Beach Club. Episcopalian. Avocations: bicycling, golf, hiking. Home (Summer): Dispute Resolution Svcs Internat 628 Little Silver Point Rd Little Silver NJ 07739-1737 Home (Winter): Dispute Resolution Svcs Internat Saguro Forest Desert Mountain 40933 N 97th St Scottsdale AZ 85262 Home Phone: 732-741-6620; Office Phone: 732-614-1366. Business E-Mail: dschmidt4@comcast.net.

SCHMIDT, DAVID A., engineering educator; b. Colby, Kans., May 10, 1953; s. Herbert J. Schmidt and Frances L. Walters; m. Linda Jean Townley, Sept. 28, 2002. PhD, Kans. State U., Manhattan, 1981. Postdoc. rschr. U. Edinburgh, 1982—83; asst. prof. Iowa State U., Ames, 1984—86; u. disting. prof. Kans. State U., 1986—. Rschr., CNRS Ecole

Polytechnique, Palaiseau, France, 2003—04. Office: Kansas State Univ 234 Nichols Hall Manhattan KS 66506 Office Fax: 785-532-7353. Business E-Mail: schmidt@cis.ksu.edu.

SCHMIDT, DAVID JOSEPH, senior resource specialist, consultant; b. Columbus, Ind., Nov. 22, 1950; s. Richard Everett and Norma Caster (Waggoner) S. BS, Ball State U., 1973, MA, 1975. Tchr. Lakeland Sch. Corp., Lagrange, Ind., 1975—. Mem. edn. adv. com. U.S. Congress 4th Dist., Ft. Wayne, Ind., 1989-94; mem. edn. com. Ind. Senate, Indpls., 1989—; pres. Assn. for Retarded Citizens, Lagrange, 1982-94, v.p., sec., Indpls., 1986-90; chmn. Ind. Adv. Coun. on Edn. of Handicapped Children and Youth, 1985—; chmn., bd. dirs. ARC Opportunities, Inc., 1994-2002, chmn. emeritus, bd. dirs., 2002—; bd. dirs. Ind. Geography Alliance, 2005-09, Weil Ops. West, LLC, 2006—; dir. Northeastern Mental Health Ctr., North East Ind. Ins. Consortium. Recipient Outstanding Alumnus award Ball State U., 1988, Alumni Achievement award Delta Chi Fraternity, 1990, Dekko Internat. Found. award for excellence, 1992. Mem. Ind. State Tchrs. Assn. (spl. edn. com. 1984—, chmn. 1986-89, legal def. panel 1981-89, chmn. 1984-89, dir. 1989-95, bd. mgmt. pers. com. 1989-95, governance com. 1995—2007, chmn. 2001—07, issues and concerns com. 2008-), Lakeland Edn. Assn. (pres. 1981-83, pres. 1999-2002, 2009-), Dallas Lake Yacht Club (commodore 1997—). Democrat. Presbyterian. Avocations: bicycling, sailing, water-skiing, scuba diving. Home: Dallas Lake 30 W 625 S Wolcottville IN 46795-9527 Office: Lakeland High Sch 805 E 75 N Lagrange IN 46761-9360 Office Phone: 260-499-2470. Business E-Mail: dschmidt@lakeland.k12.in.us.

SCHMIDT, DAVID KELSO, engineering educator; b. LaFayette, Ind., Mar. 4, 1943; s. Herbert R. and Barbara E. (Lipp) S.; m. Karalee Sue Krause, Nov. 24, 1979; children: Jeff, Kelly, Russ, Jeremy, Jillian, Kerry. BS in Aero. Engring., Purdue U., 1965; MS in Aero. Engring., U. So. Calif., LA, 1968; PhD, Purdue U., 1972. Staff engr. McDonnell Douglas Astro Corp., Huntington Beach, Calif., 1965-69; rsch. staff Stanford Rsch. Inst., Menlo Park, Calif., 1972-74; prof. of engring. Purdue U., West Lafayette, Ind., 1974-88, Ariz. State U., Tempe, 1988-93; dir. Aerospace Rsch. Ctr. Ariz. State Univ., Tempe, 1990-92; prof. aerospace engring. U. Md., College Park, 1993—, chmn. dept. aerospace engring., 1993-94. Cons. Northrop Aircraft, Hawthorne, Calif., 1985, Honeywell Systems Rsch. Ctr., Mpls., 1986, Systems Technology, Inc., Hawthorne, Calif., 1987, ARINC Rsch. Corp, Annapolis, 1995. Contbr. numerous articles to profl. jours. Assoc. fellow Am. Inst. of Aeros. and Astronauts, Am. Soc. for Engring. Edn.; mem. IEEE.

SCHMIDT, DEREK LARKIN, state legislator; b. Independence, Kans., Jan. 23, 1968; m. Jennifer Schmidt; children: Caroline, Claire. Attended., Independence C.C.; BS, U. Kans., 1990; MA in Internat. Politics, U. Leicester, Eng., 1992; JD, Georgetown U., 1996. Bar: Kans. 1996, DC 1996, US Supreme Ct 2003. Spl. counsel Gov. of Kans., Kans.; mem. legis. staff Senator Nancy Kassebaum, 1992—96; gen. counsel & legis. dir. Senator Chuck Hagel, 1996—98; asst. atty. gen. State of Kans., Kans., 1999; legis. liaison & spl. counsel Gov. Bill Graves, 2000; pvt. practice Scovel, Emert, Heasty & Chubb, Independence, 2000—; mem. Dist. 15 Kans. State Senate, 2001—, majority leader Kans., 2005—. Bd. dirs. Independence Industries, Inc.; chmn. Agr., Post Audit, Confirmation Oversight, Medicaid Reform coms. Grad. Leadership Kans., 1999; trustee, ea. Kans. br. Nat. Multiple Sclerosis Soc.; active Am. Coun. Young Polit. Leaders. Ralph Kirchner scholar U. Leicester; fellow Bowhay Inst. for Legis. Leadership Devel.; Henry Toll fellow, 2002, Simons Pub. Humanities fellow U. Kans., 2006, Aspen Inst. Rodel fellow, 2007-. Mem.: Kans. State Hist. Soc., Inc. (bd. dirs. 2000—07), Rotary. Republican. Home: Dist Office PO Box 747 Independence KS 67301 Office: Capitol Office 300 SW 10th St Rm 392-E Topeka KS 66612 Office Phone: 785-296-2497. Home Fax: 785-296-6718. Business E-Mail: Derek.Schmidt@senate.ks.gov.

SCHMIDT, EDWARD CRAIG, lawyer; b. Pitts., Nov. 26, 1947; s. Harold Robert and Bernice (Williams) Schmidt; m. Elizabeth Lowry Rial, Aug. 18, 1973; children: Harodl Robert II, Robert Rial. BA, U. Mich., 1969; JD, U. Pitts., 1972. Bar: Pa. 1972, US Dist. Ct. (we. dist.) Pa. 1972, US Ct. Appeals (3d cir.) 1972, US Ct. Appeals (DC cir.) 1975, US Supreme Ct. 1981, US Ct. Appeals (9th and 4th cirs.) 1982, US Ct. Appeals (6th cir.) 1987, US Ct. Appeals (2d cir.) 1992. Assoc. Rose, Schmidt, Hasley & Di Salle, Pitts., 1972—77, ptnr., 1977—90, Jones, Day, Reavis & Pogue, Pitts., 1990—2001, Thompson Coburn LLP, Washington, 2002—06; counsel Edward C. Schmidt LLC, Chautauqua, NY, 2006—. Mem. adv. com. Superior Ct. Pa., 1978—80; instr. NITA Duquesne U., 1998—99. Asst. editor: Antitrust Discovery Handbook, 1980; co-editor: Antitrust Discovery Handbook-Supplement, 1982; contbr. articles to profl. jours. Bd. dirs. Urban League, Pitts., 1974—77. Mem.: Acad. Trial Lawyers Allegheny County (bd. govs. 1980), Internat. Acad. Trial Lawyers, Allegheny County Bar Assn. (pub. rels. com. coun. civil litig. sect. 1977—80), DC Bar Assn., Pa. Bar Assn., Supreme Ct. Hist. Soc., We. Res. Acad. Alumni Assn. (trustee 1998—2000), Rolling Rock Club (Lignonier, Pa.). Office: PO Box 1091 20 Hazlett St Chautauqua NY 14722 Office Phone: 716-357-2448. Business E-Mail: eschmidt@ecslaw.net.

SCHMIDT, ELEANORE, library director; Assoc. dir. Long Beach Pub. Libr., Calif., 1989—98, dir. libr. svcs. Calif., 1998—. Bd. dirs. Long Beach Pub. Libr. Found. Office: Long Beach Pub Libr 101 Pacific Ave Long Beach CA 90822 Office Fax: 562-570-6016, 562-570-7408. E-mail: eschmidt@lbpl.org.

SCHMIDT, ERIC EMERSON, information technology executive; b. Washington, Apr. 27, 1955; m. Wendy Schmidt; 2 children. BSEE, Princeton U., 1976; MS in Computer Sci., U. Calif., Berkeley, 1979, PhD in Computer Sci., 1982. With Bell Labs., Zilog; research intern Xerox PARC, Palo Alto, Calif., 1979-80, mem. research staff, 1980-83; software mgr. Sun Microsystems, Mountain View, Calif., 1983-84, software dir., 1984-85, v.p., gen. mgr. software products div., 1985-88, v.p. gen. systems group, 1988-91, chief tech. officer, 1994—97; pres. Sun Tech. Enterprises, Inc., Mountain View, Calif., 1991-94; chmn., CEO Novell, Inc., Provo, Utah, 1997—2001; chmn. exec. com., CEO Google, Inc., Mountain View, Calif., 2001—. Bd. dirs. Google, Inc., 2001—, Apple Inc., 2006—09; chmn. New America Found., 2008—. Bd. trustee Princeton U. Named one of Forbes' Richest Americans, 2004—, The World's Richest People, Forbes Mag., 2006—, The 50 Who Matter Now, Business 2.0, 2007, The 50 Most Important People on the Web, PC World, 2007, The 25 Most Powerful People in Bus., Fortune Mag., 2007, The Top 200 Art Collectors, ARTnews, 2007—, The Global Elite, Newsweek mag., 2008, The Top 25 Market Movers, US News & World Report, 2009. Mem. IEEE, Assn. Computing Machinery, Sigma Xi; fellow Am. Acad. Arts & Scis. Achievements include patents in field. Office: Google Inc 1600 Amphitheatre Pkwy 41 Mountain View CA 94043-1351 Office Phone: 650-623-4000. Office Fax: 650-618-1499.*

SCHMIDT, GARY P., lawyer, personal care industry executive; b. Youngstown, Ohio, Mar. 25, 1951; BA, Miami U., 1973; JD, U. Akron, 1976. Gen. counsel Lyphomed, Inc., 1988—90; v.p., sec., gen. counsel Fujisawa USA, Inc., 1990—97; v.p., asst. sec., gen. counsel Alberto-Culver Co., Melrose Park, Ill., 1997—2000, sr. v.p., asst. sec., gen. counsel, 2000—. Mem.: ABA, Patent Law Assn., Ill. State Bar Assn., Chicago Bar Assn. Office: Alberto-Culver Co 2525 Armitage Ave Melrose Park IL 60160

SCHMIDT, GERHARD, automotive executive; b. Garmisch-Partenkirchen, Germany, 1946; Degree in Mech. Engring., U. Aachen, Germany, 1971, PhD in Mech. Engring., 1979. Joined BMW AG, 1979, head gasoline-engine activities, 1985—90, sr. v.p. powertrain devel., 1990—2000, sr. v.p. vehicle integration, 2000; v.p. rsch./advanced engring., chief tech. officer Ford Motor Co., Dearborn, Mich., also Aachen, 2001—. Bd. dirs. Automotive Fuel Cell Corp., Vancouver, British Columbia, Canada; mem. US Coun. Automotive Rsch., Ford/MIT Alliance; mem. sustainable transp. energy pathways prog. (STEPS) U. Calif. Inst. Transp. Studies, Davis; engring. adv. coun. U. Mich.; adv. bd. mem. Oakland U. Sch. Engring. & Computer Sci., Rochester, Mich.; sci. adv. coun. ATZAutoTech. mag.; adv. professorship Nanjing U. Aeronautics & Astronautics, China, 2007. Hon. com. mem. Internat. Fedn. Automotive Engring. Societies. Mem.: German Am. C. of C. (bd. dirs.). Office: Ford Motor Co N Am Hdqs 1 American Rd Dearborn MI 48126 Office Phone: 313-322-3000. Business E-Mail: gschmi19@ford.com.*

SCHMIDT, HARVEY MARTIN, economist, educator, financial analyst, consultant; b. Sept. 15, 1925; s. Joseph David and Dorothy Schmidt; m. Barbara Bebe Bloom, Nov. 25, 1961; children: Ellen Louise, Jay Stephen, Gregg Arthur. Student, U. So. Calif., 1943; BA magna cum laude, Woodbury U., 1947. Assoc. prof. bus. Woodbury U., 1947—48; pvt. practice acctg. LA, 1948—80; cons. mgmt., taxes and fins., 1965—82; econ. forecaster, internat. lectr., investment lectr. on audiotapes, 1989—. Investment lectr. on internat. cruise ships, 1992; fin. cons., Pacific Palisades, 1982—; pres. Harvey Schmidt Mgmt. Inc., 1983—, Med-Plan Operators, 1969—89, Kit Travel, 1987—. Contbr. articles to profl. jours. With USCG, 1943—44. Master: U.S. Contact Bridge League (life); mem.: Internat. Platform Assn., Bruin Athletic Club of UCLA, Exch. Club (pres. local chpt. 1953—56). Personal E-mail: bebe@usinter.net. Business E-Mail: hs@kltrav.com.

SCHMIDT, HILDRED DORIS, music educator; b. Marion County, Kans., Aug. 13, 1932; d. Rudolf B Schmidt and Susie Voth. B of Music Edn., Coll. Emporia, 1954, BA, 1954; M of music edn. with highest distinction, Ind. U., 1958. Cert. Teacher Kans. State Bd. Edn., Service Playing Certificate Am. Guild Organists. Music tchr. Mullinville Grade Sch., Kans., 1954—57, Zenda Grade and H.S., Kans., 1958—60, Inman Grade Sch., 1960—67, Lyons Jr. High, Mid. and H.S., Lyons, Kans., 1967—96; ret., 1996. Founding mem. The Silver Sounds (flute quartet); organizer music festivals Lyons Jr. High Music Dept. Mem. People to People Lifeline, Bob Larson Communicator Club. Recipient Master Teacher award, Discipline and Classroom Mgmt., 1984. Mem.: Kans. Assn. of Retired Sch. Personnel, Kans. Bandmasters Assn., Am. Guild Organists (sub-dean, Hutchinson chpt. 1988—93, 1996—98, dean Hutchinson chpt. 1998—2001, sub-dean, Hutchinson chpt. 2001—05), Music Educators Nat. Conf. (life), Kans. Music Educators Assn. So. Ctrl. Dist. (life; exec. sec. 1974—2004), Tabor Mennonite Ch., Coll. Emporia Alumni Assn. (bd. dirs. 1999—2007), Mu Phi Epsilon (pres. chpt. Phi Epsilon 1952—54). Avocations: gardening, needlecrafts, travel, photography.

SCHMIDT, JAMES CRAIG, retired bank, savings and loan association executive; b. Peoria, Ill., Sept. 27, 1927; s. Walter Henry and Clara (Wolfenbarger) S.; m. Jerrie Louise Bond, Dec. 6, 1958; children: Julie, Sandra, Suzanne. Student, Ill. Wesleyan U., 1945, 48-50, Ph.B. in Bus. Adminstrn, 1952; postgrad., U. Ill. Coll. Law, 1950-52; JD, DePaul U., 1953. Bar: Calif., Calif. Spl. agt. Fidelity & Deposit Co., Chgo., 1956-58; with Home Fed. Savs. & Loan Assn., San Diego, 1958-67; asst. sec. bus. and transp. State of Calif., 1967-69; vice-chmn., pres. Gt. Am. Bank, San Diego, 1969-88. Pres. Conf. Fed. Savs. and Loans of Calif., 1974-75; mem. Calif. Toll Bridge Authority, 1969-74; mem. Calif. State Transp. Bd., 1972-78; past chmn. San Diego Bal. Commn. Task Force. Columnist San Diego Daily Transcript. Pres. San Diego Holiday Bowl Football Game, 1986; bd. dirs. San Diego Internat. Sports Coun., San Diego Hwy. Devel. Assn.; pub. mem. San Diego County Sunset Adv. Bd.; mem. City-County Re-Investment Task Force. Mem. Calif. Bar Assn., Ill. Bar Assn., Calif. League Savs. Instns. (chmn. 1986-87), Calif. C. of C. (bd. dirs. 1987-90), U.S. Savs. Instn. League (exec. com. 1983-86), San Diego East County C. of C. (bd. dirs.), San Diego Regional C. of C. (housing, pub. policy and transp. coms.), Catfish Club, Sigma Chi, Phi Delta Phi. Office: 8383 Center Dr Ste J La Mesa CA 91942-2913 Home Phone: 619-447-5604.

SCHMIDT, JEAN, United States Representative from Ohio; b. Cin., Nov. 29, 1951; m. Peter W. Schmidt; 1 child, Emilie. BS in Polit. Sci., U. Cin., 1974. Tchg. cert. in secondary edn. U. Cin., 1986. Trustee, Miami, Ohio, 1989—2000; mem. Ohio State Ho. Reps. from Dist. 66, 2001—04, US Congress from 2nd Ohio dist., 2005—. Chmn. Clermont County Rep. Party, 1996—98, Taft for Gov., 1998; mem. agr. com. US Congress, mem. transp. and infrastructure com. Mem. Milford Miami Twp. C. of C., 1989—, Ohio Twp. Assn., 1990—, Clermont County Twp. Assn., 1990—, Clermont County 20/20 Com., 1990—, Clermont County League of Women Voters, 1990—, Clermont County Agrl. Soc., 1990—, Clermont County C. of C., 1990—, mem. econ. devel. com., 1995—2005; mem. Leukemia Soc. Team in Tng., 1994—, mentor, 1996—; bd. trustees Clermont County Libr., 1980—92, 1994—2000, 2005—; bd. mem. Clermont County Mercy Hosp. Found., 1997—, Phoenix Pl., 2005—; founder, chmn. Sauls Found. 5K Race, 1995—. Recipient Clermont County Cmty. Devel. of the Greater Cin. Found. Appreciation award, 2003, Clermont County Mental Health Svc. Recognition Award, 2003, Children's Hosp. Award of Distinction, 2003, So. Ohio Agrl. and Cmty. Devel. Found. Disting. Svc. Award, 2004; named Marriage & Family Therapy Legislator of Yr., 2003, Empowerment Coalition Legislator of Yr., 2004, Am. Liver Found. Legislator of Yr., 2004, Bioscience Legislator of Yr., 2004. Republican. Roman Catholic. Avocations: long distance running, auto racing. Office: US House Reps 238 Cannon House Office Bldg Washington DC 20515 Office Phone: 202-225-3164. Office Fax: 202-225-1992.*

SCHMIDT, JOACHIM MATTHIAS, research scientist; b. Ravensburg, Baden-Wuerttemberg, Germany, Apr. 23, 1965; s. Anneliese Frieda Schildbach and Manfred Frohwald Schmidt. Abitur, Gymnasium Corvinianum Northeim, Germany, 1984; PhD, U. Goettingen, Germany, 1993. Diploma rschr. Inst. Theoretical Physics Goettingen, Lower Saxony, Germany, 1989—90; PhD rschr. Max Planck Inst. Aeronomie, Lindau, Lower Saxony, 1991—94; rschr. Obs. Arcetri, Florence, Tuscany, Italy, 1995, U. Kiel, Schleswig-Holstein, Germany, 1996—97; scientist Imperial Coll. Sci. and Tech., London, Middle Saxony, 1998—2003; lectr. Internat. U. Bremen, Germany, 2004—06; sr. scientist NASA Goddard Space Flight Ctr., Washington, Md., 2007—; councelor NASA Hdqs., Washington, 2008—. Editor Internat. Astron. Union, Paris, 2008—. With US Army, 1984—85, Western German Army. Recipient Exchange Rschr. award, European Geophys. Union, 1995, Young Scientist Publ. award, 1996, PPARC Rsch. award, Imperical Coll. London, 1998—2003, Senior Scientist award, NASA, 2007—08. Mem.: Am. Geophys. Union (mem. advisor 2000—03). Lutherian. Avocations: swimming, travel, reading. Home: 3805 Evans Trail Ct Beltsville MD 20705 Office: NASA Goddard Space Flight Ctr 8800 Greenbelt Rd Greenbelt MD 20771 Office Fax: 301-286-1433. Personal E-mail: joachim-m-schmidt-home@t-online.de. Business E-Mail: joachim.m.schmidt@nasa.gov.

SCHMIDT, JOHN R., lawyer; b. Chgo., Nov. 24, 1943; s. Edward F. and Josephine (Roggen) S.; m. Janet Gilroy, Apr. 24, 1982; 1 child, Laura. BA, Harvard U., 1964, JD, 1967. Bar: Ill. 1967, U.S. Dist. Ct. (no. dist.) Ill. 1972, U.S. Supreme Ct. 1972. Assoc. Mayer, Brown & Platt, Chgo., 1967-73, ptnr., 1973-84, Skadden, Arps, Slate, Meagher & Flom, Chgo., 1984-93; Amb., chief US negotiator Uruguay Round, 1993—94; assoc. atty. gen. U.S. Dept. Justice, Washington, 1994—97; ptnr. Mayer, Brown, Rowe & Maw, LLP, Chgo., 1998—. Vis. scholar Northwestern U. Sch. Law, 1997—98. Contbr. articles to profl. jours. Chmn. Ill. Guardianship and Advocacy Commn., 1979-82, Met. Pier and Exposition Authority, Chgo., 1989-94; chief of staff City of Chgo., 1989; co-chmn. Citizens for Ct. Reform, Chgo., 1986-92; trustee Ill. Inst. Tech., 1991-93, 1998-, Chgo. Symphony Orch., 1978-93, 1998-; chair IIT Chgo. Kent Coll. Law Bd. Overseas, 1999-. Recipient Judge Learned Hand Human Rels. award Am Jewish Com., 1992, Edmond Randolph award, Dept. Justice, 1997, Champion Pub. Interest award, BPI, 2007. Fellow Am. Bar Found.; mem. ABA, Chgo. Coun. Lawyers (pres. 1974-76). Office: Mayer Brown Rowe Maw LLP 71 S Wacker Dr Chicago IL 60606-4637 Office Phone: 312-701-8597. Office Fax: 312-706-8397. Business E-Mail: jschmidt@mayerbrown.com.

SCHMIDT, JOSEPH DAVID, urologist; b. Chgo., July 29, 1937; s. Louis and Marian (Fleigel) S.; m. Andrea Maxine Herman, Oct. 28, 1962. BS in Medicine, U. Ill., 1959, MD, 1961. Diplomate Am. Bd. Urology. Rotating intern Presbyn. St. Luke's Hosp., Chgo., 1961-62, resident in surgery, 1962-63; resident in urology The Johns Hopkins Hosp., Balt., 1963-67; faculty U. Iowa Coll. Medicine, Iowa City, 1969-76, U. Calif., San Diego, 1976—, prof., head divsn. urology, 1976—2006; prof., emeritus, 2006—; vice-chmn. dept. surgery U. Calif., San Diego, 1985-97. Cons. U.S. Dept. Navy, San Diego, 1976—; attending urologist Vets. Affairs Dept., San Diego, 1976—; assoc. dir. for clin. rsch. U. Calif. San Diego Cancer Ctr., 1997-98. Author, editor: Gynecological and Obstetric Urology, 1978, 82, 93. Capt. USAF, 1967-69. Recipient Francis Senear award U. Ill., 1961. Fellow ACS, Am. Urol. Assn. Inc., Alpha Omega Alpha. Avocations: collecting antique medical books, manuscripts. Office: U Calif Med Ctr Divsn Urology 200 W Arbor Dr San Diego CA 92103-8897 Office Phone: 619-543-5904. Office Fax: 619-543-6573. Business E-Mail: jdschmidt@ucsd.edu.

SCHMIDT, JOSEPH W., lawyer; b. Louisville, Ky., July 6, 1946; s. A. W. and Olivia Ann Schmidt; m. Angela Petchara Apiradee, Dec. 20, 1969; children: Narissa Ann, Suriya Christine. BA in Psych., Bellarmine U., 1969; AB in Commerce, U. Md., 1972; JD, Columbia U., 1975. Bar: NY 1976. Law clk. to presiding judge US Dist. Ct. (so. dist. NY), 1975-76; assoc. Breed, Abbott & Morgan, NYC, 1976-83, ptnr., 1983-93, Whitman, Breed, Abbott & Morgan, NYC, 1993-96, Coudert Bros. LLP, NYC, 1996—2002; v.p., gen. counsel, sec. Dover Corp., NYC, 2003—. Adminstrv. editor: Columbia Jour. Law and Social Problems, 1974—75. Woodrow Wilson fellow, 1968, Harlan Fiske Stone scholar, 1975. Mem.: ABA, Assn. Corp. Coun., Soc. Corp. Secs. and Governance Profls., Assn. Bar City NY. Avocations: travel, skiing, reading. Office: Dover Corp 280 Park Ave Fl 34W New York NY 10017-1292 Office Phone: 212-922-1640. E-mail: jws@dovercorp.com.

SCHMIDT, KARL A., lawyer; b. Stockton, Calif., Sept. 18, 1947; BS, U. Calif., Berkeley, 1969, JD, 1974. Bar: Calif. 1974. Mem. Parker, Milliken, Clark, O'Hara & Samuelian, LA. Contbr. Retaliation Matters, to L.A. Daily Jour. Ann. Employment Update, 1997, USC TAx Inst. 2003: Exec. Terminations. Mem. ABA. Home Phone: 310-544-9685; Office Phone: 213-683-6518. Business E-Mail: kschmidt@pmcos.com.

SCHMIDT, KELLY L., state treasurer; b. Elmhurst, Ill. m. Chuck Schmidt; 4 children. State treas. State of ND, 2004—. Mem. ND State Investment Bd., Teachers Fund for Retirement Bd., ND Bd. Tax Equalization, ND State Hist. Soc., ND Bd. Univ. & Sch. Lands. Pres. ND Jump$tart Coalition for Personal Fin. Literacy; trustee ND State Hist. Bd. Found. Mem.: Nat. Assn. State Treas. Found. (pres., Midwest State Treas., chair, state investment bd., mem. tchrs. fund retirement bd.), AmVets Auxiliary, Am. Legion Auxiliary. Republican. Office: State Treasurer State Capitol 3rd Fl 600 E Blvd Ave Dept 120 Bismarck ND 58505-0130 Office Phone: 701-328-2643. Office Fax: 701-328-3002. Business E-Mail: treasurer@nd.gov.*

SCHMIDT, KLAUS DIETER, marketing professional, management consultant, educator; b. Eisenach, Germany, May 8, 1930; came to U.S., 1949, naturalized, 1952; s. Kurt Heinrich and Louise (Kruger) S.; m. Lynda Hollister Wheelwright, June 29, 1950; children: Karen, Claudia. BA in Econs., U. Calif., Berkeley, 1951; MBA, Stanford U., 1953; PhD in Bus. Adminstrn., Golden Gate U., 1978. Buyer, jr. mdse. mgr. Broadway Hale, 1952-54; sales mgr. Ames Harris Neville Co., 1954-56, ops. mgr., 1956-57; gen. mgr. Boise Cascade Corp., 1957-60; pres., chmn. bd. Kimball-Schmidt Inc., San Rafael, Calif., 1960-73, chmn. subs. Kalwall Pacific, 1962-67, chmn. subs. AFGOA Corp., 1966-69; asst. prof. mgmt. and mktg. San Francisco State U., 1970-75, assoc. prof. mgmt., 1975-80, prof. mgmt. and mktg., 1989-85, chmn. dept., 1979-85, prof. emeritus, 1989—, assoc. dean emeritus Sch. Bus., 1985-88; chmn. Schmidt Cons. Group, Brooklin, Maine, 1988—. Dir. Ctr. for World Bus., 1976-88, dir. U.S.-Japan Inst., 1981-88, editor-in-chief Sch. Bus. Jours., 1980-88; U.S. negotiator for Pres. Carter White House on Afghanistan issue, 1980-88; mem. Dept. Commerce Dist. Export Council, 1982-88; rsch. cons. SRI Internat. Author: (20 booklet series) Doing Business In..., Stanford Rsch. Inst., 1978-80, A Spy For Life, 2004, Living Your Life, 2005. Mem. Univ. Club (San Francisco), Alpha Delta Phi, Beta Gamma Sigma. Independent. Home and Office: PO Box 269 Brooklin ME 04616-0269 Office Phone: 207-359-4644.

SCHMIDT, KLAUS FRANZ, advertising executive; b. Dessau, Germany, May 25, 1928; came to U.S., 1951; naturalized, 1957; s. Franz and Elfriede (Klamroth) S.; m. Gisela Garbrecht, June 19, 1954; children: Dagmar Schmidt Etkin, Ena Schmidt Reynen. Student, Coll. of Journalism, Aachen, Germany, 1947-48, Sch. of Design and Printing, Bochum, Germany, 1948-50; BA, Wayne State U., 1956. Printer, compositor, 1948-56; type dir. Mogul Williams & Saylor, NYC, 1956-59, Doyle, Dane, Bernbach, NYC, 1959-61, Young & Rubicam, NYC, 1961-68, v.p., dir. print ops., 1968-75, v.p., dir. creative support, 1975-85, sr. v.p., mgr. prodn. svcs., 1985-91; advt./graphic arts cons., 1991—. Co-organizer Vision Congress Internat. Ctr. for Communications Arts & Scis., N.Y.C., 1965, 67, 69, 77; chmn., bd. trustees Internat. Ctr. Typographic Arts, N.Y.C. 1969-70 Author: Signs of the Times, 1997; Am. editor Der Druckspiegel, 1957-64; contbg. editor Print Mag., 1968-01, The Dunn Report, 1991-95 Recipient Typomundus award, 1964, Internat. Book Exhbn. award, Leipzig, Germany, 1965 Mem. Print Advt. Assn. (chmn. N.Y. chpt. 1969-71, nat. sr. v.p. 1971-75), Am. Assn.

Advt. Agys. (chmn. subcom. on phototypography 1969-75), Digital Distbn. of Advt. to Publ. Assn. (vice chmn. 1991-95), N.Y. Type Dirs. Club (pres. 1984-86, awards 1962, 64-66, 68, 69), N.Y. Art Dirs. Club (v.p. 1984-86), Advt. Prodn. Club (pres. 1982-84), Gravure Advt. Coun. (chmn. 1970-72) Home and Office: 549 Munroe Ave Sleepy Hollow NY 10591-1333 Personal E-mail: kaschmi@optonline.net.

SCHMIDT, MAARTEN, astronomy educator; b. Groningen, Netherlands, Dec. 28, 1929; came to U.S., 1959; s. Wilhelm and Antje (Haringhuizen) S.; m. Cornelia Johanna Tom, Sept. 16, 1955; children: Elizabeth Tjimkje, Maryke Antje, Anne Wilhelmina. BSc, U. Groningen, 1949; PhD, Leiden U., Netherlands, 1956; ScD, Yale U., 1966. Sci. officer Leiden Obs., The Netherlands, 1953-59; postdoctoral fellow Mt. Wilson Obs., Pasadena, Calif., 1956-58; mem. faculty Calif. Inst. Tech., 1959-95, prof. astronomy, 1964-95, exec. officer for astronomy, 1972-75, chmn. div. physics, math. and astronomy, 1975-78, mem. staff Hale Obs., 1959-80, dir. Hale Obs., 1978-80, emeritus prof. astronomy, 1996—. Co-recipient Calif. Scientist of Yr. award, 1964, Kavli prize for Astrophysics, Norwegian Acad. Sci. and Letters in partnership with the Kavli Found. and the Norwegian Ministry Edn. and Rsch., 2008. Fellow Am. Acad. Arts and Scis. (Rumford award 1968); mem. Am. Astron. Soc. (Helen B. Warner prize 1964, Russell lecture award 1978), NAS (fgn. assoc., recip. James Craig Watson Medal, 1991), Internat. Astron. Union, Royal Astron. Soc. (assoc., Gold medal 1980) Office: Calif Inst Tech MC 105 24 1200 E California Blvd Pasadena CA 91125

SCHMIDT, MARC F., neuroscientist, educator; b. Frankfurt, Germany, Feb. 29, 1964; s. Franz Schmidt and Jean Wilson; m. Catherine Tannert; children: Madeleine Tannert-Schmidt, Emilie Tannert-Schmidt. BA, Swarthmore Coll., Pa., 1986; PhD, Colo. State U., Ft. Collins, 1993. Postdoc. fellow Caltech, Pasadena, Calif., 1993—99; asst. prof. U. Pa., Phila., 1999—2005, assoc. prof., 2005—. Recipient Basil O'Connor award, Mar. Dimes, 2000—02; RO1 grant, NIH, 2000—08, fellowship, Sloan Found., 2000—03. Liberal. Achievements include research in behavioral and systems neuroscience. Office: Biology Dept Univ Pa Philadelphia PA 19104

SCHMIDT, MIKE (MICHAEL JACK SCHMIDT), retired professional baseball player; b. Dayton, Ohio, Sept. 27, 1949; m. Donna Wightman, 1973; children: Jessica Roe, Jonathan Michael. BBA, Ohio U., Athens. Player Phila. Phillies, 1972-89; co-owner Mike Schmidt's Phila. Hoagies; mgr. Clearwater Threshers, 2003—04; auxiliary coach, US nat. team World Baseball Classic, 2009. Spokesperson Participate in the Lives Am. Youth NIKE. Co-author (with Barbara Walder): Always on the Offense, 1982; co-author: (with Rob Ellis) The Mike Schmidt Study: Hitting Theory, Skills, and Technique, 1994, The Mike Schmidt Study: Building a Hitting Foundation, 1994; co-author: (with Glen Waggoner) Clearing the Bases: Juiced Players, Shrinking Ballparks, Sham Records, and a Hall of Famer's Search for the Soul of Baseball, 2006. Founder, charity fishing tournament Mike Schmidt Winner's Circle Invitational, 1999—. Named Nat. League Most Valuable Player, 1980, 1981, 1986, World Series Most Valuable Player, 1980; recipient Golden Glove award, 1976-84, 1986, Silver Slugger award, 1980-84, 86, Lou Gehrig Meml. award, 1983; named to Nat. League All-Star Team, 1974, 76, 77, 79-84, 86, 87, 89, Baseball Hall of Fame, 1995. Achievements include hitting his 500th career home run, 1987; having his uniform #20 retired by the Philadelphia Phillies, 1990.*

SCHMIDT, NANCY ANNE, psychotherapist; b. Jersey City, July 18, 1958; d. William John Lawrence and Ruth Martha (Morant) S. BA summa cum laude, Fordham U., 1986; MA summa cum laude, N.J. City State U., 1990; cert. pastoral counselor, World Christianship Ministries, 1994. Cert. social worker, criminal justice specialist, hypnotherapist, addiction counselor, eating disorders specialist; cert. domestic violence counselor, cert. crisis counselor. Adj. prof. N.J. City State U. (formerly Jersey City State Coll.), 1988-91, adj. prof. psychology, 1990-94; pvt. practice West New York, 1990—; counselor Substance Abuse Treatment Ctr., Union City, NJ, 1994-96; substance abuse program dir. Sr. Treatment and Edn. Program, Union City, 1994-96; staff psychotherapist North Hudson Cmty. Action Corp. Mental Health Ctr., West New York, 1996-98, dir. mental health, addictive svcs., social work, psychiatry, 1998—. Bd. dirs. Hudson Health Care Partnership, Jersey City; bd. dirs. Hudson County Healthy Families 2000, mem. Hudson County Task Force on Women & Addiction, co-dir. Union City Police Dept./North Hudson Cmty. Action Corp. Domestic Violence Outreach Program, Union City Police Dept. stress reduction cons.; presenter in field. Mem. APA, Am. Counseling Assn., Am. Assn. Family Counselors (cert.), Nat. Assn. Alcohol and Drug Abuse Counselors, Am. Assn. Christian Counselors, Am. Psychotherapy Assn., Alpha Sigma Lambda, Phi Kappa Phi, Psi Chi. Avocations: swimming, walking, reading, writing, poetry. Office: North Hudson Cmty Action Corp Mental Health Addictive Svc 5301 Broadway West New York NJ 07093-2622

SCHMIDT, PARBURY P., JR., chemist; b. Norwalk, Conn., Sept. 4, 1939; s. Parbury Pollen Schmidt and Marguerite Osmun Gail, Maxwell T. Gail (Stepfather); m. Pamela Lois Hottenstein, May 16, 1992; children: Jennifer Ruth, Robin Schmidt Eikenberry, Nicholas Peter. BA, Kalamazoo Coll., Mich., 1961; MA, Wake Forest U., Winston-Salem, NC, 1964; PhD, U. Mich., Ann Arbor, 1966. Postdoc. rsch. fellow U. Coll. London, 1966—67, Australian Nat. U., Canberra, 1967—68; asst. prof. chemistry U. Ga., Athens, 1968—70; prof. chemistry Oakland U., Rochester, Mich., 1970—88; program officer Office Naval Rsch., Arlington, 1988—. Fellow Postdoc. fellowship, US NSF, 1966—68; Fulbright Sr. Rsch. fellowship, Coun. Internat. Exch. Scholars, 1974—75. Mem.: AAAS, Am. Chem. Soc. Achievements include research in exciton theory, electron transfer, reaction rate theory, theory of anharmonic molecular vibrations; patents for method of inhibiting herpetic lesions by the use of platinum coordination compounds, ionization contact potential difference gyroscope.

SCHMIDT, PAUL WICKHAM, lawyer; b. Milw., June 25, 1948; s. Edmund Julian and Barbara (Wickham) S.; m. Cathryn Ann Piehl, June 27, 1970; children: Thomas Wickham, William Piehl, Anna Patchin. BA cum laude, Lawrence U., 1970; JD cum laude, U. Wis., 1973. Bar: Wis. 1973, U.S. Dist. Ct. (we. dist.) Wis. 1973, U.S. Supreme Ct. 1982, D.C. 1988. Atty. advisor Bd. Immigration Appeals, Washington, 1973-76; gen. atty. office of gen. counsel Immigration and Naturalization Service, Washington, 1976-78, acting gen. counsel, 1979-81, 86-87, dep. gen. counsel, 1978-87; assoc. Jones, Day, Reavis & Pogue, Washington, 1987-89, ptnr., 1990-92; mng. ptnr. Fragomen, Del Ray & Bernsen, PC, Washington, 1993-95; chmn. Bd. of Immigration Appeals, Falls Church, Va., 1995-2001, mem., 2001—03; judge Arlington (Va.) Immigration Ct., 2003—. Mem. ABA, D.C. Bar Assn., Wis. Bar Assn., Fed. Bar Assn. (immigration sect.). Avocations: crew volunteer, gardening, camping, history. Home: 711 S View Ter Alexandria VA 22314-4923 Office: Arlington Immigration Ct 901 N Stuart St Ste 1300 Arlington VA 22203 Business E-Mail: paul.schmidt@usdoj.gov.

SCHMIDT, RAYMOND PAUL, military officer, historian, government agency administrator; b. Western, Nebr., Sept. 14, 1937; s. Reuben Edward and Angeline Agnes (Kudlik) Schmidt; m. Roberta Ruth Schrom, June 11, 1961; 1 child, Douglas Craig. B in Edn., History and Social Sci., U. Nebr., Lincoln, 1958; postgrad., U. Md., College Park, 1960-62, The Am. U., Washington, 1975-81; M in History, U. Wis., Madison, 1966. Instr. math. and social sci. Sr. High Sch., Bellevue, Nebr., 1958-59; history instr. James Madison Meml. High Sch., Madison, Wis., 1966-68; ensign USN, 1959, historian, archivist Naval Security Group Command Washington, 1968-81, advanced through grades to capt., 1981, sr. congl. security policy rev. officer, Naval Intelligence Washington, 1981-82, sr. res. forces advisor Dept. Def., 1982-88, head Navy info. security policy, 1988-98, mgr. declassification program, 1998-00; cons., 2000—03; freelance rschr., pub. author, 2001—. Mem. Nat. Disclosure Policy Com. Team, Japan, 1989, Thailand, 89, Germany, 91, leader, Albania, 95. Author (with others): Naval Officers Guide, 1983, And I Was There, 1985; contbr. articles to profl. jours. Pres. North Ashburton Citizens Assn., Bethesda, Md., 1982—; merit badge counselor Boy Scouts Am., 1974—93; info. officer U.S. Naval Acad., Annapolis, Md., 1978—93; spkr. Pearl Harbor Symposium Adm. Nimitz Found., Tex., 1991, symposium moderator, 1992; active Montgomery County Planning Bd. Citizens Adv. Com., Md., 1989—94; ret. pers. adv. coun. Naval Dist. Washington. Named Hon. Adm. Great Navy, State of Nebr., 1983. Mem.: DAV (life), Naval Hist. Found., Lincoln Fellowship Pa., Nat. Cryptologic Mus. Found., U.S. Naval Cryptologic Vets. Assn., Naval Intelligence Profls., Am. Hist. Assn., Nat. Trust Hist. Preservation, Nat. Classification Mgmt. Soc. (editor Viewpoints 1991—96), Nat. Assn. Active and Ret. Fed. Employees, Naval Res. Assn. (life; sec./treas. 1966—68), Mil. Officers Assn. Am. (life), Res. Officers Assn. (life), Nat. Assn. Uniformed Svcs. (life), U.S. Naval Inst. (life; contbr.), Phoenix Soc., Colonial Williamsburg Found., U. Nebr. Alumni Assn. (life), U. Nebr. Found. Pres.'s Club (hon.), History Channel Club (life). Unitarian. Home: 6205 Lone Oak Dr Bethesda MD 20817-1743

SCHMIDT, ROBERT JAMES, JR., lawyer; m. Eva Marie Brault, Dec. 29, 2001; children: Matthew Jerome, Emily Elizabeth, Daniel Robert. BA, U. Va., Charlottesville, 1990; JD, U. Va., 1993; LLM, U. Wash., Seattle, 1995. Bar: Ohio 1993, US Dist. Ct. (no. & so. dists.) Ohio 1998, Ky. 2004. Asst. atty. gen. Ohio Atty. Gen., Columbus, 1996—2000; ptnr. Porter Wright Morris & Arthur, Columbus, Ohio, 2000—. Co-chair environ. law com. Columbus Bar Assn., Ohio, 1998—2000. Bd. mem. Fire Prevention Bd., Worthington, Ohio, 2006—, Worthington Pools, Ohio. Named an Ohio Rising Star, Law & Politics, 2005—07; named one of Best Lawyer in Am., 2006. Office: Porter Wright Morris & Arthur 41 S High St Columbus OH 43215 Office Phone: 614-227-2028. Business E-Mail: rschmidt@porterwright.com.

SCHMIDT, ROBERT MILTON, preventive medicine physician, educator, medical association administrator; b. Milw., May 7, 1944; s. Milton W. and Edith J. (Martinek) S.; children Eric Whitney, Edward Huntington. AB, Northwestern U., 1966; MD, Columbia U., 1970; MPH, Harvard U., 1975; PhD in Law, Medicine and Pub. Policy, Emory U., 1982; MA, San Francisco State U., 1999. Diplomate Am. Bd. Preventive Medicine, Am. Bd. Internal Medicine, Am. Bd. Hematology. Resident in internal medicine Univ. Hosp. U. Calif.-San Diego, 1970-71; resident in preventive medicine Ctr. Disease Control, Atlanta, 1971-74; commd. med. officer USPHS, 1971; advanced through grades to comdr., 1973; dir. hematology div. Nat. Ctr. for Disease Control, Atlanta, 1971-78, spl. asst. to dir., 1978-79, inactive res., 1979—; clin. asst. prof. pediatrics Tufts U. Med. Sch., 1974-86; clin. asst. prof. medicine Emory U. Med. Sch., 1971-81, clin. assoc. prof. community health, 1976-86; clin. assoc. prof. humanities in medicine Morehouse Med. Sch., 1977-79; attending physician dept. medicine Wilcox Meml. Hosp., Lihue, Hawaii, 1979-82, Calif. Pacific Med. Ctr., San Francisco, 1983—; dir. Ctr. Preventive Medicine and Health Rsch., 1983—, dir. Health Watch, 1983—; sr. scientist Inst. Epidemiol. and Behavioral Medicine, Inst. Cancer Rsch., Calif. Pacific Med. Ctr., San Francisco, 1983-88; prof. hematology and gerontology, dir. Ctr. Preventive Medicine and Health Rsch., chair health professions program San Francisco State U., 1983-99, prof. medicine, 1983—, prof. emeritus, Calif. State U. Sys., 1999—; founding dir. Health Watch Internat., 1994—, CEO, pres. Cons. WHO, FDA, Washington, NIH, Bethesda, Md., Govt. of China, Mayo Clinic, Rochester, Minn., Northwestern U., Evanston, Ill., Chgo., U. R.I., Kingston, Pan Am. Health Orgn., Inst. Pub. Health, Italy, Nat. Inst. Aging Rsch. Ctr., Balt., U. Calif., San Diego, U. Ill., Chgo., Columbia U., NYC, Harvard U., Johns Hopkins U., U. Chgo., UCLA, U. Calif. Berkeley, Brown U., Providence, U. Calif., San Francisco, Stanford U., Boston, Emory U., Atlanta, Duke U., NC, U. Tex., Houston, Ariz. State U., U. Hawaii, Honolulu, U. Paris, U. Geneva, U. Munich, Heidelberg U., U. Frankfurt, U. Berlin, Cambridge U., England, U. Singapore, others; vis. rsch. prof. gerontology Ariz. State U., 1989—90; mem. numerous sci. and profl. adv. bd., panels, com. Mem. editorial bd. Am. Jour. Clin. Pathology, 1976-82, The Advisor, 1988—, Generations, 1989—, Contemporary Gerontology, 1994—, Alternative Therapies in Health and Medicine, 1995—, Aging Today, 1997—; book and film reviewer Sci. Books and Films, 1988—, many other jours.; author: 17 books and manuals including Hematology Laboratory Series, 4 vols., 1979-86, CRC Handbook Series in Clinical Laboratory Science, 1976—; assoc. editor: Contemporary Gerontology, 1993—; contbr. more than 400 articles to sci. jours. Alumni regent Columbia U. Coll. Physicians and Surgeons, 1980—. Northwestern U. scholar, 1964-66; NSF fellow, 1964-66; Health Professions scholar, 1966-70; USPHS fellow, 1967-70; Microbiology, Urology, Upjohn Achievement, Borden Rsch. and Virginia Kneeland Frantz scholar awards Columbia U., 1970; recipient Am. Soc. Pharmacol. and Exptl. Therapy award in pharmacology, 1970, Commendation medal USPHS, 1973, Meritorious Performance and Profl. Promise award, 1989, Student Disting. Teaching and Svc. award Pre-Health Professions Student Alliance, 1992, Leadership Recognition awards San Francisco State U., 1984-89, 91-96, Meritorious Svc. award, 1992. Fellow: ACPM, AAAS (med. scis. sect.), ACP (commentator ACP Jour. Club/Annals of Internal Medicine 1993—), Internat. Soc. Hematology, Am. Soc. Clin. Pathology, Am. Coll. Preventive Medicine (sci. com.), Am. Geriat. Soc., Royal Soc. Medicine (London), Gerontol. Soc. Am.; mem.: APHA, AMA, Emory Sch. Pub. Health, Calif. Coun. Gerontology and Geriat., Nat. Assoc. Adv. for Health Professions, Internat. Health Eval. Assn. (v.p. for Ams. 1992—94, bd. dirs. 1992—, pres. 1994—96), Calif. Med. Assn., San Francisco Med. Soc., NY Acad. Sci., Am. Soc. Aging (editl. bd. 1990—, Dychtwald Pub. Speaking award 1991), Am. Soc. Microbiology, Assn. Tchr. Preventive Medicine (edn. com., rsch. com.), Am. Coll. Occupl. and Environ. Medicine, Calif. Coun. Gerontology and Geriat., Am. Assn. Med. Info., Nat. Assn. Advisors for Health Professions (bd. dirs.), Am. Assoc. Blood Banks, Acad. Clin. Lab. Physicians and Scientists, Internat. Soc. Thrombosis and Hemostasis, Am. Soc. Hematology (hon.; emeritus), Internat. Commn. Standardization in Hematology, Am. Assn. Med. Info. (chair prevention and health evaln. informatics WG), Nat. Gallery of Art (Washington), Columbia U. Club No. Calif., Circle Club (Washington), Army and Navy Club, Golden Key (hon. faculty mem.), Harvard Club (NY and San Francisco), Northwestern U. Club. No. Calif., Cosmos Club (mem. art com. 1997—), Knights of Malta, Sigma Xi, Phi Beta Kappa. Home: Whaleship Plaza 25 Hinckley Walk San Francisco CA 94111-2303 Office: Health Watch Med Ctr Calif Pacific Med Ctr San Francisco CA 94120-7999 Home Phone: 415-956-5670; Office Phone: 415-956-5670. Personal E-mail: rmschmidtmd@aol.com.

SCHMIDT, RONALD HANS, architect; b. Hoboken, N.J., Sept. 9, 1938. BArch., Syracuse U., 1961. Sr. designer Skidmore, Owings & Merrill, N.Y.C., 1963-68; ptnr., dir. archtl. design Grad. Partnership, Newark, 1968-81; pres., chief exec. officer Ronald Schmidt & Assocs., P.A., Englewood, N.J., 1981—. Chmn. Bergen County (N.J.) Econ. Devel. Corp.; mem. bd. regents Felician Coll.; mem. exec. com. Network of Opportunity. Recipient numerous awards. Office: 222 Grand Ave Englewood NJ 07631-4352 Office Phone: 201-567-5005. E-mail: rschmidt@RSAaia.com.

SCHMIDT, SHERRIE, library director, dean; BA, Ohio State U., 1970, MLS, 1974. With Ohio State U.; cataloger U. Fla., 1974—75; head user svcs. AMIGOS Bibliog. Coun., 1975—78; assoc. dir. libr. svcs. U. Tex., Dallas, 1979—82; SW US sales rep. Faxon Co., 1982—84; asst. info. sys. planning U. Tex., Austin, 1984—86; asst. dir. collections and bibliog. svcs. Tex. A&M U., 1986—90; assoc. dean libr. svcs. Ariz. State U., 1990—91, dean univ. librs., 1991—. Contbr. articles to profl. jours. Sr. fellow, UCLA, 1989. Mem.: ALA (mem. Office for Info. Tech. Policy Adv. Com. 2002—04). Office: Ariz State U 113 Hayden Libr PO Box 871006 Tempe AZ 85287-1006 Office Phone: 480-965-3956. Office Fax: 480-965-9169. E-mail: sherrie.schmidt@asu.edu.

SCHMIDT, STEFAN, mechanical engineer, economist; b. Darmstadt, Hessen, Germany, 1950; s. Josef and Elisabeth (Urnauer) S.; m. Elizabeth Anne Godwin-Schmidt, 1983; children: Rebecca Elizabeth, Benjamin Stefan Godwin. Diploma mech. engring., Fachhochschule Frankfurt, Germany, 1972; diploma indsl. engring. and mgmt., Technische U. Berlin, Germany, 1980. Profl. mech. engr. Engr. Mech. Engring. Lab., Tokyo, 1973, C & P Telephone Co. of Md., Balt., 1978-79; planning engr. Systemtechnik, Darmstadt, Germany, 1980; rsch. assoc. U. Dortmund, Germany, 1981-84; logistics, strategy, maintenance, quality assurance, and internat. mfg. engr. BMW AG, Munich, 1984—; asst. prof. tech. mgmt. and sustainable devel. U. Applied Sci., Neu Ulm, Germany, 2003—. Lectr. in field; mgmt. trainer Centre of Technol. Cooperation, Berlin, 1985—; seminar presenter C. of C., Passau and Munich, Germany, 1986—, Sabel Bus. Sch., 2000—, REFA/VDI, 2001, others. Contbr. articles to profl. jours.; pub. bus. books, 1994—. Econ. commentator Internat. Newspapers and Jours., Frankfurt, Munich, Berlin, 1990—. Recipient 1st prize Precision Instrument Maker, 1969. Fellow Verein Deutscher Wirt. ing. Home: Fritzstrasse 41 D-82140 Olching Bayern Germany Office: BMW AG D-80788 Munich Germany E-mail: stefan.sb.schmidt@bmw.de, stefan.schmidt-1@t-online.de.

SCHMIDT, STEVE (STEPHEN E. SCHMIDT), public relations executive; b. North Plainfield, NJ, 1970; m. Angela Schmidt; children: Madigan, Joseph. Attended, U. Del., Newark, 1988—93. Comm. dir. Matt Fong Senate Campaign, Calif., 1998; sr. staff mem., dep. asst. to Pres. George W. Bush The White House, Washington, spokesman, counselor to Vice Pres. Dick Cheney; media rels. cons. to Amb. Zalmay Khalilzad US Dept. State, Baghdad, Iraq; chief nomination strategist Justice Samuel A. Alito. and Chief Justice John Roberts; comm. dir. Nat. Republican Congl. Com., Washington, 2002; sr. campaign strategist Pres. George W. Bush's Re-Election Campaign, 2004; campaign mgr. Gov. Arnold Swartzenegger's Re-Election Campaign, Calif., 2006; ptnr. Mercury Pub. Affairs, Sacramento; campaign strategist, sr. advisor Senator John McCain's Presdl. Campaign, Arlington, Va., 2007—08. Republican. Office: Mercury Pub Affairs 1801 L St Ste 239 Sacramento CA 95814 Office Phone: 916-444-1380. Office Fax: 916-265-1869. Business E-Mail: sschmidt@mercuryllc.com.*

SCHMIDT, STEVEN JAMESON, library director; b. Indpls., Apr. 1, 1953; s. Lorenz Oscar Schmidt and Eleanor A. Stickney; m. Paula L. O'Maley; children: Carrie, Michael, Thomas. BA, Butler U., Indpls., 1975; MLS, Ind. U., Bloomington, 1983. Acess svcs. libr. IUPUI U. Libr., Indpls., 1983—2004; acting Herron Sch. Art Libr., Indpls., dir., 2003—04, U. Libr. Columbus, Ind., 2004—08. Author: (children's play) Purchase of Happiness (Bicentenial Playwrighting competition, 1976). Mem. Indpls. Cologne Sister Cities, Indpls., 2005—09; webmaster Ind. German Heritage Soc., Indpls., 2005—09. Fellow, Max Kade Ctr., 2005. Mem.: Ind. German Am. Soc. (editor 2007—09). Avocations: writing, photography, cooking. Office: Univ Libr Columbus 4555 Ctrl LC 1600 Columbus IN 47203 Office Fax: 812-314-8722. Business E-Mail: schmidt@iupuc.edu.

SCHMIDT, SUSAN, journalist; m. Glen Nishimura; 2 children. BA, Mary Baldwin Coll., 1975. News asst. Washington Star; reporter Herald Examiner, LA, Patriot Ledger, Quincy, Mass.; metro desk editor to bus. news reporter Washington Post, 1983—92, nat. news desk reporter, 1992—. Co-author: Truth at Any Cost, 2000. Recipient Pulitzer Prize for investigative reporting, 2006, Seldon Ring award, 2006, Worth Bingham prize, 2006; co-recipient Pulitzer Prize for nat. reporting, 2002. Office: Washington Post Nat News Desk 1150 15th St NW Washington DC 20071-0070 Office Phone: 202-334-6157. Office Fax: 202-496-3883. Business E-Mail: schmidts@washpost.com.

SCHMIDT, THOMAS CHARLES, biomedical engineer, researcher; b. Jersey City, Feb. 21, 1947; s. Ernest J. and Shirley J. Schmidt; m. Marilyn I. Karcheski, Aug. 3, 1968; 1 child, Thomas M. B in Engring., Stevens Inst. Tech., 1968, M in Engring., 1973. Registered profl. engr., Fla., Calif. Vis. lectr. physiol. psychology Stevens Inst. of Tech., Hoboken, NJ, 1974—76; engr. Perry Techs., Riviera Beach, Fla., 1976—80; sr. rsch. engr., rsch. specialist, staff engr., sr. staff engr. Lockheed-Martin, San Diego, 1980—, Riviera Beach, Fla. Participant NASA Med-Ops. Task Group (Clin. Care Capability Project), Houston, 2000; chair ASME PVHO design sub-com., 2003—. Contbr. The Underwater Handbook: A Guide to Physiology and Performance for the Engineer, 1976, articles to profl. jours.; patentee in field. Dir., pub. safety chair Clairemont Town Coun., San Diego, 1997—2008; chair Balboa Ave. Citizens Adv. Com., San Diego, 1999—2003, Healty Cmtys. & Lifestyles Initiative, County Health & Human Svcs., 2005—08; mem. Cmty. Engagement Action Forum County Health and Human Svcs., San Diego, 1999—2008, participant strategic planning process, 1999—2003; mem. Clairemont-Mesa Planning Com., San Diego, 2000—08. Recipient cert. of appreciation, State of Calif. (78th Assembly Dist.), 1999, cert. of recognition, 2000, 2001, State of Calif. (76th Assembly Dist.), 2003, 2004, spl. commendation, City of San Diego (6th Dist. Councilmember), 1998, 1999, cert. of appreciation, County of San Diego (3rd Dist. Supr.), 1999, County of San Diego (Asst Dir. Health and Human Svcs.), 2000, spl. commendation, City of San Diego (6th Dist. Councilmember), 2000, 2001, 2002, 2004, Cmty. Svc. award, City of San Diego (Dir. of Planning), 2001, 2002, commendation, Gov. of Calif., 2003, spl. commendation, City of San Diego (6th Dist. Councilmember), 2004, cert. of recognition, U. S. Congress (Calif. 50th Dist.), 2004, cert. of appreciation, ASME (Codes and Standards), 2004, cert. of aclamation, 2008. Mem.: ASME (ASME safety code com. - pressure vessels for human occupancy 1987—, chair PVHO design sub-com. 2003—), Calif. Environ. Health Assn. (exec. bd. S.W. chpt. 2000—), Undersea and Hyperbaric Med. Soc. (safety com. 1981—, submarine medicine com.

1984—). Home: 5953 Castleton Dr San Diego CA 92117 Office: Lockheed Martin MS2 100 E 17th St Riviera Beach FL 33404 Office Phone: 561-494-2064. E-mail: thomas.c.schmidt@lmco.com.

SCHMIDT, TORRANCE, horticulturist; MS in Horticulture, Wash. State U., Pullman. Rsch. assoc. WA Tree Fruit Rsch. Comm., Wenatchee, 1998—. Contbr. articles to profl. jours. (Hedrick award, Am. Pomological Soc., 2007). Student leadership sr. counselor Assn. Wash. Sch. Prins., Olympia, 1994—. Mem.: Wash. State Hort. Assn. Achievements include research in crop load management of deciduous tree fruits.

SCHMIDT, VICTOR HUGO, physics professor, researcher; b. Portland, Oreg., July 10, 1930; s. Hugo Andrew Paul and Marie Minna Henrietta (Neils) S.; m. Shirley Ann Schmidt, Sept. 13, 1958; children: Harold Jay, Lawrence Otto, Marie Denise, Gloria Mae. BSME, Wash. State U., 1951; PhD in Physics, U. Wash., 1961. Mech. design engr. Gilfillan Bros., Inc., LA, 1953-54; assoc. rsch. engr. Boeing Airplane Co., Seattle, 1955-57; asst. prof. physics Valparaiso (Ind.) U., 1961-64; assoc. prof. physics Mont. State U., Bozeman, 1964-73, prof. physics, 1973—. Mem. editl. bd. Ferroelectrics, 1997—; author: (with others) Hydrogen Bond, 1976. 1st lt. USAF, 1951—53. Grantee NSF, 1961—, Dept. Energy, 1972—, NASA, 1994—, Dept. Def., 1999— Fellow Am. Phys. Soc.; mem. IEEE (sr.), Am. Assn. Physics Tchrs., Sigma Xi. Achievements include patents for piezoelectric wind generator and pulse modified camera; explained dielectric and conductive behavior in ferroelectric (FE) KH2PO4 and discovered its tricritical point; demonstrated that LiN2H5SO4 is not FE; found antiferroelectric (AFE) phase at high pressure in tris-sarcosine calcium chloride; discovered coexistence of FE and AFE phases with paraelectric phase in proton glass; invented a piezoelectric polymer actuator. Office: Mont State U Dept Physics 264 Eps Bldg Bozeman MT 59717-0001 Home: 1429 Cherry Dr Bozeman MT 59715-5916

SCHMIDT, WILLIAM ARTHUR, JR., lawyer; s. William and Caroline (Jäger) S.; m. Gerilyn Smith, Sept. 30, 1967; children: Deborah, Dawn, Jennifer. BSBA, Kent State U., 1962; JD, Cleve. State U., 1968. Bar: Ohio 1968, Ill. 1990. Contract specialist NASA-Lewis, Cleve., 1962-66, procurement analyst, 1967-68; atty. Def. Logistics Agy., Alexandria, Va., 1968-73; assoc. counsel Naval Sea Sys. Command, Arlington, Va., 1973-75; procurement policy analyst Energy R & D Adminstrn., Germantown, Md., 1975-76; sr. atty. U.S. Dept. Energy, Germantown, 1976-78, counsel spl. projects Oak Ridge, Tenn., 1978-83; judge Agr. Bd. Contract Appeals, Wash., 1983-87; judge Bd. Contract Appeals HUD, Wash., 1987; chief legal counsel Fermilab, Batavia, Ill., 1987-92; gen. counsel Univ. Rsch. Assn., Inc., Wash., 1992—, Fermi Rsch. Alliance, Wash., 2007—. Co-author: (NASA handbook) R & D Business Practices, 1968. Founder/dir. DOE Contractor Attys. Assn.; dir. Spotsylvania Crime Solvers. Mem. ABA, Fed. Bar Assn. (past pres. East Tenn. 1978-83, 25 Yr. Svc. award 1994), Ill. Bar Assn., Bd. Contract Appeals Judges Assn. (dir.-sec. 1986-88), Sr. Execs. Assn., Delta Theta Phi (dist. chancellor 1978-83), Sigma Chi. Republican. Lutheran. Avocation: classic cars. Home: 10611 King Elder Ct Spotsylvania VA 22553-3666 Office: Fermi Rsch Alliance 1111 19th St NW Ste 400 Washington DC 20036-3627 Business E-Mail: wschmidt@ura.nw.dc.us.

SCHMIDT, WILLIAM C., retired chemicals executive; b. Niles, Mich., Sept. 27, 1938; s. Felix A. and Anna (Reifschneider) S.; m. Bethany Ann Boyd, Dec. 17, 1966; 1 child, Craig W. BBA, U. Mich., 1960, MBA, 1961. Cert. Mgmt. Acct. Various acctg. positions Dow Chem. Co., Midland, Mich., 1961-73; controller Dow Chem. Pacific Ltd., Hong Kong, 1973-78; area controller Dow Chem. Co., Midland, Mich., 1978-82, asst. corp. controller, 1982-98; v.p., chief fin. officer DowElanco, Indpls., 1989-98; chmn. bd. Wolverine Bank, F.S.B., 2004—09. Bd. dirs. Midland Hosp., 1982-89, 98-2007, chmn. bd., 1986-88, 2004-06; bd. dirs. Mid-Mich. Health Corp., 1983-89, 2001—, chmn. bd., 1986-88; treas., bd. dirs. Indpls. Symphony Orch., 1992-98; dir. West Midland Family Ctr., 2000—06; mem., vice chmn. Midland County Bldg. Authority, 2003—. Cpl. U.S. Army, 1962-64. Mem. Inst. Mgmt. Accts., Inst. Cert. Mgmt. Accts. (regent 1985-89), Am. Indsl. Health Coun. (treas. 1986-87), Ind. C. of C. (bd. dirs. 1992-98). Presbyterian. Home: 5908 Londonberrie Ct Midland MI 48640-6965

SCHMIDT, WILLIAM E., editor; b. Detroit, Mar. 15, 1947; s. E. F. and Irene E Schmidt; m. Margo Jean Doble, Nov. 4, 1972 (div. 2005); children: Jordan Alison, Lindsay Ella, Peter William. BA, U. Mich., Ann Arbor, 1967. Reporter Detroit Free Press, 1968—73; bur. chief Newsweek, Miami, Fla., 1975—76, Cairo, 1976—79, Moscow, 1979—81, corr. Chgo, 1973—75; bur. chief NY Times, Denver, 1981—83, Atlanta, 1983—87, Chgo., 1987—91, corr. London, 1991—95, dep. nat. editor NYC, 1995—97, assoc. mng. editor, 1997—2005, asst. mng. editor, 2005—08, dep. mng. editor, 2008—. Bd. dirs. Maynard Inst. Journalism Edn., Oakland, Calif., 2005—. With USAR, 1968—74. Recipient Pulitzer Prize in Nat. Reporting, Columbia U., 1988; co-recipient George Polk award for Nat. Reporting, L.I. U., 1971, Mag. Reporting award, Overseas Press Club, 1976. Mem.: Am. Corr., American Soc. of Newspaper Editors, Assn. Am. Correspondents in London (pres. 1993—94). Lutheran. Office: NY Times 620 Eighth Ave New York NY 10018 Office Fax: 646-428-6230. Business E-Mail: schmidt@nytimes.com.*

SCHMIDT, WILLIAM MAX, management consultant, marketing and business development executive; b. Danville, Pa., Nov. 23, 1947; s. Frank Wilhelm and Doris Savilla (Maurer) S.; m. Marylea O'Reilly, Sept. 20, 1980. BS, U. Pa., 1969; MBA, Northwestern U., 1971. Mktg. specialist Moody's Investors Svc., Inc., NYC, 1971-72; cons. William E. Hill & Co. Inc., NYC, 1972-74; product supr. Internat. Paper Co., NYC, 1974-79; dir. market analysis U.S. Industries, Inc., Stamford, Conn., 1979-82, mgr. corp. devel., 1982-84; dir. corp. mktg. Combustion Engring., Inc., Stamford, Conn., 1984-86, v.p. mktg., planning Union, NJ, 1986-91; pres. Pragmatics, Basking Ridge, NJ, 1991—2000, 2003—; dir. global mktg. Gemplus Internat., Montgomeryville, Pa., 2000—03. Author (newsletter): Think Again, 1995. Bd. dirs., pres. Curbing Hunger, Inc., Basking Ridge, NJ, 1995—; adv. Jr. Achievement, NYC, 1976-78; mem. governing body St. Mark's Episcopal Ch. Mem. TAPPI, Exec. Forum, Strategic Leadership Forum, Univ. Club, Sons of the Revolution, Wharton Club (N.Y.C.), Sigma Chi. Republican. Mem. United Ch. of Christ. Avocations: tennis, astronomy, canoeing, community service, coin collecting/numismatics. Office: Pragmatics 46 Quincy Rd Basking Ridge NJ 07920 Office Phone: 908-580-1259. Personal E-mail: billprag@optonline.net.

SCHMIDT-HOLTZ, ROLF, music company executive; b. Martinsreuth, Germany, Aug. 31, 1948; 2 children. Degree in Law, Polit. Sci., Psychology, U. Erlangen, U. Kiel, 1973; JD, U. Kiel, 1976. Paralegal, 1973-76; asst. prof. law U. Kiel, 1976; svc. chief Federal Press Office, 1977-80; contbr. West Deutscher Rundfunk, 1980-84; editor Tagesschau und Tagesthemen, 1980-84; TV corr. ARD Studio Bonn, WDR, 1981-84; dir. Federal Press Conf., Bonn, 1984-86; mgr. dirs. bur. info. and publicity Bertelsmann AG, Gütersloh, 1985-86; editor in chief TV program listings WDR, 1986-88; editor Der Stern Mag., Gruner & Jahr AG & Co., 1988—, Hamburger Morgenpost, Gruner & Jahr AG & Co., 1989-90; bus. dir. Gruner & Jahr Zeitschriften TV GmbH, 1990—; editor in chief Der Stern Mag., Gruner & Jahr AG & Co., 1990-94; head TV and Film Europe divsn. Bertelsmann AG, 1994—97; CEO, CLT-Ufa Luxembourg, 1997—2000; chief creative officer, mem. exec. bd. Bertelsmann AG, 2000—; chmn., pres., CEO BMG Entertainment, New York, 2001—04; chmn. Sony BMG Music Entertainment, 2004—06, CEO, 2006—; mem. supervisory bd. Gruner & Jahr AG & Co., 2000—, RTL Group, 2002—. Office: Sony BMG Music Entertainment 550 Madison Ave New York NY 10022*

SCHMIDTKE, SUZANNE DE FINE, retired social worker; d. Poul and Else de Fine Lassen; m. Edwin (Ned) C. Schmidtke, June 7, 1964; children: Peter Christian, Elizabeth de Fine Knudsen. MSW, U. Ill., Chgo., 1980. Cert. social worker NASW, 1982, diplomate NASW, 1988, Am. Bd. Examiners in Clin. Social Work, 1988, LCSW Ill. Dept. Profl. Regulation, 1989. Social worker Madden Mental Health Ctr., Ill. Dept. Mental Health, Hines, 1980—84, Ill. State Psychiat. Inst., Chgo., 1984—87, social worker adminstr., 1987—94; mgr., rsch. patient recruitment dept. psychiatry U. Ill., Chgo., 1994—2004; ret., 2004. Adj. instr., art therapy Sch. Art Inst. Chgo., 1989—93; social work field instr. Jane Addams Coll. Social Work, U. Ill., Chgo., 1992—2004. Bd. mem. Nat. Alliance on Mental Illness, Chgo., 1996—2003, pres. Springfield, 2001—03, family-to-family tchr. Ill.; pres. Nat. Alliance on Mental Illness San Fernando Valley, 2009—. Recipient Vol. of Yr., Nat. Alliance on Mental Illness, 2000. Avocations: theater, hiking, travel, films. Personal E-mail: suzned@sbcglobal.net.

SCHMIDT-NIELSEN, BODIL MIMI (MRS. ROGER G. CHAGNON), retired physiologist, educator; b. Copenhagen, Nov. 3, 1918; came to U.S., 1946, naturalized, 1952; d. August and Marie Jorgensen Krogh; m. Knut Schmidt-Nielsen, Sept. 20, 1939 (div. Feb. 1966); children: Astrid, Bent, Bodil; m. Roger G. Chagnon, Oct. 1968 (dec. 2003). DDS, U. Copenhagen, 1941, DOdont, 1946, DPhil, 1955; DS (hon.), Bates Coll., 1983; MD (hon.), U. Aarhus, Denmark, 1997. Mem. faculty Duke U., Durham, NC, 1952-64; prof. biology Case Western Res. U., Cleve., 1964-71, chmn. dept., 1970-71, adj. prof., 1971-74; trustee Mt. Desert Island Biol. Lab., Maine, rsch. scientist Maine, 1971-86, exec. com. Maine, 1978-85, v.p. Maine, 1979-81, pres. Maine, 1981-85; prof. dept. physiology U. Fla., Gainesville, 1985—. Adj. prof. Brown U., Providence, 1971-75, dept. physiol. U. Fla., Gainesville, 1986—; mem. tng. grant com. NIGMS, 1965-71. Author: August and Marie Krogh, Lives in Science, 1995, Danish edit., 1997; editor: Urea and the Kidney, 1970; assoc. editor Am. Jour. Physiology: Regulatory, Integrative and Comparative Physiology, 1978-81. Trustee Coll. of Atlantic, Bar Harbor, Maine, 1972-92. Recipient Career award NIH, 1962-64, John Simon Guggenheim Meml. fellow, 1952-53; Bowditch lectr., 1958, Jacobaeus lectr., 1974. Fellow AAAS (del. coun. 1977-79), NY Acad. Scis., Am. Acad. Arts and Scis.; mem. Am. Physiol. Soc. (coun. 1971-77, pres. 1975-76, Ray G. Daggs award 1989, Orr Reynolds award 1994, August Knogh lectr. 1994, Berliner award 1998), Soc. Exptl. Biology and Medicine (coun. 1967-71). Achievements include research, publications on biochemistry of saliva, water metabolism of desert animals, urea excretion, peristalsis of renal pelvis and concentrating mechanism, comparative kidney physiology, comparative physiology of excretory organs. Office: U Fla Dept Physiology 2015 SW 16th Ave Gainesville FL 32605 Business E-Mail: bodil@gator.net.

SCHMIEG, STEVEN JEFFREY, research and development company executive, researcher; s. Clinton Schmieg, Patricia Ann Schmieg (Stepmother); m. Heather June Hampson, Oct. 26, 1985; children: Lauren Nicole, Rachel Elaine. BS in Chemistry and Math., Adrian Coll., Mich., 1979; MBA, Oakland U., Rochester, Mich., 1985. Staff rschr. Gen. Motors R & D Ctr., Warren, Mich., 1979—. Contbr. articles to sci. publs. Recipient Charles L. McCuen Spl. Achievement award, Gen. Motors R & D Ctr., 2000. Mem.: Sigma Xi, Mich. Catalysis Soc. (sec.-treas. 2008, v.p. 2009), Catalysis Soc. (treas., 22nd North Am. Meeting), Soc. Automotive Engrs. Home: 2423 Terova Dr Troy MI 48085-3560 Office: Gen Motors R & D Ctr 30500 Mound Rd Mail Code 480-106-185 Warren MI 48090-9055 Office Fax: 586-986-8697; Home Fax: 509-357-7114. Personal E-mail: sjschmieg@aol.com. Business E-Mail: steven.j.schmieg@gm.com.

SCHMIT, LUCIEN ANDRÉ, JR., retired structural engineer; b. NYC, May 5, 1928; s. Lucien Alexander and Eleanor Jessie (Donley) S.; m. Eleanor Constance Trabish, June 24, 1951; 1 son, Lucien Alexander, III. BS, MIT, 1949, MS, 1950. Structures engr. Grumman Aircraft Co., Bethpage, NY, 1951-53; rsch. engr., aeroelastic and structures lab. MIT, 1954-58; asst. prof. engring. Case Inst. Tech., 1958-60, assoc. prof., 1961-63, prof., 1964-70; prof. engring. and applied sci. UCLA, 1970-91, Rockwell prof. aerospace engring. emeritus, 1991—; ret., 1991. Sci. adv. bd. USAF, 1977-84. Contbr. articles on analysis and synthesis of structural systems, finite elements methods, design of fiber composite components and multidisciplinary design optimization to profl. jours. Fellow AIAA (Design Lecture award 1977, Structures, Structural Dynamics and Materials award 1979, Multidisciplinary Design Optimization award 1994, Walter J. and Angeline H. Crichlow Trust prize 1999), ASCE, Am. Acad. Mechanics; mem. NAE. Home: 545 3rd Ave S Edmonds WA 98020-4103 Home Phone: 425-776-8110. Personal E-mail: schmit13@comcast.net.

SCHMIT, TIMOTHY BRUCE, musician; b. Oakland, Calif., Oct. 30, 1947; Band mem. Tim, Tom & Ron, the Contenders, New Breed, Glad, Poco, 1970—77, The Eagles, 1977—. Performed on albums with various artists including Warren Zevon, Robert Lamm, Dwight Yoakam, Ringo Starr, Tim McGraw, Jeff Larson, Dan Fogelberg, Elton John, The Wilsons, Don Henley, Beach Boys, Vince Gill, Eddie Money, Poison and many others. Musician: (albums) (solo) Playing it Cool, 1984, Timothy B., 1987, Tell Me the Truth, 1990, Feed the Fire, 2001, (with Poco) Poco, 1971, Deliverin', 1971, From the Inside, 1971, Good Feelin' to Know, 1972, Crazy Eyes, 1973, Cantamos, 1974, Seven, 1974, Head Over Heels, 1975, Very Best of Poco, 1975, Rose of Cimarron, 1976, Live, 1976, Indian Summer, 1977, Song of Richie Furay, 1979, Songs of Paul Cotton, 1979, Inamorato, 1984, Crazy Loving: The Best of Poco..., 1989, Forgotten Trail (1969-1974), 1990, (with The Eagles) Long Run, 1979, Eagles Live, 1980, Eagles Greatest Hits, Vol. 2, 1982, Hell Freezes Over, 1994, The Very Best of the Eagles, 1994, Selected Works: 1972-79, 2000, The Very Best of the Eagles, 2001, 2003, Long Road Out of Eden, 2007, (songs) How Long, 2007 (Grammy award for Best Group Vocal Country Performance, 2008), I Dreamed There Was No War, 2007 (Grammy award for Best Pop Instrumental Performance, 2009). Named to with The Eagles, Rock and Roll Hall of Fame, 1998. Office: c/o William Morris Agency 1325 Ave of the Americas New York NY 10019*

SCHMITT, BARTON DOUGLAS, pediatrician, educator; b. Chgo. Heights, Ill., 1937; married; 4 children. MD, Cornell U., Ithica, NY, 1963. Cert. in pediat. Am. Bd. Med. Specialties, 1968. Intern Minn. Hosps., 1963—64, resident, 1964—66; fellow Colo. Gen. Hosp., Denver, 1968—69; med. dir. after-hours call ctr. The Children's Hosp., Denver, 1988—; pediatrician, prof. pediat. U. Colo. Sch. Medicine, Denver. Author: The Child Protection Team Handbook, 1977, Guidelines for the Hospital and Clinic: Management of Child Abuse and Neglect, 1979, Your Child's Health, 1987, Your Child's Health: The Parents' Guide to Symptoms, Emergencies, Common Illnesses, Behavior, and School Problems, 1991, Instructions for Pediatric Patients, 1992, 1998, Pediatric Telephone Advice, 2004, Your Child's Health: The Parents' One-Stop Reference Guide, 2005, Pediatric Telephone Protocols, 2006, (computer software program) The Pediatric Advisor. Recipient Child Devel. award, Am. Acad. Pediat., 1994, Edn. award, 2004. Achievements include first to write computerized protocols for pediatric triage, 1994. Office: The Childrens Hospital 13123 E 16th Ave Aurora CO 80045-7106 Office Phone: 720-777-6179. Business E-Mail: Barton.Schmitt@uchsc.edu.

SCHMITT, BERNARD WILLIAM, bishop emeritus; b. Wheeling, W.Va., Aug. 17, 1928; Ordained priest Diocese of Wheeling-Charleston, W.Va., 1955; ordained bishop, 1988; aux. bishop Diocese of Wheeling-Charleston, 1988—89, bishop, 1989—2004, bishop emeritus, 2004—. Roman Catholic. Office: Chancery Office Box 230 1300 Byron St Wheeling WV 26003-3315 Office Phone: 304-233-0880. Office Fax: 304-233-0890.

SCHMITT, GEORGE FREDERICK, JR., materials engineer; b. Louisville, Nov. 3, 1939; s. George Frederick and Jane Limbird (Hurst) S.; m. Ann Cheatham, July 31, 1965; 2 children. BS, U. Louisville, 1962, MS, 1963; MBA, Ohio State U., 1966. Advanced engring devel. mgr. USAF Materials Lab., Wright Patterson AFB, Ohio, 1986-90, chief plans and programs br. Wright AFB, Ohio, 1989-90, asst. chief nonmetallic materials divsn., 1990-96, chief integration and ops. divsn., 1997—2005; dir. internat. programs Air Force Rsch. Lab. USAF Materials Directorate, Wright Patterson AFB, Ohio, 1966—. Guest lectr. U. Dayton, 1970, 95, Cath. U., 1973, U. Mich., 1975. Contbr. articles to profl. jours. Mem. Kettering (Ohio) Civic Band, 1965—, Affiliate Socs. Coun. Dayton, 1972-81; mem. Dayton Philharm Chorus, 1999—, Dayton Letter Carriers Band, 2000—, Windjammers Circus Music Preservation Soc., 2001—. 1st lt. USAF, 1963-66. Recipient Meritorious Civilian Svc. award, USAF, 1994, Burton award, Playhouse South Cmty. Theater, 1998, Tech. Transfer award, Fed. Lab. Consortium, 2001, Internat. Program Supr. award, USAF, 2002, Internat. Program Non-Supr. award, 2007, Internat. award, USAF Materiel Command, 2006; named Fed. Profl. Employee of Yr., Dayton, 1972; named one of Ten Outstanding Engrs., Engrs. Week, 1975. Fellow Soc. for Advancement Materials and Process Engrs. (Best Paper award 1973, nat. sec. 1975-76, nat. membership chmn. 1977-79, nat. v.p. 1979-81, nat pres. 1981-82, chmn. long-range planning com. 1983-87, trustee 1991—, chmn. Internat. SAMPE Symposium 1996, chmn. SAMPE Trophy com. 1998-2004, chmn. internat. conf., 2003, adminstr. Fellows program 1997-2007), AIAA (assoc., materials tech. com.); mem. ASTM (rec. sec. 72-75, chmn. com. on erosion and wear 1976-79, chmn. liaison subcom. 1979-83, award of merit 1981), Am. Chem. Soc., Affiliate Socs. Coun. Dayton (chmn. 1978-79). Republican. Lutheran. Home: 1500 Wardmier Dr Dayton OH 45459-3354 Office: AFRL Materials and Mfg Directorate RXO Wright-Patterson AFB 2977 Hobson Way Bldg 653 Dayton OH 45433-7733 Office Phone: 937-656-9209. Business E-Mail: george.schmitt@wpafb.af.mil.

SCHMITT, KARL MICHAEL, retired political scientist; b. Louisville, July 22, 1922; s. Edward Peter and Mary Ann (Iula) S.; m. Grace Bernadette Leary, June 18, 1949; children: Karl, Edward, Barbara, William, Michael. BA, Cath. U. Am., 1947, MA, 1949; PhD, U. Pa., 1954. Teaching asst. U. Pa., 1948-50; instr. history Niagara U., 1950-54, asst. prof., 1954-55; research analyst U.S. Dept. State, 1955-58; asst. prof. dept. govt. U. Tex., 1958-63, assoc. prof., 1963-66, prof., 1966-91, prof. emeritus, 1991—, chmn., 1975-80. Vis. prof. U. Calif., LA, 1959, Nat. War Coll., 1970-71; vis. sr. fellow U. Manchester, Eng., 1988-89; cons. Dept. of State, 1962-70 Author: Communism in Mexico; A Study in Political Frustration, 1965, Mexico and the United States, 1821-1973: Conflict and Coexistence, 1974, others. Contbr. articles to profl. jours. With US Army, 1943—45. Decorated Purple Heart. Mem. Tex. Cath. Hist. Assn. (pres. 1976-77). Roman Catholic. Home: 2603 Pinewood Ter Austin TX 78757-2136

SCHMITT, MARK FRANCIS, bishop emeritus; b. Algoma, Wis., Feb. 14, 1923; Student, Salvatorian Sem., St. Nazianz, Wis., St. John's Sem., Collegeville, Minn. Ordained priest Diocese of Green Bay, Wis., 1948, aux. bishop, 1070—1978; ordained bishop, 1970; bishop Diocese of Marquette, Mich., 1978—92, bishop emeritus, 1992—. Roman Catholic. Office: Chancery Office 444 S 4th St PO Box 550 Marquette MI 49855-0550 Office Phone: 906-225-1141.

SCHMITT, NATALIE CROHN, theater educator; b. Chgo., Aug. 10, 1936; d. Nathan N. and Lera Christina C. BA, U. Chgo., 1958, MA, 1961; PhD, Stanford U., 1968. Asst. prof. U. Ill., Chgo., 1968-72, assoc. prof. theatre, 1972-88, prof. theatre, 1988-99, prof. English, 1992-99, prof. emeritus, 1999—. Dir. theatre Brown U., Providence, 1961-63, U. Ill., 1968-98; founder Looking Glass Theater, Providence, 1962, dir., 1962-65; vis. assoc. prof. Stanford (Calif.) U., 1985. Author: Actors and Onlookers, 1990; contbr. articles to profl. jours. Sr. fellow Humanities Inst., U. Ill., 1983, NEH, 1984, 1996-97, assoc. fellow Stanford U., 1996-97. Mem.: Assn. Theatre Higher Edn. (chair theatre rsch. project 1973—74, dir. project, regional advisor 1975—78, conf. planner 1992), Assn. Soc. Theatre Rsch. (exec. com. 1999—2002, fin. com. 2000—02, treas. 2001—02). Avocation: ballet. Office: Univ Ill English Dept 601 S Morgan M/C 162 Chicago IL 60607 Business E-Mail: nschmitt@uic.edu.

SCHMITT, PATRICIA ANN, health and physical education educator; b. Crystal City, Tex., July 19, 1938; d. Joseph Frances and Clara Constance (Conring) S. BS, Tex. A&I U., 1960; MA, Tex. Woman's U., 1965, PhD, 1974. Tchr. Driscoll Jr. High Sch., Corpus Christi Ind. Sch. Dist., Tex., 1960-62, Mary Carroll High Sch., Corpus Christi, 1962-65; prof. Del Mar Coll., Corpus Christi, 1965-99, ret. 1999; waterfront dir. Heart o' the Hills Camp, Kerrville, Tex., 1960-63, 66-71. Water safety instr. trainer ARC, Nueces County, 1970—; chmn. pastor parish rels. com. Wesley United Methodist, Ch. Coun.Chair Corpus Christi, 1981-83, 1996-1998, 2001-09, Named Woman of Yr. in Edn., YWCA, 1984; recipient Disting. Service award Tex. Assn. Intercollegiate Athletics for Women, 1981, Honor award Tex. AHPERD, 1999. Mem. Tex. Assn. for Health, Phys. Edn., Recreation and Dance (life, chmn. coll. adminstrs. sect. 1981), Tex. Volleyball Ofcls. Assn. (dist. dir. 1977-83, ofcl.). Avocations: walking, gardening, travel, golf. Home: 5005 Maylands Dr Corpus Christi TX 78413-3620

SCHMITT, RICHARD, philosopher, educator; b. Frankfurt/Main, Ger., May 5, 1927; came to U.S., 1946, naturalized, 1952; s. Julius and Elisabeth Dorothea S. BA, U. Chgo., 1949, MA, 1952; PhD, Yale U., 1956. Instr. philosophy Yale U., 1956-58; mem. faculty Brown U., 1958—2001, prof. philosophy, 1968—2001, emeritus prof. philosophy, 2001—. Vis. prof. Stanford U., 1966-67, U. Calif., Santa Barbara, 1971-72, Miles Coll., summer 1964, U. Mass., Boston, 1974; adj. prof. Worcester State Coll., 2001-. Author: Martin Heidegger on Being Human, 1967, Alienation and Class, 1983, Introduction to Marx and

Engels: A Critical Reconstruction, 1987, Beyond Separateness: The Relational Nature of Human Beings, Their Autonomy, Knowledge, and Power, 1995, Alienation and Freedom, 2002, Alienacíon y Libertad, 2004; co-editor (with Anatol Anton) Toward a New Socialism, 2007, Introduction to Social and Political Philosophy, 2009; contbr. articles on phenomenology and existentialism Marxist theory. Alfred Hodder fellow, 1963-64; Guggenheim fellow, 1965-66 Mem. Am. Philos. Assn. Office: Worcester State Coll Philosophy Sullivan Hall Worcester MA 01602 E-mail: rschmitt@worcester.edu.

SCHMITT, ROBERT LEE, computer scientist; b. Astoria, NY, Oct. 1, 1948; s. Edward and Margaret Louise (Gleason) S.; m. Elsy Evagelene Burnett, June 1999; stepchildren: Eric Jason Marin, Alexis Michelle Marin. AAS in Data Processing, SUNY, Farmingdale, 1972; student, Hofstra U., 1972-73; BS in Computer Sci., SUNY, Stony Brook, 1974, MS in Computer Sci., 1975; postgrad., U. Md., 1979-80, 94-96; grad. diploma in strategic sci., U.S. Naval War Coll., 1991. Cert. computer programmer, data processor. Computer programmer U.S. Army Environ. Hygiene Agy., Aberdeen Proving Ground, Md., 1976; data sys. programmer Dept. Def., Ft. George G. Meade, Md., 1976—78, data sys. analyst, 1978—83, computer sys. analyst, 1983—85, sr. computer sys. analyst, 1985—86, computer scientist, 1986—89, mgr. sys. acquisition, 1989—94, dep. dir. for tech. fellow, 1994—95, sr. computer scientist, 1995—96, stds., tng. and verification engr., 1996—97, sys. engr., 1997—99, mgr. yr. 2000 compliance, 1999, sys. arch. implementation engr., 2000—01, sys. engr., 2001—02, dep. chief engring. divsn., 2002—03, acting dep. chief Sys. Engring Office, engr., 2003, lead sys. engr., 2003—. With Va. Summer Inst. for Math. Tchrs., 1995-96, dir. 1996-2000. With USNR, 1968-79. Home: 3002 Viburnum Pl Olney MD 20832-3073 Office: 9800 Savage Rd Fort George G Meade MD 20755-6000 Personal E-mail: robertleeschmitt@comcast.net.

SCHMITT, ROBERTA J., psychologist, educator; b. Ft. Collins, Colo. BA, Regis U., Denver, 1988; MS, Wayne State U., Nebr., 1997; EdS, U. Colo., Denver, 2003. Cert. Nat. Assoc. Sch. Psychology, Colo., 1993, profl. tchr. Colo., 1988, in profl. special svcs. Colo., 1995. Elem. sch. tchr. Thompson Sch. Dist., Loveland, Colo., 1988—95, sch. psychologist, counselor, 1995—2008. Office: Thompson Sch Dist 800 S Taft Ave Loveland CO 80537 Business E-Mail: schmittb@thompson.k12.co.us.

SCHMITT, ROLAND WALTER, retired academic administrator; b. Seguin, Tex., July 24, 1923; s. Walter L. and Myrtle F. (Caldwell) S.; m. Claire Freeman Kunz, Sept. 19, 1957; children: Lorenz Allen, Brian Walter, Alice Elizabeth, Henry Caldwell. BA in Math, U. Tex., 1947, BS in Physics, 1947, MA in Physics, 1948; PhD, Rice U., 1951; DSc (hon.), Worcester Poly. Inst., 1985, U. Pa., 1985; DCL (hon.), Union Coll., 1985; DL (hon.), Lehigh U., 1986; DSc (hon.), U. S.C., 1988, U. Tech. De Compeigne, 1991; DL (hon.), Coll. St. Rose, 1992, Russell Sage, 1993, Hartford Grad. Ctr., 1995, Ill. Inst. Tech., 1996, Rensselaer Polytechnic Inst., 1997. With GE, 1951-88, R & D mgr. phys. sci. and engring. Schenectady, 1967-74, mgr. energy sci. and engring. R & D, 1974-78, v.p. corp. R & D, 1978-82, sr. v.p. corp. R & D, 1982-86, sr. v.p. sci. and tech., 1986-88, ret., 1988; pres. Rensselaer Poly. Inst., Troy, NY, 1988-93; ret., 1993. Bd. dirs. Blasch Precision Ceramics, GlobalSpec, Logical Net, Value Innovations; chmn. NYSTAR, 2000-08; bd. advisors LearnLinc, 1996-2000; tech. adv. bd. Chrysler Corp., 1990-93; tech. adv. coun. Mobil Corp., 1997-99; mem., past pres. Indsl. Rsch. Inst., 1978-88; energy rsch. adv. bd. U.S. Dept. Energy, 1977-83; mem. Nat. Sci. Bd., 1982-94, chmn., 1984-88; chmn. CORETECH, 1988-93; mem. Com. on Japan, NRC, 1988-90, Comml. Devel. Ind. Adv. Group, NASA, 1988-90; exec. com. Coun. on Competitiveness, 1988-93; chmn. NRC Panel on Export Controls, 1989-91; mem. Dept. Commerce Adv. Commn. on Patent Law Reform, 1990-92; adv. bd. Oak Ridge Nat. Lab., 1993-98; chair Rev. NATO Sci. program, 1998; mem. NRC panel rev. state dept. use sci. tech. and health, 1999; chmn. rsch. priority panel for NRC Future of Space Sci., 1994-95; chmn. Motorola's Sci. Adv. Bd., 1995-99, ICSU, 1997. Trustee N.E. Savs. Bank, 1978-84; bd. advisors Union Coll., Schenectady, 1981-84, Argonne Univs. Assn., 1979-82, RPI, 1982-88; bd. govs. Albany Med. Ctr. Hosp., 1979-82, 88-90; bd. dirs. Sunnyview Hosp. and Rehab. Ctr., 1978-86, Coun. on Superconductivity for Am. Competitiveness, 1987-89; mem. exec. com. N.Y. State Ctr. for Hazardous Waste Mgmt., 1988-89; chmn. Office of Tech. Assessment adv. panel on industry and environment; mem. Nat. Commn. Ill. Inst. Tech., 1993-94; chair NSF Acad. Rsch. Fleet Rev., 1998-99. With USAAF, 1943-46. Recipient Rensselaer Polytechnic Inst. Cmty. Svc. award, 1982, award for disting. contbns. Stony Brook Found., 1985, Disting. Alumni award Rice U., 1985, IRI Medalist award, 1989, Royal Swedish Acad. Engring. Sci., 1990, Arthur M. Bueche award Nat. Acad. Engring., 1995, NY State Bus. Coun.'s Corning award, 2001, Tech Mentor award Ctr. Econ. Growth, 2006; named Fgn. Assn. of Engring. Acad. Japan, U. Albany Found. Acad. Laureate, 1997; named to Jr. Achievement Capital Region Bus. Hall of Fame, 1996, Rensselaer Polytechnic Inst. Hall of Fame, 1999. Fellow AAAS, IEEE (Centennial medal 1984, Engring. Leadership award 1989, Founders medal 1992, Hoover medal 1993), Am. Phys. Soc. (Pake award 1993), Am. Acad. Arts and Scis.; mem. NAE (coun. 1983-89), Am. Inst. Physics (chmn. 1993-98), Coun. Sci. Soc. Pres. (chair 1993-97), N.Y. Acad. Scis. (pres. coun. 1993—2001), Dirs. Indsl. Rsch., Rensselaer Alumni Assn. (Disting. alumni award 1993), Eta Kappa Nu (eminent mem.) Office: PO Box 240 Rexford NY 12148-0240 Office Phone: 518-384-0965. E-mail: roland@schmitt.org.

SCHMITT, WILLIAM GERARD, writer, editor, magazine manager; b. Flushing, NY, Feb. 17, 1957; s. William Thomas and Eileen Schmitt; m. Eileen Rita Schmitt, Sept. 29, 1990; 1 child, Mary. BA, Fordham U., 1978; MPA, Princeton U., 1981; cert. in theol. studies, Georgetown U. Copy editor, reporter Gannett Westchester Newspapers, Yonkers, N.Y., 1978-79; sr. editor Metals Week, NYC, 1981-85; mng. editor, Washington bur. chief Am. Metal Market, Washington, 1986-89, 93-98; assoc. editor Kiplinger Washington Letter, Washington, 1989-92; sr. editor Chem. Week Assocs., NYC, 1998—2003; comm. mgr. U. Notre Dame, South Bend, Ind., 2003—. Adj. prof. L.I. U., Brklyn., NY, 1999—2002, Fordham U., Bronx, NY, 2001—02, U. Notre Dame, 2008. Co-author: Football Weekends at Notre Dame, 2008. Mem.: Secular Franciscan Order, Phi Beta Kappa. Roman Catholic. Avocations: multimedia marketing, songwriting. E-mail: billgerards@aol.com.

SCHMITTLEIN, DAVID C., dean, marketing professor; BA magna cum laude in Math., Brown U.; M.Phil in Bus., Columbia U., PhD. Faculty mem. Wharton Sch., U. Pa., 1980—2007, Ira A. Lipman prof., prof. mktg., dep. dean, 2000—07, interim dean, 2007; John C. Head III dean MIT Sloan Sch. Mgmt., 2007—. Internat. adv. bd. Groupe HEC; academic adv. bd. China Europe Internat. Bus. Sch. (CEIBS); internat. adv. coun. Guanghua Sch. Mgmt., Peking U.; adv. bd. Sch. Econs. and Mgmt., Tsinghua U.; vis. prof. Faculty of Econs. Tokyo U.; disting. scholar in residence John M. Olin Sch. Bus., Wash. U.; mem. Global Agenda Coun. for Mktg. and Branding, World Econ. Forum. Contbr. articles to profl. jours. Mem.: Inst. for Ops. Rsch. and Mgmt. Scis. (INFORMS), Am. Statistical Assn., Am. Mktg. Assn. Office: MIT Sloan Sch Mgmt Office of the Dean 50 Memorial Dr Cambridge MA 02142 Office Phone: 617-253-2804. E-mail: dschmitt@mit.edu.*

SCHMITTMANN, BEATE, physics professor; b. 1957; Grad., U. Aachen, 1981; PhD in Physics, U. Edinburgh, 1984. Rsch. assoc. Physics Dept. U. Dusseldorf, Germany, 1984—86, rsch. asst. prof., 1991—97; vis. asst. prof. Va. Tech. U., Blacksburg, 1990—91, assoc. prof., 1991—97, prof., 1997—, chair physics dept., 2006—. Lectr. in field. Contbr. articles to profl. jours. Grantee Pro Renovanda Cultura Hungarica Fellow, Hungarian Ministry of Sci., 1995. Fellow: Am. Physical Soc. Office: Va Tech U 111 Robeson Hall Blacksburg VA 24061 Office Phone: 540-231-6518. Office Fax: 540-231-7511. E-mail: schmittm@vt.edu.

SCHMITZ, ANDREW, agricultural studies educator; b. Central Butte, Saskatchewan, Canada, Oct. 5, 1940; s. Andreas and Katherine Schmitz; m. Helen Carole Anderson, July 16, 1966; children: Troy Gordon, Katrina Laur-Ayn Funk, Andre Lloyd, Evan Denis, Dean Michael. BSA, MSc, U. of Sask., 1963; PhD, U. Wis., 1968. D. of Letters-D.Lit. U. of Sask., 1999. Prof. U. of Calif. Dept. Agrl. and Resource Econs., Berkeley, Calif., 1968—94; rsch. prof. U. of Calif., 1986—; adj. prof. U. of Sask., Saskatoon, Canada, 1986—; chair U. of Calif. Dept. Agrl. Resource Econs., Berkeley, Calif., 1989—93; eminent scholar-ben hill griffin jr. endowed chair U. of Fla. Food and Resource Economics, Gainesville, Fla., 1994—; hon. chair U. Sask. Ctr. Study of Agrl., Law, Environment, Saskatoon, Canada, 2001. Project dir. Econ. Coun. Can., Saskatoon, SK, Canada, 1986—89; fellow Am. Agrl. Economics Assn., 1985—; rsch. dir. Turkish Agrl. Econs. Rsch. Inst., Ankara, Turkey, 1998—98; cons. various govt. agencies, various legal firms. Contbr. articles to prof. jours. Recipient Best Pub. Rsch., Western Agrl. Econs. Assn., 1980, Am. Agrl. Econs. Assn., 1981, Rsch. of Enduring Quality, 1984, 1987, Best Pub. Rsch., 1970, 1978, Quality of Comm., 1979, Lifetime Achievement award, So. Agrl. Econs. Assn., 2003, Enduring Rsch. Quality award, Am. Agrl. Econs. Assn., 2003. Fellow: Am. Agrl. Econs. Assn. Office: U Fla 1130A McCarty Hall Gainesville FL 32611-0240 Business E-Mail: aschmitz@ifas.ufl.edu.

SCHMITZ, BARBARA, art preservationist; b. Cin., 1936; AM, U. Chgo., 1960; MA, PhD, NYU, 1981. Prof., advisor Lahore Coll. Women U., Pakistan, 2007—. Author: (illustrated catalogs of Islamic paintings) Islamic Manuscripts, N.Y. Pub. Libr., 1992, Islamic and Indian Manuscripts and Paintings, Pierpont Morgan Libr., 1996; co-author (with Z.A. Desai): Mughal and Persian Painting and Illustrated Manuscripts in the Raza Library, Rampur (U.P.), 2006; editor, contbr.: After the Great Mughals: Painting in Delhi and the Regional Courts in the 18th-19th Centuries, 2004. Recipient Pakistani Higher Edn. Commn. scholar, Women U. Lahore Coll. Dept. Fine Arts, 2006—09, John Paul Getty award, 2009—; Fulbright grantee, 1992—93, 1997—98, Indira Gandhi Nat. Ctr. for the Arts grantee, New Delhi, 1995, Am. Inst. Indian Studies grantee, 1998—99, Browniee Grant, Mo. Hist. Soc., 2002. E-mail: barbaraschmitz65016@yahoo.com.

SCHMITZ, DENNIS MATHEW, retired language educator; b. Dubuque, Iowa, Aug. 11, 1937; s. Anthony Peter and Roselyn S.; m. Loretta D'Agostino, Aug. 20, 1960; children: Anne, Sara, Martha, Paul, Matthew. BA, Loras Coll., 1959; MA, U. Chgo., 1961. Instr. English Ill. Inst. Tech., Chgo., 1961-62, U. Wis., Milw., 1962-66; asst. prof. Calif. State U., Sacramento, 1966-69, assoc. prof., 1969-74, prof., 1974-99; ret., 1999. Poet-in-residence, 1966-99. Author: We Weep for Our Strangeness, 1969, Double Exposures, 1971, Goodwill, Inc., 1976, String, 1980, Singing, 1985, Eden, 1989, About Night: Selected and New Poems, 1993, The Truth Squad, 2002. Recipient Discovery award Poetry Center, NYC, 1968; winner First Book Competition Follett Pub. Co., 1969; di Castagnola award Poetry Soc. Am., 1986; Shelley Meml. award Poetry Soc. Am., 1987; NEA fellow, 1976-77, 85-86, 92-93, Guggenheim fellow, 1978-79. Mem. PEN, Assoc. Writing Programs. Roman Catholic.

SCHMITZ, ELOISE E., communications executive; B in Fin., Tulane U. Corp. banker First Union; v.p., group mgr. Franchise and Comm. Group US Bank (formerly Mercantile Bank); v.p. fin. and acquisitions Charter Comm., Inc., St. Louis, 1998, sr. v.p. fin., treas., 2005, sr. v.p. strategic planning, sr. v.p., interim CFO, 2008, exec. v.p., CFO, 2008—. Office: Charter Comm, Inc 12405 Powerscourt Dr Saint Louis MO 63131

SCHMITZ, JEFFREY MICHAEL, performing arts educator; b. Evanston, Ill., Nov. 27, 1962; Instr. Columbia Coll. Chgo., 2004—, Daley Coll., Chicago, 2003—. Office: Columbia Coll Chgo 600 S Mi Ave Chicago IL 60605 Personal E-mail: schmitzjm@aol.com.

SCHMITZ, JOHN, energy and food products executive; BS in Acctg., St. Cloud State U., Minn. CPA, Minn. With Harvest States (merged with Cenex, now CHS Inc.), Inver Grove Heights, Minn., 1974—, v.p., contr., 1986—98, sr. v.p., CFO, 1999, exec. v.p., CFO. Bd. dirs. Nat. Coop. Refinery Assn., Cofina Fin., LLC. Mem. AICPA, Nat. Soc. Accts. for Coops., Minn. Soc. CPAs. Office: CHS Inc PO Box 64089 Saint Paul MN 55164-0089 Office Phone: 651-355-3778. E-mail: john.schmitz@chsinc.com.*

SCHMITZ, JOHN J., writer, educator; b. Fond du Lac, Wis., Mar. 9, 1937; s. John L. Schmitz and Josephine Knaus; children: David, Rebecca. BA, St. Francis Sem., 1963. CLU Am. Coll. Life Underwriters, 1975. Pres. John Schmitz Agy., Brookfield, Wis., 1992—; instr. Hondros Coll., Columbus, Ohio, 1994—. Cons. Bryant and Stratton Coll., Milw., 2003—04. Author: A Funny Thing Happened On My Way Out of Church, JoAnn: In Search of N.E.D., You're Not The One Who Died. Pres., founder Food for the Hungry, Wis.; bd. mem., officer Elmbrook Sch. Bd., Brookfield, Wis., 1988—92. Mem.: KC (assoc.; grand knight 1996—97). Achievements include development of insurance courses for continuing education. Avocations: writing, photography, travel. Home: 405 Lynnwood Lane Brookfield WI 53005-6134 Office: John Schmitz Agency 405 Lynnwood Lane Brookfield WI 53005-6134 Home Phone: 262-784-6591; Office Phone: 262-784-6591. Personal E-mail: jschmitz13@wi.rr.com.

SCHMITZ, MICHAEL, retired psychology professor; b. Bklyn., Jan. 13, 1949; s. William and Margaret Schmitz; m. Michele Erhardt, Oct. 4, 1974; children: Devon, Andrea. BS in Edn., U. Bridgeport, Conn.; MPS in Psychology, C.W. Post Coll., LI, 1982. Cert. in social studies NY, 1971, sch. counselor. Social studies tchr. Commack Schs., NY, 1971—85, sch. counselor, 1985—2007; Assoc. prof. psychology Suffolk Comm. Coll., Selden, NY, 1987—2009. Bd. mem. Smithtown Youth Orgn., NY, 1975—80. Named one of Coach of Yr., Suffolk County, 2000. Mem.: Suffolk County Coaches Assn. (treas. 1981—83). Independent. Roman Catholic. Avocations: basketball, baseball, softball. Home: 3 Sunreigh Ct Miller Place NY 11764 Office: Suffolk Comm Coll Selden NY 11784 Business E-Mail: schmitm@sunysuffolk.edu.

SCHMITZ, OSWALD JOSEPH, biology professor; b. Midland, Ontario, Canada; s. Heinz Karl and Clara Schmitz; m. Leslea Anne Dalrymple, Sept. 19, 1987; children: Coulter Jacob, Zachary Oswald, Cameron Oliver. BSc, U. Guelph, Canada, 1982, MSc, 1984; PhD, U. Mich., Ann Arbor, 1989. Postdoc. fellow U. BC, Vancouver, British Columbia, 1990—92; prof. Yale U., New Haven, 1992—. Author: (book) Ecology and Ecosystem Conservation. Mem.: Ecol. Soc. Am. Office: Yale Univ 370 prsopect St New Haven CT 06511 Business E-Mail: oswald.schmitz@yale.edu.

SCHMITZ, PHILIP CHARLES, editor, researcher; b. Lakewood, Ohio, Apr. 25, 1952; s. Joseph Ralph and Edna (Van Flandern) S. BA, Cornell U., 1974; MCS, Regent Coll., 1978; MA, U. Mich., 1981, PhD, 1990. Indexer, editor U. Mich., Ann Arbor, 1981-83, 89—; instr. Cen. Mich. U., Mt. Pleasant, Mich., 1983-85; editor Am. Theol. Libr. Assn., Chgo., 1985-89. Asst. editor: Anchor Bible Dictionary, 1989; editor: Index to Book Reviews in Religion, 1986-89. Mem. Soc. Bibl. Lit., Chgo. Soc. Bibl. Rsch. Democrat. Roman Catholic. Office: U Mich Program Studies Religion 445 W Engineering Bldg Ann Arbor MI 48109

SCHMITZ, ROBERT ALLEN, executive, investor; b. Chgo., Ill., Jan. 19, 1941; s. John and Lee (Zeal) S.; m. Jenny Ann Quest, Aug. 23, 1969 (div.); m. Judith Mair Grey, Oct. 25, 1997; children: Alexander, Nicholas, Lara, Maximilian. BA with distinction, U. Mich., 1963; MBA, MIT, 1965. Asst. to pres. Lima (Peru) Light and Power Co., 1965-67; acquisition analyst W.R. Grace Co., NYC, 1967-69; asst. to chmn. N.W. Industries, NYC, 1969-70; prin. McKinsey & Co., Inc., NYC, 1970-82; v.p. books Dow Jones & Co., NYC, 1982-88; chmn., pres., chief exec. officer Richard D. Irwin, Inc., Homewood, Ill., 1983-89; pres., founder Quest Capital Ltd., 1989—; investment cons. Soros Fund Mgmt., 1990-92; mgn. dir., sr. ptnr. Trust Co. of the West, 1993-97; mng. dir., founder. Quest Turnaround Advisors, 1999—; chmn., founder Headline Media Group, 2001—04; COO, PTV Inc., 2003—; CRO World Space Inc., 2008—. Mem. adv. bd. Coll. Commerce De Paul U., Chgo., 1985—; bd. dirs. Sun-Times Media Group, Chgo., Two Way Media, London, Premium TV LLC, London, Cablecom GmBH, Zurich, Adams Rite Sabre, Inc., Glendale, Calif., Superior Fireplace Co., Fullerton, Calif., Houston Foods Co., Chgo., Archibald Candy Co., Chgo., US Media Group, Inc., Crystal City, Mo., Ctrl. Valley Publ., Merced, Hobby Products Co., Inc., Penrose, Colo., Automated Bar Controls, Vacaville, Calif., Spectran Techs., Inc., Sturbridge, Mass.; non-exec. chmn. PTV Ltd., London, 2 Way Media Ltd., London. Pres. Cultural Arts Ctr. Found., Homewood, Ill. Mem. Assn. Am. Pubs. (chmn. higher edn. divsn. 1989), Nature Conservancy (trustee N.Y. state chpt.). Office: Quest Turnaround Advisors Ltd 287 Bowman Ave Purchase NY 10577 Home Phone: 914-921-3497; Office Phone: 1-914-253-8100. Business E-Mail: bschmitz@qtasvisors.com.

SCHMITZ, ROGER ANTHONY, chemical engineer, educator, academic administrator; b. Carlyle, Ill., Oct. 22, 1934; s. Alfred Bernard and Wilma Afra (Aarns) Schmitz; m. Ruth Mary Kuhl, Aug. 31, 1957; children: Jan, Joy, Joni. BSChemE, U. Ill., 1959; PhD in Chem. Engring., U. Minn., 1962. Prof. chem. engring. U. Ill., Urbana, 1962-79; Keating-Crawford prof. chem. engring. U. Notre Dame, Ind., 1979—2005, prof. emeritus, 2005—, chmn. dept. chem. engring. Ind., 1979-81, dean engring. Ind., 1981-87, v.p., assoc. provost Ind., 1987-95. Cons. Amoco Chems., Naperville, Ill., 1966—77; vis. prof. Calif. Inst. Tech., LA, 1968—69. Contbr. articles to profl. jours. With US Army, 1953—55. Fellow, Guggenheim Found., 1968. Mem.: AIChE (A.P. Colburn award 1970, R.H. Wilhelm award 1981), Am. Soc. Engring. Edn. (George Westinghouse award 1977), Nat. Acad. Engring. Roman Catholic. Home: 16865 Londonberry Ln South Bend IN 46635-1444 Office: U Notre Dame 305 Cushing Hall Notre Dame IN 46556 Office Phone: 574-631-7798. Business E-Mail: rschmitz@nd.edu.

SCHMITZ SIMON, PABLO ERVIN, bishop; b. Fond-du-Lac, Wis., Dec. 4, 1943; Ordained priest Order of Friars Minor Capuchin, 1970; missionary priest in Nicaragua; ordained bishop, 1984; aux. bishop Vicariate Apostolic of Bluefields, Nicaragua, 1984—94, vicar apostolic, 1994—. Roman Catholic. Office: Vicariate of Bluefields Apartado 8 Bluefields Zeyala Norte Nicaragua

SCHMOLKA, LEO LOUIS, law educator; b. Paris, Apr. 25, 1939; came to US, 1944; s. Francis and Irene S.; m. Lucille J. Schoenbaum, July 29, 1965; children: Andrew, Gregory. AB, Dartmouth Coll., 1960; LL.B., Harvard U., 1963; LL.M., NYU, 1971. Bar: NY 1964. Assoc. Weil, Gotshal and Manges, NYC, 1964-71, ptnr., 1971-81, of counsel, 1981—; adj. asst. prof. law NYU Sch. of Law, 1971-75; adj. assoc. prof. law NYU Law Sch., 1975-76, adj. prof., 1977-80, assoc. prof., 1981-84, prof., 1985—, mem. faculty, dir. IRS/NYU continuing profl. edn. program, 1987—. Cons. US Treasury Dept. Office Tax Policy, Washington, 1994-95, Am. Law Inst., 1979-86, U. Miami Estate Planning Inst., Fla., 1976-80; vis. adj. prof. law U. Miami Sch. Law, 1977, 80, U. San Diego Sch. Law, 1999; vis. lectr. continuing legal edn. various univs. and tax insts., 1973—. Contbr. articles to legal jours. Fellow Am. Coll. Trust and Estate Counsel; mem. ABA, NY State Bar Assn. (chmn. com. on income taxation estates and trusts 1973-75, estate and gift tax 1976-77, mem. exec. com. tax sect. 1978), Internat. Acad. Estate and Trust Law (academician). Office: NYU Sch Law 40 Washington Sq S Rm 430 New York NY 10012-1099 Personal E-mail: schmolka@optonline.net.

SCHMOLL, EDITH MARGARET, music educator; b. Boston, Mar. 10, 1924; d. William James Pruyn, Sr. and Ida Mary Langan; m. John Arthur Pickering (div.); children: Nancy Pickering, Lois Pickering, Barry Pickering; m. Mariel Theodore Schmoll, Sr., Jan. 10, 1969 (dec. 2002). Grad., Boston Clerical, Mass., 1941; student in Piano Performance, New Eng. Conservatory, Boston, 1945—46; student in Accordian Performance, Conservatory of Music, Kaiserslautern, Germany, 1954—55. Cert. tchr. music Calif. Tchr. music, LA, 1960—; br. mgr. Int. Rectifier Fed. Credit Union, Temecula, Calif., 1991—97. Concert pianist, 1940—; ch. musician, 1965—; pres. Music Songs, Sun City, Calif., 1976—. Editor: (college piano books) Creative Keyboard Experience, 1970, And Now, 2007 (Nat. Poetry award, Am. Mensa, 2008); author: Serenade, 2008—; video, Le Cygne, 2009, audio, Consolation 3, 2009, Nocturne, 2008, Chopins Raindrops and others, 2008. Mem. Legacy Soc., Mt. San Jacinto Coll. Found., Calif., 2006; past. pres. Sun City Hermosa Homeowners Assn., Calif., 1995—97. Recipient Poetry award, Am. Mensa, 2007—08. Mem.: Menifee Valley Med. Ctr. Found., Mensa. Office: Music Songs 28108 Gardena Dr Ste A Sun City CA 92586 Office Phone: 951-679-4201. Personal E-mail: musicsongs44@yahoo.com.

SCHMOLL, HANS JOACHIM, hematology and oncology educator; b. Hannover, Germany, June 21, 1946; s. Johannes and Edeltraut (Schneider) S. MD, Med. U. Hannover, 1970, PhD, 1982. Rsch. assoc. Med. U., Hannover, 1971—84, prof. medicine and hematology-oncology, 1984—95; prof. medicine and hematology, chair hematology/oncology Martin Luther U., Halle-Wittenberg, Germany, 1996—. Author, editor: Kompendium Intern Onkologie, 1986, 4th edit., 2005; assoc. editor Cancer Rsch., 2002—; editor-in-chief Onkologie, 2001—; mem. editl. bd. European Jour. Cancer Annals of Oncology. Recipient German Cancer award, 2001, Sci. award, German Assn. Med. Oncologists, 1998. Mem.: German Assn. Med. Oncology (pres., chmn. 2001—). Home: Ludwig Barnay Strasse 9 D-30175 Hanover Germany Office: Martin Luther Univ Dept Oncol Hematol Int Med IV D-06120

Halle Germany Home Phone: 0049-0171-3141667; Office Phone: 01149-345-557-2924. Personal E-mail: hjschmoll@yahoo.de. Business E-Mail: haematologie@medizin.uni-halle.de.

SCHMUDE, RICHARD WILLIS, JR., chemistry professor; b. Washington, June 18, 1958; s. Richard Willis and Winifred Forbes (Delchamps) S. PhD, Tex. A&M U., College Station; MS, BA. Prof. chemistry Gordon Coll., Barnesville, Ga., 1994—. Contbr. articles to Jour. of the Assn. Lunar and Planetary Observers, Jour. of the Royal Astron. Soc. Can., Tex. Jour. of Sci. Pres. Los Alamos Right to Life, 1990-91. Recipient Walter Haas Observing award, Assn. Lunar and Planetary Observers, 2002, Vol. of Yr. award, Lions Club Lamar County, 2005, Astronomical League award, 2008. Mem. Am. Astron. Soc. (assoc. mem.), Assn. Lunar and Planetary Observers (acting remote planets recorder 1990, remote planets recorder 1991—), British Astron. Assn. Independent. Roman Catholic. Avocation: hiking. Home: 109 Tyus St Barnesville GA 30204 Office: Gordon Coll 419 College Dr Barnesville GA 30204 Office Fax: 670-359-5850. Business E-Mail: schmude@gdn.edu.

SCHMUHL, THOMAS ROEGER, lawyer; b. Phila., Oct. 4, 1946; s. Norman George and Ethel Sandt (Roeger) Schmuhl; m. Jean Giannone, Aug. 3, 1974; children: Andrew, Deborah. AB, MA, Johns Hopkins U., Balt., 1968; JD, U. Pa. Law Sch., 1971. Bar: Pa. 1971, US Dist. Ct. (ea. dist.) Pa. 1971, Supreme Ct. Pa., US Supreme Ct. 1980. Assoc. Schnader Harrison Segal & Lewis, Phila., 1971—78, ptnr., 1979—97, chmn. bus. dept., 1984—90, chmn. internat. practice group, 1990—97; ptnr. Duane Morris LLP, Phila., 1997—. Contbr. articles to profl. jours. Active Com. of Seventy, 1976—; bd. trustees Beaver Coll., Pa., 1991—99. Officer, capt. US Army, 1968—75, commdg. officer 1070th Transp. Co., 1973—75. Mem.: ABA, Inter-Pacific Bar Assn., Am. Fgn. Law Assn., Pa. Bar Assn., Nat. Assn. Bond Lawyers (vice chmn. com. on gen. obligation bonds 1979—81), Pa. Assn. Bond Lawyers, Phila. Bar Assn., Internat. Law Assn., Multilaw (exec. coun. mem. 1990—, mem. mgmt. com. 1994—, chmn. 2000—03, Hawley award 2003), Union Internationale des Avocats. Office: Duane Morris LLP 30 S 17th St Philadelphia PA 19103 Office Phone: 215-979-1252. Office Fax: 215-689-4376. Business E-Mail: TRSchmuhl@duanemorris.com.*

SCHMULTS, EDWARD CHARLES, lawyer; b. Paterson, NJ, Feb. 6, 1931; s. Edward M. and Mildred (Moore) S.; m. Diane E. Beers, Apr. 23, 1960; children: Alison C., Edward M., Robert C. BS, Yale U., 1953; JD, Harvard U., 1958. Bar: N.Y. 1959, D.C. 1974. Assoc. White & Case, NYC, 1958-65, ptnr., 1965-73, 77-81; gen. counsel US Dept. Treasury, Washington, 1973-74, under sec., 1974-75; dep. counsel to Pres. The White House, Washington, 1975-76; dep. atty. gen. US Dept. Justice, Washington, 1981-84; sr. v.p. external rels., gen. counsel GTE Corp., Stamford, Conn., 1984-94; sr. advisor Iraqi Ministry of Justice - Coalition Provisional Authority, 2004. Lectr. securities laws. Served to 1st lt. USMC, 1953-55; capt. USMCR. Mem. Am. Bar Assn., Assn. Bar City N.Y., Adminstrv. Conf. U.S. (council 1977-84), Sakonnet Golf Club, Met. Club.

SCHMUTZ, JOHN FRANCIS, lawyer; b. Oneida, NY, July 24, 1947; s. William L. and Rosemary S. Schmutz; m. H. Marie Roney, June 7, 1969; children: Gretchen, Jonathan, Nathan. BA cum laude, Canisius Coll., 1969; JD cum laude, Notre Dame U., 1972; LLM, George Washington U., 1975. Bar: Ind. 1972, DC 1975, Tex. 1993, U.S. Ct. Mil. Appeals 1972, U.S. Tax Ct. 1973, U.S. Supreme Ct. 1975. Legislation and maj. projects officer Office Judge Adv. Gen., 1972—74; appellate atty. U.S. Army Legal Svcs. Agy., 1974—75; assoc. Ice, Miller, Donadio & Ryan, Indpls., 1976—77; staff atty. Burger Chef Sys., Inc., Indpls., 1977—78, sr. atty., 1979, asst. chief legal counsel, 1978—80, chief legal counsel, 1980, v.p., gen. counsel, sec., 1981—91; v.p.-legal Hardee's Food Sys., Inc., 1983—91; v.p., gen. counsel Sbarro, Inc., 1991—92; v.p., gen. counsel, sec. La Quinta Inns, Inc., 1992—98, gen. counsel, sec., 1998—99; sr. v.p., gen. counsel, sec. Meditrust Cos., Inc., 2000—01, La Quinta Cos., Inc., 2001—02; founding prin. Turtle Creek Group, LLC, 2002—. Dir., v.p. Bursan Credit Union; dir. Food Svc. and Lodging Inst., RIX Sys., Inc., Burger Chef Distributive Corp.; v.p. Hardee's Food Sys., Inc. Exec. editor: Notre Dame Law Rev., 1971—72. Bd. advisors Assistance League, San Antonio, 2007—; exec. bd. Boy Scouts Am.; bd. dirs. Blessed Sacrament Acad. Found. Mem.: ABA (dir. hospitality com., cmty. recreation and common interest devel. com.), Am. Corp. Counsel Assn. (bd. dirs.), Internat. Corp. Sec. Assn., Am. Hotel and Motel Assn. (gen. counsel com.), Nat. Restaurant Assn., Am. Assn. Corp. Counsel, San Antonio Bar Assn., Tex. Bar Assn., Indpls. Bar Assn., DC Bar Assn., Ind. Bar Assn., Fed. Bar Assn. Republican. Roman Catholic. Home: 17122 Eagle Star San Antonio TX 78248-1548 Personal E-mail: johnschmutz@sbcglobal.net.

SCHMUTZHART, BERTHOLD JOSEF, sculptor, educator; b. Salzburg, Austria, Aug. 17, 1928; came to U.S., 1958, naturalized, 1963; s. Berthold Josef and Anna (Valaschek) S. Student, Acad. for Applied Art, Vienna, Austria, 1956. Cert. fed. tchr., Austria. Prof. Werkschulheim Felbertal, Salzburg, 1951-58; sculptor Washington, 1959-60; tchr. Longfellow Sch., Bethesda, Md., 1960-63; prof., chmn. dept. sculpture Corcoran Sch. Art, Washington, 1963-94, prof. emeritus, 1994—; lectr. Smithsonian Instn., Washington, 1968-84. One-man shows include Fredericksburg Gallery Fine Art, Va., 1967-73, Franz Bader Gallery, Washington, 1978, 81, 83, 86, 88; group shows include Nat. Collection Fine Arts, Washington, 1961-70, High Mus. Art, Atlanta, 1965, Ark. Art Ctr., Little Rock, 1966, Birmingham Mus. Art, Ala., 1967, Hirschhorn Mus. and Sculpture Garden, Washington, 1981, Nat. Gallery Modern Art, New Delhi, 1990; represented in permanent collections Hirschhorn Collection; designer fountain, Gallery of Modern Art, Fredericksburg, 1967; author: The Handmade Furniture Book, 1981; contbr. articles to profl. jours. Fine arts panelist D.C. Commn. for Arts, 1973-79; chmn. bd. Market Five Gallery, Washington, 1978-82; bd. dirs. Franz Bader Gallery, Washington, 1981-86; trustee Arts for the Aging, Inc., Washington, 1990—98; chmn. Franz and Virginia Bader Fund, 2001-06, bd. dirs., 2006-. Recipient 1st prize Washington Religious Arts Council, 1960, for sculpture, Little Rock, 1966, Louisville, 1968, Silver medal Audubon Soc., Washington, 1971 Mem. Guild for Religious Architects, Artists Equity Assn. (pres. D.C. chpt. 1973-75), AAUP, Am. Austrian Soc. (pres. 1968-70, exec. com.), Soaring Soc. Am. Home: 32 Layline Ln Fredericksburg VA 22406-4061 E-mail: gn15bs@earthlink.net.

SCHNABEL, JULIAN, artist, film director; b. Oct. 25, 1951; m. Olatz Schnabel. B.F.A., U. Houston, 1972; postgrad., Whitney Mus. Ind. Study Program, NYC, 1973-74. Exhibited one-man shows, Contemporary Art Mus., Houston, 1976, Galerie Dezember, Dusseldorf, West Germany, 1978, Mary Boone, N.Y.C., 1979, Daniel Weinberg Gallery, San Francisco, 1979, Bruno Bischofberger, Zurich, Switzerland, Young-Hoffman Gallery, Chgo., 1980, Mary Boone-Leo Castelli, N.Y.C., 1981, Stedelijk Mus., Amsterdam, Holland, 1982, Bruno Bischofberger, Zurich, Switzerland, 1982, Los Angeles County Mus. Art, 1982, U. Art Mus., Berkeley, Calif., 1982, The Tate Gallery, London, 1982, Mary Boone, N.Y.C., 1982, Bruno Bischofberger, Zurich, Switzerland, 1983, Leo Castelli, N.Y.C., 1983, Akron Art Mus., 1983, Leslie Waddington Gallery, London, 1983, Daniel Templon Gallery, Paris, 1983, Galerie Mario Diacono, Rome, 1983, Akira Ikeda Gallery, Tokyo, 1983, Donald Young Gallery, Chgo., Martine Hamilton Gallery, N.Y.C., Pace Gallery N.Y., 1984, Whitney Mus., 1988, San Francisco Mus. Modern Art, 1988, Mus. Fine Arts, Houston, 1988, Mus. Contemporary Art, Chgo., 1990, numerous others; group shows, Hidden Houston, U. St. Thomas, 1971, La. Gallery, Houston, 1972, W.I.S.P. Exhibition, Whitney Mus. Am. Art, N.Y.C., 1974, Holly Solomon Gallery, N.Y.C., 1977, Rennaissance Soc., U. Chgo., 1979, Daniel Templon, Paris, 1980, L'Amerique Aux Indep-dendants, Grand Palais, Paris, 1980, Mary Boone, N.Y.C., 1980, La Biennale di Venezia, Venice, Italy, 1980, Indpls. Mus. Art, 1980, The Royal Acad., London, 1981, Whitney Mus. Am. Art, N.Y.C., 1981, Addison Gallery, Andover, Mass., 1981, Basel Kunstmuseum, Switzerland, 1981, Gayden Gallery, MIT, Cambridge, 1981, Kinsthallen, Goteborg, Sweden, 1981, Frankfurter Kunstverein, Frankfurt, West Germany, 1982, Inst. Contemporary Art, Boston, 1982, Whitney Mus. Am. Art, N.Y.C., 1982, Mus. Contemporary Art, LaJolla, Calif, 1982, Stedelijk Mus., Amsterdam, 1982, Art Inst. Chgo., 1982, la Biennale di Venezia, Venice, Italy, 1982, Fort Worth Art Mus., 1982, Milw. Art Mus., 1982, Stifelsen Karlsvik 10, Stockholm, 1983, Whitney Mus. Am. Art, N.Y.C., 1983, The Hirshhorn Mus., Washington, 1983, Nat. Mus. Art, Osaka, 1983, Bklyn. Mus., 1983, Mary Boone Gallery, N.Y.C., 1983, 64th Whitney Biennial, 1987, Pace Gallery, N.Y.C., 1990, Poche Gallery, Paris, 1991, Gian Ferrari Arte Contemporanea, Milan, 1993-94, Ramis Barquet Gallery, Mexico, 1995, Modern Art Gallery, Bologna, 1996-97, Thaddaeus Ropac, Salzburg, 1998-99, Galerie Forsblom, Helsinky, 2000; author: Nicknames of Maitre D's and Other Excerpts From Life, 1988; dir., screenwriter (film) Basquiat, 1996; writer, prodr. dir. (film) Before Night Falls, 2000, dir. The Diving Bell and the Butterfly, 2007 (Best Dir., Boston Film Critics Awards, 2007, Best Dir. - Motion Picture, Golden Globe award, Hollywood Fgn. Press Assn., 2008, Ind. Spirit award for Best Dir., Film Ind., 2008). Office: Pace Gallery NY 32 E 57th St Fl 4 New York NY 10022-2530

SCHNABEL, MARTA-ANN, lawyer; b. Butte, Mont., July 15, 1957; m. Kevin O'Bryon; 2 children. BA in History, with honors, Meml. U. Newfoundland, Can., 1978; JD, Loyola U., 1981. Bar: La. 1981, US Dist. Ct. (Ea. Dist. La.), US Dist. Ct. (Mid. Dist. La.), US Dist. Ct. (We. Dist. La.), US Ct. Appeals (5th Cir.). Assoc. Hammett Leake and Hammett, 1981—86, ptnr., 1986; mng. ptnr. Leake & Andersson LLP, 1987—99; shareholder O'Bryon & Schnabel PLC, New Orleans, 2000—. Mem. Alliance for Good Govt., treas., 2000—03; v.p. La. Client Assistance Found., 2003; bd. dirs. New Orleans Legal Aid Bur., 1990—94, sec., 1994—95, v.p., 1997—99; bd. dirs. New Orleans Legal Assistance Corp., 1996—99; mem. bd. trustees St. Martin's Episcopal Sch., 2001—04. Recipient Gillis Long Pub. Svc. award, Loyola Law Sch. Master: New Orleans Bar Assn. Inn of Ct.; fellow: La. Bar Found.; mem.: Def. Rsch. Inst., Assn. Def. Trial Attys., La. Assn. Def. Counsel, La. State Bar Assn. (bd. gov. 1998—2006, ethics adv. svc. com. 2000, editor-in-chief law jour. 2001—03, pres. 2006—07, practice assistance com., improvement com., co-chair access to justice com., com. rules of profl. conduct, Pres. award 1998, 2004), New Orleans Bar Assn. (pres. 1995). Office: O'Bryon & Schnabel PLC Ste 1950 1010 Common St New Orleans LA 70112 Office Phone: 504-799-4200. Office Fax: 504-799-4211.

SCHNACKENBERG, F. RICHARD, science educator, department chairman; life ptnr. John Gibbons. BA, Wabash Coll., Crawfordsville, Ind., 1965; MA, U. Wis., Madison, 1968, PhD, 1972. Chair, dept. chemistry and math. Fla. Gulf Coast U., Fort Myers, 2005—. Mem.: Am. Math. Soc., Math. Assn. America. Office: FL Gulf Coast Univ 10501 FGCU Blvd S Fort Myers FL 33965-6565

SCHNACKENBERG, GJERTRUD CECELIA, poet; b. Tacoma, Aug. 27, 1953; d. Walter Charles and Doris Ione Schnackenberg; m. Robert Nozick, Oct. 5, 1987. BA summa cum laude, Mount Holyoke Coll., 1975, LittD (hon.), 1985. Fellow The Bunting Inst., Radcliffe and Cambridge, Mass., 1979-80; lectr. in writing MIT, Cambridge, 1980-81; Hurst prof. poetry Washington U., St. Louis, 1987; Conkling writer in residence Smith Coll., Northampton, Mass., fall 1994. Vis. fellow St. Catherine's Coll., Oxford U., 1997, Getty Rsch. Inst., 2000. Author: numerous poems. Recipient Rome prize in lit. Am. Acad. Arts and Letters, 1983, Acad. award in lit. Am. Acad. Arts and Letters, 1998, Brandeis citation in poetry, 1989, Berlin prize, 2004; Nat. Endowment for the Arts fellow in poetry, 1986, Guggenheim fellow, 1987; Book Prize in Poetry, L.A. Times, 2000. Fellow: Am. Acad. Rome, Am. Acad. Arts and Scis., Am. Acad. in Berlin. Democrat.

SCHNACKENBERG, ROY LEE, artist; b. Chgo., Jan. 14, 1934; s. Elmer J. and Hazel (Bard) S.; children: Marke, Douglas; m. Shirley Goldman, 1986. B.F.A., Miami U., Oxford, Ohio, 1956. One-man shows include, Joachim Gallery, Chgo., 1962, Main St. Galleries, Chgo., 1963, 64, 66, 68-69, Michael Wyman Gallery, Chgo., 1972, Esther Robles Gallery, Los Angeles, 1973; group exhbns. include print and drawing biennial, Art Inst. Chgo., 1961, Chgo. and Vicinity Show Art Inst. Chgo., 1961, 62, 64, 66-69, 73, 78, Soc. Contemporary Art, Art Inst. Chgo., 1962, 70, New Horizons in Sculpture, Chgo., 1962, 2d ann. art dealers show, N.Y.C., 1963, Ill. Biennial Show, Champaign, 1965, 67, Twelve Chgo. Artists, Walker Mus., Mpls., 1965, also, Mulvane Art Center, Topeka, 1965, 50 States of Art Exhibit, Burpee Mus., Rockford, Ill.; Recent Aquisitions Exhbn., Whitney Mus., 1967, also, ann. exhbn. painting and sculpture, 1967, 68-69, 69-70, No. Ill. U. group exhbn., Normal, 1968-69, Western Ill. U. show, Macomb, 1968-69, Ill. Arts Council traveling Sculpture exhbn., 1968-69, Des Moines Art Center exhbn., New Am. Realists, Konsthallen, Gotenborg, Sweden, 1970, The Art of Playboy World Tour, Milan, 1971, Dept. Interior Bicentennial Exhbn., Corcoran Gallery, Washington, 1976,; nat. tour 200 Years of Illustration, N.Y. Hist. Soc.; Zriny-Hayes Gallery, Chgo., 1978, Mitchell Mus., Champaign, Ill., 1980, Continuity and Change, Chgo. Artists, 1983, Snead Gallery, Rockford, Ill., 1985, 89, 91, 93, 94, 2003, 04, 05, Chgo. Arts Club, Hyde Pk. Art Ctr., Chgo., 2004, Artichigago, 2009; executed mural Crucible, South Chgo. Savs. Bank, 1977; 2d ann. art dealers executed mural, S.E. Savs. & Loan, 1979; Artchicago, 2009, represented in permanent collections, Whitney Mus. Am. Art, N.Y.C., Art Inst. Chgo., Mus. Contemporary Art, Chgo., Burpee Art Mus., Rockford, Ill., others. Served with AUS, 1956-58. Recipient Joseph R. Shapiro award New Horizons in Sculpture, Chgo., 1962; Slobe award, 1964; Viehler award, 1965; Logan medal, 1973; Municipal award, 1974; all Art Inst. Chgo.; recipient purchase prize Burpee Mus., 1965, Copley Found. award N.Y.C., 1967 Mem. Arts Club of Chgo., Chgo. Yacht Club.

SCHNAITMAN, WILLIAM KENNETH, retired finance company executive; b. Talbot County, Md., May 12, 1926; s. William and Catherine Almeda (Cheezum) S.; m. Beverly June Marshall, July 13, 1963. Student, Strayer Bus. Sch., Balt., 1943. Clk. Comml. Credit Co., Balt., 1946-70, asst. sec., 1970-72, treas., 1972-75, dir. cash mgmt., 1976-87, ret., 1987. With AUS, 1944-46, ETO. Home: 12520 Wye Landing Ln Wye Mills MD 21679-2050

SCHNAKE, RICHARD LANE, lawyer; b. Carthage, Mo., Aug. 3, 1957; s. Ivan Eugene and Phyllis Lea (Stewart) S.; m. Kelly Dawn Barfield, Oct. 9, 1999. BA in History, S.W. Mo. State U., 1979; JD, Washington U., St. Louis, 1982. Bar: Mo., 1982, U.S. Dist. Ct. (we. dist.) Mo. 1982, U.S. Ct. Appeals (8th cir.) 1984, U.S. Supreme Ct., 1986, U.S. Ct. Appeals (7th cir.) 1989. Law clk. to Hon. Warren D. Welliver Supreme Ct. of Mo., Jefferson City, 1982-83; assoc. Neale, Newman, Bradshaw & Freeman, Springfield, Mo., 1983-87; ptnr. Neale, Newman, Bradshaw & Freeman, Neale & Newman, L.L.P., Springfield, Mo., 1988—. Mem. Mo. Supreme Ct. Civil Rules Com., Jefferson City, 1994—2002, mem. Appellate Practice Com., 2002—; spl. asst. Atty. Gen. Mo., Jefferson City, 1990-93; chmn. Springfield Metro. Bar Assn. Law Day Com., 1989-91, 2003—, sec., bd. dirs., 1992-95. Author: Civil Rules Practice, Rules 85-88, 17A Missouri Practice, 1999; contbr. articles to profl. jours. Bd. dirs., pres., sec. Ozark Counseling Ctr., Springfield, Mo., 1987-88, 89-91, 92-94, 95—. Recipient Scribes award for legal writing, 1982, David J. Dixon Appellate Advocacy award Mo. Bar Found., Jefferson City, Mo., 1990; nominee for nonpartisan appt. to Mo. Ct. Appeals, 2003. Mem. ABA, Springfield Met. Bar Assn. (seminar lectr.), Mo. Bar Assn. (seminar lectr.), Order of Coif, Phi Kappa Phi, History Ink Hist. Autographs (mng. mem.). Mem. Ch. of Christ. Avocation: autograph collecting. Office: Neale & Newman LLP 1949 E Sunshine St Ste 1-130 Springfield MO 65804-1682 Address: PO Box 10327 Springfield MO 65808-0327 Home: 4196 E Gastonbury St Springfield MO 65809 Home Phone: 417-886-7234; Office Phone: 417-882-9090. Business E-Mail: rschnake@nnlaw.com.

SCHNAPER, CARA L., diversified financial services company executive; BS, MBA, Cornell U., Ithaca, NY. Head tech. and ops., equities dept. JP Morgan Chase & Co., mng. dir., COO global markets bus.; prin. Market Resolve, LLC; exec. v.p. tech. and ops. TIAA-CREF, 2008—. Mem. operating com. CHIPCo, ServiceCo; payments risk com. Fed. Res. Bank NY; bd. dirs. Depository Trust & Clearing Corp. Treas. Summit PTA, NJ; mem. Summit Mcpl. Democratic Com., NJ. Office: TIAA-CREF PO Box 1259 Charlotte NC 28201*

SCHNAPP, DIANA CORLEY, communications educator; b. Russellville, Ark., Dec. 4, 1946; d. Robert Eston and Claudie (Cates) C. BS, Ill. State U., Normal, 1968, MS, 1970; PhD., U. Md., 1986. Tchr. Davenport Schs., Iowa, 1968-69; prof. speech communication Black Hawk Coll., Moline, Ill., 1970-92; prof. speech comm. Johnson County C.C., Overland Park, Kans., 1993—97; adj. prof. McHenry Coll., Crystal Lake, Ill., 1992—93; ret. Cons. U.S. Army Corps Engrs., Hosp. Groups, Cooperative Extension Svc., Rock Island County, 1973—; adj. prof. Coll. of DuPage, 1993, Rockhurst U., Kans. City, Mo., 2000-03 Contbr. articles to profl. jours. and mags. Vol. Sta. WQPT-TV, Luth. Hosp., Moline, 1983-85; tchr., coord. Overland Pk. Ch. of Christ, Women's Ministry Dir., 1999-02; bd. dirs. Towncrest Homeowners Assn., Moline, 1983-86, Coop. Extension Found., Women's Ministry Leader Ch. of Christ, 1993, Children's Family Svcs., Kans. City Health Ministry; Assoc. docent John Wornall House Mus. Mem. Internat. Listening Assn., Grief Counseling Am. Acad. of Bereavement. Democrat. Avocations: reading, collecting art objects, walking, theater, writing.

SCHNAPP, ROGER HERBERT, lawyer, consultant; b. NYC, Mar. 17, 1946; s. Michael Jay and Beatrice Joan (Becker) S.; m. Candice Jacqueline Larson, Sept. 15, 1979; 1 child, Monica Alexis. BS, Cornell U., 1966; JD, Harvard U., 1969; postgrad. Pub. Utility Mgmt. Program, U. Mich., 1978. Bar: NY 1970, US Ct. Appeals (2d cir.) 1970, US Supreme, 1974, US Dist. Ct. (so. dist.) NY 1975, US Ct. Appeals (4th and 6th cirs.) 1976, US Ct. Appeals (7th cir.) 1977, US Dist. Ct. (so. dist.) NY 1975, US Dist. Ct. (no. dist.) Calif. 1980, US Ct. Appeals (8th cir.) 1980, Calif., 1982, US Dist. Ct. (cen. dist.) Calif. 1982, US Ct. Dist. (ea. dist.) Calif., 1984. Atty. CAB, Washington, 1969-70; labor atty. Western Electric Co., NYC, 1970-71; mgr. employee rels. Am. Airlines, NYC, 1971-74; labor counsel Am. Electric Power Svc. Corp., NYC, 1974-78, sr. labor counsel, 1978-80; indsl. rels. counsel Trans World Airlines, NYC, 1980-81; sr. assoc. Parker, Milliken, Clark & O'Hara, LA, 1981-82; ptnr. Rutan & Tucker, Costa Mesa, Calif., 1983-84, Memel, Jacobs, Pierno, Gersh & Ellsworth, Newport Beach, Calif., 1985-86, Memel, Jacobs & Ellsworth, Newport Beach, 1986-87; pvt. practice Newport Beach, 1987—. Bd. dirs. Dynamic Constrn., Inc., Laguna Hills, Calif., 1986—; commentator labor rels. Fin. News Network; commentator Sta. KOCN Radio, 1990-91; commentator employment law Orange County Register; lectr. Calif. Western Law Sch., Calif. State U.-Fullerton, Calif. State Conf. Small Bus.; lectr. collective bargaining Pace U., NYC; lectr. on labor law Coun. on Edn. in Mgmt.; NE regional coord. Pressler for Pres., 1979-80; adv. bd. manufacturingzone Web site; dir. Orange County Bur. Jewish Edn., Friends of Fertility Found. Author: Arbitration Issues for the 1980s, 1981, A Look at Three Companies, 1982; editor-in-chief Indsl. and Labor Rels. Forum, 1964-66; columnist Orange County Bus. Jour., 1989-91; contbr. articles to profl. publs. Mem. Bus. Rsch. Adv. Coun. US Dept. Labor; trustee Chapman U., 1991-95; bd. mem., Orange County Bur. Jewish Edn. Mem. Calif. Bar Assn. (chmn.), Labor Law Consulting Group, Calif. Bd. of Legal Specialization, Jewish Cmty. Ctr. Orange County. Republican. Jewish. Office: PO Box 9049 Newport Beach CA 92658-1049 Office Phone: 949-706-7365. Business E-Mail: rhs@schnapp.com.

SCHNECK, STUART AUSTIN, retired neurologist, educator; b. NYC, Apr. 1, 1929; s. Maurice and Sara Ruth (Knapp) S.; m. Ida I. Nakashima, Mar. 2, 1956; children: Lisa, Christopher. BS magna cum laude, Franklin and Marshall Coll., 1949; MD, U. Pa., 1953. Diplomate Am. Bd. Psychiatry and Neurology (bd. dirs., sec. 1990-91, v.p. 1991-92, pres. 1992-93). Intern Hosp. U. Pa., Phila., 1953-54; resident in medicine U. Colo. Med. Center, Denver, 1954-55, 57-58, resident in neurology, 1958-61; instr. neurology U. Colo. Sch. Medicine, 1959-61; instr. neuropathology Columbia U., NYC, 1961-63; vis. fellow in neuropathology Columbia-Presbyn. Med. Ctr., NYC, 1961-63; asst. prof. neurology and pathology U. Colo., 1963-67, assoc. prof., 1967-70, prof., 1970-95, assoc. dean clin. affairs Sch. Medicine, 1984-89, emeritus prof., 1996—. Cons. Fitzsimons Army Hosp., VA, Nat. Jewish Hosp.; pres. med. bd. Univ. Hosp., Denver, 1983-89, bd. dirs., 1989-90; mem. benefits adv. bd. U. Colo., 1999—, v.p. retired faculty assn. health sci. ctr., 1998-99, pres., 1999-2001. Author (with Ida I. Nakashima) The Geezers' Guide to Colo. Hikes, 2002; contbr. articles to profl. jours. Served with USAF, 1955-57. USPHS fellow, 1961-63 Mem. Am. Acad. Neurology, Am. Assn. Neuropathologists, Am. Neurol. Assn., Univ. Srs. Assn. (chmn. bd. dirs. 1997-2002), Rocky Mountain Stroke Assn. (bd. dirs. 1998—2006), Ctr. for Personalized Edn. Physicians (bd. dirs. 1999—2008), Alpha Omega Alpha (bd. dirs. 1979-89, treas., pres. 1990-93, editl. bd. 1994—2006).

SCHNECKER, NIELS, lawyer; b. Bucharest, Romania, Jan. 1, 1960; s. Kurt and Ruth (Dankner) S. LLM, U. Paris, 1982, PhD, 1987; MBA, Nat. Sch. Bus. Studies, Washington, 1990. Floor trader Merrill Lynch Pierce Fenner & Smith, London, 1982-83; mgr., v.p. Degefa Reisen, Frankfurt, Germany, 1983-85; col. USAF, 1983—2006, ret., 2006; assoc. Chula & May, Santa Anna, Calif., 1985-85; v.p., pres., ceo Internat. Investment Bankers Group, Colorado Springs, 1986-90; gen.

mgr. rsch. & devel. Federal Express, Johannesburg, 1990-91; mng. sr. ptnr. Schnecker van Wyk & Pearson, Johannesburg, 1991—; prof., mgmt. Nat. Sch. Polit. Admin. Studies, 2002—. Of counsel The White House, Washington, 1986—87; chief counsel Phumelo Found., African Nat. Congress, Johannesburg, 1991—93; counsel Romanian Parliament, 1993—; Romanian Govt. counsel, 1993—96; prof. Am. Acad. Fin. Mgmt., NY; prof. Politic and adminstrv. studies Nat. Sch., Romania. Nat. com. U.S. Rep. Party, 1985—; prof. Nat. Sch. Polit. Adminstrv. Studies, Bucharest, Romania, 2000—. Active USAF, 1983—2006. Mem. Am. Mgmt. Assn., Am. Bank Attys. Assn., Inst. Dirs., Chartered Inst. Bankers, Jewish Lawyers Assn., Crans Montana Forum, fellow Am. Acad. Fin. Mgmt.(master fin. mgr. chartered econ. policy adv., 2004) Avocations: music, flying, skiing. Office: Schnecker van Wyk & Pearson Ion Ionescu de la Brad 4 Bucharest 1 Romania Business E-Mail: niels.schnecker@globalfininvest.com.

SCHNEEBERGER, EVELINE ELSA, pathologist, cell biologist, educator; b. The Hague, Holland, Oct. 2, 1934; came to U.S., 1952; d. Werner Friederich and Elsa (Graf) S. BA, U. Colo., 1956; MD, U. Colo., Denver, 1959; MA (hon.), Harvard U., 1990. Rsch. fellow in pathology Sir. William Dunn Sch., Oxford (Eng.) U., Harvard Med. Sch., Boston, 1966-67, instr. pathology, 1967-68, assoc. in pathology, 1968-70, asst. prof., 1970-74, assoc. prof., 1974-88, prof. pathology, 1988—. Mem. pulmonary diseases adv. com. NIH, Bethesda, Md., 1975-78, mem. pathology A study sect., 1980-83, 87-90; mem. rev. com. Nat. Inst. Environ. Health Scis., Research Triangle, N.C., 1992-96. Mem. editl. bd. Circulation Rsch., 1977-83, Tissue and Cell, 1983-94, Am. Jour. Physiology, 1990—, Am. Jour. Pathology, 1992—; contbr. chpts. to books, articles to profl. jours. Fellow AAAS; mem. Am. Soc. for Cell Biology, Am. Assn. Pathologists, Am. Thoracic Soc., Microcirculatory Soc., Phi Beta Kappa, Sigma Xi, Alpha Omega Alpha. Office: Mass Gen Hosp Molecular Pathology Unit Dept Pathology Bldg 149 13th St Fl 6 Charlestown MA 02129 Business E-Mail: eschneeberger@partners.org.

SCHNEEWEISS, SEBASTIAN, medical educator, pharmacoepidemiologist; MD, Munich U. Med. Sch., 1992; SM, Harvard Sch. Public Health, 1994, ScD, 2000. Assoc. prof. medicine, dept. epidemiology Harvard Medical Sch., Boston, 2000—; vice chief Divsn. Pharmacoepidemiology and Pharmacoeconomics Brigham and Women's Hosp.; principal investigator Developing Evidence to Inform Decisions about Effectiveness Rsch. Ctr. Brigham & Women's Hospital. Office: Brigham and Women's Hosp 1620 Tremont St Ste 2020 Boston MA 02120*

SCHNEEWIND, SARAH KATHERINE, history professor; b. Pittsburgh, Aug. 25, 1964; d. Jerome and Elizabeth Schneewind; m. Bruce Tindall, May 13, 1996; 1 child, Leo Tindall. BA, Cornell; MA, Yale; PhD, Columbia, 1999. Asst. prof. Southern Meth. U., Dallas, 1999—2005; assoc. prof. history dept. UC, San Diego, La Jolla, Calif., 2005—. Author: (book) Cmty. Schs. and the State in Ming China, A Tale of Two Melons: Emperor and Subject in Ming China; editor: Long Live the Emperor: Uses of the Ming Founder across Six Centuries of East Asian History.

SCHNEIDER, ALLAN STANFORD, biophysics, neuroscience and pharmacology educator, biomedical research scientist; b. NYC, Sept. 26, 1940; s. Harry and Edith (Gonsky) S.; m. Mary-Jane Beekman Tunis, Dec. 14, 1968; children: Henry Seth, Joseph Benjamin B.Chem. Engring., Rensselaer Poly. Inst., 1961; MS, Pa. State U., 1963; PhD, U. Calif.-Berkeley, 1968. Chem. engr. E.I. du Pont de Nemours & Co. Exptl. Sta., Wilmington, Del., 1963-64; postdoctoral fellow Weizmann Inst. Sci., Rehovot, Israel, 1969-71; staff fellow NIH, Bethesda, Md., 1971-73; assoc. Sloan-Kettering Inst. Cancer Rsch., NYC, 1974-80, assoc. mem., 1980-85; asst. prof. Cornell U. Grad. Sch. Med. Scis., NYC, 1974-80, assoc. prof. biochemistry, 1981-83, assoc. prof. cell biology and genetic, 1983-85, chmn. biochemistry unit Sloan-Kettering div., 1982-83; assoc. prof. pharmacology and toxicology Albany Med. Coll., NY, 1985-86, prof. pharmacology and toxicology, 1986-94, prof. pharmacology and neurosci., 1995—, dir. grad. studies, 1987-91. Adjunct prof. Biomedical Sci., Sch. of Public Health, St. U. N.Y., Albany, 1987—; vis. prof. Weizmann Inst. Sci., Rehovot, Israel, 1987; vis. rsch. scholar U. Bergen, Norway, 1989, 95; vis. rsch. scholar, U. of Melbourne, Australia, 1998. Contbr. chpts to books, sci. articles to profl. jours. Rsch. grantee Am. Cancer Soc., 1980-83, Am. Heart Assn., 1977-82, 90-93, NIH, 1982-93, 2001—05, NSF, 1977-79, 1997-2002, Cystic Fibrosis Found., 1980-82; established investigator Am. Heart Assn., 1977-82. Mem. Biophys. Soc., Soc. Neurosci., Soc. of Gen. Physiologist, Am. Heart Assn. (coun. on basic sci. 1977-95), Phi Lambda Upsilon, Tau Beta Pi (internat. com. for chromaffin cell biology 1987-93). Achievements include first isolation and characterization of chromaffin cells of the adrenal gland now widely used as a model neuronal cell culture system; determination of the relation between cytosolic calcium signals and neurohormone (adrenaline) secretion, relevant to cellular mechanism of hormone and neurotransmitter release; determination of hydration of biomembranes; spectroscopic characterization of protein structure in situ in biomembranes and cells; theoretical and experimental analysis of optical activity spectra of turbid biological suspensions; research on neurochemistry of adrenal chromaffin cells, regulation of cell calcium and hormone and neurotransmitter release; mechanisms of nicotine dependence and fetal nicotine syndrome and effects of maternal smoking on fetal brain development. Office: Ctr for Neuropharmacology & Neurosci Albany Med Coll MC 136 Albany NY 12208 Office Phone: 518-262-5837. Business E-Mail: schneia@mail.amc.edu.

SCHNEIDER, ALLEN MORRIS, psychology professor; BS cum laude, Trinity Coll., Hartford, Conn., 1960; PhD, Ind. U., Bloomington, 1963. Asst. to prof. psychology NYU, NYC, 1963—72; prof. psychology Swarthmore Coll., Pa., 1972—. Contbr. articles to profl. jour. Achievements include research in neurochemistry of memory. Business E-Mail: aschnei1@swarthmore.edu.

SCHNEIDER, AMANDA E., literature and language professor; b. Marietta, Ga., Mar. 30, 1976; d. Richard E. Eckert and Jane L. Rogers; m. Russell Schneider, Apr. 29, 2000; children: Kayala, Presley, Taylor. BA in Spanish, Ga. Coll. State U., Milledgeville, 1998. Youth market mgr. Coca-Cola, August, Ga., 1998—2001; Spanish tchr. North Augusta HS, 2001—03, Foxgreek HS, North Augusta, SC, 2003—. Recipient Tchr. Of Yr., Fox Greek HS, 2006, Golden Apple, WJBF News, 2009. Mem.: Internat. Club (sponsor 2009), Rotary Club (hon.).

SCHNEIDER, ARTHUR PAUL, retired videotape and film editor, author; b. Rochester, NY, Jan. 26, 1930; s. Mendell Phillip and Frieda (Bl) S.; m. Helen Deloise Thompson, June 5, 1954; children: Robert Paul, Lori Ann. Student, U. So. Calif., 1948. With NBC, 1951-68, film and videotape editor, 1953-60, developer double system method of editing video tape, 1958; pres. Burbank (Calif.) Film Editing, Inc., 1968-72, Electronic Video Industries Inc., 1977-79; supr. video tape editing Consol. Film Industries Inc., Hollywood, Calif., 1972-76, editorial supr., 1980-83; pvt. practice editing, 1983-88. Cons., lectr., author. Film and tape editor all: Bob Hope shows, 1951-67; supr. NBC kinescope and video tape editors (1966-67); video tape editor: Laugh-In Series, 1967-68; video tape editor: Comedy Shop Series, 1977-80; post-prodn. cons. to Video Systems and Broadcast Engring. mag.; video tape editor: TV series Sonny & Cher, 1973, Sonny Comedy Revue, 1974, Tony Orlando and Dawn, 1974, Hudson Bros., summer, 1974, Dean Martin Series, 1975-76, Mickey Mouse Club Series, Walt Disney Prodns., 1976, Redd Foxx Series, 1977; (author: Electronic Post Production and Videotape Editing, 1989 (pub. in Chinese 1995), Electronic Post Production Terms and Concepts, 1990; contbg. author: Association of Cinema and Video Laboratores (ACVL) Handbook, 5th edit., 1995, Focal Guide to Electronic Media CDRom Version, 1998, Jump Cut: Memoirs of a Pioneer Television Editor, 1997, (autobiography) My 50 Years of Television History: Been There, Done That, 2005; oral history interview for Acad. TV Arts and Scis. Found. Archive of Am. TV First 50 Yrs., 2001; contbr. articles to publs. in field. Recipient Broadcast Preceptor award San Francisco State U., 1975; named hon. Ky. Col. Mem. Acad. Television Arts and Scis. (Emmy nominations and Emmy award for video tape editing 1966, 68, 73, 84, gov. 1977-80, sec. 1980-81), Am. Cinema Editors (life, Life Achievement award 1999), Soc. Motion Picture and TV Engrs., Delta Kappa Alpha (life). Home: 2586 Neptune Pl Port Hueneme CA 93041 Personal E-mail: art2586@earthlink.net.

SCHNEIDER, ARTHUR SANFORD, medical educator; b. LA, Mar. 24, 1929; s. Max and Fannie (Ragin) S.; m. Edith Kadison, Aug. 20, 1950; children: Jo Ann Schneider Farris, William Scott, Lynnellen. BS, UCLA, 1951; MD, Chgo. Med. Sch., 1955. Diplomate Am. Bd. Internal Medicine, Am. Bd. Pathology. Intern, Wadsworth VA Hosp., Los Angeles, 1955-56, resident, 1956-59, chief clin. pathology sect., 1962-68; mem. faculty UCLA, 1961-75, clin. assoc. prof., 1971-75; chair dept. clin. pathology City of Hope Med. Ctr., Duarte, Calif., 1968-75; prof., chair dept. clin. pathology Whittier Coll., 1974-75; prof., chair dept. pathology Chgo. Med. Sch. Rosalind Franklin Medicine & Sci., 1975—; chief lab. service VA Med. Ctr., North Chicago, Ill., 1975-86, chief lab. hematology, 1986-94. Sr. author: BRS Pathology, 1993; sr. author 4th edit., 2009; contbr. chapters to books, articles to profl. jours. Served to capt. M.C., USAF, 1959-61. Fellow: ACP, Am. Soc. Clin. Pathologists, Coll. Am. Pathologists; mem.: AMA, AAUP, Group Rsch. in Pathology Edn., Lake County Med. Soc., Ill. Med. Soc., Am. Soc. Clin. Rsch., Am. Assn. Blood Banks, Am. Soc. Hematology, Acad. Clin. Lab. Physicians and Scientists, Assn. Pathology Chairs, Am. Assn. Investigative Pathology, Internat. Acad. Pathology, Alpha Omega Alpha, Sigma Xi, Phi Delta Epsilon. Office: Chgo Med Sch Rosalind Franklin U Medicine and Sci 3333 Green Bay Rd North Chicago IL 60064-3037 Home Phone: 847-234-5693; Office Phone: 847-578-3260. E-mail: arthur.schneider@rosalindfranklin.edu.

SCHNEIDER, BENJAMIN, psychology professor, consultant; b. NYC, Aug. 11, 1938; s. Leo and Rose (Cohen) S.; m. H. Brenda Jacobson, Jan. 29, 1961; children: Lee Andrew, Rhody Yve. BA, Alfred U., 1960; MBA, CUNY, 1962; PhD, U. Md., 1967. Lic. psychologist, Md. Asst. prof. adminstrv. scis. and psychology Yale U., New Haven, 1967-71; prof. psychology-mgmt. U. Md., College Park, 1971-79, prof. psychology and mgmt., 1982—2004, prof. emeritus, 2004—; sr. rsch. fellow Valtera Corp., 2003—; John A. Hannah prof. orgnl. psychology Mich. State U., East Lansing, 1979-82. Vis. prof. Inst. Adminstrn. and Enterprise, U. Aix-Marseille, 1993, 99, 2001, Peking U., 1988, Tuck Sch. Bus. Adminstrn., Dartmouth Coll., 1999. Author: (with D.T. Hall) Organizational Climates and Careers, 1973, Staffing Organizations, 1976, (with N. Schmitt) 2d edit., 1986, (with F.D. Schoorman) Facilitating Work Effectiveness, 1988, Organizational Climate and Culture, 1990, (with D.E. Bowen) Winning the Service Game, 1995, (with S.S. White) Service Quality: Research Perspectives, 2004, (with D.B. Smith) Personality and Organizations, 2004, (with R.E. Ployhart and N. Schmitt) Staffing Organizations, 3rd edit., 2006; co-author: (with W. Maccy, K. Barbera & S. Young) Employee Engagement: Tools for Analysis, Practice and Competitive Advantage; mem. editl. rev. bd. Jour. Applied Psychology, 1988-98, 2002-, Jour. Svc. Mgmt., 1989—, Jour. Svc. Rsch., 1998—, Orgnl. Behavior and Human Decision Processes, 2002-, Cornell Quar., 2002-. Fulbright grantee, 1973—74. Fellow APA, Am. Psychol. Soc., Soc. for Indsl. and Orgnl. Psychology (pres. 1984-85, Disting. Sci. Contbns. award 2000, Scholarly Contbn. award 2004), Acad. Mgmt. (pres. orgnl. behavior divsn. 1982-83, Haneman Career Contbns. award, Human Resource Divsn. 2009), Am. Mktg. Assn. (svcs. mktg. spl. interest group, Career Contbns. award 2006), San Diego Indsl. and Orgnl. Profls. (pres. 2005-06), Soc. Human Resources Mgmt. (Michael Losey Human Resource Rsch. award 2009). Office: 1363 Caminito Floreo Ste G La Jolla CA 92037 Office Phone: 858-488-7594. Business E-Mail: bschneider@valtera.com.

SCHNEIDER, CALVIN, physician; b. NYC, Oct. 23, 1924; s. Harry and Bertha (Green) S.; m. Elizabeth Gayle Thomas, Dec. 27, 1967. AB, U. So. Calif., 1951, MD, 1955; JD, LaVerne Coll., 1973. Intern L.A. County Gen. Hosp., 1955—56, staff physician, 1956—57; pvt. practice medicine West Covina, Calif., 1957—. Staff Inter-Community Med. Ctr., Covina, Calif. With USNR, 1943-47. Republican. Lutheran.

SCHNEIDER, CARL EDWARD, law educator; b. Exeter, NH, Feb. 23, 1948; s. Carl Jacob and Dorothy (Jones) S.; m. Joan L. Wagner, Jan. 6, 1976. BA, Harvard Coll., 1972; JD, U. Mich., 1979. Curriculum specialist Mass. Tchrs. Assn., Boston, 1972-75; law clk. to judge U.S. Ct. Appeals (D.C. cir.), Washington, 1979-80; law clk. Potter Stewart U.S. Supreme Ct., Washington, 1980-81; asst. prof. law U. Mich., Ann Arbor, 1981-84, assoc. prof. law, 1984-86, prof. law, 1986—, prof. internal medicine, 1998—, Chauncey Stillman prof. ethics, morality and practice of law; vis. prof. U. Tokyo, 1998. Disting. vis. prof. US Air Force Acad., 2007. Author: The Practice of Autonomy: Patients, Doctors and Medical Decisions, 1998, (with Margaret F. Brinig) An Invitation to Family Law, 1996, (with Marsha Garrison) The Law of Bioethics, 2003; editor: (book) The Law and Politics of Abortion, 1980, Family Law in Action: A Reader, 1999 (with Margaret F. Brinig and Lee E. Teitelbaum), Law at the End of Life: The Supreme Court and Assisted Suicide, 2000; contbr. articles to profl. jours. Mem. Pres. Coun. Bioethics, 2006—09. Fellow Am. Council of Learned Socs., Ford Found., 1985, Hastings Ctr.; life fellow Clare Coll., Cambridge. Fellow Am. Coll. Legal Medicine (hon.); mem. Order of Coif. Office Phone: 734-647-4170.

SCHNEIDER, CARL STANLEY, retired physics professor, researcher; b. Balt., Dec. 20, 1942; s. Stanley Samuel and Viola Jeannette Schneider; m. Carole Bottom, Dec. 24, 1971; children: Kathleen Schneider Sollars, James Andrew. BA, Johns Hopkins U., Balt., 1960—63; MS, MIT, Cambridge, 1963—65, PhD, 1965—68. Prof. U.S. Naval Acad., Annapolis, Md., 1968—2007; ret. Dir. sch. U.S. Naval Acad., 1986—96. Pres. Broadneck Fedn. Communities, Annapolis, 1974—76; cmty. program dir. Annapolis Rotary Club, 1995—96. Recipient Outstanding Young Men in Am., Jaycees, 1975, Meritorius Civilian Svc. award, USN, 1986—96, Frank R. Haig prize, Am. Assn. Physics Tchrs., 1998. Mem.: Mine Warfare Assn. (hon. Charles Rowzee award 1996), Phi Kappa Phi, Sigma Xi, Phi Beta Kappa. Liberal. Methodist. Achievements include patents for closed loop degaussing control system. Avocations: singing, photography, travel, hiking, gardening. Personal E-mail: carlstanleyschneider@gmail.com.

SCHNEIDER, CAROL GEARY, educational association administrator; BA in History magna cum laude, Mt. Holyoke Coll., South Hadley, Mass., 1967; postgrad. student, U. London Inst. Hist. Rsch.; PhD in Early Modern History, Harvard U. Instr. Chgo. State U., DePaul U., Boston U., U. Chgo., 1978—88, dir. Midwest Faculty Seminar, founding dir. Inst. Tchg. and Learning; exec. v.p. Assn. Am. Colls. and Univs., Washington, 1988—98, pres., 1998—. Contbr. articles to profl. jours. Bd. trustees Mt. Holyoke Coll. Woodrow Wilson fellow, Harvard U., Kent fellow, Harvard Prize fellow, Mina Shaughnessy fellow, US Dept. Edn., 1982. Mem.: Phi Beta Kappa. Office: Am Assn Colls and Univs 1818 R St NW Washington DC 20009 Office Phone: 202-387-3760 ext. 401. Office Fax: 202-265-9532. E-mail: cgs@aacu.org.

SCHNEIDER, CATHERINE CHEMIN, occupational therapist, consultant, writer; d. Anthony Joseph Chemin and Irma Gema Bizzotto; m. Daniel Patrick Schneider, Sept. 25, 1970; children: David Patrick, Patricia Marie. BSc in Occupl. Therapy, Wayne State U., 1970. Staff therapist Henry Ford Hosp., Detroit, 1971, Plymouth Ctr. for Human Devel., 1971—73, Oak Park Devel. Tng. Ctr., Mich., 1973—75; itinerant staff therapist, cons. Ingham Intermediate Sch. Dist., Mich., 1975—76; sch. therapist, cons. Birmingham (Mich.) Pub. Schs., 1978—91; cons., pres. The Positive Difference, LLC, Northville, Mich., 1992—2000; sch. therapist, cons. Bloomfield Hills (Mich.) Sch., 1992—99; presenter in field, 2003—. Author: Sensory Secrets: How to "Jump-Start" Learning in Children, 2001, 2007; co-author (with Carol Poltorak): Your Sensational Brain, 2008. Mem.: Am. Occupl. Therapy Assn. Avocations: reading, music, needlecrafts. Office Phone: 248-344-8188. Fax: 243-344-8188. E-mail: catherine_schneider@msn.com, posdiff@aol.com.

SCHNEIDER, CHARLES IVAN, newspaper executive; b. Chgo., Apr. 6, 1923; s. Samuel Hiram and Eva (Smith) S.; m. Nancy Barrier-Schneider; children: Susan, Charles I. Jr., Kim, Karen, Traci. BS, Northwestern U., 1944. Indsl. engr., sales mgr., v.p. mktg. and sales Curtis-Electro Lighting Corp., Chgo., 1945-54, pres., 1954-62, Jefferson Electronics, Inc., Santa Barbara, Calif., 1962-64; pres. 3 sub., v.p., asst. to pres. Am. Bldg. Maintenance Industries, Los Angeles, 1964-66; group v.p. Times Mirror Co., Los Angeles, 1966-88, ret.; pvt. investor and cons., 1988—. Bd. dirs. Jeppesen Sanderson, Inc., Denver, Graphic Controls Corp., Buffalo, Regional Airports Improvement Corp. Bd. regents Northwestern U., Evanston, Ill.; trustee, past pres. Reiss-Davis Child Study Center, L.A.; bd. govs., past pres. The Music Ctr.; trustee the Menninger Found.; pres. St. John's Hosp. and Health Ctr. Found., Santa Monica, Calif. Served with AUS, 1942-44. Mem. Chief Execs. Orgn. (past pres., bd. dirs.). Clubs: Standard (Chgo.); Beverly Hills Tennis (Calif.); Big. Ten of So. Calif. Avocations: tennis, squash, music, reading. Home: 522 N Beverly Dr Beverly Hills CA 90210-3318 *An individual's growth and success as a manager are in direct proportion to his or her ability to develop, motivate and lead able, capable people.*

SCHNEIDER, CYNTHIA PERRIN, former ambassador, political science professor; b. Pa., Aug. 16, 1953; m. Thomas J. Schneider; 2 children. BA in Fine Arts magna cum laude, Harvard U., 1977, PhD in Fine Arts, 1984. Asst. curator European paintings Mus. Fine Arts, Boston, unitl 1984; asst. prof. art history Georgetown U., Washington, 1984-90, assoc. prof. art history, 1990—2004; amb. to The Netherlands Am. Embassy, The Hague, 1998-2001; dir., life sciences & society initiative Georgetown U., Washington, 2003—, disting. prof. in practice of diplomacy, Pfizer Med. Humanities Initiative scholar-in-residence. Lectr. on Rembrandt and Dutch art in US and Europe; vice-chair President's Com. on Arts and Humanities. Author: Rembrandt's Landscapes, 1990; organizer, writer (catalog) Rembrandt's Landscape Print and Drawings, Nat. Gallery Art, 1990; contbr. articles to profl. jour. Mem. steering com. Creative Am., chair fed. design subcom.; coord. arts policy Clinton-Gore Campaign, 1992; bd. dir. Nat. Mus. Women in Arts, Australian-Am. Leadership Dialogue; supervisory bd. Royal Ahold, 2001—05; adv. bd. Strawberry Frog, Inc.; bd. dir. Wesley Theological Sem., Coun. Am. Ambassadors; bd. adv. Inst. for Cultural Diplomacy; internat. bd. adv., Inst. for the Study of Europe Columbia U.; Am. bd. Anne Frank House Found. Recipient Exceptional Svc. Order, Office of US Sec. of Def., 2001. Office: Distinguished Prof in Practice of Diplomacy Georgetown Univ 3300 Whitehaven St NW Ste 500 Washington DC 20057 Office Fax: 301-924-8715. E-mail: schneidc@georgetown.edu.

SCHNEIDER, DAVID ALAN, information technology manager; s. Donald Dale and Donna Margaret Schneider; m. Elizabeth Ann Robinson, May 26, 1979 (div. Apr. 1988); m. Barbara Ann Heck, Apr. 6, 1991; children: Teresa Florence, Melissa Ann, Nicholas David, Ryan Andrew. BSc in Indsl. Mgmt., Milw. Sch. Engring., 1978, degree in Applied Sci. Electronic Comm. Engring. Tech., 1976, degree in Applied Sci. Computer Engring. Tech, 1977. Computer lab asst. Milw. Sch. Engring., 1975—77, R & D coord., 1977—78, pres. alumni assn., 2007—09; account rep. ADP Network Svcs. Inc., Milw., 1978—79; info. svcs. analyst Wis. Power & Light Co., Madison, Wis., 1979—83; info. tech. sr. analyst Anaquest, Madison, 1983—85; global project mgr. S. C. Johnson & Son, Inc., Racine, Wis., 1985—; pres. MIlw. Sch. Eng. Alumni Assn., 2007—09. Mem. Racine County Line Rifle Club Inc., Racine, Wis., 2007—09. R-Conservative. Roman Catholic. Avocations: hunting, computers. Office: S C Johnson & Son Inc 1525 Howe St Racine WI 53403 Business E-Mail: daschnei@scj.com.

SCHNEIDER, DAVID C., bank executive; B in Acctg., Babson Coll., Wellesley, Mass.; MBA, Ind. U., Bloomington. CPA. Positions up to CFO Old Kent Fin. Corp., Mich., 1992—97, exec. v.p. retail banking; mng. ptnr. Stratmor Group; positions up to pres., COO CitiMortgage, Inc., St. Louis, 2001; pres. Home Loans divsn. Washington Mut., Inc., 2005—08; head retail banking WaMu segment J.P. Morgan Chase & Co., 2008—. Pres. Consumer Mortgage Coalition; mem. exec. com. Housing Policy Coun. Office: JP Morgan Chase & Co Hdqs 270 Park Ave New York NY 10017 Office Phone: 206-461-2000.*

SCHNEIDER, DON (CHARLES SCHNEIDER), museum administrator; b. Owosso, Mich., Apr. 15, 1923; s. Gordon Alexander and Kathleen Emily (Skelly) S.; m. Catherine Shuttle, 1944 (dec. 1955); life ptnr. Valerie SoRelle (dec. 1995). Student, Army Air Corps Photo Sch., Denver, 1943, Pasadena Playhouse, 1956-57; cert. in video studio prodn., Valley Cable TV Sta., 1982-83. Developer, negative cutter Technicolor, Hollywood, Calif., 1942-43; printer, timer George W. Colburn Film Lab., Chgo., 1951-54; ind. producer, editor, writer, 1952—; cameraman, dir. Sancho The Homing Steer, Disney Prodns., Burbank, Calif., 1960; film assoc. prodr., dir., editor, mixer, dubbing dir., camerman Fairway Internat., Burbank, 1961-65; lab. supr. Telefilm, Hollywood, 1965-70; Erwin Wasey Advt. Agy., 1970-71; post-prodn. supr., editor Intromedia, Hollywood, 1972; founder, CEO Movie Mus., Mich., 1979—. V.p. Internat. Puppetry Mus., North Hollywood, Calif., 1984—. Editor Movie Museum newsletter, 1979—; prodr.: (bus. film) Majestic Visitor, 1952, (film) How to Use Tools, 1958, (news documentary) Gay Rights Motorcade, 1966, (short) Dancing Lights, Magic Hands of Sculptor Rudy Mercado, 1987, (travel film) Cruise to the Falls, 1953, (musical) Broadway Comes Alive, 1999; prodr. Mardi Gras Magic

Show, 1999, Haunted Castle Movie Set, 1999; dir.: (film) Eegah, The Prehistoric Giant, 1961, (stage prodn.) The Women, 1967; composer: Sonata to a Rose, 1946; set decorator, lights They're Playing Our Song, 1984; actor Let's Do It Again, 1974, Lepke, 1975, Rocky, 1976, Funny Thing Happened On Way To Forum, 2006; film editor Incredible Creatures, 1962, Sadist, 1963, Spies A-Go-Go, 1964, Weekend of Fear, 1965, Man from Clover Grove, 1972, Our Hispanic Heritage, 1977, Norseman, 1978, Mission to Glory, 1979, Players, 1979, Brigham Young, 1984, Forty Days of Musa Dagh, 1987; set designer and cast Waltz Dream, 1939; Author (play) Madison, 2008. Recipient Award for Saving Demille Barn (Hollywood Bowl), Historic Preservation Soc., 2000. Achievements include establishing Conflict-Resolution Libr., 1956; National Endowment for the Arts, 1962; perfecting Eastman color positive/negative process, 1966; founded Separation (church and state) Day 2007 to protect churches. Avocation: counseling. Office: Movie Mus 318 E Oliver St Owosso MI 48867-2351 Office Phone: 989-725-7621.

SCHNEIDER, DUANE BERNARD, English literature educator; b. South Bend, Ind., Nov. 15, 1937; s. William H. and Lillian L. (Pitchford) S.; m. Crystal J. Gips; children: Jeffrey, Eric, Lisa, Emily. BA, Miami U., Oxford, Ohio, 1958; MA, Kent State U., 1960; PhD, U. Colo., 1965. Instr. engring. English U. Colo., 1960-65; asst. prof. English Ohio U., Athens, 1965-70, assoc. prof., 1970-75, chmn. Faculty Senate, 1981-83, chmn. dept. English, 1983-86, prof. emeritus, 1998—; dir. Ohio U. Press, 1986-95; part-time faculty New Sch. U., NYC, 2000—05. Editor, pub. Croissant & Co., 1968-2002. Author: (with others) Anais Nin: An Introduction, 1979. Mem. Thomas Wolfe Soc. (trustee, pres. 1979-81). Business E-Mail: schneide@ohio.edu.

SCHNEIDER, EDGAR ROLF GOTTFRIED, retired mathematician, application developer, writer; b. Bklyn., Apr. 9, 1932; s. Richard Bernhard Grunewald and Sylvia Goldberg, adopted s. Nathan Schneider; m. Sally Jane Mitchell, Oct. 3, 1959 (div.); children: Elisabeth Sutter, Christian, Eric; m. Alexandra Khan Kazan, June 26, 1999. BA, City Coll. of N.Y., 1954; MA, The Am. U., Washington, 1970. Mathematician, sci. computer programmer Svc. Bur. Corp., NYC, 1959—63, LA, 1963—66, IBM Corp., Bethesda, Md., 1966—70, Atlantic City, 1970—74, Harrisburg, Pa., 1974—75, Owego, NY, 1975—82. Spkr. Autism Soc. Fla., Fort Lauderdale, 1996—. Author: Discovering My Autism, 1999, Living the Good Life with Autism, 2003. Singer Fla. Philharmonic Chorus, Fort Lauderdale, 1974—2003. 2nd lt. US Army, 1954—58. Mem.: Phi Beta Kappa, Sigma Xi. Roman Catholic. Avocations: art, music, photography, history, literature. Personal E-mail: hansachsthegreat@juno.com.

SCHNEIDER, EDWARD LEE, botanist, researcher; b. Portland, Oreg., Sept. 14, 1947; s. Edward John and Elizabeth (Mathews) S.; m. Sandra Lee Alfarone, Aug. 2, 1968; children: Kenneth L., Cassandra L. BA, Ctrl. Wash. U., 1969, MS, 1971; PhD, U. Calif., Santa Barbara, 1974. From asst. to assoc. prof. botany S.W. Tex. State U., San Marcos, 1974-84, prof., 1984-94, chmn. biology dept., 1984-89, dean sci., 1989-92; pres., CEO Santa Barbara (Calif.) Botanic Garden, 1992—. Author: The Botanical World, CEOs and Trustees--Building Working Partnerships; contbr. articles to profl. jours. Bd. dirs. Ctr. for Plant Conservation; bd. dirs. Coun. Sci. Soc. Presidents, 2005-06. Recipient Presdl. Rsch. award S.W. Tex. State U., 1986, Disting. Alumnus award Ctrl. Wash. U., 1996; grantee NSF, 1980, 90. Fellow Tex. Acad. Sci. (pres. 1992-93); mem. Internat. Water Lily Soc. (bd. dirs., sec. 1989-96, inducted into Hall of Fame, Award of Appreciation 1997), Bot. Soc. Am. (bd. dirs., pres.-elect 2004, pres. 2005-06, past pres. 2006-07, Award of Merit 1998, Centennial medallion 2006), Am. Assn. Bot. Gardens and Arboreta (bd. dirs.), Internat. Pollination Congress, Nat. Coun. Deans, Am. Assn. Mus. (assessment program adv. com., nat. program com, Excellence in Peer Rev. Sev. award 2007). Home: 1140 Tunnel Rd Santa Barbara CA 93105-2134 Office: Santa Barbara Botanic Garden 1212 Mission Canyon Rd Santa Barbara CA 93105-2126 Office Phone: 805-682-4726 ext. 123. Business E-Mail: eschneider@sbbg.org.

SCHNEIDER, EDWARD LEWIS, medicine educator, research administrator; b. NYC, June 22, 1940; s. Samuel and Ann S. BS, Rensselaer Poly. Inst., 1961; MD, Boston U., 1966. Intern and resident N.Y. Hosp.-Cornell U., NYC, 1966-68; staff fellow Nat. Inst. Allergy and Infectious Diseases, Bethesda, Md., 1968-70; research fellow U. Calif., San Francisco, 1970-73; chief, sect. on cell aging Nat. Inst. Aging, Balt., 1973-79, assoc. dir., 1980-84, dep. dir., 1984-87; prof. medicine, dir. Davis Inst. on Aging U. Colo., Denver, 1979-80; dean Leonard Davis Sch. Gerontology U. So. Calif., LA, 1986—, exec. dir. Ethel Percy Andrus Gerontology Ctr., 1986—, prof. medicine, 1987—, William and Sylvia Kugel prof. gerontology, 1989—. Sci. dir. Buck Ctr. for Rsch. in Aging, 1989-98; cons. MacArthur Found., Chgo., 1985-93, R.W. Johnson Found., Princeton, N.J., 1982-87, Brookdale Found., N.Y.C., 1985-89. Editor: The Genetics of Aging, 1978, The Aging Reproductive System, 1978, Biological Markers of Aging, 1982, Handbook of the Biology of Aging, 1985, 95, 96, Interrelationship Among Aging Cancer and Differentiation, 1985, Teaching Nursing Home, 1985, Modern Biological Theories of Aging, 1987, The Black American Elderly, 1988, Elder Care and the Work Force, 1990, A Secure Old Age: Financing Long-Term Care, 1998, Ageless: Take Control of Your Age and Stay Youthful for Life, 2003. Med. dir. USPHS, 1968—. Recipient Roche award, 1964. Fellow Gerontology Soc., Am. Soc. Clin. Investigation; mem. Am. Assn. Retired Persons, U.S. Naval Acad. Sailing Squadron (coach 1980-86). Office: U So Calif Andrus Gerontology Ctr Los Angeles CA 90089-0001 E-mail: eschneid@usc.edu.

SCHNEIDER, EDWIN KAHN, research scientist; b. Philadelphia, Pa., May 6, 1948; s. Abraham and Edna May Schneider; m. Penelope Lee Ganzel, Aug. 5, 1980; children: Andrew Ganzel, Thomas Schmidt. AB, Harvard U., 1970, PhD, 1976. Postdoctoral rsch. assoc. MIT, Cambridge, Mass., 1974—77, prin. rsch. scientist, 1984—84; NATO postdoctoral fellow Reading U., England, 1977—78; rsch. fellow, assoc. Harvard U., Cambridge, Mass., 1978—83; assoc., sr. rsch. scientist U. Md., College Park, Md., 1984—93; sr. rsch. scientist Ctr. for Ocean-Land-Atmosphere Studies, Calverton, Md., 1993—; prof. climate dynamics George Mason U., Fairfax, Va., 2002—; exec. editor Climate Dynamics, 2004—. Author: (book chapter) Climate Change: An Integrated Perspective; contbr. (articles) Encyclopedia of Global Environmental Change; contbr. articles to profl. jours. Grantee, NSF, NOAA, NASA, DOE, EPRI, 1985—; fellow, NSF, 1970—72; Nat. Merit scholar, 1966—70. Fellow: Am. Meteorol. Soc.; mem.: Am. Geophys. Union. Achievements include research in Hadley circulation, El Nino/Southern Oscillation, atmospheric and oceanic dynamics, climate change. Avocations: orchestral violinist, golf. Office: Center for Ocean-Land-Atmosphere Studies 4041 Powder Mill Rd Suite 302 Beltsville MD 20705

SCHNEIDER, GERALD L., plastic surgeon; b. Mechanicsburg, Pa., Oct. 25, 1945; s. Gordon Henry and Pauline Emma (Rife) S.; 1 child, Ross Roberts. BS, No. Ariz. U., 1968; MD, U. Ariz., 1973. Intern Naval Regional Med. Ctr., San Diego, 1973-74; resident in gen. surgery U.S. Naval Hosp., San Diego, 1974-78, resident in plastic surgery Portsmouth, Va., 1978-80, staff surgeon divsn. plastic surgery San Diego, 1981-83, chief divsn. plastic surgery, 1983-84; pvt. practice Flagstaff, Ariz., 1984-90; staff surgeon La Jolla (Calif.) Cosmetic Surgery Ctr., 1990-91; surgeon Scripps Clinic & Rsch. Found., La Jolla, 1991—. Capt. USNR Fellow ACS; mem. Am. Soc. Plastic Surgeons. Avocation: golf. Office: Scripps Clinic & Rsch Found 10666 N Torrey Pines Rd La Jolla CA 92037-1092 Office Phone: 858-554-9606. Business E-Mail: schneider.gerald@scrippshealth.org.

SCHNEIDER, GISELA, art educator; b. Frankfurt, Germany, June 1, 1949; BA in Visual Art, Mont. State U., Bozeman, 1972. Cert. tchr., Mont. Instr. H.S. visual art Great Falls Sch. Dist. #1, Mont., 1972—80, Missoula County Sch. Dist., Mont., 1985—86, Colstrup Sch. Dist. #9, Mont., 1986—. Visual art workshop presenter Mont. Edn. Assn. Annual State Convs., 1988—; visual art juror and inservice presenter in field. Mem. Mont. Art Edn. Assn. (secondary art edn. com. 1972—, rep. 1989-92, Mt. Art Educator of Yr. 1993).

SCHNEIDER, GLEN WALTER, music educator, director; b. Englewood, NJ, Sept. 23, 1979; s. Walter Carlin and Judith Anne Schneider; m. Ashlee Sarah Johnson, July 12, 2003. BS in Music Edn., Duquesne U., Pitts., 1997—2001; MA in Music Edn., VanderCook Coll. Music, Chgo., 2004—06. Cert. tchr. Ill., 2001. Asst. dir. bands Oswego HS, Ill., 2003—06, dir. bands, 2006—, coord. bands, 2006—. Mem. edn. team Vic Firth, Inc., Mass., 2003—; product cons. Superscope Technologies, Geneva; with Internat. Conducting Symposium, Rome, 2008. Musician: Shawn Maxwell Quartet, 2001—; arranger (music composition) Turning Drumset Styles Into Drumset Grooves, 2006. Advisor Oswego HS Band Boosters, 2003—06. Recipient Influential Educator award, Oswego HS, 2005. Mem.: Fox Valley Music Festival (chairperson 2006—), Nat. Band Assn., Ill. Music Educators Assn. (dir. jazz ensemble II 2005, chairperson Dist. Band 2006—08), Music Educators Nat. Conf., Internat. Assn. Jazz Educators. Home: 421 Grape Vine Trl Oswego IL 60543 Office: Oswego HS 4250 Rte 71 Oswego IL 60543 Office Fax: 630-554-7160; Home Fax: 630-554-7160. Business E-Mail: gschneider0923@oswego308.org.

SCHNEIDER, HILARY A., Internet company executive; BA in Econs., Brown U., 1982; MBA, Harvard Bus. Sch., 1986. Dir. devel. The Balt. Sun Co., 1992—94, v.p. new bus. devel., 1994—95, v.p. sales, 1996—97, v.p. sales and mktg., 1997—98, gen. mgr., 1998—99; v.p. corp. fin. Drexel Burnham Lambert Inc., 1986—90; dir. bus. devel. Times Mirror Corp., 1990—92; pres., CEO Times Mirror Interactive, Balt., 1999—2000, Red Herring Comm., 2000—02; v.p., Knight Ridder Digital Knight Ridder, Inc., 2002—04, pres., CEO, Knight Ridder Digital, 2002—04, sr. v.p., 2005—06; sr. v.p. marketplaces (now called Local Markets and Commerce) Yahoo! Inc., Sunnyvale, Calif., 2006, exec. v.p., local markets and commerce divsn., Yahoo! Pub. Network, 2006—07, exec. v.p., global partner solutions, 2007—. Bd. dirs. CareerBuilder.com, Classified Ventures, Topix.net, ShopLocal; exec. sponsor and leader of significant cross-co. partnership with US publishing companies, including several daily newspapers, 2006—. Mem.: Newspaper Assn. Am. (bd. dirs.). Office: Yahoo Inc 701 1st Ave Sunnyvale CA 94089

SCHNEIDER, JAMES M., bank executive, former computer company executive; b. 1952; BS in Acctg., Carroll Coll, Waukesha, Wis., 1974. Mgmt. to ptnr. Price Waterhouse, 1974—93; sr. v.p. fin. MCI Commns., 1993—96; v.p. fin. & chief acctg. officer Dell Computer Corp., Round Rock, Tex., 1996—98, interim chief info. officer, 1999—2000, sr. v.p., CFO, 2000—07; exec. chmn. Frontier Bancshares Inc., Austin, Tex., 2007—. Bd. dirs. Lockheed Martin Corp., 2005—. Office: Frontier Bancshares Inc 4610 Chiappero Austin TX 78731

SCHNEIDER, JAN, retired obstetrics and gynecology educator; b. Prague, Czechoslovakia, Dec. 10, 1933; came to US, 1963, naturalized, 1967; s. Evzen and Erika S.; m. Sandra Wilson, May 20, 1961; children: Hana, Donald, Kathryn, Jonathan. M.B., U. London, 1957; M.P.H., U. Mich., 1967. Prof. ob-gyn, chief obstetric service dept. ob-gyn U. Mich. Med. Sch., Ann Arbor, 1963-77; prof., chmn. ob-gyn. Med. Coll. Pa. and Hahnemann U. (now Drexel U. Coll. Medicine), Phila., 1978-97, assoc. dean, 1997-99, prof. and chmn. emeritus of ob-gyn., 1999—. Editor: (with R. J. Bolognese and R. H. Schwarz) Perinatal Medicine, 2d edit, 1981. Fellow Am. Coll. Obstetricians and Gynecologists, Soc. Perinatal Obstetricians, Am. Gynecol. and Obstet. Soc., Phila. Obstet. Soc. Presbyterian.

SCHNEIDER, JANET M., arts administrator, curator, painter; b. N.Y.C., June 6, 1950. d. August Arthur and Joan (Battaglia) S.; m. Michael Francis Sperendi, Sept. 21, 1985. BA summa cum laude, Queens Coll., CUNY, 1972; spl. study fine arts Boston U. Tanglewood Inst., 1971. With Queens Mus., Flushing, N.Y.C., 1973-89, curator, 1973-75, program dir., 1975-77, exec. dir., 1977-89. Collections arranged include: Sons and others, Women Artists See Men (author catalog), 1975, Urban Aesthetics (author catalog), 1976, Masters of the Brush, Chinese Painting and Calligraphy from the Sixteenth to the Nineteenth Century (co-author catalog), 1977, Symcho Moszkowicz: Portrait of the Artist in Postwar Europe (author catalog), 1978, Shipwrecked 1622, The Lost Treasure of Philip IV (author catalog), 1981, Michaelangelo: A Sculptor's World (author catalog), 1983, Joseph Cornell: Revisited (author catalog), 1992, Blueprint for Change: The Life and Times of Lewis H. Latimer (co-author catalog), 1995. Chmn. Cultural Instns. Group, N.Y.C., 1986-87; mem. N.Y.C. Commn. for Cultural Affairs, 1991-93; bd. dirs. N.Y.C. Partnership, 1987-88, Gallery Assn. N.Y. State 1979-81; exec. dir. Cultural Inst. Group, 1995-06; cons. dir. Flushing Town Hall, 2007-08. Mem. Artists Choice Mus. (trustee 1979-82), Am. Assn. Mus., Phi Beta Kappa.

SCHNEIDER, JOANNE, artist; b. Lima, Ohio, Dec. 4, 1919; d. Joseph and Laura (Office) Federman; m. Norman Schneider, May 15, 1941; children: Melanie Schneider Tucker, Lois Schneider Oppenheim. BFA, Syracuse U., 1941. One-man shows John Heller Gallery, NYC, 1954, 55, 57, 58, Tirca Karlis Gallery, Provincetown, Mass., 1963, Frank Rehn Gallery, NYC, 1965, 66, 69, 72, 75, Elaine Benson Gallery, Bridgehampton, NY, 1972, 74, 79, 85, St. Mary's Coll., St. Mary's City, Md., 1978, Alonzo Gallery, NYC, 1978, Discovery Art Gallery, Clifton, NJ, 1978; group shows include Whitney Mus., NYC, Pa. Acad. Arts, Corcoran Galleries, Washington, Toledo Mus., U. Nebr., Everson Mus., Syracuse, NY; represented in permanent collections Met. Mus. Art, NYC, Colby Coll., Syracuse U., Butler Inst., St. Mary's Coll., U. Notre Dame, Guild Hall, East Hampton, NY Recipient Audubon Artists Stanley Grumbacher Meml. award, 1972 Address: 35 E 75th St New York NY 10021-2761 *A life spent in pursuit of creative expression is a fuller, more satisfying life.*

SCHNEIDER, JOHN ARNOLD, investor; b. Chgo., Dec. 4, 1926; s. Arnold George and Anna (Wagner) S.; m. Elizabeth C. Simpson, Oct. 20, 1951; children: Richard Ward, William Arnold, Elizabeth Anne. BS, U. Notre Dame, 1948. Exec. assignments with CBS-TV in, Chgo. and NYC, 1950-58; v.p., gen. mgr. sta. WCAU-TV, Phila., 1958-64; sta. WCBS-TV, NYC, 1964-65; pres. CBS TV Network, 1965-66, CBS/Broadcast Group, 1966-69, 71-77; exec. v.p. CBS, Inc., 1969-71, sr. v.p., from, 1977; pres., chief exec. officer MTV Networks, Inc., 1979-84. Trustee, mem. exec. com. U. Notre Dame; trustee Com. for Econ. Devel. Served with USNR, 1943-46. Mem.: Indian Harbor Yacht. Roman Catholic. Home: 155 Clapboard Ridge Rd Greenwich CT 06831-3304

SCHNEIDER, JOHN DAVID, theatre director, playwright, actor, jazz singer; b. Fond du Lac, Wis., June 7, 1948; s. David Elmer and Bernice Catherine (Pable) S. BA, St. Norbert Coll., 1970. Mem. Theatre X, Milw., 1971—; also artistic dir., 1978—; profl. playwright, 1973—; vocalist, leader John Schneider Orch., Milw., 1988—. Author: (plays) Scenarios For the Living/For the Dead, 1983; author numerous plays. Recipient New Works award Wis. Arts Bd., 1990; NEA fellow, 1988, Milwaukee County fellow, 1991, Program Devel. grantee Theatre Comms. Group-Pew Charitable Trust, 1992. Office: Theatre X 1231 E Kane Pl Milwaukee WI 53202-1630

SCHNEIDER, JOHN K., financial advisor; b. Bryn Mawr, Pa., June 30, 1964; s. Arnold C. and Dorothy A. Schneider. BS in Fin. summa cum laude, Lehigh U., 1986. Cert. chartered fin. analyst 1989. V.p. Wilmington Capital Mgmt., Del., 1986-91; sr. securities analyst DuPont Pension Fund, Wilmington, 1991; sr. v.p. Newbold's Asset Mgmt., Bryn Mawr, 1991; joined Schneider Capital Mgmt., 1996; sr. portfolio mgr., mng. dir. PIMCO Equity Advisors, 1999—2005; founder, pres., chief investment advisor JS Asset Management, LLC (JSAM), West Conshohocken, Pa., 2005; sub-advisor Touchstone Large Cap Value Fund, 2006—. Mem.: Fin. Analysts of Wilmington, Phila. Fin. Analysts Soc. (speakers com. mem.), Beta Gamma Sigma (v.p. 1986), Kappa Alpha Soc. Republican. Episcopalian. Avocations: sailing, volleyball, photography. Office: JS Asset Mgmt, LLC One Tower Bridge 100 Front St, Ste 501 West Conshohocken PA 19428 Office Phone: 610-234-2202. Office Fax: 610-825-1831.

SCHNEIDER, LISA A., lawyer; b. Bklyn., Apr. 24, 1962; BA cum laude, SUNY, Binghamton, 1984; JD, St. John's U. Sch. Law, 1987. Bar: NJ 1987, NY 1988, US Dist. Ct. (so. and ea. dists. NY) 1988, US Dist. Ct. (dist. NJ) 1988, Fla. 1994, cert.: Fla. Bd. (wills, trusts and estates) 2003. Atty. Shea & Gould; positions to shareholder pvt. wealth svcs. dept. Gunster, Yoakley & Stewart, West Palm Beach, Fla., 1994—. Contbr. articles to profl. publs. Mem. profl. adv. com. United Way of Martin County Found. Named one of Best of the Bar, South Fla. Bus. Jour., 2003—04, Fla. Legal Elite, Fla. Trend mag., 2004, Top 100 Attys., Worth mag., 2005, 2007, Top Lawyers, South Fla. Legal Guide, 2006. Mem.: Jewish Women's Found. of Jewish Fedn. of Palm Beach County (founding trustee), Found. of Jewish Fedn. of Palm Beach County (mem. profl. adv. com.), East Coast Estate Planning Coun., Treasure Coast Planned Giving Coun., Martin County Estate Planning Coun., ABA, NY State Bar Assn., NJ State Bar Assn., Martin County Bar Assn. (mem. elder law, probate and guardianship com.). Office: Gunster Yoakley & Stewart Phillips Point 777 S Flagler Dr Ste 500 E West Palm Beach FL 33401 Office Phone: 561-650-0680. Office Fax: 561-655-5677. E-mail: lschneider@gunster.com.

SCHNEIDER, MARK, political science professor; b. NYC, Oct. 28, 1946; s. Irving and Ida Schneider; m. Susan Roth, June 27, 1986; children: Johanna, Elizabeth. BA, Bklyn. Coll., 1967; PhD, U. N.C., 1974. Asst. prof. polit. sci. U. Mich., Ann Arbor, 1973-74, SUNY, Stony Brook, 1974-78, assoc. prof., 1978-85, prof., 1985—2004, chmn. dept., 1986—2004, disting. prof., 2004—. Fulbright sr. lectr., India, 1980—81; dep. commr. Inst. Edn. Scis., 2004—05. Author: The Competitive City, 1989, Public Entrepreneurs, 1995, Choosing Schools, 2000, Charter Schools: Hope or Hype, 2007; contbr. articles to profl. jours. Dep. commr. Inst. Edn. Scis., 2004—05; commr. Nat. Ctr. for Ednl. Stats., 2005—08; v.p. Am. Inst. Rsch., 2008—. Vis. scholar, Am. Enterprise Inst., 2009—. Mem. Am. Polit. Sci. Assn. (v.p. 2000-01), Midwest Polit. Sci. Assn. Office: Am Inst Rsch 1000 Thomas Jefferson St Washington DC 20007

SCHNEIDER, MARK LEWIS, foreign policy executive, retired government agency administrator; b. Newark, Dec. 31, 1941; s. Benjamin and Ruth (Kobran) S.; m. Susan Gilbert, June 20, 1965; children: Aaron Mitchell, Miriam Beth. AB in Journalism with honors, U. Calif., Berkeley, 1963; MA in Polit. Sci., San Jose State Coll., 1965; LLD (hon.), Am. U., 2000. Reporter UPI, San Francisco, 1963-64, San Francisco News Call Bull., 1965; vol. Peace Corps, El Salvador, 1966-68; reporter Washington Daily News, 1969-70; mem. staff U.S. Senate Judiciary Subcom., 1970-71; legis. asst. to Sen. Edward M. Kennedy, 1971-77, 80-81; dep. asst. sec. for human rights Dept. State, Washington, 1977-79; mem. del. UN Gen. Assembly, 1978, UN Human Rights Commn., 1979; coordinator policy planning, sr. advisor Pan Am. Health Orgn., 1981-93; adminstr. for Latin Am. and Caribbean U.S. AID, 1993-99; dir. The Peace Corps, 1999-2001; sr. v.p. Internat. Crisis Group, Washington, 2001—. Lectr. Kennedy Inst. Politics, Harvard U., 1976; adj. prof. Georgetown U., 1996. Trustee Am. U., 2006—; bd. dirs. Internat. Human Rights Law Group, 1981—92. Fulbright fellow, 1976; recipient George W. Eastman medal U. Rochestor, 2000, Bernardo O'Higgins medal Govt. Chile, 1993 Mem. Am. Polit. Sci. Assn., Latin Am. Studies Assn. Democrat. Jewish. Home: 3517 Tilden St NW Washington DC 20008-3122 Office Phone: 202-785-1601. E-mail: mschneider@crisisgroup.org.

SCHNEIDER, MARTIN AARON, photojournalist, ecologist, engineer, writer, artist, television director, filmmaker, public advocate, medical researcher, educator; b. NYC, Sept. 23, 1926; s. Morris and Florence (Frohlich) S. Student, Stuyvesant Sci., 1941-44; BC, CUNY, 1948—53. Editor Nocturne; artist, 1941—; photographer, 1954—. Photojournalist Life, Time, Newsweek, Sports Illustrated, NY Times, NBC-TV, Ency. Britannica, Mpls. Tribune, Handball Illustrated, Time Annual Year in Review, Grolier Ency., Crowell-Collier Ency., NBC Startime, Variety, Time-Life: Ecology, Saturday Review of Literature, 1960—; ecologist, USPHS, US Senate, US EPA, NYCEPA, NY State Dept. Environ. Conservation, NYC Dept. Air Pollution, 1964—; product safety engineer, designer, builder, crash-safety, pollution and radiation monitoring, multi-alternate fuel, laboratory vehicle, stereotactic radiosurgery: safer therapy delivery collimator, 1967—, univ. faculties NYU, Cornell U., Ithaca, NY, New Sch. Social Rsch. U., NYC, SUNY, Albany, Cooper Union for Advancement of Sci. and Art, NYC, CUNY, Iowa U., lectr. in field, 1969—; pub. advocate, NYC Health Dept., NY State Health Dept., NY State Dept. Environ. Conservation, Gov. Rockefeller's State Study Commission for NYC (Scott Commission), US District Ct., NY Supreme Ct., People of NYC, NYC Council, NY Atty. Gen., 1970—. TV news guest NBC Today, CBS, ABC, FOX, PBS, 1970—; radio news guest NBC, CBS, NPR, 1970; TV and radio commentator, NBC, CBS, ABC, PBS, Fox, 1970—; author: Breath of Death, 1972, Consumer Genocide: Censored Survival Kit 1992; The Schneider Tapes, 1996, War Against War, ed. 1996, CARnage: 3 Million Killed by Suppressed 100 mph Safety, 1997, The Food You Eat--Eats You: How to Get Safe Food in Same Stores at Same Price, 1998, Cataclysmathon, 2001, Cancerterias, 2002, Scars of Eternity, 2005; co-author: NBC Startime, 1963, America-Photographic Statements, 1972, Eye of Conscience, 1974 (chpt. Martin Schneider); dir., prodr., writer, videographer, cinematographer (TV documentaries) Environment Crusade, CBS, 1970, The Poisoned Air, CBS, 1970, Killers of the Environment, NBC, 1971, Censorship of Pollution Solutions by Media and Government, PBS, 1974, No Justice for Victims-Criminals Only, 1992; contbr. NY Times, Ency. Britannica, Macmillan Ency. of Photographic Artists, NY Village Voice "Whole Earth Ranger: Ecology's Batman", New World Or No World (Frank Herbert) 1970—; photography exhibited at Mus. Modern Art, NYC, 1958—, George Eastman House Mus., Rochester, NY, 1963, 64—, Libr. Congress, 1970, Smithsonian Instn., 1972—, Art Inst. Chgo., 1973—, Whitney Mus., NYC, 1978—; permanent exhibit includes NY Mus. of TV and Radio, 1999; painting exhibited at Guggenheim Mus., NYC, 1943; film exhibited at Am. Mus. Natural History, NYC, 1969-72, network TV guest appearances; dir. documentaries, 1969-. Served with US Army Paratroopers, 1944-46, PTO. Fellowship grantee Creative Artists Pub. Svc., 1977, 78; recipient TV Franny Consumer Advocacy award, 1974, for work that was a basis for the first Clean Air Act of 1970. Jewish. Achievements include advocacy for Mayo Clinic non-toxic patient-derived vaccine cancer theraphy now offered alternative to chemotherapy uniquely in US for all stages, 2004. Office: 545 8th Ave Ste 401 New York NY 10018 Office Phone: 212-840-1234. *Where millions are endangered where my work makes a difference--despite gunfire, vehicle sabotage, seizure of home and all possessions, censorship--I cannot compromise public health for private wealth- for there is no dream for me in moving mere mountains, but only in moving man to move himself.*

SCHNEIDER, MATHIEU, professional hockey player; b. NYC, June 12, 1969; married. Defenseman Montreal Canadiens, 1990-95, 2009, NY Islanders, 1995-96, Toronto Maple Leafs, 1996-98, NY Rangers, 1998—2000, LA Kings, 2000—03, Detroit Red Wings, 2003—07, Anaheim Ducks, 2007—08, Atlanta Thrashers, 2008—09, Vancouver Canucks, 2009—. Mem. Team USA, World Cup of Hockey, 1996, 2004, Team USA, Olympic Games, Nagano, Japan, 1998, Torino, Italy, 2006. Named to NHL All-Star Game, 1996, 2003. Achievements include being a member of Stanely Cup Champion Montreal Canadiens, 1993; being a member of World Cup Champion Team USA, 1996. Office: Vancouver Canucks 800 Griffiths Way Vancouver BC V6B 6G1 Canada*

SCHNEIDER, MATTHEW ROGER, lawyer; b. NYC, Nov. 7, 1948; s. Theodore David Schneider and Rosalind (Schwartz) Werner; m. Marjorie Ann Friedlander, Mar. 6, 1976; children: Adam Benjamin, Emily Beth. BA, Cornell U., 1970; student, Georgetown U., 1971; JD, Cath. U., Washington, 1974. Bar: D.C. 1976, U.S. Dist. Ct. D.C., 1994. Staff asst. U.S. Senate Jud. Com., Washington, 1973-74; counsel U.S. Senate Govt. Ops. Com., Washington, 1974-77; spl. asst. Office of Sec. Def., Washington, 1977-79; dir. legis. affairs SEC, Washington, 1979-81, sr. counsel, divsn. corp. fin., 1981-82; chief of staff U.S. Senator Jeff Bingaman, Washington, 1983-85; prin. Law Office Matthew Schneider, Washington, 1985-87; ptnr. Willkie, Farr & Gallagher, Washington, 1987-95, Garvey Shubert Barer, Washington, 1996—98, mng. dir. DC office, 1998—, mng. dir. NYC office, 2001—, mng. dir. Beijing office, 2005—06. Chmn. govt. and legal affairs com. Nat. Epilepsy Found., Washington, 1997—2003; bd. dirs. Nat. Epilepsy Found., 2000—04, mem. exec. com., 2001—04; bd. dirs Capitol Hill Hosp., Washington, 1987—95. Avocations: physical fitness training, singing, guitar. Office: Garvey Schubert Barer 5th Fl 1000 Potomac St NW Ste 5 Washington DC 20007-3501 Office Phone: 202-965-7880.

SCHNEIDER, NINA MICHELLE, nursing educator; b. Camp Hill, Pa., Sept. 25, 1964; d. Francis Albert and Donna Lee (Broome) S. ADN, Harrisburg CC, Pa., 1987; BSN, Thomas Jefferson U., Phila., 1992. BLS, ACLS, RN, Pa. Staff nurse med./surg. unit Polyclinic Med. Ctr., Harrisburg, 1987-88, staff nurse CCU, 1988-91, staff devel. instr., 1991—. Mem. AACN, MMSDO. Avocations: boating, crafts, skiing. Home: 19 Cedarhurst Ln Camp Hill PA 17011-7906 Office: Polyclinic Med Ctr 2601 N 3rd St Harrisburg PA 17110-2004

SCHNEIDER, ORREN, environmental engineer, researcher; b. Trenton, NJ, Aug. 6, 1964; s. Eugene and Anita Schneider; m. Jordana Yael Skurka; 1 child, Kaylie Rebecca. BSChemE, Cornell U., Ithaca, NY, 1987; MSEVE, U. Mass., Amherst, 1990, PhD, 1996. Cert. profl. engr., NJ, 1998. Sr. prin. engr. Hazen and Sawyer, NYC, 1996—2001; dir. water process rsch. Black & Veatch, NYC, 2001—04; mgr. water rsch. Fay, Spofford & Thorndike, West Caldwell, NJ, 2004—05; sr. environ. engr. Am. Water, Mt. Laurel, NJ, 2005—. Contbr. articles to profl. jour. Mem.: NJ Water Works Assn. (mem. rsch. and techncial transfer com. 2005—08), Am. Water Works Assn. (coagulation and filtration com. 1997—2008, chmn. plant ops. rsch. com. 2006—). Avocations: travel, kayaking. Office: Am Water 1025 Laurel Oak Rd Voorhees NJ 08043 Personal E-mail: oschneider1@comcast.net. Business E-Mail: orren.schneider@amwater.com.

SCHNEIDER, PAUL LEONARD, internist; b. LA, Feb. 24, 1964; s. George Herman and Rosa Schneider; m. Lisa Barukh, Mar. 15, 1998. BS, UCLA, 1986; MD, U. Southern Calif., 1990. Bioethicist VA Greater LA Healthcare Sys., 1994—. Pres. Southern Calif. Bioethics Com. Consortium, LA, 2007—. Contbr. scientific papers to profl. jours., chapters to books. Recipient Sherman Mellinkoff Med. Tchg. award, VA Internal Medicine Residency, 1994. Fellow: ACP (Phila.). Office: Greater LA VA Healthcare Sys 11301 Wilshire Blvd Los Angeles CA 90073 Business E-Mail: paul.schneider@va.gov.

SCHNEIDER, PETER RAYMOND, retired political scientist; b. Muskogee, Okla., Aug. 8, 1939; s. Leo Frederick and Tillie Oleta (Cannon) S.; m. Anne Larason, Jan. 22, 1964 (div. 1983); children: Christopher, Geoffrey; m. Adrienne Armstrong, Dec. 19, 1986; children: Robbie, Samantha. BS, Okla. State U., 1966, MS, 1968; PhD, Ind. U., 1974. News editor No. Va. Sun, Arlington, 1961-62; news writer AP, Balt., 1962, Balt. News-Am., 1962-65; asst. prof. U. Oreg., Eugene, 1974-76; pres. Inst. of Policy Analysis, Eugene, 1976-83; v.p. Am. Justice Inst., Sacramento, 1983; dir. Ctr. for Assessment of The Juvenile Justice Ctr., Sacramento, 1983; v.p. Nat. Partnership, Washington, 1985; sr. rsch. scientist Pacific Inst. for Rsch. and Evaluation, Bethesda, Md., 1984-92, dir. justice div., 1986-89; pres. Inst. of Policy Analysis, McLean, Va., 1992-95; CEO IPA Internat., Inc., Vienna, 1995—2007. Contbr. numerous articles to profl. jours., chpts. to books. Recipient Julia Lathrop award Am. Criminal Justice Assn., 1985. Mem. Am. Polit. Sci. Assn., Am. Restitution Assn., Pi Sigma Alpha, Sigma Delta Chi, Phi Kappa Phi, Omicron Delta Kappa, Phi Kappa Theta. Avocations: flying, tennis, selling wine, travel. Home: 1345 Woodside Dr Mc Lean VA 22102-1530 Personal E-mail: schneid703@aol.com. *In a career devoted to the pursuit of knowledge, I have learned that nothing - absolutely nothing - is worth more than lessons learned from painful personal experience. To my regret, I usually learned such lessons after the opportunities to profit from them had already passed. If I could do it over again I would be more daring and venturesome and make my mistakes early, while there was still plenty of time to invest the information.*

SCHNEIDER, PHILLIP HARRY LEONARD (PHIL SCHNEIDER), healthcare organization executive; b. Saginaw, Mich., Jan. 29, 1947; s. Leonard Franklin and Marjory Avalon (Reed) S.; m. Patricia. BA in Journalism, Ctrl. Mich. U., 1969, BS in Polit. Sci., 1969, MA in Polit. Sci., 1970. Editor-in-chief Midland Daily News, Mich., 1970—75; mgr. fin and pub. rels. Dow Chem. Co., Midland, Mich., 1975-78, mgr. media relations, 1978-82, dir. pub. rels., 1982-86; v.p. corp. comm. Medlantic Healthcare Corp., Washington, 1986—91; v.p. external rels., program devel. Nat. Assn. Chain Drug Stores, Alexandria, Va., 1991—; pres. Nat. Assn. Chain Drug Stores Found., 1991—. Comm. chmn. Am. Indsl. Health Coun., 1984-86; pub. rels. chmn. Mich. Chem. Coun., Lansing, 1984-86; dir. Am. Found. Pharm. Edn., Pub. Affairs Coun., Washington; chmn. Nat. Coun. on Patient Info. and Edn., Washington; founder, bd. dirs. Sun Safety Alliance. Contbr. articles to profl. jours. Councilman, Midland City Council, 1982-86; bd. dirs. Big Brothers, Jr. Achievement, United Way. Named Outstanding Citizen City of Midland, 1983. Mem.: Assn. Fundraising Profls., Am. Mktg. Assn., Am. Med. Writers Assn., Pub. Rels. Soc. America, Nat. Press Club, Sigma Delta Chi. Roman Catholic. Achievements include playing a key role in establishing and directing the Small Business Coalition on Health Care Reform. Avocations: golf, racquetball, biking, reading. Office Phone: 703-549-3001.

SCHNEIDER, REBECCA, librarian; b. Parkersburg, W.Va., Dec. 20, 1963; BS in Psychology, Slippery Rock U., 1987. Spl. projects coord./circulation Wilkinsburgh Pub. Libr., 1995—2001; branch mgr. Maricopa County Libr. Dist., 2001—06; overnight libr. supr. Ariz. State U., 2006—. Mem.: NOW, Women's Campaign Forum, League of Conservation Voters, Ctr. Biological Diversity, Democracy for America, Progressive Dem. America, Humane Soc. America, J Street, Emily's List, Sierra Club. Democrat. Office: 1550 E 2nd St Mesa AZ 85203-8931 also: 1970 N Harteford St Unit 1 Chandler AZ 85226 Office Phone: 480-833-5101. Personal E-mail: schneiderforcongress@gmail.com.

SCHNEIDER, RICHARD JOHN, literature and language professor; b. New Ulm, Minn., June 22, 1945; s. Richard Curtis and Myrtle Helen Schneider; m. Mary Helen Nielsen, Aug. 8, 1969; children: Eric Richard, Heidi Helen Brar, Rick Daniel. BA in English and Edn., Hamline U., St. Paul, 1967; MA in English, U. Calif., Santa Barbara, 1968, PhD in English, 1973. English tchr. Oak Grove HS, San Jose, Calif., 1969—70; prof. English Barton Coll. (Formerly Atlantic Christian Coll.), Wilson, NC, 1973—86; prof. emeritus, English Wartburg Coll., Waverly, Iowa, 1986—. Mem.: Thoreau Soc. (bd. dir. 1996—2006). Liberal. Avocations: hiking, movies. Office: Wartburg Coll 100 Wartburg Blvd Waverly IA 50677 Business E-Mail: richard.schneider@wartburg.edu.

SCHNEIDER, RICHARD T(HEODORE), optics scientist, researcher, engineer; b. Munich, July 29, 1927; came to U.S., 1961; s. Wilhelm and Martha E. (Hofmann) S.; m. Lore M. Reinhard, May 16, 1950; children: Ursula M. Schneider Long, Richard W. Diploma in physics, U. Stuttgart, Fed. Republic of Germany, 1958, PhD, 1961. Registered profl. engr. Calif. Teaching asst. U. Stuttgart, 1958-61; sect. chief Allison div. Gen. Motors Corp., Indpls., 1961-65; assoc. prof. U. Fla., Gainesville, 1965-68, prof., 1968-88, prof. emeritus, 1988-90; pres. Eye Rsch. Lab., Inc., Alachua, Fla., 1984-90; chief scientist RTS Labs., Inc., Alachua, 1984-92. Cons. Allison div. Gen. Motors Corp., Indpls., 1965-67; IPA assignment Eglin AFB, Ft. Walton Beach, Fla., 1983; liaison scientist USN Office Naval Rsch., London, 1975. Editor: Uranium Plasmas, 1971; patentee in field; contbr. articles to profl. jours. Recipient Medal for Exceptional Sci. Achievement, NASA, 1975, Outstanding Tech. Achievement award, Fla. Engring. Soc., 1978. Mem. Internat. Soc. Optical Engring., Am. Soc. Healthcare Engring., Sigms Xi, Tau Beta Pi (Eminent Engr. 1970). Home: 12903 NW 112th Ave Alachua FL 32615-6520 Home Phone: 386-462-3301. Personal E-mail: schneider-labs@att.net.

SCHNEIDER, ROB, actor; b. Pacifica, Calif., Oct. 31, 1963; s. Marvin and Pilar Schneider; m. London King, 1988 (div. 1990); 1 child, Chole Autumn. Co-owner restaurant Eleven, San Francisco. Actor: (films) Martians Go Home, 1990, Necessary Roughness, 1991, Home Alone 2: Lost in New York, 1992, Surf Ninjas, 1993, Demolition Man, 1993, The Beverly Hillbillies, 1993, Judge Dredd, 1995, Down Periscope, 1996, The Adventures of Pinocchio, 1996, Knock Off, 1998, Susan's Plan, 1998, The Waterboy, 1998, Deuce Bigalow: Male Gigolo, 1999, Big Daddy, 1999, Muppets From Space, 1999, Little Nicky, 2000, The Animal, 2001, The Hot Chick, 2002, Mr. Deeds, 2002, (voice) Eight Crazy Nights, 2002, 50 First Dates, 2004, Around the World in 80 Days, 2004, The Longest Yard, 2005, Deuce Bigalow: European Gigolo, 2005, Grandma's Boy, 2006, The Benchwarmers, 2006, Click, 2006, (voice) Shark Bait, 2006, Little Man, 2006, American Crude, 2007, Juliana and the Medicine Fish, 2007, I Now Pronounce You Chuck & Larry, 2007, Big Stan, 2007, You Don't Mess with the Zohan, 2008, (TV series) Saturday Night Live, 1990-94, Men Behaving Badly, 1996-97, (TV films) The Mummy Parody, 2001, (voice) The Electric Piper, 2003, Back to Norm, 2005.

SCHNEIDER, ROBERT, prosthodontist, educator; b. Glendale, Calif., June 2, 1949; s. John Charles and Alice Jo Schneider; m. Mary Ann Ryan, July 21, 1972; children: Robert Charles, Ryan James. DDS, U. Southern Calif., 1976; MS, U. Iowa, 1983. Diplomate Am. Bd. Prosthodontics, 1988. Prof., divison dir. maxillofacial prosthodontics U. Iowa Hosp. and Clin., 1990—. Fellow: Acad. Gen. Dentistry, Internat. Team Implantology, Acad. Osseointegration; mem.: Am. Prosthodontic Soc. (exec. dir. 2001—08). Home: 4124 Overlook Rd NorthEast Solon IA 52333 Personal E-mail: rschnei152@aol.com.

SCHNEIDER, ROBERT JAY, oncologist; b. Miami, Fla., May 31, 1949; s. Irving and Ethel (Pack) S.; m. Barbara Cunningham, June 1, 1974; children: Matthew, Kirsten. Student, Washington U., 1967-69; BA cum laude, Boston U., 1971; MD, Albert Einstein Coll. Medicine, NYC, 1975. Diplomate Am. Bd. Internal Medicine, Am. Bd. Oncology; lic. physician, N.Y. Intern, jr. and sr. resident internal medicine Bronx Mcpl. Hosp., NYC, 1975-78; fellow med. oncology Meml. Sloan-Kettering Cancer Ctr., NYC, 1978-80, adj. attending physician/cons. dept. medicine, 1981—; asst. prof. medicine N.Y. Med. Coll., Valhalla, 1980-81. Clin. instr. medicine Cornell U. Med. Coll., 1978-80; jr. clin. faculty fellow Am. Cancer Soc., 1980-81; mem. N.Y. Met. Breast Cancer Group, 1990—; cons. cancer program No. Westchester Hosp. Ctr., Mt. Kisco, N.Y., 1981-82; mem. staff Westchester County Med. Ctr., Valhalla, N.Y., No. Westchester Hosp. Ctr., Mt. Kisco, Meml. Sloan-Kettering Cancer Ctr., N.Y.C. Contbr. articles to profl. jours. Mem. adv. bd. Cancer Care, Inc. Conn., 1997-99. Recipient Clin. Fellowship award Am. Cancer Soc., 1978-79. Mem. Am. Soc. Clin. Oncology, Westchester County Med. Soc., Soc. Integrative Oncology, Am. Soc. Breast Disease, N.Y. State Med. Soc., Woodway Country Club. Republican. Presbyterian. Achievements include research in detection and treatment of early breast cancer, the human spirit in the fight against cancer, salvage chemotherapy with etoposide, ifosfamide and cisplatin in refractory germ cell tumors. Office: 101 S Bedford Rd Ste 202A Mount Kisco NY 10549-3456

SCHNEIDER, ROBERT JEROME, lawyer; b. Cin., June 22, 1947; s. Jerome William and Agnes (Moehringer) S.; m. Janice Loraine Eckhoff, Dec. 13, 1968; children: Aaron Haisley, Jared Alan, Margot Laraine. BSME, U. Cin., 1970, JD, 1973. Bar: Ill. 1973, U.S. Dist. Ct. (no. dist.) Ill. 1973, U.S. Ct. Appeals (7th cir.) 1973, U.S. Ct. Appeals (fed. cir.) 1973. Ptnr. Mason, Kolehmainen, Rathburn & Wyss, Chgo., 1973-82; ptnr., asst. chmn. patents, chmn. intellect. property dept. McDermott, Will & Emery, Chgo., 1982-94; chmn. intellectual property dept. Chapman & Cutler, Chgo., 1995—. Mem. ABA, ASME, Ill. Bar Assn., Chgo. Bar Assn., Licensing Execs. Soc., Intellectual Property Law Assn. Chgo. (sec. 1981-83), Fedn. Internat. des Conseils en Proriete Industrielle, Assn. Internationale pour la Protection de la Propriètè Industrielle, Internat. Pat-Got Assn. (treas. 2001-05, pres. 2005-), Internat. Trademark Assn., Internat. Trade Commn. Trial Lawyers Assn., Am. Intellectual Property Law Assn., Tower Club (bd. govs. 1988—, v.p. 1994-95, pres. 1995—), Univ. Club Chgo. (bd. dirs. 2001-). Republican. Roman Catholic. Home: 1609 Asbury Ave Winnetka IL 60093-1303 Office: Chapman & Cutler Chicago IL 60601 Office Fax: 312-803-3529. E-mail: iplaw@chapman.com.

SCHNEIDER, ROBERT KERRY, electric utility engineer; b. Bremerton, Wash., Jan. 11, 1949; s. Emil Kerry and Glady Elizabeth (Anderson) S.; m. Carol Anne Pfeiffer, Aug. 28, 1971; children: Steve, Jeff. BS in Physics, U. Wash., 1971, MS in Nuclear Engring., 1973, MBA, 1976. Cert. profl. engr., Wash., Calif., Ala. Engr. Bechtel Power Corp., San Francisco, 1971-72; dir. power mgmt. Snohomish Co. Pub. Utility Dist., Everett, Wash., 1977-87; sr. cons. CH2M Hill, Bellevue, Wash., 1987-95; v.p., mgr. D. Hittle & Assocs., Inc., Lynnwood, Wash., 1995—2005, pres., mgr., 2006—; mem. tech. adv. com. to Wash. State Labor and Industry Chief Elec. Insp., 2005—06. Mem. vis. adv. com. dept. mech engring. U. Wash., 1994- Mem. ASME (Disting. Svc. award, 1999, mem. bd. govt. rels. 1996-2002, v.p. region VIII, coun. mem. affairs, 1993-96, western Wash. sect. chmn., 1984-85), Puget Sound Engring. Coun. (pres. 1990-91). Avocation: skiing. Office: D Hittle and Assocs Inc PO Box 6755 Lynnwood WA 98036-0755 Office Fax: 425-744-1253.

SCHNEIDER, ROY LESTER, former Governor of Virgin Islands; b. St. Thomas, VI, May 13, 1939; s. Aluvis and Winifred Schneider; m. Barbara Watson; children: Mark, Roy Jr., Suzanne. BS, Howard U., MD, 1965, PhD (hon.), Morehouse Sch. Medicine. Diplomate Am. Bd. Surgery. Comdr. Dept. Health, St. Thomas, 1977—87; gov. US VI, St. Thomas, 1994—98. Oncology surgery fellow Mem. Sloan-Kettering Cancer Ctr., NYC; faculty mem. to prof. surgery Howard U.; assoc. dir. Cancer Rsch. Ctr. Howard U. Hosp., vice chmn. Dept. Oncology, chief Clin. Cancer; pvt. practice, 1987—94; dir. internat. policy and pub. health LifeLinkMD's Adv. Bd. Capt. US Army, 1966—68. Decorated Vietnamese Honor Medal, Bronze Star, Tech. Svc. Honor Medal; recipient Outstanding Alumnus Award, Howard U., 1984. Fellow: Am. Coll. Surgeons; mem.: Alpha Phi Alpha. Office: Lifelink Md Inc 11811 Willows Rd Ne Redmond WA 98052-2003

SCHNEIDER, SANDRA MCEWEN, emergency physician educator; b. Pitts., June 5, 1950; d. Fred Collier and Pearl Mae (Nycum) McEwen; m. Paul Gilbert Schneider, Aug. 26, 1972; 1 child, Kathryn Alexandra. BS in Chemistry, U. Pitts., 1971, MD, 1975. Diplomate Am. Bd. Internal Medicine, Am. Bd. Emergency Medicine. Resident in internal medicine Presbyn. Univ. Hosp., Pitts., 1975-78; med. dir. family health svcs. USPHS, Nat. Health Svcs. Corps, Hazard, Ky., 1978-81; asst. prof. medicine Montefiore Hosp., U. Pitts., 1981-86, assoc. prof. medicine, dir. emergency svcs., 1986-92; assoc. prof., assoc. chief divsn. emergency medicine U. Pitts. Med. Ctr., 1992-93; prof., chair dept. emergency medicine Strong Meml. Hosp., U. Rochester, NY, 1993—2007. Contbr. chpts. to books, articles to profl. jours. Grantee Upjohn Co., 1984, Smith Kline French, 1987. Mem. World Assn. Emergency and Disaster Medicine, Soc. for Academic Emergency Medicine (bd. dirs.), Nat. Assn. EMS Physicians (mem. exec. com.), Am. Coll. Emergency Physicians (fellow 1985), Am. Assn. Poison Control Ctrs., Am. Acad. Clin. Toxicology, Rochester Acad. Medicine. Democrat. Office: Univ Rochester 601 Elmwood Ave # 655 Rochester NY 14642-0001 Business E-Mail: sandra_schneider@urmc.rochester.edu.

SCHNEIDER, SCOTT MICHAEL, academic administrator; b. Bronx, NY, June 12, 1967; s. Hyman and Ruth Schneider. BS in Elem. Edn., SUNY, Cortland, 1990; MS in Spl. Edn., Coll. New Rochelle, NY, 1992; MEd in Ednl. Adminstrn., Columbia U., NY, 2003. Cert. tchr. spl. edn. NY State, 1990, tchr. day sch. NY State, 1990, sch. adminstrn. and supr. NY State, 2000, sch. dist. adminstrn. NY State, 2004, sch. bus. adminstrn. NY State, 2006. Tchr. spl. edn. pub. sch. 2X NYC Dept. Edn., Bronx, 1993—2003, reading recovery specialist pub. sch. 2X, 2000—02, coach math. pub. sch. 2X, 2003—05, lead math. specialist Region One, 2005—07; asst. prin. Pub. Sch. 51x- Bronx New Sch., 2007—. Cons. in field. Mem.: ASCD, Math. Assn. Am., Nat. Coun. Tchrs. Math., Nat. Coun. Suprs. Math., Phi Delta Kappa, Kappa Delta Pi, Alpha Epsilon Pi. Home: 2550 Independence Ave Bronx NY 10463 Personal E-mail: kiddo667@aol.com.

SCHNEIDER, STEPHEN HARLEY, medical educator; b. Neptune, NJ, Apr. 1, 1948; s. Joseph and Edith (Himmelman) S.; m. Carole Robin Lowenstein, Aug. 31, 1981; children: Ari, Rachel. BA, MD, Boston U., 1972. Cert. in internal medicine and endocrinology, N.J. Rsch. assoc. Boston City Hosp., 1975-76, fellow divsn. diabetes and metabolism, 1976-77, asst. dir. diabetes clinic, 1976-77, dir. diabetes clinic, 1977-78, dir. diabetes and metabolism svcs., 1978-79; instr. medicine Boston Univ. Sch. Medicine, 1978-79; asst. prof. medicine U. Medicine and Dentistry N.J.-Robert Wood Johnson Med. Sch., New Brunswick, NJ, 1979-85, assoc. prof. clin. medicine, 1985-88, assoc. prof. medicine, 1988-95, prof. medicine, 1995—. Mem. editl. bd. Diabetes Forcast Mag.; contbr. numerous articles to profl. jours. including Jour. Clin. Endocrinology and Nutrition, New Eng. Jour. Medicine, Diabetes Care, Atherosclerosis, Japanese Heart Jour., Diabetologia, Metabolism. Bd. dirs. Juvenile Diabetes Assn., East Brunswick Jewish Ctr. Youth Com.; founding mem. affiliate Internat. Diabetic Athlete's Assn. Recipient McKeen Cattell award Am. Coll. Clin. Pharmacology, 1986; rsch. fellow Am. Heart Assn., 1976. Fellow ACP; mem. Am. Soc. Internal Medicine, Am. Coll. Sports Medicine, Am. Fedn. Clin. Rsch., Begg Soc., Phi Beta Kappa, Alpha Omega Alpha. Jewish. Avocations: football, soccer, history, theology, bicycling. Office: UMDNJ-Robert W Johnson Med Divsn Endocrinology PO Box 19 New Brunswick NJ 08903-0019 Home Phone: 732-390-7429; Office Phone: 732-235-7751, 732-234-7219. Business E-Mail: schneide@umdnj.edu.

SCHNEIDER, STEVEN JACK, neurosurgeon; b. Bklyn., June 22, 1958; children: Samantha, Daniel, Russell, Sierra, Aspen. BA in Biology cum laude, NYU, 1979; MD magna cum laude, Baylor Coll. Medicine, 1982. Diplomate Am. Bd. Neurological Surgeons, 1992, Am. Bd. Pediatric Neurosurgery, 1997. Intern, pediatric neurological surgery Baylor Coll. Medicine and Affiliated Hosps., Houston, 1982-83, resident, pediatrics, 1983-88; fellow in pediatric neurological surgery NYU Med. Ctr., NYC, 1988-89; asst. attending physician, pediatric neurological surgery Winthrop U. Hosp., Mineola, NY, 1989—; assoc. attending physician, pediatric neurological surgery LI Jewish Med. Ctr., NY,

1989—, dir., neurosurgery residency NY, chief, pediatric neurological surgery NY, 2002—, dir., surgical services, Comprehensive Epilepsy Ctr. NY; chief attending physician neurosurgery Nassau County Med. Ctr., East Meadow, NY, 1989—; asst. attending physician North Shore U. Hosp., Manhasset, N.Y., 1992-93, head sect. pediatric neurological surgery, asst. attending physician, 1989—, chief, pediatric neurological surgery, 2002—, Schneider Children's Hosp., New Hyde Park, NY, 2002—, dir., surgical services, Comprehensive Pediatric Movement Disorder Ctr.; clin. instr., Leo M. Davidoff Dept. Neurological Surgery Albert Einstein Coll. Medicine, Yeshiva U., Bronx, NY, 1989—; clin. instr. Cornell U. Med. Ctr., NY, 1993—; clin. asst. prof. neurosurgery NYU Sch. Medicine; pediatric neurosurgeon, sr. ptnr. LI Neurosurgical Associates, PC, New Hyde Park, NY, 1989—. Contbr. articles to profl. jours.; serves as ad hoc editor for multiple scientific jours., including Pediatric Neurosurgery. Mem. adv. coun. Children's Brain Tumor Found., Epilepsy Found., Think First Found. Fellow Am. Coll. Surgeons, Am. Acad. Pediatrics; mem. Am. Epilepsy Soc., Am. Acad. Pain Medicine, Harris County Med. Soc., Tex. Med. Assn., Congress Neurol. Surgeons, Am. Assn. Neurol. Surgeons (mem. sect. on pain, mem. joint sect. on disorders spine & peripheral nerves), AMA, Am. Modulation Soc., Complex Regional Pain Syndrome Assn., Hydrocephalus Assn., Guardians of Hydrocephalus, Nat. Neurofibromatosis Found., Am. Syringomyelia Alliance Project, Congress Neurological Surgeons, Nassau County Med. Soc., NY State Neurosurgical Soc., NY Soc. Neurosurgery, Alpha Omega Alpha, Beta Lambda Sigma. Office: 410 Lakeville Rd Ste 204 New Hyde Park NY 11042 Office Phone: 516-354-3401. Office Fax: 516-354-8597. Business E-Mail: sschneid@lij.edu.

SCHNEIDER, TAPIO, environmental scientist, educator; b. Braunschweig, Germany, May 12, 1972; s. Udo and Liisa Schneider. PhD, Princeton U., NJ, 2001. Assoc. rsch. scientist Courant Inst., NYU, NYC, 2000—02; assoc. prof. environ. sci. and engring. Calif. Inst. Tech., Pasadena, 2002—. Contbr. numerous articles to profl. jours. Recipient Best Brains Sci. award, Discover Mag., 2008; Earth Sys. Sci. fellowship, NASA, 1998—2000, Rsch. fellowship, Alfred P. Sloan Found., 2004—06, Sci. and Engring. fellowship, David and Lucile Packard Found., 2005—. Mem.: Am. Meteorol. Soc., Am. Geophys. Union (James R. Holton award 2004). Office: Calif Inst Tech 1200 E California Blvd Pasadena CA 91125-2300 Office Fax: 626-585-1917.

SCHNEIDER, URSULA WILFRIEDE, author; b. Stuttgart, Germany, June 13, 1936; came to U.S., 1966; d. Kurt and Anna Schneider; children: Kurt Mihran, Yvonne Ulrike. BA in French, CUNY, 1977, MA in French Lit., 1979, ABD in Comparative Lit., 1988, PhD in Comparative Lit., 1992. Mgr. export/import of chems. A.K. Peters Co., NYC, 1967-80; asst. to sales mgr. FBA Pharms., NYC, 1981; pvt. sect. to sr. ptnr., head internat. dept. Bear Stearns, NYC, 1982-84; in-house translator for acquisition Siemens Capital Corp., NYC, 1985-86; adj. lectr. German Hunter Coll./CUNY, 1987-90, Montclair (N.J.) State U., 1991-92. Prof. World Trade Ctr./Internat. Inst. for Langs., 1988-89, UN Internat. Sch., N.Y.C., 1979. Author: Ars amandi: The Erotic of Extremes in Thomas Mann and Marguerite Duras, 1995, The Cross-Eyed God, 1995, Velvet Cages, 2001, Vernal Amours, 2004. Helena Rubinstein Found. grantee, Bd. Higher Edn. grantee; recipient Marta Retzler award. Mem. MLA, Fgn. Lang. Educators of N.J., Northeastern MLA, Am. Coun. Tchrs. English Lang., Phi Beta Kappa. Avocations: running, skiing, swimming, skating, tennis. Home: 1201 River Reach Dr Apt 204 Fort Lauderdale FL 33315-1179 Personal E-mail: uwsftlaud@aol.com.

SCHNEIDER, VALERIE LOIS, retired speech educator; b. Chgo., Feb. 12, 1941; d. Ralph Joseph and Gertrude Blanche (Gaffron) S. BA, Carroll Coll., 1963; MA, U. Wis., 1966; PhD, U. Fla., 1969; CAS, Appalachian State U., 1981. Tchr. English and history, dir. forensics and drama Montello (Wis.) H.S., 1963-64; instr. speech U. Fla., Gainesville, 1966-68, asst. prof. speech, 1969-70, Edinboro (Pa.) State Coll., 1970-71; assoc. prof. speech East Tenn. State U., Johnson City, 1971-76, prof. speech, 1976-97. Instr. newspaper course Johnson City Press Chronicle, 1979, Elizabethton Star, Erwin Record, Mountain City Tomahawk, Jonesboro Herald and Tribune, 1980; mem. investor panel USA Today, 1991-92. Editor East Tenn. State U. evening and off-campus newsletter, 1984-91; assoc. editor Homiletic, 1974-76; columnist Video Visions, Kingsport Times-News, 1984-86; book reviewer Pulpit Digest, 1986-90; contbr. articles to profl. jours. Chmn. AAUW Mass Media Study Group Com., Johnson City, 1973-74. Recipient Creative Writing award Va. Highlands Arts Festival, 1973, award Kingsport Times News, 1984, 85, Tri-Cities Met. Advt. Fedn., 1983, 84, hon. life mem. Tenn. Presbyn. Women, 2000; named Danforth assoc., 1977; finalist Money mag. contest, 1994, Writer's Digest contest, 2000. Mem.: AAUW (v.p. chpt. 1974—75, pres. 1975—76), Tenn. Basic Skills Coun. (pres. 1975—76, exec. bd. 1979—80, v.p. 1980—81), Religious Speech Comm. Assn. (Best Article award 1976), Tenn. Speech Comm. Assn. (exec. bd. 1974—77, publs. bd. 1974—78, pres. 1977—78), So. Speech Comm. Assn., Speech Comm. Assn. (Tenn. rep. to states adv. coun. 1974—75), Mensa, Presbyn. Women (hon.; life mem.), Johnson City Book Club (pres. 2001—03), Bus. and Profl. Women's Club (chpt. exec. bd. 1972—73, v.p. 1976—77), Pi Gamma Mu, Phi Delta Kappa, Tau Kappa Alpha, Delta Sigma Rho. Presbyterian.

SCHNEIDER, VIVIAN I., psychologist, researcher; b. Wichita Falls, Tex., Sept. 6, 1949; d. Robert and Vivian H. Davis; m. Robert Jordan Schneider, June 8, 1972 (dec. Mar. 13, 2002); children: Kayt, Amy J. Kim, Jay Robert. BA in Psychology, Met. State Coll. Denver, 1972; MA in Psychology, U. Colo., Boulder, 1988, PhD in Psychology, 1991. Sr. rsch. assoc. U. Colo., Boulder, 1991—. Co-author: (chpts.) Learning and Memory of Knowledge and Skills: Durability and Specificity, Foreign Language Learning: Psycholinguistic Studies on Training and Retention, The Psychology of Learning and Motivation: Advances in Research and Theory; contbr. articles to profl. jours. Ham radio operator Boulder County Amateur Radio Emergency Svcs., 1995—2009; vol. Lamb's Lunch, Boulder, 2004—; children's leader Bible Study Fellowship, Boulder, 1975—85, 2006—08; Sunday sch. tchr. Bethany Ch., Boulder, 1976—2008. Mem.: Psychonomic Soc. Avocations: reading, quilting. Office: U Colo Ucb 345 Boulder CO 80309 Home: 3010 Birch Ave Boulder CO 80305-3457 Office Fax: 303-492-8895. Business E-Mail: vivian.schneider@colorado.edu.

SCHNEIDER, WILLIAM GEORGE, chemist, research consultant; b. Wolseley, Sask., Can., June 1, 1915; s. Michael and Phillipina (Krauschaar) S.; m. Jean Purves, Sept. 2, 1940; children: Judith Schneider Saunders, Joanne Schneider Spurrier. B.Sc., U. Sask., 1937, M.Sc., 1939, D.Sc., 1969; PhD, McGill U., 1941, D.Sc., 1970; D.Sc. (hon.), York U., 1966, Meml. U., 1968, McMaster U., 1969, Laval U., 1969, Moncton U., 1969, U. N.B., 1970, U. Montreal, 1970, Acadia U., 1976, U. Regina, 1976, Ottawa U., 1978; LL.D., U. Alta., 1968, Laurentian U., 1968. Head phys. chemistry sect., div. chemistry NRC Can., Ottawa, Ont., 1946-63, dir. div. pure chemistry, 1963-65, v.p., 1965-67, pres., 1967-80; research cons., 1980—. Author: (with J.A. Pople, H.J. Bernstein) High Resolution Nuclear Magnetic Resonance, 1959; contbr. articles to profl. jours. Decorated Order of Can., 1977 Fellow Royal Soc. Can. (Henry Marshall Tory medal), Royal Soc. London, Chem. Inst. Can. (medal 1969, Montreal medal 1973); mem. Internat. Union Pure and Applied Chemistry (pres. 1983-85)

SCHNEIDER, WILLYS HOPE, lawyer; b. NYC, Sept. 27, 1952; d. Leon and Lillian (Friedman) S.; m. Stephen Andrew Kals, Jan. 21, 1979; children: Peter, Josefine. AB cum laude, Princeton U., 1974; JD, Columbia U., 1977. Bar: NY 1978, US Dist. Ct. (ea. and so. dists.) NY 1978, US Tax Ct. 1979. Law clk. to hon. Jack B. Weinstein US Dist. Ct. (ea. dist.) NY, Bklyn., 1977-78; assoc. Paul, Weiss, Rifkind, Wharton & Garrison, NYC, 1978-83, Kaye Scholer LLP, NYC, 1983-87, 1987—. Articles editor Columbia Law Rev., 1976—77; contbr. articles to profl. jours. Mem.: ABA, Internat. Tax Inst. (pres.), Assn. Bar City of NY, NY State Bar Assn. Home: 320 W End Ave New York NY 10023-8110 Office: Kaye Scholer LLP 425 Park Ave New York NY 10022-3506 Home Phone: 212-580-2124; Office Phone: 212-836-8693. E-mail: wschneider@kayescholer.com.

SCHNEIDERMAN, ANNE MERCEDES, lawyer, neurobiologist; b. Ithaca, NY; d. Howard Allen and Audrey MacLeod Schneiderman. BS in Biol. Scis. with distinction, Stanford U., Calif., 1977; PhD in Neurobiology, Harvard U., Cambridge, Mass., 1984; JD, Stanford U., Calif., 2000. Registered: US Patent and Trademark Office (patent atty.) 1998, bar: NY 2001, Calif. 2001, Washington, DC 2003; cert. Kripalu Yoga Tchr. Kripalu Ctr. for Yoga & Health, 2005. Post doctoral fellow Yale U., 1984—88; asst. prof. neurobiology Cornell U., Ithaca, 1989—96; law clk. Pennie & Edmonds LLP, NYC, 1996—2000, law clk., patent agt., 1998—2000, assoc. atty. NYC, 2000—03; legal counsel Advanced Design Consulting, USA, Lansing, NY, 2003—04; pvt. practice, 2004—. Contbr. articles to profl. jours. Recipient Best Paper Award, Am. Soc. of Zoologists, Divsn. of Devel. Biology, 1980, Nat. Merit Scholar, 1973—77, award in Neuroethology, Capranica Found., 1987; undergraduate rsch. fellowship, Calif. Heart Assn., 1977, graduate fellowship, Nat. Sci. Foun., 1977—80, fellowship, Helen Hay Whitney Found., 1984—87. Mem.: ABA, Nat. Assn. Patent Practitioners, Am. Intellectual Property Law Assn., Women's Bar Assn. State of NY, Tompkins County NY Bar Assn., Soc. Neuroscience, NY State Bar Assn., Monroe County NY Bar Assn., Kripalu Yoga Tchrs. Assn. (tchr.). Avocations: yoga, vintage sports cars. Office: 102 East State St Ste 7 PO Box 422 Ithaca NY 14851-0422 Office Fax: 815-361-9050. Business E-Mail: anne@schneidermanlaw.com.

SCHNEIDERMAN, IRWIN, lawyer; b. NYC, May 28, 1923; s. Meyer and Bessie (Klein) S.; m. Roberta Haig, Nov. 28, 1966; 1 child, Eric T. BA, Bklyn. Coll., 1943; LLB cum laude, Harvard U., 1948; DHL (hon.), Bklyn. Coll., 1993. Bar: NY 1949, DC 1952. Assoc. Cahill Gordon & Reindel, NYC, 1948-59, ptnr., 1959-89, sr. counsel, 1990—. Spl. cons. to chmn. SEC, 1981-82, mem. adv. com. on tender offers, 1983. Trustee Bklyn. Coll. Found., 1983—, NY Ctrl Park Conservancy, 2004; chmn. NYC Opera, 1993-2004; bd. dirs. WNYC Radio, 1989—, NARAL-Pro-Choice, NYC, 1990—, Lincoln Ctr. for Performing Arts, Inc., 1994-2004, dir. emeritus, 2004; chmn. NARAL-Pro-Choice NY Found., 1998-2007, chmn. emeritus, trustee, 2007; dir. Glyndebourne Assn. America, 2009. Lt. j.g. USNR, 1943—46. Mem. Harvard Club. Home: 203 E 72nd St New York NY 10021-4568 Office: Cahill Gordon & Reindel 80 Pine St New York NY 10005-1790 Home Phone: 212-988-0810; Office Phone: 212-701-3800. Personal E-mail: irwinschneiderman@yahoo.com.

SCHNEIDER-REBOZO, LISSA PRICE, literature and language professor; b. Phoenix, Apr. 17, 1960; d. Elwood H. and Lynne P. Schneider; m. Michael Alan Rebozo, Jan. 23, 1999; 1 child, Michael Joseph Rebozo. BA, Northwestern U., Evanston, Ill., 1981; MA, U. Miami, Coral Gables, Fla., 1992, PhD, 1998. Author: (book) Conrad's Narratives of Difference (Adam Gillon Book prize, 2005); contbr. articles to profl. jours. Recipient Academic Merit award, U. Miami, 1998; Seminar fellow, Nat. Humanties Ctr., 2007, Curriculum Devel. grant, U. Wis. Sys. Inst. Race and Ethnicity, 2007—08, Lesson Study Tng. grant, UWS Office Profl. & Instrnl. Devel., 2008, fellow, Wis. Tchg. Program, 2008—. Mem.: MLA, Joseph Conrad Soc. America (rev. editor 2008, bd. mem. 2002—04, 2008—, Bruce Harkness award 2007). Office: Univ Wis River Falls English Dept 410 S Third St River Falls WI 54022 Office Phone: 715-425-3124. Business E-Mail: elizabeth.schneider-rebozo@uwrf.edu.

SCHNEIER, EDWARD VINCENT, political science professor; b. Bronx, N.Y., May 25, 1939; s. Edward Vincent and Lillian (Buhr) S.; m. Janice Bernier, June 16, 1960 (div. Jan. 1974); children: Andrew, Katherine; m. Margrit Russenberger, May 13, 2000. BA, Oberlin Coll., 1960; MA, Claremont Grad. U., Calif., 1961, PhD, 1963. Rsch. fellow Brookings Instn., Washington, 1963; legis. asst. Senator Birch Bayh, Washington, 1963-64; asst. prof. The Johns Hopkins U., Balt., 1964-65, Princeton (N.J.) U., 1965-68; from asst. to assoc. prof. The City Coll., CUNY, 1968-93, prof., 1993—2002, prof. emeritus, 2002—. Ptnr. Grassroots Tavern, N.Y.C., 1975—. Author: Congress Today, 1993, Legislative Strategy, 1993, Vote Power, 1974, Party and Constituency, 1970, New York Politics, 2001, 09, Crafting Constitutional Democracies, 2005. State legis. dir. Am. for Dem. Action, Albany, 1992-2001; commr. Copake (N.Y.) Park Commn., 1991-2001; officer Downtown Ind. Dem., N.Y.C., 1975-90; trustee Roe-Jan Comty. Libr., 2003—, pres., 2005-, Columbia Greene Comty. Coll., 2008-; candidate for Congress Dem. Primary, N.Y.C., 1976; lobbyist Com. for Equity in Edn., N.Y.C., 1994-2000. Rsch. fellow NEH, U. Chgo., 1978-80, Princeton, 1996, Fulbright Found. Iceland, 1988-89, Indonesia, 2002. Mem. Am. Polit. Sci. Assn., Internat. Polit. Sci. Assn.(rsch. com. legis. Specialist). Avocations: golf, skiing, cooking. Home: 1284 Lake View Rd Copake NY 12516-1028 E-mail: nedmarg@earthlink.net.

SCHNEIER, MARC, rabbi; BA, MPhil, Yeshiva U. Cert. ordained Rabbi. Pres., founder Found. Ethnic Understanding; found. rabbi Hampton Synagogue, West Hampton Beach, NY, New York Synagogue, NYC. Author: (books) Shared Dreams, 2000; appearances: (TV and Radio incl. Good Morning America, Today Show, Good Day New York, CBS Sunday Edition, CBS Morning Show, O'Reilly Factor, Fox News, CNN, PBS, NP). Named one of The Top 50 Rabbis in America, Newsweek Mag., 2007. Mem.: Jewish Commn. for Interreligious Consultations, Hebrew Immigrant Aid Soc. (former mem. exec. com.), NY Board Rabbis (past pres.), World Jewish Congress (founder, pres, chair Am. Sect.). Jewish. Office: FFEU Ste 1C 1 East 93rd St New York NY 10128 Office Phone: 917-492-2538. Fax: 917-492-2560.

SCHNEITER, GEORGE MALAN, professional golfer, real estate developer; b. Ogden, Utah, Aug. 12, 1931; s. George Henery and Bernice Slade (Malan) S.; m. JoAnn Deakin, Jan. 19, 1954; children: George, Gary, Dan, Steve, Elizabeth Ann, Michael. BS in Banking and Fin., U. Utah, 1955. With 5th Army Championship Golf Team, U.S. Army, 1955-56; assoc. golf pro Hidden Valley Golf Club, Salt Lake City, 1957; golf pro Lake Hills Golf Club, Billings, Mont., 1957-90, sec., 1957-61, pres., 1964-90, Schneiter Enterprises, Sandy, Utah, 1974—; developer Schneiter's Golf Course, 1973—, and subdiv., 1961—; player PGA tour, 1958-78, Sr. PGA tour, 1981—. Missionary So. State Mission, LDS Ch., 1951-52. Served with U.S. Army, 1955-56. Named winner, Utah sect. Sr. Championship, Wyo., Open Super Sr. Championshio, Salt Lake City Parks Tournament, Vernal Brigham Payson Open, Yuma Open, Utah Sr. PGA Chamption, Utah Super Sr. Championshio, World Pro Am., Kona, Hawaii, Ft. Carson Golf Championship; fellow Banking & Fin. fellow, First Security Bank Utah, 1953. Mem. PGA, Salt Lake City C. of C., Intermountain Golf Courst Supertaints Assn. also: 8968 S 1300 E Sandy UT 84094 Office: 2009 Brassy Dr Las Vegas NV 89142-2033 Office Phone: 801-232-5488. Fax: 801-567-0408.

SCHNELL, GEORGE ADAM, geographer, educator, retired demographer; b. Phila., July 13, 1931; s. Earl Blackwood and Emily (Bernheimer) S.; m. Mary Lou Williams, June 21, 1958; children: David Adam, Douglas Powell, Thomas Earl. BS, West Chester U., 1958; MS, Pa. State U., 1960, PhD, 1965; postdoctoral study, Ohio State U., 1965. Asst. prof. SUNY, New Paltz, 1962-65, assoc. prof., 1965-68, prof. geography, 1968-99, founding chmn. dept., 1968-94, prof. emeritus, 1999—. Adj. prof. SUNY, 2000-05; vis. assoc. prof. U. Hawaii, summer, 1966; cons. cmty. action programming, 1965; manuscript reader, cons. to several pubs., 1967—; founder, founding bd. dirs., investigator Inst. for Devel., Planning and Land Use Studies, 1986-96; cons. Mid-Hudson Pattern for Progress, 1986, Open Space Inst., 1987, Mid-Hudson Regional Econ. Devel. Coun., 1989, Urban Devel. Corp., 1989-90, 93, Tech. Devel. Ctr., 1991, Catskill Ctr., 1991, Ednl. Testing Svc., 1993-94, 96, 97; cons. editor Exams Unltd., Albany, N.Y., 1995-99; ind. contractor and cons. Excelsior U., 2003—05; founding mem. exec. bd. dirs. Hudson Valley Study Ctr., 1995-98; ind. contractor Excelsior U., 2003; cons., presenter in field. Author: (with others) The Local Community: A Handbook for Teachers, 1971, The World's Population, Problems of Growth, 1972; contbr. Pennsylvania Coal: Resources, Technology, Utilization, 1983, West Virginia and Appalachia: Selected Readings, 1977, Hazardous and Toxic Wastes: Technology, Management and Health Effects, 1984, Environmental Radon: Occurrence, Control and Health Hazards, 1990, Natural and Technological Disasters: Causes, Effects and Preventive Measures, 1992, Conservation and Resource Management, 1993, Medicine and Health Care into the 21st Century, 1995, Forests: A Global Perspective, 1996, (with M.S. Monmonier) Ecology of the Wetlands and Associated Systems, 1998, (with M.S. Monmonier) Renewable Energy: Trends and Prospects, 2002; co-author: (with M.S. Monmonier) The Study of Population: Elements, Patterns, Processes, 1983, Map Appreciation, 1988; editor, contbr.: (with with M.S. Monmonier, G.J. Demko, and H.M. Rose) Population Geography: A Reader, 1970; contbr. articles to profl. and scholarly jours. Appt. mem. local bds. and coms. Town and Village New Paltz, New Paltz Ctrl. Sch. Dist., 1965-2007; elder Reformed Ch. New Paltz; Rep. committeeman Town of Gardiner, Ulster County, NY, 2000-01; trustee Gardiner (NY) Pub. Libr., 2005-07. With AUS, 1952-54; bd. mem. River Park Homeowners Assn., 2007—. Recipient Excellence award NY State/United Univ. Professions, 1994, Disting. Alumnus award West Chester U., 1994; named Disting. Tchr. Emeritus, SUNY New Paltz Alumni Assn., 2006. Mem. Assn. Am. Geographers, Pa. Geog. Soc. (mem. editl. bd. Pa. Geographer, Disting. Geographer award 1994), Pa. Acad. Sci. (assoc. editor jour. 1988-2005), Nat. Coun. for Geog. Edn., Paltz Club, mem. Pa., Geographer Editl. Rev. Bd., Penn. Geog. Soc. (disting. scholar award, 2008). Home: 29 River Park Dr New Paltz NY 12561-2636 Office: SUNY at New Paltz Dept Geography 75 S Manheim Blvd New Paltz NY 12561-2400

SCHNELL, ROGER THOMAS, small business owner, retired state official, military officer; b. Wabasha, Minn., Dec. 11, 1936; s. Donald William and Eva Louise (Barton) Schnell; m. Barbara Ann McDonald, Dec. 18, 1959 (div. Mar. 1968); children: Thomas Allen(dec.), Scott Douglas(dec.). A in Mil. Sci., Command and Gen. Staff Coll., 1975; A in Bus. Administn., Wayland Bapt. U., 1987. Commd. 2d lt. Alaska N.G., 1959, advanced through grades to col., 1975, shop supt. Anchorage, 1965-71, personnel mgr., 1972-74, chief of staff, 1974-87, dir. logistics, 1987; electrician Alaska R.R., Anchorage, 1955-61, elec. foreman, 1962-64; dir. support personnel mgmt. Joint Staff Alaska N.G., 1988-92, ret.; personnel mgr. State of Alaska, 1992, asst. commr. dept. mil. and vets. affairs Ft. Richardson, 1992-95, dep. commr. dept. mil. and vets. affairs, 1995-98, 2002—06, brig. gen., 2007; owner RTS Enterprises, Anchorage, 1999—. Prin., owner RTS Enterprises, 1999—; adv. bd. state joint armed svc. com. State of Alaska, 2001—06; dep. commr. dept. Mil. and Vet. Affairs, 2003—06. Chmn. Alaska Nat. Guard Mus. Trust Fund, 2001—02; appointed to Gov.'s State Seismic Hazard Safety Commn., 2005—06; chmn. pastor parish rels. com. Meth. 1st Ch., 2001—02, mem. fin. com., 2007—08; bd. dirs. Meth. Trust Fund, 2002—04, 2007—. Named Brigadier Gen. (hon.) Alaska NG, Gov. of Alaska, 2007. Mem. Fed. Profl. Labor Relations Execs. (sec. 1974-75), Alaska N.G. Officers Assn. (pres. 1976-78, bd. dirs. 1988—), Assn. U.S. Army (corp.), NG Assn. U.S. (life, retiree rep. from Alaska 1993—), Am. Legion, Amvets, Elks. Republican. Methodist. Avocations: travel, photography. Home and Office: Huntwood Park Estates 6817 Queens View Cir Anchorage AK 99504-5203 Home Phone: 907-333-8001. Personal E-mail: rogertschnell@gci.net, rtschnellenterprises@gci.net.

SCHNELLE, KARL BENJAMIN, JR., chemical engineering professor, consultant, researcher; b. Canton, Ohio, Dec. 8, 1930; s. Karl Benjamin and Kathryn Emily (Hollingsworth) S.; m. Mary Margaret Dabney, Sept. 8, 1954; children: Karl Dabney, Kathryn Chappell. BS, Carnegie Mellon U., 1952, MS, 1957, PhD, 1959. Registered profl. engr., Tenn. Chem. engr., shift foreman Organics area Pitts. Plate Glass Co., New Martinsville, W.Va., 1952-54; asst. prof. chem. engring. Vanderbilt U., Nashville, 1958—61, assoc. prof., 1961—64, assoc. prof. environ. and air resources engring., 1967—70, prof., 1970—80, chmn. divsn. socio-tech. sys., 1972—75, chmn. environ. and water resources engring., 1975—76; mgr. edn., rsch. Instrument Soc. Am., Pitts., 1964—67; chmn. environ. engring. and policy mgmt. dept. Vanderbilt U., 1976—80, chmn. chem. engring. dept., 1980—88, prof. chem. and environ. engring., 1980—2008, emeritus prof. chem. and environ. engring., 2008—; Alexander Heard disting. svc. prof., 1995-96. V.p. ECCE, Nashville, 1983-88, pres., 1989—95; mem. Air Pollution Control Bd., State Tenn., 1978-82, 82-87; Fulbright prof. U. Liege, Belgium, 1977; invited prof. Universite Catholique de Louvain, Belgium, 1982; vis. prof. chem. engring. Danish Tech. Inst., Lyngby, Denmark, 1988-89. Fellow AICE; mem. Air and Waste Mgmt. Assn. (Lyman A. Ripperton Environ. Educator award 2006), Instrument Soc. Am. (mgr. edn. and rsch. 1964-67), Am. Soc. Engring. Edn., Am. Soc. Environ. Engrs., Sigma Xi, Phi Kappa Phi, Tau Beta Pi. Office: Vanderbilt U VU Station B 351604 Nashville TN 37235-1604 Office Phone: 615-322-3370. Business E-Mail: karl.b.schnelle@vanderbilt.edu.

SCHNELLER, EUGENE STEWART, health administration and policy educator; b. Cornwall, NY, Apr. 9, 1943; s. Michael Nicholas and Anne Ruth (Gruner) Schneller; m. Ellen Stauber, Mar. 24, 1968; children: Andrew Jon, Lee Stauber. AA, SUNY, Buffalo, 1965; BA, LI U., 1967; PhD, NYU, 1973; grad. physician assoc. (hon.), Duke U., 2004. Rsch. asst. dept. sociology NYU, NYC, 1968-70; project dir. Montefiore Hosp. and Med. Ctr., Bronx, NY, 1970-72; asst. prof. Med. Ctr. and sociology Duke U., Durham, NC, 1973-75; assoc. prof., chmn. dept. sociology Union Coll., Schenectady, 1975-79, assoc. prof., dir. Health Studies Ctr., 1979-85; prof., dir. Sch. Health Mgmt. and Policy,

Ariz. State U., Tempe, 1985—91, assoc. dean rsch. and adminstrn. Coll. Bus., 1992-94; dir. L. William Seidman Rsch. Ctr., Tempe, 1992-94, counselor to pres. for health profl. edn., 1994-96; clin. prof. cmty. and family medicine U. Ariz., 1995-96, clin. prof. prevention, rsch., 1997—2002; prof., dir. Sch. Health Mgmt. and Policy W.P. Carey Sch. Bus. Ariz. State U., 1996—2002, prof. Sch. Health Mgmt. and Policy, 2002—; dir. Health Sector Supply Chain Initiatives, 2002—; prin. Health Care Sector Advances, 2004—, Dean's Coun. of 100 Disting. Rsch. Scholars, 2007—. Mem. health rsch. coun. N.Y. State Dept. Health, 1977—85; vis. rsch. scholar Columbia U., NYC, 1983—84; fellow Accrediting Commn. Edn. Health Svcs. Adminstrn., 1983—84; chmn. Western Network Edn. Health Adminstrn., Berkeley, Calif., 1987—92; commr. Calif. Commn. Future Med. Edn., 1996—97; mem. Ariz. Medicaid Adv. Bd., 1990—92, Ariz. Data Adv. Bd., 1989—91, Ariz. Health Care Group Adv. Bd., 1989; Dean's Coun. 100 Disting. Rsch. scholar Ariz. State U., 2007—. Author: The Physician's Assistant, 1980, Strategic Management of the Health Care Supply Chain, 2006; mem. editl. bd. Work and Occupations, 1975—93, Hosps. and Health Svcs. Adminstrn., 1989—92, Health Adminstrn. Press, 1991—94, Health Mgmt. Rev., 1996, Electronic Hallway, 1999; contbr. articles to profl. jours., chapters to books. Trustee Barrow Neurol. Inst., Phoenix, 1989—95; chair nat. adv. com. Investigator Awards Health Svcs. Rsch. Robert Wood Johnson Found., 1993—96. Mem.: APHA, Pharm. and Therapeutics Soc. (trustee 1999—2005, sec. 1999—2005), Assn. Univ. Health Programs Health Adminstrn. (bd. dirs. 1990—96, chmn. bd. dirs. 1994—95), Am. Sociol. Assn. Home: 11843 N 114th Way Scottsdale AZ 85259-2609 Office: Ariz State U Sch Health Mgmt and Policy WP Carey Sch Bus Tempe AZ 85287 Office Phone: 602-320-1512, 480-965-6334. Business E-Mail: gene.schneller@asu.edu.

SCHNELLER, MARINA VELENTGAS, lawyer; b. Portland, Maine, Feb. 24, 1943; d. Peter Constantine and Katherine Rena (Zolotas) Velentgas; 3 children. AB, Smith Coll., 1965; MS, U. Vt., 1968; JD, Am. U., 1972. Bar: Va. 1972, D.C. 1973, U.S. Patent & Trademark Office, U.S. Ct. Appeals (DC cir.), U.S. Supreme Ct. Atty. Cushman Darby & Cushman, Washington, 1974-80; pvt. practice, 1980-82; tech. asst. Hon. Nies US Ct. Appeals Fed. Cir., Washington, 1982—84; counsel Mobil Oil Corp., Fairfax, Va., 1984-98; ptnr.,patent prosecution, intellectual property group Venable LLP, Wash., 1998—2008. Lectr. George Mason U. Sch. Law. Adv. bd. mem. BNA U.S. Patents Quarterly, Washington; contbr. articles to profl. jours. Coach Alexandria (Va.) Soccer Assn., 1986-89, 91-93. Mem. Am. Chem. Soc. (Am. Chemists Medal 1961), ABA, Am. Intellectual Property Law Assn. (patent law com. 2005-), Patent Lawyers Club, Women Patent Lawyers Club, Hellenic Lawyers Assn. (pres.), Sigma Xi.

SCHNELLER, PAMELA, music educator; b. Chgo., Apr. 8, 1951; d. George and Marguerite Osburn; m. Roland Schneller; children: Jacqueline Whittemore, Brian Ramp. BS in Music Edn., U.Ill., Urbana, 1972; M in Ch. Music, Scarritt Grad. Sch., Nashville, 1987. Dir. First Presbyn. Ch., Nashville, 1994—99; asst. dean, sr. lectr. Blair Sch. Music/Vanderbilt U., Nashville, 2004—07, assoc. dean, 2007—. Mem.: Am. Choral Dirs. Assn. Home: 3214 Merlyn Ln Nashville TN 37214 Office: Blair Sch Music/Vanderbilt 2400 Blakemore Ave Nashville TN 37212 Business E-Mail: pam.schneller@vanderbilt.edu.

SCHNEPP, ANGELA J., secondary school educator; b. Bklyn., Mar. 17, 1951; d. Paul Michael Canino and Laura Ann Bruccoleri; m. Arthur George Schnepp, June 22, 1973; children: Deanna, Audra. BA in English, SUNY, Oneonta, 1973; MA, LI U., 1980; degree in Advanced Grad. Studies in Composition Program, Stonybrook U. English tchr. Babylon Jr./Sr. HS, NY, 1973—. Classical pianist Various nursing homes, churches and schools, 1992—2002. Mem.: Nat. Coun. of Tchrs. of English. Avocations: piano, watercolor painting, reading. Home: 106 Hobson Ave Saint James NY 11780 Office: Babylon Jr H S 50 Railroad Ave Babylon NY 11702

SCHNEPS, JACK, physics professor, department chairman; b. NYC, Aug. 18, 1929; s. Elias and Rose (Rephen) S.; m. Lucia De Marchi, Mar. 11, 1960; children: Loredana, Melissa, Leila. BA, N.Y. U., 1951; MS, U. Wis., 1953, PhD, 1956. Asst. prof. physics Tufts U., 1956-60, asso. prof., 1960-63, prof., 1963—, chmn. dept. physics, 1980-89, Vannevar Bush chair, 1995—. Vis. scientist European Orgn. Nuc. Rsch., Geneva, Switzerland, 1965-66; lectr. Internat. Sch. Elementary Particle Physics, Yugoslavia, 1968; vis. rsch. fellow Univ. Coll., London, Eng., 1973-74; vis. prof. Ecole Polytechnique, Palaiseau, France, 1982-83, The Technion, Haifa, Israel, 1989-90, Coll. de France, Paris, 1997; chmn. Internat. Neutrino Com., 2002—; vis. scholar Harvard U., 2005-06. Contbg. author: Methods in Subnuclear Physics, Vol. IV, 1970; editor Proc. of Neutrino 88, 1989; contbr. articles to profl. jours. NSF postdoctoral fellow U. Padua, Italy, 1958-59. Fellow Am. Phys. Soc.; mem. European Phys. Soc., AAUP, Phi Beta Kappa, Sigma Xi. Home: 3 Foxcroft Rd Winchester MA 01890-2407 Office: Dept Physics Tufts U Medford MA 02155 Office Phone: 617-627-3374. E-mail: jacob.schneps@tufts.edu.

SCHNIPPER, DON MARTIN, lawyer; b. Little Rock, Jan. 17, 1939; m. Mary Ann Evans, June 3, 1961; children: Caroline, Elizabeth. AB, U. Ark., 1963, JD, 1964. Bar: Ark. 1964, U.S. Supreme Ct. 1971. Ptnr. Wood, Smith, Schnipper, Clay & Vines, Hot Springs, Ark., 1964—. Spl. assoc. justice Ark. Supreme Ct., 1976-88. V.p. 1st United Meth. Ch., 1976-77, pres. 1977, vice chmn., bd. dirs. 1975-76; chmn. Ouachita Regional Counseling and Mental Health Ctr., 1977, pres., bd. dirs. 1970; bd. dirs. Hot Springs Children's Home. Fellow Am. Bar Found.; mem. ABA, Ark. Bar Assn. (chmn. young lawyers sect. 1969-70, ho. of dels. 1973-76, exec. council 1976-79, chmn. exec. council 1980-81, pres. 1985-86), Garland County Bar Assn. (pres.), Hot Springs C. of C. (bd. dirs. 1966—, pres. 1977, Disting. Svc. award 1970), U. Ark. Alumni Assn. (bd. dirs. 1978-84, nat. pres. 1982-83). Home: 850 Quapaw Ave Hot Springs National Park AR 71901-3926 Office: Wood Smith Schnipper Clay & Vines 123 Market St Hot Springs National Park AR 71901-5398 Office Phone: 501-624-1252. Personal E-mail: donschnipper@aol.com.

SCHNITZER, ALAN D., lawyer; b. Dallas, Tex., Dec. 6, 1965; BSE magna cum laude, Wharton Sch., Univ. Pa., 1988; JD, Columbia Univ., 1991. Bar: NY 1992. Assoc. Simpson Thacher & Bartlett LLP, NYC, 1991—99, ptnr., corp. law practice, 1999—; vice-chmn., chief legal officer Travelers Companies, Saint Paul, Minn., 2007—. Mem. Columbia Law Rev. Bd. dir., mem. audit com. Legal Aid Soc. Harlan Fiske Stone scholar. Mem.: ABA, NY State Bar Assn, Assn. Bar City of NY. Office: The Travelers Cos 385 Washington St Saint Paul MN 55102*

SCHNITZER, HOWARD JOEL, physics professor, researcher; b. Newark, Nov. 12, 1934; s. Albert and Helen (Ehrlich) S.; m. Phoebe Kazdin, May 22, 1966; children: Mark Jacob, Elizabeth Karen. BS in Mech. Engring., Newark Coll. Engring., 1955; PhD in Physics, U. Rochester, NY, 1960. Postdoctoral rsch. assoc. U. Rochester, 1960—61, Brandeis U., Waltham, Mass., 1961—62, asst. prof. physics, 1962—65, assoc. prof. physics, 1968, Gertrude and Edward Swartz prof. theoretical physics, 1991—, chair dept. physics, 1981—83. Vis. prof. Rockefeller U., 1969-70; hon. research assoc. Harvard U., 1974, 76—. Assoc. editor: Phys. Rev. Letters, 1978-80; contbr. articles to profl. jours. Fellow, Alfred P. Sloan Found., 1964—66, John S. Guggenheim Found., 1983—84; Predoctoral fellow, NSF, 1955—56, 1957—60. Fellow Am. Phys. Soc.; mem. Sigma Xi. Avocations: tennis, opera, travel.

SCHNOBRICH, ROGER WILLIAM, lawyer; b. New Ulm, Minn., Dec. 21, 1929; s. Arthur George and Amanda (Reinhart) Schnobrich; m. Angeline Ann Schmitz, Jan. 21, 1961; children: Julie A. Johnson, Jennifer L. Holmers, Kathryn M. Kubinski, Karen L. Holetz. BBA, U. Minn., 1952, JD, 1954. Bar: Minn. 1954. Assoc. Fredrikson and Byron, Mpls., 1956-58; pvt. practice Mpls., 1958-60; ptnr. Popham Haik, Schnobrich & Kaufman, Mpls., 1960-97, Hinshaw & Culbertson, Mpls., 1997—2004; officer Wayworth, Inc., Wayzata, Minn., 2004—. Bd. dirs. numerous corps. With US Army, 1954—56. Mem.: ABA, Order of Coif. Roman Catholic. Avocations: jogging, reading, golf. Home and Office: Wayworth Inc 530 Waycliff Dr N Wayzata MN 55391-1385 Office Phone: 952-476-8675. Personal E-mail: rnapana@aol.com.

SCHNOEBELEN, ANNE MARY, musicologist, educator; b. Tomahawk, Wis., Aug. 4, 1933; d. Herman Sabas and Katherine Alma (Yenor) Schnoebelen; m. John Albert Meixner, May 7, 1980. BA, Rosary Coll., 1958; MusM, U. Ill., 1960, PhD, 1966. From chmn. dept. musicology to prof. emerita Shepherd Sch. Music Rice U., Houston, 1974—2004, interim dean, 1981, 2002—03, prof. emerita Shepherd Sch. Music, 2004—. Author: Padre Martini's Collection of Letters in the Civico Museo Bibliografico Musicale: An Annotated Index, 1979; editor: Cantatas by Maurizio Cazzati in the Italian Cantata in the Seventeenth Century, 1985, Solo Motets from the Seventeenth Century, 10 vols., 1987—89, Seventeenth Century Italian Sacred Music, 10 vols., 1995—99; contbr. articles and reviews to profl. jours. Grantee, NEH, 1969, 1983; fellow, Fulbright, 1964; Travel grant, Am. Coun. Learned Societies, 1984. Fellow: AAUW; mem.: Am. Musicol. Soc. (coun. sec. 1986—88). Home: 2001 Holcombe Blvd #702 Houston TX 77030-4214 Office Phone: 713-348-4217. Business E-Mail: aschnoeb@rice.edu.

SCHNOEBELEN, IAN, chef; b. 1970; Sous chef Commander's Palace, Las Vegas, Lilette, New Orleans; owner, exec. chef Iris, New Orleans, 2006—. Named one of Best New Chefs, Food and Wine Mag., 2007. Office: Iris 320 Decatur St New Orleans LA 70130-1024 Office Phone: 504-299-3944.

SCHNOLL, HOWARD MANUEL, financial consultant, investment company executive; b. Milw., June 6, 1935; s. Nathan P. and Della (Fisher) Schnoll; m. Barbara Ostach, Dec. 3, 1988; children: Jordan, Terry, Jeffrey, Robert, Tammy, Daniel. BBA, U. Wis., 1958. CPA Wis.; cert. mgmt. cons., registered investment advisor. Mng. ptnr. Nankin, Schnoll & Co., S.C., Milw., 1966-86; mng. ptnr., bd. dirs. BDO Seidman, 1986-90; pres., COO Universal Med. Bldgs., L.P., Milw., 1990, also bd. dirs.; pres. Howard Schnoll & Assocs., Milw., 1991; mng. dir. Grande, Schnoll & Assocs., Milw., 1992-93; exec. mng. dir., COO Glaisner, Schilffarth, Grande & Schnoll, Ltd., Milw., 1993-98; exec. v.p., treas., bd. dirs. GS2 Securities, Inc., Milw., 1998—2004; sr. v.p. B. C. Ziegler and Co., Milw., 1999—, mng. dir., 2005—06; sr. v.p. Shilffarth-Schnoll Group, RBC Wealth Mgmt., Milw., 2006—. Bd. dirs. Milw. World Festival, Inc., 1968—, pres., 2003—05, chmn. bd., 2005—08; bd. dirs. City of Festivals Parade, Milw., 1983—89, Aurora Health Care Ventures, Milw. Heart Rsch. Found., Milw., Milw. Heart Inst., Arthritis Found.; pres. Impact, 1993—, bd. dirs.; pres., treas. Am. Heart Assn., Milw., 1978—82; capt. United Way, Milw., 1985; mem. greater Milw. com. Nat. Found. Ileitis and Colitis. Served to sgt. US Army, 1956—63. Mem.: AICPA, Acct. Computer Users Tech. Exchange, Wis. Inst. CPAs, B'nai Brith (pres. 1960—62), Boca Grove Golf and Tennis (bd. dirs. 2003—09, v.p. 2005—, treas. 2006—09), Brynwood Country Club (pres. 1988—2000, bd. dirs., treas.). Jewish. Avocations: golf, tennis. Office: RBC Wealth Mgmt 1000 N Water St Milwaukee WI 53202-4298 Office Phone: 414-347-7106. Business E-Mail: howard.schnoll@rbcdain.com.

SCHNOOR, JEFFREY ARNOLD, lawyer; b. Winnipeg, Man., Can., 1953; s. Toby and Ray. BA, U. Man., 1974, LLB, 1977. Bar: Man. 1978. Assoc. McJannet Weinberg Rich, Winnipeg, 1977-84, ptnr., 1984-86; exec. dir. Man. Law Reform Commn., Winnipeg, 1986-97; dir. criminal justice policy Man. Dept. Justice, Winnipeg, 1998—2002, exec. dir. policy devel. and analysis, 2002—05, asst. dep. min. cts. divsn., 2005—08, dep. minister justice, 2008—, dep. atty. gen., 2008—. Pres. Fedn. Law Reform Agys. Can., 1995-98; del. Uniform Law Conf. Can., 1986-2003, exec. com. 1996-2001, chair civil sect., 1996-97, v.p., 1998-99, pres., 1999-2000. Trustee United Way of Winnipeg, 1990-97, 99-2005, exec. com., 1990-97, 2001-05, treas., 1991-92, pres., 1994-95, cmty. rels. com. 1995-98, chmn. 1996-97, chair United Way 2005 com., 1997-98, hon. solicitor, 2001-05, chmn. 211 implementation com., 2001—; bd. dirs. Winnipeg Libr. Found., 1997-2001, St. Boniface Gen. Hosp., 2005-08; Man. Voluntary Sector Coun., 2001-04, U. Man. Winnipeg area study adv. group, 2001-04. Named Queen's Counsel Govt. of Man., 1992; recipient Chair's award of distinction United Way of Can., 1997. Mem. Law Soc. Man. (lectr. bar admission course 1981-96), Man. Bar Assn. (life, governing coun. 1988-96, recipient Cmty. Svc. award 1999), Can. Bar Assn. (legis. and law reform com. 1994-2000, 01—03, vice-chair 1997-2000, chair 2001-03, nat mag. editl. bd. 2002-08). Avocations: travel, languages, performing arts. Office: 110-450 Broadway Winnipeg MB Canada R3C 0V8 Home Phone: 204-475-9069; Office Phone: 204-945-8389. Business E-Mail: jeffrey.schnoor@leg.gov.mb.ca.

SCHNOOR, NEAL HENRY, music educator; b. Norfolk, Nebr., July 19, 1966; s. Walden Lowell and Ann Magdalene (Zach) Schnoor; m. Teresa Lynn Travis, Sept. 8, 1965; children: Rachel Ann, Graham Ronald. BFA in Edn., Wayne State Coll., Nebr., 1990; MusM, U. Nebr., Lincoln, 1996, PhD, 1999. Cert. tchr. Nebr., 1990. Band dir. Wakefield Pub. Sch., Wakefield, Nebr., 1990—91; dir. of bands Kearney H.S., Kearney, Nebr., 1991—94; dir. bands Lincoln Northeast H.S., Lincoln, Nebr., 1996—97; assoc. prof. music and edn., dirs bands U. of Nebr., Kearney, Nebr., 1997—. Contbr. articles to profl. jours.; guest condr. (to presentation at nat. & internat. conf.). Mem.: NEA, MENC/NMEA (pres., exec. bd. 2002—), Internat. Soc. Music Edn., U. Nebr. Kearney Edn. Assn., Nebr. State Edn. Assn., Coll. Music Soc., Nebr. State Bandmasters Assn. (past pres., Outstanding Young Band Dir. award 1994, Oustanding Young Band Dir. award 1994), Nebr. Music Educators Assn. (exec. bd. 2002—, pres.), Music Educators Nat. Conf., Phi Beta Mu, Phi Kappa Phi, Pi Kappa Lambda, Tau Beta Sigma (hon. Nat. Pk. Krinder Outstanding Band Dir. award 2009). Roman Catholic. Avocations: golf, travel, reading. Office: U Nebr Kearney 905 W 25th Kearney NE 68845-4238 Business E-Mail: schnoorn@unk.edu.

SCHNUCKER, ROBERT VICTOR, historian, educator; b. Waterloo, Iowa, Sept. 30, 1932; s. Felix Victor and Josephine (Maasdam) S.; m. Anna Mae Engelkes, Sept. 18, 1955; children: Sarai Ann, Sar Victor, Christjahn Dietrich. AB, NE Mo. State U., 1953; BD, U. Dubuque, 1956; MA, U. Iowa, 1960, PhD, 1969. Ordained to ministry Presbyn. Ch., 1956. Pastor United Presbyn. Ch. USA, Springville, Iowa, 1956-63, Meth.-Presbyn. Ch., Labelle, Mo., 1976-97; asst. prof. N.E. Mo. State U., Kirksville, 1963-65, assoc. prof., 1963-65, prof., 1969—99; interim pastor Bethany Presbyn. Ch., Grundy Center, Iowa, 1999—2001, First Presbyn. Ch., Aplington, 2002—04, Immanuel Presbyn. Ch., Waterloo, Iowa, 2004—05. Dir. Thomas Jefferson U. Press; supr. Bible exam. Presbyn. Ch. USA, Louisville, 1977-89; bd. dir. Ctr. for Reformation Rsch., St. Louis, 1984-99; pres. Conf. of Hist. Jours., 1993; adj. prof. religion U. No. Iowa, 1999—; vis. prof. religion and humanities, 2001-02. Author: A Glossary of Terms for Western Civilization, 1975, Helping Humanities Journal Survive, 1985, History Assessment Test, 1990; editor: Calviniana, 1989, Historians of Early Modern Europe, 1976-93, 97, Network News Exch., 1978-88; pres. 1st and 2d Editing History, Conf. for Hist. Jour., 1985-97; book rev. editor, mng. editor 16th Century Jour., 1972-97; pub. 16th Century Essays and Studies, 1980-97; contbr. articles to profl. jours. Recipient 16th Studies Conf. medal for Significant Achievement in Early Modern Studies, 1997, Presdl. Citation for Contbns. to the Univ., Truman State U., 1997; fellow Soc. Sci. Study of Religion, 1988, Sixteenth Century Studies conf., 1998; NEH grantee for jour. pubs., 1980. Mem. AAUP, Am. Acad. Religion, Renaissance Soc. Am., Am. History Assn. (chmn. Robinson prize com. 1987), Am. Soc. Ch. History, Soc. History of Edn., Soc. Bibl. Lit., Soc. for Reformation Rsch., Soc. Scholarly Pubs., Soc. for Values in Higher Edn., Conf. for Hist. Jour., Am. Coun. Learned Soc. (exec. bd. conf. adminstr. officers 1993-96, sec. 1994, chmn. 1995-96), Conf. Faith and History, 16th Century Studies Cons. (exec. sec. 1972-97), Humanities Iowa (bd. dirs. 1999-2003, pres. 2002-03). Office: Dept Philosophy and Religion U No Iowa Cedar Falls IA 50614-0501 Home Phone: 319-346-1244. Business E-Mail: rvs@cedarnet.org.

SCHNUR, JONATHAN, educational association administrator; b. 1966; m. Elisa Schnur; children: Matthew Sam, Elizabeth Rebecca. Grad. cum laude, Princeton U., 1989. Assoc. dir. ednl. policy, sr. edn. policy advisor to v.p. The White House, Washington; spl. asst. to sec. US Dept. Edn., Washington; co-founder, CEO New Leaders for New Schs. (NLNS), Washington, 2000—. Co-chair edn. adv. bd. Barack Obama Presdl. Campaign; spkr. in field. Democrat. Office: New Leaders for New Schs 30 W 26th St, Second Fl New York NY 10010 Office Phone: 646-792-1070.*

SCHNUR, ROBERT ARNOLD, lawyer, educator; b. White Plains, NY, Oct. 25, 1938; s. Conrad Edward and Ruth (Mehr) S.; children: Daniel, Jonathan. BA, Cornell U., 1960; JD, Harvard U., 1963. Bar: Wis. 1965, Ill. 1966. Assoc. Michael, Best & Friedrich, Milw., 1966-73, ptnr., 1973—. Chmn. Wis. Tax News, 1983-90; adj. prof. tax law U. Wis. Law Sch., 1988—; vis. prof. tax law Cornell U. Law Sch., 2006-. Capt. U.S. Army, 1963-65. Fellow Am. Coll. Tax Counsel; mem. ABA, Wis. Bar Assn. (chmn. tax sect. 1986-88), Milw. Bar Assn. Home: 3093 Timber Ln Verona WI 53593 Office: Michael Best Friedrich 100 E Wisconsin Ave Ste 3300 Milwaukee WI 53202-4108 Business E-Mail: raschnur@michaelbest.com.

SCHNURR, DENNIS MARION, archbishop; b. Sheldon, Iowa, June 21, 1948; BA, Loras Coll., Dubuque, Iowa, 1970; MA, Pontifical Gregorian Univ., Rome, 1974; JCD, Catholic Univ. Am., Washington, 1980. Ordained priest Diocese of Sioux City, Iowa, 1974, parochial vicar; mgmt. positions under apostolic nuncio to U.S., 1985—89; mgr. peace & justice projects U.S. Conf. Catholic Bishops, 1989—95, gen sec., 1995—2001; ordained bishop, 2001; bishop Diocese of Duluth, Minn., 2001—08; coadjutor archbishop Archdiocese of Cincinnati, Ohio, 2008—. Treas. U.S. Conf. Catholic Bishops. Roman Catholic. Office: Archdiocese of Cincinnati Chancery Office 100 E 8th St Cincinnati OH 45202 Office Phone: 513-421-3131. Office Fax: 513-421-6225.*

SCHOBEL, AARON ROSS, professional football player; b. Columbus, Tex., Sept. 1, 1977; s. Bob Schobel; m. June Schobel; children: Brock, John, Erika. Attended, Tex. Christian U., Fort Worth. Defensive end Buffalo Bills, 2001—. Named Defensive Player of Yr., Western Athletic Conf., 2000; named to Am. Football Conf. Pro-Bowl Team, NFL, 2006, 2007. Office: Buffalo Bills One Bills Dr Orchard Park NY 14127-2296*

SCHOCH, ALEXANDER C., lawyer, energy executive; BA, Kenyon Coll.; JD, Case Western Reserve U. Bar: Ill., Tex., Ohio, Mo. Internat. atty. Marathon Oil Co.; v.p., assoc. gen. counsel, sec. Goodrich Corp.; v.p., gen. counsel Emerson Process Mgmt.; exec. v.p., chief legal officer, sec. Peabody Energy, St. Louis, 2006—. Mem.: ABA, Am. Soc. Corp. Sec., State Bar Assn., Internat. Bar Assn. Office: Peabody Energy 701 Market St Saint Louis MO 63101*

SCHOCHET, BARRY P., health care executive; b. NYC, Mar. 13, 1951; s. George and Freda Schochet. BA in Zoology, U. Maine, 1973; MA in Health Care Adminstrn., George Washington U., 1975. Asst. adminstr. Doctors Hosp., Hollywood, Fla., 1975-76, Cypress Community Hosp., Pompano Beach, Fla., 1976-77, adminstr., 1977-78, exec. dir., 1978-79; asst. regional v.p. Nat. Med. Enterprises, St. Petersburg, Fla., 1979-80, asst. v.p. Los Angeles, 1980-81, v.p. ops. Tampa, Fla., 1981-83, sr. regional v.p., 1984-87, sr. divisional v.p., 1987-89, exec. v.p., 1989-91, sr. exec. v.p. and COO Santa Monica, Calif., 1991-93, pres., COO hosp. group, 1993-95; exec. v.p. operations Tenet Healthcare (formerly Nat. Med. Enterprises), Dallas, 1995—99; vice chmn. Tenet Healthcare, 1999—. Mem. Am. Hosp. Assn., Fedn. Am. Health Care Systems (bd. govs. 1985—, bd. dirs. 1989—, chmn. 2000), Am. Coll. Health Care Execs., Fla. League Hosps. (bd. dirs. 1981—, chmn. 1988-89), bd. dir. Healthcare leadership coun., 1999—. Office: Tenet Healthcare 13737 Noel Rd Ste 100 Dallas TX 75240-2017

SCHOCHOR, JONATHAN, lawyer, educator; b. Suffern, NY, Sept. 9, 1946; s. Abraham and Betty (Hechtor) S.; m. Joan Elaine Brown, May 31, 1970; children: Lauren Aimee, Daniel Ross. BA, Pa. State U., 1968; JD, Am. U., 1971. Bar: D.C. 1971, U.S. Dist. Ct. D.C. 1971, U.S. Ct. Appeals (D.C. cir.) 1971, Md. 1974, U.S. Dist. Ct. Md. 1974, U.S. Supreme Ct. 1986. Assoc. McKenna, Wilkinson & Kittner, Washington, 1970-74, Ellin & Baker, Balt., 1974-84; ptnr. Schochor, Federico & Staton, Balt., 1984—. Lectr. in law; expert witness to state legis. Editor-in-chief: Am. U. Law Rev., 1970—71. Mem. ABA, ATLA (state del. 1991, state gov. 1992-95), Am. Bd. Trial Advs. (membership com. 1994—), Am. Bd. Trial Advs., Am. Judicature Soc., Md. State Bar Assn. (spl. com. on health claims arbitration 1983), Md. Trial Lawyers Assn. (bd. govs. 1986-87, mem. legis. com. 1985-88, chmn. legis. com. 1986-87, sec. 1987-88, exec. com. 1987-92, v.p. 1987-88, pres.-elect 1989, pres. 1990-91), Balt. City Bar Assn. (legis com. 1986-87, spl. com. on tort reform 1986, medicolegal com. 1989-90, cir. ct. for Balt. City task force-civil document mgmt. sys. 1994-95), Bar Assn. D.C., Internat. Platform Assn., Phi Alpha Delta. Office: Schochor Federico & Staton PA 1211 Saint Paul St Baltimore MD 21202-2783 Office Phone: 410-234-1000. Business E-Mail: jschochor@sfspa.com.

SCHOCK, AARON JON, United States Representative from Illinois, former state legislator; b. Morris, Minn., May 28, 1981; Real estate mgr. Junction Mgmt., Petersen Companies, Peoria, Ill.; mem. from 92d dist. Ill. Ho. Rep., 2005—09; mem. US Congress from 18th Ill. Dist., 2009—. Mem. Peoria Bd. Edn., pres. Bd. dir. Heart of Ill. Kids Count, Youth for a Cause; mem. edn. task force Peoria C. of C.; Big Brother Heart of Ill. Big Brothers & Big Sisters, 2000—03. Republican. Office: US Congress 509 Cannon House Office Bldg Washington DC 20515-1318 also: Dist Office 100 NE Monroe Rm 100 Peoria IL 61602 Office Phone: 202-225-6201, 309-671-7027. Office Fax: 202-225-9249, 309-671-7309.*

SCHOCK, ROBERT NORMAN, geophysicist; b. Monticello, NY, May 25, 1939; s. Carl Louis and Norma Elizabeth (Greenfield) S.; m. Susan Esther Benton, Nov. 28, 1959; children: Pamela Ann, Patricia Elizabeth, Christina Benton. BS, Colo. Coll., 1961; MS, Rensselaer Poly. Inst., 1963, PhD, 1966; postgrad., Northwestern U., 1963-64. Cert. Calif. state wine judge. Jr. geophys. trainee Continental Oil Co., Sheridan, Wyo., 1960; jr. geologist Texaco In., Billings, Mont., 1961; teaching asst. Rensselaer Poly. Inst., Troy, NY, 1961-63, research asst., 1964-66; research assoc. U. Chgo., 1966-68; sr. research scientist Lawrence Livermore Nat. Lab., U. Calif., 1968—2006, group leader high pressure physics, 1972-74, sect. leader geoscis. and engring., 1974-76, div. leader earth scis., 1976-81, head dept. earth scis., 1981-87, energy program leader, 1987-92, dep. assoc. dir. for energy, 1992-98, sr. fellow Ctr. Global Security Rsch., 1998—2006. Pres. Pressure Sys. Rsch. Inc.; faculty Chabot Coll., 1969-71; dir. Alameda County Flood Control and Water Conservation Dist., 1984-86, chmn., 1985; adv. panel on geoscis. US Dept. Energy, 1985-87; chmn. adv. com. U. Calif. Energy Inst., 1992-98; rsch. adv. com. Gas Rsch. Inst., Chgo., 1995-2001; dir. studies World Energy Coun., London, 2005—; chmn. Study Group Energy Tech. in 21st Century, 1999-2004, coord. lead author intergovtl. panel on climate change, UN, 2004-07; instrumentation and facilities rev. panel NSF, 2001-04. Mem. editl. bd. Rev. Sci. Instruments, 1975-77; assoc. editor: Jour. Geophys. Rsch., 1978-80; bd. assoc. editors: 11th Lunar and Planetary Sci. Conf., 1980; mem. adv. bd. Physics and Chemistry of Minerals, 1983-97; rsch. and publs. on high pressure physics, solid state physics, physics of earth interior, rock deformation, energy R&D and energy policy. Fulbright sr. fellow U. Bonn, Germany, 1973; vis. research fellow Australian Nat. U. Canberra, 1980-81 Mem. AAAS, Am. Geophys. Union, Sigma Xi, Commonwealth of Calif. Club, Cosmos Club (Washington).

SCHOELEN, MARY JEANETTE, federal judge; b. Rota, Spain, 1968; BA, U. Calif. Irvine, 1990; JD, George Washington U. Law Sch., 1993. Law clk. Nat. Veterans Legal Services Project; staff atty., veteran's benefits program Vietnam Veterans of America, 1994; intern, com. veterans' affairs US Senate, 1994, minority counsel, com. veterans' affairs, 1997—2001, minority gen. counsel, com. veterans' affairs, 2001, dep. staff dir. benefits programs and gen. counsel, com. veterans' affairs, 2001—04; judge US Ct. Appeals Veterans' Claims, 2004—. Office: US Ct Appeals Veterans Claims 625 Indiana Ave NW Ste 900 Washington DC 20004 Office Phone: 202-501-5970.*

SCHOELLER, WOLFGANG WILHELM, chemistry educator; b. Illertissen, Bavaria, Germany, Mar. 7, 1947; s. Franz and Eleonore (Rettich) S.; m. Johanna Stabler; children: Sebastian, Friederike. Diploma in Engring., Tech. Sch., 1963; Diploma in Chemistry, U. Stuttgart, 1966, Doctorate, 1969. Postdoctoral fellow U. Tex., Austin, 1969-71; scientific asst. U. Bochum, Germany, 1971-77; prof. chemistry U. Bielefeld, Germany, 1983—. Mem. Chem. Soc. of Germany. Office: Univ of Calif at Riverside Chemical Sciences 1 434 Riverside CA 92521-0403 Business E-Mail: wolfgang.schoeller@ucr.edu. E-mail: wolfgang.schoeller@uni-bielefeld.de.

SCHOEN, JOHN W., biologist, educator; b. Anacortes, Wash., Apr. 17, 1947; s. Robert F. and Mary K. Schoen; m. Mary Beth Schoen, Sept. 6, 1970; children: Erik R., Sarah K. BA, Whitman Coll., Walla Walla, Wash., 1969; MS, U. Puget Sound, Tacoma, 1972; PhD, U. Wash., Seattle, 1977. Rsch. asst. Coll. Forest Resources, U. Wash., Seattle, 1972—76; sr. conservation biologist Alaska Dept. Fish & Game, Anchorage, 1990—97, rsch. wildlife biologist Juneau, 1990—97, game biologist, 1996—97; exec. dir. Audubon Alaska, Anchorage, 1997—99, sr. scientist, 1999—. Assoc. prof., wildlife biology U. Alaska Fairbanks, 1990—. V.p. Alaska Sea Life Ctr., Seward, 2001—07. Recipient Outstanding Conservation Leadership award, Wilburforce Found., 2008. Mem.: Wildlife Soc. (Alaska chpt. pres. 1982, fellowship 2006). Achievements include research in relationships of old growth forests to brown bear and black-tailed deer in coastal temperate rain forests. Avocations: photography, cross country skiing, flying, sailing. Office: Audubon Alaska 441 W 5th Ave #300 Anchorage AK 99501 Office Fax: 907-276-5069. Business E-Mail: jschoen@audubon.org.

SCHOEN, MARC ALAN, pension and employee benefits executive; b. Worcester, Mass., May 30, 1938; s. A. Robert and Ruth D.Schoen; m. Joanne S. Schultz, June 24, 1962; children: Elliott, Aaron, Jennifer, Matthew. BBA, BS, U. Miami, 1965. Cert. flexible compensation, enrolled retirement plan agent, fin. advisors. Asst. buyer Allied Stores, Miami, Fla., 1965-66; agt. Fidelity Mut. Ins., Miami, 1966-67, Prudential Ins. Co., Miami, 1967-68; pvt. practice registered rep., agt. Miami, 1968-73; pres. A Pension Store, Inc., Miami, 1973—2004. Cons. Criterion Funds, Inc., Houston, 1983-1987, TMG Holding LLC, Chgo., 2004-06; newspaper columnist, 1969-1976, 1984. Mem. So. Fla. Employee Benefits Coun., Dade Estate Planning Coun.; scoutmaster Boy Scouts Am., Miami, 1966-90; exec. bd. dirs. Crouse Found. to Pub. Arts at CUNY, N.Y.C., 1983—. With USN, 1957-62. Recipient Cmty. Svc. award Prudential Ins., 1968; CFC Designation, Employers Coun. on Flexible Compensation; named Outstanding Young Man Yr., Optimists, 1967; named to Rollins Coll. Sports Hall of Fame, 1987. Mem. (assoc.) Am. Soc. Pension Actuaries, Internat. Assn. Fin. Planners, Million Dollar Round Table (qualifying life), Nat. Assn. Ins. and Fin. Advisors, Employers Coun. on Flexible Compensation, Rotary, Masons; fellow: Life Underwriters Tng. Coun. Avocations: stamp collecting/philately, camping, hiking. Home: 838 Blue Heather Ct Lawrenceville GA 30045 Office Phone: 770-806-1040. E-mail: marc@apensionstore.com, maschoen@bellsouth.net.

SCHOEN, ROBERT, demographer; b. Irvington, NJ, Sept. 23, 1940; s. Bert Alan and Regina Berkowitz Schoen; m. Delores Christina Harmon, Mar. 25, 1967. PhD, U. Calif., Berkeley, 1972. Cert. Associate Soc. Actuaries Soc. Actuaries, 1968. Hoffman prof. of family sociology and demography Pa. State U., University Park, Pa., 1999—2008; prof. of population dynamics Johns Hopkins U., Baltimore, Md., 1989—99. Author: (scholarly monograph) Dynamic Population Models (Sheps Award in Math. Demography, 2004), Modeling Multigroup Populations. Capt. US Air Force, 1964—68, Glagow AFB MT. Decorated Commendation Medal US Air Force. Mem.: Population Assn. of Am. Avocations: travel, photography.

SCHOEN, ROBERT TAYLOR, rheumatologist; b. Boston, June 5, 1950; s. Donald and Barbara (Taylor) S.; m. Cynthia French; children: Alexandra, Julia. AB, Harvard U., 1972; MD, Columbia U., 1976; MBA, U. Conn., 2001. Diplomate Am. Bd. Internal Medicine, Nat. Bd. Med. Examiners; lic. physician Conn., Mass.; cert. in controlled substance, Conn., 1971. Intern in medicine Yale-New Haven (Conn.) Hosp., 1976-77, resident in medicine, 1977-79, attending physician, 1981; rsch. fellow in rheumatology and immunology Harvard Med. Sch., Brigham and Women's Hosp., Boston, 1979-81; assoc. in medicine Hosp. St. Raphael, New Haven, 1981-82, attending physician, 1982; clin. instr. medicine Yale U. Sch. Medicine, New Haven, 1982-83, asst. clin. prof., 1983-90, co-dir. Lyme Disease Clinic, 1987, assoc. clin. prof., 1995, clin. prof., 1995—. Contbr. articles to profl. jours. Recipient G. Milton Shy Essay award Am. Acad. Neurology, 1976, Wall St. Jour. prize, 2001. Fellow Am. Coll. Rheumatology (com. rheumatic disease care 1994), Am. Coll. Physicians; mem. AMA, New England Rheumatism Assn., Am. Fedn. Clin. Rsch., Am. Soc. Internal Medicine, Conn. State Med. Soc., New Haven County Med. Assn. Office Phone: 203-789-2255. Business E-Mail: robert.schoen@yale.edu.

SCHOEN, SCOTT ALAN, corporate executive; b. St. Louis, Sept. 27, 1958; s. Sheldon Simeon and Roberta Mae (Nathanson) S.; m. Laurence Maria Madeleine Gachelin, Jan. 19, 1965. BA in History, Yale U., 1980; MBA, JD, Harvard U., 1984. Bar: N.Y. 1985. Assoc. Goldman, Sachs & Co., NYC, 1984-86; v.p. Thomas H. Lee Co., Boston, 1986—; dir. Spectrum Brands, Atlanta, 2005—. Dir. AXIS Capital Holdings Ltd., Refco Grp. Ltd., LLC, Simmons Corp., Syratech Corp., TransWestern Pub. L.P., United Industries Corp. & Wyndham Internat. Inc. Vice chmn. bd. & mem. exec. com. United Way of Massachusetts Bay.; mem. bd. adv. Yale Sch. Mgmt.; mem. Yale Devel. Bd. Jewish. Avocations: skiing, tennis, golf, reading. Office: Spectrum Brands 6 Concourse Pky Ste 3300 Atlanta GA 30328 Office Phone: 770-829-6200.*

SCHOEN, STEVAN JAY, lawyer; b. NYC, May 19, 1944; s. Al and Anna (Spevack) S.; m. Cynthia Lukens; children: Andrew Adams, Anna Kim. BS, U. Pa., 1966; JD, Cornell U., 1969; MPhil, Cambridge U., Eng., 1980. Bar: N.Mex. 1970, N.Y. 1970, U.S. Supreme Ct. 1976, U.S. Tax Ct. 1973, U.S. Ct. Internat. Trade 1982. Dir. Vista law recruitment OEO, Washington, 1970-71; atty. Legal Aid Soc. of Albuquerque, 1971-73; chief atty. N.Mex. Dept. Health and Social Svcs., Albuquerque, 1973-77; ptnr. Brennan, Schoen & Eisenstadt, 1980—88, Bingham, Hurst, Apodaca, Wile & Schoen, P.C., 2001—03; prin. Stevan J. Schoen, LLC, Placitas, N.Mex., 2003—; probate judge Sandoval County, 1991—99. Arbitrator NYSE; mem. N.Mex. Supreme Ct. Appellate Rules Com., 1982—92; chmn. rules com. Com. on Fgn. Legal Cons., 1993—95; chmn. N.Mex. Supreme Ct. Com., Probate Ct. Rules and Forms, 1998—2006; mem. state bd., licensure Profl. Engrs. and Surveyors, 2004—. Mem. Mayor's Albuquerque Abd. Com. on Fgn. Trade Zone, 1992-94; v.p. Placitas Vol. Fir Dept., 1974-86; bd. edn. Bernalillo Pub. Sch. Dist., 1996-97; chair Sandoval County Dem. Party, 2001-03. Recipient Cert. for Outstanding Svc. to Judiciary, N.Mex. Supreme Ct., 1982, Outstanding Svc. award N. Mex. Supreme Ct., 1992, 2003, Cert. of Appreciation, N.Mex. Sec. of State, 1980, Pro Bono Pub. Svc. award, 1989, Cert. of Recognition Legal Aid, 1994, award Las Placitas Assn., 1996; named Outstanding Probate Judge, N.Mex State Senate, 1998. Mem. Am. Judges Assn. (ho. of dels. 1999-2002), Nat. Coll. Probate Judges, State Bar N.Mex. (past chmn. real property, probate and trust sect. 1989, Outstanding Contbn. award 1989, past chmn. appellate practice sect. 1991, past chmn. internat. law sect. 1991-92, commn. on professionalism 1992-95, organizing com. U.S.-Mex. law inst. 1992), N.Mex. Probate Judges Assn. (chmn. 1993-99, award 1998, N.Mex. state bar, chair sr. lawyers sect. 2003-04, dir. 2002-), Bench and Bar Com. (co-chair 2001-2002), Oxford-Cambridge Soc. N.Mex. (sec.), M.Mex. Assn. Counties (adv. bd. 1995-98). Office: 4 Hillside Dr Placitas NM 87043 Office Phone: 505-867-2802. Personal E-mail: schoenlaw@gmail.com. Business E-Mail: schoenlaw@comcast.net.

SCHOEN, SUZANNE, English educator; b. Chgo., July 3, 1941; d. George S. and Anne R. Thorsen; m. Raymond G. Schoen, June 13, 1964 (div. Jan. 1978); m. Gary D. Childs, Jan. 3, 1985 (dec. Feb. 13, 2007); children: Jeffrey, Valerie. BA, Rosary Coll., 1963; MA, Purdue U., 1965. Tchg. asst. Purdue U., 1963-65; reading splst. U. Wis., Madison, 1965-68; part time instr. U. Notre Dame, 1968-70; skills cons., 1970—; assoc. prof. Holy Cross Coll., Notre Dame, Ind., 1970—; founder, dir. Ctr. for Faculty Devel., 1999—; mem. planning com. Midwest Conf. on Scholarship of Tchg. and Learning, 2000—; mem. Holy Cross Self-Study for Reaccreditation, 2004—06. Caregiver to disabled man; coord. acad. integrity symposium and process. Author: Analytical Bibliography for College/Adult Reading, 1967, short stories; editor: The Irish Terriers of Notre Dame, 1992; contbr. articles to Chgo. Tribune. Mem. choir St. Matthew's Cathedral, South Bend, Ind., 1976-80; mem. adv. bd. South Bend Pub. Libr., 1988-90. Recipient Roundtable Tchg. award St. Joseph County C. of C., 1991. Mem. AAUW, Nat. Coun. Tchrs. English, North Ctrl. Reading Assn., Ctr. for Acad. Integrity, Am. Legion Aux. Avocations: reading, cinema, theater, gourmet cooking. Home: 814 S 24th St South Bend IN 46615-2116 Office: Holy Cross Coll PO Box 308 Notre Dame IN 46556-0308 Office Phone: 574-239-8415.

SCHOEN, WILLIAM JACK, finance company executive; b. LA, Aug. 2, 1935; s. Jack Conrad and Kathryn Mabel (Stegmayer) S.; m. Sharon Ann Barto, Oct. 1, 1966; children: Kathryn Lynn, Karen Anne, Kristine Lea, William Jack. BS in Fin. magna cum laude, U. So. Calif., 1960, MBA, 1963. Mktg. mgr. Anchor Hocking Glass Co., 1964-68; v.p. sales and mktg. Obear-Nester Glass Co., 1968-71; pres. Pierce Glass Co., Port Allegheny, Pa., 1971-73; pres., chief exec. officer, dir. F.&M. Schaefer Brewing Co., NYC, 1973-81; now chmn., pres. Wilshar Mgmt. Co. Inc., Naples, Fla., 1981—; chmn. Health Mgmt. Assocs. Inc., Naples, 1983—, also bd. dirs. Contbr. to indsl. publns. Founder Marine Corp. Heritage Found.; mem. Bus. Coun. of 100 of Fla.; bd. dir. Internat. Coll. Found.; chmn. Schoen Found.; mem. bd. advisors U. So. Calif. Bus. Sch.; trustee U. So. Calif., 2006-. Served with USMC, 1953-56, Korea. Mem. Hole in the Wall, Naples Yacht Club, Port Royal Club, Teton Springs Club, Phi Kappa Phi. Republican. Lutheran. Office: Health Mgmt Assocs 5811 Pelican Bay Blvd Ste 500 Naples FL 34108-2711 Office Phone: 239-598-3175.

SCHOENBERGER, JAMES EDWIN, retired federal agency administrator; b. Dayton, Ohio, Sept. 7, 1947; s. Harry Robert and Elizabeth Jane Schoenberger; m. Aura Victoria Montana, June 24, 1977; children: David, Eric. BSCE, Purdue U., 1969; MBA, Harvard U., 1971. V.p. ops. for midwestern housing developer Herman Devel. Group, Indpls., 1971-74; various positions New Communities Adminstrn. and with sec. HUD, Washington, 1974-77, assoc. dep. asst. sec., 1981-83; dir. land utilization Peabody Coal Co., St. Louis, 1977-81; sr. v.p. ops. The Investment Group, Washington, 1983-86; gen. dep. asst. fed. housing commr. HUD, Washington, 1987-89, assoc. gen., dep. asst. sec., 1990-97, ret., 1997. Pres. Temple Found., 2005—. Roman Catholic. Avocations: computers, philanthropy.

SCHOENBERGER, STEVEN HARRIS, physician, research consultant; b. Cleve., Nov. 26, 1950; s. Stanford L. and Irene (Gold) S. BA, Tulane U., 1972; MD, U. Autonoma Guadalajara, Mex., 1976. Diplomate Am. Bd. of Urology. Asst. prof. Tulane U. Sch. Medicine, New Orleans, 1983—. Rsch. assoc. Delta Regional Primate Rsch. Ctr., Covington, La., 1983-85, chief section of urology Lawrence and Meml. Hosp., New London, Conn.; chmn. laser com., Lawrence and Meml. Hosp., New London, Conn., 1989—, chief sect. urology, 2003—; rsch. cons. Pfizer Med. Group, Groton, Conn., 1989—. Fellow ACS, Am. Soc. Laser Medicine and Surgery; mem. Soc. Univ. Urologists, N.Y. Acad. Scis., New Eng. Escadrille. Office: 3 Shaws Cv Ste 206 New London CT 06320-4968 Office Phone: 860-443-0622.

SCHOENBOHM, HERBERT L., political organization administrator, radio personality; s. W.B. Shoenbohm; m. Monika Schoenbohm. Internat. sales rep. Gates Radio, Harris Corp, Collins Radio; SECC US VI, Scotland; staff aid US House Representatives; spl. asst. to Commr. Property and Procurement; radio host Freedom Forum; chmn. US VI Rep. Party, 2000—. Rep. Rep. Nat. Conv., 1980, 84, 88, 2000; mem. VI Rep. State Com. Mem.: Rep. State Com. (chmn.). Republican. Office: US VI Box 24261 Christiansted VI 00824 Office Phone: 340-773-1561. E-mail: herbs@vitelcom.net.

SCHOENER, THOMAS WILLIAM, ecologist, educator; b. Lancaster, Pa., Aug. 9, 1943; BA, Harvard Coll., 1965, PhD, 1969. Asst. prof. Harvard Coll., Cambridge, Mass., 1972-73, assoc. prof., 1973-75, U. Wash., Seattle, 1975-76, prof., 1976-80, U. Calif., Davis, 1980—, chairperson sect. evolution and ecology divsn. biol. scis., 1993-99. Mem. editl. bd. dirs. Oecologia, 1984-93; past mem. editl. bd. Evolution, Am. Naturalist, Sci., Acta Oecologia; contbr. chpts. to books, articles to profl. jours. Recipient MacArthur prize Ecol. Soc. Am., 1987; grantee NSF, 1975—, Nat. Geog. Soc., Australian Rsch. Coun., 2003-; jr. fellow Harvard U., 1969-72; Guggenheim fellow, 1992-93. Mem. NAS, Am. Acad. Arts and Scis., Am. Ornithologists Union (elective), Am. Soc. Naturalists, Ecol. Soc. Am., Am. Soc. Ichthyologists and Herpetologists, Cooper Ornithol. Soc., Am. Arachnological Soc., Soc. Study of Amphibians and Reptiles. Avocations: weightlifting, reading. Office: U Calif Sect Evolution Ecology Davis CA 95616 Office Phone: 530-752-8319. Business E-Mail: twschoener@ucdavis.edu.

SCHOENFELD, ALAN HENRY, mathematics education professor, researcher; b. NYC, July 9, 1947; s. Neil Howard and Natalie (Weinberg) S.; m. Jean Snitzer, June 14, 1970. BS in Math., Queens Coll., 1968; MS in Math., Stanford U., 1969, PhD in Math., 1973. Lectr. U. Calif., Davis, 1973-75; from asst. prof. to assoc. prof. Hamilton Coll., Clinton, NY, 1978-81, U. Rochester, NY, 1981-84; lectr. U. Calif., Berkeley, 1975-78, assoc. prof. edn., math., 1985-86, prof., 1986—, chmn. div. edn. in math., sci. and tech., 1987—98, chmn. Sch. Edn., 1994—98. Chmn. Grad. Group in Sci. and Math. Edn., U. Calif., Berkeley, 1985-87; chief organizer IV Internat. Congress Math. Edn., 1984. Author: Mathematical Problem Solving, 1985, Mathematical Association of America Notes # 1, Problem Solving, 1983; editor: Cognitive Science and Mathematics Education, 1987, A Source Book for College Mathematics Teaching, 1990, Mathematical Thinking and Problem Solving, 1994, Research in Collegiate Mathematics Education, vol. 1, 1994, vol. 2, 1996, vol. 3, 1998, vol. 4, 2000, Assessing Mathematical Proficiency, 2007, A Study of Teaching: Multiple Lenses, Multiple Views, 2008. Mem. State Calif. Math. Framework Com., 1988-90; mem. adv. panel Calif. Assessment Program, 1988—94; mem. Supt.'s Math. Task Force, 1995. Grantee NSF, 1979, 85, 87, 90-92, 96-97, 2001-06, Sloan Found., 1984, 87, Spencer Found., 1983, 93. Fellow: AAAS; mem.: Nat. Rsch. Coun. (math. sci. edn. bd. task force on K-12 1986—88, bd. testing/assessment 1993—98), Nat. Bd. for Profl. Tchg. Stds. (math. panel 1990—95), Nat. Coun. Tchrs. Math. (rsch. adv. com. 1990—93, chair 1992—93, leader prins. and stds. 1997—2000), Cognitive Sci. Soc., Am. Math. Soc. (com. on edn. 1992—97), Am. Ednl. Rsch. Assn. (exec. com. Spl. Interest Group Math. Edn. 1984—86, chair publs. com. 1994—, pres. 1998—2000), Math. Assn. Am. (chmn. tchg. undergrad. math. com. 1982—89), Nat. Acad. Edn. (exec. bd. 1995—2006, v.p. 2001—06), Kappa Delta Pi (Laureate 2006). Avocations: food, wine. Home: 830 Colusa Ave Berkeley CA 94707-1839 Office: U Calif Dept Edn Berkeley CA 94720-1670

SCHOENFELD, DAVID ALAN, statistician, educator; b. Ft. Monmouth, NJ, Apr. 19, 1945; s. Robert Louis Schoenfeld and Helene Flapan; m. Ellen Maureen Beeks, Dec. 30, 1973; children: Heather, Elizabeth, Jonathan. BA, Reed Coll., 1967; MA, U. Oreg., 1968, PhD, 1974. Postdoctoral fellow Stanford U., Calif., 1974—75; rsch. asst. prof. SUNY, Buffalo, 1975—77; from asst. to assoc. scientist Dana-Farber Cancer Inst., Boston, 1977—86; from asst. prof. to prof. dept. of biostats., Sch. Pub. Health Harvard U., Boston, 1977—, assoc. prof. to prof. dept. medicine, 1985—; dir. Biostatistics Ctr. Mass. Gen. Hosp., Boston, 1985—2009. Co-editor: (book) Aids Clinical Trials, 1995. Fellow: American Statis. Assn.; mem.: Internat. Statis. Inst., Biometric Soc., Inst. of Math. Stats. Avocation: singing. Home: 41 Brook Rd Sharon MA 02067 Office: Mass Gen Hosp 50 Staniford St Boston MA 02114 Personal E-mail: david@schoenfeld.com. E-mail: dschoenfeld@partners.org.

SCHOENFELD, HANNS-MARTIN WALTER, accounting educator; b. Leipzig, Germany, July 12, 1928; came to U.S., 1962, naturalized, 1968; s. Alwin and Lisbeth (Kirbach) Schoenfeld; m. Margit Frese, Aug. 10, 1956 (dec. Jan. 21, 2005); 1 child, Gabriele. MBA, U. Hamburg, Fed. Republic Germany, 1952, DBA, 1954; PhD, U. Braunschweig, Fed. Republic Germany, 1966; PhD (hon.), U. Graz, Austria, 2008. Pvt. practice acctg., Hamburg, 1948-54; bus. cons. Europe, 1958-62; faculty accountancy U. Ill., Champaign/Urbana, 1962—, prof. acctg., bus. adminstrn. Urbana, 1967—, Weldon Powell prof. acctg., 1976, 80-81, H. T. Scovill prof. acctg., 1985-94; prof. emeritus, 1994—; dir. Office of West European Studies, 1982-84. Lectr., cons. in bus. and acctg., Eng., Belgium, Austria, Denmark, Brazil, Mex., Germany, Poland, Indonesia, Korea, Japan, Switzerland, Hungary, Czechoslovakia, 1962—; vis. prof. Econs. U. Vienna, Austria, 1984-2002, 2006-, Handelshochschule, Leipzig, Germany, 1996-2002. Author: Management Dictionary 2 vols., 4th edit, 1971, Cost Accounting, 8th edit, 1974-95, Management Development, 1967, Cost Terminology and Cost Theory, 1974, (with J. Sheth) Export Marketing: Lessons from Europe, 1981, (with H.P. Holzer) Managerial Accounting and Analysis in Multinational Enterprises, 1986, (with L. Noerreklit) Resources of the Firm, 1996. With German Army, 1944-45. Recipient Dr. Kausch prize for internat. integration of acctg. U. St. Gall, Switzerland, 1996, Dr. h. c. U. Graz, 2008 Mem. Am. Acctg. Assn. (chmn. internat. sect. 1976-77), Acad. Acctg. Historians (v.p. 1976-77, pres. 1978-79, Hour Glass award for best book publs. 1975), Acad. Internat. Bus., German Profs. Bus. Adminstrn., German Assn. Indsl. Engring., European Acctg. Assn., Coun. of European Studies, Internat. Assn. for Acctg. Edn. and Rsch., Beta Gamma Sigma, Beta Alpha Psi. Home: 1014 Devonshire Dr Champaign IL 61821-6620 Office: U Ill Dept Acctg 360 Wohlers Hall 1206 S 6th St Champaign IL 61820-6915 Home Phone: 217-359-4433; Office Phone: 217-333-0857. Business E-Mail: hschoenf@illinois.edu.

SCHOENFELD, HOWARD ALLEN, management consultant, lawyer; b. NYC, Apr. 17, 1948; s. Irving and Muriel (Levy) S.; m. Paula Simon; 1 child, Haley Rebecca. BA, U. Pa., 1970; JD, Georgetown U., 1973. Bar: Md. 1973, U.S. Dist. Ct. Md. 1973, Wis. 1976, U.S. Dist. Ct. (ea. dist.) Wis. 1976, U.S. Dist. Ct. (we. dist.) Wis. 1987. Law clk. Md. Ct. Appeals, 1973-74; assoc. Gordon, Feinblatt, Rothman, Hoffberger & Hollander, Balt., 1974-76; ptnr. Trebon & Schoenfeld, Milw., 1976-85, Godfrey & Kahn, Milw., 1985—2002; prs. DSC Advisors, Milw., 2002—. Chmn. John Anderson Campaign for Pres., Wis., 1980; pres. Milw. Jewish Coun., 1987-89, mem., 1983—. Recipient Young Leadership award Milw. Jewish Fedn., 1983. Mem. ABA, Wis. Bar Assn., Milw. Bar Assn. Office: DSC Advisors 4101 N Port Washington Rd Milwaukee WI 53212-1029 Home Phone: 414-351-1919; Office Phone: 414-967-0579. E-mail: hasreorg@aol.com.

SCHOENFELD, JIM, professional sports team executive, professional hockey coach; b. Galt, Ont., Can., Sept. 4, 1954; m. Theresa Schoenfeld; children: Katie, Justin, Adam, Nathan. Defenseman Buffalo Sabres, 1972—81, 1984—85, Detroit Red Wings, 1981—83, Boston Bruins, 1983—84; head coach Rochester Americans, 1984, Buffalo Sabres, 1985—86, NJ Devils, 1988—89, Washington Capitols, 1994-97, Phoenix Coyotes, 1997—99; asst. coach NY Rangers, 2002—03, asst. gen. mgr. player personnel, 2007—, interim asst. coach, 2009; gen. mgr. Hartford Wolfpack, 2003—07, head coach, 2005—07. Lead analyst Nat. Hockey Night, ESPN, 1999—2002. Office: NY Rangers Hockey Club 2 Pennsylvania Plaza New York NY 10102*

SCHOENFELD, MICHAEL P., lawyer; b. Oct. 17, 1935; s. Jack and Anne Schoenfeld; m. Helen Schorr, Apr. 3, 1960; childrne: Daniel, Steven, Tracy. BS in Acctg., NYU, 1955; LLB, LLD, Fordham U., 1958. Bar: N.Y. 1959, U.S. Supreme Ct. 1963. Coun. Am. Home Assurance Co., NYC, 1958-62; ptnr. Schoenfeld & Schoenfeld, Melville, N.Y., 1959—. V.p. Interstate Brokerage Corp., 1965-84, pres., 1984-90; ptnr. Melville Realty Co., 1977-90; legal adv. various bus. orgns. V.p., trustee Temple Beth David, Commack, N.Y., 1972-75; chmn. Cmty. Action Com. of Dix Hills and Commack, 1970-72, Dix Hills Planning Bd., 1972-74; treas. Dix Hills Rep. Club, 1976-80; mem. Huntington (N.Y.) Zoning Bd. Appeals, 1980-91, chmn., 1986-89. Recipient United Jerusalem award Israel Bond Drive, 1977, City of Hope Svc. award, George Bacon award Fordham Law Sch. Mem.: Suffolk County Bar Assn., NY State Bar Assn. Home: 14 Clayton Dr Dix Hills NY 11746-5517 Office: 999 Walt Whitman Rd Melville NY 11747-3007 Office Phone: 631-673-5004.

SCHOENFELD, WALTER EDWIN, manufacturing executive; b. Seattle, Nov. 6, 1930; s. Max and Edna Lucille (Reinhardt) S.; m. Esther Behar, Nov. 27, 1955; children— Lea Anne, Jeffrey, Gary. BBA, U. Wash., 1952. Dir. Reading Railroad, 1964—68; v.p., dir. Sunshine Mining Co., Kellogg, Idaho, 1964-69, First N.W. Industries, Inc. (Seattle Super Sonics), 1968-79; chmn. bd., pres. Schoenfeld Industries, Inc. (diversified holding co.), 1968-93; vice chmn., acting pres., CEO, Vans, Inc., 1993-97, chmn., bd. dirs., 1997—2004; non-exec. chmn. Found. Bank, 2005—06, dir., 2005—, Aritzia, 2007—. Ptnr. Seattle Mariners Baseball Club, 1977-81, Seattle Sounders Soccer Club, 1974-79; bd. dirs. Hazel Bishop Cosmetics. Bd. dirs. Wash. China Rels. Coun., 1980—, Sterling Recreation Orgn., 1985-90; chmn. Access Long Distance of Washington; bd. govs. Weizmann Inst. Sci., Rehovot, Israel, 1980—; trustee Barbara Sinatra Children's Ctr., Eisenhower Hosp., Rancho Mirage, Calif., 1990—. With AUS, 1952-55, Korea. Recipient various service awards. Mem. Chief Execs. Orgn. (v.p., bd. dirs. 1987-93), Rainier Club, Broadmoor Golf Club, Tamarisk Country Club (Rancho Mirage, Calif.), Mission Hills Country Club, Alpha Kappa Psi. Office: 800 5th Ave Ste 4100 Seattle WA 98104

SCHOENHARD, WILLIAM CHARLES, JR., health system executive; b. Kansas City, Mo., Sept. 26, 1949; s. William Charles S. and Joyce Evans (Thornsberry) Bell; m. Kathleen Ann Klosterman, June 3, 1972; children: Sarah Elizabeth, Thomas William. BS in Pub. Adminstrn., U. Mo., 1971; M of Health Adminstrn. with honors, Washington U., St. Louis, 1975. V.p., dir. gen. svcs. Deaconess Hosp., St. Louis, 1975-78; assoc. exec. dir. St. Mary's Health Ctr., St. Louis, 1978-81; exec. dir. Arcadia Valley Hosp., Pilot Knob, Mo., 1981-82, St. Joseph Health Ctr., St. Charles, Mo., St. Joseph Hosp. West, Lake St. Louis, 1982—86; exec. v.p., COO SSM Health Care, St. Louis, 1986—. Adv. bd. dirs. Firstar Bank, 1998-01, Midwest Bank Ctr., 2004, Coll. Bus. Mgmt. U. Mo., Columbia, Mo., 2005-. Contbr. articles to profl. jours. Mem. Mo. Commn. on Patient Safety, 2003—04, Organ Donation and Transplantation Alliance, 2006—08; mem. adv. bd. St. Louis chpt. Lifeseekers, St. Louis, 1985—94; mem. bd. mgrs. Kirkwood-Webster (Mo.) YMCA, 1990—96, sec., 1996; mem. healthcare adv. bd. Sanford Brown Colls., 1992—94; bd. dirs. St. Andrews Mgmt. Svcs., Inc., 1994—2002, Mid Am. Transplant Svcs., 1995—, sec., 2005—09, vice chmn., 2009—; exec. com. mem. Lindenwood U., 2004—, bd. dirs., 1997—, Civic Entrepreneurs Orgn., 1997—2000, Greater St. Louis Boy Scouts Am., 1997—, Benedictine Health Sys., 2002. With USN, 1971—72, Vietnam. Fellow Am. Coll. Health Care Execs. (regent Mo.-Gateway area 1997-01, bd. govs. 2002—, chmn. 2006-07); mem. VFW, Am. Hosp. Assn. (del. regional policy bd. 1999-2005, bd. trustees, 2007—, exec. com., 2008-, ops. com. 2007—), Mo. Hosp. Assn. (bd. trustees 199-2005, chmn. 2000), Am. Heart Assn. (mem. bd. Greater St. Louis chpt. 2001-03), Cath. Health Assn. U.S. (mem. fin. com. 1999-01), Am. Legion, US Navy League, Westborough Country Club, Phi Eta Sigma, Pi Omicron Sigma, Delta Upsilon, Delta Sigma Pi. Roman Catholic. Avocations: reading, walking. Home: 420 Fairwood Ln Saint Louis MO 63122-4429 Office: SSM Health Care 477 N Lindbergh Blvd Saint Louis MO 63141-7832 Office Phone: 314-994-7810.

SCHOENHERR, JOHN (CARL), artist, illustrator; b. NYC, July 5, 1935; s. John Ferdinand and Frances (Braun) S.; m. Judith Gray; children: Jennifer L., Ian G. BFA, Pratt Inst., 1956. Painter, illustrator Owl Moon, 1987 (Caldecott medal, 1988); exhibitions include Hiram Blauvelt Art Mus., 1997. Recipient World Sic. Fiction award, World Sci. Fiction Conv., London, 1965, Silver medal, Phila. Acad. Natural Sci., 1984, purchase award, Hiram Blauvelt Art Mus., 1994. Mem.: Soc. Animal Artists (medal 1979, 1985, 2003), Am. Soc. Mammalogists (emeritus). Home and Office: 135 Upper Creek Rd Stockton NJ 08559-1209

SCHOENHUT, FREDERICK W., stock exchange executive; BS in Elec. Engring., Clarkson U. Prin. owner, pres. Copia Trading Co., Ltd., 1980—; vice chmn. NY Bd. Trade (NYBOT), 2002—03; chmn. ICE Futures, US (formerly NY Bd. Trade), 2003—; bd. dirs. IntercontinentalExchange (ICE), 2007—. Mem.: NY Cotton Exchange (NYCE), Coffee, Sugar, and Cocoa Exchange (CSCE), Commodity Floor Brokers and Traders Assn. (CFBTA). Office: ICE Futures, US One N End Ave 13th Fl New York NY 10282 Office Phone: 212-748-4040. Office Fax: 212-748-4156.*

SCHOENL, WILLIAM JAMES, history professor; b. Buffalo, Feb. 15, 1941; s. William and Erma Osborne Schoenl; m. Linda Volker, May 14, 1966; children: Karen Schoenl Carpenter, Lauren Schoenl van Loon, Mark William. BS in Math., Canisius Coll., 1963; MA in History, Columbia U., 1964, PhD in History, 1968. Prof. humanities Mich. State U., East Lansing, 1968-89, prof. history, 1989—. Mem. com. on rsch. Am. Soc. Ch. History, Chgo., 1988-93. Author: Intellectual Crisis in English Catholicism, 1982, C.G. Jung, 1998; editor: Major Issues in Jung, 1996, New Perspectives on the Vietnam War, 2002; author of poetry; contbr. articles and revs. to profl. jours. Mem., chair disbursement com. for dire needs overseas St. John Student Parish, East Lansing, Mich., 1971—; founder scholarship Meridian Non-Traditional HS, 2005-, Harry Hill Non-Traditional HS, 2009-; founder Mich. State U. Honors Coll. Dire Needs Undergraduate Grant, 2008-, Canisius Coll. Scholarship Internat. Svc., 2008-. Rsch. grantee Nat. Endowment for the Humanities, Washington, 1970, Am. Philos. Soc., Phila., 1975, global competence grantee Mich. State U., East Lansing, 1993. Mem. Am. Hist. Assn., Ctr. Jung Studies Detroit (trustee 1991-94), Kiwanis Club Okemos (chair internat. iodine deficiency disorders project 1994-98, chair Salvation Army project 1996—, chair human and spiritual values com. 1999-2002, 2004—. Avocations: fishing, walking, travel, reading mysteries, snowshoeing. Home: 2643 Roseland East Lansing MI 48823 Office: Mich State Univ Dept History East Lansing MI 48824 Office Phone: 517-355-7500.

SCHOENRICH, EDYTH HULL, internist, preventive medicine physician; b. Cleve., Sept. 9, 1919; d. Edwin John and Maud Mabel (Kelly) Hull; m. Carlos Schoenrich, Aug. 9, 1942; children: Lola, Olaf. AB, Duke U., Durham, NC, 1941; MD, U. Chgo., 1947; MPH, John Hopkins U., Balt., 1971. Diplomate Am. Bd. Internal Medicine, Am. Bd. Preventive Medicine. Intern John Hopkins Hosp., Balt., 1948-49, asst. resident medicine, 1949-50, fellow medicine, 1950-51, chief resident, pvt. wards, 1951-52; asst. chief, acting chief dept. chronic and cmty. medicine Balt. City Hosp., Balt., 1963-66; dir. svc. to chronically ill and aging Md. State Dept. Health, Balt., 1966-74; dir. divsn. pub. health adminstrn. Sch. Pub. Health, John Hopkins U., Balt., 1974-77, assoc. dean acad. affairs, 1977-86, dir. part time profl. programs and dep. dir. MPH program, 1986—, prof. dept. health policy and mgmt., 1974—, joint appointment medicine, 1978—. Contbr. articles to profl. jours. Trustee Friends Life Care Cmty., 1984—, Kennedy-Krieger Inst., Balt., 1985—, Vis. Nurses Assn., 1990-95, Md. Home and Cmty. Care Found., 1995—. Recipient Stebbins medal John Hopkins U., 1989, Disting. Med. Alumna award, 1997, Golden Apple award, 2007; named to Md. Women's Hall of Fame, 2005 Fellow ACP, Am. Coll. Preventive Medicine; mem. APHA, Assn. Tchrs. Preventive Medicine, Med. and Chirurg. Soc. Md., Balt. City Med. Soc., Phi Beta Kappa, Alpha Omega Alpha, Delta Omega. Avocations: gardening, music, theater, swimming. Home: 1402 Boyce Ave Baltimore MD 21204-6512 Office: Johns Hopkins Bloomberg Sch Sch Pub Health 615 N Wolfe St Baltimore MD 21205-2103 Office Phone: 410-955-1291. E-mail: eschoenr@jhsph.edu.

SCHOENSTADT, BARBARA LAISON, special education educator; b. Phila., Mar. 23, 1940; d. Oscar Z. and Fay (Tecker) Laison; m. Steven Ellis Schoenstadt; children: Scott, Bruce, Cori. BA in Edn., Temple U., 1962; MS in Edn., Beaver Coll., 1979. Cert. tchr., Pa. Tchr. 1st grade U.S. Army, Kaiserlautern, Germany, 1962-64; tchr. nursery sch. Temple Beth Ami, Phila., 1973-74; subs. tchr. Phila. Sch. Dist., 1974-78; tchr. 4th grade Neshaminy Sch. Dist., Langhorne, Pa., 1978-79; tchr. gifted and talented Bensalem (Pa.) Sch. Dist., 1979-82, 87—, tchr. 3rd grade, 1982-87, tchr. 2d grade, 1988—2002; ret., 2002. Coord. sci. fair Bensalem-Struble Sch., 1988—2002; adj. prof. lang. arts and reading jr. course Temple U., Phila., 2002—, student tchr. supr., 2002—; tchr. Kids on Campus Bucks County C.C., 1997—; substiute tchr. Bensalem Sch. Dist., 2008—. Sisterhood bd. dirs. Congregation Shir Ami. Mem. NEA, Pa. Edn. Assn., Pa. Assn. Gifted Edn., Bensalem Edn. Assn. Democrat. Jewish. Home: 736 Hunter Dr Langhorne PA 19053-1910 Personal E-mail: sschoenstadt@gmail.com.

SCHOEPP, DARRYLE D., pharmaceutical executive, researcher; b. June 1955; married. BS in Pharmacy, ND State U., 1978; PhD in Pharmacology and Toxicology, W.Va. U., 1982. Joined Eli Lilly and Co., 1987, v.p., global head neuroscience rsch. and early clin. investigation; sr. v.p., franchise head neuroscience Merck Rsch. Labs. (MRL), 2007—. Bd. pub. trustees ASPET, exec. editor Neuropharmacology. Recipient Pharmacia / Am. Soc. for Experimental Therapeutics (ASPET) Award for Experimental Therapeutics, 2002. Mem.: Am. Coll. Neuropsychopharmacoligy (ACNP), Pharm. Mfg. Found. (mem. Basic Pharmacology Exec. Com.). Office: Merck Rsch Labs 770 Sumneytown Pike PO Box 4 West Point PA 19486

SCHOEPS, KARL HEINZ JOACHIM, German language educator; b. Dinslaken, Germany, Dec. 8, 1935; came to U.S., 1967; s. Karl Gustav and Ella Katherina (Gruhl) S.; m. Dorothy Ann Sturdivant, Aug. 18, 1965. Staatsexamen, U. Bonn., Fed. Republic of Germany, 1962; PhD, U. Wis., 1971. Tchr. High Sch., Wipperfuth, Germany, 1964—67; from asst. prof. to prof. German U. Ill., Urbana, 1971—2000, dir. West European studies, 1985-88, prof. emeritus, 2000—. Vis. asst. prof. Mt. Holyoke Coll., South Hadley, Mass., Spring 1977. Author: Bertolt Brecht and Bernard Shaw, 1974, Bertolt Brecht, 1977, Bertolt Brecht, Life, Work, Criticism, 1989, Literatur im Dritten Reich 1933-1945, 1992, 2000, Literature and Film in the Third Reich, 2004, Holocaust and Resistance in Vilnius: Rescuers in Wehrmacht Uniforms, 2008; co-editor: DRR-Literature im Tauwetter, 3 vols., 1985, Neue Interpretationen von der Aufklärung zur Moderne, 1991. Fellow U. Wis., 1970-71, U. Ill., 1976; Fulbright grantee, 1962-63. Mem. Am. Assn. Tchrs. German (assoc. editor German Quar. 1991-94), German Studies Assn., Internat. Brecht Soc. (sec.-treas. 1980-87). Avocations: tennis, swimming, classical music, theater. Home: 905 S Orchard St Urbana IL 61801-4039 Office: U Ill Dept German Langs 707 S Mathews Ave Ste 3072 Urbana IL 61801-3643 Business E-Mail: schoeps@uiuc.edu, schorps@illinois.edu.

SCHOETTLE, ENID C.B., federal agency administrator; m. Herbert Stuart Okun, Dec. 27, 1990. BA, Radcliffe Coll.; PhD in Polit. Sci., MIT, Cambridge, Mass. Faculty polit. sci. U. Minn., Mpls., Swarthmore Coll.; staff mem. Ford Found., 1976—91, dir. internat. affairs program, 1981—91; sr. fellow Coun. on Fgn. Rels., 1991—93; nat. intelligence officer for global and multilateral issues Nat. Intelligence Coun., 1993—96; chief advocacy and external rels. unit UN Dept. Humanitarian Affairs, 1996—97; spl. advisor Nat. Intelligence Coun., Washington, 1997—. Prof. polit. sci. Univ. Minn., Swarthmore Coll. Office: Central Intelligence Agy Nat Intelligence Coun Washington DC 20505

SCHOETZ, DAVID JOHN, JR., colon and rectal surgeon, educator; b. Milw., Oct. 29, 1948; s. David John and Beverly (Rogers) S.; m. Ruthanne Brennan, Mar. 25, 1972; children: Elizabeth Anne, David John III. BA, Coll. of Holy Cross, Worchester, Mass., 1970; MD, Med. Coll. Wis., Milw., 1974. Diplomate Am. Bd. Surgery, Am. Bd. Colon and Rectal Surgery. Resident in surgery Boston U. Med. Ctr., 1974-81; resident in colon/rectal surgery Lahey Clinic Med. Ctr., Burlington, Mass., 1981-82, staff colon-rectal surgeon, 1982—, chmn. dept. colon-rectal surgery, 1987—2002; prof. surgery Med. Sch. Tufts U., Boston, 1999—, chmn. dept. med. edn., 2000—; acad. dean for Tufts Lahey Clinic, 2006—. Fellow ACS (commn. on cancer 1998-2003, gov., 2004—), Am. Bd. Colon and Rectal Surgery (sr. examiner 1996—, assoc. exec. 2005-06, exec. dir. 2006—), ABMS (bd. dirs. 2009—), Am. Soc. Colon and Rectal Surgeons (sec. 1999-2002, pres.-elect 2002-03, pres. 2003-04). Office: Lahey Clinic Med Ctr 41 Mall Rd Burlington MA 01803-4521 Office Phone: 781-744-8889.

SCHOEWE, THOMAS M., retail executive; b. 1952; BBA in Fin., Loyola U. of Chgo., 1974, MBA. Various positions including contr., CFO Beatrice Consumer Durables, Inc., 1974—86; v.p. bus. planning and analysis The Black & Decker Corp., 1986—89, v.p. fin., 1989—93, sr. v.p., CFO, 1993—99; exec. v.p., CFO Wal-Mart Stores, Inc., Bentonville, Ark., 2000—. Bd. dirs. Centex Corp., 2001—. Named a Nat. Trustee for The First Tee, 2008. Mem.: Fin. Execs. Internat. Office: Wal-Mart Stores Inc 702 SW 8th St Bentonville AR 72716-8611*

SCHOFF, DENNIS L., lawyer, insurance company executive; b. Apr. 17, 1959; m. Nina Schoff. BS in Fin., Ind. U., JD cum laude. Bar: Ind., Ohio, Pa. Atty. Taft, Stettinius & Hollister, Cin.; various positions Lincoln Nat. Corp., Phila., 1990—2000, v.p., assoc. gen. counsel, 2000—01, v.p., dep. gen. counsel, 2001—02, sr. v.p., gen. counsel, 2002—, mem. sr. mgmt. com. Mem.: ABA, Am. Corp. Counsel Assn., Exec. Bd. Gen. Counsel Roundtable, Ind. Bar Assn., Pa. Bar Assn., Allen County Bar Assn. Office: Lincoln Financial Group 150 N Radnor Chester Rd Ste A305 Wayne PA 19087-5238 Office Phone: 215-448-1400. Office Fax: 215-448-3215.

SCHOFIELD, ANTHONY WAYNE, lawyer; b. Farmington, N.Mex., Mar. 5, 1949; s. Aldred Edward and Margueriete (Knudsen) S.; m. Rebecca Ann Rosecrans, May 11, 1971; children: Josie, Matthew Paul, Peter Christian, Addie, Joshua James, M. Thomas, Jacob L., Daniel Z. BA, Brigham Young U., 1973, JD, 1976. Bar: Utah 1976, U.S. Dist. Ct. Utah 1976, U.S. Ct. Appeals (7th and 10th cirs.) 1977. Law clk. to hon. judge A. Sherman Christansen U.S. Dist. Ct. Utah, Salt Lake City, 1976-77; assoc. Ferenz, Bramhall, Williams & Gruskin, Agana, Guam, 1977-79; pvt. practice American Fork, Utah, 1979-80; assoc. Jardine, Linebaugh, Brown & Dunn, Salt Lake City, 1980-81; mem., dir. Ray, Quinney & Nebeker, Provo, Utah, 1981—93; judge 4th Jud. Dist. Ct., Provo, 1993—2007; mem. Kirton & McConkie, Orem, Utah, 2007—. Bishop Mormon Ch., American Fork, 1985-88; commr. American Fork City Planning Commn., 1980-85; trustee American Fork Hosp., 1984-93. Mem. Ctrl. Utah Bar Assn. (pres. 1987, 91). Office: Kirton & McConkie 518 West 800 North 204 Orem UT 84057 Office Phone: 801-426-2100. Personal E-mail: aschofield@kmclaw.com.

SCHOFIELD, EDMUND ACTON, JR., botanist, academic administrator, conservationist, writer; b. Worcester, Mass., Nov. 26, 1938; s. Edmund Acton and Phyllis Louise (Parslow) Schofield; m. Eileen Kathryn Carroll (div. Oct. 1972). BA in Biology, Clark U., 1962, MA in Biology, 1964; PhD in Botany, Ohio State U., 1972. Sci. editor Battelle Meml. Inst., Columbus, Ohio, 1965—67; postdoc. rsch. fellow Calif. Inst. Tech., 1972—73; ecologist Ohio Dept. Natural Resources, Columbus, 1973—76; dir. rsch. Sierra Club, San Francisco, 1976—77; staff scientist Inst. Ecology, Indpls., 1977—80; assoc. editor Horticulture Mag., Boston, 1982—85; editor Arnold Arboretum Harvard U., Boston, 1986—88; various positions Worcester, Mass., 1989—2002; dir. edn. Tower Hill Botanic Garden, Boylston, Mass., 2002—07; scholar-in-residence Am. Antiquarian Soc., Worcester, Mass., 2008—. Plant ecologist Clark U., US Antarctic Rsch. Program Hallett and McMurdo Sta., Antarctica, 1963-64, Ohio State U., US Antarctic Rsch. Program McMurdo Sta., 1967-69, Internat. Biol. Program, Barrow and Prudhoe, Alaska, 1971, Calif. Inst. Tech. Jet Propulsion Lab., Internat. Biol. Program, 1973. Editor: Earthcare: Global Protection of Natural Areas, 1978; compiler, editor: Words for Nature: A Thoreau Earthcare Reader, 1990, rev. edit., 2004; co-editor: Thoreau's World and Ours, 1993. Pres. Thoreau Country Conservation Alliance, 1992—95, Walden Forever Wild, 1993—95, Friends of Thoreau Country, 2007—; mem. Worcester Hist. Commn., Mass., 1999—2003; docent Preservation Worcester, Mass., 1999—; bd. mem. Friends of Hope Cemetery, Worcester, 2007—; tutor Vols. Worchester, 2008—. With USNR, 1956—62. Recipient Antarctic Svc. medal, U.S. Congress, 1972, Resident Rsch. associateship, NASA/NAS, 1972—73; summer fellowship, Nat. Endowment for Humanities, 1979. Mem.: Thoreau Soc. (pres. 1990—92), Hanover Theatre for Performing ARts (vol. ednl. tour guide 2008—), Worcester Hist. Mus., Worcester County Poetry Assn., Friends of Thoreau Country (pres. 2007—), English Lunch Club, Boston, Worcester History Group, Worcester County Horticultural Soc. Democrat. Congregationalist. Avocations: poetry, walking, reading, scholarly research. Mailing: 210 Park Ave #114 Worcester MA 01609 Home: The Oaks 140 Lincoln St Worcester MA 01605 Home Phone: 508-826-6866. Personal E-mail: edmundschofield@yahoo.com.

SCHOFIELD, JAMES ROY, computer programmer; b. Reedsburg, Wis., Aug. 16, 1953; s. G. C. Schofield and Margaret (Collies) Tverberg. BA, Carleton Coll., 1976. Programmer Brandon Applied Systems, San Francisco, 1977-78, Rand Info. Systems, San Francisco, 1979-83; systems programmer IBM, San Jose, Calif., 1983-91; programmer Office of Instnl. Rsch./U. Calif., Berkeley, 1991-94, Datis Corp., San Mateo, Calif., 1994-95, Compuware Corp., Los Gatos, Calif., 1995-96, Pacific Bell, San Ramon, Calif., 1996—2001, AT&T, San Ramon, Calif., 2002. Mem. Assn. for Computing Machinery, Commonwealth Club Calif., Phi Beta Kappa. Avocations: guitar, reading, swimming. Home: PO Box 25143 San Mateo CA 94402-5143 Office: AT&T 2600 Camino Ramon San Ramon CA 94583-5099

SCHOFIELD, LORNA GAIL, lawyer; b. New Haven, Ind., Jan. 22, 1956; BA, Ind. U., 1977; JD, NYU, 1981. Bar: NY 1982, US Dist. Ct. (so. and ea. dists.) NY 1982, US Ct. Appeals (11th cir.) 1983, US Ct. Appeals (2d cir.) 1985, US Tax Ct. 1991, US Dist. Ct. Fed. Claims 1992, US Ct. Appeals (10th cir.) 1993, US Ct. Appeals (6th cir.) 1995, US Supreme Ct. 1996, US Ct. Appeals (3d cir.) 1997. Assoc. Cleary, Gottlieb, Steen & Hamilton, NYC, 1981—84; asst. US atty. US Dist. Ct. (so. dist.) NY, NYC, 1984-88; assoc. Debevoise & Plimpton LLP, NYC, 1988-91, ptnr., 1991—. Contbr. articles to profl. jours. Named one of The 50 Most Influential Minority Lawyers in America, Nat. Law Jour., 2008. Mem. ABA (planning com. 1993, vice chair accts. liability subcom. 1993-94, co-chair woman advocate com. 1994, co-chair class actions and derivative suits com. 1994-97, co-chair task force on discovery 1997-2000, mem. standing com. judiciary, co-dir. divisions 2000-01, budget officer 2002-07, chair litig. sect. 2009-10), Am. Law Inst., Fed. Bar Coun., NY Coun. Def. Lawyers, Assn. of Bar of City of NY. Office: Devevoise & Plimpton LLP 919 Third Ave New York NY 10022-3904 Office Phone: 212-909-6094. Business E-Mail: lgschofield@debevoise.com.*

SCHOFIELD, REGINA BROWN, foundation administrator, former federal agency administrator; b. Natchez, Miss., Jan. 14, 1962; d. Elvia John and Velma Marie (Cameron) Brown; m. Stephen Gerard Schofield, Nov. 2, 1996. BSBA, Miss. Coll., 1983; MBA, Jackson State U., Miss., 1990. Sales rep. Philip Morris, USA, Jackson, 1983-91; spl. asst. US Dept. Edn., Washington, 1991-92, White House liaison, 1992-93; mgr. environ. issues Internat. Coun. Shopping Ctrs., Alexandria, Va.,

1993—98; mgr. govt. rels US Postal Svc., 1998—2001; dir., Office of Intergovernmental Affairs US Dept. Heath & Human Services, 2002—05, White House liaison, 2001—05; asst. atty. gen., Office of Justice Programs US Dept. Justice, Washington, 2005—07; mng. dir. pub. policy Casey Family Programs, 2008—. Bd. dirs. Nat. Wetlands Coalition, 1997—99, Va. Dept. Agrl. and Consumer Svcs., Richmond, 1995—99, Va. Fedn. Rep. Women, Richmond, 1996-98, 2001-05; bd. visitors Coll. William and Mary, Williamsburg, Va., 1997—2001, The Endowment Assn. of the Coll. of William and Mary, 2004-05; mem. Commonwealth Rep. Women's Club, Alexandria, 1995, Am. Coun. Young Polit. Leaders, 1998-2005. Roman Catholic. Avocation: reading. Office: Casey Family Programs 2001 Pennsylvania Ave NW Ste 760 Washington DC 20006

SCHOFIELD, ROBERT E. (ROBERT EDWIN SCHOFIELD), historian, educator, academic administrator; b. Milford, Nebr., June 1, 1923; s. Charles Edwin and Nora May (Fullerton) S.; m. Mary-Peale Smith, June 20, 1959; 1 son, Charles Stockton Peale. AB, Princeton U., 1944; MS, U. Minn., 1948; PhD, Harvard U., 1955. Research asst. Fercleve Corp. and Clinton Labs., Oak Ridge, 1944-46; research assoc. Knolls Atomic Power Lab., Gen. Electric Co., 1948-51; asst. prof., then assoc. prof. history U. Kans., Lawrence, 1955-60; mem. faculty Case Western Res. U., Cleve., 1960-79, prof. history of sci., 1963-72, Lynn Thorndike prof. history of sci., 1972-79; prof. history Iowa State U., Ames, 1979-93, prof. emeritus, 1993—, dir. grad. program history tech. and sci., 1979-92. Mem. Inst. Advanced Study, 1967-68, 74-75; Sigma Xi nat. lectr., 1978-80 Author: The Lunar Society of Birmingham, 1963, Scientific Autobiography of Joseph Priestley: Selected Scientific Correspondence, 1966, Mechanism and Materialism: British Natural Philosophy in an Age of Reason, 1970, (with D.G.C. Allan) Stephen Hales: Scientist and Philanthropist, 1980, The Enlightenment of Joseph Priestley: A Study of His Life and Work from 1733 to 1773, 1997, The Enlightened Joseph Priestley: A Study of His Life and Work from 1773 to 1804, 2004. Served with AUS, 1945-46. Fulbright fellow, 1953-54; Guggenheim fellow, 1959-60, 67-68 Fellow Am. Phys. Soc., Royal Soc. Arts; mem. History of Sci. Soc., Soc. History Tech., Midwest Junto History of Sci., Am. Soc. 18th Century Studies, Acad. Internat. d'Histoire des Scis. (corr.)

SCHOGGEN, PHIL H(OWARD), psychologist, educator; b. Tulsa, Aug. 28, 1923; s. Walter B. and Emma F. (Alexander) S.; m. Maxine F. Spoor, June 28, 1944; children: Leida, Christopher, Ann, Susan. AB in Psychology, Park Coll., 1946; MS, U. Kans., Lawrence, 1951, PhD in Psychology, 1954. Asst. prof. psychology U. Oreg., 1957-62, asso. prof., 1962-66; prof., chmn. dept. psychology George Peabody Coll., 1966-75; prof. York U., Toronto, Ont., Can., 1975-77; prof. human devel. and family studies N.Y. State Coll. Human Ecology, Cornell U., 1977-90, prof. emeritus, 1990—, chmn. dept., 1977-82. Author: (with R. G. Barker) Qualities of Community Life, 1973; Behavior Settings: A Revision and Extension of Roger G. Barker's Ecological Psychology, 1989. Served with USNR, 1944-46, 50-51. Mem. APA. Home: 121 Vossland Dr Nashville TN 37205-3617 Personal E-mail: schoggph@comcast.net.

SCHOLEFIELD, PETER GORDON, health facility administrator; b. Newport, Wales, June 26, 1925; emigrated to Can., 1947, naturalized, 1952; s. Tom and Margaret (Bithell) S.; m. Erna Mary Cooper, Sept. 29, 1951; children: David, John, Paul. B.Sc., U. Wales, 1944, M.Sc., 1946, D.Sc., 1960; PhD, McGill U., Montreal, Que., Can., 1949. From research fellow to prof. biochemistry McGill U., 1949-65, dir. cancer research unit, 1965-69; asst. exec. dir. Nat. Cancer Inst. Can., Toronto, 1969-80, exec. dir., 1980-91, spl. adviser to chief exec. officer, 1991-92; dir. grants and awards Alta. Heritage Found. for Med. Rsch., Edmonton, 1992-94; coord. acad. affairs Samuel Lunenfeld Rsch. Inst. Mt. Sinai Hosp., Toronto, 1994-99. Chair rsch. policy com., bd. dirs. Alzheimer Soc. of Can., 1994-2000; mem. health adv. com. Alta. Heritage Found. Med. Rsch, 1994-99; bd. dirs. Ont. Neurotrauma Found., 1999-2004, sec., 2003-04, chmn. rsch. com., 2003-04; mem. adv. bd. Inst. Neuroscis. Mental Health and Addiction, Can. Insts. Health Rsch., 2001-04, mem. standing com. on grants and awards competitions, 2005-07, mem. sub-com. on programs and peer rev., 2007-; chair Can. Tobacco Control Rsch. Initiative, 2007-09. Home: 2010 Islington Ave # 1503 Etobicoke ON Canada M9P 3S8 Personal E-mail: peter.scholefield@rogers.com.

SCHOLER, CATHERINE ROCHELLE, language educator; b. Mt. Lake, Minn., Dec. 9, 1954; d. Alfred W. and Neta H. Scholer; life ptnr. Dean S. Kliewer; 1 child, Alan Luis. BA, U. Minn., Mpls., 1981; BS, St. Cloud State U., Minn., 1991; MS, Minn. State U. Mankato, 1999. Spanish tchr. Dist. 206, Alexandria, Minn., 1991—2004; Spanish and Liberal Arts instr. Alexandria Tech. Coll., Minn., 2004—. Tchr. Fulbright Programs, Lima, Peru, 2001. Coodinator Ann. fundraiser Operation Bootstrap Africa, Alexandria, 2003—08; mem. Diversity Resource Action Alliance, Alexandria, 2004—08; choir mem. Shalom Luth. Ch., Alexandria, Minn., 2002—08; leader Women ELCA Shalom Luth., Alexandria, 2004—08. Mem.: Minn. Coun. Tchg. Lang. Culture. Dfl. Avocations: travel, skiing, golf. Home: 314 Fingal Dr Alexandria MN 56308 Office: Alexandria Tech Coll 1601 Jefferson St Alexandria MN 56308 Office Fax: 320-762-4501. Personal E-mail: catherinescholer@gmail.com. Business E-Mail: catherines@alextech.edu.

SCHOLER, SUE WYANT, state legislator; b. Topeka, Oct. 20, 1936; d. Zint Elwin and Virginia Louise (Achenbach) Wyant; m. Charles Frey Scholer, Jan. 27, 1957; children: Elizabeth Scholer Truelove, Charles W., Virginia M. Scholer McCal. Student, Kans. State U., 1954-56. Draftsman The Farm Clinic, West Lafayette, Ind., 1978—79; assessor Wabash Twp., West Lafayette, 1979-84; commr. Tippecanoe County, Lafayette, Ind., 1984-90; state rep. Dist. 26 Ind. Statehouse, Indpls., 1990—2004, ret., 2004; legis. cons. Gov.'s Office, 2007. Asst. minority whip, 1992-94, Rep. whip, 1994-2000, asst. Rep. leader, 2001—04; mem. Tippecanoe County Area Plan Commn., 1984-90; chmn. Midwestern legis. conf. CSG, 1998. Bd. dirs. Crisis Ctr., Lafayette, 1984-89, Tippecanoe Arts Fedn., 1990-99, United Way, Lafayette, 1990-93; mem. Lafayette Conv. and Visitors Bur., 1988-90. Recipient Salute to Women Govt. and Politics award, 1986, United Sr. Action award, Outstanding Legislator award, 1993, Small Bus. Champion award, 1995, Ind. Libr. Fedn. Legislator award, 1995, Disting. Legislator award Nat. Alliance for Mentally Ill, 1997, 2003, West Ctrl. Ind. Advocate award, 2003, Friend of Cmty. Action award, 1999, Disting. Pub. Svc. award Am. Legion, 2004, Family Svcs. Advocacy award Family Svcs., 2004, Sagamore of the Wabash, 2004, Order of the Griffin, Purdue U., 2004. Mem. Ind. Assn. County Commrs. (treas. 1990), Assn. Ind. Counties (legis. com. 1988-90), Greater Lafayette C. of C. (ex-officio bd. 1984-90), LWV, P.E.O., State Student Assistance Commn. Ind., Ind. Lobby Registration Commn, Purdue Women's Club (past treas.), Kappa Kappa Kappa (past pres. Epsilon chpt.), Delta Delta Delta (past pres. alumnae, house corp. treas.). Republican. Presbyterian. Avocations: golf, needlecrafts, reading. Home: 807 Essex St West Lafayette IN 47906-1534

SCHOLES, EDISON EARL, military officer; b. McCaysville, Ga., Aug. 16, 1939; s. Alvin L. and Marie (Plemmons) S.; m. Elva E. Bussey, June 4, 1961; children: Juana Kimberly Scholes, Tracy Michele Scholes Heller, Michael Lee. BS in Physics cum laude, No. Ga. Coll., 1961; MS in Ops. Rsch., Naval Postgrad. Sch., 1970; postgrad., Army War Coll., 1980, Harvard Def. Policy Seminar, 1991. Commd. 2d lt. U.S. Army, 1961, advanced through grades to maj. gen., 1991; comdr. A Detachment, 10th Spl. Forces Group U.S. ArmyEurope, 1963-66; comdr. Co. D, 2d Bn.(Abn.), 8th Cav., 1st Cav. Divsn. U.S. Army, Republic of Vietnam, 1967-68, sr. adv. I Corps. Ranger Commd. Vietnam, 1970—71, comdr. 1st Bn., 23d Inf., 2d Inf. Divsn. Republic of Korea, 1976-77, comdr. 2d Tng. Bn., Sch. Brigade, U.S. Army Inf. Sch. Ft. Benning, Ga., 1978-79, comdr. 1st Inf. Tng. Brigade, U.S. Army Infantry Tng. Ctr., 1983-85, dep. commanding gen. chief of staff 3d U.S. Army/U.S. Army Cen. Command Ft. McPherson, Ga., 1986-88, asst. divsn. comdr. 82d Airborne Divsn. Ft. Bragg, NC, 1988-89, chief of staff XVIII Airborne Corps, 1989-90, chief of staff joint task force-south, Op. Just Cause, 1989-90, dep. commanding gen. XVIII Airborne Corps, Operation Desert Shield/Desert Storm Saudi Arabia, Iraq, 1990-91, dep. commanding gen. XVIII Airborne Corps Ft. Bragg, 1991-93; dep. comdr. Allied Land Forces, S.E. Europe NATO, 1993-95; program gen. mgr. Saudi Arabia N.G. Modernization Program, Vinnell Arabia, 1996—2002; pvt. contractor numerous countries, 2002—. Decorated Dept. Def. Disting. Svc. medal, Army Disting. Svc. medal with oak leaf cluster, Silver Star, Legion of Merit with oak leaf cluster, Bronze Star with V device and 4 oak leaf clusters, Purple Heart with oak leaf cluster, 6 Air medals, Army Commendation medal with V device and oak leaf cluster, Armed Forces Expeditionary medal, Combat Infantryman badge, Expert Infantry badge; Cross of Gallantry with Silver and Bronze Stars and Palm (Republic of Vietnam); numerous other US and fgn. awards; inducted into North Ga.'s Coll., State U. Hall of Fame and S. Army Ranger Hall of Fame. Mem. 82d Airborne Divsn. Assn., Spl. Forces Assn., U.S. Army Ranger Assn., Spl. Ops. Assn. Baptist. Avocations: reading, camping, fishing. Home Phone: 615-567-6889. Personal E-mail: eescholes@comcast.net.

SCHOLES, MYRON S., financier, former law and finance educator; b. Timmins, Ont., Can., July 1, 1941; BA, McMaster U., 1959—62, MBA, 1962—64; PhD in finance, U. Chgo., 1964—69; D (hon.), U. Paris-Dauphine, 1989, McMaster U., 1990, U. Leuven, 1998. Rsch. assoc., Ctr. for Math. Studies in Bus. and Econs. U. Chgo., 1966—67, instr. in fin., grad. sch. bus., 1967—68, assoc. prof., 1973—74, prof., 1975—79, dir., Ctr. for Rsch. in Security Prices, 1975—81, Edward Eagle Brown prof. fin., 1979—82; asst. prof. in fin. MIT Mgmt. Sch., Cambridge, 1968—72, assoc. prof., 1972—73; prof. law Stanford U., Calif., 1983—96, Frank E. Buck prof. Grad. Sch. Bus., 1983—96, sr. rsch. fellow, Hoover Instn., 1988—96, Frank E. Buck prof. emeritus fin., 1996—; mng. dir., sr. advisor Salomon Bros., 1990—93; prin. Long-Term Capital Mgmt., Greenwich, Conn., 1994—98; chmn. Oak Hill Platinum Ptnrs., Rye Brook, NY, 1999—2005; mng. ptnr. Oak Hill Capital Mgmt., 1999—2005. Bd. trustees Math. Scis. Rsch. Inst.; bd. dirs. Chgo. Mercantile Exchange, 2000—, chmn. Competitive Markets Adv. Coun., 2004—; bd. dirs. Chgo. Mercantile Exchange Holdings, 2001—, Intelligent Markets, Am Century, FEP/Constellation, UNext Inc., Salomon Swapco Inc. Contbr. articles to profl. jours. Recipient Nobel Prize for econ. scis., 1997. Mem.: Am. Fin. Assn. (v.p. 1989, pres. 1990), Econometrics Soc. Office: Arbor Investors 2775 Sand Hill Rd Ste 220 Menlo Park CA 94025-7019 Address: Oak Hill Platinum Ptnrs Reckson Exec Park 1100 King St Bldg 4 Rye Brook NY 10573 E-mail: mscholes@pacbell.net.*

SCHOLLANDER, WENDELL LESLIE, JR., lawyer; b. Ocala, Fla., May 17, 1943; 1 child, Wendell Leslie III. BS, U. Pa., 1966, MBA, 1968; postgrad., Stetson U., 1969-70; JD, Duke U., 1972. Bar: NC 1977, Tenn. 1972, Fla. 1987. With Container Corp. Am., Fernandina, Fla., 1968-69; assoc. Miller, Martin, Chattanooga, 1972-75; asst. counsel R.J. Reynolds Industries, Inc., 1975-78, assoc. counsel, 1978-79, sr. assoc. counsel, 1979-82, sr. counsel, 1982-85; gen. counsel RJR Archer, Inc., Winston-Salem, NC, 1979-85; of counsel Finger, Parker & Avram, Winston-Salem, 1985-87; ptnr. Schollander, Winston-Salem, 1987—. Co-author: Forgotten Elegance, 2001, Bankruptcy for Small Business, 2008. Mem. NC Bar Assn., Forsyth County Bar Assn., Mensa, SAR, Phi Delta Phi, Kappa Sigma. Presbyterian. Office: 2000 W 1st St Ste 308 Winston Salem NC 27104-4225 Office Phone: 336-727-0900.

SCHOLLANDER, WENDELL WES, III, lawyer; b. East Ridge, Tenn., Oct. 15, 1974; BA, U. N.C., Chapel Hill, 1997; JD, Wake Forest Law Sch., Winston-Salem, NC, 2001. Missionary Presbyn. Ch., Guatemala, 1998; pvt. practice Winston-Salem, NC, 2001—; adj. prof. Wake Forest U. Sch. Law, 2009—. Co-author: Forgotten Elegance, 2001, Small Business Owner's Guide to Bankruptcy, 2002, Bankruptcy for Small Business, 2008. Scoutmaster Boy Scouts of Am., Winston-Salem, 2002—04; active Forsyth Soil and Water Commn., 2004—08, vice chmn., 2006—08. Recipient Point of Light award, Pres. George Bush, 1992, Chevron Conservation award, Chevron Award Program, 1992, Take Pride in Am. award, Dept. of Interior, 1991, 1992. Mem.: NC Bar Assn. (bankruptcy sect. 2001—, sect. coun. 2006—, young lawyers sect.), SAR (awards chair 2002—). Office: Schollander 2000 W 1st St Ste 308 Winston Salem NC 27104

SCHOLTES, LINDA MARIE, elementary school educator; b. Watertown, Wis., Apr. 19, 1948; d. Ernest Victor and Delores Marie Kubly; m. Robert Richard Scholtes, Nov. 20, 1976. Degree in libr. sci., U. Whitewater, Wis., 1970, BS in Elem. Edn., 1970, MS in Profl. Edn. Devel., 1980. Tchr. Rossman Elem. Sch., Hartford, Wis., 1970—79, Dover Elem., Fla., 1979—80, media specialist, 1980—, Plant City Adult and Cmty., Fla., 1985—. Coord. SERVE, Tampa, Fla., 2008—; sch. amb. Hillsborough Edn. Found., Tampa, 2008—. Grantee, Hillsborough Edn. Found., 2003, 2005—08. Master: AMVETS; mem.: HASLMS, HC-CIRA, HCEMC, PTA, Moose Lodge. Conservative. Methodist. Avocations: reading, fishing, sports. Office: Dover Elem Sch 3035 Nelson Ave Dover FL 33527 Business E-Mail: linda.scholtes@sdhc.k12.fl.us.

SCHOLTZ, ANDREW, music educator; b. Greenwich, Conn., Jan. 21, 1956; s. Andrew and Claudia Scholtz; m. Adrienne Nesnow; children: Paul, Clara. MusB, Boston U., 1978; MusM, Manhattan Sch. Music, NYC, 1980; PhD, Yale U., New Haven, 1997. Asst. prof. Binghamton U. SUNY, 2000—06, assoc. prof., 2006—. Author: (book) Concordia Discors: Eros and Dialogue in Classical Athenian Literature; contbr. articles to profl. jours. Home: 15 Johnson Ave Binghamton NY 13905 Office: Classical & Near Eastern Studies PO Box 6000 SUNY Binghamton Binghamton NY 13902 Office Fax: 607-777-6406. Business E-Mail: ascholtz@binghamton.edu.

SCHOLTZ, ROBERT ARNO, electrical engineering educator; b. Lebanon, Ohio, Jan. 26, 1936; s. William Paul and Erna Johanna (Weigel) Scholtz; m. Laura Elizabeth McKeon, June 16, 1962; children: Michael William, Paul Andrew. BSEE, U. Cin., 1958; MSEE, U. So. Calif., 1960; PhD, Stanford U., 1964. Co-op student Sheffield Corp., Dayton, Ohio, 1953-58; MS and PHD fellow Hughes Aircraft Co., Culver City, Calif., 1958-63, sr. staff engr., 1963-78; prof. U. So. Calif., LA, 1963—. Vis. prof. U. Hawaii, 1969, 78; cons. LinCom Corp., L.A., 1975-81, Axiomatix Inc., L.A., 1980-86, JPL, Pasadena, 1985, Tech. Group, 1987-89, TRW, 1989, Pulson Comm., 1992-93, Colley-Godward, Palo Alto, 1994-97, Time Domain Corp., 2000-01. Co-author: Spread Spectrum Comm., 3 vols., 1984, Spread Spectrum Communications Handbook, 1994, Basic Concepts in Information Theory and Coding, 1994; contbr. articles to profl. jours. Pres. South Bay Cmty. Concert Orgn., Redondo Beach, Calif., 1975—79. Fellow: IEEE (bd. govs. info. theory group 1981—86, bd. govs. communication soc. 1981—83, chmn. fin. com. NTC 1977, program chmn. ISIT 1981, Leonard G. Abraham award 1983, Donald G. Fink award 1984, Sr. Paper award Signal Processing Soc. 1992, Fred Ellersick Paper award Com. Soc. 1997, Mil. Coms. Conf. award 2001, S.A. Shelkunoff prize Antennas and Propagation Soc. 2003, Eric E. Sumner award 2006); mem.: Nat. Acad. Engring. Office: U So Calif Comm Scis Inst Dept Elec Engring Los Angeles CA 90089-2565 E-mail: scholtz@usc.edu.

SCHOLZ, PETER M., surgeon, director; MD, U. Basel, Switzerland, 1970. Diplomate Am. Bd. Surgery, 1983, Am. Bd. Thoracic Surgery, 1985. Intern in Surgery Duke U. Med. Ctr., Durham, NC, 1974—75, resident gen. and thoracic surgery, 1975—83; physician divsn. thoracic surgery Robert Wood Johnson U. Med. Group, New Brunswick, NJ, 1983—, chief divsn. cardiovasc. surgery, 2005—. Office: Clin Acad Bldg Ste 4100 125 Paterson St New Brunswick NJ 08901-1977 Office Phone: 732-235-7642.

SCHOLZ, THOMAS, plastic surgeon, researcher; s. Manfred Georg and Rose-Lore Scholz. MD, Johannes Gutenberg U., Mainz, Germany, 2003; PhD in Transplantation and Hepatobiliary Surgery, U. Mainz, 2003. Diplomate Landesärztekammer Reihnland-Pfalz, 2003. Resident physician, dept. visceral and transplantation surgery U. Hosp. Zurich, 2004, resident physician, dept. thoracic surgery, 2004—05, resident physician, dept. trauma surgery, 2005—06, resident physician, dept. intensive care medicine & trauma surgery, 2006; rsch. fellow Aesthetic and Plastic Surgery Inst., Orange, Calif., 2006—07, rsch. dir., 2007—. EMT German Arbeiter Samariter Bund, Wiesbaden, Hessen, Germany, 1995—96; intensive care med. male-nurse Interdisciplary ICU, St. Joseph's Hosp., Wiesbaden, 1999—2003; rsch. mentor, med. students U. Calif., Irvine, Orange, 2007—; jour. reviewer Clin. Physiology and Functional Imaging, Malmoe, Sweden, 2008—, Jour. Med. Case Reports, London, 2008—; sci. reviewer South African Med. Rsch. Coun., Cape Town, South Africa, 2008—. Contbr. articles to numerous med. jours. Recipient 2nd prize Resident Paper Presentation, ACS, 2002; Rsch. grant, Swiss Nat. Found., 2006, 2007. Mem.: Am. Soc. Peripheral Nerves. Avocations: skiing, running, fitness, tennis, travel.

SCHOLZE, JO S. See REYNOLDS-HUFNER, JO

SCHOMMER, JOHN JOSEPH, mathematics professor; b. New Orleans, Oct. 7, 1958; s. John Joseph and Jacqueline Cantelli Schommer; m. Anne Marie Hanigan, July 25, 1992; 1 child, Mary Catherine. PhD, Ohio U., Athens, 1992. Prof. U. Tenn., Martin, 1994—. Treas. Weakley County Habitat for Humanity, Martin, 2006—08. Mem.: Am. Math. Soc. Roman Catholic. Office: Univ Tenn Martin Dept Math and Statistics Martin TN 38238

SCHON, ISABEL, library science specialist, educator; b. Mexico City, Jan. 19; d. Oswaldo and Anita Schon; m. Richard R. Chalquest, Oct. 7, 1977; 1 child, Vera. Student, U. Nat. Autonoma de Mex.; BS cum laude, Minn. State U., Mankato, 1971; MA in Elem. Edn., Mich. State U., 1972; PhD in Edn., U. Colo., 1974. Founding dir. ednl. media ctr. Am. Sch. Found., Mexico City, 1958-72; ednl. evaluator sch. bus. adminstrn. Nat. U. Mex., 1972; evaluator bilingual ednl. materials U. Colo., 1973; asst. prof. dept. ednl. tech./libr. sci. Ariz. State U., Tempe, 1974-79, assoc. prof., 1979-83, prof. reading edn./libr. sci., 1983-89; Barahona Ctr. Study of Books in Spanish for Children & Adolescents Calif. State U., San Marcos, 1989—2008, founding faculty prof. edn., 1989—2008; dir. Isabel Schon Internat. Ctr. Spanish Books for Youth San Diego Pub. Libr., 2009—. Adminstrv. asst. materials dissemination ctr. Kettering Found., Dayton, Ohio, 1966; evaluator Southwestern Coop. Ednl. Lab., Albuquerque, 1967, Nat. Indigenous Inst., Chiapas, Mexico, 1972; vis. prof. Am. Schs., Guayaquil and Quito, Ecuador, 1971, U. Ams., Mexico, 1972; editl. cons. Macmillan Pub. Co., 1985, 87, Holt, Rinehart & Winston Inc., 1994, Harcourt Brace & Co., 1997—, Monterey Bay Aquarium, 1997—; mem. adv. bd. Parents' Choice, 1989—, Santillana Pub. Co., 1991—94; mem. lang. adv. bd. Scholastic Inc., 1992—94. Author: numerous recommended books in Spanish for children and young adults, 1991—2000, The Best of the Latino Heritage: A Guide to the Best Juvenile Books about Latino People and Culture, 1996—2002; reviewer NEH, 1981—, Jour. Nat. Assn. Bilingual Edn., 1982—85, Am. Edn. Rsch. Jour., 1983—85, Libr. Sci. Ann., 1986—, Sch. Libr. Media Quar., 1993—95, contbg. Spanish editor Sch. Libr. Jour., 1984—87, mem. editl. bd. The New Advocate, 1995—, The Reading Tchr., 1998—, columnist Booklist (ALA), 1989—; contbr. articles to profl. jours., chapters to books. Judge ALA's Nat. Libr. Writing Competition, 1977, Arroz con Leche Children's Lit. Contest, 1994—; chair internat. bd. books for young people com. Asahi Reading Promotion Award, 1997—. Recipient Herbert W. Putnam Honor award, ALA, 1979, Grolier Found. award, 1986, Denali Press award, 1992, Nat. Book award, Women's Nat. Book Assn., 1987, Dorothy C. McKenzie award, Children's Lit. Coun. So. Calif., 2005, Dist. Alumni Achievement award, Minn. State U., 2006; named a Role Model in Edn., US Mex. Found., 1992. Avocation: tennis. Office: Isabel Schon Intl Ctr, Spnsh Bks for Yth San Diego Public Library 9005 Aero Dr San Diego CA 92123 Office Phone: 619-238-6638. Office Fax: 619-236-5878.

SCHONAUER, LISA LYNN, music educator; d. David Charles Logan and Linda Lou Lurtz; m. James Christopher Schonauer, Sept. 30, 1989; children: Logan Marrie, Kaci Taylor, Dmitri Burnette. BA in Music & Counseling, Fla. Christian Coll., Kissimmee, 1994; MusM, U. Ctrl. Fla., Orlando, 2006. Pvt. practice, Mount Dora, Fla., 1991—2008; adj. asst. prof. Fla. Christian Coll., 2000—. Musician piano performance. Youth ministry & counseling Roundlake Christian Ch., Mount Dora, 1994—2004, mem. music ministry, 1994—2008. Mem.: Music Teacher's Assn. Conservative. Achievements include research in music education. Avocation: travel. Office: Fla Christian Coll 1011 Bill Beck Blvd Kissimmee FL 34744 Office Phone: 352-636-4496. Personal E-mail: llpianogrl@embarqmail.com.

SCHONBERG, ALAN ROBERT, personnel director; b. NYC, Oct. 23, 1928; s. Julius and Evelyn (Guzik) S.; m. Carole May Kreisman, Dec. 27, 1975; children: William, Evelyn, David, Jeffrey. Nat. sales mgr. Majestic Specialties, Inc., Cleve., 1953-63; pres. Internat. Personnel, Inc., Cleve., 1963-65; chmn. Mgmt. Recruiters Internat., Inc., Cleve., 1965-98, 1998—2000, chmn. emeritus, 2001—. Pres., bd. dirs. Jewish Vocat. Service, Cleve., 1983—; trustees Mt. Sinai Hosp. (now Mt. Sinai Found.), Cleve., bd. dirs. Cleve. Jewish News; gen. chmn. Welfare Fund Campaign; trustee Am. Jewish Commn., Mt. Sinai Med. Ctr., Hebrew Immigrant Aid Soc. Named one of Cleve.'s 86 Most Interesting People, Cleve. Mag., 1986, Man of Yr. local chpt. Orgn. through Rehab. and Tng., 1996, Entrepreneur of Yr. Inc. Mag., Merrill Lynch Ernst & Young,

1995; recipient Human Rels. award Cleve. chpt. Am. Jewish Com., 1998. Mem. Internat. Franchise Assn., Internat. Confederation Pvt. Employment Agys. Assns., Am. Mgmt. Assn., Assn. Human Resource Cons. (chmn. 1980—), Org. for Rehab. and Training (ORT), Assn. Am.-Israel C. of C. (pres.), Ohio Israel C. of C. (co-chmn.), Jewish Family Svcs. Assn. (v.p., pres. 1998-2002). Avocation: travel.

SCHONBERG, JEFF BRETT, literature and language professor, researcher; s. Richard and Delores Schonberg; m. Jane Elizabeth Nufer; children: Elizabeth Ann Asser, Amanda Jane. PhD, Tex. A&M, Coll. Sta., 1992. Prof. English Hardin-Simmons U., Abilene, Tex., 1980—96, Angelo State U., San Angelo, Tex., 1996—. Author: (book) Alternative Rhetorics. Mem.: Rhetoric Soc. America, Am. Dialect Soc., Linguistic Soc. America, CCCC, Nat. Coun. Tchr. Edn. Conservative. Roman Catholic. Achievements include research in endangered Chinese dialect linguistic description. Office: Angelo State Univ ASU Box 10894 San Angelo TX 76909 Business E-Mail: jeffrey.schonberg@angelo.edu.

SCHONBRUN, MICHAEL K., senior housing developer and operator; b. NYC, Jan. 26, 1948; s. Arnold Laurance and Madeline (Courland) Schonbrun; m. Michelle I. Fredson, June 6, 1971 (div. Dec. 1998); 1 child, Ethan F.; m. Susan E. Juroe, Feb. 17, 2001; children: Adam J., Theodore C. BA, Yale U., 1969; JD, U. Pa., 1973. Bar: Ohio 1973, Colo. 1975. Asst. to gov. Ohio Gov.'s Office, Columbus, 1973—74, Colo. Gov.'s Office, Denver, 1974—75; asst. dir. Colo. Dept. Health, Denver, 1976—78; pres., CEO Nat. Jewish Hosp., Denver, 1979—91; sr. v.p. Blue Cross/Blue Shield of Colo., Denver, 1991—93; exec. v.p. Vitas Healthcare Corp. Inc., Miami, Fla., 1994—95; pres. Schonbrun & assocs., Boulder, Colo., 1995—97; founder, pres., CEO Balfour Sr. Care, Boulder, 1997—. Chmn. Young Pres.'s Orgn. Healthcare Focus Forum, Dallas, 1999—2001; bd. dirs. Colo. Assn. Housing and Svcs., Denver, United Bank of Denver, 1985—91; mem. leadership coun. Assisted Living Fedn. Am., Washington, 1999—. Contbr. articles to profl. jours. Chmn. bd. dirs. Rocky Mountain Alzheimers Assn., 2002, Denver Met. Air Quality Coun., 1985—89, Internat. Med. Corp., LA, 1996—2000; mem. Colo. 2002 Winter Olympic Games Com., 1988—90. Mem.: Nat. Jewish Health (Bd.mem. 2006—). Democrat. Jewish. Avocation: travel, running, tennis, reading fiction, movies. Home: 10200 Niwot Rd Longmont CO 80504 Office: Balfour Sr Care 1331 Hecla Dr Louisville CO 80027-2325 Office Phone: 303-926-3009.

SCHÖNEMANN, PETER HANS, psychologist, educator; b. Pethau, Germany, July 15, 1929; arrived in U.S., 1960, naturalized, 2003; s. Max Paul Franz and Hertha Anna (Kahle) S.; m. Roberta Dianne Federbush, Jan. 29, 1962; children: Raoul Dieter, Nicole Deborah. Vordiplom in Psychologie, U. Munich, 1956; Hauptdiplom in Psychologie, U. Goettingen, 1959; PhD, U. Ill., 1964. Thurstone postdoctoral fellow U. N.C., 1965-66; asst. prof., then assoc. prof. Ohio State U., 1966-69; postdoctoral fellow Ednl. Testing Service, Princeton, NJ, 1967-68; vis. prof. Technische Hochschule, Aachen, Fed. Republic Germany, 1981; mem. faculty Purdue U., 1969—, prof. psychology, 1971-2001, emeritus, 2001—. Vis. prof. Univs. Munich, Bielefeld and Braunschweig, 1984-85, Nat. Taiwan U., 1992, 96, 97. Author papers in field. Recipient Found. for the Advancement of Outstanding Scholarship award, Taiwan, 1996. Office: Dept Psychol Scis Purdue U Lafayette IN 47907 Personal E-mail: pschonemann@gmail.com.

SCHONFELD, DAN, educator; b. Westchester, Pa., June 11, 1964; PhD, Johns Hopkins U., Balt., 1990. Prof. U. Ill., Chgo., 1990. Office: Univ Ill Chgo 851 S Morgan st Chicago IL 60607-7053 Business E-Mail: dans@uic.edu.

SCHONFELD, ESTHER MIRIAM, lawyer; b. NYC, Mar. 2, 1960; m. Alan Seth Schonfeld (div. 1994); children: Jeremy Adam, Alexandra; m. Benjamin Farkas, Oct. 10, 1999; 1 child, Judah Moritz Farkas; stepchildren: Esti Farkas, David Farkas, Paul Farkas. BBA, CUNY, 1981; JD summa cum laude, Touro Law Sch., 1999. Bar: NY 2000, U.S. Supreme Ct. 2003, U.S. Ct. Appeals Armed Forces 2003, U.S. Ct. Appeals (D.C. Cir.) 2003, U.S. Ct. Fed. Claims 2003. Assoc. Koopersmith & Brown, LLP, Lake Success, NY, 1999—2002; founding ptnr. Mosery & Schonfeld, PLLC, Cedarhurst, NY, 2002—07, Schonfeld & Goldring LLP, Cedarhurst, 2007—. Editor: Touro Law Rev., 1998—99. Scholarship, award, Jewish Lawyers Assn. of Nassau County, 1997. Mem.: ABA (mem. family law div.), Queens County Bar Assn. (mem. family law com.), Nassau County Bar Assn. (mem. matrimonial law com.), NY State Bar Assn. Avocations: travel, piano, cello, literature, art. Office: Schonfeld & Goldring LLP 112 Spruce St Ste A Cedarhurst NY 11516

SCHONFELD, GUSTAV, medical educator, researcher, administrator; b. Mukacevo, Ukraine, May 8, 1934; arrived in US, 1946, naturalized, 1951; s. Alexander Schonfeld and Helena Gottesmann; m. Miriam Steinberg, May 28, 1961; children: Joshua Lawrence, Julia Elizabeth, Jeremy David. BA, Washington U., St. Louis, 1956, MD, 1960. Diplomate Am. Bd. Internal Medicine. Intern. Bellevue Med. Ctr. NYU, 1960—61, resident in internal medicine, 1961—63; chief resident in internal medicine Jewish Hosp., St. Louis, 1963—64; from NIH trainee in endocrinology & metabolism to Kountz prof. medicine Washington U., St. Louis, 1964—96, Busch prof., chair medicine, 1996—99, Samuel E. Schechter prof. medicine, 2002—; rsch. assoc. Cochran VA Hosp., St. Louis, 1965—66, clin. investigator, 1968—70, cons. in internal medicine, 1972—; rsch. flight med. officer USAF Sch. Aerospace Medicine, Brooks AFB, Tex., 1966—68; from asst. physician to physician Barnes Hosp., St. Louis, 1972—96; physician-in-chief Barnes Jewish Hosp., St. Louis, 1996—99; clin. instr. medicine Harvard U. Med. Sch., Boston, 1970—72; assoc. prof. metabolism and human nutrition, asst. dir. Clin. Rsch. Ctr. MIT, Cambridge, 1970—72. Mem. rsch. com. Mo. Heart Assn., 1978-80; expert witness working group on atherosclerosis Nat. Heart, Lung and Blood Inst., 1979, Nat. Diabetes Adv. Bd., 1979; mem. endocrinologic and metabolic drugs adv. com. USPHS, FDA, 1982-86; mem. nutrition study sect. NIH, 1984-88, spl. reviewer metabolism study sect.; mem. adult treatment guidelines panel Nat. Cholesterol Edn. Program, 1986; mem. Consensus Devel. Conf. on Triglyceride, High Density Lipoprotein and Coronary Heart Disease, 1992; cons. Am. Egg Bd., Am. Dairy Bd., Inst. Shortening and Edible Oils, Ciba-Geigy, Sandoz, Fournier, Parke-Davis, Bristol-Meyers Squibb, Monsanto/Searle; adj. prof. medicine Columbia U. Coll. Physicians & Surgeons, 2006. Past editor: Atherosclerosis, past mem. editl. bd.: Jour. Clin. Endocrinology and Metabolism, Jour. Clin. Investigation, Jour. Lipid Rsch., past assoc. editor: Circulation. Recipient Berg Prize in Microbiology, 1957, 58, Faculty/Alumni award Washington U., 1995; named Physician honoree Am. Heart Assn. Mo. Affiliate, 1995; grantee MERIT status NIH, Vascular Biology Spl. Merit award, Am. Heart Assn. Fellow ACP, AAAS; mem. Assn. Am. Physicians, Am. Soc. for Clin. Investigation, Am. Physiol. Soc., Am. Soc. Biol. Chemists, Am. Inst. Nutrition, Am. Diabetes Assn., Am. Heart Assn. (program com. coun. on atherosclerosis 1977-80, 86-88, nutrition com. 1980-84, pathology rsch. com. 1980-83, budget com. 1991, awards com. 1992, exec. com. 2001—, Spl. Vascular Biology award 2005, G.L. Duff lecture award, 2006), Endocrine Soc., Alpha Omega Alpha. Democrat. Jewish. Office: Washington U Sch Medicine Box 8046 660 S Euclid Ave Saint Louis MO 63110-1010 Office Phone: 314-362-8060. Business E-Mail: gschonfe@wustl.edu.

SCHONFELD, IRVIN SAM, psychologist, educator; b. NYC; s. George and Ruth (Berson) S.; children: Emily Aviva, Daniel Reuben; m. July 12, 1981. BS, Bklyn. Coll., 1969; MA, New Sch. for Social Rsch., 1974; PhD, CUNY, 1980; MPH, Columbia U., 1987. Cert. psychologist, N.Y. Math. tchr. N.Y.C. Bd. Edn., 1969-75; rsch. assoc. Columbia U., NYC, 1981-85; prof. CUNY, 1985—. Contbr. articles on stress and psychopathology rsch., child, adolescent rsch. to profl. jours. Office: City Coll NY Dept Psychology New York NY 10031 Office Phone: 212-650-7164.

SCHONFELD, WILLIAM ROST, political science professor; b. NYC, Aug. 28, 1942; s. William A. and Louise R. (Rost) S.; m. Elena Beortegui, Jan. 23, 1964; children: Natalie Beortegui, Elizabeth Lynn Beortegui. Student, Cornell U., Ithaca, NY, 1960-61; BA cum laude with honors, NYU U. Heights Coll., NYC, 1964; MA, Princeton U., NJ, 1968, PhD, 1970. Research asst. Princeton U., 1966-69, research assoc., 1969-70, vis. lectr., 1970; asst. prof. polit. sci. U. Calif.-Irvine, 1970-75, assoc. prof., 1975-81, prof., 1981—, dean Sch. Social Scis., 1982—2002; sr. lectr. Fond. Nat. de Sci. Politique, Paris, 1973-74; researcher Centre de Sociologie des Organisations, Paris, 1976-78; dir. Ctr. for Study of Democracy, 2004—08. Author: Youth and Authority in France, 1971, Obedience and Revolt, 1976, Ethnographie du PS et du RPR, 1985 Recipient Disting. Teaching award U. Calif.-Irvine, 1984, Disting. Faculty Lectureship award for tchg., 1998, Daniel G. Aldrich Disting. Univ. Svc. award, 2000-01, Under Grad. Edn award, U. Calif., 2009; Fulbright fellow Bordeaux, France, 1964-65; Danforth grad. fellow, 1964-69; Fulbright sr. lectr. Paris, 1973-74; NSF-CNRS Exchange of Scientists fellow Paris, 1976-78; Ford Found. grantee France, Spain, 1978-79; finalist Prof. Yr. Council for Advancement and Support of Edn., 1984; Lauds & Laurels Extraordinarious award, U. Calif.-Irvine Alumni Assn., 2002., Mem. Am. Polit. Sci. Assn., Assoc. Francaise de Sci. Pol., Phi Beta Kappa. Office: U Calif Sch Social Scis Irvine CA 92697-0001 Office Phone: 949-824-8801. Personal E-mail: wrschonf@yahoo.com. Business E-Mail: wrschonf@uci.edu.

SCHONHORN, HAROLD, chemist, researcher; b. NYC, Apr. 2, 1928; s. Benjamin and Dorothy (Gitlin) S.; m. Esther Matesky, Jan. 17, 1954; children: Deborah, Jeremy. BS, Bklyn. Coll., 1950; PhD, N.Y. Polytech. U., 1959. Mem. tech. staff Bell Labs., Murray Hill, NJ, 1961-84; v.p. R & D Polyken Tech. div. Kendall Co., Lexington, Mass., 1984-93; pres. Schonhorn Consultants, 1993—. Contbr. over 100 articles to profl. jours. Pres. B'nai B'rith Lodge, Summit, N.J., 1970. With U.S. Army, 1953-55, Korea. Mem. Am. Chem. Soc. Achievements include 15 patents. Office Phone: 617-738-4742. Office Fax: 617-738-4742. Personal E-mail: HaroldSchonhorn@cs.com.

SCHOOF, ROSALIND, toxicologist; PhD, U. Cin., Ohio. Diplomate Am. Bd. Toxicology, 1986. Prin. Integral Consulting Inc., Mercer Island, Wash., 2002—. Bd. mem., pres. Wash. Women In Need, Bellevue, 2004—. Recipient Life Time Achievement award, Annual Internat. Conference Soils, Sediments and Water, 2007. Mem.: Soc. Toxicology. Business E-Mail: rschoof@integral-corp.com.

SCHOOLEY, ROBERT T., medical educator; b. Washington, Nov. 10, 1949; s. Robert Enoch and Lelia Francis (Barnhill) S.; m. Constance Benson; children: Kimberly Dana, Elizabeth Kendall. BS, Washington and Lee U., 1970; MD, Johns Hopkins U., 1974. Diplomate Am. Bd. Internal Medicine. Intern Johns Hopkins Hosp., Balt., 1974—75, resident, 1975—76; clin. assoc. lab. clin. investigation Nat. Inst. Allergy & Infectious Disease, NIH, Bethesda, Md., 1976—77, chief clin. assoc. lab. clin. investigation, 1977—78, med. officer lab. clin. investigation, 1978—79; from instr. to assoc. prof. medicine Harvard Med. Sch., Boston, 1979—90; prof. medicine U. Colo., Denver, 1990—2005, U. Calif., San Diego, 2005—, head Divsn. Infectious Diseases, 2005—. Dir. Colo. Ctr. for AIDS Rsch., 2003—05; head divsn. infectious diseases U. Calif., San Diego, 2005—, vice chair dept. medicine, 2007—. Mem. editl. bd.: Antimicrobial Agts. and Chemotherapy, 1987—2000, Biotherapy, 1987—95, Jour. Acquired Immune Deficiency Syndromes, 1988—, Clin. and Diagnostic Lab. Immunology, 1992, assoc. editor: Clin. Infectious Diseases, 2002—; contbr. articles to profl. jours. Clin. and rsch. fellow Infectious Disease Unit, Mass. Gen. Hosp., Boston, 1979-81; rsch. fellow Medicine Harvard Med. Sch., 1979-81; recipient Bonfils-Stanton award for sci. and medicine. Fellow Infectious Disease Soc. Am.; mem. AAAS, Am. Assn. Immunologists, Am. Soc. Clin. Investigation, Assn. Am. Physicians, Omicron Delta Kappa. Office: U Calif San Diego Mail Stop 0711 9500 Gilman Ave La Jolla CA 92093 Home Phone: 858-350-9610; Office Phone: 858-822-0216. Business E-Mail: rschooley@ucsd.edu.

SCHOOLFIELD, BRENDA THOMPSON, history professor; b. Wichita, Kans., July 5, 1966; d. Richard Dale and Barbara Elaine Thompson; m. William Robnett Schoolfield, Dec. 15, 1989; children: Ellis Richard, Katherine Eunice. PhD, U. SC, Columbia, 2006. Prof., divsn. social sci. Bob Jones U., Greenville, SC, 1988—. Pres. Upstate Rep. Women, Greenville, 2003—06. Mem.: Orgn. Am. Historians, Soc. Historians Early Am. Republic, Omohundro IEAHC, SC Hist. Assn. Office: Bob Jones Univ 1700 Wade Hampton Blvd Greenville SC 29614 Business E-Mail: bschoolf@bju.edu.

SCHOOMAKER, ERIC B., career military officer; b. Detroit, Sept. 15, 1948; married; 3 children. BS Commd. a 2nd Lt. as a Disting. Mil. Grad., U. Mich., Ann Arbor; MD, U. Mich. Med. Sch., 1975, PhD in Human Genetics, 1979. Cert. Am. Bd. Internal Medicine, 1979, Am. Bd. Hematology, 1982. Advanced through grades to lt. gen., 2007; intern, internal medicine Duke Univ. Med. Ctr., Durham, NC, 1976—78, fellow, hematology, 1979; rsch. hematologist Walter Reed Army Inst. Rsch., 1979—82; asst. chief, program dir., dept. medicine Walter Reed Army Med. Ctr., Washington, 1982—88, acting comdr., 2007—; med. cons. to hdqs. 7th Med. Command, Heidelberg, Germany, 1988—90; dep. comdr., clin. services Landstuhl Army Regional Med. Ctr., Germany, 1990—92; chief, program dir., dept. medicine, dir. primary care Madigan Army Med. Ctr., Tacoma, 1992—95; dir. med. edn. for the Office of the Surgeon Gen. Hdqs. US Army Med. Command (USAMEDCOM), Washington, DC and Fort Sam, Houston, Tex., 1995—97, dir. clin. ops., 1997; comdr. US Army Med. Dept. Activity (USA MEDDAC)-(Evans Army Cmty. Hosp.), Fort Carson, Colo., 1997—99; attended US Army War Coll., Carlisle Barracks, Pa., 1999—2000; command surgeon US Army Forces Command (FORSCOM), 2000—01; comdr. 30th Med. Brigade, Heidelberg, Germany, 2001—02; chief Army Med. Corps, 2002; commdg. gen. Southeast Regional Med. Command/Dwight David Eisenhower Army Med. Ctr., 2002—05, US Army Med. Rsch. and Materiel Command and Fort Detrick, Va., 2005—07; comdr. North Atlantic Regional Med. Command, 2007, Walter Reed Army Med. Ctr., 2007, US Army Med. Command, 2007—; surgeon gen. US Army, 2007—. Decorated DSM, Legion of Merit with four oak leaf clusters, Meritorious Svc. Medal with two oak leaf clusters, Joint Svc. Commendation Medal, Army Commendation Medal, Army Achiever Medal, Humanitarian Svc. Medal, Order of Mil. Med. Merit, "A" Proficiency Designator. Office: US Army Surgeon Gen Leesburg Pike Skyline 6 Falls Church VA 22041*

SCHOOMAKER, PETER JAN, retired military officer; b. Detroit, Feb. 12, 1946; m. Cynthia A Petroski, Jan. 14, 1980; 3 children. BS in Edn. Adminstrn., U. Wyo., 1969; MA in Mgmt., Ctrl. Mich. U., 1977; grad., USMC Amphibious War Sch., 1976, US Army Command/Gen. Staff Coll., 1982, Nat. War Coll., 1989; LLD (hon.), Hampden-Sydney Coll. Commd. 2d lt. US Army, 1969, advanced through grades to gen., 1997, reconnaissance platoon leader, 2nd Bn., 4th Infantry Ft. Campbell, Ky., 1970—71; comdr., Co. C, 2nd Bn., 4th Infantry US Army Europe, 1970—72, asst. S-3 (Ops.) then S-4 (Logistics), 1st Squadron, 2nd Armored Vavalry, 1972—73; comdr. troop C, 1st Squadron, 2nd Armored Cavalry Regiment US Army Europe & 7th Army, Germany, 1973-74; asst. insp. gen., 2nd Infantry Divsn. US Army, Republic of Korea, 1974, S-3, 1st Bn., 73rd armor, 2nd Infantry Divsn., 1974—75; assignment officer Officer Pers. Mgmt. Directorate US Army Mil. Pers. Ctr., Alexandria, Va., 1976-78; comdr. 1st Spl. Forces Operational Detachment US Army, Ft. Bragg, NC, 1978-81; exec. officer 2d Squadron, 2d Armored Cavalry Regiment U.S. Army Europe and 7th Army, Germany, 1982-83; spl. ops. officer J-3 Joint Spl. Ops. Command Ft. Bragg, N.C., 1984-85; served in various position within 1st Spl. Forces Operational Detachment D, 1985—88; comdr. Combat Applications Group, Ft. Bragg, NC, 1989-92; asst. divsn. comdr. 1st Cavalry Divsn., Ft. Hood, Tex., 1992-93; dep. dir. ops., readiness & mobilization Office of Dep. Chief of Staff Ops. & Plans, US Army, Washington, 1993-94; comdg. gen. Joint Spl. Ops. Command US Army Spl. Ops. Command, Ft. Bragg, NC, 1994-96, comdg. gen., 1996-97; comdg. in chief US Spl. Ops. Command, MacDill AFB, Fla., 1997—2000; chief of staff US Army, Washington, 2003—07. Bd. dir. DynCorp. Internat., 2007—, CAE USA; mem. adv. bd. Camber Corp., EWA-GSI. Decorated Disting. Svc. medal, Def. Superior Svc. medal with 3 oak leaf clusters, Legion of Merit with 2 oak leaf clusters, Bronze Star medal with oak leaf cluster, Def. Meritorious Svc. medal with oak leaf cluster, Meritorious Svc. medal with 2 oak leaf clusters, Joint Svc. Commendation medal, Joint Svc. Achievement medal

SCHOON, KENNETH JAMES, science educator, writer; b. Gary, Ind., Aug. 23, 1946; s. Lester K. and Vivian B. Schoon; m. Margaret Shipley Schoon, Nov. 22, 1969; children: Jacob Kenneth, Robert Kendall. AB in Geology, Ind. U., Bloomington, 1968, MS in Secondary Edn., 1972; PhD in Curriculum and Instrn., Loyola U., Chgo., 1989. Sci. tchr. Sch. City East Chgo., Ind., 1968—90; prof. sci. edn. Ind. U. NW, Gary, 1990—, assoc. dean edn., 1999—. Bd. mem. Ind. Dunes Environ. Learning Ctr., Porter, Ind., 2006—. Author: Calumet Beginnings: Ancient Shorelines and Settlements at the South End of Lake Michigan, 2003 (Ind. U. Outstanding Rsch. award, 2004), Portraits of a Ridge Family: The Jacob Schoons. Mem., former dir. Munster (Ind.) Hist. Soc., 1982—; mem., pres. Munster Bd. Pks. and Recreation, 1994—; chair Munster Centennial Com., 2005—07. Mem.: Munster Lions. Presbyterian. Avocations: Calumet area geology and history, genealogy, travel. Office: Ind U NW 3400 Broadway Gary IN 46408 Office Fax: 219-981-4208.

SCHOONMAKER, FRANCES G., education educator; d. Floyd G. and Aleene E. Schoonmaker; 1 child, Liesl C. Bolin. AA, Grays Harbor Coll., Aberdeen, WA, 1961; BA, U. Wash., Seattle, 1964; MA, George Peabody Coll., Vanderbilt U., Nashville, TN, 1971; EdD, Tchrs. Coll., Columbia U., NYC, 1983. Tchr. Balt. County Pub. Sch., 1973—80; prof. Tchrs. Coll., Columbia U., NYC, 1983—. Tchr. Highline Pub. Sch., Burien, Wash., 1964—65, Portland Pub. Sch., Oreg., 1965—66, Peabody Demonstration Sch., Nashville, 1966—67, David Douglas Pub. Sch., Portland, 1967—69. Author: (book) Living Faithfully: The Transformation of Washington School, Growing Up Teaching: From Personal Knowledge to Professional Practice, (textbook) Growing Up Caring, editor numerous poetry books. Elder Collegiate Ch. NY, NYC, 1992—2004; trustee Collegiate Sch., NYC, 1995—98, Plz. Head Start, NYC, 1987—92. Mem.: Coun. Profs. Supervision, Profs. Curriculum, Am. Ednl. Rsch. Assn. (sec., divsn. b 1994—96). Office: Tchrs Coll Columbia Univ 525 W 120th St New York NY 10027 Business E-Mail: schoonmaker@tc.columbia.edu.

SCHOONMAKER, SAMUEL VAIL, III, lawyer; b. Newburgh, NY, Sept. 1, 1935; s. Samuel V. Jr. and Catherine (Wilson) S.; m. Carolyn Peters, Sept. 18, 1965; children: Samuel V. IV, Frederick P. BA magna cum laude, Yale U., 1958, JD, 1961. Bar: Conn. 1961, U.S. Dist. Ct. Conn. 1961, U.S. Dist. Ct. (so. and ea. dist.) N.Y. 1964, U.S. Ct. Appeals (2d cir.) 1964, U.S. Supreme Ct. 1965. Assoc. Cummings & Lockwood, Stamford, Conn., 1961-70, co-mng. ptnr., 1987-90, mng. ptnr., 1990-94, chmn. exec. com., 1987-96; founder, pres. Schoonmaker George & Colin, P.C., Greenwich, Conn., 1996—. State trial referee Conn. Superior Ct., 1989; pres. Schoonmaker Family Assn., New Paltz, N.Y., 1975-77. Sr. topical editor Conn. Bar Jour., 1977-81; mem. editl. bd. Fairshare and Am. Jour. Family Law, 1992—; contbr. articles to profl. jours. Chmn. Conn. Child Support Commn., 1984-86; mem. Conn. Family Support Com., 1986-90; mem. Darien (Conn.) Rep. Town Com., 1974-76, rep. town meeting, 1990-98; pres. Youth Tennis Found. New Eng., Needham, Mass., 1975-77; pres. New Eng. Lawn Tennis Assn., 1977-79 (Man of Yr. award 1979); pres., trustee Huegenot Hist. Soc., 1999—. Named to New England Tennis Hall of Fame, United States Tennis Assn. Fellow Am. Acad. Matrimonial Lawyers Conn. (bd. mgrs., Disting. Svc. award 1988), Internat. Acad. Matrimonial Lawyers, Am. Bar Found.; mem. ABA (chmn. family law sect. 1982-83), Conn. Bar Assn. (chmn. family law sect. 1971-74), Conn. Bus. and Industry Assn. (bd. dirs. 1993-98), S.W. Conn. Bus. and Industry Assn. (bd. dirs. 1990-97), Pub. Defenders Assn. (chmn.), Wee Burn Country Club (Darien, Conn., asst. sec.), Yale Club (N.Y.C.), Phi Beta Kappa. Avocations: tennis, platform tennis. Home: 231 Old Kings Hwy S Darien CT 06820-5931 Office: Schoonmaker George & Colin PC PO Box 5059 81 Holly Hill Ln Greenwich CT 06831-5059 Office Phone: 203-862-5000. Business E-Mail: sus3@sqcpemlzw.com.

SCHOONMAKER POWELL, THELMA, film editor; b. Algeria, Jan. 3, 1940; m. Michael Powell, May 19, 1984 (dec. Feb. 19, 1990). Editor: (films) Who's That Knocking at My Door, 1968, Woodstock, 1970 (nominee Best Film Editing Acad. award, 1970), Raging Bull, 1980 (Best Film Editing Acad. award, 1980, Best Film Editing award Am. Cinema Editors, 1980, Best Film Editing award Brit. Acad., 1981), The King of Comedy, 1983 (nominee Brit. Acad. award for best film editing, 1983), After Hours, 1985, The Color of Money, 1986, The Last Temptation of Christ, 1988, New York Stories (Life Lessons segment), 1989, GoodFellas, 1990 (nominee Best Film Editing Acad. award, 1990, Best Dramatic Film Editing Brit. Acad. award, 1990, nominee Best Film Editing, Am. Cinema Editors, 1990), Cape Fear, 1992 (nominee Brit. Acad. award for best film editing, 1993), The Age of Innocence, 1993, A Personal Journey with Martin Scorsese Through American Movies, 1995, Casino, 1995 (nominee Best Film Editing Am. Cinema Editors, 1995), Kundun, 1997, Bringing Out the Dead, 1999, Il Mio Viaggio in Italia, 2000, Gangs of New York, 2002 (Best Dramatic Film Editing Am.

Cinema Editors award, 2003, nominee Best Film Editing Acad. award, 2003), The Aviator, 2004 (Best Film Editing Acad. award, 2005, Best Dramatic Film Editing Am. Cinema Editor award, 2005), The Departed, 2006 (Best Film Editing Acad. award, 2007, Best Dramatic Film Editing Am. Cinema Editors award, 2007). Named one of 50 Smartest People in Hollywood, Entertainment Weekly, 2007.

SCHOONOVER, BRENDA B., ambassador; BA, Morgan State U., Balt.; postgrad., Howard U. Vol. Peace Corps, Philippines, 1961, adminstr. Office Talent Search Washington, assoc. dir. Tanzania, dir. sch. partnership program Washington; affirmative action officer Govt. of Arlington County, Va.; with Fgn. Svc. U.S. Dept. State, Manila, Colombo, Sri Lanka, Tunis, Tunisia, with Bur. Near East and South Asia Washington, 1978-88, chief pers. Bur. European and Can. Affairs, 1988-91, mem. Sr. Seminar, 1996-97; adminstrv. officer, dept. dir. Office Joint Adminstrv. Svcs. Am. Embassy, Brussels, 1992-96; Capstone fellow Nat. Def. U., Washington, 1997; U.S. amb. to Togo Am. Embassy, Lome, 1998-2000; amb.-in-residence Chapel Hill, NC, 2000—01; chargé d'affaires, ad interim min. counselor Am. Embassy, Brussels, 2001—04. Vice pres. Am. Diplomacy On-line Mag. Mem. adv. bd. Carolina for Kibera; ex-officio adv. bd. Global Edn., U. N.C., Chapel Hill. Recipient Order of the Mono award, The Togolese Govt., 2000, Presdl. Meritorious award, U.S., 2003, Sec. of State Career Achievement award, 2004. Mem.: LWV (bd. dirs. Internat. Affairs Council, Triangle, NC). Office: 108 Ironwoods Dr Chapel Hill NC 27516 E-mail: RCSchoon2@aol.com.

SCHOONOVER, JACK RONALD, senior judge; b. Winona, Minn., July 23, 1934; s. Richard M. and Elizabeth A. S.; m. Ann Marie Kroez, June 18, 1965; children: Jack Ronald, Wayne J. Student, Winona State Coll., 1956-58; LLB, U. Fla., 1962. Bar: Fla. 1962. Atty. Wotitzky, Wotitzky & Schoonover, 1962-69, Schoonover, Olmsted & Schwarz, 1969-75; spl. asst. state's atty. State of Fla., 1969-72; city atty. City of Punta Gorda, Fla., city judge, 1973-74; judge 20th Jud. Cir. Ct., Ft. Myers, Fla., 1975-81, 2d Dist. Ct. Appeal, 1981-97, chief judge, 1990-92, ret., 1997. Atty. Charlotte County Sch. Bd., 1969-75, Charlotte County Zoning Bd., Charlotte County Devel. Authority; mem. unauthorized practice law com. 12th Jud. Cir., mem. grievance com. 20th Jud. Cir.; adj. prof. Edison C.C.; tchr. Charlotte County Adult Edn. Assn. Served with USAF, 1952-56. Home and Office: 14380 Olde Hickory Blvd Fort Myers FL 33912-0816

SCHOONOVER, PHILIP J., former retail executive; b. 1960; m. Cindi Schoonover; 2 children. BS in Mktg. & Fin., U. N.H.; postgrad., Boston Coll. Former sales and mktg. exec. Sony Corp. Am.; former exec. v.p., gen. merchandise mgr. TOPS Appliances; sr. v.p. digital tech. Best Buy Co., Inc., 1995—2001, exec. v.p. digital solutions, 2001—02, exec. v.p. bus. devel., 2002—04, exec. v.p. customer segments, 2004; exec. v.p., chief merchandising officer Circuit City Stores Inc., Richmond, Va., 2004—05, pres., 2005—06, pres., CEO, 2006—07, chmn., pres., CEO, 2007—08. Bd. dirs. Circuit City Stores Inc., 2005—08. Active Anti-Defamation League, United Jewish Appeal, Chabad Ho., United Way, Wayzata (Minn.) Yacht Club Youth Sailing Program. Avocation: sailing.

SCHOONOVER, STANLEY R., music educator, consultant; b. Bethesda, Md., July 27, 1955; s. William and Martha Schoonover. MusM, West Chester U., 1982. Cert. music edn. K-12 Pa. Dir. of bands Mt. Vernon HS, Alexandria, Va., 1982—92, Robinson Secondary Sch., Fairfax, Va., 1993—98; music specialist Fairfax County Pub. Schs., Fairfax, 1998—. Music cons., Va., 1990—; founding condr. Fairfax Wind Symphony, 1999. Dir.: (internat. band clinic performance) Mid-West Band and Orchestra Clinic, 1993 (5 NBA Citations of Excellence). Named to East Stroudsburg Music Hall of Fame, 2004. Mem.: Va. Band and Orch. Dirs. Assn. (pres. 1993—95), Phi Delta Kappa. Office: Alan E Leis Instructional Ctr 7423 Camp Alger Ave Falls Church VA 22042 Personal E-mail: stanschoonover@verizon.net. E-mail: stan.schoonover@fcps.edu.

SCHOPF, WILLIAM GRANT, lawyer; b. Muskegon, Mich., Sept. 7, 1948; s. William G. and June Marie (Bodine) Schopf; children: Brody A., Alexandra J., Anais M.E. AB, Princeton U., 1970; JD, Cornell U., 1973. Bar: Ill. 1973, US Dist. Ct. (no. dist. Ill.) 1973, US Supreme Ct. 1977, Tex. 1989, US Dist. Ct. (so. dist. Tex.) 1995, US Dist Ct. (ea. dist. Tex.) 1998, US Dist. Ct. (so. dist. Ill.) 2001, US Dist. Ct. (we. dist. Mich.) 2005, US Ct. Appeals (3rd, 5th, 7th, 8th, 10th and 11th cirs.). Assoc. Keck, Mahin & Cate, Chgo., 1973-79; ptnr. Reuben & Proctor, Chgo., 1979-86, Isham, Lincoln & Beale, Chgo., 1986-87, Schopf & Weiss, Chgo., 1987—. Adj. prof. John Marshall Law Sch., Chgo., 1977-78; owner Music Box Theatre & Schopf Gallery on Lake, Chgo. Author: Money in the Bank, 1988; contbr. articles, chpts. to legal publs. Named an Top 10 Trial Lawyers in Am., Nat. Law Jour., 2004. Mem. ABA, Chgo. Bar Assn., Union Internationale des Avocats, Union League Club (Chgo.), Princeton Club (NYC). Office: Schopf & Weiss 1 S Wacker Dr 28th Fl Chicago IL 60606-4617 Office Phone: 312-701-9308. E-mail: schopf@sw.com.

SCHOPPMEYER, MARTIN WILLIAM, education educator; b. Weehawken, NJ, Sept. 15, 1929; s. William G. and Madeleine M. (Haas) S.; m. Marilyn M. Myers, Aug. 9, 1958; children: Susan Ann, Martin William. BS, Fordham U., 1950; EdM, U. Fla., 1955, EdD, 1962. Tchr. Fla. pub. sch., 1955-59; instr., then asst. prof. U. Fla., 1960-63; assoc. prof., then prof. edn. Fla. Atlantic U., Boca Raton, Fla., 1963-68, dir. continuing edn., 1965-67; mem. faculty U. Ark., Fayetteville, Ark., 1968—, prof. edn., 1971-93, Univ. prof., 1993—99, Univ. prof. emeritus, 1999—, program coord. for ednl. adminstrn., 1983-90. Mem. Nat. Adv. Coun. Edn. Professions Devel., 1973-76; exec. sec. Ark. Sch. Study Coun., 1976—; evaluator instructional tng. program Nat. Tng. Fund, 1978; bd. dirs. Women's Ednl. and Devel. Inst., 1977-80, Nat. Sch. Devel. Coun., sec., 1989-90, v.p. 1990, pres., 1990-92; mem. oversight com. South Conway (Ark.) County Sch. Dist.; mem. state commn. to study effect of Amendment 59 to Ark. Constn.; cons. Lake View V. Huckabee, 1994-2002. Author books, monographs, articles in field. Mem. president's coun. Subiaco Acad., 1984-90; chmn. Subiaco Sch. Bd., 1990-93, mem., 1993-97. With U.S. Army, 1951-53, Korea. Recipient numerous fed. grants. Mem. VFW, KC (past grand knight), Ark. Edn. Assn. (past chpt. pres.), Ark. Assn. Ednl. Adminstrs., Am. Legion, Rotary, Kappa Delta Pi, Phi Delta Kappa, Delta Tau Kappa. Roman Catholic. Home: 2950 Sheryl Ave Fayetteville AR 72703-3542 Personal E-mail: mschoppmeyer@yahoo.com. *The only really sound investment for a family, a community, or a society is that money spent for the education of its youth.*

SCHOPPMEYER, MARTIN WILLIAM, JR., school system administrator; b. Ft. Lauderdale, Fla., Nov. 1, 1966; s. Martin William and Marilyn Myers Schoppmeyer; m. Carin Anne Morales. MEd in Ednl. Tech., U. Ark., Fayetteville, 1996, EdD in Ednl. Leadership and Instrnl. Design, 1999. Dir. corp. rels. Coll. Engring., U. Ark., 1999—2003; founder, supt. schs. Haas Hall Acad., Fayetteville, 2003—; founder, CEO Digi-Tell ID Sys., Fayetteville, 2000—, chmn., 2001. Adj. faculty U. Ark., 1995—2003. Contbr. articles to profl. jours., chapters to books. Chmn. The Acad., Inc., Fayetteville, 2003—. Recipient Charles and Nadine Baum Tchg. Excellence award, U. Ark., 1999; grantee Roy B. Allen Doctoral scholarship, 1998; Rsch. grant, Ark. Dept. Edn., 2003—04, 2004—05, Fed., 2004—06, Walton Family Found., 2004—06. Mem.: Am. Ednl. Rsch. Assn. (life), Rotary Internat. (life), Am. Ednl. Rsch. Assn. (life), Phi Delta Kappa (life; bd. mem. 2001—02), Rotary Club Internat. (life), Elk's Lodge (life), Phi Delta Kappa (life; bd. mem. 2000—03), Phi Kappa Phi (life; sec. 2000—03). Achievements include development and patent of iCard technology to link our clients to their digital profile; created the first only open-enrollment charter high school in the state of Arkansas, ranked by US News & World Report as one of the best in the nation. Home: 1156 East Glenn Ln Fayetteville AR 72703 Office: Haas Hall Acad 3155 North College Ave Ste 108 Fayetteville AR 72703 Business E-Mail: martinschoppmeyer@haashall.org.

SCHOR, LAURENCE, lawyer; b. Bklyn., May 3, 1942; s. Julius and Ruth (Zackowitz) S.; m. Susan Leslie Gurevitz, Dec. 26, 1965; children: Meredith Nan, Joseph Sanford, Wendy Claire, Samuel Julius. BBA, So. Meth. U., 1963; JD, U. Tex., 1966; LLM, George Washington U., 1972. Bar: Tex. 1966, D.C. 1971, Md. 1993.; U.S. Ct. Appeals (D.C., 4th, 5th, 11th cirs.). Atty. NASA, Huntsville, Ala., 1966-68; asst. gen. counsel NASA support U.S. Army C.E., Washington, 1968-70; assoc. Sellers, Conner & Cuneo, Washington, 1970-73; from assoc. to ptnr. Max E. Greenberg, Trayman, Cantor, Reiss & Blasky, Washington, 1974-80; ptnr. Schnader, Harrison, Segal & Lewis, Washington, 1981-91, ptnr.-in-charge, 1986-88; mem. Miller & Chevalier, Washington, 1991-93; ptnr. Smith, Somerville & Case, LLC, Washington, 1993-96, McManus, Schor, Asmar & Darden, LLP, Washington, 1997—. Lectr. George Washington U., others. Author: The Right to Stop Work, 1991; author: (manual) Delays, Suspensions and Acceleration, Workplace Safety and Health in the 1990's, 1992; author: Claims Against Bonding Companys, Construction Contractors' Handbook of Business and Law, 1992, How to File a Federal Contract Claim, 1998, 2007, Overview of Regulation in 43 Jurisdictions World Wick, 2009; co-author: Suing a Government: Special Considerations; Construction Disputes: Representing the Contractor, 3d edit., 2001; author, editor 50 State Lien and Bond Laws, 1993—2009, Vol. 3 Form Book rewrite, 2000, editor update, 2001—09; contbr. chapters to books, articles to profl. jours.; commentator MSNBC-TV, 2000. Founder, pres. Manor Lake Civic Assn., Montgomery County, 1969-71; precinct chmn. Montgomery County Dems., 1972-76; mem. D.C. City Coun. Procurement Reform Task Force, 1995-96. Named to Chambers Ams. Leading Lawyers for Bus., 2003—05, Super Lawyers, Met. Washington DC. Mem. ABA (chmn. region III pub. contract law sect., 1982-88, chmn. constrn. com. 1986-90, sect. budget and fin. 1990-95), D.C. Bar Assn. (chmn. divsn. 10 govt. contracts and litigation, 1981-85), Fed. Bar Assn., Am. Coll. Constrn. Lawyers (founder, bd. govs., treas. 1996-2000, pres. elect 2000, pres. 2001-02), B'nai B'rith Youth Orgn (adult adv. bd. 2001-02), Phi Alpha Delta (pres. T.C. Clark chpt. 1965-66), Nat. Panel Arbitrators Am., Arbitration Assn. Jewish. Avocations: reading, travel. Home: 7021 Mountain Gate Dr Bethesda MD 20817-3913 Office: McManus Schor Asmar & Darden LLP 1155 15th St NW 9th Fl Washington DC 20005 Office Phone: 202-296-9260. Business E-Mail: lschor@msadlaw.com.

SCHORER, SUKI, ballet teacher; b. Boston; d. Mark and Ruth (Page) S.; 1 child, Nicole. Studied with, George Balanchine. Dancer San Francisco Ballet, 1956-59, N.Y.C. Ballet, 1959-72; prin. dancer N.Y.C. Ballet Co., 1968-72, artistic assoc. lecture demonstration program, 1972-95; mem. faculty Sch. Am. Ballet, 1972—, Brown Found. sr. faculty chair, 1998—. Internat. guest tchr. and lectr. specializing in Balanchine tng. and technique; artist dir., tchr. on Balanchine Essays (videos). Author: Suki Schorer on Balanchine Technique, 1999 (de la Torre Bueno prize 2000), Put Your Best Foot Forward, 2005; created roles in Balanchine's Harlequinade, Don Quixote, Midsummer Night's Dream, Jewels, La Source, Raymonda Variations; repertory included prin. roles in Apollo, Serenade, Concerto Barocco, Symphony in C, La Sonnambula, Stars and Stripes, Tarantella, Valse Fantaisie, The Nutcracker, Brahams Schoenberg, La Valse, Western Symphony, Ivesiana, Divertimento # 15, Ballet Imperial, others. Recipient Disting. Tchr. in Arts award Nat. Found. Advancement in Arts, 1997, award Dance mag., 1998. Office: Sch of Am Ballet 70 Lincoln Center Plz New York NY 10023-6548 Office Phone: 212-769-6600. Personal E-mail: sukischorer@gmail.com.

SCHORLING, WILLIAM HARRISON, lawyer; b. Ann Arbor, Mich., Jan. 7, 1949; s. Otis William Schorling and Ruthann (Bales) Schorling Moorehead; m. Lynne Ann Newcomb, June 1, 1974; children: Katherine Pearce, Ann Oury, John Roberts. BA cum laude, Denison U., 1971; JD cum laude, U. Mich., 1975. Bar: Pa. 1975, U.S. Ct. Appeals (3d cir.) 1977, N.J. 1998, Del. 2001, U.S. Dist. Ct. (so. and ea. dists.) N.Y. 2005. Ptnr. Eckert, Seamans, Cherin & Mellott, Pitts., 1984-89, Klett Rooney Lieber & Schorling, PC, Phila., 1989—2006, Buchanan Ingersoll & Rooney, P.C., Phila., 2006—. Lectr. Pa. Bar Inst., Harrisburg, 1983—, Comml. Law League, N.Y.C., 1984—, mem. exec. coun. bankruptcy sect., 2003—, Profl. Edn. Systems, Inc., Eau Claire, Wis., 1986—, Southwest Legal Found., Dallas, 1994—; founders' coun. Comml. Fin. Assn. Edn. Found., 1991—; bd. dirs. Consumer Bankruptcy Assistance Project; adj. prof. Temple U. Beasley Sch. Law, 1999-2004. Contbr. articles to profl. jours. Trustee Pa. Acad. Fine Arts. Fellow Am. Coll. Bankruptcy, Am. Bar Found.; mem. ABA (bus. law section coun. 2000-04, chmn. bus. bankruptcy com. 1996-99, lectr. 1988—, mem. standing com. on fed. jud. improvement 2007-), Am. Banker Inst. (lectr. 1994—), Phila. Bar Assn. (lectr. 1996—), E. Dist. Bankruptcy Conf., Allegheny County Bar Assn. (chmn. bankruptcy and comml. law sect. 1991), The Com. of Seventy (chmn. 2003-04), Longue Vue Club, Duquesne Club, Presbyterian. Home: 933 S 2nd St Philadelphia PA 19147 Office: Buchanan Ingersoll & Rooney PC 50 S 16th St Ste 3200 Philadelphia PA 19102 Office Phone: 215-665-5326. Business E-Mail: william.schorling@bipc.com.

SCHORNACK, JOHN JAMES, accountant; b. Chgo., Nov. 22, 1930; s. John Joseph and Helen Patricia (Patrickus) S.; m. Barbara Anne Lelli, June 5, 1965; children: Mark Boyd, Anne Marguerite Schornack Trueman, Erin Keeley Schornack Dickes, Tracy Bevan Schornack Power. BS, Loyola U., 1951; MBA, Northwestern U., 1956; grad., Advanced Mgmt. Program, Harvard Bus. Sch., 1969. With Ernst & Young (formerly Arthur Young & Co.), 1955-91, partner, 1964-91; firm dir. personnel Ernst & Young LLP (formerly Arthur Young & Co.), NYC, 1966-71, asst. mng. ptnr. N.Y.C. office, 1971-72, mng. ptnr., 1972-74, mng. ptnr. Chgo. office, 1976-85, mng. ptnr. Midwest region, vice chmn., 1985-91; mem. mgmt. com. Arthur Young & Co. Mgmt. com. Arthur Young & Co.; vice chmn., mng. ptnr. Midwest region Ernst & Young, 1989-91; bd. dirs., chmn. Ernst & Young Found., 1981-91; chmn., bd. dirs. North Shore Bancorp, Inc., 1992-2008, Wintrust Fin. Corp., 1996-2008. Pres. Chgo. Youth Ctrs., 1979-95; bd. govs. Chgo. Symphony, 1979-85, trustee, 1985-2003, life trustee; vol. United Way, 1975-92, dir., 1989-92; vis. adv. com. sch. accountancy DePaul U., 1980-83; mem. Loyola U. Citizens Bd., 1977-94, chmn., 1993-94; mem. adv. com. Northwestern U. Grad. Sch. Mgmt., 1967-91; coun. U. Chgo. Grad. Sch. Bus., 1982-91; bd. dirs. Met. Planning Coun., 1992-95; trustee Kohl Children's Mus., 1994-2005, life trustee, 2005—; trustee Lyric Opera, 1984-92, Cath. Charities Chgo., 2004—, Cath. Theol. Union, 1992-97, Graham Found., 1992-98; trustee Barat Coll., 1983-98, life trustee, 1999-2001, vice chmn., 1985-90, chmn., 1990-97; trustee St. Francis Hosp., 1986-97, vice chmn., 1991-94; trustee Night Ministry, 1998-004 Recipient Order of the Sacred Treas., Emperor of Japan, 1999. Mem. AICPA, Am. Acctg. Assn., Ill. Soc. CPAs, Midwest-Japan Assn. (chmn. 1983-99), Japan Am. Soc., Chgo. Club, Glen View Club, The Little Club. Home: 314 Regent Wood Rd Northfield IL 60093-2762 Office: Ernst & Young LLP Great Lakes Reg Office 233 S Wacker Dr Chicago IL 60606-6306 Home Phone: 847-441-5069; Office Phone: 847-441-7383. Personal E-mail: northdel@aol.com.

SCHORR, ALAN EDWARD, librarian, publishing executive; b. NYC, Jan. 7, 1945; s. Herbert and Regina S.; m. Debra Genner, June 11, 1967; 1 son, Zebediah. BA, CUNY, 1966; MA, Syracuse U., 1967; postgrad., U. Iowa, 1967-71; MLS, U. Tex., 1973. Tchr., rsch. asst. dept. history U. Iowa, 1967-70; govt. publs. and map libr., asst. prof. Elmer E. Rasmuson Libr., U. Alaska, 1973-78; assoc. prof., dir. libr. U. Alaska, Juneau, 1978-84; prof., dean univ. libr. Calif. State U., Fullerton, 1984-86; pres. The Denali Press, Juneau, 1986—. Freelance indexer and bibliographer; vis. lectr. Birmingham (Eng.) Poly., 1981; mem. Alaska Ednl. Del. to China, 1975. Author: Alaska Place Names, 1974, 4th edit., 1991, Directory of Special Libraries in Alaska, 1975, Government Reference Books, 1974-75, 1976, 1976-77, 1978, Government Documents in the Library Literature 1909-1974, 1976, ALA RSBRC Manual, 1979, Federal Documents Librarianship 1879-1987, 1988, Hispanic Resource Directory, 1988, 3d edit., 1996, Refugee and Immigrant Resource Directory, 1990, 92, 94; editor: The Sourdough, 1974-75, Directory of Services for Refugees and Immigrants, 1987, 3d edit., 1993, Guide to Smithsonian serial publs., 1987; book reviewer, columnist: S.E. Alaska Empire, 1979-82, L.A. Times; contbr. articles to profl. jours. Mem. Auke Bay (Alaska) Vol. Fire Dept., 1978—81, Juneau Borough Libr. Adv. Com., 1981—82, Juneau Borough Cemetery Adv. Com., 1980—81, Am. Book Awards Com., 1980; chmn. program evaluation com., former chmn. facilities com., former chmn. policy com. to v.p. Juneau Bd. of Edn., 2000—; mem. Juneau Bd. Edn., 1991—94, 1995—97, 1997—2000, 2000—03, 2003—04; mem. citizens adv. coun. Juneau Empire Newspaper, 2003—. Mem. ALA (mem. reference and subscription books rev. com. 1975-86, mem. reference and adult svcs. divsn. publs. com. 1975-77, Nat. Assn. Hispanic Publs., Mudge citation commn. 1977-79, 84-86, Dartmouth Coll. Medal Commn., Governing Coun. 1977-84, mem. Dewey medal com. 1984-85, Denali Press award), Alaska Libr. Assn. (mem. exec. bd. 1974-75, mem. nominating com. 1977-79), Pacific N.W. Libr. Assn. (rep. publs. com. 1973-75), Assn. Coll. and Rsch. Librs. (mem. publ. com. 1976-80), Spl. Librs. Assn. (assoc. editor geography and map divsn. bull. 1975-76), Internat. Assn. Ind. Pubs (bd. dirs. 1990-92), True North Fed. Credit Union (bd. dirs. 1997-, treas. 2001-2002, vice chmn., 2002-04, chmn., 2004-), PEN Ctr. USA West, Explorers Club N.Y., Wash. Athletic Club (Seattle). Office: Denali Press PO Box 1535 Juneau AK 99802

SCHORR, ALVIN LOUIS, social worker, educator; b. NYC, Apr. 13, 1921; s. Louis and Tillie (Godiner) S.; m. Ann Girson, Aug. 21, 1948; children— Jessica Lee, Kenneth L., Wendy Lauren. BSS, CCNY, 1941; MSW, Washington U., St. Louis, 1943; DHL, Adelphi U., 1975. With Family Service No. Va., 1956-58; family life specialist Office Commr. Social Security, 1958-62; vis. prof. London (Eng.) Sch. Econs., 1962-63; acting chief long range research Social Security Adminstrn., 1963-64; dir. research and planning Office Econ. Opportunity, 1965-66; dep. asst. sec. Dept. Health, Edn. and Welfare, 1967-69; prof. social policy, dir. income maintenance project Brandeis U., 1969-70; dean Grad. Sch. Social Work, N.Y.U., 1970-73; gen. dir. Community Service Soc. N.Y., 1973-77; vis. prof. Cath. U. Am., 1977-79; Leonard W. Mayo prof. Case Western Res. U., 1979-92, Leonard W. Mayo prof. emeritus, 1992—. Fulbright sr. rsch. scholar, 1962-63; vist. prof. Hebrew U., Jerusalem, 1986, Fla. Internat. U., 1995, N.Mex. State U., 1996; vis. scholar London Sch. Econs., 1991-92. Author: Filial Responsibility in the Modern American Family, 1961, Slums and Social Insecurity, 1963, Social Services and Social Security in France, 1964, Poor Kids, 1966, Explorations in Social Policy, 1968, Children and Decent People, 1974, Jubilee for Our Times, 1977, Thy Father and Thy Mother, 1980, Common Decency: Domestic Policies After Reagan, 1986, Economic Development in Cleveland: A Dissenting View, 1991; The British Personal Social Services: An Outside View, 1992, Passion and Policy: A Social Worker's Career, 1997, Welfare Reform: Failure and Remedies, 2001. Recipient Disting. Service in Social Welfare award Washington U. Alumni Assn., 1969, Michael Schwerner award, 1972, Lifetime Achievement award Ohio Assn. Social Workers, 1998. Fellow Nat. Acad. Social Ins.; mem. Phi Beta Kappa. Home: 5800 Old Providence Rd No 4306 Charlotte NC 28226

SCHORR, DANIEL LOUIS, broadcast journalist, author, lecturer; b. NYC, Aug. 31, 1916; s. Louis and Tillie (Godiner) S.; m. Lisbeth Bamberger, 1967; children: Jonathan, Lisa. BSS, CCNY, 1939; doctorate (hon.), Kalamazoo Coll., Columbia Coll., Chgo., Wilkes U., Nebr. Wesleyan U., LI U., Brandeis U., Spartus Coll., Bates Coll., Haverford Coll. Asst. editor Jewish Telegraphic Agy., 1934-41; news editor ANETA (Netherlands) News Agy. in N.Y., 1941-43; freelance corr. N.Y. Times, Christian Sci. Monitor, London Daily Mail, 1948-53; Washington corr. CBS News, also spl. assignments L.Am. and Europe, 1953-55; reopened CBS Moscow Bur., 1955; roving assignments U.S. and Europe, 1958-60; chief CBS News Bur., Germany, 1960-66; Washington corr. CBS, 1966-76; Regents prof. U. Calif., Berkeley, 1977; columnist Des Moines Register-Tribune Syndicate, 1977-80; sr. Washington corr. Cable News Network, 1980-85; sr. analyst Nat. Pub. Radio, 1985—. Author: Don't Get Sick in America!, 1971, Clearing the Air, 1977, Forgive Us Our Press Passes, 1999, Staying Tuned, 2001, Come to Think of It, 2008. With U.S. Army, 1943-46, 47. Decorated officer Orange Nassau (The Netherlands), Grand Cross of Merit (Germany); recipient citations of excellence for radio-TV reporting Soviet Union Overseas Press Club, 1956, Best TV Interpretation of Fgn. News award 1963, ACLU and other awards for pub. suppressed Congsl. intelligence report, Emmy awards for coverage of Watergate, 1972, 73, 74, Peabody award for lifetime of uncompromising reporting of highest integrity, 1992, George Polk award for radio commentary L.I. U., 1994, Disting. Svc. award Am. Soc. Journalism and Mass Comm., 1994, Golden Baton award for lifetime achievement A.I. DuPont Columbia U., 1996; inducted in Hall of Fame Soc. Profl. Journalists, 1991, Comms. Hall of Fame CCNY, 1999. Mem. Am. Acad. Arts and Scis. (elected), Coun. on Fgn. Rels. N.Y.C., Nat. Press Club. Office Phone: 202-513-2277. E-mail: dschorr@npr.org. *Journalism, for more than 60 years, has been both profession and outlook on life. I have always felt myself the observer and nonparticipant, the quintessential outsider. I have pursued the sense of things behind the appearance of things, the meaning behind the manipulation. I have fought, with dubious success, against the blurring of the media line between reality and fantasy.*

SCHORR, LISBETH BAMBERGER, policy analyst; b. Munich, Jan. 20, 1931; d. Fred S. and Lotte (Krafft) Bamberger; m. Daniel L. Schorr, Jan. 8, 1967; children: Jonathan, Lisa. BA with highest honors, U. Calif.,

Berkeley, 1952; LHD (hon.), Wilkes U., 1991, U. Md., 1994, Bank St. Coll. Edn., 1999, Wheelock Coll., 2000, Lewis & Clark Coll., 2001, Whittier Coll., 2003. Med. care cons. U.A.W. and Community Health Assn., Detroit, 1956—58; asst. dir. Dept. Social Security AFL-CIO, Washington, 1958—65; acting chief CAP Health Svcs., OEO, 1965—66; chief program planning Office for Health Affairs, OEO, Washington, 1967. Cons. Children's Def. Fund, Washington, 1973—79; scholar-in-residence Inst. of Medicine NAS, 1979—80; chmn. Select Panel on Promotion Child Health, 1979—80; adj. prof. maternal and child health U. N.C., Chapel Hill, 1981—85; lectr. social medicine Harvard U. Med. Sch., 1984—; dir. project on effective interventions, 1988—2007; founder www.PathwaysToOutcomes.org; sr. fellow Ctr. for Study Soc. Policy, 2008; nat. coun. Alan Gutmacher Inst., 1974—79, 1982—85; pub. mem. Am. Bd. Pediat., 1978—84; vice chmn. Found. for Child Devel., 1978—84, bd. dirs., 1976—84, 1986—94; mem. coun. Nat. Ctr. for Children in Poverty, 1987—96; mem. children's program adv. com. Edna McConnell Clark Found., 1987—97; bd. dirs. Pub. Edn. Fund Network, 1991—93; co-chair Roundtable on Cmty. Change Aspen Inst., 1992—2006, mem. exec. com. Roundtable on Cmty. Change, 2006—; mem. bd. on children and families NAS, 1993—95; mem. Nat. Commn. State and Local Pub. Svcs., 1992—94; mem. task force on young children Carnegie Corp., 1992—94; mem. sec.'s adv. com. Head Start quality and expansion, 1993—94; mem. nat. selection com. Ford Found./Kennedy Sch. Awards for Innovations in Am. Govt., 1998—2006; dir. Pathways Mapping Initiative, Project on Effective Interventions, 2000—. Author: Within Our Reach: Breaking the Cycle of Disadvantage, 1988, Common Purpose: Strengthening Families and Neighborhoods to Rebuild America, 1997. Co-chmn. Boundaries task force Harvard Children's Initiative, 1998—2000; mem. Brookings Children's Roundtable, 1999—2002; bd. dirs. Nat. Student Partnerships, 2001—03, Eureka Cmtys., 1995—2005, Civic Ventures, 1997—99. Recipient Dale Richmond Meml. award, Am. Acad. Pediat., 1977, 9th ann. Robert F. Kennedy Book award, 1989, Nelson Cruikshank award, Nat. Coun. Sr. Citizens, 1990, Porter prize, 1993, PASS award, Nat. Coun. on Crime and Delinquency, 1997, Marian F. Langer award, Am. Orthopsychiat. Assn., 1999, Empatheia award, Vols. of Am., 1999. Mem.: Nat. Acad. on Social Ins., Inst. Medicine NAS, Phi Beta Kappa. Home and Office: 3113 Woodley Rd NW Washington DC 20008-3449 Home Phone: 202-483-7150; Office Phone: 202-462-3071. Business E-Mail: lisbeth_schorr@hms.harvard.edu.

SCHORR, S. L., lawyer; b. NYC, Feb. 19, 1930; s. Charles and Clara (Lerech) S.; m. Eleanor Daru, Mar. 23, 1956; children: Lewis, Andrew, Emily, Roberta. Student, L.I. U., 1948-50; LLB, Bklyn. Law Sch., 1953. Bar: N.Y. 1955, Ariz. 1962, U.S. Dist. Ct. Ariz. 1962, U.S. Supreme Ct. 1979. Planning commr. Pima County, Tucson, 1959-62; asst. city mgr. Tucson, 1962-63; ptnr. Lewis and Roca, Tucson, 1988—. Co-chair Continuing Legal Edn. Seminar on Ballot Box Zoning, U. Ariz., 1991, Ariz. State Bar Continuing Legal Edn. Seminar on Land Use Regulation and Litigation, 1977, 86, 89, 95. Bd. dirs. Pima Coll., 1966-67, So. Ariz. Leadership Coun., 1997—; mem. Commn. on Improved Govtl. Mgmt., Tucson, 1974-77, Gov.'s Econ. Planning and Devel. Adv. Bd., Phoenix, 1983-85, Regional Trans. Authority,2003-; Gov.'s Task Force on Seriously Mentally Ill, Phoenix, 1989-91; Ariz. State Transp. Bd., 2003-. Mem. Ariz. Bar Assn., Pima County Bar Assn. Democrat. Office: Lewis Roca 1 S Church Ave Ste 700 Tucson AZ 85701-1611 Office Phone: 520-622-2090.

SCHORSKE, CARL EMIL, historian, educator; b. NYC, Mar. 15, 1915; s. Theodore A. and Gertrude (Goldschmidt) S.; m. Elizabeth Gilbert Rorke, June 14, 1941; children: Carl Theodore, Anne (Mrs. J. L. Edwards), Stephen James, John Simon, Richard Robert. AB, Columbia U., 1936; MA, Harvard U., 1937, PhD, 1950; DLitt (hon.), Wesleyan U., 1967, Bard Coll., 1982, Clark U., 1983, New Sch. Social Rsch., 1986, Miami U., 1987, Monmouth Coll., 1994, Princeton U., 1997, SUNY, Stony Brook, 1989; DPhil (hon.), U. Salzburg, 1986, U. Graz, 1996. Prof. history Wesleyan U., Middletown, Conn., 1946-60; prof. history U. Calif.-Berkeley, 1960-69, Princeton U., 1969-80, emeritus, 1980—. Author: (with Hoyt Price) The Problem of Germany, 1947, German Social Democracy 1905-17, 1955, Fin-de-Siècle Vienna, 1980, Thinking with History, 1998. Lt. (j.g.) USNR, 1943-46; with OSS, 1941-46. Recipient Austrian Cross of Honor for arts and scis., 1979, Pulitzer prize gen. nonfiction, 1981, Grand prize cultural edn. City of Vienna, 1985, Harvard Centennial medal, 1999, Wittgenstein prize, Ministry Culture, Austria, 2004, Victor Adler prize, Austria, 2007; named Officer, French Order Arts and Letters, 1987, Great Silver medal of Honor, Austria, 1996, Gold Cross of Honor, City of Vienna, 2000; MacArthur fellow, 1981-86. Fellow Royal Acad. Fine Arts Netherlands (hon.); mem. Am. Acad. Arts and Scis., Austrian Acad. Scis. (corr.), Am. Hist. Assn. (council 1964-68, Disting. Scholar award 1992), Ctr. Advanced Study Behavioral Sci., Inst. Advanced Study., Getty Ctr. Home: 45 Meadow Lakes 01 Hightstown NJ 08520

SCHOTLAND, DONALD LEWIS, retired medical educator, neurologist; b. Orange, NJ, Sept. 21, 1930; s. Joseph Henry and Elsie (Block) S.; m. Marilyn Goldfeder, July 6, 1955 (dec. 1974); m. Estherina Shems, Jan. 11, 1976; children: John, Thomas, Peter. AB, Harvard U., 1952, MD, 1957; spl. student, MIT, 1955-56; MA (hon.), U. Pa., 1973. Diplomate Am. Bd. Psychiatry and Neurology 1964. Intern U. Ill. Research and Edn. Hosp., 1957-58; asst. resident in neurology Columbia Presbyn. Med. Center, NYC, 1958-61, asst. neurologist, 1961-65, asst. attending neurologist, 1965-66; asst. in neurology Coll. Physicians and Surgeons, Columbia U., NYC, 1960-61, vis. fellow in neurology, 1961-64, assoc. in neurology, 1964-66, asst. prof. neurology, 1966-67; assoc. prof. Sch. Medicine, U. Pa., Phila., 1967-72, prof., 1972-98, prof. emeritus, 1998—. Speaker profl. confs., U.S., Can., Italy, Japan, China, France, Israel, Finland; dir. Henry M. Watts, Jr. Neuromuscular Disease Rsch. Ctr., 1974-90. Editor: Diseases of the Motor Unit, 1982; contbr. articles, papers to profl. publs. Served to 1st lt. USAR, 1958-65. NIH postdoctoral fellow, 1961-64; recipient Research Career Devel. award, 1966-67, various grants NIH and Muscular Dystrophy Assn. Fellow Coll. of Physicians of Phila.; mem. Am. Acad. Neurology, Am. Neurol. Assn., Phila. Neurol. Soc., Muscular Dystrophy Assn. (sci. adv. com. 1974-86, chmn. fellowship com. 1974-86, chmn. 6th Internat. Conf. 1980). Home: 1310 Wyngate Rd Wynnewood PA 19096-2455 Office: Hosp of Univ Pa 3400 Spruce St Philadelphia PA 19104-4283 Personal E-mail: dlschotl@mail.med.upenn.edu.

SCHOTT, BASIL MYRON, archbishop; b. Freeland, Pa., July 21, 1939; s. Michael Schott and Mary. Attended, Immaculate Conception Coll., Troy, NY, St. Mary's Seminary, Norwalk, Conn. Ordained priest Order of Friars Minor, 1965, hegumen, protohegumen, dir. formation, dir. novices, dir. vocations, custodial councilor, custodial treas., spiritual asst. for Secular Franciscans; chaplain Holy Protection Monastery, Byzantine Nuns of St Clare, North Royalton, Ohio, Holy Annunciation Monastery, Byzantine Carmelite Nuns, Sugarloaf, Pa.; hegumen Holy Dormition Monastery, Sybertsville, Pa.; tchr. religious edn. dept. Byzantine Catholic High Sch., Parma, Ohio; syncellus for Priests and Religious Eparchy of Passaic, mem. Presbyteral Coun.; ordained bishop, 1996; bishop Eparchy of Parma (Ruthenian), 1996—2002; archbishop Archeparchy of Pitts. (Ruthenian), Pa., 2002—. Mem. Gen. Visitation Team, 1988; sec., treas., Episcopal liaison Interparochial Ecumenical, Evangelization and Youth Commissions; liaison Interparochial Religious Edn. Commn.; mem. Consecrated Life and Evangelization Committees US Conf. of Catholic Bishops, chmn. Com. on the Relationship between the Eastern and Latin Churches, mem. adminstrv. bd. Mem.: Eastern Catholic Associates (pres.). Roman Catholic. Office: Archeparchy of Pitts 66 Riverview Ave Pittsburgh PA 15214

SCHOTT, DONALD KARL, lawyer; b. Lynwood, Calif., Sept. 13, 1955; s. Otto H. and Violet M. (Reiman) S.; m. Cynthia A. Cronkrite, Aug. 9, 1980; children: Nathan Daniel, Anna Katherine, Laura Elizabeth BS in History and Polit. Sci., U. Wis., Madison, 1977; JD, Harvard U., 1980. Bar: Wis. 1980, U.S. Dist. Ct. (ea. and we. dists. Wis. 1980, no. dist. Ill. 1991), U.S. Ct. Appeals (7th cir. 1980, 9th cir. 2003), US Supreme Ct. 1995. Assoc. Quarles & Brady LLP, Milw., 1980-82, 85-87, ptnr., litig. practice Milw. & Madison, Wis., 1987—, mem. exec. com., 1999—; legis. asst. to Gov. State of Wis., Madison, 1983-85. Master: James. E. Doyle Am. Inn. Ct.; fellow: Am. Coll. Trial Lawyers; mem.: ABA, State Bar Wis. (bd. dir., young lawyers div. 1982—83), We. Dist. Bar Assn. (chmn. com. alternative dispute resolution 1992—97), Dane County Bar Assn., Phi Beta Kappa.

SCHOTT, JOHN ROBERT, international consultant, educator; b. Rochester, NY, Jan. 30, 1936; s. John and Ellen (Waite) S.; m. Diane Elizabeth Dempsey, June 19, 1963; children: Elizabeth Anne (dec.), Jennifer, Jared Reed, George Kermit Alexander. BA magna cum laude, Haverford Coll., 1957; postgrad., Oxford U., 1957-59; PhD, Harvard U., 1964. Resident tutor in govt. Eliot House, Harvard Coll., Cambridge, Mass., 1960-64; inst. polit. sci. Wellesley (Mass.) Coll., 1964-66; policy planning specialist AID, Washington, 1966-67; chief Title IX div. AID, Washington, 1967-68; vis. prof. polit. devel. Fletcher Sch. Law & Diplomacy, Tufts U., Medford, Mass., 1968-70; sr. v.p. Thunderbird Grad. Sch. Internat. Mgmt., Phoenix, 1970-71; cons. internat. affairs Francestown, NH, 1971-74; pres. Schott & Assocs., Inc., Jaffrey Center, NH, 1974-93. Mem. U.S. Del. World Assembly Internat. Secretariat for Voluntary Service, New Delhi, 1967; advisor Office Prime Minister Royal Thai Govt., Bangkok, 1978-80, Minister Cooperatives Govt. of Indonesia, Jakarta, 1983-84; research asst. spl. appointment The Brookings Inst., Washington, 1960-61 Author: Kenya Tragedy: European Colonization in East Africa, 1964, Frances' Town: History of Francestown, N.H., 1972, 2d edit., 1998, A Five-Year Comprehensive Plan for Development of Agricultural Cooperatives in Thailand, 1979, Recana-Komprehensip Pengembangan Kud, Jakarta, Indonesia, 1985; editor: An Experiment in Integrated Rural Development, 1978; contbr. articles to profl. jours. Mem. Bd. of Selectmen, Francestown, NH, 1975-78; trustee Spaulding Youth Ctr., Tilton, N.H., 1971-82, 85-89, pres. bd. trustees, 1972-75; trustee Internat. Inst. Rural Reconstrn., NYC, 1979-89, exec. com., 1985-89, bd. trustees NH Pub. Radio, 1990-96, chmn., 1993-95; spl. study commn. Coop. Extension Svc. State of NH, 1980-81, scenic and cultural by-ways com., 1993-96; forestry rep. County Extension Coun., Hillsboro County, NH, 1979-82; pres. NH Timberland Owner's Assn., 1989-90, bd. dirs., 1988-91; chmn. NH chpt. Nature Conservancy, 1990-93, hon. trustee, 1993—, chmn. NH Timber-Tourism Coalition, 1990-94; vice-chmn, Foresters Lic. Bd. State of NH, 1990-95; bd. trustees Cheshire Med. Ctr., 1992-94, RiverMead Retirement Cmty., Peterborough, NH, 1992-2000, chmn., 1996-2000; bd. overseers cmty. econ. devel. program So. NH U., 1997-2001, chmn., 1997-2000; trustee Sharon Arts Ctr., 2001-03; bd. dirs. Granite State Conservation Voters Alliance, 2004-08. Recipient The Haverford award, Haverford Coll., Pa., 1999, Global Alumni Svc. to Humanity award, Rotary Internat. Found., 2005—06; fellow, Rotary Found., 1957—58, Harvard U. Arts and Sci., 1959—60; scholar, Coslett Found., 1958—59, Fulbright Found., 1962—63.

SCHOTT, KATHARINE SUE, nursing educator; d. Francis Earl and Gertrude Betty (Brown) S. BSN, Mt. Mercy Coll., Cedar Rapids, 1975; MA, U. Iowa, 1987, PhD, 1991. Charge nurse ICU, critical care unit, recovery rm., nurse tng. officer Nursing Corp., US Army, various locations, 1975; advanced through grades to major U.S. Army, 1987; ret. lt. comdr., officer in charge fleet hosp. unit USN, 1993; instr. pathophysiology and neurological and behavioral pathology U. Iowa, 1987—; staff nurse Vis. Nurses Assn. Johnson County, Iowa City, 1993-97. Rsch. in computer-based instrn. Co-founder K-9 Potty Patrol, Milw., 1998—2003, Just Like Home Doggie Motel, Watertown, Wis., 2003—. Decorated numerous mil. awards. Home: W8264 County Road J Watertown WI 53098-3631 Personal E-mail: drschott@aol.com.

SCHOTT, ROBERT W. (BOB SCHOTT), film producer, actor, film director; b. Feb. 2, 1949; Student, Ill. Ctrl. U. Exec. prodr. Global Media Prodns., Platinum Blues Music. Founder Internat. SeaLand Enterprises, 1975—; former profl. bodybuilder. Actor: (films) Future Hunters, 1989, Head of the Family, 1996, In the Line of Fire, Fear, Force: Five, Million Dollar Mystery, VAMP, Gymkata, Blood Fist III, Aftershock, Out for Blood, Shoot Fighter, (TV episodes) Knightrider, Simon & Simon, Kaz, Eight is Enough; (TV films) Steel Cowboys, Jarret, The Norliss Tapes, Amateur Night at the Dixie Bar & Grill; prodr.: (documentaries) Adventures Beyond, The Women's Secret Weapon for Auto Buying; performer (composer (with Loretta Mears): (songs) Remembrance. Named U.S. Arm Wrestling Champion, 1981, World Arm Wrestling Champion, 1981; nominee Clio award, 1981. Mem.: AAAS, SAG, Nat. Assn. TV Programming Execs., Broadcast Music Inc. Achievements include discovery of existence of paranormal sciences with advanced technology through Department of Defense manufacturers; established paramount claim to parcel of East Pacific Ocean through US and UN; gained cooperation with NASA-DOT for new deep space commercial enterprise. Office: GMP PO Box 36773 Los Angeles CA 90036 Office Phone: 323-960-7700. Business E-Mail: isle@iwlink.com.

SCHOTT, SALLY MARIA, music publisher, arts education consultant; b. San Antonio, Feb. 7, 1943; d. Valentine Felix Schott, Jr. and Doris Faye. MusB, Okla. Coll. Women, 1964; MusM Edn., North Tex. State U., 1966. Choral dir. Jackson Intermediate, Pasadena, Tex., 1965—74, South Houston H.S., 1974—2004; founding ptnr. Alliance Music Publs., Houston, 1994—. Ednl. cons. Bay Area Chorus, Houston, 2004—; supr. student tchrs. U. Houston, 2004—, SHSU, 2008—; minority ptnr. AMC Music, Houston, 1975—2006; pres. Quaid/Schott Media Prodns., LLC, 2005—, Schott Bradshaw Publ., LLC, 2006—; cons. choral adjudicators panels, American Classic music festivals. Editor: Something to Sing About, 1981, Howard Swan: Conscience of a Profession, 1987; coord. writing team Sing, 1988. Ednl. adv. bd. Houston Chamber Choir, 2004—. Recipient Outstanding Young Educator, Pasadena Jaycees, 1974, HS Tchr. Year, Pasadena, 1986, Tchrs. Make a Difference award, KTRK, 1988, Greater Houston award in Arts, Bay Area Chorus Distinctive Svc., 2008; named to Hall Fame, U. Sci. & Arts Okla., 1996. Mem.: Tex. Choral Dirs. Assn. (state v.p. 1976—77, Choral Excellence award 2008), Am. Choral Dirs. Assn. (R&S 1994—98, pres. 2000—02, editor newsletter 2002—04), Tex. Music Educators Assn. (pres., state vocal chair 1981—86), Delta Kappa Gamma, Sigma Alpha Iota (pres. 1966, Leadership award Svc. to Music in Houston 1987). Republican. Methodist. Avocations: photography, travel, sports. Home: 62 W Thymewood Pl The Woodlands TX 77382

SCHOTT, SARAH E., lawyer; b. Sheboygan, Wis., Oct. 14, 1975; BA in Geology and Economics, magna cum laude, Lawrence U., 1997; JD cum laude, Duke U., 2000. Bar: Ill. 2000, US Dist. Ct. (No. Dist. Ill.) 2000, Wis. 2004. Assoc. Wildman Harrold Allen & Dixon, Chgo., 2000—03; v.p., asst. gen. counsel The Ziegler Cos., Inc., Milw., 2003, sr. mng. dir., gen. counsel. Mem.: Securities Industry Assn. (mem. legal and compliance divsn.), Am. Corp. Counsel Assn., ABA, Chgo. Bar Assn., Ill. Bar Assn. Office: Ziegler Companies Ste 2000 250 East Wisconsin Ave Milwaukee WI 53202 Office Phone: 414-978-6400. Office Fax: 414-978-6401.

SCHOTTENFELD, DAVID, retired epidemiologist, educator; b. NYC, Mar. 25, 1931; m. Rosalie C. Schaeffer; children: Jacqueline, Stephen. AB, Hamilton Coll., 1952; MD, Cornell U., 1956; MS in Pub. Health, Harvard U., 1963. Diplomate Am. Bd. Internal Medicine, Am. Bd. Preventive Medicine. Intern in internal medicine Duke U., Durham, NC, 1956-57; resident in internal medicine Meml. Sloan-Kettering Cancer Ctr., Cornell U. Med. Coll., NYC, 1957-59; Craver fellow med. oncology Meml. Sloan-Kettering Cancer Ctr., 1961-62; clin. instr. dept. pub. health Cornell U., NYC, 1963—65, asst. prof. dept. pub. health, 1965-70, assoc. prof. dept. pub. health, 1970-73, prof. dept. pub. health, 1973-86; John G. Searle prof., chmn. epidemiology sch. pub. health U. Mich., Ann Arbor, 1986—2004, prof. internal medicine, 1986—2004, prof. emeritus internal medicine and epidemiology Sch. Pub. Health, 2004—; adj. prof. dept. family medicine and cmty. health U. Mass. Med. Sch., Worcester, 2006—. Vis. prof. epidemiology U. Minn., Mpls., 1968, 71, 74, 82, 86; W.G. Cosbie lectr. Can. Oncology Soc., 1987. Editor: Cancer Epidemiology and Prevention, 1982, 2d. edit., 1996, 3d edit., 2006; author 10 books; contbr. more than 250 articles to profl. jours. Served with USPHS, 1959-61. Recipient Acad. Career award in Preventive Oncology, Nat. Cancer Inst., 1980-85, Disting. Achievement award Am. Soc. Preventive Oncology, 1992; vis. scholar Nat. Cancer Inst., 2007. Fellow AAAS, ACP, APHA (John Snow award 2007), Am. Coll. Preventive Medicine, Am. Coll. Epidemiology (Abraham Lilienfeld award 2002), Armed Forces Epidemiology Bd.; mem. Soc. Epidemiologic Rsch. (pres. 1998-99), Phi Beta Kappa. Office: U Mich Sch Pub Health Dept Epidemiology 109 Observatory St Ann Arbor MI 48109-2029 Home: 25 River Birch Ln Dalton MA 01226-2104 Business E-Mail: daschott@umich.edu.

SCHOTTENHEIMER, MARTY (MARTIN EDWARD SCOTTENHEIMER), former professional football coach; b. Canonsburg, Pa., Sept. 23, 1943; m. Patricia Schottenheimer; children: Kristen, Brian BA in Eng., U. Pitts., 1964. Profl. football player Buffalo Bills, 1965-68, Boston Patriots, 1969-70, Pitts. Steelers, 1971, Portland Storm, World League Football, 1974; real estate developer Miami and Denver, 1971-74; linebackers coach NY Giants, 1975-77, defensive coord., 1977; linebackers coach Detroit Lions, 1978-79; defensive coord. Cleve. Browns, 1980-84, head coach, 1985-88, Kans. City Chiefs, 1989-99, Wash. Redskins, 2001, San Diego Chargers, 2002—07; tv analyst ESPN, 1999—2000. Motivational spkr. IMG Speakers Bureau. Named Coach of the Year, UPI/AFC, 1995, AP, 2004, Pro Football Weekly, 2004.

SCHOTTER, ANDREW ROYE, economics professor, consultant; b. NYC, June 6, 1947; s. I. Harvey and Sara (Rothstein) S.; m. Anne Howland, June 7, 1970; children: Geoffrey, Elizabeth. BS, Cornell U., 1969; MA, PhD, NYU, 1974. Asst. prof. Syracuse (N.Y.) U., 1974-75, NYU, 1975-81, assoc. prof., 1981-86, prof., chmn. econs. dept. NYC, 1989-93, 96-99, chmn. C.V. Starr Ctr. for Applied Econs., 1986-89, dir. Ctr. for Experiential Social Sci., 2001—. Vis. asst. prof. Cornell U., Ithaca, 1974-75; vis. prof. U. Venice, 1993, U. Amsterdam; cons. Gulf & Western Corp., N.Y. 1987, Pegalis & Wachsman, Great Neck, N.Y., 1987-88, Nat. Econ. Rsch. Assocs., White Plains, N.Y., 1989—. Author: Economic Theory of Social Institutions, 1981, Free Market Economics: A Critical Appraisal, 1985, 2d edit., 1990, Microeconomics: A Modern Approach, 1993, 3d edit., 2000; mem. editl. bd.: Am. Econ. Rev., 1995—, Exptl. Econs., 1997; assoc. editor: Games and Econ. Behavior, (with Andrew Caplin) The Foundations of Positive Aormetics Economics, 2008, Microeconomics: A Modern Approach, 1st edit., 2008; spl. editor: Exptl. Econs. Grantee Office of Naval Rsch., 1980-85, NSF, 1988-90, 97—; recipient Kenan Enterprise award, 1993. Mem. Am. Econ. Assn., Econometric Soc., Econ. Sci. Assn. (pres.-elect 1997), Game Theory Soc. Office: NYU Dept Econs 269 Mercer St New York NY 10003-6633

SCHOTTLAENDER, BRIAN E.C., university librarian; BA in German Studies, U. Tex., Austin, 1974; MSLS, Ind. U., 1980. Past various libr. positions at Firma Otto Harrassowitz, Wiesbaden, Germany, Ind. U., U. Ariz.; from asst. head cataloging dept. to asst. univ. libr. tech. svc. UCLA, 1984—93, assoc. univ. libr. for collections and tech. svc., 1993—99; univ. libr. U. Calif., San Diego, 1999—. ALA rep. to internat. Joint Steering Com. for Revision Anglo-Am. Cataloguing Rules, 1995—2001; chair Program Coop. Cataloguing Libr. Congress, 1997—98; chair Pacific Rim Digital Alliance, 1999—2001, San Diego Libr. Circuit, 1999—. Editor: Retrospective Conversion: History, Approaches, Considerations, 1992. Sr. fellow Palmer Sch. Libr. Sci., Long Island U., 1995. Mem.: Assn. Rsch. Libr. (bd. dir. 2001—, pres. 2006—07), ALA (bd. dir. Assoc. Libr. Collections and Tech. Svc. 1996—, pres. Assoc. Libr. Collections and Tech. Svc. 2003—, recipient Margaret Mann Citation award 2001), Beta Phi Mu. Office: Adminstrv Office Geisel Libr Univ Calif 9500 Gilman Dr #0175G La Jolla CA 92093-0175 Office Phone: 858-534-3060. E-mail: becs@ucsd.edu.

SCHOULTZ, LARS, political scientist, educator; b. San Gabriel, Calif., Aug. 23, 1942; s. Ture Wilhelm and Bernice (Bowie) S.; m. Jane Volland, Jan. 18, 1969; children: Nils Gibson, Karina Anne. BA, Stanford U., 1964, MA, 1966; PhD, U. N.C., 1973. Prof. Miami U., Oxford, Ohio, 1973—77, U. Fla., Gainesville, 1977—79; William Rand Kenan Jr. prof. polit. sci. U. N.C., Chapel Hill, 1979—. Author: Human Rights and U.S. Policy Toward Latin America, 1981, National Security and U.S. Policy Toward Latin America, 1987, The Populist Challenge, 1983, Beneath the United States, 1998, That Infernal Little Cuban Republic, 2009. Sgt. U.S. Army, 1966-67. MacArthur fellow in internat. peace and security MacArthur Found., 1990-91, Fulbright fellow, Rockefeller Found. fellow, Ford Found. fellow, Social Sci. Rsch. Coun., Woodrow Wilson fellow, 1994-95, Nat. Humanities Ctr. fellow, 1999-00. Mem. Latin Am. Studies Assn. (pres. 1991-92, v.p. 1990-91). Democrat. Home: 250 Glandon Dr Chapel Hill NC 27514-3816 Office: U NC Inst Latin Am Studies Chapel Hill NC 27599-0001 Office Phone: 919-962-0422. E-mail: schoultz@unc.edu.

SCHOUMACHER, BRUCE HERBERT, lawyer; b. Chgo., May 23, 1940; s. Herbert Edward and Mildred Helen (Wagner) S.; m. Alicia Wesley (Sanchez), Nov. 4, 1967; children: Liana Cristina, Janina Maria. BS, Northwestern U., 1961; MBA, U. Chgo., 1963, JD, 1966. Bar: Nebr. 1966, U.S. Dist. Ct. Nebr. 1966, Ill. 1971, U.S. Dist. Ct. (no. dist.) Ill. 1971, U.S. Ct. Appeals (7th cir.) 1979, U.S. Supreme Ct. 1982, U.S. Ct. Fed. Claims 1986. Assoc. Luebs, Tracy, and Huebner, Grand Island, Nebr., 1966-67, McDermott, Will, and Emery, Chgo., 1971-76; ptnr. McDermott, Will,and Emery, Chgo., 1976-89, Querrey and Harrow, Ltd., Chgo., 1989—. Instr. bus. adminstrn., Bellevue Coll., Nebr.,

1967-70; lectr., U. Md. Overseas Program, 1970. Author: Engineers and the Law: An Overview, 1986; contbg. author: Construction Law, 1986, 2009, Construction Law Handbook, 1999, 2nd edit., 2008, Construction Business Handbook, 2004; co-author: Successful Business Plans for Architects, 1992; contbr. articles to profl. jour. Capt., USAF, 1967-71, Vietnam. Decorated, Bronze Star, 1971. Fellow Am. Coll. Constrn. Lawyers; mem. ABA, AIA (profl. affiliate), Nebr. Bar Assn., Ill. State Bar Assn. (ad hoc com. large law firms 1992-98), chmn. membership and bar activities com. 1988-89, coun. ins. law sect., 1986-91, mem. spl. com. on computerized legal rsch. 1986-87, mem. spl. com. constrn. law 2008-), Chgo. Bar Assn. (chmn. fed. civil procedure com. 1982-83), Def. Rsch. Inst., Ill. Assn. Def. Trial Counsel, Chgo. Bldg. Congress (bd. dirs. 1985—, sec. 1987-89, 95—, v.p. 1989-91), Soc. Ill. Constrn. Attys. (steering com. 2004-2005, sec. 2005-07, treas. 2007—), Western Soc. Engr. (assoc.), The Lawyers Club of Chgo., Tower Club, Chgo., Univ. Club Chgo., Rolling Green Country Club, Pi Kappa Alpha, Phi Delta Phi. Republican. Methodist. Office: Querrey & Harrow Ltd 175 W Jackson Blvd Ste 1600 Chicago IL 60604-2827 Office Phone: 312-540-7046. Business E-Mail: bschoumacher@querrey.com.

SCHOUTEN, RONALD, psychiatrist, educator; b. Paterson, NJ, Sept. 3, 1953; s. Neil and Charlotte Schouten; m. Evan Sue Hoffman, Aug. 21, 1977; children: Schuyler John, Alison Meg. JD, Boston U., 1978; MD, U. Ill., 1985. Diplomate psychiatry and forensic psychiatry Am. Bd. Psychiatry and Neurology. Dir. law and psychiatry svc. Mass. Gen. Hosp., Boston, 1989—; assoc. prof. of psychiatry Harvard Med. Sch., Boston, 2000—. Pres. KeyPeople Resources, Inc., West Newton, Mass., 2000—. Recipient Jonas Rappeport fellowship, Am. Acad. of Psychiatry and the Law, 1987. Mem.: Am. Coll. of Occupl. and Environ. Medicine, Acad. Orgnl. and Occupl. Psychiatry (pres. 2002—04), Am. Psychiat. Assn., Cambridge Boat Club. Office: Mass Gen Hosp WAC 812 15 Parkman St Boston MA 02114 Business E-Mail: rschouten@partners.org.

SCHOWALTER, JOHN ERWIN, child and adolescent psychiatry educator; b. Milw., Mar. 15, 1936; s. Raymond Phillip and Martha (Kowalke) S.; m. Ellen Virginia Lefferts, June 11, 1960; children: Jay, Bethany. BS, U. Wis., 1957, MD, 1960. Diplomate Am. Bd. Psychiatry and Neurology (com. on cert. in child psychiatry 1983-85, chmn. 1986-87, bd. dirs. 1993-2000, chmn. com. added qualifications forensic psychiatry 1993-97); cert. in adult and child psychiatry also psychoanalysis. Intern in pediat. Yale-New Haven Hosp., 1960-61; asst. resident in psychiatry Cin. Gen. Hosp., 1961-63; fellow in child psychiatry Yale U. Child Study Ctr., New Haven, 1963-65; psychiatrist Mental Hygiene Clinic U.S. Army, Ft. Ord, Calif., 1965-67; asst. prof. Yale U. Child Study Ctr., 1967-70, assoc. prof. Sch. Medicine, 1970-75, dir. tng., 1971-96, prof. pediat. and psychiatry, 1975-89, chief child psychiatry, 1982-90, dir. child psychiatry clin. svcs., 1990—2003, Albert J. Solnit prof. child psychiatry and pediat., 1989—2003, interim chmn., 2001—02, prof. emeritus, sr. rsch. scientist, 2003—. Mem. publ. com. Yale U. Press., 1992-97; mem. sci. adv. bd. Sophia Found. Med. Rsch., Rotterdam, The Netherlands, 1984-89; dir. mental health and substance abuse Yale Preferred Health Plan, 1995-99. Co-author: The Family Handbook of Adolescence, 1979; contbr. numerous articles, book revs.; mem. editl. bd. Pediatrics, 1976-81, Children's Health Care, 1977-2003, Jour. Am. Psychoanalytic Assn., 1978, Pediatrics in Rev., 1978-85; asst. editor: Jour. Am. Acad. Child and Adolescent Psychiatry, 1988-97; co-editor: Yearbook Psychiatry and Applied Mental Health, 1988-97. Capt. U.S. Army, 1965-67. Fellow Am. Acad. Child and Adolescent Psychiatry (sec. 1985-87, pres. 1989-91, Simon Wile award 1996, mem. fin. planning com. 2000-04, chair governance com. 2001-04, chmn. presdl. scholars com. 2005—, chmn. policy statements com. 2005—, chmn. task force policies and procedures, 2007—09, mem. fin. planning com. 2007-, mem. devel. com. 2009-), Am. Coll. Psychiatrists (chair Laughlin fellowship com. 2000-01, chair membership com. 2002-07), Am. Acad. Pediat.; mem. AMA (residency rev. com. psychiatry 1983-87, 89-94), Am. Pediatric Soc., Am. Psychoanalytic Assn. (cert. adult and child), Group Advancement Psychiatry (life fellow, com. on child psychiatry 1981, bd. dir. 1989-91, pres. 1993-95, chair life fellowship com. 2000—, mem. fin. com. 2008-), Assn. Care Children's Health (pres. 1984-86), Am. Psychiat. Assn. (chmn. McGavin award selection com., 2007—, McGavin award, 2006—), Soc. Profs. Child Psychiatry (pres. 1984-86), Western New Eng. Inst. Psychoanalysis (mem. faculty in child psychoanalysis 1984—, pres. 1986-88), Conn. Med. Soc., New Haven Med. Soc., Conn. Coun. Child Psychiatrists (pres. 1979-81), Benjamin Rush Soc. (sec., treas. 1998-99, v.p. 1999-2000, pres. 2000-02), Sigma Xi. Lutheran. Home: 256 Ives St Hamden CT 06518-2200 Office: Yale U Child Study Ctr PO Box 207900 230 S Frontage Rd New Haven CT 06520-7900

SCHOWALTER, LEO JOHN, physicist and educator; b. Detroit, Sept. 19, 1953; s. Leo John and Alice Nixon (Conn) S.; m. Rein-Ching Rachael Chieu, July 5, 1980; children: Jacob Leo, Sean Leo. BS in Math. and Physics, U. Idaho, 1975; MS in Physics, U. Ill., 1976, PhD in Physics, 1981. Staff scientist GE Co. CRD, Schenectady, N.Y., 1980-86, Si MBE program leader, 1983-86; assoc. prof. Rensselaer Poly. Inst., Troy, N.Y., 1987-93, prof., 1993—, assoc. dir. Ctr. Integrated Electronics/Electronic Mfg., 1994—. Disting. vis. scientist Jet Propulsion Lab., Pasadena, Calif., 1989-90; adv. com. NSF, 1992—. Editor/author: Proc. 2d Internat. Symposium on Silicon Molecular Beam Epitaxy, 1988, Layered Structures-Heteropitaxy, Superlattices, Strain and Metastability, 1990, Mechanisms of Heteroepitaxial Growth, 1992, Silicides, Germanides and Their Interfaces, 1994. Grantee NSF, 1991, 95, Office Naval Rsch., 1992, Air Force Office Sci. Rsch., 1993. Mem. Am. Phys. Soc. (exec. com. N.Y. State sect. 1987-91), Materials Sci. Soc. (continuing edn. com. 1993—), Am. Vacuum Soc., Sigma Xi. Achievements include research on epitaxial insulators using molecular beam epitaxy; substrate engineering with plastic epitaxial buffer layers; patent on optical detector having a plurality of matrix layers with cobalt disilicide. Office: Rensselaer Poly Inst Dept Physics Troy NY 12180

SCHOWALTER, WILLIAM RAYMOND, college dean, educator; b. Milw., Dec. 15, 1929; s. Raymond Philip and Martha (Kowalke) S.; m. Jane Ruth Gregg, Aug. 22, 1953; children: Katherine Ruth, Mary Patricia, David Gregg. BS, U. Wis., 1951; postgrad., Inst. Paper Chemistry, 1951-52; MS, U. Ill., 1953, PhD, 1957; PhD (hon.), Inst. Nat. Poly. Lorraine, France, 1996. Asst. prof. dept. chem. engring. Princeton U., 1957-63, assoc. prof., 1963-66, prof., 1966-86, Class of 1950 prof. engring. and applied sci., 1986-89, acting chmn. dept. chem. engring., 1971, chmn. dept. chem. engring., 1978-87, assoc. dean Sch. Engring. and Applied Sci., 1971-77, class of 1950 prof. engring. and applied sci. emeritus, 2000—; dean Coll. Engring. U. Ill., Urbana, 1989-2001, dean, prof. emeritus, 2001—; Mobil prof. chem. engring. Nat. U. Singapore, 1998, sr. advisor to pres., 2001—. Sherman Fairchild disting. scholar Calif. Inst. Tech., 1977-78; vis. fellow U. Salford, Eng., 1974; vis. sr. fellow Sci. Rsch. Coun., U. Cambridge, Eng., 1970; cons. to chem. and petroleum cos.; editl. adv. bd. McGraw-Hill Pub. Co., 1964-92; co-chmn. Internat. Seminar for Heat and Mass Transfer, 1970; vis. com. for chem. engring. MIT, 1979-87, Lehigh U., 1980-87; mem. vis. com. Sch. Engring., Stanford U., 1990-2001; evaluation panelist Ctr. Chem. Engring. Nat. Bur. Standards, 1982-88, chmn., 1986-88; mem. commn. engring. and tech. sys. NRC, 1983-88; engring. rsch. bd., 1984-86; adv. coun. chem. engring. Cornell U., 1983-91; adv. coun. Sch. Engring., Rice U., 1986-92; adv. com. Ill. Inst. Tech., 1992-97; adv. coun. Coll. Engring., U. Calif., Berkeley, 1997-2001, Coll. Engring. U. Mich., 1997-2001, Sch. Engring. and Applied Sci., Princeton U., 1998-2002, Carnegie Inst. Tech., 1999-2001; acad. adv. bd. Sematech Corp., 1992-2001; internat. adv. panel Nat. U. Singapore, 1996, 2002; chair, panel review Rsch. Inst. Singapore Agy. Sci. Tech. & Rsch., 2008-09, Reilly lectr. in chem. engring. U. Notre Dame, 1985, Van Winkle lectr. in chem. engring. U. Tex., Austin, 1986, David M. Mason lectr. chem. engring. Stanford U., 1987; Bird Stewart and Lightfoot lectr. chem. engring. U. Wis., 2001; R.H. Wilhelm lectr. in chem. engring. Princeton U., 2002; mem. fellowship program Packard Found. Sci. Adv. Panel, 1998—; mem. sci. adv. bd. Singapore Inst. for Chem. and Engring. Scis., 2003-07; mem. panel for U.K., Rsch. Assessment Exercise 2008, 2006-08. Author: Mechanics of Non-Newtonian Fluids, 1978; co-author: Colloidal Dispersions, 1989; mem. editl. com. Ann. Rev. Fluid Mechanics, 1974-80, Internat. Jour. Chem. Engring., 1974-94, Indsl. and Engring. Chemistry Fundamentals, 1975-78, Jour. Non-Newtonian Fluid Mechanics, 1976-2001, AIChE Jour., 1979-83; contbr. articles to profl. jours. Mem. Ill. Gov.'s Sci. Adv. Com., 1989-96. Served with U.S. Army, 1953-55. Decorated officier des Palmes Académiques (France); recipient Disting. Svc. citation Coll. Engring., U. Wis., Madison, 1983; Guggenheim fellow, 1987-88. Fellow AIChE (William H. Walker award 1982, bd. dirs. 1992-94), NAS (class membership com. 2000, 2002, class chmn. 2002-05), Am. Acad. Arts and Scis.; mem. Am. Soc. Engring. Edn. (Lectr. award chem. engring. divsn. 1971, exec. com. engr. deans coun. 1992-95, vice-chair, engring. deans coun. pub. policy com. 1998, chair engring. deans coun. pub. policy com. 1999-2001), NAE (awards com. 1986-88, chmn. 1987, acad. adv. bd. 1991-94, chmn. 1992-94, coun. 1994-2000, Draper Award com. 2001-03), Am. Chem. Soc., Soc. Rheology (exec. com. 1977-79, v.p. 1981-83, pres. 1983-85, Bingham medal 1988), Sigma Xi, Tau Beta Pi, Phi Lambda Upsilon, Phi Eta Sigma.

SCHRADE, ROBERT WARREN, classical pianist, educator; b. Walden, NY, Dec. 2, 1924; s. Louis J. and Elizabeth M. (Eitner) S.; m. Rolande M. Young, Dec. 21, 1949; children: Robelyn, Rhonda Lee, Rolisa M., Randolph R.A., Rorianne C. MusB, MusM, Manhattan Sch. Music, 1948. Mem. piano faculty Manhattan Sch. of Music, NYC, 1949-56, 68-89; mem. music faculty, artist-in-residence Chapin sch., NYC, 1948-89; pres., artistic dir. Sevenars Concerts, Inc., Worthington, Mass., 1976—. Lectr. in field. Appeared in frequent piano concerts, N.Y.C., Europe, including Carnegie Hall, Lincoln Ctr., 1977, 81, 86, with Schrade Family Pianists, 1980-93, Lincoln Ctr., N.Y.C., 2000; soloist symphony orchs. throughout Europe and South Pacific; ann. solo concerts Sevenars Music Festival, Sevenars Music Festival, Worthington, Mass., Berkshires; featured on radio and TV shows including PM Mag. film, NBC Today Show, Radio New Zealand; 50th anniversary of N.Y. adult debut Liederkranz Found. (Town Hall), N.Y.C; featured in Lifetime TV film, 2000. Cpl. USAAC, 1942-45. Avocations: tennis, fishing. Home: 30 East End Ave New York NY 10028-7053 Address: Rte 112 at Ireland St S Worthington MA 01098

SCHRADE, ROLANDE MAXWELL YOUNG, composer, pianist, educator; b. Washington, Sept. 13; d. Harry Robert and Isabelle Martha (Maxwell) Young; m. Robert Warren Schrade, Dec. 21, 1949; children: Robelyn, Rhonda Lee, Rolisa, Randolph, Rorianne. Studied with, Harold Bauer, NYC, Vittorio Giannini; student, Manhatten Sch. Music, Juilliard Sch. Music. Debut as concert pianist Town Hall, NYC, 1953, Nat. Gallery, Washington, 1954; concert pianist Constitution Hall, Washington, 1972; co-founder, dir. ann. performances, celebrating 40th anniversary Sevenars Concerts, Inc., Worthington, Mass., 1968—2008, music dir., 1975—, also broadcasts, 1984, 85; recitalist Radio Sta. WGMS-FM, Washington; mem. music faculty Allen-Stevenson Sch., NYC, 1968-89; co-founder, v.p., treas. Sevenars Music House, Inc., NYC, 1968—. Concerts include Lincoln Ctr., Alice Tully Hall, 1980, 93, Sevenars Concerts, Inc., 1968—, Lincoln Ctr., 2000; Lifetime TV film Tour, New Zealand, 1982-84; featured NBC Today Show with Schrade family pianists, 1993; named to Steinway Piano Co. Global Artist List; appearances PM Mag., TV film, 1980-81; composer, pub., recs. of over 100 songs; albums include America 76, Original and Traditional Songs for Special Days, 1988; editor: songs of Carrie Jacobs Bond, Boston Music Co.; TV feature film with Schrade Family Pianists, 1997; performed in Schrade-James Family Concert Lincoln Ctr., NYC, 2000, Lifetime TV showing. Mem.: ASCAP, DAR (Bicentennial award 1972), Mut. Artists Mgmt. Alliance (founder, bd. dirs.). Episcopalian. Home and Office: 30 East End Ave Ste 3A New York NY 10028-7053 Office: Sevenars Summer Concerts Ireland St S at Rte 112 Worthington MA 01098

SCHRADER, ALFRED EUGENE, lawyer; b. Nov. 1, 1953; s. Louis Clement and Helen Mae (Eberz) S.; m. Debra Susanne Britt-Garrett, Aug. 12, 1997. BA in Polit. Sci. magna cum laude, Kent State U., 1975; JD, Ohio State U., 1978. Bar: Ohio 1978, U.S. Dist. Ct. (no. dist.) Ohio 1978, U.S. Ct. Appeals (6th cir.) 1985, U.S. Supreme Ct. 1985. Dep. clk. Summit County Clk. of Cts., Akron, 1972-74; pvt. practice law Akron, 1978—; spl. counsel Bath Twp., Ohio, 1980-92, 95-98. Spkr. Akron Bar Assn. Akron Univ. Sch. Law CLE Seminars. Trustee Springfield Twp., Ohio, 1973-2001, pres., 1975, 79, 82, 88, 90, 95-96, 2000-01; v.p. Springfield-Akron Joint Econ. Devel. Dist., 1995-97, pres., 1997-2000; mem. adv. com. Cmty. Devel. Block, Summit County, 1985-97, Summit County Annexation Com., 1981-85; mem. Summit County Jail Study Commn., 1983, 84; mem. adv. bd. Springfield Schs., 1975; acting law dir. City of Streetsboro, Portage County, Ohio, 1997; legal coun. Reminderville Twinsburg JEDD Bd. 2000-; rep. numerous twps. State of Ohio on land use planning, annexation, revenue sharing, joint econ. devel. dist., annexation agreements, co-operative econ. devel. agreements, zoning and local govt. law matters; spl. counsel Harrison Hills Bd. Edn., Warren, Ohio Econ. Devel. Dist., 2002-2004, Lorain Co. Commr., 1999; rep. coun. dist. 8 Summit County, 2003-05, law dir. Twinsburg township, 2006-07; law dir. East Union township, Wayne County, 2007—, Chippewa township, 2007—, Confield Twp., 2008-. Mem. Akron Bar Assn. (v.p. legis. com. 1981-82, v.p. local govt. sect. 1992-93, chair local govt. sect. 1993-95, v.p. continuing legal edn. com. 2001-04, vice chair professionalism coun. 2008-), Ohio Assn. for Justice, Ohio Bar Assn., Summit County Twp. Assn. (exec. com. 1983-2001), Ohio Twp. Assn., Risk Mgmt. Authority (bd. dirs. 1996-2001, sec. 1997-2000, pres. 2000-01), Nat. Assn. Town and Twp. Attys. (bd. dirs. Ohio chpt. 1986, sec. 1987-93, v.p. 1993-97), Summit County Assn. Justice. Democrat. Roman Catholic. Fax: 330 762 2255. Home: 3344 Brunk Rd Akron OH 44312-3710 Office: Schrader Romanoski Stevenson 441 Wolf Ledges Pky Ste 400 Akron OH 44311-1039 Home Phone: 330-628-9678; Office Phone: 330-762-0765. Office Fax: 330-762-2255. E-mail: alschrader@choiceonemail.com.

SCHRADER, CAROL ANN, artist, painter; b. Elizabethtown, Pa., Dec. 19, 1939; d. Gilbert Thomas and Margaret Mary (Thomas) Steever; m. Robert F. Schrader. BS, Pa. State U., 1961, MEd, 1963; MFA, U. N.C., 1972. Instr. art Prince George's County Pub. Schs., Beltsville, Md., 1961-71; art chair, instr. U. Alaska-S.E., Sitka, 1985-86. Juror 23d Annual Exhbn. S, Tuscumbia, Ala., 1995, Ariz. Watercolor Assn. Exhbn., 2003, Contemporary Watercolorists Ariz. Exhbn., 2007, Southern Ariz. Watercolor Guild Exhbn., 2008. Contbr. Splash III, 1994, Best of Watercolor, 1995, Creative Watercolor, 1996; 200 Great Painting Ideas for Artists, 1998, Watercolor Magic, 1998, 2007, prin. works include Illinois Afternoon (Bristol-Myers Squibb award, 1991), Margaret's July (George and Beverly Ryan award, 1992), Kim's Curls (DuPage award, 1996), Between Daylight and Darkness (Arts in Miss. award, 1999), Xs (Best Show), San Diego Watercolor Soc. Internat., 2007 (best show, 2007), exhibitions include A Desert Romance: Paintings by Carol Ann Schrader, 2008, Mo. State U. Art & Design Gallery Invitational, 2009; contbr. articles to profl. jours. Recipient High Winds Medal and Honorarium, Am. Watercolor Soc., 1991, Rechenbach award Tenn. Watercolor Soc., 1995, Amy Shelton McNutt Charitable Trust award Tex. Watercolor Soc., 2001, Judith and A. Richard Cohen Meml. award, Adirondacks Exhbn. Am. Watercolor, 2007, Margaret and William Foley award, 2005, Hank McDonnell Meml. award, Calif. Watercolor Assn., 2007. Mem.: Allied Artists Am., Rocky Mountain Watermedia Soc. (Alan and Sue Provost award 2003), Phila. Water Color Soc. (Crest medal 1998), Watercolor West (Patrons award 2004), Transparent Watercolor Soc. Am. (Master Watercolorist medal 1999), Watercolor U.S.A. Honor Soc. (Jean Strauss Kramer award 2001), Nat. Watercolor Soc. (Alexander Nepote award 1989, Altfeld/Campbell award 1989, Beverly Green Meml. Collection award 2003), Am. Watercolor Soc. (Barse Miller Meml. award 2004). Avocations: running, specialty baking, collecting art and cookbooks. Home: 7435 E Thunderhawk Rd Scottsdale AZ 85255-4600 E-mail: art@carolannschrader.com.

SCHRADER, DENNIS R., former federal agency administrator; b. 1953; m. Sandra B. Schrader; 1 child, Whitney. BA, Kettering U., 1976; MA, SUNY, Buffalo. Officer US Navy Civil Engrs. Corps; dir. ops., v.p. facilities mgmt. and devel. and v.p. project planning and devel. U. Md. Med. Ctr.; dir. Homeland Security State of Md., mem. Anti-Terrorism Adv. Coun., Public Safety Comms. Interoperability Governance Work Group, Homeland Security Sr. Policy Group and Md. Pandemic Influenza Coord. Com.; dep. adminstr. for nat. preparedness, Fed. Emergency Mgmt. Agy. (FEMA) US Dept. Homeland Security, Washington, 2007—09. Ret. capt. USN.*

SCHRADER, KURT, United States Representative from Oregon, former state senator; b. Bridgeport, Conn., Oct. 19, 1951; m. Martha Schrader; 4 children. BA, Cornell U., Ithaca, NY, 1973; BS, U. Ill., 1975, DVM, 1977. Veterinarian, owner, mgr. Clackamas County Vet. Clinic, Oregon County, Oreg., West Linn, Oreg.; farmer; rsch. analyst to Gov. State of Alaska; mem. Oreg. House of Reps. from Dist. 23, 1997—2003, Oreg. State Senate from Dist. 20, 2003—08, US Congress from 5th Oreg. Dist., 2009—. Mem. emergency bd. Oreg. Senate, co-chair joint ways and means com., 2005. Past chair Canby Planning Commn.; past mem. Mayor's Future Focus Task Force, Canby; past mem. bd. dirs. South Clackamas Rec. Dist.; mem. Clackamas Rec. Task Force; mem. bd. dirs. Blue Heron Rec. Dist. Recipient Disting. Leadership by Cmty. Planner award, Am. Planning Assn. Mem.: Am. Assn. Equine Practitioners, Oreg. Vet. Assn., Am. Vet. Med. Assn., Canby C. of C., Oregon City C. of C., Oreg. Farm Bur., Nat. Fedn. Ind. Bus. Democrat. Office: US Congress 1419 Longworth House Office Bldg Washington DC 20515-3705 also: Dist Office 494 State St Ste 210 Salem OR 97302 Office Phone: 202-225-5711, 503-588-9100. Office Fax: 202-225-5699, 503-588-5517.*

SCHRADER, SUSAN RAE, elementary school educator; b. Tucson, Nov. 12, 1972; d. Edward Arthur and Nancy Young Schrader. BS, Nebr. Wesleyan U., Lincoln, 1994; M in Elem. Edn., No. Ariz. U., Phoenix, 2001. Cert. Ariz., 1995. Tchr. Tucson Unified Sch. Dist., 1995—96, Alhambra Sch. Dist., Phoenix, 1997—. Coach Peoria (Ariz.) Sch. Dist., 2004—06. V.p. Catalina Booster Club, Phoenix, 2002—04. Recipient Spirit of Catalina, Catalina Ventura Elem., 2004; named Dist. Employee of Month, Alhambra Sch. Dist.; named to Athletic Hall of Fame, Nebr. Wesleyan U., 2005. R-Consevative. Roman Catholic. Avocations: travel, gardening, home improvements, movies, reading. Office: Catalina Ventura 6331 N 39th Ave Phoenix AZ 85019 E-mail: sschrader@alhambra.k12.az.us.

SCHRADY, DAVID ALAN, civilian military employee, educator; b. Akron, Ohio, Nov. 11, 1939; s. Marvin G. and Sheila A. (O'Neill) S.; m. Mary E. Hilt, Sept. 1, 1962; children: Peter, Patrick, Matthew. BS, Case Inst. Tech., 1961, MS, 1963, PhD, 1965. Prof., chmn. Naval Postgrad. Sch., Monterey, Calif., 1974-76, dean acad. planning, 1976-80, provost and acad. dean, 1980-87, prof. ops. rsch., 1988—, Disting. prof., ops. rsch. educator, 1995—. Vis. prof. Cranfield Inst. Tech./Royal Mil. Coll. of Sci., Shrivenham, Eng., fall 1987-spring 88. Contbr. articles to profl. jours. Recipient Goodeve medal Ops. Rsch. Soc., U.K., 1992, Navy Disting. Civilian Svc. medal, 2006, Jancinto Steinhardt Memorial award, 2006. Fellow: Inst. for Ops. Rsch. and the Mgmt. Scis., Mil. Ops. Rsch. Soc., (pres. 1978—79, Wanner medal 1984); mem.: Internat. Fedn. Ops. Rsch. Socs. (hon. treas. 1988—97), Ops. Rsch. Soc. Am. (pres. 1983—84, Kimball medal 1994). Avocations: guitar, motor sports. Office: Naval Postgrad Sch Dept Ops Rsch Monterey CA 93943-5000 Business E-Mail: dschrady@nps.edu.

SCHRAG, ADELE FRISBIE, business education educator; b. Cynthiana, Ky., May 7, 1921; d. Shirley Ledyard and Edna Kate (Ford) S.; m. William Albert Schrag, Apr. 6, 1963; 1 stepchild, Marie Carol. BS, Temple U., 1942; MA, N.Y. U., 1944, PhD, 1961. Tchr. Manor Twp. High Sch., Millersville, Pa., 1942-43, Downingtown (Pa.) Sr. High Sch., 1943-50; instr., asst. prof. Temple U. Sch. Bus. and Pub. Administrn., Phila., 1950-60; prof. bus. edn. and vocat. edn. Coll. Edn., 1960-85, sr. prof. edn., 1985-88, prof. emeritus, 1988—. Vis. lectr. N.Y. U.; cons. Phila. Community Coll., 1967-82 Editor: Business Education for the Automated Office, 1964; author: (with Estelle L. Popham and Wanda Blockhus) A Teaching-Learning System for Business Education, 1975, How to Dictate, 1981, Office Procedures Update, 1982, (with Robert Poland) A Teaching System for Business Subjects, 1988; contbr. articles to profl. jours., chpts. to books. Trustee Meth. Hosp., 1981—85, Sun Cities Symphony Assn., 1988—93, Habitat for Humanity West Valley, 1994—2005, co-pres., 1999—2001; trustee Habitat for Humanity Ariz., 1999—2003. Recipient Profl. Panhellenic award, 1963; Kensington High Sch. Alumnae award, 1972 Mem. Soc. Automation in Bus. Edn. (pres. 1969-73, dir. 1974), Nat. Assn. Bus. Tchr. Edn. (pres. 1983-84), Bus. Edn. Certification Council, Phi Gamma Nu (nat. treas. 1952-54, nat. sec. 1954-56), Delta Pi Epsilon (policy commn. for bus. and econ. edn. 1975-78, dir. research found. 1978-83, pres. research found. 1983). Home: 14515 W Granite Valley Dr # 644 Sun City West AZ 85375-6021 E-mail: as107@cox.net.

SCHRAG, ANNE MICHELLE, ecologist; d. Randall and Marilyn Schrag. BS, U. Kans., Lawrence, 2001; MS, Mont. State U., Bozeman, 2006. Program coord. Nat. Pk. Svc. Inventory and Monitoring Network, Bozeman, Mont., 2003—06; climate rsch. program officer World Wildlife Fund, Bozeman, 2007—. Office: World Wildlife Fund 202 S Black Ste 3 Bozeman MT 59715 Business E-Mail: anne.schrag@wwfus.org.

SCHRAG, PETER, editor, writer; b. Karlsruhe, Germany, July 24, 1931; arrived in U.S., 1941, naturalized, 1953; s. Otto and Judith (Haas) S.; m. Melissa Jane Mowrer, June 9, 1953 (div. 1969); children: Mitzi, Erin Andrew; m. Diane Divoky, May 24, 1969 (div. 1981); children: David Divoky, Benaiah Divoky; m. Patricia Ternahan, Jan. 1, 1988. AB cum laude, Amherst Coll., 1953. Reporter El Paso (Tex.) Herald Post, 1953-55; asst. sec., asst. dir. publs. Amherst Coll., 1955-66, instr. Am. Studies, 1960-64; assoc. edn. editor Sat. Rev., 1966-68, exec. editor, 1968-69; editor Change mag., 1969-70; editor at large Saturday Rev., 1969-72; contbg. editor Saturday Review/Education, 1972-73; editl. adv. bd. The Columbia Forum, 1972-75; editl. bd. Social Policy, 1971—; contbg. editor More, 1974-78, Inquiry, 1977-80, The Am. Prospect, 1995—; editl. page editor Sacramento Bee and McClatchy Newspapers, 1978-96, contbg. editor, 1996—. Vis. lectr. U. Mass. Sch. Edn., 1970-72; fellow in profl. journalism Stanford U., Palo Alto, Calif., 1973-74; lectr. U. Calif., Berkeley, 1974-78, 90—; Pulitzer Prize juror, 1988-89; vis. scholar U. Calif. Inst. Govtl. Studies, Berkeley, 1998—. Author: Voices in the Classroom, 1965, Village School Downtown, 1967, Out of Place in America, 1971, The Decline of the Wasp, 1972, The End of the American Future, 1973, Test of Loyalty, 1974, (with Diane Divoky) The Myth of the Hyperactive Child, 1975, Mind Control, 1978, Paradise Lost: California's Experience, America's Future, 1998, Final Test: The Battle for Adequacy in America's Schools, 2003, California: America's High-Stakes Experiment, 2006; contbr. articles to profl. publs. Adv. com. Student Rights Project, NY Civil Liberties Unon, 1970-72; mem. Com. Study History, 1958-72; trustee Emma Willard Sch., 1967-69; bd. dirs. Park Sch., Oakland, Calif., 1976-77, Ctr. for Investigative Reporting, 1979-81, Ed Source, 1998—; bd. adv. Pub. Policy Inst. Calif. Guggenheim fellow, 1971-72; Nat. Endowment for Arts fellow, 1976-77 Office: 5835 Colton Blvd Oakland CA 94611-2204

SCHRAG, PHILIP GORDON, law educator; b. Chgo., Apr. 12, 1943; s. Louis Phillip and Lala D. (Fineman) S.; m. Emily Shiling, June 7, 1964 (div. Aug. 1985); children: David, Zachary; m. Lisa Gabrielle Lerman, Dec. 29, 1985; children: Samuel Lerman, Sarah. AB, Harvard U., 1964; LLB, Yale U., 1967. Bar: DC 1981. Asst. counsel NAACP Legal Def. & Edn. Fund Inc., NYC, 1967-70; consumer adv. NYC, 1970-71; assoc. prof. law Columbia U., NYC, 1971-73, prof. law, 1973-77; dep. gen. counsel ACDA, Washington, 1977-81; prof. law Georgetown U., Washington, 1981—2009, Detoney Family prof. pub. interest law, 2009—; dir. Ctr. Applied Legal Studies. Cons. Consumer Protection Bd., N.Y., 1975, Carter-Mondale Transition Planning, 1976, Gov.'s Adv. Coun., P.R., 1970. Author: Counsel for the Deceived, 1972, Behind the Scenes: The Politics of a Constitutional Convention, 1985, A Well-Founded Fear: The Congressional Battle to Save Political Asylum in America, 2000, Repay As You Earn: The Flawed Government Program to Help Students Have Public Interest Careers, 2002; co-author (with M. Meltsner): Reflections on Clinical Legal Education, 1998; co-author: (with Lisa G. Lerman) Ethical Problems in the Practice of Law, 2nd edit., 2008; co-author: (with David Ngaruri Kenney) Asylum Denied: A Refugee's Struggle for Safety in Am., 2008; co-author: (with Jaya Ramji-Nogales, Andrew I. Schoenholtz) Refugee Roulette: Disparities in Asylum Adjudication and Proposals for Reform, 2009. Del. Statehood Constnl. Conv., D.C., 1982; chair Consumer's Adv. Coun., N.Y.C., 1968-70. Office Phone: 202-662-9099. Business E-Mail: schrag@law.georgetown.edu.

SCHRAGE, ROSE, retired academic administrator; b. Montelimar, France, Apr. 15, 1942; came to U.S., 1947; d. Abraham and Celia (Silbiger) Levine; m. Samuel Schrage, Dec. 12, 1935 (dec. 1976); children: Abraham, Leon. BRE, Beth Rivkah Tchrs. Sem., Bklyn., 1968; Paralegal, Manpower Career Devel. Agy., Bklyn., 1973; MS, L.I. U., 1975; Advanced Cert. Ednl. Adminstrn., Bklyn. Coll., 1983. Cert. sch. dist. adminstr., guidance counselor, tchr., asst. prin. Sec., NYC, 1964-68; police adminstrv. aide N.Y.C. Police Dept., 1974-75; coord. state reading aid program Sch. Dist. 14, Bklyn., 1977-78, project dir. Title VII, 1978-81, asst. dir. reimbursable fed. and state programs, 1981-85, dist. bus. mgr., 1985-94, asst. prin., 1994—99, spl. edn. instrn. specialist, adminstr., 1999—; ednl. adminstr. Ctrl. Liaison Office for Impartial Hearings divsn. student support svcs. Dept. Edn., NYC, 2001—04; ret., 2004. Chmn. N.Y.C. Bd. Edn. IMPACT Com., Bklyn., 1986—. Author (poem): Never Again, 1983; contbg. editor Chai Today; contbr. articles to profl. jours. Del. Republican. Jud. Conf., 1968; founder, pres Concerned Parents, Bklyn., 1977; radio co-host Israeli War Heroes Fund-Radiothon, Bklyn.; family counselor local social agys., Bklyn.; co-founder cmty. vol. ambulance Hatzalah, 1977. Recipient Cert. of Appreciation as vol. regional coord. N.Y. State Mentoring Program N.Y. Gov. Cuomo, 1991, Proclamation, N.Y. City Coun., 2003, State of N.Y. Legis. Resolution Proclamation N.Y. State Senate, 2003, U.S. Congress Proclamation, 2003, Excellence in Fiscal Mgmt. award IMPACT. Mem. Am. Assn. Sch. Adminstrs., Assn. Orthodox Jewish Tchrs. (v.p. exec. bd., pres. 2004, Orgn. award 2003), N.Y. State Assn. Sch. Bus. Ofcls., N.Y.C. Assn. Sch. Bus. Ofcls., Coun. Suprs. and Adminstrs. Avocations: piano, reading, composing music.

SCHRAGER, IAN, hotel executive; b. NYC, July 19, 1946; s. Louis Schrager; m. Rita Narona, 1994 (div. 2001); children: Sophie Blanche, Ava Louis; m. Tania Wahlstedt, 2008. BA, Syracuse U., 1968; JD, St. John's U. Sch. Law, 1971. Co-owner (with Steve Rubell) Studio 54 (discotheque), 1977—80, Palladium, 1985—90; founder, owner Morgans Hotel Group, LLC, 1985—2005; chmn., CEO Ian Schrager Co., 2005—. Bd. dirs. Mncpl. Art. Soc., Legal Action Ctr. Office: Ian Schrager Co 818 Greenwich St New York NY 10014*

SCHRAGER, MINDY RAE, operations management specialist; b. Paterson, NJ, Jan. 18, 1958; d. Julius Maxwell and Miriam (Max) Schrager; m. Jim Flannery, 1993. BA, Dickinson Coll., 1979; MBA, Babson Coll., 1981. Integrative coaching cert. Ford Inst. JFK U., 2008, cert. NLP Master Practitioner, Aura-Soma Practitioner, Herrmann Brain Dominance Indicator facilitator. Cons. Nolan Norton & Co., Lexington, Mass., 1981—86; mgr. Logos Corp., Dedham, Mass., 1986—87; resource ctr. supr., customer satisfaction mgr., dir. quality Motorola ISG, Mansfield, Mass., 1987—95; dir. quality, dir. bill payment ops., dir. project mgmt. Fidelity Investments, Boston, 1995—99; sr. program mgr., sr. mgr. collaborative product delivery, dir. program and operational excellence Ascential Software, Westboro, Mass., 1999—2005; mgr., program dir. IBM, Westboro, 2005—, Rsch. Triangle Pk., 2007—. Mem.: NAFE, Internat. Coach Fedn., Assn. Rsch. and Enlightenment. Avocations: coaching, wellness. Home: 307 Capistrane Dr Cary NC 27519 Office: IBM 3039 E Cornwallis Rd PO Box 12195 Research Triangle Park NC 27709-2195 Office Phone: 919-337-1147. Business E-Mail: mschrager238@msn.com.

SCHRAM, MARTIN JAY, journalist; b. Chgo., Sept. 15, 1942; s. Marlo Joseph and Charleene Janice (Fidler) S.; m. Patricia Stewart Morgan, May 23, 1964; children: Kenneth Marlo, David Morgan. BA, U. Fla., 1964. Reporter The Miami (Fla.) News, 1964-65; reporter Newsday, Garden City, NY, 1965-67, mem. Washington bur., 1967-69, White House corr., 1969-73, chief Washington bur., sr. editor paper, 1973-79; writer on the presidency Washington Post, 1979-81, nat. affairs writer, 1981-86; assoc. editor, editor Sunday edits. Chgo. Sun-Times, 1986-87; asst. mng. editor, editor Sunday edits. Rocky Mountain News, Denver, 1987-88; commentator Cable News Network, 1988-98; nat. editor Washingtonian Mag., 1988-90; polit. columnist United Feature Syndicate, Newspaper Enterprise Assn., 1989-94, Scripps Howard News Svc., Washington, 1994—; news story edit., columnist Fox News, Washington, 1998-2000; mng. editor Avoiding Armageddon, PBS/Ted Turner Documentaries TV Series, 2001—03. Fellow Gannett Ctr. for Media Studies, Columbia U., 1985-86; guest scholar Woodrow Wilson Internat. Ctr., 1990-91. Author: Running for President, A Journal of the Carter Campaign, 1976, Running for President: 1976, The Carter Campaign, 1977; (with others) The Pursuit of the Presidency, 1980, The Great American Video Game: Presidential Politics in the Television Age, 1987, Speaking Freely, 1995; co-author: Cell Phonex: Invisible Hazards in the Wireless Age, 2001, Avoiding Armaegeddon: Our Future. Our Choice, 2003; co-editor: Mandate for Change, 1993. Recipient James Wright Brown Meml. award Sigma Delta Chi, 1965, Lowell Mellet award Pa. State U., 1988. Office: Scripps Howard News Svc 1090 Vermont Ave NW Ste 1000 Washington DC 20005-4906 Personal E-mail: martin.schram@gmail.com.

SCHRAM, RONALD BYARD, lawyer; b. Detroit, Sept. 7, 1942; s. Byron Canby and Mary Louise (Byard) S.; m. Carol Lorraine Anderson, July 19, 1969; children: Laura Mary, Alison Leigh. BA, Dartmouth Coll., 1964; MA in Econs., Cambridge U., England, 1966; JD, U. Mich., 1969, LLM, 1970, SJD, 1971. Bar: Mass. 1970. Assoc. Ropes & Gray, Boston, 1970-78, ptnr., 1978—2002. Author: Non-Billable Hours: A Poetic Journey Through the 1st Year of Retirement, 2005, Non-Billable Hours, 2004; editor: Sports: A Generation's Common Bond, 2007; author: Caroline and Papa: Growing Up and Growing Older, 2009. Trustee Dartmouth Coll., Hanover, NH, 1981-92, Dartmouth-Hitchcock Med. Ctr., Lebanon, NH, 1983-93, New Eng. Sports Mus., Cambridge, Mass., 1984-1999, Derby Acad., Hingham, Mass., 1982-89; trustee Ctrl. New Eng. chpt. Nat. Multiple Sclerosis Soc., Waltham, Mass., 2002—, chair, 2004-06; bd. visitors Rockefeller Ctr. of Pub. Policy, Dartmouth Coll., 2003—, chair, 2004—. Keasbey Found. fellow, Cambridge U., 1964-66; George M. Humphrey fellow in law econ. policy, U. Mich. Law Sch., Ann Arbor, 1969-70. Mem.: Phi Beta Kappa. E-mail: cschram1@aol.com.

SCHRAMM, BERNARD CHARLES, JR., retired advertising agency executive; b. Balt., Jan. 23, 1928; s. Bernard C. and Juliet Marie (Barranger) Schramm; m. Florence Mae Fangman, 1950; children: Stephanie Schramm McDaniel, Carol Schramm Molander, Bernard Charles III, Claudia Schramm Smith. Grad., Balt. Poly. Inst., 1946. Prodn. mgr. Van Sant, Dugdale & Co., Balt., 1946-52; media dir. AWL Advt., Balt., 1952-55; dir. prodn. Henry J. Kaufman Assocs., Washington, 1955-58; exec. v.p. Avalon Hill Co., Balt., 1958-64; v.p. Cargill, Wilson & Acree Advt., Richmond, Va., 1964-68; pres. William Cook Advt. Inc., Jacksonville, Fla., 1968-89, chmn. bd., 1989-97; ret., 1997. Chmn. Otis F. Smith Found., 1991—97. Mem. exec. com., v.p. United Way N.E. Fla., 1982-87, bd. dirs., 1982-93; bd. dirs. N.E. Fla. chpt. ARC, 1976-89, chmn., 1980-81; bd. dirs. Fla. C.C. Found., 1976-89. Mem.: Am. Assn. Advt. Agys. (chmn. Fla. coun. 1984—85, So. Region Bd. of Govs. 1988—92, chmn. 1989, nat. bd. dirs., agy. mgmt. com. 1989—92), Jacksonville Area C. of C., Rotary Club. Republican. Roman Catholic. Avocations: golf, reading, spectator sports, hunting.

SCHRAMM, DARRELL G.H., literature and language professor; b. Hazen, ND, Jan. 25, 1943; s. Helmuth and Alma Magdalena Schramm; life ptnr. Albert La Spina. MFA, U. San Francisco, Calif., 1989. Cert. master gardener UC Davis & Solano, 2007. Tchr. Stuart Hall, San Francisco, 1978—89; prof. U. San Francisco, 1990—. Contbr. articles to profl. jours. Hort. cons. Master Gardener Program, Fairfield, Calif., 2007—08. Avocations: writing, gardening, reading, dance. Office: Univ San Francisco 2130 Fulton St San Francisco CA 94117 Business E-Mail: schrammd@usfca.edu.

SCHRAMM, PAUL HOWARD, retired lawyer; b. St. Louis, Oct. 6, 1933; s. Benjamin Jacob and Frieda Sylvia (Goruch) Schramm; m. Sue-Ann Batson; children: Scott Lyon(dec.), Dean Andrew, Thomas Edward(dec.), Jeremy Arthur Savran. AB, U. Mo., 1955, JD, 1958. Bar: Mo. 1958, US Dist. Ct. (ea. dist.) Mo. 1963, US Dist. Ct. (we. dist.) Mo. 2003, US Ct. Appeals (8th cir.) 1967, US Tax Ct. 1970, US Supreme Ct. 1972, US Dist. Ct. (ea. dist.) Wis., 1988. Ptnr. Schramm & Schramm, St. Louis, 1959-61, Schramm & Morganstern, St. Louis, 1970-76, Schramm, Pines & Marshall, St. Louis, 1977-79, Schramm, Newman, Pines & Freyman, St. Louis, 1979-82, Schramm, Pines & Spewak, St. Louis, 1983-85, Schramm & Pines, LLC, St. Louis, 1985-2000, Edwards, Singer, Schramm, Watkins, Spoeneman & Waltrip, LLP, St. Louis, 2000—03, Edwards, Schramm, Watkins, Spoeneman, Waltrip & Beilenson, LLP, St. Louis, 2003—05, Edwards Schramm Young & Beilenson, LLP, 2006—07; of counsel Spoeneman, Watkins Waltrip & Harvell, LLP, St. Louis, 2007—09. Pros. atty. City of Ellisville, Mo., 1973-77; judge Ellisville mcpl. div. St. Louis County Cir. Ct., 1977-83; teaching faculty trial advocacy Harvard Law Sch., 1991. Mem. Bar Assn. Met. St. Louis (exec. com. 1976-77, chmn. county sect. 1976-77), St. Louis County Bar Assn. (chmn. lawyers reference service 1971, cir. ct. jud. com. 1970), M-H Bar Register Preeminent Lawyers, Phi Delta Phi. Avocations: music, sports, reading. Home: 1756 Pineberry Ct Saint Louis MO 63146-4254 Office Phone: 314-862-1110. Office Fax: 314-862-1105. Business E-Mail: pschramm@swwhlaw.com.

SCHRAMM, VERN L., biochemist, educator; B, SD State Coll., Brookings; M in Nutrition, Harvard U., Cambridge, Mass.; PhD, Australian Nat. U., Canberra. Postdoctoral rsch. assoc. NASA Ames Rsch. Ctr., Moffett Field, Calif.; mem. faculty Temple U. Sch. Medicine, Phila.; prof. Albert Einstein Coll. Medicine of Yeshiva U., Bronx, NY, 1987—, chair biochemistry dept., 1987—95, Ruth Merns chair dept. biochemistry, 1995—. Contbr. articles to profl. jours. Recipient George A. Sowell award for Excellence in Tchg., Temple U. Sch. Medicine, Rudi Lemberg award, Australian Acad. Sci., Repligen award, Am. Chem. Soc. (Biol. Chemistry Divsn.), 2006. Fellow: AAAS; mem.: NAS. Office: Albert Einstein Coll Medicine Jack and Pearl Resnick Campus 1300 Morris Park Ave Forchheimer Bldg Rm 316 Bronx NY 10461 Office Phone: 718-430-2813. Office Fax: 718-430-8565. E-mail: vern@aecom.yu.edu.

SCHRAND, RICHARD HENRY, SR., broadcast executive, advertising bureau owner, educator; b. Cin., Nov. 1, 1957; s. Edward August and Jane Marie (Scheib) S.; m. Deborah Fortner, 1979 (div. 1985); 1 child, Cynthia Lanette; m. Sharon Lynn Lassandro, Dec. 24, 1986; children: Courtney Lynne, Richard Jr., Brandon Ian. Student, Ohio State U., 1975-76, No. Ky. U., 1976-77. Intern Sta. WCPO-TV, Cin., 1971-75; producer Sta. WKRC-TV, Cin., 1975-79; pub. affairs dir., reporter, anchor Sta. WCSC-TV, Charleston, SC, 1979-83; actor Phila. Experiment, LA, 1984; asst. promotion dir. Sta. WLWT-TV, Cin., 1983-86; spl. projects coord. Sta. KXAS-TV, Dallas/Ft. Worth, 1986-87; mgr. media svcs. NBC TV Network, Burbank, Calif., 1987-89; pres. Cyn-Court Enterprises, Burbank, 1989-91; mktg. dir. Sta. WPTA-TV, Ft. Wayne, Ind., 1991-92; v.p., gen. mgr. Branson (Mo.) Broadcasting Corp., 1992-95; dir. spl. projects/nat. media, graphics and advt. creator Jim Owens & Assocs., 1995-98; gen. mgr. Jim Owens Radio, Inc., Nashville, 1995-98; pres. GRFX ByDesign, Nashville, 1996—2004, Broadsword Prod., 2002—; v.p. Komodo Studios, LA, 1999-2000; instr. computer graphics and web design Nossi Coll. Art, Nashville, 2001—, chmn. Dept. Computer Graphics, 2001—, mem. adv. bd., 2001—; co-founder Orion Agy., 2008; owner, web developer Beyondbasics.net. Instr., spkr. Graphic Design Tour, 2000—; computer design Nossi Coll. Art, 2001—, edu. bd., 2002—, adv. bd., 2003—, instr. graphic art and design, 2004—; demonstrator 3D software Siggraph, MacWorld, 2001—. Author: Canoma Visual Insight 2000, 3D Creature Workshop vol. 2, 2000, Macromedia Web Design Handbook, 2000, Adobe Golive 5F/X & Design, 2000, Adobe Live Motion Visual Jumpstart, 2000, Adobe Photoshop 6 Visual Jumpstart, 2000, Poser 4 Pro Pack F/X & Design, 2001, Final Cut Pro 3: The Complete Reference, 2002, Vue 6 Revealed, 2006, Vue 7: Beyond The Basics; contbr.: Pixels: 3D Book, 1999, Mastering Pixels: 3D, 2001; webmaster Crook & Chase Theater, Mid. Tenn. LightWave Users Group, Nossi Coll. Art, Games Plus, Handshake Productions, Elegant Diamonds. Bd. dirs. Project Graduation, Dallas/Ft. Worth, 1986-87; mem. Muscular Dystrophy Assn., Charleston, 1980-83; publicist Housing Now, L.A., 1988. Recipient Regional Emmy award NATAS, 1975, award Broadcast Promotion and Mktg. Exec., Seattle, 1992. Avocations: guitar, writing, singing, golf. Office Phone: 615-686-3594. Business E-Mail: rschrand@broadswordproductions.com, rschrand@orion-agency.com. E-mail: rschrand@beyondbasics.net.

SCHRAUZER, GERHARD NORBERT, science educator, researcher; m. Carol Ann Phipps, June 30, 1957; children: Richard Daniel, Michael Edgar. PhD with summa cum laude, U. Munich, 1957, Dr. rer. nat. Cert. in nutrition specialist Am. Coll. Nutrition, 1998. Prof. emeritus U. Calif., La Jolla, San Diego, 1967—; prof. chemistry U. Munich. Dir. Biol. Trace Element Rsch. Inst., Chula Vista, Calif. Recipient Sir Frank Macfarlane Burnet Commemorative award, 1994. Achievements include first to cancer prevention research, nitrogen fixation, vitamin B12 research, coordination chemistry discoveries. Office: Biol Trace Element Research Inst 2400 Boswell Rd Ste 200 Chula Vista CA 91914-3518 Business E-Mail: gschrauzer@ucsd.edu.

SCHREADLEY, RICHARD LEE, newswriter, retired editor; b. Harrisburg, Pa., Jan. 3, 1931; s. Harry Leroy and Flora Rebecca (McQuilken) S.; m. Doris Arlene Sheaffer, Dec. 18, 1952; 1 child, Rhys Leroy. BA, Dickinson Coll., 1952; MA, Tufts U., 1968, MAL.D., 1969, PhD, 1972. Reporter The News and Courier, Charleston, SC, 1975; asso. editor The Evening Post, Charleston, 1975-76, editorial page editor, 1976-77, editor, 1977-81; exec. editor The Evening Post and The News and Courier, 1981-88; assoc. editor and sr. writer mil. and polit. affairs The News and Courier, 1989. Author: From the Rivers to the Sea, The United States Navy in Vietnam, 1992, Valor and Virtue, The Washington Light Infantry in Peace and in War, 1996. Chmn. Fgn. Affairs Forum of Charleston, 1987-88, mem. steering com., 1989. Served to comdr. USN, 1949-52, 56-73. Mem. Navy League, Ret. Officer Assn., Washington Light Infantry, German Friendly Soc. Charleston, Army-Navy Club of Washington, Country Club of Charleston. Home: 812 Clearview Dr Charleston SC 29412-4511 Personal E-mail: rlschrea@bellsouth.net.

SCHRECKER, JOHN, historian, educator; b. Rumburk, Czech Republic, Aug. 22, 1937; s. Karl Steiner and Marian Schrecker-Heller, Franz Schrecker (Stepfather); m. Ellen Wolf, Feb. 18, 1962 (div.); m. Janet Barry, May 11, 1992; children: Michael Franz, Daniel Edwin. BA, U. Pa., 1958; MA, Harvard U., Cambridge, Mass., 1959; PhD, Harvard U., 1968. Asst. prof. of history Princeton U., NJ, 1965—71; prof. of history Brandeis U., Waltham, Mass., 1971—. Assoc. in rsch. Fairbank Ctr. for East Asian Rsch., Harvard U., Cambridge, 1971—. Author: (book) Imperialism and Chinese Nationalism, 1971, The Chinese Revolution in Historical Perspective, 1991, 2nd rev. edit., 2004; author: (with Ellen Schrecker) Mrs. Chiang's Szechwan Cookbook, 1976; editor (with Paul Cohen): Reform in Nineteenth-Century China, 1976. Fellow Fulbright, Social Sci. Rsch. Coun., NAS. Mem.: Am. Hist. Assn., Assn. for Asian Studies, Phi Beta Kappa. Avocation: classical piano. Office: History Dept MS 036 Brandeis Univ Waltham MA 02454 Office Fax: 718-736-2273. Business E-Mail: schrecker@brandeis.edu.

SCHRECKINGER, SY EDWARD, advertising executive, consultant; b. Bklyn., Jan. 10, 1937; s. Robert and Bessie (Gable) S.; m. Linda Fiarman, Mar. 4, 1962; children: Jamie Fran, Jon Gary. B.F.A., Pratt Inst., 1958. Art dir. Sudler and Hennesey, NYC, 1958-61; sr. art dir. Marschalk Co., NYC, 1961-63; group supr. Grey Advt., NYC, 1963-66; v.p., assoc. creative dir. Hicks & Greist, NYC, 1966-69; sr. v.p., assoc. creative dir. Young & Rubicam Inc., NYC, 1969-88; advt. and mktg. cons. Oceanside, NY, 1988—2008; advt.-mktg. dir. Magnificent Muffin Corp., Farmingdale, NY, 1995—. Recipient Lion Venice Internat. Film Festival, 1972, Andy Ad Club, N.Y., 1965, 86, award Internat. Bus. Assn., Best award Hollywood Radio & TV Soc., 1971, Clio Am. TV Comml. Festival, 1967, 72, 82, 85, Effy, 1985. Jewish. Office Phone: 516-536-4154.

SCHREIBER, ALAN HICKMAN, lawyer; b. Muncie, Ind., Apr. 4, 1944; s. Ephriam and Clarrisa (Hickman) S.; m. Phyllis Jean Chamberlain, Dec. 22, 1972; children: Jennifer Aline, Brett Justin. Student, DePauw U., 1962-64; BS in Bus., Ind. U., 1966, JD, 1969. Bar: Fla. 1971, U.S. Dist. Ct. (so. dist.) Fla. Asst. State Atty.'s Office, Ft. Lauderdale, Fla., 1971-76; pub. defender 17th Jud. Cir., Ft. Lauderdale, 1976—. Cons. Fla. Bar News on Criminal Law, 1982; lobbyist for indigent funding, Fla., 1980—; apptd. to Supreme Ct. Com. on Racial and Ethic Bias; co-chair Chiles-MacKay task force on criminal justice. Contbr. articles to profl. jours. Mem. Dem. Exec. Com., Ft. Lauderdale, 1980; mem. Plantation Dem. Club, 1983; campaign chmn. Goldstein for Atty. Gen. Fla., 1982. Named Young Dem. of Yr., Broward County Young Dems., 1980; Man of Yr., Jewish War Vets., 1982; recipient B'nai B'rith Pub. Servant award, 1990, Dem. of Yr. award 2000, Harry Galkin Meml. award 2002. Mem. Fla. Bar Assn., Broward County Bar Assn., ABA, Nat. Legal Aid Defenders Assn., Phi Alpha Delta. Business E-Mail: aschveiber2@ausdivv.com, aschreiber2@austin.rr.com.

SCHREIBER, BERTRAM MANUEL, mathematics professor; b. Seattle, Nov. 4, 1940; s. Isador and Amy (Hurwitz) S.; m. Rita Ruth Stusser, June 30, 1963; children: Susannah M. Schreiber Bechhofer, Deborah H. Schreiber Shapiro, Abraham D., Elisabeth T. Schreiber. BA, Yeshiva U., 1962; MS, U. Wash., 1966, PhD, 1968. Asst. prof. Wayne State U., Detroit, 1968-71, assoc. prof., 1971-78, prof., 1978—, chair dept. math., 1987-90. Vis. prof. Hebrew U., Jerusalem, 1975, 2000, 07, Mich. State U., East Lansing, 1982-83, Nat. U. Singapore, 1992, U. NSW, Sydney, 1992, Indian Statis. Inst., New Delhi and Bangalore, 1993, Tata Inst. Fund Res., Bombay, 1993, Bar Ilan U., Ramat Gan, Isreal, 1993, 2007, Tel Aviv U., 1993, U. Utrecht, The Netherlands, 1993, U. Wroclaw, Poland, 1993, 2006, U. Paris VII, 1999, U. Granada, Spain, 1999-2000, U. Wash., Seattle, 2000, Ecole Poly. Féd. Lausanne, Switzerland, 2006, U. Vienna, 2007, U. Munich, 2007. Contbr. articles to profl. jours. NSF grantee, 1968-87; Sci. and Engring. Rsch. Coun. Gt. Britain fellow U. Edinburgh, Scotland, 1976. Mem. Am. Math. Soc., Math. Assn. Am., Israel Math. Union, Edinburgh Math. Soc. Achievements include research in the fields of harmonic analysis, topological groups, and probability theory. Office: Wayne State U Dept Math Detroit MI 48202 Home Phone: 248-827-1199; Office Phone: 313-577-8838. Business E-Mail: bschreiber@wayne.edu.

SCHREIBER, BRIAN T., insurance company executive; BA, NYU; MBA, Columbia U. Cons. Booz Allen and Hamilton; investment banker Fin. Institutions Group Lehman Brothers; fin. analyst Bass Brothers, Forth Worth, Tex.; portfolio mgr. AIG Global Investment Group Am. Internat. Group, Inc. (AIG), NYC, 1997, mng. dir. Corp. Acquisitions and Investments Group, v.p. strategic planning, 2002—03, sr. v.p. strategic planning, 2003—. Office: Am Internat Group Inc (AIG) 70 Pine St New York NY 10270*

SCHREIBER, CLARE ADEL, journalist; b. Chgo., Feb. 22, 1914; d. Otto Herman Mentz and Martha Toll; m. William I. Schreiber, June 18, 1934 (dec. Jan. 1998); children: William M., James L., Ralph W.(dec.), Stephen T. BS in Journalism, U. Ill., 1935; LHD, Coll. of Wooster, 1985. Freelance writer Fairfield Iowa Ledger, 1937, The Daily Record, Wooster, Ohio, 1956; dir. Coll. of Wooster Nursery Sch., 1956—85; family life educator Cmty. Action Wayne Medina, 1985—. Exec. bd. Wayne Assn. of the Edn. of Young Children, Wooster, Ohio, 1983—. Author, editor (book) Green Grow the Children, 1984; contbr. articles. Mem. human rights group Am. Assn. for Univ. Women, Wooster, Ohio; mem. League of Women Voters, Nat. Assn. for Edn. of Young Children, Philos. Edn. Orgn. Internat. Recipient Child Advocate of the Yr., Wayne County Children's Services, 2002; fellow Paul Harris fellow, Rotary Internat., 2004. Mem.: Theta Phi Alpha, Kappa Tau Alpha. Democrat. Presbyn. Home: 1471 Cleveland Rd Wooster OH 44691 Office: Cmty Action Wayne/Medina 2375 Benden Dr Wooster OH 44691

SCHREIBER, EILEEN SHER, artist; b. Denver, 1925; d. Michael Herschel and Sarah Deborah (Tannenbaum) Sher; m. Jonas Schreiber, Mar. 27, 1945; children: Jeffrey, Barbara, Michael. Student, U. Utah, 1942-45, NYU, 1966-68, Montclair State Coll., NJ, 1975-79; also pvt. art study. Exhibited Morris Mus. Arts and Scis., Morristown, NJ, 1965-73, NJ State Mus., 1969, Lever House, NYC, 1971, Paramus Mus., 1973, NJ, Newark Mus., 1978, 1991-92, Am. Water Color Soc., Audubon Artists, N.A.D. Gallery, NYC, Pallazzo Vecchio Florence, Italy, Art Expo 1987, 1988, India Mus., 1994, 95, Athens (Greece) Mus., 1996, 97, Gaelin Gallery, Whippany, NJ, 2004, Municipal Bldg. of West Orange, NJ; represented in permanent collections Tex. A&M U., Telesoft Inc., Phoenix, State of NJ, Morris Mus., Seton Hall U., Bloomfield Coll., NJ, Barclay Bank of Eng., NJ, Somerset Coll., NYU, Morris County State Coll., Newark, Ind. Cmty. Bank, Consulting IBM, Am. Tel. Co., RCA, Johnson & Johnson, Champion Internat. Paper Co., Sony, Mitsubishi, Celanese Co., Squibb Corp., Nabisco, Nat. Bank Phila., Data Control, Ind. Cmty. Bank, Sperry Univac, Ga. Pacific Co., Pub. Svc. Co. NJ, Long Beach Island, NJ, Town Hall Libr., West Orange, NJ, Soverign Bank, 2007, Noyes Mus. NGrey, 2009others; also pvt. collections. Recipient awards N.J. Watercolor Soc., 1969, 72, 1st award in watercolor Hunterdon Art Ctr., 1972, Best in Show award Short Hills State Show, 1976, Tri-State Purchase award Somerset Coll., 1977, Art Expo, N.Y.C., 1987, 88, Lifetime Achievement & Membership award, Nat. Assn. Women, 2009, numerous others. Mem. Nat. Assn. Women Artists (chmn. watercolor jury, Collage award 1983, Marian Halpren Meml. award 1995), Nat., N.Y. Artists Equity, Printmaker Coun. Visual Artists (1st award in printmaking 1996), Women Visual Artists (Fla.). Home and Office: 10 Jackson Dr Egg Harbor Township NJ 08234 Office Phone: 609-927-0440. Personal E-mail: artess25@aol.com.

SCHREIBER, HORST, information technology manager; Diploma in Physics, Friedrich Alexander U., Erlangen, Germany, 1993, Dr. rer. nat. in Exptl. Physics, 1998. Sr. mem. tech. staff Corning Tropel Corp., Fairport, NY, 1998—2005, tech. mgr., 2005—.

SCHREIBER, HOWARD E., lawyer; b. Balt., May 18, 1959; BA in Polit. Sci., Dickinson Coll., 1981; JD with honors, Duke U., 1984. Bar: Tex. 1984. Shareholder Jenkens & Gilchrist, P.C., Dallas, 1993—, firm leader real estate practice group. Mem.: ABA, Am. Coll. Mortgage Attorneys, Dallas Bar Assn., Tex. State Bar Assn. Office: Hunton & Williams PC Ste 3200 1445 Ross Ave Dallas TX 75202-2799 Office Phone: 214-855-4370. Office Fax: 214-855-4300. Business E-Mail: hschreiber@jenkens.com.

SCHREIBER, JOHN T., lawyer; b. NYC, Mar. 30, 1960; s. Toby Schreiber and Morley Ann (Perrish) Clark; children: Zoe Cassandra Bloch Schreiber, Alana Nichole Perrish Schreiber. BA Politics, Brandeis U., 1982; JD, Santa Clara U., 1986. Bar: Calif. 1987(cert. specialist appellate law); U.S. Dist. Ct. (no. dist.) Calif. 1987; U.S. Dist. Ct. (ea. dist.) Calif. 1990; U.S. Ct. Appeals (9th cir.) 1989, U.S. Supreme Ct. 1998. Assoc. Law Offices of Wm. D. McHugh, San Jose, Calif., 1987-88, Hallgrimson, McNichols, McCann & Inderbitzen, Pleasanton, Calif., 1989-92; pvt. practice Walnut Creek, Calif., 1993—. Bd. dirs. East Bay Depot for Creative Re-use, Oakland. Field coord. Cen. Contra Costa County, Tom Bradley Campaign for Govs., Concord, Calif., 1982, Clinton-Gore Campaign, Walnut Creek, Calif., 1992; mem. Ask-A-Lawyer Program Contra Costa Legal Svcs. Found., Richmond, Calif., 1992-96; co-chair Clinton-Gore Contra Costa County, 1996. Mem. ABA, Contra Costa Bar Assn. (program dir. appellate sect. 1993-95, 2000—, pres. appellate sect. 1995-96, MCLE com. 1995—), Santa Clara Bar Assn., Am. Israeli Pub. Affairs Com. Avocations: reading, golf, softball, movies, exercising. Office: 2000 Ridgewood Rd Alamo CA 94507-1044

SCHREIBER, KAI MARKUS, neuroscientist; b. Aalen, Baden-Württemberg, Germany, Jan. 21, 1972; s. Manfred and Helga Schreiber; m. Caroline Härdter, June 9, 2001. Diploma in Phys., Eberhard-Karls-U., Tübingen, Germany, 1999, degree, 1999; PhD, U. Toronto, 2003. Postdoc. rschr. U. Calif., Berkeley, 2003—07; rsch. assoc. Rutgers U., Newark, 2007—. Editor: (radio show) Eure Tagesordnung. Candidate office lord mayor Stammtisch Unser Huhn, Tübingen, Baden-Württemberg. Recipient Grimme Online award, 2006; Emmy-Noether fellowship, Deutsche Forschungsgemeinschaft, 2003.

SCHREIBER, KURT GILBERT, lawyer; b. Milw., Aug. 22, 1946; s. Raymond R. and Mildred L. (Kleist) S.; m. Nelda Beth Van Buren, May 3, 1974; children: Katharine Anne, Matthew Edward. AB in Econs., Cornell U., 1968; JD, U. Mich., 1971; M in Theol. Studies, Vanderbilt U., 2003. Bar: Wis. 1971, Tex. 1979, Tenn. 1997. Internat. atty. Tenneco Internat. Holdings Co., London, 1974-78; atty. Tenneco Inc., Houston, 1978-80; 2d v.p., asst. gen. counsel Am. Gen. Corp., Houston, 1980-83, v.p., gen. counsel, 1983-84, sr. v.p., gen. counsel, 1984-93, sr. v.p., corp. sec., 1993-94; pvt. practice Houston, 1994-96; exec. v.p., gen. counsel Direct Gen. Corp., Nashville, 1996-98, pres., 1998—2001. Bd. dir. Cumberland Trust and Investment Co., Urban Housing Solutions. Fellow Tex. Bar Found.; mem. ABA, Wis. Bar Assn., Tex. Bar Assn., Tenn. Bar Assn. Home: 401 Bowline Ave #16 Nashville TN 37205

SCHREIBER, LIEV (ISAAC LIEV SCHREIBER), actor; b. San Francisco, Oct. 4, 1967; 2 children (with Naomi Watts) Alexander Pete Schreiber, Samuel Kai Schreiber Student, Bklyn. Tech., Royal Acad. Dramatic Arts, London; BA, Hampshire Coll., 1988; MFA, Yale Sch. Drama, 1992. Actor: (Broadway plays) In the Summer House, 1993, Betrayal, 2000—01, Glengarry Glen Ross, 2005 (Tony award for best performance by a featured actor in a play, 2005), Talk Radio, 2007 (Drama League awardd disting. performance, 2007); (films) Mixed Nuts, 1994, Denise Calls Up, 1995, Mad Love, 1995, Party Girl, 1995, Walking and Talking, 1996, The Daytrippers, 1996, Big Night, 1996, Ransom, 1996, Scream, 1996, His and Hers, 1997, Baggage, 1997, Scream 2, 1997, Phantoms, 1998, Sphere, 1998, Twilight, 1998, (voice) Desert Blue, 1998, A Walk on the Moon, 1999, Jacob the Liar, 1999, The Hurricane, 1999, Spring Forward, 1999, Hamlet, 2000, Scream 3, 2000, Dial 9 for Love, 2001, Kate & Leopold, 2001, The Sum of All Fears, 2002, Spinning Boris, 2003, The Manchurian Candidate, 2004, The Omen, 2006, The Painted Veil, 2006, The Ten, 2007, Love in the Time of Cholera, 2007, Chicago, 2008, Defiance, 2008, X-Men Origins: Wolverine, 2009; (TV films) Janek: The Silent Betrayal, 1994, The Sunshine Boys, 1995, Buffalo Girls, 1995, Since You've Been Gone, 1998, RKO 281, 1999, Young Dr. Freud, 2002, Hitler: The Rise of Evil, 2003, Lackawanna Blues, 2005, (voice only) Oil Storm, 2005,: (TV series) CSI: Crime Scene Investigation, 2006; dir.: (films) Everything is Illuminated, 2003. Avocations: basketball, fencing, bicycling. Office: c/o ID Pub Rels 8409 Santa Monica Blvd West Hollywood CA 90069

SCHREIBER, MARK TRAUDT, psychiatrist; b. Denver, Oct. 6, 1947; s. Charles William and Sophie Emily Schreiber; m. Constance Anne Rabe, Nov. 27, 1976; children: Vanessa, Laura, Charles, Anne, John. BS, U. Nebr., Lincoln, 1970; MD, Washington U., St. Louis, Mo., 1975. Diplomate Am. Bd. Psychiatry and Neurology, 1980, Am. Bd. Addictionology, 1986. Resident Barnes Hosp. Washington U., St. Louis, 1975—78; psychiatrist Hearst, Fischer & Schreiber, Virginia Beach, Va., 1978—84, Crossroads Clin., Virginia Beach, 1984—89, Atlantic Psychiatric, Virginia Beach, 1989—. Med. dir. Serenity Lodge, Chesapeake, Va., 1984—91; assoc. med. dir. Va. Beach Psychiat. Ctr., 1991—. Contbr. articles to profl. jours. Dist. coun. bd. mem. & v.p. Boys Scout America, 2008; elder Bayside Presbyn. Ch., Va. Beach, 1980—, chmn. com.; 2008—; chmn. internat. partnership com. Presbytery Ea. Va., Portsmouth, 1982—. Named Am.'s Top Psychiatrists, Consumers' Rsch. Coun. Am. Fellow: Am. Soc. Addiction Medicine (regional chmn. 2000—04), Am. Psychiat. Assn. (Disting. fellow 2005). Avocations: ballroom dancing, skiing, reading, camping, travel. Office: Atlantic Psychiatric 780 Lipshua Pkwy Ste 450 Virginia Beach VA 23452 Office Phone: 757-468-0550.

SCHREIBER, PABLO, actor; b. Apr. 26, 1978; s. Tell Schreiber. Actor: (Broadway plays) Awake and Sing!, 2006, Desire Under the Elms, 2009; (plays) Manuscript, 2005, Mr. Marmalade, 2005, Dying City, 2007, Reasons to Be Pretty, 2008 (Drama Desk award for Outstanding Featured Actor, 2009); (films) Bubble Boy, 2001, The Mudge Boy, 2003, The Manchurian Candidate, 2004, Invitation to a Suicide, 2004, Lords of Dogtown, 2005, Jimmy Blue, 2006, Quid Pro Quo, 2008, Vicky Cristina Barcelona, 2008, Nights in Rodanthe, 2008; (TV films) A Painted House, 2003, Into the Fire, 2005; (TV series) The Wire, 2003—08, Dirt, 2008, Army Wives, 2008. Office: Widescreen Mgmt 270 Lafayette St Ste 402 New York NY 10012*

SCHREIBER, PAUL SOLOMON, lawyer; b. Krakow, Poland, Mar. 29, 1941; came to U.S., 1949; s. John and Betty (Silber) S.; m. Joan A. Perlmutter, Mar. 20, 1971; children: Douglas Arun, Stacey Lauren. BS, CCNY, 1963; LLB, NYU, 1966, LLM, 1967; postgrad., U. Paris, 1967-68. Bar: N.Y. 1966. Assoc. Marshal, Bratter, Greene, Allison & Tucker, NYC, 1969-76, ptnr., 1976-82, Kramer, Levin, Naftalis, Nessen, Kamin & Frankel, NYC, 1982-94, Shearman & Sterling LLP, NYC, 1994—. Bd. dirs. Harbor Trust Co., Hoboken, N.J., 1985-92. Editor: Annual Survey Am. Law; co-author articles, papers and revs. Trustee Park Ave. Synagogue, N.Y.C., 1985—, pres., 1998-2003, hon. pres., 2003—; bd. dirs. Am. Friends of the Rambam Med. Ctr., N.Y.C., 1989-99, N.Y.C. chpt. Nat. Multiple Sclerosis Soc., 1991—2008, Sch. for Strings, 1994-96, Jr. Achievement of N.Y., 2005—; bd. overseers Rabbinical Sch. Jewish Theol. Sem., 1995-96. Arthur Garfield Hayes fellow; Ford Found. fellow. Democrat. Jewish. Office Phone: 212-848-8920. E-mail: pschreiber@shearman.com.

SCHREIBER, SALLY ANN, lawyer; b. El Paso, Tex., July 23, 1951; d. Warren Thomas and Joyce (Honey) S.; children: Amanda Honey, Ryan Thorp Luther. BBA, U. N.Mex., 1973; JD, Stanford U., 1976. Bar: Calif. 1976, Tex. 1977. Assoc. Johnson & Swanson, Dallas, 1976-81, ptnr., 1981-89; mem. firm Johnson & Gibbs, P.C., Dallas, 1989-93; of counsel Cox & Smith, Inc., Dallas, 1993-94; shareholder Munsch Hardt Kopf & Harr, P.C., Dallas, 1994—. Spkr. in field. Editor Stanford U. Law Rev., 1975-76; co-author paper Internat. Bar Assn., 1986. Bd. dirs. The Lyric Opera of Dallas, 1982-86; law sch. bd. vis. Stanford (Calif.) U., 1981-84, 2004-06; dir. Tex. Bus. Law Found., 1989—, treas. 1994-96, sec. 1996-98. Mem.: ABA, Dallas Bar Assn., Calif. Bar Assn., Tex. Bar Assn. (corp. law com. 1981—, vice-chair corp. law com. 1993—97, chair corp. law com. 1997—2001, partnership law com. 1985—, ltd. liability co. com. 1992—, opinion com. 1989—98, codification com. 1997—, bus. law sect. coun. 1996—2007, vice chmn. 2004—05, chair 2005—06). Home: 2737 Purdue Ave Dallas TX 75225-7910 Office: Munsch Hardt Kopf & Harr PC 500 N Akard St Ste 3800 Dallas TX 75201 Office Phone: 214-855-7598. Business E-Mail: sschreiber@munsch.com.

SCHREIBER, SARA, legislative staff member; d. Diane Denish. Comm. dir. to Rep. Harry Teague US House of Reps., Washington, 2008—. Democrat. Office: 1007 Longworth House Office Bldg Washington DC 20515 Office Phone: 202-225-2365. Office Fax: 202-225-9599. Business E-Mail: sara.schreiber@mail.house.gov.*

SCHREIBER, SVETLANA J., lawyer; d. Morris and Clara Schreiber; m. Allan B. Wolf (div.); children: Micel E., Orin A.; m. Billie Lawless, Dec. 29, 1994. BA, Rutgers U., NJ, 1973; MA, Kent State U., Ohio, 1980; JD, Cleve. Marshall Law Sch., 1982. Bar: Ohio 1982, NY 2002, US Dist. Ct. (no. dist.) Ohio 1982, US Ct. Appeals (6th cir.) 2002, US Supreme Ct. 1987. Atty. Svetlana Schreiber & Assocs. Co. LPA, Cleve., 1982—. Trustee bd. Cleve. Theatre, 1986—2002. Mem.: Aila-Am. Immigration Lawyers Assn., Congress Romanian Ams. (trustee bd. 2002—). Democrat. Avocations: sailing, travel, hiking, reading, writing. Office: Svetlana Schreiber & Assoc Co LPA 1370 Ontario St Ste 1620 Cleveland OH 44113

SCHREIBER HUGHES, LISA BOBBIE, United States Ambassador to Suriname; BA, JD, Rutgers U., NJ; MS in Nat. Security Strategy, Nat. Def. U. Nat. War Coll., Washington, 1997. Bar: NJ, Pa., DC. Econ officer, US fgn. svc. US Dept. State, Quito, Ecuador, 1985—86, consular officer, 1986—87, post mgmt. officer, assignments officer, office the exec. dir., bur. inter-Am. affairs, 1988—90, gen. svc. officer Havana, Cuba, 1990—92, chief agr. devel. divsn., bur. internat. orgn. affairs Rome, 1994—96, prin. officer, consul gen. Calgary, Canada, 1997—2000, dep. chief of mission Paramaribo, Suriname, 2000—02, dir. office Andean affairs, 2004—05, sr. advisor regionalization and right-sizing, bur. we. hemisphere affairs, 2005—06, US amb. to Suriname Paramaribo, 2006—; dir. consular and internat. program White House Homeland Security Coun., 2002—04. Internat. comml. arbitration rschr. Columbia U. Parker Sch. Fgn. and Comparative Law, NYC. Recipient Superior Honor awards, US Dept. State; Capstone fellow, 2006. Office: DOS Amb 3390 Paramaribo Pl Washington DC 20521-3390*

SCHREIDER, LARRY STEPHEN, director, educator; s. Elliot and Rhoda Schreider; m. Sandra DeLoney, Aug. 3, 1980; children: Stephen Alan, David Elliot, Caitlin Paige. BS in Computer Sys., Fla. Atlantic U., Boca Raton, 1974—76; MA in Orgnl. Mgmt., U. Phoenix, 1993—96. Cert. project mgmt. profl. Project Mgmt. Inst., 2006. Adj. instr. Fla. Atlantic U., 1977—78; mgr. application engring. Computer Products, Inc., Pompano Beach, Fla., 1977—86; dist. bus. mgr. Digital Equipment Corp., Huntsville, Ala., 1986—94; dir., program mgr. Computer Scis. Corp., Fairfax, Va., 1994—; sr. faculty mem. U. Phoenix, 2000—. Personal E-mail: larry.schreider@csc.com. Business E-Mail: lschreider@email.phoenix.edu.

SCHREINER, ALBERT WILLIAM, internist, educator; b. Cin., Feb. 15, 1926; s. Albert William and Ruth Mary (Neuer) S.; m. Jean Tellstrom, Dec. 12, 1953; 1 child, David William. BS, U. Cin., 1947, MD, 1949. Diplomate Am. Bd. Internal Medicine, 1958. Clin. investigator VA Hosp., Cin., 1957-59, chief med. svc., 1959-68, dir. dept. internal medicine, 1968-93; dir. resident program internal medicine Christ Hosp., Cin., 1978-87; mem. faculty U. Cin. Coll. Medicine, 1955—, assoc. prof. medicine, 1962-67, prof. internal medicine, 1967-98, emeritus prof. internal medicine, 1998—; attending physician Cin. Gen. Hosp., 1957—95. Cons. to med. dir. Gen. Electric, 1987-96; med. dirs. United Home Care Hospice, 1993-99, United Home Care Agy.; chair, instl. rev. bd. IRB Christ Hosp., 1988-2008, investigator, 2008; subinvestigator Sterling Rsch. Group, 2003-, rschr., 2008. Contbr. articles to profl. jours. Bd. dirs., chmn. health com. Cmty. Action Commn., 1968-71; trustee Drake Meml. Hosp., 1975-78, Leukemia Found. Southwest Ohio, Cancer Control, Am. Cancer Soc., bd. dirs. Hamilton County unit, 1990; bd. dirs., chair profl. affairs com. United Home Care Agy., 1998; bd. dirs. Gamble Inst. Med. Rsch., Cin., 1991-96; chmn. IRB Hilltop Rsch., 2007-. Fellow: ACP; mem.: Am. Soc. Clin. Rsch. Program Dirs. Internal Medicine, Assn. Program Dirs. Internal Medicine, Clin. Soc. Internal Medicine (pres. 1979—80), Ohio Soc. Internal Medicine (trustee 1978, sec.-treas. 1981—85, v.p. 1982—83, pres. 1984—85), Ohio Med. Assn., Am. Fedn. Clin. Rsch., N.Y. Acad. Scis., Am. Cancer Soc. (bd. dirs. Hamilton County unit 1990—92), Am. Leukemia Soc. (med. adv. exec. bd.), Phi Beta Kappa, Sigma Xi. Roman Catholic. Home: Deupree House II 3939 ERIE Ave Apt 3060 Cincinnati OH 45208-1487 Office: Sterling Rsch & Group Ltd 375 Gl enterprise Dr Springdale OH 45246 Office Phone: 513-671-8080. Office Fax: 513-671-8090. Business E-Mail: aschreiner@sterling.research.org.

SCHREINER, JOHN CHRISTIAN, economics consultant, software publisher; b. Los Angeles, Nov. 2, 1933; s. Alexander and Margaret S.; m. Marie Nielsen, June 19, 1967; children: Christian Alexander, Carl Arthur, Elizabeth, Nathan Alexander. BS in Mech. Engring., U. Utah, 1958; MBA, Harvard U., 1960; PhD, UCLA, 1970. Chartered fin. analyst. Design engr. Eimco Corp., Salt Lake City and NYC, 1957-59; credit exec. James Talcott, Inc., NYC and Boston, 1960-65; lectr. mgmt. U. Utah, 1965-66; mem. faculty Grad. Sch. Mgmt., U. Minn., Mpls., 1969-84, chmn. dept. fin. and ins., 1973-74, 76-81; pres. The Sebastian Group, Inc., 1984—. Cons. to corps. and govt. agys. Co-author: Executive Recruiting: How Companies Obtain Management Talent, 1960; contbr. articles to profl. jours. Mem. Fin. Execs. Inst., Fin. Analysts Fedn., Tau Beta Pi, Phi Kappa Phi. Republican. Mem. Ch. Jesus Christ of Latter-day Saints (missionary, Ger. 1953-56). Club: Harvard Bus. Sch. Minn. Office: The Sebastian Group Inc 2040 Douglas Dr Minneapolis MN 55422

SCHREMP, TED W., communications executive; Grad. in Econs. and Bus., U. Pitts.; MBA, Pa. State U. With Hewlett Packard, co-founder Cable, Media and Entertainment orgn.; sr. v.p., gen. mgr. Charter Telephone Charter Comm., Inc., St. Louis, 2005—08, exec. v.p., chief mktg. officer, 2008—. Office: Charter Comm, Inc 12405 Powerscourt Dr Saint Louis MO 63131

SCHRENK, GARY DALE, foundation executive; b. San Jose, Calif., Apr. 29, 1949; s. Robert Shepard and Katherine Mildred (Grant) S.; m. Rhonda Lynn King, Oct. 9, 1981 (div. Jan. 1989); children: Stephen, Kristen, James. BA in Comm., Am. U., 1970; M in Nonprofit Mgmt., Regis U., 2002. TV dir. Sta. WTOP (now WUSA), Washington, 1971-73, Sta. KBTV (now KUSA), Denver, 1973-75; with Denver Area Boy Scouts Am., 1975-80; regional dir. St. Jude Children's Rsch. Hosp., Memphis, 1980-83; dir. devel. Denver Art Mus., 1983-85; asst. dir. devel. The Children's Hosp., Denver, 1985-87; pres. North Colo. Med. Ctr. Found., Greeley, 1987—2007; dir. devel. Nat. Found. Dentistry for the Handicapped, Denver, 2007—. Dir., instr. Fast Start Course, 1985—; pres. Monfort Children's Clinic, Greeley, Colo., 1994—2001. Pres. Vision Together, Weld County, Colo., 1994—95; chmn., founding dir. Weld Citizen Action Network, 1995—98, 2000—02; founding dir. First Steps Weld County, 1993—99; chmn. Weld Cmty. Health Coalition, 1992—98; bd. dirs. North Colo. Health Alliance, 2002—06; chmn. pub. support com. Team Colo. ARC, 1997—2004; regional svc., area 2 public support com. ARC, 2004—06, bd. dirs. Centennial chpt., 2003—08. Recipient Disting. Citizen award Highlanders, Denver, 1974 Mem. Assn. Fundraising Profls. (nat. found. bd. 1998-2003, nat. assembly 1994-98, bd. dirs. Colo. chpt. 1979-2000, 03-, pres. 1984, internat. bd. dirs. 2004-07, Colo. Outstanding Devel. Profl. 2004), Colo. Assn. Nonprofit Orgns. (founding dir. 1987-92), Rotary, Tahosa Alumni Assn. (past pres., past chair). Methodist. Avocation: golf. Office: Nat Found Dentistry Handicapped 1800 15th St Ste 100 Denver CO 80202 Office Phone: 303-534-5360. Business E-Mail: gschrenk@nfdh.org.

SCHRENKO, LINDA C., former school system administrator; b. July 24, 1949; m. Frank Schrenko; 1 child, Katherine. BA in Elem. Edn., Augusta Coll., 1972, EdS in Adminstrn. and Supervision, 1986; MEd in Counseling, Ga. So. U., 1982. Tchr. 7th grade Richmond County (Ga.) Schs., 1972-74; tchr. 5th grade South Columbia (Ga.) Elem., 1974-76, tchr. Title I grades 1-6, 1976-77, tchr. 2nd grade, 1977-81, asst. prin., 1984-86; tchr. gifted program grades K-3 Columbia County Schs., 1981-82; counselor Evans Middle Sch., Columbia County, 1982-84; prin. South Columbia (Ga.) Elem., 1986-90; tchr. gifted program grades K-3 Columbia County Schs., 1981-82; counselor Evans Middle Sch., Columbia County, 1982-84; nat. and internat. edn. cons., 1990-94; supt. schs. Ga. Dept. Edn., Atlanta, 1994—2003. Bd. dirs. Coun. Sch. Performance, Edn. Commn. of States, Ga. Child Care Coun., Ga. Pub. Telecomm. Commn.; lectr. in field. Author: Teaching in the Learner Centered School. Past pres. Ctrl. Savannah Regional Area Humane Soc.; mem. Columbia County Humane Soc.; past pres. Columbia County Fedn. Republican Women; mem. Ga. Republican Found., Women Who

Win.; mem. Kiokee Bapt. Ch., Appling, Ga. Named one of 100 Most Powerful and Influential People in Ga., Ga. Trend Mag., 1995-96. Mem. ASCD, Profl. Assn. Ga. Educators, Ga. Assn. Elem. Sch. Prins., Phi Delta Kappa. Republican.

SCHREPFER, SUSAN R., history professor, director; b. San Francisco, Oct. 3, 1941; d. Robert C. and Rita M. Schrepfer; 1 child, Amy Schrepfer-Tarter. PhD, U. Calif., Riverside, 1971. Prof., history Rutgers U., New Brunswick, NJ, 1974—. Dir. Rutgers Inst. HS Tchrs. Ctr. Hist. Analysis, New Brunswick, 1988—. Author: (book) The Fight to Save The Redwoods: A History of Environmental Reform 1917-1978 (Biennial Book award, 1983), Nature's Altars: Mountains, Gender, and American Environmentalism. Recipient Blegan award, Forest History Soc., 1989; grantee, Nat. Endowment Humanities, 1980—83. Mem.: Soc. Environ. History, Am. Hist. Assn. Office: Rutgers Univ History Dept 16 Sem Pl New Brunswick NJ 08901 Business E-Mail: schrepfe@rci.rutgers.edu.

SCHREYER, CHARA, foundation administrator, art collector; Chmn. Kadima Found., Mill Valley, Calif. Trustee Mus. Modern Art, San Francisco, Contemporary Jewish Mus. Named one of Top 200 Collectors, ARTnews Mag., 2004—08. Avocation: Collector of Modern & Contemporary Art & Photography. Mailing: Kadima Foundation PMB 200 38 Miller Ave Mill Valley CA 94941

SCHREYER, LESLIE JOHN, lawyer; b. NYC, Apr. 11, 1946; s. Oscar and Greta (Loebl) S.; m. Judith Camps, Sept. 25, 1994; 1 child, Gabrielle. BA, Columbia U., 1967; LLB, Yale U., 1970; LLM in Taxation, N.Y.U., 1977. Bar: N.Y. 1971. Assoc. Chadbourne & Parke, NYC, 1970-78, ptnr., 1978-81, 83—; dep. internat. tax counsel US Treasury Dept., 1981-83; gen. counsel GLG Ptnrs. Svcs. Ltd., 2000—07; advisor GLG Ptnrs. Inc., 2007—. Adj. assoc. prof. law NYU, 1990-97; cons. Am. Law Inst., Fed. Income Tax Project on Internat. Aspects of U.S. Income Taxation, 1983-91. Author: (with others) Foreign Tax Credit, 1980; contbr. numerous articles to profl. jours. Trustee Am. Friends of the Victoria and Albert Mus., Inc. Mem. ABA, Internat. Bar Assn., Internat. Fiscal Assn., N.Y. State Bar Assn., Assn. of Bar of City of N.Y., Phi Beta Kappa. Home: 60 E End Ave New York NY 10028-7907 Office: Chadbourne & Parke 30 Rockefeller Plz Fl 31 New York NY 10112-0129 E-mail: lschreyer@chadbourne.com, les@glgpartners.com.

SCHREYER, WILLIAM ALLEN, retired finance company executive; b. Williamsport, Pa., Jan. 13, 1928; s. William L. and Elizabeth (Engel) S.; m. Joan Legg, Oct. 17, 1953; 1 child, DrueAnne Frazier. BA, Pa. State U., 1948. With Merrill Lynch, Inc. and predecessors, NYC, 1948-93; CEO Merrill Lynch & Co., NYC, 1984-92, chmn., 1985-93, chmn. emeritus, 1993—. Trustee, chmn. exec. com. Ctr. for Strategic and Internat. Studies, Pa. State U., 1986—, chmn. bd. trustees, 1993—96. With USAF, 1955—56. Mem. River Club, Links Club, Saturn Club, Springdale Golf Club, Bedens Brook Club, Eldorado Country Club, Georgetown Club, Met. Club, Nassau Club, Bond Club NY, Knights of Malta, Bay Head Yacht Club, Manasquan River Golf Club. Roman Catholic. Office: Merrill Lynch & Co Inc 14 N Harrison St Princeton NJ 08540

SCHRIEFFER, JOHN ROBERT, physics professor, science administrator; b. Oak Park, Ill., May 31, 1931; s. John Henry and Louise (Anderson) Schrieffer; m. Anne Grete Thomsen, Dec. 30, 1960; children: Anne Bolette, Paul Karsten, Anne Regina. BS, MIT, 1953; MS, U. Ill., 1954, PhD, 1957, ScD, 1974; ScD (hon.), Tech. U., Munich, 1968, U. Geneva, 1968, U. Pa., 1973, U. Cin., 1977, U. Tel Aviv, 1987, U. Ala., 1990. NSF postdoctoral fellow U. Birmingham, England, Niels Bohr Inst., Copenhagen, 1957—58; asst. prof. U. Chgo., 1958—59; asst. prof., then assoc. prof. U. Ill., 1959—62; prof. U. Pa., Phila., 1962—79, Mary Amanda Wood prof. physics, 1964—79; Andrew D. White prof. at large Cornell U., 1969—75; prof. U. Calif., Santa Barbara, 1980—91, Chancellor's prof., 1984—91, dir. Inst. for Theoretical Physics, 1984—89; Univ. prof. Fla. State U., Tallahassee, 1992—, Univ. Eminent Scholar prof., 1995—, chief scientist Nat. High Magnetic Field Lab., 1992—2004. Pres.'s com. Nat. Medal of Sci., 1996—98. Author: Theory of Superconductivity, 1964. Recipient Comstock prize, NAS, 1968, Nobel prize for Physics, 1972, John Ericsson medal, Am. Soc. Swedish Engrs., 1976, Alumni Achievement award, U. Ill., 1979, Nat. medal of Sci., 1984; fellow Guggenheim, Copenhagen, 1967, Los Alamos Nat. Lab., Exxon faculty, 1979—89. Fellow: Am. Phys. Soc. (v.p. 1994, pres.-elect 1995, pres. 1996, past pres. 1997, Oliver E. Buckley solid state physics prize 1968); mem.: NAS (coun. 1990—), Acad. Sci. USSR, Royal Danish Acad. Scis. and Letters, Am. Acad. Arts and Scis. Office: Fla State Univ NHMFL 1800 E Paul Dirac Dr Tallahassee FL 32310-3748 Business E-Mail: schrieff@magnet.fsu.edu.*

SCHRIER, ARNOLD, historian, educator; b. NYC, May 30, 1925; s. Samuel and Yetta (Levine) S.; m. Sondra Weinshelbaum, June 12, 1949; children: Susan Lynn, Jay Alan, Linda Lee, Paula Kay. Student, Bethany Coll., W.Va., 1943-44, Ohio Wesleyan U., 1944-45; BS, Northwestern U., 1949, MA, 1950, PhD (Social Sci. Research Council fellow, Univ. fellow), 1956. Asst. prof. history U. Cin., 1956-61, assoc. prof., 1961-66, prof., 1966-95, dir. grad. studies history, 1969-78, Walter C. Langsam prof. modern European history, 1972-95; Walter C. Langsam prof. history emeritus, 1995—. Vis. asst. prof. history Northwestern U., Evanston, Ill., 1960; vis. assoc. prof. history Ind. U., Bloomington, 1965-66; vis. lectr. Russian history Duke U., 1966; disting. vis. prof. US Air Force Acad., 1983-84; dir. NDEA Inst. World History for Secondary Sch. Tchrs., U. Cin., 1965; Am. del. Joint U.S.-USSR Textbook Study Commn., 1989. Author: Ireland and the American Emigration, 1958, reissued, 1970, paperback edit., 1997, The Development of Civilization, 1961-62, Modern European Civilization, 1963, Living World History, 1964, rev., 1993, Twentieth Century World, 1974, History and Life: the World and Its People, 1977, rev., 1993, A Russian Looks at America, 1979, Irish Immigrants in the Land of Canaan, 2003. Pres. Ohio Acad. History, 1973-74, Midwest Slavic Conf., 1980. Served with USNR, 1943-46, 52-54. Recipient Disting. Svc. award Ohio Acad. History, 1992; Am. Coun. Learned Socs. fgn. area fellow, 1963-64 Mem. World History Assn. (v.p. 1986-88, pres. 1988-90). Home: 10 Diplomat Dr Cincinnati OH 45215-2073 Personal E-mail: arnsond@aol.com.

SCHRIER, ROBERT WILLIAM, physician, educator; b. Indpls., Feb. 19, 1936; s. Arthur E. and Helen M. Schrier; m. Barbara Lindley, June 14, 1959; children: David, Debbie, Douglas, Derek, Denise. BA, Depauw U., Greencastle, Ind., 1957; DSc (hon.), DePauw U., Greencastle, Ind., 2004; MD, Ind. U., 1962; DSc (hon.), U. Colo., 1996, Silesian Acad. Medicine, Katowice, Poland, 1997. Intern Marion County Hosp., Ind., 1962; resident U. Wash., Seattle, 1963-65; asst. prof. U. Calif. Med. Ctr., San Francisco, 1969—72, assoc. dir. renal divsn., 1971-72, assoc. prof., 1972; prof., head renal disease U. Colo. Sch. Med., Denver, 1972-92, prof., chmn. dept. medicine, 1976—. Editor 45 textbooks in internal medicine, geriat., drug usage, and kidney disease; contbr. over 800 sci. articles to profl. jours. Pres. Western Soc. Clin. Investigation, 1981, Nat. Kidney Found., 1984-86. With US Army, 1966—69. Recipient David Hume award Nat. Kidney Found., 1987, Louis Pasteur medal U. Strasburg, 1987, Mayo Soley award Western Soc. Clin. Investigation, 1989, Robert H. Williams award Assn. Profs. Medicine, 1996, Torchbearer award 1997, Edward N. Gibbs Meml. award NY Acad. Medicine, 2000, Alexander von Humboldt Rsch award 2004, Grand Hamdan Internat. Med. Scis. award 2004. Mem. ACP (master, John Phillips award 1992), Am. Soc. Nephrology (treas. 1979-81, pres. 1983, John Peters award 1997), Internat. Soc. Nephrology (treas. 1981-90, v.p. 1990-95, pres. 1995-97, Jean Hamburger award 2003), Am. Clin. and Climatol. Assn. (v.p. 1986), Assn. Am. Physicians (pres. 1994-95, Francis Blake award 1995), Western Assn. Physicians (pres. 1982), Inst. of Medicine of NAS, Alpha Omega Alpha. Achievements include research contributions centered on the pathogenesis of acute renal failure, genetic renal disorders, mechanisms of cell injury, diabetic nephropathy and renal and hormonal control of body fluid volume; advancement of a unifying hypothesis of sodium and water regulation in health and disease which has stimulated world-wide interest in the medical science community. Office: Univ Colo Health Scis Ctr Renal Divsn C281 Aurora Arvada CO 80004 Business E-Mail: Robert.Schrier@uchsc.edu, robert.schrier@ucdenver.edu.

SCHRIER, STANLEY LEONARD, hematologist, educator; b. NYC, Jan. 2, 1929; s. Harry and Nettie (Schwartz) S.; m. Peggy Helen Pepper, June 6, 1953; children: Rachel, Leslie, David. AB, U. Colo., 1949; MD, Johns Hopkins U., 1954. Diplomate Am. Bd. Internal Medicine (chmn. subsplty. bd. hematology). Intern Osler Med. Service, Johns Hopkins Hosp., 1954-55; resident U. Mich., Ann Arbor, 1955-56, U. Chgo. Hosp., 1958-59; sr. asst. surgeon USPHS, 1956-58; instr. medicine Stanford Sch. Medicine, Calif., 1959-60, asst. prof. medicine, 1960-63, assoc. prof., 1963-72, prof. medicine, 1972-95, chief divsn. hematology, 1968-94, prof. medicine emeritus, hematology, 1996—. Vis. scientist Weizmann Inst., Rehovot, Israel, 1967-68; vis. prof. Oxford U., Eng., 1975-76, Hebrew U., Jerusalem, 1982-83 John and Mary Markle scholar, 1961; recipient Kaiser award Stanford U., 1972, Kaiser award, 1974, 75, David Rytand award, 1982, Eleanor Roosevelt Union Internationale Contre le Cancer award, 1975-76, Albion Walter Hewlett award, 1996, Walter J. Gores award, 2002. Fellow ACP; mem. Am. Soc. Hematology (pres. 2004), Am. Physiol. Soc., Soc. Exptl. Biology and Medicine, Am. Soc. Clin. Investigation, Western Assn. Physicians, Assn. Am. Physicians. Democrat. Jewish. Office: Stanford U Sch Medicine Rm 1155 MC 5156 269 Campus Dr Palo Alto CA 94305-5156 E-mail: sschrier@stanford.edu.*

SCHRIESHEIM, ALAN, science administrator; b. NYC, Mar. 8, 1930; s. Morton and Frances (Greenberg) Schriesheim; m. Beatrice D. Brand, June 28, 1953; children: Laura Lynn, Robert Alan. BS in Chemistry, Poly. Inst. Bklyn., 1951; PhD in Phys. Organic Chemistry, Pa. State U., 1954; DSc (hon.), No. Ill. U., 1991; Laureate, Lincoln Acad., 1996; PhD (hon.), Ill. Inst. Tech., Chgo., 1992, Pa. State U., 2001. Chemist Nat. Bur. Standards, 1954—56; with Exxon Rsch. & Engring. Co., 1956—83, dir. corp. rsch., 1975—79; gen. mgr. Exxon Engring., 1979—83; sr. dep. lab. dir., COO Argonne Nat. Lab., 1983—84, lab. dir., CEO, 1984—96, dir. emeritus, 1996—; prof. chemistry dept. U. Chgo., 1984—96, lectr. Bus. Sch., 1996—99; prin. Washington Adv. Group, 1996—2006; pres. Chgo. Coun. Sci. and Technol., 2007—. Karcher lectr. U. Okla., 1977; Hurd lectr. Northwestern U., 1980; Rosensteil lectr. Brandeis U., 1982; Welsh Found. lectr., 87; com. svc. NRC, 1980—; vis. com. chemistry dept. MIT, 1977—82; mem. vis. com. mech. engring. and aerospace dept. Princeton (N.J.) U., 1983—87, mem. vis. com. chemistry dept., 1983—87; mem. Pure and Applied Chemistry Com.; del. to People's Republic of China, 1978; mem. Presdl. Nat. Commn. on Superconductivity, 1989—91, U.S.-USSR Joint Commn. on Basic Sci. Rsch., 1990—93; mem. U.S. nat. com. Internat. Union Pure and Applied Chemistry, 1982—85; mem. magnetic fusion adv. com. Divsn. Phys. Scis. U. Chgo. Magnetic Fusion adv. com. to U.S. DOE, 1983—86; mem. Dept. Energy Rsch. Adv. Bd., 1983—85, Congl. Adv. Com. on Sci. and Tech., 1985—96; mem. vis. com. Stanford (Calif.) U., U. Utah, Tex. A&M U., Lehigh U.; bd. govs. Argonne Nat. Lab., 1984—96; mem. adv. com. on space sys. and tech. NASA, 1987—93; mem. nuc. engring. and engring. physics vis. com. U. Wis., Madison; mem. Coun. Gt. Lakes Govs. Regional Econ. Devel. Commn., 1987—, rev. bd. Compact Ignition Tomamak Princeton U., 1988—91; advisor Sears Investment Mgmt. Co., 1988—89; bd. dirs. HEICO, Smart Signal Corp.; adv. bd. Batterson Venture Ptnrs., Influx, UHV Aluminum, Valley Indsl. Assn., Coun. on Superconductivity for Am. Competitiveness; mem. State of Ill. Commn. on the Future of Pub. Svc., 1990—92; co-chair Indsl. Rsch. Inst. Nat. Labs./Industry Panel, 1984—87; mem. Nat. Acad. Engring. Adv. Commn. on Tech. and Soc., 1991—92, Sun Electric Corp. Bd., 1991—92, U.S. House of Reps. subcom. on Sci.-Adv. Group on Renewing U.S. Sci. Policy, 1992—96, Chgo. Acad. Scis. acad. coun., 1994—; mem. adv. bd. Chemtech; mem. sr. action group on R&D investment strategies Ctr. for strategic and Internat. Studies, 1995; bd. vis. Astronomy and Astrophysics Pa. State U., 1995—; bd. overseers Fermi Nat. Lab., 2003—. Adv. bd.: Chemtech, 1970—85, editl. bd.: Rsch. & Devel., 1988—92, Superconductor Industry, 1988—95; patentee in field. Mem. spl. vis. com. Field Mus. of Natural History, Chgo., 1987—88; trustee The Latin Sch. of Chgo., 1990—92; adv. bd. WBEZ Chicagoland Pub. Radio Cmty., 1990—96; mem. Conservation Found. DuPage County, 1983—96, Econ. Devel. Adv. Commn. of DuPage County, 1984—88, Ill. Gov.'s Commn. on Sci. and Tech., 1986—90, Inst. for Ill. Coun. Advisors, 1988—, Ill. Coalition Bd. Dirs., 1989—, Inst. for Ill. Adv. Rev. Panel, 1986—88, NASA Sci. Tech. Adv. Com. Manpower Requirements Ad Hoc Rev. Team, 1988—91, Ill. Sci. and Tech. Adv. Com., 1989—, chmn., 1997; mem. U. Ill. Engring. Vis. com., Urbana-Champaign, 1986—95; trustee Tchrs. Acad. for Math. and Sci. Tchrs. in Chgo., 1990—96; bd. visitors astronomy and astrophysics Pa. State U., 1995—; bd. dirs. LaRabida Children's Hosp. and Rsch. Ctr., 1987—95, Children's Meml. Hosp., Children's Meml. Inst. for Edn. and Rsch. Recipient Outstanding Alumni Fellow award, Pa. State U., 1985, laureate, Lincoln Acad. Ill., 1996, Disting. fellow, Poly. U., 1989, Disting. Alumni award, Pa. State U., 2005. Fellow: AAAS (coun. del. chem. sect. 1986—92, sci. engring. and pub. policy com. 1992, standing com. audit 1992, bd. dirs. 1992—96, selection com. to bring FSU scientists to ann. mtg. 1995—2000), N.Y. Acad. Scis.; mem.: AIChE (award com. 1992—2000), NAE (adv. com. tech. and soc. 1991—92, mem. program adv. com. 1992—94, chair study fgn. participation in U.S. R&D 1993—96, NRC com. on dual use tech. 1996—97, com. to assess policies and practices of Dept. of Energy to design, ma 1998—99), Chgo. Coun. on Sci. and Tech. (pres. 2007—), NASA Com. on Aeronautics Innovation Models (chmn. 2005—07), Ctr. Strategic and Internat. Studies (sr. action group 1995—96), Indsl. Rsch. Inst. (co-chmn. Nat. Labs. Indsl. Panel 1984—87, fed. adv. com. to Fed. Sci. and Tech. Com. 1992—96, sr. action group on R&D Investment Strategies), Am. Nuc. Soc., Am. Petroleum Inst. (rsch. coord. coun.), Nat. Conf. Advancement Rsch. (conf. com. 1985—, site selection com. 1994, conf. com. 50th ann. 1996), Am. Mgmt. Assn. (R&D coun. 1988—96), Am. Chem. Soc. (joint bd. coun. on sci. 1983—87, chmn. petroleum divsn. 1983—91, councilor, com. on chemistry and pub. affairs 1983—91, petroleum chemistry award 1969, 1995—96), Econ. Club, Comml. Club, Carleton Club (bd. govs. 1992—), Cosmos Club, Phi Lambda Upsilon, Sigma Xi. Home: 1440 N Lake Shore Dr Apt 31ac Chicago IL 60610-5927 Office: Argonne Nat Lab 9700 S Cass Ave Argonne IL 60439-4803 Home Phone: 312-440-9408; Office Phone: 312-630-3872. Personal E-mail: aschries@aol.com. Business E-Mail: schriesheim@anl.gov.

SCHRIESHEIM, CHESTER ARTHUR, management educator; b. NYC, Nov. 10, 1946; s. Frank Henry and Eugenia Sophia (Halley) S.; m. Janet L. Fulk, Dec. 26, 1970 (div. 1982); m. Linda Mary Shea, Sept. 4, 1982; children: Syle Richard, Joseph Frank. BS, Mich. State U., 1967, MBA, 1968; PhD, Ohio State U., 1978. Asst. prof. Kent (Ohio) State U., 1976-78; assoc. prof. U. So. Calif., LA, 1978-82; prof. mgmt. U. Fla., Gainesville, 1982-86; disting. prof. mgmt. U. Miami, 1986—, dir. PhD prog. in bus. adminstrn., 1988—. Contbr. articles to profl. jours.; author: The Introduction to Business Game, 1971, (with Howard Wicker and John Minion): Managing for Profit: A Simulation, 1974, (with Orlando Behling) Organizational Behavior: Theory, Research and Application, 1976; spl. assoc. editor Jour. Bus. Rsch., 1982-83, Mgmt. Sci., 1980; editorial bd. Acad. Mgmt. Jour., 1979-85, Leadership Quar., 1988—, Jour. Bus. Rsch., 1978—, Jur. mgmt., 1982-85, Jour. Orgn. Change Mgmt., 1987—, Tech. Report Series, 1980—, others. Mem. Acad. Mgmt., Am. Psychol. Assn., Am. Sociol. Assn., Decision Sci. Inst., Inst. Mgmt. Sci., Indsl. Rels. Rsch. Assn., Phi Kappa Phi, Beta Gamma Sigma, Alpha Zeta, Phi Theta Kappa. Avocations: swimming, tennis, computers. Office: University of Miami PO Box 249145 Miami FL 33124-9145

SCHRIVER, JOHN T., III, lawyer; b. Evanston, Ill., May 18, 1945; AB, Coll. of Holy Cross, 1967; JD, Georgetown U., 1971. Bar: Ill. 1971, Fla. 1972, US Supreme Ct., US Ct. Appeals (7th and 9th cirs.), US Ct. Appeals, fed. cir., US Dist. Ct. (no. dist.) Ill., US Dist. Ct. (so. dist.) Wis., US Dist. Ct. (so. dist.) Fla., Supreme Ct. Ill., Supreme Ct. Fla. Ptnr. McDermott, Will & Emery, Chgo., 1970—2001, Duane Morris LLC, Chgo., 2001—. Lectr. in field. Contbr. articles to law jours. Mem.: ABA, Fla. Bar, Chgo. Bar Assn. Office: Duane Morris LLP Ste 3700 190 S LaSalle St Chicago IL 60603-3433 Office Phone: 312-499-6785. Office Fax: 312-277-6942. E-mail: JTSchriver@duanemorris.com.*

SCHROCK, CHARLES A., energy executive; b. Detroit; m. Liz Schrock. BS in Nuc. Engring., U. Mich., 1975, MS in Nuc. Engring., 1978. Nuc. engring. positions Wis. Pub. Svc. Corp., 1979—88, asst. mgr. plant ops., 1988—91, mgr. nuc. engring., 1991—95, plant mgr., Kewaunee Nuc. Power Plant, 1995—98, sr. v.p. energy supply, 1998—2000; sr. v.p. ops. nuc. mgmt. co. WPS Resources Corp., 2000—01; pres. WPS Power Development Inc., 2001—03; sr. v.p., pres. generation, CEO UPPCO WPS Resources Corp., 2004—07; pres. Wis. Pub. Svc. Corp., 2007—08, pres., CEO, 2008—, Integrys Energy Group Inc., Ill., 2009—. Former bd. dirs. Wis. Valley Improvement Co., Wis. River Power Co.; bd. dirs. New North Corp., Green Bay, Wis. Pub. Svc. Corp., 2009—. Bd. dirs. Neville Pub. Mus., Green Bay; mem., exec. com. Green Bay C. of C.; mem., adv. com. U. Mich. Coll. Engring. Mem.: Am. Nuc. Soc., Assn. Electric Illuminating Companies (bd. dirs.). Office: Integrys Energy Group Inc 130 E Randolph Dr Chicago IL 60601 Office Phone: 920-433-1812. Office Fax: 920-433-1526.*

SCHROCK, RICHARD ROYCE, chemistry professor; b. Berne, Ind., Jan. 4, 1945; s. Noah J. and Martha A. Habegger S.; m. Nancy F. Carlson, 1971; children: Andrew, Eric. AB, U. Calif., Riverside, 1967; PhD, Harvard U., 1971. Rsch. chemist, Ctrl. R&D dept. E.I. du Pont de Nemours & Co., Wilmington, Del., 1972-75; asst. prof. MIT, Cambridge, 1975-78, assoc. prof., 1978-80, prof., 1980-89, Frederick G. Keyes prof. chemistry, 1989—. Assoc. editor: Organometallics; contbr. articles to profl. jours. Recipient Bailar medal, U. Ill., 1998, Sir Geoffrey Wilkinson medal, Royal Soc. Chemistry, 2002, Sir Edward Frankland prize, 2004, August Wilhelm von Hofmann medal, German Chem. Soc., 2005, Disting. Alumnus award, U. Calif., 2006, Theodore W. Richards medal, North Aheast ACS Sect., 2006, Chancellors award, U. Calif, 2006, Basolo medal, Northwestern U. & ACS Chgo. Sect., 2007; co-recipient Nobel Prize in Chemistry, 2005; NSF postdoctoral fellow, Cambridge U., 1971—72. Mem.: NAS, AAAS, Am. Chem. Soc. (award organometallic chemistry 1985, Harrison Howe award 1990, Humboldt award 1994, award inorganic chemistry 1996, Arthur C. Cope Scholar award 2001, F. Albert Cotton award in Synthetic Inorganic Chemistry 2006), Am. Acad. Arts and Scis. Office: MIT Dept Chemistry Rm 6 331 77 Massachusetts Ave Cambridge MA 02139 Office Phone: 617-253-1596. Office Fax: 617-253-7670. E-mail: rrs@mit.edu.*

SCHROCK, ROBERT D., JR., retired orthopaedic surgeon, educator; b. Omaha, Aug. 6, 1938; s. Robert D. and Elizabeth Winslow (Wetherbee) S.; m. Carolyn Gorthy, May 30, 1964; children: Robert D. III, Suzanne Bartlett Schrock Kelley. AB, Princeton U., 1960; MD, Cornell U., 1964. Cert. Am. Bd. Orthopadic Surgery. Instr. dept. orthopaedics U. Wash. Sch. Medicine, Seattle, 1969-70; clin. asst. prof. dept. orthopaedics U. Rochester (N.Y.) Sch. Medicine and Dentistry, 1972—2004. Pres. Genesee Valley chpt. Arthritis Found., Rochester, 1989-91 (Nat. Vol. award 1991, Zaia award 1993), Rochester Acad. Medicine, 1991-92. Author: (with others) Operative Surgery, 1976; contbr. articles to profl. jours. Cub master, Webelos leader Cub Scouts, Pittsford, N.Y., 1973-78 (Long House award 1977); elder Third Presbyn. Ch., Rochester, 1984-87. Maj. U.S. Army, 1970-72. Fellow ACS, Am. Acad. Orthopaedic Surgeons, Am. Acad. Cerebral Palsy and Devel. Medicine, Am. Orthopaedic Foot and Ankle Soc., Rochester Acad. Medicine (co-chair com.); mem. Med. Soc. State N.Y. (com. mem.). Presbyterian. Avocations: tennis, photography, sailing. Home: 81004 Alexander Chapel Hill NC 27517

SCHROCK, SIMON, wholesale executive; b. Oakland, Md., Dec. 28, 1936; s. Noah and Cora (Burkholder) S.; m. Eva Lena Yoder, June 7, 1959 (dec. Apr. 1962); m. Pauline Yoder, Sept. 29, 1963; children: Janice Yvonne, Eldon Laverne, Ivan Dale. With Eastern States Farm Supply Co., Oakland, Md., 1957-59, Children's Hosp., Washington, 1959-61, Copp Properties, Vienna, Va., 1961-75; pres. Choice Books of No. Va., Fairfax, Va., 1975—. Chmn. Lighthouse Lit., 1976-2001. Author: Get on With Living, 1976, Price of Missing Life, 1981, One-Anothering, 1986, Vow-Keepers Vow-Breakers, A Smoother Journey, 1994, What Shall The Redeemed Wear, 2001, Where Has Integrity Gone, 2001, Don't Throw In the Towel, 2003; contbr. articles to ch. jours. Bishop Faith Christian Fellowship, Catlett, Va., 1981—. Avocations: travel, writing, biking. Office: 10100 Piper Ln Bristow VA 20136 Business E-Mail: schrocks@nva.choicebooks.org.

SCHRODER, JACK SPALDING, JR., lawyer; b. Atlanta, July 10, 1948; s. Jack Spalding Sr. and Van (Spalding) S.; m. Karen Keyworth, Sept. 1, 1973; children: Jack Spalding III, James Edward. BA, Emory U., 1970; JD, U. Ga., 1973. Bar: Ga. 1973, U.S. Dist. Ct. (no. dist.) Ga. 1973, U.S. Ct. Appeals (11th cir.) 1982. Assoc. Alston & Bird, Atlanta, 1973-78, ptnr., 1978—2003, sr. counsel, 2004—07, of counsel, 2007—. Author: Credentialing: Strategies for a Changing Environment/BNA's Health Law and Business Series, 1996; co-editor, contbg. author: Georgia Hospital Law manual, 1979, 84, 92. Bd. dirs. Rsch. Atlanta, 1996-00, pres., 1999, co-chair bd. advisors, 2003-06; participant Leadership Ga., Atlanta, 1986. United Way (chmn. legal divsn.), Atlanta,

1980; bd. dir. Good Samaritan Health and Wellness Ctr., Jasper, Ga., 2006-, vice-chair, 2008. Decorated comdr. S.E. Commandery Mil. and Hospitaller Order of St. Lazarus of Jerusalem. Mem. ABA (vice chmn. medicine and law com. 1989-90), Am. Health Lawyers Assn. (bd. dirs. 1994-99, chmn. med. staff and physician rels. com. 1991-94, vice chair hosps. and health systems law inst. 2001-07), Ga. Acad. Healthcare Attys. (pres. 1981-82), State Bar Ga. (bd. govs. 1987-89), Atlanta Coun. Younger Lawyers (pres. 1977-78), Atlanta Bar Assn. (pres. 1982-83), Atlanta Bar Found. (pres. 1991-95), Mil. and Hospitaller Order St. Lazarus Jerusalem (comdr. S.E. commandery 2003—). Office: Alston & Bird One Atlantic Ctr 1201 W Peachtree St NW Atlanta GA 30309-3424 Office Phone: 404-881-7685.

SCHRODER, SIGRID CAROLINE, lawyer, consultant; married, 1980; 1 child, Peter; 1 child, John. BA in Geology with honors, Columbia U., NYC, 1977; JD, So. Meth. U., Dallas, 1988. Bar: Tex. 1988. V.p. PM Legal Search, Dallas, 1983—85; pvt. practice Dallas and Houston, 1989—2006; prin. Sulgrave Resources, LLC, Houston, 2001—; pres., CEO Bellevue, Mercer Island, Wash., 2007—. Sec, chair legal com., bd. Dallas Chamber Orch., 1989—91; dir. bd. Allegro Dallas (formerly known as SPA Dallas), 1989—90; devel. advisor U. Tex., Health Sci. Ctr. Biotech Incubator, Houston, 2001—03; v.p. Houston Planning Forum, 2002—03; cornerstone sponsor Houston Tech. Ctr., 2002—03; dir., adv. bd. Greater Houston Partnership, 2001—02, Houston Achievement Pl., 2003; woman, minority spkr. ABA Spkrs. Bur., 2007—. Pres. Columbia U. Alumni So. Tex., 2005—07; sec. Georgetown U. Alumni Houston, 2005—06; pres. Barnard Coll. Club, 1995—2002, Petroleum Club Houston, U. Club, Houston City Club; foreign mission oversight com. St. John the Divine, Houston, 2002—04. Recipient Alan R. Bromberg Securities award, Dedman Sch. Law, 1988. Mem.: Coll. State Bar Tex., State Bar Tex. (chair internat. law com. 2005—07, intellectual property sect.), Columbia U. Club NY (pres 1995—2006). Avocations: travel, ballet, historic preservation, photography, charity work. Office: Sulgrave Resources 800 Bellevue Way NE Ste 400 Bellevue WA 98004 Business E-Mail: caroline@sulgravellc.com.

SCHRODER, WIL, state supreme court justice; b. Ft. Mitchell, Ky., 1946; m. Susan Wahlbrink; children: Stephanie, Lydia, Wil. BA, JD, U. Ky.; LLM, U. Mo. Bar: Ky. 1970, Mo. 1972. Atty. Kansas City Legal Aid Soc., 1971; corp. atty. St. Paul Ins. Co., 1971—72; asst. law prof. Chase Law Sch., Ky., 1972—75; pvt. practice Covington, Ky., 1975—83; trial ct. judge Kenton County Dist. Ct., Ky., 1983—91; judge Ky. Ct. Appeals, 1991—2006; justice for 6th Supreme Ct. dist Ky. Supreme Ct., 2007—. Hearing officer Ky. Personnel Bd., 1981—83. Office: Supreme Ct Ky 700 Capital Ave Rm 235 Frankfort KY 40601 Office Phone: 502-564-5444.*

SCHROEDER, ALICE DAVEY, diversified financial services company executive, writer; b. Dallas, Dec. 14, 1956; d. Kenneth Roger and Susan Adele (Putman) Davey; m. Harold Schroeder Jr., May 5, 1990. BBA, U. Tex., Austin, 1978, MBA, 1980. CPA Tex. Mgr. Ernst & Whinney, Houston, 1980-86; sr. mgr. Ernst & Young, Cleve., 1986-90, NYC, 1990; project mgr. Fin. Acctg. Standards Bd., Norwalk, Conn., 1991—93; with various broker-dealer firms including Paine Webber & Co., 1993—2000; ins. analyst, mng. dir. Morgan Stanley, NYC, 2000—. Author: The Snowball: Warren Buffett and the Business of Life, 2008 (Publishers Weekly No. 1 bestseller). Chmn. charity benefit Trees for Houston, 1985; vol. Tex. Acct.'s. & Lawyers for Arts, Houston, 1982—86, Jr. League Cleve., Inc., 1988—90, Jr. League NYC, 1990—91, Jr. League Stamforn-Norwalk, 1992. Fellow: Life Mgmt. Inst.; mem.: AICPA, Tex. Soc. CPA's, Houston Jr. C. of C. (membership dir. 1985—86). Episcopalian. Avocations: reading, politics, travel, music. Home: 449 Round Hill Rd Greenwich CT 06831-2618 Office: Morgan Stanley 1585 Broadway New York NY 10036*

SCHROEDER, ARNOLD LEON, mathematics professor; b. Honolulu, May 27, 1935; s. Arnold Leon and Wynelle (Russell) S.; m. Maybelle Ruth Walker, Nov. 9, 1956; children: Steven, Michael, Wendy. BS in Math., Oreg. State U., 1960, MS in Stats., 1962; postgrad., UCLA, 1964, U. So. Calif., 1965. Prof. emeritus math./stats. Long Beach (Calif.) C.C., 1962—. Computer cons. McDonnell-Douglas Corp., 1966-74, statis. researcher and tutoring on Soc. Sci., Bio-Med, and Bus. Mgmt. using SPSS, Minitab, and Lin. Prog. Applications; dir. Schroeder's Statis. Svcs. Author: statistics/Math Note's for Colleges, 1986—. Chmn. bd. elders Grace Bible Ch., South Gate, Calif., 1985-92. With USAF, 1953-57. Mem. Am. Bowlers Tour (life). Home and Office: 5481 E Hill St Long Beach CA 90815-1923 Office Phone: 562-938-4825. E-mail: am1156@msn.com.

SCHROEDER, BRIAN S., philosopher, educator, theologian; b. Quantico, Va., June 15, 1959; s. Gary Stephen and Faye Mary (Monette) Schroeder; m. Silvia Benso, June 5, 1999; 1 child, Erik Aren. BA in Philosophy magna cum laude, Edinboro Coll., 1981; MDiv with distinction, Princeton Theol. Sem., 1984; MA in Philosophy, Stony Brook U., 1987, PhD in Philosophy, 1990. Prof. philosophy Rochester Inst. Tech., Rochester, 2001—, dir. religious studies program, 2004—, chair philosophy dept., 2008—. Faculty Collegium Phaenomenologicum, Citta' di Castello, Italy, 2000, 03, 2006—. Author: (book) Altared Ground: Levinas, History, and Violence, 1995; co-author: Pensare ambientalista: Tra filosofia e ecologia, 2000; co-editor: Thinking Through the Death of God: A Critical Companion to Thomas J.J. Altizer, 2004, Contemporary Italian Philosophy: Crossing the Borders of Ethics, Politics, and Religion, 2007, Levinas and the Ancients, 2008—; gen. co-editor SUNY Series Contemporary Italian Philosophy, 2005—; editor: (journal) Studies in Practical Philosophy, 2004—05; co-translator The Ethics of Writing, 2009. Sr. rsch., J. William Fulbright Scholarship Commn., 2000—01, Miller Rsch. Fellowship, Rochester Inst. of Techology, 2003—04, Sr. Fellowship in Religion and Soc., Princeton Theol. Sem., 1984. Mem.: Fulbright Assn., Comparative and Continental Philosophy Cir., Heidegger Cir., Soc. Asian Comparative Philosophy, Levinas Rsch. Seminar (co-dir. 2003—04, founding mem.), Wisdom Rendezvous (bd. dirs. 1992—), Found. for the Philosophy of Creativity (exec. bd. 2000—), Internat. Soc. for Universal Dialogue (treas. 2001—03), Soc. for the Philosophy of Creativity (v.p. ea. divsn. 2000—08, sec., treas. 2008—), Nietzsche Soc. (exec. com. 2001—04), Soc. for Phenomenology and Existential Philosophy (book advisory selection com. 2002—03, chair 2009—), Am. Acad. of Religion, Am. Philos. Assn., Internat. Assn. for Environ. Philosophy (chmn. bd. dirs. 2002—07, exec. co-dir. 2008—). Business E-Mail: brian.schroeder@rit.edu.

SCHROEDER, CHARLES P. (CHUCK SCHROEDER), museum director; b. Lincoln, Nebr. BS, U. Nebr., Lincoln, 1972. Former mgr., prin. Schroeder Cattle Co., Palisade; dir. Nebr. Dept. Agriculture; CEO Nat. Cattlemen's Beef Assn., 1995—2002; exec. dir. Nat. Cowboy and Western Heritage Mus., Oklahoma City, 2002—. Co-founder, pres. Heartland Ctr. For Leadership Develop. Exec. v.p., develop. dir. U. Nebr. Found. Mem.: Coun. Agricultural Rsch., Extension and Tchg. (nat. chmn.). Office: Nat Cowboy & Western Heritage Mus 1700 NE 63rd St Oklahoma City OK 73111 Office Phone: 405-478-2250. Business E-Mail: cschroeder@nationalcowboymuseum.org.

SCHROEDER, DAVID J. DEAN, retired psychologist; b. Hutchinson, Kans., Mar. 21, 1942; s. D.J.W. and Louise (Wedel) S.; m. Nevonna Joyce Thomas, May 24, 1964; children: Taryn Dee Schroeder Dye, Anita Joy Fitch. BA, Tabor Coll., 1964; MS, Kans. State Tchrs. Coll., 1967; PhD, U. Okla., 1971. Lic. psychologist, Kans. Rsch. psychologist Civil Aerospace Med. Inst., Oklahoma City, 1970-72, clin. rsch. psychologist, 1980-89, supr., 1989-90, mgr. human factors rsch. lab., 1990-91, mgr. aerospace human factors rsch. divsn., 1991—2008; intern Norfolk (Nebr.) Regional Ctr., 1972-73; clin. psychologist VA Hosp., Murfreesboro, Tenn., 1973-75, Topeka, 1975-80. Co-author: FAA Employee Survey: National Report, 1984, 86, FAA Employee Survey: Regional/Center Reports, 1984, 86, FAA Job Satisfaction Survey National Report, 1988, FAA Job Satisfaction Survey: Regional/Center/Work Group Reports, 1988; mem. adv. editl. bd. Aviation Space and Environ. Medicine, 1993-95, 99-2001, 2006-. Mem. senate adv. com. Tabor Coll., Hillsboro, Kans., 1987-89; Christian edn. com. chmn. So. Dist. Conf. Mennonite Brethren Ch., Hillsboro, 1989; Sunday Sch. tchr. Western Oaks Christian Ch., Oklahoma City, 1990—; co-chair cmty. investment subcom. Okla. City United Way, 2006-09, Okla. City Friends Libr. Bd., 2008-09, treas., 2009-; vice chair cmty. investment Okla. City United Way, 2009-. Fellow APA, Aerospace Med. Assn. (chmn. sci. program com. 1990-91, mem. coun. 1992-95, v.p. 1996-97, v.p. edn. and rsch. 1999-2002, pres.-elect, 2002-03, pres. 2003-04, program com. chair APA divsn. applied exptl. and engrng. psychology 1996-97, sec.-treas. 1998-2001, pres. 2002-03, rep. APA Coun. 2008-, chmn. aerospace human factors com. 1999-2002, Raymond F. Longacre award for outstanding accomplishmnts in psychol. and psychiat. aspects of aerospace medicine 1997), Aerospace Human Factors Assn. (pres. 1994-95, sec. 2008-, Henry L. Taylor Founders award 2001); mem. Okla. Psychol. Assn. (bd. dirs. 1988-89, pres.-elect 1991, pres. 1992), Internat. Acad. Aviation and Space Medicine, IAASM Sci. Com. 2007-. Democrat. Achievements include research in assessing the interactive effects of alcohol, age and drugs on dynamic tracking and cognitive performance, personality characteristics and training success of air traffic control students, biofeedback, anxiety and burnout in government employees, human factors of air traffic control operational errors, fatigue and shiftwork. Home: 6109 Walnut Ln Oklahoma City OK 73132 Home Phone: 405-470-1184. Personal E-mail: davids20@cox.net.

SCHROEDER, DOUGLAS FREDRICK, architect; b. Omaha, June 12, 1935; s. Walter Elmer and Ellen Ruth (Niles) S.; m. Joanne Vlecides, July 5, 1980. B.Arch., U. Mich., 1959. Registered Architect, Ill., N.C., Mich., Wis. Designer, draftsman C.F. Murphy Assocs., Chgo., 1959-63; architect, sr. architect Skidmore, Owings & Merrill, Chgo., 1964-67; architect, ptnr. Schroeder, Yamamoto & Schreiber, Chgo., 1968-69; ptnr. Hinds & Schroeder, Ltd., Chgo., 1972-74; propr. Douglas Schroeder Assocs., Chgo., 1974-83, 93—; ptnr. Siegel & Schroeder, P.C., Chgo., 1983-91; dir. SGA Planning and Constrn. Cons. Co. div. Goforth Group, Chgo., 1991-93; v.p. Yacht Harbor Mgmt. Co., South Haven, Mich., 1983-88. Dir. Inland Architect Mag. Contbr. articles to profl. jours. Bd. dirs. Chgo. Archtl. Assistance Ctr., 1982-84; chmn. Mass. Transp. Crisis Com., Chgo., 1973, Ill. Futures Forum, 1976-77; pres. Ill. Planning and Conservation League, Chgo., 1971-74; ptnr. Burnham & Bennett Plan of Chgo. 1909 Centennial Celebration. Named Outstanding Alumnus Lake Superior State U., 1971. Fellow AIA; mem. Am. Arbitration Assn. (arbitrator) Clubs: Cliff Dwellers (dir. 1971-74). Unitarian Universalist. Home: 700 W Irving Park Rd Apt 4A Chicago IL 60613-3133 Office: Douglas Schroeder Assocs Arch & Planners 980 N Michigan Ave Ste 1277 Chicago IL 60611-4523 Office Phone: 312-280-5376. Business E-Mail: dschroeder@dsa-architects.com.

SCHROEDER, EUNICE M., library director; MusB, Ft. Hays State U., Kans., 1978; MLS, Emporia State U., Kans., 1993. Cert. pub. libr. adminstr. State Libr. Kans., 2008. Sch. libr. asst. USD 210, Hugoton, Kans., 1984—88; sch. libr. media specialist Johnson Kans. Sch. Dist., 1988—92; libr. dir. Stevens County Libr., Hugoton, 1992—. Bd. dirs. Hugoton Area C. of C. Mem.: ALA, Sigma Alpha Iota, MPLA, KLA, SWKLS (bd. chmn.), PEO, Alpha Lambda Delta. Office: Stevens County Libr 500 Monroe Hugoton KS 67951-2639 E-mail: steve2lb@pld.com.

SCHROEDER, FRED ERICH HARALD, humanities educator; b. Manitowoc, Wis., June 3, 1932; s. Alfred William and Sissel Marie (Lovell) S.; m. Janet June Knope, Aug. 21, 1954; 1 child, Erich Karl. BS, U. Wis., 1960; MA, U. Minn., 1963, PhD, 1968. Elementary sch. tchr. various locations, Wis., 1952-60; asst. prof. English U. Minn., Duluth, 1968-71, assoc. prof. English, 1971-74, prof. behavioral sci., 1977-82, prof. humanities, 1974-96, dir. Ctr. for Am. Studies, 1986-87, dir. Inst. Interdisciplinary Studies, 1987-90, dir. dept. humanities and classics, 1989-90, dir. grad. liberal studies, 1992-95, prof. emeritus, 1996—. Author: Joining the Human Race: How To Teach Humanities, 1972, Outlaw Aesthetics: Arts and the Public Mind, 1977, Interdisciplinnrians:Selected Readings from Ancient Times to1950, 1990, Front Yard America: The Evolution and Meanings of a Domestic Vernacular Landscape, 1993; co-author: Encyclopedia of Modern Everyday Inventions, 2003; editor Interdisciplinary Humanities (formerly Humanities Edn. jour.), 1983-95, assoc. editor, 1995—; editor 5000 Years of Popular Culture, 1980, 20th Century Popular Culture in Museums and Libraries, 1981; lectr., writer Nat. Humanities Series, 1969-71; adv. editor Guide to U.S. Popular Culture, 2001. Mem. Minn. Humanities Commn., 1985-90. Woodrow Wilson Nat. Found. fellow, 1960-61, dissertation fellow 1963; NEH scholar, 1969-70; Inst. for Human Values in Medicine fellow, 1976; Named Alumnus Notable Achievement, Coll. Liberal Arts U. Minn., 2007. Mem. Am. Culture Assn. (pres. 1984-87), Nat. Assn. Humanities Edn. (pres. 1987-89, exec. sec.-treas. 1989-96), Am. Assn. for State and Local History (seminar instr. 1978-82), Popular Culture Assn. Avocations: collecting art, woodworking, gardening. Home: 5756 N Shore Dr Duluth MN 55804-9660 Business E-Mail: fschroed@d.umn.edu.

SCHROEDER, HORST WILHELM, food products executive; b. Schwerin, Germany, May 5, 1941; m. Gisela I. Kammin; 1 child, Bernd; stepchildren: Ralph, Isabel Lange. MBA, U. Gottingen, Hamburg, Fed. Republic Germany, 1965. Sr. auditor Price Waterhouse, Hamburg, 1966-70; fin. contr. Kellogg Co. of West Germany, Bremen, 1970-71, dir. fin., 1971-76, mng. dir., 1976-81; pres., chief exec. officer Kellogg Salada Can., Toronto, 1981-83; pres. Kellogg Internat., Battle Creek, Mich., 1983-86, Kellogg N.A., Battle Creek, 1986-88; exec. v.p. Kellogg Co., Battle Creek, 1988, pres., chief oper. officer, 1988—. Mem. adv. bd. J.L. Kellog Grad. Sch.; Bd. of govs. St. Joseph Acad. of Food Mktg., Phila., 1986-88; mem. com. external affairs U. Ill., Chgo., 1987-88. Mem. Am. Health Found. (bd. dirs. 1987—), KC (pres. 1988—, bd. dirs. 1989—). Avocations: golf, tennis. Office: Am Italian Pasta Co 1000 Italian Way Excelsior Springs MO 64024

SCHROEDER, JAMES W., JR., otolaryngologist; b. NYC, Aug. 13, 1974; s. James W. and Patricia Ann Schroeder. BA in Biology with Distinction, 1996; MD cum laude, Loyola U. Chgo., Maywood, Ill., 2000. Cert. Am. Bd. Otolaryngology, 2006, lic. physician and surgeon Ill., controlled substance Ill. Intern. gen. surgery Cook County Hosp., Chgo., 2000—01, Rush U. Med. Ctr., Chgo., 2000—01, resident, otolaryngology, head and neck surgery, 2001—05, fellow pediat., head and neck surgery, 2005—06; asst. prof., otolaryngology, head and neck surgery Northwestern U., Feinberg Sch. Medicine, Chgo., 2005—; attending physician and surgeon, dept. surgery, divsn. pediat. otolaryngology Childrens Meml. Hosp., Chgo., 2005—, North Shore U. Hosp., Evanston, 2006—. Democrat. Roman Catholic. Avocation: running. Office: Childrens Meml Hosp Divsn Pediatric Otolaryngology 2300 Childrens Plz Box 25 Chicago IL 60614 Business E-Mail: jschroeder@childrensmemorial.org.

SCHROEDER, JAMES WHITE, retired lawyer; b. Elmhurst, Ill., Apr. 19, 1936; s. Paul W. and Thelma C. (White) S.; m. Patricia N. Scott, Aug. 18, 1962; children: Scott W. and Jamie C. BA, Princeton U., 1958; JD, Harvard U., 1964. Bar: Colo. 1964, U.S. Dist. Ct. Colo. 1964, U.S. Ct. Appeals (10th cir.) 1965, U.S. Supreme Ct. 1972, U.S. Dist. Ct. D.C. 1973, U.S. Ct. Appeals (D.C. cir.) 1974, U.S. Ct. Appeals (8th cir.) 1977, U.S. Ct. Appeals (3d cir.) 1981, U.S. Claims Ct. 1983, U.S. Ct. Appeals (fed. cir.) 1983. Ptnr. Mosley, Wells & Schroeder, Denver, 1965-72, Kaplan Russin & Vecchi, Washington, 1973-92; counsel Whitman & Ransom, Washington, 1992-93; dep. under sec. U.S. Dept. Agr., 1993-2001. Arbitrator Am. Arbitration Assn. Active Ams. for Democratic Action, Smithsonian Instn.; bd. trustees Orlando Opera, 2003—. Lt. USNR, 1958-64. Am. Field Svc. scholar, 1953, NROTC scholar, 1954. Mem. ABA, Fed. Bar Assn., Denver Bar Assn., Colo. Bar Assn., D.C. Bar Assn., Cap and Gown Club, Lincoln's Inn Club, City Club Denver (pres. 1972), Princeton Club Washington (pres. 1982-84). Democrat. Home: 621 Nadina Pl Celebration FL 34747 Home Phone: 407-566-8660.

SCHROEDER, JOHN, physics professor; b. Pardan, Banat, Yugoslavia, Aug. 31, 1938; s. Stephan Schroeder and Apollonia Weissmueller; m. Mary P. Pfenninger, Aug. 8, 1964; children: Stephan Charles, Erika Ernestine Kownack. BS, U. Rochester, NY, 1962, MS, 1964; PhD, The Cath. U. Am., Washington, 1974. Physicist Naval Rsch. Lab., Washington, 1974—75; postdoctoral rsch. assoc. U. Ill., Urbana, 1975—78; rsch. physicist Gen. Electric Co. CRD Ctr., Schenectady, NY, 1978—81; prof. physics Rensselaer Poly. Inst., Troy, NY, 1982—. Contbr. scientific papers (Jerome Fischbach Travel award, 2007). Lt. USN, 1967—70, Pentagon, Washington, commd. officer USN, 1967—70. Mem.: Optical Soc. Am., Am. Phys. Soc. Roman Catholic. Achievements include patents for cataract formation in the human Lens. Home: 1030 Nott St Schenectady NY 12308-2410 Office: Rensselaer Poly Inst 110 8th St Troy NY 12180-3590 Office Fax: 518-276-6680. Business E-Mail: schroj@rpi.edu.

SCHROEDER, JOHN A., systems engineering consultant, educator; s. John Bruno and Gertrude Dorothy Schroeder; m. Joanne Louise Galt, Mar. 2, 1985; children: Sarah Louise, Jeanette Lynne. BS, Purdue U., Lafayette, Ind., 1963; MS, U. Calif., Berkeley, 1966. Cert. advanced comms. sys. engrng. U. Calif., Irvine. Sr. engr. Rockwell Internat., Anaheim, Calif., 1970—80; sys. engr. Boeing Co., San Beach, Calif., 1980—98, dir. sys. engrng. Huntington Beach, Calif., 2000—04; COO Maxsys Tech., Irvine, Calif., 1998—2000; sr. cons. Booz Allen Hamilton, LA, 2004—; part time lectr. U. So. Calif., LA, 2005—; pres. Skill Sessions Seminars, Lake Forest, Calif., 1992—96. Mem. City Redevelopment Coun., Huntington Beach, Calif., 1980, 1981; angel supporter Fred Jordan Mission, LA, 2005. Mem.: Internat. Coun. on Sys. Engrng., Am. Mensa. Avocation: Bible study. Home: 22621 Manalastas Dr Lake Forest CA 92630 Personal E-mail: jschroeder@mail.com.

SCHROEDER, JOHN H., university chancellor; b. Twin Falls, Idaho, Sept. 13, 1943; s. Herman John and Azalia (Kimes) S.; m. Sandra Barrow; children: John Kimes, Andrew Barrow. BA, Lewis and Clark Coll., Portland, Oreg., 1965; MA, U. Va., 1967, PhD, 1971. Instr. history U. Wis., Milw., 1970-71, asst. prof., 1971-76, assoc. prof., 1976-86, prof., 1986—, Am. Coun. on Edn. fellow, 1982-83, assoc. dean, 1976-82, asst. to vice chancellor, 1982-85, acting vice chancellor, 1985-87, vice chancellor, 1987-90, chancellor, 1990-98, U. Wis. sys. prof., 1998—. Louis M. Sears Meml. lectr. Purdue U., 1978. Author: Mr. Polk's War: American Opposition and Dissent, 1973, The Commercial and Diplomatic Role of the American Navy 1829-1861, 1985, Matthew C. Perry: Antebellum Sailor and Diplomat, 2001 (Theodore and Franklin Roosevelt Naval History prize 2002, John Lyman Naval History award 2002), Commodore John Rodgers: Paragon of the Early American Navy, 2006. Bd. dir. Wis. Hist. Soc., We. Golf Assn. Recipient Edward and Rosa Uhrig award U. Wis.-Milw., 1974, Disting. Teaching award AMOCO/U. Wis.-Milw., 1975. Mem. Orgn. Am. Historians, Soc. for History of Early Republic, Soc. for History Am. Fgn. Rels. Office: U Wis Dept History PO Box 413 2310 E Hartford Ave Milwaukee WI 53211-3165 Business E-Mail: jhs@uwm.edu.

SCHROEDER, JONI LYNN, secondary school educator; b. Cheverly, Md., June 20, 1958; d. James Albert and Betty Jean Schroeder. BS, Lipscomb U., Nashville, Tenn., 1983. Cert. tchr. Tenn. Tchr. health and phys. ed. Haynes Design Ctr., Nashville, 1988—. Named Tchr. of Yr., Metro Nashville Bd. Edn., 2002. Mem.: AAHPERD (assoc.). Office: Haynes Design Ctr 510 W Trinity Ln Nashville TN 37207 Personal E-mail: joni.schroeder@mnps.org.

SCHROEDER, JOYCE KATHERINE, state agency administrator, research analyst; b. Moline, Ill., Apr. 1, 1951; d. Reinhold J. and Miriam May (Schroeder). BS in Math., U. Ill., Champaign-Urbana, 1973; MA in Ops. rsch., U. Ill., Springfield, 1978. Underwriter, programmer, Springfield, Ill., 1973—76; ops. rsch. analyst Ill. Dept. Transp., Springfield, 1976—78, data analyst, 1978—80, team leader, fatal accident reporting sys., 1980—83, mgr. safety project evaluation, 1983—92, mgr. crash studies and investigation, 1992—. Sys. engrng. del. to China, China Assn. Sci. and Tech., 1986; mem. staff Driving While Intoxicated Adv. Coun. and Task Force, State of Ill., 1983-86, 89-92, Gov. Task Force on Occupant Protection, 1988-90; Ill. Traffic Safety Info. Sys. Coun., 1993-95; mem. safety engrng. tech. adv. group Ill. Ctr. Transp., 2005—; mem. Ill. Traffic Records Coord. Com., 2004-. Vol. Animal Protective League, Springfield; leader bd., co-chair LPGA Rail Classic, Springfield, 1983-87; mem. U. Ill. Sangamon Auditorium Vol. Assn., Springfield, 2007—, bd. dirs., rec. sec. 2009-. Named to Pres.'s Coun., U. Ill., 2004. Mem.: Ill. Traffic Safety Leaders, N. Am. Conf. Lions Found. (ann. conf. steering com. 2001—03, bd. dirs. 2004—, treas. 2005—), Past Dist. Gov. Assn. (sec.-treas. 1993—2006), Lions of Ill. Endowment Fund (trustee 1998—99, coord. meml. and endowments 1999—), Springfield Lincoln Land Lions Club (charter pres. 1988—90, treas. 1993—95, news editor 1995—, treas. 2002—08, sec.-treas. 2008—), Lions Ill. Found. (amb. goodwill 1993, trustee 1995—99, treas. found. bd. 1996—97, v.p. found. bd. 1997—98, chmn. long range planning com. 1997—, pres. found. bd. 1998—99, policy ad hoc com. 1999—, chmn. policy ad hoc com. 2002—, fellow 1995, fellow laureate 2002, Disting.

Svc. award 2003), Internat. Assn. Lions Clubs (life; dist. Gov. Ill. 1992—93, state membership coord. 1994—96, Melvin Jones fellow 1993), Kappa Delta Pi, Phi Kappa Phi. Avocations: travel, dogs, music, sports, humanitarian service. Office: Ill Dept Transp 3215 Exec Pk Dr Springfield IL 62703-4514 Home Phone: 217-529-8242. Personal E-mail: jksplus3@sbcglobal.net.

SCHROEDER, JULIAN IVAN, biology professor; b. Summit, NJ, June 11, 1958; s. Manfred Robert and Anny (Menschik) S.; m. Marion G. Spors, Aug. 9, 1991; children: Julia Sofia K., Nicola A.J. Dr. rer. nat., U. Gottingen, Max Planck Inst., 1987. Postdoctoral rschr. dept. physiology UCLA Sch. Medicine, 1988-90; from asst. to prof. dept. biology U. Calif. San Diego, La Jolla, 1990-2000, Novartis Endowed chair in plant scis., 2000—. Dir. U. Calif. San Diego Plant Sys. Biology Grad. Tng. Program, La Jolla, 2005—, N.Am. arabidopsis steering com, 2007—. Contbr. articles to profl. jours. Recipient Heinz Meier Leibnitz prize, Deutsche Forschungs Gemeinschaft, 1984, Presdl. Young Investigator award NSF, 1991, Blasker award in environ. sci. and engring., San Diego Found., 2001; named Highly Cited Rschr., Inst. for Sci. Info., 2002; vis. scholar guest prof., ETH Zurich, 2005; Alexander von Humboldt fellow, 1988, 1996. Fellow AAAS; mem. Biophys. Soc., Am. Assn. Plant Biologists (Charles Albert Shull award 1997). Achievements include identification of ion channels in higher plant cells, characterization of their functions and regulation in membrane signal transduction and drought stress signaling; cloning and functional roles of mineral nutrient and heavy metal transport and detoxifying enzymes in plants. Office: U Calif San Diego Div Biology Ctr Molec Gene 9500 Gilman Dr La Jolla CA 92093-0116 Home Phone: 858-459-3097; Office Phone: 858-534-7759.

SCHROEDER, LAVERNE, medical/surgical nurse; b. Dover, Colo., Mar. 2, 1925; d. Chester Albert and Thelma May (Warren) Hutchison; m. Herman D. Schroeder, Sept. 5, 1947; children: Gloria, Rodger, Colleen, Darlene. Diploma, St. Anthony Hosp. Sch. Nursing, 1947. RN Colo., Wyo. Head nurse Poudre Valley Hosp., Ft. Collins, Colo., 1948, Longmont (Colo.) Hosp., 1950, Platte County Meml. Hosp., Wheatland, Wyo., 1957—76. Contbr. poetry to anthologies; author: A Blessed Trinity, 2003, The Queen's Secret, 2005. Pres. PTA; pres. bd. dirs. Platte County Meml. Hosp., Wheatland; Platte County del. Wyo.State Rep. Conv. Mem.: Wyo. Nurse Assn., Am. Vet. Med. Assn. Aux. (pres.).

SCHROEDER, MARVIS LYNN, accountant, artist; b. Gary, Ind., June 19, 1946; d. William Isaac and Leva Marcella (Pierce) Marlatt; m. Douglas Eugene Testerman (div.); 1 child, Tiffany Lynn Courtois; m. Charles Edward Schroeder, July 19, 1988. BS in Art Edn., Ind. U., 1969, MSBA, 1984; MA in Spl. Edn., U. Wyo., Laramie, 1975. Cert. in Acctg., 1992; tchr. Wyo., Ind., Calif. Tchr. Glasgow AFB Jr. High, Mont., 1967—68; tchr. art and spl. edn. Cheyenne Pub. Schs., Wyo., 1969—71; tchr. spl. edn. NW Ind. Spl. Edn. Coop., Crown Point, 1974—80; tchr. learning disabilities Riverside Schs., Calif., 1980—81; tchr. art Hobart Schs., Ind., 1981—84; group mgr. softlines Zayre, Merrillville, Ind., 1985; fin. aid counselor Ind. U., Northwest Gary, 1986—2001; acct. Harold Sullivan CPA, Portage, Ind., 2001—03. Exhibitions include Portage Sr. Artists Exhbn., 2002—09, 1st United Meth. Ch., 2003, Chesterton Women's Art Ctr., Ind., 2003, 2005—09, Art Barn Gallery, Valparaiso, Ind., 2004, 2006, Valparaiso Art Acad. Gallery, 2005, Porter County Adminstrn. Ctr., Valparaiso, 2005—06, 170 note cards from original oil paintings, Chesterton Women's Art Ctr., 2007, exhibitions include Illiana Artists Regional Show, 2006, 2007, Illiana Artist Mems. Show. Bd. trustee Portage 1st United Meth. Ch., 2003—05, mem. fin. com., 2007. Mem.: Illiana Artists Assn., Chesterton Art Ctr. Home: 2527 Pryor Rd Portage IN 46368 E-mail: chuckandmarvis@comcast.net.

SCHROEDER, MARY MURPHY, federal judge; b. Boulder, Colo., Dec. 4, 1940; d. Richard and Theresa (Kahn) Murphy; m. Milton R. Schroeder, Oct. 15, 1965; children: Caroline Theresa, Katherine Emily. BA, Swarthmore Coll., 1962; JD, U. Chgo., 1965; LLD (hon.), Swarthmore Coll., 2006. Bar: Ill. 1966, DC 1966, Ariz. 1970. Trial atty. US Dept. Justice, Washington, 1965—69; law clk. to Hon. Jesse Udall Ariz. Supreme Ct., 1970; mem. Lewis & Roca, Phoenix, 1971—75; judge Ariz. Ct. Appeals, Phoenix, 1975—79, US Ct. Appeals (9th cir.), Phoenix, 1979—, chief judge, 2000—07. Vis. instr. Ariz. State U. Coll. Law, 1976—78. Contbr. articles to profl. jours. Recipient Disting. Achievement award, Ariz. State U. Coll. of Public Programs. Mem.: ABA (Margaret Brent award 2001), Am. Judicature Soc., Am. Law Inst. (coun. mem.), Fed. Bar Assn., Ariz. Bar Assn. (James A. Walsh Outstanding Jurist award 2004), Soroptimists. Office: US Ct Appeals 9th Cir US Courthouse Ste 610 401 W Washington St SPC-54 Phoenix AZ 85003-2156 Fax: 602-322-7320. E-mail: mary_schroeder@ca9.uscourts.gov.*

SCHROEDER, PAUL J., JR., lawyer; b. Mo., 1947; BA magna cum laude, U. Notre Dame, 1969; JD, Washington U., 1972. Bar: Mo. 1972. Ptnr. Bryan Cave, St. Louis; v.p., gen. counsel Dillard's Inc., Little Rock. Mem. ABA. Office: Dillard's Inc PO Box 486 1600 Cantrell Rd Little Rock AR 72203-0486

SCHROEDER, RAYMOND ERNEST, educational administrator; b. South Bend, Ind., Dec. 8, 1949; s. Marvin Klopsch and Jean (Hirsch) S.; m. Gail Arnsdorf, Mar. 5, 1977; children: Geneva Marie, Mary Lynn. BA in Speech, Augustana Coll., Rock Island, Ill., 1970; MS in Radio-TV, U. Ill., 1972. Reporter Sta. WOWO, Ft. Wayne, Ind., 1969; gen. mgr. Sta. WVIK, Rock Island, 1970; news reporter Sta. WILL-AM-FM, Urbana, Ill., 1971-74; instr. radio-TV U. Ill., Urbana, 1975-77; asst. prof. communication Sangamon State U., Springfield, Ill., 1977-83, assoc. prof. comm., 1983-95, dir. TV Office, 1984-97, faculty assoc. to v.p. for acad. affairs, 1984-94; prof. comm. U. Ill., Springfield, 1995—2001, prof. emeritus comm., 2001—, dir. office of technology-enhanced learning, 1997—; interim exec. dir. Inst. for Pub. Affairs, 1992-93. Part-time photographer Sta. WAND-TV, Decatur, Ill., 1975-77; coordinator community access Dimension Cable, Springfield, 1984-97; vis. scholar in online learning, U. Southern Maine, 2006-. Editor, cons. TV documentary Breadbasket or Dustbowl, 1983; tech. cons. TV documentary Illinois Prairies: Sense of Place, 1986; co-dir. TV documentary Mr. Lincoln of Illinois, 1986 (Spl. Achievement award 1987); creative cons. TV documentary The Lincolns of Springfield, Illinois, 1990 (Spl. Achievement award 1991). V.p. Holy Spirit Frat., 1986-87. Grantee Ill. State Bd. Edn., 1994, Application of Learning Technologies to Higher Edn., 1995; recipient Finalist award Nat. Fedn. Local Cable Programmers, 1987, 88, 93, Most Outstanding Achievement in Online Learning by an Individual award, Sloan Consortium, 2002. Mem. Internat. TV Assn., Broadcast Edn. Assn., Sangamon State U. Faculty Union (pres. 1993). Roman Catholic. Avocations: running, bicycling. Office: U Ill at Springfield OTEL 1 University Plz Springfield IL 62703 Home Phone: 217-629-7324; Office Phone: 217-206-7531. Business E-Mail: schroeder.ray@uis.edu.

SCHROEDER, STEVEN ALFRED, medical educator; b. NYC, July 26, 1939; s. Arthur Edward and Norma (Scheinberg) Schroeder; m. Sally B. Ross, Oct. 21, 1967; children: David Arthur, Alan Ross. BA, Stanford U., 1960; MD, Harvard U., 1964; LHD (hon.), Rush U., 1994; DSc (hon.), Boston U., 1996, U. Mass. Med. Ctr., 1997, Georgetown U., 2000; DSc, Med. Coll. Wis., 2002; DHL (hon.), U. Medicine Dentistry NJ, 2003. Diplomate Am. Bd. Internal Medicine. Intern and resident in internal medicine Harvard Med. Svc., Boston City Hosp., 1964—66, 1968—70; asst. prof., then assoc. prof. George Washington Med. Ctr., Washington, 1971—76; vis. prof. St. Thomas' Hosp. Med. Sch., London, 1982—83; prof. medicine, chief div. gen. internal medicine, mem. Inst. Health Policy Studies U. Calif., San Francisco, 1976—90; pres., CEO Robert Wood Johnson Found., Princeton, NJ, 1990—2002; clin. prof. medicine U. of Medicine and Dentistry N.J., 1990—2002; disting. prof. health and health care U. Calif., San Francisco, 2003—, dir. smoking cessation leadership ctr., 2003—. Conv. various govtl. and philanthropic health orgns.; chair internat. adv. com. faculty medicine Ben Gurion U., Israel. Sr. editor: Current Med. Diagnosis and Treatment, 1987—93, mem. editl. bd.: New Eng. Jour. Medicine Mag.; contbr. numerous articles to profl. jours. Mem. U.S. Prospective Payment Assessment Commn., 1983—88; bd. overseers Harvard Coll., 2000—06; bd. dirs. Am. Legacy Found., 2000—05, vice chair, 2001—03, chair, 2003—05; dir. James Irvine Found., Charles R. Drew U. Medicine and Sci., 2005—. Named a Nat. Pub. Health Hero, U. Calif. Berkeley, 2004. Master: ACP (James Bruce award 2007); fellow: Am. Acad. Arts & Scis.; mem.: AAAS, APHA, Assn. Am. Med. Coll. (David Rogers award 2008), Albany Med. Ctr. (Medicine prize 2000—), Soc. Gen. Internal Medicine (past pres.), Inst. Medicine, Assn. Am. Physicians, Physicians for Social Responsibility, Harvard Med. Alumni Assn. (past pres.), Alpha Omega Alpha, Phi Beta Kappa. Office: U Calif San Francisco 3333 California St Ste 430 San Francisco CA 94143-1211 Home Phone: 415-435-3872; Office Phone: 415-502-1881. Business E-Mail: schroeder@medicine.ucsf.edu.

SCHROEDER, THOMAS D., federal judge, lawyer; b. Atlanta, May 26, 1959; Attended, Conservatory of Music, U. Cin., 1977—78; BS, U. Kans., 1981; JD, Notre Dame Law Sch., 1984. Bar: NC 1984. Law clk. for Hon. George E. MacKinnon US Ct. Appeals (DC Cir.), 1984—85; assoc. Womble Carlyle Sandridge & Rice, PLLC, 1985—91, ptnr., 1991—2008, practice group leader, product liability practice group Winston-Salem, NC, 1994—2002, mem. firm mgmt. com., 1996—2007, vice chmn. firm mgmt. com., 2005—07; judge US Dist. Ct (mid. dist.) NC, 2008—. Lectr. in field; faculty, trial tng. program Womble Carlyle Sandridge & Rice, PLLC, Winston-Salem, NC. Editor-in-chief Notre Dame Law Review, 1983—84. Mem.: Joseph Br. Inn Ct., 21st Jud. Dist. Bar Assn., Forsyth County Bar Assn., NC Bar Assn., Phi Alpha Delta. Office: US Dist Ct 251 N Main St Winston Salem NC 27101

SCHROEDER, WALTER ANDREAS, physics professor; b. Johannesburg, June 15, 1962; BSc, Imperial Coll., London, 1983, PhD, 1987. Vis. asst. prof. U. Iowa, 1991—93; prof. physics U. Ill., Chgo., 1993—. Office: Univ Ill 845 W Taylor St Chicago IL 60607-7059 Business E-Mail: andreas@uic.edu.

SCHROER, GENE ELDON, lawyer; b. Randolph, Kans., Aug. 29, 1927; s. Harry Edward and Florence Lillian (Schwartz) S.; m. Edith Grace Kintner, Apr. 7, 1956 (div.); children: Kenneth G., Rebecca J., Sonya J., Connie J.; m. Anne Oliver, Dec. 21, 1988; child: Paul R., John O., Andrew M., Edward G. AB, LLB, Washburn U., 1957. Bar: Kans. 1957, U.S. Dist. Ct. Kans. 1957, U.S. Ct. Appeals (10th cir.) 1970, U.S. Supreme Ct. 1983. Pvt. practice, Topeka, 1957-68; ptnr. Schroer, Rice, P.A., Topeka, 1968—2004, pres., 1970—2004, also bd. dirs.; pvt. practice, 2004—. Contbr. articles to profl. jours. and chpts. to books. Supr. Shawnee County Soil Conservation Dist., Topeka, 1968-84. With U.S. Army, 1951-53. Mem. ABA, Kans. Bar Assn., Assn. Trial Lawyers Am. (gov. 1976-79, seminar lectr. 1973—, chmn. tort sect. 1974-75, instr. Nat. Coll. Adv. 1978, 81-88), Kans. Trial Lawyers Assn. (gov. 1972—, seminar lectr. 1974—, pres. 1974-75), Nat. Bd. Trial Advocacy (sustaining founder), Am. Bd. Trial Advs. (sec., treas. Kans. chpt. 1990-91, pres. 1991-92), Civil Justice Found. (founding sponsor), Trial Lawyers for Pub. Justice (bd. dirs. 1982-96). Democrat. Methodist. Home: 5744 SE 101st St Berryton KS 66409-9533 Office Phone: 785-357-7300. Personal E-mail: gschroer@schroer.kscoxmail.com.

SCHROERLUCKE, LESLIE JEAN, music educator; b. Boston, Nov. 29, 1962; d. Ernest Charles and Marceline Jean Gerbasi; m. Steven Wayne Schroerlucke, Aug. 17, 1991; children: Sara Kirsten, Laura Kathryn. MusB, Eastman Sch. Music, Rochester, NY, 1984; MusM, Fla. State U., Tallahassee, 1988. Clarinetist Fla. Philharm., Ft. Lauderdale, 1985—91, Miami Opera, 1985—91; instr. clarinet Fla. Internat. U., 1990—98; lectr. Broward CC, Davie, 1991—98; instr. clarinet New World Sch. Arts, Miami, 1994—98; elem. music specialist Walnut Valley Unified Sch. Dist., Calif., 2000—03; band dir. Chaparral Mid. Sch., Diamond Bar, 2004—; clarinet instr. UC Riverside, 2006—. Musician: (recording) Florida Philharmonic, Mahler's 1st Symphony, Eastman Wind Ensemble, (world premiere) Nodus by Frederick Kaufmann, Brooklyn Bridge by Ronald Weidnaar. Vol. Hope Worldwide, Guatemala City, Guatemala, 2005—05. Recipient Margaret Fox Firman award, Eastman Sch. Music, 1984, Merit award, Nat. Fedn. Music Clubs, 1989. Mem.: Am. Fedn. Musicians, Calif. Tchrs. Assn. Avocation: travel. Home: 1275 Lane Ct Claremont CA 91711 Business E-Mail: lschroerlucke@walnutvalley.k12.ca.us.

SCHROETER, MARTIN J., information technology executive; Treas. IBM Corp. Mem.: Nat. Assn. Corp. Treasurers (bd. dirs.). Office: IBM Corp 1 New Orchard Rd Armonk NY 10504 Office Phone: 914-499-4547. Office Fax: 914-499-2883. Business E-Mail: mschroet@us.ibm.com.*

SCHROPP, TOBIN, lawyer; b. 1962; BS in Fgn. Svc., Georgetown U., 1984, JD, 1987, LLM in Taxation, 1991. Bar: 1987. Sr. v.p., gen. counsel Peter Kiewit Sons' Inc., Omaha. Office: Peter Kiewit Sons Inc 1000 Kiewit Plaza Omaha NE 68131

SCHROTH, JOYCE ABLE, social worker; b. Bloomington, Ill., Apr. 4, 1948; d. Raymond Daniel Able and Lois Martha Vielhak; m. Thomas H. Schroth, July 22, 1972; children: Bradley, Michael. BA, Ill. Wesleyan U., 1971. Dir. City of Westlake, Ohio, 1998—. Mem. cmty. adv. bd. Lakewood Hosp., Ohio, 1998—, St. John West Shore Hosp., Westlake, 1998—, mem. mission & values com., 1998—; pres. adv. coun. Retired Sr. Vol. Program, Brookpark, 1999—; mem. adv. bd. Westlake Healthcare Ctr., 2002—04; pres. Cuyahoga Cnty Mcpl. Offices on Aging Assn.; mem. cmty. adv. bd. Fairview Hosp., 2003—; mem. Cuyahoga County Adv. Coun. Dept. Sr. and Adult Cmty. Svc. Chmn. citizen's adv. com. Westlake City Schs., 1985—88, chair levy com., 1988; mem. Westlake Bd. Edn., 1987—90, Cuyahoga County Adv. Coun. on Sr. and Adult Svcs., 2003; bd. dirs. Univ. Settlement, 2005—08. Recipient Cmty. Leadership award, St. John West Shore Hosp., 2002, Cleve. State U., 2005, Luth.'s Maldonado award, 2005. Mem.: Westlake Lions Club, Sigma Kappa. Republican. Mem. Lds Ch. Avocations: travel, reading, genealogy. Office: City Westlake 29694 Ctr Ridge Rd Westlake OH 44145-5114 Office Phone: 440-899-3544. Business E-Mail: jschroth@cityofwestlake.org.

SCHROTH, PETER WILLIAM, lawyer, management, educator; b. Camden, NJ, July 24, 1946; s. Walter and Patricia Anne (Page) S.; children: Laura Salome Erickson-Schroth, Julia James. AB, Shimer Coll., 1966; JD, U. Chgo., 1969; M in Comparative Law, U.Chgo., 1971; SJD, U. Mich., 1979; postgrad., U. Freiburg, Fed. Republic Germany, Faculté Internationale pour l'Enseignement de Droit Comparé; MBA, Rensselaer Poly. Inst., 1988; DHL, Shimer Coll., 2000; MSc, Sch. Oriental and African Studies, 2000. Bar: Ill. 1969, NY 1979, Conn. 1985, Mass. 1990; solicitor Supreme Ct. England and Wales 1995. Asst. prof. So. Meth. U., 1973-77; fellow in law and humanities Harvard U., 1976-77, vis. scholar, 1980-81; assoc. prof. NY Law Sch., 1977-81; prof. law Hamline U., St. Paul, 1981-83; dep. gen. counsel Equator Bank Ltd., 1984-87; v.p., dep. gen. counsel Equator Holdings Ltd., 1987-94, v.p., gen. counsel, 1994-2000. Adj. prof. law U. Conn., 1985-86, Western New Eng. Coll., 1988-92, adj. prof. mgmt. Rensselaer Poly. Inst., 1988-98, prof., 1999-2005, dir. Ctr. for Global Bus. Studies, 2000-05, pres. Internat. Rsch. and Consulting Group LLC, 2005-. Author: Foreign Investment in the United States, 2nd edit., 1977; author: (with Stiefel) Products Liability: European Proposals and American Experience, 1981; author: Doing Business in Sub-Saharan Africa, 1991; bd. editors Am. Jour. Comparative Law, 1981—84, 1991—, mem. editl. bd. Conn. Bar Jour., 1988—, sr. editor, 1993—2000, 2006—, editor-in-chief, 2000—06, recent decisions editor NY Internat. Law Rev., 1994—, mem. editl. rev. bd. Jour. Bus. in Developing Nations, 1996—2000, editor-in-chief, 2000—, co-editor-in-chief Jour. Legal Studies in Bus., 2003—. Treas., mem. bd. trustees Shimer Coll. Mem. ABA (editor in chief ABA Environ. Law Symposium 1980-82), Am. Soc. Comparative Law (bd. dirs. 1978-84, 91—), Am. Fgn. Law Assn., Internat. Bar Assn., Internat. Law Assn. (com. multinat. banking), Acad. Internat. Bus., Conn. Civil Liberties Union (bd. dirs. 1985-92), Environ. Law Inst. (assoc.), Columbia U. Peace Seminar (assoc.), Hartford Club (bd. govs. 1995-98), Am. Corp. Counsel Assn. (pres. Conn. chpt.1997-2000), Conn. Bar Assn. (chair sect. of internat. law 1997-2000). Office: PO Box 29 South Glastonbury CT 06073-0029

SCHROTH, STEPHEN TIMOTHY, education educator, researcher; b. Springfield, Ill., June 18, 1963; s. Stanley Edward and Janis Kay Schroth. BA, Macalester Coll., St. Paul, 1982—86; JD, U. Minn., Mpls., 1986—89; MA, Columbia U., NYC, 2000—03; PhD, U. Va., Charlottesville, 2003—07. Cert. elem. tchg. K-9 Ill. State Bd. Edn., 2007; profl. clear multiple subject tchr. Calif. Commn. Tchr. Credentialing, 1997, clear crosscultural, lang. & academic development tchr. Calif. Commn. Tchr. Credentialing, 1997. Literacy coach, tchr. LA Unified Sch. Dist., 1996—2003; rsch. asst. U. Va., 2003—06; asst. prof. Knox Coll., Galesburg, Ill., 2006—. Recipient Edison Internat. New Era award, 2000, Tchg. Excellence award, LA Ednl. Partnership, 2001, Gt. Books Gt. Tchrs. award, Gt. Books Found., 2003, award, Mensa Edn. Rsch. Found., 2008, Picturing America award, 2009; grantee Govs. Book Fund, Gov. & Mrs. Gray Davis, 2001, Wonder of Reading Libr. grant, The Wonder of Reading Found., 2001, 2003; Laura Bush Found. grant, Laura Bush Found. Ams. Libr., 2003, grant, Associated Coll. Ill., 2007—08. Mem.: Nat. Assn. Gifted Children (sec., treas. rsch. & evaluation divsn. 2005—). Roman Cath. Avocation: literature. Office: Knox Coll K126 2 E South St Galesburg IL 61401 Business E-Mail: sschroth@knox.edu.

SCHROYER, MICHAEL KEVIN, healthcare consultant, hospital executive; b. Kewanee, Ill., Sept. 14, 1959; s. Jesse Wayne and Shirley Ann (Brown) S.; m. Joy Anne, June 20, 1987; children: Tiffany Marie, Rebecca Ann, Adam Michael. Diploma, Moline Pub. Hosp. Sch. Nursing, 1980; BSN, Loyola U., 1984; MSN, Seton Hall U., 1987; postgrad., Rush U., 1990-91; MBA, Auburn U., 2006. Cert. hosp. exec. (CHE). Nurse mgr., CCU, ICU, PICU, CCFP Jersey Shore Med. Ctr., Neptune, NJ; assoc. dir., critical care nursing Hyde Park Hosp., Chgo.; adminstrv. dir., transplant svcs. Rush-Presbyn./St. Lukes Med. Ctr., Chgo.; adminstrv. coord., v.p. cardiovascular and med./surg. svcs. United Med. Ctr., Moline, Ill.; adminstrv. leader, v.p. Regional CardioLife Ctr., Tenet Brookwood Med. Ctr., Birmingham, Ala., 1993-96; v.p. clin. svcs. MedCath McAllen (Tex.) Heart Hosp., 1996-98, MedCath Dayton (Ohio) Heart Hosp., 1998-2000, interim CEO, 2000, v.p. ops./COO, 2000—01; pres. / CEO Okla. Heart Hosp., Oklahoma City, 2001—03; prin., cons. TRG Cardiovascular, Denver, 2001—; exec. dir. cardiac and vascular svcs. Meml. Heart & Vascular Inst., Meml. Health Sys., Springfield, Ill., 2004—07; COO St. Vincent Heart Ctr. of Ind., Indpls., 2007—; v.p. Ind. Operations, Cave Group Cardiovascular, 2008—. Author: Emergency Nursing, 1989, Nursing Spectrum, 1989, Comprehensive Nursing Care Plans, 1995. Former bd. dirs. Rock Island County chpt. Am. Heart Assn. Fellow: Am. Coll. Healthcare Executives, Am. Coll. Healthcare Execs. (cert. healthcare exec.); mem.: Am. Coll. Cardiology (cardiac care assoc. liasen Ind.), Am. Heart Assn. (bd. dirs. Oklahoma City chpt., bd. dirs. Springfield chpt., greater Indpls. chpt.), Am. Assn. Med. Cardiovasc. Adminstrs., Sigma Theta Tau. Home: 9065 Pebblepointe Cir Zionsville IN 46077 Office: St Vincent Heart Ctr of Ind 10580 N Meridian St Indianapolis IN 46290 Personal E-mail: mschroyerl@indy.rr.com.

SCHRUMP, DAVID STUART, medical association administrator, researcher; b. New Haven, Conn., Dec. 21, 1956; s. LeRoy Everett and Myra Ruth Schrump; m. Brenda Ann Willett, Mar. 13, 1984; children: Willaim David, Christopher Eldridge, Nathaniel Stuart. BA, NYU, NYC, 1979; MD, Univ. of Conn., Farmington, 1983. Diplomate Am. Bd. Thoracic Surgeons, 1994. Asst. prof thoracic surgery UT-MD Anderson Cancer Ctr., Houston, 1993—97; head thoracic oncology sect. surgery br. Nat. Cancer Inst., Bethesda, Md., 1997—. Contbr. articles to profl. jours. Hockey coach Montgomery Youth Hockey Assn., Rockville, Md., 1998. Recipient NIH Merit award for the Devel. of an Innovative Translational Rsch. Program in Thoracic Oncology, Nat. Cancer Inst., 2005, Bench to Bedside award for Outstanding Translational Lung Cancer Rsch., 2001. Fellow: ACS.; mem.: John Alexander Soc., Am. Soc. of Clin. Oncology, Internat. Assn. for the Study of Lung Cancer, Am. Assn. for Cancer Rsch., Am. Assn. forThoracic Surgery, Soc. of Thoracic Surgeons. Achievements include fundamental research pertaining to lung cancer; expert in lung cancer surgery; expert in esophageal cancer surgery; expert in pleural mesothelioma surgery. Office: National Cancer Institute Building 10 Rm 4-3942 10 Center Drive Bethesda MD 20892-1201 Office Fax: 301-451-6934. E-mail: david_schrump@nih.gov.

SCHUBART, CAREN NELSON, psychologist; b. SI, NY, Sept. 26, 1945; d. Kenneth Warwick and Carey Boone Nelson; m. Richard Douglas Schubart, July 5, 1969; children: Darcy, Lindsey, Nelson. BA in Psychology, Wittenberg U., Springfield, Ohio, 1967; MEd in Rehab. Counseling, Kent State U., Ohio, 1968; postgrad., Syracuse U., NYC, 1972—73, Boston U., 1974—88, Plymouth State U., Mass., 2001—. Lic. psychologist NH Bd. Mental Health Practice, Nat. Assn. Sch. Psychologists; cert. learning disability specialist NH Assn. Sch. Psychologists, lic. sch. psychologist NY State Edn. Dept. Rehab. counselor Ohio Bur. Vocat. Rehab., Akron, 1967—68, NY Dept. Vocat. Rehab., Syracuse, 1968—73; regional dir. spl. edn. NH Sch. Unions 16, 19, 21, Exeter, 1973—79; sch. psychologist NH Supervisory Sch. Union 16, Exeter Jr. HS, 1979—88, NH Supervisory Sch. Union 16, Exeter HS,

1989—. Contbr. articles to profl. jours. Vol. Rockingham County Family Planning, Exeter, bd. dirs. Recipient full scholarship, U.S. Govt. Dept. Rehab. Edn., 1967—68. Mem.: APA, NH Assn. Sch. Psychologists, NH Psychol. Assn., Nat. Assn. Sch. Psychologists. Independent. Episcopalian. Avocations: photography, genealogy, outdoor activities, travel. Home: 65 Court St Exeter NH 03833 Office: Exeter HS Blue Hawk Way Exeter NH 03833 Business E-Mail: cschubart@sau16.org.

SCHUBEL, JERRY ROBERT, marine scientist educator, dean; b. Bad Axe, Mich., Jan. 26, 1936; s. Theodore Howard and Laura Alberta (Gobel) S.; m. Margaret Ann Hostetler, June 14, 1958; children: Susan Elizabeth, Kathryn Ann. BS, Alma Coll., 1957; MA in Tchg., Harvard U., 1959; PhD, Johns Hopkins U., 1968; DSc (hon.), Mass. Maritime Acad., 1997. Rsch. assoc. Chesapeake Bay Inst., Johns Hopkins U., Balt., 1968-69, rsch. scientist, 1969-74, adj. rsch. prof., assoc. dir., 1973-74; dir. Marine Sci. Rsch. Ctr. SUNY, Stony Brook, 1974-83, dean, leading prof., 1983-94, acting dir. Waste Mgmt. Inst., 1985-87, provost, 1986-89, dir. COAST Inst., 1989, disting. svc. prof., 1994-95, prof. emeritus, 1995—; pres. emeritus, CEO New Eng. Aquarium, Boston, 1994—2001; vis. prof. Wash. Coll., Chestertown, Md., 2002—03, dir. Alternative Futures Forum, 2002—03; pres., CEO Aquarium of Pacific, Long Beach, Calif., 2002—. Hon. prof. East China Normal U., Shanghai, 1985—; sec. exec. com. Commn. on Food, Environ. and Renewable Resources, 1993, chair steering com., 1994; mem. governing bd. Regional Marine Rsch. Program, Greater N.Y. Bight, 1993-94; v.p., founding dir. Gulf of Maine Ocean Observing Sys., 1998-02; adv. panel Nat. Whale Conservation Fund Found., 2001-05; mem. NOAA Sci. Adv. Bd., 2008-, Nat. Sea Grant Adv. Panel, 2002-07, chair, 2004-05; bd. dirs. Internat. Resources Group, 2002—, rev. panel Census of Marine Life, U.S. Nat. Com., 2003-07, mem. NSF Edn. and Human Resources Adv. Com., 2003-05, South Bay Salt Pond Restoration, Nat. Sci. Panel, 2003-06; nat. assoc. Nat. Acads. Sci. and Engring.; mem. marine bd. NRC, 1989-94, 2002—; bd. dirs. Inst. for Learning Innovation, 2004—; mem. adv. panel Ocean Rsch. and Resources, 2006—, vice chair, 2007—, chmn., 2007-09. Author: The Living Chesapeake, 1981, The Life and Death of the Chesapeake Bay, 1 986; (with H.A. Neal) Solid Waste Management and the Environment, 1987, Garbage and Trash: Can We Convert Mountains Into Molehills?, 1992; editor: (with B.C. Marcy Jr.) Power Plant Entrainment, 1978; (with others) The Great South Bay, 1991; sr. editor Coastal Ocean Pollution Assement News, 1981-86; co-editor in chief Estuaries, 1986-88; mem. editl. bd. CRC Revs. in Aquatic Scis.; contbr. articles to profl. jours. Mem. adv. bd. Environ. Sci. Com. Outer Continental Shelf, Minerals Mgmt. Scs., 1984-86, chmn., 1986; bd. dirs. N.E. Area Remote Sensing Sys., 1983-85, L.I. Incubator Corp.; v.p. L.I. Forum for Tech., 1989-92; chair Mass. Outfall Monitoring Task Force, 1995-98; mem. sci. adv. bd. EPA, 1996-98; commr. Nat. Rsch. Coun.'s Commn. on Engring. Tech. Sys., 1996-2000; mem. vis. com. dept. ocean engring MIT, 1995-2002; trustee Natural Heritage Insts., 1995-2001; mem. Boston Artery Bus. Bd. Dirs., 1994-2001; mem. Boston Mcpl. Rsch. Bur. Bd. Dirs., 1994-2001; mem. Annenberg Challenge Adv. Com., 1995-2002; hon. trustee Sci. Mus. L.I., 2000-02. Recipient L.I. Sound Am. Environ. Edn. award, 1987, Stony Brook U. medal, 1989, Matthew Fontaine Maury award, 1990, Ocean Champion award Monmouth U. Uchan Coast Instn., 2007, Ben Gurion U. medal, 1993, sci. achievement award Sci. Mus. L.I., 2000; Alfred P. Sloan fellow, 1959; Wheaton Coll. Disting. fellow, 2000. Mem. NAS (com. on Coastal Ocean 1989-93), Nat. Assn. State Univ. and Land Grant Colls. (bd. dirs. marine divsn., chmn. 1986-88), L.I. Environ. Coun., L.I. Marine Resources Adv. Coun. (chair 1990-94), L.I. Rsch. Inst. (bd. dirs. 1992-94), L.I. Environ.-Econ. Roundtable (co-chair 1991-92), Suffolk County Recycling Commn., (chmn. 1987-88), Estuarine Rsch. Fedn. (v.p. 1982-83, pres. 1985-87), N.Y. Sea Grant Inst. (chmn. governing bd. 1988-90, mem. gov.'s task force on coastal resources 1990-91), Census Marine Life (mem. U.S. nat. com. 2003—08), The Nature Conservancy (trustee L.I. chpt. 1991-94), Franklin Electronic Pubs. (bd. dirs. 1991—), Taproot (bd. dirs. 1988-93, vice chair 1990-93), Internat. Resources Group (bd. dirs., 2002—08), Sigma Xi, Phi Sigma Pi. Avocation: photography. Office: Aquarium of the Pacific 100 Aquarium Way Long Beach CA 90802 Home Phone: 564-437-5722; Office Phone: 562-951-1608. Business E-Mail: jschubel@lbaop.org.

SCHUBERT, BARBARA SCHUELE, retired performing arts association administrator; b. Cleve., Feb. 21, 1939; d. William Edward and Mildred Marianne (Matousek) Schuele; m. John Dwan Schubert, June 15, 1963; children: William Edward, Christopher John, David Matthew. BS in Social Scis., John Carroll U, 1962, MA in English, 1967; MEd, 1980. Cert. secondary tchr., elem. remedial reading tchr., Ohio. Tchr. Sch. on Magnolia, Cleve., 1980-82, Ruffing Montessori, Cleve., 1982-83; tchr. English U. Sch., Chagrin Falls, Ohio, 1983-86; gen. mgr. Ohio Ballet, Akron, 1987-90, assoc. dir., 1990-99; ret. Bd. trustees Ohio Ballet, 1974-87, 91-99. Bd. dirs. John Carroll U., 1990—; trustee Boys Hope Girls Hope, 2001, Stratford Shakespeare Festival America. Mem.: Cleve. Skating. Roman Catholic. Personal E-mail: matousek04@yahoo.com.

SCHUBERT, BLAKE H., lawyer; b. Wheeling, W.Va., Apr. 21, 1939; s. John Arnold and Esther Elizabeth (Masters) Schubert; m. Carol Jean Cramp, Jan. 13, 1962; children: Cheryl Lynn, Charles Bradley, Elisabeth Anne. BA, Ohio Wesleyan U., Delaware, 1961; JD, U. Chgo., 1964. Bar: Ill. 1964, U.S. Dist. Ct. (no. dist.) Ill. 1968, U.S. Tax Ct. 1994. Counsel Brunswick Corp., Chgo., 1964—68; asst. group counsel FMC Corp., 1968—73; gen. counsel Dresser Tool Group, 1973—79; chmn. Schubert Securities Corp., Oak Park, 1979—84, Inter-Am. Investmemts, Inc., 1980—, Midwestern Bus. Devel. Corp., 2005—. Gen. ptnr. Investment Trust Ltd., St. Petersburg, Fla., 1981—91, Inter-Am. Fund, Oak Park, 1982—91, Inter-Am. Fund I, Oak Park, 1982—91, Inter-Am. Fund II, Oak Park, 1984—89; chmn. Compath Video Corp., Oak Park, 1984—85; lectr. Am. Inst. Banking, 1965, Chgo. Inst. Fin. Studies, 1984—85. Author: The Well-Kept Secrets of Investing, 1982. Chmn. Park Forest Co-op., Ill., 1966—70; mem. Chgo. Bd. Options Exch., 1979—83; chmn. 1st United Ch. Endowment Fund, Oak Park, 1975—80. Home and Office: 522 Linden Ave Oak Park IL 60302-1659

SCHUBERT, BRIAN, legislative staff member; b. Berlin, Conn. Grad., Boston Coll. Reporter Herald, Herald Press, Conn.; press sec., Rep. Nancy Johnson US House of Reps., Washington, 2002—07, dep. dir. external comm., Republican Conf., 2007, dir. comm., Republican Conf., 2008, chief of staff to Rep. Christopher Lee, 2008—. Republican. Office: 1711 Longworth House Office Bldg Washington DC 20515 Office Phone: 202-225-5265. Office Fax: 202-225-5910.*

SCHUBERT, DONNA CLARK, public relations educator, professional society administrator; b. Lineville, Ala., Dec. 29, 1964; d. James Marion and Eva Lee Clark; m. Christopher Louis Schubert, July 13, 1996. BA, Auburn U., 1987, MA, 1989. Assoc. prof., editor undergrad. catalog, advising coord. Troy U., Ala., 1990—. Reaffirmation exec. editor: Southern Assn. Coll. and Schs. Chair, hon. chair, multiple roles Am. Cancer Soc. Relay For Life, Troy, 1998—2006; chair Pike Animal Shelter Founder's Soc., 2007—. Mem.: Phi Kappa Phi (life; nat. v.p. 2001—07). Office: Troy Univ 105 Wallace Hall Troy AL 36082

SCHUBERT, GERI M., psychotherapist; d. Louie J. Ferguson and Mona A. Ramsey; m. Mark K. Schubert; children: Ian, Ari. BS, East Ctrl. U., 1990, MS, 1995. Lic. profl. counselor Okla. State Dept. Health, 2001, ct. appt. spl. adv. Okla. CASA Assn., 2001. Child welfare specialist Okla. Dept. Human Svcs., Sulphur, 1995—99; mental health profl. H&S Rehabilitative Treatment Svcs., Providence, Ada, 1999—2003; psychotherapist DaySpring Behavioral Health Svcs., Tulsa, Okla., 2003—; program coord. 22nd Jud. Dist. Ct. Apptd. Spl. Advocate (CASA), Inc., Ada, Okla., 2003—. Profl. mem. ACA, Alexandria, Va., 2003—. Ct. apptd. spl. adv. 22nd Jud. Dist. CASA, Ada, Okla., 2002—05; vol. Care Cottage Child Advocacy Ctr., Ada, 2003—05; acting pres. Boys & Girls Club of Ada, 2002—05. Recipient Disting. Cmty. Svc. award, CASA of Pontotoc County, 2004, Adv. Coord. of Yr. award, 2004; named Vol. Coord. of Yr., Okla. CASA, 2005. Mem.: Am. Counseling Assn. (assoc.). Office: 514 E 10th St Ada OK 74820

SCHUBERT, GUENTHER ERICH, pathologist; b. Mosul, Iraq, Aug. 17, 1930; s. Erich Waldemar and Martha Camilla (Zschitzschmann) Schubert; children: Frank, Marion, Dirk. MD, U. Heidelberg, Germany, 1957; pvt. docent in pathology, U. Tuebingen, Germany, 1966. Asst. med. dir. U. Tuebingen, Germany, 1966—76; prof. pathology, 1972; head Inst. Pathology, Wuppertal, Germany, 1976—96; chair of pathology U. Witten-Herdecke, Germany, 1985—96. Co-author: Coloratlas of Cytodiagnosis of the Prostate, 1975, Pathologie, 1984, 1997, Endoscopy of the Urinary Bladder, 1989, Textbook of Pathology, 1981, 1987. Mem. Wissenschaftlicher Beirat, Bundesarztekammer, Bonn, Germany, 1976—85; pres. Medizinisch Naturwissenschaftliche Gesellschaft, Wuppertal, 1984—85, Onkologischer Schwerpunkt, Wuppertal, 1985—93, OSP Bergisch-Land, 1992—95, Bergische Arbeitsgemeinschaft fur Gastroenterologie, Wuppertal, 1987—88, 1990—91, 1994—95. Mem.: NY Acad. Scis., Internat. Acad. Pathology, Deutsche Gesellschaft fur Urologie, Deutsche Gesellschaft fur Nephrologie, Deutsche Gesellschaft fur Pathologie, Lions. Avocations: music, diving, photography. Office: Inst Pathology Am Anschlag 71 42113 Wuppertal Germany Home Phone: 0049202 763599.

SCHUBERT, HELEN CELIA, public relations executive; b. Washington City, Wis. d. Paul H. and Edna (Schmidt) S. BS, U. Wis., Madison. Dir. pub. rels. United Cerebral Palsy, Chgo., 1961; adminstrv. dir. Nat. Design Ctr., Chgo., 1962-67; owner Schubert Pub. Rels., Chgo., 1967—. Bd. dirs. Fashion Group, Chgo., 1988—95; adj. prof. comm. Roosevelt U., 1992—. Mem. women's bd. Am. Cancer Soc., Chgo., 1988—, Art Resources in Tchg., Chgo., 1988-92. Recipient Comm. award Am. Soc. Interior Designers, Chgo., 1979, 83, 88, 94; named to Chgo. Women's Hall of Fame City of Chgo., 1990. Fellow Nat. Home Fashion League; mem. Women's Ad Club Chgo. (pres. 1981-83, Woman of Yr. award 1987), Women in Comm. (pres. 1969-70, Matrix award Lifetime Achievement 1996), Am. Advt. Fedn. (lt. gov. 1983-85). Lutheran. Personal E-mail: schube@mail.com.

SCHUBERT, RICHARD FRANCIS, social services administrator, consultant; b. Trenton, NJ, Nov. 2, 1936; s. Yaro and Frances Mary (Hustak) S.; m. Virginia Thomas Austin, Sept. 15, 2000; children: Robyn, David. BA cum laude, Eastern Nazarene Coll., 1958; LLB, Yale U., 1961. Bar: Pa. 1962, U.S. Supreme Ct 1972. Arbitration atty. Bethlehem Steel Corp., Pa., 1961-66, asst. mgr. labor relations, 1966-70; exec. asst. to undersec. labor Washington, 1970; gen. counsel labor, 1971-73; dep. sec. labor, 1973-75; asst. to v.p. indsl. relations Bethlehem Steel Corp., 1973, asst. v.p. public affairs, 1975-77, v.p. public affairs, 1977-79, pres., 1979-80, vice chmn., 1980-82; pres., CEO ARC, 1982-89, Points of Light Found., 1990-95. Bd. dirs. Internat. Ctr. for Religion and Diplomacy, Mgmt. Tng. Corp., A. Friends Czech Rep., Friends of Zambia. Exec. v.p. EXCN; chmn. emeritus Internat. Youth Found., chmn., Nazarene Compassionate Ministries; vice chmn. Leader to Leader Inst.; chmn. Nat. Job Corps Assn. Mem.: Captur N, Inc. (chmn.), Coun. on Fgn. Rels., Northampton County Bar Assn., Pa. Bar Assn., Ea. Nazarene Alumni Assn. (pres. 1969—73), Phi Alpha Delta. Mem. Ch. of Nazarene. Home: 6615 Madison McLean Dr Mc Lean VA 22101-2425 Home Phone: 703-827-5965; Office Phone: 703-416-6656. E-mail: rfs@iyfnet.org.

SCHUBERT, RUTH CAROL HICKOK, artist, educator; b. Janesville, Wis., Dec. 24, 1927; d. Fay Andrew and Mildred Wilamette (Street) Hickok; m. Robert Francis Schubert, Oct. 20, 1946; children: Stephen Robert, Michelle Carol. Student, DeAnza Coll., 1972—73; AA Scholarship, Monterey Peninsula Coll., Calif., 1974; BA with honors, Calif. State U., San Jose, 1979. Govt. employee civil svc. US NASA Moffett Field, Calif., 1953—73; owner, mgr. Casa De Artes Gallery, Monterey, Calif., 1977—86; dir. Monterey Peninsula Mus. Art Coun., 1975—76; quick-draw artist So. Oreg. Pub. TV, KSYS; leader painting workshops; demonstrator, lectr., judge in U.S., B.C. Can., New Zealand and Loreto, Baja, Mexico. One-woman shows include Aarhof Gallery, Aarau, Switzerland, 1977, Degli Agostiniani Recolletti, Rome, 1977, Wells Fargo Bank, Monterey, 1975, 1978, 1979, Seaside (Calif.) City Hall Gallery, 1979, 1989, Village Gallery, Lahaina, Hawaii, 1983, 1986, 1989, 1994, Portola Valley Gallery, 1984, 1985, Rose Rock Gallery, Carmel, 1984—86, Taupo (N.Z.) Arts Soc., 1988, Geyserland Art Mus., Rotorua, N.Z., 1988, Wanganui (N.Z.) Art Soc., 1988, Hallei Brown Ford Gallery, Roseburg, Oreg., 1991, 1995, Collection of Ann Cunningham, Carmel, 1993—95, Libr. Found., Medford, Oreg., 2005, catalog nat. group juried shows include, Sierra Nev. Mus. Art, Reno, 1980, Bard Hall Gallery, San Diego, 1980, San Diego Nat. Watercolor Show, Mid-West Nat. Watercolor Show, Rahr-West Mus., Manitowoc, Wis., 1980, Rosicrucian Mus., San Jose, 1981, 1984, Calif. State Agri-Images, Sacramento, 1984, XVII Watercolor West, Brea Civic Cultural Ctr., 1985, Watercolor West XXIII, Grand Art Galleries, Glendale, Calif., 1991, Watercolor West XXV, Riverside (Calif.) Art Mus., 1993, Watercolor West, 1994, Nat. Pen Women at Marjorie Evans Gallery, Carmel, 1986, Monterey County Juried Expo, Monterey Peninsula Mus. Art, 1986, 1987, Am. Artists Group Exhbn., 1993, 1994, 1995, Gallery Hirose, Tsukuba, Ibaragi, Japan, Internat. Art Show and End of World Hunger, Ashland, Oreg., 1990, biann. art exhbn. Sumner Mus., Washington, D.C., 1992, State of the Art, New Eng. Fine Arts, Boston, 1993, N.W. Wildlife, Nightingale Gallery, Ea. Oreg. Coll., La Grande, 1993, N.W. Visual Arts Ctr. 19th Ann., Panama City, Fla., 1993, NW Watercolor Soc. Waterworks N.W. Julie Tolles Gallery, Mercer Island, Wash., 1994, Represented in permanent collections Rogue Valley Manor Spl. Svcs., Medford, Oreg., Monterey Calif. Peninsula Mus. Art, Nat. Biscuit Co. subs. RJR Nabisco, San Jose, Waikato Mus. Art, Hamilton, N.Z., Muscular Dystrophy Assn., San Francisco, Old Sch. Hous Mus., Qualicum Bay, Vancouver Island, B.C., USS George Washington Aircraft Carrier, Adm. Robert Sprigg, Pres. Bill Clinton, Barbara Bush, George Montgomery, Marilyn Horne, Alison Krauss, also numerous pvt. collections. Recipient 1st prize, Monterey County Fair, 1979, Jade Fon Watercolor award, Hall of Flowers, San Francisco, 1980, 1st Nat. Art Show, NY Am. Artist mag., 1980, Nat. Art Appreciation award, 1984, award, Norcal State Art Fair, 1985, Watercolor award, 25 Ann. Aqueous Media Show, Salem, Oreg., 1990, award, Calif. Watercolor Soc., 2001, Silver award mem., Oreg. Watercolor Soc. Portland, 2000, numerous other awards for watercolor paintings. Mem.: Southern Oreg. Soc. Artists (Silver medal), Art Du Jour Gallery (dir. Medford, Oreg.), Women Artists Registry N.Am., Nat. Mus. Women in Arts, Art Alumni San Jose State U., Nat. League Am. Pen Women (pres. 1983—84, 1986—87), Cen. Coast Art Assn. (pres. 1982—85), Watercolor Soc., Rogue Valley Art Gallery (bd. officer 1995—96), LaHaina Arts Soc., Artists Equity Assn., Watercolor West Signature NWWS (hon. Watercolor Transparent award, Mercer Island 1994, Waterworks, Seattle 1999), Nat. Watercolor Soc. (assoc.), Am. Watercolor Soc. (assoc.). Achievements include artwork selected for inclusion in profl. pubs. including "Best of Watercolor" in Rockport Publr. and "The California Art Preview" Les Krantz. Home: 3533 Southvillage Dr Medford OR 97504-9283 Office Phone: 541-772-0136.

SCHUBERT, WILLIAM HENRY, curriculum studies educator; b. Garrett, Ind., July 6, 1944; s. Walter William and Mary Madeline (Grube) S.; children by previous marriage: Ellen Elaine, Karen Margaret; m. Ann Lynn Lopez, Dec. 3, 1977; children: Heidi Ann, Henry William. BS, Manchester Coll., 1966; MS, Ind. U., 1967; PhD, U. Ill., 1975. Tchr. Fairmount, El Sierra and Herrick Schs., Downers Grove, Ill., 1967—75; clin. instr. U. Wis., Madison, 1969—73; tchg. asst., fellow U. Ill., Urbana, 1973—75, asst. prof. Chgo., 1975—80, assoc. prof., 1981—85, prof., 1985—, coord. secondary edn., 1979—82, coord. instrnl. leadership, 1979—85, dir. grad. studies Coll. Edn., 1983—85, coord. grad. curriculum studies, 1985—2005, coord. edn. studies, 1990—94, 1996—, chair area curriculum and instrn., 1990—94, 2002—05, Univ. scholar, 2005—, coord. PhD program in curriculum and MEd program in edn. studies, 2006—. Vis. assoc. prof. U. Victoria (B.C., Can.), 1981; disting. vis. prof. U. S.C., 1986; presenter in field. Author (with Ann Lopez Schubert): Curriculum Books: The First Eighty Years, 1980; author: Curriculum: Perspective, Paradigm and Possibility, 1986, with Edmund C. Short and George Willis, 1985; author: (with J. Dan Marshall and James T. Sears) Turning Points in Curriculum: A Contemporary American Memoir, 2000; author: (with others) 2d edit., 2007; author: (with Ann Lopez Schubert, Thomas P. Thomas, Wayne M. Carroll) Curriculum Books: The First Hundred Years, 2002; editor (with Ann Lopez): Conceptions of Curriculum Knowledge: Focus on Students and Teachers, 1982; editor: (with George Willis) Reflections from the Heart of Educational Inquiry: Understanding Curriculum Teaching Through the Arts, 1991; editor: (with William Ayers) Teacher Lore: Learning From Our Own Experience, 1992, 2001; editor: (with George Willis, R. Bullugh, C. Kridel, J. Holton) The American Curriculum: A Documentary History, 1993; assoc. editor, mem. editl. bd. Ednl. Theory, mem. editl. bd. Catalyst: Voices of Chicago School Reform, Taboo: The Jour. of Culture and Edn., former mem. editl. bd. Ednl. Studies, former cons. editor Phenomenology and Pedagogy, adv. bd. Tchg. Edn., Pi Lamda Pubs., 1995—, Jour. Curriculum and Supervision, mem. editl. bd. Curriculum and Teaching, Jour. Curriculum and Pedagogy, emeritus editl. bd. Jour. Curriculum Theorizing, 1999—; editor: (book series) Student Lore, 1990—; cons. editor Jour. Curriculum Discourse and Dialogue, mem. adv. bd. Jour. Critical Issues in Curriculum and Instrn., 2000—, contbr. over 200 articles to profl. jours., chpt. to books. Mem.: ASCD (steering com. curriculum com. 1980—83, publs. com. 1987—90, internat. polling panel 1990—), Internat. Acad. Edn., Am. Assn. for Advancement of Curriculum Studies, Internat. Assn. for Advancement of Curriculum Studies, Soc. Profs. of Edn. (exec. bd. 1988—97, pres.-elect 2000—01, pres. 2001—02, Mary Ann Raywid award 2007), John Dewey Soc. (bd. dirs. 1986—95, chair awards com. 1988—90, co-chair lectures commn. 1989—91, 1989—91, pres.-elect 1990—91, pres. 1992—93), Inst. Dem. in Edn., Nat. Soc. Study Edn., World Coun. Curriculum and Instrn., Am. Ednl. Rsch. Assn. (chmn. creation and utilization of curriculum knowledge 1980—82, program chmn. curriculum studies divsn. 1982—83, sec. divsn. B 1989—91, v.p. 2000—01, Lifetime Achievement award in Curriculum Studies 2004), Am. Assn. Colls. Tchr. Edn., Soc. Study Curriculum History (sec.-treas. 1981—82, pres. 1982—83, founder), Profs. of Curriculum (factotum 1984—85), Internat. Acad. Edn., Scottish Rite, Masons, Phi Kappa Phi (pres. U. Ill. Chgo. chpt. 1981—82), Phi Delta Kappa. Office: U Ill Coll Edn M/C 147 1040 W Harrison St Chicago IL 60607-7129 Business E-Mail: schubert@uic.edu.

SCHUBERTH, JOHN M., surgeon; b. Chgo., Apr. 29, 1954; s. John E. and Jeanette A. Schuberth; m. Leigh Oshirak, July 1, 2000; 1 child, Jack Alexander. DPM, Ill. Coll. Pediat. Medicine, Chgo., 1981. Diplomate Am. Bd. Pediat. Surgery, 1985. Chief, foot and ankle surgery Kaiser Permanente Med. Group, San Francisco, 1984—. Contbr. scientific papers. Office: Dept Orthop Surgery 450 6th Ave San Francisco CA 94118 Personal E-mail: jmfoot@aol.com.

SCHUCHARD, ROBERT L., lawyer; b. LA, Feb. 14, 1952; BA in Polit. Sci., Stanford U., 1974; JD, Santa Clara U., 1977. Bar: Calif. 1977. Ptnr. Sonnenschein Nath & Rosenthal LLP, LA, 1997—2007, Davis Wright Tremaine LLP, LA, 2007—. Office Fax: 213-633-6899. Business E-Mail: robertschuchard@dwt.com.

SCHUCHAT, ANNE, federal agency administrator; BA in Philosophy, with minor in Biology, Swarthmore Coll., 1980, DS (hon.); MD, Dartmouth U., 1984. Resident in internal medicine Manhattan VA Hosp.; epidemic intelligence svc. officer Centers for Disease Control, Atlanta, 1988, chief respiratory diseases br., acting dir. Nat. Ctr. Infectious Diseases, dir. Nat. Immunization Program, 2005—, interim dep. dir. Sci. and Pub. Health Prog., 2009—; clin. asst. prof. medicine Emory U.; rear adm., asst. surgeon gen. USPHS, 2006—. Contbr. chapters to books, articles to profl. jours. Recipient Maternal and Child Health Young Investigator award, Am. Pub. Health Assn., Meritorious Svc. medal, USPHS; named Physician Rsch. Officer of Yr. Mem.: Inst. Medicine. Office: Nat Immunization Program CDC Mailstop C23 1600 Clifton Rd Atlanta GA 30333 E-mail: aschuchat@cdc.gov.*

SCHUCK, PETER HORNER, lawyer, educator; b. NYC, Apr. 26, 1940; s. Samuel H. and Lucille (Horner) S.; m. Marcy Cantor, June 26, 1966; children: Christopher, Julie. BA with honors, Cornell U., 1962; JD cum laude, Harvard U., 1965, MA, 1969; LLM, NYU, 1966; MA (hon.), Yale U., 1982. Bar: N.Y. State 1966, D.C. 1972. Practiced law, NYC, 1965-68; teaching fellow in govt. Harvard U., 1969-71; cons. Center for Study of Responsive Law, Washington, 1971-72; dir. Washington office Consumers Union, 1972-77; dep. asst. sec. for planning and evaluation HEW, Washington, 1977-79; vis. scholar Am. Enterprise Inst. for Public Policy Research, Washington, 1979; assoc. prof. law Yale U., 1979-81, prof., 1981-86, Simeon E. Baldwin prof. law, 1986—, dep. dean, 1993-94. Vis. prof. Georgetown U. Law Ctr., 1986-87, NYU Law Sch., fall 1994, N.Y. Law Sch., spring 1997, 98, 99, Fordham Law Sch., 2007. Author: The Judiciary Committees, 1975, Suing Government, 1983, Citizenship Without Consent, 1985; co-author: Agent Orange on Trial, 1986, enlarged edit., 1987, Citizens, Strangers and In-Betweens: Essays on Immigration and Citizenship, 1998, The Limits of Law: Essays on Democratic Governance, 2000, Diversity in America: Keeping Government at a Safe Distance, 2003, Meditations of a Militant Moderate: Cool Views on Hot Topics, 2006, Targeting in Social Programs: Avoiding Bad Bets, Removing Bad Apples, 2006; editor: Tort Law and the Public Interest, 1991, Foundations of Administrative Law, 1994, 2nd edit., 2004; co-editor: Paths to Inclusion, 1998, Immigration Stories, 2005,

Understanding America: The Anatomy of an Exceptional Nation, 2008; contbr. articles and revs. to profl. and popular publs. Recipient Silver Gavel award ABA, 1987; Guggenheim fellow, 1984-85; Fulbright scholar, 2004. Jewish. Office: Yale Law Sch PO Box 208215 New Haven CT 06520 Office Phone: 203-432-4967. E-mail: peter.schuck@yale.edu.

SCHUCK, THOMAS ROBERT, lawyer, farmer; b. Findlay, Ohio, Feb. 7, 1950; s. Robert Damon and Katherine Margaretta (Beynon) S. BA, DePauw U., 1972; MA, U. Kent, UK, 1974; JD, Harvard U., 1976. Bar: Ohio 1976, U.S. Dist. Ct. (no. dist.) Ohio 1977, U.S. Dist. Ct. (so. dist.) Ohio 1979, Ariz. 1990, U.S. Ct. Appeals (6th cir.) 1978, U.S. Ct. Appeals (9th cir.) 1991, U.S. Ct. Appeals Armed Forces, 2000, U.S. Supreme Ct. 2001. Law clk. U.S. Dist. Ct., Cleve., 1976-79; assoc. Taft, Stettinius & Hollister, Cin., 1979-87, ptnr., 1987—; owner, operator Rural Hill Farm. Participant Ohio Bench Bar Conf., Columbus, 1990-91, Glenmoor Justice Inst., 2000; barrister Am. Inn of Ct., 1986-87, LEAD Clermont, 1997-98; bar exam com. US Dist. Ct. (so. dist.) Ohio, MCU, panel criminal justice act, mem. criminal justice act atty. panel, 2006—; merit panel for bankruptcy judge selection US Ct. Appeals Sixth Cir., 1998, chair, 2002; life mem. Jud. Conf. of 6th Cir., mem. standing com., chair life mem. com., chair Scottish Rite Valley Cin. Found., trustee Ohio Found. Ind. Colleges Author: Federal Employment Litigation Practice Guide, 2006; contbg. author: Aids and the Law, 2d edit. 1992; contbr. articles to profl. jours. Trustee Mental Health Svcs. East, Inc., Cin., 1985-91, Ohio Found. Ind. Coll.; chair Scottish Rite Valley Cmty. Found.; sec. bd. trustees Joy Outdoor Edn. Ctr., Inc., 1999-2005; active May Festival Assocs., Cin., 1984-86, WGUC Radio Cmty. Bd., 1984-86, Clermont County Mental Health Bd., Batavia, Ohio, 1992-2000, vice-chmn., 1997-2000; steering com. Clermont County Mental Retardation Developmental Disabilities Levy, 1996, trustee, 2000-02, vice-chmn., 2002; spl. gifts com. Cin. Art Acad., 1987, Ohio Found. Ind. Colls., 1995-, bd. dir., 2003—; pres. Fed. Bar Assn. Found. Cin. Grad. fellow Rotary Internat. Found., 1972-73. Mem. Fed. Bar Assn. (pres. Cin. chpt. 1994-95, v.p. 6th cir. 1996-99, nat. membership chair 1997-99, nat. sec. 2001-2002, nat. treas., nat. v.p. 2002-03, nat. pres.-elect 2003-04, nat. pres. 2004-05, govt. rels. com., pres. Foun. of Cin.), Potter Stewart Am. Inn of Ct. (barrister 1986-87), U.S. Rowing Assn. (asst. referee), Harvard Club Cin. (pres. 1995-96), Soc. Bacchus Am., Masons (33rd degree, trustee Valley of Cin. 2003-05), Phi Beta Kappa, Delta Chi, Phi Eta Sigma, Sigma Delta Chi, Scottish Kite Valley & Cin. Found. Republican. Methodist. Avocations: reading, photography. Home: PO Box 615 189 State Route 133 Felicity OH 45120 Office: Taft Stettinius & Hollister LLP Ste 1800 425 Walnut St Cincinnati OH 45202-3957 Home Phone: 513-633-1841; Office Phone: 513-381-2838.

SCHUCKENBROCK, STEVE (STEPHEN FRANCIS SCHUCKENBROCK), computer company executive, former information technology executive; b. 1960; BBA, Elon Coll., 1982. Sales & tech. mgmt. positions IBM Corp., 1983—93; ptnr. Feld Group, 1993—95, COO, 2000—04; chief info. officer Frito-Lay, 1995—98; sr. v.p. info. tech. PepsiCo. Inc., 1998—2000; exec. v.p. global sales & client solutions Electronic Data Systems, Plano, Tex., 2003—06; sr. v.p., pres. global services, chief info. officer Dell Inc., Round Rock, Tex., 2007—09, pres. large enterprise, 2009—. Office: Dell Inc 1 Dell Way Round Rock TX 78682*

SCHUDER, JOHN CLAUDE, retired biomedical engineer, educator; b. Olney, Ill., Mar. 2, 1922; s. Charles Claude Schuder and Louise Ella Muench; m. Retha Elizabeth Sumner, July 23, 1946; children: Linda Lee Brown, Charles Wayne, Jonna Elizabeth. BSEE, U. Ill., 1943; MSEE, Purdue U., 1951, PhD, 1954. Jr. engr. Westinghouse Rsch., East Pittsburgh, Pa., 1943-44; from instr. to asst. prof. Purdue U., West Lafayette, Ind., 1949-56; assoc. prof. Doane Coll., Crete, Nebr., 1956-57; fellow, asst. prof. U. Pa., Phila., 1957-60; from assoc. prof. to prof. emeritus U. Mo. Sch. Medicine, Columbia, 1960—85, prof. emeritus, 1985—. Cons. Hewlett-Packard, Medtronics, GE, Physio Control, NIH, others. Mem. editl. bd. PACE, 1991—; contbr. articles to profl. jours. Peace activist, anti-death penalty activist Mid-Mo. Fellowship Reconciliation, 1960—. Grantee, NIH, Am. Heart Assn., Mo. Heart Assn., others. Mem.: IEEE Engring. Medicine and Biology Soc. (life). Mem. Soc. Friends. Achievements include development of transcutaneous energy transformer used with implanted artificial hearts; being the first to demonstrate the use of completely implantable cardiac ventricular defibrillator in animals; research in experimental rationale for waveforms used in cardiac defibrillators. Home: 105 Manor Dr Columbia MO 65203-1727 Home Phone: 573-445-7569.

SCHUELE, DONALD EDWARD, retired physics professor, dean; b. Cleve., June 16, 1934; s. Edward and Mildred (Matousek) S.; m. Clare Ann Kirchner, Sept. 5, 1956; children: Donna, Karen, Melanie, Judy, Rachel, Ruth. BS, John Carroll U., Cleve., 1956, MS, 1957; PhD, Case Inst. Tech., 1962. Instr. physics and math. John Carroll U., 1956-59; part-time instr. physics Case Inst. Tech., 1959-62, instr., asst. prof., assoc. prof., 1962-70; mem. tech. staff Bell Telephone Labs., 1970-72; assoc. prof. physics Case Western Res. U., 1972-74, prof., 1974—, dean undergrad. coll., 1973-76, chmn. dept. physics, 1976-78; vice dean Case Inst. Tech., 1978-83, v.p. for undergrad. and grad. studies, 1983-84, dean, 1984-86, prof. physics, 1986-88, dean math. and natural sci., 1988-89, Albert A. Michelson prof. physics, 1989—2006, Albert A. Michelson emeritus prof. physics, 2006, acting chmn. elec. engring. and applied physics, 1992-93. Cons. in field. Co-editor: Critical Revs. in Solid State Scis, 1969-84; contbr. articles to profl. jours.; patentee in field. Mem. adv. bd. St. Charles Borromeo Sch., 1970-72; pres. Seed Found., 1986-89; trustee St. Mary's Sem., 1980-93; mem. Olympic Sports Equipment and Tech. Com., 1982-93; trustee Newman Found., 1983—, Northeastern Ohio Sci. Fair, 1983—, Curriculum Adv. Com., South Eudid, Lyndhurst Sch. Sys., 2006-; mem. Diocesan Pastoral Coun., 1992-94; active Rep. Presdl. task force; bd. dirs. Beaumont Sch. Girls 2009. Recipient Disting. Physics Alumnus award John Carroll U., 1983; NSF Faculty fellow, 1961-63; Sam Givelber fellow Case Alumni Assn., 2001. Mem.: North Coast Thermal Analysis Soc., Am. Assn. Physics Tchrs., Am. Phys. Soc. (vice chair Ohio sect. 1995—96, chair 1996—97), Newman Apostolate, Case Alumni Coun. (life; 3d v.p. 2001—02, 1st v.p. 2002—03, pres. 2003—04, treas. 1992, chair Case Fund Bd. 2004—), Tau Beta Pi, Sigma Xi, Alpha Sigma Nu. Republican. Roman Catholic. Achievements include patents fluid pressure device, impact wrench torque calibrator, detection of wear particles and other impurities in industrial fluids, electrical oil analysis instrument. Home: 4892 Countryside Rd Cleveland OH 44124-2513 Office: Case We Res Univ 10900 Euclid Ave Cleveland OH 44106-1712 Home Phone: 216-382-0561; Office Phone: 216-368-4013. Business E-Mail: des3@case.edu.

SCHUELER, JOHN R., newspaper executive; b. Grosse Point, Mich. m. Linda Schueler; children: Tracie, Lindsey. BA, W. Mich. U. Dir. sales Atlanta Jour. & Constn., 1979—82; with Miami Herald, Miami, Fla., 1984—89; pres. New England Newspapers, 1989—91; v.p. consumer mktg. & circulation The Orange County Register, Santa Ana, Calif., 1991—92, exec. v.p. & gen. mgr., 1992—95, pres., COO, 1995-98; publisher Star Tribune, Mpls., 1998—2001; pub. Los Angeles Daily News, 2001—04; pres., CEO Los Angeles Newspaper Group, 2004—05; pres. Fla. Comm. Group, 2005—. Office: Media General Broadcast Group 200 S Parker St Tampa FL 33606 Office Phone: 813-221-5757.

SCHUELKE, JOHN PAUL, religious organization administrator; b. Benton Harbor, Mich., Nov. 5, 1934; s. Alwin E. and Martha M. (Schoeneberg) S.; m. Noreta H. Petersen, Sept. 9, 1956; children: Alvin, Mary, Sheryl, Brian. BS in Acctg., U. Wyo., 1957; LLD (hon.), Concordia U., Irvine, Calif., 1983. CPA. From acct. to sr. acct. Colo. Interstate Gas Co., Colorado Springs, 1957-63; staff acct. Arthur Anderson & Co., Denver, 1963-64; mgr. fin. control Colo. Interstate Corp., Colorado Springs., 1964-67, dir. fin. control, 1967-71; adminstrv. v.p. mfg. divsn. Marsh Instrument Co. subs. Colo. Mfg. Corp., Skokie, Ill., 1971-72; exec. officer bd. dirs., CAO Luth. Ch.-Mo. Synod, St. Louis, 1972-98, ret., 1999. Former chmn. Concordia Asia Ednl. Found.; lectr. in field. Asst. scoutmaster Boy Scouts Am., Colorado Springs; former mem. governing bd., sec. Luth. Svcs. in Am.; former mem. governing bd. Luth. Coun.-USA, com. Luth. Coop.; former v.p. Faith Luth Ch., Woodland Park; former mem. bd. human care ministries, sec., mem. lic. deacon com. Rocky Mountain dist. Luth. Ch.-Mo. Synod. Recipient God and Country award Eagle Scout. Mem. Alpha Kappa Psi, Gamma Delta (former pres.). Lutheran. Avocations: travel, fishing, reading.

SCHUELLER, THOMAS GEORGE, lawyer; b. Budapest, Hungary, Oct. 4, 1936; came to U.S., 1938; s. Herbert H. and Edith (Geiringer) S.; m. Sandra Burke, Sept. 3, 1960 (div. Apr. 1982), Linda W. Beech, Aug. 15, 2008; children: Katherine, Matthew, John. AB cum laude, Amherst Coll., 1958; LLB, Harvard U., 1962. Bar: N.Y. 1963. Salesman Gen. Mills. Inc., Utica, NY, 1958-59; assoc. Hughes Hubbard & Reed, NYC, 1962-69, ptnr., 1969—2006, sr. counsel, 2007—. Bd. dirs., sec. Ballet Hispanico, N.Y.C., 1987-2001. Mem. ABA, Assn. of Bar of City of N.Y., Phi Beta Kappa. Home: 335 W 70th St New York NY 10023-3525 Office: Hughes Hubbard & Reed LLP 1 Battery Park Plz New York NY 10004-1482 also: PO Box 562 108 Fairchild Rd Sharon CT 06069-2440 Office Phone: 212-837-6744. E-mail: schuelle@hugheshubbard.com.

SCHUENEMAN, BRUCE R., librarian; b. Lodi, Ohio, Apr. 23, 1955; s. Robert H. and Margaret Lois Schueneman; m. Maria de Jesus Ayala-Leon, Aug. 12, 1978; children: Sara Elisa Schueneman-Ayala, Herbert Charles Schueneman-Ayala. BA, U. Calif. Berkeley, 1977; MLS, San Jose State U., Calif., 1978; MS, Tex. A&I U., Kingsville, 1983. Head libr. sys. Tex. A&M U., Kingsville, 1997—2008, assoc. dir. sys. & tech. svcs., 2008—. Govt. docs. libr. Tex. A&I U., 1979—83, interlibrary loan libr., 1983—89, acquisitions, serials libr., 1989—95; history instr. Tex. A&M U., 1990—94, head tech. svcs., 1995—96, head collection svcs., 1996—97, co-interim dir., 1999. Co-author: (book) Barbershops, Bullets, and Ballads, College Fight Songs, State Songs of the United States; author: Minor Ballet Composers: Biographical Sketches of Sixty Six Underappreciated Yet Significant Contributors to the Body of Western Ballet Music, The French Violin School: Viotti, Rode, Kreutzer, Baillot and their Contemporaries; author: (translator) The Life and Music of Pierre Rode: containing An Account of Rode, French Violinist. Active Kingsville Symphony Orch., 2006—09. Mem.: ALA, Tex. Libr. Assn., Music Libr. Assn. Presbyterian. Office: Tex A&M Univ-Kingsville 700 Univ Blvd MSC 197 Kingsville TX 78363 Personal E-mail: bruce.schueneman@gmail.com. Business E-Mail: brs@tamuk.edu.

SCHUENEMAN, DIANE L., diversified financial services company executive; Account exec. instl. sales Merrill Lynch, 1971, head global ops. and infrastructure svcs., 2004—06, sr. v.p., head global infrastructure solutions grp., 2006—. Bd. mgrs. Omgeo; bd. dirs. Depository Trust and Clearing Corpn. Named one of The 100 Most Influential Women in NYC Bus., Crain's NY Bus., 2007. Office: Merrill Lynch 4 World Fin Ctr 250 Vesey St New York NY 10080

SCHUEPPERT, GEORGE LOUIS, financial executive; b. Merrill, Wis., July 1, 1938; s. George Henry and Eleanor Natalie (Pautz) S.; m. Kathleen Kay Carpenter, May 6, 1967; children: Steven Andrew, Stephanie Roanne, Stenning Karl BBA, U. Wis., Madison, 1961; MBA, U. Chgo., 1969. Treas., controller Steiger-Rathke Devel. Co., Phoenix, 1964-65; various positions Continental Ill. Nat., Chgo., 1965—76, 1981—86; mng. dir. Continental Ill. Ltd., London, 1977-81; sr. v.p. Continental Ill. Nat. Bank, Chgo., 1982-86; ptnr. Coopers & Lybrand, Chgo., 1986-87; exec. v.p. fin. CBI Industries Inc, Oak Brook, Ill., 1987-95, also bd. dirs., 1987-95; exec. v.p., CFO Outboard Marine Corp., Waukegan, Ill., 1996-97. Bd. dirs. Wells Mfg. Co., Barrington Bank & Trust Co. Pres. Gt. Books Found., pres. Atlas Rsch. found., West Am. Mortgage Co.; chmn., bd. dirs. De Paul U. Gov. Asst. Program. Lt. (j.g.) USN, 1961-64, trustee Village Barrington Hills. Recipient Herfurth award U. Wis., 1960 Mem. Econ. Club Chgo. (bd. dirs., chmn. membership com.). Republican. Avocations: history, architecture, travel, golf. Home: 97 Otis Rd Barrington IL 60010-5129 Office: Great Books Found 35 E Wacker Dr Ste 400 Chicago IL 60601-2298

SCHUERHOLZ, JOHN BOLAND, JR., professional baseball executive; b. Balt., Oct. 1, 1940; s. John Boland and Maryne (Wyatt) Schuerholz; m. Ellen Louise Lawson, June 21, 1963; 1 child, Regina Marie Reagan; m. Karen Louise Wiltse, Sept. 18, 1978; 1 child, Jonathan Lawrence. BE, Towson State U., 1962; postgrad., Loyola Coll., Md., 1964—66. Tchr. various schs., 1962—66; adminstrv. asst. Balt. Orioles, 1966—68, Kans. City Royals, 1968—70, asst. farm dir., 1970—75, farm dir., 1975, dir. scouting & player devel., 1976—79, v.p. player pers., 1979—81, exec. v.p., gen. mgr., 1981—90, Atlanta Braves, 1990—2007, pres., 2007—. With AUS, 1966—72. Recipient Lifetime Achievement award, Baseball America, 2004. Lutheran. Office: Atlanta Braves PO Box 4064 Atlanta GA 30302-4064

SCHUESSLER, JOHN T. (JACK SCHUESSLER), retired food service executive; b. Dec. 21, 1950; m. Patty A. Schuessler. BS, Spring Hill Coll. Mgr. trainee Wendy's franchise, Atlanta, 1974-76; joined Wendy's Internat., 1976, dist. mgr., dir. area ops., regional dir. various zones US, 1976-83, regional v.p. ea. divsn., 1983-84, zone pres., 1984-86, divsn. v.p., 1986-87, sr. v.p. N.E. region, 1987-95, exec. v.p. US ops., 1995-97, pres., COO US ops., 1997-2000, pres., COO Can., 1999-2000, pres., CEO, 2000—06, chmn., 2001—06. Trustee Wendy's Nat. Advtsg. Program.

SCHUESSLER, THOMAS FREDERICK, medical educator; b. St. Louis, Dec. 11, 1947; s. Bernice AnnaMary and Oscar Phillip Schuessler; m. Fern Ella Pflantz, June 20, 1970; children: Cheri Ann McGuire, Jon Roland, Amanda Sue Stegeman. BS in Physics, Wash. U., St. Louis, 1970; MA in Tchg., Webster U., St. Louis, 1992. Tchr. Peace Corps, Washington, 1970—72; biomed. technician Wash. U. Biomed. Lab., St. Louis, 1972—76; project engr. Sherwood Med. Industries, Maryland Heights, Mo., 1976—81; magician Self-Employed, St. Louis, 1981—92; prof. Jefferson Coll., Hillsboro, Mo., 1992—. Author: (children's play) The Wishing Machine. Named Emmerson Excellance in Tchg., Emmerson Electric Co., 1998. Mem.: Phi Delta Kappa. Lutheran. Achievements include patents for plastic medical products. Avocations: magic, spelunking. Home: 9212 Hwy BB Hillsboro MO 63050 Office: Jefferson Coll 1000 Viking Dr Hillsboro MO 63050

SCHUESSLER FIORENZA, ELISABETH, theology studies educator; b. Tschanad, Romania, Apr. 17, 1938; parents German citizens; d. Peter and Magdalena Schuessler; m. Francis Fiorenza, Dec. 17, 1967; 1 child, Chris. MDiv, U. Wuerzburg, Germany, 1962; Lic. Theol., U. Wuerzburg, 1963; DrTheol, U. Muenster, Germany, 1970, Dr. hc. mult. Asst. prof. theology U. Notre Dame, South Bend, Ind., 1970-75, assoc. prof., 1975-80, prof., 1980-84; instr. U. Muenster, 1966-67; Talbot prof. N.T., Episcopal Div. Sch., Cambridge, Mass., 1984-88; Krister Stendahl prof. Divsn. Scripture and Interpretation Harvard U., Cambridge, Mass., 1988—. Harry Emerson Fosdick vis. prof. Union Theol. Sem., N.Y.C., 1974-75, vis. prof. U. Jasel, 2003; guest prof. U. Tuebingen, Federal Republic of Germany, 1987, Cath. Theol. Faculty Luzern, Switzerland, 1990; Stiftungs prof. Humboldt U., Berlin, 1997; Ernst Troeltsch prof. U. Heidelberg, Germany, 1999. Author: Der Vergessene Partner, 1964, Priester für Gott, 1972, The Apocalypse, 1976, Invitation to the Book of Revelation, 1981, In Memory of Her, 1983, Bread not Stone, 1984, Judgement or Justice, 1985, Revelation: Vision of a Just World, 1991, But She Said - Feminist Practices of Biblical Interpretation, 1992, Discipleship of Equals: A Critical Feminist Ekklesialogy of Liberation, 1993, Jesus: Miriam's Child and Sophia's Prophet, Critical Issues in Feminist Christology, 1994, Sharing Her Word, 1998, Rhetoric and Ethic The Politics of Biblical Studies, 1999, Jesus and the Politics of Interpretation, 2000, Wisdom Ways, 2001, Grenzen uberschreiten, 2004, The Power of the Word, 2007, Democratizing Liberal Studies, 2009; editor: Searching the Scriptures, 2 vols, 1993, 94, The Power of Naming, 1996; founding co-editor Jour. Feminist Studies in Religion, The Prob of Prejudices, 2009; also editor other works. Mem.: Am. Acad. Arts and Scis., Soc. Bibl. Lit. (past pres.), Am. Acad. Religion. Office: Harvard Div Sch 45 Francis Ave Cambridge MA 02138-1911 Office Phone: 617-495-5751.

SCHUETTINGER, BRUCE MICHAEL, conservator; b. Frederick, Md., Apr. 15, 1955; s. Arthur George Schuettinger and Shirlee Price; children: Kathryn, Alison. BS in Fine Arts cum laude, Towson State U., 1978. Conservator Antique Restorations, Frederick, Md., 1983—90, Antique Restorations Ltd., New Market, Md., 1990—2007; personal property appraiser Internat. Soc. of Appraisers (Indiana U.), 1985, 1986—2008, U. Md., 1985; conservator Schuetinger Conservation Svcs., Inc., 2007—. Presenter in field. Co-author: (directory) Conservation Resources for Art and Antiques, 2001; contbr. articles to profl. jours. Mem. curitorial com. Hist. Soc. of Frederick County, Md., 2002—05. Mem.: Wash. Conservation Guild, Am. Inst. for Conservation of Historic and Artistic Wants (assoc.). Independent. Episcopalian. Avocations: painting, photography. Home: 13724 Pryor Rd Thurmont MD 21788 Office Phone: 301-865-3009. Personal E-mail: bschuettinger@verizon.net.

SCHUH, DALE R., insurance company executive; Joined Sentry Ins. Group, Stevens Point, Wis., 1972, v.p. planning, 1988, pres., COO, 1996, CEO, pres., chmn., 1997—. Office: Sentry Ins Group 1800 North Point Dr Stevens Point WI 54481

SCHUKER, STEPHEN ALAN, historian, educator; b. NYC, Feb. 16, 1939; s. Louis A. and Millicent (Milchman) S.; m. Elisabeth Glaser, 1998. AB summa cum laude, Cornell U., 1959; AM, Harvard U., 1962, PhD, 1969; children: Lauren, Daniel. Asst. head hist. rsch. naval history div. Office Chief Naval Ops., 1959-61; instr. history Harvard U., Cambridge, Mass., 1968-69, asst. prof., 1969-74, lectr., 1974-75; vis. assoc. prof. European studies Sch. Advanced Internat. Studies, Johns Hopkins U., Washington, 1977, adj. prof., 1978-83; assoc. prof. history Brandeis U., Waltham, Mass., 1977-82, prof., 1982-91; Commonwealth prof. history U. Va., Charlottesville, 1991-92, William W. Corcoran prof., 1992—; syndic U. Press New Eng., 1979-81; cons. Nat. Commn. Documents and Records Federal Ofcls., 1976, Rockefeller Found., 1981. Author: The End of French Predominance in Europe (George Louis Beer prize, Gilbert Chinard prize), 1976, American "Reparations" to Germany, 1919-1933: Implications for the Third World Debt Crisis, 1988; editor: Deutschland und Frankreich vom Konflikt zur Aussöhnung, 2000; mem. bd. editors Internat. History Rev., 2001-2004; contbr. articles to profl. jours. Lt. USNR, 1959-61. NEH fellow, 1972-73; Am. Council Learned Socs. fellow, 1976-77, 85; sr. fellow USIA-Fulbright Commn., 1984, fellow internat. security John D. and Catherine T. MacArthur Found., 1987-89, fellow Historisches Kolleg, Bayerische Akademie der Wissenschaften, 1996—, fellow German Marshall Fund, 1998-99. Mem. Am. Hist. Assn., Soc. Historians Am. Fgn. Relations, Hist. Soc. Office: U Va Corcoran Dept History University Station Charlottesville VA 22904 Office Phone: 434-924-6405. Business E-Mail: sas4u@virginia.edu.

SCHULD, SUSAN MARIE, performing arts educator; b. Auburn, Wash., Feb. 22, 1971; d. Delbert George and Margaret Ann Schuld. BA, U. Wash., Seattle, 1994; MFA, Rutgers U. Mason Gross Sch. Arts, NB, NJ, 2001; AA, Green River Coll., Auburn, 1991. Prof. voice and speech Rutgers U., NYC, 2002—, NYC Tisch Sch. Arts, 2003—, Maggie Flanigan Acting Studio, NYC, 2006—; dir. residence, mason gross sch. arts Internat. Shakespeare Globe Ctr., London, England, 2003—04. Founding mem. Lila Theater Co., Jersey City, 2001—. Recipient award, Ariz. Awards com., 1996. Democrat. Roman Cath. Avocations: yoga, singing, gardening. Office: Rutgers Univ Theater Arts 2 Chapel Dr New Brunswick NJ 08901-8577 Business E-Mail: susanschuld@gmail.com.

SCHULDT, BARBARA JEAN, school librarian; b. St. Cloud, Minn., May 6, 1945; d. Frank Anton and Marcella Rose (Schill) Laudenbach; m. Richard John Schuldt; children: Robert Paul, Ryan David, Denae Elizabeth. Degree in Bus., St. Cloud Tech. HS, 1963. Ward stenographer Vets. Adminstrn. Hosp., St. Cloud, 1963—69; ins. claims clk. Prudential Ins. Co., Golden Valley, Minn., 1969—71; med. sec. Marquette Gen. Hosp., Mich., 1972—74; clerical asst. Jeane Thorne Temp. Agy., Eagan, Minn., 1992—93; sales assoc. Penneys Dept. Store, Burnsville, Minn., 1994—96; libr. technician Dakota County Tech. Coll., Rosemount, Minn., 1995—. Libr. vol. Risen Savior Cath. Ch., Burnsville, Minn., 1992—93. Dfl. Roman Catholic.

SCHULER, ALISON KAY, lawyer; b. West Point, NY, Oct. 1, 1948; d. Richard Hamilton and Irma (Sanken) S.; m. Lyman Gage Sandy, Mar. 30, 1974, (dec. Mar. 2002); 1 child, Theodore. AB cum laude, Radcliffe Coll., 1969; JD, Harvard U., 1972. Bar: Va. 1973, D.C. 1974, N.Mex. 1975. Assoc. Hunton & Williams, Richmond, Va., 1972-75; asst. U.S. atty. U.S. Atty.'s Office, Albuquerque, 1975-78; adj. prof. law U. N.Mex., 1983-85, 90, 98—; ptnr. Sutin, Thayer & Browne, Albuquerque, 1978-85, Montgomery & Andrews, P.A., Albuquerque, 1985-88; sole practice Albuquerque, 1988—. Bd. dirs. Am. Diabetes Assn., Albuquerque, 1980—85, chmn. bd. dirs., 1984—85; bd. dirs. Chamber Music Albuquerque, 1980—2006, pres., 1983—85, 1993—94; bd. dirs. Albuquerque Conservation Trust, 1986—90, N.Mex. Osteo. Found., 1993—96; chairperson Albuquerque Com. Fgn. Rels., 1984—85; mem.

N.Mex. Internat. Trade and Investment Coun., Inc., 1986—; chartered org. rep. troop 444 Boy Scouts Am., 1997—, mem. nominating com., mem.-at-large dist. com. Sandia dist., 1998—, dist. vice chmn., 1999—2002, v.p. Great S.W. coun., 2001—05, pres. Great S.W. coun., 2006—09, mem. staff, 2002—04, wood badge course dir., 2005, western region exec. bd. and area v.p., 2008—, area pres., 2009—; bd. mem. Rotary Club Albuquerqu, 2009—; mem. coun. St. Lukes Luth. Ch., 1976—80, 1982—84, 1991—96, pres., 1994—95. Recipient Award of Merit, Sandia Dist., 2000, Svc. award, Albuquerque Astron. Soc., 2002, Silver Beaver award, Gt. S.W. Coun., 2002; named to, Best Lawyers Am., 2006. Mem. Fed. Bar Assn. (coord.), ABA, Va. Bar Assn., Dist. Columbia Bar, N.Mex. Bar Assn. (chmn. corp., banking and bus. law 1982-83, bd. dirs. internat. and immigration law sect. 1987-95, chmn. 1993-94), Albuquerque Astron. Soc. (Svc. award 2002), Harvard U. Alumni Assn. (mem. fund campaign, regional dir. 1984-86, v.p. 1986-89, chmn. clubs com. 1985-88, chmn. communications com. 1988-91), Radcliffe Coll. Alumnae Assn. Bd. Mgmt. (regional dir. 1984-87, chmn. comms. com. 1988-91), Harvard-Radcliffe Club (pres. 1980-84). Home: 632 Cougar Loop NE Albuquerque NM 87122-1808 Office: 10611 4th St NW Albuquerque NM 87114-2407 Office Phone: 505-872-0800. Personal E-mail: akschuler@aol.com. Business E-Mail: akschuler@schulerdaly.com.

SCHULER, MARY CALLAGHAN, artist, educational association administrator; b. Upper Darby, Pa., Aug. 15, 1938; d. John J. Callaghan and Catherine Graham Callaghan O'Reilly; m. Richard E. Schuler, May 12, 1962; children: Richard E., Anne E., Judith M. Cert. in Oil Painting, RI Sch. Design, Providence, 1972; BS, Cornell U., Ithaca, NY, 1979. Dir. activities Ithacare Ctr., Ithaca, NY, 1979—82; exec. staff asst. Einaudi Ctr. Internat. Studies Cornell U., Ithaca, 1983—93. Exhibitions include Logan Ridge Winery, 2002, Clinton Ho. Artspace, 2002, State of the Art Gallery, 2004—09, Artifax Gallery, 2004—09, Upstairs Gallery, 2005—09, Cmty. Sch. Music and Art, Ithaca, 2005, Tompkins Cmty. Libr., 2005, 2009, The Corners Gallery, 2007—09, Art of Friends, 2007—09, Topkins County Airport, 2009, 171 Cedar Arts Ctr. Show, 2009. Bd. dirs. State of the Art Gallery, Ithaca, 2004—08. Mem.: Cornell Alumni Assn. and Club, Cornell Campus Club, Ithaca Garden Club, Sigma Alpha Iota. Avocations: painting, reading, walking. Home: 2 Captains Walk Ithaca NY 14850-8502 Personal E-mail: mcs@lightlink.com.

SCHULER, ROBERT HUGO, chemist, educator; b. Buffalo, Jan. 4, 1926; s. Robert H. and Mary J. (Mayer) S.; m. Florence J. Forrest, June 18, 1952; children: Mary A., Margaret A., Carol A., Robert E., Thomas C. BS, Canisius Coll., Buffalo, 1946; PhD, U. Notre Dame, 1949. Asst. prof. chemistry Canisius Coll., 1949-53; asso. chemist, then chemist Brookhaven Nat. Lab., 1953-56; staff fellow, dir. radiation research lab. Mellon Inst., 1956-76, mem. adv. bd., 1962-76; prof. chemistry, dir. radiation research lab. Carnegie-Mellon U., 1967-76; prof. chemistry U. Notre Dame, Ind., 1976—, dir. radiation lab. Ind., 1976-95, dir. emeritus, 1995—, John A. Zahm prof. radiation chemistry, 1986—; Raman prof. U. Madras, India, 1985-86. Vis. prof. Hebrew U., Israel, 1980. Author articles in field. Recipient Curie medal Poland, 1992. Fellow AAAS; mem. Am. Chem. Soc., Am. Phys. Soc., Chem. Soc., Radiation Research Soc. (pres. 1975-76), Sigma Xi. Clubs: Cosmos. Office: U Notre Dame Radiation Lab Notre Dame IN 46556 Home Phone: 574-272-7723. Business E-Mail: schuler.1@nd.edu.

SCHULER, ROBERT JORDAN, language educator, writer; b. San Mateo, Calif., June 25, 1939; s. Edward Peter and Georgia Ruth Schuler; m. Carol Florence Schuler, Sept. 7, 1963; children: Sally, Edward Anthony, Michael. BA in Polit. Sci. with honors, Stanford U., 1961; MA in Comparative Lit., U. Calif., Berkeley, 1965; PhD in English, U. Minn., 1989. Instr. English Menlo Coll., Menlo Park, Calif., 1965-67; instr. humanities Shimer Coll., Mt. Carroll, Ill., 1967-77; prof. English U. Wis.-Stout, Menomonie, 1978—. Hormel prof. U. Wis.-Stout, 1995-96. Author: Seasonings, 1978, Axle of the Oak, 1978, Where is Dancers' Hill?, 1979, Morning Raga, 1980, Origins, 1981, The Red Cedar Scroll, 1981, Music for Monet, 1985; Floating Out of Stone, 1982 (award Coun. Wis. Writers 1983), Grace, 1995, Red Cedar Suite, 1999, Journey Toward the Original Mind, 1995, In Search of Green Dolphin Street, 2004, dance into heaven, 2005, Songs of Love, 2006, (collection with Janet Butler) Ekphrastic Poems, 2007; contbr. numerous poems to lit. jours. Bd. dirs. Shimer Coll. Assn., Waukegan, Ill., 1997—1999; dir. film series Menomonie Pub. Libr., 1997-2002; mem. land use planning com. Twp. of Menomonie, 1999-2002, writer land use plan, 2002—; commr. Land Use Plan Com., Menomonie, 2002—09 Recipient New Works award Wis. Arts Bd., 1999; pub. grant Ill. Arts Coun., Chgo., 1976-77, Nat. Endowment, Washington, 1978, Midwest Arts grant NEA, Menomonie Pub. Lib., 2004; fellow Danforth Found., 1969-70, lit. fellow (poetry) Wis. Arts Bd., Madison, 1997 Mem. Phi Kappa Phi. Avocations: cross country skiing, hiking, gardening. Home: E4549 479th Ave Menomonie WI 54751 Office: Dept English and Philosophy U Wis-Stout Menomonie WI 54751 Office Phone: 715-232-1454. Business E-Mail: schulerr@uwstout.edu.

SCHULER, THEODORE ANTHONY, retired civil engineer; b. Louisville, July 1, 1934; s. Henry R. and Virginia (Meisner) S.; m. Jane A. Bandy, July 29, 1979; children: Marc, Elizabeth, Eric, Ellen. BCE, U. Louisville, 1957, M Engring., 1973. Registered profl. engr. Tenn. Design constrn. engr. Brighton Engring. Co., Frankfort, Ky., 1960—65; design engr. Hensley-Schmidt Inc., Chattanooga, 1965—68, assoc., 1969—73, sr. assoc., 1973—75, prin., asst. v.p., head Knoxville office, 1975—81; chief planning engr. engring. dept. City Knoxville, 1981—96, ret., 1996. Served to lt. (j.g.) USNR, 1957-60. Fellow: ASCE. Home: 5907 Adelia Dr Knoxville TN 37920-5801 Personal E-mail: tschu30447@aol.com.

SCHULER, WALTER E., lawyer; b. Memphis, Tenn., Sept. 8, 1962; s. James D. and Clare A. Schuler. BBA magna cum laude, U. Memphis, 1993; JD cum laude with cert. in health law with hons., St. Louis U., 1996. Bar: Tenn. 1996, U.S. Dist. Ct. (Western Dist.) Tenn. 1996, U.S. Ct. Appeals (6th cir.), 1998. Assoc. The Bogatin Law Firm, PLC, Memphis, Tenn., 1996—. Contbr. articles to profl. jours., chpt. to book. Sgt. (E-5), U.S. Army, 1985-90, staff sgt. (E-6) USAR, 1990-93. Recipient Commendation Medal-1st Oak Leaf Cluster, U.S. Army, 1989, Army Achievement Medal-2nd Oak Leaf Cluster, 1989, Nat. Def. Svc. Med., 1992. Mem. Am. Health Lawyers Assn., ABA, Tenn. Bar Assn., Memphis Bar Assn. Office: Evans Petree Bogatin PC Ste 300 International Place Dr Memphis TN 38120

SCHULHOF, MICHAEL PETER, electronics company executive; b. NYC, Nov. 30, 1942; s. Rudolph B. and Hannelore (Buck) Schulhof; m. Paola Nissim, Apr. 17, 1969; children: David Kenneth, Jonathan Nissim. BA, Grinnell Coll., 1964, DSc (hon.), 1990; MS, Cornell U., 1967; PhD, Brandeis U., 1970. Lic. comml. pilot. Am. rsch. fellow Brookhaven Nat. Lab., Uptown, NY, 1969—71; asst. to v.p. mfg. CBS Records, Inc., NYC, 1971—73, exec. com., bd. dirs., 1987—88; from gen. mgr. bus. products divsn. to sr. v.p. Sony Corp., NYC, 1973—86; pres. Sony Industries, NYC, 1978—86; chmn. Digital Audio Disc Corp., Terre Haute, Ind., 1986—96; pres. Sony Software Corp., 1991—96; pres., CEO Sony Corp. Am., 1993—95. Chmn. bd. dirs. Quadriga Art Inc., 1980—, World On Line, 1998—99; bd. dirs. Sony Corp., Japan, Sony Corp. Am., Sony Pictures Entertainment, Materials Rsch. Corp., J2 Global Commn., 1997—, CBS/Sportsline; chmn. Sony Music Entertainment; former chmn. Comml. Electronics, 1998—; chmn., CEO Global Tech. Investments, 2001—; mem., coun. of fgn. rels. and investment; svcs. policy, adv. com. U.S. Trade Rep. Contbr. articles to profl. jours. Trustee Brandeis U., 1990—, Lincoln Ctr. for Performing Arts, Inc., NYC, Brookings Instn., Washington; investment and svcs. policy adv. com. U.S. Trade Rep.; active Coun. Fgn. Rels.; bd. dirs. Ctr. on Addiction and Substance Abuse at Columbia U., NYC, Am. Hosp. of Paris Found. Fellow, NSF, 1970. Master: Am. Phys. Soc. (bd. dirs. 1978); mem.: Am. Radio Relay League, Computer and Bus. Equipment Mfrs. Assn. (bd. dirs.), Whitney Mus., Guggenhiem Mus., Aircraft Owners and Pilots Assn., Atlantic Golf Club, Fenway Golf Club, Profile Club, East Hampton Tennis Club, Gipsy Trail Club, Harmony Club. Achievements include patents for audio disc apparatus. Office: 375 Park Ave New York NY 10152-0002

SCHULHOFER, STEPHEN JOSEPH, law educator; b. NYC, Aug. 20, 1942; s. Joseph and Myrelle Schullhofer; m. Laurie Wohl, May 28, 1975; children: Samuel, Jonah. AB, Princeton U., 1964; LLB, Harvard U., 1967. Bar: DC 1968, US Dist. Ct. (ea. dist.) Pa. 1973, US Supreme Ct. 1973. Law clk. to Justice Hugo L. Black US Supreme Ct., Washington, 1967—69; assoc. Coudert Freres, Paris, 1969—72; asst. prof. law U. Pa., Phila., 1972—77, assoc. prof., 1977—81, prof., 1981—85, Ferdinand Wakeman Hubbell prof., 1985—86; prof. U. Chgo. Law Sch., 1986—2001; prof. law NYU Sch. Law, 2001—, Robert B. McKay prof. law, 2002—. Speedy trial reporter US Dist. Ct. Del., Wilmington, 1975—80; cons. US EPA, Washington, 1977—78, US Sentencing Commn., 1987—94; trustee Cmty. Legal Svcs., Inc., Phila., 1981—86; vis. prof. U. Chgo., 1985, NYU, 2001; dir. Ctr. for Studies Criminal Justice, 1987—2001. Author: Prosecutorial Discretion and Federal Sentencing Reform, 1979, Unwanted Sex: The Culture of Intimidation and the Failure of Law, 1998, Rethinking the Patriot Act, 2005; editor: Criminal Law and its Processes, 1983, 2005; contbr. articles to profl. jours. Walter Meyer grantee, Am. Bar Found., 1984. Mem.: Law and Soc. Assn., ACLU (Ill. bd. dirs. 1993—97). Office: NYU Sch Law Vanderbilt Hall Rm 319 40 Washington Sq S New York NY 10012-1099 E-mail: schulhos@juris.law.nyu.edu.

SCHULHOFER-WOHL, SAMUEL, economics professor; BA, Swarthmore Coll., Pa., 1998; MA, U. Chgo., PhD, 2007. Copy editor Jour. Standard, Freeport, Ill., 1998, Birmingham Post Herald, Ala., 1998—99; copy editor to reporter Milw. Jour. Sentinel, 1999—2002; asst. prof. economics and pub. affairs Princeton U., NJ, 2007—.

SCHULHOFF, KAREN L., information specialist; b. Long Island City, NY, Dec. 11, 1959; d. Edward and Eleanor (Gillespie) S. MLS, CUNY, 1993. Tng. program coord. Chem. Bank, NYC, 1983-90; libr. Katharine Gibbs Sch., NYC, 1990-92; cons. Pfizer, NYC, 1993-2001; info. specialist, rschr. Bear, Stearns Investment Banking, NYC, 2001—; founder, owner Smack Cosmetics, Inc., 2004—. Mem.: NAFE, Am. Mgmt. Assn. Office: J P Morgan 277 Park Ave New York NY 10017

SCHULIAN, JOHN (NIELSEN SCHULIAN), screenwriter, author; b. LA, Jan. 31, 1945; s. John and Estella Katherine (Nielsen) S.; m. Paula Lynn Ellis, Aug. 20, 1977 (div. Oct. 1984). BA, U. Utah, 1967; MS, Northwestern U., 1968. Copy editor Salt Lake City Tribune, 1968; reporter Balt. Evening Sun, 1970-75; sportswriter Washington Post, 1975-77; sports columnist Chgo. Daily News, 1977-78, Chgo. Sun-Times, 1978-84, Phila. Daily News, 1984-86; staff writer Miami Vice, Universal City, Calif., 1986-87, story editor, 1987, The Slap Maxwell Story, North Hollywood, Calif., 1987-88; exec. story editor TV series Wiseguy, Hollywood, 1988-89; co-prodr. TV series Midnight Caller, Burbank, Calif., 1989-90, supervising prodr., 1990-91; co-exec. prodr. TV series Reasonable Doubts, Burbank, 1991-92; creative cons. TV series The Untouchables, LA, 1992-93; co-exec. prodr. TV series Hercules, Universal City, Calif., 1994-96; co-creator Xena: Warrior Princess, Universal City, 1995; assoc. prodr. (documentary) Ben Johnson: Third Cowboy on the Right, 1996; co-exec. prodr. (TV series) Lawless, 1996-97; consulting prodr. (TV series) JAG, 1999-2000; writer producer (TV series) The Outer Limits, Vancouver, Canada, 2000—01; culture columnist MSNBC.com, 2001—02; co-exec prodr. (TV series) Tremors, Universal City, 2002—03. Spl. contbr. Sports Illustrated, 1998—; prof. in residence U. Utah, 2004. Author: Writers' Fighters and Other Sweet Scientists, 1983, Twilight of the Long Ball Gods, 2005; contbg. editor Panorama mag., 1980-81; syndicated columnist UP Syndicate; commentator Nat. Pub. Radio, 1985-86; cons. The Reader's Catalog, 1989, Short Stories (Fiction), thuglit.com Prague Revue; contbr. articles to NY Times, Playboy, Gentlemen's Quar., Oxford Am.Mag., The National, LA Times; included in The Best Am. Sports Writing, 1994. Mem. Pacific Coast League Hist. Soc. With U.S. Army, 1968-70. Recipient Nat. Headliners Club award, 1980, Column Writing award AP Sports Editors, 1979, 82, Best Sports Stories award, 1983, 84, Nat Fleischer Excellence in Boxing Journalism award Boxing Writers Assn. Am., 1985. Mem. Writers Guild Am., Phi Beta Kappa. Office: Endeavor Talent Agy 9701 Wilshire Blvd 10th Fl Beverly Hills CA 90212 also: Sterling Lord Literistic 35 Bleecker St New York NY 10012 Personal E-mail: jschulian@aol.com.

SCHULLER, DIANE ETHEL, allergist, immunologist, educator; b. Bklyn., Nov. 27, 1943; d. Charles William and Dorothy Schuller. AB cum laude with honors in Biology, Bryn Mawr Coll., 1965; MD, SUNY, Bklyn., 1970. Diplomate Am. Bd. Allergy & Immunology, Am. Bd. Pediatrics, Nat. Bd. Med. Examiners. Intern, resident in pediats. Roosevelt Hosp., Bklyn., 1970-72; resident in allergy Cooke Inst. Allergy, 1972-74; assoc. in pediatrics Geisinger Med. Ctr., Danville, Pa., 1974-78, dir, dept. pediat. allergy, immunology & pediat. diseases, 1978-95; asst. clin. prof. pediats. Hershey Med. Coll. Pa. State U., 1974-79, assoc. clin. prof., 1979-88; clin. prof. Jefferson Med. Coll., Phila., 1989-95; dir. pediat. allergy, immunology, pulmonology Pa. State U./Hershey Med. Coll., 1995—2007, emeritus dir., 2007—, prof. pediats., 1995—. Bd. dirs. Ctrl. Pa. Lung and Health Assn.; bd. dirs., exec. com. Am. Lung Assn. Pa., sec., 1992—; chmn. Susquehanna Vly. Lung Assn., 1983—; scholarship com. Bryn Mawr Club, N.Y., 1970-75; Columbia-Montour Home Health Svcs. Adv. Group Profl. Personnel, 1975-95. Editl. bd. Annals of Allergy, Asthma and Immunology. Recipient physician's recognition award AMA, 1973-76, 74-76, 75-78, 79-82, 83-86, 87-90, 91-94, 95-98, 1999-2005. Fellow Am. Acad. Pediats. (exec. com. 1998-2004), Am. Coll. Allergy Asthma and Immunology (2d v.p. 1988, bd. regents 1989-92, exec. com. 1990-93, v.p. 1992-93, pres.-elect 1993-94, pres. 1994-95), Am. Acad. Allergy and Immunology, Am. Assn. Clin. Immunology and Allergy (regional dir., exec. com.), Joint Coun. Allergy and Immunology (bd. dirs. 1986-95, treas. joint coun. 1991-93); mem. Am. Assn. Cert. Allergists (v.p. 2002, pres.-elect 2002-03, pres. 2003-04), Pa. Allergy and Asthma Assn. (bd. dirs. 2007-), N.Y. State Allergy Soc., N.Y. State Med. Soc., N.Y. County Med. Soc., Network Mothers Asthmatics (chmn., bd. dir. 2007-), Allergy & Asthma Network Mothers Asthmatics (chair 2007-), Joint Task Force on Practice Parameters. Office: Milton S Hershey Med Coll Pa State U Hershey PA 17033 Office Phone: 717-531-1846.

SCHULLER, GUNTHER ALEXANDER, composer; b. NYC, Nov. 22, 1925; s. Arthur E. and Elsie (Bernartz) Schuller; m. Marjorie Black, June 8, 1948; children: Edwin Gunther, George Alexander. Student, St. Thomas Choir Sch., NYC; MusD (hon.), Manhattan Sch. Music, 1987, Northeastern U., 1967, U. Ill., 1968, Colby Coll., 1969, Williams Coll., 1975, Cleve. Inst. Music, 1977, New Eng. Conservatory Music, 1978, Rutgers U., 1980, Manhattan Sch. Music, 1987, Oberlin Coll., 1989. Tchr. Manhattan Sch. Music, 1950—63; head composition dept. Tanglewood, 1963—84; pres. New Eng. Conservatory Music, 1967—77; artistic dir. Berkshire Music Ctr., Tanglewood, 1969—84, Festival at Sandpoint, 1985—2000. Founder, pres. Margun Music Inc., 1975, GM Recs., 1980. French horn player Ballet Theatre, 1993, then prin. horn player Cin. Symphony Orch., 1943—45, prin. French horn Met. Opera Orch., 1945—59; composer: Suite for Woodwind Quintet, 1945, Concerto for Cello and Orchestra, Six Early Songs, 1945, Jumpin' in the Future for jazz ensemble, 1946, Quartet for Four Double Basses, 1947, Perpetuum Mobile for Four Horns & Brass, 1948, Fantasy for Unaccompanied Cello, 1951, Adagio for Flute & String Trio, 1952, Recitative and Rondo for Violin and Piano, 1953, String Quintet No.1, 1957, Music for Violin, Piano and Percussion, 1957, Contours, 1958, Woodwind Quintet, 1958, Seven Studies on Themes of Paul Klee, 1959, Spectra for Long Orch., 1960, Six Renaissance Lyrics, 1962, String Quartet No. 2, 1965, Symphony, 1965, Capriccio Stravagante, 1972, The Power Within Us, 1972, Tre Invenzioni, 1972, Three Nocturnes, 1973, Four Soundscapes, 1974, Concerto No. 2 for Orch., 1975, Triplum II, 1975, Horn Concerto No. 2, 1976, Violin Concerto, 1976, Diptych for organ, 1976, Sonata Serenata, 1978, Contrabassoon Concerto, 1978, Deaï for 3 orchs., 1978, Trumpet Concerto, 1979, Octet, 1979, Eine Kleine Posaunemusik, 1980, In Praise of Winds (Symphony for Large Wind Orch.), 1981, Symphony for Organ, 1982, Concerto Quaternio, 1983, Concerto for Bassoon and Orch., 1984, On Light Wings (piano quartet), 1984, Farbenspiel (Concerto No. 3 for Orch.), 1985; author: Horn Technique, 1962, Early Jazz: Its Roots and Development, 1968, Musings: The Musical Worlds of Gunther Schuller, 1985; composer: A Bouquet for Collage for chamber ensemble, 1988, Symphony for Brass and Percussion, 1950; Dramatic Overture, N.Y. Philharm., 1956; Concertino for Jazz Quartet and Orch., Balt. Symphony Orch., 1959; composer: Music for Brass Quintet, 1961; Concerto No. 1 for Orch., Chgo. Symphony Orch., 1966; composer: Triplum, 1967, Aphorisms for Flute and String Trio, 1967, Duologue for Violin and Piano, 1984; Concerto for Viola and Orch., 1985, String Quartet No. 3, 1986, Chimeric Images, 1988, Concerto for String Quartet and Orchestra, 1988, Concerto for Flute and Orchestra, 1988, On Winged Flight: A Divertimento for Band, 1989, Chamber Concerto, 1989, Concerto for Piano Three Hands, 1989, Phantasmata for Violin and Marinba, 1989, 5 Impromptus Eng. Horn and String Quartet, 1989, Impromptus and Cadenzas, 1990; composer: Hommage à Rayechka for 8 cellos/or multiples thereof, 1990; A Trio Setting for clarinet, violin, piano, 1990, Violin Concert No. 2, 1991, Sonata Fantasia for piano, 1992, Ritmica-Melodia-Armonia for orch., 1992, Of Reminiscences and Reflections for orch., 1993 (Pulitzer prize for music, 1994), Brass Quintet No. 2, 1993, The Past is in the Present for orch., 1994, Sextet for left hand piano and woodwind quintet, 1994, Concerto for organ and orch., 1994, Mondrian's Vision, 1994, Magnificat and Nunc Dimittis (choir), 1994, Headin Out, Movin In (jazz ensemble), 1994, Lament for M (jazz ensemble), 1994, Rush Hour an 23d St., 1994, Blue Dawn into White Heat (concert band), 1995, An Arc Ascending, 1996; composer: Bright and Sassy, 1997, Ohio River Reflections for Piano Trio and Horn, 1998, Sonata for Alto Saxophone, 1999, Fantasie Impromptu for Flutet Hpschd, 2000, Quodlibet - Vln, Cello, Oboe, Horn, and Harp, 2001, The Birth of the Cool Suite, 2001, String Quartet No. 4, 2002, Concerto da Camera No. 2, 2002, rev. Duo Concertante for Cello and Piano, 2002, Four Preludes for Harp, 2002, Encounters for Jazz Band and Large Symphony Orch., 2003, String Trio, 2003, Grand Concert for Percussion Ensemble and Three Keyboards, 2005, Nature's Way for Band/Wind Ensemble, 2006, Refrains (for ten euphoniums, twelve tubas), 2006, Where the Word Ends (for orch.), 2006, Three Little Expressions, Cello, Bass Clarinet, 2009, Adagis for Strings & Ode to the Minor Second & Major Seventh, 2007, Three Small Adventures, 2008, Three Little Expressions, Cells & Bass Clarinet, 2009, Quintet for Horn & String Quartet, 2009, (Operas) The Visitation, 1966, Fisherman and His Wife, 1970. Recipient Creative Arts award, Brandeis U., 1960, Deems Taylor award, ASCAP, 1970, Alice M. Ditson Conducting award, 1970, Rodgers and Hammerstein award, 1971, Friedheim award, 1988, William Schuman award, Columbia U., 1989, Down Beat Lifetime Achievement award, 1993, BMI Lifetime Achievement award, 1994, Gold medal, Am. Acad. Arts and Letters, 1997, Order of Merit Cross, Fed. Republic of Germany, 1997, Max Rudolf award, 1998, Adujog for Strings award, 2007; named Guggenheim fellow, 1962, 1963, MacArthur fellow, 1991, Composer of Yr., Mus. Am., 1995; named to Am. Classical Music Hall of Fame, 1998. Mem.: Am. Acad. Arts and Scis., Nat. Inst. Arts and Letters. Address: 167 Dudley Rd Newton Center MA 02459-2830 Office Phone: 617-332-6328.

SCHULMAN, ALAN, lawyer; b. Bklyn., Sept. 7, 1949; BA, NYU, 1971; JD, La. State Univ., 1974. Bar: La. 1974, Tex. 1974, Wash. 1982, Calif. 1986, US Dist. Ct. (so. dist. Calif. 1987, no. & ctrl. dist. Calif. 1989), US Ct. Appeals (5th & 11th cir. 1981, 9th cir. 1982), US Supreme Ct. 1995. Ptnr., Complex Class Action Litigation Bernstein Litowitz Berger & Grossmann, San Diego. Adj. prof. Univ. San Diego Sch. Law, 2000—; co-chmn. so. dist. Calif. Lawyer Reps. Ninth Cir. Judicial Conf., 2000—01, mem. exec. com., 2002—04, Conf. co-chmn., 2005. Editor (assoc.): La. Law Rev. Mem.: ABA (co-chmn. Securities Law com.), Fed. Bar Assn., Wash. State Bar Assn., La. State Bar Assn., State Bar Tex., State Bar Calif., Assn. Bus. Trial Lawyers San Diego (pres. 2001, mem. bd. gov. 1995—2001), Order of the Coif. Office Phone: 858-720-3185. Office Fax: 858-793-0323. Business E-Mail: alans@blbglaw.com.

SCHULMAN, AMY WEINFELD, pharmaceutical company executive, lawyer; b. NYC, Oct. 16, 1960; d. Alvin Harold and Ann Schulman; m. David Eli Nachman; children: Ezra, Gideon, Rafael. BA, Wesleyan U., 1982; JD, Yale U., 1989. Bar: NY 1990, US Dist. Ct. (so. & ea. dist. NY), US Supreme Ct. Law clk. Harold Ackerman, Newark, 1989; assoc. Cleary Gottlieb, NYC, 1990—97; of counsel Piper & Marbury, NYC, 1997; ptnr. Piper Rudnick, NYC, 1998—2004; ptnr. litigation practice, mem. exec. com., policy com. DLA Piper Rudnick Gray Cary, NYC, 2005—08; sr. v.p., gen. counsel Pfizer Inc., 2008—. Mem. steering com. DI-Drug and Med. Device, 1999—; mem. commn. on jury N.Y. State, 1999—; mem. exec. com. Yale Univ. & Yale Law Sch., 1999—; bd. dirs. N.Y. Lawyers Pub. Interest, NYC; nat. coord. counsel, trial counsel. Contbr. articles to profl. jours. Bd. dir. Bklyn. (N.Y.) Acad. Music, 2002—. Named a Top Comml. Litigator, The Am. Lawyer mag., 2006; named one of 21 Rising Female Litigators, Corp. Counsel Mags., 100 Most Powerful Women, Forbes mag., 2009; named to The 45 Under 45, The Am. Lawyer mag, 2003. Mem.: ABA (vice chmn. Products Liability com.), Internat. Assn. Def. Counsel, Def. Rsch. Inst. (vice chmn. Alternative Dispute Resolution sect.), Fed. Bar Council. Achievements include design of and implements alternative resolution programs for Fortune 500 companies and has handled nearly 750 mediations. Office: Pfizer Inc 235 E 42nd St New York NY 10017 Office Phone: 212-835-6108. Office Fax: 212-835-6001.*

SCHULMAN, CARL, surgeon, educator; married. MD, U. South Fla., Tampa, 1995; MSPH, U. Miami, Fla, 2004. Diplomate Am. Bd. Surgery, 2004. Asst. prof. surgery U. Miami Miller Sch. Medicine, 2004—. Office: Univ of Miami Miller Sch of Med PO Box 016960 (D-40) Miami FL 33101

SCHULMAN, CLIFFORD A., lawyer; b. Dec. 6, 1947; s. George and Henrietta Schulman; m. Michele Weissman, June 28, 1969; 1 child, David Michael. BS in Journalism and Comm. cum laude, U. Fla., 1969, JD, 1972. Bar: Fla. 1972, US Supreme Ct. 1981, US Ct. Appeals (5th cir.) 1975. Law clk. to Eugene P. Spellman, Miami, Fla., 1970—71; rsch. aide to Judge Nroman Hendry, 1972—73; asst. county atty. Met. Dade County, 1973—79; ptnr. Greenberg, Traurig, 1979—. Adj. prof. masters program U. Miami Law Sch.; chmn. bd. exec. com. Aventura Mktg. Coun. Editor-in-chief: continuing legal. edn. manual Environ. Rsch. Regulation and Litig. in Fla., 1981. Mem. Gov.'s Task Force on Biscayne Bay Rules, 1978; del. 57th Biennial Conf. Am. Hebrew Congregations, 1983. Served to capt. USAR, 1969—73. Mem.: Fla. Bar. (co-editor environ. law sect. newsletter 1977—80, exec. coun. environ. and land use law sect. 1979—83, sec.-treas. 1981—83, chmn. 1984—85), United Way, Alex de Touqueville Soc., Anti Defamation League (Torch of Freedom award). Office: Greenberg Traurig 1221 Brickell Ave Miami FL 33131-3224 Office Phone: 305-579-0613. Office Fax: 305-961-5613. Business E-Mail: schulmanc@gtlaw.com.

SCHULMAN, DENNIS, clinical psychologist; m. Pam Tropper; children: Holly, Julie. Grad. magna cum laude, Brandeis U., Waltham, Mass., 1972; PhD in Clin. Psychology and Pub. Practice, Harvard U., Cambridge, Mass. Ordained rabbi 2003. Clin. psychologist; instr. Fordham U., Bronx, NY; founder, Nat. Tng. Program in Contemporary Psychoanalysis Nat. Inst. the Psychotherapies, 1997—. Author: Genius of Genesis: A Psychoanalyst and Rabbi Examines the First Book of the Bible, 2003. Assoc. rabbi Chavurah Beth Shalom, Alpine, NJ. Recipient Spl. Commendation, The White House, 1972, David Aranow award for outstanding achievement in social welfare, 1972; fellow, Nat. Inst. Mental Health. Mem.: Phi Beta Kappa. Democrat. Jewish. Mailing: PO Box 3 Demarest NJ 07627 Office: Nat Inst the Psychotherapies 250 W 57th St Ste 501 New York NY 10019 Office Phone: 201-767-8162, 212-586-1566.

SCHULMAN, HAROLD, obstetrician, gynecologist; b. Newark, Oct. 26, 1930; m. Rosemarie Vincenti; children: Stanley H., Sandra C., Gina M. BS, U. Fla., 1951; MD, Emory U., 1955. Diplomate Am. Bd. Ob-Gyn., Am. Bd. Maternal and Fetal Medicine; registered diagnostic med. sonographer. Intern Jackson Meml. Hosp., Miami, Fla., 1955-56, resident, 1958-61; instr. dept. ob-gyn. U. Miami (Fla.) Sch. Medicine, 1961; instr., asst. prof. dept. ob-gyn. Temple U. Sch. Medicine, Phila., 1961-65; asst. prof. dept. ob-gyn. Albert Einstein Coll. Medicine, Bronx, 1965-67, assoc. prof., 1968-71, prof., 1971—, acting dept. chmn., 1972—80, chmn., 1973-80; assoc. dir. dept. ob-gyn Bronx Mcpl. Hosp. Ctr., 1967-70, dep. dir., 1970-72; chmn. dept. ob-gyn. Winthrop U. Hosp., Mineola, NY, 1984-93; prof. ob-gyn SUNY, Stony Brook, 1984-93; chmn. dept. ob-gyn. Lawnwood Regional Med. Ctr., Ft. Pierce, Fla., 1995-2000; cons. ob-gyn. Wyckoff Hosp. Med. Ctr., Bklyn., 2004—. Author: Tipping the Scales, 2005, Women's Secrets, Mens Muscles Unveiled, 2009; contbr. articles to profl. publs. Served to capt. U.S. Army, 1956-58. Am. Cancer Soc. fellow, 1959-60; USPHS trainee, 1965-66 Fellow ACOG (vice chmn. Dist. II 1972-75); mem. Bronx County Obstet. Soc. (pres. 1974), AAAS, Obstet. Soc. (sec. 1978-80, pres. 1982-83), N.Y. Obstetrical Soc., Soc. Maternal Fetal Medicine, Am. Gynecologic and Obstetric Soc., Am. Gynecol. Obstetrics, N.Y. Obstetics Soc. (pres. 1982), Phi Beta Kappa, Alpha Omega Alpha; hon. mem. Miami Ob-Gyn. Soc., South Atlantic Obstetricians and Gynecologists Soc., Buffalo Gynecologic and Obstetric Soc. (E.G. Winkler meml. lectr.), Croatian Ultrasound Soc. (hon.). Democrat. Jewish. Office Phone: 914-747-4168. Personal E-mail: hschulman29@optonline.net.

SCHULMAN, JOSEPH DANIEL, physician, health facility administrator, medical geneticist, educator; b. Bklyn., Dec. 20, 1941; s. Max and Miriam (Grossman) S.; m. Dixie A. King; children: Erica N., Julie K. BA, Bklyn. Coll., 1961; MD, Harvard U., 1966. Diplomate Am. Bd. Pediat., Am. Bd. Ob-Gyn., Am. Bd. Med. Genetics. Intern, then resident in pediat. Mass. Gen. Hosp., Boston, 1966-68; clin. assoc. Nat. Inst. Arthritis and Metabolic Diseases, 1968-70; resident in obstetrics and gynecology and fellow in pediatrics N.Y. Hosp.-Cornell Med. Ctr., 1970-73; Gilbert and Nat. Found. fellow Cambridge (Eng.) U., 1973-74; head sect. human biochem. genetics Nat. Inst. Child Health and Human Devel., NIH, Bethesda, Md., 1974-83; dir. med. genetics program NIH, Bethesda, 1979-1983; prof. ob-gyn., pediat., genetics George Washington U., 1983-84; CEO Genetics & IVF Inst., Fairfax, Va., 1984-98, chmn., 1984—2001, 2004—; prof. human genetics, pediat., ob-gyn. Med. Coll., Va. Commonwealth U., 1984—; with dept. ob-gyn. Fairfax Hosp., 1984—. Affiliate prof. ob-gyn. U. Cal., San Diego, 2003—; advisor to numerous govt. and pvt. orgns. Author 3 books; contbr. numerous articles to med. jours.; editorial bd. Molecular Human Reproduction, 1995—, numerous other sci. jours. With USPHS, 1968-70, 74-83. Fellow ACOG; mem. Soc. Pediat. Rsch., Soc. Gynecologic Investigation, Am. Soc. Clin. Investigation, Am. Soc. Human Genetics, Am. Fertility Soc., Harvard Club, Cosmos Club, Calif. Club, Phi Beta Kappa, Sigma Xi. Office: 3015 Williams Dr Fairfax VA 22031

SCHULMAN, MELISSA A., lobbyist, former legislative staff member; b. Detroit, Sept. 12, 1961; m. Thomas P. Mann, Aug. 12, 1990; 1 child. BA in Social Sci., Mich. State U., 1983. Staff asst. to Rep. Geraldine A. Ferraro US Ho. of Reps., 1984-85, legis. asst. to Rep. Thomas J. Manton, 1985-88, sr. legis. asst. to Rep. Steny H. Hoyer, 1988-90, policy dir.; assoc. dir., floor asst. Dem. Caucus, 1991-93, exec. dir., 1993—98; lobbyist Bockorny Group, Inc., Washington, 1998—. Office: Bockorny Group, Inc Ste 500 1101 16th St, NW Washington DC 20036 Office Phone: 202-659-9111. Office Fax: 202-659-6387.*

SCHULMAN, MICHAEL, professional sports team executive, lawyer; m. Sherry Schulman; 4 children. BA in Econs., U. Calif., Berkeley; JD, U. Santa Clara. Ptnr. McDermott, Will & Emery; chmn. bd. Anaheim Arena Mgmt. (AAM); CEO, alt. gov. Anaheim Ducks; mng. dir. H&S Ventures. Prof. law U. So. Calif.; bd. dirs. Comml. Capital Bank Corp, KDOC TV. Mem. U. Calif., Irvine Found. Bd., 1991—; bd. mem. Henry and Susan Samueli Found., Samueli Inst. for Info. Biology, Orange County Jewish Campus. Office: Anaheim Ducks Honda Ctr 2695 E Katella Ave Anaheim CA 92806

SCHULMAN, SIDNEY, neurologist, educator; b. Chgo., Mar. 1, 1923; s. Samuel E. and Ethel (Miller) S.; m. Mary Jean Diamond, June 17, 1945; children— Samuel E., Patricia, Daniel. BS, U. Chgo., 1944, MD, 1946. Asst. prof. neurology U. Chgo., 1952-57, assoc. prof., 1957-65, prof., 1965-75, Ellen C. Manning prof., divsn. biol. scis., 1975-93, Ellen C. Manning prof. emeritus, 1993—. Served with M.C. AUS, 1947-49. Mem. Am. Neurol. Assn., U. Chgo. Med. Alumni Assn. (pres. 1968-69, Norman Maclean award 1997), Chgo. Neurol. Soc. (pres. 1964-65)

SCHULTE, DAVID MICHAEL, investment banker; b. NYC, Nov. 12, 1946; s. Irving and Ruth (Stein) S.; m. Patricia Gordon, Sept. 5, 1999; children: Michael B., Katherine F. BA, Williams Coll., 1968; postgrad., Exeter Coll., Oxford U., Eng., 1968-69; JD, Yale U., 1972. Bar: DC 1973. Law clk. to Mr. Justice Stewart, US Supreme Ct., 1972-73; spl. asst. to pres. NW Industries, Inc., Chgo., 1973-75, v.p. corp. devel., 1975-79, exec. v.p., 1979-80; sr. v.p. Salomon Bros., Chgo., 1980-84; mng. ptnr. Chilmark Ptnrs., Chgo., 1984—. Editor-in-chief: Yale Law Jour, 1971-72. John E. Moody scholar Exeter Coll., Oxford U., 1968-69. Mem. Washington Bar Assn., Chgo. Club, Racquet Club, Farm Neck Golf Club, Vineyard Golf Club. Office: Chilmark Ptnrs 875 N Michigan Ave Ste 3460 Chicago IL 60611-1957 Office Phone: 312-984-9711.

SCHULTE, FRANCIS B., archbishop emeritus; b. Phila., Dec. 23, 1926; Grad., St. Charles Borromeo Sem.; MA, Univ. Pa.; postgraduate study, Harvard Univ. Ordained priest Archdiocese of Phila., Pa., 1952, tchr., Cath. schools, 1952—60, asst. supt. schools, 1960—70, supt. schools, 1970—80; pastor St. Margaret parish, Narbeth, Pa., 1980—81; ordained bishop, 1981; aux. bishop, vicar gen. Archdiocese of Phila., 1981—85; bishop Diocese of Wheeling-Charleston, W.Va., 1985—88; archbishop Archdiocese of New Orleans, 1989—2002, archbishop emeritus, 2002—. Past trustee Cath. Univ. Am.; past bd. dir. Cath. Relief Services; past chmn. Com. Bishops & Cath. Coll. & Univ. Presidents. Roman Catholic. Office: c/o 7887 Walmsley Ave New Orleans LA 70125-3431

SCHULTE, GREGORY L., United States Ambassador to United Nations, Vienna; married; 2 children. Grad. magna cum laude, U. Calif. Berkeley, 1980; MPA, Princeton U., 1983. Presdl. mgmt. intern office of sec. def., Washington, 1983—85; dir. strategic forces policy, asst. theater nuc. forces policy, 1985—92; with internat. staff NATO, Belgium, 1992—98; spl. asst. to Pres. for implementation of Dayton Peace Accords NSC, 1998—99; prin. dir. requirements, plans and counter-proliferation policy for sec. US Dept. Def., 1999—2000; sr. dir. S.E. European affairs NSC, 2000—02, exec. sec., 2003—05; permanent rep. to UN US Dept. State, Vienna, 2005—, permanent rep. to IAEA, 2005—. Recipient two Presdl. Rank awards. Address: US Dept State 2201 C Street NW Washington DC 20520 Office: US Mission to Internat Orgns IZD Tower Wagramerstrasse 17-19 1220 Vienna Austria*

SCHULTE, JEFFREY LEWIS, lawyer; b. NYC, July 24, 1949; s. Irving and Ruth (Stein) S.; m. Elizabeth Ewan Kaiser, Aug. 13, 1977; children: Andrew Riggs, Ian Garretson, Elizabeth Alexandra. BA, Williams Coll., 1971; postgrad., Harvard U., 1971-72; JD, Yale U., 1976. Bar: Pa. 1978, Ga. 1993. Law clk. to hon. John J. Gibbons U.S. Ct. Appeals (3d cir.), Newark, 1976-77; assoc. Schnader, Harrison, Segal & Lewis, Phila., 1977-84, ptnr., 1985-92, founding ptnr. Atlanta, 1992-98, exec. com., 1994-98; ptnr. Morris, Manning & Martin, Atlanta, 1998—. Chair securities law com. Ga. State Bar, 2005—07; mem. exec. com. Business Law Sect., Ga. State Bar, 2005-2007; nat. steering com. lawyers com. to end "Pay-to-Play."; bd. dir. Michael C. Carlos Mus. Emory U.,3rd adv. Cole Sch. Bus. Kennesaw State U. Contbr. articles to profl. jours. Mem.: ABA, Bus. and Tech. Alliance, Atlanta Venture Forum, Atlanta Bar Assn. (chmn. comm. and media rels. com.), Phila. Bar Assn., State Bar Ga., Pa. Bar Assn., Weekapaug Tennis Club, Yale Club of Ga. (bd. dirs. 1996—2002, pres. 2000—01, chmn. of bd. 2001—02), Weekapaug Yacht Club R.I., Williams Club N.Y.C., Williams Club Atlanta, Merion Cricket Club, Phi Beta Kappa. Office: Morris Manning & Martin Atlanta Financial Center 3343 Peachtree Rd NE Ste 1600 Atlanta GA 30326-1044 Office Phone: 404-233-7000. Business E-Mail: jls@mmmlaw.com.

SCHULTE, STEVEN C., history professor; b. Mpls., Mar. 18, 1955; s. Robert Paul and Carol Aleda Schulte; m. Tracy M. Schwoch; children: Anders Christian, Inge Carol Stollings, Kirstin Ann. BS, U. Wis.-River Falls, 1977; MA, Colo. State U., Fort Collins, 1979; PhD, U. Wyo., Laramie, 1984. Asst. prof. history U. Ozarks, Clarksville, Ark., 1984—89; dept. chair Mesa State Coll., Grand Junction, 1993—2000, prof. history, 1989—. Recipient Disting. Faculty Award, U. Ozarks, 1987, Disting. Faculty Mem. Award, Mesa State Coll., 2004. Office: Dept History 1100 N Ave Grand Junction CO 81501 Business E-Mail: schulte@mesastate.edu.

SCHULTE, TROY ANTHONY, coach, director; b. Hays, Kans., Dec. 27, 1970; s. Gary Martin and Bonita Marie Schulte; m. Sharon Sue Feauto, June 10, 1994; children: Jordan Nicole, Jackson Trey, Jaden Sue. BS in Phys. Edn., Ft. Hays State U., 1994; Masters, William Woods U., Fulton, Mo., 2004. Cert. tchr. Mo., 2002. Athletic dir. Archie R-V Sch. Dist., Mo., 2005—. Office: Archie R-V Sch Dist PO Box 106 Archie MO 64725 Office Fax: 816-293-5712; Home Fax: 816-29305712. Personal E-mail: tschulte@archie.k12.mo.us.

SCHULTER, EUGENE C., alderman; b. Chgo., Nov. 14, 1947; s. Theodore and Caroline S. Schulter; m. Rosemary Beibel; children: Philip, Monica. BA, Loyola U., 1970. Appraiser Cook County Assessor's Office, Ill.; alderman, 47th ward Chgo. City Coun., 1975—. Bd. dirs. North Cmty. Bank; chair lic. and consumer protection com. Chgo. City Coun. Bd. mem. Levy Sr. Citizens Ctr. Adv. Bd., Greening of Ravenswood Com., Common Food Pantry, St. Benedict's HS Adv. Coun., Neighborhood Boys & Girls Club Cmty. Leadership Coun. Office: 4237 N Lincoln Ave Chicago IL 60618-2953 also: City Hall 121 N LaSalle St Rm 300 Chicago IL 60602 Office Phone: 773-348-8400, 312-744-4021. Office Fax: 773-348-8480. Business E-Mail: ward47@cityofchicago.org.*

SCHULTHEIS, ADAM JOHN, music educator, consultant; b. Quebec City, Que., Canada, Apr. 23, 1962; s. August Thomas and Joan Helen Schultheis; m. Cynthia Anne Forcey, Dec. 14, 1995; children: Johnathon Michael Bohnet, Caroline Emily, Thomas Gabriel, Christopher Addison, Aidan Patrick. MusB in Edn., U. Ariz., Tucson, 1980—86; MS, Nova U., Ft. Lauderdale, Fla., 1987—89. Cert. elem. tchr. Nev., Nat. Bd. Cert. orch. Orch. tchr. McCall Elem. Sch., North Las Vegas, 1986—92, Orr Mid. Sch., Las Vegas, 1992—97, Boulder City H.S., Nev., 1997—. Music leader, cons. Boy Scouts of Am., Boulder City, Nev., 1998—; hon. composer Vincennes U., Ind., 2001—; advisor U.S. Jr. Congl. Leadership Conf., Washington, 2001—. Composer: Prayer, Vincennes U. Bicentennial, 2001, Vegas Fiddle Dance, 2005. Founder, dir. Boulder City Hometown Fiddlers, Nev., 1999—; vol. Make A Difference Day Found., Las Vegas, 1999—; chmn. Nev. Nat. Anthem Project. Recipient Disney Am. Tchr. Honoree, Disney Corp., 1999, Achievement in Edn award, Rotary Club, Boulder, City, Nev., 2001, Music For 1000 Children Award, U. Hartford, Hart Sch. Music, 2002, Nev. Cmty. award, DAR, 2006, Vol. of Yr. award, Am. Legion, 2005, Cmty. Achievement award, DAR, 2006; named Tchr. of Yr., VFW, Nev., 2006, Outstanding Am. Tchr., Nat. Honor Roll, 2005—06; named to, Clark County Sch. Dist.'s Hall of Fame, Las Vegas, 2001, Wall of Tolerance, San Francisco State U., 2004; grantee Arts in the Cmty., Target Edn. Found., 2002, 2003, 2004; Cuban Music fellow, San Francisco State U., 2001. Mem.: Sons of the Am. Legion, Music Educators Nat. Conf. (life), Am. String Tchr. Assn. (life; advisor, cons. 1986—2003), Music Tchr. Nat. Assn. (life), KC, Pi Lambda Theta, Valley Forge Freedom Found. (hon. Past George Washington Honor Medal Winner 2001). Conservative. Achievements include being Nevada's only participant in the 2001 National Independence Day Parade, Washington, D.C; being Nevada's only music participant in National World War Two Memorial Dedication, Washington, 2004; Las Vegas' centennial committee commissioned composition Vegas Fiddle Dance, 2005. Avocations: fiddling, woodworking, gardening, hiking. Home: 1327 Bayleaf Terr Ave Henderson NV 89014 Office: Boulder City HSl 1101 Fifth St Boulder City NV 89005 Personal E-mail: adamschultheis@cox.net.

SCHULTHEIS, ANN LUCIA, retired curriculum specialist; b. Kalamazoo, Aug. 22, 1946; d. Mario Salvatore Cioffari and Kathleen Loretta Mahoney; m. Patrick James Schultheis, Aug. 17, 1968 (dec.); children: Michael Patrick, Jennifer Ann O'Donoghue. BS, Western Mich. U., Kalamazoo, 1968. Tchr. elem. sch. Portage Pub. Schs., Mich., 1968—70, Allegan Pub. Schs., 1971—95; dir. arts edn. United Arts Coun., Battle Creek, 1996—98; ptnrs., edn. Kennedy Ctr.'s Performing Art Ctrs. and Schs.; asst. prin. Nat. Heritage Acads., Grand Rapids, 1998—2000, core knowledge curriculum specialist, 2000—05, state stds. specialist, 2005; ret., 2005. Co-owner, operator Hayloft Farm, Kalamazoo, 1971—2006, Celebration Hall, 1981—2003. Avocations: pottery, painting, poetry, history, gardening. Home: 8734 Oakland Hills Cir Portage MI 49024 Personal E-mail: annschultheis@yahoo.com.

SCHULTHEIS, EDWIN MILFORD, dean, business educator; b. NYC, Apr. 15, 1928; s. Milford Theodore and Lillian May (Hill) S.; m. Joan Edna Bruckner, June 23, 1956. BS, Hofstra Coll., 1950; MBA, NYU, 1958, EdD, 1972. Officer mgr., sales rep. Topton Rug Mfg. Co., NYC, 1950-54; area mgr., trainer Mobil Oil Co., NYC, 1954-62; coord. distributive edn. North Babylon (N.Y.) Pub. Schs., 1962-88, chmn. bus. mktg. and indsl. edn. depts., 1988-91; prof. bus. adminstrn. SUNY, Farmingdale, 1970-91; asst. prof. edn. NYU, 1973—; dir. edn. Syracuse (N.Y.) U., 1973-78; chmn. dept. bus. adminstrn. Five Towns Coll., Seaford, N.Y., 1991-92, divsn. chmn. bus. and tech. Dix Hills, N.Y., 1992-98, dean instrn., 1993-98, dep. dean of faculty, 1993-98, assoc. dean, 1996-97, prof. emeritus, 1998—. Test writer, cons. N.Y. State Dept. Edn., Albany, 1965—; textbook reviewer McGraw-Hill Book Co., N.Y.C., 1967-69; cons. Cornell U., 1975; dist. adviser Distributive Edn. Clubs N.Y., 1970, bd. govs., trustee, 1975-78; mem. curriculum adv. coun. Suffolk County (N.Y.) Distributive Edn. Assn., 1967—. Author: Modern Petroleum Marketing, 1971, Content and Structure of Belief-Disbelief Systems, 1972. Elder Presbyn. Ch., U.S.A. Named N.Y. State Tchr. of Yr., 1976, Outstanding Tchr. in N.Y. State, 1978; recipient Outstanding Svc. award Distributive Edn. Clubs N.Y., Suffolk County Distributive Edn. Assn., Tchr. Excellence award N.Y. State, 1980, Citation for Excellence in Edn. Gov. Mario Cuomo N.Y., 1991, Citation Excellence in Teaching Babylon Twp., 1991. Mem. Acad. Mgmt., Am. Petroleum Inst., Am. Security Coun., Suffolk County Assn. Distributive Edn. Tchrs. (mem. exec. bd. 1962-74), N.Y. State (pres. 1975-78), L.I. Distributive Edn. Assns. (hon. life, exec. bd. 1972-75), N.Y. State Occupl. Edn. Assn. (v.p. 1975-78), L.I. Bus. Edn. Chmns. Assn. (hon. life, exec. bd. 1972-75), N.Y. State Occupl. Edn. Assn. (v.p. 1975-78), L.I. Bus. Edn. Chmns. Assn. (hon. life), Distributive Edn. Clubs Am. (regional leader 1972-75, hon. life 1991), Bellport (N.Y.) Golf Club, Phi Delta Kappa, Kappa Delta Pi, Sigma Alpha Lambda, Phi Sigma Eta. Presbyterian (ordained ruling elder). Home: 14 Thorn Hedge Rd Bellport NY 11713-2616

SCHULTHEIS, PATRICIA ANN, writer, editor; b. Bridgeport, Conn., Aug. 11, 1943; d. Ralph and Clard Podufaly; m. William Christian Schultheis, Oct. 15, 1966 (dec.); children: Kurt Christian, Matthew Christian. BA, Albertus Magnus Coll., 1965; MA in Liberal Arts, Johns Hopkins U., 1973, MA in Writing, 2006. Prodn. mgr. Balt. Mag., 1976—77; rschr. Md. Pub. TV, Owings Mills, 1977—79; rsch. assoc. Changing Times Mag., DC, 1979—81; editor U. Md., Balt., 1981—85; dir. publs. CC Balt., 1985—89; copy editor The Balt. Sun, 1990; editor Skills Bank Corp., Baltimore County, 1991—95; freelance writer, 1995—; fiction editor Balt. Review, 2001—07; mem. editl. bd. Narrative Mag., 2007. Editor Mt. Wash. Newsletter, Balt., 1973—75, U. Md. Sch. Law Alumni Newsletter, Balt.; contbr. Bread Loaf Writer's Conf.; rschr. Ft. McHenry Nat. Monument. Co-author: Personal Mathematics, Media Materials; author: Baltimore's Lexington Market, 2007. Sec. Charles Village Improvement Assn., Balt., 1967—69; mentor Dickey Hill Elem. Sch., Balt., 2002—. Mem.: Hamilton St. Club. Avocations: ice skating, folk art painting, embroidery. Home: 2509 Pickwick Rd Baltimore MD 21207 Office Phone: 410-448-4211. Personal E-mail: bpschult@yahoo.com.

SCHULTHESS, CRISTIAN P., chemistry professor; b. Argentina; BS, Chemistry, U. RI, Kingston, 1978; MS in Applied Scis., Environ. Engring., U. Del., Newark, 1985; PhD, Soil Chemistry, U. Del., Newark, 1987. Cert. in capacity, chemistry CEPIA, Geneva, Switzerland, 1981. Asst. prof. U. Conn., Storrs, 1991—97, assoc. prof., 1997—. Recipient Emil Truog Soil Sci. award, Soil Sci. Soc. America, 1988. Achievements include research in developing the backtitration technique for surface charge study of solids. Office: 1376 Storrs Rd Storrs Mansfield CT 06269-4067 Business E-Mail: c.schulthess@uconn.edu.

SCHULTIS, GAIL ANN, library director; b. Freeport, Ill., May 12, 1951; d. Richard C. and Ida G. Schultis. BA, Cornell Coll., 1973; MLS, U. Mo., 1976; MA, U. Tex., San Antonio, 1989. Reference libr. U. Tex., San Antonio, 1976-79, El Paso, 1979-84, 89, head access svcs., 1984-88; reference libr. Park U., Parkville, Mo., 1989-96, dir. libr. sys., 1996—. Co-author: Best Self-Help & Self-Awareness Books, 1995. Mem. ALA, Am. Hist. Assn., Orgn. Am. Historians. Home: 10307 NW 57th Ter Parkville MO 64152-3396 Office: Park Univ Libr 8700 NW River Park Dr Parkville MO 64152-4358 Office Phone: 816-584-6704. Business E-Mail: ann.schultis@park.edu.

SCHULTZ, ALBERT BARRY, engineering educator; b. Phila., Oct. 10, 1933; s. George D. and Belle (Seidman) S.; m. Susan Resnikov, Aug. 25, 1955; children: Carl, Adam, Robin BS, U. Rochester, 1955; M.Engring., Yale U., 1959, PhD, 1962. Asst. prof. U. Del., Newark, 1962-65; asst. prof. U. Ill., Chgo., 1965-66, assoc. prof., 1966-71, prof., 1971-83; Vennema prof. U. Mich., Ann Arbor, 1983-99. Contbr. numerous articles to profl. jours. Served to lt. USN, 1955-58 Rsch. Career award NIH, 1975-80; Javits Neurosci. Investigator award NIH, 1985-92 Mem. NAE, Internat. Soc. for Study Lumbar Spine (pres. 1981-82), ASME (chmn. bioengring. div. 1981-82, H.R. Lissner award 1990), Am. Soc. Biomechanics (pres. 1982-83, Borelli award 1996), U.S. Nat. Com. on Biomechanics (chmn. 1982-85), Phi Beta Kappa Business E-Mail: aschultz@umich.edu.

SCHULTZ, ARTHUR WARREN, retired communications executive; b. NYC, Jan. 13, 1922; s. Milton Warren and Genevieve (Dann) S.; m. Elizabeth Carroll Mahan, 1949 (div. 1987); children: Arthur Warren, John Carroll (dec.), Julia Hollingsworth; m. Susan Keefe, 1988. Grad., U. Chgo.; DLitt (hon.), Rosary Coll. With Foote, Cone & Belding Comms., Chgo., 1948-82, v.p., 1957-63, sr. v.p., dir., 1963-69, exec. v.p., 1969, chmn. bd., CEO, 1970-81, chmn. exec. com., CEO, 1981-82; dir. Chgo. Sun-Times Co.; vice chmn. Chgo. Sun-Times Newspaper Co.,

1989-94. Lectr. in field. Author: In Praise of America's Collectors, 1997; co-author: Valley Club of Montecito, 1999; editor Caring for Your Collections, 1992. Pres. Cook County Sch. Nursing, 1963-64, Welfare Coun. Met. Chgo., 1965-67; mem. bus. adv. coun. Urban League Chgo., 1971-82; chmn. Nat. Com. to Save Am.'s Cultural Collections, 1990-94; mem. Pres.'s Com. Arts and Humanities, 1984-93; bd. dirs. Chgo. Crime Commn., 1965-71, Cmty. Fund Chgo., 1966-67, Better Bus. Bur., 1970-78, Lyric Opera Chgo., 1967-77, Chgo. Coun. Fgn. Rels., 1977-86, Chgo. Pub. TV, 1978-82, Chgo. Central Area Com., 1978-82; mem. milennium Com. to Save Am.'s Treasures, 1998; trustee YWCA, 1962-74, Calif. Coll. Arts & Crafts, 1985-87; trustee Art Inst. Chgo., 1975-2002, chmn. bd., 1981-84; trustee U. Chgo., 1977—, Santa Barbara Mus. Art, 1988—, pres., 1989-92. 1st lt. USAF, 1943-45. Recipient Alumni Svc. award U. Chgo., 1986. Mem. Am. Assn. Advt. Agys. (dir. 1968-71, 74-76, chmn. Chgo. coun. 1964-65, chmn. Ctrl. region 1970-71), Comml. Club, Valley Club (Montecito, Calif.), Delta Kappa Epsilon. Roman Catholic. Home and Office: 300 Hot Springs Rd Santa Barbara CA 93108-2211

SCHULTZ, CAITLIN G., psychologist, educator; b. Boulder, Colo., Apr. 12, 1982; d. Brad W. Schultz and Susan O'neill. BS in Psychology, ND State U., Fargo, 2003; MA in Clin. Psychology, U. ND, Grand Forks, 2006, PhD, 2009. Clinic assoc. Psychol. Svcs. Ctr., Grand Forks, 2005—08, Ctr. Ednl. and Psychol. Assessment, Grand Forks, 2005—08; neuropsychology technician, dept. neurosci. MeritCare Hosp., Fargo, 2006—07; tchr. U. Minn., Crookston, 2006—07; pres. Grad. Resource Alliance Students Psychology, Grand Forks, 2006—07; psychology lectr. U. ND, Grand Forks, 2006—08; psychology extern ND Sch. Blind, Grand Forks, 2007—08; clin. psychology resident U. Ala., Birmingham, 2008—, clin. psychology resident, Birmingham VAMC Internship Consortium, 2008—09, prin. investigator, rschr. blind rehab., Birmingham VAMC Internship Consortium, 2008—, asst. prof. psychology, 2009—. Student mem. ND Psychol. Assn., Fargo, 2005; assoc. mem., mediator Conflict Resolution Ctr., Grand Forks, 2005; med. psychology staff Camp Sioux Children Diabetes, Pk. River, ND, 2006; mem. APA, DC, 2007, U. Ala. Assn. Neuropsychology Students Tng., 2008—. Coord., organizer, 10k-5k race to promote tng. Grad. Resource Alliance Students Psychology, Grand Forks, 2006—08.

SCHULTZ, CARL HERBERT, real estate developer; b. Chgo., Jan. 9, 1925; s. Herbert V. and Olga (Swanson) S.; m. Helen Ann Stevesson, June 6, 1948; children: Mark Carl, Julia Ann BS Gen. Engring., Iowa State U., 1948. With Schultz Bros. Co., 1948—, mdse. mgr. and store planner Chgo., 1962—70, v.p. Lake Zurich, Ill., 1968—72, pres., 1972—2000, Ill. Schultz Bros. Co., Ind. Schultz Bros. Co., Iowa Schultz Bros. Co., Wis. Schultz Bros. Co.; chmn. Schultz Bros. Co., 2000—. Mem. Lake Bluff Zoning Bd. Appeals, Ill., 1976-85, chmn., 1978-85. Served with U.S. Army, 1944-46 Mem. Lake Zurich Indsl. Coun. (sec. 1976), Assn. Gen. Mdse. Chains (dir. 1975-86, exec. com. 1983-86, chmn. nat. conv. 1982), Ill. Retail Mchts. Assn. (dir. 1984-89), Wis. Retail Fedn. (dir. 1981-89). Presbyn. Office: 815 Oakwood Rd Unit I Lake Zurich IL 60047 Home: 1100 Pembridge Dr Apt 242 Lake Forest IL 60045-4219 Office Phone: 847-438-3900. Personal E-mail: chs701@sbcglobal.net.

SCHULTZ, DANIEL G., former federal agency administrator; b. NYC, Sept. 28, 1949; BA in Polit. Sci., CCNY, 1971; MD, U. Pitts., 1974. Cert. in Gen. Surgery and Family Practice. Intern in pediatrics and medicine U. N.Mex; gen. med. officer, clin. dir. Tuba City Indian Hosp., Navajo Reservation, Ariz., 1975—78; resident gen. surgery Pub. Health Svc. Hosp., San Francisco; fellowship in pediatric surgery Denver, 1981; med. officer Gen. Surgery Br. Ctr. Devices and Radiological Health, FDA, 1994, chief med. officer, Divsn. Reproductive, Abdominal and Radiological Devices, divsn. dir., dep. dir., dir. Office Device Evaluation, acting dir., 2004, dir., 2004—09. Fellow: Am. Coll. Surgeons.*

SCHULTZ, DANIEL R., insurance company executive; Fin. mgmt. positions Am. Family Mut. Ins. Co., Madison, Wis., 1977—99, v.p. contr. div., 1999—2006, v.p., CFO, 2006—. Office: Am Fam Mut Ins Co 6000 American Pkwy Madison WI 53783

SCHULTZ, DENNIS BERNARD, lawyer; b. Detroit, Oct. 15, 1946; s. Bernard George and Madeline Laverne (Riffenberg) Schultz; 1 child, Karanne Anne. BS, Wayne State U., 1970; JD, Mich. State U., 1977. Bar: Mich. 1977, U.S. dist. Ct. (ea. and we. dists.) Mich., U.S. Ct. Appeals (6th cir.), U.S. Dist. Ct. (we. dist.) Pa. V.p. Barkay Bldg. Co., Ferndale, Mich., to 1976; law clk. Hon. George N. Bashara, Mich. Ct. Appeals, Detroit, 1977; shareholder Butzel Long, Detroit, 1978—. Editor: Detroit Coll. Law Rev., 1977. Scholar Detroit Coll. Law Alumni Assn., 1976, Mich. Consol. Gas Co., 1977. Mem.: Mich. Bar Assn., Detroit Bar Assn. Republican. Roman Catholic. Avocations: bicycling, golf. Personal E-mail: dbs77@comcast.net.

SCHULTZ, E. EUGENE, JR., information security engineer; b. Chgo., Sept. 10, 1946; s. Earl Eugene and Elizabeth Claire Schultz; m. Cathy Brown Schultz, Aug. 9, 1975; children: Sarah Ardelle, Rachel Elizabeth, Leah Brown. BA, UCLA, 1968; MS, Purdue U., 1973, PhD, 1977. Cert. info. sys. security profl. Internat. Info. Sys. Security Cert. Consortium, info. security mgr. Info. Sys. Audit and Control Assn. Project leader, engr. Lawrence Livermore (Calif.) Nat. Lab., 1986—92; prin. Eugene Schultz and Assocs., Livermore, 1992—93; prin. security engr. ARCA Sys., San Jose, Calif., 1993—94; sr. cons. SRI Internat., Menlo Park, Calif., 1994—98; rsch. dir. Global Integrity Corp., Reston, Va., 1998—2001; prin. engr. Lawrence Berkeley Nat. Lab., 2001—05; chief tech. officer High Tower Software, 2005—. Adj. prof. Purdue U., West Lafayette, Ind., 1998—2001. Author: Internet Security for Business, 1996, Windows NT/2000 Network Security, 2000, Incident Response, 2001, Intrusion Detection and Prevention, 2004; editor-in-chief: Computers and Security, 2002—07 (Golden Page award, 2003); contbr. articles to profl. jours. Active Livermore (Calif.) Vision 2000, 2001. Recipient Tech. Innovation award, NASA, 1986. Mem.: Info. Sys. Audit & Control Assn., Computer Security Inst., Info. Sys. Security Assn. (Profl. Contbn. award, Hall of Fame). Achievements include development of decluttering method for visual displays; founding the Department of Energy's Incident Response Team. Avocations: bicycling, travel. Home: 2587 Pienza St Livermore CA 94550 Office: High Tower 26970 Aliso Viejo Pky Ste 200 Aliso Viejo CA 92656 Personal E-mail: eeschultz@sbcglobal.net.

SCHULTZ, ED (EDWARD ANDREW SCHULTZ), radio personality; b. Norfolk, Va., Jan. 27, 1954; s. George and Mary Schultz; m. Maureen Zimmerman (div. 1993); m. Wendy Schultz, 1998; 6 children. Grad., Minn. State U., Moorhead, 1977. Sportscaster Sta. WDAY, Fargo, ND; weekday radio host News & Views Sta. KFGO-AM, Fargo, ND, 1992—2003; host The Ed Schultz Show, Jones Radio Networks, 2003—, The Ed Show, MSNBC, 2009—. Author: Straight Talk from the Heartland: Tough Talk, Common Sense, and Hope from a Former Conservative, 2004; regular TV appearances include Tucker Carlson Show, Larry King Live, Hardball with Chris Matthews, O'Reilly Factor, The Situation Room, Am. Morning, Morning Joe. Recipient Eric Sevareid award (3); co-recipient Marconi award, Peabody award; named one of the Top Ten Radio Hosts in the Country, Talkers Mag., 2007, 2008. Democrat. Avocations: hunting, fishing, flying. Office: The Ed Schultz Show 1020 25th St S Fargo ND 58103-2312 Office Phone: 701-237-5948. Business E-Mail: ed@edschultzshow.com.*

SCHULTZ, FREDERICK HENRY, investor, former government official; b. Jacksonville, Fla., Jan. 16, 1929; s. Clifford G. and Mae (Wangler) S.; m. Nancy Reilly, Aug., 1951; children: Catherine G., Frederick H., Clifford G., John R. BA, Princeton U., 1951; postgrad., U. Fla. Sch. Law, 1954-56. With Barnett Nat. Bank, Jacksonville, 1956-57; owner, operator investment firm, from 1957; mem. Fla. Ho. of Reps., 1963-70, speaker of the house, 1968-70; chmn. bd. Barnett Investment Svcs., Inc.; dir. Barnett Banks Inc., to 1979; vice chmn. bd. govs. Fed. Res. System, Washington, 1979-82; sr. advisor Drexel Burnham Lambert, 1982—90; founder Schultz Ctr. Tchg. & Leadership, 2002—. Served to lt. U.S. Army, 1952-54, Korea Decorated Bronze Star Roman Catholic. Office: PO Box 1200 Jacksonville FL 32201-1200

SCHULTZ, GARY DAVID, lawyer; b. Long Beach, Calif., May 25, 1953; s. S.L. and Lorraine (Donohue) S.; m. Yvonne Y. Boyer, Sept. 17, 1982; children: Raymond A., Scott R. BA, Claremont McKenna Coll., 1975, MA, 1977; JD, Am. Coll. Law, 1982. Bar: Mont. 1986. Mgr. corp. real estate STW, Long Beach, 1977-81, asst. v.p. real estate, 1982-85; mng. ptnr. S&K Properties, Long Beach, 1981-82, S & B Properties, Long Beach, 1980—; pvt. practice Helena, Mont., 1986—. Mgr. real estate aquisitions and leasing UCLA, 1985-89; v.p. real estate acquisitions Glendale Fed. Bank, 1989-91; regional real estate mgr. Kaiser Permanente, 1991-98, svc. delivery leader, v.p., Real Estate and Transaction Svcs. Catholic Healthcare West, 1998-2000, dir. Corp. Real Estate City of Hope, 1999-. Pres. United Coun. Claremont (Calif.) Colls., 1972-73; legis. intern Calif. State Assembly, Sacramento, 1975; dep. registrar of voters County of L.A., 1971-76; v.p. Town Sq. Homeowners Assn., Santa Ana, Calif., 1986-87. Recipient Voter Registration award, L.A., 1976, Am. Jurisprudence award, 1982. Mem. ABA, Assn. Trial Lawyers Am., Am. Mgmt. Assn., Internat. Devel. Rsch. Coun., Toastmasters Internat. Avocations: travel, aquatics, music. Office: S & B Properties PO Box 3273 Long Beach CA 90803-0273 also: Law Offices Gary Schultz Power Block Bldg 4th Fl 7 W 6th Ave Helena MT 59601-5072 Office Phone: 310-521-6639. Business E-Mail: gschultz@coh.org.

SCHULTZ, HARLEY, consulting company executive; b. NYC; s. William and Rose Diane Schultz. MBA, NYU, 1981. Pres. Harley Schultz & Assocs., Cons. in Mktg., Mgmt. and Internet Bus. Devel., Scarsdale, NY, 1987—. Mem. various charitable orgns. Avocations: sailing, golf, French literature, 19th-century art, classical music. Business E-Mail: harleyschultz@consultant.com.

SCHULTZ, HARRY PERSHING, chemistry researcher, retired educator; b. Racine, Wis., Mar. 9, 1918; s. Harry Carl and Agnes (Olson) S.; m. Pearle Marie Henriksen, Sept. 25, 1943; children: Stephanie Schultz Buehler, Tor, Alison Schultz Mohns. BS summa cum laude, U. Wis., 1942, PhD, 1946. Rsch. chemist Nat. Def. Rsch. Coun., 1942-45, Merck & Co., Inc., Rahway, NJ, 1946-47; mem. faculty U. Miami, Coral Gables, Fla., 1947-91, prof. chemistry, 1952-84, chmn. chemistry dept., 1972-84, prof. emeritus, 1984—; rsch. chem. topology Big Horn, Wyo., 1991—. Vis. lectr. U. Wis., Madison, 1958; vis. prof. Mich. State U., East Lansing, 1960, 62; adv. bd. Jour. Chem. Info. and Computer Scis., Washington, 1995-99. Author: (with Popp) Organic Chemical Preparation, 1964, (with Schultz) Sir Isaac Newton, 1972, (with others) Topology in Chemistry, 2001; contbr. articles to profl. jours. Mem. Planning Commn., South Miami, Fla., 1951-55; bd. trustees Sheridan Pub. Libr., 2002-06. Grantee NIH, Walter Reed Army Inst. Rsch., Phi Beta Kappa, Sigma Xi, Phi Lambda Upsilon, Phi Kappa Phi, others. Mem. Am. Chem. Soc. (chmn. Fla. sect. 1964, gen. chmn. 153rd nat. conf. 1967, councilor 1974-77, Fla. award 1986), Lions Club. Avocations: swimming, civil war memorabilia. Home: PO Box 262 Big Horn WY 82833

SCHULTZ, HOWARD D., beverage service company executive; b. Bklyn., July 19, 1953; m. Sheri Kersch; children: Jordan, Addison. BS, No. Mich. U., 1975. Joined as saleman Xerox Corp.; v.p., gen. mgr. Hammarplast, USA, (divsn. Perstorp); dir. retail ops. & mktg. Starbucks Coffee Co., 1982—85; pres., CEO II Giornale Coffee Co., 1986—87; founder Starbucks Corp., 1987, chmn., CEO, 1987—2000, chief global strategist, 2000—04, CEO, 2008—; owner, chmn. Seattle Supersonics, 2001—06; co-founder Maveron LLC, 1998—. Bd. govs. Nat. Assn. of Securities Dealers, 1998—2001; bd. dirs. eBay Inc., 1998—2003, Potbelly Sandwich Works, 2001—, DreamWorks Animation SKG, Inc., 2004—. Author (with Dori Jones Young): Pour Your Heart Into It: How Starbucks Built a Company One Cup at a Time, 1996. Recipient Rev. Theodore M. Hesburgh award for Ethics in Bus., Mendoza Coll. Bus. U. Notre Dame, 2007; named Exec. of Yr., Restaurants & Institutions mag., 2000. Office: Starbucks Corp 2401 Utah Ave S Ste 800 Seattle WA 98134

SCHULTZ, LOUIS MICHAEL, advertising agency executive; b. Detroit, Aug. 24, 1944; s. Henry Richard and Genevieve (Jankowski) S.; children: Christian David, Kimberly Ann; m. Diane Lee; stepchildren: Vince, Andrea, Frank. BA, Mich. State U., 1967; MBA, Wayne State U., 1970. Staff Campbell-Ewald, Warren, Mich., 1967-74, v.p. group dir., 1975-77, sr. v.p., assoc. dir., 1977-82, group sr. v.p., 1982-83, exec. v.p., 1984-87, Lintas: USA, 1987-94; chmn. Lintas: WW Media Coun., 1991; mem. devel. council IPG, NYC, 1984—; pres., CEO CE Comm., 1994—; vice chmn. Campbell-Ewald, 1998-99; chmn., CEO Initiative Media N.Am., LA, 2000—; chmn. Initiative Media WW, 2000. Advisor, Detroit Renaissance Com., 1981-84. With USAR, 1967-73. Mem. NATAS, Am. Women in Radio and TV, Am. Mktg. Assn., Detroit Advt. Assn., Promotion Mktg. Assn. (bd. dirs. 1999), Ad Club N.Y. (bd. dirs.), Adcraft Club, Old Club, Hidden Valley Club, Longboat Key Club, Detroit Athletic Club, Am. Advt. Fedn. (bd. dirs.), Forest Lake Country Club, Renaissance Club, Detroit Athletic Club. Episcopalian. Avocations: golf, tennis, travel. Office: Initiative Media 5700 Wilshire Blvd Ste 400 Los Angeles CA 90036-3639 Home: 250 Bird Key Dr Sarasota FL 34236-1614

SCHULTZ, LUCINDA D., music educator; b. Dickinson, ND, Jan. 11, 1952; d. Alick and Grayce A. Dvirnak; m. David C. Schultz, Aug. 6, 1976. BS in Vocal-Choral Music Edn., Dickinson State U., Dakota, 1974; MM in Vocal Performance, Colo. State U., Fort Collins, 1976; DMA in Vocal Performance, Pedagogy and Lit., U. Colo., Boulder, 1984. Adj. instr. music U. Colo., Boulder, 1980—84; prof. music and dir. vocal studies Armstrong Atlantic State U., Savannah, Ga., 1986—; instr. music sch. music Ouachita Bapt. U., Arkadelphia, Ark. Cons. in fields, Savannah, 1990—. Singer performing artist. V.p. Savannah Onstage Festival Music, 1990—96, Ga. Chpt. Nat. Assn. Tchr. Singing, 1989—98; gov. Nat. Assn. Tchs. Singing, Ga., 1998—2004. Recipient Tchg. Excellence award, U. Colo. Coll. Music, 1984; grant, Endowment Support Classical Music, 2002—08, Disting. Alumni Fellow, Dickinson State U., 2005. Mem.: Mu Phi Epsilon (pres. 1972—74), Nat. Assn. Tchs. Singing (v.p., gov. 1989—2008), Pi Kappa Lamda. Episcopalian. Avocations: travel, gardening, reading. Home: 105 E Oglethorpe Ave Savannah GA 31401 Office: Dept of Music Armstrong Atlantic St Un 11935 Abercorn St Savannah GA 31419

SCHULTZ, NANCY JANSSON, artist; b. Kanas City, Mo., Apr. 15, 1933; d. Carl Albert Jansson and Lora Elizabeth Wilson; m. Everett Hoyle Schultz, June 24, 1955; children: Susan, Frank, Janet, Sally. Student, Park Coll., Parkville, Mo., 1951—54. Founder Women on Paper, Augusta, Ga., 1987—; exhibit organizer Art of the Sketchbook, Ga., 2005; participant Morris Mus. Artrageous. Exhibitions include Genema Gallery, Altanta, Quinlan Arts Ctr., Gainsville, Ga., Gwinnett Fine Arts Ctr., Duluth, Ga., U. SC, Aiken, Cotton Exch. Gallery, Augusta, 1998, Clayton St. Gallery, Athens, Ga., 1998, Emory U. Law Sch. Libr., Atlanta, 2000, Barnes and Noble Bookstore, Augusta, 2000, State Capitol Gallery, Ga. Arts Day, Atlanta, 2001, Aiken Ctr. Arts, 2001, State Bot. Gardens, Athens, 2002, Cork Gallery, Avery Fisher Hall, N.Y.C., 2002—05, Birmingham So. Coll. Durbin Gallery, 2006 (Merit award, 2006), Wickwire Gallery, Hendersonville, NC, McCormick Arts Coun., SC, 2007—08 (Purchase award, 2004, 2005, 2006, 2007), 20th Anniversary Show Women on Paper, Aiken Ctr. Arts, SC, 2008, 20th Anniversary Show, Sacred Heart Cultural Ctr., Augusta, Ga., 2008, Represented in permanent collections Bank Fla., Deloitte and Touche, Charlotte, N.C., Med. Coll. Ga., U. Hosp., Augusta, St. Joseph's Hosp., PAC 2000, N.H., Jud. Ctr., Ocala, Fla., Augusta Nat. Golf, Inman Pk. Festival, Atlanta, represented by, Ann Jacob Gallery, Highlands, NC, The Pheasants Eye, Lynchburg, Va., Art on Broad, Augusta, Broad Strokes Gallery, Evans. Recipient Honorable Mention, Eyes for the Art, Augusta, 1992, Merit award, Images in Art, Ocala, 1992, 1st Pl. Fine Arts for Watercolor, Blue Crab Festival, N.C., 1989, Merit award, Miss. Watercolor Soc., 1989, 1st pl. Watercolor, Columbia County Renaissance Festival, 2005, Honorable Mention, Art on Main Hendersonville, N.C., 2005, Merit award, Ala. Watercolor Soc., 2006, Images Art Festival, New Smyrna Beach, Fla., 2007; named to Archives on Women Artists, Nat. Mus. Women in the Arts, Washington, 1995. Mem.: Gertude Herbert Inst. Art, Nat. League Am. Pen Women (1st pl. 1994, 3d pl. 1997, Pres. award. 1997, Marel Brown award 1999, 1st pl. in mixed media 2002, 3d pl. 2002, 2d pl. 2005, 2d pl. Watercolor Spring Juried Show 2006), Ga. Watercolor Soc. (newsletter editor 1990—92, signature mem., Pomegranate award, Bushstrokes). Achievements include development of booklet for newcomers to Augusta area 'A Guide For Visual Artists'; design of cover and section sketches of cookbook for The Lydia Project. Avocations: aerobics, writing, reading, making hand made books. Home and Studio: 608 Aumond Rd Augusta GA 30909

SCHULTZ, NORBERT J., retired music educator; b. Gardner, Ill., Apr. 25, 1937; s. Lewis H. and Vera Schultz; m. Janet A. Schultz, Aug. 19, 1979; children: Sonia, Shelly Luppen 1 stepchild, John Bracamontes. BS in Music Edn., Ill. State U., 1959. Band, vocal and gen. music tchr., grade and H.S. Kempton and Cabrey (Ill.) Schs., 1959—61; vocal tchr. Piper City (Ill.) Grade and H.S., 1961—63; band and vocal dir. Taft Grade Sch., Lockport, Ill., 1963—67; band dir. Lyons (Ill.) Sch. Dist., 1967—70, Edwardsville (Ill.) elem, jr. high and H.S., 1970—85; gen. music tchr. Shenandoah and Woodward Elem. Schs., St. Louis, 1986—99; beginning and intermediate band dir. St. Paul's Luth. Sch., Troy, Ill., 1999—2001; ret., 2001. Profl. entertainer, band dir. Musical dir. chapel Charles Melvin Price Support Ctr. Army Facility, Granite City, Ill., 1995—2000; deacon Holy Cross Luth. Ch., Collinsville, Ill., 1988—96, elder, 1999, St. Paul's Luth. Ch., Troy, 2002—. Recipient numerous 1st pl. band awards at state competitions; named team mem. in citizen ambassador program elementary edn. del. to Vietnam, Eisenhower award, U. Toledo, 1994. Mem.: Music Tchrs. Nat. Assn., Ill. State Music Tchrs. Assn. Republican. Lutheran. Avocations: fishing, travel, private teaching. Home: Holiday Shores 846 Newport Bay Edwardsville IL 62025 Home Phone: 618-659-8736.

SCHULTZ, PHILIP, poet; b. Rochester, NY, Jan. 6, 1945; s. Samuel Benjamin and Lillian Bedina Schultz; m. Monica Banks, Jan. 28, 1995; childre: Elias, August. BA, San Francisco State U., 1967; MFA, U. Iowa, 1971. Poet-in-residence Kalamazoo (Mich.) Coll., 1971-72; writer-in-residence Newton (Mass.) Coll. of Scared Heart, 1973-74; adj. tchr. liberal arts Tufts U., Somerville, Mass., 1973-74; writing tchr. U. Mass., Boston, 1973-75; founder, dir. grad. dept. creative writing NYU, 1978-88. Adj. prof. creative writing Columbia U., N.Y., 1973-75; founder, dir. The Writers Studio. N.Y.C., 1985—. Author: Like Wings, 1978, Deep Within in the Ravine, 1984, My Guardian Angel Stein, 1986, The Holy Worm of Praise, 2002, Living in the Past, 2004, Failure, 2007 (Pulitzer Prize, 2008); contbr. poetry to various publs. Vol. tchr. poetry to troubled children Columbia-Presbyn. Hosp., 1986-87, Coalition for Homeless. Fellowship in poetry N.Y. State Coun. for Arts, 1976, 80, Nat. Endowment for Arts, 1981-82, N.Y. Found. for Arts, 1985; Fulbright fellow to Israel Hebrew U., 1983-84; recipient Am. Acad. and Inst. Arts and Letters award, 1979, Levinson prize Poetry mag., 1996-97 Mem. Pen Am. Ctr. (events com., membership com. 1979-81), Poetry Soc. of Am. (bd. govs.), Acad. Am. Poets (Lamont award), Poets House. Democrat. Jewish. Avocation: reading. Home: 88 Osborne Ln East Hampton NY 11937-2207 Office: The Writers Studio 78 Charles St Apt 2R New York NY 10014-2661 Office Phone: 212-255-7075. *I place clarity and precision above all else in my work, and if these are the modes of expression, honesty of feeling provides the substance as well as the goal. I believe the art of good writing takes place in the art of revision, which, if taxing, often enough gives me the time to get to the heart of the matter. I choose to write about only those things which I feel most passionate about: the particular circumstances of my life.*

SCHULTZ, RICHARD CARLTON, plastic surgeon; b. Grosse Pointe, Mich., Nov. 19, 1927; s. Herbert H. and Carmen (Huebner) S.; m. Pauline Zimmermann, Oct. 8, 1955; children: Richard, Lisa, Alexandra, Jennifer. MD, Wayne State U., 1953. Diplomate Am. Bd. Plastic Surgery. Intern Harper Hosp., Detroit, 1953-54, resident in gen. surgery 1954-55, U.S. Army Hosp., Ft. Carson, Colo., 1955-57; resident in plastic surgery St. Luke's Hosp., Chgo., 1957-58, U. Ill. Hosp., Chgo., 1958-59, VA Hosp., Hines, Ill., 1959-60; practice medicine specializing in plastic surgery Park Ridge, Ill., 1961-96; ret., 1996; clin. asst. prof. surgery U. Ill. Coll. Medicine, 1966-70, assoc. prof. surgery, 1970-76, prof., 1976-96, head divsn. plastic surgery, 1970-87; pres. med. staff Luth. Gen. Hosp., Park Ridge, 1977-79. Vis. prof. U. Pitts., 1972, U. Miss., 1973, U. Pisa, Italy, 1974, Jikei U. Coll. Medicine, Tokyo, 1976, Ind. U., 1977, U. Helsinki, 1977, U. N.Mex., 1978, U. Milan, 1981, So. Ill. Sch. Medicine, 1982, Tulane U. Med. Sch., 1983, Shanghai 2d Med. Coll., 1984, U. Guadalajara (Mex.), 1986, Gazi U., Turkey, 1988, U. Coll. Medicine Tsuksba, Japan, 1996, Taegu (Korea) U., 1996; sr. Fulbright lectr. U. Uppsala, Sweden, 2003; participant, guest surgeon Physicians for Peace, Turkey and Greece, 1988, Israel and Occupied Ters., 1990, Egypt, 1991, Lithuania, Estonia, 1993 (team leader); leader citizen amb. People to People Internat. Del. Plastic Surgeons to Albania & Russia, 1994, del. leader, Tibet and China, 1998. Author: Facial Injuries, 1970, 3d edit., 1988, Maxillo-Facial Injuries from Vehicle Accidents, 1975, Outpatient Surgery, 1979. Mem. sch. bd., Lake Zurich, Ill., 1966-72, pres., 1968-72; pres. Chgo. Found. for Plastic Surgery, 1966-. Served to capt. M.C., AUS, 1955-57. Fulbright Found. scholar, Sweden, 1960-61; recipient Auto Safety award Med. Tribune, 1967,

Robert H. Ivy award 1969, Disting. Sci. Achievement award Wayne U. Coll. Medicine Alumni, 1975, Sanvenero-Rosselli award, 1981; McGregor scholar, U. Mich., 1946-49; grantee Ednl. Found. Am. Soc. Plastic and Reconstructive Surgery, 1964-65. Fellow ACS (pres. local commn. on trauma 1985-87); mem. Am. Assn. Plastic Surgeons (trustee 1990-91), Am. Soc. Plastic and Reconstructive Surgeons, Midwestern Assn. Plastic Surgeons (pres. 1978-79), Chgo. Soc. Plastic Surgeons (pres. 1970-72), Midwestern Assn. Plastic Surgeons (pres. 1978-79), Am. Soc. Maxillofacial Surgeons (pres. 1988-89, award of honor 1986), Am. Assn. Automotive Medicine (pres. 1970-71, A. Merkin award 1982), Am. Cleft Palate Assn., Am. Soc. Aesthetic Plastic Surgery, Tord Skoog Soc. Plastic Surgeons (pres. 1971-75), Can. Soc. Plastic Surgery, Chilean Soc. Plastic Surgery (corr.), Japanese Soc. Plastic Surgery (corr.), Cuban Soc. Maxillofacial Surgery (corr.), Korean Soc. Plastic Surgery (corr.). Office: PO Box 357 Northport MI 49670-0357 Office Phone: 231-386-5950. Business E-Mail: schultz5@coslink.net.

SCHULTZ, RICHARD DALE, national athletic organization executive; b. Grinnell, Iowa, Sept. 5, 1929; s. August Henry and Marjorie Ruth (Turner) S.; m. Jacquilyn Lu Duistermars, June 26, 1949; children: Robert Dale, William Joel, Kim Marie. BS, Ctrl. Coll., Pella, Iowa, 1950; EdD (hon.), Ctrl. Coll., 1987; LLD (hon.), Wartburg Coll., 1988, Alma Coll., 1989, Luther Coll., 1991; PhD (hon.), U.S. Sports Acad., 1993; LLD (hon.), Daniel Webster Coll., 1997, Gettysburg Coll., 1998. Head basketball coach, athletic dir. Humboldt (Iowa) High Sch., 1950-60; freshman basketball coach U. Iowa, Iowa City, 1960-62, head baseball coach, assoc. basketball coach, 1962-70, head basketball coach, 1970-74, asst. v.p., 1974-76; dir. athletics and phys. edn. Cornell U., Ithaca, NY, 1976-81; dir. athletics U. Va., Charlottesville, 1981-87; exec. dir. NCAA, Mission, Kans., 1987-94; pres. Global Sports Enterprises, 1994-95; exec. dir. U.S. Olympic Com., Colorado Springs, Colo., 1995—2000; chmn. Mktg. Assocs. Internat., 2000—04; chmn., CEO Internat. Partnerships, 2002—. Mem. honors ct. Nat. Football Found. and Hall of Fame, Nat. Basketball Hall of Fame, 1992; chmn. bd. NCAA Found., 1989; organizer Iowa Steel Mill, Inc.; trustee Gettysburg Coll., 1996—99; bd. dirs. Hanspree Corp., Tacipe, Twaian. Author: A Course of Study for the Coaching of Baseball, 1964, The Theory and Techniques of Coaching Basketball, 1970; Contbr. articles to mags. Bd. dirs. Fellowship of Christian Athletes, 1986, chmn., 1990; chmn. Multiple Sclerosis, 1974-75; mem. Knight Found. Commn. on Intercollegiate Athletics, 1990—; mem. adv. com. on svc. acad. athletic programs Def. Dept. Recipient Disting. Alumni award Ctrl. Coll., Pella, 1970, 98, Lifetime Svc. award U. Iowa, 1994, Corbett award Nat. Assn. Collegiate Dirs. Athletics, 1994, medal of honor Ellis Island, 1997, Disting. Alumni award Ctrl. Coll., 1998, Casey award, 1999, Pres. and Mrs. Bush Cmty. Impact award 1999; mem. Basketball Hall of Fame Honor Ct., 1992, Sportsman of Yr. award Marine Corp., 1997; inducted into Iowa Baseball Hall of Fame, 1993, Ctrl. Coll. Hall of Honors, 2002, Des Moines Register Hall of Fame, 2003. Mem. Nat. Assn. Coll. Basketball Coaches, Ea. Coll. Athletic Assn. (mem. exec. com. 1980-81), Am. Basketball Coaches Assn. (Award of Honor 1994), Am. Football Coaches Assn. (internat. dir. CEO forum 2005-, lifetime membership award 1995), Levick Strategic Com. (Washington) (mem., bd. dirs. 2008-) Home: 3670 Twisted Oak Cir Colorado Springs CO 80904-4720 Office Phone: 719-685-3245, 719-331-5021. Personal E-mail: dschultzprint2@earthlink.net.

SCHULTZ, RICHARD M., biology professor; b. Malden, Mass., Mar. 20, 1949; s. Samuel and Marylyn (Schaffer) S.; m. Nicola Thomsen Neff, Oct. 20, 1979. BA, Brandeis U., Waltham, Mass., 1971; PhD, Harvard U., 1975. Postdoctoral fellow Harvard Med. Sch., Boston, 1975-78; asst. prof. biology U. Pa., Phila., 1978-84, assoc. prof., 1984-90, Patricia Williams prof. biology, 1990—, and dept. chair. Contbr. over 140 articles to profl. jours. Recipient Jan Purkinje medal Czech Acad. Sci., 1994. Fellow AAAS. Office: Dept Biology U Pa 223 Leidy Laboratories Philadelphia PA 19104

SCHULTZ, RICHARD MICHAEL, biochemistry educator, researcher; b. Phila., Oct. 28, 1942; s. William and Beatrice (Levine) S.; m. Rima M. Lunin, Mar. 7, 1965; children: Carl M., Eli J. BA, SUNY, Binghamton, 1964; PhD, Brandeis U., 1969. Rsch. fellow Harvard U. Med. Sch., Boston, 1969-71; asst. prof. Loyola U. Stritch Sch. of Medicine, Maywood, Ill., 1971-78, assoc. prof., 1978-84, prof., 1984—, chmn. dept. molecular and cellular biochemistry, 1984-2000. Mem. adv. med. bd. Leukemia Rsch. Found., Chgo., 1987-91. Co-author: Textbook of Biochemistry; contbr. articles to profl. jours., chapters to books. Recipient Rsch. grants NIH. Achievements include in vivo evidence for the role of protease enzymes and their inhibitors in regulating tumor cell metastasis, ras oncogene pathways in cancer, role of JNK and c-Jun in cancer cell protease expression, obtaining evidence on the nature of the transition-state in serine protease enzyme catalysis, regulation of gene expression by historic modification. Office: Divsn Molecular & Cellular Biochemistry Loyola U Sch Medicine Maywood IL 60153 Home Phone: 708-383-7026; Office Phone: 708-216-9378. E-mail: rschult@lumc.edu.

SCHULTZ, RICHARD OTTO, ophthalmologist, educator; b. Racine, Wis., Mar. 19, 1930; s. Henry Arthur and Josephine (Wagoner) S.; m. Diane Haldane, Sept. 29, 1990; children: Henry Reid, Richard Paul, Karen Jo. BA, U. Wis., 1950, MS, 1954; MD, Albany Med. Coll., 1956; MSc, U. Iowa, 1960. Diplomate Am. Bd. Ophthalmology. Intern, Univ. Hosps., Iowa City, 1956-57, resident in opthalmology, 1957-60; chief ophthalmology sect. div. Indian health USPHS, Phoenix, 1960-63; practice medicine specializing in ophthalmology Phoenix, 1963; NIH spl. fellow in ophthalmic microbiology U. Calif., San Francisco, 1963-64, clin. assoc., 1963-64, research assoc., 1963-64; assoc. prof., chmn. dept. ophthalmology Marquette U. Sch. Medicine (now Med. Coll. Wis.), Milw., 1964-68, prof., chmn., 1968-97, prof. ophthalmology, 1997—2000, prof. emeritus, 2000—. Mem. nat. adv. eye coun. NIH, 1984-88; cons. Froedert Hosp., Milw. Contbr. articles to profl. jours. Served with USPHS, 1960-63. Fellow: ACS (life), Am. Ophthalmol. Soc. (emeritus), Am. Acad. Ophthalmology (life); mem.: Oxford Ophthalmol. Congress (Eng.), N.Y. Acad. Scis. (emeritus), Assn. Rsch. Vision and Ophthalmology (emeritus), Pan Am. Assn. Ophthalmology (life), Milw. Ophthal. Soc., Assn. Univ. Profs. Ophthalmology (past pres., trustee). Home: 4487 Granny Smith Ct Egg Harbor WI 54209 Home Phone: 920-868-5021. Personal E-mail: eyeotto@aol.com.

SCHULTZ, STANLEY GEORGE, physiologist, educator, dean; b. Bayonne, NJ, Oct. 26, 1931; s. Aaron and Sylvia (Kaplan) S.; m. Harriet Taran, Dec. 25, 1960; children: Jeffrey, Kenneth. AB summa cum laude, Columbia U., NYC, 1952; MD, NYU, 1956. Intern Bellevue Hosp., NYC, 1956-57, resident, 1957-59; research assoc. in biophysics Harvard U., 1959-62, instr. biophysics, 1964-67; assoc. prof. physiology U. Pitts., 1967-70, prof. physiology, 1970-79; prof., chmn. dept. physiology U. Tex. Med. Sch., Houston, 1979-96, prof. dept. internal medicine, 1979—, prof. dept. integrative biol. pharm. physiology, 1997—, vice chmn., 1999—2003, Fondren chair in cell signalling, 1999—, dean Sch. Medicine, 2003—06, H. Wayne Hightower Dist. prof. biomed. sci., 2005—07, assoc. dean sch. medicine, 2007—. Cons. USPHS, NIH, 1970—; mem. physiology test com. Nat. Bd. Med. Examiners, 1974-79, chmn., 1976-79 Editor Am. Jour. Physiology, Jour. Applied Physiology, 1971-75, Physiol. Revs., 1979-85, Handbook of Physiology: The Gastrointestinal Tract, 1989-91—; mem. editl. bd. Jour. Gen. Physiology, 1969-88, Ann. Revs. Physiology, 1974-81, Current Topics in Membranes and Transport, 1975-81, Jour. Membrane Biology, 1977—, Biochim. Biophys. Acta, 1987-89; assoc. editor Ann. Revs. Physiology, 1977-81; assoc. editor News in Physiol. Scis., 1989-94, editor, 1994-2003; contbr. articles to profl. jours. Served to capt. M.C. USAF, 1962-64. Recipient Rsch. Career award NIH, 1969-74, Solomon Berson award NYU, 2003; overseas fellow Churchill Coll., Cambridge U., 1975-76, Prince Mahidol award, Thailand, 2007. Mem. AAAS, AMA (coun. on med. edn.), Am. Heart Assn. (estab. investigator 1964-68), Am. Physiol. Soc. (councillor 1989-91, pres.-elect 1991-92, pres. 1992-93, past pres. 1993-94, Guyton award 1997, Orr Reynolds award 1999, Daggs award 2003), European Acad. Sci., Fed. Am. Soc. Exptl. Biology (exec. bd. 1992-95), Biophys. Soc., Soc. Gen. Physiologists, Internat. Cell Rsch. Orgn., Internat. Union Physiol. Scis. (chmn. internat. com. gastrointestinal physiology 1977-80, chmn. U.S. nat. com. 1992-98), Assn. Am. Physicians, Am. Assn. Ob-Gyn. (hon. fellow), Assn. Chmn. Depts. Physiology (pres. 1985-86), Houston Philos. Soc., Phi Beta Kappa, Sigma Xi. Home Phone: 713-729-7660; Office Phone: 713-500-5012, 713-500-6204. Business E-Mail: stanley.g.schultz@uth.tmc.edu.

SCHULTZ, T. PAUL, economics professor; b. Ames, Iowa, May 24, 1940; s. Theodore W. and Esther (Werth) S.; m. Judith Hoenack, Sept. 16, 1967; children: Lara, Joel, Rebecca. BA, Swarthmore Coll., 1961; PhD, MIT, 1966; MA (hon.), Yale U., 1974. Cons. Joint Econ. Com., Washington, 1964; rschr. econ. dept. Rand Corp., Santa Monica, Calif., 1965-72, dir. population rsch., 1968-72; prof. econ. U. Minn., Mpls., 1972-75, Yale U., New Haven, 1974—, dir. Econ. Growth Ctr., 1983-96; prof. econ. Malcolm K. Brachman, 1977. Cons. World Bank, Rockefeller Found., InterAm. Devel. Bank; mem. com. on population NAS, Washington, 1987-89, 90-93. Author: Structural Change in a Developing Country, 1971, Economics of Population, 1981; editor: (books) The State of Development Economics, 1988, Investment In Women's Human Capital, 1995, Handbook of Development Economics, Vol. 4, 2008, (periodical) Research in Population Economics, 1985, 88, 91, 96; assoc. editor Jour. Population Econs., 1991—, Econ. of Edn. Rev., 1993-2004, China Econ. Rev., 1994-2004, Economic Development and Cultural Change, 2005-. Mem. commn. on behavioral sci. and edn. Nat. Rsch. Coun., 1997-2002. Fellow: AAAS (population resources environ. com. 1985—89, nomination com. 1987—90); mem.: Econ. Rsch. Forum for Arab Countries (trustee 1993—2001), European Soc. for Population Econs. (bd. dirs., pres. 1997), Soc. for Study Social Biology (bd. dirs. 1986—89), Internat. Union for Sci. Study Population, Population Assn. Am. (bd. dirs. 1979—81, Irene B. Taeuber award for rsch. 2007), Econometrics Soc., Am. Econ. Assn. Office: Yale U Econ Growth Ctr PO Box 208269 27 Hillhouse Ave New Haven CT 06520-8269 Office Phone: 203-432-3629. Business E-Mail: paul.schultz@yale.edu.

SCHULTZ, VICTOR M., physician; b. Pitts., Aug. 14, 1932; s. Irvin and Rose (Reiss) S. BS, Kent State U., Ohio, 1955; MD, Ohio State U., Columbus, 1958. Diplomate Am. Bd. Dermatology. Pvt. practice, Santa Monica, Calif., 1965—. Fellow Am. Acad. Dermatology, Pacific Dermatologic Assn.; mem. AMA, Am. Coll. Physicians, Calif. Med. Assn., L.A. County Med. Assn. Avocations: skiing, tennis, golf, music, swimming. Office: 2461 Santa Monica Blvd Santa Monica CA 90404-2049 Home Phone: 310-826-6832; Office Phone: 310-828-7492.

SCHULTZ, VICTORIA L., harpist, entertainer, music educator; b. Kansas City, Mo., May 12, 1952; d. Kenneth Leroy and Russie Juanita (McIntosh) S. BMusic, U. Mo., Kansas City, 1975; M Music, Drake U., 1977. Opera coach, accompanist, prof. piano U. Ctrl. Fla., Orlando, 1977-80; prof. voice and piano Valencia C.C., Orlando, 1980-86; music dir. Pine Castle (Fla.) Ctr. of the Arts, 1983-84; pianist, harpist Hyatt Regency Grand Cypress, Orlando, 1984-96; pianist Altamonte Springs (Fla.) Hilton and Towers, 1985-89; pianist, harpist Caruso's Palace, Orlando, 1990-94; harpist Sergio's Restaurant, Orlando, 1994-95; entertainer Walt Disney World, Orlando, 1996—. Adj. prof. voice Rollins Coll., Winter Park, Fla., 1991-92, Valencia CC, Orlando, 2002-04; adj. prof. harp U. Ctrl. Fla., Orlando, 1998-2006; pvt. tchr. and freelance entertainer, Fla., 1980—; clinician Harpcon, 2003, Somerset Folk Harp Festival, 2003. Composer: (music for piano and voice) Set of Songs, 1979; arranger/composer: albums Orange Blossom Tale, 1996, arranger/performer: albums Harp Dreams, 1997, Harp Favorites, 1998, Soothing Harp, 1999, Victoria Lynn-Live in Concert, 2004, composer, harpist: Harp Meditation for Chakra Attunement, 2001, Celtic Crossings with Tryskelon, 2006; author: (textbook) You CAN Play the Harp, 2002. Sponsor, Riverside Musicale Jr. Music Club, Orlando, 1991—; entertainer fund raising events for AHA, Am. Cancer Soc., Muscular Dystrophy, Am. Diabetes Assn., Cystic Fibrosis, Orlando History Ctr.; artist-in-residence Fla. Hosp. Recipient State Young Artist 1st prize, Fla. Fedn. Music Clubs, 1976, Silver medal Internat. Piano Rec. Competition, Am. Coll. Musicians, 1978, Nat. 1st Place award, Encore Prodns. Talent Competition, 1985, 1986; named Single Greatest Night Honoree, 2007. Mem. Ctrl. Fla. Musicians Assn. (local 389), Am. Harp Soc., Fla. Harpers and Friends (1st Place Composition award 2002, People's Choice award 2002), Scottish Harp Soc. Am., Ctrl. Fla. Music Tchrs. Assn. (recital chmn. 1999-2000), Orlando Music Tchrs. Nat. Assn., Fla. Fedn. Music Clubs, Orlando Music Club (founding). Democrat. Avocations: reading, movies, going to concerts, shopping. Home: 848 River Cove Ave Orlando FL 32825-8107 Office: Harpspun Prodns PMB 306 509 S Chickasaw Trl Orlando FL 32825-7852 Office Phone: 407-381-4440. Business E-Mail: victoria@victoriaschultz.com.

SCHULTZE, DEBORAH, healthcare educator; d. George S. Evans and Amy Avella Lentz; m. R. Schultze Randall, May 16, 1987 (dec. Aug. 5, 2006); m. Brian A. Hillier, Sept. 30, 1972 (div. July 0, 1986); children: Randall R. II, Jeremy W. Hillier, Elaine R. Fox, Alan E. Hillier. AAS in Health Info. Mgmt., San Jacinto Coll., North Houston Tex., 1999; BS in Health Info. Mgmt., Tex. State U., San Marcos, Tex., 2002; MS in Instrnl. Tech., U. Houston Clear Lake, Tex., 2008. Cert. Am. Health Info. Mgmt. Assn., 2002. Prof. health info. mgmt. San Jacinto Coll., Houston, 2000—. Recipient NISOD Excellence in Tchg. award, U. Tex., 2002; Faculty fellowship, San Jacinto Coll., 2006. Mem.: AHIMA, Golden Key, Phi Theta Kappa. Avocation: travel. Home: 909 Hartford Pl Saint Charles MO 63301 Office: San Jacinto Coll 5800 Uvalde Rd Houston TX 77049 Business E-Mail: debby.schultze@sjcd.edu.

SCHULZ, EKKEHARD D., metal products executive; b. Bydgoszcz, Poland, July 24, 1941; PhD in metallurgy, Clausthal U., 1971. Chmn. exec. bd. Thyssen Krupp AG; mem. sci. staff & chief engr. Clausthal U., 1967—72; with Thyssen Group, 1972, appt. dep. mem., 1985—; appt. regular mem., exec. bd. ThyssenStahl AG, 1986—, head tech. directorate, 1988—, appt. chmn. exec. bd., 1991—, mem. exec. bd., 1991—; chmn. exec. bd. Thyssen Krupp Stahl AG, 1997—, Thyssen AG, 1998—; co-chmn. exec. bd. ThyssenKrupp AG, 1999—2001, chmn exec. bd., 2001—, ThyssenKrupp Steel AG, 1999—2001. Bd. dirs. Budd Co.; mem. supervisory bds. Commerzbank AG, Hapag Lloyd AG, MAN AG, Energie AG, Strabag AG; former chmn. MAN AG, second vice chmn., 2007-; pres. Eurofer; com. mem., bd. Wirtschaftsvereinigung Stahl, VDEh. Recipient hon. professorship, Clausthal U., 1999. Office: Thyssen Krupp AG August Thyssen Str 1 40211 Düsseldorf Germany

SCHULZ, JUERGEN, art historian, educator; b. Kiel, Germany, Aug. 18, 1927; came to U.S., 1938; s. Johannes Martin Askan Schulz and Ilse (Lebenbaum) Hiller; m. Justine Hume, Sept. 1951 (div. 1968); children: Christoph (dec.), Ursula, Catherine; m. Anne Markham, May 19, 1969; 1 child, Jeremy. BA, U. Calif., Berkeley, 1950; PhD in History of Art, U. London, 1958. Reporter San Francisco Chronicle, 1950-51; copy editor UPI, London, 1952-53; from instr. to prof. history of art U. Calif., 1958-68; prof. Brown, Providence, 1968-90, Andrea V. Rosenthal prof. history art and architecture, 1990-95; Samuel H. Kress prof. Nat. Gallery of Art, 2000-2001. Mem. Inst. for Advanced Study, Princeton, N.J., 1971-72. Author: Venetian Painted Ceilings of the Renaissance, 1968, Printed Plans and...Views of Venice, 1971, La cartografia tra scienza e arte, 1990, The New Palaces of Medieval Venice, 2004; also articles. Staff sgt. U.S. Army, 1945-48. Decorated grande ufficiale Ordine della Stella della Solidarieta della Repubblica Italiana; Guggenheim fellow, 1966-67. Mem. Ateneo Veneto, Centro Internaz. di Studi di Architettura A. Palladio. Office: Brown U Dept History Art and Architecture PO Box 1855 Providence RI 02912-1855 Office Phone: 401-863-1174.

SCHULZ, KEITH DONALD, corporate lawyer, writer; b. Burlington, Iowa, Dec. 20, 1938; s. Henry Carl and Laura Iral (Bowlin) S.; m. Emily Brook Roane, Apr. 19, 1985; children: Keith Jr., Sarah, Christine, Stefan. BA, U. Iowa, 1960, JD, 1963. Bar: Iowa 1963, Ill. 1966, Wis. 1990. Dep. Sec. of State, State of Iowa, Des Moines, 1965-66; atty. AT&T, Chgo., 1966-67; sec., gen. counsel Borg-Warner Acceptance Corp., Chgo., 1967-74; asst. gen. counsel Borg-Warner Corp., Chgo., 1974-84, v.p., gen. counsel, 1984-88; of counsel Bell, Boyd & Lloyd, Chgo., 1988—. Chmn., CEO Downtown Ptnrs., Inc., 1995-96. Author: (novel) Keepers of the River, 2001; contbr. articles to Harvard Bus. Rev., Jour. for Corp. Growth. Mem. Theatre Bldg. Chgo., 1975-85, chair, 1977-82, bd. dirs., 1977-82; chmn. bd. dirs. Vol. Legal Svcs. Found., Chgo., 1984-91, pres.; bd. dirs. S.E. Iowa Symphony Orch., pres., 1998-2000, 03-08, Heritage Trust Found.; bd. dirs. Capitol Theater Found., 2006-, bd. dirs., 2006-. Mem.: Des Moines County Cmty. Found. (bd. drs. 2007—, chair 2009—, mem. bd. dir. Planned Parenthood, mem., bd. trustees Burlington Cmty., pres. 2009—), Econ. Club, Univ. Club. Avocations: tennis, bicycling, skiing. Office: Bell Boyd & Lloyd 70 W Madison St Ste 3300 Chicago IL 60602-4284 Home Phone: 312-654-0387; Office Phone: 312-372-1121. Personal E-mail: KDons@aol.com.

SCHULZ, KIRK H., academic administrator; b. Portsmouth, Va., 1963; m. Noel Nunnally; children: Tim, Andrew. BS in Chem. Engring., Va. Tech., 1986, PhD, 1991. Asst. prof. chem. engring. U. ND, Grand Forks, 1991, Mich. Tech. U., 1995—98, assoc. prof., 1998, chair Dept. Chem. Engring., 1998—2001; dir. Dave C. Swalm Sch. Chem. Engring., Earnest W. Deavenport Jr. endowed chair Miss. State U., 2001—05, dean engring. James Worth Bagley Coll. Engring., Earnest W. and Mary Ann Deavenport, Jr. endowed chair, 2005, v.p. Rsch. and Econ. Devel., 2007—09; pres. Kans. State U., 2009—. Mem. ABET Engring. Accreditation Commn. (EAC). Fellow: AAAS, Am. Soc. Engring.Educators (ASEE); mem.: AIChE, ASEE. Office: Kans State U Office of Pres 110 Anderson Hall Manhattan KS 66506 Office Phone: 785-532-6221. E-mail: kirks@k-state.edu.*

SCHULZ, RENATE ADELE, German studies and second language acquisition educator; b. Lohr am Main, Germany, Feb. 24, 1940; came to U.S., 1958; 1 child, Sigrid Diane. BS, Mankato State Coll., 1962; MA, U. Colo., 1967; PhD, Ohio State U., 1974; D (hon.), U. Leipzig, Germany, 2008. Edn. officer US Peace Corps, Ife Ezinihitte, Nigeria, 1963-65; asst. prof. Otterbein Coll., Westerville, Ohio, 1974-76, State U. Coll. NY, Buffalo, 1976-77; from asst. to assoc. prof. U. Ark., Fayetteville, 1977-81; from assoc. to prof. U. Ariz., Tucson, 1981—, head dept. German, 1984-90, chair PhD program in second lang. acquisition and teaching, 1994-97, acting head, 2008—09. Disting. vis. prof. USAF Acad., Colorado Springs, Colo., 1990-91; co-dir. Ctr. Ednl. Resources in Culture, Lang. and Literacy, 2006-07. Recipient Creative Tchg. award, U. Ariz. Found., Tucson, 1984, Stephen A. Freeman award, N.W. Conf. Tchg. Fgn. Langs., 1984, Bundesverdienstkreuz, Fed. Govt. Germany, 1990, Anthony Papalia award for excellence in tchr. edn., Am. Coun. on the Tchg. of Fgn. Langs./N.Y. State Assn. Fgn. Lang. Tchrs., 2002, Henry and Phyllis Koffler prize for outstanding accomplishments in tchg., U. Ariz., 2005, Disting. Svc. to the Profession award, ADFL, 2008. Mem.: Ariz. Lang. Assn. (Outstanding Svc. to Fgn. Edn. award 1989), Nat. Fedn. Modern Lang. Tchrs. Assns. (v.p. 2004—05, pres. 2006—07), Am. Assn. Applied Linguistics, Tchrs. of ESL, Am. Assn. Tchrs. German (v.p. 1988—90, pres. 1990—91), Am. Coun. on the Tchg. of Fgn. Langs. (exec. coun. 1979—81, Florence Steiner award 1993). Office: U Ariz Dept German Studies Tucson AZ 85721-0105 Office Phone: 520-621-1799. Business E-Mail: schulzr@u.arizona.edu.

SCHULZ, RUDOLPH WALTER, university dean emeritus; b. Chgo., Aug. 10, 1930; s. Walter Adolph and Minna Louise (Burmeister) S.; m. Charlotte Helen Adams, Sept. 8, 1956; children: Stephanie Sue, Kyle Scott. BS, Northwestern U., 1954, PhD, 1958; MA, Stanford, 1955. Lectr., research asso. Northwestern U., 1956-58, instr., 1958-59; asst. prof. psychology Carnegie-Mellon U., 1959-60; asst. prof. U. Iowa, 1960-64, asso. prof., 1964-66, prof., 1966-95, prof., chmn. dept., 1970-73, dean for advanced studies, 1976-91. Cons. in field, mem. NSF fellowship selection panel, 1962-68; NSF vis. scientist, 1962-76; bd. dirs. Midwest Univs. Consortium for Internat. Activities, Inc., 1977-91. Cons. editor: Jour. Exptl. Psychology, 1962-74, Jour. Verbal Learning and Verbal Behavior, 1964-74, Contemporary Psychology, 1970-81; editor: Psychonomic Science, 1971-72, Memory and Cognition, 1972-76; Contbr. articles to profl. jours. Served with USNR, 1950-52. Decorated Air medal.; Old Gold research fellow U. Iowa, 1963; NSF research grantee, 1964-76 Fellow Am. Psychol. Assn., AAAS (mem. council 1974-75), Am. Psychol. Soc. (charter); mem. Psychonomic Soc., Midwestern Psychol. Assn. (sec.-treas. 1973-76, pres. 1978), Sigma Xi. Home: 8 Fairview Knls NE Iowa City IA 52240-9147 Personal E-mail: profrws@aol.com.

SCHULZ, SALLY ANN, pastoral musician, conductor, educator; b. Red Oak, Iowa, Mar. 12, 1951; d. Robert Lionel and Mary Ellen Evans; m. Thomas Richard Schulz, Dec. 29, 1972; children: Matthew Thomas, Joanne Elizabeth. MusB, U. of Iowa, 1969—73. Indepent piano tchr. Schulz Studio, Bettendorf, Iowa, 1973—77; ind. piano & organ tchr. Freeport, Ill., 1977—88; dir. music St. Thomas Aquinas Ch., Freeport, Ill., 1984—90; elem. vocal music tchr. Freeport Cath. Sch., Freeport, Ill., 1988—90, Trinity Episcopal Day Sch., Baton Rouge, 1991—92; dir. music St. Ann's Ch., Long Grove, Iowa, 1993—95, 2008—; dir. music & liturgy St. John Vianney Ch., Bettendorf, Iowa, 1995—2005; dir. music Rivermont Collegiate, Bettendorf, 2006—. Mem. Diocesan Liturgical Commn., Davenport, Iowa, 2002—05; prin. organist Christ Episc. Ch., Moline, Ill., 2006—08. Mem.: Handel Oratorio Soc. Augustana Coll. Rock Island, Am. Guild of English Handbell Ringers, Am. Guild of Organists, Nat. Pastoral Musicians, Nat. Soc. Colonial Dames of Am., Delta Gamma. Achievements include Selected as a member of the MASTER CHORALE of the USA for the 2003 Festival Internazionale di Music e Arte Sacra in Rome; Selected by Paul Wilkes for his book Excellent Catholic Parishes published by Paulist Press. Home: 2993 Greenview Dr Bettendorf IA 52722

SCHULZ, WILLIAM FREDERICK, human rights scholar and advocate; b. Pitts., Nov. 14, 1949; s. William F. and Jean Smith; m. Beth Graham, 1993. AB, Oberlin Coll., 1971; MA, Meadville/Lombard Theol. Sch., 1973, DMin, 1975, DDiv, 1987; MA, U. Chgo., 1974; DHL (hon.), Nova Southeastern U., 1995, Grinnell Coll., 2004, Willamette U., 2005, Oberlin Coll., 2005, U. Cinn., 2005, Lewis and Clark Coll., 2006. Minister First Parish Unitarian Universalist, Bedford, Mass., 1975-78; dir. social responsibility Unitarian Universalist Assn., Boston, 1978-79, exec. v.p., 1979-85, pres., 1985-93; exec. dir. Amnesty Internat. USA, 1994—2006; fellow Carr Ctr. Human Rights Policy, Kennedy Sch. Govt., Harvard U., 2006—07; adj. prof. NYU, NYC, 2008—; sr. fellow Ctr. for Am. Progress, 2006—; affiliated prof. Meadville Lombard Theological Sch., Chgo., 2008—. Author: Finding Time and Other Delicacies, 1992, In Our Own Best Interest: How Defending Human Rights Benefits Us All, 2001, Making the Manifesto: The Birth of Religious Humanism, 2002, Tainted Legacy: 9/11 and the Ruin of Human Rights, 2003; editor, contbr.: Transforming Words: Six Essays on Preaching, 1984; 2d edit., 1996; editor, contbr.: The Phenomenon of Torture: Readings and Commentary, 2007, The Future of Human Rights: US Policy for a New Era, 2008. Named Humanist of Yr., Am. Humanist Assn., 2000. Mem. ACLU, Unitarian Universalist Mins. Assn., Coun. Fgn. Rels. Democrat.

SCHULZE, CHAD WILLIAM, lawyer; m. Kelly Schulze. BS in Speech Comm. and Polit. Sci., U. SD, Vermillion; JD, Hamline U. Sch. Law, St. Paul, 2002. Bar: Minn. 2002, US Dist. Ct. (dist. Minn.) 2003. Law clk. Rondoni, MacMillan & Schneider, Ltd., 2000—02; atty. Milavetz, Gallop & Milavetz, P.A., Edina, Minn., 2003—. Named a Rising Star, Minn. Super Lawyers Mag., 2006—08. Mem.: Minn. Trial Lawyers Assn., Am. Trial Lawyers Assn. (mem. Vioxx litig. group 2004—, mem. Hurricane Katrina relief group 2005—, mem. fed. litig. group 2008—), Ramsey County Bar Assn., Minn. State Bar Assn., Am. Civil Liberty Union. Avocations: hunting, fishing. Office: Milavetz Gallop & Milavetz PA 6500 France Ave South Edina MN 55435 Office Phone: 952-920-7777. E-mail: attorneyschulze@netscape.net.

SCHULZE, FRANZ, JR., critic, educator; b. Uniontown, Pa., Jan. 30, 1927; s. Franz and Anna E. (Krimmel) Schulze; m. Marianne Gaw, June 24, 1961 (div. 1975); children: F. C. Matthew, Lukas A.; m. Stephanie Mora, 1992 (div. 1996). Student, Northwestern U., Evanston, Ill., 1943; PhB, U. Chgo., 1945; BFA, Sch. Art Inst. Chgo., 1949, MFA, 1950; postgrad., Acad. Fine Arts, Munich, 1956-57. Instr. art Purdue U., 1950-52; chmn. dept. art Lake Forest (Ill.) Coll., 1952-58, artist-in-residence, 1958-61, prof. art, 1961—, Hollender prof. art, 1974-91, Hollender prof. art emeritus, 1991—; art critic Chgo. Daily News, 1962-78, Chgo. Sun-Times, 1978-85. Chgo. corr. art Christian Sci. Monitor, 1958—62; art. and arch. critic Chicagoan, 1973—74; mem. vis. com. dept. art U. Chgo., 1974—87; adj. prof. U. Ill., Chgo., 1996. Co-author: Art, Architecture and Civilization, 1969; co-author: (with Rosemary Cowler and Arthur Miller) Thirty Miles North, 2000, Philip Johnson: Life and Work, 1994; co-author: (with Kevin Harrington) Chicago's Famous Buildings, 2003; co-author: Mariotti II, 2004; author: Fantastic Images: Chicago Art Since 1945, 1972, 100 Years of Chicago Architecture, 1976, Stealing is My Game, 1976, Mies van der Rohe: A Critical Biography, 1985, The University Club of Chicago: A Heritage, 1987, Mariotti, 1988, Illinois Institute of Technology. Campus Guide, 2005, 2007; editor: Mies van der Rohe: Critical Essays, 1989, Mies van der Rohe Archive, 1993; editor: (with Kevin Harrington) Chicago's Famous Buildings, 1993; co-editor: A. James Speyer, Architect, Curator, Exhibition Designer, 1997, The Farnsworth House, 1997, Illinois Institute of Technology, Campus Guide, 2005; contbg. editor: Art News, 1973—, Inland Arch., 1975—94, corr. editor: Art in Am., 1975—. Trustee Ragdale Found., Lake Forest, 1981—. Recipient Harbison award for tchg., Danforth Found. St. Louis, 1971, Disting. Svc. award, Chgo. Phi Beta Kappa soc., 1972, Hon. Mention Hitchcock Book award, Soc. Archtl. Historians, 1987, Excellence in Architecture award, Ill. Inst. Tech., 1999; Adenauer fellow, 1956—57, Ford Found. fellow, 1964—65, Graham Found. for Advanced Studies in the Fine Arts fellow, 1971, 1981, 1993, NEH fellow, 1982, 1988, Skidmore Owings & Merrill Found. fellow, 1983. Mem.: AAUP, Soc. Archtl. Historians (Hon. Mention Hitchcock Book award), Archives Am. Art (mem. adv. com.), Coll. Art Assn. (bd. dirs. 1983—86). Office: Lake Forest Coll Young Hall Lake Forest IL 60045 Office Phone: 847-735-5084. Business E-Mail: schulze@lakeforest.edu.

SCHULZE, HORST H., hotel company executive; D in Hospitality Mgmt. (hon.), Johnson & Wales U., 1999. Various positions Hilton Hotels; positions from gen. mgr. through corp. v.p. Hyatt Hotels Corp.; charter mem., v.p. ops. Ritz Carlton Hotel Co., 1983—87, exec. v.p., 1987—88, pres., COO, 1988—2001, vice-chmn., 2001—02; founder, pres., CEO West Paces Hotels Group, 2002—, Capella Hotels & Resorts. Bd. dirs. Reliance Trust Co., Travel Inst. Bd. dirs. Cancer Treatment Ctrs. America, InfiLaw Sys., Ga. Family Coun. Recipient Ishikawa medal, 1995; named Corp. Hotelier of World, HOTELS Mag., 1991; named to Internat. Food and Beverage Hall of Fame, 2004. Office: West Paces Hotel Group/Capella Hotels & Resorts 3384 Peachtree Rd Ste 375 Atlanta GA 30326 Office Phone: 404-842-7280. Office Fax: 404-842-7288.

SCHULZE, JUERGEN HELMUT, engineering executive; b. Brockwitz, Germany, June 16, 1939; s. Helmut Bruno and Marianne (Kowalski) Schulze; m. Barbara Rueger; children: Henrik, Eric. BSME, Coll. Engring., Esslingen, 1963; MBA, Columbia U., 1972. Sales mgr. Worthington Corp., Harrison, NJ, 1963-67; sr. cons. Peat, Marwick, Mitchell & Co., NYC, 1968-72; gen. mgr. Rank Xerox, Dusseldorf, Germany, 1973-81; mng. dir. Lonza Werke, Waldshut, Germany, 1982-91; chmn., CEO Deutz motor, Cologne, Germany, 1991—2000. Prof. mktg. U. Wuppertal, Germany, 1982—94; prof. U. Oredea, 2001—; bd. dirs. No. Tech. Corp., Praecitec Corp., 1999—, Montanhydraulik Corp., LEVG GmbH; chmn. Helmut Schulze GmbH. Founding mem. Children Aids Found., Dusseldorf, 1986; mem. adv. bd. Handelshochschule, Leipzig; pres. Support Orgn. Free Dem. Party, Bonn, 1983—. Mem.: Columbia Alumni Assn., INSEAD Alumni Orgn. Avocation: golf. Home: Habichtweg 2 40670 Meerbusch Germany Office: Helmut Schulze GmbH Habichtweg 2 D 40670 Meerbusch Germany

SCHULZE, KEITH E., dermatologist, surgeon; b. Ft. Worth, Nov. 6, 1963; s. Arthur E. and Sharon E. Schulze; m. Betsy S. Nance, Apr. 29, 1989; children: Sarah E., Kristen E. BA in Chemistry summa cum laude, Tex. Luth. U., 1985; MD, U. Tex., 1989. Diplomate Am. Bd. Dermatology, 1993. Physician, ptnr. South Tex. Med. Clinics, P.A., Wharton, 1993—96, sec., treas., 1996—2000; clin. asst. prof. dept. dermatology U. Tex. Med. Sch., Houston, 2000—01; v.p., co-dir. Dermatologic Surgery Ctr., 2001—06; pres. Ft. Bend Skin Cancer Ctr., Sugar Land, Tex., 2006—. Trustee St. Thomas Episcopal Sch., Wharton, Tex., 1999—2001; dir. Wharton C. of C. and Agr., 1996—99. Recipient Eugene D.Jacobson award Highest Achievement Mammalian Physiology, U. Tex. Med. Sch., Houston, 1986, award Highest Achievement Microbiology, 1986. Fellow: Am. Soc. Dermatologic Surgery, Am. Coll. Mohs Micrographic Surgery and Cutaneous Oncology, Am. Acad. Dermatology, Am. Soc. Mohs Surgery; mem.: Houston Dermatologic Soc., Harris County Med. Soc., Tex. Dermatologic Soc., Tex. Med. Assn., Alpha Omega Alpha. Achievements include research in numerous clinical pharmacologic trials. Avocations: fishing, hunting. Office: Ft Bend Skin Cancer Ctr 15400 SW Fwy Ste 150 Sugar Land TX 77478

SCHULZE, RICHARD M., retail executive; b. St. Paul, Minn., 1941; married; 9 children. D (hon.), Univ. of St. Thomas, St. Paul, 1998. With No. States Sales Co., 1962-66; founder, chmn. Sound of Music (now Best Buy Co., Inc.), Eden Prairie, Minn., 1966—; CEO Best Buy Co., Inc., Eden Prairie, Minn., 1983—2002, chmn., 2002—. Mem. Minn. Bus. Partnership; bd. dir. Pentair Inc., Nat. Entrepreneur of Yr. Inst., 1992—; bd. of overseers Carlson Sch. of Mgmt.; bd. trustees Univ. of St. Thomas. With Minnesota Air National Guard. Recipient Nat. Entrepreneur of Yr., Ernst & Young, 1999, America's Promise Red Wagon for Cmty. Svc., Gen. Colin Powell, 1999, Outstanding Mktg. Exec of Yr., Minnesota DECA, 2000, Robert C. McDermond Medal for Excellence in Entrepreneurship, Robert C. McDermond Ctr. for Mgmt. and Entrepreneurship, 2000; named Corp. Leader of Yr., Juvenile Diabetes Assn., 1999; named one of Top CEOs, Worth Mag., 1999, Am.'s Richest People, Forbes mag., 1999—, Exec. Pay, 1999—, World's Richest People, 2001—. Office: Best Buy 7601 Penn Ave S Minneapolis MN 55423-3645*

SCHULZ-HEIK, R. JAY, medical researcher; b. New Rochelle, NY, Sept. 7, 1976; BA, Colgate U., Hamilton, NY, 1998; attending, U. Colo., Boulder, 2004—. Analyst assoc. Hudson River Group, Valhalla, NY, 1999—2002; rsch. asst. Mt. Sinai Sch. Medicine, NYC, 2002—04. Contbr. articles to profl. jours. Instl. Rsch. Tng. grant, Nat. Inst. Child Health and Human Devel., 2005—. Mem.: Internat. Soc. Traumatic Stress Studies, Behavioral Genetics Assn., Assn. Behavioral and Cognitive Therapies, Psi Chi. Office: Univ Colo Boulder UCB 345 Boulder CO 80303 Business E-Mail: jay.schulz-heik@colorado.edu.

SCHULZKE, MARGOT SEYMOUR, artist, author, educator; b. San Francisco; BA in Art, Brigham Young U., 1959; studied with, Roman Andrus and others. Lectr. Brigham Young U. Edn. Weeks., Provo, Utah, 1966-68. Instr. painting workshops; juror numerous exhibits. Exhibited in shows at Nat. Art Club, Salmagundi Club, NYC, New Orleans, San Francisco, Colo., Oreg., Nev., Calif., others, (numerous awards); at Mus. Calif., Ill., NJ, Miss., Utah; featured artist in Pastel Interpretations, Northlight, 1993, Best of Pastel, Rockport, Mass. Pubs., 1996, Landscape Inspirations, Rockport Pubs., 1997, Best of Pastel II, 1998, Pure Color: Best of Pastel, North Light, 2006; author: Painter's Guide to Design & Composition, 2006; contbg. editor, The Pastel Jour., contbr. articles to other profl. jours. Bd. dirs. Friends of Moldova Relief, Sacramento, 1992-93. Recipient Disting. Emeritus award, Brigham Young U., 2000, Pastel Laureate TM award, PSWC, 2006, Juror of Pastel 100, 2009. Mem.: Pastel USA, Emerald Art Ctr. Nat. Open Exhibn., NW Pastel Soc., Haggin Mus., Degas Pastel Soc., Calif. Art Club, Pastel Soc. West Coast (bd. dirs. 1985—, adv. bd. 1988—, founding pres. 1985—88, pres. 1995—97), Pastel Soc. Am., Am. Artists Profl. League. Mem. Lds Ch. Avocations: photography, travel, gardening, reading. Office Phone: 530-878-6502. Personal E-mail: designinart@gmail.com.

SCHULZRINNE, HENNING G., computer science educator; b. Cologne, Germany; arrived in US, 1984; m. Carol Schulzrinne; children: Nathan Paavo, Ilta Rachel. BS in Econ. and Elec. Engring., Darmstadt U. Tech., 1984; MSEE, U. Cin., 1987; PhD, U. Mass., 1992. Mem. tech. staff AT&T Bell Labs., Murray Hill, NJ, 1992-94; assoc. dept. head GMD Fokus, Berlin, 1994-96; joined dept. computer sci. and elec. engring. Columbia U., NYC, 1996—, prof. computer sci., elec. engring.; chair, dept. computer sci. Faculty, Internet Real-Time Lab Columbia U., faculty, Columbia Networking Rsch. Ctr., co-dir., Ctr. Advanced Info. Mgmt. Editor: Jour. Communications and Networks. Recipient Mayor's award for excellence in sci. and tech., NYC, VON Pioneer award. Fellow: IEEE (editor Transactions on Networking, past mem., chmn. bd. gov. Comm. Soc., past editor Internet Computing Mag.); mem.: Internet Engring. Task Force. Office: Columbia U Dept Computer Sci 450 Computer Sci Bldg New York NY 10027 Office Phone: 212-939-7004. Office Fax: 212-666-0140. Business E-Mail: hgs@cs.columbia.edu.

SCHUMACHER, BARBARA J, biology professor; d. Edward and Margaret (McNerney) Fraclose; m. William L Schumacher, June 27, 1970; children: Lynne Lafferty, David. BS in Biology, Caldwell Coll., NJ, 1969; MS in Biol. Sci., U. Houston - Clear Lake, 1982. Tchr. Immaculate Conception HS, Montclair, NJ, 1969—72; biology prof. San Jacinto Coll., Pasadena, Tex., 1982—. Mem.: Nat. Assn. Biology Tchrs., Tex. C.C. Tchrs. Assn. Office: San Jacinto Coll 8060 Spencer Hwy Pasadena TX 77505 Personal E-mail: bschum@comcast.net. Business E-Mail: barbara.schumacher@sjcd.edu.

SCHUMACHER, CYNTHIA JO, retired elementary and secondary education educator; b. Sebring, Fla., Sept. 24, 1928; d. Floyd and Espage S. BA, Fla. State U., Tallahassee, 1950, MA, 1951, postgrad., 1968-69; MS, Nova U., Ftl. Lauderdale, Fla., 1978. English tchr. Grady County Sch. System, Cairo, Ga., 1951-53; elem. tchr. Brevard County Sch. System, Melbourne, Fla., 1953-55; elem. tchr., curriculum generalist, secondary tchr. Lake County Schs., Tavares, Fla. area, 1955-85; retired, 1985. Mem. Edn. Standards Commn., Fla., 1980—85, Quality Instrn. Incentives Coun., Fla., 1983—84. Author: (poetry) Seeds from Wild Grasses, 1988, Creekstone Crossings, 1993, Soul Candles, 1998, Wellspring Legacies, 2000, Firefly Encounters, 2007; (poetry and stories) Butterfly Excursions, 1996; (children's books) Colorful Character, 1998, Searching for S, 1998. Pres. League of Women Voters of Lake County, 1989-91. Recipient Good Egg award, Leesburg Area C. of C., 1991, Lifetime Achievement award, Fla. Edn. Assn. United, 2000; named Fla. Tchr. of Yr., Fla. Fedn. Women's Clubs, 1966, Lake County Tchr. of Yr., Lake County Sch. Sys., 1985, East Cen. Fla. Tchr. of Yr. finalist, State of Fla., 1986. Mem. Lake County Edn. Assn. (pres. 1971-72, cons. 1985—). Democrat. Roman Catholic. Avocations: gardening, creative writing, macrobiotic cooking, environmental support activities. Home: PO Box 1071 Sebring FL 33871

SCHUMACHER, H(ARRY) RALPH, internist, rheumatologist, medical educator, researcher; b. Montreal, Canada, Feb. 14, 1933; s. H. Ralph and Dorothy (Shreiner) S.; m. Elizabeth Jean Swisher, July 13, 1963; children: Heidi Ruth, Kaethe Beth. BS, Ursinus Coll., 1955; MD, U. Pa., 1959. Intern Denver Gen. Hosp., 1959-60; resident in medicine Wadsworth VA Hosp., LA, 1960-62, fellow in rheumatology, 1962-63, Robert B. Brigham Hosp. and Harvard U. Med. Sch., Boston, 1965-67; chief arthritis-immunology ctr. VA Med. Ctr., Phila., 1967—2006; faculty mem. U. Pa. Sch. Medicine, Phila., 1967—, prof. medicine, 1979—, acting arthritis divsn. chief, 1978-80, 91-95, prof. orthopaedics, 1998—2002. Vis. scholar NIH, 1994-99; chmn. Govt. Group OMERACT; lectr. in field. Author: (books) Gout and Pseudogout, 1978, Essentials of a Differential Diagnosis of Rhematoid Arthritis, 1981, Rheumatoid Arthritis, 1988, Case Studies in Rheumatology for the House Officer, 1989, Atlas of Synovial Fluid and Crystal Identification, 1991, A Practical Guide to Synovial Fluid Analysis, 1991, The Spondylarthropathies, 1998, Classic Papers in Rheumatology, 2001, Crystal-induced Arthropathies, 2006; editor: Primer on Rheumatic Disease, 1981—97, Jour. Clin. Rheumatology, 1994—, Crystal Diseases Section, 2005—; mem. editl. bd. Jour. Rheumatology, 1973—, Arthritis and Rheumatism, 1981—88, Revue du Rhumatisme (now Joint, Bone, Spine), 1992—2007, Internat. Jour. Clin. Practice, 1992—, New European Rheumatology, 1993—, Asian Pacific League Against Rheumatism Jour. Rheumatology, 1997—, Current Rheumatology Reports, 1999—, Indian Jour. Rheumatology, 2000—, Portuguese Jour. Rheumatology, 2000—; mem. editl. bd. Resident and Staff Physician, 2001—08; mem. editl. bd.: Vojnosanitetski, 2005—, Chinese Jour. Integrative Medicine, 2007—, Brazilian Journal of Rheumatology, 2008—; contbr. articles to profl. jours. Pres. Ea. Pa. chpt. Arthritis Found., 1980-82; chmn., founder Phila. Garden Tours, 1987—95; bd. dirs. Hemochromatosis Rsch. Found., 1984—, Am. Bd. Med. Advancement China, 1983-99. With M.C. USAF, 1963-65. Recipient VanBreeman award Netherland Rheumatism Soc., 1988, Philip Hench award Assn. Mil. Surgeons, 1986, Hollander award Arthritis Found., 1996; named Alumnus of Yr. Ursinus Coll, 1995; named to Sports Hall of Fame, 1997; Deposition VA grantee, 1967-95, NIH grantee, 1981, 94—. Master PANLAR; fellow ACP; mem. AAAS, Am. Coll. Rheumatology (master; pres. Southeastern region 1981-82, Klemperer lectr. 2002), Phila. Rheumatism Soc. (pres. 1980), Phila. Electron Microscopy Soc. (chmn. 1975-76), Rheumatism Soc. Mex., Rheumatism Soc. Australia, Rheumatism Soc. Colombia, Rheumatism Soc. Chile, Rheumatism Soc. China, Rheumatism Soc. Argentina, Med. Soc. Argentina, Slovak Soc. Rheumatology. Office: VA Med Ctr 151 K University and Woodland Aves Philadelphia PA 19104 also: Hosp U Pa 8 Penn Tower 3400 Spruce St Philadelphia PA 19104-4206 Business E-Mail: schumacr@mail.med.upenn.edu. *I try to teach meticulous observation and questioning of dogma both in daily care of patients and in laboratory investigation of the poorly understood rheumatic diseases.*

SCHUMACHER, HARRY RICHARD, lawyer; b. June 21, 1930; s. Henry Richard and Martha (Hagenbucher) S.; m. Katherine E. Ware, June 8, 1991; children: Richard, Garry. BA, Yale U., 1951; JD magna cum laude, Harvard U., 1958. Bar: N.Y. 1959, U.S. Supreme Ct. 1964. Assoc. firm Cahill Gordon & Reindel and predecessor firms, NYC, 1958—67, ptnr., 1968—97. Chmn. Legal Svcs. for N.Y.C., Inc., 1994—2003; dir. New York Legis. Svcs., 2000—. Mem. Manhattan Borough Pres.'s Cmty. Planning Bd. 6, 1962—66; Dem. candidate N.Y. State Assembly, 1962, 1963; warden Episcopalian Ch.; bd. dirs. Incarnation Camp, Ivoryton, Conn., 1961—72. Lt. (j.g.) USNR, 1951—54. Mem.: ABA, Am. Judicature Soc., N.Y. County Lawyers Assn. (bd. dirs. 1987—93, 1996—99), Fed. Comms. Bar Assn., Assn. Bar City of N.Y., N.Y. State Bar Assn. (mem. ho. dels. 1990—94, 2001—03), Yale (N.Y.C.), Union. Home: 47 E 88th St New York NY 10128-1152 Home Phone: 212-289-3056. Personal E-mail: richard.schumacher@verizon.net.

SCHUMACHER, LAURA J., lawyer, pharmaceutical executive; b. Muskegon, Mich., 1963; m. Andy Schumacher; children: Jane, Kate. BS in Bus. Adminstrn./Mktg., U. Notre Dame, 1985; JD, U. Wis., Madison, 1988. Assoc. Schiff, Hardin & Waite, Chgo., 1988—90; atty. litig. dept. Abbott Labs., Abbott Park, Ill., 1990—93, sr. atty., 1993—95, counsel, 1995—97, sr. counsel, 1997—99, divsn. v.p. litig., 2000—03, v.p., sec., dep. gen. counsel, 2003—05, sr. v.p., sec., gen. counsel, 2005—. Bd. dirs. Chgo. Children's Mus., Clara Abbott Found. Mem.: Chgo. Network, Econ. Club Chgo. Avocations: bicycling, reading. Office: Abbott Labs 100 Abbott Park Rd Abbott Park IL 60064-3500 Office Phone: 847-937-6100. E-mail: laura.schmacher@abbott.com.*

SCHUMACHER, MABEL G., director, consultant; b. Milw., Sept. 14, 1944; d. Clarence F. and Mabel Baskin Smith; m. Vernon A. Schumacher, Nov. 1, 1984. EdB, U. Wis., Whitewater, 1968, MS in Edn., 1971; PhD, U. Wis., 1978. Cert. sch. dist. adminstr. Wis., 1975, dir. instrn. Wis., 1975, dir. spl. edn. Wis., 1975, reading specialist Wis., 1971, tchr. mentally retarded Wis., 1968, tchr. learning disabled Wis., 1971, dir. pupil svcs. Wis., 1980. Tchr. mentally retarded Racine County Handicapped Children's Edn. Bd., Burlington, Wis., 1968—73, tchr. learning disabled, 1973—74, assoc. dir. spl. edn. Union Grove, Wis., 1975—84, dir. spl. edn., 1984—88; coord. spl. edn. Wauwatosa (Wis.) Sch. Dist., 1988—90, Sheboygan (Wis.) Area Sch. Dist., 1990—92; dir. instrn. Sch. Dist. Ft. Atkinson, Wis., 1992—2002; ret. Program asst. dept. edn. U. Wis., Madison, 1974—75, adj. prof., Whitewater, 1978—84; adj. prof. programs in mgmt. for adults Cardinal Stritch U., Milw., 1980—88; rev. team mem. Sch. Evaluation Consortium, Madison, 1990; staff devel. adv. com. mem. Coop. Edn. Svc. Agy. (CESA) 2, Milton, Wis., 1994—97; rev. panel Project First View-Wis. Pub. Broadcasting, Madison, 1996; rev. team. East Troy Pub. Schs., 2005; edl. cons., 2001—; presenter in field. Bd. dirs. United Way, Ft. Atkinson, 1994—2000, campaign co-chairperson, 1995, campaign chairperson, 1996; ch. organist, instr., youth leader Ft. Atkinson, 1962—84; pres. Phi Delta Kappa, Whitewater, 1977—78; sec. Wis. Sch. Pub. Rels. Assn., Madison, 1997—99, v.p., 1999—2000, pres. elect, 2000—01, pres., 2001—02, sec., 2002—. Fellow Program Assistantship, U. Wis., Madison, 1974—75; scholar, State of Wis., 1973—75, U. Wis., Whitewater, 1967—68. Mem.: Therapy Dog, Inc., Wis. Ret. Educators Assn., Walworth County Area Ret. Educators Assn. (Vol. Yr. 2006—07), Wis. Sch. Pub. Rels. Assn. (life; sec. and past pres. 2002—, Past Pres. award 2003, 2005), Kennel Club of Ft. Atkinson. Achievements include development of variety of education-related computer databases; Facilitator of Concept-Based Curriculum Project. Avocations: travel, reading, computer, cooking, pets. Home: 848 Messmer St Fort Atkinson WI 53538

SCHUMACHER, MARGARET LYNN, not-for-profit fundraiser, director; b. Pitts., Sept. 22, 1963; d. Paul William, Sr. and Margaret Josephine Schumacher; 1 child, Crystal Lynn. BA, Chatham Coll., Pitts., 1992; MS, LaRoche Coll., Pitts., 2000. Dir. sr. programs Citizen Care, Pitts., 1995—99; devel. dir. St. Anthony Sch. Programs, Pitts., 1999—2001; dir. grants and procurement YWCA Greater Pitts., 2001—02; dir. fund devel. Redstone Presbyn. Sr. Care, Greensburg, Pa., 2002—03; devel. dir. Vets. Leadership Program, Pitts., 2003—05; exec. dir. Tampa Bay Trial Lawyers Assn., Fla., 2006—. Vol. Susan B. Koman Found., Pitts., 2001—06, Friends of DaHang, Pitts., 2006—, Voices for Children, Tampa, 2006—. Mem.: Assn. Fundraising Profls. (cert., nominating com. local chpt.), Rotary (Bethel Park Rookie of Yr.). Republican. Avocations: golf, fishing, boating, piano. Office: Tampa Bay Trial Lawyers Assn PO Box 26091 Tampa FL 33623

SCHUMACHER, PAUL MAYNARD, lawyer; b. Columbus, Nebr., Apr. 4, 1951; s. Maynard Mathew and Rita Bell (Jarosz) S.; m. Michele Suzanne Gassé, June 26, 1976; children: Nicole Suzanne, Kristen Paulette. AA, Platte Coll., 1971; BS, Fort Hays U., 1973; JD, Georgetown U., 1976. Bar: Fla. 1976, Nebr. 1977, U.S. Dist. Ct. Nebr. 1977. Mem. staff U.S. Senate, Washington, 1974-76; sole practice Miami, Fla.

and Columbus, 1976—; v.p. Community Lottery Systems, Inc., Columbus, 1990-92, pres., 1992—. V.p. Megavision Corp., Columbus, 1976—. Treas. prin. Rep. campaign com. U.S. Senate Candidate, Lincoln, Nebr., 1978-79; atty. Platte County, Columbus, 1979-87; chmn. Platte county Reps., 1988-94; mem. Nebr. Rep. State Ctrl. Com., 1994-96, 2000—; CEO Lotto Nebr., 1992—; CEO Cmty. Internet Sys., Inc., 1995-98, bd. dirs., 1995—; bd. dirs. Keep the Money in Nebr. Com. Mem. Nebr. Bar Assn., Fla. Bar Assn., Platte County Bar Assn. (pres. 1992-93), Nat. Republican small bus. adv. council, Nebr. Republican Legis. Com., Rotary, Elks. Roman Catholic. Avocation: physics. Home: 6255 Meyer Rd Columbus NE 68601-8044 Office: PO Box 122 Columbus NE 68602-0122 Home Phone: 402-563-2112. E-mail: pschumac@megavision.com.

SCHUMACHER, ROBERT DENISON, banker; b. Evanston, Ill., Dec. 16, 1933; s. Frank Ade and Dorothy Ormonde (Hilton) S.; m. Mary Ann Montgomery, Aug. 25, 1956; children: Stephen Michael, Jeffrey Hilton. BA, Williams Coll., 1956; postgrad., Grad. Bus. Sch. N.Y. U., 1957-59; MD, Harvard Bus. Sch., 1966. With Irving Trust Co., NYC, 1956-89, sr. v.p., 1977-89, mgr. adminstrv. services, 1976—89, ret., 1989. Treas. Calvary, Holy Communion and St. George's Episcopal Ch., 1976-79, warden, 1980-86, 89-93, 2001-05; clerk vestry, 2009-; trustee The Church Club, 1993-2003, treas., 1994-99; mem.summer resident's adv. com. Town of Chatham, Mass., 2001-07. Mem. The Church Club. Home: 431 E 20th St New York NY 10010-7502 Personal E-mail: rschumach@aol.com.

SCHUMACHER, TOM E., soil scientist, educator; s. Vernon R. and Lucile M. Schumacher; m. Doris A. Hamman, May 29, 1972; children: Hannah M., Glenn H. BA, Bluffton U., Ohio, 1972; MS, Mich. State U., East Lansing, 1979, PhD, 1982. Instr. mennonite ctrl. com. Howard Meml. Secondary Sch., Shenge, Sierra Leone, 1972—75; from asst. prof. to prof. SD State U., Brookings, 1983—93, prof., 1993—. Exchange prof. Chungnam Nat. U., Daechon, Republic of Korea, 2003; with Arid Lands Consortium, Tucson, 2004—; chair tillage erosion working group Internat. Soil and Tillage Rsch. Orgn., 2004—07. Contbr. over 85 articles to profl. jours. Recipient Grad. Student Assn. Faculty and Staff award, Plant Sci. Dept. SD State U., 1991, 1995, Outstanding Tchr. award, Gamma Sigma Delta, SD State U., 1992, Environ. Excellence award, SD Dept. Transp., 2004, Malo Tchg. Excellence award, 2008. Mem.: AAAS, Soil Sci. Soc. Am. (assoc. editor jour.), Pa. Soil Scientists SD (pres.), Man. Soil Sci. Soc., Internat. Soil Sci. Soc., Can. Soil Sci. Soc., Am. Inst. Biol. Scis., Soil and Water Conservation Soc., World Assn. Soil Conservation (life), Sigma Xi (Grad. Rsch. award Mich. State U. 1981). Mennonite. Achievements include research in soil structure and management; soil wettability; crop root systems; tillage erosion; soil erosion and productivity. Avocations: reading, bicycling, photography. Office: South Dakota State Univ Plant Sci Dept NPB 247D Brookings SD 57007 Business E-Mail: thomas.schumacher@sdstate.edu.

SCHUMAN, PATRICIA GLASS, publishing company executive, educator; b. NYC, Mar. 15; d. Milton and Shirley Rhoda (Goodman) Glass; m. Alan Bruce Schuman, Aug. 30, 1964 (div. 1973); m. Stanley Robert Epstein, June 14, 1997 (dec. 2005); m. Vincent C. Civello, Dec. 06, 2009. AB, U. Cin.; MS, Columbia U. Libr. trainee Bklyn. Pub. Libr.; tchr. libr. Brandeis High Sch., NYC; asst. prof. libr. N.Y. Tech. Coll., Bklyn.; assoc. editor Sch. Libr. Jour., NYC; sr. editor R.R. Bowker Co., NYC; pres. Neal-Schuman Pubs., NYC, 1976—. Vis. prof. St. John's U., Queens, N.Y., 1977-79, Columbia U., N.Y.C., 1981-90, Pratt Inst., 1993-2000, Syracuse U., 1997—; cons. N.Y. State Coun. on Arts, 1987, Office Tech. Assessment, U.S. Congress, 1982, 84, Coord. Coun. Lit. Mags., N.Y.C., 1987, NEH, 1980, Temple U., 1978-80; bd. visitors Sch. Libr. and Computer Studies Pratt Inst., 1987-2001; juror Best of Libr. Lit., 1980-88; mem. adv. bd. Sch. Libr. and Info. Studies, Queens Coll., 1989-91. Author: Materials for Occupational Education, 1973, 2d edit., 1983 (Best Edn. Book award 1973), Library Users and Personnel Needs, 1980, Your Right to Know: The Call to Action, 1993; editor: Social Responsibilities and Libraries, 1976; mem. editorial bd. Urban Acad. Libr., 1987-89, Multicultural Review, 1991-95; contbr. articles to profl. jours. Bd. dirs. Women's Studies Abstracts, Albany, N.Y., 1970-74, Pratt Inst. Sch. of Libr. and Info. Studies, 1993—2000, Ctr. for Publ., NYU, 1996—, Am. Libr. in Paris, 2004-; mem. Com. To Elect Major Owens to U.S. Congress, 1983, N.Y.C. Mayor's Com. for N.Y. Pub. Ctr., 1984-85; pres. Met. Reference and Resources Coun./Met. N.Y. Libr. Coun, Neal Schumen Found., Inc. Recipient Fannie Simon award Spl. Librs. Assn., 1984, Disting. Alumni award Columbia U., 1992, Disting. Alumni award U. Cin., 2006; U.S. Office Edn. fellow, 1969. Mem. ALA (councillor 1971-79, 84-88, exec. bd. 1984-88, 90-93, treas. 1984-88, chmn. legis. com. 1989-90, 94-96, chmn. internat. rels. com. 1998, 99, chmn. Libr. Advocacy NOW!, v.p., pres.-elect 1990-91, pres. 1991-92, Disting. Coun. Svc. award 1979, 88, Equality award 1993, hon. mem. Black Caucus, appreciation award 1993, Freedom to Read Found. Honor Roll 1999, Lippincott award for disting. svc. 2001, Eileen Cooke/James Madison award, 2007), Spl. Librs. Assn. Office: Neal-Schuman Pubs Inc 100 William St Ste 2004 New York NY 10038 Business E-Mail: pgs@neal-schuman.com.

SCHUMANN, J. PAUL, retired federal agency administrator; b. Kansas City, Mo., Dec. 10, 1937; s. Fred and Miriam E. (Penzotti) S.; m. Olva Kimmel Dorris, Dec. 23, 1960; 1 child, Robert Reynold. BA, MA, U. Miss., 1960; cert., Indsl. Coll. Armed Forces, 1966; PhD, U. Okla., 1982. Instr. polit. sci. Jacksonville (Ala.) State U., 1961-64; intelligence officer Missile and Space Intelligence Ctr., Huntsville, Ala., 1964-91, sr. intelligence officer, 1991—2006; ret., 2006. Adj. asst. prof. U. Ala., Huntsville, 1981—2000; mem. Tenn dept. Coun. on Am's Mil. Past, Huntsville, 1971—82; adj. instr. Calhoun C.C., Huntsville, 1996, Huntsville, 2006—. Contbr. articles to profl. jours. V.p. external affairs Jaycees, Jacksonville, 1963-64. Recipient achievement medal for civilian svc. U.S. Army, 1992, letter of commendation South Korean Def. Intelligence Agy., 1992, Nat. Intelligence Cert. of Distinction, 2005, superior achievement medal Def. Intelligence Agy., 2006; Dept. Def. scholar, 1971-72. Mem. Nat. Mil. Intelligence Assn., Am. Polit. Sci. Assn., Phi Alpha Theta, Phi Kappa Psi (treas. 1957-58), Pi Sigma Alpha. Avocation: military history. Home: 8204 Willowbrook Cir SE Apt A Huntsville AL 35802-3335 Personal E-mail: paulschumann@comcast.net.

SCHUMANN, LAURA ELAINE, conductor; b. Mpls., May 13, 1963; d. Aubrey Paul Schumann, Elaine Anne Topka. BMus, U. Colo., 1985; MA, U. Calif., Santa Barbara, 1988; D in Musical Arts, Tex. Tech. U., 2001. Instr. violin and string methods Wake Forest U., Winston-Salem, NC, 1990—91; instr. upper strings and music theory Winston-Salem State U., NC, 1991—92; asst. condr. orch., instr. strings Murray State U., Murray, Ky., 1992—94; asst. prof. music, dir. orchestral activities, studio strings We. State Coll., Gunnison, Colo., 1994—99; asst. prof. music, music dir., condr. SE Ohio Symphony Muskingum Coll., New Concord, Ohio, 1999—. Instr. violin and string methods Salem Coll., Winston-Salem, 1990—91; asst. condr. orch. Tex. Tech. U., Lubbock, 1997—98; music dir., condr. Ovations Youth Orch. Wheeling (W.Va.) Symphony, 2000—02; freelance violinist; competitor Jordania Internat. Conducting Competition, Kharkov, Ukraine, 2003. Condr.: Nutcracker Ballet, 2001; Musical Odyssey, 2001—02; musician (violinist): Tanglewood Inst. Orch., 1980, L.A. Philharm. Inst., 1982, Santa Barbara Symphony, 1985—87, Santa Barbara Chamber Orch., 1985—87, Salisbury Symphony, 1987—92, Winston-Salem Symphony, 1987—92, 1990—92, Colo. Music Festival, 1991—97, Memphis Symphony, 1993, 1994, Grand Junction Symphony, 1996, Lubbock Symphony, 1997, 1998, River Cities Symphony, 2000, W.Va. Symphony, 2000, 2001—06, Ohio Valley Symphony, 2001; violinist, asst. concertmaster: We. Piedmont Symphony, 1989, Paducah Symphony, 1992—94, Jackson Symphony, 1992—94, Key West Symphony, 2001—05. Recipient Women of Achievement award, YMCA/YWCA, 2001, Cambridge Heritage Leadership award, 2004. Mem.: ASCAP (Adventurous Programming award 2001), Ohio Music Educators Assn., Coll. Music Soc., Music Educators Nat. Conf., Condr.'s Guild, Am. String Tchrs. Assn., Am. Fedn. Musicians, Am. Symphony Orch. League. Office: Music Dept Muskingum Coll New Concord OH 43762 Office Phone: 740-826-8314. E-mail: schumann@muskingum.edu.

SCHUMANN, PAULA M. L., writer; b. Phila., Oct. 23, 1938; d. Paschal Francis and Paula Marie Libonati; m. Walter Francis Schumann, June 17, 1967; 2 children. MT, Philadelphia County Med. Soc., 1972. Cert. med. technologist Phila. Gen. Hosp. Sch. Med. Tech., Pa.; admitted to holy profession Secular Franciscan Order, 2004. Author and pub. Renaitre Press, King of Prussia, Pa., 1998—. Author (publisher): A Chapter in the Life of a Poet (a story in verse), 1995, With His Love, Prayers and Poems, 2002; author: (poetry) Les Saisons de la Vie, 1998. Pres. Legion of Mary, King of Prussia, Pa., 2000—02., Franklin Sch. Sci. and Arts scholar, 1960—61. Mem.: Internat. Soc. Poets (disting. mem.), Phila. Writers' Conf., Poetry Soc. Am., Acad. Am. Poets. Roman Catholic. Avocations: cooking, travel, swimming, piano, dance. Office: Renaitre Press P O Box 61163 King Of Prussia PA 19406-1163 Business E-Mail: renaitrepress@yahoo.com.

SCHUMANN, WILLIAM HENRY, III, corporate financial executive; b. Iowa City, Aug. 28, 1950; s. William Henry Jr. and Eunice Vere (Doak) S. BS, UCLA, 1972; MS, U. So. Calif., 1973. Program mgmt. analyst Hughes Helicopters, Culver City, Calif., 1973-75; mgr. fin. planning Sunkist Growers, Sherman Oaks, Calif., 1975-81; dir. N.Am. Ops. Agrl. Products Group, FMC Corp., Chgo., 1981—; treas. FMC Corp., 1987—, exec. dir. corp. development, 1990-93, v.p., 1995—, sr. v.p., CFO, 1999—2001, FMC Technologies, 2001—07, exec. v.p., CFO, 2007—. Bd. dirs. Gt. Lakes Advisors and UAP Holdings. Republican. Office: FMC Technologies 200 E Randolph Dr Chicago IL 60601

SCHUMER, CHUCK (CHARLES ELLIS SCHUMER), United States Senator from New York; b. Bklyn., Nov. 23, 1950; s. Abraham and Selma (Rosen) S.; m. Iris Weinshall, Sept. 21, 1980; children: Jessica Emily, Alison. BA magna cum laude, Harvard U., 1971, JD with honors, 1974. Bar: NY 1975. Staff mem. to Senator Claiborne Pell US Senate, 1973; assoc. Paul, Weiss, Rifking, Wharton and Garrison, 1974; mem. NY State Assembly, 1975-80, chmn. subcom. on city mgmt. and governance, 1977, chmn. com. on oversight and investigation, 1979; mem. US Congress from 16th NY Dist., 1981—83, US Congress from 10th NY Dist., 1983—93, US Congress from 9th NY Dist., 1993—99; US Senator from NY, 1998—; chmn. Democratic Senatorial Campaign Committee (DSCC), 2005—09, US Senate Rules & Adminstrn. Com., 2009—; vice chmn. US Senate Democratic Conf., 2007—, US Congressional Joint Econ. Com.; mem. US Senate Fin. Com., US Senate Judiciary Com., US Senate Banking, Housing & Urban Affairs Com., Joint Com. on the Library. Author: Positively American: Winning Back the Middle-Class Majority One Family at a Time, 2007. Bd. dirs. NY Philharmonic. Herbert Tenzer award for Pub. Service, Five Towns Jewish coun., 1995, Criminal Justice Legis. award, NY State Bar Assoc., 1999, Leadership in Govt. award, Columbia U. Bus. Sch., 1999, Travers J. Bell Mem award of Distinction, NY Dist. Econ. Edn. Found, Securities Industry, Assoc., 1999, Pub. Policy Achievement award, Amer. Cancer Society, 2000, Sound Guardian award, NY Audobon and Cons. Industry Coun. of Westchester, 2002 Mem. Jewish War Veterans, B'nai Brith, Phi Beta Kappa. Democrat. Jewish. Office: US Senate 313 Hart Office Bldg Washington DC 20515-0001 also: District Office Ste 17-02 757 Third Ave New York NY 10017 Office Phone: 202-224-6542, 212-486-4430. Office Fax: 202-228-3027, 212-486-7693. E-mail: senator@schumer.senate.gov.*

SCHUMM, STANLEY ALFRED, geologist, educator; b. Kearny, NJ, Feb. 22, 1927; s. Alfred Henry and Mary Elizabeth (Murdock) S.; m. Ethel Patricia Radli, Sept. 3, 1950; children: Brian Murdock, Mary Theresa, Christine Ann. BA, Upsala Coll., 1950; PhD, Columbia U., 1955. Research geologist U.S. Geol. Survey, Denver, 1955-67; prof. geology Colo. State U., Ft. Collins, 1967-86, Univ. disting. prof., 1986-98, acting asso. dean, 1973-74, prof. emeritus, 1998—; prin. geomorphologist Mussetter Engring., Ft. Collins, 1995—. Vis. prof. U. Calif., Berkeley, 1959-60, U. Witwatersrand, South Africa, 1975; fellow U. Sydney, Australia, 1964-65, U. New South Wales, 1988; vice chmn. U.S. Nat. Com. Quaternary Rsch., 1967-70, 75-82; dist. vis. scientist U. tex., 1970; vis. lectr. numerous univs. in U.S., vis. scientist N.Z., Europe, Can., Venezuela, Brazil; vis. scientist Polish Acad. Sci., 1969; cons. to govt. agys., engring. firms; prin. geomorphologist, dir. Water Engring. Tech., Davis, Calif., and Ft. Collins, Colo., 1980-91; sr. assoc. Ayres Assocs., Ft. Collins, 1991-2000; prin. investigator rsch. projects NSF, 1969-92, Colo. Agrl. Expt. Sta., 1970-75, Army Rsch. Office, 1970-80, 82-93, Office Water Rsch. and Tech., 1974-83, Nat. Park Svc., 1975-77, Fed. Hwy. Adminstrn., 1978-80, Soil Conservation Svc., 1980-85, NASA, 1984-88, Smithsonian Inst., 1986-87, Can. Internat. Devel. Agy., 1991-92. Author: The Fluvial System, 1977, To Interpret the Earth, 1991; co-author: Incised Channels, 1984, Geomorphology, 1985, Experimental Fluvial Geomorphology, 1987, Active Tectonics and Alluvial Rivers, 2000; editor: United States Contribution to Quaternary Research, 1969, River Morphology, 1972, Slope Morphology, 1973, Drainage Basin Morphology, 1977, Physical Geography of W.M. Davis, 1980, The Variability of Large Alluvial Rivers, 1994, River Variability and Complexity, 2005; contbr. chpts. to sci. books, articles to profl. jours. Served with USNR, 1944-45. Recipient Disting. Alumnus award Upsala Coll., 1980, L.W. Durrell award Colo. State U., 1980, Linton award Brit. Geomorphology Rsch. Group, 1981, Warren prize NAS, 1986, Outstanding Paper award Soc. Sedimentary Geology, 1996, Hydrology Days award Colo. State U., 2001; Harkness fellow U. Canterbury, N.Z., 1983; fellow Japanese Soc. for Advancement of Sci., 1983, Dept. Agr., Republic of South Africa, 1984, Australian Nat. U., 1988; named honor scientist Colo. State U. chpt. Sigma Xi, 1986, Frost lectr. U. Hull, 1999. Fellow AAAS, Geol. Soc. Am. (asso. editor 1973-75, vice chmn. geomorphology div. 1978-79, chmn. 1979-80, Kirk Bryan award 1979, Disting. Career award 1997); sr. fellow Internat. Assn. Geomorphologists; mem. (hon.) Japanese Geomorphological Union, Am. Geophys. Union (Horton award 1958, assoc. editor 1973-75), ASCE, Internat. Geog. Union, Assn. Am. Geographers, Internat. Assn. Quaternary Research, Am. Quaternary Assn. (councillor), Sigma Xi (pres. Colo. State U. chpt. 1987-88, honor scientist 1987). Home: 1308 Rollingwood Ln Fort Collins CO 80525-1946 also: Mussetter Engring 1730 S College Ave Fort Collins CO 80525-1073 Home Phone: 970-482-0680; Office Phone: 970-224-4612. E-mail: stans@mussei.com.

SCHUNICHT, SHANNON ANTHONY, retired military officer, political scientist; b. Miami, Fla., Nov. 17, 1961; s. Wayne Anthony Schunicht and Suzanne Chatin (Tindell) Fast. BA in Philosophy and Polit. Sci., Fla. State U., 1983; BA in Biology, Tex. A&M U., 1994, BS in Microbiology, 1994. Cert. real estate agt. Tex. Tchr. physics U. Mich. AAPT, 2009. Spkr. in field. With U.S. Army, 1983-90. Mem. Internat. Leprosy Assn., Am. Soc. for Microbiology. E-mail: mneumonicmind@alpha1.net.

SCHUNK, DALE HANSEN, dean; b. Chgo., Aug. 14, 1946; s. Elmer Charles and Mildred Augusta Schunk; m. Caryl Sue Cook, June 29, 1984; 1 child, Laura Christine. BS, U. Ill., Urbana, 1968; MEd, Boston U., 1974; PhD, Stanford U., Calif., 1979. Asst. prof. edn. U. Houston, 1979—85, assoc. prof. edn., 1985—86, U. NC, Chapel Hill, 1986—91, prof. edn., 1991—93; head dept. ednl. studies Purdue U., W. Lafayette, Ind., 1993—2001; dean sch. edn. U. NC, Greensboro, 2001—. Cons. chpt. 1 reading Spring Br. Ind. Sch. Dist., Tex., 1981—94; mem. bd. trustees NC Tchr. Acad., Durham, 2002—; mem. task force tchr. retention NC State Bd. Edn., Raleigh, 2004—05. Author: (textbooks) Motivation In Education, 2008, Learning Theories: An Educational Perspective, 2008; editor: (profl. book) Educational Psychology: A Century of Contributions, 2003; contbr. chapters to books, articles to profl. jours. Sec. parent coun. W. Lafayette Sch. Corp., 1997—99; girls' softball coach W. Lafayette Little League, 1997—2000. Capt. USAF, 1968—74, Sewart AFB, Tenn., Naples, Italy. Recipient Disting. Svc. award, Purdue U. Sch. Edn., 1995, Fulbright Scholar award, New Zealand-US Ednl. Found., 1997, Cmty. Honor Roll, W. Lafayette Sch. Corp., 2000. Fellow: APA (pres. divsn. ednl. psychology 1998—99, Early Career award 1982); mem.: Am. Ednl. Rsch. Assn. (program chair 1999—2000). Avocations: tennis, travel. Home: 7007 Morganshire Ct Summerfield NC 27358 Office: Univ NC-Greensboro 1000 Spring Garden St Greensboro NC 27402 Office Fax: 336-334-4120. Business E-Mail: dhschunk@uncg.edu.

SCHUNKE, HILDEGARD HEIDEL, accountant; b. Indpls., Nov. 24, 1948; d. Edwin Carl and Hildegard Adelheid (Baumbach) Schunke. BA, Ball State U., Muncie, Ind., 1971, MA in German, English, 1973, MA in Acctg., 1975. CPA Ind., Calif. Exch. tchg. grad. asst. Padagogische Hochschule, Germany, 1971-72; tchg. grad. asst. in German and acctg. Ball State U., 1972, 74-75, asst. prof. acctg., 1975-78; investing rschr. Family Partnership, Muncie, 1977-83; staff acct. Am. Lawn Mower Co., Muncie, 1984-88, G&J Seiberlich, CPAs, St. Helena, Calif., 1988-89, R.A. Gullotta, MBA, CPA, Sonoma, Calif., 1989-90; plant acct. Napa Pipe Corp., Calif., 1990—2001; sys. engr. Napa Pipe Divsn. Oreg. Steel Mills, 2002—04; freelance acct. Fairfield, Calif., 2004—; sr. fin. analyst Syar Industries, Inc., Napa, 2007—. ESOL instr. Napa County Project Upgrade, 1988—92; mem. ticketing and refreshments com. North Bay Philharm. Orch., Napa, 1988—2004, North Bay Wind Ensemble, Napa, 1988—2004; mem. steering com. Cordelia Cmty. Pk., 2005—. Named Adminstrv. Divsn. Vol. of the Yr., City of Fairfield, Calif., 2006. Mem.: AICPA, Inst. Internal Auditors, Calif. Soc. CPAs (continuing edn. instr. Redwood City 1990, bd. dirs. East Bay chpt. 1998—2000). Avocations: gardening, building computers, networks and websites. Home: 1117 Devonshire Ct Fairfield CA 94534-7443 Office: HH Schunke MA CPA 1117 Devonshire Ct Fairfield CA 94534-7443 Office Phone: 707-864-2640. Personal E-mail: hsg_1@juno.com.

SCHUNTERMANN, PETER PAUL, psychiatrist; b. Hamburg, Germany, Oct. 14, 1934; came to U.S., 1959; s. Carl Erich and Hertha (Czeczor) S.; m. Estelle S. Fieldman, June 8, 1968; children: Eric, Howard. MD, Hamburg U., 1959. Lic. psychiatrist, Mass. Instr. in child psychiatry Beth Israel Hosp., Boston, 1966-80, sr. assoc. in child psychiatry, 1980—. Staff child psychiatrist Dorchester Mental Health Clinic, Boston, 1974-76, Mystic Valley Mental Health Clinic, Arlington and Manchester, Va., Mass., 1976-81, Harvard Community Health Plan, Boston, 1982-2000, Childern's Hosp. Boston Devel. Medicine Ctr., 2000-. Maj. M.C., AUS, 1967-69. Mem. Am. Psychiat. Assn., Am. Acad. Child Psychiatry, New Eng. Coun. Child Psychiatry (bd. dirs. 1976-80, 88-91, sec. 1991-96), Mass. Psychiat. Soc., Mass. Med. Soc. Office: 200 Allen Ave Waban MA 02468-1722 Office Phone: 617-965-3740.

SCHUPAK, DONALD, merchant banker, lawyer, strategic planner; b. NYC, Apr. 2, 1943; s. Sidney and Helen (Smith) S.; m. Leslie Silverman, June 21, 1964 (div. 1981); children: Andrew, Jessica; m. Cynthia Saul, Nov. 19, 1981; children: Amanda, Andrew, Philip Nicholas. BA, Syracuse U., 1964, JD, 1966; LLM in Taxation, NYU, 1970. Bar: N.Y. 1967. Assoc. various law firms, NYC, 1966-70; ptnr. Schupak, Rosenfeld, Fishbein, et al, NYC, 1970-82; chmn. bd., chief exec. officer Donald Schupak and Co., Inc., NYC, 1982—, Safety Harbor Corp., NYC, 1985-90; mgr. Schupak Grp. Inc., NYC. Vice chmn. Horn and Hardart Co., N.Y.C., 1977-88, chmn. bd., chief exec. officer, pres., 1988—. Mem. Assn. of Bar of City of N.Y., N.Y. Bar Assn., Phi Kappa Phi, Order of Coif. Clubs: Rombout Hunt (Hyde Park, N.Y.). Office: Schupak Grp Inc 595 Madison Ave Fl 35th New York NY 10022-1907 Office Phone: 212-582-4210.

SCHUPAK, LESLIE ALLEN, public relations company executive; b. Spokane, Wash., Apr. 5, 1945; s. Leo and Henrietta (Neumann) S.; m. Dianne Barbara Goldin, June 23, 1968; 1 child, Adam J. BS, Boston U., 1967, MS, 1971. Asst. to pres., account exec. Sperber Assocs., Inc., Boston, 1968-69; account supr. Wilcox & Williams, NYC, 1969-70; v.p., mgr. Daniel J. Edelman, Inc., NYC, 1970-72; mng. ptnr. Kanan, Corbin, Schupak & Aronow, Inc. Worldwide, NYC, 1972—. Pres. Whippoorwill Lake Property Owners Assn., Chappaqua, NY, 1984-88; chmn. exec. com. Coll. Comm., Boston U., 1997-2007; dir. First Tee Met. NY, Inc. With US Army, 1968-73. Mem.: Golf Writers Am. Assn., MGA Found. (chmn.), Nat. Investor Rels. Inst., Donald Ross Soc., Met. Golf Writers Assn. (v.p.), Met. Golf Assn. (pres.), US Golf Assn. (comms. com.), Desert Mountain Club (Scottsdale, Ariz.), Metropolis Country Club (White Plains, NY). Avocations: golf, writing, fishing. Office: Kanan Corbin Schupak & Aronow Inc Worldwide 880 3rd Ave New York NY 10022 Office Phone: 212-682-6300. Business E-Mail: lschupak@kcsa.com.

SCHUPP, RUSS, computer professor, web site designer; AA, State Fair C.C., Sedalia, Mo, 1974; MusB in Edn., Ctrl. Mo. State U., Warrensburg, 1976; MA, Webster U., Whiteman Air Force Base, 2003. Lan mgr. computer programing and web devel. State Fair C.C., 1997—2000, coll. tchr., 2000—. Percussionist Sedalia Symphony, Sedalia, 1971—2008; elder Broadway Presbyn. Ch., 2004—06; percussionist Broadway Presbyn. Ch. and Antioch Fellowship Praise and Worship groups, 1996—2008. Achievements include development of a new curriculum and course requirements for computer programming, with emphasis in accounting, and web development degrees.

SCHUPPAN, DETLEF, medical educator, researcher; b. Essen, Germany, Aug. 9, 1954; s. Walther and Helga (Pahnke) S.; m. Fatuma Isaak, Oct. 21, 1959; three children. MS in Chemistry, LMU, U. Munich, Germany, 1979, PhD in Biochemistry, 1982; MD, Free U. Berlin, Germany, 1986, PhD in Medicine, 1989. Cert. in internal medicine Berlin, 1993, in gastroenterology Berlin, 1996; in biochemistry Free U. Berlin, 1992. Rsch. fellow Max Planck Institute Biochemistry, Martinsried Munich, Germany, 1979—81; instr. biochemistry & medicine U. Marburg, Germany, 1981—82, Free U. Berlin, 1982—86, fellow, 1989—93, asst. prof., 1992—96, assoc. prof., 1996—97, intern & resident, 1986—89; full prof. U. Erlangen Nuremberg, Germany, 1997—2004; assoc. prof., lectr. Harvard Med. Sch., 2007—08. Cons. gastronetrology & hepatology, Berlin, 1994-97; dir. Rsch. Labs., Free U., 1991—; cons. various pharm. cos. worldwide, 1991—. Inventor & patentee in field; contbr. articles to profl. jours. Rsch. grantee German Rsch. Assn., 1987—, German Cancer Fund, 1995—, Industry, 1984—. Mem. Am. Gastroenterol. Assn., Am. Assn. Study of Liver Diseases, Am. Soc. Cell Biology, European Assn. Study of Liver Diseases (sec. 1999—), Similar Nat. Socs. Avocations: langs., practicing music, cello. Office: Beth Israel Deaconess Med Ctr 330 Brookline Ave Boston MA 02215 Office Fax: 617-667-2767. Business E-Mail: dschuppa@bidmc.harvard.edu.

SCHUR, LUCILLE S., artist; d. Kenneth and Isabelle Breakey; m. Jeffrey Schur; children: David, Cynthia Young. AOCA, Ont. Coll. Art, Toronto, 1992. AWS Signature Member Am. Watercolor Soc., 2006, NEWS Signature Member NE Watercolor Soc., 1998, CLWAC Full Membership Catherine Lorrilard Wolfe Art Club. Watercolor, Tyna (Paul Richardson award, 2008, Old Greenwich Atr Soc. First prize, 2006, Merit award, 2006), Red Head, exhibitions include Iyme Art Assn., Lady in Waiting, Blendheim Gallery (Art Soc. of Old Greenwich 3rd Prize, 2007), exhibitions include watercolor Tyna (CLWAC 1st prize, 2008), 68th annual exhibition nwws, The New Yorker (NW Watercolor Soc. M. Graham Award, 2008), exhibitions include Flirty Red Curls, lancaster Mseum Art Pa, exhibition-blendheim gallery, Flirty Red Curls (Art Soc. of Old Greenwich 1st Prize Watercolor, 2007). Mem.: NE Watercolor Soc. (signature membership 1999, Signature Membership 1999), Am. Watercolor Soc. (signature mem. 2007, Signature Membership 2007).

SCHUR, WALTER ROBERT, physician; b. Webster, Mass., June 17, 1914; s. Robert O. and Alma L. (Gatzke) S.; m. Delta Jean Newman, June 17, 1944; children: Paul, David, Jonathan, Ruth, Timothy, Peter, Stephen, Mary, Joel, Daniel, Rhoda. Student, Valparaiso U., 1931-34; MD, Middlesex U.Sch. of Med., 1940. Resident Milford (Del.) Meml. Hosp., 1940-41, Grace Hosp., Cleve., 1942-43; intern Luth. Hosp., Cleve., 1941-42; pvt. practice Oxford, Mass., 1944—. Bd. dirs., pres. Doctors Hosp., Worcester, Mass., chmn. bd., 1978-87; bd. dirs. AdCare Hosp., 1987—, chmn. bd. dirs., 1987-91, Atlantic dist. Luth. Ch.-Mo. Synod, 1978-87, mem., sec. edn. com., missions com., 1960-77, mem. stewardship com., youth com., edn. com., 1951-57, chmn. edn. com. Atlantic dist., 1954-57, mem. commn. on mission and ministry in ch., named Dist. Layman of Yr., 1966, chmn. com. on ministry Atlantic dist., 1970; bd. dirs. Luth. Assn. Works of Mercy, assn. Evang. Luth. Chs.; bd. dirs. Valparaiso U., 1969-99, sec., 1984-99; pres., scholarship chmn. N.E. dist. Luth. Laymen's League, 1957; vice chmn. Luth. Hour Oper. Com., 1958, chmn., 1959-61; New Eng. bd. dirs. Assn. Evang. Luth. Chs., 1977-87, trustee East Coast Synod, 1977-87, mem. nat. bd. dirs., 1979-88; mem. coun. New Eng. Synod Evang. Luth. Ch. Am., 1988-94; bd. dirs., vice chmn. French River Edn. Ctr., 1985—; mem. Oxford Sch. Com., 1961-86, Mass. Commn. on Christian Unity; assoc. charter mem. Park Ridge Ctr., 1986. Recipient award of merit Internat. Luth. Laymen's League, 1963, Soli Deo Gloria award New Eng. Synod, Evang. Luth. Ch. Am., 1994. Fellow Am. Acad. Gen. Practice, Am. Acad. Family Physicians (charter); mem. AMA, Mass. Med. Soc., Worcester Dist. Med. Soc., Am. Geriatrics Assn., New Eng. Ob-gyn. Soc., Valparaiso U. Alumni Assn. (past pres.), Luth. Acad. for Scholarship (bd. dirs. 1977-86), Concordia Hist. Inst., New Eng. Luth. Hist. Soc. (charter), Internat. Platform Assn., New Eng. Huguenot Soc., Rotary (past pres.). Home: 168 Charlton St Oxford MA 01540-2008 Office: 367 Main St Oxford MA 01540-1746

SCHURENBERG, ERIC P., magazine editor; b. Cin., Aug. 23, 1953; s. Carl Joseph and Lorraine Claire (Willows) Schurenberg; m. Judith Margaret Dowd, Apr. 30, 1983; 1 child, Emilie. AB in English, Brown U., 1975. Joined Money mag., NYC, 1984, sr. editor, 1990-95, asst. mng. editor, 1995—97, Fortune mag., 1997—2000; mng. editor Goldman.com, 2000—01; editor-at-large Business 2.0, 2001, dep. mng. editor, 2001—04, Money mag., NYC, 2004—08. Commentator Nightly Bus. Report, PBS, Marketplace Morning Report, NPR; host radio prog. You and Your Money, MediaOne; former pers. fin. reporter WCBS News. Author: 401K Take Charge of Your Future, 1995. Recipient Page One award, Newspaper Guild NY, 1989, Gerald Loeb award, UCLA Anderson Sch. Mgmt., 1989, Gerald Loeb Award for distinguished bus. journalism. Mem.: Am. Soc. Mag. Editors (bd. dirs. 2007—, Nat. Mag. award 1988).*

SCHURING, ELIZABETH, lawyer; BA in English, Baylor U., 1984; JD, U. Tex. Sch. Law, 1988. Cert.: Tex. Bd. Legal Specialization (estate planning and probate law). Ptnr. Giordani, Schurig, Beckett & Tackett, LLP, Austin. Mem. faculty Investment Mgmt. Consultants Assn. Wealth Mgmt. Prog. Contbr. articles to profl. jours.; author, editor: Asset Protection: Domestic and Internat. Law and Tactics. Named a Tex. Super Lawyer, Tex. Monthly and Law & Politics mag., 2003—06; named one of Top 100 Attys., Worth mag., 2005—06. Fellow: Travis County Bar Found., Tex. Bar Found., Tex. Acad. Probate and Trust Lawyers; mem.: State Bar Tex. (mem. real estate, probate and trust law sect.), ABA (vice chair real property, probate and trust law sect. 2006—07, mem. asset protection com., real property, probate and trust law sect., mem. internat. law and practice sect.), Austin Bar Assn. (dir. estate planning and probate sect. 1995—96), Estate Planning Coun. Ctrl. Tex., Coll. State Bar Tex. Office: Giordani Schuring Beckett Tackett LLP 100 Congress Ave 22nd Fl Austin TX 78701 Office Phone: 512-370-2732. Office Fax: 512-370-2730. E-mail: eschurig@gsbtlaw.com.

SCHURING, J. KIRK, state legislator; b. Canton, Ohio, Sept. 17, 1952; s. James A. and D. Margaret (Felton) S.; m. Darlene K. Newkirk, Mar. 2, 1976; children: J. Derrick, Kristin. Student, Kent State U., Ohio, 1970-74. Sec., treas. The Schuring Agy., Inc., Canton, 1978-80, pres., 1980—93; mem. Ohio State House of Representatives, Columbus, 1993—2002; mem. Dist. 29 Ohio State Senate, Columbus, 2003—, mem. agr., health human services and aging, hwy. and transportation, judiciary on civil justice, reference, rules coms. Ins. cons. Stark Devel. Bd., Canton, 1985—. Bd. dirs., v.p. Canton Urban League, 1983—, v.p. Stark/Wayne Am. Lung Assn., 1984—; bd. dirs. Canton Players Guild, 1986—; mem. adv. bd. Walsh Coll., 1988; mem. exec. bd. Stark County Rep. Orgn., Canton, 1981—; chmn. Stark County Reagan-Bush Com., Canton, 1984. Mem. Ind. Ins. Agts. Canton (bd. dirs. 1982-85), Jaycees Internat. (Sen. 1984), US Jaycees (Charles Kulp, Jr. award 1983, Gordon B. Thomas award 1983), Ohio Jaycees (James Lammermier award 1982), Canton Jaycees (pres. 1982-83, Disting. Svc. award 1987). Republican. Mem. Ch. Christ. Clubs: Canton (pres. 1988, bd. dirs. 1986—); Brookside Country. Avocations: golf, swimming, running. Office: Senate Bldg Rm 137 Ground Fl Columbus OH 43215 Office Phone: 216-453-4200. E-mail: SD29@senate.state.oh.us.*

SCHURMAN, DAVID JAY, orthopedic surgeon, educator; b. Chgo., Apr. 25, 1940; s. Shepherd P. and Dorothy (Laskey) S.; m. Martha Ellen Rocker, Mar. 8, 1967; children: Hilary Sue, Theodore Shepherd. BA, Yale U., 1961; MD, Columbia U., 1965. Intern Baylor U., Houston, 1965-67; resident in gen. surgery Mt. Sinai Hosp., NYC, 1966-67; resident in orthop. surgery UCLA, 1969-72; asst. rsch. surgeon UCLA Med. Sch., 1972-73; asst. prof. orthopedic surgery Stanford Med. Sch., 1973-79, assoc. prof., 1979-87, prof., 1987—. Acting chief divsn. orthop. surgery Stanford U. Med. Ctr., 1990-93, fellowship dir. total joint replacement, 1983—, fellowship dir. sports medicine, 1992-95, dir. orthop. rsch. lab., 1973—. Capt. USAF, 1967-69. Fellow NIH, 1972-73; grantee NIH, 1976-96; recipient Top Dr. award, San Francisco Mag., 02, 03, 05. Mem. Am. Orthopaedic Assn. (bd. dirs. 1994-95), Clin. Orthopaedics and Related Rsch. (bd. dirs. 1994-00), Assn. Bone and Joint Surgeons (v.p. 1996-97, pres. 1997-98). Office: Stanford U Sch Medicine R145 Divsn Orthop Surgery 300 Pasteur Dr Palo Alto CA 94304-2203 Office Phone: 650-723-7608. Business E-Mail: djsortho@stanford.edu.

SCHURZ, SCOTT CLARK, newspaper executive; b. South Bend, Ind., Feb. 23, 1936; s. Franklin Dunn and Martha (Montgomery) S.; m. Kathryn Joan Foley, Aug. 5, 1967; children: Scott Clark, Alexandra Carol, John Danforth. BA, Denison U., 1957; LHD (hon.), Ind. U., 2000. Asst. instr. U. Md., 1957-58; adminstrv. asst. South Bend Tribune, 1960-66; circulation cons. Imperial Valley Press, El Centro, Calif., 1966; chmn. Hoosier Times, Inc.; dir., vice chmn. Schurz Comms., Inc., pub. Pres. Bloomington Boys' Club, 1970-71, Jr. Achievement Monroe County, 1971-73; bd. dirs. United Way Monroe County, 1979-81, Cmty. Found. Area Arts Coun. Served with U.S. Army, 1958-60. Mem.: Ind. U. Found. (bd. dirs. 1986—), Newspaper Advt. Bur. (bd. dirs. 1987—92), Internat. Press Inst. (mem. bd. US), World Press Freedom Com. (adv. bd.), Hoosier State Press Assn. (pres. 1989, 1997), Inter-Am. Press Assn. (bd. dirs. 1995—, hon. pres. life), Newspaper Assn. Am. (bd. dirs. 1992—95, found. bd. chmn. 2002—06, bd. dirs. 2002—08), Inland Daily Press Assn. (pres. 1989), Internat. Newspaper Mktg. Assn. (pres. 1986, treas. 1997—2004), World Assn. Newspapers (bd. dirs., exec. com., v.p.). Republican. Presbyterian. Office: Hoosier Times Inc 1900 S Walnut St Bloomington IN 47401-7720

SCHUSTER, CARLOTTA LIEF, psychiatrist; b. NYC, Sept. 16, 1936; d. Victor Filler and Nina Lincoln (Rayevsky) Lief; m. David Israel Schuster, Sept. 2, 1962; 1 child, Amanda. BA, Barnard Coll., 1957; MD, NYU, 1964. Cert. Am. Bd. Psychiatry and Neurology; cert. addiction psychiatry. Intern Lenox Hill Hosp., NYC, 1964-65; resident St. Luke's Hosp., NYC, 1965-68; fellow Inst. Sex Edn. U. Pa., Phila., 1968-69; instr. N.Y. Med. Coll., NYC, 1969-72; asst. attending Met. Hosp., NYC, 1969-72; assoc. attending St. Luke's-Roosevelt Hosp. Ctr., NYC, 1972-95; staff psychiatrist Silver Hill Hosp., New Canaan, Conn., 1972-95; clin. assoc. instr. Columbia U., NYC, 1990-95. Chief substance abuse svc. Silver Hill Hosp., New Canaan, 1976-95; dir. Recovery Clinic Bellevue Hosp., N.Y.C., 1995-2003; mem. faculty Dept. Psychiatry Sch. Medicine NYU, 1995—. Author: Alcohol and Sexuality, 1988; co-author: Chapter in Advances in Alcohol and Substance Abuse, 1987; contbr. chpts. to books. Mem. Am. Psychiat. Assn., Am. Med. Soc. on Addictions, Am. Acad. Addiction Psychiatry. Democrat. Jewish. Avocations: cooking, attending concerts, opera, films. Home: 130 E 30th St New York NY 10016-8230 Home Phone: 212-725-0978; Office Phone: 212-213-2513. Personal E-mail: carlotta_schuster@msn.com.

SCHUSTER, CAROL JOYCE, special education educator, consultant; d. Samuel Saul and Ruth Edna Levine; m. George M. Schuster, Sept. 18, 1964; 1 child, Robert Churchill. BS in Edn., SUNY, Oswego, 1952; MS in Edn., Queens Coll., SUNY, 1958. Lic. heath conservation for physcially handicapped NYC, 1963, tchr. orthop. handicapped NY, 1976, elem. tchr. NYC. Tchr. NYC Bd. Edn., 1953—62, tchr. physically handicapped, 1963—67, St. Francis Hosp., Roslyn; tchr. in charge Queens Gen. Hosp., Queens, NY; cons. in spl. edn. Dep. for handicapped, Huntington, NY, 1982—86; mem. adv. bd. and founding com. Dolan Family Health Ctr., Huntington, 1997—. Mem. prin. selection com. Half Hollow Hills Dist., Dix Hills, NY, 1979—80; cmty. activist Huntington, 1979—; mem. campaign com. election for US congressman Dix Hills, Huntington, LI, 1986—89; mem. Dem. campaign com. US pres. Huntington, 2003—04; youth edn. mentor AAUW; cert. instr. Literacy Vols. of Am. Recipient Lifetime award for Outstanding Achievement in Career and Cmty. Svc., SUNY, Oswego, 1997. Achievements include invention of an adjustable wheelchair desk in 1963. Avocations: reading, writing poetry and prose, painting, Sherlockian literature, travel.

SCHUSTER, E. ELAINE, lawyer; b. Oklahoma City, June 8, 1936; d. John Otto and Eula Delone (Campbell) Schuster. AB, Sweet Briar Coll., 1958; MA in Econs. and Fin., U. Okla., 1962, JD, 1968. Bar: Okla. 1968, U.S. Dist. Ct. (we. dist.) Okla. 1969, U.S. Ct. Appeals (10th cir.) 1969, U.S. Dist. Ct. (no. dist.) Okla. 1981, U.S. Dist. Ct. (ea. dist.) Okla. 1991. Prof. econs. Southeastern State U., Durant, Okla., 1961—64; assoc. Whitten & Whitten, Oklahoma City, 1968—71; asst. dist. atty. Oklahoma County, 7th Dist., 1972—78; ptnr. Jones, Schuster & Flaugher, Oklahoma City, 1978—82; prin. E. Elaine Schuster, P.C., Oklahoma City, 1982—. Lectr. in field. Founding bd. dir. Nat. Kidney Found., Okla., 1969—82; active Oklahoma County Bd. Adjustment, 1978—97, chmn., 1984—97; citizen mem. profl. liaison com. City of Oklahoma City, 1980—; bd. edn. Metro Technology Ctrs., Career Tech. Dist. No. 22, Oklahoma City, 1982—, pres., 1984—85, 1991—93, 1998—2000, 2008—, English Speaking Union, Oklahoma City Br., 2007—; scholarship com. Oklahoma City Cmty. Found., 1997—; bd. dir. University Pl. Christian Ch., 1982—86, 1989—92, elder, 1989—92, trustee, 1992; deacon Crown Heights Christian Ch., 2001—04, elder, 2004—07, bd. dir., 2001—07, 2009—; parliamentarian regional bd. Christian Ch. Disciples of Christ, Okla., 2004—; bd. dir. Sweet Briar Coll., 1986—90, trustee emerita, 2005—. Recipient Circle of Excellence, Okla. Jour. Record, 2005—; named Outstanding Bus. Woman of Okla., Town Club of Bus. and Profl. women, 1986; named one of Fifty Women Making a Difference, Okla. Jour. Record, 1997, 2001, 2005, fourteen "Ladies in the News, Okla. Hospitality Club, 2006; named to Hon. All State Sch. Bd., Okla. State Sch. Bds. Assn., 1999; grantee GE, U. Va., 1963. Mem.: AAUW (life; br. pres. 1978—80, Okla. divsn. bd. 1981—83, 1985—87, Polished Diamond award S.W. Ctrl. Region 1987), Okla. Career Tech. Adminstrv. Coun., Okla. Assn. Tech. Ctrs. (fiscal officer 2001—05, pres.-elect 2002—03, pres. 2003—04), Okla. Assn. Career Tech. Edn., Sweet Briar Coll. Alumnae Assn. (bd. dir. 1986—90, 1996—2001, Region IX dir. 1996—2001), Okla. County Bar Assn. (ethics com. 1969—71, bench and bar com. 1994—95, long range planning com. 1995—97, bd. dir. 1997—2000, CLE com. 1999—2005, Briefcase pub. com. 2005—), Okla. Bar Assn. (del. 1996—97, alt. del. 1998—99, del. 2000—01, alt. del. 2002—03, budget com. 2002—03, legal ethics com. 2003—06, professionalism com. 2003—), Oklahoma City-County Hist. Soc. (charter mem.), Kappa Beta Pi Legal Soc., Delta Kappa Gamma (hon.). Avocations: hiking, photography, travel. Office: Heritage Law Ctr 515 NW 13th St Oklahoma City OK 73103-2203 Office Phone: 405-236-8807. Business E-Mail: eeschuster@sbcglobal.net.

SCHUSTER, ELAINE, retired civil rights professional; b. Detroit, Sept. 26, 1947; d. William Alfred and Aimee Isabelle (Cote) LeBlanc; m. James William Schuster, Sept. 6, 1969; 1 child, Cambrian James. BA, Wayne State U., 1972, postgrad., 1974-75, paralegal cert., 1991; student, Bay Mills Com. Coll., 2003—. Asst. payments Mich. Dept. Social Svcs., Detroit, 1972-73; rights rep. Mich. Dept. Civil Rights, Detroit, 1973-80, 82-87, 90, asst. dir. div., 1987-90, supr., 1993-97, dir. Svc. Ctr., 1997-99, contract coord., 1999—2002, ret., 2003; ct. adminstr. Chippewa-Ottawa Conservation Ct., Bay Mills, Mich., 1980-82; quality assurance coord. State Mental Health Facility, Southgate, Mich., 1991-93; acting interim dir. Mich. Indian Commn., Detroit, 1995; proprietor Good Things to Share, 2003—; trainer HIV/AIDS health support profls., 2004—. Author: Walking in Two Worlds, Delivering Culturally Competent Care in the American Indian Community, 2004, Critique, An Indian Tours Michilimackinac, 1981, In the Track of the Bear, Discussion, Coordination of Resources to Fight HIV, 2005; contbr. articles and poems to mags. and profl. jours. Bd. dirs. Tri-County Native Ams., Warren, Mich., 1982-89, sec. Native Am. Sesquicentennial subcom., Mich., 1987; mem. Linking Lifetimes, mentor program for Native Am. youth, 1992-93; sec., newsletter editor various civic orgns.; also other polit. and civic activities. Native Am. fellow Mich. State U., 1989. Mem. NAACP (housing com. S. Oakland br. 2000), ACLU (bd. dirs. Union-Oakland county 1987-88, 2002-04). Democrat. Avocations: exploring local historical and natural places of interest, historical re-enactment, research, exercise. E-mail: ikwewe@comcast.net.

SCHUSTER, GARY BENJAMIN, academic administrator, chemistry professor; b. NYC, Aug. 6, 1946; m. Anita C. Schuster, June 16, 1968; children: Eric B., Andrew D. BS in Chemistry, Clarkson Coll. Tech., 1968; PhD in Chemistry, U. Rochester, 1971. Tchg. asst. U. Rochester, 1968-71; NIH postdoctoral fellow Columbia U., NYC, 1973-75; asst. prof. chemistry U. Ill., Champaign, 1975-79, assoc. prof. chemistry, 1979-81, prof. chemistry, 1981—94, head dept. chemistry, 1990-94; prof. chemistry, dean Coll. Sciences Ga. Inst. Tech., Atlanta, 1994—2006, provost, exec. v.p. acad. affairs, 2006—, Vasser Woolley chair of chemistry and biochemistry, interim pres., 2008—09. Symposium chmn. organic chem. physics Pacific Basin Conf., Honolulu, 1984; vice chmn. Gordon Conf. on Organic Photochemistry, 1987, chmn., 1989; vice chmn. Electron Donor Acceptor Interactions Gordon Conf., 1994, chmn., 1996; organizer symposium on photochemistry IUPAC, 1992; mem. vis. com. U. Md., 1991; lectr. in field. Mem. editl. adv. bd. Jour. Organic Chemistry, 1986-91, Advances in Phys. Organic Chemistry, Jour. Am. Chem. Soc., 1991-96; contbr. numerous articles to profl. jours. Fellow Uni-Royal, 1969-71, Alfred P. Sloan Found., 1977-79, Ctr. for Advanced Study, 1979, John Simon Guggenheim Found., 1985-86, Paul Flory fellow IBM, 1990; Dreyfus Tchr. scholar, 1979, A.C. Cope scholar, 1993; recipient Mead Imaging Pres.' award, 1987, Charles Holmes Herty medal, 2006; grantee NIH, 1991-95, NSF, 1991-94, 94-97. Mem. Am. Chem. Soc. (symposium chmn. 1979, 88), Am. Assn. Photochemistry and Photobiology, Inter-Am. Photochem. Soc. (exec. com. 1990), Sigma Xi. Office: Ga Inst Tech Office of Provost 225 N Ave NW Carnegie Bldg Atlanta GA 30332 Office Phone: 404-385-2700. E-mail: schuster@gatech.edu.

SCHUSTER, ROBERT PARKS, lawyer; b. St. Louis, Oct. 25, 1945; s. William Thomas Schuster and Carolyn Cornforth (Daugherty) Hathaway; 1 child, Susan Michele. AB, Yale U., 1967; JD with honors, U. Wyo., 1970; LLM, Harvard U., 1971. Bar: Wyo. 1971, US Ct. Appeals (10th cir.) 1979, US Supreme Ct. 1984, Utah 1990. Dep. county atty. County of Natrona, Casper, Wyo., 1971-73; pvt. practice Casper, 1973—76; assoc. Spence & Moriarty, Casper, 1976-78; ptnr. Spence, Moriarty & Schuster, Jackson, Wyo., 1978—2002; pvt. practice Jackson, Wyo., 2002—. Trustee U. Wyo., 1985-89; Wyo. Dem. nominee for US Ho. of Reps., 1994; polit. columnist Casper Star Tribune, 1987-94; pres. United Way Natrona County, 1974; bd. dirs. Dancers Workshop, 1981-83; chair Wyo. selection com. Rhodes Scholarship, 1989-98; mem. bd. visitors Coll. Arts and Scis., U. Wyo., 1991-2000; mem. Dem. Nat. Com., 1992-2000; chair Wyo. Pub. Policy Forum, 1992-98; mem. Wind River Reservation Econ. Adv. Coun., 1998-99; bd. dirs. Internat. Edn. Found., 2005—. Ford Found. Urban Law fellow, 1970-71. Mem. ABA, AJA, Wyo. Trial Lawyers Assn. (named one of Best Lawyers in Am., 2007-, Mountain States Super Lawyer, 2008-), Yale Club (pres. Wyo. chpt., 2004—). Home: PO Box 13160 Jackson WY 83002 Office: Robert P Schuster PC 250 Veronica Ln Ste 204 PO Box 13160 Jackson WY 83002 Office Phone: 307-732-7800.

SCHUSTER, SEYMOUR, mathematician, educator; b. Bronx, NY, July 31, 1926; s. Oscar and Goldie (Smilowitz) S.; m. Marilyn Weinberg, May 2, 1954; children: Paul Samuel, Eve Elizabeth. BA, Pa. State U., 1947; A.M., Columbia U., 1948; PhD, Pa. State U., 1953; postgrad. (fellow), U. Toronto, 1952-53. Instr. Pa. State U., 1950-52, Poly. U. NY, 1953—54, asst. prof., 1954—56, assoc. prof., 1956—58; vis. assoc. prof. Carleton Coll., Northfield, Minn., 1958-59, assoc. prof., 1959-63, prof. math., 1968—, chmn. dept., 1973-76, William H. Laird prof. math. and liberal arts, 1992-94, William H. Laird prof. emeritus, 1994—. Vis. assoc. prof. U. N.C., Chapel Hill, 1961; research assoc. math. dept. U. Minn., Mpls., 1962-63, assoc. prof., 1963-65; assoc. prof. Minn. Math Center, 1965-68, dir. coll. geometry project, 1964-74; dir. Acad. Year Inst. for Coll. Tchrs., 1966-67, NSF Faculty fellow, 1970-71; vis. scholar U. Calif., Santa Barbara, 1970-71, U. Ariz., 1990; guest scholar Western Mich. U., 1976, 81; vis. prof. Western Wash. U., 1983, U. Oreg., 1986. Author: (with K. O. May) Undergraduate Research in Mathematics, 1961, Elementary Vector Geometry, 1962, (with P.C. Rosenbloom) Prelude to Analysis, 1966; dir. The Coll. Geomatry Project; also research articles on geometry, graph theory, and analysis.; cons. Ency. Britanica 1965-68, cons. editor Xerox Pub. Co., 1962-71; assoc. editor, editorial bd.: Am. Math. Monthly, 1969-86; assoc. editor: Indian Jour. Math. Edn, 1976-86; co-producer 12 films on geometry. With USNR, 1944—46. Recipient Honor award Am. Film Festival, 1967, Golden Eagle award Cine Film Festival, 1967, 68; named found. fellow Inst. for Combinatorics and Applications. Mem. Math. Assn. Am., Am. Math. Soc., Nat. Assn. Math., Sigma Xi, Pi Mu Epsilon. Home: 316 Sumner St E Northfield MN 55057-2843 E-mail: schusters@charter.net.

SCHUSTER, STEPHAN CHRISTOPH, biochemist, researcher; b. Lindau, Germany, Apr. 13, 1962; BS in Chemistry, U. Konstanz, Germany, 1987; D in Natural Scis., U. Munich, 1991; PhD in Biochemistry, U. Munich, Germany, 1991; postdoctoral in Biology, Calif. Inst. Tech. Rschr. Max-Planck Inst., Munich, 1987-91, project leader, 1994; rsch. fellow Calif. Inst. Tech., Pasadena, 1991-94, vis. assoc.; assoc. prof. biochemistry and molecular biology Pa. State U. Contbr. scientific papers. Recipient Otto Hahn medal, Max Planck Soc., 1993; named one of The World's Most Influential People, TIME mag., 2009. Office: Pa State U 310 Wartik Laboratory University Park PA 16802 Office Phone: 814-863-9278. Office Fax: 814-868-6699.*

SCHUSTER, SU'A CARL, political organization administrator, bishop; Mem. Am. Samoa House of Reps., 1996—2000, 2002—04; chmn. Rep. Party of Am. Samoa, 2008—. Bishop Ch. of Jesus Christ of Latter-day Saints, 2000—08. Mem.: Lions Club (pres. 1984—2000). Office: Rep Party American Samoa PO Box 3564 Pago Pago AS 96799*

SCHUTT, DAVID L., engineering association executive; BA, Calvin Coll.; MBA, Johns Hopkins U.; MA, Princeton U., 1989, PhD in Physical Chemistry, 1992. Sci. policy fellow Am. Chem. Soc., Washington, 1992, dir. legis. & govt. affairs, 2001—02, dir. institutional devel., 2002—03, CFO, 2003—04, chief strategy officer, dir. external affairs, 2004—07; prin. DLS & Assocs., Inc., 2007; exec. v.p., COO Soc. Automotive Engineers Internat. (SAE), Warrendale, Pa., 2008—. Mem. Internat. Union of Pure and Applied Chemistry Fin. Com., US Tech. Adv. Group to ISO TC229; commr. US Nat. Commn. for the United Nat. Edn. and Cultural Orgn. (UNESCO). Office: Soc Automotive Engineers Internat (SAE) 400 Commonwealth Dr Warrendale PA 15096

SCHUTT, RUSSELL K., social studies educator, researcher; s. Robert Louis and Ruth Eleanor Schutt; m. Elizabeth Schneider; 1 child, Julia Ellen. BA, U. Ill., Chgo., 1972; PhD, U. Ill., 1977. Postdoc. fellow Yale U., New Haven, 1977—79; prof. sociology U. Mass., Boston, 1979—; lectr. sociology dept. psychiatry Harvard Med. Sch., Boston, 1990—. Author: (books) Investigating the Social World: The Process and Practice of Research, co-author numerous books; contbr. to numerous articles. Mem. Human Services Com., Lexington, Mass., 2000—04. Recipient Chancellor's Disting. Svc. award, U. Mass., 2007, Outstanding Achievement award, Coll. Arts and Sciences, U. Mass., 1986. Mem.: Eastern Sociol. Soc. (sec. 1998—2000), Am. Psychopathological Assn., Am. Sociol. Assn. Congregationalist. Avocations: swimming, running, travel, hiking. Office: Univ Mass Boston 100 Morrissey Blvd Boston MA 02125 Business E-Mail: russell.schutt@umb.edu.

SCHUTTE, DREW, publishing executive; Grad., U. Vt. East coast mgr. PC Mag. Ziff Davis Media; West coast mgr. Inc. mag.; with BusinessWeek mag. McGraw-Hill Cos., San Francisco, 1991—94; West coast advt. mgr. Wired mag. Condé Nast Publications, 1994; pub. Condé Nast Publs., 1999—2004, v.p., pub., 2004—06, v.p., pub. Wired Media, 2006—08, v.p., pub. The New Yorker, 2008—09, chief revenue officer Condé Nast Digital, 2009—; coord. ann. mini world's fair Wired NextFest, 2004. Named one of The 21 Most Intriguing, MIN mag., 2008. Office: Condé Nast Digital 4 Times Square New York NY 10036 Office Phone: 212-286-5400. Office Fax: 212-286-4168.*

SCHUTTISH, THOMAS R., oil industry executive, lawyer; b. Carmel, Calif., 1947; B in Acctg., San Jose State U., Calif.; JD, U. Calif., Davis; M in Tax Law, NYU, NYC. Sr. tax atty. to various positions in the corp. tax dept. Chevron Corp., 1980—94, asst. gen. tax. counsel, 1994—2002, gen. tax. counsel, 2002—. Mem.: Am. Petroleum Inst., State Bar of Calif., Tax Found., Tax Coun. Office: Chevron Corp Hdqs 6001 Bollinger Canyon Rd San Ramon CA 94583*

SCHUTZ, DONALD FRANK, geochemist, environmental corporate executive; b. Orange, Tex., Sept. 22, 1934; s. Theodore J. and Mildred Irene S.; m. Beatriz Valera, May 18, 1958; children: Delfino, Celita. BS in Geology cum laude, Yale U., 1956, PhD in Geology, 1964; MA in Geology, Rice U., 1958. Research staff geologist Yale U., New Haven, 1963-64; mgr. nuclear geochemistry dept. Teledyne Isotopes, Westwood, NJ, 1968-70, v.p., 1970-75, pres., 1975-93; engring. group exec. Teledyne, Inc., Westwood, 1989-92; chief scientist Teledyne Environ. Systems, 1992-93; gen. mgr. Teledyne Brown Engring. Environ. Svcs., 1993—99; v.p. Teledyne Environ., Inc., 1996-99; pres. Geonuclear, Inc., 1999—. Low level waste adv. com. N.J. Dept. Environ. Protection, Trenton, 1988-90; chmn. com. on radioactive materials N.J. BIA, Trenton, 1980-88. Pres. Children's Aid and Adoption Soc. N.J. Inc., Bogota, 1976-95, Am. Amateur Judo Found., River Vale, N.J., 1979-89; bd. visitors Berry Coll., 1985—; bd. dirs. Yale U. Alumni Fund, 1989-94; co-chmn. Children's Aid and Family Svcs. Inc., 1995-96, bd. dirs. emeritus, 2000—. Recipient Antarctic Service medal U.S. Congress, 1964. Mem.: World Fedn. Engring. Orgns. (mem. environ. com. 2005—, mem. energy com. 2006—), Am. Assn. Engring. Soc. (engrs. forum on sustainable devel. 1995—, internat. activities com.), Am. Nuc. Soc. (chmn. no. N.J. sect. 1988—89, pub. policy com. 1991—96, coord. climate change and sustainable devel. activities UN 1994—, chair environ. scis. divsn. 1995—96, vice chair 2000—01, chair 2001—02), Am. Assn. Radon Sci. and Tech. (life; pres. 1986—89, treas. 1990—95), Yale Sci. and Engring. Alumni Assn. (bd. dirs. Bergen County and vicinity chpt. 1989—), Sigma Xi. E-mail: donald.schutz@aya.yale.edu.

SCHUTZ, PAMELA S., insurance company executive; BA, Briarcliff Coll.; MS, American Univ. Mgmt. positions GE Capital Comml. Real Estate, 1978—94; pres. GE Capital Realty Group, 1994—97, Harvest Life Ins. Co., 1997—98, Genworth Life & Annuity Ins. Co. (formerly subs. of GE), 1998—; v.p. GE, 2000—04; exec. v.p., pres. & CEO retirement income & investments Genworth Fin., Richmond, Va., 2004—. Bd. mem. Nat. Assn. Variable Annuities, MIB Group Inc. Office: Genworth Financial 6620 W Broad St Richmond VA 23230

SCHUTZ, RICHARD PHILLIP, special education educator; b. Milw., Sept. 12, 1951; s. Daniel R. and Kathyrn (Hewitt) S. BS, U. Wis., 1974, MS, 1975; PhD, U. Ill., 1984. Project dir. Ctr. Devel. Disabilities, Burlington, Vt., 1981-84; asst. prof. spl. edn. U. Vt., Burlington, 1981-84; asst. prof. U. Ill., Champaign, 1984-88; project dir. Office Career Devel. For Spl. Populations, Champaign; assoc. prof. U. So. Miss., Hattiesburg, 1988-90; assoc. dir. MS-UAP, 1988-90; dir. Devel. Disabilities Inst. East Carolina U., Greenville, N.C., 1990-94; assoc. prof., co-dir. ctr. for autism and related disability U. South Fla., Tampa, 1994—2000; private cons. applied behavior analysis, spl. edn. & rehab., 2000—. Cons. New Hampshire Legal Assistance, 1983-84; mem. state adv. bd. Leadership Devel. Vocat. Edn., Champaign, 1986-89, Pa. Task Force Supported Employment, Harrisburg, 1987-90; exec. dir. K.M.S. Elder Care, 2005-. Co-author: Functional Communication in Integrated Settings for Students with Deaf Blindness, 1994, New Directions and Strategies in Habilitation Services, 1988, Establishing Community Employment Programs for Persons with Severe Disabilities, 1986, Establishing Parent Professional Partnerships, 1986, Social Integration of Severely Handicapped Students, 1984. Methodist. Avocations: fishing, skiing. Personal E-mail: richard00s@embarqmail.com.

SCHUTZ, RONALD JAMES, lawyer; b. Adrian, Minn., Nov. 15, 1955; s. Harold Henry and Joanne Dorothy (Peters) S.; m. Janet Jayne Jensen, June 4, 1977; children— Matthew, Erik, Kristin. BSME magna cum laude, Marquette U., 1978; JD, U. Minn., 1981. Bar: Minn. 1981, U.S. Dist. Ct. Minn. 1981, U.S. Ct. Mil. Appeals 1984, U.S. Supreme Ct. 1986. Atty. Merchant & Gould, Mpls., 1985—87, Robins, Zelle, Larson & Kaplan, Mpls., 1987—; ptnr. Robins Kaplan Miller & Ciresi LLP. Lectr. U. Minn. Law Sch., 1986—87; appted. by Gov. Pawlenty to chair Minn. Commn. Judicial Selection. Contbr. articles to profl. journals. Chmn. Ctr. of the American Experiment; bd. dirs. YMCA Met. Mpls., Guthrie Theater. Commd. capt. US Army, 1981, atty. JAGC, 1981—85, Ft. Ord, Calif. Recipient Army Achievement medal, 1983, 1984; named one of Attorneys of the Year, Minn. Lawyer, 2004, The Nation's Top Litigators, The Nat. Law Jour., 2008. Fellow: American Coll. Trial Lawyers; mem.: ABA, Assn. Trial Lawyers of America, Judge Advocates Assn., Minn. Bar Assn., NW Suburbs Cable Commn. Republican. Office: Robins Kaplan Miller & Ciresi LLP 2800 LaSalle Plaza Minneapolis MN 55402*

SCHUYLER, DAVID P., historian, educator; b. Albany, NY, Apr. 9, 1950; m. Marsha Sener; 1 child, Nancy. PhD, Columbia U., 1979. Prof. Am. studies Franklin & Marshall Coll., Lancaster, Pa., 1979—. Author: The New Urban Landscape, 1986, Apostle of Taste: Andrew Jackson Downing, 1996; co-editor: The Papers of Frederick Law Olmsted: vol. 2, 1982, vol. 3, 1983, vol. 6, 1992. Mem. Soc. Am. City and Regional Planning History (pres. 1998-99), Pa. Hist. Assn. (coun.), Am. Studies Assn., Orgn. Am. Historians, Soc. Winterthur Fellows. Office: Franklin & Marshall Coll 310 Stager Hall American Studies Dept Lancaster PA 17604-3003 E-mail: d_schuyler@acad.fandm.edu.

SCHVEY, HENRY I., performing arts educator; b. NYC, Aug. 10, 1948; s. Norman I. and Rita Lerner Schvey; m. Patty L Cohn, Aug. 10, 1969; children: Aram Asher, Jerusha Tamara, Natasha Avril. BS, U. Wis., Madison, 1969; MA, PhD, Ind. U., Bloomington, 1973. Asst., assoc. prof. Leiden U., Netherlands, 1974—87; prof. drama and comparative lit. Wash. U., St. Louis, 1987—. Dir. Leiden English Speaking Theatre, Netherlands, 1975—87. Author: (drama) Hannah's Shawl, (adaptation) The Awakening, (drama) Kokoschka: A Love Story, (memoir) The Poison Tree. Office: WA Univ St Louis Performing Arts Dept Box 1108 Saint Louis MO 63130 Office Fax: 314-935-4955. Business E-Mail: hischvey@wustl.edu.

SCHWAB, CHARLES ROBERT, JR., (CHUCK SCHWAB), investment company executive; b. Sacramento, July 29, 1937; m. Helen O'Neill; 5 children. BA in Economics, Stanford U., 1959, MBA, 1961. Formerly mut. fund mgr., Marin County, Calif.; founder The Charles Schwab Corp., San Francisco, 1971, chmn., CEO, 1971—2003, 2004—08, exec. chmn., 2008—. Bd. dirs. The Gap, Inc., 1986—2004, The Charles Schwab Corp., 1986—, Seibel Systems, Inc., 1994—2004; dir. U.S. Trust Corp., U.S. Trust Co. of NY; chmn. Charles Schwab Bank, N.A.; trustee Charles Schwab Family of Funds, Schwab Investments, Schwab Capital Trust, Schwab Annuity Portfolios. Author: How to be Your Own Stockbroker, 1984, Guide to Financial Independence, 1998, You're Fifty - Now What?, 2001; co-author (with Carrie Schwab Pomerantz): It Pays To Talk. Chmn. All Kinds of Minds Inst., President's Council on Fin. Literacy, 2008—; co-founder (with Helen Schwab), chmn. Charles and Helen Schwab Found., 2001—; bd. trustees Stanford U. Named one of Forbes' Richest Americans, 1999—, Forbes' Executive Pay, 1999—, World's Richest People, Forbes Mag., 1999—, Top 200 Collectors, ARTnews Mag., 2004—08, 50 Most Generous Philanthropists, BusinessWeek, 2005. Republican. Achievements include pioneer in discount brokerage business since 1974. Avocation: collector of modern & contemporary art. Office: The Charles Schwab Corp 101 Montgomery St San Francisco CA 94104-4175 E-mail: charles.schwab@schwab.com.*

SCHWAB, EILEEN CAULFIELD, lawyer, educator; b. NYC, Feb. 11, 1944; d. James and Mary (Fay) Caulfield; m. Terrance W. Schwab, Jan. 4, 1969 (dec. Apr. 25, 2004); children: Matthew, Catherine Welykoridko, Claire Vogel. BA, Hunter Coll., 1965; JD, Columbia U., 1971. Bar: N.Y. 1972, U.S. Dist. Ct. (so. and ea. dists.) N.Y. 1975, U.S. Ct. Appeals (2d cir.) 1975, U.S. Tax Ct. 1980, U.S. Ct. Appeals (10th cir.) 1993. Assoc. Poletti Friedin, NYC, 1971-72, Hughes Hubbard & Reed, NYC, 1972-75, Davis Polk & Wardwell, NYC, 1975-81; dep. bur. chief Charities Bur., Atty. Gen. of N.Y., 1981-82; counsel Sidley Austin LLP, NYC, 1983—, ptnr., 1984. Adj. prof. N.Y. Law Sch. Trustee, sec., exec. com. Caramoor Ctr. Music and the Arts; trustee Cath. Communal Fund; chair planned gifts, bequests and endowment com. Archdiocese of NY; mem. profl. adv. com. Mus. Modern Art, Met. Mus. Art, Cen. Park Conservancy, Calvary Hosp., Mus. Arts and Design, Meml. Sloan-Kettering Cancer Ctr.; co-chmn. profl. adv. com. N.Y. Pub. Libr.; chmn. adv. com. Ascension Sch.; trustee Cooke Ctr. Learning and Devel. Fellow Am. Coll. Trust and Estate Counsel; mem. N.Y. State Bar Assn., Phi Beta Kappa. Democrat. Roman Catholic.

SCHWAB, ERNEST ROE, III, physiology educator, researcher, academic administrator; b. Denver, July 19, 1950; s. Ernest Roe and Mary Ellen (Murray) S.; m. Patty Ann Millspaugh, May 16, 1974. BA, Union Coll., Lincoln, Nebr., 1975; MS, Andrews U., Berrien Springs, Mich., 1978; PhD, Loma Linda U., Calif., 1989. Assoc. prof. allied health studies, assoc. dean academic affairs Sch. of Allied Health Professions, Loma Linda U., Loma Linda, Calif., 1996—; assoc. prof. biology La Sierra U., Riverside, Calif., 1991—96; asst. prof. biology Loma Linda U., 1983—91. Contbr. articles to profl. jours. Planner, grant writer So. Calif. Young Artists Symphony, Redlands, Calif., 1998—2001; judge Calif. State Sci. Fair, L.A., Calif., 1998—2007. Recipient Godfrey T. Anderson award for Excellence in Tchg., Loma Linda U., 1990, Cert. of Merit, Nat. Acad. Advising Assn., 1994, Disting. Svc. award, Loma LInda U. Sch. Allied Health Professions, 2004; grantee Rsch. Opportunity award, NSF, 1989. Mem. Union Concerned Scientists, Scientists Action Network, N.Y. Acad. Scis., Sigma Xi (Grad. Student Research grantee 1979), Nat. Acad. Adv. Assn. (Cert. of Merit 1994), Soc. for Neurosci., Internat. Soc. for Neuroethology, Soc. Integrative and Comparative Biology. Democrat. Seventh-Day Adventist. Avocations: photography, travel, backpacking, piano. Home: 423 Marilyn Lane Redlands CA 92373 Office: Loma Linda University 11234 Anderson St Loma Linda CA 92350-0001 Personal E-mail: acheta1@earthlink.net. Business E-Mail: eschwab@llu.edu.

SCHWAB, EVAN LYNN, lawyer; b. Detroit, Apr. 13, 1938; s. Joe Schwab and Vanita Dobbs; m. Heidi Jensen, June 11, 1960 (div. Dec. 1975); children: Mari, Eric, Peter; m. Carole Fuller, Mar. 12, 1976; 1 child, William. BA, U. Wash., 1961, LLB with high honors, 1963. Bar: Wash. 1964, U.S. Dist. Ct. (we. dist.) Wash. 1966, U.S. Supreme Ct. 1967; CPA. Law clk. U.S. Supreme Ct. Justice William O. Douglas, Washington, 1963-64; assoc. Davis, Wright & Jones, Seattle, 1964-69, ptnr., 1969-88, Bogle & Gates, Seattle, 1988—99, co-chair dept. litigation, 1992—99; ptnr. trial group Dorsey & Whitney LLP, Seattle, 1999—; chair Seattle Trial Group, 2005—08. 2nd. lt. USAR, 1962-64. Fellow: Am. Coll. Trial Lawyers (chmn. Wash. state com. 2005—07); mem.: ABA, Seattle-King County Bar Assn., Wash. State Bar Assn., Fed. Bar Assn. Western Dist. Wash. (pres. 1985—86), Seattle Yacht Club (judge adv. 1986, 2005—07). Avocations: sailing, skiing. Office: Dorsey & Whitney LLP Ste 3400 US Bank Ctr 1420 Fifth Ave Seattle WA 98101-4010 Office Phone: 206-903-8858. Office Fax: 206-903-8820. Business E-Mail: schwab.evan@dorsey.com.

SCHWAB, FRANK, JR., management consultant; b. Brookline, Mass., Dec. 19, 1930; s. Frank Sr. and Phyllis (Robinson) F. BA, Rutgers U., 1952; MBA, Harvard Bus. Sch., 1956. Cert. mgmt. cons. Internal auditor Champion Paper, Inc., Hamilton, Ohio, 1956-57, mgmt. indsl. engr. Pasadena, Tex., 1957—58; cons., assoc. Booz Allen & Hamilton, NYC, 1958-65; dir. trans. planning Planning Rsch. Corp., LA, 1965; pres., CEO F.R. Schwab & Assocs., NYC, 1965-82; pres., co-CEO Fenvessy & Schwab, NYC, 1982-87; pres., CEO, Anderson & Schwab, NYC, 1987—. Bd. dirs. Sugarland Oil Corp., N.Y.C., Nat. Mining Assn. (mfrs. and svcs. divsn.), Wash., D.C. Trustee Nat. Mining Hall of Fame and Mus., Leadville, Colo., 1992—. 1st lt. U.S. Army, 1952-54, Korea. Decorated Nat. Def. Svc. medal, Korean Svc. medal with bronze star, Commendation ribbon with medal pendant, UN Svc. medal; recipient medal for merit State of NY. Mem. Inst. Mgmt. Cons. (pres. N.Y. chpt. 1975-77), Am. Arbitration Assn. (panel arbitrator), Mil. Order Fgn. Wars (vet. companion), Maidstone Club, Union Club, River Club, King Coal Club, Army and Navy Club. Republican. Avocation: tennis. Office: 230 Park Ave New York NY 10169-0005 Home Phone: 212-751-0971; Office Phone: 212-758-6800. Fax: (212) 755-9576. Business E-Mail: fschwab@andersonschwab.com.

SCHWAB, FREDERIC LYON, geologist, educator; b. Bklyn., Jan. 8, 1940; s. Herbert Sydney Schwab and Marianne Aprilliano; m. Claudia Aarons Schwab, Feb. 6, 1963; children: Kimberly Hayden Hamel, Bryan Rober, Jeffrey Lehman, Jonathan Herber. AB, Darmouth Coll., Hanover, NH, 1961; MS, U. Wis., Madison, 1963; PhD, Harvard U., Cambridge, Mass., 1967. Asst. prof. Washington & Lee U., Lexington, Va., 1967—71, assoc. prof., 1971—75, prof., 1975—2003. Examiner Ednl. Testing Svc., Princeton, NY, 1988—94; councilor Coun. Undergrad. Rsch., 1989—90. Author: (textbook) Gedsynclines: Concepts and Place Within Plate Techniques, 1982; co-author: Sedimentary Geology, 1996; contbr. scientific papers to profl. jours. Mem.: Soc. Econ. Palentologist, Internat. Assn. Sedimentilogists, Geol. Soc. Am. Earth Magazine. Avocations: running, bicycling. Home: 916 Shenandoah Rd Lexington VA 24450 Office: Dept Geology Washington and Lee Univ Lexington VA 24450 Office Fax: 540-459-8142. Business E-Mail: schwabf@wlu.edu.

SCHWAB, GEORGE DAVID, social sciences educator, writer; b. Nov. 25, 1931; s. Arkady and Klara (Jacobson) S.; m. Eleonora Storch, Feb. 27, 1965; children: Clarence Boris, Claude Arkady, Solan Bernhard. BA, CCNY, 1954; MA, Columbia U., 1955, PhD, 1968. Lectr. Columbia Coll., NYC, 1959, CUNY, 1960-68; asst. prof. history, 1968-72; assoc. prof. history, 1973-79; prof., 1980—2000; prof. emeritus, 2001—. Mem. Columbia U. Seminar on Law and Polit. Thought and Institutions; dir. Conf. History and Politics CUNY; with Nat. Com. Am. Fgn. Policy. Author: Dayez: Beyond Abstract Art, 1967, Enemy oder Foe, 1968, Switzerland's Tactical Nuc. Weapons Policy, 1969, The Challenge of the Exception: An Introduction to the Polit. Ideas of Carl Schmitt, 1970, 2nd edit., 1989, Appeasement and Detente, 1975, 81, Carl Schmitt: Polit. Opportunist?, 1975; translator: The Concept of the Polit. with Comments by Leo Strauss (Carl Schmitt), 1976, 96, Legality and Illegality as Instruments of Revolutionaries in Their Quest for Power, Remarks Occasioned by the Outlook of Herbert Marcuse, 1978, The German State in Hist. Perspective, 1978, Ideology: Reality or Rhetoric, 1978, Ideology and Fgn. Policy, 1978, 81, The Decision: Is the Am. Sovereign at Bay?, 1978, State and Nation: Toward a Further Clarification, 1980, Am. Fgn. Politics at the Crossroads, 1980, Carl Schmitt: Through a Glass Darkly, 1980, From Quantity and Heterogeneity to Quality and Homogeneity: Toward a New Foreign Policy, 1980, Toward an Open-Society Bloc, 1980, Eurocommunism: The Ideological and Political Theoretical Foundations, 1981, Am. Fgn. Policy at the Crossroads, 1982, A Decade of the Nat. Com. on Am. Fgn. Policy, 1984, (trans.) Polit. Theology: Four Chapters on the Concept of Sovereignty (Carl Schmitt), 1985, 88, 2005, The Destruction of a Family, 1987, Elie Wiesel: Between Jerusalem and New York, 1990, The Broken Vow, The Good Obtained, 1991, Thoughts of a Collector, 1991, Carl Schmitt Hysteria in the US, 1992, Contextualizing Carl Schmitt's Concept of Grossraum, 1994; (translator) The Leviathan in the State Theory of Thomas Hobbes (Carl Schmitt), 1996, Carl Schmitt, A Note on a Qualitative Authoritarian Bourgeois Liberal, 2000, The Nat. Com. on Am. Fgn. Policy's Focus on Russia, 2000, U.S. National Security Interests Today, 2003, NATO; editor Am. Fgn. Policy Interests; series Global Perspectives in History and Politics, NATO and Transatlantic Security: An Overview, 2008. Trustee, pres. mem. exec. com. Nat. Com. Am. Fgn. Policy; mem. Coun. on Fgn. Rels. Decorated Order of the Three Stars (Latvia); recipient Ellis Island medal of honor. Office: Nat Com Am Fgn Policy 320 Park Ave New York NY 10022-6815 Office Phone: 212-224-1120. Business E-Mail: george.schwab@ncafp.org.

SCHWAB, HAROLD LEE, lawyer; b. NYC, Feb. 5, 1932; s. Harold Walter and Beatrice (Braverman) S.; m. Rowena Vivian Strauss, June 12, 1953; children: Andrew, Lisa, James. BA, Harvard Coll., Cambridge, Mass., 1953; LLB, Boston Coll., 1956. Bar: NY 1957, U.S. Ct. Mil. Appeals 1958, U.S. Dist. Cts. (so. and ea. dists.) NY 1967, U.S. Dist. Ct. (no. dist.) NY 1974, U.S. Dist. Ct. (we. dist.) NY 1988, U.S. Dist. Ct. Conn. 1995, U.S. Dist. Ct. (ea. and we. dists.) Ark. 2000, U.S. Ct. Appeals (2d cir.) 1971, U.S. Ct. Appeals (DC cir.) 1986, U.S. Ct. Appeals (11th cir.) 1988, U.S. Ct. Appeals (5th cir.) 1991, U.S. Supreme Ct. 1971. V.p. H.W. Schwab Textile Corp., NYC, 1959-60; assoc. Emile Z. Berman & A. Harold Frost, NYC, 1960-67, ptnr., 1967-74; sr. ptnr. Lester Schwab Katz & Dwyer, LLP, NYC, 1974—. Lectr. NY Jud. Seminars, 2000-02, 05, NY State Bar Assn., NY County Lawyers Assn., Am. Bd. Trial Advocates; examiner, Character and Fitness Com., First Jud. Dept. Contbr. articles to legal jours.; mem. editl. bd. Jour. Products and Toxics Liability, 1976-96. Served to lt. col. USAFR. Fellow Internat. Acad. Trial Lawyers; mem. ABA, ASTM, SAE, Assn. Advancement of Automotive Medicine, NY State Bar Assn. (chmn. trial lawyers sect. 1980-81, editor sect. newsletter 1981-84), Am. Bd. Trial Advs. (pres. NY chpt. 1982-83), Fedn. Ins. and Corp. Counsel (v.p. 1979-80), NY State Trial Lawyers Assn., Def. Assn. NY, Harvard Club NY, Downtown Assn., Ft. Hamilton Officers Club. Home: 205 Beach 142 St Neponsit NY 11694 Office: Lester Schwab Katz & Dwyer LP 120 Broadway Fl 38 New York NY 10271-0071 Office Phone: 212-341-4234. Business E-Mail: hschwab@lskdnylaw.com.

SCHWAB, HERMANN CASPAR, banker; b. NYC, Jan. 8, 1920; s. Hermann Caspar and Ruth (Bliss) S.; m. Lesley Ripley, Sep 10, 1940, div. 1952, children: Henry R., Lesley Schwab Forman, Margery Schwab Weekes; m. C. Meteer Shanks, July 5, 1955; Stuart Taylor, George Bliss, Katharine Lambard Schwab Kimmick. Grad., St. Marks Sch., 1937, Yale U., 1941. With Hanover Bank, 1941-44, 46-55, asst. sec., 1949-53, asst. v.p., 1953-55; ptnr. Dick & Merle Smith, 1956; v.p. Empire Trust Co., 1957-66, sr. v.p., 1965-66; with Bank N.Y., 1966-67; sr. v.p. Schroder Trust Co., NYC, 1967-73, dir., 1970-73; pres., dir. Cheapside Dollar Fund Ltd., NYC, 1970-88; sr. v.p. Schroder Capital Mgmt. Inc., NYC, 1973-84, cons., 1984-88. Chmn., dir. Schroder Capitol Funds Inc., 1988-98, trustee dir., 1998—. Mayor Oyster Bay Cove, N.Y., 1973-85, trustee, 1965-98; trustee St. Lukes-Roosevelt Hosp. Ctr., 1969-99. 2d lt. inf., AUS, 1943-46. Mem. Piping Rock Club (Locust Valley, N.Y.), Knickerbocker Club NY, Order of St. John's Jerusalem. Home: 34 Northern Blvd Oyster Bay NY 11771-4105

SCHWAB, HOWARD JOEL, retired judge; b. Charleston, W.Va., Feb. 13, 1943; s. Joseph Simon and Gertrude (Hadas) S.; m. Michelle Roberts, July 4, 1970; children: Joshua Raphael, Bethany Alexis. BA in

History with honors, UCLA, 1964, JD, 1967. Bar: Calif. 1968, U.S. Dist. Ct. (cen. dist.) Calif. 1968, U.S. Ct. Appeals (9th cir.) 1970, U.S. Supreme Ct. 1972. Clk. legal adminstrn. Litton Industries, LA, 1967-68; dep. city atty. LA, 1968-69; dep. atty. gen. State of Calif., LA, 1969-84; judge Mcpl. Ct. L.A. Jud. Dist., 1984-85; judge Superior Ct. Superior Ct. L.A. County, LA, 1985—2006, mem., assigned judges program, 2007—. Mem. faculty Berkeley (Calif.) Judicial Coll., 1987—; adj. prof. U. So. Calif. Sch Medicine. Contbr. articles to profl. jours. Recipient CDAA William E. James award Calif. Dist. Atty.'s Assn., 1981. Mem. San Fernando Valley Bar Assn. (Appreciation award as Judge of Yr. 2002_, Inn. of Ct. Democrat. Jewish. Avocations: history, book collecting. E-mail: hschwab@lasuperiorcourt.org.

SCHWAB, JOEL GERSON, pediatrician, educator; Grad., U. Mich., 1967; MD, NY Med. Coll., 1971. Cert. in pediat. Am. Bd. Med. Specialties. Resident in pediat. Northwestern U. Children's Meml. Hosp.; asst. prof. pediat. Northwestern U.; pvt. practice Child Life Ctr., 1974—86; assoc. prof. pediat. U. Chgo. Med. Ctr., dir. med. student edn., dept. pediat.; faculty dir. health professions advising office U. Chgo. Collegiate Divsn., 2003—. Mem. admissions com. Pritzker Sch. Medicine, Chgo., mem. com. on promotions. Recipient Faculty Tchg. award, Faculty Dean Med. Edn., 1998, Outstanding Clinical Tchg. award, Pritzker Sch. Medicine, Leonard Tow Humanism in Medicine award, 2006; named Tchr. of Yr., Pediatric Residents, 1998. Mem.: Am. Assn. Pediat. Office: U Chgo Med Ctr MC3055 5841 S Maryland Ave Chicago IL 60637 Office Phone: 773-702-6169. Office Fax: 773-702-4786. Business E-Mail: jschwab@peds.bsd.uchicago.edu.

SCHWAB, JUDITH, artist, sculptor, curator, educator; b. Phila., Feb. 22, 1935; d. Henry Ellick and Eleanor Adelman; m. Ralph Schwab, 1956; children: Linda Deutsch, Andrea Cohen. BA cum laude, Kean Coll., NJ, 1975; postgrad., Rutgers U., Union, NJ, 1978—79; MFA in Sculpture, U. Del., Newark, 1986. Cert. art tchr. Pa. Substitute art tchr. Manalapan-Englishtown Pub. Schs., Englishtown, NJ, 1970—77, art tchr., 1978—79; artist Sterk Sch. Hearing Impaired, Newark, Del., 1981, art tchr., 1982; vis. artist, facilitator Xian Art Sch., Xian, China, 1998; substitute art tchr. Del. Pub. Schs., Wilmington, 1990—93; art tchr. Shortlidge Elem. Sch., Wilmington, 1994—98; artist-curator Women Collared Work, Delaplaine Arts & Edn. Ctr., Frederick, Md., 2009—, Women Collard Work Coral Springs Mus. Art, 2009, Women Collard Work Pelaplaine Arts & Edn. Ctr. Fredrick, Md., 2009. Initiator internat. exchanges Pacem in Terris, 1998; lectr. in field. One-woman shows include No. Ariz. U. Art Gallery, Flagstaff, 1985, Thompson Park Gallery, Lincroft, N.J., 1985, West Gallery and East Gallery, 1995, U. Tenn. Art Galleries I and II, Chattanooga, 1987, Susan Isaacs Gallery, Wilmington, 1990, U. Del. Clayton Hall Conv. Ctr. Gallery, 1990, Ctrl. House of Art, Tbilisi, Ga., Russia, 1991, Del. Ctr. for Contemporary Art, 1991, Jewish Cmty. Ctr. Art Gallery, 1993, Cecil CC Cultural Art Ctr., 2005, Brandeis U. Women's Com., Kings Point, Tamarac, Fla., 2007, exhibited in group shows at Del. Art Mus., 1991—92, The Lorelton Gallery, Wilmington, 1999, U. Del., 1992—94, Xian Art Sch., 1998, Artemis Gallery, Richmond, Va., 1999—2001, Synergy Gallery, West Palm Beach, Fla., 2000—01, Del. Art Mus., Wilmington, 2001—04, Grace Gallery, 2005, Cecil Cultural Arts Ctr., Cecil C.C., 2005, East of the Bay Gallery, Md., 2006, 2007—08, Ft. Lauderdale History Mus., 2006, Internat. Ctr. U. Del., 2007, Bridge of Hope, 2007, 2+3 Sacred Spaces Jewish Museum, 2007, Jewish Mus., Miami, Fla., 2008, Art-Serve, Ft. Laud, Fla., 2008, Glass Gallery, 2009, Coral Springs Mus. Art Fla., Delaplaine Art Culture, Represented in permanent collections Corp. Holding Svcs., One on One Fitness Ctr., Wilmington, Skadden Arps Slate Meagher and Flom, Salva Profl. Assn., The Arches, Del. History Mus.; prodr.:; curator Women Collared for Work, 2009—. Mem. Nat. Mus. for Women in the Arts, NOW; bd. dirs. People to People Internat., 1993—2000, Jewish Family Svc., Wilmington, 1983—84. Grantee, U. Del., 1985; Emerging Artist fellowship in Sculpture, Del. Divsn. of the Arts, 1986—87, Established Artist fellow in Sculpture, 1993—94, Art fellow, Del. State Arts Coun., 1993—94, Opportunity grantee in Painting, Del. Divsn. of the Arts, 2005, Broward County Fla. grantee, 2009. Mem.: Profl. Art Orgn., Profl. Artists Assn. Group, Del. Ctr. for Contemporary Art, Del. Art Mus., Toastmasters Club. Avocations: dance, yoga, music, voice. Office Phone: 954-452-4615. Personal E-mail: judith9325@aol.com.

SCHWAB, KLAUS MARTIN, foundation administrator; b. Ravensburg, Fed. Republic Germany, Mar. 30, 1938; m. Hilde Stoll, July 7, 1971; children: Olivier, Nicole. PhD in Engring., Swiss Fed. Inst. Tech., Zurich, 1965; PhD in Econs., U. Fribourg, 1966; MPA, Harvard U., Cambridge, Mass., 1967; DCL (hon.), Bishop U., 1991; Dr. honoris causa, U. Autonoma de Guadalajara, 1992, Swiss Fed. Inst. Tech., Lausanne, 1999, Ben Gurion U., Israel, 1999, London Sch. Econ. and Polit. Sci., 2002. Asst. to pres. German Assn. of Machine Industry, Frankfurt, Fed. Republic of Germany, 1964-66; gen. mgr. Escher Wyss Ltd., Zurich, Switzerland, 1967-71; founder, pres. World Econ. Forum, Geneva, 1971—; prof. U. Geneva, 1972—2002; co-founder The Schwab Found. for Social Entrepreneurship, 1998; founder The Forum of Young Global Leaders, 2004. Bd. advs., overseer's vis. com. JFK Sch. Govt.; mem. pres.'s coun. U. Tokyo. Author: Global Competitiveness Report, 1979—; contbr. articles to profl. jours. Decorated Légion d'Honneur France, Knight Comdr. Order St. Michael & St. George, Eng.; recipient Grand Cross, Nat. Order Merit, Germany, 1995, Golden Grand Cross, Nat. Order Austria, 1997, Medal of Freedom, Slovenia, 1997, Comdr.'s Cross with stars, Nat. Order Poland, 2002, Highest Level Order of Friendship, Kazakhstan, 2002, Order of Stara Planina First Class, Bulgaria, 2003; named an The World's Most Influential People, TIME mag., 2007. Office: World Econ Forum 91-93 route de la Capite 1223 Cologny Geneva Switzerland Business E-Mail: contact@weforum.org.

SCHWAB, STEPHEN WAYNE, lawyer; b. Washington, Jan. 25, 1956; s. A. Wayne and Elizabeth (Parsons) S.; m. Debora Zellner, May 26, 1979; children: Benjamin Earl, Jason Edward. BA, Northwestern U., 1979; JD, Pa. State U., 1982. Bar: Ill. 1982, NY 2007, U.S. Dist. Ct. (no. dist.) Ill. 1983, U.S. Ct. Appeals (7th cir.) 1985, U.S. Ct. Claims 1986, U.S. Supreme Ct. 1989, U.S. Ct. Appeals (9th cir.) 1991, D.C. 1994. Assoc. Pretzel & Stouffer, Chgo., 1982-85; ptnr. Piper Rudnick LLP, Chgo., 1985—2004; ptnr., chmn. Insurance & Reinsurance practice group DLA Piper LLP US, Chgo., 2005—. Contbr. chapters to books, articles to profl. jours. Scoutmaster Troop 5 Boy Scouts Am., Wilmette, Ill., 1999—2003; chmn.NE Ill. coun. Jamboree Com., 2003—; pres. Congl. Coun., 2009—; lay reader evang. Luth. Ch. of the Ascension, Northfield, Ill., 1998—. Recipient Nat. Scoutmaster award, Nat. Eagle Scout Assn., 2002, Potawatomi Dist. Merit award, 2003, Wood Badge award, 2003. Mem. ABA, Internat. Bar Assn., Chgo. Bar Assn., ARIAS U.S., Internat. Assn. Insurance receivers, Def. Rsch. Inst., Nat. Conf. Insurance Legislators, Nat. Assn. Insurance Commissioners, Order of Barristers, Phi Eta Sigma. Lutheran. Office: DLA Piper LLP US Fl 19 203 N LaSalle St Chicago IL 60601-1293 Home Phone: 847-251-4057; Office Phone: 312-368-2150. Office Fax: 312-630-7343. Business E-Mail: stephen.schwab@dlapiper.com.

SCHWAB, STEWART JON, dean, law educator; b. 1954; BA, Swarthmore U., 1975; MA, Mich. U., 1978; JD econ., magna cum laude, Mich. U. Law Sch., 1980; PhD econ., Mich. U., 1981. Bar: D.C. 1982. Law clk. to Hon. J. Dickson Phillips U.S. Ct. Appeals (4th cir.), 1981-82; law clk. to Hon. Sandra O'Connor U.S. Superior Ct, 1982-83; from asst. prof. to prof. law Cornell U. Law Sch., Ithaca, NY, 1983—2003, Allan R. Tessler dean, 2004—; disting. visiting prof. U. Nebr. Coll. Law, Lincoln, 2003; Fulbright sr. scholar Australian Nat. U. Ctr. for Law & Econ., Canberra, 1998. Vis. fellow Centre Socio-Legal Studies Oxford U., 1990; vis. rsch. prof. U. Va. Law Sch., 1991; vis. prof. U. Mich. Law Sch., 1988, Duke Law Sch., 1999-2000; dir. Am. Deans Law Assn., 2005-. Editor: Jour. Empirical Legal Studies, 2004—. Fellow Alcoa Found.; mem. Am. Econ. Assn., Am. Judicature Assn., Order of Coif; City of Ithaca bd. zoning appeals, 1985-88. Office: Cornell Law Sch 263 Myron Taylor Hall Ithaca NY 14853-4901 Office Phone: 607-255-3527. Office Fax: 607-255-7193. Business E-Mail: stewart-schwab@lawschool.cornell.edu, sjs15@cornell.edu.*

SCHWAB, SUSAN CARROLL, public policy educator, former federal official; b. Washington, Mar. 23, 1955; d. Gerald and Joan Inga (Newton) Schwab; m. Curtis Carroll, Nov. 20, 2006 (dec.). BA in Polit. Economy, Williams Coll., Mass., 1976; MA in Devel. Policy, Stanford U., Calif., 1977; PhD in Pub. Adminstrn. & Internat. Bus., George Washington U., DC, 1993. US trade negotiator Office US Trade Rep., Exec. Office of the Pres., Washington, 1977-79; internat. economist & trade policy officer US Embassy, Tokyo, 1980-81; chief economist, legis. asst. for internat. trade to Senator John C. Danforth US Senate, Washington, 1981-86, legis. dir., 1986—89; asst. sec., dir. gen. US & Fgn. Comml. Svc. US Dept. Commerce, Washington, 1989-93; dir. corp. bus. devel. Motorola, Inc., Schaumburg, Ill., 1993-95; dean U. Md. Sch. Pub. Policy, College Park, Md., 1995—2003, prof., 2009—; pres., CEO U. Md. Found., Adelphi, 2004—05; dep. US Trade Rep. Office US Trade Rep., Exec. Office of the Pres., Washington, 2005—06, US Trade Rep., 2006—09. Bd. dirs. Calpine Corp., 1997—2005, Caterpillar Inc., 2009—, FedEx Corp., 2009—; bd. advisors Miller Buckfire, 2009—. Author: Trade-Offs: Negotiating the Omnibus Trade Act, 1994. Bd. visitors USAF Acad.; bd. dirs. Signature Theatre. Fellow: Nat. Acad. Pub. Adminstrn. (NAPA); mem.: Coun. Fgn. Rels. Republican. Office: Maryland School of Public Policy University of Maryland 2101 Van Munching Hall College Park MD 20742 Office Phone: 301-405-6347. Office Fax: 301-403-4675. E-mail: sschwab@umd.edu.*

SCHWABER, JAMES STEPHEN, neuroscientist, director; s. Joseph H. and Frances Lindley Schwaber; m. Mary Brent Whipple, May 25, 1980; children: Jessica Lindley, Joel Bennet-Knight. PhD, U. Miami, Coral Gable, Fla., 1973. Postdoc. fellow U. Va., Charlottesville, 1973—76; asst. prof. U. Vt., Burlington, 1976—81; tech. leader and rsch. fellow E.I. DuPont de Nemours & Co., Wilmington, Del., 1981—2001; dir. Daniel Baugh Inst. Functional Genomics-Computational Biology Thomas Jefferson U., Phila.; analyst Intel, Seoul, Republic of Korea, 1968—70. Com. Arden Assessors, Del., 1994—2000. Biomed. Rsch. grant, NIH, 1975—, ONR, DARPA. Mem.: Soc. Neurosci. Achievements include patents pending for low cost high throughput digital gene sequencing. Avocations: cooking, squash, hiking, travel, bicycling. Home: 2145 Veale Rd Arden Wilmington DE 19810 Office: Thomas Jefferson Univ 1020 Locust St JAH381 Philadelphia PA 19107

SCHWANAUER, FRANCIS, philosopher, educator; b. Zsámbék, Hungary, Jan. 20, 1933; arrived in US, 1959; s. Georg and Maria (Keller) S.; m. Johanna Maria Koelln, Sept. 29, 1957; children: Stephan Michael, Miriam Frances. Maturum, Ulrich von Hutten Gymnasium, Korntal, Germany, 1954; PhD, U. Stuttgart, Germany, 1959. Asst. prof. Lebanon Valley Coll., Annville, Pa., 1960—62, U. Maine, Orono, 1962—65, U. So. Maine, Portland Gorham, 1965—67, assoc. prof., 1967—72, prof., 1972—2006, prof. emeritus, 2006—. Author: Truth is a Neighborhood with Nothing in Between, 1977, Those Fallacies by Slight of Reason, 1978, No Many is not a One (For the Case is Comparison), 1981, The Flesh of Thought is Pleasure or Pain, 1982, To Make Sure is to Cohere, 1982, Philosophical Fact and Paradox, 1987, Fables from the Fox, 1991; contbr. articles to profl. jours. Grantee, John Anson Kittredge Ednl. Fund, 1991, 1993. Mem.: New Eng. Philos. Assn. Democrat. Roman Catholic. Avocation: fishing. Home: 4 Woodmont St Portland ME 04102-2709

SCHWANDA, TOM, religious studies educator; b. East Stroudsburg, Pa., Oct. 23, 1950; s. Theodore Frank and Madlyn Betty (Backensto) S.; m. Grace Elaine Dunning, July 30, 1977; children: Rebecca Joy, Stephen Andrew. Student, Worcester Polytechnic Inst., 1968-69; BA in Econ., Moravian Coll., 1969-72; student, Gordon-Conwell Sem., 1972-74; MDiv, New Brunswick Sem., 1975; DMin, Fuller Theol. Sem., 1992. Ordained to ministry Reformed Ch. in Am., 1975. Pastor Wanaque (N.J.) Reformed Ch., 1975-87; pastor congl. care Immanuel Reformed Ch., Grand Rapids, Mich., 1987-92; interim sr. pastor Remembrance Reformed Ch., Grand Rapids, 1992-93; rsch. fellow H. Henry Meeter Ctr. for Calvin Studies Calvin Coll., Grand Rapids, 1993-95; instr. spirituality and worship Bethlehem Ctr. for Spirituality, Grand Rapids, 1993—; dir. Reformed Spirituality Network, Grand Rapids, 1992—; assoc. for spiritual formation Reformed Ch. in Am., 1995-99; prof. spiritual formation Reformed Bible Coll., Grand Rapids, Mich., 1999—2006; assoc. prof. Christian formation and ministry Wheaton Coll., Ill., 2006—. Organizer, convener Gathering Reformed Spirituality, 1993, 94, 95, 97, 99, 2001, 2004; chair spirituality com. Synod of Great Lakes, 1989-2000, mem. Christian discipleship com., 1988-94; mem. ch. life, evangelism, missions com. South Grand Rapids Classics, chair, 1992; mem. commn. on worship Reformed Ch. in Am., 1978-94; mem. care of students com. Passaic Classis, 1975, 87, chair, 1978, 83-86, pres., 1979; adj. prof. spirituality and spiritual direction and worship Fuller Theol. Sem., San Francisco Theol. Sem., No. Bapt. Theol. Sem., Western Theol. Sem., Columbia Theol. Sem., Charlotte, Orlando, Reformed Theol. Sem., Charlotte. Author: Celebrating God's Presence: The Transforming Power of Public Worship, 1995; contbr. articles to religious jours.; author poetry; manuscript reader, evaluator religious pub. co. Established, managed Wanaque Cmty. Food Pantry, 1977-87; vol. Domestic Crisis Ctr., Grand Rapids, 1988—; bd. dirs. Nat. Inst. Rehabilitation Engring., Hewitt, N.J., 1984—, pres. bd. dirs., 1986—. Recipient Barnabas award Iglesia Cristiana Ebenezer, 1987. Mem. Czechoslovak Soc. Arts and Sci., Czechoslovak Hist. Conf., Soc. for Study of Christian Spirituality, Evangelical Theol. Soc., Calvin Studies Soc. Mem. Reformed Ch. Am. Avocations: running, landscaping, genealogy, amateur radio. Home: 1999 Nottingham Ln Wheaton IL 60189 Office: Wheaton College 501 College Ave Wheaton IL 60187

SCHWANTES, ROBERT SIDNEY, international relations executive; b. Beetown Township, Wis., July 11, 1922; s. Kurt John and Lillian Ellen (Walker) S.; m. Marion Laura Miles, July 15, 1943; children: Virginia, Janet, Ingrid. AB summa cum laude, Harvard U., 1943; MA, U. Colo., 1947; PhD, Harvard U., 1950. Instr. in history Harvard U., Cambridge, Mass., 1950-52; Carnegie resch. fellow Coun. on Foreign Rels., NYC, 1952-54; various positions The Asia Found., San Francisco and Tokyo, 1954-66, dir. of programs San Francisco, 1966-69, v.p. for programs, 1969-84, exec. v.p., 1984-88; vis. rsch. scholar Hoover Inst., Stanford, 1988—. Mem. Am. adv. com. Japan Found., Tokyo, 1984-86, vis. History lectr. Harvard U., 1958. Author: Japanese and Americans, 1955, What Did You Do in the War, Daddy?, 1998; contbr. articles to profl. jours. Vestryman St. Paul's Episcopal Ch., Burlingame, Calif., 1993-95. Lt. (j.g.), USNR, 1942-46, PTO. Assn. Asian Studies, Japan Soc. No. Calif. Democrat. Avocations: reading, travel. Home: 1432 Benito Ave Burlingame CA 94010-5550 Home Phone: 650-344-9415. Personal E-mail: robertschwantes@sbcglobal.net.

SCHWARCZ, HENRY PHILIP, geologist, educator; b. Chgo., July 22, 1933; s. Arthur and Zita Elizabeth (Strauss) S.; m. Molly Ann Robinson, Dec. 20, 1964; 1 child, Joshua Arthur AB, U. Chgo., 1952; M.Sc. in Geochemistry, Calif. Inst. Tech., Pasadena, 1955, PhD in Geology, 1960. Rsch. assoc. E. Fermi Inst., U. Chgo., 1960-62; prof. geology McMaster U., Hamilton, Ont., Canada, 1962—, chmn., assoc. mem. dept. anthropology, 1998—, univ. prof., 1996-99, prof. emeritus, sch. geography and earth sciences, 1999—. Mem. assoc. com. on meteorites NRC of Can., 1978-86; vis. fellow Clare Hall Coll. Cambridge U., 1991-92, Australian Nat. U., 1995; vis. prof. Hebrew U., Jerusalem, 1992; assoc. mem. dept. anthropology U. Toronto, 1993—; mem. panel refs. Rivista di Antropologia (Roma). Assoc. editor Geochimica et Cosmochimica Acta, 1984-96, Jour. Human Evolution, 1994-2002, Geoarchaeology, 1994—, Am. Jour. Phys. Anthropology, 2004—; mem. editl. bd. Jour. Archaeol. Sci., 1986-2002; contbr. articles to profl. jours., chpts. to books. Recipient Alumni award U. Chgo., 2005; Fulbright fellow, Pisa, Italy, 1968-69, Killam fellow Can. Coun., 1993—; Johnston Medalist Can. Quality Assn., 2007. Fellow Royal Soc. Can., Geol. Soc. Am. (Archeol. Geol. Div. award 1991, Fryxell award 1999, ISI Highly Cited, 2008); mem. Geochem. Soc., Lithoprobe (NSERC 1991-94), Am. Quaternary Assn., Acad. III Sci. (mem. coun.), Geol. Soc. Am. (chmn. archeol. geol. divsn.), Soc. for Am. Archaeology, Soc. Archaeological Sci., Sigma Xi (disting. lectr. 2000-01). Avocations: playing violin, drawing, painting, cooking. Office: McMaster U Sch Geography and Earth Scis General Science Building Room 302 Hamilton ON Canada L8S 4M1 Business E-Mail: schwarcz@mcmaster.ca.

SCHWARCZ, STEVEN LANCE, lawyer, educator; b. NYC, Nov. 10, 1949; s. Charles and Elinor Schwarcz; m. Susan Beth Kolodny, Aug. 24, 1975; children: Daniel Benjamin, Rebekah Mara. BS summa cum laude in Aero. Engring., NYU, 1971; JD, Columbia U., 1974. Bar: N.Y. 1971, U.S. Dist. Ct. (so. dist.) N.Y. 1975. Assoc. Shearman & Sterling, NYC, 1974-82, ptnr., 1983-89; ptnr., chmn. structured fin. Kaye, Scholer, Fierman, Hays & Handler, 1996—; prof. Duke U. Sch. Law, Durham, NC, 1996—, Stanley A. Star prof., 2004—; spl. counsel Kaye, Scholer, Fierman, Hays & Handler, 1996—2004; faculty dir. Duke Global Capital Markets Ctr.; spl. cons. Kaye Scholer LLP, 2004—. Adj. prof. law Yeshiva U., Benjamin N. Cardozo Sch. Law, N.Y.C., 1983-92; vis. lectr. Yale Law Sch., 1992-96; lectr. Columbia Law Sch., 1992-96. Contbr. articles to profl. jours. Chmn. Friends of the Eldridge St. Synagogue, N.Y.C., 1979-96, Legis. Drafting Rsch. Fund. George Granger Brown scholar, 1971; NSF grantee in Math., 1969. Fellow Am. Coll. Comml. Fin. Lawyers; mem. Am. Law Inst., Assn. of Bar of City of N.Y. (environ. law com. 1975-78, nuc. tech. com. 1979-81, sci. and law com. 1985—, chmn. 1987-90), Am. Law and Econs. Assn., Tau Beta Pi, Sigma Gamma Tau. Jewish. Office: Duke U Sch Law Box 90360 Science Dr & Towerview Rd Durham NC 27708 Office Phone: 919-613-7060. E-mail: schwarcz@law.duke.edu.

SCHWARCZ, VERA, historian, poet, educator; d. Elmer and Katherine Savin; m. Jason Wolfe, July 31, 1983; children: Elie, Esther. BA in French Lit. and Oriental Religions, Vassar Coll., 1969; MA in East Asian Studies, Yale U., 1971; PhD in Chinese History, Stanford U., Calif., 1977. Instr. Stanford U., 1973; lectr. Chinese history Wesleyan U., Middletown, Conn., 1975-77, asst. prof. Chinese history, 1975-83, assoc. prof. history, 1983-87, prof. history, 1987—, chair East Asian studies, 1985-88, 94-96, Mansfield Freeman prof. East Asian Studies, 1987—, dir., Ctr. East Asian Studies, 1998—99, chair, Program East Asian studies, 2007. Dir. Mansfield Freeman for East Asian Studies, 1987-88, 94-96, 2007-; exch. scholar Beijing U., 1979-80, vis. scholar, 1983, 86, 89; vis. scholar Ctr. de Documentation sur la Chine Contemporaine, Paris, 1985, DAO Assn., Cluj, Romania, 1993, Miskenot Sha'ananim, Jerusalem, 1991; vis. prof. East Asian studies Hebrew U., Jerusalem, 1996-97; coun. confs. Assn. Asian Studies, 1989-; presenter, referee in field. Author: Long Road Home: A China Journal, 1984, Chinese Enlightenment: Intellectuals, and the Legacy of the May Fourth Movement in Modern China, 1986, Zhongguo de qimeng yundong, 1989, Time for Telling Truth is Running Out: Conversations with Zhang Shenfu, 1992, Bridge Across Broken Time: Chinese and Jewish Cultural Memory, 1998, Fresh Words for a Jaded World, 2000, A Scoop of Light: Poems, 2000, Zhonguo Oimeng Yundong, 2000, Zhang Shenfu Fangtan Lu, 2001, In the Garden of Memory, 2004, Truth is Woven, 2005, Garden of Flourishing Grace, Place and Memory in Singing Crane Garden, 2008; author numerous poems and books; co-editor: China: Inside the People's Republic, 1972; mem. editl. bd. Bull. Concerned Asian Scholars, 1980-, History and Theory, 1981-84, 96-99, China Rev. Internat., 1994—; contbr. articles to profl. jours., chapter to books. Fellow Danforth Found., 1971-73, NDFL, 1973-74, NAS, 1979-80, Guggenheim Found. fellow, 1989-90, Great River Arts Inst. poetry fellow, 2000, Founders fellow AAUW, 1988-89, Faculty fellow Ctr. for Humanities Wesleyan U., 1988; grantee AAUW, 1974-75, Am. Philos. Soc., 1985, Am. Coun. Learned Socs., 1978, 96; finalist Nat. Jewish Book award in History, 1999; recipient Wesleyan Writers Conf. Poetry scholarship, 1999; Poetry fellow Great River Arts Inst., Mex., 2000; recipient Poetry prize Taproot Lit. Rev., 2002-04. Mem. Assn. for Asian Studies (coun. on confs. 1989—, mem. Levenson prize com. 1991-92, chair 1992-93), New Eng. Assn. for Asian Studies (pres. 1988-89). Home: 42 Seneca Rd West Hartford CT 06117-2245 Office: Wesleyan Univ Ctr East Asian Studies Middletown CT 06459-0001

SCHWARTZ, AARON ROBERT, lawyer, former state legislator; b. Galveston, Tex., July 17, 1926; s. Joseph and Clara (Bulbe) S.; m. Marilyn Cohn, July 14, 1951; children: Richard Austin, Robert Allen, John Reed, Thomas Lee. Pre-law student, Tex. A&M U., 1948; JD, U. Tex., 1951. Bar: Tex. 1951. Mem. Tex. Ho. of Reps., 1955-59, Tex. Senate, 1960-81, past chmn. rules, jurisprudence and natural resources coms. Chmn. Tex. Coastal and Marine Coun., U.S. Coastal States Orgn.; adj. prof. legis. and cosatal mgmt. law Bates Law Sch., U. Houston, Coastal and Ocean Law, U. Tex., Sch. Law, Tex. A&M U., Corpus Christi. Contbr. articles to profl. jours. Mem. emeritus exec. com. Galveston Bay Fond.; apptd. to Tex. Oil Spill Oversight Commn., 1993. Served with USN, 1944-46, 2d lt. USAFR, 1948-53. Recipient conservation and legis. awards, Outstanding Citizen award Galveston Jr. C. of C., 1981, Man of Yr., People of Vision award Galveston chpt. Soc. for Prevention of Blindness, 1986, Disting. Service award Nat. Hurricane Conf., Tex. Coastal Mgmt. Adv. Com., 1987, Lifetime Coastal Achievement award, 1997. Mem. Tex. State Bar Assn., Galveston County Bar Assn. Democrat. Jewish. Address: 1122 Colorado St Apt 2102 Austin TX 78701-2142 Personal E-mail: ars71726@aol.com.

SCHWARTZ, ALAN DAVID, diversified financial services company executive; b. Bklyn., Mar. 23, 1950; s. Walter and Ruth Ann Schwartz; m. Nancy Seaman; children: Jennifer, Adam, Ryan. BS, Duke U., Durham, NC, 1972. Instl. salesman P.W. Pressprich & Co., NYC, 1972-74, Wertheim & Co., NYC, 1974-76; fin. mgmt. positions The Bear Stearns Companies Inc., NYC, 1976—85, exec. v.p., co-head investment banking, 1985—2001, pres., co-COO, 2001—07, pres., 2007—08, CEO, 2008; exec. chmn. Guggenheim Partners LLC, NYC, 2009—. Bd. dirs. Fuddruckers, 1984—88, Champps Entertainment, 1988—2004, Bear Stearns Companies Inc., 1987—2008, Young & Rubicam Inc., 1996. Bd. dirs. Partnership for NYC; bd. visitors Fuqua Sch. Bus., Duke U., 1986—, chmn., 2001—; bd. dirs. Robin Hood Found.; bd. trustees NYU Med. Ctr., Duke U. Recipient Banker of Yr. award, Investment Dealer's Digest, 2003; named a Top Rainmaker, Dealmaker mag., 2007. Office: Guggenheim Partners LLC 135 E 57th St New York NY 10022 Office Phone: 212-644-2876.*

SCHWARTZ, ALAN EARL, lawyer, director; b. Detroit, Dec. 21, 1925; s. Maurice H. and Sophia (Welkowitz) S.; m. Marianne Shapero, Aug. 24, 1950; children: Marc Alan, Kurt Nathan, Ruth Anne. Student, Western Mich. Coll., 1944-45; BA with distinction, U. Mich., 1947; LLB magna cum laude, Harvard U., Cambridge, Mass., 1950; LLD, Wayne State U., Detroit, 1983, U. Detroit, 1985. Bar: NY 1951, Mich. 1952. Assoc. Kelley, Drye & Warren, NYC, 1950-52; mem. Honigman, Miller, Schwartz & Cohn, Detroit, 1952—. Spl. asst. counsel NY State Crime Commn., 1951. Editor: Harvard Law Rev., 1950. Dir. Detroit Symphony Orch.; v.p., bd. dirs. United Way; bd. dirs. Detroit Renaissance, New Detroit, Jewish Welfare Fedn. Detroit, Wayne State U. Found.; trustee Cmty. Found. for Southeastern Mich.; adv. mem. Arts Commn., City of Detroit; bd. dirs., mem. investment com. Skillman Found., Wayne State U. Found. Served as ensign Supply Corps, USNR, 1945-46. Recipient Mich. Heritage Hall of Fame award, 1984, George W. Romney award for lifetime achievement in volunteerism, 1994, Max M. Fisher Cmty. Svc. award, 1997; named one of Top 200 Collectors, ARTnews, 2004-08. Mem. Mich. Bar Assn., Franklin Hills Country Club, Econ. Club (dir.). Avocation: collecting Old Masters and modern prints. Office: Honigman Miller Schwartz & Cohn 2290 1st National Bldg Detroit MI 48226

SCHWARTZ, ALAN LEIGH, pediatrician, educator; b. NYC, Apr. 25, 1948; s. Robert and Joyce (Goldner) S.; m. Judith Child, June 22, 1974; 1 child, Timothy Child. BA, Case Western Res. U., 1974, PhD in Pharmacology, 1974, MD, 1976. Diplomate Am. Bd. Pediatrics. Intern Children's Hosp., Boston, 1976-77, resident, 1976-78, fellow Dana Farber Cancer Inst., 1978-80; instr. Harvard Med. Sch., Boston, 1980-81, asst. prof., 1981-83, assoc. prof., 1983-86; prof. pediatrics, molecular biology and pharmacology Washington U. Sch. Medicine, St. Louis, 1986—, chmn. dept. pediatrics, 1995—; chmn. faculty practice plan Washington U., 1999—2001. Vis. scientist MIT, Boston, 1979-82; mem. sci. adv. bd. Nat. Inst. Child Health and Human Devel., NIH, Bethesda, Md., 1988-94; investigator Am. Heart Assn. Alumni Endowed Prof. Pediats. Wash. U. Sch. Medicine, 1987-97, Harriet B. Spoehrer Prof. Pediats., 1997—. Mem. Inst. Medicine of NAS. Office: Washington U Sch Medicine Dept Pediatrics Box 8116 One Children's Pl Saint Louis MO 63110-1093 E-mail: schwartz@kids.wustl.edu.

SCHWARTZ, ALAN VICTOR, advertising executive; b. Detroit, July 12, 1948; s. Seymour and Adeline (Goldstein) S.; children: Stacy Ilana, Andrew Robert. BS with honors, Lehigh U., 1970; MBA with highest honors, Cornell U., 1972. CPA, N.Y. Mgr. Price Waterhouse, Huntington, NY, 1972-79; v.p., dir. fin. control Doyle Dane Bernbach, NYC, 1979-81; v.p., CFO, Bernard Hodes Group, NYC, 1981-84, sr. v.p., chief oper. and fin. officer, 1984-87, exec. v.p., COO, 1987—2001, pres., CEO, 2002—; trustee The Healthcare Chaplaincy, 2005—, chmn. audit com.; bd. mem Bnai Zion, 2008—. Bd. mgrs. Evans Tower, treas. 1991-92, pres. 1992-93. Campaign vice chmn. United Way L.I., 1978. Mem. Nat. Assn. Accts. (various directorships, treas.), N.Y. State Soc. CPAs, Lehigh Alumni Assn. (pres. L.I. chpt. 1977-79, treas. 1975-77). Office: Bernard Hodes Group 220 E 42d St New York NY 10017

SCHWARTZ, ALBERT TRUMAN, chemistry professor; b. Freeman, SD, May 8, 1934; s. Albert and Edna Kaufman Schwartz; m. Beverly Beatty, Aug. 12, 1958; children: Ronald Eric, Katherine Schwartz Herrmann. BA, U. SD, 1956, Oxford U., Eng., 1958, MA, 1960; PhD, MIT, 1963; DSc (hon.), U. S.D., 1991. Rsch. chemist Procter & Gamble Co., Cin., 1963-66; asst. prof. Macalester Coll., St. Paul, 1966-72, assoc. prof., 1972-78, prof., 1978-83, DeWitt Wallace prof., 1983—2004, dean faculty, 1974-76, chair dept. chemistry, 1980-88, 94-95, DeWitt Wallace prof. emeritus, 2004—. Vis. rschr. U. Lund, Sweden, 1968, U. Mass., Amherst, 1972—73; vis. prof. U. Wis., Madison, 1979—80, U. SD, 2000; hon. vis. prof. U. York, England, 1994; dep. dir. tchr. preparation and enhancement NSF, Washington, 1986—87. Author: Chemistry: Imagination and Implication, 1973; sr. author: Chemistry in Context: Applying Chemistry to Society, 1994, 2nd edit., 1997, And Gladly Teach: A Resource Book for Chemists Considering Academic Careers, 2003; co-editor: Motion Toward Perfection: The Achievement of Joseph Priestley, 1970; contbr. articles to profl. jours. Mem. selection com. Rhodes Scholarship Trust, 1963—, sec. Minn. and Midwest dist. coms., 1993-2001. Recipient Catalyst award in chem. edn. Chem. Mfrs. Assn., 1982, Coll. Sci. Tchr. of Yr., Minn. Sci. Tchrs. Assn., 1988, Alumni Achievement award U. S.D., 2006; Rhodes scholar Oxford U., 1956-58. Fellow AAAS; mem. Am. Chem. Soc. (chair divsn. chem. edn. 1989, chair Minn. sect. 1992-93, mem. various coms., Western Conn. Sect. award 1991, Brasted award 1996, James Flack Norris award 1997, George C. Pimentel award in chem. edn. 2007). Avocations: music, photography, travel, cooking. Home: 68 Otis Ave Saint Paul MN 55104 Office: Macalester Coll 1600 Grand Ave Saint Paul MN 55105-1801 Office Phone: 651-696-6271. Personal E-mail: atandbbschwartz@gmail.com. E-mail: schwartz@macalester.edu.

SCHWARTZ, ALLAN, cardiologist; b. NYC, Mass., Jan. 22, 1947; BS magna cum laude, CCNY, 1967; MA in physics, Harvard Univ., 1968; MD, Columbia Univ. Coll. of Physicians & Surgeons, 1974. Cert. internal medicine, cardiology. Intern NY Presbyterian Hosp. Columbia Univ. Med. Ctr., 1974—75, resident in cardiology, 1975—76; vis. fellow Columbia Univ. Coll. of Physicians & Surgeons, 1974—76; rsch. fellow Harvard Univ., 1976—78; clinical cardiology fellowship Mass. Gen. Hosp., 1976—78; asst. prof. clinical med. Columbia Univ. Coll. of Physicians & Surgeons, 1978—87, assoc. prof. clinical med., 1987—90, clinical prof. med., 1990—93, dir. cardiac catheterization lab., 1990—99, Margaret Milliken Hatch clinical prof. med., 1993—99, assoc. dir. div. of cardiology, 1994—99, Harold Ames Hatch Prof. of clinical med., 1999—, chief, div. of cardiology, 1999—; asst. attending physician NY Presbyterian Hosp. Columbia Univ. Med. Ctr., 1978—87, assoc. attending physician, 1987—90, attending physician, 1990—. Asst. clin. prof. medicine U. Calif. San Francisco. Contbr. articles to profl. jours. Recipient Janeway prize, 1974, Frederick F. Gay award, 1974, Herbert J. Bartelstone award, 1974, Helen Sciarra award, 1974, Robert F. Loeb award, 1974; named Woodrow Wilson Nat. Fellow, 1967—68; named one of America's Top Doctors, Castle Connolly. Mem. Am. Coll. Cardiology, ACP, Am. Heart Assn., AMA, N.Am. Soc. Pacing and Electrophysiology. Office: NY Presbyterian Hosp Ste 5-551 161 Fort Washington Ave New York NY 10032 Office Phone: 212-305-5367. Office Fax: 212-305-3679. Business E-Mail: as20@columbia.edu.

SCHWARTZ, ALLEN R., lawyer; b. Greeley, Colo., Oct. 13, 1951; s. David L. and Margaret L. Schwartz; m. Beverly S. Stephens, Mar. 23, 1985; 1 child, Christopher; 1 stepchild, Shawn Jensen. BA in Psychology and Sociology, U. Colo., 1973, JD, 1976. Bar: Colo. 1976, US Dist. Ct. Colo. 1976, US Ct. Appeals (10th cir.) 1983. Law clk. Denver Dist. Ct., 1976-77; assoc. Fischer & Wilmarth, Ft. Collins, Colo., 1977-79; ptnr. Dean, Martin, Mitchell & Schwartz, Ft. Collins, 1979-83; mng. ptnr. Nelson & Schwartz, Ft. Collins, 1983-90; ptnr. Nelson, Reid & Schwartz, Ft. Collins, 1990-96; pvt. practice Ft. Collins, 1996—; county ct. magistrate Larimer County, Colo., 2006—. V.p., legal advisor acad. adv. com. Wingshadow Inc., Frontier HS and Frontier Mid. Sch., Ft. Collins, 1994-2005. Asst. scoutmaster Boy Scouts Am., Ft. Collins, Colo., 1991—94. Mem. Colo. Bar Assn., Larimer County Bar Assn., Overland Sertoma (pres., chmn. bd., Sertoman of the Yr. 1994-95), High Plains Dist. Sertoma (dist. gov. 1996-98, Cmty. Achievement award 1991-92). Home: 1601 Centennial Rd Fort Collins CO 80525-2418 Office: 215 W Oak St Ste 600 Fort Collins CO 80521-2729 Home Phone: 970-223-2978; Office Phone: 970-493-0456. Business E-Mail: allen@allenrschwartz.com.

SCHWARTZ, ALLYSON Y., United States Representative from Pennsylvania; b. NYC, Oct. 3, 1948; d. Everett and Renee Perl Young; m. David Schwartz, 1970; children: Daniel, Jordan. BA in Sociology, Simmons Coll., Boston, 1970; MSW, Bryn Mawr Coll., Pa., 1972. Founder, exec. dir. Elizabeth Blackwell Health Ctr. for Women, 1975-88; acting commr., 1st dep. commr. Dept. Human Svcs., 1988-90; mem. Pa. State Senate, Harrisburg, 1990—2004, minority chmn. edn. com., 1994—2004; mem. US Congress from 13th Pa. Dist., 2005—; mem. ways and means com. US Congress from 13th Pa. dist., mem. budget com. Mem. Pa. State Bd. Edn., Pa. Coun. Higher Edn., Pa. Hist. Mus. Commn., Nat. Dem. Leadership Coun.; chair instl. rev. bd. Phila. Health Mgmt. Corp.; bd. dirs. Nat. Jewish Dem. Coun.; co-chair Pa. New Dem. Coalition; bd. trustees Arcadia U., Glenside, Pa., Chestnut Hill Healthcare. Democrat. Jewish. Office: US House Reps 423 Cannon House Office Bldg Washington DC 20515-3813 Office Phone: 202-225-6111. Office Fax: 202-226-0611.*

SCHWARTZ, ANDREW B., neuroscientist, educator; PhD in Physiology, U. Minn., 1984. Fellow Johns Hopkins Sch. Medicine; researcher Barrow Neurological Inst., 1988—95, Neurosciences Inst., San Diego, 1995—2002; prof. neurobiology & researcher U. Pitts., 2002—. Achievements include development of three-dimensional trajectory representation in the motor cortex. Office: 245 McGowan Center Pittsburgh PA 15213-2536 Office Phone: 412-383-7021. E-mail: abs21@pitt.edu.*

SCHWARTZ, ANNA JACOBSON, economist; b. NYC, Nov. 11, 1915; married; 4 children. BA, Barnard Coll., 1934; MA, Columbia U., 1935, PhD, 1964; LittD (hon.), U. Fla., 1987, Emory U., 2000; ArtsD (hon.), Stonehill Coll., 1989; LLD (hon.), Iona Coll., 1992, Rutgers U., 1998; LHD (hon.), CUNY, 2000; LLD (hon.), Williams Coll., 2002; LHD (hon.), Loyola U., Chgo., 2003; ScD (hon.), City U., London, 2006. Rschr. USDA, 1936, Columbia U. Social Sci. Rsch. Coun., 1936-41; sr. rsch. staff Nat. Bur. Econ. Rsch. Inc., NYC, 1941—. Instr. Bklyn. Coll., 1952, Baruch Coll., 1959-60; adj. prof. econs. grad. CCNY, 1967-69, grad. sch. CUNY, 1986—, NYU Grad. Sch. Arts and Sci., 1969-70; hon. vis. prof. City U. Bus. Sch., London, 1984—; hon. fellow Inst. of Econ. Affairs, London, 1998. Mem. editl. bd. Am. Econ. Rev., 1972-78, Jour. Money, Credit and Banking, 1974-75, 84—, Jour. Monetary Econs., 1975—, Jour. Fin. Svcs. Rsch., 1993—; contbr. articles to profl. jours. Disting. fellow Am. Econ. Assn., 1993; hon fellow Inst. Econ. Affairs, London. Fellow Am. Acad. Arts & Scis.; mem. Western Econ. Assn. (pres. 1987-88). Office: Nat Bur Econ Research 365 Fifth Ave 5th Fl New York NY 10016-4309 Business E-Mail: aschwartz@gc.cuny.edu.

SCHWARTZ, ANTHONY, veterinary surgeon, educator, photographer; b. Bklyn., July 30, 1940; s. Murray and Miriam Sarah (Wittes) S.; m. Claudia Rosenberg, July 21, 1963; children: Thomas Frederick, Eric Leigh. Student, Mich. State U., 1957—58; DVM, Cornell U., 1963; PhD, Ohio State U., 1972. Diplomate Am. Coll. Vet. Surgeons (bd. of regents 1989-92). Gen. practice vet. medicine, Huntington, NY, 1963—66; resident in surgery Animal Med. Ctr., NYC, 1968—69, Ohio State U., Columbus, 1969—70, asst. prof., head sect. small animal surgery, 1973; asst. prof. then assoc. prof. comparative medicine Yale U. Sch. Medicine, New Haven, 1973—79; assoc. prof. then prof., chmn. dept. surgery, assoc. dean Tufts U. Sch. Vet. Medicine, Boston, 1979—89, assoc. dean clin. edn., 1989—93, prof., chmn. dept. surgery, assoc. dean acad. affairs, 1993—97, assoc. dean for acad. and outreach programs, 1997—2002, assoc. dean for continuing edu. and outreach programs, 2003—04, prof. emeritus, 2005—. Cons. U.S. Surg. Corp. Covidien, Norwalk, Conn., 1975—; mem. Bd. Tufts Animal Expo LLC, program dir., 1999-2003; mem. vet. adv. bd. PetPlace.com, Intelligent Content Corp., 2000-03; exec. dir., chair bd. dirs. N.E. Vet. Conf., 2003-05, chair program com., 2003-04. Author: (with others) Small Animal Surgery, 1989, Complications in Small Animal Surgery, 1996; editl. bd. Vet. Surgery, 1987-90, Jour. Investigative Surgery, 1987-98; assoc. editor: Textbook of Small Animal Surgery, 1985; contbr. articles to profl. jours. Capt. U.S. Army Vet Corps, 1966-68. Recipient 1st prize N.Y. State Vet. Med. Soc., 1963; Robert Wood Johnson Health Policy fellow, Washington, 1988-89; NIH grantee, 1975-84. Mem.: AVMA (legis. planning com. 1989—92, coun. on govt. affairs 1992—97), Mass. Vet. Med. Assn. (chmn. 1990—91, animal welfare com. 1990—98, Merit award for leadership in pub. rels. and colleague devel. 2002), Nat. Acads. of Practice (emeritus; co-chmn. acad. vet. medicine 2002—03), Assn. Am. Vet. Med. Colls. (treas. and exec. dir. 1992—93, Washington), Phi Kappa Phi, Sigma Xi. Democrat. Jewish. Office: Tufts U Sch Vet Medicine Dept Clin Sci 200 Westboro Rd North Grafton MA 01536-1895 Home Phone: 617-859-3948. Personal E-mail: tonyvet@comcast.net. Business E-Mail: Anthony.Schwartz@tufts.edu, tony@tonyschwartz.net.

SCHWARTZ, BARRY FREDRIC, lawyer, diversified holding company executive; b. Phila., Apr. 16, 1949; s. Albert and Evelyn (Strauss) S. AB cum laude, Kenyon Coll., 1970; JD, Georgetown U., 1974. Bar: Pa. 1974, Ill. 1974, N.Y. 1992, U.S. Dist. Ct. (ea. dist.) Pa. 1974, U.S. Dist. Ct. (no. dist.) Ill. 1975, U.S. Dist. Ct. (so. dist.) N.Y. 1992, U.S. Ct. Appeals (7th cir.) 1977, U.S. Ct. Appeals (3d cir.) 1978, U.S. Ct. Appeals (4th cir.) 1979, U.S. Ct. Appeals (6th cir.) 1981, U.S. Supreme Ct. 1981, N.Y. 1992. Assoc. Sachnoff, Schrager, Jones & Weaver, Chgo., 1974—76; ptnr. Wolf, Block, Schorr & Solis-Cohen, Phila., 1976—89, MacAndrews & Forbes Holdings, Inc., NYC, 1989—, sr. v.p., 1989—93, exec. v.p., gen. counsel, 1993—2007, exec. vice chmn., chief adminstrv. officer, 2007—. Bd. dirs. Sci. Games, 2003, REV Holdings LLC, 2004, Revlon Consumer Products, 2004, Harland Clarke Holdings Corp., 2005—, Pharma Core, Inc., 2006—, Trans Tech Pharma, Inc., 2006—, M & F Worldwide Corp., 2008, MacAndrews & Forbes Holdings Inc., 2007—; bd. visitors Georgetown U. Law Ctr., 2005—. Trustee Kenyon Coll., 2000—. Mem.: Assn. Governing Bds. of Univs. and Colls. (bd. dirs. 2004). Office: MacAndrews & Forbes Holdings Inc 35 E 62nd St New York NY 10065

SCHWARTZ, BART, lawyer; BA, Antioch Coll., 1975; JD, U. So. Calif., 1978; MBA, Vanderbilt U., 1991. Former assoc. atty. Debevoise and Plimpton, Skadden, Arps, Slate, Meagher & Flom; former exec. v.p., gen. counsel Werthan Packaging, Inc.; former sr. v.p., gen. counsel, sec. Willis Corroon Corp.; sr. v.p., gen. counsel The MONY Group, Inc., 2001—04; dep. gen. counsel Marsh & McLennan Cos., Inc., NYC, 2004; chief corp. gov. officer, corp. sec., chief securities counsel Bank NY; exec. v.p., chief legal officer, sec. Assurant, Inc., 2008—. Mem.: ABA (com. corp. gen. counsel), Coun. Chief Legal Officers, Assn. Corp. Counsel (bd. dirs. global orgn. and NY chpt.). Office: Assurant Inc One Chase Manhattan Plz New York NY 10005

SCHWARTZ, BENNETT K., dermatologist; MD, U. Vt., Burlington, 1983. Intern Thomas Jefferson U. Hosp., Phila., 1983—84; resident in dermatology Dartmouth-Hitchcock Med. Ctr., Hanover, NH, 1984—87; pvt. practice Voorhees, NJ, 1987—. Chief dermatology sect. Virtua West Jersey Hosp., Voorhees, 2007. Contbr. articles to profl. jours. Fellow: Am. Acad. Dermatology. Office: 2301 Evesham Rd Ste 403 Voorhees NJ 08043 Office Phone: 856-772-2221.

SCHWARTZ, BERNARD JULIAN, lawyer; b. Edmonton, Alberta, Can., July 29, 1960; came to U.S., 1982; s. Sol and Anne (Motkovich) S. BA, U. Alberta, 1981; JD, McGeorge Sch. Law, 1986. Bar: U.S. Supreme Ct. 1991. Atty. Ropers, Majeski, San Francisco, 1987-88, Riverside County Pub. Defenders, Riverside, Calif., 1988-89; pvt. practice Riverside, 1990—. Coach Riverside County H.S. Mock Trial Team, 1990, 96, 97. Mem. Calif. Attys. Criminal Justice, Calif. Pub. Defenders Assn., Riverside County Bar Assn., Criminal Cts. Bar Assn. (pres.).

SCHWARTZ, BRIAN MICHAEL, philosopher, think-tank executive; s. Bernard and Aileen Schwartz. BA, Oxford U., Eng., 1971; JD, Yale U., 1975. Law clk. to Hon. Irving R. Kaufman U.S. Ct. Appeals (2d cir.), NYC; famine relief coord. UNICEF, Namalu, Uganda, 1981—2002; treas. Prometheus Soc., 2003—. Author: China Off the Beaten Track, 1983, A World of Villages, 1986. Mem.: Lincoln's Inn, Lewis M. Terman High IQ Soc. (pres. 2007—), Omega Soc. (pres. 2007—), Aleph 3, Oxford Union, Polonia Club.

SCHWARTZ, CARL EDWARD, artist, printmaker; b. Detroit, Sept. 20, 1935; s. Carl and Verna (Steiner) S.; m. Kay Joyce Hofmann, June 18, 1955 (div.); children: Dawn Ellen, Cari Leigh; m. Celeste Borah, Jan. 1, 2007. BFA, Art Inst. Chgo. Sch.-U. Chgo., 1957. Past tchr. art Chgo. North Shore Art League, Suburban Fine Arts Ctr., Deerpath Art League; faculty Fla. Gulf Coast U. One-man shows include, South Bend (Ind.) Art Center, Feingarten Gallery, Chgo., 1960, Bernard Horwich Center, Chgo., Covenant Club, Chgo., Barat Coll., Chgo. Pub. Library, Alverno Coll., 1020 Art Center, Rosenberg Gallery, Peoria (Ill.) Art Guild, 1977, Ill. State Mus., 1977 Ill. Inst. Tech., 1978, Miller Gallery, Chgo., 1979, Union League Club, Chgo., 1982, Art Inst. Rental and Sale Gallery, Chgo., 1982, Horwich Gallery, Chgo., 1983, Lake Forest (Ill.) Coll., 1983, Campanile-Capponi Contemporary Gallery, Chgo., 1987, Nagata Gallery, Ft. Myers, Fla., 1988, Jan Cicero Gallery, Chgo., 1990, Neopolitan Gallery, Naples, Fla., 1996, 97; group shows include 9th Ann. Michigana Exhbt, Detroit (Cloetingh and Deman award 1959), Hyde Park Art Center, Chgo., 1960 (prize), Spectrum Exhbn. '63, Chgo. (1st prize), New Horizons Exhbt, Chgo., 1960 (Joseph Shapiro award), Nat. Design Center, Chgo., 1965 (New Horizons in Painting 1st prize), 3d Ann. Chgo. Arts Competition, 1962 (1st prize), Union League Club, Chgo., 1967 (2d prize), North Shore Art League, Chgo., 1965 (1st prize), Artists Guild Chgo., 1965 (prize), McCormack Pl., Chgo., 1965 (1st prize), Detroit Art Inst., 1965 (Commonwealth prize), Park Forest (Ill.) Art Exhbn, 1969 (Best of Show), 14th Ann. Virginia Beach (Va.) Show, 1969 (Best of Show), Suburban Fine Arts Center, Highland Park, Ill., 1970 (prize), 15th Ann. Virginia Beach Show, 1970 (prize), 32d Ann. Artists Guild, Chgo., 1970 (2d prize), North Shore Art League, 1970 (prize), 16th Ann. Virginia Beach Show, 1971 (2d prize), Ill. State Fair, 1972 (prize), Artists Guild Chgo., 1972 (1st prize), 17th Ann. Virginia Beach Exhbt, 1972 (1st prize), Artists Guild 50th Fine Art Exhbn., Chgo., 1973 (prize), Dickinson State U., 1973 (prize), North Shore Art League, 1973 (prize), Lakehurst Exhbt, 1974 (prize), Union League Art Exhbt, 1974 (1st prize), 1976 (prize), Artists Guild Fine Arts Exhbn., 1974 (best of Show), Bluegrass Painting Exhbn, Louisville, 1975 (award Washington, Art Inst. Chgo., K. Van Ella, Chgo., Gardner-Colby Gallery, Naples, Fla., Cape Coral Arts Studio, Van Liebig Art Ctr., 2005, Art League of Bonita Springs (Best of Show, Art Focus award 2007), Alliance for the Arts (award), 2007, 50 yr. Retrospective Show Fla. Gulf Coast U. Art Gallery, 2009. Recipient Logan medal, Art Inst. Chgo., 1958. Home: 5825 Briarcliff Rd Fort Myers FL 33912-4204 E-mail: carleschwartz@comcast.net. *I am a painter of light. I'm intrigued and fascinated with form. To me, there are two worlds-the one we all live in, and the one that I create. Painting is the discipline by which I constantly rediscover both of these worlds.*

SCHWARTZ, CAROL LEVITT, government official; b. Greenville, Miss., Jan. 20, 1944; d. Stanley and Hilda (Simmons) Levitt; m. David H. Schwartz (dec.); children: Stephanie, Hilary, Douglas. BS in Spl. and Elem. Edn., U. Tex., 1965. Mem. transiton team Office of Pres. Elect, 1980-81; con. office presdl. personnel The White House, Washington, 1981; cons. U.S. Dept. Edn., Washington, 1982; pres. sec. U.S. Ho. Reps., Washington, 1982-83; mem.-at-large Coun. of D.C., Washington, 1985—89, 1997—2009; candidate for mayor, Washington, 1986, 1994, 1998, 2002. Vice chmn. Nat. Edn. Commn. on Time and Learning, 1992-94, Nat. Adv. Coun. on Disadvantaged Children, 1974-79; lectr. in field; radio commentator, 1990-91; chair transp., vice-chair planning bd. Coun. Govts. Regional columnist Washington Jewish Week, 1995-97. Mem. D.C. Bd. Edn., 1974-82, v.p., 1977-80; bd. dirs. Met. Police Boys and Girls Club, 1st v.p., 1989-93, pres., 1994-96, chmn. membership com., 1984-93; mem. adv. com. Am. Coun. Young Polit. Leaders, 1982-90; mem. Nat. Coun. Friends Kennedy Ctr., 1984-91; bd. dirs. Whitman-Walker Clinic, 1988-2006, v.p., 1995-96; bd. dirs. St. John's Child Devel. Ctr., 1989-91, Hattie M. Strong Found., 1995—; trustee Kennedy Ctr. Cmty. and Friends Bd., 1991—, chmn. ednl. task force, 1993—; trustee Jewish Coun. on Aging, 1991-93; v.p. adv. bd. Am. Automobile Assn., 1988-06; bd. dirs. Washington Hebrew Congregation, 1995-98. Mem. Cosmos Club. Republican. Jewish.

SCHWARTZ, CHARLES E., medical geneticist, medical association administrator; BA in Chemistry, Colgate U.; MS in Biochemistry, Okla. State U., 1972; PhD, Vanderbilt U., 1978. NCI Postdoctoral Fellow, Dept. Biochemistry U. Vt., 1978—80; rsch. scientist La Jolla Cancer Rsch. Found., 1980—81; rsch. assoc., dept. human genetics U. Utah Sch. Medicine, 1983—85; dir. molecular genetics lab. Greenwood Genetics Ctr., 1985—95, dir., center for molecular studies, JC Self Rsch. Inst., 1996—, dir. rsch., head JC Self Rsch. Inst., 2004—. Adj. prof., dept. genetics and biochemistry Clemson U., Clemson, SC, 1987—;

asst. prof. pediatrics U. South Carolina, Columbia, 1987—, adj. asst. prof. biology, 1988—. Recipient Robert Guthrie award for Advances in Biochemical and Molecular Genetics, American Assn. Mental Retardation, 2003; named Professional of the Year, SC Chap. American Assn. Mental Retardation, 2002. Mem.: American Bd. Medical Genetics (diplomate 1993—, dir. clinical molecular genetics 2006—, treas. 2007, v.p. 2008, pres. 2009). Office: Ctr Molecular Studies JC Self Research Inst 113 Gregor Mendel Circle Greenwood SC 29646-2307*

SCHWARTZ, CHARLES WALTER, lawyer; b. Brenham, Tex., Dec. 27, 1953; s. Walter C. and Annie (Kuehn) S. BS, U. Tex., 1975, MA, 1980, JD, 1977; LLM, Harvard U., Cambridge, Mass., 1980. Bar: Tex. 1977; bd. cert. civil appellate law Tex. Bd. Legal Specialization. Law clk. U.S. Ct. Appeals (5th cir.), Austin, Tex., 1977-79; assoc. Vinson & Elkins LLP, Houston, 1980—86, ptnr., 1986—2003, Skadden, Arps, Slate, Meagher & Flom, 2003—. Contbr. articles to law revs. Fellow: Tex. Bar Found. (sustaining life), Houston Bar Found. (sustaining life), Coll. State Bar Tex., Am. Bar Found. (life; patron); mem.: ABA, Tex. Commn. Lawyer Discipline, Tex. Law Rev. Assn., Am. Law Inst., Bar Assn. of 5th Cir., State Bar Tex. (former chmn. grievance com. 1993—99, bd. dirs. 2000—04, exec. com. 2001—04, chmn. 2002—03, immediate past chmn. 2003—04). Home: 2154 Chilton Rd Houston TX 77019 Office: Skadden Arps Slate Meagher & Flom LLP 1000 Louisiana St Ste 6800 Houston TX 77002 Office Phone: 713-655-5160. Business E-Mail: charles.schwartz@skadden.com.

SCHWARTZ, DANIEL BENNETT, artist; b. NYC, Feb. 16, 1929; s. Bennett Henry and Lillian (Blumenthal) S.; m. Judith Nancy Kass, June 12, 1955 (div. 1980); 1 child, Claudia Bennet; m. Janet McCaffery, March, 1994. Grad., High Sch. of Music and Art, NYC, 1946; student, Art Students League, 1946, Y. Kuniyoshi; BFA, R.I. Sch. Design, 1949. Instr. pvt. painting class, 1965—81, 1990—2002, Parsons Sch. Design, 1983. One-man shows include Davis Galleries, NYC, 1955—56, 1958, 1960, Hirschl & Adler Galleries, 1963, Maxwell Galleries, San Francisco, 1964, Babcock Galleries, NYC, 1967, F.A.R. Galleries, 1970, Armstrong Galleries, 1985, 1987, Hammer Galleries, 1994, Hudson River Gallery, Yonkers, NY, 2001, 2007, exhibited in group shows at Albany Inst. History and Art, Am. Fedn. Arts, Butler Inst. Am. Art, Libr. of Congress, Nat. Acad. Design, Pa. Acad. Fine Art, Whitney Mus. Art, Collection Nat. Portrait Gallery, Munson-Williams-Proctor Inst., Bates Coll., Brit. Mus., Century Assn., Smithsonian Nat. Portrait Gallery, 2007, others. Louis C. Tiffany Found. grantee, 1956, 60; recipient Purchase prize Am. Acad. Arts and letters, 1964, 84, 11 Gold medals Soc. Illustrators, N.Y.C., 1960-85, Obrig prize for painting Nat. Acad. Design, 1990, winner 1st Benjamin Altman Figure prize, 1992; named to Soc. of Illustrators Hall of Fame, 2002. Mem. NAD, Century Assn. Avocation: jazz piano. E-mail: dschwartz17@nyc.rr.com.

SCHWARTZ, DANIEL C., lawyer; b. Pa., 1943; AB, Stanford U., 1965; JD, George Washington U., 1969. Bar: D.C. 1969. Asst. to dir. Bur. Competition, FTC, Washington, 1973-75, asst. dir. evaluation, 1975-77, dep. dir., 1977-79; gen. counsel Nat. Security Agy., Washington, 1979-81; ptnr., group leader Corp. Compliance and Defense Bryan Cave LLP, Washington. Mem. ABA. Office: Bryan Cave LLP 1155 F St NW Washington DC 20004 Office Phone: 202-508-6025. Business E-Mail: dcschwartz@bryancave.com.

SCHWARTZ, DAVID A., genetics, environmental sciences and pulmonology medicine physician, former federal agency administrator; m. Louise Sparks; 3 children. BA in Biology, U. Rochester, NY, 1975; MD, U. Calif., San Diego, 1979; MPH in Occupl. Medicine, Harvard U., 1985. Diplomate Nat. Bd. Med. Examiners, Am. Bd. Internal Medicine, Am. Bd. Occupl. Medicine, Am. Bd. Pulmonary Medicine, lic. NC, Iowa, DC, Tex., SC. Training in tropical medicine Walter Reed Army Inst. Rsch., 1979; pub. svc. sci. resident NSF, 1979—80; intern/resident Boston City Hosp., 1980—83, chief resident, 1983—84; rsch. fellow Robert Wood Johnson Clin. Scholars Prog., U. Wash., Seattle, 1985—87, pulmonary/critical care fellow, 1985—88; asst. prof. pulmonary disease divsn. Dept. Internal Medicine, U. Iowa, Iowa City, 1988—92, assoc. prof. pulmonary disease, critical care & occupl. medicine, 1992—96, prof., 1996—2000, dir. occupl. medicine, 1988—2000, assoc. chair prog. devel., Dept. Internal Medicine, 1996—2000; prof. medicine & genetics, chief divsn. pulmonary & critical care medicine Duke U. Med. Ctr., Durham, NC, 2000—05, dir. Ctr. Environ. Genomics, Inst. Genome Sci. & Policy, 2000—05, Walter Kempner prof. medicine, 2001—05, vice chair. rsch., Dept. Medicine, 2003—05; prof. environ. scis. & policy Duke U. Nicholas Sch. Environment & Health Scis., 2001—05, adj. prof., 2005—; dir. Nat. Inst. Environ. Health Scis., NIH, Rsch. Triangle Pk., NC, 2005—07, dir. Nat. Toxicology Prog., 2005—07; dir., pulmonary & critical care divsn., dir. Ctr. Genetics & Therapeutics, Nat. Jewish Rsch. & Med. Ctr., Denver, 2008—. Contbr. over 200 articles to profl. jours. in environ. genetics. Named one of America's Top Dr.'s, Castle Connolly Ltd., 2000—. Mem.: Am. Thoracic Soc. (Lifetime Sci. Achievement award), Assn. Am. Physicians, Am. Soc. Clin. Investigation, Am. Fedn. Clin. Rsch., Phi Beta Kappa. Office: Nat Jewish Health 1400 Jackson St Denver CO 80206 Office Phone: 303-398-1903. Business E-Mail: schwartzd@njhealth.org.

SCHWARTZ, DAVID JAY, lawyer; b. Oceanside, NY, June 30, 1967; s. Rand and Sandy Schwartz; m. Amy Roslyn Divak, June 1, 1996; 2 children. BA in economics, Duke U., 1989; JD, U. Pa., 1992; MBA, Columbia U., 1999. Bar: 1992. Corp. ptnr. Anderson, Kill & Olick PC, NYC, 1992—2001; v.p., corp. counsel Toys "R" Us Inc., Wayne, NJ, 2001—02, v.p., dep. gen. counsel, 2002—03, sr. v.p., gen. counsel, sec., 2003—. Office: Toys R Us Inc 1 Geoffrey Way Wayne NJ 07470-2030 Office Phone: 973-617-3500.*

SCHWARTZ, DONALD A., finance educator; b. NYC, Calif., June 19, 1929; s. Preston and Teryse Schwartz; m. Ann Weiner, Jan. 18, 1953; children: Terry Major, Robert. BS in Acctg., Columbia U., NYC, 1950; JD, NY U. Sch. Law, NYC, 1956. CPA Calif., 1989. Commd. officer U.S. Naval Res., U.S.S. Maury, NY, 1951—52; staff acct. CPA firms, NYC, 1953—56; ptnr. Greene & Schwartz, CPAs, Syracuse, NY, 1956—59; v.p. Divsn. Litton Industries, Orange, NJ, 1959—68, Acctg. Corp. Am., San Diego, 1968—89; prof. acctg. and dept. chair Nat. U., San Diego, 1989—. Contbr. articles jour. accountancy. Lt. jg USNR, 1951—52, U.S.S. Maury. Named Outstanding Tchr. of Yr., Nat. U., 2008. Mem.: Am. Inst. CPAs (life). Achievements include first to adapt portable microcomputer as input terminal to computerized accounting system. Home: 13554 Rostrata Rd Poway CA 92064 Office: Nat Univ 11255 North Torrey Pines Rd La Jolla CA 92037 Business E-Mail: dschwart@nu.edu.

SCHWARTZ, DONALD F., city health department administrator; BA, Brown Univ., 1977; MD, MPH, Johns Hopkins Univ., 1982; MBA, Wharton Sch. Bus. Univ. Pa., 1987. Resident in pediatrics Yale-New Haven Hosp., 1982—85; Robert Wood Johnson Found. clin. scholar Univ. Pa. Sch. Med., 1985—87; physician, fellow through dep. physician-in-chief & chief adolescent med. Children's Hosp., Phila., 1987—2008; Mary D. Ames assoc. prof. of child advocacy Univ. Pa. Med. Sch., vice-chair dept. pediatrics; health commr. & dep. mayor health & opportunity Phila. Dept. Health, 2008—. Sr. fellow Leonard Davis Inst. for Health Econ.; sr. scholar Ctr. for Clin. Epidemiology & Biostatistics; mem. gov. coun. Am. Pub. Health Assn.; adv. Mayor's Cabinet for Children, Youth Violence Task Force. Past pres. bd. dir. Phila. Citizens for Children & Youth; mem. adv. bd. Phila. Children's Network; mem. adv. com. Phila. Sch. District; mem. Pulse adv. bd. Univ. Pa. Sch. Law; bd. dir. Healthier Babies, Healthier Mothers; mem. Phila. Child Welfare Adv. bd. Office: Commr of Health Rm 600 1401 JFK Blvd Philadelphia PA 19102 Office Phone: 215-686-9009. Office Fax: 215-686-5212.*

SCHWARTZ, DONALD FRANKLIN, communication scientist; b. Jamestown, ND, 1935; m. Lois Carolyn Schwartz, June 26, 1965; children: Daria, Karin, Marc. BS, ND State U., 1957, MS, 1961; PhD, Mich. State U., 1968. Asst. dir. pub. rels. ND State U., Fargo, 1959-66, chmn. social scis., 1969-71, chmn. comm., 1967-79; instr. comm. Mich. State U., East Lansing, 1966-67; vis. scientist US Dept. Agr., Washington, 1979-80; prof. comm. Cornell U., Ithaca, NY, 1980-98, chmn. dept., 1980-85, dir. undergraduate studies, 1995-98, prof. emeritus, 1998—. Vis. scholar U. N.Mex., 1994. Contbr. articles to profl. jours. Recipient Outstanding Svc. award Future Farmers Am., 1976, Svc. award USDA, 1980, A.D. White Prof. of Yr. award, 1993; named Alumnus of Yr., Alpha Gamma Rho, 2005. Mem. Tributes Com. (chair 2007-08), AGR Epsilon Chpt. Centennial Campaign, AAUP, Internat. Comm. Assn. (sec., pub. rels. interest group 1992-93), Am. Acad. Mgmt., Am. Soc. Pers. Adminstrn. (chpt. pres. 1976-77), Pub. Rels. Soc. Am. (nat. faculty advisor student assn. 1989-90, vice-chair educators sect. 1992, Pres.'s Citation for Leadership 1990, nat. ednl. affairs com. 1993-96). Roman Catholic. Office: Cornell U Dept Communication 331 Kennedy Hall Ithaca NY 14853-4203

SCHWARTZ, DOUGLAS, public opinion poll director; BA in Govt., cum laude, Conn. Coll., New London, 1988; PhD in Polit. Sci., U. Conn., 2001. Survey assoc. news election/survey unit CBS Broadcasting Inc., NYC, election night analyst for 60 Minutes corr. Ed Bradley; dir. Quinnipiac Univ. Poll, Hamden, Conn., 1995—. Mem.: Am. Assn. Pub. Opinion Rsch. (past pres. New Eng. chpt.). Office: Quinnipiac U Polling Inst 275 Mt Carmel Ave Hamden CT 06518 Office Phone: 203-582-5201. Business E-Mail: schwartz@quinnipiac.edu.

SCHWARTZ, EDWARD ARTHUR, lawyer; b. Boston, Sept. 27, 1937; s. Abe and Sophie (Gottheim) S.; m. Sheila Kauffman, Apr. 5, 1997; children: Eric Allen, Jeffrey Michael. AB, Oberlin Coll., 1959; LLB, Boston Coll., 1962; postgrad., Am. U., 1958—59, Northeastern U., 1970; postgrad. exec. program, Stanford U., 1979. Bar: Conn. 1962, Mass. 1965. Legal intern Office Atty. Gen. Commonwealth of Mass., 1961; assoc. Schatz & Schatz, Hartford, Conn., 1962—65, Cohn, Reimer & Pollack, Boston, 1965—67; v.p., gen. coun., sec. Digital Equipment Corp., Maynard, Mass., 1967—88; pres. New Eng. Legal Found., Boston, 1990—98. Vis. prof. law Boston Coll., 1986, adj. prof., 1987—89; bd. dirs., chmn. SatelLife Corp. Editor Boston Coll. Indsl. and Comml. Law Rev, 1960-62, Ann. Survey Mass. Law, 1960-62. Home: PO Box 25 Duxbury MA 02331 Home Phone: 781-934-0099. Personal E-mail: edwschwartz@hotmail.com.

SCHWARTZ, ELEANOR BRANTLEY, academic administrator; b. Kite, Ga., Jan. 1, 1937; d. Jesse Melvin and Hazel (Hill) Brantley; children: John, Cynthia. Student, U. Va., 1955, Ga. Southern Coll., 1956-57; BBA, Ga. State U., 1962, MBA, 1963, DBA, 1969. Adminstrv. asst. Fin. Agy., 1954, Fed. Govt., Va., Pa., Ga., 1956-59; asst. dean admissions Ga. State U., Atlanta, 1961-66, asst. prof., 1966-70; assoc. prof. Cleve. State U., 1970-75, prof. and assoc. dean, 1975-80; dean, Harzfeld prof. U. Mo., Kansas City, 1980-87, vice chancellor acad. affairs, 1987-91, interim chancellor, 1991-92, chancellor, 1992-99; prof. mgmt. U. Mo. Block Sch., Kansas City, 1999—2003, prof. emeritus, 2003—. Disting. vis. prof. Berry Coll., Rome, N.Y. State U. Coll., Fredonia, Mons U., Belgium; cons. pvt. industry U.S., Europe, Can.; bd. dirs. Rsch. Med. Ctr., Waddell & Reed Funds, Inc., Toy and Miniature Mus., Menorah Med. Ctr. Found., NCAA, NCCJ, Econ. Devel. Corp. of Kansas City, Silicon Prairie Tech. Assn. Author: Sex Barriers in Business, 1971, Contemporary Readings in Marketing, 1974; (with Muczyk and Smith) Principles of Supervision, 1984. Chmn., Mayor's Task Force in Govt. Efficiency, Kansas City, Mo., 1984; mem. comm. unity planning and rsch. coun. United Way Kansas City, 1983-85; bd. dirs. Jr. Achievement, 1982-86. Recipient Disting. Faculty award, Cleve. State U., 1974, Disting. Svc. award, Kans. State U., 1992, YWCA Hearts of Gold award, 2002; named Jones Store Career Woman of Yr., Kansas City, Mo., 1989, Ctrl. Exch. Woman of Yr., 1995; named one of 60 Women of Achievement, Girl Scouts Coun. Mid Continent, 1983. Mem.: Alpha Iota Delta, Golden Key, Phi Kappa Phi. Office Phone: 816-942-1840.

SCHWARTZ, ELEANORE ANITA, retired elementary school educator, small business owner; b. Milw., Aug. 24, 1934; d. Arthur Eric Hageleit and Anna Wurth; m. James W. Schwartz, July 28, 1956; children: Ray Eric, Ted William. BA, San Francisco State Coll., 1955. Cert. tchr. Calif., 1966. Elem. sch. tchr. Millbrae Sch. Dist., Calif., 1955—59; substitute tchr. Cupertino Sch. Dist., Calif., 1960—67, elem. sch. tchr. Calif., 1961; substitute tchr. San Jose Unified Sch. Dist., 1967—85; tchr. needle art West Valley C.C., Saratoga, Calif., 1986—92; ret. Gift shop mgr. Good Shepherd Auxiliary, Saratoga, 1989—92. Chmn. bd. dirs. The Lace Mus., Sunnyvale, 1999—. Recipient Cross & Bell award, Good Sheperd Cmtys., 1992; named Citizen of the Day, Radio KABL, San Francisco, 1983. Mem.: DEA, Internat. Old Lacers, Inc., Calif., Nev., Hawaii Dist. Luth. Women's Missionary League (v.p. mission svcs. 1979—81, treas. 1981—85, v.p. conv. planning 1986—90). Christian. Avocations: lacemaking, needlecrafts. Office: The Lace Mus 552 S Murphy Ave Sunnyvale CA 94086

SCHWARTZ, ELIEZER, psychologist, educator; b. Arad, Romania, Dec. 14, 1947; came to U.S., 1974; s. George and Elka (Rothchild) S.; m. Dorota Krezolek; children: Dafna, Michal, Amitai. BA in Psychology, Hebrew U., Jerusalem, Israel, 1973; MS in Psychology, Ill. Inst. Tech., 1975, PhD in Psychology, 1977. Cert. clin. psychologist, Ill. Psychologist, chief svc. Chgo.-Read Mental Health Ctr., 1979-80; prof. Ill. Sch. Profl. Psychology, Chgo., 1981—. Clin. psychologist Ray Graham Assn. for Handicapped, Elmhurst, Ill., 1981-89; dir. clin. svcs. Michael Solomon Psychology Ctr., Chgo., 1989-91; instr. Northwestern U., Evanston, Ill., summers 1988—99; dir. neuropsychology Brownstone Ctr., Chgo., 1991-92; cons. Jewish Vocat. Svcs., Chgo., 1983-84, 91-92, North Suburban Spl. Edn. Orgn., Arlington Heights, Ill., 1985-91, Grant Hosp., Chgo., 1991-95; dir. clin. tng. Ill. Sch. Profl. Psychology, 1996-97, dean, prof., 1997—2000. Author: (with others) Severe Developmental Disabilities, 1987, The Mental Status Exam, 1989, 2d edit., 2005; contbr. articles to profl. jours. Mem. APA, ASCD, Ill. Psych. Assn., Coun. for Exceptional Children. Jewish. Avocations: reading, listening to classical music. Office Phone: 312-777-7696. Business E-Mail: eschwartz@argosyu.edu.

SCHWARTZ, ELLIOTT SHELLING, composer, writer, retired music educator; b. Bklyn., Jan. 19, 1936; s. Nathan and Rose (Shelling) S.; m. Dorothy Rose Feldman, June 26, 1960; children: Nina, Jonathan. AB, Columbia U., 1957, MA, 1958, EdD, 1962. Instr. music U. Mass., Amherst, 1960-64; from asst. prof. music to assoc. prof. Bowdoin Coll., Brunswick, Maine, 1964-75, prof. music, 1975—2007. Vis. prof. music Ohio State U., Columbus, 1988-92; vis. composer Trinity Coll. Music, London, 1967, U. Calif. Coll. Creative Studies, Santa Barbara, 1970, 73, 74; composer, pianist, commentator British Broadcast Corp, London, 1972, 74, 78, 83; vis. research musician Center Music Expt., La Jolla, Calif., 1978-79; disting. vis. prof. Ohio State U., 1985-86; music cons. Holt, Rinehart & Winston, Random House, Oxford Univ. Press, Schirmer Books, NYC, 1977—; vis. fellow Robinson Coll., Cambridge U., UK, 1993-94, 99, 2007; vis. prof. Tufts U., 2008. Composer: Island, 1970 (Internat. Gaudeamus prize 1970), Chamber Concertos I-VI, 1977-2007, Extended Piano, 1980, Dream Music With Variations, 1983, Four Ohio Portraits, 1986, Memorial in Two Parts, 1989, Elan, 1990, Rows Garden, 1993, Equinox, 1994, Timepiece, 1994, Chiaroscuro, 1995, Reflections, 1995, Rainbow, 1996, Tapestry, 1996, Alto Prisms, 1997, Vienna Dreams, 1998, Kaleidoscope, 1999, Jack O'Lantern, 2000, Mehitabel's Serenade, 2000, Rain Forest with Birds, 2001, Voyager, 2002, Downtown Crossing, 2004, Summer's Journey, 2005, Chamber Concerto VI, 2007, Cambridge Mosaic, 2007, String Quartet for Louise and Aaron; author: Electronic Music: A Listener's Guide, 1973, Music: Ways of Listening, 1982, (with Daniel Godfrey) Music Since 1945: Issues, Materials and Literature, 1993; editor: (with Barney Childs) Contemporary Composers on Contemporary Music, 1967, rev. edit., 1998; contbr. articles to profl. jours. Nat. Endowment for Arts composition grantee, 1974, 76, 82; Rockefeller Found. residence fellow Bellagio, Italy, 1980, 89; MacDowell Colony resident fellow, 1965, 66; Yaddo residence fellow, 1977; recipient Maine State award Maine Commn. Arts and Humanities, 1970, McKim Commn., 1986 Mem.: Am. Composers Alliance (governing bd. 1994—2000), Am. Soc. Univ. Composers (nat. coun. 1968—72, nat. chmn. 1983—88), Coll. Music Soc. (nat. coun. 1982—88, pres. 1988—90), Am. Music Ctr. (v.p. 1981—87). Home: PO Box 451 South Freeport ME 04078-0451 E-mail: eschwart@bowdoin.edu.

SCHWARTZ, ERIC ALEXANDER, biomedical researcher, educator; s. Daniel Schwartz and Stephanie R. Paulmeno. PhD, Rensselaer Poly. Inst., Troy, NY, 2000. Postdoc. fellow Stanford U. Sch. Medicine, Calif., 2000—04; rsch. health scientist Phoenix VA Health Care Sys., 2004—, chair, instl. animal care, 2006—08, vice-chair, instl. animal care, 2008—, rsch. safety officer, 2008—. Adj. prof. Ariz. State U., Tempe, 2006—. Contbr. articles to profl. jours. Pharmacy aide Greenwich Hosp., Conn., 1985—87; marine rm. vol. Bruce Mus., Greenwich, 1987—88; vol. Beardsley Zoo, Bridgeport, Conn., 1989—98; wildlife vol. Coyote Point Mus., San Mateo, Calif., 1999—2004; keeper aide Oakland Zoo, Calif., 2000—04; wildlife exhibit guide Phoenix Zoo, 2004—09. Grantee, NIH, 1999—2001; VISN, Pilot grant, Dept. Veterans Affairs, 2005—06. Mem.: Am. Assn. Zoo Keepers, Assn. Zoo & Aquarium Docents, Am. Diabetes Assn., Am. Heart Assn., Sigma Xi, Tau Beta Pi (corr. sec. 1992—93). Achievements include discovery of pressure-mediated, bFGF-independent activation of bFGF receptor; ability of saturated fats to amplify existing inflammation. Avocation: aviation. Office: Phoenix VA Health Care Sys 650 E Indian Sch Rd Phoenix AZ 85012 Business E-Mail: eric.schwartz@va.gov.

SCHWARTZ, ERIC PAUL, federal agency administrator; b. 1957; BA with honors in Polit. Sci., SUNY, Binghamton, 1979; JD, NYU, 1985; MA in Pub. Affairs, Princeton U., NJ. Washington dir. Asia Watch (now Human Rights Watch-Asia), 1986—89; staff cons. US House Fgn. Affairs Subcommittee Asian & Pacific Affairs, 1989—93; various positions NSC, 1993—98, spl. asst. to Pres. for nat. security affairs, sr. dir. multilateral & humanitarian affairs, 1998—2001; fellow Woodrow Wilson Ctr.; sr. fellow U.S. Inst. Peace, Washington, 2001—02; sr. fellow, dir. ind. task force on post-conflict Iraq Coun. Fgn. Rels., 2002—05; chief, exec. office, Office High Commr. for Human Rights UN, Geneva, 2003; lead expert Mitchell-Gingrich Task Force on UN Reform; dep. spl. envoy for Tsunami Recovery UN Sec.-Gen. Kofi Annan, 2005—07; exec. dir. Connect US Fund, Washington, 2007—09; asst. sec. for population, refugees, & migration US Dept. State, Washington, 2009—. Contbr. Responsibility to Protect Project Internat. Commn. Intervention and State Sovereignty; vis. lectr. pub. and internat. affairs Princeton U. Author articles and book chpts. on peace ops., humanitarian issues, and refugee policy. Office: Bur Population Refugees and Migration US Dept State 2201 C St NW Washington DC 20520*

SCHWARTZ, ESTAR ALMA, lawyer; b. Bklyn., June 29, 1950; d. Henry Israel and Elaine Florence (Scheiner) Sutel; m. Lawrence Gerald Schwartz, June 28, 1976 (div. Dec. 1977); 1 child, Joshua (dec.); m. James Frances Edward Stuart, Sept. 25, 1999 (div. Aug. 2001). JD, NYU, 1980. Mgr., ptnr. Scheiner, Scheiner, DeVito & Wytte, NYC, 1966-81; social security fraud specialist U.S. Govt., 1982—83; pensions Todtman, Epstein, et al, 1983—85; office mgr., sec. Sills, Beck, Cummis, 1985—86; office mgr., bookkeeper Philip, Birnbaum & Assoc., 1986—87; office mgr., sec. Stanley Posses, Esq., Queens, 1989—90. Owner Estaris Paralegal Svc., Flushing, N.Y., 1992—, Sutel Creative Mgmt. Agy., Flushing, 1999—. Democrat. Jewish. Avocations: needlepoint, horseback riding, tennis, bowling, writing books and cookbooks. Home and Office: 67-20 Parsons Blvd Apt 2A Flushing NY 11365-2960 Office Phone: 718-820-0432. Business E-Mail: alma62950@netzero.com.

SCHWARTZ, GARY E., psychologist, educator; PhD, Harvard U. Prof. psychology & psychiatry Yale U., dir. Psychophysiology Ctr., co-dir. Behavioral Medicine Clinic; dir. VERITAS rsch. program U. Ariz., prof. psychology, medicine, neurology, psychiatry & surgery, dir. Lab. for Advances in Consciousness & Health, dir. Ctr. for Frontier Medicine in Biofield Sci. Author: The Afterlife Experiments, The G.O.D. Experiments, The Truth About Medium; co-author: The Living Energy Universe. Office: Univ of Arizona Psychology Bldg Rm 312 1503 E University Blvd PO Box 210068 Tucson AZ 85721 Office Phone: 520-318-0286. E-mail: gschwart@email.arizona.edu.*

SCHWARTZ, GEORGE R., physician, researcher; b. Caribou, Maine; m. Colleen Jill Schwartz; children: Ruth, Rebekah, Rachel, Moses, Abigail, John Gabriel, Aaron. BS in Chemistry with honors, Hobart Coll., 1963; MD magna cum laude, SUNY, Bklyn., 1967. Diplomate Am. Bd. Family Practice, Am. Bd. Emergency Medicine; cert. CPR instr. Intern King County Hosp., Seattle, 1967-68; instr. dept. medicine U. Wash., Seattle, 1967-68; resident in psychiatry Hillside Hosp., Glen Oaks, NY, 1968-69; resident in surgery Ind. U. Med. Ctr., Indpls., 1971-72; instr. emergency medicine Med. Coll. Pa., Phila., 1972-76, dir. emergency svcs., asst. dir. emergency medicine program, 1972-74; dir. emergency medicine West Jersey Hosp., 1974-76; pvt. practice, 1977; assoc. prof., dir. divsn. emergency medicine U. N.Mex., Albuquerque, 1978-83; staff mem. emergency medicine Heights Gen. Hosp., Albuquerque, 1983-85; with Los Alamos (N.Mex.) Med. Ctr., 1985-90. Vis. assoc. prof. Med. Coll. Pa., 1991—; co-founder Allied Genomics; ptnr.

Brain Resuscitation Rsch. LLC; pres. Schwartz Pharm. and Med. Rsch. LLC. Author: Geriatric Emergencies, 1984; Co-author: (with Tandberg) Emergency Medicine Continuing Edn. Rev., 1981, 2d edit. 1984, (with Bosker) Geriatric Emergency Medicine, 1990; editor: Principles and Practice Emergency Medicine, 1978, 3d edit., 1992, 4th edit., 1999; co-editor Trauma Rounds, 1973-75; editorial bd. Annals Emergency Medicine, 1972-81, Resident and Staff Physician, 1978—, Emergency Med. Abstractrs, 1978-85, Med. Exam. Publ. Co., 1981-87; contbr. articles to profl. jours., chpts. to textbooks. Med. dir. The Bridge Counselling Ctrs., Los Alamos, N.Mex., 1988-91, N.Mex. Poison Ctr., 1978-83; dir. planning com. disaster exercise Phila. Internat. Airport, 1974, Camden County Poison Ctr., 1974-76. Recipient Gallup award, 1973, Giraffe award, 1990. Mem. AAAS, AMA, Am. Coll. Emergency Physicians (charter mem.; pres. N.Mex. chpt. 1980-81), N.Mex. Med. Soc., Univ. Assn. Emergency Physicians (chmn. socio-econ. com. 1976-77), Internat. Emergency Care Assn., Am. Trauma Soc. (founding mem.), Am. Acad. Clin. Toxicology, Am. Acad. Emergency Medicine (founding mem., sec. 1994, bd. dirs. 1998—), Internat. Assn. for Study of MSG and Food Additives (pres. 1988). Achievements include patents in field; research in computer applications in medicine, new medical diagnostic instruments.

SCHWARTZ, GERALD, public relations and fundraising agency executive; b. NYC, June 22, 1927; s. George and Martha F. S.; m. Felice P. Schwartz, June 25, 1950; children: Gary R., Gregg R., Wendy L. Student, N.C. State U., 1944-45; AB, U. Miami, Fla., 1949, BS, 1950; MS in Bus. Journalism & Mass Commn., Fla. Internat. U., Fla., 2009. Staff writer Miami Herald, 1941-44; publicity dir. U.S. Army in Europe, 1946-48; editor Miami Beach Sun, 1950-51; fund raising and pub. rels. counselor Miami, 1952-58; press sec. to Gov. Nebr., 1959—60; exec. v.p. Bar-Ilan U., Ramat Gan, Israel, 1960-61; prin. Gerald Schwartz Agy., Miami, Fla., 1962—. Editor, pub. Jewish Herald Newspaper, 1999-2000; editor, pub. emeritus Jewish Star-Times, 2000-2003. Nat. v.p. Am. Zionist Fedn., 1985—89, 1991—93; pres. Pres.'s coun. Zionist Orgn. Am., 1983—85; nat. chmn. Friends of Pioneer Women/Na'amat, 1984—98; pres. Am. Zionist Fedn. So. Fla., 1970—73, 1986—92; vice chmn. Urban League of Greater Miami, 1983—87, City of Miami Beach Planning Bd., 1953—55; bd. dirs. Greater Miami Symphony, 1982—87, Miami Beach Taxpayers Assn., 1988—89; pres. Civic League Miami Beach, 1985—87; pres. Greater Miami chpt. Assn. Welfare of Soldiers in Israel, 1983—86; chmn. City of Miami Beach Hurricane Def. Com., 1978—86, 1990—97; trustee South Shore Hosp. and Med. Ctr., Miami, 1987—2004, exec. vice-chmn. Miami Beach, 1989—2004; vice chmn. South Shore Med. Ctr. Found., 1989—2004; bd. govs. Barry U., 1985—86; chmn. Econ. Devel. Coun. City of Miami Beach, 1985—91; bd. dirs. Crimestoppers of Dade County, 1991—94; mem. exec. bd. State of Israel Bonds Orgn., 1996—; dep. chmn. Dem. Midwest Conf., 1958—60; bd. dirs. adminstrv. com. Jewish Nat. Fund of Am., 1995—, v.p. Greater Miami region, 1996—97; pres. B Nai Zion Found., Fla., 2009—; v.p. Jewish Nat. Fund., Fla., 2000—; bd. dirs. Temple Emanu-El of Greater Miami, Papanicolaou Cancer Rsch. Inst., Miami, 1962—80; bd. dirs. Fla. chpt. Boys Town of Jerusalem, 2006—08; pres. B'nai Zion Chpt. Fla., 2009—. With US Army, 1944—46. Recipient Jerusalem Peace award State of Israel Bonds, 1978, Jerusalem 3000 award State of Israel, 1996. Mem. Pub. Rels. Soc. Am. (accredited; treas. So. Fla. chpt. 1962-64), Am. Pub. Rels. Assn. (pres. chpt. 1960-61), Am. Assn. Polit. Cons., Nat. Assn. Fund Raising Execs. (pres. chpt. 1977-78), Miami Beach Taxpayers Assn. (bd. dirs. 1994-2000), Miami Internat. Press Club (bd. dirs. 1991-99), Miami Beach C. of C. (v.p. 1978-80, 81-84, 86-87, pres.-elect 1988-90, trustee 1990—), Lead and Ink, Tiger Bay Club (pres. 1986-88), Prime Minister's Club of State of Israel (Greater Miami chmn. 1997—), B'nai B'rith (pres. lodge 1964-66), Theta Omicron Pi, Omicron Delta Kappa, Alpha Delta Sigma (pres. 1965-67), Zeta Beta Tau, Sigma Delta Chi, Soc. Profl. Journalists, Investigative Reporters and Editors, Inc., Jewish War Vets. USA. Office: Gerald Schwartz Agy 21150 Point Pl Unit 406 Aventura FL 33180-4033 Personal E-mail: geraldsch62227@aol.com.

SCHWARTZ, GERALD WILFRED, business executive; b. Winnipeg, Man., Can., Nov. 24, 1941; s. Andrew O. and Lillian Arkin (Leith) S.; m. Heather Reisman, May 15, 1982; children: Carey, Jill, Andrea, Anthony. B in Commerce, U. Man., 1962, LLB, 1966; MBA, Harvard U., 1970. V.p. Estabrook & Co., Inc., NYC, 1970-73, Bear Stearns & Co., NYC, 1973-77; pres., dir., mem. exec. com. CanWest Capital Corp., Winnipeg, 1977-83; chmn., pres., CEO ONEX Corp., Toronto, 1984—; dir. RSI Home Products Inc. Bd. dirs. Celestica Internat. Holdings Inc.; dir. Indigo Books & Music, Inc., RSI Home Products Inc., hon. dir. Bank of Nova Scotia; chmn. Can. Friends of Simon Wiesenthal Ctr. Bd. dirs. Can. Coun. Christians and Jews; vice chmn., mem. exec. com. Mt. Sinai Hosp. Toronto; trustee Simon Wiesenthal Ctr.; founder, mem. adv. bd. HSEG; cofounder, vice-chmn. Can. Coun. Israel and Jewish Advocacy. With RCAF, 1958. Decorated Order of Can. Office: Onex Corp 161 Bay St 49th Fl PO Box 700 Toronto ON Canada M5J 2S1

SCHWARTZ, GIL (STANLEY BING), broadcast executive, writer; b. Ill., 1951; children: Nina, Will. BA in Theater Arts and English, Brandeis U., Waltham, Mass. Humor writer Boston Phoenix; theater co. mgr. Boston; pub. affairs assoc. Teleprompter Corp. (Westinghouse Group W HBO forerunner), 1981—84; mgr. pub. rels. Westinghouse Broadcasting, dir. comm. Group W Cable NYC, 1984—87, dir. comm. Group W TV, 1987—89, v.p. comm. Group W TV sta. group, 1989—95, v.p. corp. comm., 1995—96; sr. v.p. comm. CBS Corp., NYC, 1996—2000, 2000—04, exec. v.p. Comm. Group, 2004—05, exec. v.p. corp. comm., 2006—. Author: (plays) Ferocious Kisses, Love As We Know It; columnist (as Stanley Bing) Esquire Mag., 1984—95, Fortune Mag., 1995—; author (as Stanley Bing): (books) Crazy Bosses: Spotting Them, Serving Them, Surviving Them, 1992, Lloyd: What Happened, 1998, What Would Machiavelli Do: The Ends Justify the Meanness, 2000, Throwing the Elephant: Zen and the Art of Managing Up, 2002, You Look Nice Today, 2003, The Big Bing: Black Holes of Time Management, Gaseous Executive Bodies, Exploding Careers, and Other Theories on the Origins of the Business Universe, 2003, Sun Tzu Was A Sissy, 2004, 100 Bullshit Jobs...And How to Get Them, 2006, Rome, Inc.: The Rise and Fall of the First Multinational Corporation, 2006. Office: CBS Corp 51 W 52nd St New York NY 10019-6188 Office Phone: 212-975-4321.

SCHWARTZ, GORDON FRANCIS, surgeon, educator; b. Plainfield, NJ, Apr. 29, 1937; s. Samuel H. and Mary (Adelman) S.; m. Rochelle DeG. Krantz, Sept. 5, 1959; children: Amory Blair, Susan Leslie AB, Princeton U., 1956; MD, Harvard U., 1960; MBA, U. Pa., 1990. Intern N.Y. Hosp.-Cornell Med. Ctr., NYC, 1960-61; resident in surgery Columbia-Presbyterian Med. Ctr., NYC, 1963-68; instr. surgery Columbia U., NYC, 1966-68; assoc. in surgery U. Pa., Phila., 1968-70; dir. clin. services Breast Diagnostic Ctr., Jefferson Med. Coll., Phila., 1973-78, asst. prof. surgery, 1970-71, assoc. prof., 1971-78, prof., 1978—, dir. breast surgery fellowship, 2003—. Practice medicine specializing in surgery and diseases of breast, Phila., 1968—; founder, chmn. acad. com, sec. of Med. bd. Breast Health Inst., 1990—; edtl. bd. The Breast Jour., 1994—. Author: (with R.H. Guthrie, Jr.) Reconstructive and Aesthetic Mammoplasty, 1989, (with Douglas Marchant) Breast Disease: Diagnosis and Treatment, 1981; mem. editl. bd. The Breast-Ofcl. Jour. of the European Soc. of Mastology, 1996—, Cancer, 1997—; co-editor Seminars Breast Disease, 1997; mem. editl. bd. ONE, Oncology Econs., 1999—; contbr. mroe than 200 articles to profl. jours. Mem. Pa. Gov.'s Task Force on Cancer, 1976-82; mem. breast cancer task force Phila. chpt. Am. Cancer Soc.; mem. clin. investigation rev. com. Nat. Cancer Inst., 1992-95. Served to capt. AUS, 1961-63. NIH Cancer Control fellow, 1968-69 Mem. ACS, AMA, AAUP, Assn. for Acad. Surgery, Allen O. Whipple Surg. Assn., Soc. Surg. Oncology, Internat. Cardiovasc. Soc., Soc. for Surgery Alimentary Tract, John Jones Surg. Soc., Am. Soc. Clin. Oncology, Am. Soc. Breast Diseases (pres. 1981-83), Soc. Internat. Senologie (treas. 1982-90, v.p. 1990-92, sci. com. 1992—), Am. Soc. Breast Surgeons, N.Y. Acad. Scis., Am. Soc. Artificial Internal Organs, Am. Radium Soc., Philadelphia County Med. Soc. (chmn. com. on econs. 1999-2000, bd. dirs. 1999-2000), Internat. Sentinel Node Soc. (founding mem. 2003), Italian Soc. Senology (hon.), Greek Surg. Soc. (hon.), The Phila. Club, Union League, Princeton Club Phila. (pres. 1989-91), Princeton Club (N.Y.C.), Princeton Terrace Club, Nassau Club, Phi Beta Kappa, Sigma Xi, Alpha Omega Alpha, Nu Sigma Nu. Republican. Jewish. Office: 1015 Chestnut St Ste 510 Philadelphia PA 19107-4305 Home Phone: 215-732-1836; Office Phone: 215-627-8487.

SCHWARTZ, GREGORY JOHN, international business lawyer, business and investments transactions specialist; b. Rochester, Pa., Oct. 10, 1958; s. Louis Frederick and Helene (Kardasz) S.; m. Ann Elizabeth Salazar, Aug. 20, 1988. BA in Govt. and Politics cum laude, U. Md., 1981; JD, Cath. U. Am., 1985; postgrad., Georgetown U., 1990-93. Bar: Md. 1986, U.S. Dist. Ct. Md. 1986, D.C. 1987; lic. real estate broker, Md.; lic. title ins. agt., Md., Va., Washington, lic. securities broker. Assoc. Williams and Huffman, Chevy Chase, Md., 1985-87, Conroy, Fitzgerald, Ballman and Dameron, Gaithersburg, Md., 1987-90; mng. ptnr. Schwartz Law Firm, Washington, 1990—. Contbr. articles to profl. jours. Mem. ABA (former program Ctrl. and Ea. European Law Initiative), Md. Bar Assn., D.C. Bar Assn., Montgomery County Bar Assn., Washington Fgn. Law Soc. (former bd. dirs., rapporteur), Suburban Md. Internat. Trade Assn. (former pres. and bd. dirs.), Internat. Trade Networking Group of Washington (founder), Jaycees (bd. dirs. and legal counsel Washington br. 1987-90), Lowry Alumni Investors Club, Phi Alpha Delta, Sigma Alpha Epsilon, Omicron Delta Kappa, KC. Achievements include founded, owned and operated several entrepreneurial businesses. Avocations: horsemanship, tennis, golf, magic, flying, music, motorcycling. Home: PO Box 60675 Potomac MD 20859 Personal E-mail: bizdealmaker@aol.com.

SCHWARTZ, HEIDI K., science educator; d. Russell and Joyce Sandstrom; m. Shannon D. Schwartz, Sept. 2, 1989; children: Shandi, Wyatt. BA, Idaho State U., Pocatello, 1988; M in Learning and Tech., Western Govs. U., Salt Lake City, 2006. Cert. secondary edn.Level 2 Utah. Sci. tchr. Centerville Jr. High, Utah, 1990—. Sci. dept. chair Centerville Jr. High, 1998—2002. SB 61 Ednl. scholar, Utah State Senate, 2002. Mem.: NEA, Nat. Sci. Tchrs. Assn., Davis Edn. Assn. Office: Centerville Jr High 625 S Main Centerville UT 84014 Office Fax: 801-402-6101.

SCHWARTZ, HERBERT FREDERICK, lawyer; b. Bklyn., Aug. 23, 1935; s. Henry and Blanche Theodora (goldberg) S.; m. Gail Lubets, Jan. 23, 1960; children: Wendy Helene, Karen Anne, Peter Andrew; m. Nan Budde Chequer, Mar. 13, 1987; stepchildren: Elizabeth Guthrie, Anne Hamilton, Laura Dunham. BSEE, MIT, 1957; MA in Applied Econs., U. Pa., 1964, LLB, 1964. Assoc. Fish & Neave, NYC, 1964-70, jr. ptnr., 1970-71, mng. ptnr., 1985-91, ptnr., 1972—2004, Ropes & Gray, 2005—. Lectr. law U. Pa., Phila., 1980-89, adj. prof., 1990—, NYU Law Sch., 2003-. Author: Patent Law and Practice, Federal Judicial Center, 1988, 2d edit., 1995, Bureau of National Affairs, 2d edit., 1996, 5th edit., 2006; co-author: Principles of Patent Law, 1998, 2d edit., 2001; contbr. articles to profl. jours. Vice-chmn. Jr. Yacht Racing Assn. of L.I. Sound, 1985-88. 1st lt. U.S. Army, Signal Corps, 1957-59. Mem. Assn. of Bar of City of N.Y., Am. Intellectual Property Lawyers Assn., N.Y. Intellectual Property Lawyers Assn. (pres. 1999-00), Woods Hole Oceanographic Instn. (mem. corp. 2003-, trustee 2006-), Am. Coll. Trial Lawyers, Am. Bar Found., Am. Law Inst., Order of Coif, N.Y. Yacht Club, Riverside Yacht Club, Cruising Club of Am. Avocation: racing and cruising sailboats. Home: 24 Cherry Tree Ln Riverside CT 06878-2629 Office: Ropes & Gray LLP 1211 Avenue Of The Americas New York NY 10036-8704 Business E-Mail: herbert.schwartz@ropesgray.com.

SCHWARTZ, IRWIN H., lawyer; b. Bklyn., Mar. 25, 1948; s. Julius and Sylvia (Holzman) S.; m. Barbara T. Granett, July 3, 1971; 1 child, Matthew Lane. BA, Bklyn. Coll., 1968; JD, Stanford U., 1971. Bar: Calif. 1972, Washington 1972, U.S. Ct. Appeals (9th cir.) 1972, U.S. Supreme Ct. 1977, Internat. Criminal Ct., 2005. Asst. U.S. atty. U.S. Dist. Ct. (we. dist.) Wash., Seattle, 1972-74, exec. asst. U.S. atty., 1974-75, fed. pub. defender, 1975-81; pvt. practice Seattle, 1981—. Fellow: Am. Bd. Criminal Lawyers, Am. Coll. Trial Lawyers; mem.: NACDL (pres. 2001—02), ABA (criminal justice sect. coun. 1991—94, 2002—05), Wash. Athletic Club (Seattle). Avocations: photography, woodworking. Office: 710 Cherry St Seattle WA 98104-1925

SCHWARTZ, J. SANFORD, internist, educator; b. Detroit, Mar. 8, 1949; AB, U. Rochester, 1970; MD, U. Pa., 1974. Cert. Nat. Bd. Med. Examiners, 1975, Internal Medicine, 1977. Fellow USPHS, 1972; intern in medicine Hosp. U. Pa., Phila., 1974—75, resident, 1975—77; chief ambulatory health care Phila. VA Med. Ctr., 1977—78; Robert Wood Johnson clin. scholar U. Pa., Phila., 1976—79, prof. medicine, health care mgmt. and economics, 1989—, Robert D. Eilers prof. health care mgmt. and economics, 1989—98, exec. dir. Leonard Davis Inst. Health Economics, 1989—98, Leon Hess prof. internal medicine, 2007; dir. clin. efficiency assessment ACP, 1981—83. Mem.: Inst. Medicine. Office: Blockley Hall Ste 1120 423 Guardian Dr Philadelphia PA 19104-6021 Office Phone: 215-898-3563. E-mail: schwartz@wharton.upenn.edu.*

SCHWARTZ, JIM, professional football coach; b. Balt., June 2, 1966; m. Kathy Schwartz; children: Christian, Alison, Maria. BA in Econs., Georgetown U., Washington, 1988. Grad. asst. U. Md. Terrapins, 1989—90, U. Minn. Gophers, 1990—91; secondary coach U. NC Tar Heels, 1991—92; linebackers coach Colgate U. Raiders, Hamilton, NY, 1992; college and pro scout, coaching asst. Cleve. Browns, 1993—96; asst., quality control coach, linebackers coach Balt. Ravens, 1996—99; defensive asst., quality control Tenn. Titans, 1999, linebackers coach, 2000, defensive coord., 2001—09; head football coach Detroit Lions, 2009—. Avocation: chess. Office: Detroit Lions Inc 222 Republic Dr Allen Park MI 48101*

SCHWARTZ, JOEL DAVID, science educator; b. NYC, Dec. 12, 1947; s. Theodore and Gertrude (Greenbaum) S.; m. Ronnie Levin, Feb. 17, 1985; 1 child, Yuri Levin-Schwartz. PhD, Brandeis U., Waltham, Mass., 1980. Sr. scientist US EPA, Washington, 1979—94; prof. Harvard U., Boston, 1994—2008. Mem. NAS Com. on Lead, 1989—; mem. NAS Com. on Environ. Epidemiology, 1990—. Author: Costs and Benefits of Reducing Lead in Gasoline, 1985. MacArthur Found. fellow, Chgo., 1991; recipient Silver medal U.S. EPA, Washington, 1984, 86, Sci. Achievement award, 1989, 90, 92. Mem. Am. Statis. Assn., Am. Thoracic Soc., Soc. Epidemiologic Rsch. Democrat. Jewish. Achievements include research in getting lead out of gasoline, showing lead increase blood pressure, associating air pollution with daily mortality rate. Office: Harvard Sch Pub Health 665 Huntington Ave Boston MA 02115 Office Fax: 617-384-8745. Business E-Mail: joel@hsph.harvard.edu.

SCHWARTZ, JOHN HENRY, physician, educator; b. Fall River, Mass., Mar. 22, 1942; s. William and Sylvia Schwartz; m. Janice Halpert, 1965; children: Wendy L., Adam D. MD, NYU Sch. Medicine, NYC, 1967. Diplomate Am. Bd. Internal Medicine, 1974. Prof. medicine Boston U. Sch. Medicine, 1976—. Editl. bd. mem. Am. Jour. Physiology, Bethesda, Md., 1985—2008. Lt. col. Walter Reed Army Inst. Rsch., MC USAR, 1971—76, Washington. Grant, NIH, 1976—2008. Mem.: Am. Soc. Clin. Investigation, Am. Soc. Physiology, Am. Soc. Nephrology. Independent. Achievements include research in cell biology. Home: 241 Perkins St C201 Jamaica Plain MA 02130 Office: Boston Univ Sch Medicine 650 Albany St Boston MA 02130 Office Fax: 617-738-1290; Home Fax: 617-638-7326. Business E-Mail: jhsch@bu.edu.

SCHWARTZ, JONATHAN D., lawyer; b. LI, NY, 1961; BS in Fin. and Polit. Sci. summa cum laude, U. Pa.; JD with honors, Stanford U.; MA in Internat. Rels. with hons., Cambridge U., Eng. Bar: DC, NY. Law clk. to Judge Harry T. Edwards US Ct. Appeals DC Cir.; law clk. to Justice Thurgood Marshall US Supreme Ct., 1988—89; with Jones Day Reavis & Pogue, NYC, 1989—91; fed. prosecutor Office US Atty., Manhattan, NY, 1991—95; sr. positions Dept. Justice, Washington, 1995—2001, prin. assoc. dep. atty. gen., 2000—01; gen. counsel Napster, Inc., 2001—02; sr. v.p., dep. gen. counsel Time Warner Inc., 2002—03; exec. v.p., gen. counsel Cablevision Sys. Corp., Bethpage, NY, 2003—. Recipient Edmund J. Randolph award, Dept. Justice, 2001; named one of Top 40 Lawyers Under Age 40, Washingtonian Mag., 1998; fellow, Harvard U. Inst. Politics, 1999; Fulbright scholar, 1986—87. Office: Cablevision Sys Corp 1111 Stewart Ave Bethpage NY 11714 Office Phone: 516-803-1125.

SCHWARTZ, JONATHAN IAN, information technology executive; b. Oct. 20, 1965; Student, Carnegie Mellon U., Pitts., 1983—84; BS in Economics & Mathematics, Wesleyan U., Middletown, Conn., 1986. Cons. McKinsey & Co., Inc., 1987—89; co-founder, CEO Lighthouse Design (acquired by Sun Microsystems, Inc.), 1989—96; dir. investment group, devel. tools & Java product mktg. orgn. Sun Microsystems, Inc., Santa Clara, Calif., v.p. venture & strategic investments, 1999—2000, sr. v.p. corp. strategy & planning, 2000—02, exec. v.p. software group, 2002—04, pres., COO, 2004—06, pres., CEO, 2006—. Bd. dirs. Sun Microsystems, Inc., 2006—. Office: Sun Microsystems Inc 4150 Network Cir Santa Clara CA 95054 Office Phone: 650-960-1300, 800-555-9786. Office Fax: 408-276-3804. E-mail: jonathan.schwartz@sun.com.*

SCHWARTZ, JORDAN M., lawyer; b. NYC, Oct. 17, 1957; AB, Stanford Univ., 1978; JD, Univ. Chgo., 1981. Bar: Ill. 1981, NY 1988. V.p., gen. counsel Ticketmaster Corp., Chgo., 1985—86; assoc. Cadwalader Wickersham & Taft LLP, NYC, 1987—91, ptnr., corp. structured fin., 1991—. Mem.: ABA, Mortgage Bankers Assn. (mem. secondary & capital markets com.). Office: Cadwalader Wickersham & Taft 1 World Financial Ctr New York NY 10281 Office Fax: 212-504-6666. Business E-Mail: jordan.schwartz@cwt.com.

SCHWARTZ, JUDY ELLEN, thoracic surgeon; b. Mason City, Iowa, Oct. 5, 1946; d. Walter Carl and Alice Nevada (Moore) Schwartz. BS, U. Iowa, Iowa City, 1968, MD, 1971; MPH, Johns Hopkins U., Balt., 1996. Diplomate Am. Bd. Surgery, Am. Bd. Thoracic Surgery, Am. Bd. Med. Mgmt., cert. physician exec. Cert. Commn. Med. Mgt. Intern Nat. Naval Med. Ctr., Bethesda, Md., 1971-72, gen. surgery resident, 1972-76, thoracic surgery resident, 1976-78, staff cardiothoracic surgeon, 1979-82, chief cardiothoracic surgeon, 1982-83; chmn. cardiothoracic surg. dept. Naval Hosp., San Diego, 1983-85, quality assurance program dir., 1985-88. Exec. office Rapidly Deployable Med. Facility Four, 1986—88; asst. prof. surgery Uniformed Svcs. U. Health Sci., Bethesda, 1983—99; sr. policy analyst quality assurance Profl. Affairs and Quality Assurance, 1988—90, dep. dir. quality assurance, 1990; dir. clin. policy Health Svcs. Ops., Washington, 1990—94; head performance evaluation and improvement Nat. Naval Med. Ctr., 1994—99; cardiothoracic splty. cons. to naval med. command USN, Washington, 1983—84; Dept. Def. rep. to task force info. mgmt. Joint Commn. Accreditation Health Care Orgn., 1990—93, chmn., 1991—93, mem. task force IMS Tech., 1993—94; chmn. info. mgmt. workshop Fed. Health Care Study Commn.'s Coord. Fed. Health Care, 1993; corp. med. dir. Medcenter One Health Sys., 1999—2002, trustee, 1999—2003; corp. med. dir. ND Dept. Corrections & Rehab., 1990—2002; v.p. med. affairs Medcenter One, 2002; v.p. Surg. Svc. and Electronic Med. Records Informatics, 2003—05, Surg. Svc., 2005—06; bd. dirs. SCCI; mem. adv. com. Blue Cross Blue Shield Care Mgmt., 1999—2002, v.p. med. affairs, 2002; chmn. rsch. and bioethics com. Instnl. Rev. Bd., 2000—06; mem. exec. adv. bd. Surg. Info. Sys., 2005—08; examiner Nat. Baldridge award, 2006—09; v.p. med. affairs Knox Cmty. Hosp., 2007—. Contbr. articles to various publs. Mem. nat. physician's leadership coun. VHA, 2000—02; trustee St. Vincent's Nursing Home, 2001—05. Capt. USN, 1969—99, ret. USN, 1999. Decorated Legion of Merit, Commendation Medal Navy and Marine Corps, Meritorious Unit Commendation. Fellow: ACS (mem. com. allied health pers. 1985—91, mem. exec. com. 1987—91, mem. accreditation rev. com. edn. physician asst. 1988—94, treas. accreditation rev. com. 1991—93, sr. mem. com. allied health pers. 1991—94), Am. Coll. Cardiology; mem.: AMA, Am. Coll. Physician Execs., Am. Mgmt. Assn., Am. Med. Women's Assn., Am. Thoracic Soc.

SCHWARTZ, LEON, foreign language educator; b. Boston, Aug. 22, 1922; s. Charles and Celia (Emer) S.; m. Jeanne Gurtat, Mar. 31, 1949; children: Eric Alan, Claire Marie. Student, Providence Coll., 1939-41; BA, UCLA, 1948; certificat de phonetique, U. Paris, 1949; MA, U. So. Cal., 1950, PhD, 1962. Tchr. English, Spanish and Latin Redlands JHS, Calif., 1951—54, tchr. Spanish and French, 1954—59; prof. French Calif. State U., LA, 1959—87, chmn. dept. fgn. langs. and lit., 1970—73, prof. emeritus, 1987—; instr. Osher Learning Inst., 2006. Author: Diderot and the Jews, 1981, Poems That Sing by French Masters, 2008; co-author: Mortier-Tresson, Dictionnaire de Diderot, 1999. Served as 2d lt. USAAF, 1942-45. Decorated Air medal with 5 oak leaf clusters; recipient Outstanding Prof. award Calif. State U. LA, 1976. Mem. Calif. State U. LA Emeriti Assn. (pres. 1998-2000), Phi Beta Kappa, Phi Kappa Phi, Pi Delta Phi, Sigma Delta Pi, Alpha Mu Gamma. Home Phone: 626-791-3800.

SCHWARTZ, LILLIAN FELDMAN, artist, filmmaker, critic, nurse, writer; b. Cin., July 13, 1927; d. Jacob and Katie (Green) Feldman; m. Jack James Schwartz, Dec. 22, 1946; children: Jeffrey Hugh, Laurens Robert. BSE, U. Cin., 1947; Dr. honoris causa, Kean Coll., 1988. Nurse Cin. Gen. Hosp., 1947; head supr. premature nursery St. Louis Maternity Hosp., 1947-48; cons. AT&T Bell Labs., Murray Hill, NJ, 1968-97; pres.

Computer Creations Corp., Watchung, NJ, 1989—2005; cons. Bell Communications Research, Morristown, NJ, 1984-92, Lucent Technologies/Bell Labs. Innovations, 1996—2001. Artist-in-residence Sta. WNET, N.Y.C., 1972-74; cons. T.J. Watson Rsch. Lab. IBM Corp., Yorktown, N.Y., 1975, 82-84; vis. mem. computer sci. dept. U. Md., College Park, 1974-80; adj. prof. fine arts Kean Coll., Union, N.J., 1980-82, Rutgers U., New Brunswick, N.J., 1982-83; adj. prof. dept. psychology NYU, N.Y.C., 1985-86, assoc. prof. computer sci.; guest lectr. Princeton U., Columbia U., Yale U., Rockefeller U.; mem. grad. faculty Sch. Visual Arts, N.Y.C., 1990-91; dir. team from Rutgers U. to create world's first computer-generated 3-D model of Leaning Tower of Pisa to test structures, 1999; invited com. mem. info. tech. and creativity NAS, 2000-03; invited juror L'Oreal/Color/Internat., 2000-01; film retrospective Leeds, Eng. Lumen-Evolution, 2002, 2003-04, vis. scholar Ohio State U., 2005-. Co-author: (with Laurens R. Schwartz) The Computer Artist's Handbook, 1992, Information Technology and Creativity, 2001, (with R. Manetti) Mona Lisa: Leonardo's Hidden Face, 2007; contbd. articles to profl. jours including Scientific Am., 1995; contbr. chpts. to books, also Trans. Am. Philos. Soc., vol. 75, Part 6, 1985; one-woman shows of sculpture and paintings include Columbia U., 1967, 68, Rabin and Krueger Gallery, Newark, 1968, Computer Animation, Amsterdam, 2006, Florence, Italy, 2006, Pacific Film Archive, 20056 films shown at Met. Mus., N.Y.C., Franklin Inst., Phila., 1972, U. Toronto, 1972, am. Embassy, London, 1972, L.A. County Mus., Corcoran Gallery, Washington, 1972, Whitney Mus., N.Y.C., 1973, Grand Palais, Paris, Musee Nat. d'Art Moderne, Paris, IBM, (digital print show) Bklyn. Mus. Art, 2001, Chelsea Mus. Art, N.Y.C., 2004, Computer Animation Retrospective, U.K., U.S., 2005, Holland, Italy, U.S., 2006, Wexner Ctr. for Arts, 2005-07, others; dir.: Save the Leaning Tower;. contbr. chapters to books. Recipient numerous art and film awards, Emmy award Mus. Modern Art, 1984, Computer Graphics World Smithsonian awards for virtual reality, art analysis, inventing computer medium for art and animation, 1993; named Outstanding Alumnus, U. Cin., 1987; grantee Nat. Endowment for Arts, 1977, 81, Corp. Pub. Broadcasting, 1979, Nat. Endowment Composers and Librettists, 1981, Arts Coun. Eng., 2003. Fellow World Acad. of Art and Sci.; mem. NATAS, Am. Film Inst., Info. Film Prodrs. Am., Soc. Motion Picture and TV Engrs., Internat. Sculptors Assn., Centro Studi Pierfrancescani (Sansepolcro, Italy, founding mem.). Achievements include discovery using morphing algorithms to determine Leonardo's creative decision-making steps in transforming the Duchess of Aragon into the Mona Lisa using his own features to segue; discovery of reason for position of Christ's right hand and Judas's left hand in Leonardo da Vinci's Last Supper. Personal E-mail: lillianschwartz@lillian.com. *I have always been provoked by and concerned with the mechanical and technological world around me. I enjoy experimenting with traditional media and combining them with technology today. For example, I used computers as an art medium when computers were solely programmed for scientific purposes. By using the computer to understand the creative process I have made clear the intent of the great masters and applied their decision-making steps to my own work. The excitement in creating is to discover and to make a new world. My present success was achieved in part by being able to make new rules and not be hindered by old or obvious solutions.*

SCHWARTZ, MARINE LENORE, humanities educator; b. NYC, Oct. 23, 1948; d. Max Arthur and Barbara Oliver Schwartz; m. Jack Barsman. BA in Sociology, SUNY, Bringhamton, 1970; MA in Psychology, Sonoma Pk Stae U., Rochester, 1974; MA, TESOL Brattelboro Sch. Internat. Tng., 1998. ESL tchr. Lewis Adult, Santa Rosa, 1985—99; ELL specialist SRVUSD, San Ramon, 1999; instr. Nat. U., La Jolla, 2002—04, PDI, Anaheim, 2000—, USD, San Diego, 2002—07; ELL resource tchr. GUSD, Geyserville, 2007—. V.p. CCAE, 1988—90; adult edn. regional rep. CATESOC, Huntington, 1990—94, adult edn. asst. chair, 1994—95, adult edn. chair, 1995—96. Coord. Shomrei Torah, Calif., 1999—, pres., 1984. Mem.: CABE, CLLE, TESOL. Home: 1657 Hopper Ave Santa Rosa CA 95403

SCHWARTZ, MARSHALL ZANE, pediatric surgeon; b. Mpls., Sept. 1, 1945; s. Sidney Shay and Peggy Belle (Lieberman) S.; m. Michele Carroll Walker, Oct. 16, 1971; children: Lisa, Jeffrey. BS, U. Minn., 1968, MD, 1970. Diplomate Am. Bd. Surgery, Am. Bd. Pediatric Surgery. Intern NY Hosp., NYC, 1970—71; resident gen. surgery U. Minn., Mpls., 1971—73, 1975—76, rsch. fellow, 1974—75; jr. resident in pediat. surgery Children's Hosp. Med. Ctr., Harvard Med. Sch., 1973—74, sr. resident in pediat. surgery, 1976—77, chief resident in pediat. surgery, 1977—78; instr. Med. Sch. Harvard U., Boston, 1978—79; asst. surgery Children's Hosp. Med. Ctr., Boston, 1978—79; asst. prof. Med. Br. U. Tex., Galveston, 1979—81, assoc. prof., 1981—83, chief. pediat. surgery, 1980—83; assoc. prof. U. Calif., Davis, 1983—86, prof., 1986—92, chief pediat. surgery, 1983—92, vice chmn. faculty Sch. Medicine, 1990—91, chmn. faculty Sch. Medicine, 1991—92; prof. surgery and pediat. George Washington Sch. Medicine, 1992—96; surgeon-in-chief, chmn. dept. surgery Children's Nat. Med. Ctr., Washington, 1992—96; assoc. med. dir. Dupont Hosp. for Children, Wilmington, Del., 1996—2001, vice chmn. dept. surgery, 1996—2003; prof. surgery and pediat. Thomas Jefferson U., 1996—, vice chmn. dept. surgery, 1996—2003; sr. scholar Sch. Health Policy Thomas Jefferson U., 2005—; mem. staff St. Christopher Hosp. for Children, Phila., 2004—06, surgeon-in-chief, chief divsn. pediat. surgery, 2006—; prof. surgery and pediat. Drexel U. Sch. Medicine, Phila., 2004—; bd. dirs. Phila. Acad. Surgery, 2005—08; prof. surgery Temple U., 2008—; mem. surgery residency review com. ACGME, 2009—. Bd. dirs. Am. Bd. Surgery, 2003—09, chmn. pediat. surgery bd., 2006—09; bd. dirs. Am. Coll. Surgeon Health Policy Inst., 2008—. Mem. editl. bd. Jour. Pediat. Surgery, 1988—, Jour. ACS, 1999—. Vice chmn. Bd. of Childrens Faculty Assocs., Childrens Nat. Med. Ctr.; bd. dir. Am. Pediat. Surg. Assn., 2001—04; pres. bd. dir. Sacramento Children's Hosp. Found., 1990—92; chmn. bd. dir. Delaware Valley Transplant Program, 2000—02; bd. dirs. Gift of Life, 2005—, St. Christophers Hosp. Children, 2007—, St. Christophers Found. Children, 2007—. Recipient Basil O'Connor Rsch. award March of Dimes Found., 1981, Young Investigator award NIH, 1982, Found. for Children Rsch. award, 1982, James W. McLaughlin award U. Tex., 1983, ASPEN-Rhodes Rsch. award, 1999, Rsch. award Am. Colon and Rectal Surg. Assn., 2000. Fellow: ACS (chmn. adv. coun. pediat. surgery 2004—08, chmn. adv. coun. chairs 2005—08, mem., bd. regents 2009—); mem.: Internat. Soc. Surgery (exec. com. 2004—07), Pacific Assn. Pediat. Surgeons (pres. 1997—98), Soc. Surgery Alimentary Tract, Am. Pediat. Surg. Assn. (bd. govs. 2001—04, pres. elect 2009—), Soc. Univ. Surgeons, Am. Surg. Assn. (prog. com. 2007—09, chmn. 2008—09). Jewish. Avocations: photography, fishing, woodworking. Office: St Christopher Hosp for Children Erie Ave at Front St Philadelphia PA 19134 Office Phone: 215-427-5446. Personal E-mail: mzschwartz@msn.com. Business E-Mail: marshall.schwartz@tenethealth.com.

SCHWARTZ, MARVIN, lawyer; b. Phila., Nov. 3, 1922; s. Abe and Freda (Newman) S.; m. Joyce Ellen Sidner, Sept. 7, 1947; children: Daniel Bruce, Pamela Louise Pier. LLB, U. Pa., 1949. Bar: Pa. 1950, NY 1951, DC 1955. Law sec. to judge US Ct. Appeals, 3d Circuit, Phila., 1949—50; law sec. to Justice Burton US Supreme Ct., Washington, 1950—51; assoc. Sullivan & Cromwell, NYC, 1951-60, ptnr., 1960-92, sr. counsel, 1993—. Mediator US Dist. (so. dist.) NY, NY Supreme Ct. Comml. Divsn.; arbitrator Am. Arbitration Assn., Fin. Industry Regulatory Authority. Spl. master appellate divsn. 1st dept. Supreme Ct. NY; chmn. Zoning Bd. of Adjustment, Alpine, NJ, 1966-74; mem. Planning Bd., Alpine, 1966-67; bd. overseers emeritus U. Pa. Law Sch. With Signal Corps US Army, 1943-46. Mem. ABA, NY Bar Assn., DC Bar Assn., Am. Coll. Trial Lawyers (sec. 1986-88, bd. regents 1981-86, chmn. Downstate NY com. 1976-78), Am. Law Inst. (adviser complex litig. project), Univ. Club (NYC), Litchfield (Conn.) Country Club. Democrat. Jewish. Office: Sullivan & Cromwell 125 Broad St Fl 28 New York NY 10004-2489

SCHWARTZ, MICHAEL, academic administrator, sociology educator; b. Chgo., July 29, 1937; s. Norman and Lillian (Ruthenberg) S.; m. Ettabelle Slutsky, Aug. 23, 1959 (div. Jan. 1998); children: Monica, Kenneth, Rachel; m. Joanne Rand (Whitmore)Schwartz, Nov. 10, 1998. BS in Psychology, U. Ill., 1958, MA in Indsl. Rels., 1959, PhD in Sociology, 1962; LLD (hon.), Youngstown State U., 1990. Asst. prof. sociology and psychology Wayne State U., Detroit, 1962-64; asst. prof. sociology Ind. U., Bloomington, 1964, assoc. prof. sociology, 1966-70; prof., chmn. dept. sociology Fla. Atlantic U., Boca Raton, 1970-72, dean Coll. Social Sci., 1972-76; v.p. grad. studies and rsch. Kent State U., Ohio, 1976-78, interim pres. Ohio, 1977, acting v.p. acad. affairs Ohio, 1977-78, v.p. acad. and student affairs Ohio, 1978-80, provost, v.p. acad. and student affairs Ohio, 1980-82, pres. Ohio, 1982-91, pres. emeritus and trustee's prof., 1991; interim pres. Cleve. State U., 2001, pres., 2001—. Trustee Ctrl. State U., 1996-97; acting dir. Inst. for Social Rsch., Ind. U., 1966-67; tng. cons. Operation Head Start in Ind., 1964-70; cons. Office of Manpower, Automation and Tng., U.S. Dept. Labor, 1964-65. Cons. editor, Sociometry, 1966-70, assoc. editor, 1970; reader Am. Sociol. Rev. papers; author: (with Elton F. Jackson) Study Guide to the Study of Sociology, 1968; contbr. articles to profl. jours., chpts. to books. Chmn. Mid-Am. Conf. Coun. Pres.; rep. Nat. Coll. Athletic Assn. Pres.'s Commn.; chmn. divsn. I, 1988; corps evaluators North Ctrl. Assn. Colls. and Schs.; mem. bd. visitors Air U., USAF; mem. Akron (Ohio) Regional Devel. Bd., N.E. Ednl. TV of Ohio, Inc., N.E. Ohio Univs. Coll. Medicine; trustee Akron Symphony Orch. Assn.; mem. State of Ohio Post-Secondary Rev. Entity, 1995; mem. Assn. of Governing Bds. Commn. on Strengthening the Presidency. Recipient Disting. Tchr. award Fla. Atlantic U., 1970-71, Meritorious Svc. award Am. Assn. State Colls. and Univs., 1990; Michael Schwartz Ctr., Kent State U., named in his honor, 1991. Mem. Ohio Tchr. Edn. and Cert. Adv. Commn., Pine Lake Trout Club. Office: Office of the President Cleveland State Univ 2121 Euclid Ave Cleveland OH 44115 E-mail: mschwartz@educ.kent.edu.

SCHWARTZ, MICHAEL, professor, researcher; b. NYC, May 9, 1942; s. Leon and Beatrice Krevans Schwartz; children: Shanna, Rebecca, Joshua, Julia, Katherine. BA, U. Calif., Berkeley, 1964; PhD, Harvard U., Cambridge, Mass., 1971. Author: (book) Radical Protest and Social Structure (Hon. Mention, Sorokin award, Am. Sociol. Assn., 1978), Power Structure of American Business (Finalist, Disting. Scholarship award, ASA, 1988), The Corporate Elite as a Ruling Class, War Without End: The Iraq War In Content, 2008; contbr. articles to profl. jours. Steering com. Ad Hoc Com. to End Discrimination, San Francisco; mem., steering com. Harvard U. Student Strike, Cambridge, 1969. Grantee Math. Analysis Corp. Networks, NSF, 1974—76, Causes Indsl. Decline, 1986—89, Russell Sage Found., 1995—96; fellow, Guggenheim Found., 1980—81. Mem.: Market Cast, Inc. (founding ptnr. 1990—2000), Ea. Sociol. Soc., Am. Sociol. Assn. (editor, rose series in Sociology 2004—). Business E-Mail: ms42@optonline.net.

SCHWARTZ, MICHAEL, legislative staff member; With Operation Rescue; dir. Ctr. Social Policy Free Congress Found., Washington; exec. dir. House Family Caucus, 1995; chief of staff Representative Tom Coburn; v.p. govt. rels. Concerned Women for America, 2002—04; campaign mgr. Tom Coburn senatorial campaign, 2004; chief of staff Senator Tom Coburn, Washington, 2005—. Co-author: Gay, AIDS and You, 1998. Republican. Roman Catholic. Office: Office of Senator Tom Coburn 172 Senate Russell Office Bldg Washington DC 20510-3604 Office Phone: 202-224-5754. E-mail: michael_schwartz@coburn.senate.gov.*

SCHWARTZ, MICHAEL ROBINSON, management consultant; b. St. Louis, Mar. 18, 1940; s. Henry G. and Edith C. (Robinson) Schwartz; m. Kathleen Nowicki, Dec. 9, 1989; children from previous marriage: Christine, Richard. AB, Dartmouth Coll., 1962; MHA, U. Minn., 1964. Asst. in adminstrn. Shands Tchg. Hosp., Gainesville, Fla., 1966-67, asst. dir., 1967-68, assoc. dir., 1968-73; assoc. adminstr. St. Joseph Mercy Hosp., Pontiac, Mich., 1973-76, pres., 1976-85; exec. v.p. Mercy Health Svcs., Farmington Hills, Mich., 1985-96, COO, 1988-96; exec. v.p. Ea. Mich. region Sisters of Mercy Health Corp., 1991-92; pvt. practice Birmingham, Mich., 1996—2004, 2007—; dir. provider rels. Blue Cross Blue Shield of Mich., 2003—04, v.p. contracting, 2004—05, sr. v.p. network rels. contracting, pharmacy Mich., 2005—07. Non-resident lectr. U. Mich., 1982—93; cons. prof. Oakland U., 1980—88; asst. prof. hosp. adminstrn. U. Fla., 1967—73; pres. Eastern Mich. Regional Bd. Sisters of Mercy Health Corp., 1976—79; v.p. Lourdes Nursing Home, 1981—84, United Way-Pontiac/North Oakland, 1982—84; treas. Oakland Health Edn. Program, 1978—79; bd. dirs. Blue Cross/Blue Shield of Mich., 1982—86, coms., 1978—86, chair hosp. contingent to participating hosp. agreement adv. com., 1989—96; bd. dirs. Vis. Nurse Assn., Inc., 1997—2005, treas., 1998—2004, vice chair, 1999—2000, chair, 2000—02; chmn. bd. dirs., pres. Accord Ins. Co. Ltd., 1983—88; chmn. bd. dirs. Mercy Health Plans, 1986—96, Venzke Svc. Co., 1983—88, pres., 1983—84; chmn. bd. dirs., pres. Venzke Ins. Co. Ltd., 1988—96; mem. audit and fin. com. Am. Healthcare Sys., 1988—92; mem. S.E. Mich. Hosp. Coun., chmn. pub. rels. com., 1983—85; mem. Commonfund Healthcare Coun., 1999—2005, U. Detroit Mercy Health Professions Adv. Bd., 2002—07; trustee Sisters of Mercy Health Corp., 1991—93, sec. bd. trustees, 1993; bd. dirs. Hosp. Fund, 1986—96, Visiting Nurse Svc. Corp., 2007—, DenteMax, 2007—, vice chair, 2009. Mem. charitable trust Sisters of Mercy, Regional Cmty. Detroit, 1999—2004; bd. mem. Am. Red Cross Southeastern Mich. Blood Region, 2008—; adv. bd. mem. Global Health Svcs. Network, 2008—. With US Army, 1964—66. Fellow: Am. Coll. Healthcare Execs. (life; mem. exec. com. higher edn. 1990—93, Mich. Regent's award 1992); mem.: Comprehensive Health Planning Coun. (com. mem. 1976—81), Am. Healthcare Sys. Risk Retention Group (bd. dirs. 1990—91), Mich. Hosp. Assn. (at-large rep. corp. bd. 1990—96, exec. com. 1992—96), Pontiac Urban League (pers. com. 1979). Office Phone: 313-378-8400. Business E-Mail: mschwartzbham@aol.com.

SCHWARTZ, MILES JOSEPH, retired cardiologist; b. Richmond, Va., Aug. 7, 1925; s. Hugo and Ella ((Kramer)) Schwartz; m. Margery Baer Schwartz, June 7, 1956 (div. 1972); children: Elizabeth, James, Margaret; m. Katherine Rush, May 26, 1980. BS, Queens Coll., NYC, 1947; MD, N.Y. Univ., 1951. Diplomate Am. Bd. Internal Medicine, Am. Bd. Cardiovasc. Disease. Interne Mt. Sinai Hosp., NYC, 1951-52; resident Bronx VA Hosp., NY, 1952-53, Mt. Sinai Hosp., NYC, 1953-54; fellow Bronx VA Hosp., NY, 1954—55, asst. med. sect. chief, 1956-58; resident, to chief resident St. Luke's Hosp. Ctr., NYC, 1955-56, asst. attending physician to assoc. cardiologist, 1959-69, chief hypertension clinic, 1959-81, dir. clin. cardiology tng. program, 1966—97, attending physician, 1970-98, clin. dir. pvt. med. svc., 1974-78, assoc. dir. medicine, 1978-84, assoc. dir. cardiology divsn., 1987—97; acting dir. cardiology divsn. St. Luke's Roosevelt Hosp., NYC, 1995—96; pres. Williamsburg Healthcare Consortium, 2001—03; ret., 2003. Cons. Sharon (Conn.) Hosp., 1976—91; prof. emeritus clin. med. Columbia U., Physicians and Surgeons, NYC, 1998; mem. animal, human instl. rev. bds. Coll. of William and Mary, Williamsburg, Va., 2003—07. Served in USNR, 1944—46. Fellow: ACP, Am. Heart Assn., Am. Coll. Cardiology; mem.: Phi Beta Kappa, Alpha Omega Alpha. Jewish. Avocations: travel, history. Home: 128 Alwoodley Williamsburg VA 23188-7466 Personal E-mail: mjschwartz64@cox.net.

SCHWARTZ, MISCHA, electrical engineering educator; b. NYC, Sept. 21, 1926; s. Isaiah and Bessie (Weinstein) S.; m. Lillian Mitchnick, June 23, 1957 (div.); 1 son, David; m. Charlotte F. Berney, July 12, 1970. B.E.E., Cooper Union, 1947; M.E.E., Poly. Inst. Bklyn., 1949; PhD in Applied Physics (Sperry Gyroscope grad. scholar), Harvard U., 1951. Project engr. Sperry Gyroscope Co., 1947-52; mem. faculty Poly. Inst. Bklyn., 1952-74, prof. elec. engring., 1959-74, head dept., 1961-65; prof. elec. engring. and computer sci. Columbia U., NYC, 1974-88, Charles Batchelor prof. elec. engring., 1988-96, Charles Batchelor prof. emeritus, 1996—, dir. Ctr. for Telecommunications Research, 1985-88. Part-time tchr. Adelphi Coll., 1951-52, CCNY, 1952; cons. radiation physicist Montefiore Hosp., N.Y.C., 1954-56; vis. prof. sys. sci. dept. UCLA, 1964; vis. prof. dept. elec. engring. and computer sci. Columbia U., 1973-74; vis. prof. dept. electronic and elec. engring. U. Coll., London, 1995; vis. prof. dept. elec. and computer engring. U. Calif., San Diego, 1997; chmn. Commn. C, U.S. Nat. Com. Internat. Union Radio Sci., 1977-80; vis. scientist IBM Rsch., 1980, 94, NYNEX Sci. and Tech., 1986; vis. mem. tech. staff AT&T Bell Labs., 1995; cons. in field. Author: Information Transmission, Modulation and Noise, 4th edit., 1990, (with L. Shaw) Signal Processing, 1975, Computer Communication Network Design and Analysis, 1977, Telecommunications Networks, 1987, Broadband Integrated Networks, 1996; editor, contbr.: Communication Systems and Techniques, 1966, reissued, 1995; Mobile Wireless Comm., 2005. Trustee Gt. Neck Libr., 1997-2001, pres., 1998, 99. With US Army, 1944—46, with AUS, 1944—46. NSF sci. faculty fellow, 1965-66; recipient Disting. Vis. award Australian-Am. Ednl. Found., 1975, Vis. Scientist award Nippon Tel. & Tel., 1981, Tchg. award Columbia U., 1984, Gano Dunn award Cooper Union, 1986, Mayor's award for excellence in tech., City of N.Y., 1995; finalist Mayor's Awards for Excellence in Sci. & Tech., City of N.Y., 1992, recipient Okawa award for contbns. comm., computer networks, engring. edn., 2003. Fellow AAAS, IEEE (chmn. adminstrv. com. profl. group info. theory 1964-65, bd. dirs. 1978-79, bd. govs. Comm. Soc. 1973-79, v.p. 1982-83, pres. 1984-85, Edn. medal 1983, IEEE Centennial Hall of Fame 1984, Region 1 award for leadership in mgmt. Ctr. for Telecom. Rsch. 1990, Edwin Armstrong award for contbns. to telecomm. 1994, Millennium medal 2000); mem. NAE, AAUP (chpt. pres. 1970-72), Soc. History Tech., Tau Beta Pi, Eta Kappa Nu (eminent mem. 2001). Home: 66 Maple Dr Great Neck NY 11021-1928 Office: Columbia U Schapiro CEPSR Rm 806 New York NY 10027 Home Phone: 516-466-6076; Office Phone: 212-854-3125. Personal E-mail: mcschw66@aol.com. Business E-Mail: schwartz@ee.columbia.edu.

SCHWARTZ, NEENA BETTY, endocrinologist, educator; b. Balt., Dec. 10, 1926; d. Paul Howard and Pauline (Shulman) S. AB, Goucher Coll., 1948, DSc (hon.), 1982; MS, Northwestern U., 1950, PhD, 1953. From instr. to prof. U. Ill. Coll. Medicine, Chgo., 1953—72, asst. dean for faculty, 1968—70; prof. physiology Northwestern U. Med. Sch., Chgo., 1973—74; Deering prof. Northwestern U., Evanston, Ill., 1974—99, chmn. dept. biol. scis., 1974-78, acting dean, Coll. Arts and Scis., 1996-97, prof. emeritus, 2000—. Contbr. articles to profl. jours., chapters to books. NIH rsch. grantee, 1955—. Fellow: AAAS (exec. bd. 1998—2002, Lifetime Mentor award 2003); mem.: Soc. for Neurosci., Am. Physiol. Soc., Soc. for Study of Reproduction (dir. 1975—77, exec. v.p. 1976—77, pres. 1977—78, Carl Hartman award 1992), Endocrine Soc. (v.p. 1970—71, mem. coun. 1979—83, pres. 1982—83, Williams award 1985, Disting. Educator award 1998), Am. Acad. Arts and Scis. Home: 1511 Lincoln St Evanston IL 60201-2338 Office Phone: 847-491-5529. Business E-Mail: n-schwartz@northwestern.edu.

SCHWARTZ, NORTON A., career military officer; b. 1951; m. Suzanne Schwartz. BA in Polit. Sci. & Internat. Affairs, USAF Acad., Colorado, 1973; MBA, Cen. Mich. U., 1983; grad., Squadron Officer Sch., Alabama, 1977, Armed Forces Staff Coll., Virginia, 1984, Nat. War Coll., Washington, DC, 1989; seminar fellow, MIT, 1994. Commd. 2d lt. USAF, 1973, advanced through grades to gen., 2005, C-130E aircraft comdr. 776th & 21st tactical airlift squadrons Clark AFB, Philippines, 1975—77, C-130E/H flight examiner 61st Tactical Airlift Squadron Little Rock AFB, Ark., 1977—79, intern Air Staff Training Program, Office of the Dep. Chief of Staff for Plans, Ops, & Readiness, USAF Hdqs., 1979—80, MC-130E flight examiner, 8th Spl. ops. Squadron Hurlburt Field, Fla., 1980—83; action officer Directorate of Plans Hdqs. USAF, Office of Dep. Chief of Staff Plans & Ops., Washington, 1984-86; comdr. 36th Tactical Airlift Squadron, McChord AFB, Wash., 1986-88; dir. plans & policy Spl. Ops. Command Europe, Stuttgart-Vaihingen, Germany, 1989-91; dep. comdr. for ops., comdr. 1st Spl. Ops. Group, Hurlburt Field, Fla., 1991-93; dep. dir. ops., dep. dir. forces Office Dep. Chief of Staff for Plans and Ops., Hdqs. USAF, Washington, 1993-95; comdr. 16th Spl. Ops. Wing, Hurlburt Field, Fla., 1995-97, Spl. Ops. Command, Pacific, Camp H.M. Smith, Hawaii, 1997-98; dir. strategic planning Dep. Chief of Staff for Plans & Programs, Hdqs. USAF, Washington, 1998—2000; dep. comdr. in chief US Spl. Ops. Command, USAF, MacDill AFB, Fla., 2000; comdr. Alaskan Command, Alaskan N. Am. Def. Command Region & 11th Air Force, Elmendorf AFB, 2000—02; dir. ops. The Joint Staff, The Pentagon, Washington, 2002—04, dir., 2004—05; comdr. US Transp. Command (USTRANSCOM), Scott AFB, Ill., 2005—08; chief of staff USAF, Washington, 2008—. Decorated Def. Superior Svc. medal with oak leaf cluster, Def. Disting. Svc. medal, Disting. Svc. medal, Legion of Merit with two oak leaf clusters, Def. Meritorious Svc. medal, Meritorious Svc. medal with two oak leaf clusters, Air Force Commendation medal with oak leaf cluster, Army Commendation medal Jewish. Office: USAF 1670 Air Force Pentagon Washington DC 20330*

SCHWARTZ, RENEE GERSTLER, lawyer; b. Bklyn., June 18, 1933; d. Samuel and Lillian (Neulander) Gerstler; m. Alfred L. Schwartz, July 30, 1955; children: Carolyn Susan, Deborah Jane. AB, Bklyn. Coll., 1953; LLB, Columbia U., 1955. Bar: N.Y. 1956, U.S. Dist. Ct. (so. and ea. dists.) N.Y. 1956, U.S. Ct. Appeals (2d cir.) 1956, U.S. Dist. Ct. D.C. 1983, U.S. Supreme Ct. 1986. Assoc. Botein, Hays & Sklar, NYC, 1955-64, ptnr., 1965-89, Cooley Godward Kronish (formerly Kronish, Lieb, Weiner & Hellman), NYC, 1990—2008; sr. counsel Cooley Godward Kronish, NYC, 2009—. Bd. dirs. New Land Found., N.Y.C., 1965—. Mem. Bar Assn. City of N.Y. Home: 115 Central Park W New

York NY 10023-4153 Office: Cooley Godward Kronish 1114 Avenue Of The Americas New York NY 10036-7703 Office Phone: 212-479-6040. Business E-Mail: rschwartz@cooley.com.

SCHWARTZ, RICHARD, retired lawyer; b. NYC, Jan. 18, 1933; s. Alexander and Frances (Wexler) S. AB, Harvard U., 1954; JD, Columbia U., 1959. Bar: N.Y. 1959, Pa. 1986, Conn. 1990, U.S. Tax Ct. 1963, U.S. Dist. Ct. (so. and ea. dists.) N.Y. 1976, U.S. Ct. Appeals (2d cir.) 1976. Asst. atty. gen. State of N.Y., NYC, 1960-63; atty. James Talcott, Inc., NYC, 1963-64; sr. atty. GE, NYC, 1964-70; staff v.p. corp. law Sperry Corp., NYC, 1970-86, UNISYS Corp., Blue Bell, Pa., 1986-87; sr. v.p., sec., gen. counsel Financing for Sci. Internat., Inc., Farmington, Conn., 1988-97. Arbitrator Pa. Ct. Common Pleas, Norristown, 1987-88. Editor: Legal Aspects of Doing Business in the EEC, 1978; asst. editor in chief The Internat. Lawyer, 1979-82; author book revs.; contbr. articles to profl. jours. 1st lt. USAF, 1955-57. Mem. Hartford County Bar Assn., Assn. of the Bar of the City N.Y. Avocations: walking, stationary bicycling. Home and Office: 3106 La Mancha Way Henderson NV 89014-3684

SCHWARTZ, RICHARD BRENTON, English language educator, dean, writer; b. Cin., Oct. 5, 1941; s. Jack Jay and Marie Mildred (Schnelle) S.; m. Judith Mary Alexis Lang, Sept. 7, 1963; 1 son, Jonathan Francis. AB cum laude, U. Notre Dame, 1963; AM, U. Ill., 1964, PhD, 1967. Instr. English, U.S. Mil. Acad., 1967-69; asst. prof. U. Wis.-Madison, 1969-72, assoc. prof., 1972-78, prof., 1978-81, assoc. dean Grad. Sch., 1977, 79-81; prof. English, dean Grad. Sch., Georgetown U., Washington, 1981-98, interim exec. v.p. for main campus academic affairs, 1991-92; interim exec. v.p. for the main campus Georgetown U., Washington, 1995-96; dean Coll. Arts and Sci. U. Mo., Columbia, 1998—2006, prof. English, 1998—. Mem. exec. bd. Ctr. Strategic and Internat. Studies, 1981-87. Author: Samuel Johnson and the New Science, 1971 (runner-up Gustave O. Arlt prize), Samuel Johnson and the Problem of Evil, 1975, Boswell's Johnson: A Preface to the Life, 1978, Daily Life in Johnson's London, 1983, Japanese edit., 1990, After the Death of Literature, 1997, Nice and Noir: Contemporary American Crime Fiction, 2002, (novels) Frozen Stare, 1989, French edit., 2008, The Last Voice You Hear, 2001, After the Fall, 2002, reissued as Proof of Purchase, 2007, Into the Dark, 2002 (hon. mention genre fiction Writer's Digest), (memoir) The Biggest City in America, 1999 (Choice Mag. citation), Accidental Soldier: A Reserve Officer at West Point in the Vietnam Era, 2009—; editor: The Plays of Arthur Murphy, 4 vols., 1979, Theory and Tradition in Eighteenth-Century Studies, 1990; contbr. articles to profl. jours. Served to capt. U.S. Army, 1967-69. Decorated Army Commendation medal; recipient Presdl. medal Georgetown U., 1998; Disting. Svc. award, U. Mo. Columbia, Coll. Arts and Sci., 2007; Nat. Endowment Humanities grantee, 1970, 87; Inst. for Research in Humanities fellow, 1976; Am. Council Learned Socs. fellow, 1978-79; H.I. Romnes fellow, 1978-81. Mem. Mystery Writers Am., Johnson Soc. So. Calif., Johnson Soc. of London, Am. Soc. Eighteenth-Century Studies, Coun. Grad. Schs., N.E. Assn. Grad. Schs. (exec. com. 1986-88), Assn. Grad. Schs. in Cath. Univs. (exec. com. 1984-87), Assn. Literary Scholars and Critics, Nat. Assn. Scholars, N.Am. Conf. Brit. Studies, Jefferson Club, Mosaic Soc., Eliot Soc., University Club, Alpha Sigma Nu, Alpha Sigma Lambda. Roman Catholic. Home: 5800 Highlands Pkwy Columbia MO 65203-5125 Office: U Mo Dept English 236 Tate Hall Columbia MO 65211-6080 Home Phone: 573-442-2242; Office Phone: 573-884-7038. Business E-Mail: schwartzrb@missouri.edu.

SCHWARTZ, RICHARD EDWARD DERECKTOR, retired sociologist, educator; b. Newark, Apr. 26, 1925; s. Selig and Tillie (Derecktor) S.; m. Emilie Zane Rosenbaum, June 30, 1946; children: David, Margaret Jane, Deborah. BA, Yale U., 1947, PhD in Sociology, 1952. Rsch. fellow Inst. Human Rels., Yale U., 1951—54, instr., asst. prof. sociology and law, 1953—61; faculty Northwestern U., Evanston, Ill., 1961—71, prof. sociology, 1964—71, prof. sociology and law, 1966—71; dir. Coun. Intersocietal Studies, 1965—70, co-dir. law and social sci. program, 1967—70; dean, provost Faculty of Law and Jurisprudence, SUNY Buffalo, 1971—76; Ernest I. White rsch. prof. law Syracuse U., 1977—2004, Ernest I. White prof. emeritus, 2004—. Mem. com. law enforcement and adminstrn. justice NAS, 1975-85; fellowship referee Russell Sage Found., 1970-77, NEH, 1972-77, NSF, 1978-81; exec. dir. NESCO, 1995-2001; sr. rsch. scholar Yale Law Sch., 2002-04, 2006—. Author: (with others) Society and the Legal Order, 1970, Criminal Law, 1974, Handbook of Regulation and Administrative Law, 1994, Unobtrusive Measures, 2000; founding editor: Law and Soc. Rev., 1966-69. With USNR, 1943—45. Ctr. for Advanced Study in Behavioral Scis. fellow, 1989—90. Fellow AAAS, Am. Acad. Polit. and Social Sci.; mem. Am. Sociol. Assn. (Disting. Career award 2006), Law and Soc. Assn. (pres. 1972-75) Jewish. Home: 40 Beach Ave Milford CT 06460-8154 Home Phone: 203-874-4586; Office Phone: 203-874-4586. Personal E-mail: emnred@aol.com. *I believe that we could create a better way of life if we structured society to encourage-rather than to penalize-altruism. Although I have not yet contributed much toward achieving such a society, the effort to do so has been satisfying.*

SCHWARTZ, RICHARD FREDERICK, electrical engineering educator; b. Albany, NY, May 31, 1922; s. Frederick William and Mary Hoyle (Holland) S.; m. Ruth Louise Feldman, Oct. 25, 1945 (div. Oct. 1977); children: Kathryn Gail, Frederick Earl, Karl Edward, Eric Christian, Frieda Diane; m. Margaret Camp Boes, May 29, 1982. BEE, Rensselaer Poly. Inst., Troy, NY, 1943, MEE, 1948; PhD, U. Pa., Phila., 1959. Registered profl. engr., Pa., Mich. Instr. Rensselaer Poly. Inst., Troy, NY, 1946-48; engr. Radio Corp. Am., Camden, NJ, 1948-51; instr. U. Pa., Phila., 1951-53, rsch. assoc., 1953-59, asst. prof. electrical engring., 1959-62, assoc. prof. electrical engring., 1962-73; prof. elec. engring. Mich. Tech. U., Houghton, 1973-85, dept. head, 1973-79; prof. elec. engring. SUNY, Binghamton, 1985-95, prof. emeritus, 1995—; pvt. practice Endicott, NY, 1999—2005, Peru, NY, 2006—. Vis. asst. prof. U. Mich., Ann Arbor, 1960; cons. Pa. Bar Assn. Endowment, Armstrong Cork Co., Am. Electronics Labs., Inc., IBM, RCA, City of Phila., GE. Co-author: The Eavesdroppers, 1959; contbr. articles to profl. jours. Active Delaware County Symphony, Pa., 1967—72, Keeweenaw Symphony Orch., Houghton, 1973—85, Vestal Cmty. Band, 1993—2005, Binghamton U. Chorus, 1995—2005, Champlain Valley Oratorio Soc., 2005—; mem. exec. bd. Broome County Peace Action, 1995—2005, sec. bd., 1998—2001; active Broome County Interfaith Caregivers, 1997—2005; mentor Schs. to Career Partnership, Endicott, NY, 1995—2005, Learn and Serve Plattsburgh Schs., 2006—. With US Army, 1942—46. Fellow Acoustical Soc. Am.; mem. IEEE (sr., life, vice chmn. Binghamton sect. 2000-04), AAAS (life), NSPE (life), Am. Soc. Engring. Edn. (life), N.Y. Soc. Profl. Engrs. (life, Broome chpt., bd. dir. 2000-05, treas. 2001-04, Engr. of Yr. 1995, Contbns. to Edn. award 1996), Audio Engring. Soc. (life), Found. for Engring. Edn. Inc.(bd. dirs. 2000-04. sec. 2001-03), Order of the Engr., Sigma Xi, Eta Kappa Nu, Tau Beta Tau. Democrat. Unitarian Universalist. Patentee tuning sys., oscillator frequency control, transistor amplifier with high undistorted output. Home and Office: 19 Twin Creek Dr Peru NY 12972 Home Phone: 518-643-6594; Office Phone: 518-643-6594. Personal E-mail: richfredsch@aol.com.

SCHWARTZ, RICHARD HARVEY, pediatrician; b. Bklyn., July 6, 1938; s. Hy and Ruth (Marshak) S.; m. Rose Lynne Hass, May 29, 1960; children: Lisa, Keith, Keira. BA, George Washington U., 1960; MD, Georgetown U., 1965. Diplomate Am. Bd. Pediat., Am. Soc. Addiction Medicine. Intern U.S. Army, 1965-66, resident in pediat., 1969-71; pvt. practice, Vienna, Va., 1972—. Contbr. articles to profl. jours. Maj. U.S. Army, 1965-69. Mem. AMA (Outstanding Contbn. in Adolescent Medicine award 1990), Am. Acad. Pediatrics (rsch. award 1989). Jewish. Avocations: walking, travel. Office: Advanced Pediatrics 100 East St SE Ste 301 Vienna VA 22180 Office Phone: 703-938-5555.

SCHWARTZ, RICHARD JOHN, electrical engineering educator, researcher; b. Waukesha, Wis., Aug. 12, 1935; s. Sylvester John and LaVerne Mary (Lepien) S.; m. Mary Jo Collins, June 29, 1957; children: Richard, Stephen, Susan, Elizabeth, Barbara, Peter, Christopher, Margaret. BSEE, U. Wis., 1957; SM, MIT, 1959, ScD, 1962. Mem. tech. staff Sarnoff Rsch. Labs. RCA, Princeton, NJ, 1957-58; instr. MIT, Cambridge, 1961-62; v.p. Energy Conversions, Inc., Cambridge, 1962-64; assoc. prof. Purdue U., West Lafayette, Ind., 1964-71, prof., 1972—, head dept., 1985-95, dean engring., 1995—2001, dir. Optoelectronic Ctr., 1986-89. Co-dir. Nano Tech. Ctr. Purdue U., W. Lafayette, Ind., 2001—06; cons. solar cells, 1965—. Contbr. chpts. to books, articles to profl. jours. Served to 2nd lt. U.S. Army, 1957-58. Recipient Disting. Svc. medal U. Wis., 1989, Centennial medal, 1991. Fellow: IEEE (William R. Cherry award 1998), Internat. Electronics Con.; mem.: Nat. Elec. Engring. Dept. Heads Assn. (bd. dirs.). Achievements include development of high intensity solar cells, of surface charge transfer device, and of numerical models for solar cells. Office: Purdue U 1285 Electrical Engring West Lafayette IN 47907 Office Phone: 765-494-0619.

SCHWARTZ, ROBERT, finance educator; b. NYC, Feb. 12, 1937; s. Fred J. Schwartz and Shirley Liebowitz; m. Jody Silver Schwartz; 1 child, Emily. BA, NYU, 1959; MBA, Columbia U., NYC, 1962, PhD, 1966. Asst. prof. econs. NYU, 1965—70, assoc. prof. econs., 1970—77, prof. econs., 1977—83, prof. econs. and fin., 1983—91; prof. econs. and fin., Yamaichi Faculty fellow Stern Sch. Bus., NYU, 1991—97; Speiser prof. fin., Univ. Disting. prof. Zicklin Sch. Bus. Baruch Coll., CUNY, 1997—. Chmn. econ. adv. bd. NASDAQ, 1995—97, mem. econ. adv. bd., 1997—99. Author (with Kalman J. Cohen, Steven F. Maier and David K. Whitcomb): The Microstructure of Securities Markets, 1986; author: Equity Markets: Structure, Trading and Performance, 1988, Reshaping the Equity Markets: A Guide for the 1990s, 1991, reissue, 1993; author: (with R. Francioni) Equity Markets in Action, 2004; author: A Trading Desk's View of Market Quality, 2004; author: (with R. Francioni and B. Weber) The Equity Trader Course, 2006; editor (with Ernest Bloch): Impending Changes for Securities Markets: What Role for the Exchanges?, 1979; editor: (with Yakov Amihud and Thomas Ho) Market Making and the Changing Structure of the Securities Industry, 1985; editor: (with Henry Lucas) The Challenge of Information Technology for the Securities Markets: Liquidity, Volatility and Global Trading, 1989; editor: Global Equity Markets: Technological, Competetive and Regulatory Challenges, 1995, The Electronic Call Auction: Market Mechanism and Trading, Building a Better Stock Market, 2001; editor: (with Antoinette Colaninno) Regulation of U.S. Equity Markets, 2001; editor: (with John A. Byrne & Antoinette Colaninno) Call Auction Trading: New Answers to Old Questions, 2003; editor: Coping with Institutional Order Flow, 2004, Electronic vs. Floor Based Trading, 2006, The New NASDAQ Marketplace, 2007, Competition in a Consolidating Environment, 2008; assoc. editor Jour. Fin., 1983—88, Rev. Quantitative Fin. and Acctg. and Rev. Pacific Basin Fin. Markets and Policies, mem. adv. bd. Internat. Fin. & Jour. of Trading; contbr. articles to profl. jours. Mem.: Southern Fin. Assn., Fin. Mgmt. Assn., Am. Fin. Assn. Office: Baruch Coll CUNY One Bernard Baruch Way Box B10-225 New York NY 10010

SCHWARTZ, ROBERT M., lawyer; b. LA, 1959; BS, U. Calif., LA, 1981; JD, U. So. Calif., 1984. Bar: Calif. 1984, US Dist. Ct., Ctrl. Dist. Calif. 1984, US Ct. Appeals, 9th Cir., DC 1987, US Dist. Ct., No. Dist. Calif. 2000, US District Ct., Ea. Dist. Calif. 2001. Litig. ptnr. O'Melveny & Myers LLP, LA, co-chair entertainment and media litig. practice group, mem. class action and appellate practice group. Bd. dir., mem. exec. com. Bet Tzedek- The House of Justice, LA. Named one of 100 Power Lawyers, Hollywood Reporter, 2007. Mem.: Assn. of Bus. Trial Lawyers, ABA (mem. litig. sect.), LA County Bar Assn., Beverly Hills Bar Assn. (co-chair, entertainment law sect. 1998—99, 1999—2000). Office: O'Melveny & Myers LLP 1999 Avenue of the Stars 7th Fl Los Angeles CA 90067-6035 Office Phone: 310-246-6835. Office Fax: 310-246-6779. Business E-Mail: rschwartz@omm.com.

SCHWARTZ, ROBERT PAUL, pediatric endocrinologist; b. Lakeland, Fla., Sept. 29, 1941; s. Sydney and Edythe (Racz) Schwartz; m. Rebecca Chambers, Apr. 29, 1965; children: Sharon, Michael. BS, U. Fla., 1964, MD, 1968. Diplomate Am. Bd. Pediat. Intern, resident Charlotte Meml. Hosp., NC, 1968-70; fellowship pediat. endocrinology Duke U. Med. Ctr., Durham, NC, 1970-71, 73-74; asst. chmn. dept. pediat. Carolinas Med. Ctr., Charlotte, 1974-92; prof., chief pediat. endocrinology Wake Forest U. Sch. Medicine, Winston-Salem, NC, 1992—. Mem. editl. bd.: Jour. Pediatrics, 1996—2003; contbr. articles to profl. jours. Mem.: Pediat. Academic Soc., Lawson Wilkins Pediat. Endocrine Soc., Am. Diabetes Assn., NC Pediat. Soc. (pres. 1987—89), Am. Bd. Pediat., Am. Acad. Pediat. (chair endocrine sect. 1996—99). Office: Wake Forest U Sch Medicine Med Ctr Blvd Winston Salem NC 27157-0001 Office Phone: 336-716-3199. Office Fax: 336-716-9229. Business E-Mail: rschwrtz@wfubmc.edu.

SCHWARTZ, ROBERT TERRY, industrial designer, director; b. Irvington, NJ, Sept. 29, 1950; s. Edward Herman and Harriet Selma (Rosenstein) S.; m. Carol Fawn Mullenix, July 27, 1975; children: Zachary Jacob, Allison Lizabeth. BFA, Kansas City Art Inst., 1973; M of Indsl. Design, R.I. Sch. Design, 1975. Red Cross project dir. R.I. Sch. Design, Providence, 1975-76; head indsl. design/architecture Red Cross Nat. Hdqrs., Washington, 1976-88; dir. sci. and tech. Health Industry Mfrs. Assn., Washington, 1988-90; exec. dir., COO Worldesign Found., Great Falls, Va., 1990-96, Indsl. Designers Soc. Am., Great Falls, 1990-99; dir. indsl. design Motorola, Inc., Ft. Lauderdale, Fla., 1999—2003; v.p. new product devel. Levolor Kirsch, High Point, NC, 2003; assoc. dir. global design orgn. Procter and Gamble, 2003—07; gen. mgr. Global Design GE HealthCare. Provider expert testimony before Congress, 1994, commencement address, Kansas City Art Inst., 1995; official delegate to Nat. Medal of Arts Ceremonies, 1997-98; official state delegate for Md. and Va., Nat. Arts Advocacy Days, 1997-99; sr. tech. advisor to Peoples Republic of China, UN, 1998; appointed to curriculum adv. bd., Coll. Arts, Carnegie Mellon U., 1999-; vis. assoc. prof. design, U. Cin. Contbr. chpts. to books, articles to profl. jours.; presenter in field; holder 5 patents, 1 trademark. Recipient Project of Merit award Indsl. Design Mag., 1985, Cert. of Achievement, ARC, 1988, Louis C. Tiffany award ARC, 1987, Personal Recognition award, Industrial Designers Soc. Am., 2000, numerous others; Nat. Endowment for the Arts grantee, 1984, 92, 94; EPA grantee, 1992. Mem. Indsl. Designers Soc. Am. (Personal Recognition award 2000, Acad. Fellow 2007). Avocations: edison antiquities collecting, sailing. Office: GE Healtcare 3000 N Grandview Blvd Waukesha WI 53188

SCHWARTZ, ROBERT WILLIAM, management consultant; b. NYC, Oct. 23, 1944; s. Edward and Bertha R. S.; m. Gail Beth Greenbaum, Mar. 18, 1967; children: Jill, Evan. BS, Cornell U., 1967; postgrad., SUNY, Albany, 1970. Assoc. IBM, 1967-68; cons. Peat, Marwick, Mitchell & Co., Albany, 1970-71; v.p. Security Gen. Svcs., Inc., Rochester, 1971—77; v.p. fin. and adminstrn. Gardenway Mfg. Co., Troy, NY, 1973-77; pres. United Telecommunications Corp., Latham, 1980-82, also bd. dir.; pres., chmn. Winsource, Inc., Albany, 1982-85, Schwartz Heslin Group, Inc., 1985—. Bd. dirs. Docucon, Inc., San Antonio, State Industries for Disabled, Donnkenny, NY, Daias Analytic Corp., State Zone Capital Corp., Albany, NY, chmn., 2007—; adj. prof. Rochester Inst. Tech., 1971—73, U. Albany, SUNY Albany, 1998—, Union U., 2002—. Bd. dirs. United Cerebral Palsy of Capital Dist., 1973—, NY State Industries for Disabled, 2001-, Albany-Colonie Regional C. of C., 1999-; chair Coun. on Econ. Outreach U. Albany Found., 1998-, chair nanotech. com. Ctr. for Econ. Growth, 2001-04; trustee Newman Found., Rensselaer Poly. Inst., 1974-78, Gov. Clinton coun. Boy Scouts Am., SUNY Found. Mem. Am. Mgmt. Assn., Esarco Internat., N.Am. Tel. Assn., Assn. for Systems Mgmt., Ft. Orange Club, Econ. Club, Corenell Club (N.Y.C.). Republican. Home: 2 Myton Ln Albany NY 12204-1310 Office: 8 Airport Park Blvd Latham NY 12110-1441 Office Phone: 518-786-7733. Business E-Mail: rschwartz@shggroup.com.

SCHWARTZ, ROGER ALAN, judge; b. NYC, May 2, 1945; s. George Martin Ronald and Claire Marie (Dorsch) Schwartz; 1 child, Julia Claire. BA, Muhlenberg Coll., 1967; JD, Temple U., 1973, M in Labor Law, 1976, MPA, 1979; disting. grad., U.S. Army Command and Gen. Staff Coll.; MA in History summa cum laude, U. Scranton, 1997; postgrad., Marywood U., 1997—. Bar: Pa. 1973, N.Y. 1982, D.C. 1976, U.S. Dist. Ct. (ea. dist.) Pa. 1973, U.S. Ct. Appeals (3d cir.) 1976, U.S. Mil. Appeals 1981, U.S. Ct. Appeals (Fed cir.) 1986, U.S. Supreme Ct, 1976. Personnel mgmt. specialist CSC, Phila., 1973-74, asst. appeals officer, 1974-78; sr. adminstrv. judge U.S. Merit Systems Protection Bd., Phila., 1979-89; adminstrv. law judge Social Security Adminstrn., Wilkes-Barre, Pa., 1989—. Arbitrator Phila. Ct. Common Pleas, 1973—89; asst. prof. Inst. for Paralegal Tng., Phila., 1976—77; adj. prof. Keystone Coll., La Plume, Pa. With U.S. Army, 1968-70, Vietnam, Persian Gulf War, 1990; col. JAGC Res., ret. Decorated Legion of Merit, Bronze Star, Purple Heart, Nat. Svc. medal with svc. star, Meritorious Svc. medal with one oak leaf cluster, Meritorious Achievement medal with 1 oak leaf cluster, Army Commendation medal with 4 oak leaf clusters. Mem. ABA, Phila. Bar Assn., Am. Judicature Soc., Am. Arbitration Assn., Res. Officers Assn. (Pa. state sec. 1996-97), Assn. Adminstrv. Law Judges (v.p. region III 2000-06), Rotary (bd. dirs. Wilkes Barre chpt. 1999-2000). Avocations: computers, billiards, piano. Office: Social Security Adminstrn Office Disability Adj and Rev 7 N Wilkes Barre Blvd Wilkes Barre PA 18702-5249 Personal E-mail: rogschwartz@aol.com.

SCHWARTZ, SHEILA RUTH, education and English educator; b. NYC, Mar. 15, 1936; d. Mark Philip and Sylvia (Schwartz) Frackman; children: Nancy (dec.), Jonathan, Elizabeth. BA, Adelphi U., 1956; MA, Columbia U., 1958; EdD, NYU, 1964. Prof. SUNY, New Paltz, 1963—99. Author: How People Lived in Ancient Greece and rome, 1967, How People Live in Mexico, 1968, Earth in Transit, 1977, Like Mother, Like Me, 1978, Growing Up Guilty, 1978, Teaching the Humanities, 1979, Teaching Adolescent Literature, 1979, The Solid Gold Circle, 1980, One Day You'll Go, 1981, Jealousy, 1982, The Hollywood Writers' Wars, 1982, Bigger is Better, 1987, Sorority, 1987, The Most Popular Girl, 1987, (novels) The Little Terrorist, 2001, The Destruction of Carin, 2008, biography F. Scott Fitzgerald, 2008, 09, others; producer, writer (documentary film) The Children of Izleu; contbr. over 100 articles, book reviews, commentaries in jours. and mags. Recipient United Univ. Profl. medal N.Y. State, 1991; Fulbright fellow, Ireland, 1977. Mem. PEN (prison writing com., children's book com. 1988—, women's com. 1987—), Author's Guild, Dir. Children's Book Rev. Svc., 1970—, dir. high/low report 1979-81. Democrat. Atheist. Avocations: tennis, riding, aerobics, skiing, music, piano, travel.

SCHWARTZ, SHIRLEY E., retired chemist, researcher; b. Detroit, Aug. 26, 1935; d. Emil Victor and Jessie Grace (Galbraith) Eckwall; m. Ronald Elmer Schwartz, Aug. 25, 1957; children: Steven Dennis, Bradley Allen, George Byron. BS, U. Mich., 1957, Detroit Inst. Tech., 1978; MS, Wayne State U., 1962, PhD, 1970. Asst. prof. Detroit Inst. Tech., 1973—78, head divsn. math. sci., 1976—78; mem. rsch. staff BASF Wyandotte Corp., Mich., 1978—81, head sect. functional fluids, 1981; sr. staff rsch. scientist GM Rsch., Warren, Mich., 1981—99; part time contractor, trainee GM People, 1999—2003. Contbr. articles to profl. jours. Recipient Gold award Engring. Soc. Detroit, 1989 Fellow Soc. Automotive Engrs. (Excellence in Oral Presentation award 1986, 91, 94, Arch T. Colwell Merit award 1991, Lloyd L. Withrow Disting. Spkr. award 1995), Soc. Tribologists and Lubrication Engrs. (treas. Detroit sect. 1981, vice chmn. 1982, chmn. 1982-83, chmn. wear tech. com. 1987-88, bd. dirs. 1985-91, assoc. editor 1989-90, contbg. editor 1989—2003, Wilbur Deutsch award 1987, P.M. Ku award 1994); mem. Am. Chem. Soc., Soc. In Vitro Biology, Soc. Women Engrs. Life Achievement award 1989), Mich. Women's Hall of Fame (lifetime achievement award 1996), Women of Wayne (headliners award 2000), U.S. Nat. Acad. Engring., Mensa, Classic Guitar Soc. Mich., U.S. Power Squadrons, Detroit Navigators Engring. Soc. (Gold medal, 1989), Sigma Xi. Lutheran. Achievements include development of General Motors system that indicates when the engine oil should be changed; patents in field. *I've spent a number of very pleasant hours trying to make water behave like oil and alcohol behave like gasoline—a quest not much different from that of the ancient alchemists, who also spent their time trying to convert one substance to another.*

SCHWARTZ, SIMA M., music educator; arrived in U.S., 1995; d. Michael Shwartz and Sophia Leshchiner; m. Vladimir A. Shpachenko, June 7, 1975 (div. Oct. 1978); 1 child, Nadia Shpachenko. Grad., Music Sch. for Gifted Youth, Kharkov, 1964; MusM in Tchg. Piano, Accompanist, Performer, State Inst. Arts, Kharkov, 1969. Piano faculty Kharkov Music Schs., 1964—91; accompanist Kharkov State Philharm., 1964—91, Kharkov Inst. Arts, 1964—65; piano faculty Severodonetsk State Music Coll., 1969—72; founder, condr. Jewish Children Orch., Kharkov, 1990—91; piano tchr. Gilloh Dalled Sch., Jerusalem, 1992—95; founder, piano tchr. Sima's Music Club, Cambridge, Mass., 1996—2000; piano faculty The Music Sch., Providence, 1999—2000; founder, piano tchr. Shwartz Piano Sch., Marlborough, Mass., 2000—02; piano faculty Performing Arts Sch., Worcester, Mass., 2003—04. Mem.: Mass. Music Tchrs. Assn. (bd. dirs.), Music Tchrs. Nat. Assn. Avocations: walking, ping pong/table tennis, reading, theater. Office Phone: 774-239-1430.

SCHWARTZ, STEPHEN GREGORY, ophthalmologist; b. Queens, NY, Nov. 28, 1969; s. Charles F. and Patricia Schwartz; m. Melanie Rebak, June 15, 1996; children: Jessica Hope, Reid Alexander. BS with honors, Cornell U., Ithaca, NY, 1991; MD, NYU, NYC, 1995; MBA, J.L. Kellogg Sch. Mgmt., Evanston, Ill., 2008. Diplomate Am. Bd. Ophthalmology. Intern Lenox Hill Hosp., NYC, 1995—96; resident NYU Sch. Medicine, NYC, 1996—99; fellow Baylor Coll. Medicine, Houston, 1999—2001; asst. prof. ophthalmology Va. Commonwealth U. Sch. Medicine, Richmond, 2001—04, program dir. ophthalmology, 2002—04; asst. prof. clin. ophthalmology U. Miami (Fla.) Miller Sch. Medicine, 2004—09, assoc. prof. clin. ophthalmology, 2009—; med. dir., divsn. chief Bascom Palmer Eye Inst. Naples, Fla., 2004—. Bd. govs. Prevent Blindness Fla., Tampa, 2006—; bd. dirs. Va. Voice for Print Handicapped, Inc., Richmond, 2002—04. Grantee Investigator award, Prevent Blindness Am., 2005; Nat. Glaucoma Rsch. grantee, Am. Health Assistance Found., 2003. Fellow: Am. Acad. Ophthalmology (Achievement award 2006); mem.: AMA, Collier County Med. Soc., Fla. Soc. Ophthalmology (bd. dirs. 2006—, Outstanding Young Ophthalmologist Leadership award 2006), Fla. Med. Assn., Assn. Rsch. in Vision and Ophthalmology (members in tng. com. 2003—06), Am. Soc. Retina Specialists. Office: Bascom Palmer Eye Inst 311 9th St N # 100 Naples FL 34102 Office Phone: 239-659-3937. Office Fax: 239-659-3982. Business E-Mail: sschwartz2@med.miami.edu.

SCHWARTZ, STEPHEN LAWRENCE, composer, lyricist; b. NYC, Mar. 6, 1948; s. Stanley Leonard and Sheila Lorna (Siegel) Schwartz; m. Carole Ann Piasecki, June 6, 1969; children: Scott Lawrence, Jessica Lauren. Student, Juilliard Sch. Music, 1960—64; BFA, Carnegie-Mellon U., 1968. Composer & lyricist (Broadway plays) Butterflies Are Free, 1969, Godspell, 1971 (Most Promising Composer & Most Promising Lyricist, Drama Desk Awards, 1971), Pippin, 1972, The Magic Show, 1974, The Baker's Wife, 1976, Children of Eden, 1991, Wicked, 2003 (Drama Desk award, Outstanding Lyrics, 2004), Mit Eventyr/My Fairy Tale, 2005, writer, composer, dir. Working, 1978 (Drama Desk award, Outstanding Dir. of a Musical, 1978), lyricist Eng. Texts for Leonard Bernstein's Mass, 1971, (Broadway plays) Rags, 1986, (films) Pocahontas, 1995 (Acad. award best original score, 1996, Acad. award best original song, 1996), The Hunchback of Notre Dame, 1996, composer & lyricist The Prince of Egypt, 1998 (Acad. award best original song, 1999), Enchanted, 2007, (TV films) Geppetto, 2000; author: The Perfect Peach, 1977; composer: (albums) Reluctant Pilgrim, 1997, Uncharted Territory, 2001. Recipient Drama Desk awards, 1971, 1978, 2004, Grammy awards, 1971, 1996, 2005, Golden Globe award, 1996, star, Hollywood Boulevard, 2008. Mem.: ASCAP (bd. dirs.), Am. Motion Picture Arts Soc., Dramatists Guild (coun.). Business E-Mail: schwartz@stephenschwartz.com.

SCHWARTZ, STEVE WENDELIN, physician; b. Bethesda, Md., May 16, 1955; s. Wallace John and Gwynne June (Lingenfelter) S. AB in Chemistry summa cum laude, Duke U., 1977, MD, 1981. Diplomate Am. Bd. Family Practice. Rotating intern Med. U. S.C., Charleston, 1981-82, resident in family practice, 1982-84; emergency rm. physician Coastal Emergency Svc., 1985-86; family physician Carolina Health Care, Myrtle Beach, SC, 1984—; CEO Cactus Internat., Inc. Data processing dir. HMI, 1984—; pres. Unitrends Software Corp., 1989-2003, chief tech officer, 2004-05; rschr. Symbol Theory; programmer langs. Columnist SCO World Mag.; contbr. articles to profl. jours. Del. ann. meeting N.C. Med. Soc., 1980; participant Intramural Soccer, 1977-80; mem. Intramural Track, 1980, Blacknall Meml. Presbyn. Ch., 1977-80; coord. Boy Scouts Phys. Exam. Program, 1983; vol. cmty. health care project for poor East End Cmty. Health Ctr.; tchr. seminars on alcoholism for drug edn. project Holistic Medicine Group, 1980; Bible study coord. Valley of Achor. With USAF. 1973-75. First Place Durham Open Chess Tournament, 1974; recipient Grand Strand Leadership, 1986. Fellow Am. Acad. Family Physicians; mem. AMA (Physicians Recognition award 1986), So. Med. Assn., Horry County Med. Soc., Phi Beta Kappa, Upsilon Pi Epsilon. Avocations: chess, soccer. Office: Carolina Health Care 4605 Hwy 17 Byp S Myrtle Beach SC 29577-6681 Personal E-mail: steves@sc.rr.com.

SCHWARTZ, THEODORE H., neurosurgeon; Degree, Havard Coll., 1987; MD, Harvard Med. Sch., 1993. Internship and residency Columbia Presbyn. Med. Ctr.; dir. brain tumor surgery NY Prebyn. Hosp., NYC, 2001—. Dir. inst. minimally invasive skull base and pituitary surgery NY Presbyn. Hosp. Office: New York Presbyterian Hospital 525 East 68th St Box #99 New York NY 10021

SCHWARTZ, VICTOR ELLIOT, lobbyist, lawyer, educator; b. NYC, July 3, 1940; AB summa cum laude, Boston U., 1962; JD magna cum laude, Columbia U., 1965. Bar: NY 1965, Ohio 1972, DC 1986, US Supreme Ct., US Ct. Appeals, DC cir., US Ct. Appeals (2nd, 3rd, 4th, 5th, and 6th cir.), US Dist. Ct., DC. Law clk. to judge US Dist. Ct. (so. dist.) NY, 1965—67; from asst. to assoc. prof. law U. Cin. Coll. Law, 1967-72, prof., 1972-79, acting dean, 1973-74, dist. vis. scholar, 2002—; vis. prof. U. Va. Law Sch., 1970-71; ptnr. firm Crowell & Moring, Washington, 1980—2001; ptnr., chair Pub. Policy Group Shook Hardy & Bacon LLP, Washington, 2001—. Bd. visitors U. Cin. Sch., 1998—; disting. vis. scholar U. Cin., 2003—; gen. counsel, bd. dirs. Am. Tort Reform Assn.; chmn. Civil Justice Task Force, Am. Legis. Exch. Coun.; chmn. Dept. of Commerce Task Force on Product Liability and Accident Compensation, 1977-80. Author: Comparative Negligence, 1974, 4th edit., 2002; (with Kelly and Partlett) Cases and Materials on Torts, 1976, 11th edit., 2005, How to Prepare for the Multi-State Bar Examination, 1977, Products Liability: Cases and Trends, 1987, Products Liability: Asset Trends, 1988, (with Lee and Kelly) Multistate Legislation, 1985; editor: Columbia Law Rev., 1965; prin. draftsman: Model Uniform Product Liability Act. Recipient Sec. of Commerce award for disting. svc., Burton award for best law rev. writing in U.S., Tort Summit award, Am. Tort Reform Assn., 2002, The Jeffersonian Award, Am. Legis. Exchange Coun.; named One of 100 Most Influential Attys. in U.S., Nat. Law Jour., 1994, 97, 2006, Pvt. Sector Person of Yr., Am. Legis. Exch. Coun., 2003; named one of 50 Top Lobbyists, Washingtonian mag., 2007, One of 30 Visionaring Lawyers Legal Times Wash., 2008. Mem. ABA (chmn. products liability com. 1979, uniform laws com. 1981, torts and ins. practice sect.), Am. Law Inst. (life, adv. com. Restatement Third of Torts), Phi Beta Kappa. Office: Shook Hardy & Bacon LLP 1145 F St NW 200 Washington DC 20004 Office Phone: 202-783-4886, 202-662-4886. Business E-Mail: vschwartz@shb.com. *The greatest joys in life are found in one's relationships, be it business, romance or friendship, with other people.*

SCHWARTZ, WALLACE L., lawyer; b. Poughkeepsie, NY, 1952; BA, Harvard U., 1974; JD, Cornell U., 1977. Bar: N.Y. 1978. NY office leader Skadden, Arps, Slate, Meagher & Flom, NYC, real estate practice leader. Office: Skadden Arps Slate Meagher & Flom Four Times Sq New York NY 10036 Office Phone: 212-735-2640. Office Fax: 917-777-2640. Business E-Mail: wschwart@skadden.com.

SCHWARTZ, WILLIAM, lawyer, educator; b. Providence, May 6, 1933; s. Morris Victor and Martha (Glassman) S.; m. Bernice Konigsberg, Jan. 13, 1957; children: Alan Gershon, Robin Libby. AA, Boston U., 1952, JD magna cum laude, 1955, MA, 1960; postgrad., Harvard Law Sch., 1955-56; LHD (hon.), Hebrew Coll., 1996, Yeshiva U., 1998. Bar: DC 1956, Mass. 1962, NY 1989. Prof. law Boston U., 1955-91, Fletcher prof. law, 1968-70, Roscoe Pound prof. law, 1970-73, dean Sch. of Law, 1980-88, dir. Ctr. for Estate Planning, 1988-91; univ. prof. Yeshiva U., NYC, 1991—; of counsel Swartz & Swartz, 1973-80; v.p. for acad. affairs, chief acad. officer Yeshiva U., NYC, 1993-98; counsel Cadwalader, Wickersham and Taft, NYC, Washington, Charlotte, London, Beijing, 1988—; mem. faculty Frances Glessner Lee Inst., Harvard Med. Sch., Nat. Coll. Probate Judges, 1970, 77, 78, 79, 88; gen. dir. Assn. Trial Lawyers Am., 1968-73; reporter New Eng. Trial Judges Conf., 1965-67; participant Nat. Met. Cts. Conf., 1968; dir. Mass. Probate Study, 1976—; chmn. spl. com. on police procedures City of Boston, 1989, 91. Chmn. UST Corp., 1993—2000; bd. dirs. Viacom Inc., chmn. governance and nominating com., compensation com.; legal adv. bd. NY Stock Exch. Author: Future Interests and Estate Planning, 1965, 77, 81, 86, Comparative Negligence, 1970, A Products Liability Primer, 1970, Civil Trial Practice Manual, 1972, New Vistas in Litigation, 1973, Massachusetts Pleading and Practice, 7 vols., 1974-80, Estate Planning and Living Trusts, 1990, The Convention Method: The Unused Amending Superhighway, 1995, Jewish Law and Contemporary Dilemmas and Problems, 1997, Does Time Heal All Wrongs?, 1999, Amending Irrevocable Trusts, 2003, The Art of Effectuating a Donor's Wishes, 2005, others; note editor: Boston U. Law Rev., 1954-55; property editor: Annual Survey of Mass. Law, 1960—; contbr. articles to profl. jours. Rep. Office of Pub. Info., UN, 1968—73; chmn. legal adv. panel Nat. Commn. Med. Practice, 1972—73; examiner of titles Commonwealth of Mass., 1964—; spl. counsel Mass. Bay Transp. Authority, 1979; pres. Fifth Ave. Synagogue, NYC, 1997—2001, hon. pres., 2001—; trustee Hebrew Coll., 1975—, Salve Regina U., Yeshiva U. Recipient Homer Albers award Boston U., 1955, John Ordronaux prize, 1955, Disting. Svc. award Religious Zionists Am., 1977; William W. Treat award, William O. Douglas award Fellow Am. Coll. Probate Counsel; mem. ABA, Am. Law Inst., Mass. Bar Assn. (chmn. task force tort liability), NY State Bar Assn., Assn. Bar City NY, Nat. Coll. Probate Judges (hon.), Phi Beta Kappa. Office: Cadwalader Wickersham Taft One World Fin Ctr New York NY 10281 Office Phone: 212-504-6399. Personal E-mail: william.schwartz@cwt.com. *I have been guided by the maxim: "Ideals are like stars. You cannot touch them with your hands, but like the seafaring man, if you choose them as your guide and follow them, you will reach your destiny."*.

SCHWARTZBACH, M. GERALD, lawyer; b. Wilkes-Barre, Pa., Oct. 6, 1944; m. Susan Schwartzbach; 1 child, Micah. BA in Hist., Washington and Jefferson Coll., 1966; JD, George Washington U., 1969. Bar: Mich. 1970, US Dist. Ct. (ea. dist.) Mich. 1970, US Dist. Ct. (no. dist.) Calif. 1974, Calif. 1974, US Dist. Ct. (so. dist.) Calif. 1978, US Ct. Appeals (9th cir.) 1980, US Supreme Ct. 1982. Staff atty. Legal Aid and Defenders Office, Detroit, 1970—71, Mich. State Appellate Defender Office, Detroit, 1971, Bayview Hunter's Point Cmty. Defender, San Francisco, 1974—76; pvt. practice Detroit, 1971—72, San Francisco, 1977—87, 1989—96, Mill Valley, Calif., 1999—; assoc. Law Office of Sheldon Otis, San Francisco, 1976—77, Law Offices of Joseph W. Carcione, Jr., Redwood City, Calif., 1996—99; ptnr. Garry, McTernan, Stender, Walsh & Schwartzbach, San Francisco, 1987—89. Lectr. in field. Vol. Svc. To Am., 1969—70; bd. dirs. La Casa de Las Madres, shelter for battered women, 1981—90. Recipient Outstanding Svc. award, No. Calif. Innocence Project, 2003; named one of Best Lawyers in Am., Woodward/White, Top 10 Trial Lawyers in Am., Nat. Law Jour., 2005. Mem.: Bar Assn. San Francisco (chair criminal justice sect. 1988—91, mem. criminal justice adv. coun. 1988—92), Marin County Bar Assn., Nat. Lawyers Guild, No. Calif. Criminal Trial Lawyers Assn. (bd. govs. 1989—95), Nat. Assn. Criminal Def. Lawyers, Calif. Attys. for Criminal Justice (bd. govs. 1986—93, 2002—07, Skip Glen Outstanding Lawyer award 1986), State Bar Calif. Achievements include the successful defense of actor Robert Blake in the 2004-05 murder trial. Office: 655 Redwood Hwy Ste 277 Mill Valley CA 94941 Office Phone: 415-388-2343. Office Fax: 415-388-2353. Business E-Mail: mgs@mgslawyer.com.*

SCHWARTZBERG, ALLAN ZELIG, psychiatrist, educator; b. Cleve., Dec. 5, 1930; s. Joseph and Jeanette (Eisenman) S.; m. Katherine Weiss, June 19, 1955; children: Shana, Robert. BS cum laude, Case Western Res. U., 1951; MD, Ohio State U., 1955. Diplomate Am. Bd. Psychiatry and Neurology, Am. Bd. Forensic Medicine. Intern, resident in psychiatry Johns Hopkins Hosp., Balt., 1955—59; pvt. practice Gaithersburg, Md.; assoc. clin. prof. psychiatry Georgetown U. Sch. Medicine, Washington, 1979—89, clin. prof., 1989—. Vis. prof. faculty seminar in cmty. psychiatry Harvard U. Med. Sch., Boston, 1965-67; cons. Dept. Energy, 2002-. Editor-in-chief Internat. Annals Adolescent Psychiatry, 1988—2000; co-editor Adolescent Psychiatry, Vols. 8-19; contbr. articles to med. jours. Recipient Vicennial medal Georgetown U., 1984. Fellow AMA, Am. Psychiat. Assn. (disting. life), Am. Soc. for Adolescent Psychiatry, Am. Soc. Psychoanalytic Physicians (pres. 1986-87, 2000-01), Am. Coll. Psychiatrists; mem. Am. Group Psychotherapy Assn., B'nai B'rith, Phi Beta Kappa. Republican. Jewish. Home: 6616 Kenhill Rd Bethesda MD 20817-6014 Office: Comprehensive Behavioral Svcs 9021 Shady Grove Ct Gaithersburg MD 20877-1308 Home Phone: 301-229-3366; Office Phone: 301-590-9000. Personal E-mail: azsmd@aol.com.

SCHWARTZBERG, JOANNE GILBERT, physician; b. Boston, Nov. 30, 1933; d. Richard Vincent and Emma (Cohen) Gilbert; m. Hugh Joel Schwartzberg, July 7, 1956; children: Steven Jonathan, Susan Jennifer. BA magna cum laude, Radcliffe Coll., 1955; MD, Northwestern U., 1960. Diplomate Am. Bd. Quality Assurance and Utilization Rev. Physicians. Founder, med. dir. Chgo. Home Health Svc., 1972—95; founder, v.p., med. dir. Suburban Home Health Svc., Chgo. area, 1975—87; clin. asst. prof. preventive medicine and cmty. health U. Ill. Coll. Medicine, 1985—. Dir. Aging and Cmty. Health AMA, 1990—; pres. Inst. Medicine of Chgo., 1994—95, bd. dirs., 1990—2000, 2005—; co-chair Ill. Health and Social Svc. Caucus to the White House Conf. on Aging, 1995; presdl. appointee to adv. com. White Ho. Conf. on Aging, 2005. Contbr. articles to profl. jours. Pres. Near North Montessori Sch., Chgo., 1972—75, bd. dirs., 1970—83. Recipient Mayor's citation, City of Chgo., 1963, Physician of Year award, Nat. Assn. Home Care, 1988, Henry P. Russe Exemplary Compassion in Medicine citation, Inst. Medicine Chgo. & The Rush Presbyn. St. Luke's Med. Ctr., 2001. Mem.: Alexander Graham Bell Assn. for Deaf (bd. dirs. 1984—90, gen. chmn. internat. conv. 1986, chmn. internat. parents orgn. 1988—90), Am. Geriat. Soc, Chgo. Med. Soc., Ill. Med. Soc., Ill. Geriat. Soc. (pres. 1990—92), Am. Coll. Med. Quality, Am. Acad. of Home Care Physicians (founding bd. dirs. 1987—, pres. 1992—94, Physician of Yr. 1994). Jewish. Home: 853 W Fullerton Ave Chicago IL 60614-2412 Office: 515 N State St Chicago IL 60610-4325

SCHWARTZBERG, LEE S., internist, oncologist, hematologist; b. Oct. 14, 1952; m. Sharon Schartzberg: 2 children. BA, SUNY, Buffalo, 1973; MS, SUNY, 1974; MD, N.Y. Med. Coll., 1980. Diplomate Nat. Bd. Med. Examiners; diplomate Am. Bd. Internal Medicine; diplomate Am. Bd. Medical Oncology; diplomate Am. Bd. Hematology. Intern in internal medicine North Shore Univ. Hosp., Long Island, N.Y., 1980-81, resident in internal medicine, 1981-83; chief resident in medicine Sloan Kettering Cancer Ctr., Ithaca, N.Y., 1984-85; pvt. practice specializing in hematology and med. oncology The West Side Clinic, Memphis, 1987—; nat. med. dir. Response Techs., 1990—. Clin. instr. Cornell U. Med. Coll., 1984-85, U. Tenn. Sch. Medicine, 1987-89; clin. asst. prof. U. Tenn. Sch. Medicine, 1989—; attending staff Bapt. Meml. Hosp., Memphis; assoc. staff Bapt. Meml. Hosp., De Soto, Southaven, Miss.; consulting staff St. Francis Hosp., Memphis, Germantown Meth. Hosp., Memphis, Bapt. Meml. Hosp., Oxford, Miss. Contbr. numerous articles and abstracts to profl. jours., chapt. to book. Bd. dirs., pres. elect Am. Cancer Soc., Shelby County Div., chmn. com. on profl. edn. Recipient Am. Cancer Soc. Clin. fellowship, 1983-84, Nat. Rsch. Svc. award, 1985-86, 86-87; clin. scholar fellowship, 1986-87. Mem. Am. Soc. Clin. Oncology, Soc. for Biol. Therapy, Am. Soc. Hematology, So.Med. Assn., So. Soc. Oncology, Cancer and Acute Lukemia Group B. Home: 530 River View Rd Memphis TN 38120-2617 Office: PO Box 240728 Memphis TN 38124-0728

SCHWARTZEL, CHARLES BOONE, lawyer; b. Louisville, Jan. 4, 1950; s. Charles Joseph and Rosemary Jane (Redens) S.; m. Rose Marie Carlisi, June 20, 1980; children: Sally Ann, Charles Gerard. BA, Vanderbilt U., 1972; JD, U. Tex., 1975. Bar: Tex. 1975. Atty. Vinson & Elkins L.L.P., Houston, 1975-98, ptnr., 1983-98; pvt. practice Houston, 1998—. Contbr. articles to profl. jours. Councilman City of West University Place, Tex., 1985-89. Fellow Am. Coll. Trust and Estate Counsel; mem. Tex. Bar Assn. Roman Catholic. Office: Attorney at Law 1010 Lamar St Ste 1520 Houston TX 77002-6315 Office Phone: 713-654-1133.

SCHWARTZ-GIBLIN, SUSAN TOBY, neuroscientist, educator, dean emeritus; b. NYC, Dec. 27, 1938; d. David Jack and Anne Lila (Garfinkle) S.; m. Denis Richard Giblin, Sept. 9, 1966 (dec.); children: Vanessa Elizabeth Giblin Bibby, Timothy Norris Giblin. BA in Zoology, Columbia U., 1959; PhD in Physiology, Albert Einstein Coll. Medicine, 1965. NATO postdoctoral fellow McGill U., Montreal, Can., 1965-66; instr. exptl. psychiatry NYU Med. Ctr., NYC, 1966-75, head neurophysiology lab., 1966-72; adj. asst. prof. CUNY, 1975-78; guest investigator Rockefeller U., NYC, 1978-81, asst. prof. neurobiology and behavior, 1981-87, assoc. prof. neurobiology and behavior, 1987-93; prof. physiology, dean grad. sch. Med. Coll. Pa., Hahnemann U. (now Drexel U. Med. Sch.), Phila., 1993—97; dean, sch. grad. studies, prof. neurology SUNY Downstate Med. Ctr., 1997—2008; developer joint PhD biomedical engring. program SUNY Downstate Med. Ctr., Polytechnic U., 2004—. Lectr. in field. Reviewer jours.; contbr. numerous articles to peer-reviewed profl. jours. Recipient: Citation Classic Current Contents Jour., 1981; Mark S. Cohen fellow, 1982-85, Philip Femano fellow, 1982-86, Sandra Cottingham fellow, 1983-86, Ann Robbins Sakai fellow, 1986-90, Margaret M. McCarthy fellow, 1989-92, David Holtzman fellow, 1990-92; grantee USPHS, 1968-71, 81-87, 91-95, Whitehall Found., 1990-92. Mem. AAAS, Internat. Brain Rsch. Orgn., Soc. Neurosci., Sigma Xi. Office: SUNY Downstate Medical Ctr Sch Graduate Studies 450 Clarkson Ave Box 41 Brooklyn NY 11203 Office Phone: 718-270-2740. Office Fax: 718-270-3378. Business E-Mail: susan.schwartz-giblin@downstate.edu.

SCHWARTZMAN, ANDREW JAY, lawyer; b. NYC, Oct. 4, 1946; s. Joel Jay and Theresa (Greenhauff) S.; m. Linda Lazarus, June 8, 1986. AB, U. Pa., 1968, JD, 1971. Bar: N.Y. 1972, D.C. 1974, Temporary Emergency Ct. Appeals 1977, U.S. Dist. Ct. D.C. 1978, U.S. Ct. Appeals (D.C. cir.) 1981, U.S. Ct. Appeals (2d cir.) 1987, U.S. Ct. Appeals (2nd, 3rd, 4th, 6th, 7th, 8th cirs.) 1991, U.S. Supreme Ct. 1980. Staff counsel United Ch. of Christ Office of Comm., NYC, 1971-74; atty. adviser Fed. Energy Office, Washington, 1974-77; sr. atty. adviser U.S. Dept. Energy, Washington, 1977-78; bd. dirs. Safe Energy Comms. Coun., pres. bd. dirs., 1989—2003; dir. Media Access Project, Washington, 1978-96, pres., CEO, 1996—. Mem. adv. panel Study on Comms. Systems for an Info. Age; mem. adv. bd. Ctr. for Democracy and Tech., 1996—; lectr. Fairleigh Dickinson U., 1972-73; instr. Johns Hopkins U., 2003—; mem. comms. coun. forum Aspen Inst. on Comms. and Soc., 1992—; bd. dirs. Min. Media and Telecomms. Coalition, 1994—; mem. adv. bd. Nat. Inst. Entertainment and Media Law, Southwestern U. Sch. Law, 2000—, dist. lectr. in residence Southwestern U. Sch. Law Summer Entertainment and Media Law Program, Fitzwilliam Coll., Cambridge U., 2004; mem. adv. com. on diversity for comms. in the digital age FCC, 2007-. Contbg. author: Les Brown's Dictionary of Television, 3d edit., Ency. of the Consumer Movement, 1997; contbr. articles to legal jours. Recipient Everett Parker award United Ch. of Christ, 1994, Just Media Lifetime Achiev. award, 2004. Mem. ABA, Fed. Comms. Bar Assn., U. Pa. Alumni Assn., Sci. Am. Soc (leader in technology policy 2004). Office: Media Access Project # 1000 1625 K St NW Washington DC 20006-1604 Office Phone: 202-232-4300. E-mail: info@mediaaccess.org.

SCHWARTZMAN, JASON FRANCESCO, actor, musician; b. Los Angeles, Calif., June 26, 1980; s. Jack Schwartzman and Talia Shire; m. Brady Cunningham, July 11, 2009. Drummer, founder Phantom Planet; band mem. Coconut Records. Actor: (films) Rushmore, 1998 (Best Performance by a Young Actor in a Comedy Film, YoungStar Awards, 1999, Best Actor, Lone Star Film & TV Awards, 1999), CQ, 2001, Odessa or Bust, 2001, Julius and Friends: Hole in One, 2001, Julius and Friends: Yeti, Set, Go, 2002, Slackers, 2002, S1m0ne, 2002, Spun, 2002, Just Like Mona, 2003, I Heart Huckabees, 2004, The Hitchhicker's Guide to the Galaxy, 2005, Bewitched, 2005, Shopgirl, 2005, Marie Antoinette, 2006, Funny People, 2009, (short films) Hotel Chevalier, 2007; actor, writer (films) The Darjeeling Limited, 2007; actor: (TV series) Freaks and Geeks, 2000, Cracking Up, 2004—06.*

SCHWARTZMAN, PETER DAVID, environmental scientist, educator; s. Barbara Ann Major and David William Schwartzman; m. Huong Minh Hua, June 27, 1998; children: Camellia Nai, Juniper Rose Nai. BS in Physics, Harvey Mudd Coll., Claremont, Calif., 1991; MS in Sci. and Tech. Studies, Va. Poly. Inst., Blacksburg, Ill., 1993; PhD in Environ. Sci., U. Va., Charlottesville, 1997. Assoc. prof. environ. studies Knox Coll., Galesburg, Ill., 1998—. Exec. bd. mem. Assoc. Coll. of Midwest, Chgo., 2000—04. Author: Small is Powerful, Word Nerd Workbook #1 and #2, 2007, Word Nerd Puzzler, 2007; columnist: The Zephyr, 2001—09; contbr. articles to profl. jours. Bd. dirs. Western Ill. Nature Group, Galesburg, Ill., 2002—; vol. educator Knox County Sch. Dist. 205, Galesburg, Ill., 1998—. Recipient Honorable Mention award for original column, Ill. Press Assn. Mem.: Union of Concerned Scientists (assoc.), Amnesty Internat. (assoc.). Office: Knox Coll 2 E South St Galesburg IL 61401 Personal E-mail: drearth1@gmail.com.

SCHWARY, RONALD LOUIS, motion picture producer; b. The Dalles, Oreg., May 23, 1944; s. Mitchell Louis and Lorraine (Ablan) S.; children: Brian L., Neil L. BS, U. So. Calif., 1967. Pres. Red Truck Prodns., Inc., LA, 1985—. Prodr. (motion pictures) Ordinary People, 1980 (Golden Globe award 1981, Acad. award 1981), Absence of Malice, 1981, Tootsie, 1982, A Soldier's Story, 1984, Batteries Not Included, 1987, Havana, 1990, Scent of a Woman, 1992, Cops and Robbersons, 1994, Sabrina, 1995, Mirror Has Two Faces, 1996, Meet Joe Black, 1997, Random Hearts, 1999; (TV series) Tour of Duty, 1987, Now and Again, 1999, Medium, 2004—. Mem. Dirs. Guild Am. Republican. Roman Catholic. E-mail: ronaldschwary@mac.com.

SCHWARZ, BARBARA RUTH BALLOU, elementary school educator; b. East Orange, NJ, Aug. 8, 1930; d. Robert Ingram Ballou and Ruth Edna Sweeney; m. Eugene A. Schwarz, Jr., Dec. 24, 1954 (div. 1977); children: Ruth Ellen, Eugene A. III. BS, Trenton State Coll., 1952. Tchr. West Orange N.J. Schs., 1952-54, Franklin Sch., Ft. Wayne, Ind., 1955-56, Parliament Place Sch., North Babylon, N.Y., 1965-91. Trustee welfare trust fund North Babylon Tchrs. Orgn., N.Y., 1988-91. Vol. Safe Home, Suffolk County Coalition Against Domestic Violence, Bayshore, NY, 1979—90; sec. Victims Info. Bur., Suffolk, 1987—88, v.p., 1989—90, pres. bd. dirs., 1990—94, rep. to Women's Equal Rights Coalition, Suffolk County Human Rights Commn., 1989—94; mem. adv. bd. Suffolk County Women's Svcs., 1990—96, vice-chair, 1991—93; rep. LD 14 Suffolk County Women's Adv. Commn., 2001—06; bd. dirs. Suffolk Abortion Rights Coun., 1992—96; mem. Suffolk-Nassau Abortion Def., 1991—94; pub. affairs com. Planned Parenthood Suffolk County, 1990—92; mem. Long Islanders for Fairness and Equality, 1994—97; mem. subcom. Islip Presbyn. Ch. on Legis. Com. of N.Y. State Coalition Against Domestic Violence, 1999—2001; steering com. Save Our Svcs., Long Island, 1998—2001; mem. coun. on women L.I. Presbytery, 2002—04; sec. sr. lunch program Presbyn. Ch. of Islip, 2005—. Women's History Month Community Svc. honoree Town of Babylon, 1997. Mem. AAUW (mem. v.p. Islip area br. 1982-84, pres. 1984-88, legis. chair 1988-93, mem. com. promoting individual liberties Nassau-Suffolk dist. VI 1989-91, pro-choice coord. N.Y. state 1990-92, rep. to women on job task force 1986-98, chair dist. VI inter-br. 1991-92, chair N.Y. state pub. policy 1992-96, rep. on L.I. and N.Y. State Pro-Choice Coalitions, chair N.Y. state voter edn. campaign, 1995-98, assoc. pub. policy com. 1996-98, L.I. Achievement award 1996), N.Y. State Ret. Tchrs. Assn., Western Suffolk Ret. Tchrs. Assn., Coalition Ret. Tchrs. L.I., North Babylon Tchrs. Orgn. (retirees chpt.). Democrat. Avocations: lobbying, reading, volunteer activities. Home: 23 Wyandanch Ave Babylon NY 11702-1920

SCHWARZ, BERTHOLD ERIC, psychiatrist; b. Jersey City, Oct. 20, 1924; s. Berthold Theodore Dominick and I. Thyra W. (Ericson) Schwarz; m. Ardis Marilyn Peterson, Jan. 22, 1955; children: Lisa Thyra, Eric Rolf. AB, Dartmouth Coll., 1945; MD, NYU, 1950; MS, Mayo Grad. Sch. Medicine, 1957. Intern Mary Hitchcock Meml. Hosp., Hanover, NH, 1950-51; psychiatrist, researcher pvt. practice, Montclair, NJ, 1955-82; Mayo Found., Rochester, Minn., 1951-55; psychiatrist, researcher pvt. practice, Vero Beach, Fla., 1982—2002. Cons. Essex County Hosp. Ctr., Cedar Grove, N.J., 1965-82, Med. Correctional Assn., Ossining, N.Y., 1960-72; exec. dir. Internat. Psychosomatics Inst., Mountain Lakes, N.J., 1995—. Contbr. articles to med. jours. With USNR, 1943-45. Fellow AAAS, Am. Psychiat. Assn., Am. Soc. Psychical Rsch., Am. Geriatric Soc. Republican. Avocations: ufos, parapsychiatry, swimming, walking. Home: 1070 Reef Rd Apt 305 Vero Beach FL 32963-4342 Office: 642 Azalea Ln Vero Beach FL 32963-1832 Office Phone: 772-231-5220. Personal E-mail: ardisps@aol.com.

SCHWARZ, DAVID, retail executive; b. Metz, France, Aug. 12, 1970; s. Claude and Marie-Claude Schwarz; m. Virginie Rigaud, Sept. 12, 1998; children: Julie, Thomas, Louise. MEng, Ecole Poly., Paris, 1993, MSc; ID, Ecole des Mines, Paris, 1996. Head dept. Ministry Def., Paris, 1996—2000; adviser Min. Trade & Industry Cabinet, Paris, 2000—02; dir., dept. store mgr. Printemps, Paris, 2002—04; v.p., GMM Printemps Dept. Stores, Paris, 2004—06; v.p. Redcats USA, New York, 2006—. Advisor French MPs & Govt., Paris, 1996—2002. Contbr. articles to profl. journs. With French Parliament and Govt., Paris, 1996—2002. Comdt. French Mil. Eng. Corp, 1996—2002, Paris. Recipient First Prize, French U. Nat. Photography Contest, 1993. Avocations: photography, travel, birdwatching, skiing, fashion, history. Office: Redcats USA 463 Seventh Ave New York NY 10018 Home Phone: 917-916-7134. Personal E-mail: david.schwarz@mines.org.

SCHWARZ, EGON, language educator, writer, critic; b. Vienna, Aug. 8, 1922; arrived in U.S., 1949, naturalized, 1956; s. Oscar and Erna S.; m. Dorothea K. Klockenbusch, June 8, 1950; children: Rudolf Joachim, Caroline Elisabeth, Gabriela Barbara. PhD, Wash. U., Seattle, 1954; PhD (hon.), Wash. U., St. Louis, 2008, U. Vienna, 1997, U. Örebro, Sweden, 2002. Mem. faculty Harvard U., 1954-61; mem. faculty dept. Germanic langs. and lit. Washington U., St. Louis, 1961—, prof. German, 1963—, Rosa May Disting. Univ. prof. in the Humanities, 1975-93, prof. emeritus, 1993—. Vis. prof. U. Hamburg, Fed. Republic Germany, 1962-63, U. Calif., Berkeley, 1963-65, Middlebury Coll., 1969, U. Calif., Irvine, 1977, U. Tübingen, 1986; William Evans prof. U. Otago, Dunedin, N.Z., 1984; Disting. scholar Ohio State U., Columbus, 1987, U. Graz, Austria, 1989, 93, U. Siegen, 1993-94. Author: Hofmannsthal und Calderon, 1962, Joseph von Eichendorff, 1972, Das verschluckte Schluchzen- Poesie und Politik bei Rainer Maria Rilke, 1972, Keine Zeit für Eichendorff: Chronik unfreiwilliger Wanderjahre; an autobiography, 1979, rev., 1992, Dichtung, Kritik, Geschichte: Essays zur Literatur 1900-1930, 1983, Literatur aus vier Kulturen: Essays und Besprechungen, 1987, Ich bin Kein Freund allgemeiner Urteile über ganze Volker: Essays über österreischische, deutsche und jüdische Literatur, 2000, Die japanische Mauer: Ungewöhnliche Reisegeschichten, 2002, Refuge-Chronicle of a Flight from Hitler, 2002, Unfreiwillige Wanderjahre, 2005, Schwarz and Weiss, (essays) Mit Schwarz Listrn, 2009, others, 2007. Recipient Joseph von Eichendorff medal, 1986, Austrian Medal of Honor for Arts and Scis., 1991, Alexander von Humboldt prize for fgn. scholars, 1995; Guggenheim fellow, 1957-58, Fulbright fellow, 1962-63, sr. fellow NEH, 1970-71, fellow Ctr. for Interdisciplinary Studies, Bielefeld, Germany, 1980-81, Grosses Ehrenzeichen fur Verdienste um die Republik Osterreich, 2007; grantee Am. Coun. Learned Socs., 1962-63, Cotta prize for Literature, 2008. Mem.: MLA, German Acad. Lang. and Letters, Am. Assn. Tchrs. German, German Acad. Lang. and Lit. (hon.). Home: 1036 Oakland Ave Saint Louis MO 63122-6565 Office: Washington U German Dept Saint Louis MO 63130 Business E-Mail: eschwarz@artsci.wusl.edu. *When I was young, heroic phantasies were closer to my heart than ethical ones, desires of self-fulfillment stronger than the hopes for an equitable world. Today my horizon is broader in that I wish for a society where personal satisfactions are not achieved at the expense of others, where the earth which one generation inherits is not left more depleted to the next, a society which does not coerce other societies.*

SCHWARZ, ERNST RUEDIGER, cardiologist, researcher; s. Ernest Johann Ferdinand and Friedel Elise Schwarz; m. Juana Rocio Angel, Nov. 19, 1999; children: Aubriana d'Iwana Angel, Lujain Vanessa. MD, Philipps U. Marburg, Germany, 1987, U. Vienna, Austria, 1989; PhD, RWTH U. of Tech., Aachen, Germany, 2000. Diplomate in internal medicine German Physicians Chamber, in cardiology German Physicians Chamber, in intensive care medicine German Physicians Chamber. Assoc. prof. RWTH U. Hosp., Aachen, 1998—2000; chmn. cardiology Dr. S. Fakeeh Hosp.-Harvard Med. Internat., Jeddah, Saudi Arabia, 2000—03; prof. medicine U. Tex. Med. Br., Galveston, 2003—06, dir. cardiology clinics, 2005—06; prof. medicine UCLA, 2006—. Co-dir. cardiac transplant Cedars Sinai Med. Ctr., LA, 2006; dir. heart failure and transplantation U. Tex. Med. Br., Galveston, 2003—06, dir. heart failure fellowship program, 2004—06, dir. multidisciplinary clinic for sexual health, 2005—06; spkr. in field. Contbr. articles to profl. jours., chapters to books. Recipient Young Investigator award, Internat. Soc. Nuc. Cardiology, 1995. Fellow: Soc. Coronary Angiography and Interventions, European Soc. Cardiology, Am. Coll. Cardiology; mem.: Saudi Heart Assn., German Cardiac Soc., Heart Failure Soc. Am. Achievements include first to transesophageal echocardiography with IVUS catheters in rodent model; research in intensive invasive hemodynamic work in myocardial bridges; clinical and morphologic work in hibernating myocardium; evaluation, assessment and treatment of sexual dysfunction in patients with severe cardio-vascular diseases. Office: Cedars Sinai Med Ctr 8700 Beverly Blvd 6215 Los Angeles CA 90048 Office Fax: 310-423-1498.

SCHWARZ, FREDERICK A.O., JR., lawyer; b. NYC, Apr. 20, 1935; s. Frederick August Otto and Mary Delafield (DuBois) S.; m. Marian Ladd, June 19, 1959; children: Frederick August Otto III, Adair L., Eliza Ladd; m. Frederica Perera, May 11, 1996. BA in History magna cum laude, Harvard Coll., 1957, LLB magna cum laude, 1960; LLD (hon.), N.Y. Law Sch., 1987, CUNY, 1993. Bar: N.Y. 1961, U.S. Dist. Ct. (so. dist.) N.Y. 1963, U.S. Ct. Appeals (2nd cir.) 1978, U.S. Ct. Appeals (9th cir.) 1972, U.S. Ct. Appeals (10th cir.) 1973, U.S. Supreme Ct. 1973. Law clk. to chief judge J. Edward Lumbard U.S. Ct. of Appeals, 2d Circuit, 1960-61; asst. commr. for law revision Govt. of No. Nigeria, 1961-62; assoc. firm Cravath, Swaine & Moore, NYC, 1963-68, ptnr., 1969—81, 1987—2003, sr. counsel, 2003—; chief counsel Brennan Ctr. for Justice NYU, 2003—. Chief counsel Senate Select Com. on Intelligence, 1975—76; corp. counsel, NYC, 1982—86; chmn. Charter Revision Commn., NYC, 1989. Author: Nigeria: The Tribes, The Nation, or the Race, 1966; Editor Harvard Law Sch. Law Review., Unchecked and Unbalanced: Presidential Power in a Time of Terror, 2007; Contbr. articles to profl. jours. Chmn. Fund for the City of N.Y., 1977-81, 87-97; pres. Vera Inst. Justice, 1978-81, chmn. 1987—; mem. bd. overseers Harvard U., 1977-83; mem. Com. to Visit Harvard Coll., N.Y.-N.J. Citizens Commn. on AIDS; trustee Experiment in Internat. Living, 1965-82; bd. dirs. NAACP Legal Def. Fund. Constl. Edn. Found., Manhattan Bowery Corp., 1970-81, Lawyers for the Public Interest, 1976-81, FAO Schwarz, 1970-85; chair leadership N.Y. Adv. Coun., 1989—; trustee Nat. Resources Def. Coun., 1987-92, chmn., 1992—, Atlantee Philantropies, 1991-, 2007-, Legal Action Center, 1973-81, N.Y.C. Criminal Justice Agy., 1977-81, Town Sch., 1972-80, Am. Com. on Africa, 1965-79, Milton Acad., 1960's, NAACP Legal Def. Fund, Constitutional Edn. Found., William Nelson Cromwell Found.; chmn. N.Y.C. Campaign Fin. Bd., 2003—. Recipient Liberty award Lambda Legal Def. and Edn. Fund, 1987, The Louis Lefkowitz award Fordham Urban Law Jour. 1990, Civic Leadership award Citizens Union City of N.Y., 1990, The Whitney North Seymour Pub. Svc. award Fed. Bar Coun., 1991., Lifetime Achievement award, The Am. Lawyer mag, 2004. Fellow N.Y. Bar Found.; mem. ABA, Assn. of Bar of City of N.Y. (mem. exec. com. 1986-90, coun. on criminal justice, chmn. juvenile justice com. 1980-81, chmn. nominating com. 1983, Cardozo lectr. 1991), Am. Law Inst., Harvard Law Sch. Assn. of N.Y.C. (pres. 1983-84), N.Y. State Bar Assn., N.Y.C. Bar Assn. Office: Cravath, Swain & Moore 825 8th Ave Fl 38 New York NY 10019-7475

SCHWARZ, GERARD, conductor, musician, music director; b. Weehawken, NJ, Aug. 19, 1947; m. Jody Greitzer, June 23, 1984; children: Alysandra, Daniel, Gabriella, Julian. BS, MA, Juilliard Sch. Music, NYC, 1972; DFA (hon.), Fairleigh Dickinson U., Seattle U.; MusD (hon.), U. Puget Sound. Trumpet player Am. Symphony Orch., 1965—72, Am. Brass Quintet, 1965—73, NY Philharm., 1973—77; music dir. Erick Hawkins Dance Co., 1967—72, SoHo Ensemble, 1969—75, Eliot Feld Ballet Co., NYC, 1972—78, Princeton U. Music Sch., NJ, 1977—2002, NY Chamber Symphony, 1977—, LA Chamber Orch., 1978—86; music adv. Mostly Mozart Festival, Lincoln Ctr., NYC, 1982—84, music dir., 1984—2001, Seattle Symphony Orch., 1985—, Royal Liverpool Philharm. Orch., 2001—06. Mem. faculty Mannes Coll. Music, 1973—79, Montclair State Coll., NJ, 1975—80, Juilliard Sch., 1975—83; music dir. White Mountains Music Festival, NH, 1978—80, Music Today at Merkin Concert Hall, NYC, 1988—89; artistic adv. Tokyu Bunkamura's Orchard Hall, Japan, 1994—98; mem. Nat. Coun. on Arts, NEA, 2005—; guest condr. Phila. Orch., LA Philharm., St. Louis, Buffalo, Detroit, San Francisco, Atlanta, Houston, Pitts., Minn., Jerusalem Symphonies, Israel Chamber Orch., Moscow Philharm., Moscow Radio Orch., Orch. Nat. de France, Paris, London Symphony Orch., Helsinki Philharm., Ensemble InterContemporain, Monte Caarlo Philharm., Nat. Orch. Spain, English Chamber Orch., London Symphony, Scottish Chamber Orch., City of Birmingham Symphony, England, Sydney Symphony, Melbourne Symphony, Orchestre Nat. de Lyon, France, Orchestre Philharm. de Montpellier, France, Washington Opera, 20th Century Chamber Orch., Chamber Music Soc. Lincoln Ctr., San Francisco Opera, Rseidentie Orch., Netherlands, St. Louis Symphony, London Mozart Players, Kirov Orch., St. Petersburg, Russia, Royal Liverpool Philharm., Vancouver Symphony Orch. Rec. artist Columbia, Nonesuch, Vox, MMO, Desto, Angel, Delos Records, Season 1995. Recipient Ford Found. award for concert artists, 1973, Ditson Condrs. award, Columbia U., 1989, Seattle Mayors Arts award, 2006; named Condr. of Yr., Musical America Internat. Directory Performing Arts, 1994; nominee 10 Grammy awards. Office: Seattle Symphony Orch PO Box 21906 200 University St Seattle WA 98111-3906 Mailing: Nat Endowment for Arts 1100 Pennsylvania Ave NW Washington DC 20506*

SCHWARZ, GLENDA M., oil industry executive; b. 1965; Gen. mgr. downstream fin./performance analysis ConocoPhillips, Houston, gen. auditor, chief ethics officer, 2008—09, v.p., contr. fin., 2009—. Office: ConocoPhillips 600 N Dairy Ashford PO Box 2197 Houston TX 77252 Office Phone: 281-293-1000. Business E-Mail: glenda.m.schwarz@conocophillips.com.*

SCHWARZ, JAN, literature and language professor; m. Rebecca Lillian, Aug. 1, 1999. PhD, Columbia U., NY, 1996. Sr. lectr. U. Chgo., 2003—. Author: (book) Imagning Lives: Autobiographical Fiction of Yiddish Literature.

SCHWARZ, JOE (JOHN J.H. SCHWARZ), former congressman, physician; b. Battle Creek, Mich., Nov. 15, 1937; s. Frank William and Helen Veronica (Brennan) S.; m. Anne Louise Ennis, Jan. 16, 1971 (dec. Feb. 1990); 1 child, Brennan Louise. BA in History, U. Mich., 1959; MD, Wayne State U., 1964. Operative CIA, 1968—70; physician, surgeon Battle Creek, Mich., 1974—; commr. City of Battle Creek, 1979—85, mayor, 1985-87; mem. Mich. State Senate from 24th dist., Lansing, 1987—2002, pres. pro tempore, 1993—2002; mem. US Congress from 7th Mich. dist., 2005—07, mem. com. agr., com. armed services, com. sci.; chmn., bd. dir. Alumni Assc., U. Mich., 2005—07; lectr. Ford Sch. Pub. Policy, U. Mich. Trustee Leila Y. Post Montgomery Hosp. (now Battle Creek Health Sys.), Mich., 1980-82, Olivet Coll., 1991—, Wayland Acad., 1992-96, Libr. Mich., 1994-2003; trustee, treas. Am. Legacy Found; bd. directors Artrain, Ann Arbor, Detroit Receiving Hosp., Kellogg Cmty. Coll. Found., Univ. Musical Soc., Ann Arbor, Wayne State U. Found. Lt. Comdr. USN, 1965—67, Vietnam. Fellow ACS; mem. AMA, Am. Soc. for Head and Neck Surgery, Calhoun County Mich. Med. Soc. (pres. 1971), Mich Otolaryngological Soc., Mich State Med. Soc., Soc. Med. Consultants to Armed Forces, U. Mich. Club of Battle Creek. Republican. Roman Catholic. Business E-Mail: jschwarz@fhcrc.org.

SCHWARZ, JOHN HENRY, theoretical physicist, educator; b. North Adams, Mass., Nov. 22, 1941; s. George and Madeleine (Haberfeld) S.; m. Patricia Margaret Moyle, July 11, 1986. AB, Harvard U., 1962; PhD, U. Calif., Berkeley, 1966. Instr. physics Princeton (NJ) U., 1966-69, asst. prof., 1969-72; research assoc. Calif. Inst. Tech., Pasadena, 1972-85, Harold Brown prof. theoretical physics, 1985—. Co-author: Superstring Theory, 1987. Trustee Aspen (Colo.) Ctr. for Physics, 1982—. Recipient Dirac medal Internat. Ctr. for Theoretical Physics, 1989; Guggenheim fellow, 1978-79, MacArthur Found. fellow, 1987. Fellow NAS, Am. Acad. Arts & Scis., Am. Phys. Soc., Phi Beta Kappa (vis. scholar 1990-91). Office: Calif Inst Tech # 452 48 Pasadena CA 91125-0001

SCHWARZ, M. ROY, retired physician, administrator; b. American Falls, Idaho, July 30, 1936; s. Roy Frank and Hulda Christina (Rast) S.; m. Thelma Constance Schwarz, June 9, 1957; children: Ryan Merle, Tanna Berit. BS, Pacific Luth. U., 1959; MD, U. Wash., 1963; DS, Mont. State U., 1994, U. Idaho, 1995; DHL (hon.), Pacific Luth. U., 2002; Dr. Pub Health, Chiang Mai U., 2004; Dr. (hon.), Peking Union Med. Ctr., 2004; LHD (hon.), Johns Hopkins U., 2007. From asst. to full prof. medicine U. Wash., Seattle, 1963-79; dean, prof. U. Colo., Denver, 1979-83; sr. v.p. Am. Med. Assn., Chgo., 1984-96; pres. China Med. Bd., NYC, 1997—2006; ret., 2006. Co-author (with C. Everett Koop, Clarence E. Pearson): Critical Issues in global Health, 2001; editor: Proceedings of the VI Leukocyte Culture Conf., 1971; contbr. over 175 articles to profl. jours. Personal E-mail: tcandmr@verizon.net.

SCHWARZ, MARKUS J., psychoneuroimmunologist, neurochemist; b. Ingolstadt, Germany, Apr. 16, 1966; s. Georg and Maria (Riemer) Schwarz; divorced; 1 child, Marie Sophie. Diploma in medicine, U. Munich, 1996; MD in Exptl. Psychiatry, Ludwig-Maximilian U., Munich, 1998. Physician Ludwig-Maximilian U., Munich, 1996-97; rsch. asst. dept. neurochemistry Psychiat. Hosp., Munich, 1998—2004, head lab. sect. psychoneuroimmunology and therapeutic drug monitoring, 2004—; habilitation in exptl. psychiatry, 2005. External project ptnr. Expo 2000 Psychoneuroimmunology, Hannover, Germany, 1997—; mem. adv. bd. European Psychiatry, 1999—; mem. expert group therapeutic drug monitoring AGNP; vice chair Found. "Immunity and Soul". With Mountain Inf. German Army, 1986—87. Fellow, Arbeitsgem Neuropsychopharmacology, 1999, World Psychiat. Assn., 1999, 2001, German Soc. Biol. Psychiatry, 2001, 2002. Mem.: World Psychiat. Assn. (sec. sect. immunology and psychiatry, NY, Washington 1999—, mem. Ednl. Liaisons Network, fellow 1999, 2001), German Soc. Immunology, European Coll. Neuropsyhopharmacology (Poster award, fellow 1999), Am. Psychiat. Assn. Roman Catholic. Achievements include patents in field. Avocations: mountain biking, travel, opera, walking, skiing. Office: U Munich Psychiat Hosp Nussbaumstr 7 D-80336 Munich Germany

SCHWARZ, MICHAEL, lawyer; b. Brookline, Mass., Oct. 19, 1952; s. Jules Lewis and Estelle (Kosberg) S.; m. Rebecca Handy; 1 child, Patrick Joshua Charles. BA magna cum laude, U. No. Colo., 1975; postgrad., U. N.Mex., 1977, JD, 1980; reader in Negligence Law, Oxford U., 1978; diploma in Legal Studies, Cambridge U., 1981. Bar: N.Mex. 1980, US Dist. Ct. N.Mex. 1980, US Ct. Appeals (10th, DC and Fed. cirs.) 1982, US Ct. Internat. Trade 1982, US Tax Ct. 1982, NY 1987, US Supreme Ct. 1983, cert.: N.Mex. Supreme Ct. (Employment and Labor Law) 2000. Vol. VISTA, Albuquerque, 1975-77; rsch. fellow N.Mex. Legal Support Project, Albuquerque, 1978-79; supr. law Cambridge (Eng.) U., 1980-81; law clk. to chief justice Supreme Ct. N.Mex., Santa Fe, 1981-82; pvt. practice Santa Fe, 1982—. Spl. pros. City of Santa Fe, 1985, spl. asst. atty. gen., 1986-88; mem. west editl. adv. com. Social Security Reporting Svc., 1983-95; mem. N.Mex. Supreme Ct. Com. Profl. Responsibility, 1990-2007, chmn., 1998-2007, domestic rels. task force com., 2004—06, chmn. legal specialization com., employment and labor law, 2005, 08. Author: New Mexico Appellate Manual, 1990, 2d edit., 1996; contbr. articles to profl. jours. Vice-dir. Colo. Pub. Interest Rsch. Group, 1974; scoutmaster Gt. S.W. Area coun. Boy Scouts Am., 1977—79; mem. N.Mex. Acupuncture Lic. Bd., 1983; master's coaching level U.S.A. Hockey Assn., dir. N.Mex. coaching edn., 2004—05. Recipient Cert. of Appreciation Cambridge U., 1981, Nathan Burke Meml. award, 1980, N.Mex. Supreme Ct. Cert. Recognition, 1992, 93, 95, N.Mex. Supreme Ct. Cert. Appreciation Outstanding Svc. to Legal Sys., 2001, S.W. Super Lawyer, Law & Politics, 2007-2009, Best Lawyers In Am., 2009, NM State Bar Assn., Justice Minzner Professionalism award, 2008. Mem.: ABA (mem. profl. responsibility, mem. Ctr. Profl. Responsibility, litig. com. mem.), Am. Law Inst. (mem. restatement employment law), N.Mex. State Bar (chmn. 1990—91, bd. dirs. employment law sect. 1990—96, family law sect. bd. 1999—2001), Bar Assn. U.S. Dist. Ct. Dist. N.Mex. (1st judical dis. bar assoc. pres. 1990—91), Am. Assn. Justice, USA Hockey, Assn. Coaching Edn. (adm., assoc. coach-in-chief Rocky Mt. dist. 2004—), Santa Fe Trailrunners Hockey Assn. (bd. dirs. 2001—02). Home and Office: PO Box 1656 Santa Fe NM 87504-1656 Office Phone: 505-988-2053. Business E-Mail: barrister@pobox.com.

SCHWARZ, RICARDO B., research scientist; D in Physics, U. Va., 1972; D (hon.), Tampere U. Tech., 2002. Lab. fellow Los Alamos Nat. Lab., N.Mex., 1994. Recipient A. von Humboldt Rsch. award for sr. U.S. scientists, 2003. Fellow: Minerals, Metals and Materials Soc., Am. Soc. for Metals; mem.: NAE. Office: Los Alamos Nat Lab Materials Sci & Tech Div MST-8, MS G755 Los Alamos NM 87545 Office Fax: 505-667-8021. Personal E-mail: schwarz.ricardo@gmail.com.

SCHWARZ, RICHARD HOWARD, obstetrician, gynecologist, educator; b. Easton, Pa., Jan. 10, 1931; s. Howard Eugene and Blanche Elizabeth (Smith) S.; m. Patricia Marie Lewis, Mar. 11, 1978; children by previous marriage: Martha L., Nancy Schwarz Tedesco, Paul H., Mary Katherine Schwarz Murray. MD, Jefferson Med. Coll., 1955; MA (hon.), U. Pa., 1971. Diplomate Am. Bd. Ob-Gyn. (examiner 1977-95), Divsn. Maternal Fetal Medicine 1974. Intern, then resident Phila. Gen. Hosp., 1955-59; prof. U. Pa., Phila., 1963-78; prof., chmn. Downstate Med. Ctr., Bklyn., 1978-90, dean, v.p. acad. affairs, 1983-89, provost, v.p. clin. affairs, 1988-93, interim pres., 1993-94, prof. ob.-gyn., 1990-96, disting. Svc. prof. ob.-gyn. emeritus, 1996; chmn. ob.-gyn. N.Y. Meth. Hosp., Bklyn., 1996—2002; prof. ob.-gyn. Cornell U. Med. Coll., NYC, 1996—2002; vice chair for clin. svc. dept. Ob/GYN Maimonides Med. Ctr., 2002—; prof. ob-gyn. and reproductive sci. Mt. Sinai Sch. Medicine, NY, 2005—08. Obstetrical cons. March of Dimes Birth Defects Found., 1995-2008. Author: Septic Abortion, 1968. Editor: Handbook of Obstetric Emergencies, 1984, mem. editorial bd. jour. Ob-Gyn., Milw., 1983-87; contbr. over 200 articles to profl. jours. Bd. dirs. March of Dimes, N.Y.C., 1985-95. Capt. USAF, 1959-63. Recipient Career Achievement award, Infectious Disease Soc. Ob-Gyn., 1999, Founder's award, 2004, Wyeth Ayerest Career Achievement award, 2000. Fellow Royal Coll ObGyn (ad eundem), 1999; mem. ACOG (chmn. dist. 2 1984-87, v.p. 1989-90, pres. elect 1990-91, pres. 1991-92, Lifetime Achievement award dist. II 2005). Republican. Presbyterian. Office: Maimonides Med Ctr 967 48th St Brooklyn NY 11219-3645

SCHWARZ, SIDNEY HOWARD, rabbi; b. NYC, Oct. 8, 1953; s. Allan and Judy (Brand) S.; m. Sandra Perlstein, July 3, 1983; children: David, Joel, Jennifer. BA in Polit. Sci. summa cum laude, U. Md., 1974; MA in Modern Jewish and Am. History, Temple U., Phila., 1977, PhD in History, 1982. Ordained rabbi, 1980. Rabbi Congregatin Beth Israel, Media, Pa., 1976-83; mem. faculty Akiba Hebrew Acad., Merion, Pa., 1981-83, Gratz Coll., Wilmington and Phila., Pa., 1981-83, Reconstructionist Rabinnical Coll., Wyncote, Pa., 1982-84; exec. dir. Jewish Community Coun. of Greater Washington, 1984-87; founding rabbi Adat Shalom Reconstructionist Congregation, Bethesda, Md., 1988; founder, pres. PANIM: Inst. for Jewish Leadership and Values, 1988—. Adj. prof. of Jewish history U. Md., 1986-87; bd. dirs. Jewish Reconstructionist Found., Nat. INst. on Holocaust, Interfaith Conf. Met. Washington; mem. editorial bd. Reconstructionist mag.; mem. Washington Area Community Investment Fund; bd. govs. Reconstructionist Rabbinical Coll.; mem. steering com. Nat. Rabbinic Chevrah. Host. TV talk show Jewish Community Hour; author: Finding a Spiritual Home: How a New Generation of Jews Can Transform the American Synagogue, Judaism and Justice. The Jewish Passion to Repair the World. Recipient Covenant award, 2002; named one of The Top 50 Rabbis in America, Newsweek Mag., 2007. Mem. Reconstructionist Rabbinical Assn. (founding editor jour. Raayonot). Office: 11707 Farmland Dr Rockville MD 20852-4301 Office Phone: 301-770-5070, 301-379-2381. E-mail: rabbisid2@gmail.com.

SCHWARZ, SUSAN BOWERS YOUNG, piano teacher; b. Huntington, Ind., Feb. 2, 1928; d. Donald DeLargy and Elizabeth (Holly) Bowers; m. Jack Young; 1 child, Joshua D.; m. Ralph Schwarz. BMusic, U. Tex., 1949; MMusic, Cin. Conservatory, 1950. Instr. in piano Ind. U., Bloomington, 1950-52; music tchr. Karl C. Parrish Sch., Barranquilla, Colombia, Simon Bolivar Sch., Cali, Colombia, Am. Sch., Managua, Nicaragua, Am. Sch. US Steel Orinoco Mining Co., Puerto Ordaz, Venezuela. Pvt. piano tchr. Rosarian Acad., West Palm Beach, Fla. Mem. Palm Beach County Music Tchrs. Assn., Nat. Guild Piano Tchrs., Mu Phi Epsilon, Phi Theta Kappa, Pi Kappa Lambda. Avocations: swimming, biking, tennis, table tennis. Home: 1013 Durham A Deerfield Beach FL 33442-2501

SCHWARZ, THOMAS J., academic administrator, lawyer; b. NYC, 1945; s. Alexander and Thelma Schwarz; children: Jason, Jessica. BA, Hamilton Coll., Clinton, NY, 1966; JD, Fordham U., NYC, 1969. Bar: NY. Assoc. Skadden, Arps, Slate, Meagher & Flom LLP, NYC, 1969—76, ptnr., 1976—2003, of counsel, 2003—08; acting pres. Hamilton Coll., Clinton, 1999; interim pres. SUNY, Purchase, 2002—03, pres., 2003—. Counsel Governor's Judicial Screening Com., First Judicial Dept., 1983—87, 1988—95, Governor's Statewide Judicial Screening Com., 1988—95. Author: Federal Regulation of Campaign Finance and Political Activity; contbr. articles to profl. jours. Trustee Citizens Rsch. Found., Berkeley, Calif., 1984—2001; mayor Village, Ocean Beach, NY, 1978—87; trustee Riverside Pk. Fund, NYC, 1998—2007, The Preservation League of N.Y. State, Albany, 1998—, Arts Connection, NYC, 1998—2002; commr. Commn. to Promote Pub. Confidence in Jud. Elections, NYC, 2003—04; mem. NY State Commn. on Higher Edn., 2007—08, Hamilton Coll. Bd. of Trustees, Clinton, 1987—. Recipient Pro Bono award, Legal Aid Soc., 1998. Mem.: ABA (mem. litig. com. 1989—2006), NY State Bar Assn., Assn. Bar City of NY (sec. 1975—78, mem. N.Y. spl. com. on election law 1985—86, mem. com. on fed. legis. 1971—74). Office: Purchase College SUNY 735 Anderson Hill Rd Purchase NY 10577 Office Fax: 914-251-6014. Business E-Mail: thomas.schwarz@purchase.edu.

SCHWARZ, UDO DIETMAR, physicist, researcher; b. Göttingen, Lower Saxony, Germany, Sept. 29, 1964; s. Gerhard Walter Rudolf and Roswitha Herma Maria Schwarz. Diploma in Physics, U. Basel, Switzerland, 1989, PhD in Experimental Physics, 1993. Staff scientist U. Hamburg, Germany, 1993—2001, lectr., 1999—2001; assoc. prof. mech. engring. Yale U., New Haven, 2002—. Vis. sr. scientist Lawrence Berkeley Nat. Lab., Calif., 2001—02. Contbr. articles to profl. jours., chapters to books. Heisenberg fellow, German Rsch. Soc., 2000—02. Mem.: ASME, German Vacuum Soc. (Gaede prize 1999), German Phys. Soc., Am. Vacuum Soc., Am. Phys. Soc. Achievements include research in nanosciences.

SCHWARZENEGGER, ARNOLD ALOIS, Governor of California; b. Thal, Styria, Austria, July 30, 1947; arrived in US, 1968, naturalized, 1983; s. Gustav and Aurelia (Jedrny) Schwarzenegger; m. Maria Owings Shriver, Apr. 26, 1986; children: Katherine Eunice, Christina Aurelia, Patrick, Christopher. BA in Bus. and Internat. Econs., U. Wis., Superior; doctorate (hon.), U. Wis. Superior, 1996, Chapman U., 2002. Owner prodn., real estate cos.; gov. State of Calif., Sacramento, 2003—. Speaker Republican Nat. Convention, NYC, 2004. Actor: (films) Stay Hungry, 1976 (Golden Globe award, Best Newcomer in Films, 1976), Pumping Iron, 1977, Conan, The Barbarian, 1982, Conan, The Destroyer, 1983, The Terminator, 1984, Commando, 1985, Red Sonja, 1985, Raw Deal, 1986, Predator, 1987, Running Man, 1987, Red Heat, 1988, Twins, 1988, Total Recall, 1990, Kindergarten Cop, 1990, Terminator 2: Judgement Day, 1991, True Lies, 1994, Junior, 1994, Terminator 2: 3-D, 1996, Jingle All the Way, 1996, Eraser, 1996, Batman & Robin, 1997, End of Days, 1999, Collateral Damage, 2002, Terminator 3: Rise of the Machines, 2003, Around the World in 80 Days, 2004, The Kid and I, 2005; (TV films) The Jayne Mansfield Story, 1980, (TV spl.) Sinatra: 80 Years My Way, 1995; actor, prodr. (films) The Last Action Hero, 1993, The 6th Day, 2000; dir.: (TV series) Tales from the Crypt, 1990; (TV films) Christmas in Connecticut, 1992; author: Arnold: The Education of a Bodybuilder, 1977, Arnold's Bodyshaping for Women, 1979, Arnold's Bodybuilding for Men, 1981, Arnold's Encyclopedia of Modern Bodybuilding, 1985, 2nd. edit., 1998; editor: Muscle & Fitness Mag., Flex Mag. Nat. weight tng. coach Spl. Olympics; vol. prison rehab. programs; chmn. Pres.'s Coun. Phys. Fitness and Sports, 1990—93. Recipient Timmie award, Touchdown Club, 1990, Rave award for politics, WIRED Mag., 2007, Muhammad Ali Humanitarian award, Nat. Leadership award, Simon Wiesenthal Ctr., Father Flanagan Svc. to Youth award, Boys & Girls Town; named Jr. Mr. Europe, 1965, Best Built Man of Europe, 1966, Mr. Europe, 1966, Internat. Powerlifting Champion, 1966, German Powerlifting Champion, 1968, Mr. Internat., Internat. Fedn. Body Builders, 1968, Amateur Mr. Universe, 1969, Nat. Assn. Body Builders, 1967, Profl. Mr. Universe, 1968, 1969; named one of The World's Most Influential People, TIME mag., 2007, 50 Who Matter Now, Bus. 2.0, 2007, America's Best Leaders, US News & World Report, 2007. Republican. Roman Catholic. Office: Office of Governor State Capitol Sacramento CA 95814-4906 Office Phone: 916-445-2841. Office Fax: 916-445-4633.

SCHWARZER, WILLIAM W., federal judge; b. Berlin, Apr. 30, 1925; came to U.S., 1938, naturalized, 1944; s. John F. and Edith M. (Daniel) S.; m. Anne Halbersleben, Feb. 2, 1951; children: Jane Elizabeth, Andrew William. AB cum laude, U. So. Calif., 1948; LLB cum laude, Harvard U., 1951. Bar: Calif. 1953, U.S. Supreme Ct. 1967. Teaching fellow Harvard U. Law Sch., 1951-52; asso. firm McCutchen, Doyle, Brown & Enersen, San Francisco, 1952-60, ptnr., 1960-76; judge U.S. Dist. Ct (no. dist.) Calif., San Francisco, 1976—; dir. Fed. Jud. Ctr., Washington, 1990-95. Sr. counsel Pres.'s Commn. on CIA Activities Within the U.S., 1975; chmn. U.S. Jud. Conf. Com. Fed.-State Jurisdiction, 1987-90; mem. faculty Nat. Inst. Trial Advocacy, Fed. Jud. Ctr., All-ABA, U.S.-Can. Legal Exch., 1987, Anglo-U.S. Jud. Exch., 1994-95, Salzburg Seminar on Am. Studies; ret. disting. prof. Hastings Coll. Law U. Calif., ret. Author: Managing Antitrust and Other Complex Litigation, 1982, Civil Discovery and Mandatory Disclosure, 1994, Federal Civil Procedure Before Trial, 1994; contbr. articles to legal publs., aviation jours. Trustee World Affairs Coun. No. Calif., 1961-88; chmn. bd. trustees Marin Country Day Sch., 1963-66; mem. Marin County Aviation Commn., 1969-76; mem. vis. com. Harvard Law Sch., 1981-86. Served with Intelligence, U.S. Army, 1943-46. Recipient Edward J. Devitt Disting. Svc. to Justice award, 2004. Fellow Am. Coll. Trial Lawyers (S. Gates award 1992), Am. Bar Found.; mem. ABA (Meador Rosenberg award 1995), Am. Law Inst., San Francisco Bar Assn., State Bar Calif., Coun. Fgn. Rels.

SCHWARZKOPF, NORMAN (HERBERT NORMAN SCHWARZKOPF JR.), retired military officer; b. Trenton, NJ, Aug. 22, 1934; s. H. Norman and Ruth (Bowman) Schwarzkopf; m. Brenda Holsinger, July 6, 1968; children: Cynthia, Jessica, Christian. BS in Engring., U.S. Mil. Acad., West Point, NY, 1956; MME, U. So. Calif., Los Angeles, 1964; student, U.S. Army War Coll., Carlisle Barracks, Pa., 1972-73; LHD (hon.), U. S. Fla.; D. in Leadership (hon.), U. Richmond; D. in Pub. Svc. (hon.), U. Miami, U. Fla. Commd. 2nd lt. US Army, 1956, advanced through grades to gen., 1988; platoon leader, exec. officer 2nd Airborne Battle Group, 1957-59; platoon leader 6th Inf., Fed. Rep. Germany, 1959; aide-de-camp Berlin Command, Fed. Rep. Germany, 1960-61; assoc. prof. Dept. Mechanics US Military Acad., West Point, NY, 1965; advisor US Army, Vietnam, 1965-66; comdr. 1st Battalion, 6th Inf., 198th Inf. brigade, 23rd Inf. Div., Vietnam, 1969-70; chief, Prof. Devel. Section, Inf. branch Office Pers. Ops., Washington, 1970-72; military asst. Office Asst. Sec. Army Dept. Army, US Dept. Def., Washington, 1973-74; dep. comdr. 172d Inf. Brigade, Ft. Richardson, Alaska, 1974-76; comdr. 1st brigade 9th Inf. Divsn., Ft. Lewis, Wash., 1976-78; dep. dir. plans US Pacific Command (USPACOM), Camp Smith, Hawaii, 1978-80; asst. div. comdr. 8th Inf. Divsn. (mechanized) US Army Europe (USAREUR), 1980-82; dir. mil. personnel mgmt. US Army, Washington, 1982-83, commdg. gen. 24th Inf. Divsn. (mechanized) Ft. Stewart, Ga., 1983-85; dep. comdr. US Forces in Grenada operation (Operation Urgent Fury), 1983; asst. dep. chief staff for ops. US Army, Washington, 1985-86, commdg. gen. I Corps Ft. Lewis, Wash., 1986-87, dep. chief staff for ops. & plans Washington, 1987-88; comdr. US Ctrl. Command (USCENTCOM), MacDill AFB, Fla., 1988-91; comdr. in chief US Forces in Operation Desert Shield, Desert Storm, Saudi Arabia, 1990-91; ret. US Army, 1992. Lectr., 1993—; contbr. and analyst NBC News, 1995—; bd. dirs. Kuhlman Corp., 1994—, Home Shopping Network, 1996—, Burns International Services, Inc., 1998—2000, Remington Arms Co. Inc., 1998—2007, RACI Holding, Inc., 1999—. Author (with Peter Petre): It Doesn't Take a Hero: The Autobiography of General H. Norman Schwarzkopf, 1992. Chair Starbright Found., 1995—2003. Decorated Def. D.S.M., D.S.M. with two oak leaf clusters, D.S.M. for USN, D.S.M. for USAF, D.S.M. for USCG, Silver Star with two oak leaf clusters, Def. Superior Svc. medal, Legion of Merit, D.F.C., Bronze Star with three oak leaf clusters, Purple Heart with oak leaf cluster, Combat Infantryman badge, Master Parachutist badge, Gen. Staff Identification badge, Joint Staff Identification badge, Dept. Def. Identification badge, Presdl. Medal of Freedom; Nat. Order of Legion of Honor, hon. pfc. French Fgn. Legion (France); Order of Leopold (Belgium); knight Hon. Order of the Bath (U.K.); Decoration 1st degree (Bahrain); Sash of Independence (Qatar); Medal of Independence (United Arab Emirates); officer Order of King Abd Al Aziz 1st class (Saudi Arabia), Order of Kuwait with Sash of Most Excellent Order (Kuwait); named Father of Yr., 1991, Toastmaster Internat. Best Spkr., 1992, Humanitarian of Yr. United Cerebral Palsy, 1993, Living Legends M.D. Anderson Found., 1996; recipient Am. Patriot medal, 1993, Gilda Radner award Courage, 1995, NJ Disting. Svc. medal, 1995, Vince Lombardi award Excellence, 1995, James Ewing Layman award Soc. Surg. Oncologists, 1997, Oliver R. Grace award, 1998, Ambassador Hope award, 1998, Spirit of Hope award, 1999, Leadership award Multiple Myeloma Rsch. Found., 1999, Inspirational award U. Pitts. Med. Ctr., 2000, Harry S. Truman Good Neighbor award, 2000, Pioneer in Prostate Cancer award Fla. Cancer Edn. Network, 2000, Theodore Roosevelt Am. Experience award, 2000, Award of Excellence Ronald McDonald, 2001; named to The NJ Hall of Fame, 2007. Avocations: hunting, fishing, skeet, trap and sporting clays. Office: Care Internat Creative Mgmt Inc 40 W 57th St New York NY 10019-4001 Home: 302 Knights Run Ave Ste 910 Tampa FL 33602-5979*

SCHWARZMAN, STEPHEN ALLEN (STEVE SCHWARZMAN), private equity firm executive; b. NYC, Feb. 14, 1947; s. Joseph and Arline (Horelley) Schwarzman; m. Ellen Philips (div.); children: Teddy, Elizabeth Philips; m. Christine Hearst, Nov. 3, 1995. BA, Yale U., New Haven, 1969; MBA, Harvard U., Cambridge, Mass., 1972. With Donaldson Lufkin & Jenrette; mng. dir. Lehman Brothers Inc., NYC, 1978—84, chmn. mergers & acquisitions com., 1983—84; co-founder, chmn., CEO The Blackstone Group LP, NYC, 1985—. Adj. prof. Yale Sch. Mgmt.; mem. nat. adv. com. J.P. Morgan Chase & Co. Bd. dirs. NYC Ballet, NY Pub. Libr., New Film Soc. of Lincoln Ctr., NYC Partnership, Asia Soc., Frick Collection; mem. vis. com. Harvard Bus. Sch.; chmn. bd. trustees Kennedy Ctr. Performing Arts, Washington, 2004—. Served in USAR. Recipient Disting. Svc. award, Nat. Ctr. on Addiction & Substance Abuse, 2006, Leadership award, Yale U., 2007; named one of Forbes' Richest Americans, 2005—, World's Richest People, Forbes mag., 2006—, The World's Most Influential People, TIME mag., 2007. Mem.: Bus. Coun., Coun. Fgn. Rels. Republican. Jewish. Office: The Blackstone Grp 345 Park Ave Ste 3101 New York NY 10154-0004 Office Phone: 212-583-5823. E-mail: schwarzman@blackstone.com.*

SCHWARZSCHILD, JANE L., lawyer; b. Richmond, Va., 1949; BA, Smith Coll., 1971; JD, Univ. Va., 1974. Bar: Va. 1974. Ptnr. Armstrong Bristow Farley & Schwarzschild, PLC, Richmond, Va. Recipient Spl. Achievements and Contributions award, Va. Women Attys. Assn., 1986; named Va. Super Lawyer in Estate Planning & Probate, R. Ch Mouth Mag., 2006—09; named one of Best Lawyers in Am. Trusts and Estates, 1993—2009; named to Legal Elite in Taxes, Estates, and Trusts, Va. Bus. Mag., 2000—07. Mem.: Am. Coll. Trust & Estate Counsel, Richmond Estate Planning Coun., Va. State Bar, Va. Bar Assn. Office: Armstrong Bristow Farley and Schwarzschild PLC 1807 Libbie Ave #200 Richmond VA 23266 Office Phone: 804-282-6170. Office Fax: 804-282-6175. Business E-Mail: jschwarzschild@armstrongbristow.com.

SCHWARZTRAUBER, SAYRE ARCHIE, former naval officer, maritime consultant; b. Zion, Ill., June 23, 1929; s. Archie Douglas and Eleanor Miriam (Sayrs) S.; m. Beryl Constance Stewart, June 27, 1953; children: Sayre Archie, Beryl Ann, Heidi, Holly. BS cum laude, Maryville Coll., 1951; MA, Am. U., 1964, PhD, 1970. Commd. ensign USN, 1952, advanced through grades to rear adm., 1976; comdr. River Squadron 5, Vietnam, 1968-69, U.S.S. Decatur guided missile destroyer, 1970-71, Navy Recruiting Area 4, 1974-76; dep. chief staff Supreme Command Atlantic (NATO), 1976-79; co-dir. U.S.-Spanish Combined Staff, Madrid, 1979-81; dir. Inter-Am. Def. Coll., Washington, 1981-83; ret., 1983; apptd. rear adm. U.S. Maritime Svc., 1984; pres. Maine Maritime Acad., 1984—86. Mem. Sec. of Navy Adv. Com., 1986-90; nat. and internat. lectr. strategic naval and maritime matters, 1973—. Author: The Three-Mile Limit of Territorial Seas, 1972, Schwarztrauber, Stewart and Related Families, 1995; editor Mass. Maritime Mag., 1987-90; contbr. articles, essays and revs. to profl. jours. Ruling elder Presbyn. Ch. U.S.A., 1965-86. Decorated Def. Disting. Svc. Medal, Legion of Merit, Cross of Gallantry (Vietnam), Gran Cruz de Merito (Spain); recipient Alfred Thayer Mahan award Navy League, 1974. Mem. SAR (pres. Cape Cod chpt. 1993-95, state reg. and genealogist 1992-2003, state pres. 1998-99, nat. trustee 1999-2000), Gamewardens of Vietnam, Nat. Geneal. Soc., U.S. Naval Inst., Am. Legion, Masons (adjutant Aleppo Temple), VFW, Mil. Order World Wars, Mensa, Travelers' Century Club, Phi Kappa Phi, Pi Gamma Mu, Pi Sigma Alpha, Theta Alpha Phi. Home and Office: 60 Old Mill Rd Osterville MA 02655-1731

SCHWEBEL, MILTON, psychologist, educator; b. Troy, NY, May 11, 1914; s. Frank and Sarah (Oxenhandler) S.; m. Bernice Lois Davison, Sept. 3, 1939; children: Andrew I., Robert S. AB, Union Coll., 1934; MA, SUNY, Albany, 1936; PhD, Columbia U., NYC, 1949; Cert. in Psychotherapy, Postgrad. Ctr. Mental Health, NYC, 1958. Lic. psychologist, NY, NJ; diplomate Am. Bd. Examiners Profl. Psychology. Asst. prof. psychology Mohawk Champlain Coll., 1946-49; asst. to prof. edn., dept. chmn., assoc. dean NYU, 1949-67; dean, prof. Grad. Sch. Edn., Rutgers U., New Brunswick, NJ, 1967-77; dean emeritus Grad. Sch. Applied and Profl. Psychology, 1977—, prof., 1977-85, prof. emeritus, 1985—. Vis. prof. U. So. Calif., U. Hawaii; postdoctoral fellow Postgrad. Ctr. Mental Health, NYC, 1954-58, lectr. psychology, 1958-90; cons. NIMH, US, state and city depts. edn., UNESCO, ednl. ministries in Europe, Asia, univs. and pub. schs., UNESCO; pvt. cons. psychologist and psychotherapist, 1953—; disting. cons. & faculty Saybrook Grad. Sch. & Rsch. Ctr., 1999—, adj. rsch. faculty Inst. Transactional Psychology, 2005-. Author: A Guide to a Happier Family, 1989, Personal Adjustment and Growth, 1990, Student Teachers Handbook, 3d edit., 1996, Interests of Pharmacists, 1951, Health Counseling, 1953, Who Can Be Educated?, 1968, Remaking America's Three School System: Now Separate and Unequal, 2003; editor: Mental Health Implications of Life in the Nuclear Age, 1986, Facilitating Cognitive Development, 1986, Promoting Cognitive Growth Over the Life Span, 1990, Behavioral Science and Human Survival, 1965, The Impact of Ideology on the I.Q. Controversy, 1975; editor Peace & Conflict: Jour. Peace Psychology, 1993-2000 (vol. 9, no. 4. named Pioneer in Peace Psychology: Milton Schwebel); co-editor Bull. Peace Psychology, 1991-94; mem. editl. bd. Am. Jour. Orthopsychiatry, Readings in Mental Health, Jour. Contemporary Psychotherapy, Jour. Counseling Psychology, Jour. Social Issues, others. Mem. sci. adv. bd. Internat. Ctr. for Enhancement of Learning Potential, 1988—; trustee Edn. Law Ctr., 1973-81, Nat. Com. Employment Youth, Nat. Child Labor Com., 1967-75, Union Exptl. Colls. and Univs., 1976-78; pres. Nat. Orgn. for Migrant Children, 1980-85; pres. Inst. of Arts and Humanities, 1984-95. Served with AUS, 1943-46, ETO. Recipient Disting. Leader in Edn. award, Grad. Sch. Edn. Rutgers U., 2006; Met. Applied Rsch. Coun. fellow, 1970—71. Fellow APA, Am. Psychol. Soc., Am. Orthopsychiatry Assn., Soc. Psychol. Study Social Issues, Jean Piaget Soc. (trustee), Am. Ednl. Rsch. Assn., NY Acad. Scis., Psychologists for Social Responsibility (pres.), Sigma Xi. Home and Office: 431 S Brighton Ln Tucson AZ 85711 Office Phone: 520-745-1725. Business E-Mail: mschwebe@rci.rutgers.edu.

SCHWEBEL, RENATA MANASSE, sculptor; b. Zwickau, Germany, Mar. 6, 1930; came to U.S., 1940, naturalized, 1946; d. George and Anne Marie (Simon) Manasse; m. Jack P. Schwebel, May 10, 1955; children; Judith, Barbara, Diane. BA, Antioch Coll., 1953; MFA, Columbia U., 1961; student, Arts Students League, 1967-69. Cartographer Ecostate Inc., Ridgewood, NJ, 1949; display artist Silvestri Inc., Chgo., 1950-51; asst. Mazzolini Art Foundry, Yellow Springs, Ohio, 1952. One-woman shows include Columbia U., 1961, Greenwich Art Barn, Conn., 1975, Sculpture Ctr., NYC, 1979, Pelham Art Ctr., NY, 1981, New Rochelle Libr. Gallery, 1980, Outdoor Installations Katonah Gallery, 1986, 1989, Berman/Daferner Gallery, N.Y.C., 1992—93; artist (group shows) Stamford Mus., Conn., 1967, 1996, Hudson River Mus., Yonkers, NY, 1972, 1974, Wadsworth Atheneum, Hartford, 1974, Silvermine Art of the Northwest U.S.A: Anns., 1972, 1976, 1980, 1995, 1998, Silvermine Gallery, 1986, 1991, 2000, 2001, 2002, 2003, 2008, New Britain Mus. Am. Art, Conn., 1974, Imprimatur Gallery, St. Paul, 1985, 1986, Bergen County Mus., NJ, 1983, Sculpture Ctr., 1978—88, Katonah Gallery, NY, 1986—90, Cast Iron Gallery, NYC, 1991, 1993, Kyoto (Japan) Gallery, 1993; exhibitions include Sculptors Guild Anns., 1974—, traveling show exhibitions, in Am. cultural ctrs. in Egypt and Israel, 1981, 3 Rivers Art Festival, Pitts., 1994, FFS Gallery, NYC, 1994, 1995, Russian Consulate, 1998, Long Beach Island Assn. Arts and Scis., NJ, 1999, Grounds for Sculpture, Hamilton, NJ, 1999, Chesterwood Mus., Stockbridge, Mass., 2000, Troy Arts Ctr., NY, 2000—01, Rockland Ctr. for Arts, 2001—02, No. Westchester Arts Coun., 2002, 2003, Westport Arts Ctr., 2003, Ednl. Alliance Gallery, NYC, 2003, Carriage Barn Arts Ctr., New Canaan, Conn., 2005, Pleiades Gallery, NYC., 2006, Iona Gallery, Iona Coll., New Rochelle, NY, 2007, Broome St. Gallery, NYC, 2007, Enskilda Gallery, Stockholm, Sweden, 2008, Governors Island, NYC, 2008, Represented in permanent collections S.W. Bell, Columbia U., Colt Industries, Am. Airlines, Comcraft Industries, Nairobi, Gruber Haus, Berlin, Mus. Fgn. Art, Sofia, Bulgaria, Housatonic Mus., Jule Collins Smith Mus. Fine Art, Auburn, Ala., Hexcel Corp. Bd. dirs. Fine Arts Fedn., N.Y., 1985-87; trustee Sculpture Ctr., 1980-88, chmn. exhbn. com., 1986-88; adv. bd. Pehlham Art Ctr., 1982. Mem.: N.Y. Artists Equity, Silvermine Guild, Conn. N.Y. Soc. Women Artists, Conn. Acad. Fine Arts, Audubon Artists (Chaim Gross award 1980, Medal of Honor 1982, Rennick award 1986, 1990, 1992, 1995), Nat. Assn. Women Artists (Willis Meml. prize 1974, Medal of Honor 1981, Paley Meml. award 1979), Sculptors Guild (bd. dirs. 1975—94, pres. 1980—83, bd. dirs. 1995—2004), Katonah Gallery (artist mem. 1986—90), Ams. for Peace Now (bd. dirs. 1991—2001), Antioch Coll. Assn. (bd. dirs. 1971—77). Personal E-mail: renata99m@gmail.com.

SCHWEBEL, STEPHEN MYRON, arbitrator, mediator, legal advisor; b. NYC, Mar. 10, 1929; s. Victor and Pauline (Pfeffer) S.; m. Louise Ingrid Nancy Killander, Aug. 2, 1972; children: Jennifer, Anna. BA in Govt. magna cum laude with highest honors in govt., Harvard U., 1950; postgrad., Cambridge U., 1950—51; LLB, Yale U., 1954; LLD (hon.), Bhopal U., 1983, Hofstra U., 1997, U. Miami, 2002. Bar: N.Y. 1955, U.S. Supreme Ct. 1965, D.C. 1976. Dir. UN hdqrs. office World Fedn. UN Assns., 1950—53; lectr. Am. fgn. policy various univs. U.S. Dept. State, India, 1952; rsch., drafting asst. Trygve Lie for writing of In the Cause of Peace, 1953; assoc. White & Case, NYC, 1954—59; asst. prof.

law Harvard U., Cambridge, Mass., 1959—61; asst. legal advisor U.S. Dept. State, Washington, 1961—66, dep. legal advisor, 1973—81; exec. dir. Am. Soc. Internat. Law, Washington, 1967—72; Burling prof. internat. law Sch. of Advanced Internat. Studies, Johns Hopkins U., Washington, 1967—81; pres. Adminstrv. Tribunal IMF, Washington, 1994—; mem. World Bank Adminstrv. Tribunal, 2007—; judge Internat. Ct. Justice, The Hague, Netherlands, 1981—2000, v.p., 1994—97, pres., 1997—2000. Hon. fellow Cambridge U. Ctr. for Rsch. in Internat. Law, 1983—; mem. bd. electors Whewell Professorship in Internat. Law U. Cambridge, 1983—; hon. bencher Gray's Inn, London, 1998—; spl. rep. Micronesian claims U.S. Dept. State, 1966—71; legal adv. U.S. del. 16th-20th and 4th Spl. Gen. Assemblies UN; US assoc. rep. Internat. Ct. Justice, 1962; U.S. assoc. rep. U.S. dep. agt., 1979, U.S. counsel, 1980; U.S. rep., chmn. U.S. del. to 1st session UN Spl. Com. on Principles Internat. Law concerning friendly rels. and coop. among states, Mexico City, 1964; US rep. numerous other UN coms.; pres. So. Blue Fin Tuna Arbitration, 2000; mem. Eritrea-Yemen Arbitration Tribunal, 1998—2000, Eritrea-Ethiopia Boundary Commn., 2001—07; pres. Barbados-Trinidad & Tobago Arbitration, 2004—06; mem. Abyei Arbitration, Trinidad, 2008—09; mem. panels arbitrators and conciliators Internat. Ctr. SettlementInvestment Disputes World Bank, 2000—09; chmn. or party-apptd. arbitrator 56 internat. comml. arbitrations, 1982—2009; mem. Permanent Ct. of Arbitration, The Hague, 2006—; cons. Ford Found., 1990; chmn. supr. bd. Telders Internat. Law Moot Ct. Competition, The Hague, The Netherlands, 1993—98; chmn. Hauser Scholars Selection Bd., N.Y.U. Law Sch., 1997—2000; bd. dirs. Am. Arbitration Assn., 2006—; vis. lectr. in field. Author: The Secretary-General of the United Nations, 1952, International Arbitration: Three Salient Problems, 1987, Justice in International Law, 1994; editor: The Effectiveness of International Decisions, 1971; mem. editorial bd. Am. Jour. Internat. Law, 1967-81, hon. mem., 1996—; chmn. editorial adv. com. Internat. Legal Materials, 1967-73. Mem. UN Internat. Law Commn., Geneva, 1977—81. Frank Knox fellow Harvard U., 1950-51, Hallows Jud. fellow Marquette U. Law Sch., 2000, Hon. fellow Trinity Coll., Cambridge U., 2005; recipient Gherini prize Yale Law Sch., 1954, medal of Merit, 1997, Pres. medal Johns Hopkins U., 1992, Harold Weill medal NYU, 1992, Wolfgang Friedmann award Columbia U., 1998. Mem. ABA, Am. Soc. Internat. Law (exec. v.p. 1967-73, hon. v.p. 1982-95, hon. pres. 1996-2001, Manley O. Hudson medal 2000), Internat. Law Assn., Inst. Droit Internat., Coun. Fgn. Rels., Acad. of Experts (v.p. 1995—), Harvard Club (NYC), Athenaeum (London), Met. Club, Cosmos Club, Phi Beta Kappa. Avocation: music. Office: 1501 K St NW Washington DC 20005 Home Phone: 202-232-3114; Office Phone: 202-736-8328. Personal E-mail: judgeschwebel@aol.com.

SCHWEBER, SIMONE, education educator; d. Silvan Sam and Miriam Schweber; life ptnr. Jonathan Ivry; children: Talia Ivry, Max Ivry. BA, Swarthmore Coll.; MA in Edn., PhD in Edn., Stanford U. Goodman prof. edn. and Jewish studies U. Wis., 2000—08; fellow US Holocaust Meml. Mus., Washington. Contbr. scientific papers. Instl. fellow, NAE-Spencer Found., grant, Ctr. Advanced Holocaust Study. Office: Univ Wis-Madison 225 N Mills St Madison WI 53706 Business E-Mail: sschweber@wisc.edu.

SCHWEBLER, STEPHEN, retired chemist; b. Flemington, NJ, Dec. 5, 1928; s. Philip and Elizabeth (Pratscher) S.; m. Marian Finch, May 3, 1953; children: Bradley Stephen, Susan Elizabeth, Nancy Carol. AS, Columbia-Greene C.C., Hudson, NY, 1974; BS, SUNY, Saratoga, 1982. With Marshall's Chrysler-Plymouth, Ravena, N.Y., 1953-56; owner/mgr. Steve's Auto Svc., Coxsackie, N.Y., 1956-58; svc. mgr. Jackson & Boone Chrysler-Plymouth, West Coxsackie, N.Y., 1958-66; sr. lab. technician N.Y. State Dept. Health, Albany, 1966-72, N.Y. State Dept. Environ. Conservation, Albany, 1972-85; phys. chemist N.Y. State Office Gen. Svcs., Albany, 1985-88, specification writer, 1988-90, N.Y. State Thruway Authority, Albany, 1990-94; ret. Deacon New Baltimore Ref. Ch., N.Y., 1985-90; rsch. vol. Greene County Hist. Soc., West Coxsackie, 1996—. Democrat. Reformed Ch. Achievements include developing first confirmatory test for the birth defect, galactosemia, by paper chromatography; research in improved methods of sewage treatment and toxic substance monitoring of all bodies of water in N.Y. state. Home: 3931 Rt 51 Hannacroix NY 12087-9708 E-mail: sschweb@aol.com.

SCHWED, ROGER E., lawyer, rental company executive; b. NYC, Jan. 3, 1958; s. Peter and Antonia Holding Schwed; m. Laura F. Dukess, Feb. 26, 1989; children: Benjamin, Stephen. AB cum laude, Princeton U., 1979; JD, Columbia U., 1986. Bar: NY 1987, US Dist. Ct. (ea. dist.) NY 1987, US Dist. Ct. (so. dist.) NY 1988. Subs. rights assoc. Doubleday & Co., Inc., NYC, 1979—83; mgr. subs. rights Harper & Row, NYC, 1983—83; jud. clk. to Hon. Eugene H. Nickerson US Dist. Ct. (ea. dist.), NYC, 1986—87; assoc. Cleary, Gottlieb, Steen & Hamilton, NYC, 1987—95; counsel Skadden, Arps, Slate, Meagher & Flom, NYC, 1995—96; exec. v.p., gen. counsel Maxcor Fin. Group Inc., NYC, 1996—2005, United Rentals, Inc., 2006—. Bd. dirs. I Challenge Myself, Inc., NYC. Coach West Side Little League, NYC, 1998—2003, 2005—, West Side Soccer League, NYC, 1999—2004. Avocations: bicycling, computers, reading. Office: United Rentals, Inc Five Greenwich Office Park Greenwich CT 06831 Business E-Mail: roger@rschwed.com.

SCHWEGLER, ARMIN, language educator; b. Willisau, Luzern, Switzerland, Mar. 8, 1955; s. Armin Schwegler and Marta Vogler. Prof. U. Calif., Irvine, 1987—. Office: Univ Calif Irvine Humanities Hall Irvine CA 92697

SCHWEGLER, NANCY ANN, librarian, writer; b. Bklyn., Jan. 22, 1946; d. Richard Donald Newman and Beatrice Ella Stirba; m. Robert Andrew Schwegler, Apr. 6, 1968; children: Brian Alexander, Christopher Robert, Ashley Marie. BA, Hope Coll., Holland, Mich., 1967; MLIS, U. R.I., 1991. Libr. asst. Art Libr., U. of Chgo., Chgo., 1968—71; children's libr. Watertown (Mass.) Pub. Libr., 1971—72; cataloguer Astronomy Libr., U. Cin., 1972—73; children's libr. East Greenwich (R.I.) Free Libr., 1984—89, Bradley Hosp., Riverside, RI, 1988—. Author: (bibliography) Rhode Island Parents' Paper, Writing in Depth, 2004, Choices: Voices Values and Writing Strategies, 2006; contbr. articles to newspapers and jours. Mem.: ALA, Delta Phi Delta, Beta Phi Mu, Phi Kappa Phi. Reformed Church Of America. Avocations: lighthouse preservation advocacy, international adoption advocacy, watercolour painting. Home: 83 Darling St Warwick RI 02886 Office: Bradley Hospital 1011 Veterans Meml Pkwy Riverside RI 02915 Personal E-mail: nnschweg@aol.com. E-mail: nschwegler@lifespan.org.

SCHWEICKERT, RICHARD JUSTUS, psychologist, educator; b. Madison, Wis., July 19, 1946; s. Carl E. and Marie E. (Dilzer) S.; m. Carolyn M. Jagacinski, Dec. 27, 1980; children: Patrick, Kenneth. BS in Math., U. Santa Clara, 1968; MA in Math., Ind. U., 1972; PhD in Psychology, U. Mich., 1979. Statistician Bellevue Psychiatric Hosp., NYC, 1969-71; asst. prof. Purdue U., West Lafayette, Ind., 1978-83, assoc. prof., 1984-91, prof., 1992—. Adv. panel on human cognition and perception NSF, 1993-96. Author (with others): Handbook of Human Factors; editor Jour. Math. Psychology, 2000—04, mem. editl. bd., 1986—94, 2004—, assoc. editor Psychol. Bull. and Rev., 1993—98, mem. editl. bd. Jour. Exptl. Psychology, Learning, Memory and Cognition, 1985—89, 1991—94; contbr. articles to profl. jours. Grantee NSF, 1981-84, 92-2000, NIMH, 1983-89, Air Force Office Sci. Rsch., 2006—. Fellow AAAS, Am. Psychol. Soc.; mem. Soc. for Math. Psychology (pres. 1990-91, bd. dir.), Psychonomic Soc., Informs. Office: Purdue U Dept Psychol Scis Lafayette IN 47907

SCHWEIGERT, LYNETTE AILEEN, interior designer, consultant; b. Sacramento, July 6, 1949; d. Marvin Gerhardt and Aileen Helen (Velcoff) S.; m. Alan H. Randolph, May 1, 1976; 1 child, Tyler Mason Randolph. BS in Design, U. Calif., Davis, 1971. Display designer Weinstock's, Sacramento, 1971-72, Roos-Atkins, Sacramento, 1972-73; prin., project designer Randolph-Schweigert & Co., Reno, 1975-93; owner, project designer Hospitality Design Group, Reno, 1985—. Prin. Design Ctr. Cons., Reno, 1982-86; cons. interior design Dan Carne AIA, Reno, 1980—, Paul Huss AIA, Reno, 1985-89, U.S. West Investments, Reno, 1984-89; cons. space planning Family Counseling Svc. of No. Nev., Reno, 1986-91; instr. interior design U. Nev., Reno, 1994—. Named one of Top 60 Restaurant Designers, Contract Mag., 1985; recipient Finalist prize Sierra Arts Found., Reno, 1980, Cert. Recognition for Participation in Preprofessional Internship Program U. Nev., 1987. Mem. Inst. Bus. Designers (affiliate). Avocations: photography, skiing, vegetable gardening, water ballet. Office: Hospitality Design Gruop 2346 Palmer Ct Reno NV 89502-9746

SCHWEIKER, MARK S., former governor; b. Bucks County, Pa., Jan. 31, 1953; s. John and Mary S.; m. Katherine Schweiker; children: Brett, Eric, Kara. BS, Bloomsburg U., 1975; MA in Adminstrn., Rider U., 1983. Merrill Lynch; McGraw Hill; supr. Middletown Twp., 1979; commr. Bucks County, Pa., 1987-94; elec. lt. gov., 1994—2001; lt. gov., pres. of the Senate, chmn. of the bd. of pardons Commonwealth of Pa., 1995—2001, gov., 2001—03; former chmn. prime coun., chmn. local govt. adv. coun., chmn. gov.'s exec. coun. recycling devel. & waste reduction, dir. Pa. weed and seed program, gov., 2001—03; pres. & CEO Greater Phila. C. of C., 2003—. Former chmn. Dela. Valley Regional Fin. Authority. Former bd. dirs. Bucks County United Way. Recipient Alumnus of Yr. Bloomsburg U., 1990, Outstanding Svc. to Conservation award Nature Conservancy Pa. Branch, 1993, Tech. Advocate of Yr. Tech. Coun. Ctrl. Pa., 1996, Outstanding Achievement award Citizens Against Govt. Waste, 1997, Commitment to Excellence in Local Govt. award Pa. Economy League, 1998. Republican. Office: Greater Phila C of C 200 Broad St Ste 700 Philadelphia PA 19102

SCHWEIKER, RICHARD SCHULTZ, former trade association administrator, former United States Secretary of Health & Human Services; b. Norristown, Pa., June 1, 1926; s. Malcolm Alderfer and Blanche (Schultz) S.; m. Claire Joan Coleman, Sept. 10, 1955; children: Malcolm C., Lani, Kyle, Richard S. Jr., Lara Kristi. BA, Pa. State U., 1950; D of Pub. Svcs. (hon.), Temple U., 1970; D.Sc. (hon.), Georgetown U., 1981. Bus. exec., 1950-60; mem. US Congress from 13th Pa. Dist., 1961—69; US Senator from Pa., 1969-80; mem. appropriations com., ranking mem. Labor-HEW subcom., ranking mem. health and human resources com., ranking mem. health subcom.; sec. US Dept. Health & Human Services, Washington, 1981—83; pres. Am. Council Life Ins., Washington, 1983-94. Chmn. Partnership for Prevention, 1991—97. Alt. del. Nat. Rep. Conv., 1952, 56, del., 1972, 80; designated v.p. candidate with Reagan for Pres. of U.S., 1976. Served with USNR, World War II. Recipient Disting. Alumnus award Pa. State U., 1970, Dr. Charles H. Best award Am. Diabetes Assn., 1974, Outstanding Alumnus of Yr. award Phi Kappa Sigma, 1982, Gold medal Pa. Assn. Broadcasters, 1982, Nat. Outstanding Svc. award Headstart, 1983, Pub. Svc. Gold medal Surgeon Gen. U.S., 1988, Govt. Achievement award Juvenile Diabetes Found., 1990, Disting. Achievement award Nat. Coun. on Aging, 1991, John Newton Russell award Nat. Assn. Life Underwriters, 1992; named Outstanding Young Man of Yr., Jr. C. of C., 1960. Mem. Phi Beta Kappa.

SCHWEIKERT, EDGAR OSKAR, dentist; b. Heidelberg, Germany, Aug. 30, 1938; came to U.S., 1972; s. Oskar and Priska (Zehr) S.; m. Mary Lou Como, Apr. 7, 1969; 1 child, Marisa. Degree, Hamburg Dental Sch., 1966; Dr. Med. Dentistry, U. Munich, 1969. Lic. dentist, Calif., NY Dentist, U.S. Army, Frankfurt, Fed. Republic Germany, 1969-72; gen. practice dentistry, LA, 1972-73, Bklyn., 1973—; lectr. in field. Author: Multiple Cantilevers in Fixed Prosthesis, 1988, Spanish edit., 1990; contbr. articles to profl. jours. Served as capt. German Air Force, 1967-69. Mem. ADA, German Dental Assn., Second Dist. Dental Assn., Bay Ridge Dental Soc., Guild Dental Craftsmen. Home and Office: 429 77th St Brooklyn NY 11209-3205 Office Phone: 718-680-4717.

SCHWEIKERT, MARY LOU, elementary school educator; b. Bklyn., Aug. 6, 1938; d. Frank Salvatore Como and Angela Licciardi-Como; m. Edgar O. Schweikert, Apr. 7, 1969; 1 child, Marisa. BA in Journalism, LI U., 1962; MEd, Wagner Coll., 1978. Lic. tchr. NYC, 1965, NY, 1965. Tchr. NYC Bd. Edn., Bklyn., 1962—65, Dept. Def., 1965—72; mgr. dental office Dr. Edgar Schweikert, Bklyn., 1973—. Editor: Multiple Cantilevers in Fixed Prosthesis, 1988, Jour. Prosthetic Dentistry, 1984, Dentistry Today, 1994, 1995, 1999. Mem.: Nat. Assn. Women. Democrat. Roman Catholic. Avocations: tennis, gardening, travel. Home and Office: Dr Edgar Schweikert Dentistry 429 77th St Brooklyn NY 11209 Office Phone: 718-680-4717. Personal E-mail: mschweik@earthlink.net.

SCHWEIKERT, NORMAN CARL, retired musician; b. LA, Oct. 8, 1937; s. Carl Albert and Hilda (Meade) S.; m. Sally Hardin Haizlip, July 22, 1961; 1 son, Eric Carl. Mus.B. performer's certificate in horn, Eastman Sch. Music, 1961. Teaching assoc. Northwestern U., 1973-75, assoc. prof. (part-time), 1975-98; horn instr. Nat. Music Camp, Interlochen, 1967; curator Leland B. Greenleaf Collection Mus. Instruments, Interlochen, 1970-71 Successively 4th, 2d and 3d horn with, Rochester Philharmonic, Civic and Eastman-Rochester symphonies, 1955-62, 64-66, instr. horn, mem., Interlochen (Mich.) Arts Quintet, Interlochen Arts Acad., 1966-71, 1st horn, Rochester Chamber Orch., 1965-66, Midland (Mich.) Symphony Orch., 1969-71, 1st horn, soloist, Northwestern Mich. Symphony Orch., 1966-71, Chgo. Little Symphony, tours, 1967, 68, asst. 1st horn, soloist, Chgo. Symphony Orch., 1971-75, 2d horn, Chgo. Symphony Orch., 1975-97; appearances with, Eastman Chamber Orch., Rochester Bach Festival, Aspen Festival Orch., Moravian Music Festival, Alaska Festival, Peninsula Music Festival, Rochester Brass Quintet, Canterbury Wind Quintet, Westchester Brass Quintet, Eastman Wind Ensemble, Chgo. Symphony Winds, Quadrangle Chamber Players, Washington Island Music Festival; soloist, New Japan Philharmonic, rec. artist for, Mercury, Columbia, Everest, C.R.I., Capitol. Mark Ednl., London-Decca, DGG, RCA Victor records, Sheffield Lab, Koch; recitals, also lecture demonstrations.; Contbr. articles to profl. jours. Served with AUS, 1962-64. Recipient certificate of merit City Chgo., 1971 Mem. Internat. Horn Soc. (hon., chmn. organizing com., sec.-treas. 1970-72, adv. coun. 1972-76), Am. Mus. Instrument Soc., Phi Mu Alpha Sinfonia (life alumni mem.), Pi Kappa Lambda. Home: 1727 White Trillium Trail Washington Island WI 54246-9026

SCHWEIKERT, TIMOTHY J., industrial equipment company executive; BS in Mech. Engring., Marquette U.; MS in Engring., U. Cin. Joined GE Aircraft Engines, leadership positions (engring., product mgmt., mktg. & sales); mgr., global locomotive ops. GM, 2003; pres., China GE Transportation, 2006—; pres., CEO, China region GE Infrastructure, 2006—. Office: General Electric Co 3135 Easton Tpke Fairfield CT 06828 Office Phone: 203-373-2211. Office Fax: 203-373-3131.*

SCHWEITZER, BRIAN, Governor of Montana; b. Havre, Mont., Sept. 4, 1955; s. Adam and Kay Schweitzer; m. Nancy Hupp, 1981; children: Ben, Khai, Katrina. BS in Internat. Agronomy, Colo. State U., 1978; MS in Soil Sci., Mont. State U., 1980. Agronomist Kaercherv Agr., Libya, 1980—81; crop supt. Alfa Laval Engring. Co., Saudi Arabia, 1981—84; farm owner, rancher Flathead, Sanders Rosebud and Judith Basin counties, Mont.; mem. Mont. state farm svc. agency com. USDA, 1993—99; gov. State of Mont., Helena, 2005—. Apptd. Mont. Rural Devel. Partnership Bd., 1996, Nat. Drought Task Force. Recipient Award for outreach efforts to Native Americans, U.S. Sec. Agr., 1995. Democrat. Achievements include development of various immigration systems in Africa, Asia, Europe, and South America; over 28,000 acres of irrigated cropland in Saudi Arabia. Office: Office of the Gov PO Box 200801 Helena MT 59620-0801 Office Phone: 406-444-3111. Office Fax: 406-444-5529. E-mail: governor@mt.gov.

SCHWEITZER, GEORGE KEENE, chemistry professor; b. Poplar Bluff, Mo., Dec. 5, 1924; s. Francis John and Ruth Elizabeth (Keene) S.; m. Verna Lee Pratt, June 4, 1948; children: Ruth Anne, Deborah Keene, Eric George. BA, Central Coll., 1945, ScD in Philosophy, 1964; MS, U. Ill., 1946, PhD in Chemistry, 1948; MA, Columbia U., 1959; PhD in History, NYU, 1964. Asst. Central Coll., 1943-45; fellow U. Ill., 1946-48; asst. prof. chemistry U. Tenn., 1948-52, assoc. prof., 1952-58, prof., 1960-69, Alumni Distinguished prof., 1970—. Cons. to Monsanto Co., Proctor & Gamble, Internat. Tech., Am. Cyanamid Co., AEC, U.S. Army, Massengill, CTI-Siemens; lectr. colls. and univs.; mem. adv. bd. East Tenn. Hist. Soc. Author: Radioactive Tracer Techniques, 1950, The Doctorate, 1966, Genealogical Source Handbook, 1992, Civil War Genealogy, 1993, Tennessee Genealogical Research, 1981, Kentucky Genealogical Research, 1981, Revolutionary War Genealogy, 1982, Virginia Genealogical Research, 1982, War of 1812 Genealogy, 1983, North Carolina Genealogical Research, 1983, South Carolina Genealogical Research, 1984, Pennsylvania Genealogical Research, 1985, Georgia Genealogical Research, 1987, New York Genealogical Research, 1988, Massachusetts Genealogical Research, 1989, Maryland Genealogical Research, 1991, German Genealogical Research, 1992, Ohio Genealogical Research, 1994, Indiana Genealogical Research, 1996, Illinois Genealogical Research, 1997, Missouri Genealogical Research, 1997, Aqueous Chemistry of the Elements, 2009; also 170 articles. Faculty fellow Columbia U., 1958-60. Mem. Am. Chem. Soc., Am. Philos. Assn., History Sci. Soc., Soc. Genealogists, Phi Beta Kappa, Sigma Xi. Home: 407 Ascot Ct Knoxville TN 37923-5807

SCHWEITZER, PETRA, literature and language professor; BA, Maximilian U., 1988; MA, U. Athens, Ga., 1993; PhD, Emory U., Atlanta, 2003. Postdoc. fellow Ga. Inst. Tech., Atlanta, 2003—06; asst. prof. Shenandoah U., Winchester, Va., 2006—. Contbr. articles to profl. publs. Dean's Tchg. fellowship, Emory U., 2000—01, Jewish Studies fellowship, 2003—04. Mem.: MLA, Internat. Assn. Lit. and Philosophy, Internat. Assn. Genocide Studies, US Holocaust Mus. Office: Shenandoah Univ 1460 University Dr Winchester VA 22601 Business E-Mail: pschweit@su.edu.

SCHWEITZER, SHANNON TROY, lighting designer, design educator; b. Canton, Ohio, Mar. 29, 1979; s. David Joseph and Karen Ellain Schweitzer. BA in Theater, Mt. Union Coll., Alliance, Ohio, 2001; MFA in Lighting Design, Mich. State U., East Lansing, 2007. Electrician Playwrights Horizons, NYC, 2001—03; lighting supr., designer Ohio Light Opera, Wooster, 2001—; tchg. asst. Mich. State U., Lansing, 2004—07; coll. prof. Ctrl. Mich. U., Mt. Pleasant, 2007; asst. prof. OD design Buffalo State Coll., 2007—. Cons. Palace Theater, Lockport, NY, 2008. Light designing, If The Shoe Fits, The Children's Hour (ACTF Cert. of Merit Best Lighting Design, 2006), Tea and Sympathy (ACTF Cert. of Merit Best Lighting Design, 2006), Posed, Tartuffe, Baltimore Waltz, Antigone, Radiate, Godspell and numerous light designing, set design, The House of Blue Leaves (Thespie award for Best Set Design, 2007). Mem.: US Inst. Theatre Tech. Office: Buffalo State Coll 1300 Elmwood Ave Buffalo NY 14222 Personal E-mail: schweitzer22@gmail.com. Business E-Mail: schweist@buffalostate.edu.

SCHWEITZER, VANESSA GAYL, otorhinolaryngologist; b. Pomona, Calif., Jan. 26, 1952; d. Elford J. Nelson and Patricia Wilma (Sherman) Schweitzer. B.S. in Zoology, U. Mich., 1973; M.D., 1977. Diplomate Am. Bd. Otolaryngology. Intern in gen. surgery U. Mich., 1977-79, resident in otorhinolaryngology, 1979-83; emergency physician Chelsea Community Hosp., Mich., 1979-83, Saline Community Hosp., Mich., 1979-80, Beyer Meml. Hosp. Ypsilanti, Mich., 1980-83; sr. staff physician dept. otolaryngology, head and neck surgery Henry Ford Hosp., Detroit, 1983—; clin. prof. dept. otolaryngology, head and neck surgery U. Mich., Ann Arbor, 1984—, researcher Kresge Hearing Inst., also otology research lab. Henry Ford Hosp. and U. Mich.; lectr. in field; emergency physician Emergency Physicians' Med. Group, Inc., Ann Arbor, 1979-83. Contbr. articles to med. jours. Med. examiner Washtenaw County, Ann Arbor, 1980-84. Angell scholar, 1969-75; recipient Branstrom Freshman award, 1970, Triological Soc Fowler Rsch award, 1996. Fellow ACS; mem. AMA, ASCO, Am. Coll. Emergency Physicians, Am. Acad. Otolaryngology, Am. Acad. Facial Plastic and Reconstructive Surgery, Walter P. Work Soc. (Resident Paper Competitive award 1982), Internat. Photodynamic Therapy Assn., Phi Beta Kappa, Alpha Lambda Delta. Republican. Office: Henry Ford Health Sys 2799 W Grand Blvd Detroit MI 48202-2608 Office Phone: 313-916-3279. Business E-Mail: uschwei1@hfhs.org.

SCHWEIZER, GREGORY PAUL, music educator; b. St. Louis, Jan. 14, 1955; s. Marvin Bernard and Lois Joan Schweizer; m. Diane Marie Stipanovich, June 2, 1978; children: Matthew Gregory, Eric Michael. MusB in Edn., Webster U., St. Louis, 1981. Cert. tchr. K-12 Mo., 1981. Music dir./tchr. St. Dominic Savior Ch., St. Louis, 1978—87, Mary, Queen of Peace Sch., St. Louis, 1979—85; music dir. St. Roch Cath. Ch., St. Louis, 1986—94, St. Lucas United Ch. of Christ, St. Louis, 1994—96, Our Lady of Sorrows Cath. Ch., St. Louis, 1997—; music dir., tchr., dept. chair Visitation Acad., St. Louis, 2000—; music dir. Mo. Athletic Club Apollo Men's Chorus, St. Louis, 1985—. Adj. prof. Webster U., St. Louis, St. Louis Symphony Music Sch.; founder, dir. Camerata Singers. Composer: (composition for tv spot) Variety Club of St. Louis Promo; dir.: (theatrical) Music Director for Shooting Star Productions; condr. (chamber concert series) David & Beatrice Kornblum Concert Series, vocalist nat. comml. Chicken of the Sea Tuna, writer, performer (exercise videos) Martha Rounds; performer: (play with Vikki Carr) I'm Getting My Act Together and Taking It On the Road, G.F. Handel's Saul, St. Louis Bach Soc., St. Louis Symphony

Orch.; condr., accompanist, arranger: with Ken Page, accompanist: with Donald O'Conner, Georgia Frontierre, Lou Rawles, Tommy Tune, The Manhattan Rhythm Kings, Rita Moreno, Bernadette Peters, Kathy Rigby, pianist, condr.: VP Ball Orch., pianist: Variety Club Telethon. Mem. Ind. Sch. of St. Louis, 2004—05. Recipient Outstanding Tchr. of Yr. award, Mo., 2005, 2006, 2007, 2008; named a Tchr. of Distinction, Ind. Schs. St. Louis, 2006; named an Emerson Tchr. of Excellence, 2006. Mem.: Am. Guild Organists, Nat. Assn. of the Tchrs. of Singing (assoc.), Musicians' Assn. of St. Louis (assoc.). Avocations: photography, carpentry. Home: 5801 Westcliffe Dr Saint Louis MO 63129-4267 Office: Visitation Academy 3020 North Ballas Rd Saint Louis MO 63131 Personal E-mail: gregschweizer@hotmail.com. Business E-Mail: gschweizer@visitationacademy.org.

SCHWEIZER, KARL WOLFGANG, historian, educator, author; b. Mannheim, Germany, June 30, 1946; came to U.S., 1988; m. Pamela Schweizer. BA in History with honors, Wilfrid Laurier U., Can., 1969; MA, U. Waterloo, Can., 1970; PhD, Cambridge U., 1976. Prof. history Bishop's U., Lennoxville, Que., Canada, 1976-88, chmn. dept., 1978-79, 82-84, 86; prof., chmn. humanities dept. NJ Inst. Tech., Newark, 1988-93, prof. dept. social sci. and policy studies, 1993—, chmn. dept. humanities and social scis., 2000—03, prof. dept. humanities, 1988—2007, prof. fed. history dept., 2007—; assoc. Ctr. for Study of Global Change Rutgers U., 1995—. Grad. faculty Rutgers U., 1993—; vis. lectr. U. Guelph, Can., 1978-80; rsch. assoc. Russian Rsch. Ctr., Ill., 1979-80, 99; acad. visitor London Sch. Econs., 1986, 94, vis. scholar, 1986-87, Queens U., Ont., Can., 1986-87; vis. fellow Darwin Coll., Cambridge, 1987, 94, 2003, Princeton U., 1994, Yale U., 1994; vis. prof. dept. polit. sci. Rutgers U., 1997—; sr. rsch. assoc. Peterhouse Coll., Cambridge, 2003. Author: The Art of Diplomacy, 1983, Lord Bute: Essays in Reinterpretation, 1988, England, Prussia and the Seven Years War, 1989, Frederick the Great, William Pitt and Lord Bute, 1991, Lord Chatham, A Bibliography, 1993, François de Callières: Diplomat and Man of Letters, 1995, War, Politics and Diplomacy: The Anglo Prussian Alliance, 1756-1763, 2001, Seeds of Evil: The Gray/Snyder Murder Case, 2001, Statesmen, Diplomats and the Press, 2002, Parliament and the Press, 1689-1936, 2007, The International Thought of Herbert Butterfield, 2007, The Seven Years War: A Transatlantic History, 2008, Oligarchy, Dissent and the Culture of Print in Hanoverian Britain, 2009; co-author: The Origins of War in Early Modern Europe, 1987; co-author: (with J. Osborne) Cobbett in His Times, 1990; co-author: paperback edit., 1993, The War of the Spanish Succession, 1994, British Prime Ministers, 1997, Hanoverian Britain and Empire, 1998, A Global Encyclopedia of Historical Writing, 1998, Multiculturalism and the History of International Relations, 1999, International Military Encyclopedia, 1999, 2d edit., 2000, Oxford Dictionary of the Enlightenment, 2003, ScribnersEncyclopedia of Modern European History, 2004, Dictionary of National Biography, 2004; editor: The Devonshire Political Diary, 1757-1762, 1982, Diplomatic Thought 1648-1815, 1982, Warfare and Tactics in the 18th Century, 1984, Herbert Butterfield: Essays on the History of Science, 1998, rev. paperback edit., 2005, In Defense of Australia's Constitutional Monarchy, 2004; co-editor: Essays in European History 1648-1815 in Honour of Ragnhild Hatton, 1985, Politics and the Press in Hanoverian Britain, 1989; gen. editor: Studies in History and Politics, 1980—91, editl. cons.: Scribner's Encyclopedia of Modern European History, Oxford Dictionary of National Biography; editl. cons. Internat. Mil. Ency., Peter Lang Pub. Nat. Endowment for the Humanities, Wiley Blackwell Encyclopedia; contbr. articles to profl. jours. & ref. works. Mem. NJ Gov.'s Adv. Panel on Higher Edn. Restructuring, 1994; trustee NJ Literary Hall of Fame, 1988—92, NJ Comm. Humanities, 1989—93. Recipient Thesis Def. award, Can. Coun., 1976, travel awards, Peterhouse Coll., 1971—73, Adelle Mellen prize for outstanding contbn. to scholarship, Edwin Mellen Press, 1989, Author's award, NJ Writers' Conf., 1993, Tchg. award, NJ Inst. Tech., 2000, Congl. Order of Merit, 2005, 2007, award, Predl. Taskforce, 2006—08; named Wilfrid Laurier Proficiency scholar, 1966—69, Presdl. honoree, Rep. Inner Cir., 2006—08; grantee Inter-Univ. Ctr. for European Studies, 1978, 1981; fellow U. Waterloo, 1969—70, Can. Coun., 1970—75; Grad. Fellow, Province of Ont., 1969—70, rsch. grantee, Bishop's U., 1977, 1978, 1980, 1982, 1983, postdoctoral rsch. grantee, Can. Coun., 1977—78, 1982—83, conf. grantee, S.S.H.R.C., 1985, travel grantee, NEH, 1991, Mellon fellow, Harvard U., 1978, elected fellow, NY Acad. Scis., fellow, Internat. Biographical Assn. Cambridge. Fellow Royal Hist. Soc., Royal Soc. Arts; mem. Internat. Commn. on History of Internat. Rels., Cambridge Hist. Soc., N.Am. Conf. on Brit. Studies, Can. Assn. Scottish Studies, Can. Assn. 18th Century Studies, Inst. Hist. Rsch., Bermuda Maritime Mus. Avocations: music, writing, walking. Office: NJ Inst Tech Rutgers Federated Dept History Newark NJ 07102 Office Phone: 973-596-3274. Business E-Mail: schweizer@adm.njit.edu.

SCHWEIZER, NIKLAUS R., German educator; b. Zurich, Aug. 24, 1939; arrived in U.S., 1964; s. Rudolf Alexander Schweizer and Hedwig Louise Ulrich. BA, U. Zurich, 1964; PhD, U. Calif., Davis, 1968. Tchr. German Punahou Sch., Honolulu, 1968—70; vis. asst. prof. German Dept. European Lang. and Lit. U. Hawaii, Manoa, 1969—70, asst. prof. German, 1970—74, assoc. prof. German, 1974—83, prof. German, 1983—. Hon. consul of Switzerland, Honolulu, 1972—. Author: (novels) His Hawaiian Excellency, 1987, 1994, 2004, (book) The Ut pictura poesis Controversy in Eighteenth-Century England and Germany, 1972, A Poet Among Explorers: Chamisso in the South Seas, 1973, Hawaii und die deutschsprachigen Völker, 1982, Hawaii and the German Speaking Peoples, 1982, Seine hawaiische Exzellenz, 1990, Turning Tide: The Ebb and Flow of Hawaiian Nationality, 1999, 2002, 2005; editor: By Royal Command: Biographical Notes on Curtis Piehu Iaukea, 1988, Jour. des Malers Ludwig York Choris, 1999; contbr. articles to profl. jours., chpts. to books. Dean Consular Corps of Hawaii, 1986, historian, 1988—; pres. Friends of the Royal Hawaiian Band, 1979—99; steering com. Annexation Observance Hawai'i Loa Ku Like Kakou, 1998; bd. dirs. Friends of Iolani Palace, 1982—, chair spl. events com., 1980—2003; pres., mem. coun. Hui Hanai, aux. Queen Lili 'uokalani Children Trust, 1987, mem. coun., 1981—87; chmn. bd. Friends of the Royal Hawaiian Band, 1999—; bd. dirs. Ahahui Ka'iulani, 1990—, Moanalua Gardens Found., 1994—; del. Friends of Iolani Palace, 1996—. Recipient 1st Ann. Award, German-Hawaiian Friendship Club, 1998. Mem.: PEN Ctr. USA West, Pacific Translators, Royal Order of Kamehameha (hon.), German-Hawaiian Comm. and Friendship Club (hon.). Avocations: amateur radio, tennis, skiing, swimming. Office: Univ of Hawaii at Manoa Lang and Lit of Europe and the Ams 1890 East-West Rd Moore 483 Honolulu HI 96822 Office Phone: 808-956-4184. Business E-Mail: niklaus@hawaii.edu.

SCHWEIZER, PAUL DOUGLAS, museum director; b. Bklyn., Nov. 26, 1946; s. Alvin Charles and Marie Gertrude (Scholtz) S.; m. Jane Kulczycki, June 10, 1978 (div. 2004). BA, Marietta Coll., Ohio, 1968; MA, U. Del., 1975, PhD, 1979; postgrad. Mus. Mgmt. Inst., U. Calif., Berkeley, 1990. Instr. art history St Lawrence U., Canton, NY, 1977-78; asst. prof. St. Lawrence U., Canton, NY, 1978-80; curator St. Lawrence U. (Brush Gallery), Canton, NY, 1977-78; dir. St. Lawrence U., Canton, NY, 1979-80; dir. and chief curator Munson-Williams-Proctor Arts Inst. Mus. Art, Utica, 1980—. Bd. dirs. Remington Art Mus., Ogdensburg, NY, 1979—80, Williamstown Regional Art Conservation Lab., Mass., 1981—92, 2007—, pres. bd. trustees, 1988—92; pres. bd. dirs. Gallery Assn. NY State, 1999—2001; adj. prof. art history Pratt at Munson-Williams-Proctor, 2000—; mem. vis. com. Picker Art Gallery, Colgate U.; sr. scholar/rsch. Peale Painting Project. Author: Edward Moran (1829-1901): American Marine and Landscape Painter, 1979, Ferdinand Richardt: Drawings of America, 1855-1859, 2007; co-author (with Ellwood C. Parry III and Dan A. Kushel): The Voyage of Life by Thomas Cole: Paintings, Drawings, and Prints, 1984; co-author: (with Mary E. Murray) Life Lines: American Master Drawings, 1788-1962, 1994, Auspicious Vision: Edward Wales Root and American Modernism, 2008; editor, contbr.: Masterworks of American Art, 1989; contbr. articles to profl. jours. Rsch. grantee Nat. Endowment for Arts, 1978. Mem. Coll. Art Assn., Assn. Art Mus. Dirs., N.Y. State Assn. Art Mus. (trustee 1993-95), Mus. Assn. N.Y. (councilor 1995-2002), Gallery Assn. of N.Y. (bd. dirs. 1996-2002, pres. 1999), Otsego Sailing Club, Alpha Sigma Phi, Omicron Delta Kappa. Office: Munson-Williams-Proctor Arts Inst Mus Art 310 Genesee St Utica NY 13502-4799 Office Phone: 315-797-0000 ext. 2140. Business E-Mail: pschweiz@mwpai.org.

SCHWELB, FRANK ERNEST, Senior Judge, DC Court of Appeals; b. Prague, Czechoslovakia, June 24, 1932; came to U.S., 1947; s. Egon and Caroline (Redisch) S.; m. Taffy Wurzburg, Apr. 9, 1988. BA, Yale U., 1949-53; LLB, Harvard U., 1958. Bar: N.Y. Ct. Appeals 1958, U.S. Dist. Ct. (so. and ea. dists.) N.Y. 1960, U.S. Ct. Appeals (2d cir.) 1961, U.S. Supreme Ct. 1965, U.S. Ct. Appeals (4th cir.) 1968, D.C., D.C. Ct. Appeals, U.S. Dist. Ct. D.C. 1972. Assoc. Mudge, Stern, Baldwin & Todd, NYC, 1958-62; trial atty. Civil Rights Div. U.S. Dept. Justice, Washington, 1962-79, chief eastern sect., 1969, chief housing sect., 1969-79, spl. counsel for litigation, 1979; spl. counsel rev. panel on new drug regulation HEW, Washington, 1976-77; assoc. judge Superior Ct. D.C., Washington, 1979-88, D.C. Ct. Appeals, Washington, 1988—2006, sr. judge, 2006—. Instr. various legal edn. activities. Contbr. articles to profl. jours. With U.S. Army, 1955-57. Recipient Younger Fed. Lawyer award, Fed. Bar Assn., 1967. Mem. Bar Assn. D.C., World Peace Through Law Ctr., World Assn. Judges, Czechoslovak-Am. Orgns., De Tocqueville Soc., Order of the Battered Boot. Avocations: tennis, ping pong/table tennis, sports, gilbert and sullivan operettas, shakespeare, soccer. Office: DC Ct Appeals 430 E St NE Washington DC 20001-2138 Office Phone: 202-879-2779. Business E-Mail: fschwelb@dcappeals.gov.*

SCHWEMMER, GABRIELLE, academic administrator, coach; b. Clayton, Mo., Dec. 27, 1978; d. Daniel Lee Gagnon and Kathleen Schremp; m. Justin Michael Schwemmer, May 20, 2000; children: Jordyn Kathleen, Madelyn Joyce, Camryn Jane. BA in Elem. Edn., McKendree Coll., Lebanon, Ill., 2002; MA in Ednl. Adminstrn., Lindenwood U., St. Charles, Mo., 2006. Cert. in elem. edn. Ill., Mo., 2001, prin. 2006. Mentor, tutor Belleville Americorps, Ill., 1997—99; program dir. Jenny Craig, Fairview Heights, Ill., 1999—2001; permanent substitute Centerville Elem., Cahokia, Ill., 2001—02; tchr. 2nd grade Penniman Elem., Cahokia, 2002—03; PBIS internal coach Cahokia Sch. Dist. #187, 2003—, substitute prin., 2006—; head tchr. 4th, 5th grade Estelle Sauget Academic Ctr., Cahokia, 2003—. Named to Dean's List, McKendree Coll., 2002. Mem.: Cahokia Fedn. Tchrs. Local 1272 (union bldg. rep. 2007—08). Home: 5579 Cornestone Ct Smithton IL 62285 Office: Estelle Sauget Academic Ctr 1700 Jerome Ln Cahokia IL 62206 Personal E-mail: justobm27@yahoo.com. Business E-Mail: schwemmerg@stclair.k12.il.us.

SCHWEND, RICHARD MICHAEL, orthopedist, educator; s. Francis Richard and Shirley Lee Schwend; m. Colleen Gorman Gorman, June 17, 1977; children: Ryan Christopher, Meghan Kathleen. BA, U. Calif., Santa Barbara, 1975. Cert. Nat. Bd. Med. Examiners, 1979, diplomate Am. Bd. Pediat., 1984, Am. Bd. Orthop. Surgery, 2004. Pediat. orthop. spine surgeon to prof. dept. orthop. Children's Mercy Hosp., Kans. City, Mo., 2006—. Chief orthop. surgeon Project Perfect World Ecuador Pediat. Orthop. Surgery Program, Guayaquil, 2002. Col. USAF, 2001—08, Lackland AFB. Office: Children's Mercy Hosp 2401 Gillham Rd Kansas City MO 64108 Office Fax: 816-855-1993.

SCHWENDEMAN, PAUL WILLIAM, lawyer; b. Chgo., Apr. 7, 1945; s. Oscar and Edna Dorothy (Ellis) S.; m. Shirley Anne Starke; children: Paul A., John E., Thomas D. BA in Econs., Carleton Coll., 1966; MSJ, Northwestern U., 1967; JD, Duquesne U., 1978. Bar: Pa. 1978. Mgr. divsn. ops. Greater Waterbury (Conn.) C. of C., 1971-75; v.p. Greater Pitts. C. of C., 1975-78; assoc. Kirkpatrick & Lockhart, Pitts., 1978-84, ptnr., 1984—. Lt. USNR, 1971. Office: Kirkpatrick & Lockhart 1500 Oliver Bldg Pittsburgh PA 15222-2312

SCHWENDINGER, JULIA ROSALIND SIEGEL, sociology researcher; b. Rockaway Beach, NY, Sept. 3, 1926; d. Jacob and Lena (Pliskin) Siegel; m. Herman Schwendinger, Nov. 26, 1946; children: Jane Leni, Joseph Tom. BA, Queens Coll., 1947; MSW, Columbia U., 1950; D Criminology, U. Calif., Berkeley, 1975. Cert. tchr., Calif. Project dir. Adolescent Cmty. Survey U. Calif., Berkeley, 1963-67; dir. Women's Resource Ctr., San Francisco Sheriff's Office, 1975-76; dep. parole commr. San Francisco Bd. Parole, 1976; asst. prof. U. Nev., Las Vegas, 1976-77; vis. scholar Humboldt U., Berlin, summer 1979; adj. prof., lectr. SUNY, New Paltz, 1978-88; rsch. assoc. Inst. for Study of Social Change, Berkeley, 1986—. Vis. prof. Vassar Coll., Poughkeepsie, N.Y., spring 1980, 82; vis. scholar Moscow State U., fall 1988; cons. criminologist, Berkeley, 1988; cons. Women's Crisis Ctr., SUNY, New Paltz, 1983-86, Nat. Inst. for Juvenile Justice and Delinquency Prevention, Washington, 1981-84; criminal justice planning cons. San Francisco Sheriff's Dept., 1974. Co-author: The Sociologists of the Chair, 1974, Rape and Inequality, 1983, Delinquency and Adolescent Subcultures, 1985. Recipient Outstanding Scholarship award Soc. Study of Social Problems, 1986, Career award Women's divsn. Am. Soc. Criminology, 1994. Mem. Am. Sociol. Assn. (Disting. Scholar award 1987), Western Soc. Criminology (Paul Tappan award for Most Original and Seminal Contbn. to Criminology, 1984). Avocations: pottery, piano, singing in chorale, folk dance, gardening.

SCHWENDINGER, LAURA ELISE, composer, humanities educator; b. Mexico, Jan. 26, 1962; d. Robert Joseph and Betty Ruby Schwendinger; m. Menzie David Chinn, Sept. 2, 1991. MB, Boston Conservatory, 1980; MA, U. Calif., Berkeley, 1987, PhD, 1993. Lectr. U. Calif., Santa Cruz, 1997—98; faculty San Francisco Conservatory Music, 1989—98; asst. prof. composition and theory U. Ill., Chgo., 1998—2004, assoc. prof. composition and theory, 2004—05; assoc. prof. composition U. Wis., Madison, 2005—; Emily Mead Baldwin-Bascom prof. creative arts U. Wis. Arts Inst., 2006—. Vis. lectr. Smith Coll., Northampton, Mass., 1997. Composer: in field. Recipient Aaron Copland award, Copland House, 2007; grantee Ill. Arts Coun., 2001, Am. Music Ctr., 2003; fellow Yale Summer Sch. Music, 1995, Rockefeller Found., 1997, Am. Acad. Berlin, 1999, Bogliasco Found., 2002, North Shore MacDowell Soc., 2002, Radcliffe Inst. Advanced Study, 2002, Guggenheim Found., 2008, Yaddo Colony, 2008, AAAL, 2009; scholar Am. Acad. Arts and Letters, 1993, Nat. Endowment for the Arts, 1995; Norton Stevens fellow, MacDowell Colony Arts, 1994, resident, 2004, 2006, commn., Harvard Musical Assn., 1999, Fromm Music Found., 1999, Koussevitzky Music Found., 2001, vis. artist, Am. Acad. Rome, 2009. Office: U Wis Madison Sch Music 3561 Mosse Humanities 455 N Park St Madison WI 53706 also: c/o Carlson and Carlson 5339 Lewis St Dallas TX 75206 Office Phone: 608-263-5233. Office Fax: 608-262-8876. E-mail: lschwendinge@wisc.edu.*

SCHWENGER, WILBUR JOHN, mathematics educator; s. John William and Helen Elizabeth Schwenger; m. Barbara Ann Silvis, Aug. 15, 1970; children: Karin Christine, Lauralee Ruth, John Daniel, William James. AA, Palm Beach CC, West Palm Beach, Fla., 1967; BA, U. Fla., Gainesville, 1969, MEd, 1971. Tchr. St. Lucie County Sch. Bd., Fort Pierce, Fla., 1971—. Scoutmaster Boy Scouts Am., Ft. Pierce, 1973—88, cubmaster, 1988—94, scoutmaster, 1995—; jr. civitan advisor Civitan, 1973—90. A1C USAF, 1961—65. Recipient Dist. award of Merit, Boy Scouts Am., Silver Beaver, Civitan, Outstanding Jr. Civitan Advisor Fla. Dist., 2001, Dist. award of Merit, 1976, Silver Beaver award, 1976, Tchr. of Yr. award, St. Lucie County Sch. Bd., 1983, Lamb award, Lutheran Ch. Mem.: Am. Math. Assn., Math. Ass. Ft. Pierce, Nat. Coun. Tchrs. Math. Lutheran. Avocations: hiking, camping, scouting. Home: 5207 Citrus Ave Fort Pierce FL 34982 Personal E-mail: schwenw@netscape.net.

SCHWENINGER, LOREN, history professor; b. Culver City, Calif., Jan. 7, 1941; s. Ivan Franklin Schweninger and Wanda Wolmuth; m. Patricia Jean Eames, Aug. 21, 1965; children: John Franklin, Michael Ivan, James Lee, Emily Jean. BA, U. Colo., Boulder, 1958; MA, U. Colo., 1966; PhD, U. Chgo., 1972. Prof. history U. NC, Greensboro, 1971—2002, Elizabeth Rosenthal excellence prof., 2003—. Author: (books) Runaway Slaves: Rebels on the Plantation (Lincoln Prize, 2000), (book) James T. Rapier and Reconstruction, 1978, From Tennessee Slave to St. Louis Entrepreneur: The Autobiography of James Thomas, 1984, Black Property Owner in the South: 1790-1915, 1990, Black Property Owner in the South, 1790-1915, 1997. Recipient Fellowship, Rsch. Grants, Nat. Endowment for the Humanities, 1985, 1995-2008. Home: 807 Rankin Pl Greensboro NC 27403 Office: Univ NC Greensboro 1100 Spring Garden St Greensboro NC 27412 Business E-Mail: llschwen@uncg.edu.

SCHWENK, THOMAS L., physician; b. Kalamazoo, Mich., Oct. 26, 1949; s. Lee G. and Katherine J. Schwenk; m. Jane K. Kindig, Dec. 22, 1970; children: Sarah J., Andrew T. BChE, U. Mich., 1971, MD, 1975. Cert. Am. Bd. Family Medicine, Am. Bd. Sports Medicine. Residency family medicine U. Utah, 1975—78, fellow family medicine, 1980—82; prof., George A. Dean chair dept. family medicine U. Mich., Ann Arbor, 1986—, prof. dept. med. edn., assoc. dir., Depression Ctr. Contbr. chapters to books, several articles to publications; writer Journal Watch, 1994—. Fellow: Am. Coll. Sports Medicine; mem.: Inst. of Medicine, Am. Bd. Family Practice (former v.p. bd. dirs.). Office: U Mich Dept Family Medicine 1500 E Med Ctr Dr Ann Arbor MI 48103 also: Briarwood Family Medicine Bldg 10-Ann Arbor 1801 Briarwood Circle Ann Arbor MI 48109-5734 Office Fax: 734-615-2687. Personal E-mail: tschwenk@umich.edu.*

SCHWENN, LEE WILLIAM, retired health facility administrator; b. Morrisonville, Wis., Dec. 23, 1925; s. LeRoy William and Vivian Mae (Kramer) S.; m. Glenna Edith Mehne, Jan. 16, 1947; 1 son, William Lee. BS, U. Wis., 1948; M.P.H., U. N.C., 1956. Tchr. pub. schs., Appleton, Wis., 1948-52; teaching cons. Wis. Health Dept., 1952-53; adminstrv. asst. Madison (Wis.) Health Dept., 1953-57; adminstrv. cons. U.S. Children's Bur., Atlanta Regional Office, 1957-58; adminstr. USPHS, Washington, 1958-66; assoc. dir. D.C. Dept. Health, 1966-70, D.C. Dept. Human Resources, 1970-71; exec. v.p. Maimonides Med. Center, Bklyn., 1971-88, pres., 1988-89, spl. cons. Bd. Trustees, 1989-96. Recipient Distinguished Pub. Service award D.C. Govt., 1970 Mem. Delta Omega. Home: 1007 Westminster Dr Greensboro NC 27410-4551

SCHWERDTNER, FREDERICK HOWARD, lawyer, retired police commander, real estate broker; b. Chgo., Oct. 13, 1949; s. Fred and Lydia (Tatz) S.; m. Julie Anne Carramusa, Oct. 21, 1990; 1 child, Sarah Elizabeth. BS, Loyola U., Chgo., 1973, JD, 1989; MBA with distinction, DePaul U., 1983. Bar: Ill. 1989, U.S. Ct. Appeals (7th cir.) Ill. 1989. Officer Oak Park (Ill.) Police Dept., 1973-93, commdr., 1989-93; with DuPage County Vets. Assistance Commn., 1995—, pres., 1997—99; lawyer Pvt. Practice, Ill. Contbr. articles to profl. jours. Tutor inner city high sch. students, Chgo., 1988; apptd. local bd. mem. Selective Svc. Sys., police commr. Bd. Police Commr., Village of Glendale Heights, Ill., 1999-, chmn., 2002-. Served USMC, 1965-69, Vietnam, 1967-68. Mem. ABA, Fraternal Order Police, Marine Corps League (Band of Bros. Detachment), VFW, Vietnam Vets of Am., Ill. State Bar Assn., Chgo. Bar Assn., DuPage County Bar Assn., Beta Gamma Sigma. Lutheran. Avocations: hiking, tennis, racquetball, golf. Office Phone: 630-653-3494. Personal E-mail: vet-star@comcast.net.

SCHWERIN, HORACE S., marketing research consultant; b. NYC, Jan. 18, 1914; s. Paul and Rose (Lewis) S.; m. Lorraine Roth, June 14, 1941 (div. Dec. 1969); children: Barbara, Bruce; m. Enid May Highton, Apr. 28, 1973. BS, Lafayette Coll., 1935; MA, London U., 1936; MS, U. Paris, 1937. Gen. mgr., research dir., cons. N.Y. advt. agys., 1936-41; pres. Research Analysts, Inc., 1946; chmn. bd. Schwerin Research Corp., NYC, Toronto, London, Hamburg, to 1968; chmn., pres. Horace Schwerin & Assos., Englewood Cliffs, NJ, 1968-72; dir. marketing devel. Campbell Soup Co., Camden, NJ, 1972—, v.p. market planning Canned Food div., 1977-82, mktg. strategy cons., 1982—; CEO, chmn. Schwerin Murphy, Inc., 1991-98; ret., 1998. Author: (with Henry H. Newell) Persuasion in Marketing, 1981; also articles on market research, nutrition, use of govt. data bases. Served as capt. U.S. Army, 1946. Decorated Legion of Merit with oak leaf cluster; inducted into Market Rsch. Coun. Hall of Fame, 1992. Mem. Am. Mktg. Assn., Market Rsch. Coun., Can. Club (NYC), Penn Club (NYC). Methodist. Home: 5D Toll Gate Of Moorestown 633 E Main St Moorestown NJ 08057-3059 Office: 633 E Main St Moorestown NJ 08057-3059

SCHWERIN, KARL HENRY, anthropology educator, researcher; b. Bertha, Minn., Feb. 21, 1936; s. Henry William and Audrey Merle (Jahn) S.; m. Judith Drewanne Altermatt, Sept. 1, 1958 (div. May 1975); children: Karl Frederic, Marguerite DelValle; m. Partha Louise, Jan. 25, 1979; stepchildren: Tamara, Brent, Taryn. BA, U. Calif., Berkeley, 1958; PhD, UCLA, 1965. Instr. Los Angeles State Coll., 1963; asst. prof. anthropology U. N.Mex., Albuquerque, 1963-68, assoc. prof., 1968-72, prof., 1972-2001, asst. chmn. dept. anthropology, 1983-85, chmn. dept. anthropology, 1987-93, prof. emeritus, 2001—. Prof. invitado Inst. Venezolano de Investigaciones Cientificas, Caracas, 1979. Author: Oil and Steel Processes of Karinya Culture Change, 1966, Antropologia Social, 1969, Winds Across the Atlantic, 1970; editor: Food Energy in Tropical Ecosystems, 1985; contbr. articles to profl. jours. V.p. Parents without Ptnr., Albuquerque, 1976-77. Grantee Cordell Hull Found., Venezuela, 1961-62, N.Y. Zool. Soc., Honduras, 1981; Fulbright scholar Cañar, Ecuador, 1969-70, Paris, 1986; founded Karl H. Schwerin Fellowship in Ethnology. Fellow Am. Anthropol. Assn.; mem. Am. Ethnol. Soc., Am. Soc. Ethnohistory (pres. 1975), Southwestern Anthropol. Assn. (co-editor Southwestern Jour. Anthropology 1972-75), N.Mex. Cactus and Succulent Soc. (v.p. 1970-71), Internat. Congress of Americanists (35th-40th, 43d, 46th, 48th, 49th, 50th), Netherwood Pk. Neighborhood Assn. (pres. 2005-07, U. N. Mex. Retiree Assn. Bd., 2007-), Sigma Xi (chpt. pres. 1980-81) Avocations: photography, gardening, hiking, travel, bicycling. Office: U NMex Dept Anthropology MSC01-1040 Albuquerque NM 87131-0001 Office Phone: 505-277-4614. Business E-Mail: schwerin@unm.edu.

SCHWERING, FELIX KARL, electronics executive, researcher; b. Cologne, Nordrhein-Westfalen, Federal Republic of Germany, June 4, 1930; came to U.S., 1964; s. Felix Bernhard and Maria (Heinrichs) S. BS, U. Aachen, Federal Republic of Germany, 1951, Diplom-Ingenieur, 1954, PhD, 1957. Asst. prof. U. Aachen, Federal Republic of Germany, 1956-58; electronic scientist U.S. Army R & D Labs., Fort Monmouth, NJ, 1958-61; project leader AEG-Telefunken, Ulm, Federal Republic of Germany, 1961-64; rsch. scientist U.S. Army Communication Electronics Command (CECOM), Fort Monmouth, NJ, 1964-96, ret., 1996, cons., 1996—. Vis. lab. assoc. US Army Rsch. Office, Rsch. Triangle, NC, 1984-85; vis. prof. NJ Inst. Tech., Newark, 1986—, Rutgers U., New Brunswick, NJ, 1973-87, Monmouth U., 1996—99. Author: (with others) Millimeter Wave Antennas, 1988; author, editor (with others) Microwave Antennas, 1989; mem. editl. bd. Microwave and Optical Tech. Letters, 1988—; contbr. articles to profl. jours.; patentee in field. Fellow: IEEE (Best Paper award Antennas and Propagation Soc. 1961, 82); mem.: Internat. Sci. Radio Union, Am. Geophys. Union, Armed Forces Comm. Electronics Assn., Sigma Xi. Roman Catholic. Office: US Army CERDEC Attn AMSRD-CER-ST-WL Fort Monmouth NJ 07703-5203 Office Phone: 732-532-0469. Business E-Mail: felix.schwerin@us.army.mil.

SCHWERTFEGER, TIMOTHY R., investment company executive; b. Mar. 28, 1949; BA in Econs. and Fin., Northwestern U.; JD, Georgetown U.; student, Harvard Bus. Sch., Stanford U. Nat. dir. health care investment banking svcs. Nuveen Investments, Inc. (div. St. Paul Co., Inc.), 1977—86, head corp. mktg., 1987—89, exec. v.p., 1989—96, chmn. Nuveen Mutual Funds & Exch.-traded Funds, 1996—, chmn., CEO, 1996—2007, non-exec. chmn., 2007—. Pres. Hubbard St. Dance Chgo.; bd. dirs. Better Boys Found., Lyric Opera Chgo., Mus. Contemporary Art, Providence St. Mel Sch. Office: Nuveen Investments Inc 333 W Wacker Dr Chicago IL 60606

SCHWETHELM, OTTO C., oil industry executive; B acctg., Univ. Tex., Austin. CPA. Mgmt. positions Saudi Aramco; mgmt. positions through v.p. Tesoro Corp., San Antonio, 1998—2003, v.p., contr., 2003—06, v.p. fin., treas., 2006—07, v.p., CFO, 2007—08, sr. v.p., CFO, treas., 2008—. Office: Tesoro Corp 300 Concord Plz San Antonio TX 78216-6999

SCHWEYEN, STEPHEN GREGORY, engineering company executive; b. Berthold, ND, Aug. 12, 1951; s. Theodore Francis Schweyen and Elizabeth Mae Smith; m. Lauri Ellen Reed, Nov. 12, 1973; children: Rachel, Leah, Sarah, Rebekah, Stephen, Nicholas, Charles. BA in Zoology, U. Wash., Seattle, 1976. Cert. spl. inspector Wash. Assn. Bldg. Ofcls. Inspector and tech dir. engring. svcs. Profl. Svc. Industries, Pitts. Testing Lab., Pitts., 1976—. Tech. dir. Am. Concrete Inst., Farmington Hills, Mich., 1994—; chief, Seattle Coun. Thunderbird Dist., 2006—08, dist. chmn., tng. Author: Family History, 2000. Scoutmaster, troop 7 Boy Scouts Am., 1992—2008. With US Army, 1971—72. Recipient Scoutmaster of Yr., Boy Scouts Am., Seattle Coun., 2003, Dist. award of merit, Boy Scouts Am., 2005, Troop of Yr., 2006; named Family of Month, KC, 2006. Mem.: Knights of Columbus (named Knight of Month), U. Wash. Alumni Assn., St. Vincent de Paul Soc., KC, 82nd Airborne Divsn. Assn., Am. Legion, Boy Scouts Am. (Scoutmaster Appreciation award 2008). Roman Catholic. Avocations: collecting rare books and maps, coin collecting/numismatics, hiking, camping, genealogy. Home: 5514 22nd Ave S Seattle WA 98108 Office: Profl Svc Industries 24413 56th Ave W Mountlake Terrace WA 98043 Personal E-mail: remeor@aol.com.

SCHWIEBERT, DEBORAH JOHNSON, marketing executive; b. Moline, Ill., Apr. 26, 1952; d. Robert B. and Ruth E. Cronin; m. Mark W. Schwiebert, Oct. 10, 1987. BA in English, St. Mary's Coll., 1974; MA in Organizational Leadership, St. Ambrose U., 2007; attending in Humanities (hon.), saint Mary's, Notre Dame, Indiana, 2009. Dealer mgmt. rep. John Deere Co., East Moline, Ill., 1975—77, territory mgr., 1977-85; mktg. cons. John Deere Info. Systems, East Moline, Ill., 1985-91, mgr. quality assurance, 1991-93; project mgr., product safety mktg. Deere & Co., Moline, Ill., 1993-97, divsn. mgr. retail customer, 1997-98, mgr. Deere.com, 1998—2005, dir. communication svcs., 2005—. Deere & Co. Credit Union, 1996-2001 Mem. St. Mary's Coll. Alumni (pres. 1998-2000, bd. dirs. 1994-2000, bd. trustees 1998—2009, chair bd. trustees 2004-07) Roman Catholic. Avocations: reading, travel. Home: 3913 14th St Rock Island IL 61201-6016 Office: Deere & Co One John Deere Pl Moline IL 61265-1373

SCHWIETZ, ROGER L., archbishop; b. St. Paul, Minn., July 3, 1930; MA in Philosophy, U. Ottawa; MA in Sacred Theology, Loyola U.; STL in Sacred Theology, Gregorian U., Rome; HHD (hon.), Lewis U., 1998. Ordained priest Oblates of Mary Immaculate, 1967; assoc. pastor St. Thomas Aquinas Parish, International Falls, Minn., 1975—78; dir. Coll. Seminary prog. for Oblates of Mary Immaculate Creighton U., Omaha, 1978—84; pastor Holy Family Parish, Duluth, Minn., 1984—89; ordained bishop, 1990; bishop Diocese of Duluth, 1990—2000; coadjutor archbishop Archdiocese of Anchorage, Alaska, 2000—01, archbishop Alaska, 2001—; apostolic adminstr. Diocese of Juneau, Alaska, 2008—09. Episcopal moderator Teens Encounter Christ (TEC) movement, 1991—; chmn. vocation com. Nat. Conf. Cath. Bishops, 1998; bd. dir. Cath. Relief Services, 1997—2003; mem. adminstrv. bd. Nat. Conf. Cath. Bishops, 1994—97, 1998—2002; regional bd. rep. Am. Coll., Leuven, Belgium. Roman Catholic. Home and Office: Archdiocese of Anchorage 225 Cordova St Anchorage AK 99501-2409*

SCHWIMMER, DAVID, actor; b. Queens, NY, Nov. 12, 1966; BS in Speech/Theater, Northwestern U., 1988. Co-founder The Lookingglass Theater Co., Chgo., 1988. Actor (films) Flight of the Intruder, 1991, Crossing the Bridge, 1992, The Waiter, 1993, Twenty Bucks, 1993, The Party Favor, 1995, The Pallbearer, 1996, Breast Men, 1997, The Thin Pink Line, 1998, Kissing a Fool (also exec. prodr.), 1998, Six Days Seven Nights, 1998, Apt Pupil, 1998, All the Rage, 1999, Picking Up the Pieces, 2000, Hotel, 2001, Duane Hopwood, 2005, (voice) Madagascar, 2005(voice) Madagascar: Escape 2 Africa, 2008, Nothing But the Truth, 2008, (TV films) A Deadly Silence, 1989, Since You've Been Gone, 1998, Uprising, 2001, (TV miniseries) Band of Brothers, 2001, (TV series) The Wonder Years, 1992, Friends, 1994-2004, Monty, 1994, (stage appearances) West, The Odyssey, Of One Blood, In the Eye of the Beholder, The Master and Margarita, Some Girls, 2005; dir. (films) Run Fatboy Run, 2007, (TV series) Little Britain USA, 2008-; (TV appearances) LA Law, NYPD Blue, 1993, L.A. Law, 1992, 93, ER, 1996, The Single Guy, 1997, Curb Your Enthusiasm, 2004; exec. prodr. Humanoid, 2003, Shoot the Moon, 1996*

SCHWIND, WILLIAM F., JR., lawyer, oil industry executive; b. Chgo., 1944; BS, JD, Loyola U., Chgo. Bar: Tex. 1969. With Marathon Oil Corp., Findlay, Ohio, 1974—83; comml. contract mgr. Jakarta, Indonesia, 1983—84; gen. atty. Marathon Oil Corp., Houston, 1984—91; sr. v.p. adminstrn., gen. counsel, sec. Dehli Gas Pipeline Corp., Dallas, 1991—92; v.p., gen. counsel, sec. Marathon Oil Corp., Houston, 1992—. Mem.: ABA, Am. Petroleum Inst. (chmn. gen. com. law), Am. Corp. Counsel Assn. Office: Marathon Oil Co PO Box 4813 5555 San Felipe Rd Houston TX 77210-4813

SCHWINGER, DAVID, lawyer; b. Phila., Nov. 8, 1956; BS summa cum laude, U. Pa., 1977; JD with high honors, George Washington U., 1982. Bar: DC 1982. Mng. ptnr. Katten Muchin Zavis Rosenman, Washington, Locke Liddell & Sapp PLLC, Washington, 2007—. Mem.: Nat. Reverse Mortgage Lenders Assn., Mortgage Bankers Assn. of Am. Office: Locke Liddell & Sapp PLLC 401 9th St NW Ste 400 S Washington DC 20004 E-mail: dschwinger@lockeliddell.com.

SCHWINGHAMER, MARY DENISE, veterinarian; b. Jasper, Ind., Aug. 25, 1953; DVM, Auburn U., 1978. Preceptor Brentwood Vet. Clinic, Tenn., 1978—79; staff veterinarian Birmingham Humane Soc., Ala., 1980—81; emergency animal clinician Emergency Animal Clinic, Birmingham, 1980—83; small animal clinic propr. Companion Animal Clinic, Irondale, Ala., 1981—94; tech. writer, 1994—. Contbr. articles to profl. jours. Roman Catholic. Achievements include invention of; research in treatment for canine parvovirus enteritis; treatment for HIV-AIDS and Systemic Viremias in human population with companion animals as in vivo models. Avocations: swimming, dog and horse care and breeding. Home: 7313 Martha Dr Huntsville AL 35802 Office Phone: 256-881-5500.

SCHWITTERS, KATHLEEN CHANTELL, school psychologist specialist; b. El Paso, Tex., Jan. 17, 1978; d. Jim and Suzanne Schwitters. BA in Psychology, Tex. A&M U., Coll. Station, 2000, MS in Ednl. Psychology, 2004. Lic. sch. psychologist specialist Tex. State Bd. Exams. Psychologists, 2005. Lic. specialist, sch. psychology Pflugerville Ind. Sch. Dist., Tex., 2002—. Mem.: NASP, Phi Kappa Phi Nat. Honor Soc., Kappa Delta Pi Internat. Honor Soc. Office: Pflugerville Ind Sch Dist 1401 W Pecan Pflugerville TX 78660 Personal E-mail: kathleen00@sbcglobal.net.

SCIAME, FRANK J., real estate developer, construction executive; BS in architecture, CUNY: City Coll.; DFA (hon.), 2004. Founder, CEO F. J. Sciame Construction Co., 1975—; founder Sciame Devel., Inc., 1996—. Bd. dirs., former pres. City Coll. Alumni Assn.; bd. dirs. City Coll. Fund, NYC, Actor's Ctr., NYC, South Street Seaport Mus.; chmn. NY Landmarks Conservancy, Seaport North Cmty. Bus. Assn. Morgan Libr. and Mus., NYC, Pratt Inst. Sch. Architecture, Bklyn., NY, Historic Front St. restoration, NYC, Ctrl. Synagogue restoration, Harvard Club of NYC, South court addition to NY Pub. Libr. main br., Seamen's Church Inst., NYC, Bear Stearns specialty floors at 383 Madison Ave. Recipient NYC Entrepreneur of Yr. award in construction, Ernst & Young, 1996, Construction Mgr. of Yr., Construction Mgmt. Assn. America, 1997, Chmn.'s award, NY Landmarks Conservancy, 1997, Pillar of NY award, Preservation League of NY State, 2003. Mem.: AIA (former pub. dir. of NYC chapt.), NY Bldg. Congress (former chmn.), NY State chapt. of AIA (hon.), NYC chapt. of AIA (hon.). Office: FJ Sciame Construction Co Inc/Sciame Devel Inc 14 Wall St New York NY 10005 Office Phone: 212-232-2200. E-mail: info@sciame.com.*

SCIAME, JOSEPH, university administrator; b. Bklyn., Sept. 9, 1941; s. Joseph and Sophie (Pintacuda) S. EdB, St. John's U., 1971. Fin. aid officer, asst. to dean of admissions St. John's U., Jamaica, NY, 1967-71, dir. fin. aid, 1971-82, dean fin. aid, 1982, v.p. fin. aid and student svcs., 1982-94, v.p. for govt. and cmty. rels., 1994—2002, v.p. for cmty. rels., 2002—. Mem. Gov. Commn. on Sch. Achievement, 1971—, chairperson, 1993—; pres. N.Y. Assn. Student Fin. Aid Adminstrn., 1980-82, Ea. Assn. Student Fin. Aid Adminstrn., 1986-87. Mem. Town of North Hempstead, N.Y., 1975, chmn. bd. ethics, 1984—; nat. chmn., bd. dirs. Garibaldi-Meucci Mus., N.Y., 1987-93, 97-99, pres., CEO, 1999-2007; mem. Providence Rest, 1995-, chmn., 2007-09; bd. dirs. St. John's Prep, 1996—; bd. mem. Queens Symphony Orch., 2000—, Boy Scouts Am., 2000—, v.p. membership, 2001-07; bd. mem. Holocaust Resource Ctr., 2002—, chmn. 2008-. Decorated Cavaliere Ufficiale del Merito della Repubblica Italiana, Commendatore Order Merit House of Savoy, Cavaliere SS Maurice Lazarus, 2007; recipient Lifetime Membership award Ea. Assn., 1995, Achievement award N.Y. State Fin. Aid Adminstrs., 1982, Congl. Record award, 1979, 91, 93, 94, 95. Mem. Nat. Assn. Student Fin. Aid Adminstrs. (chmn. 1987-88, Disting. Svc. award 1988, Leadership award 1994), Assn. Equestrian Order Holy Sepulchre (knight grand cross 1991, knight invested 1980), Order Sons of Italy in Am. (lodge pres. 1974-75, state pres. 1993-97, nat. v.p. 1997—2003, nat pres. 2003-05), Futures in Edn. Found. (vice chair 1991-93, chair 1994-97), Jamaica C. of C. (bd. dirs) Roman Catholic. Avocations: walking, cooking, gardening, reading, lecturing. Home: 6 Jones St New Hyde Park NY 11040-1616 also: Trout Ln Southampton NY 11968 Office: St John's Univ Off Vp Cmty Rels 8000 Utopia Pky Jamaica NY 11439-0001 Office Phone: 718-990-1486. Business E-Mail: sciamej@stjohns.edu.

SCIANCE, CARROLL THOMAS, chemical engineer, educator; b. Okemah, Okla., Feb. 16, 1939; s. Carroll Elmer and Winifred (Black) Sciance; m. Anita Ruth Fischer, Jan. 30, 1960; children: Steven, Frederick, Thomas, Erica. BSChemE, U. Okla., 1960, M in Chem. Engring., 1964, PhD, 1966. With E.I. duPont de Nemours & Co., Inc., 1966-95, planning mgr. nylon intermediates divsn., petrochem. dept. Wilmington, Del., 1978-80, tech. mgr., 1980-83, dir engring. rsch., engring. dept., 1983-87, prin. cons. corp. rsch. and devel. planning divsn., 1987-89; mgr. petroleum products R & D divsn. Conoco, Inc., 1989-93; dir. environ. tech. partnerships ctrl. R & D dept. DuPont, 1993-95; pres. Sci. Cons. Svcs., Inc., 1995—. Math. scis. and edn. bd. NRC, 1987—89; adv. bd. chem. sci. and tech. NIST, 1988—94; sr. lectr. U. Tex., Austin, 1996—; mem. Travis County Appraisals Rev. Bd., Tex., 1999—2004; instr. U. Phoenix, Austin, Tex., 2005—07. Pres. Hudson Bend Colony Homeowners Assn., 2004—06. Officer USAR, 1961—63. Fellow: AIChE (bd. dirs. material engring. and scis. divsn. 1986—92, chmn. new tech. com. 1990—92, mem. govt. rels. com. 1993—96); mem.: Am. Chem. Soc. (mem. environ. R & D com. 1995—99), Fedn. Materials Soc. (v.p. 1988—92, pres. 1993—94), Sigma Xi. Home: 16658 Forest Way Austin TX 78734-1110 Personal E-mail: scscorp@earthlink.net.

SCIARRA, JOHN J., obstetrician, gynecologist, educator; b. West Haven, Conn., Mar. 4, 1932; s. John and Mary Grace (Sanzone) S.; m. Barbara Crafts Patton, Jan. 9, 1960; chidren: Vanessa Patton, John Crafts, Leonard Chapman. BS, Yale U., 1953; MD, Columbia U., NYC, 1957, PhD, 1963. Asst. prof. Columbia U., NYC, 1964-68; prof., dept. head U. Minn. Med. Sch., Mpls., 1968-74; prof. Northwestern U. Med. Sch., Chgo., 1974—; chmn. ob-gyn Northwestern Meml. Hosp. and Northwestern U. Med. Sch., Chgo., 1974—2003. Guest prof. Peking U., China, 2005. Editor Gyn-Ob Reference Series, 1973-2005, Internat. Jour. Gyn-Ob, 1985-2006. V.p. med. affairs Chgo. Maternity Ctr., Chgo., 1974—2003; treas. Soc. Family Planning, 2005-. Fellow ACS, Am. Coll. Ob-Gyn. (chmn. internal affairs com. 1985-89), Royal Coll. Ob-Gyn. (ad eundem); Internat. Fedn. Gyn-Ob. (pres. 1991-94, pres. Supporters Assn. 1994-2000); mem. Assn. Profs. Gyn-Ob. (sec. 1976-79, pres. 1980-81, Achievement award 1998, Tchg. award 2003), Am. Assn. Maternal and Neonatal Health (pres. 1980-89), Coun. Resident Edn. in Ob-Gyn., Am. Fertility Soc. (Hartman award 1965, bd. dirs. 1971-73), Assn. Profs. Gyn-Ob. Med. Edn. Found. (sec.-treas. 1987-91, pres. 1991-93), Ctrl. Assn. Ob-Gyn. (trustees 1986-90, pres. 1990-91), Chgo. Gynecol. Soc. (pres. 1990-91), Internat. Soc. Gynecol. Endoscopy (hon. 2005, v.p. 1997-99, pres. 1999-01), Am. Gynecol. Club (pres. 2007-08), Internat. Acad. Human Reprodn., Yale Club N.Y.C., Carleton Club (Chgo.). Avocations: photography, travel. Office: Northwestern U Med Sch Dept Ob-Gyn 680 N Lake Shore Dr Ste 1015 Chicago IL 60611-8702 Office Phone: 312-695-5107. Business E-Mail: jsciarra@northwestern.edu.

SCIESZKA, JON, children's author; b. Flint, Mich., Sept. 8, 1954; s. Louis and Shirley Scieszka; m. Jerilyn Hansen; children: Casey, Jake. BA in Writing, Albion Coll., Mich., 1976; MFA, Columbia U., 1980. Elem. sch. tchr. The Day Sch., NYC; founder nonprofit lit. orgn. Guys Read. Nat. Amb. Young People's Lit. Libr. of Congress, 2008—. Author: (children's books) The True Story of the Three Little Pigs, 1989, The Frog Prince, Continued, 1991, Knights of the Kitchen Table, 1991, The Stinky Cheese Man and Other Fairly Stupid Tales, 1992 (Caldecott Medal honor book, 1993), Math Curse, 1995, The Book That Jack Wrote, 1997, Squids Will Be Squids, 1998, Summer Reading Is Killing Me!, 2000, Baloney, (Henry P.), 2001, It's All Greek to Me, 2001, Sam Samurai, 2002, Science Verse, 2004, Seen Art?, 2005, Cowboy and Octopus, 2007; editor: Guys Write for Guys Read, 2005. Office: c/o Viking Penguin 375 Hudson St New York NY 10014-3658*

SCIFRES, DENISE CELIA LE BLANC, historian, educator; b. Shreveport, La., Aug. 31, 1949; d. Lowney Lewis and Bonnie Bell (Childress) Le Blanc; m. Robert Lynn Scifres, July 3, 1971; children: Chandra, Scott, Leslie. AA, Hinds Jr. Coll., 1969; BS, U. So. Miss., 1971; M Social Sci., Miss. Coll., 1979, EdS, 1986. Tchr. Pearl (Miss.) Jr. High Sch., 1972-79; instr. history Hinds C.C., Raymond, Miss., 1981—. Cons. Magnolia Pub. Co., Brandon, Miss., 1980-87, Internat. Geographic, Jackson, Miss., 1983, Miss. Dept. Archives and History, Jackson, 1984-86, Silver-Burdett Co., Morristown, N.J., 1986; summer wilderness ranger U.S. Forest Svc. Editor, editorial cons. Mississippi's People and Past, 1980, author student workbook, 1981, tchrs. guide, 1981; editor Mississippi Life Past and Present, 1986. Mem. Miss. Hist. Assn., So. Hist. Assn., Delta Kappa Gamma. Roman Catholic. Avocations: mountain climbing, piano, singing, sewing, lace making. Office: Hinds Community Coll PO Box 1269 Raymond MS 39154-1269

SCILACCI, W. JAMES, JR., utilities executive; BA in Econs., UCLA; MBA, Santa Clara U., Calif. Fin. assoc. Getty Oil Co., Bank of America; treasurer's org. and positions in corp. fin., investor rels. fin. analysis, and cash mgmt. So. Calif. Edison, 1984—93, asst. treas., 1993—95, dir. qualifying facilities resources, 1995—2000, v.p., CFO, 2000—03, gen. rate case team leader, 2003, sr. v.p., CFO, 2003—05, Edison Mission Group, 2005—08; exec. v.p., CFO, and treas. Edison Internat., 2008—. Office: Edison Internat 2244 Walnut Grove Ave Rosemead CA 91770 Office Phone: 626-302-2222.

SCILEPPI, JOHN A., psychologist, educator; b. Bklyn., Aug. 30, 1946; s. Adolph G. and Marie Theresa (Saccaro) S.; m. Lynn A. Ruggiero, Nov. 27, 1982; 1 child, Luke M.R. BA magna cum laude in Psychology, Marist Coll., Poughkeepsie, 1967; MA, Loyola U., Chgo., 1969, PhD in Social Psychology, 1973. Lic. psychologist, N.Y. NDEA rsch. and tchg. fellow Loyola U., Chgo., 1969—71; asst. prof. St. Xavier Coll., Chgo., 1971—73; v.p. acad. affairs Oglala Sioux C.C., Pine Ridge, SD, 1975—76; assoc. prof. psychology Marist Coll., Poughkeepsie, NY, 1973-75, 76-88, prof., 1988—, chair psychology dept., 2005—08. Dir. MA Psychology program, 1990-2002; psychol. cons. for program evaluation, survey research and interpersonal communication. Abstractor: Psychological Abstracts, 1977-81; author: A Systems View of Education: A Model of Change, 1984, rev. edit., 1988, Community Psychology: A Common Sense Approach to Mental Health, 2000, The Community Mental Health System: A Navigational Guide for Providers, 2007, Applications Of A System Approach to Education: Models tor Change, 2007. Chmn. bd. Sch. of the New Cmty. of Chgo., 1970-72; bd. dirs. Rehab. Programs Inc., Poughkeepsie, 1981-94, Hyde Park Free Libr., 1996-2002, pres. 2001-02, Anderson Ctr. for Autism, Staatsburg, N.Y., 2003—; mem. planning com. United Way of Dutchess County (N.Y.), 1979-80. Mem. Am. Psychol. Assn., Eastern Psychol. Assn., Psi Chi, Alpha Sigma Nu. Democrat. Roman Catholic. Office: Marist Coll Psychology Dept Poughkeepsie NY 12601 Office Phone: 845-575-3000. Business E-Mail: john.scileppi@marist.edu.

SCINTO, MICHAEL JOSPEPH, broadcast executive; b. Joseph Francis and E. Adele Scinto; m. Katherine Gail Jessup, Aug. 9, 1975; children: Zachary Michael, Carly Rose. Attended, Wright State U., Dayton, Ohio, 1971—76. Radio talk show host WAVI Radio, Dayton, 1977—85, WCOL Radio, Columbus, Ohio, 1985—86, WING Radio, Dayton, 1986—87, WDAO Radio, Dayton, 1999—, Mike Gallagher Show, Irving, Tex., 2001—; assignmnet editor Wdtn TV-2, Dayton, 1979—80; radio & TV talk show host WHIO Radio & TV, Dayton, 1987—92; newspaper columnist Ind. Voice, Greater Dayton, Ohio, 2000—. Contbr. articles to publs. Host & past pres. Tipp-Monroe Optimist Club, Tipp City, Ohio, 1989—2009; mem. Tipp-Monroe Twp. Pks. Adv. Com., Tipp City, 1994—2000. Sgt. USAF, 1972—76, Lackland Air Force Base, Tex. Recipient Mil. Tng. Instr. Honor Grad. award, ITB Instr. Tng. Br., 1972. Conservative. Methodist. Avocation: soccer. Home and Office: Mike Scinto Show PO Box 112 Vandalia OH 45377 Office Fax: 866-375-6934. Business E-Mail: mike@themikescintoshow.com.

SCIORSCI, ADAM Q., sales executive; b. Denville, Nj, Dec. 16, 1978; s. Nicholas A. and Susan M. Sciorsci; m. Erin M. Coyne, Oct. 11, 2008. BS, Ithaca Coll., NY, 2000. Group sales mgr. Lakewood BlueClaws, NJ, 2005—06; dir. group sales & hospitality Colo. Springs Sky Sox, 2006—. Mem. North Colo. Springs Rotary Club, 2007—08. Mem.: Sigma Alpha Mu Frat. (chpt. pres. 1997—98). Roman Catholic. Office: Colorado Springs Sky Sox 4385 Tutt Boulevard Colorado Springs CO 80922 Office Fax: 719-597-2491. Business E-Mail: asciorsci@skysox.com.

SCIORTINO, ANTONELLA, engineering educator; b. Italy; Laurea in Civil Engring., Poly. di Bari, Italy; MCE, U. Calif., LA, 2000, PhD in Civil Engring., 2000. Cert. profl. engr., Italy, 1993. Grad. rsch. asst. U. Calif., 1996—99, tchg. asst., 1998—99, lectr. and postdoc. fellow, 2000—01; vis. rschr. CNR, Bari, 2002—03; project engr. Watershed Authority, Apulia Region, Bari, 2003; asst. prof. Calif. State U., Long Beach, 2004—, undergrad. advisor, 2008—. Named Faculty of Yr., CSULB Assoc. Engring. Student Body, 2006; Fulbright Scholarship, 1996—97. Mem.: ASCE, Chi Epsilon (faculty advisor 2008—). Office: Calif State Univ Long Beach 1250 Bellflower Blvd Long Beach CA 90840 Business E-Mail: asciorti@csulb.edu.

SCIPIO, L. ALBERT, II, (LOUIS ALBERT SCIPIO II), retired aerospace science engineering educator, historian; b. Juarez, Mex., Aug. 22, 1922; s. Louis Albert and Marie Leona (Richardson) Scipio; m. Katherine Ruth Jones, Aug. 15, 1942; children: Louis Albert, Karen R. BS, Tuskegee Inst., 1943; B.Civil Engring., U. Minn., 1948, MS, 1950, PhD, 1958. Archtl. draftsman McKissack & McKissack, Tuskegee, Ala., 1943; instr. Tuskegee Inst., 1946; designer Long & Thorshov, Mpls., 1948-50; lectr. U. Minn., Mpls., 1950-59; research physicist Hughes Aircraft Co., Culver City, Calif., 1954; Fulbright prof. Cairo U., Giza, Egypt, 1955-56; assoc. prof. mechanics Howard U., Washington, 1959-61; Fulbright prof. Cairo U., Giza, Egypt, 1955-56; dir. grad. studies for engring. and architecture, prof. aerospace engring. Howard U., Washington, 1967-70, Univ. prof. space scis., 1970-87, Disting. Univ. prof. emeritus, 1987—2008; prof. phys. scis. U. PR, Mayaguez, 1961-63; prof. aerospace engring. U. Pitts., 1963-67; pub. Roman Publs., Silver Springs, Md., 1981—2008; cons. in field. Author: Compendium of Aircraft Stress Analysis and Design, 1956, Principles on continua with Applications, 1966, Structural Design Concepts, 1967, E. M. Collar Insignia 1907-1926, 1981, Last of the Black Regulars, 1983, With the Red Hand Division, 1985, The 24th Infantry at Fort Benning, 1986, Pre-War Days at Tuskegee, 1987, The Collar Dist Story (1907-1999), 1999. Bd. visitors Air Force Inst. Tech., 1979—83. With US Army, 1943—46. Mem.: NSPE, AAAS, AIAA, Coun. Am. Mil. Past, Co. Mil. Historians, Am. Phys. Soc., Soc. Natural Philosophy, Internat. Assn. Bridge and Structural Engrs., NY Acad. Scis., Sigma Xi, Phi Beta Kappa, Pi Tau Sigma, Sigma Gamma Tau, Sigma Pi Sigma, Pi Mu Epsilon, Alpha Kappa Mu. Home: 12511 Montclair Dr Silver Spring MD 20904-2053

SCIRICA, ANTHONY JOSEPH, federal judge; b. Norristown, Pa., Dec. 16, 1940; BA, Wesleyan U., 1962; JD, U. Mich., 1965; postgrad. Fulbright Scholar, Central U., Caracas, Venezuela, 1966. Bar: Pa. 1966, US Dist. Ct. (ea. dist.) Pa. 1984, US Ct. Appeals (3d cir.) 1987. Ptnr. McGrory, Scirica, Wentz & Fernandez, Norristown, Pa., 1966—80; asst. dist. atty. Montgomery County, Pa., 1967—69; mem. Pa. Ho. of Reps, Harrisburg, 1971—79; judge Montgomery County Ct. Common Pleas, Pa., 1980—84, US Dist. Ct. (ea. dist.) Pa., Phila., 1984—87, US Ct. Appeals (3rd cir.), Phila., 1987—, chief judge, 2003—. Chmn. Pa. Sentencing Commn., 1980—85, com. on rules of practice & procedure, Jud. Conf. of US; prof. Penn State U. Sch. of Law, 2004—; mem. US Jud. Panel on Multidistrict Litig., 2006—. Scholar Fulbright scholar, Ctrl. U., Caracas, Venezuela, 1966. Mem.: ABA, Am. Law Inst., Montgomery Bar Assn., Pa. Bar Assn. Office: 22614 US Courthouse Independence Mall W Philadelphia PA 19106-1715*

SCISM, DANIEL REED, lawyer; b. Evansville, Ind., Aug. 27, 1936; s. Daniel William and Ardath Josephine (Gibbs) S.; m. Paula Anne Sedgwick, June 21, 1958; children: Darby Claire, Joshua Reed. BA, DePauw U., 1958; JD, Ind. U., 1965. Bar: Ind. 1965, U.S. Dist. Ct. (so. dist.) Ind. 1965, U.S. Ct. Appeals (7th cir.) 1967, U.S. Supreme Ct. 1976. Reporter Dayton (Ohio) Jour.-Herald, 1958-59; editor Mead Johnson & Co., Evansville, 1961; first assoc., then ptnr. Roberts, Ryder, Rogers & Scism and predecessor firms, Indpls., 1965—86; ptnr. Barnes & Thornburg, Indpls., 1987—2002, of counsel, 2003—. Cons. Ind. Pers. Assn., 1984-2002. Treas. Marion County chpt. Myasthenia Gravis Found., Indpls., 1970; v.p. Marion County Mental Health Assn., Indpls., 1970-71; pres. The Suemma Coleman Agy., Indpls., 1973-74; bd. dirs. Ind. Humanities Coun., 1995-00, chmn. bd., 1997-98; trustee Indpls. Mus. Art, 2001—07; bd. dirs. Westminster Village North, Inc., 2003-06; pres. Persimmon Woods Homeowners Assn., 2001-03, sec. 2003-. With US Army, 1959—62. Edwards fellow Ind. U., 1964. Mem. ABA, Ind. Bar Assn., Woodland Country Club (bd. dirs. 1984-88, sec. 1998-99). Methodist. Home: 10909 300 Yard Dr Fishers IN 46037-9306 Office: Barnes & Thornburg 11 S Meridian St Indianapolis IN 46204-3535

SCITOVSKY, ANNE AICKELIN, economist, researcher; b. Ludwigshafen, Germany, Apr. 17, 1915; arrived in U.S., 1931, naturalized, 1938; d. Hans W. and Gertrude Margarete Aickelin; 1 child, Catherine Margaret. Student, Smith Coll., 1933—35; BA, Barnard Coll., 1937; postgrad., London Sch. Econs., 1937—39; MA in Econs., Columbia U., 1941. Mem. staff legis. reference svc. Libr. of Congress, 1941—44; mem. staff Social Security Bd., 1944—46; with Palo Alto (Calif.) Med. Found./Rsch. Inst., 1963—, chief health econs. div., 1973—94, sr. staff scientist, 1994—. Lectr. Inst. Health Policy Studies, U. Calif., San Francisco, 1975—94; mem. Inst. Medicine of NAS, Nat. Acad. Social Ins., Pres.'s Commn. for Study of Ethical Problems in Medicine and Biomed. and Behavioral Rsch., 1979—82, U.S. Nat. Com. on Vital and Health Stats., 1975—78, Health Resources and Svcs. Adminstrn., AIDS adv. com., 1990—94; cons. HHS, Inst. Medicine Coun. on Health Care Tech. Assessment, 1986—90. Home: 161 Erica Way Portola Valley CA 94028-7439 Office: Palo Alto Med Found Rsch Inst Ames Bldg 795 El Camino Real Palo Alto CA 94301-2302 Personal E-mail: ascitovsky@aol.com.

SCIUTTO, JIM, news correspondent; b. 1970; s. Ernest and Elizabeth Sciutto; m. Gloria Riviera, Oct. 27, 2006. BA in History, Yale U., 1992. Prodr. PBS; news corr. Asia Bus. News, Hong Kong, ABC News, Chgo., 1998, news corr., anchor Wash., sr. foreign corr. London, 2002—. Fulbright fellow, Hong Kong, 1993—94. Recipient Emmy for best story in regularly scheduled newscast, 2004, 2005, George Polk award for television reporting, 2007; fellow, Pierson Coll., Yale, 2002. Mem.: Coun. Foreign Rels. Mailing: ABC News Hdqs 77 W 66th St New York NY 10023

SCIUVA, MARGARET W., counselor; b. Cleve., Dec. 22, 1962; d. Joseph Aloysius and Katharine Elizabeth Williams; m. James Salvatore Sciuva, May 23, 1987; children: James Jr., Anthony, Richelle. BA in Comm. and Psychology, John Carol U.; postgrad. in counseling, John Carroll U.; MA in Counseling, Webster U. Rape crisis counselor Safe Homes Rape Crisis Ctr., Lauren, SC; family preservation therapist Spartanburg Mental Health, HSA, Cayce, SC; founder, exec. dir. SC Mental Health Counselors Assn. Treas. Polk County Mid. Sch. PTA, Tryon, NC, 2000; active Polk County Hist. Soc., Tryon, 2003. Mem.: SC Lic. Profl. Counselors, Nat. Bd. Cert. Counselors, NC Lic. Profl. Counselors. Avocations: reading, travel, gardening. Personal E-mail: mwsciuv@attglobal.net.

SCLAFANI, ANTHONY PAUL, plastic surgeon, educator, biomedical researcher; b. Bklyn., Oct. 3, 1963; BA, Columbia U., 1985; MD, U. Pa., 1989. Diplomate Am. Bd. Otolaryngology, Am. Bd. Facial Plastic and Reconstructive Surgery. Intern in gen. surgery Beth Israel Med. Ctr., NYC, 1989-91; from resident in otolaryngology, head and neck surgery to prof. N.Y. Eye and Ear Infirmary, NYC, 1991—2004, prof., 2004—, dir. facial plastic surgery, 1996—, surgeon dir., 2005—; fellow in facial plastic and reconstructive surgery St. Louis U. Sch. Medicine, 1995-96; pvt. practice NYC, 1996—, Chappaqua, NY, 1998—. Editor-in-chief Facial Plastic Surgery; assoc. editor Facial Plastics Clinics N.Am.; contbr. articles to profl. jours. Fellow ACS, Am. Acad. Facial Plastic and Reconstructive Surgery (Sir Harold Delf Gillies award 1996, Ira Tresley Rsch. award 2002, 04), Am. Acad. Otolaryngology and Head and Neck Surgery; mem. Am. Soc. Laser Medicine and Surgery, Sociol. Soc., Triological Soc. Office: NY EE Infirm/Facial Pl Surg Dept Otolaryng/Head Neck 310 E 14th St 6th Fl New York NY 10003-4201 also: 59 S Greeley Ave Chappaqua NY 10514-3321 also: 330 West 58th St 610 New York NY 10019 Office Phone: 914-238-5500. Personal E-mail: docs@nyface.com.

SCLAFANI, KAREN C., lawyer; BA, LeMoyne Coll.; JD, NYU. Corp. assoc. Mudge, Rose, Guthrie and Alexander, NYC; v.p., dep. gen. counsel Avis Budget Group Inc., Parsippany, NJ, sr. v.p., gen. counsel, 1998—2006, exec. v.p., gen. counsel, 2006—. Office: Avis Budget Group, Inc 6 Sylvan Way Parsippany NJ 07054 Office Phone: 973-496-3500. Office Fax: 973-496-3444.

SCLAFANI, LISA, surgeon, educator; d. Anthony Joseph and Paula Giunta Sclafani; m. Joseph Sorrento; children: Alessandra Grace Sorrento, Cristina Maria Sorrento, Gina Kathryn Sorrento. BA, NYU, 1978, MD, 1982. Attending surgeon Meml. Sloan Kettering Cancer Ctr., NYC, 2001—; assoc. prof. clin. surgery Cornell U. Med. Coll., NYC, 2003—. Bd. dir. Am. Soc. Breast Diseases, Dallas, 2002—. Contbr. articles to profl. jours. Recipient Lillian Solotoroff award, NYU, 1977, award, 1979, Davidson award, Albert Einstein Coll. Medicine, 1987; Clin. fellow, Am. Cancer Soc., 1987—88. Fellow: ACS, Phi Beta Kappa, Soc. Surg. Oncology. Achievements include research in new approaches to breast cancer surgical treatments. Office: Meml Sloan Kettering Cancer Ctr 1275 York Ave New York NY 10021

SCLAFANI, SUSAN K., educational consultant, former federal agency administrator; b. Albany, NY, Sept. 22, 1944; AB in German and Math., Vassar Coll., 1966; MA in German Lang. and Lit., U. Chgo., 1967; ME in Ednl. Adminstrn., U. Tex., Austin, 1985, PhD, 1987. Cert. Tchr.Math. Ill., N.Y., Lifetime Tchr. Math. and German 6-12 Tex., Adminstr., Supt., Supr., Midmgr. Tex. Tchr. Ctrl. YMCA H.S., Chgo., 1971—72, Woodson Jr. H.S. Houston Ind. Sch. Dist., Tex., 1972—74, H.S. for Engring. Professions, Houston Ind. Sch. Dist., Tex., 1975—78; coord. magnet sch. Washington H.S. Houston Ind. Sch. Dist., 1978—83; ctrl. office coord. instrnl. tech. Houston Ind. Sch. Dist., Tex., 1983—84, exec. dir. curriculum devel., 1987—89, asst. supt. constrn. mgmt. and program planning, 1989—92, assoc. supt. dist. adminstrn., 1992—94, chief of staff, 1994—96, chief of staff ednl. svcs., 1996—2001; counselor to sec. US Dept. Edn., Washington, 2001—06, acting sec., vocational & adult edn., 2003—04, asst. sec., vocational & adult edn., 2004—06; mng. dir. Chartwell Education Group LLC, NYC, 2006—. V.p. and gen. mgr. Quantum Access, Inc., 1986—87; adj. prof. dept. curriculum and instrn. U. Houston, Tex., 1988—94, adj prof. dept. ednl. leadership, 1999—2001; presenter to numerous ednl. groups. Co-author (with R. Paige): (Book) Strategies for Reforming Houston's Schools; School Choice or Best Systems, What Improves Education, 2001; contbr. articles to profl. jours. Vol. Star of Hope Women and Family Shelter, Houston, 1988—90; mem. com. Tex. Alliance for Minorities in Engring., Houston, 1975—85; activity vol., conf. spkr. Coun. for Exceptional Children, Houston, 1989—91; com. mem. Tex. Task Force for the Homeless, 1990—92; mem. Hispanic Youth Leadership Forum Steering Com., Houston, 1990—. Pub. Policy, Comty. and Agy. Support, Success by Six Coms., United Way, Houston, 1987—2001; chair Children's Policy Com. United Way, Houston, 1987—2001. Office: Chartwell Edn Group LLC 1900 M St NW Ste 310 Washington DC 20036 Business E-Mail: sclafani@chartwelleducation.com.

SCOBEY, MARGARET, former ambassador; b. Memphis, 1949; d. James and Delores Scobey. BA in History, U. Tenn., 1971, MA in History, 1973. Consular US Dept. State, Lima, Peru, 1981—83, polit. officer Peshawar, Pakistan, 1983—86, chief polit. sect. Jerusalem, 1990—91, polit. counselor Kuwait City, Kuwait, 1994—96, dep. chief of mission Sanaa, Yemen, 1996—99, dir. Office of Arabian Peninsula Washington, 2000—01; dep. chief of mission US Dept State, Riyadh, Saudi Arabia, 2001—03; US amb. to Syria US Dept. State, Damascus, 2003—05; polit. counselor US Dept State, Baghdad, Iraq, 2005—07; sr. adv. to under sec. for pub. diplomacy & pub. affairs US Dept. State, Washington, 2007—. Staff asst. to asst. sec. Near East and South Asian Affairs; watch officer Operation Ctr.; polit. mil. officer Office of Israeli and Arab-Israeli Affairs, dep. dir. of sec. staff.

SCOBLIC, J. PETER, magazine editor; b. NYC, July 29, 1974; s. Joseph Michael and Barbara Scoblic. BA, Brown U., 1997. Editor-in-chief Brown Jour. World Affairs, Providence, 1994-96; rsch. dir. Hedrick Smith Prodns., Bethesda, Md., 1998-99; editor Arms Control Today, Washington, 1999—2003; mng. editor The New Republic, Washington, 2003—04, exec. editor, 2004—. Vis. scholar Carnegie Endowment Internat. Peace, Washington, 2006—. Author Book. Office: The New Republic 1331 H St NW Ste 700 Washington DC 20005

SCOFIDIO, RICARDO, artist, architect, educator; m. Elizabeth E. Diller. Ptnr. Diller & Scofidio (now Diller Scofidio & Renfro), NYC, 1979—; prof. arch. The Cooper Union for the Advancement of Sci. and Art, NY. Works include Inst. Contemporary Art, Blur Bldg. (Progressive Architecture Design award), designed viewing platform for Ground Zero, NYC, media pavillion for Swiss EXPO 2002, Brasserie Restaurant, NY (James Beard Found. award for Best New Restaurant Design), Slither, Gifu, Japan, Loophole, Mus. Contemporary Art, Chgo., 1992, Apparatus Drawing, Mus. of Modern Art, NY, 1993, Case #00-17164, New Mus., 1993, Dysfunction, Ctr. d'Art Contemporian de Castres, France, 1993, Desiring Eye, I'dentity and Difference, Triennale, Milan, 1994, Pelts, Thaddeus Ropac Gallery, Paris, France, 1997, Non-Place, San Francisco Mus. Modern Art, 1997, Slow House, At the End of the Century: One Hundred Years of Architecture, Mus. Contemporary Art, LA, 1998, The American Lawn: Surface of Everyday Life, Canadian Centre for Architecture, Montreal, 1998, Public Faces/Private Places, Pusan Internat. Arts Festival, Korea, 1998, His/Her Bathroom, Thomas Healy Gallery, NY, 1998, Dress Code, Landesmuseum, Linz, Austria, 1998, (permanent collections) Travelogues, Internat. Arrivals Terminal 4, JFK Airport, NY, (installation) The Desiring Eye: Reviewing the Slow House, Gallery MA, Tokyo, 1992, Master/Slave, Fondation Cartier, Paris, InterClone Hotel, Ataturk Airport for Istanbul Biennial, 1997, (dance collaborations with the Lyon Ballet Opera of France and Charlerol/Danses of Belgium (touring exhbn.) EJM1: Man Walking at Ordinary Speed and EJM2:Inertia, 1998, (web project) Refresh, Dia Art Found., (video installation) Pageant, Johannesburg Biennial & Rotterdam Film Festival, 1997, (permanent installation) X,Y, Kobe, Japan, 1997, (multi-media work for stage in collaboration with Builders Assn.) Jet Lag, 1998 (Obie award for Creative Achievement), (pub. art commn., permanent video marques) Jump Cuts, United Artists Cineplex, San Jose, Calif., (collaborative dance work with Charlerol/Danses) Moving Target, (collaborative theater work with Dumb Type and Hotel Pro Forma) Business Class, Copenhagen Cultural Capital, (interactive video installation) Indigestion, Barbican Art Gallery, London, Walter Phillips Gallery, Banff, Canada, Biennial Nagoya, Japan, 1997, (electronic project) Subtopia, ICC Gallery, Tokyo, 1997, and several others, (installations commissioned by) Mus. of Modern Art, Whitney Mus., New Mus. of Contemporary Art, Walker Art Ctr., Minn., Cartier Found., Palais des Beaux-Arts Brussels, and Gallery Ma Tokyo, (works are in permanent collections of) Mus. of Modern Art, Mus. of Modern Art San Francisco, Fond Nat. d'Art Contemporian, several FRACs in France, Musee de la Mode in Paris, and many private collections, co-pub. with Elizabeth Diller Back to the Front: Tourisms of War, FRAC Basse-Normandie, 1994, Flesh: Architectural Probes, Princeton Architectural Press, 1995, Blur: The Making of Nothing, Abrams, 2002. Recipient Chrysler award for Innovation in Design, 1988—89, MacArthur Found. award, 1999, Brunner prize in Arch., AAAL, 2003, MacDermott award for Creative Achievement, MIT; named one of The World's Most Influential People, TIME mag., 2009; fellow, N.Y. Found. Arts, 1998—99, Graham Found. Fellowship, 1998—99, Chgo. Inst. for Architecture and Urbanism Fellowship. Address: The Cooper Union for the Advancement Dept Arch Cooper Sq New York NY 10003-7120 Office: Diller Scoffidio & Renfro 601 W 25TH St RM 1815 New York NY 10001-1152 Office Phone: 212-260-7971.*

SCOFIELD, GORDON LLOYD, mechanical engineer, educator; b. Huron, SD, Sept. 29, 1925; s. Perry Lee and Zella (Reese) S.; m. Nancy Lou Cooney, Dec. 27, 1947; children: Cathy Lynn, Terrence Lee. B.M.E., Purdue U., 1946; M.M.E., U. Mo., Rolla, 1949; PhD in M.E, U. Okla., 1968. Instr. mech. engring. S.D. State Coll., Brookings, 1946-47; successively grad. asst., instr., asst. prof., asso. prof., prof. U. Mo., Rolla, 1947-69; prof., head mech. engring.-engring. mechs. dept. Mich. Technol. U., Houghton, 1969—80; disting. prof. mech. engring. S.D. Sch. Mines and Tech., Rapid City, 1981-88, asst. v.p. for acad. affairs, 1981-83, v.p., dean engring., 1984-86; pres. S.D. Sch. Mines and Tech. Found., 1982-90. Cons. U.S. Naval Ordnance Test Sta., China Lake, Calif., 1956-71; bd. dirs. Accreditation Bd. for Engring. and Tech., 1994-2000; cons. to industry. Served with USNR, 1943-46. NSF sci. faculty fellow, 1966-67; recipient alumni achievement award U. Mo., Rolla, 1975 Mem. ASME, Soc. Automotive Engrs. (pres. 1977, Excellence in Engring. Edn. award, 1999), Am. Soc. Engring. Edn., Sigma Xi, Tau Beta Pi, Pi Tau Sigma, Phi Kappa Phi. Home: PO Box 1085 Rapid City SD 57709-1085 *Satisfaction comes from sharing achievements. By acknowledging and sharing the importance of others in our success it is possible to accomplish more that is worth remembering.*

SCOFIELD, LOUIS M., JR., lawyer; b. Brownsville, Tex., Jan. 14, 1952; s. Louis M. and Betsy Lee (Aiken) S.; children: Christopher, Nicholas, Emma. BS in Geology with highest honors and high distinction, U. Mich., 1974; JD with honors, U. Tex., 1977. Bar: Tex. 1977, US Dist. Ct. (ea. and so. dists.) Tex., US Ct. Appeals (5th cir.) 1981, US Supreme Ct. 1984. Ptnr. Mehaffy/Weber, Beaumont, Tex., 1982—. Spkr. CNA Ins., Dallas, Jefferson County Ins. Adjusters, SE Tex. Ind. Ins. Agts., Gulf Ins. Co., Dallas, Employers Casualty Co., Beaumont, Tex. Employment Commn., Jefferson County Young Lawyers Assn., Jefferson County Bar Assn., South Tex. Coll. Law, John Gray Inst., Lamar U., 1991, Tex. Assn. Def. Counsel, 1991, 2007, Mfr.'s Alliance, 2007; cert. arbitrator Nat. Panel Consumer Arbitrators; presenter Forest Park HS, Martin Elem. Sch., St. Anne's Sch. Contbr. columns in newspapers, articles to profl. jours. Patron Beaumont Heritage Soc., John J. French Mus.; bd. dirs. Beaumont Heritage Soc., 1983-84, endowment fund com., 1988; chmn. lawyers divsn. United Appeals Campaign, 1984; grand patron Jr. League of Beaumont, 1989-90. Recipient Tex. Super Lawyer, Tex. Monthly Mag., 2005, 2006—09. Fellow: Tex. Bar Found. (life); mem.: ABA, Jefferson County Bar Assn. (disaster relief project 1979, outstanding young lawyer's com. 1980, dir. 2005), Def. Rsch. Inst., Tex. Assn. Defense Counsel (dir. at large 1986—87, v.p. 1987—89, program chmn. San Diego 1989, adminstrv. v.p. 1989—90), Assn. Defense Trial Attys. (exec. coun. 1999—2002, chmn. Tex. membership com. 1999—, conv. host 2005, columnist Assoc. Press 2004—09), State Bar of Tex. (mentors com. 1995), Beaumont County Country Club, Phi Beta Kappa. Democrat. Episcopalian. Avocations: golf, reading, fishing. Home: 4790 Littlefield St Beaumont TX 77706-7748 Office: Mehaffy & Weber PO Box 16 Beaumont TX 77704-0016 Office Phone: 409-835-5011. Business E-Mail: louscofield@mehaffyweber.com.

SCOFIELD, VIRGINIA LEE, research scientist; b. Lincoln, Nebr., May 14, 1948; d. Louis Morris and Betsy Aiken Scofield. BA, U. Tex., Austin, 1970, PhD, 1977. Asst. prof. UCLA Sch. Medicine, 1984—89; rsch. assoc. prof. U. Southern Calif., LA, 1995—2000; faculty scientist M.D. Anderson Cancer Ctr. Sci. Park, Smithville, Tex., 2000—. Vis. prof. dept. biology and english Pomona/Claremont Colls., Calif., 1995—97. Mem. editl. bd.: Biol. Bull., 1984—88, Frontiers in Biol. Sci., 2006—; contbr. articles to profl. jours. Grantee, NIH, 1987—90, US CDC, 1987—90, U. Calif. Task Force AIDS, 1985—90, Am. Cancer Soc., 1987—90; fellow, Stanford U. Sch. Medicine, Calif., 1977—83, NIH, 1978—81. Mem.: Am. Soc. Cell Biology, Am. Assn. Immunologists, Sigma Xi, Phi Kappa Phi, Angel Flight (sec. 1969—70), Alpha Phi (pledge class pres. 1967—68). Liberal. Episcopalian. Achievements include patents for sperm as immunogen carriers; genital-mucosal vaccines against HIV and other STDs. Home: 303 Quail Run Smithville TX 78957 Office: MD Anderson Cancer Science Park 1808 Park Road 1-C PO Box 389 Smithville TX 78957 Office Fax: 512-237-2444. Business E-Mail: vscofield@mdanderson.org.

SCOGGINS, M. W. (BILL SCOGGINS), academic administrator; Grad., U. Tulsa; M in Petroleum Engring., U. Okla.; PhD in Petroleum Engring., U. Tulsa. With Mobil, 1970—99; mem., exec. com. Mobil Oil; pres. Internat. E & P, Global Exploration; exec. v.p. ExxonMobil Prodn. Co., 1999—2004; pres. Colo. Sch. Mines, 2006—. Mem., exec. com. U. Tulsa Bd. Trustees, 2005, mem., fin., investment, audit com., mem., faculty and curriculum com.; mem., bd. dirs. Questar Corp., Trico Marine Services, Inc., Colo. Renewable Energy Authority. Sec. Bapt. Found. Colo. Named to Coll. Engring. Hall of Fame, 1998. Mem.: Colo. Oil and Gas Assn. Office: Office of Pres Colorado School of Mines 1500 Illinois St Golden CO 80401-1887*

SCOGGINS, ROB, choreographer, director; b. East St. Louis, Dec. 3, 1956; s. Paul and Carol Scoggins; m. Sarah Shepherd, Dec. 14, 2001; children: Holly, Ariel, Miller, Maggie. MFA, Lindenwood, St. Charles, 1986. Dir. dance Lindenwood U., 1995—2005. Choreographer (dance piece) Many Feet Bring Houses (Am. Coll. Nat. Dance Festival award, 1990, 2002). Recipient Proclamation award, City St. Charles Mayor, 2002. Master: Jeté (advisor 2006—). Office: Univ Missouri St Louis 1 University Blvd Saint Louis MO 63121 Business E-Mail: scogginsro@umsl.edu.

SCOGLAND, WILLIAM LEE, lawyer; b. Moline, Ill., 1949; s. Maurice William and Harriet Rebecca S.; m. Victoria Lynn, 1976; 1 child, Thomas. BA magna cum laude, Augustana Coll., 1971; JD cum laude, Harvard U., 1975. Bar: Ill. 1975, U.S. Dist. Ct. (no. dist.) Ill. 1975. From assoc. to ptnr. Jenner & Block, Chgo., 1981—. Lectr. in law U. Chgo. Law Sch., 2000—; bd. dirs. Am. Benefits Coun., 2004—; adv. coun. employee welfare and pension benefit plans US Dept. Labor, 2006—08. Author: Fiduciary Duty: What Does It Mean?, 1989; co-author Employee Benefits Law, 1987; contr. Tort and Ins. Law Jour., 1989, and others. Fellow: Am. Coll. Employee Benefits Counsel; mem.: Omicron Delta Kappa, Phi Beta Kappa. Republican. Office: Jenner & Block LLP 330 N Wabash Chicago IL 60611 Office Phone: 312-923-2878. Business E-Mail: wscogland@jenner.com.

SCOGNAMIGLIO PASINI, CARLO, economics and finance professor, former senator, defense minister; b. Varese, Italy, Nov. 27, 1944; s. Luigi and esther (Pasini) S.; m. Cecilia Pirelli, May 28, 1980; children: Filippo, Elisabetta Thea. D.Econs., U. Bocconi, Milan, Italy, 1968; spl. student, London Sch. Econs., 1970-71. Asst. prof. U. Bocconi, 1968-73, prof., 1973-79, U. Rome-Luiss, 1979—, dean and rector, 1984—. Senator Constituency of Milan, 1992—, pres. of senate, acting pres. of Republic, 1994-96, defense minister, 1998-99; pres. Corriere della Sera, 1983, Aspens Inst. Italia, 1995—. Author: The Stock Exchange, 1973, Industrial Crises, 1976, Industrial Economics, 1987, Theory of Finance, 1987, The Liberal Project, 1996. Winner prize for econs. French Acad., 1988. Avocations: golf, sailing, skiing. Office: Senato della Repubblica 00100 Rome Italy Office Fax: 3906 67063825. E-mail: c.scognamiglipasini@senato.it.

SCOLA, LUIS, professional basketball player; b. Buenos Aires, Apr. 30, 1980; Forward, center Ferro Carril Oeste, Argentina, 1995—98, Gijón Baloncesto, Spain, 1998—2000, TAU Cerámica, Spain, 2000—07, Houston Rockets, 2007—. Mem. Argentine Olympic Men's Basketball Team, Athens, Greece, 2004, Beijing, 08. Recipient Silver medal, Internat. Basketball Fedn. World Championship, USA, 2002, Internat. Basketball Fedn. Americas Championship, 2007, Gold medal, men's basketball, Athens Olympic Games, 2004, Bronze medal, men's basketball, Beijing Olympic Games, 2008; named Most Valuable Player, Asociación de Clubs de Baloncesto, Spain, 2005, 2007; named to NBA All-Rookie First Team, 2008. Office: Houston Rockets 1510 Polk St Houston TX 77002*

SCOLES, CLYDE SHELDON, library director; b. Columbus, Ohio, Apr. 14, 1949; s. Edward L. and Edna M. (Ruddock) Scoles; m. Diane Francis, July 14, 1976; children: David, Kevin, Karen, Stephen. BS, Ohio State U., 1971; MLS, U. Mich., 1972. Libr. Columbus Pub. Libr., 1972-74; libr. dir. Zanesville Pub. Libr., Ohio, 1974-78; asst. dir. Toledo-Lucas County Pub. Libr., 1978-85, dir., 1985—. Adj. lectr., libr. bldg. cons. U. Mich.; v.p. bd. dirs. Read for Literacy. Mem.: ALA, Maumee Hist. Soc., Com. of 100, Toledo C. of C., Ohio Libr. Coun., Ohio Libr. Assn., Rotary, Torch. Office: Toledo-Lucas County Pub Libr 325 N Michigan St Toledo OH 43604 Office Phone: 419-259-5256. Business E-Mail: clyde.scoles@toledolibrary.org.

SCOLES, EUGENE FRANCIS, lawyer, educator; b. Shelby, Iowa, June 12, 1921; s. Sam and Nola E. (Leslie) S.; m. R. Helen Glawson, Sept. 6, 1942; children— Kathleen Elizabeth, Janene Helen. AB, U. Iowa, Iowa City, 1943, JD, 1945; LLM, Harvard U., Cambridge, Mass., 1949; JSD, Columbia U., NYC, 1955. Bar: Iowa 1945, Ill. 1946. Assoc. Seyfarth-Shaw & Fairweather, Chgo., 1945-46; asst. prof. law Northeastern U., 1946-48, assoc. prof., 1948-49, U. Fla., 1949-51, prof., 1951-56, U. Ill., Champaign, 1956-68, Max Rowe prof. law, 1982-89, prof. emeritus, 1989—; vis. prof. McGeorge Law Sch. U. Pacific, Sacramento, 1989-92; prof. U. Oreg., 1968-82, dean Sch. Law, 1968-74, disting. prof. emeritus, 1982—. Vis. prof. Khartoum U., Sudan, 1964-65; reporter Uniform Probate Code Project, 1966-70; mem. joint editorial bd. Uniform Probate Code, 1972—, Uniform Law Com., 1970-82. Author: (with H.F. Goodrich) Conflict of Laws, 4th edit., 1964, (with R.J. Weintraub) Cases and Materials on Conflict of Laws, 2d edit., 1972, (with E.C. Halbach, Jr., P.G. Roberts, H.D. Begleiter) Problems and Materials on Decedents' Estates and Trusts, 7th edit., 2006, Problems and Materials on Future Interests, 1977, (with P. Hay, P.J. Borchers, S.C. Symeonides) Conflict of Laws, 4th edit., 2004; contbr. articles to profl. jours.; notes and legislation editor Iowa Law Rev., 1945. Mem. ABA, Soc. Pub. Tchrs. Law, Am. Law Inst., Ill. Bar Assn., Assn. Am. Law Schs. (pres. 1978), Order of Coif Office: U Oreg Sch Law 1515 Agate St Eugene OR 97403-1221 Office Phone: 541-346-3862.

SCOLES, MARIE Y., elementary school educator; d. Richard and Doris Scheg; m. Thomas E. Scheg, Oct. 26, 1991; children: Ian, Courtney. BS in Secondary Edn. Math., SUNY, 1985, MS in Secondary Edn. in Math., 1991. Cert. secondary education mathematics educator N.Y., 1985. Mid. sch. math. tchr. South Seneca H.S., Ovid, NY, 1985—2003, math. tchr., 1985—. Adivsor Jr. Nat. Honor Soc., Ovid, 1997—98. Mem.: Assn. of N.Y. State Math. Tchrs. (assoc.). Office: South Seneca High School 7263 Main St Ovid NY 14521 Personal E-mail: courian@aol.com. E-mail: mscoles@southseneca.k12.ny.us.

SCOLESE, CHRISTOPHER J., federal agency administrator; b. 1956; m. Dianne Scolese; 4 children. BSEE, SUNY, Buffalo, 1978; MSEE, George Washington U. Earth Observing Sys. (EOS) program mgr., dep. dir. flight programs and projects for earth sci. Goddard Space Flight Ctr., Greenbelt, Md., EOS Terra Project mgr., EOS sys. mgr., dep. dir.; dep. assoc. adminstr. Office Space Sci. NASA, Washington, chief engr., 2005—07, assoc. adminstr., 2007—, acting adminstr., 2009. Spkr. in field. With USN, 1978—83. Recipient Calspan Aeronautics award, 1973, Presdl. Rank award of Meritorious Exec., NASA Outstanding Leadership medal (2), Nat. Capital Section Young Engineer/Scientist of the Yr. award, Am. Inst. Aeronautics & Astronautics. Fellow: AIAA (assoc.; mem. astrodynamics com., chmn. nat. capitol sect. guidance navication and control tech. com., Young Engr./Scientist of Yr. award nat. capitol sect.); mem.: IEEE, Tau Beta Pi, Eta Kappa Nu. Office: NASA Hdqrs Mail Code S 300 E St SW Washington DC 20546 Business E-Mail: christopher.j.scolese@nasa.gov.*

SCOLLANS, CAROL G. J., art educator; b. Boston; d. Annestasia C. and James F. Scollans; married; children: Erin A., Liana F. MA in Art History, U. Mass., Amherst, 1988. Ind. curator, 1988—; sr. lectr. U. Mass., Boston, 1989—. Rsch. fellow Brit. Cultural Coun., Belfast, Northern Ireland, 1992—96. Author: (art historical) Two Lives, One Passion; contbr. articles to profl. jours. Trustee Stearns Burton Found., New Ipswich, NH, 2006—08, New Ipswich Hist. Soc., NH, 1999—2008. Cultural Coun. grant, New Eng. Cultural Coun., 2003, grant, NEA, 1988—90. Office: Univ Mass Art 100 Morrissey Blvd Boston MA 02115 Business E-Mail: carol.scollans@umb.edu.

SCOLLARD, PATRICK JOHN, hospital executive; b. Chgo., Apr. 20, 1937; s. Patrick J. and Kathleen (Cooney) S.; m. Gloria Ann Carroll, July 1, 1961; children: Kevin, Maureen, Daniel, Thomas, Brian. BS in Econs., Marquette U., 1959; grad. sr. exec. program, MIT, 1976. With Equitable Life Assurance Soc. U.S., NYC, 1962-79, asst. v.p., 1969-71, v.p., personnel dir., 1971-75, v.p. corp. adminstrv. svcs., 1975-79; sr. v.p. Chem. Bank, NYC, 1979-80, exec. v.p., 1980-87, chief adminstrv. officer, 1987-92; pres., CEO St. Francis Hosp., Roslyn, NY, 1992-99; pres. Scollard Assocs. LLC, Garden City, NY, 1999—; pres., CEO Cath. Health Svcs. of L.I., Melville, NY, 2003—04, also bd. dirs. Bd. dirs. Ctr. Productive Longevity, Cath. Health Svcs. L.I., North Fork C.C., LI Healthcare Network; chmn. Scollard Family Found. Inc., 1999—.

SCOMMEGNA, ANTONIO, obstetrician, gynecologist, educator; b. Barletta, Italy, 1931; came to U.S., 1954, naturalized, 1960; s. Francesco Paola and Antonietta S.; m. Lillian F. Sinkiewicz, May 3, 1958; children: Paola, Frank, Roger. BA, State Lyceum A. Casardi, Barletta, 1947; MD, U. Bari, Italy, 1953. Diplomate: Am. Bd. Obstetrics and Gynecology, also sub-bd. endocrinology and reprodn. Rotating intern New Eng. Hosp., Boston, 1954-55; resident obstetrics and gynecology Michael Reese Hosp. and Med. Center, Chgo., 1956-59, fellow dept. research human reprodn., 1960-61, research asso., 1961; fellow steroid tng. program Worcester Found. Exptl. Biology, also Clark U., Shrewsbury, Mass., 1964-65; asso. prof. obstetrics and gynecology Chgo. Med. Sch., 1965-69; mem. staff Michael Reese Hosp. and Med. Center, 1961—89, attending physician obstetrics and gynecology, 1961—89, dir. sect. gynecologic endocrinology, 1965-81; dir. ambulatory care obstetrics and gynecology Mandel Clinic, 1968-69, chmn. dept., 1969-89; attending, chief svc. U. Ill. Chgo. Hosp. and Med. Ctr., 1989-98; trustee Michael Reege Med. Ctr., 1977—80; prof. dept. ob-gyn. Pritzker Sch. Medicine, U. Chgo., 1969-89; prof., head dept. ob-gyn. Coll. Medicine, U. Ill. Chgo., 1989-98, prof. emeritus, 1999—. Contbr. articles to profl. jours. Fulbright fellow, 1954-55 Fellow Am. Coll. Obstetricians and Gynecologists, Endocrine Soc., Chgo. Inst. Medicine, Am. Gynecol. and Obstet. Soc.; mem. AMA, Ill., Chgo. med. socs., Am. Fertility Soc., Chgo. Gynecol. Soc. (sec. 1976-79, pres. 1981-82), Soc. Study Reprodn., AAAS, Soc. for Gynecologic Investigation. Home: 2645 N Dayton Chicago IL 60614 Office Phone: 312-996-0222. Business E-Mail: anmis@uic.edu.

SCOPPETTA, NICHOLAS, fire commissioner; b. NYC, Nov. 6, 1932; m. Susan Scoppetta; children: Andrea, Eric. BS, Bradley U., 1958; JD, Bklyn. Law Sch., 1962. Investigator Soc. Prevention of Cruelty to Children; asst. dist. atty. NY County, 1962—69; asst. U.S. atty. (so. dist.) NY US Dept. Justice, 1969—71; commr. of investigation NYC, 1972—76, dep. mayor for criminal justice, 1976—78; founding ptnr. Scoppetta & Schieff LLP, 1980—96; commr. Adminstrn. for Children's Svcs., NYC, 1996—2001, NYC Fire Dept., 2001—. Assoc. counsel The Knapp Commn. (Commn. to Investigate Alleged Police Corruption), 1971; prof. law, dir. Inst. Jud. Adminstrn. NYU, 1978—; mem. Waterfront Commn. of NY Harbor, 1979; chmn. Commn. to Combat Police Corruption, 1994—96; founder, pres. New Yorkers for Children, 1996—. Past pres., former chmn. bd. trustees Children's Aid Soc. Served in US Army. Recipient Hugo-Morgenthau award, Hugo Morgenthau Associates, 1997.

SCORCIONI, RUGGERO, research scientist; b. Pavullo, Modena, Italy, Feb. 22, 1971; s. Francesco Scorcioni and Ida Giberti. Degree in Software Engring., U. Modena, 1995; PhD in Computational Neurosci., George Mason U., Fairfax, Va., 2003. Cert. State Registration, Italy, 1996. Cons. CINECA Interuniversity Supercomputing Ctr., Bologna, Italy, 1997—99; software design engr. IBM, Rome, 1999—2000; rsch. asst. prof. George Mason U., Fairfax, 2000—08; assoc. fellow Neurosci. Inst., San Diego, 2008—. Mem.: Soc. Neurosci. Achievements include patents pending for neuronal measurement tool; arborization reconstruction. Office: Neuroscis Inst 10640 John Jay Hopkins Dr San Diego CA 92121 Business E-Mail: scorcioni@nsi.edu.

SCORGIE, KATHRYN, education educator; d. Albert E. and Carolyn Fath Thielen; m. Glen Given Scorgie, May 13, 1978; children: Claire Louise Maurer, Catherine Abigail, Sarah. PhD, U. Alta., Edmonton, Alberta, Can., 1996. Cert. Alta., Can., 1992. Prof., sch. edn. Azusa Pacific U., Calif., 1997—; lectr., dept. spl. edn. San Diego State U., 2002—. Contbr. articles to profl. jours., chapters to books. Faculty Rsch. Coun. grant, Azusa Pacific U., 2000, 2007, Creative Tchg. grant, 2009. Mem.: Internat. Assn. Sci. Study Disability, Coun. Exceptional Children, Am. Ednl. Rsch. Assn. Office: Azusa Pacific Univ Ste 300 5353 Mission Center Rd San Diego CA 92108 Office Fax: 619-718-9659. Personal E-mail: kscorgie@mail.sdsu.edu.

SCORNAIENCHI, JOAN WEBB, educational association administrator, consultant; b. Johnstown, Pa. d. Calvin John and Amelia Maystrovich Webb; m. John Joseph Scornaienchi, Apr. 19, 1997. BSc, Ind. U. Pa., 1981, MA, 1982. Specialist drug and alcohol prevention Highland Ctr. of Mercy Hosp., Johnstown, Pa., 1982—83; adminstr. Kent State U., Ohio, 1983—94; bus. and industry liaison officer Cambria County CC, Johnstown, 1995—96; customer svc. rep. Caterpillar Fin. Svcs., Columbia, Md., 1997—2000; edn. program specialist Md. State Dept. Edn., Balt., 2001—, spkr. character edn. spkrs. bureau, 2008—; co-founder, etiquette and protocol cons. Ambassador Protocol, Columbia, 2005—. Presenter in field. Mem. Balt./Wash. C. of C., 2005—; vol. Balt. City Teen Ct., 2003—, mem. adv. com., 2003—. Recipient Diversity award, Kent State U., 1991, Orientation Week Creative Program award, 1992, citation, City of Balt. Mayor's Office, 2004, Emerging Leader award, South Atlantic Region Soroptimist Internat., 2006. Mem.: Soroptomist Internat. Howard County (treas. 2004—06, com. chair 2004—06, pres. 2006—08, past-pres. 2008—), Nat. Assn. Multicultural Edn., Nat. Grants Mgmt. Assn. Avocations: travel, reading, writing, etiquette training, bicycling. Home: 6209 Bird Race Columbia MD 21045 Personal E-mail: joanwebbs@comcast.net.

SCORSESE, MARTIN, film director, film producer; b. Flushing, NY, Nov. 17, 1942; s. Charles and Catherine (Cappa) Scorsese; m. Laraine Marie Brennan, May 15, 1965 (div.); 1 child, Catherine Terese Glinora Sophia; m. Julia Cameron, 1975 (div. 1977); 1 child, Domenica Elizabeth; m. Isabella Rosellini, Sept. 29, 1979 (div. 1983); m. Barbara DeFina, Feb. 9, 1985 (div. 1991); m. Helen Morris, 1999; 1 child, Francesca Kingsland. BS in Film Comm., NYU, 1964, MA in Film Comm., 1966, Doctorate (hon.), Princeton U., Wesleyan U., Bard Coll., Williams Coll., Royal Coll. Art. Faculty asst., then instr. film NYU, NYC, 1963-70; founder World Cinema Found., 2007—. Dir.: (films) (writer, assoc. prodr., actor) Who's That Knocking at My Door?, 1968, (actor) Boxcar Bertha, 1972, (co-writer, actor) Mean Streets, 1973, Alice Doesn't Live Here Anymore, 1975, (actor) Taxi Driver, 1976 (Palme d'Or award, Cannes Internat. Film Festival), New York, New York, 1977, The Last Waltz, 1978, Raging Bull, 1980, The King of Comedy, 1983, After Hours, 1985, The Color of Money, 1986, The Last Temptation of Christ, 1988, New York Stories, 1989, (co-writer) Goodfellas, 1990, Cape Fear, 1991, (co-writer) The Age of Innocence, 1993, (writer) Casino, 1995, Kundun, 1997, Bringing Out the Dead, 1999, The Gangs of New York, 2002, (exec. prodr.) The Aviator, 2004, (prodr.) The Departed, 2006 (NY Film Critics Circle award, Best Dir., 2006, Nat. Bd. Review award, Best Dir., 2006, 2006 Critics Choice award, Broadcast Film Critics Assn., 2007, Golden Globe award, Best Dir., 2007, Outstanding Directorial Achievement in Feature Film for 2006, Directors Guild of America, 2007, Academy award, Best Dir., 2007), Shine a Light, 2008; prodr.: The Grifters, 1990, Mad Dog and Glory, 1993; exec. prodr.: Naked in New York, 1994, Clockers, 1995, Grace of My Heart, 1996; (documentaries); dir.: Street Scenes, 1970, Italianamerican, 1974, American Boy: A Profile of Steven Price, 1979, Made in Milan, 1990; (dir., writer) The Big Shave, 1968, (editor, asst. dir.) Woodstock, 1970, (assoc. prodr.) Medicine Ball Caravan, 1971, (editor) Elvis on Tour, 1973, (dir. prodr.) No Direction Home: Bob Dylan, 2005 (Banff Rockie award, 2006, Grammy award, 2006, Columbia-DuPont Journalism award, 2007), (co-dir.) A Personal Journey with Martin Scorsese Through American Movies, 1997, Il Mio Viaggio in Italia, 1999, The Blues, 2002, (other film appearances include) Cannonball, 1976, Pavlova: A Woman for All Seasons, 1983, 'Round Midnight, 1986, Akira Kurosawa's Dreams, 1990, Guilty by Suspicion, 1991, Quiz Show, 1994, (prodr.) Search and Destroy, 1995, La Memoire Retrouvee, 1996, The Muse, 1999; exec. prodr.: Kicked in the Head, 1997, The Hi-Lo Country, 1998; appeared in (TV series) Entourage, 2008. Decorated Legion d'Honneur France; recipient Edward L. Kingsley Found. award, 1964, Screen Prodrs. Guild prize, 1965, Am. Cinematheque award, 1991, Britannia award, Brit. Acad. Film & TV Arts, 1993, Golden Lion award, Venice Film Festival, 1995, Wexner prize, Wexner Ctr. for Arts, Columbus, Ohio, 1996, Life Achievement award, Am. Film Inst., 1997, Lifetime Career award, Lincoln Ctr. Film Soc., 1998, Ray of Light award, Dalai Lama, 1998, Evelyn F. Burkey award, Writers Guild America East, 2003, Lifetime Achievement award, Dirs. Guild America, 2003, Ellis Island Family Heritage award, 2004, Kennedy Ctr. Honors, John F. Kennedy Ctr. Performing Arts, 2007; named one of The World's Most Influential People, TIME mag., 2007. Fellow: Am. Acad. Arts & Scis.; mem.: AAAL (hon.).

SCOTCHMER, SUZANNE ANDERSEN, economics professor; b. Seattle, Jan. 23, 1950; d. Toivo Mathias and Margaret A. BA in Econ., U. Wash., 1970; MA in Stats., U. Calif., Berkeley, 1979, PhD in Econ., 1980. Asst., assoc. prof. econ. Harvard U., Cambridge, Mass., 1981—86; prof. econs. and pub. policy U. Calif., Berkeley, 1986—. Vis. prof. U. Toronto, 1993, Tel Aviv U., 1994, U. Paris, Sorbonne, 1992, New Sch. of Econs., Moscow, 1993, U. Auckland, 2002; Stockholm Sch. Econs., 2006, U. Calif., 2007, NYU, 2008, prin. investigator, NSF, 1986-2002; mem. Toulouse Network on Info. Tech., 2005-; mem. sci. tech. econ. policy bd., NAS, 2005-. Author: Innovation and Incentives, 2004; mem. editl. bd. Am. Econ. Rev., 1991-95, Jour. Pub. Econ., 1986-01, Jour. Econ. Perspectives, 1994-97, Regional Sci. and Urban Econ., 1991—, Jour. Econ. Lit., 1998-01; contbr. articles to profl. jours. Sloan fellow, 1979, Phi Beta Kappa fellow, 1978, Hoover Nat. fellow Stanford U., 1989, Olin fellow Yale Sch. Law, 1993, and Sch. Law U. So. Calif., 2005; France/Berkeley Fund grantee, 1994-95; Kaufmann Found. grantee, 2005. Office: Univ Calif 2607 Hearst Ave Berkeley CA 94720-7320 Business E-Mail: scotch@berkeley.edu.

SCOTLAND, S. J. (SUSAN ROSE SCOTLAND), artist, educator; b. Oakland, Calif., Feb. 01; 1 child, Spencer Joseph. BA, U. Tex., 1992; studied painting with Neal Wilson and Jill Penke, Tex. State U. Cert. tchr. Tex., CNA Maine, 2009. Tchr. Waco (Tex.) Sch. Dist., 1993—. Author various poetry; exhibitions include Amsterdam Whitney Gallery, N.Y.C., 2005, 2006, 2007, 2008, 2009, Montserrat Gallery, 2005—07, Gallerie Gora, Montreal, Can., 2005. Mem.: Portland Mus. Art, Art House at Jones Ctr., Women and Their Work. Independent. Avocations: theater, tennis, travel, painting, golf. Personal E-mail: scotland_88@hotmail.com.

SCOTT, ADAM, professional golfer; b. Adelaide, Australia, July 16, 1980; Student, UNLV. Amateur tour golfer, 1996—2000; profl. golfer PGA Tour, 2001—. Mem. Australian Team World Cup, 2002; mem. Internat. Team Pres.'s Cup, 2002, 03, 05, 08. Achievements include winning PGA Tour events including the Deutsche Bank Championship, 2003, Players Championship, 2004, Booz Allen Classic, 2004, Tour Championship, 2006, Houston Open, 2007; winning international events including the Alfred Dunhill PGA Championship, 2001, Qatar Masters, 2002, 2008 Gleneagles Scottish PGA Championship, 2002, Scandic Carlsberg Scandinavian Masters, 2003, Johnnie Walker Classic, 2005 Singapore Open 2005, 2006; top ten World Ranking, 2006. Mailing: PGA Tour 112 PGA TOUR Blvd Ponte Vedra Beach FL 32082

SCOTT, ANNE BYRD FIROR, history professor; b. Montezuma, Ga., Apr. 24, 1921; d. John William and Mary Valentine (Moss) Firor; m. Andrew Mackay Scott, June 2, 1947; children: Rebecca, David MacKay, Donald MacKay. AB, U. Ga., 1941; MA, Northwestern U., 1944; PhD, Radcliffe Coll., 1958; LHD (hon.), Lindenwood Coll., 1968, Queens Coll., 1985, Northwestern U., 1989, Radcliffe Coll., 1990, U. of the South, 1990, Cornell Coll., 1991; LLD (hon.), Wake Forest U., 2007. Congressional rep., editor LWV of U.S., 1944-53; lectr. history Haverford Coll., 1957-58, U. N.C., Chapel Hill, 1959-60; asst. prof. history Duke U., Durham, N.C., 1961-67, assoc. prof., 1968-70, prof., 1971-80, W.K. Boyd prof., 1980-91, W.K. Boyd prof. emerita, 1992—, chmn. dept., 1981-85; Gastprofessor Universität, Bonn, Germany, 1992-93. Vis. prof. Johns Hopkins U., 1972-73, Stanford U., 1974, Harvard U., 1984, Cornell Coll., 1993, Williams Coll., 1994, U. Miss., 2000; Times-Mirror scholar Huntington Libr., 1995; vice chmn. Nat. Humanities Ctr., 1991-98; mem. adv. com. Schlesinger Libr.; lectr. in field. Author: The Southern Lady, 1970, 1995; author: (with Andrew MacKay Scott) One Half the People, 1974; author: Natural Allies, 1991; editor: Jane Addams, Democracy and Social Ethics, 1964, The American Woman, 1970, Women in American Life, 1970, Women and Men in American Life, 1976, Unheard Voices, 1993, Pauli Murray and Caroline Was, 2006; mem. editl. bd.: Revs. in Am. History, 1976—81, Am. Quar., 1974—78, Jour. So. History, 1978—84; contbr. articles to profl. jours. Chmn. Gov.'s Commn. on Status of Women, 1963-64; mem. Citizens Adv. Council on Status of Women U.S., 1964-68; trustee Carnegie Corp., 1977-85, W.W. Ctr. for Scholars, 1977-84; chmn. bd. dirs. Nat. Cmty. Investment Fund, 1996—2002. AAUW fellow, 1956-57; grantee NEH, 1967-68, 76-77, Nat. Humanities Ctr., 1980-81; grad. medal Radcliffe Coll., 1986, Duke U. medal, 1991, John Caldwell medal N.C. Humanities Coun., 1994; fellow Ctrl. Advanced Study in Behavioral Sci., 1986-87; Fulbright scholar, 1984, 92-93. Fellow Am. Acad. Arts & Sci; mem. Am. Antiquarian Soc., Orgn. Am. Historians (exec. bd. 1973-76, pres. 1983, Disting. Pub. Svc. award 2002), So. Hist. Assn. (exec. bd. 1976-79, pres. 1989), Soc. Am. Historians Assn. (Disting. Scholarly Achievement award, 2008), Phi Beta Kappa. Democrat. Office: Duke U Dept History Durham NC 27708 Personal E-mail: annefiror@gmail.com. Business E-Mail: ascott@email.unc.edu.

SCOTT, BENJAMIN, retired electrical engineer; b. Maringoulin, La., Nov. 30, 1929; s. Harry Scott, Sr. and Sarah (London) Scott; m. Doretha L. Scott, June 27, 1959; children: Benjamin Eric Jr., Daryl Deion. AA, Pasadena City Coll., Calif., 1954; BS, Pacific State U., LA, 1959; M in Mgmt. Sci., UCLA, China Lake, 1969. Project elec. engring. Defense Dept., China Lake, 1952—69, dir. Sylmar, Calif., 1964—67, spl. projects electronics Pasadena, Calif., 1969—74; CEO, chief cons. Benjamin Scott & Assocs., Inc., San Francisco, 1977—78, LA, 1978—80, Pasadena, 1981—2001; ret. Author: (manuscript) South Africa, An Emerging Democracy, 1990, (book) Perspectives of Aparthied South African One Man's Journey. Cmty. organizer NAACP, Pasadena and China Lake, Calif., 1952—; internat. organizer for Africa People to People, LA, 1972; bd. mem. ARC, Inglewood and LA, 1997—2003; coord. Pasadena Urban Coalition, 1966—74, Congress Racial Equality, LA, 1962—97; cons. Black and Minority Businesses, LA, 1977—79; contbr. South African Peace Negotiations, 1986—90. Master sgt. US Army, 1945—47, PTO. Decorated Heroism During Korean War award US Army; recipient Recognition award, Civil Rights Field-Time Mag. Feature, 1963, Pres. Richard M. Nixon, 1972, LA City Coun., 1977, Einsenhower Commn., 1998, Superior Achievement award, Def. Dept., 1966, Humanitarian award, William R. Tolbert, Jr. Pres., Liberia, 1972, Humanitarian for Peace award, Vista U., South

Africa, 1990. Mem.: Clare Barton Soc., Mystic Shrine, Masons, Am. Disabled Vets., Am. VFW, Am. Legion. Republican. Episcopalian. Avocations: water-skiing, boating, tennis, golf.

SCOTT, BETSY SUE, lawyer; b. Chgo., July 3, 1951; d. Leo and Regina Mackta; m. Thomas Jefferson Scott Jr., Apr. 25, 1981; children: Elspeth Watts, Marghuerita Taylor, Thomas Jefferson Scott III. Cert. in French lang., U. Paris, 1971; BA, Hamilton Coll., 1972; JD, Cumberland Coll., 1976. Bar: Pa. 1976, N.Y. 1980, D.C. 1984. Trust adminstr. Mfrs. Hanover Trust, NYC, 1976-78; assoc. Fink, Weinberger et al, NYC, 1978-80; employee benefits officer 1st Va. Bank, Falls Church, 1982-83; mem. Hill, Betts & Nash, Washington, 1983-85; sole practice, litigation cons. Washington, 1985-86; employee benefits atty., Pension and Welfare Benefits Adminstrn. US Dept. Labor, Washington, 1986-90; atty. Office Fgn. Assets Control, US Treasury Dept., Washington, 1990—2006; of counsel Patton Boggs LLP, 2006—08; sole practice, 2008—. Translator French-English litigation, Washington, 1985—. Mem. Great Falls Womens Club, River Bend Golf and Country Club. Republican. Avocations: sailing, fencing, gardening. Office: 11710 Plaza America Dr Reston VA 20190 Office Phone: 703-871-5070. Business E-Mail: betsysuescott@bsscottlaw.com.

SCOTT, BOB (ROBERT SCOTT), retired chemical engineer, educator; b. Knoxville, Tenn., Dec. 1, 1934; s. Bob and Katherine Scott; m. Julia Scott; children: Robert, Joseph. BS in Chem. Engring., U. Tenn., 1957; MS in Chem. Engring., U. Cin., 1964. Chem. engr. Dupont, Olin, Shell Chem. Co.; staff mem. Oak Ridge Nat. Lab., US Army Signal Corps R&D Lab.; prof. Pellissippi State Tech. Cmty. Coll. Mem. Ch. of the Savior - United Ch. of Christ. Mem.: Audubon Soc., Am. Assn. Retired People, Mensa, Am. Inst. Chem. Engrs., Tenn. Ornithol. Soc., Tech. Soc. Knoxville, Sierra Club. Democrat. Office: 2216 Delta Way Knoxville TN 37919 Office Phone: 865-310-8710. Business E-Mail: scottforcongress@aol.com.*

SCOTT, BOBBY RANDOLPH, biomedical researcher, writer; b. Minden, LA, Dec. 21, 1944; s. Bobby Lee and Ethel Scott; children: Robin, Renee Walker. BS, Southern U., Baton Rouge, La.; MS, PhD, U. Ill., Urbana. Biophysicist Inhalation Toxicology Rsch. Inst., Albuquerque, 1977—96; staff scientist Lovelace Respiratory Rsch. Inst., Albuquerque, 1996—2005, sr. scientist, 2005—. Mem. US, Russian Fedn. Working Group on MAYAK Studies, 1994—2004; cons. EPA Sci. Adv. Bd. Radiation Adv. Com., 2000—04; assoc. editor Nonlinearity Biology, Toxicology, & Medicine, 2004—05, Dose Response Jour., 2005—. Contbr. chapters to books to profl. jours. Mem.: Internat. Dose Response Soc., Environ. Mutagen Soc., Soc. Risk Analysis, Health Physics Soc., Radiation Rsch. Soc. Achievements include first to developed quantitative model for assessing the health risks to humas from exposure of to large radiation doses as might occur during a radiological terrorism incident & developed a novel cancer risk model which explains the protective effects of low doses of radiation. Office: Lovelace Respiratory Rsch Inst 2425 Ridgecrest Dr SE Albuquerque NM 87108 Business E-Mail: bscott@lrri.org.

SCOTT, BRIAN WALTER, management consultant; b. Melbourne, Victoria, Australia, Apr. 23, 1935; s. Walter and Dorothy Ada (Ransom) S.; m. Dorothy Yvonne Allen, Aug. 15, 1959; children: David, Mark, Jennifer, Susan. B of Econs., Sydney U., Australia, 1955; MBA, Stanford U., 1959; D of Bus. Adminstrn., Harvard U., 1963. Asst. prof. U. So. Calif., Los Angeles, 1961-62; cons. mgmt. W.D. Scott and Co. Pty. Ltd., Sydney, 1963-69, dir., 1969-74, mng. dir., 1974-79, chmn., 1979-85; dep. chmn. A.C.I. Internat. Ltd., Sydney, 1985-86, chmn., 1986-88; dir., mgmt. rev. Edn. Portfolio, New South Wales, 1988-90. Chmn. Mgmt. Frontiers Pty. Ltd., Sydney, 1985—, Found for Devel. Cooperation Ltd., Brisbane, 1990-2007; bd. dirs. Metrobank Card Corp., 2002-, PNG Microfinance Ltd., 2003-, James N. Kirby Found. Ltd., 1981-. Chmn. Trade Devel. Coun., Canberra, 1984-90, chmn. Australian-Korean Found., 1992-2000; chmn. coun. Knox Grammar Sch., Sydney, 1981-89, Australia-Asean Bus. Coun., Canberra, 1980-82; mem. governing bd. Asian Inst. Mgmt., Manila, 1990—; co-chmn. Australia-Korea Forum, 1989-91. Named Officer, Order of Australia, 1985; recipient Australian Mfrs. Export Coun. award, 1989. Fellow Inst. Dirs. Australia (fed. pres. 1982-86), Internat. Acad. Mgmt., Australian Inst. Mgmt., Inst. Mgmt. Cons.; mem. Trade Policy Rsch. Ctr. (coun. mem. 1985-90), Sydney U. (senate 1990-95), Royal Sydney Yacht Squadron Club, Am. Club (Sydney). Avocations: reading, travel. Home: PO Box 829 Avalon Beach NSW 2107 Australia Office: Mgmt Frontiers Pty Ltd PO Box 494 North Sydney 2059 Australia E-mail: brianwscott@aol.com.

SCOTT, BYRON, professional basketball coach, retired professional basketball player; b. Ogden, Utah, Mar. 28, 1961; m. Anita Scott; children: Thomas, LonDen, DaRon. Student, Ariz. State U., 1979-85. Draft pick San Diego Clippers (now LA Clippers), 1983; player LA Lakers, 1983—93, 1996—97, Ind. Pacers, Indpls., 1993—95, Vancouver Grizzlies, 1995—96, Pananthinaikos, Greece, 1997—98; asst. coach Sacramento Kings, 1998—2000; head coach NJ Nets, East Rutherford, 2000—04, New Orleans Hornets, 2004—. Head coach NBA Ea. Conf. All-Star Team, 2002. Named NBA Coach of Yr., 2008. Achievements include winning NBA Championships as a member of the Lakers, 1985, 87, 88. Office: New Orleans Hornets 1250 Poydras St Ste 101 New Orleans LA 70113-1804

SCOTT, CARLA ANNE, musician, educator; b. Elmhurst, Ill., Feb. 6, 1951; d. William Frederick and Clara Lou Sommer; m. Kinney Duane Scott, Dec. 22, 1984; 1 child, Joelle Lynn Jewell. BA, Adams State Coll., Alamosa, Colo., 1973; Kodaly level 1, Colo. Coll., 1998; Kodaly Level 2, U. Colo., Boulder, 1999. Asst. libr., music instr. Lamar CC, Colo., 1974—75; tchr. elem. band and gen. music Harrison Sch. Dist. 2, Colorado Springs, 1975—2006; elem. band and orch. tchr. Sch. Dist. 11, Colorado Springs, 2006—. Prin. oboist Pueblo Symphony Orch., 1973—2006, orch. rep., 1988—2006; prin. oboist Pikes Peak Philharm.; 2d oboe and English horn Chamber Orch. of the Springs; free lance musician, Colo.; presenter in field. Pres. Pikes Peak Philharm., Colorado Springs, 2002—. Recipient 25 Yr. award, Colo. Music Educators Assn., 2004. Home: 3031 Fascination Cir Colorado Springs CO 80917 Office: Midland Internat Elem Sch 2110 W Broadway Colorado Springs CO 80904 Personal E-mail: casoboe@pcisys.net.

SCOTT, CAROL, science educator; MEd, Southwestern Okla. State U., Weatherford, 1997. Cert. Nat. Bd. Profl. Tchg. Stads., 2002. Media and tech. dir. Mustang Pub. Schs., Okla., 1997—. Pres. Mustang Area Reading Coun., 2007—. Grant, Nat. Geog., 2007—08. Mem.: Internat. Soc. Tech. in Edn.

SCOTT, CATHERINE DOROTHY, library and information scientist, consultant; b. June 21, 1927; d. Leroy Stearns Scott and Agnes Frances (Meade) Scott Schellenberg. AB in English, Cath. U. Am., 1950, MS in Libr. Sci., 1955. Asst. libr. Export-Import Bank USA, Washington, 1951-55, Nat. Assn. Home Builders, 1955-62, reference libr., 1956-62; founder, chief tech. libr. Bellcomm, Inc., subs. AT&T, 1962-72; chief libr. Nat. Air, Space Mus. Smithsonian Instn., 1972-82, chief libr. Mus. Reference Ctr., 1982-88, sr. reference libr., 1989-95; info. cons., 1995—. Presdl. appointee, mem. Nat. Commn. Librs., Info. Sci., 1971—76; bd. visitors Cath. U. Am. Libr. Sci. Sch., Librs., 1984—93. Editor: International Handbook of Aerospace Awards and Trophies, 1980, 81; guest editor: Aeronautics and Space Flight Collections, 1985, in Spl. Collections, 1984. Vice chmn. DC Rep. Com., Washington, 1960—68; del. Rep. Nat. Conv., San Francisco, 1964; mem. platform com. Rep. Nat. Com., 1968, sec., 1964; del. Rep. Nat. Conv., Miami, Fla., 1968, mem. Inaugural Com., 1969, 1972. Named to Hon. Order Ky. Cols., 1968; recipient Sec.'s Disting. Svc. award Smithsonian Instn., 1976, Alumni Achievement award Cath. U. Am., 1977, Century Circle, 1998—, Disting. Fed. Svc. Nat. Commn. Libr. and Info. Sci. medal, 1985. Mem.: Cath. U. Am. The Lumen Soc., Cath. U. Am. Saint Thomas Aquinas Soc., Am. Soc. Info. Sci., League Rep. Women DC (bd. dirs. 1995—97, nominating com. 1996—97, contbg. 1999—), Nat. Fedn. Rep. Women, Cath. U. Am. Devel. Com., Friends of Cath. U. Librs. (founder, pres. 1984—88, exec. coun. 1984—96, sustaining 1998—), Internat. Fedn. Libr. Assns. (del. 1976, 1983, 1985, 1988—89), Nat. Mus. Women in Arts, Am. Soc. Assn. Execs., Spl. Librs. Assn. (Washington chpt. pres. 1973—74, chair aerospace divsn. 1974—75, cons. com. 1976—91, assn. dir. 1987—90, bd. dirs. 1987—94, award com. 1990—91, pres.-elect 1991—92, bd. dirs. 1991—94, pres. 1992—93, past pres. 1993—94, immediate past pres. 1993—94, chair assn. awards and honors 1994—95, chpt. cons. com. 1994—98, conf. planner 1996—, convenor ret. caucus 1997—99, conf. program facilitator 1998—2008, Hall of Fame 1996), Cath. U. Century Club, Spl. Librs. Assn. Legacy Club, Capital Yacht Club. Office Phone: 202-554-3928. Fax: 202-488-9223.

SCOTT, CHARLES DAVID, chemical engineer, consultant; b. Chaffee, Mo., Oct. 24, 1929; s. Charles Perry and Alma Gertrude (Kendall) S.; m. Alice Reba Bardill, Feb. 11, 1956; children: Timothy Charles, Mary Alice, Lisa Ann. BS in Chem. Engring., U. Mo., 1951; MS in Chem. Engring., U. Tenn., 1961, PhD, 1966. Registered profl. engr., Tenn. Devel. engr. Union Carbide Corp., Oak Ridge, 1953-57; rsch. engr. Oak Ridge Nat. Lab., 1957-73, sect. chief, 1973-76, assoc. divsn. dir., 1976-83, rsch. fellow, 1983-86, sr. rsch. fellow, 1987-94; dir. bioprocessing rsch. and devel. ctr., 1991-94; engirng. R&D cons. Oak Ridge, 1994—. Adj. prof. chem. engring. U. Tenn., Knoxville. Contbr. articles to profl. jours.; patentee in field. 1st lt. AUS, 1951-53. Recipient U.S. Dept. Energy E.O. Lawrence award, 1980, U. Tenn. Nathan W. Doughtery award, 1987, U. Mo. Honor award, 1988, David Perlman award Am. Chem. Soc., 1994; Union Carbide Corp. fellow, 1983; Martin Marietta Sr. Corp. fellow, 1987. Mem. Am. Chem. Soc. (chmn. separation sci. subdivsn.), Am. Assn. Clin. Chemistry (chmn. com. advanced analytical concepts, nat. award 1980), Am. Inst. Chem. Engrs. (bd. dirs.), Nat. Acad. Engring., Sigma Xi, Alpha Chi Sigma. Lutheran. Personal E-mail: cdscott1@aol.com.

SCOTT, CHARLES LEWIS, retired photojournalist; b. Grayville, Ill., Aug. 18, 1924; s. Marvin Joseph and Prudence (Blood) S.; m. Jane Turner, Jan. 14, 1945 (dec. 1983); children: Lyntha Ann, Thomas Marvin; m. Martha McDonald, Aug. 23, 1986. BS in Journalism, U. Ill., 1948; MS, Ohio U., 1970. Photographer Champaign-Urbana (Ill.) Courier, 1946-50, chief photographer, 1953-56; photographer Ill. Natural History Survey, 1946-51, Binghamton (N.Y.) Press, 1951-53; asst. picture editor Milw. Jour., 1956-58; picture editor, 1958-66; graphics dir. Chgo. Daily News, 1966-69; instr. Sch. Journalism, Ohio U., Athens, 1969-70, asst. prof., 1971-72, asso. prof., 1972-74, 76-77, prof., 1977—; dir. Sch. Visual Communication, 1978-95, prof. emeritus visual comm., 1995; picture editor Chgo. Tribune, 1974-76; dir. photography Rocky Mountain News, Denver, 1987-88; ret., 1995. Served with U.S. Navy, 1942-45. Decorated D.F.C., Air medal (3); recipient numerous awards in regional and nat. news photo contests; inductee Illini Media Hall of Fame, U. Ill., 2006. Mem. Nat. Press Photographers Assn. (charter mem., Newspaper Photographer of Yr. 1952, Editor of Yr. 1966, Joseph Sprague Meml. award 1975, Robin F. Garland Educator award 1979), Soc. Profl. Journalists, Ohio News Photographers Assn. (Lifetime Achievement award 1995). Presbyterian. Home: 8559 Lavelle Rd Athens OH 45701-9190

SCOTT, CHARLOTTE H., business educator; b. Yonkers, NY, Mar. 18, 1925; d. Edgar B. and Charlotte Agnes (Palmer) Hanley; m. Nathan Alexander Scott, Jr., Dec. 21, 1946; children: Nathan Alexander III, Leslie Kristin Scott Ashamu. AB, Barnard Coll., 1947; postgrad., Am. U., 1949-53; MBA, U. Chgo., 1964; LL.D., Allegheny Coll., 1981. Research asso. Nat. Bur. Econ. Research, NYC, 1947-48; economist R.W. Goldsmith Assos., Washington, 1948-55, U. Chgo., 1955-56, Fed. Res. Bank, Chgo., 1956-71, asst. v.p., 1971-76; prof. bus. adminstrn. and commerce, sr. fellow Tayloe Murphy Inst., U. Va., Charlottesville, 1976-86; prof. commerce and edn. U. Va., Charlottesville, 1986-98, prof. emeritus, 1998—. Bd. dir. Atlantic Rural Expn., Inc.; mem. adv. bd. NationsBank Charlottesville, 1991-93; mem. nat. adv. bd. coun. SBA, 1979-82; mem. consumer adv. coun. bd. govs. FRS, 1979-82, vice chmn., 1980-81, chmn., 1981-82. Mem. editorial bd. Jour. Retail Banking, 1978-85, Jour. Internat. Assn. Personnel Women, 1981-85; contbr. articles to profl. jours. Pres. women's bd. Chgo. Urban League, 1967-69; mem. Va. Commn. on Status of Women, 1982-85, Gov.'s Commn. on Va.'s Future, 1982-85, Gov.'s Commn. on Efficiency in Govt., 1985-87; treas. Va. Women's Cultural History Project, 1982-85; bd. dirs. Boys and Girls Club of Charlottesville Area Cmty. Found.; governing bd. Charlottesville Area Cmty. Found., 1993-2004; mem. adv. bd. Ash Lawn-Highland Mus.; treas. Episcopal Diocese, Coun. Region XV, 1999-2004. Mem. Internat. Assn. Personnel Women (v.p. mems.-at-large 1980-82), Assn. Study of Higher Edn., Va. Assn. Econs., Acad. Mgmt., Barnard Coll./Columbia U. Alumnae Assn. (bd. dirs. 1977-81, trustee 1977-81). Episcopalian. Home: Apt 5317 250 Pantops Mountain Rd Charlottesville VA 22911 Office: U Va McIntire Sch Commerce Monroe Hall Charlottesville VA 22903 Business E-Mail: scott_c@forbes2.comm.virginia.edu.

SCOTT, CHARNETA CLAUDETTA, psychologist, educator; b. Jacksonville, Fla., May 3, 1963; d. Charles Alexander Scott and Venetia Lemar McLemoure. BS, U. of Fla., 1981—85; MA, Ea. N.Mex U., 1985—86; PhD, Howard U., 1992—2003. Lic. Professional Counselor D.C. Dept. of Health Health and Licensing, 2004. Clin. psychologist D.C. Dept. of Mental Health, 1996—; coord. of ct. services, therapist Francis and Associates, P.C., Washington, 2001—; adj. faculty Trinity U., Washington, 2000—. Assoc. dir. for conf. adminstrn. WBC Learning Conf., Washington, 2005—. Team mem. Capitol Area Crisis Response Team, Washington, 2004. Recipient Dedication to Work with Children, Francis and Associates, 2004, U. of Fla. Hall of Fame, 1984—85; Walter and Theodora Daniel Endowed Ednl. Rsch. Grant, Walter and Theodora Daniel Ednl. Rsch. Fund, 1998. Mem.: APA, Assn. for Play Therapy, Inc., The Am. Acad. of Experts in Traumatic Stress. D-Liberal. Roman Cath. Avocation: dance. Home: 722 Varnum St NW Washington DC 20011-7230 Personal E-mail: charneta@aol.com.

SCOTT, CHERYL M., foundation administrator, healthcare educator; BA, U. Wash., 1975, MA in Health Adminstrn., 1977. Joined Group Health Coop., Seattle, 1979, regional v.p., exec. v.p., COO, pres., CEO, 1997—2004, pres. emerita, 2004—; COO Bill and Melinda Gates Found., Seattle, 2006—. Clin. assoc. prof. Dept. Health Svcs. U. Wash. Sch. Pub. Health and Cmty. Medicine, 2004—; past bd. mem. Am.'s Health Insurance Plans; past chair Alliance of Cmty. Health Plans and Healthcare Forum; bd. chair Health Tech. Ctr.; mem. Com. on Redesigning Health Insurance Benefits, Payment and Performance Improvement Programs Inst. Medicine. Past chair Alliance for Edn. U. Wash. Health Adminstrn. Program, chair External Adv. Com.; chair King County's Blue Ribbon Com. on Election Reform; trustee Wash. State Life Scis. Discovery Fund. Office: Bill and Melinda Gates Found 1551 Eastlake Ave E Seattle WA 98101 Office Phone: 206-448-6755. Office Fax: 206-448-6464. E-mail: scott.cm@ghc.org.

SCOTT, CHRISTINA LYNN, psychology professor; d. Walter Brandt and Carol Ann Scott. PhD, Kans. State U., Manhattan, 2000. Vis. asst. prof. Pepperdine U., Malibu, Calif., 2002—04; Psi Chi advisor St. Mary's Coll. Calif., Moraga, Calif., 2006—09, asst. prof. psychology, 2005—. Mem.: Soc. Sci. Study Sexuality. Office: Saint Mary's Coll Calif 1928 Saint Mary's Rd Moraga CA 94575 Office Fax: 925-631-8520. Business E-Mail: cls4@stmarys-ca.edu.

SCOTT, CROUTER, medical educator; b. Walla Walla, Wash., June 17, 1976; s. Mike and Bev Crouter. BS, Linfield Coll., McMinnville, Oreg, 1998; MS, U. Wis., La Crosse, 2000; PhD, U. Tenn., Knoxville, 2005. Diplomate exercise specialist Am. Coll. Sports Medicine, 2000. Lab technician El Camino Coll., Torrence, Calif., 2000—02; postdoc. assoc. Cornell U., Ithaca, NY, 2005—07; asst. prof. U. Mass., Boston, 2007—. Mem.: Am. Coll. Sports Medicine. Office: Univ Mass Boston 100 Mo Blvd Boston MA 02125 Business E-Mail: scott.crouter@umb.edu.

SCOTT, DAVID ALBERT, United States Representative from Georgia; b. Aynor, SC, June 27, 1945; s. Albert and Mamie (Polite) Scott; m. Alfredia Aaron, Oct. 26, 1969; children: Dayna Dorienda, Marcye Michelle. BA, Fla. A&M U., 1967; MBA, U. Pa., 1969. Pres., owner Dayn-Mark Advt., Atlanta; mem. Ga. House of Reps., Atlanta, 1975-82, Ga. Senate, Atlanta, 1983—2002, chmn. edn. com., 1993, chmn. rules com., 1994—2002; mem. US Congress from 13th Ga. dist., 2003—; mem. Agriculture com., Fin. Svcs. Com. Chmn. Atlanta Fulton Senate Del., 1992—94. Creator, prodr., dir. (film) Langston! (4 Emmy awards, best cultural affairs program award NATAS, spl. recognition Congl. Black Caucus, Bronze Jubilee award), (nat. radio program) Inside Black America (spl. cmty. svc. award Mayor of Chgo., James Weldon Johnson journalism award NAACP, spl. citation City of Highland Park, Mich., spl. broadcasting cmty. svc. award Detroit City Coun., spl. tribute Mich. Ho. of Reps.). Mem. exec. bd. dirs. U. Pa. Wharton Sch. Bus. Recipient Silver Microphone award, 1986, 1992, 1993, 1994, Telly award, 1994; named one of Most Influential Black Americans, Ebony mag., 2006; named to Power 150, 2008. Mem.: NAACP, Black Caucus, Nat. Assn. Black Elected Ofcls., Ga. C of C. (bd. dirs.), Ga. Bus. Coun., Alpha Phi Alpha. Democrat. Baptist. Avocations: reading, writing, movies, theater. Office: US Ho Reps 417 Cannon Ho Office Bldg Washington DC 20515-1013 Office Phone: 202-225-2939. Office Fax: 202-225-2939.*

SCOTT, DAVID ALBERT, biomedical researcher, dental educator; s. Albert Ernest and Irene Scott; m. Christopher Gertig; children: Sean Paul, Liam Patrick. BSc, Heriot Watt U., Edinburgh, Scotland, 1987; PhD, McGill U., Montreal, Quebec, 1997. Assoc. prof., oral health and systemic disease U. Louisville Sch. Dentistry, 2004—, dir., oral biology grad. programs, 2006—. Editl. bd. mem. Tobacco Induced Diseases, Essen, Germany, 2002—, treas. Internat. Soc. Prevention, 2008—; assoc. prof., microbiology and imunology U. Louisville Sch. Medicine, 2008—. Musician (guitarist): (musical recordings) Motorcycle Boy, (riverhead) Musical Recordings; editor (with xing li wang): (book) Molecular Mechanisms of Tobacco-Induced Diseases. Rsch. grants, NIH, 1997—2008, NSERC, 1997—2008, CIHR, 1997—2008, Welcome Trust, 1997—2008. Mem.: Soc. Leukocyte Biology, Internat. Assn. Dental Rsch. Jain. Achievements include patents for infrared spectroscopy for inflammatory periodontal diseases and cotinine as an anti inflammatory therapeutic. Office: Sch Dentistry 501 S Preston St Louisville KY 40292

SCOTT, DAVID CLINTON, research scientist; b. Brighton, Colo., Sept. 5, 1960; s. Robert Glenn and Janice Elizabeth (Smith) S.; children: Clinton P., Alexander J., Eric O. BA, U. Colo., 1986; PhD, U. So. Calif., 1993. R & D chemist ICI, Hawthorn, Calif., 1987-88; rsch. asst. chemistry dept. U. So. Calif., LA, 1988-93; rsch. scientist Jet Propulsion Lab, Pasadena, Calif., 1993-2000; sr. mem. tech. staff Atmospheric Scis., Pasadena, Calif., 2000—. Contbr. articles to profl. jours. Mem. AAAS, Am. Geophys. Union, Am. Chem. Soc., Applied Optics, Phi Beta Kappa. Avocations: mountain biking, running, swimming, skiing, hiking. Office Phone: 818-354-8095. Business E-Mail: david.c.scott@jpl.nasa.gov.

SCOTT, DAVID EDMUND, music educator, conductor, consultant; b. Tucson, Sept. 9, 1960; s. Douglas Edmund and Marian Eileen (Dick) S.; m. Debra Christene Dane, June 27, 1987; 1 child, Lori Christina. B in Music Edn., Baylor U., 1982, MusB, 1983; MusM, Ohio State U., 1989, PhD, 1992. Band dir. J. Frank Dobie H.S., Pasadena, Tex., 1983-88; grad. tchg. assoc. Ohio State U., Columbus, 1988-92; assoc. prof. music U. Wis., Superior, 1992—. Cons., clinician, 1993—; presenter Music Educators Nat. Conf. Conv., 1994. Music dir., conductor Red Cedar Symphony Orch., Rice Lake, Wis., 1995—; conductor Duluth (Minn.)-Superior Youth Orch., 1995-96. Presbyterian. Office: Dept Music U Wis-Superior 1800 Grand Ave Superior WI 54880-2873

SCOTT, DAVID J., lawyer, medical products executive; B, St. Lawrence U., Canton, NY; JD, Cornell Law Sch., Ithaca, NY. Pvt. practice lawyer; with RJR Nabisco, Inc., Grand Met. PLC; sr. v.p., gen. counsel Internat. Distillers & Vintners, London, 1996—97; gen. counsel United Distillers & Vintners, London, 1997—99; sr. v.p., gen. counsel Medtronic, Inc., 1999—2004, sec., 2000—04; sr. v.p., gen. counsel, sec., mem. exec. com. Amgen, Inc., Thousand Oaks, Calif., 2004—. Office: Amgen Inc One Amgen Ctr Dr Thousand Oaks CA 91320-1799 Office Phone: 805-447-1000. Office Fax: 805-447-1010.*

SCOTT, DAVID RODICK, retired lawyer, educator; b. Phila., Dec. 30, 1938; s. Ernest and Lydia Wister (tunis) S.; m. Ruth Erskine Wardle, Aug. 20, 1966; children: Cintra W., D. Rodman. AB magna cum laude, Harvard U., 1960, JD, 1965; MA, Cambridge U., 1962. Bar: Pa. 1966, D.C. 1977, U.S. Dist. Ct. (ea. dist.) Pa. 1966, U.S. Ct. Appeals (3rd cir.) 1966, U.S. Ct. Appeals (D.C. cir.) 1977, U.S. Supreme Ct. 1977. Law clk. to assoc. justice Supreme Ct. Pa., Phila., 1965-66; assoc. Pepper, Hamilton & Scheetz, Phila., 1966-69, 72-76; asst. dist. atty. City of Phila., 1970-72; sr. trial atty. criminal divsn. U.S. Dept. Justice, Washington, 1976-80; chief counsel, acting dir. Office Govt. Ethics, Washington, 1980-84; univ. counsel Rutgers U., New Brunswick, NJ, 1984—2004, ret., 2004. Acting dir. U.S. Office Govt. Ethics, 1982-83; tchr., lectr. in law Cath. U. Am., Washington, 1977-81, Inst. Paralegal Tng., Phila., 1970-74; instr. faculty of arts and scis. Rutgers U.; adj. prof. Rutgers Law Sch., Camden, 2004; lectr. in field. Contbr. chpts. to textbooks, articles to profl. jours. Trustee United Way Greater Mercer County, 1990-2005, Princeton Area Cmty. Found., Inc., 1991-2002, 2005—, Planned Parenthood Assn. Mercer Area Inc., 2004—, Internat. Lawn Tennis Club USA, 2004—; bd. mgrs. Episc. Acad., Merion, Pa., 1970-74 Keasbey Found. fellow, 1960-62. Mem Pa. Bar Assn., Nat. Assn. Coll. and Univ. Attys. (bd. dirs. 1993-96), Am. Friends Cambridge U. (head N.J. chpt. 1987-93). Home: 255 Russell Rd Princeton NJ 08540-6733

SCOTT, DEBRA LAURETTE, trombone professor; MusD, U. North Tex., Denton, 2004. Dir. bands Wharton County Jr. Coll., Wharton, Tex., 1992—2000. Office: Stephen F Austin State Univ Box 13043 SFA Station Nacogdoches TX 75962 Home Phone: 936-564-7720; Office Phone: 936-468-1186. Office Fax: 936-468-5810.

SCOTT, DONALD LAVERN, city manager, librarian, former army officer; b. Hunnewell, Mo., Feb. 8, 1938; s. William Edward and Amanda Beatrice (Dant) S.; m. Betty Jean Forte, Mar. 3, 1962; children: Jeffrey Jerome, Merriell Edward Lavern. BA in Graphic Arts, Lincoln U., 1960; MA in Counseling and Human Devel., Troy State U., 1982. Commd. 2d lt. U.S. Army, 1960, advanced through grades to brig. gen., 1991; bn. comdr. 3d Bn., 47th Inf. Div., Ft. Lewis, Wash., 1978-80; prof. mil. sci. Tuskegee (Ala.) U., 1980-81; dep. insp. gen. U.S. Army Europe, Heidleberg, Fed. Republic Germany, 1982-83; comdr. Hohenfels (Germany) Tng. Ctr., 1983-85; insp. gen. VII U.S. Corps, Stuttgart, Fed. Republic Germany, 1985-86; asst. div. comdr. 1st Cav. Div., Ft. Hood, Tex., 1986-88; chief of staff 2d U.S. Army, Ft. Gillem, Ga., 1988-91; ret. U.S. Army, 1991; chief of staff City of Atlanta, 1991, COO, 1991—; dir., founder AmeriCorps Nat. Civilian Cmty. Corps, 1993—96; mem. Five Star Coun., Vets. History Project, 1996—. Bd. dirs. Atlanta Conv. and Bus. Bur., 1991—; advisor Jimmy Carter's Atlanta Project, 1992; mem. 100 Blackmen, Atlanta, 1992; dep. Libr. of Congress, 1996-; mem. Leg. Br. Coun. Chief Adminstrn. Officers, 1996-. Decorated D.S.M., Legion of Merit, Bronze Star (6), Meritorious Svc. medal. Mem. Assn. U.S. Army, Atlanta C. of C., Kappa Alpha Psi (reporter 1980-82). Avocations: golf, reading, jogging. Office: City of Atlanta Office of Mayor 55 Trinity Ave SW Atlanta GA 30303-3520 Home Phone: 703-698-9799. E-mail: dscott@loc.gov.

SCOTT, DOUGLAS EDWARD, lawyer; b. Evanston, Ill., Jan. 20, 1957; BA in Economics, magna cum laude, U. Ill., 1979, MBA, 1981; JD, UCLA, 1984. Bar: Calif., 1984; U.S. Dist. Ct. (cen. dist.) Calif.; CPA, Ill. Assoc. O'Melveny & Myers, 1984-87; atty. Sci. Applications Internat. Corp., San Diego, 1987—92, corp. v.p., gen. counsel, 1992—97, sr. v.p., gen. counsel, 1997—2003, sr. v.p., sec., gen counsel, 2003—07, exec. v.p., sec., gen. counsel, 2007—. James scholar. Mem. ABA, State Bar of Calif. (sr. v.p., gen. counsel and asst. sec.), Phi Beta Kappa. Office: Sci Applications Internat Corp Mail Stop F 3 10260 Campus Point Dr San Diego CA 92121

SCOTT, EDWARD WILLIAM, JR., retired computer company executive & philanthropist; b. Panama City, Panama, May 25, 1938; s. Edward William and Janice Gertrude (Grimison) S.; m. Cheryl S. Gilliland, apr. 23, 1988; children: Edward William, Heather Yolanda Deirdre, Reece Donald; 1 stepson, Erik Veit. BA, Mich. State U., 1959, MA, 1963; BA, Oxford U., Eng., 1962. Personnel specialist Panama Canal Co., 1962-64, staff asst. to dir. personnel, 1964-66; personnel officer IRS, Detroit, 1966-68; staff personnel mgmt. specialist U.S. Dept. Justice, Washington, 1968-69, chief personnel systems and evaluation sect., 1970-72, dir. Office Mgmt. Programs, 1972-74, assoc. dep. commr. planning and evaluation U.S. Immigration and Naturalization Svc., 1974-75, dep. asst. atty. gen., 1972-75, asst. sec. for adminstrn. Trans. Dept., 1977-80; pres. Office Power, Inc., Washington, 1980-81; dir. mktg. Computer Consoles, Inc., 1981-84; v.p. mktg. Dest Systems, 1984-85; dir. govt. mktg. Sun Microsystems, Mountain View, Calif., 1985-88; exec. v.p. Pyramid Tech., Mountain View, 1988-95; founder, pres. BEA Sys., Inc., San Jose, Calif., 1995—. Founder, chmn. Ctr. for Global Devel., Washington, (with Bill Gates and George Soros) Data-Debt, AIDS, and Trade-Africa; founder, chmn., Friends of the Global Fight, Wash.; founder, pres. escottVentures, Inc.; owner, chmn., Fla. Bear Com.; owner, Kiz Tennis Club; pres. U.S. Dept. Justice Fed. Credit Union, 1970-73. Bd. mem. Malaria No More, VOXIVA, Holy Trinity Episcopal Acad., Fla. Inst. Tech., King Ctr. Performing Arts. Recipient Presdl. Mgmt. Improvement certificate, 1971; Spl. Commendation award Dept. Justice, 1973; also Spl. Achievement award, 1976; William A. Jump Meml. award, 1974; presdl. sr. exec. service rank of Disting. Exec., 1980; Mich. State U. scholar, 1957-60. Mem.: Phi Kappa Phi, Phi Eta Sigma. Office: Bea Software 5450 Great America Pkwy Santa Clara CA 95054-3644 Business E-Mail: ed@escottventures.com.

SCOTT, ERIC, paleontologist, educator; b. Burbank, Calif., Aug. 3, 1962; s. James Robert and Helen Louise Scott; m. Kim Marie Cooper, July 27, 1996. MA, U.Calif., LA, 1990. Chief excavator George C. Page Mus.La Brea Discoveries, L A, 1985—91; curator paleontology San Bernardino County Mus., Redlands, Calif., 1991—; adj. prof. Calif. State U., San Bernardino, 2005—. Contbr. chapters to books, articles to profl. jours. Coun. mem.; occasional chmn. Bloomington Mcpl. Adv. Coun., Bloomington, Calif., 2005—09. Mem.: Soc. of Vertebrate Paleontology (chmn., info. mgmt. com. 2007—09). Conservative. Achievements include discovery of first record of extinct horse Equus conversidens from the Rancho La Brea tar pits; first record of extinct short-faced bear, Arctodus Simus, from Riverside County; co-author newly named Genus Aiolornis. Office: San Bernardino County Mus 2024 Orange Tree Ln Redlands CA 92374 E-mail: escott@sbcm.sbcounty.gov.

SCOTT, EUGENIE CAROL, science foundation director, anthropologist; b. LaCrosse, Wis., Oct. 24, 1945; d. Allen K. and Virginia Meliss (Derr) S.; m. Robert Abner Black, Oct. 18, 1965 (div. 1970); m. Thomas Charles Sager, Dec. 30, 1971; 1 child, Carrie Ellen Sager. BS in Anthropology, U. Wis., Milw., 1967, MS in Anthropology, 1968; PhD in Anthropology, U. Mo., Columbia, 1974; DSc (hon.), McGill U., 2003, Ohio State U., 2005, Mt. Holyoke Coll., 2006, U. Wis., Milw., 2006, Rutgers U., New Brunswick, NJ, 2007, U. New Mex., 2008. Asst. prof. anthropology U. Ky., Lexington, 1974-82; postdoctoral fellow U. Calif., San Francisco, 1983-84; asst. prof., dept. anthropology U. Colo., Boulder, 1984-86; exec. dir., pub. newsletter NCSE Reports, Nat. Ctr. Sci. Edn., Oakland, Calif., 1987—. Vis. prof., U. Kans., 1976; bd. dirs. Biol. Scis. Curriculum Study, Colorado Springs, Colo., 1993-99; pub. Bookwatch Revs., 1988-92. Author, editor: Biology Textbooks, The New Generation, 1990, Evolution and Creationism: An Introduction, 2004, 2nd edit 2009; co-author: Teaching About Evolution and the Nature of Science, 1998; co-editor: Not In Our Classrooms: Why Intelligent Design is Wrong for Our Schools, 2006; prodr.: (videotape series) How Scientists Know About... Mem. nat. adv. bd. Ams. United for Separation of Ch. and State, Washington, 1995—; mem. nat. adv. coun. Am. Civil Liberties Union, 2005-. Recipient Pub. Sci. and Edn. award Com. for Sci. Investigation Claims of Paranormal, 1991, Disting. Alumnus award U. Mo. Arts and Scis., 1993, Isaac Asimov Sci. award Am. Humanist Assn., 1998, James Randi Skeptic of Yr. award Skeptic Soc., 1999, Bruce Alberts award Am. Soc. Cell Biology, 1999, 1st Amendment award Playboy Found., 1999, Outstanding Svc. award, Am. Inst. Biol. Scis, 2002, Pub. Svc. award, Nat. Sci. Bd., 2003, Geol. Soc. Am. Pub. Svc. award, 2001, Margaret Nicholson Dist. Svc. award Calif. Sci. Tchr. Assn., 2002, Ctr. for Inquiry Def. Sci. award, 2003, Anthropology in Media award Anthrop. Assn., 2006, Scientific Freedom and Responsibility award, Am. Assoc Adv. Sci., 2007, Outstanding Educator award, Exploratorium, 2007, UCSF medal, 2008. Fellow Com. Scientific Investigation, Calif. Acad. Scis. (elected 1994), AAAS; mem. Am. Assn. Phys. Anthropology (bd. dirs., exec. com. 1988-93, sec.-treas. 1993-97, pres. 2001-2003), Am. Anthropol. Assn., Nat. Assn. Biology Tchrs. (hon.), Nat. Sci. Tchrs. Assn., Sigma Xi. Office: Nat Ctr Sci Edn PO Box 9477 Berkeley CA 94709-0477 also: Nat Ctr Sci Edn 420 40th St Ste 2 Oakland CA 94609-2509

SCOTT, FREDERICK ISADORE, JR., editor, management consultant; b. Balt., Oct. 27, 1927; s. Frederick Isadore and Rebecca Esther (Waller) S.; m. Viola Fowlkes, Feb. 4, 1949 (dec. Sept. 2006). B.E. in Chem. Engring, Johns Hopkins, 1950; MS in Mgmt. Engring, Newark Coll. Engring., 1956. Chem. process engr. in r&d RCA, Harrison, NJ, 1951-59; with Kearfott div. Gen. Precision Aerospace, Little Falls, 1960-62; asst. sales mgr. Isotopes, Inc., Westwood, NJ, 1964-66; mgr. capacitor sect. Wellington Electronics, Inc., Englewood, NJ, 1967-68; owner F.I. Scott & Assocs. (med. equipment), Montclair, NJ, 1968-80; tech. product mktg. and editorial svcs. F.I. Scott & Assocs., Check, Va., 1980-86; editor instrumentation publ. Am. Lab. and Internat. Lab., Fairfield, Conn., 1968-80, cons. editor, 1980—; pres. Group Tech., Ltd., 1979—2002; editor Am. Clin. Lab., 1990—2002. Served with AUS, 1946-47. Mem. Am. Chem. Soc. (sr.), AAAS, NY Acad. Sci., IEEE (editor newsletter No. NJ sect. 1957-58, chmn. publs. com. 1958-59), NY Micros. Soc. Home and Office: 1 E Chase St Apt 410 Baltimore MD 21202-2597 Office Phone: 410-625-2065. Personal E-mail: fiscott@ziplink.net. *Perhaps the most significant aspect of my life is a long-felt realization that each person is ultimately responsible for his or her condition in life. Application of this principle continually requires that the individual assess a failure in such a way as to determine how his or her actions might have avoided it or, if unavoidable, how its recurrence can be obviated. Accepting responsibility in this manner can, I believe, lead the way toward a society based on a federation of autonomous individuals delegating authority to units of government when appropriate but clearly retaining the capability to recall that delegated authority should it be abused.*

SCOTT, G. JUDSON, JR., lawyer, federal judge; b. Phila., Nov. 16, 1945; s. Gerald Judson and Jean Louise S.; m. Ildiko Kalman, Mar. 21, 1971; children: Nathan Emory, Lauren Jean. AA, Foothill Jr. Coll., Los Altos, Calif., 1965; BA, U. Calif., Santa Barbara, 1968; JD cum laude, U. Santa Clara, 1975. Bar: Calif. 1975, U.S. Dist. Ct. (no. dist.) Calif. 1975, U.S. Ct. Appeals (9th cir.) 1975, U.S. Supreme Ct. 1981. Assoc. Feldman, Waldman & Kline, San Francisco, 1975-76, Law Offices John Wynne Herron, 1976-80; of counsel Haines & Walker, Livermore, Calif., 1980; ptnr. Haines Walker & Scott, 1980-84; officer, dir., shareholder Smith, Etnire, Polson and Scott, Pleasanton, 1984-88; pvt. practice, 1988—2009. Judge pro tem Livermore-Pleasanton Mcpl. Ct., 1981-83; settlement commr. Alameda County Superior Ct., 1994—09, judge pro tem, 2001-08; lectr. Calif. Continuing Edn. of Bar. Contbg. author: Attorney's Guide to Restitution, 1976; editor: The Bottom Line, 1989-91. Pres. Walnut Creek Open Space Found., Calif., 1981—83. Rear adm. USN, 1968—2001. Fellow: Nat. Conf. Bar Pres., Am. Bar Found.; mem.: ABA (house dels. 2003—), Alameda-Contra Costa County Trial Lawyers Assn. (bd. dirs. 2005—06, treas. 2007, sec. 2008, pres. elect 2009), Alameda County Bar Assn. (chmn. law office econs. com. 1986—87, mem. jud. nomination evaluation com. 1996—97, chair task force 1997, bd. dirs. 1997—98, v.p. 1999, pres.-elect. 2000, pres. 2001), Calif. State Bar (mem. standing com. on lawyer referral svcs. 1985—88, mem. exec. com. law practice mgmt. sect. 1988—93, chair 1992—93), Ea. Alameda County Bar Assn. (v.p. 1981—82), Coll. Master Advs. and Barristers (sr. counsel), Consumer Attys. Calif. (reviewer pending legis.), Am. Assn. Justice, Pleasanton C. of C., Livermore C. of C. (past chmn. growth study 1983), Million Dollar Advs. Forum. Republican. Office Phone: 925-460-0800. Business E-Mail: gjs@scott-law.com.

SCOTT, GARY KUPER, retired academic administrator; b. Jefferson City, Mo., Jan. 3, 1933; s. Ralph Elmer and Lillian Rachel (Kuper) S.; children— Tina Marie, Lisa René, Corey Kuper. AA, Jefferson City Jr. Coll., 1953; B.Ed., Western Wash. State Coll., 1960, M.Ed., 1962; PhD, U. Minn., 1965. Dir. student counseling center Minot (N.D.) State Coll., 1965-67; faculty, head dept. psychology Lincoln U., Jefferson City, 1967-77, chmn. dept. edn. and psychology, 1979-83, dean Sch. Edn. and Grad. Studies, 1983-85, dir. grad. and continuing edn., 1985-88, dean grad. and continuing edn., 1988-95; ret., 1995. Pres. Cole County Mental Health Assn., 1969-70; Bd. dirs. YMCA.; mem. Jefferson City Sch. Bd., 1985-87; mem. Cole County Democratic Com., 1968-70. Mem. Am., Mo. psychol. assns. Clubs: Rotary. Home: 1002 Roseridge Cir Jefferson City MO 65101-3640

SCOTT, GARY M., engineering educator, department chairman; b. Fond du Lac, Wis., Nov. 5, 1964; s. John H. and JoAnn F. (Hull) S. m. Kay Alane Shulta, Jan. 12, 1991. BS in Paper Sci. and Engring. & Computer Info. Sys., U. Wis., Stevens Point, 1988; MS in Computer Scis., U. Wis., Madison, 1991, PhD in Chem. Engring., 1993. Rsch. fellow U. Wis., 1988—93; rsch. chem. engr. USDA Forest Svc. Products Lab., Madison, 1993—98; prof. Dept. Paper and Bioprocess Engring. SUNY ESF, Syracuse, NY, 1998—, chair, 2007—. Lectr. dept. chem. engring., U. Wis., 1994—97. Contbr. articles to profl. jours. Bd. dirs. Syracuse Pulp and Paper Found., 2006—. Mem. AIChE, TAPPI. Avocations: trumpet, bicycling, triathons, skiing. Office: SUNY ESF One Forestry Dr Syracuse NY 13210 Business E-Mail: gscott@esf.edu.

SCOTT, GEORGE GALLMANN, accountant; b. Hattiesburg, Miss., July 8, 1928; s. John Havers and Rebecca Evelyn (Gallmann) S.; m. Patsy T. Womack, June 27, 1953; 1 child, George Gallmann. BS, Millsaps Coll., 1949. Accredited bus. acct., tax advisor, 1992; accredited in acctg. and taxation Nat. Accreditation Coun. for Accountancy. Clk. Spanish Trail Transport, Mobile, Ala., 1949—50, asst. auditor, 1953—55; bookkeeper Met. Engraving & Electrotype Co., Richmond, Va., 1952—53; chief clk. Mobile (Ala.) office Ctrl. Truck Lines of Tampa, Fla., 1955—56; gen. auditor M.R.&R. Trucking Co., Crestview, Fla., 1956—66, sec.-treas., 1967—77; pub. acct. enrolled represent Taxpayers IRS, 1979—2008. Mem. data processing adv. com. Okaloosa-Walton Col., Niceville, Fla., 1965- 66, 72-73; mem. Okaloosa County Gen. Advisory Com. for Devel. Vocat. Edn., 1973, 79. Bd. dirs. Okaloosa Cmty. Concert Assn., 1982-87; chmn. Crestview Downtown Devel. Bd., 1988-89; bass-baritone soloist, 1953—, choir dir. Meth. Ch., 1966-83, chmn. ofcl. bd., 1971-73, chmn. fin. com., 1974-75, 79-81, audit com., 1977-86, mem. com. on lay personnel, 1979-87, chmn., 1983-87, 89-90, mem. com. on pastor-parish rels., 1980-86, coun. on ministries, 1985, trustee, 1985-87, treas., 1990-95; mem. Walton Co. C. of C. With U.S. Army, 1950-52. Mem. Nat. Assn. Accts., Nat. Assn. Enrolled Agts., Am. Trucking Assn. (nat. acctg. and fin. coun. 1956-77), Southeastern Acctg. and Fin. Coun. (bd. dirs. 1974-77), Fla. Assn. Enrolled Agts., Crestview Downtown Mchts. Assn. (bd. dirs. 1980-84, treas. 1980-84), Greater Crestview C. of C. (chmn. bus. ethics com. 1973-74, bd. dirs. 1981-83, treas. 1982-83), Fla. Accts. Assn. (bd. govs. 1979-80, pres. N.W. Fla. chpt. 1979-80), DeFuniak Springs Bus. and Profl. Assn., Kiwanis (past treas., past sec., past pres.), Pi Kappa Alpha. Home: 244 Seminole Trail Crestview FL 32536-2326

SCOTT, GERALD WESLEY, retired American diplomat; b. Oklahoma City, Aug. 7, 1940; s. Charles Wesley and Dorothy Bernadine (Heidlage) S.; m. Frances Helen Gardner-Brown, Aug. 9, 1975; children: Charles Alan, Michael Tacon. BS in Fgn. Svc., Georgetown U., 1962; MA, Johns Hopkins U., 1969, Naval War Coll., 2000. Commd. fgn. svc. officer, 1969; vice consul Am. Consulate Gen., Danang, Viet Nam, 1973-75; polit. officer Am. Embassy, Rome, 1980-83; advisor polit. and security affairs U.S. Mission to UN, NYC, 1983-85; dep. chief of mission Am. Embassy, Mbabane, Swaziland, 1985-88, polit. counselor Kinshasa, Zaire, 1988-92, Nairobi, Kenya, 1992-93, dep. chief of mission Kinshasa, 1993-95; ambassador to The Gambia, Banjul, 1996-98; State Dept. rep. Naval War Coll., Newport, RI, 1998-2000; ret., 2000. Cons. internat. and security affairs, 2000—; sr. advisor US delegation to UN Gen. Assembly, 2001, 02, 03, 04, 05, 06, 07, 08; adv. US delegation to 58th session of UN Commn. Human Rights, 2002. Lt. USNR, 1962-67. Decorated Air medal, Navy Commendation medal. Mem. Am. Fgn. Svc. Assn. (William R. Rivkin award 1992), Sovereign Mil. Order of Malta, SAR, Sons of the Revolution, Lotos Club (NYC), Army and Navy Club (Washington). Roman Catholic. Office: G W Scott PO Box 4915 Buena Vista CO 81211

SCOTT, GLORIA RANDLE, former college president; b. Apr. 14, 1938; d. Freeman and Juanita (Bell) Randle; m. Will Braxton Scott. AB, Ind. U., 1959, MA, 1960, PhD, 1965, LLD, 1977; DHL, Fairleigh Dickinson U., 1978, Westfield State Coll., 1992, Wilson Coll., 1992, Mt. Vernon Coll., Marian Coll., 1999. Rsch. assoc. in genetics Inst. Psychiat. Rsch. Ind. U. Med. Ctr., Indpls., 1961-63; instr. biology Marian Coll., Indpls., 1961-65; dean students Knoxville Coll., Tenn., 1965-67; asst. to pres. N.C. Agrl. and Tech. State U., 1967-68, prof., 1967-76, dir. planning Inst. Rsch., 1973-76; prof. Tex. So. U., 1976-78; v.p., prof. Clark Coll., 1978-86; prof. Grambling State U., 1987; pres. Bennett Coll., Greensboro, NC, 1987-2001, founder Women's Leadership Inst., 1989; owner Scott's Bay Enterprises on Baffin Bay, Riviera, Tex., 1973—. Founding sec. bd. dirs. Africa U., Mutare, Zimbabwe, 1988-97; bd. dirs. Loew Corp.; vice chair Women's Coll. Coalition, 1990-94; bd. dirs. Nat. Assn. Ind. Colls. and Univs., 1992-96, Nat. Assn. Schs. and Colls. of the United Meth. Ch., 1993-95. Del. UN Decade for Women Internat. Forum, Nairobi, Kenya, 1985; chmn. del. UN Decade for Women Conf., Beijing, 1995; chmn. bd. Nat. Scholarship Fund for Negro Students, 1984-85; 1st v.p. Girl Scouts U.S., 1972-75, pres., 1975-78; bd. dirs. Wilson Coll., 1978-83, Nat. Urban League, 1976-85, Neal Marshall Club, Indian U. Alumni; mem bd. visitors Ind. U. Sch. Edn., Bloomington, 1988-94; bd. dirs. United Negro Coll. Fund, 1993-95, chair golden anniversary com., 1992-95; chair edn. adv. com. Delta Sigma Theta, 1989—; mem. adv. bd. James McGregor Leadership Acad., Md., 2000-05; mem. divsn. III pres.'s coun. NCAA, 1998-2001; founder Nat. African Am. Women's Leadership Inst., 1999; mentor Leadership Inst., 1997-98; mem. Internat. Women's Forum; chmn. Coun. Presidents Black Coll. Fund, UMC, 1997-99. Recipient Drum Major for Justice award, 1993, N.C. Gov's. award for Outstanding N.C. Women, 1991, Achievement award Delta Sigma Theta, 1994. Mem. Rotary (organizing founder East Greensboro 2000-01). Home: 4422 S Alameda St Apt 52 Corpus Christi TX 78412-2442 Home Phone: 361-297-5233. E-mail: randle@rivnet.com.

SCOTT, GREGORY KELLAM, former state supreme court justice, lawyer; b. San Francisco, July 30, 1943; s. Robert and Althea Delores Scott; m. Carolyn Weatherly, Apr. 10, 1971; children: Joshua Weatherly, Elijah Kellam. BS in Environ. Sci., Rutgers U., 1970, EdM in Urban Studies, 1971; JD cum laude, Ind. U., Indpls., 1977. Asst. dean resident instrn. Cook Coll. Rutgers U., 1972-75; trial atty. U.S. SEC, Denver, 1977-79; gen. counsel Blinder, Robinson & Co., Inc., Denver, 1979-80; asst. prof. coll. law U. Denver, 1980-85, assoc. prof., 1985-93, prof. emeritus, 1993—, chair bus. planning program, 1986-89, 92-93; justice Colo. Supreme Ct., Denver, 1993-2000; gen. counselor Kaiser-Hill Co., Golden, Colo., 2000—; judge trial referee Colo. Supreme Ct., Colo., 2000. Of counsel Moore, Smith & Bryant, Indpls., 1987-90; v.p., gen. counsel Comml. Energies, Inc., 1990-91; presenter in field. Author: (with others) Structuring Mergers and Acquisitions in Colorado, 1985, Airport Law and Regulation, 1991, Racism and Underclass in America, 1991; contbr. articles to profl. jours. Mem. ABA, Nat. Bar Assn., Nat. Assn. Securities Dealers, Inc., Nat. Arbitration Panel (arbitrator), Colo. Bar Found., Sam Cary Bar Assn., Am. Inn Ct. (founding mem. Judge Alfred A. Arraj inn). Avocations: golf, reading, travel. Office: Kaiger Hill 11025 Dover St Unit 1000 Westminster CO 80021-5573

SCOTT, HAL S., law educator; b. Chgo., Nov. 25, 1943; AB, Princeton U., 1965; MA, Stanford U., 1967; JD, U. Chgo., 1972. Bar: Mass. 1982. Law clk. to Hon. Harold Leventhal US Ct. Appeals DC. cir., Washington, 1972—73; law clk. to Justice Byron R. White US Supreme Ct., 1973—74; acting prof. law U. Calif., Berkeley, 1974—75; asst. prof. law Harvard Law Sch., Cambridge, Mass., 1975—80, prof., 1980—90, Nomura prof. internat. fin. sys., 1990—, dir. program internat. fin. sys., 1986—. Cons. IBM, NYC, 1977; bd. dirs. Lazard Ltd., 2006—. Author: Euro: Law and Market Practices, 1999, International Finance: Law and Regulation, 2004; co-author (with Philip A. Wellons): International Securities Regulation, 2002; co-author: International Finance: Transactions, Policy and Regulation, 2001, 2004; contbr. articles to profl. pubs. Mem.: Internat. Acad. Consumer and Comml. Law (past pres.). Office: Harvard Law Sch 1563 Massachusetts Ave Cambridge MA 02138 Office Phone: 617-495-4590. Office Fax: 617-495-9593. Business E-Mail: hscott@law.harvard.edu.

SCOTT, HILLARY, singer, musician; d. Linda Davis and Lang Scott. Founding band mem. Lady Antebellum, 2006—. Singer: (albums) Lady Antebellum, 2008. Recipient Top New Group of Yr. award, Acad. Country Music, 2008, New Artist of Yr. award, Country Music Assn., 2008. Office: Capitol Records Nashville 3322 W End Ave #11 Nashville TN 37203 Office Phone: 615-269-2000.*

SCOTT, J. LENNOX, real estate company executive; s. W. Lennox Scott. BBA, U. Washington. Cert. residential broker. Pres. John L. Scott Real Estate, Bellevue, Wash., 1980—2002, chmn., CEO, 2002—. Author: Next Generation Real Estate, 2002. Active John L. Scott Found.; bd. dirs. Econ. Develop. Coun., Seattle/King County, Wash. Wildlife & Recreation Coalition. Named one of Five Most Admired Individuals' in Real Estate, REAL Trends Inc., 2005, Real Estate's 25 Most Influential Thought Leaders, Realtor Mag., 2006; named to Hall of Leaders, Coun. Real Estate Brokerage Mgrs., 2005. Mem.: Realty Alliance, Young Pres.'s Alumni Orgn., Nat. Assn. Home Builders, Seattle King County Assn. Realtors (former pres., Realtor of Yr. 2002, Pres.'s award 2003), Nat. Assn. Realtors (bd. dirs., Pacesetter award), Rotary Internat. Office: John L Scott 3380 146th Pl SE Ste 450 Bellevue WA 98007 Office Phone: 206-230-7600. Office Fax: 206-230-7650.*

SCOTT, JACK ALAN, academic administrator, former state senator; b. Sweetwater, Tex., Aug. 24, 1933; m. Lacreta Isbell Scott; children: Sharon Mitchell, Sheila Head, Amy Schones, Greg, Adam(dec.). BA, Abilene Christian U., 1954; MDiv, Yale U., 1962; MA, Claremont Graduate U., 1967; PhD, Claremont U., 1970; LLD (hon.), Pepperdine U., 1991. Mem. faculty Pepperdine U., 1962-72, provost, 1970-73; dean Orange Coast Coll., 1973-78; pres. Cypress Coll., 1978-87, Pasadena City Coll., 1987-95, pres. emeritus, 1995—; prof. higher edn. Pepperdine U., 1995—; mem. Calif. State Assembly from 44th Dist., 1996—2000, Calif. State Senate from 21st Dist., 2000—08, past chair Accreditation Commn. of Western Assn. of Schs., mem. budget, ins. and transp. coms., chair edn. com. and edn. budget subcommittee; chancellor Calif. CC Sys., 2009—, CEO bd. govs. Co-founder Coalition for a Non-Violent City; past chair Am. Heart Assn. Mem.: Calif. Healthcare Assn., Assn. Calif. C.C. Adminstrs. (past pres.), Pasadena Rotary, Rubio Canon Land and Water Assn. Democrat. Church Of Christ. Office: Calif CC Sys Office 1102 Q St, 4th Fl Sacramento CA 95814 Office Phone: 916-322-4005. E-mail: jscott@cccco.edu.*

SCOTT, JAMES ARTHUR, radiologist, educator; b. Cleve., Aug. 23, 1950; s. Robert James and Margaret Emma (Hinz) S.; m. Phyllis Virginia Gauthier, Oct. 3, 1981. SB, MIT, 1972; MD, Boston U., 1976. Diplomate Am. Bd. Radiology, Am. Bd. Nuc. Medicine. Resident Harvard U. Med. Sch.-Mass. Gen. Hosp., Boston, 1976-80, fellow, 1980-81, instr., 1982-83, asst. prof., 1984-93, assoc. prof., 1994—. Mem. editl. adv. bd. Jour. Nuc. Medicine, Am. Jour. Roentgen. Recipient New Investigator Rsch. award NIH, 1984-87. Mem. Soc. Sci. Exploration, Sigma Xi, Am. Coll. Radiology, AAAS, Phi Lambda Upsilon, Theta Xi. Lutheran. Avocations: writing, golf, history. Office: Div Nuclear Medicine Mass Gen Hosp Boston MA 02114 Personal E-mail: jas.scott@verizon.net. Business E-Mail: scott@helix.mgh.harvard.edu.

SCOTT, JAMES L., dean, emergency physician, educator; MD, U. Ariz., 1983. Diplomate Am. Bd. Emergency Physicians, Nat. Bd. Med. Examiners. Internal medicine intern U. Ariz.; resident Georgetown U.; emergency medicine resident George Washington U.; with George Washington U. Sch. Medicine and Health Sciences, Washington, 1986—, residency dir., asst. dean grad. med. edn., asst. dean student affairs, prof. Dept. Emergency Medicine, 1998—, assoc. dean, 2000—03, interim dean, 2003—04, dean, 2004—. Recipient Nat. Tchg. award, Am. Coll. Emergency Physicians, 1998. Mem.: Soc. Acad. Emergency Medicine, Am. Coll. Emergency Physicians. Office: GWU Sch Med and Health Science 2300 Eye St NW Ross Hall 713 West Washington DC 20037 Office Phone: 202-994-2977. Office Fax: 202-741-2921. E-mail: jscott@gwu.edu, msdijls@gwumc.edu.*

SCOTT, JANICE WILKIE, museum director; b. New Haven; d. Valleau Wilkie. Attended, Knox Coll., Galesburg, Ill. Riding instr., NH and Ind.; dir., collections mgr. Sid Richardson Mus., 1982—. Office: Sid Richardson Mus 309 Main St Fort Worth TX 76102 Office Phone: 817-332-6554. Business E-Mail: jan@sidrichardsonmuseum.org.

SCOTT, JILL, poet, musician; b. Phila., 1952; Founder, pres. Blues Babe Found. Singer (with Eric Benet, Will Smith, Roots, Common); musician: (albums) Who is Jill Scott? Words & Sounds, Vol. 1, 2000, Experience: Jill Scott 826+, 2001, Beautifully Human: Words and Sounds, Vol. 2, 2004, The Real Thing, 2007, (songs) God Bless the Child, 2007 (Grammy award for Best Traditional R&B Performance, 2007), Daydreamin', 2007 (Grammy award for Best Urban/Alternative Performance, 2008); co-prodr.(with Dr. Cornel West et. al.): (albums) Never Forget: A Journey of Revelations, 2007; actor: (plays) Rent. Founder Blues Babe Found., Phila. Recipient Grammy Award, 2003. Office: Hidden Beach Recordings 3030 Nebraska Ave Santa Monica CA 90404

SCOTT, JOAN WALLACH, historian, educator; b. Bklyn., Dec. 18, 1941; d. Samuel and Lottie (Tanenbaum) Wallach; m. Donald M. Scott, Jan. 30, 1965; children: Anthony Oliver, Elizabeth Rose. BA, Brandeis U., 1962; MA, U. Wis., 1964, PhD, 1969; LittD (hon.), SUNY, Stony Brook, 1989, Brown U., 1992, John Jay Coll. Criminal Justice, City U. NY, 2005; D honoris causa (hon.), U. Bergen, Norway, 2004; LLD (hon.), Harvard U., 2007. Asst. prof. history U. Ill., Chgo., 1970—72; asst. prof. Northwestern U., 1972—74; assoc. prof. U. NC, Chapel Hill, 1974—77, prof., 1977—80; Nancy Duke Lewis prof. history Brown U., Providence, 1980—85; prof. social sci. Inst. for Advanced Study, Princeton, NJ, 1985—, Harold F. Linder prof., 2000—. Dir. Pembroke Ctr. for Tchg. and Rsch. on Women, 1981—85, NEH Seminar for Coll. Tchrs., 1977, 1980—81; mem. Inst. for Advanced Study, Princeton, 1978—79; mem. editl. bd. Jour. Modern History, 1980—83; chair adv. com. Princeton U. Women's Studies Program, 1985—97; adv. com. Stanford Humanities Ctr., 1987; adj. prof. history Rutgers U., New Brunswick, NJ, 1993—2005; vis. prof. Humanities Ctr., Johns Hopkins U., 1996—98; bd. govs. U. Calif. Humanities Rsch. Inst., 1998—2000; adv. bd. Rutgers U. Ctr. Cultural Analysis, 2005—. Author: The Glassworkers of Carmaux, 1974, Gender and the Politics of History, 1988, Only Paradoxes to Offer: French Feminists and the Rights of Man, 1996, Parité: Sexual Equality and the Crisis of French Universalism, 2005, The Politics of the Veil, 2007; co-author (with Louise Tilly): Women Work and Family, 1978, rev. edit., 1987; co-editor (with Brian Tierney): Western Societies: A Documentary History, 1984; co-editor: (with Jill Conway and Susan Bourque) Learning About Women: Gender, Power and Politics, 1987; co-editor: (with James Gilbert) The Myth Making Frame of Mind: Social Imaginations of American Culture, 1992; co-editor: (with Judith Butler) Feminists Theorize the Political, 1992, Love and Politics in Wartime: Letters to My Wife, 1943-45, 1992 (Benedict S. Alper); co-editor: (with Cora Kaplan and Debra Keates) Transitions, Environments, Translations: Feminisms in International Politics, 1997; co-editor: (with Debra Keaates) Schools of Thought: Twenty-five Years of Interpretive Social Science, 2001; co-editor: (with Debra Keates) Going Public: Feminism and the Shifting Boundaries of the Private Sphere, 2004; contbr. articles to profl. jours. Recipient Hans Sigrist prize, U. Bern, 1999, Academic Freedom award, Middle East Studies Assn., 2006; grantee, Am. Coun. Learned Socs., 1978; fellow NEH, 1975—76; Rsch. Tng. fellow, Social Sci. Rsch. Coun., 1966—68. Fellow: Am. Acad. Arts and Sciences, Sch. Criticism and Theory (sr.); mem.: AAUP (mem. Com. Acad. Freedom and Tenure 1993—2006, chmn. Com. Acad. Freedom and Tenure 1999—2005), Soc. French Hist. Studies, Berkshire Conf. Women Historians, Am. Hist. Assn. (chair com. on women historians 1978—80, Joan Kelly prize com. 1987—88, sec. Mod. European Sect. 1988—89, Joan Kelly prize 1989), Phi Beta Kappa. Office: Inst for Advanced Study Sch Social Sci Einstein Dr Princeton NJ 08540-1914 Office Phone: 609-734-8280. Office Fax: 609-951-4457. E-mail: jws@ias.edu.

SCOTT, JOHN BROOKS, retired research and development company executive; b. Morenci, Ariz., Aug. 8, 1931; s. Brooks and Lucile (Slagle) S.; m. Jo Ann Rohrbach, June 5, 1987; children from previous marriage: Janice, Steven, Sarah. BS, U. Ariz., 1957, MA, 1959. Asst. prof. systems engrng. U. Ariz., Tucson, 1959—61; mgr. Bell Aerosystems Co., Tucson, 1961—62; sr. v.p. IIT Rsch. Inst., Annapolis, Md., 1963—90, pres. Chgo., 1990-97. Author papers on computer software, electromagnetic compatibility. Past pres. bd. dirs. Md. Hall for Creative Arts, Inc.; past chmn. Md. Hall Found.; past mem. bd. govs. IIT Rsch. Inst.; past trustee Ill. Inst. Tech. Mem. Greater Annapolis C. of C. (pres. 1987); mem. Phi Kappa Phi, Sigma Pi Sigma, Pi Mu Epsilon. Home: Apt 903 3145 S Atlantic Ave Daytona Beach FL 32118-6045 E-mail: jscott2030@cfl.rr.com.

SCOTT, JOHN D., pharmacologist; b. Edinburgh, Apr. 13, 1958; married; 2 children. BSc in Biochemistry with honors, Herriot-Watt U., Edinburgh, 1980; PhD in Biochemistry, U. Aberdeen, 1983. NIH postdoctoral fellow dept. pharmacology U. Wash., Seattle, 1983—86, rsch. asst. prof. dept. biochemistry, 1986—88; asst. prof. dept. physiology and biophysics, dept. biol. chemistry U. Calif., Irvine, 1988—89; asst. scientist Ctr. Rsch. Occupl. & Environ. Toxicology Oreg. Health Scis. U., 1989—90, asst. scientist Vollum Inst. Advanced Biomed. Rsch., dept. biochemistry and molecular biology, 1990—92, scientist, 1993—97, sr. scientist, 1997—; investigator Howard Hughes Med. Ctr. (known as Vollum Inst.), 1997—. Spkr. in field. Mem. editl. bd. Jour. Biol. Chemistry; contbr. articles to profl. jours. Recipient John J. Abel award, Am. Soc. Pharmacology and Exptl. Therapeutics, 1996; scholar Med. Endowments Hon., U. Aberdeen, 1980—83. Fellow: Royal Soc.; mem.: Protein Soc., Biochem. Soc., Am. Soc. Biochemistry and Molecular Biology (William C. Rose award 2008). Office: Vollum Inst Oreg Health Scis U 3181 SW Sam Jackson Park Rd Portland OR 97239-3011

SCOTT, JOHN JOSEPH, lawyer; b. Chgo., Dec. 30, 1950; s. John Joseph and Alice S.; m. Maria Crawford, Aug. 17, 1974. BA, Yale U., 1972; JD, U. Chgo., 1975. Bar: Ill. 1975, U.S. Dist. Ct. (no. dist.) Ill. 1976. Assoc. Kirkland & Ellis, Chgo., 1975-82, ptnr., 1982-91; asst. gen. counsel CF Industries Holdings, Inc., Deerfield, Ill., 1991—2006, sr. litig. counsel, 2006—. Mem. ABA, Chgo. Bar Assn., Order of Coif. Roman Catholic. Avocations: reading, swimming, bike riding, playing tennis. Office: CF Industries Holdings Inc 4 Parkway North Ste 400 Deerfield IL 60015-2590

SCOTT, JOHN PAUL, medical educator; b. Kamunting, Malaysia, June 26, 1956; came to U.S., 1991; s. Joseph and Agnes (Beldon) S.; m. Lesley Carol Poole, Dec. 5, 1981; children: Christopher Michael, Elizabeth Mary, David Matthew, Emily Rose. MB ChB, Otago U., Dunedin, New Zealand, 1979, MD, 1990; MS, Cambridge U., England, 1992; MS in Econs., U. London, 1999; LLB in Econs. with honors, U. Wolverhampton, 2000, LLM, U. Glasgow, 2002; MSc, U. Oxford, England, 2007. Resident Otago U., Dunedin, New Zealand, 1979-83; assoc. prof. transplantation Mayo Clinic, Rochester, Minn., 1991-96, prof., 1996—. Vis. fellow Oriel Coll., Oxford, England, 2008—; med. dir. Lung Transplantation, Mayo Clinic, Rochester, Minn., 2008—. Contbr. articles to profl. jours. Fellow dept. pulmonary medicine Otago U., 1984-85, Cambridge U., 1985-88, sr. fellow, 1988-91. Fellow Royal Coll. Physicians (internat. advisor 2000—, assoc. dir. 2004-08), Royal Australian Coll. Physicians, Am. Coll. Physicians, Royal Statis. Soc.; mem. Am. Thoracic Soc. (Minn. rep. 1993-96), Royal Soc. New Zealand, Internat. Soc. Philosophical Enquiry, Mayo Thoracic Soc. (pres. 1996-99). Avocations: philosophy, economics, chess, climbing, travel. Office: Mayo Clinic 200 1st St SW Rochester MN 55905-0002 Business E-Mail: scott.john@mayo.edu.

SCOTT, JOHN TONER, retired lawyer; b. Indpls., July 12, 1935; s. John Elmer and Jane (Toner) Scott; m. Cecilia Ann Drilling, Sept. 9, 1961; children: Jeffrey, John, Greg. BS in Accting., Ind. U., 1958, LLB, 1961. Bar: Ind. 1961, U.S. Dist. Ct. (so. dist.) Ind. 1979. Assoc. Peck, Scott & Shine, Anderson, Ind., 1963—68, Scott & Shine, Anderson, 1968—70; ptnr. Scott & Scott, Anderson, 1970—. Pres. Shadow Trails, Inc., 1965—80; asst. city atty. City of Anderson, 1968—71; editor, pub. Anderson Herald, Ind., 1981—86. Mem. Family Svc. Madison County, Anderson, 1964, pres., 1967; mem. Urban League of Madison County, Anderson, 1973—77, pres., 1976—77; active mem. Maplewood Cemetery Bd., Madison County, 1996—, treas., 1998; dist. chmn. Hillis for Congress Com., Anderson, 1970—80; del. Ind. State Rep. Convention, Indpls., 1970—92; bd. dirs. ARC, Anderson, 1981, 1988—94, 1997—, v.p. bd. dirs., 1981, pres. bd. dirs., 1993; pres. UN Assn., Anderson, Ind., 1964—70. Capt. US Army, 1961—63. Mem.: Anderson C. of C., Ind. Defense Lawyers Assn. (com. chmn.), Ind. Trial Lawyers Assn., Assn. Ins. Attys., Ind. State Bar Assn. (past com. chmn., del. Madison County 1980—97), Madison County Bar Assn. (pres. 1970—71), Ind. U. Alumni Assn. (bd. dirs. Alumni Club Madison County 1993—96, pres. 1995—96, Disting. Alumni award 1998), Internat. Platform Assn., Sertoma (v.p., bd. dirs. Anderson chpt. 1966—68), Lincoln Lodge, Delta Theta Pi (sec.-treas. 1957—58), Blue Key, Alpha Kappa Psi (treas. 1957—58), Sigma Delta Chi, Phi Gamma Delta (bd. chpt. advisors Delta Colony, Ball State U. 1998—2001, pres. bd. chpt. advisors 1998—2001, legate Beta Sigma chpt. 2001). Republican. Presbyn. Home: 928 Winding Way Anderson IN 46011-1629 Office: Scott & Scott 931 Merdian St Ste 505 Anderson IN 46016 Home Phone: 765-642-3130. E-mail: thescottfamily@insightbb.com.

SCOTT, JONATHAN P., think-tank executive; b. Providence, Nov. 4, 1966; 1 adopted child, Christopher. Attended, U. RI. Counselor Whitmarsh Corp., 1992—2005; chmn. RI State GOP Platform Com.; bd. chmn. Ocean State Policy Rsch. Inst. With George H.W. Bush Presdl. Campaign, John Chafee Senatorial Campaign. Bd. mem. Furball Farms, Moses Brown Alumni Assn. Republican. Episcopalian. Office: 18 Mayflower St Providence RI 02906 Office Phone: 401-301-6322.

SCOTT, JOYCE, writer; d. Charles William and Emma Reardon; m. Edward Dale Scott, Sept. 13, 1971; 1 child, Tonia Louise. Student, Inst. Children's Lit., 1984, student, 1993, Long Ridge Writers Group, 1994. Mem.: The Internat. Women's Writing Guild, Soc. Children's Book Writers and Illustrators.

SCOTT, JOYCE ALAINE, academic administrator; b. Long Beach, Calif., May 21, 1943; d. Emmett Emery Scott and Grace (Evans) Wedum. BA, U. Conn., 1964; MA, U. Va., 1966; PhD, Duke U., 1973. From instr. to assoc. prof. U. Wyo., Laramie, 1971-74, asst. dean, 1974-78, asst. v.p. acad. affairs, 1976-81, assoc. v.p. acad. affairs, 1981-84; provost, v.p. SUNY-Potsdam, 1984-86; exec. v.p. Wichita (Kans.) State U., 1986-90, v.p. on spl. assignment, 1990-91; sr. cons. Am. Assn. State Colls. and Univs., 1991-92, v.p. acad. and internat. programs, 1992-97; dep. commr. Mont. U. Sys., Helena, 1998—2003; provost, v.p. acad. and student affairs Tex. A&M U., Commerce, 2003—06, assoc. prof. dept. ednl. leadership, 2004—. Mem. Commn. on Ednl. Credit and Credentials of Am. Coun. on Edn., Washington, 1982-87; cons. faculty Am. Open U., Lincoln, Nebr., 1981-82. Contbr. articles to profl. jours. Trustee Jones Internat. U. Mem. MLA, Am. Assn. Tchrs. French, Phi Beta Kappa, Phi Kappa Phi, Phi Sigma Iota. Republican. Presbyterian. Office: Dept Educational Leadership PO Box 3011 Commerce TX 75429-3011 Office Phone: 903-886-5503. Business E-Mail: Joyce_Scott@tamu-commerce.edu.

SCOTT, KAMELA KOON, psychologist, educator; b. Carson City, Nev., July 28, 1964; d. Ray Harold and Bert Gardner Koon; m. David Keitt Scott, Feb. 13, 1993; children: Nicolas Keitt, Isaac David. BA, Baylor U., Waco, Tex., 1986; PhD, U. No. Tex., Denton, 1992. Lic. Clin. Psychologist Divsn. Med. Quality Assurance, Fla., 1994. Psychology intern U. Tex. Med. Br. and Shriner's Burns Inst., Galveston, Tex., 1991—92; instr. dept. psychiatry Emory U. Sch. Medicine, Atlanta, 1992—93; asst. prof. dept. of Pediat. U. Fla. Coll. Medicine, Jacksonville, Fla., 1993—96, asst. prof., 1996—2002, assoc. prof. dept. surgery, 2002—. Program dir., psychol. svcs. U. Fla., Dept. Pediat., Dist. Hematology/Sickle Cell Program, Jacksonville, 1993—96, U. Fla. Regional Trauma Sys., Jacksonville, 2001—; chmn. Sexual Harassment Com. U. Fla., Jacksonville, 1997—; mem. Jacksonville Pediat. Injury Control Sys., 1996—; bd. mem. Shands Jacksonville Ethics Com., 1996—, Shands Jacksonville Emergency Preparedness Com., 1998—; adv. bd. mem. Shands Jacksonville Clin. Pastoral Edn. Adv. Bd., 1998—2004; supervising psychologist Shands Jacksonville Trauma Psychology Post-Doctoral Fellowship, 1998—; site reviewer Fla. Brain and Spinal Cord Injury Program, Tallahassee, 1998—; lectr. U. Fla. Risk Mgmt. Ednl. Series, Gainesville, 2002—. Author: (book chapter) Surg. Clinics of North Am., (book chapters (2) Behavioral Aspects of Pediatric Burn Injuries, (jour. article) Current Surgery, Jour. of Trauma, Jacksonville Medicine. Adv. bd. mem. Partnerships for Preventing Violence, Jacksonville, 1998—2003, Serving Child Victims of Traumatic Abuse, Jacksonville, 2002—03; active mem. Compassionate Families, Inc., Jacksonville, 1998—2003. Named Outstanding Alumnae of Yr., U. North Tex., 2005; grantee, City of Jacksonville, Fla., 2001—05, State of Fla. Byrne Grant, 2001-2002, The Blue Found. for a Healthy Fla., 2001—05, The Jacksonville Jaguars Found., 1999-2001, U. of Fla. Dean's Fund, 1997-1998; scholar, Pres. U.S., Washington, D.C., 1982. Mem.: APA. Republican. Baptist. Avocations: scuba diving, skiing, deep sea fishing, camping. Office: U Fla Surgery 655 West 8th St Jacksonville FL 32209 Business E-Mail: kamela.scott@jax.ufl.edu.

SCOTT, KAREN ELIZABETH, advocate; b. Buffalo, July 21, 1957; children: James Kenneth-Mark, Alexis Victoria Scott-Davis. BA, Empire State Coll., Buffalo, NY, 2002. Adminstrv. asst. WNY Libr. Resources Coun., Buffalo, 1990—97; rsch. adminstr. U. Buffalo, travel specialist. Civil rights and human rights advocate; bd. dirs. Langston Hughes Inst., Buffalo, 2000. Avocations: interior decorating, fashion design, current affairs.

SCOTT, KAREN N., language educator; d. George M. and Patricia D. W. Scott. Attending, U. Wis., Madison, 2004—. Cert. TEFL Hamline U., 2003. Grad. tchg. asst. U. Wis., Madison, 2005—. Fgn. lang. tchr. Pvt., Madison, Wis., 2004—. FLAS, U. Wis., 2007. Mem.: MLA, ACTFL, AATG.

SCOTT, KENNETH EUGENE, lawyer, educator; b. Western Springs, Ill., Nov. 21, 1928; s. Kenneth L. and Bernice (Albright) S.; m. Viviane H. May, Sept. 22, 1956 (dec. Feb. 1982); children: Clifton, Jeffrey, Linda; m. Priscilla Gay, July 30, 1989; children: Ashley (dec. Apr. 2002), Shaler. BA in Econs., Coll. William and Mary, 1949; MA in Polit. Sci., Princeton U., 1953; LLB, Stanford U., 1956. Bar: N.Y. 1957, Calif. 1957, D.C. 1967. Assoc. Sullivan & Cromwell, NYC, 1956-59, Musick, Peeler & Garrett, LA, 1959-61; chief dep. savs. and loan commr. State of Calif., LA, 1961-63; gen. counsel Fed. Home Loan Bank Bd., Washington, 1963-67; Parsons prof. law and bus. Stanford (Calif.) Law Sch., 1968-95, emeritus, 1995—; sr. rsch. fellow Hoover Instn., 1978-95, emeritus, 1995—; fellow Am. Acad. Berlin, 2001. Mem. Shadow Fin. Regulatory Com., 1986—, Fin. Economists Roundtable, 1991—. Author: (with others) Retail Banking in the Electronic Age, 1977; co-editor: The Economics of Corporation Law and Securities Regulation, 1980. Mem. Calif. Bar Assn., Phi Beta Kappa, Order of Coif, Pi Kappa Alpha, Omicron Delta Kappa. Home: 610 Gerona Rd Stanford CA 94305-8453 Office: Stanford Law Sch Stanford CA 94305-8610 Home Phone: 650-325-0909; Office Phone: 650-723-3070. E-mail: kenscott@stanford.edu.

SCOTT, LEE (HAROLD LEE SCOTT JR.), retail executive; b. Joplin, Mo., Mar. 14, 1949; s. Harold Lee and Avis Viola (Parsons) S.; m. Linda Gale Aldridge, June 7, 1969; children: Eric Sean, Wyatt Parson. BBA, Pitts. State U., Kans., 1971. Br. mgr. Yellow Freight System, Springdale, Ark., 1972-78; mgr. Queen City Warehouse, Springfield, Mo., 1978-79; dir. transp. Wal-Mart Stores, Inc., Bentonville, Ark., 1979-83, v.p. distbn. to sr. v.p. logistics, 1983—93, exec. v.p. logistics, 1993—95; exec. v.p. merchandise & sales Wal-Mart Stores USA, 1995—98, pres., CEO, 1998—99; vice chmn., COO Wal-Mart Stores, Inc., Bentonville, Ark., 1999—2000, pres., CEO, 2000—09, chmn. exec. com., 2009—. Bd. dirs. Pvt. Truck Council, 1985—86, Wal-Mart Stores, Inc., 1999—, Cooper Industries, 2000—04. Named an Outstanding Alumni, Pitts. State U., 1995; named one of The World's 100 Most Influential People, TIME mag., 2005, The 25 Most Powerful People in Bus., Fortune mag., 2007. Republican. Methodist. Avocations: reading, quail hunting. Office: Wal-Mart Stores Inc 702 SW 8th St Bentonville AR 72716-6299*

SCOTT, LEIGHTON REEVES, interior designer, artist, writer; b. Columbus, Ind., Sept. 9, 1942; AB, U. Md., 1968, Knox Coll., 1964. Scientist NASA, Greenbelt, Md., 1968—73; sys. analyst NOAA, Suitland, Md., 1973—76; sr. physicist Johns Hopkins Applied Physics Lab., Laurel, Md., 1976—81; computer software cons. Westinghouse Def. Sys., Linthicum, Md., 1982—84; computer scientist Nat. Security Agy., Ft. George G. Meade, Md., 1984—94; cons., creativity trainer Mt. Airy, Md., 1995—2003. ADA program mgr. Nat. Security Agy., Ft. Meade, 1983—88. Author: (book) The Search for Manhood, 1992, Museum of the Mind, 2009. Achievements include invention of software blueprints; Vented Bennett Ion Mass Spectrometers orbiting Earth and Venus; design of National Security Agency's first electronic systems support system; U.S. government's first walk-in on-site store for disabled employees. Avocations: art, interior and product design, model building. Office: Lee Scott Design 594 Shannon Dr N Greencastle PA 17225 Home: 594 Shannon Dr N Greencastle PA 17225 Home Phone: 717-597-3902; Office Phone: 301-318-3731. Business E-Mail: leescottdesign@gmail.com.

SCOTT, LESLI, psychologist; b. Reedsburg, Wis., Feb. 15, 1981; d. Greg and Cheryl Whitaker; m. Erik Scott, June 27, 2003; 1 child, Taylen. BA in Psychology, U. Wis., La Crosse, 2003; MS in Edn., Sch. Psychology, U. Wis., Stout, Menomonie, 2004, EdS in Sch. Psychology, 2008. Sch. psychologist Borman Mid. Sch., Phoenix, 2005—07, Gilbert HS, Gilbert, Ariz., 2007—. Office Fax: 480-507-1636. Personal E-mail: lesli215@hotmail.com. Business E-Mail: lesli_scott@gilbert.k12.az.us.

SCOTT, LOUIS EDWARD, advertising executive; b. Waterbury, Conn., June 17, 1923; s. Louis Arthur and Ellen (Eckert) S.; m. Phyllis Corrine Denker, Jan. 27, 1942; children: Susan Louise, Eric Richard, Jane Lynn. BS, U. Calif., Berkeley, 1944. Sr. account exec. McCarty Co., LA, 1946-50; from mem. staff to dir. Foote, Cone & Belding, 1950—61; dir. Foote, Cone & Belding/Honig, 1961—98. Bd. dirs. Smart and Final Corp., Casino Internat., True North Comm. Chmn.

publicity com. Los Angeles Community Chest, 1960; patron mem. Los Angeles YMCA; mem. Freedoms Found.; chmn. So. Calif. advisory bd. Advt. Council; mem. exec. advisory bd. Art Center Coll. Design. Served with U.S. Maritime Service, also USNR, World War II. Named Western Advt. Man of Year, 1972 Mem. Am. Assn. Advt. Agys. (dir., past chmn. Western region), Rio Verde Country Club, Seattle Yacht Club, Cruising Club Am. Home: 19119 E Tonto Trail Rio Verde AZ 85263 Address: Crown Isla Marina 4000 Coronado Bay Rd Coronado CA 92118

SCOTT, LOUISE H., music educator; d. William H. and Jean E. Hohmeyer; m. Frank E. Scott, June 16, 1970; children: Jared M., Kevin M. DMA, U. Ariz., Tucson, 1980. Prof. music Sch. Music, Northern Ariz. U., Flagstaff, 1977—. Musician (concert master): Arizona Opera and Flagstaff Symphony. Mem.: MENC, SAA, ASTA. Office: Northern Ariz Univ Sch Music Box 6040 NAU Flagstaff AZ 86011 Office Phone: 928-523-3879. Business E-Mail: louise.scott@max.edu.

SCOTT, MADELEINE, performing arts educator; d. John F. Scott and Denise Lavedan; m. Ronald Polsky; children: Linda Yeung, Jennifer Mancuso. MA, U. Calif. LA, 1974. Cert. movement analyst Laban Bartentieff Inst. Movement Studies, NY, 1987, movement pattern analyst Motus Humanus, Colo., 2007. Lectr., dance UCLA, 1974—79; prof., dance Ohio U., Athens, 1980—. Choreographer dancer Repertory, Solo and Group Dances (Ohio Arts Coun. Individual Artist fellowship, 1986), dancer Manuel ALum Dance Company, Douglas Nielsen Dance Company. Recipient Excellence Tchg. award, Ohio U., 1984. Mem.: Motus Humanus. Office: Dance Ohio Univ Putnam Hall Athens OH 45701 Office Fax: 740 593-0749. Business E-Mail: scottm@ohio.edu.

SCOTT, MAKEDA, legislative staff member; Attended, St. Augustine's Coll., 1990—94, Clark Atlanta U., 1994—96. Pub. affairs ast. Sta. WSB-TV, 1995—97; comm. coord. The Enterprise Found., 1999—2004; North Am. campaign officer Brit. Fgn. & Commonwealth Office, Washington, 2004—06; media and PR chief Balt. Housing Authority, 2006—07; sr. campaign strategist AFSCME, 2006—07; comm. dir. to Rep. John Sarbanes US House of Reps., Washington, 2007—. Democrat. Office: 426 Cannon House Office Bldg Washington DC 20515 Office Phone: 202-225-4016. Office Fax: 202-225-9219.*

SCOTT, MARGARET SIMON, retired mortgage broker; b. Boston, May 12, 1934; d. Frank A. and Margaret Alice (Gotham) Simon; m. Walter Neil Scott, Nov. 21, 1959 (div. June 1997); 1 child, Walter David Kimbley; m. Stephen E. Michelman, Feb. 8, 2003. BA in Physics, Wellesley Coll., Mass., 1956; MA in Polit. Sci., Boston U., 1965; MS in Human Resources Mgmt., U. Utah, Salt Lake City, 1974. Rsch. asst. Bell Tel. Labs., Whippany, NJ, 1956—58; rsch. asst. med. sch. U. Louisville, 1959-60, Harvard U., Boston, 1960-64; instr. polit. sci. Trinity U., San Antonio, 1966-67; cons. info. systems US Dept. Labor, Washington, 1968; dir. manpower planning NYC Human Resources Adminstrn., 1968—71; asst. v.p. First Nat. City Bank, NYC, 1972—77; v.p. Citibank, N.A., NYC, 1978-86, AMEV Asset Mgmt., Inc., NYC, 1986-88; pres. Mortgage Adv. Svcs., Inc., NYC, 1988-99. Vol. Jr. League, Louisville, 1957; bd. mgr. NY Jr. League, NYC, 1970—74; sec. 1095 Park Ave Corp., NYC, 1977—86; bd. mgrs. McBurney YMCA, NYC, 1995—2000, chmn., 1998—2000; trustee United Adult Ministries, 1998—, mem. exec. com., 1999—, chair, fin. com., 1999—; mem. Housing Health and Human Svcs. Com. of NY City Cmty. Bd. 4, 2006—08; trustee First Presbyn. Ch. in City NY, 1995—98, pres., 1997—98; trustee NY City Presbytery, 1996—98, treas., 1998—2002, chair coun. adminstrn. and support svcs., 2003—05, mem. com. on ministry, 2006—07; ruling elder First Presbyn. Ch., 2000—03; mem. steering com. Presbyn. Welcome, 1999—2004, co-moderator, 2001—03; trustee Presbyn. Synod of Northeast, 2002—05; bd. dirs. YWCA, NYC, 1980—85. Named Outstanding Vol. of Yr., Jr. League of City of NY, Inc., 2005. Mem.: Wellesley Club. Democrat. Home: 884 W End Ave Apt 41 New York NY 10025-3515 E-mail: margaretsnyc@mac.com.

SCOTT, MARIANNE FLORENCE, retired librarian, educator; b. Toronto, Dec. 4, 1928; d. Merle Redvers and Florence Ethel Scott. BA, McGill U., Montreal, Que., Can., 1949, BLS, 1952; LLD (hon.), York U., 1985, Dalhousie U., 1989; DLitt (hon.), Laurentian U., 1990. Asst. librarian Bank of Montreal, 1952-55; law librarian McGill U., 1955-73, law area librarian, 1973-75, dir. libraries, 1975-84, lectr. legal bibliography faculty of law, 1964-75; nat. librarian Nat. Library of Can., Ottawa, Ont., 1984-99, ret., 1999. Co-founder, editor: Index to Can. Legal Periodical Lit, 1963—; contbr. articles to profl. jours. Decorated officer Order of Can.; recipient Queen Elizabeth II Silver Jubilee medal, 1977, IFLA medal, 1996, Queen Elizabeth II Golden Jubilee medal, 2002. Mem. Internat. Assn. Law Libraries (dir. 1974-77), Am. Assn. Law Libraries, Can. Assn. Law Libraries (pres. 1963-69, exec. bd. 1973-75, honored mem. 1980—), Can. Library Assn. (coun. and dir. 1980-82, 1st v.p. 1980-81, pres. 1981-82), Corp. Profl. Librarians of Que. (v.p. 1975-76), Can. Assn. Rsch. Librs. (pres. 1978-79, past pres. 1979-80, exec. com. 1980-81, sec.-treas. 1983-84), Can. Writers Found. (bd. dirs. 1999—, treas. 2003-08, pres. 2008-), Ctr. for Rsch. Librs. (dir. 1980-83), Internat. Fedn. Libr. Assns. (honor com. for 1982 conf. 1979-82, chair com. on copyright and other legal matters 1998-2003, hon. fellow 2003), Conf. of Dirs. of Nat. Libraries (chmn. 1988-92), Friends of Lib. and Archives Can., 2008 Home: 119 Dorothea Dr Ottawa ON Canada K1V 7C6 E-mail: mfscott@rogers.com.

SCOTT, MARK C., biologist, educator; b. Augusta, Ga., Sept. 24, 1964; s. John L. and Helen R. Scott; m. Tina Waters, Sept. 3, 1988. BS, Wofford Coll., Spartanburg, SC, 1987; MS, Va. Tech, Blacksburg, 1994; PhD, U. Ga., Athens, 2001. Adj. asst. prof. Clemson U., SC, 2003—; rsch. biologist SC Dept. Natural Resources, Clemson, 2003—. Grant, US Fish & Wildlife Svc., US EPA, US Forest Svc., Nat. Pk. Svc., US Geol. Survey. Mem.: Am. Fisheries Soc., Soc. Conservation Biology. Avocations: travel, cooking, scuba diving, guitar. Office: SC Dept Natural Resourses 311 Natural Resources Dr Clemson SC 29631 Business E-Mail: scottm@dnr.sc.gov.

SCOTT, MARY SUE, education educator; b. Elk City, Okla., Dec. 11, 1948; d. Alford Veal and Reta Green Isbell; m. John M. Scott, Jan. 28, 1995; children: Nathan Shaw, Aaron Shaw, Julianna Shaw, David Shaw. BS in Elem. Edn., North Tex. State U., Denton, 1971; MEd, U. Tex., Tyler, 1983. Classroom tchr. Tyler ISD, 1977—80, 1986—90, East Tex. Christian Acad., Tyler, 1983—86; prof., reading Sch. of Coll. Prep. Studies Tyler Jr. Coll., 1990—, dept. chair, english & reading, 2008—. Recipient Mattie Alice Scroggin Baker Excellence Tchg. award, Tyler Jr. Coll., 2007. Mem.: Nat. Assn. Devel. Edn., Tex. Assn. Devel. Edn., Nat. Inst. Staff & Orgnl. Devel. (Excellence award 2005), Tex. CC Tchrs. Assn. Office: Tyler Jr Coll 1400 E 5th St Tyler TX 75701

SCOTT, MATTHEW PETER, biology educator; b. Boston, Jan. 30, 1953; s. Peter Robert and Duscha (Schmid) S.; m. Margaret Tatnall Fuller, May 13, 1990; children: Lincoln Fuller, Julia Fuller. BS, MIT, 1975, PhD, 1980. Postdoctoral tng. Ind. U., Bloomington, 1980-83; from asst. prof. to assoc. prof. U. Colo., Boulder, 1983-90; prof. Stanford (Calif.) U., 1990—, chmn. dept. devel. biology, 1997-98, assoc. chmn. dept. devel. biology, 1999—; assoc. investigator Howard Hughes Med. Inst., 1989-90, investigator, 1993—. Vis. prof. genetics Harvard Med. Sch., 1994-95. Recipient Passano Young Investigator award Passano Found., 1990. Mem. NAS, Inst. Medicine, Am. Acad. Arts and Scis. Achievements include research in developmental genetics, in particular, homeotic genes, signaling systems, and cancer biology. Office: Stanford U Sch Med Dept Devel Biology 279 Campus Dr Beckman B300 Stanford CA 94305-5329*

SCOTT, MCGREGOR W., lawyer, former prosecutor; b. 1962; m. Jennifer Urbanski Scott; 3 children. BA in History, Santa Clara U.; JD, U. Calif. Dep. dist. atty. Contra Costa County, 1989—97; dist. atty. Shasta County, 1997—2003; US atty. (ea. dist.) Calif. US Dept. Justice, Sacramento, 2003—09; ptnr., mem. Litig. Group Orrick, Herrington & Sutcliffe LLP, Sacramento, 2009—. Chair Rural Counties Commn., Calif. Dist. Atty. Assn.; bd. dirs. Calif. Dist. Atty. Assn.; mem. US Atty. Gen. Adv. Com. Lt. col. USNG. Avocations: reading, basketball, golf, exercise, college football, hunting. Office: Orrick, Herrington & Sutcliffe LLP 400 Capitol Mall, Ste 3000 Sacramento CA 95814-4497 Office Phone: 916-329-7982. Office Fax: 916-329-4900. E-mail: mscott@orrick.com.*

SCOTT, MELLOUISE JACQUELINE, retired media specialist; b. Sanford, Fla., Mar. 1, 1943; d. Herbert and Mattye (Williams) Cherry; m. Robert Edward Scott, Jr., July 1, 1972; 1 child, Nolan Edward. BA, Talladega Coll., 1965; MLS, Rutgers U., 1974, EdM, 1976, EdS, 1982. Media specialist Seminole County Bd. Edn., Sanford, 1965-72, Edison (N.J.), 1972-98; ret. Edison (N.J.) Bd. Edn., 1999. Mem. ALA, N.J. Ret. Educators Assn., NEA. Baptist. Home: PO Box 1771 Sanford FL 32772-1771

SCOTT, MICHAEL DENNIS, lawyer; b. Mpls., Nov. 6, 1945; s. Frank Walton and Donna Julia (Howard) S.; children: Michael Dennis, Cindal Marie, Derek Walton. BS, MIT, 1967; JD, UCLA, 1974. Bar: Calif. 1974, U.S. Dist. Ct. (no., so. and ctrl. dists.) Calif. 1974, U.S. Patent Office 1974, U.S. Ct. Appeals (9th cir.) 1974, U.S. Supreme Ct. 1978, U.S. Ct. Appeals (fed. cir.) 1989. Systems programmer NASA Electronics Rsch. Lab., Cambridge, Mass., 1967-69, Computer Scis. Corp., El Segundo, Calif., 1969-71, Univac, Valencia, Calif., 1971; from assoc. to ptnr. Smaltz & Neelley, LA, 1974-81; exec. dir. Ctr. for Computer/Law, LA, 1977-94; pvt. practice LA, 1981-86, 88-89; pres. Law and Tech. Press, 1981-94; ptnr. Scott & Roxborough, LA, 1986-88, Graham & James, 1989-93; v.p., gen. counsel Sanctuary Woods Multimedia, Inc., San Mateo, Calif., 1993-94; of counsel Steinhart & Falconer, San Francisco, 1995-97; ptnr. Hosie Wes Sacks & Brelsford, Menlo Park, Calif., 1997-98, Perkins Coie LLP, 1998—2003; prof. law Southwestern U., LA, 2003—. Adj. assoc. prof. law, Southwestern U., LA, 1975-80, 01-03, Loyola U., L.A., 1997-99, 02-04, Pepperdine U., LA, 2001-03; chmn. World Computer Law Congress, LA, 1991, 93; co-chmn. Internat. IT Law Conf., 2005, 2007. Author: (with David S. Yen) Computer Law Bibliography, 1979, Computer Law, 1984, Scott on Computer Law, 1991, Multimedia: Law and Practice, 1993, Scott on Multimedia Law, 1996, (with Warren S. Reid) Year 2000 Computer Crisis: Law Business Technology, 1998, Internet and Technology Law Desk Reference, 1999, Intellectual Property and Licensing Law Desk Reference, 2001, Telecommunications Law Desk Reference, 2003, Scott on Outsourcing Law and Practice, 2006, Scott on Information Technology Law, 2007; editor-in-chief: Computer/Law Jour., 1978-94, Software Protection, 1982-92, Software Law Jour., 1985-94, Internat. Computer Law Adviser, 1986-92, Cyberspace Lawyer, 1996—, E-Commerce Law Report, 1998—. Mem. Computer Law Assn. (bd. dirs. 1994-99), Calif. State Bar Assn.

SCOTT, MIMI KOBLENZ, psychotherapist, actress, journalist, playwright; b. Albany, NY, Dec. 15, 1940; d. Edmund Akiba and Tillie (Paul) Koblenz; m. Barry Stuart Scott, Aug. 13, 1961 (dec. Nov. 1991); children: Karen Scott Zantay, Jeffrey B. BA in Speech and English Edn., Russell Sage Coll., 1962; MA in Speech Edn., SUNY, Albany, 1968; M in Social Welfare, SUNY, 1985; PhD in Psychology, Pacific Western U., Encino, Calif., 1985. Cert. tchr., social worker. Tchr. English, speech Albany Pub. Schs., 1961-63; hostess, producer talkshow Sta. WAST-TV 13, Albany, 1973-75; freelance actress NYC, 1975-77; producer, actress Four Seasons Dinner Theater, Albany, 1978-82; instr. of theatre Albany Jr. Coll., 1981-83; pvt. practice psychotherapy Albany, NY, 1985-92, NYC, 1992—2007; actor Off Broadway show Hollywood, 2008—; exec. prodr. City of Albany Park Playhouse, 1989-92; actor self-employed NYC, 1992—; actor Off Broadway show Grandma Sylvia's Funeral, 1996-98, Split Ends, 2004, Grease, Albany, 2007. Guest psychotherapist Sally Jessy Raphael Show, 1992, 93, Jane Whitney Show, 1994, A Current Affair, 1995, News Talk TV, 1995; founder, producing artistic dir. Manhattan Playwrights Inc., 2001—07; group therapist Women's Health and Resource Ctr. South Fla., Hollywood, 2008—. Scriptwriter, dir., actor (TV films) To Liberty and Justice for All, 1985, featured writer Backstage, 1995—96, featured in ind. film Mr. Vincent, Sundance, 1997, book and lyricist (musical) Dressing Room, Soho Playhouse, N.Y.C., 2000; author: Mind Tricks, 2003; dir.: Mind Tricks, 2003; featured on NBC Dateline, 2005, VH1's So Jewtastic, 2006; author, dir., prodr.: SPLIT! Tales from Children of Divorce in Upstate New York, 2008. Event organizer AmFar, 1985; co-chmn. March of Dimes Telethon, 1985-86; fundraiser Leukemia Found., 1987, AIDS Benefit, North Miami Beach, Fla., 1988; elected to SUNY Albany U. Found., 1990. Recipient FDR Nat. Achievement award March of Dimes, 1985, Recognition Cert. Capital Dist. Psychiat. Ctr., 1983-85; named Woman of Yr. YWCA, 1986, Commr. Albany Tricentennial Celebration, 1986; named Mimi Scott Day in her honor Mayor of Albany, 1989. Mem.: NASW, AFTRA, AEA, SAG, Hollywood Fla. C. of C., Drama League of N.Y., N.Y. League Profl. Theatre Women. Jewish. Avocations: golf, tennis, writing. Home and Office: 1830 Radius Dr #714 Hollywood FL 33020 Home Phone: 954-926-0133; Office Phone: 954-926-0133. Personal E-mail: mscott13@aol.com.

SCOTT, NORMAN ROSS, electrical engineering educator; b. NYC, May 15, 1918; s. George Norman and Lillias B.H. (Ogg) S.; m. Marjorie M. Fear, Apr. 6, 1950; children: Mari, George, Ian, Charles. BS, MS, MIT, 1941; PhD, U. Ill., 1950. Asst. prof. elec. engring. U. Ill., Urbana, 1946-50; asst. prof. to prof. elec. engring. U. Mich., Ann Arbor, 1951-87, assoc dean Coll. Engring., 1965-68, dean Dearborn Campus, 1968-71, prof. emeritus of elec. engring. and computer sci., 1987—. Cons. Nat. Cash Register Co., Dayton, 1956-65; mem. math. and computer sci. rsch. adv. com. AEC, Washington, 1961-63. Editor-in-chief IEEE Trans. on Computers, N.Y.C., 1961-65; author: Analog and Digital Computer Technology, 1959, Electronic Computer Technology, 1970, Computer Number Systems and Arithmetic, 1985. Maj. U.S. Army, 1941-46. Fellow IEEE. Home: 2260 Gale Rd Ann Arbor MI 48105-9512 Office: U Mich EECS Dept Ann Arbor MI 48109

SCOTT, OLOF HENDERSON, JR., priest; b. Phila., May 13, 1942; s. Olof Henderson and Julia Irene (Rutroff) S.; m. Eva Jakowenko, Sept. 13, 1969; children: Lisa Ann, Christopher Olof, Timothy Nicholas. BA in Physics, Franklin and Marshall Coll., 1964; MS in Nuclear Engring., Pa. State U., 1966; postgrad., St. Vladimir's Orthodox Theol. Sem., 1975-76. Ordained deacon Antiochian Orthodox Christian Ch., 1975, priest, 1976, archpriest, 1988. Ops. engr. S3G ops. Knolls Atomic Power Lab., GE Co., Schenectady, N.Y., 1966-68, project engr. S3G ops., 1968-69; lead nuclear engr. Seabrook Nuclear project Pub. Svc. Co. of N.H., Manchester, 1969-70; project engr. VEPCO projects Nuclear Energy Sys. divsn. Westinghouse Elec. Co., Monroeville, Pa., 1970-72, project mgr. VEPCO projects Nuclear Energy Sys. divsn., 1972-74, regional sales mgr. mktg., 1974-75; dean St. George Orthodox Cathedral, Charleston, W.Va., 1976—; dean of clergy Appalachian-Ohio Valley Deanery, 1976—2005, Virginias Deanery, 2005—. Spiritual advisor NAC-SOYO of Archdiocese, 1977-82, vice-chmn. inter-orthodox and inter-faith rels., 1987-2005, chmn., 2005—; exec. bd. W.Va. Coun. Chs., 1977—; bd. govs. Nat. Coun. Chs., 1977-2005, nominating com., 1979-81, exec. com., 1985-96, membership com., 1988-91, unity and rels., 1989-92, ch. world svc., 1997-2005; active West Va. Ecumenical Coalition on Infant Mortality, 1992-96; rep. Christian Chs. Together in the US, 2006—, Steering Comm., 2008-. Contbr. articles to profl. jours. Bd. dirs. Religious Coalition for Cmty. Renewal in Charleston, 1987-95, Charleston Ch. Recreation Assn., 1998—, Kanawha Home for Children, 1986-89, pres., 1989; long-range planning com. W.Va. State Rep. Exec. Com., 1985-87; adv. bd. Nat. Ctr. for Human Rels., 1997-98, Charleston Area Religious Leaders Assn., 2004—; del. 8th Assembly of WCC, Harare, Zimbabwe, 1998. Named Hon. West Virginian, 2001; Olof H. Scott Day named in his honor, City of Charleston, W.Va., 2001. Mem. Acad. Parish Clergy (pres. W.Va. chpt. 1983-85), Am. Nuclear Soc., St. Vladimir's Theol. Found., Charleston Ministerial Assn., Order of St. John of Jerusalem-Knights Hospitellers (chaplain 1985—), Order of St. Ignatius of Antioch, Soc. for Preservation and Encouragement Barbershop Quartet Singing in Am. Inc. (v.p. 1984-85), Pa. State Club W.Va. (pres. 1984-88), Alden Kindred of Am., Order DeMolay, Sigma Pi Sigma, Delta Sigma Phi. Avocations: camping, barbershop quartet, motorcycling. Office: St George Orthodox Cathedral PO Box 2044 Charleston WV 25327-2044 Home: 823 Sherwood Rd Charleston WV 25314-1833 Personal E-mail: frolof@suddenlink.net. *My thoughts on life are but mere recitations of the Holy Scripture and my feeble attempts at making Those words and Thoughts my own.*

SCOTT, P. MARK, musician, educator; b. Amarillo, Tex., June 16, 1953; s. Peter Mark and Margie Mayfield (Ingham) Scott. MusB in Organ Performance, Tex. Chrstian U., Ft. Worth, 1975, MusB in Sacred Music, 1975; attended, Royal Sch. Ch. Music, Croydon, Eng., 1980, attended, 1985, attended, 1990, Abbey of St. Pierre, Solesmes, France, 2000, Monastery of Christ in Desert, N.Mex., 2000, Ampleforth Abbey, York, Eng., 2000. Min. music, organist St. Stephen Presbyn. Ch., Ft. Worth, 1975—; instr. sacred music U. N. Tex., Denton, 2004—. Arranger: Awake Thou Wintry Earth, 1992, Lord, Let Your Angels Shelter Me, 1992. Dir. spl. series events St. Stephen Presbyn. Ch., Ft. Worth, 1975—. Nordan Fine Arts fellow, Tex. Christian U., 1971—75. Mem.: Tex. Choral Dirs. Assn., Am. Guild Organists (former dean Ft. Worth chpt.), Am. Choral Dirs. Assn. Avocation: history of World War II. Office: Saint Stephen Presbyn Ch 2700 McPherson Ave Fort Worth TX 76109-1450 Office Phone: 817-927-8411. Business E-Mail: muspms@ststephen-pcusa.com.

SCOTT, PAMELA J., educational consultant; b. Chehalis, Wash., Dec. 24, 1948; d. Jean Jones; m. Paul Alan Scott, June 6, 1970; children: Craig A., Ryan T., Eric J., Meghan. MEd, Heritage U., Toppenish, Wash., 1991. Nat. Bd. Cert. Tchr. 2004. Educator Kennewick Sch. Dist., Wash., 1987—2005, consulting peer educator, 2005—. Adj. prof. Heritage U., Toppenish, 2005—. Recipient Curriculum Quill award, Kennewick Sch. Dist., 2004. Mem.: ASCD, Nat. Coun. Tchrs. Math. Office: Kennewick Sch Dist 524 S Auburn St Kennewick WA 99336 Personal E-mail: pscott2b@charter.net. E-mail: pam.scott@ksd.org.

SCOTT, RALPH MASON, retired radiologist, educator; b. Leemont, Va., Nov. 23, 1921; s. Benjamin Thomas and Marion Hazel (Mason) S.; m. Alice Latine Francisco, Dec. 21, 1946; children: Susan Taylor, Ralph Mason, John Thomas. BA, U. Va., 1947; MD, Med. Coll. Va., 1950. Diplomate Am. Bd. Radiology (trustee 1965-76, treas. 1969-70, v.p. 1970-72, pres. 1972-74). Intern Robert Packer Hosp., Sayre, Pa., 1953-54, resident, 1954-57, dir. radiation therapy and nuclear medicine sect., 1957-59; fellow Christie Hosp. and Holt Radium Inst., Manchester, England, 1956-57; asst. prof. radiology U. Chgo. Med. Sch., 1959-60; assoc. prof. radiology, dir. radiation therapy and radioisotopes U. Louisville Med. Sch., 1960-64, prof., dir. radiation therapy, 1964-77; prof. and chmn. dept. rad. oncology U Louisville, 1974-77; prof. radiation therapy U. Louisville Med. Sch., 1981-82; prof. emeritus U. Louisville, 1995; dir. J. Graham Brown Regional Cancer Ctr., Health Scis. Ctr. U. Louisville Med. Sch., 1981-82; dir. dept. radiation medicine Christ Hosp., Cin., 1982-93; ret. Clin. prof. radiology U. Cin. Coll. Medicine, 1982-93; prof., chmn. dept. therapeutic radiology U. Md. Sch. Med., 1977-80; dir. radiation therapy program div. cancer rsch. resources and ctrs., Nat. Cancer Inst. (on leave from U. Louisville), 1976-77. Pres. Ky. divsn. Am. Cancer Soc., 1972-73; bd. dirs. Living Arrangements for the Developmentally Disabled, 1993-95, No. Ky. Assn. for the Retarded, 1993-95, Day Spring Inc., 1993-95, United Health Care, 1994-95, Seven Counties Svcs., Inc., 1997-2003, J. Graham Brown Regional Cancer Ctr. Corp., 1997—. Lt. (j.g.) USNR, 1943-46, PTO. Mem. Am. Roentgen-Ray Soc. (exec. coun. 1968—, chmn. exec. coun. 1972-73), AMA, Am. Coll. Radiology (vice chmn. commn. on cancer 1968-69), Am. Radium Soc., Am. Soc. Therapeutic Radiologists, Assn. U. Radiologists, Radiol. Soc. N.Am., Pi Kappa Alpha, Phi Chi. Home: Treyton Oak Towers 211 W Oak St Apt 922 Louisville KY 40203 Home Phone: 502-568-9485. Personal E-mail: ramsco1@earthlink.net.

SCOTT, RAYMOND E., manufacturing executive; Pres. GM divsn. Lear Corp., 2000—04, 2005, pres. European Customer Focused Divsn., 2004—05, sr. v.p., pres. North Am. Customer Group, 2005—06, sr. v.p., pres. North Am. Seating Systems, 2006—08, sr. v.p., pres. global elec. & electronic systems, 2008—. Office: Lear Corp 21557 Telegraph Rd PO Box 5008 Southfield MI 48086 Office Phone: 248-447-1500. Office Fax: 248-447-1722.

SCOTT, REBECCA J., law and history educator; AB, Radcliffe Coll.; MPhil in Econ. History, London Sch. Econs.; PhD, Princeton U. Charles Gibson disting. univ. prof. history and law U. Mich. Law Sch., Ann Arbor. Author: Degrees of Freedom: Louisiana and Cuba after Slavery, 2005; contbr. articles to profl. jours. Recipient Frederick Douglass prize, 2006; grantee Guggenheim fellowship, 2004. Mem.: Am. Acad. Arts and Scis. Office: Mich U Law Sch 969 Legal Rsch 625 S State St Ann Arbor MI 48109-1215 Office Phone: 734-615-2082. Office Fax: 734-764-8309. E-mail: rjscott@umich.edu.

SCOTT, RENAY MARIE, academic administrator, educator; d. Douglas and Joan Scott. BA, Calvin Coll., Grand Rapids, Mich., 1984; MA, Mich. State U., Lansing, 1988; PhD, Wayne State U., Detroit, 1995. Cert. in secondary tchg. Mich., 1988. Tchr. secondary social studies Freedom Bapt. Acad., Hudsonville, Mich., 1984—89; instr. Grand Rapids Sch. Bible, Grand Rapids, 1990—94; asst. prof. Grace Bible

Coll., Wyoming, Mich., 1994—96; assoc. prof. Cornerstone U., Grand Rapids, 1996—98; chairperson Ctrl. Mich. U., Mt. Pleasant, 2003—06, prof., 1998—2006; dean Owens CC, Toledo, 2006—. Adj. faculty Lourdes Coll., 2006—. Editor: Mich. Social Studies Jour., 2001—08. Recipient Provost award, Cornerstone U., 1998, Outstanding Adminstr. award, Owens CC, 2008. Mem.: Orgn. Am. Historians, Nat. Coun. Social Studies (bd. dirs. 2006—07, leadership taleds 2008—), Mich. Coun. Social Studies (pres. 2001—06, bd. dirs. 2007). Avocations: bicycling, running, travel, reading, photography, birdwatching. Office Phone: 567-661-7179.

SCOTT, RICHARD LYNN (RICK SCOTT), investment company executive, former health and medical products company executive; b. Kans. City, Mo., 1952; married; 2 children. BSBA, U. Mo.; JD, So. Meth. U. Bar: Tex. Chmn., CEO, Columbia/HCA Healthcare Corp., Nashville, 1987-97; pres., CEO Richard L. Scott Investments, LLC, Naples, Fla., 1997—; co-founder, chmn. Solantic Corp., Jacksonville, Fla., 2001—; founder Conservatives For Patients' Rights (CPR), 2009—. Bd. dirs. Associated Industries of Fla., CyberGuard, 2001—03, Solantic Corp., 2001—, Secure Computing Corp., 2006—, Envestnet Asset Mgmt. Inc., Continental Structural Plastics, Inc. Mem. nat. bd. The United Way, 1997—2003. Recipient Second Century award for Excellence in Health Care, Columbia U. Sch. Nursing, 1995, Entrepreneurship award, George Washington U., 2007; named CEO of the Yr., Financial World mag., 1995; named one of The Top 25 Performers, US News & World Report, 1995, America's 25 Most Influential People, TIME mag., 1996. Mem.: Bus. Coun., Bus. Roundtable, Healthcare Leadership Coun. Office: Richard L Scott Investments LLC 1400 Gulfshore Blvd N Ste 148 Naples FL 34102 also: 28 W 44th St Ste 1111 New York NY 10036 Office Phone: 239-263-9030, 212-398-2020. Office Fax: 239-263-9031, 212-398-2033.

SCOTT, RICHARD MALACHI, psychologist; b. Bklyn., Dec. 15, 1968; s. David Malachi and Olive Scott. AA in Gen. Studies, Mira Costa Coll., 1990, AS in Psychology, 1990, AA in Visual Arts, 1990; BA in Psychology, U. Calif., San Diego, 1991; MA in Clin. Psychology, We. Am. U., 1993; PhD in Clin. Psychology, Saybrook Inst., 2000; postgrad., Coll. Medicine & Health Scis., St. Lucia; D Clin. Hypnosis, Nat. Bd. Ethical Stds., 2008. Lic. clin. psychologist. Social worker, case worker Salvation Army, Family Svcs. Divsn., San Diego, 1993—2000; social worker Dept. Pub. Social Svcs., Riverside, Calif., 1996—98; psychol. asst. various orgns., Calif., 1997—2009; clin. psychologist Calfi. Dept. Corrections, Chino, Calif., 2000—08; pvt. practice San Diego, 2004—. Project and clin. dir. So. Calif. Alcohol and Drug Program, Inc., Downey, Calif., 2004; clin. psychologist Geriatric Cons., Inc., San Diego, 2003—08, Dept. of Corrections, San Diego. Mem.: Nat. Acad. Sports Medicine, San Diego Psychol. Assn., APA. Avocations: dance, drawing, painting, sculpting, singing. Home: 11672 Ramsdell Ct San Diego CA 92131-3607 Personal E-mail: research2005@hotmail.com.

SCOTT, RIDLEY, film director; b. South Shields, Tyne and Wear, Eng., Nov. 30, 1937; m. Felicity Heywood, 1964 (div.); 2 children; m. Sandy Watson, 1979 (div. 1989); 1 child. BA, Royal Coll. Art; grad., London Internat. Film Sch. Dir.: (films) The Duellists, 1977, Alien, 1979, Legend, 1985, Black Rain, 1989; prodr.: The Browning Version, 1994, Clay Pigeons, 1998, Where the Money Is, 2000, Six Bullets from Now, 2002, All the Invisible Children, 2005, In Her Shoes, 2005, A Good Year, 2006, The Assassination of Jesse James by the Coward Robert Ford, 2007; exec. prodr.: Monkey Trouble, 1994, The Hire: Hostage, 2002, The Hire: Beat the Devil, 2002, The Hire: Ticker, 2002, Tristan & Isolde, 2006; dir., prodr. (films) Thelma & Louise, 1991, 1492: Conquest of Paradise, 1992, G.I. Jane, 1997, Black Hawk Down, 2001, Matchstick Men, 2003, Kingdom of Heaven, 2005, American Gangster, 2007, Body of Lies, 2008, writer, dir., prodr. Boy on a Bicycle, 1965; dir.(and co-prodr.): Blade Runner, 1982, (and exec. prodr.): Someone to Watch Over Me, 1987, White Squall, 1996, Gladiator, 2000; dir., prodr., exec. music prodr. Hannibal, 2001; dir.: (TV series) Z Cars, 1962, Adam Adamant Lives, 1966, The Informer, 1966; exec. prodr.: The Hunger, 1997, AFP: American Fighter Pilot, 2002, Numb3rs, 2005—; (TV films) RKO 287, 1999, The Last Debate, 2000, The Gathering Storm, 2002 (Emmy award, 2002). Winner Design scholarship, N.Y.; named one of 50 Most Powerful People in Hollywood Premiere mag., 2004, 2005. Address: William Morris Agency One William Morris Pl Beverly Hills CA 90212

SCOTT, ROBERT, state official, school system administrator; children: Katie, Jonathon. JD, U. Tex. Sr. policy advisor to Gov. Perry, State of Tex., 2003; chief exec. Tex. Edn. Agency, 2003—04, chief dep. commr., 2004—07, commr. edn., 2007—. Mem.: Tex. Bar Assn. Office: Tex Edn Commn William B Travis Bldg 1701 N Congress Ave Austin TX 78701 Office Phone: 512-463-9734. Office Fax: 512-463-9838. E-mail: commissioner@tea.state.tx.us.*

SCOTT, ROBERT ALLYN, academic administrator; b. Englewood, NJ, Apr. 16, 1939; s. William D. and Ann F. (Waterman) S.; children: Ryan Keith, Kira Elizabeth. BA, Bucknell U., 1961; PhD, Cornell U., 1975; LLD, Ramapo Coll., 2000. Mgmt. trainee Procter & Gamble Co., Phila., 1961-63; asst. dir. admissions Bucknell U., Lewisburg, Pa., 1965-67; asst. dean Coll. Arts and Scis. Cornell U., Ithaca, 1967-69, assoc. dean, 1969-79, anthropology faculty, 1978-79; dir. acad. affairs Ind. Commn. for Higher Edn., Indpls., 1979-84, asst. commr., 1984-85; pres. Ramapo (N.J.) Coll., 1985-2000, Adelphi U., 2000—. Cons. Sta. WSKG Pub. TV and Radio, 1977-79, also to various colls. and univs., pubs., 1966—; mem. curriculum adv. com. Ind. Bd. Edn., 1984-87, Lilly Endowment Think Tank, 1984-86; mem. nat. adv. panel Ind. 21st Century Schooling Project, 1990-92; U.S. rep. to creation of U. Mobility Asian-Pacific, 1993—; U.S. rep. to meetings of Coun. European Rectors, 1991—; sr. advisor to U.S. State Dept. on Higher Edn. in Unesco European Region, 1997—; U.S. del. to UNESCO N.Am. and World Confs. on Higher Edn., 1998; sr. cons., chair N.J. Higher Edn. Restructuring Team, 1994. Author books and monographs; editl. bd. Cornell Rev., 1976-79; book rev. editor Coll. and Univ., 1974-78; cons. editor Change mag., 1979-95, Jour. Higher Edn., 1985-98; exec. editor Saturday Evening Post book div. Curtis Pub. Co., 1982-85; contbr. articles to sociols., ednl. and popular publs. Trustee Bucknell U., 1976-78, First Unitarian Ch., Ithaca, 1970-73, 78-79, chmn., 1971-73, Unitarian Universalist Ch. of Indpls., 1980-85. With USNR, 1963-65. Spencer Found. rsch. grantee, 1977; recipient Sagamore of the Wabash award, 1986, Leader of Yr. award Prudential Found., 1987, Disting. Svc. award West Bergen Mental Health Ctr., 1991, Presdl. medal NYU, 1994, Sci. and Edn. award Boy Scouts Am., 1993, Raoul Wallenberg Humanitarian Leadership award, 2000, Disting. Svc. award ACIT, 2002, Disting. Svc. award Harbor Child Care, 2003, Excellence in Higher Edn. award Huntington Chamber, 2003, Telly award for Excellence in Cable TV Programming, 2003, 06, 08, Cmty. Svc. award Garden City Chamber, 2004, Annual Svc. award Hispanic Counseling Ctr., 2004, Martin Luther King, Jr. Cmty. Svc. award, 2005, Outstanding Paper Excellence award Emerald Group Publishing, Ltd., 2003, 04, Suffolk Child Care Coun. honoree, 2006, David Excellence award Networking Mag., 2007, Chief Exec. award, CASE, 2008, Cmty. Svc. award Mineola-Garden City Rotary Club, 2009. Fellow Am. Anthrop. Assn.; mem. Am. Sociol. Assn., Am. Assn. Higher Edn., Coun. on Liberal Arts and Scis. (chair 1990-93), Am. Coun. on Edn. Commn. On Internat. Edn. (chair 1991-93), L.I. Assn., Global Kids, Inc., Coun. Fgn. Rels., Regional Plan Assn., Nat. Fgn. Lang. Ctr., Brookings Instn. Study Group, Higher Edn. Colloquium (chmn. 1982-84, 96-98), N.J. Assn. of Coll. and Univs. (chair 1991-92), Bucknell U. Alumni Assn. (bd. dirs. 1971-80, pres. 1976-78, Outstanding Achievement 1991), Indian Trail Club, Century Assn., Cornell Club, The Econ. Club of NY, Phi Kappa Psi, Phi Kappa Phi. Office: Adelphi U Garden City NY 11530 Office Phone: 516-877-3838.

SCOTT, ROBERT CORTEZ, United States Representative from Virginia, lawyer; b. Washington, Apr. 30, 1947; s. Charles Waldo and Mae (Hamlin) Scott. BA, Harvard U., Cambridge, Mass., 1969; JD, Boston Coll. Sch. Law, 1973; LLD (hon.), Commonwealth Coll., Hampton, Va., 1988. Lawyer pvt. practice, Newport News, 1973—91; mem. Va. State Ho. Dels., Richmond, 1978—83, Va. State Senate, Richmond, 1983—93, US Congress from 3rd Va. dist., 1993—, mem. edn. and the workforce com., mem. judiciary com., ranking minority mem. crime, terrorism and homeland security subcommittee. Bd. pres. NAACP, Newport News; pres. bd. Peninsula Legal Aid Ctr., Hampton, 1977—81; chmn. 1st dist. Dem. Party Va., 1980—85; adv. com. Peninsula Boy Scouts America; bd. dirs. Hampton Roads March of Dimes; mem. state exec. bd. March of Dimes, Va., 1987. Served in USAR, 1970—74, served in Mass. N.G., 1974—76. Recipient Brotherhood Citation award, Nat. Conf. Christians & Jews, 1985, Child Adv. award, Va. Acad. Pediat., 1987, Disting. Svc. award, Va. State Fraternal Order Police, 1987; named an Outstanding Legislator, So. Health Assn., 1989; named one of 100 Most Influential Black Americans, Ebony mag., 2006. Mem.: Peninsula C. of C., Sigma Pi Phi, Alpha Phi Alpha. Democrat. Episcopalian. Office: US House Reps 1201 Longworth House Office Bldg Washington DC 20515 Office Phone: 202-225-8351.*

SCOTT, ROBERT LANE, chemist, educator; b. Santa Rosa, Calif., Mar. 20, 1922; s. Horace Albert and Maurine (Lane) S.; m. Elizabeth Sewall Hunter, May 27, 1944; children: Joanna Ingersoll (dec.), Jonathan Armat, David St. Clair, Janet Hamilton. S.B., Harvard U., 1942; MA, Princeton U., 1944, PhD, 1945. Sci. staff Los Alamos Lab., 1945-46; Frank B. Jewett fellow U. Calif., Berkeley, 1946-48; faculty UCLA, 1948—, prof. chemistry, 1960-92, prof. emeritus, 1993—, chmn. dept., 1970-75. Author: (with J.H. Hildebrand) Solubility of Nonelectrolytes, 3d edit, 1950, rev., 1964, Regular Solutions, 1962, Regular and Related Solutions, 1970; Contbr. articles to profl. jours. Guggenheim fellow, 1955; NSF sr. fellow, 1961-62; Fulbright lectr., 1968-69 Fellow AAAS, Am. Phys. Soc.; mem. Am. Chem. Soc. (Joel Henry Hildebrand award 1984), Royal Soc. Chemistry (London), Sigma Xi. Home: 11128 Montana Ave Los Angeles CA 90049-3509 Business E-Mail: scott@chem.ucla.edu.

SCOTT, ROSA MAE, artist, educator; b. East Hampton, NY, Apr. 12, 1937; d. James Alexander and Victoria (Square) Nicholson; m. Frank Albert Hanna, Apr. 1, 1957 (div. Mar. 1985); 1 child, Frank Albert Hanna III; m. Warner Bruce Scott, Aug. 3, 1985 (dec. Oct. 2002); children: Bernadine, John, Patricia, Charlene, Lawrence. AA, Dabney Lancaster, 1989; BA, Mary Baldwin, 1992. Cosmetologist Rosa's Beauty Shop, East Hampton, 1962-68; sec. Frank Hanna's Cleaning Co., East Hampton, 1962-77; cashier, clk. Brook's Pharmacy, East Hampton, 1992; lead tchr. East Hampton Day Care, 1992-94, 97-98; substitute tchr. Lexington (Va.) Schs., 1994—; lead tchr. Suffolk C.C. Child Care Ctr., River Head, N.Y., 1999; substitute tchr. East Hampton Sch., 2000—03; lead tchr. after sch. program Springs Sch., 2000—02, 2004—05, substitute tchr., 2000—03. Substitute tchr. East Hampton Sch., 1996-97, 2000-04; sec. Lylburn Downing Cmty. Ctr., Inc., Lexington, 1985-92; arts and crafts tutor, supr. East Hampton Town Youth After Sch. Program, 1996—. Pres. Rockbridge Garden Club, Lexington, 1996; co-organizer Va. Co-op. Ex. Garden Clubs, Lexington, 1995; bd. dirs. Rockbridge Area Pres. Homes, 1996, Fine Arts of Rockbridge, 1985-92, Friends of Lime Kiln, Lexington, 1985-92. Mem.: Guild Hall, East End Arts, Montauk Artists Assn. (receptionist 2003—05), Artist Alliance East Hampton, L.I. Black Artists (v.p. 2000—05), Rockbridge Arts Guild (pres. LI Black Artists 2006—). Avocations: collecting emmett kelly clowns, art, reading, theater, tennis. Home: PO Box 1265 East Hampton NY 11937-0708 Personal E-mail: rosahannascott@aol.com.

SCOTT, RUPERT NEIL, professor and capitalize university librarian; b. Montgomery, Ala., Oct. 27, 1952; s. John Taylor and Ruby Winston Scott; m. Sheila Berry Scott; children: Stephanie Gravely, Sherry Shrewsbury, David Winston. BA, U. South Fla., Tampa, 1975; MS, Fla. State U., Tallahassee, 1976; MBA, Stetson U., DeLand, Fla., 1982. Assoc. sys. writer Burroughs Corp., Atlanta, 1976—77; pub. svcs. libr. William Carey Coll., Hattiesburg, Miss., 1977—80; head, reference svcs. Stetson U., 1980—86; mgmt. cons. KPMG-Peat Marwick, Washington, 1986—87; assoc. libr. dir. Ga. Coll. State U., Milledgeville, 1987—2003; libr. dir. Beacon U., Columbus, Ga., 2003—04; user svcs. libr. Mid. Tenn. State U., Murfreesboro, 2004—. Co-founder MTSU Sci. & Spirituality Forum, Murfreesboro, 2007—. Author: (book) Postmarked Milledgeville, 2001, Flannery O'Connor: An Annotated Reference Guide to Criticism, 2002 (Outstanding Academic Title, 2002), Flannery O'Connor: The Contemporary Reviews, 2009. Pres. DeLand Pub. Libr. Trustees, 1983—87, Eagle Scout, 1970. Recipient BSA Order of Arrow, 1970, Outstanding Svc. award, Volusia County (Fla.) Commrs., Daytona Beach, 1987; named Outstanding Young Men of America, 1978; NEH grant, 1989. Mem.: Am. Libr. Assn., Beta Phi Mu, Themis Honor Soc. Avocations: writing, travel, history. Office: Mid Tenn State Univ Box 13 1301 E Main St Murfreesboro TN 37132 Business E-Mail: rnscott@mtsu.edu.

SCOTT, SHERRY J., psychologist; b. Lowell, Mass., Feb. 6, 1972; d. Bruce E. and Marilyn J. Scott. BS, Fla. State U., Tallahassee, MS, EdS, Fla. State U., Tallahassee, 1998. Registered scho. psychologist State Fla. Dept. Edn., 1999. Intervention specialist Brighter Pathways, Inc., Orlando, Fla., 1998—99; psychologist Polk County Schs., Bartow, Fla., 1999—, crisis intervention team leader to trainer, 2001—. Recipient Psychologist of Yr., Polk County Schools, 2008; nominee Psychologist of Yr., Fla. Assn. Sch. Psychologists, 2008. Mem.: Fla. Assn. of Sch. Psychologists, NASP, Golden Key, Phi Kappa Phi, Phi Beta Kappa. Independent. Avocations: reading, travel, theater. Home: 349 Winter Ridge Blvd Winter Haven FL 33881 Personal E-mail: sherry.scott@polk-fl.net.

SCOTT, STANLEY DEFOREST, real estate company executive; b. Hudson County, NJ, Nov. 2, 1926; s. Stanley DeForest and Anne Marie (Volk) Scott; m. Mary Elizabeth Forbes Hazard, Dec. 30, 1953. BA, U. So. Calif., LA, 1950. Gen. mgr. Alfred Scott Pubs., NYC, 1951-56; chmn., pres. S.D. Scott Printing Co., Inc., NYC, 1956-92; gen. ptnr. 145 Hudson St. Assocs. Co-chmn. mus. and art com. Fraunces Tavern Mus., 1973—87, 1998—2007; assoc. J. Carter Brown Libr.; former mem. Mayor's Industry Adv. Com.; former bd. dirs. Bus. Relocation Com. With USNR, 1944—46. Mem.: Friends of Canterbury Cathedral in US, Am. Assocs. Royal Acad. Arts (patron), Am. Antiquarian Soc., Am.-Scottish Found., Mt. Vernon Ladies Assn. (adv. com.), Am. Mus. Britain (coun. 1986—), Mus. Modern Art, Am. Friends Hermitage Mus., Am. Friends Brit. Mus. (patron), English-Speaking Union NY (patron), Royal Oak Found., Am. Friends English Heritage, Sir John Soane's Mus. Found. (patron), Met. Mus. Art, Morgan Libr. (patron), N.Y. Hist. Soc., Am. Trust for the Brit. Libr., World Monuments Fund (internat. coun.), NY Philharmonic (patron), Sons of the Revolution (bd. mgrs., hon. past pres.,), Am. Numismatic Soc. (trustee), Carnegie Hall Soc. (patron), Church Club N.Y., Union Club, Knickerbocker Club, Grolier Club, St. George's Soc., Pilgrims US, Soc. Colonial Wars (mem. coun.), Soc. Mayflower Descs. Republican. Episcopalian. Home: One Sutton Pl South New York NY 10022-2471 Office: 145 Hudson St New York NY 10013-2103 Personal E-mail: sctthudson@hotmail.com, sctthudson@aol.com.

SCOTT, STEPHANIE D., city official; b. 1966; 2 children. Ph.D in Environ. Psychology, CUNY. Researcher Urban Inst., 1998—2003; chief of staff to Councilman Adrian Fenty DC City Coun., 2003—04; chief of staff Adrian Fenty's Re-Election Campaign, 2004; sec. dist. DC Govt., Washington, 2007—. Democrat. Office: Office Dist Sec John A Wilson Bldg 1350 Pennsylvania Ave Ste 419 Washington DC 20004 E-mail: stephanie.scott@dc.gov.

SCOTT, STEPHEN, composer, musician, educator; b. Corvallis, Oreg., 1944; BA, U. Oreg., 1967; MA, Brown U.; fieldwork in African musics, Ghana, Tanzania, Zimbabwe, 1970. Prof. music Colo. Coll., Colorado Springs, 1989—, founder, dir. Bowed Piano Ensemble, 1977—, Nancy Bryson Schlosser and C. William Schlosser prof. arts, 2003—06, assoc. chair, 2007—08, with, 1969—. Composer: (albums) Portraits, Vikings of the Sunrise, New Music for Bowed Piano, 1999, Minerva's Web/The Tears of Niobe, The Deep Spaces, 2006. Recipient Chamber Music prize, New England Conservatory/Rockefeller Found., 1980; grantee Peter S. Reed Found.; Composer's fellowship, Nat. Endowment Arts, 1985—86, US Artists Simon fellow, 2008. Office: Colo Coll Music Dept Packard 111 14 E Cache La Poudre Colorado Springs CO 80903 also: c/o New Albion Records Box 25 Elizaville NY 12523 Office Phone: 719-389-6557. E-mail: sscott@coloradocollege.edu.*

SCOTT, SUSAN CRAIG, plastic surgeon; b. NYC, 1948; m. Norman Scott; children: Eric, William, Kelly. MD, Columbia U., 1974. Diplomate Am. Bd. Plastic Surgery with subspecialty in hand surgery. Intern Roosevelt Hosp., NYC, 1974—75, resident in gen. surgery, 1975—79; resident in plastic surgery NYU Med. Ctr., 1979—81; fellow in hand surgery Roosevelt Hosp., 1981—82; pvt. practice plastic surgery NYC, 1987—. Cons. team physician NY Liberty. Achievements include assisting in the wrist surgery of Patrick Ewing in 1997; has performed surgery on Allan Houston, Latrell Sprewell, John Starks, Charles Oakley and Herb Williams. Office: 150 E 77TH St New York NY 10021-1922 Office Phone: 212-288-9922. Personal E-mail: smcscott@verizon.net.

SCOTT, T. GORDON, chemistry and math educator, writer; b. Laconia, NH, Nov. 27, 1941; s. William Stafford and Jeanne Richardson Scott; m. Elizabeth Mary Winterberg, Mar. 11, 1995. BA, U. Pa., 1963; BA with honours, Cambridge U., England, 1965, MA, 1970; PhD, U. Ill., 1969. Profl. tchg. cert., Pa.; postgrad. tchg. lic., Va. Tchg. asst. U. Ill., Champaign-Urbana, 1965-66; asst. prof. chemistry Oberlin Coll., Ohio, 1969-70; lectr. biochemistry U. Calif., Santa Barbara, 1971; cons. Sci-Math Cons., Uniontown, Pa., 1972-75; supr. secondary studies Westminster Acad., Carmichaels, Pa., 1975-79; asst. prof. chemistry Alderson-Broaddus Coll., Philippi, W.Va., 1981-84; assoc. prof. chemistry Bryan Coll., Dayton, Tenn., 1984-86, Knoxville Coll., Tenn., 1987-89, Union Coll., Barbourville, Ky., 1989-91, Jarvis Christian Coll., Hawkins, Tex., 1992-98; with Chem. Edn. Cons. USA, Hawkins, Tex., 1998-2000; instr. math. Winona Ind. Sch. Dist., Tex., 1998-99; instr. math, chemistry and astronomy Pittsylvania County Schs., Va.; tchr. Dan River HS, Ringgold, Va., 2000—02; adj. prof. chemistry and natural sci.-biochemistry Danville CC, Va., 1999—2004; adj. instr. pharmacology Nat. Coll., Danville, 2001—03; assoc. prof. chemistry Winston-Salem State U., NC, 2004—09. Rsch. assoc. DuPont Chem. Co., Inc., Phila., 1963, EPA, Phila., 1988, Edgewood-Aberdeen Rsch. US Army, Aberdeen Proving Ground, Md., 1993; vis. prof. La. Coll., Pineville, 1992; adj. sci. instr. Hargrave Mil. Acad., Chatham, Va., 2003; undergrad. rsch. mentor NSF, New Orleans, 2004; cons. with Transition State Assocs., Danville, Va. Author: (with others) Synthetic Procedures in Nucleic Acid Chemistry, 1968, Spectroscopic Model Studies of NAD, 1969; contbr. articles to Jour. Am. Chem., Soc., 1967, 1970, 1972, 2003. Musician with Danville Recorder Consort, Danville Area Choral Arts Soc. Thouron fellow to Cambridge U., 1963-65; Thouron scholar Gonville & Caius Coll., Cambridge U.; grantee NSF, 1996-97, Army Rsch. Orgn., 1993-95, Robert A. Welch Found., 1996-98, NSF, 1997-99. Mem. Am. Chem. Soc., Cambridge U. Chem. Soc., Am. Sci. Affiliation (dir. 1998), Rotary Internat. (chmn. internat. edn. com. 1977-81). Achievements include determined the fluorescent lifetime of coenzyme NADH. Avocations: baritone vocal solos, exploring ideas, renaissance music (treble and tenor blockflute), astronomy. Office Phone: 336-750-3179. Business E-Mail: scottg@wssu.edu.

SCOTT, TERRY LEE, communications executive; b. Rockford, Ill., Oct. 21, 1950; s. Wilson C. and Marie G. (Bunger) S.; divorced; children: Andrea, Brady, Tiffany. BS in Acctg. magna cum laude, Bradley U., 1972. CPA Ill., Tex. Audit prin. Arthur Young and Co., Dallas, 1972-82; v.p. fin. and adminstrn., treas. Paging Network Inc., Dallas, 1982-90; sr. v.p. Paging Network, Inc., Dallas, 1990-92, pres., CEO, bd. dirs., 1993-95, Terion Inc., Melbourne, Fla., 1995-97, chmn., CEO, 1997-99, Terry Scott Enterprises, Plano, Tex., 1997—; dir. Chameleon Tech., Inc., Seattle, 2000—03, Metasolv Software, Inc., Dallas, 2003—06; CFO, v.p. Fin. of Chase Med., Inc., 2003—04; pres., CEO, dir. Airimba Wireless, Inc., Plano, Tex., 2004—06. Mem. AICPA, Tex. Soc. CPAs, Phi Kappa Phi, Zeta Pi. Methodist. Home: 5816 Gallant Fox Ln Plano TX 75093-2910 Home Phone: 214-713-7614; Office Phone: 214-718-8927. Personal E-mail: tscott1704@aol.com.

SCOTT, THOMAS JEFFERSON, JR., lawyer, electrical engineer; b. Montgomery, Ala., Dec. 30, 1943; s. Thomas Jefferson Sr. and Irene (Feagin) S.; m. Betsy Sue Mackta, Apr. 25, 1981; children: Elspeth Watts, Marghuerita Taylor, Thomas Jefferson III. BEE, Yale U., 1966, BA in Econs., 1967; JD, Vanderbilt U., 1974. Bar: Va. 1974, D.C. 1975, N.Y. 1980, U.S. Dist. Ct. D.C. 1986, U.S. Dist. Ct. (ea. dist.) Va. 1993, U.S. Tax Ct. 1981, U.S. Ct. Fed. Claims, 1982, U.S. Ct. Appeals (fed. cir.) 1982, U.S. Ct. Appeals (4th cir.) 1993, U.S. Supreme Ct. 1984. Trial atty. civil div. U.S. Dept. of Justice, Washington, 1974-78; assoc. Cooper & Dunham, NYC, 1978-80, sr. trial counsel civil div., 1980-85; ptnr. Pennie & Edmonds, Washington, 1985—90, Howrey & Simon, Washington, 1990—97, Hunton & Williams, Washington, 1997—2007, Goodwin Procter LLP, Washington, 2007—. Capt. USNR, 1966-71. Decorated D.F.C. Mem. ABA, Am. Intellectual Property Law Assn. Office: Goodwin Procter LLP 901 New York Ave NW Washington DC 20001 Office Phone: 202-346-3442. Business E-Mail: tscott@goodwinprocter.com.

SCOTT, THOMAS WALLACE, entomologist, director; BS, Bowling Green State U., 1973, MS, 1977; PhD, Pa. State U., State Coll., 1981. Prof., entomology U. Calif., Davis, 1996—, dir., mosquito rsch. lab., 1996—. Contbr. scientific papers to profl. jours. Fellow: AAAS; mem.: Soc. Vector Biology, Entomol. Soc. America, Am. Soc. Tropical Medicine and Hygiene, Am. Mosquito Control Assn., Am. Com. Med. Entomology, Am. Com. Arthropod-Borne Viruses. Achievements include research in food and biotechnology. Office: Univ Calif Davis 1 Shields Ave Davis CA 95616 Business E-Mail: twscott@ucdavis.edu.

SCOTT, TONY, computer software company executive; BS in Info. Sys. Mgmt., U. San Francisco; JD in Intellectual Property and Internat. Law, Santa Clara U., Calif. Engr. Gt. Am. Pk., Santa Clara, 1976; v.p. ops. Bristol-Meyers Squibb; chief tech. officer GM, 1999; sr. v.p., chief info. officer The Walt Disney Co., 2005—08; corp. v.p., chief info. officer Microsoft Corp., 2008—. Office: Microsoft Corp 1 Microsoft Way Redmond WA 98052-6399

SCOTT, TROY M., microbiologist, director; b. Toledo, Mar. 20, 1975; s. Dale F. and Debbie K. Scott; 1 child, Langston T. BS, U. Fla., Gainesville, 1997, MS, 2000, PhD, 2002. Dir. BCS Labs., Inc., Gainesville, 2000—, Hydros Coastal Solutions, Inc., Miami, Fla., 2008. Adj. prof. U. Miami, 2008—. Contbr. scientific papers. Mem.: Am. Soc. Microbiology. Office: BCS Labs Inc 4641 NW 6th St Ste C Miami FL 32609

SCOTT, VICKI SUE, retired school system administrator; b. Pine Bluff, Ark., Feb. 16, 1946; d. John Wesley and Ruby Gray (Whitehead) and Hannah (Lewis) S. BA, Hendrix Coll., 1968; MS in Edn., U. Cen. Ark., 1978, postgrad., 1979-84, U. Ark., 1983-85, Ark. State U., 1993-94. Cert. dist. adminstr., secondary sch. prin., mid. sch., secondary health and phys. edn. Tchr., coach Brinkley (Ark.) Pub. Schs., 1968-76, Lonoke (Ark.) Jr. and Sr. High Schs., 1976-77, S.E. Jr. High Sch., Pine Bluff, 1978-92, asst. prin., 1992-2000, dir. summer sch., 1991, 92; prin. White Hall (Ark.) Jr. H.S., White Hall, Ark., 2000—08. AIDS educator Arkansas River Edn. Svc. Coop., Pine Bluff, 1989-92. Active Leadership Pine Bluff, 1993-94. Scholar Assn. Women Ednl. Suprs., 1985; named Outstanding Young Women of Am., 1974, Ark. Leadership Acad., 2000. Mem.: DAR, ASCD, Ark. Ret. Tchrs. Assn., Nat. Mid. Sch. Assn., Nat. Assn. Sch. Secondary Prins., Ark. Assn. Ednl. Adminstrs., Ark. Assn. Mid. Level Adminstrs. (bd. dirs. 2002—04), Order Ea. Star, Phi Delta Kappa, Delta Kappa Gamma (Epsilon chpt. pres., scholar 1994). Baptist. Avocations: reading, hiking, travel, golf. Home: 3215 S Cherry St Pine Bluff AR 71603-5983 Personal E-mail: foghorn@cablelynx.com.

SCOTT, WALTER, JR., telecommunications industry executive; b. May 21, 1931; m. Suzanne Scott. BS, Colo. State U., 1953; LittD, U. Nebr., 1983; LHD, Coll. St. Mary, 1988; D of Commerce, Bellevue U., 1996. With Peter Kiewit Sons, Inc., Omaha, 1953—, engr., project engr., dist. engr., Cleve. dist., 1959—61, asst. dist. mgr., Cleve. dist., 1961—62, dist. mgr. Cleve. dist. Omaha, 1962-64, v.p., 1964, exec. v.p., 1965-79, chmn. bd., 1964, pres., 1979, chmn. bd. dirs., pres., CEO, 1979-97, chmn. emeritus, 1997—; chmn. Level 3 Communications Inc. (former subs. PKS), Broomfield, Colo., 1997—. Bd. trustee Open World Leadership Ctr.; dir. Berkshire Hathaway, Burlington Resources, Commonwealth Telephone Enterprises, MidAmerican Energy Holdings, RCN Corp., Valmont Industries. Served with USAF, 1954-56. Recipient Nebr. Builder award, U. Nebr., 1983, Outstanding Achievement in Construction award, The Moles, 1986, Brotherhood award, Nat. Conf. Christians and Jews, 1986, Horatio Alger award, Horatio Alger Assn., 1997, Spirit Youth award, Uta Halee Girls Village, 1988, Perry W. Branch Disting. Svc. award, U. Nebr. Found., 1989, Golden Beaver for Mgmt., The Beavers, 1990, Order of Tower, U. Nebr., Omaha, 1991, Golden Plate award, Am. Acad. Achievement, 1991, Golden Apple award, Met. Cmty. Coll. Found., 1993, Headliner award, Greater Omaha C. of C., 1996, Nebraskalander award, Nebraskaland Found., 1998, Manresa award, Creighton U., 1998, Cmty. Builder award, Greater Omaha C. of C., 1999, Bus. Vol. of Yr., Nat. Alliance Bus., 1999, Midlander of Yr., Omaha World-Herald, 2000; named Philanthropist of Yr., Nat. Soc. Fund-Raising Execs., 1987, Man of Yr., Mid-Am. Coun. Boy Scouts Am., 1988, King Ak-Sar-Ben XCII, Knights of Ak-Sar-Ben, 1988, Disting. Eagle Scout, Boy Scouts Am., 1991, Citizen of Yr., United Way of the Midlands, 1993, Air Force Assn., 1993, Person of Yr., Pmaha Club, 1996; named one of Forbes Richest Americans, 2006; named to Nebr. Bus. Hall Fame, Nebr. C. of C. and Industry, 1995, Omaha Bus. Hall Fame, Greater Omaha C. of C., 1995. Mem.: Chi Epsilon Soc. (hon.). Office: Peter Kiewit Sons Inc 1000 Kiewit Plz Omaha NE 68131-3302 also: Joslyn Art Mus 2200 Dodge St Omaha NE 68102-1208 Office: Level 3 Communications Inc 1025 Eldorado Blvd Broomfield CO 80021

SCOTT, WALTER, JR., business consultant; b. Balt., July 24, 1925; s. Walter and Margaret Catherine (Pfeiffer) S.; m. Barbara Main, July 6, 1946 (dec. 1964); children: Stephen Walter, Susan Marjorie, Cynthia Margaret, Christopher Main; m. Mary Joan Braun, Aug. 5, 1966 (dec. 1986); m. Helene Lyda Burke, May 1, 1987. AB, Duke U., 1945; MBA with distinction, Harvard U., 1949. Advtg. mgr. The Quaker Oats Co., Chgo., 1950-57; v.p. mktg. J.H. Filbert, Inc., Balt., 1957-67, pres., 1968-77; div. gen. mgr. Cen. Soya Co., Ft. Wayne, Ind., 1972-77; exec. v.p. Fairmont Foods Co., Des Plaines, Ill., 1978-81; pres. McKeon, Scott, Woolf & Assocs., Palo Alto, Calif., 1982-84; chmn. bd. Integral Cons. Group, Mill Valley, Calif., 1986-87, Scott, Woolf & Assocs., Palo Alto, 1984—2001, Mulford Moreland & Assocs., San Jose, Calif., 1986-89. Chmn., speaker pres. courses, Am. Mgmt. Assn., N.Y.C., 1970-90; trustee Calif. Inst. Integral Studies, San Francisco, 1983-89; bd. dirs. West Marine, Inc., Watsonville, Calif., 1995-2001. With USNR, 1943-46, PTO. Mem. Phi Beta Kappa. Home and Office: 1450 Redford Dr Palm Springs CA 92264 Home Phone: 760-416-1451; Office Phone: 760-416-0851.

SCOTT, WALTER DILL, management educator; b. Chgo., Oct. 27, 1931; s. John Marcy and Mary Louise (Gent) S.; m. Barbara Ann Stein, Sept. 9, 1961; children: Timothy Walter, David Frederick, Gordon Charles. Student, Williams Coll., Williamstown, Mass., 1949-51; BS, Northwestern U., Evanston, Ill., 1953; MS, Columbia U., NYC, 1958. Cons. Booz, Allen & Hamilton, NYC, 1956—58; assoc. Glore, Forgan & Co., NYC, 1958—63, ptnr. Chgo., 1963-65; pntr. Lehman Bros, Chgo., 1965-72, sr. ptnr., 1972-73, also bd. dirs.; assoc. dir. econs. and govt. Office Mgmt. and Budget, Washington, 1973-75; sr. v.p. internat. and fin. Pillsbury Co., Mpls., 1975-78, exec. v.p., 1978-80, also bd. dirs.; pres., CEO, Investors Diversified Svcs., Inc., Mpls., 1980-84; group mng. dir. Grand Met. PLC, Mpls., 1984-86, also bd. dirs.; chmn. Grand Met USA, Mpls., 1984-86; prof., sr. Austin fellow Kellogg Sch. Mgmt., Northwestern U., Evanston, Ill., 1988—. Mem. adv. bd. dirs. Chgo. Cmtys. in Schs.; mem. adv. bd. good city, bd. dirs. Ctr. Exec. Women. Lt. (j.g.) USN, 1953—56. Office: Northwestern U Kellogg Sch Mgmt 2001 Sheridan Rd Evanston IL 60208-0814 Business E-Mail: wds@kellogg.northwestern.edu.

SCOTT, WILL T., state supreme court justice; b. Ratliff's Creek, Ky., July 20, 1947; s. John H. H. and Betty (Thompson) Scott. Attended, Eastern Ky. U.; BA, Pikeville Coll.; JD, U. Miami, 1974, MS in Taxation, 1975. Bar: Ky., Fla. With trust dept. Pikeville Nat. Bank, 1975—76; atty. priv. practice, 1976—2004; asst. atty. Pike County, 1981—82; judge Pike County Cir. Ct., 1984—88; justice Ky. Supreme Ct., 2005—, dep. chief justice, 2006—. Served to First Lt. US Army, 1966—69. Decorated Bronze Star, Vietnamese Cross of Gallantry, Combat Infantryman's Badge. Mem.: Ky. Circuit Judges' Assn. (second v.p. 1986). Office: Ky Supreme Ct 700 Capital Ave Frankfort KY 40601 Office Phone: 502-564-4168.*

SCOTT, WILLIAM CLEMENT, III, investor; b. NYC, Apr. 25, 1934; s. William Clement and Susan L. (Cameron) S.; m. Cindy L. Taylor, Dec. 5, 1981; children by previous marriage: Katherine Louise, David Campbell. AB, Coll. William and Mary, Williamsburg, Va., 1956. Self-employed, 1956-64; v.p. Booz-Allen & Hamilton, NYC, 1964-69; group v.p. Cordura Corp., Los Angeles, 1969-72; exec. v.p. Western Pacific Industries, NYC, 1972-76, pres., chief operating officer, 1976-87; pvt. investor NYC, 1987-88; chmn., CEO Panavision Inc., NYC, 1988-98. Bd. dirs. Edison Control Corp. With Opera Orch. NY, pres., 1988-97; with Met. Opera Club NYC, pres., 2002-04. Mem. Met. Opera Club, Racquet and Tennis Club, Knickerbocker Club, Hay Harbor Club, Fishers Island Country Club, Coral Beach Club (Bermuda), Royal Bermuda Yacht Club. Republican. Episcopalian. Office: 445 Park Ave Ste 1905 New York NY 10022 Office Phone: 212-688-4748. E-mail: wcscott@att.net.

SCOTT, WILLIAM FLOYD, accountant; b. Woodland, Miss., Feb. 26, 1936; s. Robert Fulton and Sarah Etta (Watson) S.; m. Carolyn Marie Pierce, Dec. 12, 1958; children: David, Ricky, Stephen, Julie. BS in Bus. Adminstrn., Delta State U., Cleveland, Miss., 1957. Staff acct. Reynolds Elec. & Engring., Las Vegas, Nev., 1957-62, sr. auditor, 1962-65, dir. internal auditing, 1965-70; sr. staff acct. Davis & Mosher, CPAs, Pasadena, Tex., 1970-72; owner Scott & Co., CPAs, Pasadena, 1972—2001; mng. dir. Scott, Forrest, Adams & Co., PLLC, CPAs, Pasadena, 2002—07. Chmn. fin. com. Meml. Bapt. Ch., Pasadena, Pasadena, 1974—80, treas., 1974—. Mem. AICPA, Tex. Soc. CPAs, Pasadena Noon Optimist Club (treas. 1973-75), Neighborhood Assn. Three Villas (treas. 2000-2007). Avocations: reading, gardening, sports. Office: Scott & Co PLLC CPA 3954 Bolivia Dr Pasadena TX 77504-2509 Office Phone: 281-487-2501. E-mail: wmfscott@swbell.net.

SCOTT, YVONNIE MICHELLE, special education educator, diagnostician, paralegal; b. Rochester, NY, Jan. 18, 1963; d. Harry Scott and Mary Jean Crews-Scott; m. Myron E. Miles (div.). BSc, Troy State U., Fort Rucker, Ala., 1987; MEd, Clark Atlanta U., 2002. Cert.: Ga. (paralegal) 2005; edn. specialist Clark Atlanta U., 2003, in ednl. leadership Clark Atlanta U., 2004, tchr. NY, Va., Ga. Kindergarten tchr. Rochester City Schs., 1985—86; tng. instr. Dept. Def., US Army, 1987—91; job coach John Odom Work Ctr., Dothan, Ala., 1992; spl. edn. tchr. asst. Dale County Bd. Edn., Ozark, Ala., 1995—97; spl. edn. tchr., diagnostician Cobb County Bd. Edn., Marietta, Ga., 2000—. Owner Scott's Enterprises, Alexandria, Va., 2001—; mentor, tchrs., students; workshop attendee in field. Named Tchr. of Month, Dept. Def., Fort Rucker, 1988; Academic scholarship, Ozark Hospitality, 1981. Mem.: Coun. Exceptional Children, Nat. Educators Assn., Order of the Eastern Star, Alpha Kappa Alpha (mem. health com. 2004). Democrat. Baptist. Avocations: piano, cooking, travel. Office: South Coff HS 1920 Clay Rd SW Austell GA 30106 Office Phone: 770-355-1531.

SCOTT-ALLEN, CYNTHIA, psychologist; b. NJ; d. Ruth Scott; 1 child, Brianna Hoyrd. MEd, Jersey City State Coll., NJ, 1887. Cert. sch. psychologist Jersey City State Coll., 1990. Sch. psychologist Jersey City Pub. Schs., 1991—. Baptist. Avocations: reading, travel. Office: Jersey City Pub Schs 346 Claremont Ave Jersey City NJ 07305 Business E-Mail: cscott-allen@jcboe.org.

SCOTT-BATTLE, GLADYS NATALIE, retired social worker; b. Cambridge, Mass., Sept. 16, 1933; d. Dudley Fairfax and Bessie Mae (Mitchell) Scott; m. James Henry Battle, Jr., Oct. 18, 1953 (div. 1975); children: Gregory, James, Jameel. BA, Fordham U., Lincoln Ctr., NY, 1975; MSW, Columbia U., NYC, 1978. Lic. psychiat. social worker; cert. social worker, tchr., NY. Program dir. Cmty. Svc. Soc., NYC, 1978—79; corp. liaison cities and schs., NYC, 1979—80; psychotherapist Harlem Interfaith Counseling, NYC, 1980—82; psychiat. social worker Met. Hosp., NYC, 1982—93; psychiat. social worker Bronx clin. divsn. N.Y.C. Bd. Edn., 1982—92; ret., 1992. Cons. NY State Disability Determinations, 1992—, NYC Family Ct., 1987-92, family and criminal ct.-selected cases. V.p. Women Who Help Other People, NYC, 1985; bd. dirs. Morningside Gardens Coop., NYC, 1986-88; vol. Met. Mus. Art. Mem. NASW, Nat. Assn. Black Social Workers, United Fedn. Tchrs., Internat. Assn. Social Workers, Bus. and Profl. Women's Club Riverside Ch. Democrat. Avocations: visiting museums and art galleries, painting, theater, travel, exploring Hudson Valley landmarks and museums.

SCOTT-BURTON, JENNIFER MARIE, special education educator; b. Royal Oak, Mich., Dec. 10, 1973; d. Bruce Craven and Mary Helen Best Scott. BA in sci. and Psychology, Purdue U., 1996; MS in Edn., Ind. U., 1998, EdD, 2009—. Cert. tchr. learning disabled/mentally handicapped Ind., dist. adminstr. Ind. Paraprofessional spl. edn. Paoli (Ind.) Jr. Sr. H.S., 1996—97; ADL supr., instr. Orange County Devel. and Rehab. Ctr./First Chance Ctr., Paoli, 1997—98; spl. edn. tchr. K-12 Medora (Ind.) Cmty. Schs., 1999; spl. edn. tchr. K-6 New Albany-Floyd County Schs., Georgetown, Ind., 1999—2002; assoc. instr., field experience supr. Ind. U., Bloomington, 2002—03; spl. edn. tchr. 9-12 Westfield (Ind.) Washington Schs., 2003—04; program coord. N.W. Ind. Spl. Edn. Coop., Crown Point, 2005, spl. edn. adminstr., 2005, R.I.S.E. Spl. Svcs., Indpls., 2005—, assoc. dir., 2005—. Corp. joint spl. edn. adv. com. New Albany/Floyd County Sch. Corp., 2001—02; mem. leadership team com. Georgetown Elem. Sch., 2001—02. RCIA sponsor St.Paul's Cath. Ch., Bloomington, 2002—03. Mem.: Ind. Coun. Spl. Edn. (adminstr. 2004—, ctrl. roundtable mem. 2005—), Ind. U. Sch. Adminstrs. Assn., Assn. Supervision and Curriculum, Coun. for Exceptional Children (polit. action com. 2003), Nat. Alliance for Mentally Ill, Pi Lambda Theta, Phi Delta Kappa. Democrat. Roman Catholic. Avocations: skiing, running, travel, reading. Personal E-mail: jenstarski7@hotmail.com.

SCOTTI, DENNIS JOSEPH, educator, researcher, consultant; b. NYC, Apr. 20, 1952; s. Joseph Charles and Theresa (Giancola) S. BS, Stony Brook U., 1974; MBA, Adelphi U., 1977; MS, Temple U., 1980, PhD, 1982. Bd. cert. in healthcare mgmt.; cert. managed care and healthcare fin. profl. Dep. chief adminstr. Dept. Mental Health Devel. Ctr., Suffolk, N.Y., 1975-77; asst. prof. Rutgers U., N.J., 1980-83; assoc. prof. Fairleigh Dickinson U., N.J., 1983-88, prof., 1989—, sr. prof. Ctr. Healthcare Mgmt. Studies, 2001—06, Alfred E. Driscoll endowed prof., 2006—. Exec. v.p. Presscott Assocs., Ltd., Avon, Conn., 1989—. Author: Strategic Management in the Health Care Sector, 1988; contbr. articles to profl. jours. Mem. Regents Adv. Coun. N.J.; bd. trustees, quality of paitent com. CentraState Healthcare Sys., N.J. Recipient Tchg. Excellence award Exec. MBA, 1997. Fellow Am. Coll. Healthcare Execs., Healthcare Fin. Mgmt. Assn. (William G. Fulmer Bronze award 1997, Robert H. Reeves Silver award 2001, Frederick T. Muncie award 2004, co-recipient Helen M. Yerger Spl. Recognition award 2002); mem. Med. Group Mgmt. Assn., Health Planning and Mktg. Soc., Acad. Mgmt. (co-recipient Best Theory to Practice award 2003), Health Decisions Assembly, Phi Theta Kappa, Delta Mu Delta. Office: Fairleigh Dickinson U 1000 River Rd Teaneck NJ 07666-1996 Personal E-mail: djs341@comcast.net.

SCOTTON, CAROL ROBINSON, economist, educator; b. Buffalo, June 27, 1953; d. George A. and Alvera M. Robinson; m. Robert Vinson Scotton. BA, U. Tenn., Chattanooga; MEd, Ga. State U., Atlanta, PhD, 2000. Proofreader Dittler Bros. Printing Co., Atlanta, 1978—80; trainer, instrnl. designer and developer Life Office Mgmt. Assn., Atlanta, 1988—89; mgr. Byers Engring. Co., Atlanta, 1980—88; cmty. health planner US Ctrs. Disease Control & Prevention, Atlanta, 1989—2000, economist, 2000—05; asst. prof. Knox Coll., Galesburg, Ill., 2005—. Bd. mem. Knox County Bd. Heath, Galesburg, Ill., 2006—; bd. dirs. Atlanta Soto Zen Ctr., 2000—05, Nat. Soc. Performance and Instrn., Washington, 1991—93, Atlanta, 1988—91. Mem.: Assn. Evolutionary Economics, Am. Econ. Assn. Buddhist. Office: Knox Coll Box K-43 2 E South St Galesburg IL 61401-4999 Business E-Mail: cscotton@knox.edu.

SCOTT-THOMAS, KRISTIN, actress; b. Redruth, Cornwall, Eng., May 24, 1960; m. Francois Olivennes, 3 children, Hannah, Joseph, George. Student, Cen. Sch. Speech and Drama, Ecole Nat. des Arts. Stage debut in Schnitzler's La Lune Déclinante Sur 4 ou 5 Personnes Qui Danse; stage appearances include La Terre Etrangère, Naive Hirondelles, Yes Peut-Etre, Bérénice, 2001, Three Sisters, 2003, As You Desire Me, 2005, The Seagull, London, 2007 (Best Actress, Laurence Olivier Awards, 2008), Broadway, 2008; appearances on French, German, Australian, U.S. and Brit. TV include L'Ami d'Enfance de Maigret, Blockhaus, Cameleon La Tricheuse, Sentimental Journey, The Tenth Man, Endless Game, Framed, Titmuss Regained, Look at it this Way, Body and Soul; film appearances include Djamel et Juliette, L'Agent Troubé, La Méridienne, Under the Cherry Moon, A Handful of Dust, Force Majeure, Bille en Tete, The Bacheloir, Bitter Moon, Four Weddings and a Funeral (BAFTA award), Angels and Insects (Evening Standard Film award), Richard III, 1995, Angels & Insects, 1996, Somebody to Love, 1996, The Pompatus of Love, 1996, Mission: Impossible, 1996, The English Patient, 1996, Amour et confusions, 1997, Souvenir, 1998, The Revenger's Comedies, 1998, The Horse Whisperer, 1998, Up at the Villa, 1999, Random Hearts, 1999, Life as a House, 2001, Gosford Park, 2001, The Golden Compass (voice), 2007, The Walker, 2007, Il ya a longtemps que je t'aine, 2008, The Other Boleyn Girl, 2008, Seuls two, 2008, Easy Virtue, 2008, Confessions of a Shopaholic, 2009. Office: Creative Artists Agency 2000 Avenue Of The Stars Los Angeles CA 90067-4700

SCOTT-WILLIAMS, WENDY LEE, library and information scientist; b. Buffalo, Jan. 22; d. Arthur Raymond and June Amelia Schutt; m. Nigel Simon Scott-Williams, Feb. 29, 1980. BA cum laude, SUNY, Buffalo, 1975; MA with honors, Cambridge U., 1979; MLIS with honors, CUNY-Queens Coll., 1987. Applications rep. Barrister, NYC, 1982-83; coord. computer systems Stroock & Stroock & Lavan, NYC, 1983-87; tech. svcs. mgr. Batten, Barton, Durstein & Osborn (BBDO) Worldwide, NYC, 1987-92; adminstr., mgr. info. resources Fairchild Publs., NYC, 1992-96; info. resource mgr. March of Dimes, White Plains, NY, 1996—. Active Buffalo Zool. Soc. Mem. Spl. Librs. Assn., Med. Libr., Cambridge Union Soc., Oxford-Cambridge Soc., Nature Conservancy, Greenpeace. Presbyterian. Avocations: travel, gardening. Office: March of Dimes Nat Hdqs 1275 Mamaroneck Ave White Plains NY 10605-5298

SCOUTT, LESLIE M., medical educator; d. Will Jerrold and Nancy Howard Scoutt; m. Joseph Glassford Garner; children: Will Garner, Matthew Garner, Katherine Garner. BA, Wesleyan U., 1974; MD, U. Rochester, NY, 1978. Lic. med. Conn. State, 1985. Residency in internal medicine Univ. Hosp., Boston U., 1978—81; residency in diagnostic radiology Beth Israel Hosp., Boston, 1978—81; emergency rm. physician Leominster Hosp., Mass., 1982—83; instr. diagnostic imaging Yale U. Sch. Medicine, New Haven, 1985—87, clin. asst. prof. diagnostic imaging, 1987—88, asst. prof. diagnostic radiology, 1988—94, assoc. prof. diagnostic imaging, 1994—2002, clin. chief, sect. ultrasound, 1999—2003, prof. diagnostic radiology, 2002—, chief, sect. ultrasound, dept. diagnostic imaging, 2003—, co-dir., vascular lab., 2003—08. Contbr. articles to profl. jours. Mem.: Am. Coll. Radiology, Am. Bd. Radiology (co-dir., US sect. written diagnostic radiology bd. exam 1999—2005, chair US sect. core exam and maintainance cert. exam 2008—, mem. oral exam com. 1999—), Am. Assn. Women Radiologists, Soc. Radiologists Ultrasound, Am. Inst. Ultrasound in Medicine, Am. Roentgen Ray Soc., Radiol. Soc. N.Am. Office: Yale Univ Sch Medicine 333 Cedar St PO Box 208042 New Haven CT 06520-8042 Office Phone: 203-785-2688. Office Fax: 203-785-4328. Business E-Mail: leslie.scoutt@yale.edu.

SCOVANNER, DOUGLAS A., retail executive; BS, Washington and Lee U., 1977; MBA, U. Va., 1979. With Coca-Cola Enterprises and affiliates, Atlanta, 1980-92, v.p., treas., 1989-92; sr. v.p. fin. Fleming Cos., Oklahoma City, 1992-94; sr. v.p. fin., CFO Target Corp., Mpls., 1994—2000, exec. v.p., CFO, 2000—. Trustee Darden Sch. Found. U. Va. Darden Grad. Sch. Bus. Adminstrn.; vice chmn. exec. com. Minn. Orchestral Assn.; bd. mem. Greater Met. Housing Corp. Office: Target Corp 1000 Nicollett Mall Minneapolis MN 55403-2467*

SCOVEL, CALVIN L., III, federal agency administrator; b. 1952; m. Cathy Scovel; children: Carey, Thomas. BA, U. NC; MA, Naval War Coll.; JD, Duke U. Advanced through grades to brigadier Gen. USMC; legal adv. to sec. USN; first counsel to insp. gen., chief def. counsel USMC; sr. judge USN Marine Corps Ct. Criminal Appeals; insp. gen. US Dept. Transp., Washington, 2006—. Office: US Dept Transp 1200 New Jersey Ave SE 7th Fl Washington DC 20590 Office Phone: 202-366-1959. Office Fax: 202-366-3912.

SCOWCROFT, BRENT, former national security advisor, retired military officer; b. Ogden, Utah, Mar. 19, 1925; s. James and Lucile (Ballantyne) S.; m. Marian Horner, Sept. 17, 1951 (dec. 1995); 1 dau., Karen. BS, U.S. Mil. Acad., 1947; MA, Columbia U., 1953, PhD, 1967; postgrad., Georgetown U., 1958. Commd. 2d lt. USAF, 1947, advanced through grades to lt. gen., 1974; asst. prof. dept. social sci. U.S. Mil. Acad., 1953-57; asst. air attache Am. Embassy, Belgrade, Yugoslavia, 1959-61; assoc. prof. dept. polit. sci. USAF Acad., Colorado Springs, Colo., 1962-63, prof., head dept., 1963-64; mem. staff long range planning div. Office Dep. Chief Staff Plans and Ops., Washington, 1964-67; assigned Nat. War Coll., 1967-68; staff asst. Western Hemisphere region Office Asst. Sec. Def. Internat. Security Affairs, Washington, 1968-69; dep. asst. dir. plans for nat. security matters office Dep. Chief Staff Plans and Ops., Washington, 1969-70; spl. asst. to dir. Joint Staff, Joint Chiefs of Staff, Washington, 1970-71; mil. asst. to the Pres. The White House, Washington, 1972-73; dep. asst. to the Pres. for nat.

security affairs NSC, Washington, 1973-75, asst. to the Pres. for nat. security affairs, 1975-77, 1989-93; mem. Pres.'s Gen. Adv. Com. on Arms Control, Washington, 1977-80; vice chmn. Kissinger Associates., Inc., Washington, 1982-89; pres. Forum for Internat. Policy, Washington, 1993—. Bd. dirs. Nat. Bank Washington, Qualcomm, Inc., Am. Coun. on Germany; chmn. Pres.'s Commn. on Strategic Forces; mem. Pres.'s Commn. on Def. Mgmt., Pres. Spl. Rev. Bd. on Iran/Contra Affair; pres. The Scowcroft Group, 1994—. Co-author (with George H.W. Bush): A World Transformed, 1998; co-author: (with Zbigniew Brzezinski & David Ignatius) America and the World: Conversations on the Future of American Foreign Policy, 2008. Bd. dirs. Atlantic Coun. U.S., 1977—; bd. visitors U.S. Air Force Air U., 1977-79; bd. dirs. Internat. Rep. Inst., 1994—; chmn. Pres. Fgn. Intelligence Adv. Bd., 2000-05; chmn. Am.-Turkish Coun., 2000—, Eisenhower Inst., 2004-05; mem. adv. bd. Georgetown Ctr. for Strategic and Internat. Studies; pres. George Bush Presdl. Libr. Foun.; bd. dirs. Gerald R. Ford Found., Nat. Def. U.; mem. Internat. Rep. Inst. Decorated D.S.M. with two oak leaf clusters, Legion of Merit with oak leaf cluster, Air Force Commendation medal, D.S.M. Dept. Def., Nat. Security medal; recipient Medal of Freedom, 1991; named Hon. Knight Brit. Empire, 1993. Mem. Coun. Fgn. Rels. (bd. dirs.), UN Assn. U.S. (vice chmn.), Am. Polit. Sci. Assn., Acad. Polit. Sci. Mem. Ch. Jesus Christ of Latter-day Saints. Office: The Scowcroft Group # 500 900 17th St NW Ste 500 Washington DC 20006-2507

SCRABECK, JON GILMEN, retired dental educator; b. Rochester, Minn., Dec. 6, 1938; s. Clarence and Nancy Alma (Brown) S.; m. DeAnn Louise Jacks, June 16, 1962; children: Joan Louise, Erik Jon. Student, Contra Costa Coll., San Pablo, Calif., 1964-66, U. Calif., Berkeley, 1966-67; DDS, UCLA, 1971; MA in Edn., U. Colo., 1985. Pvt. practice, Santa Rosa, Calif., 1971-78; sr. instr. U. Colo. Sch. Dentistry, Denver, 1978-79, asst. prof., 1980-86, dir. patient care, 1979-80, acting dir. clin. affairs, 1980-81, acting assoc. dean, acting div. chmn., 1984-85; dept. chmn. Marquette U. Sch. Dentistry, Milw., 1986-90, assoc. prof., 1986—2003, assoc. prof. tenure, 1989, curricular head, 1990—2003; ret., 2003. Cons. Dental Student mag.,1983-86, Colo. Bd. Dentistry, Denver, 1985-86, Dentist mag., 1986-90, VA, Milw., 1987-90. Editor Jour. Colo. Dental Assn., 1980-86; contbr. articles and abstracts to dental jours. Mem. vol. staff Morey Dental Clinic, Denver, 1982-85, Health Fair, Denver, 1983-85; ofcl. judge S.E. Wis. Sci. Fair, Milw., 1988—. Fellow Internat. Coll. Dentists, Acad. Dental Materials, Am. Coll. Dentists, Pierre Fauchard Acad.; mem. ADA (coun. on journalism 1984-86, coun. on dental rsch. 1986-88, manuscript reviewer 1988—), Acad. Operative Dentistry, Wis. Dental Assn. (assoc. editor Jour. 1987—), Omicron Kappa Upsilon, Alpha Gamma Sigma. Roman Catholic. Avocations: foreign and domestic travel, photography, boating, fishing, water-skiing. Home: 2895 W Long Cir Unit E Littleton CO 80120 E-mail: jgscrabeck@aol.com.

SCRANTON, GEORGE ALFRED, theater educator; b. Pasco, Wash., Oct. 25, 1944; m. Claire Elaine Markham; children: Trevor Markham, Lindsey Melia Scranton Astrup. Diploma, Briercrest Bible Inst., Caronport, Saskatchewan, 1965; BA in Bibl. Lit. & Speech, Drama, Seattle Pacific Coll., 1968, MA in Bibl. Lit., 1971; MA in Theatre History & Criticism, U. Wash., Seattle, 1975; PhD, Grad. Theol. Union, Berkeley, Calif., 1994. Ordination in specialized ministry Evang. Covenant Ch., 2004. Prof. theatre Seattle Pacific U., 1970—. Dir.(actor, author): (numerous plays & prodns.). Chair worship & prayer 1st Covenant Ch., Seattle, 2006—08; chair New Life Puppeteers, Auburn, Wash., 1979—2008; chair bd. Taproot Theatre Co., Seattle, 2009—. Mem.: Assn. Theatre Higher Edn. (Chgo.) (chair, religion & theatre focus group 1996—2002). Office: Seattle Pacific Univ 3307 3rd Ave W Seattle WA 98119

SCRANTON, PIERCE EDWARD, orthopedist, department chairman; m. Elaine Diane Donner, June 9, 1972; children: Russell, pierce III. PhD in Sci. (hon.), Kenyon Coll., Gambier, Ohio, 1968; MD, U. Cin. Med. Sch., 1972. Diplomate Am. Bd. Orthop. Surgery, Chgo., 1980. Asst. prof., Dept. Orthop. U. Pitts., 1977—79; pres. NFL Physicians Soc., NY, 1996—97, Am. Orthop. Foot & Ankle Soc., Chgo., 2001—02, founder & chmn., outreach & edn. found., 2002—05; chmn. Nat. Orthop. Ednl. Soc., Cin., 2003—08. Author: (novel) Death on the Learning Curve. Bd. mem. Prosthetic Outreach Found., Seattle, 2002—08. Named one of Humanitarian of Year, Kenyon Coll, 2008; finalist USA Book News award, 2008. Avocations: fly fishing, skiing, golf. Office: Orthop Internat Ltd 12333 NE 130th Ln #400 Kirkland WA 98034

SCRIBNER, CHARLES, III, art historian, writer; b. Washington, May 24, 1951; s. Charles and Joan (Sunderland) S.; m. Ritchie Harrison Markoe, Aug. 4, 1979; children: Charles IV, Christopher Markoe. AB, Princeton U., 1973, MFA, 1975, PhD, 1977. Editor Charles Scribner's Sons, NYC, 1975—2004, dir. subs. rights, 1978-82, pub. paperback divsn., 1982-83, exec. v.p., 1983-84; v.p. Macmillan Pub. Co., NYC, 1984-94. Instr. dept. art and archaeology Princeton U., 1976-77; mem. adv. coun. Princeton U. Libr., 1981-90; mem. adv. coun. dept. art and archaeology Princeton U., 1983-91, 99-2003, 05-09; trustee Princeton U. Press, 1984-90, Homeland Found., 1987—; bd. advisors Wethersfield Inst., 1985—; bd. dirs. Met. Opera Guild, 1990-92; dir. Cath. Edn. Inst., 2004-07. Author: The Triumph of the Eucharist-Tapestries by Rubens, 1982, Rubens, 1989, Bernini, 1991, The Shadow of God, 2006. Trustee St. Paul's Sch., Concord, NH, 1994-2006. Mem. Assn. Princeton U. Press, NYC Racquet and Tennis Club, Ivy Club (Princeton). Roman Catholic. Office: 155 E 72d St #5D New York NY 10021-4371 Office Phone: 917-623-0890. E-mail: cscribner3@yahoo.com.

SCRIGGINS, LARRY PALMER, lawyer, director; b. Englewood, NJ, Nov. 27, 1936; s. Thomas Dalby and M. Patricia (Fowler) S.; m. Victoria Jackola, Feb. 17, 1979; children: Elizabeth J., Thomas P. AB, Middlebury Coll., 1958; JD, U. Chgo., 1961. Bar: Md. 1962. Law clk. to chief judge Md. Ct. Appeals, 1962; assoc. Piper & Marbury, LLP, Balt., 1962-69, ptnr., 1969-98, vice chmn., 1988-93, mem. exec. com., CFO, 1993-98; sr. counsel Piper Rudnick, LLP, Balt., 1999-2001; ptnr. emeritus DLA Piper US LLP, Balt., 2001—. Mem. legal adv. com. N.Y. Stock Exch., 1992-96; bd. dirs. USF & G Corp., 1979-98, Center Stage Assocs., 1979-89, Balt. Choral Arts Soc., 1979-96, Balt. Conv. Bur., 1982-95, YMCA of Greater Balt., 1987-94, Fund for Ednl. Excellence, 1990-98, chmn. bd. trustees, 1993-98; bd. dirs. Nat. Aquarium in Balt., bd. govs. 1987-93; bd. dirs. Balt. Symphony Orchestra, 1996-2001. Contbr. articles to profl. jours. Fellow: Am. Bar Found.; mem.: ABA (sect. on bus. law coun. 1972—76, chmn. law and acctg. com. 1985—88, vice chair and editor-in-chief The Bus. Lawyer 1989—90, chair 1991—92, chmn. com. corp. laws 1996—2000, chmn. ad hoc com. on ethics 2000 1999—2002, sr. advisor 2000—), AICPA (planning com. 1989—92), Fin. Acctg. Stds. Bd., Task Force in Fin. Instruments, Am. Law Inst., Am. Judicature Soc., Md. Bar Assn. (coun. 1976—78, chmn. 1977—78, mem. com. on corp. laws 1981—84). Office: DLA Piper US LLP 6225 Smith Ave Baltimore MD 21209-3600 Office Phone: 410-580-4252. Office Fax: 410-580-3001. Business E-Mail: larry.scriggins@dlapiper.com.

SCRIMGEOUR, ANDREW DAVID, library director; b. Medicine Hat, Alberta, Can., Aug. 8, 1945; s. David Henry and Sylvia Irene Scrimgeour; m. Dorothy Jean Hancock, June 15, 1968; children: Drew Hancock, Meghan Brewer. BA, Nyack Coll., NY, 1967; MDiv, Princeton Theol. Sem., NJ, 1971; MTh, Princeton U., NJ, 1975; MLS, Rutgers U., New Brunswick, NJ, 1976; PhD, Drexel U., Phila., 1999. Rsch. asst. Princeton Theol. Sem., 1974—76; libr. dir. Iliff Sch. Theology, Denver, 1980—84, cons., 1984—85; dir. libr. devel. Boston Theol. Inst., Cambridge, Mass., 1976—80; dean librs. Regis U., Denver, 1984—2000, 1984—2000, assoc. v.p. academic affairs, 1992—94; dean librs. Drew U., Madison, NJ, 2000—. Archivist Soc. Bibl. Lit., Atlanta, 1982—; cons. Am. Coun. Learned Socs., Washington, 1987; chair Conf. SJ Coll. and U. Libr. Dirs., 1987—89; cons. Rsch. Librs. Group, Washingtnon, 1988; exec. com. Colo. Alliance Rsch. Librs., Denver, 1992—2000; bd. mem. Scholars Press, Atlanta, 1993—95; cons. Boston U., 1993—94; exec. com. Virtual Academic Libr. Environment, NJ, 2000—; bd. mem. Westar Inst., Santa Rosa, Calif., 2005—. Author: (book) Just Call Me Bob: The Wit and Wisdom of Robert W. Funk, Guide to Research Funding in Religious Studies. Sec. Jacob Landau Inst., Roosevelt, NJ. Travel grant, Nat. Endowment Humanities, 1985, Am. Coun. Learned Socs., 1988—90, Rsch. grant, Kasper Found., 2008. Mem.: Assn. Coll. & Rsch. Librs., Am. Acad. Religion (Atlanta) (archivist 1982—2000), Soc. Bibl. Lit., Colo. Calligraphers Guild (hon.). Episcopalian. Home: 1 High View Dr High Bridge NJ 08829 Office: Drew Univ 36 Madison Ave Madison NJ 07940 Office Fax: 973-408-3770. Business E-Mail: ascrimge@ddrew.edu.

SCRIMGEOUR, GARY JAMES, writer, educator; b. Auckland, New Zealand, Jan. 15, 1934; came to U.S., 1957; s. Colin Graham and Caroline Lenna (Hardie) S. BA with honors, U. Sydney, Australia, 1954; MA in English, Wash. U., 1959; PhD, Princeton U., 1968. Asst. personnel officer Dexion Ltd., London, 1956-57; mem. faculty dept. English Fla. U., Gainesville, 1959-61, Rutgers U., New Brunswick, NJ, 1963-64, Ind. U., Bloomington, 1964-69, Nat. Jud. Coll., 1974—94; editor, writer Benjamin Blom, Inc., NYC, 1969-70; chief social sys. divsn. and head editl. office Sch. Pub. and Environ. Affairs, Ind. U., 1970-74; dir. Profl. Studies Assocs., Bloomington, 1973—; editor Coll. Engring. U. Nev.-Reno, 1992-94, sr. editor Coll. Bus. Adminstrn., 1994—2001; ind. editor for sci./engring. faculty, 2001—. Faculty coord. Nat. Jud. Coll., 1973-93; cons. for rsch. in alcoholism, ct. systems, hwy. safety and design of seminars to various govt. agys., schs. and social orgns., 1970—. Author: A Woman of Her Times, 1982, The Garden Inspector, 1993, The Quilting Women, 1995; contbr. numerous manuals on ct. sys. and alcohol safety to profl. publs. and articles on lit. criticism to lit. jours. Jane E. Procter fellow Princeton U., 1968. Office: 369 Bret Harte Ave Reno NV 89509 Office Phone: 775-786-1442. Business E-Mail: gscrim@unr.nevada.edu.

SCRIMSHAW, NEVIN STEWART, physician, nutritionist, educator; b. Jan. 20, 1918; m. Mary Ware Goodrich, 1941; 5 children. BA with honors, Ohio Wesleyan U., 1938; MA in Biology, Harvard U., 1939, PhD in Physiology, 1941, MPH, 1959; MD with honors, U. Rochester, 1945. Intern Gorgas Hosp., 1945-46; Rockefeller postdoctoral fellow U. Rochester, NY, 1946—47, Merck NRC fellow NY, 1947—49; asst. resident in ob-gyn. Strong Meml. Hosp., Genesee Hosp., NY, 1948—49; dir. Inst. Nutrition C.Am. and Panama, Guatemala, 1949—61, cons. dir., 1961—65, cons., 1965—. Cons. nutrition Pan-Am. San Bur. WHO, 1948—49, regional advisor on nutrition, 1949—53; dir. Clin. Rsch. Ctr. MIT, 1962—66, 1979—83, dir. internat. food and nutrition program, 1976—88, prof. human nutrition, 1961—76, head dept. nutrition and food sci., 1961—79, inst. prof., 1976—87, emeritus, 1988—; vis. prof. Columbia U., NYC, 1976—88, vis. lectr., 1961—66, Harvard U., 1968—85; adj. prof. Tufts U.; mem. govt. adv. com. NIH; chmn. internat. com. NRC; dir. devel. studies divsn. UN U., 1985—86, food nutrition program, 1975—97, sr. advisor, 1998—; mem. adv. com. WHO, Nutrition Found., others. Editor (with others): Amino Acid Fortification of Protein Foods, 1971, Nutrition, National Development and Planning, 1973, The Economics, Marketing and Technology of Fish Protein Concentrate, 1974, Development: Significance and Potential for the Tropics, 1976, Single-Cell Protein: Safety for Animal and Human Feeding, 1979, Nutrition Policy Implementation: Issues and Experience, 1983, Diarrhea and Malnutrition: Interactions, Mechanisms and Interventions, 1983, Chronic Energy Deficiency, 1987, Acceptability of Milk and Milk Products in Populations with Lactose Intolerance, 1988, Nutrition in the Elderly, 1989, Activity, Energy Expenditure and Energy Requirements of Infants and Children, 1990, RAP: Rapid Assessment Procedures: Qualitative Methodologies for Planning and Evaluation of Health Related Programs, 1992, Protein-energy Interactions, 1992, Community-based Longitudinal Nutrition and Health Studies: Classical Examples from Guatemala, Haiti, and Mexico, 1995, The Effects of Improved Nutrition in Early Childhood: The Institute of Nutrition of Central American and Panama Follow-up Study, 1995, The Nutrition and Health Transition of Democratic Costa Rica, 1995, Energy and Protein Requirements, 1996, Causes and Consequences of Intrauterine Growth Retardation, 2000; contbr. articles to profl. jours. Trustee Rockefeller Found., 1971—83, Pan-Am. Health and Edn. Found., 1986—92; pres. Internat. Nutrition Found. for Developing Countries, 1982—. Recipient Osborne and Mendal award, 1960, Internat. award, Inst. Food Technologists, 1969, medal of honor, Fundacion F. Cuenca Villoro, Spain, 1978, Bristol-Myers prize, 1988, Alan Shawn Feinstein award, 1991, World Food prize, 1991, Kellogg award in internat. nutrition, 2002, Lifetime Achievement award, UN, 2004. Fellow: APHA (v.p. 1978, award of excellence in promoting and protecting health of people 1974), AAAS, Am. Soc. Clin. Nutrition, Royal Soc. Health, Am. Soc. Nutritional Scis.; mem.: NAS (chair applied biol. sect. 1973—76, 1988—91), Nat. Inst. Medicine, others, Internat. Epidemiol. Assn., Internat. Union Nutritional Scis. (pres. 1978—81), Am. Epidemiol. Soc., Am. Physiol. Soc., Mass. Med. Soc., New Eng. Pub. Health Assn., Mass. Pub. Health Assn., Am. Bd. Nutrition, Am. Coll. Preventive Medicine, Am. Coll. Nutrition, Am. Acad. Arts and Scis., Inst. Medicine NAS. Home and Office: Sandwich Mountain Farm 115 Sandwich Notch Rd PO Box 330 Campton NH 03223-0330 Office Phone: 603-726-4200. Office Fax: 603-726-4614. Business E-Mail: nscrimshaw@inffoundation.org.

SCRIPA, ROSALIA, engineering educator, researcher; b. NYC, July 1, 1948; d. Rosario and Bridget Nastasi; m. Louis Scripa. BS in Ceramic Engring., Alfred U., NY, 1970; MS in Ceramic Engring., Pa. State U., State Coll., 1972; MS in Materials Sci. Engring., U. Fla., Gainesville, 1974, PhD in Materials Sci. and Engring., 1976. Lic. in profl. engring., State Ala. Bd. Licensure, 1984. Prof. materials sci. and engring. U. Ala., Sch. Engring., Birmingham, 1976—, assoc. dean, 1977—78, adj. prof. biomed. engring., 1984—, assoc. dean academic and student affairs, 1996—2000, adj. prof. materials and metall. engring. Tuscaloosa, 1986—; assoc. provost undergrad. programs U. Ala., Provost Office, 2000—01, assoc. provost undergrad. programs and faculty affairs, 2001—05, assoc. provost faculty devel. and faculty affairs, 2005—06; summer faculty fellow NASA/Marshall Space Flight Ctr., Huntsville, Ala., 1985—86; program scientist materials sci. NASA, Microgravity Sci. and Applications Divsn., Washington, 1995—96. Mem. proposal rev. panels NSF, Washington, 1978—; mem. US symposium com. Third Internat. Symposium on Ceramic Materials and Components for Engines, Oak Ridge, Tenn., 1987—88; chair and mem. NCAA, Indpls., 1993—97, mem. postgrad. scholarship com., 1996—2001; mem. space studies bd. com. microgravity NRC, Washington, 1996—2000; chair and mem. several proposal rev. panels NASA, NSF, 1997—2001. Contbr. chapters to books, articles to profl. publs. Vol. ARC Disaster Relief, Birmingham, 2007—08. Recipient Disting. Engring. Educator award, Nat. Soc. Women Engrs., 1986, Presdl. award, U. Ala. Pres., 1992, Enhancement Tech. Awareness award, Materials Info. Soc., 1993, Outstanding Achievement award, U. Fla., 1997, Outstanding Svc. award, NRC Space Studies Bd., 1998, Success award, Golden Key, 2000, Lifetime Achievement award, World Congress Arts, Scis. and Comm., 2005, U. Ala. Alumni Assn., 2007, Disting. Alumni award, Dept. Materials Sci. & Engring., U. Fla., Gainesville, 2009; named Woman of Yr., Am. Biog. Soc., 1999, Outstanding Woman, Bd. Internat. Rsch., 2001; grant, NSF, 1983, NASA/Marshall Space Flight Ctr., 1985—93, Steel Founder's Soc. America, 1986—88, NASA, 1994—2006, numerous grants. Mem.: AAAS, Am. Ceramic Soc., Soc. Women Engrs., Am. Soc. Engring. Edn. (chair numerous nat. and internat. profl. conf. tech. sessions 1976—, mem. minorities in engring. com. 1977—78, mem. new engring. educator's com. 1977—81, mem. campus liason bd. 1980—81), Am. Assn. Crystal Growth (chair numerous nat. and internat. profl. conf. tech. sessions 1976, chair, awards com. 1996—97, exec. bd. mem. 1996—, treas. 2002—03, editor peer reviewed procs., jour. crystal growth), Am. Soc. Crystal Growth (bd. mem. 2000—), Ala. Soc. Profl. Engrs., Materials Rsch. Soc., Tau Beta Pi (Prof. of Yr. 1982), Sigma Xi, Omicron Delta Kappa. Avocations: reading, travel. Office: Univ Ala Birmingham 1075 10th St S Birmingham AL 35294 Office Fax: 205-934-8485. Business E-Mail: rscripa@uab.edu.

SCRIPPS, DOUGLAS JERRY, musician, educator, conductor; b. Grand Rapids, Mich., Aug. 25, 1942; s. Kenneth Witvoet and Marguerite F. (Rottier) Scripps; m. Betty Ann Broersma Porter, July 24, 1963 (div. Aug. 1974); children: Elisabeth Ann Scripps Blue, Theodore Jon; m. Merilee Evelyn Collins, Apr. 5, 1975; children: Daniel Collins, Taylor Douglas, Adam Rottier. Student, Eastman Sch. Music, 1961-62; BA, Calvin Coll., 1965; student, U. Music and Dramatic Art, Vienna, 1965—66; MM, U. Mich., 1970. Prin. trumpet Grand Rapids Symphony Orch., 1961—65, assoc. conductor, 1976—85; dir. music Grand Rapids CC, 1967—78; conductor Lake St. Clair Symphony, Detroit, 1970—72, Alma (Mich.) Symphony Orch., 1985—2002; music dir. Grand Rapids Ballet, 1979—99; asst. prof. music Ctrl. Mich. U., Mt. Pleasant, 1981—84; prof. music, dept. chair Alma Coll., 1985—2002, prof. emeritus, 2003—. Guest condr. Interlochen Ctr. Arts, Joffrey Balley, Bay View Music Festival, Blue Lake Fine Arts Camp, Czech Music Camp; vis. prof. Grand Valley State U., Calvin Coll., 1977—81; condr. Ctrl. European Youth Symphony Orch., 2004—05. Recipient Am. Heritage Assn. study abroad lectr., Vienna, 1999. Avocations: reading, travel, sailing. Home: PO Box 476 Northport MI 49670-0476 Business E-Mail: scripps@alma.edu.

SCRIVEN, MARY STENSON, federal judge; b. Atlanta, 1962; d. Marshall and Mary Stenson. BA, Duke U., Durham, NC, 1983; JD, Fla. State U. Coll. Law, 1987. Bar: Fla. 1987. Assoc. atty. Carlton Fields, PA, Fla., 1987—95, shareholder Fla., 1995—97; magistrate judge US Dist. Ct. (mid. dist.) Fla., 1997—2008, judge, 2008—. Assoc. prof. Stetson U. Coll. Law, Gulfport, Fla., 1996—97. Office: US Courthouse Orlando Divsn 401 W Ctrl Blvd Ste 1200 Orlando FL 32801 Office Phone: 407-835-3840.*

SCRIVENER, LOIS DOING, retired principal, educator; b. Mineola, NY, Oct. 10, 1945; d. Park Atkinson and Mary Houser Doing; m. James W. Scrivener, Jan. 21, 1967; children: Patricia, James Jr., Andrew. BA in English and Edn., St. Bonaventure U., 1967; MA in Theology, Immaculate Conception, 1982; EdS in Ednl. Leadership, U. Ctrl. Fla., 1996; MS in Brain Rsch., Nova Southeastern U., 2006. Cert. tchr. N.Y., tchr. English, ednl. leadership Fla. Substitute tchr. Nassau County, NY, 1970—82; tchr. St. Edward the Confessor, Syosset, NY, 1982—84; tchr., part-time adminstr. Holy Child, Old Westbury, NY, 1984—89; tchr. theology Ctrl. Cath. H.S., Melbourne, Fla., 1989—92; prin. Holy Name of Jesus, Indiatlantic, Fla., 1992—. Adj. prof. Barry U., Miami, Fla., 2000—04; mem. salary scale com. Brevard County Cath. Sch., 1993—2004. Regent NSDAR, Satellite Beach, Fla., 1974—2006; youth min. St. William the Abbot, Seaford, NY, 1975—88. Recipient St. Piux X CCD award, 1988, Schs. of Tomorrow Innovations in Tech. award, Today's Cath. Tchr., 1999, Outstanding Sch. Bd. award, NABE, 2000; named Catechist Prin. of Yr., Diocese Orlando, 1996, Nat. Disting. Prin., U.S. Dept. Edn., 2001, Blue Ribbon Sch. Excellence, 2001, U.S. Dept. Edn. No Child Left Behind, 2003. Mem.: Nat. Cath. Edn. Assn. (Disting. Home and Sch. award 2000, Disting. Prin. 2001, Oustanding Sch. Bd. award 2001). Home: 421 Mallard Ln Indialantic FL 32903

SCRIVEN-YOUNG, DAVID JOSEPH, lawyer; b. Berwyn, Ill., Nov. 17, 1978; s. David Michael and Marie Elizabeth Young; m. Katherine Lynn Scriven, July 29, 2000; children: Henry Francis, Charles Laurence. BA, Marquette U., Milw., 2000; JD, DePaul U., Chgo., 2003. Bar: Ill. 2003, US Dist. Ct. (no. dist.) Ill. 2003. Atty. Jenner & Block LLP, Chgo., 2003—05, McDermott Will & Emery LLP, 2005—. Recipient Gt. Lakes Stewardship award Adv. of Yr., Lake Mich. Fedn., 2005. Mem.: ABA (young lawyers divsn. chair law practice mgmt. com. 2005—06, young lawyers divsn. chair environment, energy, and resources law com. 2006—07, young lawyers divsn. liasion to standing com. environ. law 2006—). Office: McDermott Will & Emery LLP 227 West Monroe St Chicago IL 60606-5096 Office Fax: 312-984-7700. Business E-Mail: dscriven-young@mwe.com.

SCRIVER, CHARLES ROBERT, medical researcher, human geneticist, retired medical educator; b. Montreal, Que., Can., Nov. 7, 1930; s. Walter deM. and Jessie (Boyd) S.; m. E.K. Peirce, Sept. 8, 1956; children: Dorothy, Peter, Julie, Paul. BA cum laude, McGill U., Montreal, 1951, MDCM cum laude, 1955; DSc (hon.), U. Man., 1992, U. Glasgow, 1993, U. Montreal, 1993, Utrecht U., 1999, U. B.C., 2002, U. We. Ont., 2007, McGill U., 2007. Intern Royal Victoria Hosp., Montreal, 1955-56; resident Royal Victoria and Montreal Children's Hosps., 1956-57, Children's Med. Ctr., Boston, 1957-58; McLaughlin travelling fellow Univ. Coll., London, 1958-60; chief resident pediat. Montreal Children's Hosp., 1960-61; asst. prof. pediat. McGill U., 1961, prof. biology Faculty of Sci., prof. pediat. Faculty of Medicine, 1969—, Alva prof. human genetics, 1994—2002, prof. emeritus, 2002—. Mem. med. adv. bd. Howard Hughes Med. Inst., 1981-88; dir. Med. Rsch. Coun. Group in Genetics, 1972-94; assoc. dir. Can. Genetic Diseases Network, 1989-98. Co-author: Amino Acid Metabolism and Its Disorders, 1973, Garrod's Inborn Factors in Disease, 1989; sr. online editor Metabolic and Molecular Bases Inherited Disease, 1986—2008; sr. editor emeritus, 2008-, contbr. more than 600 rsch. publs. in field. Decorated Order of Can., Que., Mont.; recipient Wood Gold medal, McGill U., 1955, Gairdner Internat. award, Gairdner Found., 1979, Prix Michel-Sarrazin, Club de Rech Clin du Que., 1988, Ross award, Can. Pediatric Soc., 1990, Award of Excellence, Genet Soc. Can., 1992, Prix d'Excellence, Inst. Rsch. Clin. de Montreal, 1993, Prix du Quebec, Wilder Penfield, 1995, Lifetime Achievement award, Montreal Children's Hosp., 1995, Medal of Merit, Can. Med. Assn., 1996, Lifetime Achievement award, March of Dimes Birth Defects Found., 1997, Querci Found. prize, Italy, 2001, Founders award, Can. Coll. Med. Geneticist, 2003; named Royal Coll. lectr., 1992, Disting. Scientist, Med. Rsch. Coun., 1995—; named to Can. Med. Hall of Fame, 2001, Can. Sci. Engring. Hall of Fame, 2001; Markle scholar, 1962—67. Fellow: AAAS, Royal Soc. London (Can. Rutherford lectr. 1983), Royal Soc. Can. (McLaughlin medal 1981), Royal Coll. Physicians of Ireland (hon.), Am. Coll. Med. Genetics (hon.); mem.: Am. Acad. Pediat. (Mead Johnson award for rsch. in pediat. 1968), Soc. Francaise de Pediat., Brit. Pediat. Assn. (50th Anniversary lectr. 1978), Assn. Am. Physicians, Am. Soc. Clin. Investigation, Am. Pediat. Soc. (pres. 1994—95), Am. Soc. Human Genetics (dir. 1971—74, pres. 1986—87, William Allan award 1978, Award of Excellence in Human Genetics Edn. 2001), Soc. Pediat. Rsch. (pres. 1975—76), Can. Soc. Clin. Investigation (pres. 1974—75, G. Malcolm Brown Meml. award 1979, Henry Friesen award 2001). Office: McGill Univ-Montreal Childrens Hosp Rsch Inst 2300 Tupper St Montreal PQ Canada H3H 1P3 Business E-Mail: charles.scriver@mcgill.ca.

SCRIVNER, ELLEN M., psychologist; d. John P. O'Shea and Dorothy Mary O'Shea-Hanley; m. Peter C. Scrivner, Aug. 25, 1962; children: Anne Collins (Scrivner) Kuban, Thomas C. BS, St. Louis U., 1961, MS, 1963; PhD in Psychology, Cath. U. Am., 1986. Lic. psychologist Bd. of Examiners, Md. Police psychologist, Fairfax County, Va., Prince Georges County, Md.; dep. dir. COPS Office, U.S. Dept. of Justice, Washington, 2000—02; sr. advisor FBI Office Law Enforcement Co-ords., 2002—04; dep. supt. bur. of adminstrv. svcs. Chgo. Police Dept., 2004—07; dir. John Jay Coll. Criminal Justice Leadership Acad., 2007—. Pres. Pub. Safety Innovations, Washington, 2003—04; vis. fellow Nat. Inst. Justice, U.S. Dept. Justice. Author: Law Enforcement Families: Issues and Answers, 1994, Police Psychology Into The 21st Century, 1995. Mem. adv. bd. Local Initiatives Support Corp., NYC, 2003—05. Recipient Women of Courage and Vision award, U.S. Dept. of Justice, 2001, Lifetime Achievement award, 2000. Mem.: APA (life; divsn. pres. 1991—92, Disting. Svc. award 1990). Achievements include research in excessive force/violence, community policing, police psychology. Home: 700 New Hampshire Ave NW Washington DC 20037 Personal E-mail: ellenscrivner284@msn.com. Business E-Mail: escrivner@jjay.cuny.edu.

SCROGGS, LARRY KENNETH, lawyer, state legislator; b. Beebe, Ark., Oct. 8, 1941; s. Kenneth Chalmers and Mildred Lorene (McDonald) S.; m. Mary Patricia Rushing, Aug. 25, 1967; children: Larry Kenneth Jr., James Kevin, Michael Kyle. BA, Harding U., 1963; JD, Vanderbilt U., 1971. Bar: Tenn. 1971, U.S. Dist. Ct. (we. dist.) Tenn. 1971, U.S. Ct. Appeals (8th cir.) 1982, U.S. Ct. Appeals (6th cir.) 1989, U.S. Supreme Ct. 1981. Assoc. Law Firm of Leo Bearman, Memphis, 1971-72, Holt, Batchelor, Spicer, Memphis, 1972-76, ptnr., 1976-80, Less & Scroggs, Memphis, 1980-92; pvt. practice, Germantown, Tenn., 1992-96; ptnr. Scroggs & Rogers, Collierville, Tenn., 1997—2003, Burch, Porter & Johnson, Memphis, 2003—06; chief adminstrv. officer, chief counsel Juvenile Ct. Memphis and Shelby County, 2006—. Mcpl. ct. judge City of Germantown, 1980-86; atty. for County Trustee, Shelby County, Memphis, 1990—06. Mem. Tenn. Ho. Reps., Nashville, 1996-2002; Lt. U.S. Navy, 1964-67, Vietnam. Mem. ABA, Tenn. Bar Assn., Memphis Bar Assn. (bd. dirs. 1990-91). Republican. Mem. Ch. of Christ. Avocations: photography, boating, tennis. Office: Juvenile Ct Memphis and Shelby County 616 Adams Ave Memphis TN 38105 Office Phone: 901-405-8518. Business E-Mail: Larry.Scroggs@shelbycountytn.gov.

SCRUGGS, ELAINE M., Mayor, Glendale, Arizona; m. Larry Scruggs; 1 child, Jennifer. Former mgmt. specialist; elected mem. Glendale City Coun., Ariz., 1990-93; mayor City of Glendale, Ariz., 1994—. Past chmn. Maricopa Assn. Govts., past chmn. regional coun.; chmn. Regional Pub. Transp. Authority, Maricopa Assn. Govt. Regional Aviation Systems policy com., Ariz. Mcpl. Tax Code Commn.; chair bd. dirs. Valley Metro Regional Pub. Transportation Authority; bd. dirs., past chmn. Westmarc. Dir. Glendale Leadership Program, 1984-89; mem. Ariz. Coalition for Tomorrow, Ariz. Women in Mcpl. Govt.; active mem. youth adv. commn., Mayor's Alliance Against Drugs and Gangs; adv. bd. YWCA. Recipient Tribute to Women's Pub. Sector Leadership award, YWCA Advisory Board, 2001; named Top 100, Ariz. Woman Mag., 1998, Woman of Yr., 2003. Mem. Glendale C. of C., Ariz. Mcpl. Water Users Assn. (past chair). Office: Office Mayor 5850 W Glendale Ave Glendale AZ 85301-2563*

SCRUGGS, RICHARD F. (DICKIE SCRUGGS), lawyer; b. Brookhaven, Miss., May 17, 1946; m. Diane Scruggs. BA, U. Miss., 1969, JD, 1976. Bar: Miss. 1977, US Dist. Ct., So. and No. Dist. Miss., US Dist. Ct., So. Dist. Alaska, US Ct. Appeals, Fifth Circuit. Note editor Miss. Law Jour., 1975—76; editor-in-chief Miss. Lawyer, 1976; ptnr. Scruggs, Millette, Bozeman & Dent, P.A., Scruggs Law Firm, P.A. Mem. Big Brothers Big Sisters Miss. Carrier pilot USN, 1969—74. Named one of 100 Most Influential Lawyers, Nat. Law Jour., 2006. Fellow: Internat. Acad. Trial Lawyers; mem.: Miss. Bar. Assn., Am. Bar Assn., ABA, Phi Delta Phi. Office: Scruggs Law Firm PO Box 1135 Oxford MS 38655-1135 Office Phone: 662-281-1212. Office Fax: 662-281-1312.

SCRUGGS, SAMUEL D., lawyer, chemicals executive; b. San Francisco, Sept. 6, 1959; BA, U. Utah, Salt Lake City, 1984; JD, Columbia U., NYC, 1987. Bar: NY 1989. Atty. LeBoef, Lamb, Greene & MacRae, NYC, 1987—89, Skadden, Arps, Slate, Meagher & Flom, NYC, 1989—95; v.p., assoc. gen. counsel, then v.p. corp. tax, then exec. v.p. legal tax & corp. devel. Huntsman Cos., 1995—2002, exec. v.p., corp. gen. counsel, mem. office of chmn., 2002—. Office: Huntsman Corp Legal Dept 500 Huntsman Way Salt Lake City UT 84108 Office Phone: 801-584-5700.

SCUDDAY, ROY GEORGE, lawyer; b. Odessa, Tex., Sept. 29, 1946; s. Roy Sheppard and Letitia Roselyn (Keith) Scudday; m. Linda R. Reed, Jan. 16, 1999; children: Roy Keith, John Andrew. BA in History, Rice U., 1968; JD, U. Tex., 1971; MA in History, SW Tex. U., 2001. Bar: Tex. 1971, Tex. (US Dist. Ct. (so. dist.)) 1979, Tex. (US Dist. Ct. (we. dist.)) 1980, (US Ct. Appeals (5th cir.)) 1980. Hearing examiner. Tex. Water Quality Bd., Austin, 1971—73; staff atty. Gulf Coast Waste Disposal Authority, Houston, 1973—79; ptnr. Fielder & Scudday, Lockhart, Tex., 1979—88; hearings atty., comptroller of pub. accounts, 1988—96; adminstrv. law judge, comptr., 1996. Home: 502 W Prairie Lea St Lockhart TX 78644-2623

SCUDDER, THAYER, anthropologist, educator; b. New Haven, Aug. 4, 1930; s. Townsend III and Virginia (Boody) S.; m. Mary Eliza Drinker, Aug. 26, 1950; children: Mary Eliza, Alice Thayer. Grad., Phillips Exeter Acad., 1948; AB, Harvard U., 1952, PhD, 1960; postgrad., Yale U., 1953-54, London Sch. Econs., 1960-61. Rsch. officer Rhodes-Livingstone Inst., No. Rhodesia, 1956-57, sr. rsch. officer, 1962-63; asst. prof. Am. U., Cairo, 1961-62; rsch. fellow Ctr. Middle East Studies, Harvard U., 1963-64; asst. prof. Calif. Inst. Tech., Pasadena, 1964-66, assoc. prof., 1966-69, prof. anthropology, 1969-2000, prof. emeritus, 2000—; dir. Inst. for Devel. Anthropology, Binghamton, NY, 1976—2002; commr. World Commn. on Dams, 1998-2000. Cons. UN Devel. Program, FAO, IBRD, WHO, Ford Found., Navajo Tribal Coun., AID, World Conservation Union, Lesotho Highlands Devel. Authority, South China Electric Power Joint Venture Corp., U.S. Nat. Rsch. Coun., Que.-Hydro, Environ. Def. Fund, Ministry of Energy & Mines, Lao People's Dem. Republic, Nature Conservancy Author: The Ecology of the Gwembe Tonga, 1962, The Future of Large Dams: Dealing with Social, Environmental, Institutional and Political Costs, 2005; co-author: Long-Term Field Research in Social Anthropology, 1979, Secondary Education and the Formation of an Elite: The Impact of Education on Gwembe District, Zambia, 1980, No Place to Go: The Impacts of Forced Relocation on Navajos, 1982, For Prayer and Profit: The Ritual, Economic and Social Importance of Beer in Gwembe District, Zambia, 1950-1982, 1988, The IUCN Review of the So. Okavango Integrated Water Development Project, 1993. Recipient (1st) Lucy Mair medal for applied anthropology, Royal Anthropol. Inst., 1998, John Phillips award, Phillips Exeter Acad, 2005; John Simon Guggenheim Meml. fellow, 1975. Mem. Am. Anthrop. Assn. (1st recipient Solon T. Kimball award for pub. and applied anthropology 1984, Edward J. Lehman award 1991), Soc. Applied Anthropology (Bronislaw Malinowski award 1999). Office: Calif Inst Tech # 228 77 Pasadena CA 91125-0001 Office Phone: 626-395-4207. Business E-Mail: tzs@hss.caltech.edu.

SCUDERI, ROB, professional hockey player; b. Syosset, NY, Dec. 30, 1978; s. Robert and Leslie Scuderi. Grad., Boston Coll., 2001. Defenseman Wilkes-Barre/Scranton Penguins (AHL), 2001—05, Pitts. Penguins, 2004, 2005—09, LA Kings, 2009—. Achievements include being a member of NCAA National Championship Team, Boston College, 2001; being a member of Stanley Cup Champion Pittsburgh Penguins, 2009. Office: LA Kings 1111 S Figueroa St, Ste 3100 Los Angeles CA 90015*

SCUDIERE, DEBRA HODGES, lawyer; b. Columbus, Ohio, Sept. 18, 1954; d. L.L. and Anita Lillian (Campbell) Hodges; m. William A. Scudiere, July 16, 1988; 1 child, Rachel Giovanna. BA magna cum laude, W.Va. U., 1976, JD, 1982. Bar: W.Va. 1982, U.S. Dist. Ct. (no. and so. dists.) W.Va. 1982, U.S. Supreme Ct. 1989. With Furbee, Amos, Webb & Critchfield, Morgantown, W.Va., 1982—2001; atty. Kay Casto & Chaney, PLLC, Morgantown, W.Va., 2001—. Mem. W.Va. Law Rev., 1981-82; adj. lectr. trial advocacy W.Va. U., Morgantown, 1991—. Staff mem. W.Va. Law Rev., 1981-82; rsch. editor Jour. Coll. and Univ. Law, 1981-82. Pres., chmn. bd. dirs. North Cen. W.Va. Legal Aid Soc., Morgantown, 1989-95; bd. dirs. W.Va. Sr. Legal Aid, Inc., 1999—. Mem. Def. Rsch. Inst., Def. Trial Counsel W.Va., Marion County Bar Assn., Monongalia County Bar Assn., W.Va. Bar Assn., W.Va. State Bar (mem. bd. govs., v.p., pres.-elect 2004-05, pres. 2005-06), So. Conf. Bar Pres. (pres. 2005-06), Nat. Conf. Bar Pres., Order of Barrister, Pi Delta Phi, Phi Delta Phi. Mem. Lds Ch. Office: 215 Don Knotts Blvd Ste 310 Morgantown WV 26501 Office Phone: 304-296-1100.

SCULCO, THOMAS PETER, surgeon; b. NYC, Feb. 20, 1944; s. Alfred Francis and Mary Jacqueline Sculco; m. Cynthia Davis, June 4, 1966; children: Sarah Jane, Peter. BA in Classics, Brown U., 1965; MD, Coll. of Physicians and Surgeons Columbia U., 1969. Intern in gen. surgery Roosevelt Hosp., NYC, 1969-70, resident in orthopedic surgery, 1970-71; orthop. fellowship London Hosp., 1974—75; asst. attending orthopedic surgery Meml. Hosp., NYC, 1977-83; resident in orthopedic surgery Hosp. for Spl. Surgery, 1971-74, asst. attending orthopedic surgery, 1977-83, assoc. attending orthopedic surgery, 1983-91, attending surgeon in orthopedics, 1991—, Korein-Wilson prof. orthopedic surgery, surgeon-in-chief, med. dir.; asst. attending orthopedic surgery NY Hosp., 1977-83, attending surgeon in orthopedics, 1991—; cons. orthopedic surgeon Mary Manning Walsh Nursing Home, 1978—, Meml. Hosp., 1983—, Bronx Vets. Adminstrn. Hosp., 1987—; from asst. to assoc. prof. clin. surgery Cornell U., 1977-91; dept. chmn., prof. clin. surgery in orthopedics Weill Med. Coll., Cornell U., 1991—. Chief surg. arthritis svc. Hosp. for Spl. Surgery, 1993-2003, dir. orthopedic surgery, 1993-2003, surgeon-in-chief, 2003—; sr. scientist Hosp. for Spl. Surgery, 1996—. Mem. editl. bd. Surg. Blood Mgmt. Forum, 1997. Trustee NY chpt. Arthritis Found., 1997—; mem. Carnegie Hill Assn., St. Bernard's Sch.; bd. dirs. Westerley (RI) Cmty. Chorus, 190-96; sponsor Westerley Pub. Libr., 1996; patron Met. Opera, Carnegie Hall. MC maj. USAF, 1975—77. Recipient Clint Compere award Twentieth Century Orthopedic Assn., 1997, Lifetime Achievement award Arthritis Found., 1999,; recipient numerous grants; named Best Doctors in NY, NY Mag., 2003 Mem. AMA, NY County Med. Soc., Am. Acad. Orthopedic Surgeons (com. on data svcs. chmn. 1981-85, coun. musculoskeletal specialty socs. 1986-90, coord. com. on health policy 1986-89, task force on data chmn. 1987, com. on clin. policies 1991—, patent edn. com. 1999—, liaison to bd. trustees Arthritis Found. 1999—, bd. dirs. 1999-2001), NY Acad. Medicine, NY State Orthopedic Soc., Eastern Orthopedic Soc., Am. Orthopedic Soc., Austrian Orthop. Soc. (hon.), Interurban Orthopedic Assn., Am. Rheumatism Assn., Orthopedic Rsch. and Edn. Found., Knee Soc. (founding mem. 1983, exec. com. 1983-84, program chmn. 1986, membership com. 1986-93, chmn. 1992-93, edn. com. 1990-94, chmn. 1993-94), Assn. VA Orthopedic Surgeons (founder 1986, sec.-treas. 1986-88), Assn. for Arthritis Hip and Knee Surgery, Acad. Orthopedic Soc., Physicians Sci. Soc., Med. Strollers, Internat. Soc. Tech. in Arthroplasty, Am. Austrian Found. (bd. dirs. 2000—), Hip Soc. (membership com. 2000—, Otto Aufranc Rsch. award 1991, Charnley Rsch. award 1995), Austrian Orthop. Assn. (hon.). Office: The Hosp for Spl Surgery 535 E 70th St New York NY 10021 Address: Belaire Bldg 525 East 71st St 2nd Fl between York Ave and East River New York NY 10021 Office Phone: 212-606-1475. Office Fax: 212-734-9572. Business E-Mail: sculcot@hss.edu.

SCULLEY, JOHN, investment company executive, former computer company executive; b. NYC, Apr. 6, 1939; s. John and Margaret Blackburn (Smith) S.; m. Carol Lee Adams, Mar. 7, 1978; children: Margaret Ann, John Blackburn, Laura Lee. Student, R.I. Sch. Design, 1960; BArch, Brown U., 1961; MBA, U. Pa., 1963. Asst. account exec. Marschalk Co., NYC, 1963-64, account exec., 1964-65, account supr., 1965-67; dir. mktg. Pepsi-Cola Co., Purchase, NY, 1967-69, v.p. mktg., 1970-71, sr. v.p. mktg., 1971-74, pres., CEO, 1977-83; pres. PepsiCo Foods, Purchase, NY, 1974-77; pres., CEO Apple Computer Inc., Cupertino, Calif., 1983-1993; chmn., CEO Spectrum Info. Technologies, 1993—94; ptnr. Sculley Brothers LLC, 1995—2004; chmn. Live Picture Inc., 1997—98; venture ptnr. Rho Ventures, Palo Alto, 2004—. Co-author (with John A. Byrne): Odyssey: Pepsi to Apple...a Journey of Adventure, Ideas & the Future, 1987. Chmn. Wharton Grad. Exec. Bd., 1980; mem. art adv. com. Brown U., 1980; bd. dirs. Keep Am. Beautiful.; mem. bd. overseers Wharton Sch., U. Pa. Mem. U.S. C. of C. Clubs: Indian Harbor, N.Y. Athletic; Coral Beach (Bermuda); Wharton Bus. Sch. of N.Y. (bd. dirs.); Camden (Maine) Yacht. Republican. Office: Rho Ventures 525 University Ave Ste 1350 Palo Alto CA 94301

SCULLEY, PATRICK DAVID, retired army officer, director; b. Jamestown, NY, Sept. 12, 1947; s. Claude Francis and Hildegarde Ruth (Anderson) S.; m. Peggy Ann Carroll, Aug. 26, 1967; children: Patricia, Paul, Perry, Peter. BA, Wash. and Jefferson Coll., Pa., 1969; DDS, SUNY, Buffalo, 1973; MA in Health Svcs. Mgmt., Webster U., St. Louis, 1994. Diplomate Fed. Svcs. Bd. Gen. Dentistry, Am. Bd. Oral Medicine, Am. Bd. Gen. Dentistry; cert. Am. Coll. Health Care Execs., Am. Soc. Assn. Execs. Commd. US Army, advanced through grades to maj. gen., 1999; gen. practice resident Kimbrough Army Hosp., Ft. Meade, Md., 1973-74; gen. dentist US Army MEDDAC, White Sands Missile Range, N.Mex., 1974-76; gen. dentistry resident US Army DENTAC, Ft. Knox, Ky., 1977-79, clinic chief Ft. Riley, Kans., 1979-81; comdr. 576th Med. Detachment, Bad Kreuznach, West Germany, 1982-85; staff officer US Army Health Svcs. Command, Ft. Sam Houston, Tex., 1985-86, asst. inspector gen., 1986-88; dental cons. Dept. Army Surgeon Gen.'s Office, Washington, 1988-90; student US Army War Coll., Carlisle Barracks, Pa., 1990-91; comdr. US Army Dental Activity, Ft. Bragg, NC, 1991-92; dir. dental svcs. Health Svcs. Command US Army, 1992-93, comdr. Dental Command, 1993-95, asst. surgeon gen. pers., 1996, commdg. gen. US Army Ctr. Health Promotion and Preventive Medicine, 1996-99, acting dep. surgeon gen., 1998-99, dep. surg. gen./chief Army Dental Corps, chief of staff US Army Med. Command, 1999—2002, ret., 2002; exec. dir. Sigma Xi, 2002—06; dir. sci. and tech. Ctr. for Applied Tech., Tex. A&M U., San Antonio, 2006—. Instr. oral medicine gen. practice residency, Ft. Riley, 1980-81; mem. bd. examiners Fed. Svcs. Bd. Gen. Dentistry, Washington, 1986-90; mem. bd. examiners Am. Bd. of Gen. Dentistry, 1991-95. Asst. high sch. football coach Bad Kreuznach Am. H.S., 1982-83; basketball coach Vienna Youth Inc., Va., 1988-89, Cath. Youth Orgn., San Antonio, 1985-86; softball coach Girls Recreation Softball League, Manhattan, Kans., 1981; mem. adv. coun. Raleigh-Durham USO, 2004-06; mem. steering com. NC Project Lead the Way, 2004-06. Fellow: Internat. Coll. Dentists; mem.: ADA (alt. del. Ho. Dels. 1999—2000), Assn. Mil. Surgeons US (Fed. Healthcare Adminstr. of Yr. 2001), Am. Bd. Gen. Dentistry, Acad. Gen. Dentistry (chmn. self-assessment com. 1988—91, pres. Army chpt. 1988—91, ho. of dels. 1988—91, examination coun. 1988—92, chmn. reference com. on adminstrn. comm. and constrn. bylaws 1990, long range planning coun. 1997—98, chmn. long range planning coun. 1998—99, chmn. strategic advancement com. 1999—2002, Disting. Svc. award 1999), Am. Coll. Health Care Execs., Triangle Area's Rsch. Dirs. Club (vice chmn. 2004—, chmn. 2005), Sigma Xi, Omicron Kappa Upsilon. Independent. Roman Catholic. Avocation: history. Office: Texas Ctr Applied Tech 9350 S Presa St San Antonio TX 78223-4733 Business E-Mail: patrick-sculley@tamu.edu.

SCULLIN, DOROTHY DODWORTH, artist, writer; b. Pitts., Jan. 22, 1929; d. James Russell and Dorothy Thompson Dodworth; m. Richard J. Scullin; children: Laura, Charlotte, Richard III. BA, Chatham U., Pitts., 1951; BFA, RI Sch. Design, Providence, 1952; attended, Boston U. Grad. Sch. Edn., 1955. Asst. children's libr., Boston, 1953—55, Robbins Libr., Arlington, Mass., 1955—57; tchr. Williams Coll., Williamstown, Mass., 1970, Mass. Coll. Liberal Arts, N. Adams, 1975; writer N. Adams Transcript, Mass., 1976, illustrator Mass., 1976. Author (book): A Dangerous Day for Mrs. Doodlepunk, 1954, Mrs. Doodlepunk Trades Work, 1957, Look Out, Mrs. Doodlepunk, 1961; painter (commissioned oil portraits of children); exhibitions include oil paintings solo and group shows in US & Can. Leader Girl Scouts US, Mass. coun.; vol. tour guide Clark Art Inst., Williamstown, Mass. Mem.: Puppeteers America. Republican. Episcopalian. Avocations: puppetry, boating, needleart. Home: 280 Stone Hill Rd PO Box 42 Williamstown MA 01267

SCULLIN, FREDERICK JAMES, JR., federal judge; b. Syracuse, NY, Nov. 5, 1939; s. Frederick James and Cleora M. (Fellows) S.; m. Veronica Terek, Aug. 31, 1984; children: Mary Margaret, Kathleen Susan, Kellie Anne, Rebecca Rose; 1 stepchild, Angel Jeanette Godleski. BS in Econs., Niagara U., 1961; LLB, Syracuse U., 1964. Bar: NY 1964, Fla. 1976, US Dist. Ct. (no. dist.) NY 1967, US Supreme Ct. 1971. Assoc. Germain & Germain, Syracuse, 1967-68; asst. dist. atty. Onondaga County, Syracuse, 1968-71; asst. atty. gen. Organized Crime Task Force, State of NY, Albany, 1971-78, dir. regional office, 1974-78; chief prosecutor, dir. Gov.'s Coun. on Organized Crime State of Fla., Tallahassee, 1978—; sole practice Syracuse, 1979-82; US atty. (no. dist.) NY US Dept. Justice, Syracuse, 1982-92; judge US Dist. Ct. (no. dist.) NY, 1992—2006, chief judge, 2000—06, sr. judge, 2006—; judge Fgn. Intelligence Surveillance Ct. (FISC), 2004—. With US Army, 1964-67, Vietnam; col. USAR. Decorated Air medal, 2 Bronze Stars; Cross of Gallantry (Vietnam); recipient Meritorious Svc. Cross, Vietnam Svc. medal, Vietnam Campaign medal, 5 stars; Nat. Def. medal, NY State Dist. Svc. medal, various others. Mem. Am. Judicature Soc., Fla. Bar Assn., Fed. Bar Assn., Fed. Bar Coun., Onon City Bar Assn., Fgn. Intelligence Surveillance Ct. Office: US Dist Ct US Courthouse 100 S Clinton St Syracuse NY 13261-6100 Office Phone: 315-234-8560.*

SCULLION, ANNETTE MURPHY, lawyer, educator; b. Chgo., Apr. 6, 1926; d. Edmund Patrick and Anna (Nugent) Murphy; 1 child, Kevin. BEd, Chgo. Tchrs. Coll., 1960; JD, DePaul U., 1964, MEd, 1966, Loyola U., Chgo., 1970; EdD, No. Ill. U., 1974. Bar: Ill. 1964, U.S. Dist. Ct. (no. dist.) Ill. 1965, U.S. Ct. Appeals (D.C. cir.) 1978. Lectr. Chgo. C.C., 1964-68; pvt. practice Chgo., 1964—; from asst. prof. bus. edn. to prof. Chgo. State U., 1966-98. Founder, adviser Bus. Edn. Students Assn., Chgo. State U., 1976—; sch. law workshop coord. Ill. Divsn. Vocat. and Tech. Edn., 1981, coord. edn. workshops, 1990—. Mem. ABA, Nat. Bus. Edn. Assn., Womens Bar Assn. Ill., Am. Tchr. Edn., Beta Gamma Sigma. Home: 386 Muskegon Ave Calumet City IL 60409-2347

SCULLION, MARY (SISTER MARY SCULLION), nun, advocate; Student in math., Temple U., Phila. Tchr. St. Malachy, North Phila.; nun Sisters of Mercy; staff mem. Mercy Hospice, Phila.; co-founder Woman of Hope, Phila., 1985, Outreach Coordination Ctr., Phila., 1988; co-founder, exec. dir., pres. Project H.O.P.E, Phila., 1989—. Recipient Liberty Bell award, Philadelphia Bar Assn., Nat. Nonprofit Leadership award, Prudential, Philadelphia award, 1992, Leadership for a Changing World award, Ford Found., 2002; named one of The World's Most Influential People, TIME mag., 2009; grantee Eisenhower Fellowship, 2002. Roman Catholic. Office: Project H.O.M.E 1515 Fairmount Ave Philadelphia PA 19130 Office Phone: 215-232-7272. Office Fax: 215-232-7277.*

SCULLY, JOHN CARROLL, life insurance marketing research company executive; b. Springfield, Mass., Mar. 16, 1932; s. James and Frances (Carroll) S.; m. Barbara A. Fougere, Sept. 7, 1953; children: Kathleen, Margaret, John, James, Patricia, Mary Ellen, Susan. BA, Holy Cross Coll., 1953; C.L.U., Boston U., 1963; postgrad., Dartmouth Inst., 1977. With John Hancock Mut. Life Ins. Co., 1953-92, gen. agent Indpls., 1966-75, sr. v.p. agency dept. Boston, 1975-80, pres. retail sector, 1980-92; pres. emeritus Life. Ins. Mktg. Rsch. Assoc., Windsor, Conn., 1992-97. Bd. dirs. Greater Boston YMCA, 1975-91; chmn. Mass. campaign Holocaust Meml. Mus., 1985—; div. chmn. United Way, 1985—; bd. dirs. Cath. Charities, 1986—; trustee Springfield Coll., 1986, Suffolk U., 1986, Am. United Life Ins. Co. With U.S. Army, 1954-56. Mem. Am. Coll. Life Underwriters, Nat. Assn. Life Underwriters (v.p. Ind. 1973-75), Life Ins. Mktg. and Rsch. Assn. (past chmn.), Gen. Agts. and Mgrs. Assn. (past pres. Indpls. Nat. Mgmt. award

1973-75), Life Underwriter Tng. Coun. (past chmn.), Greater Boston C. of C. (bd. dirs. 1985—), Wellesley Club, Executives Club (past pres.), Algonquin Club (bd. dirs.), KC. Roman Catholic. Home: Unit 414 4800 N AIA Vero Beach FL 32963 Office: Limra Internat PO Box 208 Hartford CT 06141-0208 Personal E-mail: johnscully1@comcast.net.

SCULLY, MARLAN ORVIL, physics professor; b. Casper, Wyo., Aug. 3, 1939; s. Orvil O. and Thelma G. (Thoms) Scully; m. Judith Bailey, Aug. 16, 1958; children: James, Robert, Steven. AS, Casper Coll., 1959; BS, U. Wyo., 1961; MS, Yale U., 1963, PhD, 1966. Instr. Yale U., New Haven, 1967-69; asst. prof. MIT, Cambridge, 1969-71, assoc. prof., 1971-72; prof. U. Ariz., Tucson, 1972-80; disting. prof. physics U. N.Mex., Albuquerque, 1980—92; Burgess disting. prof. Tex. A&M U., 1996—, prof. physics, 1992—96, prof. elec. engring., 1999—; dir. Ctr. Theoretical Physics, Tex. A&M U., 1995—, Inst. Quantum Studies, Tex. A&M U., 2001—; disting. rsch. chair TEES, 2000—; vis. prof. chemistry Princeton U., 2003—05, prof. mechanical and aerospace engring. and materials sci., 2005—. Dir., co-founder Radtech, 1984; mem. Joint coun. on Quantum Electronics, Internat. Commn. on Optics; mem. program com. VIIth and VIIIth Internat. Conf. on Quantum Electronics (co-chmn. program com.); panel mem. Internat. Conf. on Hot Electrons in Semiconductors, North Tex. State U.; co-dir. VIIth Course of NATO Internat. Sch. Quantum Electronics; mem. program com. for OSA sponsored topical meeting on Picosecons Phenomena, Hilton Head, S.C., 1978; invited lectr. U.S.-Japan Coop. Seminar on Laser Spectroscopy, Hakone, Japan, 1977; mem. NRC panel on electron, atomic and molecular physics; advisor to ARO Nat. Acad. Panel, Los Alamos Physics Div. Author: (with others) Laser Physics, 1974; contbr. articles to profl. jours. Recipient Elliott Cresson medal The Franklin Inst., 1990; John S. Guggenheim fellow, 1970, Alfred P. Sloan fellow, 1972. Fellow AAAS, Am. Acad. Arts and Scis., Optical Soc. Am. (dir. at large 1978-80, publs. com. 1972, Ives medal com. 1976, chmn. Wood prize com. 1978, Adolph E. Lomb medal 1970, Townes award, 1990), Am. Phys. Soc. (Arthur L. Schawlow prize for Laser Sci., 2005); mem. NAS, IEEE (Quantum Electronics award, 2003) Max Planck Soc, Academia Europa. Avocations: cattle ranching, inventing.

SCULLY, MARTHA SEEBACH, speech and language pathologist; b. S.I., Nov. 1, 1951; d. Henry F. and Rose Anne (Callahan) Seebach; m. Roger Tehan Scully, Dec. 29, 1979; 1 child, Roger Tehan. BA, Trinity Coll., 1972; MS, George Washington U., 1974; postgrad., Syracuse U., NY, 1976-79. Lic. speech-lang. pathologist, Md. Clin. supr. Syracuse U., 1976-79; speech-lang. pathologist Fairfax (Va.) County Pub. Schs., 1979—. Bd. dirs. Trinity Coll., Washington, Nat. Children's Choir, 1987-91; trustee Davis Meml. Goodwill Industries, 1994-96, bd. dirs. Goodwill Guild, 1990—, chair ball; docent Folger Shakespearean Libr.; chmn. Nat. Challenge Com. of Disabled, 1985; mem. Ear Ball, 1988, 89; mem. Internat. Children's Festival, 1990, 91; co-chmn. Jr. League of Washington Capital Collection, 1990; chmn. Salvation Army Garden Party, 1992, Washington Embassy Tour, 1993; mem. bd. edn. Holy Cross Sch., Garrett Park, Md., 2001-. Recipient First Order Affiliation Order of Franciscans mirror, 1985; named Outstanding Woman in Am., 1987, 88. Mem. Am. Biog. Inst., Am. Speech-Lang.-Hearing Assn., Coun. for Exceptional Children, Montgomery County Assn. for Hearing Impaired Children, Benevolent and Protective Order Elks (mem. Washinton-Rockville lodge, lecturing knight 1999, esteemed loyal knight 2000, 2008-; chaplain, 2006-07), Christ Child Soc., John Caroll Soc., Chevy Chase Women's Republican Club, Junior League Wash. Home: 10923 Wickshire Way Rockville MD 20852-3220

SCULLY, ROBERT WILLIAM (BOB SCULLY), retired diversified financial services company executive; b. Boston, Feb. 5, 1950; m. Nancy Beth Peretsman, Sept. 17, 1988. AB, Princeton U., 1972; MBA, Harvard Bus. Sch., 1977. Joined Salomon Brothers, 1979, v.p. domestic products capital markets svc. group, mng. dir., 1984—88; co-founder Scully Brothers & Foss, 1988—93; mng. dir. industrials investment banking, mem. investment banking mgmt. com. Lehman Brothers Holdings, Inc., 1993—96; joined Morgan Stanley, 1996, vice chmn. investment banking, 1999—2006, chmn. global capital markets, 2004—06, co-pres., 2006—07, mem. Office of Chmn., 2007—09. Bd. dirs. GMC Financial Services, 2006—09, MSCI Inc., 2008—09, Bank of America Corp., 2009—. Bd. dirs. Global Fund for Children.*

SCULLY, ROGER TEHAN, II, lawyer; b. Washington, Jan. 10, 1948; s. James Henry and Marietta (Maguire) S.; m. Martha Anne Seebach, Dec. 29, 1979. BS, U. Md., 1977; JD, Cath. U., 1980. Bar: Md. 1980, D.C. 1981, U.S. Tax Ct. 1982, U.S. Supreme Ct. 1988. V.p. Bogley Related Cos., Rockville, Md., 1971-75; law clk. to presiding justice Superior Ct. of D.C., Washington, 1979-81; assoc. Lerch, Early & Roseman, Bethesda, Md., 1981-82; gen. counsel Laszlo N. Tauber, M.D. & Assocs., Bethesda, 1982-94, Jefferson Meml. Hosp., Alexandria, Va., 1982-94; spl. counsel Venable, Baetjer, Howard & Civiletti, Washington, 1991-96. Cons. in real estate Order of Friar Minor, N.Y.C., 1977—; lectr. Mortgage Bankers Assn., Washington, 1984—; bd. dirs. Nozzoli Constrn. Co., Washington; exec. com., spl. counsel to bd. dirs., bd. dirs. Chromachron Technology Corp., Toronto; bd. dirs. MusicWorks, N.Y.C.; vice chair Sayett Tech., Inc., Rochester, N.Y.; vice chair, bd. dirs., exec. com. MediaShow, Inc., Rochester; mng. dir. Jefferson Meml. LLC, Washington. Author: (with Quarles & Howard) Summary Adjudication Dispositive Motions and Summary Trials, 1991. Mem. pres.'s coun. St. Bonaventure U., Olean, N.Y., 1995—, chmn. pres.'s coun., 1986-96; trustee Belmont Abbey Coll., Charlotte, N.C., 1993-95; bd. trustees Edmund Burke Sch., Washington, 1984-2001, trustees emeritus, 2001-; bd. dirs. Nat. Children's Choir, Washington, 1980-94. Recipient First Order Affiliation Order of Friars Minor, 1985; named one of Outstanding Young Men in Am., 1982. Fellow D.C. Bar Assn.; mem. ABA, ATLA, FBA, Md. Bar Assn. (chmn. corp. counsel sect.), Am. Judicature Soc., Assn. Governing Bd. of Univs. and Colls., Am. Inns of Ct., Irish Legal Soc., Selden Soc., U.S. Jud. Conf. of 4th Cir. (permanent mem.), U.S. Jud. Conf. Fed. Cir. (del.), Jud. Conf. of D.C. (del.). Office: 7712 Greentree Rd West Bethesda MD 20817-1428 Personal E-mail: rts2esq@yahoo.com.

SCULLY, SEAN PATRICK, orthopaedic surgeon, educator; s. Michael A. and Anne Rita Scully; m. Kristi Griffin Scully, Aug. 11, 1979; children: Patrick, Colin. BS in Biochemistry, SUNY, Binghamton, 1978; MD, PhD in Biophysics, U. Rochester, 1986. Cert. Am. Bd. Orthop. Surgery, 1995. Residency Duke U., Durham, NC, 1986—92; intramural rsch. fellowship Nat. Inst. Health, Bethesda, Md., 1989—90; asst. prof. cell biology Duke U. Medical Ctr., 1994—2000, assoc. prof. orthop., 1997—2000; clin. orthop. oncology fellow Mass. Gen. Hosp., Boston, 1992—93; assoc. prof. orthop. Mayo Medical Sch., Rochester, Minn., 2001—03, prof. orthop., 2003—04; prof. orthop., cell biology and cellular molecular pharmacology U. Miami, 2004—. Mem. advisory panel Musculoskeletal Transplant Found., 1994—2001; vice-chmn. Shriners Rsch. Advisory Bd., 1996—; Ad Hoc reviewer, orthop. study section NIH, 1997—, OBM-2, NIH, 2001—; presenter in field. Dep. editor Clinical Orthopaedics and Related Research, 2003—; contbr. articles to prof. jours., chpts. to books. Recipient William F. Neuman award in biophysics, 1984, George H. Whipple award, 1986, Marshall R. Urist award, 1999; named one of America's Top Doctors for Cancer, Cantle Connolly's LTD, 2005; grantee John J. Fahey N.Am. Traveling fellowship, 1993. Mem.: Austriah Swiss German, Nat. Inst. Arthritis, Musculoskeletal and Skin Diseases Nat. Inst. Health (FDA panel on cartilage repair 2005—), Internat. Skeletal Soc., Internat. Soc. Limb Salvage, Soc. Surgical Oncologists, Am. Orthop. Assn. (Howard Hatcher fellowship com. 2000, ASG fellowship com. 2000, Austrian Swiss German Traveling fellowship 2000), Assn. Bone and Joint Surgeons (co-chair symposium on gene therapy in orthop. 2000, awards com. 2002—), Musculoskeletal Tumor Soc. (strategic planning com. 2001, specialty day organizer 2001), Orthop. Rsch. Soc., Am. Acad. Orthop. Surgeons (subcom. basic sci. evaluation 1995—, program com. 1999—, clinician scientist com. 2001—, fellowship issues task force 2003—, Howard Hatcher pathology fellowship com. 2003—, ASG fellowship exchange com. 2003—). Achievements include research in tumor biology. Office: U Miami 1400 NW 12th Ave Miami FL 33136 Office Fax: 305-325-4784.

SCULLY, TERRENCE J., retail executive; V.p. Target Fin. Svcs. Target Corp., Mpls., 1998—2003, pres. Target Fin. Svcs., 2003—. Former bd. mem. Greater Twin Cities United Way. Office: Target Corp 1000 Nicollet Mall Minneapolis MN 55403-2467 Office Phone: 612-304-6073. Office Fax: 612-370-5502.*

SCULLY, THOMAS A., lawyer, former federal agency administrator; b. 1957; BA, U. Va., 1979; JD, Cath. U., 1986. Staff asst. Fed. Election Commn., 1979—81, U.S. Senator Slade Gorton, 1981—85; atty. Akin, Gump, Strauss, Hauer & Feld, LLP, 1986—88; comm. staff Bush-Quayle Campaign, 1988, dep. dir. congl. affairs; assoc. dir. human resources, vets. and labor Office Mgmt. & Budget, Washington, 1989—92, counselor to the dir., 1992—93; pres., CEO Fedn. Am. Hosps., 1995—2001; ptnr. Patton Boggs, LLP, Washington; dep. asst. to the pres. The White House, Washington, 2001—03; CEO, adminstr. Centers. for Medicare and Medicaid Services US Dept. Health & Human Services, Washington, 2001—03; sr. counsel Alston & Bird LLP, Washington, 2003—. Mem.: bd. dirs., SHPS, Inc., 2004-. Republican. Office: Alston & Bird LLP 10th Fl N Bldg 950 F St NW Ste 1 Washington DC 20004-1439 Office Phone: 202-756-3459. Business E-Mail: tscully@alston.com.

SCURICH, KELLY LEMOS, music director; b. Sharon, Pa., Sept. 21, 1960; d. John and Mildred Novak Lemos; m. Thomas Michael Scurich, Oct. 10, 1987; children: Jenna Christine, Jonathan Frank. MusB, Youngstown State U., Ohio, 1983; MusM, Youngstown State U., 1985. Tchr. St. Mary's Mid. Sch., Warren, Ohio, 1985—86; dir. music Holy Trinity Luth. Ch., Hermitage, Pa., 1983—88; choral music dir. West Branch HS, Beloit, Ohio, 1987—93, Hickory HS, Hermitage, 1993—94, Canfield HS, Ohio, 1994—; dir. music First Covenant Ch., Boardman, Ohio, 1988—94. Named Tchr. of the Yr., Mahoning County Fine Arts Coun., 1992. Mem.: Ohio Choral Dirs. Assn. (show choir chair, bd. dirs. 1988—92), Ohio Music Educators Assn., Am. Choral Dirs. Assn., Nat. Assn. Tchrs. Singing, Music Educators Nat. Conf. Office: Canfield High School 100 Cardinal Dr Canfield OH 44406

SCYTHES, JAMES MICHAEL, history professor; b. Bridgeton, NJ, Aug. 12, 1971; s. Mervin and Virginia Scythes; 1 child, Isabella Rose. MA, Villanova U., Pa., 1997. Instr. history West Chester U. Pa., 1999—, Thomas Jefferson U., Phila., 2005—. Trustee Gloucester County Hist. Soc., Woodbury, NJ, 2002—09. Recipient Excellence Tchg. award, Thomas Jefferson U., 2006—07. Home: 473 Griscom Dr Woodbury NJ 08096 Office: West Chester Univ Pa High St West Chester PA 19383 Business E-Mail: jscythes@wcupa.edu.

SCZUDLO, WALTER JOSEPH, lawyer; s. Walter and Dolores J. Sczudlo; children: Lauren Hall, Elizabeth Fairbanks, Walter Christopher; m. Rebecca Grey Tucker. AB, Middlebury Coll.; JD, Golden Gate U.; LLM, Georgetown U.; post grad., U. Calif., Santa Barbara, Tulane U., Vt. Law Sch. Bar: Alaska, Calif., DC, US Ct. Appeals (9th cir.), US Ct. Appeals (DC cir.), US Dist. Ct. (no., cen., ea. and so. dists.) Calif., US Dist. Ct. Alaska, US Ct. Claims, US Tax Ct. Law clk. to presiding justice Alaska Supreme Ct.; assoc. atty. Merdes, Schaible, Staley and Delisio, Anchorage; legis. dir., gen. counsel U.S. Senator Murkowski, Washington; sr. tax assoc. Schramm and Raddue, Santa Barbara, Calif.; dir. congl. rels., counsel Natural Gas Supply Assn., Washington; Washington counsel Shell Oil Co.; v.p., Washington counsel Intercontinental Energy Corp.; gen. counsel, exec. v.p. Assn. Fundraising Profls., Washington, 1999—; prin. ptnr. WEBK Broadcasting 105.3 FM, Killington, Vt., 1985—. Dir., exec. com. mem. pub. affairs coun., Washington, 2003-, dir. Pacific & Western Energy, Inc., Fairbanks, Alaska, 1980-, Sun's Edge, Inc., Santa Barbara, 1987—, Natural Gas Roundtable, Washington, 1987—. Author: (with other) Washington Legal Foundation, 1988. Com. chmn. Steve Cowper for Gov., Anchorage, 1982. Recipient Am. Jurisprudence award Bancroft-Whitney Pub. Co. Office Phone: 800-666-3863.

SEABOLT, RICHARD L., lawyer; b. Chgo., Aug. 28, 1949; BGS with distinction, U. Mich., 1971; JD, U. Calif., Hastings, 1975. Bar: Calif. 1975. Ptnr. Duane Morris LLP, San Francisco, 1981—. Mem. Calif. Civil Jury Instr. Adv. Com. Author: Matthew Bender Practice Guides, California Pretrial Civil Procedure and Civil Discovery, 2004. Mem.: Assn. Bus. Trial Lawyers (bd. govs.), State Bar Calif. (chair litig. sect. 2006). Office: Duane Morris LLP One Market Spear Tower San Francisco CA 94111 Office Phone: 415-957-3212. Business E-Mail: rlseabolt@duanemorris.com.

SEABOLT, ROBERT D., lawyer; b. Newport News, Va., 1955; BA magna cum laude, Univ. Richmond, 1977; JD, Univ. Va., 1980. Bar: Va. 1980. Adminstrv. ptnr. Troutman Sanders LLP, Richmond, Va., and mem. exec. com. Named one of Virginia's Legal Elite, Civil Litig. Mag., 2003. Mem.: ABA, Va. State Bar, Va. Bar Assn., Richmond Bar Assn. Office Phone: 804-697-1328. Office Fax: 804-698-5100. Business E-Mail: bob.seabolt@troutmansanders.com.

SEABORG, DAVID MICHAEL, evolutionary biologist; b. Berkeley, Calif., Apr. 22, 1949; s. Glenn Theodore and Helen Lucille (Griggs) S.; m. Adele Fong Yee, June 17, 1990. BS, U. Calif., Davis, 1972; MA, U. Calif., Berkeley, 1974. Biology tchr. U. Calif., Berkeley, 1972-73; biol. rschr., photographer Trans Time Labs, Berkeley, 1978; pvt. practice, 1974—; hypnosis and self-hypnosis tchr. Open Edn. Exchange, Oakland, Calif., 1978—81; biol. tchr. Oakland Mus., Calif., 1983-87; rsch. biologist, dept. ecology and evolutionary biology U. Calif., Irvine, 1987; pres. dir. Rsch. Found. for Biol. Conservation and Rsch., Walnut Creek, Calif., 1983—; radio talk show host Sta. KPFA, Berkeley, 1996; biology and life sci tchr. Phillip and Sala Burton Acad. H.S., San Francisco, 1996-97; lab. Chem. Biodynamics U. Calif., Berkeley, 1975; comedian, 1969—. Vol. asst. to curator Smithsonian Instn. 1966-67; sci. philos., environ. issues, 1974—; Inventor game, Sum-It, 1981; originator, theory of evolution based on organisms as integrated systems; chmn. Com. for Arts and Lectures, U. Calif., Berkeley, 1974-75; chmn. Bastille Day, Lafayette (Calif.)-Langeac Soc., 1982, master of ceremonies, 1982-86, 98-2000. Contbr. articles to profl. sci. jours.; author: (poetry book) Honor Thy Soubug, 2008. Environ. organizer; founder, pres. U Turn Soc., Glenn Seaborg Open Space Fund, World Rainforest Fund, Found. for Biol. Conservation and Rsch.; creator, organizer press conf. on global environ. and social issues 100th Nobel Prize Festivities, Stockholm, 2001, alternate del. Dem. Party Nat. Convention, Denver, 2008. Recipient Meritorius Svc. award Smithsonian Inst., 1967, Animal Photograph award Soc. Photographic Scientists and Engrs., 1967, Best of Show Photo Contest award Klamath Basin Audubon Soc., 1991; award Nat. Libr. Poetry, 1995, 99, 2006, 07, award Big Yr. Environ. Competition, 2008. Mem.: UN Assn. of USA (East Bay chpt. bd. dirs. 2006—09), Nat. Resources Def. Coun., Earth Island Inst., World Wildlife Fund, Desert Tortoise Preserve Com., Population Connection, Save the Bay Assn., Greenpeace, Rainforest Action Network, Nature Conservancy, Calif. Alumni Assn., Calif. Aggie Alumni Assn., Sierra Club, Club of Rome USA (bd. dirs. 1995—2008, v.p. 1998—2001). Democrat. Address: 1888 Pomar Way Walnut Creek CA 94598-1424 Office Phone: 925-938-9206. E-mail: davidseaborg@juno.com.

SEABROOK, LARRY B. (LAWRENCE B. SEABROOK), city councilman, former state legislator; b. Jacksonville, Fla., July 16, 1951; AAS, Kingsborough Cmty. Coll.; BA, John Jay Coll. Criminal Justice; MA, Long Island Univ.; JD, CUNY Law Sch. Instr. Malcolm King Coll., Monroe Bus. Coll.; mem. dist. 83 N.Y. State Assembly, Albany, 1983-96; senator N.Y. State Senate, Albany, 1996—2000; city councilman Dist. 12 NY City Coun., 2002—. Chmn. Civil Rights com. NY City Coun.; adj. prof. John Jay Coll. Criminal Justice. Recipient Man of Yr. award, NAACP, Williamsbridge Branch & Nat. Coun. Negro Women, Legis. Leadership award, Assn. Med. Schools, Disting. Svc. award & Presdl. medal, John Jay Coll. Mem. Williamsbridge NAACP Democrat. Baptist. Mailing: 3687-A White Plains Rd Bronx NY 10467-5708 Office Phone: 718-994-9900, 212-788-6873. Office Fax: 718-652-0703. Business E-Mail: seabrook@council.nyc.ny.us.*

SEABROOK, RAYMOND J., corporate financial executive; b. Toronto, Canada, Mar. 1, 1950; married; 2 children. B in Bus., McMaster U., Hamilton, Ontario, 1975. Cert. arch., Humber Coll., Toronto, 1972. With Coopers and Lybrand, Toronto, Canada, 1976—85; v.p. fin. control Onex Packaging and Am. Can Can., 1985—88; sr. v.p., CFO Ball Packaging Products Canada, 1988—92; v.p., treas. Ball Corp., Broomfield, Colo., 1992—96, v.p. planning & control, 1996—98, sr. v.p. fin., 1998—2000, sr. v.p., CFO, 2000—06, exec. v.p., CFO, 2007—. Bd. dir. Andersen Corp., 2004—. Office: Ball 10 Longs Peak Dr Broomfield CO 80021

SEABROOK, RENITA L., criminal justice professor; b. Augusta, Ga., Oct. 4, 1968; d. Frederick Seabrook and Gloria J. Youmans. PhD, Rutgers U., Newark, NJ Campus, 2007. Counselor Ga. State Bd. Pardons & Paroles, Atlanta, 2000—06; program devel. cons. Ga. Dept. Corrections-Risk Reductions Svcs., Atlanta, 2006—06; vis. lectr. U. Md. Ea. Shore, Princess Anne, 2006—07, asst. prof., 2007—. Cons. Riverside Regional Jail, Hopewell, Va., 2008—. Contbr. chapters to books, articles to profl. jour. Mem.: Jour. Prisoners Prisons (editl. bd. mem. 2008), Delta Sigma Theta Sorority. Avocations: travel, reading. Office: Univ Md Eastern Shore 3025 Hazel Hall Princess Anne MD 21853 Business E-Mail: rlseabrook@umes.edu.

SEACREST, RYAN (RYAN JOHN SEACREST), television and radio personality, entrepreneur; b. Atlanta, Dec. 24, 1976; s. Gary and Connie Seacrest. Attended, U. Ga., 1994—95. DJ WSTR/Star 94, Atlanta, 1992—94, 102.7 KIIS-FM morning show, LA. Launched fashion line, R Line, 2005; part owner at Katana, Sushi Roku and Boa. Host (TV series) Gladiators 2000, 1994, Radical Outdoor Challenge, ESPN, 1995, The New Edge, 1996, The Click, 1997, American Juniors, 2003, American Idol, 2002—, host, exec. prodr. On-Air With Ryan Seacrest, 2004, corr. Extra Weekends, 2002, The Tonight Show, 2005—, host (TV) Wild Animal Games, 1995, (radio) Live from the Lounge, Star 98.7, 1995—2001, Ryan Seacrest for the Ride Home, Star 98.7, LA, 1995—2004, American Top 40, 2004—, On-Air With Ryan Seacrest, 102.7 KIIS-FM, 2004—, New Year's Eve: Live From Times Square With Ryan Seacrest, NYC, 2003—; exec. prodr.: New Year's Eve: Live From Times Square With Ryan Seacrest, 2004, New Year's Rockin' Eve 2006, 2005; actor: (TV series) Reality Check, 1995; voice Hey Arnold!, 1999, Robot Chicken, 2005, guest appearances Beverly Hills, 90210, 2000, Mad TV, 2002, 2005, Player$, 2003, guest host Good Day Live, 2003, Larry King Live, 2003, 2004, 2005. Named Marconi Radio award for Personality of Yr. (major market size), Nat. Assn. Broadcasters, 2008; named a Maverick, Details mag., 2007; named one of 50 Most Beautiful People, People Mag., 2003, The 100 Most Powerful Celebrities, Forbes.com, 2007, 2008. Office: William Morris Agy 1 William Morris Pl Beverly Hills CA 90212 Business E-Mail: Ryan@kiisfm.com, ryan@eonline.com. E-mail: Ryan@AT40.com.

SEADEN, GEORGE, civil engineer; b. Cracow, May 26, 1936; s. Simon and Mary (Guttman) S.; m. Linda Helen Mutch, Mar. 18, 1978; children: Amy Elisabeth, Maia Claire. BE, McGill U., Montreal, Que., Can., 1958; MS, Harvard U., 1968; postgrad., Northwestern U., 1992. Engr. Gatineau Power, Hull, Que., 1958-59, Ent. Fougerolle, Paris, 1960-62; mgr. Warnock Hersey Ltd., Montreal, 1959-60; assoc. Cartier, Coté, Piette, Montreal, 1962-67; sr. advisor Ministry Urban Affairs, Ottawa, Ont., Canada, 1969-71; pres. Archer, Seaden & Assoc., Inc., Montreal, 1971-84; dir. gen. Inst. Rsch. in Constrn. Nat. Rsch. Coun., Ottawa, 1985-97, chief Constrn. Tech. Group, 1995-97; exec.-in-residence Faculty Adminstrn. U. Ottawa, 1997—2001. Vis. prof. U. Ottawa, 1968-73; mem. Can. Constrn. Rsch. Bd., 1985-91, Constrn. Industry Devel., Can., 1988-93, Civil Engring. Rsch. Found., 1993—, Rsch. Bd. Am. Pub. Works Assn., 1994-97; dir. Continental Automated Bldg. Assn., 1995-97, Can. Rsch. Mgrs. Assn., CERIU; pres. Conseil Internat. du Batiment, Rotterdam, The Netherlands, 1989-92; vice chair Constrn. for Sustainable Devel. in the Twenty First Century Conf., Washington, 1996; chair INFRA 2000, Montreal; mem. jury to select best Can. Constrn. projects and engring. design; lectr. numerous univs. and rsch. ctrs.; chmn. Internat. Symposium on Innovation, Ottawa, 2001. Contbg. author: Buildings, Culture and Environment, 2003; co-editor: Trends in Building Construction Worldwide, 1989, Innovation in Construction, 2001; mem. editl. bd. Bldg. Rsch. and Practice, Constrn. Bldg. Rev., 1991—; contbr. numerous articles to profl. publs. Chmn. bd. dirs. St. Andrew's Sch., Westmount, Que., 1975-82; dir. SJCC, 2002—. Fellow Am. Soc. Civil Engrs. E-mail: george.seaden@rogers.com.

SEADER, JUNIOR DEVERE (BOB SEADER), retired chemical engineering professor; b. San Francisco, Aug. 16, 1927; s. George Joseph and Eva (Burbank) S.; m. Joyce Kocher, Aug. 12, 1950 (div. 1960); m. Sylvia Bowen, Aug. 11, 1961; children: Steven Frederick, Clayton Mitchell, Gregory Randolph, Donald Jeffrey, Suzanne Marie, Robert Clark, Kathleen Michelle, Jennifer Anne. BS, U. Calif., Berkeley, 1949, MS, 1950; PhD, U. Wis., 1952. Instr. chem. engring. U. Wis., Madison, 1951-52; group supr. chem. process design Chevron Rsch. Corp., Richmond, Calif., 1952-57, group supr. engring. rsch., 1957-59; prin. scientist heat transfer and fluid dynamics rsch. Rocketdyne div. N.Am. Aviation, Canoga Park, Calif., 1959-65, sr. tech. specialist, summer 1967; prof. chem. engring. U. Idaho, 1965-66, U. Utah, Salt

Lake City, 1966—2003, chmn. dept. chem. engring., 1975-78. Tech. cons.; trustee CACHE Corp., Austin, Tex., 1969—2002. Author 15 books; assoc. editor IEC Rsch. jour., 1986-99; contbr. more than 100 articles to tech. publs. With USNR, 1945—46. Recipient Disting. Tchg. award U. Utah, 1975, Donald L. Katz lectureship, 1990, Dean's Tchg. award U. Utah, 1998, CACHE award for excellence in computing in chem. engring. edn. Am. Soc. Engring. Edn., 2004. Fellow: AIChE (Inst. lectr. 1983, bd. dirs. 1983—85, Computing in Chem. Engring. award 1988, Warren K. Lewis award for chem. engring. edn. 2004). Heat transfer research connected with the development of rocket engines associated with the Apollo and Space Shuttle projects, 1960-65; recognition of Separation Process Principles by Seader and Henley as out of 30 ground breaking chemical engineering book 2008. Home Phone: 801-523-8870. E-mail: j.seader@utah.edu.

SEAFORD, JOHN NICHOLAS, clergyman, retired dean; b. Middlesbrough, Eng., Sept. 12, 1939; s. Nicholas and Kathleen (Longbotham) S.; m. Helen Marian Webster, Aug. 2, 1967; children: Nicholas, Charles, Katherine. BA, Durham U., Eng., 1967, diploma in theology, 1968. Ordained to ministry Anglican Ch., 1968. Curate St. Mark's Ch., London, 1968-71, St. Luke's Ch., Winchester, Eng., 1971-73; vicar Chilworth and North Baddesley, Hampshire, Eng., 1973-78, Highcliffe and Hinton Admiral, Dorset, Eng., 1978-93; rural dean Christ Ch., Dorset, 1988-93; hon. canon Winchester Cathedral, 1993—2005, canon emeritus, 2005—; rector St. Helier Ch., Jersey, Channel Islands, 1993—2005; dean of Jersey, 1993—2005; mem., legislature States of Jersey, Parliament of Jersey, 1993—2005; chaplain H.M. Prison, Jersey, 2004—05. Mem. Gen. Synod, Ch. of Eng., 1993-95, 2000-05. Home: Claremont Buffetts Rd Sturminster Newton DT10 1DT England

SEAGLE, EDGAR FRANKLIN, environmental engineer, consultant; b. Lincolnton, NC, June 27, 1924; s. Franklin Craig and Lillie Mae (James) S.; m. Doris Elaine Long, Mar. 23, 1958; children: Rebecca Jane, Mary Elaine, James Craig, William Franklin. AB in Chemistry, U. N.C., 1949, MS in Pub. Health, 1954; BCE, U. Fla., 1961; DPH, U. Tex., 1974. Registered profl. engr., Ala. Sr. sanitarian Health Dept., City of Charlotte, NC, 1950-52, chief indsl. hygiene sect. NC, 1956-59; sanitation cons. N.C. State Bd. Health, Raleigh, 1954-56; engr. dir. USPHS, Rockville, Md., 1961-78; asst. dir. Fellowship Office Nat. Acad. Scis., Washington, 1978-83; pub. health engr. Dept. of Environ., State of Md., Balt., 1985-88; ind. engring. cons. Rockville, 1984-85, 88—. Contbr. articles to profl. publs. With USN, 1943-46, PTO. Mem. ASCE, APHA, Am. Acad. Environ. Engrs. (diplomate). Methodist. Home and Office: 14108 Heathfield Ct Rockville MD 20853-2760 Personal E-mail: edgarseagle@comcast.net.

SEAGLE, J. HAROLD, lawyer; b. Marion, NC, May 9, 1947; s. Rufus James and Alma Rhoda (McMahan) S.; m. Linda Jean Cranford, June 3, 1967; 1 child, James Mark. BA, U. NC, Chapel Hill, 1973, JD, 1977. Bar: N.C. 1977; U.S. Dist. Ct. (ea., middle, we. dists.) N.C. 1977, 88, 92; U.S. Ct Appeals (4th cir.) 1982; U.S. Supreme Ct. 1982. Assoc. atty. Rountree & Newton, Wilmington, NC, 1977-79; ptnr. Rountree & Seagle, L.L.P., Wilmington, 1979—2001. Past pres. Fifth Jud. Dist. Bar. Active Ctrl. United Meth. Ch.; past moderator Wilmington Baptist Assn.; bd. dirs. Rescue Mission of Cape Fear; past adv. Bd. Coastal Bioethics Network; past chmn. annual fund drive Am. Cancer Soc.; past sect. chmn. Cape Fear United Way. Mem.: 28th N.C. Jud. Dist. Bar, N.C. Bar Coun. of Pres. Wilmington Inns of Ct. (exec. com., master), Maritime Law Assn. of U.S. (proctor), Southeastern Admiralty Law Inst. (past chmn., chmn. adv. coun.), N.C. Coll. of Advocacy, N.C. Acad. Trial Lawyers, N.C. State Bar, N.C. Bar Assn., New Hanover County Bar Assn. Avocations: motorcycle racing, guitar. Home and Office: 311 Bradenton Knoll Fletcher NC 28732 Office Phone: 828-545-7777. Personal E-mail: haroldseagle@charter.net.

SEAGLE, MARY JANE, educational association administrator; b. Jefferson City, Mo., Sept. 24, 1949; d. Edith Irene Houchin; life ptnr. Paul Lemuel Tucker; children: Rae Christine Wansing, Paige Elizabeth Jones, John Wesley. Mentor, McNair scholars program U. Montevallo, Ala., 2007—, chair, welcoming com. OSP, 2008—. Home: 835 N Boundary St 3 Montevallo AL 35115 Office Fax: 205-665-6112. Business E-Mail: seaglem@montevallo.edu.

SEAGLE, MIKE, theater educator; MFA, U. Ill., Urbana, 1991. Author: (plays) Rituals & Recollections, Redemption: A Dream Play about the Herrin Massacre, The Bachelor's Excuse...or a Bedfull of Lesbians. Mem.: Theatre Comm. Group. Liberal. Home: 708 Rusty Ln Carterville IL 62918 Office: John A Logan Coll 700 College Rd Carterville IL 62918

SEAGREN, ALICE, state official, school system administrator, former state legislator; b. 1947; m. Fred Seagren; 2 children, Christina and Greg. BS in Mktg., SE Mo. State U. Mem. Bloomingdale Sch. Bd., 1989—92; Minn. state repr., Dist. 41A Minn. Ho. of Reps., 1992—2002, chmn. K-12 edn. fin. com., 1999—2004, former mem., Edu. Policy, Local Govt & Met. Affairs & Ways & Means, Transportation Policy Committees; former chair Edu. Com., Nat. Coun. of State Legislatures, Assembly of State Issues; commr. of edn. State of Minn., 2004—. Active Bloomington (Minn.) Sch. Bd., 1989-92; bd. dir. Normandale Cmty. Coll. Found., Fraser Cmty. Services Mem. Bloomington C. of C. (bd. dirs. 1990-92), Phi Gamma Nu, Alpha Chi Omega. Republican. Home: 9730 Palmer Cir Bloomington MN 55437-2017 Office: Minn Dept Children, Famlies, Learning 1500 Highway 36 W Roseville MN 55113-4035 Office Phone: 651-582-8204. E-mail: mde.commissioner@state.mn.us.*

SEAL, ROBERT A., library director; b. Canton, Ohio, June 9, 1948; s. Merle E. and Evelyn L. (Baker) S.; m. Adela M. Rosca, July 10, 1971; children: Katherine Anne, Corinne Marie. BA, Northwestern U., 1971; MLS, U. Denver, 1972. From circulation libr. to sci.-tech. circulation libr. U. Va., Charlottesville, 1972-76; head adminstrv. svcs. U. Va. Librs., 1976-81; dir. libr. svcs. U. Okla., Norman, 1981-85; libr. U. Tex., El Paso, 1985-94, Tex. Christian U., Ft. Worth, 1994—2005; dean of libraries Loyola U., Chgo., 2005—. Chmn. bd. trustees Amigos Bibliographic Coun., Dallas, 1993-97; cons. Acad. for Ednl. Devel., Washington, 1996-97, Banco Ctrl. de Nicaragua, 1997-98; bd. trustees Online Computer Libr. Ctr. Author: Guide to the Literature of Astronomy, 1977, Bibliography of Astronomy 1970-79, 1982. Elder First Presbyn. Ch., El Paso, 1989-91, Fort Worth, 1999-2001. Mem. ALA, Tex. Libr. Assn., Assn. Coll. & Rsch. Librs., Libr. Adminstrn. & Mgmt. Assn., Internat. Rels. Roundtable, Downtown Lions Club (v.p. 1993-94, bd. dirs. 1991-93). Office: Loyola U Chgo Cudahy Libr Rm 105 1032 W Sheidan Rd Chicago IL 60626 Office Fax: 773-508-8691. E-mail: rseal@luc.edu.

SEAL, (SEAL HENRY OLUSEGUN OLUMIDE ADELO SAMUEL), musician; b. London, Feb. 19, 1963; s. Frances and Adebisi Samuel; m. Heidi Klum, May 10, 2005; children: Henry Gunther Ademola Dashtu Samuel, Johan Riley Fyodor Taiwo Samuel 1 stepchild, Helene Klum. Singer: (albums) Seal, 1992, 1994, Human Being, 1998, Waiting for You, 2003, Seal IV, 2003, The Acoustic Session, 2003, Live in Paris, 2005, One Night to Remember, 2006, System, 2007, Soul, 2008, (songs) Crazy, Killer, 1991, Kiss From a Rose, 1995 (Best Male Pop Vocal Performance, Record of Yr., Song of Yr., Grammy Awards, 1995). Office: c/o Mitch Rose Creative Artists Agy LCC 200 Ave of the Stars Los Angeles CA 90067

SEALE, JAMES LAWRENCE, JR., agricultural studies educator, trade association administrator, researcher; b. Memphis, Mar. 12, 1949; s. James Lawrence and Mary Helen (Keefe) S.; divorced. BA, U. Miss., 1972; postgrad., U. Chgo., 1978-79; PhD, Mich. State U., 1985. Agrl. vol. Peace Corps, Tondo, Zaire, 1973-75; agrl. advisor Harvard Inst. for Internat. Devel., Abyei, Sudan, 1978; specialist Mich. State U., Fayoum, Arab Republic of Egypt, 1980-83; asst. prof. agrl. econs. U. Fla., Gainesville, 1985-90, assoc. prof. agrl. econs., 1990-95, prof. agrl. econs., 1995—. Vis. prof. U. Leicester (Eng.), 1992, 94, hon. vis. fellow, 95. Author: (with H. Theil and C.F. Chung) International Evidence on Consumption Patterns, 1989; editor: Journal of Agricultural and Applied Economics, 1998-2001, spl. edit., 2002-03; contbr. articles to profl. jours. Vol. Farmer to Farmer, UOCA, Namibia, 1994, Farmer to Farmer, Wenrock Internat., 1994; vol. agrl. bus. svcs. Wenrock Internat., Far Eastern Russia, 1998. NIMH scholar U. Chgo., 1978-79; traveling scholar U. Mich., 1979; rsch. fellow Cairo U., 1980-83; McKethan-Matherly rsch. fellow, 1986-88, McKethan-Matherly sr. rsch. fellow, 1991-94. Mem. Am. Econs. Assn., Am. Agrl. Econs. Assn., Internat. Assn. Agrl. Economists, Econometrics Soc., Caribbean Agro-Econ. Soc., Internat. Agrl. Trade Rsch. Consortium, Gamma Sigma Delta. Episcopalian. Avocations: scuba diving, Karate. Office: U Fla Dept Food and Resource G-125 McCarty PO Box 110240 Gainesville FL 32611-0240 Home: 406 NE 7th Ave Gainesville FL 32601 Office Phone: 352-256-5917. Business E-Mail: jseale@ufl.edu.

SEALE, JAMES MILLARD, retired religious organization administrator, minister; b. Middlesboro, Ky., Oct. 4, 1930; s. Albert Tyler and Edith Josephine (Buchanan) S.; m. Mary Dudley Harrod; children: William Alan, Ann Lynn Seale Hazelrigg. BA, Transylvania U., 1952; BD, Lexington Theol. Sem., 1955, MDiv, 1963, D Ministry, 1981. Ordained to ministry Christian Ch. (Disciples of Christ), 1951. Student pastor various Christian Chs., Ky., 1949-54; pastor 1st Christian Ch., Pikeville, Ky., 1954-58, Erlanger (Ky.) Christian Ch., 1958-61; sr. minister 1st Christian Ch., Mt. Sterling, Ky., 1961-70, Paris, Ky., 1978-82; stewardship sec. Gen. Office Christian Ch., Indpls., 1970-74; adminstr. Christian Ch. Home of Louisville, 1974-78; dir. devel. Christian Ch. Homes Ky., Louisville, 1978; pres. Disciples of Christ Hist. Soc., Nashville, 1983-95, pres. emeritus, 1995. Author: A Century of Faith and Caring, 1983, Forward From The Past, 1991; editor: (jour.) Discipliana, 1983—92. Pres. Kiwanis Club, Pikeville, 1957, Mt. Sterling, 1963, lt. gov., Ctrl. Ky., 1965. Mem. Christian Ch. Avocations: writing, photography, golf, fishing.

SEALE, JAMES PAUL, medical educator, researcher; b. Baytown, Tex., Dec. 16, 1953; s. Thomas Frederick Seale and Elizabeth Louise Davis; m. Dana Paulette McDaniel, June 12, 1976; children: Josiah David, Julie Elizabeth Martin, Jonathan Paul, Jenni Kathryn. BA, U. Tex., Austin, 1975; MD, Baylor Coll. Medicine, Houston, 1978. Diplomate family physician Am. Bd. Family Medicine, 2004, addictionologist Am. Soc. Addiction Medicine, 1998. Rsch. dir., family medicine Mercer U. Sch. Medicine, Macon, Ga., 2003—, prof. family medicine, 2004—. Cons. Pan Am. Health Orgn., Washington, 2005—; lectr. U. Tex. Health Sci. Ctr., Houston, 2006. Author: (book) Substance Abuse: A Patient-Centered Approach. Recipient Humanism Medicine award, Mercer U. Sch. Medicine, 2007; Subtance Abuse Faculty Devel. fellowship, Nat. Inst. Alcohol Drug Abuse & Alcoholism, 1987—88, Generating Project fellowship, N.Am. Primary Care Rsch. Group & AAFP, 1999—2000. Mem.: Rsch. Soc. Alcoholism, Ga. Acad. Family Physicians, Internat. Soc. Biomed. Rsch. Alcoholism, Soc. Tchrs. Family Medicine, N.Am. Primary Care Rsch. Group, Am. Acad. Family Physicians, Alpha Omega Alpha. Achievements include research in Georgia-Texas improving brief intervention project. Office: Mercer Univ Sch Medicine FHC 3780 Eisenhower Pkwy Macon GA 31206 Office Fax: 478-784-5496. Business E-Mail: seale.paul@mccg.org.

SEALE, ROBERT ARTHUR, lawyer; b. Shreveport, La., July 17, 1942; s. Robert Arthur Sr. and Lucille (Frank) S.; m. Chalon Fontaine; children: Robert A. III, John Meyers. BBA, La. State U., 1964, JD, 1967. Bar: La. 1967, Tex. 1969. Mem. La. Law Rev., 1965—67; rsch. asst. La. Law Inst. for La. Mineral Code, Baton Rouge, 1967; law clk. U.S. Dist. Ct. (WD-LA), Shreveport, 1967-68; atty./ptnr. Vinson & Elkins, Houston, 1968—97; ptnr. Phelps Dunbar LLP, Houston, 2002—04; of counsel Liskow & Lewis, Houston, 2005—. Former trustee and gen. counsel Mus. of Fine Arts, Houston, 1981-89 Mem. devel. bd. U. Tex. Health Sci. Ctr., Houston, 1995—; trustee Episcopal H.S., Houston, 1985—88. Named one of Best Lawyers in Am. Fellow: Houston Bar Fedn. (life); mem.: ABA, Tex. Bar (sustaining life fellow), Omicron Delta Kappa. Avocations: civic and charitable activities, golf, travel. Office: Liskow & Lewis First City Tower 1001 Fannin Ste 1800 Houston TX 77002 Business E-Mail: raseale@liskow.com.

SEALEY-LARAGH, JEAN E., emeritus medical educator, researcher; d. Ivor P. and Elizabeth Wylie Sealey; m. John H. Laragh, Sept. 22, 1975; 1 child, Robert Sealey Laragh. BSc in Biochemistry, Glasgow U., Scotland, 1959, DSc in Biochemistry, 1975. Rsch. assoc. medicine Columbia U., Coll. Physicians & Surgeons, NYC, 1966—75; asst. prof. physiology in medicine Cornell U. Med. Coll., NYC, 1975—82, rsch. prof. physiology/biophysics in medicine, 1983—2000; rsch. prof. emerita physiology/biophysics in medicine Weill Cornell Med. Coll., NYC, 2000—. Dir., cardiovasc. Ctr. Labs. Cornell U. Med. Coll., 1975—95; mem. adv. com. Nat. Heart, Lung & Blood Inst., NIH, 1985—89. Contbr. scientific papers to over 250 profl. publs. Recipient Chavez Meml. award, Internat. Soc. Hypertension, 1982. Mem.: Am. Soc. Hypertension (chmn. sci. awards com. 1990—98, chmn. fin. com. 2003—04, pres.-elect 2004—06), Endocrine Soc., Am. Soc. Nephrology, Internat. Soc. Hypertension. Office: Weill Cornell Med Coll Box 266 1300 York Ave New York NY 10065-4805 Home Fax: 561-369-3479. Business E-Mail: jsealey@med.cornell.edu.

SEALL, STEPHEN ALBERT, lawyer; b. South Bend, Ind., Oct. 24, 1940; s. Stephen Henry and Mildred Rita (MacDonald) S.; m. Barbara Ann Halloran, June 25, 1966; children: John Paul, Edward Andrew, Ann Marie. BA, Purdue U., 1963; postgrad., Cornell U. Grad. Sch. Bus. Adminstrn., 1963; LLB, U. Notre Dame, 1966. Bar: Ind. 1966, U.S. Claims Ct. 1973, U.S. Tax Ct. 1968, U.S. Ct. Appeals (6th cir.) 1980, U.S. Ct. Appeals (7th cir.) 1969, U.S. Supreme Ct. 1973. Assoc. Thornburg, McGill, Deahl, Harman, Carey & Murray, South Bend, 1966-71; ptnr. Barnes & Thornburg LLP and predecessor firm Thornburg, McGill, Deahl, Harman, Carey & Murray, 1972—2005, vice chmn. and mgmt. com., mng. ptnr. South Bend office, 1985—2001. Spkr. in field. (Mem. editl. bd.) Notre Dame Law Rev., 1964—66. Mem. Mayor's Com. on Downtown Devel., South Bend, 1975-77, Mayor's Com. on Utilization of Downtown Bldgs., South Bend, 1988-96; trustee Project Future, South Bend, 1986-2002; exec. com. Meml. Hosp. South Bend, Inc., 1999-2003; dir. Meml. Health Found., 1992-98, Meml. Health Sys., 1997-2003, United Way of St. Joseph County, Inc., 1992-98, Conv. and Tourism Industry Coun., 1994-2000, CASIE Ctr., Inc., 1998-2006, Home Mgmt. Resources, Inc. 2003-06. Fellow Am. Coll. Tax Counsel, Am. Bar Found., Ind. Bar Found.; mem. ABA (taxation sect.), Ind. State Bar Assn. (chmn. taxation sect. 1977-78), Summit Club (chmn. 1976-77), Morris Park Country Club (bd. dirs., sec. 1998-2001). Democrat. Roman Catholic. Avocations: golf, softball, weightlifting. Office: Barnes & Thornburg LLP 600 1st Source Bank Ctr 100 N Michigan St Ste 600 South Bend IN 46601-1632 Home: 245 Martellago Dr North Venice FL 34275-6710 Office Phone: 574-233-1171.

SEALS, MARGARET LOUISE CRUMRINE, retired journalist; b. Buckhannon, W.Va., Oct. 27, 1944; d. James Richard and Helen Margaret (Brown) Crumrine; m. Harry Eugene Seals, Jan. 10, 1975. BS in journalism, W. Va. U., 1966; MS in mass. comm., Va. Commonwealth U., 1983. Reporter, copy editor Democrat & Chronicle, Rochester, NY, 1966-67, Dayton (Ohio) Daily News, 1967-68; copy editor Richmond (Va.) Times-Dispatch, 1968-75, copy desk slot editor, 1975-81, exec. news editor, 1981, asst. mng. editor, 1982-92, dep. mng. editor, 1992-93, mng. editor, 1994—2006. Adj. intr. Va. Commonwealth U. Mass Comm. Sch., 2007—08. Mem. Leadership Metro Richmond, 1986, seminar days co-chair, 2007-08, curriculum com., 2007-08; mem. adv. bd. sch. mass. comm. Va. Commonwealth U., 1988-93, mem. alumni adv. bd. 04-; mem. adv. com. Sch. Journalism, W.Va. U., 1999—. Named Outstanding Woman in Comms. YWCA Met. Richmond, 1989; recipient Perley Isaac Reed award W.Va. U. Journalism Sch. Alumni Assn., 1996; inducted into Va. Comm. Hall of Fame, 2003. Mem.: Ctrl. Va. Chpt. W.Va. U. Alumni Assn. (treas. 2008—), Richmond Tree Steward (mem. adv. panel 2009—), Va. Press Assn. (dir. 2001—03, treas. 2003—04, sec. 2004—05, v.p. 2005—06), AP Mng. Editors (editor APME News 1993—94, dir. 1993—95, treas. 1996—97, dir. 1998—2001, Disting. Svc. award 2002, 75th anniversary editor 2008), Va. Press Women Found. (treas. 1986—88, 2d v.p. 1988—90, pres. 1990—92, 2008—, Press Woman of Yr. 1986, Communicator of Achievement award 1997), Soc. Profl. Journalists (bd. dirs. Va. profl. chpt. 1998—2003, pres. Va. profl. chpt. 2000—02), Nat. Fedn. Press Women (bd. dirs. 1990—92, Communicator of Achievement award 1997), Phi Kappa Phi. Avocations: history, hiking, travel, gardening. Personal E-mail: louise.seals@comcast.net.

SEAMAN, ALFRED BARRETT, journalist, writer; b. Rockville Center, NY, July 4, 1945; s. Alfred Jarvis and Mary Margaret (Schill) S.; m. Laura Powers Maxwell, Apr. 25, 1970; children: Katherine Maxwell, Margaret Elise, Elizabeth Barrett. BA, Hamilton Coll., 1967; MBA, Columbia U., 1971. Reporter Life mag., NYC, 1971-72, Fortune mag., NYC, 1972; corr. Time mag., NYC, 1973, Chgo., 1973-76, Bonn, Germany, 1976-78, bur. chief Detroit, 1978-81, dep. bur. chief Washington, 1981-83, White House corr., 1984-88, dep. chief corrs. NYC, 1988-91, sr. editor, 1991-94, spl. projects editor, 1994—2001. Co-author: Going for Broke: The Chrysler Story, 1981; author: Binge: Campus Life in an Age of Disconnection and Excess, 2005. Alumni trustee Hamilton Coll., Clinton, N.Y., 1990-93, 94-95, charter trustee, 1997—; trustee Village of Irvington, N.Y., 1992-94. With USNR, 1969-71. Mem.: U.S. Sr. Golf Assn., Univ. Glee Club N.Y.C. Episcopalian. Avocations: tennis, golf. Home: Ardsley Ave W Ardsley On Hudson NY 10503

SEAMAN, ALFRED JARVIS, retired advertising agency executive; b. Hempstead, L.I., NY, Sept. 17, 1912; s. Alfred J. and Ellen (Delaney) S.; m. Mary M. Schill, Sept. 26, 1937 (dec. June 1975); children: Marilyn Hollingsworth, Susan, Barry, Deborah; m. Honor S. Mellor, July 16, 1977. BS, Columbia U., 1935; LittD, L.I. U., 1987. Account exec. Fuller & Smith & Ross, Inc., NYC, 1937-41; partner Knight & Gilbert. Inc., Boston, 1941-43; with Compton Advt., Inc., NYC, 1946-59, exec. v.p., creative dir., dir., 1954-59; vice chmn. bd., chmn. exec. com. SSC & B, Inc., 1959-60, pres., chief exec. officer, 1960-79, chmn., chief exec. officer, 1979-81. Dir., mem. exec. com. Interpublic Group of Cos., Inc. Hon. bd. dirs., adv. council, founding chmn. Advt. Ednl. Found.; bd. dirs., hon. dir. com. Advt. Council.; chmn. planning bd., 1962—, mayor Village Upper Brookville, 1966-98; chmn. emeritus Samuel Waxman Cancer Research Found.; dir. Jupiter Hosp., 1991-2002. Lt. USNR, 1943-46. Named to Advt. Hall of Fame, 1983 Mem.: U.S. Sr. Golf Assn., Creek (Locust Valley, L.I.) (pres.), Piping Rock (Locust Valley, L.I.), Racquet and Tennis (N.Y.C.), Jupiter Island (Fla.), Nat. Golf Links Am. (Southampton, N.Y.), Seminole (Fla.), Hobe Sound Yacht (Fla.). Home: Wolver Hollow Rd Upper Brookville Oyster Bay NY 11771 also: Jupiter Island 126 Gomez Rd Hobe Sound FL 33455-2424 Office: 220 E 42nd St New York NY 10017-5806

SEAMAN, ARLENE ANNA, retired musician; b. Pontiac, Mich., Jan. 21, 1918; d. Roy Russell and Mabel Louise (Heffron) S. BS, life cert., Ea. Mich. U., 1939; MMus, Wayne State U., 1951; postgrad., Colo. Coll., 1951-52, Acad. Music, Zermatt Switzerland, 1954-58, U. Mich. Guest conductor Shepherds and Angels, Symphonie Concertante, 1951; asst. conductor Detroit Women's Symphony, 1960-68; adjudicator Mich. State Band and Orch. Festivals, Solo and Ensemble Festivals, 1950-70, Detroit Fiddler's Band Auditions, 1948-52, Mich. Fedn. Music Clubs, 1948-55; tchr. Ea. Mich. U., 1939-42, Hartland Sch. Music, 1939-42, Pontiac (Mich.) Pub. Schs., 1942-45, Detroit Pub. Schs., 1945-73, pvt. studio, 1973-90. Performer cello South Oakland Symphony, 1958-65, Detroit Women's Symphony, 1951-68, Riviera Theatre Orch., 1959, 60, Masonic Auditorium Opera, Ballet Seasons, 1959-65, Toledo Ohio Symphony, 1963-70, others; performer trumpet Detroit Brass Quartet, 1974-78; piano accompanist various auditions, recitals, solo and ensemble festivals; composer: Let There Be Music, 1949, Fantasy for French Horn and Symphonic Band, 1951. Mem. Quota Internat., Delta Omicron. Home: 6231 N Montebella Rd #347 Tucson AZ 85704

SEAMAN, IRVING, JR., banker; b. Milw., July 14, 1923; s. Irving and Anne (Douglas) S.; m. June Carry, June 24, 1950, (dec. 2001); children: Peter Stewart, Marion Carry, Terry Osborne, Anne Douglas; m. Barbara P. Gardner, May 22, 2002. BA, Yale U., 1944. With Continental Ill. Nat. Bank & Trust Co., Chgo., 1947-61, v.p., 1959-61; pres., chief exec. officer, dir. Nat. Boulevard Bank, Chgo., 1961-65, chmn. exec. com., chief exec. officer, dir., 1966-76; vice chmn. bd., dir. Sears Bank and Trust Co., Chgo., 1976-77, pres., chief operating officer, dir., 1977-82; sr. cons. Burson-Marsteller, Chgo., 1982-94. Chmn. bd. Associated Bank Chgo., 1985-05. Mem. Northwestern U. Assn.; life mem. bd. dirs. Lake Forest Hosp.; bd. dirs. United Way of Chgo., 1975-89, pres., 1979; bd. dirs. United Way/Crusade of Mercy, 1980-89, 94-95, vice chmn., 1980-81; trustee Chgo. Symphony Orch., 1987—. Lt. (j.g.) USNR, WWII. Mem. Commonwealth Club, Econ. Club, Chgo. Club, Comml. Club, Racquet Club, Onwentsia Club, Old Elm Club, Shoreacres Club, Augusta Nat. Golf Club, Sawgrass Country Club. Home: 666 N Sheridan Rd Lake Forest IL 60045-1410

SEAMAN, SCOTT M., lawyer; b. Chgo. m. Charlene Mc Mann; 1 child, Danielle. BA, Barat Coll., Lk. Forest, 1984; JD Magma cum Laude, Loyola U. Chgo. Sch. Law, 1987. Bar: US Supreme Ct. 1993, Ill. 1987, US Ct. Appeals (7th cir.) 1988, US Ct. Appeals (10th cir.), US

Dist. Ct. (Northern Dist. Ill.) 1987, US Dist. Ct. (Ctrl. Dist. Ill.) 1989, US Dist. Ct. (Northern Dist. Fla.). Attorney Skadden, Arps, Slate, Meagher & Flom, Chgo., 1987—94; ptnr. Meckler Bulger Tilson Marick & Pearson LLP, Chgo., 1994—. Expert content prodr. & commentator Lexis-Nexis, 2008. Co-author: (book) Allocation Of Losses In Complex Insurance Coverage Claims, 2006, 2nd Ed., 2008; contbg. editor: Wrongfull Death And Survival Action, 2007; contbr. chapters to books, articles in numerous profl. jours. Co-founded Chgo. Chap.,Co-Chair. Lymphoma Rsch. Found., 2002—08; Key Note Adderess North Am. Forum Lymphoma, LA, 2006; mem. Nat. Bd. Selectors Jefferson Awards Pub. Svc., 2008. Recipient AV rated, Martindale Hubbell, 1995, Inaugural Tribute award, Lymphom Rsch. Found., 2007; named one of Ill. Super Lawyers, Law & Politics, 2005—09. Mem.: Am. Bar Assoc. (past v.chair Tort Trial & Insurance Practice Sec., Litigation Practice Sec., Comml. & Bus. Litigation oom.), Defense Rsch. Inst. (Alternative Dispute Resolution Com., Insurance Com., Comml. Litigation Com., Internat. Law Com., Climate Change Litigation Task Force, Bus. Torts Substantive Law Group). Office: Meckler Bulger Tilson Marick & Pearson LLP 123 North Wacker Dr Ste 1800 Chicago IL 60606 Office Phone: 312-474-7139. Business E-Mail: scott.seaman@mbtlaw.com.

SEAMAN, SHEILA LYNNE, librarian; b. Mich., 1950; d. William Henry and Delight Anne Seaman; m. John P. Nee, Aug. 14, 1976. BA, Colby Coll., Waterville, Maine, 1972; MLS, Case Western Res. U., Cleve., 1973. Asst. libr. Greenfield CC, Mass., 1973—77; coord. pub. svcs. U. South, Sewanee, Tenn., 1977—81; asst. reference libr. Coll. Charleston, SC, 1981—84, asst. dean pub. svcs., 1984—. Contbr. articles to profl. jours. Mem.: ALA, Am. Coll. & Rsch. Librs. Office: Coll Charleston 205 Calhoun St Charleston SC 29401 Office Fax: 843-953-6319. Business E-Mail: seamans@cofc.edu.

SEAMANS, WILLIAM, writer, retired reporter, commentator; b. Providence, July 8, 1925; s. William and Mary Seamans; m. Jane Kingsbury, Sept. 15, 1951; children: Laurie, Jonathan, Adam. AB, Brown U., 1949; MS, Columbia U., 1952. Freelance journalist, 1952-53; journalist CBS News, 1953-63; producer evening news ABC News, 1963-65, European producer London, 1965-70, field producer NYC, 1970-72, corr., bur. chief Tel Aviv, 1972-92; commentator Vt. Pub. Radio, lectr., freelance writer, 1992—. Producer Nightline in Israel Week (including Palestinian-Israeli town meeting) (Emmy award, Dupont award). Served with inf. AUS, 1942-45. Decorated Bronze Star medal; CBS Murrow News fellow Columbia U., 1961-62. Mem. Writers Guild Am., Nat. Acad. TV Arts and Scis. (Emmy award 1961, 89), Overseas Press Club Am. (award for best radio reporting invasion of Cyprus 1974, award for best fgn. affairs documentary Yitzhak Rabin biography 1975), Nat. Press Club (Washington), Fgn. Corrs. Assn. in Israel. E-mail: wmseamans@verizon.net.

SEAPKER, JANET KAY, museum administrator, architectural historian, consultant; b. Pitts., Nov. 2, 1947; d. Charles Henry and Kathryn Elizabeth (Dany) Seapker; m. Edward F. Turberg, May 24, 1975. BA, U. Pitts., 1969; MA, SUNY, Cooperstown, 1975. Park ranger Nat. Park Svc., summers 1967-69; archtl. historian N.C. Archives and History, Raleigh, 1971—76, hist. preservation adminstr., 1976—77, grant-in-aid adminstr., 1977—78; dir. Cape Fear Mus. (formerly New Hanover County Mus.), Wilmington, NC, 1978—2000, ret.; archtl. historian-preservation/mus. cons.; curator U. N.C. Wilmington's Kenan House, 2003—04, Minnie Evans Study Ctr., Cameron Art Mus., 2008—09. Bd. dirs. Bellamy Mansion Found., Wilmington, 1986-89, 91-97, Lower Cape Fear Hist. Soc., Wilmington, 1985-88; N.C. rep. S.E. Mus. Conf., 1986-90; bd. dirs. Cape Fear Coast Conv. and Vis. Bur., 1997-2001, sec., 2001, Wrightsville Beach Mus., 2004-05; field reviewer Inst. Mus. Svcs., 1982-2001 Contbr. articles to profl. jours. Bd. dirs. Downtown Area Revitalization Effort, Wilmington, 1979-81, Thalian Hall Ctr. for Performing Arts, 1996-98; bd. dirs. Hist. Wilmington Found., 1979-84, pres., 1980-81; mem. Cmty. Appearance Commn., Wilmington, 1984-88, 250th Anniversary Commn., Wilmington, 1986-90; mem. Wilmington Historic Preservation Commn., 2005-2008, vice chair Historic Preservation Commn.; pres. Friends of Oakdale Cemetery, Inc., 2004-08. Grad. program fellow SUNY, Cooperstown, 1969-70; recipient Profl. Svc. award N.C. Mus. Coun., 1982, Woman of Achievement award YWCA, 1994, Historic Wilmington found. Katherine Howell Lifetime Achievement award, 2008. Mem. Am. Assn. Mus. (accreditation vis. com. 1983-2001, reviewer mus. assessment program 1982-2002), Nat. Trust Hist. Preservation, Southeastern Mus. Conf. (N.C. state rep. 1986-90), N.C. Mus. Coun. (sec.-treas. 1978-84, pres. 1984-86; recipient William T. Anderson award 2004), Hist. Preservation Found N.C. (sec. 1976-78). Presbyterian. Home and Office: 307 N 15th St Wilmington NC 28401-3813 Office Phone: 910-762-6301. Personal E-mail: jseapker@ec.rr.com.

SEARCY, MARSHALL MAYES, JR., lawyer; b. San Diego, Calif., Oct. 30, 1946; s. Marshall Mayes and Evelyn Williamson Searcy; m. April Annette Thomas Giroir, Dec. 27, 1995; children: Marshall Mayes III, Kyle Eric Giroir, Amy Meredith, Dustin Nils Giroir, Alisa Holland Giroir, Rebecca Merrill, Timofee Wallace. BA with honors, U. Tex., Austin, 1969; JD with honors, U. Tex., 1972. Bar: Tex., US Ct. Appeals (5th cir. and fed. cir.), Tex. (fed. dist. cts.). Ptnr. Rain Harrell Emery, Dallas, 1972—87, Locke Purnell Rain Harrell, Dallas, 1987—93, Kelly Hart & Hallman LLP, Fort Worth, Tex., 1993—. Recipient Law Good Scout award, Boy Scouts of Am. Longhorn Coun., 2006; named one of Best Lawyers in Am. Super Lawyers, Tex. Monthly Mag. Fellow: Am. Coll. Trial Lawyers; mem.: Fort Worth Bar Found., Tex. Bar Found., Am. Bd. Trial Advocates. Avocation: Russian lang. & hist. Home: 1517 Hillcrest St Fort Worth TX 76107-1575 Office: Kelly Hart & Hallman LLP 201 Main St Ste 2500 Fort Worth TX 76102-3105 Business E-Mail: marshall.searcy@khh.com.

SEARCY, WILLIAM NELSON, lawyer, director; b. Moultire, Ga., June 26, 1942; s. Floyd Hartsfield and Anna (Pidcock) Searcy; m. Camille Heery, June 17, 1967; 1 child, Amelia Ashburn. AB, U. Ga., 1964, JD, 1967; LLM in Taxation, Washington U., St. Louis, 1968. Bar: Ga. 1967, U.S. Dist. Ct. (so. dist.) Ga. 1970, U.S. Ct. Appeals (5th and 11th cirs.) 1976, U.S. Tax Ct. Assoc. Bouhan, Williams & Levy, Savannah, Ga., 1970-73; ptnr. Brannen, Searcy & Smith LLP, Savannah, 1973—. Sec. Am. Fed. Savs. and Loan Assn., 1978—81; mem. adv. bd. Liberty Savs. Bank, 1984—88; chmn. bd. dirs. Citizens Bank, 1991—. Pres. Chatham-Savannah Voluntary Action Ctr., Inc., 1978—80; bd. trustees Mighty Eighth USAF Mus., 2005—. U. Ga. Found., 2006—. Served to maj. gen. Ga. N.G. USAF, 1967—2004, comdr. Ga. N.G. USAF, 2000—04. Mem.: ABA (sec. spl. liaison tax com. S.E. region 1983—85, chmn. 1984—85), Inst. Continuing Legal Edn., Savannah Estate Planning Coun., Am. Judicature Soc., Savannah Bar Assn. (pres. Younger Lawyers sect. 1975—76), State Bar Ga. (mem.-at-large exec. coun. Young Lawyers sect. 1975—78, chmn. conf. with Ga. Soc. CPAs 1979—81, chmn. sect. taxation 1983—84, Ga. commn. continuing lawyer competency 1989—95, vice chmn. 1995), N.G. Assn. U.S. (chmn. air resolution com. 2001—03, bd. dirs. 2002—04, chmn. resolutions com. 2003—05, spl. adv. com. 2005—), Georgian Club, Savannah Golf Club, Oglethorpe Club, Rotary (pres. Savannah West 2004—05). Office: PO Box 8002 Savannah GA 31412-8002

SEARLE, RODNEY NEWELL, state legislator, farmer, insurance agent; b. Camden, NJ, July 17, 1920; s. William Albert and Ruby Marie (Barrus) S.; m. Janette Elizabeth Christie, May 17, 1941 (dec.); children: R. Newell Jr., Linda Jennison Grant, Alan John; m. Ruth Anne Bartlett, May 6, 2001. BA, Mankato State U., 1960; DHL, Winona State U., 2001. Prodn. coordinator Johnson & Johnson, New Brunswick, NJ, 1940-47; farmer Waseca, Minn., 1947—; spl. agt. John Hancock Mut. Ins. Co., Waseca, Minn., 1961-84; mem. Minn. Ho. of Reps., St. Paul, 1957-80, speaker, 1979—. Bd. pres. Minn. Legis. Soc., 1996—. Author: Minnesota Standoff-The Politics of Deadlock, 1990. Lay reader St. John's Episcopal Ch., 1952—; chmn. Upper Mississippi River Basin Commn., 1981-82; pres. Minn. State U. Bd., 1981-92; chmn. Minn. Higher Edn. Bd., 1991-92; bd. dirs. Minn. Wellsprings, 1984-90; emeritus mem. adv. bd. Hubert H. Humphrey Inst.; emeritus mem. coun. Minn. Hist. Soc.; bd. dirs. Minn. Agrl. Interpretive Ctr., 1983-02; mem. Waseca County Hist. Bd., 1995—; capt. Minn. Wing of the Civil Air Patrol. Named Minn. State Tree Farmer of Yr., 1978 Mem. Am. Tree Farm Sys., Nat. Conf. State Legislators, Minn. Forestry Assn. (bd. dirs. 1991-01), Masons, Rotary (pres. club 1968). Independent.

SEARLS, EILEEN HAUGHEY, retired lawyer, librarian, educator; b. Madison, Wis., Apr. 27, 1925; d. Edward M. and Anna Mary (Haughey) S. BA, U. Wis., 1948, JD, 1950, MS in LS, 1951. Bar: Wis. 1950. Cataloger Yale U., 1951-52; instr. law St. Louis U., 1952-53, asst. prof., 1953-56, assoc. prof., 1956-64, prof., 1964-2000, law libr., 1952-2000. Chmn. Coun. Law Libr. Consortia, 1984-90; sec. Bd. of Conciliaton and Arbitration, Archdiocese of St. Louis, 1986-98. Named Woman of Yr. Women's Commn., St. Louis U., 1986. Mem. ABA, ALA, Wis. Bar Assn., Bar Assn. Met. St. Louis, Am. Assn. Law Librs. (Marian Gould Gallagher Disting. Svc. award 1999), Mid Am. Assn. Law Librs. (pres. 1984-86), Mid Am. Law Sch. Libr. Consortium (chmn. 1980-84), Southwestern Assn. Law Librs., Altrusa Club. Office: 3700 Lindell Blvd Saint Louis MO 63108-3412 Business E-Mail: searlseh@slu.edu.

SEARS, DAVID O'KEEFE, psychology professor; b. Urbana, Ill., June 24, 1935; s. Robert R. and Pauline (Snedden) S.; married; children: Juliet, Olivia, Meredith. BA in History, Stanford U., 1957; PhD in Psychology, Yale U., 1962. Asst. prof. to disting. prof. psychology and polit. sci. UCLA, 1961—, dean social scis., 1983-92. Dir. Inst. for Social Sci. Rsch., 1993-2008. Author: Public Opinion, 1964, Politics of Violence, 1973, Tax Revolt, 1985, Political Cognition, 1986, Social Psychology, 12th edit., 2005, Racialized Politics, 2000, Oxford Handbook of Political Psychology, 2003, The Diversity Challenge, 2008. Recipient Edward L. Bernays award, Soc. for Psychol. Study of Social Issues, 1979, Warren E. Miller Career award, Am. Polit. Sci. Assn., 2003; fellow, Guggenheim, 1988—89. Fellow Am. Acad. Arts and Scis.; mem. Soc. for Advancement Socio-Econs. (pres. 1991-92), Internat. Soc. Polit. Psychology (pres. 1994-95, Harold D. Lasswell award 1994). Office: UCLA Psychology Dept Los Angeles CA 90095-0001 Office Phone: 310-825-2160. Business E-Mail: sears@psych.ucla.edu.

SEARS, DONNA MAE, writer, illustrator; b. St. Paul, Oct. 23, 1951; d. Raymond and Shirley Marie (Dupre) Waldoch; m. Mark D. Sears, Sept. 4, 1993. BA in Art and Edn., Cardinal Stritch Coll., Milw., 1969-73; postgrad., Rock Valley Coll., Rockford, Ill., 1985, 87, 89-90, So. Ill. U., 1983; cert. of tng., Computervision Tech. Ctr., Itasca, Ill., 1986-88. Electronic assembler Warner Electric Co., Marengo, Ill., 1973-75, machine hand, 1976-78, quality assurance lead insp., 1978-80, draftswoman, 1980-86, CAD-sr. draftswoman, 1986-87; tchr. art Stephen Mack Sch. Dist., Rockford, 1975, Harrison Sch. Dist., Wonder Lake, Ill., 1975-76; CAD specialist Greenlee Textron Inc., Rockford, 1988-89; asst. buyer Ingersoll Milling, Rockford, 1989-90; asst. office mgr. and sign maker Shake-A-Leg Signs, Rockford, 1990-92; tech. writer and illustrator Mathews Co., Crystal Lake, Ill., 1992; engring. CAD illustrator Clinton Electronics, Loves Park, Ill., 1993-2000; from sr. CAD designer to coord. mfg. engring. Pacific Bearing Co., Roscoe, Ill., 2000—06, engr. sys. adminstrn., process engr., 2006—. Author: (with others) Treasured Poems of America, 1990, Poetic Voices of America, spring 1992, Anthology of American Poetry, fall 1991 (awards of Poetic Excellence 1992), Distinguished Poets of America, spring 1993, The Sound of Poetry, spring 1993. Vol. Boone County Conservation Dist., 1990-92; mem. choir St. James Ch., Belvidere, Ill., 1985-93; assoc. mem. Spl. Olympics; mem. Macktown Living Hist. Edn. Ctr., 1999-2004, 2008-. Recipient Leadership award YWCA, Rockford, 1988. Mem. Am. Bus. Women's Assn., Macktown Living History Edn. Ctr. (bd. dirs., sec. 1999-2002). Roman Catholic. Avocations: bicycling, art, gardening, fishing, camping. Office: Pacific Bearing Co 6402 Rockton Rd Roscoe IL 61073 Business E-Mail: donna.sears@pacific-bearing.com.

SEARS, HELEN, city councilwoman; Dir. govt. & cmty. affairs Health & Hosp. Corp. Elmhurst Med. Ctr., Queens, NY; city councilwoman Dist. 25 NY City Coun., 2002—. Chmn. Women's Issues com. NY City Coun. Co-founder, dir. Catherine Sheridan Sr. Ctr.; bd. mem. NYC Health Sys. Agy. Named Woman of Yr, 115th Precinct Community Coun. Democrat. Mailing: Dist Off 37-32 75th St Queens NY 11372 Office Phone: 718-803-6373, 212-788-7066. Office Fax: 718-803-9832. Business E-Mail: sears@council.nyc.ny.us.*

SEARS, JAMES WALTER, geologist, educator; b. Champain, Ill., Feb. 10, 1949; s. Robert Carver and Mary Hoch Sears; m. Debra Burnette, May 24, 1981; children: Robert David, Stephen Carver, Kathryn Elayne, Leila Marie, Adam James, Ellen Anne. BS, Northern Ariz. U., Flagstaff, 1971; MS, U. Wyo., Laramie, 1973; PhD, Queen's U., Kingston, Can., 1979. Asst. prof. Auburn U., Ala.; prof. U. Mont., Missoula, 1982—, geology field sch. dir., 1991—. Contbr. scientific papers (Disting. Scholar, U. Mont., 2008). Rsch. grant, NSF, 2001, 2003. Mem.: Geol. Soc. America. Office: Univ Montana Campus Dr Missoula MT 59812 Business E-Mail: james.sears@umontana.edu.

SEARS, JIM (JAMES M. SEARS), pediatrician; m. Diane Sears; children: Lea, Jonathan. MD, St. Louis U., 1996. Pediatric resident Northeastern Ohio U. Coll. Medicine and Tod Children's Hosp., Youngstown, 1996—99; pvt. practice Capistrano Beach, Calif.; med. expert The Doctors, 2008—. Lectr. in field. Co-author: The Baby Book, 2003, The Premature Baby Book, 2004, The Healthiest Kid in the Neighborhood, 2006, Father's First Steps-Twenty-Five Things Every New Father Should Know, 2006, The Baby Sleep Book, 2006; contbr. Parenting mag., Baby Talk mag. Avocations: bicycling, skiing, hiking. Office: Sears Family Pediatrics 26933 Camino De Estrella Capistrano Beach CA 92624*

SEARS, JOHN PATRICK, lawyer; b. Syracuse, NY, July 3, 1940; s. James Louis and Helen Mary (Fitzgerald) Sears; m. Carol Jean Osborne, Aug. 25, 1962; children: James Louis, Ellen Margaret, Amy Elizabeth. BS, Notre Dame U., 1960; LLB, JD, Georgetown U., 1963. Bar: N.Y. 1963. Clk. N.Y. Ct. Appeals, 1963-65; assoc. Nixon, Mudge, Rose, Guthrie, Alexander & Mitchell, 1965-66; mem. staff Richard M. Nixon, 1966-69; dep. counsel to U.S. Pres. Richard Nixon Washington, 1969-70; ptnr. Gadsby & Hannah, Washington, 1970-75, Baskin & Sears, Washington, 1977-84; pvt. practice Washington, 1984—. Polit. analyst NBC Today Show, 1984—89; mem. bd. polit. experts Wall St. Jour., 1984—. Columnist: LA Times, Newsday, 1992—. Mgr. Ronald Reagan's Presdls. Campaign, 1975—76, 1979—80; sr. advisor Jack Kemp for V.P. Campaign, 1996. Fellow, Kennedy Inst. Politics, Harvard U., 1970. Home and Office: 3350 SW 27th Ave Apt 1203 Miami FL 33133

SEARS, JOHN WINTHROP, lawyer; b. Boston, Dec. 18, 1930; s. Richard Dudley and Frederica Fulton (Leser) S.; m. Catherine Coolidge, 1965 (div. 1970). AB magna cum laude, Harvard U., Cambridge, Mass., 1952, JD, 1959; MLitt, Oxford U., Eng., 1957; D Polit. Sci. (hon.), Bridgewater State Coll., Mass., 2006. Bar: Mass. 1959, U.S. Dist. Ct. Mass. 1982. Rep. Brown Bros. Harriman, NYC, 1959-63, Boston, 1963-66; mem. Mass. Ho. Reps., 1965-68; sheriff Suffolk County, Mass., 1968-69; chmn. Boston Fin. Commn., 1969-70, Met. Dist. Commn., 1970-75; councilor-at-large Boston City Coun., 1980-82; trustee Sears Office, Boston, 1975—. Contbr. articles to profl. jours. Apptd. bd. dirs. Fulbright Scholarship, 1991-93; trustee Christ's Ch., Longwood, Brookline, Mass., 1965—, Sears Trusts, Boston, 1975—; hon. trustee J.F. Kennedy Libr., 1991—2003; bd. dirs. Am. Mus. Textile Heritage, 1987-97, Shirley-Eustis Assoc., Environ. League, Mass., 1994-97; Rep. candidate Sec. State, Mass., 1978, Gov. of Mass., 1982; vice chmn. Ward 5 Rep. Com., 1965-69, 75-85; chmn. Rep. State Com., 1975-76, mem., 1980-85; del. Rep. Nat. Conv., 1968, 76, State Conv., 1966-92; mem. U.S. Electoral Coll., 1984; bd. dirs. United South End Settlements, 1966—, chmn., 1977-78. Lt. comdr. USNR, 1952-54, 61-62. Recipient Outstanding Pub. Servant award Mass. Legis. Assn., 1975; Rhodes scholar, 1955 Mem. Mass. Bar Assn., New Eng. Hist. and Geneal. Soc. (bd. dirs., councillor 1977-82), Mass. Hist. Soc., Handel and Haydn Soc. (gov. 1982-87), Signet Soc., Boston Atheneum, Tennis and Racquet Club, Somerset Club, The Country Club (Brookline), St. Botolph Club, Club of Odd Vols., Wednesday Evening Club of 1777, Thursday Evening Club of 1846 (pres. 1999-2004), Spee Club (Cambridge) (pres., trustee), Longwood Cricket Club (hon.), Phi Beta Kappa, Beacon Hill Seminars. Republican. Home: 7 Acorn St Boston MA 02108-3501 *As the working years come to an end, some of us look for ways to teach, to help neighbors, especially those in need, to build up the beauty and excellence we may have encountered in our own lives, and do our best to pass them on to others.*

SEARS, MARY HELEN, lawyer; b. Syracuse, NY; d. James Louis and Helen Mary (Fitzgerald) Sears. AB, Cornell U., Ithaca, NY, 1950; JD with honors, George Wash. U., Washington, DC, 1960. Bar: Va. 1960, DC 1961, US Supreme Ct. 1963. Chemist Allied Chem. and Dye Corp., Syracuse, 1950-52, Hercules Powder Co., Wilmington, Del., 1952-55; patent examiner US Patent Office, Washington, 1955-60; pvt. practice Washington, 1960—64; assoc. Irons, Birch, Swindler & McKie, Washington, 1969—81; mem. firm Irons & Sears, Washington, 1981—84; chmn. trade regulation practice dept. Memel, Jacobs, Pierno, Gersh & Ellsworth, Washington, 1984-87; ptnr., chmn. intellectual property and unfair competition practice dept. Ginsburg, Feldman & Bress, Washington, 1987-91; ptnr., chmn. intellectual property and telecomm. practice group Reid & Priest, Washington, 1991-94; founder, chmn. M. H. Sears Law Firm, 1994—2007. Mem. adv. bd. Boardroom Reports, Inc., NYC, 1980-85; mem. Cornell U. Coun., 1981-87, 89-93, life mem., 1995—, mem. adminstrv. bd., 1984-86. Contbr. articles to various publs. Recipient Outstanding Performance award, US Dept. Commerce, 1957, World's Leading Patent Law Experts, Euromoney Publs., PLC, 2001, Belva Lockwood prize, George Wash. U. Law Sch. Assn. for Women, 2007; named one of World's Leading Patent Law Experts, Euromoney Publs., PLC, 1995, 1997, 2003, 2005, 2007. Mem.: ABA (co-chmn. appellate practice com., litigation sect. 1989—92), DC Bar Assn., Va. State Bar Assn., Am. Soc. Internat. Law, Am. Intellectual Property Law Assn., George Wash. U. Law Alumnae Assn. (bd. dirs. 1995—2001), Order of Coif, Phi Alpha Delta. Republican. E-mail: mhsears@mhsears.com, mhsears@verizon.net.

SEARS, PATRICIA MARIE, elementary school educator, consultant; b. Portsmouth, Va., Aug. 19, 1952; d. Peter Paul and Esther Marie Vispo; 1 child, Stephanie Marie. BS magna cum laude in Elem. Edn., Old Dominion U., 1974; MEd, Campbell Coll., 1979. Cert. early edn. Va., gifted edn. Va., elem. sch. prin. Va., elem. sch. supr. Va. Tchr. Norfolk Pub. Sch., Va., 1974—75, 1979—80, Wake County Pub. Sch., Raleigh, NC, 1975—79; gifted tchr. Virginia Beach City Pub. Sch., 1980—87, gifted resource tchr., 1987—89, early childhood coord., 1989—2003, lang. arts. coord., 2005—08; cons. Pearson Edn., Old Tappan, NJ, 2005—. Assoc. prof. Tidewater CC, 1994—95; pres. Reel Connections, Ltd., 1997; reviewer Pearson Learning Group, Parsippany, NJ, 1999—; presenter in field. Author: Language Arts Birth-5, 1998. V.p. Princess Anne Rep. Women's Club, Virginia Beach, 2002—03; mem. Friends of Libr., Virginia Beach, 2000—. Mem.: Nat. Assn. Gifted Children, Delta Kappa Gamma. Roman Catholic. Avocations: reading, travel. Home: 4768 Red Coat Rd Virginia Beach VA 23455

SEARS, ROBERT STEPHEN, finance educator, former dean; b. Odessa, Tex., May 27, 1950; s. William Bethel and Leola Vernon (Little) S.; Reva Dana Flournoy, Aug. 17, 1973; children: Matthew Stephen, Elizabeth Rea. AAS, Odessa Jr. Coll., 1970; BA summa cum laude, Tex. Tech. U., 1973, MS, 1976; PhD, U. N.C., 1980. Supr. Bethel Enterprises, Odessa, 1973—74; tchg. asst. Tex. Tech U., Lubbock, 1974—76, dir. Inst. Banking and Fin. Studies, 1988—98; tchg. asst. U. N.C., Chapel Hill, 1976—79; asst. prof. U. Ill., Champaign, 1979—85, assoc. prof., 1985—88; rsch. prof. Bur. Econ. and Bus., Champaign, 1984; tchg. asst. Lubbock Bankers Assn., 1990—2005; chmn. dept. fin. Tex. Tech U., Lubbock, 1997—2001, interim dean Coll. Bus., 2000, sr. exec. assoc. dean, Coll. Bus, 2001—03; Milan Puskar dean Coll. Bus. & Economics W.Va. U., Morgantown, 2005—08, prof. fin., 2005—. Cons. Cameron Brown Mortgage Co., Raleigh, N.C., 1978-80, Howard Savs. Bank, Livingston, N.J., 1980; asset mgr., trustee, pvt. investors, 1984—. Author: Investment Management, 1993, (chpt) Modern Real Estate, 1980, 84; assoc. editor Rev. of Bus. Studies, 1989-95, Jour. Fin. Rsch., 1990-96, Internat. Chmn. fin. com. Temple Bapt. Ch., Champaign, Ill., 1982, bd. deacons, 1982-88, chmn. deacons, lay leader, 1983; Sunday sch. tchr. Carrboro (NC) Bapt. Ch., 1977-79; bd. deacons Ind. Ave. Bapt. Ch., Lubbock, 1989-96, Sunday sch. tchr., 1991-92, master design com., 1993-96; trustee All Saints Episcopal Sch., 1995-2003, treas., 2000-03; bd. deacons Southcrest Bapt. Ch., Lubbock, 1998-2005 Rsch. grantee Cameron Brown Mortgage Co., Raleigh, N.C., 1978-80, U. Ill, Champaign, 1980-84, 86-87, Investors in Bus. Edn., Champaign, 1980-81, 84; recipient Excellence in Undergrad. Tchg. award U. Ill. Champaign, 1984-85, Award for Outstanding Coll. Educator Champaign-Urbana, Ill. Jaycees, 1983-84, Coll. of Commerce Alumni Assn. Undergrad. Excellence in Tchg. award U. Ill., 1981-82; Mortar Bd., Omicron Delta Kappa Leadership scholarship and Svc. award Tex. Tech U., 1997-98, Pres.'s Excellence in Tchg. award Tex. Tech U., 1993-94, Acad. Achievement award Tex. Tech U., 1994-95. Mem. Am. Fin. Assn., Southwestern Fin. Assn. (pres. 1989-90, v.p., program chmn. 1988-89, sec., treas. 1986-88, bd. dirs. 1984-86, program com. 1985-86, 89-2005, Outstanding Educator 2006), Fin. Mgmt. Assn. (program com. 1986, 89-94, 97, 99-2004), So. Fin. Assn. (program com. 1986), We. Fin. Assn. (program com.

1986), Ea. Fin. Assn., Lake Ridge Country Club Republican. Baptist. Avocations: golf, walking, sports. Office: West Virginia U Coll Bus and Econ Office 449 Morgantown WV 26506-6025 Office Phone: 304-293-7800, 304-293-7797.

SEARS, SANDRA JONES, medical/surgical nurse, consultant; b. Auburn, Mass., 1945; d. Harold Douglas Jones and Margaret Catherine Buckley; m. Raymond R. Johnson (div.); 1 child, Sharon Rae; m. Norman Allen Sears, June 22, 1980. AS with hons., Quinsigamond CC, 1975; BS in Psychology with hons., Worcester State Coll., Mass., 1978; BSN, Fitchburg State Coll., 1981. RN Mass., Ariz., cert. operating room nurse, Ariz., 2004, legal nurse consultant, Ariz., 2002. Registered nurse Meml. Hosp., Worcester, 1975—81; staff nurse John C. Lincoln Hosp., Phoenix, 1982—83, Paradise Valley Hosp., 1983—, charge nurse, 1985—86; owner Horizon Light Legal Nurse Cons., Phoenix. Lectr. in field; prin., owner HorizonLight Legal Nurse Cons. Mem.: Assn. Operating Rm. Nurses, Nat. Alliance Certified Legal Nurse Cons., Am. Assn. Legal Nurse Cons., Assn. Perioperative Nurses. Roman Cath. Avocations: reading, baseball, travel, history of lighthouses, stamp collecting/philately. Personal E-mail: horizonlightlnc@gmail.com, horizonlightlegalnurseconsulting@gmail.com.

SEARS, WILLIAM, pediatrician; Resident Harvard Med. Sch. Children's Hosp.; assoc. ward chief Hosp. for Sick Children, Toronto, assoc. prof. pediatrics; assoc. clinical prof. pediatrics U. Calif. Sch. Medicine, Irvine. Med. & parenting cons. BabyTalk mag., Parenting mag.; pediatric cons. Parenting.com. Fellow: Royal Coll. Pediatricians, Am. Acad. Pediatrics. Office: 26933 Camino De Estrella Ste A Capistrano Beach CA 92624 Office Phone: 949-493-5437. Office Fax: 949-493-0535.*

SEARY, JENNIFER, language educator; d. Wendy De Jesus. BA in English Lit. and Rhetoric, Binghamton U., NY, 2000; MS in Adolescent Edn., Mercy Coll., Dobbs Ferry, NY, 2005. Cert. provisional tchr. Dept. of Edn. Paralegal Rosenberg & Estis PC, NYC, 2000—01; tchr. Herbert H. Lehman HS, Bronx, NY, 2001—03, CES Vanguard HS, NYC, 2003—. Adj. prof. Monroe Coll., New Rochelle, NY, 2005—. Vol. NY Cares, NYC, 2001—06. Recipient Ron Parham Fund Scholastic Excellence, Manhattan Ctr. Sci. and Math., 1995, cert. of Merit for Acad. Achievement, Ednl. Opportunity Program Ctr./Binghamton U., 2000, Sr. Svc. award, 2000, cert. for Exceptional Commitment and Svc., Sponsors for Ednl. Opportunity, 2002, cert. of Appreciation, 2003; Tchrs. of Tomorrow grantee, US Dept. Edn. Mem.: Latina Exec. Women, 100 Hispanic Women, Ednl. Opportunity Program Alumni Orgn., Sigma Lambda Upsilon/Señoritas Latinas Unidas (advisor 2005—06, Cacique for Leadership 2005).

SEARY, LAWRENCE ANTHONY, cinematographer, television producer; b. NYC, June 13, 1951; m. Phyllis Cole, Oct. 2, 1976; children: Tara Ann, Paul Anthony. BFA, NYU, 1973. News cameraman, assignment desk supr., prodr. NBC, NYC, 1974—2007. Recipient N.Y. State Broadcast award UPI, 1987. Mem. Nat. TV Acad. (bd. govs. 1996-2000, 03-05, nat. bd. trustees 2003-06, awards com., 9 Emmy award nominations 1978, 82, 94, 95, 2003, 05, Emmy awards 1978, 2 Emmy awards 2003), Mensa, N.Y. Press Club (1st v.p., 2002—, Feature Video award 1994). Democrat. Roman Catholic. Office: NBC 30 Rockefeller Plz Rm 728E New York NY 10112-0002 Personal E-mail: larryseary@aol.com. Business E-Mail: larry.seary@newyorkpressclub.org.

SEASE, GENE ELWOOD, communications executive; b. Portage, Pa., June 28, 1931; s. Grover Chauncey and Clara Mae (Over) S.; m. Joanne D. Cherry, July 20, 1952; children: David Gene, Daniel Elwood, Cheryl Joanne. AB, Juniata Coll., 1952; BD, Pitts. Theol. Sem., 1956, ThM, 1959; PhD, U. Pitts., 1965, MEd, 1958; LLD, U. Evansville, 1972, Butler U., 1972; LittD, Ind. State U., 1974; DD, U. Indpls., 1989. Ordained to ministry United Methodist Ch., 1956; pastor Grace United Meth. Ch., Wilkinsburg, Pitts., 1952-63; conf. dir., supt. Western Pa. Conf. United Meth. Ch., Pitts., 1963-68; lectr. grad. faculty U. Pitts., 1965-68; mem. staff U. Indpls., 1968-89, asst. to pres., 1968-69, pres., 1970-88, chancellor, 1988-89, pres. emeritus, 1989—; chmn. Sease, Gerig & Assocs., Indpls., 1989—. Bd. dirs. Bankers Life Ins. Co. of NY Author: Christian Word Book, 1968; also numerous articles. Pres. Greater Indpls. Progress Com., 1972-75, Marion County Sheriff's Merit Bd.; mem. Ind. Scholarship Commn.; cons. Time Warner; bd. dirs. Indpls. Conv. Bur., Ind. Law Enforcement Tng. Acad., 500 Festival, Crossroads coun. Boy Scouts Am., Community Hosp. Indpls., St. Francis Hosp.; chmn. Ind. State Fair Commn. Mem. Internat. Platform Assn., English Speaking Union, Japan-Am. Soc. Ind., Ind. C. of C. (bd. dirs.), Indpls. C. of C. (bd. dirs.), Ind. Schoolmen's Club, Ind. State Fair Commn. (chmn.), Econ. Club of Indpls. (bd. dirs.), Skyline Club (bd. dirs.), Phi Delta Kappa, Alpha Phi Omega, Alpha Psi Omega. Clubs: Mason (33 deg., Shriner), Kiwanian, Columbia. Office Phone: 317-634-1171.

SEASHORE, MARGRETTA REED, physician, educator; b. Red Bank, NJ, June 20, 1939; d. Robert Clark and Lillie Ann (Heaviland) Reed; m. John Seashore, Dec. 26, 1964; children: Robert H., Carl J., Carolyn L. BA, Swarthmore Coll., 1961; MD, Yale U., 1965. Diplomate Am. Bd. Pediatrics, Am. Bd. Med. Genetics, Nat. Bd. Med. Examiners. Intern in pediat. Yale U. Sch. Medicine, New Haven, 1965-66, asst. resident in pediat., 1966-68, postdoctoral fellow in genetics and metabolism, depts. pediat. and medicine, 1968-70, asst. clin. prof. human genetics and pediat., 1974-78, from asst. prof. to assoc. prof., 1978-90, prof. genetics and pediatrics, 1990—; clin. asst. prof. pediat. U. Fla. Coll. Medicine, Gainesville, 1970-71, asst. prof., 1971-73; attending physician Duvall Med. Ctr., U. Hosp. Jacksonville, 1970-73, asst. prof., 1970-71; attending physician Hope Haven Children's Hosp., Jacksonville, Fla., 1970-73, Shands Tchg. Hosp., Gainesville, 1971-73, Danbury (Conn.) Hosp., 1977—, Yale-New Haven Hosp., 1974—, dir. Genetic Consultation Svc., 1977-86, 1989—; cons. physician Bridgeport (Conn.) Hosp., 1974—, Lawrence and Meml. Hosp., New London, Conn., 1979—, Norwalk (Conn.) Hosp., 1981—. Contbr. chapters to books. Fellow: Am. Coll. Med. Genetics (founding fellow), Am. Acad. Pediat. (mem. screening com. Conn. chpt. 1977—, mem. genetics com. 1989—94, chair com. genetics 1990—94); mem.: AAAS, AMA, New Eng. Genetics Group (chmn. outreach com. 1979—89, mem. steering com. 1979—98, chmn. screening com. 1989—93, co-dir. 1992—95), Soc. Study Inborn Errors of Metabolism, Am. Bd. Med. Genetics (bd. dirs. 2004—), Soc. Inherited Metabolic Disorders (bd. dirs. 1989—, sec. 1991—96, pres. 1997), Am. Soc. Human Genetics (mem. genetic svcs. com. 1986—91). Avocations: music, gardening, sewing, computers. Office: Yale U Sch Med Dept Genetics 333 Cedar St New Haven CT 06510-3289 Home Phone: 203-565-6267; Office Phone: 203-785-4938. Business E-Mail: margretta.seashore@yale.edu.

SEATON, EDWARD LEE, editor, publishing executive; b. Manhattan, Kans., Feb. 5, 1943; s. Richard Melvin and Mary (Holton) Seaton; m. Karen Mathisen, Sept. 4, 1965; children: Edward Merrill, John David. AB cum laude, Harvard U., 1965; postgrad., U. Ctr., Quito, Ecuador, 1965-66, U. Mo., 1966—67. Staff writer Courier-Jour., Louisville, 1968—69; editor-in-chief, pub. Manhattan Mercury, 1969—. Bd. dirs., officer 8 newspaper and broadcasting affiliates; mem. Pulitzer Prize Bd., 1992—2001, chmn., 2001; mem. adv. com. Knight Internat. Press Fellowship Program, 1994—2006; mem. Cabot Awards bd. Columbia U., 1995—2003. Contbr. articles to profl. jours. Chmn. Alfred M. Landon lecture patrons Kans. State U.; chmn. Latin Am. Scholarship Program Am. Univs., Cambridge, Mass., 1986—87. Decorated comendador Order Christopher Columbus (Dominican Republic); recipient Cabot prize, Columbia U., 1993; Fulbright scholar, 1965. Mem.: World Press Freedom Com. (bd. dirs. 1989—2009), Internat. Press Inst., Internat. Ctr. Journalists (bd. dirs. 1990—2001), Inter-Am. Press Assn. (exec. com. 1976—, pres. 1989—90), Am. Soc. Newspaper Editors (Found. pres. 1994—, pres. 1998—99), Kans. C. of C. and Industry (pres. 1987), Fly Club (Harvard U.). Avocations: tennis, cooking. Office: 318 N 5th St Manhattan KS 66505-0787

SEATON, JEAN ROBARTS, psychology educator; b. Atlanta, Apr. 1, 1931; d. Faye Huntington and Helen (Hooker) Robarts; m. Robert Finlayson Seaton, Apr. 18, 1954; children: Scott Ward, Sandra Jean. BA, Agnes Scott Coll., 1952; MEd, U. Cin., 1968; PhD, Case Western Res. U., 1982. Pers. dir. Macy's Calif., Hillsdale, 1954-59; instr. U. Cin., 1968-72; prof. psychology Ursuline Coll., Cleve., 1973-96, head psychology dept., 1973-96, chair div. natural and social scis., 1984-92. Trustee St. Luke's Med. Ctr., Cleve., 1981-95; coun. mem. Garfield Ch., Pepper Pike, Ohio, 1973-; mem. coun. City of Pepper Pike, 1981-97. Lt. WAVES USNR, 1952-54. Recipient Outstanding Teaching award Ursuline Coll., 1990. Democrat. Methodist. Avocation: travel. Home: 16 Pepper Creek Dr Pepper Pike OH 44124-5248

SEATON, LYNN, music educator; b. Tulsa, Okla., July 18, 1957; s. Earl and Reba Seaton; m. Marianna Seaton; 1 child, Aubrey. Pvt. practice, 1979—; prof. U. North Tex., Denton, 1998—. Performer (musician) over 100 recordings with many famous persons in more than 35 countries. Bd. mem. Internat. Soc. Bassists, Dallas, 2007—. Recipient Grammy winner; named Jazz Artist of Yr., Sammons Ctr. for Arts, 2008; named to Hall of Fame, Okla. Jazz Soc., 2006; nominee 2 Grammy Recordings. Mem.: Am. Fedn. Musicians, Internat. Assn. Jazz Edn. Unitarian Universalist. Avocations: fishing, reading. Office: Univ North Tex 1155 Union Cir 305040 Denton TX 76203-5017 Business E-Mail: lynn.seaton@unt.edu.

SEATON, SHIRLEY SMITH, academic administrator, consultant; b. Cleve. d. Kibble Smith and Cecil Wright; m. J. Lawrence Seaton, Oct. 2, 1965; 1 child, Eric Dean BA, MA in History, Howard U., 1949; MEd, Case We. Res. U., 1956; EdD, U. Akron, 1981; cert. Chinese history and culture, Beijing Normal U. Tchr. Cleve. Dist., 1950—59, dir. social studies, 1976—87; prin. Lafayette, Dike, Cleve., 1959—63, 1965—75; with Stas. WEWS-TV, WVIZ-TV, Cleve., 1963—67; adj. prof. Cleve. State U., 1988—90; adminstr. John Carroll U., University Heights, Ohio, 1990—. Program dir. OEO, Cleve., 1965; peer rev. Ohio Proficiency Test, 1986—2005; cons. Basics and Beyond, Cleve., 1990— Coord. Ctr. Civic Edn., 11th Congress Dist., 1987—; peer interview chair Fulbright tchr. exch. U.S. Dept. State, 1994-99, 2001-07; trustee We. Res. Hist. Soc., Cleve., 1996—, Ret. Vol. Program, Cleve., 1997-2003; commr. City of Cleveland Heights, 1997— Recipient Ohio Humanitarian award Govt. of Ohio, 1992; Fulbright grantee USIA, 1959, 82. Mem. AAUW, Fulbright Assn., Nat. Alliance Black Edn., Coalition 100 Black Women, Phi Delta Kappa, Alpha Kappa Alpha, Phi Beta Delta, Alpha Sigma Nu. Episcopalian. Avocation: bridge. Home: 3680 Bendemeer Rd Cleveland Heights OH 44118 Office: John Carroll U 20700 North Pk Blvd University Heights OH 44118 Office Phone: 216-397-1604. Personal E-mail: ssseaton@sbcglobal.net.

SEATS, PEGGY CHISOLM, public affairs executive; b. Lisman, Ala., Oct. 12, 1951; d. William H. and Bernice (Berry) Chisolm; m. Melvin Seats (dec.). BA in Communications cum laude, Lewis U., 1974; grad. cert. in event mgmt., George Washington U., 1995; MA in Pub. Comm., Am. U., 1997; grad. cert. in intercultural comm., Vaxjo (Sweden) U., 1997; Master's cert. in Pub. Affairs & Exec. Non-profit mgmt., Georgetown U., 2005. Account exec. Globe Broadcasting, Chgo., 1976-78, Merrill Lynch, Chgo., 1978-79, Transp. Displays, Inc., Chgo., 1979-81; with Reverie, Inc., 1981—; nat. accounts mgr. Soft Sheen Products Co., Chgo., 1981-83; mktg. cons. Reverie, Inc., Chgo., 1983-85; pub. rels., mktg. mgr. Proctor & Gardner Advt., Chgo., 1985-86; dir. pub. rels., mktg. Morris Brown Coll., Atlanta, 1986-87; mgr. mktg. Howard U. Press, Washington, 1989-90; cons. White House Initiative on Historically Black Colls., Univs., 1990-92. State advisor U.S. Congl. Adv. Bd., Ill., 1982. Contbr. numerous articles to newspapers and mags. Founder Benjamin Banneker Meml. Found., Washington, 1996; organizer S.W. Waterfront Initiative, 2000—; facilitator L'Enfant Plaza Revitalization Project, 1997—; bd. dir. Congl. Award Found. Recipient Kizzie award Black Women Hall of Fame, Chgo., 1981, Svc. award Nat. Assn. Women in Media, Chgo., 1982. Mem. Internat. Platform Assn., Internat. Assn. Bus. Communicators, Internat. Spl. Events Soc., Pub. Rels. Soc. Am., Black Pub. Rels. Soc. (founder Atlanta chpt.), Nat. Assn. Market Developers, World Affairs Coun., Comittee of 100, Lewis U. Alumni Assn. (bd. dirs. Ill. 1979), Washington Interdependence Coun. (founder, CEO 1996), Benjamin Banneker Inst. Math. and Sci. (founder). Unitarian Universalist. Avocations: music, art collecting, reading. Home: 2020 Pennsylvania Ave NW Washington DC 20006-1811 Office Phone: 202-387-3380. Business E-Mail: info@bannekermemorial.org.

SEAU, JUNIOR (TIANA BAUL SEAU JR.), professional football player; b. San Diego, Jan. 19, 1969; s. Tiaina Baul and Luisa Seau; m. Gina Deboer (div.); children: Sydney Beau, Jake Ryan, Hunter Tiaina. Student, U. So. Calif., 1987—90. Linebacker San Diego Chargers, 1990—2003, Miami Dolphins, 2003—06, New Eng. Patriots, 2006—08, 2008. Founder, pres. The Junior Seau Found., San Diego, 1992—; owner SEAU's the Restaurant, 1996—. PSA spokesman Nat. Beer Wholesaler's Assn. Recipient Walter Payton Man of Yr. award, 1994, Emil Karas award for Most Inspirational Player, 2002, Spirit San Diego award, San Diego C. of C., 2003, Don Shula Leadership award, 2003, 2004, Volunteer Svc. award, The White House, 2005; named First Team All-Pro, AP, 1992—94, 1996, 1998, 2000, Profl. Star of Yr., San Diego Chargers Hall Champions, 1992, San Diego Chargers Team MVP, 1993, 1997—2001, Linebacker of Yr., NFL Alumni Assn., 2000, Cmty. Partner of Yr., Ctr. Cmty. Solutions, 2007; named one of Most Influential Asian-Americans the 1990's; named to All-Am. Team, Walter Camp Found., 1989, The NFL's 1990's All Decade Team, Am. Football Conf. Pro Bowl Team, 1991—2002, Nat. Boys and Girls Club Hall of Fame, 1999. Office: Junior Seau Found 8787 Complex Dr Ste 200 San Diego CA 92123 E-mail: info@juniorseau.org.*

SEAVERS, DEAN S., security firm executive; married; 2 children. BBA summa cum laude, Kent State U., 1984; MBA, Stanford U., 1987. Mem., advt. & product planning groups Ford Motor Co.; ops. mgr., KFC nat. mgmt. co. PepsiCo, 1990—92; mng dir. & co-owner Flex-Tech Comm., 1992—96; mgr., brand transformation Allied Domecq Retailing, 1996—99; dir., ops. planning & strategy Burger King Corp., 1999—2000; regional v.p., ops. ADT Security Services, 2000—01, sr. v.p., ops., 2001—04; pres. SimplexGrinnell, 2004—07; pres. & CEO GE Security, Bradenton, Fla., 2007—. Recipient CareerFocus Eagle award, Nat. Eagle Leadership Inst., 2001. Mem.: Alpha Kappa Mu. Office: GE Security 8985 Town Center Pkwy Bradenton FL 34202 Office Phone: 941-739-4200.*

SEAVEY, CHRISTOPHER GORDON, psychotherapist, alcohol/drug abuse services professional; b. Syracuse, NY, Dec. 4, 1942; s. Gordon Crowell and Shirley Edith Seavey; m. Eudene Sawyer, Aug. 8, 1965 (div. Mar. 1983); children: Sandra, Sherry, Gordon; m. Nancy Bowen, 1983. BA in Human Svcs., U. Mass., 1986; MA in Rehab. Counseling, U. South Fla., 1991; PhD in Psychotherapy, Internat. U. Grad. Studies, 2001. Sr. counselor Project Turnabout, Hingham, Mass., 1982—86; counselor Coastal Cmty. Counseling, Braintree, Mass., 1986—87, South Shore Coun. on Alcoholism, Quincy, Mass., 1987; chem. dependency counselor II David Lawrence Ctr., Naples, Fla., 1989—90; cons. vocat. rehab. Intracorp, Naples, 1990—96; acting dir. Addiction Recovery Ctr., Ft. Myers, Fla., 1993—98; clin. dir. Assisted Addiction Recovery, Naples, 1995—2004; dir. Christopher Seavey LMHG PA, 2004—. Mem. adv. bd. Naples Rehab. Inc., 1994-97. Chmn. Collier County Depression Coalition, Naples, 1997. Recipient Book award U. Mass., Boston, 1986; U. Calif. San Francisco fellow, 1986; Tobacco Coalition grantee, 1998. Mem. NADAAC, ACA, Internat. Assn. Rehab. Profls., Internat. Coun. on Alcohol and Addictions, Fla. Rehab. Assn. (pres. S.W. Fla. chpt. 1994-95, Svc. award 1999), Fla. Mental Health Counselors, Gulf Coast Mental Health Counselors Assn. (past pres.), Internat. Soc. Study Women's Sexual Health, Am. Assn. Sexuality Educators, Counselors and Therapists, Phi Kappa Phi. Office: 9853 N Tamiami Trail Ste 213 Naples FL 34108 Office Phone: 239-595-7775. Business E-Mail: chriseavey@earthlink.net.

SEAVEY, WILLIAM ARTHUR, lawyer, vintner; b. LA, Aug. 28, 1930; s. Arthur Jones and Dorothy (Keyes) S.; m. Mary van Beuren, June 25, 1955, (dec. Aug. 29, 2008); children: Dorothy K., Arthur V.B., William G., Frederic A., Charles K. AB, Princeton U., 1952; LLB, Harvard U., 1955; grad. Inst. Internat. Studies, U. Geneva, Switzerland, 1956, D in Polit. Sci., 1970. Bar: Calif. 1957, U.S. Dist. Ct. (so. and no. dist.) Calif. 1957, U.S. Ct. Appeals (9th cir.) 1957. Assoc. Luce, Forward, Kunzel & Scripps, San Diego, 1956-57; asst. U.S. atty. U.S. Dist. Ct. (so. dist.) Calif., 1957-59; pvt. practice San Diego, 1959-65; lectr. in internat. law and econ., asst. to pres. Mills Coll., Oakland, Calif., 1968-74; ptnr. Richards & Seavey, San Francisco, 1974-76, Davis, Stafford, Kellman & Fenwick, San Francisco, 1976-78; of counsel Friedman, McCubbin, Spalding, Bilter, Roosevelt etal, San Francisco, 1987—2004. Founder, proprietor Seavey Vineyard, St. Helena, Napa County, 1981—. Author: Dumping Since the War: The Gatt and National Laws, 1970. Councilman City of Coronado, Calif., 1960-62, mayor 1962-64; trustee French-Am. Internat. Sch., San Francisco, 1968-96; pres. English Speaking Union, San Francisco, 1982-85, Alliance Francaise, San Francisco, 1979-81; chair Javits Fellowship Bd., Washington, 1989-92; mem. Columbus Fellowship Found. Bd., Washington, 1993-99; dir. San Francisco Com. on Fgn. Rels., 1995-98, 2001—, chmn., 1998-2001. Mem. ABA, Calif. Bar Assn., Am. Soc. Internat. Law, Pacific Union Club, Cercle de l'Union, Met. Club (Washington). Republican. Avocations: hiking, piano. Home and Office: 1310 Conn Valley Rd Saint Helena CA 94574-9624 E-mail: info@seaveyvineyard.com.

SEAWELL, DONALD RAY, lawyer, performing company executive; b. Jonesboro, NC, Aug. 1, 1912; s. A.A.F. and Bertha (Smith) S.; m. Eugenia Rawls, Apr. 5, 1941; children: Brook Ashley, Donald Brockman. AB, U. N.C., 1933, JD, 1936, DLitt, 1980; LHD, U. No. Colo., 1978. Bar: NC 1936, NY 1947. With SEC, 1939-41, 45-47, Dept. Justice, 1942-43; chmn. bd., dir., pub., pres. Denver Post, 1966-81; chmn. bd., dir. Gravure West, LA, 1966-81; dir. Swan Prodns., London; of counsel firm Bernstein, Seawell, Kove & Maltin, NYC, 1979—2006; chmn. bd. Denver Ctr. Performing Arts, 1972—2006, chief exec. officer, 1972—2006; chmn. emeritus, 2007—. Ptnr. Bonfils-Seawell Enterprises, NYC; bd. vis. U. NC Chmn. bd. ANTA, 1965—; theatre panel Nat. Coun. Arts, 1970-74; bd. govs. Royal Shakespeare Theatre, Eng.; trustee Am. Acad. Dramatic Arts, 1967—, Hofstra U., 1968-69, Cen. City Opera Assn., Denver Symphony; bd. dirs., Air Force Acad. Found., Nat. Ints. Outdoor Drama, Walter Hampden Meml. Library, Hammond Mus.; pres. Helen G. Bonfils Found., 1972-97, pres. emeritus, 1997—, Denver Opera Found.; Population Crisis Com., 1982-91; bd. dirs. Family Health Internat., Found. for Internat. Family Health; bd. visitors NC Sch. Arts, 1992-98; pres. Frederick G. Bonfils Found., 1972-92; chmn. Civilian Mil. Inst. Recipient Am. Acad. Achievement award, 1980, Tony award for producing, On Your Toes, 1983, Vocie Rsch. and Awareness award, Voice Found., 1983, Arts and Entertainement Cable Network award, 1987, Third Millennium Leadership award, Am. Diabetes Assn., 1996, Colo. Tourism Hall of Fame award, 1999, Thomas Degaetani award, U.S. Inst. for Theatre Tech., 2000, Benjamin F. Stapleton, Jr. award, 2000, Disting. Svc. award, U. Colo., 2000, Downtown Denver award for Tantalus, 2001, AWARE Honoree award, 2001, Donald Seawell Outstanding Achievement in Theatre award, Colo. Festival World Theatre, 2005, Founders award for Outstanding Contbn. to Am. Theater, Theater Hall Fame, NYC, 2005, Theatre Hall Fame, NYC, 2006; named Officer, Most Excellent Order of the Brit. Empire, 2002. Mem. Bucks Club (London), Dutch Treat Club (NYC), Denver Country Club, Denver Club, Cherry Hills Country Club, Mile High Club (Denver), Garden of Gods Club (Colorado Springs, Colo.). Office: Denver Ctr for Performing Arts 1101 13th St Denver CO 80204 Business E-Mail: dseawell@dcpa.org.

SEAWELL, THOMAS ROBERT, artist, retired educator; b. Balt., Mar. 17, 1936; s. Robert James and Cynthia Edith (Bass) S.; m. Barbara Louise Frey, Nov. 30, 1985; children: James Bradford, Lee Thomas, Gustin Charles, Jay Turner Frey. B.F.A., Washington U., 1958; M.F.A., Tex. Christian U., 1960. Mem. faculty dept. art SUNY-Oswego, 1963-91, prof., 1973-91; tchg. adj. Tex. A&M, Commerce, 1999—2006. Juror 50th Cooperstown Nat., 1985, Nat. Print Exhbn. Minot State U., ND, 1985, Rochester Print Club Ann. Meml. Art Gallery U., Minn., 1988; vis. artist Ox Bow Print Symposium, 1985, Ann. Matrix Artist U. Dallas, 1989, Midwestern State U., Wichita Falls, 1993, East Tenn. State U., Knoxville, 1997; guest spkr. L.A. Coll., 2004. One-man exhbns. include retrospective U. Md., Baltimore County, 1983, Retrospective Tyler Art Gallery, SUNY, Oswego, 1991, Univ. Gallery, Tex. A&M U., Commerce, 1995, Brazos Gallery, Dallas, 1997, La. Coll., Pineville-Alexandria, 2004; group exhbns. include Contemporary Am. Prints in Leningrad, USSR, 1983-84, The Collagraph, U. Mont., 1987, The Streets Suite, Rochester Meml. Art Gallery, 2005; traveling exhbn. So. Arts Fedn. Traveling Exhbn. "A Sense of Place," 1986—, Columbia Coll., 1996-97, Art in the Metroplex, J.M. Moudy Gallery, Ft. Worth, Tex., 1997, Contemporary Tex. Clay, Dallas Visual Arts Ctr., 1997, To Have and to Hold, Irving (Tex.) Arts Ctr. Main Gallery, 1998, Kennedy-Douglass Ctr. for the Arts Nat. Ceramic Competition, 1999, Woodmere Art Mus., 1999, San Angelo Mus. Fine Arts, 2000, 2004, Ark. State U., 2000, U. Wis., Parkside, 2000, 2003, 2005, Oxford Gallery, Rochester, N.Y., 2000; represented in permanent collections Bklyn. Mus., DeCordova Mus. Art, Rochester Meml. Art Gallery, Pushkin Mus., USSR, Brit. Mus., Munson-Williams-Proctor Inst., Library of Congress, Portland Art

Mus., Ark. Arts Ctr., Alexandria Mus. Art, La., Phila. Watercolor Soc., 2005, Roberson Art Mus., Binghamton, NY, 2005, Phila. Water Color Soc., Berman Mus., 2005; commd. print editions: Geldermann Securities Ltd., 1985-92, 8 Stock Exchange Images, The Print Club Albany, N.Y., 2004. Recipient Joseph A. Cain Meml. Purchase award for sculpture Del Mar Coll., 1999, 2d prize 15th Internat. Miniature Print Exhbn. Roberson Art Mus., Binghamton, N.Y., 2005, 08. Mem. Boston Printmakers, Phila. Water Color Soc., Soc. Am. Graphic Artists, Tex. Sculpture Assn. Office Phone: 903-886-3102. Personal E-mail: tseawell@9plus.net.

SEAWRIGHT, JAMES L., JR., sculptor, educator; b. Jackson, Miss., May 22, 1936; s. James L. and Josephine (Power) S.; m. Mabelle M. Garrard, June 22, 1960; 1 child, James Andrew. Student, U. of South, 1953-54, Delta State Coll., 1954-55; BA in English, U. Miss., 1957; postgrad., Art Students League of N.Y., 1961-62. Tech. supr. Columbia-Princeton Electronic Music Center, NYC, 1963-69; tchr. Sch. Visual Arts, 1967-69; dir. visual arts program Princeton U., 1972-2001, prof. coun. of humanities and visual arts, 1992—; prof. visual arts Lewis Ctr. for Arts, emeritus prof., 2009. Asst. to choreographer, Henry St. Playhouse, N.Y.C., 1962-63, spl. effects, tech. cons., Mimi Garrard Dance Co., N.Y.C., 1964—; sculptor represented in permanent collections, Mus. Modern Art, N.Y.C., Whitney Mus., N.Y.C., N.J. State Mus., Trenton, Guggenheim Mus., N.Y.C., Wadsworth Atheneum, Hartford, Conn., others; pub. commns. for SEA-TAC Internat. Airport, Seattle, Logan Internat. Airport, Boston; also pvt. collections. Served with USN, 1957-61. Recipient Theodoron award Guggenheim Mus., 1969, Am. Acad. Arts and Letters Art award, 1997, Lifetime Achievement award Miss. Inst. Arts and Letters, 2003, Howard T. Behrman award for disting. accomplishment in humanities Princeton U., 2004; Graham Found. Advanced Study in Arts fellow, 1970. Mem. Am. Abstract Artists, Phi Delta Theta. Democrat. Episcopalian. Office: 185 Nassau St Princeton NJ 08544-2003 Home Phone: 845-386-4883. Personal E-mail: james@seawright.net. Business E-Mail: jims@princeton.edu.

SEAY, CHARLOTTE J., artist; d. Charles Ervin and Imogene Touchstone Craig; m. John Randolph Seay, Mar. 20, 1964; children: Daniel Thomas, Steven Lee, Sheri Lynn Smith, Scott Craig. Student, Midland Coll., Tex., 1986—88, U. of Tex. of the Permian Basin, Odessa, 1988—90. Designer Midland Country Club/Wildscatter, 1976—77; painter, printmaker, 1980—; curator Midland/Wirral, Eng. art exhbn. City of Midland, 1999—2000; cover designer Tumbleweed Publs. Jr. League of Midland, 2003; label designer Messina Hof Winery, Bryan, Tex., 2005—. Tchr. Pecos Arts Assn., Snyder Arts Assn., Paint and Palette, West Texas Area, 1992—2001; juror Monahans Art Assn., Tex., 1994; lectr. Del Rio Old Firehouse Art Mus., Tex., 1997; juror Watercolor Horizons Group, Odessa, Tex., 1998; instr. secondary sch. art tchrs. workshop Midland Ind. Sch. Dist., 1999; illustrator Sweet Mischief Press, Midland, 2001—02, Midland, 2003—04; juror Carlsbad Art Assn., N.Mex., 2003; illustrator Author's Pub. House, Midland, 2005, Midland, 06. Contbr. essays to publs. Bd. dirs. Midland Tourism Bd., 2003—04; chmn. hotel/motel tax adv. bd. Midland City Coun., 2002—06; mem. City of Midland and Chamber Planning Retreat, 2004—06, Visions 2000 of Midland, 1999; elder Grace Presbyn. Ch., Midland, 2001—04; pres. Midland Opera Theater, 2003—04, Opportunity Ctr. of Midland, 1973—74. Recipient Merit award, Midland Arts Assn. and Midland Coll., 2005, Daniel Smith award, So. Watercolor Soc., 1998, Paul Harris fellowship, Dist. 5530, Rotary Clubs Internat., 1994, Swartz Framing award, Midland Arts Assn. and Mus. of the S.W., 2005; named Disting. Artist, Arts Assembly of Midland, 1997, Best In Show, Odessa Arts Assn., 1994, Best in Show, 1995, Best In Show, Arts Assembly of Midland/Celebration of the Arts, 1992. Mem.: Midland Arts Assn. (pres. 1995—96), Tex. Watercolor Soc. (chmn. 47th ann. exhbn. 1996—97), Tex. Watercolor Soc. (pres. 1996—97), Arts Assembly of Midland (Vol. of the Yr./Midland Opera Theater 2004), Midland Country Club Ladies Assn. (bd. of directors 1998—99). Republican. Presbyterian. Avocations: travel, writing essays, writing poetry, photography, reading. Home Fax: 432-570-1875. Personal E-mail: seayart@sbcglobal.net.

SEAY, STEPHANIE, elementary school educator; b. Spartanburg County, SC; B in Early Childhood Edn., Univ. SC-Upstate; M in Early Childhood Edn., Furman Univ. Tchr., 1995—, Wellford (SC) Elem. Sch., 2004—. Adj. prof., mentor, early childhood edn. Presbyn. Coll. Named SC Tchr. of Yr., 2006. Office: Wellford Elem Sch 684 Syphrit Rd Wellford SC 29385 Business E-Mail: seays@spart5.k12.sc.us.

SEAY, SUZANNE, financial planner, educator; b. Tulsa, May 3, 1942; d. James Paul and Ann (Maxey) S. BS, Hardin-Simmons U., 1964; MA, Ariz. State U., 1966. CFP, 1986. Tchr. Baker (Oreg.) Pub. Schs., 1964-65, Govt. of Guam, Agana, 1966-68, Hollister, Calif., 1968-74, Tehran (Iran) Am. Sch., 1974-75, Am. Sch. Isfahan, Iran, 1975-78; internat. pubs. rep. World Editions, Hollister, 1978-87; fin. planner, investment adviser Clock Tower Fin. (name now Royal Alliance), Monterey, Calif., 1984—; tchr. fin. planning Gavilan Coll., Gilroy, Calif., 1988-95, Monterey Peninsula Coll., 1988-94, Hartnell Coll., Salinas, Calif., 1989-94. Spkr. in field. Fin. columnist RVing Women mag., 1995-2004; talk show host Fin. Planning for Peace of Mind, Phoenix, 2002. Mem. Am. Field Svc., Hollister, 1987-96; treas. San Benito Hospice, Hollister, 1987-91; bd. trustees. St. Bonaventure Indian Mission and Sch., 1998-2001. Mem.: Fin. Planning Assn., RVing Women (bd. dirs. 2000—02). Independent. Avocations: motorhome, travel, reading. Home and Office: 2571 N Avenida San Valle Tucson AZ 85715-3404 Office Phone: 520-886-5621. Personal E-mail: suzyseay@aol.com. Business E-Mail: sseay@royalaa.com.

SEAY, WILLIAM CLAUDE, JR., history professor, geography educator; MPhil, U. London, postgrad, 2005—. Adj. instr. history Va. State U., Ettrick, 2002—04; adj. instr. history and geography John Tyler C.C., Midlothian, Va., 2002—; vis. prof. global fin. history John Molson Sch. Bus., Concordia U., Montreal, Que., Canada; vis. prof. global history and cultural geography Bishop's U., Sherbrooke, Que. Textbook reviewer Prentice Hall, Saddle River, NJ, 2004, Houghton Mifflin, Boston, 2004. Author: (textbook) Religious Minorities in British America and an Global History Text; co-author: The Student Ancillary for Western Civilisation. Mem.: World Hist. Assn., Am. Polit. Sci. Assn., Am. Hist. Assn., The Inst. Hist. Rsch., London. Office: John Tyler CC 800 Charter Colony Pkwy Midlothian VA 23114 Office Phone: 804-706-5086. Business E-Mail: wseay@jtcc.edu.

SEBASTIAN, PETER, political scientist, consultant, retired diplomat; b. June 19, 1926; m. Harvel Huddleston, Dec. 11, 1951; 1 child, Christopher. BA, U. Chgo., 1950; postgrad., U. d'Aix-Marseille, Nice, France, 1949, New Sch. for Social Research, NYC, 1950, Nat. War Coll., 1969-70. Dir., owner cons. co., NYC, 1950-57; U.S. Fgn. Service officer Dept. State, Washington, 1957-76, dep. exec. sec., 1976-77, sr. seminar, 1977-78; U.S. consul gen. Casablanca, Morocco, 1978-80; minister, counselor Am. embassy, Rabat, Morocco, 1980-82; dir. for North Africa Dept. State, Washington, 1982-84; ambassador to Tunisia Tunis, 1984-87; ambassador-in-residence Ctr. for Strategic Internat. Studies, Georgetown U., Washington, 1987-88; cons in fgn. affairs to the public and pvt. sector, lectr., 1988—. Mem. V.P. Bush's task force on border control, 1988—89. Contbr. poems to Osmose, 1949; author studies for the pvt. sector U.S. Dept. State and other U.S agys. Bd. dirs. Santa Fe Coun. on Internat. Rels., 2005. Sgt. AUS, 1944-46. Decorated Ouissam Alaouite (Morocco), numerous U.S. mil. decorations; recipient Presdl. Meritorious Service award, 1985. Mem. Am. Group Seminar Assn., Nat. Geog. Soc., Mid. East Inst. Episcopalian. Avocations: painting, drawing, photography. Home Phone: 505-983-6364; Office Phone: 505-992-3402. Personal E-mail: Batuta@aol.com.

SEBASTIAN, THOMAS, language educator; b. Oberhausen, Germany, Oct. 26, 1956; s. Walter Sebastian and Margarete Wilting; m. Judith Geerke, Dec. 12, 1982; children: Antonia, Cecilia. PhD, Johns Hopkins U., Balt., 1992. Prof. German Trinity U., San Antonio, 1992—. Office: Trinity Univ One Trinity Pl San Antonio TX 78212-7200

SEBAT, JONATHAN, geneticist, educator; Grad., U. Calif., Santa Barbara, 1995; PhD, U. Idaho, 2002. Adj. prof. biology Stony Brook U.; assoc. prof. genetics Cold Spring Harbor Lab.; founding mem. Stanley Ctr. for Psychiatric Genomics. Office: One Bungtown Rd Cold Spring Harbor NY 11724 Office Phone: 516-422-4196. E-mail: sebat@cshl.edu.*

SEBEK, MICHAEL, research scientist, entrepreneur, educator; b. Prague, Czech Republic, Jan. 25, 1954; s. Antonín and Jana (Hanzlová) S.; m. Ivana Ornestová, Nov. 21, 1992; children: Michael, Natalie. Diploma in elec. engring., Czech Tech. U., Prague, 1978; PhD, Czech Acad. Scis., Prague, 1981, DSc, 1995. Scientist Inst. Info. Theory and Automation, Prague, 1981-88, sr. scientist, 1988-90, chief scientist, 1991-98, head control theory dept., 1998—2005; prof. Czech Tech. U., 2000, head control engring. dept., 2003—. Vis. prof. U. Twente, Netherlands, 1990-91, Swiss Fed. Inst. Tech., Zurich, 1994-95; mem. policy com. Internat. Fedn. Automatic Control, 1993—2005, adminstrv. and finance com., 2005-; coord. of EUROPOLY (European Network of Excellence for Indsl. Applications of Polynomial Methods) 1998; co-founder and CEO of PolyX, Ltd. (world-wide producer of software for polynomial methods in systems, signals and control), 1998; mgr. Ctr. applied cyberntics Conrol, Czech Tech. U. Prague, 2000—; lectr. in field. Contbr. numerous articles to profl. jours.; co-author Polynomial Toolbox software, Metlab. Mgr., coach Medicina Baseball Club, Prague, 1985-90. Recipient Czech Nat. prize Czech Parliament, 1989. Mem. IEEE (sr., mem. exec. com. Czech sect. 1996—), IEEE Control Sys. Soc. (mem. conf. editl. bd. 1994-2000, chmn. Czech chpt. 1996-2000), Am. Math. Soc., N.Y. Acad. Scis, Soc. Indsl. and Applied Math. Achievements include invention of 2D and nD polynomial equations with application to 2D and 3D systems; new techniques for robust controller design; research in computational algorithms for polynomials and polynomial matrices; contribution to polynomial methods for systems, signals and control. Avocations: jogging, baseball, photography. Home: Jarní 4 16000 Prague 6 Czech Republic Office: Czech Tech U Prague Technicka 2 166 27 Prague 6 Czech Republic also: Inst Info Theory & Automation 18208 Prague 8 Czech Republic Personal E-mail: m.sebek@polyx.cz. Business E-Mail: m.sebek@c-a-k.cz.

SEBELIUS, KATHLEEN GILLIGAN, Secretary of Health and Human Services, former Governor of Kansas; b. Cin., May 15, 1948; d. John J. and Mary K. (Dixon) Gilligan; m. Keith Gary Sebelius, 1974; children: Edward Keith, John McCall. BA, Trinity Coll., 1970; MA in Pub. Adminstrn., U. Kans., 1977. Dir. planning Ctr for Cmty. Justice, Washington, 1971—74; spl. asst. Kans. Dept. Corrections, Topeka, 1975—78; exec. dir. Kans. Trial Lawyers Assn., 1978—86; mem. Kans. House of Reps. from Dist. 56, 1987-95; ins. commr. State of Kans., 1995—2002, gov., 2003—09; sec. US Dept. Health & Human Services, Washington, 2009—. Founder Women's Polit. Caucus; precinct committeewoman, 1980-86; mayor, City of Potwin, 1985-87; mem. Presdl. Advisory Commn. on Consumer Protection & Quality in Health Care, 1997. Recipient Breaking the Glass Ceiling award, Women in Govt., 1997, Svc. award, Kansas City YMCA; named Outstanding Elected Officer, Nat. Fedn. of Dem. Women, 1996; named one of 100 Most Powerful Women, Forbes mag., 2009. Mem.: Kans. Women's Political Caucus (founder), Nat. Assn. Ins. Commrs. (chair), Common Cause (state bd., nat. gov. bd. 1975—81), Kans. Kids Count (bd. mem.), Friends of Cedar Crest (bd. mem.). Democrat. Roman Catholic. Office: US Department Health & Human Services 200 Independence Ave SW Rm 615 F Washington DC 20201*

SEBHATU, MESGUN, physics professor; b. Menoxeito, Eritrea, Ethiopia, Jan. 6, 1946; came to U.S., 1970; s. Sebhatu and Mehret (Tesfay) S.; m. Almaz Yilma, July 21, 1984; children: Emnet, Temnete. BS in Physics, Haile Selassie I U., Addis Ababa, Ethiopia, 1969; PhD in Physics, Clemson U., SC, 1975. Vis. asst. prof. N.C. State U., Raleigh, 1975-76; asst. prof. physics Pensacola (Fla.) Jr. Coll., 1976-78, Winthrop Coll., Rock Hill, S.C., 1978-84, assoc. prof. physics, 1984-91; King-Chavez-Parks vis. prof. physics Mich. State U., East Lansing, 1991-92; prof. Winthrop U., Rock Hill, 1992—. Textbook reviewer Prentice Hall, 1987, Little Brown, 1989, Jones and Bartlet, 2006; contbr. articles to profl. jours. Rsch. initiation and devel. grantee NSF, 1989, Cottrel grantee Rsch. Corp., 1982; Kavli Inst. for Theoretical Physics scholar U. Calif., Santa Barbara, 2002-04. Fellow African Sci. Inst.; mem. Am. Phys. Soc., Am. Assn. Physics Tchrs. Democrat. Roman Catholic. Achievements include derivation of two-nucleon solitary wave exchange potentials. Office: Winthrop Univ 101 Sims Bldg Rock Hill SC 29733-0001 Office Phone: 803-323-4935. Business E-Mail: sebhatum@winthrop.edu.

SEBO, STEPHEN ANDREW, electrical engineer, educator, researcher, consultant; b. Budapest, Hungary, June 10, 1934; s. Emery Sebo and Elizabeth Thieben; m. Eva Agnes Vambery, May 25, 1968. MSEE, Budapest Poly-tech. U., 1957; PhD, Hungarian Acad. Sci., 1966. Engr. Budapest Elec. Co., 1957-61; asst. prof. Budapest Poly. U., 1961-66, assoc. prof., 1966-68, Ohio State U., Columbus, 1968-74, prof., 1974—82, Am. Electric Power prof. in power sys. engring., 1982—2003, Neal A. Smith prof., 1995—2003, prof. emeritus, 2003—. Recipient Power Educator award Edison Elec. Inst., 1981, Tech. Person of Yr. award Columbus Tech. Coun., 1994. Fellow IEEE (Prize Paper award 1981). Office: Ohio State U Elec Engring 2015 Neil Ave Columbus OH 43210-1272 Office Phone: 614-292-7410. Business E-Mail: sebo.1@osu.edu.

SEBOLD, RUSSELL PERRY, III, romance languages educator, writer; b. Dayton, Ohio, Aug. 20, 1928; s. Russell Perry and Mary (Kiger) Sebold; m. Jane Norvell Hale, Nov. 24, 1955; children: Mary Norvell, Alice Hale. Student, U. Chgo., 1945—47; BA, Ind. U., 1949; MA (Woodrow Wilson fellow), Princeton U., 1951, PhD, 1953; D.Phil. and Letters (hon.), U. Alicante, Spain, 1984. Instr. Spanish, Duke U., 1955-56; instr. Spanish, U. Wis., 1956-58, asst. prof., 1958-62, assoc. prof., 1962-66; prof. Spanish, chmn. dept. fgn. langs. and lits. U. Md., 1966-68; prof. Spanish, U. Pa., 1968-88, chmn. dept. Romance langs., 1968-78, Edwin B. and Leonore R. Williams prof. Romance langs., 1988—. Mem. adv. com. Soc. Ibero-Am. Enlightenment, 1968—, treas., 1969—; mem. steering com. Am. Soc. Eighteenth Century Studies, 1970—; corr. academician Royal Spanish Acad., 1993—, Royal Acad. Humane Letters of Barcelona, 1993—. Author: Tomás de Iriarte: poeta de rapto racional, 1961, El rapto de la mente, 1970, 1989, Colonel Don José Cadalso, 1970, Cadalso: el primer romántico europeo de España, 1974, Novela y autobiografía en la Vida de Torres Villarroel, 1975, Trayectoria del romanticismo español, 1983, Descubrimiento y fronteras del neoclasicismo español, 1985, Bécquer en sus narraciones fantásticas, 1989, De Ilustrados y románticos, 1992, La novela romantica en España, 2000, La perduración de la modalidad clásica, 2001, Lírica y poética en España, 1536-1870, 2003, Ensayos de meditacion y critica literaria, 2004, En el principio del movimiento realista, 2007; author, editor Fray Gerundio de Campazas (José Francisco de Isla), 4 vols., 1960—64, 2d edit., 1992, Visiones y visitas de Torres con don Francisco de Quevedo por la Corte (Diego de Torres Villarroel, 1966, 2d edit., 1991, Numancia destruida (Ignacio López de Ayala, 1971, 2d edit., 2005, Poética (Ignacio de Luzán), 1977, 2nd edit, 2008, Comedias (Tomás de Iriarte), 1978, 2d edit., 1986, Gustavo Adolfo Bécquer (antologia critica), 1985, Vida (Diego de Torres Villarroel), 1985, Rimas (Gustavo Adolfo Bécquer), 1991, author, editor (with David T. Gies) Ilustración y neoclasicismo, 1992, Noches lúgubres (José de Cadalso), 1993, author, editor (with Jesus Perez Magallon) El hombre practico (Conde de Fernán Nuñez), 1996, Cartas marruecas, Noches lúgubres (Jose de Cadalso), 1999, 7th edit., 2008, El delincuente honrado(Gasper Melchor de Jovellanos), 2008, translator Lugubrious Nights(Cadalso), 2008, gen. editor Hispanic Rev., 1968—97, adv. editor Eighteenth Century Studies, 1983—, Cuadernos para Investigación de la Literatura Hispánica, 1987—, El Gnomo, 1992—, Dieciocho, 1994—, Siglo XIX, 1995—, Salina, 1999—, columnist ABC newspaper, Madrid, 1985—; contbr. articles to profl. jours. Recipient Elio Antonio de Nebrija Internat. prize, U. Salamanca, 2001; grantee, Am. Philos. Soc., 1971, 1976, 1982; Guggenheim fellow, 1962—63, Am. Coun. Learned Socs. fellow, 1979—80. Mem.: Hispanic Soc. Am., Sociedad de Literatura Española del Siglo XIX, Ctr. 18th Century Studies (Oviedo, Spain), Am. Assn. Tchrs. French, Am. Assn. Tchrs. Spanish and Portuguese, Sigma Delta Pi, Phi Gamma Delta, Phi Beta Kappa. Episcopalian. Home: 16 Flintshire Rd Malvern PA 19355-1108 Office: U Pa Dept Romance Langs Philadelphia PA 19104-6305 Personal E-mail: rpsebold@verizon.net.

SEBOLT, STEPHANIE ANN, literature and language professor; b. Heidelberg, Germany, Apr. 11, 1964; d. Herman Kenneth and Ruth Eugenie Doswald; m. Daniel Joseph Sebolt, July 15, 1996; children: Alexander Klaus, Maximilian Heinrich, Nicholas Mark. BA in French, Mary Wash. Coll., Fredericksburg, Va., 1986; MA in Curriculum & Instrn., Va. Poly. Inst. and State U., Blacksburg, 1991. Cert. pk-4 tchg. Va., 1986, k-12 French Va., 1991, k-12 ESL Va., 1991. 6-12 ESL tchr. Roanoke County Pub. Schs., Va., 1993—95, k-5 ESL tchr., 1995—. Vis. instr. Roanoke Coll., Salem, 2007—08. Contbr. columns in newspapers. Bd. mem. Cmty. Sch., Roanoke, 2005—08; bd. sec. New Vista Montessori Sch., Roanoke, 2003—05. Mem.: Va. Edn. Assn., VATESOL, TESOL. Avocations: travel, reading, hiking. Home: 1733 High Gate Ln Salem VA 24153 Office: Burlington Elem Sch 6533 Peters Creek Rd Roanoke VA 24019 Personal E-mail: stephsebolt@verizon.net. Business E-Mail: ssebolt@rcs.k12.va.us.

SEBORA, TERRENCE, finance educator; b. Oshkosh, Wis., Oct. 14, 1946; s. Clifford and Lucille Sebora; m. Colleen Murphy, July 24, 1971; children: Christopher, Carrie, Caitlin Bauch. PhD, U. NC, Chapel Hill, 1990. Co-owner Sebora Stores Inc., Oshkosh, Wis., 1977—91; assoc. prof. U. Nebr., Lincoln, 1991—. Dir. religion edn. St. Paul's Cath. Parish, Combined Locks, Wis., 1973—77. Office: Univ Nebr 1234 R St Lincoln NE 68588-0491 Office Fax: 402-472-5855. Personal E-mail: tsebora@aol.com. Business E-Mail: tsebora1@unl.edu.

SEBRING, MARJORIE MARIE ALLISON, former home furnishings company executive; b. Burnsville, NC, 1926; d. James William and Mary Will (Ramsey) Allison Shockey; 1 child, Patricia Louise Banner Krohn (dec.). Student, Mars Hill Coll., 1943, Home Decorators Sch. Design, NYC, 1948, Wayne State U., 1953; cert. home furnishings rep., U. Va., 1982. Dir. decorating divsn. Robinson Furniture, Detroit, 1949—57; head buyer Tyner Hi-Way House, Ypsilanti, Mich., 1957—63, Town and Country, Dearborn, Mich., 1963—66; instr. Nat. Carpet Inst., 1963—71; owner Adams House, Inc., Plymouth, Mich., 1966—72; exec. v.p. mktg. and sales, regional sales and mktg. mgr. Triangle Industries, LA, 1972—89; co-owner Markham-Sebring, Inc., St. Petersburg, Fla., 1983—89. Co-owner Accessories, Etc., 1985-89, Talamanca Pipeline Ltd., Costa Rica; chmn. bd. dir. U.S. Homes, Heritage Lakes, 1990-1992, 2002-04, 06, 08. Vol. coord. Pasco County Clk. Ct., Suncoast Theatre; adv. bd. Webster Coll.; charter mem. Presdl. Task Force, 1980-2008; elder pres. Presbyn. Ch. Seven Springs, 1985-2008; bd. dir. Fla. Presbyn. Homes, 1985-2008, Gills Trinity YMCA, 2001-05; mem. Tampa Bay Presbytery Rev. and Evaluation, Pasco County Planning Com., 2002-08; bd. dir. James P. Gills Suncoast YMCA, 2001-05; citizens adv. com. Pasco County, 2001-08. Recipient recognition for work with youth and aged; named to Fla. Finest List, Gov. of Fla., 1994. Mem. Internat. Home Furnishings Assn., Fla. Home Furnishings Rep. Assn. (officer), Am. Security Coun. (coun.), Williamsburg Found., USCG Aux., Nat. Audubon Soc., Internat. Platform Assn. (jouvenile justice coun. 2003-05), Heritage Lake Assn. (bd. dir. 2002-08, chmn.), II Westminster Assn.(chmn. bd. 1992-95, 97-99, 2001-08, pres. 2002-08), Pasco Rep. Club (pres. 2002-08). Republican. Achievements include contbr. creative display to Better Homes & Gardens, 1957-64. Home: 2701 Regency Oaks Blvd # A 506 Clearwater FL 33759-1529 Home Phone: 727-793-0747; Office Phone: 727-808-7992.

SEBRIS, ROBERT, JR., lawyer; b. NYC, May 20, 1950; s. Robert and Ruth Sebris; m. S. Lawson Hollweg, Sept. 8, 1973; children: Jared Matthew, Bryan Taylor. BS in Indsl. Labor Rels., Cornell U., 1972; JD, George Washington U., 1978. Bar: DC 1978, Wash. 1980. Labor rels. specialist Onondaya County Office labor rels., Syracuse, NY, 1973-74, U.S. Dept. Labor, Washington, 1972-75; labor rels. mgr. U.S. Treasury Dept., Washington, 1975-78, employee rels. mgr., 1978-80; assoc. Davis, Wright, Todd, Riese & Jones, Seattle, 1980-84; ptnr. Davis, Wright, Tremain, Bellevue, Wash., 1985-92, Sebris Busto James, Bellevue, 1992—. Expert witness Amendments NLRA US Senate hearing, 1997. Co-author: (book) Employer's Guide to Strike Planning, 1985; contbr. articles to profl. jours. Mem. Bellevue CC Found., 1988—95, pres., 1995—96; chair employment law cert. program U. Wash. Law Sch., 1996—97. Mem.: ABA (health law forum, labo and employment law sect., mem. com. employee rights), Soc. Human Resource Mgmt., Am. Health Lawyers Assn., Pacific Coast Labor Law Conf. (planning com. 1980—93, chmn. 1991—92), Seattle/King County Bar Assn. (chmn. labor law sect. 1991—92), DC Bar Assn., Wash. Bar Assn. Avocations: golf, writing. Home: 16301 Mink Rd NE Woodinville WA 98072-9463 Office: Sebris Busto James Ste 325 14205 SE 36th St Bellevue WA 98006 Office Phone: 425-450-0300. Business E-Mail: rsebris@sebrisbusto.com.

SECCHIA, PETER F., forest products executive, former United States ambassador to Italy; b. Englewood, NJ, Apr. 15, 1937; s. Charles P. and Valerie Margaret (Smith) Secchia; m. Joan Peterson, 1964; children: Mark, Charles, Sandra, Stephanie. BS in Econ., Mich. State U., 1963,

HHD (hon.), 1997; AA (hon.), Grand Rapids Cmty. Coll., 1993; LLD (hon.), Grand Valley State U., 1990, Davenport Coll., 1993, Cooley Law Sch., 1993. Positions through v.p. sales Universal Forest Products, Grand Rapids, Mich., 1962—71, dir., 1967—, chmn., pres., CEO, 1971—89, chmn., 1993—2006, chmn. emeritus, 2006; U.S. Amb. to Italy, 1989—93. Chmn. River City Food Co.; mng. ptnr. SIBSCO LLC. Mem. exec. com. Gerald R. Ford Found., past chmn. endowment com.; trustee Bush Presdl. Libr. Found., James A. Baker III Inst. Pub. Policy, Rice Univ, John Cabot Univ., Rome; Mich. del. Rep. Nat. Convention, 1976, 1980, 1984; mem. Rep. Nat. Com., 1980—89, vice chmn. Midwest region, 1984—89; co-chmn. Dole for Pres. Nat. Campaign, 1995—96. Served to sgt. USMC, 1956—59. Recipient Cavaliere di Gran Croce, Govt. of Italy, Disting. Honor award, U.S. Dept. State, 1993, Louis A. Smith Disting. Jurist award, Cooley Law Sch., 1993, Michelangelo D'Oro Children of the World award, 1993, Peace award, Internat. Commn. for Peace; named Master Entrepeneur of the Year for Mich., 1994, Businessman of the Year, Econ. Club We. Mich., 1995. Mem.: Council of Am. Ambassadors. Republican. Methodist. Office: Universal Forest Products 2801 East Beltline NE Grand Rapids MI 49525

SECCHIUTTI, RONALD, electrical engineering designer; b. East Liverpool, Ohio, Aug. 4, 1943; s. Mario Secchiutti and Mary Sialino; m. Karen Chimley, Aug. 20, 1964; children: Lynette, Ronald Jr. Attended, Youngstown U., Ohio, 1970—72. Lineman Duquesne Light Co., Pitts., 1963—70; elec. field engr. Hope Creek Nuc. Plant Bechtel Corp., Salem, NJ, 1970—75; lead elec. designer Nine Mile Nuc. Plant Stone & Webster Corp., Cherry Hill, NJ, 1975—82; lead elec. and instrumentation designer Designer Contractor, Newark, Del., 1982—95; lead elec. designer Merck West Point Jacobs Engring., Conshohocken, Pa., 1995—2000, Shaw Group, Trenton, NJ, 2000—. V.p. Parvin State Pk. Appreciation Com., Pittsgrove, NJ, 1991—92; walkathon com. Assn. for Retarded Citizens, Vineland, NJ, 2003—; ofcl. Spl. Olympics, Trenton, 2004—; state exec. com. United We Stand Am., Edison, NJ, 1993—94; state conv. spkr. United We Stand Am. NJ. Chpt., Marilton, 1994. Quartermaster USNR, 1960—63, USS Kidd. Recipient World Weightlifting Record Holder for Powercurl Master Divsn., World Natural Powerlifting Fedn., 2003. Master: Free & Accepted Masons (worshipful master 2007—); mem.: Order Sons Italy in Am., Highlander Unit at NUR Shriners Ancient Arabic Order Nobles Mystic Shrine (clan chief 1996), Am. Mensa (life), Clown Unit at NUR Shriners Ancient Arabic Order Nobles Mystic Shrine (unit pres. 2005). Achievements include created map for Parvin State Park use that identified and named the trails. Avocations: hiking, bicycling.

SECHE, STEPHEN A., United States Ambassador to Yemen; m. Susan Canning. BA in Journalism, U. Mass., Amherst, 1974; completed Arabic lang. tng., US Fgn. Svc. Inst. Field Sch., Tunis, Tunisia, 1999. Journalist, 1974—78; joined US Fgn. Svc., 1978; fgn. svc. assignments US Dept. State, Guatemala, Peru, Bolivia, info. officer, US Embassy Ottawa, Canada, 1989—93, press attache, US Embassy New Delhi, 1993—97, counselor pub. affairs and dir. Am. Cultural Ctr. Damascus, Syria, 1999—2002, dir. office Egypt and Levant affairs Washington, 2002—04, dep. chief of mission Damascus, 2002—05, charge d'affaires, US Embassy, 2005—06, US amb. to Yemen Sana'a, 2007—. Vis. fellow U. So. Calif., LA, 2006—07. Office: DOS Amb 6330 Sanaa Pl Washington DC 20521-6330*

SECHRIST, CHALMERS FRANKLIN, JR., electrical engineering educator; b. Glen Rock, Pa., Aug. 23, 1930; s. Chalmers F. and Lottie V. (Smith) S.; m. Lillian Beatrice Myers, June 29, 1957; children: Jonathan A., Jennifer N. BE in Elec. Engring., Johns Hopkins U., 1952; MS, Pa. State U., 1954, PhD in Elect. Engring., 1959. Sr. engr. Bendix Corp., summers 1952, 53, 54; instr. elec. engring. Pa. State U., 1954-55; staff engr. HRB-Singer, Inc., State College, Pa., 1959-65; from asst. prof. to prof. elec. engring. U. Ill., Urbana, 1965-96, assoc. head instructional programs dept. elec. and computer engring., 1984-86, asst. dean engring., 1986-96, prof. Emeritus, 1996—; program dir. divsn. undergrad. edn. NSF, Washington, 1992-96; adj. prof. engring. Fla. Gulf Coast U., 1998—2006; mem. adv. bd. Whitaker Sch. Engring., Fla. Gulf Coast U., 2006—. Acting sci. sec. Sci. Com. on Solar-Terrestrial Physics, 1981; chmn. publs. com. Middle Atmosphere Program, 1980-86, editor handbook, 1981-86; mem. adv. com. on tech. edn. Fla. Dept Edn., 2001-2005 Editor: Proc. Aeronomy Confs, 1965, 69, 72; contbr. articles to profl. jours. Grantee NSF. Fellow: IEEE (edn. activities bd. 1990, tech. activities bd. 1991—92, edn. activities bd. 1992—93, chmn. com. on pre-coll. edn. ednl. activities bd. 1997—99, edn. activities bd. 1997—99, awards and recognition com. edn. activities bd. 2000—01, oversight subcom. Virtual Mus. 2000—02, precoll. edn. coord. com. edn. activities bd. 2000—03, Millennium medal 2000); mem.: Internat. Tech. Edn. Assn., Am. Soc. Engring. Edn., Am. Geophys. Union, Edn. Soc. of IEEE (v.p. 1989—90, pres. 1991—92, Achievement award 1993). Office Phone: 239-454-0640. Personal E-mail: csechrist@comcast.net.

SECK, OUSMANE, economics professor; b. Lambaye, Senegal, Jan. 20, 1969; s. Cheikh Seck and Fatime Faye; m. Koumba Ndiaye, Feb. 10, 2002; 1 child, Fatime. Baccalauréat, Lycee Seydina Limamou Laye, Pikine- Dakar-Senegal, 1990; Maîtrise, U. Cheikh Anta Diop, Dakar, Senegal, 1995, diplôma in d'Etudes Approfondies, 1997; PhD, MA, U. Kans., Lawrence, 2006. Lectr. U. Cheikh Anta Diop, 1997—2000, Calif. State U. Fullerton, 2006—. Cons. Ctr. Rsch. Economie Appliquee, Dakar, 1997—2000. Contbr. articles to profl. jours. Bourse d'Excellence fellow, Programme Troisieme Cycle Interuniversitaire Economie, 1996. Office Fax: 714-278-3097. Business E-Mail: oseck@fullerton.edu.

SECKLER, BERNARD DAVID, retired mathematics professor, translator; b. NYC, Feb. 14, 1925; s. Samuel and Anna Seckler; m. Evelyn Aida Mehler, Nov. 25, 1953; children: Judith, Stephen. BA, Bklyn. Coll., 1945; MA, Columbia U., NYC, 1948; PhD, NYU, 1958. Instr. math. Sch. Gen. Studies, Bklyn. Coll., 1947—55, instr., 1957—58, LIU, Bklyn., 1948—54, prof. math. C.W. Post Coll., Brookville, NY, 1964—94, chmn. dept., 1968—72; rschr. math. Courant Inst., NYU, 1954—58; assoc. prof. math. Pratt Inst., Bklyn., 1958—64. Sr. translator Russian SIAM Theory of Probability jour., Phila., 1964—90, co-editor Russian transls., 1986—90. Author: The Programmable Hand Calculator in the Classroom, 1983; editor 8 math. book transls. from Russian, editor, pres. Jour. Fine Arts Philately, 1995—2006. Vol. Recording Blind and Dyslexic, NYC, 1973—2003. Served with US Army, 1945—46. Mem.: Pi Mu Epsilon. Home: 19 Ramsey Rd Great Neck NY 11023-1611 Personal E-mail: ebs19@optonline.net.

SECREST, BETH ANNE, accounting educator; d. Robert Warren and Marie Theresa Secrest. BA summa cum laude, Walsh U., North Canton, Ohio, 1980; MS in Acctg., U. Va., Charlottesville, 1981. Assoc. prof. Walsh U., 1981—. V.p. Wellington Woods Homeowners Assoc., Canton, Ohio, 2004—06; adv. bd. mem. Aultcare, Canton, 2004—05; phys. com. mem., bd. dirs. North Canton YMCA, 1996. Recipient Excellence Tchg. award, Kent State U. Stark Campus, 1985, Fantastic Female Faculty award, Walsh U., 2009. Mem.: Assn. Cert. Fraud Examiners, Am. Acctg. Assn., Am. Inst. CPAs, U. Va. Alumni Assn., Sigma Beta Delta, Beta Alpha Psi. Roman Catholic. Avocations: gardening, reading, cooking. Office: Walsh Univ 2020 East Maple St North Canton OH 44720 Office Phone: 330-490-7049. Business E-Mail: bsecrest@walsh.edu.

SECREST, GEORGE MCCALL, JR., (MAC), lawyer; b. Laredo, Tex., Jan. 5, 1952; BA, U. Houston, 1974; JD with distinction, St. Mary's U. Sch. Law, 1977. Admitted: Tex. 1977, US Ct. Appeals, 5th Cir. 1981, US Dist. Ct., No., So., Ea. & We. Dists. Tex. 1982, US Supreme Ct. 1984, US. Ct. Appeals, 11th Cir. 1989, US Ct. Appeals 6th Cir. 1990. Briefing atty. Tex. Ct. Criminal Appeals, 1977—78; asst. dist. atty. Harris County, Tex., 1978—81; asst. fed. pub. defender So. Dist. Tex., 1981—83; adj. prof. law So. Tex. Coll. Law, 1984, U. Houston, 1994—2003, 2007, Bennett & Secrest, PLLC, Houston. Mem. Gov.'s Ad Hoc Com. to Revise the Tex. Code of Criminal Procedure, 1995—96, Tex. Bd. Legal Specialization Exam Commn., Criminal Law. Named one of Best Lawyers in Am., 1997—2008. Mem.: Harris County Criminal Lawyers Assoc. (Lawyer of Yr. 2007), Nat. Assn. Criminal Def. Lawyers, Tex. Criminal Def. Lawyer's Assn., Harris County Criminal Lawyers Assn. (treas. 1996—97), Houston Bar Assn., State Bar Tex. (Criminal Def. Lawyer of Yr. 1998), Bar Assn. 5th Fed. Cir., John Harlan Soc. Office: Bennett & Secrest PLLC 24th Fl Esperson Bldg 808 Travis St Houston TX 77002 Office Phone: 713-757-0679. Office Fax: 713-650-1602.

SECREST, JAMES SEATON, SR., lawyer; b. Middletown, Ky., Dec. 9, 1930; s. Elmer S. and Linney (Witherbee)S.; m. Mary Sue Corum, Sept. 2, 1950; children: James Seaton, Lynne Suzanne. JD, U. Louisville, 1954. Bar: Ky. 1954. Ptnr. Goad & Secrest, Scottsville, Ky., 1955-62; solo practice Scottsville, Ky., 1962-77; ptnr. Secrest & Secrest, Scottsville, 1977—. City judge pro tem Scottsville, 1955-58; judge Allen County, 1958-61; city atty. Scottsville, 1962-66; atty. Allen County, 1966-89, dep. judge-exec., 1990-99; bd. dir. Barren River Area Devel. Dist., 1970, mem. regional bd. ethics; mem. adv. bd. dir. Starbank, Scottsville, 1998; bd. dir. Commonwealth Health Corp., YMCA Scottsville and Allen County, 2006-. Recipient William H. Natcher award for Disting. Svc. in Govt., Barren River Area Devel. Dist. Mem. Scottsville C. of C. (pres. 1962), Ky. County Attorneys Assn. (pres. 1973), Ky. Assn. Counties (bd. dir. 1985-86), ABA, Ky. Bar Assn. (awared of Sr. Counselor), Rotary (pres. 1960). Republican. Methodist. Home: 714 Secrest Ln Scottsville KY 42164 Office: Secrest & Secrest 210 W Main St PO Box 35 Scottsville KY 42164-1123 Office Phone: 270-237-3616. Personal E-mail: jsecrest@nctc.com.

SECRETAN, JIMMY, application developer, researcher; s. Jim Secretan and Secretan Rose. BS in Computer Engring., U. Ctrl. Fla., Orlando, 2004, MS in Computer Engring., 2007. Rsch. asst. U. Ctrl. Fla., 2004—07; sr. software engr. Distributed Simulation Techs., Orlando, 2008—. Grad. Rsch. fellowship, NSF, 2005—08. Mem.: IEEE. Personal E-mail: jimmy@thepublicgrid.org.

SECUNDA, EUGENE, marketing professional, educator; b. Bklyn., June 15, 1934; s. Sholom and Betty (Almer) Secunda; m. Shirley Carol Frummer, Sept. 23, 1961; children: Ruthanne, Andrew. Comml. degree, N.Y. Inst. Photography, 1955; BS, NYU Sch. Bus., 1956; MS, Boston U., 1962; PhD, NYU, 1988. News editor Sta.-WBMS, Boston, 1956-57; reporter New London (Conn.) Daily Day, 1958-59; publicist various Broadway shows, 1959-62; sr. publicist 20th Century Fox Film Corp., NYC, 1962-65; with J. Walter Thompson Co., NYC, 1965-73, dir. corp. and pub. affairs, 1974-78, sr. v.p., dir. entertainment group, 1978—80, dir. entertainment divsn., 1978-80; sr. v.p., dir. comm. svcs. N.W. Ayer Internat., NYC, 1980-82; pres. Barnum/Secunda Assocs., NYC, 1982-85, Secunda Mktg. Comm., NYC, 1985—2005. Adj. prof. media studies NYU, NYC, 1972—2003, prof. mktg. and advt. Grad. Sch. Bus., 1985—88, prof. mktg., 1993—96, adj. prof. mktg. and media studies, 1996—; prof. mktg. and advt. Baruch Coll. CUNY, 1988—93; prof. mktg. Adelphi U., Garden City, NY, 1993—96; guest lectr. FBI Acad., Columbia U., UCLA; Fulbright scholar U. Ljubljana, Slovenia, 2006—. Contbr. articles to profl. jours. Mem. Greenwich Village Trust. With USAR, 1957—63. Mem.: NATAS, Am. Mktg. Assn., Mcpl. Arts Soc., Am. Acad. Advt., Internat. Advt. Assn., Internat. Comm. Assn., Greenwich Village Preservation Soc., Soc. of Silorians. Address: 30 5th Ave New York NY 10011-8859

SEDAGHAT, HASSAN, mathematician, educator; b. Aug. 19, 1959; s. Ali and Zahra Sedaghat. PhD, George Wash. U., 1990. Math. prof. Va. Commonwealth U., Richmond, Va., 1990—. Author: Nonlinear Difference Equations: Theory with Applications to Social Science Models; book rev. editor: Jour. Difference Equations and Applications, 2004—. Mem.: Am. Math. Soc. Office: Virginia Commonwealth University Dept of Math Box 842014 Richmond VA 23284-2014 E-mail: hsedagha@vcu.edu.

SEDARIS, DAVID RAYMOND, writer, comedian; b. Johnson City, NY, Dec. 26, 1956; s. Lou and Sharon Sedaris. Student, Kent State U.; BFA, Art Inst. Chgo., 1987. Tchr. writing Art Inst. Chgo., 1987—90; commentator Nat. Pub. Radio, 1992—. Author: (essays) SantaLand Diaries, 1992, (books) Barrel Fever: Stories and Essays, 1994, Holidays on Ice, 1997, Naked, 1997, Me Talk Pretty One Day, 2000 (Thurber Prize for Am. Humor, 2001), Dress Your Family in Corduroy and Denim, 2004 (Publishers Weekly Bestseller), When You Are Engulfed in Flames, 2008 (Publishers Weekly Bestseller); co-author (with sister Amy under the name The Talent Family): (plays) Stump the Host, 1993, Stitches, 1994, One Woman Shoe, 1995 (Obie award, 1995), Incident at Cobbler's Knob, 1997, The Little Freida Mysteries, 1997, The Book of Liz, 2001; writer: (TV series) Exit 57, 1995; performer: (comedy albums) The David Sedaris Box Set, 2002, David Sedaris: Live at Carnegie Hall, 2003; editor: (short stories) Children Playing Before a Statue of Hercules, 2005; contbg. writer Esquire, The New Yorker. Recipient Lambda Award, 2001; named Humorist of Yr., TIME mag., 2001. Office: c/o Don Congdon Assocs 156 5th Ave Ste 625 New York NY 10010-7002

SEDDON, JOHANNA MARGARET, ophthalmologist, epidemiologist; b. Pitts. BS, U. Pitts., 1970, MD, 1974; MS in Epidemiology, Harvard U., 1976. Intern Framingham (Mass.) Union Hosp., 1974-75; resident Tufts New Eng. Med. Ctr., Boston, 1976-80; fellow ophthalmic pathology Mass. Eye and Ear Infirmary, Boston, 1980-81, clin. fellow vitreoretinal Retina Svc., 1981-82; instr. clin. ophthalmology Harvard Med. Sch., Boston, 1982-84, asst. prof., asst. surgeon ophthalmolgy, 1984, assoc. prof., 1989—; assoc. surgeon, dir. ultrasound svc. Mass. Eye and Ear Infirmary, Boston, 1989—, founder, dir. epidemiology rsch. unit, 1984—85, dir. epidemiology unit, 1985—, surgeon in ophthalmology, 1992—2007; assoc. prof. faculty dept. epidemiology Harvard Sch. Pub. Health, Boston, 1992—; founding dir. ophthalmic epidemiology and genetics svc. New Eng. Eye Ctr., Tufts Med. Ctr., 2007—; prof. ophthalmology Tufts U. Sch. Medicine, 2007—. Mem. com. vision Commn. Behavioral and Social Scis. and Edn., NRC, NAS, Washington, 1984; mem. divsn. rsch. grants NIH, 1987-89, 94—; mem. sci. adv. bd. Found for Fighting Blindness, 1994—, Macular Degeneration Internat., 1994—, adv. panel, Age-Related Macular Degeneration Alliance Internat.; spkr. in field; lectr. in field. Author books and articles in field, especially in field of ocular tumors and macular degeneration; mem. editl. staff ophthalmic jours. Recipient NIH Nat. Svc. Rsch. awards, 1975, 80-81, Lewis R. Wasserman Merit award Rsch. to Prevent Blindness for seminal findings in ophthalmic rsch., 1996, 1st Maurice Rabb, Jr. award Prevent Blindness Am. Orgn., 2005; Inaugural Gold fellow, Assn. rsch. Vision & Ophthalmology, grantee, Prin. Investigation award Nat. Eye Inst., 1984—, Nat. Cancer Inst., 1986; med. sch. scholar, 1970-74, Henry H. Clark Med. Edn. Found. scholar, 1973, voted one of Am.'s top ophthalmologists, Consumer Rsch. Coun. Am., 2004. Mem. AMA (Sr. Honor award 2003), APHA, Am. Acad. Ophthalmology (Honor award 1990, Sr. Honor award 2003), Am. Med. Women's Assn., Assn. Rschr. Vision & Ophthalmology (elected, chair epidemiology sect. 1990, trustee clin. vision epidemiology sect. 1992-97. v.p. 1996-97, Spl. Recognition award 1997, Gold fellow 2009), Soc. Epidemiologic Rsch., New Eng. Ophthal. Soc., Am. Coll. Epidemiology, Retina Soc., Macula Soc. (mem. com. 2006—), Mass. Soc. Eye Physicians and Surgeons (v.p. 2000-02, mem. com. 2006—), Am. Epidemiol. Soc., Am. Soc. Ret. Surgeons (Hon. award 2005). Achievements include discovery of association between nutrition, dietary antioxidants, and systemic inflammatory biomarkers and age-related macular degeneration; genetic markers associated with progression of age-related macular degeneration; novel genetic variants associated with age related macular degeneration. Home: 4 Louisburg Sq Boston MA 02108-1203 Office Phone: 617-636-9000. Personal E-mail: jseddon@earthlink.net.

SEDEI RODDEN, PAMELA JEAN, psychologist, director; b. Johnstown, Pa., Jan. 31, 1956; d. Joseph and Betty Ruth (Watkins) Sedei; m. William Eugene Rodden, Dec. 4, 1982; 1 child, Gretchen Jean Rodden. BA, Southwestern Coll., Winfield, Kans., 1977; MS, Pitts. State U., Kans., 1979; PhD, Western Colo. U., 1983. Lic. profl. counselor Colo., diplomate in psychotherapy, cert. cognitive behavior therapist, nat. cert. counselor, domestic violence counselor, criminal justice specialist. Staff psychologist Autumn Manors Inc., Florence, Kans., 1982-83; clin. psychologist Richmond (Tex.) State Hosp., 1984-86; unit psychologist Wheat Ridge (Colo.) Regional Ctr., 1986-89, acting unit dir., 1989; dir. behavioral svcs. Colo. State Divsn. Devel. Disabilities, Denver, 1989-97; dir. Forensic Mental Health Svcs., Boulder, Colo., 1997—2001, Pamela JS Rodden & Assocs., Fort Collins, Colo., 2001—. Dir. Rodden Consultants, Longmont, Colo., 1986—90, Rodden Assocs., 2001—. Co-author: A Model For Interdisciplinary On Site Evaluation of People Who Have Dual Diagnosis, 1991. Fellow: Am. Coll. Forensic Examiners; mem.: ACA. Republican. Roman Catholic. Address: 1420 Blue Spruce Dr Ste G Fort Collins CO 80524 Office Phone: 970-482-8553. E-mail: Pjsrodden@juno.com.

SEDELMAIER, JOHN JOSEF, filmmaker; b. Orrville, Ohio, May 31, 1933; s. Josef Heinrich and Anne Isabel (Baughman) S.; m. Barbara Jean Frank, June 6, 1965; children: John Josef, Nancy Rachel, Adam Frederich. BFA, Art Inst. Chgo. at U. Chgo., 1955. Dir. art Young and Rubicam, Chgo., 1955-61; dir. art, assoc. creative dir. Clinton E. Frank, Chgo., 1961-64; dir. art, producer J. Walter Thompson, Chgo., 1964-67; pres. Sedelmaier Film Prodns., Chgo., 1967—. Spkr. Brit. design and art direction Lectr. Series, London, 1998; spkr. Harvard Bus. Sch., 2003. Exhibitions include Mus. Broadcast Comms., Chgo., 1988, Mus. Broadcasting, LA, 1991, Mus. TV and Radio, NYC, 1992, Represented in permanent collections Acad. TV Arts and Scis. Archive; dir.: (films) OpenMinds, 2003 (Sundance Film Festival Official Selection, 2003). Recipient Golden Ducat award for short film MROFNOC Mannheim Film Festival, 1968, Golden Gate award for short film Because That's Why, San Francisco Film Festival, 1969, 82 Clio awards, 1968-92, numerous Gold, Silver and Bronze Lion awards Cannes Film Festival, 1972-90, Gold Hugo award Chgo. Film Festival, 1976, 91, 2d Ann. IDC Creative award, Chgo., 1980, Internat. Broadcasting award for world's best TV comml., 1980, 86, Clio award for dir. of yr., 1981, London Internat. Advt. awards, 1986-88, numerous awards Internat. Festival of NY, 1984-93, Ann. Achievement award Assn. Ind. Comml. Producers, 1988; named Advt. Person of Yr., Chgo. Advt. Club, 1984, Jewish Communicator of Yr., 1985; named one of 50 Pioneers & Visionaries Who Made TV America's Medium, Advt. Age Mag., 1995; profiled in Communication Arts mag., Mar. 1976, Print mag., Jan. 1982, Fortune mag., June 1983, Newsweek mag., Nov. 1986, numerous others; featured on 60 Minutes, 48 Hours; subject of cover story Esquire mag., Aug. 1983; included in Arts & Entertainment's Top 10 Greatest Commls. of All Time, 1999; inducted The Art Dirs. Hall Fame, 2000; body of work and interview made part of permanent collections Acad. TV Arts and Scis. Archive, 2006.

SEDEÑO, EUGENE RAYMOND, electronics engineer, consultant; b. Honolulu, Aug. 31, 1952; s. Josephine Marie Sedeño Rosa; m. Theresa Ann Contreras, Dec. 28, 1980; children: Roxanne Guadelupe, Raymond Contreras. ASET, Heald Engring. Coll., 1974; BSEE, Coll. Allied Sci., 1980; MBA, Calif. Coast U., 2002. Field svc. engr. Bausch & Lomb, San Leandro, Calif., 1974—81; project mgr. Tylan Corp., Carson, Calif., 1981—85; field svc. supr. Sci. Atlanta, Santa Fe Springs, Calif., 1985—86; facilities and systems engr. Refractory Composities, Inc., Whittier, Calif., 1986—90, cons., 1985—91; supr. test and integration Thermco Systems, Orange, Calif., 1989—90; field engring. So. Calif. Edison, 1990—. With US Army, 1970—76. Mem. Am. Mgmt. Assn., Mensa. Democrat. Roman Catholic. Avocations: kenpo karate, kobudo, kajukenbo, photography, collecting antique books. Home: 16137 Minnetonka St Victorville CA 92395-9146 Office: So Calif Edison 12353 Hesperia Rd Victorville CA 92395-4797 Office Phone: 760-951-3132. Office Fax: 760-951-3115. Business E-Mail: Eugene.Sedeno@sce.com.

SEDER, SAM (SAMUEL LINCOLN SEDER), radio personality, comedian, writer; b. NYC, Nov. 28, 1966; m. Nikki Seder; 1 child, Myla Rae. Co-host The Majority Report, Air America Radio, 2004—05, host The Sam Seder Show, 2005—07, host Seder on Sunday, 2007—08; co-host (webcast) Breakroom Live with Maron & Seder, 2009—. Sub. host The Randi Rhodes Show, The Mike Malloy Show. TV/film appearances include All-American Girl, 1994, The Show, 1996, The Big Fall, 1996, Spin City, 1997, Next Stop Wonderland, 1998, Home Movies, 1999, Sex and the City, 2000, Happy Accidents, 2000, Endsville, 2000, Saddle Rash, 2002, Man About Town, 2005, America Undercover, 2005, Lucy, the Daughter of the Devil, 2007, actor, prodr., writer, dir. (films) Who's the Caboose?, 1997, (TV series) Pilot Season, 2004, actor, writer, prodr. (films) Beat Cops, 2001; dir.: (TV series) I'm with Busey, 2003; co-author (with Stephen Sherrill): F.U.B.A.R.: America's Right-Wing Nightmare, 2006. Office: Air Am Radio 641 Sixth Ave 4th Fl New York NY 10011*

SEDGHIZADEH, PARISH PAYMON, dentist, oral and maxillofacial pathologist, educator; s. Parvin Javadi. DDS, U. So. Calif., 2001—01; MS, Ohio State U., 2003. Lic. dentist Calif. Dental Bd., 2001. Tchg. assoc. Ohio State U., Columbus, 2001, asst. instr., 2001—. Instr. Kaplan Test Prep, Inc., Columbus, Ohio, 2002—. Contbr. chapters to books, articles to profl. jours. Recipient RL Fowkes and LJ Fogel Meml. award, So. Calif. Acad. Oral and Maxillofacial Pathology, 2001, Excellence in Oral and Maxillofacial Surgery award, Am. Acad. Oral and Maxillofacial Surgery, 2001, Merit award, Am. Acad. Oral Medicine, 2001; grantee, NIH, 2003—; fellow, Am. Cancer Soc., Ohio Divsn., 2002—,

Am. Acad. Oral and Maxillofacial Pathology, 2003—, NIH, 2003—; scholar, U. of So. Calif., 1998—99. Achievements include research in characterizing a novel gene (DESC1) in precancerous and cancerous mucosa of the head and neck.

SEDGWICK, ALEXANDER, retired historian, educator; b. Boston, June 8, 1930; s. William Ellery and Sarah (Cabot) S.; m. Charlene Mary Maute, June 24, 1961; children— Catherine Maria, Alexander Cameron BA, Harvard U., 1952, PhD in History, 1963. Asst. prof. history Dartmouth Coll., 1962-63; assoc. prof. U. Va., Charlottesville, 1963-66, 1966-74, prof., 1974—, chmn. history dept., 1979-85, dean Coll. Arts and Scis., 1985-90, dean grad. studies Charlottesville, 1990-95, univ. prof., 1995-97, univ. prof. emeritus, 1997—; ret., 1997. Mem. adv. com. in history Sr. Fulbright Awards Council for Internat. Exchange of Scholars. Author: The Ralliment in French Politics 1890-98, 1965, The Third French Republic, 1870-1914, 1968, Jansenism in Seventeenth Century France, Voices in the Wilderness, 1977, The Travails of Conscience. The Arnauld Family and the Ancien Regime, 1998; co-author: Church, State and Society Under the Bourbon Kings of France, 1982, For Want of a Horse, 1985, That Gentle Strength, 1980, Les Discour sur les Révolutions, 1991, History Today, 1991, Chroniques de Port-Royal, 1993, 95. Served with U.S. Army, 1952-54. Fulbright fellow, 1960-62; recipient Am. Coun. Learned Socs. grant-in-aid, 1967-68, Am. Philos. Soc. grant-in-aid, 1971. Mem. AAUP (nat. council 1976-79), Soc. French Hist. Studies (sec. 1979-83, pres. 1983-84), Am. Hist. Assn. Home: 1409 Rugby Rd Charlottesville VA 22903-1240 E-mail: as6d@virginia.edu.

SEDGWICK, KYRA, actress; b. NYC, Aug. 19, 1965; m. Kevin Bacon, Sept. 4, 1988; children: Travis, Sosie. Appeared in off-Broadway prodns. Time Was, 1981, Dakota's Belly Wyoming, 1989; stage appearances in Ah Wilderness!, 1988 (Theatre World award), Maids of Honor, 1990, Oleanna, 1994; Actress (films) War and Love, 1985, Tai-Pan, 1986, Kansas, 1988, Born on the Fourth of July, 1989, Mr. and Mrs. Bridge, 1990, Pyrates, 1991, Singles, 1992, Heart and Souls, 1993, Murder in the First, 1995, Something to Talk About, 1995, Losing Chase, 1996, Phenomenon, 1996, Montana, 1997, Critical Care, 1997, Twelfth Night, 1998, The Red Door, 1999, Labor Pains, 1999, What's Cooking, 2000, Just a Kiss, 2002, Behind the Red Door, 2002, Secondhand Lions, 2003, The Woodsman, 2004, Loverboy, 2005, The Game Plan, 2007; (TV movies) The Man Who Broke 1,000 Chains, 1987, Women & Men II, 1991, Hallmark Hall of Fame, 1992 (Golden Globe award nomination 1993), The Wide Net, 1997, Door to Door, 2002, Cavedweller, 2004, Something the Lord Made, 2004, (TV series) Another World, 1982-83, Talk to Me, 2000, Queens Supreme, 2003-07, The Closer, 2005- (Best Performance by an Actress in a TV Series-Drama, Golden Globe award, Hollywood Fgn. Press Assn., 2007, Favorite TV Drama Diva, People's Choice Awards, 2009); (mini-series) Family Pictures, 1983; (TV appearances) ABC Afternoon Spls., 1985, Am. Playhouse, 1987, 88, Miami Vice, 1985, Amazing Stories, 1986, Ally McBeal, 2002. Named one of Top 25 Entertainers or Yr., Entertainment Weekly, 2007. Office: c/o Handprint Entertainment 9100 Wilshire Blvd Ste 700E Beverly Hills CA 90212-3423

SEDIGHI, ARTIN, application developer, researcher; b. Shiraz, Iran, July 13, 1976; arrived in U.S., 1990; s. Mousa and Flora Sedighi. BSEE, Rensselaer Poly Inst., Troy, NY, 1998, MS, 2004. Software engr. GTE, Waltham, Mass., 1999—2000, Lavastorm.com, Waltham, Mass., 2000—01; cons. Tibco Software, NYC, 2001—03; software arch. SIAC/NYSE, NYC, 2003—04, Tibco Software, NYC, 2004—05, DataSynapse, NY, 2005—06; cto, founder Soft Module, NYC, 2006—. Contbr. articles to profl. jour., scientific papers to meetings, workshops and confs. Mem.: IEEE, Assn. for Computing Machinery, Eta Kappa Nu, Chi Phi. Republican. Jewish. Avocations: jazz, photography. Office Phone: 917-696-4834. Business E-Mail: sediga@alum.rpi.edu.

SEDIN, DANIEL, professional hockey player; b. Ornskoldsvik, Sweden, Sept. 26, 1980; m. Marinette Sedin; 1 child, Ronja. Left wing MoDo Hockey (Swedish Elite League), 1997—2000, 2004—05, Vancouver Canucks, 2000—. Mem. Swedish Olympic Hockey Team, Torino, Italy, 2006. Achievements include being a member of gold medal winning Swedish Hockey Team, Torino Olympics, Italy, 2006. Avocations: golf, tennis. Office: Vancouver Canucks 800 Griffiths Way Vancouver BC V6B 6G1 Canada*

SEDIN, HENRIK, professional hockey player; b. Ornskoldsvik, Sweden, Sept. 26, 1980; m. Johanna Sedin; 1 child, Valter. Center MoDo Hockey (Swedish Elite League), 1997—2000, 2004—05, Vancouver Canucks, 2000—. Mem. Swedish Olympic Hockey Team, Torino, Italy, 2006. Named to NHL All-Star Game, 2008. Achievements include being a member of gold medal winning Swedish Hockey Team, Torino Olympics, Italy, 2006. Avocations: boating, golf. Office: Vancouver Canucks 800 Griffiths Way Vancouver BC V6B 6G1 Canada*

SEDLAK, VALERIE FRANCES, retired English language and literature educator, academic administrator; b. Balt., Mar. 11, 1934; d. Julian Joseph and Eleanor Eva (Pilot) Sedlak; 1 child, Barry. AB in English, Coll. Notre Dame of Md., 1955; MA, U. Hawaii, 1962; PhD, U. Pa., Phila., 1992. Grad. tchg. fellow East-West Cultural Ctr. U. Hawaii, 1959-60; adminstrv. asst. Korean Consul Gen., 1959-60; tchr. Boyertown Sr. H.S., Pa., 1961-63; asst. prof. English U. Balt., 1963-69; assoc. prof. Morgan State U., Balt., 1970-2000, assoc. prof. English emerita, 2001—, asst. dean Coll. Liberal Arts, 1995-2000, sec. to faculty, 1981-83, faculty rsch. scholar, 1982-83, 92-93, comm. officer, 1989-90, dir. writing for TV program, 1990-97; exec. dir. Renaissance Inst. Coll. of Notre Dame of Md., 2000—03, ret., 2003—. Cons. scholar Md. Humanities Coun., 1992—; adj. prof. York Coll., Pa., 2004-05. Author numerous poems and lit. criticism; editor Liberal Arts Rev., 1996-2000; assoc. editor Md. English Jour., 1994-2000; assoc. editor Morgan Jour. Rsch., 1995-2000, CEA mag., 2002-05; mem. editl. bd. CEA Critic, 2003-06; contbr. articles to lit. jours. Coord. Young Reps., Berks County, Pa., 1962-63; chmn. Md. Young Reps., 1964; election judge Baltimore County, Md., 1964-66; regional capt. Am. Cancer Soc., 1978-79; mem. adv. bd. Md. Our Md. Anniversary, 1984, The Living Constitution: Bicentennial of the Fed. Constitution, 1987. Morgan-Penn Faculty fellow, 1977-79, NEH fellow, 1984; named Outstanding Tchg. prof., U. Balt. Coll. Liberal Arts, 1965, Outstanding Tchg. Prof. in English Dept., Morgan State U., 1987. Mem. MLA, South Atlantic MLA, Coll. Lang. Assn., Coll. English Assn. (Mid-Atlantic Group v.p. 1987-90, pres. 1990-92, exec. bd. 1992-2005, nat. bd. dir. 2001-04, nat. liaison officer 1993-2004), Women's Caucus for Modern Langs., Md. Coun. Tchrs. English, Md. Poetry and Lit. Soc., Md. Assn. Depts. English (bd. dir. 1992-2006), Mid. Atlantic Writers' Assn. (founding 1981, exec. assoc. editor Mid. Atlantic Writers' Assn. Rev. 1989-2000), Delta Epsilon Sigma (v.p. 1992-94, pres. 1994-96), Pi Kappa Delta Roman Catholic. Home: 17049 Keeney Mill Rd New Freedom PA 17349 Personal E-mail: vfsedlak@aol.com.

SEDLER, ROBERT ALLEN, law educator; b. Pitts., Sept. 11, 1935; s. Jerome and Esther (Rosenberg) S.; m. Rozanne Friedlander, Jan. 24, 1960; children: Eric, Beth. BA, U. Pitts., 1956, JD, 1959. Bar: D.C. 1959, Ky. 1968, Mich. 1979; U.S. Supreme Ct. 1969. Asst. prof., assoc. prof. law St. Louis U., 1961-65; assoc. prof. law, asst. dean Addis Ababa U., Ethiopia, 1963-66; assoc. prof. to prof. law U. Ky., Lexington, 1966-77; prof. law Wayne State U., Detroit, 1977—, disting. prof. law, 2000—05; Gibbs chair civil rights and civil liberty Wayne State Acad. Scholars, Detroit, 2000—05, pres., 2007—08. Author: Across State Lines, 1989: Applying the Conflict of Law to Your Practice, 1989, American Constitutional Law, 2005; (with R. Cramton) The Sum and Substance of Conflict of Laws, 1987, Ethiopian Civil Procedure, 1968; contbr. articles to profl. jours. Gen. counsel ACLU Ky., 1971-76. Named Gershenson Disting. Faculty fellow, Wayne State U., 1985—87. Mem. ABA, AAUP, Phi Beta Kappa, Order of the Coif. Democrat. Jewish. Home: 18851 Capitol Dr Southfield MI 48075-2680 Office: Wayne State U 471 W Palmer Detroit MI 48202-3620 Home Phone: 248-569-3966; Office Phone: 313-577-3968. Personal E-mail: rsedler@aol.com. Business E-Mail: rsedler@wayne.edu.

SEDMAK, DANIEL D., academic administrator; b. Columbus, Ohio, Apr. 18, 1952; m. Peggy Sedmak; 5 children. BS in biology, U. Cin.; MD, Ohio State U., 1980. Resident in pathology Cleve. Clinic Found., 1980—84, fellow in immunopathology, 1984—85; joined faculty Ohio State U., 1985; dir. nephropathology and transplant pathology programs Ohio State U. Hosp.; prof. and chair pathology Coll. Medicine and Pub. Health, Ohio State U., 1997, interim dean, sr. assoc. v.p. health sci. and exec. vice dean; exec. dean Georgetown U. Sch. Medicine, 2003—04, exec. v.p. health sci., 2003—04; exec. vice dean, assoc. v.p. health sciences Ohio State Med. Ctr., Columbus, 2003—. Office: Ohio State Univ Med Ctr 200 Meiling Hall 370 West 9th St Columbus OH 43210 Office Phone: 202-687-4600. Business E-Mail: sedmak@georgetown.edu.

SEDO, MANUEL ARTURO, psychologist, researcher; b. Barcelona, 1932; arrived in US, 1972; s. Manuel Sedo and Manuela Garcia-Tunon; m. Asuncion Sastre, July 10, 1965; children: Silvia Johnson, Natalia C., Arturo. PhD, Boston Coll., Chestnut Hill, 1978; diploma, Inst. Psychology, Sorbonne, 1960. Lic. psychologist, sch. psychologist Commonwealth of Mass. Staff psychologist Children's Hosp. Med. Ctr., Boston, 1975—78; sch. psychologist Boston Pub. Schs., 1980—2000; dir. of test devel. Plurilingual Testing, Natick, Mass., 2000—. Author, rschr.: language and test psychol. tests with low lang.-load and high-processing oral naming test. Recipient Fulbright Fellowships, 1990, 1991; fellow, Harvard Coll., 1972, Harvard U., 1972—73. Mem.: APA, Mass. Neuropsychol. Soc. (mem. bd.). Achievements include design of Neuropsych tests of prefrontal maturity 3 to 11 based on simple curriculum contexts; early language neutral attention and language tests. Office: Lang Neutral Testing 9 Ingleside Rd Natick MA 01760 Office Phone: 508-655-6970. Business E-Mail: manuel@sedo.net.

SEDRA, ADEL SHAFEEK, engineering educator, academic administrator; b. Assouut, Egypt, Nov. 2, 1943; arrived in Can., 1966; s. Chafik and Hélène (Monsour) S.; m. Doris M. Barker, May 5, 1973; children: Paul Douglas, Mark Andrew. BSEE, Cairo U., 1964; MASc in Elec. Engring., U. Toronto, Ont., Can., 1968, PhD in Elec. Engring., 1969; DSc (hon.), Queen's U., 2003; LLD (hon.), U. Toronto, 2005; DSc (hon.), McGill U., Montreal, 2007. Registered profl. engr., Ont. Instr. Cairo U., 1964-66; asst. prof. elec. engring. U. Toronto, 1969-72, assoc. prof., 1972-78, prof., 1978—2003, chmn. dept., 1986-93, v.p., provost, chief acad. officer, 1993—2002; prof. elec. engring., dean faculty of engring. U. Waterloo, Ont., Canada, 2003—. Pres. Elec. Engring. Consociates Ltd., Toronto, 1979-81; bd. dirs. Info. Tech. Rsch. Ctr., Toronto, 1988-93; mem. rsch. coun. Can. Inst. for Advanced Rsch., 1994—; del. Oxford U. Press, 1995—2007. Co-author: Filter Theory and Design, 1978, Microelectronic Circuits, 1982, 5th edit., 2004 (also Spanish, Korean, Greek, Italian, Portuguese, Chinese, Persian, and Hebrew transls.), SPICE, 1997; contbr. over 120 articles to sci. jours. Operating grantee Nat. Scis. and Engring. Rsch. Coun. Can., 1970—2002; Ryerson Poly. Inst. fellow, 1988. Fellow IEEE (Darlington best paper award 1984, Edn. medal 1996, Cir. and Sys. Soc. Edn. award 1994, Guillemin Cauer Best Paper award 1987, Golden Jubilee medal 2000, 3d Millennium medal 2000), Can. Acad. Engrs., Royal Soc. Can., Am. Soc. Engring. Edn. (Terman award 1988); mem. Info. Tech. Assn. Can. (Tech. Achievement award 1993), Assn. Profl. Engrs. Ont. (Excellence award 2002). Office: U Waterloo Dean of Faculty of Engring 200 University Ave W Waterloo ON Canada N2L 3G1 Home: 1704-4 Willow St Waterloo ON N2J 4S2 Canada Office Phone: 519-888-4567 ext. 33348. Business E-Mail: sedra@uwaterloo.ca.

SEE, CAROLYN, English language educator, writer, book critic; b. Pasadena, Calif., Jan. 13, 1934; d. George Newton Laws and Kate Louise (Sullivan) Daly; m. Richard Edward See, Feb. 18, 1955 (div. June 1959); 1 child, Lisa Lenine; m. Tom Sturak, June 11, 1959; 1 child, Clara Elizabeth Marya. BA, Calif. State U., LA, 1958; PhD, UCLA, 1963. Prof. English Loyola Marymount Coll., LA, 1970-85, UCLA, 1985—; book critic L.A. Times, 1981-93, Washington Post, 1993—. Author: Rhine Maidens, 1980, Golden Days, 1986, Making History, 1991, Dreaming: Hard Luck and Good Times In America, 1995, The Handyman, 1999, Making a Literary Life, 2002, There Will Never Be Another You, 2006 Bd. dirs. Calif. Arts Coun., L.A., 1987-91, Day Break, for homeless, Santa Monica, Calif., 1989—, Friends of English, UCLA, 1990—; buddy for life AIDS Project L.A., AIDS relief, L.A., 1990—. Recipient award Sidney Hillman Found., 1972, Robert Kirsch award L.A. Times, 1994; PEN Ctr. USA West Lifetime Achievement award 1998; grantee Nat. Endowment for Arts, 1980, Guggenheim fellow, 1990-91. Mem. Writers Guild Am., Libr. Found. Calif., PEN Ctr. USA West (pres. 1990-91), Nat. Book Critics Cir. (bd. dirs. 1986-90). Democrat. Avocations: gardening, sailing, dance, brush clearing. Address: Ms Carolyn See 930 3rd St 203 Santa Monica CA 90403 Home Phone: 310-395-4282. Business E-Mail: csee@ucla.edu.

SEEBA, JOHN M., federal agency administrator, accountant; BS in Accounting, Rochester Inst. Tech. CPA Md. Internal auditor IRS; with Office of Inspector Gen., US Dept. Defense, Washington; dep. asst. inspector gen. fin. audits Office of Inspector Gen., US Postal Svc.; asst. inspector gen. auditing US Dept. Commerce, 2005; inspector gen. FTC, 2008—. Recipient Nat. Exec. Award, US Postal Svc. Office: FTC Office of Inspector Gen, Rm 1110 600 Pennsylvania Ave, NW Washington DC 20580 Office Phone: 202-326-2800. Office Fax: 202-326-2034. E-mail: OIG@ftc.gov.*

SEEBACH, DIETER, chemistry professor; b. Karlsruhe, Federal Republic of Germany, Oct. 31, 1937; s. Kurt E. and Erika (Weisert) S.; m. Ingeborg Ria Reichling, June 23, 1961; children: Jorg D., Petra I., Lutz V. BS in Chemistry, U. Karlsruhe, 1961, PhD in Natural Scis., 1964, Habilitation, 1969; D. (hon.), U. Montpellier, Montpellier, France, 1989. Asst. U. Karlsruhe, 1961-64, 66-70; lectr. Harvard U., Cambridge, Mass., 1965-66; vis. prof. U. Wis., Madison, 1969-70, Calif. Inst. Tech., Pasadena, 1974, Max Planck Inst., U. Kaiserslautern, Cornell U., Harvard U.; prof. chemistry U. Giessen, Giessen, Fed. Republic Germany, 1971-77, Eidgenoessische Technische Hochschule, Zurich, Switzerland, 1977—. Cons. Sandoz AG, Basel, Switzerland, 1978—; lectr. in field. Author: Four-membered Rings, 1970, Modern Synthetic Methods Series, 1976, 80, 83, 86; author rsch. papers in field; patentee in field. Elected mem. Akad. der Naturforscher, Leopoldina, Halle, Fed. Republic Germany, 1984, Akademie der Wissenschaften und der Lit. in Mainz, Fed. Republic Germany, 1990. Recipient Karl-Ziegler prize Ges. Deutscher Chemiker, 1987, Havinga medal U. Leiden, The Netherlands, 1985, Fluka prize Reagent of Yr. Fluka-AG, Switzerland, 1987, Award for Creative Work in Organic Synthesis Am. Chem. Soc., 1992, Allan R. Day award 1995, Hamilton award 1996, Roger Adams award, ACS, 1999, King Faisal Internat. prize for sci. 1999, Yamada prize Japan Rsch. Found. Optically Active Compounds, 2000, Marcel Benoist prize Eidg. Wissenschaftspreis Marcel Benoist Stiftung, 2000, Chirality medal, 2002, Nagoya medal, 2002, A.W. Von Hoffman medal, Tetrahedron prize, 2003, du Vigneaud award, 2004, Ryoji Noyori prize, 2004. Fellow: Royal Soc. Chemistry Gt. Britain; mem.: Chemische Gesellschaft, Schweiz, Academica Mexicana de Ciencias (corr. Chirality Medal 2002), Academia Europeae, Nat. Acad. Sciences (fgn. assoc). Avocations: reading, music, swimming, travel, cars, gourmet cuisine. Office: Eidgenossische Tech Hochsch Wolfgang-Pauli-Str 10 HCI CH-8093 Zurich Switzerland Office Phone: 41 1 632 29 90. Business E-Mail: seebach@org.chem.ethz.ch.

SEEBACH, LYDIA MARIE, physician; b. Red Wing, Minn., Nov. 9, 1920; d. John Henry and Marie (Gleusen) S.; m. Keith Edward Wentz, Oct. 16, 1959; children: Brooke Marie, Scott. BS, U. Minn., 1942, MB, 1943, MD, 1944, MS in Medicine, 1951. Diplomate Am. Bd. Internal Medicine. Intern Kings County Hosp., Bklyn., 1944; fellow Mayo Found., Rochester, Minn., 1945-51; pvt. practice Oakland, Calif., 1952-60, San Francisco, 1961—. Asst. clin. prof. U. Calif., San Francisco, 1981—; mem., vice chmn. Arthritis Clinic, Presbyn. Hosp., San Francisco, 1961-88, pharmacy com., 1963-78; chief St. Mary's Hosp. Arthritis Clinic, San Francisco, 1968-72; exec. bd. Pacific Med. Ctr., San Francisco, 1974-76. Contbr. articles to med. jours. Fellow ACP; mem. AMA, Am. Med. Womens Assn. (pres. Calif. chpt. 1968-70), Am. Rheumatism Assn., Am. Soc. Internal Medicine, Pan Am. Med. Womens Assn. (treas.), Calif. Acad. Medicine, Calif. Soc. Internal Medicine, Calif. Med. Assn., San Francisco Med. Soc., San Francisco Med. Assn., San Francisco Soc. Internal Medicine, No. Calif. Rheumatism Assn., Internat. Med. Women's Assn., Mayo Alumni (bd. dirs. 1983-89), Iota Sigma Pi. Republican. Lutheran. Avocations: music, cooking, gardening, needlepoint. Office: 490 Post St Ste 1536 San Francisco CA 94102-1414 Office Phone: 415-362-6398. Personal E-mail: lseebach@sbcglobal.net.

SEEBER, FREDRICK PAUL, emeritus physics professor; s. Fredrick Woodrow and Columbia Seeber; m. Ellen Patricia Warren; children: Colleen Patricia Seeber-Combs, Patricia Susan Santos, Fredrick Charles. BA, NJ City U., Jersey City, 1963; MA, NJ City U., 1966; EdD in physics, Rutgers U., New Brunswick, 1981. Prin. investigator Natinal Sci. Found., Wash., Md., 2000—; emeritus prof. physics Camden County Coll., Blackwood, NJ, 2002—. Course instr. laser physics Laser Inst. Am., Orlando, Fla., 1980—. Contbr. to numerous articles (NSF Grant, 2000, Rutgers Disting. Alumni award, 1996). Councilman-coun. pres. Stafford Twp., Manahawkin, NJ, 1986—. State NJ. Work Grant, 1980. Fellow: Inst. Applied Laser Surgery (fellow-instr. 1980), Laser Institue Am. (dir. 1990—2000). Roman Catholic. Avocations: boating, fishing, travel. Office: Camden County Coll Box 200 Blackwood NJ 08012 Office Fax: 856-734-4959. Personal E-mail: fredpseeber@comcast.net. Business E-Mail: fseeber@camdencc.edu.

SEEBORG, MICHAEL C., economics professor; s. Roy Rudolph and Marjorie Jean Seeborg; m. Rong Wu, May 13, 1989; children: Kurt Thomas, Andres Paul, Melissa Tiffany. BA, U. Oreg., Eugene, 1969; PhD in Economics, U. Utah, Salt Lake City, 1976. Asst. & assoc. prof. economics Ball State U., Muncie, Ind., 1976—89; Robert S. Eckley disting. prof. economics Ill. Wesleyan U., Bloomington, 1989—. Chair Provost Search Com., Bloomington, 2005—06, John Wesley Powell Rsch. Conf. Com., Bloomington, 2009—, Ill. Wesleyan U. Dept. Economics, 1989—95, 2001—05, Ill. Wesleyan U. Coun. Program and Policies, 2006—07; pres. IWU Fed. Credit Union, 2006—. Contbr. to numerous profl. jours. Recipient Best Paper award, Tchg. and Learning Conf., 2007, Internat. Bus. & Economics Conf., 2001, 2002, 2003, Du Pont award, Ill. Wesleyan U., 1999; vis. scholar, Warsaw Agrl. U., 1986; Technos Internat. Week Travel Grant, Tanaka Ikueikai Ednl. Trust, 2005. Mem.: Mo. Valley Econ. Assn. (dir. 2004—05), Midwest Econ. Assn., Am. Econ. Assn., Phi Kappa Phi, Phi Beta Delta.

SEEDS, NICHOLAS WARREN, neuroscience educator, researcher; BS, U. N.Mex., Albuquerque, 1964; PhD in Biochemistry, U. Iowa, Iowa City, 1968. NSF fellow Lab. Biochem. Genetics, NIH, Bethesda, Md., 1968-70; asst. prof. biophysics and genetics U. Colo. Med. Ctr., Denver, 1970-75, assoc. prof. biochemistry, biophysics and genetics, 1975-81, prof., 1981—, dir. neurosci. program, 1989-97, dir. Neurosci. Ctr., 1990-97. Med. genetics course dir., cons. NIH, 1974-2003; bd. mem. NY Spinal Cord Grant Review, 2002-09, MDA Sci. Adv. Bd., 2004; lectr. over 100 nat. and internat. orgns., 1970—. Mem. editl. bd. Internat. Jour. Devel. Neurosci., 1976-80, Jour. Biol. Chemistry, 1980-85; contbr. over 100 articles to sci. jours., chpts. to books. Fogarty sr. internat. fellow NIH, 1979, Humboldt internat. fellow, 1979; Jacob Javits disting. investigator grantee NIH, 1989—. Mem. Am. Soc. Cell Biology (program com. 1987, 88, chmn. local arrangements 1991, 92), Soc. for Neurosci., Am. Soc. Biochemistry and Molecular Biology, Soc. for Neurochemistry (ann. meeting com. 1998). Office: U Colo Health Sci Ctr MS 8315 PO Box 6511 Aurora CO 80045 Business E-Mail: nicholas.seeds@ucdenver.edu.

SEEGER, LAUREEN E., lawyer, health products executive; BBA, U. Wis., Eau Claire, 1983; JD, U. Wis., Madison, 1986. Atty. Jones, Day, Reavis & Pogue, 1986—92; ptnr.-in-charge tech. litigation sect. Morris, Manning & Martin, LLP, 1992—2000; v.p., gen. coun. McKesson Provider Technologies, 2000—06; exec. v.p., gen. counsel, sec. McKesson Corp., San Francisco, 2006—. Office: McKesson Corpn 1 Post St San Francisco CA 94104*

SEEGER, PETE, folk singer, songwriter; b. NYC, May 3, 1919; s. Charles Louis and Constance de Clyver (Edson) Seeger; m. Toshi-Aline Ohta, July 20, 1943; children: Daniel Adams, Mika Salter, Tinya. Student, Harvard U., 1936-38. Co-founding mem. The Weavers, 1948—59. Singer: (albums) American Industrial Ballads, 1957, Dangerous Songs, 1966, Abiyoyo, 1967, World of Pete Seeger, 1973, Essential, 1978, Greatest Hits, 1987, Traditional Christmas Carols, 1989, Children's Concert at Town Hall, 1990, Folk Music of the World, 1991, Pete Seeger's Family Concert, 1992, Singalong-Live at Sanders Theatre, 1992, Darling Corey/Goofing Off Suit, Live at Newport, Waist Deep in the Big Muddy, 1993, Clearwater Classics, Link in the Chain, 1996; musician Pete, 1996 (Grammy award for Best Traditional Folk Album, 2006); singer American Favorite Ballads, 1997, Birds, Beasts, Bugs & Fishes, For Kids & Just Plain Folks, God Bless the Grass, If I Had a Hammer-Songs of Hope & Struggle, 1998, Headlines & Footnotes, 1999, American Folk Game & Activity, Stories & Songs for Little Children, 2000, Song and Play Time, 2001; co-author (with Paul DuBois Jacobs): (children's book) The Deaf Musicians, 2006 (Schneider Family Book award); singer: (albums) Brothers and Sisters, 2006, At 89, 2008

(Grammy award for Best Traditional Folk Album, 2009). With US Army, 1942—45. Recipient Nat. Medal of the Arts, 1994, Kennedy Center Honor, 1994; named to Rock and Roll Hall of Fame, 1996. Subject of book: How Can I Keep from Singing: Pete Seeger, by David King Dunaway, 1981. Office: care Harold Leventhal 250 W 57th St New York NY 10107*

SEEHAUSEN, RICHARD FERDINAND, architect; b. Indpls., Mar. 17, 1925; s. Paul Ferdinand and Melusina Dorothea (Nordmeyer) S.; m. Phyllis Jean Gates, Dec. 22, 1948; children: Lyn, Dirk. Student, DePauw U., 1943, Wabash Coll., 1944, State U. Iowa, USN Pre Flight, 1944; BArch, U. Ill., 1949. Registered profl. arch., 1951. Pilot training Norman Naval Air Base, 1945; ptnr. Johnson, Kile, Seehausen & Assocs., archs., engrs., Rockford, Ill., 1955-82, pres., 1974-82, Richard F. Seehausen-Arch., Inc., Rockford, Ill., 1983—2001. Mem. com. jail planning and constrn. stds. Bur. Detention Facilities, Ill. Dept. Corrections, 1970-73; analyst Dept. Def., 1962-66; analyst Fed. Fall-Out Shelter, 1962—. Prin. works include No. Ill. U. Ctr., Harrison Hall, Lorado Taft, Oreg., Health Svc. Bldg., No. Ill. U., (Renovation) Old Winnebago County Pub. Safety Bldg., Rockford, Ill., St. Mark Luth. Ch., Christ Meth. Ch., Forest Hills Free Ch., Page Park Spl. Edn. Sch., Winnebago County Courthouse, Court Street Meth. Ch., Willows Personal Care Ctr., 1st Presbyn. Ch., Rochelle, Ill., Messiah Luth. Ch., Rock Falls, Ill., Rockford Mut. Ins. Home Office Bldg., Ch. of the Nazarene, Freeport, Ill., Stephenson County Courthouse, LDS Temple, McHenry County Ct. House, Woodstock, Ill., Ogle County Pub. Safety Bldg., Oreg., DeKalb H.S., Freeport YWCA Bldgs., renovation Carroll County Ct. House, DeKalb Area Retirement Ctr., Oak Crest Retirement Ctr., Sycamore/DeKalb, Ill., St. Paul Ch. of Christ, Davis, Ill., Savanna Meth. Ch., Savanna, Ill., others. Bd. dir. Rockford Boys Club, Lincoln Pk. Boys Club, past dir.; trustee Emmanuel Luth. Ch., Rockford, 1989-92; mem. Nat. Trust Hist. Preservation, 2000—. Served with USN, 1943-45, USNR, 1945-47, lt. USAF, 1949-55. Mem. AIA (dir. No. Ill. chpg. 1966-68, 75-77, pres. chpt. 1978-79, nat. design com. 2005—), Ill. Coun. of Am. Inst. Archs., U. Ill. Alumni Assn., Mason (Shriner), Kiwanian, Forest Hills Country Club (gov. 1970-72), Saddle Brooke Country Club, Saddle Brooke Arc. Com., Lambda Chi Alpha. Lutheran. Office: Richard F Seehausen Arch Inc 65297 E Emerald Ridge Dr Tucson AZ 85739-1434

SEELAM, SEETHARAMI, research scientist; s. Laxma and Saraswathi Seelam; m. Prathima Bedaala. BE, Osmania U., Hyderabad, 1999; MS, U. Tex., El Paso, 2002, PhD, 2006. Postdoc. staff IBM Rsch., Yorktown Heights, NY, 2006—. Contbr. scientific papers. Mem.: IEEE (Outstanding Paper award), ACM, Upsilon Pi Epsilon. Personal E-mail: seelam@gmail.com.

SEELAND, ARTHUR DAVID, bishop; b. Jersey City, Oct. 31, 1931; s. Theodore Arthur and Dorothea Augusta (Thomas) Seeland; m. Mary Ann Hove, Apr. 10, 1954; children: John Robert, Eric David, Tellef Martin, Karen Victoria. BA, Houghton Coll., 1953; MDiv, Temple U., 1958; D Ministry, McCormick Theol. Sem., 1978; grad. with highest distinction, U.S. Naval War Coll., 1981; ThM, Princeton Theol. Sem., 1973. Diplomate Am. Bd. Med. Psychotherapists. Pastor NJ United Meth. Conf., 1953—64; commd. lt. (j.g.) USN, 1963, advanced through grades to comdr., 1975, chaplain, 1964—87; clin. dir. Family and Psychol. Svcs., Cherry Hill, NJ, 1987—90; rector Holy Sacraments Anglican Cath. Ch., King of Prussia, Pa., 1988—93; archdeacon Diocese of the Resurrection, Quakertown, Pa., 1990—93; bishop Diocese of the Pacific and SW of the Anglican Rite Cath. Ch., LA, 1993—. Lectr. med. ethics Med. Sch. Uniformed Services U., Bethesda, Md., 1980—84; lectr. ethics U.S. Nat. War Coll., Washington, 1980—84; asst. prof. Pa. State U., Hershey; pres. Holy Cross Seminary, Hereford, Ariz., 2005—. Contbr. articles to profl. jours. Editl. bd. Jour. of Christian Bioethics, Waco, Tex., 1994—99; pres. Houghton (NY) Coll. Alumni, 1981—83. Master: Mason (life; grand chaplain NJ 1963—, grand chaplain France 1977—); mem.: Assn. of Mil. Surgeons of the U.S. (life), NY Acad. of Scis. (life). Anglican Catholic. Avocations: sailing, travel, hiking, hunting. Home: 764 West Bay Ave Barnegat NJ 08005 Office: Diocese of the Pacific and Southwest 6752 East Ramsey Rd Hereford AZ 85615

SEELER, RUTH ANDREA, pediatrician, educator; b. NYC, June 13, 1936; d. Thomas and Olivia Seeler. BA cum laude, U. Vt., 1959, MD, 1962. Diplomate Am. Bd. Pediat., Am. Bd. Pediatric Hematology/Oncology. Intern Bronx (N.Y.) Mcpl. Hosp., 1962—65; pediats. hematology/oncology fellow U. Ill., 1965—67; dir. pediatric hematology/oncology Cook County Hosp., 1967—84; prof. pediatrics and pediatric edn. Coll. Medicine U. Ill., Chgo., 1984—; assoc. chief pediatrics Michael Reese Hosp., Chgo., 1990—97, acting chief pediatrics, 1997—99; pediatrician St. Anthony's Hosp./U. Ill. Coll. Medicine, 1999—2001. Course coord. pediatrics Nat. Coll. Advanced Med. Edn., Chgo., 1987-96; mem. subboard Pediatric Hematology/Oncology, Chapel Hill, 1990-95; chief Midwest Am. Bd. Pediat., 1990-, Mem. editl. bd. Am. Jour. Pediat. Hematology/Oncology, 1985-95. Founder med. dir. camp for hemophiliacs Ill. Hemophilia Found., 1973—2000, pres. Ill., 1981—85; jr. and sr. warden, treas. Ch. Our Saviour, Chgo., 1970—92. Mem.: U. Vt. Med. Sch. Alumna Assn. (pres 2008—), Phi Beta Kappa, Gamma Phi Beta Found. (trustee 1994—, 2002—08, grantas chair). Avocations: triathalons, biking, swimming. Office: U Ill Coll Medicine Pediats M/C 856 840 S Wood St Chicago IL 60612-7317 Office Phone: 312-355-1021. Business E-Mail: seeler@uic.edu.

SEELEY, CATHY LYNN, director, secondary school educator, consultant; b. SI, NY, Sept. 26, 1948; d. Mervil John and Katharine Virginia (Bissell) S.; children: Dawn Rebecca Peavler, Kelly Nicole Peavler, Miranda Jean Peavler. BS, Va. Polytech. Inst., 1969; postgrad., U. Wyo., 1972-79; MA, U. No. Colo., 1974; EdD, U. Houston, 1985. Tchr. maths. Bennett (Colo.) Schs., 1970-71, Jefferson County (Colo.) Pub. Schs., 1971-79; maths. coord. LaPorte (Tex.) Ind. Sch. Dist., 1979-83; instructional computer specialist Austin (Tex.) Ind. Sch. Dist., 1983-84; dir. maths. Tex. Edn. Agy., Austin, 1984—91; dir., prof. U. Tex., Dana Ctr., 1991—99, sr. fellow, 2006—; math tchr. Peace Corps, Burkina Faso, 1999—2001; sr. advisor U. Tex., Distance Edn., 2002—03; pres. Nat. Council Tchrs. Math, 2004—06. Instr. U. Wyo., 1974-79, Sioux Falls (S.D.) Coll., 1975, U. Houston, Clear Lake, 1980, Tex. A&M U., 1986-88; one of 24 writers Nat. Coun. Tchrs. Math. Curriculum and Evaluation Standards; mem. adv. co. Tex. Higher Edn. Coordinating Bd. EESA Title II Program, 1986-88; cons. Gov.'s Coun. on Sci. and Tech. Subcom. on Edn., 1986; nat. selection panel Presdl. Awards for Excellence. Contbr. articles to profl. jours. Named one of Outstanding Young Women in Am., 1986. Mem. Tex. Alliance for Sci., Tech. and Maths. Edn. (exec. bd. 1986-88, steering com. 1986-89), Math. Assn. Am. (pres. 2006), Adminstrv. Women in Edn. (pres. 1986-87), Assn. State Suprs. of Maths., Tex. Computer Edn. Assn., Women and Maths. Edn., Nat. Coun. Tchrs. of Maths. (com. Denver chpt. ann. meeting 1975, conf. co-chair 1984, Houston conf. 1982-84, profl. devel. and status adv. com. 1985-88, testing and evaluation task force, 1986-88, commn. on standards for sch. maths. 1987-89, mem. editoral panel 1988-91, bd. dirs. 1988-91, various other coms., pres.).

SEELIG, GERARD LEO, management consultant; b. Schluchtern, Germany, June 15, 1926; came to U.S., 1934, naturalized, 1943; s. Herman and Bella (Bach) S.; m. Lorraine Peters, June 28, 1953; children: Tina Lynn, Robert Mark and Carol Ann (twins). BEE, Ohio State U., 1948; MS in Indsl. Mgmt, N.Y. U., 1954. Registered profl. engr., Ohio. Electronics engr. Martin Corp., Balt., 1948-50; sr. engr. Fairchild Aircraft Co., Farmingdale, NY, 1950-54; program mgr. RCA, Moorestown, NJ, 1954-59, Van Nuys, Calif., 1959-61; div. mgr. Missile & Space Co. div. Lockheed Aircraft Corp., Van Nuys, 1961-63; v.p., gen. mgr. Lockheed Aircraft Corp. (Lockheed Electronics div.), Los Angeles, 1963-68; exec. v.p. Lockheed Electronics Co., Inc., Plainfield, NJ, 1968-69, pres., 1969-71; group exec., exec. asst. to office of pres. ITT, NYC, 1971-72, corp. v.p., 1972-79, sr. v.p., 1979-81, exec. v.p., 1981-83; pres. indsl. and tech. sector Allied Corp., exec. v.p. Morristown, NJ, 1983-87; bd. trustees Opera San Jose, Calif. Disting. exec. lectr. Rutgers Grad. Sch. Mgmt.; exec.-in-residence, vis. prof. Columbia U. Grad. Sch. Bus.; bd. dirs. 5 corps., Cardiac Therapy Found.; cons. various investment firms. Served with AUS, 1944-46. Recipient Disting. Alumnus award Ohio State U., 1987. Fellow AIAA (assoc.); mem. IEEE (sr.).

SEELIG, JILL, publishing executive; MBA, Fordham U., NY. Various positions in fin. svcs. industry including mktg. dir. for Mastercard, 1984—89; advt. sales rep. NY Mag.; advt. sales rep. Self Mag. Condé Nast Publs., 1993—94, beauty dir., 1994—95, nat. sales mgr., 1996—99, advt. dir. Vanity Fair, 1998—99; v.p., pub. O, The Oprah Mag. Hearst Corp., 2000—, pub. O at Home, 2004—. Office: O Mag 1700 Broadway New York NY 10019*

SEELIG, TINA L., entrepreneurship program director, educator; PhD, Stanford U. Med. Sch., 1985. Entrepreneur, mgmt. cons., author, & scientist; created and taught courses including The History and Philosophy of Brain Function; rsch. assoc. Technology Mus.; tech. and mktg. cons. for several biotechnology companies; mgmt. cons. Booz, Allen and Hamilton; founder BookBrowser, 1991—93; multimedia prodr. Compaq Computer Corp., 1993; exec. dir., Stanford Technology Ventures Program Stanford U., Calif.; Fenwick and West Entrepreneurship educator on creativity & innovation, dept. mgmt. sci. and engring. Stanford U. and Hasso Plattner Inst. for Design, Calif.; dir. Stanford Entrepreneurs Network; co-dir. Mayfield Fellows Program. Written several popular science books, has designed a series of educational games; author: The Epicurean Laboratory: Exploring the Science of Cooking, 1991, Incredible Edible Science (Scientific American Mysteries of Science), 1994 (Internat. Children's Choice award); designer (ednl. card games) Games for Your Brain (12 games) (winner of several awards, including Parents Guide to Children's Media Outstanding Achievement for 1999). Recipient award for Excellence in Undergraduate Tchg., Stanford U., Tau Beta Pi, 2005; co-recipient with Tom Byers, Nat. Olympus Innovation award, Nat. Collegiate Inventors and Innovators Alliance, 2008, with Tom Byers, Bernard M. Gordon prize, NAE, 2009. Office: Stanford U Management Science & Engring Terman Engineering Ctr 3rd Fl Rm 411 380 Panama Way Stanford CA 94305-4026 Office Phone: 650-725-1627. Office Fax: 650-723-1614. Business E-Mail: tseelig@stanford.edu.*

SEELING, JONI M., biology professor; d. Richard M. and Elizabeth A. Seeling. BS, Iowa State U., Ames, 1987; PhD, Iowa State U., 1992. Postdoc. rsch. assoc. Dept. Human Genetics, U. UT, Salt Lake City, 1992—96, Dept. Oncological Sci., U. UT, 1996—2000; rsch. assoc. Huntsman Cancer Inst., U. UT, 2000—02; asst. prof. CUNY, Queens Coll., Flushing, NY, 2003—. Contbr. articles to profl. jours. Chair U. UT, Postdoc. Scholars Assn., 1997—2002; active Am. Assn. Med. Coll. Gt. Conf. V, Palm Springs, Calif.; facilitator CUNY, Queens Coll., 2008; active U. UT, Postdoc. Task Force. Mem.: AAAS, Alpha Lambda Delta Honor Soc., Golden Key Honor Soc., Iota Sigma Pi Honor Soc., Phi Eta Sigma Honor Soc., Phi Kappa Phi Honor Soc., Phi Beta Kappa Honor Soc., Soc. Devel. Biology. Office: City Univ NY Queens Coll 65-30 Kissena Blvd Flushing NY 11367 Office Fax: 718-997-3908.

SEELOW, DAVID D., family therapist; b. Gloversville, NY, Oct. 23, 1954; s. Donald Robert Seelow and Doris Helen (Fernandez) Faulkner. BA, SUNY, Stonybrook, 1977, PhD, 1990; MA, Columbia U., 1987. Family therapist Family Counseling Ctr. Inc., Westhampton Beach, N.Y., 1989-90; community svcs. worker Berkshire Family Ctr. and Svcs., Melville, N.Y., 1991—; adj. asst. prof. SUNY, Old Westbury, N.Y., 1991—. Lectr. in field. Contbr. articles to profl. jours. Mem. Internat. Assn. of Lit. and Philosophy, Modern Lang. Assn., Northeast Modern Lang. Assn. Avocations: tennis, writing, exercise, travel. Office: Dept Comparative Humanities SUNY Old Westbury NY 11568

SEELY, DENNIS M., secondary school educator; m. Vivian D. Gaden, July 4, 1996. BA in Speech and Theater, U. LaVerne, La., 1971; postgrad., Ball State U., 1975, U. Okla., Norman, 1987; MS in Comm., Lacross U., Covington, La., 2004, PhD, 2005. Cert. tchr. Ariz. Commd. 2d lt. US Army, 1971, advanced through grades to maj., 1991; congrl. press sec. Rep. Jim Kolbe, Tucson, 1991—92; tchr. Santa Rita HS, Tucson, 1994, Blue Ridge HS, Lakeside, Ariz., 1994—. Mem.: US Inst. Theater Tech., Nat. Coun. Tchrs. English, Alpha Psi Omega. Office: Blue Ridge HS 1200 W White Mountain Blvd Lakeside AZ 85929 Mailing: Po Box 1479 Show Low AZ 85902-1479

SEELY, JAMES MICHAEL, retired military officer, defense consultant, small business owner; b. LA, Oct. 15, 1932; s. Louis K. and Mary Edith (Gleason) S.; m. Gail Margaret Deverman, July 13, 1957; children: Ted Andrew, Nina Marie. BS, UCLA, 1955; MS, George Washington U., 1976. Commd. ensign USN, 1955, advanced through grades to rear adm.; student pilot, 1955-56; attack pilot, 1957-75; comdg. officer Attack Squadron 165, Naval Air Sta. Whidbey Island, Wash., 1972-73; comdr. Carrier Air Wing 9, Naval Air Sta. Lemoore, Calif., 1974-75; comdg. officer U.S. Naval Air Sta., Whidbey Island, 1977-79; dep. dir. DCNO (Air Warfare, OP-50), Pentagon, Washington, 1979-82; dir. Joint Analysis Directorate, Office Joint Chiefs Staff, Washington, 1982-84; comdr. Medium Attack Tactical Electronic Warfare Wing, Pacific Fleet, Naval Air Sta. Whidbey Island, 1984-86; dir. DCNO (Air Warfare, OP-50), Pentagon, 1986-88; dep. comptr. of Navy, Pentagon, 1988-89; ret., 1989; with RRP Def. Cons. Assocs., Arlington, Va., 1989—2002; owner, pres. JMS Cons., 2002—. Vietnam combat duty with Attack Squadrons 93, 152, 165 flying from aircraft carriers USS Enterprise, Hancock, Bon Homme Richard, Shangri-La and Constellation; 447 combat missions. Decorated Defense Superior Service, Legion of Merit (3), D.F.C. (4), Bronze Star, Air Medal (43), Navy Commendation medal with combat v (7). Mem. Naval Inst., Tailhook Assn., Assn. Naval Aviation, Marine Corps Aviation Assn., Red River Valley Fighter Pilots Assn., Navy League, Assn. Old Crows, Golden Eagles, Sigma Pi. Republican. Roman Catholic. Avocations: sports, automobiles. Home: 15552 Legacy Way Haymarket VA 20169-6117 Home Phone: 703-753-2618; Office Phone: 703-753-2618. E-mail: jimseely@comcast.net.

SEELY, ROBERT DANIEL, cardiologist, medical association administrator; b. Woodmere, NY, Nov. 4, 1923; s. Harry and Ethel (Weil) S.; m. Marcia Ann Wells, June 19, 1953; children: Ellen Wells, Anne Wells. BS, NYU, 1943; MD, Columbia U., 1946. Intern Mt. Sinai Hosp., NYC, 1946-47, asst. resident in medicine, 1950-51, resident in pathology, 1951-52, chief resident in medicine, 1952-53; Sara Welt fellow in cardiovascular research Presbyn. Hosp., NYC, 1953-54; instr. dept. physiology, cardiovascular research Western Res. U., Cleve., 1947-48; chief rheumatic heart disease clinic Mt. Sinai Hosp., NYC, 1961-70, attending physician medicine and cardiology, 1978—, chief of service dept. medicine, 1979—, clin. prof. medicine, cardiology Sch. Medicine, 1970—; practice medicine specializing in cardiovascular disease NYC, 1953—. Contbr. articles to profl. jours. Served to capt. M.C. AUS, 1948-50. Recipient Solomon Berson Meml. award Mt. Sinai Hosp., 1977 Fellow Am. Coll. Cardiology, ACP; mem. N.Y. Heart Assn., AMA, N.Y. County Med. Soc., Soc. Cert. Internists N.Y., Phi Beta Kappa, Alpha Omega Alpha, Beta Lambda Sigma Office: 49 E 96th St # 11D New York NY 10128-0782 Personal E-mail: billybobseedy@gmail.com.

SEEMAN, MELVIN, sociologist, educator; b. Balt., Feb. 5, 1918; s. Morris and Sophie (Kostman) S.; m. Alice Ruth Zerbola, June 30, 1944; children— Teresa E., Paul D. BA, Johns Hopkins U., 1944; PhD, Ohio State U., 1947. Asst. prof. sociology Ohio State U., 1947-52, assoc. prof., 1953-59; prof. UCLA, 1959-88, prof. emeritus, 1988—. Mem. Am. Sociol. Assn. Home: 21532 Paseo Serra St Malibu CA 90265-5112 Office: UCLA Dept Sociology 405 Hilgard Ave Los Angeles CA 90095-9000 E-mail: mseeman@conet.ucla.edu.

SEEMANN, ROSALIE MARY, international business and foreign policy association executive; b. St. Louis, July 30, 1942; d. Ulysses Sylvester and Helen Maire (Hootselle) Simon; m. Richard Vaughn, Jan. 20, 1968 (dec.); 1 child, Heather Elizabeth. Student, Lindenwood Colls., St. Charles, Mo., 1973-76, Harris Tchrs. Coll., St. Louis, 1961, U. Fla., Gainesville, 1964. Vol. U.S. Peace Corps, Brazil, 1964-66; tech. analyst, group leader Conductron-Mo., St. Charles, 1966-71, bus. mgr., 1971-77; maintenance engr. McDonnell Douglas Astronautics, St. Louis, 1977-78; mgr. supply support Northrop Def. Systems Divsn., Rolling Meadows, Ill., 1978-80; logistics mgmt. cons. Logistic Support Svcs., Spring Grove, Ill., 1980-85; mgr. reliability, maintainability, integrated logistic Recon/Optical, Inc., Barrington, Ill., 1985-90; v.p., exec. dir. Mid-Am. Com. Internat. Bus. & Govt. Coop., Chgo., 1991-97; exec. dir. World Affairs Coun., St. Louis, 1997-99; founder, pres. Mid-West Inst. Internat. Exch., 1999—; v.p. global initiatives World Trade Ctr., St. Louis, 1999—2001. Bd. dirs. Libr. Internat. Rels., Chgo.-Kent Coll. Law, Prime Med. Products. Bd. dirs. U. Mo.-St. Louis Chancellor's Coun., internat. affairs com.; bd. dirs. World Affairs Coun. Am.; mem. women's bd. Goodman Theatre, Chgo.; active Girl Scouts U.S.A.; master gardener Mo. Bot. Garden, 2005. Recipient commendation Conductron-Mo., 1967, pres. award Recon-Optical, 1989. Mem. Am. Soc. Assn. Execs. (internat. sect. coun. 1996—), Nat. Coun. Internat. Visitors, Am. Women Internat. Understanding, Soc. Logistics Engrs. (Mem. of Yr. award, sr. mem.), English Speaking Union, Japan Am. Soc., Chgo. Coun. Fgn. Rels. (Chgo. com.), Assn. Old Crows, Coun. Women Leaders, Execs. Club Chgo., Arts & Edn. Coun. Greater St. Louis, Internat. Trade Assn., Senate Constantine Prophyrogenetus Internat. Assn. (Greece, hon. pres.), Inst. Mid. East Studies Al-Mamun, Mo. Botanical Garden (named master gardner 2005) Home Phone: 636-745-8533; Office Phone: 636-745-2352. Office Fax: 636-745-2352.

SEENITH, SIVASUNDARAM, mathematician, educator; s. Sam Seenith and Tham Kanaga; m. Irene M Siva, May 21, 1973; 1 child, Diantha A Siva. PhD, U. Tex., 1987. Prof. Embry-Riddle Aero. U., Daytona Beach, Fla., 1989—. Organizer, gen. chair various profl. confs. Author: Vector Lyapunov Functions and Stability Analysis of Nonlinear Systems, 1991, College Mathematics for Aviation I, 1992, College Mathematics for Aviation II, 1993, Dynamics Systems on Measure Chain, 1996, Advances in Nonlinear Dynamics, 1997, Nonlinear Problems in Aviation and Aerospace, 2000, Advances in Dynamics and Control, 2004; editor-in-chief Jour. Nonlinear Studies; editor-in-chief: Nonlinear Systems in Aviation, Aerospace and Astronautics Book Series; editor-in-chief Nonlinear Systems in Aviation, Aerospace and Astronautics Series; editor: Proceedings of Nonlinear Problems in Aviation Aerospace, Proceedings of Mathematical Problems in Engineering and Aerospace Sciences, Jour. Aerospace Engineering, Global Jour. Mathematical Analysis, Scientific Journal of Actual Problems of Aviation and Aerospace Systems; author: Advances in Mathematical Problems in Engineering, also Space & Sciences, 2009, Advances in Nonlinear Analysis: Theory Method and Applications, 2009, Advances in Dynamics And Control: Theory Methods And Applications, 2009, World Congress 2010 ICNPAA.COM. Mem.: AAUP, Soc. Indsl. and Applied Math., Internat. Fedn. Nonlinear Analysts (charter), Math. Assn. Am. (charter math. for bus., industry and govt. 1999), Acad. Nonlinear Scis., Am. Math. Soc. Avocations: travel, cricket. Office: Embry-Riddle Aero U 600 S Clyde Morris Blvd Daytona Beach FL 32114 Personal E-mail: seenithi@gmail.com. Business E-Mail: siva@erau.edu.

SEEP, DOROTHY M., music educator; d. Frederick Henry and Estelle May Muller; m. Ralph Vincent Seep, Nov. 11, 1978; children: Jessica, Jeremy. MusB, Eastman Sch. Music, 1969, MusM, 1972. Music tchr. Taft Elem. Sch., Washingtonville, NY, 1969—71, Wayne Ctrl. Sch., Ontario, NY, 1972—81, Rochester Christian Sch., Penfield, NY, 1987—92; sr. choir dir. Rochester Christian Reformed Ch., Penfield, NY, 1988—91; music tchr. Annapolis Area Christian Sch., 1999—. Founder and dir. children's chorale Annapolis Area Christian Sch., Md., 1999—2008; founder and dir. adult cmty. choir and orch., 2003. Mem. choir Nat. Presbyn. Ch., Washington, 2004—; music dir. Safe Harbor Presbyn. Ch., 1999—2002. Mem.: Am. Choral Dir. Assn., Phi Kappa Lambda, Sigma Alpha Iota. Presbyterian. Avocations: sewing, gardening, reading, cooking. Office: Annapolis Area Christian Sch 710 Ridgely Ave Annapolis MD 21401 Office Phone: 410-266-8255.

SEERY, CAROL HUBBARD, communication sciences educator; PhD, U. Wash., Seattle, 1992. Assoc. prof. U. Wis., Milw., 1993—. Office: Univ Wis Milw Communication Scis and Disorders Dept PO Box 413 Enderis Hall 873 Milwaukee WI 53201-0413 Business E-Mail: cseery@uwm.edu.

SEETHALER, WILLIAM CHARLES, high technology manufacturing executive; b. NYC, Dec. 4, 1937; s. William Charles and Catherine Frances (Flaherty) Seethaler. Student, Quinnipiac Coll., Conn., 1955-56, Ohio State U., 1956-58; BSBA, U. San Francisco, 1977; MBA in Global High Tech., Pepperdine U., 1982; grad. tech. mktg. program, Stanford U., 1990; grad. global enterprise mgmt. program, Oxford U., Eng., 2000. Lic. real estate salesperson Calif., cert. in nanotechnology Calif. Inst., San Jose, 2008, in clean techs. Clean Tech. Inst., San Jose, 2008. Asst. to v.p. sales & asst. to chief engr. T. Sendzimir, Inc., Waterbury, 1960—66; mgr. internat. ops. Dempsey Indsl. Furnace Co., East Longmeadow, Mass., 1966-67; mgr. internat. sales Yoder Co., Cleve., 1967-74; mng. dir., owner Seethaler & Assocs., Palo Alto, Calif., 1974—; owner, chief exec. officer Seethaler Internat. Ltd., Palo Alto, Calif., 1982-92; ptnr. DFS Computer Assocs., San Jose, Calif., 1976-87; v.p. mktg. and sales Telewave Inc., Mountain View, Calif., 1996—2001; regional mgr. IMSM, Malmesbury, Wiltshire, England, 2002—; rep. Spacesonic, San Carlos, Calif., 2004—06; assoc. prof. Internat. Mktg.,

Bus., Global Exporting & Importing Mission Coll., Santa Clara, Calif., 2006—. Bd. dirs. Palo Alto Fund, 1979—93, chmn., 1986—88; cmty. rels. advisor Stanford U., 1986—2003; mem. Friends of Rewley House, Oxford U., 2001—. Mem.: Soc. Mfg. Engrs., Joint Venture: Silicon Valley (bd. dirs. 1992—95), Assn. MBA Execs., Assn. Iron and Steel Engrs. (life), Inst. Indsl. Engrs. (sr.; v.p. profl. rels. Peninsula chpt. 1988—90, bd. dirs. 1988—, del. to Silicon Valley Engrng. Coun. 1991—97), Oxford Alumni Assn., Stanford U. Alumni Assn. (life), Palo Alto C. of C. (bd. dirs. 1975—79, v.p. orgn. affairs 1976—77, pres. 1977—78), Ohio State U. Alumni Assn., Pepperdine U. Alumni Assn., U. San Francisco Alumni Assn., Stanford Buck Club. Office: PO Box 51115 Palo Alto CA 94303

SEFERIAN, EDWARD G., medical educator; BS, Tufts U., Medford, Mass., 1980—84; MD, Ind. U., Indpls., 1988—92; MS, U. Chgo., 1998—2000. Diplomate Am. Bd. Internal Medicine, 1996, Am. Bd. Pediat., 2004. Chem. engr. W.R. Grace & Co., Lexington, Mass., 1985—88; resident in internal medicine, pediat. U. Chgo. Med. Ctr., Chgo., 1992—96, pediat. critical care fellow, 1996—99; clin. asst. prof. pediat. Ind. U. Sch. Medicine, Indpls., 1999—2002; asst. prof. pediat. Mayo Med. Sch., Rochester, Minn., 2002—. Mem.: Am. Acad. Pediat., Acad. Health Svcs. Rsch., Am. Thoracic Soc., Soc. Critical Care Medicine. Office: Mayo Clinic 200 First St SW Rochester MN 55905 Business E-Mail: seferian.edward@mayo.edu.

SEFF, KARL, zeolite chemist, chemistry educator; b. Chgo., Jan. 23, 1938; s. Joseph and Rose (Hauser) S. BS, U. Calif., Berkeley, 1959; PhD, MIT, 1964. Asst. rsch. chemist UCLA, 1965—67; asst. prof. chemistry U. Hawaii, Honolulu, 1968—73, assoc. prof. chemistry, 1973—75, prof. chemistry, 1975—2006, emeritus prof. chemistry, 2007—. Cons. Filtrol Corp., L.A., 1966-73, Mitsubishi Heavy Industry, Nagasaki, Japan, 1992-94; vis. scholar Princeton (N.J.) U., 1974-75, Oxford (Eng.) U., 1988, 89, Pusan and Kyungpook Nat. Univs., Korea, 1996; assoc. rschr. U. Mex, 1981-82; vis. prof. U. Leuven, Belgium, 1975, Dartmouth U., 1989; lectr. Tokyo Inst. Tech., 1980, 91, Los Alamos Nat. Lab., 1985, U. Bristol, 1988, ETH, Zurich, Switzerland, 1988, Goethe U., Frankfurt, Germany, 1988, Imperial Coll., London, 1989, Cambridge U., 1989, Kyungpook Nat. U., Korea, 1990, Acad. Sci. Leningrad, 1990, Pusan Nat. U., Korea, 1990, Northwestern U., 1994, others; assoc. chair chemistry dept. U. Hawaii, 2000, chair, 2000-03. Contbr. numerous articles to profl. jours. NATO sr. fellow, NSF, 1975, Rsch. Travel award, 1988-90; grantee Army Rsch. Office, 1969-72, NIH, 1972-75, 75-78, NSF, 1973-76, 75, 77, 78-81, Petroleum Rsch. Fund, 1974-76, 95-98, Gordon Conf., 1976, U.S.-Korea Coop. Rsch., NSF, 1982, 84-86, Mitsubishi Industries, 1992-93. Mem. Am. Chem. Soc. (local sect. pres., award 1983, councilor 1992-94, 2005-07), Am. Crystallographic Assn., Vegetarian Soc. Hawaii (exec. com. 1993—), Internat. Zeolite Assn., Sigma Xi. Democrat. Avocations: travel, gardening, cacti. Office: U Hawaii Dept Chemistry 2545 The Mall Honolulu HI 96822-2275 Business E-Mail: seff@hawaii.edu.

SEFFRIN, JOHN REESE, health science association administrator, educator; b. Hagerstown, Ind., May 19, 1944; s. Theodore H. and Mary Ellen (Reese) Seffrin; m. Carole Sue Washburn, Apr. 16, 1966; 1 child, Mary. BS in Edn., Ball State U., Muncie, Ind., 1966, DSc (hon.), 1994; MS, U. Ill., Champaign-Urbana, 1967; PhD in Health Edn., Purdue U., West Lafayette, Ind., 1970, D (hon.) in Social Sci., 2003; DSc (hon.), Thomas Jefferson U., Med. Coll. Phila., 2008, Ind. U., Bloomington, 2008. Asst. prof. health edn. Purdue U., 1970—76, assoc. prof., chair health & safety edn., 1976—79; prof., chmn. dept. applied health sci. Ind. U., Bloomington, 1979—92; exec. v.p., chief staff officer Am. Cancer Soc., Atlanta, 1992—95, CEO, 1995—. Trustee Am. Cancer Soc. Found., 1992—; commr.-at-large Nat. Commn. Health Edn. Credentialing, 1995—2000; charter mem., mem. steering com. C-Change (formerly Nat. Dialog on Cancer), 1999; mem. subcom. on cessation HHS, Washington, 2002—03; bd. dirs. Healthcare Inc. Nat. bd. dirs. Am. Lung Assn., 1980—90; treas. Partnership for Prevention of Premature Death, Disease and Disability, 1991—; mem. Pres.'s Commn. on Improving Econ. Opportunity in Cmtys. Dependent on Tobacco Prodn. While Protecting Pub. Health, 2000—01; trustee Ctr. Advancement Health, 2003—05; pres. State Welfare Bd. Ind. Dept. Pub. Welfare, 1979—80, 1982—84; treas. Midwest Nuc. Bd., 1973—75; chmn. cmty. edn. com. Am. Lung Assn., 1981—83, v.p., 1980, pres., 1982; bd. dirs. Nat. Ctr. Tobacco-Free Kids, 1996—; chmn. bd. dirs. Nat. Health Coun., 1998—2000; past pres. Internat. Union against Cancer; bd. dirs. Wabash Ctr. for the Mentally Retarded, 1970—73. Recipient Outstanding Alumnus award, Ball State U., 1982, Surgeon Gen.'s Cert. appreciation, USPHS, 1992, Presdl. citation, Soc. Pub. Health Edn., 2007; named Sagamore of Wabash, State of Ind., 1980, 1988. Fellow: Am. Sch. Health Assn. (mem. governing coun. 1979—81, 1982—89, pres. 1987—88, Howe award 1991); mem.: NAS (Nat. Cancer Policy Bd. 1997—2002), AMA, Am. Acad. Family Physicians (pub. adv. bd. 1999—), Rsch. Am. (bd. dirs. 1996—), Independent Sector (bd. dirs. 1997—2006), Nat. Interagy. Coun. on Smoking and Health (bd. dirs. 1979—), Internat. Union Against Cancer (ex-officio mem. US nat. com. 2000—, pres. 2002—06), Ind. Assn. for Health, Phys. Edn. and Recreation (pres. 1976, Cert. of Appreciation 1977, Honor award 1982), Am. Cancer Soc. (dir. Ind. Divsn. 1977—90, chmn. Ind. Divsn. 1982—85, dir.-at-large to nat. bd. dirs., chmn. nat. pub. edn. com. 1984—87, nat. v.p. 1986—87, chmn. nat. bd. dirs. 1989—91), Ind. Thoracic Soc. (mem. governing coun. 1977—84), Ind. Family Health Coun. (dir. 1979—81, v.p. 1980—81, pres. 1981), Ind. Assn. Health Educators (pres. 1975—76, chair 1997—2000), Assn. for Advancement Health Edn. (bd. dirs. 1989—92), Nat. Assn. State Bds. of Edn. (commn. on sch. cmty. role in improving adolescent health 1989—90), Eta Sigma Gamma, Phi Delta Kappa. Roman Catholic. Office: Am Cancer Soc Inc 250 Williams St NW Atlanta GA 30303 Business E-Mail: john.seffrin@cancer.org.

SEFKOW, SUSAN BENNETT, psychology professor; b. St. Paul, Mar. 20, 1949; d. Richard W. and Ruthanne Evans Bennett; m. Thomas W. Sefkow; children: Adam B., Ryan B., Elizabeth Anne B. BA, Yale U., New Haven, 1971; MS, U. Mass., Amherst, PhD, 1978. Prof. psychology & women and gender studies Winona State U., Minn., 1978—. Office: Winona State Univ Psychology Dept 231 Phelps Winona MN 55987 Business E-Mail: ssefkow@winona.edu.

SEFTON, JAMES EDWARD, history professor; b. San Francisco, July 29, 1939; s. Edward and Kathryn Sefton. PhD, U. Calif., LA, 1965. Prof. history Calif. State U., Northridge, 1965—. Photographic exhibition, California 166, Textures of the Night; author: (photographic exhibition) Remote Roads: Photographs Along the Way; contbr. articles to profl. jours.; author: (book) The United States Army and Reconstruction, 1865-1877, Andrew Johnson and the Uses of Constitutional Power. Recipient Disting. Tchg. award, Calif. State U., 1970, Intercollegiate Athletics Disting. Svc. award, 1998, CSUN Dorsey award Excellence in Mentoring Students, 2007. Mem.: Phi Sigma Kappa (Devoted Svc. award 1994). Office: Calif State Univ 18111 Nordhoff St Northridge CA 91330-8250

SEGA, A. CHRISTOPHER, lawyer; b. Frankfurt, Germany, Oct. 12, 1954; BA, Dartmouth Coll., 1976; MBA, George Wash. U., 1981; JD in Comparative & Internat. Law, Cath. U. America, 1991. Bar: Md. 1991, DC 1992, US Tax Ct. 1993. Ptnr., Trusts & Estates, Taxation practices Venable LLP, Washington. Adj. prof. Catholic Univ. Am., 1993—95, Georgetown Univ., 2004—. Contbr. articles to profl. jours. Named a Top Washington Lawyer, Washingtonian Mag., 2004. Fellow: Am. Coll. Trust & Estate Counsel; mem.: Estate Planning Coun. (pres. 2006—07), ABA (chmn. com. fiduciary income tax, chmn. subcom. grantor trusts), DC Bar Assn. Office: Venable LLP 575 7th St NW Washington DC 20004 also: Venable LLP 5th Fl 1 Church St Rockville MD 20850 Office Phone: 202-344-8565, 301-217-5658. Office Fax: 202-344-8300. Business E-Mail: acsega@venable.com.

SEGA, RONALD MICHAEL, civilian military employee, former dean; b. Cleve., Dec. 4, 1952; m. Bonnie Dunbar. BS in Math. and Physics, USAF Acad., 1974; MS in Physics, Ohio State U., 1975; grad., Squadron Officers Sch., 1979; PhD in Elec. Engring., U. Colo., 1982; grad., Air Command and Staff Coll., 1985, Air War Coll., 1991; Ph.D (hon.), Clarkson U., 1993; grad. Mgmt. Inst., Harvard U., 1997; Ph.D (hon.), Bridgewater State Coll., 1998; exec. program in global security, Harvard U., 2001. Commd. 2d lt. USAF, 1974, advanced through grades to maj. gen., 2001, ret., 2005, instr. pilot Williams AFB, Ariz., 1976—79; mem. faculty USAF Acad., 1979—82, asst. prof., 1982—85, assoc. prof., 1985—90, tech. dir. Lasers & Aerospace Mechanics Directorate, Frank J. Seiler Rsch. Lab, 1987—88; astronaut Space Shuttle Discovery, 1990; dir. ops. Gagarin Cosmonaut Training Ctr. NASA, Russia, 1994—95; payload comdr. 3d Shuttle/Mir docking mission Atlantis, 1996; dean Coll. Engring. & Applied Sci. U. Colo., Colorado Springs, 1996—2001; dir. def., rsch. & engring. US Dept Def., Washington, 2001—05, under sec. Dept. Air Force, 2005—. Contbr. articles to tech. publs. Decorated Legion of Merit, Def. Meritorious Svc. medal, Meritorious Svc. medal with oak leaf cluster; recipient Outstanding Leadership medal, NASA, 1997; named a Air Force rsch. fellow, Air Force Office Sci. Acad., 1980; named to, Ohio Vets. Hall of Fame, 1994. Fellow: AIAA (assoc. Achievement award 1996), Inst. for Advancement of Engring.; mem.: IEEE (sr.), Aerospace Edn. Found. (trustee 2000). Office: USAF 1670 Air Force Pentagon Rm 4E886 Washington DC 20330

SEGAL, BERNARD LOUIS, cardiologist, educator; b. Montreal, Feb. 13, 1929; came to U.S., 1961, naturalized, 1966; s. Irving and Fay (Schecter) S.; m. Idajane Fischman, Feb. 17, 1963; 1 dau., Jody Segal Reinbold. BSc cum laude, McGill U., 1950, postgrad., 1950-51, MD, C.M. high standing, 1955. Diplomate Am. Bd. Internal Medicine. Intern Jewish Gen Hosp., Montreal, 1955-56; resident Balt. City Hosp., 1956-57, Beth Israel Hosp., Boston, 1957-58, Georgetown Med. Ctr., Washington, 1958-59, St. George's Hosp., London, 1959-61; pvt. practice internal medicine and cardiology Phila., 1961—; prof. medicine Med. Coll. Pa., Hahnemann U., 1996—; prof. medicine, sr. attending physician Jefferson Med. Coll./Thomas Jefferson U., 1998—2008. Dir. emeritus cardiology Thomas Jefferson U., 1998 Author: Auscultation of the Heart, 1965; Editor: Theory and Practice of Auscultation, 1964, Engineering in the Practice of Medicine, 1966, Your Heart, 1972, Arteriosclerosis and Coronary Heart Disease, 1972; mem. editl. bd. Am. Jour. Cardiology, 1970—, Clin. Echocardiography, 1978; contbr. articles to profl. jour. Fellow ACP, Am. Coll. Cardiology (chmn. scholar-trainee com., trustee 1969-71), Am. Coll. Chest Physicians; mem. NY Acad. Sci., Alpha Omega Alpha. Home: 1156 Red Rose Ln Villanova PA 19085-2121 Office: Jefferson Heart Inst 925 Chestnut St Mezzanine Philadelphia PA 19107-4824 also: 401 E City Line Ave Ste 525 Bala Cynwyd PA 19004-1125 Office Phone: 215-955-8145.

SEGAL, ERICH, author, educator; b. Bklyn., June 16, 1937; s. Samuel Michael and Cynthia (Shapiro) S.; m. Karen James, June 10, 1975; 2 dau., 1 son (dec.). AB, Harvard U., 1958, A.M., 1959, PhD, 1965. Teaching fellow humanities Harvard U., 1959-63; vis. lectr. Yale U., 1964-65, asst. prof., 1965-68, assoc. prof. classics and comparative lit., 1968-73; vis. prof. classical philology U. Munich, Germany, 1973; vis. prof. classics Princeton U., 1974-75, Tel Aviv U., spring 1976; vis. prof. comparative lit. Dartmouth Coll., fall 1976-80; vis. fellow Wolfson Coll., Oxford U., 1978, 79, 80; adj. prof. classics Yale U., 1981-88; hon. research fellow University Coll., London, 1983—; supernumerary fellow Wolfson Coll., Oxford U., 1986—; hon. fellow Wolfson Coll., London, 1999—. Mem. exec. com. Nat. Adv. Council, Peace Corps, 1970; jury mem. Cannes Film Festival, 1971, Nat. Book Award (Arts and Letters), 1971; lectr. Am. Comparative Lit. Assn., 1971, Am. Philos. Assn., 1971, 72, German Classical Assn., 1974, Boston Psychoanalytic Inst., 1974, Ist. Nazionale del Dramma Antico, Sicily, 1975, Brit. Classical Assn., 1977; William Kelley Prentice Meml. lectr. Princeton U., 1981, Inaugural Andrea Rosenthal Meml. lectr. Brown U., 1992. Author, narrator: TV spl. The Ancient Games, 1972, rebroadcasted 1976; TV commentator track and field events Olympics, 1972, 76; occasional commentator: Wide World of Sports, ABC, Sports World, NBC; host: Mourning Becomes Electra (Masterpiece Theatre), Pub. Broadcasting System, 1978; radio commentator: (in French) Olympics, RTL Radio, Paris, 1972, 76; author: TV spl. Olympathon '80; novels Love Story, 1970, Fairy Tale, 1973, Oliver's Story, 1977, Man, Woman and Child, 1980, The Class, 1985 (Prix Deauville, France, 1986, Premio Bancarella Selezione, Italy), Doctors, 1988, Acts of Faith, 1992, Prizes, 1995, Only Love, 1997; book and lyrics Sing Muse, 1961-62; play Odyssey, 1974; lyrics with various composers including Charles Aznavour, Michel Legrand, (acad. books) Oxford Readings in Aristophanes, 1996, Oxford Readings in Menander, Plautus and Terence, 2001, The Death of Comedy, 2001; co-author: screenplays (with others) The Beatles' Yellow Submarine, 1968, author: The Games, 1970, Love Story, 1970 (Golden Globe award Hollywood Fgn. Press Assn., Acad. award nomination best screenplay, Writers Guild nomination, Best Screenplay, 1970), R.P.M, 1970, Jennifer on my Mind, 1971, Oliver's Story, 1978, A Change of Seasons, 1981, Man, Woman and Child, 1983; author: over 70 articles, revs. in profl. jours. including Am. Jour. Philology, Classical Rev.; also N.Y. Times Book Rev., New Republic, Times Literary Supplement (London), The Independent (London); Washington Post Book Rev., Yale Rev., acad. books; Roman Laughter: The Comedy of Plautus, 1968, rev. edit., 1987; editor: Euripides: A Collection of Critical Essays, 1968, Oxford Readings in Greek Tragedy, 1983, Plato's Dialogues, 1986; co-editor: (with Fergus Millar) Caesar Augustus: Seven Essays, 1984; editor, translator: Plautus: Three Comedies, 1969, reprinted 1985, Plautus: Four Comedies, 1996. Co-recipient (with Mother Theresa and Sir Peter Ustinov) Premio San Valentin di Terni award, 1989; Guggenheim fellow, 1968; recipient Presidential Commendation for service to Peace Corps, 1971, Humboldt Stiftung award West Germany, 1973, Chevalier de l'Ordre des Arts et des Lettres (France), 1998. Mem. ASCAP, Acad. Lit. Studies, Am. Philol. Assn., Am. Comparative Lit. Assn., Writers Guild of Am.-West, Authors League, Soc. Roman Studies (U.K.), PEN, Harvard Club (London), Athenaeum (London). Avocations: walking, swimming.

SEGAL, FREDERICK LESLIE, lawyer; b. NYC, Oct. 7, 1947; children: Sabrina Meredith, Elysia Meghan. BS, U. Pitts., 1970; JD, Hofstra U., 1973; LLM, NYU, 1979. Bar: Pa. 1979, NY 1974, US Patent and Trademark Office 1975, US Supreme Ct. 1978, US Ct. Appeals (2d cir.) 1974, US Dist. Ct. (we. dist.) Pa. 1979, US Dist. Ct. (ea. and so. dists.) NY 1974, US Ct. Customs and Patent Appeals 1976, US Ct. Claims 1976, US Ct. Appeals D. 1982, US Customs Ct. 1976, US Tax Ct. 1976. Clk. U.S. Dist. Ct. (ea. dist.) N.Y., Bklyn., 1973—74; assoc. Mendes & Mount, NYC, 1974—78, Hart & Hume, NYC, 1978—79, Rosenberg & Kirschner, Pitts., 1979—81, Berger Kapetan, Malakoff & Meyers, Pitts., 1981—82; pvt. practice Pitts., 1982—. Patent agt., atty. U.S. Patent and Trademark Office, Washington, 1982—; arbitrator Am. Arbitration Assn., 1983—, Ct. Common Pleas Allegheny County, Pitts., 1981—. With N.G. US Army, 1970—72., NY State scholar, 1971—73. Mem.: ATLA, ABA, Vintage Triumph Register (nat. judge 2008), Pa. Trial Lawyers Assn., Allegheny County Bar Assn., Pa. Bar Assn., U. Pitts. Golden Panther Alumni Assn. (bd. dirs. 1983—), Men of Achievement, Packard Automobile Club (nat. judge 2002), Lincoln and Continental Owner's Club (nat. judge 2001). Democrat. Jewish. Home: 1740 Beechwood Blvd Pittsburgh PA 15217-1714 Office: Manor Complex 564 Forbes Ave Ste 1011 Pittsburgh PA 15219-2903 Home Phone: 412-421-8602; Office Phone: 412-391-2263. Fax: 412-421-5734. Personal E-mail: pittdaddy@aol.com.

SEGAL, JACK, mathematics professor; b. Phila., May 9, 1934; s. Morris and Rose (Novin) S.; m. Arlene Stern, Dec. 18, 1955; children: Gregory, Sharon. BS, U. Miami, 1955, MS, 1957; PhD, U. Ga., 1960. Instr. math. U. Wash., Seattle, 1960-61, asst. prof., 1961-65, assoc. prof., 1965-70, prof., 1970-1999, prof. emeritus, 2000—, chmn. dept., 1975-78. Author: Lecture Notes in Mathematics, 1978, Shape Theory, 1982. NSF postdoctoral fellow Inst. Advanced Study, Princeton, N.J., 1963-64; Fulbright fellow U. Zagreb, Croatia, 1969-70, U. Coll. London hon. rsch. fellow, 1988; NAS exch. prof. U. Zagreb, 1979-80. Mem. Am. Math. Soc. Home: 8711 25th Pl NE Seattle WA 98115-3416 Office: U Washington Dept Mathematics Seattle WA 98195-0001 Office Phone: 206-543-1914. Business E-Mail: segal@math.washington.edu.

SEGAL, JONATHAN A., lawyer; b. Phila., 1961; BA summa cum laude, U. Pa., JD. Bar: Pa. 1985, NY 2005. Law clk. US Dist. Ct. (Ea. Dist.) Pa.; legis. dir. Pa. State Coun. SHRM, Inc.; cons. Fed. Jud. Ctr., Washington; ptnr. Duane Morris LLP; mng. ptnr. Duane Morris Inst. Contbg. editor: HRMagazine, The Met. Corp. Counsel; host (TV Special) The Sexual Harassment Quiz. Named to Pa. Super Lawyers, 2005—09, America's Leading Bus. Lawyers, Chambers USA, 2007—09. Mem.: Nat. Assn. Coll. and U. Attys. Office: Duane Morris LLP 30 South 17th St Philadelphia PA 19103 Office Phone: 215-979-1869. Office Fax: 215-405-2628. Business E-Mail: jsegal@duanemorris.com.*

SEGAL, LORE, writer; b. Vienna, Mar. 8, 1928; came to US, 1951, naturalized, 1956; d. Ignatz and Franzi (Stern) Groszmann; m. David I. Segal, Nov. 3, 1960 (dec.); children: Beatrice Ann, Jacob Paul. BA in English, Bedford Coll., U. London, Eng., 1948. Prof. writing div. Sch. Arts, Columbia U., also Princeton U., Sarah Lawrence Coll., Bennington Coll.; prof. English U. Ill., Chgo., 1978-92, Ohio State U., 1992-97. Author: Other People's Houses, 1964, (children's book) Tell Me A Mitzi, 1970, All the Way Home, 1973, Lucinella, 1976, Tell Me a Trudy, 1977, The Story of Mrs. Brubeck and How She Looked for Trouble and Where She Found Him, 1981, Her First American, 1985, The Story of Mrs. Lovewright and Purrless Her Cat, 1985, Morris the Artist, 2003, Why Mole Shouted and Other Stories, 2004, More Mole Stories and Little Gopher Too, 2005, Shakespeare's Kitchen, 2007; translator: (with W.D. Snodgrass) Gallows Songs, 1968, The Juniper Tree and Other Tales from Grimm, 1973, The Book of Adam to Moses, 1987, The Story of King Saul and King David, 1991; contbr. short stories, articles to N.Y. Times Book Rev., Partisan Rev., New Republic, The New Yorker, others5 Guggenheim fellow, 1965-66; Council Arts and Humanities grantee, 1968-69; Artists Public Service grantee, 1970-71; CAPS grantee, 1975; Nat. Endowment Arts grantee, spring 1982, 1987; NEH grantee, 1983; Acad. Arts and Letters award, 1986. Fellow: Acad. Arts & Scis. Address: 280 Riverside Dr New York NY 10025-9010 Business E-Mail: lore@usa.net.

SEGAL, MARTIN ELI, retired actuarial and consulting company executive; b. Vitebsk, Russia, Aug. 15, 1916; came to U.S., 1921, naturalized, 1928; s. Isidor and Anna (Title) S.; m. Edith Levy, June 17, 1937; children: Susan Segal Rai, Paul. LHD (hon.), Pratt Inst., 1976; MusD (hon.), Mannes Coll. Music, 1976; LHD (hon.), Grad. Ctr. CUNY, 1979, L.I. U., 1986, NYU, 1988, The Juilliard Sch., 2006; D in Music (hon.), Manhattan Sch. Music, 1999. Various positions ins. industry, 1935-39; founder The Segal Co., consultants and actuaries, NYC, 1939, pres., CEO, 1939-67, chmn. bd., 1967-91, cons., 1991—. Pres. Wertheim Asset Mgmt. Svcs., Inc., N.Y.C., 1972-75, chmn., bd., 1975-82; ptnr. Wertheim & Co., investment bankers, N.Y.C., 1967-82. Former columnist: Associated Press. Founding chmn. NY Internat. Festival of the Arts, Inc., 1985-02; chmn. bd. Lincoln Ctr. Performing Arts, Inc., 1981-86, chmn. emeritus, 1986—; gen. chmn. Night of 100 Stars (first ever AIDS Benefit), Actors' Fund Am., 1985; organizing co-chmn. Internat. Conf. on Future of Arts Edn., 1999; bd. dirs., founding mem. Pub. Radio Internat., 1981-94, dir. emeritus, 1994-98; counselor at large, 1998—; co-chmn. Conf. on Intellectual Property The Arts and Tech., 1994; chmn. arts and culture com., NY92, NY93, NY94, NY95; nat. bd. dirs. Nat. Urban League, 1961-70, chmn. First Equal Opportunity Day Dinner, 1961, v.p. 1967-70; bd. dirs. Nat. Bldg. Mus., 1983-91; founding mem., bd. advisers Libr. of Am., 1984—, sole hon. mem. bd. dirs., 2005—; trustee Am.-Scandinavian Found., 1986-91, adv. trustee, 1991—; bd. visitors Grad. Sch. and Univ. Ctr., CUNY, 1983-96; bd. trustees Grad. Ctr. Found., Inc., 1996—2008, vice chmn. bd. trustees, 2003—08; bd. dirs. ASCAP Found., 1997-03, S.L.E. Lupus Found., 2000—; adv. com. arts Harvard, 1993-99, coun. mem., 1999—; bd. trustees, chmn. exhbns. com. Mus. Modern Art, 1978-81; trustee Inst. for Advanced Study, Princeton, NJ, 1972-91, trustee emeritus, 1991—; bd. dirs. City Ctr. Music and Drama, 1971-74, trustee NY City Ctr., 1974—; founder, pres. Cultural Assistance Ctr., Inc., 1974-82, chmn., 1982-84, hon. chmn., 1984—; founding pres. Film Soc. of Lincoln Ctr., 1968-78, pres. emeritus, 1978—; adv. com. Tony voter Am. Theater Wing, 2000—08; adv. coun. Theatre Devel. Fund, 1992—, Town Hall Found., 1986-; nat. bd. Young Audiences, Inc., 1979—; adv. bd. Concert Artists Guild, 1983-00; founding mem. publs. com. The Pub. Interest, 1965-2002; vis. com. Harvard U. Sch. Pub. Health, 1979-92, dean's coun. Sch. Pub. Health, 1990-2006; adv. bd. Studio in a Sch. Assn., 1988—; bd. dirs. Helena Rubinstein Found., 1972-95; chmn. Mayor's Com. on Cultural Policy, 1974; founding chmn. Commn. for Cultural Affairs City of NY, 1975-77; chmn. pub. svc. awards com. Fund for City of NY, 1978-79, bd. dirs., 1978-87; co-chair China cultural exch. mission, Ctr. US-China Arts Exchange, 1979; bd. dirs. Bd. Hosps. City NY, 1962-70, NY City Health and Hosps. Corp., chmn. fin. com., exec. com. mem., 1970-72; founder Film Guild N.Y., 1940-41. Decorated Royal Swedish Order of Polar star; recipient Cert. of Merit, Mcpl. Art Soc., 1974, award for Svc. to Music, Third Street Music Sch. Settlement, 1981, award of Honor for Arts and Culture, N.Y.C. Mayor, 1982, Ann. award of Distinction, Mus. City of N.Y., 1982, Concert Artists Guild award, 1983, Edn. Fund award, LWV of NYC, 1984, Disting. Am. Fgn. Birth award, Internat. Ctr. NYC, 1985, John H. Finley medal, Alumni Assn. CCNY,

1985, Annual Arts Leadership award, Alumni and Friends of LaGuardia H.S., 1985, Friend of the Arts award, Town Hall, 1987, Dirs. Emeriti award, Lincoln Ctr. for Performing Arts, Inc., 1987, Patron of the Arts award, Songwriters Hall of Fame, 1988, NY State Gov.'s Arts award, 1989, Presdl. Citation award, Nat. Fedn. Music Clubs, 1989, Pub. Spirit award, Creative Arts Rehab. Ctr., 1989, Pres.'s award, Grad. Sch. and Univ. Ctr. of City Univ. of N.Y., 1990, Honor medal, Nat. Arts Club, 1992, Laureate award, Lincoln Ctr., 1997, Our Town Treasure award, Mus. City of N.Y., 1998, Civic Leadership award, Citizens Union of City of N.Y., 1998, award of Honor, Arts Roundtable, 1998, CUNY Graduate Ctr., Martin E. Segal Theatre Ctr., 2000, Acting Co. Joan Warburg Humanitarian award, 2001, S.L.E. Lupus Found. award, 2001, Honoree, Am.-Scandinavian Found., 2004, Alliance for Arts, 2004, Chamber Music Soc. Lincoln Ctr., 2005, Living Landmark Honoree, NY Landmarks Conservancy, 2005; named comdr. Order Arts and Letters, Ministry Culture French Govt., 2005, officer Order Arts and Letters, 1984—2005. Mem.: The Pilgrims of the U.S., Century Assn. Democrat. Jewish. Office: 1 Park Ave 8th Fl New York NY 10016

SEGAL, ROBERT MARTIN, lawyer; b. Atlantic City, Apr. 7, 1935; s. Nathan Albert and Edna (Dutkin) S.; m. Rhoda Sue Luber, June 8, 1958; children: Deborah Ann, William Nathan, Elizabeth Ann Student, Cornell U., 1953-54; BS in Econs., U. Pa., 1957; LLB cum laude, Harvard Law Sch., 1960. Bar: Pa. 1961. Assoc. Wolf, Block, LLP, Phila., 1960—69, ptnr., 1969—2007, sr. counsel, 2007—09, chmn., exec. com., 1978-79, 82-83, 86-87, 89-98. Hon. pres. Jewish Employment and Vocat. Svc.; bd. dirs. Orleans Homebuilders, Inc., Goodman Co. Contbr. articles to profl. jours. and mags. Constable of elections Lower Merion Twp., Pa., 1970-72; bd. dirs. Jewish Family and Children's Agy., Am. Jewish Com., Feinstein Ctr. for Am. Jewish History at Temple U.; bd. govs. Rep. Jewish Coalition; past trustee Hahnemann U., Fedn. Jewish Agys., Phila. Rehab. Plan, Inc., Rosenbach Mus. and Libr., Grater Phila. Urban Affairs Coalition. Mem. ABA, Pa. Bar Assn., Phila. Bar Assn., Internat. Coun. Shopping Ctrs., Urban Land Inst. (assoc.), Am. Coll. Real Estate Lawyers, Phila. Bar Found. (trustee 1981-87), Am. Law Inst., Harvard Law Sch. Assn. Phila., Federalist Soc., Wharton Club, Chaine des Rotisseurs, Societe Mondiale du Vin, Anglers Club of Absecon Island, Sunday Breakfast Club, La Coquille Club, Harvard Club, Beta Gamma Sigma. Avocations: golf, swimming. Office: Orleans Homebuilders, Inc 1 Greenwood Square 3333 Street Road Ste 101 Bensalem PA 19020 Office Phone: 215-977-2230. Business E-Mail: rsegal@wolfblock.com.

SEGAL, SCOTT H., lawyer, lobbyist; BA summa cum laude, Emory U., 1986; JD, U. Tex., 1989. Bar: DC, Tex. Dir. forensics U. Tex., Austin; co-head fed. govt. rels. and advocacy practice Bracewell & Giuliani LLP. Tchr. law, policy devel. and comm. U. Md., Johns Hopkins U. Mem.: ABA, DC Ct. Internat. Trade. Office: Bracewell & Giuliani LLP 2000 K St NW, Ste 500 Washington DC 20006-1872 Office Phone: 202-828-5845. Office Fax: 202-857-2127. E-mail: scott.segal@bgllp.com.*

SEGAL, SHELDON JEROME, biologist, educator, foundation administrator; b. NYC, Mar. 15, 1926; s. Morris M. and Florence (Bogen) S.; m. Harriet Ellen Feinberg, May 22, 1961; children: Amy Robin, Jennifer Ann, Laura Jane. BA, Dartmouth Coll., 1947; postgrad., U. Geneva, 1947-48; MS, U. Iowa, 1951, PhD, 1952; MD (hon.), U. Tampere, Finland, 1984, U. Upssala, Sweden, 1985; LHD (hon.), Mercy Coll. Rsch. scientist William S. Merrill Co., Cin., 1952-53; rsch. assoc., asst. prof. U. Iowa, 1953-56; asst. med. dir. Population Coun., NYC, 1956-63, med. dir., 1963-78, v.p., 1969-76, sr. v.p., 1976-78; affiliate Rockefeller U., NYC, 1956-76, adj. prof., 1977-87; dir. population scis. Rockefeller Found., 1978-91; disting. scientist Population Coun., NYC, 1991—. Lectr. Columbia U., 1959-61; vis. prof. All-India Inst. Med. Scis., New Delhi, 1962-63, Amir Chand lectr., 1975; mem. Marine Biol. Lab, Woods Hole, Mass.; cons. World Bank, WHO, NIH, Ford Found., Indian Govt., UN Office Sci. and Tech., UN Fund Population Activities; mem. com. on contraceptive tech. NAS, 1977-80, com. on health effects of marijuana Inst. Medicine, 1981-82, NAS com. on demographic impact of contraceptive tech., 1988-89, nat. rsch. con., overview com. for Indo-U.S. sci. initiative, 1985-89; adv. com. on human reproduction FDA; cons. to dir. Nat. Inst. Child Health and Human Devel., 1978-80; plenary lectr. 3d World Congress Endocrinology, 1968, Upjohn lectr. Am. Fertility Soc., 1971, plenary lectr. World Fertility Congress, 1975, Sigma Xi lectr. U. Idaho, 1976, plenary lectr. World Congress on Ob-Gyn., 1976, lectr. Chinese Acad. Scis., 1977, Carl Gemzell lectr. U. Upssala, 1982, Pierre Soupart lectr. Axel Munthe Found., 1988, Alpha Omega Alpha lectr. U. Pa. Coll. Medicine, 1989, plenary lectr. World Congress on Human Reproduction, 1990, 2005; hon. prof. Peking Union Med. Coll., Beijing, 1987, Chinese Acad. Scis., 1988; trustee Marine Biol. Lab., 1985—, chmn. bd. trustees, 1991-2004; pres. 10th World Congress on Human Reproduction, 1999, 2004. Co-editor 8 books; author 3 books; contbr. 300 articles to profl. jours. Trustee Rye Country Day Sch., 1979-85, pres. bd. trustees, 1981-85; trustee Ctr. for Reproductive Law and Policy, 1992—. Lt. (j.g.) USNR, 1943-45. Decorated Order Comdr. of Lion (Finland); recipient Honor award Innsbruck U., Austria, hon. citation Pres. of India, 1978, Clarence J. Gamble award World Acad. Arts and Scis., 1980, Joseph C. Wilson award Rochester Assn. for UN, 1981, UN Population award, 1984, Axel Munthe award in medicine Axel Munthe Found., Italy, 1985, Sci. award Planned Parenthood Fedn. Am., 1990, Dmitirus N. Chorafas award in medicine Swiss Acad. Scis., 1995, Joseph Bolivar DeLee Humanitarian award, U. Chgo. Hosps., 2007. Fellow AAAS, Royal Coll. Obstetricians and Gynecologists (hon.); mem. Am. Reproductive Med. Soc. (hon. v.p. 1975-76, trustee found. 1975-77), Endocrine Soc., Internat. Soc. for Study Reprodn. (pres. 1968-72), Coun. Fgn. Rels., Internat. Acad. Human Reproduction (hon. pres. 2005), Mexican Acad. Medicine (hon.), Inst. Medicine, Dartmouth Club N.Y., Woods Hole Yacht Club. Home: 525 E 72nd St New York NY 10021 Office: Population Coun One Dag Hammarskjold Plz New York NY 10017 E-mail: ssegal@popcouncil.org.

SEGAL, THEODORE D., lawyer; b. Washington, Aug. 7, 1955; BA magna cum laude, Duke U., 1977; JD magna cum laude, Georgetown U., 1984. Bar: Md. 1985, DC 1986. Law clk. Chief Judge William C. Pryor, DC Ct. Appeals, 1984—86; ptnr. DLA Piper, Washington. Mem.: ABA, Am. Health Lawyers Assn. Office: DLA Piper 1200 19th St NW Washington DC 20036-2412 Office Phone: 202-861-3838. Office Fax: 202-223-2085. Business E-Mail: theodore.segal@dlapiper.com.

SEGAL, VLADIMIR M., retired metallurgist, researcher; b. Barashi, Russia, Oct. 3, 1936; arrived in U.S., 1989; s. Miron S. and Rahei N. (Volfovich) S.; m. Galina M. Freidlina, Feb. 20, 1962; children: Svetlana, Leonid. MSME, Tech. U., Minsk, Russia, 1959, PhD in Metallurgy, 1965; ScD in Metallurgy, Acad. Scis., 1974. Devel. engr. Minsk Tractor Plant, Minsk, Belarus, 1959-65; sr. scientist Acad. Scis., Minsk, Belarus, 1965-86; prof. Engring. Inst., Lygansk, Ukraine, 1986-89; design engr. Interstate Forging Industry, Navasota, Tex., 1990-92; rsch. engr. Texas A&M U., College Station, Tex., 1992-95; prin. rsch. scientist Honeywell Electronics, Spokane, Wash., 1996—2000. Author: 8 books in Russian, 1966-95. Achievements include invention of new metalworking techniques for materials processing for properties; over 50 patents in field. Home Phone: 517-548-3417. Personal E-mail: vladimirsegal@comcast.net, vladimir_segal@msn.com.

SEGALL, ROBERT D., lawyer; b. Chgo., 1946; BA, Vanderbilt U., Nashville, 1968; JD summa cum laude, U. Ala., Tuscaloosa, 1971; LLM, Harvard U., Cambridge. Law clerk Hon. Frank M. Johnson Jr., 1971—72; shareholder Copeland, Franco, Screws & Gill PA, Montgomery, Ala. Mem.: ABA, Am. Coll. Trial Lawyers, Ala. Bar Assn. (pres.-elect 2004—05, pres. 2005—06), U.S. Supreme Ct., 1975, U.S. Ct. of Appeals 11th Cir., U.S. Ct. of Appeals 5th Cir., 1974, U.S. Dist. Ct. Middle Dist. Ala., 1972, Am. Bd. Trial Advocates, Ala. Bd. of Bar Commrs., Montgomery Bar Assn. (pres. 1989), Ala. Law Found. (life). Office: Copeland Franco Screws & Gill PA PO Box 347 Montgomery AL 36101-0347 Office Phone: 334-834-1180. Business E-Mail: segall@copelandfranco.com.

SEGALLA, THOMAS FRANCIS, lawyer; b. Lee, Mass., Apr. 7, 1943; s. Stanley John and Ann (Finnegan) S.; m. Mary Louise, Aug. 5, 1967. BBA, U. Miami, Coral Gables, Fla., 1965; JD cum laude, SUNY-Buffalo, 1972. Bar: N.Y. 1973, U.S. Dist. Ct. (we.dist.) N.Y. 1973, U.S. Supreme Ct. 1983. Prodn. mgr. UniRoyal Inc., Naugatuck, Conn., 1966-69; law asst. N.Y. Atty. Gen., Buffalo, 1971; ptnr. Saperston & Day, PC, Buffalo, 1972-2001, Goldberg Segalla, Buffalo, 2001—. Lectr. Erie C.C., Buffalo, 1970-73, Bryant & Stratton Inst., Buffalo, 1975; assoc. prof. SUNY, 1985-90. Editor SUNY Buffalo Law Rev., 1971-72. Mem. ABA, Def. Rsch. Inst., Erie County Bar Assn., Fed. Def. and Corp. Counsel, Internat. Assn. Def. Counsel, Kappa Sigma (pres. Miami 1964-65). Roman Catholic. Home: 25 Westfield Rd Buffalo NY 14226-3492 Office: Goldberg Segalla 665 Main St Ste 400 Buffalo NY 14203 Office Phone: 716-566-5480. Business E-Mail: tsegalla@goldbergsegalla.com.

SEGARS, KELLY SCOTT, SR., physician, banker; b. Red Bay, Ala., Mar. 11, 1930; s. Dock and Ora (Sims) S.; m. Martha Ann Thompson, oct. 3, 1952; children: kelly Scott, Jr., Mark Thompson, Leigh Ann. BS in Pharmacy, Auburn U., 1952; MD, U. Miss.-Jackson, 1959. Diplomate Am. Bd. Fam. Practice. Intern USPHS Hosp., Norfolk, Va., 1959-60; physician Segars Clinic, Iuka, Miss., 1960—. Founder. pres., chmn. First Am. Nat. Bank, Iuka, 1964—; pres. Segars Communications, Iuka, 1970—, S & G Cablevision, Iuka, 1978—; pres. Tri-State Savs. & Loan, 1963-64; chief med. staff Tishominga County Hosp., Iuka, 1968, 76, 82, dir. coronary care unit, 1970—; chmn. constrn. com. Kelly Segars Field, 1964, Iuka Mcpl. Library, 1971. Exec. coun. Boy Scouts Am., Tupelo, Miss., 1971—. 1st lt. U.S. Army, 1953-55. Decorated Army Commendation medal. Fellow Am. Acad. Family Physicians; mem. AMA, Miss. Med. Assn., Flying Physicians assn., Ole Miss Med. Alumni, Rotary (paul Harris Fellowship). Republican. Methodist. Office Phone: 662-423-3656. Personal E-mail: ksegars@fanb.net.

SEGEL, JASON JORDAN, actor; b. LA, Jan. 18, 1980; Actor: (films) Can't Hardly Wait, 1998, Dead Man on Campus, 1998, SLC Punk!, 1998, New Jersey Turnpike, 1999, Slackers, 2002, 11:14, 2003, Certainly Not a Fairytale, 2003, LolliLove, 2004, The Good Humor Man, 2005, Bye Bye Benjamin, 2006, Knocked Up, 2007; (TV series) Freaks and Geeks, 1999—2000, Undeclared, 2001—02, Harry Green and Eugene, 2004, CSI: Crime Scene Investigation, 2004—05, How I Met Your Mother, 2005—08; (TV films) North Hollywood, 2001; actor, writer (films) Forgetting Sarah Marshall, 2008. Office: c/o BWR Pub Rels 6th Fl West Tower 9100 Wilshire Blvd Beverly Hills CA 90212

SEGELCKE, ELKE, literary scholar; b. Lueneburg, Germany; d. Helmut Segelcke and Marietta Segelcke-von Seydlitz und Ludwigsdorf; m. James Marshall Boswell Rev. PhD, U. NC, Chapel Hill, 1987. Wissenschaftliche mitarbeiterin U. Augsburg, Germany, 1982—85; vis. asst. prof. Wash. U., St. Louis, 1987—89; temp. asst. prof. San Diego State U., 1989—91; asst.-assoc. prof. Ill. State U., Normal, 1992—. Contbr. articles to profl. publs. Grantee, DAAD, U. Pa., 1988, Am. Coun. Learned Socs., 1993; Summer Seminar grant, NEH, Berlin, 1994, Faculty Rsch. Visit grant, DAAD, German Academic Exch. Svc., 1997, 2009. Mem.: GSA, MLA, H. Mann-Gesellschaft, Marieluise Fleisser-Gesellschaft, WiG, AATG, NeMLA, IVG. Achievements include research in German, European studies, literature of classical modernity and the avant-garde in Weimar Germany, unification literature & transcultural literature. Home: 309 Florence Ave Normal IL 61761 Office: Ill State Univ Stevenson Hall Campus PO Box 4300 Normal IL 61790-4300 Office Fax: 309-438-8038. Business E-Mail: esegelc@ilstu.edu.

SEGELMAN, ALVIN BURTON, pharmaceutical executive, educator, research scientist; b. Boston, Sept. 27, 1931; s. Joseph Theodore and Anna (Klein) Segelman; m. Florence Hannah Pettler, Apr. 27, 1972 (dec. Jan. 7, 1994); children: Lauren Beth, Sheera Toba. BS, Mass. Coll. Pharmacy, 1954, MS, 1967; PhD, U. Pitts., 1971. Registered pharmacist Mass., cert. nutritional specialist Am. Coll. Nutrition. Chief pharmacist Kenmore Pharmacy, Boston, 1954—61; pres. Bell Pharmacy, Somerville, Mass., 1961—67; instr. pharmacognosy and microbiology pharmacognosy dept. U. Pitts., 1967—71; asst. prof. pharmacognosy dept. Rutgers U., Piscataway, NJ, 1971—74, assoc. prof., chmn. pharmacognosy dept., 1974—90; v.p. R&D health scis. Nature's Sunshine Products, INc., Provo, Utah, 1990—2000; CEO Pharmacognosy Rsch. Inst., Orem, Utah, 2001—. Prin. investigator rsch. Rutgers Biomed. Rsch. Grants, New Brunswick, 1972—85, U.S. Pub. Health Svc. Grant, Washington, 1973; co-prin. investigator rsch. Am. Cancer Soc., Washington, 1987—88; expert med. cons. U.S. Congress Select Com. on Aging, Washington, 1981—83; vis. prof. Jagellonian U., Cracow, Poland, 1989, Patrice Lamumbe U., Moscow, 1999; cons. in field. Co-author: Antibiotics in Historical Perspective, 1981; contbr. articles to profl. jours.; sci. reviewer: various profl. and sci. jours. Mem. various coms. Acad. Pharm. Scis., Washington, 1976—89; mem. med. adv. com. Planned Parenthood Middlesex County, New Brunswick, NJ, 1979—90. Served to 2d lt. U.S. Army N.G., 1949—59. Avocations: small arms pistol competition, ethnopharmacognosy research and writing, mountain climbing. Home and Office: Pharmacognosy Rsch Inst 54 West 680 South Orem UT 84058 Office Phone: 801-226-2184. Personal E-mail: herbdoctoralvin@aol.com. E-mail: chattiecathe@aol.com.

SEGER, MARK, molecular biologist; b. Trier, Germany, June 15, 1978; s. Ted M. Lee and Ingrid Caesar, Larry and Bernidette Caesar, Adolph Britt. BS in Biology and Animal Sci., N.Mex State U., Las Cruces, 2002, MS in Molecular Biology, 2005; PhD in Molecular Biology, N.Mex State U., Las Cruces, New Mexico, 2009. Tutor N.Mex State U., 1998—2002, rsch. asst., 2002—. Office: N Mex State Univ University Ave Las Cruces NM 88003 Personal E-mail: segerm@hotmail.com.

SEGERSTEN, ROBERT HAGY, lawyer, investment banker; b. Boston, June 24, 1941; s. Wendell C. and Claire H. Segersten; m. Marie E. Makinen, Feb. 13, 1965; children: Amanda Beth, Vanessa Bryce. AB, Bates Coll., 1963; JD, Boston U., 1970. Bar: Mass. 1970. Assoc. Nessen & Csaplar, Boston, 1970-75; v.p. March Co., Boston, 1975-77; pres. March-Eton Corp., Concord, Mass., 1977-82; ptnr. Nessen, Goodwin & Segersten, Concord, 1977-82, Kane & Segersten, Dedham, Mass., 1983-85; pres. Woodbine Optical Corp., Boston, 1990—2006; pres., CEO Solos Endoscopy, Boston, 2006—. Officer, bd. dirs. Friends of Jimmy Fund, Boston. Served to lt. USN, 1963—67. Mem.: ACLU, Mass. Bar Assn. Democrat. Episcopalian. Home: 64 Folsom Ave Hyannis MA 02601-4823 Business E-Mail: rsegersten@solosendoscopy.com.

SEGERSTRALE, ULLICA CHRISTINA, social sciences educator, researcher; d. Curt Olof Segerstrale and Dagny Cecilia Flodin; m. Val Jason Martin, Dec. 6, 1991. MS in Sociology, U. Helsinki, Finland, 1973; MA in Comm., U. Pa., Phila., 1975; PhD, Harvard U., Cambridge Mass., 1983. Vis. asst. prof. Smith Coll., Northampton, Mass., 1984—86; prof. and acting chair Abo Akademi U., Finland, 1986—87; sr. rschr. Acad. of Finland, Helsinki, 1988—91; asst. prof. Ill. Inst. Tech., Chgo., 1988—93, assoc. prof., 1993—2000, chair dept. social sci., 2000—, prof. sociology, 2003—. Adv. bd. Ctr. for the Study of Ethics in the Professions, IIT, Chgo., 1989—; sr. fellow Ctr. on Nanotechnology and Soc., IIT, Chgo., 2005—; assoc. editor Sci. Studies, Helsinki, 1988—; mem. editl. bd. Social Epistemology, Pitts., 2002—, Jour. Bioscis., Bangalore, India, 2002—05. Author: Defenders of the Truth: The Battle for Science in the Sociobiology Debate and Beyond, 2000, Nature's Oracle: An Intellectual Biographu of William D. Hamilton, 2007; editor: Nonverbal Communication: Where Nature Meets Culture, 2000, Beyond the Science Wars, 2000. Recipient Julia Beveridge award, Ill. Inst. Tech., 2006, Hon. Fgn. Mem., Finnish Soc. of Sciences and Letters, 2003; grantee, Sloan Found., 2004; fellow, Salzburg Seminar in Am. Studies, 1974, Fulbright Program, 1974, Guggenheim Meml. Found., 2002—03, Am. Philos. Soc., 2002—03, Bellagio Residency, Rockefeller Found., 2003. Mem.: AAAS, Am. Sociol. Assn., Soc. for the Social Studies of Sci., Sigma Xi. Achievements include research in underlying reasons for the sociobiology controversy. Avocations: travel, languages. Office: Ill Inst Tech 3301 S Dearborn Ste 116 Chicago IL 60616 Office Fax: 312-567-6821. Business E-Mail: segerstrale@iit.edu.

SEGGELKE, MARTIN HEINRICH, conductor, music professor; b. Hamburg, Germany, Nov. 6, 1975; s. Barbara and Heinrich F. A. B. Seggelke. Diploma in Conducting, U. Calgary, Can., 2003; MusM in Music Edn., U. Bremen, Germany, 2003, MS in Geography, 2003; MusM in Conducting, SUNY, Fredonia, 2004; DMA in Conducting, Eastman Sch. Music, U. Rochester, NY, 2006. Clarinetist German Marine Band, Kiel, Schleswig-Holstein, 1995—97; instr. U. Bremen, 1999—2003; tchg. asst. SUNY, Fredonia, 2003—04; assoc. conductor Eastman Wind Ensemble Eastman Sch. Music, Rochester, 2004—06; prof. music; dir. wind ensembles and orchestras, coord. music discipline U. Minn., Morris, 2006—. Music dir., condr. New Opera and Theatre Ensemble, Bremen, 1999—2003; condr. Symphonic Wind Band Norderstedt, 2002—03; condr., bd. mem. OSSIA New Music Ensemble, Rochester, 2004—06; Reiki master tchr., Morris, Minn., 2005—; conductor, faculty mem. Performing Arts Inst. Wyoming Sem., Pa., 2008—; presenter at internat., nat., & regional profl. confs. Contbr. articles to profl. jours. and mags. Recipient Tchg. Asst. prize for excellence in tchg., Eastman Sch. Music, 2006, Fundamental award, U. Minn., 2009, Imagine Fund award, McKnight Found., 2009; Faculty Enrichment grant, U. Minn., 2007, 2008—09, Morris Academic Ptnrs. Grant, 2008—, Faculty Rsch. Enhancement grant, 2009. Mem.: Minn. State HS League, Coll. Music Soc., Minn. Band Directors' Assn., Minn. Music Educators' Assn. (Outstanding Svc. cert. 2008), Internat. Soc. for the Rsch. and Promotion of Wind Music, Nat. Band Assn., Music Educators' Nat. Assn., Coll. Band Directors' Nat. Assn., World Assn. of Symphonic Bands and Ensembles (bd. mem., German sect. 2002—06). Avocation: music. Home: 205 W 7th St Morris MN 56267 Office: U Minn Morris 600 E 4th St Morris MN 56267 Business E-Mail: seggelke@morris.umn.edu.

SEGGER, MARTIN JOSEPH, museum director, educator, art historian; b. Felixtowe, Eng., Nov. 22, 1946; s. Gerald Joseph and Lillian Joan (Barker-Emery) S.; m. Angele Cordonier, Oct. 4, 1968; children: Cara Michelle, Marie-Claire, Margaret Ellen. BA, U. Victoria, 1969, diploma in edn., 1970; MPhil, U. London, 1973. Prof. art history U. Victoria, BC, Canada, 1970—74; museologist Royal B.C. Mus., Victoria, 1974—77; dir. Maltwood Art Mus., prof. art history U. Victoria, 1977—, dir. cmty. rels., 2001—. Cons. Nat. Mus. Corp., Ottawa, 1977, UNESCO, O.E.A., Cairo, 1983; bd. dirs. Canadian Cultural Rsch. Network, Victoria Coll. Art, Can. Rsch. Alliance; bd. advisors Greater Victoria Econ. Devel. Commn.; pres. Pacific northwest chpt. Soc. Archtl. Historians, 2002— Author: exhbn. catalogue House Beautiful, 1975, Arts of the Forgotten Pioneers, 1971, Victoria: An Architectural History, 1979, (commendation Am. Assn. State and Local History 1980), This Old House, 1975, This Old Town, 1979, British Columbia Parliament Buildings, 1979, The Heritage of Canada, 1981, Samuel Maclure: In Search of Appropriate Form, 1986 (Hallmark award 1987, 98), (a guide) St. Andrew's Cathedral, 1990, The Development of Gordon Head Campus, 1988, An Introduction to Museum Studies, 1989, An Introduction to Heritage Conservation, 1990, Botswana Live, 1994, Exploring Victoria's Architecture, 1996; contbr., cons. British Columbia Encyclopedia, 2000, Victoria Modern, 2006. Mem. heritage policy rev. com. Govt. Can., 2001—; Canadian Decorative Arts Soc., 2001—; mem. cultural diversity experts com. Govt. Can., 2002—; v.p. Commonwealth Museums Assn., 2003—; bd. govs. Heritage Can. Found., 1979—83; chmn. City of Victoria Heritage Adv. Com., 1975—79; bd. dirs. Downtown Victoria Cmty. Alliance, Heritage Trust, 1977—86, B.C. Touring Coun., Sta. CFUV Radio, B.C. Govt. Ho. Found., Royal B.C. Mus., 1996—99; co-chair B.C. Arts Festival; mem. B.C. Heritage Adv. Bd., 1973—83; councillor City of Victoria, 1987—93; vice-chair Provincial Capital Commn., 1991—2001; pres. Assn. Vancouver Island Municipalities, 1993—94; chmn. B.C. Festival of the Arts, 1999; bd. dirs. Internat. Coun. Mus.-Can., 1999, Victoria Coll. Art, 2001—, Victoria Harbour Authority, 2002—, dir.; bd. chair Queenswood Soc., 2007—. Decorated knight Equestrian Order of Holy Sepulchre of Jerusalem; recipient award, Heritage Can. Comm., 1976, Heritage Conservation award, Lt. Gov. B.C., 1989, Harley J. McKee award, Assn. Preservation Tech., 1994, Queen's Golden Jubilee medal; named Hon. Citizen, City of Victoria, 2000, Arts Citizen of Yr., 2001. Fellow Royal Soc. Arts, Can. Mus. Assn. (counsellor 1975-77); mem. Internat. Coun. Mus. (chair internat. com. for tng. pers. 1995-98), Internat. Coun. Monuments and Sites (bd. dirs. 1980-82), Soc. Study Architecture Can. (bd. dirs. 1979-81), Can Mus. Dirs. Orgn., Commonwealth Assn. Museums (pres. 2005—), Union Club Victoria. Roman Catholic. Avocations: travel, motor mechanics, water color painting. Home Phone: 250-384-3694; Office Phone: 604-721-8298. Business E-Mail: msegger@uvic.ca.

SEGLER, CHRISTOPHER PAIGE, surgeon, researcher; s. David Otis and Julia Cate Segler; m. Paige Elizabeth Clem, May 29, 2004. BA in English, U. Houston, 1996; DPM in podiatric medicine, Calif. Coll. Podiatric Medicine, 2003. Rsch. asst. U. Houston, Dept. Chemistry, 1994—97; hospice vol. Hospice at the Tex. Med. Ctr., Inpatient Unit, Houston, 1994—95; psychiat. tech. Sharpstown Gen. Hosp., Houston,

1995—97; psychiat. technician Harris County Psychiat. Ctr., Houston, 1997—98; med. illustrator Calif. Coll. Podiatric Medicine, Dept. Basic Scis., San Francisco, 2000—02; sr. editor Nat. Foot and Ankle Rev., Oakland, Calif., 2002—03; podiatric surg. resident Dept. Veterans Affairs Health Care Sys., Salt Lake City, 2003—; design prin., co-founder Orthovation, LLC, Houston, 2003—; pvt. practice Chattanooga, 2006—. Chief resident U. Utah/VAMC, 2005—06. Contbr. articles to profl. jours., chapters to books. Recipient Excellence in Rsch. award, Calif. Coll. of Podiatric Med., 2003; named 1st place, Outstanding Resident Rsch Abstract Competition, Am. Podiatric Med. Assn., 2006; grantee, Gilkey Meml. Fund, 2000. Mem.: Soc. for Exptl. Biology and Medicine, Am. Podiatric Med. Writers Assn., Utah Podiatric Med. Assn., Am. Podiatric Med. Assn., Am. Coll. Foot and Ankle Surgeons (assoc. 2nd pl. Sci. Rsch. Post Competition, Instnl. Category 2005, 3rd pl. Sci. Rsch. Post Competition, Instnl. Category 2006, others), Omicron Delta Kappa (life), Alpha Epsilon Delta (life), Sigma Tau Delta (life). Achievements include invention of Tarsal Joint Space Distractor, surgical instrument for use in foot and ankle surgery. Avocations: rock climbing, kayaking, writing, painting, running. Office: Ankle & Foot Ctr Chattanooga 531 Signal Mountain Rd Chattanooga TN 37405 Business E-Mail: drsegler@anklecenter.com.

SEGRAVES, JAMIE NICOLE, language educator; b. Houston, May 13, 1985; d. James Gordon and Jane Lynn Segraves. BA, U. Tex., Austin, 2006; MA, Middlebury Coll., Vt., 2007, Middlebury Coll., Madrid, 2007; attending, Georgetown U., Washington, 2007—. Spanish instr. George Washington U., Washington, 2008—, Georgetown U., 2008—. Mem.: GSPSO. Avocation: travel. Office: Dept Spanish and Portuguese Georgetown Univ Box 571039 Washington DC 20057-1039 Personal E-mail: jamiesla@gmail.com. Business E-Mail: jns33@georgetown.edu.

SEGREST, LINDA HUDSON, music educator; d. James Edward and Lois Lanelle Hudson; m. Thomas Louis Segrest; children: Thomas James, Sarah Lauren, Jeff Hudson. MusM, Miss. Coll., Clinton, 1975. Instr. Miss. U. Women, Columbus, 1980—. Office: Miss Univ Women 1100 College St Columbus MS 39701 Business E-Mail: lsegrest@as.muw.edu.

SEGRETO, LINDA MARY JANECZEK, special education educator, librarian; b. Troy, NY, July 2, 1948; d. Walter John and Margaret Angela (Catallozzi) Janeczek; m. Anthony Joseph Segreto; children: Anthony Walter, Amanda Margaret. AAS, Maria Coll., 1968; BS in Bus. Edn., SUNY, Albany, 1970, M in Libr. Sci., 1976; spl. edn. credentials, Calif. State U., Long Beach, 1999. Tchr. Calif., C.C. tchr. Calif., tchr. N.Y. Bus. tchr. Lansingburgh Ctrl. Sch. Dist., Troy, NY, 1970—78; bus. adminstr. TRW Def. and Space Sys., Redondo Beach, Calif., 1978—87; bus. instr. Cypress (Calif.) Coll., 1980—82; spl. edn. tchr./transition specialist Manhattan Beach (Calif.) Unified Sch. Dist., 1997—; sch. librarian Robert M. Finley Middle Sch., Clen Cove, NY, 2009—. Sch. host, coord., vol. Best Buddies Calif., LA, 1999—. Active PTA, Palos Verdes, Calif., 1990—, Friends of the Libr., Palos Verdes, 1990—; mem., vol. L.A. Mission, 2000—. Mem.: NY State Tchrs. Assn., Calif. Tchrs. Assn., Coun. for Exceptional Children, Pi Lambda Theta. Avocations: travel, music, dramatics, yoga, golf.

SEGROVE, DAVID ANTHONY, information technology manager; b. Rochford, Essex, Eng., Aug. 9, 1969; m. Jill Ann Rivera, Dec. 10, 1999; 1 child, Erin Lynn Bartel. Analyst, programmer Security Pacific, London, 1987—88; pc support supr. Brit. & Commonwealth Mcht. Bank, London, 1988—90; pc support mgr. Credit Suisse Fin. Products, London, 1990—92; cons. Bankers Trust, London, 1992—93, asst. v.p. NYC, 1993—95; v.p. Lehman Bros., NYC, 1995—97; software devel. mgr. OrthoLogic, Tempe, Ariz., 1997—99; cons. Stone Age Innovations, Cave Creek, Ariz., 1999—2002; project mgr. Remuda Ranch, Wickenburg, Ariz., 2002—05; systems analyst Sun Health, Sun City, Ariz., 2005—06; prin. Jde Ltd., Phoenix, 2006—. Avocations: writing, photography, fishing, travel. Personal E-mail: dave.segrove@click-done.com.

SEHILI, MAHMOUD, artist; b. Tunis, July 27, 1931; m. Gabriele Buth, Apr. 11, 1959; children: Thouraya, Lilia, Raouf. Student, Fine Arts Sch., Tunis; diploma supérieur des arts plastiques, Ecole des Beaux-Arts, Paris. Tchr. Inst. Technol. Art, Arch., Urbanisme, Tunis; dir. Irtissem Art Gallery, Tunis, 1977—. Recipient Golden medal, Cagnes sur Mer, 1st prize, Town of Tunis, 1963, others. Avocations: music, playing the luth, composition of arabic music, fishing. Home: 4 Rue Victor Hugo Carthage Tunisia Office Phone: 00216-99312066.

SEHRING, ADOLF, artist, sculptor; came to the U.S., 1949; s. George Henry M. and Clair (Burstin) S.; married, 1992; children: Nina, Marc. Student, Acad. Fine Arts, Germany. Pres. A. Sehring Studio Inc., Orange, Va., 1970—, Am. Artist Portfolio Inc., Orange, 1987—. Lectr. in field. One man shows include Grand Palais, Paris, 1980, Bayley Mus., Va., 1983, Va. Mus., 1984, World Bank, Washington, 1985, Yokohama, Japan, 1989, Newport Beach, Calif., 1993, Palm Desert, Calif., 1994; commd. by the Vatican to paint the ofcl. portrait of Pope John Paul II, Hearst Castle, Calif., to sculpt Pocahontas bronze, Town of Gloucester, Va., bronze in collection of Pres. Bush; represented in permanent collections Chrysler Mus., Am. Embassy, Stockholm, Bayly Mus., Victoria and Albert Mus.; represented in 10 galleries; art is now available at art auctions on Carnival and Princess Cruise Lines worldwide.; www.adolfsehring.com. Recipient Stalin medal for art, Rias award, 1946. Avocations: antiques, gardening, birds. Personal E-mail: lsregina@msn.com.

SEHRING, HOPE HUTCHISON, library science educator; b. Akron, Ohio; d. Welsey Harold and Jane (Brown) Hutchison; m. Frederick Albert Sehring, July 15, 1978. BS, Slippery Rock U., Pa., 1968; MEd, U. Pitts., Pa., 1973, MLS, 1984; postgrad. studies, Seton Hill U., Greensburg, Pa., 2002. Cert. instrnl. media specialist. Reference libr.-intern Carnegie Mellon U., Pitts., 1981; libr. media specialist Gateway Sch. Dist., Monroeville, Pa., 1968—2003; dir. Jeannette Pub. Libr., 2006—. Mem. pub. rels. com. Westmoreland County Federated Libr. Sys.; assoc. Wal-Mart, Delmont, Pa., 2006. Contbr. articles to profl. jours. Active Pa. Citizens Better Librs., Friends of Monroeville Pub. Libr., Monessen Adv. Coun., Westmoreland Libr. Network; pub. rels. com. Westmoreland County Libr. Network. Recipient Gift of Time Tribute, Am. Family Inst., 1992, 1996; Henry Clay Frick Found. scholar, U. London, 1969, 1973. Mem.: Jeannette Rotary (v.p. 2008—, pres. 2008—), Gateway Edn. Assn., Pa. State Edn. Assn., Sch. Librs. Assn. (treas. 1982—84), Rotary, Alpha Xi Delta. Avocation: culinary arts. Home: 265 Fenneltown Rd New Alexandria PA 15670 Office Phone: 724-523-5702. Personal E-mail: gg7495@yahoo.com.

SEIBEL, CATHY, federal judge; b. West Islip, NY, 1960; m. Barron Lerner. AB, Princeton U., NJ, 1982; JD, Fordham U. Sch. Law, NYC, 1985. Bar: NY 1986. Law clk. to Hon. Joseph M. McLaughlin US Dist. Ct. (ea. dist.) NY, 1985—87; spl. asst. US atty. (we. dist.) Wash. US Dept. Justice, 1991—93, asst. US atty. (so. dist.) NY, 1987—91, 1993—97, asst. US atty.-in-charge, 1997—99, sr. trial coun., 1999—2005, dep. US atty., 2005—08; judge US Dist. Ct. (so. dist.) NY, 2008—. Office: US Courthouse 500 Pearl St New York NY 10007*

SEIBEL, CHARLES BURGESS, accountant, educator; b. Annapolis, Md., May 31, 1950; s. John Edward and Amelia Lucille (Tucker) Seibel; m. Teresa Mae McCauley, Sept. 15, 1979; children: Charles Laundle, Daniel Lee. AA in Fin. Acctg., Anne Arundel CC, Arnold, Md., 1975; BS in Acctg., Bowie State U., 1997. Asst. br. acct. Internat. Harvester Co., Tuxedo, Md., 1970—77; chief acct. Am. Gas Assn., Arlington, Va., 1977—84; sr. cost acct. Honeywell, Inc., Annapolis, 1984; accounts receivable supr., credit mgr. Mash's Inc., Landover, Md., 1985—86; comptr. Gateway Ford Tractor, Inc., Upper Marlboro, Md., 1986—87; pvt. practice acct. West River, Md., 1987—95; acct. Alcoholism Recovery, Inc., Crownsville, Md., 1995—99; substitute tchr. Anne Arundel County Pub. Schs., Annapolis, 1999—2002; tchr. Riverdale Bapt. Sch., Upper Marlboro, 2002—. Fellow: Lions (pres. 1988—89, 1989—90, Melvin Jones fellow 2004); mem.: Delta Mu Delta (sec. 1977, 1997). Democrat. Methodist. Avocations: golf, umpiring, hunting, farming, singing. Home: 4824 Sudley Rd West River MD 20778 Office: Riverdale Bapt Sch 1133 Largo Rd Upper Marlboro MD 20774 Personal E-mail: cbtmseibel@msn.com.

SEIBEL, MACHELLE MAYER, gynecologist, educator; b. Galveston, Tex., Apr. 29, 1949; s. Tony N. and Elaine (Farb) S.; m. Sharon Elaine Glazier, June 1, 1987; children: Amy Nicole, Sherry Rene, Alexander Nathan. BA, U. Tex., 1971; MD, U. Tex., Galveston, 1975. Diplomate Am. Bd. OB/GYN, 1982, divsn. of reproductive endocrinology and infertility, 1983. Resident Emory U., Atlanta, 1975-79; fellowship in reproductive medicine Harvard Med. Sch., Boston, 1979-81; dir. gynecology endocrine labs. Beth Israel Hosp./Harvard Med. Sch., Boston, 1981-85, dir. in vitro fertilization, 1985-87, dir. reproductive medicine, 1987-90; dir. Faulkner Ctr. for Reproductive Medicine Faulkner Hosp./Harvard Med. Sch., Boston, 1990-98; assoc. clin. prof. gynecology Harvard Med. Sch., Boston, 1985-97; clin. prof. gynecol. obstetrics Boston U. Sch. Medicine, 1998—; practice ob-gyn. Fertility Ctr. New Eng., 1998—; med. dir. Inverness Med. Author: (textbook) Infertility: A Comprehensive Text, 1990, 2d edit., 1997, Technology and Infertility, 1993, Ovulation Induction, 1994, Gamete Donation, 1995, Infertility: Your Questions Answered, 1995. Mem. Am. Coll. Ob/gyn. (Searle Donal Richardson award 1983, Focus on Patient Edn. award Mead Johnson 1993), and others. Office: 1153 Centre St Boston MA 02130-3446

SEIBER, RICHARD ALLAN, retired chaplain United States Air Force; b. LA, Nov. 15, 1932; s. Edward Maurice and Dorothy Mildred (Ball) S.; m. Wilma Ellen Shook, Sept. 24, 1955; children: Bruce Wayne, Roger Kent, Dale Eugene, Michael Allan. BA in History, U. Puget Sound, 1958; MDiv, Garrett Bibl. Inst., 1960; grad., Air Command & Staff Coll., 1962, Air War Coll., 1970, Army Command and General Staff Coll. Ordained elder United Meth. Ch., 1960. Enlisted USAF, 1950, advanced through grades to lt. col., ret., 1976, chaplain, 1960—76; student pastor Meth. Ch., Algona-Pacific, Wash., 1955—57, Sciota-Friendship, Ill., 1957—60; pastor United Meth. Ch., Spanaway, Wash., 1976—83, Epworth-LeSourd United Meth. Ch., Tacoma, 1983—97; ret. United Meth. Ch., Tacoma, 1997. Mem. editl. bd. Meth. History United Meth. Ch., Madison, NJ, 1982—86, mem. gen. conf. archives and history, 1980—88, mem. jurisdictional conf. archives and history, 1980—, pres. jurisdictional conf. archives and history, 1980—84; chmn. com. on chaplains Pacific N.W. Conf., 1977—88, archivist, 1978—2004. Editor: Memoirs of Puget Sound: David Blaine, 1978 (Wash. Gov.'s Writer's award), Methodist History Index: Oct. 1962-July 1982, 1984, Jour. Henry Bridgeman Brewer, 1839-48, 1986; contbr. Sprague, Lamont, Edwall, WA, 1881-1981, 1982; contbr. Religious Heritage of Washington State, 1988, Illustrated History of Methodism, 1999; co-editor: William Roberts: Circuit Riding Superintendent of the Oregon-California Mission Conference, 1847-1853, 2004. Mem. Tacoma Mayor's Task Force on Vets. Affairs, 1986-91; chmn. Ministry with Service People—Co-NeXion, Tillicum, Wash., 1976-79, 87-90; mem. Wesley Homes Corp., Des Moines, Wash., 1984—; v.p. exploring, exec. com. Mount Rainier Coun., Boy Scouts Am., 1976-81, v.p. rels., 1981-92, mem. nat. coun., rep. Pacific Harbors coun., 1999-2009. Recipient Silver Beaver award Boy Scouts Am., 1977, God and Svc. recognition award Boy Scouts Am., 1988, James E. West fellow, 1997, Ministry of Memory award, United Methodist Ch. Gen. Commn. on Archives and History, 2008. Mem.: SAR (life; chpt. pres. 1989—91, Meritorious Svc. medal 2009), Hist. Soc. The United Meth. Ch. (charter), Air Force Hist. Found., Air War Coll. Alumni Assn. (life), Scouting Heritage Soc. (life; charter), Air Force Assn. (life; chpt. pres. 1980—84, state pres. 1994—98, Exceptional Svc. award 1999, 2005, Presdl. citation 2006), Nat. Eagle Scout Assn. (life), Mil. Officers' Assn. (life), Mil. Chaplains' Assn. (Puget Sound chpt. pres. 1985—93, 2002, chmn. Pacific NW Nat. Security Forum 2006—08, hon. vice comdr. We. Air Def. Sector 2007—09), Sigma Chi (life). Avocations: stained glass, genealogy, clocks, early northwest church history, collecting royal doulton. Home: 5514 89th Avenue Ct W University Place WA 98467-1532 Home Phone: 253-564-3757. Personal E-mail: raseiber@nventure.com.

SEIBERG, NATHAN, physics professor; b. Israel, Sept. 22, 1956; married; two children. BSc with high distinction, Tel-Aviv U., 1977; PhD, Weizmann Inst. Sci., Israel, 1982. Sr. scientist Weizmann Inst., 1985-86, assoc. prof., 1986-89, prof., 1989-91, Rutgers U., 1989-90, prof. II, 1990-97; prof. Inst. Advanced Study, Princeton, NJ, 1997—. Vis. mem. Inst. for Advanced Study, 1994-95. With Israeli Def. Force, 1977-82. Recipient Israel Phys. Soc. prize, 1976, Mifal Hapais prize, 1979, Michael Landau prize, 1981, J.F. Kennedy prize, 1982, N.J. Pride award N.J. Monthly Mag., 1996, Bd. Trustees award Rutgers U. for Excellence in Rsch., 1996, Dannie Heineman prize Am. Inst. of Physics, 1998; named Racah lectr. Weizmann Inst. Sci., 1985, Oskar Klein lectr. and Oskar Klein medal, 1995, Disting. IFT lectr. U. Fla., 1996; Amos de-Shalit Found. scholar, 1976; John D. and Catherine T. MacArthur Found. fellow, 1996, Wolfgang Pauli Lectr. award ETH, 2002, Einstein Lectr. award Weizmann Inst. Sci., 2008. Fellow: Am. Acad. Arts and Scis. 2001; mem.: Nat. Acad. Scis. Office: Inst for Advanced Study Sch Natural Sci Einstein Dr Princeton NJ 08540 Business E-Mail: seiberg@ias.edu.

SEIBERT, GREGG GEORGE, communications executive, former investment company executive; b. Mineola, NY, June 1, 1955; s. George and Wilma (Churchill) S.; m. Mara Kurka, May 19, 1979. BA, SUNY, Stony Brook, 1978; MBA, U. Pa., 1980. Asst. v.p. Morgan Guaranty Trust Co., NYC, 1980-83; assoc. dir. Bear, Stearns & Co., Inc., NYC, 1983—89; mng. dir., head global media group Merrill Lynch & Co., Inc., NYC, co-head global corp. fin., co-head global industries and comm. group, head Americas corp. banking, 2003—04, vice chmn., mem. exec. client coverage group., 2004—08; exec. v.p. Cablevision Systems Corp., Bethpage, NY, 2009—. Office: Cablevision Systems Corp 1111 Stewart Ave Bethpage NY 11714-5310*

SEIBLE, FRIEDER, structural engineer, educator; b. Schwaebisch Gmuend, Germany, 1952; m. Betsy Seible; children: Michael, Daniel, Anika. Dipl. Ing. in civil engring., U. Stuttgart, Germany, 1976; MCE, U. Calgary, Alta., Can., 1978; PhD in civil engring., U. Calif., Berkeley, 1982. Registered profl. engr., 1985. Mem. faculty U. Calif.-San Diego, La Jolla, 1983—, founding chair dept. structural engring., 1995—2001, Eric and Johanna Reissner Prof. Applied Mechanics and Structural Engring., dir. Charles Lee Powell Structural Rsch. Laboratories, prof. Structural Engring., interim dean Irwin & Joan Jacobs Sch. Engring., 2002—03, dean, 2003—. Mem. seismic adv. bd. Calif. Dept. Transp. (Caltrans). Recipient Best paper award Can. Soc. Civil Engring., 1982, K.B. Woods award Transp. Rsch. Bd., 1983, 92, Presdl. Young Investigator award Pres. Reagan, 1986, Japanese Govt. Rsch. award for fgn. rsch. specialists Sci. and Tech. Agy., 1987, Outstanding Paper award N.Am. Masonry Conf. award, 1990, 93, Best Paper award Internat. Conf. on Short and Medium Span Bridges, 1990, Raymond C. Reese Rsch. prize ASCE, 1992, Outstanding Jour. Paper award Masonry Soc., 1993, Shiley Achievement award Chancellor's Assocs., 1994, Outstanding Concrete Project award Am. Concrete Inst., 1994, Orchid award for design of Scripps Crossing pedestrian bridge San Diego Cmty. Awareness Program, 1994, citation for Lighting Design, Internat. Assn. Lighting Designers, 1994, Alan H. Yorkdale award ASTM, 1994, Concrete Bridge award Portland Cement Assn., 1994, Moisseiff award ASCE, 1995, Charles Pankow award for innovation CERF, 1996, Best Paper award ASCE, 1997. Mem.: NAE. Achievements include being one of the world's foremost seismic structural engineers.

SEIDE, PAUL, civil engineering educator; b. NYC, July 22, 1926; s. Julius David and Sylvia (Eiler) S.; m. Joan Cecilia Matalka, Jan. 7, 1951; children: Richard Laurence, Wendy Jane Seide Kielsmeier. B.C.E., CCNY, 1946; M. Aero. Engring, U. Va., 1952; PhD, Stanford U., 1954. Aero. research scientist Nat. Adv. Commn. for Aeros., Langley AFB, Va., 1946-52; research asst. Stanford Calif. U., 1952-53; research engr. Northrop Aircraft Co., Hawthorne, Calif., 1953-55; head methods and theory sect. TRW Inc., Los Angeles, 1955-60; head methods and research sect. Aerospace Corp., El Segundo, Calif., 1960-65; prof. civil engring. U. So. Calif., LA, 1965-91, prof. emeritus, 1991—, assoc. chmn. dept. civil engring., 1971-73, 81-83; Albert Alberman vis. prof. Technion-Israel Inst. Tech., Haifa, 1975; vis. prof. U. Sydney, Australia, 1986, U. Canterbury, N.Z., 1986. Cons. Northrop Inc., 1972-77, Aerospace Corp., 1966-68, Rockwell Inc., El Segundo, 1982-85 Author: Small Elastic Deformations of Thin Shells, 1975; contbr. numerous articles to profl. jours. NSF fellow, 1964-65 Fellow (life) ASME, Am. Acad. Mechanics; mem. ASCE (life), Tau Beta Pi, Sigma Xi. Democrat. Jewish. Home: 300 Via Alcance Palos Verdes Estates CA 90274-1105 Home Phone: 310-375-6364. Personal E-mail: paulseide@verizon.net.

SEIDEL, ARTHUR HARRIS, lawyer; b. NYC, May 25, 1923; s. Philip and Pearl (Geller) S.; m. Raquel Eliovich, Aug. 21, 1949; children: Stephen A., Paul B., Mary Beth Sharp. BS, CCNY, 1942; A.M., U. Mich., 1943; JD with honors, George Washington U., 1949. Bar: DC149, Pa. 1956, NY 1957. Atty. patent dept. Gulf Oil Corp., Washington and Pitts., 1947-52; individual practice law, 1952-64; sr. ptnr. firm Seidel & Gonda, 1964-68, Seidel, Gonda & Goldhammer (P.C.), Phila., 1968-72, pres., 1972-84, Seidel, Gonda, Goldhammer & Abbott, P.C., Phila., 1984-88, Seidel, Gonda, Lavorgna & Monaco, Phila., 1988-2001; of counsel Drinker, Biddle & Reath, Phila., 2001—. Lectr. in Intellectual Property Temple U. Law Sch., 1973-86, Am. Law Inst. Editor: George Washington Law Rev, 1949; author: (with others) Trademark Practice, 2 vols, 1963, Monographs on Patent Law and Practice, 5th edit, 1993, Trademarks and Copyrights, 6th edit., 1992, Trade Secrets and Employment Agreements 3d edit, 1995; also articles. Mem. Adv. Com. for Restatement of Law of Unfair Competition. Mem. ABA, Am. Law Inst., Pa. Bar Assn., Phila. Bar Assn., Am. Intellectual Property Law Assn., Phila. Intellectual Property Law Assn. (1st Ann. Outstanding Achievement award 2009), Order of Coif. Home: The Quadrangle C104 3300 Darby Rd Haverford PA 19041-1095 Office: Drinker Biddle & Reath LLP Ste 300 1000 Westlakes Dr Berwyn PA 19312-2409 Office Phone: 610-993-2218. Personal E-mail: arthurseidel@comcast.net. Business E-Mail: arthur.seidel@dbr.com. *My entire professional career has been devoted to the question of innovation, patents for inventions, trademarks for new businesses and copyrights for new writings. I have seen the United States become the world's leader in technology and business.*

SEIDEL, GEORGE ELIAS, JR., zoology educator; b. Reading, Pa., July 13, 1943; s. George E. Sr. and Grace Esther (Heinly) S.; m. Sarah Beth Moore, May 28, 1970; 1 child, Andrew. BS, Pa. State U., 1965; MS, Cornell U., 1968, PhD, 1970; postgrad., Harvard U. Med. Sch., Boston, 1970-71. Asst. prof. physiology Colo. State U., Ft. Collins, 1971-75, assoc. prof., 1975-83, prof., 1983-93, univ. disting. prof., 1993—. Vis. scientist Yale U., 1978-79, MIT, 1986-87; mem. bd. on agr. NRC. Co-editor: New Technologies in Animal Breeding, 1981; contbr. articles to profl. jours. Recipient Alexander Von Humboldt award, N.Y.C., 1983, Animal Breeding Research award Nat. Assn. Animal Breeders, Columbia, Mo., 1983, Clark award Colo. State U., 1982, Upjohn Physiology award, 1986; Gov's. award for Sci. and Tech., Colo., 1986. Mem. AAAS, NAS, Am. Dairy Sci. Assn., Am. Soc. Animal Sci. (Young Animal Scientist award 1983, Physiology, Endocrinology award, 2008), Soc. for Study of Reprodn., Internat. Embryo Transfer Soc. (pres. 1979, disting. svc. award 2001, Pioneer award 2008). Home: 3248 Arrowhead Rd Laporte CO 80535-3022 Office: Colo State U Animal Repro Biotech Lab Fort Collins CO 80523-1683 Office Phone: 970-491-5287. Business E-Mail: gseidel@colostate.edu.

SEIDEL, JAMES P., manufacturing executive; s. Robert A. and Mary Ann Seidel; m. Deborah J. Aziz, Nov. 14, 1998; children: Allison J., Grace C. BS, U. Wis., LaCrosse, 1989. Regional fleet mgr. Bridgestone Corp., Nashville, 1991—2002; nat. sales mgr. Gt. Am. Tire & Auto, Denver, 2002; dir. sales Continental Tire N.Am., Charlotte, NC, 2003—05; v.p., COO Stamford Tires & Wheels, Inc., Charlotte, 2005—, also sec., bd. dirs. Avocations: bicycling, running, gardening, antique cars, cooking. Office: Stamford Tires Wheels Inc PO Box 823438 Pembroke Pines FL 33082-3438 Business E-Mail: jseidel@stamford-tires.com.

SEIDEL, JOAN BROUDE, securities dealer, investment advisor; b. Chgo., Aug. 16, 1933; d. Ned and Betty (Treiger) Broude; m. Arnold Seidel, Aug. 18, 1957; children: David, Craig. BA, UCLA, 1954; postgrad., N.Y. Inst. Fin. Registered prin., investment advisor Morton Seidel & Co. Inc., LA, 1970-74, v.p., 1974-93; pres., 1993—; also bd. dirs. Morton Seidel & Co. Inc., LA. Instr. UCLA Extension, 1979—84; bd. overseas Hebrew Union Coll. Treas. City of Beverly Hills, Calif., 1990-2001, chmn. rent adjustment bd., 1989-90, mem., 1983-89; investment com. YWCA of greater LA, 1987-2002, treas. 1992-95; bd. dirs. Discovery Fund for Eye Rsch., LA, 1987—, treas., 1999—; corp. bd. dirs. Queen's Care, 1999-2005, fin. com., 1999-2005, audit com., 2004-05; bd. dirs. LA Opera, 2002—; CFO Maple Couns. Ctr., 2002-04; bd. govs. Cedars Sinai Med. Ctr. Named Citizen of Yr. Beverly Hills C. of C., 1993. Fellow Assn. for Investment Mgmt. and Rsch., Israel Inst. Tech. (hon.); mem. Am. Technion Soc. (v.p. 1998-2002, pres. So. Calif. chpt. 2001-04, nat. bd. dirs. 2002—, internat. bd. 2003—, nat. pres.

2006—), Nat. Assn. Security Dealers (dist. bus. conduct com. 2S 1993-95, 98-2000, small firm adv. bd. 1998-2000, chair dist. 2 1999-2000), L.A. Soc. Fin. Analysts, LA Opera Fin. Investment Com., Orgn. Women Execs., Rotary, Phi Sigma Alpha. Avocations: reading, travel. Office: Morton Seidel & Co Inc 8730 Wilshire Blvd Ste 530 Beverly Hills CA 90211-2792 Office Phone: 310-360-7541. Personal E-mail: seidel350@aol.com.

SEIDEL, RICHARD L., artist; b. Upper Arlington, Ohio, Dec. 18, 1949; s. Conrad Richard and Elizabeth Mary Seidel. BBA, Nothwood U., Mich, 1972. Cert. in art Ohio State U., 1968. Artist Seidel Gallery, Belleair Bluffs, Fla., 1988—. Oil painting, Midnight Sail. Mem.: PPFA. Home: P0 Box 362 Largo FL 33779 Office: Seidel Gallery 562 Indian Rocks Rd N Ste C Largo FL 33770 Business E-Mail: seidelgallery@hotmail.com.

SEIDEL, ROBERT WAYNE, science historian, educator; b. Kansas City, Mo., June 9, 1945; s. Wayne Herman and Harriet Anita (Day) S.; m. Alison Publicover, Aug. 26, 1972 (div. 1989); 1 child, Mary Ruth; m. Christine Ruth Stack, July 1, 1993. BA, Westmar Coll., 1967; MA, U. Calif., Berkeley, 1968, PhD, 1978. Exhibit designer Lawrence Hall Sci., Berkeley, 1970-72; specialist Poland 4-city tour USIA, Warsaw, 1971-72; grad. rsch. and teaching asst. U. Calif., 1972-78; asst. prof. Tex. Tech U., Lubbock, 1978-83, dir. rsch. history of engrng. program, 1979-83; rsch. historian U. Calif., Berkeley, 1980-82, Laser History Project, Albany, Calif., 1983-85; adminstr. Bradbury Sci. Mus., Los Alamos, N.Mex., 1985-90, overview project leader, 1990-92; sr. staff mem. Ctr. Nat. Security Studies, Los Alamos, N.Mex., 1992-94; dir. Charles Babbage Inst., U. Minn., Mpls., 1994-99; ERA Land Grant prof. History of Tech. U. Minn., Mpls., 1994-99, prof. chem. engrng., 1999—; rsch. dir. IT 75th History Project, 2008—. Author: Lawrence and His Laboratory: A History of the Lawrence Berkeley Laboratory, 1989, Los Alamos and the Making of the Atomic Bomb, 1995. Mem. N.Mex. Sci. Ctr. Commn., 1989-92; bd. dirs. The Bakken Mus., 1994-2004. Woodrow Wilson fellow, 1967, U. Calif. Regent's fellow, 1968, German Marshall Fund fellow, Grenoble, France, 1975, Sr. fellow Dibner Inst., MIT, 2001; recipient Bicentennial Essay prize Nat. Sci. Tchrs. Assn., 1976. Mem. AAUP, History Sci. Soc., Soc. for History Tech. Democrat. Avocation: computer simulations. Home: 5625 Woodlawn Blvd Minneapolis MN 55417-2667 Office: 151 Amundson Hall/U Minn Minneapolis MN 55455 Home Phone: 612-722-7591; Office Phone: 612-624-8003. Business E-Mail: rws@tc.umn.edu.

SEIDEL, SELVYN, lawyer, educator; b. Long Branch, NJ, Nov. 6, 1942; s. Abraham and Anita (Stoller) S.; m. Deborah Lew, June 21, 1970; 1 child, Emily. BA, U. Chgo., 1964; JD, U. Calif., Berkeley, 1967; diploma in law, Oxford U., 1968. Bar: N.Y. 1970, D.C. Ct. Appeals 1982. Ptnr. Latham & Watkins, NYC, 1985—2006; chmn. and CEO Burford Advisors LLC. Adj. prof. Sch. Law, NYU, 1974-84; instr. Practicing Law Inst., 1980-81, 84. Contbr. articles to profl. jours. Bd. dirs. Citizen Scholarship Fund Am., 1995-2000. Mem. ABA, N.Y. County Bar Assn., N.Y.C. Bar Assn. (mem. fed. cts. com. 1982-85, internat. law com. 1989-92, 95-96, art law com. 1997-2000), Boalt Hall Alumni Assn. (bd. dirs. 1980-82). Home Phone: 646-522-6168. Business E-Mail: s.seidel@burfordadvisors.com.

SEIDELMAN, SUSAN, film director; b. Pa., Dec. 11, 1952; Student, Drexel U., NYU. Dir. films, including: Smithereens, 1982, Desperately Seeking Susan, 1985, Making Mr. Right, 1987, Cookie, 1989, She-Devil, 1990, The Dutch Master (nominee Acad. award in dramatic short category), 1994, The Barefoot Executive, 1995; directorial debut with short film: You Act Like One, Too (Student Film award AMPAS), 1997, HBO Sex and The City, 1999, A Cooler Climate, 1999. Mem.: Boynton Beach Club. Office: care Michael Shedler 350 5th Ave New York NY 10118-0110

SEIDEN, MICHAEL V., hospital administrator, physician; b. NYC, Oct. 9, 1958; s. Stanley and Patricia (Guzewicz) Seiden; m. Jean A. Lambert, Oct. 6, 1981; children: Stanley, Stephanie. BA, Oberlin Coll., 1980; MA, MD, Washington U., 1986, PhD in Humoral Immunology, 1986. Diplomate Am. Bd. Internal Medicine. Intern, resident Mass. Gen. Hosp., Boston, 1986-89, chief med. resident, 1991, asst. in medicine, 1992, chief clin. rsch. unit Divsn. Cancer Medicine; oncology fellow Dana Farber Cancer Inst., Boston, 1990; post-doctoral fellow Brigham and Women's Hosp., Boston, 1992; chmn. clin. rsch. com. Gynecologic Cancer Program Dana-Farber/Harvard Cancer Ctr., Boston, coord. cancer stem-cell project; pres., CEO Fox Chase Cancer Ctr., Phila., 2007—. Instr. Harvard U. Med. Sch., 1991; asst. to the dir. Mass. Gen. Hosp. Cancer Ctr., 1993. Mem. editl. bd. Clin. Cancer Rsch., Jour. Clin. Oncology, The Oncologist; contbr. articles to profl. jours. Recipient Mass. Breast Cancer Scholar, 2001; named, 1995, 2000. Office: Fox Chase Cancer Ctr 333 Cottman Ave Philadelphia PA 19111-2497*

SEIDEN, STEVEN ARNOLD, executive search consultant; b. NYC, Feb. 18, 1936; s. Leon and Eleanor (Troy) S.; m. Katherine Cohen, June 8, 1965; children: Lisa Brooke, Hilary Anne. AB, Yale U., New Haven, Conn., 1958. Pres. Seiden Krieger Assocs., 1984—. Mem. NY Stock Exch. Regulatory Adv. Com., 1981-83, policy com. Am. Coun. for Capital Formation, 1982-87. Mem. adv. bd. Registered Rep. Mag., 1982-84. With US Army, 1961—62. Mem.: US C. of C. (small bus. coun. 1985—89), Internat. Assn. Corp. and Profl. Recruiters (editl. bd. 1993—95), NY Biotech. Assn., Turnaround Mgmt. Assn. (program co-chair NY chpt. 1991—92), NY Soc. Security Analysts, Securities Industry Assn. (bd. dirs. 1981—83), Assn. Corp. Growth (asst. v.p. 1987—88, bd. dirs.), Wall St. Tax Assn. (bd. dirs. 1981—83), Bond Club, Century Country Club. Republican. Office: Seiden Krieger Assocs 375 Park Ave New York NY 10152-0002 Business E-Mail: steven@seidenkrieger.com.

SEIDENBERG, IVAN G., telecommunications industry executive; b. NYC, Dec. 10, 1946; s. Howard and Kitty (Zaretsky) S.; m. Phyllis A. Maisel, Dec. 13, 1969; children: Douglas, Lisa. BS in Math., CUNY, 1972; MBA in Mktg. Mgmt., Pace U., 1980. Various engring. positions NY Tel., 1966-74; dist. mgr. transmission design AT&T, Basking Ridge, NJ, 1974-76, dist. mgr. tech. planning, 1976-78, div. mgr. fed. regulatory NYC, 1978-81, asst. v.p. mktg., 1981-83; v.p. fed. relations Nynex Corp., Washington, 1983-86, v.p. external affairs, pres., vice chmn., chmn., CEO, 1995-98, Bell Atlantic Corp, NYC, 1999-2000; pres., co-CEO Verizon Comm., NYC, 2000—02, pres., CEO, 2002—05, chmn., CEO, 2005—; chmn. Bus. Roundtable. Bd. dirs. Boston Properties Inc., CVS Corp., Honeywell, Wyeth, Viacom, Inc. Bd. dirs. NY Hall Sci., Nat. Urban League., Pace U., Mus. TV and Radio, Verizon Found., NY Presbyterian Hosp.; past chmn. corp. fund bd. John F. Kennedy Ctr. for the Performing Arts. Sgt. US Army, 1966—68, Vietnam. Mem. US Telephone Assn. (bd. dirs. 1985—), Rockland Bus. Council (trustee 1987). Office: Verizon Communications Ste 200b 1095 Avenue of the Americas New York NY 10036-6704 also: Business Roundtable 1717 Rhode Island Ave NW Ste 800 Washington DC 20036 Office Phone: 212-395-2121, 202-872-1260. Office Fax: 202-466-3509. E-mail: info@businessroundtable.org.*

SEIDENMAN, NEIL ARNOLD, interpreter; b. Balt., Apr. 3, 1933; s. Louis J. and Bertha Lapidus Seidenman; m. Agnese Fois Seidenman (div.); children: Nathan Louis, Steven Attile, Kenneth Joseph. BS in Langs., Georgetown U., DC, 1955. Sr. staff interpreter US State Dept., DC, working in Spanish, Portuguese and Italian, 1958—87, asst. chief interpreter, 1977—87; ret., 1988; freelance interpreter, 1988—. With US Army, 1955—58. Recipient Hall of Fame award, Balt. City Coll., 2005. Mem.: Am. Assn. Lang. Specialists, Pentagon Ski Club, Ski Club Washington, DC. Democrat. Avocations: languages, travel, piano, tennis, skiing.

SEIDENSTAT, PAUL, retired economics professor; b. Wilmington, Del., June 1, 1933; s. Julius and Ida Seidenstat; m. Linda Denenberg, Sept. 2, 1961; children: Mindye Hughes, Terri Lucier, Marla Minestrella. PhD, Northwestern U., Evanston, Ill., 1964. Asst. prof. economics U. Del., Newark, 1961—67; assoc. prof. economics Temple U., Phila., 1968—2006. Cons. City Coun., Wilmington, 1978—80; fin. dir. New Castle County, Wilmington, 1981. Author: (book) New Businesses & Urban Employment Opportunities; editor: Protecting Airline Passengers in the Terrorist Era, Privatizing the US Justice System, Privatizing Correctional Instutitions, Educational Choice & Privatizing Education, Privatizing Transportation Systems, Contracting Out Government Services, Competition & Privatization in Water & Wastewater Industries, Reinventing Water & Wastewater Systems, Management Innovation in US Public Water & Wastewater Systems. 1st lt. US Army, 1956—58, Brooke Army Med. Ctr. Home: 116 Delview Dr Wilmington DE 19810

SEIDL, R(OBERT) BRYCE, museum director, former manufacturing company executive, city official; b. Madison, Wis., July 21, 1946; s. Robert Joseph and Gwen (Bryce) Seidl; m. Christina Russell Seidl, May 10, 1969; children: Andrew Joseph, Kathryn Lynn. AB in Ecology, U. Calif.-Berkeley, 1968; MBA, U. Mich., 1971. Indsl. engr. Simpson Timber Co., Shelton, Wash., 1971—72; tech. rep. Simpson Chems. Divsn., Portland, Oreg., 1973, prodn. mgr., 1980; mgr. planning & control Simpson Columbia Door Divsn., Vancouver, Wash., 1974—79, divsn. mgr., 1981—83; COO, pres., CEO Fisher Mills, Inc., 1998—2003; pres., CEO Pacific Sci. Ctr., 2003—. City councilman, Vancouver, 1978—83; mayor, Vancouver, 1984—87; active Wash. State Local Governance Study Commn., 1985—; pres. Vancouver Area Devel. Authority, 1986—; bd. dirs. ShoCraft Sheltered Workshop, Vancouver, 1980—82, Columbia River Econ. Devel. Coun., Vancouver, 1982—, Pilchuch Glass Sch., 1996—, pres., 2003; bd. dirs., chmn. Clark County Pub. Transit Sys., Vancouver, 1981—83; trustee Pacific U., Calif. Coll. Arts & Crafts. Avocation: gardening. Office: Pacific Sci Ctr 200 Second Ave N Seattle WA 98109 Office Phone: 206-443-2001. Office Fax: 206-443-3631.

SEIDLER, ALAN, composer, musician, music company executive; b. NYC, Dec. 4, 1947; s. Jack and Martha (Kahn) Seidler; m. Jean Godden Seidler, Feb. 16, 1977 (div. 1980). Student, Juilliard Sch., NYC. Adj. instuctor musical theatre Inst. for Arts Iona Coll., New Rochelle, NY, 1970; chmn., pres. Ook Ook Productions, Inc., NYC, 1974—75; faculty voice and piano NY Schs. Music, NYC, 1978—79; chmn., pres. New Classics Entertainment, NYC, 1995—; chmn. artistic dir. FHE Creative & Performing Artists, Inc., 2001—; chmn., pres. Hoove Ape Records, 2006—. Cons. programming Radio Pacifica WBAI-FM, NYC, 1971—72; musical dir. Roundabout Theatre, NYC, 1967—68. Composer: (films) He Outta Be Committed (Audience Appreciation award Louisville Film Festival, 2000), Tracks for Orchestra, 1970-71, Overture: Homaze to Ives(1970), The Last Invocation, 1984, Five English Poems For High Voice, 1977-80, Oh, On An Early MOrning, 1987, Complaint Team Chamber of Soc., 1989, Playthings For Several & chamber Ensemble, 1990, The Mystic Trumpeter, 1999-2006, Choral Symphany(Pubs. prize 2006), & Numerous others. Scholar, Young Artists New Rochelle, N.Y., 1969. Mem.: Orchestra of Our Time (bd. mem. 2008—), Soc. Composers, Inc., Chamber Music Am., Am. Music Ctr., Am. Fedn. TV and Radio Artists, Am. Soc. Composers, Authors and Publishers (grantee 1997—2008). Office: c/o George T Gilbert Esq 100 Fifth Ave Fl 11 New York NY 10011 Office Phone: 212-277-7196.

SEIDLER, B(ERNARD) ALAN, lawyer; b. NYC, Nov. 26, 1946; s. Aaron H. and Ethel T. (Berkowitz) S.; m. Lynne Aubrey, Jan. 21, 1978; children: Jacob A., Morgan H., Lily R. BA, Colgate U., 1968; JD, Seton Hall U., 1972. Bar: NY 1973, US Dist. Ct. (ea., no. and so. dists.) NY 1975, US Ct. Appeals (1st cir.) 2007, US Ct. Appeals (2d cir.) 1976, US Ct Appeals (3d cir.) 1984, US Ct Appeals (4th cir.) 2004, US Ct. Appeals (11th cir.), 2008, US Supreme Ct. 1977. Staff atty. NY Legal Aid Soc., NYC, 1972-75; sole practitioner NYC, 1975—. Mem. Snedens Landing Tennis Assn. (Palisades, NY), Palisades Swim Club. Office: 580 Broadway New York NY 10012 Office Phone: 212-334-3131. Personal E-mail: seidlerlaw@gmail.com. Business E-Mail: snedens66@aol.com.

SEIDLER, DORIS, artist; b. London, Nov. 26, 1912; m. Bernard Seidler, Sept. 5, 1935; 1 child, David. Exhibited in group shows at Bklyn. Mus. Bi-Ann., Vancouver Internat., Honolulu Acad. Arts, Pa. Acad. Fine Arts, Phila., Soc. Am. Graphic Artists, Assoc. Am. Artists Gallery, Jewish Mus., N.Y.C., Albright-Knox Mus., 1994, Brit. Mus. Recent Acquisitions, 1997, Whitworth Gallery, Manchester, Eng., 2003, Represented in permanent collections Libr. of Congress, Smithsonian Instn., Washington, Phila. Mus. Art, Bklyn. Mus., Seattle Mus. Art, Whitney Mus., Nat. Gallery Art, Nassau County (N.Y.) Mus. Fine Arts, Brit. Mus., London, Victoria and Albert Mus. London, Pallant House Coll., Eng., Portland Mus. Art, Oreg., Birmingham Mus., Eng. Address: 14 Stoner Ave Great Neck NY 11021-2101

SEIDMAN, BARBARA R., mathematics educator; b. Bklyn., Apr. 3, 1947; d. Celia Cohen Imber and Harry Adelman; children: Jennifer S., David H. BA, Bklyn. Coll. CUNY, 1967. Cert. elem. sch. tchr. NY, 1967, math. tchr. NJ Dept. Edn., 1984; lic. real estate agt. Elem. sch. tchr. PS 5, Bklyn., 1967; ops. asst. mfrs. Hanover Corp., NYC, 1969—71; realtor Various Real Estate Orgns., NJ, 1983—93; math. tchr. Middlesex County Vocat. & Tech. Schs., Woodbridge, NJ, 2008—. Mem.: NEA, Middlesex County Edn. Assn., NJ Edn. Assn., Math. tchrs. Assn. NJ, Nat. Assn. Tchrs. Math., Sisterhood Congl. B'nai Tikvah, Hadassah (fundraising v.p. 1983—85). Avocations: reading, needlecrafts, cooking, computers. Office: Academy Woodbridge 1 Convery Blvd Woodbridge NJ 07095 Business E-Mail: seidmanb@mcvts.net.

SEIDMAN, DAVID N(ATHANIEL), materials scientist, engineer, educator; s. Charles and Jeanette (Cohen) S.; m. Shoshanah Cohen-Sabban, Oct. 21, 1973; children: Elie, Ariel, Eytan. BS, NYU, 1960, MS, 1962; PhD, U. Ill., Urbana, 1965. Postdoc. assoc. Cornell U., Ithaca, NY, 1964-66, asst. prof. materials sci. and engring., 1966-70, assoc. prof. materials sci. and engring., 1970-76, prof. materials sci. and engring., 1976-85, Northwestern U., Evanston, Ill., 1985-96, Walter P. Murphy prof. materials sci. and engring., 1996—; founding dir. Northwestern U. Ctr. for Atom-Probe Tomography, Evanston, Ill., 2004—. Vis. prof. Technion, Haifa, 1969-70, Tel-Aviv U., Ramat-Aviv, 1972, 2009; Lady Davis vis. prof. Hebrew U., Jerusalem, 1978, 80-81, prof. materials sci., 1983-85; vis. scientist C.E. de Grenoble, 1981, C.N.E.T.-Meylan, 1981, C.E. de Scalay, 1989, U. Goettingen, 1989, 92; sci. cons. Argonne Nat. labs., Ill., 1985-94, prin. bd. mem., NanoLife, 2009-. Editor: Jour. Materials Sci., 2004—06, Materials Rsch. Soc. Bulletin, 2007—; editor-in-chief (jour.) Interface Sci., 2002—04, mem. editl. bd., editor spl. issues, 1993—2001, mem. editl. bd. Materials Sci. Forum, 1996—; contbr. numerous articles to profl. jours. Recipient Max Planck Rsch. prize Max-Planck-Gesellschaft and the A. von Humboldt-Stiftung, 1993; Guggenheim fellow, 1972-73, 80-81, Humboldt fellow, 1989, 92; named chair for phys. metallurgy Gordon Conf., 1982. Fellow Am. Phys. Soc., TMS (mem. fellows award com. 2002-2005, chair, 2006, Hardy Gold medal 1966), Am. Soc. Materials Internat. (Grossman and Howe awards com. 2005-07, Albert Sauveur Achievement award, 2006,Sauveur award Com.,2009-); mem. AAAS, Materials Rsch. Soc. (editl. bd. Materials Rsch. Bulletin, 2007—,David Turnbull Lctr. award, 2008), Microscopy Soc. Am., A. von Humboldt Soc. Am., Internat. Field-Emission Soc. (mem. steering com. 1997-2002, pres. 2000-2002), Böhmische Phys. Soc. Democrat. Jewish. Achievements include research in micro-structural temporal evolution of microstructures in metallic alloys and phase transformations; high temperature structural, metals, semiconductor-metal alloy reactions, internal interfaces, atomic-scale imperfections in metals and semiconductors; three-dimensional atom-probe tomography, field ion microscopy and electron microscopy. Avocations: reading, history, travel. Office: Northwestern Univ MS&E Dept Cook Hall 2220 Campus Dr Evanston IL 60208-3108 Office Phone: 847-491-4391. Business E-Mail: d-seidman@northwestern.edu.

SEIDMAN, ELLEN SHAPIRO, lawyer, former federal agency administrator; b. NYC, Mar. 12, 1948; d. Benjamin Harry Shapiro and Edna (Eysen) Stern; m. Walter Becker Slocombe, June 14, 1981; 1 child, Benjamin William. AB, Radcliffe Coll., 1969; JD, Georgetown U., 1974; MBA, George Washington U., 1988. Bar: D.C., 1975. Law clk. US Ct. of Claims, Washington, 1974-75; assoc. Caplin & Drysdale, Washington, 1975-78; atty., advisor US Dept. Transp., Washington, 1978-79, dep. asst. gen. counsel, 1979-81; assoc. gen. counsel Chrysler Corp Loan Guaranty Bd., Washington, 1981-84; atty., adv. US Dept. Treasury, Washington, 1981-86, spl. asst. to under sec. fin., 1986-87; dir. strategic planning Fed. Nat. Mortgage Assn., Washington, 1987-88, v.p., asst. to chmn., 1988-91, sr. v.p. regulation rsch. and econs., 1991-93; spl. asst. to the Pres. for econ. policy The White House, Washington, 1993-97; dir. Office Thrift Supervision US Dept. Treasury, Washington, 1997—2001; sr. counsel, Minority Staff, fin. svcs. com. US Congress, Washington, 2002; sr. mng. dir. nat. practice ShoreBank Adv. Svcs., 2002—05; exec. v.p. nat. policy & partnership devel. ShoreBank Corp., 2006—; dir. fin. svcs. & edn. project, asset building program New Am. Found., 2007—. Office: The New Am Found 1630 Connecticut Ave NW 7th Fl Washington DC 20009 Office Phone: 202-822-9146. Business E-Mail: ellen_seidman@sbk.com.

SEIDMAN, JONATHAN G., geneticist, educator; m. Christine Edry, 1973; 3 children. BA in Biochemistry, Harvard U., 1971; PhD, U. Wis. Postdoctoral studies Nat. Inst. Child Health and Human Develop.; Henrietta B. and Frederick H. Bugher Prof. Cardiovascular genetics Harvard Med. Sch., Boston; investigator Howard Hughes Med. Inst. Contbr. articles to profl. jours. Recipient (with wife) Bristol-Myers Squibb award for Disting. Achievement in Cardiovascular Rsch., 2002. Mem.: Inst. Medicine, NAS. Avocations: sailing, gardening. Office: Havard Med Sch, Seidman Lab Dept Genetics 77 Avenue Louis Pasteur Boston MA 02115 Business E-Mail: seidman@genetics.med.harvard.edu.*

SEIDMAN, STEPHEN BENJAMIN, dean, computer science educator; b. NYC, Apr. 13, 1944; s. Sylvan and Anne (Levine) S.; m. Barbara Heidemarie Koppe, Aug. 24, 1969; children: Miriam, Naomi. BS, CCNY, 1964; AM, U. Mich., 1965, PhD, 1969. Asst. prof. math. NYU, 1969—72, George Mason U., Fairfax, Va., 1972—76, assoc. prof. math., 1976—84, prof. computer sci., 1984—90; prof., dept. head computer sci., engrng. Auburn U., Ala., 1990—96; prof., chair dept. computer sci. Colo. State U., Ft. Collins, 1996—2001; dean Coll. Computing Sci. N.J. Inst. Tech., Newark, 2001—05, prof. info. sys., computer sci., 2005—06; dean Coll. Natural Sci. and Math., U. Ctrl. Ark., 2006—09; dean Coll. Sci., Tex. State U., San Marcos, 2009—. Author: Assembly Language programming in Compass, 1987, IEEE Computer Society Real-World Software Engineering Problems: A Self-Study Guide for Today's Software Professional, 2006. Mem.: CSAB (bd. dirs. 2005—), IEEE Computer Soc. (bd. govs. 2003—05, sec. bd. govs. 2005, treas. 2006, v.p. ednl. activities 2007—08), Arkansas Sci. & Tech. Authority (bd. dirs. 2006—09), Assn. Computing Machinery. Business E-Mail: seidman@txstate.edu.

SEIFE, CHARLES, communications educator; b. NYC, July 7, 1972; s. Burton and Tama Seife; m. Meridith Walters Walters, Aug. 6, 2005. AB in Math., Princeton U., NJ, 1993; MS in Math., Yale U., New Haven, 1995; MS in Journalism, Columbia U., 1996. Corr. New Scientist Mag., Washington, 1997—2000; writer Sci. Mag., Washington, 2000—05; assoc. prof. NY U., NYC, 2005—. Author: (non-fiction book) Zero: The Biography of a Dangerous Idea (Pa. Martha Albrand award, 2000), Alpha and Omega, Decoding the Universe, Sun in a Bottle. Office: NY Univ 20 Cooper Sq New York NY 10003

SEIFERT, BETTY L., conservator, consultant; d. Marvin Leon Morris and Cleo Mae Bird; m. Walter Seifert, May 31, 1970; children: Eli, Sara Marguerite. BA, BS, Tex. Woman's U., 1962; MLS, Rutgers U., 1964. Libr. N.Y. Pub. Libr., NYC, 1962—64, Bronx Vet.'s Hosp., NYC, 1965—68; exhibit preparator Maine State Mus., Augusta, 1975—76, conservation technician, 1976—82; conservator Profl. Svc. Industries, Groton, Mass., 1982—85; cons. conservator various orgns., 1985—89; chief conservator Jefferson Patterson Pk. and Mus., St. Leonard, Md., 1989—; dep. dir. Md. Archaeol. Conservation Lab., St. Leonard, 1997—2007; curator Jefferson Patterson Pk, Museum, 2007—. Weaving instr. Riverside Ch. Arts and Crafts, NYC, 1968—73. Author: (manual) Standards and Guidelines for Archaeological Investigations in Maryland: Technical Update No. 1 - Collections and Conservation Standards. Adv. bd. mem. for conservation of the USS Monitor Mariner's Mus., Newport News, Va., 2003—06; bd. mem. adv. coun. for underwater archaeology Soc. for Hist. Archaeology, 1990—2001. Recipient full tuition and textbooks scholarship, N.Y. Pub. Libr., 1962—64, Gov.'s Disting. Svc. award, Gov. of Maine, 1978, 2004 Spl. Recognition award, Md. Dept. of Housing and Cmty. Devel., 2004. Mem.: Am. Inst. for Conservation. Achievements include development of Standards and Guidelines for Curation and Conservation of Archaeological Collections; Technical Lead in Design of the Maryland Archaeological Conservation Laboratory. Avocations: weaving, spinning, basketry. Office: Jefferson Patterson Pk Museum 10515 Mackall Rd Saint Leonard MD 20685 Office Fax: 410-586-0080. E-mail: bseifert@mdp.state.md.us.

SEIFERT, CAROLINE HAMILTON, community health nurse; b. Warren, Ohio, May 28, 1937; d. Oliver L. and Martha (Moran) Hamilton; m. Dale E. Seifert, Sept. 5, 1959; children: Brian Dale, Joan Kimberly. Diploma, Youngstown Hosp., Ohio, 1959; BSN, U. Cin., 1964, MEd, 1979. Cert. sch. nurse, health educator, spl. edn. educator. Caseworker Children's Svcs. div. Dept. Health and Human Svcs.,

Batavia, Ohio, 1966-68; dir. Happy Days Nursery Sch. Bethel (Ohio) United Meth. Ch., 1970-73; social worker Clermont County Bd. Mental Retardation/Devel. Disabilities, Batavia, 1973-97; sch. nurse, health educator Thomas A. Wildey Sch., Owensville, Ohio, 1973-97; retired, 1997. Instr. Sch. Health Svcs. U. Cin., 1976, preceptor nursing students, 1992-97. Mem. Hamilton/Clermont Sch. Nurses Orgn. (v.p.), S.W. Ohio Sch. Nurses Assn. (program chmn.), Profl. Assn. for Retardation (v.p. nursing div., Nurse of Yr.). Home: 2631 Oldforge Ln Cincinnati OH 45244-2831 Office: Thomas A Wildey Sch PO Box 8 Owensville OH 45160-0008

SEIFERT, FRANK C., thoracic surgeon; b. Chgo., Feb. 27, 1948; MD, U. Chgo. Pritzker Sch. Medicine, 1974. Cert. Thoracic Surgery, Surgical Critical Care. Intern, gen. surgery U. Chgo. Hospitals, 1974—75, resident, cardiothoracic surgery, 1976—80; resident, anatomy Stanford U. Med. Ctr., 1980—83; fellow U. Goteborg, 1977—78; hosp. appt. U. Hosp., Stony Brook, NY; assoc. prof. surgery SUNY-Stony Brook, NY. Named one of Medical Marvels, New York Mag., 2006. Fellow: Am. Coll. Cardiology, Am. Coll. Surgeons. Office: Health Sciences Center T19-080 SUNY Stony Brook Surgery Stony Brook NY 11790 Office Phone: 631-444-1820. Business E-Mail: fseifert@notes.cc.sunysb.edu.

SEIFERT, GEORGE, mathematician, educator; b. Jena, Germany, Mar. 4, 1921; s. Max and Frieda Seifart; m. Bertha Elizabeth Scheffel, Feb. 4, 1948 (dec.); children: Curt, Edward. PhD in Math., Cornell U., Ithaca, NY, 1950. Asst. prof. U. Nebr., Lincoln, 1950—54; prof. Iowa State U., Ames, 1954—, chmn., dept. math., 1964—66. Mathematician Rsch. Inst. Advanced Studies, Balt., 1959—60. Contbr. articles to profl. jour. Mem. Green Hill Retirement Cmty., Ames, Iowa, 2004—08. Lt. (j.g.) Res. USN, 1943—46. Mem.: Am. Math. Assn. Democrat. Avocations: travel, hiking, theater, classical music, ballet. Home: 2421 Hamilton Dr Ames IA 50014 Office: Iowa State Univ Ames IA 50011 Personal E-mail: goaseifert@hotmail.com.

SEIFERT, JEFFREY W., political scientist, researcher; BA summa cum laude, Towson State U., Md., 1992; MA, Syracuse U., NY, 1995, PhD, 2001. Global programs coord. Syracuse (N.Y.) U., 1999—2000; specialist info. sci. and tech. policy Congl. Rsch. Svc., Washington, 2000—. Vis. instr. Va. Tech. U., Blacksburg, Va., 2001—. Contbg. author: The New International Studies Classroom, 2000, Comparative Perspectives on E-Government, 2006, mem. editl. bd.: Govt. Info. Quar., 2003—, Jour. E-Gov., 2004—06, assoc. editor: Jour. Info. Tech. & Politics, 2007—; contbr. articles to profl. jours. Mem.: Midwest Polit. Sci. Assn., Internat. Studies Assn. (active learning internat. affairs sect. 2000—01, Jr. scholar 1999), Internat. Soc. Polit. Psychology, Assn. Am. Geographers, Am. Polit. Sci. Assn. (bd. dir. info. tech. politics sect. 2002—04, pres. info. tech. politics sect. 2005—06), Gamma Theta Upsilon. Office: Congressional Research Service 101 Independence Avenue SE Stop 7450 Washington DC 20540-7450 Office Fax: 202-707-7000.

SEIFERT, NANCY FAYE ESHELMAN, retired special education educator, consultant; b. Cleve., Sept. 25, 1941; d. Russell H. and Neva Marie (Keener) Eshelman; 1 child, James Russell Callahan; m. Harold Allen Seifert, Feb. 21, 1976. BS in Elem. Edn., Ashland U., Ohio, 1969; MS in Spl. Edn., Kent State U., Ohio, 1975; postgrad., Ohio State U., Ashland U., Ohio U., Bowling Green U. Cert. mentally retarded, elem. and spl. edn. tchr., Ohio. Substitute tchr. Ashland City Schs., 1962-66, 78-83, tutor, 1968-69; tchr. 2d grade South Cen. Schs., Greenwich, Ohio, 1966-68, pre sch. tchr. head, 1969; instr. in primary class Dale-Roy Sch., Ashland, 1969—71, instr. in pre-sch., home tng. cons., 1971—77; substitute tchr. Ashland County Schs., 1978-83, Ashland County/West Holmes Joint Vocat. Sch., 1978-84, spl. needs coord., 1984—95; ret., 1995; bd. mem. & dir. devel. Pediat. Devel. Ctr.(now Raintree Home for Disabled Children), 1979—82; advisor & asst. mgr. MR Flowers Greenhouse, Mansfiels, 2009. Advisor child care Ashland County-West Holmes Joint Vocat. Sch., 1973-88, Vocat. Evaluation Ctr., Mansfield, Ohio, 1986-05; cons. com. Employability Skills Project, State of Ohio, 1986-89; dir. devel. Pediatric Devel. Ctr., Mansfield, 1977-78. Choir mem. Womans Assn., 1950-2006; mem. Govs. com. Employment Handicapped, 1969-76; mem. C.A.C., 1969-96; supporter Echoing Hills Village, Warsaw, Ohio, 1976—, Friends of Ashland U. Libr., 1985—, Ashland Co. Reading Proficiency Remediation Com., 1989-91, Friends of Echoing Ridge, Canal Fulton, Ohio, 1992—; contbr., tour guide Ashland Hist. Soc., 1986—, Easter Seal Assn., 1961-, George Washington's Mt. Vernon, Va., 2005-, Restoration Soc., Williamsburg, Va., 2005-; bd. dirs. Ch.-in-the-Park, Ashland, summers 1983-86, contbr., Ashland Symphony Orch., 1985-, mem., Ashland Symphony Womens Assn., 1994-, libr., Ashland Symphony Youth Chorus, 1994-1998, historian & head Hist. Eshelman Family, vol. Harrisville Masonic Mem. Nat. Vocat. Assn., Ohio Vocat. Assn., Ohio Vocat. Educators (spl. needs pers.), Ohio Assn. Suprs. and Work Study Coords. (pres. dist. V 1989-90), Learning Disabilities Assn., Ohio Ret. Tchrs. Assn. (life), Ashland Ret. Tchrs. Assn. (life), Order of Eastern Star (worthy matron 1971, past matron dist. 4), Ashland U. Alumni Assn., Friday Club of Ashland (pres. 1997-99, 2001-02, 03—), Ashland Cmty. Chorus, Presby. Ch. (bd. deacon's, bd. elders, chmn. worship, music com. PNC cir.), Mantz & S.P. Warner Family Reunions(pres.), Eastern Star(Corn Festival Flower Sales Lodi Ohio) Republican. Presbyterian. Avocations: reading, embroidery, swimming, travel, crafts, crocheting. Home: 524 Katherine Ave Ashland OH 44805-3840 also: 1319 Park St Ashland OH 44805

SEIFERT, RACHEL A., lawyer; b. New Brunswick, NJ, 1959; BA, U. Md., 1981, JD, 1985. Bar: Md. 1985. Atty. priv. practice, Dallas, 1985—92; v.p., assoc. gen. counsel Columbia/HCA, 1992—98; sr. v.p., sec., gen. counsel Cmty. Health Sys. Inc., Brentwood, Tenn., 1998—. Bd. mem. Women Bus. Leaders of U.S. Health Care Industry Found. Mem.: ABA, Federation of Am. Hospitals, Am. Health Lawyers Assn. Office: Community Health Sys 4000 Meridian Blvd Franklin TN 37067

SEIFERT, SHELLEY JANE, bank executive; b. Aug. 12, 1954; BS in Consumer Econs. and Journalism, U. Mo., 1976; MBA with honors in Fin., U. Louisville, 1980. Fin. analyst Nat. City Bank, Ky., 1979-81, compensation analyst, 1981-85, mgr. compensation, 1985-86, mgr. compensation, recruiting and tng., 1986-91; mgr. compensation and devel. Nat. City Corp., Cleve., 1988-91, human resource dir., 1991-94, sr. v.p., 1994—2000, corp. human resource dir., 1994—2004, exec. v.p. corp. svcs., 2000—. Spkr. in field.; bd. dirs., Blair Corp., 2006-. Grad. Leadership Cleve.; vice chair bd. dirs. Bus. Vols. Unlimited, Vis. Nurse Assn. Greater Cleve.; bd. dirs. Arthritis Found.; mem. Cleve. Commn. on Econ. Partnership and Inclusion. Recipient Woman of Distinction award YMCA. Mem. Urban League (bd. dirs., chair employment com., Ohio labor adv. com.). Office: Nat City Corp Nat City Ctr 1900 E 9th St Cleveland OH 44114-3401 Office Phone: 216-222-2000.

SEIFERT, THOMAS LLOYD, lawyer; b. Boston, June 6, 1940; s. Ralph Frederick and Hazel Bell (Harrington) S.; m. Ann Cecelia Berg, June 19, 1965. BS cum laude, Ind. U., Bloomington, 1962; JD cum laude, Ind. U., 1965. Bar: Ill. 1965, Ind. 1965, N.Y. 1979. Assoc. law firm Keck, Mahin & Cate, Chgo., 1965-67; atty. Essex Group, Inc., Ft. Wayne, Ind., 1967-70, Amoco Corp., Chgo., 1970-73; assoc. gen. counsel, asst. sec. Canteen Corp., Chgo., 1973-75; sec., gen. counsel The Marmon Group, Inc. (and predecessor cos.), Chgo., 1975-78; v.p., gen. counsel, sec. Hanson Industries, Inc., NYC, 1978-82; sr. v.p. law, chief fin. officer Petrie Stores Corp., NYC, 1982-83; mem. Finley, Kumble, Wagner, Heine, Underberg, Manley, Myerson & Casey, NYC, 1983-87, Paul, Weiss, Rifkind, Wharton & Garrison, NYC, 1987-91; gen. counsel, chief legal officer Sterling Grace Capital Mgmt., L.P. and affiliated cos., NYC, 1991—. Note editor Ind. Law Jour., 1964-65. Named to Ind. Track and Cross Country Hall of Fame, 1993. Mem. ABA, N.Y. State Bar Assn., Order of Coif, The Creek, Beta Gamma Sigma. Home: Museum Tower 15 W 53d St Apt 31 E New York NY 10019-5401 Office: Sterling Grace Capital Mgmt 405 Park Ave Ste 1203 New York NY 10022 Home Phone: 212-757-8821; Office Phone: 212-644-5067. Personal E-mail: tlseifert@msn.com.

SEIFF, ERIC A., lawyer; b. Mt. Vernon, NY, Apr. 25, 1933; s. Arthur N. and Mathilde (Cohen) S.; m. Sari Ginsburg, June 26, 1960 (div. Oct. 1983); children: Judith C., E. Kenneth, Dean A.; m. Meredith Feinman, Jan. 15, 1984; children: Abigail, Sarah. BA, Yale U., 1955; LLB, Columbia U., 1958. Bar: N.Y. 1958, U.S. Dist. Ct. (so. dist.) N.Y. 1960, U.S. Dist. Ct. (ea. dist.) N.Y. 1981, U.S. Ct. Appeals (2d cir.) 1965, U.S. Supreme Ct. 1967. Assoc. Bower and O'Connor, NYC, 1959-60, Yellin, Kramer & Levy, NYC, 1961; asst. dist. atty. N.Y. County Dist. Atty.'s Office, 1962-67; asst. counsel Agy. for Internat. Devel., Washington, 1967-70, regional legal advisor Rio de Janeiro, 1970-72; gen. counsel N.Y. State Divsn. Criminal Justice Svcs., 1972-74; dep. chief atty. Legal Aid Soc. Criminal Def., NYC, 1974-75; first dep. commr. N.Y. State Investigation Commn., 1975-77, chmn. NYC, 1977-79; ptnr. Seiff, Kretz & Abercrombie (formerly Scoppetta & Seiff), NYC, 1981—; spl. dist. atty. Bronx County, 1986-89. Spl. asst. atty. gen. State of N.Y., Gov.'s Task Force Investigating Conduct of Attica Prosecutions, 1975. Gen. counsel Friends of Van Cortlandt Pk., 1989—; bd. dirs. Legal Aid Soc., NYC, 1994—2000, Prisoners' Legal Svcs., NYC, 1988—, Lawyers Fund for Client Protection, NY, 1980—. Recipient Frank S. Hogan Meml. award, Frank S. Hogan Assn., 1994. Mem.: N.Y. State Assn. Criminal Def. Lawyers (bd. dirs. 2001—08), Bar Assn. City N.Y. (chmn. project on the homeless 1999—2003), N.Y. Criminal Bar Assn. (bd. dirs. 1980—, past pres.). Office: Seiff Kretz & Abercrombie 444 Madison Ave 30th Fl New York NY 10022 Office Phone: 212-371-4500.

SEIFY, HISHAM, plastic surgeon, researcher; b. Cairo, June 27, 1968; m. Lilly Seify. MD, Emory U., Atlanta, PhD, 2005. Diplomate Am. Bd. Plastic Surgery, 2007. Pres. Newport Plastic Surgery, Newport Beach, Calif., 2006—; asst. clin. prof. U. Calif., Irvine, 2006—, UCLA, 2006—; v.p. Future Care IPA, Calif., 2008. Contbr. scientific papers (Shereel Aston award, 2007). Bd. dirs. United Doctors Inc., Calif., 2007—. Sci. grant, Emory U. Ctr. Endoscopic Surgery, 1999. Mem.: Am. Soc. Plastic Surgeons. Achievements include research in projects on a variety of topics related to plastic surgery. Office: Newport Plastic & Reconstructive Surgery 20072 SW Birch St Newport Beach CA 92660 Personal E-mail: drseify@gmail.com. Business E-Mail: drseify@newportplastic.com.

SEIGEL, JERROLD EDWARD, historian, writer; b. St. Louis, June 9, 1936; s. William and Katherine (Ginsberg) S.; m. Jayn Rosenfeld, Aug. 28, 1966; children: Micol, Jessica. AB, Harvard U., 1958; PhD, Princeton U., 1963. Instr. Princeton (N.J.) U., 1962-65, asst. prof., 1965-68, assoc. prof., 1968-78, prof. history, 1978-88, NYU, NYC, 1988—, Kenan prof., 1994—2006, emeritus, 2006—. Vis. prof. history Maitre d'Etudes, Ecoles des hautes études, Paris, 1988-94; finalist Nat. Book Critics Cir., 1987. Author: Rhetoric and Philosophy, 1968, Marx's Fate, 1978, Bohemian Paris, 1986, Private Worlds of Marcel Duchamp, 1995, The Idea of the Self, 2005. Fulbright fellow Inst. Internat. Edn., 1961-62; NEH fellow, 1979-80, 87-88; resident Am. Acad. Rome, 2000; Guggenheim fellow, 2004-05. Mem. N.Y. Inst. for Humanities, Phi Beta Kappa. Home: 48 Horatio St New York NY 10014-1614 Business E-Mail: jes3@nyu.edu.

SEIGEL, JONAS KEARNEY, prosecutor; b. Ridgewood, NJ, Dec. 28, 1977; s. Jan Kearney and Judy Lynn Seigel. BA, Goucher Coll., Balt., 2000; JD, Thomas M. Cooley Law Sch., Lansing, Mich., 2007. Intern Passaic County Prosecutor's Office, Paterson, 2007, Balt. County Office Pub. Defender, 1999; atty. Seigel Law Firm, Ridgewood, 2007—; spl. prosecutor Ridgewood Mcpl. Ct., 2008—. Vol. Habitat Humanity, New Orleans, 2006. Mem.: NJ Assn. Justice, Passaic County Bar Assn., Bergen County Bar Assn., NJ State Bar Assn., Am. Bar Assn. Office: Seigel Law Firm LLC 505 Goffle Rd Ridgewood NJ 07450

SEIGEL, STUART EVAN, lawyer; b. NYC, Mar. 25, 1933; s. Philip Herman and Betty Sarah (Leventhal) S.; m. Joyce Roberta Meyers (div.); children: Charles Meyers, Lee Bennett, Suzanne Marcie; m. Sherry Diane Jackson,Sept. 24, 1989. BS, NYU, 1953, LLB, 1957; LLM in Taxation, Georgetown U., 1960. Bar: N.Y. 1958, D.C. 1958. Atty. Office Chief Counsel, IRS, Washington, 1957—65, Office Tax Legis. Counsel, Dept. Treasury, Washington, 1965—69, assoc. tax legis. counsel, 1968—69; ptnr. Cohen and Uretz, Washington, 1969—77; chief counsel IRS, Washington, 1977—79; ptnr. Williams and Connolly, Washington, 1979—89, Arnold and Porter, NYC, 1989—2002; chmn., CEO Seigel & Assocs., LLC, NYC, 2006—. Lectr. George Washington U. Sch. Law, 1970-73; adj. prof. law Antioch Sch. Law, 1973-76, Georgetown U. Sch. Law, 1981. Mem. ABA, Am. Law Inst., Am. Coll. Tax Counsel, N.Y. State Bar Assn., Met. Club Washington Office: 100 Park Ave 23rd Fl New York NY 10017 Business E-Mail: stuart@seigel-llc.com.

SEIGENTHALER, JOHN LAWRENCE, retired newspaper executive; b. Nashville, July 27, 1927; s. John and Mary (Brew) Seigenthaler; m. Dolores Watson, Jan. 3, 1955; 1 child, John Jr. Staff corr. Nashville Tennessean, 1949-60, editor, 1962-72, pub., 1973-82, pres., 1979-82, chmn., 1982-92; editorial dir. USA Today, 1982-92, ret., 1992. Chmn. freedom forum First Amendment Ctr., Vanderbilt U., Nashville, 1992—; adminstrv. asst. to atty. gen. U.S., 1961; dir. Tennessean Newspapers, Inc., 1963—79, 1978—83. Mem. U.S. Adv. Commn. Info., 1962—64, Pres.'s Jud. Nominating Commn., 1978—79, Nat. Commn. Electoral Reform, 2001—02. Nieman fellow, Harvard U. Mem.: Am. Soc. Newspaper Editors (dir., pres.), Sigma Delta Chi. Office Phone: 615-385-5006. Business E-Mail: johns@fac.org.

SEIGENTHALER, JOHN MICHAEL, public relations executive, former newscaster; b. Nashville, Dec. 21, 1955; s. John Lawrence and Dolores (Watson) S.; m. Kerry Lynn Brock, Jan. 4, 1992. BA in Pub. Policy, Duke U., 1978. Reporter Nashville Tennessean, 1978-79; advance rep. Kennedy for Pres., Washington, 1979-80; writer WDCN-TV, Nashville, 1980; prodr. WNGE-TV, Nashville, 1980-81; reporter, anchor WSMV-TV, Nashville, 1981-90, KOMO-TV, Seattle, 1990—99; weekend anchor, NBC Nightly News WNBC-TV, NYC, 1999—2007; CEO SPR NY Seigenthaler Pub. Rels., Inc., NYC, 2008—. Reporter, producer documentaries: An Eye for An Eye, 1984 (ABA award), Reflections in Black and White, 1986 (Robert F. Kennedy Journalism award), Breaking Down the Barriers, 1990 (Pres.'s Com. on Employment for Disabled award); reporter, producer pub. affairs programs: Prison Riots, 1985 (Am. assn. TV Program Execs. award). Recipient 2 local Emmy awards, 1986. Mem. NATAS, Soc. Profl. Journalists. Roman Catholic. Avocations: tennis, skiing, water-skiing. Office: Seigenthaler Public Relations Inc 115 29th Ave Nashville TN 37212

SEIGLER, DAVID STANLEY, botanist, educator, chemist; b. Wichita Falls, Tex., Sept. 11, 1940; s. Kenneth R. and Floy M. (Wilkinson) S.; m. Janice Kay Cline, Jan. 20, 1961; children: Dava, Rebecca. BS in Chemistry, Southwestern State Coll., Okla., 1961; PhD in Organic Chemistry, U. Okla., 1967. Postdoctoral assoc. USDA No. Regional Lab., Peoria, Ill., 1967-68; postdoctoral fellow dept. botany U. Tex., Austin, 1968-70; asst. prof. botany U. Ill., Urbana, 1970-76, assoc. prof., 1976-79, prof. botany, 1979—, head dept. plant biology, 1988-93. Curator U. Ill. Herbarium, 1993—. Author: Plant Secondary Metabolism, 1999; editor: Crop Resources, 1977, Phytochemistry and Angiosperm Phylogeny, 1981; contbr. numerous articles to profl. jours. Recipient Fulbright Hays Lecturer award Fulbright Commn., Argentina, 1976, (alternate) Germany, 1995-96, study award Deutsche Akademischer Austauschdienst, Germany, 1995, Rupert Barneby award NY Bot. Garden, 1997. Mem. Phytochem. Soc. N.Am. (pres. 1988-89), Bot. Soc. Am., Am. Chem. Soc., Am. Soc. Plant Taxonomists, Internat. Soc. Chem. Ecology (pres. 1990-91). Mem. Assembly of God Ch. Avocation: genealogy. Home: 510 W Vermont Ave Urbana IL 61801-4931 Office: U Ill Dept Plant Biology 265 Morrill Hall 505 S Goodwin Ave Urbana IL 61801-3707 Home Phone: 217-384-1192; Office Phone: 217-333-7577. Business E-Mail: seigler@life.uiuc.edu.

SEIGLER, MICHAEL EDWARD, lawyer, librarian; b. Tallahassee, Oct. 14, 1948; s. Claude Milo and Roberta Bradford (Whitfield) S.; m. Janet Cummings, Feb. 19, 1971; children: Kelly Elizabeth, Megan Whitfield. AA, Lake Sumter C.C., 1968; BS, Fla. State U., 1970, MS, 1974; JD, Atlanta Law Sch., 1980. Bar: Ga. 1980, U.S. Ct. Appeals (5th cir.) 1980, U.S. Ct. Appeals (11th cir.) 1980, U.S. tax Ct. 1985, U.S. Supreme Ct. 1985, Cert. tchr. Libr., tchr. Sumter Correctional Inst., Bushnell, Fla., 1970—73; asst. libr. dir. Leesburg Pub. Libr., Fla., 1974—75, libr. dir., 1975—77, Atlanta Law Sch., 1979—81; atty. Brooks & Brock, Marietta, Ga., 1981—83; libr. Port Charlotte Pub. Libr., 1983—84; assoc. Brooks & Brock, Marietta, 1985, Brock & Barr, Marietta, 1985—86, Brock & Clay, 1987; judge pro hoc vice State Ct. of Cobb County, 1986; pvt. practice, 1986—. Asst. dir. Pine Mountain Regional Libr., 1988-95; libr. dir. Smyrna Pub. Libr., 1995—; design judge Ben Franklin Awards, 2001, 03-. Columnist Smyrna Vinings Living, 2000-02; contbr. articles to jours. Vol. worker ACLU, Atlanta, 1979; mem. Fla. State U. Libr. Com., Tallahassee, 1974, Children's Program Com., Port Charlotte, 1983, Port Charlotte Cultural Ctr. Adv. Com., 1984, Pine Mountain Arts Coun., past bd. dirs.; mem. Cobb County Dem. Exec. Com., 1986-87; exec. com. Cobb Christmas, 1986-87; com. mem. Smyrna Cmty. Culture, 2000-2002, Smyrna Edn. Task Force, 2008; sec. program com. WRFG Cmty. Radio, 2002, bd. dirs., 2003-07, chair fin. com., 2003-07. Named Tchr. of Yr., Sumter Correctional Inst., 1973. Mem. Nat. Libr. Assn. (com. chmn. 1975-76), Fla. Libr. Assn. (caucus chmn. 1976-77), Ga. Libr. Assn. (mem. com. chmn. 1992—, sec. 1993-94, parliamentarian 1997, 1st v.p. 1999, pres. 2000, bd. dirs. 2008), Metro Atlanta Libr. Assn. (v.p. 1997, pres. 1998), Southeastern Libr. Assn. (mem. com. 1988—, convention chair 2000, com. chair 2001—, Ga. bd. rep. 2008, v.p. 2009, pres. elect 2009-), ALA (con. spkr.), Atlanta Law Sch. Alumni Assn. (treas. 1986-90), Fla. State U. Alumni Assn. (life), Ga. Libr. Video Assn. (pres. 1991-92), Mensa (sec. 1987, 89, pres. Ga. chpt. 1988, mediator Ga. chpt. 2000-02, regional vice chmn. 2003-07, trustee Mensa Edn. and Rsch. Found. (v.p. 1993), Ga. Coun. Media Orgn. (chair steering com. 2000), Leadership Meriwether (pres. 1993), Smyrna Edn. Task Force. Office: 100 Village Green Cir SE Smyrna GA 30080-3478 Home: 192 Katrina Dr Powder Springs GA 30127 Office Phone: 770-431-2860. Personal E-mail: mjseigler@msn.com. Business E-Mail: mseigler@ci.smyrna.ga.us.

SEIGLER, RUTH QUEEN, college nursing administrator, educator, consultant; b. Conway, SC, July 31, 1942; d. Charles Isaac and Berneta Mae (Weaks) Queen; m. Rallie Marshall Seigler, Sept. 1, 1963; children: Rallie Marshall Jr., Scot Monroe. ADN, Lander Coll., 1962; BSN, U. S.C., 1964, M of Nursing, 1980. Pub. health nurse Richland County Health Dept., Columbia, SC, 1964—66; dir. nurses Columbia Area Mental Health Ctr., 1966—69; program nurse specialist Midlands Health Dist., 1969—72; discharge planner Richland Meml. Hosp., 1972—73, clin. dir., 1973—75; exec. dir. S.C. State Bd. Nursing, 1976—83; v.p. nursing dept. Self Meml. Hosp., Greenwood, SC, 1983—86; exec. dir. S.C. Commn. on Aging, Columbia, 1986—95; asst. dean Coll. Nursing U. S.C., Columbia, 1995—96, assoc. clin. prof., 1996—. Cons. intergenerational family studies, 1999—; dir. Cockcroft Leadership Program for Nurse Execs., 2002—, Ctr. for Nursing Leadership, 2004-05, sr. cons., 2005—; bd. dirs. Queen Gas Co., Barnwell, S.C.; nurse cons. Creative Nursing Mgmt., Mpls., 1984—. Advisor: The Role of Cmty. Mental Health Nurse, 1971. Moderator Trinity Presbytery, 2003—. Recipient Disting. Alumni award Lander Coll., 1978, Career Woman Recognition award Columbia YWCA, 1980, William S. Hall award S.C. Assn. Residential Care Homes, 1988, U. S.C. Coll. Nursing Disting. Alumni award, 1993, award for excellence S.C. League for Nursing, 1995, Svc. Recognition award S.C. AARP, 1995; named one of Ten Women of Achievement, S.C. March of Dimes, 1987, hon. fellow AVC Leadership, 2002, Excellence in Leadership award, 2004, Ordie P. Taylor Humanitarian award, 2005, Palmetto Gold award Top 100 Nurses in S.C., 2006. Mem. ANA, APHA, S.C. Nurses Assn. (sec. 1965-68, bd. dirs. 1986-88, Excellence award 1984, Recognition award 1984), S.C. Hosp. Assn., S.C. Gerontol. Soc., S.C. Nurses Found., S.C. Healthy People 2000 (vice chair), Partnership for Older South Carolinians (founder, chair bd. dirs.), Columbia Luncheon Club (pres. 1997-98), S.C. Fedn. Older Ams., Evening Mission Action Group, Bd. Nursing Home Examiners, Pilot Club, Inc. (pres. 1988-89, 97-98), Vols. of Am.-Carolinas (bd. dirs., chair, 1998-00, elder, 1999-01), Rotary Internat., Sigma Theta Tau, Beta Sigma Phi (pres. chpt. 1997-98). Presbyterian. Avocations: gardening, travel. Home: 6 Beaver Dam Ct Columbia SC 29223-3100 Office: U SC Coll Nursing Ctr Nursing Leadership Columbia SC 29208-0001

SEIL, FREDRICK JOHN, retired neuroscientist; b. Nove Sove, Yugoslavia, Nov. 9, 1933; s. Joseph and Theresa (Krieger) S.; m. Daryle Faith Wolfers, July 2, 1955; children: Jonathan Fredrick, Joel Philip Timothy. BA, Oberlin Coll., 1956; MD, Stanford U., 1960. Intern Kaiser Found. Hosp., San Francisco, 1960-61; resident in neurology Stanford U., Calif., 1961-64, fellow in neurology, 1964-66; staff neurologist VA Med. Ctr., Palo Alto, Calif., 1969-76, clin. investigator Portland, Oreg., 1976-79, staff neurologist, 1979-81, dir. VA office regeneration research programs, 1981—2001, ret., 2001. Asst. prof. neurology Stanford U., 1969-75, assoc. prof. neurology Oreg. Health and Sci. U., Portland, 1976-78, prof. neurology, 1978-2001, prof. cell and devel. biology, 1990-2001, prof. emeritus neurology, 2001—. Editor: Nerve, Organ and Tissue Regeneration: Research Perspectives, 1983, Neural Regeneration, 1987, 94, Current Issues in Neural Regeneration Rsch., 1988, Neural Regeneration and Transplantation, 1989, Advances in Neural Regeneration Research, 1990, Neural Injury and Regeneration, 1993, Multiple Sclerosis: Current Status of Research and Treatment, 1994, Neural

Regeneration, Reorganization, and Repair, 1997, Neural Plasticity and Regeneration, 2000; contbr. articles to profl. jours. Capt. US Army Med. Corps, 1966—68. Grantee VA, 1970-2001, NIH, 1986-95. Mem. Internat. Brain Rsch. Orgn., Internat. Soc. Develop. Neurosci., Am. Neurol. Assn., Am. Assn. Neuropathologists, Soc. Neurosci., Soc. Exptl. Neuropathology. Democrat. Achievements include founding of biennial International Symposium on Neural Regeneration; co-founding of biennial Asia Pacific Symposium on Neural Regeneration. Home: 1 Twain Ave Berkeley CA 94708 Personal E-mail: seilf@comcast.net.

SEILER, CHARLOTTE WOODY, retired education educator; b. Thorntown, Ind., Jan. 20, 1915; d. Clark and Lois Merle (Long) Woody; m. Wallace Urban Seiler, Oct. 10, 1942 (dec. Aug. 2002); children: Patricia Anne Seiler, Janet Alice Seiler Sawyer. AA, Ind. State U., 1933; AB, U. Mich., 1941; MA, Ctrl. Mich. U., 1968. Tchr. elem. schs., Whitestown, Ind., 1933-34, Thorntown, 1934-37, Kokomo, Ind., 1937-40, Ann Arbor, Mich., 1941-44, Willow Run, Mich., 1944-46; instr. English divsn. Delta Coll., University Center, Mich., 1964-69, asst. prof., 1969-77; ret., 1977. Organizer, dir. Delta Coll. Puppeteers, 1972—77. Mem. Friends of Grace A. Dow Meml. Libr., 1974-2000, treas., 1974-75, 77-79, corr. sec., 1975-77; leader Sr. Ctr. Humanities program Midland (Mich.) Sr. Ctr., 1977-94; vol. Quality Health Care, North Port, Fla., 2001—; leader Bridge Refresher Harbor Cove, North Port, 2002—. Fellow AAUW; mem. Mich. Libr. Assn., Harbor Cove Civic Assn., Pi Lambda Theta, Chi Omega. Presbyterian. Home: 3000 Aston Gardens Dr Unit 215 Venice FL 34292

SEILER, JACK P., Mayor, Ft. Lauderdale, Florida, prosecutor; b. Fort Collins, Colo., May 27, 1963; m. Susan Rimes; children: Marianna, Jacqueline, Preston, Susanne. BA in Bus. Adminstrn., U. Notre Dame, 1985; JD, U. Miami, 1988. Bar: DC 1988, Fla. Supreme Ct. 1988, US Dist. Ct. (so. Fla. dist.) 1989. Atty. Seiler, Sautter, Zaden, Rimes & Weihe; councilman City of Wilton Manors, Fla., 1993—96, vice mayor, 1996—98, mayor, 1998—2000; mem. Fla. House of Reps. from Dist. 92, Ft. Lauderdale, 2000—06; mayor City of Ft. Lauderdale, 2009—. Com. mem. Policy and Budget, Rules and Calendar, Constitution and Civil Law, Standards of Official Conduct, 2007—08; chmn. Broward Legislative Delegation, 2007—08; gen. counsel Promenade in the Park/Beaux Arts of Ft. Lauderdale Mus. Art, Inc.; guardian ad litem 17th Dist. Cir. Ct. Broward County. Former chmn. City of Wilton Manors Bd. of Adjustments and Appeals, Island City Found. Inc.; former mem. Wilton Manors Visioning Com. and Stakeholders Forum, Ft. Lauderdale High Sch. Pub. Affairs Cluster Adv. Bd., Waiver Review Com. Sch. Bd. of Broward County; mem. Orange Bowl Com., 1994—, Kids in Distress Broward Adv. Coun., Downtown Coun. Steering Com., Marine Industries of South Fla. Manatee Pub. Awareness Team, 2001—02; chmn. Orange Bowl Found.; bd. dirs. Brian Piccolo Chpt. Nat. Football Found. and Coll. Hall Fame Inc., 1988—; bd. dirs. Orange Bowl Com., 1999—; bd. trustees Ft. Lauderdale Mus. Discovery & Sci.; dir. PACE Ctr. for Girls; dir. & adv. Providence Pl. Shelter for Homeless Women and Children, 1998—; lector St. John the Bapt. Cath. Ch. Mem.: Wilton Manors Bus. Assn. (dir.), Broward County Bar Assn. (bench & bar com., chmn. lawyer referral com., profl. responsibility com.), Wilton Manors Elem. PTA, Notre Dame Club Greater Ft. Lauderdale (bd. dirs. 1989—98), Dem. Club (Pompano, Tri-Cities, North Broward, Pine Island & Ft. Lauderdale), St. Thomas More Soc. (bd. dirs.). Democrat. Roman Catholic. Avocations: coaching, golf, fishing. Office: 100 N Andrews Ave Fort Lauderdale FL 33301 Office Phone: 954-828-5000.*

SEIMS, LA RUE K., public health service officer; d. Beverly Burton Davis and Doris Muriel Richison. MA, Ind. U., Bloomington, 1977; MPH, Johns Hopkins U., Balt., 1994. Monitoring evaluation advisor CARE, Atlanta, 2000—01; program rsch. evaluation advisor Save Children, Washington, 2001—. Sch. health advisor WHO, Geneva, 1996—97. Vol. Palestine Human Rights Campaign, Chgo., 1980—83. Mem.: Mensa. Democrat. Achievements include design of introducing HIV/AIDS into the Bangladesh high school curricula. Avocations: swimming, scuba diving, travel, theater. Office: Save Children 2000 L St NW Washington DC 20036

SEINFELD, JERRY, comedian, actor, television producer, scriptwriter; b. Bklyn., Apr. 29, 1954; s. Kalman and Betty S.; m. Jessica Sklar, Dec. 25, 1999; children: Sascha, Julian, Shepherd Kellen Grad. with degree in theatre communications, Queens Coll., NY, 1976. Former salesman. Stand-up comedian, 1976—; joke-writer (TV series) Benson, ABC, 1980; actor, co-writer, prod. (TV series) Seinfeld, NBC-TV, 1990-97 (Emmy award Outstanding Comedy Series, 1993, Emmy nomination, Lead Actor - Comedy Series, 1994, Golden Globe winner, 1994, best actor comedy series), (TV movie) The Ratings Game, 1984, I'm Telling You for the Last Time, 1999; (TV specials) The Tommy Chong Roast, 1986, The Seinfeld Chronicles, 1989; (film) exec. prodr. Comedian, 2002, writer, actor A Uniorm Used to Mean Something, 2004, Hindsight is 20/20, 2004, actor The Thing About My Folks, 2005, writer, prodr., actor Bee Movie, (voice), 2007; writer Jerry Seinfeld-Stand-Up Confidential, 1987; author: Sein Language, 1993; guest appearances The Larry Sanders Show, 1992, News Radio, 1995. Recipient Am. Comedy award funniest male comedy stand-up, 1988, funniest actor in a TV series, 1992, 1993; Screen Actors Guild award, Outstanding Performance by an Ensemble in a Comedy Series, 1994, 1996, 1997; People's Choice award, Favorite TV Comedy Series, 1998; named one of The 100 Most Powerful Celebrities, Forbes.com, 2008 Jewish. Avocations: zen, yoga.

SEINFELD, JOHN HERSH, chemical engineering professor; b. Elmira, NY, Aug. 3, 1942; s. Ben B. and Minna (Johnson) S. BS, U. Rochester, 1964; PhD, Princeton U., 1967; DSc honoris causa, U. Patras, Greece, 2002, Carnegie Mellon U., 2002; DSc, Clarkson U., 2009. Asst. prof. chem. engring. Calif. Inst. Tech., Pasadena, 1967-70, assoc. prof., 1970-74, prof., 1974—, Louis E. Nohl prof., 1980—, exec. officer for chem. engring., 1973-90, chmn. engring. and applied sci. div., 1990-2000. Allan P. Colburn meml. lectr. U. Del., 1976; Camille and Henry Dreyfus Found. lectr. MIT, 1979; mem. coun. Gordon Rsch. Confs., 1980-83; Donald L. Katz lectr. U. Mich., 1981; Reilly lectr. U. Notre Dame, 1983; Dean's Disting. lectr. U. Rochester, 1985; Katz lectr. CUNY, 1985; McCabe lectr. N.C. State U., 1986; Lewis lectr. MIT, 1986; Union Carbide lectr. SUNY, Buffalo; Van Winkle lectr. U. Tex., 1988; Bicentennial lectr. La. State U., 1988; Ida Beam lectr. U. Iowa, 1989, David Mason lectr. Stanford U., 1989; Julian Smith lectr. Cornell U., 1990; Merck lectr. Rutgers U., 1991; Henske Disting. lectr. Yale U., 1991; lectr. AIChE, 1980; Centennial lectr. U. Pa., 1993; Miles Disting. lectr. U. Pitts., 1994; Kelly lectr. Purdue U., 1996; Disting. rsch. lectr. Carnegie Mellon U., 1998; Berkeley lectr. U. Calif., Berkeley, 1998; Sigma Xi lectr., 1998—, Merck Sharp & Dohme lectr. U. P.R., 1998; Hess lectr. U. Va., 1998; inaugural disting. lectr. U. Toledo, 1999; Priestley lectr. Commonwealth Sci. and Indsl. Rsch. Orgn., 2000; Amundson lectr. U. Houston, 2002, Hottel lectr. MIT, 2002, Lowrie lectr. Ohio State U., 2004; Fingerson/TSI lectr. U. Minn., 2004; Frontiers lectr. U. Conn., 2005; ICI disting. lectr. U. Alta., 2005; Mah lectr. Northwestern U., 2006; Holtz lectr. Johns Hopkins U., 2006, Quinn lectr. U. Penn., 2008, Friendlander lectr. UCLA, 2009. Author: Numerical Solution of Ordinary Differential Equations, 1971, Mathematical Methods in Chemical Engineering, Vol. III, Process Modeling, Estimation and Identification, 1974, Air Pollution: Physical and Chemical Fundamentals, 1975, Lectures in Atmospheric Chemistry, 1980, Atmospheric Chemistry and Physics of Air Pollution, 1986, Fundamentals of Air Pollution Engineering, 1988, Distributed Parameter Systems--Theory and Applications, 1989, Atmospheric Chemistry and Physics, 1998, 2nd edit., 2006; assoc. editor Environ. Sci., Tech., 1981-97; mem. editorial bd. Computers, Chem. Engring, 1974-96, Jour. Colloid and Interface Sci, 1978-95, Advances in Chem. Engring, 1980-03, Revs. in Chem. Engring, 1980—, Aerosol Sci. and Tech., 1981-93; assoc. editor: Atmospheric Environment, 1976—. Recipient Donald P. Eckman award Am. Automatic Control Coun., 1970, Pub. Svc. medal NASA, 1980, Disting. Alumnus award U. Rochester, 1989, Nev. medal Desert Rsch. Inst., 2001, Haagen-Smit Clean Air award Calif. Air Resources Bd., 2003, Haagen-Smit award, Atmos Environ., 2004; Camille and Henry Dreyfus Found. Tchr. Scholar grantee, 1972. Fellow AIChE (bd. dirs. 1988-91, mem. editl. bd. jours. 1985—, Allan P. Colburn award 1976, William H. Walker award 1986, Warren K. Lewis award 2000), NAE, AAAS, Japan Soc. Promotion Sci., Am. Geophysical Union; mem. Am. Soc. Engring. Edn. (Curtis W. McGraw Rsch. award 1976, George Westinghouse award 1987), Assn. Aerosol Rsch. (bd. dirs. 1983—, v.p. 1988-90, pres. 1990-92), Am. Acad. Arts and Scis., Am. Chem. Soc. (Svc. through Chemistry award 1988, Creative Advances in Environ. Sci. and Tech. award 1993), Internat. Aerosol Rsch. Assembly (Fuchs award 1998), Sigma Xi, Tau Beta Pi. Home: 4409 Beulah Dr La Canada CA 91011 Office: Calif Inst Tech Divsn Chemical and Chemical Engring 210-41 Pasadena CA 91125-0001 E-mail: seinfeld@caltech.edu.

SEIPEL, PETER, physical education educator, athletic director; b. St. Thomas, VI, Feb. 3, 1970; Degree in sports mgmt., St. Leo U., Fla., 1994. Phys. edn. tchr., athletic dir. Ivanna Eudora Kean HS, St. Thomas, 1996—. Mem.: AAHPERD, Nat. Interscholastic Athletic Adminstr. Assn., Am. Football Coaches Assn., Nat. HS Baseball Coaches Assn., US Golf Assn., Athletic Equipment Mgrs. Assn., Am. Fedn. Tchrs., Sigma Phi Epsilon. Home: PO Box 301914 St Thomas VI 00803 Office: Ivanna Eudora Kean HS 6501 Red Hook Plz Ste 3 St Thomas VI 00802 Office Fax: 340-779-1948. Personal E-mail: bigseip@hotmail.com.

SEIPLE, JOHN W., JR., corporate financial executive; b. July 20, 1958; married; 3 children. BA in Econs., Davidson Coll.; MBA, Tex. Christian U. With Interfirst Bank Dallas, N.A.; ptnr., sr. v.p. Trammell Crow Co.; v.p., market officer Prologis, Houston, 1993—94, sr. v.p., regional dir., 1994—97, mng. dir. S.E. region, 1997—99, COO, 1999, pres., chief investment officer N.Am. Denver, 2004—, chair N.Am. mgmt. com., chair N.Am. investment com., mem. Office of the Chmn.

SEITEL, ALAN LEWIS, speech pathology educator; b. Jersey City, June 24, 1947; s. Robert and Helen Seitel; m. Kathleen Ann Koop, Oct. 18, 1984; children: Bryce Reynolds, Abbey Jennelle. PhD, U. Tex., Austin, 1975. Cert. clin. competence Am. Speech-Language-Hearing Assn., 1971. Exec. dir. & ceo Ctr. Communication & Learning, Bangor, Maine, 1989—96; pres. Apex Speech & Rehab. Svcs., Brewer, 1999—2004; dir. rehab. svs. Sebasticook Valley Hosp., Pittsfield, Maine; chief clin. officer InSpeech, Tuscan, Ariz., 2004—06; assoc. prof. & program dir. Tex. A & M Internat. U., Laredo, Tex., 2007—. V.p., communication disorders Am. Assn. Mental Retardation, Washington, 1982—84; legislative counselor-me Am. Speech-Lang.-Hearing Assn., Rockville, Md., 1996—98; mem. chair Ariz. Speech-Lang.-Hearing Assn., Phoenix, 2005—06. Dir. United Way Penobscot Valley, Bangor, Maine, 1995—97. Fellow, Am. Assn. Mental Retardation, 1985. Achievements include research in disorders, dialects and differences in bilingual language learners. Avocations: bicycling, skiing. Home: 3020 Anejo Dr Laredo TX 78045 Office: Tesas A&M Internat Univ 5201 University Blvd Laredo TX 78041-1900

SEITMAN, JOHN MICHAEL, arbitrator, mediator, lawyer; b. Bloomington, Ill., Feb. 9, 1942; BS, U. Ill., 1964, JD, 1966. Bar: Calif., U.S. Dist. Ct. (so., ctrl., no. and ea. dists.) Calif., U.S. Ct. Appeals (9th cir.). Prin. Lindley, Lazar & Scales, San Diego, 1966-97; full-time neutral affiliated with JAMS, 1997—. Lectr. in continuing legal edn. Bd. dirs. San Diego County Bar Found., 1983-89, treas., 1983-84, pres., 1988-89; del. to 9th Cir. Jud. Conf., 1986, 88. Fellow Am. Bar Found.; mem. ABA, State Bar Calif. (pres. 1991-92), San Diego County Bar Assn. (pres. 1986). Office: PO Box 2156 Del Mar CA 92014-1456 Home Phone: 858-793-4426; Office Phone: 858-793-4555. Personal E-mail: jseitman@pacbell.net.

SEITTER, JULIE E., psychologist; b. Kans. City, Mo., Sept. 22, 1960; d. Paul E. Bower. BA in Psychology, U. Kans., Lawrence, 1982. Cert. edn. specialist U. Iowa Sch. Psychology, 1984. Psychologist Kans. Pub. Sch., 1984—90, Blue Valley Sch., Overland Pk., Kans., 1990—, dist. diversity coun., 2006—. Diversity coun. sponsor Blue Valley Northwest High Sch., Overland Pk., 2005—, cmty. svc. sponsor, 2005—. Organizer Ch. Resurrection, Leawood, Kans., 2004—08. Office: Blue Valley Northwest HS 13260 Switzer Rd Overland Park KS 66213 Office Fax: 913-681-7035. Business E-Mail: jseitter@bluevalleyk12.org.

SEITTER, KEITH L., professional society administrator, meteorologist; m. Julie Seitter. Grad. in Meteorology, Pa. State U.; D in Geophys. Scis., U. Chgo., 1982. Postdoctoral rschr. Air Force Geophys. Lab. Hanscom AFB, Bedford, Mass.; faculty mem. U. Lowell (now U. Mass. Lowell); asst. to exec. dir. Am. Meteorol. Soc., Boston, 1991, dep. exec. dir., 1999—2004, exec. dir., 2004—. Mem. adv. bd. Can. Inst. Sci. and Tech. Info. Contbr. articles to sci. jours. Fellow: Royal Meteorol. Soc., Am. Meteorol. Soc. Office: Am Meteorol Soc 45 Beacon St Boston MA 02108-3693 Office Phone: 617-227-2426 ext. 220. Office Fax: 617-742-8718. E-mail: kseitter@ametsoc.org.

SEITZ, KARL RAYMOND, editor; b. Corpus Christi, Tex., Sept. 26, 1943; s. Kerlin McCullough and Martha Elisabeth (Tillman) S.; m. Patricia Jean Floyd, June 13, 1970; 1 child, Lee Kerlin. BA, Birmingham So. Coll., 1970. Copy editor Birmingham (Ala.) Post-Herald, 1967-70, asst. news editor, 1970-73, chief editorial writer, 1973-78, editor editorial page, 1978—2005. Dir. Birmingham Post-Birmingham Typographical Union Pension Plan, 1983-90, chmn., 1986-90; v.p. Goodfellow Fund, Inc., Birmingham, 1986—2005. Active exec. in residence Birmingham So. Coll., 1987, Leadership Birmingham, 1986—, mem. mem.'s coun., 1998—2001. With USN, 1961—64. Mem. Nat. Conf. Editl. Writers, Acad. Polit. Sci. Home: 1212 30th Street S Birmingham AL 35205-1910 E-mail: kseitz@earthlink.net.

SEITZ, MARY LEE, mathematics professor; BS in Edn. summa cum laude, SUNY, Buffalo, 1977, MS in Edn., 1982. Cert. secondary tchr., N.Y. Prof. math. Erie C.C.-City Campus, Buffalo, 1982—. Reviewer profl. jours. and coll. textbooks. Vol. Buffalo (N.Y.) Philharmonic Orch. Mem. NY Maths. Assn. Two Yr. Colls., Assn. Maths. Tchrs. NY, NY Assn. Two Yr. Colls., Inc., Buffalo (N.Y.) Philharmonic Orch. Soc., Commerative AF, Pi Mu Epsilon. Avocations: gardening, photography, bird watching. Office: Erie C C-City Campus 121 Ellicott St Buffalo NY 14203-2601 E-mail: seitzm@ecc.edu. *Quotable quote from Alfred Lord Tennyson, "To strive, to seek, to find, and not to yield".*

SEITZ, NICHOLAS JOSEPH, editor, journalist; b. Topeka, Jan. 30, 1939; s. Frank Joseph and Lydia Natalie (Clerico) S.; m. Velma Jean Pfannenstiel, Sept. 12, 1959; children: Bradley Joseph, Gregory Joseph. BA, U. Okla., 1966. Sports editor Manhattan (Kans.) Mercury, 1960-62, Norman (Okla.) Transcript, 1962-64, Okla. Jour., Oklahoma City, 1964-67; staff Golf Digest mag., Norwalk, Conn., 1967—, editor, 1973-82; editorial dir. Golf Digest and Tennis, 1982-90; editorial dir. Sports/Leisure divsn. N.Y. Times Co. Mag. Group, 1991-92, sr. v.p., editor in chief, 1992-98, editor at large, 1999—. Syndicated golf instrn. and commentary CBS Radio Network; commentary ESPN TV Network. Author: Superstars of Golf, 1978; (with Dave Hill) Teed Off, 1977; (with Tom Watson) Getting Up and Down, 1983, Getting Back to Basics, 1991, Tom Watson's Strategic Golf, 1993; contbr. articles to profl. jours.; anthologized in: Best Sports Stories. Named Okla. Sports Writer of Year Nat. Sportswriters and Sportscasters Assn., 1965; winner contests Nat. Basketball Writers Assn.; winner contests Golf Writers Assn.; recipient Lincoln A. Werden award for outstanding contbn. to golf journalism, 1993, Meml. Tournament Golf Journalism award, 2000, PGA Lifetime Achievement in Journalism award, 2002, Major Achievement award The Masters, 2007. Home: 36 Hunt St Norwalk CT 06853-1015 Office: 20 Westport Rd Wilton CT 06897-0850 Personal E-mail: nseitz@optonline.net.

SEIVERS, LANA C., educational association administrator, former state official; b. Clinton, Tenn, 1951; BEd, Middle Tenn. State U.; MA in Ednl. Adminstrn., U. Tenn., D in Ednl. Leadership. Speech pathologist Spl Edn. Oak Ridge Sch. System, Tenn.; adminstr. early childhood and edn programs Oak Ridge Sch. System, prin. Linden Elem. Sch.; supt. Clinton City Schs., Tenn., 1989—2003; commr. Tenn. Dept. Edn., Nashville, 2003—08; exec. dir. Miss. Ctr. Edn. Innovation, Jackson, 2008—. Design cons. Inst. Sch. Leaders; mem. adv. coun. Edn of Childen with Disabilities. Mem.: Assn. Ind. and Mcpl. Schs. (bd. dirs.), Tenn. Orgn. Sch. Supts. (treas.), E. Tenn. Supts. Stidy Coun. (chair), So. Assn. Colls. and Schs. (chair). Office: Miss Ctr Edn Innovation 200 S Lamar St Jackson MS 39201 Office Phone: 601-354-3356.*

SEIWALD, ROBERT J., retired inventor; b. Ft. Morgan, Colo., Mar. 26, 1925; BS in Chemistry, U. San Francisco; PhD in Organic Chemistry, St. Louis U., 1954. Prof. organic chemistry U. San Francisco, 1957-89; ret., 1989. Served in WWII. Inducted Nat. Inventors Hall of Fame, 1995. Achievements include invention of first patented antibody labeling agent. Office: Nat Inventors Hall of Fame 221 S Broadway St Akron OH 44308-1505*

SEJNOWSKI, TERRENCE JOSEPH, science educator; b. Cleve., Aug. 13, 1947; s. Joseph Francis and Theresa (Cudnik) Sejnowski; m. Beatrice Alexandra Golomb, Mar. 24, 1990. BS, Case Western Res. U., 1968; PhD, Princeton U., 1978. Rsch. fellow Harvard Med. Sch., Boston, 1979-82; prof. biophysics Johns Hopkins U., Balt., 1982-90; prof. Salk Inst. U. Calif. San Diego, La Jolla, 1988—, dir. computational neurobiology tng. program, 2001—; Francis Crick prof. Salk Inst., 2005—. Investigator Howard Hughes Med. Inst., 1991—; bd. dirs. San Diego McDonnell-Pew Ctr. for Cognitive Neurosci., 1990-98, Inst. for Neural Computation, U. Calif. San Diego., 1990—. Editor-in-chief Neural Computation, 1989—; co-inventor: (with others) the Boltzmann machine and NET talk; mem. editl. bd. Sci. Mag., 1990—. Pres. Neural Info. Processing System Found. Recipient Presdl. Young Investigator award NSF, 1984, Wright prize Harvey Mudd Coll., 1996; Sherman Fairchild Disting. scholar Calif. Inst. Tech., 1993. Fellow IEEE (Neural Network Pioneer award 2002), AAAS, Soc. Neurosci.; mem. Inst. Medicine, Am. Phys. Soc. (sr. mem.), Internat. Neural Network Soc. (governing bd. 1988-92, Hebb prize 1999), Am. Math. Soc., Assn. Rsch. in Vision and Ophthalmology, Am. Assn. Artificial Intelligence, Biophys. Soc., Optical Soc. Am., Am. Psychol. Soc., Am. Psychol. Assn., N.Y. Acad. Scis., Fedn. Am. Soc. Exptl. Biophysics, Soc. Neuroscience, Internat. Soc. Neuroethology, Soc. Math. Biology, Johns Hopkins U. Soc. Scholars. Achievements include co-invention of the Boltzmann machine, of NETtalk, a neural network for text-to-speech. Office: Salk Inst PO Box 85800 San Diego CA 92186-5800 Home Phone: 858-587-0423. E-mail: sejnowski@salk.edu.

SEKERKA, ROBERT FLOYD, physics and mathematics professor; b. Wilkinsburg, Pa., Nov. 27, 1937; s. John Jacob and Vivian Mae (Smith) S.; m. Dianne Thompson, Apr. 30, 1960 (div. Apr. 1981), m.; children: Lee Ann Sekerka Loew, Robert Thompson; m. 2d Carolyn Lee Confer, Esqire, May 24, 1981. BS in Physics summa cum laude, U. Pitts., 1960; AM in Physics, Harvard U., Cambridge, Mass., 1961, PhD in Physics, 1965; PhD (hon.), U. Timisora, Romania, 1996. Technician, Dept. Metallurgy Westinghouse Rsch. Labs., Pitts., 1955—58, jr. engr., Crystallogenics, 1962—63, sr. scientist, Dept. Theoretical Physics, 1965—68, mgr. materials growth and properties Dept., 1969; jr. rsch. metall. engr. Carnegie Inst. Tech., Pitts., 1960—61; assoc. prof. metallurgy and materials sci., Carnegie Mellon U., Pitts., 1969—72, prof. metallurgy and materials sci., 1972—76, prof. and head Dept. Metall. Engring. and Materials Sci., 1976—82, u. prof. physics and math., 1991—, prof. physics and math. and dean, Mellon Coll. Sci., 1982—91. Mem. space studies bd. NRC, 1989-91. Assoc. editor Jour. Crystal Growth, 1971-94; Metallurgical Trans., 1970-76; editorial bd. Applied Microgravity Tech., 1987-90. Past bd. dirs. Forbes Health Sys., Pitts., Pitts. Regional Ctr. for Sci. Tchrs.; past vice chmn. bd. dirs. NMR Inst.; past mem. rsch. com. Allegheny Singer Rsch. Inst., Pitts. Recipient A.G. Worthing award U. Pitts., 1959, Philip M. McKenna Meml. award, 1980, Bruce Chalmers award TMS, 1998; Woodrow Wilson fellow, 1960, NSF fellow, 1962-65. Fellow: Am. Phys. Soc., Am. Soc. Metals, Japanese Soc. for Promotion of Sci.; mem.: Internat. Orgn. Crystal Growth (pres. 2001—07, Frank prize 1992), Am. Assn. Crystal Growth (mem. exec. com. 2007—), Minerals Metals Materials Soc., Edgewood Country Club, Sigma Xi, Phi Beta Kappa, Omicron Delta Kappa. Home: 307 S Dithridge St Atrium 911 Pittsburgh PA 15213-3519 Office: Carnegie Mellon Univ Dept Physics and Math 6416 Wean Hall Pittsburgh PA 15213-3890 Office Phone: 412-268-2362. Business E-Mail: sekerka@cmu.edu.

SEKOWSKI, CYNTHIA JEAN, health products executive, medical consultant; b. Chgo., Feb. 14, 1953; d. John L. and Celia L. (Matusiak) S. PhD in Health Svcs. Adminstrn., Columbia Pacific U., 1984, PhD in Health Scis., 1984; grad., Realtor Inst., 1998. Chief contact lens dept. Lieberman & Kraff, Chgo., 1974—87; pres., CEO Seko Eye Care, Inc., Chgo., 1988—; realtor Country Club Realty Group, Naples, Fla., 1995—2002, John R. Wood, Inc. Realtors, 2002—. Rschr., technologist U. Ill., Chgo., 1976-78. Active Chgo. Zool. Soc., 1984—, Little City Inner Cir., 1991—, Aurora Lakeland Med. Ctr. Found.; sponsor Save the Children Orgn., 1983—; asst. to campaign mgr. Rep. state senatorial candidate, Chgo., 1972; mem. Am. Mensa; pres. Compass Point Condo Assn., Naples, 1996-99; budget com. Windstar Country Club Master Homeowner's Assn., Naples, 1996-99; mem. ptnrs. coun. Habitat for Humanity, mem. Dem. Nat. Com. Fellow: Contact Lens Soc. Am.;

mem.: Winners Cir. Spl. Olympics, Women's Coun. Realtors, Naples Area Bd. Realtors, Nat. Assn. Realtors, Fla. Assn. Realtors, Nat. Contact Lens Examiners, Better Vision Inst., Opticians Assn. Am., Ill. Soc. Opticianry, Am. Fedn. Police and Concerned Citizens (sustaining mem.), Wis. Hist. Soc., Soc. of the Little Flower, Nat. Wildlife Fedn. (charter mem. Guardians of the Wild), SW Fla. Conservancy, Nat. Geog. Soc., US Golf Assn., Columbia Pacific U. Alumnae Assn., The Phoenix Soc. (med. profl.), Geneva Lakes Conservancy, Bear's Paw Country Club (mktg. com. 2002—), Vanderbilt Country Club (residents adv. bd. 1999—2001, vice-chmn. adminstrn. com. 2001—03). Roman Catholic. Avocations: gardening, reading, photography, golf, writing poetry. Office: John R Wood Inc Realtors 3255 Tamiami Trl N Naples FL 34103 Office Phone: 239-269-5000. E-mail: luvfla@mindspring.com.

SEKULA, DAVID JOSEPH, lab administrator, researcher; b. Bklyn., Sept. 26, 1966; s. Edward Joseph Sekula Jr. and Carol Lee Sekula; m. Gina Marie Sekula, Apr. 6, 2002; children: Nicholas, Tyler. BS, Lebanon Valley Coll., Annville, Pa., 1988. Lab asst. Princeton U., NJ, 1988—92, rsch. asst., lab. mgr., 1992—94; sr. rsch. asst., lab. mgr. Meml. Sloan Kettering Cancer Ctr., NYC, 1995—98; rsch. asst., lab. mgr. Dartmouth Med. Sch., Hanover, NH, 1998—2005, 2005—. Contbr. articles to peer reviewed jour. Leader Boy Scouts Am., Manchester, NH, 1998—, Denville, NJ, 1984—98. Recipient Eagle Scout, Boy Scouts Am., 1984, Silver Beaver, 1998. Mem.: Alpha Phi Omega, Nat. Eagle Scout Assn. Home: PO Box 1717 Grantham NH 03753 Office: Dartmouth Med Sch N Coll St Hanover NH 03755 Business E-Mail: david.sekula@dartmouth.edu.

SEKULER, ROBERT WILLIAM, science educator; b. Elizabeth, NJ, May 7, 1939; s. Sidney and Mary (Siegel) Sekuler; m. Susan Pamela Nemser, June 25, 1961; children: Stacia, Allison, Erica. AB, Brandeis U., 1960; MSc, Brown U., 1963, PhD, 1964; postgrad. (NIH postdoctoral fellow), MIT, 1964-65. Prof. psychology Northwestern U., Evanston, Ill., 1973-89, prof. ophthalmology Med. Sch., 1978-89, prof. neurobiology and physiology, 1982-89, John Evans prof. neuroscience, 1986-89, chmn. dept., 1975-79, assoc. dean Coll. Arts and Scis., 1985-89; v.p. Optronix, Inc., 1980-82; Louis and Frances Salvage prof. psychology Brandeis U., Waltham, Mass., 1989—, provost, dean faculty, 1989-91, dir. program cognitive scis., 1998—, chair program on neurosci., 2003—; mem. Ctr. Complex Sys., 1990—. Rsch. prof. biomed. engring. Boston U., 1992—2001, adj. prof. cognitive and neural sys., 1994—; vis. prof. psychology U. Toronto, 2000; cons. NSF, NIH, AAAS, USAF, U. Calif., APA, U. Pa.; chmn. vision com. NRC-NAS; chmn. working group on visual function and aging NRC, chmn. working group on aging workers and visual impairment; scientist Rotman Inst. Baycrest Geriatric Ctr., 2000. Author (with D. Kline and K. Dismukes): (book) Aging and Human Visual Function, 1981; author: Star Trek on the Brain, 1998, Star Trek on the Brain, paperback edit., 1999, Star Trek on the Brain, Japanese edit., 2000; author: (with R. Blake) Perception, 1985, Perception, Hungarian edit., 2000, Perception, 5th edit., 2005; editor: Perception & Psychophysics, 1971—86, Jour. Exptl. Psychology, 1973—74, Vision Rsch. Jour., 1974—79, 1980—92, Optics Letters, 1977—79, Am. Jour. Psychology, Ophthalmic and Physiol. Optics, 1986—99, Intelligent Sys., 1986—92, Psychology and Aging, 1987—92; co-author: Oxford Textbook of Geriatric Medicine, 1992, 1999, Ency. Psychology, 1999; contbr. articles to profl. jours. Grantee, Nat. inst. Neurol. Diseases and Stroke, USAF, NSF, Nat. Eye Inst., Nat. Inst. Aging, USN, James McDonnell Found., Alzheimer's Found. Fellow: AAAS, Am. Psychol. Soc., Optical Soc. Am.; mem.: Vision Sci. Soc., New Eng. Coll. Optometry (bd. trustee 2007—), New England Coll. Optometry, Knowles Inst. for Hearing Rsch. (bd. dirs. 1988—90), Psychonomic Soc., Neurosci. Soc., Assn. Rsch. in Vision and Ophthalmology, Sigma Xi. Home: 64 Strawberry Hill Rd Concord MA 01742-5502 Office: Brandeis Univ Volen Ctr Ctr for Complex Systems Waltham MA 02454

SEKULIC, DUSAN P., science and engineering educator, researcher; b. Novi Sad, Vojvodina, Yugoslavia, June 21, 1949; arrived in US, 1993; s. Petar and Djurdjinka Sekulic; m. Gorana Jesic, Dec. 17, 1949; children: Visnja, Aleksandar. B in Engring., U. Novi Sad, 1972, BS in Physics, 1976; MME, U. Belgrade, 1976, DSc, 1981. Cert. profl. mech. engr., Yugoslavia, 1973. Prof. U. Novi Sad, 1976—95; vis. rschr. Tech. U. Munich, 1977; vis. scholar Duke U., Durham, NC, 1988—89; vis. scientist MIT, Cambridge, Mass., 1989; vis. prof. U. Tenn., Knoxville, 1993, Marquette U., Milw., 1994—96; sr. rsch. scientist U Ky. Ctr. for Mfg., Lexington, 1997—; prof. U. Ky., Lexington, 2002—, dir. grad. studies, MFS program. Author: Fundamentals of Heat Exchanger Design, 2003; contbr. articles to profl. jours. Grantee Materials Sci. and Advanced Mfg., NSF, 1999—2003, Heat Exch. and Boundary Layer Phenomena, KFA-Julich, Germany, 1989—91, Ky. Sci. and Engring. Found., 2003—; Cryogenics Rsch. grant, Dept. of Energy, 1988—91, Sr. Fulbright scholar, 1988—89. Fellow: ASME; mem.: Soc. Natural Philosophy, Minerals, Metals and Materials Soc., Yugoslav Soc. Physicists, Mathematicians and Astronomers, Yugoslav Assn. Engrs., Am. Welding Soc. Avocations: rowing, scuba diving, skiing. Home: 1064 Albert Ln Lexington KY 40514 Office: Univ Ky 210 CRMS Bldg Lexington KY 40506 Business E-Mail: sekulicd@engr.uky.edu.

SEKULOW, JAY ALAN, lawyer; b. Bklyn., June 10, 1956; m. Pam Sekulow; 2 children. BA cum laude, Mercer U., Macon, Ga.; JD, Mercer U, Macon, Ga.; PhD in Am. Legal History, Regent U., Virginia Beach. Bar: Ga. 1980. Mem., lawyer Jews for Jesus; chief counsel Am. Ctr. for Law and Justice, Virginia Beach, 1990—, European Ctr. for Law and Justice, 1998—; host Jay Sekulow Live!. Adj. prof. law Regent U. Author: From Intimidation to Victory, 1990, Knowing Your Rights, 1993, Students Rights and the Public School, And Nothing But The Truth, 1996, Christian Rights in the Workplace, 1997; The Christian, The Court, and The Constitution, 2000. Bd. trustees Supreme Ct. Hist. Soc., Washington. Named one of 25 Most Influential Evangelicals in America, Time Mag., 2005, 100 Most Influential Lawyers in America, Nat. Law Journ., 1994, 1997, 45 Leading Pub. Sector Lawyers, Am. Lawyer mag., 1997. Office: Am Ctr for Law & Justice 1000 Regent Univ Dr Virginia Beach VA 23464-5037

SELA, MICHAEL, immunologist, chemist; b. Tomaszow, Poland, Mar. 6, 1924; arrived in Israel, 1941; s. Jakob and Roza (Aleskowski) Salomonowicz; m. Margalit Liebmann, June 20, 1948 (dec. Jan. 1975); children: Irit, Orlee; m. Sara Kika, Jan. 25, 1976; 1 child, Tamar. Grad., Ecole de Chimie, U. Geneva, 1947; MS, Hebrew U., Jerusalem, 1946, PhD in Biochemistry, 1954, D (hon.), 1995, U. Bordeaux II, 1985, Nat. Autonomous U. Mex., 1985, Tufts U., Mass., 1989, Colby Coll., Maine, 1989, U. Tel Aviv, 1999, Ben-Gurion U., Israel, 2001. Faculty Weizmann Inst. Sci., Rehovot, Israel, 1950—, chmn. dept. immunology, 1963-75, W. Garfield Weston prof. immunology, 1966—, v.p., 1970-71, dean faculty biology, 1970-73, bd. govs., 1970—, pres., 1975-85, dep. chmn. bd. govs., 1985—2005. Vis. scientist NIH, Bethesda, Md., 1956—57, 1960—61; vis. prof. molecular biology U. Calif., Berkeley, 1967—68; chmn. Coun. European Molecular Biology Orgn., 1975—79; pres. Internat. Union Immunol. Socs., 1977—80; chmn. sci. adv. com. European Molecular Biology Lab., 1978—81; spl. program rsch. & tng. tropical diseases WHO, 1979—81; staff dept. biology MIT, Cambridge, Mass., 1986—87; sci. adv. group experts Programme Vaccine Devel., 1987—92; adv. bd. Tables Rondes Roussel UCLAF, France, 1980—; mem. coun. Paul Ehrlich Found., Frankfurt, 1980—97; mem. intern guidance panel Israel Inst. Gifted Children, 1987; founding mem., bd. dirs. Internat. Found. Survival & Devel. Humanity, Moscow, Washington, 1988—92. Mem. editl. bd. numerous sci. pubs.; contbr. articles to profl. jours., chapters to books. Decorated Comdr.'s Cross Order of Merit Germany, 1986, officer l'Ordre de la Legion d'Honeur France, 1987; recipient Israel prize in natural scis., 1959, Rothschild prize in chemistry, 1968, Emil von Behring prize, Germany, 1973, Otto Warburg medal, German Soc. Biol. Chem., 1968, Gairdner Found. Internat. award, 1980, prix de l'Institut de la Vie, France, 1984, Albert Einstein Golden medal, UNESCO, 1995, Cabellero Order de San Carlos, 1997, Interbrew-Baillet Latour Health prize, Belgium, 1997, Wolf Found. prize in medicine, Israel, 1998; Fogarty Internat. scholar, 1973—74. Fellow: AAAS (hon. fgn.); mem.: NAS (assoc.; fgn.), Italian Acad. Sci. (fgn. assoc.), French Acad. Scis. (fgn.), Am. Philos. Soc. (fgn.), Internat. Coun. Scientific Unions, Pontifical Acad. Scis., Israel Acad. Scis. & Humanities, Max Planck Soc. (fgn., Harnack medal 1996), Acad. Medicine Mex. (hon.), Am. Acad. Arts & Scis. (hon.; fgn.), Romanian Acad. (hon.), Chilean Soc. Immunology (hon.), French Soc. Immunology (hon.), Am. Assn. Immunologists (hon.), Scandinavian Soc. Immunology (hon.), Am. Soc. Biol. Chemists (hon.). Office: Weizmann Inst Sci Wolfson Bldg 708 Box 26 Rehovot 76100 Israel Office Phone: 972 8 934 4022. E-mail: michael.sela@weizmann.ac.il.*

SELANDER, LARRY, lawyer; b. Chgo., May 28, 1946; BSChemE, U. Notre Dame, Ind., 1967; JD, U. Ill. Coll. Law, 1972. Bar: Ill. 1972. Formerly with Keck, Mahin & Cate, Chgo.; now ptnr. Duane Morris LLP, Chgo. Contbr. articles to profl. jours., chapters to books. Mem.: ABA, Chgo. Bar Assn., Ill. State Bar Assn. Office: Duane Morris LLP 190 S LaSalle St Ste 3700 Chicago IL 60603 Office Phone: 312-499-0147. Office Fax: 312-277-6954. Business E-Mail: LSelander@duanemorris.com.*

SELANDER, ROBERT WILLIAM, finance company executive; b. Oct. 9, 1950; s. Herbert Selander; m. Candice James, Jan. 31, 1981. BS, Cornell U., 1972; MBA, Harvard U., 1974; D in Internat. Bus. (hon.), Richmond The Am. U. in London, 2005. Mgmt. positions through dir. global retail strategy Citicorp., 1974—94; exec. v.p., pres. Europe, Middle East/Africa & Canada regions MasterCard Inc., 1994—97, pres., CEO, 1997—2009, CEO, 2009—; pres., CEO MasterCard Internat., 1997—. Bd. dirs. MasterCard Internat., 1997—, The Hartford Fin. Services Group, Inc., 1998—, MasterCard Inc., 2002—. Mem. Com. to Encourage Corp. Philanthropy. Office: MasterCard Inc 2000 Purchase St Purchase NY 10577*

SELANNE, TEEMU, professional hockey player; b. Helsinki, Finland, July 3, 1970; m. Sirpa Vuorinen; children: Eemil, Eetu, Leevi, Veera Johanna. Right wing Winnipeg Jets, 1992—95, Phoenix Coyotes, 1995—97, Anaheim Ducks (formerly Mighty Ducks of Anaheim), 1997—2001, 2005—07, 2008—, San Jose Sharks, 2001—03, Colo. Avalanche, 2004—05. Mem Finnish Nat. Olympic Team, 1992, 98, 2002, Finnish Nat. Team, World Cup of Hockey, 1996, 2004, Finnish Nat. Team, World Championships, 1996, 99. Recipient Calder Meml. Trophy, 1993, Maurice Richard Trophy, 1999, Bill Masterton Trophy, 2006; named World Championships Tournament MVP, 1999, NHL Rookie of Yr., Sporting News, 1993; named to All-Rookie Team, 1993, First All-Star Team, NHL, 1993, 1997, NHL All-Star Game, 1993, 1994, 1996—2000, 2002, 2003, 2007. Achievements include being a member of Stanley Cup Champion Anaheim Ducks, 2007. Office: Anaheim Ducks 2695 E Katella Ave Anaheim CA 92806-5904

SELBER, JESSE CREED, plastic surgeon, researcher; b. Phila., June 26, 1974; s. Gerald Selber and Judith Creed. MPH, Harvard, Boston, 2001; MD, U. Rochester Sch. Medicine, NY, 2002, Tex., 2008. Surgery house officer Hosp. U. Pa., Phila., 2003—08; microvascular fellow MD Anderson Cancer Ctr., Houston, 2008—. Contbr. scientific papers to publs. Office: MD Anderson Cancer Ctr 1400 Holcombe Blvd Houston TX 77030 Office Phone: 713-794-1247.

SELBY, CECILY CANNAN, dean, science educator; b. London, Feb. 4, 1927; d. Keith and Catherine Anne Cannan; m. Henry M. Selby, Aug. 11, 1951 (div. 1978); children: Norman, William, Russell; m. James Stacy Coles, Feb. 21, 1981. AB cum laude, Radcliffe Coll., 1946; PhD in Phys. Biology, MIT, 1950. Teaching asst. in biology MIT, 1948-49; adminstrv. head virus study sect. Sloan-Kettering Inst., NYC, 1949-50, asst. mem. instr., 1950-55; instr. microscopic anatomy Cornell U. Med. Coll., 1955-57; tchr. sci. Lenox Sch., NYC, 1957-58, headmistress, 1959-72; nat. exec. dir. Girl Scouts U.S.A., NYC, 1972-75; adv. com. Simmons Coll. Grad. Mgmt. Program, 1977-78; mem. Com. Corp. Support of Pvt. Univs., 1977-83; spl. asst. acad. planning N.C. Sch. Sci. and Math., 1979-80, dean acad. affairs, 1980-81, chmn. bd. advisors, 1981-84; prof. sci. edn. NYU Sch. Edn., 1985—92. Cons. U.S. Dept. Commerce, 1976-77; dir. Avon Products Inc., RCA, NBC, Loehmanns Inc., Nat. Edn. Corp., 1977-83, pres. Am. Energy Ind., 1976; co-chmn. commn. pre-coll. math. and sci. Nat. Sci. Bd., 1982-83; mem. policy steering com. Gov. Cuomo's Conf. on Sci. and Engring., 1989-90; co-chair Nat. Sci. Bd. Commn. on Pre-Coll. Sci., Math. and Tech., 1982-83; chair NY Acad. Sci. Conf. on Women in Sci. and Engring., 1998; affil. scholar Steinhardt Sch. Edn., NYU, 1993-, Radcliffe Inst., Harvard U., 2000-2001; trustee emeritus NY Hall Sci., 2006. Contbr. articles to profl. jours., chapters to books. Founder, chmn. NY Ind. Schs. Opportunity Project, 1968-72; mem. invitational workshops Aspen Inst., 1973, 75, 77, 79; bd. dir. RCA, NBC, 1973-86; trustee MIT, Bklyn. Law Sch., Radcliffe Coll., Woods Hole Oceanographic Instn., Women's Forum N.Y., NY Hall of Sci., 1982—, vice chmn., 1989—, trustee Girls Inc., 1992—, Nat. Coun. Women in Medicine, 1990-94; bd. dir. Avon Products, 1973-97; mem. Yale U. Peabody Mus. Adv. Coun., 1981-89; v.p. NY Hall Sci., 1986-99; chair NY Hall of Sci. Coun., 1999-; co-chair program in sci., soc. and gender Radcliffe Inst. of Harvard U., 1999-2001. Recipient Woman Scientist of Yr. award, N.Y. chpt. Am. Women in Sci., 1992, Alumnae Achievement award, Radcliffe Coll., 2001. Fellow: Am. Women Sci., NY Acad Scis.; mem.: Century Assn. Club, Woods Hole Golf Club, The Explorers Club, Cosmopolitan Club, Sigma Xi, Phi Delta Kappa. Home and Office: 1 E 66th St New York NY 10065-5854 Business E-Mail: selbyc@aol.com.

SELBY, CORA NORWOOD, retired elementary school educator; b. Nassau, Del., July 15, 1920; d. Clarence Paige and Martha Loretta (Maull) Norwood; m. Paul Myron Selby, Sr., May 26, 1945; children: Paul M.N., Clarence P.N., Clyde L.N., Clyde L.N., Adrian L.N., Terence P.N. BS in Elem. Edn., Del. State U., 1940; MS in Edn., U. Del., 1959, degree (hon.), 1987. Tchr. Ross Point 215-C, Laurel, Del., 1941—64, Paul Laurence Dunbar, Laurel, 1964—66, N. Laurel Sch., 1964—68, faculty adv. Head Start, 1968—80; adult educator Laurel Sch. Dist., 1968—2002, migrant specialist, 1980—87; ret., 2002. Mentor Read Aloud N. Laurel, 1998—; tchr. Elem. Start Program Lake Forest, 1993—2002. Bd. trustees Del. State U., Dover, Del., 1997—; pres. Laurel Sr. Ctr., 2000—; mem. Laurel C. of C.; bd. dirs. Laurel Gardens, 1999—. Mem.: Nat. Assn. Equal Opportunity Higher Edn., Retired Educators Assn., Delaware Assn. Adult and Continuing Edn. (life), Exchange Club, Phi Delta Kappa, Alpha Delta Kappa. Home: 34385 Whaleys Rd Laurel DE 19956

SELBY, DIANE RAY MILLER, retired fraternal organization administrator; b. Lorain, Ohio, Oct. 11, 1940; d. Dale Edward and Mildred (Ray) Miller; m. David Baxter Selby, Apr. 14, 1962; children: Elizabeth, Susan, Sarah. BS in Edn., Ohio State U., 1962. Sec. Kappa Kappa Gamma Frat., Columbus, Ohio, 1962-63, editor, 1972-86; tchr. Hilliard (Ohio) High Sch., 1963-65; exec. dir. Mortar Bd., Inc. Nat. Office, Columbus, Ohio, 1986—2007; ret., 2007. Editor The Key of Kappa Kappa Gamma Frat, 1972-86 (Student Life award, 1983, 84, 85). Founding officer Cmty. Coordinating Bd., Worthington, Ohio, 1983; pres. PTA Coun., Worthington, 1984, Worthington Band Boosters, 1985; sec., treas. Sports and Recreation Facilities Bd., Worthington, 1986-90; mem. sustaining com. Jr. League Columbus, 1991-93, docent Kelton House, 1979—; libr. fundraising com. Ohio State U. Mortar Bd. Alumni Coun., 2006-. Mem.: Assn. Coll. Honor Soc. (exec. com. 1999—2001, 2003—04, 2004—07, chmn. bylaws com., trustee 2004—07, v.p. 2005—06, pres. 2006—07), Mortar Bd., Inc. (hist. com., grad. fellowship 2007—08), Docent Kelton House, Jr. League Columbus, Mortar Bd. Alumni Columbus Chpt. (pres. 2007—09), Twig 53 Children's Hosp., Ladybugs and Buckeyes, Ohio State U. Retiree's Assn. (conf. co-chair 2007—08, benefit's com. 2007—), Worthington Women's Club, Kappa Kappa Gamma (house bd. v.p. 1997—2000, v.p. heritage museum guild 2007—). Republican. Lutheran. Home: 6750 Merwin Pl Columbus OH 43235-2838 Business E-Mail: selby.1@osu.edu.

SELBY, JEROME M., mayor; b. Wheatland, Wyo., Sept. 4, 1948; s. John Franklin and Claudia Meredith (Hudson) S.; m. Gloria Jean Nelson, June 14, 1969; children: Tyan, Cameronn, Kalen. BS in Math., Coll. Idaho, 1969, MA in Ednl. Adminstrn., 1974; MPA, Boise State U., 1978. Assoc. engr. Boeing Co., Seattle, 1969-71; dir. evaluation WICHE Mountain States Regional Med. Program, Boise, 1971-74; dir. rsch., evaluation Mountain States Health Corp., Boise, 1974-76, with health policy analysis and accountability, 1976-78; dir. health Kodiak (Alaska) Area Native Assn., 1978-83; mgr. Kodiak Island Borough, 1984-85, mayor, 1985-98, 2004—, mcpl. and fisheries cons., 1998—; regional dir. planning and devel. Providence Health System, 1998—2003. Propr. Kodiak Tax Svc., 1978—, Registered Guide, Kodiak, 1987—; cons. Nat. Cancer Inst., Washington, 1973-78, others. Contbr. articles to profl. jours. Treas. ARC, Kodiak, 1978-93, bd. dirs., 1978-95, chmn., 1989-90, mem. western ops. hdqrs. adv. bd., 1986-92, mem. group IV and V nat. adv. coj., 1986-89, nat. bd. govs., 1989-95, chmn. chpt. rels. com., 1994-95, mem. Alaska statewide chpt. bd. dirs., 2002—; pres. S.W. Alaska Mcpl. Conf., Anchorage, 1988-89, v.p., 1986-87, treas., 1996-98, bd. dirs., 1986-98; pres. Alaska Mcpl. League Investment Pool, Inc., 1992-98; v.p. Alaska Mcpl. League, 1988-90, pres., 1990-91, bd. dirs., 1988-98, 2004—; bd. dirs. Alaska Mcpl. League Jt. Ins. Assn. Bd., 1995—, v.p., 1996-98, pres., 1998-2000; mem. Coun. on Econ. Policy for Rural Alaska, 2006-07; mem. Alaska Resource Devel. Coun., 1987-2001, exec. com., 1989-2000; bd. dirs. Alaska State C. of C., 2000-07, exec. com., 2002-06; mem. policy com. of outer continental shelf adv. bd. US Dept. Interior, 1990-2004, vice chair, 1996-98, chair, 1998-2000; chmn. Natural Gas Subcom., 2000-01; co-chair Alaska Task Force, 1995-2004; mem. Com. on Oil Pollution Act, 1995; mem. Nat. Assn. Counties, Cmty. and Econ. Devel. Steering Com., 1990-98, Alaska govtl. roles task force, 1991-92; mem. Alaska state/local govt. task force, 1996-98; chmn. Kodiak Island Exxon Valdez Restoration Com., 1991-95; bd. dirs. Kodiak Health Care Found., 1992—, v.p. 1992—; co-chmn. Arctic Power, 1993-2005; bd. dirs. Western Interstate Region Nat. Assn. Counties, 1993-98, 2007-; bd. dirs. Alaska Oceans, Seas, Fisheries Rsch. Found., 1998-2005, pres., 1998-2005; mem. environment, energy and land use steering com. Nat. Assn. Counties, 1997-98; mem. grad. med. edn. com. Alaska Family Practice Residency, 2000-01; mem. Koniag Edn. Found., 2002-03; mem. Oiled Regions of Alaska, 2001—, pres., 2002—. Paul Harris fellow, 1987, 88, 91, 92, 96, 2005; recipient Outstanding Contbn. award Alaska Mcpl. League, 1994, Disting. Alumni award Albertson Coll. of Idaho, 1997, Lifetime Achievement award Alaska Mcpl. League, 1998, Mem. Yr., Kodiak C. of C., 2005. Mem. Alaska Conf. Mayors, Nat. Soc. Tax Profls., Acad. Polit. Sci., Alaska Mcpl. Mgrs. Assn., Kodiak C. of C. (dir. 1983-99, Mem. of Yr. 2005), Rotary (bd. dirs. 1989-97, 2004—, treas. 1989-93, v.p. 1993-94, pres.-elect 1994-95, pres. 1995-96, 2009-, v.p. 2007-08, pres. elect 2008-09, pres 2009-). Office: Kodiak Tax Svc 1120 Baranof St Kodiak AK 99615 Home Phone: 907-486-4833; Office Phone: 907-486-4833.

SELBY, JOHN BAYNE, SR., retired radiologist, medical educator; b. Cheyenne, Wyo., Feb. 17, 1924; s. John Edwin Selby and Caroline Lansdale Duckett; m. Jane Claire Dentry, June 11, 1950; children: John Bayne Jr., Henry Gordon, Rebecca Jane. BS, U. Tenn., 1948, MD, 1946; MS in Medicine, U. Minn., 1957. Diplomate Am. Bd. Internal Medicine, Am. Bd. Nuc. Medicine. Asst. in pathology Johns Hopkins U., Balt., 1950—51; intern Evanston (Ill.) Hosp., 1947—48; resident Garfield Hosp., Washington, 1948—50; fellow in pathology Johns Hopkins U., Balt., 1950—51, Mayo Clinic, Rochester, Minn., fellow in medicine, 1954—57, asst. staff mem., 1957; assoc. prof. medicine U. Ky., Lexington, 1958—75; chief nuc. medicine VA Hosp., Lexington, 1966—75, Charleston, SC, 1975—89; prof. radiology Med. U. SC, Charleston, 1995—2000, emeritus prof. radiology, 2001—. Mem. editl. bd. Clin. Nuc. Medicine, Phila., 1985—2005, Jour. SC Med. Assn., Columbia, 2000—06. Author: Self Assessment Nuclear Medicine, 1977, 1981, Mission in Space, 1994. Mem. Med. Discipline Commn., SC, 1985—88; pres. Ky. Diabetes Assn., Lexington, 1968—69; bd. dirs. Sch. Applied Radiol. Sci., Med. U. SC, Charleston, 1984—86. Capt. US Army, 1952—54, Korea, col. USAR, 1956—74. Fellow: ACP; mem.: Soc. Nuc. Medicine, Endocrine Soc., Alpha Omega Alpha. Avocation: tennis. Home: 2602 Atlantic Ave Sullivans Island SC 29482 Personal E-mail: selbysr2@aol.com.

SELBY, LELAND CLAY, lawyer; b. Granite City, Ill., July 4, 1944; s. William Edward and Agnes (Newell) Selby; m. Diane Schryver, Aug. 20, 1966; children: L. Clay, Timothy S., Amanda E. Henry. BA, U. Richmond, 1966; LLB, U. Va., 1969. Bar: Conn. 1969, NY 1989. Assoc. Hirschberg, Pettengill & Strong, Greenwich, Conn., 1969-74; ptnr. Hirschberg, Pettengill, Strong & Nagle, Greenwich, 1974-78, Whitman & Ransom, Greenwich, 1978-93, Whitman Breed Abbott & Morgan, Greenwich, 1993-95; mem. Fogarty Cohen Selby & Nemiroff LLC, Greenwich, 1995—. Chmn. bd. govs. Greenwich Found. for Cmty. Gifts, 1980—90; pres. United Way of Greenwich, 1978—80; co-pres. Greenwich chpt. English-Speaking Union, 2001—06; bd. dirs., v.p. Stamford Ctr. for Arts, Conn., 1989—2003, chmn. adv. coun., 2003—05; bd. dirs. Retirement Sys., Town of Greenwich, 1993—2001, Greenwich Symphony Orch., 1986—95; bd. dirs. exec. com. English-Speaking Union US, 2001—07. Named Greenwich Young Man of Yr., Greenwich Jaycees, 1974. Fellow Am. Coll. Trust and Estate Counsel; mem. ABA, Conn. Bar Assn., NY State Bar Assn., Greenwich Bar Assn., Preston Mountain Club (sec. 1999-04), Riverside Yacht Club, Indian Harbor Yacht Club (bd. dir.), Va. Club NYC, Harpoon Club of Greenwich.

Episcopalian. Avocations: fly fishing, sporting clays, hiking, reading, travel. Office: Fogarty Cohen Selby & Nemiroff 88 Field Point Rd Greenwich CT 06836-2508 Home: 303 W Lyon Farm Dr Greenwich CT 06831-4356

SELBY, ROBERT RICK, surgeon; Diplomate Am. Bd. Surgery, Calif. Chief USC Surgeons, La., 1995—. Office: USC Surgeons 1510 San Pablo St Ste 200 Los Angeles CA 90033 Office Phone: 323-442-5908. Office Fax: 323-442-5721. Business E-Mail: rselby@surgery.usc.edu.

SELBY, RONALD M., orthopedic surgeon; b. New Brunswick, NJ, Feb. 24, 1951; s. Raymond V. and Louise Selby; m. Rosemary Selby. AB, Rutgers U., 1973; postgrad., U. Vt., 1974; MD, Autonomous U. Guadalajara, Mex., 1979. Diplomate Am. Bd. Orthop. Surgery, Am. Bd. Forensic Medicine, cert. advanced shoulder arthroscopy. Intern Muhlenberg Hosp., Plainfield, NJ, 1979—80; resident in gen. surgery NY Med. Coll./Westchester County Med. Ctr. and Met. Hosp. Ctr., 1980—81; resident, chief resident in orthop. surgery St. Vincent's Hosp. and Med. Ctr. NY, 1981—84; James A. Dickson fellow in adult reconstructive surgery Cleve. Clinic Found., 1984—85; clin. asst. prof. orthop. surgery N.Y. Med. Coll., Valhalla, 1988—2008; attending dept. surgery divsn. orthop. surgery St. Peter's U. Hosp., New Brunswick, NJ; attending CARES Ambulatory Surgery Ctr., New Brunswick; attending dept. orthop. surgery Robert Wood Johnson U. Hosp., New Brunswick. Team physician N.Y.C. Marathon, Spl. Olympics World-Wide Games, NC, 1999; orthop. surgery team cons. St. Bartholomew's Pop Warner Football and Cheerleaders, 1992—; orthop. surgery cons. jr. divsn. U.S. Tennis Assn., 1998—; orthop. team cons. New Brunswick (NJ) H.S. Athletics, 1998—; instr. Coll. Medicine Drexel U., Phila., 2005—; orthop. cons. various athletic orgns. and teams.; presenter in field. Assoc. editor Arthroscopy: The Jour. Arthroscopic and Related Surgery, 2003—09; contbr. articles to profl. jours. Hon. co-chmn. physician's adv. bd. Nat. Congl. Com. Recipient Nat. Leadership award, Physician's Adv. Bd., Nat. Congl. Com., Order of Merit cum laude, Orthop. Rsch. and Edn. Found., Honors, Arthritis Found.; named Physician of Yr., Nat. Congl. Com.'s Physician's Adv. Bd., 2002; named one of Am.'s Top Surgeons, Consumer's Rsch. Coun. Am., 2002—09, Best Drs., Better Living Mag., 2002—03; named to Best Doctors, Better Living mag., 2002—03. Fellow: Royal Soc. Medicine, Am. Acad. Orthop. Surgeons (spkr. mgr. 2004, mem. comms. coun. 2005—, chmn. sports medicine/arthroscopy program subcom. 2005—, mem. ctrl. program subcoms. 2005—, mem. sports medicine evaluation subcom., chmn. subcom. arthroscopy and sports medicine), Am. Coll. Sports Medicine; mem.: Nat. Assn. Sports Physicians, Athletic Trainers' Soc. NJ, Irish Am. Orthop. Assn., Internat. Fedn. Sports Medicine, European Soc. Sports Traumatology, Knee Surgery and Arthoscopy, Nat. Athletic Trainer's Assn., Internat. Cartilage Repair Soc., Am. Med. Soc. Sports Medicine, Osteoarthritis Rsch. Soc. Internat., Internat. Soc. Arthroscopy, Knee Surgery and Orthop. Sports Medicine (mem. program com. 2005—07, mem. editl. bd. 2005—, chmn. comms. com. 2005—07, bd. dirs.), Am. Orthop. Soc. for Sports Medicine (mem. subcom. of edn. com.), Arthroscopy Assn. N.Am. (advisor comms. com. 2005—, presenter, bd. dirs., archives com., rsch. com, learning ctr. com., edn. com., Cert. for Dedication and Svc.), St. Vincent's Hosp. and Med. Ctr. NY Alumni Assn., Cleve. Clinic Found. Alumni Assn. Office: 330 Livingston Ave New Brunswick NJ 08901 Office Phone: 732-846-4900.

SELCEN, DUYGU, physician; d. Vural and Ayse Ozel Selcen. MD, Hacettepe U., Ankara, Turkey, 1988. Mayo found. scholar Mayo Clinic, Rochester, Minn., 2001—02, cons., 2002—. Recipient Best Oral Presentation award, World Muscle Soc., 2005, Pres.'s Young Myologist of Yr. prize, 2007. Mem.: World Muscle Soc., Soc. Neurosci., Child Neurology Soc., Am. Acad. Neurology. Achievements include research in mutations in myotilin causes myofibrillar myopathy pathology; mutations in Zasp causes adult onset muscular dystrophy; discovery of mutation in a BAG family of proteins causes severe childhood onset muscular dystrophy and cardiomyopathy. Office: Mayo Clinic 200 1st St SW Rochester MN 55905

SELCO, JODYE ISABEL, chemistry professor; b. LA, June 12, 1957; d. Marlow I. Selco and Letty Jo (Baron) Randell. PhD, Rice U., Houston, 1983. Asst. prof. Miss. State U., Starkville, 1985—87; asst. through prof. U. Redlands, Calif., 1987—2001; prof. Cal Poly Pomona, Calif., 2001—. Cons. Battelle, U.S. Army, Redstone Arsonal, Ala., 1986, 87, 89-92, Universal Energy Systems, USAF, Edwards AFB, Calif., 1988. Contbr. articles to profl. publs. Grantee Parson's Found., 1988, U. Redlands, 1988-93. Mem. AAUP, AAUW, Am. Women In Science, Am. Chem. Soc., Am. Phys. Soc., Coblenz Soc., Iota Sigma Pi. Office: CEEMaST Cal Poly Pomona 3801 W Temple Ave Pomona CA 91768 Business E-Mail: jiselco@csupomona.edu.

SELDEN, ANNIE, mathematics professor; b. Torrington, Conn., Feb. 1, 1938; d. Adolf Laurer and Annie (Wopperer) Anderson; m. Herbert Lloyd Alexander Jr., Oct. 7, 1961 (div. July 1970); children: Neil Brooks, Kim Anne; m. John Selden, May 24, 1974. BA, Oberlin Coll., 1959; MA, Yale U., 1962; PhD, Clarkson U., 1974. Instr. SUNY, Potsdam, 1969-71; sr. lectr. Bayero U., Kano, Nigeria, 1978-85; asst. prof. Hampden Sydney Coll., Va., 1973-74, Bosphorus U., Istanbul, Turkey, 1974-78, Tenn. Technol. U., Cookeville, 1985-90, assoc. prof., 1990—95, prof., 1995—2003, emerita, 2003—. Vis. scholar edn. in math., sci. and tech. U. Calif., Berkeley, 1993; sec.-treas. Math. Edn. Resources Co., 1994—; external examiner Fed. Advanced Tchrs. Coll., Katsina, Nigeria, 1979-82, Gumel, Nigeria, 1981-82; reader advanced placement calculus exams., 1990-92; vis. scholar Ctr. for Rsch. in Math. and Sci. Edn., San Diego State U., 1995-96; vis. prof. Ariz. State U., 1999-2000; adj. prof. N.Mex. State U., 2003—. Dept. editor: UME Trends: News and Reports on Undergrad. Math. Edn., 1989—96, MAA Online's Tchg. and Learning Sect., 1996—; mem. editl. bd. Jour. Computers in Math. and Sci. Teaching, 1992—96, Jour. for Rsch. in Math. Edn., 1997-2000; assoc. editor for tchg. and learning MAA Online, 1997—; assoc. editor Media Highlights sect. Coll. Math. Jour., 1994-2006; contbr. articles to profl. jours. Fulbright scholar, 1959—60, Woodrow Wilson fellow, 1960—61, NSF grad. trainee Clarkson U., 1972—73, NSF grantee, 1971, 1994—96. Fellow: AAAS; mem. AAUP (Tenn. Tech. chpt. sec. 1991-92, v.p. 1992-93, pres. 1994—95), Am. Math. Soc., Math. Assn. America(life)(dept. rep. 1986—2000, coord.-elect spl. interest group on rsch. in undergrad. math. edn. 1999-2000, coord. 2000-02, past coord. 2002-03, editl. bd. mem.), Assn. Women in Math. (Louise Hay award for contbns. to math. edn. 2002), Nat. Assn. Math., Am. Math. Assn. Two-Yr. Colls., Benjamin Banneker Assn., Nigerian Math. Soc. (organizer 5th ann. conf. 1984), Internat. Group for Psychology Math. Edn., Am. Edni. Rsch. Assn., Nat. Coun. Tchrs. Math., Rsch. Coun. for Math. Learning, Tenn. Acad. Sci., Women in Higher Edn. Tenn. (Tenn. Tech. chpt. pres. 1990-92, state 1st v.p. 1991-92, state pres. 1992-93), Women Organizing Women (treas. 1992-93), Am. Coun. Edn. (nat. indentification program for women com. 1992-93), Assn. for Sci. Study of Consciousness(life), Phi Beta Kappa, Sigma Xi, Pi Mu Epsilon, Kappa Mu Epsilon, Internat. Program Com. 19th Internat. Commn. Math. Instrn. Study Conf. (Taiwan). Office: NMex State U Dept Mathematical Scis PO Box 30001 Las Cruces NM 88003-0001 Business E-Mail: aselden@math.nmsu.edu.

SELDEN, ROBERT WENTWORTH, physicist, consultant; b. Phoenix, Aug. 11, 1936; s. Edward English and Mary Priscilla (Calder) S.; m. Mary Tania Hudd, June 1958 (div. 1976); 1 child, Ian Scott; m. Marjorie Anne Harmon, Feb. 20, 1977; children: Brock, Thane, Shawna, Kirsten. BA in Physics cum laude, Pomona Coll., 1958; MS in Physics, U. Wis., 1960, PhD in Physics, 1964. Rsch. assoc. Lawrence Livermore Nat. Lab., Calif., 1965—67, staff mem. Calif., 1967—73, group leader Calif., 1973—78, asst. assoc. dir., 1978—80; div. leader applied theoretical physics Los Alamos Nat. Lab., N.Mex., 1980—83, dep. assoc. dir. strategic def. rsch. N.Mex., 1983—84, assoc. dir. theoretical and computational physics, 1984—86, dir. Ctr. for Nat. Securities Studies, 1986—88, assoc. dir. for lab. devel., 1991—94; chief scientist USAF, Washington, 1988—91, panel chmn. sci. adv. bd., 1984-88, 91-96, 1991—96, 2002—05, chmn. sci. adv. bd., 1999—2002, mem., 2002—05; cons. Los Alamos, 1994—. Chmn. study group on reactor materials and nuclear explosives U.S. Dept. Energy, 1976-78; mem. ballistic missile def. techs. adv. panel U.S. Congress Office Tech. Assessment, 1984-85, The Pres.'s Defensive Tech. Study Team, Washington, 1983; strat. adv. group U.S. Strat. Command, 1996—, panel chair, 2003-; strat. adv. group jt. adv. com. Sec. Def., Sec. Energy, 1996—. Editor Rsch. Jour. Lawrence Livermore Nat. Lab., 1976-77; contbr. sci. and tech. papers to profl. jours. Pres. Livermore Cultural Arts Coun., 1969-72; chmn. Livermore Sister City Orgn., 1973, Planning Commn. City of Livermore, 1971-76; bd. dirs. Orch. of Santa Fe, 1986-88. Capt. U.S. Army, 1964-67. Grad. fellow Edward John Noble Found., 1958-62; recipient Theodore von Karman award for outstanding contbn. to def. sci., 1989, medal for outstanding pub. svc. U.S. Sec. Def., 1996; decorated for exceptional civilian svc. USAF, 1988, 91, 96, 2005. Mem. AAAS, Am. Phys. Soc., N.Y. Acad. Sci., Air Force Assn. Avocations: tennis, hiking, music. Office: 624 La Bajada Los Alamos NM 87544-3805 E-mail: selden@cybermesa.com.

SELDERS, JEAN E., retired psychology professor; b. La Junta, Colo., Nov. 6, 1942; d. Samuel Allen and Dorothy Jean Selders; m. Paul J. Fraker (div.); m. James R. Powell (div.). BA, U. No. Colo., 1964, MA, 1967; PhD, U. Denver, 1980. Cert. Colo. Dept. Edn., Colo. Soc. Sch. Psychologists, Nat. Assn. Sch. Psychologists, Nat. Cert. Sch. Psychologist. Spl. edn. tchr. Jefferson Co. Pub. Schs., Lakewood, Colo., 1964—65; elem. tchr. Mt. Calm Pub. Schs., Tex., 1965—66; spl. edn. tchr. Dept. Def. Overseas Schs., Tokyo, 1967—70, Cumberland County Schs., Fayetteville, NC, 1970—72; Ednl. diagnostician NC Dept. Pub. Health, 1972—78; sch. psychologist Littleton Pub. Schs., Littleton, Colo., 1980—2004; coll. instr. Arapahoe CC, 1990—2004; ret., 2005. Bd. dirs. Nat. Fragile X Found., Denver, 1988—92; pres., bd. dirs. Arapahoe Assn. Retarded Citizens, Littleton, 1980—88; state sec.,. bd. Colo. Soc. Sch. Psychologists, 1984—89. Vol. Opera Corado, Denver, 1980—, Central City Opera, Central City, 1980—. Recipient State Champion-Toastmistress, NC, 1976, Colo. Sch. Psychologist Yr., Colo. Soc. Sch. Psychologists, 1985. Mem.: APA, Arapahoe/Douglas Mental Health Assn., Colo. Soc. Sch. Psychologists (state bd. sec. 1980—85), Alpha Gamma Delta (rec. sec. 1963—64, panhellenic del. 1982—84). Republican. Lutheran. Avocations: travel, reading, theater, opera.

SELDES, MARIAN, actress; b. NYC, Aug. 23, 1928; d. Gilbert and Alice (Hall) S.; m. Julian Claman, Nov. 3, 1953 (div.); 1 child, Katharine; m. Garson Kanin, June 19, 1990 (dec. Mar. 1999). Grad., The Dalton Sch., NYC, 1945, Neighborhood Playhouse, 1947; DHL, Emerson Coll., 1979; DFA (hon.), Juilliard Sch., 2003. Faculty drama and dance divsn. Juilliard Sch. Lincoln Ctr., NYC, 1969-91; adj. faculty drama dept. Fordham U., 2003, 2005. Appeared with Cambridge (Mass.) Summer Theatre, 1945, Boston Summer Theatre, 1946, St. Michael's Playhouse, Winooski, Vt., 1947-48, Bermudiana Theatre, Hamilton, Bermuda, 1951, Elitch Gardens Theatre, Denver, 1953, The Cretan Woman, Lysistrata, 1955 (actress/artist-in residence Stanford U.), The Flowering Peach, L.A., 1956, Witness for the Prosecution, The Players' Ring, L.A., 1957; Broadway appearances include Medea, 1947, Crime and Punishment, 1948, That Lady, 1949, Tower Beyond Tragedy, 1950, The High Ground, 1951, Come of Age, 1952, Ondine, 1954, The Chalk Garden, 1955, The Wall, 1960, A Gift of Time, 1962, The Milk Train Doesn't Stop Here Any More, 1964, Tiny Alice, 1965, A Delicate Balance, 1967 (Tony award for best supporting actress), Before You Go, 1968, Father's Day, 1971 (Drama Desk award, Tony nomination), Mendicants of Evening (Martha Graham Co.), 1973, Equus, 1974-77, The Merchant, 1977, Deathtrap, 1978 (Tony nomination), Ivanov (Drama Desk nomination), 1997, Ring Round the Moon, 1999 (Tony nomination), 45 Seconds from Broadway, 2001 Dinner At Eight, 2003 (Tony nomination), Deuce, 2007; off-Broadway appearances include Diff'rent, 1961, The Ginger Man, 1963 (Obie award), All Women Are One, 1964, Juana LaLoca, 1965, Three Sisters, 1969, Am. Shakespeare Festival, Stratford, Conn., Mercy Street at Am. Place Theater, N.Y.C., 1969, Isadora Duncan, 1976 (Obie award), Other People, Berkshire Theatre Festival, 1969, The Celebration, Hedgerow Theater, Pa., 1971, Richard III, N.Y. Shakespeare Festival, 1983, Remember Me, Lakewood Theatre, Skowhegan, Maine, Painting Churches, 1983, 84 (Outer Critics Circle award 1984), Gertrude Stein and a Companion, White Barn Theatre, Westport, Conn., 1985, Lucille Lortel Theatre, N.Y.C., 1986, Richard II, N.Y. Shakespeare Festival, 1987, The Milk Train Doesn't Stop Here Anymore, WPA Theatre, N.Y.C., 1987, Happy Ending, Bristol (Pa.) Riverside Theatre, 1988, Annie 2 John F. Kennedy Ctr., Washington, 1989-90, Goodspeed Opera House, Chester, Conn., 1990, A Bright Room Called Day, N.Y. Shakespeare Festival, 1991, Three Tall Women, River Arts, Woodstock, N.Y., 1994, Another Time, Am. Jewish Theatre, 1993, Breaking the Code, Berkshire Theatre Festival, 1993, Three Tall Women, Vineyard Theatre, N.Y.C., 1994, Promenade Theatre, 1994-95, nat. tour, 1995-96, Boys From Syracuse, City Ctr., N.Y.C., 1997, Dead End: Williamstown, 1997, Dear Liar, Irish Repertory Theater, 1999, The Matchmaker: Williamstown, 1998, Tongue of a Bird, Mark Taper Forum, 1998, Sail Away, Carnegie Hall, 1999, Mad About The Boy, Carnegie Hall, 1999, The Torch-Bearers, 2000, Ancestral Voices, 2000, The Skin of our Teeth, 2000, Williamstown, The Play About the Baby, Alley Theatre, Houston, 2000, The Butterfly Collection, Playwrights Horizons, NY, 2000, The Play About the Baby, Century Ctr. Theatre, Helen, NY Shakespeare Festival, 2001, Play Yourself, N.Y. Theater Workshop, 2002, Beckett/Albee, Century Ctr. Theatre, N.Y.C., 2003, The Royal Family Ahmanson Theatre, L.A., 2004, Dedication or the Stuff of Dreams, Primary Stages, 2005; nat. tour Three Tall Women, 1995-96, La Fille du Regiment, Met. Opera, 2008; The Torch Bearers Williamstown, 2009, film appearances include The True Story of Jesse James, 1957, The Light in the Forest, 1958, The Greatest Story Ever Told, 1965, Gertrude Stein and a Companion, 1988, In a Pig's Eye, 1988, The Gun in Betty Lou's Handbag, 1992, Tom and Huck, 1995, Digging to China, 1997, Home Alone 3, 1997, Affliction, 1997, Celebrity, 1998, The Haunting, 1999, Town and Country, 1999, Duets, 1999, Hollywood Ending, 2002, Mona Lisa Smile, 2003, (documentary) Golden Age of Broadway, 2005, (narrator documentary) Ballet Russes, 2005, August Rush, 2006, The Visitor, 2007, (voice) The Toe Tactic, 2008, Home, 2008, Suburban Girl, 2008, Miriam, 2008, Leatherheads, 2008, The Extraman, 2009; (TV) Good and Evil, 1991, Murphy Brown, 1992, Truman, 1995, Cosby, 1996, 98, Trinity, Sex and the City, 1998, Remember WENN, 1999, The Others, 2000, If These Walls Could Talk 2, 2000, Nero Wolfe, 2001 (A&E), The Education of Max Bickford, 2002, American Masters PBS "Juilliard Documentary, 2003", Plainsong Hallmark Hall of Fame, 2004, (narrator) Tracking the Lion in Winter, 2004, Frasier, 2004, The Book of Daniel, 2005, In From the Night, 2006, Big Day, 2006, Law and Order SVU, 2006; also appearedon radio CBSMystery Theater, 1976-81, Theatre Guild on The Air; author: The Bright Lights, 1978, Time Together, 1981; appeared in soap operas One Life to Live, Guiding Light, 1998. Bd. dirs. Neighborhood Playhouse, The Acting Co., Nat. Repertory Theatre; bd. trustees Broadway Cares/Equity Fights Aids. Winner Ovation award Theater L.A. for Three Tall Women, 1996, Conn. Critics award for Three Tall Women, 1996, Theatre Hall of Fame, 1996, Players Hall of Fame, 2008; recipient Madge Kennedy/Sidney Kingsley award Dramatists Guild Fund, 2000, Obie award for sustained achievement, Lucille Lortel award for Sustained Achievement, 2003, Edwin Booth award, Players Club, 2003, Lifetime Mem. award Theatre Libr. Assn., 2003, Breukelein Inst. Gaudium award, 2003, Julliard Sch. medal svc. to arts, 2005, Drama League award sustained achievement, 2006, Dutch Treat Gold medal award, 2006, Rebekah Koht award Nat. Coun. Jewish Women, 2006. Mem. Players Club, Women's City Club, Century Assn. Home: 210 Central Park S Apt 19D New York NY 10019-1426

SELDNER, BETTY JANE, environmental engineer, aerospace transportation executive, consultant; b. Balt., Dec. 11, 1923; d. David D. and Miriam M. (Mendes) Miller; m. Warren E. Gray, June 20, 1945 (div. 1965); children: Patricia, Deborah; m. Alvin Seldner, Nov. 15, 1965; children: Jack, Barbara. BA in Journalism, Calif. State U., Northridge, 1975, MA in Communications, 1977. Dir. pub. info. United Way, Van Nuys, Calif., 1958-63, dir. edn. Los Angeles, 1963-68; dir. pub. relations, fin. San Fernando Valley Girl Scout Council, Reseda, Calif., 1968-73; asst. dir. pub. info. Calif. State U., Northridge, 1973-75; dir. environ. mgmt. HR Textron Corp., Valencia, Calif., 1975-87; environ. engr. Northrop Aircraft, Hawthorne, Calif., 1987-88, EMCON Assocs., Burbank, Calif., 1988-92, Atkins Environ., 1992-93, Seldner Environ., Valencia, Calif., 1993—; pres. Seldner Environ. Svcs., 1993—. Author non-fiction. Named Woman of Yr., Santa City C. of C. and vol. orgns., 2000. Mem. Santa Clarita Valley Environ. Mgrs. Soc. (chmn. bd. dirs. 1984), San Fernando Valley Round Table (pres. 1971-72), Hazardous Materials Mgrs.' Assn., Zonta Internat., Valencia Indsl. Assn. (environ. chair). Republican. Jewish. Avocation: sailing. Office Phone: 661-255-6427. Personal E-mail: Betty13ix@ca.rr.com.

SELECKY, MARY C., state agency administrator; BA, Univ. Pa. Adminstr. NE Tri-County Health District, Colville, Wash., 1979—99; sec. Wash. Dept. Health, Olympia, 1999—. Mem.: Assn. State & Territorial Health Officials (past pres., McCormack award 2004), Nat. Assn. City & County Health Officials (bd. dir.), Wash. State Assn. Local Public Health Officials (past pres.). Office: Dept Health 101 Israel Rd SE Olympia WA 98501*

SELEEM, SUZANNE, chemistry professor; PhD, U. West London, 1992. Lectr. Yale U., New Haven, 1999—2001; assoc. prof. Ctrl. State U., Wilberforce, Ohio, 2004—. Fellow: RCS; mem.: Rotary Club (fgn. projects coord. 2006, bd. mem. 2001—08). Liberal. Avocations: travel, reading. Home: 2420 Shafor Blvd Dayton OH 45419 Office: Ctrl State Univ 1400 Brush Row Rd Wilberforce OH 45384 Personal E-mail: sseleem1@aol.com. Business E-Mail: sseleem@centralstate.edu.

SELELYO, PAT, biology professor; m. William E. Selelyo, Oct. 28, 1978. MS in Entomology and Applied Ecology, U. Del., Newark, 1974. Rsch. tech. U. Idaho, Kimberly, 1980—89; prof. Coll. Southern Idaho, Twin Falls, 1989—. Recipient Tchg. Excellence award, Coll. Southern Idaho, 1993—94. Office: Coll Southern Idaho Biology Dept 315 Falls Ave Twin Falls ID 83301

SELES, MONICA, retired professional tennis player; b. Novi Sad, Yugoslavia, Dec. 2, 1973; arrived in US, 1996; d. Karolj and Esther Seles. Profl. tennis player, 1989—2008. Mem. U.S. Fed Cup Team, 1996, 99, 2000, WTA Tour Players' Coun., 1998—99. Co-author (with Nancy Ann Richardson): Monica: From Fear to Victory, 1996; author: Getting a Grip, 2009; performer: (TV series) Dancing with the Stars, 2008. Active Spl. Olympics. Recipient Ted Tinling Diamond Award, 1990, Rado Topspin Award, 1990, Comeback Player of Yr. Award, WTA Tour, 1995, 1998, Committment to Cmty. Award, Fla. Times-Union, 1999, Flo Hyman Meml. Award, Women's Sports Found., 2000, Sanex Hero of Yr. Award, WTA Tour, 2002; named Sportswoman of Yr., Yugoslavia, 1985, Female Rookie of Yr., TENNIS Mag./Rolex Watch, 1989, Most Improved Player, WTA Tour, 1990, Player of Yr., 1991, Female Athlete of Yr., AP, 1991, 1992, Comeback Player of Yr., TENNIS Mag., 1995, Female Pro Athlete of Yr., Fla. Sports Hall of Fame, 1998, Player Who Makes a Difference, Family Circle Cup, 1999. Achievements include 3rd player in the Open-era to capture the Australian and Roland Garros in same calendar year; World #1 ranked player, 1991, 92, 95; youngest #1 ranked player in tennis history for women and men at 17 years, 3 months, 9 days; Winner Grand Slam titles: Roland Garros, 1990, 91, 92, French Open, 1990, 91, 92, U.S. Open, 1991, 92, Australian Open, 1991, 92, 93, 96; Winner 53 Career Singles Titles and 6 Career Doubles Titles, WTA Tour. Office: c/o Internat Mgmt Group 1 Erieview Plz Cleveland OH 44114-1715

SELETZ, JULES M., surgeon; b. Chgo., 1930; BA in Biology, Va. Mil. Inst., 1953; MD, U. Health Scis., Chgo., 1958. Diplomate Am. Bd. Surgery, FACS. Intern, then resident in gen. surgery Boston City Hosp., 1958-63, mem. staff, 1963-74; mem. faculty Sch. Medicine Tufts U., 1963-82; mem. staff Newton Wesleslev Hosp., 1963-82; mil. surgeon U.S. Army, 1982-94; mem. staff Keller Army Cmty. Hosp., West Point, N.Y., 1990-94; physician surveyor Joint Com. Accreditation Healthcare Orgn., 1994-01. Author mystery/med. thriller novels and hist. fiction. Home: PO Box 1087 Lincoln NH 03251-1087 Office Phone: 781-631-4317. E-mail: jseletz@earthlink.net.

SELEZNEV, VADIM EUGENJEVICH, mathematician, researcher; b. Orel, Russia, June 24, 1962; s. Eugeny Mihaylovich Seleznev and Nina Petrovna Selezneva; 1 child, Jana Vadimovna Selezneva. MD in Aircraft Constrn., Aviation Inst., Kharkov, Ukraine, 1985; PhD in Computational Mechanics, All Russian Sci. Rsch. Inst. Exptl. Physics, Sarov, 1991; DSc in Computational Mechanics, Moscow Power Engring. Inst., 2003. Cert. prof., Russia, 2006. Head of dept. Russian Fed. Nuc. Ctr., All-Russian Sci. Rsch. Inst. Exptl. Physics, Sarov, Nizhny Novgorod Region, 1996—2000, sr. sci. rschr., 1992—95, dep. chief designer, 2001—05, mathematician, 1985—91; head ctr. Sci. Prodn. Enterprise All-Russian Sci. Rsch. Inst. Exptl. Physics, Sarov, Computational Mechanics Tech. Ctr., 2001—05; first dep. dir. Joint Stock Co. Phys. and Tech. Ctr., Sarov, 2006—. Author: (book) Numerical Simulation of Gas Pipline Networks: Theory Computational Implementation and Industrial Applications., 2005, Mathematical Simulation of Pipeline Networks and Open Channel Systems: Methods, Models and Algorithms, 2007, Modern Computer Training Systems in Pipeline Transmission, 2007, Mathematical Simulation of Trunk Pipeline Networks: Supplementary Notes, 2009, Fundamentals of Numerical Simulation of Trunk Pipeline Networks: 2nd edit. rev. & expanded, 2009. Grantee Grant, Gov. Nizhny Novgorod Region, 1996. Mem.: Nuc. Engring. Assn. (assoc.). Conservative. Russian Orthodox. Achievements include development of pipeline integrity management system ALFARGUS; AMADEUS software for high accuracy numerical estimation and optimization of natural gas transmission. Avocation: travel. Office Fax: 7 (83130) 7-44-37. Business E-Mail: sve@ptc.sar.ru.

SELF, BILL, men's college basketball coach; b. Okmulgee, Okla., Dec. 27, 1962; m. Cindy Self; children: Lauren, Tyler. BSBA, Okla. State U., 1985, M in Athletic Adminstrn., 1989. Asst. coach U. Kans., 1985-86, head coach, 2003—; asst. coach Okla. State U., 1986-93; head coach Oral Roberts U., 1993-97, U. Tulsa, 1997—2000, U. Ill. Champaign-Urbana, 2000—03. Mem. competition com. USA Men's Basketball, 2005—; bd. mem. Nat. Assn. Basketball Coaches. Finalist Naismith Coach of Yr. award 2000, 01, 02, 03; named Don Haskins Coach of Yr., Western Athletic Conf., 2000, John and Nellie Wooden Coach of Yr., Utah Tipoff Club, 2000, Nat. Coach of Yr., The Sporting News, 2000, 2009, AP, 2009; Big 12 Coach of Yr., 2006, 2009; recipient Henry Iba award USBWA, 2009. Achievements include coaching the Univeristy of Tulsa to Western Athletic Conference regular season championship, 1999, 2000; coaching the University of Illinois to Big Ten regular season championship, 2001, 2002; coaching the University of Kansas to Big 12 regular season championship, 2005-09; head coach of the NCAA Men's Basketball National Championship winning University of Kansas Jayhawks, 2008. Office: Univ Kans Men's Basketball Allen Fieldhouse 1651 Naismith Dr Lawrence KS 66045 Office Phone: 785-864-7929.*

SELF, BRIAN P, engineering educator; b. Lynchburg, Va., Mar. 15, 1966; s. Samuel and Betsy Self; m. Eileen Joseph. BS in Engrng. Sci. & Mechanics, Va. Poly. Inst. & State U., Blacksburg, 1988, MS in Engrng. Mechanics, 1991; PhD in Bioengring., U. Utah, Salt Lake City, 1996. Rsch. engr. Air Force Rsch. Labs., San Antonio, 1996—99; prof. USAF Acad., Colorado Springs, Calif., 1999—2006; assoc. prof. Calif. Poly. State U., San Luis Obispo, Calif., 2006—. Contbr. articles to profl. jours. Vol. Big Brother-Big Sister, San Antonio, 1997—2003. Grantee grant, NSF, 2008—. Mem.: Aerospace Med. Assn. (Outstanding Aerospace Physiology Rschr. Paul A. Bert award 2006), Am. Soc. Engrng. Edn. (zone iv chair, sect. chair, mechanics divsn. treas. 2001—, bd. dirs. 2008—, Jr. Outstanding New Mechanics Educator award 2002, Mechanics Divsn. Best Paper award 2005), Tau Beta Pi. Office: Calif Poly State Univ 1 Grand Ave Mech Engrng Dept San Luis Obispo CA 93407-0358

SELFE, EDWARD MILTON, lawyer; b. St. Paul, Sept. 26, 1921; s. Edward Milton and Eleanor (Moen) S.; m. Rena Hill McMurry, July 10, 1950 (div. Oct. 1979); children: Murry, Edward, James; m. Jane Comer Bowron, Dec. 31, 1979. BA, Presbyn. Coll., Clinton, SC, 1943; LLB, U. Va., 1950. Bar: N.Y., Va., Ala. Asst. prof. law Law Sch., U. Va., Charlottesville, 1950-51; assoc. Shearman & Sterling, NYC, 1951-52, Bradley Arant Rose White, Birmingham, Ala., 1952-57, ptnr., 1957-2000, of counsel, 2000—; vice chmn. Secor Bank, Birmingham, 1988-91, gen. counsel, 1991-93. Lectr. Law Sch., U. Ala., Tuscaloosa, 1968—90. Chmn. Birmingham-Jefferson County Transit Authority, 1972-82. Served to capt., inf. U.S. Army, 1943-47, ETO. Decorated Silver Star, Bronze Star (V) with oak leaf cluster, Purple Heart. Fellow Am. Coll. Tax Counsel; mem. ABA, Ala. Bar Assn., Birmingham Bar Assn. Democrat. Avocation: tennis (ranked 5th nationally by USTA in men's singles-age 85). Home: 84 Arlington Crest 2600 Arlington Ave S Birmingham AL 35205-4167 Office: Bradley Arant Boult Cummings LLP One Federal Pl 1819 Fifth Ave N Birmingham AL 35203-2119 Office Phone: 205-521-8280. Business E-Mail: eselfe@bradleyarant.com.

SELFE, TERRY KIT, medical researcher; d. Robert Ross and Shirley Jean Selfe. D in Chiropractic, Palmer Coll. Chiropractic, Davenport, Iowa, 1988; MSLS, U. Ky., Lexington, 1995; PhD, U. Va., Charlottesville, 2007. Cert. clin. rsch. profl. Soc. Clin. Rsch. Assocs., 2009. Reference libr. Life U., Marietta, Ga., 1996—97, asst. libr. dir., 1997—98, dir. libr. svcs., 1998—2004; rsch. scientist U. Va., 2007—, postdoc. fellow, 2004—07. Contbr. articles tp profl. jours. Recipient Oscar & Ruth Lanford Meml. award, U. Va., Valedictorian, Palmer Coll. Chiropractic; fellowship, NIH. Fellow: Internat. Acad. Med. Acupuncture; mem.: Soc. Clin. Rsch. Assocs., Beta Phi Mu, Pi Tau Delta. Office: Univ Va 202 Jeanette Lancaster Way Charlottesville VA 22903

SELFRIDGE, GEORGE DEVER, retired dentist, retired military officer; b. Pitman, NJ, Sept. 24, 1924; s. William John and Edith (Gorman) S.; m. Ruth Motisher, 1948; children: Pamela Ruth, Kimberly Dawn, Cheryl Beth. Student, Gettysburg Coll., 1942-43, Muhlenburg Coll., 1943-45; DDS, U. Buffalo, 1947; MA, George Washington U., 1974. Commd. lt. (j.g.) USN, 1948, advanced through grades to rear adm., 1973; intern Naval Dental Sch., Bethesda, Md., 1948-49, Naval Hosp., St. Albans, NY, 1949-50; asst. dental officer U.S.S. Midway, 1949-51; with USN, 1951-64; sr. dental officer U.S.S. Randolph, 1958-60, U.S.S. Cadmus, 1964-65, U.S.S. Vulcan, 1965-66, Svc. Force, 1964-66, Submarine Force, Atlantic Fleet, 1967-69; from asst. dir. grad. edn. to comdg. officer Navy Grad. Dental Sch., Bethesda, 1969-76; exec. officer Norfolk (Va.) Navy Dental Clinic, 1972-73; ret. USN, 1976; dean Dental Sch., Washington U., St. Louis, 1976-86; dir. dental services Barnes Hosp., St. Louis, 1976—87, Children's Hosp., St. Louis, 1976-87; exec. dir. Am. Bd. Orthodontics, 1986-97; ret., 1998. Adv. bd. VA Hosp., St. Louis, 1977-79; mem. exec. coun. Cen. Region Testing Svc., 1976-86; adv. com. St. Louis Jr. Coll. Dist., 1976-86. Contbr. articles to med. jours. Decorated Legion of Merit; recipient commendation medals, Greater St. Louis Gold Medallion award, 1995, Spl. Recognition award Am. Bd. Orthopedics, 1996. Mem. ADA, Am. Coll. Dentists (past pres.), Internat. Coll. Coll. Dentists (dep. registrar, sec. U.S. sect., Spl. Recognition award), Assn. Mil. Surgeons U.S., Omicron Kappa Upsilon. Republican. Home: 14545 Foxham Ct Chesterfield MO 63017-5620

SELFRIDGE-FIELD, ELEANOR, educator; b. New Orleans, June 29, 1940; BA magna cum laude, Drew U., 1962; MSc, Columbia U., 1963; PhD, Oxford U., Eng., 1969. Tchr. musical info. and representation U. Pitts., Drew U.; with CCARH Stanford (Calif.) U., 1984—, cons. prof., 1995—. Cons. in field; mem. adv. bd., tech. com. IEEE Coumpter Soc.; mem. tech. com. Am. Musicological Soc.; co-chair Internat. Musicological Soc. Author: Venetian Instrumental Music, 1974, 80, 94, Pallade Veneta, 1985, The Music of B. and A. Marcell, 1990, Beyond MIDI, 1997, Song and Season:Science,Culture and Theatrical Time in Early Modern Venice and numerous others; co-editor: Computing in Musicology, 1985-00; editor: Melodic Similarity: Concepts, Procedures, and Applications (Computing in Misicology 11), 1998; contbr. numerous articles to profl. jours. Co-founder, adv. bd. mem. Humanities West, San Francisco; U.S. Rep. Instituto Internazionale A. Vivaldi (Venice). Office: CCARH Stanford U Braun #128 Stanford CA 94305-3076 Office Phone: 650-725-9242.

SELI, EMRE UTKU, reproductive endocrinology and infertility specialist, physician researcher; s. Kemal Ali Seli and Ayla Zeliha Hungen; m. Meltem Solak, Dec. 10, 1994; children: Devin Murat, Denis Aydin. MD, Istanbul U., Turkey, 1984—92. Postdoctoral rsch. fellow dept. ob-gyn. Divsn. Reproductive Endocrinology and Infertility, Yale U. Sch. Medicine, New Haven, 1995—97, resident dept. ob-gyn., 1997—2001, instr. and fellow dept. ob-gyn., 2001—04, asst. prof. dept. ob-gyn. Contbr. articles to profl. jours. Recipient Outstanding Laparoendoscopic Surgeon Award, Soc. Laparoendoscopic Surgeons, 2001; grantee, Am. Coll. Obstetrics and Gynecology, 1999, 2000, N.Am. Menopause Soc., 1999, 2000, NIH, 2004—. Achievements include discovery of a mammalian embryonic polyA binding protein that regulates gene expression during mammalian oocyte and embryo development; non-invasive metabolomic embryo assessment; research in gene expression during gamete and embryo development; infertility; and fertility preservation in women with cancer; development of non-invasive metabolic embryo assessment technology for assisted reproductive technologies. Business E-Mail: emre.seli@yale.edu.

SELIB, JONATHAN, legislative staff member; BA in History with honors, Trinity Coll., Hartford, Conn., 1997; JD, Am. U. Coll. of Law, Washington, 2003. Tax counsel, Dem. staff US Senate Fin. Com., Washington, 2003—06; legis. dir., Senator Max Baucus US Senate, Washington, 2006—08, chief of staff to Senator Max Baucus, 2008—. Articles editor: Internat. Law Rev. Democrat. Office: 511 Hart Senate Office Bldg Washington DC 20510-2602 Office Phone: 202-224-2651. Business E-Mail: jon_selib@baucus.senate.gov.*

SELIG, BUD (ALAN HUBER SELIG), Major League Baseball commissioner; b. Milw., July 30, 1934; s. Ben and Marie Selig; m. Suzanne Lappin Steinman, Jan. 18, 1977; children: Sari, Wendy. B in Am. History and Polit. Sci., U. Wis., Madison, 1956; LHD (hon.), Lakeland Coll., 1989. With Selig Ford (became Selig Chevrolet 1982), West Allis, Wis., 1959-90, pres., owner, 1966-90; with Selig Exec. Leasing Co., West Allis, 1959—, pres., owner, 1977—; part owner Milw. Braves, 1963-65; co-founder Teams, Inc., 1964; co-owner, pres., CEO Milw. Brewers Baseball Club, Inc., 1970-98; interim commr. Maj. League Baseball, 1991-98, commr., 1998—. Bd. dirs. Green Bay Packers Profl. Football Team., Marcus Corp., Oil-Dri Corp. Am.; coord. World Baseball Classic, 2006 Co-founder Child Abuse Prevention Fund, 1988. With U.S. Army, 1956-58. Recipient Maj. League Exec. of Yr. award UPI, 1978, Sportsman of Yr. award Internat. B'nai B'rith, 1981, Sportsman of Yr. award US Olympic Com., 1983, August A. Busch, Jr. award Maj. League Baseball Ownership, 1989, Baird award for mgmt. excellence, 1989, Disting. Citizen award Boy Scouts America, 1990, Good Scout award, 1999, Ellis Island Congl. Medal of Honor, 1993, World of Difference award Anti-Defamation League, 1994, Herbert Hoover Humanitarian award for outstanding svc. to benefit Am.'s youth Boys and Girls Clubs America, 1998, Champion of Youth award, 2005, Disting. Svc. award US Sports Acad., 1998, Sports Leadership award March of Dimes NYC Chpt., 2000, Master of the Game award Marquette U. Sports Law Inst., 2000, Human Rels. award Nat. Conf. Cmty. and Justice, 2001, Sports Torch of Learning Am. Friends of Hebrew U., 2001, Big Bat/Frank Slocum award Baseball Assistance Team, 2003, Urban Hero award, 2003, Honor award Nat. Bldg. Mus., 2003, Judge Emil Fuchs award Boston Chpt. Baseball Writers Assn. America 2004, Centennial Nat. Human Rels. award Am. Jewish Com., 2006, Gold Medal award United Svcs. Org., 2006, Frederick Douglass Medallion NY Urban League, 2007, Award of Excellence Sports Lawyers Assn., 2007, Hank Greenberg Meml. award, 2008, Lifetime Achievement award for his commitment to Milw. cmty. and dedication to his social responsibility Jewish Family Svcs., 2008, Maj. League Baseball Lifetime Achievement award AT&T Nat. Sportsmanship Awards, 2008, Woodrow Wilson award for pub. svc. The Woodrow Wilson Internat. Ctr. Scholars, 2008; named Exec. of Yr. Sports Bus. Jour., Sports Bus. Daily, 2006; named one of Most Influential People in the World of Sports Bus. Week, 2007, 08; named to Wis. Bus. Hall of Fame, 2000, Wis. Athletic Hall of Fame, 2001. Office: Office of the Commr Major League Baseball 245 Park Ave New York NY 10167-0002*

SELIG, KARL-LUDWIG, literature and language professor; b. Wiesbaden, Germany, Aug. 14, 1926; naturalized, 1948; s. Lucian and Erna (Reiss) S. BA, Ohio State U., 1946, MA, 1947; postgrad., U. Rome, Italy, 1949—50; PhD, U. Tex., 1955. Asst. prof. Romance langs. and lit. Johns Hopkins U., Balt., 1954-58; assoc. prof. U. N.C., Chapel Hill, 1958-61, U. Minn., Mpls., 1961-63; vis. prof. U. Tex., Austin, 1963-64, prof. Romance langs. and lit., 1964-65; Hinchliff prof. Spanish lit. Cornell U., Ithaca, NY, 1965-69, dir. grad. studies in Romance lit., 1966-69; prof. Spanish lit. Columbia U., NYC, 1969—. Brown Found. fellow, vis. prof. Spanish and comparative lit. U. of the South, Sewanee, Tenn., 1990; vis. prof. U. Munich, 1963-64, U. Berlin, 1967; vis. prof. U. Greifswald, Germany, 1991-96, hon. prof., 1996—; cons. prof. Ohio State U., Columbus, 1967-69; vis. lectr. U. Zulia, Maracaibo, Venezuela, 1968; dir. summer seminar NEH, 1975, cons., 1975-77; vis. scholar Ga. U. Sys., 1977; vis. rsch. scholar Fondation Hardt, Vandoeuvres, Switzerland, 1959, Herzog August Bibliothek Wolfenbüttel, Fed. Repubic Germany, 1979—; mem. com. grants-in-aid Am. Coun. Learned Soc., 1969-73; chmn. Comparative Lit. Program and Colloquia, Columbia Coll., 1976-88. Author: (books) The Libr. of Vincencio Juan de Lastanosa, Patron of Gracián, Geneva, 1960, Studies on Alciato in Spain, 1990, Studies on Cervantes, 1993, also numerous articles, revs.; editor: (books) (Thomas Blundeville) of Councils and Counselors, 1963; editor: (with A.G. Hatcher) Studia Philologica et Litteraria in Honorem L. Spitzer, 1958; editor: (with J.E. Keller) Essays in Honor of N.B. Adams, 1966; editor: (with R. Brinkmann) Theatrum Europaeum. Festschrift E.M. Szarota, 1982; editor: (with S. Neumeister) Theatrum Mundi Hispanicum, 1986; editor: (with R. Somerville) Florilegium Columbianum: Essays in Honor of Paul Oskar Kristeller, 1987; editor: (with E. Sears) The Verbal and the Visual: Essays in Honor of William Sebastian Heckscher, 1990; editor: Polyanthea Essays on Art and Lit. in Honor of William Sebastian Heckscher, 1993, Mira de Amescua, La hija de Carlos Quinto, 2002; assoc. editor: Modern Lang. Notes, 1955—58, mng. editor: Romance Notes, 1959—61; editor: U. NC Studies in Comparative Lit., 1959—61, Bull. Comediantes, 1959—64; assoc. editor:, 1964—68, mem. editl. bd.:, 1979—88; co-editor: Yearbook of Comparative Lit., vol. IX, 1960; mem. editl. bd.: Colección Támesis, 1962—79, Romanic rev., 1969—89, Yale Italian Studies, 1976—80, Tchg. Lang. Through Lit., 1978—88, Edición Reichenberger, 2002—, assoc. editor: Hispania, 1969—74, Ky. Romance Quar., 1973—85, gen. editor: Revista Hispánica Moderna, mem. nat. adv. bd.: MLA Internat. Bibliography, 1978—88. Recipient Mark Van Doren award Columbia, 1974, spl. citation Columbia Coll. Alumni Assn., 1991, Festschrift, Über Texte, 1997; fellow Fulbright Found., Rome, 1949-50, Newberry Libr., 1958, Folger Shakespeare Libr., 1959, 63, Belgian Am. Ednl. Found., 1961, 62; sr. fellow Mediaeval and Renaissance Inst. Duke U., 1978; Fulbright rsch. scholar Utrecht, The Netherlands, 1958-59; DAAD rsch. grantee, 1979; Karl-Ludwig Selig scholarship named in his honor, Columbia Coll., 2001. Mem. MLA (sec., then chmn. Romance sect. 1965-66, chmn. comparative lit. 1973, James Russell Lowell prize com. 1989-90, chmn. 1990), Internat. Assn. Hispanists, Acad. Lit. Studies, Am. Friends Herzog August Bibliothek (bd. dirs. 1996—), Phi Beta Kappa (hon.). Home: 333 W 86th St Apt 406 New York NY 10024

SELIG, STEFAN M., bank executive; With First Boston, 1984—88; assoc. Wasserstein Perella & Co., 1988; mng. dir., co-head mergers & acquisitions UBS Securities LLC; mng. dir., mng. dir. Banc of America Securities, vice chmn. global investment banking, global head mergers & acquisitions; exec. vice chmn. global corp. & investment banking Bank of America Merrill Lynch, 2009—. Adv. Limited Brands Inc., Computer Assocs., RR Donnelley. Office: Bank of America Corp 100 North Tryon St Charlotte NC 28255*

SELIG, WILLIAM GEORGE, academic administrator; b. Prince Rupert, BC, Can., Sept. 25, 1938; s. George Oliver Selig and Minerva Junuetta (Brand) Goodale; m. Judith Margaret Sprague, June 20, 1964; children: Cheryl, Cynthia. BA, Cen. Washington State Coll., 1961, MA, 1968; CAGS, U. Mass., 1972, EdD, 1973. Tchr. Ketchikan Alaska HS, 1961—62, Sharon (Mass.) High Sch., 1963-64, Hydaburg (Alaska) Grade Sch., 1964-65, W. Puyallup (Wash.) Jr. High Sch., 1966-69; dir. spl. edn. Northampton (Mass.) Schs., 1969-73, 1974-76; asst. prof. Westfield (Mass.) State Coll., 1973; dir. pupil svcs. Longmeadow (Mass.) Pub. Schs., 1976-80; prof. Regent U., Virginia Beach, Va., 1980-83, dean, prof., 1984-89, provost, 1989-2000; Disting. prof. ednl. leadership, 2000—. Bd. dirs. Set Net, Virginia Beach; pres. Motivational Teaching Systems, Inc.; spl. edn. adv. bd. dirs. Virginia Beach Pub. Schs.; bd. trustees Klingberg Family Ctrs., New Britain, Conn., 1991—2000. Author: Training for Triumph, 1984, Loving Our Differences, 1989, Handbook of Individualized Strategies for Classroom Discipline, 1995, Handbook of Individualized Strategies for Building Resilience in At Risk Students, 2005; contbr. chpt. to book. Episcopalian. Avocations: skiing, tennis. Office: Regent University 1000 Regent University Dr Virginia Beach VA 23464-9800 Office Phone: 757-352-4137. Business E-Mail: georsel@regent.edu.

SELIG, WILLIAM PAUL, advocate; b. Ridgewood, NY, Sept. 19, 1949; s. Joseph Peacc Lewis and Janet Lucille Selig; m. Donna R. McIntyre, July 1, 1982; 1 child, Hannah Jo He-Young; m. L. Scazzero Benjamin. BA, U. Md., College Park, 1972; MRE, Unification Theol. Sem., Barrytown, NY, 1981. Prin., owner Good Health Food Stores, Washington, 1977—80; dir. office of strategic affairs CAUSA Internat., NYC, 1980—84; sr. v.p. Summit Coun. for World Peace, Washington, 1981—; COO Internat. Security Coun., NYC, 1983—87; adminstrv. dir. Assn. for the Unity of L.Am., NYC, 1984—; gen. mgr. Global Affairs Jour., NYC, 1985—88; adminstrv. dir. Fedn. for World Peace, Washington, 1991—; sr. v.p. World Inst. for Devel. and Peace, Washington, 1996—; dir. dept. cultural affairs Washington Times Found., Washington, 1997—98; v.p. Young Gruppe, Inc., Washington, 1998—; sr. v.p. Universal Cultural Found., Washington, 2005—; dep. dir. internat. office of govt. rels. Universal Peace Fedn., Washington, 2006—08. Author: Founding CAUSA Instruction Manual, World Peace, Freedom and Justice; reviewer: films and books The New York City Tribune. Active Rockville Millennium Coun., Md., 1999—2000; vol. Peace Corps, Bogota, Colombia, 1972—75; dep. dir. Lit. Fedn. for World Peace, 1998—99; dir., comm. & logistics World Peace Pilgrimage, Jerusalem, 2003—08; dep. sec. gen. N.Am. chpt Interreligious and Internat. Fedn. for World Peace, Washington, 1999—2006; metro chaircouple Blessed Family Assn. 8000, Washington, 1993—95; dist. leader Family Fedn. for World Peace and Internat., Rockville, Md., 1996—2002; elder Montgomery Family Ch., Rockville, 2002—; exec. dir. Montgomery County chpt. Am. Clergy Leadership Conf., Rockville, 1999—; dir. Nat. Won Jeon Shrine of Am., Washington, Md., 2001—. Recipient Cheon Il Guk award, CheongPyeong Heaven & Earth Tng. Ctr., 2003; named Amb. for Peace, Interreligious and Internat. Fedn. for World Peace, 2001. Mem.: World Assn. Non-Govtl Orgns. (assoc.), Nat. Coun. Returned Peace Corp Vols. (assoc.). Republican. Office: Summit Council World Peace 1112 16th ST NW Ste 540 Washington DC 20036

SELIGMAN, BRAD, lawyer; b. Cin., Aug. 25, 1951; s. Selig J. and Muriel (Bienstock) S.; children: Corina Kasten, Mariana Campos, Sofia Maya Campos. BA, Sonoma State U., Calif., 1975; JD, U. Calif., San Francisco, 1978. Bar: Calif. 1978, US Dist. Ct. (no. dist.) Calif. 1978, US Dist. Ct. (ea. dist.) Calif. 1979. Teaching fellow Law Sch. Stanford U., Calif., 1978-79; sr. law clk. to Hon. Lawrence K. Karlton US Dist. Ct. (ea. dist.) Calif., Sacramento, 1979-80; assoc. Farnsworth, Saperstein & Brand, Oakland, Calif., 1981-85; ptnr. Farnsworth, Saperstein & Seligman, Oakland, 1985-89; mng. dir. Saperstein, Seligman & Mayeda, Oakland, 1989-91; of counsel Saperstein, Mayeda, Larkin & Goldstein, Oakland, Calif., 1991-94; exec. dir. The Impact Fund, Berkeley, Calif., 1992—. Advisor Disability Rights Edn. and Def. Fund, Inc., 1992—; trustee Calif. Rural Legal Assistance, San Francisco, 1982-88; bd. dirs. Equal Rights Advisors, San Francisco, 1989-92. Author: (with others) CEO: Wrongful Employment Termination Practice, 1987, Tax Aspects of Litigation and Settlements, 1989. Named one of 100 Most Influential Lawyers, Nat. Law Jour., 2006. Office: The Impact Fund 125 University Ave Berkeley CA 94710 Business E-Mail: bs@impactfund.org.

SELIGMAN, JOEL, academic administrator; b. NYC, Jan. 11, 1950; s. Selig Jacob and Muriel (Bienstock) Seligman; m. Friederike Felber Seligman, July 30, 1982; children: Andrea, Peter. AB in polit. sci. magna cum laude, UCLA, 1971; JD, Harvard U., 1974. Bar: Calif. 1975. Atty., writer Corp. Accountability Rsch. Group, Washington, 1974-77; prof. law Northeastern U. Law Sch., 1977-83, George Washington U., 1983-86, U. Mich., Ann Arbor, 1987—95; dean law sch. U. Ariz., Tucson, 1995-99, Samuel M. Fegtly prof. law, 1995—99; dean law sch. Washington U., St. Louis, 1999—2005, Ethan A. H. Shepley prof. law, 1999—2005; pres. U. Rochester, NY, 2005—. Cons. Fed. Trade Commn., 1979—82, US Dept. Transp., 1983, Office Tech. Assessment, 1988—89; chair adv. com. on mktg. info. SEC, 2000—01; reporter Nat. Conf. of Commrs. on Uniform State Laws, Uniform Securities Act, 2002; bd. dirs. Eastman Kodak Co. Co-author: Constitutionalizing the Corporation: The Case for the Federal Chartering of Giant Corporations, 1976, The High Citadel: The Influence of Harvard Law School, 1978, The Transformation of Wall Street: A History of the Securities and Exchange Commission and Modern Corporate Finance, 1982, The SEC and the Future of Finance, 1985, Securities Regulation, The New Uniform Securities Act, 2002; contbr. articles to profl. jour. Mem.: Eastman Kodak Co. (bd. dir.), Am. Law Inst. (adv. com., adv. corp. governance project), State Bar Calif., Fin. Industry Regulatory Authority (bd. govs.), AICPA (profl. ethics exec. com. 2000—02). Office: Office of Pres U Rochester 240 Wallis Hall Rochester NY 14627 Office Phone: 585-275-8356. Office Fax: 585-256-2473. E-mail: seligman@rochester.edu.

SELIGMAN, NICOLE KAY, broadcast executive, lawyer; b. 1956; m. Joel Irwin Klein, 2000. BA magna cum laude, Harvard Coll., Radcliffe, 1978; JD magna cum laude, Harvard Law Sch., 1983. Assoc. editl. page editor The Asian Wall St. Jour., Hong Kong, 1978—80; law clk. to Hon. Harry T. Edwards US Ct. Appeals (DC Cir.), Wash., DC, 1983—84; law clk. to Justice Thurgood Marshall U.S. Supreme Ct., 1984—85; ptnr., litig. Williams & Connolly LLP, Wash., DC; exec. v.p., gen. counsel Sony Corp. of America, 2001—; corp. exec. Sony Corp., Tokyo, 2003—, group deputy gen. counsel, 2003—. Named one of 50 Women to Watch, The Wall St. Jour., 2008.*

SELIGMANN, WILLIAM ROBERT, lawyer, author; b. Davenport, Iowa, Oct. 10, 1956; s. William Albert and Barbara Joyce (Carmichael) S.; m. Carole Lee Francis; children: D Anna, Matthew. BA, U. Calif.,

Santa Barbara, 1979; JD, Santa Clara U., 1982. Bar: Calif. 1983, U.S. Dist. Ct. (no. dist.) Calif. 1983. Assoc. Office of J.R. Dempster, Cupertino, Calif., 1983-85; city atty. City of Campbell, Calif., 1985—; ptnr. Dempster, Seligmann & Raineri, Los Gatos, Calif., 1985—2001, pvt. practice, 2001—. Reviewer: California Municipal Law Handbook, 1997—98, 2007, cons.: Continuing Education of the Bar, California Land Use Practice, 2006. Bd. dirs. Los Gatos C. of C. Mem. Santa Clara County Bar Assn. (civil practice com., judiciary com.), State Bar Calif. (exec. bd. pub. law sect. 2001—, chair 2004-05, advisor 2005—), Calif. League Cities (fair polit. practices com., city atty. divsn.). Avocations: cross country skiing, scuba diving, swimming, writing, Aikido. Office: 333 Church St Santa Cruz CA 95060 Home Phone: 831-438-8595; Office Phone: 831-423-8383. Business E-Mail: bill@southbaylaw.com.

SELIGSON, CARL HAROLD, corporate financial executive; b. NYC, Feb. 25, 1935; s. Harold P. and Lilian (Yohalem) Seligson; m. Bonnie Laskin, Mar. 6, 1983; children: Susan S. Pattenaude, Barbara S. Zweig, Nina Priven, Eric M. Drath. AB, Brown U., 1956; postgrad., NYU Grad. Sch. Bus. Adminstrn., 1961—63. Textile salesman Cohn, Hall, Marx Co., Montreal, Canada, 1958—61; security analyst Burnham & Co., NYC, 1961—67, Kuhn, Loeb & Co, NYC, 1967—71; mng. dir. Merrill Lynch, NYC, 1971—87, Kidder, Peabody & Co., NYC, 1987—90; sr. exec. cons. regulated industries Deloitte & Touche, NYC, 1990—92; mng. dir. Prudential Securities, NYC, 1992—95; sr. advisor Andersen Consulting, NYC, 1996—2000; sr. v.p. energyLeader.com, NYC, 2000; sr. advisor Prospect St. Ventures, NYC, 2001, K Rd. Power, NYC, 2002—05; fin. cons. Edison Electric Inst., Washington, 2003—. Contbr. articles to profl. jours. including Pub. Utilities Fortnightly, Telephony, Fin. Exec., The So. Banker, Coal Monthly and Energy News. Chmn. Regulatory Industry Com., Securities Industry Assn., 1985—87; mem. strategic issues com. and adv. coun. Elec. Power Rsch. Inst., Palo Alto, Calif., 1998—2006; mem. adv. coun. Nat. Assn. Registry Utilities Commrs. Edn. & Rsch. Found., 2005—07; bd. dirs. Nuc. Energy Inst., Washington, 1988—95. With Counter Intelligence Corps US Army. Fellow Fin. Analysts Fedn.; mem. Univ. Club. NY. Avocations: water sports, travel, theater. Personal E-mail: cseligson@nyc.rr.com.

SELIGSON, MITCHELL A., political science educator; b. Hempstead, NY, Nov. 12, 1945; m. Susan Berk, June 18, 1967; 1 child, Amber Lara. BA cum laude, Bklyn. Coll., 1967; MA, U. Fla., 1968; PhD, U. Pitts., 1974. Vol. U.S. Peace Corps, Costa Rica, 1968-70; asst. prof./assoc. prof. U. Ariz., Tucson, 1974-85; prof. U. Pitts., 1986-93, Daniel H. Wallace prof. polit. sci., 1994—2004, dir. Latin Am. studies, 1986-92, rsch. prof., 1992—2004; Centennial prof. polit. sci. Vanderbilt U., Nashville, 2004—. Fellow Ctr. Ams.; dir. L.Am. pub. opinion project; cons. to World Bank, UN Devel. Program, US AID, Inter-Am. Devel. Bank, Guatemala, Honduras, Nicaragua, Costa Rica, Colombia, Dominican Republic, Mex., Ecuador, Jamaica, Panama, El Salvador, Peru, Bolivia, Paraguay, 1980—. Author, editor: Peasants of Costa Rica and the Development of Agrarian Capitalism, 1980, The Gap Between Rich and Poor, 1984, Authoritarians and Democrats, 1987, Elections and Democracy in Central America, 1989, rev. edit. 1995, Development and Underdevelopment, 1993, The Political Economy of Global Inequality, 2003, The Legitimacy Puzzle in Latin America. Fulbright fellow, Costa Rica, 1986, Rockefeller Found. fellow, 1985-86; grantee Social Sci. Rsch. Coun., Ford Found., NSF, Mellon Found., Heinz Endowment. Mem. Am. Polit. Sci. Assn., Latin Am. Studies Assn. (chmn. fin. com. 1991). Office: Vanderbilt U Dept Polit Sci Nashville TN 37235 Office Phone: 615-322-6938. Business E-Mail: m.seligson@vanderbilt.edu.

SELIGSON, THEODORE H., architect, interior designer, urban planner; b. Kansas City, Mo., Nov. 10, 1930; s. Harry and Rose (Haith) S.; m. Jacqueline Rose, Dec. 27, 1964 (div. 1976). BArch, Washington U., St. Louis, 1953. Registered architect, Mo., Kans. Intern Marshall & Brown, Kansas City, Mo., 1949-54; designer, head design Kivett & Myers, Kansas City, Mo., 1954-62; prin. Design Assocs., 1955—, Atelier Seligson, Kansas City, Mo., 1962-64; pres. Seligson, Eggen, Inc., Kansas City, 1964-73, Seligson Assocs., Inc., Architects Planners, Kansas City, 1973-97; prin. Foss, Seligson, Lafferty, 1997—. Vis. lectr. adult edn. U. Mo.-Kansas City, 1958-61, vis. prof. arch., 1989—, vis. prof. urban design, 2002--; tchr., critic Kansas City Art Inst., Mo., 1961-64, 71-72, adj. prof., 1986, 89, 91, 92; adj. prof. Kans. State U., 1991-92, 97; vis. prof. Washington U., St. Louis, 1975, 77, 78, 81, 86, 91, U. Kans., Lawrence, 1978, 79, 80, 91, 92; art cons. Design Assocs., Kansas City, Mo., 1955—. Projects pub. in archtl. jours. V.p. Friends of Art Nelson-Atkins Mus. Art, Kansas City, bd. dirs. 1963-67, chmn. selections com., 1981, vis. curator, 1972, 87; chmn. Capitol Fine Arts Commn. Mo., 1983-90, Kansas City Worlds Fair goals and themes subcom., 1985-90; bd. dirs. Westport Tomorrow, Kansas City, 1980-87, Hist. Kansas City Found., 1984-90; pres. Native Sons of Kansas City, 1989, bd. dirs. 1978-94, Westport Cmty. Coun., 1973-75; bd. govs. Truman Med. Ctr., Kansas City, 1998-2002, mem. bd. advisors, 2002--; mem. Kansas City Key to City Commn., 2001-02; bd. dirs. Sacred Structures, 2003—. Recipient Urban Design award Kansas City Mcpl. Art Commn., 1968, 74, 78; Nat. Archtl. award Am. Inst. Steel Constrn., 1970; Nat. award ASID/DuPont Corian, 1989. Fellow AIA (Kansas City chpt. pres. 1983, bd. dirs. 1979-84, Design Excellence award 1966, 68, 70, 74, Ctrl. States Regional award 1974, 78, Honor award for outstanding svc. to chpt. and profession 1982-83); mem. Mo. Coun. Archs., Am. Soc. Interior Designers, Nat. Coun. Archtl. Registration Bds. (task analysis adv. com. 1988-90), Soc. Archtl. Historians (pres. 1973-75, bd. dirs. 1994-97). Jewish. Office: Foss Seligson Lafferty 450 E 4th St Kansas City MO 64106

SELIN, IVAN, entrepreneur; b. NYC, Mar. 11, 1937; s. Saul and Freda (Kuhlman) Selin; m. Nina Kallet, June 8, 1957; children: Douglas, Jessica. BE, Yale U., 1957, ME, 1958, PhD, 1960; DSc, U. Paris, 1962. Rsch. engr. Rand Corp., Santa Monica, Calif., 1960-65; sys. analyst Dept. Def., Washington, 1965-67, dep. asst. sec. def., 1967-69, acting asst. sec. for systems analysis, 1969-70; founder, chmn. bd. Am. Mgmt. Systems, Inc., Arlington, Va., 1970-89; undersec. state Dept. State, Washington, 1989-91; chmn. Nuc. Regulatory Commn., Washington, 1991—95; chmn., CEO Phoenix Internat., Washington, 1995—; chmn. Enumerale Solutions, Inc., 1998—. Lectr. UCLA, 1961-63; chmn. mil. econ. adv. panel to CIA, 1978-89; bd. dirs. BZL Biologics, Inc. Author: Detection Theory, 1964; contbr. articles to profl. jours. Pres. Corp. Against Drug Abuse, 1988-95; bd. dirs., gov. UN Assn. U.S., 1979-89; exec. com. Greater Washington Research Ctr., Fed. City Council; trustee Asia Soc., 1996-98; chmn., bd. dirs. Smithsonian Nat. Mus. of Am. History, 1996—, Yale U. Coun., 2000—. Recipient Disting. Civilian Svc. medal, 1970, Disting. Svc. medal Sec. of State, 1991; Fulbright scholar, 1959-61; Ford Found. grantee, 1952-54. Mem. IEEE (editor Trans. on Info. Theory 1960-65), Coun. Fgn. Rels., Yale Club, Sigma Xi, Tau Beta Pi. Home: 1455 Ocean Dr Apt 1602 Miami FL 33159 Office Phone: 202-337-2337. Business E-Mail: ixs@phnx-intl.com.

SELIN, LISA K., physician; b. Helsinki, Finland, Apr. 8, 1952; d. Lauri Oscar and Hilma K Selin. BSc, Dalhousie Univ, 1970—74; MD, Dalhousie U., 1974—79, FRCP, 1980—84; PhD, Univ. Man., 1986—93. Med. intern Dalhousie U., Halifax, Canada, 1979—80, resident in internal medicine, 1980—84; fellow in infectious diseases Univ. of Man., Winnipeg, Canada, 1984—86; doctoral student Univ of Man., 1986—91; postdoctoral fellow Univ. Mass. Med. Sch., 1992—95, instr., 1995—96; asst. prof. Univ. Mass. Med Sch., 1996—2001; assoc. prof. Univ. Mass. Med. Sch., 2001—08, prof., 2008—. Contbr. articles to profl. jours. Med. Coun. of Can. Student fellowship, Med. Coun. of Can., 1986—91, Dalhousie Entrance schoarship, Dalhousie Univ, 1970, Izaak Walton Killam scholarship, Izaak Walton Killam Found., 1984—86, Clin. Investigator award, Nat. Inst. of Health, 1996—99, Rsch. grant, NIH- NIAID, 2000—, NIH-NIAID, 2001—, 1999—2003. Mem.: Can. Infectious Disease Soc., Am. Assn. of Immunologists. Achievements include research in T cell-mediated heterologous immunity in viral infections. Avocations: painting, cross country skiing, swimming, gardening, travel. Office: Univ Mass Med Sch 55 Lake Ave North Worcester MA 01655 E-mail: liisa.selin@umassmed.edu.

SELINGER, JERRY ROBIN, lawyer; b. Peekskill, NY, Nov. 3, 1947; s. Philip R. and Helen D. (Klein) S.; m. Barbara D. Wax, Aug. 2, 1969; children: Elise, Scott. BS in Engring. Sci., SUNY, Buffalo, 1969; MS, Columbia U., 1971; JD, George Washington U., 1975. Bar: Md. 1975, D.C. 1976, U.S. Ct. Appeals (fed. cir.) 1977, U.S. Supreme Ct. 1978, Tex. 1980, U.S. Ct. Appeals (5th cir.) 1981, U.S. Ct. Appeals (3d cir.) 1982. Atty. Arent, Fox, Kintner, Plotkin & Kahn, Washington, 1975-79, Richards, Harris & Medlock, Dallas, 1979-82; mem., dir. Baker, Mills & Glast, Dallas, 1982-90; ptnr. Vinson & Elkins LLP, Dallas, 1990-97; 1997shareholder Jenkens & Gilchrist, Dallas, 1997—2005; ptnr. Morgan Lewis & Bockius LLP, Dallas, 2005—08, Patterson & Sheridan LLP, Dallas, 2008—. Contbr. articles to profl. jours. Bd. trustees Dallas Bar Found., 2001—08. Fellow Dallas Bar (chair 2007); mem. ABA, Tex. Bar Assn. (chair intellectual property law sect. 1996-97, bd. dirs. 1998-01), Dallas Bar Assn. (bd. dirs. 1995-96), Tex. Young Lawyers Assn. (bd. dirs. 1984-86, Pres. award 1986), Am. Intellectual Property Law Assn. (bd. dirs. 2002-05), Dallas Assn. Young Lawyers (sec. 1983, treas. 1984), Order of Coif, Phi Delta Phi. Home: 10414 Woodford Dr Dallas TX 75229-6317 Office: Patterson & Sheridan LLP 1700 Pacific Ste 2650 Dallas TX 75201 Office Phone: 214-272-0957. Business E-Mail: jselinger@attersonsheridan.com.

SELINGO, JEFFREY J., editor, reporter; BA in Journalism, Ithaca Coll., 1995; MA in Govt., Johns Hopkins U. Bus. tech. reporter Arizona Republic; environ. reporter Wilmington Star-News, NC; bus. and politics editor Chronicle of Higher Edn., Washington, asst. mng. editor, editor, 2007—. Recipient Nat. Award for Edn. Reporting, Edn. Writers Assn., Dateline Award, Soc. Profl. Journalists; finalist Livingston Award; grantee Pulliam Journalism Fellowship. Office: Chronicle of Higher Edn 1255 23Rd St, NW Washington DC 20037 Office Phone: 202-466-1000. Office Fax: 202-452-1033.

SELIX, KAREN ELIZABETH, writer, artist, vocalist; b. Alice, Tex., Jan. 10, 1960; d. LeRoy Albert; 3 children. Owner, designer Spark a Link, Inc., 1999—. Author: (children's stories) Rainbow's End, 2000, Black Rainbow, 2003; co-author (with LeRoy Selix): (cassette recording) The Easter Bunny That Wasn't a Rabbit, 1988; musician: (albums) I'll Be There, 2005, Until We Meet Again, 2005, Wedding Bells and Wedding Rings, 2009. Recipient Gift of Life award, Ben Taub Gen. Hosp., 1973. Roman Catholic. Home: 145 Galaxy Dr Hot Springs AR 71913

SELKE-KERN, BARBARA ELLEN, university official, writer; b. Houston, Dec. 14, 1950; d. Oscar Otto Jr. and Edith Hicks (Hardey) Selke; m. Homer Dale Kern, May 31, 1985. BS, U. Colo., 1973; MA, U. Tex., 1981, PhD, 1986. Cert. elem. and secondary tchr., Tex. Co-owner Colo. Sound, Denver, 1972-76; tchr. Jefferson County Schs., Lakewood, Colo., 1974-76; dir. Harvest Time Day Care Ctr., Austin, 1976-77; mgr. TourService, Inc., Austin, 1977-82; from curriculum specialist to ednl. resources coord. U. Tex., Austin, 1982-88, ednl. resources dir., 1988-92; coord. adult vocat. and apprenticeship programs Austin CC, 1992—94, lead coord. for career programs, 1994, coord. grant devel., 1994—95, exec. asst. to pres., 1995-97, dean bus. svcs. and continuing edn., 1997-98; dir. orgnl. advancement Tex. State Tech. Coll. Sys., 1998-99, vice chancellor, 1999—2002, exec. vice chancellor, 2002—06. Author: Retail Travel Marketing, 1983, Communication Skills, 1984, Orientation to Cosmetology Instructor Training, 1984, Resumes and Interviews, 1984, Competency in Teaching, 1985, Guidelines for the Texas Cosmetology Commission Instructor Licensing Examination, 1985, Effective Communication, 1986, Effective Teaching, 1986, Balancing the Curriculum for Marketing Education, 1987, Bulletin Board Designs for Marketing Education, 1987, Marketing Education I, 1988, Flashcards for Marketing Education, 1988, Glossary for Marketing Education, 1988, Validated Task Lists for Apparel And Accessories Marketing, 1991; co-author: Higher Level Thinking in Marketing Education, 1990; author (computer software): Emergency Aid, 1986, 2nd edit., 1989, Measuring Employee Productivity, 1986, Retail Pricing in Action, 1987, Marketing Fibers and Fabrics, 1989, Physical Distribution, 1991; editor: Training Plans for Marketing Education, 1987, Correspondence, 1988, Instructional Planning, 1988; contbr. articles to profl. jours. Am. Bus. Women's Assn. scholar, 1985.

SELKIRK, JAMES KIRKWOOD, retired biochemist; b. NYC, Dec. 3, 1938; s. James Kirkwood and Doris (Schuler) S.; m. Carole Ann Bozzone, Sept. 16, 1961; children: James Kirkwood, David Edward. BS in Biochemistry, Coll. Environ. Sci. and Forestry, Syracuse U., NY, 1964; BS in Environ. Sci., Chemistry, Syracuse U., NY, 1964; PhD in Biochemistry, Syracuse U. Upstate Med. Ctr., Syracuse, 1969. Postdoctoral fellow McArdle Lab. Cancer Rsch., U. Wis., Madison, 1969-72; staff fellow Nat. Cancer Inst., NIH, Bethesda, Md., 1972-74, sr. staff fellow, 1974-75; sr. staff scientist unit leader chem. carcinogenesis biology divsn. Oak Ridge (Tenn.) Nat. Lab., 1975-85; chief carcinogenesis and toxicology evaluation br. nat. toxicology program Nat. Inst. Environ. Health Scis., 1985-89, assoc. dir. divsn. toxicology rsch. and testing, 1989-92, chief carcinogen mechanism group Lab. Molecular Carcinogenesis, 1992—97; spl. asst. to sci. dir. for technology devel. Nat. Inst. Evniron. Health Scis., 1997-2000; deputy dir. Nat. Ctr. Toxicogenomics, 2000—09; adj. prof. Oak Ridge Biomed. Grad. Sch., U. Tenn., 1975-85; mem. breast cancer task force NIH, 1979-82; mem. com. on pyrenes and analogs NAS, 1981-83; chmn. Interagy. Testing Commn., 1986-90. Author rsch. articles, chpts. in books; mem. editl. bd. Carcinogenesis Jour., 1984-87, 91-93, Cancer Rsch., 1981-86, Environ. Health Perspectives, 1993-98, contbg. editor, 2003—. Mem. Orange County Planning Bd., 1997—; chmn. Weaver Dairy Precinct, Dem. Party Orange County, 1996-99. With AUS, 1959-61. With chem. corps US Army, 1959—60. Recipient U.S. Interagy. Testing Com. Exemplary Svc. award, 1992. Mem. Am. Cancer Soc. (carcinogenesis study sect. 1975-78, 92-96). Avocations: scuba diving, coin collecting/numismatics, marksmanship. Home: 30119 Settle Dr Chapel Hill NC 27517 Home Phone: 919-967-0017. Personal E-mail: jselkirk@nc.rr.com.

SELKOE, DENNIS JESSE, neurologist, researcher, educator; b. NYC, Sept. 25, 1943; s. Herbert E. and Mary P. (Lille) S.; m. Polly Ann Strasser, June 24, 1967; children: Gregory, Kimberly. BA, Columbia U., 1965; MD, U. Va., 1969. Diplomate Am. Bd. Psychiatry and Neurology, Nat. Bd. Med. Examiners. Intern in medicine Hosp. U. Pa., Phila., 1969-70; rsch. assoc. NIH, Bethesda, Md., 1970-72; resident in neurology Peter Bent Brigham/Children's Hosp., Boston, 1972-74, chief resident in neurology, 1974-75; rsch. assoc. Harvard Med. Sch., Boston, 1975-78, asst. prof. neurology, 1978-82, assoc. prof., 1982-85, assoc. prof. neurology and neurosci., 1985-90, faculty mem. divsn. on aging, 1980—, prof. neurology and neurosci., 1990—, Vincent and Stella Coates prof. neurol. diseases, 2001—; co-dir. Ctr. Neurologic Diseases Brigham and Women's Hosp., Boston, 1985—. Mem. sci. adv. bd. Alzheimer's Disease Assn., Chgo., 1983-89; mem. Gov.'s Commn. on Alzheimer's Disease, Mass., 1985-87; neurosci. adv. com. Howard Hughes Med. Inst., 1996—. Author over 200 articles, book chpts. on biochemistry and molecular biology of Alzheimer's Disease. Recipient Wood-Kalb Found. prize Alzheimers Disease Assn., 1984, Med. Rsch. award Met. Life Found., 1986, LEAD award Nat. Inst. on Aging, 1988, NIH Merit award, 1991—, Arthur Cherkin award UCLA, 1995, Mathilde Solowey award in neurosci. Found. for Advanced Edn. in Scis., NIH, 1998, Rita Hayworth award Alzheimer's Assn., 1995, Boerhaave medal U. Leiden, 1998, Pioneer award Alzheimer's Assn., 1999, Lifetime Achievement award, Alz Assn., 2008; grantee Bristol-Myers Squibb Neurosci., 1990. Fellow AAAS, Am. Acad. Neurology (Potamkin prize 1989, Dr. A.H. Heineken prize for Medicine 2002, Lifetime Achievement award, Alzheimers Assn., 2008); mem. Am. Neurol. Assn., Soc. for Neurosci., Am. Assn. Neuropathologists, World Fedn. Neurologists, Inst. Medicine NAS, Assoc. Am. Physicians. Office: Harvard Med Sch Brigham & Womens Hosp 77 Avenue Louis Pasteur Boston MA 02115-5727

SELKOWITZ, ARTHUR, retired advertising executive; b. NYC, May 26, 1943; s. Harry and Anne (Lichten); m. Betsey Wattenberg, Apr. 15, 1967; children: Adam, Jed. AB, Syracuse U., NY, 1965. Account exec. Dancer Fitzgerald Sample, 1969-71; with Benton & Bowles, Inc., NYC, 1971-82, v.p., account supr., 1972-75, sr. v.p., mgmt. supr., 1975-81, sr. v.p., account dir., 1981-82; founder, pres. Penchina, Selkowitz Inc., NYC, 1982-90; exec. v.p. internat. D'Arcy, Masius, Benton & Bowles, NYC, 1990-94, pres. Asia and Pacific, 1995-96, pres. N.Am., 1996-97, chmn., CEO, 1997-2000; vice chmn., chief client officer BCom3 Group, Inc., NYC, 2001—02, Publicis Groupe, 2002. Lectr. Columbia U., 2003—06; mem. adv. bd. Spot Runner, Inc. Dancer Fitzgerald Sample, N.Y.C., 1966—71. Chmn. Mill River Collaborative, Stamford, Conn.; bd. mem. Stamford Mus. and Nature Ctr., Conn.; Lupus Rsch. Inst., NYC. Mem.: Lotos (N.Y.) Club.

SELL, CLAY (JEFFREY CLAY SELL), energy company executive, former federal agency administrator; b. 1967; s. George and Judy Sell; m. Alisa M. Sell; children: Jack, Robert, Mary Margaret. BS in Bus. Adminstrn., Tex. Tech. U., 1989; JD, U. Tex. Staff mem. to Rep. Mac Thornberry US House of Reps., Washington, 1995—97, adminstrv. asst., 1997—99; majority clk. & staff dir. for energy & water sub com. of the Senate Com. on Appropriations US Senate Appropriations Com. Energy & Water Sub Com., Washington, 2000—03; spl. asst. to the Pres. for econ. policy The White House, Washington, 2003—04, spl. asst. to Pres. for legis. affairs, 2004—05; dep. sec. US Dept. Energy, Washington, 2005—08; pres. Hunt Energy Horizons, LLC, Dallas, 2008—; sr. v.p. Hunt Oil Co., Dallas, 2008—. Office: Hunt Energy Horizons LLC 1900 N Akard St Dallas TX 75201 Office Phone: 214-978-8689. Office Fax: 214-978-8671.*

SELL, LEELOU, retired elementary school educator; d. Werner William and Lydia Veryl Sell. BA, Long Beach State Coll., Calif., 1960; postgrad., Pepperdine U., Calif. State U., Fullerton, U. Calif., Irvine. Cert. tchr. Calif. Tchr. Anaheim City Sch. Dist., Calif., 1960, 1961—97; chpt. counselor Zeta Tau Alpha, 1960—61; ret., 1997—. Co-author: Math for Kindergartners, 1970. Vol. Braille Inst., Anaheim, 1997—; vol., bd. dirs., mem. com. Pacific Symphony, Orange County, Calif., 1997—; bd. dirs., mem. com. Am. Heart Assn., Orange County, 1998—2001. Named Hon. Life Mem., Jefferson PTA, Anaheim, 1970, Price PTA, Anaheim, 1986. Mem.: AAUW, Calif. Ret. Tchrs. Assn., Zeta Tau Alpha (pres., v.p., sec. membership 1955—60), Delta Kappa Gamma (2d v.p., sec. rec. sec., chmn. various coms. 1985—). Avocations: reading, theater, needlecrafts, herb gardening, travel.

SELL, STEWART, pathologist, immunologist, educator; b. Pitts., Jan. 20, 1935; s. Oliver Martin and Mary Myra (Stewart) S.; m. Patricia Damon King, June 20, 1958 (div. 1985); children: Sherri Lynn Phillips, Stacy L. Klinke, Sean Stewart, Stephaine King Kinzel; m. Ilze Mara Klavins, Feb. 16, 1991; 1 child, Philip Janus. BS, Coll. of William and Mary, 1956; MD, U. Pitts., 1960. Diplomate Am. Bd. Pathology, Am. Bd. Med. Lab. Immunologists. Intern, asst. resident in pathology Mass. Gen. Hosp., Boston, 1960-62; rsch. assoc. germfree animal rsch. lab. NIAID, NIH, Bethesda, Md., 1962-64; spl. fellow dept. exptl. pathology U. Birmingham (Eng.) Med. Sch., 1964-65; instr., asst. prof., then assoc. prof. pathology U. Pitts. Sch. Medicine, 1965-69; assoc. prof., then prof. pathology U. Calif., San Diego, 1970-82; prof. U. Tex. Med. Sch., Houston, 1982—96, chmn. dept. pathology, 1982-87; prof., dip. exptl. pathology Albany Med. Coll., 1997—2002; rsch. physician Wadsworth Ctr. and Rsch. Sci., Albany, NY, 2002—, Ordway Rsch. Inst. Adj. prof. lab. medicine U. Tex.-M.D. Anderson Cancer Ctr., Houston, 1983-97; mem. pathology B study sect. NIH, 1972-77; mem. immunology adv. com. Am. Cancer Soc., 1983-88; mem. bd. sci. counsel divsn. cancer biol. diagnosis Nat. Cancer Inst., 1982-86. Author: Immunology, Immunopathology & Immunity, 1972, 5th rev. edit., 1996, 6th edit., 2001, BasicImmunology, 1987; editor: Seriological Cancer Markers, 1992, Monoclonal Antibodies in Cancer, 1985, Stem Cells Handbook, 2004, 7 other oncology books. Recipient disting. alumnus award, U. Pitts., 1998, Disting. Scientist award, Internat. Acad. of Oncobiology and Medicine, 1998, NIH grantee, 1964—, Philip S. Hench Disting. Alumnus award, U. Pitts. Sch. Medicine, 1988, Gary J. Miller Meml. award, AACR, 2002, Rudolph L.K. Virchow award, Leadership Medica, Italy, 2005, Abbott award. Mem. Am. Assn. Immunologists, Am. Soc. Exptl. Pathology, Am. Assn. Cancer Rsch. (Gary Miller Meml. award 2002, Spl. Svc. award, 2005), Internat. Soc. Oncodevel. Biology and Medicine (bd. dirs. 1972-85, Abbott award, 2007), Internat. Acad. Tumor Market Oncology (bd. dirs. 1984-2005, Disting. Scientist award, 1998), Am. Soc. Microbiology, Internat. Acad. Pathology (Athens, Greece) (keynote spkr., 2008). Achievements include discovery of immunoglobulin on surface of lymphocytes, activation of B-cells by antibody to surface immunoglobulin; identification of promoter-enhancer region of alphafetoprotein in gene expression, of liver stem cell, of role of delayed hypersensitivity in immunity to syphilis, cancer stem cell hypothesis, experimental model of aflatoxin carcinogenesis. Office: Wadsworth Ctr NY State Dept Health Empire State Plaza Albany NY 12201

SELLARS, CHRISTI VON LEHE, music educator; b. Charleston, SC, July 30, 1954; d. Diedreich Peterman and Fay Johnson von Lehe; m. Robert Marion Sellars, Mar. 21, 1981; children: Katharine Elizabeth, Patrick Grayson. MusB in Edn., Converse Coll., 1976, MusM in Edn., 1986. Choral dir. Spartanburg HS, SC, 1977—82; music instr. Spartanburg Day Sch., 1992—2001; prof. music Wofford Coll., Spartanburg, 1993—. Choir dir. Cannon's Meth. Ch., Spartanburg, 1998—; asst. pianist Spartanburg Little Theatre, 1992—98; founder Spartanburg Day Sch. Singers, 1994, STARTS- Wofford Students in the Arts, 2003.

Performer Spartanburg (S.C.) Repertory Co., 1989—92; pres. Spartanburg (S.C.) Little Theatre, 1992—98, Spartanburg (S.C.) Philharm., 1985—87; bd. dir. Spartanburg (S.C.) Little Theatre, 1992—98, Music Found., Spartanburg, 1991—95. Named Spartanburg (S.C.) City Young Career Woman, Bus. and Profl. Women, 1980. Mem.: Am. Choral Dirs. Assn., S.C. Music Educators Assn. Meth. Avocations: reading, composing. Home: 3213 Hwy 56 PO Box 132 Pauline SC 29374 Office: Wofford College Box H 429 N Church St Spartanburg SC 29303 E-mail: sellarscv@wofford.edu.

SELLARS, NIGEL ANTHONY, historian, writer; b. Birmingham, England, Oct. 2, 1954; came to U.S., 1963; s. Robert William and Florence (Thompson) S.; m. Victoria Susan Brown, Dec. 17, 1981 (div. Jan. 1989); m. Nancy Lee Phillips Sellars, Jan. 1, 1990. BA in Psychology, U. Okla., Norman, 1977, BA in Journalism, 1980, MA in Journalism, 1985, PhD in History, 1994. Reporter Moore Monitor, Sooner Pub. Co., Moore, Okla., 1981-84, Daily Okla., Okla. Pub. Co., Oklahoma City, 1984-88; editor Yukon Review Newspaper, Yukon, Okla., 1988; adjunct prof. Dept. Journalism, U. Okla., Norman, Okla., 1990—; grad. teaching asst. Dept. History, U. Okla., Norman, Okla., 1988-94; instr. dept. history U. Okla., 1994—. Author twelve short stories, 1982-94; music album Dougherty's Fancy, 1989; contbr. articles to profl. jours. Recipient Donnell M. Owings award, Dept. History, U. Okla., Norman, 1990, Marshall Gregory award, Okla. Edn. Assn., Oklahoma City, 1986, 88, Carl Rogan award, Okla. AP, Oklahoma City, 1987. Mem. Orgn. Am. Historians, Western History Assn., Okla. Hist. Soc., Am. Hist. Assn., Small Press Writers and Artists Orgn. Avocations: folk music, cooking. Office: University of Oklahoma Dept History Norman OK 73019-0001

SELLECK, TOM, actor; b. Detroit, Jan. 29, 1945; s. Robert D. and Martha S.; m. Jacquelyn Ray, 1970 (div. 1982); 1 stepson, Kevin; m. Jillie Joan Mack, Aug. 7, 1987; 1 child, Hannah Margaret. Ph.D (hon.), Pepperdine U. Actor: (films) Myra Breckinridge, 1970, The Seven Minutes, 1971, Midway, 1976, Coma, 1982, High Road to China, 1983, Lassiter, 1984, Runaway, 1985, Three Men and a Baby, 1987, Her Alibi, 1989, An Innocent Man, 1989, Quigley Down Under, 1990, Three Men and a Little Lady, 1990, Folks!, 1992, Christopher Columbus: The Discovery, 1992, Mr. Baseball, 1992, In and Out, 1997, The Love Letter, 1999, Angus Magillicutty, 2003, (voice) Meet the Robinsons, 2007; (TV films) The Sacketts, 1979, Divorce Wars, 1982, Louis L'Amour's "The Shadow Riders", 1982, Broken Trust, 1995, Ruby Jean and Joe, 1996, Last Stand at Saher River, 1998, Louis l'Amour's Crossfire Trail, 2000, Monte Walsh, Reversible Errors, Ike: Countdown to D Day, 2004, Stone Cold, 2005, Jesse Stone: Night Passage, 2006; (TV series) The Young and the Restless, 1973-74, Magnum P.I. 1980-88, Las Vegas, 2007-; (TV appearances) Lancer, 1969, Bracken's World, 1969, Sarge, 1971, THe F.B.I., 1973, Marcus Welby, M.D., 1974-75, The Streets of San Francisco, 1975, The Rockford Files, 1978-79, Simon & Simon, 1982, Friends, 1996, 2000, Boston Legal, 2006 Bd. mem. Michael Josephson Inst. Ethics. Mem.: NRA. Office: Creative Artists Agy 2000 Ave of the Stars Los Angeles CA 90067 Office Phone: 323-962-5704.

SELLER, GREGORY EROL, marketing executive, consultant, writer; b. Denver, Oct. 4, 1953; s. Otto Gustave and Dolores Louise (Crawford) S. BBA, U. Colo., 1975. Account exec. Gt.-West Life, LA, 1975-79, asst. v.p. group devel. Denver, 1980-84; v.p. govt. mkts. and nat. accts. Great-West Life, LA, 1988—; pres., chief exec. officer Benefits Communication Corp., Denver, 1985-87, sr. v.p. govt. mkts., 1991—. Bd. dirs. Benefits Communication Co., Fascorp, Emjoy Corp, Advised Assets Group LLC. Editor newsletter Focus on 457, 1988—. Mem. vestry, treas. St. Thomas Episc. Ch., Hollywood, Calif., 1990-93 Mem. Delta Upsilon. Democrat. Office: Great West Life Ste 560 18111 Von Karman Ave Irvine CA 92612-7131

SELLER, JEFFREY, theatre producer; b. Oak Park, Mich. Grad., U. Mich., 1986. Co-founder The Booking Office, NYC; theatre prodr. Prodr.: (Broadway plays) Rent, 1996— (Drama Desk award, Outstanding Musical, 1996, Tony award, Best Musical, 1996), De La Guarda, 1998, La Bohéme, 2002—03 (Drama Desk award, Outstanding Revival of a Musical, 2003, Tony award, Best Revival of a Musical, 2003); prodr.: (Broadway plays) Private Lives, 2002 (Drama Desk award, Outstanding Revival of a Play, 2002, Tony award, Best Revival of a Play, 2002); prodr.: (Broadway plays) Avenue Q, 2003— (Tony award, Best Musical, 2004), High Fidelity, 2006, In the Heights, 2008— (Tony award, Best Musical, 2008), , 2008—, West Side Story, 2009. Achievements include producing the Broadway musical RENT, winner of the Pulitzer Prize for Drama, 1996. Office: Nederlander Theatre c/o RENT 208 W 41st St New York NY 10036-7298

SELLER, ROBERT HERMAN, cardiologist, physician; b. Phila., Mar. 21, 1931; s. David and Elsie (Straussman) S.; m. Maxine Schwartz, June 3, 1956; children: Michael, Douglas, Stuart. AB, U. Pa., 1952, MD, 1956. Intern. Grad. Hosp. of U. Pa., Phila., 1956-57; research asst. dept. pharmacology U. Pa., 1953-55; resident in cardiology, research fellow Am. Heart Assn., Phila. Gen. Hosp., 1957-58; resident in internal medicine Albert Einstein Med. Ctr., Phila., 1958-59, chief resident, 1959-60; instr. medicine Hahnemann Med. Coll. and Hosp., Phila., 1960-64, asst. prof., 1964-69, assoc. prof., 1969-72, dir. Service F, 1962-67, asst. coordinator mil. edn. for nat. def., 1961-64, dir. div. family medicine, 1967-72, acting chmn. dept. family medicine and community health, 1972-74, prof. medicine, family medicine and community health, 1973-74; practice medicine, specializing in cardiology Buffalo, 1974—; prof., chmn. dept. family medicine, prof. medicine SUNY-Buffalo, Deaconess Hosp., 1974-82, chmn. dept. family practice and dir. family practice residency program, 1974-82; prof. medicine and family medicine SUNY-Buffalo, 1974-2000; emeritus prof. medicine and family medicine, 2000—. Author: Differential Diagnosis of Common Complaints, 1986, 5th edit., 2007, Diagnosis of Common Complaints, 2004; contbr. articles to profl. jours. NIH grantee, 1972-75; Deaconess Hosp. family practice resident tng. grantee, 1975-; health professions spl. projects grantee, 1975- Fellow ACP, Am. Coll. Cardiology, Am. Acad. Family Physicians, Phila. Coll. Physicians; mem. AMA, N.Y. Med. Soc., Erie County Med. Soc., Am. Fedn. Clin. Research, Am. Heart Assn., Soc. of Tchrs. of Family Medicine, N.Y. Acad. Sci., N.Y. Acad. Family Physicians. Home Phone: 716-381-8000.

SELLERS, BAKARI T., state legislator; b. Sept. 18, 1984; Congl. intern with Congressman Jim Clyburn, 2003; mayoral intern with mayor Shirley Franklin, 2004; mem. Med. Com., Mil. Com., Pub. & Munic Affairs Com.; mem. house rep. SC; state rep. Dist. 90 SC, 2007—. Named to Power 150, Ebony Mag., 2008. Mem.: Student Govt. Assn. (pres. 2004—05), Morehouse Coll. (bd. trustee 2004—05), St. Philip's Episcopal Ch. Democrat. Address: PO Box Box 428 Denmark SC 29042 Office: 314A Blatt Bldg Columbia SC 29201 Home: 4231 Voorhees Rd Denmark SC 29042 Home Phone: 803-793-3637; Office Phone: 803-734-3003. Business E-Mail: SellersB@schouse.org.

SELLERS, ELLA JO, literature and language professor; d. Joe Carmi and Eloise Hooks Sellers. BA in English, U. NC, Wilmington, 1980; MA in Folk Studies, Western Ky. U., Bowling Green, 1981. Cert. devel. edn. specialist Appalachian State U., Boone, NC, 2008. English tchr. Sch. Extended Hope, Elizabethtown, NC, 1996—2000; English instr. Bladen CC, Dublin, NC, 2000—. Advisor BCC Drama Club, Dublin, 2006—. Recipient award, NC Governor's Office, 1998; named Tchr. of Yr., Sch. Extended Hope, Bladen County Sch., 1998—99; Kellogg fellowship, Nat. Ctr. Devel. Edn., 2007—08. Mem.: NC Folklore Soc., NC CC Faculty Assn., Sigma Kappa Delta (life; advisor 2000—). Liberal. Home: 506 E Oliver St Whiteville NC 28472 Office: Bladen CC 7418 NC Hwy 41 W Dublin NC 28332 Business E-Mail: esellers@bladencc.edu.

SELLERS, FRED EVANS, accounting educator; b. Lexington, Mo., Feb. 28, 1941; s. James MacBrayer and Rebekah Hall (Evans) S.; m. Katherine Ann Griggs, May 3, 1969; children: Mark Griggs, Rebekah Field. BA in History, Yale U., 1965; MBA, U. Kans., 1976, PhD in Bus., 1984. CPA Tex. Reporter Kansas City Star, Kansas City, Mo., 1965—66, copy editor, 1966—70, Washington Star, 1970—72, asst. nat. editor, 1972—73; asst. prof. U. Tulsa, 1979—87; assoc. prof. Southwestern U., Georgetown, Tex., 1987—. Sec., treas. planning com. U. Tulsa Conf. Accts., 1980—87; chmn. dept. econ. and bus. Southwestern U., Georgetown, Tex., 1994—2004, sec. of faculty, 2004—. Contbr. articles to profl. jours. Trustee Wentworth Mil. Acad., Lexington, Mo., 1986—, pres., 1990-92; trustee Williamson County (Tex.) Literacy Coun., 1989-91; treas., bd. dirs. St. John's Presch., Tulsa, 1984-87; conv. del. Episc. Diocese Okla., 1984, 85; audit com. St. John's Episc. Ch., Tulsa, 1983-87; bishop's com. Grace Episc. Ch., 1989, jr. warden, 1989, bishop's warden, 1990, chmn. audit com., 2004, treas., 2004-05, mem. rector search com., 2004; alt. Tex. State Rep. Conv., 1988; treas. Georgetown Area United Way, 1993-99, treas., bd. mem. Georgetown Symphony Soc., 2007-; mem. Georgetown Ethics Commn., 2004—07, vice chair, 2004-06, chair, 2006—07. Mem. Inst. Mgmt. Accts. (dir. manuscripts Austin chpt. 1988-96), Am. Acctg. Assn. (membership com. 1980-81), AICPA, Tex. Soc. CPAs (ednl. instns. com. Austin chpt.), Rotary. Avocations: bridge, piano, trombone, singing, jogging. Home: 1610 E 15th St Georgetown TX 78626-7206 Office: Southwestern U Dept Econs and Bus Adminstrn Georgetown TX 78627-0770 Home Phone: 512-863-7720; Office Phone: 512-863-1574. Business E-Mail: sellersf@southwestern.edu.

SELLERS, GREGORY JUDE, physicist; b. Far Rockaway, NY, June 20, 1947; s. Douglas L. and Rita R. (Dieringer) S.; m. Lucia S. Kim, Nov. 26, 1983; 1 child, Kristin Kim. AB in Physics, Cornell U., 1968; MS, U. Ill., 1970, PhD, 1975. Sr. scientist B-K Dynamics, Inc., Rockville, Md., 1974-76; with Allied-Signal Corp., Morristown, NJ, 1976-88, applications physicist, 1977-88; product supr. Amphenol Fiber Optic Products, Naperville, Ill., 1985-88; mgr. Cinch Connectors, Elk Grove, Ill., 1988-91; pres. Forss, Inc., Naperville, 1991-96, Fotron, Inc., Naperville, 1995—. Bd. dirs. Fotron; lectr. Benedictine U., 2004—, instr. DeVry U., 2008-. Mem. AAAS, IEEE, Am. Phys. Soc. Achievements include development and commercialization of electronic connectors and fiber optic products; development of applications for polymeric materials and glassy metals in the electrical and electronics arena. Co-inventor adhesive bonding metallic glass, electromagnetic shielding, testing of thermal insulation, amorphous antipilferage marker, amorphous spring-shield, multiple fiber positioner for optical fiber connection, raised rib waveguide ribbon for precision optical interconnects. Home and Office: Fotron Inc 7S 515 Oak Trails Dr Naperville IL 60540 Home Phone: 630-983-4146; Office Phone: 630-983-4146. E-mail: fotron1gs@aol.com.

SELLERS, PETER HOADLEY, mathematician, educator; b. Phila., Sept. 12, 1930; s. Lester Hoadley and Therese (Tyler) S.; m. Lucy Bell Newlin, June 21, 1958; children: Mortimer, Therese, Mary, Lucy Bell BA, U. Pa., 1953, MA, 1958, PhD, 1965. Math. tchr. Kangaru Sch., Embu, Kenya, 1961-63; programmer U. Pa., Phila., 1958-61; mem. faculty Rockefeller U., NYC, 1966—. Johnson Found. postdoctoral fellow, 1963-65 Mem. editl. bd. Genomics, 1986-97; author: Combinatorial Complexes, 1979; contbr. articles to profl. jours. Trustee Coll. of the Atlantic, Bar Harbor, Maine, 1985-96; curator Rockefeller Hist. Instrument Collection, 1997—. Lt (j.g.) USNR, 1953-55 Mem. Am. Math. Soc., Math. Assn. Am., Soc. Indsl. and Applied Math. Democrat. Episcopalian. Avocations: boat building, sailing. Home: 413 W Stafford St Philadelphia PA 19144-4407 Office: Rockefeller Univ 1230 York Ave New York NY 10065-6399 Business E-Mail: sellers@rockefeller.edu.

SELLERS, SHEILA RENEA, special education educator; b. Claremore, Okla., Aug. 5, 1965; d. Kathy L. Perry; m. Alfred L. Sellers, Oct. 6, 2002; children: Russell R. Howard, Austin L. Howard, Jasmine L., Jerald L., Jessica L. A in Arts & Sci., Rogers State Coll., Claremore, 1990; BE in Elem. Edn., Northeastern State U., Tahlequah, Okla., 1991; MEd in Early Childhood Spl. Edn., U. Anchorage Alaska, 2004. Cert. in tchg. Okla., Alaska. Tchr. Claremore Pub. Schs., 1991—2002; devel. specialist Programs Infants & Children, Anchorage, 2002—04, infant learning program mgr., 2004—06; asst. prof. U. Anchorage Alaska, 2006—. Ednl. cons., Anchorage, 2004—; early intervention coun. mem. Govs. Disability Spl. Edn., Anchorage, 2006—, Govs. Disability Coun., Anchorage, 2007—. Vol. I Know I Can, Anchorage, 2009, Dem. Party, Anchorage, 2008—09; v.p. Autism Partnership Project, Anchorage, 2007—09. Recipient Outstanding Parental Communication & Advocacy award, Okla. Edn. Dept., 2000, Outstanding Alumni award, U. Anchorage Alaska, 2008; named Outstanding Tchr. of Yr., 2001; Lang. to Literacy Classroom Material grant, Clarmore Pub. Sch. Found., 1996—98, 2000. Mem.: NEA, Assn. Play Therapy, Claremore Classroom Tchrs. Assn. (v.p. 2000—02), Nat. Assn. Edn. Young Child, Coun. Exceptional Children, Kappa Delta Pi Honor Soc. (historian 2008—). Liberal. Office: Univ Anchorage Alaska 3211 Providence Dr Anchorage AK 99508 Office Fax: 907-786-4474. Business E-Mail: ssellers@uaa.alska.edu.

SELLES, ROBERT HENDRIKUS, retired actuary; b. Amsterdam, Nov. 8, 1938; arrived in U.S., 1969; s. Albertus Henrikus and Jansje Suzanna (Cordes) Selles; m. Manuela Ioana Comnene, Aug. 26, 1966 (div. Mar. 1978); 1 child, Melina Joanna. B of Commerce with honors, U. Manitoba, 1961. Actuarial asst. Can. Premier Life Ins. Co., Winnipeg, Man., Canada, 1961-62; asst. actuary Sun Life Assurance Co. Can., Montreal, 1962-69; sr. v.p. Hay/Huggins Co., Inc., Phila., 1969—2004, ret., 2004. Fellow: Soc. Actuaries; mem.: Gavel Soc., Western Pension and Benefits Conf., Am. Acad. Actuaries, Conf. Cons. Actuaries, Netherlands Am. Assn. Delaware Valley (bd. dirs. 1993—96), Rainbow River Inc. (pres. 1995—2005), Netherlands Soc. Phila. (bd. dirs. 1991—, pres. 1993—96, 1999—2000), Internat. Benefits Found., Actuaries Club San Francisco. Home: 1420 Locust St Apt 34-A Philadelphia PA 19102-4220 Personal E-mail: rselles@aol.com. Business E-Mail: robert@sellers.us.

SELLEY, MICHAEL L., pharmaceutical company executive; b. Woking, Surrey, U.K., Jan. 20, 1948; s. Stanley John and Rosina Lillian Selley; m. Angela Grace Charlton, July 30, 1966 (div. Sept. 1976); 1 child, Michelle Louise; m. Pamela Kay Foulser, Oct. 29, 1977; 1 child, Timothy Michael. BSc, U. London, 1968; MSc, U. Alta., Edmonton, 1971; PhD, U. Sydney, 1975. Sr. rsch. scientist Sandoz Pharma Ltd., Basle, Switzerland, 1975-84; sr. rsch. fellow John Curtin Sch. Med. Rsch. Inst. Advanced Studies, Australian Nat. U., Canberra, 1985-95; chief of staff Office of the Min. for Sci., Parliament Ho., Canberra, 1996-97; chmn. and mng. dir. Pan Australia Labs Pty. Ltd., Symonston, 1997—99; chmn., CEO Angiogen Pharms. Pty. Ltd., Sydney, 1999—2006; chief sci. officer Nuon Therapeutics Inc., San Mateo, 2006—08; chmn. & CEO Xenexus Pharm., North Ryde, 2008—. Contbr. articles to profl. jours. Anutech Canberra Tech. Partnership grantee, 1991-93. Fellow Royal Australian Chem. Inst. Achievements include patents for new drugs for the treatment of autoimmune and neurodegenerative diseases. Avocations: horseback riding, golf, classical music, wine. Home: 19 Holmes St Turramurra NSW 2074 Australia Office: Level 9 Avaya House 123 Epping Rd North Ryde NSW 2113 Australia Home Phone: 61 2 9440 0764; Office Phone: 612 8985 7317. Office Fax: 612 8875 7777; Home Fax: 612 9144 3175. Business E-Mail: mlselley@xenexuspharma.com.

SELLIN, JOSEPH HENRY, gastroenterologist; b. NYC, Mar. 25, 1948; s. Stephen and Regina Sellin; m. Rena Sellin; children: Angela, Jonathan. BA magna cum laude, Amherst Coll., 1969; MD, Albert Einstein Coll. Medicine, 1973. Diplomate Am. Bd. Internal Medicine, sub-bd. in Gastroenterology. Med. intern Montefiore Hosp., Bronx, N.Y., 1973-74, resident in medicine, 1974-76; rsch. fellow in medicine Albert Einstein Coll. Medicine, Bronx, 1976-77; fellow in medicine U. Chgo., 1977-79, rsch. assoc., instr., 1979-80; asst. prof. medicine U. Tex. Med. Sch., Houston, 1980-87, asst. prof. medicine and physiology, 1986-87, assoc. prof. medicine and physiology, 1987-94, prof. medicine and integrative biology, 1994—, dir. div. gastroenterology, 1990—. Mem. staff Hermann Hosp., chief gastroenterology, 1990—, chmn. gastrintestinal endoscopy com., 1992—; mem. staff Lyndon Baines Johnson Hosp., St. Joseph's Hosp., Methodist Hosp. Contbr. numerous articles to profl. jours. John Woodruff Simpson fellow, 1969; AGA Marion rsch. scholar, 1984-87; NIH grantee, 1982-85,86-89, 86-90, 89—; recipient several awards. Fellow Am. Coll. Gastroenterology Investigation; mem. Am. Gastroent. Assn., Am. Physiol. Soc., Am. Soc. for Clin. Investigation, Crohn's and Colitis Found. Am. (regional med. advisor 1991-94), Gastrointestinal Rsch. Group, Harris County Med. Soc., Houston Gastroent. Soc., Houston Gulf Coast Ileitis and Colitis Found. (co-chair med. adv. com. 1990-92), Soc. for Exptl. Biology and Medicine, Tex. Med. Assn., Tex. Soc. for Gastroenterology and Endoscopy, Phi Beta Kappa. Office: U Tex Med Sch 6431 Fannin St 4234 MSB Houston TX 77030-1501

SELLIN, THEODORE, diplomat, consultant; b. Phila., June 17, 1928; s. Thorsten and Amy (Anderson) S.; m. Taru Jarvi, July 10, 1965; 1 child, Derek. Student, U. Uppsala, Sweden, 1946-48; BA, U. Pa., 1951, MA, 1952. Joined Fgn. Svc., Dept. State, 1952; vice consul Copenhagen, 1952-56; rsch. analyst Dept. State, Washington, 1956-58; program officer Office Internat. Confs., 1965-67; acad. tng. staff U. Ind., 1958-59; 2d sec. Am. Embassy, Helsinki, Finland, 1959-64, 1st sec., polit. officer, 1971-73, 1st sec., labor-polit. officer Oslo, 1967-71; polar affairs officer Dept. State, 1975; consul gen. Goteborg, Sweden, 1978-80; fgn. rels. cons. Dept. State, Washington, 1980—. Office: Dept State A/GIS/IPS/CR/EAN Washington DC 20520

SELLINGSLOH, HULDA KNIPLING, retired artist; b. Port Lavaca, Tex., Nov. 29, 1912; d. Henry John and Hulda (Rasch) Knipling; m. August Sellingsloh, May 1, 1943 (dec. Apr. 1998); children: Susan Louise, Marian Kay, Ellen Agnes, John August. LLB, Houston Law Sch., 1939. Bar: Tex. 1940. Sec. draftsman Calhoun County Abstract Co., Port Lauaca, 1933—34; sec. to pres. Tex. Luth. Coll., Seguin, 1935—36; legal sec., draftsman Fohs Oil Co., Houston, 1936—43; draftsman, asst. engr. U.S. Coast & Geodetic Survey, Balt., 1943—45; civic leader various civic and religious orgns., Beacon and Fishkill, NY, 1945—72; profl. visual artist NY, N.Mex., and Tex., 1973—99. Leader, pres. various chs., clubs, Beacon and Fishkill, 1950—72; artist Eastside Creative Art Club, 1960—72; pres. Santa Fe chpt. Artists Equity, N.Mex., 1973—78. Author: (life history) Top Crop, 1999—2000. Pres. Houston Women Lawyers, 1943, Santa Fe Artists Assn., 1974—76, St. John's Women's Club, Beacon, 1959—60, 1966—69; pres., leading minister St. Clare Secular Franciscan Fraternity, Crowley, Tex. Recipient numerous awards, various regional art assns., 1960—, Best of Show awards, Santa Fe, N.Y., Tex., 1960—, Editors Choice award, Nat. Libr. Poets, 1998, 2008. Mem.: Tex. Bar Assn., Pastel Soc. Am. (juried assoc.), Tarrant County Women's Section, Internat. Soc. Poets. Democrat. Roman Catholic. Home: 5 Oak Dr Hopewell Junction NY 12533

SELLKE, FRANK WILLIAM, cardiothoracic surgeon, researcher; b. Ft. Wayne, Ind., Feb. 5, 1956; s. Erwin A. and Anna Luise (Schumacher) S.; m. Amy Marie Brill, Jan. 31, 1987; children: Michelle, Eric, Nicholas, Amanda. AB summa cum laude, Wabash Coll., 1978; MD, Ind. U., Indpls., 1981. Diplomate Am. Bd. Thoracic Surgery, Am. Bd. Surgery. Intern Ind. U. Hosp., Indpls., 1981-82; emergency physician Culver Union Hosp., Crawfordsville, Ind., 1982-83; resident in surgery Akron (Ohio) City Hosp., 1983-87; postdoctoral fellow cardiac surgery U. Iowa, Iowa City, 1987-90; from instr. to asst. prof. surgery Harvard Med. Sch., Boston, 1990-95, assoc. prof. surgery, 1995—2000, prof. surgery, 2000—; cardiothoracic surgeon Beth Israel Hosp., Boston, 1990—; chief cardiothoracic surgery Beth Israel Deaconess Med. Ctr., Boston, 1999—2006, chief cardiothoracic surgery rsch., 2006—08; chief cardiothoracic surgery & prof. Brown Med. Sch., 2009—. Chmn. dept. cardiovascular surgery and medicine Landmark Med. Ctr., 2005—08. Mem. editl. bd. Jour. Thoracic and Cardiovascular Surgery, Jour. Cardiac Surgery, Shock; contbr. rsch. articles to profl. jours. Fellow Am. Coll. Cardiology, Am. Coll. Surgeons; mem. AMA, Am. Surg. Assn., Am. Heart Assn., Am. Physiol. Soc., Am. Coll. Chest Physicians, Soc. Univ. Surgeons, Assn. Acad. Surgeons, Am. Assn. for Thoracic Surgery, Soc. Thoracic Surgeons, Phi Beta Kappa. Lutheran. Home: 121 Monadnock Rd Chestnut Hill MA 02467-1136 Office: Beth Israel Deaconess Med Ctr 110 Francis St Boston MA 02215 Office Phone: 617-632-8385, 401-444-2732. Business E-Mail: fsellke@bidmc.harvard.edu, fsellke@lifespan.org.

SELLMYER, DAVID JULIAN, physicist, researcher; b. Joliet, Ill., Sept. 28, 1938; s. Marcus Leo and Della Louise (Plumhoff) S.; m. Catherine Joyce Zakas, July 16, 1962; children: Rebecca Ann, Julia Maryn, Mark Anthony. BS, U. Ill., 1960; PhD, Mich. State U., 1965. Asst. prof. MIT, Cambridge, 1965-72, assoc. prof., 1972; U. Nebr., Lincoln, 1972-75, prof., 1975—, chmn. dept. physics, 1978-84, George Holmes disting. prof., 1987—, dir. Nebr. Ctr. Materials and Nanosci., 1988—. Contbr. articles, book revs. to refereed jours. Recipient tech. award NASA, 1972; disting. vis. prof. S.D. Sch. Mines and Tech., Rapid City, 1981. Fellow Am. Phys. Soc. Office: U Nebr Lincoln Nebr Ctr Materials and Nanosci 112 Brace Lab Lincoln NE 68588-0111 Business E-Mail: dsellmyer@unl.edu.

SELLS, BOAKE ANTHONY, private investor; b. Ft. Dodge, Iowa, June 24, 1937; s. Lyle M. and Louise (Gadd) S.; m. Marian S. Stephenson, June 20, 1959; children: Damian, Brian, Jean Ann. BSc, U. Iowa, 1959; MBA, Harvard U., 1969. Bus. office mgr. Northwestern Bell Tel., Des Moines, 1959-63; salesman Hydraulic Cos., Ft. Dodge,

1964-67; pres. Cole Nat. Corp., Cleve., 1969-83; vice chmn. Dayton Hudson Corp., Mpls., 1983-84, pres., 1984-87; chmn., pres., chief exec. officer Revco D.S., Inc., Twinsburg, Ohio, 1987-92. Trustee Cleve. Play House, Mus. Contemporary Art, Cleve., dir.

SELMAN, ALAN LOUIS, computer science educator; b. NYC, Apr. 2, 1941; s. Dan and Rose (Grass) S.; m. Sharon Jevotovsky, July 7, 1963; children: Jeffrey, Heather. BS in Math. cum laude, City Coll., CUNY, 1962; MA, U. Calif., Berkeley, 1964; PhD, Pa. State U., 1970. Asst. prof. computer sci. Fla. State U., Tallahassee, 1972-77; assoc. prof. Iowa State U., Ames, 1977-82, prof., 1982-86, Northea. U., Boston, 1986-90, acting dean, 1988-89; prof., chmn. dept. computer sci. U. Buffalo, Buffalo, 1990-96; prof. dept. computer sci. SUNY, Buffalo, 1990-98, prof. dept. computer sci. and engring., 1998—. Editor: Complexity Theory Retrospective, 1990; assoc. editor Jour. Computer and Sys. Scis.; mem. editl. bd. Chgo. Jour. Theoretical Computer Sci.; co-editor: Complexity Theory Retrospective II, 1997; editor-in-chief Theory Computing Sys. Fulbright award, 1981-82; recipient Humboldt Rsch. award, 2005. Fellow Assn. Computing Machinery, Invitation Fellowship Japan Soc. Promotion Rsch. Office: U Buffalo Dept Computer Sci-Engring 201 Bell Hall Buffalo NY 14260-2000 Business E-Mail: selman@buffalo.edu.

SELMAN, JAY E., neurologist; b. 1945; AB in Polit. Sci., Washington U., St. Louis, 1967, MS in Speech and Hearing, 1969; MD, U. Tex. Southwestern Med. Sch., Dallas, 1973. Diplomate Am. Bd. Pediat., Am. Bd. Psychiatry & Neurology with added qualification in clin. neurophysiology, special competence in child neurology. Intern pediat. Albert Einstein Coll. Medicine/Bronx Mcpl. Hosp., NY, 1973—77, resident pediat. and neurology NY, 1974—78, fellowship pediat. neurology NY, 1976—77; assoc. clin. prof. neurology Columbia U. Coll. Physicians and Surgeons, NYC, 1992—; attending neurologist No. Westchester Hosp., Mount Kisco, NY. Head Stroke Liaison Com. No. Westchester Hosp.; mem. profl. adv. bd. Epilepsy Found.; mem. learning network Jewish Bd. Family and Child Svcs. NY; vis. clin. asst. prof. neurology Albert Einstein Coll. Med.; neurological cons. Blythedale Children's Hosp., Valhalla, NY, 2002—, chief pediat. neurology, 2008—. Contbr. articles to profl. jours. Named one of NY's Top Dr.'s, Castle Connolly Med. LTD. Mem.: Epilepsy Soc. So. NY, Child Neurology Soc., Am. Acad. Neurology and Movement Disorders, Am. Epilepsy Soc. Home: 95 Bradhurst Ave Valhalla NY 10595-1637 Office Fax: 914-666-7371. Personal E-mail: jay_selman@yahoo.com.

SELMAN, RUSSELL BERTRAM, lawyer, department chairman; b. Oceanside, NY, May 31, 1954; s. Leon Daniel and Lorraine Thelma (Leichter) S.; m. Elizabeth Friedgut. BA, New Coll., 1975; MPA, Syracuse U., 1978; JD, Washington U., 1980. Bar: Ill. 1987, D.C. 1981, Mo. 1980. Asst. enforcement counsel U.S. Environ. Protection Agy., Washington, 1980-82, atty., advisor, 1983; atty. McKenna, Conner & Cuneo, Washington, 1983-86, Schiff, Hardin & Waite, Chgo., 1986-88, Bell, Boyd & Lloyd, Chgo., 1988-93; ptnr., chmn. environ. law dept. Katten Muchin Rosenman, Chgo., 1993—. Contbr. Chicago Lawyer mag. Office: Foley & Lardner 321 N Clark St Chicago IL 60654 Office Phone: 312-832-9405. Business E-Mail: russell.selman@kattenlaw.com.

SELMORE, DAMETRIA SUZANNE, actor; d. Damon Edward Selmore and Earnestine Jeanette Ganzy. BA in Theatre Performance, Fla. A&M U., Tallahassee, 2008. Parlimentarian Essential Theatre Union, Tallahassee, 2007—08; pres., black grad. student orgn. U. Fla., Gainesville, 2008—. Dir.(actor): (play) For Colored Girls Who Have Considered Suicide When The Rainbow Is Enuf, A Raisin in the Sun (Best Actress nominee, 2002); actor, actor: The Vagina Monologues, Wit, And Baby Makes 7, The Laramie Project, The Piano Lesson (Best Actress award, 2003), To Kill A Mockingbird (Best Supporting Actress award, 2004), The Guys, Flyin' West; dir.: Yellowman by Dael Orlandersmith; actor: Dearly Departed, 365 Days 365 Plays, Living in Colour; singer (actor): (musical) Little Shop of Horrors, Dreamgirls, School House Rock! Live!; actor: The Colored Museum, 2009. Founder Black Artists Movement, Tallahassee, Fla.; counselor Dept. Childrens & Families, Fla.; mem. Mt. Mariah Primitive Bapt. Ch., Lamont, Fla., 2005—08. Mem.: Zeta Phi Beta. Democrat. Baptist. Avocations: singing, swimming, guitar, reading, piano. Office: Univ Fla Sch Theatre PO Box 115900 Gainesville FL 32611 Home: 2959 Apalachre Pkwy Apt B24 Tallahassee FL 32301 Office Fax: 352-392-5114. Personal E-mail: dametriaselmore@yahoo.com. Business E-Mail: dselmore@ufl.edu, sotd@arts.ufl.edu.

SELOVER, R. EDWIN, lawyer, utilities executive; b. Norman, Okla., Aug. 18, 1945; BA, Union Coll., 1967; JD, U. Minn., 1972. Bar: NJ 1972. Atty. Pub. Svc. Electric & Gas Co. (PSE&G), Newark, 1972-75, asst. gen. counsel, 1975-79, assoc. gen. counsel, 1979-80, gen. counsel, 1980-83, v.p., gen. counsel, 1983-88, sr. v.p., gen. counsel, 1988—; v.p., gen. counsel Pub. Svc. Enterprise Group Inc. (PSEG), Newark, 1988—2002, sr. v.p., gen. counsel, 2002—06, exec. v.p., gen. counsel, 2006—; sr. v.p., gen. counsel PSEG Services Corp., 1999—2006. Bd. trustees NJ Conservation Found., NJ Future, 1998—, Stockton Alliance, NJ; nuc. ind. sector chmn., Infrastructure Adv. Com. NJ Office of Counterterrorism. Served US Army, 1969—71. Mem.: NJ Bar Assn., ABA. Office: Pub Svc Enterprise Group Inc PO Box 570 Newark NJ 07101 Office Phone: 973-430-7000.*

SELTSER, RAYMOND, epidemiologist, educator, preventive medicine physician; b. Boston, Dec. 17, 1923; s. Israel and Hannah (Littman) S.; m. Charlotte Frances Gale, Nov. 16, 1946; children: Barry Jay, Andrew David. MD, Boston U., 1947; MPH, Johns Hopkins U., 1957. Diplomate Am. Bd. Preventive Medicine (trustee, sec.-treas. 1974-77), Am. Bd. Med. Specialties (mem. exec. com. 1976-77). Asst. chief med. info. and intelligence br. U.S. Dept. Army, 1953-56; epidemiologist divsn. internal health USPHS, 1956-57; from asst. prof. to prof. epidemiology Johns Hopkins U. Sch. Hygiene and Pub. Health, Balt., 1957-81, assoc. dean, 1967-77, dep. dir. Oncology Ctr., 1977-81; dean U. Pitts. Grad. Sch. Pub. Health, 1981-87, prof. epidemiology, 1981-88, emeritus dean, emeritus prof. epidemiology, 1988—; assoc. dir. USPHS Ctrs. for Disease Control, Rockville, Md., 1988-90; assoc. dir. Ctr. for Gen. Health Svcs. Extramural Rsch. Agy. for Health Care Policy and Rsch., Rockville, 1990-95, sr. advisor spl. population rsch. Ctr. Primary Care Rsch., 1995-98; med. and healthcare advisor Dept. Va Office Inspector Gen. Office Health Care Inspections, Chevy Chase, Md., 1997—2000. Cons. NIMH, 1958-70, also various govtl. health agys., 1958-79; expert cons. Pres.'s Commn. on Three Mile Island, 1979-80; mem. Three Mile Island Adv. Panel Health, Nat. Cancer Inst. Cancer Control Grant Rev. Com., Pa. Dept. Health Preventive Health Service Block Grant Adv. Task Force, Gov.'s VietNam Herbicide Info. Commn. Pa.; chmn. Toxic/Health Effects Adv. Com., 1985-87. Trustee, exec. com., chmn. profl. adv. com. Harmarville Rehab. Ctr., Pitts., 1982-87; bd. dirs. Health Edn. Ctr., Media Info. Svc.; chmn. USPHS Task Force on Improving Med. Criteria for SSA Disability Determination, 1988-92. Capt. AUS, 1951-53, Korea Decorated Bronze Star; recipient Centennial Alumni citation Boston U. Sch. Medicine, 1973; elected to Johns Hopkins Soc. of Scholars, 1986. Fellow AAAS, APHA (mem. governing coun. 1975-77, chmn. EPI sect. coun. 1979-80), Pa. Pub. Health Assn. (bd. dirs. 1985-88, pres.-elect 1986-88), Am. Coll. Preventive Medicine, Am. Heart Assn.; mem. Am. Epidemiol. Assn., Internat. Epidemiol. Assn., Am. Soc. Preventive Oncology, Am. Cancer Soc. (bd. dirs. Pa. divsn. 1985-87, exec. com. 1986-87), Assn. Schs. Pub. Health (sec. 1969-71, exec. com., chmn. edn. com. 1983-87), Soc. Med. Cons. Armed Forces, Soc. Epidemiologic Rsch., Nat. Coun. Radiation Protection and Measurements (consociate), Johns Hopkins Alumni Coun. (exec. com. 1994-97), Sigma Xi, Delta Omega, Nat. Acad. Practice, Nat. Acad. Practice Medicine. E-mail: rseltser@comcast.net.

SELTZER, BARRY S., federal judge; b. 1954; BA magna cum laude, Hamilton Coll., 1976; MBA, JD, NYU, 1980, LLM in Taxation, 1984. Atty. Trenam, Simmons, Kemker, Scharf, Barkin, Frye & O'Neill, Tampa, Fla., 1980-82; asst. U.S. atty. So. Dist. Fla., 1984-88; judge Broward County Ct., 1988-91; magistrate judge U.S. Dist. Ct. (so. dist.) Fla., Ft. Lauderdale, 1991—. Comment editor NYU Law Rev. of Law and Social Change. Recipient Spl. Achievement award Dept. Justice, plaques and commendations Drug Enforcement Agy., US Secret Svc., Bur. of Alcohol, Tobacco and Firearms, Postal Inspection Svc., US Customs Svc., USDA. Mem. ABA, Fed. Bar Assn., Fla. Bar, Broward County Bar Assn., Fed. Magistrate Judges Assn., Stephen Booher Inn of Ct. (past pres.), B'nai B'rith Justice Unit (past pres.), Beta Gamma Sigma. Office: 109 US Courthouse 299 E Broward Blvd Fort Lauderdale FL 33301-1944

SELTZER, BENJAMIN, neurologist, educator; b. Phila., Aug. 5, 1945; s. Albert P. and Sylvia (Superstein) S.; m. Natalie C. Ross, Oct. 13, 1974; children: Daniel, Jennifer, Peter, Nathan. AB, U. Pa., 1965; MD, Jefferson Med. Coll., 1969. Fellow in neurology Harvard Med. Sch., Boston, 1970-73, lectr. on neurology, 1978-88, assoc. prof. neurology, 2008—; staff neurologist Boston City Hosp., 1973-75, Beth Israel Hosp., 1975-88; chief dementia study unit VA Hosp., Bedford, Mass., 1978-88; from asst. to assoc. prof. neurology and psychiatry Boston U. Sch. Medicine, 1978-88; prof. neurology, psychiatry and anatomy, dir. divsn. behavioral neurosci. Tulane U. Sch. Medicine, New Orleans, 1988—2006, vis. prof., 2006—. Adj. prof. psychology U. New Orleans, 1990—2000. Contbr. numerous articles to med. and sci. jours. Fellow Am. Acad. Neurology, Royal Soc. Medicine (London); mem. Soc. for Neurosci., Gerontol. Soc. Am, Brigham Behavioral Neurology Group, 2006-. Home: 30 Longwood Ave Brookline MA 02446

SELTZER, VICKI LYNN, obstetrician, gynecologist; b. June 2, 1949; d. Herbert Melvin and Marian Elaine (Willinger) Seltzer; m. Richard Stephen Brach, Sept. 2, 1973; children: Jessica Lillian Brach, Eric Robert Brach. BS, Rensselaer Poly. Inst., 1969; MD, NYU, 1973. Diplomate Am. Bd. Ob-Gyn. (examiner 1988-2001). Intern Bellevue Hosp., NYC, 1973—74, resident ob-gyn., 1974—77; fellow gynecol. cancer Am. Cancer Soc., NYC, 1977—78, Meml. Sloan Kettering Cancer Ctr., NYC, 1978—79; assoc. dir. gynecol. cancer Albert Einstein Coll. Medicine, NYC, 1979—83, prof. ob-gyn., 1989—. Assoc. prof. ob-gyn SUNY, Stony Brook, 1983—89; Edie and Marvin H. Shur prof. ob-gyn and women's health Albert Einstein Coll. Medicine, NYC, 2003—; dir. ob-gyn. Queens Hosp. Ctr., Jamaica, NY, 1983—93, pres. med. bd., 1986—89; chair ob-gyn L.I. Jewish Med. Ctr., 1993—; v.p. women's health svcs. North Shore-L.I. Jewish Health Sys., 1999—; chair ob-gyn North Shore U. Hosp., 1999—, chair med. bd., 2001—; mem. steering com. N.Y. State Coun. Grad. Med. Edn., 2005—, chair subcom. primary care; mem. U.S. Coun. Grad. Med. Edn., 2006—. Author: Every Woman's Guide to Breast Cancer, 1987; editor: Women's Primary Health Care, 1995, 2000; editor-in-chief: Primary Care Update for the Ob-Gyn, 1993—; mem. editl. bd. Women's Life mag., 1980—82, Jour. Jacobs Inst. Women's Health, 1990—95, Ob-Gyn. Survey, 2005—, Jour. Reproductive Medicine, 2005—, mem. internat. editl. bd. Jour. Soc. Obstreticians and Gynecologists Can., 2000—; contbr. articles to profl. jours.; host (TV series) Weekly Ob-Gyn. program, Lifetime Med. TV. Mem. Mayor Beame's Task Force on Rape, NYC, 1974—76; chair health com. Nat. Coun. Women, NYC, 1979—84; bd. govs. Nat. Coun. Women's Health, 1985—94; chair Coun. Resident Edn. Ob-Gyn., 1987—93. Recipient citation, Nat. Safety Coun., 1978, Achiever award, L.I. Ctr. Bus. and Profl. Women, 1987; Galloway Fund fellow, 1975. Fellow: ACOG (gynecol. practice com. 1981, v.p. 1993—94, pres.-elect 1996—97, pres. 1997—98), N.Y. Obstet. Soc. (pres. 1999—2000); mem.: Am. Hosp. Assn. (governing coun. maternal and child health 2004—, chair-elect 2007, chair 2008), N.Y. Cancer Soc., Am. Med. Women's Assn. (com. chair 1975—79, editl. bd. jour. 1986—2002, citation 1973), Internat. Fedn. Gynecology and Obstetrics (internat. steering com. to reduce maternal mortality 2000—02), Women's Med. Assn. (v.p. N.Y. 1974—79, resident rev. com. ob-gyn 1993—98, Lila Wallis Lifetime Achievement award 2002), NYU Sch. Med. Alumni Assn. (bd. govs. 1979—, v.p. 1987—91, pres. 1992—93), Alpha Omega Alpha.

SELTZER, WILLIAM, statistician, social science administrator; b. NYC, Sept. 22, 1934; s. William B. Seltzer and Edith S. (Goldman) Alt.; m. Jane E. Berger, Nov. 20, 1970; children: Benjamin, Ezra. BA, U. Chgo., 1956. Rsch. asst. Health Info. Found., NYC, 1957-60; statistician U.S. Bur. Census, Suitland, Md., 1960-64; advisor Pakistan Inst. Devel., Econs. and Cen. Statis. Office, Karachi, 1964-68; staff assoc. Population Coun., NYC, 1968-74; br. chief UN Statis. Office, NYC, 1974-86, dir., 1986-94; sr. advisor to under-sec.-gen. Dept. Econ. and Social Info. and Policy Analysis, NYC, 1993-94; sr. rsch. schlar Fordham U., NYC, 1995—. Mem. com. on population and demography, chair panel on data collection NAS, Washington, 1977-82, mem. Roundtable on the Demography of Forced Migration, 2001-04; cons. UN Population Fund, 1995, Internat. Criminal Tribunal for Rwanda, 1996, UN Stats. Divsn., 1996-98, Internat. Labor Office, 1997, World Bank, 1997-98; mem. panel of Ind. Experts, Metagora Project Orgn. for Econ. Cooperation and Devel., 2005—07. Author: Poems, 1960, Politics and Statistics, 1994; co-author: Population Growth Estimation, 1973; also various UN documents, jour. articles, reports. Fellow Am. Statis. Assn. (chair social stats. sect. 1983-84, chair com. on internat. rels. 1986-87, chair com. on profl. ethics 2000—05), Scientific Freedom and Human Rights Com. (chair), Royal Statis. Soc. (hon.;); mem. Population Assn. Am., Internat. Statis. Inst., Internat. Assn. Ofcl. Statisticians. Mem. Soc. Of Friends. Office: Fordham U Dept Sociology and Anthropology 441 E Fordham Rd Bronx NY 10458-5149 Office Phone: 718-817-3868. E-mail: seltzer@fordham.edu.

SELVA, PAUL JOSEPH, career military officer; b. 1958; BS in Aeronautical Engring., US Air Force Acad., Colo. Springs, Colo., 1980; Grad., Squadron Office Sch., Maxwell AFB, 1983; MS in Mgmt. & Human Rels., Abilene Christian U., Abilene, Tex., 1984; Disting. Grad., Air Command & Staff Coll., Maxwell AFB, 1992; MS in Polit. Sci., Auburn U., Montgomery, Ala., 1992; Nat. Def. Fellow, Sec. Def. Strategic Studies Group, Rosslyn, Va., 1996. Advanced through grades to lt. gen. USAF, 2008, undergraduate pilot training Reese AFB, Tex., 1980—81; co-pilot, aircraft comdr. 917th Air Refueling Squadron, Dyess AFB, Tex., 1981—84; co-pilot, aircraft comdr., instructor pilot and flight comdr. 32nd Refueling Squadron, Barksdale AFB, La., 1984—88; company grade adviser to comdr. Strategic Air Command, mgr. offensive aircraft sys., exec. officer, dep. chief staff plans and resources Strategic Air Command (SAC), Offutt AFB, Nebr., 1989—91; instr. pilot, fight comdr. 9th Air Refueling Squadron, March AFB, Calif.; comdr. 722nd Ops. Support Squadron, March AFB, Calif., 1992—94, 9th Air Refueling Squadron, Travis AFB, Calif.; dep. condr. 60th Ops. Group, Travis AFB, Calif., 1994—95, comdr., 1998—2000; asst. to dir. Office of Sec. of Defense for Net Assessment The Pentagon, Washington, 1996—98; comdr. 62nd Airlift Wing, McChord AFB, Wash., 2000—02; vice comdr. Tanker Airlift Control Ctr., Scott AFB, Ill., 2000—03, comdr., 2003—04; dir. ops. US Transp. Command (USTRANSCOM), Scott AFB, Ill., 2004—06; dir. Air Force Strategic Planning, dep. chief staff strategic plans and programs USAF, Washington, 2006—08, dir. Air Force Quadrennial Defense Review, Office of Air Force Chief of Staff, 2007—08; asst. to chmn. of Joint Chiefs of Staff US Dept. Def., 2007—. Decorated Defense Superior Svc. Medal, Legion of Merit with two oak leaf clusters, Defense Meritorious Svc. Medal, Meritorious Svc. Medal with three oak leaf clusters, Air Force Commendation Medal, Air Force Achievement Medal, Combat Readiness Medal with two oak leaf clusters, Nat. Defense Svc. Medal with oak leaf cluster, Armed Forces Expeditionary Medal with two bronze stars, S.W. Asia Svc. Medal with bronze star, Global War on Terrorism Svc. Medal; recipient Armed Forces Svc. Medal; Nat. Def. Fellow, Sec. of Def. Strategic Studies Group, 1996. Office: Joint Chiefs of Staff US Dept Def 9999 Joint Staff Pentagon Washington DC 20318-9999*

SELVADURAI, ANTONY PATRICK SINNAPPA, civil engineer, mathematician, educator, consultant; b. Matara, Sri-Lanka, Sept. 23, 1942; arrived in Can., 1975; s. Kanapathiyar Sinnappa and W. Mary Adeline (Fernando) S.; m. Sally Joyce; children: Emily, Paul, Mark, Elizabeth. Diploma in Engring., Brighton Poly., 1964; Diploma, Imperial Coll./London U., 1965; MS, Stanford U., 1967; PhD in Theoretical Mechanics, U. Nottingham, 1971, DSc in Theoretical Mechanics, 1986. Registered profl. engr., Can.; chartered mathematician, UK. Staff rsch. engr. Woodward Clyde Assoc., Oakland, Calif., 1966-67; rsch. assoc. dept. theoretical mechanics U. Nottingham, 1969-70; lectr. dept. civil engring. U. Aston, Birmingham, England, 1971-75; asst. prof. civil engring. Carleton U., Ottawa, Ont., Canada, 1975-76, assoc. prof., 1976-81, prof., 1982-93, chmn. dept., 1982-90, Davidson Dunton Rsch. lectr., 1987; prof., chmn. dept. civil engring./applied mechanics McGill U., Montreal, Canada, 1993-96, William Scott prof., 2004, James McGill prof., 2005. Vis. rsch. sci. Bechtel Group, Inc., San Francisco, 1981-82; vis. prof. U. Nottingham, 1986, Inst. de Mécanique de Grenoble, France, 1990; cons. Atomic Energy of Can. Ltd., Pinawa, Man., 1983-96—, Ministry of Transp. Ont., Toronto, 1984-97, Fleet Tech., Ottawa, 1988—, Atomic Energy Control Bd., 1987—. Author: Elastic Analysis of Soil Foundation Interaction, 1979, (with R.O. Davis) Elasticity and Geomechanics, 1996, (with R.O. Davis) Plasticity and Geomechanics, 2002; editor: Mechanics of Structured Media, 1981, (with G.Z. Voyiadjis) Mechanics of Material Interfaces, 1986, Developments of Mechanics, 1987, (with M.M. Zaman and C.S. Desai) Recent Accomplishments and Future Trends in Geomechanics in the 21st Century, (with M.J. Boulon) Mechanics of Geomaterial Interfaces, 1995, Mechanics of Poroelastic Media, 1996, Partial Differential Equations in Mechanics, Vol. 1, Fundamentals, Laplace's Equation, Diffusion Equation, Wave Equation, 2000, Vol. 2, The Biharmonic Equation, Poisson's Equation, 2000, (with J.M. Hill) Mathematics and Mechanics of Granular Materials, 2005. King George VI Meml. fellow English Speaking Union of Commonwealth, 1965, Rsch. fellow SRC, UK, 1969, Erskine fellow U. Canterbury, New Zealand, 1992, 98, Killam Rsch. fellow Can. Coun. for Arts, 2000-02; recipient Rsch. award Alexander von Humboldt Found., 1997, Gold medal Can. Congress Applied Mechanics, 2007. Fellow Royal Soc. Can., Am. Acad. Mechanics, Can. Soc. Civil Engring. (Leipholz medal 1991), Assoc. Profl. Engrs. Ont. (Engring. medal 1993), Engring. Inst. Can., Inst. Math. and Its Applications, Can. Acad. Engring.; mem. Internat. Assn. for Computer Methods and Advances in Geomechanics (award for significant paper in the category theory computational analytical 1994, paper prize computational and analytical theory category 1997, John Booker medal 2001), Max Planck Soc. (Max Planck Rsch. prize 2003), Can. Coun. for Arts (Killam prize 2007), Canadian Congress for Applied Mechanics (Gold medal 2007), Internat. Assn. Computer Methods and Advances Geomechanics (Outstanding Accomplishments award). Roman Catholic. Office: McGill U Dept Civil Engring Montreal PQ Canada H3A 2K6 E-mail: patrick.selvadurai@mcgill.ca.

SELVARAJU, RAGHURAM, medical researcher; s. Muthusamy Selvaraju and Sadhonadevi Gunaratnam. BS, Carnegie Mellon U., Pitts., 1999; MS, U. Geneva, 2001, PhD, 2004; MBA, Cornell U., Ithaca, NY, 2005. NASD Series 7, 63, 86 and 87 NY, 2005. Pharm. rschr. Serono S.A., Geneva, 2000—04; biotech. equity rsch. analyst Rodman & Renshaw LLC, NYC, 2005—08; sr. v.p. & head healthcare rsch. Hapoalim Securities USA, Inc., NYC, 2009—. Fin. dir. Flamenco Latino, NYC, 2005—09. Recipient Inventorship Award, Serono S.A., 2002. Mem.: Am. Neurol. Assn., Soc. Neurosci., AAAS. Achievements include discovery of remyelinating properties of the secreted protein osteopontin, a potential therapy for the neurodegenerative diseases multiple sclerosis and peripheral neuropathy; establishment of the myelination-stimulating properties of various chemokine proteins, signaling molecules that may be therapeutically applicable in dysmyelinating disorders such as multiple sclerosis. Home Phone: 646-784-2027; Office Phone: 212-898-6301.

SELVER, PAUL DARRYL, lawyer; b. NYC, May 28, 1947; s. Rene T. Selver and Marilyn (Steiner) Pomerance; m. Ellen J. Roller, Jan. 22, 1984; children: Adam, Max, Katelyn. BA magna cum laude, Harvard U., 1969, JD, 1972. Bar: N.Y. 1973. Assoc. Hale Russell & Gray, NYC, 1972-74; ptnr. Brown and Wood (formerly Tufo and Zuccotti), NYC, 1974-94, Battle Fowler, NYC, 1994-2000, Paul Hastings Janofsky & Walker, NYC, 2000—05, Kramer Levin Naftalis & Frankel LLP, NYC, 2005—. Lectr. law Columbia U. Law Sch., 1994-97; assoc. adj. prof. Sch. Architecture, Planning and Preservation Columbia U., NYC, 1986-88; chmn. zoning and design com. Real Estate Bd. NY, 2000—. Edit. bd. Metropolis Mag., 1983-86; author: (guide book) Real Estate: Land Use Regulations, 1986. Mem. Borough Mountain Lakes Planning Bd., 2005—; mem. adv. bd. Cityland, Ctr. for N.Y.C. Law at N.Y. Law Sch., 2004—; mem. bd. dirs. Citizens Housing and Planning Council, 2005—. Mem.: ABA, Assn. of Bar of City of N.Y. Office: Kramer Levin Naftalis & Frankel LLP 1177 Avenue of the Americas New York NY 10036 Office Phone: 212-715-9199. Business E-Mail: pselver@kramerlevin.com.

SELVY, BARBARA, dance instructor; b. Little Rock, Jan. 20, 1938; d. James Oliver and Irene Balmat Banks; m. Franklin Delano Selvy, Apr. 15, 1959; children: Lisa Selvy Yeargin, Valerie Selvy Miros, Lauren Kroll, Franklin Michael, Madison Banks Selvy. Student, U. Ctrl. Ark., Conway, 1955—57. Founder, dir. Carolina Ballet Theater, Greenville, SC, 1973—; pres. Dance Arts Inc. and Incentives, Inc. Mem. adv. bd. dirs. Met. Arts Coun., and S.C. Govs. Sch., St. Marys Cath. Sch. Appeared in numerous TV commls., on Goodson-Toddman game show Play Your Hunch, 1958-59; toured Far East with TV show Hit Parade, 1958; named Miss Ark., 1956, Mrs. S.C., 1981; dir. and staged Mrs. Va., Mrs. N.C., Mrs. S.C. pageants; choreographed Little Theater prodns., Furman U. Opera. Mem. Nat. Rep. Congl. Com., 2003, Pres. Bush Small

Bus. Adv. Coun., 2003; Thrift Jhoplon adv. bd. com. mem. St. Francis Cath. Sch. Mem. So. Assn. Dance Masters (ballet adviser, regional dir.), Dance Educators Am., Dance Masters of Am., Profl. Dance Tchrs. Home: 18 Oglethorpe Lane Hilton Head Island SC 29926 Personal E-mail: barbarabselvy@aol.com.

SELWAY, JANET SMALL, family nurse practitioner; b. Balt., July 15, 1950; d. John Joseph Selway, Jan. 23, 1971; children: Stephanie, Jay. RN, St. Joseph Hosp. Sch. Nursing, 1971; BSN, Coll. Notre Dame, 1986; MSN, U. Md., 1988, PNP, 1991. Cert. adult nurse practitioner, ANCC. Emergency rm. staff nurse St. Joseph Hosp., Towson, Md., 1971-81; primary nurse shock trauma unit U. Md.-Md. Inst. Emergency Med. Svcs. Sys., Balt., 1981-86; emergency dept. nurse practitioner Johns Hopkins Hosp., Balt., 1988-90; nurse practitioner Melvin Kordon M.D., Columbia, Md., 1990-91, Family Medicine Specialists, Balt., 1991-93, Family & Children's Health Ctr., Balt., 1991-93, David Hartig, M.D., Cockeysville, Md., 1993—. Mem. Nurse Practitioners Assn. Md. (founding mem., pres. 1993-96, v.p. 1991-93), Md. Nurses Assn. (coun. nurse practitioners corr. sec. 1989-91), Sigma Theta Tau. Democrat. Office: Hunt Valley Med Ctr 10 Warren Rd Ste 110 Cockeysville MD 21030-2518 Home: 1718 Hunter Mill Rd White Hall MD 21161-9430

SELWAY, PHILLIP JAMES, musician; b. Huntingdon, England, May 23, 1967; married. Student in English and History, Liverpool Poly, Eng. Drummer touring musicals; sub-editor; tchr. English; drummer Radiohead, 1992—. Musician: (albums) Pablo Honey, 1993, The Bends, 1995, OK Computer, 1997 (Grammy award for Best Alternative Music Performance, 1997), Kid A, 2000 (Grammy award for Best Alternative Music Performance, 2000), Amnesiac, 2001, I Might Be Wrong: Live Reocrdings, 2001, Hail to the Thief, 2003, In Rainbows, 2007 (Grammy award for Best Alternative Music Album, 2009). Office: Capital Records 1750 North Vine St 10th Fl Hollywood CA 90028*

SELYA, BRUCE MARSHALL, federal judge; b. Providence, May 27, 1934; s. Herman C. and Betty (Brier) S.; children: Dawn Meredith Selya Sherman, Lori Ann Selya Young. BA magna cum laude, Harvard U., Cambridge, Mass., 1955, JD magna cum laude, 1958. Bar: DC 1958, RI 1960. Law clk. US Dist. Ct. RI, Providence, 1958-60, judge, 1982-86; assoc. Gunning & LaFazia, Providence, 1960-62; ptnr. Gunning, LaFazia, Gnys & Selya, Providence, 1963-74, Selya & Iannuccillo, Providence, 1974-82; judge US Ct. Appeals (1st Cir.), Providence, 1986—2006, sr. judge, 2006—; judge Fgn. Intelligence Surveillance Ct. (FISC), 2005—. Judge Lincoln Probate Ct., RI, 1965-72; mem. RI Jud. Council, 1964-72, sec., 1965-70, chmn., 1971-72; mem. Gov.'s Commn. on Crime and Adminstrn. Justice, 1967-69; del. Nat. Conf. on Revisions to Fed. Appellate Practice, 1968-82; judge Panel on Multi-District Litigation, 1989-2004; mem. various spl. govtl. commns. and adv. groups Chmn. bd. trustees Bryant U., Smithfield, RI, 1986-92,chair emeritus, 1993-; bd. dirs. Lifespan Health Sys., 1993-2000, chair emeritus, 2000-, chmn. bd. dirs., 1994-; mem. bd. trustees RI Hosp. subs. Recipient Louis Dembitz Brandeis medal for disting. legal svc. Brandeis U., 1988, Neil Houston award Justice Assistance of Am., 1992. Mem. ABA, FBA, Fed. Judges Assn., RI Bar Assn. (chmn. various coms.), RI Bar Found., US Jud. Conf. (mem. com. on jud. br.), Am. Arbitration Assn., Am. Judicature Soc. (bd. dirs.). Jewish. Home: 224 George St Providence RI 02906-3115 Office: US Ct Appeals US Courthouse 1 Exchange Terr Rm 316 Providence RI 02903*

SELZ, NAN, museum director; BA in English, Vassar Coll., Poughkeepsie, NY, 1961; MA in English, U. Ark., Fayetteville, 1967. Cert. fund raising exec. 1990. Exec. dir. ACLU, Ark., 1975—78, Pulaski County Coun. on Aging, Inc., 1978—85, Ark. Sesquicentennial Commn., Inc., 1985—86, Mus. of Discovery, 2004—; dir., devel. Ark. Easter Seal Soc., Inc., 1986—88; pres. Arthritis Found., Ariz., 1988—92, St. Vincent Found., 1992—2004. Mem. women's health adv. bd. St. Vincent Ctr. for Women and Children, 1999—2003; mem. Ark. steering com. Leave a Legacy, 2001—03; bd. dirs. Susan G. Komen Found., 1999—2004. Named an Outstanding Ark. Fund Raising Exec., 1995; named one of Top 100 Women in Ark., 1996—98. Mem.: Nat. Soc. Fund Raising Execs. (pres. Ark. chpt. 1991), Am. Assn. Mus., Aesthetic Club. Office: Mus of Discovery 500 President Clinton Ave Ste 150 Little Rock AR 72201 Office Phone: 501-396-7050 ext. 207. Business E-Mail: nselz@amod.org.

SELZ, PETER HOWARD, art historian, educator; b. Munich, Mar. 27, 1919; arrived in US, 1936, naturalized, 1942; s. Eugene and Edith S.; m. Thalia Cheronis, June 10, 1948 (div. 1965); children: Tanya Nicole Eugenia, Diana Gabrielle Hamlin; m. Carole Schemmerling, Dec. 18, 1983 Student, Columbia U., U. Paris; MA, U. Chgo., 1949, PhD, 1954; DFA, Calif. Coll. Arts and Crafts, 1967. Instr. U. Chgo., 1951-56; asst. prof. art history, head art edn. dept. Inst. Design, Ill. Inst. Tech., Chgo., 1949-55; chmn. art dept., dir. art gallery Pomona Coll., 1955-58; chief curator dept. painting and sculpture exhbns. Mus. Modern Art, 1958-65; dir. univ. art mus. U. Calif., Berkeley, 1965-73, prof. history of art, 1965—; Zaks prof. Hebrew U., Jerusalem, 1976. Vis. prof. CUNY, 1987; vis. prof. grad. theol. union, 2007-; pres.'s coun. on art and architecture Yale U., 1971-76 Author: German Expressionist Painting, 1957, New Images of Man, 1959, Art Nouveau, 1960, Mark Rothko, 1961, Fifteen Polish Painters, 1961, The Art of Jean Dubuffet, 1962, Emil Nolde, 1963, Max Beckmann, 1964, Alberto Giacometti, 1965, Directions in Kinetic Sculpture, 1966, Funk, 1967, Harold Paris, 1972, Ferdinand Holder, 1972, Sam Francis, 1975, The American Presidency in Political Cartoons, 1976, Art in Our Times, 1981, Art in a Turbulent Era, 1985, Chillida, 1986, Twelve Artists from the GDR, 1989, Max Beckmann: The Self Portraits, 1992, William Congdon, 1992, Beckmann, 1996, Gottfried Helnwein, 1997, Beyond the Mainstream, 1997; co-author: Theories and Documents of Contemporary Art, 1996, Beyond the Mainstream, 1998, Barbara Chase-Riboud, 1999, Nathan Oliviera, 2001, The Art of Engagement, 2006; editor: Art in Am., 1967—, Art Quar., 1969-75, Arts, 1981-92, Cross-Currents in Modern Art, 2000; contbr. articles to profl. jours. Trustee Am. Crafts Coun., 1985—89; mem.adv. coun. archives Am. Art, 1971—; mem. acquisitions com. Fine Arts Mus., San Francisco, 1993; pres. Berkeley Art Project, 1988—93; project dir. Christo's Running Fence, 1973—76; commr. Alameda County Art Commn., 1990—95; bd. dirs. Richmond Art Ctr., 1998—2004; chair Berkeley Arts Festival, 1997—2000; trustee Neue Galerie, New York, 2002—, Kala Inst., Berkley, Calif., 2001—. Decorated Order of Merit Fed. Republic Germany; Fulbright grantee Paris, 1949-50; fellow Belgian-Am. Ednl. Found.; Sr. fellow NEH, 1972; resident Rockefeller Found. Study Ctr., Bellagio, 1994. Mem. Coll. Art Assn. Am. (dir. 1959-64, 67-71, Charles Rufus award 2007), AAUP, Internat. Art Critics Assn. Office: U Calif Dept Art History Berkeley CA 94720-0001 Home Phone: 707-459-6152; Office Phone: 510-524-5402.

SELZNICK, BRIAN, illustrator, writer; b. East Brunswick, NJ, July 14, 1966; Grad., RI Sch. Design, 1988. Former staff Eeyore's Books for Children, NYC. Author, illustrator: books The Houdini Box, 1991 (Tex. Bluebonnet award, RI Children's Book award), The Invention of Hugo Cabret, 2007 (Caldecott medal, 2008), illustrator: books Amelia and Eleanor Go for a Ride, 1999, Riding Freedom, 1999, Frindle, 2000 (Christopher award, 1997), The Dinosaurs of Waterhouse Hawkins, 2001, When Marian Sang, 2002, The School Story, 2002, Wingwalker, 2002, The Doll People, 2003, The Dulcimer Boy, 2003, The Meanest Doll in the World, 2003, Walt Whitman: Words for America, 2004, The Landry News, 2005. Mailing: c/o Scholastic 557 Broadway New York NY 10012*

SEMAK, MICHAEL WILLIAM, photographer, educator; b. Welland, Ont., Can., Jan. 9, 1934; s. John and Lena (Roketsky) S.; m. Annette Antoniuk, Jan. 30, 1960; children: James, Arlene. Student archtl. tech., Ryerson Poly. Inst., 1956-58. Freelance photographer Toronto-Pickering, 1961—; mem. faculty York U., Toronto, 1971—, assoc. prof. photography, 1977—. Exhibitor one-man shows, Image Gallery, NYC, 1972, Il Diaframma Canon Gallery, Milan, Italy, 1976, Enjay Gallery, Boston, 1977, Ukraina Soc., Kiev, U.S.S.R., 1980, 81, Can. Mus. Contemporary Photography, Ottawa, 2005, Mus. Contemporary Photography, Fed. Govt. Can., Ottawa, Ont., 2005; group shows, Ont. Art Gallery, 1967, Expo '67 Internat. Exhbn., Montreal, 1967, Neikrug Gallery, NYC, 1971; represented in permanent collections, Nat. Film Bd. Can., Ottawa, Nat. Gallery Can., Ottawa, Mus. Modern Art, NYC, UN, Geneva. Recipient Photo Excellence Gold medal Nat. Film Bd., 1969; recipient Excellence award Pravda newspaper, Moscow, 1970, 71, Excellence diploma Fedn. Intenationale de l'art Photographique, Switzerland, 1972 Achievements include first to be included in a speech of the federal government's member of parliament regarding photographs at solo show at The Canadian Museum of Contemporary Photography in Ottowa, 2005. Home: 1796 Spruce Hill Rd Pickering ON Canada L1V 1S4 Office: Dept Photography York U 4700 Keeles St Toronto ON Canada M3J 1P3 *I see many contradictions around us, social realities which I believe rob us of our self-esteem and individuality. Must we continually accept and succumb to the never-ending hot baths for the mind society offers us? I wish my photography and words to disturb the complacent and the sleeper. I offer you cold showers for the mind.*

SEMANCIK, STEPHEN, physicist; BS in Physics, Rensselaer Poly. Inst., Troy, NY, 1974; MSc in Physics, Brown U., Providence, RI, 1976, PhD in Physics, 1980. Postdoc. fellow Nat. Bur. Standards, Gaithersburg, 1980—82; physicist Nat. Inst. Standards and Tech., Gaithersburg, Md., 1982—88, project leader, 1988—2004, supervisory project leader, 2004—08. Selected mem. edtorial bd. sensors and actuators b Elsevier, 2003—09; selected mem. edtorial bd. sensor letters Am. Sci. Publishers, 2003—08. Contbr. chapters to books. Recipient Tech. Achievement award, NIST Chem. Sci. and Tech. Lab., 1995, Bronze medal, US Dept. Commerce, 1991, Silver medal, 2006; Rsch. fellowship, NRC, 1980. Mem.: Internat. Meeting Chem. Sensors (steering com. mem. 2006—08, Elected to Fellowship 2006), Am. Phys. Soc., Am. Vacuum Soc. Achievements include patents for Author or Co-Author of 5 US Patents: 5, 330, 855 5, 345, 213 5, 356, 756 5, 464, 966 6, 095, 681.

SEMANKO, NORMAN M., political organization administrator; BS, U. Idaho; JD, Georgetown U., 1992. Bar: 1993. Legis. asst. to Rep. Larry E. Craig US House of Reps., Washington; legis. asst. and field rep. to Senator Larry E. Craig US Senate, Washington; exec. dir. and gen. counsel Idaho Water Users Assn., Boise; of counsel Barker, Rosholt & Simpson, LLP, Boise; Idaho rep. Western States Water Coun.; mem. city coun. City of Eagle, Idaho, 2008—09; chmn. Idaho Republican Party, Boise, 2008—. Mem.: Idaho State Bar Assn. (past pres. Water Law sect.). Republican. Roman Catholic. Office: Idaho Water Users Assn 1010 W Jefferson Ste 101 Boise ID 83702 also: Idaho Republican Party 802 West Bannock Lower Plz 103 Boise ID 83702 Office Phone: 208-344-6690, 208-343-6405. Office Fax: 208-344-2744, 208-343-6414. E-mail: norm@iwua.org, info@idgop.org.*

SEMAS, PHILIP WAYNE, editor; b. Gilroy, Calif., Feb. 23, 1946; s. Louis Alexander and Marian (Crapper) S.; m. Robin Lucille Tuttle, Sept. 7, 1967; children: Katherine Lucille, Anna Marian, Ellis Jeremy. Student, U. Oreg., 1963-67. Editor Coll. Press Service, Washington, 1967-68; free-lance writer Berkeley, Calif., 1968-69; asst. editor Chronicle of Higher Edn. Inc., Balt. and Washington, 1969-76, 1976-78, mng. editor, 1978-88; editor Chronicle of Philanthropy, Washington, 1988—95; editor, new media Chronicle of Higher Edn. Inc., Washington, 1995—2002, editor in chief, 2002—. Recipient Higher Edn. Writers award, AAUP, 1974 Mem. Am. Soc. Mag. Editors Office: Chronicle of Higher Edn 1255 23rd St NW Ste 700 Washington DC 20037-1125 Home Phone: 301-422-2859; Office Phone: 202-466-1000.

SEMEL, TERRY S., retired Internet company executive; b. NYC, Feb. 24, 1943; s. Ben and Mildred S.; m. Jane Bovingdon, Aug. 24, 1977; children: Eric Scott, Courtenay Jane, Lily Bovingdon Semel, Kate Bovingdon Semel. BS in Acctg., L.I.U., 1964; postgrad. in market research, CCNY, 1966-67; LHD (hon.), Emerson Coll., 2004. Domestic sales mgr. CBS Cinema Center Films, Studio City, Calif., 1970-72; v.p., gen. mgr. Walt Disney's Buena Vista, Burbank, Calif., 1972-75; pres. W.B. Distbn. Corp., Burbank, 1975-78; exec. v.p., COO Warner Bros., Inc., Burbank, 1979-80, pres., COO, 1980-94, chmn., co-CEO, 1994-99, Warner Music Group Inc., 1995-99; chmn. Windsor Media, Inc, 1999—2001; chmn., CEO Yahoo! Inc., 2001—07, non-exec. chmn., 2007—08. Bd. dirs. Polo Ralph Lauren Corp., 1997-, Yahoo! Inc., 2001-08 Vice chmn. Pres.'s Com. for the Arts and Humanities; vice chair San Diego Host Com. for 1996 Rep. Nat. Conv.; bd. trustee Solomon R. Guggenheim Mus., Edn. First, Cedars Sinai Med. Ctr., Environ. Media Assn., Emerson Coll.; bd. dir. Mus. TV and Radio, LA County Mus. Art. Named Pioneer of Yr., 1990, Found. of Motion Pictures Pioneers; named one of the 50 Most Important People on the Web, PC World, 2007; recipient UCLA medal, 2005, Yale Legends in Leadership award, 2005.

SEMENOV, ANDREI YURIEVICH, research scientist; s. Yuri Semenov and Alla Semenova; m. Irina Semenova, July 8, 1994. MS in Physics, Moscow State U., 1987; PhD, Joint Inst. Nuc. Rsch., Dubna, Russia, 1998. Scientist Joint Inst. Nuc. Rsch., Dubna, 1987—99; rsch. scientist Kent State U., Ohio, 1999—2005, rsch. assoc., 1999—2005, Iowa State U., Ames, 2005—07; rsch. scientist, physics dept. U. Regina, Saskatchewan, Canada, 2007—. Mem.: Sigma Xi Sci. Rsch. Soc. (assoc.). Achievements include research in electromagnetic structure of neutron; development of detector systems for nuclear physics experiments. Office: Univ Regina Physics Dept 3737 Wascana Pky Regina SK S4S 0A2 Canada

SEMIN, ALEXANDER, professional hockey player; b. Krasnojarsk, Russia; Left wing Washington Capitals, 2003—04, 2006—, HC Lada Togliatti, Russia, 2004—06. Mem. Team Russia, World Championships, 2005, 06, 08. Office: Washington Capitals 627 N Glebe Rd, Ste 850 Arlington VA 22203 also: MCI Center 601 F St NW Washington DC 20004*

SEMINACK, RICHARD STEPHEN, bishop; b. Phila., Pa., Mar. 3, 1942; BA, St. Basil's Coll., Stamford, Conn., 1963; SEOB, Pontifical Oriental Inst., Rome, 1968; attended, Catholic Univ. Am., Washington. Ordained priest Archeparchy of Phila. (Ukrainian), Pa., 1967; parochial vicar Holy Ghost Church, Chester, Pa., 1968—71, Presentation Church, Lansdale, Pa., 1971—72, St. Anne Church, Warrington, Pa., 1972—77; chaplain Sisters of St. Basil the Great, Phila., 1977—82; parochial vicar Assumption of the Blessed Virgin Mary Church, Miami, Fla., 1982—84; pastor Holy Trinity Church, Carnegie, Pa., 1984—2003; ordained bishop, 2003; bishop St. Nicolas of Chgo. (Ukrainian), 2003—. Roman Catholic. Office: St Nicolas Ukrainian Cath Eparchy 2245 W Rice St Chicago IL 60622

SEMINARA, LYNDA ANNE, editor; b. Needham, Mass., Jan. 17, 1961; d. Donald Cecil Garaventi and Lois Ann Pichulo Garaventi; children: Daniel Joseph, Robert James. BA cum laude, U. Pa., 1985. Writer, editor, tour coord. Cultural Heritage Alliance, Phila., 1985—88; from prodn. editor to sr. ops. mgr. W.B. Saunders Co., Phila., 1988—93; self-employed editor and writer, 1993—; pres. and owner The Word-Shop, Cherry Hill, NJ, 1993—; sr. editor OCC N.Am., NYC, 2003—. Game creator Senior Sez trivia games, 2002—. Vol. sr. citizens and children, 1996—2001; sponsor Children Internat., 2003—; music ministry, 1974—. Mem.: Internat. Scleroderma Network (sr. editor 2004—), Soc. Children's Book Writers and Illustrators. Roman Catholic. Avocations: volunteer work, writing, guitar, languages.

SEMINOFF, JEFFREY ALEKSANDR, ecologist, educator; b. Sacramento, Calif., Nov. 28, 1967; s. Carole Jones and Serje Geoffrey Seminoff; m. Jennifer Grae Gilmore, Mar. 26, 2000; children: Quin Aleksandra, Graeson Lee. BS in Ecology and Evolutionary Biology, U. Ariz., Tucson, 1989, MS in Ecology and Evolutionary Biology, 1994, PhD, 2000. Lectr., dept. zoology U. Fla., Gainesville, Fla., 2000—02, adj. faculty, 2002—; ecologist NOAA SW Fisheries Sci. Ctr., La Jolla, Calif., 2002—. Co-founder Coastal Conservation Found., Tucson, 1994—2000; adj. prof. Indiana-Purdue U., West Lawfayette, Ind., 1999—; mem., bd. dirs. Drylands Inst., Tucson, 1995—2006, Pro Peninsula, San Diego, 2008—. Contbr. articles to profl. sci. jours. Mem. Drylands Inst., Tucson Arizona, Ariz., 1995—2006, ProPeninsula, San Diego. Achievements include research in sea turtle ecology. Home: 4539 Onondaga Ave San Diego CA 92117 Office: NOAA-Southwest Fisheries Sci Ctr 8604 La Jolla Shores Dr La Jolla CA 92037 Office Fax: 858-546-7003. Business E-Mail: jeffrey.seminoff@noaa.gov.

SEMLER, WILLIAM LUDWIG, retired obstetrician, retired gynecologist; b. Racine, Wis., Dec. 21, 1922; s. Rudolph and Ida Frederica (Schmidt) Semler; m. Ellen Natalie Poulson, July 8, 1956; children: David William, Karen Lorraine, Barbara Jean. BS, U. Wis., Madison, 1944, MD, 1949. Lic. Wis., 1952. Intern Jersey City Med. Ctr., 1949—50; resident, ob-gyn. Mt. Sinai Hosp., Milw., 1952—54, St. Lukes Hosp., Milw., 0195—4195; pvt. practice ob-gyn. Miw., 1955—99; ret., 1999. Mem. exec. com. St. Michael's Hosp., Milw., 1976—88, chmn. credentials com., 1976—84, chmn. dept. ob-gyn., 1980—84, chmn. quality assurance com., 1980—84, chmn. exec. com., 1984—86, pres. med. staff, 1984—86, chmn. quality assurance com., 1986—95, chmn. family practice residency adv. com., 1988—99; staff St. Lukes Hosp., Milw., St. Joseph's Hosp., Milw., Mt. Sinai Hosp., Milw., Good Samaritan Med. Ctr., Milw., Columbia Hosp., Milw., Family Hosp., Milw; clin. instr. Med. Coll. Wis., 1990—2003; ret. tchg., 2004. Contbr. articles to profl. jours. With med. corp US Army, 1943—46, flight surgeon USAF, 1950—52. Mem.: AMA, Am. Coll. Physician Execs., Am. Menopause Soc., Soc. Laparoscopic Surgeons, Can.-Am. Med.-Dental Assn., Milw. Soc. Ob-gyn., Wis. Soc. Ob-gyn., Am. Coll. Physicians, Sports Car Club Am. Lutheran. Avocations: golf, photography, jewelry, travel, stained glass.

SEMMEL, STUART, historian; s. Bernard and Maxine Semmel; m. Tina Lu. AB, Harvard Coll., 1988; AM, Harvard U., 1988, PhD, 1997. Asst. dir. history and lit. Harvard U., Cambridge, Mass., 1995—98; fellow Penn Humanities Forum, Phila., 1999—2000; vis. asst. prof. dept. history Am. U., Washington, 2000—01; asst. prof. dept. history U. Del., Newark, Del., 2001—06, assoc. prof., 2006—09; vis. assoc. prof., dept. history Yale U., 2008—09, sr. lectr., 2009—. Author: Napoleon and the British, 2004. Fellow, Nat. Humanties Ctr., 2005—06. Mem.: Am. Hist. Assn., North Am. Conf. Brit. Studies. Office: Yale Univ Dept History New Haven CT 06511 Business E-Mail: stuart.semmel@yale.edu.

SEMO, JOSEPH, lawyer; b. Pitts., June 6, 1951; s. Ramon and Eleonora Semo; m. Judith Jurin Semo, Dec. 21, 1975; children: Davina, Daniel. BS in Econs., U. Pa., Phila., 1973; JD, George Washington U., Washington, 1976. Bar: D.C. 1977, Va. 1976, Md. 1985, Wis. 1995, U.S. Supreme Ct. Shareholder Seifman Semo & Slevin PC, Washington, 1977—89; ptnr. Pepper Hamilton & Sheetz, Washington, 1989—91; shareholder Reinhart Boerner, Washington, 1991—97, Feder Semo and Bard PC, Washington, 1998—2005; prin. Semo Law Group, Bethesda, Md., Washington, 2005—. Lectr. in field. Contbr. articles to profl. jours. Chmn. City of Annapolis Police and Fire Retirement Commn., Md., 1985—; bd. dirs. D.C. Employment Justice Ctr., 2004—, Partnership for Jewish Life and Learning, Rockville, Md., 2005—, Wharton Sch. Club, Washington, 1985—. Capt. Quartermaster Corps USAR. Recipient Joseph Wharton award, Wharton Sch. Club of Washington, 2003. Office: Semo Law Group 1800 M St Washington DC 20036

SEMON, MARK DAVID, physicist, researcher; b. Milw., Mar. 27, 1950; s. Milton K. and Joyce Gloria (Kupper) S. Student, Imperial Coll., London, 1973-74; AB magna cum laude, Colgate U., 1971; PhD, U. Colo., 1976. Rsch. asst. Kitt Peak Nat. Obs., Tucson, 1970, Los Alamos (N.Mex.) Sci. Lab., 1974; asst. prof. physics Bates Coll., Lewiston, Maine, 1976-83, assoc. prof., 1983-88, prof. physics, 1990—. Vis. prof. physics Amherst (Mass.) Coll., 1988-90; accident reconstructionist Med. and Tech. Cons., Portland, Maine, 1986—; referee Am. Jour. Physics, 1988—, Founds. of Physics, 1989—. Asst. editor Am. Jour. Physics, 1988-90; contbr. articles to Phys. Rev., Il Nuovo Cimento, other profl. jours. Woodrow Wilson fellow, 1971; grantee NSF, 1980, Nat. Rsch. Corp., 1978. Mem. Am. Phys. Soc., Am. Acad. Forensic Scientists, Am. Assn. Physics Tchrs., Am. Coll. Forensic Examiners, Coun. Undergrad. Rsch., Soc. Woodrow Wilson Fellows. Achievements include evaluation of expectation values in Aharonov-Bohm Effect; co-authoring new equation of state for liquid/gas systems near critical point, alternative formulation of quantum electrodynamics; new interpretation of the electromagnetic vector potential, new geometric model of velocity addition in special relativity, simplified derivation of Thomas pressesion and a discussion of its experimentals confirmations. Office: Bates Coll Dept Physics 44 Campus Ave Lewiston ME 04240-6018 Home Phone: 406-575-4499; Office Phone: 207-786-6324. Business E-Mail: msemon@bates.edu.

SEMON, WARREN LLOYD, information scientist, educator; b. Boise, Idaho, Jan. 17, 1921; s. August and Viola Lorreta (Eastman) S.; m. Ruth Valerie Swift, Dec. 1, 1945; children— Warren Lloyd, Nolan David, Jonathan Richard, Sue Anne. Student, Hobart Coll., 1940-43; S.B., U. Chgo., 1944; MA, Harvard, 1949, PhD, 1954. Instr. math. Hobart Coll., 1946-47; lectr. applied math. Harvard U., Cambridge, Mass., 1956-61, asst. dir. computation lab., 1954-61; head applied math. dept. Sperry Rand Research Ctr., Sudbury, Mass., 1961-64; mgr. computation and analysis lab. Burroughs Research Ctr., Paoli, Pa., 1964-67; prof. computer sci. Syracuse (N.Y.) U., 1967-84, prof. emeritus, 1984—, dir.

system and information sci., 1968-76, dean Sch. Computer and Info. Sci., 1976-84. Cons. USAF, 1957, NSA, 1957, Lockheed Electronics Corp., 1967, Monsanto Co., 1972. Contbr. articles to profl. jours. Served to 1st lt. USAAF, 1943-46, MTO. Fellow IEEE; mem. Assn. Computing Machinery, Math. Assn. Am., IEEE Computer Soc. (chmn. publs. com. 1972-74, bd. govs. 1973-74, editor-in-chief 1975-76), Sigma Xi. Home: 1035 Scott Drive Apt 224 Prescott AZ 86301

SEMONIN, RICHARD GERARD, retired state official; b. Akron, Ohio, June 25, 1930; s. Charles Julius and Catherine Cecelia (Schooley) S.; m. Lennie Stuker, Feb. 3, 1951; children: Cecelia C., Richard G. Jr. (dec.), James R., Patricia R. BS, U. Wash., 1955. With Ill. State Water Survey, Champaign, 1955-91, chief, 1986-91, chief emeritus, 1991—; co-chmn. Ill. Water Rsch. & Land Use Planning Task Force, 1992-94. Adj. prof. U. Ill., 1975-91; chmn. Ill. Low-Level Radioactive Waste Task Group, 1994-96. Contbr. chpts. to books and articles to profl. jours.; co-editor: Atmospheric Deposition, 1983. Staff sgt. USAF, 1948-52. Grantee, NSF, 1957—76, US Dept. Energy, 1965—90. Fellow: AAAS, Am. Meteorol. Soc. (councilor 1983—86); mem.: Ill. Acad. Scis., Weather Modification Assn., Nat. Weather Assn. (councilor 1978—81), Sigma Xi. Roman Catholic. Avocations: civil war, golf, fishing, genealogy. Home: 1002 Devonshire Dr Champaign IL 61821-6620 Office: Ill State Water Survey 2204 Griffith Dr Champaign IL 61820-7495 E-mail: semonin@uiuc.edu.

SEMOUCHKINA, ELENA, physicist, researcher; b. Tomsk, Russia, May 1, 1956; arrived in US, 1997; m. George Semouchkin, Apr. 26, 1985; children: Alex Semouchkin, Vassilissa Semouchkin. A in German, Tomsk State U., Russia, 1974, A in Modern Dance, 1978, MS in Engring. with highest distinction, 1978, PhD in Physics and Math., 1986; PhD in Materials, Pa. State U., Univ. Pk., 2000. Rsch. asst. Physics-Tech. Inst., Tomsk, 1979-83, sr. rschr., 1984-92; sci. cons. NEOS Co., St. Petersburg, Russia, 1992-94; sr. rschr. State Tech. U., St. Petersburg, 1994-97; rsch. asst. Pa. State U., University Park, 1997-2000, rsch. assoc., 2001—05, sr. rsch. assoc., assoc. prof., 2006—. Contbr. articles to sci jours. Recipient Young Siberian Scientist award, 1985, Xerox Rsch. award, Pa. State U., 2001; fellow, NSF, 2004; scholar Lenin, Tomsk State U., 1974—78. Russian Orthodox. Avocations: downhill skiing, dance, reading, drawing, painting. Home: 1632 Oxford Cir State College PA 16803 Office: Pa State U 266 Materials Rsch Lab University Park PA 16802 Business E-Mail: eas203@psu.edu.

SEMPLE, JAMES WILLIAM, lawyer; s. Calvin James and Marie Robinson; m. Ellen Burns; children: Megan Semple Greenberg, Luke Robinson. AB, St. Josephs U., Phila.; JD, Villanova U., 1974. Bar: Del. 1974, U.S. Dist. Ct. Del. 1974, D.C. 1975, U.S. Ct. Appeals (3d cir.) 1982. Ptnr. Morris, James, Hitchens & Williams, Wilmington, 1983—. Lectr. numerous seminars; mediator Superior Ct. Voluntary Mediation Program. Mem.: ABA, Fedn. Defense and Corp. Counsel, Am. Bd. Trial Advs. Office: Morris James LLP PO Box 2306 Wilmington DE 19899-2306 Office Phone: 302-888-6800. Business E-Mail: jsemple@morrisjames.com.

SEMPLE, JANE FRANCES, health facility director; b. Lakewood, Ohio, Feb. 14, 1951; d. Frank Joseph and Margaret Eleanor (Carpenter) Semple; m. Nick N. Morana, June 24, 1977 (div. Sept. 1981). AAB, Cuyahoga CC, Cleve., 1977; BA, Baldwin-Wallace Coll., 1980; MBA, Case Western Res. U., 1984; ND, Trinity Coll. Natural Health, 1999. Diplomate Am. Bd. Naturopaths. Adminstrv. asst. DeVilbiss Co., Cleve., 1969—77; project dir. Nat. Survey Rsch. Ctr., Cleve., 1977—80; market rsch. mgr. Sherwin-Williams Co., Cleve., 1980—85; instr. Cuyahoga CC, Cleve., 1986—92, Baldwin-Wallace Coll., Berea, Ohio, 1992—93; dir. Alternative Healing Inst., 1989—. Author: Naturopathic Health Series. Mem. S. B. Anthony Soc. Womenspace, Cleve., 1980—88. Mem.: Coalition for Natural Health, Am. Botanic Coun., Am. Assn. Nutritional Cons., Am. Naturopathic Med. Assn. Democrat. Home: 26969 Greenbrooke Dr Olmsted Falls OH 44138 Office: Alternative Healing Inst 4965 Doven Ctr Rd North Olmsted OH 44070 Office Phone: 440-777-2665. Personal E-mail: drjane@bright.net.

SEMPLE, ROBERT BAYLOR, JR., editor, journalist; b. St. Louis, Aug. 12, 1936; s. Robert B. and Isabelle Ashby (Neer) S.; m. Susan Riker Kirk, Aug. 19, 1961 (div. Feb. 1980); children: Robert Baylor III, Elizabeth, William, Mary; m. Lisa Pulling, Jan. 10, 1981. Grad., Phillips Acad., 1954; BA, Yale U., 1959; MA, U. Calif., Berkeley, 1961. Reporter Nat. Observer, 1961-63; corr. New York Times, 1963-68, White House corr., 1968-72, dep. nat. editor, 1973-75, London bur. chief, 1975-77, fgn. editor NYC, 1977-82, op-ed page editor, 1982-88, assoc. editor editl. page, 1988—, and editl. bd. mem. Recipient Pulitzer prize for editl. writing on environ. issues, 1996; Carnegie fellow, 1959-60; Woodrow Wilson fellow, 1960-61. Mem. Century Assn. (NYC), Yale Club (NYC). Episcopalian. Office: New York Times 620 8th Ave New York NY 10018 E-mail: semple@nytimes.com.

SEMRAU, SUE, women's college basketball coach; b. Seattle; Attended, U. Pugent Sound; BS in Comms., U. Calif., San Diego, 1985; MS in Athletic Adminstrn., U. So. Calif., 1988. Pub. rels. dir. Seattle Storm, 1985—86; asst. basketball coach Santa Monica HS, 1986-87; pub. rels. and promotions dir. LA Heat, 1986-87; head women's basketball coach, asst. athletic dir. Occidental Coll., LA, 1987-91; asst. coach No. Ill. U., 1991-93; top asst. coach, recruiting coord. U. Wis., 1993-96; head coach women's basketball Fla. State U., 1997—. Head coach coll. alumni Athletes in Action Spring Australian Tour, 1997; bd. dirs. Women's Basketball Coaches Assn. Office: Fla State Athletic PO Box 2195 Tallahassee FL 32316-2195*

SEMYONOV, OLEG G., research scientist; b. Abakan, Siberia, Russia, Jan. 3, 1944; arrived in U.S., 1997; s. Gabriel P. and Anna G. Semyonov; m. Eugenia V. Khorochilova, Oct. 15, 1971; children: Xenia, Nick. MS, Moscow State U., 1967; PhD, Lebedev Inst. Physics, Moscow, 1981. Rsch. scientist VNIIEF, Arzamas, Russia, 1967—70, Inst. Atomic Energy, Moscow, 1970—71; sr. scientist Lebedev Inst. Physics, Moscow, 1971—97; sr. rsch. engr. Applied Laser and Fusion Tech., Hull, Que., Canada, 1999—2001; sr. rsch. scientist SUNY, Stony Brook, 2001—. Cons. ALFT, Inc., Hull, 2001; tech. transl. KAHOT, Inc., Bklyn., 1998. Contbr. articles to profl. publs. Russian Orthodox. Achievements include discovery of effect of polarization of x-ray lines of highly ionized atoms in a high-current discharge and suggested a theoretical model to explain it; microrelief and internal structure modification of solid films irradiated by pulsed x-rays; fluorescent biomedical imaging of tumors in vivo; optical powering of sensors and actuators; fluroescence sensors; patents in field. Avocations: tennis, guitar, composing. Home Phone: 631-736-2565; Office Phone: 631-632-1402. Business E-Mail: osemyonov@ece.sunysb.edu.

SEN, ALPER, engineering educator; PhD, U. Tex., Austin, 2004. Tech. staff mem. Freescale Semiconductor Inc., Austin, 2004—; adj. prof. U. Tex., 2008—. Program com. mem. Internat. Conf. Formal Methods Computer Aided Design, Internat. Conf. Distributed Computing and Networking. Contbr. articles to profl. jours. Mem.: IEEE.

SEN, AMARTYA KUMAR, economist, educator; b. Santiniketan, India, Nov. 3, 1933; s. Ashutosh and Amita Sen. BA, Calcutta U., 1953, Cambridge U., Eng., 1955; PhD, 1959; more than 90 hon. degrees including: DLitt (hon.), Visva-Bharati U., 1983; DLitt (hon.), U. Essex, 1984, Georgetown U., 1989, Jødavpur U., 1990, Williams Coll., 1991, New Sch. Social Rsch., 1992, Calcutta U., 1992, Oberlin Coll., 1993, Syracuse U., 1994, Wesleyan U., 1995, Oxford, 1996; DSc (hon.), U. Edinburgh, 1995; D (hon.), U. Caen, 1987, Louvain, 1989, U. Zurich, 1994, U. Stockholm, 1996, Bard Coll., 1997, Kiel U., 1997; dottore ad honorem, U. Bologna, 1988; LLD (hon.), U. Tulane, 1990, Queen's U., 1993; LLD (hon.), Wesleyan U., 1995, Harvard U., 2000, U. Tokyo, 2002, Yale U., 2003, Gottingen U., 2005, Michigan U., 2006, Sorbonne, 2007, U. Coll. Dublin, 2007. Prof. econs. Jadavpur U., Calcutta, 1956-58; fellow Trinity Coll., Cambridge U., 1957-63; prof. econs. Delhi U., 1963-71, London Sch. Econs., 1971-77, Oxford (Eng.) U., 1977-80, Drummond prof. polit. economy, 1980—87; prof. econs. and philosophy Harvard U. Lamont, Cambridge, Mass., 1987—98, 2004—; master Trinity Coll., Cambridge U., 1998—2004. Vis. prof. U. Calif., Berkeley, 1964-65; Andrew D. White prof.-at-large Cornell U., Ithaca, N.Y., 1978-84; chmn. expert group role advanced skill and tech. UN, 1967; hon. fellow Trintiy Coll., Cambridge Inst. Social Studies, The Hague, Inst. Devel. Studies, U. Sussex, London Sch. Econs., U. London. Author: Choice of Techniques, 1960, Collective Choice and Social Welfare, 1970, Growth Economics, 1970, Guidelines for Project Evaluation, 1972, On Economic Inequality, 1973, Employment, Technology and Development, 1975, Poverty and Famines: An Essay on Entitlement and Deprivation, 1981, Utilitarianism and Beyond, 1982, Choice, Welfare and Measurement, 1982, Resources, Values and Development, 1984, Commodities and Capabilities, 1985, On Ethics and Economics, 1987, The Standard of Living, 1987, Hunger and Public Action, 1989, The Political Economy of Hunger, 1990, Inequality Reexamined, 1992, Quality of Life, 1993, India: Economic Development and Social Opportunity, 1995, Indian Development: Selected Regional Perspectives, 1997, On Economic Inequality, 1997, Development as Freedom, 1999, Rationality and Freedom, 2002, The Argumentative Indian, 2005, Identity and Violence: The Illusion of Destiny, 2006; contbr. articles to profl. jours. Recipient Adam Smith Prize, Cambridge U., 1954, Stevenson Prize, 1956, Mahalanobis award, 1976, Rank E. Seidman Disting. award in Polit. Economy, 1986, Agnelli Internat. prize, 1990, Alan Shawn Feinstein World Hunger award, 1990, Jean Mayer Global Citizenship award, 1993, Indira Gandhi Gold Medal award, Asiatic Soc., 1994, Edinburgh Medal, 1997, 9th Catalonia Internat. prize, 1997, Nobel prize in econ. scis., 1998; co-recipient Wassily Leontief prize for advancing frontiers econ. thought Tufts Global Inst. for Environ. and Devel., 2000; George C. Marshall award US Agy. Internat. Develop., 2005. Fellow Brit. Acad., Econometric Soc. (past pres.); mem. AAAS (fgn. hon.), Am. Econ. Assn. (past pres.), Indian Econ. Assn. (past pres.), Royal Econ. Soc. (v.p.), Indian Econometric Conf., Devel. Studies Assn. (past pres.), Internat. Econ. Assn. (pres. 1986-89, hon. pres.), Accademia Nazionale dei Lincei, Am. Philosophical Assn. Office: Lamont U Prof Dept Econs Harvard U Cambridge MA 02138*

SEN, AYUSMAN, chemistry professor; b. Calcutta, India, Jan. 5, 1951; came to U.S., 1973; s. Amiya Kumar and Geeti (Datta) S.; m. Suchismita Roomjhoom Gupta, July 29, 1979; 1 child, Deepa Amrita. BSc with honors, U. Calcutta, India, 1970; MS, Indian Inst. Tech., Kanpur, India, 1973; PhD, U. Chgo., 1978. Rsch. fellow Calif. Inst. Tech., Pasadena, 1978-79; asst. prof. Pa. State Univ, University Park, Pa., 1979-84; assoc. prof. Pa. State Univ., University Park, Pa., 1984-89, prof., 1989—, chem. dept. chmn. Imperial Oil disting. lectr. Univ. Toronto, 1993; Iberdrola vis. prof. Univ. Valladolid, Spain, 1999—2000; Gerhard Closs lectr. Univ. Chgo., 2002. Contbr. numerous articles to profl. jours. Recipient Young Investigator award Chevron Rsch. Co., 1982-84, Paul J. Flory Sabbatical award IBM, 1987-88, Faculty Scholar medal Pa. State U., 2003; Alfred P. Sloan Rsch. fellow, 1984-88. Fellow AAAS; mem. Am. Chem. Soc. Office: Pa State U Chemistry Dept 404 Chemistry Bldg University Park PA 16802

SEN, BISAKHA PIA, performing arts educator; b. Kolkata, West Bengal, India, Oct. 8, 1969; d. Samindra Mohan and Sugata Sen; m. Sanjeev Chaudhuri Sen. PhD, Ohio State U. Assoc. prof. U. Ala. Birmingham, Ala., 2006—. Dancer & dance tchr (indian classical-folk fusion dance) Notinee Indian Dance Group. Achievements include established Alabama's first Indian classical-folk fusion dance group. Avocation: acting. Office: UnivAlabama at Birmingham RPHB 330 1665 Univ Blvd Birmingham AL 35294 Business E-Mail: bsen@uab.edu.

SEN, DIPANKAR, technology manager, principal; s. S. Sen; m. Rini Ghose, Apr. 18, 1995; 1 child, Amelie. Degree in Agrl. and Process Engring.; B.Tech with honors, Indian Inst. Tech., Kharagpur, West Bengal, 1985; MS in Environ. Engring., Va. Tech., Blacksburg, 1987, PhD in Civil and Environ. Engring., 1995; MBA, Wharton Sch. U. Pa., Phila., 2000. Cert. profl. engr., Va., 1991, Calif., 2008. Prin. Aquaregen-Aquifas, Mountain View, Calif., 2000—08; sr. project mgr. Santa Clara Valley Water Dist., San Jose, Calif., 2002—. Sr. rsch. assoc. & faculty Va. Tech, Manassas, 1988—93; sr. assoc. Stearns Wheler, Cazenovia, NY, 1996—2000; founding advisor Entex Inc., Raleigh, NC, 2004—07; advisor Suganit Sys., Reston, Va., 2008—09. Co-author: (book) RFID for Energy and Utility Industries; contbr. scientific papers. With IIT Kharagpur, 1983—85. Recipient Freedom R.K. Hall award, IIT Kharagpur, 1985, Silver medal, 1985; fellow, Civil Engring., Va. Tech, Blacksburg, 1993—95. Mem.: Water Environment Fedn. Achievements include first to integrated fixed film activated sludge system; development of open source IFAS modeling tools; high rate cellulosic ethanol. Business E-Mail: dsen@valleywater.org.

SEN, KAUSTAV, finance educator, consultant; BTech, Indian Inst. Tech., Kharagpur, 1985; PhD, Rutgers U., New Jersey, MBA, 1994. Cert. informations sys. auditor, Info. Sys. Audit and Control Assn., 2000. Mktg. exec. Wipro Ltd., Kolkata, India, 1986—87; grad. asst. Rutgers U., 1987—91; asst. prof. Montclair State U., NJ, 1992—95, Pace U., NYC, 1996—2001, assoc. prof., 2002—. Cons. GE Capital, Conn., 1995—97, Chase Manhattan Bank, NY, 1997—98, Prudential Ins., NJ, 1998—2000, Ny Life Ins., NY, 2000—01, Quantitative Mgmt. Assoc., NJ, 2006—; vis. faculty Indian Inst. Mgmt., Kolkata, 2003—04, City U. Hong Kong, 2005—05, Hong Kong Poly. U., 2006—06. Contbr. articles to profl. jours. Recipient SAP Curriculum Devel. award, Innovation Tchg. award. Mem.: Am. Acctg. Assn., Info. Sys. Audit and Control Assn. Office: Pace Univ One Pace Plaza New York NY 10038 Business E-Mail: ksen@pace.edu.

SEN, KOUSHIK, science educator; b. Bankura, West Bengal, India; s. Rakhahari and Sibani Sen; m. Aditi Sen; 1 child, Gunjan. BTech, Indian Inst. Tech., Kanpur, India, 1999; PhD, U. Ill., Champaign, 2006. Asst. prof. U. Calif., Berkeley, 2006—; cons. Parallocity Inc., Sunnyvale, Calif., 2008. Recipient C.L. and Jane W-S. Liu award, U. Ill., 2004, C.W. Gear Outstanding Grad. award, 2005, Disting. Paper award, Assn. Computing Machinery, 2005, Career award, NSF, 2008. Mem.: Assn. Computing Machinery. Achievements include research in concolic testing an automated testing tool for programs. Office: Univ Calif Berkeley 581 Soda Hall #1776 Berkeley CA 94720 Home Fax: 510-642-2420. Business E-Mail: ksen@cs.berkeley.edu.

SEN, LAURA J., wholesale distribution executive; b. Mass., July 7, 1956; BA in Romance Languages, Boston Coll., 1978. Exec. trainee handbag dept. Jordan Marsh Co., 1978—79; mgmt. positions Zayre Corp., Framingham, Mass., 1979—89, BJ's Wholesale Club, Inc., Natick, Mass., 1989—94, sr. v.p. gen. merchandising, 1994—97, exec. v.p. merchandising, 1997—2003; prin. Sen Retail Consulting, 2003—06; exec. v.p. merchandising & logistics BJ's Wholesale Club, Inc., Natick, Mass., 2007—08, pres., COO, 2008—09, pres., CEO, 2009—. Bd. dirs. Abington Bancorp, Inc., 2001—, BJ's Wholesale Club, Inc., 2008—. Bd. mem. St. Coletta Sch., Cardinal Cushing Schools. Avocation: crossword puzzles. Office: BJs Wholesale Club Inc 1 Mercer Rd Natick MA 01760-2400*

SEN, PRANAB, computer scientist, researcher; b. Thane, Maharashtra, India, May 8, 1973; s. Gouranga Deb and Sulekha Sen. PhD, Tata Inst. Fundamental Rsch., Mumbai, Maharashtra, 2001. Postdoc. rschr. Lab. Rsch. Informatique, U. Paris-Sud, Orsay, France, 2001—02, Inst. Quantum Computing, U. Waterloo, Ontario, Canada, 2003—05; rsch. staff mem. NEC Labs. America, Princeton, NJ, 2005—06; reader Tata Inst. Fundamental Rsch., Mumbai, 2006—. Achievements include research in various areas of quantum computation and information. Office: Tata Inst Fundamental Rsch Homi Bhabha Rd Colaba Mumbai Maharashtra 400005 India

SEN, SHUKDEB, biology professor; s. Satyendra Prasad and Bani Sen; m. Sulakshana Patnaik, May 8, 1991; 1 child, Susan. PhD, Atlanta U., 1977. Prof. dept. biology Bethune Cookman U., Daytona Beach, Fla., 1977—. Contbr. scientific papers to profl. jours. Grant, NIH, 1980—95. Mem.: AAAS, Am. Soc. Plant Biologists. Office: Bethune Cookman Univ 640 Mary McLeod Bethune Blvd Daytona Beach FL 32114-3099 Business E-Mail: sens@cookman.edu.

SENA, CHARALENA, dental office executive; d. Charles Howard Huntley and Linda Gayle Helms; m. Bartholomew Sena; children: David Wayne Williams, Sena Rhyan Joshua children: Ricky Darrell Williams. BA in Bus., Appalachian State U., NC, 1981, MBA, 1981; PhD in Math., Camborne U., Eng., 1984, PhD in Arts, 1986; BA in Pub. Rels., Weybridge U., Del., 2002; MBA in Criminal Justice, Felton U., New Castle, Del., 2004; D Clin. Psychology, Williamstown U., Wilmington, Del., 2006, PhD in Clin. Psychology and Behavioral Sci., 2006. Office mgr., fin. mgr. Office of Dr. Jeffrey F. West, Charlotte, NC, 1989—94; bus. mgr. Lee & Associates, Charlotte, 1996—2001; bus. cons., fin. mgr. Charles Payet, DDS, Charlotte, 2000—01; CFO Viken, Inc., Bound Brook, NJ, 2001—05, R&S Mgmt. Corp. (formerly Viken, Inc.), Flushing, NY, 2005—06; CEO CS Exec. Cons., Raritan, NJ, 1988—. Contbr. articles to profl. publs. Mem.: AADOM (cons. 2003—07), CPMM. Republican. Achievements include taking Fortune 100 and 500 companies to the next level. Business E-Mail: charalena2006@yahoo.com.

SENAT, JOEY, communications educator; BA, La. State U., Baton Rouge, 1984; MA, U. Memphis, 1993; PhD, U. NC, Chapel Hill, 1998. Reporter Tulsa World, Okla., 1984—89, Comml. Appeal, Memphis, 1989—92; instr. Elon Coll., NC, 1993—95; faculty OSU Sch. Journalism, Stillwater, Okla., 1998—. Bd. dirs. FOI Okla. Inc., Edmond, 2003—, pres., 2008. Author: (book) Mass Communication Law in Oklahoma; contbr. articles to jours.;, editor rsch. jours. Recipient Second Pl. award, History, Law, and Newspaper Divsns. AEJMC, 1996, John B. Adams award, UNC Sch. Journalism and Mass Comm., 1997, First Amendment award, Okla. Soc. Profl. Journalists, 2005, Marian Opala First Amendment award, FOI Okla. Inc., 2007, Golden Torch award, OSU Coll. Arts & Scis., 2005; named Outstanding Prof., 2000. Mem.: Investigative Reporters & Editors, Assn. Edn. Journalism and Mass Comm., Kappa Tau Alpha. Office: Okla State Univ 206 Paul Miller Stillwater OK 74078-4053 Office Fax: 405-744-7104. Business E-Mail: joey.senat@okstate.edu.

SENAY, GABRIEL BOGALE, research scientist, educator; m. Yodit Mengeste Lulseged, Sept. 13, 1996; children: Eden Gabriel, Melak Gabriel. PhD, Ohio State U., Columbus, 1996. Profl. engr., NSPE/OSPE, Ohio, 2002. Prin. scientist SAIC/USGS-EROS, Sioux Falls, SD, 2000—. Author: (paper) Developing Index Maps of Water-Harvest Potential in Africa (Best Paper award, 2004); author: (and co-author) numerous other papers and book chpts. in field. Recipient Best Publ., ESTC, 2004, Peer award, EROS, 2004, STAR award, 2005, Group Achievement award, 2005; grantee, USDA, 2003, NASA, 2006. Mem.: AGU (corr.), ASABE (corr.). Home: 4927 E Brennan Dr Sioux Falls SD 57110 Business E-Mail: senay@usgs.gov.

SENCZUK, ANNA MARIA, cell biologist, researcher; b. Czestochowa, Poland, Nov. 3, 1965; arrived in US, 2000, permanent resident, 2006; d. Janusz and Halina Senczuk; m. Miroslaw Josef Studzinski, Dec. 29, 1990; children: Tom Studzinski, Lukas Studzinski. Attended, Academia Medyczna, Wroclaw, Poland, 1990; BS in Cell, Molecular and Microbiology, U. Calgary, Alta., Can., 1996, MS in CMMB, 1999. Assoc. U. Calgary, 1999—2000; assoc. scientist Amgen, Seattle, 2000—. Presenter in field. Contbr. articles to profl. jours. Mentor Sci. Expo., Seattle, 2002—08. Mem.: Sigma Xi. Achievements include patents for HIC dual salt. Office: Amgen 1201 Amgen Ct West AW2D2152 Seattle WA 98119 Personal E-mail: senczukowa@hotmail.com. Business E-Mail: senczuka@amgen.com.

SENDAULA, HENRY MUSOKE, engineering educator; PhD, U. Conn., Storrs, 1972. Cert. elec. engr., Tenn., 1986. Assoc. prof. U. Tenn., Chattanooga, 1976—86; prof. engring. Temple U., Phila., 1986—. Cons. TVA, Chattanooga, 1976—86. Author: (book) Power Quality Control Techniques. Achievements include patents in field. Business E-Mail: musoke@temple.edu.

SENDAX, VICTOR IRVEN, dentist, educator, dental implant researcher; b. NYC, Sept. 14, 1930; s. Maurice and Molly R. S.; m. Deborah deLand Cobb, Dec. 17, 1969 (div. June 1976); 1 child, Jennifer Reiland; m. Marcia Ayer Pearson, Dec. 13, 1986; children: Anneliese Chase, Cordelia Ayer. Grad., Tanglewood Music Ctr., 1953; BA, NYU, 1951, DDS, 1955; postgrad., Harvard U. Sch. Dental Medicine, Cambridge, Mass., 1969-72. Diplomate Am. Bd. Oral Implantology/Implant Dentistry (pres. 1996, dir.). Commr. NY State Dental Svc. Corp., 1969-73; pres., dir. BioDental Rsch. Found., Inc., NYC, 1975—; pres. Victor I. Sendax, D.D.S., P.C., NYC, 1972—, Sendax Mini Dental Implant Ctrs. Mgmt., Inc., 1985—; assoc. attending oral implantologist mini-dental implant program St. Lukes-Roosevelt Hosp., NYC, 1979—. Adj. assoc. prof. implant prosthodontics Columbia U. Sch. Dental and Oral Surgery, NYC, 1974-92; vis. lectr. dept. implant dentistry Harvard U. Sch. Dental Medicine, NYU Coll. Dentistry; faculty NY County Dental Soc. Sch. for Continuing Dental Edn.; mem. dental implant rsch. programs adv. com. Nat. Inst. Dental Rsch., HHS; cons. Julliard Sch.

Voice and Drama, NYC, 1972—90, Vocal Dynamics Lab. Dept. Otolaryngology, Lenox Hill Hosp., NYC, 1970-90; founder Sendax Seminars; 1st dir. implant prosthodontics resident program Columbia U. Sch. Dental and Oral Surgery and Columbia Presbyn. Hosp. Editor: Dental Clinics of North America: HA-Coated Dental Implants, 1992; mem. editl. bd. Oral Implantology, 1979-98; patentee in mini-implants, oral implant magnetics, implant abutments and sinus graft implant stabilizers; co-developer IMTEC/SENDAX mini-dental implant system, author: (profl. text book) Mini Dental Implant Innovations, 2009. Mem. bd. dirs. City Ctr. Music and Drama, Inc. divsn. Lincoln Ctr. Performing Arts, NYC, 1966-75; mem. adv. bd. Amagansett (N.Y.) Hist. Assn., 1969-89; trustee Leukemia Soc. Am., NYC, 1967; bd. dirs. Schola Cantorum, 1980-90, Soc. Asian Music, 1965-76. Capt. Dental Corps USAF, 1955-57. Recipient Cert. of Honor, Brit. Dental Implant Assn., 1988., Aaron Gershkoff Meml. award for Outstanding Contbns. and Dedication to Oral Implantology Am. Acad. of Implant Dentistry, 1996. Fellow: Royal Soc. Medicine Gt. Britain, Am. Acad. Implant Dentistry (nat. pres. 1981), Internat. Coll. Dentists, Am. Coll. Dentists; mem.: ADA (ho. of dels. 1969), Japan Soc., N.Y. Acad. Scis., Internat. Assn. Dental Rsch., Am. Assn. Dental Rsch. (implant group), Fedn. Dentaire Internat., Am. Analgesia Soc., Acad. of Osseointegration, Am. Dental Edn. Assn. (former chmn. spl. interest group on dental implant edn.), Century Assn. Home: 70 E 77th St Apt 6A New York NY 10075-1811 Office: Mini Dental Implant Ctr 30 Central Park S Ste 14B New York NY 10019-1628 Office Phone: 212-753-2775. Business E-Mail: vis@sendax-minidentimpl.com. *I stand in awe of mankinds' eternal need to innovate and push back the frontiers of knowledge, while tempering the harsher realities of existence with a perspective born of our cultural heritage.*

SENDEK, HERB, men's college basketball coach; b. Pitts., Feb. 22, 1963; m. Melanie Scheuer; children: Kristin, Catherine, Kelly. BA in Indsl. Mgmt. summa cum laude, Carnegie-Mellon U., Pitts., 1985. Asst. coach Ctrl. Cath. HS, Pitts., 1984—85; grad. asst. coach Providence Coll. Friars, 1985—86, asst. coach, 1987—89, U. Ky. Wildcats, 1989—93; head basketball coach Miami U. Red Hawks, Ohio, 1994—96, NC State U. Wolfpack, 1996—2006, Ariz. State U. Sun Devils, 2006—. Named Ohio Coach of Yr., 1995, Coach of Yr., Mid-Am. Conf., 1995, Atlantic Coach Conf., 2004, Dist. 5 Coach of Yr., Nat. Assn. Basketball Coaches, 2002, 2004, Dist. IX Coach of Yr., US Basketball Writers, 2008; named to Penn Hills Hall of Fame, Pa., Pa. Hall of Fame, East Boros Chpt., We. Pa. Chpt., Five-Star Basketball Camp Hall of Fame; finalist Naismith Nat. Coach of Yr., 2002. Office: Ariz State Univ Athletics Carson Ctr PO Box 872505 Tempe AZ 85287-2505*

SENDER, ADAM D., investment company executive, art collector; Gen. ptnr. Exis Capital Mgmt., NYC, 1998—. Named one of Top 200 Collectors, ARTnews Mag., 2004—08. Avocation: Collector of Contemporary Art. Office: Exis Capital Mgmt 33rd Fl 767 Third Ave New York NY 10017

SENDLINGER, SHAWN CROWLEY, chemistry professor, department chairman; b. The Dalles, Oreg., Mar. 27, 1963; s. Robert Julius and Dorothy Eileen Sendlinger; m. Jennifer Lynn Garst, May 25, 1997; children: Shelby Garst, Jack Garst. BS, Oreg. State U., Corvallis, 1985; MS, PhD, Cornell U., Ithaca, NY, 1990. Assoc. prof. Dept. Chemistry, NCCU, Durham, 2000—08, interim chair, 2007—. Edn. cons. Shodor Edn. Found., Durham, 1999—2008. Contbr. articles to profl. jour. Grant, Office Pres. U. NC Sys., 2004—06. Mem.: Am. Chem. Soc. (alt. councilor 2002—05).

SENDO, TAKESHI, mechanical engineering educator, researcher, writer; b. Ena City, Japan, Aug. 5, 1917; s. Shigeyoshi and Michie (Yamamoto) S.; m. Hide Okamoto, Apr. 16, 1945; children: Mitsuyoshi, Sachiko, Kazuyasu. B of Engring., Tokyo U., 1941. Prof. mech. engring. Meijo U., Nagoya City, Japan, 1959-90, hon. prof., 1990—. Curator libr. Meijo U., Nagoya City, 1975-80. Author: Treatise of High Speed Deformation of Metal, 1993, 2nd edit., 1994, Experiment: Behavior of Al Column by Drop Hammer Test, 1959-90; contbr. over 60 articles to profl. jours. Mem. cmty. activity com. Local Self-Governing Orgn., Moriyama City, Japan, 1990, 91. Served to lt. comdr. Japanese Navy, 1941-45. Fellow Japan Soc. Mech. Engring., Japan Soc. Precision Engring. Avocations: composing haiku and tanka, trying essay, jogging. Home: 21-8 Choei Moriyama-ku Nagoya 463 Japan

SENER, STEPHEN FRANCIS, oncologist, surgeon; b. Chgo., Jan. 30, 1950; s. Charles J. and Helen Sener; m. Sherri Abbott, June 21, 1971; children: Matthew Charles, Michael Stephen. BA in Chemistry, Northwestern U., Evanston, Illinois, 1972; MD, Northwestern U., Chgo., 1977. Lic. surgeon Am. Bd. Surgery, 1983, surg. oncologist Soc. of Surg. Oncology, 1988. Asst. prof. surgery Northwestern U., Chgo., 1987—92, assoc. prof. surgery, 1992—98; prof. of surgery Northwestern U. Dept. of Surgery, 1998—; head, divsn. gen. surgery Evanston Northwestern Healthcare, 1996—2001, attending surgeon, 1984—, vice-chairman, dept. surgery, 1999—. Contbr. articles to profl. jours. Recipient Departmental Honors award, Northwestern U. Dept. Chemistry, 1972, Faculty Tchr. Yr., Northwestern U. Dept. Surgery, 1998. Fellow: Soc. Surg. Oncology; mem.: Am. Surg. Assn., Midwest Surg. Assn. (mem. exec. com. 2003—), Am. Cancer Soc. (Ill. pres. 1992—94, nat. bd. dirs. 1992—2006, nat. pres. 2004—05, pres. 2004—05, immediate past pres. 2005—06, St. George medal 1998), Chgo. Surg. Soc. (sec. 1999—2003), Am. Soc. Clin. Oncology, Ctrl. Surg. Assn. Achievements include first to organize and lead six surgical teams from Evanston Northwestern Healthcare on humanitarian surgical missions to Moscow State University, Latvia Cancer Inst., and Peking University. Office: Evanston Northwestern Healthcare 2650 Ridge Walgreen Bldg Rm 2507 Evanston IL 60201

SENERCHIA, RORY ELIZABETH, language educator; b. New Haven, Sept. 22, 1977; d. Kevin Michael Walsh; m. Marcus Anthony Senerchia, June 26, 2004; children: Sydney Marie, Marcus Anthony IV. MA in Comparative Lit. & Cultural Studies, UCONN, Storrs, 2001. English tchr. Blackstone Millville Regional HS, Mass., 2001—03; asst. prof. English Johnson & Wales U., Providence, 2003—. Cmty. svc. learning cons. RI & MA Campus Compact, Providence, 2005—. Grant, RI & MA Campus Compact, 2005—. Mem.: RICTE (pres. 2007—). Office: Johnson @ Wales Univ 8 Abbott Pk Pl Providence RI 02903 Business E-Mail: rsenerchia@jwu.edu.

SENESE, SUZANNE MARIE, art and music educator, performance artist; b. Chgo., Dec. 6, 1950; d. Louis Michael and Angeline Mary Olivo Senese. Student, Quincy Coll., Ill., 1968—70; BS in Music Edn. and Vocal, No. Ill. U., DeKalb, 1972; MA in Interdisciplinary Arts, Columbia Coll., Chgo., 2003. Music educator St. John Vianney Sch., Northlake, Ill., 1973—76, St. Pius X Elem. Sch., Lombard, Ill., 1976—85; choir/orch. dir. Seton H.S., South Holland, Ill., 1985—87; choir, orch., music and theatre educator Regina Dominican H.S., Wilmette, Ill., 1984—99; fine arts and choir educator Fenwick HS, Oak Park, Ill., 1999—, dir., 2008—, condr.; chapter sponsor Tri M Music Honor Soc. Student tchr. supr. Columbia Coll. Chgo. MAT Program. Vol. St. Leonard's House; mem. Park Ridge Civic Orch. Chorus, Northwestern U. Summer Chorus; dir. Choir Concert Tour, Italy; music dir., cantor, organist Santa Lucia Ch., Chgo., 1983—91. Recipient Heart of Sch. Arts award, Archdiocese of Chgo., 2001. Mem.: Nat. Assn. Art Edn., Nat. Assn. Pastoral Musicians, Nat. Cath. Edn. Assn., Ill. Arts Edn. Assn., Am. Choral Dir. Assn., Music Educators Nat. Conf. Roman Catholic. Avocations: theater, reading, crossword puzzles, baseball. Office: Fenwick High Sch 505 Washington Blvd Oak Park IL 60302 Office Phone: 708-386-0127 198. Personal E-mail: ssenese@msn.com.

SENEY, ERIN E., biologist, marine biologist; b. Lexington, Ky., Oct. 1, 1978; d. Franklin D. Sene Jr. and Rebecca A. Mazzarella; m. Bryan M. Smouther. BA, U. Va., Charlottesville, 2000; MS, Coll. William & Mary, Williamsburg, Gloucester Point, Va., 2003; PhD, Tex. A & M U., College Sta., Galveston, 2008—. Contractor and fishery biologist NOAA Fisheries Sea Turtle Facility, Galveston, 2005—08. Bd. mem. and v.p. fundraising and pub. rels. Friends of the Virgina Pep Band Inc., Charlottesville, 2003—08. Mem.: Am. Soc. Ichthyologists and Herpetologists, Internat. Sea Turtle Soc. (Archie Carr Student award 2008). Personal E-mail: eeseney@gmail.com.

SENEY, RONALD JOE, speech educator, theater educator; b. Robbstown, Tex., Oct. 5, 1943; s. Alva Paul and Inez Idell Seney. BE, Mo. State U., Springfield, 1968, MA, 1978; ABD, La. State U., Baton Rouge, 1984. Tchr. speech and theatre Nev. HS, Mo., 1970—76, Parkview HS, Springfield, Mo., 1977—81; prof. speech, dir. forensics Stephen F. Austin State U., Nacogdoches, Tex., 1984—90; prof. speech, asst. dir. forensics Mankato State U., Minn., 1990—96; prof. speech and theatre Lincoln Land CC, Springfield, Ill., 1996—. Actor: (performer) USO Tours to the Orient (Outstanding Tchr. of Yr., 1975, 1981), Summer Stock, Community Theatre. Bd. govs. Mo. State Speech Assn., 1980, Tex. State Speech Assn., 1988—90, Minn. State Speech Assn., 1994; v.p. Tex. Forensic Assn., 1984—88, pres., 1988—90; Dist. III chair Nat. Individual Event Tournament, 1988—90. Office: Lincoln Land CC 5250 Shepherd Rd PO Box 19256 Springfield IL 62794-9256 Office Fax: 217-786-2866. Business E-Mail: ron.seney@llcc.edu.

SENFT, MASON GEORGE, musician; b. Bklyn., Nov. 1, 1942; s. Arthur and Ann (Nagel) S. BA cum laude, Adelphi U., 1964. Pvt. practice accompanist/vocal coach, Roslyn Heights, NY, 1964—. Tchr. Adelphi U., Garden City, NY, 1964-73; dir. Nat. Scholastic Aptitude Tng. Inst., Garden City, 1966-69; musical dir. Tibbits Opera House, Coldwater, Mich., 1972-73, Canal Fulton Playhouse, Ohio, 1974-84, Island Lyric Opera, Garden City, 1980—, A Small Co. in America, Glen Cove, NY, 1984—; cons. Island Chamber Symphony Orch., Glen Head, NY, 1985—, Nat. Grand Opera, Tilles Ctr., Greenvale, NY, 1988—, PBS TV spl. Christmas with Flicka, 1988, Dark Summer debut by Christine Berl, Lincoln Ctr. Chamber Soc., Alice Tully Hall, NY, 1989, Glimmerglass Opera, 1992—; accompanist to Frederica von Stade 350th Convocation Celebration, Harvard U., Cambridge, Mass., 1986; accompanist ARC benefit concert In Concert, Carnegie Hall, 1989, Met. Opera Gala, NYC, 1994; music coach The Aspern Papers, Dallas Opera, debut 1988; cons. NY Virtuoso Chamber Symphony, 1989—; music coach DiCapo Opera Co., 1975-90; accompanist concert in honor of Queen Margrethe II of Sweden, The White House, 1991, hist. gala concert at Steinway Hall, NY, 1991, gala concert for Met. Opera Four Seasons Hotel, 1993. Author: Chimera, 1997, Elusive Thought, 1998, Windows, 1998; orchestrator: (films) Liberty Heights, 1998; prodr.: (CD) A Memorial Tribute-To the Fallen Heroes of September 11, 2001, Three Tenors-Home for the Holidays, 2004; musician (with violinist Jeremy Cushman): (TV broadcast) Madison Sq. Garden, NYC, 2003; prodr.(orchestrator): (CD) Tutto Morena, 2008; acoompanist: Historic Concert Mikve Isreal-Emanuel Curacao, 2009; lyricist, orchestrator Music of Alfred Morena, 2009. Apptd. to the Rep. Presdl. Task Force, 2001. Recipient citation for lifetime achievement NY State Assembly, 1994. Mem. Musicians Union Local 802, LI Singers Soc. (accompanist 1985-96), Mensa. Avocations: travel, writing, metaphysics. Home: 18 Osborne Ln Greenvale NY 11548 Personal E-mail: msenft@optonline.net.

SENG, COLEEN JOY, church administrator, director, former mayor; b. Council Bluffs, Iowa, Feb. 8, 1936; d. Otis A. and Helen V. (Anderson) McElwain; m. Darrel E. Seng, Oct. 22, 1960 (dec. 1993); children: Marcee Lee, Christopher Charles, Phillip Scott. BA, Nebr. Wesleyan U., 1958. Dist. dir. Girl Scouts USA, Saginaw, Mich., 1958-60, Lincoln, Nebr., 1960-62; cmty. ministry 1st United Meth. Ch., Lincoln, 1977-97; mem. Lincoln City Coun., 1987—2003; mayor City of Lincoln, 2003—07; dir. cmty. ministries First United Methodist Ch., 2007—. Mem. Mayor's first multi-cultural task force, co-chair of Gov. Nelson's urban adv. team, chmn. railroad transp. safety dist. Lincoln/Lancaster county joint budget com., mem. Lincoln/Lancaster county homeless coalition; active U. Place Cmty. Orgn. N.E. Family Resource Ctr.; past chair Lincoln/Lancaster county family resource ctr. bd.; past pres. Lincoln Fellowship of Chs.; mem. Lincoln Interfaith Coun.; mem Lincoln Urban Ministries com.; past pres. Homestead Girl Scouts Coun., Planned Parenthood Vets. Nebr., bd. ordained ministries United Methodist Annual Conf., 2008- Democrat. United Methodist. Avocations: reading, movies, gardening. Home: 6101 Walker Ave Lincoln NE 68507-2467 Office: First United Methodist Church 2723 North 50th St Lincoln NE 68504

SENGER, JEFFREY M., lawyer; b. 1962; AB magna cum laude, Harvard U.; JD cum laude, Harvard Law Sch. Law clerk for Hon. Earl B. Gilliam U.S. Dist. Ct., So. Dist, Calif.; dir. training civil and appellate dept. lawyers U.S. Dept. Justice; sr. trial atty.; spl. asst. U.S. atty. U.S. Dept. Justice, asst. U.S. atty., sr. coun. Office Dispute Resolution, sr. coun., office assoc. atty. gen.; dep. chief coun. US FDA. Fed. mediator U.S. Dist. Ct.; civil, family, and criminal misdemeanor mediator Superior Ct., Washington, DC; arbitrator Better Bus. Bur., DC Bar Assn.; tchr. negotiations Harvard Law Sch.; tchr. trial techniques Nat. Inst. Trial Advocacy, Harvard Law Sch. Author: Federal Dispute Resolution: Using ADR with the United States Government; contbr. chapters to books, articles to law jours. Fellow: Am. Bar Found.; mem.: Am. Law Inst. Office: FDA 5600 Fishers Ln Rockville MD 20857

SENGERS, JOHANNA M. H. LEVELT, physicist; b. Amsterdam, The Netherlands, Mar. 4, 1929; arrived in US, 1963, naturalized, 1977; m. Jan V. Sengers, 1963; 4 children. Drs, U. Amsterdam, 1954, PhD in Physics, 1958; PhD (hon.), Delft U. Tech., 1992. Rsch. assoc. U. Amsterdam, Van der Waals Lab, 1954-58, 59-63, U. Wis., Inst. Theoretical Chemistry, Madison, 1958-59; physicist heat divsn. Inst. Basic Stds., Nat. Bur. Stds., Gaithersburg, Md., 1963-78; group leader thermophysics divsn. Nat. Engring. Lab., 1978-87; sr. fellow thermophysics divsn. Nat. Inst. Standards and Tech., 1983-95, scientist emeritus, 1995—. Lectr Cath. U., Louvain, Belgium, 1971; rsch. assoc. Inst. Theoretical Physics, U. Amsterdam, 1974—75; regent's prof. chemistry U. Calif., LA, 1982; Alexander von Humboldt rschr. Ruhr U., Bochum, 1991; co-chair Interacad. coun. adv. panel Women for Sci., 2005—06. Author: How Fluid Unmix: Discoveries by the School of Van der Waals and Kamerlingh Onnes, 2002; contbr. chapters to books, archival pubs., reports, and 3 books. Chair working group A Internat. Assn. Properties Steam, 1985-90; pres. Internat. Assn. Properties Water and Steam, 1991-92. Recipient Silver medal U.S. Dept. Commerce, 1972, Gold medal, 1978, Wise award Interagy. Com. Women in Sci. and Engring., 1985, Alexander von Humboldt Rsch. award Alexander von Humboldt-Stiftung, Bonn, Germany, 1991, L'Oreal-UNESCO Women in Sci. award, 2003. Fellow: AAAS, ASME (Yeram S. Touloukian award 2006), Am. Phys. Soc., Internat. Assn. Properties Water and Steam (hon.); mem.: AIChE, Assn. Women in Sci., Royal Holland Soc. of Scis. and Humanities, Dutch Phys. Soc., Netherlands Royal Acad. Arts and Sci. (corr.), European Phys. Soc., Nat. Acad. Engring., Nat. Acad. Sci., Cosmos Club. Democrat. Unitarian Universalist. Office: Phys & Chem Properties Div Nat Inst Stds & Tech 100 Bureau Dr Stop 8380 Gaithersburg MD 20899-8380 Home Phone: 301-424-8089; Office Phone: 301-975-2463. Business E-Mail: johanna.sengers@nist.gov.

SENGPIEHL, PAUL MARVIN, lawyer, former state official; b. Stuart, Nebr., Oct. 10, 1937; s. Arthur Paul and Anne Marie (Andersen) S.; BA, Wheaton (Ill.) Coll., 1959; MA in Pub. Adminstrn., Mich. State U., 1961; JD, Ill. Inst. Tech.-Chgo. Kent Coll. Law, 1970. Lic. min., 2007. m. June S. Cline, June 29, 1963; children— Jeffrey D., Chrystal M. Bar: Ill. 1971, U.S. Supreme Ct. 1982. Adminstrv. asst. Chgo. Dept. Urban Renewal, 1962-65; supr. Ill. Municipal Retirement Fund, Chgo., 1966-71; mgmt. officer Ill. Dept. Local Govt. Affairs, Springfield, 1971-72, legal counsel, Chgo., 1972-73; spl. asst. atty. gen. Ill. Dept. Labor, Chgo., 1973-76; asst. atty. gen. Ct. of Claims div. Atty. Gen. of Ill., 1976-83; hearing referee Bd. Rev., Ill. Dept. Labor, 1983-84; local govt. law columnist Chgo. Daily Law Bull., 1975-84; instr. polit. sci. Judson Coll., Elgin, Ill., 1963. Republican candidate for Cook County Recorder of Deeds, 1984; dep. committeeman Oak Park Twp Rep. Orgn.; elected alt. del., served del. Rep. Nat. Conv., 1992; People's Choice candidate pres. Oak Park Village, 1993; Rep. alt. state ctrl. committeeman 7th Congl. Dist., elected commiteeman Oak Park Rep., 1994-98, elected rep. committeeman, 1994-96; elected del. Rep. Nat. Convention, 1996; co-chmn. Cook County Jail Ministry Bd., chmn. 2003-; treas. Cook County Correctional Chaplaincy Coun., 2003-06, chmn., 2006-, lic. min., 2007-, Ordination Min., 2009-. Mem. Ill. Bar Assn. (local govt. law sect. council 1973-79, vice chmn. 1976-77, co-editor local govt. newsletter 1976-77, chmn. 1977-78, editor newsletter 1977-78, state tax sect. council 1979-82, 84-85), Chgo. Bar Assn. (local govt. com., chmn. legis. subcom. 1978-79, sec. 1979-80, vice chmn. 1980-81, chmn. 1981-82, state and mcpl. tax com.), John Ericsson Rep. League Ill. (state sec. 1983-85, 95—, hon. past pres. Cook County 1982-97, pres. 1997—), Oak Park-River Forest C. of C. (small bus. coun. 1991-2000). Baptist (vice chmn. deacons 1973-76, 79-80, moderator 1983-86, supt. Sunday sch. 1986-93). Home and Office: 727 N Ridgeland Ave Oak Park IL 60302-1735 Office Phone: 708-383-8859. Personal E-mail: sengpiehllaw@yahoo.com. Business E-Mail: sengpiehllaw@aol.com.

SENGUPTA, ABHIJIT, molecular and optical physicist; PhD, Stanford U., 1995. Rsch. asst. Stanford U., Calif., 1989—95; NSF postdoctoral fellow Mass. Inst. Tech., Cambridge, Mass., 1995—97; rsch. scientist Eastman Kodak Co., Rochester, NY, 1997—99; asst. prof., rsch. Jefferson Lab. Consortium, Old Dominion U., Norfolk, Va., 1999—2001; sr. scientist, project leader Bell Labs., Lucent Tech., Norcross, Ga., 2001—02, OFS, Norcross, Ga., 2002—03; prin. rsch. scientist SYSTIMAX Solutions, Richardson, Tex., 2004—; founder, pres. FEMTONIX, Alpharetta, Ga., 2003—. Vis. scientist Inst. Optics, U. Rochester, 1998—99; adj. asst. prof., physics Old Dominion U., 1999—2003, adj. asst. prof., elec. computer engring., 1999—2001; cons. SOLAREX, Toano, Va., 1999—2000, Laser Ctr. Va., Ctr. Anti-Aging Rsch., Va. Beach., 2000—01; panel reviewer NSF, Arlington, Va., 1999—2000; peer reviewer Internat. Sci. Tech. Ctr., Wash., DC, 2000—. One-man shows include Stanford U. Tressidor Union Gallery; co-author: Laser Techniques in Chemistry, 1995. Recipient Innovation award, Va. Ctr. Innovative Tech., 2000, US Patent award in Optical Comms. Mem.: AAAS, OSA, IEEE. Office Phone: 678-528-5109. E-mail: asengupta@femtonix.com.

SENGUPTA, ANITA, aerospace engineer, researcher; d. Shyamal and Faye Sengupta; life ptnr. Abraham Antonio Anderson. BS in Aerospace Engring., Boston U., 1998; MS in Aerospace Engring., U. South Calif, 2000; PhD in Aerospace Engring., U. South Calif., LA, 2005. Cert. in private pilot single engine land, FAA, 2002. Propulsion engr. Boeing Space & Comm., Huntington Beach, Calif., 1998—2001; sr. sys. engr. mars sci. lab. mission NASA Jet Propulsion Lab., Pasadena, Calif., 2005—, sr. mech. engr., 2001—05, sr. engr. venus lander mission, 2007—. Mem. bd. dirs. ASEI, LA, 2006—08. Contbr. articles to profl. jours. Vol. spkr. LA's best, 2003—08, JPL Speaker's Bur., Pasadena, 2008; canvasser Obama Campaign, Cleve., 2008. Recipient Woman Engr. of the Yr., ASEI, 2006, NASA Tech award, NASA, 2007, Best Paper award, AIAA, 2004. Mem.: NSS, Sigma Gamma Tau: Nat. Honor Soc. Aerospace Engring., Tau beta Pi: Nat. Honor Soc. Engring., IEEE, AIAA. Democrat. Avocations: travel, scuba diving, bicycling. Office: NASA Jet Propulsion Lab 4800 oak Grove Dr Pasadena CA 91109 Personal E-mail: anita.aerospace@gmail.com. Business E-Mail: anita.sengupta@jpl.nasa.gov.

SENGUPTA, ARUP KUMAR, engineering educator, researcher; b. Calcutta, Bengal, India, June 11, 1951; came to US, 1980; s. Ajay K. and Ranu S.; m. Susmita Chanda, Jan. 19, 1983; children: Neal and Sohan. BSChemE, Jadavpur U., Calcutta, 1973; MS in Environ. Engring., U. Houston, 1982, PhD in Environ. Engring., 1984. Registered profl. engr., Pa. Process devel. engr. Kuljian Corp., Phila. and Calcutta, 1973-80; grad. rsch. asst. U. Houston, 1980-84; asst. prof. Lehigh U., Bethlehem, Pa., 1985—90, assoc. prof., 1990—94, prof., 1994—, chair dept. civil and environ. engring., 1998—2005. Contbr. articles to profl. jours. Recipient Indsl. Ecology Fellowship award, NSF and Lucent Technologies, 1999, Profl. Rsch. award, Pa. Water Environment Assn., 2001, Frontier Rsch. award, Assn. Environ. Engring. and Sci. Profs. and Malcolm Pirnie, 2001, Internat. Ion Exch. award in Cambridge U., Soc. Chem. Industry (Separation Sci. and Tech. Divsn.), UK, 2004, Mondialogo Sustainable Engring. award, Daimler-Chyrsler and UNESCO, 2005; co-recipient Grainger Challenge Silver award, NAE, 2007; grantee, NSF, 1985, 1986, EPA, 1988, 1990. Mem. NSPE, ASCE (Rudolph Hering medal 1994), AIChE, Am. Chem. Soc., Pa. Soc. Profl. Engrs., Assn. Environ. Engring. and Sci. Profs., Sigma Xi. Avocations: playing tennis, reading history. Office: Dept Civil and Environ Engring Lehigh U 13 E Packer Ave Bethlehem PA 18015 Office Phone: 610-758-3534. E-mail: arup.sengupta@lehigh.edu.

SENGUPTA, ATANU, research scientist; s. Tapas and Joyashree Sengupta; m. Arunima Bandyopadhyay, Dec. 25, 2001. BS in Chemistry, U. Calcutta, 1996; B.Tech in Fiber, U. Calcutta, India, 2001; PhD, U. Wash., Seattle, 2006. Rsch. scientist Real-Time Analyzers Inc, Middletown, Conn., 2006—; grad. rsch. asst. U. Wash., 2002—06. Recipient SBIR grant, NSF, 2006, 3rd best project award, Alps Industries, 2002; fellow, U. Wash., Seattle, Initiatives Fund, 2003—04; grants, NSF, 2008. Mem.: Am. Chem. Soc. Achievements include research in controlling binding and orientation of proteins on nanoparticles; Bioaerosol detection and characterization by surface-enhanced Raman spectroscopy; surface-enhanced Raman spectroscopy of soft-landed polyatomic ions and molecules; detection of bacteria by surface enhanced Raman spectroscopy; comparison of psychroactive arctic marine bacteria and common mesophillic bacteria; Surface-Enhanced Raman Spectroscopy of Bacteria and Pollen; bioaerosol characterization by surface-enhanced Raman spectroscopy. Office: Real-Time Analyzers Inc 362 Indsl Pk Rd Ste 8 Middletown CT 06457 Personal E-mail: atanu_sengupta@yahoo.com.

SENGUPTA, PARTHO P., cardiologist, educator; s. Pradeep Kumar and Monika Pradeep Sengupta. MBBS, Govt. Med. Coll., Nagpur, 1993, MD, 1996; DM, All India Inst. Med. Scis., New Delhi, 2000. Diplomate Am. Bd. Internal Medicine, 2007. Asst. prof. dept. medicine Mayo Clinic, Scottsdale, Ariz., 2007—. Contbr. articles to numerous profl. publs. Office: Mayo Clinic Ariz 13400 E Shea Boulevard Scottsdale AZ 85259 Business E-Mail: sengupta.partho@mayo.edu.

SENGUPTA, SHRAMIK, science educator; s. Ajit Kumar and Ruma Sengupta; m. Koyeli Ganguli, May 29, 2008. BTech with Honors, Indian Inst. Tech., Kharagpur, 1998; MS, U. Colo., Boulder, 2000; PhD, U. Minn., Mpls., 2004. Rsch. assoc. U. Notre Dame, Ind., 2005—07; asst. prof. U. Mo., Columbia, 2007—. External cons. Techshot, Inc., Greenville, Ind., 2005—06. Mem.: Am. Electrophoresis Soc. Achievements include patents for multistage electrophoresis apparatus; research in rapid detection of viable bacteria present at low concentrations; sorting bacteria by species using dielectrophoresis; microfluidic flow sensors; micro-reactors for controlled protein crystallization; electrophoretic cell sorting. Office: U MO Dept Biological Enging 1406 E Rollins St Columbia MO 65211 Business E-Mail: senguptas@missouri.edu.

SENGUPTA, SUNANDO, economics professor; m. Paramita Sengupta. Asst. prof. Bowie State U., Md., 2005—. Recipient Outstanding Rsch. award, IBFR, 2007. Mem.: Fin. and Economics Club (hon.). Office: Bowie State Univ 14000 Jericho Pk Rd Bowie MD 20715 Business E-Mail: ssengupta@bowiestate.edu.

SENIA, GRACE MELANIE, language and music educator; d. Gibson Kenyon Davis and Gertrude Mae Cook; m. Anthony Joseph Senia, June 26, 1971; children: Carmella Grace Bullick, Filene Marie Travis. BA, U. Buffalo, 1965; MS in Reading summa cum laude, Marywood U., 2001; postgrad. concert level oratorios with orchestra, SUNY, Binghamton. Cert. tchr. Latin and English NY, 1974, tchr. Latin Pa., 1980, English Pa., 1990, instr. reading NY, 2001, tchr. Latin NJ, 2001. Tchr. Latin and English Greene Ctrl. Sch., NY, 1964—68; tchr. English East HS, Rochester, NY, 1970—71, Hancock Ctrl. Sch., NY, 1971—87; tchr. Latin and English Scranton HS, Pa., 1993—94, Honesdale HS, Pa., 1999; adj. tchr. SUNY, Binghamton, 2001; instr. Latin Binghamton City HS, 2005—09. Tchr. after sch. program Hancock Cmty. Edn. Found., 2003—06; scholarly rsch., Latin. Past conf. del. Emory United Meth. Ch.; mem. adult concert chorus Binghamton U., appeared with Binghamton Philharm. Orch. on WSKG Pub. TV Sta. Mem.: Internat. Honor Soc. in Edn., Nat. Scholars Honor Soc., Kappa Delta Pi. Avocations: piano, golf. Home: 257 E Main St Hancock NY 13783 Office: Binghamton City Sch Dist 31 Main St Hancock NY 13783 Home Phone: 607-637-2695.

SENIOR, DONALD PAUL, religious organization administrator; b. Phila., Jan. 1, 1940; s. Vincent Edward and Margaret (Tiernan) S. BA in Philosophy, Passionist Sem. Coll., Chgo., 1963; Licentiate in Sacred Theology, U. Louvain, Belgium, 1970, STD, 1972. Prof. New Testament Cath. Theol. Union, Chgo., 1972—, dir. Israel program, 1980-88, acting dean, 1986-87, acting pres., 1988, pres., 1988—. Author books and articles on New Testament; assoc. editor The Bible Today, New Theology Rev., New Testament Message (22 vols.); gen. editor The Cath. Study Bible; writer, commentator, host radio and TV programs, Chgo. Mem. Cath. Bibl. Soc. Am., Soc. Bibl. Lit., Soc. for New Testament Studies, Cath. Theol. Soc. Am., Chgo. Soc. Bibl. Rsch. Democrat. Home and Office: 5401 S Cornell Ave Chicago IL 60615-5664

SENIOR, RICHARD JOHN LANE, linen and uniform services executive; b. Datchet, Eng., July 6, 1940; arrived in U.S., 1972, naturalized, 1977; s. Harold Dennis Senior and Jane Lane Dorothy (Chadwick) Senior Rigg; m. Diana Morgan, Dec. 19, 1966; children: Alden, Alicia, Amanda. BA, Oxford U., 1962, MA, 1966; MIA, Yale U., 1964. Jr. mgr. Tate & Lyle, London, 1964—66; mgmt. cons. McKinsey & Co., Inc., London, Chgo., 1967-74; pres., CEO Morgan Svcs., Inc., Chgo., 1974—2004, chair, CEO, 2004—. Bd. dir. Northwestern Meml. Healthcare, 1992-2001, Chgo. Crime Commn., 1994-99, Ball Hort. Co., 1996-, Near South Planning Bd., 2001-2003, Northwestern Meml. Found., 2001-; regional adv. bd. Kemper Ins. Cos., 1994-96. Pres. bd. trustees Latin Sch., Chgo., 1979-83. Hon. scholar Christ Ch., Oxford U., 1960-1962; Fulbright travel fellow, Yale U., 1962-64. Mem. Uniform and Textile Svc. Assn. (bd. dirs. 1996-99, exec. com. 2001-06, chmn. 2002-04), Textile Rental Svcs. Assn. Am. (pres. 1983-85, dir., exec. com. 1978-86), Racquet Club (bd. govs. 1983-91, 2006-09), Chgo. Club, Glen View Club, Casino (bd. govs. 1991-96, treas. 1993-94), Econ. Club, Yale Club Chgo. (bd. dirs. 1991-95, AYA del. 1992-95, chmn. grad. sch. task force 1990-95). Home: 1500 N Lake Shore Dr Chicago IL 60610-6657 Office: Morgan Svcs Inc 323 N Michigan Ave Chicago IL 60601-3798 Office Phone: 312-346-3184. Business E-Mail: senior@morganservices.com.

SENIOR, ROBERT THOMAS, retired military officer; b. Phila., June 18, 1944; s. Matthew John and Julia Mary Senior. Cert. in bus., Pierce Jr. Coll., Phila., 1963; AS, SUNY, Albany, 1980; BA, Widener U., Chester, Pa., 1993, postgrad., 1994. Clk. Phila. Electric, 1963—64; chief hosp. corps USN, 1964—89; combat medic 2d Marine Divsn., Camp LeJeune, NC, 1966, 2d Marine Air Wing, Beaufort, SC, 1966—67, 3d Batallion 1st MAR, Vietnam, 1967—68, USS Coranado, 1977—78, USS Independence, 1979—80, USS Sylvania, 1981—82, 1st Platoon Truck Co., Connellsville, Pa., 1982—85; ret., 1989. EMT, Chgo. Jr. Coll., 1981; ind. med. technician Portsmouth VA Hosp., 1969—85. Vol. USO Phila. Airport. Decorated Combat Action Ribbon, Marine Combat Insignia, 3 Presdl. Unit Citations, 1 Navy Unit Citation, Surface Warfare Pin, Fleet Marine Force Pin. Mem.: KC (4th degree), VFW (Americanism recorder 1991—), DAV (life), Naval Inst., Navy League, Marine Corps League, Am. Vets. (life). Avocations: reading, exercise, volunteer work, music. Home: 201 President Ave Rutledge PA 19070 Personal E-mail: rts0200mail@widener.edu.

SENIOR, THOMAS BRYAN A., electrical engineering educator, researcher, consultant; b. Menston, Yorkshire, Eng., June 26, 1928; arrived in U.S., 1957; s. Thomas Harold and Emily Dorothy (Matthews) Senior; m. Heather Margaret Golby, May 4, 1957; children: Margaret, David, Hazel, Peter. B.Sc., Manchester U., 1949, M.Sc., 1950; PhD, Cambridge U., 1954. Sr. sci. officer Royal Radar Establishment, Malvern, Eng., 1952-57; rsch. scientist U. Mich., Ann Arbor, 1957-69, prof. elec. engring., 1969-84, prof. elec. and computer sci., 1984-98, Arthur F. Thurnau prof., 1990-98, prof. emeritus, 1998—, dir. radiation lab., 1975-87, assoc. chmn. elect. engring. & computer sci. dept., 1984-90, acting chmn., 1987-88, assoc. chmn. acad. affairs, 1991-98. Cons. in field. Author: (with Bowman and Uslenghi) Electromagnetic and Acoustical Scattering by Simple Shapes, 1969; Mathematical Methods in Electrical Engineering, 1986; (with Volakis) Approximate Boundary Conditions in Electromagnetics, 1995; contbr. articles to profl. jours. Fellow IEEE (3d Millennium medal, AP-S Disting. Achievement award 2000); mem. Internat. Sci. Radio Union (chmn. U.S. nat. com. 1982-84, vice chmn. Com. B. 1985-87, chmn. 1988-90, pres. 1996-99, Van der Pol Gold medal 1993). Home: 1919 Ivywood Dr Ann Arbor MI 48103-4527 Office: U Mich Dept Elec Engring Comp S Ann Arbor MI 48109 E-mail: senior@eecs.umich.edu.

SENIOR, TIMOTHY C., bishop; b. Phila., Pa., Mar. 22, 1960; s. James Harwood and Elise (Rockwell) Senior. BA, St. Charles Borromeo Sem., Overbrook, Pa., 1981, MA, MDiv, St. Charles Borromeo Sem., Overbrook, Pa., 1988; MBA, MSW, Boston Coll., 1992. Ordained priest Archdiocese of Phila., 1985; asst. pastor Assumption parish, Feasterville, Pa., 1985—88; religion tchr. Archbishop Kennedy High Sch., Conshohcoken, Pa., 1988—89; dep. sec. Catholic Human Services Archdiocese of Phila., 1992—97, sec. Catholic Human Services, 1997—2004, vicar for clergy, 2004—; ordained bishop, 2009; aux. bishop Archdiocese of Phila., 2009—. Chaplain Divine Providence Village, Springfield, Pa. Roman Catholic. Avocation: piano. Office: Archdiocese of Phila 222 N 17th St Philadelphia PA 19103-1299 Office Phone: 215-587-4507. Office Fax: 215-587-4545.*

SENKAYI, ABU LWANGA, environmental scientist; b. Mpigi, Uganda, Oct. 16, 1943; came to U.S., 1973; s. Alamanzane Buza and Manjeri (Nalwoga) Abalyawo; m. Sunajeh Nansamba, Dec. 27, 1969; children: Ali K., Sala N. BS, Makerere U., Kampala, Uganda, 1971, MS, 1973; PhD, U. Calif., Davis, 1977. Rsch. scientist Tex. A&M U., College Station, 1977-87; sr. soil chemist Ebasco Environ. Svcs., Dallas, 1987-90; soil chemist PRC Environ. Mgmt., Inc., Dallas, 1990-96; sr. soil scientist Railroad Commn. of Tex. (Surface Mining/Reclamation Divsn.), Austin, Tex., 1996-97; environ. scientist U.S. EPA, Dallas, 1997—. Author 7 book chpts.; contbr. articles to Soil Sci. Soc. Am. Jour., Soil Sci. Jour., Clays and Clay Minerals Jour. Recipient PRC-EMI Exceptional Performance award, 1991, Fed. Ingeragy. Recognition award, 2000. Mem. Soil Sci. Soc. Am., Clay Mineral Soc., Mineral. Soc. Gt. Britain, Sigma Xi. Achievements include research on the chemistry and mineralogy of lignite, mineralogical weathering processes in soils, and problems associated with reclamation of surface-mined lands. Home: 1122 De Havilland Ave Duncanville TX 75137-4742 Office: US EPA Region 6 Compliance Assurance and Enforcement Divsn Dallas TX 75202-2733 E-mail: senkayi.abu@epa.gov.

SENKLER, ROBERT L., insurance company executive; BA in Math. and Stats., Minn. Duluth Coll., 1974. Began Minn. Life Ins. Co., 1974—, v.p. Individual Ins. Divsn., 1987-94; pres. Securian Fin. Group (Minn. Life Ins. Co.), 1994—2007, CEO, 1994—, chmn., 1995—. Past chmn. Ins. Fed. Minn.; pres. Minn. Bus. Prtnrshp., 2003; chmn. Cap. City Partnership. Recipient Univ. Minn.-Duluth Acad. Sci. Engring., 2003. Fellow Soc. Actuaries. Office: Securian Fin Group 400 Robert St N Saint Paul MN 55101-2015

SENKOV, OLEG N., physicist, researcher, materials scientist; b. Nesterov, Ukraine, Mar. 28, 1952; s. Nikolai I. and Olga N. Senkov; m. Svetlana V. Perevoshchikova, July 15, 1989; children: Alex, Tatiana. MSc in Physics, Moscow State U., 1975; PhD in Solid State Physics, Russian Acad. Sci., 1981. Engr. Inst. of Solid State Physics, Chernogolovka, Russia, 1975—81, scientist, 1981—91, sr. scientist, 1991—96; asst. dir., rsch. prof. U. Idaho, Moscow, Idaho, 1996—2000; sr. scientist UES, Inc., Dayton, Ohio, 2000—. Assoc. prof. Moscow State Acad. Instrument Engring. and Informatics, Moscow, 1989—94; vis. scientist McGill U., Montreal, Quebec, Canada, 1994—96; dir. NATO Rsch. Workshop, 2003; spkr. in field. Contbr. articles to profl. jours. Recipient numerous rsch. awards. Fellow: ASM Internat.; mem.: The Minerals, Metallurgical and Materials Soc. Achievements include patents in field. Office: UES Inc 4401 Dayton-Xenia Rd Dayton OH 45432-1894 Personal E-mail: osenkov@msn.com.

SENNEMA, DAVID CARL, arts consultant; b. Grand Rapids, Mich., July 6, 1934; s. Carl Edward and Alice Bertha (Bieri) S.; m. Martha Amanda Dixon, Feb. 22, 1958; children: Daniel Ross, Julia Kathryn, Alice Dixon. BA, Albion Coll., 1956. Mgr. Columbia Music Festival Assn., 1964-67; exec. dir. S.C. Arts Commn., Columbia, 1967-70; assoc. dir. Fed.-State Partnership and Spl. Projects program Nat. Endowment for the Arts, Washington, 1971-73; prof. arts adminstrn., dir. cmty. arts mgmt. program Sangamon State U., Springfield, Ill., 1973-76; dir. SC State Mus., Columbia, 1976-85; bus. mgr. Palmetto Mastersingers, 1988—96. Cons. in field, 1996-. Co-author: Columbia, S.C. A Postcard History, 1997. Mem. adv. panel Nat. Endowment for the Arts Music, 1968-70; chmn. Springfield Arts Commn., 1975-76. Served with U.S. Army, 1957-58. Recipient Verner Lifetime Achievement award, 2006, Short Story Winner, SC Fiction Project, 2009; named to Order of Palmetto, SC, 1986. Mem. Rotary. Avocation: singing. Office Phone: 803-782-3581. Personal E-mail: dsennema@sc.rr.com.

SENNET, CHARLES JOSEPH, lawyer; b. Buffalo, Aug. 7, 1952; s. Saunders M. and Muriel S. (Rotenberg) S. AB magna cum laude, Cornell U., 1974; JD with high honors, George Washington U., 1979. Bar: Ill. 1979, U.S. Dist. Ct. (no. dist.) Ill. 1979, U.S. Ct. Appeals (7th cir.) 1982, U.S. Ct. Appeals (D.C. cir.) 1993. Assoc. Reuben & Proctor, Chgo., 1979-83; assoc. counsel Tribune Co., Chgo., 1984-91, sr. counsel, 1991—2009, asst. gen. counsel, 2009—. Adj. faculty Medill Sch. Journalism, Northwestern U., 1991-94, 2004—08; chmn. Television Music Lic. Com., 1995—. Contbr. articles to profl. jours. Chmn. cable royalty distbn. com. Nat. Assn. Broadcasters, 2005—. Mem. ABA (spkr. 1984-88, 91-97, 2000-08, mem. gov. bd. Forum on Comms. Law 1995-98), NATAS, Ill. Bar Assn. (chmn. media law com. 1989-91), Chgo. Bar Assn., Fed. Comms. Bar Assn. Office: Tribune Co 435 N Michigan Ave Chicago IL 60611-4066

SENNETT, JOHN O., lawyer; b. Broken Bow, Nebr., Apr. 10, 1948; BS, Univ. Nebr., 1970, JD, 1972. Bar: Nebr. 1972, US Dist. Ct. (Dist. Nebr.) 1972, US Supreme Ct. 1975, US Ct. Appeals (8th Cir.) 1976. Ptnr. Sennett Duncan Borders & Jenkins PC, LLO, Broken Bow, Nebr. Mem.: ABA, Assn. of Trial Lawyers of Am., Nebr. Trial Lawyers Assn., Custer County Bar Assn., Nebr. State Bar Assn. (Ho. of Del. 1986—92, chmn. 1991—92, bd. trustees 1992—98, pres. 2004—05). Office: Sennett Duncan Borders & Jenkins PC LLO 425 S 7th St Broken Bow NE 68822 Office Phone: 308-872-6868. Office Fax: 308-872-2191. Business E-Mail: jsennett@adb-law.com.

SENNETT, MICHAEL, lawyer; b. Chgo., Oct. 24, 1951; BA with honors, Quincy U., 1973; JD cum laude, Loyola U., 1977. Bar: Ill. 1977, (US Supreme Ct.) 1984. Assoc. Bell, Boyd & Lloyd, Chgo., 1977—83, ptnr., 1984—2007; chair antitrust and trade regulation Bell, Boyd & Lloyd, LLP, Chgo., 1996—2007; ptnr. antitrust and competition law Jones Day, 2007—. Exec. editor Loyola U. Chgo. Law Jour., 1976—77; adj. law faculty Loyola U., 1996—; bd. advisors Inst. for Consumer Antitrust Law Studies, Chgo., 1998—. Contbr. chpt. to book. Trustee Children's Home and Aid Soc. of Ill., Inc., Chgo., 2004—, Quincy U., Ill., 2006—. Mem.: Internat. Bar Assn., Chgo. Bar Assn. (chair, antitrust law com. 1996—97), ABA, Lawyers Club Chgo. Office: Jones Day 77 W Wacker Chicago IL 60601 Office Phone: 312-269-4243. Office Fax: 312-782-8585. Business E-Mail: msennett@jonesday.com.

SENNETT, NANCY J., lawyer; b. Milw., Nov. 26, 1951; BS in English & comm. arts with honors, U. Wis., 1973; JD cum laude, Northwestern U., 1979. Bar: Wis. 1979. With Foley & Lardner LLP, Milw., 1979—, chair securities litig. practice group, mng. ptnr. Milw. office. Chair merit selection com. reappointment magistrate judges Ea. Dist. Wis. Notes and comments editor Northwestern U. Law Rev., 1978-79. Active Jr. Achievement. Mem.: ABA (securities litig. com.), Securities Industry Assn. (compliance & legal divsn.), State Wis. Bar Assn., Milw. Bar Assn. (Lawyer Year 2003), ABCD, Inc. (bd. dirs.), Betty Brinn Children's Mus. (founding bd. dirs.), Greater Milw. Com., Tempo & Rotary, U. Wis. Alumni Assn. (bd. dirs., Distinguished Alumni Award 2003). Office: Foley & Lardner LLP US Bank Ctr 777 E Wisconsin Ave Milwaukee WI 53202-5367 Office Phone: 414-297-5522. Business E-Mail: nsennett@foley.com.

SENOR, DANIEL SAMUEL, investment company and think-tank executive; b. NY, Nov. 6, 1971; s. James Mayer Senor; m. Campbell Brown, Apr. 2, 2006; children: Eli James, Asher Liam. BA, U. We. Ontario; student, Hebrew U., Jerusalem; MBA, Harvard Bus. Sch., 2001. Intern Am. Israel Pub. Affairs Com. (AIPAC), 1993; fgn. policy adv., comm. dir. to Senator Spencer Abraham US Senate; venture capitalist The Carlyle Group, 2001—03; dep. to press sec. Scott McClellan The White House, Washington, 2003; Pentagon & White House adv. US Ctrl. Command Forward, Doha, Qatar, 2003, Baghdad, Iraq, 2003—04; ptnr. Rosemont Solebury Capital Mgmt. LP, NYC; co-founder, bd. dirs. Fgn. Policy Initiative, Washington, 2009—. Adj. sr. fellow Mid. East studies Coun. Fgn. Rels., 2008—. Analyst Fox News, 2005—, reg. contbr. Wall St. Jour., NY Times, Washington Post, NY Post, Weekly Standard. Recipient Disting. Civilian Svc. award, US Dept. Def. Republican. Jewish. Office: Rosemont Solebury Capital Mgmt LP 375 Greenwich St Ste 711 New York NY 10013 Mailing: Fgn Policy Initiative 1718 M St NW #234 Washington DC 20036*

SENRA, JENNY, psychologist; b. Jamaica, NY, Apr. 25, 1979; d. Francisco and Ana Senra. MS in Sch. Psychology, Mercy Coll., Dobbs Ferry, 2006. Cert. sch. psychologist NY, 2006. Sch. psychologist NYCDOE, Bronx, NY, 2006—; lacrosse coach Bronxville HS, NY, 2007—. Mem.: UFT. Office: NYCDOE E Tremont Ave Bronx NY 10460

SENS, ALEXANDER, classicist, educator; s. Richard and Osna Sens; life ptnr. Serena Darsey Schorr; m. Christina McNamara Sens, Sept. 1, 1990 (dec. Oct. 14, 2005); children: Emilia Rachel, Jonah Nicholas. PhD, Harvard U., Cambridge, Mass., 1991. Asst. prof. Georgetown U., Wash., 1991—97, assoc. prof., 1997—2002, prof., 2002—, joseph durkin sj prof. classics, 2006—.

SENSE, EDGAR H., language educator; s. Herbert Karl and Cecelia Maria Sense; m. Jeannette Anne Orford; children: Kathleen Mason, Kristina Sabalino. MA in English Lit., CSU Fresno, Calif., 1994. Prof. English Coll. Sequoias, Visalia, Calif., 1994—. Pres. Coll. Sequoias Tchrs. Assn., 2007—. Office: Coll Sequoias 915 Southern Mooney Blvd Visalia CA 93277

SENSENBRENNER, FRANK JAMES, JR., United States Representative from Wisconsin; b. Chgo., June 14, 1943; s. James and Margaret Sensenbrenner; m. Cheryl Warren, Mar. 26, 1977; children: James Frank IV, Robert Alan Frank. AB in Polit. Sci., Stanford U., Calif., 1965; JD, U. Wis., Madison, 1968. Bar: Wis. 1968, US Supreme Ct. 1972. State rep. Wis. State Assembly, Madison, 1969-75; mem. Wis. State Senate, Madison, 1975-79, asst. minority leader, 1976-79; mem. US Congress from 5th Wis. dist., 1979—, chmn. sci. com., 1997—2001, chmn. judiciary com., 2001—07. Ranking mem. select com. energy independence and global warming Riveredge Nature Ctr., 2007—. Mem.: Capitol Hill Club, Am. Philatelic Soc., Chenequa Country Club. Republican. Office: US House Reps 2449 Rayburn House Office Bldg Washington DC 20515-4905 Office Phone: 202-225-5101.*

SENSENIG, ARTHUR LLOYD, economist, consultant; b. Ehprata, Pa., Oct. 5, 1952; s. Russell Issac and Lucy Catharine Sensenig; m. Barbara Ann Zimmerman, June 24, 1972; children: Rachael Erin Lundquist, David Andrew, Kathryn Ann Hunt. MA in Applied Economics, Am. U., Washington, 1981. Economist Bur. Econ. Analysis, Washington, 1978—93, Office of Actuary, CMS, Dept. HHS, Balt., 1993—. Contbr. to academic papers and govt. reports (Best Descriptive Paper award, 2007). Mem. St. Luke Luth. Ch., Silver Spring, Md., 1980—. Mem.: Conf. Rsch. Income and Wealth. Avocation: fishing. Home: 304 Hannes St Silver Spring MD 20901 Office: Office of Actuary CMS Dept HHS 7500 Security Blvd Baltimore MD 21244-1850

SENSENIG, DAVID MARTIN, retired surgeon; b. May 4, 1921; s. Wayne and Elizabeth Long (Crawford) S.; m. Constance Campbell, June 6, 1947; children: Philip Campbell, David Martin, Andrew Wilson, Thomas O'Brien; m. Bernice Evans, Dec. 20, 1975. BS, Haverford Coll., 1942; postgrad., U. Pa., 1942-43; MD, Harvard U., 1945; JD, Temple U., 1998. Diplomate Am. Bd. Surgery, Am. Bd. Thoracic Surgery. Rotating intern Allentown (Pa.) Hosp., 1945-46; surg. ho. officer, jr. asst. resident Peter Bent Brigham Hosp., Boston, 1948-50; sr. asst. resident, resident surgeon New Eng. Ctr. Hosp., Boston, 1950-52; surg. resident Westfield (Mass.) State Sanatorium, 1952-53; asst. chief surg. svc., dir. surg. rsch. lab. VA Med. Tchg. Group Hosp., Memphis, 1953-55; asst. chief surg. svc. VA Hosp., Albany, N.Y., 1955-57; resident in thoracic and cardiac surgery Univ. Hosp. State U. Iowa, Iowa City, 1957-59, instr. in surgery, 1957-58, assoc. in surgery, 1958-59, from asst. prof. to assoc. prof., 1960-62; chief thoracic surgery sect. VA Hosp., Phila., 1959-60, asst. chief surg. svc., 1963-66; cardiothoracic surgeon Pa. Hosp., Phila., 1962-63; asst. prof. surgery U. Pa., Phila., 1962-66, supr. Animal Rsch. Lab., 1963-66; pvt. practice medicine specializing in surgery Bangor, Maine, 1966-88; attending surgeon Ea. Maine Med. Ctr., Bangor, 1966-88, St. Joseph Hosp., Bangor, 1966-88, chief surg. svc., 1974-79, VA Hosp., Togus, Maine, 1988-95, ret., 1995. Contbr. articles to profl. jours. Capt. US Army, 1943—48. Mem. ACS (gov. at large 1985-91), Am. Thoracic Soc., Internat. Cardiovasc. Soc., Am. Geriatric Soc., Am. Coll. Chest Physicians, New Eng. Surg. Soc., New Eng. Soc. Vascular Surgery v.p. 1991), Maine Vascular Soc. (pres. 1978), Iowa Acad. Surgery, Pa. Assn. Thoracic Surgery, N. Am. Soc. Pacing and Electrophysiology, Penobscot County Med. Soc. (pres. 1974), Phila. Acad. Surgery, Bangor Med. Club (pres. 1970). Republican. Lutheran. Home: 101 Sunset Dr Lansdale PA 19446-1706 Home Phone: 215-393-3409.

SENSIPER, SAMUEL, electrical engineer; b. Elmira, NY, Apr. 26, 1919; s. Louis and Molly (Pedolsky) S.; m. Elaine Marie Zwick, Sept. 10, 1950; children: Martin, Sylvia, David. BSEE, MIT, 1939, ScD, 1951; EE, Stanford U., 1941. Asst. project engr. to sr. project engr., cons.

Sperry Gyroscope, Garden City, Great Neck, NY, 1941-51; sect. head and sr. staff cons. Hughes Aircraft, Culver City, Malibu, Calif., 1951-60; lab. divsn. mgr. Space Gen. Corp., Glendale, Azuza, L.A., 1960—67; lab. mgr. TRW, Redondo Beach, Calif., 1967—70; cons. elec. engr. LA, 1970—73; dir. engring. Transco Products, Venice, Calif., 1973—75; cons. elec. engr. in pvt. practice LA, 1975—95; cons., 1995—. Faculty U. So. Calif., L.A., 1955-56, 79-80. Contbr. articles to profl. jours.; patentee in field. Recipient Cert. of Commendation U.S. Navy, 1946; indsl. electronics fellow MIT, 1947-48. Fellow IEEE (life), AAAS (life); mem. Calif. Soc. Profl. Engrs., MIT Alumni Assn., Stanford Alumni Assn., U. Calif. Alumni Assn., Electromagnetics Acad., Sigma Xi, Eta Kappa Nu, Nat. Soc. Profl. Engr.(life). Home and Office: 3775 Modoc Rd #117 Santa Barbara CA 93105-4466 Office Phone: 805-879-5560. Personal E-mail: sensiper1@ieee.org.

SENTELLE, DAVID BRYAN, federal judge; b. Canton, NC, Feb. 12, 1943; s. Horace Richard Jr. and Maude (Ray) Sentelle; m. Jane LaRue Oldham, June 19, 1965; children: Sharon Lewis, Regan Herman, Rebecca. BA, U. NC, 1965, JD with honors, 1968. Bar: NC 1968, NC (US Dist. Ct. (we. dist.)) 1969, (US Ct. Appeals (4th cir.)) 1970. Assoc. Uzzell & Dumont, Asheville, NC, 1968—70; asst. US atty. (we. dist.) NC US Dept. Justice, 1970—74; dist. judge City of Charlotte, NC, 1974—77; ptnr. Tucker, Hicks, Sentelle, Moon & Hodge, P.A., Charlotte, 1977—85; judge US Dist. Ct. (we. dist.) NC, Charlotte, 1985—87, US Ct. Appeals (DC Cir.), 1987—, chief judge, 2008—. Adj. prof UNC, 1991—92; adj. prof. Fla. State U. Coll. Law, 1993; presiding judge Spl. Divsn. for Appointment of Ind. Counsels, 1992—; Disting. adj. prof. Geroge Mason U. Sch. Law. Author: Judge Dave and the Rainbow People, 2002; contbr. articles to profl. jours. Chmn. Mecklenburg County Rep. Com., 1978—80, NC State Rep. Conv., 1979—80. Fellow, Dameron Found., 1967. Mem.: Mecklenburg County Bar Assn., Shriners, Masons (Scottish Rite), Am. Inn of Ct. Found. (bd. dir.), Edward Bennett Williams Inn of Ct. (pres.). Baptist. Office: US Court of Appeals 333 Constitution Ave NW Washington DC 20001-2866*

SENTELL-PEREZ, JO, psychologist; d. James Pritchard Williams and Jimmie Sue Wirt, Morgan Edward Wirt (Stepfather); m. Brent Gerard Perez, July 30, 1992; children: Travis Sentell, Brianna Pepiton, Alexis Perez. BA, La. State U., Baton Rouge, 1978; MS, U. New Orleans, 1983. ESA Wash. State Bd. Edn., 2006. Clin. asst. Dr. Robert McFarlane, New Orleans, 1980—81, Baton Rouge Psychol. Assocs., Baton Rouge, 1984—87; sch. psychologist East Baton Rouge Parish, 1987—98, Bellevue Sch. Dist., Wash., 2006—07, Lake Washington Sch. Dist., Redmond, 2007—. Vol. Stop Rape Crisis Ctr., Baton Rouge, 1975—79. Mem.: NASP. Independent. Avocations: travel, literature, exercise, art.

SENTENNE, JUSTINE, corporate ombudsman consultant; b. Montreal, Que., Can. d. Paul Emile and Irene Genevieve (Laliberte) Sentenne. MBA, U. Que., Montreal, 1993; postgrad., McGill U., Ecole Nat. d'Adminstrn. Publique, 1989—91. Fin. analyst, assoc. mgr. portfolio Bush Assocs., Montreal, 1970-82; city councillor, mem. exec. com. City of Montreal and Montreal Urban Com., 1978-82; adminstrv. asst. Montreal Conv. Ctr., 1983; dir. sponsorship Ctrl. Com. for Montreal Papal Visit, 1984; dir. pub. rels. Coopers & Lybrand, Montreal, 1985-87; exec. dir. Que. Heart Found., 1987-89; corp. ombudsman Hydro-Que, Montreal, 1991—. Tchr. DSA program Concordia U.; mem. jury John Labatt Ltd., London, 1982—86. V.p., bd. dirs. Armand Frappier Found., Canada, Chateau Dufresne Mus. Decorative Arts, Montreal, 1985—90; chmn. bd. dirs. Wilfrid Pelletier Found., Montreal, 1986—91; bd. govs. Youth and Music Can., Montreal, 1981—86; chmn. bd. dirs. Women's Ctr., Montreal, 1986—88, Vol. Bur. Montreal, 1986—87; bd. dirs. Palais des Congres de Montreal, 1981—89, Port of Montreal, 1983—84, Can. Ctr. Ecumenism, Montreal, 1968—85, 2006—, Montreal Diet Dispensary, 1989—2001, treas., 1996; bd. mgmt. Saidye Bronfman Ctr. Arts, 1994—99; Notre Dame de Grace v.p. riding assn. Liberal Party of Can., chairperson women's commn., 2000—; mem. Liberal Party, Westmount Valle, Canada; bd. dirs. Pathways to Faith, 1990—2000. Recipient Silver medal, ville de Paris, 1981, Women's Kansas City Assn. Internat. Rels. and Trade medal, 1982; named Career Woman of the Yr., Sullivan Bus. Coll., 1979. Fellow: Montreal Soc. Investment Analysts, Inst. Fin. Analysts, Fin. Analysts Fedn. N.Y.; mem.: Health and Welfare Svcs. Ctr. Cavendish (chair, bd. dirs. 2004—06), Internat. Ombudsman Assn. (bd. dirs. 1996—99, 2000—03, founding mem. Forum of Can. Ombudsmen, bd. dirs. 2001—, sec.). Roman Catholic.

SENTERS, MELINDA, history professor; PhD, U. Ky., Lexington. Asst. prof. history Lindsey Wilson Coll., Columba, Ky., 2000—. Mem.: Filson Club Hist. Soc., Orgn. Am. Historians. Office: Lindsey Wilson Coll 210 Lindsey Wilson St Columbia KY 42728

SENZEL, MARTIN LEE, lawyer; b. Rochester, NY, June 21, 1944; s. Albert Benjamin and Besse (Lipson) S.; m. Dagni Maren Belgum, Feb. 17, 1979; 1 child, Whitney. BA, Yale U., 1966, LLB, 1969. Bar: N.Y. 1971, U.S. Dist. Ct. (so. dist.) N.Y., U.S. Ct. Appeals (2nd cir.) 1973. Assoc. Cravath, Swaine & Moore LLP, NYC, 1969—77, ptnr., 1977—2000. Bd. dir. Medinol Ltd. Mem.: ABA, N.Y. State Bar Assn., Assn. Bar City N.Y. Home: Apt 4-E 101 Central Park W New York NY 10023-4204 Office: Cravath Swaine & Moore LLP Worldwide Plz 825 8th Ave Fl 36 New York NY 10019-7475 Office Phone: 212-474-1520. E-mail: msenzel@cravath.com.

SEO, DONG CHEOL, wetland biogeochemist, environmental chemist; b. Sacheon, Gyeongsangnam-do, Republic of Korea, July 3, 1974; s. Bu Ung Seo and Chang Sang Jeon. BS, Gyeongsang Nat. U., Jinju, Gyeongsangnam-do, 2000, MS, 2002, PhD, 2005. Cert. in wordprocess 1st class Korea C. of C. & Industry, 2001, in computer info. lit. 2002; wastewater environment indsl. engr., Human Resources Devel. Svc. Korea, 2002. Rschr. Inst. Agr. and Life Scis., Gyeongsang Nat U., Jinju, 2005—06; postdoc. rschr., dept. oceanography & coastal scis. Wetland Biogeochemstry Group, La. State U., Baton Rouge, 2006—. Instr. Jinju Nat. U., 2003—06. Contbr. numerous articles to profl. jours. Sgt. Korean Army, 1994—96, Gyeonggi, Republic of Korea. Recipient Outstanding Profl. award, Am. Biog. Inst., 2008; named Outstanding Intellectuals of 21st Century, Internat. Biog. Ctr., 2008, Gt. Minds of 21st Century, Am. Biog. Inst., 2008. Mem.: Korean Soc. Agriculture and Environment (Promising Scientist award 2006), Korean Soc. Soil Sci. and Fertilizer, Korean Soc. Applied Biol. Chemistry. Achievements include development of sewage treatment plant for a detached house in an agricultural village by natural purification method; research in relationship between molecular diversity of denitrifier community composition and denitrification potential in sediment of louisiana wetlands under different redox potentials; relative contributions of bacteria and fungi to denitrification in wetland sediment under various redox potential; alternative of optimum management and analysis of removal efficiency for treating the wastewater in constructed wetland to upper region of Juam lake; design of constructed wetlands for treating agricultural non-point sources pollution in greenhouse area; research in changes of physico-chemical characteristics of sand in constructed wetland for sewage treatment in long term period; screening of the optimum filter media in constructed wetland for treatment of ammonium nitrogen and phosphorus; applicability of the simultaneous treatment process for biological nitrogen and phosphorus using the dpao in constructed wetland; development of simultaneous treatment process of biological nitrogen and phosphorus in sewage treatment plant by natural purification system. Home: 449-3 Gajwa-dong Jinju Gyeongsangnam-do 660-300 Republic of Korea Office: La State Univ 3165 Energy Coast & Environ Bldg Baton Rouge LA 70803 Office Fax: 225-578-6423. Personal E-mail: ga-93@hanmail.net. Business E-Mail: dseo@lsu.edu.

SEO, DONGWON, communications engineer, design scientist; b. Choong-Ju, Choong-Buk, Republic Of Korea, Oct. 2, 1966; s. Inseok Seo; m. Eunju Kang, Oct. 21, 1991; children: Minjeong, Elliot. PhD, U. Ill., Urbana-Champaign, 2000. Prin. scientist Qualcomm Inc., San Diego, 2000—. Contbr. articles to profl. publs. Recipient Upendra Patel Achievement award, 2007. Mem.: IEEE (sr.). Achievements include invention of low power wireless transmitter design and high-voltage tolerant circuits implementation; patent; 7 pending patent applications; first to a concept of class-AB digital-to-analog converter and commercialized. Office: Qualcomm Inc 5775 Morehouse Dr San Diego CA 92121 Personal E-mail: dwseo_us@yahoo.com. Business E-Mail: dseo@qualcomm.com.

SEO, KYUNGHEE, computer scientist, educator; b. Daejeon, Republic of Korea, June 3, 1963; d. IkSun Jeong; m. JaeSeung Lee, Dec. 22, 1988; 1 child, Jiho Lee. BS in Math., Sogang U., 1986, BS in Computer Sci., 1989, MS in Computer Sci., 1991, PhD in Computer Sci., 1998. Invited prof. Sungshin Women's U., Seoul, 1999—2006, Cath. U. Korea, Bucheon, Republic of Korea, 2006—. Mem.: Korean Inst. Comm. Scis., Korean Info. Sci. Soc. Avocation: cooking. Home: 453 HonJe-4Dong SeodaemunGu Seoul 120-786 Republic of Korea Office: Computer Dept Catholic Univ 43-1 Yoekgok 2-dong Wonmi-Gu Bucheon Gyeonggi 420-743 Republic of Korea Personal E-mail: khseo63@gmail.com. Business E-Mail: khseo@catholic.ac.kr.

SEO, SEONG S., chemistry professor, researcher; PhD, U. Ark., Feyetteville, 2000. Asst. prof. Albany State U., Ga., 2002—08, assoc. prof., 2008—. Mem.: ACS. Office: Albany State Univ 504 College Dr Albany GA 31705

SEO, YOO-JIN, occupational health educator; b. Pusan, Republic of Korea, May 1, 1952; s. Seo Soo-hak and Shin Yeon-rae; m. Kim Yang-sook; children: Seo Yong-hoon, Seo Soo-yeon. PhD, Toua U., Shimoseki, Japan, 1997. Vis. prof. dept. ergonomics U. Eivnron. Health, Kitakyushu, Japan, 1989—93; dir. gen., Office Pub. Rels. Kyungnam U., Masan, Republic of Korea, 1999—2002, dean acad. affairs, 2006—. Home: Doosan Apt 207-1201 Gyungsangnamdo Masan 631-763 Republic of Korea Office: Dept Exercise Sci Sport Studies 449 Weolyoung-dong Gyungsangnamdo Masan 631-701 Republic of Korea Office Phone: +82-11-586-7787. Business E-Mail: yoojin@kyungnam.ac.kr.

SEOANE-VAZQUEZ, ENRIQUE, research scientist; b. Pontevedra, Spain; PhD, U. Minn., 2002. Rschr. Ctr. Health Outcomes & Evaluation Studies, Columbus, Ohio, 2002—. Contbr. scientific papers to profl. jours. Office: Ohio State Univ 500 W 12th Ave Columbus OH 43210 Office Fax: 614-292-1335. Business E-Mail: pharmacoeconomics@osu.edu.

SEOK, JAEWOOK, materials and polymer scientist; s. Jong Ku Seok and Qyu Sun Song; m. Su Jin Kim, Oct. 10, 1974; 1 child, Yeon Seo. BEng in Polymer Sci., Kyungpook Nat. U., Taegu, Republic of Korea, 1997, MEng in Polymer Sci., 1999; MEng in Materials Sci. and Engring., Cornell U., Ithaca, NY, 2006; postgrad., NC State U., Raleigh, 2004—. Rsch. engr. Anam Semiconductor, Seoul, 1999—2000; sr. rschr. Amkor Tech. CZ, Ariz., 2000—04. Contbr. scientific papers to profl. jours. Nat. rschr. Korean Army, 1999—2004, Seoul. Mem.: Semiconductor Equipment and Materials Internat., Internat. Microelectronics and Packaging Soc., Polymer Soc. Korea. Democrat. Roman Catholic. Achievements include patents for innovative fabrication method of organic substrates for semiconductor micro-system-packaging to have enhanced reliability performance; high molecular weight polymeric photoinitiator for flat panel liquid display application. Avocations: tennis, classical music, painting. Home: 202-603 Bosung Apt Bummul dong Susung gu Taegu 706-100 Republic of Korea Office Phone: 919-515-8147. Business E-Mail: jseok@ncsu.edu, js554@cornell.edu.

SEOL, DAI-WU, geneticist, educator; PhD, U. Pitts., Pitts., Pa., 1998. Asst. prof. U. Pitts., 2000—. Cons. Genenmed Inc., Seoul, Republic of Korea, 2000—. Dir. Sunday Sch. Korean Ctrl. Ch. Pitts., 2003. Achievements include patents for cancer gene therapy using a secretable trimeric TRAIL. Office: Kyungwon Univ San 65 Sujeong Seongnam 461-701 Republic of Korea Business E-Mail: seold@kyungwon.ac.kr.

SEON, YVONNE, retired cultural educator, minister; d. George Raymond and Beatrice M. Reed; 3 children. BA, Allegheny Coll., Meadville, Pa., 1959; MA, Am. U., 1960; PhD, Union Inst., 1974; MDiv, Howard U., 1981. Exec. dir. High Commn. Inga Dam Project, Kinshasa, Democratic Republic of Congo, 1961—63; program officer Office Internat. Confs., US Dept. State, Washington, 1964—67; dir. student life programs Wilberforce U., Ohio, 1967—71; dir. Bolinga Black Cultural Resources Ctr. Wright State U., 1971—73; student svcs. program coord. Prince Georges CC, Largo, Md., 1993—96, prof. African Am. studies, 1996—2006. Sec. US Del. 14th Gen. Assembly UNESCO, Paris, 1966; disting. elected vis. dir. Bolinga Black Cultural Resources Ctr., 2005—06, dir., 2007—08. Pres. Capitol Hill Group Ministries, Washington, 1987—89; ordained min. Unitarian Universalist Assn., Boston, 1981—; bd. dirs. Africare, DC, 1977—2000, vice-chair, 2002—04, 2006—08; bd. dirs. Prince George's County So. Christian Leadership Conf., Largo, 1994—2006; mem. Bretton Woods Com., Washington, 2000—07; trustee Allegheny Coll., 2007—. Mailing: PO Box 467 Yellow Springs OH 45387

SEOW, STEVEN C., research scientist; b. Singapore, Apr. 20, 1973; married. PhD in Exptl. Psychology, Brown U., Providence, 2005. User rschr. Microsoft, Redmond, Wash., 2005—. Author: (book) Designing and Engineering Time: The Psychology of Time Perception in Software.

SEPEHR, ALI, physician; s. Cyrus and Shokrieh Mohammadzadeh. MD, U. Calif., LA, 2004. Physician U. Calif. Irvine, Orange, 2004—. Contbr. articles to profl. jour. Recipient For Outstanding Patient Care, Tchg. and Rsch., U. Calif., Irvine, 2005, 2006, 2007; Regents Scholar, U. Calif., LA, 2000—04. Mem.: Am. Acad. Otolaryngology. Achievements include research in New Imaging Technology.

SEPINWALL, ALYSSA, history professor; BA, U. Pa., Phila., 1991; MA, Stanford U., Calif., 1993, PhD, 1998. Instr. & tchg. asst. Stanford U., 1993—95; Lucius N. Littauer postdoc. fellow Ctr. Advanced Judaic Studies U. Pa., 1998; asst. prof., history Calif. State U., San Marcos, 1999—2004, assoc. prof., history, 2004—. Contbr. articles. Office: Calif State Univ San Marcos History Dept San Marcos CA 92096

SEPÚLVEDA, JOHN U., federal agency administrator; b. NYC, 1954; m. Awilda Rodriguez. BA, Hunter Coll., 1977, LHD (hon.), 2000; MA, MPhil, Yale U. Spl. asst. to asst. sec. Fed. Housing Adminstrn., US Dept. Housing and Urban Devel., Washington, 1993, dir. Office of Insured Health Care Facilities; with Office of Presdl. Pers. The White House, 1996—97; dep. dir. US Office Pers. Mgmt. (OPM), 1998—2001; dir. Dept. Housing and Industry Outreach Fed. Home Loan Mortgage Corp. (Freddie Mac), McLean, Va., 2001; CEO Nat. Assn. Hispanic Real Estate Profls.; sr. v.p, ops. Nat. Assn. Mortgage Brokers; asst. sec. for human resources & adminstrn. US Dept. Veterans Affairs, 2009—. Tchr. polit. sci. Hunter Coll., Yale U.; former mem. White House Interagency Task Force on Asian Am. and Pacific Islanders, Pres.'s Coun. for Y2K Conversion, Pres.'s Coun. on Integrity and Efficiency. Recipient Hammer Award; named to Hunter Coll. Hall of Fame, 2001. Office: US Dept Veterans Affairs 810 Vermont Ave NW Washington DC 20420*

SEPULVEDA, SONJA MARIAN ATKINSON, choral director, accompanist; b. Lancaster, SC, May 15, 1952; d. Leo Laten and Mary Lou Hatfield Atkinson; m. Juan Pablo Sepulveda, June 10, 1972; children: Dru Adrian, Brys Kristofer. MusB in Edn., Winthrop U., Rock Hill, SC, 1974; MusM in Choral Conducting, Winthrop U., 1975; D in Mus. Arts, U. S.C. Cert. tchr. music edn., choral edn. S.C., 1975. Choral dir. Wilder Fine Arts and Elem. Sch., Sumter, SC, 1975—81, Sumter H.S., SC, 1981—99, Clarendon Sch. Dist. 1, Summerton, SC, 2000—02, DuBose Mid. Sch., Summerville, SC, 2002—; condr. Carolina Alive and Renaissance Singers of U. S.C., 2005—. Choral dir. Palmetto Choirs, Sumter, 2000—; choral dir. and organist St. John Meth. Ch., Sumter, 2002—; dance tchr. Freed Spirits Dance Co., Sumter, 1979—89; piano tchr., Sumter, 1975—81; music edn. tchr. U. S.C., Sumter, 1979—83; choral dir. First Presbyn. Ch., Sumter, 1985—2001, Shaw Heights Bapt. Ch., Sumter, SC, 1978—81, Crosswell Bapt. Ch., Sumter, 1965—78. Composer: (musical) Robin Hood. Recipient Ivey Reuben Edn. award, NAACP, 1990, Paul Harris fellow, Rotary Internat., 1992; named SC. Outstanding Educator of the Yr., Jaycees, 1987, Tchr. of the Yr., Wilder Elem. Sch., 1981. Mem.: PTA (life), Music Educators Nat. Conf. (chmn. S.C. all state com. 1994—98), Am. Choral Dirs. Assn. (jazz choir chmn. S.C. 1995—96), Delta Kappa Gamma (music chmn. 1991—2002). R-Consevative. Presbyterian. Achievements include Choral Director for mini seriesNorth and South; Singer in the Robert Shaw Festival Chorus, 1991-1997; Solo performance at the Lincoln Center; Montreat Chamber Singer, 1988-2001; Singer in the National American Choral Directors Multicultural Choir, 2001; Solo performance for the National Television in Mexico. Avocations: travel, bicycling. Home: 618 Antlers Dr Sumter SC 29150 Office: U SC Sch Music Columbia SC 29208 Personal E-mail: sonjasepulveda@hotmail.com.

SEPÚLVEDA AMOR, JAIME, public health service officer; b. Mexico City, 1954; married; 2 children. MD, Nat. Autonomous U. Mex., 1978; MPH, Harvard Sch. Pub. Health, 1980, MS, 1981, PhD, 1985. Dir. gen. epidemiology, Mexico, 1985—91; vice-min. health, 1991—94; dir. Nat. Pub. Health Inst., Cuernavaca, Mexico, 1995—2003; dean Nat. Sch. Pub. Health, Mexico, 1995—2003; dir. NIH, Mexico, 2003—. Founder Nat. AIDS Coun., 1986, Nat. Immunization Coun.; chair adv. bd. epidemiology in Mex., 1988—91, AIDS & Reproductive Health Networks; founding pres. Coun. Health Rsch. for Devel., 1993—96; mem. bd. Internat. Network Clin. Epidemiology, 1997—; mem. Harvard Bd. Overseers, 2002—; mem. adv. coun. NIH Fogarty Internat. Ctr. Recipient Red Cross award, 1989. Mem.: Inst. Medicine (fgn. assoc.). Office: Institutos Nacionales de Salud Periférico 4118 Edif Zafiro 1 1er piso Col Jardines del Pedregal Deleg 01900 Alvaro Obregon Mexico Office Phone: (55)5135-2229 5568-0754. Office Fax: (55)5135-1980 ext 298. E-mail: jsepulveda@salud.gob.mx.

SEQUEIRA, LEON R., federal agency administrator; b. June 7, 1968; B, Northwest Mo. State U.; JD with honors, George Washington U. Bar: Mo., Ill. Legal counsel com. rules and adminstrn. US Senate, Washington, legal counsel to US senator Mitch McConnell, 2003—05; dep. asst. sec. policy US Dept. Labor, Washington, asst. sec. policy, 2007—. Office: US Dept Labor Rm S2006 200 Constitution Ave NW Washington DC 20210 Office Phone: 202-693-6151. Office Fax: 202-693-5960.*

SÉQUIN, CARLO H., computer science educator; b. Winterthur, Switzerland, Oct. 30, 1941; arrived in US, 1970, naturalized, 1994; s. Carl R. and Margrit (Schaeppi) S.; m. Margareta Frey, Oct. 5, 1968; children: Eveline, André. BS, U. Basel, Switzerland, 1965, PhD, 1969. Mem. tech. staff Bell Labs., Murray Hill, NJ, 1970-76; vis. Mackay lectr. U. Calif.-Berkeley, 1976-77, prof. elec. engring. computer scis., 1977—, assoc. chmn. computer sci., 1980-83, assoc. dean capital projects, 2001—. Author: First Book on Charge-Coupled Devices, Charge Transfer Devices, 1975; sculpture designer: Pax Mundi II; H&R Block Headquarters, Kansas City, 2007, Hyperbolic Heragon II, Sutardja Dai Hall, U. Calif. Berkeley; contbr. articles to profl. jours. Fellow IEEE (Tech. Achievement award 2003), Assn. Computing Machinery, Swiss Acad. Engring. Scis. Achievements include patents for integrated circuits. Office: U Calif Dept EECS Computer Scis Divsn Soda Hall Berkeley CA 94720-1776 Office Phone: 510-642-5103. Business E-Mail: sequin@cs.berkeley.edu.

SERAFIN, DONALD, plastic surgeon, educator; b. NYC, Jan. 18, 1938; s. Stephen Michael and Julia (Sopko) S.; m. Patricia Serafin; children: Allison Elizabeth, Christina Julia, Donald Stephen, Lara Leigh. AB, Duke U., 1960, MD, 1964. Diplomate Am. Bd. Surgery, Am. Bd. Plastic Surgery. Surg. intern Grady Meml. Hosp., Atlanta, 1964-65; resident in surgery Emory U. Hosp., Atlanta, 1965-69; asst. resident in plastic and reconstructive surgery Duke U. Med. Ctr., Durham, NC, 1971-73, chief resident, 1973-74; Christine Kleinert fellow in hand surgery U. Louisville Hosp., 1972-73; practice medicine specializing in plastic surgery, Durham. Mem. staff N.C. Splty. Hosp., Durham Regional Hosp., Maria Parham Hosp.; asst. prof. plastic, reconstructive and maxillofacial surgery Duke U., 1974-77, assoc. prof., 1977-81, prof., 1981-2000, prof. emeritus, 2000—, chief divsn. plastic reconstructive and maxillofacial and oral surgery, 1985-95, chmn. Plastic Surgery Rsch. Coun., 1983. Assoc. editor Jour. Reconstructive Microsurgery; contbr. articles to profl. jours. Ret. col. USAR, 2004. Decorated Air Force Commendation medal, Army Commendation medal, Army Achievement medal, Army Meritorious Svc. medal. Fellow ACS; mem. AMA, Internat. Soc. Reconstructive Microsurgery, Am. Soc. Plastic Surgeons, Am. Assn. Plastic Surgeons, Am. Soc. Aesthetic Plastic Surgery, Am. Soc. Surgery Hand, Am. Assn. Hand Surgery, Am. Burn Assn., Plastic Surgery Rshc. Coun., N.C. Soc. Plastic, Maxillofacial and Reconstructive Surgeons, Southeastern Soc. Plastic and Reconstructive Surgeons. Office: 511 Ruin Creek Rd Ste 104B Henderson NC 28350 Office Phone: 252-438-8252, 919-220-7711. Personal E-mail: seradonald@aol.com.

SERAFINE, MARY LOUISE, psychologist, lawyer, educator; b. Rochester, NY, July 2, 1948; BA in Music with honors, Rutgers U., 1970; PhD, U. Fla., 1975; JD, Yale U., 1991. Bar: Calif. 1992, DC 1993, US Tax Ct. 1995, NY 1999, Tex. 2005. Tchg. and rsch. fellow U. Fla., Gainesville, 1970-76; vis. asst. prof. U. Tex., San Antonio, 1976-77, asst. prof. Austin, 1977-79; postdoctoral fellow dept. psychology Yale U.,

New Haven, 1979-83, lectr., 1981-83; asst. prof. dept. psychology Vassar Coll., Poughkeepsie, N.Y., 1983-88; with O'Melveny & Myers, LA, 1991-96, Chadbourne & Parke, LA, 1996-97, Fried, Frank, Harris, Shriver & Jacobson, LA, 1997-99; pvt. practice, 1999—. Author: Music as Cognition: The Development of Thought in Sound, 1988; editl. reviewer Child Devel., Devel. Psychology, Am. Scientist, Jour. Exptl. Child Psychology, Jour. Applied Developmental Psychology, Yale Law Jour.; contbr. articles to profl. jours. Grantee State of Fla., 1974-75, U. Tex.-Austin, 1977, Spencer Found., 1979-85. Office: PO Box 4342 Austin TX 78765 Office Phone: 512-220-5452. Business E-Mail: mlserafine@earthlink.net.

SERAG, ENGY, claims consultant; b. Cairo, Sept. 17, 1977; d. Samy Serag and Soheir Hassib. BS, Am. U., Cairo, 2000, MS, 2003; PhD in Civil Engring., U. Ctrl. Fla., Orlando, 2006. Rsch. asst. U. Ctrl. Fla.; asst. prof. San Diego State U., 2006—08. Recipient Outstanding Tchg. award, U. Ctrl. Fla., 2006; Lab. fellowship, Am. U. Cairo, 2001—03, Rsch. fellowship, U. Ctrl. Fla., 2004—06. Mem.: Nat. Assn. Women Constrn., Am. Soc. Civil Engrs. Achievements include research in model to quantify construction labor productivity. Business E-Mail: eserag@mail.sdsu.edu.

SERBAROLI, FRANCIS J., lawyer, educator, writer; b. NYC, Feb. 8, 1952; AB, Fordham U., 1973, JD, 1977. Bar: NY 1978, US Dist. Ct. (ea. and so. dists.) NY 1978, US Ct. Appeals (2d and DC cirs.) 1979, US Supreme Ct. 1983. Asst. atty. gen. NY State Dept. Law, 1978-80; ptnr. Cadwalader Wickersham & Taft, NYC, 1995—. Vice chmn. NY State Pub. Health Coun., 1995—; health law columnist The NY Law Jour. Author: The Corporate Practice of Medicine Prohibition in the Modern Era of Health Care, 1999. Chmn. bd. trustees Loyola Sch., NYC, 1999—2006; mem. bd. trustees Cath. Healthcare Sys., Archdiocese of NY. Fellow NY Acad. Medicine; mem. Am. Health Lawyers' Assn., NY State Bar Assn., Assn. Bar City NY Office: Cadwalader Wickersham Taft LLP One World Fin Ctr New York NY 10281

SERCHUK, IVAN, lawyer; b. NYC, Oct. 13, 1935; s. Israel and Freda (Davis) S.; children: Camille, Bruce Mead, Vance Foster. BA, Columbia U., 1957, LLB, 1960. Bar: N.Y. 1961, U.S. Dist. Ct. (so. dist.) N.Y. 1963, U.S. Ct. Appeals (2d cir.) 1964, U.S. Tax Ct. 1966. Law clk. to judge U.S. Dist. Ct. (so. dist.) N.Y., NY, 1961-63; assoc. Kaye, Scholer, Fierman, Hays & Handler, 1963-68; dep. supt., counsel N.Y. State Banking Dept., NYC, Albany, 1968-71; ptnr. Berle & Berle, 1972—73; spl. counsel N.Y. State Senate Banks Com., 1972; ptnr. Serchuk & Zelermyer LLP, White Plains, NY, 1976—2003; mem. Todtman, Nachamie, Spizz & Johns, PC, NYC, 2003—. Lectr. Practising Law Inst., 1968-71. Mem. N.Y. State Bar Assn., Assn. of Bar of City of N.Y. Office: Todtman Nachamie Spizz & Johns PC 425 Park Ave New York NY 10022 Home: 100 United Nations Plaza New York NY 10017 Office Phone: 212-754-9400. Business E-Mail: iserchuk@tnsj-law.com.

SEREBRIER, JOSÉ, musician, composer, conductor; b. Montevideo, Uruguay, Dec. 3, 1938; came to U.S., 1956; s. David and Frida (Wasser) S.; m. Carole Farley, Mar. 29, 1969; 1 child, Lara Adriana Francesca. Diploma, Nat. Conservatory, Montevideo, 1956, Curtis Inst. Music, 1958; BA, U. Minn., 1960; studied with Aaron Copland, Anatal Dorati, Pierre Monteux. Ind. composer, condr., 1955—. Apprentice condr. Minn. Orch., 1958-60; assoc. condr. Am. Symphony Orch., N.Y.C., 1962-66; music dir. Am. Shakespeare Festival, 1966; composer-in-residence Cleve. Orch., 1968-71; artistic dir. Internat. Festival of Ams., Miami, 1984—, Festival Miami, 1985—; guest condr. numerous orchs. including London Symphony, London Philharm., Paris Radio, Cleve. Symphony Orch., Phila. Symphony Orch., Pitts. Symphony Orch.; founder, artistic dir. Festival Miami (internat. arts festival), 1984. Composer: (for orch.) Variations on a Theme from Childhood, (for chamber) Symphony for Percussion, Concerto for Violin and Orch. (recorded by Royal Phila. Orch. on ASV), (concerto for harp and orch.) Colores Magicos, 1970, Symphonie Mystique, 2003 (5 Grammy nominations including best new composition 2004), Symphony No. 3 (Grammy nomination for best new competition 2004), also works for chorus, voice, keyboard; recs. for RCA, CRI, ASV, KEM, Disc, Trax Classique, EMI, Tioch, Chandos, Varese-Sarabande Decca, IMG, Pickwick, BMG, BIS Records, Vox, Dinemec, Conifer Classics, Decca, Warner Classics, Naxos, with various orchs.; condr. for many recs. including Sibelius Symphony No. 1, Holst's The Planets, Carmen, Poulenc's opera La Voix Humaine, Shostakovich Film Suites vol. 1, 2 and 3(Deutsche Schallplatten award 1988), Carole Farley Sings French Songs (Deutsche Schallplaten award 1988), (home video) Kultur, Prokoviev's Alexander Nevsky, Beethoven's Eroica and Tchaikovsky Symphony No. 1 with Sydney and Melbourne Symphony Orch., Mendelssohn Symphonies, Beethoven Symphonies, Bloch's Violin Concerto and Serebrier's Poema Elegiaco CD, 1992, Le Orchestral Music of Tchaikovsky (several vols.), Laserdisc of Operas The Telephone by Menotti and La Voix Humaine by Poulenc with Scottish Chamber Orch., 1992, Royal Philharm. Orch., 1992, Dvörak Symphonies with Czech State Philharm. for Conifer/BMG, Music of Janacek and Chadwick (4 CDs) for R.R., Hindemith CD with Philharmonia Orch. for ASV; (first complete recording) Partita, Ned Rorem For Naxos; (world-premiere recordings) Winterreise, Fantasia; solo-violin sonata with London Philharm. Orch.; Gershwin CD with Royal Scottish Nat. Orch. for Dinemic; Delius songs and orch. works, Grieg songs, London Philharmonic Orch. recording for Dinemic; conductor Grammy Awards, 2003; recordings: music by William Schuman (2 Grammy nominations), Ives Symphony No. 4 (Grammy nomination), Carmen Symphony (Latin Grammy for best classical album 2004). Recipient Ford Found. Condr.'s award, Alice M. Ditson award, 1976, commn. award Nat. Endowment Arts, 1978, Deutsche Schall Platten Critics award, Music Retailers Assn. award for Best Symphony Rec., 1991, 2002; Guggenheim fellow, 1958-60; Rockefeller Found. grantee, 1968-70. Mem. Am. Symphony Orch. League, Am. Music Ctr., Am. Fedn. Musicians. Home: 270 Riverside Dr New York NY 10025-5209 Personal E-mail: caspi123@aol.com. *A composer has the duty to communicate with his audience. The academic-intellectual composer of the 50's has become obsolete. Writing just for one's colleagues has fortunately been proven a dead-end.*

SERENBETZ, ROBERT, manufacturing executive, financial planner; b. Rockville Centre, NY, Apr. 18, 1944; s. Raymond Robert Serenbetz and Mildred (Egner) Clapp; m. Karen Jeanne Jackson, Dec. 30, 1967; children: Todd, Gregg, Kathryn. AB, Dartmouth Coll., 1966; MBA, Harvard U., 1968. Cert. fin. planner. Mktg. staff asst. to group product mgr. Colgate-Palmolive Co., NYC, 1968-75; dir. mktg. Colgate-Palmolive Colombia, Cali, Colombia, 1975-77; v.p. mktg. Colgate-Palmolive Canada, Toronto, Ont., Canada, 1977-81; v.p. mktg. western hemisphere Warner-Lambert Co., Morris Plains, NJ, 1981; pres. Warner-Lambert Can., Toronto, 1981-85; pres. Latin Am., Asia, Australia Warner-Lambert Co., Morris Plains, 1986-89; pres. Am. Chicle, Morris Plains, 1989-91; pres., COO DNA Plant Tech. Corp., Cinnaminson, NJ, 1991-92, pres., CEO Oakland, Calif., 1992-94, chmn., CEO, 1994-96; COO DNAP Holding Corp., Oakland, Calif., 1996-98; pvt. practice CFP, 2003—. Mem. adv. bd. Coun. Ams., N.Y.C., 1987-89; mem. steering com. Pharm. Mfrs. Assn., Washington, 1987-89; bd. dirs. Caribbean/Cen. Am. Com., Washington, 1989; mem. adv. bd. Coun. for Internat. Unity, N.Y.C., 1987-89; alumni coun. Dartmouth Coll., 2002-05, student life com. chmn., 2004-05; pres, newsletter editors assn, Darmouth Coll. 2006-2008 Bd. dirs. Notch Brook Resort Gen. Ptnrs. Condominium Assn., Stowe, Vt., 1988-94; pres. bd. dirs. Seaside Homeowners Assn., Isle of Palms, S.C., 1997—; mem. U.S. Postal Svc. Mktg. Adv. Bd., 1990-2004, vice chmn., 1998-2004. Mem. Nat. Candy Wholesalers Assn. (bd. dirs. 1989-91), Morris County C. of C. (bd. dirs. 1989-91), Leadership Inc. (bd. dirs. Phila. br. 1993-94), Fin. Planning Assn., Wild Dunes Club (Isle of Palms, SC), Trillium Links and Lake Club (Cashiers, NC). Republican. Episcopalian. Avocations: golf, stamp collecting/philately, photography, tennis. E-mail: bobserenbetz@prodigy.net.

SERENSON, LYNN ANN, mathematics educator; d. Roy William and Marie Elizabeth Eden; m. Peter Martin Serenson, Aug. 3, 1975; children: Traci Lynn, Heather Lisa. BSc, Ctrl. Mich. U., Mt. Pleasant, 1974; M in Curriculum Edn., Oakland U., Rochester, Mich., 1979. Tchr. math. Novi Cmty. Schs., Mich., 1974—. Recipient Edith Slyth award, Am. Math. Coun., 2006. Mem.: Mich. Assn. Mid. Sch. Educations, Detroit Area Coun. Tchrs. Math. (v.p. 1992—94), Mich. Coun. Tchrs. Math. (h.s. proficiency test bd.), Nat. Coun. Tchrs. Math. Catholic. Avocations: reading, travel, swimming, racquetball, jet ski. Home: 3572 Loon Lake Rd Wixom MI 48393 Office: Novi Middle Sch 49000 11 Mile Novi MI 48374

SERFAS, RICHARD THOMAS, architecture educator, urban planner, municipal official; b. Reading, Pa., Nov. 24, 1952; s. Clifford Donald and Helen Catherine (McGovern) S. Student, Jacksonville U., 1970—72; BA, Colo. State U., 1974; MPA, Pa. State U., 1977; MS in Real Estate Devel., Columbia U., 1995. Project coord. ACTION Peace Corps, VISTA, Gary, Ind., 1974—75; city adminstr. City of Beverly Hills, Mo., 1975; grad. rsch. asst. dept. pub. adminstrn. Pa. State U., Middletown, 1976—77; community planner St. Louis County Dept. Planning, 1977—79; mgmt. analyst Clark County Sanitation Dist., Las Vegas, Nev., 1978—79; environ. planner Clark County Dept. Comprehensive Planning, Las Vegas, 1979—80, prin. planner, 1980—84, asst. coord. planning, 1984—85, coord. advance planning, 1985—89, asst. dir., 1989—94; project mgr. Focus 2000, Las Vegas, 1996—99; v.p. comml. planning and design Am. Nev. Corp., Henderson, Nev., 2000—. Instr. U. Nev. Sch. Architecture, Las Vegas, 1989-94; student advisor Las Vegas chpt. AIA, 1989-94. Staff advisor Clark County Comprehensive Plan Steering Com., 1980-94, Environ. Task Force, Las Vegas, 1984-94, Archtl. Design Task Force, Las Vegas, 1984-94, Devel. Sector Task Force, Las Vegas, 1984-94; mem. Transit Tech. Com., Las Vegas, 1989-94. Recipient achievement award Nat. Assn. Counties, 1983-90. Mem. Am. Inst. Cert. Planners, Urban Land Inst., Comml. Retail Coun., Nat. Assn. Corp. Real Estate Execs., Nat. Coun. for Urban Econ. Devel., Am. Planning Assn. (treas. Nev. chpt. 1979-91, pres. 1992-96, Appreciation award 1981, 83, 85, 87, 89, 91, Outstanding Pub. Sector Planning Accomplishment award 1987, 88, 90, 91), Cmty. Assns. Inst. So. Nev. (bd. dirs. 1990-92, sec. 1993-95), Las Vegas Coun. Boy Scout America (bd. dirs. 2007-, chmn. 2007-, City Henderson Devel. Agy. (commr. 2007-, adv. com. 2006-). Democrat. Roman Catholic. Avocations: tennis, skiing, hiking, photography. Home: 2129 Stone Croft St Las Vegas NV 89134-2543 Office Phone: 702-990-2157. Personal E-mail: richard.serfas@aol.com. Business E-Mail: richard.serfas@anclv.com.

SERFATY, DANIEL, human systems engineer; b. Fes, Morocco, Oct. 31, 1954; came to U.S., 1981; s. Jacques and Viviane; m. Irene Mizrahi, July 9, 1980; children: Nastasha, Gabriel. DUES in Math. and Physics, U. de Paris, 1973; BS, Technion, IIT, Haifa, Israel, 1977, MS in Aero. Engring., 1981; MBA in Internat. Mgmt., U. Conn., 1985. Lectr. elec. engring. U. Conn., Storrs, 1985-86; group leader human-machine and decision systems Alphatech, Inc., Burlington, Mass., 1986—95; prin. founder, pres. Aptima, Inc., Woburn, Mass., Wash., 1995—. Educator computer literacy The Learning Clin., Brooklyn, Conn., 1982-85; bd. dirs. New Eng. Tax Svcs., Inc., Malden, Mass., Net Train Solutions, Newton, Global Wisdom, Inc., Wash., Qualtech Sys. Inc., Conn. Author: (with others) Teams: Their Training and Performance, 1991, Command and Control, 1988, guide to computer literacy for gifted children, 1985; contbr. over 100 articles chpts. to profl. jours. and books. With Internat. Sephardic Edn. Found., NYC, 1981—. Recipient Wohl award Alphatech, 1989. Mem. AIAA, IEEE (gen. coord. internat. conf. on SMC, 1989), Judgment and Decision Making Soc., Human Factors and Ergonomics Soc. (Cognitive Engring. and Decision Making Tech. Group), Eta Kappa Nu, Sigma Chi (chair 2004-06). Office: Aptima Inc 12 Gill St Ste 1400 Woburn MA 01801 Office Phone: 781-496-2411. E-mail: serfaty@aptima.com.

SERGI, VINCENT A.F., lawyer; Grad., Beloit Coll.; JD with honors, Northwestern U. With fin. and reorganization dept. Katten Muchin Zavis Rosenman, 1974, dept. head, nat. mng. ptnr., 1996—, mem. bd. dirs., mem. exec. and operating com., chmn. compensation com. Bd. dirs. Goodman Theatre, Joffrey Ballet, Providence-St. Mel Sch. Office: 525 W Monroe St Chicago IL 60661-3693 Office Phone: 312-902-5255. Business E-Mail: vincent.sergi@kmzr.com.

SERGUEEVA, ALLA VLADIMIROVNA, materials scientist, researcher; d. Vladimir Leonidovich Sergueev and Nina Ivanovna Sergueeva; m. Iouri Alexandrovich Sergueev, Nov. 8, 1985; 1 child, Dennis Iouriyevich Sergueev. BS (hon.), Tech. Coll., Nijnii Novgorod, Russia, 1983; MS (hon.), Ufa State Aviation Tech. U., Russia, 1989, PhD, 1998. Tech. designer Ufa Engine Constrn. Plant, Russia, 1983—84; mgr. metallography lab. Tantal, Spl. Design Engring. Office, Ufa, 1989—95; co-mgr. med. equipment prodn. Medicor, Co., Ufa, 1995—97; rsch. assoc. Inst. Physics Advanced Materials, Ufa, 1997—99, Chem. Engring. and Material Sci. Dept., Davis, Calif., 1999—. Contbr. articles to profl. jours. Grantee, Pres. Republic of Bashkortostan, Ufa, Russia, 1995, Pres. Russian Fedn., 1996; Spl. grants for young investigators, U.S. Civilian R & D Found., 1998, Russian Found. Basic Rsch., 1998. Mem.: Minerals, Metals, and Materials Soc., Materials Rsch. Soc. Achievements include research in superplasticity of the materials, nanostucture development, plasticity in nanocrystalline materials, shear band deformation in metallic glasses. Office: Univ Calif One Shields Ave Davis CA 95616

SERKES, JEFFREY D., former energy executive; b. Dec. 24, 1950; BBA in Acctg., George Washington U.; MBA in Fin., Rutgers U. With RJR Nabisco; from v.p. fin, sales and distbn. to v.p., treas. IBM, 1995—2002; pres. JDS Opportunities, LLC, 2002—03; sr. v.p., CFO Allegheny Energy, Inc., Hagerstown, Md., 2003—06. Bd. adv. Rutgers U.; dir., chmn., audit com., compensation com. REFAC.

SERKIS, ANDY, actor; b. London, Apr. 20, 1964; m. Lorraine Ashbourne, July 22, 2002; children: Ruby, Sonny, Louis. With Duke's Playhouse, Lancaster, England, 1985, Royal Exchange Theater, Manchester, England, 1989. Actor: (plays) Hush, 1992, Cabaret, 1993, The Queen and I, 1993, Punchbag, 1993, King Lear, 1993, Mojo, 1995, Hurlyburly, 1997, A Lie of the Mind, 2001, Othello, 2002; dir.: The Double Bass, 2003; actor: (films) Prince of Jutland, 1994, The Near Room, 1995, Stella Does Tricks, 1996, Loop, 1997, Career Girls, 1997, Mojo, 1997, Insomnia, 1998, Clueless, 1998, Among Giants, 1998, The Tale of Sweety Barrett, 1998, Five Seconds to Spare, 1999, Topsy-Turvy, 1999, The Jolly Boys' Last Stand, 2000, Pandaemonium, 2000; actor: (films) Shiner, 2000, The Escapist, 2001, The Lord of the Rings: The Fellowship of the Ring, 2001, 24 Hour Party People, 2002, Deathwatch, 2002, The Lord of the Rings: The Two Towers, 2002, The Lord of the Rings: The Return of the King, 2003, Standing Room Only, 2004, 13 Going on 30, 2004, Blessed, 2004, King Kong, 2005, Stories of Lost Souls, 2006, (voice) Stingray, 2006, Stormbreaker, 2006, The Prestige, 2006, (voice) Flushed Away, 2006, Extraordinary Rendition, 2007, The Cottage, 2008, Inkheart, 2008; (TV films) Grushko, 1994, The Pale Horse, 1997, The Jump, 1998, Shooting the Past, 1999, Arabian Nights, 2000, Longford, 2006, Einstein and Eddington, 2008; (TV miniseries) Touching Evil III, 1999, Oliver Twist, 1999, Little Dorrit, 2008. Office: c/o Larry Taube Principal Entertainment 1964 Westwood Blvd Los Angeles CA 90025*

SERKOVA, NATALIE JULIA, medical educator, researcher; b. Kiev, Ukraine, Aug. 17, 1970; d. Gala Anne Vaysman, Alex Gregory Vaysman (Stepfather). PhD, U. Bremen, German, 1996. Cert. in radiol. scis. U. Colo., 2002. Asst. prof. U. Bremen, Low Saxony, 1999—2002; assoc. prof. anesthesiology and radiology, dir., Bioimaging Cancer Ctr. U. Colo., Anschutz Med. Ctr., Aurora. Exec. advisor SIDMAP, LA. Contbr. articles to med. jours. Reviewer Can. NIH, Toronto, 2005—07, NIH, Bethesda, Md., 2005—07, Brit. Sci. Found., London, 2006—08, NASA, US Dept. Energy, Oak Ridge, Tenn., 2008, South African Med. Rsch. Coun., Capetown, 2008. Recipient Emmy Noether award, German Sci. Found., 1999—2002, award, Colo. Cancer Generation, 2006; Shared Instrumentation grant, NIH, 2005, R21 grant, NCI, 2005. Mem.: Soc. Molecular Imaging, U. Colo. Cancer Ctr., Internat. Soc. Magnetic Resonance Medicine. Achievements include patents for use of nanoparticles for molecular imaging. Home: 210 S Garfield St Denver CO 80209 Office: Univ Colo Anschutz Med Ctr 12631 E 17th Ave Mail Stop 8202 Aurora CO 80045 Office Fax: 303-724-1761. Business E-Mail: natalie.serkova@ucdenver.edu.

SERLET, BERTRAND, information technology executive; PhD in computer sci., U. Orsay, France. Rsch. engr. Xerox PARC, 1985—89; engring./managerial positions NeXT, 1989—97; sr. v.p. software engring. Apple Computer Inc., Cupertino, Calif., 1997—. Achievements include key player in the definition, development and creation of Mac OS X, the world's most advanced operating system. Office: Apple Computer Inc 1 Infinite Loop Cupertino CA 95014 Office Fax: 408-996-1010.

SERLING, JOEL MARTIN, educational psychologist; b. Seneca Falls, NY, Feb. 8, 1936; s. Philip and Cecil Serling; children: Meredith Anne, Rebecca Lynne, Heather Lee. AA, U. Buffalo, 1957; BS in Edn., Ohio Northern U., 1959; MA, Columbia U., 1960. Cert. sch. psychologist NY, NC. Instr. psychology West Liberty State Coll., W.Va., 1961—63; vocat. psychologist Divsn. Child Welfare, Cleve., 1963—64; sch. psychologist Steuben County Bd. Coop. Ednl. Svcs., Bath, NY, 1964—65, Chenango County Bd. Coop. Ednl. Svcs., Norwich, NY, 1965—67, Delaware County Bd. Coop. Ednl. Svcs., Walton, NY, 1967—68, Vestal Ctrl. Sch., NY, 1968—70, Whitesboro Ctrl. Sch., NY, 1970—92. Bd. edn., bd. dirs Hillel Day Sch., Utica-Rome, 1971—75; instr. psychology Am. Inst. Banking, 1971—; bd. profl. advisors Mohawk Valley Learning Disabilities Assn., 1972—76; cons., mentor Empire Coll., SUNY, 1975—; adj. prof. psychology Utica Coll., Syracuse U., 1971—75, 1986—, Mohawk Valley CC, 1971—91, SUNY Coll. Tech., Utica-Rome, NY, 1975—, CC Southern Nev., 1995—; presenter in field. Co-author, co-developer: Early Identification Screening Index, 1971; contbr. articles to profl. publs. Recipient Cert. recognition, Mohawk Valley Learning Disabilities Assn., 1973. Mem.: APA, Phi Delta Kappa, Whitesboro Tchrs. Assn., NY State United Tchrs. Assn., United U. Professions, Ctrl. NY Psychol. Assn., Sch. Psychologists Upper NY, NY Assn. Sch. Psychologists (cert. of recognition 1977), Nat. Assn. Sch. Psychologists (charter), Odd Fellows Club, Zeta Beta Tau. Jewish. Home Phone: 702-792-6211. E-mail: jssp@cox.net.

SERMYAGIN, KONSTANTIN, petroleum engineer; b. Ufa, Republic of Bashkortostan, Russia, June 16, 1979; s. Vladimir Sermyagin and Florida Dulatova; m. Ekaterina Khanukaeva, June 24, 2006. BS with honors, Bashkirian State U., Ufa, 2001; MS, Heriot-Watt U., Edinburgh, Eng., 2002. Rsch. fellow YuganskNIPIneft, Ufa, 1999—2001; project mgr. YUKOS Oil Co., Moscow, 2002—05; petroleum engr. DeGolyer & MacNaughton Corp., Moscow, 2005—07, reservoir simulation project mgr. Dallas, 2007—. Scholar, Pres. Republic Bashkortostan, 2000—01. Mem.: Soc. Petroleum Engrs. Russian Orthodox. Office: DeGolyer & MacNaughton Corp 5001 Spring Valley Rd Ste 800 E Dallas TX 75244

SERNA, PATRICIO, state supreme court justice; b. Reserve, N.Mex., Aug. 26, 1939; m. Eloise Serna; children: Elena Patricia, Anna Alicia 1 stepchild, John Herrera. BSBA with honors, U. Albuquerque, 1962; JD, U. Denver, 1970; LLM, Harvard U., 1971; postgrad., Nat. Jud. Coll., 1985, postgrad., 1990, postgrad., 1992, postgrad., 1994; LLD (hon.), U. Denver, 2002. Bar: N.Mex. 1970, Colo. 1971, U.S. Dist. Ct. N.Mex. 1970. Probation and parole officer State of N.Mex., Santa Fe, Las Cruces, 1966—67; spl. asst. to commn. mem. Equal Opportunity Commn., Washington, 1971—75; asst. atty. gen. State of N.Mex., Santa Fe, 1975—79; pvt. practice Santa Fe, 1979—85; dist. judge First Jud. Dist., Santa Fe, 1985—96; justice N.Mex. Supreme Ct., Santa Fe, 1996—, chief justice, 2001—02. Adj. prof. law Georgetown U., Washington, 1973, Cath. U., Washington, 1974—75; faculty advisor Nat. Jud. Coll., Reno, 1987. Bd. dirs. Santa Fe Group Homes Inc. With US Army, 1963—65. Mem.: Santa Fe Bar Assn., No. N.Mex. Am. Inns of Ct., Nat. Hispanic Bar Assn. (Judge of Yr. award 2002, Judge of Yr. 2002), N.Mex. Hispanic Bar Assn., N.Mex. Bar Assn., Elks, Phi Alpha Delta. Avocations: hiking, fishing, Ping Pong, chess, painting. Office: NMex Supreme Ct PO Box 848 Santa Fe NM 87504-0848 Office Phone: 505-827-4886. Business E-Mail: suppms@nmcourts.com.*

SERNETT, RICHARD PATRICK, lawyer; b. Mason City, Iowa, Sept. 8, 1938; s. Edward Frank and Loretta M. (Cavanaugh) S.; m. Janet Ellen Ward, Apr. 20, 1963; children: Susan Ellen, Thomas Ward, Stephen Edward, Katherine Anne. BBA, U. Iowa, 1960, JD, 1963. Bar: Iowa 1963, Ill. 1965, U.S. Dist. Ct. (no. dist.) Ill. 1965, U.S. Supreme Ct. 1971. House counsel, asst. sec. Scott, Foresman & Co., Glenview, Ill., 1963-70, sec., legal officer, 1970-80; v.p., law sec. SFN Cos., Inc., Glenview, 1980-83, sr. v.p., sec., gen. counsel, 1983-85, exec. v.p., gen. counsel, 1985-87; pvt. practice Northbrook, Ill., 1988-90; v.p., sec., gen. counsel Macmillan/McGraw-Hill Sch. Pub. Co., 1990-92; ptnr. Sernett & Blake, Northfield, Ill., 1993-95; ret., 1995. Mem. U.S. Dept. State Adv. Panel on Internat. Copyright, 1972-75. Chmn. bd. dirs. Iowa State U., Broadcasting Co., 1987-94. Mem. ABA (chmn. copyright divsn. 1972-73, com. on copyright legis. 1967-70, com. on copyright office affairs 1966-67, 79-81, com. on program for revision copyright law 1971-72), Am. Intellectual Property Law Assn., Am. Soc. Corp. Secs., Ill. Bar Assn. (chmn. copyright com. 1971-72), Chgo. Bar Assn., Patent Law Assn. Chgo. (bd. mgrs. 1979-82, chmn. copyright law com.

1972-73, 77-78), Copyright Soc. U.S.A. (trustee 1972-75, 77-80), Wyndemere Country Club, Naples, Fla., Mission Hills Country Club, Northbrook, Ill. Home: 3741 Mission Hills Rd #409 Northbrook IL 60062

SERNOFFSKY, MICHAEL A., elementary school educator; b. Buffalo, June 17, 1953; s. Max A. and Mildred B. Sernoffsky; m. Elaine S. Simmons, June 21, 1986; children: Jared M., Janae B. BS in Edn., Medille Coll., Buffalo, 1979. Cert. in elementary edn. Commonwealth of Pa. Tchr. Iroquois Ctrl. Sch., Elma, NY, 1979—82, Gettysburg Area Sch., Pa., 1982—83; aquatic dir. Lancaston YMCA, Pa., 1976—85; supr., mgr. Aeco Mgt Svcs. Henshey, 2000—; tchr., coach Ellizabeth Town Area Sch., Pa., 1983—. Youth coach soccer Rheems AA, 1993—2003; trng. dir. Destination Imagination, Pa., 2004—; Sunday Sch. Tchr. Trinity Lutharean Church, Ephrata, Pa., 1995—2008. Recipient Eagle Scout, BSA, South Wales, 1968; named Wrestling coach of Yr., Lancaston Lebanon League, 1996—. Mem.: Wrestling Coaches Assn.

SEROKA, JAMES HENRY, social studies educator, academic administrator; b. Detroit, Mar. 5, 1950; s. Henry S. and Mary (Wyoral) S.; m. Carolyn Marie White, June 27, 1970; children: Mihail, Maritsa. BA, U. Mich., 1970; MA, Mich. State U., 1972, PhD, 1976. Labor mkt. analyst U.S. Dept. of Labor, Washington, 1970-71; asst. prof. U. N.C., Greensboro, 1976-77, Appalachian State U., Boone, N.C., 1977-79, So. Ill. U., Carbondale, 1979-81, assoc. prof., 1981-87, prof., dir., 1987-88; prof., head div. humanities and social scis. Pa. State U., Erie, 1988-90; prof. U. North Fla., Jacksonville, 1990-98; dir. Ctr. for Pub. Leadership, Jacksonville, 1991-98; vis. prof. internat. security studies U.S. Air War Coll., Maxwell AFB, Ala., 1997-98, 2005—09; prof. Auburn (Ala.) U., 1998—; dir. Ctr. for Govtl. Svcs., Auburn, 1998—2005. Dir. Master of Pub. Affairs Program Soc. Ill. U., 1987-88, Rural and Small Town Adminstrn. Project, 1980-85; asst. dir. Appalachian Regional Bur. Govts., Boone, N.C., 1977-79; manpower planning analyst U.S. Dept. Labor, Washington, 1970-71; exchange prof. Fakultet Politickih Nauka, Univerzitet u Beogradu, Yugoslavia, 1986; vis. prof. Air War Coll., Montgomery, Ala.; sr. researcher Coun. for the Internat. Exchange Scholars Yugoslavia, 1980; mem. state adv. com. Gov.'s Rural Affairs Coun. for State of Ill., 1988; dir. Ctr. Govt. Svcs., Auburn, 1998—. Co-author: Political Organizations in Social Yugoslavia, 1986 (Choice award 1987); editor Rural Public Adminstration, 1986; co-editor: Developed Socialism, 1982, Comparative Political Systems, 1990, Yugoslavia: The Failure of Democratic Transformation, 1992; contbr. numerous articles to profl. jours. Recipient Akademischer Austausch Dienst Lang. scholar Fed. Republic of Germany, 1988 and numerous other grants, traveling fellows. Mem. Am. Soc. Pub. Adminstrn., Am. Polit. Sci. Assn., Internat. Polit. Sci. Assn., Midwest Polit. Sci. Assn., So. Polit. Sci. Assn., Southwestern Polit. Sci. Assn., Western Polit. Sci. Assn., Policy Studies Orgn., Acad. Polit. Sci., Internat. Studies Assn., Am. Assn. Advancement of Slavic Studies, Western Social Sci. Assn., Cmty. Devel. Soc., Hon. Order of Ky. Colonels. Office: Auburn Univ Dept Political Sci 7080 Haley Ctr Auburn AL 36849 Business E-Mail: jseroka@auburn.edu.

SEROT, BRIAN DAVID, physics professor; b. NYC, Feb. 1, 1955; s. Marvin Michael and Betty Serot; m. Rose Aleman, Aug. 1, 1985. PhD, Stanford U., Calif., 1979. Asst. prof. physics Stanford U., 1980—83; prof. physics Ind. U., Bloomington, 1984—. Fellow: Am. Phys. Soc. (fellowship 1993). Home: 2707 E Brigs Bnd Bloomington IN 47401 Office: Ind Univ Swain W 117 Bloomington IN 47405 Business E-Mail: serot@indiana.edu.

SEROTA, GILBERT ROSS, lawyer; s. Max and Mildred Becker Serota; m. Dagmar Serota, July 25, 1998; children: Natalie, Dylan, Kyle Ross. AB cum laude, Princeton U., NJ, 1973; JD, Columbia U., NYC, 1976. Bar: Calif. 1977. Ptnr. Orrick, Herrington, Sutcliffe, San Francisco, 1983—91; dir., ptnr. Howard Rice Nemerovski Canady Falk & Rabkin, 1991—. Office: Howard Rice Nemerovski Canady Falk & 3 Embarcadero Center San Francisco CA 94111 Business E-Mail: gserota@howardrice.com.

SEROTA, JAMES IAN, lawyer; b. Chgo., Oct. 20, 1946; s. Louis Henry and Phyllis Estelle (Horner) S.; m. Susan Perlstadt, May 7, 1972; children: Daniel Louis, Jonathan Mark. AB, Washington U., St. Louis, 1968; JD cum laude, Northwestern U., 1971. Bar: Ill. 1971, US Dist. Ct. (no. dist.) Ill. 1972, DC 1978, US Supreme Ct. 1978, US Ct. Appeals (DC cir.) 1978, U.S. Dist. Ct. (DC dist.), US Ct. Claims 1980, NY 1981, US Dist. Ct. (so. and ea. dists.) NY, 1981, US Dist. Ct. (no dist.) NY, 2003, US Ct. Appeals (2d cir.) 1983. Trial atty. Antitrust div. US Dept. Justice, Washington, 1971—77; assoc. Bell, Boyd & Lloyd, Washington, 1977—81; ptnr. Werner, Kennedy & French, NYC, 1982—85, Levitsky & Serota, 1985-86, Huber, Lawrence & Abell, NYC, 1987—98, Vinson & Elkins, NYC, 1998—2002; shareholder Greenberg Traurig, NYC, 2003—. Contbr. articles to profl. jours.; editor Law Rev.; ed bd., antitrust columnist CCH Power and Telecom Law jour. Mem. law bd. Northwestern U. Law Sch. Recipient Spl. Achievement award U.S. Dept. Justice, 1976. Mem. ABA (chmn. ins. industry com. 1987-90, vice chair program com. 1990-91, chair annual mtg. program 1991-94, chair fuel & energy com. 1994-97, coun. 1997-2000), N.Y. State Bar Assn., Assn. of Bar of City of N.Y. (antitrust and trade regulation com. 1988-91), Fed. Bar Council. Office: Greenberg Traurig LLP 15th Fl 200 Park Ave Met Life Bldg New York NY 10166 Office Phone: 212-801-2277. Business E-Mail: serotaj@gtlaw.com.

SEROTA, SUSAN PERLSTADT, lawyer, educator; b. Chgo., Sept. 10, 1945; d. Sidney Morris and Mildred (Penn) Perlstadt; m. James Ian Serota, May 7, 1972; children: Daniel Louis, Jonathan Mark. AB, U. Mich., 1967; JD, NYU, 1971. Bar: Ill. 1971, DC 1972, NY 1981, US Dist. Ct. (no. dist.) Ill. 1971, US Dist. Ct. (so. dist.) NY 1981, US Dist. Ct. (ea. dist.) NY 1985, US Ct. Claims 1972, US Tax Ct. 1972, US Ct. Appeals (DC cir.) 1972. Ptnr. Pillsbury Winthrop Shaw Pittman LLP, NYC, 1982—, ptnr., chmn. Exec. Compensation & Benefits practice, 2001—. Adj. prof. Sch. Law, Georgetown U., Washington, 1974-75; mem. faculty Practicing Law Inst., NYC, 1983—; mem. Internal Revenue Svc. Adv. Com. on Tax Exempt and Govtl. Entities, 2008-. Editor: ERISA Fiduciary Law, 1995, 2006; assoc. editor Exec. Compensation Jour., 1973—75, dep. editor Tax Mgmt., Estate and Gift Taxation and Exec. Compensation, 1973—75, mem. editl. adv. bd. Benefits Law Jour., 1973—, Tax Mgmt. Compensation Jour., 1993—, mem. bd. editors ERISA and Benefits Law Jour., 1992—; contbr. articles to profl. jours. Fellow: Am. Coll. of Employee Benefits Counsel (pres. 2004—05, dir., charter fellow), Am. Coll. Tax Counsel (regent 1999—2005); mem.: ABA (chmn. joint com. employee benefits 1987—88, chmn. com. employee benefits 1991—92, vice-chair taxation sect. 1999—2001, chair taxation sect. 2006—07), Am. Tax Policy Inst. (dir. 2008—), Am. Bar Retirement Assn. (dir. 1994—2004, pres. 1999—2000), NY State Bar Assn. (exec. com. tax sect. 1988—92), Internat. Pension and Employee Benefit Lawyers Assn. (co-chair 1993—95). Democrat. Office: Pillsbury Winthrop Shaw Pittman 1540 Broadway New York NY 10036 Office Fax: 212-858-1500. Business E-Mail: susan.serota@pillsburylaw.com.

SERRA, MATTHEW D., consumer products company executive; b. 1945; With R.H. Macy & Co., 1962—69, Bloomingdale's, 1969—76; divisional merchandising mgr. men's wear Lord & Taylor, 1976; v.p. & divisional merchandise mgr. Saks Fifth Ave, NYC, 1976—78, assoc. gen. merchandise mgr. men's and boys' wear, 1978—79, sr. v.p. & gen. merchandise mgr. men's and boys' wear, 1979—83; pres. Gimbels NY divsn., 1983, Gimbels East, 1983—86, CEO, 1985—86; pres. Sibleys, Rochester, NY, 1986—90, CEO, 1987—90; pres. CEO Seaman's Furniture Co., NY, 1991—92; chmn., CEO Sterns divsn. of Federated Dept. Stores Inc., 1993-98; pres., CEO Foot Locker Worldwide, 1998—2000; COO Foot Locker Inc. (formerly Venator Group Inc.), 2000—01, pres., 2000—09, CEO, 2001—09, chmn., 2004—. Office: Foot Locker Inc 112 W 34th St New York NY 10120*

SERRA, RICHARD, sculptor; b. San Francisco, Nov. 2, 1939; m. Clara Weyergraf-Serra. BA in English Lit., U. Calif., 1961; BFA, MFA, Yale U., 1964; DFA (hon.), Calif. Coll. Arts and Crafts, 1994. One-man shows include Galleria La Salita, Rome, 1966, Kunsthalle Tübingen, Germany, 1978, Richard Hines Gallery, Seattle, 1979, Venice Biennale, 1981, Pace Gallery, Leo Castelli Gallery, 1987, Musée Nat. d'art Moderne, Paris, 1984, Mus. Haus Lange, Krefeld, Germany, 1985, Mus. Modern Art, NYC, 1986, Bonnefantenmuseum, Maastricht, 1990, Pace Gallery, 1992; exhbns. include Stedelijk Mus., Amsterdam, 1969, Kunsthalle, Bern, Switzerland, 1969, Solomon R. Guggenheim Mus., NYC, 1969, Pasadena Art Mus., Calif., 1970, Leo Castelli Gallery, NYC, 1970, 72, 74, 82, 84, ACE Gallery, LA, 1970, 72, 74, Whitney Mus. Am. Art, NYC, 1973, Akira Ikeda Gallery, Nagoya, Japan, 1982, Margo Levin Gallery, 1984, Visual Arts Mus., 1985, Mus. Modern Art, NYC, 1986; group shows include Tony Shafrazi Gallery, 1991-92, Pace Gallery, 1992, Dia Ctr. for Arts, NYC, Whitney Biennial: Day for Night, Whitney Mus. Am. Art, 2006; represented in permanent collections: Mus. Modern Art, NYC, Whitney Mus. Am. Art, NYC, Guggenheim Mus., NYC, Pasadena Mus. Art, LA County Mus. Art, Art Gallery Ont., Toronto, Stedelijk Mus.; also filmmaker. Recipient Chevalier, Order Arts and Letters, France, 1985, Comdr., 2008, Sculpture Ctr. award for Distinction in Sculpture, 1992, Praemium Imperiale, Japan Art Assn., 1994, Gold Medal for Sculpture, Am. Acads. Arts and Letters, 2001, Internat. Art award, Cristóbal Gabarrón Found., 2005. Fellow: Am. Acad. Arts and Sciences. Office: 173 Duane St Fl 5 New York NY 10013-3334

SERRANO, ELENA LIDIA, nutritionist, educator; b. Madrid, Dec. 4, 1967; d. Jon Francis (Stepfather) and Virginia Burton Jedda; m. Theodore Eliot Tod, Aug. 8, 2004; children: Jon Henry Distler, Paul Wyatt Distler. PhD, Colo. State U., Fort Collins, 2001. Assoc. ext. specialist Colo. State U., 1998—2001; assoc. prof. Va. Tech, Blacksburg, 2002—. Chair Va. Action Healthy Kids, 2002—06. Recipient Outstanding Svc. Learner Educator award, Va. Tech, 2004, State Early Career award, Epsilon Sigma Pi, 2006, Healthy Sch. Hero award, Action Healthy Kids, 2006, Excellence Rsch. award, NEAFCS, 2007. Democrat-Npl. Office: Virginia Polytech Inst & State Univ 201 Wallace Annex Blacksburg VA 24061-0430 Business E-Mail: serrano@vt.edu.

SERRANO, HELEN, art educator; d. Victor Serrano and Ana Inés Méndez. BS in Art Edn., NYU, 1975—79; MS in Studio Art, Coll. New Rochelle, NY, 1982—84; MA in Art History, CUNY, 1988—91. Cert. art tchr. NY State Dept. Edn., 1984, Nat. Bd. Profl. Tchg. Standards, 1996. Art tchr. Diana Sands Intermediate Sch. 147, Bronx, NY, 1980—92, John Philip Sousa Mid. Sch. 142, Bronx, 1992—2003, Pub. Sch./Mid. Sch. 194, Bronx, 2003—. Mem. early adolescence to young adulthood art standards com. Nat. Bd. Profl. Tchg. Standards, 1999—2001, mem. early adolescent to young adulthood art assessment devel. team, 2001—02, mem. early adolescence to young adulthood art benchmarking team, 2002—03; facilitator blueprint for tchg. and learning arts profl. devel. NYC Dept. Edn., 2004—. Recipient Disting. Educator award, NY State Dept. Edn., 1996, Art Educator award, NYC Art Tchrs. Assn., 1996, Region 8 Art Educator of Yr. award, NY State Art Tchrs. Assn., 1999. Mem.: NYC Art Tchrs. Assn. (chair 1996—99, Nat. Mid. Level Educator of Yr. award 2001), Nat. Art Edn. Assn. Office: Pub Sch/Mid Sch 194 1301 Zerega Ave Bronx NY 10462

SERRANO, JOSÉ ENRIQUE, United States Representative from New York; b. Mayagüez, PR, Oct. 24, 1943; arrived in US, 1950; s. Jose E. and Hipolita (Soto) Serrano; m. Mary Staucet; children: Lisa Marie, Jose Marco, Justine, Benjamin; 1 child, Jonathan. Student, CUNY Lehman Coll., 1961. With Mfrs. Hanover Trust Co., 1961-69; mem. Bd. Edn., NYC, 1969-74, NY State Assembly, 1975—90, US Congress from 16th (formerly 18th) NY dist., 1990—, mem. appropriations com., 1993—95, 1996—, chmn. subcommittee on fin. svcs. and gen. govt., mem. Congl. Hispanic Caucus. With 172nd Support Bn. Med. Corps US Army, 1964—66. Recipient Congl. Recognition award, Nat. Coun. La Raza, 1993, Evelina Lopez Antonetty award, Disting. Pub. and Cmty. Svc., Hunter Coll. Ctr. Puerto Rican Studies, 2003, Man of Yr. award, Bronx Puerto Rican Day Parade, 2003, Friend of the Nat. Pks. award, Nat. Pks. Conservation Assn., 2005. Democrat. Roman Catholic. Office: US House Reps 2227 Rayburn House Office Bldg Washington DC 20515-3216 Office Phone: 202-225-4361. Office Fax: 202-225-6001.*

SERRANO GUERRA, DAMARIS ELIZABETH, language educator; d. Beliss Serrano and Oderay Serrano De. PhD in Hispanic Cultural Studies, Mich. State U., East Lansing, 2005. Asst. prof. U. Panama, 1999—2000; assoc. prof. spanish Wright State U., Dayton, Ohio, 2005—. Rschr. Proyecto CIICLA, San José, Costa Rica, 2001—. Contbr. articles to profl. jours. Recipient Johannes Sachse Meml. award, Mich. State U., Presdl. award, Wright State U., 2007; fellow, Smithsonian Rsch. Inst., 2001. Mem.: Latin Am. Assn. Dayton. Roman Catholic. Avocations: travel, dance, writing, reading. Office: Wright State Univ 3640 Colonel Glenn Highway Dayton OH 45435 Office Fax: 937-775-2820; Home Fax: (937)775-2820.

SERRATELLI, ARTHUR JOSEPH, bishop; b. Newark, Apr. 18, 1944; Attended, Immaculate Conception Sem.; BA, Seton Hall Univ., 1965; STL, Pontifical Gregorian Univ., Rome, 1969, STD, 1977; SSL, Pontifical Biblical Inst., Rome, 1976. Ordained priest Archdiocese of Newark, 1968, aux. bishop, 2000—04, vicar for ministries, regional bishop for Essex County, vicar gen. for apostolates, 2000—02, vicar gen., moderator of the curia, 2002—04; parochial vicar St. Anthony's Parish, Belleville, NJ, 1968—69; prof. theology Immaculate Conception Sem., 1969—71, 1977—2002; rector St. Andrews Coll. Sem., Seton Hall Univ., 1997—2000; ordained bishop, 2000; bishop Diocese of Paterson, NJ, 2004—. Trustee Seton Hall Univ., Assumption Coll.; bd. overseers Immaculate Conception Sem. Mem.: US Conf. Cath. Bishops (chmn. com. doctrine, com. for rev. scripture translations). Roman Catholic. Office: Diocese of Paterson 777 Valley Rd Clifton NJ 07013

SERRATO, DARLENE B., finance educator; d. Edward and Mathilda Bohac; m. Antonio Serrato, Sept. 23, 1995; children: Magdalen Jane, Anthony Edward. BS, U. Houston, 1972; MBA, U. Houston-Ctrl. Campus, 1980; PhD, U. Houston-Univ. Pk., 1987. Asst. prof. U. Houston-Clear Lake, 1982—87; asst.-assoc. prof. Houston Bapt. U., 1987—. Named Outstanding Advisor, NACADA. Office: Houston Baptist Univ 7502 Fondren Rd Houston TX 77074-3298 Business E-Mail: dserrato@hbu.edu.

SERRE, JEAN-PIERRE, mathematician, scholar; b. Bages, France, Sept. 15, 1926; s. Jean and Adèle (Diet) S.; m. Josiane Heulot, Aug. 10, 1948; 1 child, Claudine. Baccalauréat, Lycée de Nîmes, France, 1944; agrégation, Ecole Normale Supérieure, France, 1948; PhD, Sorbonne, 1951; PhD (hon.), Cambridge U., Eng., 1978, U. Stockholm, 1980, U. Glasgow, Scotland, 1983, U. Athens, 1996, Harvard U., 1998, Durham U., 2000, London U., 2001, U. Oslo, 2002, U. Oxford, 2003, Acad. Bucharest, 2004, U. Barcelona, 2004, U. Madrid, 2006, Mcgill U., 2008. With Centre Nat. de la Recherche Scientifique, Paris, 1948—54, U. Nancy, 1954—56; prof. Coll. de France, Paris, 1956—94, prof. emeritus. Author: Groupes algébriques et corps de classes, 1959, Corps Locaux, 1962, Lie Algebras and Lie Groups, 1965, Représentations linéaires des groupes finis, 1968, Cours d'arithmétique, 1970, Trees, 1980, Galois Cohomology, 1997, Local Algebra, 2000, Collected Papers, 1986, 2000. Recipient Fields medal, 1954, prix Balzan, 1985, Leroy P. Steele prize Am. Math. Soc., 1995, Wolf prize in math., Israel, 2000, Abel prize, Norway, 2003. Mem. Acad. Sci. Paris, Royal Soc. London (hon. fellow), London Math. Soc. (hon.), Nat. Acad. Sci. U.S. (fgn.), Nederland Acad. Sci. (fgn.), Acad. Sci. Stockholm (fgn.), Russian Acad. Sci. (fgn.), Norwegian Acad. Sci. (fgn.). Home: 6 Ave de Montespan 75116 Paris France Office: Coll de France 75005 Paris France Business E-Mail: serre@dma.ens.fr.

SERRIE, HENDRICK, retired anthropology and international business educator; b. Jersey City, July 2, 1937; s. Hendrick and Elois (Edge) S.; m. Gretchen Tipler Ihde, Sept. 3, 1959; children: Karim Jonathan, Keir Ethan. BA with honors, U. Wis., 1960; MA, Cornell U., 1964; PhD with distinction, Northwestern U., 1976. Dir. Solar Energy Field Project, Oaxaca, Mex., 1961-62; instr. U. Aleppo, Syria, 1963-64; asst. prof. Beloit (Wis.) Coll., 1964-69, Calif. State U., Northridge, 1969-70, Purdue U., West Lafayette, Ind., 1970-72, New Coll./U. South Fla., Sarasota, 1972-77; tchr. Pine View Sch., Sarasota, 1978; prof. anthropology, internat. bus. Eckerd Coll., St. Petersburg, Fla., 1978—2002, dir. internat. bus. overseas programs, 1981—2002; ret., 2002. Sr. rsch. assoc., Human Resources Inst., St. Petersburg, 1988—. Author, editor: Family, Kinship, and Ethnic Identity Among the Overseas Chinese, 1985, Anthropology and International Business, 1986, What Can Multinationals Do for Peasants, 1994, The Overseas Chinese: Ethnicity in National Context, 1998; writer, dir. films: Technological Innovation, 1962, Something New Under the Sun, 1963; contbr. articles to Wall Street Jour. and Wall Street Jour. Europe. Tchr. Sunday sch., North United Methodist Ch., Sarasota, 1977—. Exxon scholar, So. Ctr. for Internat. Issues, Atlanta, 1980-81; Presdl. fellow Am. Grad. Sch. Internat. Mgmt., 1991; recipient Leavy award, Freedoms Found., Valley Forge, Pa., 1989. Fellow Am. Anthrop. Assn., Soc. Applied Anthropology; mem. So. Ctr. Internat. Issues, Acad. Internat. Bus., Tampa Bay Internat. Trade Coun., Internat. Soc. Intercultural Edn., Tng. and Rsch. Republican. Avocations: singing, drawing, beach walking, bicycling, sailing. Personal E-mail: serrieh@gmail.com.

SERRIN, JAMES BURTON, mathematics professor; b. Chgo., Nov. 1, 1926; s. James B. and Helen Elizabeth (Wingate) S.; m. Barbara West, Sept. 6, 1952; children: Martha Helen Stack, Elizabeth Ruth, Janet Louise Sucha. Student, Northwestern U., 1944-46; BA, Western Mich. U., 1947; MA, Ind. U., PhD, 1951; DSc, U. Sussex, 1972; DSc in Engring., U. Ferrara, Italy, 1992; DSc in Math., U. Padova, Italy, 1992; DSc, U. Tours, France, 2004. With MIT, Cambridge, 1952-54; mem. faculty U. Minn., Mpls., 1955—, prof. math., 1959-95, Regents prof., 1968—, head Sch. Math., 1964-65; emeritus, 1995. Vis. prof. U. Chgo., 1964, 75, Johns Hopkins U., 1966, U. Sussex, 1967-68, 72, 76, U. Naples, 1979, U. Modena, 1988, Ga. Inst. Tech., 1990. Author: Mathematical Principles of Classical Fluid Mechanics, 1957. Mem. Met. Airport Sound Abatement Council, Mpls., 1969—. Recipient Disting. Alumni award Ind. U., 1979 Fellow AAAS; mem. NAS, Am. Math. Soc. (G.D. Birkhoff prize 1973), Math. Assn. Am., Soc. for Natural Philosophy (pres. 1969-70), Finnish Acad. Sci. and Letters. Home: 4422 Dupont Ave S Minneapolis MN 55419-4739 Office Phone: 612-624-9530.

SERRITELLA, JAMES ANTHONY, lawyer; b. Chgo., July 8, 1942; s. Anthony and Angela (Deleonardis) S.; m. Ruby Ann Amoroso, Oct. 3, 1981. LLD, North Park U., 1996; BA, SUNY-S.I., 1965, Pontifical Gregorian U., Rome, 1966; postgrad., DePaul U., 1966-67; MA, U. Chgo., 1968, JD, 1971. Bar: Ill. 1971, U.S. Dist. Ct. (no. and ea. dist.) Ill. 1971, U.S. Supreme Ct. 1976, U.S. Tax Ct. 1985, U.S. Ct. Appeals (fifth cir.) 1995, U.S. Ct. Appeals (sixth cir.) 1992, U.S. Ct. Appeals (seventh cir.) 1993, U.S. Ct. Appeals (ninth cir.) 1996. Ptnr. Kirkland & Ellis, Chgo., 1978; ptnr. Reuben & Proctor, Chgo., 1978-86, Mayer, Brown & Platt, Chgo., 1986-97, Burke, Warren, MacKay & Serritella, PC, Chgo., 1997—. Lectr. in field. Contbr. articles to profl. jours. Exec. bd. govt. rels. com. United Way of Chgo., 1979-84; bd. dirs. Child Care Assn. Ill., 1975-79, Lyric Opera Guild, 1979-84; v.p. Comprehensive Community Svcs. of Met. Chgo., 1976-81; chmn. adv. bd. DePaul U. Coll. Law Ctr. Ch./State Studies, 1982—, dean's vis. com., 1982—; trustee Mundelein Coll., 1982-86, St. Xavier Coll., St. Mary of the Lake Sem., 1982-83, Sta. WTTW Chgo. Pub. TV, 1978-81, Loretto Hosp., 1989-91; mem. geriatrics/gerontology steering com. McGaw Med. Ctr. Northwestern U., 1981-82; adv. bd. N.Am. Coll., 1990-92; mem. Bus. Execs. for Econ. Justice, 1988-94, State wide citizens com. on Child Abuse and Neglect, 1988-94; bd. advisors Alzheimer's Ctr. Rush-Presbyn.-St. Luke's Med. Ctr., 1990—; cons. Union of Bulgarian Founds., 1992, Internat. Acad. for Freedom of Religion and Belief, Budapest, Hungary, 1992. Recipient St. Joseph Sem. Rerum Novarum award, 1999. Fellow Am. Bar Found.; mem. ABA, FBA, NCCJ (adv. com. on ch., state and taxation), Am. Assn. homes for Aging, Nat. Health Lawyers Assn., Ill. State Bar Assn. (bd. govs., spl. com. on jud. redistricting), Ill. Bar Found. (charter), Chgo. Bar Assn. (com. on evaluation of jud. candidates), Cath. Lawyers Guild (bd. govs.), Canon Law Soc. Am. (active mem.), Diocesan Attys. Assn. (exec. com.), Nat. Cath. Cemetery Conf., Cath. Health Assn., The Chgo. Club, Econ. Club, Tavern Club. Office: Burke Warren MacKay & Serritella PC IBM Plaza 22nd Fl 330 N Wabash Ave Chicago IL 60611-3603 E-mail: jserritella@burkelaw.com.

SERRITELLA, WILLIAM DAVID, lawyer; b. Chgo., May 16, 1946; s. William V. and Josephine Dolores (Scalise) S. JD, U. Ill., Champaign, 1971. Bar: Ill. 1971, US Dist. Ct. (no. and cen. dists.) Ill. 1972, US Dist. Ct. (ea. and we. dists.) Wis. 1995, US Ct. Appeals (7th cir.) 1974, US Supreme Ct. 1979, US Dist. Ct. (so. dist.) Ind. 1997. Law clk. U.S. Dist. Ct., Danville, Ill., 1971-72; ptnr. Ross & Hardies, Chgo., 1972—2003, McGuire Woods, Chgo., 2003—07, Johnson & Bell, Ltd., Chgo., 2007—. Arbitrator Am. Arbitration Assn. Named to Leading Lawyers Network, Ill. Super Lawyers, Top Best Lawyers Network. Fellow Am. Bar Found.; mem. ABA, Ill. Bar Assn., Chgo. Bar Assn., Internat. Assn. Def. Counsel, Soc. Trial Lawyers, Defense Rsch. Inst., Trial Lawyers

Club (Chgo.), Lawyers Club Chgo. Office: Johnson & Bell Ltd Ste 2700 33 W Monroe St Chicago IL 60603-5404 Office Phone: 312-984-0272. Business E-Mail: serritellaw@jbltd.com.

SERRY, CYRUS, medical educator; MD, Tehran Med. U., Iran, 1962. Bd. cert. cardio thoracic surgery and vascular surgery. Sr. attending, assoc. prof. Rush U., 1972—; chief sect. cardiac surgery Elmhurst Hosp., Ill., 1988—98; chief divsn. thoracic surgery Cook County Hosp., Chgo., 1993—98. Mem.: ACS, Chgo. Surg. Soc., Soc. Thoracic Surgeons. Office: 310 Ottawa Ln Oak Brook IL 60523 Office Phone: 312-563-2762.

SERULLE, YAFELL, medical researcher; b. Santo Domingo, Dominican Republic, Nov. 22, 1977; s. Haffe Serulle and Sonia Espaillat; m. Sabine Chlosta, May 6, 2006. MD, U. Nat. Pedro Henriquez Urena, Santo Domingo, 2001; PhD, NY U., NYC, 2007. Grad. asst. NYU Sch. Medicine, NYC, 2002—07, postdoc. fellow, 2007—. Contbr. articles to profl. jours. (Alzforum Paper of Week). Mem.: NY Acad. Sci., Biophysical Soc., Soc. Neuroscience. Office: Dept Phys and Neuroscience NYU SoM 550 First Ave New York NY 10016 Home Phone: 646-209-6496; Office Phone: 212-263-5433. Personal E-mail: yafell.serulle@gmail.com.

SERVAN-SCHREIBER, DAVID, psychiatrist; b. Paris, Apr. 21, 1961; MD, Laval U., Quebec, Canada, 1984; PhD, Carnegie Mellon U., 1991. Diplomate Am. Bd. Psychiatry and Neurology. Intern Royal Victoria Hosp., Montreal, 1984-85; resident in Psychiatry Western Psychiatric Inst., U. Pitts., 1990-93; mem. staff U. Pitts. Med. Ctr., 1993—, Shadyside Hosp., Pitts., 1994—, U. Pitts., 1993—. Mem. AMA, Soc. Biological Psychiatry. Office: 5215 Centre Ave Pittsburgh PA 15232

SERVODIDIO, PAT ANTHONY, broadcast executive; b. Yonkers, NY, Nov. 9, 1937; s. Pasquale and Catherine (Verdisco) S.; children: Christian, Alexa. BS, Fordham U., 1959; postgrad., St. John's U., NYC, 1960-63. Asst. to bus. mgr. Sta. WCBS-TV, NYC, 1960-64; account exec. Sta. WTNH-TV, New Haven, 1964-66; account exec., N.Y. sales mgr. RKO TV Reps., NYC, 1967-74; v.p., N.Y. sales mgr. Sta. WOR-TV, NYC, 1974-79, v.p., gen. sales mgr., 1979-81; v.p., gen. mgr. Sta. WHDH-TV, Boston, 1981—82; pres. RKO TV, NYC, 1982-87, RKO Gen., Inc., NYC, 1987—91, also bd. dirs.; v.p., gen. mgr. Sta. WKYC-TV, Cleve., 1991-92; pres. Multimedia Broadcasting Co., Cin., 1992-94; broadcast cons., 1995—. Bd. regents St. Peter's Coll., 1983-99; mem. com. future financing Rutgers U., New Brunswick, N.J., 1983-85; dir. TV bur. Advt. Bd., 1993-94; bd. dirs. Internat. Radio and TV Found., 1983-93, Assn. for Maximum Svc. TV, Inc., 1993-95. With U.S. Army, 1959-62.

SERVODIDIO, THOMAS GERARD, lawyer; b. SI, NY, Sept. 14, 1962; s. Francis and Nina Servodidio; m. Julie Ann Luybli, Aug. 15, 1987; children: David, Daniel, Maria BA magna cum laude, Bucknell U., 1984; JD cum laude, U. Pa., 1987. Bar: Pa. 1987, NJ 1988, DC 1989, US Dist. Ct. Ea. Pa. 1987, US Dist. Ct. Dist. NJ 1988, US Ct. Appeals 3rd Cir. 1991, US Ct. Appeals 4th Cir., Supreme Ct. Pa., Supreme Ct. NJ. Assoc. Duane Morris LLP, Phila., 1987—96, ptnr., 1997—, chair legal recruitment & retention com., 1998—2000, chair firm employment, and immigration dept. Spkr. in field. Contbr. articles to law jours. Mem.: ABA, DC Bar, Phila. Bar Assn., Pa. Bar Assn., Phi Beta Kappa. Republican. Office: Duane Morris LLP 30 S 17th St Philadelphia PA 19103-4196 Office Phone: 215-979-1844. Office Fax: 215-979-1020. Business E-Mail: tgservodidio@duanemorris.com.*

SERWATKA, JUDY ANN, computer and information systems educator; d. Carl Daniel and Mary Ellen Penovich; m. Conrad Mitchell Serwatka, Oct. 4, 1997. BS in Computer Tech., Purdue U. Calumet, Hammond, Ind.l, 1978, MS in Mgmt., 1983; EdD in Bus. Edn., No. Ill. U., 1993. Sys. engr. Bethlehem Steel Corp., Burns Harbor, Ind., 1979—85; assoc. prof. info. sys. and computer programming Purdue U. Calumet, Hammond, 1985—2002; assoc. prof. computer and info. tech. Purdue U. North Ctrl., Westville, Ind., 2002—06, prof. computer and info. tech., 2006—, dir. MBA program, 2006, chair dept. computer and info. tech., 2007—. Author: Business Data Communications: Introductory Concepts and Techniques, 2004; contbr. articles to profl. jours. Recipient cert. recognition, Ind. Partnership for Statewide Edn., 2002, 2004, Merlot Vol. of the Yr. award, Project Merlot, 2005. Mem.: Assn. Computing Machinery, Internat. Assn. Computer Info. Sys., Network and Sys. Profls. Assn. (dir. 2002—04), Sigma Xi. Office: Purdue U North Ctrl 1401 S US 421 Westville IN 46391 E-mail: jserwatka@pnc.edu.

SERWATKA, WALTER DENNIS, publishing executive; b. Irvington, NJ, July 19, 1937; s. Walter F. and Grace R. (Sheehan) S.; m. Beverly M. Farrell, Aug. 10, 1963 (div. Feb. 1988); children: David, Nora, Nancy; m. Constance L. Holcomb, May 10, 1991. BBA in Acctg., Upsala U., 1959; MBA in Fin., Fairleigh Dickinson U., 1966; postgrad., Harvard U., 1978, Columbia U., 1979, Stanford U., 1985. With treas.'s dept. WESTVACO, NYC, 1964-68; dir. fin. analysis Random House Co., NYC, 1968-72; with McGraw-Hill Info. Systems Co., 1972-83; from contr. Sweet's divsn. to asst. contr. McGraw-Hill, Inc., NYC, 1972-76, sr. v.p., contr., 1976-79, group v.p. real estate info. svcs., 1979-83, sr. v.p. group mfg. and circulation svcs., 1985, exec. v.p., CFO, 1985-88, exec. v.p. ops., 1989—92; exec. v.p. fin. and svc. McGraw-Hill Publ. Co., NYC, Nebr., 1983-84; pres. McGraw-Hill Info. Svc., NYC, 1988-89; sr. advisor Whitestone Comm., Inc., 1993—. Trustee Upsala Coll., East Orange, NJ; bd. dirs. Am. Cancer Soc. With US Army, 1959—62. Mem. Fin. Exec. Inst., Mag. Pubs. Assn., Am. Inst. Accts., Planning Execs. Inst., Pvt. Sector Council.

SERWER, ANDY (ANDREW E. SERWER), editor, journalist; b. Sept. 16, 1959; BA in Hist., with honors, Bowdoin Coll., Brunswick, Maine, 1981; MBA, Emory U., Atlanta, 1984; M in Journalism, Columbia U., NYC. Reporter Fortune mag. Time Inc., NYC, 1984, assoc. editor, sr. writer, 1995—98, editor-at-large, 1998—2006, mng. editor, 2006—. Contbg. writer Money, Time, Sports Illus. SLAM mags. Host (TV series) CNN's American Morning, CNN's In the Money. Named Bus. Journalist of Yr., TJFR Bus. News Reporter, 2000; named one of 100 Most Influential Bus. Journalists, NewsBios.com, 2007. Office: Fortune 1271 Ave of Americas New York NY 10020-1393 also: In the Money 1 CNN Ctr Atlanta GA 30303 Office Phone: 212-275-7820, 212-522-4668. Office Fax: 404-827-1784.*

SESONSKE, ALEXANDER, nuclear and chemical engineer; b. Gloversville, NY, June 20, 1921; s. Abraham and Esther (Kreitzer) S.; m. Marjorie Ann Mach, Apr. 17, 1952 (dec. Jan. 1995); children: Michael Jan, Jana Louise. B.Chem. Engring., Rensselaer Poly. Inst., 1942; MS, U. Rochester, 1947; PhD, U. Del., 1950. Engr. Chem. Constrn. Corp., NYC, 1942; chem. engr. Manhattan Project, 1943-45, Columbia Chem. Corp., 1945-46; staff Los Alamos Sci. Lab., 1950-54, 60-61, cons., 1961-63; faculty Purdue U., Lafayette, Ind., 1954, prof. nuclear and chem. engring., 1959-86, prof. emeritus, 1986—, asst. chmn. dept. nuclear engring., 1966-73. Cons. Oak Ridge Nat. Lab., 1963-67, Electric Power Research Inst., 1974; mem. rev. com. Argonne (Ill.) Nat. Lab., 1965-67, 75-81; ind. cons. 1986—. Author: (with Samuel Glasstone) Nuclear Reactor Engineering, 1963, 4th edit., 1994, Nuclear Power Plant Design Analysis, 1973; mem. editorial bd. Advances in Nuclear Sci. and Tech., 1972—; contbr. numerous articles to profl. jours. Recipient Wall of Fame award U. Del., 1988. Fellow Am. Nuclear Soc. (Arthur H. Compton award 1987); mem. Am. Inst. Chem. Engrs., Am. Soc. Engring. Edn., Sigma Xi, Omega Chi Epsilon. Achievements include research on nuclear fuel mgmt., liquid metal heat transfer and nuclear reactor engring. Home and Office: 700 Black Lake Blvd SW Apt 109 Olympia WA 98502 Office Phone: 360-943-5467.

SESSIONS, ALICE, biology professor, department chairman; children: Emily, Michael. PhD, Johns Hopkins U., Balt., 1979; MAT, Boston U., Mass., 1989. Chair, biology dept. Austin CC, Tex., 2006—. Office: Austin CC 1212 Rio Grande Austin TX 78701 Business E-Mail: asession@austincc.edu.

SESSIONS, JEFF (JEFFERSON BEAUREGARD SESSIONS III), United States Senator from Alabama, former state attorney general; b. Hybart, Ala., Dec. 24, 1946; s. Jefferson Beauregard and Abbie (Powe) S.; m. Mary Montgomery Blackshear, Aug. 9, 1969; children: Mary Abigail, Ruth Blackshear, Samuel Turner BA, Huntingdon Coll., Montgomery, Ala., 1969; JD, U. Ala., 1973. Bar: Ala. 1973. Assoc. Guin, Bouldin & Porch, Russellville, Ala., 1973-75; asst. US atty. (so. dist.) Ala. US Dept. Justice, Mobile, Ala., 1975-77, US atty., 1981-93; assoc. then ptnr. Stockman & Bedsole Attorneys, Mobile, Ala., 1977-81; ptnr. Stockman, Bedsole & Sessions, Mobile, 1993-94; atty. gen. State of Ala., Montgomery, 1995—97; US Senator from Ala., 1997—; mem. US Senate BudgetCom., US Senate Energy & Nat. Resources Com., US Senate Armed Forces Com.; ranking mem. US Senate Judiciary Com., 2009—. Mem. U.S. Atty. Gen's. adv. com., 1987-89, vice-chmn. 1989 Presdl. elector State of Ala., 1972; trustee, mem. exec. com. Mobile Bay Area Partnership for Youth, 1981-95; chmn. adminstrv. bd. Ashland Pl. United Meth. Ch., Mobile, 1982; 1st v.p. Mobile Lions Club, 1993-94. Capt. USAR, 1975-85 Recipient U.S. Atty. Gen's. award for significant achievements in the war against drug trafficking, US Dept. Justice, 1992, George (Buck) Gillespie Congl. award, Blinded Americans Veterans Found., 2000, Nat. Leadership award, Civil War Preservation Trust, 2004, Disting. Eagle Scout award, Guardian of Small Bus. award, Minuteman of the Yr. award, Reserve Officers Assn., Svc. to Agrl. award, AL Farmers Fedn., Teddy Roosevelt Environ. award, Watchdog of the Treasury award Mem. ABA, Ala. Bar Assn., Mobile Bar Assn. Republican. Methodist. Office: US Senate 335 Senate Russell Office Bldg Washington DC 20510-0001 also: Regions Ctr Ste 802 200 Clinton Ave Huntsville AL 35801 Office Phone: 202-224-4124. Office Fax: 202-224-3149. E-mail: senator@sessions.senate.gov.

SESSIONS, JOAN T., administrator, educator; d. David Pyper and Rose Smith Thomas; children: Linda Ann Hadley, Gina Louise. BS in Edn., Kent State U., 1962; postgrad., U. Akron, 1970; MA in Edn., Ohio State U., 1966; PhD in Edn., Kent State U., 1975; postgrad., U. Chgo., 1996, St. Michael's Coll., Burlington, Vt., 1998. Cert. elem. tchr., elem. prin. Ohio. Rsch. asst. Ohio State U., 1965—66; tchr. pub. schs., Wooster, Ohio, 1962—64, Elyria City Schs., 1966—67; dir. of info. systems, planning quality assurance Ctr. for Human Services, Cleve., 1974—91; program specialist UN Volunteers, Beijing, 1991—96; tutoring program dir. U. Chgo., 1998—2005; Headstart dir. Elyria City Schs., 1967—70, elem. prin. Ohio, 1970—72; tchg. fellow Ohio State U., 1972—73; rsch. assoc. Bur. Ednl. Rsch., 1973—74; dir. evaluation Ctr. for Human Svcs., Cleve., 1974—91; instr. John Carroll U., 1985—90; vol. UN, Beijing; lang. evaluation cons. Beijing Diplomatic Svc., 1991—96. Grad. sch. lectr. John Carroll U., Cleve., 1987—89; grad. tchg. fellow Kent State U., 1972—74; cons. and lectr. in field; tutor program dir., mgr. VISTA and AmeriCorps, 1999—2005; primary literacy tutoring cons. City Yr. Chgo., 2001—05; USI primary literacy tutor program tng. materials evaluation methodology Dept. Neighborhood Schs., U. Chgo., 2006—; adj. prof. Loyola Chgo., 2006—. Pres. Ohio City Redevelopment Assn., Cleve., 1986—91; treas., pres., deacon, trustee and elder Fairmont Presbyn. Ch.; mission cons. Fourth Presbyn. Ch., Chgo., 2007—; with Peace Moley Task Force, Chgo. Presbytory, 2008—; bd. dirs. 5000 S Cornell Condominium Assn., 2001—, Literacy Vols. of Ill. Recipient Deacons award, Fairmont Presbyn. Ch., 1984, award, Luth. Med. Ctr. Women's Bd., 1988, Cmty. Svc. award, Mayor George Voinovich, City of Cleve., 1991, Moccasin award for cmty. svc., City Yr. Chgo., 2004; grantee, Cleve. Found., United Way of Cuyahoga County, Gund Found., Luth. Med. Ctr. Found., 1989, BP Am. Found., numerous others. Mem.: Wooster Edn. Assn., Ohio Fedn. Women, Wooster Jr. Women's Club. Avocations: collecting art, studying Chinese language and culture. Home: 141 N La Grange Rd Apt 403 La Grange IL 60525-2049 Personal E-mail: joansessions@comcast.net.

SESSIONS, JUDITH ANN, dean, university librarian; b. Lubbock, Tex., Dec. 16, 1947; d. Earl Alva and Anna (Mayer) S. BA cum laude, Cen. Fla. U., 1970; MLS, Fla. State U., 1971; postgrad., Am. U., 1980, George Washington U., 1983. Head libr. U. S.C., Salkehatchie, 1974-77; dir. Libr. and Learning Resources Ctr. Mt. Vernon Coll., Washington, 1977-82; planning and systems libr. George Washington U., Washington, 1981-82, asst. univ. libr. for adminstrn. svcs., acting head tech. svcs., 1982-84; univ. libr. Calif. State U., Chico, 1984-88; univ. libr., dean of libr. Miami U., Oxford, Ohio, 1988—. Cons. Space Planning, SC, 1976, DataPhase Implementation, Bowling Green U., 1982, TV News Study Ctr., George Washington U., 1981; asst. prof. dept. child devel. Mt. Vernon Coll., 1978—81; mem., lectr. U.S.-China Libr. Exch. Del., 1986, 91; lectr., presenter in field; mem. coord. com. OhioLink Adv. Coun., 1995—2003, v.p., 1996—97, chair, 1998—2000; mem. gov. bd. OhioLink, exec. com., 1998—2001; mem. OCLC Users Coun., 1998—2001; convenor Pub. Acad. Libr. Group, 1999—2000; mem. OCLC Preservation Resources Interest Group, 1999—2001, chmn., 2001; mem. Olionet Alternet, 2002—08. Contbr. articles, book revs. to profl. jours. Trustee Christ Hosp., Cin., 1990-94, Deaconness Gamble Rsch. Ctr., Cin., 1990-94, OhioNet, 1990-94, treas. 1993; bd. dirs. Hamilton (Ohio) YWCA, 1994-98, pres., 1995-96, v.p., 1996-97, 97-98; mem. OCLC user's coun., 1998—; mem. steering com. Tri City Reading Initiative, 2002-03. Recipient award for outstanding contbn. D.C. Libr. Assn., 1979, Disting. Svc. award Miami U., 2008; rsch. grantee Mt. Vernon Coll., 1980, Am. Assn. Colls. and U. grant, 2007-; recipient Fulbright-Hayes Summer Travel fellowship to Czechoslovakia, 1991. Mem. ALA (Olofson award 1978, councillor-at-large policy making group 1981-94, coun. com. on coms. 1983-84, intellectual freedom com. 1984-88, directions and program rev. com. 1989-91, fin. and audit subcom. 1989-90, mem. exec. bd. 1989-94, mem. del. to Zimbabwe Internat. Book Fair 1997), Assn. Coll. and Rsch. Librs. (editorial bd. Coll. and Rsch. Librs. jour. 1979-84, nominations and appointments com. 1983-85, faculty status com. 1984-86), Libr. and Info. Tech. Assn. (chair legis. and regulation com. 1980-81), Libr. Adminstrn. and Mgmt. Assn. (bd. dirs. libr. orgn. and mgmt. sect. 1985-87), Calif. Inst. Librs. (v.p., pres. elect 1987-88), Mid-Atlantic Regional Libr. Fedn. (mem. exec. bd. 1982-84), Jr. Mems. Round Table (pres. 1981-82), Intellectual Freedom Round Table (sec. 1984-85), Freedom to Read Found. (trustee 1984-88, v.p. 1985-86, treas. 1986-87, pres. 1987-88), Rotary, Beta Phi Mu. Office: Miami U Edgar W King Oxford OH 45056 Office Phone: 513-529-2800. Business E-Mail: sessioja@muohio.edu. E-mail: judith@lib.muohio.edu.

SESSIONS, PETE (PETER ANDERSON SESSIONS), United States Representative from Texas; b. Waco, Tex., Mar. 22, 1955; s. William Steele and Alice June (Lewis) Sessions; m. Juanita Diaz, 1984; children: Bill, Alex. BS in Polit. Sci., Southwestern U., Georgetown, Tex., 1978. Dist. mgr. mktg. Southwestern Bell Tel. Co., 1978—94; v.p. pub. policy Nat. Ctr. Policy Analysis, Dallas, 1994—95; mem. US Congress from 5th Tex. Dist., 1997—2003, US Congress from 32nd Tex. Dist., 2003—, US House Rules Com.; chmn. Nat. Republican Congressional Com. (NRCC), 2009—. Bd. mem. YMCA; mem. exec. bd. circle ten coun. Boy Scouts America; active United Meth. Ch. Recipient Nat. Disting. Eagle Scout award, 1999. Mem.: Rotary Club. Republican. Methodist. Avocations: hiking, mountain climbing, running. Office: US Congress 1514 Longworth Ho Office Bldg Washington DC 20515-4305 also: Park Ctrl VII 12750 Merit Dr Ste 1434 Dallas TX 75251 Office Phone: 202-225-2231.*

SESSIONS, ROY BRUMBY, otolaryngologist, educator; b. Houston, July 28, 1937; s. Roy Brumby and Elizabeth (Compton) S.; m. Mary Cousart, Aug. 28, 1976: children: Kate, Elizabeth, Abigail, Matthew. BS, La. State U., Baton Rouge, 1958; MD, La. State U., New Orleans, 1962. Resident gen. surgery and otolaryngology Washington U. Sch. Medicine, St. Louis, 1965-69; asst. prof. Baylor Coll. Medicine, Houston, 1969-73, assoc. prof., 1973-83; prof. head and neck surgery Meml. Sloan Kettering Cancer Ctr., NYC, 1983-89; prof., chmn. dept. otolaryngology, head and neck surgery Med. Sch. Georgetown U., Washington, 1989-97; chmn. dept. otolaryngology, head and neck surgery Beth Israel Med. Ctr., NYC, 1998—, assoc. dir. Cancer Ctr., co-dir. Inst. Head and Neck Surgery, 1998—. Contbr. articles to profl. jours., chpts. to books; author one textbook. Lt. comdr. USN, 1962-65. Roman Catholic.

SESSIONS, WILLIAM K., III, federal judge; b. Hartford, Conn., 1947; BA, Middlebury Coll., 1969; JD, George Washington U., 1972. Bar: 1973; Ct. of Appeals, DC, 1973; Ct. of Appeals (2nd circut) 1975; US Dist. Ct., Vt., 1973; US Supreme Ct., 1992. Law clk. Honorable Hilton Dier, Jr. Addison (Vt.) Dist. Ct., 1973; exec. dir. Addison County Youth Svcs. Bur., 1973-74; staff Addison County Public Defender, 1974-78; pvt. practice Middlebury, Vt., 1978-80; ptnr. Sessions, Keiner, Dumont & Barnes, P.C., Middlebury, Vt., 1980-95; judge US Dist. Ct., Burlington, 1995—, chief judge, 2002—. Adj. prof. law Vt. Law Sch., 1978-95; vice chmn. US Sentencing Commn., 1999—; chair Vt. State com. of selection for Rhodes Scholarship Trust, 2000; trustee Vt. Law Sch., 1999-2001. 1st Lt. US Army, 1972—77. Mem.: Friends Children's Art Exch. Office: US Dist Ct PO Box 928 Burlington VT 05402-0928 Office Phone: 802-951-6350.*

SESSIONS, WILLIAM STEELE, lawyer, former FBI director; b. Ft. Smith, Ark., May 27, 1930; s. Will Anderson and Edith A. (Steele) S.; m. Alice June Lewis, Oct. 5, 1952; children: William Lewis, Mark Gregory, Peter Anderson, Sara Anne. BA, Baylor U., 1956, LLB, 1958; degree (hon.), John C. Marshall Law Sch., St. Mary's U., 1989; LLD (hon.), Dickinson Coll., 1988, Flager Coll., 1990, Davis & Elkins Coll., 1992, McMurry U., 1997. Bar: Tex. 1959; U.S. Dist Ct. (Western Dist.) Tex.; Ct. Appeals (5th Cir.). Ptnr. McGregor & Sessions, Waco, Tex., 1959-61; assoc. Tirey, McLaughlin, Gorin & Tirey, Waco, 1961-63; ptnr. Haley, Fulbright, Winniford, Sessions & Bice, Waco, 1963-69; sect. chief, govt. ops sect. criminal divsn. US Dept. Justice, Washington, 1969-71; US atty. (we. dist.) Tex. US Dept Justice, San Antonio, 1971-74; judge US Dist. Ct. (we. dist.) Tex., San Antonio, 1974-87, chief judge, 1980-87; dir. FBI, Washington, 1987-93; ptnr. Sessions & Sessions, San Antonio and Washington, 1995-2000, Holland & Knight, LLP, San Antonio and Washington, 2000—; arbitrator, mediator Am. Arbitration Assn., Internat. Ctr. Dispute Resolution, Nat. Panelist Disting. Neutrals, Arbitration Appeal Panel. Bd. dirs., chmn. benchbook com. Fed. Jud. Ctr., Washington, 1981—84; mem. Tex. Commn. on Judicial Efficiency, 1995, Tex. Commn. on a Representative Student Body, 1998, Gov.'s Task Force on Homeland Security, Gov.'s Anti-Crime Commn., Tex., 2002, ABA Standing Com. on the 21st Century Judiciary, ABA Standing Com. on the Libr. of Congress; mem. steering com. of coastal Tex.; mem. George W. Bush presdl. lib. steering com. Baylor U.; serves on initiatives of Constitution Project; served as signatory The Ctr. for Study of Presidency; served as commr. Commn. on Safety & Abuse in America's Prisons. Contbr. articles to profl. jours. Active Dr. Martin Luther King Jr. Fed. Holiday Commn., 1991-96, hon. bd. dirs., 1993-94; bd. trustees Nat. Environ. Edn. & Tng. Found., Inc., 2001—. Lt. USAF, 1951-55; capt. USAFR. Recipient Rosewood Gavel award St. Mary's U. Sch. Law, San Antonio, 1982, Disting. Alumni award Baylor U., Golden Plate award Am. Acad. Achievement, 1988, Law Enforcement Leadership award Assn. Fed. Investigators, 1989, medal of honor DAR, 1989, Disting. Eagle Scout award Boy Scouts Am., 1990, Person of Yr. award Am. Soc. for Indsl. Security, 1990, Magna Charta award Baronial Order of Magna Charta, 1990, Price Daniel Disting. Pub. Svc. award Baylor U., 2002, The Best Lawyer, 2005, 06, 07, 10th Anniversary Constitutional Cramprон award, The Constn. Project, 2008, Holland & Knight LLP's Chesterfield Smith award, 2008; named Lawyer of Yr., Baylor Law Sch., 1988, Father of Yr., Nat. Fathers Day Com., 1988, Ellis Island Congl. Medal of Honor, 1992; inducted into Eagle Scout Hall of Fame, 1998, Outstanding Fifty Yr. Lwyer award, Tex. Bar Found., 2009. Fellow ABA (chmn. spl. com. on judicial independence 1997—, Nat. Law Day chmn. 2000-02, hon. co chmn., pres. commn. on the 21st Century Judiciary, 2002-, mem. commn. on civic edn. and separation of powers); mem. Jud. Conf. U.S. (com. on ct. adminstrn., chmn. jud. improvements subcom. 1983-85, ad hoc com. on automation to subcom. 1984-87, mem. ad hoc ct. reporter com. 1984-87), San Antonio Bar Assn. (bd. dirs. 1973-74), Fed. Bar Assn. (pres. San Antonio sect. 1974), Am. Judicature Soc. (exec. com. 1982-84), Dist. Judges Assn. of 5th Cir. (pres. 1982-83), State Bar of Tex. (chmn. com. to develop procedures for cert. state law questions to Supreme Ct. by Fed. Cts. 1983-85), Waco McLennan County Bar Assn. (pres. 1968), San Antonio Inns of Ct. (pres. 1986), William S, Nat. Assn. of Former US Attys., DC Bar, Bd. for Mid-Atlantic Innocence Project (hon.), Adv. Bd. for Innocence Commn., Va., ABA. Sessions Inns of Ct. Republican. Methodist. Avocations: hiking, climbing, canoeing. Office: Holland & Knight LLP Ste 100 2099 Pennsylvania Ave NW Washington DC 20006 Office Phone: 202-955-3000, 202-419-2410. Office Fax: 202-955-5564. Business E-Mail: william.sessions@hklaw.com.

SESSLE, BARRY JOHN, adult education educator, researcher; b. Sydney, NSW, Australia, May 28, 1941; arrived in Can., 1971; s. Frederick George and Sadie Isobel (Lawson) S.; m. Mary Baldwin; children from previous marriage: Erica Jane, Claire Marie. BDS, Sydney U., New South Wales, 1963, MDS, MSc, Sydney U., New South Wales, 1965; PhD, U. New South Wales, 1969, DSc (hon.), 2000, DSc (hon.), 2008. Scholar Dental Found. Sydney U., 1963-64; tchg. fellow U. New South Wales, 1965-68; vis. assoc. U.S. Nat. Inst. Dental Rsch., Bethesda, Md., 1968-70; assoc. prof. U. Toronto Dental Sch., Ont., Canada, 1971-76, prof., 1976-85, chmn. divsn. biol. scis., 1978-84, assoc. dean rsch., 1985-90, dean, 1990-2001. Mem. com. on dental scis. Can. Med. Rsch. Coun., Ottawa, 1979-82, 1990, 1992, 1994, 2002-03, 2006-08; mem. com. grants rev. U.S. NIH, Bethesda, 1976-. Author: The Neural Basis of Oral and Facial Function, 1978; editor: Mastication and Swallowing, 1976, Oro-facial Pain and Neuromuscular Dysfunction, 1985, Effects of Injury of Trigeminal and Spinal Somatosensory Systems, 1987, Trigeminal Neuralgia: Current Concepts Regarding Pathogenesis and Treatment, 1991, Temporomandibular Joint and Masticatory Muscle Disorders, 1994, Temporomandibular Disorders and Related Pain Conditions, 1995, Neurobiology of Mastication, 1999, Orofacial Pain, 2001, 2nd edit., 2008, Sleep and Pain, 2007; mem. editl. bd. Arch. Oral Biol. Jour., 1988—, Pain Jour., 1986-90, Jour. Dental Rsch., 2003-05, Dysphagia Jour., 1990—, Pain Rsch. and Mgmt. Jour., 1995—, Oral Bioscis. and Medicine, 2003-2005, Jour. of Oral Rehab., 2003—; editor-in-chief Jour. Orofacial Pain, 1997—. Can. rsch. chair, 2001—. Recipient Tchr. award Can. Fund for Dental Edn., 1977, Disting. Career award Can. Pain Soc., 1999, Nat. Recognition award Am. Acad. Orofacial Pain, 2004; grantee Med. Rsch. Coun., Can. Inst. Health Rsch. 1971—, NIH, 1974—, Inst. Musculoskeletal Health and Arthritis Quality Life award Can. Inst. Health Rsch., 2005. Fellow Royal Soc. Can., Can. Acad. Sci., Internat. Coll. Dentists, Can. Acad. Health Scis.; mem. Internat. Assn. Study Pain (hon., sec. Can. chpt. 1982-87, mem. coun. 1993-96, pres.-elect 1997-99, pres. 1999-2002, chmn. orofacial pain group 2002-05, pres. Can. chpt. 2007-09), Soc. Neurosci. (pres. South Ont. chpt. 1982-83), Internat. Assn. Dental Rsch. (pres. Can. divsn. 1977-78, sec.-treas. 1976-79, chmn. neurosci. group 1985-86, pres. 1994-95, Oral Sci. award 1976, Pindborg Oral Biol. prize 1994), Internat. Union Physiol. Sci. (sec. oral physiology commn. 1983-90). Office: Faculty Dentistry U Toronto 124 Edward St Toronto ON Canada M5G 1G6 Office Phone: 416-979-4921.

SESSLER, ANDREW MARIENHOFF, physicist; b. Bklyn., Dec. 11, 1928; s. David and Mary (Baron) S.; m. Gladys Lerner, Sept. 23, 1951 (div. Dec. 1994); children: Daniel Ira, Jonathan Lawrence, Ruth. BA in Math. cum laude, Harvard U., 1949; MA in Theoretical Physics, Columbia U., 1951, PhD in Theoretical Physics, 1953. NSF fellow Cornell U., Ithaca, NY, 1953—54; asst. prof. Ohio State U., Columbus, 1954, assoc. prof., 1960; on leave Midwestern Univs. Rsch., 1955—56; vis. physicist Lawrence Radiation Lab., 1959—60; vis. physicist, summer Niels Bohr Inst., Copenhagen, 1961; rschr. theoretical physics Lawrence Berkeley Lab. U. Calif., Berkeley, 1961—73, rschr. energy and environment Lawrence Berkeley Lab., 1971—73, dir. Lawrence Berkeley Lab., 1973—80, sr. scientist plasma physics Lawrence Berkeley Lab., 1980—94, disting. sr. staff scientist Lawrence Berkeley Lab., 1994—2001, disting. vis. scientist Lawrence Berkeley Lab., 2001—02, disting. scientist Lawrence Berkeley Lab., 2002—, dir. emeritus, 2002—. U.S. advisor Panjab U. Physics Inst., Chandigarh, India; mem. U.S.-India Coop. Program for Improvement Sci. Edn. in India, 1966, high energy physics adv. panel to U.S. AEC, 1969-72, adv. com. Lawrence Hall Sci., 1974-78; chmn. Stanford Synchrotron Radiation Project Sci. Policy Bd., 1974-77, EPRI Advanced Fuels Adv. Com., 1978-81, BNL External Adv. Com. on Isabelle, 1980-82; mem. sci. pol. bd. Stanford Synchrotron Radiation Lab., 1991-92; L.J. Haworth dist. scientist Brookhaven Nat. Lab., 1991-92; spokesperson Neutrino Factory and Muon Collider Collaboration, 1999-2002, assoc. spokesperson 2002—. Mem. editl. bd. Nuc. Instruments and Methods, 1969—2000, correspondent Comments on Modern Physics, 1969—71; contbr. articles to profl. jours. Mem. Superconducting Super Collider Sci. Policy Com., 1991—93; mem. radiation effects rsch. bd. Nat. Rsch. Coun., 2001—04, mem. nuclear radiation studies bd., 2005—. Recipient E.O. Lawrence award US Atomic Energy Commn., 1970, US Particle Accelerator Sch. prize, 1988, Nicholson Medal for Humanitarian Svc., 1994, Robert R. Wilson prize 1997; fellow Japan Soc. for Promotion Sci. at KEK, 1985. Fellow AAAS (nominating com. 1984-87), Am. Phys. Soc. (chmn. com. internat. freedom scientist 1982, study of directed energy weapons panel 1985-87, chmn. panel pub. affairs 1988, chmn. divsn. physics of beams 1990, chmn. com. applications of physics 1993, councilor for divsn. physics of beams 1994-97, pres.-elect 1997, pres. 1998, past pres. 1999, vice-chmn. forum on physics and soc. 2001, chmn.-elect 2002, chmn. 2003), N.Y. Acad. Sci.; mem. NAS (bd. on radiation effects rsch. 2002-05, nuclear radiation studies bd., 2005-), IEEE (sr.), Fedn. Am. Scientists Coun. (vice chmn. 1987-88, chmn. 1988-92), Assoc. Univ. Inc. (bd. dirs. 1991-98), Sigma Xi. Avocations: skiing, hiking, jogging, exercise, flute. Office: Lawrence Berkeley Lab Univ Calif MS 71R0259 1 Cyclotron Rd Bldg Berkeley CA 94720-8211 Office Phone: 510-486-4992. Business E-Mail: AMSessler@lbl.gov.

SESSOMS, ALLEN LEE, academic administrator, physicist, educator, retired diplomat; b. NYC, Nov. 17, 1946; s. Albert Earl and Lottie Beatrice (Leff) Sessoms; m. Karley Allison Sessoms; children: Manon Elizabeth, Stephanie Csilla, Avery Danielle, Reid Allen. BS in Physics with hon., Union Coll., Schenectady, NY, 1968; MS in Physics, U. Wash., Seattle, 1969; PhD in Physics, Yale U., 1972; DSc (hon.), Union Coll., 1998; PhD (hon.), Soka U., Japan, 2000. Sci. assoc. CERN, Geneva, 1973-78; asst. prof. physics Harvard U., Cambridge, Mass., 1974-81; sr. tech. advisor OES, State Dept., Washington, 1980-82; dir. Office Nuclear Tech. & Safeguards, State Dept., Washington, 1982-87; counselor for sci. and tech. US Embassy, Paris, 1987-89, polit. minister, counselor Mexico City, 1989-91, dep. chief of mission, 1991-93; exec. v.p., v.p. for acad. affairs U. Mass. Sys., Boston, 1993-95; pres. CUNY Queens Coll., Flushing, NY, 1995-2000; lectr., fellow Belfer Ctr. for Sci. and Internat. Affairs, JFK Sch. Govt., Harvard U., Cambridge, Mass., 2000—03; pres. Del. State U., 2003—08, U. DC, 2008—. Adv. com. U.S. Sec. Energy, 1995-2002; mem. NCAA Pres. Coun., 1996-2000; nuc. energy adv. com. U.S. Dept. Energy. Contbr. articles to profl. jours. Bd. dirs. Milestone Capital, Drawing Ctr.; mem. adv. coun. Toda Internat.; mem. bd. trustees Chapman U. Travel/study grant Ford Found., 1973-74; Alfred P. Sloan Found. fellow, 1977-81; recipient Wilbur Cross medal Yale Grad. Sch. Alumni, 1999, Medal of Highest Honor, Soka U., Japan, 1999; officer dans l'Order des Palmes Académiques, France, 1999. Fellow: Am. Phys. Soc.; mem: AAAS, NY Acad. Sci., Cosmos Club. Office: Office of the Pres Univ DC 4200 Connecticut Ave NW Washington DC 20008 Office Phone: 202-274-6016. Personal E-mail: allensessoms@aol.com. Business E-Mail: asessoms@udc.edu.

SESSOMS, WILLIAM D., JR., Mayor, Virginia Beach, Virginia, bank executive; Grad., Va. Commonwealth U. Banker Sovran Bank, Virginia Beach, Va., 1976—84, Wachovia Bank, Virginia Beach, Va., 1984—2004; Virginia Beach pres. TowneBank, 2005—; mem. at-large Virginia Beach City Coun., 1988—92; vice mayor City of Virginia Beach, Va., 1992—2002, mayor, 2009—. Mem. Va. Pub. Sch. Authority, Local Health Benefits Adv. Com., Va., Gov.'s Commn. on Environ. Stewardship, Va. Recipient First Citizen award, Virginia Beach, 2006. Office: City Hall Bldg #1 2401 Courthouse Dr Ste 234 Virginia Beach VA 23456 Office Phone: 757-385-4581, 757-385-4242. Office Fax: 757-427-5626. E-mail: wsessoms@vbgov.com.*

SESSUMS, T. TERRELL, lawyer; b. Daytona Beach, Fla., June 11, 1930; m. Neva Ann Steeves, Aug. 16, 1958; children: Thomas T. Jr., Richard H., Sandra Sessums Mooneyham. BA in polit. sci., U. Fla., 1952; JD, U. Fla. Coll. Law, 1958; grad., Fla. Exec. Mgmt. Program, 1993; LLD (hon.), Fla. So. Coll., 1973; D of pub. adminstrn. (hon.), Rollins Coll., 1974; LLD (hon.), Flagler Coll., 1988; LHD (hon.), U. So. Fla., 1995. Assoc. atty. Hardee & Ott, Tampa, 1958—60; legis. aide/legal asst. to State Senator Sam Gibbons, Fla. Senate, 1959—61; ptnr. Albritton, Sessums Gordon & Ryder, Tampa, 1961—84; shareholder, mng. ptnr. Macfarland Ferguson & McMullen, 1984—97; ptnr. Salem Saxon, P.A., 1998—2003; of counsel Salem Law Group, P.A., Tampa, 2003—. Spkr. Fla. Ho. Rep., 1972—74; adj. prof. U. So. Fla., Tampa, 1974—75; gen. coun. Tampa Port Authority, 1974—89; colloquium bd., lectr., ednl. policy issues Harvard U. Grad. Sch. Edn., 1977; chmn. Fla. Bar Legis. Com., 1977—78; coun. Fla. Conf. Cir. Judges, 1978; spl. coun. Fla. Bar/Workers' Compensation Section, 1978—79, chmn., 1979—80; served on Fla. Bd. Regents, 1979—88, chmn., 1986—88; spl. coun. to US Senator Bob Graham, 1995; dir. GTE Fla., 1986—93; dir. region II, cons. bd. Southeast Bank, N.A., Tampa Bay, 1973—91; dir. Blue Cross Fla., 1977—78; trustee, exec. com., gen. coun. Time Warner Trust, Tampa, 1983—98; dir. Family TV Co. (WFTV, Channel 28), 1978—84; pres. Ashley St. Properties, Inc., 1986—89, Golden Pond Groves, Inc., Tampa, 1986—89, Halifax Mgmt. Co., 1994—97; v.p. Trouble Creek Properties, Inc., 1988—2001; mem. Tampa Bay Area Com. on Fgn. Rels., 1982—; state dir., sr. mem. Orange Bowl. Com., 1991—; dir. Mus. Sci. and Industry (MOSI), Tampa, 1990—94, adv. coun., 1994—; founding pres. Ga. Seagle Alumni Assn., Inc., 1982—84, dir., 1984—94, adv. coun., 1994—2004. Contbr. articles to jour. Bd. trustees exec. com. U. So. Fla. Found., 1979—89; bd. dir. Moffitt Cancer Ctr., Inc., 1984—91; ednl. mission to coll. and U. in China and Japan U. So. Fla., 1986, life mem. pres. coun.; trustee Found. Eye Rsch., Inc., 1987—91; dir. Fla. State Fair Authority, 1995—96; pres. Greater Tampa C. of C., 1983—84, gen. coun., 1979—87, exec. com., 1988—91, chmn. com. of 100, 1986; dir. Fla. C. of C., 1987—96, v.p. pub. affairs, 1988—89, mem. project cornerstone adv. com., 1988—89, vice chmn. programs, 1989—90, chmn. rsch. and info. coun., 1990—91, chmn., 1992—93, exec. com., 1988—94, bd. gov., 1996—; pres. alumni coun. U. Fla. Coll. Law, 1984—85, mem. major gifts com./Hillsborough County chmn., 1989—91; trustee U. Tampa, 1978—91, chmn. strategic planning com., 1987—88, vice chmn. bd. trustees, 1987—88, chmn. bd. trustees, 1988—90, bd. overseers; trustee Fla. So. Coll., 1989—, chmn. long range planning com., 1990—2003, pres. coun., 1983—85, chmn. bd. trustees, 1993—2003, emeritus chmn. bd.; parents' coun. Wofford Coll., 1981—85, pres. coun., 1982—85; trustee Inter Am. Scholarship Found., Inc.; asst. scoutmaster Boy Scouts Am., Tampa, 1976—79; organizing com. mem. Tampa Bay Performing Arts Ctr., 1980, trustee, 1980—88; mem. Found. Excellence in Edn., 1987—90; dir. Fla. Independent College Fund, 1988—90; fed. judicial nom. com. Fla. (Middle Dist. Panel), 1997—2001; chmn. adv. coun. Tampa United Meth. Ctr., 1989—94; trustee United Meth. Found. Higher Edn., 1998—2006; conf. lay leader United Meth. Ch., 2000—04; dir. Nat. Conf. Christians and Jews, Tampa Bay Chpt., 1990—94. 2nd lt. USAF, 1952, capt. USAF, 1954—56. Recipient Disting. Alumnus award, U. Fla., 1973, CHIEF award (Champion Higher Independent Edn. in Fla.), Pres. Independent Coll. and U. in Fla., 1974—75, Pres. Disting. Citizen award, U. So. Fla., 1975, Don L. and Ruth E. Smith Founders award, 1980, Nat. Football Found. award, Contbn. to Cmty. and Football Tampa Chpt., 1982, Person of Vision award, Nat. Soc. Prevent Blindness, 1986, "Class of 56" award, U. So. Fla. Alumni Assn., 1988, Silver Medallion award, Nat. Conf. Christians and Jews, 1990, Disting. Svc. award, Fla. Assn. Coll. and U., 1993, Francis Asbury award, Fla. Annual Conf., United Meth. Ch., 1998; named diplomat, Fla. Demolay Hall Fame, 1995. Mem.: Fla. Bar Assn., Hillsborough Bar Assn., Tampa Bar Assn., Hall Fame Bowl Assn. (founding dir. 1986—88), Tampa Kiwanis Club, U. Club Tampa, Omicron Delta Kappa. Achievements include having the Terrell Sessums Elementary School and Terrell Sessums Mall at University of South Florida named in his honor. Office Phone: 813-224-9000.

SESTAK, JOE (JOSEPH A. SESTAK JR.), United States Representative from Pennsylvania, retired military officer; b. Springfield, Pa., Dec. 12, 1951; m. Susan L. Clark; 1 child, Alexandra. BS, US Naval Acad., 1974; MPA, Harvard U., PhD in Polit. Economy and Govt. Advanced through ranks to vice adm. USN, 2005, ret., 2005, served six sea tours Atlantic and Pacific Fleets, comdr. Cruiser Destroyer Group 2 Arabian Gulf and MTO, comdr. George Washington Battle Group, joint staff Force Structure Resources and Assessment Directorate, dir. Strategy and Policy Divsn. on staff of Chief of Naval Ops., dir. Navy Quadrennial Def. Rev., dir. Navy Ops. Group, dir. Assessment Divsn./Capability Analysis Group, dep. chief. naval ops. for warfare requirements & programs., comdr. USS Samuel B. Roberts, 1991—93, head Strategy and Concepts Br. on staff of Chief of Naval Ops., 1993—94; dir. def. policy NSC, 1994—97; comdr. Destroyer Squadron 14 USN, 1997; mem. US Congress from 7th Pa. dist., 2007—, mem. armed services com., edn. & labor com., small bus. com. Decorated Def. Disting. Svc. medal, Legion of Merit with Gold Star, Meritorious Svc. medal with Gold Star, Navy Commendation medal with two Gold Stars, Def. Superior Svc. medal, Joint Svc. Commendation medal, Navy Achievement medal. Democrat. Roman Catholic. Achievements include being the highest ranking military officer to ever serve in the US Congress. Office: 600 N Jackson St Ste 203 Media PA 19063 also: 1022 Longworth House Office Bldg Washington DC 20515 Office Phone: 610-892-8623, 202-225-2011. Office Fax: 610-892-8628.*

SESTINA, JOHN E., financial planner; b. Mar. 17, 1942; s. John J. and Regina Sestina; m. Mary Barbara Jezek, Dec. 20, 1970; 1 child, Alison. BS, U. Dayton, 1965; MS in Fin. Svc., Am. Coll., 1982. Cert. fin. planner, chartered fin. cons. With John E. Sestina and Co., Columbus, Ohio, 1967—. Author: Complete Guide to Professional Incorporation, 1970, Managing To Be Wealthy, 1988, 2d edit. 2000, Fee-Only Financial Planning, How to Make It Work For You, 1991, 2d edit. 2000; (video tape series) Managing To Be Wealthy (4 series), 1987; contbr. articles to profl. jours.; contbr. weekly fin. planning segment AM Columbus, WOSU-AM, 1979—. Named one of Nation's 200 Best Fin. Advisors of 1996-98, Worth Mag. Mem. Soc. Ind. Fin. Advisors (past pres., Fin. Planner of Yr. award 1982), Internat. Assn. Fin. Planners, Nat. Assn. Personal Fin. Advisors (founder, pres.), Inst. Cert. Fin. Planners, Fin. Planning Clubs Internat. (founder). Office: 1161 Bethel Rd Ste 201 Columbus OH 43220-2606 Office Phone: 614-326-3077. Business E-Mail: jsestina@sestina.com.

SESTRIC, ANTHONY JAMES, lawyer; b. St. Louis, June 27, 1940; s. Anton and Marie (Gasparovic) Sestric; m. Carol F. Bowman, Nov. 24, 1966; children: Laura Antonette, Holly Nicole, Michael Anthony. Student, Georgetown U., Washington, DC, 1958-62; JD, Mo. U., 1965. Bar: Mo. 1965, Minn. 1996, US Ct. Appeals (8th cir.) 1965, US Ct. Appeals (7th cir.) 1984, US Dist. Ct. Mo. 1966, US Dist. Ct. (no dist.) Tex. 1985, US Dist. Ct. Ill. 1994, US Tax Ct. 1969, US Supreme Ct. 1970, US Claims Ct. 1986. Law clk. US Dist. Ct., St. Louis, 1965-66; ptnr. Sestric, McGhee & Miller, St. Louis, 1966-77, Fordyce and Mayne, 1977-78, Sestric & Garvey, 1978-96, Sestric Law Firm, St. Louis, 1996—. Spl. asst. to Mo. atty. gen., St. Louis, 1968; spl. asst. cir. atty., 2001—08; mem. Fed. Jud. Selection Commn., 1993, US Jud. Selection Commn., 1993—94, US Magistrate Merit Selection Commn., 2005; gen. chmn. 22d jud. cir. bar com., 1995; mem. Region XI Disciplinary Com., 2001—, gen. chmn., 2008. Contbr. articles to profl. jours. Hearing officer St. Louis Met. Police Dept.; active St. Louis Air Pollution Bd. Appeals and Varience Rev., 1966-73, chmn., 1968-73; active St. Louis Airport Commn., 1975-76; dist. vice-chmn. Boy Scouts Am., 1970-76; bd. dirs. Full Achievement, Inc., 1970-77, Legal Aid Soc. St. Louis, 1976-77, Law Libr. Assn. St. Louis, 1976-78, Thomas Dunn Memls., 1995-98, Marquette Learning Ctr., 1995-98; v.p. bd. St. Elizabeth Acad., 1985-86 Mem. ABA (state chmn. judiciary com. 1973-75, cir. chmn. com. condemnation, zoning and property use 1975-77, standing com. bar activities 1982-88), Nat. Conf. Bar Pres.'s (exec. coun. 1987-90), Mo. Bar Assn. (vice-chmn. young lawyers sect. 1973-76, bd. govs. 1974-77, chmn. law practice mgmt. com. 1997-99), Bar Assn. Met. St. Louis (chmn. young lawyers sect. 1974-75, exec. com. 1974-83, 94-95, pres. 1981-82, bd. govs. 1995-98, chmn. survey com. 1999). Home: 3967 Holly Hills Blvd Saint Louis MO 63116-3135 Office Phone: 314-351-2512.

SETFORD, DAVID F., museum director; BA with honors, Leicester U., Eng., 1979; MA, U. Manchester, 1980. Chief curator Norton Mus. Art, West Palm Beach, Fla., 1990—99; founder, dir. ArtReach Internat., 1999; dir. Palm Beach! America's Internat. Fine Art & Antique Fair; dir. curatorial affairs Naples Mus. Art, Fla., 2005—08; dir. Hyde Collection, Glens Falls, NY, 2008—. Mem.: Eng. Museums Assn. (assoc.). Office: Hyde Collection 161 Warren St Glens Falls NY 12801 Office Phone: 518-792-1761 ext. 19. Office Fax: 518-792-9197. E-mail: dsetford@hydecollection.org.

SETHI, ARJINDER P. S., program director; s. Gurcharan Singh Bakshi and Santosh Sethi; m. Harneet Bhatti, Mar. 20, 1988; children: Mansha, Anshuman. MBBS, U. Delhi, 1986, MD, 1991. Lic. internal medicine Scranton-Temple Residency Program, 2005. Gen. duty med. officer Hindu Rao Hosp., Delhi, 1991—92; cons. physician Healing Touch Med. Ctr., Delhi, 1992—2002; emergency rm. physician Marian Cmty. Hosp., Carbondale, Pa., 2005—06; assoc. program dir. Scranton-Temple Residency Program, Pa., 2005—; hospitalist Moses Taylor Hosp., Scranton, 2006—07. Organizer health screening camps, free vaccination camps & blood donation camps Indian Med. Assn., Delhi, 1993—2002. Recipient Cert. Merit award, Ministry Edn. & Culture, Govt. India, 1982, First prize in dramatics, Maulana Azad Med. Coll. Cultural Soc., 1983, Best Cmty. Svcs. award, Indian Med. Assn., 1996, Pres. Appreciation award, 1997, Golden Stethoscope award, Moses-Taylor Hosp., 2005, Resident's Tchg. award, 2007; grantee Nat. Talent Search Exam. scholarship & Cert. Merit award, Nat. Coun. Edn., Rsch. & Tng., Govt. India, 1991. Fellow: Am. Coll. Physicians; mem.: ACP, Pa. Med. Soc., Indian Med. Assn. Acad. Med. Specialties (life), Assn. Physicians India (life), Indian Med. Assn. (life), Assn. Program Dirs. Internal Medicine. Achievements include development of a new medical college in Norteastern Pennsylvania called The Commonwealth Medical College; a new competency-based curriculum for Scranton-Temple residency program per accreditation council of graduate medical education requirements; house staff portfolio for Scranton-Temple residency program per accreditation council of graduate medical education requirements. Office: Scranton-Temple Residency Program 746 Jefferson Ave Scranton PA 18510

SETHI, RAJAT, cardiologist, educator; b. New Delhi, Sept. 2, 1964; arrived in US, 2005; s. Prabhu Dayal Sethi; m. Manjit Dhalla, Aug. 25, 1990; children: Vishal, Akshay. Pharm D, U. Delhi, India, 1985, MSc, 1987; PhD, U. Man., Winnipeg, Canada, 1994. Registered pharmacist Delhi. Asst. rsch. officer NRC, Canada, 1994—96; dir. preclin. rsch. Medicure Inc., Canada, 1996—2000; sr. scientist U. Manitoba, Canada, 2000—05; mem. faculty Tex. A&M Health Sci. Ctr., Irma Lerma Rangel Coll. Pharmacy, Kingsville, 2005—. Co-author: book; contbr. chapters to books, more than 150 articles to profl. jours. Recipient Best Rsch. Trainee award, Heart and Stroke Found. Can., 1991—92, Prize for excellence in rsch., Man. Med. Svc. Found., 1993; scholar, U. Delhi, 1985—87, Man. Health Rsch. Coun., 1990—91, Heart and Stroke Found. Can., 1990—94; Rsch. Ctr. scholar, St. Boniface Gen. Hosp., 1989—90. Mem.: Can. Pharmacy Assn., Internat. Soc. Heart Rsch., Am. Assn. Colls. of Pharmacy. Achievements include beneficial effect of distiller's grain in cardiovascular disease; treatment of cardiovascular and related pathologies; adenine based inhibitors of adenylyl cyclase. pharmaceutical compositions and other methods of use; treatment of cerebrovascular disease; treatment of cardiovascular and related pathologies; treatment of diabetes and related pathologies; treatment of iatronic and age-related hypertension and pharmaceutical compositions. Office: Tex A&M Health Sci Ctr Irma Lerma Rangel Coll Pharmacy MSC 131 Kingsville TX 78363 Business E-Mail: rsethi@pharmacy.tamhsc.edu.

SETHI, SHYAM SUNDER, management consultant; b. Rawalpindi, Pakistan, July 11, 1942; s. Balraj and Shakuntala (Sawhney) Sethi; m. Kiran Nair, Oct. 17, 1972; children: Seema, Shana. B.E. in Mech. Engring., Birla Inst. Tech., Ranchi, India, 1964; MSI.E., U. Wis., 1970. Cert. mgmt. cons. V.p. Drake Sheahan/Stewart Dougall, NYC, 1970-80; pres., ptnr. Distbn. Mgmt. Assocs., Inc., Princeton, NJ, 1980-96; exec. dir. Dechert-Hampe & Co./DMA, 1996-2000; pres. Distbn. Mgmt. Assocs., Inc., 2001—. Cons. in supply chain, logistics, inventory mgmt., ops. for maj. consumer goods, indsl. and retail cos., Europe, S.Am. and US; spkr. internat. logistics conf. Contbr. articles to profl. jours. Pres. NJ chpt. Coun. Logistics Mgmt., 1987-88, NJ chpt. Inst. Mgmt. Consultants, 1987-88. Mem. Yacht Assn. India. Hindu. Avocations: tennis, sailing. Home: 4 Haelig Ct Bridgewater NJ 08807-2377 Office: DMA Inc PO Box 6843 Bridgewater NJ 08807-0843 Office Phone: 732-469-1885. Personal E-mail: sethinj@optonline.net.

SETHI, YASH PAL, radiologist, consultant; MBBS, U. Delhi, India, 1987, MD, 1992. Diplomate Am. Bd. Radiology, 2001. Resident physician internal medicine SUNY Health Sci. Ctr., Bklyn., 1995—96; resident radiology Wayne State U. Med. Ctr., Detroit, 1996—98; radiology resident and chief resident St. Vincents Cath. Med. Ctr., NY, 1998—2000; clin. instr. imaging fellow U. Mo., Columbia, 2000—01, asst. prof., 2001—; staff radiologist Harry S Truman VA Med. Ctr., Columbia, 2001—04. Dir., residency program U. Mo., Columbia, Mo., 2006—, dir. med. students radiology curriculum, 2002—06, dir., MRI fellowship Hosp. and clin. radiology dept., 2005—. Contbr. scientific papers in field. Recipient Physician Recognition, 2001, Order of Socrates award, 2005, Svc. Quality Hero, U. Mo., 2002, 2004; named Tchr. of Year, 2002, 2003, 2004. Mem.: AMA, Mo. State Radiol. Soc. (bd. dirs. 2005—), Assn. Program Dirs., Assn. U. Radiologists, N Am. (Marconi Phillips Aur award Faculty Devel. 2004), Mo. State Med. Assn., Clin. Magnetic Resonance Soc., N.am., Am. Roentgen Ray Soc., Am. Coll. Radiology, Radiol. Soc. N. Am., Soc. Gastrointestinal Endoscopists (life). Office: Univ Missouri Hosp One Hospital Dr Columbia MO 65212

SETHNA, BEHERUZ NARIMAN, academic administrator, educator, management consultant; b. Bombay, July 31, 1948; came to U.S., 1973; s. Nariman Dhanjishaw and Mithu Nariman (Mistry) S.; m. Madhavi Kaji, May 25, 1974; children: Anita B., Shaun B. B in Tech. with honors, Indian Inst. Tech., Bombay, 1971; MBA, Indian Inst. Mgmt., Ahmedabad, 1973; MPhil, Columbia U., 1975, PhD in Bus., 1976; student, Ind. U., 1986, Harvard U., 1991. Cert. computing profl. Inst. for Cert. Computing Profls. Engring. and mgmt. trainee various corps., Bombay, 1968-69, 70-72; case writer, trainee Clarion Advt., Bombay, 1973; project mgr., cons. Lever Bros. Co., NYC, 1974-76; prof., chair mktg. and mgmt. info. systems Clarkson U., Potsdam, NY, 1976-89, dir. grad. programs, 1978-80; mktg., rsch. and strategic planning mgr. Procter & Gamble (India)/Richardson Hindustan (Vicks), Bombay and Westport, Conn., 1980-81; interim exec. v.p. acad. and student affairs; dean Coll. of Bus., chief acad. officer Lamar (Tex.) U., 1989-94, Gulf States Utilities prof. bus., 1991-94; pres. West Ga. Coll., Carrollton, 1994—96, State U. West Ga., 1996—2005, U. West Ga., 2005—; interim sr. vice chancellor Univ. Sys. Ga., 1999—2000, interim exec. vice chancellor, chief acad. officer, 2006—07; pres. Ga. Assn. Colls., Carrollton, 2000—01, Gulf South Conf., 2008—; chair Atlanta Regional Coun. Higher Edn., 2008—, vice chair, 2008—. Mem. adv. coun. SUNY-Canton (N.Y.) Coll., 1975-89; cons. in field. Author: Research Methods in Marketing, 1984; contbr. articles to profl. jours. Scoutmaster Boy Scouts Am., Potsdam, 1987—89, pack com. chair, den leader, 1987—89, mem. dist. bd., 1991—94, mem. exec. bd. Atlanta Area coun., 1997—2003, Pres.'s Scout, Gold Cord, 1966; leader Girl Scouts U.S., Beaumont, 1989—94. Recipient Minority Achiever's award, Role Model award, 1991, Dean's Leadership award, Acad. Bus. Adminstrn., 1993, Nat. Svc. award, 1996, Alumnus award (hon.), 1999, Disting. Alumnus award, Indian Inst. Tech., Bombay, 2000, Carroll County Citizen of Yr., 1999, rated 1st among Carroll County's Movers, Shakers and Newsmakers, 2002, Resolution of Commendation, State Senate, 2003, Instructional Innovation award (hon.), 1984—89, 2004, Cornerstone award, Bd. Regent, 2007, Empowerment award, Ctr. Student Leadership, 2007; named one of 100 Most Influential Georgians, Ga. Trend, 2003, 2006, 2009; grantee, US Dept. Energy, 1980, IBM Corp., 1984, AT&T, 1985; Fulbright scholar, U.S. Info. Agy., 1986—87, Paul Harris fellow, Rotary Internat., 1997. Mem. Rotary (polio plus edn. chair). Avocation: scouting. Home: 107 Windsong Ct Carrollton GA 30117-8978 Office: U W Ga Office Pres Carrollton GA 30118-0001 Office Phone: 678-839-6442. Business E-Mail: bsethna@westga.edu.

SETHNA, JAMES PATARASP, physicist; b. Ann Arbor, Mich., Aug. 23, 1955; s. Patarasp Rustomji and Shirley Sue (Smith) S.; m. Carol Margaret Devine, Apr. 1, 1989. BA in Physics, Harvard U., 1977; M in Physics, Princeton U., 1978, PhD in Physics, 1981. Postdoctoral fellow Inst. Theoretical Physics U. Calif., Santa Barbara, 1981-82, 83-84; postdoctoral fellow Lab. Atomic and Solid-State Physics Lab. Atomic and Solid-State Physics, Cornell U., Ithaca, N.Y., 1982-83, asst. prof., 1984-89, assoc. prof., 1989-95, prof., 1995—. Recipient Sloan Rsch. fellow Sloan Found., 1985, Presdl. Young Investigator award NSF, 1985. Achievements include research in Barkhausennoise in magnets using a critical point in the shape of the hysteresis loop; onset of chaos from quasiperiodic motion; elastic theory has zero radius of convergence using thermodynamics of cracks; modeled the cholesteric blue phase of liquid crystals as a network of disclination lines. Office: Cornell Univ Lab Atomic and Solid State Physics Clark Hall Ithaca NY 14853

SETIA, PANKAJ, management educator; s. T. C. and Usha Setia. PhD, Mich. State U., East Lansing, 2008. Cert. java2 profl. Sun Microsys., 2000, in object oriented programming using C++ Computer Soc. India, 2000, in artificial intelligence and software engring. Ministry of IT, Govt. of India, 2001. Bus. exec. Tata Telesvcs. Ltd., New Delhi, 2001—03; asst. prof. U. Ark., Fayetteville, 2008—. Editl. asst. Info. Sys. Rsch., E Lansing, Mich., 2004—08. Contbr. articles to profl. jours. Reviewer. Recipient Student Excellence Rsch. award, Acctg. & Info. Sys. Dept., Eli Bd. Coll. Mgmt., Mich. State U., 2007, Chan Hahn Best Paper Finalist award, Acad. Mgmt. Conf., 2007; Fellowship, Ctr. Leadership Digital Enterprise. Mem.: INFORMS Soc., Prodn. & Ops. Mgmt. Soc., Assn. Info. Sys. Office: Univ Ark 224 Bus Bldg Fayetteville AR 72701 Office Phone: 479-575-5653. Business E-Mail: psetia@uark.edu.

SETLOW, JANE KELLOCK, biophysicist; b. NYC, Dec. 17, 1919; d. Harold A. and Alberta (Thompson) Kellock; m. Richard Setlow, June 6, 1941; children: Peter, Michael, Katherine, Charles. BA, Swarthmore Coll., 1940; PhD in Biophysics, Yale U., 1959. With dept. radiology Yale U., 1959-60; with biology div. Oak Ridge Nat. Lab., 1960-74; biophysicist Brookhaven Nat. Lab., Upton, N.Y., 1974—. Mem. recombinant DNA molecule program adv. com. NIH, chmn., 1978-2005. Editor: Genetic Engineering, Principles and Methods; mem. editl. bd. various jours.:; contbr. articles to profl. jours. Predoctoral fellow USPHS, 1957-59; postdoctoral fellow, 1960-62 Mem. Biophys. Soc. (pres. 1977-78), Am. Soc. Microbiology. Democrat. Home: 57 Valentine Rd Shoreham NY 11786-1243 Office: Biology Dept Brookhaven Nat Lab Upton NY 11973 Office Phone: 631-344-3420.

SETLOW, RICHARD BURTON, biophysicist, researcher; b. NYC, Jan. 19, 1921; s. Charles Meyer and Elsie Setlow; children: Peter, Michael, Katherine, Charles; m. Neva Delihas, Mar. 3, 1989. AB, Swarthmore Coll., 1941; PhD, Yale U., 1947; DSc, U. Toronto, 1985; MD, U. Essen, 1993. Assoc. prof. Yale U., 1956-61; biophysicist Oak Ridge (Tenn.) Nat. Lab., 1961-74, sci. dir. biophysics and cell physiology, 1969-74; dir. U. Tenn.-Oak Ridge Grad. Sch. Biomed. Scis., 1972-74; sr. biophysicist Brookhaven Nat. Lab., Upton, NY, 1974—2006, chmn. biology dept., 1979-87, assoc. dir. life scis., 1985-98, assoc. lab. dir., 1998, sr. biophysicist emeritus, 2007—. Prof. biomed. scis. U. Tenn., 1967-74; adj. prof. biochemistry SUNY, Stony Brook, 1975—. Author: (with E.C. Pollard) Molecular Biophysics, 1962; editor: (with P.C. Hanawalt) Molecular Mechanisms for Repair of DNA, 1975; contr. books to chap. Recipient Finsen medal Internat. Assn. Photobiology, 1980, Enrico Fermi award U.S. Dept. Energy, 1988, Environ. Mutagen Soc. award, 2002. Mem. NAS, Am. Acad. Arts and Scis., Biophys. Soc. (pres. 1969-70), Internat. Com. Photobiology (pres. 1972-76), Radiation Rsch. Soc., Am. Soc. Photobiology, Am. Assn. Biochemistry and Molecular Biology, Am. Soc. Cancer Rsch., Environ. Mutagen Soc., 11th Internat. Congress on Photobiology (hon. pres. 1992), Phi Beta Kappa. Home: 4 Beachland Ave East Quogue NY 11942-4941 Office: Brookhaven Nat Lab Dept Biology Upton NY 11973 Home Phone: 631-728-3391; Office Phone: 631-728-5136. Personal E-mail: setlow@optonline.net. Business E-Mail: setlow@bnl.gov.

SETO, THEODORE PAUL, lawyer, educator; b. Kermanshah, Iran, Feb. 18, 1951; came to U.S., 1951; s. Paul Susumu and Genevieve (Reynolds) S.; m. Lenore T. Rothman, Aug. 2, 1980 (div. 1999); 1 child, Kira Rothman Seto; m. Sande Lynn Buhai, July 8, 2000; children: Samantha Elizabeth, Genevieve Danielle. BA, Harvard U., 1973, JD, 1976. Bar: Mass. 1977, U.S. Dist. Ct. Mass. 1978, U.S. Dist. Ct. (ea. dist.) Pa. 1983, U.S. Tax Ct. 1985, U.S. Ct. Appeals (1st cir.) 1983, U.S. Ct. Appeals (3d cir.) 1990, U.S. Supreme Ct. 1983, U.S. Claims Ct. 1990. Law clk. to Hon. Judge Mansfield U.S. Ct. Appeals (2nd cir.), NYC, 1976-77; assoc. Foley, Hoag & Eliot, Boston, 1977-83, Drinker Biddle & Reath, Phila., 1983-86, ptnr., 1986-91; assoc. prof. Loyola Law Sch., LA, 1991-97, prof., 1997—. Vis. prof. U. Paris X, 1998, Cornell Law Sch., 2005; mem. Tax Adv. Com., 2008. Author: A Uniform System of Citation, 12th edit. 1976; contbr. articles to profl. jours. Democrat. Office: Loyola Law Sch 919 Albany St Los Angeles CA 90015-1211 Home Phone: 323-255-6195; Office Phone: 213-736-1154. Business E-Mail: tseto@lls.edu.

SETRAKIAN, BERGE, lawyer; b. Beirut, Apr. 14, 1949; came to U.S. 1976; s. Hemayak and Arminee S.; m. Vera L. Nazarian, Nov. 22, 1975; children: Ani, Lara. Diplome d'Etudes de Doctorat, U. Lyons, France, 1973; Diplome d'Etudes de Doctorat Droit Compare, F.I.E.D.C., Strasbourg, France, 1974; Licence en Droit Francais, U. St. Joseph, Beirut, 1972, Licence en Droit Libanais, 1972. Bar: Beirut 1972, N.Y. 1983. Assoc. Tyan & Setrakian, Beirut, 1972-76; ptnr. Whitman & Ransom, NYC, 1976-93, Whitman, Breed, Abbott & Morgan, NYC, 1993-2000, Winston & Strawn, NYC, 2000—05, LeBoeuf, Lamb, Greene & MacRae, 2005—07; Dewey and LeBeuf, 2007—. Bd. dirs. Cedars Bank, Calif., 1987—2005, Interaudi Bank, NY, 1991, Altadis SA, Imperial Tobacco Plc, 2008—. Pres. Armenian Gen. Benevolent Union, N.Y.C., 2002-; bd. dirs. Armenian Assn. of Am., Washington, 1978-87; bd. dirs. Am. Task Force for Lebanon, 1988—; bd. dirs. Am. U. Armenia, 1992—. Mem. ABA, N.Y. Bar Assn., Beirut Bar Assn., Am. Fgn. Law Assn., Englewood Field Club. Office: Dewey & Leboeuf LLP 1301 Ave Americans New York NY 10019 Office Phone: 212-259-8399.

SETSER, CAROLE SUE, food scientist, educator; b. Warrenton, Mo., Aug. 26, 1940; d. Wesley August and Mary Elizabeth (Meine) Schulze; m. Donald Wayne Setser, June 2, 1969; children: Bradley Wayne, Kirk Wesley, Brett Donald. BS, U. Mo., 1962; MS, Cornell U., 1964; PhD, Kans. State U., 1971. Grad. asst. Cornell U., Ithaca, NY, 1962-64; instr. Kans. State U., Manhattan, 1964-72, asst. prof., 1974-81, assoc. prof., 1981-86, prof., 1986-2001, prof. emeritus, 2001—. Vis. prof. Bogazici U., Istanbul, Turkey, 2000—01. Recipient Rsch. Excellence award, Coll. of Human Ecology, Manhattan, 1990. Mem.: Inst. Food Techs. (chmn. sensory evaluation divsn. edn. com. 1989—92, continuing edn. com. 1992—95, sec. product devel. divsn. 1997—99, also other offices), Am. Assn. Cereal Chemists (assoc. editor 1989—93), Kappa Omicron Nu (Excellence for Rsch. award 1987), Sigma Xi, Phi Tau Sigma (Outstanding Food Scientist 1998), Gamma Sigma Delta, Phi Upsilon Omicron, Phi Kappa Phi (Scholar award 1998). Home Phone: 785-537-9449. Business E-Mail: setser@ksu.edu.

SETSER, CHRISTIE ELAINE, auditor; d. James David and Helen Emma Setser; m. Norman Bodenstein (div.). BA in History, Pittsburg State U., Kans., 1977, MS in Sociology, 1979. Social worker Mo. Dept. Social Svcs., St. Louis, 1979—97; tax auditor Mo. Dept. Labor, St. Louis, 1999—. Adj. prof. Columbia Coll., Mo., 1980. Mem.: Internat. Assn. Workforce Profls. (zone sec. 2000—), Mensa, Daus. Union Vets. (past state pres.). Avocations: reading, writing, genealogy, mathematics. Office: Mo Dept Labor 505 Washington Ave Saint Louis MO 63101

SETSER, DONALD WAYNE, chemistry professor; b. Great Bend, Kans., Jan. 2, 1935; s. Leo Wayne and Velma Irene (Hewitt) S.; m. Carole Sue Schulze, June 2, 1969; children: Bradley Wayne, Kirk Wesley, Brett Donald. BS, Kans. State U., 1956, MS, 1958; PhD, U. Wash., 1961. Asst. prof. Kans. State U., Manhattan, 1963-66, assoc. prof., 1966-68, prof. chemistry, 1968-2000, Alumni Disting. prof. chemistry, 1984-2000, prof. emeritus, 2000—. Vis. prof. U. Grenoble, France, 1981, 84, 87, 91, Bogazici U., Turkey, 2000. Editor Reactive Intermediates, 1976; contbr. more than 300 articles to profl. jours. Recipient Rank prize electro-optics divsn., 1992. Fellow Am. Phys. Soc.; mem. Am. Chem. Soc. (Midwest award St. Louis sect. 1984). Home: 414 Wickham Rd Manhattan KS 66502-3751 Office: Kans State U Dept Of Chemistry Manhattan KS 66506 Home Phone: 785-537-9449; Office Phone: 785-532-6665. Business E-Mail: setserdw@ksu.edu.

SETSER, PATRICIA A., music educator; b. Kansas City, Mo., June 29, 1951; d. Flo Daulton and George Sterling Waugh; m. Michael W. Setser, Sept. 9, 1972. MusB Edn., Ctrl. Mo. State U., 1973, MA in Music Edn., 1978. Cert. tchr., life - music coord. K-12, history K-8 Mo., 1973. Coord. music North Kansas City Sch. Dist., 1996—; band dir. Winnetonka HS, Kansas City, 1983—. Guest condr., adjudicator Heart of Am. Wind Symphony, Mo., 1978—, musician, Mo., 2001—; musician, guest conductor Kansas City Wind Symphony, Shawnee Mission, Kans., 2002—. Condr. (music contest) St. Louis Music Festival (Grand Champions, 2001, 2005), Nat. Adjudicators Nat. Festival, Va. (Grand Champions, 2002), Chgo. Music Festival (Grand Champions, 2000); instr. (tchg.) Tchg. (Excellence in Tchg. Award, 1994); condr. (orch. condr.) State Contest (First Pl. Ratings), band condr. (conducting) State Music Contests (First Pl. Ratings - all years); composer: (entry level jazz for young band students) Musical composition. Bd. mem. Warrensburg Cmty. Band, Mo., 2001—. Named Disting. Music Alumnus, Ctrl. Mo. State U., 2005—06. Mem.: Mo. Music Educators Assn. (assoc.), Music Educators Nat. Conf. (assoc.), Am. Quarter Horse Assn. (assoc.), Epsilon Omega - Sigma Alpha Iota (assoc.; pres., v.p, sec. 1970—73, Sword of Honor - Leadership 1974). Avocations: antique automobiles, gardening, genealogy. Office: North Kansas City Sch Dist 1950 NE 46th St Kansas City MO 64116 E-mail: psetser@nkcsd.k12.mo.us.

SETTERHOLM, JEFFREY MILES, systems engineer; b. Rochester, NY, May 8, 1946; s. Vernon Miles and Grace Lorraine (Bogema) S.; m. Donna Jean Stollenwerk, July 6, 1974; children: Gregory Todd, Vincent Michael. BS in Engring., Applied Sci. cum laude, Yale U., 1968; MS in Sys. Sci. and Math., Washington U., 1976. Electronic engr. McDonnell Douglas Aircraft Divsn., St. Louis, 1974, sr. engr. flight simulation, 1976-78; prin. devel. engr. mil. avionics divsn. Honeywell Inc., Mpls., 1978-84; prin. engr. aerospace divsn. Rosemount, Inc., Burnsville, Minn., 1984-92; ind. software tech. cons. Lakeville, Minn., 1992-94; geodetic scientist Geospan Corp., Maple Grove, Minn., 1994—2003, contract engr., 2006—09, Alliant Techsys., Plymouth, Minn., 2005—06. Author: The Philosophy Works Manual, 1993, Learning Together in a Diverse World, 2004. Capt. USAF, 1969-73. Decorated DFC. Mem. AIAA, Soc. Automotive Engrs. Lutheran. Achievements include patents in field; origination of the computer configurable six-axis hand controller concept; invention of surveying from non-coplanar images; research in virtual cockpit concepts. Home: 8095 230th St E Lakeville MN 55044-8287 Personal E-mail: jeff@setterholm.com.

SETTERLUND, TINA A.M., music educator; b. Belleville, Ill., Mar. 3, 1955; d. William L. and Elizabeth A. Marietta; m. D. Phillip Setterlund, Dec. 29, 1973 (div.); children: Reid, Lauren; m. Grady A. White, Dec. 21, 1992. AA, Belleville Area Coll., 1987; B in Music Edn., So. Ill. U., 1989. Music dir. St. John U.C.C., Mascoutah, Ill., 1971—; tchr. High Mt. Sch., Swansea, Ill., 1989—95; dir. vocal music Belleville East HS, Ill., 1995—2005; pvt. practice vocal coach Belleville. Dir. Belleville Philharm. Chorale, 1983—91; asst. dir., accompanist Masterworks Children's Chorale, Belleville, 1990—95; dir. Metro-East Cmty. Chorale, Belleville, 1991—94, Coca-Cola Choir, St. Louis, Olympic Torch Relay Festivities; music dir. St. John's U., 1971—. Recipient Excellence in Tchg. award, So. Ill. Univ., 2003. Mem.: St. Clair County Music Dirs. Assn. (treas. 2004—05, v.p. 2005—07), Music Educators Nat. Conf., Ill. Music Educators Assn., Pi Kappa Lambda. Avocations: interior decorating, reading, gardening, harp. Home: 57 W State Mascoutah IL 62258 Personal E-mail: tamsetterlund@yahoo.com.

SETTERSTROM, JAMES ROBERT, agricultural studies educator; b. Rockford, Ill., July 4, 1950; s. Robert and Carolyn Setterstrom; m. Dianna Kay Barker, Aug. 22, 1970; children: Scott, Brian, Carl. BS, U. Wis., Platteville, 1973. Vo- ag instr. Lena Winslow HS, Ill., 1973—76; agr. instr. Highland CC, Freeport, Ill., 1983—. Twp. supr. Oneco Twp., Orangeville, Ill., 2005—08; mem. Pk. Hills Evang. Free Ch., Freeport, 1996—2008; dir. Conservation Agr. Partners, Freeport, Ill., 2000—08, Stephenson Co. 4-H Found., Freeport, Ill., 2004—08; mem. Stephenson Co. Farm Bur., Freeport, 2000—08. Recipient Faculty Excellence award, Highland CC, 1997—98. Master: Orangeville Lodge 687 (Lodge Builder award 2002, 2005). Office: Highland CC 2998 W Pearl City Rd Freeport IL 61032 Business E-Mail: jim.setterstrom@highland.edu.

SETTLE, BENJAMIN HALE, federal judge; b. Olympia, Wash., 1947; BA, Claremont McKenna Coll., 1969; JD, Willamette U. Coll. Law, 1972. Bar: Washington 1972. Assoc. Don Miles Attorneys, 1972; judge adv., gen. corps US Army, 1973—76; assoc. Don Miles Attorneys, 1976—77; ptnr. Settle & Johnson, P.L.L.C., 1977—2007; judge US Dist. Ct. (we. dist.), Wash., 2007—. Capt., active duty USAR, 1973—76. Office: US Courthouse 1717 Pacific Ave Tacoma WA 98402-3234 Office Phone: 253-882-3850.

SETTLE, MARK, information technology executive; BS Earth and Planetary Sci., MS Earth and Planetary Sci., MIT; PhD Geol. Sci., Brown U. CIO Occidental Petroleum, 1997—99; exec. v.p., systems and processing Visa Internat., 1999—2001; v.p., CIO Arrow Electronics, Inc., Melville, NY, 2001—. Retired USAF. Office: Arrow Electronics Inc 50 Marcus Dr Melville NY 11747-4210

SETTLES, F. STAN, JR., engineering educator, manufacturing executive; b. Denver, Oct. 3, 1938; s. Frank S. and Dorothy Marie (Johnson) S.; m. Evelyn Brown, June 10, 1961; children: Frank S. III, Richard, Charles, Michael. BS in Prodn. Tech., Indsl. Engring., LeTourneau Coll., Longview, Tex., 1962; MS in Indsl. Engring., Ariz. State U., Tempe, 1967, PhD in Indsl. Engring., 1969. Sr. systems analyst AiResearch Mfg. Co., Phoenix, 1968-70, project mgr., 1970-74, mgr. operational planning, 1974-80; mgr. indsl. engrs. Garrett Pneumatic Systems, Phoenix, 1980-83; mgr. indsl. mfg. engring. Garrett Turbine Engring. Co., Phoenix, 1983-85; v.p. mfg. ops. AiResearch Mfg. Co., Torrance, Calif., 1985-87; dir. indusl. mfg. engring. The Garrett Corp., Phoenix, 1987-88; dir. planning Garrett Engine Div., Phoenix, 1988-92; asst. dir. White House Office of Sci. and Tech. Policy, 1992-93; program dir. NSF, 1992-94; prof., chmn. indsl. and systems engring. dept. U. So. Calif., LA, 1994—2003, IBM prof. engring. mgmt., dir. sys. arch. & engring. program, 2003—. Faculty assoc. Ariz. State U., Tempe, 1974-85, 90-92, rsch. prof., 1992-94. Mem. sch. bd. Tempe Elem. Sch. Dist., 1976-80; mem. YMCA Indian Guides, nat. chief, 1978-79. Fellow Inst. Indsl. Engrs. (pres. 1987-88, Ops. Rsch. award 1980), Inst. Ops. Rsch. and Mgmt. Sci., Nat. Acad. Engrs., Soc. Mfg. Engrs. (sr.), IEEE Engring. Mgmt. Soc., Am. Soc. Quality Control, Am. Soc. Engring. Edn. Republican. Presbyterian. Home: 1310 E Ocean Blvd Unit 1602 Long Beach CA 90802-6917 Office: U So Calif Dept Indsl Sys Engring Los Angeles CA 90089-0193 Office Phone: 213-740-0263. Business E-Mail: settles@usc.edu.

SETTLES, JEANNE DOBSON, retired librarian; b. Covington, Tenn., Nov. 21, 1928; d. Garrett Edward and Lula Mai (Birmingham) Dobson; m. Andrew Settles, Dec. 26, 1948; children: Thomas E., Anthony Dobson. BS, Memphis State U., 1966, MEd, 1977. Cert. tchr., Tenn. Libr. Memphis City Schs., 1966—72, 1977—91; ret., 1991. Mem. Delta Kappa Gamma (treas.). Avocations: painting, writing, sewing, travel.

SETZLER, MARK H., political science professor; s. James David and Susan Audrey Setzler; m. Heather Nicole Jones, 1993; children: Hunter Thomas, Austin Phillip. PhD, U. Tex., Austin, 2000. Legis. corr. US Congress, Washington, 1993; tchg. fellow U. Tex., 1993—97; instr. polit. sci. U. Portland, Oreg., 1999—2001; asst. prof. polit. sci. Lewis and Clark Coll., Portland, 2001—02, High Point U., NC, 2004—, dept. chair, 2007—. Contbr. articles to profl. jour. (Best Article of Yr., 2000). Named Tchr. of Yr., U. Portland, 2001. Office: High Point Univ 883 Montlieu Ave High Point NC 26272

SETZLER, WILLIAM EDWARD, retired chemicals executive; b. Bklyn., Dec. 20, 1926; s. William Edward and Gertrude A. (Seyer) S.; m. Dorothy C. Kress, Dec. 2, 1950 (dec. Mar. 1987); children: William John, Heather A.; m. Lenore Kelly, July 13, 1991. B of Chem. Engring., Cooper Union, 1950; MS in Liberal Studies, Columbia U., 1993. V.p. ops. Argus Chem. Corp., NYC, 1950-66; v.p. engring., then group v.p. Witco Chem. Corp. (now Crompton Corp.), NYC, 1966-75, exec. v.p., 1975-90, ret., 1990, also bd. dirs.; chmn. and CEO Faimount Chem. Inc., 1993-97. Author and patentee in field. Served with USAAF, 1945-46. Mem. Am. Inst. Chem. Engrs., Soap and Detergent Assn. (bd. dirs.), The Dorothy Setzler Fund (pres. 1991—). Home: 3921 Lincoln St Seaford NY 11783-2115 Home Phone: 516-785-8948. Personal E-mail: billchair@att.net.

SEUM, JACK F., legislative staff member; b. Chgo., June 2, 1946; m. Carol S. Thompson, 1977; 2 children. BA, Southern Ill. U., 1969; MPA, George Washington U., 1984. Campaign aide for Senator Charles Percy US Senate, Washington, 1972; legis. asst. for Rep. Alphonzo Bell US House of Reps., 1973—74, legis. asst. for Rep. Marvin Esch, 1975—76, legis. asst. for Rep. Cooper Evans, 1981—87, adminstrv. asst. for Rep. John J. Rhodes III, 1987—93, chief of staff for Rep. Clifford B. Stearns, 1993—; advance worker Percy Exploratory Com., 1974—75; Washington dir. Nat. Field Rsch. Ctr., 1976—80. With US Army, 1969, 1st lt., 1972. Office: Office of Congressman Clifford B Stearns 2370 Rayburn House Office Bldg Washington DC 20515 Office Phone: 202-225-5744. Business E-Mail: jack.seum@mail.house.gov.*

SEVART, DANIEL JOSEPH, lawyer; b. Oswego, Kans., June 25, 1944; s. Vernon Joseph and Alma Bridget (Carland) S.; m. Shoko Kato, Apr. 17, 1968; 1 child, Eric J. AA, Parsons Jr. Coll., 1964; BA, Washburn U., 1973, JD with honors, 1975. Bar: Kans. 1976, U.S. Dist. Ct. Kans. 1976, U.S. Ct. Appeals (10th cir.) 1976. Assoc. Render & Kamas, Wichita, Kans., 1976-78, ptnr., 1978-82, Schartz & Sevart, Wichita, 1982-83, Sevart & Sevart, Wichita, 1983—. Bd. dirs. Wichita Symphony Soc., Inc., 1989—. Served to staff sgt. USAF, 1965-72. Mem. Assn. Trial Lawyers Am., Kans. Bar Assn. (bd. govs. 1995-98, 2000-01, sec.-treas. 1998-99, v.p. 2001-02, pres.-elect 2002-03, pres. 2003-04, Kans. Trial Lawyers Assn. (bd. govs. 1989—), Wichita Bar Assn. (bd. govs. 1988-90, sec.-treas. 1990-91, v.p. 1991-92, pres.-elect 1992-93, pres. 1993-94), Wichita C. of C. Democrat. Roman Catholic. Avocations: classical music, gardening, fishing, camping, travel. also: 1900 L St NW Ste 500 Washington DC 20036-5031

SEVCENKO, IHOR, history and literature professor; b. Radosc, Poland, Feb. 10, 1922; came to U.S., 1949, naturalized, 1957; s. Ivan and Maria (Cherniatynska) S.; m. Oksana Draj-Xmara, Apr., 1945 (div. 1953); m. Margaret M. Bentley, July 16, 1953 (div. 1966); m. Nancy Patterson, June 18, 1966 (div. 1995); children: Catherine, Elisabeth. Dr.Phil., Charles U., Prague, 1945; Doct. en Phil. et Lettres, U. Louvain, Belgium, 1949; PhD (hon.), U. Cologne, Germany, 1994; D in Hist. Scis. (hon.), U. Warsaw, Poland, 2001; D in Liberal Arts (hon.), Cath. U., Lublin, Poland, 2005. Fellow in Byzantinology Dumbarton Oaks, 1949-50, dir. studies, 1966, prof. Byzantine history and lit., 1965-75, sr. research assoc., 1975—; lectr. Byzantine and ancient history U. Calif., Berkeley, 1950-51; fellow Byzantinology and Slavic lit., research program USSR, 1951-52; instr., then asst. prof. Slavic langs. and lit. U. Mich., 1953-57; mem. faculty Columbia U., 1957-72, prof., 1962-65, adj. prof., 1965-72; vis. prof. Harvard U., 1973-74, prof., 1974-92, emeritus, 1992. Vis. fellow All Souls Coll., Oxford U., 1979—80, Wolfson Coll., Oxford U., 1987, 93, Onassis Found., Athens, 2002; vis. mem. Princeton Inst. for Advanced Study, 1956; vis. prof. Munich U., 1969, Coll. de France, 1985, Cologne U., 1992, 96, Ctrl. European U., Budapest, 1995, 97; treas., acting treas., bd. dirs. Am. Rsch. Inst. in Turkey, 1964—66, 1967, 1975—; assoc. dir. Harvard Ukrainian Rsch. Inst., 1973—89, acting dir., 1977, 1985—86; chmn. US Nat. Com. Byzantine Studies, 1966—77; mem. Internat. Com. for Greek Paleography, 1983—; hon. pres. Byzantine studies Ukrainian Nat. Com., 1993—; guest of the rector Collegium Budapest, 1998. Author: Etudes sur la polémique entre Théodore Métochite et Nicéphore Choumnos, 1962, Society and Intellectual Life in Late Byzantium, 1981, Ideology, Letters and Culture in the Byzantine World, 1982, Byzantium and the Slavs in Letters and Culture, 1991, Ukraine Between East and West, 1996; co-author: Der Serbische Psalter, 1978, Life of St. Nicholas of Sion, 1984; contbr. articles to profl. jours. Recipient Hruševs'kyj medal, Sci. Ševcenko Soc., 1996, Antonovych Lit. prize, Kiev, 2000; Guggenheim fellow, 1963, Humboldt-Forschungspreistraeger, 1985. Fellow Mediaeval Acad. Am., Brit. Acad. (corr.); mem. Am. Philos. Soc., Am. Acad. Arts and Scis., Ukrainian Acad. Arts and Scis. US (hon. pres. 2003-), Sci. Sevcenko Soc., Société des Bollandistes Belgium (adj.), Accademia di Palermo (fgn.), Accademia Nazionale dei Lincei (fgn.), Internat. Assn. Byzantine Studies (v.p. 1976-86, pres. 1986-96, hon. pres. 1996—), Christian Archeol. Soc. Athens (hon.), Austrian Acad. Sci. (corr.), Accademia Pontaniana Naples (fgn.), Acad. Humanities Rsch. (Moscow), Polish Acad. Arts and Scis. (fgn.), Cosmos Club (Washington), Harvard Club (NYC), Signet Soc., Phi Beta Kappa (hon.) Office: Harvard Univ 204 Boylston Hall Cambridge MA 02138 Office Fax: 617-496-6720. Business E-Mail: sevcenko@fas.harvard.edu.

SEVENING, DIANE KAY, alcohol/drug abuse studies educator, researcher; b. Platte, SD, July 27, 1951; d. James Clayton (Stepfather) and Florence June Rommen; m. Douglas Lee Sevening, Aug. 15, 1981; children: Rodney Justin, Ryan Lee. D of edn., U. SD, 1998—99. Instr. U. SD Arts & Sciences Alcohol & Drug Abuse Studies Dept., Vermillion, 1984—89, 1989—99, asst. prof. Internat. pres. Internat. Coalition for Addiction Studies Edn. (INCASE), Vermillion, SD, 2000—02. Contbr. articles to profl. jours.; co-author: A Comparison of Traditional Teaching Methods and Problem-Based Learning in Addictions Studies Class, 2002. Sec. U. SD Student Affairs Com., 2001—03; mem. U. SD Academic Integrity Task Force, 2002—03; presenter Internat. Coalition for Addiction Studies Edn. (INCASE) Conf., Portland, Oreg., 2003, Nat. Drug and Alcohol Recovery Month, Sioux Falls, SD, 2003, Vol. Am., Sioux Falls, SD, 2003—03. Mem.: Internat. Coalition for Addiction Studies Educators (assoc.; immediate past pres. 2002—03), Gamma Sigma Delta (assoc.), Phi Delta Kappa (assoc.). Home: 602 W Dartmouth St Vermillion SD 57069 Office: Univ SD 414 E Clark St Vermillion SD 57069 Business E-Mail: dsevenin@usd.edu.

SEVER, JOHN LOUIS, medical researcher, educator; b. Chgo., Apr. 11, 1932; s. John Louis and Harriet (Link) Sever; m. Gerane Werle, Mar. 3, 1956; children: Kimberly, Beverly, Valerie. BA, U. Chgo., 1952; BS, MD, MS, PhD, Northwestern U., 1957. Head sect. infectious diseases NINDS, NIH, Bethesda, Md., 1960—71, chief infectious diseases, 1971—88; chmn. pediat. Children's Nat. Med. Ctr., Washington, 1988—90, prof. pediat., ob-gyn., immunology, microbiology and tropical medicine, 1988—. Cons. Rotary Internat., Evanston, Ill., 1964—, NIH, Bethesda, 1988—, WHO, Geneva, 1991—. Editor: 11 med. books; contbr. more than 600 articles to profl. jours. Capt. USPHS, 1960—88. Recipient Kimbel award, Am. Soc. for Microbiology, 1979, Wellcome Diagnostics award, Pan Am. Med. Virology, 1989, Meritorious Alumni award, Northwestern U., 1989, Pasteur award, Microbiology Soc., 1987, Abbott award, 1996, Soc. for Biomolecular Screening award, 2001. Mem.: Pan Am. Soc. Rapid Viral Diagnosis (pres. 1995—96), Assn. Med. Lab. Immunologists (pres. 1994—95, Erwin Niter award 1997), Teratology Soc. (pres. 1976—77), Assn. Med. Clin. and Lab. Immunologists (pres. 1992—94), Infectious Disease Soc. of Ob-gyn. (pres. 1994—96, Ortho-McNeill award 1998), Country Glen Club, Potomac Rotary Club. Avocation: gardening.

SEVERANCE, JERI-LYNNE WHITE, elementary school educator; b. El Paso, Tex., Nov. 30, 1965; d. James Claude and Carol Ann (Magee) White; m. Scot Clark Severance, Dec. 30, 1989; children: Jacie, Jared. BA in Music Edn., Eckerd Coll., 1987; M in Music Edn., U. Tex., Austin, 1989; degree in Ednl. Leadership, Nat. Louis U., 2006. Cert. music tchr. K-12 Fla., TESOL K-12, exceptional student edn. and ednl. leadership K-12. Music tchr. Dunnellon (Fla.) H.S., 1989—90, Gateway H.S., Kissimmee, Fla., 1990—91, Grover C. Fields Middle Sch., New Bern, NC, 1991—92; pres-sch. tchr. 1st Alliance Ch., Orlando, Fla., 1992—93; fine arts tchr. Vanguard Sch., Lake Wales, Fla., 1993—94; music tchr. Midway Elem., Sanford, Fla., 1994—95; instr. Barry U., Orlando, Fla., 1995—97; music tchr. Pleasant Hill Elem., Kissimmee, 1995—98, tchr. exceptional student edn., 1998—. Co-founder, co-chair Pleasant Hill Elem. Festival of Arts, Kissimmee. Chamber singers choir dir. First United Meth. Ch., Kissimmee. Mem.: AAUW (sec., com. chair 1995—2001), Coun. for Exceptional Children (com. chair 2000—02), Phi Delta Kappa (com. chair 2003—04, exec. bd. 2003—), Alpha Delta Kappa (chaplain, pres.-elect 1996—2002, pres. 2003—04). Democrat. Methodist. Avocations: reading, sewing, dancing. Office: Pleasant Hill Elem Sch 1253 Pleasant Hill Rd Kissimmee FL 34741 Office Phone: 407-935-3700. Business E-Mail: severancej@osceola.k12.fl.us.

SEVERDIA, ANTHONY GEORGE, chemistry researcher; b. Sharon, Pa., Sept. 20, 1946; s. George Anthony and Angela Mary (Tomich) S. BS, Pa. State U., U. Park, 1968; MS, Case Western Res. U., Cleve., 1971, PhD, 1974. Rsch., teaching assoc. Rensselaer Poly. Inst., Troy, NY, 1975-77; chemist NYU, 1977-79, 82-83, Columbia U., NYC, 1979-82; analytical chemist Mallinckrodt Group, Terre Haute, Ind., 1983-92; prin. chemist analytical sci. Sanofi-Aventis Rsch., Gt. Valley, Pa., 1992—. Presenter in field. Contbr. articles to profl. jours. Summer fellow NSF, Cleve., 1971. Mem. Am. Chem. Soc. (exec. com., treas. Terre Haute sect. 1991-92), Soc. Applied Spectroscopy, The Internat. Soc. for Optical Engring. Home: 301 Pritchard Ln Wallingford PA 19086-6104 Home Phone: 610-627-1601; Office Phone: 610-889-6103. Personal E-mail: aseverdia@comcast.net.

SEVERE, KIM LYNETTE, psychologist; b. Orange, NJ, Apr. 19, 1967; d. Dennis and Yvonne Houston; m. Carl Severe, July 6, 1996; 1 child, Kiana Lynn. BS in Psychology, Howard U., Washington, 1989; MA in Counseling, NJ City U., 2004. Cert. sch. psychology NJ, 2005. Records mgr. Richards & O'Neil Law Firm, NYC, 1990—2000. Mem.: NASP, NJ Assn. Sch. Psychologists. Office: East Orange Sch Dist 715 Park Ave East Orange NJ 07017 Office Fax: 973-266-3473. Business E-Mail: k.severe@eastorange.k12.nj.us.

SEVERIN, EZRA B., musician; b. San Francisco, Calif., Sept. 21, 1971; s. Walter Clifford Barney and Susan Severin. BA, Sonoma State U., Rohnert Pk., 1994; MFA, NC Sch. Arts, Winston-Salem, 2000. Tech. dir. Sir Francis Drake HS, San Anselmo, Calif., 1995—97, So. Oreg. U., Ashland, 2003—; carpenter, welder Oreg. Shakespeare Festival, Ashland, 2000—03. Campaign vol. Obama '08, Ashland, Oreg., 2008. Recipient award, Sonoma State U., 2004. Mem.: USITT, IATSE, BPO Elks. Quaker. Office: Southern Oregon Univ 1250 Siskiyou Blvd Ashland OR 97520

SEVERINI, THOMAS ALAN, statistician, educator; b. Butler, Pa., Aug. 15, 1959; s. Carl Thomas and Rose (Morozowich) Severini; m. Karla Jean Engel, Aug. 11, 1988; children: Katherine, Anthony, Joseph, Elisabeth. BS, Pa. State U., 1981; MS, U. Mich., 1982; PhD, U. Chgo., 1987. Reliability engr. IBM, Rochester, Minn., 1982—83; asst. prof. statistics U. Wis., Madison, 1987—89; cons. Arthur D. Little, Washington, 1989—90; asst. prof. statistics Northwestern U., Evanston, Ill., 1990—94, assoc. prof., 1994—2000, prof., 2000—. Dept. chair Northwestern U., Evanston, 2001—; cons. in field. Author: Likelihood Methods in Statistics, 2000, Elements of Distribution Theory, 2005; contbr. articles to profl. jours. Mem.: Inst. Math. Statistics, Am. Statis. Assn., Phi Beta Kappa. Office: Northwestern Univ 2006 Sheridan Rd Evanston IL 60208-0852 Home Phone: 847-856-0298; Office Phone: 847-467-1254. Business E-Mail: severini@northwestern.edu.

SEVERINO, ROBERTO, language educator, academic administration executive; b. Catania, Italy, July 19, 1940; s. Giuseppe and Alba (Scroppo) S. Student, State U. Catania, Italy, 1960-62; BA, Columbia Union Coll., 1967; MA, U. Ill., 1969, PhD, 1973. Head acct., pers. dir. Industria Nazionale Apparecchiature Scientifiche, Milan, 1961-63; teaching asst., lang. lab. supv. Columbia Union Coll., Takoma Park, Md., 1965-67; grad. teaching asst. U. Ill., Urbana, 1967-70, coord. Corr. Sch., 1970-71; instr. dept. French and Italian U. Mass., Amherst, 1971-73; prof. dept. Italian Georgetown U., Washington, 1973—, acting chmn., 1987, chmn. dept., 1988—93; pres., co-founder Nat. Inst. Contemporary Italian Studies, 1986—; co-founder Associazione Internazionale del Diritto e dell'Arte, 1994—; pres. emeritus Am. U. of Rome, 1990-93, chair. Lit. dir. Georgetown U. Elec. Text Repository, Italian Archive, 1988-91, Ultramarina, 1992-96; mem. adv. bd. Nat. Italian Am. Found. Nat. Christopher Columbus 1992 Celebration; mem. U.S. delegation to 1st Conf. on Italian lang. and culture in U.S., 1987; founder Georgetown Poetry Series; pres. Coun. Promotion of Italian Lang. in Am. Schs., 1999—; hon. pres. U.S. Assn. Internat. Antonietta Labisi, 2000—; pres. Italian Muse Found., Washington, 2003—; inst. dir. NEH "The Art of Tchg. Italian Through Italian Art", 2004; elected mem. exec. com. Lista Unitalia Com. of Italians Residing Abroad; mem. selecting com. Washington Post Ednl. Found.; lectr., spkr. in field Author: Le soluzioni immaginarie, 1985, The Signs and Sounds of Italian, 1985, A carte scoperte, 1990, Presente imperfetto ed altri tempi, 1992, The Battle for Humanism, 1994, A Dumas: Mariano Stabile Sindaco di Palermo, 1994, My Dream-The Paintings of Gaetano N. Musto, 2002, Uga Martinotti, Io sono un pittore, 2005, Campania, Land of Myth and History, 2005; co-author: Periscopio, 1986, International Nuclear Agreements Multilingual Glossary, 1988, United Nations Organization Multilingual Glossary, 1988, Regularizing the Irregular Italian Verb, 1990, Preserving and Promoting Italian language and Culture in North America, 1997, Napoleon: One Image, Ten Mirrors, 2002; translator: The Next 6000 Days by Saverio Avveduto, 1987; editor: (serials) Segni, 1985-88, Hispano-Italic Studies, 1976, 79; mem. editorial bd. Educazione Comparata, 1993—; contbr. articles to profl. jours.; translator: Angelo Scandurra: The Hot-Tempered Musician and Other Poems, 1996, M. Rotelli's E. Sanguineti, If, For Me, You Write a Poem, 1999, Francesco Battiato: Amnesia of the Blue, 2000; editor: Giuseppe Severino: Ricordi di Castelnuovo primi '900. Scene di vita paesana, 1992; co-founder, U.S. editor: Colophon, An Internat. Jour. Arts and Letters, 1997-2003 Trustee Joel Nafuma Refugee Ctr., Rome, 1993—; chmn. Strega Lit. Prize, Washington D.C. Jury, 1997-2001; mem. jury Prima Parete in Concerto, Lion's Internat. Art Prize, Catania, 1998—, Spoleto Poetry Prize, 1999—. Rsch. grantee Interuniversity Ctr. European Studies, 1977; recipient Accademia Internazionale di Lettere, Scienze, Arti medal, 1983, Internat. Poetry prize, 1986, Gold Cross Cavaliere dell'Ordine al Merito della Repubblica Italiana, 1983, Gold medal Italian Ministries of Univs. and Sci. Rsch., 1988, Marranzano d'Argento prize, 1989, Gold Commander class Cross al Merito della Repubblica Italiana, 1990, Georgetown U. Vicennial Disting. Svc. medal, 1994, Telamone prize, 1995, Top Sprint: Siciliani nel Mondo award, 2000, Premio Internazionale "Castello di Pietrarossa" Caltanissetta, 2001, Gold Comdr. Cross Order "Stella della Solidarieta Italiana" by decree of Pres. of Italy, 2004 Mem. MLA, So. Atlantic Modern Lang. Assn., Nat. Assn. Secondary Sch. Prins. (mem. sch. partnerships internat. Italian adv. coun. 1988—), Italian Am. Cultural Found., Italian Cultural Soc. (pres. 1979-81, 83-85, Outstanding Svc. award 1983, chmn. acad. policy com. 1981—), Assn. Internationale Critiques Literaires and Associazione Italiana Critici Letterari, Greater Washington Assn. Tchrs. Fgn. Langs. (mem. award selection com. 1983-85), Manuscript Soc., Renaissance Soc. Am., Circolo Culturale Italiano (hon.), Am. Club (Rome), Touring Club Italiano (hon.), Gamma Kappa Alpha (v.p. 1990—, sec.-treas. and chpt. advisor 1985-90), World Jurist Assn. Ctr. Assocs. (U.S. pres. 1993—, chmn. program devel. and fin. com. 2000—), Associazione Internazionale del Diritto e dell'Arte (v.p. 1994—), Nat. Italian Am. Found. Coun. of 1,000, Napoleonic Soc. Am., Soc. di Studi Valdesi, Istituto Internazionale di Epistemologia la Magna Grecia, Unione Nazionale per la lotta contro l'Analfabetismo, Sons of Italy. Home: 4949 Quebec St NW Washington DC 20016-3230 Office: Georgetown U Dept Italian 37th And O Sts NW ICC 307 Washington DC 20057-0001 E-mail: Severiro@georgetown.edu.

SEVERNS, KAREN S., family court services administrator; d. Dan Vassar and Susan Darlene Peckham; m. Michael Martin Karen Vassar, Apr. 7, 1986; children: Camilla, Hannah, Joshua Michael. AA, U. Alaska, 1995; BS, Wayland Bapt. U., Alaska, 1998; MSW, Boston Coll., 2003. Asst. prof., Title IV-E coord. Lewis & Clark State Coll., Lewiston, Idaho, 2004—; family ct. svcs. coord. 2d Jud. Dist. Nez Perce, Lewiston, 2005—, CASA Program Mgr., 2007—. Psycho-social rehab. social worker Child and Family Enrichment Ctr., Moscow, 2004—. Mental health profl. Red Cross, Lewiston, Idaho, 1981—2006. Recipient Nat. Mil. Important Patriot: donned frosted flakes cereal box, Nat. Mil. Family Assn., 1998-1999. Mem.: NASW (life). Avocations: international travel, Native American art, swimming, singing karaoke, dancing. Home: 1060 Fiddlers Ridge Loop Potlatch ID 83855-8724 Personal E-mail: karensevern s@yahoo.com.

SEVERO, NORMAN C., retired statistics professor; b. Buffalo, May 31, 1928; s. John Anthony and Mary Severo. BA, U. Buffalo, 1950; PhD, Carnegie Inst. Tech., Pitts., 1955. Joint Fulbright & Swedish govt. fellow U. Stockholm, 1955—56; mathematician Nat. Bur. Standards, Washington, 1955—59; assoc. prof. U. Buffalo, 1959—61, prof., 1961—96, prof. emeritus, 1996—; vis. prof biomath. Cornell Grad. Sch. Med. Scis., NYC, 1966; vis. prof. math. U. Campinas, Brazil, 1973—73; vis. scholar biostatistics Dana-Farber Cancer Inst. & Harvard U., Boston, 1995. Contbr. articles to profl. jours. Fellow: AAAS, Inst. Math. Stats., Am. Statis. Assn.; mem.: Internat. Statis. Inst., Sigma X, Pi Mu Epsilon, Phi Kappa Phi. Home: 150 Meadowview Ln Williamsville NY 14221 Business E-Mail: severo@buffalo.edu.

SEVERO, RICHARD, writer; b. Newburgh, NY, Nov. 22, 1932; s. Thomas and Mary Theresa (Farina) S.; m. Emöke Edith de Papp, Apr. 7, 1961. BA, Colgate U., 1954; postgrad., NYU Inst. Fine Arts, 1955-56, Columbia U. Sch. Architecture and Urban Planning, 1964-65. News asst. CBS, NYC, 1954-55; reporter Poughkeepsie New Yorker, NY, 1956-57, A.P., Newark, 1957-61, NY Herald Tribune, 1961-63; writer TV news CBS, NYC, 1963-66; reporter Washington Post, 1966—68; reporter, fgn. correspondent, feature writer, feature obituary reporter, sci. and environ. reporter NY Times, NYC, 1968—2006. Assoc. Seminar on the City, Columbia U., 1966-69; vis. lectr. Am. culture Vassar Coll., 1985-99; bd. dirs. Hudson Valley Philharm., 1998-99, Colgate U. Alumni Corp., 1988-92. Author: Lisa H., 1985; (with Lewis Milford) The Wages of War, 1989 (Am. Legion Nat. Comdr.'s award 1990); contbr. articles to mags. Established Thomas and Mary Severo Scholarship funds for majors in music and Italian Vassar Coll., 2002. Poynter fellow-in-residence Vassar Coll., 1974-75; CBS News fellow, 1964-65; Recipient Front Page award Washington-Balt. Newspaper Guild, 1967; Journalistic award H.A.V.E.N., 1969; Schaeffer Gold Typewriter award NY Newspaper Reporters Assn., 1969; Page One award Newspaper Guild of N.Y., 1970; hon. mention Mike Berger award Columbia U., 1970; Leone di San Marco award Italian Heritage and Culture Com., 1982; George Polk Meml. award L.I. U. Sch. Journalism, 1975; Hudson River Fisherman's Assn. award, 1976; Mike Berger award Columbia U., 1976; James Wright Brown award Deadline Club, Sigma Delta Chi, NYC, 1976; Feature award NY Press Club, 1977; Page One award Newspaper Guild NY, 1977, 82; Media award Am. Cancer Soc., 1977; hon. mention Heywood Broun Meml. award Am. Newspaper Guild, 1977; Penney-Mo. Newspaper award U. Mo. Sch. Journalism, 1978; Media award Agt. Orange Victims Internat., 1982; Page One award NY Newspaper Guild, 1982; Gift of Life award NY Blood Ctr., 1991, Spl. Writing award Soc. of the Silurians, 1992. Avocations: music, cello. Personal E-mail: richard.severo2@verizon.net.

SEVERS, CHARLES A., III, lawyer; b. NYC, Sept. 16, 1942; s. Charles A. and Gertrude (O'Neill) S.; m. Regina Ferrone, Sept. 4, 1965; children: Charles A. IV, Cornelius Forsythe, Rudyard Pierrepont, Olivia Consuelo Poor. BA, Georgetown U., 1964, JD, 1967. Bar: N.Y. 1968, D.C. 1985. Ptnr. Dewey Ballantine, NYC, 1967-96; gen. counsel, exec. v.p. Nat. Madison Group, NYC, 1996—2007. Lectr. various continuing legal edn. programs. Contbr. articles to profl. jours. Dir., trustee various orgns. Fellow Am. Coll. Trust and Estate Counsel; mem. ABA, N.Y. State Bar Assn., Assn. of Bar of City of N.Y., D.C. Bar Assn., Union Club. Address: High Meadow Old Chatham NY 12136

SEVERS, WALTER BRUCE, pharmacology educator, researcher; b. Pitts., June 10, 1938; s. Walter Bruce and Pauline Marie (Sever) S.; m. Anne Elizabeth Daniels, Apr. 25, 1970; children: Mary, Jane, Steven, William, Katherine. BS, U. Pitts., 1960, MS, 1963, PhD, 1965. Postdoctoral fellow NIH, Bethesda, Md., 1966-68; asst. prof. pharmacology Coll. Medicine, Pa. State U., Hershey, 1968-71, assoc. prof., 1971-77, prof., 1977-99, prof. emeritus, 1999—. Cons. pharmacology/toxicology, 1999—; v.p. for sci. affairs Ednl. Horizons, Inc., Lemoyne, Pa., 1998—; ad hoc grant cons. NIH, U.S. Army, NSF; vis. prof. physiology U. Belgrade Med. Sch., 1994—. Mem. editl. Bd. Am. Jour. Physiology, 1978-98; assoc. editor Pharmacology, 1998-2000; contbr. numerous articles, chpts., revs. to profl. publs. Recipient Disting. Alumnus award U. Pitts., 1978, I.M. Setchenov medal Acad. Med. Sci. USSR, 1983, Blue medal for sci. Acad. Med. Sci., Bulgaria, medal for sci. U. Belgrade; NASA grantee, 1976-98. Fellow Am. Coll. Clin. Pharmacology; mem. Am. Physiol. Soc., Am. Soc. Pharmacology and Exptl. Therapeutics, Soc. for Neurosci., Soc. for Exptl. Biology and Medicine, Sigma Xi (pres. Pa. State U. chpt. 1981-82), Kiwanis (pres. Hershey area 1980, bd. dirs.). Republican. Roman Catholic. Avocations: reading, camping, hiking. Home: 1011 Grubb Rd Palmyra PA 17078-3510 Office: Pa State U Coll Medicine Dept Pharm Mail Code H78 500 University Dr Hershey PA 17033-2360 Office Phone: 717-531-8291. Business E-Mail: wbs2@psu.edu.

SEVERS, WILLIAM FLOYD, actor; b. Britton, Okla., Jan. 8, 1932; s. Harry Lysander Fletcher and Katherine Lucinda (McAuliffe) S.; m. Mary Anne Proctor, Jan. 18, 1964 (div. 1971); 1 child, Pilar; m. Barbara Alice Schonger, Sept. 9, 1978; children: Katherine Meghan, Erin Christine. AA, Pasadena Playhouse Coll., 1956. Appeared on Broadway in Cut of the Axe, 1959-60, The Moon Is Blue, 1962, On Borrowed Time, 1991-92, nat. tour Look Homeward, Angel, 1960; co-star nat. tour Spoon River, 1964; actor Secret Storm, All My Children, One Life to Live, Guiding Light, Texas, Search for Tomorrow, Another World, Loving, 1963-93; other TV appearances include Armstrong Circle Theatre, 1963, The Defenders, 1964, World War II, A GI Diary, 1978, Nurse, 1980, Muggable Mary, 1986, Law and Order, recurring role as Hon. Henry Fillmore, 1990-2004, Hallmark Hall of Fame, Grace and Glorie, 1998, Law and Order: Criminal Intent, 2000, The Sopranos, 2007; appeared in films including Funny Farm, 1988, Regarding Henry, 1991, Meet the Parents, 2000, Revolution #9, 2000, 13 Conversations About 1 Thing, 2001, The Departed, 2005; actor European tour West Side Story, 1990-91, 94, Asian tour West Side Story, 1999; actor, voice artist numerous commls., 1964— Staff sgt. USAF, 1946-53. Mem. SAG, AFTRA, Actors Equity Assn., Pasadena Playhouse Alumni Assn. Democrat. Avocations: reading, golf. Home: 8309 Rancho Paraiso NW Albuquerque NM 87120 Personal E-mail: wfsevers@gmail.com.

SEVERSON, GLEN ARTHUR, state supreme court justice; b. Sioux Falls, SD, Mar. 9, 1949; s. Arthur and Muriel S.; m. Mary K. Schweitzer, May 24, 1975; children: Thomas, Kathryn. BS, U. SD, 1972, JD, 1975. Bar: SD 1975, US Dist. Ct. SD, 1976, US Ct. Appeals (8th cir.) 1989, Minn. 1990. Dep. state atty. Beadle County, Huron, SD, 1975-76; ptnr. Benson, Wehde, Martin & Severson, Huron, SD, 1976-82, Fingerson, Severson & Nelson, Huron, SD, 1982-93; cir. ct. judge Sioux Falls, 1993—2002; presiding judge of cir., 2002—08; assoc. justice SD Supreme Ct., 2008—. City atty. City of Huron, 1977-92; pres. SD Mcpl. Attys. Assn., Pierre, 1985. Bd. dirs. SD Bd. Water and Natural Resources, Pierre, 1986-92, Huron Area C. of C., 1983-86. Mem. ABA, SD Bar Assn., Minn. Bar Assn., SD Judges Assn. (pres. 2000-2001, presiding judge, 2002). Roman Catholic. Avocations: flying, fishing, hunting, reading. Office: SD Supreme Ct 500 E Capitol Ave Pierre SD 57501 Office Phone: 605-773-3474.*

SEVERSON, KATIE LEANN, music educator; b. Rugby, ND, Feb. 6, 1978; d. Sherman Wayne and Louisa Lorraine Severson. BA in Secondary Edn., Dickson State U., ND, 2003. Cert. tchr. NDEA, 2003. Spanish instr. Dickinson Cath. Schs., 2003—; adj. spanish instr. Dickinson State U., 2005—.

SEVERSON, ROGER ALLAN, bank executive; b. Thief River Falls, Minn., Sept. 2, 1932; s. Alfred Gerhard and Esther Olga (Landro) S.; m. Beverly Diane Hays, Aug. 30, 1953; children: Eric Hays, Holle Diane. BS, U. Minn., 1954. Group v.p. First Nat. Bank, Mpls., 1952-73; pres. FBS Fin., Inc., Mpls., 1974-77; exec. v.p. F&M Savs. Bank, Mpls., 1977-82; sr. v.p. First Nat. Bank, St. Paul, 1983-85; exec. v.p. Shelard Nat. Bank, Mpls., 1985-86, TCF Bank Savs., Mpls., 1986-92; ret., 1992. Mem. Robert Morris Assocs., 1980-92; trustee Heitman Mortgage Investors, Chgo., 1970-71, Mass. Mut. Mortgage Realty Investors, Springfield, 1972-85. Vice chmn. bd. of trustees The Am. Luth. Ch. Synod, Mpls., 1976-81; trustee Children's Health Ctr., Mpls., 1971-72; bd. dirs. Goodwill Industries, Mpls., 1967-70. Fellow Versterheim Mus.; mem. Ethics in Pub. Policy Ctr., Ctr. for Am. Experiment. Home: 8321 Essex Rd Chanhassen MN 55317-8705

SEVIER, MICHAEL CHRISTOPHER, engineer; b. Antioch, Calif., June 25, 1979; s. John Scott and Patricia Lee Sevier; m. Meghan Andrea Kerner. PhD, U. Calif. Santa Barbara, 2007. Grad. rschr. UC Santa Barbara, 2001—07; project engr. ATA Engring., El Segundo, Calif., 2007—. Rsch. fellow, NASA, 2002—04. Democrat. Avocations: surfing, running, painting.

SEVIGNY, CHLOË, actress; b. Darien, Conn., Nov. 18, 1974; d. Paul Sevigny. Actor: (films) Kids, 1995, Trees Lounge, 1996, Gummo, 1997, Palmetto, 1998, The Last Days of Disco, 1998, Boys Don't Cry, 1999, Julien Donkey-Boy, 1999, A Map of the World, 1999, American Psycho, 2000, Ten Minutes Older: The Trumpet, 2002, Demonlover, 2002, Party Monster, 2003, Death of a Dynasty, 2003, Dogville, 2003, The Brown Bunny, 2003, Shattered Glass, 2003, Melinda and Melinda, 2004, Manderlay, 2005, Broken Flowers, 2005, 3 Needles, 2005, Lying, 2006, Sisters, 2006, Zodiac, 2007; (TV films) Mrs. Harris, 2005, If These Walls Could Talk 2, 2000; (TV series) Big Love, 2006—, (TV appearances) Will & Grace, 2004. Named one of The 50 Most Powerful Women in NYC, NY Post, 2008. Office: Endeavor Talent Agy 9601 Wilshire Blvd 10th Fl Beverly Hills CA 90212

SEVILLA, CARLOS ARTHUR, bishop; b. San Francisco, Aug. 9, 1935; Student, Gonzaga U., Santa Clara U., Jesuiten Kolleg, Innsbruck, Austria, Cath. Inst. Paris. Ordained priest Society of Jesus, 1966, solemn professed, 1974; aux. bishop Archdiocese of San Francisco, 1988—96; ordained bishop, 1989; bishop Diocese of Yakima, Wash., 1996—. Roman Catholic. Office: Diocese of Yakima 5301-A Tieton Dr Yakima WA 98908-3493 Office Phone: 509-965-7117. Office Fax: 509-966-8334.

SEVILLA, EMERITA NEPOMUCENO, writer; b. Manila, Philippines, Dec. 7, 1926; arrived in U.S., 1979; d. Perfecto Jardiniano and Dolores Mapa (Alvarez) Nepomuceno; m. Victor Jocson Sevilla, Dec. 10, 1949 (dec. May 20, 1993); children: Mary Therese Victoria, Victor, Mary Enid, Vincent, Vidal, Virgil, Valentin, Vinci, Mary Elaine. BA in Journalism, U. Santo Tomas, Manila, 1949. Writer, rschr. Red Cross Philippines, Manila, 1947—48; reporter Evening News, Manila, 1948—49; sec. to dept. head Dept. Commerce and Industry, Manila, 1949—51; owner, co-founder, treas. Sevilla Bookshop, Davao City, Philippines, 1951—67; mgr. Ency. Britannica, Manila, 1968—71; cons. Philamlife Ins. Co., Manila, 1972—92. Author: (poetry) Springs of Joy, 1992, Silver and Gold, 1995, Soaring Beyond Sunshine and Shadow, 2006, (prayerbook) Treasures from Heaven, 1997. Mem.: DAV, Rancho Cucamonga Pub. Libr., Help Hospitalized Vets. (Donor of Yr. 2004), Trinitarians, Perpetual Rosary Assn. (life; Regina Coeli divsn.), Priests Sacred Heart, Rancho Cucamonga Sr. Citizen Club. Roman Catholic. Avocations: reading, book collecting.

SEVIN, DIETER HERMANN, literature and language professor; b. Mühlanger, Germany, Nov. 5, 1938; arrived in USA, 1958, naturalized, 1963; s. Wolf-Dieterich and Erna (Brockmann) Sevin; m. Ingrid Antje Dirks, June 15, 1963; children: Sonja, Karen. BA, San Jose State U., 1963; MA, U. Wash., Seattle, 1964, PhD, 1967. Asst. prof. Pacific Lutheran U., Tacoma, 1967-68, Vanderbilt U., Nashville, 1968-73, assoc. prof., 1973-82, prof., 1982—, chair dept., 2002—. Author: Individuum und Staat, 1972, Zur Diskussion: A Modern Approach to German Conversation, 3d edit., 1987, The Resonance of Exile. Successful and Unsuccessful Reception Of German Exile, 1992, Text Strategies in GDR Prose Fiction Between the Building and Fall of the Berlin Wall, 1994, Christa Wolf: Divided Heaven/The Quest for Christa T. Interpretations, 4th rev. edit., 2000; author: (with Ingrid Sevin) Wie Geht's? An Introductory German Course; editor: Georg Büchner: New Perspectives On His International Reception, 2007; co-editor (with Richard E. Schade): Practicing Progress: The Promise and Limitations of Enlightenment, 2007; contbr. articles to profl. jours. Recipient The Cross of the Order of Merit, Fed. Republic Germany, 2007; named Lit. in Century Totalitarianism, 2008. Fellow: German Acad. Exch. Svc. (grantee 1980), Am. Coun. Learned Socs. (grantee 1981—82), Am. Philos. Soc. (grantee 1991). Lutheran. Avocations: travel, reading, music. Office: Vanderbilt U Dept Germanic And Slav Nashville TN 37235 Office Phone: 615-322-2611.

SEWARD, GEORGE CHESTER, lawyer; b. Omaha, Aug. 4, 1910; s. George Francis and Ada Leona (Rugh) S.; m. Carroll Frances McKay, Dec. 12, 1936 (dec. 1991); children: Gordon Day, Patricia McKay (Mrs. Dryden G. Liddle), James Pickett, Deborah Carroll (Mrs. R. Thomas Coleman). BA, U. Va., 1933, LLB, 1936. Bar: Va. 1935, NY, Ky., DC, US Supreme Ct. With Shearman & Sterling, NYC, 1936-53, Seward & Kissel LLP, NYC, 1953—. Dir. Witherbee Sherman Corp., 1952-66, pres. 1964-66, Howmet Corp., 1955-75, Chas. P. Young Co., 1965-72, Howmedica Inc., 1970-72, Benson Mines, Inc., 1980-85; trustee Benson Iron Ore Trust, 1969-80. Author: Basic Corporate Practice, 1977, Seward and Related Families, 1994; co-author: Model Business Corporation Act Annotated, 1960, We Remember Carroll, 1992. Trustee Arts and Scis. Coun. U. Va., 1983-93, pres., 1991-93; trustee Edwin Gould Found. for Children, 1955-96, Nature Conservancy of Ea. LI, 1969-80, NY Geneal. and Biog. Soc., 1991-2006. Named to Louisville Male HS Alumni Assn. Hall of Fame, 1991; commd. Ky. Col., 1993. Fellow: NY State Bar Found., Am. Bar Found.; mem.: ABA (chmn. sect. com. corp. laws 1952—58, chmn. bus. law sect. 1958—59, ho. of dels. 1959—60, chmn. sect. banking com. 1960—61, ho. of dels. 1963—74, joint com. with Am. Law Inst. on continuing legal edn. 1965—74), Internat. Bar Assn. (hon. life pres., lectr. series by heads of state named in his honor, New Delhi 1988, Lisbon 1992, Budapest 1993, Geneva 1994), Downtown Assn. (NYC), Athenaeum Lit. Assn. (Louisville), Greencroft Club (Charlottesville, Va.), Univ. Club (Chgo.), Met. Club (Washington), Bohemian Club (San Francisco), Gardiner's Bay Country Club (Shelter Island, NY), NY Yacht Club, Knickerbocker Club, Delta Sigma Rho, Theta Chi, Phi Beta Kappa, Phi Beta Kappa Fellows (pres. 1969—75), Order of Coif, Raven Soc., Cum Laude Soc. Home: 48 Greenacres Ave Scarsdale NY 10583-1436 Office: Seward & Kissel LLP One Battery Park Plz New York NY 10004 also: Internat Bar Assn 1 Stephen St London W1T 1AT England

SEWARD, JAMES PICKETT, internist, educator; b. NYC, Oct. 14, 1949; s. George C. and Carroll Frances (McKay) S. AB, Harvard U., 1971; M of Pub. Policy, U. Calif. Berkeley, 1977; MD, U. Calif. San Francisco, 1977; M of Med. Mgmt., Tulane U., 2003. Diplomate Am. Bd. Internal Medicine, Am. Bd. Occupational Medicine, Am. Bd. Med. Mgmt. Resident U. Calif. Hosps., San Francisco, 1977—80; Robert Woods Johnson postdoctoral fellow U. Calif., San Francisco, 1980—82; med. dir. health svcs. Lawrence Livermore Nat. Lab., Calif., 1994—; dir. preventive medicine residency U. Calif., Berkeley, 1991—95, clin. prof. San Francisco, 1983—, clin. prof. Sch. Pub. Health Berkeley, 1986—2005. Fulbright scholar, 1972-73. Fellow Am. Coll. Preventive Medicine (occupl. med. regent 2005-07), Am. Coll. Occupl. an Environ. Medicine, Am. Coll. Physicians Execs., Calif. Acad. Preventive Medicine (past pres.), We. Occupl. and Environ. Med. Assn. (past pres.), Calif. Med. Assn. Office: HSD L723 LLNL PO Box 808 Livermore CA 94551-0808

SEWARD, JOHN EDWARD, JR., insurance company executive; b. Kirksville, Mo., June 12, 1943; s. John Edward and Ruth Carol (Connell) S.; children: Mitch, Justina. BS in Fin., St. Joseph's Coll., 1968. CLU, CPCU, cert. profl. ins. agt. Mgr. acctg. svcs. Guarantee Res. Life Ins. Co., Hammond, Ind., 1965-69; asst. contr. Gambles Ins. Group, Mpls., 1969-71, N.Am. Cos., Chgo., 1971-73; v.p., treas. Home & Auto Ins. Co., Chgo., 1973-75, bd. dirs., 1974-83; pres., chief exec. officer, dir. Universal Fire & Casualty Ins. Co., 1983-88, acting chmn. bd., pres., chief exec. officer, 1988, chmn. bd., pres., chief exec. officer, 1989-92; co-founder, pres., CEO J&J Underwriting Svcs., Inc., 1992-93, chmn., CEO, 1994; v.p. Concord Gen., 1993—; pres. Classictire & Marine Ins. Co., 1994; chmn., CEO Bus. Risk Svcs., Inc., Schererville, Ind., 1995—. Bd. dirs., v.p., treas., v.p. fin. Calumet Coun. Boy Scouts Am., 1981-85; mem. Shriners Hosp.-Teddy Bear Club, 1980; mem. exec. com. Chgo. Baseball Cancer Charities, 1981—; co-chmn. Ron Kittle's Ind. Sports Charities, 1989. Named to Wall of Fame, T.F. South H.S., 1993. Fellow Life Mgmt. Inst., Am. Biog. Inst. (dep. gov.). Office: Bus Risk Svcs 1124 Lisa Ln Schererville IN 46375-1183 Office Phone: 219-865-6370.

SEWARD, RUDY RAY, sociology educator; b. Quincy, Ill., Nov. 3, 1944; s. Otis Ray and Corine Doris (Nelson) S.; m. Jean Ann Otte, Sept. 6, 1969; children: Rudy Allyn, Erik Russell. BS, N.E. Mo. U., 1966; MA, So. Ill. U., 1969, PhD, 1974. Rsch. fellow Stockholms Universitat, Stockholm, 1971-72; instr. So. Ill. U., Carbondale, 1972-73; asst. prof. sociology U. North Tex., Denton, 1973-80, assoc. prof., 1980-90, prof., 1990—, mem. grad. faculty, 1982—, grad. advisor dept. sociology, 1987—, assoc. chmn. sociology and social work, 1992—. Author: The American Family: A Demographic History, 1978, Determinants of Family Culture; Effects on Fatherhood, 1991; contbg. author: Fatherhood and Families in Cultural Context; adv. editor Sociol. Quar., 1982-84; also articles. Asst. scoutmaster Boy Scouts Am., 1985—. Recipient President's Coun. Teaching award U. North Tex., 1989; named Top Prof., Mortar Bd., 1989, Student Assn. Honor Prof., 1991. Mem. Am. Sociol. Assn. (membership coord. S.W. region 1994—), Nat. Coun. Family Rels., Tex. Coun. Family Rels. (exec. coun. 1994—), Southwestern Social Sci. Assn. (program chmn. sociology 1992-93, pres. sociology 1993-94), Midwest Sociol. Soc., Tex. Assn. Coll. Tchrs., Internat. Sociol. Assn. (com. on family rsch.). Avocations: collecting baseball cards and stamps, bicycling, camping. Office: U North Tex PO Box 13675 Denton TX 76203-6675

SEWELL, CAROL ANN, artist; b. Dodge City, Kans., June 12, 1944; d. John Elbert and Mary Claire (Wetmore) Frazier; m. Herbert Carey Zortman, Aug. 21, 1960 (div. Jan. 1989); children: Elaine Marie, Anita Louise, Stanley Dale; m. George D. Rosel, Sept. 22, 1990 (dec. June 1995), m. Maurice Sewell, June 4, 2004. Student, Ctrl. Coll., McPherson, Kans., 1961; BFA cum laude, Ft. Hays State U., 1994. Cert. machine embroidery instr. Dress designer Ms. Cosmo Ltd., Wichita, Kans., 1975-76; designer artistic embroidery garments, 1977-80, 99; owner Carol Ann's Gallery, Liberal, Kans.; part time music tchr. W. Mid. Sch., 1999—; co-owner Maurice and Carol Ann Sewell, Inc. Part-time art tchr. U.S. D 443, Dodge City, part-time music tchr. One-woman show Ft. Hays Libr., 1993; singer: A Touch of Class; developer: The Tour (the Life of Christ); performer: Wild West Dinner Theater. Mem. Baker Art Ctr., Liberal, 1989—, Hays (Kans.) Arts Coun., 1993, Carnegie Ctr. of Arts, Dodge City, Kans.; solo pianist ch. weddings and comty. functions; mem. Glory Rd. Singers, 1999; mem. cast Wild West Show, 2001—, Touch of Class Ladies Group; vol. Make A Wish Found., Operation Christian Child, 2008; tchr. Sunday sch. Recipient All Am. Scholar Collegiate award, 1994, Grand Champion award State Fair, 1989, 90, 95, 97, 98, Purple Champion award, 1990, 06, others; named Woman of World, 1995-96, Internat. Women of World, 1996-97, Internat. Woman of Yr., 1995-96. Mem.: So. Gospel Music Assn., Baker Art Ctr., Mid. Am. Arts and Crafts Assn., Christian Womens Club, Lions Club, Art Club, Pinnacle Honor Soc. Republican. Avocations: piano, singing, dramatics, painting. Home and Office: 2901 Westview Dodge City KS 67801 Personal E-mail: carolannsewell@ymail.com.

SEWELL, D. BRUCE (BRUCE SEWELL, DURWARD BRUCE SEWELL), lawyer; b. 1958; B, U. Lancaster, UK, 1979; JD, George Washington U., 1986. Bar: Calif. 1986, DC 1987, US Ct. Appeals, Fed. cir. Assoc. Schnader Harrison Segal & Lewis; ptnr. Brown & Bain PC; sr. atty. Intel Corp., Santa Clara, Calif., 1995—2001, v.p. legal & govt. affairs, dep. gen. counsel, 2001—04, v.p., gen. counsel, 2004—05, sr. v.p., gen. counsel, 2005—. Office: Intel Corp 2200 Mission College Blvd Santa Clara CA 95052*

SEWELL, DANIEL D., psychiatrist, educator; b. Des Moines; MD, U. Iowa, 1985. Cert. Nat. Bd. Psychiatry and Neurology, 1991, geriatric psychiatrist 1992. Clin. prof. psychiatry U. Calif., San Diego, 2007—. Med. dir. UCSD Sr. Behavioral Health Program, San Diego, 1997—. Contbr. scientific papers. Recipient Humanism Medicine award, Arnold P. Gold Found., 2005. Fellow: Am. Psychiat. Assn.; mem.: Am. Assn. Geriatric Psychiatry.

SEWELL, GLORIANA, music educator; b. Huntington, NY, June 6, 1948; d. Reavis Staggs and Evelyn (Vilches) Kurlowich; m. C. Eugene Sewell, Aug. 8, 1969; children: Keren Ligowski, Daniel Sewell. BA in Piano, Bob Jones U., 1970. Piano tchr. in pvt. practice, Santa Barbara, Calif., 1970-71, Sodus, N.Y., 1971-78; Suzuki piano tchr. in pvt. practice Quakertown, Pa., 1979-86, Milford Square, Pa., 1986—; Kindermusik tchr. Milford Square Music Studio, 1996—. Piano accompanist ch. choir Assembly of the Word, Milford Square, 1993—. Recipient Tchr. award for 1st Pl. Winner, Baldwin Jr. Keyboard Competition, 1985, 1992, 2000, Tchr. of Yr. award, 1989, award, Music Tchrs. Nat. Assn. Student Composition Competition, 1993, 1994, 2001, Tchr. award 1st Pl., Yamaha H.S. Keyboard Competition, 2002. Mem.: Dalcroze Soc. Am., Nat. Guild Piano Tchrs., Am. Orff-Schulwerk Assn., Kindermusik Educations Assn., Suzuki Assn. of Ams., Pa. Music Tchrs. Assn. (pres. Lehigh Valley chpt. 1991—92, co-dir. spring music festival 1997, v.p. 1999—2001, pres. 2001—03, immediate past pres. 2003—07, past pres. at large 2007—09), Music Tchrs. Nat. Assn. (Disting. Svc. award 2003). Avocation: gardening. Home and Office: Milford Square Music Studio PO Box 199 2244 Milford Square Pike Milford Square PA 18935 Office Phone: 215-536-8142. Personal E-mail: gloriana.s@comcast.net.

SEWELL, WILLIAM GEORGE, III, electronics engineer, writer; b. Roanoke, Va., Dec. 14, 1950; s. William George Jr. and Elizabeth Marie (Morrison) S.; m. Verna Landry, Aug. 25, 1970 (div. 1974); children: Ronald Allen, Bryan Joseph; m. Nancy A. Levy, Dec. 31, 2005. BS in Engring., U. Ill., Chgo., 1980; PhD, Calif. U., Modesto, 1983. Electronic technician 928 Airlift Group, Chgo., 1972-74; with FAA, Chgo., 1974-85, staff engr. Wheeling, Ill., 1980-82, regional nav. and landing systems engr. Chgo., 1982-85, nat. program mgr., 1985—87; with Jerry Thompson & Assocs., Kensington, Md., 1987-88; v.p. Navcom Systems, Inc., 1988-89; founder, CEO The Think Corp., 1988-89, Software Coalition, 1989—90. Cons. engr. W.G. Sewell & Assocs., Internat., Niles, Ill., 1981—88; dir. comm. and info. systems group SEMA, Inc., 1990—93; dir. comm. solutions Jacobs Facilities, Inc., 1993—2000; chair TIA Indsl. Telecoms Standards Body, 1995—2001; Sverdrup fellow, 1998; v.p. Holmes & Narver, Inc., 2000—01; sr. v.p. DMJM Holmes & Narver, Inc., 2001—08, gen. mgr., 2003—; mem. joint venture bd. Lawa Assoc., 2001—07; pres. GEOLINK, 2002—04; sr. v.p. AE Com, 2008—. Contbr. articles to profl. jours., chapters to books. Mem. Chgo. Coun. Fgn. Rels., 1976-80. With USAF, 1970—76, Vietnam. Recipient 1st prize, Am. Soc. Electro-Surgery, 1982. Mem. IEEE, Am. Soc. Indsl. Security Internat., Bldg. Indsl. Cons. Svcs. Internat. Achievements include invention of high speed turn control for land vehicles, 1980; co-inventor child's hidden identification and location device, 1990. Office: 515 S Flower St Los Angeles CA 90071 Office Phone: 213-593-8487. E-mail: bill.sewell@aecom.com.

SEWRIGHT, CHARLES WILLIAM, JR., mortgage banking advisory services company executive; b. Great Lakes, Ill., Feb. 22, 1946; s. Charles William Sewright Sr. and Selma Joy Kester; m. Bonnie Joyce Knight, July 2, 1967; children: Kimberly Ann, Traci Lynn, Megan Paige. BS in Acctg., Calif. State U., Long Beach, 1969, MBA, 1974. Fin. analyst aeronautic div. Philco-Ford Corp., Newport Beach, Calif., 1969-73; sr. acctg. analyst Calif. Computer Products, Anaheim, 1973-74; product line controller McGaw Labs. div. Am. Hosp. Supply Corp., Irvine, Calif., 1974-75, div. acctg. mgr., 1975-76, fin. planning dir., 1976-80; v.p., controller critical care div. McGaw Park, Ill., 1980-85; v.p., controller EZ Painter Corp., Milw., 1985-86; v.p. dept. mgr. automotive fin. services secondary mkts. Marine Midland Bank, Buffalo, N.Y., 1986-87; pres., chief exec. officer Marine Midland Mortgage Corp., Buffalo, 1987-91, Anchor Mortgage Svcs., Inc., Wayne, NJ, 1991-95; exec. v.p., COO Avondale Fed. Savs. Bank, Chgo., 1997—2000; founder, chmn., CEO Quest Advisors, Inc., Northbrook, Ill., 1995—. Chair credit com. Am. Employees Fed. Credit Union, McGaw Park, Ill., 1980-85; vice chmn. Bd. Am. Employees Fed. Credit Union, 1981-85; mem. Fannie Mae Adv. Bd., 1990-92; speaker in field; mem. bd. trustees Medaille Coll., 1989-92; dir. Avondale Fed. Savs. Bank. Mem. Nat. Assn. Accts., Inst. of Cert. Mgmt. Accts. (cert.), Mortgage Bankers Assn. Am. (legis. com. 1990—), Mortgage Bankers Assn. Am. (bd. govs. 1990-98), Beta Gamma Sigma, Phi Kappa Phi. Avocation: golf. Office: Quest Advisors Inc 75407 Rowan Chapel Hill NC 27517 Business E-Mail: csewright@questadvisors.com.

SEXAUER, CORNELIA F., history professor; b. St. Louis, Sept. 14, 1945; d. George H. and Connie F. Fields; children: Angela M. Kolkmeier, Michelle A. Lewis, Michael G. Degree summa cum laude, U. Mo., St. Louis, 1992; MLS, U. Mo., Columbia, 2002; PhD, U. Cin., Ohio, 2003. Cert. in women's studies U. Cin., 2002; hist. preservation 2002. Assoc. prof. U. Wis. Marathon County, Wausau, 2002—. Contbr. articles to profl. jours. Recipient 1st Pl., Phi Alpha Theta, 1994; named Exceptional Adj. Faculty, U. Mo., 2002; Taft Advanced Competitive fellowship, U. Cin., 1998—99, History Tchg. Alliance grant, Fed. Govt., 2002—05, Chancellor's Tchg. fellowship, U. Wis. Colls., 2007, Summer Rsch. grant, U. Wis. Marathon County, 2007, Nat. Endowment Humanities, 2007—08. Office: Univ Wis Marathon County 518 S 7th Ave Wausau WI 54401

SEXTON, EDMUND M., federal agency administrator; BA, U. Ala.; attended, Livingston U. Lic. comml. instrument multi-engine rotorcraft pilot. Sheriff Tuscaloosa County, Ala., 1991—2008; asst. sec. state and local law enforcement US Dept. Homeland Security, 2008—. Mem. dir.'s law enforcement adv. com. Ala. Homeland Security; chair Ala. Mutual Aid Task Force; sitting commr. Ala. Peace Officers Standards and Tng. Commn.; chmn. Ala. E.M.A. Mutual Aid Formation Com.; mem. US Atty. Northern Dist. Ala. Terrorism Task Force, Sentencing Review Commn., Governor's Sch. Violence Task Force. Pres. YMCA, pres. met bd.; bd. mem. E911; mem. bd. visitors Coll. Continuing Studies U. Ala.; mem. Character First Com. Mem.: Nat. Sheriffs' Assn. (pres. 2005—06, Nation's Outstanding Sheriff of Yr. 2007), Tuscaloosa Rotary Club. Office: US Dept Homeland Security 12th & C St SW Washington DC 20024*

SEXTON, JARED, African American studies professor; s. Charles and Deborah Sexton. BA, U. NH., Durham, 1996; PhD, U. Calif., Berkeley, 2002. Postdoc. fellow U. Calif., Berkeley, 2002—04, asst. prof. Irvine, 2004—08, assoc. prof., 2008—. Office: Univ Calif Irvine 3000 Humanities Gateway Irvine CA 92697-6850

SEXTON, JOHN EDWARD, academic administrator, law educator; b. Bklyn., Sept. 29, 1942; s. John Edward and Catherine (Humann) S.; m. Lisa Ellen Goldberg; children: Jed, Katherine. BA in History, Fordham U., 1963, MA in Comparative Religion, 1965, PhD in History of Am. Religion, 1978; JD magna cum laude, Harvard U., 1979; Ph.D (hon.), Fordham U., 2005; degree (hon.), St. Francis Coll., Katholieke Universiteit, Leuven. Bar: NY 1981, US Supreme Ct. 1984. Prof. religion St. Francis Coll., Bklyn., 1966—75, religion dept. chair, 1970—75; law clk. to Hon. Harold Leventhal and Hon. David L. Bazelon US Ct. Appeals DC Cir., Wash., 1979—80; law clk. to Chief Justice Warren E. Burger US Supreme Ct., Wash., DC, 1980-81; assoc. prof. law NYU Sch. Law, NYC, 1981—84, prof., 1984—, Warren E. Burger prof. constl. law, 1994—2001, Benjamin F. Butler prof. law, 2001—, dean, 1988—2002, dean emeritus, 2002—; pres. NYU, 2002—. Dir. Washington Sq. Legal Services, NYC, 1983-2002, Pub. Interest Law Found., NYC, 1983-85, dep. chmn., Fed. Res. Bank NY, 2002-04, chmn., 2004-; past founding chmn. NASD Dispute Resolution; mem. exec. com. Consortium Ind. Colleges and Universities. Author: Modern Federal Jury Instructions-Civil, 1985, How Free Are We: A Non-Lawyer's Guide to the Constitution, 1986, Redefining the Supreme Court's Role: A Theory of Managing the Federal Court System, 1986, Civil Procedure, Cases and Materials, 1988. Dir. Root-Tilden Scholarship Program, 1984-88; chair bd. gov. NY Acad. Scis., 2007-. Recipient Golden Plate award, Acad. Achievement, 2005; named one of NY Influentials, NY Mag., 2006. Fellow Am. Acad Arts & Sciences; mem. Assn. Am. Law Schs. (pres.

1997-98), Assn. Am. Univ. Presidents, Coun. Fgn. Rels. Office: NYU Sch Law Vanderbilt Hall Rm 316 40 Washington Sq S New York NY 10012-1099 Office Phone: 212-998-2345. E-mail: john.sexton@nyu.edu.*

SEXTON, RANDY J., professional sports team executive; b. Brockville, Ont., Canada, July 24, 1959; m. Jo-Ann Sexton; children: Michael, Ben, Patrick. BS, St. Lawrence U.; MBA, Clarkson U. Asst. coach St. Lawrence U. Hockey Team, 1983—85; mgr. ops. Terrace Investments Ltd., 1985-87, v.p., 1987-90; pres., CEO, gen. mgr. Ottawa Senators, 1988—96; exec. dir. Capital Sports Mgmt. Inc. (CSMI); asst. gen. mgr. Fla. Panthers, 2007—, acting gen. mgr., 2009—. Office: Fla Panthers One Panther Parkway Sunrise FL 33323*

SEXTON, ROBERT FENIMORE, educational organization executive; b. Cin., Jan. 13, 1942; s. Claude Fenimore and Jane (Wisenall) S.; m. Pam Peyton Papka, Sept. 15, 1985; children: Rebecca, Robert B., Ouita Papka, Paige Papka, Perry Papka. BA, Yale U., 1964; MA in History, U. Wash., Seattle, 1968, PhD in History, 1970; DHL (hon.), Berea Coll., 1990, Georgetown Coll., Ky., 1993, Eastern Ky. U., 2000. Asst. prof. history Murray (Ky.) State U., 1968-70; dir. Office Acad. Programs, Commonwealth of Ky., Frankfort, 1970-73; assoc. dean, exec. dir. Office Exptl. Edn. U. Ky., Lexington, 1973-80; dep. exec. dir. Ky. Coun. Higher Edn., Frankfort, 1980-83; exec. dir. Prichard Com. for Acad. Excellence, Lexington, 1983—; founder, pres. Ky. Ctr. Pub. Issues, Lexington, 1988—94. Vis. scholar Harvard U., Cambridge, Mass., 1992, 94; chair Nat. Ctr. for Internships, Washington, 1973-80, Coalition for Alternatives in Post-Secondary Edn., Washington, 1977-80; bd. dirs. Editl. Projects in Edn., Consortium Policy Rsch. in Edn., Ky. Long Term Policy Rsch. Ctr., Edn. Trust, Trust for Early Edn., 1992-94. Pub. The Ky. Jour., 1988-2001; editor book series: Public Papers of Governors of Kentucky, 1973-86, Mobilizing Citizens for Better Schools, 5 books, 2004; contbr. articles to profl. jours. Co-chmn. Carnegie Ctr. for Literacy, Lexington, 1990-93; mem. Gov.'s Task Force on Health Care, Frankfort, 1992-99; bd. dirs. Ky. Inst. Edn. Rsch. Fund for Improvement in Postsecondary Edn., 1993-2000; chair Bluegrass Edn. Work Coun., Lexington, 1978-80; founder, steering com. Gov.'s Scholars Program, Frankfort, 1983-85. Recipient Charles A. Dana award for pioneering achievement, 1994. Mem. Am. Assn. Higher Edn. (bd. dirs. 1979-83). Democrat. Avocations: fishing, travel. Office: Prichard Com Acad Excell 167 W Main St Ste 310 Lexington KY 40507-1702

SEXTON, SCOTTY EUGENE, music educator, gifted and talented educator; b. Somerset, Ky., Apr. 19, 1973; s. Isaac Roy and Verna Gussie (Hunley) Sexton. BA of Music Edn. summa cum laude, Cumberland Coll., 1996; MA in Edn., Ea. Ky. U., 1999. Dir. band, tchr. music Hart County Schs., Munfordville, Ky., 1996—98; dir. band, gifted & talented resource specialist Wayne County Schs., Monticello, 1998—2006. Chmn. adv. bd. Family Pl. Resource Ctr., Monticello, 2002—06. Founder, dir. Cardinal Chorus, Monticello, 1998—2006, Cardinal Drama Club, 1998—2006; coach Turner Intermediate Sch. Acad. Team, 1998—2006. Mem.: NEA, Nat. Band Assn., Ky. Music Educatos Assn. (chair elem./mid. sch. band 2004—06), Hon. Order Ky. Cols. Democrat. Nazarene. Avocations: music, scrapbooks, reading, exercise. Home: 130 Golden Pond Rd Monticello KY 42633 Office: Pulaski County Schs University Dr Somerset KY 42503 Business E-Mail: scott.sexton@pulaski.kyschools.us.

SEXTON, WADE J., oncologist, educator; b. Lake City, Tenn., May 16, 1967; s. Curtis C. and Carol J. Sexton; m. Angel V. Varsalona, July 18, 1992; children: Samuel S., Benjamin C., Noah T. BS, Furman U., Greenville, SC, 1989; Med. Degree, Emory U. Sch. Medicine, Atlanta, 1993. Urology resident Wake Forest U. Bapt. Med. Ctr. Bowman Gray Sch. Medicine, Winston-Salem, NC, 1993—99; chief, urology 82nd Med. Group, Sheppard AFB, Wichita Falls, Tex., 1999—2000; fellow, urologic oncology U. Tex. MD Anderson Cancer Ctr., Houston, 2000—01; dir., urologic oncology Wilford Hall Med. Ctr. Lackland AFB, San Antonio, 2001—04; assoc. mem. Moffitt Cancer Ctr., Tampa, Fla., 2004—; assoc. prof., dept. oncologic scis. U. South Fla., Tampa, 2004—. Contbr. articles to profl. jours., chapters to books. Maj. USAF, 1999—2004. Decorated Meritorius Svc. medal USAF. Mem.: Am. Urol. Assn., Quaternion Club. Office: Moffitt Cancer Ctr 12902 Magnolia Dr Tampa FL 33612 Office Fax: 813-745-8494. Business E-Mail: wade.sexton@moffitt.org.

SEYFERTH, DIETMAR, chemist, educator; b. Chemnitz, Germany, Jan. 11, 1929; arrived in U.S., 1933; s. Herbert C. and Elisabeth (Schuchardt) S.; m. Helena A. McCoy, Aug. 25, 1956; children: Eric Steven, Karl Dietmar, Elisabeth Mary. BA summa cum laude, U. Buffalo, 1951, MA, 1953; PhD, Harvard, 1955; D honoris causa, U. Aix-Marseille, 1979, Paul Sabatier Univ., Toulouse, France, 1992, Tech. U. Chernnitz, Germany, 2007. Fulbright scholar Tech. Hochschule, Munich, Germany, 1954-55; postdoctoral fellow Harvard U., 1956-57; faculty MIT, 1957—, prof. chemistry, 1965-2000, prof. emeritus, 2000—, Robert T. Haslam and Bradley Dewey prof., 1983-99. Cons. to industry, 1957—. Author: Annual Surveys of Organometallic Chemistry, 3 vols, 1965, 66, 67; regional editor: Jour. Organometallic Chemistry, 1963-81; coordinating editor revs. and survey sects., 1964-81; editor: Organometallics, 1981—; contbr. research papers and articles to profl. lit. Recipient Disting. Alumnus award U. Buffalo, 1964, Alexander von Humboldt Found. sr. award, 1984, Clifford C. Furnas Meml. award SUNY-Buffalo, 1987; Guggenheim fellow, 1968. Fellow AAAS, Am. Inst. Chemists, Inst. Materials, Am. Acad. Arts and Scis.; mem. NAS, Am. Chem. Soc. (Frederic Stanley Kipping award in organosilicon chemistry 1972, disting. svc. award advancement inorganic chemistry 1981, award in organometallic chemistry, 1996, Arthur C. Cope Sr. Scholar award 2003), Materials Rsch. Soc., Am. Ceramic Soc., Royal Soc. Chemistry, Gesellschaft Deutscher Chemiker, German Acad. Scientists-Leopoldina, Phi Beta Kappa, Sigma Xi. Office: MIT 77 Massachusetts Ave Rm 4-382 Cambridge MA 02139-4307 Office Phone: 617-253-1861. Business E-Mail: seyferth@mit.edu.

SEYFRIED, AMANDA LOUISE, actress; b. Allentown, Pa., Dec. 3, 1985; Actress (TV series) As the World Turns, 2000—01, All My Children, 2002—03, Veronica Mars, 2004—06, Wildfire, 2006, Big Love, 2006—07, (films) Mean Girls, 2004 (Best On-Screen Team, MTV Awards, 2005), Nine Lives, 2005 (Bronze Leopard award for Best Actress, 2005), America Gun, 2005, Alpha Dog, 2006, Gypsies, Tramps & Thieves, 2006, Solstice, 2008, Mamma Mia!, 2008. Office: c/o Innovative Artists LA 1505 10th St Santa Monica CA 90401

SEYMOUR, B(ARBARA) J(EAN), social worker; b. Chgo., Feb. 7, 1930; d. Louis C. and Amelia (Potasch) Jacobson; m. Douglas Seymour, Sept. 15, 1963 (div. 1984); children: Colin, Leif. PhB, U. Chgo., 1948, MA in Social Service Adminstrn. with honors, 1962; MA in English, Portland State U., 1982; PhD in English, U. Oreg., 1985. Caseworker Oreg. Pub. Welfare Commn., Portland, 1950-51, 54-60, asst. to adminstr. Salem, 1963-71; info. dir. Oreg. Dept. Environ. Quality, Portland, 1971-74; lobbyist Tri-Met Transit Dist., Portland, 1974-76, Oreg. Environ. Council, Portland, 1977; dir. social services Pacific U. Optometry Clinics, Portland, 1978-86; pvt. practice psychotherapy Portland, 1976—; pvt. practice in gender identity, 1987—; asst. prof. social work, English Pacific U., Forest Grove, Oreg., 1986—90. Lectr. social work Portland State U., 1972, 76; adj. prof. Pacific U., Forest Grove, Oreg., 1986; cons. in field. Bd. dirs. Columbia-Willamette Planned Parenthood, Portland, 1975-81, 1st v.p., 1978, Downtown Neighborhood Assn., Portland, 1988-94, 2000-06, v.p. 2005-06. Grantee Met. Arts Commn., 1978. Mem. Nat. Assn. Social Workers (cert., chmn. local chpt. 1978-79), Am. Pub. Welfare Assn. (bd. dirs. 1969-70), World Profl. Assn. Transgender Health, Mensa (Oreg. local sec. 1990-93), U. Chgo. Alumni Assn. (local pres. 1983-86, v.p. programs 1986-94). City Club Portland (rsch. bd. 1993-96, 2003-06). Avocations: theater, poetry, literature. Home and Office: Apt 34 1405 SW Park Ave Portland OR 97201-3455 E-mail: bjseymour@spiritone.com.

SEYMOUR, DANIEL KEITH, human services administrator; b. London, May 6, 1971; s. Andrea Louise and John Peter William Rivers (Stepfather); m. Gabrielle Helene Cooper, June 15, 2000; children: Ella Sadie, Jessica Rose. Degree in Politics, Philosophy and Economics, Merton Coll. Oxford U., 1992; degree in Human Rights Theory and Practice, Essex U., 1995. Head office Orgn. for Security & Cooperation Europe, Djakove, Peje, 1999—2000; chief, planning & social policy UNICEF, Hanoi, Vietnam, 2004—07, capacity bldg. officer NYC, 2001—04, chief, gender & human rights, 2007—; rep. Children Advisor, 2000—01; child rights advisor Fgn. & Commonwealth Office, London. Contbr. articles to profl. jours.

SEYMOUR, DOROTHY Z. See **MILLS, DOROTHY**

SEYMOUR, EVERETT HEDDEN, JR., lawyer; b. Tuxedo Park, Apr. 16, 1958; s. Everett Hedden and Deborah (Robinson) S.; m. Pamela Joy Schirmeister, June 11, 1994; children: Sara Isabel, Charles Nathaniel. BA, Yale U., 1980; JD, U. Va., 1986. Bar: NY 1988, US Dist. Ct. (so. and ea. dists.) NY 1988, Conn. 1988, US Dist. Ct. Conn. 1988. Law clk. to justice US Dist. Ct., New Haven, 1986—87; assoc. Davis Polk & Wardwell, NYC, 1987—97; mng. dir., assoc. gen. counsel J.P. Morgan Chase & Co., NYC, 1997—. Articles rev. editor U. Va. Law Rev., 1984-86. Office: JP Morgan Chase & Co 245 Park Ave 11th Fl New York NY 10017-2014

SEYMOUR, JEFFREY ALAN, governmental relations consultant; b. LA, Aug. 31, 1950; s. Daniel and Evelyn (Schwartz) S.; m. Valerie Joan Parker, Dec. 2, 1973; 1 child, Jessica Lynn. AA in Social Sci., Santa Monica Coll., 1971; BA in Polit. Sci., UCLA, 1973; MPA, 1977. Councilman aide LA City Coun., 1972-74; county supr.'s sr. dep. LA Bd. Suprs., 1974-82; v.p. Bank of LA, 1982-83; prin. Jeffrey Seymour & Assocs., LA, 1983-84; ptnr. Morey/Seymour & Assocs., LA, 1984—2002, Seymour Consulting Group, 2002—. Mem. comml. panel Am. Arbitration Assn., 1984—90; mem. bd. overseers Hebrew Union Coll., 2008—; bd. visitors, dept. polit. sci. UCLA, 2008, adv. bd., Sch. Pub. Affairs, 09. Chmn. West Hollywood Parking Adv. Com., LA, 1983-84; chmn. social action com. Temple Emanuel of Beverly Hills, 1986-89, bd. dirs. 1988-93, v.p. 1990-93; v.p. Congregation N'Vay Shalom, 1994-95; mem. Pan Pacific Park Citizens Adv. Com., LA, 1982-85; bd. dirs. William O'Douglas Outdoor Classroom, LA, 1981-88; mem. bd. regents U. Calif., 2001-02; pres. Alumni Assns. U. Calif., 2000-02; chair UCLA Fund, 2002-04; friends com. LA Free Clin., 2006—07; mem. govtl. affairs com. Venice Family Clin., 2005—; mem., bd. dirs. UCLA Found., 2007—; pres. UCLA Alumni Assn., 1998-00. Recipient plaques for svcs. rendered Beverlywood Cheviot Hills Dem. Club, LA, 1981, Jewish Fedn. Coun. Greater LA, 1983, certs. of appreciation, LA Olympic Organizing Com., 1984, County of LA, 1984, City of LA, 1987, Santa Monica Mountains Conservancy, 1999, UCLA Alumni Assn., 2002, others; commendatory resolutions, rules com. Calif. State Senate, 1987, Calif. State Assembly, 1987, 96, County of LA, 1987, City of LA, 1987; mem. bd. Regents of U. Calif., 2000-2002. Mem. ASPA, UCLA Alumni Assn. (mem. govtl. steering com. 1983-97, bd. dirs. 1995—, chair govtl. rels. steering com. 1995-97, pres. 1998-2000, Svc. medal 2008); exec. sect. Calif. Fedn. Young Dems., 1971; mem. Calif. Dem. Cen. Com., 1979-82; pres. Beverlywood-Cheviot Hills Dem. Club, LA, 1978-81; co-chmn. Westside Chancellor's Assocs. UCLA, 1986-88; mem. LA Olympic Citizens Adv. Com.; mem. liaison adv. commn. with city and county govt. for 1984 Olympics, 1984; v.p. comty. rels. metro region, Jewish Fedn. Coun. of LA, 1985-87, co-chmn. urban affairs commn., 1987-89, vice chmn., 1989-90, subcom. chmn. local govt. law and legislation commn., 1990, chmn. campus outreach task force, 1994; mem. adv. bd. Nat. Jewish Ctr. for Immunology & Respiratory Medicine, 1991-93; bd. dirs. Hillel Coun. of LA, 1991; mem. platform on world peace and internat. rels. Calif. Dems., 1983; pres. 43d Assembly Dist. Dem. Coun., 1975-79; arbitrator BBB, 1984; trustee UCLA Found., 1989-97; pres. UCLA Jewish Alumni, 1992-95; mem. Santa Monica Mountains Conservancy adv. com., 1996-99; mem. cabinet Jewish Cmty. Rels. Com. Greater LA, 1994, chair campus outreach task force, 1994-95, govtl. rels. commn., 1995-96, v. chair Jewish Cmty. Rels. com. Jewish Fedn. Coun. Greater LA, 1998; mem. bd. dirs., Century City C of C, 1998-2000, adv. bd. LA Peace Now, mem. adv. com. 2004—); mem., bd. dirs. UCLA Found., 2007—; mem., bd. dirs. West Hollywood Library Fund, 2008—. Office: 2815 Townsgate Rd Ste 140 Westlake Village CA 91361 Office Phone: 818-905-0283. Business E-Mail: jeff@jseymourgroup.com.

SEYMOUR, JOSEPH JOHN, air transportation executive; b. Herkimer, NY, July 11, 1947; s. John Edward and Julia (Crough) S.; m. Susan Elizabeth LathburySept. 19, 1970; children: Abigail, Christopher. BBA, Northeastern U., 1970; M in City Planning, U. R.I., 1976. Dir. urban renewal City of East Rochester, N.Y., 1967-76; spl. asst. for downtown devel. City of Rochester, N.Y., 1977-78; dir. planning and devel. City of Peekskill, N.Y., 1978-82; commr. planning and devel. City of Yonkers, 1983-84; city mgr. City of Peekskill, 1984—89; commsr. of general services NY, 1990—95; exec. dep. commsr. NY Dept. of Motor Vehicles, 1995—2001; exec. dir. NY Port Authority, 2001—. Ind. cons. Village of Hilton, Village of East Rochester, Village of Fairport, Town of Webster, City of Naughatuck, Conn.; corp. dir. Unique Homes of N.Y. Inc. Mem. Internat. City Mgrs. Assn., Am. Planning Assn., Nat. Assn. Housing and Renewal Ofcls. Avocations: skiing, sailing, bicycling.

SEYMOUR, KAREN PATTON, lawyer, former prosecutor; b. Big Springs, Tex. m. Samuel Seymour; 2 children. BA, So. Methodist U., 1983; BS, So. Meth. U., 1986; JD, U. Tex., 1986; LLM, U. London, 1987. Bar: NY 1988. Fed. prosecutor US Attys. Office, So. Dist. NY, 1990—96, Asst. US Atty., Criminal Div. Chief, 2002—04; ptnr. Sullivan & Cromwell, NY, NY, 1987—90, 1996—2002, 2004—. Office: Sullivan & Cromwell 125 Broad St New York NY 10004-2498

SEYMOUR, LESLEY JANE, editor-in-chief; b. San Juan; BA, Duke U., 1978. Reporter Women's Wear Daily, 1978, NY Daily News Tonight, 1981—82; writer, sr. editor Vogue, 1982—91; beauty dir. Glamour, 1994—97; editor-in-chief YM/Young & Modern, NYC, 1997—98, Redbook, NYC, 1998—2001, Marie Claire mag., NYC, 2001—06, More mag., 2008—. Achievements include guiding Redbook magazine to a National Magazine award for public service. Office: Meredith Corp 125 Park Ave New York NY 10017

SEYMOUR, MCNEIL VERNAM, lawyer; b. St. Paul, Dec. 21, 1934; s. McNeil Vernam and Katherine Grace (Klein) S.; children: Margaret, McNeil Vernam, James, Benjamin; m. Mary Katherine Velner, May 15, 1993. AB, Princeton U., 1957; JD, U. Chgo., 1960. Bar: Minn. 1960, U.S. Dist. Ct. Minn. 1960. Mem. Seymour & Seymour, St. Paul, 1960-71; mem. firm Briggs & Morgan, St. Paul, 1971—, ptnr., 1976—2005, of counsel, 2005—. Pres. Thomas Irvine Dodge Nature Ctr., 2006—08, dir., 2006—; sec., bd. dirs. Ramsey County Law Libr., 1972—76; past pres. White Bear Unitarian Ch., past treas.; trustee Oakland Cemetery Assn., 2006—. With US Army, 1960—62. Mem. Minn. Bar Assn., Ramsey County Bar Assn., Somerset Country Club. Unitarian Universalist. Home: 886 S Highview Cir Mendota Heights MN 55118-3686 Office: Briggs & Morgan W-2200 1st Nat Bank Bldg Saint Paul MN 55101 Office Phone: 651-808-6601. Business E-Mail: mseymour@briggs.com.

SEYMOUR, RICHARD DEMING, technology educator; b. Shelby, Ohio, Oct. 3, 1955; s. G. Deming and Elizabeth (Peterson) S.; m. Vicki Stebleton; 1 child, Ryan. BS in Edn., Ohio State U., 1978; MA, Ball State U., 1982; EdD, W.Va. U., 1990. Tchr. Crestview Sr. High Sch., Ashland, Ohio, 1978-81; from instr. to assoc. prof. Ball State U., Muncie, Ind., 1982—. Vis. instr. W.Va. U., Morgantown, 1985, Oreg. State U., 1990-91. Co-author: Exploring Communications, 1987, rev. edit., 2000; co-editor: Manufacturing in Technology Education, 1993. Advisor 4-H Clubs, Richland County, Ohio, 1978-81; dir. tech. in-svc. workshops Ind. Dept. Edn., Indpls., 1988-2000. Named technology tchr. educator of yr. Coun. on Technology Tchr. Edn., 1998. Mem.: Tech. Edn. Collegiate Assn. (internat. advisor 1990—92, nat. contest coord. 1992—), Am. Soc. Engring. Edn., Tech. Educators Ind. (pres. 1995—96), Ind. Math., Sci., Tech. Alliance (bd. dirs. 1994—), Coun. on Tech. Tchr. Edn. (v.p. 2003—05, pres. 2007—), Soc. Mfg. Engrs., Internat. Tech. Edn. Assn. (bd. dirs. 1992—94, chmn. internat. conf. 1999, award of distinction 1999), Phi Delta Kappa, Epsilon Pi Tau. Methodist. Avocations: model railroads, sports, travel. Office: Ball State Univ Dept Tech Muncie IN 47306-0255 E-mail: rseymour@bsu.edu.

SEYMOUR, STEPHANIE KULP, federal judge; b. Battle Creek, Mich., Oct. 16, 1940; d. Francis Bruce and Frances Cecelia (Bria) Kulp; m. R. Thomas Seymour, June 10, 1972; children: Bart, Bria, Sara, Anna. BA magna cum laude, Smith Coll., 1962; JD, Harvard U., 1965. Bar: Okla. 1965. Practice, Boston, 1965—66, Tulsa, 1966—67, Houston, 1968—69; assoc. Doerner, Stuart, Saunders, Daniel & Anderson, Tulsa, 1971—75, ptnr., 1975—79; judge US Ct. Appeals (10th cir.), Tulsa, Okla., 1979—, chief judge, 1994—2000, sr. judge, 2006—. Mem. US Jud. Conf., 1994—, com. defender svcs., 1985—90, chmn., 1987—90, com. to review cir. council conduct and disability, 1996—; joint fed. tribal rels. com. 9th and 10th cirs., 1993—; mem. Okla. State Fed. Tribal Judicial Coun., 1993—94. Task force Tulsa Human Rights Commn., 1972—76; legal adv. panel Tulsa Task Force Battered Women, 1971—77; trustee Tulsa County Law Libr., 1977—78. Mem.: ABA, Am. Inns of Ct. (Council Oak chpt.), Nat. Assn. Women Judges, Fed. Judges Assn., Tulsa County Bar Assn., Okla. Bar Assn. (assoc. bar examiner 1973—79), Phi Beta Kappa. Office: US Courthouse 333 W 4th St Ste 4-562 Tulsa OK 74103-3819*

SEYMOUR, THADDEUS, language educator; b. NYC, June 29, 1928; s. Whitney North and Lola Virginia (Vickers) S.; m. Polly Gnagy, Nov. 20, 1948; children: Elizabeth Halsey, Thaddeus, Samuel Whitney, Mary Duffie, Abigail Comfort AB, U. Calif., 1950; MA, U. N.C., 1951, PhD, 1955; D.H.L. (hon.), Wilkes Coll., 1968; LL.D. (hon.), Butler U., 1971, Ind. State U., 1976; LLD (hon.), Wabash Coll., 1984, U. Cen. Fla., 1990, Stetson U., 1990; DHL (hon), Rollins Coll., 1990. Mem. faculty Dartmouth Coll., 1954-69, prof. English, dean coll., 1959-69; pres. Wabash Coll., Crawfordsville, Ind., 1969-78, Rollins Coll., Winter Park, Fla., 1978-90, prof. English, 1978—. Pres. Ind. Conf. Higher Edn., 1977; v.p. Assoc. Colls. Ind., 1978; vice-chmn. Fla. Ind. Colls. Fund Past mem. Ind. Bicentennial Commn.; trustee Park-Tudor Sch., 1970-78, Bach Festival Soc., Winter Park Pub. Libr., 1998—2004; chmn. Fla. selection com. Rhodes Scholarship Trust, 1983-88; chmn. Habitat for Humanity of Winter Park, 1994—; sec.-treas. Winter Park Health Found., 1998—2005. Mem. Cmty. Found. Ctrl. Fla. (bd. dirs.), Ring 219 (charter), Internat. Brotherhood Magicians, Century Assn., Rotary, Omicron Delta Kappa. Home: 1804 Summerfield Rd Winter Park FL 32792 Office Phone: 407-646-1985. Business E-Mail: tseymour@rollins.edu.

SEYON, PATRICK L. N., social sciences educator, educational consultant; s. Thomas Toh Seyon and Florence Elizabeth Johnson; m. Barbara Greene, Nov. 29, 1991; children: Donald, Marina, Lord Tuan, Letecia Juah, Florence Desiree, Gwyn Thomas. BA, U. Liberia, Monrovia, 1961; MS, Kans. State U., Emporia, 1967; MA, Stanford U., Palo Alto, Calif., 1975, PhD, 1977. V.p. adminstrn. U. Liberia, 1981—84, pres., 1991—96; vis. scholar Ctr. Internat. Affairs, Harvard U., Cambridge, Mass., 1984—86; dir., outreach program African Studies Ctr., Boston U., 1996—2000, rsch. fellow, 1996—; dean liberal arts Roxbury CC, Roxbury Crossing, Mass., 2004—07, assoc. prof., 2007—. Edn. cons. Nat. Summit on Africa, Washington, 1996. Mem., bd. dirs. Internat. Inst. Boston, 1996—2004. Fulbright scholar, Stanford U., 1972—77. Mem.: African Studies Assn. Episcopalian. Avocation: travel. Business E-Mail: pseyon@rcc.mass.edu.

SEYOUM, BERHANE, medical educator; MD, Wayne State U., Detroit, MPH, 2007. Cert. in endocrinology Wayne State U., 2007. Asst. prof. Wayne State U., 2006—. Office Phone: 313-745-3320. Business E-Mail: bseyoum@med.wayne.edu.

SEZNEC, ALAIN, dean, language educator; b. Paris, Mar. 20, 1930; came to U.S., 1941; s. Jean Joseph and Genevieve (Dunan) S.; m. Janet E. Grade, June 15, 1950; children: Anne, Peter J., Catherine G., Dominique M., Michael A. Licence es lettres, U. Paris, 1951, Diplome d'Etudes Superieures, 1953. Instr. French Harvard U., Cambridge, Mass., 1953-55, 57-58; asst. prof. Cornell U., Ithaca, NY, 1958-63, assoc. prof., 1963-69, prof., 1969—, assoc. dean Coll. Arts and Scis., 1969-73, vice provost for humanities and performing arts, 1970-73, chmn. dept. Romance studies, 1976-78, dean, 1978-86, Carl A. Kroch Univ. librarian, 1999—, prof. Romance studies emeritus, 1996—. Editor: Princesse de Cleves (de Lafayette), 1961; author: Diderot and Pope's Essay on Man, 1975. Trustee Wells Coll., 1998—. Served with French Army, 1955-57. French Nat. fellow, 1965; recipient Clark award Cornell U., 1968 Mem. Modern Lang. Assn., Am. Assn. Tchrs. French. Home: 131 Kline Rd Ithaca NY 14850-2114 Office: Cornell U 210 Olin Library Ithaca NY 14853-5301

SFEKAS, STEPHEN JAMES, lawyer, educator; b. Balt., Feb. 12, 1947; s. James Stephen and Lee (Mesologites) S.; m. Joanne Lorraine Murphy, May 27, 1973; children: James Stephen, Andrew Edward Stephen, Christina Marie; m. Elizabeth Ruff, Nov. 1, 1997. BS in Fgn. Svc., Georgetown U., 1968, JD, 1973; MA, Yale U., 1972. Bar: Md. 1973, U.S. Dist. Ct. Md. 1974, U.S. Ct. Appeals (4th cir.) 1974. Law clk. U.S. Dist. Ct., Balt., 1973-74; assoc. firm Frank, Bernstein, Conaway & Goldman, Balt., 1974-75; asst. atty. gen. State of Md., Balt., 1975-81;

assoc. firm Tydings & Rosenberg, Balt., 1981-82, ptnr., 1983-86; with firm Miles & Stockbridge, Balt., 1986-90; ptnr. Weinberg & Green, Balt., 1991-98, Saul, Ewing, LLP, Balt., 1998—2001; counsel Cook & Di Franco, LLC, 2001—05; sole practice Balt., 2005—. Instr. legal writing C.C. Balt., 1976-79; instr. legal ethics Goucher Coll., Balt., 1979; adj. prof. adminstrv. law U. Md., Balt., 1981-93, health, 1993—, law sch. U. Balt., 1993—. Editor Georgetown Law Jour., 1972-73, The Project for Orthodox Renewal, 1993; contbr. articles to legal publs. Bd. dirs. Md. region NCCJ, 1981-89, co-chmn. Md. region, 1986-89, bd. dirs., Orthodox Christian Laity, 1990—98, Ctrl. Md. Ecumenical Coun., 1991—93, The ARC of Balt., 1999-, Vol. for Med. Engring., 2001-05; mem. Piraeus Sister City Com., City of Balt., 1983-89; mem. parish coun. Greek Orthodox Cathedral of Annunciation, Balt., 1981-84; pres. Greek Orthodox Counseling and Social Svcs. of Balt., 1984-88; mem. bylaw com. Girl Scouts Ctrl. Md., 1989-91, Md. Leadership Program, 1997; mem. pres.'s adv. coun. U. Md., Baltimore County, 1999-2002; mem. human rights com. The ARC of the U.S., 2002-07, co-chair, Gov.'s Transition Work Group on Disabilities, 2007-08. Danforth fellow, Woodrow Wilson fellow, WHO fellow, London, 1979. Fellow: Md. Bar Found., Soc. for Values in Higher Edn. (bd. dir. 2002—08); mem.: ABA (forum com. on health law, Grant Morris fellow 1979), Am. Health Lawyers Assn., Bar Assn. Balt. City, Md. Bar Assn. (sec. treas. health law sec. 2009—). Democrat. Greek Orthodox. Avocations: sailing, Ju Jitsu, Judo. Home Phone: 410-448-0548; Office Phone: 410-385-5322. Business E-Mail: stephen@sfekaslaw.com.

SFIROUDIS, GLORIA TIDES, library and information scientist, educator; d. George and Mary Despotides; m. Harry Sfiroudis, June 30, 1957; children: Steven, Christina. BA in Geography and Geology, Hunter Coll., 1954, MS in Edn., 1957; Profl. Diploma in Adminstrn. and Supervision, Queens Coll., 1981. Cert. tchr. effectiveness instrn. N.Y. Tchr. North Babylon Sch., LI, NY, 1954—55, P.S. 123, Bklyn., 1955—61; tchr. 2nd and 3rd grade P.S. 229, Queens, NY, 1970—72, tchr., libr., 1972—74, corrective reading tchr., 1974—82, talented and gifted tchr., 1982—89, acting asst. prin., 1989—90, ednl. enrichment specialist, 1991—2000, tchrs. coll. literacy coach, 2000—04, libr./rsch. tchr., 2004—. Chairperson sch. bd. William Spyropolous Sch. of St. Nicholas, Flushing, NY, 1982—2000; mem., participant Law in a Free Soc., Albany, NY, 1985—89. Co-author: (handbook) The Opera, 1990. Vol. Hosp. Audiences, Inc., NYC, 1975—; active fundraiser Reading Olympics, March of Dimes, UNICEF, Am. Cancer Soc.; mem. exec. bd. St. Nicholas Shrine Ch., Flushing, 1995—. Recipient Vol. Cmty. Action award, Hosp. Audiences, Inc., award, Audubon Soc., 1995; CVS Innovations Charitable Trust Inc. grant, TPI Philanthropic Initiative, 2002—05, Greenwich Conn. fellow, Korean Summer Inst. Yale U. fellow, 1997. Mem.: St. Nicholas Ladies Philoptochos Soc. (sec. 1999—, Pastor's award 2002). Avocations: piano, swimming. Office: Emanuel Kaplan Sch PS 229 67-25 51st Rd Woodside Woodside NY 11377 Office Phone: 718-446-2120.

SFORZINI, RICHARD HENRY, aerospace engineer, educator; b. Rochester, NY, July 25, 1924; m. Corinne Lorenz, 1947; children: Richard Jr., Suzanne Simonelli, Deborah Pugh, Michael, Stephen, Andrew, Mark. Degree of Mech. Engr., MIT, 1954; BS, U.S. Mil. Acad., 1947. Instr. ordnance U.S. Mil. Acad., 1954-56, asst. prof., 1956-57; project dir. anti-tank missile sys. R&D Army Rocket and Guided Missile Agy., Redstone Arsenal, Ala., 1958-59; engr. Huntsville divsn. Thiokol Chem. Corp., Ala., 1959-62, mgr. engring. dept. Ala., 1962-64, dir. engring. space booster divsn. Brunswick, Ga., 1964-66; vis. prof. Auburn (Ala.) U., 1966-67, prof., 1967-85, prof. emeritus aerospace engring., 1985—. Home and Office: 912 Cherokee Rd Auburn AL 36830-2723

SGANGA, JOHN B., retired furniture holding company executive; b. Bronx, NY, Nov. 21, 1931; s. Charles and Marie (Crusco) S.; m. Evelyn Joan Battilana, Jan. 19, 1957; children: Mark, John B. Jr., Matthew. BS in Acctg. cum laude, Bklyn. Coll., 1961; postgrad., Bernard Baruch Coll. Systems analyst DIVCO, Wayne, NY, 1965-67; mgr. mgmt. cons. svcs. Coopers & Lybrand, CPAs, NYC, 1967-74; sr. v.p. fin. and adminstrn. Aurora Products Co. subs. RJR Nabisco, West Hempstead, NY, 1974—78; contr. Gt. Lakes Carbon Corp., NYC, 1979-80, v.p., 1980-81, sr. v.p. fin., CFO, 1981-86; v.p. Cunard Line, Ltd., NYC, 1988; exec. v.p. CFO Consolidated Furniture Corp. (formerly Mohasco Corp.), NYC, 1989—2001, also bd. dirs., mem. Various Othol Furniture Co., 2001—05. Contbr. articles to profl. jours.; editl. adv. to Financial Management mag. Served with USNR, 1950-54. Mem. Inst. Cert. Mgmt. Cons. (a founder), Inst. Mgmt. Accts., Fin. Execs. Internat. (past chmn. com. M.I.S.), Treas.'s Club. Home: 21311 Canea Mission Viejo CA 92692-4992 Personal E-mail: sganga-sr@cox.net.

SGARRO, DOUGLAS A., retail executive, lawyer; b. NY, 1959; m. Breda Sgarro; 3 children. Grad, Hamilton Coll., 1981; law degree, Univ. of Va. Sch. of Law, 1984. Assoc. Brown & Wood LLP, New York, NY, 1984—93, ptnr., 1993—97; sr. v.p. and chief legal officer CVS Pharmacy, Woonsocket, RI, 1997—2004; pres. CVS Realty Co., Woonsocket, RI, 1999—; sr. v.p. and chief legal officer CVS Corp., Woonsocket, RI, 2000—04; exec. v.p. strategy, chief legal officer CVS Corp., CVS Pharmacy, Woonsocket, RI, 2004—07; exec. v.p., chief legal officer, pres. CVS Realty CVS Caremark Corp., Woonsocket, RI, 2007—. Dir. Providence Children's Mus., United Way, Rye, NY. Mem.: Am. Bar Assoc. Bus. Law Sect., Internat. Assoc. of Atty. Exec. in Corp. Real Estate. Avocations: reading, exercise. Office: CVS Caremark Corp One CVS Dr Woonsocket RI 02895*

SHA, BEVERLY E., medical educator; BS, U. Chgo., 1982; MD, Johns Hopkins U., Balt., 1986. Diplomate Am. Bd. Internal Medicine, 1989, in infectious diseases 2002. Clin. instr. Rush U. Med. Ctr., Chgo., 1991—92, asst. prof., medicine, 1992—99, assoc. prof., medicine, 1999—. Office: Rush Univ Med Ctr 600 S Paulina Ste 140 Chicago IL 60612

SHA, WILLIAM T., senior nuclear scientist, consultant; Grad. in Mech. Engring., Poly. Inst., Brooklyn, 1958; Dr. Engring. Sci., Columbia U., NYC, 1964. Mech. engr. Combustion Engring. Inc.; fellow scientist Westinghouse Atomic Power Divsn.; positions including dir. Analytic Thermal Hydraulic Rsch. Prog., dir. Multiphase Flow Rsch. Inst. and spl. cons. to lab. dir. Argonne Nat. Lab., Ill., 1968—97; pres. Sha and Assocs., Inc., 1997—. Vis. prof. Tsinghua U., Xian Jiaotong U.; cons. Heat Transfer Rsch. Facility, Columbia U., Lungmen Nuc. Power Plant Project of Taiwan Power Co., China Guangdong Nuc. Power Holding Co. Contbr. articles to sci. jours.; mem. editl. bd.: Internat. Jour. Nuc. Engring. and Design. Recipient Outstanding Asian Am. award, Asian Am. Heritage Coun., 1984, Argonne Pacesetter award, 1986. Fellow: Am. Nuc. Soc. (Thermal Hydraulics Divsn. Tech. Achievement award 2005, Seaborg medal 2006, Samuel Untermyer II award 2007). Achievements include patents in field.

SHA, XUEYAN, agricultural studies educator; b. Zhangjiagang, Jiangsu, China, Jan. 12, 1964; s. Wenru Sha and Yuxiu Chen; m. Xue Jin, Oct. 21, 1987; children: Sha, Devin. BAS, Nanjing Agrl. U., Jiangsu Province, China, 1984, MAgr, 1987; PhD, La. State U., Baton Rouge, 1998. Asst. prof. La. State U. AgCtr., Rayne, 2002—08, assoc. prof., 2008—. Rice prodn. task force U. Trinidad and Tobago, Arima, 2009—. Contbr. chapters to books, articles to profl. jours. Recipient Tipton Rsch. Team award, La. Agrl. Expt. Sta., 2003, Disting. Rsch. & Edn. Team award, 31st Rice Tech. Working Group, 2006. Mem.: Rice Tech. Working Group, Crop Sci. Soc. America, Am. Soc. Agronomy, Kappa Phi Kappa. Home: 103 Efferson Ln Rayne LA 70578-8646 Office: Louisiana State Univ AgCtr 1373 Caffey Rd Rayne LA 70578 Office Fax: 337-788-7553. Business E-Mail: xsha@agcenter.lsu.edu.

SHABANA, YASSER M., plant pathologist professor, research scientist; PhD, Mansoura U., Egypt, 1992. Cert. plant pathologist Mansoura U., Egypt, U. Fla., 1992. Program mgr. weed biocontrol U. Fla., Gainesville, 2006—; demonstrator Mansoura U., 1981—87, rsch. asst., 1987—92, asst. prof., 1992—98, assoc. prof., 1998—2003, prof., head dept. plant pathology, 2003—. Rsch. fellow U. Hohenheim, Stuttgart, Germany, 1999—2001, guest lectr., 2000; vis. scholar U. Fla., Gainesville, 1989—91; vis. prof. Perdue U., West Lafayette, Ind., 2005—06; program mgr. weed biocontrol U. Fla., Gainsville, 2006—; invited spkr. and cons. in field; co inventor US Patents. Contbr. 18 sci. & profl. Socs. Advisor spkr trainer panel mem. IFS, Sweden. Recipient Professorship award, Sauerborn Lab. U. Hohenheim Germany, 2004; grantee, Higher Edn. Enhancement Project Fund, 2004; vis. scholar, U. Fla., Gainsville, 1994—97; Rsch. grant, Third World Acad. Scis., Italy, 1993, Rsch. and Traval grants, Mansoura U., Egypt, 1994, Travel grant, U. Fla., Gainsville, 1998, Equipment grant, Supreme Coun. Egyptian Univs., 1999, Rsch. grant, Danida, Denmark, Cabi Biosci., UK, 2001—02, Equipment grant, Alexander von Humboldt Found., Germany, 2003, Travel grant, U. Hohenheim, Germany, 2000. Mem.: Weed Sci. Soc. America (com. mem. biological control), Internat. Found. Sci. (sci. advisor 1998—, Rsch. grants 1989, 1991, 1994, 2005, Travel grant 1998), Egypt Agrl. Scis. Soc. (assoc.), Egyptian Mycol. Soc. (assoc.), Egyptian Phytopath. Soc. (assoc.), Arab Soc. Plant Protection (assoc.), Internat. Parasitic Plant Soc. (assoc.), Fla. Weed Sci. Soc. (assoc.), Internat. Orgn. Biol. Control (assoc.), Am. Phytopath. Soc. (assoc.), Nat. Profl. Assn. Agriculturists Egypt (assoc.), Egyptian Soc. State Sci. Award Winners (assoc.). Achievements include patents for broad-spectrum bioherbicide for controlling pigweed species; phomopsis species fungus useful as a broad-spectrum bioherbicide to control several species of pigweeds. Office: Univ Fla 1453 Fifield Hall Plant Pathology Dept Gainesville FL 32611 Home Phone: 352-373-4221; Office Phone: 352-392-9055. Personal E-mail: yassershabana2@yahoo.com.

SHABANEH ALTAMIMI, HAMED A., medical educator, consultant; s. Abdulsalam A. Shabaneh and Ida A. Shawar; m. Abeer S. Abu Snaineh, June 23, 1994; children: Obadeh H. Shabaneh, Layan H. Shabaneh, Hala H. Shabaneh, Jana H. Shabaneh. MD (hon.), Tex. Tech U. Health Scis. Ctr., Lubbock, 2003. Diplomate Am. Bd. Internal Medicine, 2000. Assoc. prof. Patient Friends Soc., Hebron, Tex., 1994—97; asst. prof. medicine and gastroenterology Tex. Tech U. Health Scis. Ctr., 2003—. Cons. U. Med. Ctr., Lubbock, 2003—. Contbr. scientific papers. Independent. Avocation: astronomy. Home: 5804 91st St Lubbock TX 79424 Office: Tex Tech Univ Health Scis Ctr 3601 4th St Lubbock TX 79430 Office Fax: 806-743-3148; Home Fax: 806-743-1183. Business E-Mail: hamed.shabanehaltamimi@ttuhsc.edu.

SHABANI, JAVAD, research scientist; b. Tehran, Iran; Attending, Princeton U., NJ, 2009. Cert. engr., NJ. Rschr. U. Calif., Santa Cruz, 2004—05, Princeton U., 2005—. Achievements include research in real-time 3D thermal imaging using Raman spectroscopy, correlated states of electrons in wide quantum wells at low fillings, strain-induced Fermi contour anisotropic of GaAs 2D holes.

SHABAZ, JOHN C., judge; b. West Allis, Wis., June 25, 1931; s. Cyrus D. and Harriet T. Shabaz; children: Scott J., Jeffrey J., Emily D., John D. LLB, Marquette U., 1957; BS in Polit. Sci., U. Wis., 1999. Comd. 2d. lt. US Army, 1953, assigned to inactive reserves as capt., 1964; pvt. practice law West Allis, Wis., 1957—82; mem. Wis. Assembly, 1965—81; judge US Dist. Ct. (we. dist.) Wis., 1982—96, chief judge, 1996—2001. Office: US Dist Ct PO Box 591 Madison WI 53701-0591

SHABESTARI, KHOSROW TOUTOUNCHI (T. SHABESTARI), research scientist; arrived in US, 2003; s. Javad Shabestari; m. Azam Akhtari, Sept. 19, 1973; children: Neda, Nika. BSc in Geophys. Engring., Istanbul Tech. U., Turkey, 1989, MS, 1993; PhD, U. Tokyo, Tokyo, 1999. Geophysical, Istanbul Tech. U./Istanbul, 1989. Rsch. assistance Istanbul Tech. U., Turkey, 1990—91; rsch. assoc. Internat. Inst. of Earthquake Engring. and Seismology, Tehran, Iran, 1993—96; post doctoral fellowship U. Tokyo, 1999—2000; rsch. scientist Earthquake Disaster Mitigation Rsch. Ctr., Nat. Inst. Earth Sci. & Disaster Prevention, Kobe, 2000—03, Air Worldwide, Boston, 2003—. Referee Earthquake Engring. Rsch. Inst., Oackland, Calif., 2003—, Seismology Soc. of Am., Los Alamos, N.Mex., 2004—. Contbr. scientific papers pub. to profl. jour. Scholar (monbusho) rsch. scholarship, Japanese govtl., 1996—99. Mem.: Seismol. Soc. of Japan (assoc.), Japan Assn. for Earthquake Engring. (assoc.), Japan Soc. of Civil Engring. (assoc.), Seismol. Soc. of Am. (assoc.), Earthquake Engring. Reseach Inst. (assoc.). Achievements include first to time develop JMA intesity attenuation equation for Japan site application for entire Japans rapid generation of GM maps. Office: Air Worldwide Corp 131 Dartmouth st Boston MA 02116-5134 Office Fax: 617-267-8284. Business E-Mail: kshabestari@air-worldwide.com.

SHABICA, CHARLES WRIGHT, retired geologist, earth science educator; b. Elizabeth, NJ, Jan. 2, 1943; s. Anthony Charles and Eleanor (Wright) S.; m. Susan Ewing, Dec. 30, 1967; children: Jonathan, Andrew, Dana. BA in Geology, Brown U., 1965; PhD, U. Chgo., 1971. Emeritus prof. earth sci. Northeastern Ill. U., Chgo., 1971—; disting. prof., 1991; pres. Shabica & Assocs. Coastal Cons., Inc., Northfield, Ill., 1985—. Chmn. bd. dirs. Aesti Corp., 1991-96; rsch. collaborator Nat. Park Svc., 1978-82, 89—; adj. prof. Coll. V.I., St. Thomas, 1980, adj. prof. environ. sci. Northwestern U., Evanston, 1999-2003; Kellogg fellow Northeastern Ill. U., 1979—; chmn. Task Force on Lake Michigan, Chgo., 1986-89; mem. Chgo. Shoreline Protection Commn., 1987-88; cons. Shedd Aquarium, Chgo., 1991; mem. Ft. Sheridan Commn., 1989-90; bd. dirs. Winnetka (Ill.) Hist. Soc. Editor: (with Andrew A. Hay) Richardson's Guide to the Fossil Fauna of Mazon Creek, 1997. Commr., packmaster Boy Scouts Am., Winnetka, Ill., 1984-88. Coop. Inst. for Limnology and Ecosystems Rsch. Lab. fellow. Mem. ASCE, Internat. Assn. for Great Lakes Rsch., Am. Shore and Beach Preservation Assn. (bd. dirs., pres. Great Lakes chpt.), Sigma Xi. Home: 326 Ridge Ave Winnetka IL 60093-3842 Office: 550 W Frontage Rd Ste 3735 Northfield IL 60093-1246 Office Phone: 847-446-1436. Personal E-mail: charles@shabica.com, cshabica@comcast.net.

SHABOT, MYRON MICHAEL, hospital administrator; b. Houston, Aug. 5, 1945; s. Sam and Mona Doris (Stalarow) S.; 1 child, Samuel Laib. Student, Tulane U., 1963-64; BA, U. Tex., Austin, 1966; MD, U. Tex., Dallas, 1970. Intern Parkland Meml. Hosp., Dallas, 1970—71; resident Harbor Gen. Hosp., Torrance, Calif., 1973—78; lectr. surgery UCLA Sch. Medicine, 1977-78, asst. prof., 1978-82, clin. assoc. prof. surgery and anesthesiology, 1983-97, prof. surgery, 1997—; dir. surg. ICU, LA County Harbor Med. Ctr.-UCLA Sch. Medicine, 1980-82; med. dir. Enterprise Info. Svcs. Cedars-Sinai Med. Ctr., LA, dir. surg. ICU, 1982—, vice chief of staff, 2000—01, chief of staff, 2002—03, also bd. dirs. Sec. Cedars-Sinai Med. Ctr. Attending Staff, 1999-2000; bd. dirs. eHealth Initiative and Found., 2006—; adj. prof. U. Tex. Health Scis. Ctr., Houston; supr. sys. chief quality officer Meml. Hermann Healthcare Sys., Houston, 2007, sr. v.p., sys. chief medcial officer, 2007-. Contbr. articles to profl. jours. Served to lt. comdr. USPHS, 1971-73. Fellow ACS (So. Calif. chpt. bd. dirs. 1988—, pres. 1992-93, gov., 1992—), Am. Coll. Critical Care Medicine, Am. Coll. Med. Informatics; mem. Western Surg. Assn., Pacific Coast Surg. Assn., Soc. Critical Care Medicine, Am. Assn. Surgery of Trauma, Soc. Computers in Critical Care and Pulmonary Medicine (bd. dirs. 1988—, treas. 1989—, pres., 1993-94), Soc. Clin. Data Mgmt. Systems (pres. 1985-86), L.A. Surg. Soc. (pres. 1997-98), Phi Eta Sigma. Jewish. Home Phone: 713-647-9894. Business E-Mail: michael.shabot@memorialhermann.org.

SHACHMUT, KENNETH MICHAEL, retail executive; m. Daria Shachmut; children: Spike, Chris. BSEE with honors, Princeton U., NJ, 1970; grad. student in ops. rsch., Columbia U., NYC; MBA, Stanford U., Calif., 1976. Gen. mgmt. cons. Booz Allen Hamilton, San Francisco, McKinsey & Co., San Francisco, London, Amsterdam; exec. officer Safeway, Inc., 1994—99, sr. v.p. strategic initiatives, health initiatives and re-engring., 1999—. Spkr. World Health Care Congress. Lt. (jr. grade) US Navy Civil Engr. Corps, 1971—74. Mem.: Princeton Club No. Calif. Office: Safeway Inc 5918 Stoneridge Mall Rd Pleasanton CA 94588 Office Phone: 925-467-3000. Office Fax: 925-467-3323.*

SHACK, ROBERT BRUCE (BRUCE SHACK), plastic surgeon, department chairman; b. Vernon, Tex., Oct. 7, 1947; s. Nathan Lee and Patsy Lee (Holliday) S.; m. Sharon Summers Frazier, Aug. 16, 1969 (div. 1982); children: Robert David, Nathan Andrew; m. Wanda Kaye, Nov. 11, 1984; children: Jerion Elizabeth, Austin Ryan. BS, Midwestern U., Wichita Falls, Tex., 1969; MD, U. Tex., Galveston, 1973. Diplomate Am. Bd. Surgery, Am. Bd. Plastic Surgery with added qualifications in surgery of the hand. Extern St. Paul's Hosp., Dallas, 1971, St. Bartholomew's Hosp., London, 1971; intern surgery Vanderbilt U. Med. Ctr., Nashville, 1973—74, asst. resident surgery, 1974—77, chief resident surgery, 1977—78, resident plastic surgery, 1978—79, chief resident plastic surgery, 1979—80, asst. prof. plastic surgery, 1982—87, assoc. prof. plastic surgery, 1987—96, interim chmn., assoc. prof. dept. plastic surgery, 1996, chmn. and prof. dept. plastic surgery, 1997—; asst. prof. plastic surgery Johns Hopkins Hosp., Balt., 1980—82, U. Md. Sch. Medicine, Balt., 1981—82. Attending surgeon Children's Hosp. and Ctr. for Reconstructive Surgery, Balt., 1980—82; attending surgeon plastic surgery Md. Inst. for Emergency Medicine, 1980—82, Children's Hosp., Balt., 1980—82, Vanderbilt U. Med. Ctr., Nashville, 1982; attending head and neck surgeon John Hopkins Hosp., Nashville, 1980—82; staff privileges Baptist Hosp., 1982, Centennial Med. Ctr., Nashville, 1982; courtesy privileges in surgery Nashville Gen. Hosp., 1982—93; prof., chmn. dept. plastic surgery Vanderbilt Ctr. for Cosmetic Plastic Surgery; cons. head and neck surgery VA Hosp., 1982—; mem. instrnl. course com. Plastic Surgery Ednl. Found., 1985—86, 1986—87, 1987—88, mem. in svc. exam com., 1985—86, 1987—88, chmn. breast/aesthetic subcom. in-svc. exam. com. plastic surgery, 1988—94, chmn. in-svc. exam com., 1994—97, assoc. vis. prof., 1996; mem. adv. bd. Tenn. chpt. Neurofibromatosis Found., 1990—; sr. guest examiner Am. Bd. Plastic Surgery, 1999—2002, CAQSH exam cons., 1999—2002; mem. carrier adv. com. Tenn. Medicare Part B, 2004—; vis. prof. plastic surgery Scott-White Clinic, Tex. A&M, Temple, 1996; vis. prof. dept. plastic surgery U. Miss., Jackson, 1997; XV Marzoni lectr. and vis. prof. U. Ala., Birmingham, 2000; IX Ann. Coleman lectr. and vis. prof. U. Va., 2001; vis. prof. plastic surgery So. Ill. Sch. Medicine, 2003, Baylor Coll. Medicine, 2003; presenter and lectr. in field. Contbr. chapters to books, articles to profl. jours. Recipient Disting. Alumnus award, Midwestern State U. Divsn. Scis., 1998; named one of Outstanding Young Men in Am., 1969; grantee, LPG, Inc., 1998—99, Aesthetic Surgery Edn. and Rsch. Found., 1998, 1999, Southeastern Soc. for Plastic Surgeons, 2002—03. Fellow: ACS (mem. Tenn. dist. 2 com. on applicants 1990—2000); mem.: AMA, Am. Soc. Plastic and Reconstructive Surgeons (treas. practice rels. commn. 1983—84, mem. fin. com. 1983—84, treas. practice rels. commn. 1984—85, mem. fin. com. 1984—85, 1985—86, socioeconomic com. 1985—86, mem. fin. com. 1986—87, socioeconomic com. 1986—87, 1987—88, v.p. associated mgmt. svcs. 1988—90, chmn. fin. com. 1988—90, mem.-at-large bd. dirs. 1991—93, chmn. profl. liability ins. com. 1991—94, pres. associated mgmt. svcs. 1991—98, chmn. mktg. com. 1995—97, asst. sect. 1997), Tenn. Soc. Plastic and Reconstructive Surgery (pres. 2002—), Tenn. Med. Assn., So. Surg. Assn., So. Med. Assn. (asst. sec. plastic surgery sect. 1984—85, sec. plastic surgery sect. 1986—88, assoc. councilor State of Tenn. 1986—, chmn. elect plastic surgery sect. 1989, chmn. plastic surgery sect. 1990, councilor 2004—, pres. 2008—, pres. elect 2008—09), Southeastern Soc. Plastic and Reconstructive Surgeons (resident and rsch. com. 1984—85, chmn. So. Med. Assn. liaison com. 1986—90, chmn. resident and rsch. com. 1993—95, trustee bd. dirs. 1995—, chmn. spl. edn. com. 1998, 2001—02, pres. 2007, grantee 1998—99), Nashville Surg. Soc. (sec.-treas. 1993—96, pres.-elect 1996, pres. 1996—97), Nashville Acad. Medicine, John Staige Davis Soc. Plastic Surgeons Md., John B. Lynch Soc. (v.p. 1984—85, pres. 1985—), H. William Scott, Jr. Soc. (sec. 1993—97, pres.-elect 1999, pres. 2000—01), Am. Soc. for Aesthetic Plastic Surgery (grantee 1997—98), Am. Soc. for Reconstructive Microsurgery, Am. Soc. Plastic Surgeons (sec. 1998—2001, alt. del. AMA 2000—02, practice commr. 2000—, chmn. by-laws com. 2001—, v.p. 2002), Am. Soc. Maxillofacial Surgeons (mem. fin. com. 1993—98), Am. Cancer Soc., Am. Burn Assn., Am. Assn. Plastic Surgeons, Sigma Xi, Mu Delta, Beta Beta Beta. Republican. Methodist. Avocations: golf, shooting. Office: Vanderbilt U Med Ctr Dept Plastic Surgery 1161 21st Ave S D-4207 MCN Nashville TN 37232-2345 Office Phone: 615-936-0169. Business E-Mail: bruce.shack@vanderbilt.edu.

SHACKELFORD, GEORGE T. M., curator; b. La., 1955; BA summa cum laude, Dartmouth Coll., 1977; MA in Art, Yale U., 1978, MA in Philosophy, 1980, PhD, 1986. Asst. curator European art Mus. Fine Arts, Houston, 1984—88, curator European painting & sculpture, 1988—95; curator European Paintings Mus. Fine Arts, Boston, Boston, 1996—99, chair Art of Europe dept., 1999—, Arthur K. Solomon curator of modern art. Mem.: Assn. Art Mus. Curators (trustee 2003—06, pres. 2006—). Office: Mus Fine Arts Boston 465 Huntingdon Ave Boston MA 02115-5597 also: Assn Art Mus Curators 174 E 80th St New York NY 10021 Office Phone: 617-369-3400. E-mail: gshackelford@mfa.org.

SHACKELFORD, JAMES FLOYD, materials science educator, researcher; b. Springfield, Mo., Sept. 1, 1944; s. Amos Franklin and Opal Leona Shackelford; m. Penelope Lea Openshaw, Dec. 11, 1971; 1 child, Scott. BS, U. Wash., Seattle, 1966, MS, 1967; PhD, U. Calif., Berkeley, 1971. Postdoctoral fellow U. Calif., Berkeley, 1971, McMaster U., Hamilton, Ont., Canada, 1972—73; asst. prof. U. Calif., Davis, 1973—79, assoc. prof., 1979—84, prof., 1984—, assoc. dean,

1984—2001, dir. integrated studies honors program, 2001—. Author: Introduction to Materials Science for Engineers, 1984, 7th edit., 2009, (book) Bioceramics, 1999; editor: CRC Handbook of Materials Science and Engineering, 1992, CRC Practical Handbook of Materials Selection, 1995, CRC Materials Science and Engineering Handbook, 2nd Edition, 1994, Bioceramics - Applications of Ceramic and Glass Materials in Medicine, 1999, CRC Handbook of Materials Science and Engineering, 3rd Edition, 2001, Ceramic and Glass Materials: Structure, Properties and Processing, J.F. Shackelford and R.H. Doremus, Eds., Springer, 2008. Fellow: Am. Ceramic Soc. (Outstanding Educator 1996); mem.: ASM Internat. Office: U Calif Dept Chem Engring and Materials Sci Davis CA 95616 Business E-Mail: jfshackelford@ucdavis.edu.

SHACKELFORD, LOTTIE HOLT, political organization administrator; b. Pulaski County, Ark., Apr. 30, 1941; d. Curtis and Bernice Linzy Holt; m. Calvin H. Shackelford Jr. (div.); children: Russell, Karla, Karen. BS, Philander Smith Coll., Little Rock, Ark., 1979, LHD (hon.), 1988; student, Harvard U., Cambridge, Mass., 1983, U. Ark., Little Rock; LHD (hon.), Shorter Coll., Rome, Ga., 1987. City dir. City of Little Rock, 1978—87, mayor, 1987—91; dir. Overseas Private Investment Corp., 1993—2002; vice chmn. DNC, 1989—; sr. exec. v.p. Global USA, Inc., Washington. Del. Italian Econ. Trade Mission, 1987, U.S.-Soviet Women's Wilderness Dialogue, USSR, 1987; panelist Harvard U. Inst. Polits. Pub. Affairs Forum, 1987; bd. dirs. Little Rock Advt. and Promotion, Econ. Opportunity Agy., Little Rock Job Corps, Elizabeth Mitchell's Children Ctr., Links, Inc., Medicis Pharm. Corp., Phoenix; adv. com. Ark. Vocat. and Tech. Edn., Sta. KARK-TV; speaker in field. Del. Dem. Nat. Conv., 1980, 84, 88, 92, 2000, 04, 08, co-chair, 1988; co-chair platform com., Dem. Nat. Com., 1984, co-chair rules com., 1988, mem. resolutions com.; mem. Dem. Policy Commn.; bd. dirs. Nat. League Cities, Ark. Mcpl. League, Ark. Women's Polit. Coun., Urban League, ARC, Ark. PTA, YWCA; bd. dirs. So. Regional Coun., pres., 1988-90; regional bd. dirs. Nat. Black Caucus Local Elected Ofcls., 1979-92; youth dir. St. Peter's Bapt. Ch., 1969-73; pres. Little Rock PTA Coun., 1973; coord. human and civil rights workshops, 1975-77, others. Recipient Women of Style award, Pulaski County Coun., 1987; fellow, Ark. Inst. Politics, Harvard U. Kennedy Sch. Govt. Mem. NAACP, Nat. Urban League, Nat. Assn. State Dem. Chairmen (sec.), Links, Inc., Delta Sigma Theta, Gamma Phi Delta, Alpha Kappa Mu. Democrat. Office: Global USA Inc 1990 M St NW Ste 200 Washington DC 20036*

SHACKELFORD, SCOTT ADDISON, air force officer, chemist; b. Long Beach, Calif., Aug. 11, 1944; s. Richard Walter and Phyllis Marian (Pearson) S.; m. Alpha Marilyn Coon, Aug. 23, 1969; children: Laura DeAnna, Vicki LeAnna. Student Colo. State U., 1962-64; BA, Simpson Coll., 1964-66; MA, No. Ariz. U., 1968; PhD, Ariz. State U., 1973. Second lt. US Air Force, 1972, advanced through grades to major, 1992; rsch. chemist F.J. Seiler Rsch. Lab., U.S. Air Force Acad., Colo., 1972-74, rsch. group chief, 1974-77,instr., asst. prof. dept. chemistry and biol. scis., 1977-78; lang. student Nat. Def. Lang. Inst., Monterey, Calif., 1978; exchange scientist DFVLR-Institut fuer Chemische Antriebe und Verfahrenstechnik, Hardthausen A.K., Fed. Republic Germany, 1978-80; rsch. sect. chief Air Force Rocket Propulsion Lab., Edwards AFB, Calif., 1980-84; rsch. liaison officer European Office Aerospace Rsch. and Devel., London, 1984-87; dir. Aerospace Rsch. Liaison, 1986-88; sr. scientist F.J. Seiler Rsch. Lab. USAF Acad., Colo., 1987—92, rsch. fellow, Alliance Pharm. Corp., San Diego, 1992-1994, prin. scientist, 1994-1996, adj. assoc. prof., dept. chemistry Point Loma Nazarene U., 1997-2003, sr. scientist I and II Pfizer Inc., La Jolla, Calif., 1998-2003, sr. rsch. chemist, rsch. advisor propellant chemistry Air Force Rsch. Lab., Edwards AFB, Calif., 2003—; sec. Tri-Svcs. Joint Tech. Coordinating Group/Munitions Devel./Working Party for Explosives, Washington, 1975-77; lab. rsch. task mgr. to Air Force Office Sci. Research, Washington, 1981-84, 88-1992; nat. propellant survey cons., 1981-82; mem. sci. adv. com. Simpson Coll., Indianola, Iowa, 1983-87; chmn. Jannaf combustion sub-com. panel Chem. Combustion Kinetics, 1990-1991; chemistry cons. Technica Inc., Orlando, Fla., 1997-1998; sr. chemistry rsch. cons., Turin Shroud Ctr., Colo., 2005-; vp. USAF Acad. Jr. Officer Coun, 1974-1975; lectr. in field. Contbr. articles to profl. publs. Patentee in field. Co-mgr. Tee Ball Youth Baseball Team, Fort Collins, Colo., 1964; asst. coach Am. Legion Summer Baseball Team, Pacifica, Calif., 1967, 68; Sunday school tchr. Village Christian Ch., Colorado Springs, Colo., 1975-77; adult bible study tchr. Warton Barracks Base Chapel, Heilbronn, Germany, 1979-1980; adult class leader Base Protestant Chapel, Edwards, Calif., 1984, chmn. community christian ch. permanent relocation com, 1989—; deacon Torrey Pines Christian Ch., La Jolla, 1995-1997, elder, 1997-2003; Recipient Tech. Achievement award, Air Force Sys. Command, 1977, R&D award USAF Chief-of-Staff, 1982, Alumni Achievement award Simpson Coll. Alumni Assn., 1985; Rsch. grant, Office Naval Rsch., 2005—; chief scientist entrepreneurial rsch. grant, Air Force Rsch. Lab. Propulsion, 2008, dir., 2008-. Mem. NRC (mentor), Am. Chemical Soc. (fluorine divsn., chair San Diego sect. 1998-99). Mem. Disciples of Christ. Ch. Current work: In-situ mechanistic studies of thermochemical decomposition and combustion processes with deuterium isotope effects, energetic material sensitivity, anhydrous nitration reactions, heterocyclic solid salt synthesis. Subspecialties: Organic chemistry; Condensed Phase Reaction Mechanisms Iniviation Sensitivity Heterocyclic Salts. Home Phone: 661-718-2665; Office Phone: 661-275-5847. Personal E-mail: s.m.shackelford2@gmail.com.

SHACKLEFORD, GREGORY M., cancer researcher, molecular and cell biologist, educator; s. Norma M. and James W. Shackleford. BS in Chemistry, U. Ga., Athens, 1975; PhD in Microbiology, U. Tex., Austin, 1983. Postdoc. fellow U. Calif., San Francisco, 1983—89; asst. prof. pediat. and molecular microbiology & immunology Keck Sch. Medicine, U. Southern Calif., LA, 1989—96, assoc. prof. rsch. pediat. and molecular microbiology & immunology, 1996—. Contbr. articles to profl. jours., chapters to books. Recipient award, Nat. Rsch. Svc., 1985—88, Jr. Faculty Rsch. award, Am. Cancer Soc., 1992—94, Rsch. Excellence award, Childrens Hosp. LA, 1993—96, Gold Std. award, US Dept. Def., 1995; grantee, Zumberge Research and Innovation Fund, 1990—91, Wright Found., 1990—91, 2000—01, NIH, 1991—95, T.J. Martell Found., 1992—, Calif. Breast Cancer Rsch. Program, 1995—98, US Dept. Def. Breast Cancer Rsch. Program, 1996—2002, Susan G. Komen Breast Cancer Found., 2000—02, Calif. Cancer Rsch. Program, 2003—05, Pediat. Brain Tumor Found., 2006—; Postdoc. fellow, Damon Runyon-Walter Winchell Cancer Fund, 1983—85, Rsch. scholar, Jean Perkins Found., 2007—09. Mem.: Am. Assn. Cancer Rsch., Soc. for Neuro-Oncology. Achievements include discovery and characterization of multiple genes involved in cancers of the breast and other tissues and genes involved in embryonic development; development of animal models for human cancers. Office: Childrens Hosp LA Divsn Hematology-Oncology 4650 W Sunset Blvd Los Angeles CA 90027-6062 Business E-Mail: shacklef@usc.edu.

SHACKLEY, DOUGLAS JOHN, fire alarm company executive; b. Oakland, Calif., Sept. 21, 1938; s. Floyd H. and Margret I. Shackley; m. Chloe Jeanne Olson, Sept. 11, 1965; children: Derek Todd, Darren James, Daniel John, Christina Louise. Student, San Jose State U., 1957, Chabot Coll., 1962-63; diploma in bus. mgmt., LaSalle Extension U., 1972. Officer mgr. service dept. Am. Dist. Telegraph Co., Oakland, 1961-67; office mgr. Pacific Aux. Fire Alarm Co., San Francisco, 1967-69, mgr., 1969-73, gen. mgr., 1974—2004, pres., CEO, 2004—, also bd. dirs. Mem. task force improved fire protection Gov. of Calif., 1989; contbg. mem. Alarm Industry Telecom. Com.; pres. Dad's Club Chabot Sch., 1969—70, pres. Paren'ts Club, 1971—72; mem. Eden area YMCA, San Francisco YMCA, Boy Scouts Am.; sustaining mem. Calif. Rep. Com.; mem. Rep. Presdl. Task Force, 1994—95; moderator Eden United Ch. of Christ, 1980—81, vice moderator, 1987—88. With USMC, 1957—61. Mem.: Calif. Automatic Fire Alarm Assn. (bd. dirs. 1986—87, v.p. No. Calif. 1987—88, pres. 1988—89, bd. dirs. 1994—95, v.p. No. Calif. 1996—2000, pres. 2003, 2003—, v.p. No. Calif. 2004—, Art Kane Meml. award 2000), Nat. Automatic Fire Alarm Assn. (bd. dirs. 2003—), Nat. Fire Prevention Assn., San Francisco C. of C. (mem. code com.), Lake Mont Pine Home Owners Assn. (bd. dirs. 1988—89), Rotary (Paul Harris fellow). Home: 1380 Carlton Pl Livermore CA 94550-6400 Office: Pacific Aux Fire Alarm Co 95 Boutwell St San Francisco CA 94124-1903 Office Phone: 415-467-9393. Business E-Mail: doug@pafa.com.

SHACTER, DAVID MERVYN, lawyer; b. Toronto, Ont., Can., Jan. 17, 1941; s. Nathan and Tillie Anne (Schwartz) S. BA, U. Toronto, 1963; JD, Southwestern U., 1967. Bar: Calif. 1968, US Ct. Appeals (9th cir.) 1969, US Supreme Ct. 1982. Law clk., staff atty. Legal Aid Found., Long Beach, Calif., 1967-70; asst. city atty. City of Beverly Hills, Calif., 1970; ptnr. Shacter & Berg, Beverly Hills, 1971-83, Selwyn, Capalbo, Lowenthal & Shacter Profl. Law Corp., 1984-99; pvt. practice, 1999—. Del. State Bar Conf. Dels., 1976-2000; lectr. Calif. Continuing Edn. of Bar, 1977, 82-83, 86; judge pro tem LA and Beverly Hills mcpl. cts.; arbitrator LA Superior Ct., 1983—, judge pro tem; disciplinary examiner Calif. State Bar, 1986. Bd. dirs. and pres. Los Angeles Soc. Prevention Cruelty to Animals, 1979-89. Mem.: City of Hope Med. Ctr. Aux., Am. Arbitration Assn. (nat. panel arbitrators, neutral arbitrator, panel chmn.), Beverly Hills Bar Found. (pres. 1995—97, bd. govs. 1998—2001), Beverly Hills Bar Assn. (bd. govs. 1985—90, sec. 1987—88, treas. 1988—89, v.p. 1989—90, pres.-elect 1990—91, pres. 1991—92, editor-in-chief jour.), Nat. Assn. Securities Dealers (arbitrator 1998—), West LA C. of C. Office: 10801 National Blvd Ste 608 Los Angeles CA 90064 Office Phone: 310-474-4115. Business E-Mail: david@shacterlaw.com.

SHACTER, JOHN, technology management and education consultant; b. Vienna, Sept. 26, 1921; came to U.S., 1938; s. Jacob and Regina (Bursten) S.; m. Kathleen Williams, Mar. 6, 1947; children: Suzanne, Linda. BSChemE, U. Pa., 1943. Rsch. devel. engr. Manhattan atomic project Union Carbide Corp., NYC, 1943-44, ops. supr. Oak Ridge, Tenn., 1944-46, process design, analysis mgr., 1946-55, corp. projects and new ventures NYC, 1956-58, mgr. corp. planning and mgmt. systems, 1958-66, founder, dir. multi-co. combined ops. planning Atomic En. Commn. Oak Ridge, 1966-72, asst. to pres., cons. Man. systems, 1972-76, sr. cons., 1976-83; founder, pres. JS Assocs. Mgmt., Tech. Strategic Planning and Edn. Cons., Kingston, Tenn., 1983—; internat. process analysis Frankfurt, Germany, 1955. Adj. prof. grad. engring. design, econs. U. Tenn.; mem. U.S. Acad. Scis. Adv. Panel on Mgmt. and Tech., cons. Internat. Inst. for Applied Sys. Analysis in Laxenburg, Austria. News columnist and host TV and radio discussions; contbr. numerous articles to profl. jours. Named Outstanding Boss of Yr. Soc. of Profl. Secs. Fellow AIChE (past pres., Outstanding Engr.), AAAS, Am. mgmt. Assn. (seminars chmn., lectr.); mem. Tenn. Soc. Profl. Engrs. (State's Outstanding Engr. 1992), Torch Club (past pres.), Rotary Club (past pres.), Profl. Soc. (past pres.), Soc. Profl. Journalists, Tenn. Soc. Ret. Tchrs., Oak Ridge Inst. Continued Learning(chair BRICL). Achievements include contributed basic designs for new multi-billion dollar US uranium enrichment plants, new methods of corp. planning, investment analyses and performance evaluation; incorporating new time-value-of-money concepts and implementations and multinational research and development planning; investment planning this new methods have since been adopted by the world largest corporations. Avocations: water sports, dance, music. Office: John & Kathleen Shacter 458 Foremast Rd Kingston TN 37763-7114 Office Phone: 865-376-7600. Personal E-mail: jsplg@comcast.net.

SHAD, ARTHUR (ART), councilman; m. Virginia Shad; children: Cole, Isaac, Nathan. BA in Bus. & Fin. with honors, U. North Fla., 1994. Cert. financial planner. V.p. investments UBS Fin. Svcs. Inc.; councilman, Dist. 5 Jacksonville City Coun., 2003—. Mem. Rules Com.; vice chmn. Transp., Energy & Utilities Com.; coun. liaison Cultural Coun. Greater Jacksonville; mem. Cultural Svc. Grant Com. Sgt. USMC, Persian Gulf (1990-1992). Recipient Charles D. Webb award, Jacksonville City Coun., 2004. Republican. Office: 117 W Duval St Ste 425 Jacksonville FL 32202 Office Phone: 904-630-1386, 904-630-1382. Business E-Mail: ashad@coj.net.*

SHADDOCK, CARROLL SIDNEY, lawyer; b. Beaumont, Tex., July 7, 1940; s. Carroll Bitting Jr. and Hulda Martha (Gaertner) S.; m. Dorothea Schulze, Nov. 30, 1963; children: Carroll Christian, Peter Eric, Matthew Nolan. BA, Rice U., 1962; JD, Yale U., 1965. Ptnr. Locke Lord Bissell and Liddell LLP, Houston, 1967—. Chmn. Scenic Am., Washington, 1985-92, Scenic Tex., 1992—, Trees for Houston, 1982—, Billboards Limited, Houston, 1982-92. Republican. Lutheran. Avocations: music, golf, travel. Office: Locke Lord Bissell and Liddell LLP 600 Travis St Ste 3400 Houston TX 77002-3095 Home: 2310 Underwood St Houston TX 77030 E-mail: cshaddock@lockelord.com.

SHADE, GEORGE HENRY, JR., obstetrician, gynecologist, educator; b. Detroit, Jan. 4, 1949; s. George Henry Shade, Sr. and Julia M. Bullard-Shade; m. Carlotta Ann Johnson, July 24, 1976; children: Carla Nicole, Ryan McNeal. BS in Psychology, Wayne State U., Detroit, 1971, MD, 1974. Diplomate Am. Bd. Ob-gyn., 1980. Resident physician dept ob-gyn. Wayne State U., 1974—78; ptnr. Vincent, Combs, Massé & Shade, MD, PC, Detroit, 1978—2000; chmn. physicians adv. coun. St. John Health, 2000—02; chief dept. ob-gyn. Sinai-Grace Hosp. Detroit Med. Ctr., 2002—07, v.p. med. affairs Sinai-Grace Hosp., 2005—. Clin. instr. Wayne State U., 1978—82, asst. prof., 1982—2002, assoc. prof., 2002—; asst. prof. Mich. State U., 1982—2002, assoc. prof., 2002—; nat. spkrs. bureau Wyeth Pharm. Corp., 2000—; vice chmn. bd. medicine State Mich., Lansing, 2006—. Contbr. articles to profl. jours. Bd. dirs. Omnicare Health Plans, Detroit, 2001—03. Recipient Psi Chi Nat. honor Soc., Dept. of Psychology-Wayne State U., 1971. Mem.: Sigma Pi Phi, Kappa Alpha Psi (life). Democrat. Baptist. Achievements include research in pelvic endometriosis in the African American female. Avocations: horseback riding, music, photography, art, sports cars and auto racing. Office: Sinai Grace Hosp Wayne State U 6071 W Outer Dr Ste M541 Detroit MI 48235 Office Fax: 313-966-4296. Business E-Mail: gshade@dmc.org.

SHADEGG, JOHN BARDEN, United States Representative from Arizona; b. Phoenix, Oct. 22, 1949; s. Stephen and Eugenia Shadegg; m. Shirley Shadegg; children: Courtney, Stephen. BA, U. Ariz., 1972, JD, 1975. Advisor U.S. Sentencing Commn.; spl. asst. atty. gen. State of Ariz., 1983-90; spl. counsel Ariz. State Ho. Rep. Caucus, 1991-92; pvt. practice; mem. U.S. Congress from 4th Ariz. dist., 1995—, asst. whip, mem. commerce com., fin. svcs. com., homeland sec. com. Mem. Victims Bill of Rights Task Force, 1989-90; mem. Fiscal Accountability and Reform Efforts Com., 1991-92; counsel Arizonian's for Wildlife Conservation, 1992; chmn. Proposition 108-Two-Thirds Tax Limitation Initiative, 1992. Rep. Party Ballot Security chmn., 1982; active Corbin for Atty. Gen., 1982-86; Rep. Precinct committeeman; chmn. Ariz. Rep. Caucus, 1985-87; chmn. Ariz. Lawyers for Bush-Quayle, 1988; mem. steering com., surrogate spkr. Jon Kyl for Congress, 1988-92; former pres. Crime Victim Found.; founding dir. Goldwater Inst. Pub. Policy; chmn. Ariz. Juvenile Justice Adv. Coun.; mem. adv. bd. Salvation Army; mem. vestry Christ Ch. of Ascension, 1989-91; mem. class II Valley Leadership; bd. dirs. Ariz. State U. Law Soc. Republican. Episcopalian. Office: US Ho Reps 306 Cannon Ho Office Bldg Washington DC 20515-0001*

SHADER, RICHARD IRWIN, psychiatrist, pharmacologist, educator; b. Mt. Vernon, NY, May 27, 1935; s. Myer and Beatrice (Epstein) Shader; m. Aline Brown, Sept. 21, 1958 (dec. Aug. 10, 2002); children: Laurel Beth, Jennifer Robin, Robert Andrew; m. Cynthia H. Livingston, Dec. 6, 2003. Student, Harvard U., Cambridge, Mass., 1952-56; MD, NYU, 1960; grad., Boston Psychoanalytic Inst., 1970. Diplomate Am. Bd. Psychiatry and Neurology (dir. 1977-84, treas. 1982-83, pres. 1984). Intern Greenwich Hosp., Conn., 1960-61; resident in psychiatry Mass. Mental Health Ctr., Boston, 1961-62, 64-65, NIMH, Bethesda, Md., 1962-64; assoc. prof. psychiatry Harvard Med. Sch., 1970-79; psychiatrist in chief New Eng. Med. Ctr. Hosp., Boston, 1979-91; prof. dept. psychiatry Tufts U. Med. Sch., Boston, 1979—2007, prof. emeritus, 2007—, chmn. dept., 1979-91, prof. pharmacology, 1989—2007, prof. emeritus, 2007—, chmn. dept. pharmacology and exptl. therapeutics, 1991-93, dir. grad. program dept. pharmacology and exptl. therapeutics, 1999—, sr. rsch. fellow, med. cons. Ctr. for the Study of Drug Devel., 2007—. Author (with A. DiMascio): Psychotropic Drug Sides Effects, 1970; author: (with D. J. Greenblatt) Benzodiazepines in Clinical Practice, 1974; author: Manual of Psychiatric Therapeutics, 1975, 1998, 2003; editor: Psychiatric Complications of Medical Drugs, 1972; editor: (with A. DiMascio) Clinical Handbook of Psychopharmacology, 1970, Butyrophenones in Psychiatry, 1972; editor: (with D. J. Greenblatt) Pharmacokinetics in Clinical Practice, 1985, MAOI Therapy, 1988; editor: (with J. P. Tupin and D. S. Harnett) Handbook of Clinical Psychopharmacology, 1988; editor: (with D.A. Ciraulo) Pharmacotherapy of Depression, 2004; editor: 2d edit., 2007; editor: (with others) Drug Interactions in Psychiatry, 1989, 3d edit., 2005; editor: Clinical Manual of Chemical Dependence, 1991; editor-in-chief Jour. Clin. Psychopharmacology, 1980—. Bd. dirs. Med. Found., Inc., 1980—87. With USPHS, 1962—64. Recipient Seymor Vestermark award, Am. Psychiat. Assn., 1988, 1990; fellow, Ctr. Advanced Study Behavioral Scis., Stanford, Calif., 1990—91; Joseph J. Michaels Merit scholar, 1968—69. Fellow: Am. Coll. Neuropsychopharmacology (v.p. 1984, pres. 1990, emeritus 2005, life emeritus); mem.: AMA (emeritus), Am. Soc. Pharmacology and Exptl. Therapeutics, Am. Soc. Clin. Pharmacology and Therapeutics (emeritus), Mass. Med. Soc. (emeritus,). Democrat. Jewish.

SHADLE, STEVEN CURTIS, librarian; b. Spokane, Wash., Sept. 23, 1959; s. Donald Herbert and Elinor Devine Shadle; married. M in Librarianship, U. Wash., Seattle, 1980, BA in Linguistics, 1987. Tech. svcs. libr. US AID, Washington, 1990—91; ISSN cataloger Libr. Congress, Washington, 1991—95; serials cataloger U. Wash. Libraries, Seattle, 1995—2004, serials access libr., 2004—. Workshop developer Serials Cataloging Coop. Tng. Program, Washington, 2001—01, trainer, 1999—. Contbr. chapters to books, articles to profl. jours. Higher Edn. Act fellow, US Dept. Edn., 1993—94. Mem.: ALA (Bogle-Pratt award 2004), North Am. Serials Interest Group, Phi Beta Kappa, Beta Phi Mu. Avocation: music. Office: Univ Washington Librs Box 352900 Seattle WA 98195-2900 Business E-Mail: shadle@u.washington.edu.

SHADLEY, ROBERT D., retired army officer; b. Circleville, Ohio, Aug. 5, 1942; BS in Indsl. Engring., MS in Indsl. Engring., Purdue U.; M of Mil. Arts and Scis., Army Command/Gen. Staff Coll. Commd. 2d lt. U.S. Army, 1965, advanced through grades to maj. gen., 1997; served in Vietnam and Desert Shield/Desert Storm; exec.officer to the comdg. gen. U.S. Army Materiel Command, 1992-94; dir. for logistics U.S. Atlantic Command, 1994-95; chief of ordnance, comdg. gen. U.S. Army Ordnance Ctrs. and Schs., 1995-97; dep. comdg. gen. for ordnance U.S. Army Combined Arms Support Command, Aberdeen Proving Ground, Md.; dep. chief of staff for logistics Hdqrs. U.S. Army Forces Command, Ft. McPherson, Ga., 1997-2000. Decorated Disting. Svc. medal, Legion of Merit with 2 oak leaf clusters, Bronze Star medal with oak leaf cluster, others. Address: Alliant Techsystems MN07-ME10 4700 Nathan Ln North Plymouth MN 55442-2512

SHADOAN, WILLIAM LEWIS, retired judge; b. Galesburg, Ill., July 12, 1931; s. William Parker and Hortense (Lewis) S.; m. Katherine E. Thomson, 1961; children: Ann-Wayne Harlan, Kate, Tom. BS, U. Ky., 1955; JD, U. Louisville, 1961. Bar: Ky. 1961, U.S. Dist. Ct. (we. dist.) Ky. 1961. City atty., Wickliffe, Ky., 1963; county atty. Ballard County, Ky., 1963-76; chief regional judge 1st cir. Wickliffe, Ky., 1983—2006; ret., 2006. Chmn. Ballard County Dem. Party, 1963; trustee Meth. Ch., Wickliffe, 1961-84; advisor Selective Svc., Peducah, Ky., 1968; chmn. Wickliffe C. of C., 1967-71; mem. exec. com. Ky. Hist. Soc., Frankfort; vice chmn. Ky. Cert. of Need and Lic. Bd., 1973-84; named assoc. justice Ky. Surpeme Ct., 1984. Capt. U.S. Army, 1955-59. Mem. ABA, Ky. Health Systems Assn. (vice chmn. 1976-82), Ky. Bar Assn. (Outstanding Judge 1997), Assn. Trial Lawyers Am., Ky. County Ofcls. Bd. (chmn. 1976-80), Miss. River Commn. (chmn. 1976-83), Ky. County Attys. Assn. (pres. 1966-77), First Dist. Bar Assn. (pres.), Masons (Wickliffe, 32 degree), Shriners (Madisonville, Ky.), Orer Ea Star, Elks. Home: RR 2 Wickliffe KY 42087-9804

SHADOW, RUBY L. WESLEY, nursing educator, administrator, researcher; b. Detroit, Nov. 25, 1949; d. David Williams and Leatrice (Gragg) Williams; 1 child, Nathaniel Rogers Wesley III. Diploma, Providence Hosp. Sch. Nursing, Southfield, Mich., 1971; BS in Nursing, Wayne State U., Detroit, 1974, MEd, 1977; PhD, U. Md., Balt., 1987. Clin. instr. U. Tenn. Sch. Nursing, 1978-79; community health nursing instr. U. Md., Balt., 1984-85; assoc. prof. Bowie State U., 1985-89; asst. dean Coppin State Coll., Balt., 1989-90; asst. prof. Wayne State U., 1991—; nurse researcher Rehab. Inst. Mich., 1992, dir. nursing practice Detroit, 1992-93, dir. nursing, 1993-96; asst. v.p. med./surg. rehab. nursing Sinai Hosp., Detroit, 1996—98; chief oper. officer Detroit Inst. for Children, 1998—99; pres., CEO Big Bros./Big Sisters of Metro Detroit, 2000—02; v.p. programs Detroit Urban League, 2002—03; exec. dir. Wayne County Patient Care Mgmt. Sys., 2003—06; assoc. chief nursing edn. and rsch. VA Med. Ctr., Washington, 2006—. Henry C. Welcome fellow, 1986-87; Nat. Inst. Disability and Rehab. rsch. fellow, 1991-92. Office: Washington VA Med Ctr 50 Irving St NW Washington DC 20422-0002 Office Phone: 202-745-8486. Personal E-mail: drrlwesley@hotmail.com.

SHAEFFER, CHARLIE WILLARD, JR., cardiologist; b. Phila., Feb. 8, 1938; s. Charlie Willard and Lucy Virginia (Chambliss) S.; m. Claire Brightwell, Feb. 24, 1959; children: Charlie Willard III, James Robert. BS, Fla. State U., 1960; MD, Washington U., St. Louis, 1964. Diplomate Am. Bd. Internal Medicine, Am. Bd. Cardiovascular Disease, Am. Bd. Critical Care Medicine. Rotating intern Naval Hosp., Bethesda, Md., 1964-65, resident in internal medicine Oakland, Calif., 1965-68, fellow cardiology Bethesda, 1968-70, staff cardiology Portsmouth, Va., 1970-71, chief, cardiology, 1971-74; cardiologist, corp. sec. Desert Cardiology Cons., Inc., Rancho Mirage, Calif., 1974—. Cons. Naval Hosp., San Diego, 1974-75; head cardiology Eisenhower Med. Ctr., Rancho Mirage, Calif., 1976-78, pres., med. staff, 1982-83, bd. dirs., 2002—; instr. Advanced Cadiopulmonary Life Support, Am. Heart Assn., Dallas, 1983—; Am. Bd. Lipidology, 2007. Contbr. articles to profl. jours. Pres. Riverside (Calif.) County Heart Assn., 1978—79; Calif. affiliate Am. Heart Assn., Burlingame, Calif., 1984—85, Desert divsn. Palm Desert, Calif., 1989—90, chmn. S.W. Region, 1989—90, 1992—93, vol. advocate, 2006, chmn. pub. policy subcom., 1996—99, chair tobacco issues subcom., 1998—; bd. dirs. Eisenhower Med. Ctr., Rancho Mirage, 1990—93, 2002—09, Eisenhower Meml. Hosp., Rancho Mirage, 1990—93. Recipient Bronze Svc. award Calif. affiliate Am. Heart Assn., 1982, Silver Svc. award 1983, 85, 87, Gold Svc. award 1988, Sol Azteca award La Prensa Hispansa, 2000, Cmty. Svc. award Riverside County Med. Assn., 2002; named Physician Vol. of Yr., 1996; honoree Eisenhower Med. Ctr. Aux., 1999, Am. Heart Assn. Desert Divsn., 2004. Fellow ACP, Clin. Cardiology Am. Heart Assn. (Jefferson award, 2005, named Advocacy Vol. Yr. 2006), Am. Coll. Cardiology, Am. Coll. Chest Physicians. Avocations: jogging, music, reading, travel. Office: Desert Cardiology Cons 39000 Bob Hope Dr Rancho Mirage CA 92270-3221 E-mail: cshaeffer@desertcard.com.

SHAEVITZ, JOSHUA WILLIAM, physics professor; m. Sarita Sudhir Shah, July 8, 2001; children: Maina Tsipora, Rishi Sudhir. PhD, Stanford U., Calif., 2004. Miller rsch. fellow U. Calif., Berkeley, 2004—07; asst. prof. Princeton U., NJ, 2007—. Sloan Rsch. fellowship, A. P. Sloan Found., 2008—.

SHAEVSKY, MARK, lawyer; b. Harbin, Manchuria, China, Dec. 2, 1935; came to U.S., 1938, naturalized, 1944; s. Tolio and Rae (Weinstein) S.; m. Lois Ann Levi, Aug. 2, 1964; children: Thomas Lyle, Lawrence Keith. Student, Wayne State U., Detroit, 1952—53; BA with highest distinction, U. Mich., Ann Arbor, 1956; JD with highest distinction, U. Mich., 1959. Bar: Mich. 1959. Law clerk to presiding judge US Dist. Ct., Detroit, 1960-61; assoc. Honigman, Miller, Schwartz & Cohn, Detroit, 1961-64, ptnr., 1965-69, sr. ptnr., 1969—2001, of counsel, 2001—05; prin., owner Mark Shaevsky & Assocs., LLC, Farmington Hills, 2006—. Instr. law Wayne State U. Law Sch., Detroit, 1961-64; comml. arbitrator Am. Arbitration Assn., Detroit; bd. dir. Charter One Fin. Inc.1995-2004, Charter One Bank, 1995-2004, H.W. Kaufman Fin. Group, Inc., Freya Fanning Mgmt., LLC, USF Ins. Co., 1911 Trust Co. Contbr. Wayne State U. Law Rev., U. Mich. Law Rev., 1957-59, asst. editor, 1958-59. Dir. Detroit Mens Orgn. of Rehab. through Tng., 1969—79; trustee William Beaumont Hosp., 1997—, Beaumont Found., 1997—2005, Jewish Vocat. Svcs., 1973—76; mem. exec. bd. Am. Jewish Com., 1965—74; sec., dir. Am. Friends Hebrew U., 1976—84; mem. capital needs com. Jewish Welfare Fedn., 1986—97; bd. dir. William Beaumont Hosp., 2002—, Beaumont Indemnity Co., 2007—, Shaevsky Family Found., 2000—. With US Army, 1959—60. Burton Abstract fellow, 1959. Mem. ABA, Mich. Bar Assn., Franklin Hills Country Club, Detroit Athletic Club, Order of the Coif, Phi Beta Kappa. Home: The Hills of Lone Pine 4750 N Chipping Gln Bloomfield Hills MI 48302-2390 Office: 30883 Northwestern Hwy Ste 200 Farmington MI 48334 Office Phone: 248-737-0808. Business E-Mail: advisors@mshaevsky.com.

SHAFER, BYRON EDWIN, political science professor; b. Hanover, Pa., Jan. 8, 1947; s. Byron Henry and Doris Marguerite (von Bergen) S.; m. Wanda Kathleen McErn, Aug. 22, 1981. BA, Yale U., 1968; PhD, U. Calif., Berkeley, 1979; MA, Oxford U., 1985. Andrew W. Mellon prof. Am. govt. Oxford (Eng.) U., 1985-2001; Hawkins prof. polit. sci. U. Wis., Madison, 2001—. Author: Presidential Politics, 1983, Quiet Revolution, 1983, Bifurcated Politics, 1988, Is America Different?, 1991, The End of Realignment?, 1991, The Two Majorities, 1995, Postwar Politics in the G-7, 1996, Present Discontents, 1996, Partisan Approaches to American Politics, 1998, Contesting Democracy, 2001, The State of American Politics, 2002, The Two Majorities and the Puzzle of Modern American Politics, 2003, The End of Southern Exceptionalism, 2006. Resident scholar Russell Sage Found., N.Y.C., 1977-85; recipient Schattschneider prize Am. Polit. Sci. Assn., 1980, Burdette prize, 1990, Party Politics prize, 2001, 2003, Race & Ethnicity prize, 2006, V.O. Key prize, 2007-08. Mem.: Phi Beta Kappa. Lutheran. Avocations: gardening, livestock management, furniture restoration. Home: Nether Blenheim 10621 W Blue Mounds Rd Blue Mounds WI 53517 Office: U Wis Dept Polit Sci Madison WI 53706-1389 Office Phone: 608-263-1909. Business E-Mail: bshafer@polisci.wisc.edu.

SHAFER, SCOTT L., library director; b. Salem, Ohio, Aug. 5, 1960; s. R. Lee and Betsy L. Shafer. BA, Kent State U., Ohio, 1982, MLIS, 1984. Dir. Wellsville Carnegie Pub. Libr., Ohio, 1985—89; head pub. svcs. Lima Pub. Libr., Ohio, 1989—93, asst. dir., 1993—2000, dir., 2001—. Pres. Columbiana County Librs.' Assn., Lisbon, Ohio, 1987—89, NOLA Regional Libr. Sys., Youngstown, Ohio, 1989, v.p., 1987—89; coord. mgmt. and adminstrn. divsn. Ohio Libr. Coun., Columbus, 1992—93, treas., 2007, v.p. to pres. elect, 2008—; pres. NORWELD Regional Libr. Sys., Bowling Green, Ohio, 1994—95; class advisor Ohio State Bar Found., Columbus, 2000—01; charter mem. Allen County Untied Tax Entities, Lima, 2002—; citizen rep. Lima City Records Commn., 2002—; fellow Oxford Round Table, Oxfordshire, England, 2005—05; mem. exec. com. Lima Area Regional Devel. Dirs. Roundtable, 2006—; mem. bd. dirs. Ohionet, Columbus, 2008—. Contbr. articles to profl. jours. Mem. Rotary, Lima, 2002—08; deacon Market St. Presbyn. Ch., Lima, 1996—99, elder, 1999—2005, chmn. PNC, 2005—07; mem. Lima Symphony Orch., 1995—2005, v.p., 2003—05, pres., 2005—07; mem. exec. com. Ohio Chautauqua Program, Lima, 2001, Ohio and Its People, Lima, 2003. Mem.: ACLU, ALA, Ohio Libr. Coun., Human Rights Campaign, Lima Area Torch Club (pres. 2006—07), Elks, Rotary. Presbyterian. Avocations: art, music, hiking. Home: 260 S Primrose Pl Lima OH 45805 Office: Lima Pub LIbr 650 W Market St Lima OH 45805 Office Fax: 419-224-2669. Business E-Mail: shafers@limalibrary.com.

SHAFER, YVONNE, theater educator, writer; b. LA, Sept. 20, 1936; d. Harvey Jordan and Hazel Bonsall; m. Thomas Shafer, Apr. 4, 1964 (div. 1985); m. Robert B. Chamberlain. BA Speech and Theatre, U. Calif., Santa Barbara, 1958; MA Speech and Theatre, U. Iowa, 1959, PhD Speech and Theatre, 1965; postgrad., Stanford U., 1961—62. Tchr. Reedley H.S., Calif., 1959—60, San Lorenzo H.S., Calif., 1960—61; asst. prof. Humboldt State Coll., Calif., 1965—67, dir. upward bound theatre program Calif., 1967; asst. prof. Bowling Green State U., 1967—70; with U. Del. Honors Program, 1975—80; assoc. prof. Ohio State U., Columbus, 1980—83, Fla. State U., 1984—87, U. Southern Maine, 1988—89, U. Colo., Boulder, 1989—94; Fulbright prof. U. Libre, Brussels, 1995; with U. Md. Overseas Program, 1995—96; assoc. prof. St. John's U., 1996—2006, prof. emerita, 2006—. Vis. prof. U. Ga., Athens, 1974—75, U. Calif., Santa Barbara, 1983—84; disting. vis. prof. Nanjing U., China, 1987. Author: (theatre histories) American Women Playwrights, 1995, August Wilson, 1997, Performing O'Neill, 2000, The Changing American Theatre, 2002; mem. editl. bd. (jours.) Western European Stages, 1995—, Jour. Dramatic Theory and Criticism, 1996—; contbr. articles to profl. jours. Mem.: Eugene O'Neill Soc. (exec. bd.), Ibsen Soc. Am., Am. Soc. Theatre Rsch. Democrat. Avocations: tennis, golf, swimming. Home: 120 2nd St New Castle DE 19720-4806 Personal E-mail: shafery@comcast.net.

SHAFERT, TIM D., science educator; s. Dwite Warren and Lola Catherine Shafer. MA, IUP, Ind., Pa., 1976. Cert. EPA refrigerant, RSES, 1995. Asst. prof. Shafer HVAC, Kittanning, Pa., 1980—90, WCCC, Youngwood, Pa., 1990—. With USNR, 1968—70, Lower Burell, Pa. Home: 703 N Mckean St Kittanning PA 16201 Office: WCCC 415 Pavillion Ln Youngwood PA 15697 Office Fax: 724-925-1150. Personal E-mail: sirteachyou@yahoo.com. Business E-Mail: shafert@my.wccc.edu.

SHAFF, KAREN E., lawyer, insurance company executive; BA, Northwestern U., Evanston, Ill.; JD, Drake U., Des Moines. Atty. Austin and Gaudineer, Des Moines, 1979—82, Principal Fin. Group, 1982—83, asst. counsel, 1983—86, assoc. counsel, 1986—90, sr. v.p., gen. counsel, 1999—2004, exec. v.p., 2004—, gen. counsel, 2004—. Bd. dir. Sargasso Mut. Ins. Co., GuideOne Mut. Ins. Co., GuideOne Specialty Mut. Ins. Co. Bd. mem. Hospice of Ctrl. Iowa Found., Sci. Ctr. of Iowa; trustee Grinnell Coll.; mem. Greater Des Moines Partnership. Mem.: ABA, Assn. Life Ins. Counsel (bd. mem., pres. elect), Am. Corp. Counsel Assn., Polk County Bar Assn., Iowa State Bar Assn. (mem. bd. gov. 1989—95). Office: Principal Fin Group 711 High St Des Moines IA 50392

SHAFFER, ANITA MOHRLAND, counselor, educator; b. Racine, Wis., Apr. 5, 1939; d. Milton Arthur and Gudrun Amanda Stoffel. BS magna cum laude, U. Wis., 1961; MEd, U. Wash., 1966; postgrad., Ariz. State U., 1971-76. Cert. in elem. edn., social sci. secondary edn., spl. edn., Tex.; lic. profl. counselor, Tex. Tchr. Racine Unified Dist. 1, 1961-63, Edmonds Sch. Dist. 15, Lynnwood, Wash., 1963-70, Ariz. Dept. Corrections, Phoenix, 1971-77; tchr. spl. edn. Pasadena (Tex.) Ind. Sch. Dist., 1977-78, spl. edn. counselor, 1978-90, elem. counselor, 1990-98; univ. supr. U. Houston, 1998—. Ednl. cons., 1998—. Mem. Tex. Counseling Assn., Houston Counseling Assn., Mus. Fine Arts Houston (patron), Houston Lic. Profl. Counselors Assn., Pi Lambda Theta, World Affairs Coun. Home: 5905 Woodway Place Ct Houston TX 77057-2005

SHAFFER, BENJAMIN SCOTT, surgeon; b. Mansfield, Ohio, Apr. 22, 1958; s. Sheldon and Dianne Shaffer; m. Jill Rara Duryea, Feb. 4, 1970; children: Emma Rose, Noah Charles. BS, U. Fla., Gainesville, 1980, MD, 1984. Diplomate Am. Bd. Orthop. Surgeons, 1992. Sports medicine fellow Kerlan Jobe Orthop. Clinic, LA, 1989—90; orthop. surgeon Kaiser Permanente Med. Group, LA, 1990—92; chief, dept. orthop. Georgetown U. Med. Ctr., Washington, 1992—2000; surgeon Wash. Orthops. and Sports Medicine, Washington, 2000—. Head team physician Georgetown U. Athletic Dept., Washington, 1992—2000, Wash. Capitals NHL Hockey Club, Washington, 1999—2008, Wash. Freedom Pro Womens Soccer Team, Washington, 2001—03; cons. Arthrex, Naples, Fla., 2006—08; head team physician Wash. Nationals MLB Baseball Club, Washington, 2006—08. Health care com. Barack Obama Healthcare Com., Washington, 2008—08. Recipient Alonzo Neufeld award, Western Orthop. Soc., 1991; named one of Top Doctor, Wash. Mag., 2003; named to Hall of Fame, U. Fla., Gainesville, 1980. Mem.: NHL Team Physicians Soc. (v.p. 2007—, pres. 2009—), Am. Soc. Shoulder and Elbow Surgeons, Am. Orthop. Soc. Sports Medicine, Arthroscopy Assn. N.Am. Achievements include invention of intra-articular measuring device for ACL knee reconstruction. Avocations: running, tennis, video editing. Office: Wash Orthop and Sports Medicine 2021 K St NorthWest Ste 516 Washington DC 20007 Office Fax: 202-296-2515.

SHAFFER, BERNARD WILLIAM, mechanical and aerospace engineering educator; b. NYC, Aug. 7, 1924; s. Abraham and Eva (Ellinsky) S.; m. Florence Solow, Feb. 23, 1947 (dec. Oct. 29, 1986); children: Janet Ilene, Roberta Franceen. BME, CCNY, 1944; MSME, Case Inst. Tech. (now Case W. Res. U.), 1947; PhD, Brown U., 1951. Registered profl. engr., N.Y., R.I. Aero. rsch. scientist flight propulsion rsch. lab. NACA (now NASA), Cleve., 1944-47; spl. lectr. applied mechanics Case Inst. Tech. (now Case Western Reserve Univ.), Cleve., 1946-47; rsch. assoc., grad. div. applied math. and engring. instr. Brown U., Providence, 1947-50; asst. prof. mech. engring. NYU, NYC, 1950-53, assoc. prof., 1953-58, prof., project dir. rsch. divsn., 1958-73; prof. dept. mech. and aerospace engring. Poly. Inst. NYU, Bklyn., 1973—93, Farmingdale, prof. emeritus Bklyn., 1993—. Cons. in field; mem. adv. coun. Coll. Aeros., N.Y.C., 1982—; vis. rsch. prof. mech. engring. Fla. Atlantic U., Boca Raton, 1992, Disting. vis. rsch. prof., 1993-95, 97—. Contbr. articles to profl. jours. Bd. dirs. Harbor Hills Civic Assn., Great Neck, N.Y., 1968-71. With USAAF, 1944-47. Recipient various govt. grants. Fellow ASME (Richards Meml. award 1968); mem. AIAA (assoc. fellow), Sigma Xi, Tau Beta Pi, Pi Tau Sigma. Avocations: golf, swimming.

SHAFFER, BRENDA JOYCE, minister; b. Somerset, Pa., Oct. 29, 1944; d. James Howard and Eva Lorene (Olsen) Folk; m. Thomas Neil Shaffer, June 11, 1966; children: Michael Alan, Christopher James. BS Elem. Edn., Indiana U. Pa., 1966, MS Ednl. Psychology, 1974, postgrad., 1992, Duke U., 2003—07. Cert. elem. prin. Tchr. Prince George's County Sch., North Forestville Elem., Lanham Elem., Md., 1966—69; tchr. elem. schs. Anne Arundel County Schs., Md., 1969—70, Shade-Ctrl. Sch. Dist., Cairnbrook, Pa., 1971—91, tchr. instrnl. support, 1991—98; min. Beulah United Meth. Ch., Friedens, Pa., 2003—. Computer assoc. U. Pitts., 1987—; mem. Oxford U. Roundtable, Eng., 2007; presenter computer workshops Sunday sch. tchr., chair edn. com. Otterbein United Meth. Ch., Wilbur, Pa., 1990—; mem. Central City (Pa.) Choir, 1991, Somerset (Pa.) Cmty. Choir, 1992, Johnston (Pa.) Choraleers, 1993, Johnstown Symphony Chorus, 1994-95; com. Red Ribbon Campaign, Somerset, 1991, We. Pa. Minister's Chorus, 2002-, Duke U. Course of Study Choir, 2003-07; mem. Western Pa. UMC Coun. Fin. and Adminstrn., children's ministry team United Meth. Ch.; mem. Connellsville Dist. Lay Ministry Com. Mem. ASCD, NEA, Pa. ASCD, Pa. State Edn. Assn., Shade Edn. Assn. (v.p. 1980-81), Nat. Coun. Tchrs. Math., Kappa Delta Pi Avocations: reading, walking, choir. Home: 3023 Whistler Rd Stoystown PA 15563-9802 Office: Beulah United Meth Ch 433 Bicycle Rd Friedens PA 15541

SHAFFER, HARRY GEORGE, retired economics professor; b. Vienna, Aug. 28, 1919; arrived in U.S., 1940; s. Max Schaffer and Teofilia (Infeld) Schaffer Weissman; m. Betty Rosenzweig, June 7, 1987; children by previous marriages: Bernard Charles, Ronald Eric, Len Joseph, Tanya Elaine; stepchildren: Rene Carlis, Jamie Paul. BS, NYU, 1947, MA, 1948, PhD, 1958. Instr. Concord Coll., Athens, W.Va., 1948-50, U. Ala., Tuscaloosa, 1950-56; from asst. prof. to prof. U. Kans., Lawrence, 1956-69, prof. econs. and Soviet and East European studies, 1969—90, prof. emeritus, 1990—. Vis. prof. Portland State Coll., Oreg., summer 1963, U. Calif.-Davis, 1973-74. Author: English-Language Periodic Publications on Communism, 1971, Periodicals on the Socialist Countries and on Marxism, 1977, Women in the Two Germanies, 1981, American Capitalism and the Changing Role of Government, 1999; author booklet: The U.S. Conquers the West, 1974; editor: The Soviet Economy, 1963, rev. edit., 1969, The Soviet System in Theory and Practice, 1965, 2d edit., 1984, The Communist World: Marxist and Non-Marxist Views, 1967; (with Jan Prybyla) From Under-Development to Affluence: Western, Soviet and Chinese Views, 1968; editor, contbg. author: The Soviet Treatment of Jews, 1974, Soviet Agriculture, 1977; contbr. articles to profl. jours. Served with M.I., US Army, 1943-44 Mem. Am. Econ. Assn., Assn. Comparative Econ. Studies, AAUP, Ams. for Dem. Action, Common Cause, NAACP, Unity Ch., Beta Gamma Sigma Democrat. Jewish. Home: 2510 Jasu Dr Lawrence KS 66046-4537 Office: U Kans Dept Econs 355 Snow Hall Lawrence KS 66045-7522 Office Phone: 785-864-3501.

SHAFFER, JOYE COY, reading specialist; b. Lorain, Ohio; d. Harold Russell and Rose Marie (Uhrig) Jenkins; m. Robert H. Shaffer; children: John Coy, William Coy, Connie Coy Weeks, Teri Coy McLean. BS in Edn. cum laude, Kent State U., 1966; MA in Edn. summa cum laude, Calif. State U., Long Beach, 1971; EdD in Edn., U. No. Colo., 1975; postgrad., Oxford U., summer 1987, 89. Evaluator Colo. Dept. Edn., 1978; dir. Summer Reading Clinic U. Sask., Saskatoon, 1974; dir. U.S. Office Edn. Right-to Read Project U. No. Colo., Greeley, 1975-78; external evaluator ERIC Clearinghouse on Reading and Comm. Ind. U., Bloomington, 1989; asst. to dean Fla. State U., Panama City, 1982-86, dir. info. svcs., 1987-89; reading resource specialist, tchr. Orange County Schs., Orlando, Fla., 1989-95. Vis. prof. adult literacy summers Columbia U. Tchrs. Coll., NYC, 1976—77; vis. scholar Ind. U., Bloomington, 1988—89. Contbr. articles to profl. jours. Exhibiting mem. Fla. com. Nat. Mus. Women in the Arts, 2006—; exhibiting mem. Beaux Arts of Volusia County, Fla.; bd. mem. Women's Resource Ctr. Gulf Coast Cmty. Hosp., 1986—89. Grantee Right-To-Read, 1975-78; recipient Cert. of Distinction Colo. Assn. Adult and Continuing Edn., 1978, Cert. of Appreciation City of Greeley Human Rels. Commn., 1979. Mem. LWV (program chairperson Bay County, Fla. 1987-89), Fla. Reading Assn. (v.p. 1990-91, pres. 1992-93), Internat. Reading Assn. (chairperson basic edn. and reading com. 1978-79, pres. Weld County coun. 1975-76), Fla. Literacy Coalition, AAUW Hist. Preservation Project. Avocations: art, golf, tennis, travel. Home: Seascape Towers # 426 5207 S Atlantic Ave New Smyrna Beach FL 32169

SHAFFER, KITT, radiologist, educator; b. Kans. City, Mo., Apr. 9, 1954; d. William Elias and Anna Mae Johnston Shaffer; m. Timothy Paul Titcomb, Feb. 14, 1980. MD, Tufts Sch. Medicine, Boston, 1983; PhD, U. Kans., 1983—83. Diplomate Am. Bd. Radiology, 1987. Co-dir., thoracic imaging Brigham & Women's Hosp., Boston, 1991—92, dir., med. student edn. radiology, 1996—2005, radiology ednl. cons., 2008—; asst. chief radiology Dana-Farber Cancer Inst., Boston, 2001—04; dir., human body course anatomy Harvard Med. Sch., Boston, 2005—07, lectr. radiology, 2008—; dir. Cambridge Health Alliance, Cambridge, Mass., 2005—08; vice-chair Dept. Radiology, Boston Med. Ctr., 2008—; prof. radiology Boston U. Med. Sch. Radiology ednl. cons. Brigham and Women's Hosp., Boston, 2008—; vis. prof. radiology Dartmouth Med. Ctr., Hanover, NH, 2003—07, U. Wash., Seattle, 2007; vis. prof. radiology St. Luke's Healthcare Sys., Kans. City, Mo., 2008, U. Ind., Indpls., 2009—, U. Western Ont., London, 2009—, U. Md., Balt., Emory U., Atlanta; anatomy question writer Nat. Bd. Med. Examiners, Phila., 2006—08; thoracic bd. examiner Am. Bd. Radiology, Louisville, 2000—; chair, edn. com. Alliance Med. Student Educators Radiology, 2006—. Panelist Dana-Farber Cancer Inst., Boston, 2002—04. Recipient Warren Widrich Edn. award, Boston Va. Med. Ctr. Dept Radiology, 1988, Faculty prize, Harvard Med. Sch., 2005, Profl. Leadership award, Am. Assn. Women Radiologists, 2004, Outstanding Tutor award, Acad. Harvard Med. Sch., 2007; named one of Best First Yr. Tutor, Harvard Med. Sch., 2003, Tutor of Yr., 2004; fellowship, Harvard Macy Insst., 1999, Bok Ctr. Edn., Harvard U., 2000, fellow, Shapiro Ctr. Beth Israel, Boston, 2001, Provost IT Innovation grant, Harvard U., 2000, Provost Equipment grant, 2005. Mem.: Soc. Breast Imaging, Soc. Thoracic Radiologists, Am. Coll. Radiology, Am. Roentgen Ray Soc. (mem. edn. com.), Alliance Med. Student Educators Radiology (pres., founding mem. 2005—06), Assn. U. Radiologists, Am. Assn. Women Radiologists, New Eng. Roentgen Ray Soc., Radiologic Soc. North America, Alpha Omega Alpha. Achievements include first to development of web-based teaching modules of radiologic anatomy. Avocations: painting, ceramics. Office Fax: 617-638-6602; Home Fax: 617-638-6602. Business E-Mail: kitt.shaffer@bmc.prg.

SHAFFER, LEIGH S., psychology professor; d. Edward Wesley and Ruth D. Shaffer; m. Barbara Anne Benskin, Aug. 14, 1971; 1 child, Victoria Anne. BA, Wichita State U., 1969, MA, 1971; DPhil, Pa. State U., 1974. Asst. prof. psychology Pa. State U., McKeesport, 1974—77, Nebr. Wesleyan U., Lincoln, 1977—80, West Chester U., Pa., 1980—. Acting assoc. provost West Chester U., 2002. Co-author: Voices From the Pagan Census, 2003; contbr. articles to profl. jours. Avocation: golf. Office: West Chester U 407 Old Libr Bldg West Chester PA 19383

SHAFFER, RICHARD JAMES, lawyer, retired manufacturing executive; b. Pe Ell, Wash., Jan. 26, 1931; s. Richard Humphrys and Laura Rose (Faas) S.; m. Donna M. Smith, May 13, 1956; children: Leslie Lauren Shaffer Litsinger, Stephanie Jane Athenton. BA, U. Wash.; LL.B., Southwestern U. Bar: Calif. Various positions in mfg. and contracts adminstrn. depts. N. Am. Aviation Inc./Rockwell Corp.; western regional counsel The Bendix Corp., 1968—73; v.p., gen. counsel Norris Industries Inc., Long Beach, Calif., 1974—81; v.p., gen. counsel, sec. NI Inc., Long Beach, Calif., 1981—89; gen. counsel Masco Bldg. Products Corp., 1985—89; pvt. practice, 1989—98; internat. ops. officer Newport Fin. Group, 2003; CFO Dreamquest Entertainment Ltd., 2004; cons., 2005—. Chmn. Calif. State Senate Ltd. Liability Co. Act drafting com., mem. task force Calif. State Bar, 1992-94; lectr. in field. Co-author: Practicing Under the Limited Liability Company Act. Trustee Ocean View Sch. Dist., 1965-73, pres., 1966, 73; mem. fin. adv. com. Orange Coast Coll., 1966; mem. Long Beach Local Devel. Corp., 1978-89, Calif. Senate Commn. on Corp. Governance, Shareholders' Rights and Securities Transactions, 1986-97, chmn. drafting com. ltd. liability co. act for senate com., 1991-93; mem. Pers. Commn. City of Huntington Beach, 1996-98; mem. Huntington Beach clean water subcom. Huntington Harbour; bd. dirs. Huntington Beach Libr. Patrons, 1996-98. Ensign and lt. j.g. USN, 1954—57. Mem. ABA, Am. Arbitration Assn.(bd. arbitrators), Calif. Bar Assn. (exec. com. corp. law dept. com. bus. sect. 1981-88), Orange County Bar Assn., Trinidad Island Homeowners Assn. (pres.), Huntington Harbour Yacht Club, Catalina Island Yacht Club, Wanderlust Skiers of Huntington Harbour. Avocations: skiing, yachting.

SHAFFER, RICHARD PAUL, financial planner, real estate company executive, military officer; b. Ft. Worth, Oct. 12, 1949; AA in Bus., Coll. of the Mainland, 1975; BBA in Bus., Sam Houston State U., Huntsville, Tex., 1975, MBA in Bus., 1976. Pers. technician U.S. Govt., Houston, 1968-75; pers. recruiter M.D. Anderson Cancer Hosp., Houston, 1976-79; acctg. auditor State of Tex., Galveston, 1979-82; owner, fin. planner Co. Benefits, Galveston, 1982—; owner Shaffer & Assocs. Real Estate, Galveston, 1982—. Master sgt. USAFR, 1967—87. Mem.: N.G. Assn. Tex., Modern Woodmen Am. (No. 2 Agt. Calif. 2004, No. 7 Agt. Annuity Sales 2004, No. 10 Agt. Pres.' Cabinet 2004, Million Dollar Round Table). Republican. Methodist. Avocations: pilot, swimming, fishing, dance, reading. Home: 743 Marlin Bayou Vista Hitchcock TX 77563-2611 Office: Co Benefits 743 Marlin St Hitchcock TX 77563-2611 E-mail: rpshaffer@woodmen.org.

SHAFFER, SCOTT A., biology professor, researcher; b. San Diego, 1966; s. Ernest and Mae Shaffer; m. Kelly L. Rankin. BS, San Diego State U., 1993; MS, U. Calif., Santa Cruz, 1996, PhD, 2000. Rsch. faculty U. Calif., 2000—07; asst. prof. Calif. State U., San Bernardino, 2008—. Educator Nat. Audubon Soc., Local chpt., Walnut Creek, Calif., 2000. Recipient Elton prize, Jour. Animal Ecology, Antarctic Svc. medal; grantee, Calif. Sea Grant, Moore Found., Packard Found.; Rsch. fellowship, NSF REU. Fellow: Ecol. Soc. America; mem.: AAAS, Am. Physiol. Soc. Office: Univ Calif Long Marine Lab 100 Shaffer Rd Santa Cruz CA 95060-5730 Business E-Mail: shaffer@ucsc.edu.

SHAFFER, SHERRILL LYNN, economist; b. Tyler, Tex., Aug. 1, 1952; s. Douglas Marsene and Ethel Elizabeth (Green) S.; m. Margaret Jane Ahrens, Jun 20, 1987; 1 child, David Carsten. BA, Rice U., Houston, 1974; MA, Stanford U., Calif., 1978, PhD, 1981. Rsch. asst. Stanford U., Calif., 1976—79, instr., 1979—80; from economist to chief Fed. Res. Bank NY, NYC, 1980—88; from rsch. officer, economist to asst. v.p./discount officer Fed. Res. Bank Phila., 1988—97; John A. Guthrie disting. prof. banking and fin. svcs. U. Wyo., Laramie, 1997—. Vis. scholar Stanford U., 2004; chmn. tenure and promotion com., grad. coun., 2000-02, MBA adv. com., grad. admissions com., 1999-2000, grad. program rev. com., 2000-02; violinist solo and with orchs., Calif., NY, 1976-88; cons. asst. Rosse & Olszewski, Palo Alto, Calif., 1978-80; rsch. assoc. Ctr. for Applied Macroecon. Analysis Australian Nat. U., 2008-; cons. in field. Contbr. articles to profl. jours.; assoc. editor to editor Jour. Econs. and Bus., 1993—, mem. editl. bd. Jour. Regulatory Econs., 2002—. Sec. bd. dirs. NY Arts Group, NYC, 1982—83; mem. program com. So. Fin. Assn., 1996; exec. adv. coun. mem. dept. fin. Temple U., 1996—97; bd. advisors cultural programs series U. Wyo., 1999—; mem. fin. com. St. Matthew's Cathedral, Laramie, Wyo., 1998—2004, mem. vestry, 1999—2002; bd. dirs. artist selection com. Tri-County Concerts Assn., 1996—. Recipient Messier cert. Astron. League, 1993, Anbar Citation of Excellence for published rsch., 1996, 1998, Outstanding Sr. Svc. award, U. Wyo. Coll. Bus., 2000—01, 2002—03, Outstanding Sr. Rsch. award, 2006—07; vis. scholar, Stanford Univ., 2004. Mem. AAAS, Am. Econ. Assn., Am. Math. Soc., Math. Assn. Am., N.Am. Econs. and Fin. Assn., Indsl. Orgn. Soc., NY Acad. Scis., Fin. Mgmt. Assn. (program com. 1991, 01, 03, 04, 05, 07, nat. awards com. 2000, 01), So. Fin. Assn. (program com. 1996), Del. Valley Amateur Astronomers (observing chmn. 1993, publicity chmn. 1994-96), Chamber Music Am. Episcopalian. Avocations: hiking, astronomy, bicycling, theology, number theory. Office: U Wyo Dept Econs and Fin Dept 3985 1000 E Univ Ave Laramie WY 82071 Home: 2062 Red Tail Ct Laramie WY 82072-5924

SHAFFER, THOMAS H., medical educator, consultant; s. Thomas H. and Alice V. Shaffer; m. Catherine Leigh Myers, Aug. 3, 1974; children: Thomas Derek, Kurt Thomas. BS, Drexel U., Phila., 1968, MSE, 1970, PhD, 1972; Degree in Math., Pa. State U., State Coll., 1968. Cert. DEA Fed., 2004. Instr., mech. engring. Penn. State U., 1968; asst. prof. physiology & medicine U. Pa., Phila., 1976—77; prof. physiology & pediat. Temple U., Phila., 1987—; assoc. dir., biomed. rsch. Alfred I duPont Hosp. Children, Wilmington, Del., 2001—, dir., 2001—, dir., ctr. pediatric rsch., 2004—; prof. pediat. Thomas Jefferson Med. Coll., Phila., 2001—. Sys. engr. Gen. Electric Space Divsn., Valley Forge, Pa., 1968—70, engring. cons., 1970—72; sys. cons. AVCO Everett Rsch. Lab., Everett, Mass., 1970—74; pulmonary cons. Children's Hosp. Phila., 1975—2000, Veterans Adminstrn. Med. Ctr., 1980—85, Pa. Hosp., Phila, 1981—89, Alliance Pharm., San Diego, 1991—2001, Intertek Testing, Chgo., 1999—, Hill-Rom, Hatboro, Pa., 1999—2004; physiology cons. CryoFluor Therapeutics, Tucson, 2000—04; perfluorochem. cons. Benechill Inc., San Diego, 2001—08. Contbr. articles to profl. jours. Sci. bd. Benechill, San Diego, 2001—08. Mem.: NY Acad. Scis., Am. Pediatric Soc., Am. Physiology Soc., Am. Thoracic Soc., Am. Assn. Advancement Sci. Achievements include first to liquid ventilation in preterm infants. Avocations: music, guitar. Office: Temple Univ Sch Medicine Dept Physiology Philadelphia PA 19140 Office Phone: 215-707-3239. Business E-Mail: tshaffer@temple.edu.

SHAFFER, THOMAS LINDSAY, lawyer, educator; b. Billings, Mont., Apr. 4, 1934; s. Cecil Burdette and Margaret Jeanne (Parker) S.; m. Nancy Jane Lehr, Mar. 19, 1954; children: Thomas, Francis, Joseph, Daniel, Brian, Mary, Andrew, Edward. BA, U. Albuquerque, 1958; JD, U. Notre Dame, 1961; LLD, St. Mary's U., 1983, Valparaiso U., 2008. Bar: Ind. 1961. Assoc. Barnes, Hickam, Pantzer, & Boyd, Indpls., 1961-63; prof. law U. Notre Dame, Ind., 1963-80, assoc. dean, 1969-71, dean, 1971-75, Robert and Marion Short prof., 1988-97; Robert and Marion Short prof. emeritus, 1997—; supervising atty. Notre Dame Legal Aid Clinic, 1991—; prof. law Washington and Lee U., 1980—88, Robert E.R. Huntley prof. law, 1987-88. Vis. prof. UCLA, 1970-71, U. Va., 1975-76, U. Maine, 1982, 87, 98, Boston Coll., 1992; mem. Ind. Constl. Revision Commn., 1969-70, Ind. Trust Code Study Commn., 1968-71; reporter Ind. Jud. Conf., 1963, 67; adj. prof., law Valparaiso U., 2005. Author: Death, Property, and Lawyers, 1970, The Planning and Drafting of Wills and Trusts, 1972, 5th edit., 2007, On Being a Christian and a Lawyer, 1981, American Legal Ethics, 1985, Faith and the Professions, 1987, Moral Memoranda From John Howard Yoder, 2002; co-author: Lawyers, Law Students, and People, 1977, Cases in Legal Interviewing and Counseling, 1980, American Lawyers and Their Communities, 1991, Property Cases, Materials and Problems, 1992, 3rd edit., 2006, Lawyers, Clients, and Moral Responsibility, 1994, 2nd edit. 2009, Legal Interviewing and Counseling, 1976, 4th edit., 2004; co-editor: The Mentally Retarded Citizen and the Law, 1976; contbr. articles to profl. jours. Served with USAF, 1953-57. Frances Lewis scholar Washington and Lee U., 1979; recipient Emil Brown Found. Preventive Law prize, 1966, Presdl. citation U. Notre Dame, 1975, St. Thomas More award St. Mary's U., 1983, Law medal Gonzaga U., 1991, Reinhold Niebuhr award U. Notre Dame, 1991, Jour. Law and Religion award, 1993. Cardinal O' Hara award, Notre Alumni Assn., 2009. Mem. Ind. State Bar Assn., Jewish Law Assn. Roman Catholic. Home: 1865 Champlain Dr Niles MI 49120-8935 Office: Notre Dame Legal Aid Clinic 725 Howard St South Bend IN 46617-1529 Office Phone: 574-631-7250. Personal E-mail: tshaffer0404@aol.com.

SHAFFER, WAYNE EUGENE, lawyer; b. Wauseon, Ohio, June 25, 1922; s. Chalmer L. and Leva Louella (Rashley) Shaffer; m. Georgia Grace Frey, June 4, 1949; children: Julie Anne, Wayne Daniel(dec.). BA, Ohio No. U, Ada, 1946; JD, Ohio No. U., 1949. Bar: Ohio 1949. Ptnr. Newcomer, Shaffer, Spangler & Breininger, Bryan, Ohio, 1949—. Founding mem., pres. Nat. Assn. State Bds. Edn., Washington, 1963; mem. Ohio State Bd. Edn., Columbus, 1955—92, pres.; founding mem., pres. Bryan Area Found., 1974. Lt. (j.g.) USN, 1942—46, ETO, PTO. Recipient Good Citizenship award, Bryan C. of C., 2005; named 3 time winner, Capt. Budd Carr Sailfish Tournament. Fellow: Ohio State Bar Assn. (life; chmn. legal edn. com. 1965); mem.: ABA, Ohio Cmty. Sch. Assn., Ohio Supts. Assn. (Ohio Educator of Yr.). Republican. Home: 604 Circle Dr Bryan OH 43506 Office: Newcomer Shaffer Spangler & Breininger 117 W Maple St Bryan OH 43506 Office Phone: 419-636-3196.

SHAFFER SOLOVAY, SUSAN, investment company executive; married; 2 children. B, U. Pa., Phila., 1981. Instl. broker Fimat Bank USA, Prudential Securities; trader E.F. Hutton; founder, CEO Pomegranate Capital Mgmt., LLC, 2007—. Founder P.S. 6 Alumni Found., NYC, 2002; vol. The Penn Fund, 2006—07. Named one of Top 20 Nonbank Women in Fin., US Banker, 2007, 2008. Office: Pomegranate Capital Mgmt LLC 145 E 57th St 11th Fl New York NY 10022 Office Phone: 212-981-4918.*

SHAFFERT, KURT, retired lawyer, chemical engineer; b. Vienna, July 20, 1929; s. Rudolph nee Schafranik and Irma (Altar) S.; m. Judith Pytel, June 12, 1955; children: Elona Ruth, Robin Laurette. BChemE, CCNY, 1951; LLB cum laude, NYU, 1963. Bar: N.Y. 1963, D.C. 1965, U.S. Supreme Ct. 1967, U.S. Patent and Trademark Office 1964. Chem. engr. Diamond Alkali Co., Newark, 1951-54; process devel. engr. Am. Cyanamid Co., Stamford, Conn., 1957-59; patent liaison engr. Uniroyal Inc., 1959-63; assoc. Arthur, Dry & Kalish, NYC, 1963-66, Office of Robert F. Conrad, Washington, 1966-69; sr. ptnr. Shaffert, Miller & Browne, Washington, 1970-74; sr. trial atty. intellectual property sect. Antitrust divsn. Dept. of Justice, Washington, 1974-85, professions and intellectual property sect., 1985-94, intellectual property guidelines task force, 1994, civil task force, 1994-2000; ret., 2000. Mem. Bethesda-Chevy Chase Jewish Comm. Group, 1965, pres., 1973-74, v.p. 1972-73, treas. 1971-72; mem. Jewish Comm. Ctr. of Greater Wash., 1970-78, bd. dirs., 1973-78; provided tape recorded Holocaust recollections for Stephen Spielberg Holocaust Archive Survivors of the Shoa Visual History Found., 1998. With U.S. Army, 1955-56. Mem. ABA (antitrust sect., patent, trademark and copyright sect.), Profl. Assn. Antitrust Divsn. Dept. of Justice (pres. 1978-79), Bar Assn. D.C. (council del. 1972-74), D.C. Bar Assn, Classic Residence by Hyatt (resident coun., 2006-08).

SHAFFNER, RANDOLPH PRESTON, shop owner, educator, writer, publisher; b. Winston-Salem, NC, Jan. 17, 1940; s. Emil Nathaniel and Anna Jackson (Preston) S.; m. Margaret Farmer Rhodes; children: Eric Randolph, Edward David, Joseph Andrew, Thomas Matthew, Jackson Rhodes. Student, Davidson Coll., NC, 1958-60; BA in English with honors in writing, U. NC, Chapel Hill, 1962, MA in Comparative Lit., 1969, PhD, 1973. Surveyor's lineman Joyce Mapping Co., Winston-Salem, 1955-58, 62; counselor, scoutmaster Camp Sequoyah, Weaverville, NC, 1959; track repairman Alaska R.R., Anchorage, 1960; case handler Emard Packing Co., Anchorage, 1960, AYR Canneries, Seldovia, Alaska, 1961; tchr. US Peace Corps., Chiengrai, Thailand, 1963-65, St. Christopher's Sch., Richmond, Va., 1969-71; instr. U. NC, 1968-69, 71-73; asst. prof. Fairfield U., Conn., 1973-78, Western Carolina U., 1984, 87, Continuing Edn. program World Masterpieces, Highlands, NC, 1987—89; moderator Highlands lecture series Western Carolina U., 1989-92. Instr. Carolina environ. program U. NC, Chapel Hill, 2003; editor John F. Blair Pub., Winston-Salem, 1966-68; bookseller, owner Cyrano's Bookshop, Highlands, NC, 1978-05; founder, pub. Faraway Pub., 2001; asst. to dean Sch. Libr. Scis. U. NC, Chapel Hill, 1973-74; literary mag. adv., various subcoms. Dept. Eng. Fairfield U., 1973-78. Author: Apprenticeship Novel, 1984, Tree Ordinance for Town of Highlands, 1987, Good Reading Material, Mostly Bound and New: The Hudson Library 1884-1994, 1994, Heart of the Blue Ridge: Highlands, North Carolina, 2001, 2d edit., 2004, Highlands Heritage Trail: A Walking Tour of Many Highlands Historical Buildings and Landmarks, 2003, Highlands Images of America, 2008; (with others) Nineteenth Century Literature Criticism, Vol. 21, 1989; contbr. poetry to NC Poetry Soc. anthology Here's to the Land, 1992; contbr. short stories to mags; contbr. Heritage of Macon Co., NC, Vol. 2, 1999. Lectr. with Alexander, String Quartet, Words & Music, 1989, 92, 94, for Western Carolina U., Highlands lectr. series, 1991-93, 2000; inaugural lectr. Chattooga Watershed Cultural Heritage Series, 2005, Zahner Conservation Lecture Series, 2009; instr. Ctr. for Life Enrichment, 2000, 06-; chmn. ARC Disaster Svcs., Fairfield, 1974-78, Zoning Bd. of Adjustment, Highlands, 1981-83, 85-90; pres., bd. trustees Hudson Libr., Inc., Highlands, 1987-90, 99-2001, chmn. libr. com., 1995-99; trustee Hudson Libr. Bascom-Louise Art Gallery, 1987-90, 95-99, Highlands Land Trust, Inc., 1995-96; bd. dirs. ARC, Fairfield, 1974-78, Highlands Cultural Art Ctr., 1987; fundraising com. Highlands Permanent Endowment Scholarships, 1987-89; Town of Highlands Millennium Com., 1999; historian Highlands Hist. Soc., Inc., 1999—, adv. com., 2001—, archivist, 2005—; founding mem., v.p. Highlands Plateau Greenway, Inc., 2007-, mem. Macon County Hist. Preservation Commn. Task Force, 2006, Macon County Heritage Coun., 2006—; bd. dirs. Friends Mtn. Hist., 2006—, vice chmn., 2007—, editor Mtn. Hist. Museums-in-Partnership Newsletter, 2007-; vice-chmn. bd. missions Greenfield Hill Congl. Ch., Fairfield, Conn., 1977, chmn. scholarship co., 1975-77; chaperon Am. Inst. for Fgn. Study, Grenoble, France, 1970. Recipient God and Country award, 1955, Outstanding Pres. and Trustee award Hudson Libr. and Bascom-Louise Gallery, 1990, Daniel Boone Coun. Boy Scouts Am. Disting. Citizen award, 2002, Gertrude and Dolly Harbison award, Hudson Libr., 2004; Goethe Inst. scholar German Embassy, Munich, Fed. Rep. Germany, 1965, Univ. Besançon, France, 1965, Named Trail Worker of Yr. Highlands Plateau Greenich, 2009 Mem.: NC Writers' Network, Am. Assn. for State and Local History (ann. award for Heart of the Blue Ridge 2005), Highlands Biol. Found. (trustee 1981—2006, fund raising com. 1986, environ. protection com. 1986—88, exec. com. 1986—2004, treas. 1990—2004, adv. com. on Nature Ctr. 1992, hon. trustee 2006—), Highlands Mchts. Assn. (chmn. fin. com., treas. 1984—87, chmn. tree com. and beautification com. 1984—89, greenways com. 2004—), Am. Acad. Poets, NC Poetry Soc., Writers' Workshop, Am. Comparative Lit. Assn., Internat. Comparative Lit. Assn., NC Literary and Historical Assn., Soc. NC Archivists, Highlands-Cashiers Land Trust, Nat. Peace Corps Assn., Highlands Hist. Soc., Highlands C. of C., Clan Morrison Soc., NC Soc. Historians (History Book award 2002, Paul Green Multimedia award 2007), Trail Hikers Am., Rotary (Outstanding Vol. award 1989), Lambda Iota Tau (faculty moderator Delta Omicon Ch. 1975—80, founder). Democrat. Moravian. Avocations: construction, reading, travel, hiking, writing. Office: Highlands Hist Soc 524 N 4th St Highlands NC 28741-0670 Home: PO Box 765 189 Cowee Gap Ln Highlands NC 28741-0765 Office Phone: 828-787-1050. Business E-Mail: highlandshistory@nctv.com.

SHAFIPOUR, POUYA, physician, dermatologist; s. Hamid Reza Shafipour and Fereshteh Amin; m. Pantea Tahouri, May 18, 2003. BA, U. Calif., Berkeley, 1998; MS, Georgetown U., Washington, 1999; MD, Loma Linda U., Calif., 2003. Lic. physician Calif., 2004. Resident physician U. Calif. Irvine, Orange, Calif., 2003—04, Kaiser Permanente, LA, 2005—. Fellow: Am. Acad. Family Physicians; mem.: AMA, Calif. Med. Assn., Am. Soc. Laser Medicine and Surgery (assoc.), Am. Acad. Cosmetic Surgery (assoc.), Am. Soc. Bariatric Physicians. Home: 901 Teakwood Rd Los Angeles CA 90049-1331 Home Fax: 319-937-0206. Personal E-mail: pshafipourmd@gmail.com.

SHAFIR, ROBERT S., finance company executive; BA, Lafayette Coll.; MBA, Columbia U. With Morgan Stanley & Co., 1985—90; sr. mgmt. positions Lehman Brothers Holdings Inc., 1990—2000, co-head, global equities, 2000—05; CEO Americas Credit Suisse, 2007—. Mem. exec. com. Lehman Brothers Holdings Inc. Office: Credit Suisse 11 Madison Ave New York NY 10010

SHAFIRO, VALERIY, audiologist, educator; b. Odessa, Ukraine, Sept. 22, 1970; s. Leonid and Galina Shafiro; m. Tatyana Perlovskaya; children: Samuel, Benjamin. PhD, CUNY, NYC, 2004. Nurse City Hosp., Petropavlovsk-Kamchatsky, Russia, 1989—89; rsch. assoc. CUNY, 1996—2004; asst. prof. audiology Rush U. Med. Ctr., Chgo., 2003—. Contbr. scientific papers. Sgt. Soviet Army, 1989—91, Russia, Germany. Recipient Nat. Rsch. Svc. award, NIH, NIDCD, 2003; grantee Rsch. grant, Am. Speech Hearing Found., 2008; New Investigator Rsch. Grant, 2007, Rsch. grant, Deafness Rsch. Found., 2007. Office: Rush Univ Med Ctr 600 S Paulina Str 1015 AAC Chicago IL 60612

SHAFRITZ, DAVID ANDREW, physician, research scientist; b. Phila., Oct. 5, 1940; s. Saul and Ethel (Kohn) S.; m. Sharon C. Klemow, Aug. 16, 1964; children: Gregory S., Adam B., Keith M. AB in Chemistry with honors, U. Pa., 1962, MD, 1966. Diplomate Nat. Bd. Med. Examiners, Am. Bd. Internal Medicine. Intern, then asst. resident U. Md. Hosp., Balt., 1966-68; rsch. assoc. NIH, Bethesda, Md., 1968-71; clin. and rsch. fellow Mass. Gen. Hosp., Boston, 1971-73; instr. Harvard Med. Sch., Boston, 1971-73, asst. prof. medicine, 1973; asst. prof. medicine and cell biology Albert Einstein Coll. Medicine, Yeshiva U., Bronx, NY, 1973-76, assoc. prof., 1976-81, prof. medicine and cell biology, 1981—, dir. Marion Bessin Liver Rsch. Ctr., 1985—, Herman Lapota prof. liver disease rsch. (endowed chair), 1992—. Cons. integrated Genetics, Inc., Framingham, Mass., 1981-86, Immuno, Vienna, Austria, 1986-91, Innovir, Inc., N.Y.C., 1991-98, Eugenetech Internat., Inc., Ramsey, N.J., 1991-93, Ctrs. for Med. Innovation, 1997-2001; temp. advisor WHO, Geneva, 1983; mem. Nat. Com. for Clin. Lab. Stds., Villanova Pa., 1983—, Renaissance Techs., 1996—, Affymetrix, Inc., 1997—; sci. adv. bd. com. liver cancer program Inst. for Cancer Rsch., Fox Chase and Phila., 1987—, mem. rev. panel C. study sect. Nat. Inst. Diabetes and Digestive and Kidney Diseases, 1988-92, chmn., 1991-92; mem. cen. coord. com. Liver Tissue Procurement and Distbn. Sys., 1986-95, Nat. Inst. Health Metabolic Pathology Study sect., 1995-99; mem. Nat. Bd. Med. Examiners and U.S. Med. Exam. Com., 1996-98. Co-author: The Liver: Biology and Pathobiology, 1982, 4th edit., 2001, Hepatobiliary Diseases, 1991; assoc. editor Hepatology, 1981-86; mem. editl. bd. Jour. Med. Virology, 1982-93, Hepatology, 1990-96, Jour. Virology, 1992-98; contbr. numerous rsch. articles and revs. to profl. publs.; contbr. chpts. to books; patentee in field. Trustee Westchester Jewish Ctr., Mamaroneck, N.Y., 1980-86. Lt. comdr. USPHS, 1968-71. Recipient Merck award U. Pa., 1962, Morton McCutcheon Meml. Rsch. prize Sch. Medicine, 1966, Career Scientist award Irma T. Hirschl Trust, N.Y.C., 1974-79, NIH Merit award, 1994, Disting. Rsch. Achievement award Am. Liver Found., 2000, AGA Rsch. Mentor award, 2007; European Molecular Biology Orgn. fellow, 1978; recipient Rsch. Career Devel. award NIH, 1975-80, spl. rsch. fellow, 1971-73, rsch. grantee, 1974—. Mem. Am. Assn. for Study of Liver Diseases, Internat. Assn. for Study of Liver, Am. Gastroenterol. Assn. (Mentors award 2007), Am. Soc. Biochemistry and Molecular Biology, Am. Soc. Investigative Pathology, Am. Soc. Clin. Investigation, Assn. Am. Physicians, N.Y. Acad. Scis., Harvey Soc., Interurban Clin. Club (sec./treas. 1996-99, pres. 1999-2000). Democrat. Jewish. Avocations: jogging, tennis. Home: 4 Pheasant Run Larchmont NY 10538-3423 Office: Yeshiva U Albert Einstein Coll Med Marion Bessin Liver Rsch Ctr 1300 Morris Park Ave Bronx NY 10461-1926 Office Phone: 718-430-2098. Business E-Mail: shafritz@aecom.yu.edu.

SHAFRITZ, KEITH MICHAEL, psychology professor; b. Boston, Dec. 29, 1972; s. David A. and Sharon K. Shafritz; m. Donna J. Lutz, May 30, 1999; children: Matthew, Riley. BA, Haverford Coll., 1995; MPhil, Yale U., 1999, PhD, 2002. Rsch. asst. Albert Einstein Coll. Medicine, Bronx, NY, 1996—97; grad. rsch. fellow Yale U., New Haven, 1997—2002, grad. tchg. fellow, 1998—2000, postdoctoral rsch. fellow, 2002—03; rsch. assoc. Duke U., Durham, NC, 2003—05; asst. prof. Drew U., Madison, NJ, 2005—06, Hofstra U., Hempstead, NY, 2006—. Adj. prof. Quinnipiac U., Hamden, Conn., 2002; cons. children and adults with attention deficit hyperactivity disorder, 2006—; rsch. affiliate Yale U., Conn., 2007—; faculty advisor Hofstra U. Neurosci. Club, 2007—; sci. reveiwer various profl. jours. Contbr. articles to profl. jours. Contbr. donations to Haverford Coll., 1996—, Bryn Mawr Coll., 1996—; vol. Beth El Synagogue, Bellmore, NY, 2007—. Recipient Rsch. Travel award, Yale U., 1997—99, Nat. Rsch. Svc. award, NIMH, 2002—03, Rsch. Travel award, Drew U., 2005, Hofstra U., 2007; fellow, Yale U., 1997—2002, 2000, Duke U., 2003—05; Faculty Rsch. and Devel. grant, Hofstra U., 2007, 2008. Mem.: AAAS, Cognitive Neurosci. Soc., Soc. Neurosci., Sigma Xi. Democrat. Achievements include advances in the brain basis of Attention Deficit Hyperactivity Disorder and Autism. Avocations: photography, piano. Office: Hofstra Univ Dept Psychology Hempstead NY 11549 Office Phone: 516-463-4856. Office Fax: 516-463-6052. Business E-Mail: keith.shafritz@aya.yale.edu.

SHAFROTH, FRANK H., JR., legislative staff member; Various positions Nat. League of Cities, Washington, 1981—84, dir. fed. rels., 1984—91, dir. Ctr. Policy & Fed. Rels., 1991—99; dir. state-fed. rels. Nat. Governors' Assn., Washington, 1999; chief of staff to congressman Jim Moran US House or Reps., Washington, 2007—, asst. to rep. Moran, House Appropriations Com., 2007—. Adj. prof. George Mason U. Bd. dirs. Alexandria Soccer Assn. Inc. Democrat. Mailing: US House Reps 2239 Rayburn House Office Bldg Washington DC 20515 Office Phone: 202-225-4376. Office Fax: 202-225-0017. Business E-Mail: frank.shafroth@mail.house.gov.*

SHAGAM, JANET YAGODA, educator, microbiologist; b. Washington, July 7, 1949; d. Herman Joseph and Dorothy Muriel (Cohen) Yagoda; m. Richard Noel Shagam, June 30, 1974; children: Leah, Joshua, Michael. BA, U. Mass., 1972; MS, U. Ariz., 1976; PhD, U. N.Mex., 1986. Insr. Albuquerque Tech. Vocat. Inst. Coll. of Arts and Sci., 1987—; tech. cons. Monteverde Environ., Albuquerque, 1992—. Cons. Albuquerque Tech. Vocat. Inst., Technologies Dept., 1992—. Author: Laboratory Manual for Biophysical Science, 1989; contbr. articles to profl. jours. Bd. mem. Albuquerque Childrens Mus., 1992—. Mem. N.Mex. Hazardous Waste Mgmt. Soc., Am. Soc. for Microbiology, Nework for Women in Sci. and Engring., Sigma Xi.

SHAGAM, MARVIN HÜCKEL-BERRI, private school educator; b. Monongalia, W.Va. s. Lewis and Clara (Shagam) S. AB magna cum laude, Washington and Jefferson Coll., 1947; postgrad., Harvard Law Sch., 1947—48, Oxford U., 1948—51. Tchr. Mount House Sch., Tavistock, England, 1951—53, Williston Jr. Sch., Easthampton, Mass., 1953—55, Westtown Sch., Pa., 1955—58, Thacher Sch., Ojai, Calif., 1958—; head English dept. Kurasini Internat. Edn. Centre, Dar-es-Salaam, Tanzania, 1966—67; head dept. Nkumbi Internat. Coll., Kabwe, Zambia, 1967—68. Vol. visitor Prisons in Calif., 1980-95, Calif. Youth Authority, 1983-93; sr. youth crisis counsellor InterFace, 1984-94. With U.S. Army, 1942-46, 1st lt. M.I. res.,1946-57. Danforth Found. fellow, 1942; Coun. for the Humanities fellow, Tufts U., 1983. Mem. We. Assn. Schs. and Colls. (accreditation com.), Great Tchg. (Cooke chair 1977—), Phi Beta Kappa, Delta Sigma Rho, Cum Laude Soc. Republican. Avocations: hiking, camping, travel. Home: 5025 Thacher Rd Ojai CA 93023-8304 Office: The Thacher Sch 5025 Thacher Rd Ojai CA 93023-9001 Office Phone: 805-646-4377. Fax: 805-646-4377. E-mail: mshagam@thacher.org.

SHAGAN, BERNARD PELLMAN, endocrinologist, educator; b. Bklyn., Sept. 29, 1935; s. Samuel David and Pearl (Pellman) S.; m. Maureen Helen Oshever Amster, June 24, 1957 (div. 1970); children: Ellen Ruth Basch, Brian Ross; m. Phoebe Orange, Aug. 24, 1972; 1 child, Adam Irwin. AB, Harvard U., 1956; MD, NYU, 1960. Diplomate Am. Bd. Internal Medicine; bd. cert. endocrinology and metabolism. Chief sect. endocrinology Coney Island Hosp., Bklyn., 1968-79; chief sect. endocrinology, assoc. prof. medicine East Tenn. State U. Quillen Dishner Coll. Medicine, Johnson City, 1979-84; assoc. chmn., then acting chmn. dept. medicine Nassau County Med. Ctr., East Meadow, NY, 1984-87; assoc. prof. clin. medicine SUNY, Stony Brook, 1985-87; chmn., program dir. dept. medicine Monmouth Med. Ctr., Long Branch, NJ, 1987-96, dir. Diabetes Edn. Ctr., 2002—06; pvt. practice in endocrinology and metabolism Shrewsbury, NY, 1997-98, West Long Branch, NJ, 1998—2002; pvt. practice of endocrinology Long Branch, NJ, 2002—04; clin. prof. medicine Drexel U. Med. Ctr.; chief med. dir. Health Pia Am., Newark, 2004—06. Clin. prof. medicine Med. Coll. Pa. Hahnemann U., Phila., 1988—2002; clin. prof. medicine Coll. Medicine Drexel U., Phila., 2004—. Contbr. articles to med. jours. Capt. M.C., U.S. Army, 1966-68. Master ACP (gov. N.J. 1996-2000, fellowship); fellow Am. Coll. Endocrinologists; mem. Am. Assn. Clin. Endocrinologists, Am. Diabetes Assn., Endocrine Soc. Jewish. Avocations: music, singing, piano. Office Phone: 732-276-5326. Business E-Mail: bshagan@optonline.net.

SHAGAN, STEVE, scriptwriter, film producer; b. NYC, Oct. 25, 1927; m. Elizabeth Florance, Nov. 1956. Film technician Consol. Film, Inc., NYC, 1952-56, RCA, Cape Canaveral, Fla., 1956-59; asst. to publicity dir. Paramount Pictures, Hollywood, Calif., 1962-63. Prodr.: (TV series) Tarzan, 1966; prodr., writer movies for TV, Universal and CBS, Hollywood, Calif., 1968-70; writer original screenplay: Save the Tiger, 1972 (Writers Guild award, Acad. award nominee 1973); prodr. film, author screenplay: City of Angels (produced as movie Hustle), 1975, novel, screenplay The Formula, 1979, screenplay Voyage of the Damned, 1976 (Acad. award nominee); writer, prodr. film The Formula, 1980; author: (novels) Save the Tiger, 1972, City of Angels, 1975, The Formula, 1979, The Circle, 1982, The Discovery, 1985, Vendetta, 1986, Pillars of Fire, 1989, A Cast of Thousands, 1993, (screenplays) Primal Fear, 1996, Gotti, 1996 (Emmy nominee Best Screenplay). Served with USCG, 1944-46. Mem. Writers Guild Am. (bd. dirs. West chpt. 1978-82). Office: RBZ Mgmt 11755 Wilshire Blvd 9th Fl Los Angeles CA 90025-1586

SHAH, ANIL R., plastic surgeon; b. Joliet, Ill. m. Sameea Shah. MD, Loyola Stritch. Clin. instr. NY U., 2005—, asst. prof. Adv. SAAKHI, NYC, 2005—, vol. Mem.: FACS (assoc.). Achievements include discovery of three facial anatomic structures necessary for facial rejuvenation. Office: 845 N Michigan Ave Ste 934 E Chicago IL 60611 Business E-Mail: shah@shahfacialplastics.com.

SHAH, BIMAL, financial advisor, small business owner; arrived in US, 1993; m. Ami B. Mehta, Mar. 4, 1998; children: Rajvi B., Parthvi B. BCom (hon.), Bombay U., 1993; BS in Advt. (hon.), Fla. U., Gainesville, 1995. ChFC, Am. Coll., Pa., 2000; CLU Am. Coll., Pa., 2000. Sole propr. Bimal Shah Ins., Fort Lauderdale, Fla., 1996—2003; pres. Rajparth Adv. Group, LLC., Boca Raton, Fla., 2003—. Mem. South Fla. Hindu Temple, Weston, 2000—, Shiva Vishnu Temple, Fla., 2000—, India Religious Cmty. Ctr., Fort Lauderdale, JAINA South Fla., Weston, 2000—. Recipient Nat. Sale Achievement award, Nat. Assn. Insurance and Fin. Advisors, 1996—2000, Nat. Quality award, 1996—2000, Eagle award, 1996—2005, Nat. Ethics award, Nat. Assn. for Ethics for Agents and Advisors; named Rookie of Yr., Agt. of Yr., Time mag., Sports Illustrated, Top of Table award, Million Dollar Round Table, 2008. Mem.: Million Dollar Round Table (life; qualifiying mem., mem. ct. of table 1999—2000, Ct. of Table award 1996—), Palm Beach India Assn. Hindu. Avocations: travel, horseback riding. Office: Rajparth Advisory Group LLC 55 NE Fifth Ave Ste 402 Boca Raton FL 33432 Office Phone: 886-975-2669. Office Fax: 561-391-7755. Business E-Mail: bimalshah@bellsouth.net.

SHAH, BIPIN CHANDRA, banker; b. Bombay, July 23, 1938; s. Manilal and Keshar Shah; m. Fay Shah, 1962 (div. 1985); m. Ellen T. Dever, Sept. 20, 1985 (div. 1992); children: Nelie, Sarah Lynn, Genevieve. BA, Baldwin-Wallace Coll., 1962; MA, U. Pa., 1965. Pres. Vertex Systems, Inc., King of Prussia, Pa., 1970-74; sr. v.p. Fed. Res. Bank, Phila., 1974-78, Am. Express, NYC, 1979-80; exec. v.p. Phila. Nat. Bank, 1980-84, CoreStates Fin. Corp., Phila., 1984-86, vice chmn., 1986-89, COO, 1990-91; pres., CEO Gensar Holdings, Inc., Ft. Washington, Pa., 1992-96; CEO, pres. Genpass, Inc. (formerly Shahdill, Inc.), Fort Washington, Pa., 1996—2005. Bd. dirs. VISA, USA, San Matteo, Calif., Franklin Inst., Phila., Phila. Internat. Bank, N.Y.C., U.S. Pro Indoor Tennis, Phila.; chmn. bd. dirs. CoreStates Bank Del., Wilmington. Fund raiser Phila. Indoor Tennis, 1985-88. Mem. Union League. Republican. Avocations: reading, golf, tennis, fishing. Home Phone: 610-527-1150; Office Phone: 610-716-1830.

SHAH, FARHED, economics educator; BA, Columbia U., NYC, 1982; PhD, U. Calif., Berkeley, 1990. Asst. prof. U. Conn., Storrs, 1991—96, assoc. prof., 1996—. Author: (book) Reservoir Conservation: The RESCON Approach & Model; contbr. chapters to books. Recipient Best Investigative Rsch. award, Assn. Argentina de Economía Agraria, 2004; TOKTEN fellowship, UN Devel. Program, 1998, 2001, grant, Conn. Dept. Environ. Protection, 1994—97, World Bank, 1999—2002, US Forest Svc., 1999—2000, US Dept. Agr., 2002—. Mem.: Gamma Sigma Delta (pres. Conn. chpt. 1996—99). Office: Univ Conn 1376 Storrs Rd Storrs CT 06269-4021 Office Fax: 860-486-1932.

SHAH, HEMANG J., systems engineer; b. Mumbai, Maharashtra, India, Jan. 21, 1981; s. Jayant M. and Bina J. Shah; m. Ruchita N. Vora. BE in Electronics and Telecom. Engring., U. Mumbai VESIT, 2002; MS in Elec. and Telecom. Engring., Drexel U., Phila., 2004, PhD, 2007. Grad. rsch. fellow Drexel U., 2003—07, grad. tchg. asst., 2003—07; grad. summer fellow Nat. Inst. Stds. and Tech., Gaithersburg, Md., 2003; sr. engr. Qualcomm MEMS Techs., San Diego, 2007—. Contbr. articles to profl. jours. Recipient Rsch. Excellence award, Drexel U., 2007. Mem.: IEEE, Soc. Info. Display, Internat. Soc. Optics, Toastmasters (v.p. to pub. rels. 2009—), Sigma Xi. Office: Qualcomm MEMS Techs Inc 5775 Morehouse Dr BB130-O San Diego CA 92121 Personal E-mail: hemangshah.linkedin@gmail.com. Business E-Mail: hemangs@qualcomm.com.

SHAH, JATIN PREMANAND, head and neck surgeon, educator; b. Visnagar, Gujarat, India, Dec. 31, 1940; came to U.S., 1967; s. Premanand C. and Sarla P. (Mehta) S.; m. Bharti N. Gandhi, May 11, 1967; 1 child, Mili MD, Baroda Med. Coll., India, 1964, MS in Surgery, 1967; PhD (hon.), U. Athens, Catholic U. Louvain, Belgium. Diplomate Am. Bd. Surgery. Attending surgeon Meml. Sloan Kettering Cancer Ctr., NYC, 1974—, chief head and neck svc., 1992—, E.W. Strong chair in head and neck oncology; prof. surgery Cornell U. Med. Coll., NYC, 1987—. Vis. prof. Royal Soc. Medicine, London, 1997. Author: Head and Neck Surgery, 1996 (prize Royal Soc. Medicine 1996), rev. edit., 1997 (1st prize Brit. Med. Assn. 1997), 3d edit., 2003 (George D. Howells prize U. London 2003). Hon. fellow in dental surgery Royal Coll. Surgeons Eng; Blokhin Gold medal Russian Acad. Scis., Ellis Island Medal of Honor, 2009 Fellow ACS, Royal Coll. Surgeons Edinburgh (hon.), Royal Australian Coll. Surgeons (hon.); mem. Soc. Head and Neck Surgeons (pres. 1991), Internat. Fedn. Head and Neck Oncological Socs. (bd. dirs. 2002), NY Cancer Soc. (pres. 1984), NY Head and Neck Soc. (pres. 1985), North Am. Skull Base Soc. (pres. 2003), Internat. Acad. Oraloncology (pres. 2005) Office: Meml Sloan Kettering Cancer Ctr 1275 York Ave New York NY 10021-6094 Office Phone: 212-639-7604.

SHAH, KAUSHAL J., thoracic surgeon; b. Kolkata, India, Apr. 8, 1973; s. Jatin G. and Mina J. Shah; m. Purvi C. Panchal, Aug. 10, 2003; children: Ria K., Sahil K. MD, Robert Wood Johnson Med. Sch., Piscataway, NJ. Diplomate in vascular surgery & gen. surgery Am. Bd. Surgery, 2007, registered physician in vascular interpretation Am. Registry Diagnostic Med. Sonography, 2008. Asst. prof. surgery U. Pitts. Med. Ctr., Pitts., 2005—07; attending surgeon Ohio Heath - Ctrl. Ohio Vascular Svcs., Columbus, 2007—; clin. asst. prof. surgery Ohio State U. Coll. Medicine, Columbus, 2008; clin. asst. prof.surgery Ohio U. Coll. Osteo. Medicine, Athens, 2009—. Med. student UMDNJ - Robert Wood Johnson Med. Sch., 1991—95; resident U. Md. Med. Ctr., Balt., 1998—2004; rsch. resident R Adams Cowley Shock Trauma Med. Ctr., Balt., 2000—01; fellow Duke U. Med. Ctr., Durham, NC, 2004—05. Computer digital art for music album; contbr. articles to profl. jour. Named one of Top Surgeons, Consumers' Rsch. Coun. America, 2007. Mem.: Assn. Acad. Surgery, Am. Mem. Assn., Ohio State Med. Assn., Columbus Med. Assn., Soc. Vascular Surgery, Golden Key. Hindu. Avocations: travel, sailing, skiing, photography. Office: Ctrl Ohio Vascular Svcs 285 E State St Ste 260 Columbus OH 43215 E-mail: kshah00@hotmail.com.

SHAH, MANISH HARIKANT, plastic surgeon; b. Edmonton, Alberta, Oct. 14, 1970; arrived in US, 1973, naturalized, 1991; s. Harikant Chandrakant and Kunjlata Harikant Shah; m. Korinne Danielle Kirkpatrick, May 22, 1999; children: Anisa Darai Manish, Anya Kashi Manish, Aidan Kabir Manish. BSE, U. Pa., Phila., 1992; MD, U. Va., Charlottesville, 1997; MD in Gen. Surgery, Emory U., Atlanta, 2000, Med. Coll. Ga., Augusta, 2002; MD in Plastic Surgery, U. Tenn., Chattanooga, 2004; MD in Aesthetic Surgery, Manhattan Eye, Ear, and Throat Hosp., NY, 2005. Diplomate Nat. Bd. Med. Examiners, 1998, Am. Bd. Plastic Surgery, 2006. Chief plastic surgery Denver Health Med. Ctr., 2005—06, attending plastic surgeon, 2005—09; med. dir. wound care program Triumph Hosp., Aurora, Colo., 2006—08; surg. cons. Lifestyle Lift, Denver, 2007—. Cons. Gerson-Lehman, NYC, 2006—. Author: (med. rsch.) Annals of Plastic Surgery. Fed. adv. Am. Soc. Plastic Surgeons Govt. Affairs Coun., Carol Stream, Ill., 2006—. Recipient Eagle Scout, Boy Scouts Am., 1988; fellow Aesthetic Surgery, NYU Med. Ctr., 2005. Mem.: Internat. Soc. Aesthetic Plastic Surgery, Denver Med. Soc., Colo. Med. Soc., Colo. Soc. Plastic Surgeons, Am. Soc. Plastic Surgeons, Tau Beta Pi. Democrat. Hindu. Avocations: travel, music, theater, auto racing. Office: Ctr Plastic Aesthetic Surgery 125 Inverness Dr E Ste 200 Englewood CO 80112 Home Fax: 303-649-9694. Personal E-mail: drshah@drmanishshah.com.

SHAH, NIKHIL L., urologist, surgeon; BA, MPH, U. Mich.; MD, Kirksville Coll. Osteopathic Medicine. Fellow Henry Ford Hosp. Vattikuti Urology Inst., chief resident; dir. minimally invasive & robotic urology St. Joseph's Ctr. for Robotic Surgery. Mem.: AMA, AUA. Office: Saint Joseph's Hospital 5665 Peachtree Dunwoody Rd NE Atlanta GA 30342*

SHAH, PREDIMAN K., cardiologist, educator; MBBS, Govt. Med Coll. Srinagar, India, 1969. Diplomate Am. Bd. Internal Medicine. Intern, cardiology Mt. Sinai Hosp., Milw., 1971-72; resident All India Inst. Med. Scis., New Delhi, 1970-71, Montefiore Hosp., NYC, 1973-74, fellow cardiology, 1974-76; hosp. apptd. Cedar Sinai Med. Ctr., LA, dir., divsn. cardiology, dir., Atherosclerosis Rsch. Ctr., Shapell and Webb Family Endowed Chair, Cardiology; prof. medicine UCLA Sch. Medicine. Mem. scientific adv. bd. Larry King Cardiac Found.; nat. chmn. Entertainment Industry Found. Nat. Cardiovascular Rsch. Initiative, 2001—; vis. prof. Cleveland Clinic, Mayo Clinic, Tex. Heart Inst., U. Utah, U. Va., U. Calif., San Diego, U. Calif., San Francisco, U. Tex. Galveston Med. Branch, U. San Antonio & Mass. Gen. Hosp. Harvard Med. Sch.; Fullbright vis. prof. to Japan, Argentina, Chile and Taiwan; spkr. in field. Contbr. scientific papers; mem. editl. bd. Circulation, Am. Jour. Cardiology, Internat. Jour. Heart Failure, Indian Heart Jour., Jour. Preventative Cardiology, Reviews in Cardiovascular Medicine, Current Cardiology Reports, Jour., Jour. Am. Coll. Cardiology, Arteriosclerosis, Thrombosis and Vascular Biology, Cardiovascular Pharmacology &Therapeutics. Named one of Top Cardiovascular Specialist, Am. Health Mag. Fellow Am. Coll. Cardiology (mem. of several committees including Ann. Scientific Program Com., chairperson Clin. Cardiology Spotlight Program (ClinCard), ACP, Coll. Chest Physicians; mem. Am. Heart Assn. (vol., chmn. ednl. task force, LA bd., mem. Western Regional Bd., pres. LA chpt. 2001-2002 (Lifetime Achievement award, 2002, mem. rsch. com., chmn. fall symposium, mem. Young Investigators Award Group, mem. Western Regional Peer-Review Group), European Acad. Scis. Office: Cedars-Sinai Med Ctr 8700 Beverly Blvd Rm 5531 Los Angeles CA 90048-1865 Office Phone: 310-423-3884. Office Fax: 310-423-0144. Business E-Mail: shahp@cshs.org.

SHAH, PREMAL, non-profit microloan company executive; BA in Economics, Stanford U. Strategy cons. Mercer Mgmt. Consulting, NY; prin. product mgr. PayPal, 2000—06; pres. Kiva.org, 2006—. Co-founder Silicon Valley Microfinance Network; featured spkr. Clinton Global Initiative and Global Microcredit Summit, 2006. Named one of Agenda Setters-2007, silicon.com, Young Global Leaders, World Econ. Forum, 2009; Grant to Rsch. Microfinance in Gujarat, India, 1997. Office: Kiva 3180 18th St Ste 201 San Francisco CA 94110 Office Phone: 415-358-7524. Office Fax: 415-552-5780. Business E-Mail: premal@kiva.org.

SHAH, RAJAL B., pathologist; arrived in U.S., 1995; s. Bipin S. and Sharmishtha Shah; m. Ami R. Patel, June 15, 1995; children: Ansh R., Alay R. MD, Gujarat U., Ahmedabad, Gujarat, India, 1989. Bd. cert. in anatomic and clin. pathology Am. Bd. Pathology, 2000. Resident physician dept. pathology Gujarat Cancer and Rsch. Inst., India, 1989—93, lectr. Ahmedabad, 1993—95; resident anatomic and clin. pathology St. John Hosp. and Med. Ctr., Detroit, 1995—99; fellow genitourinary/surg. pathology dept. pathology U. Mich., Ann Arbor, 1999—2001, asst. prof. pathology and urology, 2001—07, assoc. prof. pathology and urology, 2007—. Prin. investigator and dir. Specialized Program of Rsch. Excellence in Prostate Cancer, Tissue Core Program U. Mich., Ann Arbor, 2004—. Contbr. articles to profl. jours. Grantee Specialized Program Rsch. Excellence in Prostate Cancer, Nat. Cancer Inst., 2003—. Fellow: Am. Coll. Pathologist; mem.: Am. Urology Assn., U.S. and Can. Acad. Pathology. Home: 360 Fairways Ln Chelsea MI 48118 Office: Univ Michigan Hospital 1500 East Medical Center Dr Ann Arbor MI 48109 Office Fax: 734-763-4095. Business E-Mail: rajshah@umich.edu.

SHAH, RAJIV JANA, federal agency administrator; b. 1973; BA, U. Mich.; MS in Health Economics, U. Pa., MD; attended, London Sch. Econs. Co-founder Health Sys. Analytics, Project IMPACT for South Asian Am.; mem. transition com. on health for Gov. Ed Rendell; health care policy advisor Gore 2000 Presdl. Campaign; joined Bill & Melinda Gates Found., 2001, dir. strategic opportunities, dep. dir. policy and fin. Global Health Program, dir. agrl. devel. Global Devel. Program; under sec. for rsch., edn. & economics USDA, Washington, 2009—. Policy aide British Parliament; with WHO. Contbr. articles to profl. jours. Bd. mem. Alliance for a Green Revolution in Africa (AGRA), Seattle Pub. Libr., Seattle CC Dist. Named Young Global Leader, World Econ. Forum, 2007. Office: USDA 1400 Independence Ave, SW Washington DC 20250*

SHAH, SHAMIR, architect; b. Kenya; BA in Architecture, Yale U., 1987. Arch. Costas Kondylis and Assocs., NYC, 1987—99; founder Shamir Shah Design, NYC, 1999—. Named one of Best of the Best, Met. Home Mag., 2000. Office: Shamir Shah Design 10 Greene St New York NY 10013 Office Phone: 212-274-7476. Office Fax: 212-274-7477. E-mail: shamirshah@earthlink.net.*

SHAH, SHIRISH KALYANBHAI, computer science, chemistry and environmental science educator; b. Ahmedabad, India, May 24, 1942; came to U.S., 1962, naturalized, 1974; s. Kayyanbhai T. and Sushilaben K. S.; m. Kathleen Long, June 28, 1973; 1 son, Lawrence. BS in Chemistry and Physics, St. Xavier's Coll. Gujarat U., 1962; PhD in Phys. Chemistry, U. Del., 1968; cert. in bus. mgmt., U. Va., 1986; PhD in Cultural Edn. (hon.), World U. West, 1986. Asst. prof. Washington Coll., Chestertown, Md., 1967-68; dir. quality control Vita Foods, Chestertown, Md., 1968-72; asst. prof., assoc. prof. sci., adminstr. food, marine sci. and vocat. programs Chesapeake Coll., Wye Mills, Md., 1968-76; rsch. grant Food Tech. Program, 1973—75; assoc. prof., prof. sci., chmn. dept. tech. studies CC Balt., 1976—91; assoc. prof. chemistry Coll. Notre Dame Md., 1991—2002. Cons. joint apprentice com. Balt. City Govt., 1980-91; chmn. computer sys. and engring. techs. CC Balt., 1979-89, project facilitator telecom. curriculum and lab., 1985-89, coord. tech. studies, 1989-91; mem. Balt. City Adult Edn. Adv. Com., 1982-89, Distance Learning Task Force, 1996-97, chmn. Coll. wide computer user com., 1985-91; higher edn. eval. team Mid. Atlantic States Assn., 1987-2008; adj. prof. Phys. Sci. Coppin State Coll., 1996-98; coun. mem. Faculty R&D, 1994-97; reviewer AAAS, 1996-2005, NIH Edn. grant, 2000-02; adj. prof. chemistry Villa Julie Coll., 2002-05; lectr., prof. chemistry Towson U., 1998—, FYE advisor, 1999-, Morgan State U., 1999—. Contbr. numerous sci. projects, articles to profl. jours. Permanent mem. Rep. Senatorial Com.; charter mem. Rep. Presdl. Task Force; mem. Congl. Adv. Com., 1983—; tchr., developer prison programs Patuxent Inst., Jessup, Md., 1982-91; developer joint program for computer aided design between Coll. and HS, 1989-91; adviser Young Reps., 1992-2002; vol. Gilchrist Hospice Ctr. Recipient award, Am. Chem. Soc., 2007; Comm. grant, Mayor's Manpower Office for release of prisoners, 1980—81, Md. Dept. Transp. grant, 1981—82. Fellow Am. Inst. Chemists (co-chair internat. com. 2002); mem. IEEE, APHA, NSTA, Am. Lung Assn. (chair environ. affairs com., 1976-80), Am. Lung Assn. Md. (bd. dir. 1971-80), Am. Chem. Soc. (chmn.-elect Md. sect. 1995-96, chmn. 1996-98, chair kids and chemistry program Md. sect. 1996-99, sec. Mid-Atlantic regional conf., 2002-04, chmn. com. govt. rels. Md. sect. 1998-, chair pub. rels. com. 2000-, pres.-elect Chesapeake sect. 2002-03, co-coord. chemagination program 2005, Phoenix award 1996-97, Pub. Rels. award, 1996, Sci. Policy award, 2000, Salute to Excellence award, 2004, Outstanding Coord. Chemagination, 2005), Indsl. Hygiene Assn. (pres. Chesapeake sect. 2003-04), Nat. Environ. Tng. Assn., Nat. Assn. Indsl. Tech. (dir. local region, bd. dir. 1989-95), Md. Pub. Health Assn. (bd. dir., chair pub. health nursing edn. 2005), Am. Vocat. Assn., Am. Tech. Edn. Assn., Am. Fedn. Tchrs., Md. State Tchrs. Assn., Md. Assn. Cmty. and Jr. Colls. (v.p. 1977-78, pres. 1978-97), Moose Lodge, Pub. Relations Nat. Am. Chem. Soc., Sigma Xi, Epsilon Pi Tau, Iota Lambda Sigma Nu. Roman Catholic. Home: 5605 Purlington Way Baltimore MD 21212-2950 Office: Chemistry Dept Towson University Towson MD 21252- Office Phone: 410-704-2720. Personal E-mail: dr.shah@juno.com. Business E-Mail: sshah@towson.edu.

SHAH, SYED FAISAL ALI, communications engineer; married. BS, NED U. Engring. & Tech., Karachi, 1998; MS, King Fahd U. Petroleum and Minerals, Dhahran, Saudi Arabia, 2001; PhD, U. Minn., Mpls., 2008. Lectr., dept. elec. engring. U. Sharjah, United Arab Emirates, 2001—04; rsch. asst., dept. elec. engring. U. Minn., 2004—06; DSP intern Key Eye Comm. Inc., Mpls., 2006—07; sr. DSP engr. Azimuth Sys. Inc., Acton, Mass., 2008—. Reviewer IEEE Transactions Wireless Commn. Contbr. articles to profl. jours. Office: Azimuth Sys Inc 35 Nagog Pk Acton MA 01720

SHAH, SYED-WAQAR, science educator; m. Ulfat Zahara Bukhari; children: Syed Hassan Waqar, Syed Ahsan Bilal, Syed Annis Waqar, Mansoora Marriam Bukhari, Shala Sharif Bukhari. Faculty of Sci., Govt. Coll., Lahore, Pakistan, 1970; BSc Biology, Govt. Saadiq Egerton Coll., Bahawalpur, Pakistan, 1973; B.Ed. in Sci. Edn., B. Zakariya U., Multan, Pakistan, 1977; M.Ed. in Secondary Edn., U. Punjab, Lahore, 1980; M.Ed. in Ednl. Leadership, Wayne State U., 1996. Tchr. sci., botany, zoology and gen. sci. Govt. H.S., M.Ghar, Pakistan, 1977-79; tchr. sci., math. and social studies U. Lab. Sch. IER, Lahore, Pakistan, 1980-83; assoc. prof. U. Punjab, Lahore, 1984-99; tchr. Wayne County RESA, Mich., 1990-91; substitute tchr. Dearborn and Hamtramck Pub. Schs., Mich., 1995-96; faculty. U. Punjab Inst. Edn. and Rsch., Lahore, 1999—. Chmn. acad. affairs com. U. Punjab, Lahore, 1997-99, mem. acad. staff assn., 1983-99, chmn. estate and maintenance com., 1993-94, mem. budget and purchase com., 1994-94. sec. student affairs com., 1986-88. Scholar Sch. Bd. Edn., Multan, Pakistan, 1965. Mem. Wayne State Alumni Assn. Home: PO Box 4244 Falls Church VA 22044 E-mail: waqara@yahoo.com.

SHAH, UDAYAN KANAIYALAL, surgeon; b. Lexington, Va., Mar. 6, 1968; s. Kanaiyalal Ramanlal and Daksha Kanaiyalal Shah; m. Barbara Ziv; children: Henry S.U., Silas L.U. MD, Boston U. Sch. Medicine, 1992. Cert. Am. Bd. Otolaryngology-Head & Neck Surgery, 1998. Attending surgeon Children's Hosp. Phila. & U. Pa. Sch. Medicine, 1998—2007; attending surgeon, dir., of fellow resident edn. Nemous Alfred I duPont Hosp. for Children & Thomas Jefferson U. Sch. Medicine, Wilmington, Del., 2007—, assoc. prof., 2007—; chair Medical Devices Drugs Com., Am. Acad. Otolaryngology. Author: sci. papers in field; editor: Tonsil and Adenoid Techniques. Treas. Soc. Ear, Nose and Throat Advances in Children, 2004—. Fellow: ACS, Am. Soc. Pediatric Otolaryngology; mem.: Am. Soc. Pediat. (chair devel. com.), Am. Acad. Pediatrics. Office: Alfred I duPont Hosp for Children Divsn Otolaryngology 1600 Rockland Rd Wilmington DE 19803 Office Phone: 302-651-5895. Business E-Mail: ushah@nemours.org.

SHAH, VIVEK R., publishing executive; BA, Tufts U. Gen. mgr. dir. fin. exec. grp. Fortune Grp. (now The Fortune/Money Grp.), gen. mgr. Fortune Americas; sr. v.p. CNNMoney.com; pres. digital publ. bus./fin. network Fortune/Money Grp. Time Inc., 2005—, pres. bus. and finance network, 2007—. Recipient Consumer Mktg. Achievement award, Time Inc.; named one of 40 Under 40, Crain's NY Bus., 2006. Office: Fortune Money Grp One Time Warner Ctr New York NY 10019-8016*

SHAHA, MAYA, nursing educator; d. Debi Prosad Shaha and Ursula Elisabeth Shaha-Mueller. MSN, City U. St Bartholomew Sch. Nursing & Midwifery, London, 1997, PhD in Nursing, 2003. Diploma in gen. nursing and sick children's care, Schule fuer Integrierte Krankenpflege, Zuerich, Switzerland, 1993. Nurse Stadtspital Waid, Zuerich, 1993—94, U. Hosp., Zuerich, 1994—2002; lectr. U. Applied Scis. Health, Aarau, Aargau, Switzerland, 2000—01, Freiburg, Switzerland, 2001—, Johns Hopkins U. Sch. Nursing, Balt., 2005—. Rsch. fellow City U. St Bartholomew Sch. Nursing & Midwifery, 2004—05; vis. lectr. U. Witten-Herdecke, Nordrhein-Westfalen, Germany, 2007—, U. Vienna, 2008—, U. Lausanne, Vaud, Switzerland, 2008—. Contbr. articles to profl. publs. Expert Liberal Dem. Party, Bern, Switzerland, 1993—2008. Grant, Dorothy Evans Lyne Fund, 2006—07. Mem.: Oncology Nurses Assn., Swiss Assn. Nurses, Akademische Fachgesellschaft Onkologie, Verein zur Foerderung der Pflegewissenschaft (bd. mem. 2002—08), Sigma Theta Tau Nu Beta. Avocations: fencing, flute, reading. Office: Head Office Nursing & Allied Health Profls Dept Nursing Devel & Rsch Inselspital Univ Hosp Bern Bern Switzerland Office Phone: 41316322255. Business E-Mail: maya.shaha@hefr.ch.

SHAHBAZI, SHAHBAZ, finance and business educator; b. Kermanshah, Iran, Aug. 10, 1946; m. Jamileh Zendehnam, Aug. 23, 1976; children: Ali, Maryam. BS in Polit. Sci., Tehran U., Iran, 1970; MA in Acctg., N.I.O.C. Coll. Accountancy, Tehran, 1974; PhD in Internat. Bus. Mgmt., U. Tex. Dallas, Richardson, 1980. CFO Iran Air, Tehran, 1980—86, gen. dir. mktg. & comml. agreements, 1986—2002; prof. Tehran U., 1985—2002; coll. prof. Merritt Coll., Oakland, Calif., 2004—, DVC, Pleasant Hill, Calif., 2005—, GG U., 2009. Author several books. Home: 14 Sharmar Ct Alamo CA 94507 Office: Diablo Valley Coll 321 Golf Club Rd Pleasant Hill CA 94523-1544 Personal E-mail: sh.shahbazi@sbcglobal.net. Business E-Mail: sshahbazi@dvc.edu.

SHAHEEN, GERALD L., retired manufacturing executive; B in Mktg., Bradley U., 1966, M, 1968. With Caterpillar Inc., Peoria, Ill., 1967—, mng. dir. Geneva, 1995, v.p. engring. products divsn. Peoria, 1995, group pres., 1998—2008. Bd. dir. Ford Motor Co., 2007—, Nat. City Corp., AGCO Corp. Past chmn., bd. dir. US C. of C.*

SHAHEEN, GREG A., sports association executive; b. 1967; B in Bus. with distinction, Ind. U. V.p., Divsn. I men's basketball and championship strategies NCAA, sr. v.p., basketball and bus. strategies, 2006—. Pres. Nat. Invitational Tournament; mem. bd. advisors Inocon Group; program dir., Opportunities to Learn About Bus. Wabash Coll.; bd. dirs. Ind. Sports Corp. Bd. dirs. Thomas Page Ctr. for Entrepreneurship, Miami U., Boy's and Girl's Clubs Indpls., Carmel-Clay Edn. Found. Named one of Forty Under 40, Sports Bus. Jour., 2005, 2006, 10 Most Powerful People in Coll. Sports. Mem.: Nat. Assn. Basketball Coaches, Nat. Assn. Collegiate Dirs. of Athletics (mem. bd.). Office: Nat Collegiate Athletic Assn 700 W Washington St PO Box 6222 Indianapolis IN 46206-6222 Office Phone: 317-917-6222. Office Fax: 317-917-6888.

SHAHEEN, JACK GEORGE, communications educator; b. Pitts., Sept. 21, 1935; s. Jack and Nazara (Jacob) S.; m. Bernice Marie Rafeedie, Jan. 22, 1966; children: Michael A., Michele L. BFA, Carnegie Inst. of Tech., 1957; MA, Pa. State U., 1964; PhD, U. Mo., 1969. Entertainment dir. U.S. Spl. Svcs., Berlin, Germany, 1960-63; spl. programs dir. UCLA, 1965-67; asst. instr. mass communications U. Mo., Columbia, 1967-69; prof. mass communications So. Ill. U., Edwardsville, 1969-94. Cons. Inst. for Internat. Rsch. Inc., Washington, 1986—; cons. mid. east affairs CBS News, 1994—. Author: The TV Arab, 1984 (Outstanding Book of Yr., Choice Mag. 1984), Reel Bad Arabs: How Hollywood Vilifies A People, 2001, Guilty: Hollywood's Verdict on Arabs After 9/11, 2007; editor: Nuclear War Films, 1978; contbr. more than 300 articles, essays to newspapers and mags. Scholar-diplomat Dept. State, 1980; Fulbright scholar, 1975, 82; Oxford Rsch. fellow, 2004. Democrat. Mem. Eastern Orthodox Ch. Avocations: tennis, swimming. Home: One Dahlgren Ln Hilton Head Island SC 29928-3939 Personal E-mail: jackg_s@yahoo.com.

SHAHEEN, JEANNE, United States Senator from New Hampshire, political scientist, former governor; b. St. Charles, Mo., Jan. 28, 1947; d. Ivan and Belle Bowers; m. William H. Shaheen; children: Stefany, Stacey, Molly. BA, Shippensburg U., 1969; M of Social Sci. in Polit. Sci., U. Miss., 1973. Campaign mgr. Pres. Jimmy Carter, NH, 1980, Gary Hart, 1984, Gov. Paul McEachon, 1986, 1988; mem. NH Senate, 1991-96; gov State of NH, Concord, 1997—2003; vice chair Dem. Nat. Convention Com., 2004; nat. chair John Kerry Presidl. Campaign, 2004; dir. Inst. Politics Harvard U., Cambridge, Mass., 2005—07; US Senator from NH, 2009—. Chair Edn. Commn. States, 2000—01. Democrat. Protestant. Office: PO Box 1510 Manchester NH 03105-1510 also: G53 Dirksen Senate Office Bldg Washington DC 20510 Office Phone: 202-224-2841.*

SHAHEEN, NICHOLAS J., epidemiologist, educator; Grad., Harvard U.; MD, U. Chgo. Pritzker Sch. Medicine; MPH, U. NC Sch. Pub. Health. Fellow in epidemiology Nat. Inst. Health; assoc. prof. medicine & epidemiology U. NC Sch. Medicine, dir. Ctr. for Esophageal Diseases & Swallowing. Fellow: Am. Coll. Physicians, Am. Coll. Gastroenterology, Am. Gastroenterological Assn.; mem.: NC Med. Soc., Am. Med. Soc., Am. Soc. Gastrointestinal Endoscopy. Office: University of North Carolina Center for Functional GI Bioinformatics Bldg CB #7080 Chapel Hill NC 27599-7080*

SHAHEEN, ROBERT JOSEPH, bishop; b. Danbury, Conn., June 3, 1937; Attended, Our Lady of Lebanon Maronite Sem, Cath. Univ., Washington. Ordained priest Eparchy of Our Lady of Lebanon of LA (Maronite), 1964; pastor St. Raymond's Maronite Cath. Church, St. Louis; ordained bishop, 2001; bishop Eparchy of Our Lady of Lebanon of LA (Maronite), 2001—. Roman Catholic. Office: Our Lady of Lebanon 333 S Vicente Blvd Los Angeles CA 90048 Mailing: Our Lady of Lebanon PO Box 16397 Beverly Hills CA 90209

SHAHEEN, SUSAN ALISON, research faculty; d. Joseph and Pauline (Menz) S. BA in English and Polit. Sci., Nazareth Coll., 1988; MS in Pub. Policy, U. Rochester, 1990; grad. cert. in constl. history, U. Oxford, 1988; french proficiency cert., U. Paris, 1990; PhD in Ecology, U. Calif., Davis. Environ. grants analyst Environ. Data Rsch. Inst., Rochester, N.Y., 1989-90; assoc. ICF, Inc., Fairfax, Va., 1990-91; environ. cons., assoc. Energetics, Inc., Washington, 1991—. Eisenhower scholar English Speaking Union, 1988. Avocations: biking, travel, music. Office: Transp Sustainability Rsch Ctr Univ Calif Berkeley CA 94720

SHAHIDULLAH, MOHAMMAD, medical researcher, educator; b. Village Ruhuli, Bangladesh, Nov. 1, 1959; s. Akkel Ali Mondal and Saleha Khatun; m. Sadequn Nahar, Aug. 19, 1988; children: Asif, Archie. PhD, U. Glasgow, 1994; DVM, Bangladesh Agrl. U., 1982. Lectr. pharmacology Bangladesh Agrl. U., Mymensingh, 1983—87, asst. prof., 1987—94, U. Ariz., 2005—, U. Louisville, 2005—06; postdoctoral rsch. fellow U. Glasgow, 1994—2001; rsch. fellow, lectr. Hong Kong Poly. U., Kowloon, 2001—05. Contbr. articles to profl. jours. Recipient U. Prize, Bangladesh Agrl. U., 1985, Rsch. Louisville award, 2005; Merit scholar, Dhaka Edn. Bd., Bangladesh, 1975, Bangladesh Agrl. U., 1977—83, Commonwealth scholar, Assn. Commonwealth Univs. UK, 1990. Mem.: Am. Physiol. Soc., Internat. Soc. Eye Rsch., Fedn. U. Tchrs. Bangladesh, Assn. U. Tchrs. UK, Assn. Rsch. Vision and Ophthalmology. Achievements include development of isolated eye preparation as an experiemtal model for diverse ocular research; in vitro eye model to study retinal physiology using multifocal electroretinogram; discovery of link between intracellular calcium movement and aqueous humor formation; first to show in the isolated whole eye preparation that chloride ion is involved in the secretion of eye's aqueous humor; development of novel method of isolating and culturing ocular nonpigmented ciliary epithelial cells. Office: U Ariz Dept Physiology Tucson AZ 85724 Office Phone: 520-626-7351. Office Fax: 620-626-2382. Business E-Mail: shahidua@email.arizona.edu.

SHAHIED, ISHAK I., science educator; BA, Ea. Nazarene Coll., 1959; MS, U. Tenn., 1964; PhD, Colo. State U., 1973. Sr. rsch. chemist Aerospace Med. Rsch. Lab. USAF, Dayton, 1973—74; prof., dept. chmn. St. George's Med. Coll., Grenada, 1977—86; prof. Cleveland Coll., Kansas City, Mo., 1986—89; prof., head biochemist Life U., Marietta, Ga., 1989—94; prof. St. Matthew's Med. Coll., Belize, 1997—98, Ctrl. Bapt. Coll., Conway, Ark., 2001—02; prof., dean basic scis. St. James Sch. Medicine, Bonaire, Netherlands Antilles, 2002—. Tchr. Cleve. Coll., Kansas City, Mo., 1976-77, 86-89. Author: Biochemistry of Foods and the Biocatalysts, 1977, (textbook) Physiology, 1980. Named Hon. fellow Truman Libr. Inst.; recipient Best Instr. award, 1984. Mem. NY Acad. Sci. Avocations: writing, swimming. Office Phone: 011 599 717 2150. Personal E-mail: shahiedishak@hotmail.com.

SHAHN, EZRA, science educator; b. YC, Nov. 12, 1933; s. Ben and Tillie Shahn; 1 child, Zachary. BA, Bard Coll., Annandale-on-Hudson, NY, 1955; PhD, U. Pa., Phila., 1965. Biophysicist NIH, Bethesda, Md., 1958—60. Office: Biol Scis Hunter Coll 695 Pk Ave New York NY 10065 Business E-Mail: eshahn@hunter.cuny.edu.

SHAHN, JUDITH, voice educator; b. NYC, Nov. 30, 1955; d. Joseph and Ruth Goldman, Arthur McDonell (Stepfather); m. Jay Lurie, July 22, 2001; 1 child, Ella. MFA, Carnegie-Mellon U., Pitts., 1977. Cert. voice tchr. Kristin Linklater, NY, 1991. Voice tchr. Cornish Coll. Arts, Seattle, 1986—90; sr. lectr. U. Wash. Sch. Drama, Seattle, 1990—. Dialect coach Seattle Repertory Theatre, Intiman Theatre, ACT Theatre, 1986—. Mem.: VASTA. Jewish. Office: Univ Wash Box 353950 Hutchinson Hall Seattle WA 98195 Personal E-mail: jshahn@comcast.net. Business E-Mail: jshahn@u.washington.edu.

SHAHRESTANI, HAMID, economics professor; s. Shahrestani; m. Ladan Salehi ala; children: Nasir Seyed, Sameam Seyed, Naeem Seyed. PhD, U. Cin., 1983. Assoc. prof. economics Ohio U., Chillicothe, 1982—. Contbr. articles to profl. jours. Editl. mem. Clute Inst. Academic Rsch., Littleton, Colo., 2007—08. Faculty Rsch. Grant, Ohio U., 2005—08. Office: Ohio Univ Chillicothe 101 University Dr Chillicothe OH 45601 Business E-Mail: shahrest@ohio.edu.

SHAHRUR, HUSAYN K., finance educator; PhD, Ga. State U., Atlanta, 2003. Asst. prof. fin. Bentley U., Waltham, Mass., 2003—. Contbr. articles to profl. jour. Office: Bentley Univ 175 Forest St Waltham MA 02453

SHAICH, RONALD M., food service executive; b. Newark, Dec. 30, 1953; s. Joseph and Pearl (Kalfus) S. AB in Govt., Clark U., 1976; MBA, Harvard U., 1978. Ea. regional mgr. Cole Nat. Corp., Cleve., 1978-80; pres. Targeting Systems, Inc., Washington, 1980-81; owner, pres. The Cookie Jar, Boston, 1981-82; co-founder, co-chmn., co-CEO Au Bon Pain Co., Inc., Boston, 1982—98; co-founder, chmn., CEO Panera Bread Co. (formerly Saint Louis Bread Co.), Richmond Heights, Mo., 1998—. Bd. dirs. Store 24, Inc., Boston. Trustee Clark U., Worcester, Mass., 1989—; incorporator Mt. Auburn Hosp., Cambridge, Mass.; treas. Mass. Dem. Party, Boston, 1990—. Recipient Golden Plate award, Internat. Foodservice Mfrs. Assn., 2005. Jewish. Avocation: swimming. Office: Panera Bread Co 6710 Clayton Rd Richmond Heights MO 63117

SHAIK, SHAVALI, medical researcher; s. Nabisahib and Zaibunbee Shaik; m. Mahaboobbi Shaik, Sept. 25, 1994; 1 child, Fawaz M. PhD, Banaras Hindu U., India, 1992. JSPS rsch. fellow Hamamatsu U. Sch. Medicine, Shizuoka, Japan, 1996—98; rsch. instr. U. ND Sch. Medicine & Health Scis., Grand Forks, 2000—04, rsch. asst. prof., 2004—08; rschr. Beth Israel Deaconess Med. Ctr., Harvard Med. Sch., Boston, 2008—. Contbr. articles to sci. jours. Postdoc. fellowship, Japan Soc. Promotion Sci. Award, Tokyo, 1996—98. Mem.: NY Acad. Sci., Soc. Toxicology, Soc. Neurosci. Achievements include discovery of endogenous neurotoxins which can cause dopaminergic neuron loss in Parkinson's disease; growth factors like IGF-1, that can protect dopaminergic neurons in Parkinson's disease. Office: Beth Israel Harvard Med Sch 3 Blackfan Cir Boston MA 02115

SHAIKH, BAHU SULTAN, physician, educator; b. Karachi, Sind, Pakistan, 1945; came to US, 1969; s. Noor Mohammad and Shahkhatoon Shaikh.; m. Yasmeen Khamisani, 1972 (div. Nov. 1995); children: Maheen, Sasha Ghulam Mohammad; m. Mona Sayed, July 1996; 1 child: Aneesa. Student, St. Patrick's Coll., Karachi, Pakistan, 1963; MBBS, Dow Med. Coll., Karachi, 1968. Intern Ellis Hosp., Schenectady, NY, 1969; resident in internal medicine Thomas Jefferson U., Phila., 1970-72, rsch. fellow, 1972-74; asst. prof. coll. medicine Penn State U., Hershey, Pa., 1974-80; assoc. prof. Med. Coll. Ohio, Toledo, 1980-87, clin. assoc. prof., 1987—99, clin. prof., 1999—. Cons. Toledo Clinic, Ohio, 1987—. Contbr. several chpts. in books related to cancer and AIDS, 1983-87, numerous articles to prof. jours. Recipient Key to the Golden Door award, Internat. Inst. Greater Toledo, 1999. Fellow. ACP, Pakistan Acad. Med. Scis.; mem. Am. Soc. Clin. Oncology, Am. Soc. Hematology, Assn. Internat. Physicians of NW Ohio, Assn. Pakistani Physicians N.Am. Office: Toledo Clinic 4235 Secor Rd Toledo OH 43623-4299

SHAIKH, SABINA LEE, economist, educator; BA, U. Wis., Madison, 1992; MA, Colo. State U., Ft. Collins, 1995; PhD, U. Calif., Davis, 1999. Sr. rsch. economist RCF Econ. and Fin. Consulting, Chgo., 2001—08; lectr. U. Chgo., 2003—. Contbr. chapters to books, articles to profl. jours. Office: Univ Chgo 5828 S University Ave Chicago IL 60637 Business E-Mail: sabina@uchicago.edu.

SHAIMAN, MARC, composer, arranger, orchestrator; b. Newark, Oct. 22, 1959; s. William Robert and Claire (Goldfein) Shaiman; life ptnr. Scott Wittman. Vocal arranger for Bette Midler, musical dir. & co-prodr. Arranger, musical dir.: (Broadway concerts/revues) Peter Allen: Up in One, 1979, Bette! Divine Madness, 1979, Andre De Shield's Harlem Nocturne, 1984, An Evening with Harry Connick Jr. & His Orchestra, 1990, Patti LuPone on Broadway, 1995, (Broadway plays) Leader of the Pack, 1985, composer & lyricist: Hairspray, 2002 (Drama Desk awards for Outstanding Music & Lyrics, 2003, Tony award for Best Original Score, 2003, Grammy award for Best Musical Show Album, 2003, Best New Musical award for London prodn., Laurence Olivier Awards, 2008), Martin Short: Fame Becomes Me, 2006, composer: The Odd Couple, 2005; Arranger (films) Beaches, 1988, When Harry Met Sally, 1989 (ASCAP award, 1990), composer: Misery, 1990, Scenes from a Mall, 1991, City Slickers, 1991 (ASCAP award, 1992), The Addams Family, 1991 (ASCAP award, 1992), Sister Act, 1992 (ASCAP award, 1993), Mr. Saturday Night, 1992, A Few Good Men, 1992 (ASCAP award, 1993), Sleepless in Seattle, 1993 (Acad. award nominee), Heart & Souls, 1993, Addams Family Values, 1993, City Slickers II: The Legend of Curly's Gold, 1994, North, 1994, Speechless, 1994, Stuart Saves His Family, 1995, Forget Paris, 1995, The American President, 1995 (Acad. award nominee), Bogus, 1996, Mother, 1996, The First Wives Club, 1996 (ASCAP award, 1996, Acad. award nominee), Ghosts of Mississippi, 1996, George of the Jungle, 1997 (ASCAP award, 1997), In & Out, 1997, My Giant, 1998, Simon Birch, 1998, Patch Adams, 1998 (ASCAP award, 1998, Acad. award nominee), The Out-of-Towners, 1999, South Park: Bigger, Longer & Uncut, 1999 (Acad. award nominee, LA Film Critics Assn. award for Best Music, 1999, Chgo. Film Critics Assn. award for Best Original Score, 2000, Online Film Critics Soc. Award for Best Original Score, 2000), The Story of Us, 1999, The Kid, 2000, One Night at McCool's, 2001, Down with Love, 2003, Alex & Emma, 2003, Rumor Has It, 2005, Hairspray, 2007, (TV series) What's Alan Watching?, 1989, (TV miniseries) From the Earth to the Moon, 1998, (TV movies) Jackie's Back!, 1999, 61*, 2001; Assoc. prodr. (films) Sister Act 2: Back in the Habit, 1993, exec. prodr.: Hairspray, 2007; Actor: (TV series) Saturday Night Live, 1986-89, (films) Broadcast News, 1987, Beaches, 1988, Scenes from a Mall, 1991, Hot Shots!, 1991,The Addams Family, 1991, Mr. Saturday Night, 1992, Heart & Souls, 1993, North, 1994, The Wedding Planner, 2001, Down with Love, 2003; Albums include: (with Bette Midler) Thighs & Whispers, 1979, Mud Will Be Flung Tonight, 1985, Some People's Lives, 1990, For the Boys, 1991, Experience the Divine, 1993, Bathhouse Betty, 1998, 3 for One, 2000, Bette, 2000, (with Harry Connick, Jr.) We Are in Love, 1990, It Had to be You, 1999, Come by Me, 2000. Recipient Emmy award for Outstanding Individual Achievement in Writing a Variety or Music Program, 1992, Hollywood Film award for Outstanding Achievement in Music in Film, Hollywood Film Festival, 2002, Harry Mancini Career Achievement award, ASCAP, 2007. Address: Kelly Bush Pub Rels 2047 Glencoe Way Los Angeles CA 90068-3129 also: The Kraft-Benjamin Agency 345 N Maple Dr Ste 385 Beverly Hills CA 90210-3869

SHAIN, HAROLD I., publishing executive; b. Apr. 27, 1953; BA in Economics & Acctg., Bklyn. Coll.; Grad., Stanford U. Exec. MBA Program, 1990. Acct. Fairchild Productions, 1976; circulation bus. mgr. Times-Mirror mag.; circulation mgr. New York mag., 1981—83; circulation dir. Family Computing, 1983—84; v.p. circulation, fulfillment, mktg. manufacturing & prodn. Boardroom Reports, 1984—86; circulation dir. Newsweek, 1986—87, v.p. circulation, 1987—89, sr. v.p., 1989—91, exec. v.p., gen. mgr., 1992—98, US pub., 1993—98, pres., COO, 1998—2007; pres., CEO Budget Travel, 2007—. Office: Budget Travel 530 Seventh Ave 2nd Fl New York NY 10018

SHAIN, IRVING, retired chemicals executive, academic administrator; b. Seattle, Jan. 2, 1926; s. Samuel and Selma (Blockoff) S.; m. Mildred Ruth Udell, Aug. 31, 1947; children: Kathryn A., Steven T., John R., Paul S. BS in Chemistry, U. Wash., 1949, PhD in Chemistry, 1952. From instr. to prof. U. Wis., Madison, 1952-75, vice chancellor, 1970-75, chancellor, 1977-86; provost, v.p. acad. affairs U. Wash., Seattle, 1975-77; v.p. Olin Corp., Stamford, Conn., 1987-92, ret., 1992, also bd. dirs. Mem. tech. adv. bd. Johnson Controls, Inc., Milw., 1980-2003; trustee Univ. Rsch. Park, Inc., Madison, pres., 1984-86, v.p., 1987—; mem. Nat. Commn. on Superconductivity, 1989-90. Contbr. articles on electroanalytical chemistry to profl. jours. Bd. dirs. Madison Gen. Hosp., 1972-75; v.p. Madison Cmty. Found., 1984-86; mem. CEO adv. bd. Kamehameha Schs./Bishop Estates, 2002-04; mem. bd. dirs. Madison Symphony Orch., 2006-. With U.S. Army, 1943-46, PTO. Fellow AAAS, Wis. Acad. Scis., Arts and Letters; mem. Am. Chem. Soc., Electrochem. Soc., Conn. Acad. Sci. and Engring., Phi Beta Kappa, Sigma Xi, Phi Kappa Phi, Alpha Chi Sigma (Chemistry Hall of Fame 2006-). Home: 2820 Marshall Ct # 8 Madison WI 53705-2270 Office Phone: 608-441-8000. E-mail: i.shain@att.net.

SHAINMAN, IRWIN, musician, educator; b. NYC, June 27, 1921; s. Samuel and Gussie (Pollack) S.; m. Bernice Cohen, Aug. 29, 1948; children— Joan, Jack. BA, Pomona Coll., 1943; MA, Columbia, 1948; Premier Prix, Conservatoire Nat. de Musique de Paris, France, 1950. Prof. music, curator Paul Whiteman collection Williams Coll., Williamstown, Mass., 1948-91, prof. emeritus, 1991—; chmn. music dept., 1971-77; dean faculty, 1972-73; coordinator performing arts, 1973-76; Class of 1955 prof. music, 1980-91. Tchr. ext. U. Mass., 1952-55, Mass. State Coll., North Adams, 1957, Bennington Coll. Composer's Conf. and Chamber Music Ctr.; cons. advanced placement program Coll. Entrance Exam. Bd., 1969-75; edn. com. Saratoga Performing Arts Ctr., 1967-68; pres. Williamstown Theatre Found., 1972-77, South Mountain Concert Assn., 1980-96; lectr. J.F. Kennedy Ctr. for Performing Arts,

Washington, 1994-2006. Condr., Berkshire Symphony, 1950-65, Williams Coll. band, brass ensemble and woodwind ensemble, 1st trumpet, Albany (N.Y.) Symphony Orch., 1960-65, Vt. Symphony Orch., 1954-58; contbr. articles to profl. jours.; columnist: Berkshire Eagle; author: Avoiding Cultural Default and Other Essays, 1991. Mem. merit aid panel Mass. Arts Council, 1984. Served with AUS, 1942-45. Decorated Bronze Star, Purple Heart, Combat Inf. badge.; N.Y. Philharmonic scholar, 1934-35; Recipient Danforth Found. Tchrs. award, 1957-58 Mem. Am. Musicological Soc., Coll. Music Assn., Music Critics Assn. Home: 88 Baxter Rd Williamstown MA 01267-2111 Home Phone: 413-458-4461.

SHAINWALD, SYBIL, lawyer; b. NYC, Apr. 27, 1928; d. Samuel and Anne; m. Sidney Shainwald; children: Robert, Louise, Laurie, Marsha. BA, Coll. William and Mary, 1948; MA, Columbia U., 1972; JD, N.Y. Law Sch., 1976, LLD (hon.), 2000. Bar: N.Y. 1976. Pvt. practice, NYC, 2005—. Legal advisor Am. Found. for Maternal Child and Health; adj. prof. dept. law Baruch Coll., 1981—82. Co-editor: Jour. Women and Health; contbr. articles to profl. jours. Active Abortion Rights Action; co-founder, bd. mem. Trial Lawyers for Pub. Justice, 1982—88; bd. mem. Hysterectomy Edn. Resources and Svcs., 1985—, Dalkon Shield INfo. Network, Nat. Network to Prevent Birth Defects, No. Ariz. Sch. Midwifery, 1989—; bd. advisors Med. Legal Aspects of Breast Implants; bd. dirs. Consumer Interest Rsch. Inst.; fellow Roscoe Pound Inst., Morgan Libr.; trustee Civil Justice Found., 1998—99; bd. dirs. Am. Friends of Tel Aviv Mus., 2000, Friends of Tel Aviv Mus., 2000-; trustee N.Y. Law Sch., 2000—; adv. bd. Southampton The Hamptons Shakespeare Festival, 2000—; co-chair Take Home a Nude N.Y. Acad. Art, 2001; active Sybil Shainwald Charitable Found., N.Y.C. Comptrs. Health Task Force. Recipient Susan B. Anthony award, NOW; grantee, Nat. Endowment for the Humanities, Rockefeller Found., Gov. W. Averell Harriman; scholar Pres. Bryan scholar, Coll. of William and Mary, Edward Coles scholar. Mem.: ATLA (chair environ. and toxic tort sect. 1988—89, co-chair breast implant litigation group 1992—2000, mem. Dalkon shield litigation group 1995, mem. contraceptive implant litigation group 1995, co-chair DES litigation group, environ. law adv. com.), N.Y. State Trial Lawyers (bd. govs.), Assn. of the Bar of the City of N.Y. (judge nat. moot ct. competition 1988—2003), Soc. Med. Jurisprudence, Health Action Internat.-U.S. (co-founder, mem. steering com.), Lawyers Com. for Human Rights, Am. Soc. Law, Medicine and Ethics, Nat. Women's Health Alliance (pres.), Nat. Women's Health Network (bd. mem. 1980—86, chair litigation svc. 1980—86, chair health law and regulation 1981—88, chmn. bd. dirs. 1982—86, chair N.Y. state affiliate), Phi Beta Kappa. Avocations: art, music. Home: 955 5th Ave 15B New York NY 10021 Business E-Mail: shainwaldlaw@aol.com.

SHAKER, MARCUS SIDNEY, pediatrician; MD, U. Va. Sch. Medicin, Charlottesville, 1998. Diplomate Am. Bd. Pediat., 2001, Am. Bd. Allergy and Immunology, 2003. Asst. prof. pediat. Children's Hosp. Dartmouth, Lebanon, NH, 2004—. Fellow: Am. Acad. Allergy, Asthma, and Immunology, Am. Acad. Pediat. Office: Dartmouth-Hitchcock Med Ctr One Med Ctr Dr Lebanon NH 03756

SHAKER, WILLIAM HAYGOOD, marketing professional, public policy reformer; b. Downey, Calif., Apr. 22, 1938; s. Elmer S. and Marylee Shaker; m. Joanna Drummond, Jan. 28, 1966; children: Catherine Patricia, Marylee, Marcus, Matthew. BS in Engring., U. So. Calif., 1964; MS in Engring., U. Mich., 1969. Registered profl. engr., Calif. Exec. Dow Chem. Co., Midland, Mich., 1966-78; v.p. Nat. Legal Ctr. for the Pub. Interest, Washington, 1979; exec. v.p. Nat. Tax Limitation Com., Washington, 1980-86; pres. Am. Coun. for Health Care Reform, Arlington, Va., 1982—, Heart to Heart Found., Arlington, 1982—; CEO Washington Mktg. Group, Arlington, 1987—, The List Store, Arlington; pres. Health PAC, Arlington, 1994—. Pres. RepublicanPac.com, 2000—, Rule of Law Com., 2000-, Children of Heroes Fund, 2004-. Author: Health Care Reform, 1994, also legis. and govt. publs.; editor: Electric Power Reform, 1979; editor: Electric Power Reform, 1974, (pub. millennium edit.) The Man of Galilee, 2001,; contbr. articles to profl. jours. Founder, chmn. Taxpayers United, Mich., 1972-84; mem. Repub. State Ctrl. Com. Mich., 1974-1978, Pres. Ronald Reagan's Transition Team, 1980; founder, pres. Hear to Heart Found., 1983-, Children of Heroes Fund, 2004-; found Conservative Party Mich., 1972. With Calif. Nat. Guard USAR, 1960—67. Mem. Govtl. Rsch. Assn. (most effective presentation of govtl. rsch. award 1973), Direct Mktg. Assn. (Echo award 1982-97, Maxi award 1987-2006), Pub. Rels. Soc. (Silver Anvil 1979), Am. Conservative Union (Health Care Reform award 1995), Am. Assn. Polit. Consultants (Silver and Bronze Pollie awards 2007). Republican. Lutheran. Avocation: history. Office Phone: 703-534-9331. E-mail: william.shaker@twmg.com.

SHAKESPEARE, FRANK, ambassador; b. NYC, Apr. 9, 1925; s. Francis Joseph and Frances (Hughes) S.; m. Deborah Anne Spaeth, Oct. 9, 1954; children: Mark, Andrea, Fredricka. BS, Holy Cross Coll., 1945; D.Eng. (hon.), Colo. Sch. Mines, 1975; DCS (hon.), Pace U., 1979; LLD (hon.), Del. Law Sch., 1980, Sacred Heart U., 1985, U. Dallas, 1987, Pepperdine U., 1990, Nichols Coll., 1991, Marquette U., 1993; D of Pub. Svc. (hon.), Hillsdale Coll., 1996. Formerly pres. CBS-TV Services; exec. v.p. CBS-TV Stas.; dir. USIA, 1969-73; exec. v.p. Westinghouse Electric Corp., 1973-75; pres. RKO Gen. Inc., NYC, 1975-85, vice chmn., 1983-85; U.S. ambassador to Portugal Lisbon, 1985-87; U.S. ambassador to The Holy See Vatican City, 1987-89. Chmn. Heritage Found., 1975-85, dir., 1989—; chmn. Radio Free Europe/Radio Liberty, Inc., 1976-85; dir. Bradley Founhd., 1989—. Served to lt. (j.g.) USNR, 1945-46. Mem.: Union League. Home: 303 Coast Blvd La Jolla CA 92037-4630

SHAKESPEARE, VALERIE MONROE, curator, director, art gallery owner; b. Kalamazoo, Mar. 30, 1947; d. Monroe Shakespeare and Martha Ellen Wright; m. R. Tery Fugate-Wilcox, Nov. 1, 1963. Student, Ariz. State U., Tempe, 1961—63. Owner Little Rm. Gallery, Galesburg, Mich., 1964—68, Fvlcrvm Gallery, SoHo, NY, 1993—97, Shakespeare's Fvlcrvm, SoHo, 1997—2001, Trbeca, NY, 2001—05; dir./curator Candlewood Lake Art Ctr., New Fairfield, Conn., 2005—. Chmn. ann. arts festival Kalamazoo C. of C., 1965; jr. com. Guggenheim Mus., New York, 1978—89; exec. dir. Actual Art Found., NYC, 1982—2009; guest curator Gallery of City of NY, 1987; pres. New Art Found., New York, 1990—; bd. dirs., moderator Artists Talk on Art, New York, 1990—99; dir. Onion Ring Art Ctr., Pine Island, NY, 2009—. Contbr. articles to profl. jours.; co-author (with Tery Fuqute-Wilcox): (autobiography memoir) It's The Artist Life For Me, 2008. Vol. aux. policewoman NYPD, 1979—97; benefit com. Mothers for More Halfway Houses, New York, 1980—85, Night of 100 Trees, New York, 1985—90, Vols. for Schs., New York, 1983—89, South St. Seaport for Muscular Dystrophy, New York, 1986—86. Fellow: Mus. Modern Art (patron 1978—), Whitney Mus.; mem.: Aldrich Mus., Guggenheim Mus. (assoc.; patron 1979—). Avocations: cooking, sewing, horseback riding.

SHAKIR, HUZEFA, research scientist; s. Ismail and Sabera Shakir; m. Zahabiya Shakir, Jan. 6, 2004; 1 child, Hasnain H. BTech with honors, Indian Inst. Tech., Kharagpur, 2000; PhD, Tex. A&M U., Coll. Sta., 2007. Asst. mgr. Suzuki Motor Corp., Gurgaon, Haryana, India, 2000—02; sr. scientist Halliburton, Houston, Tex., 2007—. Reviewer Tex. A&M U., 2002—, mentor, 2002—06; gen. sec. Indian Insts. Tech. Alumni Greater Houston, 2008—. Contbr. articles to jours. Recipient award, Indian Inst. Tech., 1999, Hall Color award, 2000, Best Paper award, Am. Control Conf., 2005; fellowship, Ctr. Tchg. Excellence, 2005, Internat. Tex. Pub. Edn. grant, Tex. A&M U., 2006. Fellow: Ctr. Tchg. Excellence; mem.: IEEE, ASME, Soc. Petroleum Engrs., Phi Kappa Phi. Achievements include patents pending for method and apparatus for surveying a borehole while rotating; research in large angle rotation sensing with modified michelson interferometer; invention of multiaxis magnetic levitation system. Home: 7700 Willow Chase Blvd Apt 1223 Houston TX 77070 Office: Halliburton 3000 N Sam Houston Pkwy E Houston TX 77032

SHAKIROV, ZAIR SAATOVICH, biologist, researcher; b. Tashkent, Uzbekistan, Nov. 1, 1955; s. Saat Shakirov and Muborak Bakhadirova; m. Akida Zakirovna Nazarova, Aug. 20, 1983; children: Sodiq Zairovich, Rustam Zairovich, Suhrob Zairovich. MSc in Biology, Tashkent State U., 1981; PhD, Uzbekistan Acad. Scis., Tashkent, 1989. Jr. rsch. scientist Inst. Microbiology Uzbekistan Acad. Scis., Tashkent, 1986—91, sr. rsch. scientist, 1991—2003, head lab., 2003—. Supr. PhD student Inst. Microbiology Uzbekistan Acad. Scis., Tashkent, 1993—96, Tashkent, 2001—06. Grantee, European Commn., 1998—2002, Cooperative Devel. Rsch., Ctrl. Asian Republics, US Agy. Internat. Devel., 1998—2002, 2003—07, Sci. Tech. Ctr. Ukraine Found., USDA, 2005—, 2006—. Fellow: Uzbekistan Soc. Biochemistry (assoc.), Uzbekistan Soc. Microbiology (assoc.); mem.: Internat. Union Microbiol. Socs. (assoc.). Pacific. Muslim. Achievements include research in structure and physical- chemical properties of glutamine synthetase of Ankistrodemus braunii; comparative analysis of nitrogen-fixators of Uzbekistan arid Yemen soils; bacteria of Azospirillum genus from salt-affected soils of Uzbekistan; biotechnology for the improved adaptation of leguminous trees to stress conditions; use of symbiotic biodiversity to enhance plant tolerance to environmental stresses; adaptation of Onobrychis, a salt and drought tolerant perennial legume grass species of Central Asia deserts, for crop production and to combat desertification. Avocations: singing, science, high technology, travel, computers. Home: Jangoh C-15 h-12a flats 56-57 100128 Tashkent Uzbekistan Office: Uzbekistan Acad Scis Inst Microbiology A Kadyri Build 7 B 100128 Tashkent Uzbekistan Office Phone: 998 71 1427120. Office Fax: 998 71 1427129. Personal E-mail: zair@dostlink.net. Business E-Mail: info@microbio.uz.

SHAKLEY, ELAINE M., organist, department chairman; b. Boswell, Pa., Dec. 23, 1922; d. John Henry and Pearl Beatrice Morrison; m. Glenn Huling Shakley; children: Susan, Bonnie, Pam. MusB, Heidelberg Coll., Tiffin, Ohio, 1944; MA, Case Western Res. U., Cleve., 1965. Music supr. K-1 Northfield Pub. Schs., Ohio, 1944—45, music supr. K-12, 1959—74; music tchr. Roosevelt Jr. HS, Cleveland Heights, Ohio, 1944—46; music cons. Cleveland Heights, 1959—74; adj. prof. Cleve. State U., 1961—99; music tchr. Chagrin Falls Pub. Schs., Ohio, 1974—83; tchr. WVIZ-TV, Cleve., 1965—66; organist Fed. Ch. Chagrin Falls, Ohio, 1965—93, Chagrin Falls United Meth. Ch., 1993—2004; music dir. First English Luth. Ch., Cleveland Heights, 1959—63; bell choir dir. Federated Ch., Chagrin Falls, Ohio, 1974—93. Chmn. Chagrin Valley Nat. Piano Auditions, Cleve., 1998—2009. Composer: (songs) April, 1944, Mass in Pentatonic, 1970; prodr., writer script for songs; author: various music courses of study. Chmn. Musical Club Jr. Divsn., Cleve., 1996—2006, Fortnightly Chagrin Valley Jr. Divsn., Cleve., 1998—2009. Recipient Alumni Excellence award, Heidelberg Coll., 2002; grantee, Martha Holden Jennings Found., 1966. Achievements include restarting string education in Chagrin Falls school system. Avocations: knitting, swimming, walking. Home and Office: 7662 Birchmont Dr Chagrin Falls OH 44022 Personal E-mail: eshakley@aol.com.

SHAKNO, ROBERT JULIAN, hospital and social services administrator; b. Amsterdam, Holland, Aug. 15, 1937; came to U.S., 1939, naturalized, 1944; s. Rudy C. and Gertrude S.; m. Linda, June 10, 1962; children: Steven Lee, Deborah Sue. BBA (scholar 1955), So. Methodist U., 1959; M.H.A., Washington U., St. Louis, 1961. Adminstrv. asst. Mt. Sinai Hosp., Chgo., 1961—63; asso. adminstr. Tex. Inst. Rehab. and Research, Houston, 1963—65; asst. adminstr. Michael Reese Hosp., Chgo., 1965—70, v.p., hosp. dir., 1970—73; asso. exec. dir. Cook County Hosp., Chgo., 1973—75; pres. Hackensack Med. Center, NJ, 1975—85, Mt. Sinai Med. Ctr., Cleve., 1985—96; dir. nat. strategy practice KPMG Peat Marwick, 1996-98; v.p. med. affairs, vice dean sch. of medicine Case Western Res. U., 1998—2002; pres., CEO Jewish Family Svc., Cleve., 2002—05; ptnr. Tatum Ptnrs., LLC, Deerfield, Ill., 2005—; adv. bd. Med. Svcs. Co., Cleveland, Ohio, 2005; ptnr. exec. svc. corp., Chgo., 2007—. Bd. dirs. Ohio Hosp. Inc. Co. Mem. editorial bd. Mgmt. Series, Am. Coll. Healthcare Execs. Mem. Leadership Cleve.; bd. dirs. Premier Hosp. Alliance, chmn., 1994-96; bd. dirs. The New Cleve. Inc., Univ. Circle Inc., Cleve., Cleve. Sight Ctr.; trustee Hope Lodge, Cleve. chpt. Am. Cancer Soc.; chmn. elect, bd. dirs. Jewish Family Svcs.; chmn. social svcs. divsn. United Jewish Appeal, Cleve., 1987-88, chmn. health cabinet, 1990, gen. co-chmn., 1990—; chmn. Hosp. Pacesetter campaign United Way, chmn. health svcs. portfolio, 1988-89, oversight comm., 1992-93; bd. trustees Mount Sinai Health Sys., Chgo., 2006-. Served to 1st lt. USAR, 1960-66. Named Young Adminstr. of Yr., Washington U., 1968 Fellow Am. Coll. Hosp. Adminstrs.; mem. Am. Hosp. Assn. (coun. urban hosps., del. coun. on met. hosps., rep. regional policy bd.), Washington U. Alumni Assn. (past pres.), Greater Cleve. Hosp. Assn. (bd. dirs.), Ohio Hosp. Assn. (bd. dirs.), Cleve. Sight Ctr. (trustee, bd. dirs.), Sigma Alpha Mu (past pres.). Home: 908 Island Ct Deerfield IL 60015 Office Phone: 312-909-2022. Personal E-mail: lbs1shak@sbcglobal.net.

SHAKOOR, ABDUL, geologist, educator; s. Ata and Zainab Muhammad; m. Roohi Mukhtar, Apr. 11, 1971; children: Najia, Qasim. MSc, Punjab U., Lahore, 1964, Leeds U, Eng., 1968; MS, Purdue U., West Lafayette, Ind., 1978, PhD, 1982. Cert. Am. Inst. Profl. Geologists, 1985, registered Profl. Geologist Pa., 1996. Site geologist, mangla dam WAPDA, Lahore, Punjab, 1964—65; asst. prof. Punjab U., Lahore, 1965—77, grad. student West Lafayette, 1977—82; prof. engring. geology Kent State U., Ohio, 1982—. Cons., engring. geology Pvt. Cons., Kent, 1982—. Contbr. sci. papers (AEG Floyd T. Johnston Svc. award, 2004). Recipient Outstanding Alumnus award, Dept. Geosciences, Purdue U., 2001, Glenn W. Frank Outstanding Tchg. award, Dept. Geology, Kent State U., 1987, 1993, 2006; named one of Outstanding Prof. Yr., ASCE, Pitts. Sect., 1997; grant, IDOT, 1979, 1981, NSF, 1990, ODOT, 1994, 2001, 2006. Fellow: Geol. Soc. Am.; mem.: Engring. Geology Divsn., GSA (chair 2008), Am. Inst. Profl. Geologists, ASCE, Internat. Assn. Engring. Geologists, Assn. Environ. and Engring. Geologists. Business E-Mail: ashakoor@kent.edu.

SHAKTINI, NAMASCAR, language educator; d. Edgar and Clarice Orr. PhD, U. Calif., Santa Cruz, 1981. Assoc. prof., French & comparative lit. Fla. Atlantic U., Boca Raton, 1988—. Contbr. articles to profl. jours.

SHALALA, DONNA EDNA, academic administrator, former United States Secretary of Health and Human Services; b. Cleve., Feb. 14, 1941; d. James Abraham and Edna (Smith) S. AB, Western Coll., 1962; MSSC, Syracuse U., 1968, PhD, 1970; 39 hon. degrees, 1981-91. Vol. Peace Corps, Iran, 1962-64; asst. prof. polit. sci. CUNY, 1970-72; assoc. prof. politics and edn. Tchrs. Coll. Columbia U., 1972-79; asst. sec. for policy devel. & rsch. US Dept. Housing & Urban Devel., Washington, 1977-80; prof. polit. sci., pres. Hunter Coll., CUNY, 1980-87; prof. polit. sci., chancellor U. Wis., Madison, 1987-93; sec. US Dept. Health & Human Services, Washington, 1993-2001; pres. U. Miami, 2001—. Dir., treas. Mcpl. Assistance Corp. NYC, 1975—77; co-chair Pres. Commn. on Care for Am. Returning Wounded Warriors, 2007—. Author: Neighborhood Governance, 1971, The City and the Constitution, 1972, The Property Tax and the Voters, 1973, The Decentralization Approach, 1974. Mem. Trilateral Commn., 1988—92, Knight Commn. on Intercollegiate Sports, 1989—91; bd. govs. Am. Stock Exch., 1981—87; trustee TIAA, 1985—89, Com. Econ. Devel., 1982—92, Brookings Inst., 1989—92; bd. dirs. Children's Def. Fund, 1980—93, Am. Ditchley Found., 1981—93, Spencer Found., 1988—92, M&I Bank of Madison, 1991—92, NCAA Found., 1991, Inst. Internat. Econs., 1981—, Gannett Co., Inc., McLean, Va., United Health Group, Mpls., Lennar Corp., Miami; trustee emeritus Kennedy Ctr. Bd. of Trustees, Washington. Recipient Disting. Svc. medal, Columbia U. Tchrs. Coll., 1989, Presdl. Medal of Freedom, The White House, 2008; Ohio Newspaper Women's scholar, 1958, Western Coll. Trustee scholar, 1958—62, Carnegie fellow, 1966—68, Guggenheim fellow, 1975—76. Mem. ASPA, Am. Polit. Sci. Assn., Nat. Acad. Arts and Scis., Nat. Acad. Pub. Adminstrn., Coun. Fgn. Rels., Nat. Acad. Edn. (Spencer fellow 1972-73), Inst. Medicine (coun. mem. 2006-). Office: U Miami Office Pres 230 Ashe Bldg Coral Gables FL 33146 E-mail: dshalala@miami.edu.*

SHALES, THOMAS WILLIAM, television and film critic, writer, journalist; b. Elgin, Ill., Nov. 3, 1953; s. Clyde LeRoy and Hulda Louise (Reko) S. BA, Am. U., 1973. Entertainment editor Washington Examiner, 1968-71; writer style sect. Washington Post, 1972—77, chief TV critic, 1977—, TV editor, 1979—; film critic, modular arts service Nat. Public Radio, 1970-79, film critic, Morning Edit., 1979—. Adj. prof. Am. U., 1978; syndicated columnist On the Air, Washington Post Writers Group, 1979— Author: The American Film Heritage, 1972, On the Air!, 1982, Legends, 1989; Co author: Live from New York: An Uncensored History of Saturday Night Live, 2002. Recipient Disting. Alumnus award Am. U., 1978. Recipient Pulitzer Prize for criticism, 1988, Disting. Writing Award, Am. Soc. Newspaper Editors, 1988. Office: Washington Post Co 1150 15th St NW Washington DC 20071-0002

SHALIKASHVILI, JOHN MALCHASE, former Chairman of the Joint Chiefs of Staff; b. Warsaw, June 27, 1936; s. Dimitri and Maria (Ruediger) S.; m. Joan E. Zimpelman, Dec. 27, 1966; 1 child, Brant. BSME, Bradley U., 1958; attended, Naval War Coll., 1969—70, U.S. Army War Coll., 1977—78; MA in Internat. Affairs, George Washington U., 1970; LLD (hon.), U. Md., 1993, Bradley U., 1994. Joined U.S. Army, 1958, advanced through grades to gen., 1992, ret., 1997, various troop and staff assignments Alaska, U.S., Fed. Republic of Germany, Vietnam, Korea, Italy, Belgium, 1959-75, commdr. 1st bn. 84th field arty. Ft. Lewis, Wash., 1975-77; dep. chief of staff ops. So. European Task Froce U.S. Army, Vicenza, Italy, 1978-79; comdr. div. arty., 1st Armored Div. U.S. Army, Nuernberg, Fed. Republic of Germany, 1979-81, chief., politico-mil div., later dep. dir. ODCSOPS Washington, 1981-84, asst. div. comdr. 1st. Armored div. Nuernberg, Fed. Republic of Germany, 1984-86, dir. strategy, plans, policy ODCSOPS Washington, 1986-87; comdg. gen. 9th inf. div. Ft. Lewis, Wash., 1987-89; dep. comdr.-in-chief Hdqrs. USAREUR and 7th Army, Heidelberg, Fed. Republic of Germany, 1989-91; asst. to chmn. Joint Chiefs of Staff US Dept. Def., Washington, 1991-92; Supreme Allied Comdr. Europe (SACEUR), Comdr.-in-Chief NATO, Brussels, 1992-93; chmn. Joint Chiefs of Staff, US Dept. Def., Washington, 1993-97. Vis. prof. Ctr. Internat. Security and Cooperation, Stanford U.; bd. dirs. L-3 Comm. Holdings, Inc., 1998—, Boeing Co., 2000—06, Frank Russell Trust Co., Plug Power Inc. Bd. trustees Bradley U.; mem. Buffalo Soldier Meml. Hon. Com. Decorated Def. D.S.M. with 3 oak leaf clusters, D.S.M. (Army) with oak leaf cluster), D.S.M. (Navy), D.S.M. (Air Force), D.S.M. (Dept. Trans.), Legion of Merit with 2 oak leaf clusters, Bronze Star medal with V device, Meritorious Svc. medal with 3 oak leaf clusters, Air medal, Joint Svc. Commendation medal, Army Commendation medal, Nat. Def. Svc. medal with bronze svc. star, Armed Forced Expeditionary medal, Republic of Vietnam Svc. medal with silver service star, S.W. Asia Svc. medal with bronze svc. star, Humanitarian Svc. medal, Army Svc. Ribbon, Overseas Svc. Ribbon with bronze Arabic numeral 5, Inter-Am. Def. Bd. medal, Kuwait Liberation medal, Order of Combat Infantryman badge, Parachutist badge, Joint Chiefs of Staff Identification badge, Army Staff Identification badge, Brazilian Order of Mil. Merit with 1st and 2d award, French Grand Officer of Nat. Merit, Belgian Grand Cordon of Order of Leopold, German Order of Merit with star and sash, Japanese Order of Rising Sun, Argentine Order of May in Grade of Gt. Cross for Mil. Merit, Korean Order of Nat. Security Merit, Tong-IL medal, Bintang Yudha Dharama Utama Hon. Decoration (Indonesia), Kuwait Def. medal, Grand Cross of Royal Norwegian Order of Merit, Grand Cross of Mil. Merit medal of Portuguese Republic, Republic of Vietnam Gallantry Cross with 2 silver and 1 bronze star, Republic of Vietnam Armed Forces Honor medal 1st class, Republic of Vietnam Armed Forces Honor medal 1st class, Republic of Vietnam Campaign medal, Republic of Vietnam Chung My medal 2d class, Tng. Svc. medal 1st class, Netherlands Comdr. Order Orange Nassau with swords, Mexican U.S. Mil. Merit 1st class, Great Cross Repub. Poland; recipient Chilean Bernardo Higgins award, Dwight D. Eisenhower Dist. Svc. award Vets. Fgn. Wars, Dist. Alumni Achievement award George Washington U., Presdl. Medal of Freedom award, The White House, 1997*

SHALITA, ALAN REMI, dermatologist; b. Bklyn., Mar. 22, 1936; s. Harry and Celia; m. Simone Lea Baum, Sept. 4, 1960; children: Deborah (dec.) and Judith (twins). AB, Brown U., 1957; BS, U. Brussels, 1960; MD, Bowman Gray Sch. Medicine, 1964; DSc (hon.), L.I. U., 1990. Intern Beth Israel Hosp., NYC, 1964-65; resident dept. dermatology NYU Med. Ctr., 1967-68, NIH tng. grant fellow dept. dermatology, 1968-70, instr. dermatology, 1970-71; asst. prof. NYU, 1971-73, Columbia U., 1973-75; assoc. prof. medicine, head divsn. dermatology SUNY Downstate Med. Ctr., Bklyn., 1975-79, prof., 1979—, head divsn. dermatology, 1979-80, chmn. dept. dermatology, 1980—, asst. dean, 1977-83, acting dean Queens campus, 1983-84; assoc. dean clin. affairs SUNY Health Sci. Ctr., Bklyn., 1989-92, assoc. provost for clin. affairs, 1992-93, assoc. v.p. clin. affairs, 1993—2005, assoc. dean grad. med. edn., 1999—2006. Disting. tchg. prof. SUNY Health Sci. Ctr., Bklyn., 1996—; asst. attending in dermatology U. Hosp., NYC, 1970-73, Bellevue Hosp. Ctr., 1970-73, Manhattan VA Hosp., 1971-73, Presbyn. Hosp., 1973-75; bd. dirs. Kings County Hosp. Ctr.; cons. dermatology Bklyn. VA Hosp., 1975—; chief dermatology U. Hosp. Bklyn., 1975—, Brookdale Med. Ctr., 1977-90, Kings County Hosp. Ctr., Bklyn., 1975—, acting med. dir., 1989-92; med. dir. U. Hosp. Bklyn., 1992-96. Pres. Temple Shaaray Tefila, N.Y.C., 1982-86, chmn.

bd. trustees, 1987-95. Lt. M.C. USNR, 1965-67. Recipient Torch of Liberty award Anti-Defamation League, 1987, Surg. and Pediat. awards Beth Israel Hosp., NYC, 1965, Leah Dickstein Man of Good Conscience award Women's Med. Assn. NY, 1999, Leadership in Urban Med. Edn. award Arthur Ashe Inst. for Urban Health, 1999; Spl. fellow NIH, 1970-73. Mem.: AMA, Venezuelan Dermatology Soc., Argentina Dermatology Soc., Brit. Assn. Dermatologists, N.Y. Dermatol. Soc. (pres. 1989—90), Dermatol. Soc. Greater N.Y. (pres. 1980—81), N.Y. State Dermatol. Soc., N.Y. Acad. Medicine, N.Y. State Med. Soc., N.Y. Acad. Scis., Internat. Soc. Dermatology, Assn. Profs. Dermatology (sec.-treas. 1988—94, pres. 1996—98), Am. Soc. Dermatol. Surgery (past bd. dirs.), Dermatology Found. (past trustee), Soc. Investigative Dermatology, Am. Acad. Dermatology (bd. dirs. 1983—87, v.p. 1995—96), Polish Dermatology Soc. (hon.), Soc. Francaise de Dermatology (hon.), Am. Dermatol. Assn. (hon.; sec.-treas. 1996—2001, pres. 2001—02), Alpha Omega Alpha. Republican. Home: 70 E 77th St Apt 9B New York NY 10021-1811 Office: 450 Clarkson Ave Brooklyn NY 11203-2056 Office Phone: 718-270-1229. Business E-Mail: ashalita@downstate.edu. *Treat others with compassion, dignity and respect, add a little humor to everyone's life. Speak up for what you truly believe, be charitable.*

SHALL, MARY SNYDER, physical therapist, educator; b. Wichita, Kans., Mar. 18, 1954; d. Melvin Henry Snyder and Jeanne M. King, adopted d. Cathleen Ann Collins; m. Mark L. Shall, July 13, 1991 (dec. July 7, 2008). BA, Creighton U., Omaha; MS, Duke U., Durham, NC, 1978; PhD, Va. Commonwealth U., Richmond, 1991. Lic. phys. therapist Va., 1988. Phys. therapist Barnes Rd. Phys. Therapist, Portland, Oreg., 1978—79, William A. Callahan Ctr., Wilsonville, Oreg., 1979—81; lectr. U. Calif., San Francisco, 1981—87; grad. student and rsch. assoc. Va. Commonwealth U., 1987—90, prof., 1990—. Pres. MCVAA, Richmond. Contbr. scientific papers. Vol. make quilts for hurricane victims Richmond Quilting Guild, 1992—2008. Grantee Neuromuscular Devel., NIH, 2001-2004. Mem.: Am. Phys. Therapy Assn., Soc. Neurosci. (local pres. 1996—98), Sigma Xi Sci. Rsch. Soc. Office: Va Commonwealth Univ Dept Phys Therapy Box 980224 Richmond VA 23298-0224 Office Fax: 804-828-8111.

SHALLCROSS, DORIS JANE, education educator; b. Cranford, NJ, Feb. 28, 1933; d. John William and Ethel Belle (Ruth) S. BA, Montclair State Coll., NJ, 1955; MA, Wesleyan U., Middletown, Conn., 1962; EdD, U. Mass., Amherst, 1973. Tchr. Hunterdon Ctrl. H.S., Flemington, NJ, 1955-61, Roosevelt Jr. H.S., Cleveland Heights, Ohio, 1961-65, Cleveland Heights H.S., 1965-67; adminstr. Cleveland Heights Pub. Schs., 1967-69; dir. humanistic edn. Montague Pub. Schs., Mass., 1972-75; program devel. specialist Tchr. Corps., SUNY, Oneonta, NY, 1976-78; asst. prof. edn. divsn. home econs. U. Mass., Amherst, 1978-82, prof., dir. grad. studies in creativity, 1982-95; pres. Shallcross Creativity Inst., Haydenville, Mass., 1995—. Pres. bd. trustees Creative Edn. Found., Buffalo, 1988-94, trustee emerita, 2006; co-dir. Global Odyssey, 1992—; bd. dir. Ctr. for Critical and Creative Thinking, Hartford, Conn., 1989-92, 95—; prof. internat. grad. program in creativity U. Santiago, Santiago de Compostela, Spain, 1999. Author: Teaching Creative Behavior, 1981; co-author: The Growing Person, 1985, Leadership: Making Things Happen, 1987, Intuition: An Inner Way of Knowing, 1989, Celebrating the Soul of CPSI, 2004; cons. editor Jour. Creative Behavior, 1967—; contbr. articles to profl. jours. Mem. Planning Bd., Town of Williamsburg, 1981-89; v.p. bd. dirs. Pioneer Valley Performing Arts H.S., 1995-98, pres., 1998—; chair edn. com. Arts in Edn. Ctr., 1997—, pres. 2002—; bd. dirs. Mass. Charter Schs. Assn., 2001-, v.p., 2007—, Enchanted Cir. Theater, 2007-; mem. Creative Problem Solving Inst. Coun., co-chair, 2004-05; mem. Ctr. Charter Pub. Sch. Excellence, bd. dirs., mem. bd. dir., Mass. Ctr. Charter Pub. Sch. Excellence, 2007-. Recipient Disting. Leader award Creative Edn. Found., 1986; named to Creative Problem Solving Inst. Hall of Fame, 2004; named Trustee Emeritus Creative Edn. Found.; grantee, NSF, 1987-89, U. Mass., Amherst, 1987-89. Mem. NEA, Mass. Soc. Profs., Inst. for Noetic Scis., Am. Creativity Assn. (bd. dirs. 1990-93). Avocations: music, golf, reading, gardening. Home: 26 S Main St Haydenville MA 01039-9735 E-mail: dshallx@comcast.net.

SHALOM, GALIT, psychologist; b. Béer-Sheva, Israel, Dec. 26, 1969; arrived in US, 1992; d. Emil and Nourit Assor; m. Moshe Shalom, July 7, 1996; children: Nathan, Brit. BA in Edn. & Behavioral Scis., Ben-Gurion U. Negev, 1995; MA in Clinical Psychology, Forest Inst. Profl. Psychology, 1998, PsyD in Clinical Psychology, 2000. Lic. psychologist Fla., 2002. Evening news anchor ICS, Beer-Sheva, 1991—92; psychologist-in-tng. Forest Human Svcs. Ctr., Springfield, Mo., 1997—99, Neuropsychological & Assocs. SW Mo., 1999; intern Forest Inst. Profl. Psychology, Springfield, Mo., 1999—2000, tchg. asst., 1999—2000, clinical supr., 1999—2000; clinical psychologist Greene County Jail, Springfield, 2000; adj. prof. psychology Fla. Internat. U., Miami, 2001—02, post-doctorate residence, 2001—02; postdoctoral resident Fla. Internat. U. Counseling and Psychol. Svcs. Ctr., Miami, 2001—02; licensed clinical psychologist S. Fla. State Hosp., Atlantic Shores Healthcare, Inc., Pembroke Pines, Fla., 2003, pvt. practice, Boca Raton, Fla., 2003—, Jewish Family Svc., Inc. Broward County, Plantation, Fla., 2004—. Guest spkr. various seminars & presentations, 1999—2001. With Israeli mil., comdr. naval divsn. Israeli Defence Force, 1988—90. Recipient Outstanding Psychological Trainee of Month, The Resident Com., Forest Human Svcs. Ctr., 1998. Mem.: APA, Soc. for Psychology of Women. Jewish. Avocation: reading. Office: 370 W Camino Gardens Blvd Ste 204 Boca Raton FL 33432 Home: 16493 Sw 27Th St Miramar FL 33027-5205 E-mail: drshalom@bellsouth.net.

SHALOWITZ, ERWIN EMMANUEL, civil engineer; b. Washington, Feb. 13, 1924; s. Aaron Louis and Pearl (Myer) S.; m. Elaine Mildred Langerman, June 29, 1952; children: Ann Janet, Aliza Beth, Jonathan Avram. Student, U. Pa., U. Notre Dame, 1944-45; BCE, George Washington U., 1947, postgrad., 1948-49; grad. soil mechanics, Cath. U., 1951; MA in Pub. Adminstrn. (fellow U.S. Civil Service Commn.), Am. U., 1954. Registered profl. engr., Washington. Engr. Klemitt Engrng. Co., NYC, 1947; with cons. firm Whitman, Requardt & Assos., Balt., 1947-48; chief structural rsch. engr., head def. rsch. sect., project officer and tech. adviser for atomic tests Bur. Yards and Docks, Dept. Navy, Washington, 1948-59; supervisory gen. engr. spl. asst. for protective constrn. programs, project mgr. for bldg. systems, chief rsch. br., chief mgmt. info, chief contracting procedures and support, chief contract evaluation and analysis, team leader/project mgr. acquisition sys., acquisition/procurement exec., Pub. Bldg. Svc., Gen. Svcs. Adminstrn., Washington, 1959—98; mgr. ednl. svc. for individual improvement Silver Spring, Md., 1998—. Chmn. fed. exec. tng. program U.S. Civil Service Commn., 1950; fallout shelter analyst Dept. Def.; chmn. GSA Fire Safety Com., GSA Fallout Protection Com., GSA Bldg. Evaluation Com.; mem. Interagy Com. on Housing Rsch. and Bldg. Tech.; mem. Nat. Evaluation Bd. Architect-Engr. Selections; mem. standing com. on procurement policy Nat. Acad. Sci. Bldg. Research Adv. Bd. and Interagency Com. on Procurement Curriculum Rev.; coordinator pub. bldgs. design and constrn. Small Bus. Program and Minority Enterprise and Minority Subcontracting Programs. Contbr. articles profl. jours. Served to engrng. and cmdg. officer USNR, 1944-46. Recipient Commendable Svc. award GSA, 1968, Outstanding Performance recognition, 1976, 77, 79, 83, 87, 93-96, Superior Accomplishment award, 1995, others; Engr. Alumni Achievement award George Washington U., 1985. Fellow ASCE, Am. Biog. Inst.; mem. Soc. Advancement Mgmt., Am. Biog. Inst. (nat. bd. advisors), Soc. Am. Mil. Engrs., Sigma Tau, Pi Sigma Alpha. Jewish. Avocations: Bible study, ping pong/table tennis. Home: 3122 Gracefield Rd Apt 108 Silver Spring MD 20904-5801 Personal E-mail: eshalowitz@aol.com. *PRINCIPLES: Look beyond the material for lasting values and meaning, optimize managerial effectiveness by creating an objective and challenging climate in an organization, delve into the underlying causes of problem areas for meaningful solutions, and persevere in spite of obstacles. IDEAS: Cultural pluralism; the intrinsic potential of each individual; and love, appreciation, and support of one's family as indispensable for real accomplishment. GOALS: To attain the highest level of professional accomplishment within my capabilities and to continue to have a rich, happy, and fulfilling family life. STANDARDS OF CONDUCT: To be fair, consistent, and straightforward; and to avoid over-reacting.*

SHAM, JAMES S.K., medical educator; s. Yung-Ping Sham and Lai-Ming Lee; m. Joanna C.H. Kai; children: Jonathan Ian Yin, Jeffrey Thomas Yuen. BSc, Chinese U. Hong Kong, 1981, MPhil, 1983; PhD, Johns Hopkins U., Balt., 1989, U. Pa., Phila., 1992. Asst. prof. medicine Johns Hopkins U., Balt., 1992—2000, assoc. prof. medicine, 2001—. Contbr. articles to profl. jours., chapters to books. Recipient Spl. Investigator award, AHA, 1992—94; grant, 1994—97, NIH, 1995—2000, 2000—04, 2002—, 2004—, AHA, 2007—. Mem.: Cardiac Muscle Soc., Am. Heart Assn., Am. Thoracic Soc., Biphysical Soc., Am. Physiol. Soc. Office: Johns Hopkins Med Insts 5501 Hopkins Bayview Cir Rm 4B43 Baltimore MD 21224 Office Fax: 410-550-2612. Business E-Mail: jsks@jhmi.edu.

SHAM, LU JEU, physics professor; b. Hong Kong, Apr. 28, 1938; s. T. S. and Cecilia Maria (Siu) Shen; m. Georgina Bien, Apr. 25, 1965; children: Kevin Shen, Alisa Shen. GCE, Portsmouth Coll., Eng., 1957; BS, Imperial Coll., London U., Eng., 1960; PhD in Physics, Cambridge U., Eng., 1963. Asst. rsch. physicist U. Calif., San Diego, 1963-66, assoc. prof., 1968-75, prof., 1975—, chair dept. physics, 1995-98, dean div. natural scis., 1985-89, Disting. physics prof., 2005—, asst. prof. physics Irvine, 1966-67; rsch. physicist IBM Corp., Yorktown Heights, NY, 1974-75. Reader Queen Mary Coll., U. London, 1967—68. Assoc. editor: Physics Letters A, 1992—; contbr. articles to profl. jours. Recipient Churchill Coll. studentship, Eng., 1960—63, U.S. Scientist award, Humboldt Found., 1978, Faculty Rsch. Letter award, 2000, Lamb medal, 2004, Chancellor Assocs. award for Excellence in Rsch., 1995; fellow, Guggenheim Found., 1984. Fellow: Am. Phys. Soc.; mem.: NAS, AAAS, Optical Soc. Am., Acad. Sinica Republic of China. Democrat. Avocations: tennis, folk dancing. Office: U Calif San Diego Dept Physics 0319 La Jolla CA 92093-0319 Office Phone: 619-534-3269. E-mail: lsham@ucsd.edu.

SHAMASH, YACOV, dean, electrical engineering educator; b. Iraq, Jan. 12, 1950; BSEE, Imperial Coll., London, 1970; PhD in Control Systems, Imperial Coll., 1973. Postdoctoral fellow in elec. engring. Tel-Aviv U., 1973—75, from lectr. elec. engring. to sr. lectr. elec. engring., 1975-78; prof. elec. engring. Fla. Atlantic U., Boca Raton, 1977-85; prof., chair dept. elec. engring. dept. Wash. State U., Pullman, 1985-92; dean engring. SUNY, Stony Brook, 1992—. Bd. dirs. KeyTronic, Spokane, Wash., 1990—; vis. asst. prof. U. Pa., Phila., 1976-77. Contbr. over 100 articles to profl. jours., book chpts. Fellow IEEE (sr.). Office: SUNY Coll Engring & Applied Sci Stony Brook NY 11794-2200

SHAMBAUGH, DAVID LEIGH, political scientist, educator, writer; b. Chgo., Jan. 18, 1953; s. George E. Shambaugh, Jr. and Genevieve (Krum) Shambaugh; m. Ingrid Larsen, Aug. 7, 1982; children: Christopher Leigh, Alexander George. BA in East Asian Studies, George Washington U., 1977; MA in Internat. Affairs, Johns Hopkins U., 1980; PhD in Polit. Sci., U. Mich., 1989. Prof. U. London, 1988—96, George Washington U., Washington, 1996—; sr. fellow Brookings Instn., 1998—. Cons. in field. Editor China Quar., 1991—96, mem. editl. bd., 1989—, Studies on Contemporary China, 1991—, Internat. Security, 2003—, China Perspectives, 1998—, Current History, 1999—; author: The Making of a Premier: Zhao Ziyang's Provincial Career, 1984, Beautiful Imperialist: China Perceives America, 1991, China and Europe, 1996, 2008, Modernizing China's Military Progress, Problems, and Prospects, 2002, The Odyssey of China's Imperial Art Treasures, 2005; editor, contbr. American Studies of Contemporary China, 1993, Greater China: The Next Superpower?, 1995, Deng Xiaoping: Portrait of a Chinese Statesman, 1995, China's Military in Transition, 1997, Contemporary Taiwan, 1998, The Modern Chinese State, 2000, Is China Unstable?, 2000, co-editor Chinese Foreign Policy: Theory and Practice, 1994, co-editor, contbr. China's Military Faces the Future, 1999, The China Reader: The Reform Era, 1999, Making China Policy: Lessons from the Bush and Clinton Administrations, 2001, Power Shift: China and Asia's New Dynamics, 2005, China Watching, 2006, China's Communist Party, 2008, International Relations of Asia, 2008. Grantee, Brit. Acad./Econ. & Social Rsch. Coun. China Exch. Program, 1990, 1994, Chiang Ching-kuo Found., 1998—2000, Smith Richardson Found., 1998—99, 2005—06; Rsch. fellow, Pacific Cultural Found., 1998—2000, Woodrow Wilson fellow, 2002—03, others. Mem.: Pacific Coun. on Internat. Policy, Coun. on Fgn. Rels., Asia Soc., Internat. Studies Assn., Assn. for Asian Studies, Coun. on Security Coop. in the Asia Pacific, Nat. Com. U.S.-China Rels., Internat. Inst. Strategic Studies, World Econ. Forum. Avocations: travel, basketball, tennis, canoeing, bluegrass music. Office: George Washington Univ Elliott Sch Internat Affairs 1957 E St NW Ste 503 Washington DC 20052 Office Phone: 202-994-5887. Business E-Mail: shambaug@gwu.edu.

SHAMBAUGH, IRVIN CALVIN, JR., aptitude test firm executive, consultant; b. Harrisburg, Pa., June 7, 1943; s. Irvin Calvin and Viola Mary (Deibler) Shambaugh; m. Amy Wilcox Shambaugh, Jan. 3, 1975. BS in Geol. Sci., Pa. State U., 1964; postgrad., MIT, Cambridge, Mass., 1964—65, Tex. Christian U., Ft. Worth, 1974—76, East Tex. State U., 1976—77. Rsch. coord. Johnson O'Connor Rsch. Found., Ft. Worth, 1965—76; pres., chief scientist Aptitude Inventory Measurement Svc., Dallas, 1976—; pres. Aptitude Expertise, Inc., 2009—. Centennial fellow Coll. Earth and Min. Scis., Pa. State U., 1996. Author: The Test-Taker's Guide to Career Literature, 1982, Test Manual for Selected AIMS Worksamples, 1986, Books About Careers, 1986, Career Facts: Where to Find Them and How to Use Them, 1992, The AIMS Guide to Career Facts, 1997; co-author: AIMS Information About Aptitudes, 1979, The Aptitude Handbook: A Guide to the AIMS Program, 1996, 2004, Career Facts: In Print and on the World Wide Web, 2003, AIMS Guide to Career Information, 2009; co-prodr.: (e-pub.) AIMS Information Disk, 2004; editor: You and Your Aptitudes, 1983; developer Activity Preference Questionnaire, 1994, psychometric instrument lll Interest Inventory, 1996; contbr. articles to profl. jours.; developer AIMS test battery, 1976—, digital version, 2005—, AIMS Measure of Color Perception, 2005—, AIMS Reasoning Measure, 2006, rev. edit., 2008, 3-D Mental Gymnastics Worksample, 2006, rev. edit., 2008. With USMC, 1966—68. Mem.: AAAS, ACA, APA (assoc.), Nat. Assn. Test Dirs., Nat. Assn. Coll. Admissions Counselors, Nat. Coun. Measurement in Edn., Am. Psychol. Soc., Assn. Assessment in Counseling and Edn. Achievements include development of psychometric instruments. Home: 934 Westbrook Dr Garland TX 75043-5243 Office: Aptitude Inventory Measurement Svc 12160 Abrams Rd Ste 314 Dallas TX 75243-4525

SHAMBAUGH, STEPHEN WARD, lawyer; b. South Bend, Ind., Aug. 4, 1920; s. Marion Clyde and Anna Violet (Stephens) S.; m. Marilyn Louise Pyle (dec. 1993); children: Susan Wynne Shambaugh Hinkle (dec. 1998), Kathleen Louise Shambaugh Thompson; m. Virginia W. Roberts Dec. 28, 2007. Student, San Jose State Tchrs. Coll., 1938-40, U. Ark., 1951; LLB, U. Tulsa, 1954. Bar: Okla. 1954, Colo. 1964. Mem. staff Reading & Bates, Inc., Tulsa, 1951-54; v.p., gen. mgr., legal counsel Reading & Bates Drilling Co. Ltd., Calgary, Alta., Canada, 1954-61; sr. ptnr. Bowman, Shambaugh, Geissinger & Wright, Denver, 1964-81; sole practice Denver, 1981-97; now ret. Dir., fin. counsel various corps. Col. USAF. Mem. Colo. Bar Assn., Okla. Bar Assn., P-51 Mustang Pilots Assn., Mil. Officers Assn. Am. (life), Am. Legion, Masons, Elks, Phi Alpha Delta. Personal E-mail: swscolonel@aol.com.

SHAMBUREK, ROLAND HOWARD, physician; b. Adell, Wis., June 7, 1928; s. William and Catherine (Illig) Shamburek; m. Gladys Irene Gibbons, June 21, 1952; children: Steven J., Robert D., Daniel J. Grad., Monroe HS, Wis., 1946; BS, U. Wis., 1950, MD, 1953; MPH, Harvard U., 1960; grad., U.S. Army War Coll., Carlisle Barracks, Pa., 1972. Diplomate Am. Bd. Preventive Medicine. Commd. 1st lt. M.C., U.S. Army, 1953, advanced through grades to col., 1968; intern St. Joseph's Hosp., Marshfield, Wis., 1953-54; grad. U.S. Naval Sch. of Aviation Medicine, Pensacola, Fla., 1957; resident in preventive (aerospace) medicine USAF Sch. Aerospace Medicine, Brooks AFB, 1960-63; service in 216th Field Artillery (Atomic) Battalion, 1954—56, 1966, Office of Army Surgeon Gen., Washington, 1966—70, 1972—75; comdr. 67th EVAC Hosp., Vietnam, 1970-71, U.S. Army Med. Pers. Support Agy., 1975-77; ret. U.S. Army, 1977; exec. v.p. Aerospace Med. Assn., 1977-79; clin. practice Pentagon Health Clinic, Washington, 1981-85; med. researcher Office of Army Surgeon Gen., 1985-87. Med. monitor Canary Island Tracking Sta. for Gemini missions NASA, 1965—66. Contbr. scientific papers in field. Decorated Legion of Merit with oak leaf cluster, Army Commendation medal, Meritorious Svc. medal; recipient Gold Palm Eagle Scout award, Boy Scouts Am., 1945. Mem.: AMA (del. 1978), Internat. Acad. Aviation and Space Medicine, Soc. NASA Flight Surgeons, U.S. Army Flight Surgeons, Soc. Med. Cons. Armed Forces, Aerospace Med. Assn. (v.p. 1968—69), Am. Coll. Preventive Medicine (v.p. 1968—69), Assn. Mil. Surgeons (John Shaw Billings award 1968). Address: 3700 Moss Dr Annandale VA 22003-1915

SHAMMAS, NAZIH KHEIRALLAH, environmental engineer, consultant, engineering educator; b. Homs, Syria, Feb. 18, 1939; arrived in US, 1991; s. Kheirallah Hanna and Nazha Murad (Hamwi) Shammas; m. Norma Massouh, July 28, 1968; children: Sarmed Erick, Samer Sam. Degree in engirng. with distinction, Am. U., Beirut, 1962; MS in Sanitary Engring., U. NC, Chapel Hill, 1965; PhD in Civil Engring., U. Mich., Ann Arbor, 1971. Instr. civil engring. Am. U., Beirut, 1965-68; tchg. fellow U. Mich., Ann Arbor, 1968-71; asst. prof. civil engring. Am. U., Beirut, 1972-76, King Saud U., Riyadh, Saudi Arabia, 1976-78, assoc. prof., 1978-91; prof. environ. engring. Lenox Inst. Water Tech., Mass., 1991-2001, dean edn., 1992-93. Cons., ptnr. Cons. and Rsch. Engrs., Beirut, 1973—76; cons. Ar-Riyadh Devel. Authority, 1977—93, Riyadh Water and Sanitary Drainage Authority, 1979—83, Assoc. Cons. Engrng. Team, 1994—99, Vikakis Internat., 1995—2002; adj. prof. environ. sci. Berkshire Cmty. Coll., 1995—; planning assoc. Berkshire Regional Planning Commn., 1999—2003. Co-author: Environmental Sanitation, 1988, Wastewater Engineering, 1988, Physicochemical Treatment Processes, 2005, Advanced Physicochemical Treatment Processes, 2006, Advanced Physiochemical Treatment Technologies, 2007, Biosolids Treatment Processes, 2007, Biosolids Engineering Management, 2008; contbr. articles to profl. jours. and confs.; co-author: Biological Treatment Process, 2009, Advanced Biological Treatment Processes, 2009, Advanced in Hazardous Industrial Waste Treatment, 2009, Waste Treatment in the Metal Manufacturing, Forming, Coating & Finishing Industries, 2009. Recipient Excellence in Tchg. award, King Saud U., 1981, 1984; Block grantee, U. Mich., 1968—70. Mem.: ASCE, Assn. Environ. Engrng. and Sci. Profs., Internat. Water Assn., New Eng. Water Works Assn., New Eng. Water Environ. Assn., Am. Water Works Assn., Water Environ. Fedn. Achievements include research in biological and physiochemcial remediation processes; mathematical modeling of nitrification process; water and wastewater management in developing countries; water conservation; wastewater treatment and reuse; appropriate technology for developing countries; multidisciplinary studies in environmental management and planning. Home: 35 Flintstone Dr Pittsfield MA 01201 Personal E-mail: nazihshammas@aol.com.

SHAMMASH, JONATHAN, medical educator; Assoc. prof. clin. medicine Weill Cornell Med. Coll., NYC, 2003—; med. dr. dept. medicine Eaglewood Hosp. & Med. Ctr. Office: Eaglewood Hosp & Med Ctr 350 Engle St Englewood NJ 07631

SHAMOIAN, CHARLES ANTHONY, psychiatrist, educator; b. Worcester, Mass., Oct. 5, 1931; s. Garabed Sarkis and Anna (Varjabedian) S.; m. Paula Baker, Oct. 8, 1961; children: Paula Ann, Charles Raymond. AB, Clark U., 1954, MA, 1956; PhD, Tufts U., 1960, MD, 1966. Diplomate Am. Bd. Psychiatry and Neurology. Intern Bellevue Hosp., NYC, 1966-67; resident Payne Whitney Psychiat. Clinic-N.Y. Hosp., NYC, 1967-70, chief resident, 1970-71, unit chief, 1975-79; asst. prof. psychiatry Cornell U. Med. Coll., NYC, 1970-75, assoc. prof., 1979-84, prof. clin. psychiatry, 1984—; practice medicine specializing in psychiatry White Plains, N.Y., 1979—. Dir. geriatric services N.Y. Hosp.-Cornell U. Med. Ctr., White Plains, 1979-89, dir. partial hospitalization program, 1995—. USPHS postdoctoral fellow, 1960-61. Fellow Gerontol. Soc. Am. (vice chmn. clin. medicine sect. 1984-85), Am. Psychiat. Assn. (chmn. coun. aging 1985—); mem. Am. Assn. Geriatric Psychiatry (bd. dirs. 1983-84, sec. 1984-85, pres.-elect 1985). Office: New York Hosp-Cornell Med Ctr 21 Bloomingdale Rd White Plains NY 10605-1504

SHAMOO, ADIL ELIAS, biochemist, educator; b. Baghdad, Iraq, Aug. 1, 1941; came to U.S., 1964, naturalized, 1973; s. Elias M. and Mariam T. (Mansour) S.; m. Joan Hutchison, Dec. 16, 1967 (div. Dec. 1997); children: Abraheem, Zachary, Jessica. B.Sc. in Physics, U. Baghdad, 1962; MS in Physics (grad. fellow), U. Louisville, 1966; PhD in Biophysics, CUNY, 1970. Instr. engring. physics Speed Sch., U. Louisville, 1965-68; asst. prof. physiology City U. N.Y., 1971-73; guest worker Lab. Biophysics and Neurochemistry, NIH, Bethesda, Md., 1972-73; asst. prof. radiation biology and biophysics U. Rochester, 1973-75; guest prof. Max-Planck Inst. Biophysics, Frankfurt, West Germany, 1977-78; assoc. prof. radiation biology and biophysics U. Rochester, 1975-79; prof., chmn. dept. biol. chemistry U. Md., Balt., 1979-82, prof. biochemistry and molecular biology, 1982—, prof. epidemiology and preventive medicine, 2003—, head membrane biochemistry research lab., 1982-90. Cons. div. biol. scis. Kodak Co., Rochester, 1976-77; NIH tng. fellow U. Louisville, 1967; investigator Am. Heart Assn., 1976-79; Neurosci. Rsch. Program fellow, Boulder, Colo., summer 1977; chmn. symposia, various coms. in field; mem. organizing coms. workshops in field; adj. profl. dept. physics East Carolina U., Greenville, N.C., 1996-2000; bd. dirs. Friends Rsch. Inst., 1994-2001; ethics cons. Armed Forces Epidemiol. Bd.; chair ethics adv. group GlaxoSmithKline Co., 2003. Editor (with M.W. Miller) Membrane Toxicity, 1977, Carriers and Channels in Biological Systems, 1975, Carriers and Channels in Biological Systems-Transport Proteins, 1980, Regulation of Calcium Transport Across Muscle Membranes, 1985, Principles of Research Data Audit, (with R. Verna) Biotechnology Today, 1995, Ethics in Neurobiological Research with Human Subjects, 1997; editor in chief Membrane Biochemistry, 1977-93, Accountability in Research: Policies and Quality Assurance, 1988—; mem. editl. bd. Molecular and Cellular Biochemistry, 1987-94, Quality Assurance: Good Practice Regulation and Law, 1991-2000; contbr. articles and abstracts to profl. jours., chpts. to books. Bd. dirs. Alliance for Mentally Ill of Md., 1990-93, Friends Rsch. Inst. Inc., 1994-2002; mem. rsch. monitoring com. Nat. Alliance for Mentally Ill, bd. dirs. 1994-97; pres. faculty senate U. Md., Balt., 1993-94; mem. coun. univ. systems U. Md., 1994-97; mem. adv. com. Vantage Pl., 1995-97; bd. dirs. Howard County Mental Health Authority, 1997-00, pres., 1997-2000; bd. dirs. Citizens for Responsible Care and Rsch., 1998—, v.p., 1998—; mem. Nat. Human Rsch. Protections Adv. Com., 2000-02; mem. Def. Health Bd., 2006—. Recipient Advocacy award Mental Health Assn. Md., 1994, Disting. Svc. award Alliance for Mentally Ill of Md., 1994, Howard County Mental Health Auth., 1999. Mem. AAAS, AAUP (chpt. sec. 1971-72), Basic Sci. Council of Am. Heart Assn., Am. Soc. Biol. Chemists and Mol. Biol., Am. Coll. Sports Medicine, Am. Assn. Physics Tchrs., Am. Soc. Bioethics and Human Values, Am. Physiol. Soc., Biophys. Soc. (Cole Membrane Award Com. 1983-84, chmn. biophysics subgroup 1982-83, council 1986-89), Membrane Biophys. Group (chmn. 1982-83, sec.-treas. 1983-85, co-chmn. U.S. bioenergetics group 1979-80), Md. Acad. Scis. (chmn. com. programs and exhbns. 1986-87, sci. council 1985-89), N.Y. Acad. Scis., Coun. of Biology (editor 1989—), Soc. Quality Assurance, Defence Health Bd., 2006- Achievements include patents for liquid scintillators. Office: 108 N Greene St Baltimore MD 21201-1503 E-mail: ashamoo@umaryland.edu.

SHAMPO, MARC ANTHONY, retired editor; b. Green Bay, Wis., Oct. 20, 1924; s. Norman Joseph Shampo and Antoinette Rondou; m. Norma Eileen Beyea, Oct. 23, 1945 (div. Oct. 1965); 1 child, Teresa; m. Lila Irene Mayhew, July 29, 1967 (dec. Jan. 27, 2008); children: Barbara, Charles, Nancy, Scott. BS, U. Wis., 1948, MS, 1949; PhD, U. Wis., Madison, Wis., 1960. H.S. tchr., Pewaukee, Wis., 1949—51, Racine, Wis., 1951—58; prof. Duquesne U., Pitts., 1958—62; med. editor Mayo Clinic, Rochester, Minn., 1962—89; ret., 1989. Contbr. articles to profl. jours., chpts. to books. With US Army, 1943—46, ETO. Decorated Combat Inf. Badge, Purple Heart, Bronze Star. Mem.: Phi Delta Kappa, Phi Eta Sigma. Home: 211 2d St NW Rochester MN 55901

SHAMRELL, RICHARD T., physics professor; BS in Physics, USAF Acad., Colo., 1973; MA in Mgmt. & Human Rels., Webster U., St. Louis, Mo., 1977; MS in Physics, So. Ill. U., Edwardsville, 1998. Instr. pilot & acad. instr. Laughlin AFB, Tex., 1975—78, student br. chief & instr. pilot Del Rio, Tex., 1981—86; aircraft comdr. RAF Upper Heyford, 1978—81; air ops. officer, pilot US Logistic Group, Ankara, Turkey, 1986—88; air ops. officer,instr. pilot Mather AFB, Sacramento, 1988—91; base ops. officer McClellan AFB, 1991—93; instr. physics Clark Coll., Vancouver, Wash., 1998—, co-divisn chair, phys. sci. & engring. divsn., 2004—06. Recipient Exceptional Faculty award, Clark Coll., 2005. Office: Physics Dept Clark Coll 1933 Fort Vancouver Way Vancouver WA 98663 Business E-Mail: rshamrell@clark.edu.

SHAMS, ALICIA MARIE, microbiologist; b. St. Paul, Apr. 30, 1979; d. Albert Edward and Susan Francis Peterson; m. Ryan I. Shams. BS, U. Minn., Mpls., 2001; MPH, Emory U., Atlanta, 2003. Student worker Minn. Dept. Health, Mpls., 1996—97, CDC, Atlanta, 2001—02, microbiologist, 2002—. Contbr. articles to profl. jours. Mem.: Delta Gamma Frat. (honor bd. mem. 1995—96). Dfl. Office: CDC 1600 Clifton Rd NE MS C-16 Atlanta GA 30329 Business E-Mail: ashams@cdc.gov.

SHAMSUDDIN, ABULKALAM MOHAMMED, medical educator; MD, U. Dhaka, Bangladesh, 1972; PhD, U. Md., Balt., 1979. Cert. Am. Bd. Pathology, 1977. Prof. pathology U. Md. Sch. Medicine, Balt., 1988—; pres. IP-6 Rsch. Inc., Balt., 1999—. Chmn. IP-6 Found. Inc., Balt., 2005—. Chmn. Kamolpur Janakallyan Trust, Dhaka, 2004—08. Grantee Colon Carcinogenesis, Am. Cancer Soc., 1985—87. Achievements include patents for cancer screening tests and anti-cancer medicine. Avocations: skiing, music, opera. Office: IP-6 Rsch Inc 15 Charles Plaza Ste 2508 Baltimore MD 21201-3931 Business E-Mail: research@ip-6.net.

SHAN, XI, research scientist; BS, Tsinghua U., Beijing, 1993; PhD, Case Western Res. U., Cleve., 2004. Engr. Ctrl. Iron and Steel Rsch. Inst., Beijing, 1993—98; sr. rsch. assoc. Case Western Res. U., Cleve., 2004—. Mem.: Electrochem. Soc., NACE Internat., ASM Internat. Achievements include patents for hydrogen storage for micro-fabricated electrochemical devices.

SHAN, YING, computer scientist; s. Tinghua Shan and Zhaoxia Chen; m. Hui Liu, Mar. 19, 1994; children: Amy Cheng, Larry Hao. Sr. mem. tech. staff Sarnoff Corp., Princeton, NJ, 2001—07; applied rschr. Microsoft Corp., Redmond, Wash., 2007—. Contbr. scientific papers. Mem.: IEEE. Business E-Mail: ying.shan@microsoft.com.

SHAN, YUFENG, research scientist; Faculty mem. Shandong U., Jinan, China, 1995—2000; vis. prof. French Nat. Inst. for Rsch. in Computer Sci. and Control, Sophia Antipolis, 2000; rsch. scientist U. Calif., Berkeley, 2001—02. Author: more than 20 rsch. papers. Mem.: IEEE. Office: Rensselaer Polytechnic Inst 110 8th St Troy NY 12180 Home: 284 Great Rd Apt D7 Acton MA 01720-4732 Personal E-mail: yfshan@yahoo.com. Business E-Mail: shany@rpi.edu.

SHAN, ZUYAO, medical researcher; s. Shan Qingfang and Fan Xinrui; 1 child, Serana. PhD, Cleve. State U., 2003. Rsch. assoc. St. Jude Children's Rsch. Hosp., Memphis, 2003—06, asst. mem., 2006—. Grantee Thrasher Rsch. Fund, 2004—06. Mem.: ISMRM, IEEE Soc. (memphis sect. chair 2006—07). Achievements include research in medical image computing. Office: St Jude Children's Research Hosp 262 Danny Thomas Pl Memphis TN 38105 Personal E-mail: zuyao_shan@hotmail.com. Business E-Mail: zuyao.shan@stjude.org.

SHANAHAN, BETTY, professional society administrator; BSEE, Mich. State. U.; M of Software Engring., Wang Inst. of Grad. Studies; MBA in Strategic Mgmt., U. Chgo. Grad. Sch. of Bus. Cert. assn. exec. Various positions in devel., engring. mgmt. and mktg. Data Gen., Alliant Computer Sys., 1978—90; mktg. mgmt., including v.p., prod. mgmt. and mktg., software computers divsn. Stellent, Inc., 1990—2002; exec. dir. Soc. of Women Engr., Chgo., 2002—. Bd. dir. Women in Engring. Programs and Adv. Network; bd. dirs. JETS; champions bd. Nat. Girls Collaborative Project. Fellow: Soc. Women Engr. (life); mem.: IEEE, Am. Soc. of Assn. Execs., Assn. for Computing Machinery. Office: Exec Dir Soc of Women Engr 230 E Ohio St Chicago IL 60611

SHANAHAN, BRENDAN FREDERICK, professional hockey player; b. Mimico, Ont., Can., Jan. 23, 1969; s. Donal and Rosaleen Shanahan; m. Catherine Shanahan, July 4, 1998; children: Jack, Maggie, Catherine Rosaleen. Left wing NJ Devils, 1987—91, 2009—, St. Louis Blues, 1991—95, Hartford Whalers, 1995—97, Detroit Red Wings, 1997—2006, NY Rangers, 2006—08. Recipient King Clancy Meml. Trophy, 2003, Mark Messier Leadership Award, 2006; named to First All-Star Team, NHL, 1994, 2000, Second All-Star Team, 2002, NHL All-Star Game, 1994, 1996—2000, 2002, 2007. Achievements include being a member of Stanley Cup Champion Detroit Red Wings, 1997, 1998, 2002; being a member of gold medal Canadian Hockey team, Salt Lake City Olympic Games, 2002. Office: NJ Devils Prudential Ctr 165 Mulberry St Newark NJ 07102*

SHANAHAN, ELLEN C., music educator; married. MA in Music, Smith Coll., Northampton, Mass. Instr. music Berkshire CC, Pittsfield, Mass., 1983—2000, prof. music, 2000—. Office: Berkshire CC 1350 West St Pittsfield MA 01201 Business E-Mail: eshanahan@berkshirecc.edu.

SHANAHAN, MAUREEN GABRIELLE, academic administrator; d. Louise and Edmund Shanahan. BA, Duke U., Durham, NC, 1981; JD, Loyola U. Sch. Law, LA, 1985; PhD, U. Mich., Ann Arbor, 2000. Lic.: Calif. State Bar 1986. Assoc. dir., honors program James Madison U., Harrisonburg, Va., 2004—. Mem.: Women's Caucus Art (fundraising chair 2008), Coll. Art Assn., Phi Kappa Phi. Office: James Madison Univ Honors Program 800 So Main St MSC 1501 Harrisonburg VA 22807 Office Fax: 540-568-8079. Business E-Mail: shanahmg@jmu.edu.

SHANAHAN, MIKE (MICHAEL EDWARD SHANAHAN), former professional football coach; b. Oak Park, Ill., Aug. 24, 1952; m. Peggy, children: Kyle, Krystal. BS Phys. Edn., Ea. Ill. U., Charleston, 1974, MS Phys. Edn., 1975. Grad. asst. Ea. Ill. U., 1973—74; asst. coach U. Okla., 1975-76; offensive coord. No. Ariz. U., 1976—77, Ea. Ill. U., 1977—78, U. Minn., 1979—80, U. Fla., Gainesville, 1980—84, asst. head coach, 1983—84; receivers coach Denver Broncos, 1984-87; head coach L.A. Raiders, 1988-89; asst. coach Denver Broncos, 1989-91; offensive coord. San Francisco 49ers, 1992-94; head coach Denver Broncos, 1995—2008. Achievements include head coach of the Super Bowl Championship winning Denver Broncos, 1998, 1999. Avocations: golf, travel.*

SHANAHAN, SHEILA ANN, pediatrician, educator; m. Justin Laurence Cashman Jr., Sept. 14, 1968; children: Justin III, Gillis. BA, Trinity Coll., 1963; MD cum laude, Med. Coll. Pa., 1969. Diplomate Nat. Bd. Med. Examiners, Am. Bd. Pediats. Intern Presbyn. Hosp., NYC, 1969-70, resident in pediats., 1970-72, asst. in clin. pediats., 1972-75, assoc. clin. pediats., 1975-78; pvt. practice specializing in pediats. Greenwich, Conn., 1972-78; asst. attending Greenwich Hosp., 1972-73, assoc. attending, 1973-78; from instr. to assoc. Columbia Coll. Physicians and Surgeons, NYC, 1972-78; asst. prof. pediats. George Washington U. Sch. Medicine, Washington, 1980—, Georgetown U. Sch. Medicine, Washington, 1984—; pvt. practice specializing in pediats. Washington, 1984—. Attending dept. ambulatory medicine Children's Hosp. Nat. Med. Ctr., Washington, 1980—84; courtesy staff Georgetown U. Hosp., Washington, 1984—, Sibley Meml. Hosp., Washington, 1984—, Children's Hosp. Nat. Med. Ctr., 1984—. Fellow Am. Acad. Pediats.; mem. Am. Women's Med. Assn. Office: 4900 Massachusetts Ave NW Washington DC 20016-4358

SHANBHAG, ABHIJIT G., semiconductor company executive; B in Tech. in Elec. Engring., Indian Inst. Tech., Bombay; PhD in Elec. Engring., U. So. Calif., 1996. Leadership positions Qualcomm, Ericsson; group leader Morphics Tech. (acquired by Infineon); co-founder Scintera Networks, Inc., San Jose, Calif., 2001, chief tech. officer, 2001—. Contbr. articles to internat. jours. and conf. proceedings. Adv. bd. Viterbi Sch. Engring., U. So. Calif. Achievements include holds patents in communications systems and signal processing. Office: Scintera Networks Inc 1154 Sonora Ct Sunnyvale CA 94086 Home Phone: 408-735-5960; Office Phone: 408-636-2613 18. Business E-Mail: ags@scintera.com. E-mail: ashanbhag@scinteranetworks.com.

SHANBHAG, SACHIN, science educator, researcher; b. Belgaum, Karnataka, India, Apr. 1, 1977; s. Prakash and Shobha Shanbhag; m. Priya Pai, Sept. 1, 2003. BTech, IIT, Mumbai, 1999; PhD, U. Mich., Ann Arbor, 2004. Asst. prof. dept. sci. computing Fla. State U., Tallahassee, 2006—; postdoc. rsch. fellow U. Mich., Ann Arbor. Contbr. articles to profl. jours. Judge k-12 Sci. Fair, Tahassee, 2007—08. Recipient New Faculty award, Petroleum Rsch. Fund, 2007—, First Yr. Asst. Prof. award, Fla. State U., 2007. Independent. Achievements include first to primitive path analysis of polymer networks. Avocations: camping, baking.

SHANE, JEFFREY, physics professor; married. BSEE, Ohio No. U., Ada, 1987; MA in Tchg., Kent State U., Ohio, 1990. Cert. to profl. tchg. stds. Nat. Bd. Dirs., 2002, in physics & math. tchg. Ohio Dept. Edn., 2002. Physics tchr. Revere Local Sch., Richfield, Ohio, 1990—; phyiscs instr. U. Akron, Ohio, 1995—. Business E-Mail: jshane@revere.k12.oh.us.

SHANE, JEFFREY NEIL, lawyer; b. NYC, Mar. 27, 1941; s. Albert and Ann (Semanoff) S.; m. Dzing J. Wu, June 27, 1992; 1 child Ann Wu. AB, Princeton U., 1962; LLB, Columbia U., NYC, 1965. Bar: D.C. 1966. Trial atty. FPC, Washington, 1966-68, US Dept. Transp., Washington, 1968-70, spl. asst. to gen. counsel, 1970-72; traveled in Africa, Europe, 1972-73; researcher Environ. Law Inst., Washington, 1974-75; mem. UN Task Force on Human Environ., Bangkok, 1975-77; atty., cons. environ. law in developing countries, Washington, 1978-79; asst. gen. counsel internat. law US Dept. Transp., Washington, 1979-83, dep. asst. sec. for policy & internat. affairs, 1983-85, asst. sec. for policy & internat. affairs, 1989—93; dep. asst. sec. for transp. affairs US Dept. State, Washington, 1985-89; counsel Wilmer, Cutler & Pickering LLP, Washington, 1993-96, ptnr., 1997-2000, Hogan & Hartson LLP, Washington, 2000—02, 2008—; assoc. dep. sec. US Dept. Transp., Washington, 2002—03, under sec. for policy, 2003—08. Adj. prof. law Georgetown U., Washington, 1985-89; mem. Archl. and Transp. Barriers Compliance Bd., 1989-93, 2005-06, vice-chmn., 1992-93; vice chmn. Adv. Com. on Confs. in Ocean Shipping, 1990-91; chmn. commn. on air transport Internat. C. of C., Paris, 1994-2001, chmn. mil. airlift com. Nat. Defense Transport Assn.; mem, Air Transp. Stabilization Bd., 2004-07; pres. 36th Assembly Internat. Civil Aviation Orgn., Montreal, 2007; chair Internat. Air Transport Assn. Agenda Freedom Summit, 2008. Co-author: Developing Economies and the Environment, 1978; co-author-editor: NEPA in Action: The Impact of the National Environmental Policy Act on Federal Decision-Making, 1975, Environmental and Natural Resource Management in Developing Countries, 1979. With USAR, 1965—71. Recipient Presdl. Meritorious Rank award, Dept. of State, 1988, L. Welch Pogue award for Lifetime Achievement in Aviation, 2006, Sec. Transp. Gold medal, 2007, Disting. Svc. award, Dept. Transp., 2008; named Transportation Person of Yr., U. Md. Sch. Bus., 2006. Mem.: ABA (chmn. forum on air and space law 2001), Cosmos Club (Wash.), Met. Club, Columbia Country Club (Chevy Chase, Md.), Wings Club (N.Y.C. bd. govs. 1995—98), Internat. Aviation Club (Washington pres. 1999—2000), Aero Club (Washington bd. govs. 1984—86). Jewish. Office Phone: 202-637-6851.

SHANE, JOHN MARDER, endocrinologist; b. Kans. City, Mo., Oct. 5, 1942; s. Henry Kamsler and Ruth (Marder) S.; m. Eileen Goodart, June 18, 1967; children: Robert M., Edward G. BS, U. Okla., 1964, MD, 1967. Diplomate Am. Bd. Ob-Gyn., Am. Bd. Reproductive Endocrinology; cert. master gardener. Resident Harvard Med. Sch., Boston, 1970-73, fellowship, 1973-75, instr., 1970-75, asst. prof., 1975-78; pvt. practice Tulsa, 1978-99. Lectr., cons. Tutorial Svcs. Internat., England, 1984—; bd. dirs. St. Francies G.I.F.T. Lab., Tulsa; cons. to preimplantation genetics project Chapman Genetics Inst., Children's Med. Ctr., Tulsa. Author: CIBA Symposium Infertility: Diagnosis and Treatment; contbr. articles to profl. jours. and publs.; exhibitions include Okla. Woodturners, The Philbrook Mus. Active Tulsa Garden Ctr., 1988—; bd. dirs. Temple Israel, Tulsa, 1985-86, Up With Trees Found., 2000—, Tulsa, master gardener. Capt. USAF, 1967-69. Recipient Annual award Boston Obstet. Soc., 1977; named one of Best Doctor's in Am., Tulsa's Best Doctors, Tulsa People Mag. Mem. ACS, Tulsa Gynecol. Soc. (past pres. 1986-87), Soc. Reproductive Endocrinologists, Tulsa bonsai Soc. (bd. dirs. 1988—), Am. Coll. Ob-Gyn. (v.p. 1971-92, pres. New England Jr. divsn. 1972-73), Am. Bonsai Soc. (nat. bd. dirs.), Chanie des Rotisseurs (l'Ordre Mondial, Tulsa v.p., advisor to bd., Bronze Star 2001), Southside Rotary of Tulsa (bd. dirs., pres. 1997-98, Nat. Arboretum Bonsai Pavillion (nat. bd. dirs.), Rotary Club Tulsa (past pres. Southside club). Independent. Jewish. Avocations: gardening, cooking, bonsai, collector Oriental arts, woodturning.

SHANE, PETER MILO, law educator; b. Oceanside, NY, July 12, 1952; s. Albert and Ann (Semanoff) S.; m. Martha Elisabeth Chamallas, June 27, 1981; 1 child: Elisabeth Ann. AB, Harvard U., 1974; JD, Yale U., 1977. Bar: N.Y. 1978, U.S. Ct. Appeals (5th cir.) 1978, D.C. 1979, U.S. Ct. Appeals (8th cir.) 1983, U.S. Supreme Ct. 1984, Pa. 1995. Law clk. to judge U.S. Ct. Appeals (5th cir.), New Orleans, 1977-78; atty., advisor office of legal counsel U.S. Dept. Justice, Washington, 1978-81; asst. gen. counsel Office of Mgmt. and Budget, Washington, 1981; assoc. prof. law U. Iowa, Iowa City, 1981-85, prof., 1985-94; dean U. Pitts., 1994-98, prof., 1994—2001; Disting. Service prof. law & pub. policy, dir. Inst. for Study of Info. Tech. and Soc., Carnegie Mellon U., 2001—03, Disting. Service prof. law & pub. policy (adj.), 2003—, chair adv. bd., 2003—06; Joseph S. Platt-Porter, Wright, Morris and Arthur prof law, dir. Ctr. Interdisciplinary Law & Policy Studies, Ohio State U., 2003—07; Jacob E. Davis and Jacob E. Davis II chair in law Ohio State U., 2007—, dir. project law and democratic devel., 2007—; exec. dir. Knight Commn. on the Info. Needs of Cmtys. in a Democracy, 2008—09. Adj. lectr. Am. U., Washington, D.C., 1979-80; vis. prof. law Duke U., Durham, N.C., 1986, Boston Coll., Newton, Mass., 1999, Villanova (Pa.) U., 1999, Carnegie Mellon U., 2000-01; cons. U.S. Dept. Edn., Washington, D.C., 1980, MacArthur Justice Found., Chgo., 1987; active Adminstrv. Conf. U.S., 1991, pub. mem., 1995; cons. Nat. Commn. Jud. Discipline and Removal, 1992-93; cooperating atty. Iowa Civil Liberties Union, Des Moines, 1982-94, bd. dirs., 1987-89; active Coun. on Legal Edn. Opportunity, 1996-2004; reporter Civil Justice Adv. Group, U.S. Dist. Ct. (we. dist.) Pa. Author: (with H.H. Bruff) The Law of Presidential Power: Cases and Materials, 1988, (with H.H. Bruff) Separation of Powers Law, 1996, 2005, (with J. Mashaw and R. Merrill) Administrative Law: The American Public Law System, 2009, Democracy Online: The Prospects for Political Renewal Through the Internet, 2004, (with John Podesta and Richard C. Leone) A Little Knowledge: Security, Privacy and Public Information After September 11, 2004, Madison's Nightmare: How Executive Power Threatens American Democracy, 2009. Mem. Dem. cen. com. Johnson County, Iowa, 1982-88. Recipient citation for outstanding svc. Pa. House of Reps., 1998, Cleo Disting. Svc. award, 2004; named Young Leader of Higher Edn., Am. Assn. Higher Edn., 1998; Old Gold Summer fellow U. Iowa, 1981-84, Mellon Found. fellow, 1982. Mem. ABA (coun. sect. adminstrv. law and regulatory practice 1993-96, chmn. com. on govt. orgn. and separation of powers 1987-91), Assn. Am. Law Schs. (chair adminstrv. law 1990, chair remedies 1992, chair law sch. deans 1997), Am. Law Inst. Jewish. Office: Ohio State U Moritz Coll Law 55 W 12th Ave Columbus OH 43210 Office Phone: 614-688-3014. Business E-Mail: shane.29@osu.edu.

SHANE, PHILIP BARRY, accounting educator; b. Chgo., Feb. 6, 1949; s. Orville Saul and Lois Elayne (Herr) S.; m. Sharon Kay O'Neal, Aug. 31, 1978; children: Jacob, Adam, Bethan. BS, U. Ill., 1971; PhD, U. Oreg., 1982. Audit staff sr. Coopers and Lybrand, Chgo., 1972-74, supervising tax specialist, 1974-75; asst. prof. U. Kans., Lawrence, 1981-84; assoc. prof. U. Mont., Missoula, 1985-90; vis. assoc. prof. U. Ariz., Tucson, 1989-90; asst. prof. Pa. State U., University Park, 1990—. Vis. assoc. prof. U. Auckland, New Zealand, 1995-96. Contbr. articles to profl. jours. Dir., treas. Big Bear Resources, Missoula, 1985-88. Mem. AICPA, Am. Acctg. Assn., Am. Fin. Assn., Acctg. Assn. Australia and New Zealand, Canadian Academic Accounting Assn. Avocations: hiking, backpacking, cross country skiing, rafting. Office: Pa State U 203 Beam BAB University Park PA 16802

SHANE, WILLIAM WHITNEY, astronomer; b. Berkeley, Calif., June 3, 1928; s. Charles Donald and Mary Lea (Heger) S.; BA, U. Calif., Berkeley, 1951, postgrad., 1953-58; ScD, Leiden U., The Netherlands, 1971; m. Clasina van der Molen, Apr. 22, 1964; children: Johan Jacob, Charles Donald. rsch. assoc. Leiden U., 1961-71, sr. scientist, 1971-79; prof. astronomy, dir. Astron. Inst., Cath. U. Nijmegen, The Netherlands, 1979-88; guest prof. astronomy Leiden U., 1988-93; C.H. Adams fellow Monterey Inst. Rsch. Astronomy, Calif., 1994—. With USN, 1951-53. Fellow AAAS; mem. Internat. Astron. Union (commns. 33, 34), Am. Astron. Soc., Astron. Soc. Netherlands, Astron. Soc. of the Pacific, Phi Beta Kappa. Achievements include rsch. on structure and dynamics of galaxies, observational astronomy. Home: 9095 Coker Rd Prunedale CA 93907-1401 Office: Monterey Inst Rsch Astronomy 200 8th St Marina CA 93933-6002 Office Phone: 831-883-1000.

SHANER, DALE L., weed scientist; b. Kewanee, Ill., Jan. 11, 1948; s. Dale L. Shaner and Naomi W. Shaner-Vereecke; m. Diana J. Haltom; 1 child, Nathan C. BS, DePauw U., Greencastle, IN, 1970; MS, U. Colo., Boulder, 1970; PhD, U. Ill., Urbana, 1976. Asst. prof. U. Calif., Riverside, 1976—79; rsch. fellow Am. Cyanamid, Princeton, NJ, 1979—2000, BASF, Princeton, 2000—01; plant physiologist USDA-ARS, Fort Collins, Colo., 2001—. Pres. Weed Sci. Soc. Am., Lawrence, Kans., 2006—07. Author: (book) Herbicide Resistance and World

Grains. Fellow: Weed Sci. Soc. Am. (pres. 2006—07, Industry award 1993). Office: Udsa-Ars 2150 Ctr Ave Bldg D Ste 320 Fort Collins CO 80526 Office Fax: 970-492-7408. Business E-Mail: dale.shaner@ars.usda.gov.

SHANES, JEFFREY GLENN, cardiologist; b. Elkhart, Ind., Nov. 14, 1949; s. Harry and Doris Shanes; m. Mara Davis, Sept. 5, 1999; children: Ira Gary, Morris Mordecai, Fran Merzel, Yehuda Poupko, Chaim Poupko, Eli Sheva Schreiber, Chaya Segal. BS, Roosevelt U., Chgo., 1972; MD, Finch U. Health Scis./Chgo. Med. Sch., 1976. Diplomate Am. Bd. Internal Medicine, 1979, in cardiovasc. disease 1981. Chmn. cardiology dept. Gottlieb Hosp., Melrose Park, 1991—2001; instr. medicine Wash. U., St. Louis, 1979—81, U. Ill., Chgo., 1982—83, asst. prof. medicine, 1983—88, dir. cardiac catheterization lab, 1982—88, assoc. prof. medicine, 1988—2004, Rosalind Franklin U. Medicine and Sci., Chigo., 2004—; pres. Cons. in Cardiovasc. Medicine, Melrose Park, Ill., 1990—. Contbr. articles to profl. jours. Recipient Lange Med. Publs. award, 1976; Studies Left Ventricular Dysfunction grant, NIH, 1986. Mem.: ACP, Am. Heart Assn., Am. Coll. Cardiology. Avocations: photography, travel, scuba diving. Office: Consultants in Cardiovascular Medicine 675 W North Ave Melrose Park IL 60160 Office Fax: 708-344-0508.

SHANFIELD, STEPHEN B., psychiatrist, educator; b. Toronto, Ont., Can., Aug. 14, 1939; s. Joseph P. and Mildred Lenore (Neiman) S.; m. Carmen Lynn Kight, Aug. 15, 1971 (div. Mar. 1990); 1 child, Jason Gabriel; m. Alicia Debra Leff, Sept. 1, 2000. BA, UCLA, 1961; MD, U. So. Calif., 1965. Intern Montefiore Hosp. and Med. Ctr., NYC, 1965-66; resident in psychiatry Sch. of Medicine Yale U., New Haven, 1966-69; maj. USAF, 1969-79; staff physician Wilford Hall USAF Med. Ctr., San Antonio, 1969-71; from asst. prof. to prof. Coll. Medicine U. Ariz., Tucson, 1973-85; prof. Health Sci. Ctr. U. Tex., San Antonio, 1985—2006, prof. emeritus, 2006—. Contbr. articles to prof. jours. Fellow Am. Psychiat. Assn. (life), Am. Coll. Psychiatrists; mem. Group Advancement Psychiatry. Home: 122 Chester St # 2 San Antonio TX 78209-5679 Personal E-mail: stephen.shanfield@gmail.com.

SHANGRAW, ROBERT EDWARD, medical educator, researcher; b. Troy, NY, Mar. 16, 1954; s. Robert Dixon and M. Janice (Bonacker) S.; m. Patricia Mary Ford, May 25, 1985; children: Kirsten Celanire, Sarah Elizabeth, Kathleen Ford. BS, Rensselaer Poly. Inst., 1976; PhD, Albany Med. Coll., NY, 1981, MD, 1985. Resident in surgery U. Wash., Seattle, 1985-86; rsch. assoc. U. Tex. Med. Br., Galveston, 1986-87; resident in anesthesia Hosp. U. Pa., Phila., 1987-90; asst. prof. anesthesiology Oreg. Health and Sci. U., Portland, 1990—96, assoc. prof., 1996—2001, prof., 2001—. Cons. NIH Study Sects., 1998—. Contbr. articles on biomedicine to profl. jours. Fellow NIH, 1977-80, 82, 83. Mem. AMA, Am. Physiol. Soc., Am. Soc. Anesthesiologists, Internat. Anesthesia Rsch. Soc., Biochem. Soc., Assn. Univ. Anesthesiologists, Sigma Xi, Alpha Omega Alpha. Roman Catholic. Avocations: skiing, sailing, hiking, kayaking, swimming. Home: 5776 SW Calusa Loop Tualatin OR 97062-9757 Office: Oreg Health and Sci U Dept Anesthesiology and Periop Medicine 3181 SW Sam Jackson Park Rd Portland OR 97239-3098 Office Phone: 503-494-7641. Business E-Mail: shangraw@ohsu.edu.

SHANIES, STANLEY ALVIN, cardiologist; b. NYC, Oct. 21, 1938; s. William and Helen (Friedman) S.; m. Ellen Shanies, Sept. 8, 1968; 1 child, Julie Nicole. BA, Hofstra U., Hempstead, NY, 1961; MD, U. Bologna, Italy, 1967. Intern L.I. Jewish Med. Ctr., New Hyde Park, N.Y., 1968, resident, 1971, fellow cardiology, 1975, pvt. practice, 1975—. Asst. clin. prof. medicine Albert Einstein Coll. Medicine, N.Y.C., 1980-97; assoc. prof. biology Hofstra U., Hempstead, N.Y., 1997. Contbr. articles to profl. jours. Pres. Shelter Rock Jewish Ctr., Roslyn, N.Y., 1997; pres. Heart Coun. L.I., Hicksville, N.Y., 1990-91. Maj. U.S. Army, 1970-72. Named Outstanding Alumni Hofstra U., 1996. Fellow Am. Coll. Angiology; mem. Am. Heart Assn., Am. Coll. Cardiology. Avocation: photography. Office: Lake Success Medical Associates 1300 Union Tpke New Hyde Park NY 11040 Home: 5 Woods Lane Roslyn NY 11576 Fax: 516-328-8450. Personal E-mail: stanshan@optonline.net. Business E-Mail: lksuccessmedical@aol.com.

SHANK, FRED ROSS, food scientist; b. Harrisonburg, Va., Oct. 11, 1940; m. Peggy Anne Westbrook, June 1967; children: Virginia Anne, Fred Ross III. BS in Agriculture, U. Ky., 1962, MS in Nutrition, 1964; PhD, U. Md., 1969. Dep. dir. Office Nutrition and Food Sci. FDA, Washington, 1979-86, dir. Office Phys. Sci., 1986-87, dep. dir. Ctr. for Food SAfety and Applied Nutrition, 1987-89, dir., 1989-98, sr. advisor to FDA commr., 1998-99; sr. v.p. sci. Chocolate Mfrs. Assn., McLean, Va., 1999—2000; v.p. Sci. Inst. Food Tech., Washington, 2000. Fellow Inst. Food Technologists; mem. Am. Assn. Cereal Chemists, Am. Soc. for Nutrition. Home: 2621 Steeplechase Dr Reston VA 20191-2130 Home Phone: 703-620-3133; Office Phone: 202-466-5980. E-mail: fred_shank001@comcast.net.

SHANK, J. WILLIAM, art conservator; Studied art history and art conservation, Villa Schifanoia, Florence, Italy; grad. studies, NYU Inst. Fine Arts; advanced tng. in art conservation, Harvard U. With We. Ctr. for the Conservation of Fine Arts; mem. staff San Francisco Mus. Modern Art, 1985—2000, chief conservator, 1991—2000; now with Conservation Resources Mgmt. Founder Rescue Pub. Murals (in cooperation with Heritage Preservation). Curator (conservation based exhbn.) A Hidden Picasso, Guggenheim Mus., Bilbao, Spain, 2004. Booth Family Rome Prize Fellowship for Historic Preservation and Conservation, Am. Acad. in Rome, 2004—05. Address: P O Box 410266 San Francisco CA 94141-0266 also: Rambla de Catalunya 74 4° P150 Barcelona 8007 Spain Office Phone: 415-920-9966. Business E-Mail: willshank@earthlink.net.

SHANK, MAURICE EDWIN, aerospace engineer, consultant; b. NYC, Apr. 22, 1921; s. Edwin A. and Viola (Lewis) S.; m. Virginia Lee King, Sept. 25, 1948; children: Christopher K., Hilary L. Shank-Kuhl, Diana L. Shank. BS in Mech. Engring., Carnegie-Mellon U., 1942; D.Sc., MIT, 1949. Registered profl. engr., Mass. Assoc. prof. mech. engring. MIT, Cambridge, 1949-60; dir. advanced materials R&D Pratt & Whitney, East Hartford, Conn., 1960-70; mgr. materials engring. and rsch., 1971-72; dir. engring. tech., 1972-80; dir. engine design and structures engring. Pratt & Whitney, East Hartford, Conn., 1980-81, dir. engring. tech., 1981-85, dir. engring. tech. assessment, 1985-86; v.p. Pratt Whitney of China, Inc., East Hartford, 1986-87; pvt. exec. cons. to industry and govt., 1987—. Cons. editor McGraw-Hill Book Co., N.Y.C., 1960-80; adv. com. to mechanics div. Nat. Bur. Standards, Washington, 1964-69; vis. com. dept. mech. engring. Carnegie-Mellon U., Pitts., 1968-78; corp. vis. coms. depts. materials sci. and engring., dept. aeros. and astronautics MIT, 1968-74, 79-92; mem. rsch. and tech. adv. coun. com. on aero. propulsion NASA, Washington, 1973-77, mem. aero. adv. com., 1978-86; mem. aero. and space engring. bd. NRC, 1989-92; lectr. in field. Contbr. articles to profl. jours. Served to maj. U.S. Army Corps. of Engrs., Ordnance Corps, 1942-46, Middle East/North Africa. Fellow AIAA, ASME, AIME, Am. Soc. Metals; mem. Nat. Acad. Engring., Conn. Acad. Sci. and Engring. Clubs: Cosmos. Episcopalian. Avocations: boating, fishing.

SHANK, RUSSELL, librarian, educator; b. Spokane, Wash., Sept. 2, 1925; s. Harry and Sadie S.; m. Doris Louise Hempfer, Nov. 9, 1951 (div.); children: Susan Marie, Peter Michael, Judith Louise. BS, U. Wash., 1946, BA, 1949; MBA, U. Wis., 1952; DrLS, Columbia U., 1966. Reference libr. U. Wash., Seattle, 1949; asst. engring. libr. U. Wis.-Madison, 1949-52; chief pers. Milw. Pub. Libr., 1952; engring.-phys. scis. libr. Columbia U., NYC, 1953-59, sr. lectr., 1964-66, assoc. prof., 1966-67; asst. univ. libr. U. Calif.-Berkeley, 1959-64; dir. sci. libr. N.Y. Met. Reference and Rsch., 1966-68; dir. librs. Smithsonian Instn., Washington, 1967-77; univ. libr. prof. UCLA, 1977-89, asst. vice chancellor for libr. and info. svcs. planning, 1989-91, univ. libr., prof. emeritus, 1991—. Cons. Indonesian Inst. Sci., 1970; bd. cons. Pahlavi Nat. Library, Iran, 1975-76; pres. U.S. Book Exchange, 1975; bd. trustees Freedom to Read Found., 1989—. Trustee OCLC, Inc., 1978-84, 87, chmn., 1984; mem. library del. People's Republic of China, 1979; bd. dirs. Am. Council on Edn., 1980-81. Served with USNR, 1943-46. Recipient Disting. Alumnus award U. Wash. Sch. Librarianship, 1968, Role of Honor award Freedom to Read Found., 1990, Disting. Alumnus award Columbia U. Sch. Libr. Sci., 1992; fellow Coun. on Libr. Resources, 1973-74. Fellow AAAS; mem. ALA (pres. 1978-79, coun. 1961-65, 74-82, exec. bd. 1975-80, chmn. internat. rels. com. 1980-83, pres. info. sci. and automation div. 1968-69), Assn. Coll. and Rsch. Librs. (pres. 1972-73, Hugh Atkinson award 1990), Assn. Rsch. Librs. (bd. dirs. 1974-77), Beta Phi Mu. Home: 12919 Montana Ave Apt 101 Los Angeles CA 90049-4843 Business E-Mail: rshank@ucla.edu. *Intellectual freedom is the paramount human right. It is the American's premier heritage. Without it the claim to democracy is a sham. Should the principles of our society fade or perish, the survival of this freedom alone would justify the nation's experience. The freedom to think, to read, and to speak will be our enduring monument. Their diffusion throughout the world must be our unending crusade.*

SHANKAR, RAVI, composer, musician; b. Apr. 7, 1920; m. Sukanya Rajan; children: Shubho, Geetali, Anoushka. Studied under, Ustad Allauddin Khan of Maihar; trained in Guru-Shishya tradition, pupil of Ustad Allauddin Khan, 1938. Solo sitar player; former dir. music All India Radio; founder Nat. Orch.; founder, dir. Kinnara Sch. Music, Bombay, 1962, LA, 1967. Vis. lectr. U. Calif., 1965; fellow Sangeet Natak Akademi, 1976; responsible for music and choreography for ASIAD, 1982. Musician: numerous albums in India, UK & US, including 3 Ragas, 1956, India's Master Musician, 1963, Ragas & Talas, 1964, Sound of the Sitar, 1965, Menuhin Meets Shankar, 1966, West Meets East, 1967, The Sounds of India, 1968, Concerto for Sitar & Orchestra, 1971, Transmigration Macabre, 1973, Shankar Family & Friends, 1974, Pandit Ravi Shankar, 1986, Tana Mana, 1987, Inside the Kremlin, 1988, The Genius of Ravi Shankar, 1990, Farewell, My Friend, 1992, Concert for Peace: Royal Albert Hall, 1995, Sublime Sounds of Sitar,k 1996, Mantram, 1997, 4 Ragas, 2000, Full Circle: Carnegie Hall, 2001, East Meets West 2, 2002, The Best of Ravi Shankar, 2003, Ahir Lalit, 2004, Sitar Concertos & Other Works, 2005; concert tours in Europe, US, The East; composer: (film scores) Pather Panchali, 1946, The Flute and the Arrow, 1957, The Sword and the Flute, 1959, Godaan, 1963, The Psychedelics, 1966, Charly, 1968, Meera, 1979, Ghandi, 1982, Genesis, 1986, Yehudi Menuhim: The Violin of the Century, 1996, Tenussian Vacuvasco, 2000, Ravi Shankar: Between 2 Worlds, 2001; actor (films) Chappaqua, 1966, Unterwegs nach Katchmandu, 1971, Hit for Six, 2007; composer numerous ragas and talas; author: My Music, My Life, 1969, Rag Anurag (Bengali), (autobiography) Raga Mala, 1997. Recipient Deshikottam award, 1982; Silver Bear of Berlin; award of Indian Nat. Acad. Music, Dance and Drama, 1962; award of Padma Bhushan, 1967, Padma Vibushan, 1981, Internat. Music Coun. UNESCO award, 1975; elected to the Rajya Sabha, India, 1986; recipient 16 hon. doctorates around the world; recipient Grand prize Fukuoka Asian Cultural Prizes, Japan, 1991, Ramon Magsaysay award, The Philippines, 1992, Bharatiya Vidya Bhavan Mahatma Gandhi award, 1992, U.K. Ho. of Commons Shield, 1995, Crystal award, Switzerland, 1995, Premium Imperial Arts award, Japan, 1997, Light of Asia award, U.S., 1997, Juliet Hollister award, U.S., 1998, The Polar Music prize, Sweden, 1998, Bharat Ratna, India, 1999, Hon. KBE, 2000; named Commdr. of Legion of Honour, France, 2000. Address: Sulivan Sweetland 1a Hillgate Pl Balham Hill London SW12 9ER England

SHANKARAN, NISHANTH, application developer; s. Shankaran Nagaswami and Maithili Shankaran. BS, U. Madras, 2002; MS, U. Calif., Irvine, 2004; PhD, Vanderbilt U., Nashville, Tenn., 2008. Software devel. engr. Amazon.com, Seattle, 2008—, intern, 2008. Intern BBN Technologies, Cambridge, Mass., 2005, IBM Rsch., New Delhi, 2007. Contbr. articles to profl. jours. (IEEE Transactions award). Office: Amazon Dot Com 605 5th Ave S Ste 100 Seattle WA 98104

SHANKEL, DELBERT MERRILL, microbiologist, biologist, educator; b. Plainview, Nebr., Aug. 4, 1927; s. Cecil Wilfred and Gladys Dalton (Dodd) Shankel; m. Carol Jo Mulford, Sept. 10, 1962; children: Merrill, Jill, Kelley. BA, Walla Walla Coll., 1950; PhD, U. Tex., 1959. Tchr. Walla Walla Coll. Acad., College Place, Wash., 1950-51; instr. San Antonio Coll., 1954-55; asst. prof., assoc. prof. microbiology and biology U. Kans., Lawrence, 1959-68, prof., 1968—, asst. dean, assoc. dean arts and sci., 1966-72, acting dean, 1973, exec. vice chancellor, 1974-80, 86, 90-92, acting chancellor, 1980-81, chancellor, 1994-95, chancellor emeritus, 1996. Commr. N. Ctrl. Assn. Colls. and Schs., Chgo., 1991—95, cons., evaluator, 1969—96, NW Comm. Coll., 1997—. Editor: Artimutagenesis and Anticarcinogenesis: Mechanisms vols. I-III, 1986, 1988, 1993; assoc. editor: Mutation Rsch., 1992—95. Active numerous civic orgns. With US Army, 1952—54. Recipient Outstanding Educator award, Mortar Bd., U. Kans., 1982, 1985, 1990; named Disting. Alumnus of the Yr., Walla Walla Coll., 1989; numerous rsch. grantee. Fellow: Am. Acad. Microbiology; mem.: Radiation Rsch. Soc., Soc. Gen. Microbiology (Eng.), Genetics Soc. Am., Environ. Mutagen Soc. (chmn. pub. policy com. 1991—93, mem. nat. coun. 1994—97), Am. Soc. Microbiology (past chmn. edn. com., chmn. numerous coms.), U. Kans. Alumni Assn. (interim pres., CEO 2004), Sigma Xi (pres. U. Kans. chpt. 1967). Republican. Unitarian Universalist. Avocations: sports, music, theater, reading. Office: U Kans 1002 Haworth Hl Lawrence KS 66045-0001 Office Phone: 785-864-3150. Business E-Mail: shankel@ku.edu.

SHANKEL, LYNNE, conductor, composer; Grad., U. Mich. Bd. evaluators Nat. Music Theater Network, Inc., NYC. Assoc. condr. (Broadway plays) You're a Good Man, Charlie Brown, 1999, music supr. Company, 2006—07, composer, arranger, musical dir., condr. Cry-Baby, 2008, musical dir. (off-Broadway shows) Summer of '42, 2001, 2005, The Thing About Men, 2003, Altar Boyz, 2005, (regional shows) Tom Jones, 2005. Office: Nat Music Theater Network 11th Fl 242 W 38th St New York NY 10018 Office Phone: 212-664-0979.

SHANKLIN, CAROL W., dietician, educator; BS in Home Econs. Edn., U. Tenn., Martin, 1973; MS in Food Sys. Adminstrn., U. Tenn., Knoxville, 1974, PhD in Food Sys. Adminstrn., 1976. Asst. prof. foods and nutrition Tex. Tech. U., 1977—78; asst. food svc. dir. Highland Hosp., Lubbock, Tex., 1978; asst. prof. food sys. mgmt. Tex. Women's U., 1978—82, assoc. prof. food sys. mgmt., 1982—88, assoc. prof., chair dept. nutrition and food scis., 1985—87, prof., chair dept. nutrition and food scis., 1987—90; tech. advisor, cons. Miss. Inst. Higher Learning, 1988—89; grad. program dir., prof. dept. hotel, restaurant, instn. mgmt. and dietetics Kans. State U., Manhattan, 1990—2001, asst. dean. Grad. Sch., prof. dept. hotel, restaurant, instn. mgmt. and dietetics, 2001—04, assoc. dean. Grad. Sch., prof. dept. hotel, restaurant, instn. mgmt. and dietetics, 2004—07, prof. Grad. Sch., prof. dept. hotel, restaurant, instn. mgmt. and dietetics, 2007—09, interim dean, Grad. Sch., prof. dept. hotel, restaurant, instn. mgmt. and dietetics, 2008—, dean grad. sch., prof. dept. hospitality mgmt. & dietetics, 2009—. Contbr. articles to profl. jours. Recipient Michael Olsen Rsch. Achievement award, U. Del. Mem.: Am. Dietetic Assn. (Medallion award 2001). Achievements include research on environmental issues in the food service and hospitality industry; dietetics and hospitality education; quality service in food service operations; research in food service management, food safety and security in food service operations. Office: Kansas State U Graduate Sch 103 Fairchild Manhattan KS 66502-1404 Office Phone: 785-532-7927. Business E-Mail: shanklin@k-state.edu.

SHANKLIN, DOUGLAS RADFORD, physician; b. Camden, NJ, Nov. 25, 1930; s. John Ferguson and Muriel (Morgan) S.; m. Virginia McClure, Apr. 7, 1956; children: Elizabeth, Leigh, Lois Virginia, John Carter, Eleanor. Student, Wilson Tchrs. Coll., 1949; AB in Chemistry, Syracuse U., 1952; MD, SUNY, Syracuse, 1955. Intern in pathology Duke U., 1955-56, resident, 1958; resident in pathology SUNY, Syracuse, 1958-60; practice medicine specializing in pathology Gainesville, Fla., 1960-67, 78-83; mem. faculty U. Fla., 1960-67; prof. pathology, ob-gyn. U. Chgo., 1967-78; prof. dept. pathology U. Tenn., Memphis, 1983—, prof. obstetrics, 1986—, vice chmn. dept. pathology, 1983-90. Vis. prof. U. Okla., 1967, Duke U., Mich. State U., 1969, Leeds U., Dundee U., Karolinska, 1974, Leeds U., 1978, 85, Emory U., 1980, London U., Edinburgh U., 1981, 85, U. Brit. Coll., 1987; jr. investigator Marine Biol. Lab., Woods Hole, Mass., 1951-54, sr. investigator, 1966—, mem. corp., 1970—; parliamentarian, 1990-94; mem. Marine Resources Adv. Com., 1988-90, mem. election com., 1994-96; chmn. nat. adv. com. W-I-C evaluation U.S. Dept. Agr., 1979-86; lectr. Coll. Law U. Fla., 1963-67, 77-83; cons. Pan Am. Health Orgn., 1973-89; sr. cons. Santa Fe Found., 1976-79, exec. dir., 1979-83; course dir. Ctr. Continuing Edn., U. Chgo., 1980-82. Author: Syllabus for Study of Gynecologic-Obstetric-Pediatric Disease, 1961, Diseases of Woman, Pregnancy, Child, 1964, Maternal Nutrition and Child Health, 1979, 2nd edit., 2000, Tumors of Placenta and Umbilical Cord, 1990; editor Interscience Devel. Disorders, 1971-80; assoc. editor Jour. Reproductive Medicine, 1968-70, 79-85, editor in chief, 1970-75; mem. editl. bd. Exptl. Molecular Pathology, 1999—; contbr. articles to profl. jours. Trustee Coll. Light Opera Co., Falmouth, Mass., 1970—, Hippodrome Theatre, Gainesville, 1975-83, Opera Memphis, 1989-92. With M.C., USNR, 1956-58. Recipient Best Basic Sci. Tchg. award U. Fla., 1967, Excellence in Tchg. award, Grad. Coll. Med. Scis., U. Tenn., 2002; named freeman citizen of Glasgow, 1981. Fellow: Royal Soc. Medicine (london); mem.: AAAS, Coll. Physicians and Surgeons Costa Rica, Internat. Physicians for Prevention Nuc. War, Physicians Social Responsibility, Am. Coll. Ob-gyn., N.Y. Acad. Scis., So. Med. Assn., So. Soc. Pediat. Rsch., Math. Assn. Am., Internat. Acad. Pathologists, Soc. Pediat. Rsch., Am. Coll. Rheumatology (spl. study com. 1995—96), Hosp. Assn., Am. Chem. Soc., Am. Soc. Molecular Marine Biology and Biotech., Am. Soc. Exptl. Pathology, Cosmos Club, Pediat. Pathology Club (sec.-treas. 1970—75, pres. 1981—82), Navy League, Sigma xi, Phi Beta Kappa. Home: PO Box 1267 Gainesville FL 32602-1267 also: PO Box 511 Woods Hole MA 02543-0511 Fax: (901) 683-7461. E-mail: radfordcrawford@juno.com.

SHANKLIN, ELIZABETH E., secondary school educator; b. Nashville, July 23, 1934; d. J. Gordon and Emily (Shacklett) S. BS, Columbia U., 1956; MA, Sarah Lawrence Coll., 1990. Tchr. N.Y.C. Bd. of Edn., 1968—. Author: The Answer is Matriarchy, 1978, Toward Matriarchy: The Radical Struggle of Women in the United States to Reconstruct Motherhood 1785-1925, 1990, Authorizing Mothers, 1824-1833, 2004. Mem. AAUW, AFT, Am. Hist. Assn., Orgn. Am. Historians, The Feminists. Green Party. Home: 2600 Netherland Ave Bronx NY 10463-4801

SHANKLIN, KENNETH DALE, plastic surgeon; b. Toluca, Ill., Dec. 21, 1931; s. Walter Arthur and Elsie Ida Josephine (Holz) S.; m. Doris Gay Minton, July 24, 1955 (div. Jan. 21, 1971); 1 child, Steven Dale; m. Colleen Jean Wheeler, July 30, 1978. BS, U. Ill., 1954; MD, U. Utah, 1967. Diplomate Am. Bd. Med. Specialists in gen. surgery, plastic surgery; lic. Calif. Commd. 2d lt. USAF, 1954, advanced through grades to lt. col., ret., 1977; intern Wilford Hall USAF Med. Ctr., San Antonio, 1967-68, resident in plastic surgery, 1972-74, resident in gen. surgery Travis AFB, Calif., 1968-72; assoc. clin. prof. plastic surgery U. Tex., San Antonio, 1974-77; asst. clin prof. plastic surgery U. Calif., Davis, 1977-84, assoc. clin. prof. plastic surgery San Francisco, 1984—2004; pvt. practice plastic surgery Fresno, Calif., 1977-93; acting chief med. officer Mil. Entrance Processing Sta., Sacramento, 1994—2001. Bd, dirs., pres. Valley Children's Hosp. Med. Staff, Fresno; bd. dirs. Liga Flying Physicians, Fresno, 1995-98. Prodr., dir. films sci. meetings (Outstanding award 1976). Mem. Am. Soc. Plastic Surgeons, Internat. Congress Plastic and Reconstructive Surgeons (bd. dirs. 1983-91), Am. Med. Soc. Vienna, Mil. Order of the World Wars (dept. N. Calif. comdr. 1996-97, region 14 comdr. 1998-99, nat. surgeon gen. 2004—, Disting. Chpt. Comdr. 1997, Silver Patrick Henry Patriotism award, 1997), Am. Legion (dist. vice comdr. 1998-99, dist. comdr. 1999-2000, vice comdr. Calif. 2001-02), Rotarian, Comml. Pilot Single Multi Engine Airplane Rotorcraft Helicopter, Instrument Airplane (Lic.) Avocations: teaching, flying. Home and Office: Mil Order World Wars 5100 John D Ryan Blvd 2211 San Antonio TX 78245-3513

SHANKMAN, STEWART A., psychologist, educator; m. Alexandra Levit, Mar. 1, 2004; 1 child, Jonah. PhD, Stony Brook U., NY, 2005. Lic. clin. psychologist Ill., 2007. Asst. prof. U. Ill., Chgo., 2005—. Contbr. articles to profl. jours. Recipient Young Investigator award, NARSAD, 2008—. Mem.: Soc. Rsch. Psychopathology (assoc.). Liberal. Jewish. Office: Univ Ill Chgo 1007 W Harrison St Rm 1062D Chicago IL 60607

SHANKS, HERSHEL, editor, writer; b. Sharon, Pa., Mar. 8, 1930; s. Martin and Mildred (Freedman) S.; m. Judith Alexander Weil, Feb. 20, 1966; children: Elizabeth Jean, Julia Emily. BA, Haverford Coll., Pa., 1952; MA, Columbia, 1953; LLB, Harvard, 1956. Bar: D.C. 1956. Trial atty. Dept. Justice, 1956-59; pvt. practice Washington, 1959-88; ptnr. Glassie, Pewett, Beebe & Shanks, 1964-88; editor Bibl. Archaeology Rev., Washington, 1975—. Pres. Bibl. Archaeology Soc., 1974—2004, Jewish Ednl. Ventures Inc., 1987—. Author: The Art and Craft of Judging, 1968, The City of David, 1973, Judaism in Stone, 1979, Jerusalem--An Archaeological Biography, 1995, The Mystery and

Meaning of the Dead Sea Scolls, 1998, Jerusalem's Temple Mount, From Solomon to the Golden Dome, 2008, The Copper Scroll and the Search for the Temple Treasure, 2008, also articles; co-author: (with Ben Witherington III) The Brother of Jesus, 2003; co-editor: Recent Archaeology in the Land of Israel, 1984; editor: Ancient Israel, A Short History, 1988, revised edit., 1999, Christianity and Rabbinic Judaism, 1992, Understanding the Dead Sea Scrolls, 1992; editor Bible Rev., 1985—2004, Moment mag., 1987—2004, Archaeology Odyssey, 1998—2004; contbr. articles to profl. jours. Fellow Royal Asiatic Soc.; mem. ABA, D.C. Bar Assn., Am. Schs. Oriental Rsch., Soc. Bibl. Lit., Cosmos Club, Phi Beta Kappa. Home: 5208 38th St NW Washington DC 20015-1812 Office: Bibl Archaeology Soc 4710 41st St NW Washington DC 20016-1706 Office Phone: 202-966-9888. E-mail: hshanks@bib-arch.org. *I try to take time to identify what is important in my life, to focus on that and ignore the rest when it conflicts. It takes conscious effort not to dissipate energy on activities and attitudes that don't matter in the big picture of my priorities. Free to concentrate on what I value most, I try to accomplish something each day in a regular, habitual way.*

SHANKS, ROBERT L., automotive executive; B in Fgn. Svc., Georgetown U., 1975; M, Am. Grad. Sch. Internat. Mgmt., 1979. Joined Ford Motor Co., 1977, various fin. positions including head bus. devel. activities Asia-Pacific ops., head fin. function Ford Lio Ho Taiwan, CFO Mazda Motor Corp., CFO Premier Automotive Grp. (PAG), 2002—04, v.p. ops. support, fin. & strategy Ford of Europe & PAG, 2004, v.p. & controller, the Americas, 2005—. Office: Ford Motor Co N Am Hdqs 1 American Rd Dearborn MI 48126*

SHAN KUO-HSI, PAUL CARDINAL, cardinal, bishop emeritus; b. Puyang, China, Dec. 3, 1923; Degree, St. Joseph Regional Sem., Chiughsien, China, Berchmans Coll., Manila, Philippines, Bellarmine Coll., Baguio, Philippines; PhD in Theology, Pontifical Gregorian U., Rome. Professed Soc. Jesus, 1946, ordained priest, 1955; asst. master of novices Jesuit Noviaiate, Thuduc, Vietnam, 1961—63; master of novices, rector Manresa House, Changhua, Taiwan, 1963—70; rector St. Ignatius Inst., Taipei, Taiwan, 1970—76; pres. Kuangchi Programe Service, 1976—79; episcopal vicar Archdiocese of Taipei, 1976—79; ordained bishop, 1980; bishop Diocese of Hualien, Taiwan, 1980—91, Diocese of Kaohsiung, Taiwan, 1991—2006, bishop emeritus, 2006—; elevated to cardinal, 1998; cardinal-priest S. Crisogono, 1998—. Roman Catholic. Office: 125 Szu-wei 3rd rd 80203 Kaohsiung Taiwan Office Phone: (07)331.01.69. Office Fax: (07) 33.34.583.

SHANLEY, JOHN PATRICK, playwright, screenwriter; b. NYC, 1950; s. Nicholas and Frances Shanley; m. Jayne Haynes (div.); adopted children: Nick, Frank. Grad., NYU. Disting. artist-in-residence The New Sch. for Drama, NYC, 2006—. Writer (plays) Rockaway, 1982, Welcome to the Moon, 1982, Danny and the Deep Blue Sea, 1984, Savage in Limbo, 1985, the dreamer examines his pillow, 1985, Women of Manhattan, 1986, All for Charity, 1987, Italian-American Reconciliation, 1988, The Big Funk, 1990, Beggars in the House of Plenty, 1991, Four Dogs and a Bone, 1993, Psychopathia Sexualis, 1996, Missing/Kissing, 1997, Cellini, 1998, Where's My Money, 2001, Dirty Story, 2003, Doubt, 2004 (Pulitzer Prize for drama, 2005, Tony Award for best play, 2005), Sailor's Song, 2004, Defiance, 2006, Down and Out, The Red Coat, Let Us Go Out Into the Starry Night, Out West, A Lonely Impulse of Delight, (screen adaptations) Alive, 1993, Congo, 1995, (teleplay) Live From Baghdad, 2002, (screenplays) Moonstruck, 1987 (Acad. Award for best writing- screenplay written directly for the screen, 1988), January Man, 1989, We're Back! A Dinosaur's Story, 1993, writer, assoc. prodr. Five Corners, 1987, writer, dir. Joe Versus the Volcano, 1990, Chain of Command, 2005, Doubt, 2008, Appeared in film Crossing Delancey, 1988. Served USMC. Recipient Ian McLellan Hunter Lifetime Achievement award, Writers Guild America, 2009. Fellow: Am. Acad. Arts & Scis. Office: c/o William Morris Agy 151 S El Camino Dr Beverly Hills CA 90212-2704*

SHANLEY, THOMAS PATRICK, medical educator; b. Berea, Ohio, Jan. 22, 1963; s. Thomas Joseph and Patricia Irene Shanley; m. Maureen Garrity, Sept. 19, 1987; children: Lauren Elizabeth, Molly Rose, Ashleigh Noel, Matthew Thomas. MD, U. Chgo., 1989. Cert. FCCM Am. Coll. Critical Care Medicine, 2004. Asst. and assoc. prof. Cin. Children's Hosp. Med. Ctr., 1997—2004; Ferrantino prof. U. Mich., Ann Arbor, 2004—. Co-editor: (book) Pediatric Critical Care Medicine: Basic Science and Clinical Evidence (Best Drs. in Am., 2007). KO8 and RO1 grant, NIH, 2000—08. Fellow: Soc. Pediat. Rsch. (sec. & treas. 2008—). Office: Univ Mich 1500 E Med Ctr Dr Ann Arbor MI 48109 Office Fax: 734-647-5624. Business E-Mail: tshanley@med.umich.edu.

SHANMAN, JAMES ALAN, lawyer; b. Cin., Aug. 1, 1942; s. Jerome D. and Mildred Louise (Bloch) S.; m. Marilyn Louise Glassman, June 11, 1972; 1 child, Ellen Joan. BS, U. Pa., 1963; JD, Yale U., 1966. Bar: NY 1967, Conn. 2004, US Ct. Appeals for the Armed Forces, 1971, US Supreme Ct. 1971, US Ct. Appeals (2d cir.) 1972, US Dist. Ct. (so. and ea. dists.) NY 1972, US Ct. Internat. Trade 1976, US Ct. Appeals (fed. cir.) 1987, US Dist. Ct. (ea. dist.) Mich. 1989, US Ct. Appeals (7th cir.) 1999, US Dist. Ct. Conn. 2006. Assoc. Cahill Gordon & Reindel, NYC, 1971-74, Freeman, Meade, Wasserman, Sharfman & Schneider, NYC, 1974-76; mem. firm Sharfman, Shanman, Poret & Siviglia, P.C., NYC, 1976-95; ptnr. Camhy Karlinsky & Stein LLP, NYC, 1995-96; mem. firm Sharfman, Siviglia, Poret, Kook, Ross & Shanman, P.C., NYC, 1996-98; ptnr. Edwards, Angell, Palmer & Dodge LLP (formerly Edwards & Angell LLP), NYC and Stamford, 1998—. Speaker on reins. law topics. Contbr. articles to profl. jours. Capt. USAF, 1966-71. Mem.: ARIAS.US (cert. arbitrator), Assn. of Bar of City of N.Y. (com. ins. law 1985—88, com. profl. liability ins. 1988—92, com. on assn. ins. plans 1989—, com. ins. law 1990—92, 1998—2001), N.Y. State Bar Assn. Office: Edwards Angell Palmer & Dodge LLP Three Stamford Plz 301 Tresser Blvd Stamford CT 06901 Office Phone: 203-975-7505. Business E-Mail: jshanman@eapdlaw.com.

SHANMUGAM, VICTORIA KATE, medical educator; m. Kannon K. Shanmugam, 2003; children: Thomas, William. BA, U. Oxford, Eng., 1996; MBBS, Imperial Coll. Sch. Medicine, London, 1999. Asst. prof. medicine Georgetown U. Hosp., Washington, 2007—. Recipient Physician Scientist Devel. award, Am. Coll. Rheumatology, 2007—; Disting. fellow, 2007. Mem.: RCP (London). Office: Georgetown Univ Hosp 3800 Reservoir Rd NW Washington DC 20007 Office Fax: 202-444-6217. Business E-Mail: vks4@gunet.georgetown.edu.

SHANNON, CAREEN BRETT, lawyer, educator, writer; b. Oakland, Calif., Dec. 11, 1958; d. Larry Richard and Janet Loretta Shannon; life ptnr. William Considine; 1 child, Rachel Vineberg Shannon-Solomon. BA, Oberlin Coll., 1981; JD, CUNY, 1989. Bar: N.J. 1989, U.S. Dist. Ct. N.J. 1989, N.Y. 1990, U.S. Dist. Ct. (so. dist.) N.Y. 1990. Motions law clk. U.S. Ct. Appeals (2nd cir.), NYC, 1989—90, pro se law clk., 1990—91; staff atty. The Legal Aid Soc., NYC, 1991—92; assoc. Satterlee, Stephens, Burke & Burke, NYC, 1992—94, Whitman, Breed, Abbott & Morgan, NYC, 1994—95, Reid & Priest, NYC, 1995—96; legal editor Matthew Bender & Co., NYC, 1996—98; of counsel Fragomen, Del Rey, Bernsen & Loewy, LLP, NYC, 1998—. Adj. prof. law Benjamin N. Cardozo Sch. Law, NYC, 2004—; spkr. in field. Author (and co-author): handbooks; contbr. chapters to books, articles to profl. jours. Pro bono atty. N.Y. Lawyers for the Pub. Interest, NYC, 2002—04, NYC Bar Justice Ctr., 2009—. Recipient Oberlin Study Abroad Program in France, Oberlin Coll., 1980; scholar Yr. Abroad Program in Denmark, Am. Field Svc., 1976—77; Grad. fellow in Japan, Oberlin Shansi Meml. Assn., 1981—83, Grad. fellow at Oberlin Coll., 1984, Robert Masur fellow in Civil Liberties, The Nation Inst., 1988—99. Mem.: ABA (mem. steering com. internat. law sect. ann. conf. 2002—03), Am. Immigration Lawyers Assn. Avocations: fly fishing, rock climbing, skydiving, weightlifting, skiing. Office: Fragomen Del Rey Bernsen & Loewy LLP 7 Hanover Sq New York NY 10004 Business E-Mail: cshannon@fragomen.com.

SHANNON, DANIELLE, coach; d. Rick and Katie Bifulco; m. Michael Shannon, July 7, 2007. BS in Athletic Tng. & Exercise Sci., Ithaca Coll., NY, 2002; MS in Athletic Tng., W.Va. U., Morgantown, 2004. Cert. athletic trainer Nat. Athletic Trainer's Assn. Bd. Certification, 2002. Grad. asst. W.Va. U., 2002—04; asst. athletic trainer St. John Fisher Coll., Rochester, NY, 2004—. Mem.: Nat. Athletic Trainer's Assn. Office: St John Fisher Coll 3690 E Ave Rochester NY 14618 Business E-Mail: dbifulco@sjfc.edu.

SHANNON, DONALD HAWKINS, retired editor; b. Auburn, Wash., Feb. 1, 1923; s. Ernest Victor and Fern (McConville) S.; m. Sally van Deurs, June 13, 1952; children— John McConville, Susanna Shepard. BA, Stanford, 1944; postgrad., Law Sch., 1946-47. Reporter Brazil Herald, Rio de Janeiro, 1947-48; Reporter UPI, London, 1949-51, Western Reporters, Washington, 1951-53; mem. staff L.A. Times, 1954-92, bur. chief Paris Paris, 1962-65, bur. chief Africa, 1965-66, bur. chief Tokyo Tokyo, 1966-71; bur. chief UN, NYC, 1971—75, Washington, 1975—92; sr. editor Georgetown and Country, Washington, 1996-99; ret., 1999. Served with AUS, 1944-46, PTO. Mem. Nat. Press Club, City Tavern Club, Overseas Press Club (NYC), Phi Gamma Delta. Address: 1068 30th St NW Washington DC 20007-3822

SHANNON, GEORGE RAYMOND, gerontologist, educator; b. Chgo., Dec. 30, 1939; m. Ellen Levine, Dec. 31, 1978; m. Elizabeth Mary Elkin, Oct. 31, 1959 (div. Aug. 25, 1965); children: Mary Ellen Shannon-Amenda, Elizabeth Mary Shannon-Reedy, Margaret Mary, Catherine Mary. BA, Antioch U., LA, 1997; M in Gerontology, U. So. Calif., 1999, PhD in Gerontology, 2004. Post-doctoral fellow VA Ctr. Excellence, Sepulveda, Calif., 2004—06; rsch. assoc. Ptnrs. in Care Found., San Fernando, Calif., 2006—. Lectr. in field. Contbr. articles to profl. jours. Recipient Poster of Yr. award, Am. Acad. Home Care Physicians, 2006; Mary Pickford scholarship, Davis Sch. Gerontology U. So. Calif., 1997—99. Mem.: AFTRA, SAG, Am. Geriat. Soc. (Presdl. Poster of Yr. award 2006), Am. Soc. Aging, Gerontol. Soc. Am., Actors Equity Assn., Sigma Phi Omega, Phi Kappa Phi. Liberal. Avocations: reading, exercise, travel, acting. Office: Ptnrs in Care Found 732 Mott St Ste150 San Fernando CA 91340 Office Fax: 562-622-3892; Home Fax: 323-850-8809. Personal E-mail: gshannon@usc.edu, georgershannon@aol.com.

SHANNON, HOLDEN E., air transportation executive; Grad., Rice U., Houston, 1985. V.p. corp. real estate and environ. affairs Continental Airlines, Inc., Houston, 1995—2004, sr. v.p. global real estate & security, 2004—. Office: Continental Airlines Inc PO Box 4607 Houston TX 77210 Office Phone: 713-324-5000. Office Fax: 713-324-2637.

SHANNON, JOHN SANFORD, lawyer, retired rail transportation executive; b. Tampa, Fla., Feb. 8, 1931; s. George Thomas and Ruth Evangeline (Garrett) S.; m. Elizabeth Howe, Sept. 22, 1962; children: Scott Howe, Elizabeth Garrett, Sandra Denison. AB, Roanoke Coll., 1952; JD, U. Va., 1955. Bar: Va. 1955. Assoc. Hunton Williams Gay Powell & Gibson, Richmond, Va., 1955-56; solicitor Norfolk & Western Ry., Roanoke, Va., 1956-60, asst. gen. solicitor, 1960-64, gen. atty., 1964-65, gen. solicitor, 1965-68, gen. counsel, 1968-69, v.p. law, 1969-80, sr. v.p. law, 1980-82; exec. v.p. law Norfolk (Va.) So. Corp., 1982-96, ret., 1996. Bd. dirs. Norfolk So. Ry. Co., Pocahontas Land Corp., Va. Holding Corp., Norfolk and Western Ry. Co. Editor-in-chief: Va. Law Rev, 1954-55. Chancellor Episcopal Diocese Southwestern Va., 1974-82; pres. bd. trustees North Cross Sch., Roanoke, 1973-82; trustee, past chmn. exec. com. Roanoke Coll., Salem, Va., 1974-2005; bd. dirs. Legal Aid Soc., Roanoke Valley, 1969-80, pres., 1970-79; trustee Chrysler Mus., Norfolk, 1982-94, Norfolk Acad., 1987-99. Mem. Va. Bar Assn., Norfolk and Portsmouth Bar Assn., Shenandoah Club, Norfolk Yacht and Country Club, Order of Coif, Sigma Xi, Omicron Delta Kappa, Phi Delta Phi. Home: 7633 Argyle Ave Norfolk VA 23505-1701

SHANNON, KATHLEEN E., insurance company executive; AB, Wilson Coll.; MA in Am. Studies, Boston Coll., JD; LLM in Corp. Law, NYU. Bar: NY, Pa. Atty. Am. Internat. Group, Inc. (AIG), NYC, 1976, sec., assoc. gen. counsel, 1986, v.p., 1989, dep. gen. counsel, 2002, sr. v.p., dep. gen. counsel, sec., 2003—. Mem.: Stockholder Rels. Soc. of NY (former pres.), Soc. Corp. Secretaries & Governance Profls. (former mem. bd. dirs., former chair Audit and Pub. Com. Affairs Coms., treas.). Office: Am Internat Group Inc (AIG) 70 Pine St New York NY 10270*

SHANNON, MARGARET BARRETT, lawyer; b. 1949; BA, Baylor U., 1971; JD, Southern Methodist U., 1976. Bar: 1976. Ptnr. Andrews Kurth LLP, 1984—94; v.p., sec., gen. counsel BJ Services Co., Houston, 1994—. Mem. United Way Women's Initiative of Alexis de Tocqueville Soc., 2003—04; mem. bd. dirs. St. Luke's Episcopal Health Charities, Houston; mem. Exec. Women's Partnership Greater Houston Partnership. Mem.: ABA, Harris County Health Alliance (bd. dirs.), South Tex. Coll. Law (bd. dirs.). Office: BJ Services Co 4601 Westway Park Blvd Houston TX 77041

SHANNON, MARILYN MCCUSKER, biologist, educator; b. McKeesport, Pa., June 16, 1952; d. David Edward and Margaret Ellen McCusker; m. Ronald Ellis Shannon, Jan. 8, 1977; children: John, Rosemary Shannon Imrick, Stephen, Gregory, Regina, Ellen, Vahn, Monica, Lucia. BA, U. Pitts., 1974; MA, Ind. U., Bloomington, 1979. Instr. biology Alverno Coll., Milw., 1979—80, Ind. U.-Purdue U., Ft. Wayne, Ind., 1983—. Vol. tchr. Couple to Couple Legue, Cin., 1982—, faculty Ann. Physician's Conf., 1998—; spkr. in field. Author: Fertility, Cycles and Nutrition, 1990, 4th edit., 2008, (booklet) Managing Morning Sickness, 1996; co-author (with Jay Wile and Marilyn Shannon): (textbook) The Human Body, 2002. Bd. dirs., key leader Allen County 4-H Clubs, Ft. Wayne, Ind., 2001—, bd. dirs., 2006—; parish coun. Sacred Heart Cath. Ch., Ft. Wayne, Ind., 2005—. Recipient Edward M. Keefe award, Couple to Couple League, 1992. Roman Catholic. Avocations: gardening, hiking, cooking, writing. Business E-Mail: shannon@ipfw.edu.

SHANNON, MARY LOU, adult health nursing educator; b. Memphis, Apr. 4, 1938; d. Sidney Richmond Shannon and Lucille (Gwaltney) Shannon Cloud. BSN, U. Tenn., 1959; MA, Columbia U., 1963, MEd, 1964, EdD, 1972. Staff nurse City of Memphis Hosps., 1959—60, instr. Sch. Nursing, 1960—62; asst. prof. U. Tenn., Memphis, 1964—70, assoc. prof., 1970—73, prof., 1973—89; prof., chair adult health dept. Sch. Nursing U. Tex., Galveston, 1989—98, prof., 1989—2000, prof. emeritus, 2000—. Bd. dirs. Nat. Pressure Ulcer Adv. Panel, Buffalo, 1987-96; vis. prof. U. Alta., Edmonton, Can., 1982, Union U., Memphis, 2001, Bapt. Coll. Health Scis., 2003, U. Tex., Galveston, 2004; mem. project adv. bd. RAND, Santa Monica, Calif., 1994. Contbr. chpts. to books in field and to periodicals; mem. editl. bd. Advances in Wound Care, 1987-2000. Trustee Nurses Edn. Funds, N.Y.C., 1972-86. Mem. AAAS, ANA, Nat. League Nursing (bd. of rev. 1983-86), Orthopedic Nurses Assn., So. Nursing Rsch. Soc., Am. Assn. for History of Nursing, Sigma Xi, Sigma Theta Tau, Phi Kappa Phi. Avocations: travel, reading.

SHANNON, MOLLY HELEN, actress; b. Shaker Heights, Ohio, Sept. 16, 1964; m. Fritz Chestnut, May 29, 2004; children: Stella Shannon Chestnut, Nolan Shannon Chestnut. BFA in Drama, NYU, 1987. Actor: (films) The Phantom of the Opera, 1989, Return to Two Moon Junction, 1995, Lawnmover Man 2: Beyond Cyberspace, 1996, Dinner and Driving, 1997, The Thin Pink Line, 1998, A Night at the Roxbury, 1998, Happiness, 1998 (Best Acting by Ensemble, Nat. Bd. Review, 1998), Daydream Believer, 1998, Analyze This, 1999, Never Been Kissed, 1999, Superstar, 1999, My 5 Wives, 2000, How the Grinch Stole Christmas, 2000, Wet Hot American Summer, 2001, Osmosis Jones, 2001, Serendipity, 2001, Shallow Hal, 2001, The Santa Clause 2, 2002, American Splendor, 2003, My Boss's Daughter, 2003, Good Boy!, 2003, Shut Up and Sing, 2006, Scary Movie 4, 2006, Marie Antoinette, 2006, Little Man, 2006, Talladega Nights: The Ballad of Ricky Bobby, 2006, Gray Matters, 2006, Year of the Dog, 2007, Evan Almighty, 2007, (voice) Igor, 2008,: (TV films) SNL Fanatic, 2000, Saturday Night Live Primetime Extra 1, 2001, The Music Man, 2003, The Twelve Days of Christmas Eve, 2004, (voice) The Amazing Screw-On Head, 2006, The Mastersons of Manhattan, 2007; (TV series) Saturday Night Live, 1995—2001, Cracking Up, 2004—06, Kath and Kim, 2008—09. Office: c/o Innovative Artists 1505 10th St Santa Monica CA 90401

SHANNON, PATRICIA D., theology studies educator; b. Bellefonte, Pa., Mar. 5, 1953; m. Michael H. Shannon; children: Meredith E. Burrows, Michael D. PhD, Grad. Theol. Union, Berkeley, Calif., 2006. Instr. Chabot Coll., Hayward, Calif., 2002—. Office: Chabot Coll 25555 Hesperion Blvd Hayward CA 94552 Business E-Mail: pshannon@chabotcollege.edu.

SHANNON, PETER MICHAEL, JR., lawyer; s. Peter Michael Sr. and Marian Shannon. BA, St. Mary of the Lake, Mundelein, Ill., 1949, MA, 1952, STL, 1953; JCL, Gregorian U., Rome, 1958; JD, U. Calif., Berkeley, 1971. Bar: Calif. 1972, D.C. 1972, Ill. 1988, U.S. Dist. Ct. Md. 1972, U.S. Dist. Ct. D.C. 1972, U.S. Dist. Ct. (no. dist.) Ill. 1988, U.S. Ct. Appeals (1st, 2d, 3d, 4th, 5th, 6th, 7th, 8th, 9th, 10th and D.C. cirs.) 1972-75, U.S. Supreme Ct. 1975. Supervisory atty. litigation U.S. Dept. of Justice, Washington, 1971-75; sr. appellate atty. ICC, Washington, 1975-77, dir. enforcement, 1977-80; ptnr. Shannon, et al, Washington, 1980-82, Keck, Mahin & Cate, Chgo., 1982-96, Arnstein & Lehr, Chgo., 1996—2001; pvt. practice Western Springs, Ill., 2001—. Author: Energy and Transportation Implications of Ratemaking Policy Concerning Sources of Energy, 1980, Disposition of Real Estate by Religious Institutions, 1987, The Dual Approach of Civil Law Courts to Ecclesiastical Related Disputes, 1988. Mem. ABA (chmn. transp. com., adminstrv. law and regulatory practice sect. 1984-87, coun. mem. 1988-91), Ill. Bar Assn., Chgo. Bar Assn., Canon Law Soc. (pres. 1965-66), Ctr. for Disability and Elder Law (pres. 1997-99).*

SHANNON, RANDY LANNARD, college football coach; b. Miami, Feb. 24, 1966; s. Dorleatha Johnson; children: Ty, Xavier, Randy Jr., Steven. BS, U. Miami, 1989. Linebacker Dallas Cowboys, 1989—91; grad. asst. U. Miami, 1991, defensive line, 1992, linebackers coach, 1993—97, 2000, defensive asst., 1998—99, defensive coord., 2001—06, head football coach, 2006—. Recipient Christopher Plumer award for Most Inspirational Player, 1988, Frank Broyles award for Nat. Asst. Coach of Yr., 2001. Achievements include being mem. of coaching staff in 10 Bowl Games. Office: U Miami Dept Athletics 5821 San Amaro Dr Miami FL 33146

SHANNON, THOMAS A., JR., federal agency administrator; BA, Coll. William and Mary; M in Politics, Oxford U., doctorate. Consular/polit. rotational officer U.S. Embassy, Guatemala City, Guatemala, 1984—86; country officer Cameroon, Gabon, Sao Tome, Principe, 1987—89; spl. asst. to amb. U.S. Embassy, Brasilia, Brazil, 1989—92; regional labor attache U.S. Consulate General, Johannesburg, 1992—96; polit. counselor U.S. Embassy, Caracas, Venezuela, 1996—99; dir. Inter-Am. affairs Nat. Security Coun., 1999—2000; U.S. dep. permanent rep. OAS, 2000—01; dir. Andean affairs US Dept. State, 2001—02, dep. asst. sec. we. hemisphere affairs, 2002—03, asst. sec. for we. hemisphere affairs, 2005—; sr. dir. we. hemisphere affairs Nat. Security Coun., 2003—05; spl. asst. to Pres. The White House, 2003—05. Career mem. Sr. Fgn. Svc. Office: US Dept State 2201 C St NW Washington DC 20520*

SHANNON, THOMAS ALFRED, retired educational association administrator emeritus; b. Milw., Jan. 2, 1932; s. John Elwood and Eleanor Ann (Mitchell) S.; m. Barbara Ann Weidner, June 26, 1954; children: Thomas Alfred, Paul J., Suzanne L., Terrence D. BS, U. Wis, 1954; JD, U. Minn., 1961. Bar: Minn. 1961, Calif. 1963, U.S. Supreme Ct. 1965, D.C. 1977, Va. 1984; Life cert. as sch. adminstr., Calif.; cert. assoc. exec. Am. Soc. Assn. Execs. Pvt. practice law, Mpls., 1961-62; schs. atty. San Diego City Schs., 1962-73; dept. supt., gen. counsel, 1973-77; exec. dir. Nat. Sch. Bds. Assn., Washington, 1977-97, ret., 1997. Adj. prof. law and edn. U. San Diego; vis. prof. edn. U. Va.; adv. mem. Edn. Commn. of States; prof. Nat. Acad. Sch. Execs., 1971-77; legal counsel Am. Assn. Sch. Adminstrs., 1973-77; adj. prof. ednl. adminstrn. George Washington U., 1996-97. Exec. pub. The Am. Sch. Bd. Jour., 1977-96, Exec. Educator, 1978-96, Sch. Bd. News, 1981-96. Chmn. San Diego County Juvenile Justice Commn., 1973-74; mem. nat. coun. Boy Scouts Am., 1979-97; bd. dirs. Found. for Teaching Econ., San Francisco, 1993-2003. With USN, 1954—59. Mem. VFW (life), Am. Bar Assn. (chmn. com. public edn. 1978-82), Nat. Orgn. on Legal Problems of Edn. (pres. 1973), Nat. Sch. Bds. Assn. (chmn. council sch. attys. 1967-69) Home: 21125 Cardinal Pond Ter Apt 406 Ashburn VA 20147 Personal E-mail: tombar2@juno.com.

SHANNON, THOMAS FREDERIC, German language educator; b. Cambridge, Mass., Mar. 16, 1948; m. Christine D. Höner. BA in German summa cum laude, Boston Coll., 1969; MA in German Lit., SUNY, Albany, 1973; MA in Theoretical Linguistics, Ind. U., 1975, PhD in Germanic Linguistics, 1982. Instr. in German Boston Coll., 1969-70; tchg. fellow in German SUNY, Albany, 1971-73; univ. fellow Ind. U., Bloomington, 1973-74, assoc. instr., 1974-76, 79-80; acting asst. prof. in Germanic linguistics U. Calif., Berkeley, 1980-82, asst. prof., 1982-87, assoc. prof., 1987-94, prof., 1994—, dir. lang. lab., 1989-92, assoc. dir. Berkeley Lang. Ctr., 1994-95, dir. abroad study ctr. Germany, 2000—02. Co-organizer Berkeley Confs. on Dutch Lang. and Lit., 1987, 89, 91, 93,

95, 97, 2005, 10th Interdisciplinary Conf. Netherlandic Studies, 2000; econs. presenter and spkr. in field. Mem. editl. adv. bd. Jour. Germanic Linguistics, 1998—; contbr. articles to profl. jours. With USAR, 1970-76. Grantee Fulbright Found., 1976-78, U. Calif. Berkeley, 1983-84, 94-95, ACLS, 1987, Internat. Assn. Netherlandic Studies, 1988, 91, 94, 97, 06, German Acad. Exch. Svc., summer 1996; NDEA fellow, 1969; Fulbright rsch./lectr. grantee Rijksuniversiteit Groningen, Netherlands, 1992-93; Inst. fuer deutsche Sprache summer rsch. grantee, Mannheim, Germany, 1997. Mem. MLA (exec. com. discussion group in Germanic philology 1989-94, discussion group for Netherlandic Studies 1995-99, divsn. on lang. change 1995-99), Am. Assn. Netherlandic Studies (exec. com. 1988—, editor newsletter 1989-95, series editor publs. 1994-2006), Am. Assn. Tchrs. German, Internat. Assn. Netherlandic Studies, Linguistic Soc. Am., Pacific Ancient and Modern Lang. Assn., European Linguistic Soc., Soc. Germanic Philology (v.p. 1991-92, 95-99), Internat. Cognitive Linguistics Soc., Maatschappij der Nederlandse Letterkunde, Alpha Sigma Nu. Home: 770 Rose Dr Benicia CA 94510-3709 Office: U Calif Dept German 5319 Dwinelle Hall Berkeley CA 94720-3243 Home Phone: 707-748-1493; Office Phone: 510-642-2004. E-mail: tshannon@berkeley.edu.

SHANNON, THOMAS O., plastic surgeon; b. Pottstown, Pa., Aug. 25, 1962; s. John H. and Rosemary E. Shannon; m. Kelly R. Shannon, Nov. 4, 1995; children: Sydney, Mitchell, Lauren. BA in Chemistry, U. Rochester, 1984; MD, Pa. State U., 1988. Diplomate Am. Bd. Surgery, lic. physician Tex., Pa. Surg. resident Lankenau Hosp. and Med. Rsch. Ctr., Phila., 1988—93; resident in plastic surgery U. Tex. Med. Br., Galveston, 1993—96; plastic surgeon Keystone Plastic Surgery, Conroe, Tex., 1996—2007, Woodlands, Tex., 1996—. Med. dir. Woodlands Meml. Woundcare Ctr., 1998—2001; med. dir. wound care Triumph N.W. Hosp., 2002—05, 2007—; med. dir. woundcare Nexus Hosp., 2006—07; presenter in field. Contbr. articles to profl. jours. Capt. US Army, 1986—2004. Ames Rsch. Lab. fellow, 1983, Std. Oil Rsch. Profl. Program trainee, 1984, summer fellow, NIH, 1985. Fellow: Am. Soc. Laser Medicine & Surgery; mem.: AMA, Am. Burn Assn., Tex. Med. Assn., Montgomery County Med. Soc., Blocker-Lewis Plastic Surg. Soc., Singleton Surg. Soc., Galveston Hist. Found., Mixed Volleyball League, The Woodlands Mixed Bowling League. Presbyterian. Avocations: tennis, skiing, volleyball, bowling, choir, swimming. Office: Keystone Plastic and Reconstructive Surgery LLC 3115 College Park Dr Bldg 101 The Woodlands TX 77384 also: 13628 Michael Rd Tomball TX 77375 also: 18955 Memorial N Ste 530 Humble TX 77338 Office Phone: 936-321-4345. Business E-Mail: tshannon@keystoneplasticsurgery.com.

SHANNON, WILLIAM NORMAN, III, college educator, food service executive; b. Chgo., Nov. 20, 1937; s. William Norman Jr. and Lee (Lewis) S.; m. Bernice Urbanowicz, July 14, 1962; children: Kathleen Kelly, Colleen Patricia, Kerrie Ann. BS in Indsl. Mgmt., Carnegie Inst. Tech., 1959; MBA in Mktg. Mgmt., U. Toledo, 1963. Sales engr. Westinghouse Electric Co., Detroit, 1959-64; regional mgr. Toledo Scale, Chgo., 1964-70; v.p. J. Lloyd Johnson Assoc., Northbrook, Ill., 1970-72; mgr. spl. projects Hobart Mfg., Troy, Ohio, 1972-74; corp. v.p. mktg. Berkel, Inc., La Porte, Ind., 1974-79; gen. mgr. Berkel Products, Ltd., Toronto, Canada, 1975-78; chmn. Avant Industries, Inc., Wheeling, Ill., 1979-81; chmn., pres. Hacienda Mexican Restaurants, South Bend, Ind., 1978—95; chmn. Ziker Shannon Corp., South Bend, 1982-88, Hacienda Franchising Group, Inc., South Bend, Ind., 1987—92. Assoc. prof. mktg. and internat. bus. St. Mary's Coll., Notre Dame, Ind., 1982—; chmn. Hacienda Franchise Group, Inc., 1987-96, Hacienda Mex. Restaurants Mgmt., Inc., 1994-96; sr. chmn. Hacienda Mex. Restaurants, 1996-2004; mem. London program faculty, 1986, 89, 92, 94, 97, coord. internat. bus. curriculum, 1989—, mktg. curriculum, 1983; advisor Coun. Internat. Bus. Devel., Notre Dame, 1991-2005; mng. dir. Alden & Torch Lake Railway, 1995—. Co-author: Laboratory Computers, 1971; columnist Bus. Digest mag., 1988-1994; mem. editl. bd. Jour. Bus. and Indsl. Mktg., 1986-1992, South Bend Tribune Business Weekly, 1990-1994; contbr. articles to profl. jours. V.p. mktg. Jr. Achievement, South Bend, Ind., 1987-90; pres. Small Bus. Devel. Coun., South Bend., 1987-90; bd. dirs. Ind. Small Bus. Coun., Indpls., 1986—, Mental Health Assn., South Bend, 1987-90, Michiana World Trade Orgn., Internat. Bus. Edn., 1989-91; Entrepreneurs Alliance Ind., 1988-92, Nat. Small Bus. United, Washington, 1989-92, Women's Bus. Initiative, 1986-90, dir. ednl. confs., 1986-90; chmn. bd. trustees, Holy Cross Coll., Notre Dame, Ind., 1987-1993, chmn. edn. com., 1993-1993; chmn. St. Joseph County Higher Edn. Coun., 1988-91, Nat. Coun. Small Bus., Washington, 1988-1994; Midwest region adv. coun. U.S. SBA, 1988-91; at-large mem. U.S. Govt. Adv. Coun. on Small Bus., Washington, 1988-90, 1994-1996, chmn. Bus. and Econ. Devel. Com., 1988-90, 1994-1996; vice chmn. Internat. Trade Com., 1994-1996; nat. adv. coun. Women's Network for Entrepreneur Tng., 1991-1994; vice chmn. State of Ind. Enterprise Zone Bd., 1991-1994; elected del. White House Conf. Small Bus., Washington, 1986; bd. dirs. Ind. Small Bus. Devel. Ctrs. Adv. Bd.; co-pres. Helena Twp. Downtown Devel. Authority, 2002—. Named Small Bus. Person of the Yr., City of South Bend, 1987, Small Bus. Advocate of the Yr., State of Ind., 1987, Ind. Entrepreneur Advocate of the Yr., 1988. Mem. Am. Mktg. Assn. (chmn. Mich./Ind. chpt., pres. 1985-86), U.S. Assn. Small Bus. and Entrepreneurship (nat. v.p. for entrepreneurship edn. 1991-92, nat. v.p. entrepreneurship devel. 1992-1996), Ind. Inst. New Bus. Ventures (mktg. faculty 1987-91), Michiana Investment Network (vice chmn. 1988-91), SBA (adminstrn. adv. coun. 1988-1992, contbg. editor Our Town Michiana mag. 1988-91), U.S. C. of C., Nat. Coun. Small Bus. (Washington), South Bend C. of C. (bd. dirs. 1987-1996, vice chmn. membership 1993-1996), Assn. for Bus. Communications (co-chmn. Internat. Conf. 1986), Univ. Club Notre Dame (vice chmn.), Shamrock Club Notre Dame (exec. dir., trustee 1993-1996), Rotary. Roman Catholic. Office: Saint Mary's Coll Dept Bus Adminstrn Eco Notre Dame IN 46556 Office Phone: 574-284-4508. *Enjoy good fortune resulting from LUCK, an acronym for (L) Learning how to (U)Use your talents with genuine (C) Concern on how your (K) Knowlege can benefit others.*

SHAO, LIN, physicist, director; b. Yunnan, China; m. Huan Mo; 1 child, Kelsey. PhD, U. Houston, 2001. Postdoctoral fellow U. Houston, 2001—04; dir. funded postdoctoral fellows Los Alamos (N.Mex.) Nat. Lab., 2004—. Recipient Rsch. Achievement award, Sigma Xi, 2000, First prize, TCSUH, 2000. Mem.: Material Rsch. Soc., Am. Electrochem. Soc., Am. Phys. Soc. Achievements include patents for 6 U.S. Patents on deivice fabrication; first to ultrashallow junction formation by defect engineering; ultrathin layer transfer by ion cutting technique. Office: Los Alamos National laboratory Ms G755 Los Alamos NM 87545

SHAO, OTIS HUNG-I, retired political science professor; b. Shanghai, July 18, 1923; came to U.S., 1949, naturalized, 1956; s. Ming Sun and Hannah (Chen) S.; m. Marie Sheng, Apr. 2, 1955. BA, St. John's U., 1946; MA, U. Colo., 1950; PhD, Brown U., 1957. From instr. to prof. polit. sci. Moravian Coll., Bethlehem, Pa., 1954-62; assoc. prof., then prof. polit. sci. Fla. Presbyn. Coll., St. Petersburg, 1962-68; prof. internat. politics, dean (Grad. Sch., U. Pacific), 1968-74; dir. Pub. Affairs Inst., 1969-74; provost Callison Coll., 1974-76; dean faculty, v.p. Occidental Coll., 1976-78; asso. exec. dir. sr. commn. Western Assn. Schs. and Colls., 1978-80; v.p., dean Hawaii Loa Coll., 1980-85; pres. Sheng Shao Enterprises Calif., 1985-92; CEO, chmn. D.S. Capital Internat., Calif., 1993-94. Mem. grad. students relations com. Council Grad. Schs. U.S., 1970-73; mem. exec. council undergrad. assessment program Ednl. Testing Service, 1978-80. Contbr. articles to profl. jours. Chmn. bd. dirs. Fgn. Policy Assn. Lehigh Valley, 1961-62; bd. dirs. World Affairs Council, San Joaquin County, 1969-77; trustee Inst. Med. Scis., Pacific Med. Center, San Francisco, 1968-72, optical scis. group of Profl. and Pub. Service Found., 1969-72; Resident fellow Harkness House, Brown U., 1953-54, Danforth Asso., 1958-85. Recipient Distinguished Service award Fgn. Policy Assn. Lehigh Valley, 1962 Mem. AAUP (pres. Fla. Presbyn. Coll. chpt. 1965-66), Am. Assn. Higher Edn., Rho Psi, Tau Kappa Epsilon. Democrat. Presbyterian. Home: 1784 Curtner Ave San Jose CA 95124

SHAO, QIUXIA, literature and language professor; children: Yancheng Zhang, Xiaolin Zhang. BA, Dalian Inst. Fgn. Languages, China, 1982; EdM, SUNY, Buffalo, 1994, PhD, 2000. Asst. prof. Dalian U., Liaoning, 1982—91; lectr. chinese lang. SUNY, Buffalo, 1997—2000; sr. lectr. chinese lang. NY U., NYC, 2000—. Author: (text books) Chinese for Tomorrow. Recipient Golden Dozen award, NY U., Coll. Art and Sci., 2005. Office: NY Univ 715 Brodway 3rd fl New York NY 10003

SHAO, ZHENHUA, electrical engineer, consultant; arrived in U.S., 1989; s. Jinrui Shao and Rujing Hua. Diploma in elec. engring., Shanghai Jiao Tong U., 1983, MSME, 1989; MSEE, Wichita State U., 1991; PhD Elec. Engring., U. Kans., 1994. Registered profl. engr., Calif. Elec. engr. Shanghai Jiao Tong U., 1983—86; rsch. asst. Nat. Inst. Aviation Rsch., Wichita, 1990—92; tchg. asst. U. Kans., Lawrence, 1993—94; elec. design engr. Eastman Kodak, Kansas City, 1995; chief engr. NGK Insulators Inc., Torrance, Calif., 1996—2002; circuit design mgr. L.A. divsn. Ibiden USA Inc., Torrance, Calif., 2003—. Cons. Lawrence Paper Co., 1994—95; cons. engring., San Gabriel, Calif., 1997—; reviewer IEEE and Inst. Elec. Engring. Contbr. articles to profl. jours. Named Outstanding Rschr., Shanghai Jiao Tong U., 1985; named one of Top 50 Pairs in Open Pair Game, N.Am. Bridge Championships U.S., Am. Contract Bridge League, 1998, Top 50 Pairs in Open Pair Game, N.Am. Bridge Championships Can., 1999. Achievements include patents in field; design of high frequency integrated circuits. Home: PO Box 1083 San Gabriel CA 91778 E-mail: zshao2001@yahoo.com.

SHAOMAN, YIN, research scientist; married. Rsch. assoc. Case Western Res. U., Cleve., 2004—. Achievements include research in human prion protein,test for diease-associated prion,prion protein with insertion mutation; discovery of normal cellular prion protein with a methionine.

SHAPEERO, LORRAINE G., physician, researcher, educator; d. Ezra and Goldine Shapeero. BA, U. Calif., Berkeley, 1964; MD, U. Calif., San Francisco, 1968. Diplomate Am. Bd. of Radiology, 1974. Resident to faculty U. Pa., Phila., 1970—74; fellowship Inst. of Orthop. Royal Nat. Orthop. Hosp., London, 1975—76; faculty U. Calif., San Francisco, 1977—82, 1984—95, Columbia U., NY, 1982—84, Institut Gustave Roussy, France, 1990—; chief Musculo-skeletal Radiology sect. Uniformed Svcs. U., Bethesda, Md., 1995—; attending radiologist Walter Reed Army Med. Ctr., Wash., 1995—; dir. Bone and Soft Tissue Sarcoma Program US Mil. Cancer Inst., Wash., 2000—. Contbr. articles various profl. jours. and rsch. publs. Mem.: Musculoskeletal Radiology (mem. editl. bd. 1999—2002), Investigative Radiology (mem. editl. bd. 1990—94), Internat. Skeletal Soc., Radiology (mem. editl. bd., cons. to editor 1995—2001), Acad. Radiology (mem. editl. bd. 1994—), Assn. U. Radiologists (bd. dirs.), Alliance Med. Student Educators in Radiology (exec. com.), Am. Roentgen Ray Soc., Am. Coll. Radiology, Radiol. Soc. North Am., Internat. Soc. Magnetic Resonance in Medicine, Connective Tissue Oncology Soc., Radiology Rsch. Alliance (pres. 2005—06), Phi Beta Kappa. Office: Uniformed Svcs U 4301 Jones Bridge Rd Bethesda MD 20814

SHAPER, C. PARK, energy executive; BA, BS, Stanford Univ.; MBA, Northwestern Univ. Cons. Boston Consulting Group, 1995—97; v.p., CFO First Data Corp., 1997—99; pres., bd. dir. Altair Corp., 1999; v.p., CFO Kinder Morgan Inc., Kinder Morgan Energy Partners LP, Kinder Morgan Mgmt. LLC, Houston, 2000—04, exec. v.p., CFO, 2004—05, pres., 2005—. Bd. dir., treas. Children's Fund, Houston. Office: Kinder Morgan Inc Ste 1000 500 Dallas St Houston TX 77002

SHAPERE, DUDLEY, philosophy educator; b. Harlingen, Tex., May 27, 1928; s. Dudley and Corinne (Pupkin) S.; m. Hannah Hardgrave; children: Hannah Elizabeth, Christine Ann; children by previous marriage: Alfred Dudley, Catherine Lucretia. BA, Harvard U., 1949, MA, 1955, PhD, 1957. Instr. philosophy Ohio State U., 1957-60; asst. prof. U. Chgo., 1960-65, assoc. prof., 1965-67, prof., 1967-72, mem. com. on evolutionary biology, 1969-72, chmn. undergrad. program in history and philosophy of sci., 1966-72, chmn. com. on conceptual founds. sci., 1970-72; prof. U. Ill., Urbana, 1972-75, chmn. program in history and philosophy of sci., 1972-75; prof. U. Md., College Park, 1975-84; Z. Smith Reynolds prof. philosophy and history of sci. Wake Forest U., 1984—2002; ret., 2002. Mem. com. on history and philosophy of sci. U. Md., 1975-84, chmn. program in history and philosophy of sci., 1983-84.; vis. prof. Rockefeller U., 1965-66, Harvard U., 1968; mem. Inst. Advanced Study, Princeton, N.J., 1978-79, 81, 89, Otto Neugebaur fellow, 2001; spl. cons. (program dir.) program in history and philosophy of sci. NSF, 1966-75; Sigma Xi nat. bicentennial lectr., 1974-77. Author: Philosophical Problems of Natural Science, 1965, Galileo: A Philosophical Study, 1974, Reason and the Search for Knowledge, 1984; editorial bd.: Philosophy of Sci., Studies in History and Philosophy of Sci.; rev. bd.: Philosophy Research Archives; contbr. articles to profl. jours. Served with AUS, 1950-52. Recipient Quantrell award for excellence in undergrad. tchg. U. Chgo., 1968; Disting. Scholar-Tchr. award U. Md., 1979-80. Fellow AAAS (sec. sec. 1972); mem. APA, Philosophy of Sci. Assn., History of Sci. Soc., Am. Philos. Assn., Acad. Internat. de Philosophie des Scis. Home: 3125 Turkey Hill Ct Winston Salem NC 27106-4951 E-mail: shapere@wfu.edu.

SHAPIRO, ANDREW JOSEPH, federal agency administrator; b. 1967; s. Lawrence R. and Miriam Shapiro; m. Yael Weinman, Feb. 17, 2002; children: Samuel, Zachary. BA cum laude in Diplomatic History, U. Pa., Phila., 1989; JD, Columbia U., NYC, 1994; M in Internat. Affairs, Columbia U., 1995. Sr. rsch. asst. Washington Inst. Near East Policy; assoc. atty. Covington & Burling LLP, Washington, 1995—98; counsel internat. competition policy adv. com. US Dept. Justice; legis. asst. to sr. def. and fgn. policy advisor to Senator Hillary Clinton US Senate, 2001—09; sr. advisor to Sec. State Hillary Clinton US Dept. State, Washington, asst. sec. for polit. & military affairs, 2009—. Mem. Obama-Biden Dept. of Def. Agy. Rev. Team; mem. confirmation and transition team Sec. State Hillary Clinton. Recipient Appreciation Award, Gold Star Wives of Am., Patrick Henry Award, Nat. Guard Assn. Mem.: Internat. Inst. Strategic Studies, Coun. Fgn. Rels. Office: US Dept State Bur Polit Mil Affairs 2201 C St NW Washington DC 20520*

SHAPIRO, ANNA D., theater director; BA, Columbia Coll., Chgo.; MFA, Yale Sch. Drama. With Steppenwolf Theatre Co., Chgo., 1995—, dir. New Plays initiative, resident dir., assoc. artist; assoc. prof., dir. MFA directing prog. Northwestern U. Sch. Communication, Chgo., 2002—. Dir.: (plays) The Viewing Room, 1996, Wolf Lullaby, 1998, Three Days of Rain, 1999, Side Man, 1999, The Infidel, 2000, The Ordinary Yearning of Miriam Buddwing, 2001, The Drawer Boy, 2001, Purple Heart, 2002, Until We Find Each Other, 2002, Man From Nebraska, 2003, I Never Sang For My Father, 2004, The Pain and the Itch, 2005, A Blameless Life, 2005, The Unmentionables, 2006, The Crucible, 2007; (Broadway plays) August: Osage County, 2007 (Outstanding Dir., Outstanding Play, Drama Desk Awards, 2008, Best Direction of a Play, Best Play, Tony Awards, 2008). Recipient Princess Grace award, 1996. Office: Northwestern U Sch Communication Theater and Interpretation Ctr Rm 217 1949 Campus Dr Evanston IL 60208-2430 also: Steppenwolf Theatre Co 4th Fl 758 W North Ave Chicago IL 60610 Office Phone: 847-491-3285. E-mail: anna-shapiro@northwestern.edu.

SHAPIRO, BETH, biology professor; b. Allentown, Pa., Jan. 14, 1976; d. I. Robert and Kathleen Shapiro; m. David Capel, June 3, 1974. BS, MS, U. Ga., Athens, 1999; PhD, Oxford U., Eng., 2003. Welcome trust rsch. fellow Oxford U., 2004—06, rsch. fellow royal soc., 2006—07; Shaffer asst. prof. dept. biology Pa. State U., State Coll., 2007—. Mem.: AAAS. Office: Pa State Univ 208 Mueller Lab University Park PA 16802-5301

SHAPIRO, BURTON LEONARD, dentist, maxillofacial pathologist, geneticist, educator; b. NYC, Mar. 29, 1934; s. Nat Lazarus and Fay Rebecca (Gartenhouse) S.; m. Eileen Roman, Aug. 11, 1958; children: Norah Leah, Anne Rachael, Carla Faye. Student, Tufts U., Medford, Mass., 1951-54; DDS, NYU, 1958; MS, U. Minn., 1962, PhD, 1966. Faculty U. Minn. Sch. Dentistry, Mpls., 1962—, assoc. prof. div. oral pathology, 1966-70, prof., chmn. div. oral biology, 1970-79, prof., chmn. dept. oral biology, 1979-88, prof. dept. oral pathology and genetics, 1979-88, dir. grad. studies, mem. grad. faculty genetics, 1966—, prof. dept. oral sci., 1988—2006, mem. grad. faculty pathobiology, 1979; prof. dept. lab. medicine and pathology U. Minn. Sch. Medicine, 1985—; prof. emeritus U. Minn. Sch. Dentistry, 2006; mem. Human Genetics Inst. U. Minn. Sch. Medicine, 1988—, univ. senator, 1968-72, 88-93; also mem. med. staff U. Minn. Health Scis. Center; exec. com. Grad. Sch. U. Minn., chmn. health scis. policy rev. council, chmn. univ. faculty consultative com., 1988-92; chmn. univ. fin. and planning com. Grad. Sch. U. Minn., 1988. Hon. research fellow Galton Lab. dept. human genetics Univ. Coll., London, 1974; spl. vis. prof. Japanese Ministry Edn., Sci. and Culture, 1983 Mem. adv. editorial bd.: Jour. Dental Research, 1971—; Contbr. articles to profl. jours. Served to lt. USNR, 1958-60. Am. Cancer Soc. postdoctoral fellow, 1960-62; advanced fellow, 1965-68; named Century Club Prof. of Yr., 1988. Fellow Am. Acad. Oral Pathology, AAAS; mem. Internat. Assn. Dental Research (councilor 1969), Am. Soc. Human Genetics, Craniofacial Biology Soc. (pres. 1972), Sigma Xi, Omicron Kappa Upsilon. Office: U Minn Sch Dentistry Dept Oral Sci Minneapolis MN 55455 Business E-Mail: burt@umn.edu.

SHAPIRO, DAVID JOEL, poet, art critic, educator; b. Newark, Jan. 2, 1947; s. Irving Shapiro and Fraida Chagy; m. Lindsay Stamm, Aug. 30, 1970; 1 child, Daniel Jonathan Stamm. BA magna cum laude, Columbia U., 1968, PhD in English with distinction, 1973; BA with 1st honours, Cambridge U., Eng., 1970, MA, 1974. Lectr., instr., asst. prof. Columbia U., NYC, 1972-81, vis. prof., 1987, 88; assoc. prof. art history William Paterson U., Wayne, N.J., 1980-96, prof., 1996—. Vis. prof. creative writing Bklyn. Coll., CUNY, 1979; vis. lectr. visual arts Princeton (N.J.) U., 1982-83; vis. adj. prof. Cooper Union, N.Y.C., 1980—; editorial assoc. Res, Harvard mag. in anthropology and aesthetics. Author: January, 1965, Poems from Deal, 1969, A Man Holding an Acoustic Panel, 1971, The Page Turner, 1973, Lateness, 1977, House (Blown Apart), 1988, Introduction to John Ashbery's Poetry, (chapbook, with Terry Winters) After a Lost Original, numerous others; author critical books on Jasper Johns, Mondrian's Flowers, Jim Dine; mem. editl. bd. Blvd.; former mem. editl. bd. Little Mag. Bd. advisors Poet's House, N.Y.C. Recipient poetry prize Gotham Book Mart, 1962, Triennial Zabel prize Nat. Acad. and Inst. Arts and Letters, 1977; grantee Merrill Found., 1967, NEH and Nat. Endowment for Arts, 1978-80; Kellett fellow Cambridge U.; grantee Graham Found., 1996-97, Found. for Continuing Performance Art, 1996-97. Jewish. Avocations: playing tennis and writing poetry with his son, violinist, chamber music. Home: 3001 Henry Hudson Pky Bronx NY 10463-4717

SHAPIRO, DAVID L., lawyer; b. Corsicana, Tex., May 19, 1936; s. Harry and Alice (Laibovitz) S. BA, U. Tex., Austin, 1967; JD, St. Mary's U., 1970. Bar: Tex. 1970, U.S. Dist. Ct. (we. dist.) Tex. 1972, U.S. Supreme Ct. 1975, U.S. Ct. Appeals (5th cir.) 1981. Assoc. Law Office Jim S. Phelps, Houston, 1971; pvt. practice, Austin, 1972—. Spl. counsel com. human resources Tex. Ho. Reps., Austin, 1973-74; counsel subcom. health svcs. Tex. Senate, Austin, 1983-87. With U.S. Army, 1959-61. Mem.: Am. Legion, Austin Criminal Def. Lawyers Assn., Coll. of State Bar of Tex., State Bar Tex. (chmn. lawyer referral svc. com. 1980—82, contbr. Media Law Handbook supplement 1986, adminstrn. of justice com. 1990—93, jury svc. com. 1998—2001). Democrat. Avocations: automobiles, football. Office: 505 W 18th St Austin TX 78701-1243 Office Phone: 512-626-3920. Personal E-mail: daveinaustintexas@yahoo.com.

SHAPIRO, DAVID LOUIS, law educator; b. NYC, Oct. 12, 1932; s. Louis and Sara (Grabelsky) Shapiro; m. Jane Wilkins Bennett, June 19, 1954; 1 child: Lynn Mayson. Grad., Horace Mann Sch., 1950; AB magna cum laude, Harvard U., 1954, LLB summa cum laude, 1957. Bar: DC 1957, Mass. 1964. Assoc. Covington & Burling, Washington, 1957-62; law clk. to Justice John M. Harlan US Supreme Ct., 1962-63; asst. prof. law Harvard Law Sch., Cambridge, Mass., 1963—66, prof., 1966—84, William Nelson Cromwell prof. law, 1984—2006, emeritus, 2006—, assoc. dean, 1971-76; dep. solicitor gen. US Dept. Justice, Washington, 1989—91. Vis. prof. U. Pa., 1968, U. Stanford, 1969, NYU, 2003, 05, U. Ariz., 2004. Author: Federalism: A Dialogue, 1995, Civil Procedure: Preclusion in Civil Actions, 2001; co-author: The Federal Courts and the Federal System, 1973, 88, 96, 2003, 09; editor: The Evolution of a Judicial Philosophy: Selected Opinions of Justice John M. Harlan, 1969, The Judicial Code and the Rules of Procedure in the Federal Courts, annually 1988-2000. Mem.: Am. Law Inst. Office: Harvard Law Sch 1563 Massachusetts Ave Cambridge MA 02138 Office Fax: 617-495-1950. Business E-Mail: dshapiro@law.harvard.edu.

SHAPIRO, DEBRA L., finance educator, consultant; b. Washington, Mar. 29, 1960; d. Herbert Shapiro and Madelyn Hope Rubinstein Shapiro. BA in Psychology with honors, U. Md., Coll. Pk., 1982; MS, Northwestern U., Evanston, Ill., 1983, PhD in Orgn. Behavior, 1986. Asst. prof. mgmt. U. NC, Chapel Hill Kenan-Flagler Bus. Sch., 1986—91, assoc. prof. mgmt., 1992—95, prof. mgmt., 1996—99, assoc. dean PhD programs, 1998—2001, Willard J. Graham disting. prof. mgmt., 2000—03; prof. mgmt. U. Md., Robert H. Smith Sch. Bus., Coll.

Pk., 2003—05, Clarice Smith prof. mgmt., 2006—, assoc. dean PhD programs, 2008—. Author: (book) Managing Multinational Teams: Global Perspectives; contbr. articles to profl. jours. Cato fellow, U. NC's Kenan-Flagler Bus. Sch., 1999—2001. Mem.: Acad. Mgmt. (chair conflict mgmt. divsn. 1995—96, rep.-at-large bd. govs. 2002—05, assoc. editor 2005—07), Soc. Orgnl. Behavior. Avocations: piano, theater, singing. Office: Robert H Smith Sch Bus Univ Md 4520 Van Munching Hall College Park MD 20742 Office Fax: 301-314-8787. Business E-Mail: dshapiro@rhsmith.umd.edu.

SHAPIRO, EDWARD MURAY, dermatologist; b. Denver, Oct. 6, 1924; s. Isador Benjamin and Sara (Berezin) Shapiro; m. Ruth Young, Oct. 14, 1944; children: Adrian Michael, Stefanie Ann; m. Dorothy Rosmarin, July 22, 1990. Studied, U. Colo., 1941—43; AB with honors, U. Tex., 1948, MD, 1952. Diplomate Am. Bd. Dermatology. Intern Jefferson Coll. Medicine Hosp., Phila., 1952—53; resident in dermatology U. Tex. Med. Br., Galveston, 1953—55, Henry Ford Hosp., Detroit, 1955—56, assoc. in dermatology divsn., 1956—57; clin. instr., dermatology Baylor U. Coll. Medicine, Houston, 1957—68, assoc. clin. prof., 1968—, Columbia Bayshore Hosp., 1962—; active staff mem. Meml. Hosp. S.E., Houston, 2000. Contbr. articles to profl. jours. With USAAF, 1943—46. Grantee, Henry J.N. Taub, 1958—60. Fellow: Am. Acad. Dermatology; mem.: AMA, Am. Physicians Art Assn., Am. Physicians Art Assn. (v.p. 1993, pres. 2003—04, 2003—04, 2004—05), Houston Dermatology Assn., Harris County Med. Assn. (pres., S.E. br. 1968—69), South Ctrl. Dermatol. Assn. (bd. dirs. 1987—88), Tex. Dermatol. Soc. (pres.-elect 1988, pres. 1989—90), Tex. Med. Assn., Rotary Internat. (Paul Harris fellow 1995, 1997), B'nai B'rith. Republican. Jewish. Avocations: painting, sports. Office: 4419 Crenshaw Pasadena TX 77504 Office Phone: 281-991-5944.

SHAPIRO, EDWARD ROBERT, psychiatrist, educator, health facility administrator, psychotherapist; b. Boston, Sept. 13, 1941; s. Jacob and Ruth (Yankelovich) S.; m. Donna Elmendorf; 1 child, Joshua Jackson; 1 child from previous marriage, Jacob Matthew; 1 stepchild, Zachary Andrew Robbins. BA magna cum laude, Yale U., 1962; MA in Anthropology, Stanford U., 1966; MD, Harvard U., 1968. Diplomate Am. Bd. Psychiatry and Neurology. Intern in medicine Beth Israel Hosp., Boston, 1968-69; resident in psychiatry Mass. Mental Health Ctr., Boston, 1969-72, chief resident in psychiatry, 1971-72; clin. assoc. NIMH, Bethesda, Md., 1972-74; dir. Adolescent and Family Treatment and Study Ctr. McLean Hosp., Belmont, Mass., 1974-89, dir. Psychosocial Tng. and Consultation, 1989-91; bd. dirs. Ctr. for Study of Groups and Social Systems, Boston, 1983-90, A.K. Rice Inst., Washington, 1983-90, dir. Nat. Group Rels. Conf., 1989-91; faculty mem. Boston Psychoanalytic Inst., 1978—; assoc. clin. prof. psychiatry Harvard Med. Sch., Boston, 1982—; med. dir., CEO The Austen Riggs Ctr., Stockbridge, Mass., 1991—; tng. and supr. analyst Psychoanalytical Inst. of the Berkshires, 2003—; clin. prof. psychiatry Yale U. Sch. Medicine, 2009—. Dir. The Erik H. Erikson Inst. for Edn. and Rsch., 1994-2000. Co-author: (with A.W. Carr) Lost in Familiar Places: Creating New Connections Between the Individual and Society, 1991; editor: The Inner World in the Outer World: Psychoanalytic Perspectives, 1997; mem. editorial bd. Jour. Adolescence, 1977-82, Psychiatry, 1988—; assoc. editor Jour. Adolescence, 1982-84; contbr. articles to profl. jours. Mem. Yale Russian Chorus. With USPHS, 1972-74. Recipient Isenberg Teaching award McLean Hosp., 1980, Rsch. prize Soc. for Family Therapy and Rsch., 1984, Felix and Helen Deutsch Sci. prize Boston Psychoanalytic Inst., 1980, Outstanding Psychiatrist for Advancement of the Profession award Mass. Psychiat. Assn., 2007. Fellow Am. Psychiat. Assn. (disting. life), Am. Coll. Psychoanalysis, A.K. Rice Inst.; mem. Am. Psychoanalytic Assn. Achievements include helping develop the Erik H. Erikson Inst. for Edn. and Rsch. as a vehicle for applying the clinical insights developed at Riggs to larger social issues. Avocation: music. Office: The Austen Riggs Ctr PO Box 962 25 Main St Stockbridge MA 01262-0962

SHAPIRO, ELI, business consultant, educator, economist; b. Bklyn., June 13, 1916; s. Samuel and Pauline (Kushel) S.; m. Beatrice Ferbend, Jan. 18, 1946 (dec. July 1999); 1 child, Laura J. AB, Bklyn. Coll., 1936; A.M., Columbia U., 1937, PhD, 1939. Instr. Bklyn. Coll., 1936-41; rsch. assoc. Nat. Bur. Econ. Rsch., 1938-39, cons., 1939-42, mem. rsch. staff, 1955-62; asst. prof. fin. U. Chgo., 1946-47, assoc. prof., 1948-52, prof., 1952; prof. fin. Mass. Inst. Tech., 1952-61; assoc. dean Mass. Inst. Tech. (Sch. Indsl. Mgmt.), 1954-58, Alfred P. Sloan prof. mgmt., 1976-84, Alfred P. Sloan prof. emeritus, 1984—; prof. fin. Harvard Bus. Sch., 1962-72, Sylvan C. Coleman prof. fin. mgmt., 1968-72; chmn. fin. com., dir. Travelers Ins. Cos., Hartford, Conn., 1971-78, vice chmn. bd., dir., 1976-78; chmn. bd. Mass. Co., 1971-72; pres. Nat. Bur. Econ. Research, 1982-84. Chmn. bd. Fed. Home Loan Bank Boston, 1970-89; econ. analyst div. monetary rsch. US Dept. Treasury, 1941-42; economist rsch. div. OPA, 1941-42; staff cons. Com. Econ. Devel., 1950-51, mem. rsch. adv. com., 1961-64, 69—, project dir., 1966-69; cons. sec. treasury; mem. enforcement commn. WSB, 1952-53; cons. Inst. Def. Analyses; dep. dir. Rsch. Com. Money Credit, 1959-61. Author: (with others) Personal Finance Industry and Its Credit Standards, 1939, (with Steiner) Money and Banking, 1941, Development of Wisconsin Credit Union Movement, 1947, Money and Banking, 1953, (with others), 1958, (with D. Meiselman) Measurement of Corporate Sources and Uses of Funds, 1964, (with others) Money and Banking, 1969, (with Wolf) The Role of Private Placement in Corporate Finance, 1972; Editor: (with W.L. White) Capital for Productivity and Growth, 1977. Served from ensign to lt. USNR, 1942-46. Recipient Econ. Dept. award Bklyn. Coll., 1936, Honors Day award distinguished alumni, 1949 Fellow Am. Acad. Arts and Scis.; mem. Nat. Bur. Econ. Research (pres.), Am. Econ. Assn., Council Fgn. Relations, Am. Fin. Assn. Home and Office: 180 Beacon St Boston MA 02116-1408 Office Phone: 617-266-5512.

SHAPIRO, EUGENE DAVID, pediatrician, epidemiologist, educator; s. Jonah R. and Rita R. Shapiro; m. Susan K. Bowers; children: Lauren R., Amy E., Daniel J. BA, Yale Coll., New Haven, Conn., 1970; MD, U. Calif., San Francisco, 1976. Resident Children's Hosp. Pitts., 1976—79; asst. prof. pediat. Yale Sch. Medicine, New Haven, 1983—89, assoc. prof. pediat., 1989—93, prof. pediat., 1993—. Grantee, NIH, 1983—; fellow, Children's Hosp. Pitts., 1979—81; Robert Wood Johnson scholar, Yale Sch. Medicine, 1981—83. Fellow: Am. Acad. Pediat.; mem.: Am. Epidemiologic Assn., Pediatric Infectious Disease Soc., Infectious Disease Soc. Am., Soc. Pediatric Rsch., Am. Pediatric Soc., Am. Bd. Pediatrics-Infectious Diseases. Achievements include research in assessment of clinical effectiveness of vaccines. Office: Yale U Dept Pediatrics 333 Cedar St PO Box 208064 New Haven CT 06520-8064

SHAPIRO, EVE ILANA, medical researcher; b. Framingham, Mass., Apr. 6, 1976; d. Paul and Ania Shapiro; life ptnr. Mindy Stevens. BA, Ind. U., Bloomington, 1998; MA, U. Calif., Santa Barbara, 2002, PhD, 2005. Author: (book) Gender Circuits: The Evolution of Bodies in the Technological Age; contbr. articles to profl. jours. Recipient Phi Beta Kappa award, Ind. U., 1998; Humanities and Social Scis. Rsch. grant, U. Calif., 2004, Grad. Divsn. Dissertation fellowship, 2005, Gen. Edn. Course Devel. grant, U. Conn., 2007—. Mem.: Am. Sociol. Assn. (coun. mem. 2008—, Martin Levine Dissertation fellowship 2004, Grad. Paper award 2005, Grad. Student Paper award 2007). Jewish. Office: Univ Conn Storrs 354 Mansfield Dr Storrs Mansfield CT 06269 Business E-Mail: eve.shapiro@uconn.edu.

SHAPIRO, FRED DAVID, lawyer; b. Cleve., Nov. 10, 1926; s. Isadore R. and Lottie (Turetsky) S.; m. Helen Solomon, Sept. 5, 1948; children— Gary N., Ira R., Diane S. BA cum laude, Ohio State U., 1949; LL.B., Harvard U., 1954. Bar: Ohio 1954. Since practiced in, Cleve.; sr. ptnr. Shapiro and Lodwick, Co., L.P.A, 1994—. Served with USNR, 1945-46. Mem. Ohio State Bar Assn., Cleve. Met. Bar Assn., The Rowfant Club, Phi Beta Kappa. Jewish. Home: 29226 S Woodland Rd Cleveland OH 44124-5737 Office Phone: 216-378-9730. Personal E-mail: fshapo@aol.com.

SHAPIRO, GARY EVAN, newspaper journalist; b. Lewiston, Maine, Feb. 5, 1964; s. Sherman George and Charlotte (Cominsky) S. AB, Harvard U., 1986; JD, Columbia U., 1993. Assoc. Skadden Arps Slate Meagher & Flom, NYC, 1993-94; writer, event prodr. NYC, 1994-99; journalist Forward newspaper, NYC, 1999—. Contbg. editor Am. Scholar, 2000—; note editor Columbia Jour. Environ. Law, 1993; contbr. numerous articles to profl. jours.; prodr. numerous programs on diplomacy, history, arch., bus., arts and lit., politics and econs., sci., edn., philosophy. Recipient Charles William Eliot medal for Citizenship, 1986, Cox Medal, Phillips Exeter, 1982; John Finley Traveling fellow, 1986. Mem. Overseas Press Club, Nat. Arts Club (lit. com. 1997—), Harvard Club (program com. 1995-2000). Avocation: book collecting. Home: 27 W 44th St # 50 New York NY 10036-6613 Office: Forward Newspaper 45 E 33rd St New York NY 10016-5336

SHAPIRO, GEORGE HOWARD, retired lawyer; b. St. Louis, Nov. 10, 1936; s. Isadore T. and Alice (Schucart) S.; m. Mary Kenney Leonard, 1977 (div. 1994); m. Ray Ann Kremer, 1999; 1 child, Ellen. BA, Harvard U., 1958, LLB, 1961; postgrad., London Sch. Econs., 1961-62. Bar: Ga. 1960, D.C. 1963. Atty. U.S. Dept. Labor, Washington, 1962-63; assoc. Arent Fox Kintner Plotkin & Kahn, Washington, 1963-69, ptnr., 1970-99; ret., 2000. Co-author: 'Cable Speech' The Case for First Amendment Protection, 1983; editor: New Program Opportunities in the Electronic Media, 1983, Current Developments in CATV, 1981. With USAR, 1962-68. Frank Knox Meml. fellow Harvard U., 1961-62. Mem. D.C. Bar Assn., Fed. Communications Bar Assn. Democrat. Jewish. Avocation: skiing. Home: Apt 906 3180 Mathieson Dr NE Atlanta GA 30305-1871 E-mail: GHSinATL@aol.com.

SHAPIRO, HAROLD TAFLER, economics professor, former academic administrator; b. Montreal, Que., Can., June 8, 1935; s. Maxwell and Mary (Tafler) Shapiro; m. Vivian Bernice Rapoport, May 19, 1957; children: Anne, Marilyn, Janet, Karen. BComm, McGill U., Montreal, 1956; PhD in Econs. (Harold Helm fellow, Harold Dodds sr. fellow), Princeton U., NJ, 1964. From asst. prof. to assoc. prof. econ. U. Mich., Ann Arbor, 1964—70, prof., 1970—76, prof. econ. and pub. affairs, 1977, chmn. dept. econ., 1974—77, v.p. acad. affairs, 1977—79, pres., 1980—87; rsch. adv. Bank Can., 1965-72; pres. Princeton U., 1988—2001, pres. emeritus, prof. economics & pub. affairs Woodrow Wilson Sch., 2001—. Mem. exec. com. Assn. of Am. Universities, 1985—89; trustee NJ Commn. Sci. and Tech., 1988—91; mem. Pres.'s Coun. Advisors Sci. and Tech., 1990—92, Stem Cell Inst. of NJ Joint Bd. Mgrs., 2005—; chmn. com. employer-based health benefits Inst. Medicine, 1991, Nat. Acad. Sci. Com. Americas Energy Future, 2007—; bd. overseers Robert Wood Johnson Med. Sch., 2000—; bd. dir. The Hastings Ctr., Reading is Fundamental, Knight Found. Comm. on Intercollegiate Athletics, Merck Vaccine Adv. Bd., Princeton Healthcare Sys.; bd. trustees U. Medicine & Dentistry NJ, 2006—; trustee tech. Israel Inst. Tech., 2002—; chmn. Orgn. NIH Nat. Sci., 2000—03, mem. adv. com. Human Embryonic Stem Cell Rsch., 2006—; chmn. bd. DeVry Inst., 2008—. Author: A Larger Sense of Purpose: Higher Education and Society, 2005; editor (with William G. Bowen): Universities and Their Leadership, 1998; editor: (with James F. Childress & Eric M. Meslin) Belmont Revisited: Ethical Principles for Research With Human Subjects, 2005. Chair Nat. Bioethics Adv. Commn., 1996—2001; chmn. spl. Presdl. com. Rsch. Librs. Group, 1980—89; mem. Gov.'s High Tech. Task Force, Mich., 1980—87, Gov.'s Commn. Jobs and Econ. Devel., Mich., 1983—87, Carnegie Commn. Coll. Retirement, 1984—86; dir. Am. Coun. Edn., 1989—91; mem. Pres. Bush Coun. Advisors Sci. and Tech., 1990—93; trustee Alfred P. Sloan Found., 1980—, Interlochen Ctr. Arts, 1988—95, U. Pa. Med. Ctr., 1992—, Univ. Corp. Advanced Internet Devel., 2000, Am. Jewish Com., 2002—, Ednl. Testing Svc., 1994—2000. Recipient Lt. Gov.'s medal in commerce, McGill U., 1956, William D. Carey Lectureship award Leadership in Sci. Policy, 2006. Fellow: AAAS, Mich. Soc. Fellows (sr.); mem.: Am. Philos. Soc., Inst. Medicine of NAS/NRC, Univs. Rsch. Assn. (trustee 1988—2001). Office: Princeton Univ Woodrow Wilson Sch 359 Wallace Hall Princeton NJ 08544 Office Phone: 609-258-6184. Business E-Mail: hts@princeton.edu.

SHAPIRO, HARRY DEAN, lawyer; b. Louisville, June 21, 1940; s. Herman Shapiro and Toby (Spector) Levy; m. Linda Siegel, Dec. 19, 1970; 1 child, Deborah Anne. BS, U. Louisville, 1962, JD, 1964. Bar: Ky. 1964, D.C. 1968, Md. 1970. Trial and appellate atty. U.S. Dept. Justice, Washington, 1964-70; assoc. Venable, Baetjer & Howard, Balt., 1970-74, ptnr., 1975-87; sr. ptnr., head of tax practice Weinberg & Green, Balt., 1987—98, chmn. corp. dept., 1993-95; transaction group coord., 1995-98; head tax practice Saul Ewing LLP (formerly Saul, Ewing, Remick & Saul LLP), 1998-99; chmn. tax group Saul Ewing LLP (formerly Saul, Ewing, Remick & Saul LLP), 1999—. Author: Federal Tax Liens, 1981, The Successful Practice, 2005; contbr. articles to profl. jours. Mem. Md. State Bd. Edn., 1990-97; v.p. Assoc. Jewish Charities of Balt., Inc. 1991-94; vice chmn. The Assoc. Jewish Cmty. Fedn. Balt. 1987-89, asst. treas., 1989-91, mem. exec. com., 1993-97; trustee Sinai Hosp., Balt., 1987-90; counsel Balt. Mus. Art, 1984-97, trustee, 1984-96, sec., 1985-92, v.p., sec., 1992-94, v.p., 1994-96; dir., 1989-96; chmn. Joint Budgeting Coun., 1993-96, Coun. Jewish Fedns.; trustee Acad. Art Mus., Easton, 1998-2005. Capt. USAR, 1967-70. Recipient Disting. Alumni award Brandeis Sch. of Law, 1996, Chmn.'s award Balt. Mus. Art, 1996, Named One Of Md. Super Lawyer, Law & Politics Mag. and Balt. Mag., 2007-. Mem. ABA (tax sect.), Md. State Bar Assn., Ky. Bar Assn., D.C. Bar Assn., Md. Club, Center Club. Home: 717 S President St Unit 602 Baltimore MD 21202 Office: Saul Ewing LLP Lockwood Pl 500 E Pratt St Baltimore MD 21202-3133 Office Phone: 410-332-8658. Business E-Mail: hshapiro@saul.com. *Our country is at a crossroads in its history, and it is becoming clear that a sea change is necessary. Basic reforms must occur in our governmental and educational structures. The question is whether we have the intelligence to reject the cries for bigger government and more taxes to solve these problems when fundamental action is required.*

SHAPIRO, HARVEY, poet; b. Chgo., Jan. 27, 1924; s. Jacob J. and Dorothy (Cohen) S.; m. Edna Lewis Kaufman, July 23, 1953 (div.); children: Saul, Dan. BA, Yale U., 1947; MA, Columbia U., 1948. Instr. English Cornell U., 1949-50, 51-52; creative writing fellow Bard Coll., 1950-51; mem. editl. staff Commentary, New Yorker, 1955-57, N.Y. Times Mag., NYC, 1957, asst. editor, 1964-75; editor N.Y. Times Book Rev., 1975-83; dep. editor N.Y. Times Mag., 1983-96, consulting editor, 1996—2002. Author: The Eye, 1953, The Book and Other Poems, 1955, Mountain, Fire Thornbush, 1961, Battle Report, 1966, This World, 1971, Lauds, 1975, Nightsounds, 1978, The Light Holds, 1984, National Cold Storage Company, 1988, A Day's Portion, 1994, Selected Poems, 1997, How Charlie Shaver Died and Other Poems, 2001; editor: Poets of World War II, 2003, The Sights Along the Harbor: New and Collected Poems, 2006. With USAAF, World War II. Decorated D.F.C., Air medal with 3 oak leaf clusters.; Rockefeller Found. grantee in poetry, 1967 Club: Elizabethan (New Haven), Century (N.Y.).

SHAPIRO, HOWARD M., lawyer, former prosecutor; b. May 8, 1960; BA magna cum laude, Williams Coll., 1982; JD, Yale Univ., 1985. Bar: NY 1986, DC 1997. Law clk. Judge Pierre N. Leval, US Dist. Ct. (so. NY dist.), 1985—87; asst. U.S. atty. U.S. Dept. Justice, so. NY dist., 1987—92; gen. counsel FBI, Washington, 1993—97; ptnr., co-chmn. Litigation dept., co-chmn. investigations & criminal litigation group Wilmer Cutler Pickering Hale & Dorr, Washington. Assoc. prof. Cornell Law Sch. Contbr. articles to newspapers. Recipient Nat. Intelligence Disting. Svc. medal, dir. of Ctrl. Intelligence, 1997; named one of Top DC Lawyers, Washingtonian mag., 2002, 2004, DC Go-to Litigators, Legal Times, 2003. Office: Wilmer Cutler Pickering Hale & Dorr 1875 Pennsylvania Ave NW Washington DC 20006 Office Phone: 202-663-6606. Office Fax: 202-663-6363. Business E-Mail: howard.shapiro@wilmerhale.com.

SHAPIRO, IRWIN IRA, physicist, researcher; b. NYC, Oct. 10, 1929; s. Samuel and Esther (Feinberg) S.; m. Marian Helen Kaplun, Dec. 20, 1959; children: Steven, Nancy. AB, Cornell U., 1950; A.M., Harvard U., 1951, PhD, 1955. Mem. staff Lincoln Lab. MIT, Lexington, 1954-70; Sherman Fairchild Distinguished scholar Calif. Inst. Tech., 1974; Morris Loeb lectr. physics Harvard, 1975; prof. geophysics and physics MIT, 1967-80, Schlumberger prof., 1980-84; Paine prof. practical astronomy, prof. physics Harvard U., 1982-97; sr. scientist Smithsonian Astrophys. Obs., 1982—; dir. Harvard-Smithsonian Ctr. for Astrophysics, 1983—2004; prof. Harvard U./Timken, 1997—. Cons. NSF, NASA. Contbr. articles to profl. jours. Recipient Albert A. Michelson medal Franklin Inst., 1975, award in phys. and math. scis. N.Y. Acad. Scis., 1982, Einstein medal Einstein Soc. Bern, 1994, Joseph Henry medal Smithsonian Instn., 2004; Guggenheim fellow, 1982. Fellow AAAS, Am. Geophys. Union (Charles A. Whitten medal 1991, William Bowie medal 1993), Am. Phys. Soc.; mem. AAAS, NAS (Benjamin Apthorp Gould prize 1979), Am. Astron. Soc. (Dannie Heineman award 1983, Dirk Brouwer award 1987, Gerard Kuiper award 1997), Am. Philos. Soc., Internat. Astron. Union, Phi Beta Kappa, Sigma Xi, Phi Kappa Phi. Home: 17 Lantern Ln Lexington MA 02421-6029 Office: Harvard-Smithsonian Ctr Astrophysics 60 Garden St Cambridge MA 02138-1516 Business E-Mail: ishapiro@cfa.harvard.edu.

SHAPIRO, ISAAC, lawyer; b. Tokyo, Jan. 5, 1931; arrived in U.S., 1946, naturalized, 1951; s. Constantine and Lydia (Chernetzky) S.; m. Jacqueline M. Weiss, Sept. 16, 1956; children: Tobias, Alexandra, Natasha. AB, Columbia U., 1954, LLB, 1956; postgrad., U. Paris, 1956—57. Bar: N.Y. 1957, U.S. Supreme Ct. 1971, Paris 1991. Assoc. Milbank, Tweed, Hadley & McCloy, NYC, 1956-65, ptnr., 1966-86, resident ptnr. Tokyo, 1977-79; ptnr. Skadden Arps Slate Meagher & Flom LLP, NYC, 1986—2001; resident ptnr. Skadden Arps Slate Meagher & Flom, Hong Kong, 1989-90, Paris, 1990—2001; of counsel Skadden Arps Slate Meagher & Flom LLP, NYC, 2001—; ptnr. Skadden Arps Slate Meagher & Flom (Europe) LLP, 2006—; tchg. fellow comparative law NYU, 1959-61. Lectr. Soviet law, 1961-67; adj. asst. prof. NYU, 1967-69, adj. assoc. prof., 1969-71, 74-75; adj. prof., dir. Russian legal studies Columbia Law Sch., 1999-2000. Author: (with Hazard and Maggs) The Soviet Legal System, 1969, Japan: The Risen Sun (in Japanese), 1982, Edokko: Growing Up a Foreigner in Wartime Japan, 2009; editor: The Middle East Crisis-Prospects for Peace, 1969; contbr. articles to profl. jours. Mem. Joint Com. US-Japan Cultural and Ednl. Cooperation, Washington, 1972—78, Japan-US Friendship Commn., 1976—78; mem. svcs. policy adv. com. to US Trade Rep., 1982—91; trustee Nat. Humanities Ctr., Triangle Park, NC, 1978—89, Bank of Tokyo Mitsubishi Found., 1986—; trustee, v.p. Chamber Music Soc. Lincoln Ctr., 1980—86; pres. Japan Soc., NYC, 1970—77; trustee Isamu Noguchi Zaidan, Japan, 1999—, Isamu Noguchi Found., NY, 1985—, pres., 1985—2005; trustee, chmn. Ise Cultural Found., 1984—90; bd. advisors Trust for Mutual Understanding, NYC, 1985—; dir. Bank of Tokyo-Mitsubishi Trust Co., NY, 1975—77, 1980—2001, Japan Soc., 1969—77, 1979—80; bd. dirs. Bus. Coun. for Internat. Understanding, 1989—95, Nat. Com. US-China Rels., 1989—95, Asian Cultural Coun., 1980—. With US Army, 1950—52. Fulbright scholar, 1956-57; decorated Order of the Rising Sun gold rays and neck ribbon Emperor Japan, 2006. Mem.: ABA, N.Y. State Bar Assn., Coun. Fgn. Rels., Japan Soc. N.Y. (trustee 1969—77, 1979—80, pres. 1970—77), Century Assn. (N.Y.C.), Cercle de l'Union Interalliee (Paris), Royal Automobile Club (London). Office: Skadden Arps Slate Meagher & Flom LLP 4 Times Sq New York NY 10036-6522 Office Phone: 212-735-3480. Business E-Mail: isaac.shapiro@skadden.com.

SHAPIRO, JAMES EDWARD, judge; b. Chgo., May 28, 1930; BS, U. Wis., 1951; JD, Harvard U., 1954. Bar: Wis. 1956, U.S. Dist. Ct. (ea. dist.) Wis. 1956, U.S. Ct. Appeals (7th cir.) 1962, U.S. Supreme Ct. 1971. Sole practice, Milw., 1956-57; resident house counsel Nat. Presto Industries, Eau Claire, Wis., 1957-60; ptnr. Bratt & Shapiro, Milw., 1960-64; sole practice Milw., 1964-74; ptnr. Frank, Hiller & Shapiro, Milw., 1974-82; judge U.S. Bankruptcy Ct., Milw., 1982—, chief judge, 1996-2000. Mem. Bayside Bd. Appeals, Wis., 1969-77; Milwaukee County Ct. commr., 1969-78; dir. Milw. Legal Aid Soc., 1969-77. Served to 1st lt. U.S. Army, 1954-56. Jewish. Office: US Courthouse 140 Fed Bldg 517 E Wisconsin Ave Milwaukee WI 53202-4500 Office Phone: 414-297-3291 ext. 3201. Business E-Mail: james_e_shapiro@wieb.uscourts.gov.

SHAPIRO, JEFFREY A., legislative staff member; BA in Polit. Sci., U. Ill., Urbana-Champaign, 2001. Washington rep. Gen. Mills, Inc., 2002—06; sr. legis. aide for Rep. Lee Terry US House of Reps., Washington, 2001—02, chief of staff for Rep. Adrian Smith, 2007—. Office: Office of Congressman Adrian Smith 503 Cannon House Office Bldg Washington DC 20515 Office Phone: 202-225-6435. Business E-Mail: jeff.shapiro@mail.house.gov.*

SHAPIRO, JEFFREY HOWARD, electrical engineering professor, consultant; s. Reuven Paul and Eve Shapiro; m. Ellen Arlene Kirschenbaum, June 21, 1969; children: Lisa Ann Rindler, David Michael. SB in Elec. Engring., MIT, Cambridge, Mass., 1967, SM in Elec. Engring., 1968, EE in Elec. Engring., 1969, PhD in Elec. Engring., 1970. Asst. prof. elec. engring. and applied physics Case Western Res. U., Cleve., 1970—73; assoc. prof. elec. engring. MIT, Cambridge, Mass., 1973—85, prof. elec. engring., 1985—, assoc. head dept. elec. engring. and computer sci., 1989—99, Julius A. Stratton prof. elec. engring., 1999—, dir., rsch. lab. electronics, 2001—. Cons. Lincoln Lab. MIT, Lexington, 1977—; corp. mem. C. S. Draper Lab., Cambridge, 2001—.

Contbr. over 100 articles to profl. jours. Recipient Tchg. award, MIT Grad. Student Coun., 1979, Quantum Electronics award, IEEE Lasers & Electro Optics, 2008, Quantum Communication award, 2008. Fellow: IEEE (assoc. editor, ieee transactions on info. theory 1979—82), Am. Phys. Soc., Inst. Physics, Optical Soc. of Am. (assoc. editor, jour. of the optical soc. of am. 1980—83); mem.: SPIE, Eta Kappa Nu, Sigma Xi, Tau Beta Pi. Achievements include patents for microchannel spatial light modulator; patents pending for converting optical information encoding; selecting optical waves; phase conjugate optical coherence tomography methods and apparatus; research in field. Avocations: travel, ballroom dance, philately. Office: MIT 77 Massachusetts Ave Cambridge MA 02139 Office Fax: 617-253-1301. Business E-Mail: jhs@mit.edu.

SHAPIRO, JOAN ISABELLE, lab administrator, medical/surgical nurse; b. Aug. 26, 1943; d. Macy James and Frieda Lockhart; m. Ivan Lee Shapiro, Dec. 28, 1968; children: Audrey, Michael. Diploma, Peoria Meth. Sch. Nursing, 1964. RN. Nurse Nurse Grant Hosp., Columbus, Ohio, 1975—76, Cardiac Thoracic and Vascular Surgeons Ltd., Geneva, Ill., 1977—97, mgr. non-ivasive lab., 1979—97. Owner operator Shapiro's Mastiff's 1976-82; sec.-treas. Sounds Svcs., 1976—, Mainstream Sounds Inc., 1980-84; co-founder Cardio-Phone Inc., 1982-99, Edgewater Vascular Inst., 1987-89, Associated Profls., 1989-92; v.p. Computer Specialists Inc., 1986-89; founder, pres. Vein Ctr., Edema Ctr. Ltd. Mem. DAR (sec. Katahdin Valley-Lydia Putman chpt. 2004—08), Soc. Noninvasive Technologists, Soc. Peripheral Vascular Nursing (cmty. awareness com. 1984-2004), Kane County Med. Soc. Aux. (pres. 1983-84, adviser, 1984-85), Katahdin Valley Putnam Cpt. of DAR (sec. 2004-08). Lutheran. Home: Cardiac Thoracic/Vas Surg PO Box 325 Fort Fairfield ME 04742-0325 Business E-Mail: joan@ivanshapiro.com.

SHAPIRO, JUDITH R., former academic administrator, anthropology educator; b. NYC, Jan. 24, 1942; Student, Ecole des Haute Etudes Inst. d'Etudes Politiques, Paris, 1961—62; BA, Brandeis U., 1963; PhD, Columbia U., 1972, LLD (hon.), 2008. Asst. prof. U. Chgo., 1970—75; fellow U. Calif., Berkeley, 1974—75; Rosalyn R. Schwartz lectr., asst. prof. anthropology Bryn Mawr Coll., Pa., 1975—78, assoc. prof. Pa., 1978—85, prof. Pa., 1985—94; pres. Barnard Coll., 1994—2008. Chmn. dept. Bryn Mawr Coll., 1982—85, acting dean undergrad coll., 1985—86, provost, 1986—94; bd. dir. Fund for City of NY; ptnr. NYC Partnership and C. of C.; exec. com. NY Bldg. Congress. Contbr. articles to profl. jours. Nat. adv. com. Woodrow Wilson Nat. Fellowship Found.; chair bd. dirs. Consortium on Financing Higher Edn.; bd. dirs. Fund for the City of N.Y.; chair bd. dirs. Women's Coll. Coalition. Recipient Gold Medal, Nat. Inst. of Social Sciences, 2002, Barnard Medal of Distinction, 2008; grantee Summer Field Tng. grant, NSF, 1965, Ford Found., 1966, NIMH, 1974—75, Social Sci. Rsch. Coun., 1974—75; fellow, Woodrow Wilson Found., 1963—64, Columbia U., 1964—65, Younger Humanist fellow, NEH, 1974—75, Am. Coun. Learned Socs., 1981—82, Ctr. for Advanced Study in the Behavioral Scis., 1989. Fellow: Am. Acad. Arts & Scis.; mem.: NY State Leadership Coun. (devel. of World's Mus., NYC), Am. Philos. Soc., Social Sci. Rsch. Coun. (com. social sci personnel 1977—80), Am. Anthrop. Assn. (ethics com. 1976—79, bd. dirs. 1984—86, exec. com. 1985—86), Am. Ethnol. Soc. (nominations com. 1983—84, pres. elect 1984—85, pres. 1985—86), Phila. Anthrop. Soc. (pres. 1983), Morningside Area Alliance (pres. 2003—04), adv. com, Save the Children, Women's Forum, Sigma Xi, Phi Beta Kappa. Office Phone: 212-854-2021.

SHAPIRO, KEITH J., lawyer; b. Chgo., Nov. 14, 1958; BS, Univ. Ill., 1980; JD, Emory Univ., 1983. Bar: Ill. 1983. Former chmn., pres. Am. Bankruptcy Inst.; co-mng. shareholder, co-chair nat. bus. reorganization and bankruptcy practice Greenberg Traurig LLP, Chgo. Fellow: Am. Coll. Bankruptcy; mem.: INSOL Internat. (bd. dirs.), Am. Bankruptcy Bd. of Certification (founder, first chmn. 1992—95), R3, London, Chgo. Bar Assn. (chair, bankruptcy and reorganization com. 1999—2000), Am. Bankruptcy Inst. (pres. 2000—01, chmn.bd. 2002—03). Office: Greenberg Traurig LLP Ste 3100 77 W Wacker Dr Chicago IL 60601 Office Phone: 312-456-8405. Office Fax: 312-456-8435. Business E-Mail: shapirok@gtlaw.com.

SHAPIRO, LARRY J., dean, educator, pediatrician; b. July 6, 1946; s. Philip and Phyllis Shapiro; m. Carol-Ann Uetake; children: Jennifer, Jessica, Brian. AB, Washington U., St. Louis, 1968, MD, 1971. Diplomate Am. Bd. Pediat., Am. Bd. Med. Examiners, Am. Bd. Med. Genetics. Intern St. Louis Children's Hosp., 1971—72, resident, 1971—73; rsch. assoc. NIH, Bethesda, Md., 1973—75; asst. prof. Sch. Medicine UCLA, 1975—79, assoc. prof., 1979—83, prof. pediat. and biol. chemistry, 1983—91; investigator Howard Hughes Med. Inst., 1987—91, investigator, W.H. and Marie Wattis Disting. prof.; prof., chmn. dept. pediat. U. Calif.-San Francisco Sch. Medicine, 1991—2003; chief pediat. svcs. U. Calif.-San Francisco Med. Ctr., 1991—2003; Spencer T. and Ann W. Olin Disting. prof., exec. vice chancellor for med. affairs, dean Washington U. Sch. Medicine, St. Louis, 2003—. Contbr. numerous articles to profl. publs. Served to lt. comdr. USPHS, 1973—75. Fellow: AAAS, Am. Acad. Pediat. (E. Mead Johnson award in rsch. 1982); mem.: Am. Acad. Arts and Scis., Am. Pediatric Soc. (coun. mem. 1999—2001, pres. 2003—04), Am. Soc. Clin. Investigation, Am. Soc. Human Genetics (coun. 1985—88, pres.-elect 1995, pres. 1997), Assn. Am. Physicians, Soc. for Inherited Metabolic Disease (coun. 1983—88, pres. 1986—87), Western Soc. for Pediatric Rsch. (coun. 1983—87, pres. 1989—90, Ross award in rsch. 1981), Soc. Pediatric Rsch. (coun. 1984—87, pres. 1991—92), Inst. Medicine (coun. mem.). Office: Wash U 660 S Euclid campus box 8106 Saint Louis MO 63110

SHAPIRO, LEO J., social researcher; b. NYC, July 8, 1921; m. Virginia L. Johnson, Feb. 9, 1952; children: David, Erik, Owen, Amy. BA, U. Chgo., 1942, PhD, 1952. Survey specialist Fed. Govt. Agy., Washington, 1941-45, Sci. Rsch. Assn., Chgo., 1948-52; prin., founder Leo J. Shapiro and Assocs., Chgo., 1952-91; pres. SAGE LLC Survival & Growth Enterprise, Tucson, 2002—. Bd. dirs. Field of Flowers. Fellow U. Chgo., 1949. Fellow Social Sci. Rsch. Coun.; mem. Am. Sociol. Assn., Phi Beta Kappa.

SHAPIRO, LIZA J., anthropologist, educator; BA in Anthrop. & Psychology summa cum laude, SUNY, Albany, 1983; PhD in Anthrop., SUNY, Stony Brook, 1991. Asst. prof. dept anthrop. U. Tex., 1990—97, assoc. prof. dept. anthrop., 1997—2008, prof. dept. anthrop, 2008—. Assoc. editor Jour. Human Evolution, 2004—07, Am. Jour. Physical Anthrop., 2005. Mem.: Soc. Integrative & Comparative Biology, Am. Assn. Physical Anthropologists, Phi Beta Kappa. Office: University of Texas Dept Anthropology 1 University Sta C3200 Austin TX 78712-1086 Office Phone: 512-471-7533. Office Fax: 512-471-6535. E-mail: liza.shapiro@mail.utexas.edu.*

SHAPIRO, LOUIS A., hospital administrator; BA, U. Pitts., M in Health Adminstrn. Diplomate Am. Coll. Healthcare Execs. Exec. v.p., chief adminstrv. officer Grad. and Mt. Sinai Hosps., Phila.; v.p. Allegheny Hosp., Pitts.; sr. practice cons. McKinsey and Co.; chief adminstrv. officer Geisinger Clinic, Danville, Pa., 2002—04; exec. v.p., clin. enterprise COO Geisinger Health Sys., Danville, Pa., 2004—06; pres., CEO Hosp. for Spl. Surgery, NYC, 2006—. Office: Hosp for Spl Surgery 535 E 70th St New York NY 10021*

SHAPIRO, LUCY, molecular biology educator; b. NYC, July 16, 1940; d. Philip and Yetta (Stein) Cohen; m. Roy Shapiro, Jan. 23, 1960 (div. 1977); 1 child, Peter; m. Harley H. McAdams, July 28, 1978; stepchildren: Paul, Heather. BA, Bklyn. Coll., 1962; PhD, Albert Einstein Coll. Medicine, 1966. Asst. prof. Albert Einstein Coll. Medicine, NYC, 1967-72, assoc. prof., 1972-77, Kramer prof., chmn. dept. molecular biology, 1977-86, dir. biol. scis. divsn., 1981-86; Eugene Higgins prof., chmn. dept. microbiology, Coll. Physicians and Surgeons Columbia U., NYC, 1986-89; Joseph D. Grant prof. devel. biology Stanford (Calif.) U. Sch. Medicine, 1989-97, chmn. dept. devel. biology, 1989-97, Virginia and D.K. Ludwig prof. cancer rsch., dept. devel. biology, 1998—; dir. Beckman Ctr. Molecular and Genetic Medicine, Stanford U., 2001—. Mem. bd. sci. counselors NIH, Washington, 1980—84; mem. bd. sci. advisors G.D. Searle Co., Skokie, Ill., 1984—86; trustee Scientists Inst. for Pub. Info., 1990—94; mem. sci. adv. bd. SmithKline Beecham, 1993—2000, Anacor Pharms., Inc., 2001—, PathoGenesis, 1995—2000, Ludwig Inst. Cancer Res., 2000—, Glaxo Smith Kline, 2001—07, Hatteras Ventures, 2008—09, Pasteur Inst., Paris, 2009—; mem. adv. bd. Biodesign Inst., Ariz. State U., 2006—08, Singapore Inst. Molecular & Cell Biology, 2006—08, Lawrence Berkeley Nat. Labs., 2006—; bd. dirs. Anacor Pharms. Inc., 2001—, Gen-Probe Inc., 2008—; Hitchcock prof. U. Calif., Barkeley, 2008. Editor: Microbiol. Devel., 1984; mem. editl. bd. Jour. Bacteriology, 1978-86, Trends in Genetics, 1987—, Genes and Development, 1987-91, Cell Regulation, 1990-92, Molecular Biology of the Cell, 1992-98, Molecular Microbiology, 1991-96, Current Opinion on Genetics and Devel., 1991—; contbr. articles to profl. jours. Mem. sci. bd. Helen Hay Witney Found., N.Y.C., 1986-94, Biozentrum, Basel, 1999-2001, Hutchinson Cancer Ctr., Seattle, 1999; mem. grants adv. bd. Beckman Found., 1999—; co-chmn. adv. bd. NSF Biology Directorate, 1988-89; vis. com., bd. overseers Harvard U., Cambridge, Mass., 1987-90; mem. sci. bd. Whitehead Inst., MIT, Boston, 1988-93; mem. sci. rev. bd. Howard Hughes Med. Inst., 1990-94, Cancer Ctr. of Mass. Gen. Hosp., Boston, 1994; mem. Presidio Coun. City of San Francisco, 1991-94; mem. pres. coun. U. Calif., 1991-97. Recipient Hirschl Career Scientist award, 1976, Spirit of Achievement award, 1978, Alumna award of honor Bklyn. Coll., 1983, Excellence in Sci. award Fedn. Am. Soc. Exptl. Biology, 1994, Hitchcock award UC Berkeley, 2008, Gairdner Found. Internat. award, 2009, Swedish Royal Acad. Sci., 2008, John Scott award 2009; Jane Coffin Child fellow, 1966; resident scholar Rockefeller Found., Bellagio, Italy, 1996. Fellow AAAS, Am. Acad. Arts and Scis., Am. Acad. Microbiology, Calif. Coun. on Sci. and Tech.; mem. NAS (Selman A. Waksman award 2005), Inst. Medicine of NAS, Am. Philos. Soc., Am. Soc. Biochemistry and Molecular Biology (nominating com. 1982, 87, coun. 1990-93), Am. Heart Assn. (sci. adv. bd. 1984-87). Avocation: watercolor painting. Office: Stanford U Sch Medicine Beckman Ctr Dept Devel Biology Stanford CA 94305 Office Phone: 650-725-7678.

SHAPIRO, MARC ROBERT, retail executive; b. North Hollywood, Calif., Apr. 1, 1959; s. Mel and Sally Shapiro; children: Julie Joseph Jack, Shapiro Shapiro. AA in Bus. Adminstrn., LA Harbor Coll., Wilmington, Calif., 1987; BSBA, U. Phoenix, 2006. Ops. mgr. Name Bears, Inc., Victorville, Calif., 1989—92; exec. v.p. Retail Project Mgrs., LLC, Irvine, Calif., 1992—2007; v.p., mng. dir. Crossmark, 2007. Mem.: Am. Numis. Assn. (life). Jewish. Avocations: travel, languages, home remodeling.

SHAPIRO, MARK HOWARD, physicist, educator, dean; b. Boston, Apr. 18, 1940; s. Louis and Sara Ann (Diamond) S.; m. Anita Rae Lavine, June 8, 1961; children: David Gregory, Diane Elaine, Lisa Michelle. AB with honors, U. Calif., Berkeley, 1962; MS (NSF coop. fellow), U. Pa., 1963, PhD, 1966. Research fellow Kellogg Radiation Lab., Calif. Inst. Tech., Pasadena, 1966-68; vis. assoc. divsn. math., physics and astronomy Calif. Inst. Tech., 1976—; research assoc. Nuclear Structure Research Lab. U. Rochester (N.Y.), 1968-70; mem. faculty Calif. State U., Fullerton, 1970—2002, prof. physics, 1978—2002, acting assoc. dean Sch. Math., Sci. and Engring., 1985-86, acting dir. Office Faculty Research and Devel., 1986-87, chmn. physics dept., 1989-96, 98-01, prof. physics emeritus, 2002—; dir. tchr. enhancement program NSF, Washington, 1987-88. Tour speaker Am. Chem. Soc., 1983—85. Editor, pub.: The Irascible Professor, 1999; webmaster Calif. State U. Fullerton Emeriti Assn.; contbr. over 125 articles to profl. jours, amateur radio. Mem. pub. info. and edn. com. Calif. Task Force on Earthquake Preparedness, 1981—85; dist. team leader Fullerton Cmty. Emergency Response Team, 2007—; pres. Pasadena Young Democrats, 1967—68; bd. dirs. Calif. State U. Fullerton Found., 1982—85. Grantee Research Corp., 1971-74, Calif. Inst. Tech., 1977-78, U.S. Geol. Survey, 1978-85, Digital Equipment Corp., 1982, NSF, 1985-87, 90—; named Vol. of Yr. Cal State Fullerton Emeriti Assn. Fellow Am. Phys. Soc., Materials Rsch. Soc., Coun. on Undergrad. Rsch. (physics/astronomy councillor 1993-2002), Calif. State U. Emeritus and Retired Faculty Assn. (webmaster 2007—, treas. 2008—). Achievements include research in experimental nuclear physics, experimental nuclear astrophysics, geophysics and atomic collisions in solids. Office: Calif State Univ Physics Dept Fullerton CA 92834-6866 Business E-Mail: mshapiro2@roadrunner.com.

SHAPIRO, MARK S., theme park company executive; b. Chgo., Feb. 25, 1970; BA in Polit. Sci., Comm., U. Iowa, 1992. Intern NBC Sports TV, 1989, prodn. asst. 1990—91, assoc. prodr., 1991—92; prodn. asst ESPN TV, 1993—94, prodr., 1994, v.p., gen. mgr. classic & original entertainment, sr. v.p., gen mgr. programming, 2001—02, exec. v.p. programming, prodn., 2002—04; pres., CEO Red Zone LLC, 2004—05, Six Flags, Inc., 2005—. Mem. Abu Dhabi Investment House Adv. Bd., US Travel & Tourism Adv. Bd.; bd. dirs. Tribune Co. Recipient 2 Peabody awards, 16 Emmy awards, Disting. Alumni award, U. Iowa, 2004; named one of 35 Promising Execs. on the Rise, The Hollywood Reporter, 2001, 101 Most Powerful People in Show Bus., Entertainment Weekly, 2003, Top 40 Under 40, Sports Bus. Daily, 2003—05; named to The Power 100, The Sporting News, 2003—04. Mailing: Six Flags Corp Offices 1540 Broadway New York NY 10036 also: Six Flags Corp Offices 924 Ave J East Grand Prairie TX 75050 Office Phone: 212-652-9403. Office Fax: 212-354-3038.

SHAPIRO, MARK S., neuroscientist, educator; b. Atlanta, Ga. PhD, Rush U. Med. Ctr., Chgo., 1991. Assoc. prof. U. Tex. Health Sci. Ctr., San Antonio, 2000—. Contbr. articles to profl. jours. RO1 Rsch. grant, NIH, 2002—, grant in Aid, Am. Heart Assn., 2007—09. Mem.: Physiol. Soc., Am. Physiol. Soc., Soc. Gen. Physiologists (councillor 2006—), Biophysical Soc. Office: Univ Tex Health Sci Ctr 7703 Floyd Curl Dr San Antonio TX 78258 Business E-Mail: shapirom@uthscsa.edu.

SHAPIRO, MARVIN LINCOLN, communications company executive; b. Erie, Pa., Feb. 12, 1923; s. Hyman and Flora (Burstein) S.; m. B. Gertrude Berkman, Oct. 25, 1946; children: Susan Jo, Barbara Ann, Jonathan David. BS, Syracuse U., 1948; postgrad., Williams Coll., 1966, Columbia U., 1975. Account exec. WSYR, Syracuse, 1948-50; account exec. sta. WCAU-TV, Phila., 1950-55, nat. sales mgr., 1956-58; account exec. CBS TV Spot Sales, Chgo., 1955-56, NYC, 1958-60; with TV Advt. Reps., Inc., NYC, 1961-66, exec. v.p., 1965-66, pres., 1968-69, dir., vice chmn., 1969-77, chmn., 1978; pres. Radio Advt. Reps., Inc., NYC, 1966-68, dir., vice chmn., 1969-77; exec. v.p., COO, pres. sta. group Westinghouse Broadcasting Co., Inc., NYC, 1969-77, sr. v.p., 1978-83, also dir., 1969-83; pres., dir. Foxwood Comm. Inc., NYC, 1983—; mng. dir. Veronis Suhler Stevenson, NYC, 1983—; dir. Queen City Broadcasting, 1986—95; pres., dir. Farragut Comm., Inc., NYC, 1992-99, Columbia Empire Broadcasting Corp., Yakima, Wash., 1992-96. Dir. Broadcasting Ptnrs. Holdings, L.P., 1996-00, VS&A Spectrum, Inc., 1997-2000, dir. Riviera Broadcasting Group, LLC, 2005-, ITN Networks, LLC, 2006-; chmn. bd. Micro-Relay, Inc., 1974-83; chmn. bd. dirs., pres. CATV Enterprises, Inc., 1970-83. Boxing official Pa. Athletic Commn., 1952-55; Bd. dirs. TV Bur. Advt., 1974-81, chmn., 1977-79; bd. dirs. Radio Advt. Bur., 1970-77; With USAAF, 1942-45. Decorated Air medal with 9 oak leaf clusters.; recipient Communications Alumni award Syracuse U., 1960 Mem. Internat. Radio and TV Soc., DAV, Alpha Epsilon Rho (hon.). Clubs: Long Ridge (Stamford). Home: 26 Foxwood Rd Stamford CT 06903-2207 Office: Veronis Suhler Stevenson 350 Park Ave New York NY 10022-6022

SHAPIRO, MATTHEW DAVID, economist, educator; b. Mpls., Apr. 11, 1958; s. Irving and Janet (Reinstein) S.; m. Susan L. Garetz, Oct. 21, 1989; children: Benjamin Avigdor, Molly Kendall. BA summa cum laude, Yale U., 1979, MA, 1979; PhD, MIT, 1984. Jr. staff economist Coun. Econ. Advisers, Washington, 1979-80, sr. economist, 1993-94; asst. prof. Yale U., New Haven, 1984-89; assoc. prof. U. Mich., Ann Arbor, 1989-95, prof., 1995—, L.R. Klein Collegiate prof., 2004—, sr. rsch. scientist, 2000—, chair, 2003—07. Rschr. Nat. Bur. Econ. Rsch., Cambridge, Mass., 1986—; mem. acad. adv. coun. Fed. Res. Bank Chgo., 1995-; mem. com. on nat. stats. NAS, 1999-2002; mem. Fed. Econ. Stats. Adv. Com., 2000—, chmn., 2006—, mem. Am. Economic Assn. Com. Statistics, 2005-, chair, 2009-. Bd. editors Am. Econ. Rev., 1993-96, 2000-02, co-editor, 1997-2002; contbr. articles to profl. jours. Recipient Paul A. Samuelson Cert. of Excellence, TIAA-CREF, 1997; Olin fellow Nat. Bur. Econ. Rsch., Cambridge, 1986-87, Alfred P. Sloan fellow Sloan Found., 1991-93. Mem. Am. Econ. Assn., Econometric Soc., Phi Beta Kappa. Office: U Mich Dept Econs 611 Tappan Ave Ann Arbor MI 48109-1220

SHAPIRO, MERYL, lawyer; d. Robert M. and Thelma Shapiro. JD, NY Law Sch., 1978. Atty. Guggenheimer & Untermyer, NYC, 1978—79, Law Offices of Henry R. Simon, NYC, 1979—81, Toberoff & Tessler, NYC, 1981—86, Katz, Katz & Brand, NYC, 1986—87, Law Offices of Henry R. Simon, White Plains, NY, 1988—91, Wiesen, Gurfein & Jenkins, NYC, 1991—93, Weinstein, Chase, Messinger & Peters, P.C., Bklyn., 1995—2005; founder Meryl Shapiro, Atty.-at-Law, NYC, 2005—. Supporter Sylvia Rivera LAw Project, NYC, Soka U. of Am., Aliso Viejo, Calif.; com. mem. Dem. Party County Com., 74th Asssembly Dist., NYC; NE zone legal divsn. chair, women's divsn. chpt. leader Soka Gakkai Internat.-USA, NYC. Mem.: Nat. Lesbian and Gay Law Assn., Bars of the So. and Ea. Dists. of NY, NY State Trial Lawyers' Assn., NY State Bar Assn. (com. on women in the law 2006—), Assn. of Bar of City of NY (civil rights com. 2001—03). Buddhist. Office: Meryl Shapiro Atty at Law Ste 7F 305 East 24th St New York NY 10010 Business E-Mail: mshapiro@merylshapiro.com.

SHAPIRO, MICHAEL, lawyer; b. NYC, Jan. 21, 1950; s. Howard H. and Rita (Pearlman); m. Marica J. Cardarelli, July 7, 1979; 2 children: Rebecca, Benjamin. BA cum laude, CCNY, 1970; JD, NYU, 1973. Bar: NY 1974, US Dist. Ct. (so. and ea. dists.) NY 1975, US Supreme Ct. 1980, US Ct. Appeals (2d cir.) 1986, US Ct. Appeals (11th cir) 1989, US Dist. Ct. (ea. dist) Mich. 2006, US Ct. Appeals (6th cir.) 2006. Asst. dist. atty. Queens County Dist. Atty. Office, Queens, NY, 1973-75; spl. asst. atty. gen. Health and Social Svcs., NYC, 1975-77, NYC Corruption, 1977-85; counsel Slotnick & Baker, NYC, 1985-88; ptnr. Slotnick, Shapiro & Crocker, NYC, 1989—2005, Buchanan Ingersoll & Rooney, Pitts., 2005—06, Carter Ledyard & Milburn, NYC, 2006—; legal analyst In Depth with Chris Matthews, 1994—95; faculty mem. intensive advocacy trial prog. Benjamin N. Cardozo Sch. Law, 2000—. Mem. Nat. Assn. Criminal Def. Lawyers, NY State Bar Assn., NY Criminal Bar Assn., NY County Lawyers Assn., Westchester Bar Assn. Avocations: tennis, skiing, foreign travel. Office: Carter Ledyard & Milburn 2 Wall St New York NY 10005 Office Phone: 212-238-8676, 212-732-3200. Office Fax: 212-732-3232. Business E-Mail: mshapiro@clm.com.

SHAPIRO, MICHAEL BRUCE, lawyer; b. Akron, Ohio, 1947; BBA summa cum laude, Kent State U., 1969; JD magna cum laude, U. Mich., 1972. Bar: Mich. 1972. Ptnr. Honigman Miller Schwartz & Cohn, LLP, Detroit. Mem. citizens property tax commn. Mich. Senate, 1986-87. Mem. ABA, Am. Property Tax Counsel, State Bar of Mich., Inst. Property Taxation, Order of the Coif, Beta Alpha Psi, Pi Sigma Alpha, Beta Gamma Sigma (Best Lawyers of America, 1996). Office: Honigman Miller Schwartz & Cohn LLP 2290 1st Nat Bldg Detroit MI 48226 Office Phone: 313-465-7622. Business E-Mail: mbs@honigman.com.

SHAPIRO, MICHAEL EDWARD, museum director; b. NYC, Nov. 15, 1949; s. Edward Aaron and Sylvia (Fishman) S.; m. Elizabeth Harvey, 1977; 2 children. BA, Hamilton Coll., 1972; MA, Williams Coll., 1976, Harvard U., 1978, PhD, 1980. Asst. prof. dept. art history Duke U., Durham, NC, 1980-84; curator 19th-20th century art St. Louis Art Mus., 1984-92, chief curator, 1987-92; dir. Los Angeles County Mus. Art, 1992-93; dir. mus. programs, chief curator High Mus. Art, Atlanta, 1994-95, dep. dir., chief curator, 1996-99, dir., 2000—. Author: Bronze Casting and American Sculpture, 1985; contbg. author: Frederic Remington: The Masterworks, 1988, George Caleb Bingham, 1990; mng. curator, editor Rings: Five Passions in World Art, 1996; co-curator Impressionism: Paintings Collected by European Museums, 1998, mng. curator, 1999. Recipient Chevalier, Order Arts & Letters, France, 2005. Office: High Museum Art 1280 Peachtree St NE Atlanta GA 30309

SHAPIRO, NEAL, broadcast executive, television producer; s. Sumner and Mildred Shapiro; m. JuJu Chang, Dec. 2, 1995; 3 children. BA in History and Polit. Sci., Tufts U., 1980. With ABC News, 1980—93; spl. segment prodr. World News Tonight, 1986—89; broadcast prodr. Prime-Time Live, 1989—93; exec. prodr. NBC News, Dateline, NYC, 1993—2001; pres. NBC News, NYC, 2001—05, Sta. WNET Channel 13, 2007—. Recipient George Polk award, 1992, 2000, 23 Emmy awards, 3 Investigate Reporter and Editor award. Office: Thirteen/WNET 450 W 33rd St New York NY 10001

SHAPIRO, NELSON HIRSH, lawyer; b. Feb. 3, 1928; s. Arthur and Anna (Zenitz) S.; m. Helen Lenora Sykes, June 27, 1948; children: Ronald Evan, Mitchell Wayne, Jeffrey Mark, Julie Beth. BEE, Johns Hopkins U., 1948; JD, George Washington U., 1952. Bar: D.C. 1952, Va. 1981. Patent examiner U.S. Patent Office, 1948-50; patent advisor U.S. Signal Corps, 1950-52; mem. Shapiro & Shapiro, Arlington, Va., 1952-98, Vorys, Sater, Seymour and Pease LLP, Washington, 1998-2001, Miles & Stockbridge, McLean, Va., 2001—. Patentee; contbr. articles to legal publs. and Ency. of Patent Practice and Invention Mgmt.,

1964. Mem. ABA, Am. Patent Law Assn., Bar Assn. DC, Order of Coif, Tau Beta Pi. Home: 7001 Old Cabin Ln Rockville MD 20852-4531 Office: 1751 Pinnacle Dr Ste 500 Mc Lean VA 22102-3833 Home Phone: 301-881-0841; Office Phone: 703-610-8687. E-mail: nshapiro@milesstockbridge.com.

SHAPIRO, NORMA SONDRA LEVY, federal judge; b. Phila., July 27, 1928; d. Bert and Jane (Kotkin) Levy; m. Bernard Shapiro, Aug. 21, 1949; children: Finley, Neil, Aaron. BA in Polit. Theory with honors, U. Mich., 1948; JD magna cum laude, U. Pa., 1951. Bar: Pa. 1952, U.S. Supreme Ct. 1978. Law clk. to presiding justice Pa. Supreme Ct., 1951-52; instr. U. Pa. Law Sch., 1951-52, 55-56; assoc. Dechert Price & Rhoads, Phila., 1956-58, 67-73, ptnr., 1973-78; judge U.S. Dist. Ct. 3rd circuit (ea. dist.) Pa., 1978—98, sr. judge, 1998—. Assoc. trustee U. Pa. Law Sch., 1978-93; former trustee Women's Law Project, Albert Einstein Med. Ctr.; v.p. Jewish Pub. Soc.; trustee Fedn. Jewish Agys., 1980-83; mem. lawyers adv. panel Pa. Gov.'s Commn. on Status of Women, 1974; legal adv. regional Coun. Child Psychiatry, bd. dirs. Women Judges' Fund for Justice. Guest editor: Shingle, 1972. Mem. Lower Merion County (Pa.) Bd. Sch. Dirs., 1968-77, pres., 1977, v.p., 1976; v.p. Jewish Community Relations Council of Greater Phila., 1975-77; chmn. legal affairs com., 1978; pres. Belmont Hills Home and Sch. Assn., Lower Merion Twp.; legis. chmn. Lower Merion Sch. Dist. Intersch. Council; mem. Task Force on Mental Health of Children and Youth of Pa.; treas., chmn. edn. com. Human Relations Council, Lower Merion; v.p., parliamentarian Nes Ami Penn Valley Congregation, Lower Merion Twp. Named Woman of Yr., Oxford Circle Jewish Community Center, 1979, Woman of Distinction, Golden Slipper Club, 1979; Gowen fellow, 1954-55; recipient Hannah G. Solomon award Nat. Coun. Jewish Women, 1992; Disting. Daughter of Pa.; Liberty Bell award, Berks County Bar Assn. Mem. Am. Law Inst., Am. Bar Found., ABA (ho. dels. 1990-96, coun./chmn. conf. fed. judges 1986-87, chmn. jud. divsn. 1996-97, Margaret Brent Women Lawyers Achievement award 1999, bd. gov. 2003-), Pa. Bar Assn. (ho. of dels. 1979-81), Phila. Bar Assn. (chmn. com. women's rights 1972, 74-75, chmn. bd. govs. 1977-78, chmn. pub. rels. com. 1978, Sandra Day O'Connor award), Fed. Bar Assn. (Bill of Rights award 1991), Nat. Assn. Women Lawyers, Phila. Trial Lawyers Assn., Am. Judicature Soc., Phila., Nat. Assn. Women Judges (exec. comm. bd. dir.), Fellowship Commn., Order of Coif (chpt. pres. 1973-75), Tau Epsilon Rho. Office: US Dist Courthouse Independence Mall West 601 Market St Rm 10614 Philadelphia PA 19106-1714

SHAPIRO, PAUL D., sociologist, educator; PhD, U. Nev., Las Vegas, 2000. Assoc. prof. sociology Ga. Southwestern State U., Americus, 2003—. Office: Ga Southwestern State Univ 800 Wheatley St Americus GA 31709 Business E-Mail: shapiro@canes.gsw.edu.

SHAPIRO, PAULA, retired maternal/women's health nurse; b. Pitts., Nov. 16, 1927; d. Ben and Esther (Halpert) Cohn; m. Bernard Shapiro, July 17, 1982; children: Eugene Hershorin, Abby Hershorin, Marc Hershorin, Jay Hershorin, Ellen Fenerty, Kenneth, Fred, Stacy Pierce. RN, Montefiore Hosp. Sch. Nursing, 1948; BS, Phila. U., 1987. RN, Pa. Nursing care coord. Thomas Jefferson U. Hosp., Phila.; asst. supr. operating rm. Wakefield (R.I.) Gen. Hosp.; staff RN operating rm. Jefferson Hosp., Phila., ret., 1993. Contbr. articles to profl. jours. Vol. Thomas Jefferson U. Hosp., gift shop Nat. Mus. Am. Jewish History; vol. o.r. nurse Tel Aviv, Israel, 1977; election judge. Home: 1500 Locust St Apt 2216 Philadelphia PA 19102-4317 Personal E-mail: paulashapiro@hotmail.com.

SHAPIRO, PERRY, economics educator; b. LA, Jan. 15, 1941; s. Abraham and Ann (Warshaw) Shapiro; m. Jody Silverstein Shapiro, June 25, 1994; children: Elizabeth Naomi, Samuel Robert, Sarah Gertrud. BA in Econ., U. Calif.-Berkeley, 1962, PhD in Econ., 1968. Postdoc. fellow urban econ. Wash. U., St. Louis, 1967—68; lectr. London Sch. Econ., 1968—69; asst. prof. econ. U. Calif.-Santa Barbara, 1969—74, assoc. prof., 1974—78, prof., 1978—, chair dept. econ., 1987—93; vis. prof. U. Mich., Ann Arbor, 1979—80; adj. prof. Rsch. Sch. Social Scis., 1994—. Author: An Analytical Framework for Regional Policy, 1970. Grantee, NSF, 1979—, Nat. Inst. Justice, 1980—85; vis. scholar, Federalism Rsch. Ctr. Australian Nat. U., 1992, US Bur. Labor Stats., Wash., 1975—76; Fulbright sr. rsch. scholar, Australia Nat. U., 1990—91. Mem.: Nat. Tax Assn., Econometric Soc., Am. Econs. Assn.

SHAPIRO, PHILIP ALAN, lawyer; b. Chgo., May 14, 1940; s. Joe and Nettie (Costin) Shapiro; m. Joyce Barbara Chapnick, May 29, 1966 (dec. Feb. 2006); children: David Ian, Russell Scott, Mindi Jennifer. AA, Wilson Coll., 1960; BS in Fin., So. Ill. U., 1965; MBA, Nat. Univ., San Diego, Calif., 1975; MBA in Mktg. with distinction, San Diego State U., San Diego, 1977; JD, Western State U., 1985. Bar: Calif. 1988. With US Marine Corps, 1958—66; spl. agt. U.S. Secret Svc., Washington, 1965-67, Chgo., 1967-77; mgr. divsn. sales Roche Labs. divsn. Hoffman-La Roche, Inc., Chgo.; assoc. Law Office Jeffrey S. Schwartz, 1988-91; pvt. practice, 1991—. Chair gen. and solo practice sect. State Bar of Calif. Editor (law rev.): We. State U. Coll. Law. Mem. adv. bd. Spreckes Elem. Sch., San Diego, 1976—77; mem. Univ. City Town Coun., San Diego, 1977; pres. Congregation Beth El, La Jolla, Calif., 1976—79; bd. dirs. Mt. Hope Cemetery. Recipient Merit award, U.S. Treasury Dept., 1965, Israel Solidarity award, 1977, U. Judaism award, 1978; named Alum of Yr., Thomas Jefferson Sch. Law, 2006—07. Mem.: ABA (vice chmn. gen. practice sect.), Fed. Law Enforcement Officers Assn., Assn. Former Agts. of U.S. Secret Svc., San Diego Bus. Referrals (pres. 1998—99), San Diego County Bar Assn., State Bar Calif. (exec. com. gen. practice sect. chair, Wiley W. Manuel award 1990—91), Calif. Trial Lawyers Assn., Thomas Jefferson Sch. of Law Alumni Assn. (pres. 2004—, bd. dirs.), Congregation Beth El Club (La Jolla, Calif.) (Man of Uacok award 2009). Office: The Law Offices of Shapiro and Clamon 110 W C St Ste 2208 San Diego CA 92101 Office Phone: 619-239-1511. Office Fax: 619-239-1007. Business E-Mail: shapiroclamon@gmail.com.

SHAPIRO, PHILIP EDWIN, dermatologist, dermatopathologist, educator; b. New Hyde Park, NY, Mar. 30, 1959; s. Lewis and Suzanne Marie (Bassewitz) Shapiro; m. Kimberly Ann Bouchard, Oct. 4, 1998; m. Jacklyn Marie Trimble (div.); children: Adam Henry, David Alexander. BS magna cum laude, Rensselaer Polytech. Inst., Troy, NY, 1982; MD, Albany Med. Coll., NY, 1982. Diplomate Am. Bd. Dermatology, 1986, Am. Bd. Dermatology and Pathology (Dermatopathology), 1988, lic. physician Conn., NY, Fla. Intern Albany Med. Ctr. Hosp., 1982—83; resident in dermatology Columbia-Presbyn. Hosp., NYC, 1983—86; postdoctoral fellow dermatology Yale U. Sch. Medicine, New Haven, 1986—87; fellow dermatopathology NYU Med. Ctr., 1987—88; asst. prof. dermatology, dir. dermatopathology lab. Yale U. Sch. Medicine, 1988—91, asst. prof. dermatology and pathology, dir. dermatopathology fellow tng. program, 1991—95, assoc. clin. prof. dermatology, 1996—. Dir. Dermatopathology Lab. New Eng., Meriden, Conn., 1995—; attending physician Yale-New Haven Hosp., New Haven, 1988—; asst. attending physician St. Francis Hosp., Hartford, Conn., 1995—; lectr., presenter in field. Contbr. articles to profl. jours., chapters to books. State chmn. Dermatology Foun., Evanston, Ill., 2003—07. Fellow: Am. Soc. Dermatopathology, Am. Acad. Dermatology; mem.: AMA, Am. Soc. Clin. Pathologists, New Eng. Dermatol. Soc., US and Can. Acad. Pathology, New Haven County Med. Assn., Conn. State Med. Soc., Internat. Soc. Dermatopathology. Achievements include research in melanocytic neoplasia, delineating new entities or diagnostic criteria through clinicopathologic correlation. Avocations: tennis, cello, boating. Office: Dermatopathology Lab New England 140 Green Rd Meriden CT 06450

SHAPIRO, RICHARD GERALD, retail executive, consultant; b. NYC, Apr. 24, 1924; s. David and Sophie (Hayflich) S.; m. Lila Eig, July 27, 1951; children: Judith, Amy, Donald. BA, U. Mich., 1946; MBA, Harvard, 1948. With Lord & Taylor, NYC, 1948-64, v.p., 1959-63, sr. v.p., 1963-64; also mem. adv. bd.; pres. Wm. Filene's Sons Co., Boston, 1965-68, chief exec. officer, chmn. bd., 1968-73; pres. Gimbel Bros. Corp., NYC, 1973-76; v.p. W.R. Grace & Co., pres. sporting goods div., 1977-79, pres. splty. store div., 1979-84; pres. Richard Shapiro Assocs., 1979—; sr. v.p. Montgomery Ward, Inc., 1986-88. Bd. dirs. Assoc. Merchandising Corp., Nitrotec Corp., Capital Market Fund; retail chmn. Greater N.Y. Fund, 1963; chmn. merc. div. Mass. Bay United Fund, 1967 Mem. corp. Simmons Coll., Boston Mus. Fine Arts (permanent); bd. dirs. Mass. Mchts.; bd. dirs Family Counseling and Guidance Centers, 1969-72, v.p., 1970; trustee Brandeis U. Served with AUS, 1942-46. Mem.: Harvard Bus. Sch. Assn. (gov.). Home: 10019 Gable Manor Ct Potomac MD 20854-5000 Personal E-mail: rgsle@webtv.net.

SHAPIRO, RICHARD MICHAEL, lawyer; b. New Haven, Feb. 7, 1951; s. Robert and Pearl Edith (Glassman) S. BA, U. South Fla., 1978; JD, Southwestern U., 1980. Bar: Conn. 1981, Fla. 1981, U.S. Dist. Ct. (mid. dist.) Fla. 1982. Jud. intern to presiding judge U.S. Dist. Ct. for Conn., 1979; assoc. Mitzel, Mitzel and Feegel, Tampa, Fla., 1981; asst. pub. defender State of Fla., Bradenton, 1981; pres. and prin. Shapiro Law Group, Bradenton, 1981—. Fellow Roscoe Pound Found., 1994—; lectr. in field. Mem. FBA, ABA, ATLA (sustaining mem., bd. govs. 1997—, med. quality assurance com. 1994—, co-chmn. spkrs. bur./people's law sch. com. 1999-2000, stalwarts/endowment com. 1999-2000, key persons com. 1999-2000), Am. Judicature Soc., Fla. Bar Assn. (jud. selection, nomination and tenure com. 1989—, exec. coun. trial lawyers sect. 1997-2000), Acad. Fla. Trial Lawyers (Eagle founder 2000-01, F.L.A.G. trustee 1995—, co-chmn. med. malpractice taskforce 1996-97, pres. 2003-2004, Jon E. Krupnick award for perseverance 2001), Conn. Bar Assn., Hillsborough County Bar Assn., Tampa Bay Trial Lawyers Assn. (founder, bd. dirs. 2000—), So. Trial Lawyers Assn. (bd. govs. 1996—, pres. 2003-04), Trial Lawyers for Pub. Justice (Fla. state coord. 1992-97). Democrat. Jewish. Avocations: tennis, volleyball, scuba diving, boating. Office: Shapiro Law Group 1732 Manatee Ave W Bradenton FL 34205-5925 Business E-Mail: rshapiro@shapirolawgroup.com.

SHAPIRO, RICHARD N., lawyer; Degree, U. Md., 1980; JD with honors, George Mason U., 1984. Cert.: Nat. Bd. Trial Advocacy (civil trial adv.), bar: Va., W.Va., DC, NC, US Supreme Ct. With US Dist. Ct. (fed. dist.), Norfolk, Va.; ptnr. Shapiro, Cooper Lewis & Appleton, P.C., Va. Beach, Va. Lectr. in field. Contbr. chapters to books. Mem.: Acad. Rail Labor Attys., Va. Trial Lawyers Assn., Va. Beach Bar Assn., Norfolk-Portsmouth Bar Assn., Am. Assn. Justice (chmn. RR law sect. 2005—06). Office: Shapiro Cooper Lewis & Appleton PC 1294 Diamond Springs Rd Virginia Beach VA 23455

SHAPIRO, ROBERT FRANK, investment company executive; b. St. Louis, Dec. 19, 1934; s. Eugene J. and Clara (Katz) S.; m. Anna Marie Susman, Dec. 21, 1960; children: Albert Andrew, Robert Jr., Jeanne Savitt. Grad., St. Louis Country Day Sch., 1952; BA, Yale U., 1956. Assoc. Lehman Bros., NYC, 1956-67, ptnr., 1967-73, dir., sr. mng. dir., 1970-73; ptnr. Wertheim & Co., 1974; exec. v.p. Wertheim & Co., Inc., NYC, 1974-75, pres., 1975-86; co-chmn. Wertheim Schroder & Co., Inc., 1986-87; chmn. RFS and Assocs., Inc., NYC, 1988—2004, New Street Capital Corp., 1992-94; vice-chmn. Klingenstein, Fields & Co., L.P., NYC, 1997—. Bd. dirs. TJX Cos., Inc., The Burnham Fund, chmn. nominating com. N.Y. Stock Exch., 1980, mem. regulatory adv. com., 1988—, surveillance com., 1989—; bd. govs. Am. Stock Exch., 1970-76. Trustee Lenox Hill Hosp., Skowhegan; mem. gov. bd. Yale U. Art Gallery, New Haven, 1993—; trustee Louis Comfort Tiffany Found. Mem. Securities Industry Assn. (chmn. 1985, Bond Club N.Y. (pres. 1987-88, Yale Club, Century Country Club, Knickerbocker Club. Avocation: Collector of Contemporary Art, especially American. Office: Klingenstein Fields & Co LLC 787 7th Ave New York NY 10019-6018 Office Phone: 212-492-6143.

SHAPIRO, ROBERT JACOB, economic advisory firm executive; b. Balt., Oct. 4, 1948; AB, U. Chgo., 1970; MS, London Sch. Econs. and Polit. Sci., 1972; MA, Harvard U., 1980, PhD. Legis. dir. to Senator Daniel Patrick Moynihan US Senate; dir. econ. studies, co-founder Progressive Found., Washington; dep. nat. issues dir./chief econ. policy Dukakis-Bentsen Presdl. Campaign, 1988; prin. econ. adv. Gov. Bill Clinton presdl. campaign, 1991-92; sr. advisor to sec. US Dept. Commerce, Washington, under sec. for econ. affairs, 1997—2001; v.p., co-founder Progressive Policy Inst., Washington, 1998—; sr. econ. adviser Al Gore's Presdl Campaign, 2000; co-founder, chmn. Sonecon LLC, Washington; co-chmn. Am. Task Force Argentina, Arlington, Va., 2006—; advisors Barack Obama Transition Team, Washington, 2008. Sr. fellow Georgetown U. Bus. Sch. Assoc. editor U.S. News and World Report; contbg. editor The New Rep., Internat. Economy, Intellectual-Capital.com.; contbr. articles to profl. jours. Bd. dirs. Axson Johnson Found., Ctr. for Internat. Polit. Economy. Fellow: Nat. Bur. Econ. Rsch., The Brookings Instn., Harvard U. Office: Sonecon LLC 633 Pennsylvania Ave NW Ste 400 Washington DC 20004 also: American Task Force Argentina PO Box 3197 Arlington VA 22203*

SHAPIRO, ROBERT L., lawyer; b. Plainfield, NJ, Sept. 2, 1942; m. Linell Shapiro; children: Brent(dec.), Grant. BS in Fin., UCLA, 1965; JD, Loyola U., LA, 1968. Bar: Calif. 1969, U.S. Ct. Appeals (9th cir.) 1972, U.S. Dist. Ct. (ctrl., no. and so. dists.) Calif. 1982. Dep. dist. atty. Office of Dist. Atty., LA, 1969-72; sole practice LA, 1972—87; of counsel Bushkin, Gaims, Gaines, Jonas, LA, 1987-88, Christensen, Glaser, Fink, Jacobs, Weil & Shapiro (now Glaser, Weil, Fink, Jacobs, Howard & Shapiro, LLP), LA, 1988—95, ptnr., 1995—. Co-founder Legalzoom.com, Inc., 1999—; lectr. in field. Author: When The Press Calls: A Lawyer's View, 1991, The Search For Justice: A Defense Attorney's Brief on the O.J. Simpson Case, 1996; co-author: (with Walt W. Becker) Misconception, 2001; frequent guest on network and cable TV shows and is called upon for legal expertise. Bd. dirs. Brent Shapiro Found. for Drug Awareness. Recipient Am. Jurisprudence award Bancroft Whitney, 1969; named Pro-bono Lawyer the Yr., State of Nevada; named one of 100 Super Lawyers, LA Daily Jour. Mem. Nat. Assn. Criminal Def. Lawyers, Calif. Attys. for Criminal Justice, Trial Lawyers for Pub. Justice (founder 1982), Century City Bar Assn. (Best Criminal Def. Atty. 1993). Avocation: avid sport fan to basketball and boxing. Office: 10250 Constellation Blvd Fl 19 Los Angeles CA 90067 Office Phone: 310-553-3000, 310-556-7886. Office Fax: 310-556-2920. Business E-Mail: rs@glaserweil.com.*

SHAPIRO, ROBYN SUE, lawyer, educator; b. Mpls., July 19, 1952; d. Walter David and Judith Rae (Sweet) S.; m. Charles Howard Barr, June 27, 1976; children: Tania Shapiro-Barr, Jeremy Shapiro-Barr, Michael Shapiro-Barr. BA summa cum laude, U. Mich., 1974; JD, Harvard U., 1977. Bar: D.C. 1977, Wis. 1979, U.S. Supreme Ct. 1990. Assoc. Foley & Lardner, Washington, 1977-79; ptnr. Barr & Shapiro, Menomonee Falls, Wis., 1980-87; assoc. Quarles & Brady, Milw., 1987-92; ptnr. Michael Best & Friedrich, Milw., 1992—2005, chair health law practice, 2003—05; ptnr. Gardner Carton & Douglas LLP, Milw., 2005—06, Drinker Biddle Gardner Carton, Milw., 2006—07, Drinker Biddle & Heath, 2007—. Adj. asst. prof. law Marquette U., Milw., 1979-83; assoc. dir. bioethics ctr. Med. Coll. Wis., Milw., 1982-85, dir., 1985—; asst. prof. bioethics Med. Coll. Wis., 1984-89, assoc. prof. bioethics, 1989-97, prof. bioethics, 1997—, Ursula Von der Ruhr prof. bioethics, 2000—; dir. Wis. Ethics Com. Network, 1987-98, Midwest Ethics Com. Network, 1998-2004, Med. Ethics Com. Network, 2004—; bd. dirs. Wis. Health Decisions, 1990-93; drug safety and risk mgmt. adv. com. FDA, 2003-2007; mem. data and safety monitoring bd. Med. Coll. Wis., 2003-; mem. recombinant DNA adv. com. NIH, 2005—, mem. Biosafety Working Group NIH Recombihant DNA adv. com. 2007-, mem. Clinical Trails Working Group NIH Recombihant DNA adv. com. 2007-. Mem. editl. bd. Cambridge Quar., 1991—, HEC Forum, 1988—91, Human Rights, 1998—2007; contbr. articles to profl. jours. Mem. ethics com. St. Luke's Med. Ctr., Milw., 1983—, Elmbrook Meml. Hosp., Milw., 1983-86, Cmty. Meml. Hosp., Menomonee Falls, 1984—, Aurora Sinai Med.Ctr., Milw., 1986—, Milw. County Mental Health Complex, 1984—, Froedtert Meml. Luth. Hosp., 1985—; mem. subcom. organ transplantation Wis. Health Policy Coun., Madison, 1984, bioethics com., 1986-89; mem. com. study on bioethics Wis. Legis. Coun., Madison, 1984-85; bd. dirs. Jewish Home and Care Ctr., 1994-2005, chair ethics com., 1994—; chair Bayside Ethics Bd., 1994—; bd. dirs. Milw. area chpt. Girl Scouts U.S., Am. Bioethics Assn., 1995-97, Wis. Perinatal Found., 1996-99, Am. Soc. Bioethics and Humanities, 1997-00, Manor Park Found., 2002—; mem. sec.'s adv. com. on xenotransplantation U.S. Dept. Health and Human Svcs., 2001-05; mem. sci. adv. com. Alzheimer's Assn. Southeastern Wis., 1997—; mem. data and safety monitoring bd. GlaxoWellcome, 1995-03; mem. med. and cmty. adv. bd. After Breast Cancer Diagnosis, 1999—. James B. Angell scholar, 1971—72. Fellow: Am. Bar Found.; mem.: ABA (coordinating com. on bioethics and law 1993—, individual rights and responsibilities sect., health rights com. chair 1994—99, vice chair clin. ethics group 1998—2001, coun. 1999—, working group on health info. privacy 2000—02, misuse genetic info study group 2002—, AIDS coordinating com. 2003—, health law sec. 2004—, health law sect. 2004—, sec. individual rights and responsibilites vice chair 2005—06, chair-elect 2006—07, chair 2007—, adv. nat. conf. of commrs. on uniform state laws), Profl. Dimensions (Golden Compass award 1994), Internat. Bioethics Assn. (chair task force on ethics coms.), Am. Soc. Transplant Surgeons (ethics com. 1999—), Milw. AIDS Coalition (steering com. 1988—91), Milw. Acad. Medicine (coun. 1992—98, chair bioethics com. 1992—98), Am. Soc. Law, Medicine and Ethics, Assn. Post-Doctoral Programs in Clin. Neurophysiology (bd. dirs.), Wis. Found. (Atty. of Yr. 1988), Assn. Women Lawyers, Wis. Bar Assn. (individual rights sect. coun. 1987—90, chair health law sect. 1988—89), Am. Hosp. Assn. (spl. com. HIV practitioners 1991—93, bioethics tech. panel 1991—94), Am. Health Lawyers Assn., Susan G. Komen Breast Cancer Found., Phi Beta Kappa (Wis. chpt. scholarship com. chair 1990—93). Home: 9474 N Broadmoor Rd Milwaukee WI 53217-1309 Office: Med Coll Wis Bioethics Ctr 8701 Watertown Plank Rd Milwaukee WI 53226-3548 Office Phone: 414-221-6040. Business E-Mail: rshapiro@mcw.edu, robyn.shapiro@dbr.com.

SHAPIRO, SANDRA, lawyer; b. Providence, Oct. 17, 1944; d. Emil and Sarah (Cohen) S. AB magna cum laude, Bryn Mawr Coll., Pa., 1966; LLB magna cum laude, U. Pa., 1969. Bar: Mass. 1970, U.S. Dist. Ct. Mass. 1971, U.S. Ct. Appeals (1st cir.) 1972, U.S. Supreme Ct. 1980. Law clk. U.S. Ct. Appeals (1st cir.), Boston, 1969-70; assoc. Foley, Hoag & Eliot LLP, Boston, 1970-75, ptnr., 1976—. Mem. bd. bar overseers Mass. Supreme Judicial Ct., 1988-92, mem. gender bias study com., 1986-89; dir. Mass. Govt. Land Bank, 1994-96; dir. Lex Mundi, 2004-08. Contbr. articles to profl. jours. Bd. dirs. Patriots' Trail coun. Girl Scouts U.S., 1994—97; mem. bd. overseers Boston Lyric Opera, 1993—99, New Eng. Conservatory of Music, 1995—2001, Celebrity Series of Boston, 1997—, chair, 2003—. Woodrow Wilson fellow, 1966. Mem.: ABA (ethics, profl. and pub. edn. com. 1994—), U. Pa. Law Sch. Alumni Assn. (bd. mgrs. 1990—94), Boston Bar Assn. (mem. coun.), Mass. Bar Assn. (chmn. real property sect. coun., com. on profl. ethics), Nat. Women's Law Ctr. Network, New Eng. Women in Real Estate, Women's Bar Assn. Mass. (pres. 1985—86), Boston Club, Order of Coif. Office: Foley Hoag LLP 155 Seaport Blvd Boston MA 02210-2600 Office Phone: 617-832-1156. Business E-Mail: sshapiro@foleyhoag.com.

SHAPIRO, STEPHEN MICHAEL, lawyer; b. Chgo., May 3, 1946; s. Samuel H. and Dorothy A. (D'Andrea) S.; m. Joan H. Gately, Oct. 30, 1982; children: Dorothy Henderson, Michael Clifford. BA magna cum laude, Yale U., 1968, JD, 1971. Bar: Ill. 1971, Calif. 1972, DC 1991, US Dist. Ct. (no. dist. trial bar Ill.) 1992, US Ct. Appeals (all cirs.), US Supreme Ct. 1975. Law clk. US Ct. Appeals (9th cir.), San Francisco, 1971—72; with Mayer, Brown & Platt, Chgo., 1972—78; asst. to solicitor gen. US Dept. Justice, Washington, 1978-80, dep. solicitor gen., 1981—83; sr. mem. Supreme Ct. and Appellate Ct. practice Mayer, Brown LLP, Chgo., 1983—, ptnr., 1977—. Former trustee Product Liability Adv. Found. Co-author: Supreme Ct. Practice, 2007; contbr. articles to profl. jours. Mem. Am. Law Inst. (life), Am. Acad. Appellate Lawyers, 7th Cir. Bar Assn., Inst. Jud. Adminstrn. (bd. dirs.), Phi Beta Kappa. Republican. Jewish. Office: Mayer Brown LLP 71 S Wacker Dr Ste 4430 Chicago IL 60606 Office Phone: 312-701-7327. Office Fax: 312-706-8684. E-mail: sshapiro@mayerbrown.com.

SHAPIRO, STEVEN R., legal association administrator; JD, Harvard U., 1975. Law clk. to Hon. J. Edward Lumbard US Ct. Appeals 2nd Cir., 1975—76; with ACLU, 1976—, staff counsel Children's Rights Project, gen. staff counsel, assoc. legal dir., 1987—93, legal dir., 1993—. Adj. prof constl. law Columbia U.; bd. dirs. Human Rights First (previously Lawyers Com. for Human Rights); mem. Asia Adv. Com. Human Rights Watch, mem. policy com. Named Civil Rights Lawyer of Yr., Am. Lawyer, 1981. Office: ACLU 125 Broad St 18th Fl New York NY 10004

SHAPIRO, STUART CHARLES, computer scientist, educator; b. NYC, Dec. 30, 1944; s. Louis M. and Bertha (Rubinstein) S.; m. Caren Dee Knight, July 16, 1972. BS, MIT, 1966; MS, U. Wis., 1968, PhD, 1971. Lectr. computer scis. dept. U. Wis., Madison, 1971; vis. asst. prof. Ind. U., Bloomington, 1971-72, asst. prof., 1972-77, assoc. prof., 1977-78; asst. prof. SUNY, Buffalo, 1977-78, assoc. prof., 1978-83, prof., 1983—, chmn., 1984-90, 96-99, dir. Ctr. Cognitive Sci., 2004—08. Pres. Principles of Knowledge Representation and Reasoning, Inc., 1998-2000; rsch. scientist Nat. Ctr. for Geographic Info. and Analysis, 1989—. Author: Techniques of Artificial Intelligence, 1979, LISP: An Interactive Approach, 1986, Common Lisp: An Interactive Approach, 1992; editor: Encyclopedia of Artificial Intelligence, 1987, paperback edit., 1990, 2d edit., 1992, (with Lucja Iwanska) Natural Language Processing and Knowledge Representation: Language for Knowledge and Knowledge for Language, 2000; contbr. articles to profl. jours. Grantee NSF, 1971—; recipient numerous grants for computer sci. research, 1971—. Fellow Am. Assn. Artificial Intelligence; mem. IEEE (sr.), Assn. Computing Machinery (chmn. spl. interest group on artificial intelligence 1991-95, Disting. Scientist 2006—), Assn. Computational Linguistics, Cognitive Sci. Soc., Assn. Computing Machinery Disting. Scientist, Sigma Xi. Home: 142 Viscount Dr Buffalo NY 14221-1770 Office: Univ at Buffalo Dept of Comp Sci & Engring 201 Bell Hall Buffalo NY 14260-2000 Home Phone: 716-636-0816; Office Phone: 716-645-3180 ext. 125. Personal E-mail: shapiro@roadrunner.com. Business E-Mail: shapiro@buffalo.edu.

SHAPIRO, THEODORE, psychiatrist, educator; b. NYC, Feb. 26, 1932; s. Herman Alexander and Nettie (Rosenblatt) S.; m. Joan May Itkin, June 26, 1955; children: Susan, Alexander Herman. BA, Wesleyan U., 1953; MD, Cornell U., 1957. Diplomate Am. Bd. Psychiatry and Neurology, Am. Bd. Child Psychiatry, Am. Psychoanalytic Assn. Intern Montefiore Hosp., NYC, 1957—58; resident in psychiatry NYU-Bellevue Hosp., 1958—61; instr. to prof. NYU Sch. Medicine, 1960—76; rsch. assoc. child psychiatry NYU-Bellevue Hosp., 1961—65; asst. lectr. N.Y. Psychoanalytic Inst., NYC, 1970—86; prof. psychiatry and pediatrics Cornell U. Med. Coll., NYC, 1976—2002; tng. and supervising analyst N.Y. Psychoanalytic Inst., NYC, 1986—; vice chair for child and adolescent psychiatry, 1995—2002; emeritus prof. Cornell U. Med. Coll., NYC, 2002—. Cons. alcohol, drug abuse and mental health adminstrn. WHO, Washington, Geneva and Copenhagen, 1980—82; chair com. on stewardship Task Force Future, 1980—82, acad. sec., 1981—83, chair work group on sci. issues, 1988—89, chair com. editorship and stewarship of jour., 1984—86, 1990—92; participant APA bilateral exch. in Ea. Europe, 1992; mem. reviewer child psychopathology and treatment rev. com. NIMH, 1994—98; lectr. Jefferson Med. Coll., 2007; lectr. in field; spkr. in field. Author: Clinical Psycholinguistics, 1979; co-editor: Infant Psychiatry, 1976; editor: Psychoanalysis and Contemporary Science, 1976, Structure in Psychoanalysis, 1991, Affect: Psychoanalytic Perspectives, 1992; co-author: Manual of Panic-Focused Psychodynamic Psychotherapy, 1996, Psychodynamic Treatment of Depression, 2004, Psychodynamic Approaches to the Adolscent with Panic Disorder, 2004; editor Jour. Am. Psychoanalytic Assn., 1984-93; book rev. editor Internat. Jour. Psychoanalysis, 1993-2002; co-editor Research in Psychoanalysis, 1995; contbr. articles to profl. jours. Keynote lectr. Am. Psychoanalytic Assn., Boston, 2003, H. Hartmann Meml. NY Psychoanalytic Inst., 2004. Recipient Wilfred C. Hulse award, N.Y. Coun. Child Psychiatry, 1982, Harry Bakwin Meml. award, NYU, 1982, Heinz Hartmann award, N.Y. Psychoanalytic Inst., 2004; grantee, NIMH, 1976—86. Fellow Am. Acad. Child Psychiatry (sec. 1981-83), Am. Psychiat. Assn.; mem. Internat. Acad. Child/Adolescent Psychiatry (chmn. com. 2006), Soc. Profs. Child Psychiatry (chmn. com. on edn. 1982-90), Group for Advancement of Psychiatry (chmn. com. on child psychiatry 1985-90, elected GAP bd., 2008-), Am. Bd. Psychiatry & Neurology (com. on child and adolescent psychiatry 1987-93, chmn. 1992-93), N.Y. Psychoanalytic Soc. Jewish. Office: Weill Med Coll Cornell U Payne Whitney Clinic PO Box 140 New York NY 10021-0012 Office Phone: 212-746-5713. E-mail: tshapiro@med.cornell.edu.

SHAPIRO, VICTOR LENARD, mathematics professor; b. Chgo., Oct. 16, 1924; s. Joseph E. and Anna (Grossman) S.; m. Florence Gilman, Mar. 21, 1948; children: Pamela Sue Shapiro Baer, Laura Fern Shapiro Young, Charles R., Arthur G. BS, U. Chgo., 1947, MS, 1949, PhD, 1952. Mem. faculty Rutgers U., 1952-60, prof. math., 1959-60; mem. Inst. Advanced Studies, Princeton, N.J., 1953-55, 58-59; mem. faculty U. Oreg., Eugene, 1960-64; prof. math. U. Calif., Riverside, 1964—, faculty research lectr., 1978. Author: Topics in Fourier and Geometric Analysis, 1961, Contemporary Mathematics, Vol. 208, 1997, Singular Quasilinearity and Higher Eigen Values, 2001; contbr. articles to profl. jours. and publs. Served with AUS, 1943-46. NSF postdoctoral fellow, 1954-55 Fellow AAAS; mem. Am. Math. Soc., Math. Assn. Am., Am. Soc. Indsl. and Applied Math. Office: U Calif Math Dept Riverside CA 92521-0001 Office Phone: 951-827-3113. Business E-Mail: shapiro@math.ucr.edu.

SHAPIRO, WALTER ELLIOT, columnist; b. NYC, Feb. 16, 1947; s. Salem Seeley and Edith Geraldine (Herwitz) S.; m. Meryl Gordon, Aug. 24, 1980. BA, U. Mich., 1970, postgrad., 1970-71. Reporter Congl. Quarterly, Washington, 1969-70; editor Washington Monthly, 1972-76; spl. asst. U.S. Sec. Labor, Washington, 1977-78; Presdl. speechwriter The White House, Washington, 1979; reporter Washington Post, 1979-83; gen. editor Newsweek, NYC, 1983-87; sr. writer Time Mag., NYC, 1987-93; White House corr. Esquire mag., 1993-97; polit. columnist USA Today, 1995—2004; fellow Joan Shorenstein Ctr. on the Press, Politics and Pub. Policy Kennedy Sch. Govt. Harvard U., Boston, 2005; chief Washington bur. Salon.com, 2006—. Contbg. editor Washington Monthly, 1976—. Author: (book) One-Car Canavan: On the Road with the 2004 Democrats Before America Tunes In", 2003. Leadership fellow Japan Soc., U.S.-Japan, 1991. Mem.: White House Correspondents Assn., Judson Welliver Soc., Author's Guild. Jewish. Avocations: standup comedy, rotisserie baseball. Office: Salon Media Group 3417 1/2 M St NW Washington DC 20007 Home Phone: 212-580-0928; Office Phone: 202-333-5695. Business E-Mail: wshapiro@salon.com.

SHAPIRO, WARREN, anthropologist, educator; b. Bklyn., Jan. 11, 1941; s. Charles and Esther Shapiro; m. Fiona Powell, May 28, 1968 (div. Apr. 1970). BA, Bklyn. Coll., 1961; MA, U. Chgo., 1963; PhD, Australian Nat. U., 1969. Instr. Anthropology Adelphi U., Garden City, NY, 1965; asst. prof. Anthropology Calif. State U., LA, 1968—69; asst. prof., assoc. prof. Anthropology Rutgers U., New Brunswick, NJ, 1969—83, prof. Anthropology, 1983—. Disting. lectr. U. Manchester, England, 1988. Author: Social Organization in Aboriginal Australia, 1979, Miwuyt Marriage, 1981; contbr. Internat. Ency. Social and Behavioral Scis. Fellow Inst. Cross Cultural Rsch., U. Pitts., 1964; scholar, London Sch. Econs., 1988—89. Fellow: Am. Anthropol. Assn.; mem.: AAUP, Australian Inst. aboriginal Studies (corr.). Achievements include discovery of previously unknown systems of kin-classification in central Arnhem Land, Australia & solutiore of the murngin controversy. Avocations: bodybuilding, baseball, stamp collecting/philately. Office: Rutgers Univ Dept Anthropology 131 George St New Brunswick NJ 08901 E-mail: WS1369@aol.com.

SHAPIRO-MATHES, ANGELA, former broadcast executive; b. 1950; BA, St. Peter's Coll. Co-owner Brookville Mktg/Greybark Advt.; owner, oper. several businesses; co-founder, pub. Soap Opera Digest, 1975, Soap Opera Update, 1988; co-prodr. Soap Opera Awards; sr. v.p. mkg. and promotion ABC Daytime, 1995, pres., 1998, Buena Vista Prodns., 2000; pres. ABC Family Channel Walt Disney Co., Burbank, Calif., 2002—03; pres. Fox TV Studios, 2004—07; pres., gen. mgr. TLC, LA, 2007—08. Named one of The 100 Most Powerful Women in Entertainment, Hollywood Reporter, 2006, 2007.

SHAPLEY, ROBERT MARTIN, neurophysiology and perception educator; b. NYC, Oct. 7, 1944; s. Benjamin and Florence Edith (Rosenthal) S.; m. Laurie Rose Sigal, July 31, 1966; children: Nina Claire, Alice Eve. AB, Harvard U., 1965; PhD, Rockefeller U., 1970. Postdoctoral fellow Northwester U., Evanston, 1970-71, Cambridge U., Eng., 1971-72; asst. prof. Rockefeller U., NYC, 1972-76, assoc. prof., 1976-87; prof. neural sci. NYU, NYC, 1987—, Spencer prof. for sci., 1992—, dir. Ctr. for Neural Sci., 1991-94, dir. Ctr. for Theoretical Neurobiology, 1994—. Chmn. Visual Scis. B, Study Sect., Bethesda, Md., 1990-92. Assoc. editor Jour. Gen. Physiology, 1983-95, Visual Neurosci., 1988-91; sensory editor Exptl. Brain Rsch. (Hamburg, Fed. Republic Germany), 1990-1997; editor Contrast Sensitivity, 1993; contbr. articles to profl. jours. Recipient Career Devel. award NIH, 1977-82; Helen Hay Whitney Found. fellow, 1970-72; John and Catherine MacArthur Found. fellow, 1986. Mem.: Soc. Neurosci. Jewish. Avocations: tennis, history of art. Home: 1 Washington Square Vlg New York NY 10012-1632 Office: NYU Ctr for Neural Sci 4 Washington Pl New York NY 10003-6621

SHAPO, MARSHALL SCHAMBELAN, lawyer, educator; b. Phila., Oct. 1, 1936; s. Mitchell and Norma (Schambelan) S.; m. Helene Shirley Seidner, June 21, 1959; children: Benjamin, Nathaniel. AB summa cum laude, U. Miami, 1958, JD magna cum laude, 1964; AM, Harvard U., Cambridge, Mass., 1961, SJD, 1974. Bar: Fla. 1964, Va. 1977, Ill. 1993. Copy editor, writer Miami News, Fla., 1958-59; instr. history U. Miami, 1960-61; asst. prof. law U. Tex., 1965-67, asso. prof., 1967-69, prof., 1969-70; prof. law U. Va., 1970-78, Joseph M. Hartfield prof., 1976-78; Frederic P. Vose prof. Northwestern U. Sch. Law, Chgo., 1978—; of counsel Sonnenschein, Nath & Rosenthal, Chgo., 1991-2001. Vis. prof. Juristisches Seminar U. Gottingen (Fed. Republic Germany), 1976; cons. on med. malpractice and tort law reform U.S. Dept. Justice, 1978-79; mem. panel on food safety Inst. Medicine, NAS, 1978-79; vis. fellow Centre for Socio-legal Studies, Wolfson Coll., Oxford, vis. fellow of Coll., 1975, Wolfson Coll., Cambridge, 1992, 2001; mem. Ctr. for Advanced Studies, U. Va., 1976-77; cons. Pres.'s Commn. for Study of Ethical Problems in Medicine and Biomed. and Behavioral Rsch., 1980-81; reporter Spl. Com. on Tort Liability System ABA, 1980-84; del. leader People to People Citizen Amb. program delegation to East Asia Tort and Ins. Law, 1986; lectr. seminar Kobe U., Osaka Bar Assn., Ritsumeikan U., U. Girona, U. Pompeu Fabra, U. Pisa, Brazilian Bar Assn., U. Bremen, U. Coimbra; lectr. appellate judges' seminars ABA, 1977, 83, 90; reporter symposium on legal and sci. perspectives on causation, 1990; advisor Restatement of the Law, Third, Torts: Products Liability, 1992-97. Author: Towards a Jurisprudence of Injury, 1984, Tort and Compensation Law, 1976, The Duty to Act: Tort Law, Power and Public Policy, 1978, A Nation of Guinea Pigs, 1979, Products Liability, 1980, Public Regulation of Dangerous Products, 1980, The Law of Products Liability, 1987, Tort and Injury Law, 1990, (with Richard Peltz) 3d edit., 2006, The Law of Products Liability, 2 vols., 2d edit., 1990, 4th edit., 2001, supplements, 1991, 92, 93, 95, 96, 97, 98, 99, 2002, 03, 04, 05, 06, 07, 08, Products Liability and the Search for Justice, 1993, (with Helene Shapo) Law School Without Fear, 1996, 2d edit., 2002, Basic Principles of Tort Law, 1999, 2d edit., 2003, Tort Law and Culture, 2003, Compensation for Victims or Terror, 2005, Experimenting with the Consumer, 2008; (with Page Keeton) Products and the Consumer: Deceptive Practices, 1972, Products and the Consumer: Defective and Dangerous Products, 1970, (with D. Jacobson & A.N. Weber) International e-Commerce: Business & Legal Issues, 2001, (with G. Hernandez & others) eBusiness & Insurance, 2001, Concise Hornbook on Tort Law, 2003; mem. editl. bd. Jour. Consumer Policy, 1980-88, Products Liability Law Jour.; author: A Representational Theory of Consumer Protection: Doctrine, Function and Legal Liability for Product Disappointment, 1975; mem. adv. bd. Loyola Consumer Law Reporter; contbr. articles to legal and med. jours. Recipient Andrew J. Hecker award Fedn. Ins. and Corp. Counsel, 2001, Robert B. McKay Prof. award Am. Bar Assn., 2005, Disting. Alumnus award U. Miami Sch. Law, 2005; NEH sr. fellow, 1974-75 Mem. Am. Law Inst., Am. Assn. Law Schs. (chmn. torts compensation systems sect. 1983-84, torts round table coun. 1970). Home: 1910 Orrington Ave Evanston IL 60201-2910 Office: Northwestern U Sch Law 357 E Chicago Ave Chicago IL 60611-3059 E-mail: m-shapo@law.northwestern.edu.

SHAPOURY, ALIREZA, research scientist; BS, Shahid Beheshti U., Tehran, 1994; MS, Iran U. Sci. and Tech., Tehran, 1997; D, Tex. A & M U., Coll. Sta., 2007. Cert. grad. tchg. acad., Tex. A & M U., 2004. Lectr. Shahid Beheshti U., Tehran, 1996—99; design engr. Tom Co., Tehran, 1999—2000; engring. rsch. asst. Tex. Engring. Expt. Sta., 2000—05, 2007; rf test engr. Wireless Facilities Inc., San Diego, 2006—07; rf engring. cons. Pro Media Telecom. Inc., San Diego, 2006—07; rsch. scientist Phys. Optics Corp., Torrance, Calif., 2007—. Contbr. articles to profl. jours. Pres. and cofounder Persian Student Assn., Coll. Sta., 2001—02; pres. U. Apartments Cmty. Coun., Coll. Sta., 2004—05. Recipient Weirus Spirit award, Tex. A & M U., 2005, Small Bus. Innovative Rsch. award, US Navy, 2008, US Air Force, 2008. Mem.: IEEE (Travel grant 2001, Best paper grant 2003).

SHAPPELL, SCOTT ALLEN, engineering educator, consultant; PhD, U. Tex. Med. Br., Galveston, 1990. Capt. USN, 1988—2007. Contbr. scientific papers (Adm. Louis de Florez award, Flight Safety Found., Inc., 2002). Recipient Sonny Carter Meml. award, Soc. US Naval Flight Surgeons., 1996, Williams E. Collins award, Aerospace Human Factors Assn., 2002. Fellow: Aerospace Med. Assn. (Harry G. Moseley award 2003); mem.: APA (pres. divsn. 21 2008—), Human Factors & Ergonomics Soc. Conservative. Achievements include research in human factors analysis and classification system. Office: Clemson Univ 130 Freeman Hall Clemson SC 29634 Office Fax: 864-656-0795. Business E-Mail: hfeng@clemson.edu.

SHAPPERT, GRETCHEN C.F., lawyer, former prosecutor; b. 1956; AB, Duke U.; JD, Washington & Lee U. Bar: 1980. Assoc. Maupin, Taylor, & Ellis, P.A., Raleigh, 1980—81, Tucker, Hicks, Sentelle, Moon, & Hodge, P.A., Charlotte, 1981—83; asst. pub. defender Mecklenburg County, NC, 1983—88, asst. dist. atty., 1988—90; asst. US atty. (we. dist.) NC US Dept. Justice, 1990—2004, acting US atty., 2004—05, US atty. (we. dist.) NC, 2005—09, with Exec. Office for US Attys. (EOUSA) Washington, 2009—. Republican. Office: Exec Office for US Attys US Dept Justice 950 Pennsylvania Ave, NW, Rm 2242 Washington DC 20530-0001 Office Phone: 704-344-6222.*

SHAPSHAY, SANDRA LYNNE, philosopher, educator; b. Boston, May 27, 1969; m. Steven Wagschal, June 14, 1998. PhD, Columbia U., NYC, 2001. Asst. prof. philosophy Ind. U., Bloomington, 2003—. Recipient Year-long award, German Academic Exch. Svc., 1996—97; Year-long Faculty fellowship, Poynter Ctr. Study Ethics and Am. Insts., 2005—06. Mem.: Am. Philos. Assn. Liberal. Office: Ind Univ 1033 E Third St Bloomington IN 47405 Business E-Mail: sshapsha@indiana.edu.

SHAPSHAY, STANLEY M., otolaryngologist, educator; b. Bklyn., Dec. 22, 1942; s. Samuel and Mollie Shapshay; m. Ruth E. Shapshay, Oct. 1, 1967; children: Sandra Lynne, Mara Rachelle. BS, Bklyn. Coll., 1964; MD, Med. Coll. Va., Richmond, 1968. Diplomate Am. Bd. Othlaryngology. Intern surgery Boston City Hosp., 1968-69; resident otolaryngology Tufts-New Eng. Med. Ctr., Boston, 1969-71, 1972-75; fellow otolaryngical head & neck surgery Serafimer Hosp., Karolinska Med. Sch., Stockholm, 1971-72; asst. prof. otolaryngology Boston U. Sch. Medicine, 1977-86, clin. assoc. prof. otolaryngology, 1986—91, prof. otolaryngology, 1991—2005; prof., chair dept. otolaryngology Tufts U. Sch. Medicine, Boston, 1994—2001; prof. otolaryngology-head & neck surgery Mt. Sinai Sch. Medicine & Med. Ctr., NYC, 2005—06; prof. dept. otolaryngology Albany Med. Coll., NY, 2006—; staff Univ. Ear, Nose & Throat of Northeastern NY, LLP, 2006—. Clin. instr. U. Wash., Seattle, 1975—77; chief otolaryngology dept. VA Med. Ctr., Boston, 1977—80, attending otolaryngologist, 1980—82; asst. vis. surgeon otolaryngology Univ. Hosp., Boston, 1977—82; vis. surgeon Children's Hosp. Med. Ctr., Boston, 1977—87; chief ambulatory surgery/otolarygology Boston City Hosp., 1980—82; staff dept. otolaryngology/head & neck surgery Lahey Clinic Med. Ctr., Burlington, Mass., 1982—94, chmn. clin. laser com., 1984—93, bd. govs., 1993—94, New Eng. Med. Ctr. Hosps., 1995—97; vis. prof. Stanford U., Calif., 1995, Vanderbilt U. Med. Ctr., Nashville, 1995, U. Istanbul, Turkey, 1997; adj. prof. dept. surgery/otolaryngology Brown U. Sch. Medicine, Providence, 1997—; vis. scientist spectroscopy lab. MIT, 1996—. Mem. editl. bd. Lawers in Surgery and Medicine, Medical Laser Industry Report, Otolaryngoloty-Head & Neck Surgery; contbr. articles to profl. jours., chapters to books; spkr. in field. Maj. US Army, 1975—77. Fellow: ACS, Am. Rhinological Soc., Am. Coll. Chest Physicians, Am. Broncho-Esophagol. Assn. (coun. mem. 1985—, chmn. prevention fgn. body accidents and caustic ingestion com. 1988—89), Am. Soc. Head & Neck Surgery (mem. prevention com.), Am. Acad. Otolaryngology & Ophthalmology; mem.: AMA, Am. Laryngological Assn., Am. Coun. Otolaryngology (subcom allied health pers. 1975—76), Am. Acad. Otolaryngology (Young Otolaryngologist 1981—82), Triological Soc. (coun. mem. 1997—, pres 2005—06, Edmund Prince Fowler award), Biomed. Optics Soc., Am. Bd. Laser Surgery (founding mem.), New Eng. Otolaryngol. Soc. (sec.-treas. 1984—88, pres. 1990—91), Am. Soc. Laser Medicine & Surgery (chmn. postgrad. edn. com. 1986—87, membership/awards com. 1989—90, v.p. 1989—90). Avocations: reading, tennis, ballroom dancing. Office: Albany Med Coll Dept Otolaryngology 43 New Scotland Ave Albany NY 12208 also: Univ ENT Northeastern NY 35 Hackett Blvd Albany NY 12208 Office Phone: 518-262-3125, 518-262-5575. Office Fax: 518-262-3165, 518-262-6670.*

SHAQFEH, ERIC STEFAN G., engineering educator; b. Pottsville, Pa., Nov. 23, 1959; m. Terhilda S. Garrido, July 23, 1983; children: Stefan Garrido-Shaqfeh, Elena Garrido-Shaqfeh. PhD, Stanford U., Calif., 1986. Postdoc. rschr. Cambridge U., 1986; tech. staff mem. ATT Bell Labs., Murray Hill, NJ, 1987—90; prof. Stanford U., 1990—. Recipient Presdl. Young Investigator award, NSF, 1990—95, award, Camile & Henry Dreyfus Found., 1994, Curtis W. McGraw Rsch. award, ASEE, 1998, Hougen Professorship award, U. Wis. Madison, 2004; fellow, David & Lucile Packard Found., 1991—96. Home: 921 Aquarius Way Oakland CA 94611 Office: Stanford Univ 488 Escondido Mall Stanford CA 94305 Business E-Mail: esgs@stanford.edu.

SHARAPOVA, MARIA, professional tennis player; b. Nyagan, Russia, Apr. 19, 1987; d. Yuri and Yelena Sharapova. Trained, Bollettieri's Acad., 1996. Prof. tennis player WTA Tour, 2001—; model IMG Modeling Agy., 2003—; winner Wimbledon, 2004, US Open, 2006, Australian Open, 2008. Recipient ESPY award, Best Female Tennis Player, ESPN, 2008; named Newcomer of Yr., WTA, 2003, Most Improved Player of Yr., 2004, Player of Yr., 2004, Female Choice Athlete, Teen Choice Awards, 2006, 2007, Female Athlete of Yr., US Sports Acad., 2006, Whirlpool 6th Sense Player of Yr., 2006; named one of The Most Influential People in the World of Sports, Bus. Week, 2007, The 100 Most Powerful Celebrities, Forbes.com, 2008. Achievements include winning 19 career singles WTA championships; 3 career doubles championships; 4 career ITF Women's Circuit singles titles; winner of 3 Grand Slam singles titles; first Russian woman to win at Wimbledon, 2004; signed endorsement deals with Parlux Fragrances Inc and Motorola; mem. Russian Fed Cup Team, 2008. Avocations: singing, reading, stamp collecting/philately, fashion, Russian music. Mailing: WTA Tour One Progress Plz Ste 1500 Saint Petersburg FL 33701

SHARARA, FADY IHSAN, reproductive endocrinologist, infertility specialist; b. Beirut, Feb. 26, 1962; s. Ihsan A. Sharara and Samia R. Mouneimneh; m. Roula Mohsen Dalloul; children: Yasmeen, Noora. BS, Am. U. Beirut, 1982, MD, 1986. Asst. prof. U. Ill., Chgo., 1994—95; co-dir. divsn. reprodn. endocrinology and infertility Michael Reese Hosp. and Fertility Ctr., 1995—96; asst. prof., assoc. prof. U. Md. Sch. Medicine, Balt., 1996—2000; dir. assisted reproductive techs. Fertility and Reproductive Health Ctr., Annandale, Va., 2000—01; founder, med. dir. Va. Ctr. Reproductive Medicine, Reston, 2001—; clin. assoc. prof. George Washington U. Sch. Medicine, Washington, 2001—. Dir. asst. reproductive techs. U. Md. Sch. Medicine, 1997—2000. Recipient Serono Young Investigator award, Chgo. Area Reproductive Endocrinologists, 1995. Fellow: ACOG; mem.: ESHRE, ASRM, Am. Infertility Assn. (bd. dirs. 2001—03), Mid. East Fertility Soc., Endocrine Soc. Office: Va Ctr Reproductive Medicine 11150 Sunset Hills Rd Ste 100 Reston VA 20190 Home Phone: 301-320-9320; Office Phone: 703-437-7722. Business E-Mail: fsharara@ucrmed.com.

SHARDA, RAMESH, management science-information systems educator; b. Bijainagar, Rajasthan, India, June 1, 1953; came to U.S., 1975; s. Kanhaiya Lal and Gorjya Devi (Nyati) S.; m. Usha Rathi, Feb. 19, 1980; children: Rohit, Ruchy. BEng with honors, U. Udaipur, India, 1975; MS in Agrl. Engring., Ohio State U., 1976; MBA, U. Wis., 1978, PhD, 1981. Grad. rsch. assoc. Ohio State U., Columbus, 1975-76; grad. teaching assoc. U. Wis., Madison, 1976-78, lectr., 1978-80; asst. prof. mgmt. sci. and info. systems Okla. State U., Stillwater, 1980-84, assoc. prof., 1984-89, prof., 1989—. Presenter in field; cons. TMS, Inc., Cushing, Okla., 1981-83, Conoco, Ponca City, Okla., 1986, Memorex Telex, Tulsa, 1988-89, Purolator Products Co., Tulsa, 1990—; reviewer Mgmt. Sci., Jour. Mgmt., Interfaces, Journal of Intelligent Mfg., Decision Scis. Editor: (with others) Impacts of Recent Computer Advances on Operations Research, 1989; column editor OR-MS Today, 1990—, Neural Network News, 1989—, AI Week, 1990—; contbr. articles to profl. jours. Vol. fund raiser Sta. KOSU, Stillwater, 1989; faculty advisor India Student Assn., Stillwater, 1989-90. Recipient Faculty Achievement award Burlington-No. Found., 1987; Nat. Sci. Talent Search scholar, India, 1970; grantee Univ. Ctr. for Water Rsch., 1980-90, U.S. Geol. Survey, 1990, Memorex-Telex Corp., 1988, NSF, 1989-90. Mem. Ops. Rsch. Soc. Am. (gen. chmn. conf. 1989, vice chmn., chmn.-elect computer sci. tech. sect. 1990—), Inst. for Mgmt. Scis., Decision Sci. Inst., IEEE Computer Soc., Internat. Neural Network Soc., Phi Kappa Phi, Beta Gamma Sigma, Alpha Epsilon. Avocations: movies, cards, ping pong/table tennis, stamp collecting/philately. Home: 4103 W 15th Ave Stillwater OK 74074-1670 Office: Okla State U Coll Bus Adminstrn Stillwater OK 74078-0001

SHARE, RICHARD HUDSON, lawyer; b. Mpls., Sept. 6, 1938; s. Jerome and Millicent Share; m. Carolee Martin, 1970; children: Gregory Share, Jennifer Share Frolik, Ashley Share Jakubowsky. BS, UCLA, 1960; JD, U. So. Calif., 1963. Bar: Calif. Sup. Ct. 1964, U.S. Dist. Ct. (cen. and so. dists.) Calif., U.S. Supreme Ct. 1974. Field agt. IRS, 1960—63; mem. law divsn., asst. sec. Avco Fin. Svcs., 1963—72; founder Frandzel and Share, A Law Corp., LA, 1972—99, Richard Hudson Share & Assocs., 1999—. Lectr. Nat. Bus. Inst., Creditor's Rights; adj. prof. Loloya Law Sch., 1999. Office: PO Box 1003 Pacific Palisades CA 90272-1003 also: 150 N Santa Anita Ave Ste 530 Arcadia CA 91006-3127 Office Phone: 800-771-0104. E-mail: sharelaw@aol.com.

SHARER, JOHN DANIEL, lawyer; b. Bklyn., Sept. 19, 1950; s. Albert Robert and Alda Loretta (Tapiro) S.; m. Kathleen Gail Donaldson, Feb. 14, 1981; 1 child, Stephanie Erin. AB summa cum laude, Dartmouth Coll., Hanover, NH, 1972; JD, U. Pa., Phila., 1975. Bar: Pa. 1975, NJ 1975, DC 1976, NY 1989, Va. 1994. Law clk. Superior Ct. Pa., Hon. Edmund B. Spaeth, Jr., Phila., 1975-76; assoc. Sutherland, Asbill & Brennan, Washington, 1976-82, ptnr., 1982-94; counsel Christian & Barton, L.L.P., Richmond, Va., 1994-95, ptnr., 1996-99; sr. counsel Dominion Resources Svcs. Inc., Richmond, 1999—2001, mng. counsel electric delivery, 2001—06, asst. gen. counsel, 2006—. Faculty Va. State Bar Professionalism Course, 2001—04; mem. Third Dist. Disciplinary Comm. Sect. III, 2003—06; grader Va. State Bar Examination, 2003—; mem. Va. State Bar Standing Com. on Professionalism, 2004—, Va. State Bar Coun., 2005—; bd. govs. Va. State Bar Com. on the Edn. Lawyers, 2007—. Bd. dirs. Wakefield Sch., Marshall, Va., 1990-94; pres. Dartmouth Club of Cen. Va., 1997-2003. Named Va. Super Lawyers, 2009. Fellow Va. Law Found. (Va. Super Lawyers 2009); mem. Phi Beta Kappa. Republican. Avocations: classical music, judicial biographies, computers, Norfolk. Home: 12317 Northlake Ct Richmond VA 23233-6635 Office: 120 Tredegar St PO Box 26532 Richmond VA 23261-6532 Office Phone: 804-819-2271. Business E-Mail: john.d.sharer@dom.com.

SHARER, KEVIN W., medical products executive; b. Clinton, Iowa, Mar. 2, 1948; m. Faye M. Sharer (div.); children: Heather, Keith; m. Carol Sharer. BS in Aero. Engring., US Naval Acad., 1970; MS in Aero. Engring., US Naval Postgraduate Sch., 1971; MBA, U. Pitts., 1982. Commd. lt. to lt. comdr. USN, 1970—78; with AT&T, 1978-82; cons. McKinsey & Co., 1982-84; pres., CEO Gen. Electric Co., Princeton, NJ, 1984-89; exec. v.p., pres. bus. markets divsn. MCI Communications, Washington, 1989—92; pres., COO Amgen Inc., Thousand Oaks, Calif., 1992-2000, pres., CEO, 2000—01, chmn., pres., CEO, 2001—. Bd. dirs. Amgen Inc., 1992—, 3M Corp., 2001—07, Northrup Grumman Corp., 2003—, Chevron Corp., 2007—. Chmn. bd. trustees LA County Mus. Natural Hist.; bd. trustees U. So. Calif. Office: Amgen Inc 1 Amgen Ctr Dr Thousand Oaks CA 91320-1799 Office Phone: 805-447-1000. Office Fax: 805-447-1010.*

SHARF, STEPHAN, automotive executive; b. Berlin, Dec. 30, 1920; arrived in USA, 1947, naturalized, 1952; s. Wilhelm and Martha (Schwartz) S.; m. Rita Schantzer, 1951, (dec. 2001). Degree in Mech. Engring., Tech. U., Berlin, Fed. Republic Germany, 1947; PhD, Oakland U., Rochester, Mich., 2007, DSc with honors, 2007. Tool and die maker Buerk Tool & Die Co., Buffalo, 1947-50; foreman Ford Motor Co., 1950-53, gen. foreman Chgo., 1953-58; with Chrysler Corp., Detroit, 1958-86, master mechanic Twinsburg stamping plant, 1958-63, mfg. engring. mgr., 1963-66, mrg. prodn. Twinsburg stamping plant, 1966-68, plant mgr. Warren stamping plant, 1968-70, plant mgr. Sterling stamping plant, 1970-72, gen. plants mgr. stamping, 1972-78, v.p. Engine and Casting div., 1978-80, v.p. Power Train div., 1980-81, exec. v.p., mfg., dir., 1981-85, exec. v.p. internat., 1985-86, also bd. dirs.; pres. SICA Corp., Bloomfield Hills, Mich., 1986—. Columnist Ward's Auto World Common Sense mag., 1987—. Bd. dirs. Jr. Achievement, Detroit council Boy Scouts Am.; trustee, v.p. Oakland U. Mem. Soc. Auto Engrs., Detroit Engring. Soc. Clubs: Wabeek Country. Avocations: golf, travel, charity. Home: 966 Adams Castle Dr Bloomfield Hills MI 48304-3713 Office: SICA Corp President 725 Adams Rd Ste 230 Birmingham MI 48009 Personal E-mail: sharfsteve@yahoo.com.

SHARFSTEIN, JOSHUA MOSES, federal agency administrator, pediatrician; b. Sept. 26, 1969; s. Steven Sharfstein and Margaret Shiling; m. Yngvild Olsen; 2 children. Grad., Harvard, 1991; MD, Harvard Med. Sch., 1996. Pediatrics resident Boston Med. Ctr., 1999, Boston Children's Hosp., 1999; gen. pediatrics fellow Boston U. Sch. Med., 2001; pediatrician Children's Nat. Med. Ctr., Mt. Wash. Pediatric Hosp.; sr. public health aide for Rep. Henry A. Waxman Calif.; commr. Balt. Health Dept., 2005—09; prin. dep. commr. FDA, 2009—. Named Pub. Official of Yr., Governing Mag., 2008. Office: Balt City Health Department 1001 E Fayette St Baltimore MD 21202-4715*

SHARFSTEIN, SUSAN T., engineering educator; b. Palo Alto, Calif., 1965; married. BS with honors, Calif. Inst. Tech., Pasadena, 1987; PhD in Chem. Engring., U. Californa, Berkeley, 1993. Acting instr., biochemical engring. U. Calif., 1992, postdoc. rsch. asst., 1993—94, LA, 1994—96; asst. prof. bioengineering U. Toledo, 1996—2001; vis. scientist Wadsworth Labs., NY State Dept. Health, Albany, 2000—02; asst. prof. chem. and biol. engring. Rensselaer Poly. Inst., Troy, NY, 2001—. Mem. com. chair Congregation Agudat Achim, Niskayuna, NY, 2003—06. Recipient Early Career Devel. award, NSF, 2000—05, Class 51 Outstanding Tchg. award, Rensselaer Poly. Inst., 2007, Sch. Engring. Excellence in Edn. award, 2007. Mem.: Internat. Soc. Stem Cell Rsch., Am. Soc. Engring. Edn., Am. Soc. Biochemistry and Molecular Biology, AIChE (Travel award 2007), Am. Chem. Soc. (ann. meeting session co-chair 2004—), Sigma Xi. Office: Rensselaer Poly Inst 110 8th St Biotech 2nd Fl Troy NY 12180

SHARGEL, GERALD L., lawyer; b. New Brunswick, NJ, Oct. 5, 1944; BA, Rutgers U., 1966; JD, Bklyn. Law Sch., 1969. Bar: NY 1969, US Dist. Ct. (ea. and so. dists.) NY 1969, US Ct. Appeals (2nd, 3rd, 5th and 9th cirs.) 1969. Pvt. practice, NYC, 1970—. Faculty mem. Practising Law Inst., 1976—77; adj. assoc. prof. law NYU, 1977—82; mem. adv. bd. NYU Sch. Law, Ctr. for Rsch. in Crime and Justice, 1984—88; practitioner in residence Bklyn. Law Sch. Mem.: ABA, Fed. Bar Coun., NY State Trial Lawyers Assn., NY County Lawyers Assn., Assn. Bar City NY, NY State Bar Assn., Criminal Bar Assn. Office: 570 Lexington Ave 45th Fl New York NY 10022 also: Bklyn Law Sch 250 Joralemon St Rm 808 Brooklyn NY 11201 Office Phone: 212-446-2323, 718-780-7546. Business E-Mail: gerald.shargel@brooklaw.edu.*

SHARIATI, MEHDI SEZAVAR, social sciences educator; MA in Economics, U. Mo. Kans. City, 1983, PhD, 1994; MA in Sociology, U. Kans., Lawrence, 1986. Chmn. social sci. divsn. Donnelly Coll., Kans. City, Kans., 1996—2001; prof. Kans. City Kans. CC, 2001—. Contbr. articles to profl. jours. Adv. Mental Health Organs., Kans. City, 1982—2008. Recipient Tchg. Excellence award, NISOD, 2008. Master: Kans. City Kans. CC Economics Club. Office: Kans City Kans CC 7250 State Ave Kansas City KS 66112

SHARIFI, NEDA A., scientist; m. Ali M. Lankar Sharifi; children: Ava Ilene, Sophie Ilene. BS in Physiology & Neurobiology, U. Md., Coll. Pk., 1999; PhD in Human Genetics & Molecular Biology, Inst. Genetic Medicine, John Hopkins U. Sch. Medicine, Balt., 2007, attending, 2007—. Registered US patent agt. Pepper Hamilton LLP, 2008. Rsch. asst. U. Md., 1997—2000; lab instr.neurobiology dept. Nat. Inst. Neurological Disorders & Strokes, Bethesda, Md., 2000—01; tchg. asst., human genetics John Hopkins U. Sch. Medicine, 2003—04; with Inst. Genetic Medicine, John Hopkins U. Sch. Medicine, Balt., 2001—. Recipient Poster award, Nat. Inst. Health, Md., 2000; finalist Predoc. Presentation award, Am. Soc. Human Genetics, New Orleans, 2006; grant, Golden Key Nat. Honor Soc., 1997. Mem.: US Patent & Trademark Bar Assn., Tehran Woman's Skiing Team, Tehran Woman's Swimming Team. Personal E-mail: nsharifi@gmail.com.

SHARIFI, NIMA, oncologist, researcher; s. Mohammad and Roghieh Sharifi. BS, Va. Tech., Blacksburg, 1992—95; MD, U. Pitts., Pa., 1996—2001. Res. Cleve. Clinic Found., Cleve., 1998—99; res., internal medicine Yale New Haven Hosp., Conn., 2001—03; oncologist UT Southwestern Med. Ctr., Dallas, asst. prof. medicine. Grantee fellowship, Howard Hughes Med. Inst., 1998, Med. Oncology fellowship, NIH, 2006. Mem.: AAAS, Am. Assn. Cancer Rsch., Am. Soc. Clin. Oncology. Office: Nat Cancer Inst Bldg 560 Rm 21-81 Frederick MD 21702 Home: 2506 Worthington St Dallas TX 75204

SHARIFOV, ROVSHAN CHINGIZ, lawyer; b. July 19, 1974; BA in Polit. Sci., NYU, NYC, 1997, JD, 2002. Legal aide NY State Atty. Gen.'s Office, NYC, 2001—02; asst. dist. atty. Dist. Atty.'s Office Nassau County, Mineola, NY, 2002—06; mng. ptnr. Sharifov & Russell, LLP, Hempstead, NY, 2006—. Pub. Svc. fellow, NYU, 2001. Mem.: Nassau County Former Asst. Dist. Atty.'s Assn., NY State Trial Lawyers Assn., NY State Bar Assn. Office: Sharifov and Russell LLP 50 Main St Hempstead NY 11550

SHARIFY, NASSER, librarian, educator, writer; b. Tehran, Iran, Sept. 23, 1925; came to U.S., 1953, naturalized, 1972; s. Ebrahim and Eshrat (Saghafy) S.; m. Homayoun Taslimy, June 14, 1950 (div. 1978); children: Sharareh, Shahab. Licencie es Lettres, U. Tehran, 1947; MS, Columbia U., 1954, Dr. L.S., 1958. Editorial staff Teheran jours. Rah-e Now, Jahan-e Now, Saba, Jonb va Jush, 1943-51; translator, announcer All India Radio, 1948-49; librarian, dep. dir. Library of Parliament Iran, Tehran, 1949-53; cataloger Library of Congress, 1954-55; program asst. libraries devel. sect. UNESCO, Paris, 1959-61; acting chief servicing sect. Dept. Edn., 1962-63; dir. gen. Ministry Edn., Tehran, 1961-62; asst. prof. library and info. scis. and internat. edn. U. Pitts., 1963-66; founder, dir. Internat. Library Info. Center, 1964-66; vis. lectr. SUNY Albany Sch. Library Sci., summer, 1966; dir. internat. librarianship and documentation, internat studies and world affairs SUNY, Oyster Bay, 1966-68; dean, prof. grad. sch. library and info sci. Pratt Inst., Bklyn., 1968-87, chmn. inst. research council, 1971-89, disting. prof., dean emeritus sch. computer, info. and library scis., 1987—; pres. B.E.L.T., Inc., internat. planning cons., 1981—. Dir. Grad. Library Tng. Program, UNESCO Mission, Nat. Tchrs. Coll., Tehran, 1960; Iran's Ofcl. del. to UNESCO Conf. Ednl. Pubs., Geneva, 1961, SE Asia Edn. Secs. Conf., Murree, Pakistan, 1961, Internation Conf., on Cataloging Prins., Paris, 1961, CENTO Libr. Devel. Conf., Ankara, Turkey, 1962; chmn. standing com. for preparation reading materials for new literates UNESCO, Tehran, 1961-62; mem. U.S. AID Mission, Turkey, Iran, Pakistan, 1966; dir. Conf. on Internat. Responsibility Coll. and Univ. Librarians, Oyster Bay, 1967; U.S. del. 33d Conf. and Internat. Congress on Documentation, Tokyo, 1967; ALA del. UN Conf. on Non-Govtl. Orgn., 1969; cons. U.S. AID, Conf. on Book Devel., 1967; mem. adv. bd. Ency. Libr. and Info. Scis., 1969—; chmn. Pre-Am. Library Assn. Conf. Inst. on Internat. Libr. Manpower, Edn. and Placement in N.Am., Detroit, 1970; mem. Am. del. Internat. Fedn. Libr. Assn. Conf., Liverpool, Eng., 1971, Budapest, 1972, Grenoble, France, 1973, Washington, 1974, Brussels, 1977, Montreal, 1982, Chgo., 1985, Barcelona, 1992; organzier USAID sponsored Global Info. Village Conf., Rabat, Morocco, Bklyn., N.Y., 1997, spkr., 1997; bldg. cons. Learning Resources Center, Nat. Tchrs. Coll., Iran, 1972-73, cons. campus planning, 1972-73; UNESCO cons. missions to plan and evaluate Nat. Sch. Info. Sci., Morocco, 1973-74, 79-81, 89, 96-; cons. U.S. Info. Agy., Morocco, 1991, 92, 95; chmn. Conf. on Orgn. and Control of Info for Islamic Research, 1982; chmn. bd. cons. to Nat. U. Iran, 1974-75, Pahlavi Nat. Library of Iran, 1975-77; speaker Symposium Internat. sur l' information Economique, Casablanca, Morocco, 1990; inaugural speaker Ctr. Documentation et D'Information Multimedia, Rabat, Morocco, 1995. Author: cataloging of Persian works Including Rules for Transliteration Entry and Description, 1959, Book Production, Importation and Distribution in Iran, Pakistan and Turkey, 1966; Beyond the National Frontiers: The International Dimension of Changing Library Education for a Changing World, 1973; The Pahlavi National Library of the Future, 17 vols., 1976, other books; contbr. to Ency. of Library and Info. Sci., 1969, ALA World Ency. Library and Info. Services, 1980, 86, library jours., 1973—, Bookmark, 1972, Library Education in the Middle East, 1991, Remembering Rangathan: A Sentimental Reflection, 1992; contbr. poetry to various jours. and anthologies, 1947-51, 67, 91-93 lyrics to Iranian motion pictures and recs., 1948-52; works on display at Archieves of Hoover Inst. on War Revolution and Peace, Stanford U.; Contbr. to: film script for motion picture Morad, 1951-52. Trustee Bklyn. Public Library, 1970-82; pres. Maurice F. Tauber Found., 1981—. Recipient Taj (crown) medal and citation for disting. svc. Mohammad Reza Shah Pahlavi, Shah of Iran, 1978, Kaula Gold medal and citation for disting. svc. to internat. librarianship, 1985; named for Annual Nasser Sharify Lecture Series, Sch. of Computer Info. and Libr. Scis., Pratt Inst., 1988—; writings by and about Nasser Sharify are preserved at Archives of Hoover Instn. on wars, revolutions and peace., Stanford U., Stanford, Calif. Mem. ALA (chmn. com. equivalencies and reciprocity 1966-71, mem. UNESCO panel, mem. nominating com. 1970-71, chmn. Pakistan, Iran, Turkey, Morocco, and Middle East Resource panels, internat. libr. edn. com. 1973—, mem. com. internat. libr. schs. div. libr. edn. 1968-72, coord. country resources panels, internat. libr. edn. com. libr. edn. div. 1973-78, Citiation extraordinary and exemplary svc. internat. librarianship 1999, John Ames Humphry OCLC Forest Press award 2004), NY Libr. Assn. (dir. library edn. sect. 1969-72), Pub. Libr. Assn. (task force on internat. relations 1981-86), Am. Assn. Libr. Schs. (chmn. govtl. relations com., 1984-88), Am. Soc. Info. Sci., Spl. Libr. Assn., Internat. Fedn. Libr. Assns. (adv. group libr. edn. 1971-73, v.p. libr. schs. sect. 1973-77). Home: 252 Jericho Tpke Westbury NY 11590-1213 Office: Pratt Inst Sch Info and Libr Sci 144 W 14th St New York NY 10011-7301 Personal E-mail: nsharify@aol.com, nassersharify@gmail.com. *If I am asked to wash a car, I try to make it spotless. If I am to write a book, I try to make it faultless. But it seems that I always find spots on the shining surface of the car, and faults in many well-written pages of the book. This gives me another reason to live for another day.*

SHARKEY, ANDREW G., III, science association director; b. Pitts. m. Debbie Sharkey. BA in Polit. Sci., Yale U., New Haven, 1968; MA, Duquesne U., Pitts., 1970. Pres. Steel Svc. Ctr. Inst., 1981—93; with Am. Iron and Steel Inst., 1993—, pres., CEO, 2005—. Mem.: NAM Coun. Mfg. Assns., Key Industries Assn. Com. of Am. Soc. Assn. Execs., US Chamber Com. of 100, Am. Iron and Steel Inst. Office: Am Iron and Steel Inst Ste 705 1140 Connecticut Ave NW Washington DC 20036 Office Phone: 202-452-7100.

SHARKEY, CATHERINE MOIRA, law educator; b. Balt., May 1, 1970; BA in Economics, summa cum laude, Yale U., 1992; JD, Yale U., 1997; MS in Economics for Devel., Oxford U., 1994. Bar: Md. 1998, DC 2000, NY 2000. Law clk. to Hon. Guido Calabresi US Ct. Appeals (2nd Cir.), New Haven, 1997—98; law clk. to Hon. David H. Souter US Supreme Ct., Washington, 1998—99; Supreme Ct. & appellate litig. assoc. Mayer, Brown Rowe & Maw, NYC, 2000—02, cons., 2002; assoc. prof. law Columbia U., NYC, 2003—07, NYU Sch. Law, 2007—. Rhodes Scholar, 1992—94. Office: NYU Sch Law 40 Washington Sq S New York NY 10012

SHARKEY, (JOHN) MICK, biology educator; BS in Biology, Boise State Univ., 1989. Formerly in retail grocery industry; biology tchr. Parma (Idaho) H.S., 1989—. Recipient John 'Mick' Sharkey Day in Idaho, Feb. 27, 2006, Idaho Gov.; named Idaho Tchr. of Yr., 2006; named one of nation's top 5 percent of biology tchrs., Dolan DNA Learning Ctr., 2002; finalist GenzymeInvitrogen Biotech Educator award, 2007; grantee summer fellowship, Cold Spring Harbor Lab., NY. Office: Parma High Sch 908 N 8th Parma ID 83660 Business E-Mail: jsharkey@parmaschools.org.

SHARKEY, ROBERT EMMETT, lawyer; b. Chgo., Oct. 21, 1942; s. Edward Francis and Catherine Christine (Grundhoefer) S.; m. Phoebe Dadakis, July 28, 1963 (div.); children: Siobhan, Edward, Catherine, James. BA, Georgetown U., 1964, JD, 1967. Bar: Md. 1967, D.C. 1995, U.S. Dist. Ct. Md. 1967, U.S. Ct. Appeals (4th cir.) 1972, U.S. Ct. Appeals (2nd cir.) 1973, U.S. U.S. Supreme Ct. 1973, U.S. Ct. Appeals (fed. cir.) 1986, U.S. Ct. Fed. Claims 1986, D.C. 1995, D.C. Ct. Appeals 1995, U.S. Dist. Ct. D.C. 1996. Mem. staff subcom. fed., state, local rels. Commn. for Re-orgn. Exec. Branch Md. Govt., College Park, 1967; law clerk for Chief Judge Edward S. Northrop U.S. Dist. Ct. Md., Balt., 1967-68; assoc. Gordon, Feinblatt, Rothman, Hoffberger & Hollander, Balt., 1968-74, ptnr., 1974—. Mem. counsel Balt. Hist. Soc., 2000. Mem. Md. Bar Assn. (profl. ethics 1987—, vice chmn. com. profl. ethics 1991-93, chmn. com. profl. ethics 1993), Bar Assn. Balt. City (com. profl. ethics 1984-86), St. Thomas More Soc. Md. (pres. 1982-83), Georgetown U. Alumni Assn. (law alumni rep. 1992), Ice Club Balt. (v.p. 1981-83), Phi Delta Phi. Avocation: figure skating. Home: 4514 Foxhall Cres NW Washington DC 20007-1055 E-mail: rsharkey@gfrlaw.com.

SHARKEY, THOMAS DAVID, biochemist, educator; b. Detroit, Jan. 28, 1953; s. Robert Hugh and Patricia June (Elliott) S.; m. Paulette Marie Bochnig June 21, 1974; 1 child, Jessa Sung. BS in Biology with honors, Mich. State U., 1974, PhD in Botany and Plant Pathology, 1980. Postdoctoral fellow Australian Nat. U., Canberra, 1980-82; assoc. rsch. prof. Desert Rsch. Inst., Reno, 1982-87; asst. prof. U. Wis., Madison, 1987-88, assoc. prof., 1988-91, prof., 1991—2008, Dept. Biochemistry and Molecular Biology, Mich. State U., 2008—, chair, 2008—. Assoc. dir. Biolog. Scis. Ctr., Reno, Nev., 1983-87; chmn. dept. botany U. Wis., Madison, 1992-94; dir. Inst. Cross-Coll. Biology Edn., 2004-07. Editor: Trace Gas Emissions from Plants, 1991, Photosynthesis: Physiology and Metabolism, 2000; contbr. more than 160 articles to profl. peer-reviewed jours. Mem.: AAAS, Internat. Soc. Photosynthesis Rsch., Am. Soc. Plant Biologists. Office: MI State Univ Dept Biochemistry Mol Biology 210 Biochemistry Bldg East Lansing MI 48824 Home: 1210 Prescott Drive East Lansing MI 48823 Office Phone: 517-353-3257. Business E-Mail: tsharkey@msu.edu.

SHARKEY, TINA, Internet company executive; m. Seth Goldstein; 2 children. BA in Internat. Rels. & Telecomm., U. Pa., 1986. V.p. mktg., then v.p. programming Q2 Inc. (divsn. QVC), 1993—95; co-founder, chief cmty. architect iVillage.com, 1995—97; head online expansion Sesame Workshop (formerly Children's TV Workshop or CTW), 1997, group v.p., gen. mgr. CTW online, then group pres. online svcs., 1999; launch team mem. Adobe Acrobat/NY1 brands, Frankfurt Balkind Ptnrs., NYC; prin. Majestic Ptnrs., NYC; sr. v.p. lifestyle & cmty. programming America Online Inc., 2003—05, sr. v.p. network programming, 2006, sr. v.p. instant messaging & social media, 2006—07; chmn., global pres. BabyCenter, LLC, San Francisco, 2007—. Founding bd. mem. BabyBuggy, Inc., NYC, 2001; bd. dirs. Vonage, 2008—, Interactive Advt. Bur., Online Pubs. Assn. Named a Woman to Watch, Advt. Age, 2009; Henry Crown Fellow, Aspen Inst., 2004. Office: BabyCenter LLC 163 Freelon St San Francisco CA 94107 Office Phone: 415-537-0900. Business E-Mail: tsharkey@babycenter.com.*

SHARKEY, VINCENT JOSEPH, finance company executive; b. Newport, RI, May 25, 1944; s. Vincent Joseph and Dorothy (Auvil) S.; m. Joyce Toomey, Dec. 27, 1969; children: Alison Greeley, Christina Geist, John, Julia. BA in Econs., Yale U., 1966; JD, U. Va., 1971. Bar: N.J. 1971, U.S. Ct. Appeals (3d cir.) 1985. Asst. prosecutor Bergen County Prosecutor's Office, Hackensack, NJ, 1971-72; pvt. practice, Bergen County, 1972-75; ptnr. Riker, Danzig, Scherer, Hyland & Perretti, Morristown, NJ, 1979—2006; sr. v.p. Fidelity Nat. Fin., 2007—. Lt. U.S. Army, 1966-68. Mem. Yale U. Alumni Assn. (pres. Bergen County chpt. 1986-88). Business E-Mail: vincent.sharkey@fnf.com.

SHARMA, BHAVENDER PAUL, biotechnologist; b. Patiala, Punjab, India, Oct. 22, 1949; s. Tribhawan Nath and Parkash Wati Sharma; m. Kathryn Ann Bilinski, Aug. 15, 1973; children: Anjana, Nealinder. BSChemE, Punjab U., 1969; MPhil, Rutgers U., 1974, PhD, 1977; MBA, Syracuse U., 1985. Instr. Rutgers U., New Brunswick, NJ, 1975—76; sr. project engr. Corning Inc., NY, 1976—83; dir. tech. and strategic planning Genencor Internat., Inc., South San Francisco, Calif., 1983—91; pres. InterSpex Products, Inc., Foster City, Calif., 1991—94; exec. dir. CV Therapeutics, Inc., Palo Alto, Calif., 1994—2001; v.p. Telik, Inc., Palo Alto, 2002—07, Geron Corp., Menlo Park, Calif., 2007—. Editor newsletter INSAF, West Orange, N.J., 1996—. Office: Geron Corp 230 Constitution Dr Menlo Park CA 94025 Office Phone: 650-566-7245. Business E-Mail: bsharma@geron.com.

SHARMA, BHAVNEESH K., internist, researcher; s. Krishan Kumar and Prem Lata Sharma; m. Manisha Kaushik, Aug. 23, 2001; 1 child, Bhavya. B in Medicine and Surgery, U. Delhi, New Delhi, 1998; MD in internal medicine, U. Delhi, 2003. Lic. Indian Med. Assn., 1998, foreign grad. Ednl. Commn. Fgn. Med. Grads., 2003. Rsch. investigator Lok Nayak Hosp., New Delhi, 1998—2000, resident physician, 2000—03, chief resident, 2003—04; resident physician Brookdale U. Hosp., Bklyn., 2004—. Contbr. articles to profl. jours. Recipient Young Investigator award, Am. Coll. Chest Physicians, 2003; scholar Nat. Sci. Scholarship, NSF, 1992. Mem.: AMA, ACP (assoc.), Soc. Gen. Internal Medicine, Am. Thoracic Soc., Soc. Critical Care Medicine, Com. Interns & Residents (dept. rep. 2005—), Indian Med. Assn. (life; mem. 1998—). Achievements include research in the association between gastroesophageal reflux disease and bronchial asthma; esmolol on the oxidant and antioxidant activity during myocardial infarction; the effect of vitamin E supplementation on the oxidant and antioxidant activity in chronic obstructive pulmonary disease; pulmonary dysfunction in type 2 diabetes; the role of serum B-natriuretic pepetide and troponon I as prognostic markers in septic shock patients; autoimmune phenomenon in chronic hepatitis C infection. Office: Brookdale Univ Hosp One Brookdale Plz Brooklyn NY 11212 Home: 4370 Kissena Blvd Apt 20c Flushing NY 11355-3740 Personal E-mail: bhavneesh@hotmail.com.

SHARMA, BRAHAMA D., chemistry professor; b. Sampla, Punjab, India, June 5, 1931; naturalized Am. citizen; s. Des Raj and Kesara Devi (Pathak) S.; m. Millicent M. Hewitt, Dec. 22, 1956 (div. 1996); children: Nalanda V. Sharma Bowman, Renuka D; m. Katharine A. McAfee, June 17, 2001. BS with honors, U. Delhi, India, 1949, MS, 1951; PhD, U. So. Calif., 1961. Registered parliamentarian. Chemist Govt. Opium Factory, Ghazipur, India, 1951-52; lab. assoc., sci. asst. Nat. Chem. Lab., Poona, India, 1952-55; lab. assoc. U. So. Calif., LA, 1955-61; research fellow Calif. Inst. Tech., Pasadena, 1961-65; asst. prof. chemistry U. Nev., Reno, 1963-64, Oreg. State U., Corvallis, 1965-70, Calif. State U., Northridge, 1973-75, assoc. prof., 1975-76; prof. L.A. Pierce Coll., Woodland Hills, Calif., 1976-96. Part-time assoc. prof. chemistry Calif. State U., L.A., 1973-85, prof., 1985—; vis. assoc. Calif. Inst. Tech., 1979, 82; pres. L.A. Pierce Coll. Senate, 1981-82, chmn. profl. and acad. stds., 1989-92. Contbr. articles to profl. jours. Key leader sci. and tech. 4-H U. Calif., San Luis Obispo County. Grantee E.I. duPont de Nemours, L.A., 1961, NSF, 1967-69. Mem. Am. Chem. Soc. (chmn. edn. com. So. Calif. chpt. 1981-82, rsch. grantee 1965-69), Royal Soc. Chemistry (chartered chemist),Am. Crystallographic Assn., Am. Inst. Physics (assoc.), Am. Inst. Parliamentarians (sec., adminstr., lt. gov. region VII, exec. lt. gov. region VII), Nat. Assn. Parliamentarians (registered parliamentarian, life), Calif. Assn. Parliamentarians (pub. rels. chmn., statewide edn. chmn. So. area, pres. Calif. Sigma unit), San Luis Obispo Gem and Mineral Club Inc. (pres. 1998, sec. 1999, v.p. 2000). Avocations: playing bridge, reading, history, classical music, crystal models. Personal E-mail: mercury610@aol.com.

SHARMA, DEEPAK, bank executive; b. Amla, India, May 4, 1954; s. Kamer Nath and Khalatamka (Devi) S.; m. Radhika Kalra, Jan. 13, 1984; children: Priyanka, Arjun. BS in Chemistry, Delhi U., 1973; MBA, Indian Inst. Mgmt., Ahemdabad, India, 1976. Loans officer Citibank, Bombay, 1976-78, treas. Seoul, Korea, 1979; ops. head Saudi Am. Bank, Riyadh, Saudi Arabia, 1980-86, global pvt. bank head, 1987-92; global pvt. bank head Middle East Citibank, Geneva, 1993; CEO global wealth mgmt., Asia-Pacific and Middle East region Citigroup, Singapore, 2005—07, CEO Citi global wealth mgmt. internat., 2007—. Co-founder, trustee Indiapore Trust; trustee Singapore Indian Devel. Assn.; bd. mem. Singapore Tyler Print Inst.; mgmt. bd. Middle East Inst. Office: Citigroup 399 Park Ave New York NY 10043*

SHARMA, DEVEN, financial information company executive; b. Oct. 20, 1955; BS, Birla Inst. Tech., India; MS, U. Wis.; D in Bus. Adminstrn., Ohio State U. With Anderson Strathclyde, Dresser Industries; ptnr. Booz-Allen & Hamilton, 1988—2002; exec. v.p. global strategy The McGraw-Hill Companies, Inc., 2002—07; exec. v.p. investment svc. & global sales Standard & Poor's, NYC, 2007, pres., 2007—. Bd. dirs. 800-Flowers Inc., CRISIL, The US-China Bus. Coun., Asia Soc. Bus. Coun. Office: Standard & Poor's 55 Water St New York NY 10041 Office Phone: 212-438-1000. Office Fax: 212-438-2000.*

SHARMA, DINESH KUMAR, management science educator; arrived in U.S., 1988; s. Phool W. Sharma; m. Preeti R. Rani; children: Amit K., Rajat K. BS in Math., M.D. U., Rohtak, India, 1985; PhD, Chaudhary Charan Singh U., India, 1999. Asst. prof. U. Md. Ea. Shore, Princess Anne, 1999—2002, assoc. prof., 2002—. Contbr. articles to profl. publs. (Received 6 Best Paper awards). Mem.: N.E. Decision Scis. Inst., S.E. Decision Scis. Inst., Decision Sciences Inst., Operational Rsch. Soc. India (life), Acta Ciencia Indica (life), Sigma Beta Delta (hon.; chpt. pres.). Office: U Md Ea Shore Dept Bus Mgmt and Acctg Princess Anne MD 21853

SHARMA, DIVESH SHANKAR, finance educator; s. Daya Shankar and Sarita Sharma; m. Vineeta Chand, Jan. 16, 1988; 1 child, Nivita Divya. B in Commerce, U. Canterbury, New Zealand, 1988, M in Commerce, 1991; Degree in Higher Edn., Griffith U., Queensland, Australia, 1994, PhD, 1999. Cert. Inst. Chartered Accountants, Australia, 1998. Auditor KPMG, Christchurch, New Zealand, 1988; assoc. prof. Nanyang Technol. U., Singapore, 2001—05; lectr. to sr. lectr. Griffith U., Brisbane, Australia, 1992—2001; prof. Auckland U. Tech., New Zealand, 2005—07; assoc. prof. Fla. Internat. U., Miami, 2007—. Recipient Excellence award, Inst. Chartered Accountants, 1993. Mem.: Am. Acctg. Assn.

SHARMA, GAURAV, imaging scientist, electrical engineer; b. Dehradun, India, Oct. 12, 1968; came to U.S., 1992; s. Sohan Lal and Santosh Sharma. B Engring., Indian Inst. Tech., Roorkee, India, 1990; M Engring., Indian Inst. Sci., Bangalore, 1992; MS in Applied Math., NC State U., Raleigh, 1995, PhD in Elec. Engring., 1996. Rsch. engr. Ctr. for Devel. Telematics, Bangalore, 1992; rsch. asst. NC State U., Raleigh, 1992—96, tchg. asst., 1995; summer rsch. intern Webster Rsch. Ctr. Xerox Corp, NY, 1993, 94, 95, mem. rsch. staff, Digital Imaging Tech. Ctr. Webster, 1996—2003; assoc. prof. U. Rochester, 2003—; dir. Ctr. Electronic Imaging Sys. (CEIS), 2008—. Editor Digital Color Imaging Handbook, 2003; contbr. articles to profl. jours. Mem. IEEE (sr.; referee trans. on signal/image processing/coms. 1995—; chair Rochester sect., 2007), Soc. Imaging Sci. and Tech., Sigma Xi, Phi Kappa Phi, Pi Mu Epsilon. Achievements include 38 patents on digital imaging and image processing; over 10 patents pending. Office: ECE Dept U Rochester PO Box 270126 Rochester NY 14627-0126 Business E-Mail: gaurav.sharma@rochester.edu.

SHARMA, GAURAV, finance company executive; b. New Delhi, Nov. 27, 1981; s. Mangat Ram Sharma and Santosh Kumari; m. Pooja Batra, Dec. 3, 2007. BS in Tech., Indian Inst. Tech, Delhi, 2002; PhD, Purdue U., West Lafayette, 2006. Summer intern IBM India Rsch. Lab, New Delhi, 2001, Microsoft Rsch. Lab., Cambridge, England, 2004; quantitative analyst D. E. Shaw & Co., NYC, 2007—. Mem.: IAFE. Home: 423 W 45th St #1FE New York NY 10036 Office: D E Shaw & Co 120 W 45th St New York NY 10036 Business E-Mail: sharmag@deshaw.com.

SHARMA, JAYENDRA, pediatrician, cardiologist; b. Ahmedabad, Gujrat, India, Oct. 16, 1961; s. Ramakant Sharma and Aruna Tiwari; m. Swati Dave-sharma, May 8, 1991; children: Chinmayi J., Yash J. MBBS, Smt. NHL Mcpl. Med. Coll., Ahmedabad, 1985; MD, NY Presbyn. Hosp. Cornell, NYC, 1998; MD in Pediat., Maiminides Med. Ctr., Bklyn., 1995. Cert. Am. Bd. Pediat., 1995, 2002, Am. Bd. Pediat. Cardiology, 2005. Dir., pediat. cardiology Lincoln Med. Ctr., Bronx, NY, 1998—2002, Children Hosp., Downstate, Bklyn., 2002—06, Jamaica Hosp. Med. Ctr., NY, 2006—. Contbr. articles to profl. jours. Named Best Tchr., Pediat. Residents, 1998—99, 2002, 2005. Fellow: Am. Coll. Cardiology. Office: Jamaica Hosp Med Ctr 8900 Van Wyck Expressway Jamaica NY 11418 Office Fax: 718-206-7144. Business E-Mail: jsharma@jhmc.org.

SHARMA, KRISHNA KATHRIBAIL, biochemist, educator; b. Mudnor, Karnataka, India, July 18, 1955; came to U.S., 1990; s. Shankaranarayana and Parvathi Bhat;m. Sandhya Noojibail, Nov. 27, 1987; children: Sangitha, Nikhilesh. BSc, St. Philomena Coll., Karnataka, India, 1974; MSc, Kasturba Med. Coll., 1978; PhD, Kasturba Med. Coll., Karnataka, 1982. Jr. rsch. fellow Kasturba Med. Coll., Manipal, India, 1978, lectr., 1979-81, asst. prof., 1982, reader, 1987-89; rsch. assoc. U. Mo., Columbia, 1983-86, rsch. asst. prof., 1990-94, asst. prof. biochemistry, 1994—. Rsch. grantee NIH, 1993, Fight for Sight, 1996. Mem. AAAS, Am. Soc. Biochemistry and Molecular Biology, Assn. for Rsch. in Vision and Ophthalmology, Sigma Xi. Office: Mason Eye Inst 1 Hospital Dr Columbia MO 65201-5276

SHARMA, NUTAN, neurologist, educator; b. Dunkirk, NY, Mar. 3, 1965; d. Moti Lal and Krishan Kanta Sharma. AB, Stanford U., Palo Alto, Calif., 1986; MD, SUNY, Stony Brook, PhD, 1995. Cert. Bd. Psychiatry and Neurology, 2000. Asst. prof. neurology Harvard Med. Sch., Cambridge, Mass., 2005—. Mem.: Soc. Neurosci., Movement Disorder Soc., Am. Acad. Neurology, Am. Neurol. Assn. Office: Mass Gen Hosp 149 13th St Rm 6407 Charlestown MA 02129 Office Fax: 617-726-4101.

SHARMA, PRASHANT, physicist, educator; s. Ram Swaroop and Kanchan Sharma; m. Sapna Sharma, Aug. 31, 2004. PhD, Boston U., 2002. Postdoc. fellow Cornell U., Ithaca, NY, 2002—04; postdoc. assoc. Argonne Nat. Lab., Ill., 2004—06; asst. prof. Suffolk U., Boston, 2006—. Office: Suffolk Univ 41 Temple St Boston MA 02114 Office Fax: 617-367-5063; Home Fax: 617-573-8013. Business E-Mail: psharma@suffolk.edu.

SHARMA, RAJ KISHORE, research scientist, educator; s. Ramesh Chand and Sheela Sharma. PhD, Delhi U., 2001. Rschr & developer Yonsei U. Korea, Seoul; rsch. prof. UCF, Orlando, Fla., 2001—. Achievements include research in energy related materials. Office: NanoSci Tech Ctr UCF 12424 Resarch Pkway Ste 400 Orlando FL 32826 Office Phone: 305-282-3325. Personal E-mail: drrajksharma@yahoo.co.in. Business E-Mail: rsharma@mail.ucf.edu.

SHARMA, RAJENDRA, chemist, educator; s. M. L. and Kamal Sharma; m. Abha Sharma, Jan. 31, 1982; children: Abhishek, Akanksha. PhD, Rajasthan U., Jaipur, 1979. Jr. rsch. fellow, dept. chemistry U. Rajasthan, Jaipur, 1975—78; sr. rsch. fellow Indian Coun. Med. Rsch., Jaipur, 1978—79. Rsch. assoc. All India Inst. Med. Sci., New Delhi, 1980—81; chemist Oil and Natural Gas Corp., Dehradun, Uttaranchal, India, 1981—89, suptd. chemist, 1991—2000; postdoc. fellow U. Tex. Med. Br., Galveston, 1989—91, visting scientist, 2000—03, instr., 2006—; assoc. prof. U. North Tex. HLTH Sci Ctr., Fort Worth, 2007. Recipient Best Achievement award, Dir., Keshav Dev Malviya Inst. Petroleum Exploration, 1991, Bd. Mem. Exploration, Oil and Natural Gas Corp., 1993. Mem.: Am. Assn. Biochemistry and Molecular Biology, Assn. Rsch. Vision and Ophthalmology, Am. Chem. Soc. Office: Univ North Tex HLTH Sci Ctr 3500 Camp Bowie Blvd Fort Worth TX 76107 Office Fax: 817-735-2118. Business E-Mail: rsharma@hsc.unt.edu.

SHARMA, RAMASWAMY, microbiologist, researcher; married. BS in Microbiology, U. Bombay, 1992, BS in Biochemistry and Chemistry, 1993, MS in Microbiology and Immunology, 1995; PhD, Wayne State U., Detroit, 2006. Cert. Pentasoft, 1999, HDSE Aptech, 2001. Rsch. asst. UDCT and Hoechst Pharms., Mumbai, 1992, U. Bombay, 1993—95, Wayne State U., 2001—06, founding pres. Michbio student chpt., 2004—06; microbiologist Wyeth Lederle Ltd., Mumbai, 1995—2001; postdoc. fellow Forsyth Inst., Boston, 2006—08, asst. rsch. investigator, 2008—. Recipient Ctr. Molecular Medicine and Genetics Travel award, Wayne State U., 2003, 2006, Dean's Academic and Rsch. Excellence award, Wayne State U. Sch. Medicine, 2005. Mem.: HMS/HSDM Postdoc. Assn., Am. Soc. Neurochemistry, Soc. Neurosci., Nat. Postdoc. Assn., Internat. Assn. Biol. and Med. Rsch., Sigma Xi, Internat. and Am. Assn. Dental Rsch. Achievements include research in study of stress-pathways and genes involved in dental fluorosis and characterization of enzymes involved in enamel formation. Office: Forsyth Inst 140 The Fenway Boston MA 02115 Office Fax: 617-892-8303. Business E-Mail: rsharma@forsyth.org.

SHARMA, SAMIN KUMAR, internist, interventional cardiologist, educator; b. Alwar, India, May 28, 1955; Undergraduate degree, Maharaja Coll., India, 1972; MD, SMS Med. Coll., Rajasthan U., Jaipur, 1978. Cert. Internal Medicine, Cardiovascular Disease, Interventional Cardiology. Intern, internal medicine SMS Hosp., Jaipur, India, 1978—79, resident, internal medicine, 1979—82, NYU Downtown Hosp., 1983—86; fellow, cardiology City Hosp. Ctr. at Elmhurst, 1986; prof., medicine, cardiology Mt. Sinai Med. Sch., NY; dir., interventional cardiology Mt. Sinai Med. Ctr., NY. Serves on Cardiac Adv. Bd. NY State; travels to India 4 to 6 times a yr. to teach the art of angioplasty to Indian cardiologists; founder, dir. Live Symposium of Complex Coronary Cases, 1998—. Contbr. several articles to profl. jours.; featured on or in Today Show, NY Times, Wall Street Journal, NY Mag., Barron's, Forbes, Newsweek, Washington Post, Crain's NY Bus., Newsday, NY Post, NY Sun, Earthtimes, India Abroad and India Today. V.p. Rajasthan Develop. Found., India. Recipient Best Med. and Chief Resident, NY Infirmary-Beekman Downtown Hosp., Ctr. of Excellence award for Rotational Coronary Atherectomy, 1996—2000, Simon Dack award for Best Tchr., Cardiovascular Inst., Mt. Sinai Hosp., 2000, Prestigious Jaipur, Rajasthan Govt. India, 2002, Governor's award Excellence, NY State, 2006, Jacobi Medallion award, 2007, Mt. Sinai Physician Yr. award, 2007; named one of Best Doctors, US News and World Report, Top Physicians, Consumer Rsch. Coun. America, Castle Connelly. Office: 5 E 98th St 3rd Fl New York NY 10029 Office Phone: 212-427-1540. Business E-Mail: samin.sharma@mountsinai.org.*

SHARMA, SANJEEV, engineer, researcher; s. Maheshwor and Radha Kumari Sharma; m. Anupama Panta, May 14, 2002. MS in Aeroelectrical Engring., Kiev Inst. Civil Aviation Engr., USSR, 1991; PhD, U. Newcastle, Australia, 2001. Airworthiness engr. Dept. Civil Aviation, Kathmandu, Nepal, 1991—96; part-time lectr., staff mem. U. Newcastle, 1996—99; human factors specialist Tenix Def. Aerospace Divsn., Melbourne, Australia, 2001—03; lead human factors engring. specialist BAE Systems Australia, Adelaide, 2004—. Contbr. articles to profl. jours. Mem.: Soc. Nonlinear Dynamics in Human Factors (founder), Human Factors and Ergonomics Soc. Achievements include first to use nonlinear dynamical system/chaos theory in empirical human factors research; use dynamic spectrogram and slope of the regression line fitted to the spectral curve as fractal-like self-similar measures of human perception. Home: 8 Declivity St Highbury Adelaide SA 5089 Australia Office: BAE Systems Australia Taranaki Rd Edinburgh Pks Adelaide SA 5111 Australia Personal E-mail: sanjeevnewcastle@hotmail.com. Business E-Mail: sanjeev.sharma@baesystems.com.

SHARMA, SANJIV, cardiologist; s. Sohan Lal and Inder Mohini Sharma; m. Geetanjali Sharma, May 2, 1994; children: Rohan, Rhea. Degree in Premed., Multani Mal Modi Coll., Punjabi U., 1983; MBBS, All India Inst. Med. Scis., New Delhi, India, 1988, MD, 1993. Diplomate Am. Bd. Internal Medicine, 1996, Am. Bd. Cardiovasc. Disease, 1999, Am. Bd. Interventional Cardiology, 2000. Jr. resident All India Inst. Med. Scis., New Delhi, 1989—91, sr. resident, 1992—93; resident Mass. Gen. Hosp., Harvard Med. Sch., Boston, 1993—94, Boston U. Sch. Med., 1994—96; cardiology fellowship West LA VA Med. Ctr., 1996—99; interventional cardiology fellowship Cedars Sinai Med. Ctr., LA, 1999—2000; interventional cardiologist Bakersfield Heart Hosp., Calif., 2000—. Dir. rsch. and edn., chmn. health edn. and continuing med. edn. com. Bakersfield Heart Hosp., Calif., 2000—; instr. clinical medicine UCLA, 2005. Fellow: Am. Coll. Cardiology, Soc. Cardiac Angiography and Intervention. Achievements include invention of guiding catheter for coronary intervention-patent pending; research in novel strategy for preventing the complication of slow-flow and no-reflow phenomena in saphenous vein graft interventions; first to use of drug eluting stent and filter-wire in vertebral artery percutaneous intervention; research in status paper advocating the use of intracoronary administration of abciximab in percutaneous coronary interventions; intragraft administration of abciximab and verapamil prevents slow-flow and no-reflow phenomena during saphenous vein graft percutaneous coronary interventions. Office: Ctrl Cardiology Medical Clinic 2901 Sillect Ave Ste 100 Bakersfield CA 93308 Personal E-mail: sanjiv1122@yahoo.com.

SHARMA, SANTOSH DEVRAJ, obstetrician, gynecologist, educator; b. Kenya, Feb. 24, 1934; arrived in US, 1972; d. Devraj Chananram and Lakshmi (Devi) S. BS, MB, B.J. Medical Sch., Pune, India, 1960. House surgeon Sasson Hosp., Poona, India, 1960-61; resident in ob-gyn. various hosps., England, 1961-67; house officer Maelor Gen. Hosp., Wrexham, U.K., 1961-62; asst. prof. ob-gyn. Howard U. Med. Sch., Washington, 1972-74; assoc. prof. John A. Burns Sch. Med., Honolulu, 1974-78, prof., 1978—. Fellow Royal Coll. Ob-Gyn., Am. Coll. Ob-Gyn. Avocations: travel, photography, environmental protection. Office: 1319 Punahou St Rm 824 Honolulu HI 96826-1032 Office Phone: 808-203-6501. Business E-Mail: santosh@hawaii.edu.

SHARMA, SATISH KUMAR, engineering educator; s. Rama Naresh and Tarawati Sharma; m. Mamta Sharma, Feb. 24, 1993; children: Shiva Shree, Shruti Shree. BTech, Kamla Nehru Inst. Tech., Sultanpur, 1991; PhD, Inst. Tech., Banaras Hindu U., India, 1997. Jr., sr. rsch. fellow Banaras Hindu U., Inst. Tech., Varanasi, 1993—99; postdoc. fellow U. Man., Winnipeg, Manitoba, Canada, 1999—2001, rsch. assoc., 2001—06; sr. antenna engr. Info. Magnetics Technologies Corp., Winnipeg, 2001—06; asst. prof. San Diego State U., 2006—. Contbr. articles to profl. jours. Recipient Young Scientist award, URSI Commn. B, Field and Waves, EMTS, 2004. Mem.: IEEE, USNC/URSI Commn. B, ASEE. Office: San Diego State Univ ECE 5500 Campanile Dr San Diego CA 92182 Office Fax: 619-594-2654. Personal E-mail: satish.sharma@lycos.com. Business E-Mail: ssharma@mail.sdsu.edu.

SHARMA, SURENDRA PRASAD, technical manager, scientist; b. Gorakhpur, India, Feb. 3, 1943; came to U.S., 1971; s. Suresh Dutt and Dhanpati (Devi) S.; m. Prabha Durgapal; 1 child, Seema. BS, U. Gorakhpur, 1962; MS in Engring., Peoples' Friendship U., Moscow, USSR, 1968; PhD, MIT, 1978. Scientist Scientists' Pool, Coun. of Sci. and Indsl. Rsch., New Delhi, 1968-70; lectr., Dept. of Aeronautics Indian Inst. Tech., Bombay, 1970-71; rsch. asst. MIT, Cambridge, Mass., 1972-78; adj. rsch. prof. aeronautics Naval Postgrad. Sch., Monterey, Calif., 1979; rsch. engr. U. Tenn. Space Inst., Tullahoma, Tenn., 1979-81; sr. engr. Brown & Root, Inc., Houston, 1981-82, Sii Drilco, Smith Internat., Houston, 1982-85; tech. mgr. & ctr. Rep. Exploration Tech. Devel. Program NASA Ames Rsch. Ctr., Moffett Field, Calif., 1986—. Contbr. articles profl. jours. Mem. PTA, Cupertino, Calif. Assoc. fellow Am. Inst. Aeronautics and Astronautics; mem. Soc. Petroleum Engrs., IEEE, Sigma Xi (MIT chpt.). Avocations: gardening, classical music. Home: 20309 Silverado Ave Cupertino CA 95014-4437 Office: MS 269-2 NASA Ames Rsch Ctr Moffett Field CA 94035-1000 Office Phone: 415-604-3432. E-mail: spsharma@pacbell.net.

SHARMA, SUSHIL K., medical educator; b. Bharmar, India, Dec. 2, 1952; arrived in Can., 1988, naturalized, 2000; s. Shri Ram and Ram Piari Sharma; m. Kusum Sharma, June 27, 1983; 1 child, Aditya. BSc with honors in biophysics, Panjab U., India, 1974; MSc with honors in biophysics, Panjab U., 1976; PhD in neuroscience, All India Inst. of Med. Scis., India, 1986; postgraduate diploma in med. radio tech. (hon.), Bhabha Atomic Rsch Ctr., India, 1978. Rsch. officer All India Med. Inst., New Delhi, 1979—88; rsch. assoc. U. Manitoba, Winnipeg, 1988—93; sr. scientist U. Montreal, Montreal, Canada, 1993—97; deputy dir. Defence Inst. Physiology, New Delhi, 1997; rsch. scientist U. Manitoba, Winnipeg, 1997—2000; assoc. prof. U. ND Sch. Medicine, Grand Forks, ND, 2000—; dir. Cyclotron /microPET Labs. Author: (med. rsch. operation) Reputed Internat. Jours. of Med. Rsch. Certified, 1978. Mem.: Soc. of Neuroscience.

SHARMA, VANSHDEEP, psychiatrist; s. Manohar Sharma; life ptnr. Deborah Marin. MD, Maulana Azad Med. Coll., New Delhi, 1981. Diplomate Am. Bd. Psychiatry and Neurology, 1991, in child psychiatry Am. Bd. Psychiatry and Neurology, 1993. Vice chair, psychiatry Mt. Sinai Med. Ctr., New York, NY, 2003—. Office: Mt Sinai Med Ctr 1 Gustave Levy Pl New York NY 10029 Business E-Mail: vansh.sharma@mssm.edu.

SHARMA, VENKATANARAYANAN, professor; s. Sreekrishna and Kamalam Sharma; m. Sunita Subramanian, Feb. 10, 1991; children: Adrika V, Arvind V. PhD, Cancer Inst., U. Madras, India, 1989. Pre-doctoral fellow Cancer Inst., U. Madras, Chennai, 1986—89; project investigator MD Anderson Cancer Ctr., Houston, 1989—92; rsch. scientist Ohio State U., Columbus, 1992—95; asst. prof. U. West Fla., Pensacola, 1995—97, assoc. prof., 1999—2005, prof., 2005—. Head, lab. cytokine rsch. U. West Fla., 1995—, dir., health sci. adv. programs, 2001—, adminstrv. fellow, 2006—. Contbr. articles to profl. jours.; mem. editl. bd. Jour. of Alternative and Complementary Medicine. Pres. India Cultural Ctr., Inc., Pensacola, 2004—08. Recipient Awards for excellence in tchg., U. West Fla., 1998, 2003, Disting. U. Rsch. and Creative Activities award, 2001, Excellence in Undergrad. Tchg. and Advising award, 2005, 2001, Escambia County Father of Yr. award, Chief Judge's Children's Coun., Pensacola, 2002, Nautilus Excellence award, U. West Fla., 2004, Ann. Disting. Tchg. award, U. West Fla. Student Govt. Assn., 2005, Pres.'s award for Leadership in Diversity, U. West Fla., 2006; fellowship, U. Grants Commn., India, 1986—89, grants, Merck Pharm. Co., 2004. Mem.: Nat. Assoc. Advisors Health Profession Inc. Independent. Hindu. Achievements include research in identification of B-cell secreted cytokines and MNP transcription factor. Avocations: travel, gardening, woodworking. Home: 3243 Moss Point Lane Cantonment FL 32533-4844 Office: U West Fla 11000 University Parkway Pensacola FL 32514 Office Fax: 850-474-2749. E-mail: vsharma@uwf.edu.

SHARMA, VIRENDER, medical educator, director; s. Ravinder Lal and Salochana Devi Sharma; m. Sarah M. Garrett, Dec. 10, 2000; children: Kunal M., Keshav S. MBBS, All India Inst. Med. Sciences, New Delhi, India, 1992. Cert. physician Med. Coun. India, 1992. Assoc. prof. medicine Mayo Clinic Ariz., Scottsdale, 2002—07, prof. medicine, 2007—, dir. esophageal clinic, 2005—. Fellow: ACG, AGA, ASGE; mem.: Phenix GI Soc. (pres. 2009—). Achievements include patents for gastrointestinal neurostimulation. Office: Mayo Clinic 13400 E Shea Blvd Paradise Valley AZ 85253 Office Fax: 480-301-8673. Business E-Mail: sharma.virender@mayo.edu.

SHARMA, VIVEK, finance educator; s. Charanjit Lal and Bimla Sharma; m. Nirmala Somasundram, Feb. 2, 1997; children: Vatsala Bhardwaj, Neal Bhardwaj. BTech with honors, Indian Inst. Tech., Kharagpur, 1989; PGDM, Indian Inst. Mgmt. Lucknow, 1992; PhD, Va. Tech. U., Blacksburg, 2004. Grad. engr. Tata Steel, Jamshedpur, Bihar, India, 1989—90; asst. mgr. credit control SIEL, Delhi, 1992—93; asst. prof. IMS-BIMTECH, Delhi, 1993—95; sr. lectr. fin. TMC Stansfiled Coll., Singapore, 1995—99; asst. prof. fin. U. Mich., Dearborn, 2004—. Cons. IDA, Singapore, 2000. Contbr. to publs. Merit scholarship, Govt. India, 1985—89, grant, U. Mich., 2005—. Mem.: FMA Internat.

SHARMAN, ROBERT D., meteorologist, researcher; b. Long Beach, Calif. s. Oliver A. Sharman and Grace I. Schrader; m. Teddie Sharman; 1 child, Chris J. BS, UCLA Sch. Engring., 1969, MS, 1971; PhD, UCLA Atmosphere Sci., 1981. Sr. engr. Logicon Inc., San Pedro, Calif., 1983—96; rsch. scientist NCAR, Boulder, Colo., 1996—. Contbr. articles to rsch. jours. Named one of Top 50 Scientists, Rsch. Leader in Aerospace, Sci. Am., 2003. Mem.: Royal Meteorol. Soc., Am. Meteorol. Soc. Achievements include research in aviation turbulence forecasting and detection. Business E-Mail: sharman@ucar.edu.

SHARMAN, WILLIAM, professional basketball team executive; b. Abilene, Tex., May 25, 1926; m. Joyce Sharman; children from previous marriage: Jerry, Nancy, Janice, Tom. Student, U. So. Calif. Basketball player Washington Capitols, 1950-51, Boston Celtics, 1951-61; coach LA/Utah Stars, 1968-71, LA Lakers, 1971-76, gen. mgr., 1976-82, pres., 1982-88, spl. cons., 1991—. Author: Sharman on Basketball Shooting, 1965. Named to All Star 1st Team, NBA, 1956-59, 2nd Team, 1953, 55 (game MVP), 60, All League Team, 7 times, named Coach of Yr., 1972, One of Top Players in NBA History, league 50th anniversary, 1997, league leader free-throw percentage, 7 times; named to Basketball Hall of Fame, 1976, Naismith Basketball Hall of Fame (as player), 2004, as coach (3d man ever as both player and coach), 2004; named All-Am., twice; inductee U. So. Calif. Hall of Fame, 1994; Porterville H.S. gymnasium renamed in his honor, 1997; recipient John Wooden All-Time All-Am. award, 2003.

SHARON, YITZHAK YAAKOV, physicist, educator; b. Tel Aviv, Feb. 29, 1936; came to U.S., 1948; s. Abraham Sharon-Schwadron and Dina Freidenberg; m. Sandra Brook, Jan. 13, 1991; 1 child, Dina Avrahama Jennie. AB with highest honors, Columbia U., 1958; MA in Physics, Princeton U., 1960, PhD in Physics, 1966. Asst. Inst. for Advanced Study, Princeton, NJ, 1965-66; asst. prof. Northeastern U., Boston, 1966-72; assoc. prof. Richard Stockton Coll., Pomona, NJ, 1972-75, prof. physics, 1975—, trustee fellow in scis., 2000-01, Weinstein prof. Jewish studies, 2008—. Cons. Ednl. Svcs., Inc. Phys. Sci. Study Commn., 1962-63; vis. prof. Temple U., Phila., 1970-71, U. Montreal, 1970; vis. fellow Princeton U., 1980-82, 91-92; summer physicist Nat. Bur. Standards, Washington, 1971, Oak Ridge (Tenn.) Nat. Lab., 1969, Lawrence Radiation Lab., Berkeley, Calif., 1968; vis., cons., vis. scholar, vis. scientist, Rutgers U., 1995—. Contbr. articles to profl. jours. Grantee NSF, N.J. Dept. Higher Edn., Ctr. for Theology and Natural Scis. Mem. Am. Phys. Soc., Am. Assn. Physics Tchrs. (NJ exec. bd., NJ Lifetime Contbn. Physics Edn. award 2005), Sigma Xi, Phi Beta Kappa. Jewish. Home: 19 James Ave Kendall Park NJ 08824-1620 Office: Richard Stockton Coll NJ Dept Physics Pomona NJ 08240 Home Phone: 732-297-8146; Office Phone: 609-652-4500. Business E-Mail: sharon@physics.rutgers.edu.

SHARP, ANNE CATHERINE, artist, educator; b. Red Bank, NJ, Nov. 1, 1943; d. Elmer Eugene and Ethel Violet S. BFA, Pratt Inst., Bklyn., 1965; MFA, Bklyn. Coll., CUNY, 1973. Tchr. art Sch. Visual Arts, 1978-89, NYU, 1978, SUNY, Purchase, 1983, Pratt Manhattan Ctr., N.Y.C., 1982-84, Parsons Sch. Design, N.Y.C., 1984-90, Visual Arts Ctr. of Alaska, Anchorage, 1991, Anchorage Mus. Hist. and Art, 1991, 93, 94, 95, U. Alaska, Anchorage, 1994-96, Fashion Inst. Tech., SUNY, 1997-98; lectr. AAAS, The 46th Arctic Divsn. Sci. Conf., U. Alaska, Fairbanks, 1995, Cmty. Ch., Ho-Ho-Ku, N.J., 2005. One-person shows Pace Editions, N.Y.C., Ten/Downtown, N.Y.C., Katonah (N.Y.) Gallery, 1974, Contemporary Gallery, Dallas, 1975, Art in a Public Space, N.Y.C., 1979, Eatontown Hist. Mus., N.J., 1980, N.Y. Pub. Library Epiphany Br., 1988, Books and Co., N.Y., 1989, The Kendall Gallery, N.Y.C., 1990, Alaska Pacific U., Carr-Gottstein Gallery, Anchorage, 1993, Internat. Gallery Contemporary Art, Anchorage, 1993, Art Think Tank Gallery, N.Y.C., 1994, U.S. Geol. Survey, Reston, Va., 1994, Stonington Gallery, Anchorage, 1994, on TV Ltd. Benefit, N.Y.C., 1998-2000; group shows include Arnot Art Mus., Elmira, N.Y., 1975, Bronx Mus., 1975, Mus. Modern Art, N.Y.C., 1975-76, Nat. Arts Club, N.Y.C., 1979, Calif. Mus. Photography, Riverside, 1983-92, Jack Tilton Gallery, N.Y.C., 1983, Lincoln Ctr., N.Y.C., 1983, Cabo Frio Print Biennale, Brazil, 1983, Pratt Graphic Ctr., N.Y.C., 1984, State Mus. N.Y., Albany, 1984, Kenkeleba Gallery, N.Y.C., 1985, Hempstead Harbor Art Assn., Glen Cove, N.Y., 1985, Mus. Mod. Art, Weddel, Fed. Republic of Germany, 1985, Kenkeleba Gallery, N.Y.C., 1985, Paper Art Exhbn. Internat. Mus. Contemporary Art, Bahia, Brazil, 1986, Mus. Salon-de-Provence, France, 1987, Mus. Contemporary Art, Sao Paulo, Brazil, 1985-86, Salon de Provence, France, 1987, Adirondack Lakes Ctr. for Arts, Blue Mountain Lake, N.Y., 1987, Kendall Gallery, N.Y.C., 1988, Exhibition Ctr. Parsons Sch. Design, N.Y.C., 1989, F.M.K. Gallery, Budapest, Hungary, 1989, Galerie des Kulturbundes Schwarzenberg, German Dem. Republic, Q Sen Do Gallery, Kobe, Japan, 1989, Anchorage Mus. History and Art, 1990-91, 94, U. Alaska, Anchorage, 1990, 91, Coos Art Mus., Coos Bay, Oreg., 1990, Spaceship Earth, Mus. Internat. de Neu Art, Vancouver, Can., 1990, Courcourse Gallery, Emily Carr Coll. Art and Design, 1990, Nat. Mus. Women in the Arts, Washington, 1991, Visual Arts Ctr. Alaska, 1991, 92, Nomad Mus., Lisbon, Portugal, 1991, Mus. Ostdeutsche Gallery, Regensberg, Germany, 1991, Mcpl. Mus. Cesley Krumlov (So. Bohemia) CSFK, Czechoslovakia, 1991, Böltmiche Dörter Exhbn. Hochstrass 8, Munich, 1992, BBC-TV, Great Britain, U.K., Sta. WXXI-TV, Rochester, N.Y., 1992-93, Site 250 Gallery Contemporary Art., Fairbanks, 1993, Santa Barbara (Calif.) Mus. Art, 1993, The Rochester (N.Y.) Mus. and Sci. Ctr., 1990-94, Space Arc: The Archives of Mankind, Time Capsule in Earth Orbit, Hughes Comm., Divec TV Satellite Launch, 1994, Stonington Gallery, Anchorage, 1994, 95, UAA Art Galley U. Alaska, 1995, Arctic Trading Post, Nome, Alaska, 1995, Allan P. Kikbuarts Ctr. Gallery at the Lawrenceville (N.J.) Sch., 1996, Blue Mountain Gallery, N.Y., 1998, The Book Room, Jersey City, 2000, 01, A.I.R. Gallery, NY, 2002, 03, 04, 05, 06, 07, 08, 09, others; represented in permanent collections Smithsonian Instn., Nat. Air and Space Mus., Washington, Albright Knox Gallery, Buffalo, St. Vincent's Hosp, N.Y.C., N.Y. Pub. Libr., N.Y.C., U.S. Geol. Survey, Reston, Va., White House (Reagan, Bush adminstrns.), Libr. of Congress, Washington, Site 250 Gallery Contemporary Art, Fairbanks, Alaska, Schooner J. & E. Riggin, Camden, Maine, Libr. Congress, Washington, New Rivers Press, NYC, Anchorage Mus. History and Art, in embassies Program, Washington, others; Moon Shot series to commemorate moon landing, 1970-76, Cloud Structures of the Universe Painting series, 1980-86, Am. Landscape series, 1987-89, Thoughtlines, fall 1986, Swimming in the Mainstream with Her, U. Va., Charlottesville; author: Artist's Book - Travel Dreams U.S.A., 1989, Artworld-Welt Der Kunst, Synchronicity, 1989—, Art Think Tank: Projects in Art and Ecology, 1990—, The Alaska Series, 1990—, Portraits in the Wilderness, 1990—, Family History Project J. Lindemann, 2004—,; columnist: Anchorage Press, 1995. Sponsor Iditorod Trail Com., Libby Riddles. Tchg. fellow Bklyn. Coll., 1972; Artist-in-residence grantee Va. Ctr. for Creative Arts, 1974, Artpark, Lewiston, N.Y., 1980, Vt. Studio Colony, 1989; recipient Pippin award Our Town, N.Y.C., 1984, certificate of Appreciation Art in Embassy program U.S. Dept. State, 1996. Mem. Mus. Women in Arts, Pratt Inst. Alumni Assn., Internat. Assn. *As an active painter I explore the mysteries of the 21st century space adventure in my American landscapes, painted directly from nature and in planetary landscapes, fantastic pictures of the cosmos. I believe it is in the reconciliation between inner and outer experience, through a personal sense of humor and use of universal symbols that a mystical or cosmic harmony can be expressed in art.*

SHARP, BARRY J., school system administrator; BBA, Coll. William and Mary, 1981. CPA. Dir. fin. and adminstrn. The AES Corp., Arlington, Va., 1986—87, v.p., CFO, 1987—2006, sr. v.p., 1998, exec. v.p., 2001—06, COO, 2002, cons., 2006—; bd. dirs. Imagine Schools, Arlington, Va., 2005—, CFO, 2006—. Bd. mem. Coll. William and Mary Bus. Found. Office: Imagine Schools 1005 N Glebe Rd Ste 610 Arlington VA 22201 Office Phone: 703-527-2600. Office Fax: 703-527-0038.

SHARP, DAN STEVEN, epidemiologist; s. Darrell Dean Sharp and Stella Louise Morrison-Sharp; m. Carol Lee Thomas, Dec. 26, 1996; m. Caroline Stanley Johnson, June 20, 1970 (div. Apr. 16, 1996); children: Sarah Elizabeth, David Henry. BS in Chemistry, U. Redlands, Calif., 1972; MD, U. Calif., Irvine, 1975; MPH, U. Calif., Berkeley, 1984; PhD in Epidemiology, U. Calif., 1987. Board Certified in Public Health and General Preventive Medicine Am. Bd. of Preventive Medicine, 1990, diplomate Nat. Bd. of Med. Examiners, 1977, Physician's and Surgeon's Certificate Bd. of Med. Quality Assurance, State of Calif., 1977, Certificate of Registration as a Visiting Overseas Doctor Gen. Med. Coun., UK, 1989. Flight surgeon US Army, Natick, Mass., 1977—80; sr. med. epidemiologist Med. Rsch. Coun., Cardiff, Wales, 1988—90; dir., Honolulu heart program Nat. Heart, Lung and Blood Inst., 1992—97; assoc. dir. sci. Health Effects Lab., Nat. Inst. for Occupl. Safety and Health, Morgantown, W.Va., 2000—. Contbr. scientific papers. Capt. US Army, 1977—80, Natick, Massachusetts. Mem.: Soc. for Epidemiologic Rsch. Achievements include research in cardiovascular disease in populations.

SHARP, DAVID HOWLAND, physicist; b. Buffalo, Oct. 14, 1938; s. Russel Howland and Margaret (Dorries) E.; m. Gloria Evanitsky, Jan. 9, 1982; children: Lisa E., Michelle L.; stepchildren: Brian P. Riepe, Michael A. Riepe. BA in Physics, Princeton U., 1960; PhD in Theoretical Physics, Calif. Inst. Tech., 1964. Asst. prof. U. Pa., 1967—74; mem. staff Los Alamos Nat. Lab., N.Mex., 1974—84, fellow, 1984—, group leader complex systems group, theoretical divsn., 2002—04, sr. sci. advisor applied physics divsn., 2002—04, dep. chief sci. officer, 2004—06, chief scientist, 2006—07. Vis. fellow Princeton U., 1963—64, rsch. assoc., 1964—65, instr., 1966—67; rsch. fellow Technische U. München, 1965—66, Calif. Inst. Tech., 1966—; lab. fellow Los Alamos Nat. Lab., 1984—; vis. fellow Ctr. Theoretical Neurosci., Salk Inst., 1995—98; mem. indsl. adv. bd. Inst. Math. and Its Applications, 2002—, mem. bd. gov., 2007—; mem. N. Mex. Rsch. Coun., 2005—, Coun. on Rsch., U. Calif., 2006—, Nat. Lab. Rsch. Adv. Bd. U. Calif., Davis, 2007—. Mem. editl. bd.: Jour. Math. Physics, 1985—87. Recipient def. programs award of excellence, U.S. Dept. Energy, 2001; Postdoctoral fellow, NSF, 1963—64. Fellow AAAS, Am. Phys. Soc., Soc. Indsl. and Applied Math.; mem. Am. Math Soc. (mem. editl. bd. Jour. Procs. 1992-2003), Internat. Assn. Math. Physicists, Internat. Soc. Gen. Relativity and Gravitation, NY Acad. Scis., Soc. Petroleum Engrs., N.Mex. Acad. Scis., Internat. Neural Network Soc. Home: 174 Laguna St Los Alamos NM 87544-2603 Personal E-mail: davidandglory@msn.com. Business E-Mail: dcso@lanl.gov.

SHARP, JAMES E., lawyer; b. Tulsa, Okla., 1940; Grad., U. Ariz.; JD, U. Okla. Bar: Okla. 1965, DC 1969. Asst. US atty. DC US Dept. Justice, DC; ptnr. Sharp & Associates PLLC. Lt. JAGC USNR. Recipient Spl. Achievement award, US Dept. Justice. Fellow: Am. Coll. Trial Lawyers; mem.: Okla. Bar Assn., DC Bar Assn., The Barristers. Office: Sharp & Associates PLLC 1215 19th St NW Washington DC 20036 Office Phone: 202-467-4114. Office Fax: 202-467-1625.*

SHARP, J(AMES) FRANKLIN, finance educator, portfolio manager; b. Johnson County, Ill., Sept. 29, 1936; s. James Albert and Edna Mae (Slack) S. BS in Indsl. Engring., U. Ill., 1960; MS, Purdue U., 1962, PhD, 1966, cert. mgmt. acctg., 1979. Chartered fin. analyst, 1980; cert. in fin. mgmt., 1997. Asst. prof. engring., econs. Rutgers U., New Brunswick, NJ, 1966-70; assoc. prof. NYU Grad. Sch. Bus., NYC, 1970-74; supr. bus. research AT&T, NYC, 1974-77, dist. mgr. corp. planning, 1977-81, dist. mgr. fin. mgmt. and planning, 1981-85; prof. fin. Grad. Sch. Bus. Pace U., NYC, 1975-91; chmn. Sharp CFA Rev. & Inst. for Investment Edn., 1987-96, Sharp Seminars, 1996—. Speaker, moderator meetings, 1965—; cons. Sharp Investment Mgmt., 1967—. Contbr. numerous articles to profl. publs.; corr.: Interfaces, 1975-78; fin. editor: Planning Rev., 1975-78. Mem. N.Am. Soc. Corp. Planning (treas. 1976-77, bd. dirs. at large 1977-78), Inst. Mgmt. Sci. (chpt. v.p. acad. 1972-74, chpt. v.p. program 1974-75, chpt. v.p. membership 1975-76, chpt. pres. 1976-77), Internat. Affiliation Planning Socs. (coun. 1978-84), N.Y. Soc. Security Analysts (CFA Rev. 1985-87), Ops. Rsch. Soc. Am. (pres. corp. planning group 1976-82), AAUP (v.p. Pace U. chpt. 1988-90), Theta Xi. Republican. Office: 315 E 86th St Apt 7H New York NY 10028-4740

SHARP, JANE PRICE, retired editor; b. Marlinton, W.Va., Oct. 14, 1919; d. Calvin W and Mabel Elizabeth (Milligan) Price; m. Basil Clair Sharp (dec.); children: Basil P.(dec.), John C., Jane Jessee. Student, Davis Elkins Coll., 1936-37. Legal sec. Prosecution atty. office, Marlinton, 1937-1939; acct. Pocahontas Prodrs., Marlinton, 1945-57; acct., reporter Pocahontas Times, Marlinton, 1937-57, editor, owner, 1957-82, editor emeritus, 1982—. Chmn. Planning Commn. Pocahontas County, 1970, Town Coun. Marlinton; legis. W.Va., 1989-90; former chmn. Pocahontas County Dem. Exec. Com.; elder, sunday sch. tchr. Marlinton Presbyn. Ch.; sec. Pioneer Days. Mem. W.Va. Press Assn. (life; pres. 1978, Adam Kelley award 1996), Pocahontas County Hist Soc. (dir. 1963—, pres. 1970-71, sec. 1994-2005), Marlinton Woman's Club (sec., past pres., Woman of Yr. 1996—). Presbyterian. Avocations: gardening, genealogy. Home: 1118 2nd Ave Marlinton WV 24954-1012 Office: Pocahontas Times 810 2nd Ave Marlinton WV 24954-1091

SHARP, LEWIS INMAN, museum director, curator; b. NYC, Dec. 22, 1941; BA, Lewis & Clark Coll., 1965; MA, U. Del., 1968, PhD. Asst. curator paintings & sculpture Met. Mus. Art, NYC, 1972—75, assoc. curator, 1975—82, curator, adminstr. Am. Wing, 1982—89; dir. Denver Art Mus., 1989—. Office: Denver Art Mus 100 W 14th Ave Pkwy Denver CO 80204-2749 Office Phone: 303-640-2793.

SHARP, PHILIP RILEY, think-tank executive, former congressman; b. Balt., July 15, 1942; s. Riley and Florence S.; m. Marilyn Kay Augburn, 1972; children: Jeremy Beck, Justin Riley. BS cum laude, Sch. Fgn. Service, Georgetown U., 1964; PhD in Govt., 1974; postgrad., Exeter Coll., Oxford U., Eng., summer 1966. Legis. aide to Senator Vance Hartke US Senate, 1964-69; from asst. to assoc. prof. polit. sci. Ball State U., Muncie, Ind., 1969-74; mem. US Congress from 10th Ind. Dist., 1975-83, US Congress from 2nd Ind. Dist., 1983—95, mem. energy & commerce com., interior & insular affairs com., oversight and investigation com.; lectr. pub. policy John F. Kennedy Sch. Govt., Harvard U., 1995—; pres. Resources for the Future, 2005—. Democrat. Methodist. Office: Resources for the Future 1616 P St NW Washington DC 20036 Office Phone: 202-328-5103.*

SHARP, PHILLIP ALLEN, biologist, educator; b. Ky., June 6, 1944; s. Joseph Walter and Katherin (Colvin) S.; m. Ann Christine Holcombe, Aug. 29, 1964; children: Christine Alynn, Sarah Katherin, Helena Holcombe. BA, Union Coll., Barbourville, Ky., 1966; PhD, U. Ill., 1969; LHD (hon.), Union Coll., Barbourville, Ky., 1991; DSc (hon.), U. Ky., 1994, Bowdoin Coll., 1995, U. Tel Aviv, Israel, 1996, Albright Coll., 1996; degree (hon.), U. Glasgow, 1998, U. Uppsala, 1999, Thomas Moore Coll., 1999, U. Buenos Aires, 1999, No. Ky. U., 1999, PhD (hon.), 2001. NIH postdoctoral fellow Calif. Inst. Tech., 1969—71; sr. research investigator Cold Spring Harbor (N.Y.) Lab., 1972—74; assoc. prof. MIT, Cambridge, 1974—79, prof. biology, 1979—99, dir. Ctr. Cancer Rsch., 1985—91, head dept. biology, 1991—99, inst. prof., 1999—. Bd. dirs. Biogen Idec Inc., 1978—2009; chmn. sci. bd. BIOGEN IDEC, 1987—2002, pres. adv. coun. sci. and tech., 1991—97; chmn. GM Cancer Rsch. Found. Awards Assembly, 1994—2007; mem. presdl. appt. Nat.Cancer Adv. Bd. NIH, 1996—2000; mem. sci. bd. Ludwig Inst., 1998—2009; mem. bd. sci. govs. Scripps Rsch. Inst., 1999—; trustee Mass. Gen. Hosp., 2001—; co-founder, chair of sci. bd. and mem. of bd. dirs. Alnylan Pharm. Inc., 2002—; bd. advisors Polaris Venture Ptnrs., 2002; mem. Corp. Ptnrs. HealthCare Systems, Inc., 2003—; sci. adv. bd. Fidelity Bioscis. Group, 2004—; dir. sci. bd. Sirtris Pharm. Inc., 2005—. Mem. editl. bd.: Cell, 1974—95, Jour. Virology, 1974—86, Molecular and Cellular Biology, 1974—85, RNA, 1995—. Trustee Alfred P. Sloan Found., 1995—2004. Recipient award, Am. Cancer Soc., 1974—79, Eli Lilly, 1980, NAS/US Steel Found., 1980, Gairdner Found. Internat., 1986, NY Acad.Scis., 1986, Howard Ricketts award, U.Chgo., 1985, Alfred P. Sloan Jr. prize, Gen. Motors Rsch. Found., 1986, Louisa Horwitz prize, 1988, Albert Lasker Basic Med. Rsch. award, 1988, Dickson prize, U. Pitts., 1990, Fourth Ann. Biotech. Heritage award, 2002, Alumni Achievement award, U. Ill., 2003, Nat. Sci. medal in Biol. Scis., 2004, Winthrop-Sears award, Chemists' Club NY, 2007; co-recipient Nobel Prize in Physiology or Medicine, 1993; named Class of '41 chair, MIT, 1986—87, John D. MacArthur chair, 1987—92, Salvador E. Luria chair, 1992—99. Fellow: AAAS, Royal Soc. Edinburgh (hon.); mem.: NAS (councilor 1986, Nat. Medal of Sci. 2004, Double Helix medal 2006), Alfred P. Sloan Mgmt. Soc. of MIT, Corp. Ptnrs. HealthCare Systems, Inc., Inst. Medicine of NAS (elected mem.), Am. Philos. Soc. (elected mem., The Benjamin Franklin medal 1999), European Molecular Biology Orgn. (assoc.), Am. Soc. Biochemistry and Molecular Biology (elected mem. coun.), Am. Acad. Arts and Scis., Am. Soc. Microbiology, NAS Republic of Korea (hon.). Office: MIT Rm E17529B Koch Inst 40 Ames St Cambridge MA 02139-4307 Business E-Mail: sharppa@mit.edu.

SHARP, ROBERT GENE, history professor; b. Spokane, Wash., July 18, 1943; married. PhD, U. N.Mex, Albuquerque, 1970. Cert. prof. Tex., 1970. TA, counselor Purdue U., West Lafayette, Ind., 1965—66; fellow U. Denver, 1966—67. Grad. instr. U. N.Mex. Heath safety com. mem. Heath Police Dept., Tex., 2006—08. Recipient Tchg. Excellence award, U. Tex., 1987. Mem.: Whitworth U. Crimson Club (named Outstanding Sr. Writer of Coll. 1965), Gonzaga U. Bulldog Club, Mustang Club. Independent. Avocations: tennis, reading, politics, bicycling, sports, travel, history. Home: 804 Country Club Dr Heath TX 75032 Office: Eastfield Coll 3737 Motley Dr Mesquite TX 75150 Business E-Mail: rgs4475@dcccd.edu.

SHARP, RON, secondary school educator; b. Shawnee, Okla., May 15, 1952; s. Halbert K. and Virginia Pauline Sharp; m. Debbie Marie Buckmaster (div.); 1 child, Kara Meli. BA in Social Studies, Southeastern Okla. State U., Durant, 1974; MEd in Polit. Sci., U. Ctrl. Okla., Edmond, 1979; PhD in Polit. Sci., Kensington U., Glendale, Calif., 1988. Cert. tchr. Okla. Instr. social scis. Shawnee (Okla.) Pub. Schs., 1974—. Instr. U.S. Profl. Tennis Assn., Shawnee, 1978—; mem. adv. bd. Pottawatomie County Jail Trust, Shawnee, 2002—06. Author: Clarisa Leflore/Choctaw Princess, 2004. Adv. Nat. Youth Leadership Forum, Washington, 2005; honorary role Nat. Tchr., 2007; parliamentarian Rep. Party, Pattawatomie, Okla., 1996—99, chmn. precinct, 1996—2004. Recipient Pres.'s award, U.S. Interpreunmenal and Interagency Affairs, 2001, Leadership award, Heritage Found., 2002, Am. Medal Hon., 2002; named Tennis Coach of Yr., Okla. State Tennis Coaches Assn., 1976, 1977, 1979, 1984, 1996, Nat. Tennis Coach of Yr., Nat. H.S. Athletic Coaches Assn., 1987, All-American Tennis Coach of Yr., 1987, Tchr. of Yr., Shawnee (Okla.) H.S., 1996, 1997, 1998, Masonic Lodge, 1998. Mem.: Nat. Coun. Social Studies, Okla. States Tennis Coaches Assn. (pres. 1977—82), U.S. Profl. Tennis Assn. (mentor 1983—), Shawnee Assn. Classroom Tchrs. (legis. liaison 1996—2004). Republican. Bapt. Avocations: tennis, genealogy, politics. Home: 1835 N Oklahoma Shawnee OK 74804 Office: Shawnee High School 1001 N Kennedy Shawnee OK 74801 Office Phone: 405-275-3084. Business E-Mail: rsharp@shawnee.k12.ok.us.

SHARP, RONALD ALAN, language educator, writer, former dean; b. Cleve., Oct. 19, 1945; s. Jack Trier and Florence (Tenenbaum) S.; m. Inese Brutans, June 22, 1968; children: Andrew Janis, James Michael. BA, Kalamazoo Coll., 1967; MA, U. Mich., 1968; PhD, U. Va., 1974. Instr. in English Western Mich. U., Kalamazoo, 1968-70; from instr. to prof. English Kenyon Coll., Gambier, Ohio, 1970—2002, assoc. provost to provost, acting pres., 1998—2003; prof. English Vassar Coll., Poughkeepsie, NY, 2003—, dean faculty, 2003—08. Dir. Keats Bicentennial Conf., Harvard U., 1995. Author: Keats, Skepticism and the Religion of Beauty, 1979, Friendship and Literature: Spirit and Form. 1986; translator: Teatro Breve (Garcia Lorca), 1979, editor (with Eudora

Welty) The Norton Book of Friendship, 1991, (with Nathan Scott) Reading George Steiner, 1994, (with Robert Ryan) The Persistence of Poetry: Bicentennial Essays on John Keats, 1998, Selected Poems of Michael Harper, 2002; co-editor Kenyon Rev., 78-82; contbr. articles to profl. jours. Recipient award for editl. excellence Ohioana Assn., 1980; fellow Nat. Humanities Ctr., 1981, 86, NEH, 1981, 84-87, 93, 94, 96, 98, Ford Found., 1971, Mellon Found., 1980, Danforth Found., 1971, English Speaking Union, 1973, Am. Coun. Learned Socs., 1986. Mem. MLA, NEH (chmn's. adv. group humanities edn. 1987), Wordsworth-Coleridge Assn., Keats-Shelley Assn. Jewish. Office: Vassar Coll Eleanor Butler Sanders Hall Box 0744 Poughkeepsie NY 12604 Office Phone: 845-437-7000. Business E-Mail: sharp@vassar.edu.

SHARP, WALTER L. (SKIP SHARP), career military officer; b. 1952; m. Joanne R. Caporaso; children: Elizabeth, Steven, Kevin. Grad., US Mil. Acad., 1974; MS in Ops. Analysis and Engring., Rensselaer Poly. Inst., 1981; grad., Command and Gen. Staff Coll., 1986, Army War Coll. Advanced through grades to gen. US Army, 2008, platoon leader A Company, later exec. officer, B Company, later S-3 (Air), 1st Bn., 67th Armor, 2d Armored Divsn. Fort Hood, Tex., 1975—77; armor co. comdr. 1st Bn., 67th Armor, 2nd Armored Divsn., Fort Hood, Tex., 1978—80; combat devel. analysis officer Office of Dir. Combat Developments US Army Armor Sch., Fort Knox, Ky., 1981—84; combat devel. officer, Deep Attach Programs Office, Office Dep. Chief of Staff for Ops. & Plans US Army, 1984—85; exec. officer, 2nd Squadron, 11th Armored Cavalry Regiment US Army Europe/Seventh Army, Germany, 1986—88; combat devel. analysis officer, A3 Task Force, Office Chief of Staff US Army, Washington, 1988—89, dir. analysis, Force Devel. Divsn, Office Dep. Chief of Staff for Ops. & Plans., 1989—90; comdr., 7th Cavalry Squadron, 1st Cavalry divsn., Desert Shield/Storm, 1990—93; dir., models & simulations directorate US Army Combined Arms Command, Nat. Simulations Ctr., Fort Leavenworth, 1993—94; comdr., 2d Armored Cavalry Regiment Operation Uphold Democracy, Haiti, 1994—96; exec. officer to comdr.-in-chief UN Combined Forces Command/US Forces Korea, Republic of Korea, 1996—97; asst. divsn. comdr. for maneuver 2nd Infantry Divsn., Camp Red Cloud, Republic of Korea, 1997—98; comdr. 3rd Infantry Divsn. (Mechanized), Fort Stewart, 1999—2001; dep. dir. for Global/Multilateral Issues/Internat. Am. Affairs (J-5) The Joint Staff, Washington, 1998—99, vice dir. for force structure, resources & assessment (J-8), 2001—03, dir. strategic plans & policy (J-5), 2003—05, dir., 2005—08; comdg. gen. UN Command, Republic of Korea / US Combined Forces Command, US Forces Korea, Seoul, Republic of Korea, 2008—. Decorated DSM, Defense Superior Svc. Medal with Oak Leaf Clusters, Bronze Star, Legion of Merit with Oak Leaf Cluster, Meritorious Svc. Medal with 5 Oak Leaf Clusters, Army Commendation Medal, Army Achievement Medal. Office: US Forces Korea Bldg 2310 96205 Seoul Republic of Korea*

SHARP, WILLIAM, retired advertising executive; b. Chgo., Aug. 1, 1929; s. William and Essie Mae (Kendall) Sharp; m. Doris Ellen Wooten, May 16, 1952; children: William Gregory, Dianne, Michael. Student, Woodrow Wilson Jr. Coll., Chgo., Roosevelt U. Owner, mgr. Card Gifters & Sharp Advt. Agy., Chgo., 1957-65; copywriter Tatham-Laird & Kudner Advt. Agy., 1965-67; copy supr. Leo Burnett Advt. Agy., 1967-68; group creative supr. J. Walter Thompson Advt., 1968-69; dir. communications OEO, Washington, 1969-72; v.p., advt. mgr. Coca-Cola USA, Atlanta, 1972-81; ptnr. Kaiser, Kuhn, Bennett & Sharp Advt. Agy., Atlanta, 1981-83; sr. v.p., gen. mgr. Burrell Advt., Atlanta, 1983—90; founder, pres. Sharp Advt., Inc., Atlanta, 1990; ret. Past chmn. bd. dirs. Am. Advt. Fedn.; adj. mktg. prof. Emory U. Goizueta Bus. Sch., Atlanta. Author: How To Be Black and Get a Job in Advertising Agency Anyway, 1969. Adv. Citizens for Michael Lomax, 1981—89; bd. dirs. Atlanta Coll. Art, Ballethnic Dance Co.; chmn. Atlanta Ednl. Telecomm. Collaborative. Served with US Army, 1952. Recipient NY Art Dir.'s Club award; named Ad Man of Yr., Southern Mag.; named to Advt. Hall of Fame, Am. Advt. Fedn., 2009. Mem.: NAACP (mem. Atlanta branch exec. bd.), Assn. Nat. Advertisers (past. bd. dirs.).

SHARPE, KEITH YOUNT, retired lawyer, writer; b. Hiddenite, NC, July 11, 1930; s. Ruel Yount and Eileen Lois (Lackey) S.; m. Margaret Joyce Land, Aug. 27, 1955 (div.); children: Jonathan, Matthew, Leonora, Felicia. AB, Duke U., 1952; JD, Wake Forest U., 1957, MBA, 1982; MLA, U. NC, Asheville, 2001. Bar: NC 1957. Pvt. practice law, Winston-Salem, NC, 1957-62, 82-94; asst. solicitor Mcpl. Ct. of Winston-Salem, 1958-60; with Pilot Freight Carriers Inc., Winston-Salem, 1962-82, sr. v.p., 1967-76, exec. v.p., 1976—82, also dir.; v.p., dir. Comml. Automotive Co., 1967-76, Terminal Warehouse Corp., 1967-82. Bd. govs. So. Motor Carriers Rate Conf., 1977-81. Served with inf. U.S. Army, 1952-54. Mem. Assn. Transp. Practitioners, Phi Alpha Delta, Theta Chi. Democrat. Episcopalian. Home: 5932 Fox Ridge Ln Winston Salem NC 27104

SHARPE, PHIL, nuclear scientist; b. Reidsville, NC, Jan. 22, 1972; s. Ray and Sandra Sharpe; m. Tina Sharpe, Dec. 31, 1994; 1 child, Sam Liz. PhD in Nuc. Engring., NC State U., Raleigh, 2000. Mgr. Thermal Sci. and Safety Analysis Dept. Idaho Nat. Lab., Idaho Falls, 2001—, group leader, fusion safety program, 2001—. Treas. Snake River Montessori Sch., Idaho Falls, 2007—. Office: Idaho Nat Lab 2525 Fremont Ave Idaho Falls ID 83415-3860

SHARPE, ROBERT FRANCIS, JR., lawyer, food products executive; b. Long Branch, NJ, Mar. 9, 1952; s. Robert Francis and Audrey Carolyn (Rembe) Sharpe; m. Maria Renna, Sept. 9, 2000; 1 child, Robert Francis III. BA, DePauw U., Greencastle, Ind., 1974; JD, Wake Forest U., Winston-Salem, NC. Bar: NC 1978. V.p. Tyco Internat. Ltd.; with RJR Nabisco Holdings Corp., sr. v.p., gen. counsel; sr. v.p. pub. affairs, gen. counsel, sec. Pepsico Inc., Purchase, NY, 1998—2002; ptnr. Brunswick Group, LLP, 2002—05; exec. v.p. legal & external affairs ConAgra Foods, Inc., Omaha, 2005—08, exec. v.p. external affairs & pres. comml. foods, 2008—. Bd. dirs. Ameriprise Fin. Mem.: ABA, Am. Corp. Counsel Assn., NC Bar Assn. Republican. Episcopalian. Avocations: golf, fishing. Office: ConAgra Foods Inc 1 ConAgra Dr Omaha NE 68102 Office Phone: 402-595-4000.*

SHARPE, ROLAND LEONARD, structural engineer, consultant; b. Shakopee, Minn., Dec. 18, 1923; s. Alfred Leonard and Ruth Helen Sharpe; m. Jane Esther Steele, Dec. 28, 1946; children: Douglas Rolfe, Deborah Lynn, Sheryl Anne. BSCE, U. Mich., 1947, MSE, 1949. Registered civil engr., structural engr. Designer Cummins & Barnard, Inc., Ann Arbor, Mich., 1947-48; instr. engring. U. Mich., 1948-50; exec. v.p. John A. Blume & Assocs., engrs., San Francisco, 1950-73; chmn., founder Engring. Decision Analysis Co., Inc., Cupertino, Calif., 1974-87; cons. earthquake engr. Sharpe Structural Engrs., Los Altos, Calif., 1987—. Mng. dir. EDAC, GmbH, Frankfurt, Germany, 1974—82; pres. Calif. Devel. & Engring. Co., Inc., Las Vegas, Nev., 1973—81; mem. nat. earthquake hazard reduction program adv. com. overviewing Fed. Emergency Mgmt. Agy., U.S. Geol. Survey, NSF and Nat. Inst. Stds. and Tech., 1990—93. Author (with J. Blume, E. G. Kost): (book) Earthquake Engineering for Nuclear Facilities, 1971; co-author: DOE Seismic Safety Manual, 1996; contbr. articles to profl. jours. Mem. Planning Commn., Palo Alto, 1955—60; mng. dir. Applied Tech. Coun., Palo Alto, 1973—83; dir. Earthquake Engring. Rsch. Inst., 1972—75, mem.; project dir., editor Tentative Provision Devel. Seismic Regulations Bldgs., 1978; tech. mgr., contbr., editor Data Processing Facilities: Guidelines Earthquake Hazard Mitigation, 1987. With USMC, 1942—46. Recipient citation for contbn. to constrn. industry, Engring. News Record, 1978—79, 1986—87, chmn. U.S. Joint Com. Earthquake Engring., 1982—88, citation for devel. of improvements in structural design and constrn. practices, Applied Tech. Coun., Japan Structural Cons. Assn., 1990. Fellow: Assn. Consulting Civil Engrs., India (hon.); mem.: ASCE (hon.; chmn. dynamic effects com. 1978—80, exec. com. structural divsn. 1980—84, chmn. 1983, exec. com. structural divsn. 1989—93, mgmt. group B 1989—93, Earnest E. Howard award 1994), Structural Engrs. World Congress (pres. 1995—2007, chair 1998), Structural Engrs. Assn. Calif. (coll. of fellows dir. 1971—73, chmn. seismology com. 1972—74), Earthquake Engring. Rsch. Inst. (hon.; dir. 1972—75), Am. Concrete Inst. (life), Structural Engrs. No. Calif. (hon.; dir. 1969—71), Japan Structural Cons. Assn. (hon.). Avocations: gardening, hiking, fly fishing. Home: 10320 Rolly Rd Los Altos Hills CA 94024-6568 Office: Sharpe Struct Engrs 10320 Rolly Rd Ste 1 Los Altos Hills CA 94024-6568 Office Phone: 650-948-9095. Personal E-mail: rsharpe3@mindspring.com. *Personal philosophy: One's conduct should be beyond reproach both morally and ethically and I should serve each of my clients to the best of my ability.*

SHARPE, VIRGINIA DEEGAN, educational consultant; b. Chgo., Mar. 2, 1935; d. Phillip Joseph Deegan and Edna (Farrar) Carroll; m. William Gibson Sharpe, May 6, 1961; 1 child, Michael Philip. BEd, U. Miami, Fla., 1956; MEd, Fla. Atlantic U., 1970; EdD, U. Fla., 1988. Cert. tchr., Fla. Tchr. Dade County Sch. System, Miami, 1956-62, Volusia County Sch. System, De Land, Fla., 1966-78, dir. health and phys. edn., 1978-90, dir. curriculum, 1985-90; prin. St. James Episcopal Sch., Ormond Beach, Fla., 1990-92; ednl. cons., De Land, 1990—; founder Reading Edge Charter Sch., DeBary, Fla., 1998—. Adj. prof., sr. practicum advisor Nova U., Port Orange, Fla., 1992-2000; adj. prof. Stetson U., De Land, 1990-97. Asst. min. St. Barnabas Episcopal Ch., DeLand, 1975-89, Holy Presence Episcopal Ch., DeLand, 1989-95, Chapel Divine Mercy, DeLand, 2002-; trainer cons. Fla. Performance Measurement Sys., 1982-; pres. Fla. Assn. Health, Phys. Edn., Recreation and Dance, 1987, mem. ICCEC Catechism Comm., chair CEC Philosophy Edn. comm. Recipient Honor award Fla. Assn. Health, Phys. Edn., Recreation and Dance, 1988; named Outstanding Religious Leader, DeLand Jaycees, 1985. Fellow Inst. Devel. Edn. Activities; mem. ASCD, Phi Delta Kappa, Sigma Kappa (pres. alumnae Ctrl. Fla. 2002-, Pearl Ct. award 2006), Delta Psi Kappa, Kappa Delta Pi, Sigma Kappa (Beta Tau chpt. corp. bd. 2007-09, sec. 2007-09). Home and Office: 323 N Blue Lake Ter Deland FL 32724-4699 Office Phone: 386-736-8573. Business E-Mail: wsharpe1@cfl.rr.com.

SHARPE, WILLIAM FORSYTH, economics professor; b. Cambridge, Mass., June 16, 1934; s. Russell Thornley Sharpe and Evelyn Forsyth (Jillson) Maloy; m. Roberta Ruth Branton, July 2, 1954 (div. Feb. 1986); children: Deborah Ann, Jonathan Forsyth; m. Kathryn Dorothy Peck, Apr. 5, 1986. AB, UCLA, 1955, MA, 1956, PhD, 1961; DHL (hon.), DePaul U., 1997; D (hon.), U Alicante, Spain, 2003, U. Vienna, Austria, 2004. Economist Rand Corp., 1957—61; asst. prof. econs. U. Wash., 1961—63, assoc. prof., 1963—67, prof., 1967—68, U. Calif., Irvine, 1968—70; Timken prof. fin. Stanford (Calif.) U., 1970—89, Timken prof. emeritus, 1989—92, prof. fin., 1993—95, STANCO 25 prof. fin., 1995—99, prof. emeritus, 1999; prin. William F. Sharpe Assocs., 1986—92; chmn. Fin. Engines, Inc., 1996—2003. Author: The Economics of Computers, 1969, Portfolio Theory and Capital Markets, 1970; co-author: Fundamentals of Investments, 1989, 3d edit., 2000, Investments, 6th edit., 1999. With US Army, 1956—57. Recipient Graham and Dodd award, Fin. Analysts' Fedn., 1972, 1973, 1986—88, Nicholas Molodovsky award, 1989, Nobel prize in econ. scis., 1990, UCLA medal, 1998. Mem.: Am. Econ. Assn., Ea. Fin. Assn. (Disting. Scholar award 1991), Western Fin. Assn. (Enduring Contbn. award 1989), Am. Fin. Assn. (v.p. 1979, pres. 1980), Phi Beta Kappa.*

SHARPEE, RHODA ANDERSON, social worker; b. Cleve., May 11, 1938; d. Elmer F. and Ruth M. (Swanson) Anderson; m. Dale F. Sharpee, Sept. 5, 1964; children: Marc K., Sara L. BA, U. Dubuque, 1963; MSW, George Williams Coll., 1977; student, Sch. Social WorkDist. 79, 2000. Lic. clin. social worker, Ill. Sch. social worker Sch. Dist. 15, Palatine, Ill., 1982—94; police social worker Hanover Twp. Youth Commn., Bartlett, Ill., 1977—91; case worker Fla. State Welfare, Miami, 1967—69; social worker Mendota State Hosp., Madison, Wis., 1964—66; regional rep. Inst. Noatic Scis. Mem. NASW, Am. Humanistic Pscyh., Ill. Sch. Social Workers Assn., Inst. of Noetic Scis. Address: PO 925 Land O Lakes WI 54540 Personal E-mail: rhodale2@yahoo.com. E-mail: rhodale@alphacomm.net.

SHARPLESS, JOSEPH BENJAMIN, retired county official; b. Takoma Park, Md., Feb. 4, 1933; s. William Raiford and Julia Maude (Rouse) Sharpless; m. Nancy Kathleen Steffen, July 28, 1962 (dec. Feb. 1988); 1 child, Carole Marie. BA, Earlham Coll., 1955; MS, Pa. State U., 1960. Instr. recreation Montgomery County Recreation Dept., Rockville, Md., 1957—58; from program supr. to dir. Recreation and Parks Dept., Livingston, NJ, 1959—70; chief recreation svc. Md.-Nat. Capital Park and Planning Commn. Prince George's County, Riverdale, Md., 1970—77, parks and recreation div. chief, 1977—95; ret., 1995. Mem. bd. regents, instr. Sch. Sports Mgmt. N.C. State U., 1989—92. Contbr. articles to profl. jours. Dir. volleyball Spl. Olympics Inc., 1994—2007; tech. del. Spl. Olympics World Summer Games, 1995, 1999, 2003, 2007, USA Nat. Spl. Olympics Games, 2006, Spl. Olympics Global Sports Res. Team, 2008; trustee U.S. Volleyball Edn. Found., 1976—2005, sec., 1996—2005; nat. volleyball chmn. AAU, 1966—69, 1972; nat. commr. U.S. Volleyball, 1976—81; mem. volleyball games staff 1996 Olympic Games, Atlanta; staff World Volleyball Congress, Atlanta, 1996; v.p. Montpelier Cmty. Assn., South Laurel, Md., 1983—84, pres., 1985; mem. Md. Sports Adv. Com., 1988—92, Md. State Games Commr., 1986—91; pres. NJAAU, 1968—70, volleyball chmn., 1961—70, Potomac Valley AAU, 1971—73. Recipient Pioneer Volleyball award, AAU, 1998, Breitkeutz Leadership award, 1972; named to, Earlham Coll. Athletic Hall of Fame, 2005. Fellow: Nat. Recreation Pks. Assn. (life Berman Profl. Citation award Mid-Atlantic Regional Coun. 1995, Disting. Svc. award 1995, Disting. Fellow award 1996); mem.: NJ Soccer Ofcls. Assn. (sec., treas. 1966—70), Nat. Capitol Area Bd. Volleyball Ofcls. (sec. 1985—89), Sch. and Coll. Soccer Ofcls. Assn. (sec., treas. 1965—70, del. Mid-Atlantic NRPA regional coun. 1969—79), Md. Recreation and Pk. Assn. (v.p. 1975—77, pres. 1977—78, Mem. of the Yr. 1975, citation 1985), NJ Recreation and Pks. Assn. (sec. 1965, v.p. 1966, pres. 1967, Disting. Fellow 1996), Am. Pk. and Recreation Soc. (bd. dirs. 1977—80, nat. coun., coun. affiliate pres.), Nat. Intercollegiate Soccer Ofcls. Assn. (sec. 1966—68, treas. 1968—70), US Volleyball Assn. (regional commr. 1965—78, nat. ofcl. 1967—96, bd. dirs. 1973—2008, v.p. 1974—90, exec. com. 1976—80, 1985—89, 1992—96, exec. cons. 1989—2004, corp. sec. 1992—96, mng. editor pubs. 1994—98, v.p. 1996—2004, 1996—2004, regional commr., referee, scorekeeper emeritus 2000, numerous awards). Independent. Mem. Soc. Of Friends. Home: 26205 S Cedarcrest Dr Sun Lakes AZ 85248-7206 Personal E-mail: chessycrab@aol.com.

SHARPLESS, K. BARRY, chemist, educator; b. Phila., Apr. 28, 1941; m. Jan Dueser, Apr. 28, 1965; children: Hannah, William, Isaac. BA, Dartmouth Coll., 1963; PhD, Stanford U., 1968; doctorate (hon.), Dartmouth Coll., 1995, Swedish Royal Inst. Tech., 1995, Tech. U. Munich, 1995, Cath. U. Louvain, Belgium, 1996. Postdoctoral assoc. Harvard U., Stanford U., to 1970, faculty dept. chemistry, 1977-80; faculty MIT, Cambridge, 1970-77, 1980-90; W. M. Keck prof. chemistry Scripps Rsch. Inst. and Skaggs Inst. of Chem. Biology, La Jolla, Calif., 1990—. Recipient Pual Janssen prize for Creativity in Organic Synthesis, Chem. Pioneer award, Am. Inst. Chemists, 1988, Prelog medal, Swiss Fed. Inst. Tech., Zurich, 1988, Scheele medal and prize, Swedish Acad. Pharm. Scis., Tetrahedron prize for Creativity in Organic Chemistry, 1993, King Faisal Internat. prize for sci., 1995, Microbial medal, Kitasato Inst., Tokyo, 1997, Harvey medal, Technion-Israel Inst. Tech., 1998, Carothers award, 1999, John Scott Medal, City of Phila, 2001, Benjamin Franklin medal in chemistry, 2001, Wolf prize in chemistry, Wolf Found., Israel, 2001, Nobel prize in Chemistry, 2001; fellow A. P. Sloan, 1987—88, Guggenheim, 1987—88; scholar Camille and Henry Dreyfus Tchr. Fellow: AAAS, Am. Acad. Arts and Scis., Royal Soc. Chemistry (hon.); mem.: NAS (Award in Chemical Sciences 2000), Am. Chem. Soc. (Creative Work in Synthetic Organic Chemistry award 1983, Harrison Howe award Rochester chpt. 1987, Remsen award Md. sect. 1989, Arthur C. Cope award 1992, Roger Adams award 1997, Richards medal Northeastern sect. 1998, Top 75 Contbrs. to Chem. Enterprise 1998). Office: Scripps Rsch Inst BCC 315 10550 N Torrey Pines Rd La Jolla CA 92037-1000*

SHARPTON, AL (ALFRED CHARLES SHARPTON JR.), minister, political activist, radio talk show host; b. Bklyn., Oct. 3, 1954; s. Alfred Charles and Ada Sharpton; m. Kathy Lee Jordan, Oct. 31, 1980 (separated 2004); children: Dominique, Ashley. Student, Bklyn.Coll. Lic. Ordained Pentecostal min. 1964, Baptist min. 1994. Youth dir. Operation BreadBasket, 1969; founder Nat. Youth Movement, 1971; road mgr. James Brown concert tours, 1973—80; founder, pres., CEO Nat. Action Network, Inc., Bklyn., 1991—; dir. ministers divsn. Nat. Rainbow Push Coalition, 1994—98; host daily nat. talk radio program Keepin It Real with Al Sharpton, 2006—. Candidate NY State Senate, 1978, US Senate, 1988, 92, 94, NYC mayor, 1997, Pres., 2004. Co-author: (with Anthony Walton) Go Tell the Pharaoh: The Autobiography of Reverend Al Sharpton, 1996, (with Karen Hunter) Al on America, 2002; host Spike TV's reality show I Hate My Job, 2004—05, TV appearances include NY Undercover, Law & Order: Special Victims Unit, Girlfriends, My Wife and Kids, Rescue Me, Boston Legal, film appearances include Cold Feet, Bamboozled, Mr. Deeds, Malcolm X, regular appearances on Fox News, CNN, MSNBC. Named one of 100 Most Influential Black Americans, Ebony mag., 2006; named to Power 150, 2008. Baptist. Home: Nat Action Network Inc 104 W 145TH St Frnt 1 New York NY 10039-4103 E-mail: show@sharptontalk.net.*

SHARROCK (WRENTMORE), ANITA KAY, information technology specialist; b. Logan, Ohio, Dec. 3, 1955; d. Lloyd Earl and Gayle Irene (Daubenmier) W. BS, Ohio U., Lancaster, 1978; MS, Ohio U., Athens, 1979; postgrad., Ohio State U., Columbus, 1985, Ctrl. Ohio Tech. Coll., Newark, 1987. Cert. tchr. Vis. lectr. Denison U., Granville, Ohio, 1980; lectr. Ohio State U., Newark, 1980-83; instr. Cen. Ohio Tech. Coll., Newark, 1983-86; substitute tchr. Newark City Schs., 1986-87, Northfork Sch. Dist., Utica, Ohio, 1987, Lakewood Sch. Dist., Hebron, Ohio, 1987; with Kelly Services, Reynoldsburg, Ohio, 1986-87; computer specialist Def. Constrn. Supply Ctr., Columbus, Ohio, 1987—92, DLA Sys. Automation Ctr., 1992—2000, DLA Sys. Integration Office, 2000—04, DLA Info. Ops., Columbus, 2004—06, mgmt. and program analyst, 2006—07; info. tech. specialist, 2007—. Mem. exec. bd. Newark-Licking County Coun. Tchrs. Math., Newark, 1985-88. Mem. IEEE Computer Soc., Nat. Coun. Tchrs. Math., Ohio Coun. Tchrs. Math., Am. Math. Soc., Assn. for Computing Machinery, Phi Kappa Phi, Kappa Delta Pi. Independent. Methodist. Avocations: swimming, dance, hiking, reading. Home: 103 Ramona Ave Newark OH 43055-1334 Home Phone: 740-522-4421; Office Phone: 614-692-8347. Business E-Mail: anita.sharrock@dla.mil.

SHARROW, MARILYN JANE, library administrator; b. Oakland, Calif. d. Charles L. and H. Evelyn Sharrow; m. Larry J. Davis. BS in Design, U. Mich., 1967, MALS, 1969. Libr. Detroit Pub. Libr., 1968-70; head fine arts dept. Syracuse U. Librs., NY, 1970-73; dir. libr. Roseville Pub. Libr., Mich., 1973-75; asst. dir. librs. U. Wash., Seattle, 1975-77, assoc. dir. librs., 1978-79; dir. librs. U. Man., Winnipeg, Canada, 1979-82; chief libr. U. Toronto, Canada, 1982-85; univ. libr. U. Calif., Davis, 1985—. Chair bd. North Regional Libr. Facility, 1999—2001; bd. dirs. Press U. Calif., 2005—08. Named Woman of Yr. in mgmt., Winnipeg YWCA, 1982; named a Woman of Distinction, U. Calif. Faculty Women's Rsch. Grp., 1985. Mem.: ALA, Can. Assn. Rsch. Libr. (pres. 1984—85), Calif. State Network Resources Libr. Com., OCLC-Rsch. Librs. Adv. Com. (vice-chair 1992—93), Assn. Rsch. Librs. (pres.-elect 1989—90, pres. 1990—91, chair sci. tech. work grp. 1994—98, leadership devel. task force 2006—07, rsch. collections com. 1993-95, 2000-2002, preservation com. 1997-99, 2003-05, chair membership com. 2007—). Office: U Calif Shields Libr 100 NW Quad Davis CA 95616-5292 Office Phone: 530-752-2110. E-mail: mjsharrow@ucdavis.edu.

SHARTLE, STANLEY MUSGRAVE, engineering executive, consultant, surveyor; b. Brazil, Ind., Sept. 27, 1922; s. Arthur Tinder and Mildred C. (Musgrave) Shartle; m. Anna Lee Mantle, Apr. 7, 1948; 1 child, Randy. Student, Purdue U., 1947—50. Registered profl. engr., land surveyor. Ind. chief dep. surveyor Hendricks County, Danville, Ind., 1941—42, dep. county surveyor, 1944—50, county engr., surveyor, 1950—54, county hwy. engr., 1975—77; asst. hydrographer Fourteenth Naval Dist., Pearl Harbor, Hawaii, 1942—44; staff engr. Ind. Toll Rd. Commn., Indpls., 1954—61; chief right of way engring. Ind. State Hwy. Commn., Indpls., 1961—75; owner, civil engr. Shartle Engring., Indpls., 1977—89; prin. Parsons Cunningham & Shartle Engrs., Inc., Indpls., 1990—. Right of way engring. cons. Gannett Fleming Transp. Engrs., Inc., Indpls., 1983—88; part-time lectr. Purdue U. Ind. State Hwy. Commn., 1965—67. Author: Shartle Genealogy, 1955, 2d edit., 2005, Musgrave Family History, 1961, 2d edit., 1995, Right of Way Engineering Manual, 1975, (novel) Her Word of Honor, 2001; contbr. articles to profl. jours. Ex-officio mem., charter mem. exec. sec. Hendricks County Planning Commn., 1951—54; mem. citizen adv. com. Hendricks County Subdivision Control Ordinance, 1988—. Recipient Outstanding Contbn. award, Hendricks County Soil and Water Conservation Dist., 1976; named Stanley Shartle Day, Hendricks County, 1997. Mem.: Geog. and Land Info. Soc., Internat. Right of Way Assn. (founder chpt. 10), Ind. Toll Rd. Employees Assn. (pres. 1959—60), Nat. Soc. Profl. Surveyors, Ind. Soc. Profl. Land Surveyors (life; bd. dirs. 1979), Am. Congress Surveying and Mapping (life). Avocations: astronomy, genealogy, geodesy. Office Phone: 317-272-7912.

SHASHKIN, PAVEL NIKOLAYEVICH, biochemist; b. Ulyanovsk, Russia, Sept. 23, 1957; s. Nikolay I. Shashkin and Maria Ya Shashkina; m. Tamara S. Shashkin; children: Alexey, Alice Shashkina, Veronika. M in Physics, M.V. Lomonosov Moscow State U., 1980; PhD in Biology, Cancer Rsch. Ctr., Moscow, 1990. Rsch. scientist Cancer Rsch. Ctr., Moscow, 1991—97, sr. rsch. scientist, 1997—99; vis. instr. U. Md., Balt., 1998—2000; rsch. assoc. U. Winnipeg, Man., Canada, 2000—01, U. Va., Charlottesville, 2002—04, Cleve. Clinic, 2004—07; sr. scientist BPS Biosci,. Inc., 2008—. Contbr. articles to profl. jours. Grantee, Karolinska Inst. Stockholm, Sweden, 1995, 1996. Mem.: Am. Heart Assn., Am. Diabetes Assn. Avocations: tennis, travel. Home: 12766 Torrey Bluff Dr #122 San Diego CA 92130 Office: BPS Bioscience Inc 11526 Sorrento Valley Rd #A2 San Diego CA 92121 Office Phone: 858-523-9968. Business E-Mail: pshashkin@bpsbioscience.com.

SHASTEEN, DONALD EUGENE, retired government official, small business consultant; b. Englewood, Colo., Dec. 3, 1928; s. George Donald and Frances True (Meyers) S.; m. Shirley Mae Johnson, Aug. 8, 1954; children: Jon Randolph, Ron Winston, Sherilyn Sue Kosman. BA in Journalism, U. Colo., 1950. Reporter Omaha World-Herald, Des Moines, 1954-58, Lincoln, Nebr., 1958-66; exec. asst. to Senator Carl T. Curtis of Nebr., Washington, 1966-73, adminstrv. asst., 1973-78, to Sen. Gordon J. Humphrey, 1979-80; with transition group Senate Republican Conf., 1980; dep. under sec. for legislation and intergovtl. rels. Dept. Labor, 1981-83, dep. asst. sec. for vets. employment, 1983-85, asst. sec. for vets. employment and tng., 1985-89; small bus. cons. pvt. practice, 1989—. Pres. Shasteen Assocs. Rep. nominee for U.S. Senate Nebr., 1978. Served with U.S. Army, 1951-52. Mem. Am. Legion, VFW, Am. Vets., Disabled Am. Vets., Phi Delta Theta. Republican. Lutheran. Home Phone: 301-983-0264; Office Phone: 240-876-3366. Personal E-mail: shasteen@msn.com.

SHATILA, AHMAD HUSSAIN, surgeon, oncologist; arrived in U.S., 1970; s. Hussain Ahmad and Yisir Omar Shatila; m. Bonnye Lynn Oliver, June 24, 1972; children: Suzanne, Sarah, David. BS in Biology, Am. U. Beirut, 1965, MD, 1970. Diplomate Am. Bd. Surgery. Resident surgery U. Louisville, 1970—72, SUNY, Syracuse, 1972—75; fellow surg. oncology Luth. Med. Ctr., Cleve., 1975—76, Cleve. Met. Health Med. Ctr., Case We. Res. U., 1976—78; pvt. practice Cleve., 1976—2008. Mem. med. staff MetroHealth Med. Ctr., Case Western Res. U., Divsn. Surg. Oncology, 1976—2008, emeritus staff, 2008—; asst. clin. prof. surgery Case Western Res. U., Cleve., 1984—; chmn. dept. surgery S.W. Gen. Health Ctr., Middleburg Heights, Ohio, 1989—91, chief surg. oncology, 1990—2008, co-founder cancer program; pres. med. staff S.W. Med. Corp., 2000—08; founder Cleve. Breast Clinic, Middleburg Heights; presenter in field. Contbr. articles to profl. jours. Com. mem. S.W. Cmty. Health Found., Middleburg Heights, 1990—. Fellow: ACS, U.S. Soc. Surg. Oncology; mem.: Ea. Coop. Oncology Group (investigator 1976—2005, mem. breast steering com. 1980—86, vice chair toxicity com. 1983—88, mem. surgery steering com. 1984—87), Ohio State Med. Assn., Am. Cancer Soc. (med. adv. com.), Am. Soc. Clin. Oncology. Conservative. Muslim. Achievements include being the surgical oncology co-chair of the first US Intergroup clinical trial: Efficacy of Adjuvant Chemotherapy in High Risk Node Negative Breast Cancer. Avocations: golf, photography, boating, gardening. Office: For Corresponder PO Box 30849 Middleburg Heights OH 44130 Office Phone: 440-263-8746.

SHATIN, JUDITH, composer, educator; b. Boston, Nov. 11, 1949; d. Leo and Harriet Evelyn (Sommer) S.; m. Michael Kubovy, June 28, 1992. AB, Douglass Coll., 1971; MM, Julliard Sch., 1974; PhD, Princeton U., 1979. Asst. prof. U. Va., Charlottesville, 1979-85, assoc. prof., 1985-92, prof., 1992—, chmn. McIntire dept. music, 1995—2002, William R. Kenan, Jr. prof., 1999—. Dir. Va. Ctr. Computer Music, 1988—. Composer: (orch.) Aura, 1981, (piano concerto) Passion of St. Cecilia, 1985, (flute concerto) Ruah, 1985, (piano trio) View from Mt. Nebo (commd. by Garth Newel Chamber Players), 1985, (piano trio) Ignoto Numine (commd. Monticello Trio), 1986, (flute, clarinet, violin, cello) Secret Ground (commd. by Roxbury Chamber Players), 1990, (soprano and tape) Three Summers Heat, 1989 (Barlow Found. Commn.), (orch.) Piping the Earth (commd. by Women's Philharm.), 1990, (flute and piano) Gabriel's Wing (commd. by Julia Bogorad and the Upper Midwest Flute Assn.), 1990, (flute and electronics) Kairos (Commd. Va. Commn. for the Arts), 1991, (chorus, brass quintet, tympani) We Hold These Truths (commd. U. Va., for Thomas Jefferson's 250th birthday), 1992, (string orch.) Stringing the Bow (commd. Va. Chamber Orch.), 1992, COAL (commd. as part of 2-yr. retrospective of work, sponsored by Lila Wallace- Readers Digest Arts Ptnrs. Program), 1994, (piano and percussion) 1492 (commd. Arioso Ensemble), 1992, (piano) Chai Variations on Eliahu HaNavi, 1995, (flute and guitar) Dreamtigers (commd. Ekko!), 1996, (chorus) Adonai Roi, 1995, (string quartet) Janus Quartet (commd. for the Arcata Quartet), 1994, (string quartet and electronic playback) Elijah's Chariot (commd. Kronos Quartet), 1995, (amplified clarinet with PVC extensions effects processor, foot pedals and playback sys.) Sea of Reeds (commd. F. Gerard Errante), 1997, (chorus and piano) Songs of War and Peace, 1998, (brass quintet) Fantasia sobre el Flamenco, 1998, (piano, cello, percussion) Houdini: Memories of a Conjurer, 1999 (commd. Core Ensemble), (wind quintet and piano) Ockeghem Variations (commd. Hexagon Ensemble), 2000, Run (piano quartet) (commd. Currents) 2001, (SATB chorus) Allelulia, 2001, Singing the Blue Ridge (commd. Wintergreen Performing Arts through Ams. for the Arts), 2002, Animating Democracy Project, Tree Music (commd. U. Va. Art Mus., interactive electronics), 2003, Penelope's Song (viola and electronics), 2003, Amulet (commd. N.Y. Treble Singers, SSA Chorus), 2005, Civil War Memories (commd. Jane Franklin Dance, electronics), 2005, Clave (commd. New Ear, flute, clarinet, saxophone, violin, viola, piano, percussion), 2006, Jabberwocky, 2006 (commd. Va. Glee Club), (amplified cello and electronics) For the Birds (commd. Madeleine Shapiro), 2006, Why the Caged Bird Sings (commd. Young People's Chorus NYC), 2007, violint piano Tower of the Eight Winds Command Libr. Congress, 2008. Nat. Endowment for Arts Composer fellow, 1980, 85, 89, 92; recipient award Va. Commn. for the Arts, 1989, 02, 07. Mem. Am. Music Ctr., Am. Women Composers (pres. 1989-93), Am. Composers Alliance (bd. dirs. 1993-98), Internat. Alliance for Women in Music (chair nominating com. 1996-98, adv. bd. 1999-). Business E-Mail: shatin@virginia.edu, asst@judithshatin.com.

SHATKIN, AARON JEFFREY, biochemistry educator; b. Providence, July 18, 1934; s. Morris and Doris S.; m. Joan A. Lynch, Nov. 30, 1957; 1 son, Gregory Martin. AB, Bowdoin Coll., 1956, DSc (hon.), 1979; PhD, Rockefeller Inst., 1961. Sr. asst. scientist NIH, Bethesda, Md., 1961-63, rsch. chemist, 1963-68; vis. scientist Salk Inst., La Jolla, Calif., 1968-69; assoc. mem. dept. cell biology Roche Inst. Molecular Biology, Nutley, N.J., 1968-73, full mem., 1973-77, head molecular virology lab., 1977-86, head dept. cell biology, 1983-86; dir. N.J. Ctr. Advanced Biotech. Medicine, 1986—; prof. molecular genetics UMDNJ, 1986—; univ. prof. molecular biology Rutgers U., New Brunswick, N.J., 1986—. Adj. prof. cell biology Rockefeller U.; vis. prof. molecular biology Princeton U. Mem. editl. bd. Jour. Virology, 1969-82, Archives of Biochemistry and Biophysics, 1972-82, Virology, 1973-76, Comprehensive Virology, 1974-82, Jour. Biol. Chemistry, 1977-83, 94-99, RNA Jour., 1995-96, Procs. of NAS, 1997-2001; editor Advances in Virus Rsch., 1983—, Jour. Virology, 1973-77; founding editor-in-chief Molecular and Cellular Biology, 1980-90. Served with USPHS, 1961-63. Recipient U.S. Steel Found. NAS prize in molecular biology, 1977, N.J. Sci. and Tech. Pride award, 1989, Thomas Edison Sci. award State of N.J., 1991, award for Disting. Rsch. in the Biomed. Scis., Assn. Am. Med. Colls., 2003, Edward J. H Excellence Medicine Outstanding Scientist award, 2009; Rockefeller fellow, 1956-61 Fellow AAAS, Am. Acad. Arts and Scis., Am. Acad. Microbiology, N.Y. Acad. Scis.; mem. NAS, Am. Soc. Microbiology, Am. Soc. Biol. Chemists, Am. Soc. Virology, Am. Chem. Soc., Am. Soc. Cell Biology, Harvey Soc. Home: 1381 Rahway Rd Scotch Plains NJ 07076-3452 Office: Ctr Advanced Biotech and Medicine 679 Hoes Ln Piscataway NJ 08854-5627 E-mail: shatkin@cabm.rutgers.edu.

SHATTER, SUSAN LOUISE, artist, museum administrator, educator; b. NYC, Jan. 17, 1943; d. Aubrey and Florence (Breines) S.; m. Paul Brown (div. June 1975); 1 child, Scott Brown. Student, Skowhegan Sch. Sculpture, Maine, 1964; BFA, Pratt Inst., 1965; MFA, Boston U., 1972. Artist in residence Skowhegan (Maine) Sch Painting and Sculpture, 1977, 79; art instr. Sch. Visual Arts, NYC, 1980-84, Tyler Sch. of Art, Phila., 1985, San Francisco Art Inst., 1989, Vt. Studio Ctr., Johnson, 1989, Bklyn. Coll., 1991-95. Vis. critic, U. Pa., 1974-85, acting co-chair, 1983-84; bd. govs. Skowhegan Sch. Painting and Sculpture, 1979—, chair, 1988-91. One-woman shows include Catalogue by D. Kuspit, SUNY Fine Arts Ctr., 2003, Fischbach Gallery, NYC, 1973-97, Harcus Gallery, Boston, 1975-87, Mattingly Baker Gallery, Dallas, 1981, John Berggruen Gallery, San Francisco, 1986, Heath Gallery, Atlanta, 1987, SECCA, Winston-Salem, NC, 2001, Lyons Wier Gallery, NYC, 2002, Staller Ctr. Arts, 2003, Lyonswier Gallery, 2005, Ancocisco Gallery, Portland, Maine, 2006, DFN Gallery, NYC Catalogue by David Cohen, 2006; works reproduced in America '76: A Bicentennial Exhibition, 1976, Boston Watercolor Today, 1976, Realist Drawings and Watercolors: Contemporary Works on Paper, 1980, Contemporary Realism Since 1960, 1981, Perspectives on Contemporary American Realism: Works of Art on Paper from the Collection of Jalane and Richard Davidson, 1983, Eireland, McMullen Mus. of Art, Boston Coll., 2003, New Vistas: Contemporary American Landscapes, 1984, American Realism: Twentieth Century Drawings and Watercolors from the Glenn C. Janss Collection, 1984, A Graphic Muse: Prints by American Women, 1987, Spirit of Place: Contemporary Landscape Painting & the American Tradition, 1989, Twentieth Century Watercolors, 1990, American Realism and Figurative Art: 1991, 1991, (catalogue) Meridian Shift, 12 yrs. of paintings by Susan Shatter, U. Tex., San Antonio, 1998; represented in permanent collections Art Inst. Chgo., Mus. Fine Arts, Boston, MIT, Cambridge, Currier Gallery of Art, Manchester, NH, Hood Art Mus., Dartmouth Coll., Hanover, NH, Phila. Mus. Art, Utah Mus. Fine Art, Salt Lake City, Farnesworth Mus., Maine, Buffalo Bill Hist. Soc., Cody, Wyo., U. Tex., San Antonio, Nat. Mus. Am. Art, Washington, Yale U. Art Gallery, Boise (Idaho) Mus., Colby Mus., Maine, Walker Art Mus., Brunswick, Maine, Nat. Acad. Mus., NYC, U. Maine, Bangor. Grantee Mass. Creative Artists Humanities, Radcliff Inst., Ingram-Merrill Found., NEA, NY State Found. the Arts, Yaddo Corp., Ballinglen Artists Fellowship, Ireland, 1999, Pollock-Krasner Found, 2004-05; Brittany fellow Rochefort-en-Terre, 2002, Bogliasco Found. Fellowship, Italy, 2008; recipient Childe Hassam Purchase award, Am. Acad. Arts and Letters, 2003; Yaddo resident, Saratoga Springs, NY, 2001, 02. Mem. NAD (treas. 1998-05, pres. 2005-09, W. Paten prize 2003), The Century Club Office: DFN Gallery 210 W 11th Ave New York NY 10001 also: Nat Acad Design 1083 Fifth Ave New York NY 10128 Office Phone: 212-369-4880. Office Fax: 212-360-6795. Personal E-mail: sshatter@mindspring.com.

SHATTUCK, GEORGE CLEMENT, retired lawyer; b. Syracuse, NY, Sept. 2, 1927; s. Frank M. and Geneveive Mary (Hannon) S.; m. Sheila Eagan, Sept. 21, 1957 (div. 1985); children: Edward, George, Frank, Mark, Patrick; m. Carla A. Amussen, June 16, 1987; 1 dau., Morgan. BS in Mgmt., Syracuse U., 1950, JD, 1953. Bar: N.Y. 1954, U.S. Supreme Ct. 1973. Retired ptnr., estate planning splty. practice group Bond, Schoeneck & King Law Firm, Syracuse, 1954—94. Author: Oneida Land Claims, 1991. Mem. Syracuse Bd. Edn., 1968-75. Roman Catholic. Avocations: writing, reading, fishing. Home: 5158 W Lake Rd Cazenovia NY 13035-9616

SHATTUCK, JOHN, foundation administrator, former ambassador; b. Pasadena, Calif., Sept. 22, 1943; s. H. Francis Jr. and Ruth (Murphy) S.; m. Petra Tölle, May 17, 1970 (dec. Mar. 1988); m. Ellen Hume, Feb. 14, 1991; children: Jessica, Rebecca, Peter, Susannah. BA magna cum laude, Yale U., 1965, JD, 1970; MA with 1st class hon. in internat. law, Cambridge U., Eng., 1967; doctorate (hon.), CUNY, 1995, Kenyon Coll., 2001, U. R.I., 2002, U. Western Bohemia, Czech. Rep., 2002. Law clk. to Hon. Edward Weinfeld U.S. Dist. Ct. (so. dist.) N.Y., 1970-71; nat. counsel ACLU, 1971-77, dir. Washington office, 1977-84; v.p. govt., community and pub. affairs Harvard U., 1984-93, sr. assoc. sci. tech. and pub. policy program John F. Kennedy Sch. Govt., 1984-93; asst. sec. for democracy, human rights and labor US Dept. State, Washington, 1993-98, US amb. to Czech Republic Prague, 1998-2000; CEO John F. Kennedy Presdl. Libr. Found., 2001—09. Lectr. Harvard Law Sch., 1986—93; sr. fellow and lectr. Tisch Coll. Pub. Svc., Tufts U., 2007—09; pres. & rector Ctrl. European U., Budapest, 2009—. Author: Freedom on Fire: Human Rights Wars and America's Response, 2003; contbr. articles to profl. jours. Bd. dir. The Petra Fedn., Am. Friends of Czech Republic, ABA Ctrl. & E. Law Inst., Common Cause. Recipient UN Assn. Human Rights award 1998, Am. Bar Assn. Ambassador award 2000, H.L. Mencken award Free Press Assn. 1988, Pub. Svc. award Yale U. Law Sch. 1988, Roger Baldwin medal 1984, Global Leadership award Tufts U., 2003. Fellow Am. Acad. Arts Scis. Office: Ctrl Europaen Univ Nador 9 1051 Budapest Hungary Home Phone: 617-332-6002; Office Phone: 0113613273004. Personal E-mail: john.shattuck@ifklfoundation.org, jhshuttuck@gmail.com.

SHATTUCK, MAYO ADAMS, III, utilities executive; b. Boston, Oct. 7, 1954; s. Mayo Adams Jr. and Jane (Bergwall) S.; m. Molly Anne George, Sept. 29, 1997; children: Mayo Adams IV, Kathleen Elizabeth, Spencer George, Wyatt Augustus, Lillian Jessie. BA, Williams Coll., 1976; MBA, Stanford U., 1980. Analyst Morgan Guaranty Trust Co., NYC, 1976-78; mgr. Bain & Co., Menlo Park, Calif., 1980-83; v.p. to mng. dir. and head of corp. fin. Alex Brown & Sons, San Francisco, 1985-91, pres. and COO Balt., 1991-97; co-chmn., CEO BT Alex Brown Inc., from 1997; vice chmn. Bankers Trust N.Y., from 1997; co-chmn., co-CEO, Deutsche Banc Alex Brown Inc., Balt., 1999—2001; pres., CEO, chmn. bd. Constellation Energy Group, Balt., 2001—02, chmn., pres., CEO, 2002—. Bd. dir. Constellation Energy, Gap Inc., Edison Electric Inst., Capital One Fin.; bd dir., mem. exec. com. Nuclear Energy Inst. Adv. dir. U. Md. Balt. County, Johns Hopkins Medicine. Avocations: tennis, golf. Office: Constellation Energy Group 750 E Pratt St 18th Floor Baltimore MD 21202*

SHATTUCK, SCOTT HARLAN, performing company executive; b. Denver, Aug. 23, 1960; s. Harlan Louis Jr. and Gloria Mae (Evick) S. BA, Colo. State U., 1983; MFA, U. Tex., Austin, 1988. Prodn. stage mgr. Colo. Shakespeare Festival, Boulder, Colo., 1983-84; prodn. asst. Denver (Colo.) Center Theatre Co., 1983-85; dir. prodn. Tex. Shakespeare Festival, Kilgore, 1988-92; asst. prof. dramatic arts Dickinson Coll., Carlisle, Pa., 1988-92, chair dramatic arts, 1991-92; producing dir. Jean Cocteau Repertory, NYC, 1992-94, artistic dir., 1994-96, producing artistic dir., 1996—. Bd. advisers Theatre Insight, Austin, 1989—; cons. Region VII Edn. Svc. Ctr., K ilgore, 1989-92, Nancy Quinn Fund for Emerging Theatres of Alliance of Resident Theatres, N.Y.C., 1996—; artistic assoc. Vortex Repertory Co., Austin, Tex., 1991—; adj. asst. prof., Marymount Manhattan Coll., N.Y.C., 1993—. Mem. Assn. Theatre in Higher Edn., Theatre Comm. Group. Democrat. Office: Jean Cocteau Repertory 330 Bowery New York NY 10012-2414

SHATZ, CARLA J., biology professor, researcher; b. NYC; BA in Chemistry, Radcliffe Coll., 1969; MPhil, Univ. Coll., London, 1971; PhD, Harvard U., 1976, postdoc., 1976—78. Assoc. prof. neurobiology Sch. Medicine Stanford U., Palo Alto, Calif., 1985—89, prof. neurobiology, 1989—92; investigator Howard Hughes Med. Inst., 1994—2000; Class of 1943 prof. neurobiology U. Calif., Berkeley, 1992—2000; prof., chair dept. neurobiology Harvard Med. Sch., Boston, 2000—07, Nathan Marsh Pusey prof. neurobiology; head Bio-X program, prof. biological scis. and neurobiology Stanford U., 2007—. Mem. commn. on life scis. NRC, 1990—96; nat. adv. NIH, 1996—99; mem. coun. NAS, 1998—2001. Fellow: Inst. Medicine, Am. Philos. Soc., NAS, AAAS. Office: Clark Ctr 318 Campus Dr W 1 1 Rm W157 Stanford CA 94305-5437 Office Phone: 650-723-0534. Business E-Mail: cshatz@stanford.edu.

SHATZ, MARILYN JOYCE, psychologist, educator; b. NYC, Mar. 4, 1939; d. Morris and Freida Reva (Levinthal) Karpman; m. Stephen Sidney Shatz, Dec. 21, 1958 (div. July 1977); children: Geoffrey Ian, Adria Beth; m. Richard Feingold, Jan. 1, 1995. BA, U. Pa., Phila., 1971, MA, 1973, PhD, 1975. Asst. prof. Grad. Ctr. NYU, 1975-77; asst. prof. to prof. U. Mich., Ann Arbor, 1977—2009, dir. linguistics program, 1995—2001; adj. prof. U. NC, 2007—. Assoc. editor Lang. Jour. Linguistic Soc. Am., Washington, 1991-93; vis. scholar Inst. Human Devel., Berkeley, Calif., 1991-92. Author: A Toddler's Life: Becoming a Person, 1994; co-editor: Handbook of Language Development, 2007; contbr. articles to profl. jours. Fellow Guggenheim, Harvard U., 1980, Nat. Inst. Edn., U. Wis., 1981; Fulbright scholar Cambridge U., 1985; named First Alternate James McKean Cattell, 1991. Home: 2730 Maitland Dr Ann Arbor MI 48105-1565 Office: 530 ChurchSt Ann Arbor MI 48109 Office Phone: 734-647-3712. Business E-Mail: mshatz@umich.edu.

SHAUGHNESSEY, GAIL, educator; d. Mary Ellen Carter; m. Michael M. Shaughnessey, May 18, 1974; children: Ian, Evan. MA, Calif. State U. Dominquez Hills, LA, 2000. Faculty Cochise Coll., Sierra Vista, Ariz., 2001—.

SHAUGHNESSY, ALLEN F., pharmacist, educator; b. Plainfield, NJ, Jan. 11, 1959; s. Francis Henry and Dorothy Suzanne (Allen) S.; m. Rebecca Joan Clark, July 26, 1980; children: Christopher, Joshua, m. Andrea Esther Gorden; children Add Jesse Student, Gettysburg Coll., 1977-79; BS in Pharmacy, Temple U., 1982; PharmD, Med. U. of S.C., 1984. Registered pharmacist; bd. cert. pharmacotherapy specialist. Cons. pharmacist Sandlapper Cons. Pharmacists, Lexington, S.C., 1984-85; poison info. Med. U. of S.C., Charleston, 1983-84, asst. prof., 1987-89; clin. pharmacist Lexington Family Practice-Irmo, Columbia, S.C., 1984-87; asst. prof. U. S.C., Columbia, 1985-87; dir. pharmacologic edn. St. Margaret Meml. Hosp., Pitts., 1989-92; asst. prof. U. Pitts. Coll. Pharmacy, 1990—; dir. rsch./assoc. dir. ed. Harrisburg (Pa.) Family Practice Residency, 1992—; clin. assoc. prof. Med. Coll. Pa./Hahnemann U., 1995—2002; adj. prof. Pa. State Coll. Medicine, 2002—04; prof. family medicine Tufts U. Sch. Medicine, 2006—; assoc. program dir. Tufts U. Family Medicine Residency, 2005—. Fellow Am. Coll. Clin. Pharmacy; mem. Soc. Tchrs. Family Medicine, Rho Chi. Republican. Presbyterian. Personal E-mail: afshaughnessy@verizon.net. Business E-Mail: allen.shaughnessy@tufts.edu.

SHAUGHNESSY, TIMOTHY S., information technology executive; Various positions IBM Corp., including gen. mgr. global svcs. Asia-Pacific, v.p. & controller, then sr. v.p. svcs. delivery, 2008—. Office: IBM Corp 1 New Orchard Rd Armonk NY 10504 Office Phone: 914-499-5407. Business E-Mail: tshaugh@us.ibm.com.

SHAVELL, STEVEN M., law educator; b. Wash., May 29, 1946; AB in Math. and Economics, U. Mich., 1968; PhD in Economics, MIT, 1973. Lt. j.g. US Pub. Health Svc. Centers for Disease Control, 1968—70; asst. prof. economics Boston Coll., 1973—74, Harvard U., Cambridge, Mass., 1974—79, assoc. prof., 1979—80; asst. prof. law and economics Harvard Law Sch., 1980—82, prof., 1982—, Samuel R. Rosenthal prof., 2000—, dir. John M. Olin Ctr. for Law, Economics, and Bus., 1985—. Vis. prof. U. Chgo. Law Sch., 1984—85, NYU Law Sch., 1999; assoc. editor Geneva Risk and Ins. Rev., 1990—; bd. editors Internat. Rev. Law and Economics, 1987—, Jour. Law, Economics, and Orgn., 1989—, Rsch. in Law and Economics, 1990—, Am. Law and Economics Rev., 1999—, Ency. Law and Economics, 1999—; bd. advisors Ctr. for Law, Economics, and Fin. Institutions, Copenhagen Bus. Sch., 2001—; bd. faculty advisors Jour. Law, Economics, and Policy, 2003—. Author: Economic Analysis of Accident Law, 1987, Foundations of Economic Analysis of Law, 2004; co-author: Fairness versus Welfare, 2002, Analytical Methods for Lawyers, 2003. NSF Grad. Fellowship, 1968, NSF Nat. Needs Postdoctoral Rsch. Fellowship, 1977—78, Harvard Law Sch. Liberal Arts Fellow, 1977, Liberty Fund Summer Fellow in Law and Economics, 1979, Guggenheim Meml. Found. Fellowship, 1983—84. Fellow: Econometric Soc.; mem.: Am. Law and Economics Assn. (bd. dirs. 1990—94, pres. 2001—02), Am. Acad. Arts and Sciences. Office: Harvard Law Sch 1563 Massachusetts Ave Cambridge MA 02138 Office Phone: 617-495-3668. Office Fax: 617-496-2256. Business E-Mail: shavell@law.harvard.edu.

SHAVER, JAMES PORTER, retired education educator, dean; b. Wadena, Minn., Oct. 19, 1933; BA magna cum laude, U. Wash., Seattle, 1955; MAT, Harvard U., Cambridge, Mass., 1957, EdD, 1961. Instr. Grad. Sch. Edn., Harvard U., 1961-62; asst. prof., dir. Social Studies Curriculum Ctr., Ohio State U., Columbus, 1964-65; assoc. prof. Utah State U. Coll. Edn., Logan, 1962-64, prof., 1965—, chmn. Bur. Rsch. Svcs., 1965-93, assoc. dean rsch., 1978-93, acting dean Sch. Grad. Studies, 1990-91, 92-93, dean, 1993-99, prof. emeritus secondary edn., 1999—. Mem. Commn. Youth Edn. for Citizenship, ABA, 1975-81; mem. edn. task force Am. Hist. Assn.-Am. Polit. Sci. Assn. Project '87, 1981-84; tech. advisor Nat. Ctr. on Effective Secondary Schs., 1988-91; mem. adv. bd. program in civic and moral edn. Inst. for Philosophy and Pub. Policy, U. Md., 1992—; mem. steering com. Nat. Assessment Edn. Progress Civics Consensus Project, 1995-96. Co-author: Teaching Public Issues in the High School, 1966, 2d edit., 1974, Facing Value Decisions: Rationale-building For Teachers, 1976, 2d edit., 1982; editor:

Building Rationales for Citizenship Education, 1977, Handbook of Research on Social Studies Teaching and Learning, 1991; co-editor: Democracy, Pluralism, and the Social Studies, 1968; also others. Recipient Outstanding Svc. and Tchg. award, Utah Coun. for the Social Studies, 1975, 1978, Lifetime Achievement award, 1998. Mem. AAAS, AAUP, Nat. Coun. Social Studies (pres. 1976, Exemplary Rsch. award 1977, Exemplary Rsch. Editor award 1991), Am. Ednl. Rsch. Assn., Phi Beta Kappa, Phi Kappa Phi. Home: 11 Bridger Mountain Rd N Montana City MT 59634-9641 Business E-Mail: jim.shaver@usu.edu.

SHAVER, JOAN LOUISE FOWLER, dean, women's health nurse; b. Can. 1 child. BS in Nursing, U. Alberta, Can., 1966; M in Nursing, U. Wash., 1968-70, PhD in Physiology and Biophysics, 1976. Nursing instr. chair med. surgical prog. Holy Cross Hosp. Sch. Nursing, Calgary, Canada, 1966-68; staff nurse Virginia Mason Hosp., Seattle, 1970-71; asst. prof. Sch. Nursing U. Ariz., Tucson, 1976-77; assoc. prof. U. Calgary, Canada, 1977-80; asst. prof. Dept. Physiological Nursing U. Wash., Seattle, 1980-85, rsch. affil. Regl. Primate Rsch. Ctr., 1983-86, assoc. prof., 1985-89, chair Dept. Physiological Nusring, 1988-95, prof., 1989-95, prof., chair Dept. Biobehavioral Nursing & Health Systems, 1995-96, co-dir. Ctr. Women's Health Rsch., 1989-96; prof. biobehavioral health sci., dean Coll. Nursing U. Ill., Chgo., 1996—, co-dir. Rsch. Core Nat. Ctr. Excellence in Women's Health, 1997—. Bd. dirs. Advocate HealthCare, Chgo.; ednl. adv. coun. Select Comfort Corp.; pres. Am. Acad. Nursing, 2003—05. Mem. editl. bd. Health Care for Women Internat., 1984—, Heart and Lung: The Jour. Critical Care, 1988-90, Jour. Applied Nursing Rsch., 1988-91, IMAGE: Jour. Nursing Scholarship, editl. adv. bd. Nursing Rsch., 1997—, Biol. Rsch. for Nursing, 1999—, Jour. Nursing Scholarship, 2000—; contbr. articles to profl. jours. Mem. nat adv. coun. NIH Nat. Inst. Nursing Rsch.; mem. governing coun. Advocate Ill. Masonic Med. Ctr.; mem. health adv. com. Alberta Heritage Found. Med. Rsch. Abe Miller Meml. scholar Alberta Assn. Registered Nurses, 1968-69; Kathryn McLaggen Meml. fellow Can. Nurses Found. Fellow: Am. Acad. Nursing Am. Nurses Assn.; mem.: Inst. Medicine Chgo., Sigma Theta Tau Internat. Office: U Ill Chgo Coll Nursing MC 802 845 S Damen Ave Chicago IL 60612-7350 Business E-Mail: jshaver@uic.edu.*

SHAW, ALAN, lawyer; b. Long Branch, NJ, July 23, 1930; m. Margaret Knight, Oct. 15, 1959; children: Andrew Macbeth, Adriane Macbeth. AB, U. Mich., 1952; LLB, Harvard U., 1955. Bar: Mass. 1955, N.Y. 1958. Atty. Skadden, Arps, Slate, Meagher & Flom, NYC, 1958-65; v.p., gen. counsel, sec. Athlone Industries Inc., Parsippany, NJ, 1966-93, also bd. dirs. Adj. prof. law Fordham U.; arbitrator Am. Arbitration Assn., FINRA Dispute Resolution, N.Y. Stock Exch.; panelist Contract Dispute Resolution Bd., N.Y.C. With U.S. Army, 1955-57. Mem. ABA (sect. on corps., litig., alt. dispute resolution sect.), NJ Gen. Counsel Group, Assn. Bar City NY, Soc. Profls. Dispute Resolution, Morristown (NJ) Club, Washington Assn. Morristown (trustee, 2d v.p.), Morris County Golf Club, Harvard Club, Churchill Ctr. (charter mem.), Alexander Hamilton Hist. Soc., Franklin and Eleanor Roosevelt Inst. Home: 490 S Maple Ave Basking Ridge NJ 07920-1327 Office: 1812 Front St Scotch Plains NJ 07076

SHAW, ALAN BOSWORTH, geologist, retired paleontologist; b. Englewood, NJ, Mar. 28, 1922; s. Carroll Harper and Natalie Frederique (Howe) S.; m. Helen Louise Wilson, Nov. 2, 1945 (div. Apr. 1952); m. Marian Tavenner Stoll, Mar. 11, 1954 (dec. Apr. 1981); children: Nancy Jeanne, Sally Ann; m. Mary Elizabeth Merrem, Sept. 3, 1982. AB magna cum laude, Harvard Coll., 1946; AM, PhD, Harvard U., 1949. Asst. prof. geology U. Wyo., Laramie, 1949-55; paleontologist Shell Oil Co., Denver, 1955-60; owner Nat. Elec. Svc., NYC, 1960-61; freelance cons. geologist Denver, 1961; supr. Pan Am. Rsch. (now BP), Tulsa, Okla., 1961-68; various positions Pan Am. Petroleum, Denver, 1968-76; chief paleontologist Amoco Prodn., Chgo., 1976-77, chief geologist, 1977-81; geol. rsch. cons. Amoco Rsch., Tulsa, 1981-85; ret., 1985. Oil industry rep. NRC Com. on Paleontology, Washington, 1963-69; mem. Com. on Paleontology and Stratigraphy Deep Sea Drilling Program, 1973-75. Author: Time in Stratigraphy, 1964; contbr. numerous articles to profl. jours. Served to 1st lt., USAAF, 1943-45. Recipient Disting. Flying Cross, Moore Paleontology medal Soc. Sedimentary Geology, 1996. Achievements include invention of graphic correlation system for use of fossils in making time correlations of sedimentary rocks. Home: 210 Kamira Kerrville TX 78028 Personal E-mail: shaw99@ktc.com.

SHAW, ALAN ROGER, finance educator, retired company executive; b. Bklyn., July 7, 1938; s. Sewall S. and Vera (Dimmick) S.; children: Stephen S., Todd J., Bradley C.; m. Mary Elizabeth Hogg, May 30, 1987. Student, Susquehanna U., 1957, Adelphi U., 1963-66; LLD (hon.), Susquehanna U., 1999. Analyst Harris Upham & Co., NYC, 1958-71, asst. v.p., 1971-73, v.p., 1973-75; 1st v.p. Smith, Barney, Harris, Upham & Co., NYC, 1975-80; sr. v.p., mng. dir. Smith Barney, NYC, 1980—2004. Tchr. N.Y. Inst. Fin., 1966— Mem. Market Technicians Assn. (pres. 1974), N.Y. Soc. Security Analysts, Securities Industry Assn. Inst. (trustee 1986-92), Unqua Corinthian Yacht Club (commodore 1988-90), Shelter Island Yacht Club. Home: PO Box 322 79 N Midway Rd Shelter Island NY 11964 E-mail: almed@optonline.net.

SHAW, ALBERT CHENG-GIN, medical educator, researcher; s. David and Katharine Shaw; m. Pauline Lin; children: William, Emily. AB Summa Cum Laude, Harvard Coll., Cambridge, Mass., 1983; MD, Harvard Med. Sch., Harvard MIT Health Scis. and Tech., Boston, 1991; PhD, Harvard U., Cambridge, 1991. Diplomate Am. Bd. Internal Medicine, infectious diseases. Internship and residency Mass. Gen. Hosp., Boston, 1991—94, infectious diseases fellow, 1994—97; post-doc. rsch. fellow Harvard Med. Sch., Boston, 1995—98, instr., medicine, 1998—2001; asst. prof., medicine Yale U. Sch. Medicine, New Haven, 2001—07, biomed. rschr., tchg. and patient care, 2001—, assoc. prof., medicine, 2007—. Recipient L.J. Henderson prize, Harvard Coll., 1983, T.J. Hoopes prize, 1983, James Tolbert Shipley prize, Harvard Med. Sch., 1991; Postdoc. fellowship, Howard Hughes Med. Inst., 1995—98, Nat. fellow, Brookdale Found., 2003—05. Fellow: Infectious Disease Soc. America; mem.: Soc. Leukocyte Biology, Am. Assn. Immunologists, Phi Beta Kappa. Office: Yale Univ Sch Medicine 300 Cedar St Box 208022 New Haven CT 06520

SHAW, ANDREA ELIZABETH, literature and language professor, director; d. Burchel Reginald and Kathleen Maude Shaw; m. Harold Dean Nevins, Apr. 1, 1989; children: Harold Dean Nevins, Iris Kathleen Nevins. PhD, U. Miami, Coral Gables, 2004; MFA, Fla. Internat. U., Miami, 2007. Asst. prof. & asst. dir. Nova Southeastern U., Fort Lauderdale, Fla., 2005—. Contbr. articles to profl. jours. Bd. mem. Women's Internat. Film Festival, Miami, 2007—09; sec. St. Andrew HS Girls Old Girls' Assn., Miami, 2008—09. Office: Nova Southeastern Univ 3301 College Ave Fort Lauderdale FL 33314-7796 Business E-Mail: andrshaw@nova.edu.

SHAW, ANNITA LOUISE, art educator; b. Scottsbluff, Nebr., Feb. 13, 1941; d. Harold Kenneth and Velma Loraine Shaw; m. Max Le Roy Shaw, June 29, 1968; 1 child, Justin Owen. BS in Elem. Edn., Chadron State Coll., Nebr., 1963; MA in Art Supervision and Direction, NYU, 1969. Tchr. 2d grade Bridgeport Sch. Dist., Nebr., 1961—64; tchr. 3rd grade Geneva Sch. Dist., Nebr., 1964—66; elem. art specialist Omaha Sch. Dist., 1966—68; tchr. jr. high sci. New London Sch. Dist., Conn., 1968—70; tchr. jr. and sr. high visual arts and visual arts curriculum specialist Ctrl. Kitsap Sch. Dist., Silverdale, Wash., 1974—2003; owner A.Shaw Originals, Kenneth Shaw Family Farms, Nebr., Neb. Panhandle Farm. Mem. adv. com. Wash. State Commn. on Student Learning, Olympia, 1993—95; mem. assessment cert. team Nat. Bd. Profl. Tchg. Stds., San Francisco, 1996; mem. People to People Am. Program Art Edn. Delegation to Russia, 2006; presenter in field. Prodr.: (videos) Whistle Wisdom, 1993, Perspective: More than Converging Line, 1999, Roll, Pinch, Shake and Rattle, 2001; contbr. articles to mags. and profl. jours. Mem.: Chariot Awareness Edn. Found. (founder 2008), Nat. Art Edn. Assn. (mem. dels. assembly 1994, pres. Wash. chpt., treas. Wash. chpt., historian and ret. rep. Wash. chpt., Pacific Region Elem. Art Educator 1988, Christa McAliffe Excellence in Edn. 1990, Pacific Region Mid. Level Art Educator 2001, Wash. Art Educator of Yr. 2000, Nat. Mid. Level Art Educator of the Yr. 2002), Women in the Arts (charter mem.). Avocations: sculpting, designing pins and medallions, writing. Home: PO Box 737 Silverdale WA 98383-0737 Personal E-mail: mashaw@mindspring.com.

SHAW, ANTHONY, pediatric surgeon, retired educator; b. Shanghai, Oct. 31, 1929; s. Bruno and Regina (Hyman) S.; m. Iris Violet Azian, Mar. 12, 1955; children: Brian Anthony, Diana Shaw Clark, Daniel Aram. BA cum laude, Harvard Coll., 1950; MD, NYU, 1954. Diplomate Am. Bd. Surgery; cert. spl. competence pediat. surgery. Intern and resident in surgery Columbia-Presbyn. Med. Ctr., NYC, 1954-56, 58-62; resident in pediat. surgery Babies Hosp., NYC, 1962; asst. prof. surgery Columbia U. Coll. Physicians and Surgeons, NYC, 1965-70; chief pediat. surgery St. Vincent's Hosp., NYC, 1963-70, Harlem Hosp. Ctr., NYC, 1965-70; prof. surgery U. Va., Charlottesville, 1970-81, chief pediat. surgery Med. Ctr., 1970-81; prof. surgery UCLA, 1981-2001, emeritus prof. surgery, 2001—; chief pediat. surgery Olive View-UCLA Med. Ctr., Sylmar, 1986-2001, cons. surgeon, 2003—. Expert witness on child abuse L.A. Superior Ct., 1986—; chmn. gov.'s adv. com. child abuse and neglect Commonwealth of Va., 1975-80; vis. prof. pediat. surgery People's Republic of China, 1985. Contbr. more than 220 articles to profl. jours. Mem. Gov.'s Task Force on Child Abuse Va., 1973-74. Capt. U.S. Army, 1956-58. Recipient Commrs. award Va. Dept. Social Svcs., 1980, award Gov.'s Adv. Bd., Cert. of Recognition HEW, 1978. Fellow Am. Pediat. Surg. Assn. (sec. 1982-85), ACS (v.p. 1987-89); mem. AMA, Pacific Coast Surg. Assn. (v.p. 1989-90), Am. Soc. Law, Medicine, and Ethics, Am. Profl. Soc. on Abuse of Children, Alpha Omega Alpha. Avocation: writing humor. Home and Office: One S Orange Grove Blvd # 9 Pasadena CA 91105 Home Phone: 626-796-8588; Office Phone: 626-796-8588. Personal E-mail: shawpas@pacbell.net.

SHAW, BRIAN K., professional basketball coach, retired professional basketball player; b. Oakland, Calif., Mar. 22, 1966; m. Nikki Shaw; 2 children. Attended, St. Mary's Coll., Calif.; B, U. Calif., Santa Barbara, 1988. Guard Boston Celtics, 1988-89, 90-91, Il Messaggero Roma, Italy, 1989-90, Miami Heat, 1991-94, Orlando Magic, 1994-96, Phila. 76ers, 1997-98, Portland Trailblazers, 1998-99, LA Lakers, 1999—2003, scout, 2003—04, asst. coach, 2004—. Recipient Gold medal, FIBA World Championship, 1986; named Player of Yr., Pacific Coast Athletic Assn., 1988; named to All-Rookie 2d Team, NBA, 1989. Achievements include member of NBA Finals championship winning Los Angeles Lakers, 2000-02. Avocations: fishing, playing cards. Office: LA Lakers Staples Ctr 1111 S Figueroa St Los Angeles CA 90015-1300*

SHAW, CAROLE, editor, publisher; b. Bklyn., Jan. 22, 1936; d. Sam and Betty (Neckin) Bergenthal; m. Ray Shaw, Dec. 27, 1957; children: Lori Eve Cohen, Victoria Shaw Locknar. BA, Hunter Coll., 1962. Singer Capitol Records, Hilton Records, Rama Records, Verve Records, 1952-65; TV appearances Ed Sullivan, Steve Allen, Jack Paar, George Gobel Show, 1957; owner The People's Choice, LA, 1975-79; founder, editor-in-chief Big Beautiful Woman mag., Beverly Hills, Calif., 1979—93; on air fashio cons. NBS S Home Show, 1993—95; with Carole Shaw Collectibles The Home Shopping Club, 1993—95; actress Nashville, 2000—; mem. Moonlight & Memories, 2003—. Creator Carole Shaw and BBW label clothing line for large-size women. Author: Come Out, Come Out Wherever You Are, 1982. Avocations: piano, painting, swimming, travel. Office: BBW Mag 6666 Brookmont Ter Ste 412 Nashville TN 37205-4622 Personal E-mail: bibewa@comcast.net.

SHAW, CECELIA, retired chef; b. Mankato, Minn., Feb. 18, 1959; d. Maxine Adele and Robert Cyril Shaw; m. Steve Schept, Sept. 15, 1990. Degree in Culinary Arts, Mankato Tech. Coll., Minn., 1984. Owner, head chef Soupstone, Mankato, 1980—81; pvt. practice Mankato, 1981—83; salad and prep cook Maggies Cafe, Mankato, 1983; asst. kitchen mgr. Phoenix Restaurant, Mankato, 1983—84; 1st commis chaud Hotel Sofitel, Bloomington, Minn., 1984—86; supr., chef Ebenezer Soc., Mpls., 1986—87; dietary mgr. Mar. Ho., Mpls., 1987—90; kitchen mgr. Table of Contents, St. Paul, 1990—91; line chef Azur Restaurant, Mpls., 1991—92; sous chef Blue Point Restaurant, Wayzata, Minn., 1992—94; prep chef D'Amico Cucina, Mpls., 1994—96; ret., 1996. Vol. Hope Now, Arlington Heights, Ill., 2002—04. Avocations: languages, travel, gardening, cooking. Home: 2300 Glen Oaks Ct Algonquin IL 60102-4275 Personal E-mail: ceceliasrd2@earthlink.net.

SHAW, CHARLES RAYMOND, journalist; b. Phila., Feb. 2, 1951; s. Charles Raymond Sr. and Dorothy Blanche (Buckman) S.; m. Francine Ruth Pennock, Jan. 14, 1983. BS in Journalism, Temple U., 1972; MS in Journalism, Columbia U., 1973. Staff writer Intelligencer Jour., Lancaster, Pa., 1973-83, asst. news editor, 1983-88, news editor, 1989-97, editor, 1997—. Mem. Pa. Soc. of Newspaper Editors, Am. Soc. Newspaper Editors, Pa. Assoc. Press (bd. dirs.). Office: Lancaster Newspaper PO Box 1328 Lancaster PA 17608-1328 Office Phone: 717-291-8650. E-mail: rshaw@lnpnews.com.

SHAW, DANIEL STEPHEN, psychology professor, department chairman; b. Washington, Feb. 8, 1958; s. Milton and Natalie Jane (Bisguyer) S.; m. Ann Caroline Plough, May 9, 1987; three children. BA, Oberlin Coll., 1980; MA, U. Va., 1985, PhD, 1988. Lic. clin. psychologist, Pa. Rsch. asst. Children's Hosp. Nat. Med. Ctr., Washington, 1980-82; clin. intern in psychology dept. psychology U. Va., Charlottesville, 1984-85, clin. intern in psychology dept. family practice, 1986-87; clin. intern Med. Coll. of Hampton Roads, Norfolk, Va., 1987-88; asst. to full prof. clin. and devel. psychology U. Pitts., 1989—, asst. to full prof. psychiatry, 1989—, dir. psychology clinic, 1990, 1992, 1997—98, dir. grad. admissions, 1990—92, 1995, 1997, dir. Pitt early steps project, 2000—, faculty assoc., Univ. Ctr. Social and Urban Rsch., 2000—, chmn. dept. psychology; behavioral scientist, child and family ctr. U. Oreg. Dept. Psychology, 2002—. Divorce mediator L.A. Conciliation Ct., 1983; rsch. asst. U. Va., 1983-86, teaching asst., 1986-87. Bd. dirs. SUPPORT, Inc., Pitts., 1989-91. Grantee U. Pa., 1988-91, Buhl Found., Jewish Health Found., NIMH, 1994—, recipient Mid-career Rsch. Svc. award, 1999-2009, SR. Rsch. Svc. award NIDA, 2009-. Mem. APA (div. devel. psychology, Boyd McCandless Young Investigator award 1995), Pa. Psychol. Assn., Greater Pitts. Psychol. Assn. (task force 1988-89), Soc. for Rsch. in Child Devel., Soc. for Rsch. on Child and Adolescent Psychopathology, Life History Rsch. Soc. (Young Scholar award 1990). Democrat. Jewish. Avocations: tennis, photography, computers. Office: U Pitts Dept Psychology Sennott Sq Bldg Rm 4101 210 S Bouquet St Pittsburgh PA 15260-0001 Office Phone: 412-624-1836. Office Fax: 412-624-8827. Business E-Mail: casey@pitt.edu.

SHAW, DAVID ELLIOT, computer scientist, hedge fund manager; b. Chgo., Mar. 29, 1951; s. Charles B. Jr. and Marilyn (Baron) Shaw. BA, U. Calif., San Diego, 1972; MS, Stanford U., 1975, PhD, 1980. Pres. Stanford Systems Corp., Palo Alto, Calif., 1976-79; assoc. prof. Columbia U., NYC, 1980-86; v.p. Morgan Stanley & Co., NYC, 1986-88; founder, chmn., pres., CEO D.E. Shaw & Co., NYC, 1988—; chief scientist D.E. Shaw Rsch., LLC, 2001—. Sr. rsch. fellow Columbia U. Ctr. Computational Biology & Bioinformatics; adj. prof. biomed. informatics Columbia U. Coll. Physicians & Surgeons. Contbr. articles to profl. jours. Mem. subcom. tech./fin, chmn. mayor's panel NYC Partnership, 1987; appt. com. advs. on sci./tech. for Pres. Clinton, 1994, chmn. panel ednl. tech., 1995. Named one of 400 Richest Americans, Forbes mag., 2006—, 25 Leaders Reshaping NY, Crain's NY Bus. mag., 2008. Fellow: Am. Acad. Arts & Scis.; mem.: AAAS (bd. dirs. 1998—, treas.), Coun. on Competitiveness (exec. com. 1998—), NY Acad. Scis. (bd. govs. 1993—95). Democrat. Jewish. Office: DE Shaw Rsch LLC 120 W 45th St 39th Fl New York NY 10036 Office Phone: 212-849-0880. Business E-Mail: david.shaw@deshaw.com.*

SHAW, DAVID TAI-KO, electrical and computer engineering educator, academic administrator; b. China, Mar. 13, 1938; came to U.S., 1960, naturalized, 1972; m. Katharine Lin-Yee Yang; children: Albert, Stanley. BSM.E., Nat. Taiwan U., Taipei, 1959; MS in Nuclear Engring., Purdue U., 1961, PhD, 1964. Asst. prof. div. interdisciplinary studies and research Sch. Engring., SUNY-Buffalo, 1964-67, assoc. prof. faculty engring. and applied scis., 1967-74, prof. elec. engring. and nuclear engring., aerospace and engring. sci., 1974-77, prof. elec. engring., 1974—, dir. lab. for power and environ. studies, 1978—90. Exec. dir. State Inst. on Superconductivity, 1987-97; vis. prof. U. Paris, 1976-77; vis. scientist Centre d'Etudes Nucleairs de Fontenay-aux-Roses (France) Commissariat a L'Energie Atomique, 1976-77; vis. assoc. dept. environ. health engring. Calif. Inst. Tech., 1970-71; mem. U.S. del. French Commissariat a L'energie Atomique, 1974, U.S. del. Joint Nuclear Energy Agy. IAEA Internat. Liaison Group on Thermionic Elec. Power Generation, Paris, 1974; mem. U.S. vis. team USSR Acad. Scis. Editor: Fundamentals of Aerosol Science, 1978, Recent Developments in Aerosol Science, 1978, Assessment of Airborne Radioactivity, 1978, Jour. Nanoparticle Rsch. North and South America Regions, 1999-; editor-in-chief: Jour. Aerosol Sci. and Tech., 1982-93; contbr. articles to profl. jours. Mem. IEEE, ASME, AAAS, Am. Assn. Aerosol Rsch. (pres. 1982-85, Assn. award 1984, Internat. Aerosol Fellow award 1994), Sigma Xi, Sigma Pi Sigma. Office: Ctr Innovation Engring Learing 330 Bonner Hall Amherst NY 14260-1900 E-mail: dshaw@buffalo.edu.

SHAW, DENNIS FREDERICK, former library director, chartered physicist, consultant; b. Teddington, Middlesex, Eng., Apr. 20, 1924; s. Albert and Lily Florence (Hill) S.; m. Joan Irene Chandler, June 25, 1949; children: Peter James, Margaret Denise, Katherine Joan, Deborah Mary. BA in Physics, U. Oxford, 1945, MA, 1950, DPhil in Nuc. Physics, 1950. Sr. rsch. officer Oxford (Eng.) U., 1950-75; tutor in physics Keble Coll., 1956-75, professorial fellow, 1977—, keeper of sci. books, 1975-91, emeritus, 1991. Vis. scientist CERN, Geneva, 1961-62; vis. prof. U. South Tenn., 1974; chmn. IFLA Sci. and Tech. Librs., 1987-91, hon. treas. spl. librs. div., 1991-93, cons., 1993—; mem. Home Office Sci. Adv. Coun., London, 1966-78; mem. Home Def. Sci. Adv. Com., London, 1978-95; mem. Hebdomadal Coun., Oxford U., 1980-89; mem Com. for the Internat. Coun. of Sci. Unions Press, 1991-96, mng. editor electronic pub., 1997-2002. Author: Introduction to Electronics, 1962, 70, Information Sources in Physics, 1985, 95; editor: Proceedings of ICSU/UNESCO Internat. Conferences on Electronic Publishing in Sci., 1996, 2001, Guidelines for Scientific Publishing, 1999; contbr. articles to profl. jours. Gov. Christ's Hosp., London, Almoner, 1980-98, chmn. edn. com., 1993-96; mem. Oxford City Coun., 1963-67; freeman City of London, 1998. Decorated Comdr. Brit. Empire, 1974. Fellow Inst. Physics, Zool. Soc.; mem. Am. Inst. Physics (sr.), Internat. Assn. Tech. Univs. Librs. (hon., sec. 1983-85, pres. 1986-90, chmn. pub. bd. 1991-93), N.Y. Acad. Sci., Oxford and Cambridge Club. Anglican. Home: 29 Davenant Rd Oxford OX2 8BU England Office: Keble Coll Parks Rd Oxford OX1 3PG England Business E-Mail: dennis.shaw@keb.ox.ac.uk.

SHAW, DIANE, artist, educator; d. Charlotte Carolyn Styers; children: Victoria Leigh, Stuart Neal. MFA, U. Memphis, 1991. Adj. prof. U. Tenn., Martin, 2000—04, asst. prof., 2005—. Contbr. articles to art jours. Treas. Weakley Co. Arts and Humanities Coun., Martin, 2000—08, Arts Coop., Martin, 2008. Mem.: Tenn. Arts Edn. Assn. Avocation: art.

SHAW, DONALD LESLIE, Spanish language educator; b. Feb. 11, 1930; s. Stephen Leslie and Lily (Hughes) S.; m. Maria Concetta Cristini, June 30, 1958; children: Andrew Leslie, Sylvia Maria Pierina. BA, U. Manchester, Eng., 1952, MA, 1953; PhD, U. Dublin, Ireland, 1960. Asst. lectr. U. Dublin, 1955-57, U. Glasgow, Scotland, 1957-64, U. Edinburgh, Scotland, 1964-69, sr. lectr., 1969-72, reader, prof. spanish, 1972-86; prof. spanish U. Va., Charlottesville, 1986—. Vis. prof. Brown U., Providence, 1967, U. Va., Charlottesville, 1983. Author: Historia de la Literatura Española, Siglo XIX, 1973, La Generación del 98, 1977, Nueva Narrativa Hispanoamericana, 1981, Alejo Carpentier, 1985, Borges' Narrative Strategies, 1992, Antonio Skármeta and the Post-Boom, 1994, The Post-Boom in Spanish American Fiction, 1998, A Companion to Spanish American Fiction, 2001, Spanish American Poetry After 1950, 2007. Served with RAF, 1953-55. Avocation: cycling. E-mail: dls6h@vriginia.edu. Office: U Va 115 Wilson Hall Charlottesville VA 22903-3238 Home: 102 Shamrock Rd #16 Charlottesville VA 22903 Home Phone: 434-296-4528; Office Phone: 434-924-4658. Business E-Mail: dls6h@virginia.edu.

SHAW, ELEANOR JANE, newspaper editor; b. Columbus, Ohio, Mar. 23, 1949; d. Joseph Cannon and Wanda Jane (Campbell) S. BA, U. Del., 1971. With News-Jour. newspapers, Wilmington, Del., 1970-82, editor HEW desk, asst. met. editor, 1977-80, bus. editor, 1980-82; topics editor USA Today, 1982-83; asst. city editor The Miami Herald, 1983-85; projects editor The Sacramento Bee, 1985-87, news editor, 1987-91, exec. bus. editor, 1991-93, editor capitol bur. news, 1993-95, state editor, 1995-99; mgr. employee comm. The McClatchy Co., Sacramento, 1999—2004; associate TMT Worldwide, 2004—08; pres. Shaw Media Consulting, 2008—. Bd. dirs. Del. 4-H Found., 1978—83, Safety Ctr., Inc., Sacramento, 2003—, chair, 2007—08. Mem. Calif. Soc. Newspaper Editors (bd. dirs. 1990-96), No. Calif. Wine Soc. (v.p. 1987-93, pres. 1993-2002). Office Phone: 916-849-6781. Personal E-mail: ellieshaw@sbcglobal.net. Business E-Mail: elliejshaw@gmail.com.

SHAW, FRANK X., computer software company executive; BJ, U. Oreg., Eugene; grad., US Dept. Def. Info. Sch. Pub. rels. mgr. Gelman & Grey Comm., Knoll & Co., Inc.; v.p. Insync Comm., 1996—98; gen. mgr. Microsoft platform team Waggener Edstrom Worldwide, pres. Microsoft account worldwide; corp. v.p. corp comm. Microsoft Corp., 2009—. Pub. affairs officer USMC. Office: Microsoft Corp One Microsoft Way Redmond WA 98052-6399*

SHAW, HAROLD, retired performing arts association administrator; b. Hebron, NY, June 11, 1923; Student, Ithaca Coll., 1942, Columbia, 1944, N.Y. U. Extension, 1948. Former assoc. Hurok Concerts, Inc., NYC; chmn., owner Shaw Concerts, Inc., NYC, 1969-99; ret., 1999; performing arts dir. Seattle World's Fair, 1961-62. Former concert mgr. Nathan Milstein, Vladimir Horowitz, Dame Janet Baker, Jessye Norman, Helen Donath, Jacqueline duPre, Wolfgang Holzmair, Jard van Nes, Mitsuko Uchida, Garrick Ohlsson, Shura Cherkassky, Horacio Gutiérrez, Julian Bream, John Williams, Elmar Oliveira, Kyoko Takezawa, Robert Shaw, Andrew Davis, and over 100 artists and attractions; exec. dir. President's Shakespeare Ann. Com., 1964. Dir. exec. staff, mem. performing arts com. Cultural Commn., N.Y.C., 1966; nat. chmn. Performing Arts Energy Commn., 1974; chmn. bd. trustees Am. Shakespeare Theatre, Stratford, Conn., 1974. With USAAF, 1942-43. Mem.: Am. Summer Stock Mgrs. Assn. (co-founder), Actors Equity Assn., Assn. Coll., Univ. and Cmty. Arts Adminstrs., Am. Symphony Orch. League, Internat. Performing Arts Adminstrs., Athletic Club, Phi Mu Alpha Sinfonia. E-mail: hshaw611@msn.com.

SHAW, HELEN LESTER ANDERSON, nutrition educator, researcher, retired dean; b. Lexington, Ky., Oct. 18, 1936; d. Walter Southall and Elizabeth (Guyn) Anderson; m. Charles Van Shaw, Mar. 14, 1988. BS, U. Ky., Lexington, 1958; MS, U. Wis., Madison, 1965, PhD, 1969. Registered dietitian. Dietitian Roanoke (Va.) Meml. Hosp., 1959-60, Santa Barbara (Calif.) Cottage Hosp., 1960-61; dietitian, unit mgr. U. Calif., Santa Barbara, 1961-63; rsch. asst., NIH fellow U. Wis., Madison, 1963-68; from asst. prof. to prof. U. Mo., Columbia, 1969-88, assoc. dean, prof., 1977-84; prof., chair dept. food and nutrition U. N.C., Greensboro, 1989-94, dean Sch. Human Environ. Scis., 1994-2000; ret., 2000. Cluster leader Food for 21st Century rsch. program U. Mo., 1985-88. Contbr. articles to rsch. publs. Elder First Prebsbyn. Ch., Columbia, Mo., 1974—89, Greensboro, NC, 1992—. Recipient Teaching award Home Econ. Alumni Assn., 1981, Gamma Sigma Delta, 1984, Centennial Legacy medallion U. Ky., 2007; rsch. grantee Nutrition Found., 1971-73, NIH, 1972-75, NSF, 1980-83. Mem. Am. Soc. for Nutrition, Am. Bd. Nutrition, Am. Soc. for Clin. Nutrition, Am. Dietetic Assn., Sigma Xi, Phi Upsilon Omicron, Kappa Omicron Nu. Democrat. Avocations: tennis, singing, volunteering, watercolor painting. Personal E-mail: shaw713helen@aol.com.

SHAW, JACK ALLEN, communications company executive; b. Auburn, Ind., Jan. 1, 1939; s. Marvin Dale and Vera Lucille (Harter) S.; m. Martha Sue Collins, Aug. 24, 1963; 1 child, Mark Allen. BSEE, Purdue U., 1962; DSc (hon.), Capitol Coll., 1994, DSc (hon.), 1995; D in Engrig. (hon.), Purdue U., 1998. Project engr. Hughes Aircraft Co., El Segundo, Calif., 1962-69; dir. program mgmt. ITT Space Comms., Ramsey, NJ, 1969-74; v.p., corp. devel. Digital Comms. Corp., Gaithersburg, Md., 1974-78, exec. v.p., COO Germantown, Md., 1978-81, pres., CEO, 1981-84, M/A-com Telecom divsn., Germantown, Md., 1984-87; chmn., CEO Hughes Network Sys., Inc., 1988—, chmn., also bd. dirs., 1978—, Germantown, 1987-2000, corp. sr. exec. v.p. enterprise sector, 2000—; pres., CEO Hughes Elecs., 2001. Bd. dirs. XM Satellite Radio, Guidant Corp.; exec. v.p. Hughes Electronics, 1999. Mem.: IEEE (sr.), Radio Club Am. (hon.). Republican. Personal E-mail: jackbrasshat@aol.com.

SHAW, JAMES GREGORY (GREG), state supreme court justice; b. 1957; s. James Hubert and Ruth (Cooper) Shaw; m. Samantha Shaw, Aug. 1980; children: Gregory, Christopher. BS, Auburn Univ., 1979; JD, Samford Univ., 1982; LLM, Univ. Va., 2004. Bar: Ala. 1982. Atty., private practice, 1982—84; staff atty. Ala. Supreme Ct. Justice Janie Shores, 1984—85, Ala. Supreme Ct. Justice James Gorman Houston, 1985—2000; judge Ala. Ct. Criminal Appeals, 2000—09; chief judge Ala. Ct. of Judiciary, 2007—09; assoc. justice Ala. Supreme Ct., 2009—. Mem. Ala. Chief Justice's Commn. on Professionalism, Ala. State Bar Com. on Archives & History, Jud. Liaison com., Pattern Jury Instructions com., adv. com. criminal procedure. Master: Hugh Maddox Inn of Ct. (hon.); mem.: Kiwanis Club of Montgomery. Methodist. Office: Ala Supreme Ct 300 Dexter Ave Montgomery AL 36104 Office Phone: 334-229-0700.*

SHAW, JANE ELIZABETH, electronics company executive, retired pharmaceutical company executive; b. Droitwich, Eng., Feb. 3, 1939; came to U.S., 1964; m. Peter Fredrick Carpenter, Sept. 25, 1982; 1 son, Jonathan. BS, U. Birmingham, Eng., 1961, PhD in Physiology, 1964. Rsch. scientist Worcester Found., Shrewsbury, Mass., 1964-70; asst. prof. Stanford U., Palo Alto, Calif., 1970-72; prin. scientist ALZA Corp., Palo Alto, 1970-71, project/program dir., 1972-80, v.p. R & D, 1980-84, exec. v.p. rsch., 1984-87, pres., COO, 1987—94; founder Stable Network, 1995—; chmn., CEO Nektar Therapeutics (formerly Aerogen Inc.), 1998—2005; exec. chmn. Intel Corp., 2009—. Bd. dirs. McKesson Corp., 1992—, Intel Corp., 1993—, OfficeMax Inc., 1994—2006, Nektar Therapeutics (formerly, Aerogen Inc.), 1998—2005. Contbr. over 110 sci. papers to profl. publs.; patentee in field. Med. Rsch. Coun. scholar U. Birmingham, 1961-64; hon. rsch. fellow U. Birmingham, 1966. Mem. AAAS, Am. Physiology Soc., Am. Soc. Clin. Pharmacology and Therapeutics, Am. Assn. Pharm. Scientists, N.Y. Acad. Scis., Sigma Xi. Office: Intel Corp 2200 Mission College Blvd Santa Clara CA 95054*

SHAW, JEANNE OSBORNE, editor, poet; b. Stone Mountain, Ga., June 1, 1920; d. Virgil Waite and Daisy Hampton (Scruggs) Osborne; m. Harry B. Shaw, Dec. 10, 1982; children from previous marriage: Robert Allan Gibbs, Marilyn Osborne Gibbs Barry. BA, Agnes Scott Coll., Atlanta/Decatur, 1942. Editl. staff Atlanta Constitution, 1942; feature writer New London Day, Conn., 1943; book reviewer Atlanta Constitution, 1940—42, Atlanta Jour., 1945—48; poetry Banner Press Emory U., Atlanta, 1957—59; book editor Georgia Mag., Decatur, 1957—73. Author: The Other Side of the Water, 1970 (author of yr. in poetry award Dixie Coun. Authors and Journalists), From Cowslip to Cobalt, 1971, Unravelling Yarn, 1979, Faithbuilders, 1982—84, Third Millennium Christmas, 2001, The First Easter Parade, 2003; co-author: Noel: Poems of Christmas, 1979, They Continued Steadfastly, History of Druid Hills Baptist Church, 1987; contbr. poems, pen and ink sketches to mags.; author: Serious Poem, 2005; author: (poems collection) (easter book) Druid Hills Baptist Church Atlanta, 2009. Mem. nat. arts and humanities com. Learning Life Boy Scouts Am., 2000—; pres. Newton class Druid Hills Bapt. Ch., 1973—74, dir. ch. tng., 1978—79, ch. clk., 1995—2001. Recipient Internat. Narrative Poem award, Poets and Patrons, Inc., 1992, Robert Martin, Burke, Otto in Praise of Poetry award, N.Y. Poetry Forum, 1973, 1979, 1981, Westbrook award, Ky. Poetry Soc., 1976, Ariz. award, 1981, Ind. State Fedn. Poetry Clubs award, Ala. State Poetry Soc. award, 1990, Rev. Earl M. Smith Meml. award, 1997, Joseph V. Hickey Meml. award, Nat. Fedn. State Poetry Socs., 1998. Mem.: Ga. Poetry Soc. (artistic dir. 2000, judge Nat. River of Words Contest 2002—05, 2007—08, founding mem. 2009, Traditional award 1984, Cole and Ledford award 1986, Goreau award 1987, Melissa Henry award 1989, Charles and Virginia Dickson award 1990, Jo Ann Yeager Adkins award 1991, Poem About Atlanta award 1992, Goreau award 1993, Free Verse award 1993, My Very Best Poem award 1995, Traditional award 1997, Jabberwocky award 1997, Annette Peery award 1998, 1999, Charles Bruehler award 2000, Annette Peery award 2001, 22d Anniversary award 2002, Mikki Morris award 2002, Reece award 2002, Poems Reach Song award 2004—08, Formal prize 2008), Atlanta Writers Club (pres. 1949—50, Aurelia Austin Writer of Yr. in poetry 1971, Wyatt award 1986, Light Verse award 1989, 1990, Daniel Whitehead Hicky award 1991, F. Levering Neely award 1991, Poet Laureate's award 1993, Wyatt award 1995, Daniel Whitehead Hicky award 1995, Gerry Crocker award 1995, Villanelle award 1997, 1998, Virginia Cole Veal award 1999, Light Verse award 2001, 2005, Serious Poetry award 2005, Formal Verse award 2006—08, Ben Willingham award), Poetry Soc. Ga. (John Clare prize 1955, Katharine H. Strong prize 1975, Eunice Thomson prize 1976, Jimmy Williamson prize 1977, Capt. Frank Spencer prize 1985, Conrad Aiken prize 1987, 1988, Capt. Frank Spencer prize 1988, Sarah Cunningham prize 1989, Soc. prize 1989, Lucy McEntire prize 1990—2007, Grace Schley Knight prize 1991, Gerald Chan Sieg prize 1991, Eunice Thomson prize 1992, Grace Schley Knight prize 1993, Sarah Cunningham prize 1994, Harriet Ross Colquitt prize 1994, Lucy McEntire prize 1994, Gerald Chan Sieg prize 1995, Harriet Ross Colquitt prize 1995, Eva Tennyson Forbes Meml. prize 1996, Sarah Cunningham prize 1997, About Holes prize 1998, Soc. prize 2001, Formal prize 2005, Grace Schley Knight prize 2005, Monday prize 2005, Conrad Aiken prize 2006, Critics' Com. prize 2006, Conrad Aiken prize 2007, Lucy McEntire prize 2007, Formal prize 2007, 2008—09, Soc. prize 2008—09), Ga. Writers Assn. (Lit. Achievement award 1971, Ga. Sr. Poet Laureate award 2006, Formal prize 2009), Phi Beta Kappa. Home: 809 Pinetree Dr Decatur GA 30030-2332 also: PO Box 916 Decatur GA 30031 Home Phone: 404-373-9892.

SHAW, JEFFREY WILLIAM, gas industry executive; b. Salt Lake City, Nov. 9, 1958; s. William R. Jr. and Janet (Engar) S.; m. Cynthia Roberts, July 3, 1984; children: Morgan, Lauren, Catherine, Michael. BA in Acctg., U. Utah, 1983. CPA, Nev. With audit div. Arthur Andersen & Co., Dallas, 1983-85, Las Vegas, Nev., 1985-88; dir. internal audit SW Gas Corp., Las Vegas, Nev., 1988—91, controller, chief acctg. officer, 1991—93, v.p., controller, chief acctg. officer, 1993—94, v.p., treas., 1994—2000, sr. v.p. fin., treas., 2000—02, sr. v.p. gas resources & pricing, 2002—03, pres., 2003—04, CEO, 2004—. Active Boy Scouts Am., Dallas, 1985, Las Vegas, 1987—. Mem. AICPA, Am. Law Assn. (bd. dirs.), Nev. Soc. CPAs., U. Nev. Las Vegas Found. (bd. trustees). Republican. Mem. Lds Ch. Avocations: writing, guitar, composing music, golf, basketball. Office: SW Gas Corp PO Box 98510 Las Vegas NV 89193-8510

SHAW, JOHN FREDERICK, retired naval officer; b. Dallas, Oct. 14, 1938; s. John Frederick and Sarah E. (Crouch) S.; m. Janice Muren, July 14, 1962; children: Elizabeth Lee, Suzanne Michele. BS, U.S. Naval Acad., 1960; MS in Mgmt. with distinction, Naval Postgrad. Sch., Monterey, Calif., 1970; grad., Armed Forces Staff Coll., 1971. Commd. ensign USN, 1960, advanced through grades to rear adm., 1983; exec. officer USS Long Beach (CGN 9), 1978-79; comdg. officer USS Bainbridge (CGN 25), 1980-83; dir. guided missile destroyer 51, Arleigh Burke program Comdr. Naval Sea Systems Command, Washington, 1983-85, mgr. AEGIS shipbldg. program, 1985-87; comdr. Cruiser-Destroyer Group One, San Diego, 1987-88; dep. chief staff plans and policy Supreme Allied Comdr., Atlantic, Norfolk, Va., 1988-89, chief staff, 1989-91; ret., 1991; prof. joint mil. ops. Coll. Continuing Edn., Naval War Coll., San Diego, 1992-94. Bd. advisors United Svc. Benefit Assn., Kansas City, Kans., 1987-93; mem. cmty. bd. advisors Sam and Rose Stein Inst. for Rsch. on Aging, 1998-2004; membership chmn., 1999-2000, sec.-treas., 2000-2004, emeritus bd. mem., 2006—; tax. cons. for elderly, AARP, 2000-07,09 Trustee Coronado Libr., 1998—2005, exec. sec., 2001—02, pres., 2002—04. Decorated Def. D.S.M., Legion of Merit with two gold stars, Meritorious Svc. medal with gold star, Navy Commendation medal with gold star, Meritorious Unit Commendation (civilian) USN. Mem. AARP, U.S. Naval Inst. (life), U.S. Naval Acad. Alumni Assn. (life, pres. Washington chpt. 1986, bd. govs. San Diego/Coronado chpt. 1996-99), Surface Navy Assn. (life), San Diego Navy League (dir. 1997-2002), Coronado Men's Golf Club, San Diego Class of 60 Representative. Avocations: golf, reading, economics, travel. Personal E-mail: jshaw14@aol.com.

SHAW, JOHN M., oncologist; b. Newark, Aug. 31, 1942; MD, U. Md., Balt., 1968. Cert. in internal medicine, in oncology, lic. Calif. Intern Northwestern U., Chgo., 1968-69, resident, 1969-72; attending staff Northwestern Meml. Hosp., Chgo., 1972—; oncologist Hematology Oncology Associates Ill., 1976—; asst. prof. hematology/oncology Northwestern U. Author of articles in New England Jour. of Medicine, Clinical Pharmacology and Therapeutics, Lancet. Hematology-Oncology fellow Temple U., Phila., 1974-76. Mem. Am. Coll. Clin. Oncology. Office: Hematology Oncology Associates Ill 676 N Saint Clair St Ste 2140 Chicago IL 60611-2919*

SHAW, JOHN W., lawyer; b. Mo., 1951; m. Cynthia Shaw; children: Sarah Ann, Katherine Kennan, Amy Elizabeth. BA, MA, U. Mo., 1973, JD, 1977. Bar: Mo. 1977. Ptnr. Lathrop & Norquist, 1983-92, Bryan Cave LLP, 1992-98, Berkowitz Oliver Williams Shaw & Eisenbrandt LLP (formerly Berkowitz Stanton Brandt Williams and Shaw LLP), Kansas City, 1998—. Bd. advisors, dept. personal fin. planning U. Mo.-Columbia, bd. advisors, Coll. Arts and Sci., Mo. 100 adv. group of bus. leaders to pres. Recipient Disting. Alumni award, Coll. Arts and Sci., U. Mo.-Columbia, 2005; named Commencement Keynote Spkr., 2003, Best of the Bar, Kansas City Bus. Jour., 2003; named one of Mo. Super Lawyers, Law and Politics, 2006—09, Best Lawyers in Am., 2007—09. Mem. ABA, Securities Industry Assn. (legal and compliance group), Mo. Bar, Def. Rsch. Inst. (chmn. firearms litigation subcom.), Order of Coif. Office: Berkowitz Oliver Williams Shaw & Eisenbrandt LLP 2600 Grand Blvd Ste 1200 Kansas City MO 64108 Home Phone: 913-491-9332; Office Phone: 816-561-7007. Business E-Mail: jshaw@bowse-law.com.

SHAW, JON ANGUS, psychiatrist; s. Leland Burdette Shaw and Vena Catskill; children: Deborah, Daniel, David. BA in Gen. Sci., U. Oregon, Eugene, 1959; MS in Psychology, U. Oregon, Portland, 1964, MD, 1964. Cert. Oregon, 1965, Md., 1968, DC, 1973, Fl., 1990, Wash. Sch. Psychiatry, 1968, diplomate Am. Bd. Psychiatry and Neurology, 1972, Am. Bd. Child & Adolescent Psychiatry and Neurology, 1974, Am. Psychoanalytic Assoc. Bd., 1983. Col. US Army, 1964—89; assoc. prof. psychiatry Georgetown U.W, Wash., 1975—89; chief, child & adolescent disorder res. br. NIMH, Rockville, 1986—89; vis. prof. psychiatry Uniformed Svcs., U. Health Scis., Bethsda, Md., 1989—; Psychiatry & Neurology Cons. Office Surgeon Gen., Pentgon, 1984—86; chief dept. psychiatry Walter Reed Army Med. Ctr., Wash., 1980—84; prof. clin. pediatrics U. Miami, Sch. Medicine; clin. prof. psychiatry Miami Sch. Medicine, 1989—. Chmn. Education Com., Fla. Psychoanalytic Ins., 2009—; med. dir. State Inpatient Psychiatry Program, 2007—. Col. US Army. Recipient Meml. award, Am. Acad. Child Psychiatry, 1970, Lewis B. Hill award, Balt. DC Inst. Psychoanalysis, 1977; named one of Top Psychiatrists, Consumer's Rsch. Coun. America, 2002—03. Avocations: hiking, golf. Home: 2532 Lake Ave Miami Beach FL 33150

SHAW, JUDY BROWDER, engineer; BS in Chemistry, Harding Coll.; postgrad, Texas Tech U. Process devel. engr. then process engr. mgr. Texas Instruments, 1978—2000, mgr. Silicon Tech. Devel. Process Engrng. teams, 2000—07, dir., adv. process modules, 2007—. Cofounder SiTD Women's Network, 2002, Women Tex. Instruments Fund, 2003; mem. SiTD Business Diversity Team, Leadership Tex., 2004; bd. dirs. Real Options for Women, Plano, Tex. Named to Hall of Fame, WITI, 2004.

SHAW, KATHLEEN M. TROUTNER, retired librarian; b. Waverly, Iowa, May 17, 1935; d. Bert Clifton and Kathleen Marjorie Troutner; m. Robert Einar Shaw (div.); children: Robert Belden(dec.), Ellen Katherine Shaw Karnes. BA in Edn., Western Wash. U., Bellingham, 1970; MS in Ednl. Media, Western Oregon State U., Monmouth, 1978. Tchr. Corvallis Sch. Dist., Oreg., 1970—73, resource tchr., 1973—76; media specialist Salem Sch. Dist., Oreg., 1978—82; libr. Saudi-Aramco Schs., Dhahran, Saudi Arabia, 1982—92; ret., 1992. Pres. Oak Harbor Libr. Bd., Wash., 1999—; bd. dirs. Sr. Svcs. Island County, Island County, Wash., 2004—. Mem.: AAUW (pres. Whidbey Island, Wash. br. 1997—98, named gift honoree 1998), Whidbey Island Cmty. Chorus. Avocations: singing, reading, knitting. Home: 790 SW Echo Loop Oak Harbor WA 98277 Personal E-mail: putsy8@hotmail.com.

SHAW, KENDALL (GEORGE), artist, educator; b. New Orleans, Mar. 30, 1924; s. George Kendall and Florence Gladys (Worner) Shaw; m. Frances (Glenn) Fort, Oct. 31, 1955 (dec. 2007). Student, Ga. Inst. Tech., 1944-46; BS in Chemistry, Tulane U., 1949, MFA, 1959; postgrad., La. State U., 1950. Instr. Columbia U., 1961-66, Hunter Coll., 1966-68, Parsons Sch. Design, N.Y.C., 1966-86, Lehman Coll., 1968-70, Bklyn. Mus. Art Sch., 1970-76; US del. to UNESCO Conf., London, 1965. One-man shows include Orleans Gallery, New Orleans, 1960, 61, 63, Columbia U., 1962, 65, Bienville Gallery, New Orleans, 1968, Tibor de Nagy Gallery, NYC, 1964, 65, 67, 68, Southampton Coll., 1969, John Bernard Myers Gallery, 1972, Alessandra Gallery, 1976, Lerner Heller Gallery, NYC, 1979, 81, 82, Nature Morte, NYC, 1983, Bernice Steinbaum Gallery, NYC, 1991, Artists Space, NYC, 1992, The Gallery of South Orange, NJ, 1997, U. Richmond, Va., 1999, Tulane U., 2001, Ogden Mus. So. Art, New Orleans, 2007, Ruskin Gallery, Cambridge U., Eng., 2007; group shows include Downtown Gallery, New Orleans, 1959, Orleans Gallery, 1959, 60, 61, Mus. Contemporary Art, Nagaoka, Japan, 1965, Alessandra Gallery, NYC, 1976, Albright-Knox Gallery, Buffalo, 1970, PS 1, NYC, 1977, curator Rice U., Houston, 1977, Gladstone Villani Gallery, NYC, 1978, Galerie Habermann, Cologne, 1979, Modern Art Gallery, Vienna, 1980, Contemporary Art Ctr., New Orleans, 2002, Jacksonville Art Mus., Fla., 1983, The Ogden Mus. So. Art, New Orleans, 2001-04, Leslie/ Lohman Gallery, NYC, 2007, others; represented in permanent collections Sammlung Ludwig, Aachen, Bklyn. Mus., Mus. Contemporary Art, Nagaoka, Japan, Everson Mus., Syracuse, Chase Bank, NYC, NYU, NYC, Polk Mus. Art, Lakeland, Fla., Orlando Mus. Art, Weatherspoon Art Gallery, Greensboro, NC, Marsh Art Gallery, Richmond, Va., Tulane U., New Orleans, New Orleans Mus. Art, Miss. Mus. Art, Jackson, The Ogden Mus. So. Art, New Orleans; curator: Gallerie Simonne Stern, New Orleans, 1968, Ill. Wesleyan U., Bloomington, 1980, contbr. articles to profl. jours. Vol. Prospect Pk. Alliance, Bklyn., 2006—. Served in USN, 1943—46. Named Disting. Alumnus, Tulane Coll., 2001. Mem.: Art Group, NY Artists Equity Assn., Coll. Art Assn. Address: 916 President St Brooklyn NY 11215-1604 Personal E-mail: kendallshaw@aol.com.

SHAW, KENNETH ALAN, former university president; b. Granite City, Ill., Jan. 31, 1939; s. Kenneth W. and Clara H. (Lange) Shaw; m. Mary Ann Byrne, Aug. 18, 1962; children: Kenneth William, Susan Lynn, Sara Ann. BS, Ill. State U., 1961, DHL, 1987; EdM, U. Ill., 1963; PhD, Purdue U., 1966, EdD (hon.), 1990; DHL, Towson State, 1979, Ill. Coll., 1986. Tchr. history, counselor Rich Twp. High Sch., Park Forest, Ill., 1961-63; residence hall dir., instr. edn. Ill. State U., 1963-64; counselor Office Dean of Men, Purdue U., 1964-65, Office Dean of Men, Purdue U. (Office Student Loans), 1965-66; asst. to pres., lectr. sociology Ill. State U., 1966-69; v.p. acad. affair, dean Towson State U., Balt., 1969-76; pres. So. Ill. U., Edwardsville, 1977-79; chancellor So. Ill. U. System, Edwardsville, 1979-86; pres. U. Wis. System, Madison, 1986-91; chancellor, pres. Syracuse U., 1991—2004. Bd. dirs. Unity Mutual Life Ins. Co. Trustee Am. Coll. Testing, 1990; mem. NY Gov.'s Commn. Ednl. Reform, 2003—04. Recipient Young Leader in Edn. award, 1980, Silver Anniversary award, NCAA, 1986, Coaches Silver Anniversary award, Nat. Assn. Basketball, 1986; named Citizen of Yr., So. Ill. Inc., 1985; named to Ill. Basketball Hall of Fame, 1983. Mem.: Am. Assn. Higher Edn. (chmn.), State Higher Edn. Exec. Officers Assn., Am. Higher Edn. Assn., Am. Social. Assn., Am. Coun. Edn. (com. on minorities in higher edn. 1987—91), Met. Devel. Assn. (bd. dirs. 1991, chmn. bd. dirs.), Pi Gamma Mu, Phi Delta Kappa.

SHAW, L. EDWARD, JR., investment company executive, lawyer; b. Elmira, NY, July 30, 1944; s. L. Edward and Virginia Anne (O'Leary) S.; m. Irene Ryan; children: Christopher, Hope, Hillary, Julia, Rory BA in Econs., Georgetown U., Washington, 1966; JD, Yale U., New Haven, 1969. Bar: N.Y. 1969. Assoc. Milbank, Tweed, Hadley & McCloy, NYC, 1969—76, ptnr., 1976—82; sr. v.p., gen. counsel Chase Manhattan Corp., NYC, 1982—85, exec. v.p., gen. counsel, 1985-96; vice chmn., gen. counsel Natwest Markets, NYC, 1996-97, pres., 1997-99; exec. v.p., gen. counsel Aetna Inc., Hartford, Conn., 1999—2004; of counsel Gibson Dunn & Crutcher LLP, NYC, 2004—; sr. mng. dir. Richard C. Breeden & Co., Greenwich, Conn., 2006—. Bd. dirs. HealthSouth Corp., Birmingham, Ala., 2005—, H&R Block, 2007—. Mem.: Am. Law Inst., Phi Beta Kappa. Roman Catholic. Office: Gibson Dunn & Crutcher LLP 200 Park Ave 47th Fl New York NY 10166 Office Phone: 212-351-3846. Business E-Mail: eshaw@Gibsondunn.com.

SHAW, LEONARD GLAZER, retired electrical engineering educator, consultant; b. Toledo, Aug. 15, 1934; s. A. Daniel and Mary (Glazer) S.; m. Susan Gail Weil, Dec. 24, 1961; children: Howard Benjamin, Mitchell Bruce, Jenny Louise. BSEE, U. Pa., 1956; MSEE, Stanford U., 1957, PhD, 1961. From asst. to assoc. prof. Polytech. U. N.Y., Bklyn., 1960-75, prof., 1975—99, prof. emeritus, 1999—, head dept. elec. engrng. and computer sci., 1982-90, dean Sch. Elec. Engrng. and Computer Sci., 1990-94, vice provost for undergrad. studies, 1995-96. Vis. prof. Tech. U., Eindhoven, Netherlands, 1970, Ecole Nationale Superieure de Mecanique, Nantes, France, 1977, U. Sussex, Brighton, Eng., 1998; cons. Sperry Systems Mgmt. Div., Great Neck, N.Y.; mem. grant rev. panels NSF, 1986-98. Co-author: Signal Processing, 1975; contbr. articles to profl. jours. Rsch. grantee NSF, 1973, 81. Fellow: IEEE (mem. pub. bd. 1961—92, mem. various coms., editor-in-chief

IEEE Press 1988—91, gen. chmn. Conf. of Decision and Control 1989, chmn. Tech. Field Award Coun. 1995—97), Control Sys. Soc. of IEEE (fin. v.p. 1992—93, 2000, pres.-elect 2001, pres. 2002). Business E-Mail: lpshaw@poly.edu.

SHAW, LEROY ROBERT, retired language educator, writer; b. Medicine Hat, Alta., Can., Jan. 15, 1923; arrived in US, 1923; s. Roy Albert and Ruby Eda Cecilia Shaw; m. Ida Rosmarie Mannaberg, July 1959; children: Dion Desmond, Melissa Amanda. BA, U. Calif., Berkeley, 1946, MA, 1948, PhD, 1954; postgrad., U. Zurich, Switzerland, 1949, U. Vienna, Austria, 1949. Instr. Reed Coll., Portland, Oreg., 1951—53, U. Tex., Austin, 1953—57, asst. prof., 1957—59, assoc. prof., 1959—64; prof. U. Wis., Milw., 1965—68; prof. German U. Ill., Chgo., 1968—93, head dept., 1977—85; ret., 1993. Vis. prof. U. Calif., Berkeley, 1955, Trinity Coll., Dublin, 1967—68; dir. modern German theater symposium U. Tex., Austin, 1963; dir. Wagner in retrospect symposium U. Ill., Chgo., 1983; writer, instr. 30 audio-visual tapes Tex. Ednl. Project, 1961—62. Author: Witness of Deceit: Gerhart Hauptmann as Critic of Society, 1958, Focus on German for Beginners, 1965, Focus...for Intermediates, 1965, The Playwright and Historical Change, 1970; co-author (with Robert A. Jones): Frank Wedekind: A Bibliographic Handbook, 2 vols., 1996; editor: Wagner in Retrospect, 1983; contbr. numerous articles to profl. publs. Fellow, Am. Philos. Soc., 1955; Alexander von Humboldt fellow, Munich, 1962—64, 1972, Fulbright fellowship, Trinity Coll., Dublin, 1966—67, Deutscher Akademischer Austausch Dienst fellowship, Munich, 1981. Mem.: MLA, Wagner Soc. America. Home: 1137 N Euclid Ave Oak Park IL 60302 Home Phone: 708-386-7618.

SHAW, MICHAEL, biologist, educator; b. Barbados, W.I., Feb. 11, 1924; s. Anthony and Myra (Perkins) S.; m. Jean Norah Berkinshaw, Oct. 16, 1948; children: Christopher A., Rosemary E., Nicholas R., Andrew L. BSc, McGill U., 1946, MSc, 1947, PhD, 1949, DSc (hon.), 1975, U. B.C., 2003, U. Saskatchewan, 2008. NRC Can. postdoctoral fellow Botany Sch., Cambridge U., 1949-50; assoc. prof. biology U. Sask., Canada, 1950-54, prof., 1954-67, prof., head dept. biology, 1961-67; dean faculty agrl. scis. U. B.C., Canada, 1967-75, v.p. acad. devel., 1975-81, acad. v.p., provost, 1981-83, univ. prof., 1983-89, univ. prof. emeritus, 1989—. Mem. Sci. Coun. Can., 1976-82, Natural Scis. and Engring. Rsch. Coun. Can., 1978-80. Contbr. articles to profl. jours. Recipient Queen's Silver Jubilee medal, 1977, Gold medal Biol. Coun. Can., 1983. Fellow Royal Soc. Can. (Flavelle medal 1976), Can. Phytopath. Soc., Am. Phytopath. Soc.; mem. AAAS, Can. Bot. Assn., Can. Soc. Plant Physiologists (Gold medal 1971), Am. Soc. Plant Biologists. Home: 1792 Western Pky Vancouver BC Canada V6T 1V3

SHAW, MICHAEL, mortgage company executive; BA in Econs., Case Western Reserve U., Cleve.; MBA in Fin., NYU. Various risk mgmt. roles including chief credit officer mortgage bus. Citibank; chief risk officer Fin. Guaranty Ins. Co. (subs. GE Capital); sr. risk mgr. global risk mgmt. GE/GE Capital; sr. consumer credit exec. Chase Fin. Svcs.; sr. consumer banking credit exec., sr. risk exec. J.P. Morgan Chase & Co.; sr. v.p. credit risk oversight Fannie Mae (Fed. Nat. Mortgage Assn.), 2006—08, chief risk officer, 2008—. Office: Fannie Mae 3900 Wis Ave NW Washington DC 20016 Office Phone: 202-752-7000.*

SHAW, NANCY RIVARD, museum curator, art historian, consultant; b. Saginaw, Mich. d. Joseph and Jean Marcotte; m. Danny W. Shaw, Feb. 29, 1980; 1 stepchild, Christina Marie. BA magna cum laude, Oakland U., 1969; MA, Wayne State U., 1973. Asst. curator Am. art Detroit Inst. Arts, 1972-75, curator, 1975-98, curator emeritus, 1998—. Adj. prof. art and art history Wayne State U., Detroit, 1991-98; lectr. in field.; organizer exhibns. Contbg. author: American Art in the Detroit Institute of Arts, Vol. I, 1991, Vol. II, 1997, Vol. III, 2005; contbr. articles to exhbn. catalogues and profl. jours. Mem. Wayne State U. Alumni Assn. Avocations: painting, singing. Personal E-mail: nrivardshaw@yahoo.com.

SHAW, NAOMI, sales consultant, insurance agent, management consultant; AA, Cabillo Coll.; AS, Coll. Siskiyous; BSc, U. Wash. Cert. CPR 1978, emergency responder team 2006, med. emergency stds. trainer 2007; disaster preparedness instr. 1988, Wilton cert. instr. 1992, sales specialist Citrix, 1995, sales trainer Microsoft, 1997, amateur cert. HAM radio operator, 2006, cert. video surveillance operator 2008, military tax specialist 2008, small bus. tax specialist 2008, merchandising agent 2009, sales demonstrator 2009. Coord. USAF Family Svcs., Barrigada, Guam; recreational therapist Shriners Hosp., Sacramento; occupl. therapist Shreveport, La.; phlebotomist Schumpert Hosp.; prof. Am. arts Bossier CC; media film cons. Consumnes Coll.; screenwriter UNLV Film Studies; prodr. KGTF-TV, 1986—88; sales mgr. High Desert Sys., 1993—97; v.p. bus. devel. Genesis Assocs., 1997—2004; regional mgr. Eastern Intrepid Sys., 1997—2000; agt. Lincoln Heritage, 2003—, Old Mut. Life, 2004—, Fidelity, 2004—, Am. Progressive, 2005—, Humana, 2005—; XBox field support rep. Microsoft Corp., 2005—08; regional mgr. Mosaic Sales Solutions, 2005—08, Procter & Gamble, 2006—08; sales rep. Allianz, 2006—; fin. cons. Sunlife, 2006—; fin. sales rep. ING, 2006—; sales rep. U Oughtta Be on Chocolates, 2007—; field rep. Kodak, 2005—08; agent Unicare, 2006—; v.p. bus. devel. Pink Angel Designs, 2008—; sr. bus. dir. Simply Living, 2008—; mng. ptnr. SunPillars, 2008—; agent AFLAC, 2008—; field rep. RMX, 2007—; fin. advisor WFG, 2008—; field rep. Choice Retail, 2007—, Omega Solutions, 2007—; agent Tritus Bus. Solutions, 2008—; lic. agent NAA, 2005—; field agent Safeway Fin., 2007—; agent MOH, 2007—; fin. advisor Safeway Fin., 2007—, Legacy Group, 2008—; fin. cons. AHCP, 2008—; tax specialist III H&R Block, 2008—. Agrl. rschr. Burpee Seed, 1979—83; dir. High Desert Sys., Nev.; dir. fundraising March of Dimes, La.; case mgr. Easter Seals, La.; Senate liaison for spl. edn., Nev., 1993—95; mem. adv. coun. Family Fun Mag., 1995—2005; adj. prof. Merced Coll.; Vt. sales mgr. Am. Inst. Integrated Medicine; mem. adv. bd. Crayola, 1997—; adj. prof. BNU, 2004—08; field svc. provider Acosta, 2005—07; merchandiser Nintendo, 2005—08; field rep. Archco, 2005—08; mfrs. rep. Nike, 2005—08; merchandiser Siena, 2005—08; sales rep. Lawrence Svcs., 2006—08; field sales Quest Svcs., 2006—08; field rep. Handlemans, 2006—08, Timex, 2006—08; field sales rep. Lantis, 2007—08; mktg. asst. Good News Garage, 2006—; fin. dir. PAD Inc., 2007—; field svc. rep. Liz & Co., 2006—08; agent Lawrence Svcs., 2005—08; field svc. provider BDS, 2006—08; ICCP auditor, 2007—; ptnr. Home Fires, Wild Horses, 2008—; ops. mgr. Get Stoned, 2008—; strategic mktg. mgr. Renegade Kidz, 2008—; family room vol. Shriners Hosp., 1991—, World AIDS Cure, 1993—, Ronald McDonald House, Burlington, 2004—; resource asst. Duncan Holbert Found., 1986—90; IT resource mgr. St. Jude's Ranch, 1992—2003, North Star project, 2009—. Editor: Family Focus, 1983—85; prodr.: Guam Today, 1985—87, Farm and Home Mag., 1989; photographer: Atwater News, 1993—97, features editor: Winton Times, 1994—97; co-author: IT Security, 2001; contbr. articles to various publs. Mem. fin. com. ITsAlive, 1993—97; nat. coord. Angel Wings, 2007—; regional dir. We Are The World, 2008—; leader Girl Scouts America, 1983—, 4-H, 1990—; grant writer Wild Mustang Rescue, 1995—, First Nations Coun., 2006—; quilter Project Linus, 1995—, Splashes of Hope, 2000—, Afghan Relief Effort, 2001—; vol. First Night, 1997—, NICSI, San Francisco, 2004—, Cultural Canvas Thailand, 2005—, Katrina's Angels, 2005—, Cmty. Health Ctr. Burlington, 2006—, Stone Mountain Hospice, 2007—, Art Aids Art, 2007—; vol., HAM operator, EMT SANMA, Arlington, Va., 2002—, Tour de Cure, 2004—, Harvest of Love, Detroit, 2006—, Ruckus Nation, 2007—08; translator BYE, 2002—, Action Against Hunger, 2003—; Wash. Reading Corps., 2006—; web asst. Asia-Pacific Cultural Ctr., 2003—; project mgr. Domestic Rabbit Rescue, 2003—; case worker Armed Forces Emergency Comms., 2006—; holiday project vol. Operation Gratitude, 2005—, Indego Africa, 2004—; regional dir. Pass It On, 2007—; dir. Angel's Foundation, 2007—; mem. Organic Gardening Farm Rsch. Coun., 1983—85; bd. dirs. Atwater Water Dist., 1993—95, Beanies for Baghdad, 2006—; emergency mgr. Am. Red Cross, 1995—2004; project asst. Childhelp, Okla. City, 1996—; camp counselor Easter Seals Soc., 1975—81, 1994—98, 2003—08; fin. coord. asst. Project Darfur, 2006—; webmaster Mountain Sch., 2005—; web designer Native Am. Edn. Svcs., 2007—; translator Hope Internat., 2004—; Webmaster Kenya Edn. Fund., 2007—; bd. mem. Compassionate Kids, 2005—; case asst. Project Polaris, 2008—. Recipient 5000 hr. svc. pin, Family Support Ctrs., 1995; named Vol. of Yr., USAF Families, 1988, 1988, 1992, Nat. Chili Champion, 1996. Mem.: ASTD, West Valley Execs., ASBA, Nat. Grange, Nat. Assn. Women Bus. Owners, Vermont Horse Coun., Nat. PTO, Soc. Mfg. Engrs., Women's Environment and Devel. Orgn., Bus. Women's Network, Girl Scouts (life), Am. Bus. Women's Assn., Hike Vt., Foothills Dance Assn., Amateur Radio Relay League, Soroptomist Internat., Svc. Club. Avocations: gardening, needlecrafts, art, hiking, cooking. Home and Office: 70 S Winooski Ave 284 Burlington VT 05401 Business E-Mail: naomi_shaw@sunpillars.com, naomi_shaw@us.aflac.com, naomi@pinkangeldesign.com.

SHAW, R. DANIEL, anthropology professor; b. Seattle, Wash., Nov. 19, 1943; s. R. Stanley and Laurel M. Shaw; m. Karen A. Perona, July 30, 1966 (dec. Oct. 23, 2005); m. Georgia R. Grimes, Aug. 19, 2006; children: Richard D., Ryan S., Robert J. BA in Anthropology & Oriental Studies, U. Ariz., Tucson, 1967, MA in Anthropology, 1968; PhD in Anthropology, U. Papua New Guinea, Port Moresby, 1976. Consulting anthropologist US Pub. Health Svc., Tucson, 1966—68; anthrop. linguist, bible translator Summer Inst. Linguistics, Ukarumpa, Papua New Guinea, 1969—81, internat. anthropology cons. Dallas, 1978—; prof. anthropology and transl. Fuller Grad. Sch. Intercultural Studies, Pasadena, Calif., 1982—. Editor: (book) Kinship Studies in Papua New Guinea, 1974; author: Samo Social Structure: A Socio-Linguistic Approach to Understanding Interpersonal Relationships, 1976, Health Concepts and Attitudes of the Papago Indians, 1968, Transculturation: The Cultural Factor in Translation and Other Communication Tasks, 1988 (Top Ten List, 1988), Kandiya: Samo Ceremonialism and Interpersonal Relationships, 1990, From Longhouse to Village: Samo Social Change, 1996; co-author: Understanding Folk Religion: A Christian Response to Religious Belief and Practice, 1999 (Top Ten List, 2000), Communicating God's Word in a Complex World: God's Truth or Hocus-Pocus?, 2003 (Top Ten List, 2004); contbr. articles to profl. jours., papers at soc. meetings, and confs. on anthropology, translation, and mission. Dir. Mission Aviation Fellowship, Redlands, Calif., 1994—2003, Nampa, Idaho, 2005—; internat. trustee MAF Internat., Ashford, Kent, 2007—; dir. Providence Mission Homes, Pasadena, Calif., 1997—. Recipient Peer Recognition, Directory Am. Scholars, 2002, C. Davis Weyerhaeuser award for Faculty of Yr., Fuller Theol. Sem., 2006, Twenty-five yr. Svc. award, 2007; vis. scholar, U. Stellenbosch, 2004—05. Fellow: Polynesian Soc. (life), Am. Anthrop. Assn. (life); mem.: Summer Inst. Linguistics, Assn. of Evang. Professors of Mission, Am. Soc. Missiologists. Achievements include partnerships with academic institutions in India, Indonesia, Papua New Guinea and Central Africa. Office: Fuller Grad Sch Intercultural Studies 135 N Oakland Ave Pasadena CA 91182 Office Phone: 626-584-5200. Business E-Mail: danshaw@fuller.edu.

SHAW, RHOD, lobbyist; m. Emily Shaw; 3 children. BS in Geology, Franklin & Marshall Coll. Chief of staff, legis. dir. to Rep. Jimmy Hayes US Ho. of Reps., Washington, 1987—93, chief of staff, legis. dir. to Rep. Sherrod Brown, 1993—95; prin. Alpine Group, Inc. Office: Alpine Group, Inc Ste 201 660 Pennsylvania Ave, SE Washington DC 20003 Office Phone: 202-547-1831. Office Fax: 202-547-4658.*

SHAW, RICHARD EUGENE, cardiovascular researcher; b. Springfield, Ohio, Jan. 20, 1950; s. Eugene Russell and Marjorie Caroline Shaw; m. Nov. 26, 1976; 2 children. BA, Duquesne U., 1972; MA, U.S. Internat. U., San Diego, 1977; PhD, U. Calif., San Francisco, 1984. Cert. nuc. med. technologist. Nuclear Medicine Tech. Cert. Bd. Staff nuc. med. technologist Scripps Meml. Hosp., La Jolla, Calif., 1975-79; rsch. asst. U. Calif. San Francisco Sch. Medicine, 1980-85; mgr. rsch. programs San Francisco Heart Inst., Daly City, Calif., 1985-87, dir. rsch., 1988-90, dir. rsch. and ops., 1991—2003; dir. rsch., quality and edn. Sutter Pacific Heart Ctrs., 2003—08, Calif. Pacific Med. Ctr.'s Heart & Vascular Ctr., 2009—. Sr. advisor steering com. for databases Daus. of Charity Nat. Health Sys., St. Louis, 1993-96. Editor-in-chief Jour. Invasive Cardiology, 1989—; contbr. articles to profl. jours; chpts. to books. Coach Am. Youth Soccer Orgn. and Youth Baseball Assn., bd. dirs., Burlingame, Calif., 1990-94; pres. Burlingame H.S. Athletic Boosters, 2000—. Named Impact Player of Yr. award, Mi-Co Corp., 2005. Fellow Am. Coll. Cardiology (nat. cardiac database com., outcomes assessment subcom. 1998—, NCDR task force 2001—, publs. subcom. 2001—), Am. Coll. Angiology; mem. Am. Heart Assn., Soc. for Clin. Trials, N.Y. Acad. Scis., Am. Statis. Assn., Am. Med. Informatics Assn., Soc. Behavioral Medicine. Avocation: music. Office: Sutter Pacific Heart Ctr CPMC 2200 Webster # 303 San Francisco CA 94115 Home Phone: 650-678-2375. Business E-Mail: shawr@sutterhealth.org.

SHAW, RICHARD THOMAS, humanitarian, retired federal agent, retired military officer; b. Manchester, NH, Nov. 22, 1943; s. Elwood Barton and Carmella (DiGennaro) Shaw; m. Carla Ann Harnden, July 14, 2003; children: Steven S., Michael J. BBA, MPA, Nat. Coll. Arts and Sci., Tulsa, Okla., 1980; HHD, Sussex Coll. Tech., Eng., 1984; RHD, Universal Ministries Sch. Theology, Milford, Ill., 2009. Sr. sgt. mil. pers. US Army, 1961—67; sr. claims adjudicator US HHS, 1967—74, fed. agy. adminstr., 1968—74; mil. pers. officer USAR, 1968—2003; ret., 2003; ordained min. Universal Ministries, Milford, Ill., 2009. Motivational spkr. Mem. Internat. Platform Assn. Pub. Spkrs.; nat. chmn. Pride in Am. Found. Mil. officer US Army, 1961—87, res. US Army, 1987—2003. Decorated Army Commendation medal, cert. appreciation US Army Reserve, cert. of recognition Sec. of Defense; named life fellow, Sussex Coll. Tech., Eng., 1991, elected, Orgn. Amazing Men, 2003. Mem.: Nat. Assn. Ret. Fed. Employees (life), Am. Legion (life; past chmn., prisoner of war, missing in action), VFW (life), Jaycees (life, past state pres. Maine Jaycees, 1974-75, attained Number 1 status, US Jaycees Parade of States, 1974-75, Recipient Clayton Frost award, elected nat. v.p. US JCI Senate 1979, received Number 1 US JCI Senator award 1980), Lions Club Internat. (life mem.; past zone chmn., past regional chmn., Outstanding Zone Chmn. award Dist. 41L, 1996, Outstanding Regional Chmn. award Dist. 41L, 1997, conferred Melvin Jones fellow 2006). Democrat. Roman Catholic. Avocations: travel, golf, reading, antiques.

SHAW, ROBERT GILBERT, state legislator, food service executive; b. Erwin, NC, Nov. 22, 1924; s. Robert Gilbert B. and Annie Elizabeth (Byrd) S.; m. Grace Lee Wilson, Jan. 29, 1951 (div. 1976); children: Ann Karlen, Barbara Jean; m. Linda Owens, May 27, 1982. AA, Campbell U., 1948; postgrad., U. N.C., 1948-50. Restaurateur, 1951-. County commr. County of Guilford, Greensboro, N.C., 1968-76; chair N.C. Rep. Party, Raleigh, 1975-77; minority leader N.C. Senate, Raleigh, 1984-2002; chair Guilford County Rep. Party, 1973-75; mem. Rep. Nat. Com., Washington, 1975-77. With USAAC, 1943-46. Named Legislator of Yr. Nat. Fedn. Wildlife, 1990. Mem. Elks (life, bd. govs. 1953—). Presbyterian. Avocations: fishing, hunting, politics. Home: 5105 Bennington Dr Greensboro NC 27410 Home Phone: 336-855-7533. Personal E-mail: RGB112224@aol.com.

SHAW, ROBERT WILLIAM, JR., management consultant, venture capitalist; b. Ithaca, NY, Aug. 10, 1941; s. Robert William and Charlotte G. (Throop) Shaw; m. Anne P. Meads, Aug. 29, 1964; children: Mark Andrew, Christopher Matthew. B of Engring. Physics, Cornell U., 1964, MSEE, 1964; PhD, Stanford U., 1968; MPA, Am. U., 1981. Postdoctoral fellow Cavendish Lab., Cambridge, England, 1968-69; mem. tech. staff Bell Tel. Labs., Murray Hill, NJ, 1969-72; with Booz Allen Hamilton, Bethesda, Md., 1972-83, sr. v.p. energy and environ. divsn., 1979-83, mem. oper. coun., 1981-83, also bd. dirs.; pres. Arete Ventures, Inc., 1983-97, Utech Venture Capital Corp., 1985—2003, Utech, LLC, 2003—05; gen. ptnr. Utech Venture Capital Corp. Fund I, 1985—2000, Utech Venture Capital Corp. Fund II, 1988—2003, Utech Venture Capital Corp. I Parallel Fund L.P., 1988—2001, Utech Venture Capital Corp. II Parallel Fund, L.P., 1991—2003, Utech Climate Challenge Fund, LLC, Bethesda, 1995—2005; v.p. Can. Energy and Environment Ventures, Inc., 1993-95; pres. Arete Corp., Center Harbor, NH, 1997—; ptnr. Atrium Capital/Honda Ventures, 2004—. Spl. ltd. ptnr. Nth Power Techs. Fund II; mem. investment com. Sustainable Asset Mgmt. Pvt. Equity Fund, Commons Capital LLC; mng. ptnr. Micro-Generation Tech. Fund, LLC, 1997—2009; mng. mem. SC Green Tech Ventures, LLC, 2007—; mem. bd. energy and environ. sys. Nat. Rsch. Coun., 1998—2004; mem. energy com. Aspen Inst. Humanistic Studies, Investor's Cir., Solar Cir.; bd. councillors China-US Ctr. Sustainable Devel.; chmn. bd. dirs. CTP Hydrogen Corp., 1998—2007, Distributed Energy Systems, 1996—2007, Evergreen Solar, 1994—2005; bd. dirs. H2Gen Innovations, Inc., 2001—; mem. adv. coun. Cornell U. Engring. Coll., 2005—, chmn., 2009—; mem. hydrogen tech. adv. com. US Dept. Energy, 2006—, vice chair, 2008—; dir. Soc. Sci. & Pub., 2008—. Contbr. articles to profl. jours. Named NASA trainee; Office Sci. Rsch. fellow, USAF, 1968—69. Mem.: AAAS, Social Venture Network, Inst. Noetic Scis., Assn. Humanistic Psychology, Orgnl. Devel. Network, Nat. Venture Capital Assn., Am. Phys. Soc., Tau Beta Pi, Sigma Xi, Kappa Delta Rho, Pi Alpha Alpha, Phi Kappa Phi. Home: PO Box 1664 Center Harbor NH 03226-1664 Office: PO Box 1299 Center Harbor NH 03226-1299 Office Phone: 603-253-9797. Business E-Mail: aretecorp@roadrunner.com.

SHAW, RONALD AHREND, physician, educator; b. Toledo, July 20, 1946; s. Harold Michael and Eve Helen (Ganch) S.; m. Carol Ann Rapp, June 13, 1970; children: Robert, Benjamin, Daniel. BS, U. Toledo, 1968; MD, Washington U., 1972. Diplomate Am. Bd. Emergency Medicine. Intern, then resident in surgery St. Luke's Hosp., St. Louis, 1972-73, resident in surgery, 1973; mem. staff Bapt. Med. Ctr.-Montclair, Birmingham, Ala., 1976-81, chief emergency svc., 1979-81; assoc. dir. lifesaver flight ops. Caraway Meth. Med. Ctr., Birmingham, 1981-85; dir. emergency svc. sch. medicine U. Ala., 1985-89; asst. dir. emergency svc. R.I. Hosp., Providence, 1989-95; attending physician emergency dept. Bapt. Med. Ctr., Montgomery, Ala., 1996—; med. dir. emergency dept. Jackson Hosp., 2000—01; sec.-treas., med. staff Bapt. Med. Ctr., 2001—03. Cons. U. Tex., Houston, 1986, Bell Helicopter, Ft. Worth, 1986, Mut. Assurance, Birmingham, 1986-89, NYU, 1988-89, R.I. State Med. Examiners Office, 1991-96, Fla. Dept. Health, EMS Office, 1991—, Joint Underwriters Assocs. of R.I., 1991-96; chmn. adv. bd. emergency svc. Ala. Dept. Pub. Health, 1986-89; med. dir. Emergency Med. Svcs. div. R.I. Dept. Health, 1990-95; med. dir. Health Care Rev., Inc., 1995-96. Bd. dirs. MADD, Ala., 1986, Univ. Emergency Medicine Found., 1995-96; mem. planning com. Youth Baseball, Vestavia Hills, ala., 1986, 87; mem. disaster com. City of Birmingham, 1984-89; mem. 911 Commn., State of R.I., 1991-96. Recipient Disting. Achievement award Birmingham Emergency Med. Svc., 1988. Fellow Am. Coll. Emergency Physicians (bd. dirs. Ala. chpt. 1984-89, steering com. EMS sect. 1991-94, sec.-treas. R.I. chpt. 1995-96); mem. AAAS, ACS (state com. on trauma R.I. chpt. 1990-96), N.Y. Acad. Sci., Med. Assn. Ala. (mem. coun. med. svc. 1985-86). Republican. Avocations: hunting, stamp collecting and computer programming. Office Phone: 334-272-1050. Personal E-mail: kd1hp@msn.com.

SHAW, RUSSELL BURNHAM, writer, journalist; b. Washington, May 19, 1935; s. Charles Burnham and Mary (Russell) S.; m. Carmen Hilda Carbon, July 19, 1958; children: Mary Hilda, Emily Anne, Janet, Charles, Elizabeth. BA, Georgetown U., 1956, MA, 1960. Staff writer Cath. Standard, Washington, 1956-57; reporter Nat. Cath. News Svc., Washington, 1957-66; dir. publs., pub. info. Nat. Cath. Ednl. Assn., Washington, 1966-69; dir. Nat. Cath. Office for Info., Washington, 1969-73; assoc. sec. for communication U.S. Cath. Conf., Washington, 1973-74, sec. for pub. affairs Nat. Conf. Cath. Bishops, 1975-87; dir. pub. info. KC, New Haven, 1987-97; assoc. prof. Pontifical U. Holy Cross, Rome, 1996—, Cath. Distance U., Washington, 2006—. Consultor Pontifical Coun. for Social Comms., 1984—89, 2001—; editor The Pope Speaks, 1998—2005. Author: The Dark Disciple, 1961, Abortion on Trial, 1968, Church and State, 1979, Choosing Well, 1982, Why We Need Confession, 1986, Renewal, 1986, Signs of the Times, 1986, Does Suffering Make Sense?, 1987, To Hunt, To Shoot, To Entertain, 1993, Understanding Your Rights, 1994, Papal Primacy in the Third Millennium, 2000, Ministry or Apostolate—What Should the Catholic Laity Be Doing?, 2002, Catholic Laity in the Mission of the Church, 2005, Nothing to Hide, 2008, A popular History of Vatican Council II, 2009, Writing The Way:The Story of a Spritual Classic, 2009; co-author: S.O.S. for Catholic Schools, 1970, Beyond the New Morality, 3d edit., 1988, Fulfillment in Christ, 1991, Personal Vocation, 2003, Good News, Bad News, 2007, others; editor Ency. of Cath. Doctrine, 1997; columnist Washington Report, 1966-2006,Cath. Herald, 1999—; contbg. editor Crisis Mag., 2002-07, Columbia Mag., 2002-06, Our Sunday Visitor, 2006-. Mem. Equestrian Order of Holy Sepulchre of Jerusalem, Phi Beta Kappa. Roman Catholic. Home and Office: 2928 44th Pl NW Washington DC 20016-3555 Home Phone: 202-363-9566; Office Phone: 202-363-9566. Personal E-mail: rshaw10290@aol.com.

SHAW, RUTH G., energy company executive; b. Feb. 19, 1948; m. Colin Stuart Shaw; 2 children. BA in English magna cum laude, East Carolina U.; PhD, U. Tex. Pres. El Centro Coll., Dallas, 1984—86, Central Piedmont Cmty. Coll., 1986—92; v.p. corp. comms. Duke Energy Corp., Charlotte, NC, 1992-94, sr. v.p. corp. resources, 1994-97, exec. v.p., chief adminstrv. officer, 1997—2003, pres. Duke Power Co., 2003—06, group exec. pub. policy, pres. Duke Nuclear, 2006, exec. adv. to chmn. & CEO, 2006—, pres. Duke Energy Found., 1994—2003. Bd. dirs. Wachovia Corp., 1990—, MedCath Corp., 2003—, The Dow

Chemical Co., 2005—, DTE Energy, 2007—, Edison Electric Inst., Nuclear Energy Inst., S. E. Electric Exchange; chair Charlotte Rsch. Inst.; mem. Palmetto Bus. Forum. Mem. Order of the Long Leaf Pine; trustee U. N.C., Charlotte; bd. dirs. Rsch. Triangle Found. of N.C.; mem. Conf. Bd. Chief Adminstrv. Officer's Coun.; chmn. Found. for the Carolinas; elder 1st Presbyn. Ch., Charlotte; active United Way, Arts and Scis. Coun., YMCA, Boy Scouts Am. Named Outstanding Alumni, East Carolina U., disting. grad. U. Tex., Charlotte Woman of Yr., 1992, Businesswoman of Yr., 1995; recipient award for comms. excellence, 1997. Office: Duke Energy Corp 526 S Church St Charlotte NC 28202-1802

SHAW, STANLEY MINER, retired pharmacist, educator; b. Parkston, SD, July 4, 1935; s. George Henry and Jensina (Thompson) S.; m. Excellda J. Watke, Aug. 13, 1961; children: Kimberly Kay, Renee Denise, Elena Aimee. BS, S.D. State U., 1957, MS, 1959; PhD, Purdue U., 1962. Instr. S.D. State U., 1960-62; asst. prof. bionucleonics Purdue U., West Lafayette, Ind., 1962-66, assoc. prof., 1966-71, prof. nuclear pharmacy, 1971—2005, prof. emeritus nuclear pharmacy, 2005—, head. divsn. nuclear pharmacy, 1990—2004, acting head Sch. Health Scis., 1990-93. Bd. pharm. spltys. Splty. Council Nuclear Pharmacy, 1978-82. Contbr. articles to profl. jours. Recipient Lederle Pharmacy faculty award, 1962, 1965, Parenteral Drug Assn. Rsch. award, 1970, Henry Heine Outstanding Tchr. award, Sch. Pharmacy Purdue U., 1989, 1993, 1999, Disting. Alumnus award, S.D. State U., 1991, Coll. Pharmacy Disting. Alumnus award, 2006, Disting. Pharmacy Educator award, Am. Assn. Colls. Pharmacy, 1994. Fellow Acad. Pharmacy Practice (chmn. sect. nuclear pharmacy 1979-80, historian 1981-85, mem.-at-large 1993-95, chmn.-elect 1995-96, chmn. 1996-97, Disting. Achievement award 1998), Am. Soc. Hosp. Pharmacy, Am. Pharm. Assn. (ho. of dels. 1977, 79, 86, 92, Founder's award, Daniel B. Smith Practice Excellence award 2000); mem. Health Physics Soc., Sigma Xi, Phi Lambda Upsilon, Phi Lambda Sigma, Rho Chi. Home: 7208 W Greenview Dr Battle Ground IN 47920-9732 Office: Purdue Univ Sch Pharmacy West Lafayette IN 47907-1336 Business E-Mail: sshaw@pharmacy.purdue.edu.

SHAW, STEVEN A., information technology executive; BBA, MBA, Univ. So. Calif. Mgmt. positions with Volt Info. Sciences Inc., NYC, 1995—97, pres. ProcureStaff subs., 1997—2005, bd. dir., 1998—, sr. v.p., 2000—05, exec. v.p., COO, 2005, co-CEO, 2005—06, pres., CEO, 2006—. Office: Volt Info Sciences 560 Lexington Ave New York NY 10022

SHAW, SUE ANN, medical transcriptionist; b. Van Nuys, Calif., Oct. 7, 1938; d. Harry Herbert and Elizabeth (Allison) Nesbit; m. Gerald Cargile Shaw (dec.); children: Deanna Christine Rushing, Jody Ray Rushing(dec.), John Paul Rushing. Cert. med. transcriptionist Am. Assn. Med. Transcription. Med. transcriptionist Meth. Hosps. of Dallas, 1975—2005. Vol. Meals on Wheels, Waxahachie, Tex., 2003, Charlton Meth. Hosp., Dallas, 2005—. Mem.: Am. Assn. Med. Transcription (founding officer, corr. sec. Greater Dallas chpt. 1979—82, com. mem. 1989—92). Republican. Baptist. Avocations: embroidery, stained glass, quilting, painting, gardening. Home: 110 Sunglow Loop Red Oak TX 75154

SHAW, THEODORE MICHAEL, former legal association administrator; b. NYC, Nov. 24, 1954; s. Theodore and Jean Audrey (Churchill) Shaw; m. Cynthia E. Muldrow; children: T. Winston, Zora Jean. BA with honors, Wesleyan U., 1976; JD, Columbia U., 1979. Bar: Calif., NY. Trial atty. Civil Rights Divsn. US Dept. Justice, 1979—82; dir. ednl. docket NAACP Legal Def. & Ednl. Fund, Inc., 1982—87, assoc. dir.-counsel NYC, 1993—2004, pres., dir.-counsel, 2004—08; founder, counsel Legal Def. & Edn. Fund's Western Regional Office, 1987—90. Asst. prof. law U. Mich. Law Sch., 1990—93; adj. prof. Columbia U. Sch. Law, 1993—. Recipient Lawrence A. Wein prize for social justice, Columbia U., Baldwin medal, Wesleyan U.; named one of Most Influential Black Ams., Ebony mag., 2006. Mem.: ABA, Langston Bar Assn., LA County Bar Assn., Nat. Bar Assn. (A. Leon Higginbotham Jr. Meml. award Young Lawyers Divsn.).

SHAW, THOMAS M., art historian, educator; b. Greenwich, Conn., Apr. 4, 1944; s. Hugh and Cordella Shaw. BA, Wesleyan U., Conn., 1966; MA, Syracuse U., NY, 1967; PhD, Columbia U., NY, 1981. Lectr., Summer session Columbia U., NYC, 1983—2003; vis. assoc. prof. Lafayette Coll., Easton, Pa., 1986—87; prof. art history Kean U., Union, NJ, 1987—, coord. art history program, 1994—2000, 2006—. Cons. African collections Lincoln U., Oxford, Pa., 2006—07. Author: (book) Irony and Illusion in the Architecture of Imperial Dakar, The Fulani Matrix of Beauty and Art in the Djolof Region of Senegal, What Manner of Men?. Adv. Art Across the River, Pa., 2004—06. Mem.: Soc. Architectural Historians, Coll. Art Assn., Phi Kappa Phi, Delta Tau Delta. Democrat. Baptist. Avocations: antiques, bridge, fishing, gardening. Office: Kean U Morris Ave Union NJ 07083

SHAW, TIMOTHY MILTON, political science professor; b. Frimley, Surrey, Eng., Jan. 27, 1945; came to Can., 1971; s. Arnold J. and Margaret E. (Milton) S.; m. Jane L. Parpart, Sept. 2, 1983; children: Laura, Lee Parpart; m. Susan M. Sturt, July 8, 1967 (div. 1980); children: Benjamin, Amanda. BA, Sussex U., 1967; MA, East Africa U., 1969, Princeton U., 1971, PhD, 1975. Prof. polit. sci. Dalhousie U., Halifax, Canada, 1971—2002; dir. Ctr. African Studies, Halifax, 1983—89, Ctr. for Fgn. Policy Studies, Halifax, 1993—2000, Internat. Devel. Studies Program, 1986—89, dir. BA and MA program, 1998—2000; dir. Pearson Inst., Halifax, 1985—87, Inst. Commonwealth Studies, U. London, 2001—06; prof. Royal Roads U., Victoria, Canada, 2006—07; prof., dir. Inst. Internat. Rels., UWI, T&T, 2007—. Vis. faculty Makerere U., Kampala, 1968-70, U. Zambia, Lusaka, 1973-74, Carleton U., Ottawa, Ont., Can., 1978-79, U. Ife, Nigeria, 1979-80, U. Zimbabwe, 1989, Rhodes U., South Africa, 1993, 2002-03, Warwick U., U.K., 1997, U. Western Cape & Stellenbosch U., South Africa, 1998—, Mbarara U. Sci. and Tech., 1998—, Aalborg U., 2000-01, Bus. Sch., Makerere U., 2006-; cons. UN Econ. Commn. for Africa, Addis Ababa, Ethiopia, 1983-88. Editor: Palgrave Macmillan Internat. Polit. Economy Series, 1984—, Ashgate Publishing Series on the International Political Economy of New Regionalisms, 2001—; author: Reformism and Revisionism in Africa's Political Economy in the 1990s, 1993, Commonwealth: Inter- and Non-State Contributions to Global Governance, 2008; author: (with Julius Ihonvbere) Illusions of Power: Nigeria in Transition, 1998; co-editor (with Julius Nyangoro): Beyond Structural Adjustment in Africa, 1992; co-editor: Corporatism in Africa, 1988; co-editor: (with Kevin Dunn) Africa's Challenge to International Relations Theory, 2001; co-editor: (with Sandra Maclean & John Harker) Advancing Human Security & Development in Africa, 2002; co-editor: (with Fredrik Soderbaum) Theories of New Regionalism: A Palgrave Reader, 2003; co-editor: (with Natalie Mychajlyszyn) Twisting Arms & Flexing Muscles: Humanitarian Intervention & Peacebuilding in Perspective, 2005; co-editor: (with Morten Boas & Marianne Marchand) The Political Economy of Regions & Regionalisms, 2005; co-editor: (with Sandra Maclean and David Black) A Decade of Human Security, 2006; co-editor: (with Andrew F. Cooper) The Diplomacies of Small States. Between Vulnerability and Resilience; co-editor: others. Mem. New Dem. Party, Halifax, 1984—. Grantee, Social Sci. & Humanities Rsch. Coun. Can., Africa, 1981—2006, Ford Found., 1999—2001. Mem. Can. Assn. Devel. Studies (pres. 1993-94), European Assn. Devel. Inst. (co-chmn. working group on new regionalisms), Can. Assn. African Studies (pres. 1984-85), Internat. Studies Assn. (pres. global devel. sect. 1995-96). Avocations: jogging, cooking, swimming, travel. Home: 5A Poolside #2 Maracas Valley St Joseph Trinidad and Tobago Office: Inst Internat Rels Univ West Indies Saint Augustine Trinidad and Tobago Office Phone: 868 662 2002 ext. 2010. Fax: 868-469-0715. Business E-Mail: timothy.shaw@sta.uwi.edu.

SHAW, WILLIAM FREDERICK, statistician; b. Bklyn., Feb. 24, 1920; s. Charles Peter and Josephine Veronica (Seusing) S.; m. Josephine Cannington Kerbey, Jan. 18, 1947; children: William Frederick, Teresa Anne. BBA, U. Miami, 1949; MA, George Washington U., 1953; postgrad. studies in econometrics, math. and computer scis., U.S. Dept. Agr. Grad. Sch., 1964-74; PhD (fellow), Walden U., 1977. Rsch. asst. U. Miami, 1948—49; with Rsch. and Stats. divsn. FHA, Washington, 1950—73, chief statistician Rsch. and Stats. divsn., 1969—; chief statistician, dir. Advanced Statis. Analysis and Computer Applications Staff HUD, 1974—82, chief statistician, dir. housing stats. divsn., 1982—89, chief statistician, dir. info. sys. divsn., 1990—91, chief statistician, dir. Office of Evaluation, 1991—. Pres. Kerbey-Shaw Assos. Served with F.A. AUS, 1943-45. Decorated Bronze Star; recipient Superior Performance award HUD, 1977; named by Info. Resources Adminstrn. Coun. as Fed. Office Sys. Profl. of Yr., 1983. Mem. AAAS, Am. Statis. Assn., Am. Risk and Ins. Assn., Am. Real Estate and Urban Econ. Assn., Am. Econ. Assn., Am. Fin. Assn., N.Y. Acad. Scis., Nat. Assn. Rev. Appraisers and Mortgage Underwriters, Soc. Cost Estimating and Analysis, Res. Offcers Assn. U.S., 101st Airborne Divsn. Assn., Air Force Assn., Alpha Kappa Psi. Roman Catholic. Home: 6527 Byrnes Dr Mc Lean VA 22101-5227 Office: HUD 7th and D Sts SW Washington DC 20411-0001

SHAW, WILLIAM J., hotel executive; b. Arlington, Va., Oct. 3, 1945; married; 3 children. BBA, U. Notre Dame, 1967; MBA, Washington U., 1972. With Arthur Andersen & Co., 1972-74, Marriott, 1974-79, corp. controller, 1979-82, corp. v.p., 1982-85, sr. v.p. fin., head dept. tax & risk mgmt., 1985-88, treas., 1986, exec. v.p., CFO, 1988-92; pres. Marriott's Svc. Group, 1992-97; pres., COO Marriott Internat., Inc., Bethesda, 1997—2009, vice chmn., 2009—; chmn. bd. Host Marriott Services Corp., Bethesda, Md., 1995-99, Sodexho Marriott Services, Gaithersburg, Md., 1998. Bd. dirs. Marriott Internat., Inc., 1997—, Sodexho, Inc., 1998—2001. Bd. trustees Suburban Hosp. Found., U. Notre Dame, South Bend, Ind.; mem. NCAA Leadership Adv. Bd.; bd. dirs. Wolf Trap Found. for Performing Arts. Office: Marriott International Inc 10400 Fernwood Rd Bethesda MD 20817*

SHAW, WILLIAM J., religious organization administrator; BA in Philosophy and Religion summa cum laude, Bishop Coll.; MDiv, Union Theol. Seminary; DMin, Colgate Rochester Div. Sch. Supply pastor New Bethel Baptist Church, Marshall, Tex.; pastor White Rock Baptist Church, 1956—; pres. Nat. Baptist Conv. USA, Inc., 1999—. Chmn. bd. dir. Jr. Achievement Del. Valley, Inc., Cmty. Legal Svcs. Phila., Med. Ctr. Univ. Penn., Phila. Airport Adv. Bd. Named one of 100 Most Influential Black Americans, Ebony mag., 2006; named to Power 150, 2008. Mem.: Baptist Min. Conf. Phila. (pres.), Greater Phila. Urban Affairs Coalition. Office: White Rock Baptist Church Office 5240 Chestnut St Philadelphia PA 19139 Office Phone: 215-474-5785. Office Fax: 215-474-3332. E-mail: president@nationalbaptist.com.

SHAWCROSS, JOHN THOMAS, English educator; b. Hillside, NJ, Feb. 10, 1924; s. Ernest Edward and Lillian Anderson (Kuncken) S. AM, NYU, 1950, PhD, 1958; DLitt, Montclair State U., 1975, St. Bonaventure U., 1995. Prof. English Rutgers U., New Brunswick, N.J., 1963-67; prof. English U. Wis., Madison, 1967-70, CUNY, 1970-79, U. Ky., Lexington, 1979—94. Author: John Milton: The Self and the World, 1992 (Milton Soc. award 1993), The Arms of the Family: The Significance of John Milton's Relatives and Associates, 2004, Rethinking Milton Studies: Time Present and Time Past, 2005, A Milton Bibliography, 1624-1799, 2006. With Devel. John Milton's Thought: Law, Govt., Religion, 2008; Lt. (j.g.) U.S. Navy, 1942-46 Home: 690 Mason Headley Rd Apt 318 Lexington KY 40504-2386

SHAWGER, DAVID C., set designer, educator; b. Summit, NJ, Nov. 17, 1047; s. David C. and Helen Ellis Shawger; m. Carma L. Shawger; children: Michelle Shawger O'Keefe, Kathleen Shawger Cotton. MA, Bradley U., Peoria. Ill., 1973. Recipient Gold medal, Kennedy Ctr., 2001. Office: Ball State Univ 2000 University Ave Muncie IN 47306 Office Fax: 765-285-4030.

SHAWN, GILBERT R., orthopedist, educator; b. Greensboro, NC, Feb. 28, 1970; married. BS, U. NC, Chapel Hill, 1992; MD, U. NC Sch. Medicine, 1996. Asst. prof. U. Ala., Birmingham, 2003—. Vol. Brookwood Bapt. Ch., Birmingham. Rsch. Grant, NIH, 2007, 2008. Fellow: Pediatric Orthop. Soc. North America, Am. Acad. Orthop. Surgery; mem.: Orthop. Rsch. Soc. Achievements include research in promoting blood vessel growth to improve bone healing. Office: UAB Orthop Surgery 1600 7th Ave South ACC Suite 316 Birmingham AL 35233 Business E-Mail: shawng@uab.edu.

SHAWN, WALLACE, playwright, actor; b. NYC, Nov. 12, 1943; s. William and Cecille (Lyon) S; m. Twink Caplan. BA., Harvard U., 1965; BA, Oxford U., Eng., 1968, MA, 1975. Instr. English Indore Christian Coll., Madhya Pradesh, India, 1965-66; tchr. English, Latin, drama Ch. of Heavenly Rest Day Sch., NYC, 1968-70; shipping clk. Laurie Love Ltd., NYC, 1974-75; machine operator Hamilton Copy Ctr., NYC, 1975-76. Author: (plays) Our Late Night, 1975 (Obie award for disting. playwriting 1975), Summer Evening, 1976, The Youth Hostel, 1976, Mr. Frivolous, 1976, (libretto) In the Dark, 1976, (trans.) The Mandrake, 1977, Marie and Bruce, 1980, The Hotel Play, 1981, Aunt Dan and Lemon, 1985, The Music Teacher, 2006; (monologue) The Fever, 1990 (Obie award for best play 1991); (screenplay) My Dinner with Andre, 1981; actor: (theatre) The Mandrake, 1977, The Master and Margarita, 1978, Chinchilla, 1979, The First Time, 1983, Ode to Napoleon Bonaparte, 1984, Aunt Dan and Lemon, 1985, The Fever, 1991; (films) Manhattan, 1979, Starting Over, 1979, All That Jazz, 1979, Simon, 1980, Atlantic City, 1981, My Dinner with Andre, 1981, A Little Sex, 1982, The First Time, 1983, Deal of the Century, 1983, Lovesick, 1983, Strange Invaders, 1983, Saigon-Year of the Cat, 1983, Crackers, 1984, The Hotel New Hampshire, 1984, The Bostonians, 1984, Micki and Maude, 1984, Heaven Help Us, 1985, Head Office, 1986, Radio Days, 1987, The Bedroom Window, 1987, Nice Girls Don't Explode, 1987, Prick Up Your Ears, 1987, The Princess Bride, 1987, The Moderns, 1988, She's Out of Control, 1989, Scenes From the Class Struggle in Beverly Hills, 1989, We're No Angels, 1989, Shadows and Fog, 1992, Mom and Dad Save the World, 1992, Nickel and Dime, 1992, The Cemetary Club, 1993, Un-Becoming Age, 1993, The Meteor Man, 1993, Vanya on 42nd Street, 1994, Mrs. Parker and the Vicious Circle, 1994, Canadian Bacon, 1995, Clueless, 1995, (voice) Toy Story, 1995, All Dogs Go to Heaven 2, 1996, House Arrest, 1996, Vegas Vacation, 1997, Critical Care, 1997, My Favorite Martian, 1999, (voice) Toy Story 2, 1999, The Prime Gig, 2000, The Curse of the Jade Scorpion, 2001, Love Thy Neighbor, 2002, Duplex, 2003, The Haunted Mansion, 2003, Melinda and Melinda, 2004, (voice) The Incredibles, 2004, Chicken Little, 2005, Southland Tales, 2006, (voice) Happily N'Ever After, 2007; (TV films) How to Be Perfect In Three Days, 1983, Saigon: Year of the Cat, 1983, Just Like Dad, 1995, Blind Men, 1998, Noah, 1998, Mr. St. Nick, 2002, Monte Walsh, 2003, Karroll's Christmas, 2004, (TV series) One Life to Live, 1992, Clueless, 1996-97, (voice) The Lionhearts, 1998. Fulbright scholar, India, 1956-66, PEN/Laura Pels Found. award for drama, 2005. Mem.: Am. Acad. Arts and Letters. Office: care Rosenstone/Wender 3 E 48th St New York NY 10017-1027

SHAY, ALBERT W., lawyer; b. Cherry Hill, NJ, May 17, 1959; BA, U. Md., 1982; MHA, St. Louis U., 1987, JD magna cum laude, 1987. Bar: Va. 1987, DC 1988. Ptnr., health care practice group Sonnenschein Nath & Rosenthal LLP, Washington. Mem.: Am. Health Lawyers Assn. Office: Sonnenschein Nath & Rosenthal LLP Ste 600, E Tower 1301 K St NW Washington DC 20015 Office Phone: 202-408-6401. Office Fax: 202-408-6399. Business E-Mail: ashay@sonnenschein.com.

SHAY, JONATHAN, psychiatrist, writer; b. 1941; BA, Harvard U., 1963; MD, U. Pa., 1971, PhD, 1972. Staff psychiatrist US Dept. Vet. Affairs Outpatient Clinic, Boston, 1987—. Invited spkr. for active duty mil. audiences on prevention of psychological and moral injury on mil. svc.; invited lectr.; visiting lectr. in ethics US Mil. Acad., US Naval Acad.; guest lecture of Sec. Navy, 2000; completed sa study for the Commandant of the Marine Corps. known as the Trust Study, 00; visiting scholar-at-large Naval War Coll., Newport, RI, 2001; chair ethics, leadership and personnel policy Office US Army Dep. Chief Staff for Personnel, 2004—05. Author: Achilles in Vietnam: Combat Trauma and the Undoing of Character, 1994, Odysseus in America: Combat Trauma and the Trials of Homecoming, 2002. Named a MacArthur Fellow, John D. and Catherine T. MacArthur Found., 2007. Achievements include written works being pioneering in the field of Classics, resulting in many honors and speaking engagements throughout the world. Office: Dept Veteran Affairs Outpatient Clinic Boston MA 02114 E-mail: jshay@world.std.com.

SHAY, KATHLEEN M., lawyer; b. Drexel Hill, Pa., Feb. 21, 1952; AB, Villanova U., 1974, JD, 1977. Bar: Pa. 1977, US Ct. Appeals 3rd Cir., US Dist. Ct. Ea. Dist. Pa., Supreme Ct. Pa. Ptnr. Duane Morris LLP, Phila., chair firm corp. practice group, 1998—. Bd. consultors Villanova U. Sch. Law, 1992—, vice chair, 2001—04, chair, 2004—; bd. trustees Acad. Notre Dame de Namur, 1995—2001, 2004—, chair, 1998—2001. Mem.: ABA (bus. law sect.), Phila. Bar Assn. (exec. com. bus. sect. 2001—, sec. 2002, treas. 2003, vice chair 2004, chair 2005), Pa. Biotech. Assn., Pa. Bar Assn. (corp., banking & bus. law sect.), Tech. Coun. Ea. Pa., Women's Investment Network (bd. dir. 2000—06), Greater Phila. Venture Group, Assn. Corp. Growth (bd. dir. Phila. chpt. 2004—), Order of Coif. Office: Duane Morris LLP 30 S 17th St Philadelphia PA 19103-4196 Office Phone: 215-979-1210. Office Fax: 215-979-1020. Business E-Mail: kmshay@duanemorris.com.*

SHAY, ROSHANI CARI, political science professor and healthcare professional; b. Milw., Oct. 5, 1942; d. Walter John and Dorothee May (Dahnke) O'Donnell; 1 child, Mark Sather. Student, Willamette U., 1960—63; BA, U. Oreg., 1968, MA, 1971, PhD, 1974. Adminstrv. asst. Dept. of Youth Svcs., Lubbock, Tex., 1963; tchg. asst., instr. U. Oreg., Eugene, 1969-72; vis. asst. prof. Oreg. State U., Corvallis, 1973-74, Willamette U., Salem, Oreg., 1973-79, Lewis and Clark Coll., Portland, Oreg., 1976, 78; from asst. prof. to prof. Western Oreg. U., Monmouth, 1979—2003, chair history, polit. sci., pub. adminstrn. dept., 1991-94, chair social sci. divsn., 1994-2000; exec. dir. Hawaii Wellness Inst., Honolulu, 2003—. Author: (with others) The People of Rajneeshpuram, 1990, Annual Yearbook in the Sociology of Religion, 1995, (simulation) European Unity Project, 1982; co-prodr., actress: Aging Is Not for Sissies, 2006-. Co-founder, v.p., sec.-treas Ind. Opportunities Unltd., Salem, 1986—; co-founder, sec. Inst. for Justice and Human Rights, San Francisco, 1988-94; bd. dirs. Oreg. UN Assn., Portland, 1982-00, Salem UN Assn., 1982-91; v.p., pres., bd. dirs. Garten Svcs. Inc. for Disabled, Salem, 1989-03; pres. Assn. Oreg. Faculties, 1989-91; adv. bd. Connections Program for Disabled Deaf, Salem, 1989-03; pres., bd. dirs. Model UN of the Far West, San Francisco, 1981-84, 86-88, 95-00, 02-03; Hawaii Alliance Nonprofit Orgns., 2006-, bd. dir., Friends Oreg. Sch. Deaf, 2009-. Danforth Found. fellow, 1968-74; named Woman of Achievement YWCA Tribute, Salem, 1990, Mem. of Yr., Oreg. Rehab. Assn., 1995. Mem. AAUW, Am. Fedn. Tchrs. (v.p., legis. officer local 2278 1982-88), Western Polit. Sci. Assn., Communal Studies Assn., Mental Health Assn. Oreg., Oreg. Acad. Sci., Soc. for Utopian Studies, Oreg. Hosp. Found., Oreg. Internat. Coun., Oreg. Mediation Assn., Phi Kappa Phi (pres., sec., treas.), Phi Alpha Delta (Outstanding Faculty Advisor in USA, 2000), Oreg. Women's Polit. Caucus. Democrat. Avocations: volunteer work with multiply disabled deaf, reading, meditation. Office: Hawaii Wellness Inst 3670 Kalihi St Honolulu HI 96819 Home: 106 Independence Way Independence OR 97351 Office Phone: 808-228-9028. Business E-Mail: shayr@wou.edu, hwi@earthlink.net.

SHAYE, ROBERT KENNETH, film company executive; s. Max and Dorothy S.; m. Eva Lindstern, 1970; children: Katja, Juno. BBA, U. Mich., 1960; postgrad., Sorbonne U., 1961; JD, Columbia U., 1964. Bar: N.Y. 1967. Founder, co-chmn., co-CEO New Line Cinema, NYC, 1967—2008. Recipient 1st prize Rosenthal competition Soc. Cinematologists, 1964, cert. of merit Inst. Copyrights and Patents, U. Stockholm, 1966, award ASCAP/Nathan Burkan Meml. competition, 1964; Fulbright scholar, 1964-66. Mem. Motion Picture Pioneers (bd. dirs.). *Life is a lot tougher than television watching in the '50's led me to believe.*

SHAYER, ZEEV, research scientist, educator; s. Yrachmieal Yhuda Shayer; children: Assaf, Chezy. PhD, Tel Aviv U., 1985. Rsch. prof. U. Denver, 2008, Colo. Sch. Mines, Golden, Colo., 2008—. Cons., Littleton, Conn., 2008. Achievements include patents for multifunctional material for radiation space. Office: Colo Sch Mines 1523 Ill Golden CO 80401-1887 Office Fax: 303-273-3919. Business E-Mail: zshayer@mines.edu.

SHAYS, CHRISTOPHER H., former United States Representative from Connecticut; b. Stamford, Conn., Oct. 18, 1945; m. Betsi DeRaismes, 1968; 1 child, Jeramy Alice. BA in Am. Hist. and Polit. Sci., Principia Coll., Elsah, Ill., 1968; MBA, NYU, 1974, MPA, 1978. Real estate broker, 1984—87; mem. Conn. House of Reps. from Dist. 147, Stamford, 1975—87, US Congress from 4th Conn. Dist., Washington, 1987—2009, mem. fin. services com., oversight & govt. reform com., homeland security com. Co-chair UN Working Grp., Non-Proliferation Task Force, Congl. Friends of Animals Caucus, Congl. Arts Caucus;

co-founder Congl. Nat. Svc. Caucus; chair Govt. Reform Subcom. Nat. Security & Vets. Affairs; US chair Global Legislators Organized for Balanced Environment. Vol. US Peace Corps, 1968—70. Republican. Christian Scientist.*

SHCHERBAKOVA, ESTELLA, chemist, mathematician, educator; b. Dnepropetrovsk, Ukraine, Oct. 15, 1938; arrived in Russia, 1951, arrived in U.S., 1994; d. Stepan and Fira (Poltorak) Masko; m. Stanislav Shcherbakov; 1 child, Yuriy Shcherbakov. MA math and drawing, State Pedagogical Inst., Moscow, Russia, 1956—61; PhD chem. sci., Post grad. Sch. of L. Karpov Rsch. Physical Chem. Inst., Moscow, Russia, 1968—74. Math tchr. HS #79, Moscow, 1961—62; engr. State Inst. of Caouchouc, Moscow, 1962—64; sci. worker from jr. to maj. L. Karpov Rsch. Phys. Chem. Inst., Moscow, 1964—94. Cons. and joint rsch. Inst. of Thin Chem. Tech., Moscow, 1971—89, State External Polytech. Inst., Moscow, 1978—90. Co-author: 113 articles, SU Jour. Miscellaneous reports, 1961—91, (book, monograph) Math Matters of Investigation of Chem. Equilib., 1978, From Newton to Present Days: Minimization of Nonlinear Functions of Several Variables, 2007, (3 inventions) SU Bull. of Inventions, 1985, 1992—93. Recipient Semicentennial, L. Karpov Inst./ Moscow, Russia, 1988. Finding common math technology for investigation of the multiple equilibriums in solutions and applying it to various chemical systems, including solutions of bromine and iodine that brought to inventions of industrial modus of their deriving from a leach. Finding the method for nonlinear optimizations, as to apply non-equilibrium thermodynamics to processes of polymerizations. Home: 2820 W 32nd St Apt 3E Brooklyn NY 11224 E-mail: shchest@aol.com. *She evacuated in Kuybishev (Samara) Russia, 1941-1945; resided in Moscow from 1951 because of father's job in aerospace engineering.*

SHE, CHIAO-YAO, physics professor, researcher; s. Young-Chi She and I-Jung Fang; m. Lucia Shumai Yein, Feb. 8, 1964; children: Colleen Suelie Kirtland, Fannie Camille. BS, Taiwan U., 1957; MS, N.D. State U., 1961; PhD, Stanford U., 1964. Asst. prof. elec. engring. U. Minn., Mpls., 1964—68; from asst. to prof. physics Colo. State U., Fort Collins, 1968—. Editor: (book) Selected Papers on Laser Applications in Remote Sensing, SPIE Milestone Series, MS 141 (1997); contbr. articles to profl. jours. Recipient, Fulbright scholarship, 2000, Lecture prize, NSF/Coupling, Energetics and Dynamics of Atmospheric Regions Sci. Steering Com., 2003. Fellow: Optical Soc. of Am.; mem.: Am. Phys. Soc., Am. Geophys. Union. Achievements include invention of Two high-spectral-resolution atmospheric lidars. Office: Colo State U Dept Physics 200 W Lake St Fort Collins CO 80523-1875 Office Fax: 970-491-7947.

SHEA, BERNARD CHARLES, retired pharmaceutical executive; b. Bradford, Pa., Aug. 7, 1929; s. Bernard and Edna Catherine (Green) S.; m. Marilyn Rishell, Apr. 12, 1952; children: David Charles, Melissa Leone. BS in Biology, Holy Cross Coll., Worcester, Mass. Dir. mktg. Upjohn Co., Kalamazoo, 1954-80; pres. pharm. div. Pennwalt Corp., Rochester, NY, 1980-86, v.p. health div. Phila., 1986, sr. v.p. health div., 1987-88, sr. v.p. chemicals, 1988-89; group pres. Atochem N.Am., Inc., Phila., 1989-90, pharm. cons., 1990-93. Served to lt. (j.g.) USN, 1951-54, Korea Home: 5231 Highgate Ct Zephyrhills FL 33541 Personal E-mail: berniemari@comcast.com, berniemari@msn.com, berniemari@sbcglobal.net.

SHEA, BRENT MACK, social sciences educator; b. Oneida, NY, June 3, 1946; s. Mack Evered and Alice May (Meeker) Shea. BA, SUNY, Binghamton, 1968, MA, 1972, PhD, 1977. Vis. instr. Harpur Coll. SUNY, Binghamton, 1975-76, resident dir. Coll.-in-the-Woods, 1976-78, rsch. assoc., 1977-78; from asst. prof. to prof. Sweet Briar Coll., Va., 1978—92, chmn. dept. anthropology and sociology, 1986—90, 1996—99, 2005—06, chmn. dept. sociology, 2007—, prof., 1992—. Vis. fellow Yale U., New Haven, 1984—85, postdoctoral fellow, 1985—86; sci. collaborator Centro studi per l'Evoluzione Umana, Rome, 1990—; vis. scholar Summer Inst. Survey Rsch. U. Mich., 1991; presenter, rschr. in field. Co-editor, contbg. author: Social Psychiatry across Cultures, 1995; editor: conf. procs. Work and Mental Health, 1996; mem. editl. bd. Internat. Scope Rev., 1999—; co-editor: Internat. Scope Rev., 2000—01; contbr. articles to profl. jour., chapters to books. Regents scholar, Harpur Coll. SUNY, 1964—68, Faculty Rsch. fellow, Sweet Briar Coll., 1984—85, 1992—93, NIMH Postdoctoral Rsch. fellow, Instn. Social and Policy Studies, Yale U., 1985—86. Mem.: AAUP (chpt. pres. 1996—99, chair state com. on coll. and univ. governance 1998—2001, state exec. com. 1998—2001), Va. Sociol. Assn. (mem. exec. com. 1980—81, pres., co-chmn. conf. program), Ea. Ednl. Rsch. Assn. (dir. rsch. ethics 1979—83, bd. dirs. 1979—85, gen. sec. 1983—85), Ius Primi Viri Internat. Assn., Rome (v.p. bd. 1994—, NGO rep. economic and social coun., United Nations Hdqs. 2005—), Internat. Sociol. Assn. (v.p. exec. bd. 1994—98, mental health and illness rsch. com.), Am. Sociol. Assn. (task force on internat. focus of Am. sociology 1999—2003), Soc. Automotive Historians. Avocations: classical piano, classic cars. Home: PO Box 1 Sweet Briar VA 24595-0001 Office: Sweet Briar Coll Dept Sociology Sweet Briar VA 24595 Office Phone: 434-381-6193.

SHEA, CHRISTOPHER, chemicals executive, director; MA in Pastoral Studies, Wash. Theol. Union. Cert. in rational addictions Nat. Assn. Cognitive Behavioral Therapists; assoc. counselor Alcohol Drug, Md. Adj. prof. Balt. City CC, Md.; clin. dir. Father Martins Ashley, Havre de Grace, Md., 2002—. Bd. chair Nat. Coun. Acloholism & Drug Dependence-Md. Chpt. Personal E-mail: chrismd104@yahoo.com.

SHEA, EDWARD EMMETT, lawyer, educator, writer; b. Detroit, May 29, 1932; s. Edward Francis and Margaret Kathleen (Downey) S.; m. Ann Marie Conley, Aug. 28, 1957; children: Michael, Maura, Ellen. AB, U. Detroit, 1954; JD, U. Mich., 1957. Bar: Mich. 1957, Fla. 1959, N.Y. 1961. Assoc. Simpson Thacher & Bartlett, NYC, 1960-63. Dykema, Wheat, Spencer, Detroit, 1963-69, Cadwalader Wickersham & Taft, NYC, 1969-71; v.p., gen. counsel, chmn. Reichhold Chems., White Plains, NY, 1971-81; adj. prof. Pace U. Grad. Sch. Bus., NYC, 1982—; counsel, ptnr. Windels, Marx, Davies & Ives, NYC, 1982-84; ptnr. Windels, Marx, Lane & Mittendorf, NYC, 1986—; sr. v.p., gen. counsel GAF Corp., 1984-86. Sec. Peridot Chems., 1988-97; lectr. N.Y. Inst. Fin., 1995-; trustee Pearl Theatre Co., 2008-; bd. mem. Theater for New City, 2009-. Author: An Introduction to the U.S. Environmental Laws, 1995, The Lead Regulation Handbook, 1996, 2d edit., 2007, The McGraw-Hill Guidebook to Acquiring and Divesting Businesses, 1998, Environmental Law and Compliance Methods, 2002; editor: The Acquisitions Yearbook, 1991-93; contbr. articles to profl. jours. Mem. adv. bd. N.Y. State Small Bus. Ctr. Program, 1988-93. 1st lt. JAGC, USAF, 1957-60. Mem. N.Y. Athletic Club. Office: Windels Marx Lane & Mittendorf 156 W 56th St Fl 23 New York NY 10019-3867 Office Phone: 212-237-1140. Business E-Mail: eshea@windelsmarx.com.

SHEA, JAMES L., lawyer; b. Balt., June 19, 1952; Ab cum laude, Princeton U., 1974; JD, U. Va., 1977. Bar: Md. 1977, DC 1998. Law clk. to Hon. Joseph H. Young US Dist. Ct. Md., 1977-78; asst. atty. gen. State of Md., 1981-83; mng. ptnr. Venable LLP, Washington, 1994—2006, chmn., 2006—. Past chmn. bd. Empower Balt. Mgmt. Corp.; chmn. bd. Downtown Partnership of Balt., Downtown Mgmt. Authority; bd. mem. Greater Balt. Com.; regent U. Systems. Md., College Park. Recipient Leadership in Law Award, The Daily Record; named Power 50: The Men and Women Who Rule award, Balt. Mag., 2003, 2006. Fellow Am. Coll. Trial Lawyers; mem. ABA, Md. State Bar Assn., Bar Assn. Balt. City, Order of Coif. Address: Venable LLP 750 E Pratt St Baltimore MD 21202 Office Phone: 410-244-7734. Office Fax: 410-244-7742. E-mail: jshea@venable.com.

SHEA, KATHERINE MARIE, physician, consultant; b. Portland, Oreg., Dec. 4, 1952; d. Robert Lyle and Margaret Dawn Dressler; m. Thomas Charles Shea; children: Margaret Eileen, Joseph Thomas. BA, Brown U., Providence, Rhode Island, 1974; MD cum laude, U. Oreg. Health Scis. Ctr., Portland, 1978; MPH, U. NC Sch. Pub. Health, Chapel Hill, 1995. Diplomate Nat. Bd. Med. Examiners, 1981, Am. Bd. Pediat., 1984. Resident, pediat. NC Meml. Hosp., Chapel Hill, NC, 1978—81; fellow cmty. pediat. Boston City Hosp., 1981—82; pediatrician Whittier St. Neighborhood Health Ctr., Roxbury, Mass., 1981—82, Dorchester House Neighborhood Health Ctr., Mass., 1982, East Boston Neighborhood Health Ctr., 1983—86, West Roxbury Harvard Cmty. Health Plan, Mass., 1986—88, Children's Med. Ctr., Escondido, Calif., 1988—89, Wake County Health Dept., Raleigh, 1993; staff physician San Diego State U. Student Health Ctr., 1989—92, NC State U. Student Health Ctr., Raleigh, 1996—; preventive medicine resident U. NC Med. Sch., Chapel Hill, 1993—95; fellow clin. rsch.; gcrc-niehs program Nat. Inst. Environ. Health Scis., Research Triangel Park, NC, 1994—96, vis. scholar, 1996—97; cons. children's environ. health Ind. Contractor, Chapel Hill, 1999—. Mem. expert panel, phthalates Nat. Toxicology Program, Ctr. Evaluation Risks Human Reproduction, Research Triangel Park, 1999—2000; project dir., aap atsdr coop. agreement; partnership develop an environ. safety net children Agy. Toxic Substances and Disease Registration, Atlanta, 1999—2004; tech. editor, modules children's environ. health and climate change WHO, Geneva, 2001—; med. cons. Environ. Def., Washington, 2000—02, Physicians Social Responsibility, Washington, 2003—05; tech. cons., writer and editor, children's environ. health Intergovernmental Forum Chem. Safety, Geneva, 2003—; project dir., health cmty. responding climate change Inst. Environment U. NC, Chapel Hill, 2007—08; raporteur, inter-regional workshop environ. health impacts from exposure to metals Ctr. Disease Control and Prevention, Atlanta, 2005. Contbr. articles to profl. jours. Com. mem. Sch. Health Adv. Com., Chapel Hill, 2000—05; mem. and current chair Toxic Free NC, Raleigh, 2003—. Mem.: APHA, NC Pediatric Soc., Alpha Omega Alpha. Avocations: singing, yoga, reading. Office: NC State Univ SHS 2815 Cates Ave Raleigh NC 27695 Business E-Mail: kmshea2@gw.fis.ncsu.edu.

SHEA, MARTIN M., broadcast executive; BS, U. Hartford, West Hartford, Conn. Various positions up to v.p. investor rels. Paramount Comm. Inc. (formerly Gulf & Western), 1977—94; sr. v.p. corp. comm. Triarc Cos., Inc., 1994—95, 1995—97; mng. dir. Edelman Worldwide, 1995; sr. v.p. investor relations Viacom, Inc., 1998—2004, exec. v.p. investor relations, 2004—05; exec. v.p. investor rels. CBS Corp., 2005—. Named Number One Investor Rels. Office in Media Industry, Instl. Investor, 2003, Number One Investor Rels. Officer Across All Industries, Investor Rels. Mag., 2003. Mem.: Nat. Inst. Investor Relations (past pres. NY chpt.). Office: CBS Corp 51 W 52nd St New York NY 10019-6188 Office Phone: 212-975-4321.

SHEA, PAUL, museum association administrator, curator; Various positions West Yellowstone and Yellowstone Nat. Pk., 1979—93; pres. West Yellowstone Hist. Soc., 1993—, Mus. Assn. of Mont.; curator Yellowstone Hist. Ctr. and Mus., exec. dir., 2002—. Office: Yellowstone Historic Ctr PO Box 1299 West Yellowstone MT 59758 Office Phone: 406-646-1100. Business E-Mail: pshea@yellowstonehistoriccenter.org.

SHEA, WILLIAM RENE, historian, history and philosophy professor; b. Gracefield, Que., Can., May 16, 1937; s. Herbert Clement and Jeanne (Lafreniere) S.; m. Evelyn Fischer, May 2, 1970; children: Herbert, Joan-Emma, Louisa, Cecilia, Michael. BA, U. Ottawa, 1958; LPh, Gregorian U., Rome, 1959; LTh, Gregorian U., 1963; PhD, Cambridge U., Eng., 1968. Assoc. prof. U. Ottawa, 1968-73; fellow Harvard U., Cambridge, Mass., 1973-74; prof. history and philosophy of sci. McGill U., Montreal, 1974—; dir. d'etudes Ecole des Hautes Etudes, Paris, 1981-82. Sec.-gen. Internat. Union of History and Philosophy of Sci., 1981-89, pres., 1990-93; mem. gen. com. Internat. Coun. of Sci. Union, Paris, 1983-89; cons. Killam Found., Ottawa, Ont., 1983-85; mem. McGill Centre for Medicine, Ethics and Law, 1990-95; Hydro Que. prof. environ. ethics, 1992—; vis. prof. U. Rome, 1992; dir. Inst. History of Sci., U. Louis Pasteur, Strasbourg, 1995-2003; Galileo chair history of sci. U. Padua, 2003—. Author: Galileo Intellectual Revolution, 1972, The Magic of Numbers and Motion, 1991, Copernico, 2001, Designing Experiments and Games of Chance, 2003, Coffee with Galileo, 2007; co-author: Galileo Florentine Residences, 1979, Galileo in Rome, 2003, Galileo Observed: The Politics of Belief, 2006; editor: Nature Mathematized, 1983, Otto Hahn and the Rise of Nuclear Physics, 1983, Revolutions in Science, 1988, Creativity in the Arts and Science, 1990, Persuading Science: The Art of Scientific Rhetoric, 1991, Interpreting the World, Science and Society, 1991, Energy Needs in the Year 2000: Ethical and Environmental Perspectives, 1994, Science and the Visual Image in the Enlightenment, 2000, Campanus of Novara's Theorica Planetarum, 2007, Galileo's Sideral Message, 2009. Recipient The Alexandre Koyre medal, Internat. Acad. of History of Sci., 1993, Knight of the Order of Malta, 1993; Can. Coun. fellow, 1965—68, Can. Cultural Inst. fellow, Rome, 1973, Social Scis. and Humanities Rsch. Coun. Can., 1980—81, Inst. of Advanced Studies in Berlin fellow, 1988—89. Fellow Royal Soc. Can.; mem. Royal Swedish Acad. Scis. (fgn.), Acadmie D'Alsace, Academia Europaea (mem. coun., 2003-07), History of Sci. Soc. (coun. 1973-76), European Sci. Found. (standing com. for humanities 1989-95, chmn. 1999-2003), Can. Nat. Com. of History and Philosophy of Sci. (coun. 1982-93), Can. Philos. Assn., Internat. Acad. History of Sci. (pres. 1997-2001), Rotary. Home: 35 Via Guglielmo Marconi 35122 Padua Italy Office Phone: 39-049-827-5073. Fax: 39-049-827-5068. E-mail: william.shea@unipd.it.

SHEAFFER, CRISTAL S., music educator; b. Mechanicsburg, Pa., Feb. 3, 1960; d. Claude P. and Louise B. Swartzbaugh; m. Joel C. Sheaffer, July 29, 2006; children: Jessica L Janderchick, Julie L Janderchick. BS in Music Edn., Indiana U. of Pa., 1982; MEd in Ednl. Psychology, Temple U., Phila., 2000. Level 2 tchr. cert. Pa. Woodwind instr., accompanist, colorguard instr. Milton Hershey Sch., Hershey, Pa., 1985—90, elem. gen./instrumental/vocal instr., 1990—93, h.s. vocal/classroom music instr., 1993—; children's choir dir. Hershey 1st United Meth. Ch., 1990—98. Prin. flutist Ctrl. Pa. Symphony, Hershey, 1987—; flutist Ctrl. Pa. Woodwind Quintet, Hershey, 2001—. Mem.: NEA, Milton Hershey Edn. Assn. (bldg. rep. 2000—03), Pa. State Edn. Assn., Dauphin County Music Educators Assn., Pa. Music Educators Assn., Music Educators Nat. Conf. Office: Milton Hershey Sch 851 Spartan Ln Hershey PA 17033 Personal E-mail: janderchick6374@comcast.net. E-mail: sheafferc@mhs-pa.org.

SHEAFFER, M. P. A., educator; d. Joseph M. Sheaffer and Annie P. Moore. BS, MA, PhD. Educator Millersville U., Pa. Author: (poetry book) Lacquer Birds and Leaves of Brass; contbr. numerous poetry books. Recipient numerous awards, Nat. Fedn. Poetry Socs., 1990—2008. Mem.: Poetry Soc. America. Independent. Avocations: travel, hiking, photography, theater, gardening. Home and Office: Millersville Univ Pa Chryst Hall New Holland PA 17557 Business E-Mail: mpa.sheaffer@millersville.edu.

SHEAFFER, RICHARD ALLEN, electrical engineer; b. Bronxville, NY, May 30, 1950; BSEE, Pa. State U., 1972; MSEE, U. So. Calif., 1975; MBA, Pepperdine U., 1996. Registered profl. engr., Calif., Fla. Elec. engr. So. Calif. Edison Co., Rosemead, 1973-79, 80-90, Harris Controls divsn., Melbourne, Fla., 1979-80; cons. San Diego Gas & Elec., 1990-91, sr. transmission planner, 1991-2000, prin. engr., 2004—; rep. for decommissioning San Onofre Nuc. Generating Sta. Unit 1, 2000—; rep. for steam generator replacement project Units 2 and 3, 2005—. Project leader nomogram study for Pacific and S.W. transfer subcom. Western Systems Coordinating Coun., 1988, 91; project leader Ariz.-Calif. 7550 NW Path Rating, 1994-97. Author: 1984 West-of-the-River Operating Study, 1985, December 22, 1982 Disturbance Study, 1983. Mem. IEEE (Power Engring. Soc., Engring. Mgmt. Soc.), Am. Nuc. Soc., Phi Eta Sigma.

SHEAFFER, SUZANNE FRANCES, geriatrics nurse; b. Harrisburg, Pa., Feb. 8, 1963; d. Walter Richard and Catherine Frances (Mourawski) Markham; children: William Chester, Sarah Suzanne, Katye Iona; m. Paul L. Sheaffer Jr. ADN, Harrisburg CC, Pa., 1984; BSN, York Coll., Pa., 1997; B in Criminal Justice Adminstrn., Ctrl. Pa. Coll., Summerdale, 2005; postgrad. in Criminal Justice, St. Leo U., Fla., 2005—06; postgrad., North Ctrl. U., 2007—; PhD student, 2009—. RN; lic. nursing home adminstr., Pa. Nurse ICU and critical care unit Meml. Hosp., York, Pa., 1987-88; staff nurse emergency dept. Polyclinic Med. Ctr., Harrisburg, 1988-91; assoc. prof. Nat. Edn. Ctr.-Jr. Coll., Harrisburg, 1991; dir. nursing Camp Hill Care Ctr., Pa., 1991-92; resident assessment supr. Susquehanna Ctr., Harrisburg, 1992-94; dir. nursing Susquehanna Luth. Village, Millersburg, Pa., 1994-95; asst. adminstr. Dauphin Manor, Harrisburg, 1995—; mgr. clin. svcs. ea. divsn. HCR Manor Care; med. analyst Medicaid Fraud Control Unit Pa. Atty. Gen. Office, 2003—. ACLS, CPR instr. Am. Heart Assn., Harrisburg, 1989—; BCLS, CPR instr. ARC, Harrisburg, 1992—; RN, paramedic Lebanon County First Aide and Safety Patrol, Pa., 1992-. Sec. Little People PTA, Harrisburg, 1991-92; pres. Student Human Resource Mgmt. Club, York Coll., Pa., 1992—; v.p. Prince of Peace PTO, 1997-98; cheerleading coach, Midget Footbal Assoc., 2002—; cheerleading coord. Susquehanna Twp. Midget Football Assn., 2003, HNJ, 2006-; acad. adviser Eta Sigma Alpha Chi Beta chpt., 2003-05; home room parent Holy Name Jesus Sch., 2002-, cheer coord., 2006-09. Recipient Nurse of Hope award Am. Cancer Soc., Dauphin County, Harrisburg, 1983-84. Mem. AACN, Pa. Nurses Assn., Pa. Dir. Nursing Assn. for Long Term Care, PANPHA (advocate), York Coll. Alumni Assn. (bd. dirs. Susquehanna Valley), Pa. Homesch. Assn., Ctrl. Pa. Alumni Assn. Roman Catholic. Avocations: ceramics, ballet, flute. Office Phone: 717-712-2033. Personal E-mail: sheafferfam@msn.com.

SHEAFFER, WILLIAM JAY, lawyer; b. Carlisle, Pa., Jan. 18, 1948; s. Raymond Jay and Barbara Jean (Bell) S.; m. Carol Ann Madison, Jan. 5, 1974. BA cum laude, U. Cen. Fla., 1975; JD, Nova U., 1978. Bar: Fla. 1978, U.S. Dist. Ct. (mid. dist.) Fla. 1979, U.S. Dist. Ct. (so. and no. dists.) Fla. 1981, U.S. Ct. Appeals (5th and 11th cirs.) 1981, U.S. Supreme Ct. 1983. Atty. State of Fla., Orlando, Fla., 1978-79; pvt. practice, 1979—. Apptd. to merit selection panel to consider U.S. Magistrate Judge Applicants, 1995, 97, 99. Pres. City Coun. Edgewood, Fla., 2000—02, coun. mem., 2003—04. Served to ensign class 4 USN, 1967—71. Named one of Legal Elite, Fla. Trend Mag., 2004, 2005, Orlando's Top Lawyers, Orlando Mag., 2004, 2005, 2006, 2007, 2008, Top Lawyers in Fla., Super Lawyers Mag., 2006, 2007, 2008. Mem.: ACLU, NACDL, ABA, The Federalist Soc., Assn. Fed. Def. Attys., Ctrl. Fla. Assn. Criminal Def. Attys., Nat. Bd. Trial Advocacy (bd. cert. criminal trial specialist), Fed. Trial Lawyers Assn., Fla. Assn. Criminal Def. Lawyers Inc., Fed. Bar Assn., Orange County Bar Assn. (Guardian Ad Litem of Yr. 1994, award of excellence 1995), Fla. Bar Assn. (vice chmn. 9th jud. cir. grievance com. 1997, 1998, cert. criminal trial specialist). Democrat. Avocations: boating, running, skiing. Office: 609 E Central Blvd Orlando FL 32801-2916 Home Phone: 407-240-0302; Office Phone: 407-423-1066. Fax: 407-648-0683. Business E-Mail: mail@defenselaw.net.

SHEAHAN, JOHN BERNARD, economist, educator; b. Toledo, Sept. 11, 1923; s. Bernard William and Florence (Sheahan) S.; m. Denise Eugénie Morlino, Nov. 29, 1946; children: Yvette Marie, Bernard Eugene. BA, Stanford U., Calif., 1948; PhD, Harvard U., Cambridge, Mass., 1954. Econ. analyst Office Spl. Rep. in Europe, ECA, Paris, 1951-54; mem. faculty Williams Coll., Williamstown, Mass., 1954—94, prof. economics, 1966—94, prof. emeritus. Mem. devel. adv. service Colombia adv. group Harvard, 1963-65; nat. research prof. Brookings Instn., 1959-60; vis. prof. El Colegio de México, Mexico City, 1970-71; Fulbright research scholar Institut de recherche économique et de planification, Université de Grenoble, France, 1974-75; vis. scholar Inst. Devel. Studies, U. Sussex, 1981-82; vis. fellow Ctr. for U.S.-Mexican Studies, U. Calif. at San Diego, 1991. Author: Promotion and Control of Industry in Postwar France, 1963, The Wage-Price Guideposts, 1967, An Introduction to the French Economy, 1969, Patterns of Development in Latin America, 1987, Conflict and Change in Mexican Economic Strategy, 1992, Searching for a Better Society: The Peruvian Economy from 1950, 1999. Mem. Presdl. Price Adv. Com., 1979-80 Mem. Latin Am. Studies Assn., New England Coun. Latin Am. Studies (pres. 1989-90), Phi Beta Kappa. Home: PO Box 751 Williamstown MA 01267

SHEAKS, BARCLAY, artist; b. Oct. 22, 1928; s. Earl Leroy and Jeanie Rice Sheaks; m. Deborah Mae Joyner; 1 child, Owen James. BFA, Va. Commonwealth U., 1948; LHD (hon.), Christopher Newport U., 1997. Disting. resident artist Va. Wesleyan Coll., Norfolk, 1990—2005. Author: (poetry book) Stretching the Eyes Distance, 1980, (book) The Acrylics Book, 1995; Represented in permanent collections Va. Mus. Fine Arts, Chrysler Mus., Butler Inst. Am. Art, Valentine Mus., Mobile Mus., Med. Coll. Va., Christopher Newport U., others. Mem.: Peninsula Fine Arts Ctr. Avocation: boating. Home: 51 Hopkins St Newport News VA 23601

SHEALY, HARRY E., JR., biology professor, consultant; s. Harry E. and Margaret E. Shealy; m. Margaret Grubbs; children: Margaret S. Garrick, John C. PhD, U. SC., Columbia, 1972. Postdoc. fellow U. Man., Winnipeg, Manitoba, Canada, 1972—73; prof. biology U. SC, Aiken, 1973—. Pres. H and D Environ. Svc. Inc., Aiken, 1993—2008. Vice-chair Hitchcock Woods Found., Aiken, 1980—2008; founding mem. and past pres. Aiken Land Conservancy, Aiken, 1990—2008; bd. mem. Conservation Voters SC, Columbia, 2004—08. Episcopal. Business E-Mail: hshealy@usca.edu.

SHEAPENTUKH, DMITRY V., history professor; b. Kiev, Ukraine, May 31, 1950; s. Valdimir Emanuilovinch Sheapentukh and Lubov Alievskaia; m. Mogileva Nataliia; children: Leon, Anna. MA, Moscow State U., Mich. State U., 1980; PhD, U. Chgo., 1988. Vis. asst. prof. SUNY, Oswego, 1987—88; fellow, Russian Rsch. Ctr. Harvard U., Cambridge, 1990—91; assoc. prof. Indiana U., South Bend, 1991—. Contbr. articles to profl. jours. Home: Hoover Ave 1534 South Bend IN 46634-7111 Office: Indiana Univ-South Bend Dept History PO Box 7111 South Bend IN 46634-7111 Business E-Mail: dsheapen@iusb.edu.

SHEA-PORTER, CAROL, United States Representative from New Hampshire, social worker; b. NYC, Dec. 2, 1952; d. William and Peggy Shea; m. Gene Porter; 2 children. BS in Social Services, U. NH, 1975, MPA, 1979. Instr. The Charter House, 1987—2001; history instr. Prince George's C.C., 1987—89; dir. The Shepard's Ctr., Multi-Purpose Sr. Ctr.; mem. Mayor's Taskforce on us housing, Washington, US Congress from 1st NH dist., 2007—, mem. armed svcs. com. and edn. & labor com. NH regional coord. Wesley Clark for Presdl. Campaign. Democrat. Roman Catholic. Office: 1508 Longworth House Office Bldg Washington DC 20515 also: 104 Washington St Dover NH 03820*

SHEAR, ALAN JAMES, theologian; m. Deirdre J. Robinson, Apr. 1, 2004; children: Joel Anders, Melissa Callahan Stanley. BA, Wilmington Coll., Ohio, 1977; MDiv, McCormick Theol. Sem., Chgo., 1980. Pvt. practice, Frederick, Md.; clergy Presbyn. Ch. USA, Providence, 1981—86; press sec. US House Representatives, Washington, 1988—90; pub. rels. profl. various, 1990—2002. Ceremonialist Four Quarters Interfaith Sanctuary Earth Religion, Artemas, Pa., 1996—. Office: Marquette Univ Coughlin Hall Milwaukee WI 53202 Business E-Mail: alan.shear@marquette.edu.

SHEAR, NATALIE PICKUS, conference and event management executive; b. NYC, Oct. 18, 1940; d. Sam and Mildred (Shulman) Pickus; m. Daniel H. Shear, Dec. 14, 1968 (dec. Apr. 1989); children: Adam Brian, Tamara Beth; m. Henry D. Lewis, Jan. 10, 1999. BA in Journalism, Fairleigh Dickinson U., 1962. Editl. asst. Show Bus. Newspaper, NYC, 1962-64, Jewish News, Newark, 1964-66; dir. Manhattan women's divsn., program asst. Am. Jewish Congress, NYC, 1966-68; mng. editor Jewish Week, Washington, 1968-71; dir. pub. rels. United Jewish Appeal, Washington, 1973-74; pub. affairs dir. Leadership Conf. Civil Rights, Washington, 1977-83; pres. Natalie P. Shear Assocs., Inc., Washington, 1983—. Editor: (newspaper) Books Alive, 1973—74; editor, pub.: newsletter Trends, Inc., 1989—94. V.p. Nat. Child Rsch. Ctr., Washington, 1974—76; bd. dirs. Urban Philharm. Soc., 1998—99; vol., bd. dirs. Nat. Jewish Dem. Coun., Washington, 1996—; vol. nat. bd. Ams. Dem. Action, 2001—; pres. Ohr Kodesh Sisterhood, Chevy Chase, Md., 1980—82; chairperson women's task force Am. Jewish Congress, Washington, 1984—86. Mem.: Nat. Press Club. Avocation: needlecrafts. Home: 4701 Willard Ave Chevy Chase MD 20815-4643 Office: 1730 M St NW Ste 801 Washington DC 20036 Home Phone: 301-986-0421; Office Phone: 202-833-4456. Business E-Mail: natalie@natalieshear.com.

SHEAR, THEODORE LESLIE, JR., archaeologist, educator; b. Athens, Greece, May 1, 1938; s. Theodore Leslie and Josephine (Platner) S.; m. Ione Doris Mylonas, June 24, 1959; children: Julia Louise, Alexandra. AB summa cum laude, Princeton U., NJ, 1959, MA, 1963, PhD, 1966. Instr. Greek and Latin Bryn Mawr Coll., Pa., 1964-66, asst. prof., 1966-67; asst. prof. art and archaeology Princeton U., 1967-70, assoc. prof., 1970-79, chmn. program in classical archaeology, 1970-85, assoc. chmn. dept. art and archaeology, 1976-78, 82-83, prof. classical archaeology, 1979—; prof. archaeology Am. Sch. Classical Studies, Athens, 1988-94. Mem. mng. com. Am. Sch. Classical Studies, Athens, 1972—; mem. archaeol. expdns. to Greece and Italy, including Mycenae, 1953-54, 1958, 1962-63, 1965-66, Eleusis, 1956, Perati, 1956, Corinth, 1960, Morgantina, Sicily, 1962; mem. Ancient Agora of Athens, 1955, 1967, field dir., 1968-94; trustee William Alexander Procter Found., 1982-89, Princeton Jr. Sch., 1983-2006, pres., 1994-2006. Author: Kallias of Sphettos and the Revolt of Athens in 286 B.C., 1978; contbr. articles to profl. jours. White fellow Am. Sch. Classical Studies, 1959-60. Mem. Archaeol. Inst. Am., Am. Philol. Assn., Coll. Art Assn., Archaeol. Soc. Athens (hon.), Century Assn. Club (NYC); Nassau Club (Princeton), Princeton Club (NYC), Hellenic Yacht Club (Piraeus, Greece), Phi Beta Kappa. Republican. Episcopalian. Home: 87 Library Pl Princeton NJ 08540-3015 also: 30 Deinokratous St Athens Greece

SHEARD, TIM, science educator; s. Franklin and Anita Sheard; m. Barbara Seagle; children: Samuel John Seaver, Caleb Franklin. BA in Chemistry, Harvard U., Cambridge, Mass., 1977; MS, U. Vt., Burlington, 1979; PhD, U. Mass., Amherst, 1985. Assoc. prof. Oreg. Grad. Inst., Beaverton, 1991—2004; prof. computer sci. Portland State U., Oreg., 2004—. Programmer MetaML. Mem.: ACM. Mem. Soc. Of Friends. Achievements include development of Omega programming and logic system. Office: Portland State Univ 1900 SW Fourth Ave Ste 120-04 Portland OR 97201

SHEARER, DEREK NOCROSS, political science professor, diplomat, academic administrator; b. LA, Dec. 5, 1946; s. Lloyd and Marva (Peterson) S.; m. Sue Toigo; 1 child, Casey (dec.); stepchildren: Anthony, Julie, Molly. BA, Yale U., 1968; PhD, Union Grad. Sch., Yellow Springs, Ohio, 1977. Lectr. U. Calif., LA, 1979-81; dir. internat. and pub. affairs ctr., prof. of pub. policy Occidental Coll., LA, 1981-94, 98—; dep. undersec. U.S. Dept. Commerce, Washington, 1993; U.S. amb. to Finland U.S. Dept. State, Washington, 1994-97; prof. internat. affairs Occidental Coll., LA, 1997—; internat. advisor Ziff Bros. Investments, 1998—. Fellow Econ. Strategy Inst., Washington, 1993; policy adv. to Presidential Candidate Bill Clinton, 1990-92; adv. on NATO peace keeping USN, 1997—; pub. policy fellow Woodrow Wilson Internat. Scholars Ctr., 1999-2000; dir. global affairs Occidental Coll., 2001—, Chevalier prof. diplomacy and world affairs, 2002—; founder Pacific Coun. Internat. Policy, 1994—; sr. fellow USC Inst. Public Diplomacy. Contbr. articles to profl. publs. Planning commr. City of Santa Monica (Calif.), 1984; bd. mem. Nat. Consumer Bank, Washington, 1991. Fellow Guggenheim Found., 1984, U.S.-Japan Leadership fellow Japan Soc., 1991. Democrat. Avocations: basketball, tennis, travel, mysteries. Office: Global Affairs Occidental Coll Los Angeles CA 90041 Office Phone: 323-259-2681. Business E-Mail: lima@oxy.edu.

SHEARER, LINDA, museum director; b. LI, NY, Feb. 13, 1946; BA, Sarah Lawrence Coll., Bronxville, NY, 1968. Assoc. curator Solomon R. Guggenheim Mus., NYC, 1969—80; exec. dir. Artists Space, NYC, 1980—85; curator painting and sculpture Mus. Modern Art, NYC, 1985—89; dir. Williams Coll. Mus. Art, Williamstown, Mass., 1989—2004; Alice & Harris Weston dir. Contemporary Arts Ctr., Cin., 2004—06; interim dir. Contemporary Arts Mus Houston, 2007—. Tchr. contemporary art Williams Coll., Sch. Visual Arts, NYC. Bd. trustees Am. Fedn. of Arts; adv. com. Skowhegan Sch. of Painting and Sculpture; chair Phila. Exhibition Initiative, 2003. Mem.: Am. Fedn. of Arts (former trustee), Assn. Art Mus. Dirs. (former trustee). Office: Contemporary Arts Mus Houston 5216 Montrose Blvd Houston TX 77006-6598 Office Phone: 713-284-8250. Office Fax: 713-284-8275.

SHEARER, LINDA RAE, English educator; b. Connellsville, Pa., Aug. 3, 1954; d. Randall Wilbur and Gertrude Elizabeth Shearer. BA, Alderson-Broaddus Coll., Philippi, WV, 1976; MEd, Calif. U., California, Pa., 1980. Tchr. Connellsville Area Sch. Dist., Pa., 1978—. Advisor Nat. Honor Soc. Connellsville Area HS, 1988—98, 2007—; activities dir. Connellsville Area Sr. HS, 1988—98, 2007—, founder and sponsor Patriots, 2003—. Decorated Army Commendation Medal; recipient Citation from Senate of Pa., Senators Jane Orie and Richard Kasunic, 2003, Disting. Alumni award, Alderson Broaddus Coll., 2005, Elks Disting. Citizen award, Connellsville Elks # 503, 2006, Individual Award for Vol. Svc., Connellsville C. of C., 2006, Presdl. Vol. Svc. award, 2007; named Fayette County Tchr. of the Yr., Fayette County C. of C., 1998, 2007, Vets. Fgn. Wars Tchr. of Yr., Pa., 2008—09. Mem.: NEA, Connellsville Area Edn. Assn., Pa. State Edn. Assn. Baptist. Home: 304 Stadium Rd Connellsville PA 15425-1964 Office: Connellsville Area Senior High School 201 Falcon Dr Connellsville PA 15425 Personal E-mail: teddy@cvzoom.net. E-mail: lshearer@casdfalcons.org.

SHEARER, RICHARD EUGENE, educational consultant; b. Connellsville, Pa., Dec. 30, 1919; s. H.D. and Florence (Prinkey) S.; m. Ruth Mansberger, June 16, 1944 (dec. Mar. 1993); children: Patricia (Mrs. Richard Wilson), Suzanne (Mrs. Terry Jones), Richard J.; m. Marilyn Likeness Erdman, May 7, 1994. AB, Eastern Bapt. Coll. and Sem., Phila., 1943, D.D., 1953; B.D., New Brunswick Theol. Sem., 1945; MA, Columbia, 1948, Ed.D., 1959; LL.D., Denison U., 1958; H.H.D., Bishop Coll., 1977. Ordained to ministry Bapt. Ch., 1943; minister Atlantic Highlands, N.J., 1943-45, New Brunswick, N.J., 1945-5O; pres. Alderson-Broaddus Coll., Philippi, W.Va., 1951-83; ind. cons., 1983—; cons., interim dir. W.Va. Found. Ind. Colls.; prin. resdl. devel. Bridgeport, W.Va., 1983—; v.p., exec. dir. United Health Found., Clarksburg, W.Va., 1987—; pres. R. Shearer & Assocs., Philippi, W.Va., 1984. Lectr. Mex. Pastor's Conf., summer 1955; past pres. W.Va. Found. Ind. Colls.; mem. Commn. on Instnl. Funding, Am. Bapt. Chs., U.S.A.; coordinator (Central Europe Coll. Program); pres. Am. Bapt. Assn. Sch. and Coll. Adminstrs., 1977; mem. W.Va. Ednl. Found., W.Va. State Scholarship Commn. Bd. regents W.Va. Assn. Pvt. Colls.; bd. dirs. W.Va. Found. Independent Colls.; sr. min. Bridgeport (W.Va.) Bapt. Ch., 1988-93; bd. dirs. Eastern Bapt. Theol. Sem., Phila. Named Phi Delta Kappa Profl. Educator of Year, 1964 Mem. Am. Assn. Sch. Adminstrs., W.Va. Assn. Coll. and Univ. Presidents (sec. mem. exec. com. 1963—), Assn. Am. Colls. (comm. coll. and soc.), Kiwanis. Office: 300 Shearerwood Dr Philippi WV 26416 Personal E-mail: rmshearer1@aol.com. *The joint impact of good religion and good education has been the dominant theme of my life and work. I feel that education is a powerful force which can be directed in either constructive or destructive directions. Good religion can assure that the power in education is constructive, and good education can assure that religion has depth.*

SHEARER, ROBERT K., apparel executive; BA, Catawba Coll. Asst. contr. VF Corp., Greensboro, NC, 1986—89, contr., 1989—94, v.p., contr., 1994—98, v.p. fin., CFO, 1998—2003, v.p. fin. & global processes, CFO, 2003—05, sr. v.p., CFO, 2005—. Office: VF Corp 105 Corporate Ctr Blvd Greensboro NC 27408

SHEARER, RONALD ALEXANDER, economics professor; b. Trail, BC, Can., June 15, 1932; s. James Boyd and Mary Ann (Smith) S.; m. Renate Elizabeth Selig, Dec. 20, 1956 (dec.); children: Carl, Bruce. BA, U. B.C., 1954; MA, Ohio State U., 1955, PhD, 1959. Asst. prof. econs. U. Mich., 1958-62; economist Royal Commn. Banking and Fin., Toronto, Canada, 1962-63; mem. faculty U. B.C., Vancouver, 1963—, prof. econs., 1970-98, emeritus prof., 1998—, head dept., 1972-76. Co-author: Money and Banking, 1975, The Economics of the Canadian Financial System, 1994; editor: Trade Liberalization and a Regional Economy, 1971. Mem. Can. Econs. Assn. Office: U BC Dept Econs Vancouver BC Canada Home Phone: 604-266-2852. Business E-Mail: rshearer@interchange.ubc.ca.

SHEARER, VELMA MILLER, clergywoman; b. Hines, Minn., Jan. 2, 1921; d. Floyd and Mary (Ross) M.; m. Byron C. Shearer, Nov. 3, 1946; 1 child, Mary Jane. RN, Rockford Meml. Hosp., Ill., 1944; BFA, U. Dayton, Ohio, 1968; MDiv, United Theol. Sem., Dayton, 1984, DMin, 1987. Ordained to ministry Ch. of the Brethren, 1987. Staff nurse, supr. Castaner (P.R.) Gen. Hosp., 1945-47; staff nurse, oper. rm. supr. Dettmer Hosp., Troy, Ohio, 1954-58; nursing instr. Miami Valley Hosp., Dayton, 1970-72; clergy So. Ohio Dist. Ch. of the Brethren, 1983—2003, clergy So. Ctrl. Ind. dist., 2003—; clergy So. Ohio Dist. Neighbors in Need, 1990—2003. Field edn. supervisor Bethany Theol. Sem., Richmond, Ind., 1994-2003; mem. issues caucus com. Ohio Coun. Chs., 1988-96. Author: Nuc Radiation and Cancer, 1981, poems; artist numerous paintings and drawings. Mem. nuclear study com. Ch. of Brethren, So. Ohio, 1978-92; bd. dirs. Ohio Environ. Coun., 1994-2000; mem. adv. bd. Ohio Coalition, 1995-01; petitioner to stop disposal of low-level radioactive wastes from other states in Ohio, 1995-97; mem. interfaith com. on global warming Ohio Coun. Chs., 1998—2001; fellowship of reconciliation rep., Historic Peace Ch. Commn., 2005-. Recipient Ann. Peace award Wright State U.; Ohio Humanities Coun. grantee, 1989-90. Mem. Internat. Assn. Women Mins., Nat. Coun. Fellowship Reconciliation. Home and Office: 1100 West 4th St #16 North Manchester IN 46962 Home Phone: 260-982-1351.

SHEARER, WILLIAM THOMAS, pediatrician, educator; b. Detroit, Aug. 23, 1937; BS, U. Detroit, 1960; PhD, Wayne State U., 1966; MD, Washington U., St. Louis, 1970. Diplomate Am. Bd. Pediat., Am. Bd. Allergy and Immunology (chmn. 1994-95, dir. 1990-95, chair nominations com., clin. immunology soc.), Nat. Bd. Med. Examiners, cert. in diagnostic lab. immunology. Post-doctoral fellow in biochemistry dept. chem. Indiana U., Bloomington, 1966—67; intern in pediat. St. Louis Children's Hosp., 1970—71, resident in immunology in pediat., 1971—72, dir. divsn. allergy and immunology, 1974—78; fellow in immunology in pediat. Barnes Hosp., Washington U., St. Louis, 1972—74; spl. USPHA sci. rsch. fellow in medicine dept. medicine Washington U., 1972—74, assoc. prof., 1978, prof., 1978; prof. pediat., microbiology, immunology Baylor Coll. Medicine, Houston, 1989—, dir. AIDS rsch. ctr., 1991—; head sect. allergy & immunology Tex. Children's Hosp., Houston, 1978—, med. dir. AIDS ctr. Mem. ACTU Cmty. Adv. Bd. Tex. Children's Hosp., Houston, 1991—; chmn. pediat. core com. pediat. AIDS clin. trial group Nat. Inst. Allergy and Infectious Diseases, NIH, Bethesda, Md., 1989—, ad hoc reviewer, 1991, mem. therapeutics subcom. AIDS rsch. adv. com., 1993—, chmn. pediat. AIDS clin. trial group immunology com., 1994—, mem. pediat. AIDS clin. trials group exec. Com., 1991—95, mem. spl. rev. com. persons affected by chronic granulomatous disease, 1992; site visitor Gen. Clin. Rsch. Ctr. NIH, Bethesda, Md., 1993, vice chmn. pediat. AIDS clin. trials group exec. com., 1996—; chmn. study populatoin/patient mgmt. com. Clin. Ctrs. for the Study of Pediat. Lung and Heart Complications of HIV Infection, Nat. Heart, Lung and Blood Inst., NIH, Bethesda, Md., 1989—, mem. AIDS ad hoc work group, 1991; dir. Pediat. HIV/AIDS Clin. Rsch. Ctr., Houston, 1988—; chmn. exec. com. clin. trial intravenous gammaglobulin in HIV infected children Nat. Inst. Child Health and Human Devel., Bethesda, 1989—; dir. Am. Bd. Allergy and Immunology, 1990—95, chair, 1994—95; vice-chair exec. com. Pediat. AIDS Clin. Trials Group, 1996—2001. Editor: Pediatric Asthma, Allergy, and Immunology, 1989—2001; editl. bd. Jour. Allergy and Clin. Immunology, 1993—, Clin. and Diagnostic Lab. Immunology, 1994—, editor Pediatric Allergy and Immunology, 1995—, Allergy and Immunology Tng. Program Dir.; assoc. editor: Jour. Allergy and Clin. Immunology, 2003—; guest editor Seminar Pediatric Infectious Disease, 1990, contbr. intro. Allergy: Princples and Practice, 1992, contbr. articles to profl. jours. including New Eng. Jour. Medicine. AIDS cons. Houston Ind. Sch. Dist., 1986—; med. adv. Spring Br. Ind. Sch. Dist., Houston, 1987—; chmn. cmty. HIV/AIDS adv. group Tex. Med. Ctr., 1991—. Recipient faculty rsch. award, Am. Cancer Soc., 1977—79, Myrtle Wreath award, Hadassah, 1985, spl. recognition award, Am. Acad. Allergy and Immunology, 1994; grantee NIH, 1988—; scholar rsch., Cystic Fibrosis Found., 1974—77. Mem.: Clin. Immunology Soc. (chair Am. Bd. Allergy and Immunology nominations com. 1994—96, pres. 2001—02), Am. Acad. Allergy, Asthma and Immunology (assoc. chmn. for planning of 1997-98 internat. meetings, profl. ednl. coun.), Am. Acad. Allergy and Immunology (chmn. clin. and lab. immunology com. 1994—96, chmn. tng. program dirs. nat. issues subcom. 1994—96), Tex. Allergy and Immunology Soc. (chmn. nat. issues com. 1992—96, pres. 1994—96), Tex. Allergy Soc. (exec. com. 1990—), Am. Acad. Pediat. (exec. com. sect. allergy and immunology 1991—), Am. Soc. Clin. Investigation. Achievements include research in half-matched T-cell-depleted bone marrow transplants; membrane signal pathway of human B lymphcytes. Office: Baylor Coll Med Allergy/Immun Clinic 6621 Fannin MC FC 330 01 Houston TX 77030-2600 E-mail: wshearer@bcm.tmc.edu.

SHEARING, MIRIAM, retired state supreme court chief justice; b. Waverly, NY, Feb. 24, 1935; BA, Cornell U., 1956; JD, Boston Coll., 1964. Bar: Calif. 1965, Nev. 1969. Justice of peace Las Vegas Justice Ct., 1977-81; judge Nev. Dist. Ct., 1983-92, chief judge, 1986; justice Nevada Supreme Ct., Carson City, 1993—2005, chief justice, 1997, 2004, sr. justice, 2005—. Mem. ABA, Am. Judicature Soc. (chair 2001-03), Nev. Judges Assn. (sec. 1978), Nev. Dist. Ct. Judges Assn. (sec. 1984-85, pres. 1986-87), State Bar Nev., State Bar Calif., Clark County Bar Assn. Democrat. Personal E-mail: shearing@nvcourts.state.nv.us.

SHEARMUR, ALLI, film company executive; m. Edward Shearmur; 1 child, Imogen. Grad., U. Pa.; JD, U.So. Calif. Law Ctr. V.p. Stewart Pictures; v.p. prodn. Walt Disney Pictures, 1994—97; exec. v.p. prodn. Universal Pictures, Paramount Pictures, co-pres. prodn., 2005—07; pres. motion picture prodn. Lionsgate, 2008—. Named one of The 100 Most Powerful Women in Entertainment, The Hollywood Reporter, 2006. Mem.: Calif. Bar Assn. Office: Lionsgate 2700 Colorado Ave Santa Monica CA 90404 Office Phone: 323-956-5000.

SHEATHER, SIMON JAMES, management educator; b. Melbourne, Victoria, Australia, Nov. 21, 1958; s. Kevin James and Margaret Millicent (O'Keefe) S. BSc, U. Melbourne, Victoria, Australia, 1981; PhD, LaTrobe U., Australia, 1986. Lectr. U. Melbourne, 1986-87, Australian Grad. Sch. Mgmt., U. NSW, 1987-88, sr. lectr., 1989-93, assoc. prof., 1994—, dir. MBA program, 1994—. Author: Robust Estimation and Testing, 1990; contbr. articles to profl. publs. Office: Texas A&M Univ Dept of Statistics 3143 College Station TX 77843-3143 Business E-Mail: sheather@tamu.edu.

SHEBEL, HEATHER A., editor; d. Jack Raymond and Martha Ann Heminger; m. Shebel John M., Oct. 10, 2001. BA in math., U. Chgo., 1996. Rsch. tech. U. Chgo. Hosp., 1996—2001; sr. manuscript editor Jour. AMA, Chgo., 2001—. Editor (copy editor): (cd-rom) Multimedia Textbook of Coronary Arteriography and Interventions, 1997; co-author: Journal of Hand Surgery, 2002 (Joseph H. Boyes award, 1998). Mem.: Coun. Sci. Editors (cert.). Office: Am Med Assn 515 N State St Chicago IL 60654

SHEBILSKE, WAYNE LAWRENCE, psychology professor, researcher; b. Appleton, Wis., Mar. 17, 1947; s. Lawrence and Eileen Shebilske; m. Joan Page, May 2, 1947; children: Lisa Koza, Laurie George, Michael Page, Ben Page. PhD, U. Wis., Madison, 1974. Prof. U. Va., Charlottesville, 1974—85, Tex. A&M U., Coll. Sta., 1985—99, Wright State U., Dayton, Ohio, 1999—; study dir. Nat. Acad. Sci., Washington, 1974—85. Author: (textbook) Psychology: Principles and Applications; contbr. scientific papers to rsch. publs. Office: Wright State Univ 3640 Colonel Glenn Hwy Dayton OH 45435-0001 Office Fax: 937-775-3347. Business E-Mail: wayne.shebilske@wright.edu.

SHEBITZ, DANIELA JOY, biology professor; married. PhD, U. Wash., Seattle, 2006. Asst. prof. Kean U., Union, NJ, 2006—. Faculty advisor Biology Club & Tri Beta Biol. Honor Soc., Union, 2006—; co-chair Sustainability Task Force, Inst. Urban Ecosystem Studies & Sustainability Program Devel. Com., Union, 2007—. Contbr. scientific papers to profl. jours. Mem. Cranford Environ. Commn., NJ, 2008—09. Mem.: Soc. Ethnobiology, Ecol. Soc. Am. Office: Kean Univ 1000 Morris Ave Union NJ 07083 Office Fax: 908-737-3666. Business E-Mail: dshebitz@kean.edu.

SHEBLE, BRIAN A., psychologist, consultant, educator; s. Barbara and David Sheble; m. Heather Tichy, July 19, 2003. BA in Edn., Lindenwood U., St. Charles, Mo., 1999, MA in Sch. and Profl. Counseling, 2003. Cert. sch. counselor Mo., sch. psychologist Mo., Ill., edn. specialist in sch. psychology Mo. Sch. psychologist intern Jefferson County Spl. Svcs. Coop., Hillsboro, Mo., 2005—06; sch. psychologist Belleville Area Spl. Svcs. Coop., Ill., 2006—. Rschr, presenter in field. Mem.: NASP, Ill. Assn. Sch. Psychologists, Mo. Assn. Sch. Psychologists (grad. rep. 2005—06, recipient intern scholarship 2005—06), Pi Gamma Mu, Kappa Delta Pi (v.p. 1999—2003, Chpt. Svc. award 2000—01). Home: 405 Caleb Pl Fenton MO 63026 Personal E-mail: bsheble2@yahoo.com. Business E-Mail: bsheble@stclair.k12il.us.

SHECTER, HOWARD LEE, lawyer; b. Boston, May 13, 1943; AB, Harvard U., 1965; JD, U. Pa., 1968. Bar: Pa. 1968, N.Y. 1996. Assoc. Morgan, Lewis & Bockius LLP, Phila., 1968-73, ptnr. NYC, 1973—2007, mng. ptnr., bus. and fin. practice group leader, 1979—84, chmn., 1985—86; ptnr. Orrick, Herrington & Sutcliffe LLP, NYC, 2007—, head M & A practise. Founder & former chmn. seminar series, Acquiring or Selling the Privately Held Company, Practicing Law Inst. Office: Orrick Herrington & Sutcliffe LLP 666 Fifth Ave New York NY 10103 Office Phone: 212-506-5155. E-mail: hshecter@orrick.com.

SHEDAKER, KATHLEEN EDITH, publishing executive; b. Boston, May 2, 1953; d. Richard Flave Shedaker and Jessica Mae Gould; m. Jon Patterson Speller Sr.; 1 child, Jon Patterson Speller Jr. AAS in Bus. Adminstrn., Monroe Coll., 2001, BBA in Bus. Mgmt., 2003. Rschr. Press Office Saudi Arabia, NYC, 1986-96, Bosniac Nat. Coun. of

Sanjak, NYC, 1996, Backster Rsch. Found., San Diego, 1985; pub. Morning Star Chapel & Press, NYC, 1986—; v.p. Robert Speller & Sons, Pubs., 2006—. Dir. microgenepools.com, NYC, 2000—; coord. Becky Barrymore Rsch. Project, 2005—; v.p. Robert Speller & Sons, Pubs., 2006—, exec. sec., Royalty Rsch. Ctr., 2007-. Author: The American Dynasty Database, 1998, The Classic Seed Money in Action, 2003, Psychic Cat Becky Barrymore, 2006; contbr. microgenepools rsch. monograph. Exec. dir. Anti-Communist Internat., NYC, 1985-; exec. sec. Royalty Rsch. Ctr., 2007. Recipient Cold War Victory medal Anti-Communist Internat., 2000. Mem.: NY Geneal. and Biog. Soc., Morning Star Chapel (co-founder, Interfaith award 1996). Avocations: genealogy, music, art, poetry. Business E-Mail: kshedaker@yahoo.com.

SHEDD, ARTHUR B., retired school system administrator; b. Sherbrooke, Que., Can., Sept. 19, 1920; s. Burton D. and Jennie Ellis Shedd; m. Patricia Truman Thompson, Nov. 25, 1943; children: Candace Vancko, Wendy Rivera, Arthur Jr. EdB, Keene Tchrs. Coll., NH, 1943; MA, Columbia U., NYC, 1947, EdD, 1950. Cert. adminstr. NH, NY, tchr. NH. Tchr. Bergenfield HS, NJ, 1946—48; dir. NH secondary sch. svcs. NH Dept. Edn., Concord, 1949—51; HS prin. Scotia-Glenville Sch. Dist., NY, 1951—54; prin. Bedford Ctr. Dist., Mt. Kisco, 1954—61; supt. schs. Clarence Ctrl. Schs., 1961—63, North Shore Schs., Sea Cliff, NY, 1963—69, Cortland City Schs., NY, 1969—80; adj. prof. edn. SUNY, Cortland, 1984—2005; ret., 2005. Mem. commr.'s adv. bd. NY State Dept. Edn., Albany, 1961—64; pres. Syracuse Sch. Study Coun. Syracuse U., 1972—74. Pres. CAPCO Opportunities for Cortland, 1969—72; bd. dirs. Cortland Boy Scouts, 1972—76; pres. bd. dirs. YMCA, 1976—78. Lt. j.g. USNR, 1943—46. Mem.: Am. Assn. Sch. Adminstrs. (licentiate). Avocations: fly fishing, skiing. Home Phone: 860-426-0038.

SHEDD, DAVID R., federal official; BA, Geneva Coll., Beaver Falls, Pa.; MA in Latin Am. Studies, Georgetown U. Sch. Fgn. Svc., Washington. Fgn. svc. post US Embassy, Costa Rica, Mex., 1984—93; various sr. mgmt. assignments including chief Congl. liaison CIA; intelligence policy positions Nat. Security Coun., Washington, 2001—05, spl. asst. to the Pres., sr. dir. intelligence programs and reform; chief of staff, acting dir. intelligence staff to the dir. nat. intelligence Office the Dir. Nat, Intelligence, Washington, 2005—07, dep. dir. nat. intelligence policy, plans, and requirements, 2007—. Office: Office the Dir Nat Intelligence Washington DC 20511*

SHEDD, DENNIS W., federal judge; b. Cordova, SC, Jan. 28, 1953; BA, Wofford Coll., 1975; JD, U. SC, 1978; LLM, Georgetown U., 1980. Bar: SC. Law clerk Harry Dent & Assoc., 1977—78; admin. asst. US Senator Strom Thurmond, 1978—88; chief counsel US Senate Jud. Com., Washington, 1985-86; of counsel Bethea, Jordan & Griffin, Columbia, S.C., 1988-90; pvt. practice, 1989-90; judge US Dist. Ct. SC, Greenville, 1990—2002, US Ct. Appeals (4th cir.), 2002—. Adj. prof. U. SC, 1989-92. Mem. SC Bar Assn., Richland County Bar Assn., Phi Beta Kappa. Office: US Courthouse 1100 Laurel St Columbia SC 29201-2431

SHEDD, DONALD POMROY, surgeon; b. New Haven, Aug. 4, 1922; s. Gale and Marion (Young) S.; m. Charlotte Newsom, Mar. 17, 1946 (dec. Apr. 28, 2007); children: Carolyn, David, Ann, Laura BS, Yale U., New Haven, Conn., 1944, MD, 1946. Diplomate Am. Bd. Surgery. Intern Yale New Haven Hosp., 1946-47, asst. resident, resident, 1949-53; instr. surgery Yale U. Med Sch., New Haven, 1953-54, asst. prof., 1954-56, assoc. prof., 1956-67; chief dept. head and neck surgery Roswell Park Cancer Inst., Buffalo, 1967-96, prof. emeritus, 1996—; rsch. prof. emeritus SUNY at Buffalo, 1996—. Co-editor: Surgical and Prosthetic Speech Rehabilitation, 1980, Head and Neck Cancer, 1985, (with Prof. Abel Fink) The Early History of Hospice Buffalo, 2003; author: Historical Landmarks in Head and Neck Cancer Surgery, 2000; contbr. numerous articles to profl. jours. Founding bd. dirs. Hospice Buffalo, Inc., 1973—83. Capt. US Army, 1947—49. Mem. Am. Head and Neck Soc., Soc. Univ. Surgeons, Soc. Surg. Oncology, New Eng. Surg. Soc., Soc. Head and Neck Surgeons (pres. 1976-77). Avocations: sailing, windsurfing, tennis, history of medicine.

SHEDLIN, GARY STEPHEN, investment banker; b. Nov. 8, 1963; s. Victor and Susan S.; m. Deborah Rae Winograd, Mar. 23, 1991. Grad. summa cum laude, Colgate Univ.; MBA, Harvard Univ. Assoc. to ptnr. Lazard Freres & Co. LLC, NYC, mng. dir., 1997—2004; mng. dir., co-head global fin. institutions Citigroup Inc., NYC, 2004—08, chmn. Fin. Institutions Group (FIG), 2008—. Recipient Rainmaker prize, fin. sector, Dealmaker mag., 2006. Mem.: Phi Beta Kappa. Office: Citigroup Inc 399 Park Ave New York NY 10043 Office Phone: 212-559-1000. Office Fax: 212-793-3946.

SHEDRINSKY, ALEXANDER MIKCHAIL, chemistry professor, conservator, consultant; b. Leningrad, USSR, Mar. 27, 1943; arrived in USA, 1980. s. Mikchail Alexander Shedrinsky and Mussa A. (Gordon) Tsipkina; m. Raissa A. (Bekker), Oct. 16, 1965 (div. Apr. 1975); one child, Mikchail Alexander; m. Maria G. (Kurbatova), June 30, 1982; one child, Maria Antonia. MS in Chemistry, Leningrad U., 1965; MS in Organic Chemistry, N.Y. Univ., 1983, PhD in Organic Chemistry, 1986. Rsch. asst. State Sci. Rsch. Inst. Pulp and Paper, Leningrad, 1971—72; asst. prof. chemistry Leningrad N.W. Poly. Tech., 1972—75, LI Univ., Bklyn., 1988—92; lectr. in organic chemistry Leningrad Pharm. Sch., 1976—79; tchg. fellow NY Univ., NYC, 1981—83, postdoctoral fellow Conservation Ctr. Inst. Fine Arts, 1986—88; assoc. prof. chemistry LI Univ., Bklyn., 1992—97; adj. assoc. prof. Conservation Ctr. Inst. Fine Arts NY Univ., NYC, 1993—97; cons. Met. Mus. Art, NYC, 1994—; prof. chemistry LI Univ., Bklyn., 1997—; adj. prof. Conservation Ctr. Inst. Fine Arts NY Univ., NYC, 1998—99; cons. internat. coun. Mus. Modern Art, 2001—. Vis. scientist Am. Mus. Natural History, NYC, 1995—; vis. prof. Forchheimer, 1997, Hebrew U. Jerusalem; Fulbright prof. USIA, St. Petersburg (Russia) Acad. Art, 1995, 2001-02. Contbr. chpt. to book, articles to internat. scientific journals; reviewer, Jour. Analytical and Applied Pyrolysis, Curator, Archeometry, 1989—. Andrew W. Mellon Fellow Met. Mus. Art, Dept. Object Conservation, 1988-90, Charles and Francis Atkins Fellow Met. Mus. Art, Dept. Paintings Conservation, 1984-86. Mem. Am. Chem. Soc. (tour spkr.) Washington,1992-, Internat. Inst. Conservation, NY Acad. Sci. Achievements include synthesis of new synthetic varnish for the purpose of painting conservation; introducing analytical pyrolysis in the field of art conservation (first rev. on the subject in 1989); devel. of new analytical approach (Py-GC and Py-GC-MS) to analysis of different ambers. Office: LIU 1 Univ Plz Brooklyn NY 11201-5301 Office Phone: 718-488-1208. Personal E-mail: alexandershedrinsky43@gmail.com.

SHEDROFF, SHARON D., psychologist, anthropologist, researcher, consultant; b. Middletown, Conn. d. Leon and Sylvia Shedroff. BA summa cum laude, Syracuse U., NYC, 1974; MA, Calif. Sch. Profl. Psychology, San Diego, 1979. Lic. marriage, family and child counselor Calif., 1981. Psychology intern T.R.I. Cmty. Svcs., San Diego, 1978—81, marriage, family & child counselor, 1981—82; rsch. psychologist Grid Rsch., San Diego, 1983—85; founder, ptnr. Edwards Assocs., San Diego, 1985—, Strategic Vision Inc., San Diego, 1989—, Inst. for Value-Centered Life, San Diego, 1999—. Author: (novels) Dakota Dreams, 2003; contbr. articles to profl. jours. Mem.: Am. Morgan Horse Assn., U.S.A. Equestrian. Avocations: skiing, competitive horseback riding. Home: PO Box 420036 San Diego CA 92142 Office: The Edwards Assocs PO Box 420429 San Diego CA 92142 Office Phone: 858-576-7141.

SHEEAN, PATRICIA M., nutritionist, educator; BA in Nutrition & Dietetics, U. Ariz., 1992; MA in Nutrition, U. Ill., Chgo., 1999, PhD in Nutrition Epidemiology, 2005. Prof. dept. preventive medicine Feinberg Sch. Medicine Northwestern U., 2005—. Rsch. editor Jour. Am. Dietetic Assn. Mem.: Am. Soc. for Parenteral & Enteral Nutrition, Am. Dietetic Assn. Office: Northwestern University Dept of Preventive Medicine 680 N Lake Shore Dr Ste 1102 Chicago IL 60611 Office Phone: 312-503-3438. E-mail: p-sheean@northwestern.edu.*

SHEEDER, ROBERT ELWOOD, lawyer; b. Ind., Pa., Apr. 8, 1951; s. Elwood B. and Alice (Poole) Sheeder; m. Martha Ann Painter. BA with high honors, U. Va., 1973; JD cum laude, U. Mich., 1976. Bar: Tex. 1976, Pa. 1978, US Dist. Ct. We. Dist. Pa. 1980, US Ct. Appeals 3rd Cir. 1981, US Dist. Ct. No. Dist. Tex. 1985, US Dist. Ct. Ea. Dist. Tex. 1986, US Ct. Appeals 5th Cir. 1988, US Dist. Ct. So. Dist. Tex. 1989, US Dist. Ct. We. Dist. Tex. 1991, US Supreme Ct. 1996. Assoc. Reed, Smith, Shaw & McClay, Pitts., 1977-84; ptnr. Winstead, McGuire, Sechrest & Minick, Dallas, 1984-92; shareholder Jenkens & Gilchrist, P.C., Dallas, 1992—2007, Bracewell & Guiliani, Dallas, 2007—. Lectr. labor law So. Meth. U., 1988-90. Editor-in-chief: Tex. Labor Letter, 1994-01. Fellow: Coll. Labor and Employment Lawyers; mem.: ABA, Dallas Bar Assn., Tex. State Bar Assn. (governing coun. labor & employment law sect. 2002—04, Best Lawyers in Am. 2001—), Chambers USA. Republican. Presbyterian. Office Phone: 214-758-1643. Business E-Mail: roebrt.sheeder@bgllp.com.

SHEEHAN, CHARLES VINCENT, investment banker; b. London, Dec. 19, 1930; came to U.S., 1931; s. Charles Vincent and Mary Margaret (Stokes) S.; m. Susan Ellen Rosar, May 5, 1962. BS, Georgetown U., 1952. Chief fin. officer Gen. Electric Co., Tokyo, Sydney, Australia and Sao Paulo, Brazil, 1962-64, 64-66, 67-71, staff exec. Fairfield, Conn., 1972-83, v.p. corp. exec. office, 1983-87; sr. v.p., chief fin., adminstrn. officer Kidder, Peabody Group, Inc., NYC, 1987-90. Bd. dirs. Fleet Trust Co., Highlands-Cashiers Hosp.; chmn. bd. dirs. Indian River Meml. Hosp. Chmn. Non-partisan Polit. Action Com. for Gen. Electric Co. employees, Fairfield, 1982-83. Served to lt. USN, 1952-54. Mem. Johns Island Club (Vero Beach, Fla.), Quail Valley Golf Club (Vero Beach, Fla.), Wildcat Cliffs Country Club (Highlands, N.C.) (pres. 1998-99). Republican. Roman Catholic. Avocations: golf, boating. Home (Winter): 560 Whiteside Mountain Rd Highlands NC 28741-7361 E-mail: gecharlie@earthlink.net.

SHEEHAN, DEBORAH HARDICK, lawyer; b. Glens Falls, NY, July 11, 1961; d. Frank Clark and Jean Ogden Hardick; m. John Francis Sheehan, Nov. 5, 1994; 1 child, Hannah Elizabeth. BA cum laude, Coll. New Rochelle, NY, 1983; JD, Union U. Albany Law Sch., NY, 1986. Bar: NY 1987, US Supreme Ct. 2003. Lawyer Duggan Crotty & Dunn, P.C., New Windsor, NY, 1987—88, Law Office of Paul M. Whitaker, Albany, 1988—98; sole practice Albany, 1998—. Pro bono atty. The Legal Project, Inc., Albany, 1993—; mem. Harriet Tubman March 10 Coalition, Albany, 2000—03; mem., cookie coord. Girl Scouts USA Troop 593, Albany, 2003—; bd. dirs. The Women's Bldg., Inc., Albany, 1998—2003. Recipient Pro Bono award, The Legal Project, Inc., 1994—95. Mem.: Exec. Women's Golf Assn. Democrat. Methodist. Home and Office: 20 W Meadow Dr Albany NY 12203 Office Phone: 518-456-5644. Fax: 518-456-4512. E-mail: deblawofc@aol.com.

SHEEHAN, GREGORY D., lawyer; AB magna cum laude, Harvard U., 1977; JD, U. Calif., Berkeley, 1980. Bar: Mass. 1980, Calif. 1981. Law clk. Judge Walter J. Skinner, US Dist Ct. (Mass.), 1980—81; ptnr. corp. dept. & chmn. investment mgmt. practice group Ropes & Gray, Boston. Editor (exec.): Calif. Law Rev. Pres. French-Am. C. of C. of New England, 1993—95. Mem.: Phi Beta Kappa, Order of the Coif. Office: Ropes & Gray 1 International Pl Boston MA 02110-2624 Office Phone: 617-951-7621. Office Fax: 617-951-7050. Business E-Mail: gsheehan@ropesgray.com.

SHEEHAN, JAMES JOHN, historian, educator; b. San Francisco, May 31, 1937; s. James B. and Sally W. (Walsh) S.; m. 1960; 1 child, Michael L.; m. Margaret L. Anderson, Sept. 2, 1989. BA, Stanford U., 1958; MA, U. Calif., Berkeley, 1959, PhD, 1964. From asst. to assoc. prof. Northwestern U., Evanston, Ill., 1964-79; prof. Stanford (Calif.) U., 1979-86, chmn. dept., 1982-89, Dickason prof. in humanities, 1986—. Author: Lujo Brentano, 1966, German Liberalism, 1978, German History 1770-1866, 1989, Der Ausklang des alten Reiches, 1994, Museums in German Artworld, 2000; editor: The Boundaries of Humanity, 1991; contbr. articles to profl. jours. Decorated officer's cross Order of Merit; fellow Am. Coun. Learned Socs., 1981-82, NEH, 1985-86, Wissenschaftskolleg Berlin; Guggenheim fellow, 2000—. Fellow AAAS (Humboldt Rsch. prize 1995), Am. Acad. Berlin; mem. Royal Hist. Soc. (corr.), Am. Hist. Assn. (nominating com. 1979-81, chmn. conf. group on Ctrl. European history 1985-86, pres. 2005), Am. Philos. Soc. (Orden pour le Mérite). Office: Stanford U Dept History Stanford CA 94305 Home Phone: 510-649-8910. Business E-Mail: sheehan@stanford.edu.

SHEEHAN, JOHN D., automotive executive; b. Trumbull, Conn. BBA in Acctg., St. Bonaventure U., NY. CPA. Chief acctg. officer, contr. Delphi Corp., Troy, Mich., 2002—, acting CFO, 2005, chief acctg. officer, chief restructuring officer, contr., 2005—08, v.p., CFO, 2008—. Mem.: Am. Inst. Cert. Pub. Accts. Office: Delphi Corp World Headquarters 5725 Delphi Dr Troy MI 48098-2815*

SHEEHAN, LAWRENCE JAMES, lawyer; b. San Francisco, July 23, 1932; AB, Stanford U., 1957, LLB, 1959. Bar: Calif. 1960. Law clk. to chief judge U.S. Ct. Appeals 2d Cir., NYC, 1959-60; assoc. O'Melveny & Myers, LA, 1960-68, ptnr., 1969-94, of counsel, 1995—2004. D. dirs. FPA Mut. Funds, Source Capital, Inc. Mem. ABA, Los Angeles County Bar Assn., Calif. Bar Assn., Order of Coif. Office: O Melveny & Myers 1999 Avenue Of The Stars Los Angeles CA 90067-6035 also: 400 S Hope St Los Angeles CA 90071-2801 Office Phone: 310-246-6895. Business E-Mail: lsheehan@omm.com.

SHEEHAN, MICHAEL ANDREW, former protective services official, former federal agency administrator; b. Red Bank, NJ, Feb. 10, 1955; s. John M. and Janet M. (Purcell) S.; m. Sita Sheehan; children: Alexandra, Michael BS, US Mil. Acad., 1977; MS in Fgn. Svc., Georgetown U., 1988. Commd. 2d lt. U.S. Army, 1977-97, advanced through grades to lt. col., ret., 1997; intelligence analyst The White House, Washington, 1989-91; dir. internat. programs NSC, Washington, 1992-93, dir. global issues, 1995-97; dir. POLMIL affairs U.S. Mission to UN, NYC, 1993-95; dept. asst. sec. for internat. org. affairs US Dept. State, Washington, 1997-98, coord. for counter terrorism, 1998-2000; asst. sec. gen. Dept. Peacekeeping Ops. UN, NYC, 2001—03; dep. commr. counter-terrorism NY Police Dept., NYC, 2003—06; Disting. Fellow, Ctr. for Law & Security NYU Sch. Law, NYC, 2006—. Mem.: Coun. on Fgn. Rels., Spl. Forces Assn. Roman Catholic. Office: NYU Sch Law 110 W 3rd St Ste 224/5 New York NY 10012

SHEEHAN, MICHAEL JARBOE, archbishop; b. Wichita, Kans., July 9, 1939; s. John Edward and Mildred (Jarboe) Sheehan. MST, Gregorian U., Rome, 1965; D in Canon Law, Lateran U., Rome, 1971. Ordained priest Diocese of Dallas-Ft. Worth, 1964; asst. gen. sec. Nat. Coun. Cath. Bishops, Washington, 1971—76; rector Holy Trinity Sem., Dallas, 1976—82; pastor Immaculate Conception Ch., Grand Prairie, Tex., 1982—83; ordained bishop, 1983; bishop Diocese of Lubbock, Tex., 1983—93; archbishop Archdiocese of Santa Fe, N.Mex., 1993—; apostolic adminstr. Diocese of Phoenix, 2003. Bd. dirs. Tex. Conf. of Chs.; past chmn. Am. Bd. Cath. Missions, 1989—91. Contbr. articles to profl. jours. Trustee St. Mary Hosp., Lubbock, Tex., 1983—89, Cath. Relief Svcs., 1992—. Mem.: Serra Club (chaplain 1983—93, chmn. NCCB com. on Evangelization 1996—99, NCCB adminstv. com. Washington). Roman Catholic. Avocations: skiing, racquetball. Office: Archdiocese Santa Fe 4000 Saint Josephs Pl NW Albuquerque NM 87120-1714

SHEEHAN, NEIL, reporter, writer; b. Holyoke, Mass., Oct. 27, 1936; s. Cornelius Joseph and Mary (O'Shea) Sheehan; m. Susan Margulies, Mar. 30, 1965; children: Maria Gregory, Catherine Fair. AB cum laude, Harvard, 1958; LittD (hon.), Columbia Coll., Chgo., 1972; LHD (hon.), Am. Internat. Coll., 1990, U. Lowell, 1991. Vietnam bur. chief UPI, Saigon, 1962—64; reporter N.Y. Times, NYC, Djakarta, Saigon, Washington, 1964—72. Author: The Arnheiter Affair, 1972, A Bright Shining Lie: John Paul Vann and America in Vietnam, 1988 (Nat. Book award, 1988, Pulitzer Prize for gen. non-fiction, 1989, Robert F. Kennedy Book award, 1989, Vetty award Vietnam Vets. Ensemble Theatre Co., 1989, Spl. Achievement award Vietnam Vets. Am., 1989, Outstanding Investigative Reporting award Investigative Reporters and Editors Inc. of U. Mo. Sch. Journalism, 1989, Amb. award English Speaking Union, 1989, John F. Kennedy award Holyoke, Mass., 1989, selected by Modern Libr. as one of the 100 best works of non-fiction of the 20th century 1999), After the War Was Over: Hanoi and Saigon, 1992; contbr. articles and book revs. for popular mags., The Pentagon Papers, 1971. With US Army, 1959—62. Recipient Louis M. Lyons award for conscience and integrity in journalism, 1964, Silver medal, Poor Richard Club, Phila., 1964, Cert. of Appreciation for best article on Asia, Overseas Press Club Am., 1967, 1st Ann. Drew Pearson prize for excellence in investigative reporting, 1971, Columbia Journalism award, 1972, 1989, Sidney Hillman Found. awards, 1972, 1988, Page One award, Newspaper Guild N.Y., 1972, Disting. Svc. award and Bronze medallion, Sigma Delta Chi, 1972, Citation of Excellence, Overseas Press Club, 1972, Lit. Lion award, N.Y. Pub. Libr., 1992; Guggenheim fellow, 1973—74, Adlai Stevenson fellow, 1973—75, Lehrman Inst. fellow, 1975—76, Rockefeller Found. fellow in humanities, 1976—77, Woodrow Wilson Internat. Ctr. for Scholars fellow, 1979—80. Mem.: Am. Acad. Achievement, Soc. Am. Historians, Lansdowne Club (London). Achievements include obtaining Pentagon Papers, 1971. Home and Office: 4505 Klingle St NW Washington DC 20016-3580 Office Phone: 202-363-3433.

SHEEHAN, ROBERT C., lawyer; b. NYC, Oct. 12, 1944; s. John Edward and Mary Elizabeth (Trede) Sheehan; m. Elizabeth Mary Mammen, Aug. 17, 1968; children: Elizabeth, Robert, William. BA, Boston Coll., 1966; LLB, Univ. Pa., Phila., 1969. Bar: NY 1970. Joined Skadden, Arps, Slate, Meagher & Flom LLP, 1969, ptnr. NYC, 1978—94, exec. ptnr., 1994—2009. Head, founder, Financial Institutions Merger & Acquisition Group Skadden, Arps, Slate, Meagher & Flom LLP; counsel for fin. institutions in connection with their rels. with various state and fed. banking regulatory authorities; bd. dir. Lawyers' Com. for Civil Rights Under Law; co-chair, Law Firm Pro Bono Project Pro Bono Inst. Mem. bd. overseers U. Pa. Law Sch.; bd. dir. Harlem RBI; bd. dir., vol. Legal Svc., Inc. Mem.: Assn. of the Bar of City of NY. Office: Skadden Arps Slate Meagher Flom LLP 4 Times Sq New York NY 10036-6595 Office Phone: 212-735-3350. Office Fax: 212-735-2000, 917-777-3350. Business E-Mail: rsheehan@skadden.com.

SHEEHAN, ROBERT JAMES, II, retired management and market research consultant; b. Pitts., May 13, 1937; s. Regis James and Helen Lillian (O'Leary) S.; m. Marie Elizabeth Yoskovich, Apr. 24, 1964; children: Stephanie Ann, Robert James III. AB in Econs., U. Pitts., 1967, MA, 1970; postgrad., Am. U. Cert. mgmt. cons. Rsch. analyst Action Housing Inc., Pitts., 1960-63; from project rep. to dir. rehab. Urban Redevel. Authority Pitts., 1963-73; assoc. chief economist, dir. econ. rsch. Nat. Assn. Homebuilders, Washington, 1973-82, v.p econ. policy analysis, 1982-83; v.p. Regis J. Sheehan & Assocs., McLean, Va., 1983-96, pres., 1997—2008. Founding dir. Georgetown Cons., Inc., 1993—; vice-chmn. Fairfax County Housing and Redevel. Authority, 1988-92, chmn. 1993-95. cons. in field. Author: The Basics of Land Acquisition, 1985; co-pub., prin. contbr. Mgmt./Econs. & Constrn. Real Estate newsletters; contbr. articles to profl. jours. Pres. bd. dirs. Touchstone Theatre Co., 1984-2003; pres. Caths. for Housing, 1998-2003; founding mem. Superior Bus. Roundtable. Mem. Nat. Economists Club, Inst. Mgmt. Cons. (pres. Washington chpt. 1989-96), Nat. Assn. Bus. Econs., KC. Roman Catholic. Avocations: walking, jogging, reading. Personal E-mail: rjscmc@comcast.net.

SHEEHAN, SUSAN, writer; b. Vienna, Aug. 24, 1937; arrived in U.S., 1941, naturalized, 1946; d. Charles and Kitty C. (Herrmann) Sachsel; m. Neil Sheehan, Mar. 30, 1965; children: Maria Gregory, Catherine Fair. BA, Wellesley Coll., Mass., 1958; DHL (hon.), U. Lowell, Mass., 1991. Editl. rschr. Esquire-Coronet, NYC, 1959-60; freelance writer NYC, 1960-61; staff writer New Yorker mag., NYC, 1961—; contbg. writer Archtl. Digest, 1997—. Writer-in-residence, lectr. Georgetown U., 1999. Author: Ten Vietnamese, 1967, A Welfare Mother, 1976, A Prison and a Prisoner, 1978, Is There No Place on Earth for Me?, 1982, Kate Quinton's Days, 1984, A Missing Plane, 1986, Life For Me Ain't Been No Crystal Stair, 1993, The Banana Sculptor, the Purple Lady, and the All-Night Swimmer, 2002; contbr. articles to various mags., including N.Y. Times Sunday Mag., Washington Post Sunday Mag., Harper's, Atlantic, New Republic, McCall's, Holiday, Boston Globe Sunday Mag., Life. Mem. lit. panel DC Commn. on Arts and Humanities, 1979-84; mem. pub. info. and edn. com. Nat. Mental Health Assn., 1982-83; mem. adv. com. on employment and crime Vera Inst. Justice, 1978-86; chair Pulitzer Prize nominating jury in gen. non-fiction for 1988, 1994, mem., 1991; juror Parkman Prize Com., Soc. Am. Historians, 2008; bd. dirs. Brides Against Breast Cancer, 2006—. Recipient Sidney Hillman Found. award, 1976, Gavel award ABA, 1978, Individual Reporting award Nat. Mental Health Assn., 1981, Pulitzer prize for gen. non-fiction, 1983, Judge Robert F. Kennedy Journalism awards, 1980, 84, Feature Writing award NY Press Club, 1984, NY Pub. Libr. Lit. award, 1992, Alumnae Assn. Achievement award Wellesley Coll., 1984, Carroll Kowal Journalism award NASW, 1993, Disting. Grad. award Hunter Coll. H.S., 1995, Pub. Awareness award Nat. Alliance for Mentally Ill, 1995, Casey medal for meritorious journalism, 1997; Durant scholar Wellesley Coll., 1958; fellow Guggenheim Found., 1975-76, Woodrow Wilson Internat.

Ctr. for Scholars, 1981, Open Soc. Inst., 1998-99. Mem.: Soc. Am. Historians, Authors Guild, Lansdowne Club (London), Phi Beta Kappa. Home: 4505 Klingle St NW Washington DC 20016-3580 Office: New Yorker Mag 4 Times Sq New York NY 10036-7441

SHEEHAN, TIMOTHY J., lawyer; b. Beacon, NY, Apr. 28, 1959; BA magna cum laude, SUNY, Buffalo, 1981; JD, U. Buffalo, 1984. Bar: NY 1985, US Dist. Ct. Ea. Dist. NY, US Dist. Ct. So. Dist. NY. Ptnr. Wilson, Elser, Moskowitz, Edelman & Dicker LLP, White Plains, NYC. Mem.: NY State Med. Malpractice Def. Bar, NY State Bar Assn., Westchester County Bar Assn. Office: Wilson Elser Moskowitz Edelman & Dicker LLP 3 Gannett Dr White Plains NY 10604 Office Phone: 914-323-7000 ext. 4243. Office Fax: 914-323-7001. Business E-Mail: sheehant@wemed.com, timothy.sheehan@wilsonelser.com.

SHEEHAN, WILLIAM PATRICK, psychiatrist, astronomer; b. Mpls., June 18, 1954; s. Bernard Leroy and Minnie Joyce Sheehan; m. Deborah Ann Nelson; children: Brendan Patrick, Ryan William. BA, U. Minn., Mpls., 1977; AM, U. Chgo., 1978; MD, U. Minn. Med. Sch., 1987. Diplomate Am. Bd. Neurology and Psychiatry. Med. dir. Woodlands Cmty. Mental Health Ctr., Willmar, Minn., 1993—98; head divsn. psychiatry Dept. Neurosci., U. ND, Fargo, 1998—99; cons. psychiatrist Kensington Ctr., Timaru, New Zealand, 1999—2000; psychiat. cons. Putting All Cmtys. Together Families, Willmar, 2000—04; psychiatrist Rice Meml. Hosp., Willmar, 2004—06, Child and Adolescent Behavioral Health Svc., Willmar; co-founder Geneva Med. Imaging, Lake Geneva, Wis., med. dir. Cons. Dept. Vets. Affairs, Mpls. Author: (book) Planets and Perception (Book of Yr., Astron. Soc. Pacific, 1988), Worlds in the Sky, 1992, The Immortal Fire Within: the life and work of Edward Emerson Barnard, 1995, The Planet Mars, 1996, In Search of Planet Vulcan, 1997, Epic Moon, 2001, Mars: the lure of the red planet, 2001, Transits of Venus, 2004, A Passion for Planete, 2009. Mem., planning com. Minn. Brain Injury Assn. Recipient Gold medal, Oriental Astron. Assn., 2004, Career Svc. award, Minn. Brain Injury Assn., 2007. Fellow: John Simon Guggenheim Meml. Found., Royal Astron. Soc. Can. (hon.). Achievements include patents pending for infrared brain imaging technology; use of functional brain imaging (SPECT) in psychiatry; research in low cholesterol and violence, structure and evolution of the Milky Way, also in perception and planetary observation. Avocations: running, painting, photography, travel. Office: Steehan Neurosci 1700 Technology Dr NE Willmar MN 56201

SHEEHEY, PATRICIA ANN, secondary school educator; b. Des Moines, Sept. 25, 1946; d. James Michael Sheehey and Elizabeth Ann Markunas; m. William Elwin McConnell, June 24, 1978 (dec. Aug. 1999). BA English, Marycrest Coll., Davenport, Iowa, 1968; MA English, We. Ill. U., 1970; postgrad., U. Iowa, 1971—2000, U. London, 1971. Instr. West H.S., Davenport, 1969—, head dept. lang. arts, 1998—. Mem. alumni bd. Marycrest Coll., Davenport, 1980—84. Recipient Golden Apple Outstanding Tchr. award, Scott County, 1980. Mem.: NEA, Iowa State Edn. Assn., Davenport Edn. Assn., Nat. Coun. Tchrs. English (regional judge), Alpha Delta Kappa (sec., treas., pres. 1978—82, scholarship chair 1983—86, state bylaws chair 2004—, internat. bylaws com. 2006—). Roman Catholic. Avocations: writing, antiques, reading. Home: 5 Birchwood Dr Blue Grass IA 52726 Office: West High Sch 3505 W Locust Davenport IA 52804 Personal E-mail: sheeheyp@aol.com.

SHEEHY, BETTY JO, real estate company executive, investment advisor; b. Baileysville, W.Va., Oct. 1, 1936; d. Virgil and Virginia Graham Lester; m. John D. Sheehy, Sept. 21, 1963 (div. 1976); children: John, Peter, Barbara. Student, Marshall U., 1956; lic. in real estate, Southampton Coll., 2002. Fin. cons. Merrill Lynch, Short Hills, NJ, 1984—90; fin. adv., assoc. v.p. Morgan Stanley, Southampton, NY, 1991—2002; owner, broker Betty Jo Sheehy Real Estate, Southampton, 2002—; v.p. investments Newbridge Securities, West Palm Beach, Fla., 2006—. Chpt. pres. NJ Symphony Women League, Short Hills, 1977—81; vol. Red Cross of the Oranges, NJ, 1970; benefactor Parish Art Mus., Southampton, 1999—. Recipient Leadership Devel. award, Merrill Lynch, 1985—86; named Bus. Woman of Yr., Nat. Congressional Com., 2006. Avocations: golf, music, reading, running. Home: 39 County Rd 39 Southampton NY 11968 Office Phone: 516-318-5647. Personal E-mail: bettyjosheehy@gmail.com.

SHEEHY, RICK, Lieutenant Governor of Nebraska, former mayor; b. Hastings, Nebr., Oct. 3, 1959; m. Connie Sheehy; children: Maggie, Joel. Attended, Ctrl. CC, U. Nebr.-Lincoln. City coun. mem. City of Hastings, Nebr., 1994—2005, mayor, 2000—05; lt. gov. State of Nebr., Lincoln, 2005—. Market gen. mgr., paramedic Rural/Metro Ambulance, 1982—. Exec. com. mem. Cottonwood Festival; mem. Nebr. State Trauma Adv. Bd., Mary Lanning Hosp. Found. Bd., Crane Meadows Bd. Dirs., Nebr. Rural Health Assn. Mem.: Hastings C. of C. (former chair), Hastings Noon Rotary, Hastings Sertoma Club (past pres.). Republican. Office: Lt Gov State Capitol, Rm 2315 PO Box 94863 Lincoln NE 68509-4863 Office Phone: 402-471-2256. Office Fax: 402-471-6031.

SHEEKEY, KEVIN J., city official; b. June 12, 1966; s. Arthur and Kathleen Sheekey; m. Robin Sheekey; children: Dillon Arthur, Samantha Ryan. Grad., Washington U., St. Louis. Chief of staff to Rep. James H. Scheuer; scheduler for Senator Daniel Patrick Moynihan, 1992—94, dep. campaign mgr., 1994—96, chief of staff, 1996—97; chief lobbyist Bloomberg LP, 1997; spl. adv. to Mayor Michael Bloomberg NYC, 2002; pres. NYC Host Com. for 2004 Rep. Nat. Convention, 2003—04; campaign mgr. Bloomberg for Mayor, 2005; dep. mayor for govt. affairs NYC, 2006—. Named one of Esquire 100, 2007. Office: City Hall 52 Chambers St New York NY 10007-1222*

SHEELER, JIM, journalist, educator; b. Houston, 1969; m. Annick Sheeler; 1 child, James. BA in Journalism, Colo. State U., 1990; MA in Journalism, U. Colo. With Boulder Daily Camera, Colo., 1991—96; sr. staff writer Boulder Planet, 1996—2000; freelance writer Denver Post, 1999—2003; staff writer Rocky Mountain News, Denver, 2004—; scholar-in-residence U. Colo. Sch. Journalism & Mass Comm., Boulder. Author: Obit, 2007, Final Salute, 2008; contbr. Best Newspaper Writing 2006-2007, Life on the Death Beat. Recipient Pulitzer prize for feature writing, 2006. Office: Rocky Mountain News 101 W Colfax Ave # 500 Denver CO 80202-5315 Office Phone: 303-892-2561, 303-868-2386. Office Fax: 303-892-2841. Personal E-mail: jsheeler@mac.com. Business E-Mail: sheelerj@rockymountainnews.com.

SHEEN, CHARLIE (CARLOS IRWIN ESTEVEZ), actor; b. NYC, Sept. 3, 1965; s. Ramon (Martin Sheen) and Janet Estevez; m. Donna Peele, Sept. 3, 1995 (div. Nov. 19, 1996); m. Denise Richards, June 15, 2002 (div. Nov. 17, 2006); children: Sam, Lola Rose; m. Brooke Mueller, May 31, 2008; children: Max, Bob; 1 child, Cassandra Jade Estevez (with Paula Profit). Actor: (films) Grizzly II: The Predator, 1984, Red Dawn, 1984, The Boys Next Door, 1985, Ferris Bueller's Day Off, 1986, Lucas, 1986, Platoon, 1986, Wisdom, 1986, The Wraith, 1986, A Life in the Day, 1986, Wall Street, 1987, No Man's Land, 1987, Three for the Road, 1987, Eight Men Out, 1988, Young Guns, 1988, Major League, 1989, Never on Tuesday, 1989, Comicitis, 1989, Courage Mountain, 1990, Navy SEALS, 1990, Backtrack, 1990, Hot Shots!, 1990, Men At Work, 1990, The Rookie, 1990, Cadence, 1991, Beyond the Law (aka Fixing the Shadow), 1992, Hot Shots, Part Deux, 1993, The Three Musketeers, 1993, Loaded Weapon I, 1993, Deadfall, 1993, Major League 2, 1994, Terminal Velocity, 1994, The Shadow Conspiracy, 1995, Shockwave, 1995, Loose Women, 1996, (voice only) All Dogs Go to Heaven 2, 1996, The Arrival, 1996, Postmortem, 1997, Bad Day On the Block, 1997, Money Talks, 1997, Mission to Mars, 1997, Free Money, 1998, Letter From Death Row, 1998, Five Acres, 1999, Being John Malkovich, 1999, Rated X, 2000, Famous, 2000, Good Advice, 2001, Scary Movie 3, 2003, Deeper Than Deep, 2003, The Big Bounce, 2004, Scary Movie 4, 2006; actor, exec. prodr. (films) The Chase, 1994, No Code of Conduct, 1998; actor: (TV movies) Execution of Private Slovik, 1974, Silence of the Heart, 1984, The Fourth Wise Man, 1985, Out of the Darkness, 1985; (TV series) Sugar Hill, 1999, Spin City, 2000-02 (Golden Globe award bext actor, 2001), Two and a Half Men, 2003- (Actor in a television series, comedy, ALMA Awards, 2008). Named one of The 100 Most Powerful Celebrities, Forbes.com, 2008.*

SHEEN, MARTIN (RAMON ESTEVEZ), actor; b. Dayton, Ohio, Aug. 3, 1940; s. Francisco and Mary Ann (Phelan) Estevez; m. Janet Sheen, Dec. 23, 1961; children: Emilio, Ramon, Carlos, Renee. Grad. high sch. Made NY stage debut as mem. Living Theatre in The Connection, 1959; Broadway debut in Never Live Over a Pretzel Factory, 1964; other stage appearances include The Subject Was Roses, 1964-66, The Wicked Crooks, 1967, Hamlet, 1967, Romeo and Juliet, 1968, Hello and Goodbye, 1969, The Happiness Cage, 1970, Death of a Salesman, 1975, Julius Caesar, 1988; film appearances include The Incident, 1967, The Subject Was Roses, 1968, Catch-22, 1970, No Drums, No Bugles, 1971, Rage, 1972, Badlands, 1973, The Legend of Earl Durand, 1974, The Cassandra Crossing, 1976, The Little Girl Who Lives Down the Lane, 1977, Apocalypse Now, 1979, The Final Countdown, 1980, Gandhi, 1982, That Championship Season, 1982, The King of Prussia, 1982, No Place to Hide, 1983, The Dead Zone, 1983, Man, Woman, and Child, 1983, Enigma, 1983, Eagle's Wing, 1983, Firestarter, 1984, The Believers, 1987, Wall Street, 1987, Siesta, 1987, Judgement in Berlin, 1988, Walking After Midnight, 1988, Da, 1988 (exec. producer, dir.), Beverly Hills Brats, 1989, Cadence, 1991 (dir.), JFK, 1991 (narrator), Hot Shots, Part Deux!, 1993 (cameo), Hear No Evil, 1993, Gettysburg, 1993, The Break, 1995, The American President, 1995, The War At Home, 1996, Truth or Consequences, 1997, Spawn, 1997, Letter From Death Row, 1998, Stranger in the Kingdom, 1998, Storm, 1998, Monument Avenue, 1998, Free Money, 1998, Catch Me If You Can, 2002, The Departed, 2006, Bobby, 2006; TV series include As the World Turns, The Edge of Night, The West Wing, 1999-2006 (Golden Globe award, 2001, SAG award, 2001, 2002); TV movies and miniseries include Then Came Bronson, 1969, The Subject Was Roses, 1969, Mongo's Back in Town, 1971, Welcome Home, Johnny Bristol, 1972, That Certain Summer, 1972, Catholics, 1973, The Execution of Private Slovik, 1974, The California Kid, 1974, The Story of Pretty Boy Floyd, 1974, The Missiles of October, 1974, Sweet Hostage, 1975, The Last Survivors, 1975, Blind Ambition, 1979, Taxi!!, 1978, The Long Road Home, 1980, Fly Away Home, 1981, Kennedy, 1982, Choices of the Heart, 1983, The Atlanta Child Murders, 1985, Consenting Adult, 1985, Out of Darkness, 1985, Shattered Spirits, 1986, Samaritan, 1986, News at Eleven, 1986, Babies Having Babies (dir.), 1986, Conspiracy: The Trial of the Chicago 8, 1987, No Means No (exec. producer), Night Breaker, 1989, Project Alf, 1996, Marlon Brandon: The Wild One, 1996, D.R.E.A.M. Team, 1999; TV appearances include Mannix, 1967, The Streets of San Francisco, 1972, Murphy Brown, 1988 (Emmy award, Guest Actor - Comedy Series, 1994), The Simpsons (voice), 1989, The Great War, 1996, The Elevator, 1996, Entertaining Angels, 1996, Spin City, 1996, Medussa's Child, 1997, 187 Documented, 1997, Titanic: Anatomy of a Disaster (narrator), 1997, Tudjman (narrator), 1997 Babylon 5: The River of Souls, 1998, Letter From Death Row, 1998, Ambrose Chapel, 1998, Gunfighter, 1998, No Code of Conduct, 1998, Shadrach (voice), 1998, Stranger in the Kingdom, 1998, Talk of the Town, 1998, Voyage of Terror, 1998, Celebrity Poker Showdown, 2003. Recipient Lifetime Achievement award, Imagen Found., 1998, Laetare medal, U. Notre Dame, 2008; named Favorite Actor in a New Series, TV Guide Awards. Roman Catholic.

SHEEN, MICHAEL, actor; b. Gwent, Wales, Feb. 5, 1969; one child, Lily (with Kate Beckinsale) Grad., Royal Acad. Dramatic Art. Actor: (TV films) Gallowglass, 1993, Lost In France, 1998, Dirty Filthy Love, 2004, Essential Poems for Christmas, 2004, Kenneth Williams: Fantabulosa!, 2006; (films) Othello, 1995, Mary Reilly, 1996, Wilde, 1997, Heartlands, 2002, The Four Feathers, 2002, Bright Young Things, 2003, Underworld, 2003, The Deal, 2003, Timeline, 2003, Laws of Attraction, 2004, The Banker, 2004, Dead Long Enough, 2005, Kingdom of Heaven, 2005, The League of Gentlemen's Apocalypse, 2005, Underworld: Evolution, 2006, The Queen, 2006 (Award for Best Supporting Actor, LA Film Critics Assn., 2006), HG Wells: War with the World, 2006, Blood Diamond, 2006, Music Within, 2007, Airlock, or How to Say Goodbye in Space, 2007, Frost/Nixon, 2008, Underworld: Rise of the Lycans, 2009; voice (TV films) Beowulf, 1998, Doomwatch: Winter Angel, 1999; actor: (TV miniseries) The Battle for Rome, 2006; guest appearance Ancient Rome: The Rise and Fall of an Empire, 2006; performer: (songs) (theatre) When She Danced, 1991, Le Livre de Spencer, 1994, The Dresser, 1995, 1999, The Seagull, 1995, The Ends of the Earth, 1996, The Home Coming, 1996, Look Back in Anger, 1999 (nominee for Laurence Olivier Theatre award for Best Actor, 2000), Amadeus, 1999 (nominee for 1999 Laurence Olivier Theatre award for Best Supporting Performance of 1998), (Broadway plays), 2000, Frost/Nixon, 2007, (theatre) Caligula (nominee for 2004 Laurence Olivier Theatre award for Best Actor of 2003, 2003 London Critics Circle Theatre award for Best Actor), Charley's Aunt, Peer Gynt. Recipient Variety award, Brit. Ind. Film Awards, 2008. Mem.: Royal Acad. Dramatic Art (assoc.). Office: c/o Roxane Vacca Mgmt 73 Beak St London W1R 3LF England

SHEEN-AARON, JULIA, state agency administrator, public health service officer; MPH, Emory U., Atlanta; grad. pub. health cert. program, U. Wash. Sch. Pub. Health and Cmty. Medicine. Dir. chronic disease program VI Dept. Health, St. Thomas, 1993—2004, project mgr., cardiovascular health program, 1993—2004, project coord., behavioral risk factor surveillance systems, 1994—2004, project mgr., breast and cervical cancer program, 1995—98, project mgr., tobacco prevention and control program, 1995—2005, territorial asst. commr., St. Croix dist., 2007—, acting commr., 2009—. Office: VI Dept Health 48 Sugar Estate St Thomas VI 00802 Office Phone: 340-774-0117. Office Fax: 340-773-6551. Business E-Mail: julia.sheen@usvi-doh.org.*

SHEERAN, MICHAEL JOHN LEO, priest, academic administrator; b. NYC, Jan. 24, 1940; s. Leo John and Glenna Marie (Wright) Sheeran. AB, St. Louis U., 1963, PhL, 1964, AM in Polit. Sci., 1967, AM in Theology, 1971, STL, 1971; PhD, Princeton U., 1977. Joined Soc. of Jesus, 1957, ordained priest Roman Cath. Ch., 1970. Exec. editor Catholic Mind, NYC, 1971-72; assoc. editor Am. Mag., NYC, 1971-72; assoc. chaplain Aquinas Inst., Princeton, NJ, 1972-75; asst. dean Regis U., Denver, 1975-77, dean, 1977-82; v.p. acad. affairs Regis Coll., Denver, 1982-92, acting pres., 1987-88, pres., 1993—. Retreat dir., cons. governance religious cmtys., 1970—. Author: Beyond Majority Rule, 1984; contbr. articles and editls. to publs. Trustee Regis Jesuit HS, 1999—2005; chmn. Mile High United Way, Denver, 1999—2000; nat. bd. dirs. Campus Compact, 2002—06; trustee Rockhurst Coll., Kansas City, Mo., 1982—91, Creighton U., Omaha, 1985—95, U. San Francisco, 1985—94, 2001—, Loyola U., New Orleans, 1994—96, Rocky Mountain Coll. Art and Design, Denver, 1994—99; mem. adv. bd. Cmty. Coll. Aurora, Colo., 2001—; bd. dirs. Colo. Inst. Tech., 2001—06. Ford Found. scholar, 1963. Democrat. Roman Catholic. Home: 3333 Regis Blvd Denver CO 80221-1099 Office: Regis U 3333 Regis Blvd Denver CO 80221-1099 Office Phone: 303-458-4190. Business E-Mail: president@regis.edu.

SHEESLEY, MARY FRANK, art educator; b. Redwood Falls, Minn., Aug. 1, 1947; d. Wencel and Lois (Dooner) Frank; m. Gary James Sheesley, Apr. 30, 1966 (div. Mar. 25, 1985); children: Jason, John. AA summa cum laude, Chipola Jr. Coll., 1984; BS magna cum laude, Troy State U., 1986; MS, Fla. State U., Panama City, 1991; PhD, Fla. State U., 2000. Child devel. assoc. credential Washington, 1976. Co-owner Qurly-Q Pork Farm, Buffalo Lake, Minn., 1969—79, Bonifay, Fla., 1979—84; editor Nat. Drillers Buyers Guide, Bonifay, Fla., 1982; art educator Bay Dist. Schs., Panama City, 1986—2003, 2005—; tchg. asst. Fla. State U., Tallahassee, 1991—92; adj. prof. U. West Fla., Ft. Walton Beach, 1992; art educator Frankfurt Internat. Sch., Oberursel, Germany, 1995—96; adj. prof. Gulf Coast C.C., Panama City, 2002; asst. prof. U. West Ga., Carrollton, 2003—05. Mem. adv. bd. Region 6E Head Start, Willmar, Minn., 1975—79; chair Fla. State Art Textbook Adoption Com., Tallahassee, 1993—94; founder Global Art Exch. Program, 1994—; mem. tchr. edn. adv. coun. com. U. West Ga., 2003—05, mem. tchr. edn. field experience evaluation com., 2003—05, mem. assessment adv. com., 2003—05; presenter of various workshops and numerous inservice sessions, 1993—. V.p. Minn. Porkettes, 1978—79; treas. V.F.W. Auxiliary, Hutchinson, Minn., 1973—78; sch. restructuring task force com. Bay Dist. Sch. Sys., Panama City, Fla., 1989—91; chairperson Cath. Charities, Hector, Minn., 1977—79; mem. ch. coun., lector Blessed Trinity Cath. Ch., Bonifay, 1982—84; euchristic minister Our Lady of Perpetual Help, Carrollton, Ga., 2005; mem. sch. bd. St. John's Cath. Sch., Panama City, 2002—03; bd. dirs. Panhandle Alcoholism Coun., Panama City, 1980—84. Recipient Arrowmont Scholarship, 1987; grantee Fulbright Meml. Tchr. Scholarship, Tokyo, 1997; Art scholar, Chipola Jr. Coll., 1982, Returning Woman scholar, Marianna Jr. Women's Club, 1981, Acad. scholar, Troy State U., 1984—86, scholar, Fla. Ctr. for Tchrs., 1993, 2002, Ednl. grant, Truth About Tobacco, 1997. Mem.: Alpha Delta Kappa, Fla. Art Edn. Assn., Fla. League Art Tchrs. (charter mem.), Bay County Art Tchrs. Assn. (pres. 1996—2001), Nat. Art Edn. Assn., Internat. Soc. for Edn. through Art, Garnet Key Honor Soc., Gamma Beta Phi, Phi Theta Kappa. Independent. Roman Catholic. Avocations: travel, painting, reading, gardening, scuba diving. Office Phone: 850-872-7540 ext. 4829. Business E-Mail: sheesmf@bay.k12.fl.us.

SHEETS, JEFF W., oil industry executive; b. Bossier City, La., 1958; BS in Chem. Engring., U. Mo., Rolla, 1980; MBA, U. Houston, 1989. Process engr. exploration & prodn. divsn. Conoco Inc., 1980, staff fin. dir., 1990—93, staff fin. dir. exploration & prodn. divsn. Norway, 1993, comml. services mgr. Stavanger, Norway, 1994—97, asst. treas. Houston, 1998—2001, v.p., treas., 2001, ConocoPhillips, Houston, 2002—08, sr. v.p. planning & strategy, 2008—. Bd. dirs. OIL Investment Corp. Ltd. Office: ConocoPhillips PO Box 2197 Houston TX 77252-2197*

SHEFF, DAVID, writer, editor; married; 3 children. Grad., U. Calif., Berkeley. Contbg. editor Playboy; editor New West mag., California mag.; founding editor Men's Life, Yahoo Internet Life; journalist Rolling Stone, Fortune, Wired. Author: The Playboy Interviews with John Lennon & Yoko Ono, 1981, Game Over: How Nintendo Zapped an American Industry, Captured Your Dollars, and Enslaved Your Children, 1993, Game Over Press Start To Continue, 1999, All We Are Saying: The Last Major Interview with John Lennon and Yoko Ono, 2000, China Dawn: Culture and Conflict in China's Business Revolution, 2003, Beautiful Boy: A Father's Journey Through His Son's Addiction, 2008 (#1 NY Times best seller, Entertainment Weekly Best Nonfiction Book, 2008, Barnes and Noble Discover award, 2009). Named one of The World's Most Influential People, TIME mag., 2009. Office: c/o Houghton Mifflin Pubs 222 Berkeley St Boston MA 02118*

SHEFFER, JAMES THOMAS, music educator; b. Phila., May 27, 1970; s. James F. and Antoinette Patricia Sheffer; m. Terri Lynn Huffman, June 25, 1994; children: Victoria Lynn, Jamie Lynn. BS in Music Edn., West Chester U., 1992; MA in Edn. Adminstrn. and Supervision, U. Phoenix, 2004, MA in Edn. Curriculum and Instrn., 2005. Cert. music tchr. grades K-12 State of NJ., 1992, Commonwealth of Pa., 1992. Tchr. music, band dir. Medford Lakes Neeta Sch., NJ, 2001—04; dir. instrumental music Medford Meml. Mid. Sch./Haines 6th Grade Ctr., 2004—. Dir. instrumental music Manchester Twp. H.S., Lakehurst, NJ, 1996—2001. Dir.: (marching band director) Salute to the 50s and 60s (US Scholastic Band Assn. Group I Champions, 2001). Grantee Excellence in Edn., Medford Lakes Edn. Found., 2003. Mem.: ASCD, NAESP, N.J. Music Educators Assn., Music Educators Nat. Conf., Olympic Conf. Band Dirs. Assn., Internat. Assn. Jazz Edn., South Jersey Band and Orch. Dirs. Assn. (treas. 1996—2000). Roman Catholic. Achievements include development of Scales, Chorales, and Arpeggios for Band Warm-up. Avocations: music, fishing, swimming, travel. Home: 218 Kihade Trail Medford Lakes NJ 08055 Office: Medford Township Memorial Middle Sch 55 Mill St Medford NJ 08055 Home Fax: 609-953-6929. Personal E-mail: jimsheffer@aol.com. E-mail: jsheffer@medford.k12.nj.us.

SHEFFEY, RUTHE T., language educator; m. Vernon R. Sheffey, Dec. 29, 1950; children: Illona Sheffey Rawlings, Renata Sheffey Strong. BA, Morgan State U., Balt., 1947; MA, Howard U., 1949; PhD, U. Pa., 1959. Prof. English Morgan State U., Balt., 1949—, chair dept. English, 1970-76. Author: Impressions in Asphalt, 1969, Trajectory (My Collected Essays), 1989; editor Zora Neale Hurston Forum, 1986—. Named Md. Outstanding Faculty Mem. of Yr., 1994, Disting. Scholar in African-Am. Studies for Yr., Towson State U., 2002, Sheroe as Honor, Women for Responsive Govt., Inc., 2003; named to Morgan State U. Hall of Fame, 2000. Mem. Nat. Coun. Tchrs. English (past mem. coll. bd.), Coll. English Assn. (past pres. Mid. Atlantic Group), Zora Neale Hurston Soc. (founder, 1984, pres.), Langston Hughes Soc. (past pres.), other lit. socs., Alpha Kappa Alpha (Golden mem.). Mem. United Ch. of Christ. Avocations: reading, theatre-going, dance.

SHEFFIELD, GARY ANTONIAN, professional baseball player; b. Tampa, Fla., Nov. 18, 1968; s. Betty and Harold Jones (Stepfather); m. DeLeon Sheffield, Feb. 5, 1999; children: Ebony, Carissa, Gary Jr. Outfielder Milw. Brewers, 1986-92, Fla. Marlins, 1993-98, LA Dodgers, 1999—2001, Atlanta Braves, 2002—03; third baseman San Diego Padres, 1992-93; outfielder, designated hitter NY Yankees, 2004—06,

Detroit Tigers, 2006—09; outfielder NY Mets, 2009—. Co-author (with David Ritz): Inside Power, 2007. Founder Gary Sheffield Found., 1995—. Recipient Silver Slugger award, 1992, 1996, 2003-05; named Player of Yr. Sporting News, 1992, Nat. League Comeback Player of Yr., 1992; named to Nat. League All-Star Team, 1992-93, 1996, 1998-2000, 2003, Am. League All-Star Team, 2004, 2005. Achievements include leading the National League in: batting average (.330), 1992. Office: NY Mets Citi Field 126th St & Roosevelt Ave Flushing NY 11368*

SHEFFIELD, JEFFREY T., lawyer; b. Oct. 1954; BA phi beta kappa, U. Chgo., 1976; JD, Harvard Law Sch., 1979. Bar: Ill. 1980. Law clk. Mass. Supreme Jud. Ct., Mass., 1979—80; ptnr., mem. firm mgmt. com. Kirkland & Ellis LLP, Chgo. Former adj. prof. IIT/ Chgo. Kent Coll. Law; former lecturer U. Chgo. Sch. Law. Contbr. articles to profl. jours. Office: Kirkland & Ellis LLP 200 E Randolph Dr Chicago IL 60601 Home: 125 Laurel Ave Wilmette IL 60091-2830 Home Phone: 847-251-1270; Office Phone: 312-861-2454. Office Fax: 312-861-2200. Business E-Mail: jsheffield@kirkland.com.

SHEFFIELD, LEWIS GLOSSON, physiologist; b. Adel, Ga., Oct. 30, 1957; s. Eugene Davis and Martha Sue (Sinclair) S.; m. Mary Frances Tanner, July 18, 1980. MS, Clemson U., 1980; PhD, U. Mo., 1983. Rsch. asst. Clemson (S.C.) U., 1978-80, U. Mo., Columbia, 1980-83; postdoctoral assoc. Mich. State U., East Lansing, 1983-86; asst. prof. dairy sci. dept. U. Wis., Madison, 1986-91, assoc. prof. dairy sci., 1991—, dir. endocrinology-reproductive physiology program, 1990—. Contbr. articles to profl. jours. Recipient First award NIH, 1988. Mem. Am. Dairy Sci. Assn. (milk synthesis chair 1991-92), Com. on Mammary Gland Biology, Endocrine Soc., Sigma Xi. Achievements include demonstration that epidermal growth factor interacts with estrogen and progesterone to regulate mammary devel. and are working to understand the cellular and molecular basis of that interaction; that prolactin causes a decrease in epidermal growth factor-induced growth responses, which appears to be related to mammary gland differentiation. The molecular regulation of this response is also under investigation. Office: U Wis 864 Animal Scis Bldg 1675 Observatory Dr Madison WI 53706-1205

SHEFFIELD, NANCY, city agency administrator; b. Mpls. BA in Sociology and Psychology, U. Minn., 1969; postgrad., U. Wis., 1992. Participant City of Aurora (Colo.) Supervisory Cert. Series Program, 1988-90. Social worker LeSueur County Human Svcs., Le Centre, Minn., 1969-71; quality control reviewer Minn. Dept. Human Svcs., St. Paul, 1971-74, quality control supr., 1974-75; neighborhood planner City of Aurora, 1987, neighborhood support supr., 1987-94, acting mgr. Original Aurora Renewal, 1994-95, acting mgr. neighborhood support divsn., 1995, dir. neighborhood svcs., 1996—. Office: City Aurora Dept Neighborhood Svcs 15151 E Alameda Pkwy Aurora CO 80012 Office Phone: 303-739-7280. Business E-Mail: nsheffie@auroragov.org.

SHEFFIELD, SCOTT D., oil industry executive; BS in Petroleum Engring., U. Tex. Prodn. and reservoir engr. Amoco Prodn. Co.; petroleum engr. Parker & Parsley Devel. Co., 1979—85, v.p. engring., 1981—85, pres., bd. dirs., 1985—89, chmn., CEO, 1989; pres., bd. dirs. Parker & Parsley Petroleum Co., 1990—97, chmn., CEO, 1990—97; pres., CEO Pioneer Natural Resources, Irving, Tex., 1997—99, chmn., pres., CEO, 1999—2004, chmn., CEO, 2004—. Office: Pioneer Natural Resources 5205 N O'Connor Blvd Irving TX 75039

SHEFTEL, ROGER TERRY, merchant banker; b. Denver, Sept. 10, 1941; s. Edward and Dorothy (Barnett) S.; m. Phoebe A. Sherman, Sept. 7, 1968; children: Tisha B., Ryan B. BS in Econs., U. Pa., 1963. Comml. lending officer Provident Nat. Bank, Phila., 1963-65; asst. to pres. Continental Fin. Corp., Denver, 1965-68; v.p. Eastern Indsl. Leasing Corp., Phila., 1968-71, exec. v.p., dir., 1971-73, HBE Leasing Corp., Phila., 1971-73; dir. Kooly Kupp, Inc., Boyertown, Pa., 1974-77, pres., dir., 1977; prin. Trivest, Phila., 1973-77, pres., 1977-78, 1670 Corp., 1978-82, Am. Cons. Group, Inc., 1982-83; exec. v.p., dir. Argus Rsch. Labs., Inc., 1982-83; pres. Leasing Concepts, Inc., 1983-87, Brice Capital Corp., 1987-92, Rhodes Fin., Inc., 1992—. Dir. strategic planning Wharton Sch., U. Pa., 1999; pres. AttendByWeb, Inc., 1999—, AssignByWeb, Inc., 1999—; CEO, chmn. FlyOff, Inc., 1998—. Mem.: Friars Club. Home: 414 Barclay Rd Bryn Mawr PA 19010-1218 Office: Rhodes Fin Inc PO Box 7338 Saint Davids PA 19087-7338 Personal E-mail: rtsheftel@comcast.net.

SHEHAB, TARIQ, engineering educator, researcher; BS, King Fahd U., Saudi Arabia, 1991, MS, 1996; PhD, Concordia U., Can., 2001. Structural engr. Concordia U., Montreal, Canada, 1991—97, rsch. asst., 1997—2001, postdoc. fellow, 2002—04; asst. prof. engring. Calif. State U., Long Beach, 2004—. Contbr. articles to profl. jours.; peer reviewer in field:. Mem.: ASCE, Internat. Assn. Engrs., Constrn. Industry Inst., Constrn. Specification Inst. Achievements include patents for automated inspection technologies; research in field of automation, rehabilitation of infrastructure systems, intelligent construction systems and improving construction technologies and practices. Avocations: swimming, bicycling, reading.

SHEHADI, SAMEER IBRAHIM, plastic surgeon; b. Zahle, Lebanon, Mar. 3, 1931; came to U.S., 1984; s. Ibrahim A. and Mounira D. (Dumit) S.; m. Leila A. Nassif, June 18, 1960; children: Ramzi Richard, Kamal Sameer, Imad Edward. BA, Am. U. Beirut, 1952, MD, 1956. Diplomate Am. Bd. Surgery, Am. Bd. Plastic Surgery. Intern. Am. U. Hosp., Beirut, resident gen. surgery, 1956-59, chief resident gen. surgery, 1959-60; resident plastic surgery St. Louis U. Hosps., 1960-62; fellow hand surgery Pitts. U. Hosps., 1962; resident head and neck surgery Roswell Park Meml. Inst., Buffalo, 1963; clin. asst. prof. Am. U. Beirut, 1963-79, clin. prof. surgery, 1979-84, chmn. dept. surgery, 1976-79, 81-84; prof., dir. div. plastic surgery St. Louis U., 1984-97, emeritus prof. surgery, 1997—. Contbr. articles to profl. jours. Recipient Chevaliers award Order of the Cedars, Govt. Lebanon, 1968. Fellow ACS (gov. at large Lebanon chpt. 1981-84); mem. AMA, St. Louis Met. Med. Soc., St. Louis Surg. Soc., Mo. Med. Assn., Lebanese Order of Physicians, Am. U. Beirut Med. Alumni Assn., Am. Soc. Plastic and Reconstructive Surgeons, Am. Assn. Maxillofacial Surgeons, Am. Assn. Chmn. Plastic Surgery, Am. Assn. Plastic Surgeons, Am. Assn. Hand Surgeons, Lebanese Soc. Plastic and Reconstructive Surgeons (pres. 1974-84), Internat. Soc. Burn Injuries (Lebanon rep. 1968-84). Home: Shabshab Bldg Cairo St Hamra Beirut Lebanon Office: Nassif Bldg Sourati Hamra Beirut Lebanon Office Phone: 961-1746345. E-mail: sshehadi@gmail.com.

SHEIK, DUNCAN, singer, songwriter; b. Montclair, NJ, Nov. 18, 1969; Degree in semiotics, Brown U., New Providence, RI, 1992. Performed with bands His Boy Elroy, 1993, Liz and Lisa. Singer, musician, co-prodr. (albums) Duncan Sheik, 1996; singer, musician, co-prodr.: albums Humming, 1998, Phantom Moon, 2001, Daylight, 2002, White Limousine, 2006, songs "Wishful Thinking", 1998; TV Appearances: Boston Public, 2003, American Dreams, 2003; composer: (plays) (musical score) The Nightingale, 2006, Nero (Another Golden Rome), 2006, Spring Awakening, 2006 (Drama Desk award outstanding music, 2007, Tony award best original score written for the theatre, 2007, Tony award best orchestrations, 2007, Grammy award for Best Musical Show Album, 2008). Office: Gold Mountain Entertainment 11 Music Sq E Apt 103 Nashville TN 37203-4353

SHEIKH, AAMER, accounting educator; b. Rawalpindi, Punjab, Pakistan, July 21, 1971; arrived in US, 1990; s. Arif Anwar Sheikh and Parveen Rozina. BBA, Coll. William and Mary, Williamsburg, Va., 1994; M of Acctg. Sci., U. Ill., Urbana-Champaign, 1996; PhD, U. Ga., Athens, 2001. CPA Va., 1995. Asst. prof. acctg. Coll. William and Mary, Williamsburg, 2001—06, Quinnipiac U., Hamden, Conn., 2006—. Mem.: Am. Mensa (life). Office: Quinnipiac U Sch Bus SB-DNF 275 Mount Carmel Ave Hamden CT 06518-1908 Business E-Mail: aamer.sheikh@quinnipiac.edu.

SHEIKH-TAHA, MARWAN, medical educator, researcher; b. Beirut, Lebanon, Dec. 14, 1973; s. Taha Sheikh-Taha and Nadia Agha. PharmD, Lebanese Am. U., 1999. Cert. in BCPS (AQ cardiology) Am. Pharmacist Assn., 2006. Assoc. prof. Lebanese Am. U., Byblos, Lebanon, 2002—. Author: (research) Thalassemia / Cardiology / Pharmacy. Recipient, Order of Pharmacy, Lebanon, 1999. Mem.: ASHP. Home: Lebanon Office: Lebanese Am Univ Byblos PO Box 36 Lebanon Office Fax: 18017612883.

SHEILD, CAROLYN JEAN, science educator; b. Redfield, SD, Oct. 19, 1961; d. John Morgan and Jean Jordan (Powers) Sheild. BS summa cum laude, U. Wis., Eau Claire, 1984; MS, Northeastern U., 1990. Cert. tchr. Salem State Coll., 1990. Lab & field asst. Ctr. Limnology, Madison, Wis., 1985; natural resource specialist Dept. Natural Resources, Madison, 1985—86; tchr. oceanography Acadia Inst. Oceanography, Seal Harbor, Maine, 1992; tchr. biology Souhegan HS, Amherst, NH, 1992—93; tchr. sci. Clarke Mid. Sch., Lexington, Mass., 1994—. Presenter Benthic Ecology Meeting, Mobile, Ala., 1988, 90, Mass. Libr. Assn., Worcester, 1996, Woods Hole Oceanographic Instn., 2001, Boston Harbor Educators Conf., 2003, Nat. Sci. Tchr. Assn. Conference, Boston, 2008, Mass. Marine Educators Conference, Woods Hole, Mass., 2007—08; faculty rep. Jonas Clarke Sch. Assn., Lexington, 1996—2001; pilot tchr. Ridge 2000 Office, University Park, Pa., 2003—. Contbr. articles to profl. jours. Asst. sci. Sea Edn. Assn., Woods Hole, 1989, 1992—94, alumni coun. chair, 1997—2001, bd. trustees, 2004—; harvester Food Project, Acton, Mass., 2003, 2008; Sunday sch. tchr. Wellesley Hills Congl. Ch., Mass., 1997—2000, music com., 2001—03, outreach com., 2006—. Recipient Cmty. Svc. award, Rotary Club, Madison, 1980, Acad. All Am. award, Nat. Assn. Intercollegiate Athletics, 1981—83, Track & Field Scholar Athlete award, Wis. Women's Intercollegiate Athletic Conf., 1983—84; named to Hall of Fame, U. Wis., Eau Claire, 1988; grantee Grant-in-aid Rsch., Sigma Xi Rsch. Soc., Boston, 1988. Mem.: NSTA (presenter 1999, 2003, 2004), Nat. Assn. Intercollegiate Athletics (Dist. 14 Hall of Fame 1994), Madison Sports Hall of Fame Club (Hall of Fame 2005). Avocations: flying trapeze, scuba diving, photography.

SHEILS, DENIS FRANCIS, lawyer; b. Ridgewood, NJ, Apr. 7, 1961; s. Denis Francis and Anna Marie (Clifford) Sheils; m. Harriet A. Bonawitz, Sept. 17, 1988 (div. Aug. 7, 2007); children: Denis F., Dylan L, Matthew D. BA, La Salle Coll., 1983; JD, Fordham U., 1986. Bar: NY 1987, Pa. 1987, US Dist. Ct. (ea. dist.) Pa. 1987, US Ct. Appeals (3d cir.) 1987, US Dist. Ct. (so. and ea. dists.) NY 1992, US Supreme Ct. 1994, US Dist. Ct. (no. dist.) NY 1997, US Ct. Appeals (2d cir.) 1999, Nev. 2003, US Dist. Ct. Nev. 2003. Assoc. Kohn, Swift & Graf, PC, Phila., 1987—97, shareholder, 1997—. Mem.: ABA, Phila. Bar Assn. Roman Catholic. Office: Kohn Swift & Graf PC 21st Fl One South Broad St Philadelphia PA 19107 Home: The Dorchester Unit Number 1613 226 W Rittenhouse Sq Philadelphia PA 19103 Office Phone: 215-238-1700. Business E-Mail: dsheils@kohnswift.com.

SHEIMAN, RONALD LEE, lawyer; b. Bridgeport, Conn., Apr. 26, 1948; s. Samuel Charles and Rita Doris Sheiman; m. Deborah Joy Lovitky, Oct. 16, 1971; children: Jill, Laura. BA, U. Mich., 1970; JD, U. Conn., 1973; LLM in Taxation, NYU, 1974. Bar: Conn. 1973, US Ct. Appeals (2d cir.) 1975, US Supreme Ct. 1977, DC 1978, NY 1981. Tax atty. Office Regional Counsel IRS, Phila., 1974-78; pvt. practice Westport, Conn., 1978—. Mem.: ABA, Conn. Bar Assn., Fed. Bar Assn. Home: 128 Random Rd Fairfield CT 06825-1408 Office: 1804 Post Rd E Westport CT 06880-5607 Home Phone: 203-371-4941.

SHEINBAUM, MARC X., bank executive; Grad., NYU, 1981—84. Tech. auditor and mgmt. cons. Coopers & Lybrand; chief risk officer Gen. Electric, 1992, pres., gen. mgr. Montgomery Ward credit-card bus., sr. v.p. client devel., chief mktg. officer consumer fin. in the Americas, pres. money svcs., 2004—07; CEO retail auto and edn. fin. JP Morgan Chase & Co., NYC, 2007—, sr. v.p. Office: JPMorgan Chase Bank Retail Fin Svcs 900 Stewart Ave 6th FL Garden City NY 11530-4855 Office Phone: 516-745-3838. Office Fax: 516-745-4040. Business E-Mail: Marc.X.Sheinbaum@jpmchase.com.*

SHEINDLIN, JUDITH (JUDGE JUDY), television personality, judge; b. Bklyn., Oct. 21, 1942; d. Murray and Ethel Blum; m. Ronald Levy, 1964 (div. 1976); children: Jamie, Adam; m. Gerald Sheindlin, 1977 (div. 1990); stepchildren: Greg, Jonathan, Nicole; m. Gerald Sheindlin, 1991. BA, Am. U., Wash., DC, 1963; JD, NY Law Sch., 1965; LLD (hon.), Elizabethtown Coll. Pros. atty. Family Ct., NYC, 1978—82, judge Bronx, 1982—86; supervising judge Manhattan, NYC, 1986—96. Appeared as herself (TV films) ChiPs '99, 1998, (TV series) Judge Judy, 1996— (nominee Daytime Emmy for outstanding special class series, 1999, 2000, 2001, 2002, 2003); author: Don't Pee on My Leg and Tell Me It's Raining: America's Toughest Family Court Judge Speaks Out, 1996, Beauty Fades, Dumb is Forever: The Making of a Happy Woman, 1999, Keep It Simple, Stupid: You're Smarter Than You Look: Uncomplicating Families in Complicated Times, 2000, Judge Judy Sheindlin's Win or Lose by How You Choose, 2000, You're Smarter Than You Look: Uncomplicating Relationships in Complicated Times, 2001, Judge Judy Sheindlin's You Can't Judge a Book By Its Cover: Cool Rules for School, 2001. Internat. spokesperson North Shore Animal League America. Recipient Gracie Allen Tribute award, Am. Women in Radio and TV; named one of The 100 Most Powerful Celebrities, Forbes.com, 2007, 2008.*

SHEINGOLD, DANIEL H., electrical engineer; b. Boston, Sept. 26, 1928; s. Louis S. and Elsie Sheingold; m. Ann Silverman, Aug. 2, 1953 (dec. Feb. 1995); children: Mark J., Laura S. Duffy. BSEE with distinction, Worcester Poly. Inst., 1948; MSEE, Columbia U., 1949. Engr. George A. Philbrick Rschs. Inc., Boston, 1949-55, application engring. mgr., 1957-63; v.p. George A. Philbrick Researches, Inc., Dedham, Mass., 1964-67; staff cons. Teledyne Philbrick, Dedham, 1967-68; tech. mktg. mgr. Analog Devices, Inc., Norwood, Mass., 1969—. Editor: Analog-Digital Conversion Handbook, 1972, 3d edit., 1986, Nonlinear Circuits Handbook, 1974, Transducer Interfacing Handbook, 1980; editor Analog Dialogue jour., 1969—, others. Vol. reader Rec. for Blind and Dyslexic, 2003—. With AUS, 1955-57. Fellow IEEE (life); mem. IEEE Instrumentation and Measurement Soc. (sec.-treas. 1976, v.p. 1977, pres. 1978), AAAS. Jewish. Avocations: music, walking, reading. Office: Analog Devices Inc PO Box 9106 3 Technology Way Norwood MA 02062-9106 Office Phone: 781-461-3294. Business E-Mail: dan.sheingold@analog.com.

SHEINKOP, MITCHELL, orthopedist, surgeon, educator; BS, Univ. Ill., Champaign-Urbana, 1963; MD, Chgo. Med. Sch., 1967. Cert. Ill., Orthopedic Bd., 1974, Am. Bd. Orthopedic Surgery, 1983. Intern Cook County Hosp., Chgo., 1967—68; resident in orthopedic surgery Northwestern U. Sch. Medicine, Chgo., 1968—71, orthodontic and prosthesis rsch., 1973—78; asst. prof. surgery, orthopedics Univ. Chgo. Hosp. and Pritzker Sch. Medicine, Chgo., 1972—73; hosp. chief Univ. Chgo. Hosp. Childrens Orthopedic Clin., 1972—73; sr. attending surgeon Rush Presbyn. St. Lukes Med. Ctr., 1973—; orthopedic surgeon Chgo. Police Dept., 1985—87; attending surgeon Oak Park Hosp., 1994—; dir., adult reconstruction program Rush Affiliated Network Orthopedic Residency Program, 1995—; attending surgeon Ill. Masonic Hosp., 1996; faculty dir. The Nat. Ctr. Advanced Med. Edn., 1997—98; prof. orthopedics, prof. emeritus Rush Univ., 1999—; prof., dept. orthopedics Neurologic & Orthopedic Hosp. Chgo., dir. joint replacement program. Fellow in pediatric orthopedics and trauma Hadassah Med. Ctr., Jerusalem; fellow in hand surgery Passavant Meml. Hosp., Chgo.; orthopedic cons. Ill. State Pediatric Inst., 1973—74. Vol. attending surgeon Children's Meml. Hosp. First lt., capt. USAF, 1967—76. Mem.: AMA, Inst. Medicine Chgo., Ill. Orthopedic Soc., Chgo. Rheumatism Soc., Am. Acad. Orthopedic Surgeons, Am. Coll. Surgeons, Chgo. Com. Trauma, Chgo. Med. Soc. Office: Midwest Orthopedics Ste 1063 1725 W Harrison St Chicago IL 60612 also: Neurologic & Orthopedic Hosp Chgo 4501 N Winchester Ave Chicago IL 60640 Office Phone: 773-250-0000.*

SHEKA, KEDAMBADY P., surgeon; b. Bellare, India, Sept. 8, 1942; s. Marayana and Rukmini N. Sheka; married; children: Karthik, Satya. B Medicine, B Surgery, Kasturba Med. Coll., Mangalore, India, 1965, MS, 1971. Diplomate Am. Bd. Thoracic Surgery. Chmn. surg. svcs. Coney Island Hosp., Bklyn., 1993—2009; pres. Univ. Group Med. Assocs., Bklyn., 2000—09. Fellow: ACS, Royal Coll. Surgeons; mem.: Assn. Surgeons India, Soc. Thoracic Surgery. Avocation: tennis. Home: 366 Ramona Ave Staten Island NY 10312 Office Phone: 718-616-3445.

SHEKHAR, STEPHEN S., obstetrician, gynecologist; b. New Delhi, Jan. 13, 1944; arrived in U.S., 1972; s. S.P. Jain and Shakuntala Mithal; m. Claudette Dorita, Jan. 6, 1978; children: Sasha, Stephen. MBBS, Punjabi U., Patiala, India, 1966. Surgeon Nat. Health Svc. U.K., 1966-72; intern Roosevelt Hosp.-Columbia Coll. Physicians and Surgeons, NYC, 1972-73; resident in ob-gyn. St. Clare's Hosp., N.Y. Med. Coll., NYC, 1973-76, Harlem Hosp.-Columbia U., NYC, 1976-77; pvt. practice Studio City, Calif., 1977—. Mem. staff L.A. County-U. So. Calif. Med. Sch.; clin. prof. ob-gyn. and family medicine U. So. Calif. Sch. Medicine, Oreg. Health Scis. U. Sch. Medicine. Fellow ACS, Am. Coll. Ob-Gyn., L.A. Soc. Ob-Gyn.; mem. AMA, Calif. Med. Assn., L.A. County Med. Assn., Oreg. Med. Assn., Jackson County Med. Assn. Home and Office: PO Box 1742 Medford OR 97501-0136 Office Phone: 541-608-6199. Personal E-mail: drssshekhar@yahoo.com.

SHELBURNE, D. AUDELL, adult education educator; s. Gene P. and Anita F. Shelburne; m. Theresa A. Darcy; children: David P. children: Nicholas J., William D., Peter J., Thomas A., Katherine E., Megan E. BA, U. Dallas, 1987; MA, U. Houston, 1991; PhD, Tex. Tech U., Lubbock, 1997. Asst. prof. U. Mary Hardin-Baylor, Belton, Tex., 1998—2002, chair, assoc. prof., 2002—07, chair, prof., 2008—09, prof., 2009—. Dir. Writers' Festival U. Mary Hardin-Baylor, 2002—; vis. asst. prof. Tex. Tech U., Lubbock, 1997—98. Editor: Windhover: A Jour. Christian Lit., 2002—; asst. textual editor The Variorum Edit. of the Poetry of John Donne, 1998—. Recipient Helen Hodges Ednl. Trust award, 1993, 1994, George T. Prigmore award, Tex. Tech U., 1994, Summer Rsch. award, 1997, Faculty award Excellence Tchg., U. Mary Hardin-Baylor, 2005, Sabbatical award, 2007; William Bryan Gates fellow, Tex. Tech U., 1993, 1995. Mem.: Modern Lang. Assn., John Donne Soc. (mem. exec. bd. 2004), Phi Kappa Phi, Sigma Tau Delta. Office: University of Mary Hardin-Baylor 900 College St Belton TX 76513 E-mail: ashelburne@umhb.edu.

SHELBURNE, JOHN DANIEL, pathologist; b. Washington, Aug. 27, 1943; s. Clarence Daniel and Edith (McDaniel) S.; m. Katherine Howard Parrish, June 17, 1966; children: Mark, Kerri. BA, U. N.C., 1966; PhD, Duke U., 1971, MD, 1972. Intern, then resident Duke U. Med. Ctr., Durham, NC, 1972-76; asst. prof. Duke U., Durham, 1973-78, assoc. prof., 1978-85, prof. pathology, 1985—; dir. electron microscopy lab. VA Med. Ctr., Durham, 1976-92, chief lab. svc., 1983-99, chief of staff, 1999—. Adv. WHO, Manila, 1990; panel mem. VA Program, Washington, 1987—; participant Nordrhein/Westfalen Exchange, Germany, 1988. Editor: Basic Methods in Biological X-Ray Microprobe, 1983; author, editor: Microprobe Analysis in Medicine, 1989, Biomedical Applications of Microprobe Analysis, 1999. Mem. Appalachian Trail Conf., Harpers Ferry, West, Va., 1970—; bd. dirs. Cen. Carolina Youth Soccer, Durham, 1987-90; founding mem. N.C. Soc. for Electron Microscopy and Microprobe, Research Triangle Park, N.C., 1980—. Recipient Morehead scholarship, 1961-66, AOA Med. Honorary Duke Med. Sch., 1970; named Med. Scientist Tng. Program participant NIH, 1966-72, Shelley Meml. lectr., 1985, Florey Meml. lectr., 1988. Fellow Coll. Am. Pathologists; mem. Am. Assn. Pathologists, Microscopy Soc. Am., Microbeam Analysis Soc. Democrat. Episcopalian. Home: 4302 Malvern Rd Durham NC 27707-5451 Office: Duke U Dept Pathology PO Box 3712 Durham NC 27710-3712

SHELBY, CARROLL HALL, automotive designer; b. Leesburg, Tex., Jan. 11, 1923; s. Warren Hall Shelby and Eloise Lawrence; m. Jeanne Fields (separated 1960); children: Sharon Anne, Michael Hall, Patrick Burke. Profl. race car driver Cad-Allard, Aston Martin, and Maserati teams, 1954—60; founder Carroll Shelby Sports Cars, Dallas, 1957, Shelby School of High Performance Driving, 1961, Shelby-Dowd Wheel Co., 1973, Shelby-Am. Automobile Club, 1975, Carroll Shelby Internat., Inc., LA; automobile designer, 1961—, Shelby-Am., 1962—, Ford Motor Co., Chrysler Corp., GM; tech. advisor Ford GT project, 2003. Co-founder Original Tex. Chili Co., 1969, Internat. Chili Soc. Founder Carroll Shelby Children's Found., 1991. 2nd lt. US Army Air Corps. Recipient Kruse Internat. Collector Car Hall of Fame Award, 2002, Robert E. Petersen Lifetime Achievement Award, 2003; named winner, Torrey Pines, 1955, 24 Hours of LeMans, 1959, Continental Divide Raceways, 1960, Sports Car Driver of Yr., Sports Illustrated, 1956, 1957; named to Internat. MotorSports Hall of Fame, 1991, Automotive Hall of Fame, 1992. Achievements include design of original Shelby Cobra Roadster, Ford Motor Co., 1962; Shelby Mustang, 1964; Dodge Viper, 1989; Shelby GT500, 2005. Office: Carroll Shelby Children's Found 19021 S Figueroa St Gardena CA 90248 also: Carroll Shelby Licensing Inc 19021 S Figueroa St Gardena CA 90248-4510*

SHELBY, JAMES ELBERT, materials scientist, educator; b. Memphis, Mar. 11, 1943; s. James Elbert and Jessie Mae (Morris) S.; divorced; 1 child, Cleo. BS, U. Mo., 1965, MS, 1967, PhD, 1968, degree (hon.), 1994. Mem. tech. staff Sandia Nat. Lab., Livermore, Calif., 1968-82; prof. glass sci. N.Y. State Coll. Ceramics, Alfred, 1982—; McMahon prof. ceramic engring. NY State Coll. Ceramics, Alfred, 1997—2008. Cons. Corning (N.Y.) Inc., 1987-90, 2005, Delco, Milw., 1991-92, Praxair, N.Y., 1991-92, Molten Metal Tech., Mass., 1992-95; chair Gordon conf. on glass Gordon Rsch. Found., 1985. Author: Handbook of Gas Diffusion in Solids and Melts, 1996, Introduction to Glass Science of Technology, 1997, 2d edit., 2004; editor: Rare Elements in Glasses, 1994; contbr. over 270 articles to profl. jours. Fellow Am. Ceramic Soc. (George W. Morey award 1975); mem. Soc. Glass Tech. Independent. Achievements include leading authority on interaction of gases with glasses and melts; recognized authority on preparation and properties of glasses; discovery of many new glassforming systems; invention of method for crating magnolic oxide glasses; discovery of photo-enhanced hydrogen diffusion and application to hydrogen storage. Office: NY State Coll Ceramics 2 Pine St Alfred NY 14802-1214 Business E-Mail: shelbyje@alfred.edu.

SHELBY, JAMES STANFORD, surgeon, researcher; b. Ringgold, La., June 15, 1934; s. Jesse Audrey and Mable (Martin) S.; m. Susan Rainey, July 15, 1967; children: Bryan Christian, Christopher Linden. BS in Liberal Arts, La. Tech. U., New Orleans, 1956; MD, La. State U., Houston, 1958. Diplomate Am. Bd. Surgery, Am. Bd. Thoracic Surgery. Intern Charity Hosp. La., New Orleans, 1958-59, resident in surgery and thoracic surgery, 1959-65; fellow in cardiovasc. surgery Baylor U. Coll. Medicine, Houston, 1965-66; practice medicine specializing in cardiovasc. surgery Shreveport, La., 1967—2004; ret., 2004. Mem. staff Schumpert Med. Ctr., Highland Hosp., Willis-Knighton Med. Ctr.; assoc. prof. surgery La. State U. Sch. Medicine, Shreveport, 1967—; pres. Shelby Oil and Gas. With M.C., AUS, 1961-62. Recipient Medallion award La. Tech. U., 1982. Mem. AMA, Am. Coll. Cardiology, Soc. Thoracic Surgeons, Am. Heart Assn., Southeastern Surg. Congress, So. Thoracic Surgery Assn. Home: 6003 E Ridge Dr Shreveport LA 71106-2425 Office: 2751 Albert Bicknell Dr Ste 5C Shreveport LA 71103-3970 Office Phone: 318-632-9438. Personal E-mail: jshelby@worldnet.att.net.

SHELBY, KARLA JANE, music company executive, director; d. Elmo Bo Woodrow and Opal Lorene Cannon; m. Terry Greg Shelby; children: Dylan James, Bo Weston. BS in edn., U. Okla., Norman; MEd in adminstrn., Southwestern Okla. State U., Weatherford. Singer (musician & songwriter): (recording) The Cannons (billboard charts). Mem. & dir. cotton pickin C. of C.; pianist, sunday sch. tchr., youth activites vol. First Bapt. Ch. Recipient Entertainers of Yr., Okla. Opry Assn., Group of Yr. Mem.: Okla. Music Educators' Assn., Am. Choral Dirs. Assn., Kappa Delti Pi, Kappa Delti Pi, Philanthropic Educators' Orgn. Office: Western Oklahoma State Coll 2801 N Main Altus OK 73521 Office Fax: 580-477-7733. Business E-Mail: karla.shelby@wosc.edu.

SHELBY, NINA CLAIRE, special education educator; b. Weatherford, Tex., Oct. 23, 1949; d. Bill Hudson and Roselle (Price) S.; m. Richard Dean Powell, May 29, 1971 (div. 1973); 1 child, Stoney Hudson. BA in English, Sul Ross State U., 1974, MEd, 1984; MA in English, U. Tex., 1995. Cert. ednl. diagnostician Sul Ross State U., 2008. Jr. high lang. arts educator Liberty Hill, Tex., 1974-75; H.S. resource educator Georgetown (Tex.) I. S. D., 1976-77; intermediate resource educator Raymondille (Tex.) I. S. D., 1977-81; educator of severe profound Napper Elem. Pharr (Tex.) San Juan Alamo Ind. Sch. Dist., 1981-90; H. S. life skills educator Pharr (Tex.) San Juan Alamo ISD North H.S., 1990-93; intermediate inclusion educator Carman Elem. Pharr (Tex.) San Juan Alamo Ind. Sch. Dist., 1993—2000, chair dept. spl. edn. Carman Elem., 1998—2000; primary resource/inclusion educator Elgin (Tex.) Elem. Sch., 2008, chair dept. spl. edn., 2002—; educator, ednl. diagnostician Elgin I.S.D., 2008—. Coach asst. Tex. Spl. Olympics, Pharr, 1981-2000, sponsor vocat. adj. club, 1990-93, adaptive asst. device team, Edinburg, Tex., 1993-95; spl. edn. rep. to Elgin Primary Campus Performance Adv. Coun., 2000— Asst. cub scout leader Boy Scouts Am., 1994-95, sec. parental com. bd. rev., 1997—; parent vol. boy's and girl's Club McAllen, 1992-96. Mem. DAR, Daus. Republic of Tex., Assn. Tex. Profl. Educators, Tex. Ednl. Diagnosticians Assn., Alpha Delta Kappa. Democrat. Mem. Ch. Of Christ. Avocations: reading, horticulture, piano, opera. Home: PO Box 426 Elgin TX 78621-0426 Office: Elgin Elem Sch Elgin ISD 1001 W 2d St Elgin TX 78621 Office Phone: 512-281-3457. Business E-Mail: nshelby@elginisd.net.

SHELBY, PAULUS P., JR., biology educator; s. Paulus P. and Neva Jo Shelby; m. Diane B. Bynum, Aug. 5, 1977; 1 child, Rebekah R. PhD, U. Tenn., Knoxville, 1988. Adj. biology instr. Pellissippi State Tech. CC, Knoxville, 1997—. Office: Pellissippi State Tech CC 10915 Hardin Valley Rd PO Box 22990 Knoxville TN 37933-0990 Personal E-mail: ppshelby@pstcc.edu.

SHELBY, RICHARD CRAIG, United States Senator from Alabama; b. Birmingham, Ala., May 6, 1934; s. O.H. and Alice L. (Skinner) S.; m. Annette Nevin, June 11, 1960; children: Richard Craig, Claude Nevin. AB, U. Ala., 1957, LLB, 1963. Bar: Ala. 1961, DC 1979. Law clk. Supreme Ct. of Ala., 1961-62; practice law Tuscaloosa, Ala., 1963—78; prosecutor City of Tuscaloosa, 1963—71; spl. asst. atty. gen. State of Ala., 1968—71; U.S. magistrate No. Dist. of Ala., 1966—70; mem. Ala. State Senate, 1971—78, 96th-99th Congresses from 7th Ala. dist., 1979-87; mem. energy and commerce com.; mem. vets. affairs com.; US Senator from Ala., 1987—; chmn. Banking, Housing & Urban Affairs Coms., 2003—07; mem. Spl. Com. on Aging and Appropriations Com. Mem. com. appropriations US Senate, chmn. com. banking, housing, and urban affairs, spl. com. aging. Active Boy Scouts Am.; pres. Tuscaloosa County Mental Health Assn., 1969-70; bd. govs. Nat. Legis. Conf., 1975-78. Recipient Taxpayer's Friend award, Nat. Taxpayers Union, 1998, Congressional Leadership award, Airports Coun. Internat.-N.Am., 2003. Mem. ABA, Ala. Bar Assn., Tuscaloosa County Bar Assn., DC Bar Assn., Am. Judiciary Soc., Exch. Club, Tuscaloosa County Mental Heatgh Assn.(former pres.) Republican. Presbyterian. Office: US Senate 110 Hart Senate Bldg Washington DC 20510-0001 also: Federal Bldg Ste 240 1118 Greensboro Ave Tuscaloosa AL 35401-2816 Office Phone: 202-224-5744, 205-759-5047. Office Fax: 202-224-3416, 205-759-5067. E-mail: senator@shelby.senate.gov.*

SHELBY, ROSELLE PRICE, writer, retired special education educator; b. Granbury, Tex., Sept. 6, 1929; d. Ernest Blanton and Alice Parthenia (Merrill) Price; m. Billy Hudson Shelby, May 5, 1948; 1 child, Nina Claire. AA, Weatherford Coll., 1948; BA, Tex. Wesleyan U., Ft. Worth, 1960; NDEA diploma, U. Minn., 1963; MEd, Sul Ross State U., Alpine, Tex., 1974. Cert. tchr., Tex. Tchr. Waka Ind. Sch., Tex., 1956-57, 60-65, 69-72, Hart Ind. Sch., Tex., 1957-60, Eagar Ind. Sch., Ariz., 1966-67, New Waverly Ind. Sch., Tex., 1967-68, Willis Ind. Sch., Tex., 1968-69, Georgetown Ind. Sch., Tex., 1972-87. Author: Frogs in the Milk, 1967; editor: Quick and Easy Way to Riches, 1980. Active local Democratic Party, 1968—, precinct chair, Georgetown, 1980-90, election judge, 1991-2000; mem. sch. bd., Alpine, Ariz. Fulbright scholar U. Costa Rica, 1964; Reynolds fellow U. NC, 1971. Mem. AAUW (br. pres. Perryton 1971-72, state bd. dirs. 1971-73, 75-77, br. pres. Georgetown 1975-77), DAR, Daughters of Republic of Tex. (charter mem. Brazos River Chpt.), Am. Assn. Ret. Persons, Beta Sigma Phi, Delta Kappa Gamma (v.p. 1979-81), Phi Theta Kappa. Mem. Ch. of Christ. Avocations: bible study, reading, cooking, travel. Home: 2006 Terry Ln Georgetown TX 78628-3338

SHELDON, DEBORAH ANN, music educator, consultant; d. John Anthony and Judith Ann Capperella; 1 child, Marie Joelle. PhD, Fla. State U., Tallahassee, 1991. Asst. prof. music edn. Ill. State U., Normal, 1991—94; assoc. prof. music edn. U. Ill., Urbana, 1994—2002; prof. music edn. Temple U., Phila., 2002—. Cons. FJH Music, Ft. Lauderdale, Fla., 2001—, author, 2001—, clinician, 2001—. Office: Temple Univ 2001 N 13th St Philadelphia PA 19122 Business E-Mail: dsheldon@temple.edu.

SHELDON, DEENA LYNN, television camera operator, film producer; b. Groveland, Mass., Mar. 10, 1962; d. Frederic J. and Penny Margolis. BS, Boston U., 1984. Co. mem. Body Lang. Dancers, 1986; mem. Michael Macchio's Jazz Co., 1980-85, Danny Sloan's Repertory, 1980-82, Celtic's Green Gang, 1980-82, Dean Brittenham's Shiley Elite Athletic Program. Camera operator Redsox and Bruins, Sta. WSBK-TV, Boston, 1985, Am.'s Cup, Maj. League Baseball and postseason play, Homerun Derby, Boston Marathon, Extreme Games, ESPN, 1986—; NY Mets and NY Islanders, Sportschannel, 1987-92; NY Mets, Sta. WWOR-TV, 1987-92; Monday Night Football, Superbowl XXXIV, Superbowl XXXVII, Acad. Awards, NBA Championship, Ky. Derby, Triple Crown, Indy 500, Rose Bowl, Pro Bowl, NFL Hall of Fame game, Superbowl XXIX halftime show, Dem. and Rep. convs., Presdl. inaugurations, 1993, 96, 97, 2004, 05, 09, ABC, 1992—, Late Night with David Letterman, NFL, Triple Crown, Olympics, Phil Donahue Show, Macy's Day Parade, Sunday Night Football Superbowl XLIII, NBC, 1986—, Sunday Night Football; Superbowl XXXVIII, NFL and championship games, Daytona 500, Joan Rivers Show, Major League Baseball and postseason play, CBS, 1987—; Superbowl XXXI, World Series, NFL, NHL, Fox Sports, 1994—; robotic camera operator Met. Life and Fuji blimps, NFL championship and playoff games, Daytona 500, Indy 500, 1989—; first asst. camera (films) U2 3D Feature; pace prodr.: (films) Hannah Montana/Miley Cyrus: Best of Both Worlds Concert Tour Film; Jonas Brothers: 3D Feature; prodr.: (TV) 3D HD NBA Finals, 2007.College Football in 3D,2008, NBA Allister Weekend in 3D, 2006, 09, English Nat. Ballet & House Parliament in 3D, 2009, pres. v.p., Barack Obama's Innugurt, 2009, v.p. Predsl. Debacks, 204.4 Youth counselor and instr. athleticism. Recipient Emmy awards for CBS's Postseason Major League Baseball, 1990, CBS's Daytona 500, 1993, ESPN's Extreme Games, 1995-98, NY Emmy for NY Mets, 1992-93, 93-94, Fox's Postseason Maj. League Baseball, 1999, Sunday Night Football, 2007; Emmy nominee for ESPN's Am.'s Cup, 1995. Mem. NABET, Internat. Brotherhood Elec. Workers, Internat. Alliance Theatrical Stage Employees. Avocations: trail running, dance, sunshine, instructing in athleticism. Home: 70445 Mottle Cir Rancho Mirage CA 92270 Office Phone: 760-522-1020. Personal E-mail: deenasheldon@mac.com.

SHELDON, ELEANOR HARRIET BERNERT, sociologist, writer; b. Hartford, Conn., Mar. 19, 1920; d. M.G. and Fannie (Myers) Bernert; m. James Sheldon, Mar. 19, 1950 (div. 1960); children: James, John Anthony. AA, Colby Jr. Coll., 1940; AB, U. N.C., 1942; PhD, U. Chgo., 1949. Asst. demographer Office Population Rsch., Washington, 1942-43; social scientist USDA, Washington, 1943-45; assoc. dir. Chgo. Community Inventory, U. Chgo., 1947-50; social scientist Social Sci. Rsch. Coun., NYC, 1950-51, rsch. grantee, 1953-55, pres., 1972-79; rsch. assoc. Bur. Applied Social Rsch. Columbia U., 1950-51, lectr. sociology, 1951-52, vis. prof., 1969-71; social scientist UN, NYC, 1951-52; rsch. assoc., lectr. sociology UCLA, 1955-61; assoc. rsch. sociologist, lectr. Sch. Nursing U. Calif., 1957-61; sociologist, exec. assoc. Russell Sage Found., NYC, 1961—72; vis. prof. U. Calif., Santa Barbara, 1971. Author: (with L. Wirth) Chicago Community Fact Book, 1949, America's Children, 1958, (with R.A. Glazier) Pupils and Schools in N.Y.C, 1965; editor: (with W.E. Moore) Indicators of Social Change, Concepts and Measurements, 1968, Family Economic Behavior, 1973; contbr. articles to profl. jours. Bd. dirs. Colby-Sawyer Coll., 1979-85, UN Rsch. Inst. for Social Devel., 1973-79; trustee Rockefeller Found., 1978-85, Nat. Opinion Rsch. Ctr., 1980-87, Inst. East-West Security Studies, 1984-88, Am. assembly, 1976-95. William Rainey Harper fellow, U. Chgo., 1945—47. Fellow AAAS, Am. Acad. Arts and Scis., Am. Sociol. Assn., Am. Statis. Assn.; mem. U. Chgo. Alumni Assn. (Profl. Achievement award), Sociol. Rsch. Assn. (pres. 1971-72), Coun. on Fgn. Rels., Am. Assn. Pub. Opinion Rsch., Ea. Sociol. Soc., Internat. Sociol. Assn., Internat. Union Sci. Study of Population, Population Assn. Am. (2d v.p. 1970-71), Inst. of Medicine (chmn. program com. 1976-77), Cosmopolitan Club. Home and Office: 630 Park Ave New York NY 10021-6544 E-mail: ehbsheldon@aol.com.

SHELDON, GEORGE FRANK, medical educator; b. Dec. 20, 1934; s. Richard Robert and Helen Irene (Zerzan) S.; m. Ruth Guy, Aug. 28, 1959; children: Anne Anderson, Elizabeth, Julia. BA, U. Kans., Lawrence, 1957, MD, 1961; postgrad., Mayo Clinic Grad. Sch., 1965. Asst. instr. we. civilization U. Kans., 1955—57; intern Kans. U. Med. Ctr.; resident in surgery U. Calif., San Francisco, 1965-69; fellow in surg. biology Harvard Med. Sch. of Peter Bent Brigham Hosp., 1969-71; from asst. to prof. U. Calif., 1971-82; Dr. Zack D. Owens Disting. prof. surgery, dept. chmn. U. NC, Chapel Hill, 1984—2001. Chmn. residency rev. com. accreditation Coun. Grad. Med. Edn.; mem. Coun. Grad. Med. Edn. of Health and Human Svcs., 1986, chmn. 1998; mem. adminstrv. bd. Coun. Acad. Socs., chair, 1998-99; chmn. Merit Rev. Bd. Surgery Va., AAMC, 2000, 01; pres. vis. bd. UN Formed Svcs. U. Health Scis., 2002-03; mem. Coun. on Physician and Nurse Shortage Wharton Sch. Bus. U. Penn. Author: (with J.B. Runnell) Pictorial History of Kansas Medicine, 1961; (with Jill Ridky) Managing in Academics, 1993; editor: (with J.B. Davis) Clinical Surgery, 1995; editor-in-chief: E-Facs.org. With USPHS, 1962-64. Recipient Surgeon's Dist. award for Svc. to Safety, Nat. Safety Coun., 1993, Douglass Stubbs award Nat. Med. Assn., 1991, Disting. Faculty award Med. Alumni Assn. U. N.C., 2001; named Disting. Med. Alumnus, Kans. U., 2000. Fellow Royal Coll. Surgeons of Edinburgh (hon.), Royal Coll. Surgeons Eng., European Surg. Assn., Assn. of Surgeons of Gt. Britain and Ireland, Phila. Acad. Surgeons (Hunterian Orator 2001); mem. ACS (sec. bd. govs., regent 1984-93, pres. 1998, editor-in-chief e.facs.org web portal 2004—, dir. Inst. Health Policy Rsch., Surgeon of Yr. 2001, Fitts Orator, 1987, Scudder Orator Honored Surgeon, editor E facs.org web ponta 2004-), Am. Bd. Surgery (chmn. 1989-90), Nat. Bd. Med. Examiners (test com. 1981-84), Am. Assn. Surgery of Trauma (pres. 1984, Fitts medal), Am. Surg. Assn. (sec. 1989-94, pres. 1994-95), Assn. Am. Med. Colls. (exec. com., chair elect 1999, chair 2000-01, disting. svc. mem.), Soc. Surg. Chmn. (pres.), Coun. Acad. Socs. (chmn. 1998—, com. on gender equity and com. on health workforce), Inst. Medicine (sec. com. on employer based health ins. and tech. assessment edn. bds., Fluid Resuscitation com. on Nation's Physician Workforce 1996, Reviewer Poison Ctrs), Hunter Soc. (172nd Hunterian Orator). Achievements include being recognized as the leading authority on surgical workforce. Office: U NC at Chapel Hill Dept Surgery Campus Bx 7050 4006 Burnett-Womack Bldg Chapel Hill NC 27599-7050 Office Phone: 919-900-4053. Business E-Mail: gsheldon@med.unc.edu.

SHELDON, GILBERT IGNATIUS, bishop emeritus; b. Cleve., Sept. 20, 1926; s. Ignatius Peter and Stephanie Josephine (Olszewski) Sheldon. Student, John Carroll U.; M.Div., St. Theol. Sem., 1970; D.Min., St. Mary Sem. and Ohio Consortium of Sems., 1974; HHD, Jesuit U. of Wheeling, 1993; STD, Franciscan U., Steubenville, 1994. Ordained priest Diocese of Cleve., 1953, assoc. pastor, 1953-64, diocesan dir. propagation of faith, 1964-74; pastor, Episcopal vicar Lorain County, Ohio, 1974-76; pastor Sacred Heart Ch., Oberlin, Ohio, 1974—76; aux. bishop Diocese of Cleve., 1976—92; ordained bishop, 1976; vicar for Summit County, 1979-80, So. Region, 1980-92; bishop Diocese of Steubenville, Ohio, 1992—2002, bishop emeritus Ohio, 2002—. Bd. dirs. Soc. Propagation of Faith, 1968-74, Diocesan Presbyteral Coun.; instr. theology St. John Coll.; clergy adv. bd. econ. edn. Akron U.; mem. Bishop's Com. Latin Am.; adv. bd., Franciscan U.; bd. trustees St. Mary Seminary, Diocesan Health Ins. Adv. Bd., Cath. Charities Corp.; former mem. bd. trustees Borromeo Coll.; mem. acad. bd. St, Mary Seminary; bd. dirs. Bishops' Com. Latin Am., adminstrv. com. Nat. Conf. Cath. Bishops/USCC, Nat. Adv. Coun., Bishops' Com. for Missions, Nat. Bd. Soc. for Propagation of Faith; bd. trustees Pontifical Coll. Josephinum, Bishop Emeritus of Steubenville, 2002, Adj. Faculty, Franciscan U. of Steubenville, 2003. Goals for Greater Akron. With USAF, 1944—45. Mem. Nat. Conf. Cath. Bishops (adminstrv. bd. 1985—, adv. bd. 1985-87), Am. Legion, Cath. War Vets., Knights of Columbus, Order of Alhambra., Rotary Club Akron and Steubenville. Clubs: K.C. Lodges: Rotary (Akron). Roman Catholic. Avocations: golf, astronomy, photography, history, travel. Home: 609 N 7th St Steubenville OH 43952-1748 Home Phone: 740-283-9608. Business E-Mail: lnichols@diosteub.org, gsheldon@diosteub.org.

SHELDON, INGRID KRISTINA, retired mayor, controller; b. Ann Arbor, Mich., Jan. 30, 1945; d. Henry Ragnvald and Virginia Schmidt Blom; m. Clifford George Sheldon, June 18, 1966; children: Amy Elizabeth, William David. BS, Eastern Mich. U., 1966; MA, U. Mich., 1970; doctorate (hon.), Cleary U., 2001. Cert. tchr., Mich. Tchr. Livonia (Mich.) Pub. Schs., 1966-67, Ann Arbor Pub. Schs., 1967-68; bookkeeper Huron Valley Tennis Club, Ann Arbor, 1978—; acct. F.A. Black Co., Ann Arbor, 1984-88; coun. mem. Ward II City of Ann Arbor, 1988-92, mayor, 1993-2000. Commr. Housing Bd. Appeals, Ann Arbor, 1988—91; vice chmn. fin. and budget com. S.E. Mich. Coun.Govts.; treas. Huron Valley Child Guidance Clinic, Ann Arbor, 1984—, Ann Arbor Hist. Found., 1985—, Parks Adv. Commn., 1987—92, Ann Arbor Planning Commn., 1988—89; excellence com. Ann Arbor Pub. Schs. reorgn., 1985; treas. SOS Cmty. Crisis Ctr., Ypsilanti, Mich., 1987—93; chair United Meth. Retirement Cmty., Ann Arbor, 2003—06; trustee Cmty. Found., 2001—05; chair Ann Arbor Summer Festival, 2005; treas. Dixboro United Meth. Ch., 2006—, Ann Arbor Thrift Shop. Recipient Cmty. Svc. award Ann Arbor Jaycees, 1980, DAR Cmty. Svc. award, 1997; AAUW fellow, 1982. Mem.: Mich. Mcpl. League (life; del. 1989—97, hon. life mem. 1994, trustee 1997—2000, pres. 1999—2000), Ann Arbor Rotary (pres.-elect 2006—, pres. 2006—07), Ann Arbor Women's City Club (fin. com. 1987—90, chair endowment com. 1989—90, treas. 2003), Alpha Omicron Pi, Kappa Delta Pi. Republican. Methodist. Avocation: musical theatre. Home: 1416 Folkstone Ct Ann Arbor MI 48105-2848 Personal E-mail: aasheldon@aol.com.

SHELDON, J. MICHAEL, lawyer, educator; b. Mt. Carmel, Pa., Sept. 01; s. Lloyd Loomis and Helen Roberta (Sosnowski) S. AA, Harrisburg CC, Pa., 1978; BS, Pa. State U., 1980; M in Journalism, Temple U., 1991; JD, Widener U. Sch. Law, 1996. Bar: U.S. Ct. Appeals 2004, U.S. Surpeme Ct. 2006. News announcer Sta. WNUE-AM, Ft. Walton Beach, Fla., 1974-76, Sta. WFEC-AM, Harrisburg, 1977-78; announcer Sta. WCMB-AM, Wormleysburg, Pa., 1979-80; writer newspaper Pa. Beacon, Harrisburg, 1982-85; media specialist Commonwealth Media Svcs., Harrisburg, 1982-86; dir. communications Pa. Poultry Fedn., Harrisburg, 1986-89; news anchor Sta. WGAL-TV, Lancaster, Pa., 1989-90; dir. pub. rels. Profl. Ins. Agts. - Pa., Md., Del., Mechanicsburg, Pa., 1990-92; v.p. comm. and mktg. United Way of the Capital Region, Harrisburg, Pa., 1992-93, Widener U. Sch. of Law, 1994-96; pres. Open Mike Comm., Harrisburg, 1994—; criminal def. lawyer NBG Mag., 2007—08; pvt. practice, 1999—. Mem. adj. faculty dept. journalism Temple U., 1992; mem. faculty dept. humanities Pa. State U., 1995-97, 99-04. Contbg. author: Pa. 12th Annual Civil Litigation Update, Spoliation of Evidence: Why You Can't Have Your Cake and Eat it Too, 1999; contbg. editor: A Practical Guidebook to Massachusetts Aviation Law, 1999; Contbr. articles to profl. jours. Pub. rels. advisor Cen. Pa. Leukemia Soc., Harrisburg, 1989-90; media advisor Polit. Campaign, Hershey, Pa., 1990. With USAF, 1969-73. Mem. Pa. Bar Assn., Pa. Criminal Def. Lawyers Assn., Dauphin County Bar (bd. dirs. 2006-08), VFW (life), Am. Legion (life), Loyal Order of Moose, Chi Gamma Iota, Delta Tau Kappa. Republican. Roman Catholic. Avocations: motorcycles, music, electronics, martial arts. Office: 6059 Allentown Blvd Harrisburg PA 17112-2672

SHELDON, JEANNE, computer software company executive; m. Marvin Sheldon; 1 child. BA in History & Physical Sci., San Jose State U. Section mgr., software quality assurance divsn. Software Publ. Corp.; with Microsoft Corp., 1989—, software test mgr., 1989, gen. mgr. Microsoft Office sustaining engring. services, corp. v.p. Office authoring applications, Microsoft bus. divsn. Avocations: photography, hiking. Office: Microsoft Corp Bus Divsn 1 Microsoft Way Redmond WA 98052-6399

SHELDON, MARIANNE BUROFF, history professor; d. Archer Clark and Stefania Buroff; 1 child, Meredith Julia. PhD, U. Mich., Ann Arbor, 1975. Prof. history Mills Coll., Oakland, Calif. Contbr. articles to profl. jours. Sec. bd. trustees Mills Coll., 2005—08. Mem.: Am. Hist. Assn. Office: Mills Coll 5000 MacArthur Blvd Oakland CA 94613 Office Fax: 510-430-2256. Business E-Mail: mshel@mills.edu.

SHELDON, RICHARD ROBERT, retired literature and language professor; b. July 12, 1932; s. Richard Robert and Helen Irene (Zerzan) S.; m. Karen Ryden Sears, Feb. 8, 1964; children: Katherine Palmer, John Ryden, Robert Charles, Rebecca Ann. BA, U. Kans., 1954; JD, U. Mich., 1960, MA, 1962; PhD, Mich. U., 1966. Chmn. Russian dept. Grinnell (Iowa) Coll., 1965-66; asst. prof. Dartmouth Coll., Hanover, NH, 1966-70, assoc. prof., 1970-75, prof. Russian lang. and lit., 1975—, chmn. dept., 1970-81, 90-00, formerly dir. fgn. studies programs, chmn. com. on orgn. and policy, com. on admissions, com. on diversity, com. on off-campus study, dean of humanities, 1984-89, acad. dir. alumni coll., 1990—2003. Vis. prof. U. Calif. Berkeley, 1968, Stanford (Calif.) U., 1974; cons. Coun. Internat. Ednl. Exchange, N.Y.C., 1967-83, Dept. Edn., Washington, 1979—, Cornell U. Press, Ithaca, N.Y., 1970—; sr. assoc. mem. St. Antony's Coll., Oxford, Eng., 1983-84. Translator, editor: (books by V. Shklovsky) A Sentimental Journey, 1970, Zoo or Letters Not About Love, 1971, Third Factory, 1977; compiler: Viktor

Shklovsky: An International Bibliography of Works by and about Him, 1977, Knight's Move, 2005; co-editor: Soviet Society and Culture, 1988; author articles, book revs., other transls. Chmn. bd. Norwich (Vt.) Day Care Ctr., 1980-81. Pfc. U.S. Army, 1955-57. Summerfield scholar, 1952-54; Nat. Def. Act fellow Dept. Edn., Washington, 1961-64, Alfred P. Lloyd fellow U. Mich., Ann Arbor, 1964-65, Ctr. Advanced Study fellow U. Ill., Urbana, 1969-70, Am. Coun. Learned Socs. fellow, 1970; Internat. Rsch. and Exchanges Bd. study grantee, USSR, 1964-65. Mem. Am. Assn. Advancement of Slavic Studies, Am. Assn. Tchrs. Slavic and East European Langs., Coun. of Mem. Instns. (exec. com., adv. com. to pres., vice chair 1995-97, subcom. priorities), Phi Beta Kappa, Phi Alpha Theta, Phi Delta Theta (pres. 1953), Delta Sigma Rho. Democrat. Episcopalian. Home: 86 S Main St Hanover NH 03755-2029

SHELDON, ROY ALBERT, literature and language professor; b. Elyria, Ohio, Mar. 11, 1948; s. Floyd Carl Sheldon and Elsie Emma Rehg; 1 child, Emily Rose. BA summa cum laude, Kent State U., Ohio, 1974; MA, Bowling Green U., Ohio, 1976; PhD, Purdue U., West Lafayette, Ind., 1982. Grad. tchg. asst. Bowling Green U., 1974—76, Purdue U., 1976—81, instr., 1981—82; asst. prof. English Franklin Coll., Ind., 1982—83, Washburn U., Topeka, 1983—89, assoc. prof. English, 1989—. Bus. writing cons., Topeka, 1984—. Editor: Business Writing Samples, 1993, Business Writing Guidelines, 1995, Grammar and Writing Exercises, 1998. Recipient Scholarship Recognition award, Washburn U. Student Assn., 1990—91; named Outstanding Undergrad. Alumnus, Kent State U., 2005. Mem.: Popular Culture Assn., Am. Mensa Ltd. (proctor 1993—), Phi Kappa Phi. Avocations: genealogy, coin collecting/numismatics. Office: Washburn U 1700 SW College Topeka KS 66621

SHELDON, SARA A., museum director, writer; Ed. in Fine Art and Art History, Colo. Coll., Colorado Springs; ed. in Chinese Lang. and Politics, U. Colo., U. Wis.; degree, Grad. Sch. Internat. Studies, U. Denver, 1956. Past dir. Leanin' Tree Mus. and Sculpture Garden of Western Art, curator, assoc. dir. Owner White Sand Lake Press. Author: (books) Operation Restore America, 1998, The Few. The Proud.: Women Marines in Harm's Way, 2007. Office: Leanin Tree Museum 6055 Longbow Dr Boulder CO 80301 also: White Sand Lake Press 750 S 41st St Boulder CO 80305 Office Phone: 303-530-1442 ext. 4299, 303-499-7260. Office Fax: 303-581-2152. Business E-Mail: sheldos@leanintree.com.

SHELDON, STEPHEN, pediatric sleep medicine educator, researcher; b. Miami Beach, Fla., Nov. 4, 1947; s. Murray M. and Sally (Lee) Sheldon; m. Rebecca Sheldon, May 17, 1996; children: David Patrick, Susan Victoria, Mara Elyn, Amy Michel. BS, U. Fla., 1969; DO, Chgo. Coll. Osteo. Medicine, 1975. Diplomate Am. Bd. Physicians and Surgeons, Am. Bd. Sleep Medicine, Am. Bd. Pediat. Resident in pediatrics Rush-Presbyn.-St. Luke's Med. Ctr., Chgo., 1975-78, chief pediatric resident, 1977-78, coord. pediatric residency, 1978-80, dir. pediatric residency, 1980-83; dir. pediatric research Mt. Sinai Hosp. Med. Ctr., Chgo., 1983-85; chmn. dept. pediatrics Chgo. Coll. Osteo. Medicine, 1985—. Cons. pediatrician Rush-Presbyn.-St. Lukes Med. Ctr., 1983—; prof. pediat. Feinberg Sch. Medicine Northwestern U., 2006—; assoc. dept. neurology U. Chgo., 1986—. Author: Pediatric Differential Diagnosis, 1979, 1986, Manual of Practical Pediatrics, 1981, Diagnosis and Management of the Hospitalized Child, 1984, Pediatric Sleep Medicine, 1992, Atlas of Sleep Medicine in Infants and Children, 1999, Evaluating Sleep in Infants and Children, 1996; sr. editor: Principles and Practice of Pediatric Sleep Medicine. Fellow: Am. Acad. Pediat. (cert. merit 1985); mem.: AMA, Ambulatory Pediatric Assn., Am. Acad. Sleep Medicine. Avocations: painting, ship building, cabinetry, writing, photography. Business E-Mail: ssheldon@northwestern.edu.

SHELDON, TERRY EDWIN, lawyer, investment advisor; b. Sacramento, June 22, 1945; s. Earl M. and Christine M. S.; m. Jan L. Winters, Aug. 26, 1966; children: Jeffrey, Tiffini, Melissa. BS magna cum laude, Abilene Christian U., 1967; JD, So. Meth. U., 1970. Bar: Calif. 1970. Assoc. Bronson, Bronson & McKinnon, San Francisco, 1970-74; gen. counsel, also dir. Consol. Capital Cos., Emeryville, Calif., 1974-83, exec. v.p., chief oper. officer, 1984-85, cons., advisor, 1986-87; pres., trustee Consol. Capital Spl. Trust, 1980-85; exec. v.p., trustee Consol. Capital Realty Investors, 1975-85, Consol. Capital Income Trust, 1978-85, Consol. Capital Income Opportunity Trust, 1983-85, Consol. Capital Income Opportunity Trust 2, 1985; chmn. Nat. Syndication Forum (a div. of RESSI), 1981-82; real estate securities specialist RESSI. V.p., prin. Alpha Venture Corp., Walnut Creek, Calif., 1987; bus. cons., 1988—. Chmn. bd. visitors adv. com. Coll. of Bus. Adminstrn. Abilene Christian U., 1990. Mem. ABA, Calif. Bar Assn., Nat. Assn. Securities Dealers (direct participation programs com., real estate com., standing adv. com. to bd. govs. 1980-83), Nat. Syndication Forum. Republican. Mem. Ch. of Christ.

SHELDON-MORRIS, TIFFINI ANNE, clinical psychologist, consultative examiner; b. Berkeley, Calif., Apr. 20, 1976; d. Terry E. and Jan L. Sheldon; m. John Christopher Morris, Aug. 6, 2000. BS in Psychology, Abilene Christian U., 1997; MS in Psychology, Fla. Inst. Tech., 2001, D of Psychology, 2001. Licensed Clinical Psychologist Tex., 2004. Postdoctoral fellow Houston Veterans Affairs Med. Ctr., Houston, 2001—02; team leader and counselor Sr. Connections, Houston, 2003—04; clin. psychologist VeriCare, 2004—. Consultative examiner Dept. of Assistive and Rehabilitative Svcs., Austin, Tex., 2004—. Active mem. Monterey Ch. Christ, Lubbock, Tex., 2004—. Scholar Grad. Student Tchg. Assistantship, Fla. Inst. of Tech., 1998-2000. Mem.: APA, Alpha Kappa Delta Internat. Hon. Soc., Alpha Chi Nat. Honor Soc., Girls Aiming Toward Achievement. Avocations: travel, reading, swimming, music, theater. Home: 6508 89th St Lubbock TX 79424 Office: VeriCare 4715 Viewridge Ave Ste 230 San Diego CA 92123 Office Fax: 800-819-1655; Home Fax: 806-698-8994. Personal E-mail: drtiffini@yahoo.com.

SHELL, (PETERSON) JUANITA, psychologist, educator; b. Winston-Salem, NC, Apr. 21, 1940; d. Douglas James and Sallie (Sanders) Shell; m. Alonza Peterson, Dec. 24, 1961; children: Lisa Peterson, Jason Peterson. BA, CCNY, 1971; PhD, CUNY, 1977; postgrad., NYU, 1980—91. Libr. asst. Bklyn. Pub. Libr., 1959-64; sec. Haryou-Act, NYC, 1965-67; psychotherapist Psychol. Ctr., NYC, 1971-74; cons.-therapist Hale House, NYC, 1974-77; psychology intern NYU-Bellevue Med. Ctr., NYC, 1974-75; staff psychologist Bellevue Psychiat. Hosp., 1978—. Clin. instr. dept. psychiatry NYU Sch. Medicine, 1978—85, asst. clin. prof. Dept. Psychiatry Sch. Medicine NYU, 1985—; mem. faculty Bklyn. Coll., 1976-78; cons. Bklyn. Cmty. Counseling Ctr., 1976—86; mem. N.Y.C. Mayor's Adv. Subcom. on Mental Retardation and Devel. Disabilities, 1978-1982; cons. in field. Contbr. articles to profl. jours. Chairperson health com. N.Y.C. Cmty. Bd. 4, 1979-81. Black Analysis Inc. fellow 1975-76; NIMH grantee, 1971-74. Mem. APA, Metro. Jack and Jill Am. (v.p. Met. chpt. 1984-86, pres. Met. chpt. 1987-1989), Jack and Jill Alumni Inc. (founding mem., pres. 1989-), Woman's Aux. of North Gen. Hosp., NYU Bellevue Soc., NYU Psychoanalytic Soc., N.Y. State Divsn. Women, Harlem Toastmasters (founding mem., 2002—, sec., v.p., 2009). Democrat. Episcopalian. Office: Dept Psychiatry NYU-Bellevue Med Ctr 462 First Ave at 27th St New York NY 10016 Office Phone: 212-562-4509. Personal E-mail: juanita.shell@att.net.

SHELL, OWEN GLADSTONE, JR., retired bank executive; b. Greenville, SC, June 19, 1936; s. Owen and Katherine S.; m. Mary Ruth Trammell, Aug. 9, 1980; children: Katherine Sloan, Mary Carroll, Robert Owen, James Walker. BS, U. S.C., 1960; postgrad., Stonier Grad. Sch. Banking, 1971; grad., Advanced Mgmt. Program, Harvard U., 1979. V.p. Citizens & So. Nat. Bank S.C., Columbia, 1968-71, sr. v.p., 1971-74, exec. v.p., 1974-79; pres., dir., chief exec. officer First Am. Nat. Bank, Nashville, 1979-86; vice chmn. bd., dir. First Am. Corp., 1979-86; chmn., pres., chief exec. officer Sovran Bank/Tenn., Nashville, 1986-91; pres. Nations Bank of Tenn. (formerly Sovran Bank), Nashville, 1992-96; pres. asset mgmt. group NationsBank Corp., St. Louis, 1997-99; pres. Asset Mgmt. Bank of Am., Charlotte, 1997—2002; ret., 2002. Bd. dirs. Nashville br. Fed. Res. Bank, Atlanta, Ctrl. Parkine, Inc., chmn. bd., Lifepoint Hosp. Inc. Chmn. Leadership Nashville, Tenn. Performing Arts Found., Mid. Tenn. coun. Boy Scouts Am., Vanderbilt U. Owen Grad. Sch. Mgmt.; trustee Met. Nashville Pub. Edn. Found.; chmn. bd. INROADS/Nashville; bd. dirs. Tenn. Bus. Roundtable, Tenn. Tomorrow. Mem.: Assn. Res. City Bankers, Old Warson Country Club (St. Louis), Harvard Club N.Y.C., Belle Meade Country Club (Nashville), Kappa Alpha. Presbyterian. Home: 4412 Chickering Ln Nashville TN 37215-4915 also: 114 Tern Dr Anna Maria FL 34216

SHELLER, JOHN WILLARD, lawyer; b. LA, Oct. 29, 1950; s. Willard and Barbara S.; m. Mary Elizabeth Hodor, Aug. 9, 1975(dec. 2008); children: Matthew John, James Henry. BA, Stanford U., 1972; JD, Loyola U., LA, 1975. Bar: Calif. 1975. Ptnr. in charge Hinshaw & Culbertston, LA. Mem. Am. Bd. Trial Advs. Contbr. articles to profl. jours. Mem. Calif. State Bar Assn., LA County Bar Assn., LA Country Club. Avocation: golf. Office: Hinshaw & Culbertson 11601 Wilshire Blvd Ste 800 Los Angeles CA 90025 Home: 16 Park Ave Venice CA 90291-3222 Office Phone: 310-909-8000. Business E-Mail: jsheller@hinshawlaw.com.

SHELLEY, BONNIE J., retired voice educator; b. Sullivan, Mo., Nov. 15, 1926; d. Earl William Sperry and Erma Laura Trout; m. Peter Lipkan (dec.); children: Kathleen, Michael, Christopher(dec.), Charissa, Brian; m. Clark C. Shelley (dec.); m. Dean F. Hollister, Nov. 15, 1990. MusB, U. Ariz., Tucson, 1965; MA in Music, Calif. State U., Fullerton, 1976. Adj. prof. voice Yavapai Coll., Prescott, Ariz., 1986—93, 1998—2007, No. Ariz. U., Flagstaff, 1989—93; ret., 2007. Youth choir dir. St. Francis Episcopal Ch., Palos Verdes, Calif., 1982—85; choir dir., bell dir. 1st Congl. Ch./St. Lukes Episcopal, Prescott, 1989—93, Prescott, 1994—96; choir dir. United Meth. Ch., Prescott Valley, 2000—05, Mingus View Presbyn. Ch., 2005—. Mem.: Nat. Assn. Tchrs. Singing. Home: 5325 N Bremont Way Prescott Valley AZ 86314

SHELLEY, CAROLE, actress; b. London, Aug. 16, 1939; arrived in U.S., 1964; d. Curtis and Deborah (Bloomstein) Shelley; m. Albert G. Woods, July 26, 1967 (dec.). Student, Arts Ednl. Sch., 1943-56, Prepatory Acad. Royal Acad. Dramatic Art, 1956-57; studies with Iris Warren and Eileen Thorndike. Trustee Am. Shakespeare Theatre, 1974—82. Actor: (plays) The Odd Couple, 1965, Absurd Person Singular, 1973, The Norman Conquests (L.A. Drama Critics Cir. award, 1975), As You Like It, King Lear, She Stoops to Conquer, 1972, The Country Wife, 1973, A Doll's House, Man and Superman, 1977, Misalliance, 1980, Grand Hunt, 1980, The Play's the Thing, 1978, Lion in Winter, 1987, The Elephant Man (Outer Critics Cir. award, 1979, Tony award for Best Actress, 1979), What the Butler Saw, 1989, Broadway Bound, 1987—88, Lettice and Lovage, 1989—90, The Miser, 1990, Cabaret Verboten, 1991, The Destiny of Me, 1992—93, Later Life, 1993 (Outer Critics nominee), Richard II, 1994, London Suite, 1995, Show Boat, 1995—96, 1998, The Film Society, 1997, The Last Night of Ballyhoo, 1997—98, Cabaret, 1999—2002, Wicked, 2002—04, 2005—, The Importance of Being Earnest, 2005—, Ring Round the Moon, 2006, Billy Elliot, 2008; (films) The Boston Strangler, The Odd Couple, 1968, The Super, 1990, Devlin, 1991, Quiz Show, 1993, The Road to Wellville, 1993, Bewitched, 2005, others; (TV series) The Odd Couple, 1965, Robin Phillips Grand Theatre Co., 1983—84, Nat. Co. The Royal Family (L.A. Drama Critics Cir. award, 1977); (Broadway plays) Noises Off, 1985, Stepping Out, 1986 (Tony nominee, 1986), Waltz of the Toreadors, 1986, Oh Coward, 1986—87, Broadway Bound, 1987—88; voice actor: (films) Robin Hood; The Aristocats; Hercules. Recipient Obie award for Twelve Dreams, N.Y. Shakespeare Festival, 1982. Jewish. Office: Robert Duva 277 W 10th St New York NY 10014 Office Phone: 212-807-8344.

SHELLEY, CHARLES ARTHUR, JR., retired academic administrator; b. Hagerstown, Md., Mar. 17, 1948; s. Charles Arthur Shelley Sr. and Esther Marie Shelley; m. Ruth Ann Raskinis, May 14, 1999; children: Rebecca Elisabeth Moore, Daniel Charles, Kathryn Amy Brown. Degree in German Studies, Phillips U., Marburg, Germany, 1969; BA, Alma Coll., Mich., 1970; MA, Mich. State U., East Lansing, 1973, PhD, 1984. Prin. Saginaw Pub. Schs., Mich., 1970—2005; internat. student advisor Saginaw Valley State U., Univ. Ctr., 2007—. Actor: (cmty. theatre) 24 Roles;, singer ch. and cmty. choirs, solo parts. Scoutmaster Troop 366, BSA, Saginaw, 1987—93; deacon, elder 1st Presbyn. Ch., Saginaw; pres. Pit and Balcony Cmty. Theatre, Saginaw. Recipient Eagle Scout, Boy Scouts America, 1966. Mem.: Local and Regional Affiliates NAESP (pres.), Saginaw Rotary Club (pres.). Presbyterian. Avocations: hiking, singing, acting, camping, theater.

SHELLEY, LEO EUGENE, retired librarian; b. Snyder County, Pa., Feb. 26, 1942; s. Oscar William Shelley and Elva Pearl (Smith) Shelley; m. Mary Virginia Weatherlow; children: Andrew Penn, Sarah Virginia Lopez. BS in Edn., Millersville U., Pa., 1964; MLS, U. Pitts., Pa., 1970. Peace corps vol. libr. Cuttington U. Coll., Suacoca, Bong County, Liberia, 1964—67; reference libr. Millersville U., Pa., 1967—2008, faculty senator, 1981—94, chair libr., 1995—2008, assoc. prof. emeritus, 2009. Historian, vestry mem., people's warden, treas. St. James Episcopal Ch., Lancaster, Pa., 1982—. Mem.: Friends Ganser Libr. (pres. 1982—84), Lancaster County Libr. Assn. (pres. 1972—73). Episcopal. Avocations: reading, gardening, walking. Home: 225 Redwood Dr Lancaster PA 17603

SHELLEY-TREMBLAY, JOHN FONTAINE, psychology professor; s. William and Cynthia Tremblay; m. Shannon Shelley-Tremblay, Aug. 6, 1994; children: Sean, Alexander, Gabriel. MA, New Sch. U. Grad. Faculty, NYC, 1998; PhD, CUNY Grad. Ctr., NYC, 2003. Adj. prof. psychology CCNY, NYC, 1998—2002; asst. prof. psychology U. South Ala., Mobile, Ala., 2003—. Contbr. articles to profl. jours. Mem. Mobile Pops Symphonic Band, Ala., 2002—05; mentor Ind. Living Ctr. Mobile, Ala., 2003—04; mem. Literacy Coalition South Ala., Mobile, 2004—08. Grantee, Juvenile Justice and Delinquency Prevention., 2003—07. Mem.: APA, Soc. Psychophysiological Rsch., Southeastern Psychol. Assn., Assn. Psychol. Sci. Avocations: trombone, martial arts, theater. Office: Univ S AL Life Scis Rm 384 Mobile AL 36688-0002 Business E-Mail: jstremblay@usouthal.edu.

SHELLMAN-LUCAS, ELIZABETH C., special education educator, researcher; b. Thomas County, Ga., Feb. 5, 1937; d. Herbert and Juanita (Coleman) Smith; m. John Lee Lucas, Jr. (dec.); 1 child, Sandie Juanita Lucas Boyce; m. Eddie Joseph Shellman; 1 child, Eddie Joseph Shellman, Jr. MS in Edn., CUNY, 1990. Cert. tchr. NY. Pvt. practice cosmetologist, NYC, 1959—; tchr. dept. edn. NYC High Sch. Dist., 1984—. Vol. various cmty. orgns.; citizen amb. del. People to People Internat., 1994; ch. sch. tchr., supt. Canaan Bapt. Ch., Harlem, 1990-2002; with rec. sec. Missionary Ministry, 2007-. Recipient Unsung Heroine award, 2007, Excellence in Scholarship & Career Devel.; named Woman of Yr., 2000. Mem. Coun. for Exceptional Children. Avocations: reading, music, dance, jogging, languages.

SHELNUTT, JOHN A., physicist, researcher; s. George Washington Shelnutt; m. Yan Qiu, Jan. 8, 1998; children: John Judson, Julian Yao-Ting. PhD in Physics, Ga. Inst. Tech., 1975. Cons. AT&T Bell Labs., Murray Hill, NJ, 1977—79; disting. mem. of tech. staff Sandia Nat. Labs., Albuquerque, 1979—; adj. prof. U. Ga., Athens, 2002—. Mem.: AAAS, Biophysical Soc., Am. Chem. Soc., Am. Phys. Soc., Sigma Xi. Office: Sandia Nat Labs 1001 University Blvd SE Albuquerque NM 87106 Office Fax: 505-272-7077. Business E-Mail: jasheln@unm.edu.

SHELOR, BELVA JEAN, psychologist; b. Radford, Va., June 22, 1969; d. Frank Jefferson and Ileda Blackwell Shelor. EdS., James Madison U., Harrisonburg, VA, 1995. Cert. in pupil personnel svcs. Va., 2006. Sch. psychologist Lynchburg City Schs., Va., 1995—. After-sch. program tchr. JIFF, Lynchburg, 1995—2008. Mem.: NASP. Liberal. United Methodist. Avocation: travel.

SHELOV, STEVEN PATRICK, pediatrician, educator; b. Honolulu, Nov. 19, 1944; s. Sidney M. and Faith R. S.; m. Marsha Liberman, Aug. 30, 1968; children: Joshua, Danielle, Eric. BS, Yale, 1966; MD, Med. Coll. Wisc., 1971; MS in Med. Admin., U. Wisc., 1995. Diplomate Am. Bd. Pediatrics. Intern, then resident Montefiore Med. Ctr., Bronx, 1971-74, chief resident, 1974-75; asst. dir. amb. pediat. Albert Einstein Coll. Med., Bronx, NY, 1977-79; dir. pediat. edn. Montefiore Med. Ctr., Bronx, 1980—, prof. and vice chmn. pediat., 1989-97; chmn. pediat. Infants and Children's Hosp. of Bklyn., Maimonides Med. Ctr., Bklyn., 1997—; prof. Mt. Sinai Sch. Medicine. Editor: Caring for Your Baby and Young Child: Birth to 5, 1991, 1996, 2004, Pediatrics for Medical Students, 2003, Guide to Your Child's Symptoms, 1997, The First Year of Life, 2004. Bd. trustees NACHAF, 2008. Recipient Geo. Armstrong award Ambulatory Pediat. Assn., 1996, Lifetime Achievement in Edn. award Am. Acad. Pediat., 2002. Mem.: Vis. Nurse Svc. (Lillian Wald award 2008), Nat. Assn. Children's Hosps. (bd. trustees 2008—), Am. Acad. Pediats. (Holroyd-Sherry award 2004, Clifford Grulee award 2009). Office: Maimonides Med Ctr 4802 10th Ave Brooklyn NY 11219-2844 Home Phone: 914-472-2714; Office Phone: 718-283-6150. Business E-Mail: sshelov@maimonidesmed.org.

SHELTON, AMY ELIZABETH, health facility administrator; b. Cin., Ohio, Dec. 6, 1973; d. William Marshall and Rebecca Sue Duke; m. Bryan Michael Shelton, Sept. 30, 2000; children: Bennett, Lucas. BBA, Trevecca Nazarene U., Nashville, 1996. Budget acctg. analyst Vanderbilt U. Med. Ctr., Nashville, 2002—04, chief bus. adminstr., 2004—. Mem.: Nat. Coun. U. Rsch. Administrators, MGMA. Conservative. Office: Vanderbilt U Med Ctr 536 Robinson Rsch Bldg Nashville TN 37232-6602 Business E-Mail: amy.shelton@vanderbilt.edu.

SHELTON, BESSIE HUNTER, music educator, director; b. Tuskegee, Ala., Aug. 12, 1947; d. Winzer and Ruth Idell Hunter; 1 child, Martin. BA in English, Tuskegee U., Ala., 1969; MusB in Voice, U. Mich., Ann Arbor, 1973; MusM, U. Montevallo, Ala., 1985. Music instr., choir dir. Lawson State Cmty. Coll., Birmingham, Ala., 1983—. Singer solo vocal competition, solo performances, Lexington Philharmonic Orchestra, Ala. Mus. Fine Arts. Min. music New Mt. Moriah Bapt. Ch., Hueytown, Ala., 2002—. Named Tchr. of Yr., Lawson State Cmty. Coll. Mem.: Ala. Assn. Coll. Music Administrs., Music Educators Nat. Assn. Home: 720 Owen Ave Bessemer AL 35020 Office: Lawson State Cmty Coll 3060 Wilson Rd Birmingham AL 35221 Personal E-mail: bsbessemer@aol.com. Business E-Mail: bshelton@lawsonstate.edu.

SHELTON, CHARITY FAITH, speach language pathologist; d. Barry and Betty Gayle Fielder; m. Rob D. Shelton, June 12, 1992; children: Matilyn R., Erin N., Eden G. MS in Communication Scis. and Disorders, SW Mo. State U., Springfield, 1997. Cert. in clin. speech-lang. pathology Am. Speech Lang. Hearing Assn., 1998. Speech-lang. pathologist Nat. Health Care Corp., Springfield, 1997—98, Mo. Rehab. Ctr., Mt. Vernon, 1998—. Contbr. scientific papers to numerous jours. Recipient Outstanding Health Educator of Yr., U. Mo. Med. Sys., 2004. Mem.: Mo. Head Injury Adv. Coun. (Jefferson City, Mo.) (past chair), Am. Speech Lang. Hearing Assn. (Mt. Vernon) (coord., Profl. Jour. Club 2005—). Office: Mo Rehab Ctr 600 N Main St Mount Vernon MO 65712 Business E-Mail: sheltoncf@health.missouri.edu.

SHELTON, DARLENE, psychologist, consultant; d. Harvey Clinton and Opal Lyles Shelton; m. David Weinberg, Oct. 10, 2003. BA in Psychology, So. Ill. U., 1979, MA in Psychology, 1986, PhD in Behavioral Medicine and Psychology, 1990. Lic. clin. psychologist State of Ky., State of Conn. Dir., coord. psychol. svcs. Econ. Opportunity Family Health Ctr., Miami, 1991—94; rsch. asst. prof. dept. psychiatry U. Miami Sch. Medicine, 1993—94; assoc. prof., dir. diversity and minority affairs Spalding U. Sch. Profl. Psychology, Louisville, 1995—2003; assoc. rsch. scientist dept. psychiatry Yale U. Sch. of Medicine, New Haven, 2003—04; exec. dir. Emancipation Inst., Inc., Guilford, Conn., 2004—; sr. fellow Garrison Inst., NY, 2005—; assoc. of the Chaplain's Office, Yale U., New Haven, 2006—. Rsch. cons. U.S. HHS, Pub. Health Svc., Health Resources and Svcs. Adminstrn., Bur. Health Resources Devel., Washington, 1991—93; forensic psychology cons. Thematix Group, Guilford, Conn., 2001—; program cons. Garrison Inst., Garrison, 2004—; rsch. cons. Ctr. for Women Policy Studies, Washington, 1993; mem. adv. com. Pediat. AIDS Health Care Demonstration Project of U. Miami/Jackson Meml. Hosp., 1992—94; grant reviewer Women's Initiative for HIV Care and Reduction of Perinatal HIV Transmission, Maternal and Child Health Bur., Health Resources and Svcs. Adminstrn., Rockville, Md., 1995; mem. Ky. HIV Prevention Cmty. Planning Group, State of Ky. Dept. of HIV Prevention, Frankfort, 1996—98; mem. African-Am. adv. com. Ky. HIV Prevention Cmty. Planning Group, State of Ky., Dept. HIV Prevention, Frankfort, 1996—98, advisor, 1998—99; psychol. cons. State of Fla. Dept. Juvenile Justice Dist. XI, Miami, 1994—95; rsch. cons. R.E.A.C.H., Louisville, 1995—96, Coun. on Prevention and Edn.: Substances, Inc. (COPES) Family Connection Demonstration Project, Louisville, 1996—2000; psychologist U. Louisville Sch. Medicine WINGS

(HIV/AIDS) Clinic Aux. Support Team, Louisville, 1996—2000; co-process evaluator Ky. Incentives for Prevention, Louisville, 1997—2000; psychologist site supr. Americana Cmty. Ctr., Louisville, 1999—2003; adj. asst. prof. dept. psychology Barry U., Miami Shores, Fla., 1995; presenter, lectr., spkr. in field. Author: (nonfiction book) Babies Mamas, (booklet) Health Care Utilization and Medical Adherence Issues Among Prenatal HIV Seropositive African American Women in Miami: The Role of The Family and The Extended Kinship Networks.; panelist (television program) KENTUCKY TONIGHT: Coping Emotionally with the Aftermath of September 11th; author: (public service television script) Make Your Next Move Count, (public service TV script) Child Abuse: Sticks and Stones and Words Can Hurt; contbr. articles to scholarly jours. Mem. planning com. Ann. Nat. Conf. on the Black Family in Am., Louisville, 2001—03; judge panelist ABA Regional Client Counseling Competition, Louisville, 2002; facilitator One Louisville, 2001—02; bd. dirs. Ctr. for Haitian Studies, Miami, 1993—95. Recipient White Ho. Briefing Honoring World AIDS Day invitation, 2005, NIMH Postdoctoral fellowship in psychoimmunology, Ctr. for the Biopsychosocial Study of AIDS, Dept. Psychiatry, U. Miami Sch. of Medicine, 1990—91, Cert. Appreciation for Contbns. in Devel. of Creative AIDS Edn. Programs, U.S. Dept. VA, 1990, Ill. Minority Grad. Incentive Program fellowship, State of Ill., 1986—90, So. Ill. U. Grad. Dean's fellowship, 1984—85, Cert. of Appreciation, Omega Psi Phi, 1997, 1998, 1999, 2000; named Outstanding Leader and Mentor, Spalding U. Black Student Assn., 1997, Nat. Inst. of Drug Abuse Sponsored Jr. Minority Investigator, APHA, 1992; grantee Ongoing Program of Stress Mgmt. for Spl. Immunology Unit Staff., U.S. Dept. VA, Office Acad. Affairs, and Regional Med. Edn. Ctr., 1989, Five-year Plan for Ethnic Minority Recruitment, Retention and Tng. in Psychology, APA, 2002, Qualitative studies addressing the sexual behaviors and biopsychosocial issues of patients in the Women's HIV/AIDS Clinic at the U. of Miami, U. Miami Sch. of Medicine Ctr. for Comprehensive Study of HIV/AIDS, 1990—92; scholar Non-Traditional Student Scholarship award, Delta Sigma Theta, Carbondale Alumnae Chpt., 1989. Mem.: APA, Inst. Noetic Scis., Kentuckiana Assn. of Black Psychologists (pres. 2002—03), Ky. Psychol. Assn., Conn. Psychol. Assn. (ethnic diversity task force 2004, co-chair 2005—), Nature Conservancy. Achievements include research in Ethnographic Study of Miami-area HIV Positive Expectant Mothers with Previous Children. Office: Emancipation Inst Inc Deep River Ctr 3 Taliar Ridge Rd Guilford CT 06437 E-mail: darlene.shelton@chiglobal.org.

SHELTON, HAL TERRY, history professor; b. Brownwood, Tex., July 26, 1935; s. William and Myrtle Shelton; m. Sutthida Chantrasri, July 23, 1976. BE, Tex. A & M U., 1958; MEd, U. Houston, 1972, MA in History, 1985, PhD, 1991. Lt. col. US Army, 1958—79; prof. & assoc. prof., dept. mil. sci. Rice U., Houston, 1969—72; tchg. rsch. fellow, dept. history U. Houston, 1982—89, lectr., dept. history, 1989—91; prof., history San Jacinto Coll., Pasadena, Tex., 1991—, Am. Mil. U., Manassas, Va., 1994—2003. Adj. instr., dept. history North Harris Coll., 1986—88. Author: (books) General Richard Montgomery and the American Revolution, The Use of Site History in Urban Studies, 1988, The Shamrock Hotel Revisited: An Urban History, 1989, (books) From Redcoat to Rebel: General Richard Montgomery and the American Revolution, 1994; assoc. editor: book American History Reader, vol. II, 1992, contbg. editor: book The American Revolution: An Encyclopedia, 1993, Encyclopedia of the American Political Parties and Elections, 1990; contbr. chapters to books & sci. papers. Decorated US Army Meritorious Svs. medal Rice U.; recipient Robert Giesberg award, U. Houston, 1988; David Libr. of Am. Revolution Rsch. grant, 1988. Home: 3414 Summer Bay Dr Sugar Land TX 77478 Office: San Jacinto Coll Ctrl Campus Dept History 8060 Spencer Hwy PO Box 2007 Pasadena TX 77501-2007

SHELTON, HUGH (HENRY HUGH SHELTON), former Chairman of the Joint Chiefs of Staff; b. Tarboro, NC, Jan. 2, 1942; m. Carolyn L. Johnson; children: Jon, Jeff, Mark. BS, N.C. State U.; MS, Auburn U.; grad., Air Command and Staff Coll., Nat. War Coll. Commd. 2d lt. US Army, 1963, advanced through grades to gen., 1996, ret., 2001; with 5th Spl. Forces Group, Vietnam, 173d Airborn Brigade, Vietnam; comdr. 3d Bn., 60th Infantry, 9th Infantry Divsn., Ft. Lewis, asst. chief of staff for ops.; comdr. 1st Brigade, 82d Airborne Divsn., Ft. Bragg, N.C.; chief of staff 10th Mountain Divsn., Ft. Drum, N.Y.; with ops. directorate Joint Staff, Washington, 1987—89; asst. divsn. comdr. for ops. 101st Airborne Divsn., 1989-91; comdr. 82d Airborne Divsn., Ft. Bragg, N.C., XVIIIth Airborne Corps., 1993, US Spl. Ops. Command (USSOCOM), 1996—97; chmn. Joint Chiefs of Staff, US Dept. Def., Washington, 1997—2001; pres., internat. ops. M.I.C. Industries, 2002—06; chmn. Protective Products of America, Inc., 2009—. Bd. dirs. Anheuser-Busch Companies Inc., 2001—08, Anteon Internat. Corp., 2002—06, Red Hat, Inc., 2003—, Protective Products of America, Inc., 2006—, CACI Internat. Inc., 2007—. Decorated Def. D.S.M. with two oak clusters, D.S.M., Bronze Star with V device with three oak clusters, Purple Heart, Legion of Merit with oak leaf cluster.

SHELTON, JAMES D. (DENNY SHELTON), hospital investment company executive; BA in Polit. Sci. and History, La. State U.; MS in Pub. Adminstrn., U. Mo. Hosp. adminstr. La., Iowa, NC, Ga., Ill., Mo.; exec. dir. Westbank Hosp. Ops. Nat. Med. Enterprises (now Tenet Healthcare Corp.), New Orleans, 1984—86, v.p. ops., 1986—90, sr. v.p. ops., 1990—93, exec. v.p. ctrl. divsn., 1993—94; pres. ctrl. group Columbia/HCA, 1994—98, pres. Pacific group, 1998—99; chmn., CEO Triad Hosps. Inc., 1999—2007; chmn. Legacy Hosp. Partners, Inc., 2007—; sr. advisor CCMP Capital Advisors, LLC. Chmn. Fedn. Am. Hosps., 1999, mem. bd. govs., 1999—2002; bd. dirs. Am. Hosp. Assn., Ventas, Inc., Omnicare, Inc. Office: Legacy Hosp Partners Inc 2800 N Dallas Pky Ste 200 Plano TX 75093*

SHELTON, JAMES DOUGLAS, banker; b. Boynton Beach, Fla., Feb. 28, 1939; s. Clarence Wilton and Lou Anna (Ward) S.; m. Claudia Ellen Marshall, Oct. 20, 1973; children: Christopher John, Ryan Marshall. BA, Duke U., 1961; MDiv, Union Sem., 1965; STM, Boston U., 1966; SEP, Stanford U., 1975. Adj. prof. NY Sem., NYC, 1966-68; asst. treas. Bankers Trust Co., NYC, 1968-71; v.p. Chase Manhattan Bank, NYC, 1971-84; sr. v.p. Conn. Bank & Trust, Hartford, Conn., 1984-88; chmn., pres., chief exec. officer First Fed. Savs., East Hartford, Conn., 1988-2001. Bd. dirs. Conn. On-Line Computer Ctr., Avon, chmn., 1989-2001; bd. dirs. Cmty. Bank League of New Eng., Boston, chmn., 1989-96; mem. Conn. Legislature Interstate Banking Task Force, Hartford, 1989-90. Bd. dirs. Jr. Achievement North Ctrl. Conn., Windsor, 1986-90, Sci. Ctr. Conn., West Hartford, 1988-94, Riverfront Recapture, Inc., Hartford, 1994-98, Charter Oak State Coll. Found., New Britain, Conn., 2004—; corporator Am. Sch. for the Deaf, West Hartford, 1986-2001; trustee Noah Webster House, West Hartford Hist. Soc., 2005— Mem. Am. Cmty. Bankers Assn. (bd. dirs. 1995-2001), New Eng. Automated Clearing House Assn. (bd. dir. 1983-98), The Country Club of Farmington, Old Guard of West Hartford.

SHELTON, JIM (JAMES H. SHELTON), federal agency administrator, former educational association administrator; m. Sonia Shelton; children: Justice, Jameson. B in Computer Sci., Morehouse Coll.; MBA, Stanford U. Sr. mgmt. cons. McKinsey & Co., Atlanta; with Knowledge Universe, Inc.; co-founder LearnNow; ptnr., East Coast lead NewSchools Venture Fund, San Francisco; program dir. edn. divsn. Bill & Melinda Gates Found.; asst. dep. sec. innovation and improvement US Dept. Edn., Washington, 2009—. Office: US Dept Edn Office of Innovation and Improvement 400 Maryland Ave, SW Washington DC 20202*

SHELTON, KATHRYN H., retired librarian; d. Bruce Whittington and Edna Poyas (Hall) Martin; m. L. Jev Shelton, Aug. 27, 1970; children: Kirsten Anna, Martin Harold, Andrew Olaf. BA in English, Randolph-Macon Woman's Coll., Lynchburg, Va., 1963; MS in Libr. Sci., Simmons Coll., Boston, 1966; MA in Am. Studies, U. Minn., 1969; student, U. Alaska. Cert. Modern Archives Inst., 1986. Profl. libr. asst. Boston Pub. Libr., 1965-67; substitute libr. Mpls. Pub. Libr., 1967-68; tchg. assoc. Gen. Coll. U. Minn., Mpls., 1968-69; asst. libr. reader svcs. Carleton Coll., Northfield, Minn., 1969-70; part-time libr. III Dept. Environ. Conservation & Edn. Alaska State Libr., Juneau, 1975-76; assoc. prof. libr. sci., head libr. U. Alaska, Juneau, 1970-75, 76-78; libr. II. State Legislature, Juneau, 1979—85; archivist I Alaska State Archives Dept. Adminstrn., Juneau, 1985-86; libr. III head pub. svcs. sect. Dept. Edn. Alaska State Libr., 1986-87, libr. III head Hist. Libr. Dept. Edn., 1987—2005, Alaska state libr., dir. divsn. librs., archives and museums, 2005—08; ret., 2008. Spkr. in field. Editor: Alaskana Books, 1993; contbr. articles to profl. jours. Mem. Alaska Geographic Names Bd., 1987—93, Gold Rush Centennial Task Force, 1993—2003; dir. Alaska Newspaper Project, 1991—98. Recipient Kudo award, State of Alaska, 1985. Mem.: ALA, Acad. Cert. Archivists, Soc. Am. Archivists, Gastineau Channel Hist. Soc. (sec. 1991), Alaska Hist. Soc. (pres. 2000—02), Alaska Libr. Assn. (ann. conf. prog. chmn. 1973, pres. 1973—74, continuing edn. com. 1984, collection devel. com. 1986—88, Alaskana subcom. 1987—95). Office Phone: 907-465-2911.*

SHELTON, KENNETH R., JR., real estate company executive, artist; b. Galveston, Tex., Aug. 29, 1946; Pres. Moore Climatic Inc., 1984—87; gen. ptnr. Various Real Estate Ltd. Partnerships, 1978—, Moore-Shelton, LP, 1984—; pres. Polybus, Inc., 1989—; gen. ptnr. Video Lane Ltd., 1983—. Exhibited in group shows at Rosenberg Libr., Galveston, 1982, one-man shows include Galveston Art Ctr., 1991, exhibited in group shows at Island Inspired, Galveston Art Ctr., 1992. Mem. Galveston Bd. Realtors, 1983—; pres. Galveston County Apt. Assn., 1984—85; chmn. Cancer Crusade, 1983—84; pres. Galveston Acad. Excellence Booster Club, 2000—03, v.p., 1999—2000, 2003—; founding pres. Galveston Fencing Club, 1999—2001, Knights of Momus, 1984—85. Mem.: Galveston Fencing Club (dir.). Episcopalian. Avocations: painting, fencing, furniture making. Office: 2002 45th St Ste 103 Galveston TX 77550 Mailing: PO Box 3123 Galveston TX 77552

SHELTON, LAWRENCE G., social sciences educator; b. Rushville, Ill., 1942; s. Jake R. Shelton and Marjorie A. Stapleton; married. AB, Harvard U., Cambridge, Mass., 1964; PhD, U. Minn., Mpls., 1970. Asst. prof. psychology U. Pitts., 1968—71; assoc. prof. human devel. & family studies U. Vt., Burlington, 1971—. Chair Mt. Mansfield Union Sch. Dist., Underhill, Vt., 1986—92. U. Design Consulting Team grant, US Dept. Edn., Office Post Sec. Edn., 2008—. Mem.: APA, Nat. Assn. Edn. Young Children, Soc. Rsch. Child Devel., Soc. Rsch. Adolescence, Nat. Coun. Family Rels. Office: Univ Vt Living Learning C-150 633 Main St Burlington VT 05405-0384 Business E-Mail: lawrence.shelton@uvm.edu.

SHELTON, ROBERT NEAL, academic administrator, physics professor, researcher; b. Phoenix, Oct. 5, 1948; s. Clark B. and Grace M. (McLaughlin) S.; m. Adrian Ann Millar, Aug. 30, 1969; children: Christian, Cameron, Stephanie. BS, Stanford U., 1970; MS, U. Calif., San Diego, 1973, PhD, 1975. Postdoctoral researcher U. Calif.-San Diego, La Jolla, 1975-76, asst. rsch. physicist, 1976-78; asst. prof. Iowa State U., Ames, 1978-81, assoc. prof., 1981-84, prof. physics, 1984-87; prof. physics, chmn. dept. U. Calif.-Davis, 1987-90, vice chancellor for rsch., 1990-96, vice provost for rsch., 1996-2001; exec. vice chancellor, provost U. N.C., Chapel Hill, 2001—06; pres. U. Ariz., Tucson, 2006—. Contbr. over 200 articles to profl. jours. Fellow Am. Phys. Soc., Calif. Coun. on Sci. and Tech.; mem. AAAS, Materials Rsch. Soc., Sigma Xi, Phi Beta Kappa. Office: Univ Ariz Adminstrn Bldg Rm 712 PO Box 210066 Tucson AZ 85721-0066

SHELTON, SAMANTHA, psychologist; b. Chgo., July 16, 1974; d. Emmett and Marie Shelton. BS, Xavier U. La., New Orleans, La., 1996; Clin. Psychology, Forest Inst. of Profl. Psychology, Springfield, Mo., 2000. Mental health provider Sinai-Mile Sq. Mental Health Clinic, Chgo., 2000—01; clin. psychologist Fed. Bur. of Prisons, Beaumont, Tex., 2001—03, drug abuse program coord. Las Vegas, Nev., 2003—. Treas. Fed. Bur. of Prisons Non Profit Orgn., Las Vegas, Nev., 2003—04. Contbr. scientific papers. Mem.: APA, Black Psychologist Assn. Office: Fed Bureau of Prisons Metropolitan Detention Ctr Los Angeles CA 90012 Home: 1449 East 3rd St #302 Long Beach CA 90802 Business E-Mail: sshelton@bop.gov.

SHELTON, STEPHANI, broadcast journalist, consultant; b. Boston; d. Phil and Babette (Belloff) Saltman; m. Frank Herold. BS, Boston U. Corr. CBS News, NYC, 1973—84; news corr. WWOR-TV, NYC, 1984—88; corr., anchor Fin. News Network, NYC, 1989—91. Freelance reporter Sta. WPIX-TV, 1991-95, Sta. WNBC-TV, 1993-96, WWOR-TV, 1999-02; writer, prodr., radio anchor CNBC, 2003—; cons. trainer Ctrl. and Eastern Europe broadcast journalists, 1998—; med. health prodr.-reporter PBS, The Learning Channel, 1997-99; owner The Fred Group Ltd., video/internet prodn. co., 1998—; freelance radio documentary writer Westinghouse Group W Broadcasting, NYC, 1970-73. Recipient Peabody award, 1972, N.J. Best Spot News award AP, 1987, 88, N.J. Working Press award, 1993-94; Emmy nominee, 1995, 96, 99, 2000. Mem. Soc. Profl. Journalists (award 1999), Radio and TV News Dirs. Assn., N.Y.C. Press Club, Investigative Reporters and Editors, Com. to Protect Journalists. E-mail: backbay38@aol.com, fred@fredgroupltd.com. *Guiding principles: a questioning mind, a refusal to take no for an answer and the memory of 28 marathons. If you don't ask "why", you are not a journalist.*

SHELTON, WILLIAM L., career military officer; b. 1954; BS, USAF Acad., 1976; MS in Astronautical Engring., USAF Inst. Tech., 1980; grad., Armed Forces Staff Coll., 1986; MS in Nat. Security Strategy, Nat. War Coll., 1995. Commd. 2d. lt. USAF, 1976, advanced through grades to lt. gen., 2007; launch facilities mgr., launch dir. and tech. asst. to commr. Space and Missile Test Ctr., Vandenberg AFB, Calif., 1976—79; space shuttle flight controller Johnson Space Ctr., Houston, 1981—85; staff officer, dep. chief of staff for ops. Air Force Space Command, Peterson AFB, Colo., 1986—88, exec. officer to vice comdr., 1992—93, dir. requirements, 2000—02, dir. plans and programs, 2002—03, dir. air and space ops., 2003, comdr. 14th Air Force (Air Force Strategic), 2005—08; staff officer Office of Space Plans and Policy, Office of Sec. of Air Force, Washington, 1988—90; comdr. 2nd Space Ops. Squadron, Falcon AFB, Colo., 1990—92, 50th Ops. Group, Falcon AFB, Colo., 1993—94; dep. program mgr., exec. asst. Cooperative Threat Reduction Program Office, Office of Asst. to Sec. of Def. for Nuclear, Chem. and Biological Defense Programs, Washington, 1995—97; comdr. 90th Space Wing, Francis E. Warren AFB, Wyo., 1997—99; chief Space Superiority Divsn. Office of Dep. Chief of Staff for Plans and Programs, USAF Hdqs., Washington, 1999—2000, dir. manpower and orgn., 2000; dir. capability and resources integration (J8) US Strategic Command (USSTRATCOM), Offutt AFB, Nebr., 2003—05, dir. plans and policy (J5), 2005, comdr. Joint Functional Component Command for Space Vandenberg AFB, Calif., 2005—08; chief warfighting integration and chief info. officer Office of Sec. of Air Force, US Dept. Def., Washington, 2008—09; asst. vice chief staff, dir. Air Force Staff USAF, Washington, 2009—. Decorated Disting. Svc. Medal, Defense Superior Svc. Medal (with Oak Leaf Cluster), Legion of Merit (with Oak Leaf Cluster), Defense Meritorious Svc. Medal (with Oak Leaf Cluster), Meritorious Svc. Medal (with 4 Oak Leaf Clusters), Air Force Commendation Medal, Joint Meritorious Unit Award (with 2 Oak Leaf Clusters), Air Force Outstanding Unit Award (with Silver and 2 Bronze Oak Leaf Clusters), Air Force Organizational Excellence Award (with Oak Leaf Cluster); fellow Seminar XXI, MIT, 1997. Office: USAF 1670 Air Force Pentagon Washington DC 20330*

SHEMESH, LORRAINE R., painter; b. Jersey City; d. Murray Shemesh and Mildred Behar-Nissim; m. Jack Bashkow, Sept. 12, 1993. BFA in Painting magna cum laude, Boston U., 1971; postgrad., Tyler Sch. Art, Rome, 1971-72; MFA in Painting, Tyler Sch. Art, Elkins Park, Pa., 1973. Asst. prof. fine arts R.I. Sch. Design, Providence, 1973-80, Amherst (Mass.) Coll., 1980-81. One-woman shows include R.I. Sch. Design, 1976, Alpha Gallery, Boston, 1978, Allan Stone Gallery, N.Y.C., 1983, 85, 88, 91, 95, 2000, 04, Solo Show Allan Stone Gallery, 2009, Butler Inst. Am. Art., Ohio, 2006; exhibited in selected group shows at Inst. Contemporary Art, Boston, 1977, DeCordova Mus., Lincoln, Mass., 1979, Mus. RI Sch. Design, 1974,76,78, Mead Art Mus., Amherst Coll., 1981, Mus. City of N.Y., 1983-84, 95, San Francisco Mus. Modern Art, 1985-86, Nasher Mus. Art, Nasher Mus. Art Duke U., Durham, N.C., 1987, Akron (Ohio) Art Mus., 1987, Bronx Mus. Arts, N.Y.C., 1988, ABC, 1990, Sotheby's, N.Y.C., 1993, Arnot Art Mus., 1995, Musée de Carouge, Switzerland, 1999, Frye Art Mus., Seattle, Wash., 2002, Nat. Acad. Design Mus., N.Y.C., 2002, 06, 07, 09, Frye Art Mus., Seattle, 2002; represented in pub. collections Mus. City of N.Y., DeCordova Mus., Butler Inst. Am. Art, Youngstown, Ohio, Mus. R.I. Sch. Design, AT&T, Chgo., Boise (Idaho) Art Mus., Morgan Stanley, N.Y.C., Montgomery Securities, San Francisco, Nat. Acad. Mus., N.Y.C., Novartis Corp., Basel, Switzerland; selected publs. include Art in America, 1988, 95, 2000, 07, A Guide to Drawing 4th edit., 1988, American Realism: 20th Century Drawing and Watercolors, 1986, Art & Auction, 2000; publs. include N.Y. Times, 1995, 2000, 04, 07, 09, Harper's Mag., The New Yorker, 1995, 2000. Grantee R.I. State Coun. for the Arts, Providence, 1979, Disting. Alumni award Sch. Visual Arts/Boston U., 1992; fellow Tyler Sch. Art, 1972-73, Corp. Yaddo, Saratoga Springs, N.Y., 1981; finalist painting NEA/MAAF Regional Fellowship, 1996, recipient Watershed Residency, 2000, 05. Mem.: Nat. Acad. N.Y.C. Office Phone: 212-684-2189. E-mail: lshemesh@aol.com.

SHEMIN, RICHARD JAY, cardiothoracic surgeon, educator; b. Little Rock, Sept. 25, 1950; s. Saul and Beverly (Newfield) S.; m. Susan Helaine Packer, Aug. 25, 1971; children: Stephanie Leigh, Michael Andrew, Michelle Elizabeth. BA magna cum laude, Boston U., 1970, MD magna cum laude, 1974. Cert. Am. Bd. Thoracic Surgery. Intern, gen. surgery Peter Bent Brigham Hosp./Harvard Med. Sch., Boston, 1974—75, resident, cardiothoracic vascular surgery, 1975—76, 1978—80; asst. prof., cardiothoracic surgery Harvard Med. Sch., Boston, 1982—87; fellow in cardiothoracic surgery NYU Sch. Medicine, NYC, 1980-82; clin. assoc., cardiothoracic surgery NHLBI/NIH, The Clinical Ctr., Bethesda, Md., 1976-78; sr. resident in surgery Brigham and Women's Hosp./Harvard Med. Sch., Boston, 1978-80, assoc. surgery, cardiac surgeon, prof., 1982-87; med. dir., cardiac surgery, ICU Brigham and Women's Hosp., Boston, 1984—87; assoc. cardiothoracic surgery Children's Hosp. Med. Ctr., Boston, 1984; prof., chmn. Boston U. Sch. Medicine, 1987—2007, chief, cardiothoracic surgery, 1995—2007, vice chair dept. cardiothoracic surgery, 1997—2007; chair dept. cardiothoracic surgery Boston Med. Ctr., 1987—2007, co-dir., Cardiovascular Ctr., 2000—07; prof., surgery David Geffen UCLA Sch. Medicine, 2007—; vice-chmn., dept. surgery UCLA Med. Ctr., 2007—, chief cardiothoracic surgery, chmn. cardiothoracic surgery, 2007—, co-dir., Cardiovascular Ctr., 2007—. Cons. Dana Farber Canc Inst, Boston, MA, 1983, Baxter Healthcare, Orange County, Calif., 1990-; pres., Boston U. Cardiothoracic Surgery Found., Inc.; presenter in the field Contbr. several articles to profl. jours; assoc. editor Circulation, Jour. Cardiac Surgery; reviewer for several jours. including Annal of Thoracic Surgery, Jour. Thoracic and Cardiac Vascular Surgery. Lt. comdr. USPHS, 1996-98. Recipient Roche award Boston U. Med. Sch., 1974, Boston U. Sch. Medicine Alumni award, 1987, Outstanding Leadership, Thoracic Surgery Found. for Rsch. and Edn. Fellow ACS (coun. Mass. Chpt.), Am. Surg. Assn., Am. Coll. Cardiology (coun. Mass. Chpt.), Am. Heart Assn. (pres. greater Boston divsn.), Am. Coll. Chest Physicians; mem. Soc. Thoracic Surgeons (chair workforce com. 1998-), Am. Assn. Thoracic Surgery, Thoracic Surgery Tng. Dirs. Assn. (exec. com., editor Adult Cardiac Surgery), Algonquin Club Boston (exec. com., bd. dirs.), Northeast Cardiac Surgery Soc. (immediate past pres.), Phi Beta Kappa, Alpha Omega Alpha. Avocations: sailing, hunting, golf, reading history and biographies. Office: UCLA Divsn Cardiothoracic Surgery 10833 LeConte Los Angeles CA 90095 Office Phone: 310-206-8232. Office Fax: 310-825-7473.

SHEMMERI, THAFUR, pediatric dentist; m. Nida Kazzaz, July 17, 1977; children: Ealaf, Esel, Aws. BDS, Baghdad U., 1977; DMD, Boston U., 1991, MSc in Dentistry, 1990, DSc in Dentistry, 1991. Cert. in pediatric dentistry Boston U., 1988. Pvt. practice, Baghdad, Iraq, 1977—86; pvt. practice in pediatric dentistry Mass., 1992—. Mem.: Mass. Dental Soc., Am. Orthodontic Soc., Am. Acad. Pediatric Dentistry, ADA, Am. Acad. Pediat. (assoc.). Office: Wachusett Pediatric Dentistry 100 Whalon St Fitchburg MA 01420 Office Fax: 978-343-5979. Personal E-mail: thafurshemmeri@hotmail.com.

SHEMS, ESTHERINA, retired child psychiatrist; b. Tel Aviv, Apr. 15, 1932; came to US, 1950; d. Aaron and Rachel (Yehuda) S.; m. Donald L. Schotland, Jan. 11, 1976. BS cum laude, Lynchburg Coll., 1954, DSc (hon.), 2003; MD, Woman's Med. Coll. Pa., 1958; DSc (hon.), Lynchburg Coll., 2009. Rotating intern Lankenau Hosp., Phila., 1958-59; fellow in adult psychiatry U. Pa., Phila., 1960-63; child psychiatry affiliate Child Study Ctr. Phila., 1961-63; asst. instr., dept. psychiatry U. Pa. Sch. Medicine, Phila., 1962-63, Irving Schwartz Inst. for Children and Youth, 1964-66, various staff, adminstrv. positions Phila. Psychiat. Ctr. Phila., 1964-81; clin. assoc. in psychiatry U. Pa. Sch. Medicine, Phila., 1979-81; cons. early intervention programs Cmty. Coun. for Mental Health/Mental Retardation, Inc., Phila., 1981—2002; ret. Numerous cons. and tchg. positions in field including invited lectr., Inst. Pediatrics Chinese Acad. Med. Scis., Beijing, People's Republic of China. Exec. bd. Trust Fund of Alumnae/i Assn. Woman's Med. Coll., Med. Coll. Pa., 2001—, vice-chair., 2003—. Named one of Outstanding Young Women of America, 1967, one of Outstanding Young Women of

Pa., 1967; recipient T. Gibson Hobbs Outstanding Alumni award Lynchburg Coll., 1969, Disting. Alumni award, 1990, Richard H. Thornton award for Excellence, 1995, Lifetime Achievement award, Va. Found. Ind. Colls., 2002. Fellow Am. Orthopsychiat. Assn., Coll. Physicians Phila.; mem. Med. Women's Internat. Assn. (US del. and session co-chmn. XIX Internat. Congress 1984, XX Internat. Congress 1987, XXII Congress 1995, mem. sci. rsch. com. 1990-98, nat. coord. for USA 1992-98, v.p. N.Am., exec. bd. 1998-2001), Am. Psychiat. Assn. (life mem.), Am. Med. Women's Assn. (life, mem. exec. com., bd. dirs. 1986-88, 92-98, councilor of orgn. 1986-88, mem. various coms. and task forces 1970—, Bertha Van Hoosen MD award 2002), Psychiat. Physicians Pa., Phila. Psychiat. Soc., Phi Kappa Phi, Chi Beta Phi (various offices), others. Avocations: travel, photography, music, reading. Home: 1310 Wyngate Rd Wynnewood PA 19096-2455

SHEMWELL, ROBERT H., federal judge; b. 1941; BA, La. State U., 1963, JD, 1967. Assoc. Seale, Smith, Baine & Phelps, 1967-70; asst. U.S. atty. U.S. Dist. Ct. (we. dist.) La., 1970-75, clk. of ct., 1975—, part-time magistrate judge Shreveport, 1984—; acting clk. of ct. U.S. Bankruptcy Ct., 1986-87. Office: US Dist Ct We Dist 1167 US Courthouse 300 Fannin St Shreveport LA 71101-3141 Fax: 318-676-3966.

SHEN, ALFRED C., neurosurgeon; b. Ithaca, NY, Oct. 5, 1964; s. C. C. and Helen H. Shen; m. Kim Nguyen, Feb. 12, 2000; children: Eric Y., Erin Y. BSEE, Rice U., Houston, 1987; MD, U. Tex., Dallas, 1991. Diplomate Am. Bd. Neurol. Surgery, 2004. Spine fellow U. Tenn., 1999; neurosurgeon Desert Spine and Neurosurg. Inst., Rancho Mirage, Calif., 2002—; cheif neurosurgery Eisenhower Med. Ctr., 2008—. Mem.: AMA, Congress Neurol. Surgeons, Am. Assn. Neurol. Surgeons. Office: 39000 Bob Hope Dr W410 Rancho Mirage CA 92270

SHEN, BO-WEN, research scientist; arrived in US, 2007, naturalized; s. Kuan-Hua Shen and Shu-Mei Shen Chiu; m. De-Mei Meng, June 5, 1996; 1 child, Alexander. PhD, NC State U., Raleigh, 1998. Atmospheric scientist NASA, Goddard Space Flight Ctr., Sci. App. Internat. Corp., Greenbelt, Md., 1999—2006; rsch. scientist NASA, Goddard Space Flight Ctr., U. Md. Earth Sys. Sci. Interdisciplinary Ctr., Greenbelt, Md., 2006—. Mem.: IEEE Computer Soc., Am. Geophys. Union, Am. Meteorological Soc. Achievements include hurricane forcasts in 2004 and 2005 hurricane seasons with an ultra-high resolution global model on the NASA Columbia Supercomputer; research in joint project "coupling NASA advanced multi-scale modeling visualization systems for improving prediction high-impact tropical weather". Avocations: travel, computers. Office: UMCP/ESSIC and NASA/GSFC Laboratory for Atmospheres Code 613 Greenbelt MD 20771 Personal E-mail: bowen.shen@gmail.com.

SHEN, CHUN-YEN, mathematics professor; PhD, Ind. U. Bloomington, 2009. Assoc. instr. Ind. U. Dept. Math., 2005—. Office: Dept Math 831 E 3rd St Rawles Hall Bloomington IN 47405

SHEN, DAVID, orthodontist; married; 1 child. BS, SUNY, Stony Brook; DDS, U. Pa., Phila., 1981. Cert. in orthodontic specialty U. Pa., 1981, phase II Am. Bd. Orthodontics. Faculty mem. U. Calif., San Francisco; orthodontist OrthoWorks, San Francisco, 1983—. Spkr. in field. Fellow: Acad. Dentistry Internat.; mem.: Calif. Dental Assn., Am. Assn. Orthodontics, Am. Dental Assn., San Mateo County Dental Soc. (past chmn. mem. com.), No. Calif. Asian Dental Assn. (past pres.), Align Century Club. Avocations: photography, water sports, travel. Office: OrthoWorks Ste 2418 450 Sutter St San Francisco CA 94108*

SHEN, HUI, engineering educator; PhD, Pa. State U., State Coll., 2003. Rschr. Northwestern U., Evanston, Ill., 2004—06; asst. prof. Ohio Northern U., Ada, 2006—. Achievements include research in biomechanics and advanced materials. Office: Ohio Northern Univ 525 S Main St Ada OH 45810 Business E-Mail: h-shen@onu.edu.

SHEN, JIANQIANG, research scientist; Attending, Oreg. State U., Corvallis, 2009. Rsch. asst. Oreg. State U., 2003—; rsch. intern IBM Rsch., Cambridge, Mass., 2006. Fellowship, Nanjing U., China, 1997—2002. Mem.: Assn. Advancement Artificial Intelligence, Upsilon Pi Epsilon, Phi Kappa Phi. Office: Sch EECS Oreg State Univ 2040 Kelley Engring Ctr Corvallis OR 97331 Business E-Mail: shenj@eecs.oregonstate.edu.

SHEN, JIE, engineering educator; PhD, U. Sasktoon, Saskatchewan, Can., 2000. Assoc. prof. U. Mich., Dearborn, 2008. Contbr. articles to profl. jours. Laser Sensor grant, NSF, 2005, CT Sys. grant, Nat. Sci. Found., 2007. Office: Univ Mich Dearborn 4901 Evergreen Rd Rm 207 CIS Dearborn MI 48128

SHEN, MICHAEL, lawyer; b. Nanking, Jiangsu, Peoples Republic of China, Aug. 15, 1948; came to U.S. 1951; s. James Cheng Yee and Grace (Pai) S.; m. Marina Manese (div.); m. Pamela Nan Bradford, Aug. 12, 1983; 1 child, Jessica Li. BA, U. Chgo., 1969; MA, U. Pa., 1970; JD, Rutgers U., 1979. Bar: U.S. Dist. Ct. N.J. 1979, N.Y. 1980, U.S. Dist. Ct. (so., no. and ea. dists.) N.Y. 1980, N.J. 1981, U.S. Ct. Appeals (2d cir.) 1987, U.S. Supreme Ct. 1988, U.S. Ct. Appeals (3rd cir.) 1996. Staff atty. Bedford Stuyvesant Legal Svcs., Bklyn., 1979-80, Com. for Interns and Residents, NYC, 1980-81; ptnr. Michael Shen & Assocs., PC, NYC, 1981—. Past bd. dirs. past pres. Asian Am. Legal Def. and Edn. Fund, NYC; pres. bd. dirs. Anti-Discrimination Ctr. Metro New York; past bd. dirs. Nat. Employment Law Project, past pres. Past bd. dirs. N.Y. Civil Liberties Union, N.Y.C., Nat. Asian Pacific Am. Legal Consortium. Mem. Internat. Platform Assn., Nat. Employees Lawyers Assn., N.Y. State Bar Assn., N.Y. County Bar Assn., Nat. Lawyers Guild. Avocations: arts, reading. Office: Michael Shen PC 150 W 80th St Ste 6B New York NY 10024 Home Phone: 917-359-8035; Office Phone: 212-227-0300. E-mail: mslaw@alumni.uchicago.edu.

SHEN, MICHAEL YUE-HUA, cardiologist; b. Harbin, China, Apr. 25, 1958; arrived in US, 1987; s. Ho-Fu Shen and Hong-Yun Liu; m. Jennifer Fang-Yin Lin, 2001; children: Alexander David, Annabelle Ellian. MD, Jiamusi Med. Coll., Jiamusi, Heilongjiang, China, 1982; MS in Exercise Physiology, Beijing Inst. Phys. Edn., 1987. Diplomate Cardiovascular Disease Am. Bd. of Internal Medicine, 1999, Internal Medicine Am. Bd. of Internal Medicine, 1996, Certification Bd. of Nuc. Cardiology, 1997. Dir., nuc. cardiology and dir., ctr. for cardiovasc. informatics UMDNJ - Robert Wood Johnson Med. Sch. South Campus, Camden, NJ, 1999—2003; head, sect. of cardiac imaging Cleve. Clinic Fla., Ft Lauderdale/Weston, Fla., 2003—. Bd. dirs. Am. Soc. of Nuc. Cardiology, Bethesda, Md., 2005—; coding and reimbursement com. Am. Coll. of Cardiology, Bethesda, Md., 2005—; epiccare steering com. Cleve. Clinic Found., Cleveland, Ohio, 2003—. Contbr. scientific papers pub. to profl. jour. Grantee Referral Analysis on Cardiac Imaging, Fujisawa Healthcare, 2003, Effect trial, IVIVI Technologies, 2005, 5A Trial, Astellas, 2005; FACC, Am. Coll. of Cardiology, 2001. Mem.: Healthcare Info. Mgmt. Sys. Soc. Achievements include patents for Healthcare informatics. Office: Cleve Clin Fla 2950 Cleve Clin Blvd Fort Lauderdale FL 33331 Office Fax: 954-659-5291; Home Fax: 954-434-7789. Personal E-mail: drmikeshen@aol.com. Business E-Mail: shenm@ccf.org.

SHEN, PATRICK P., lawyer; b. Tainan, Taiwan, Oct. 10, 1966; BA, Brigham Young U., 1990, JD, 1994. Bar: Colo. 1995, Supreme Ct. Colo., US Ct. Appeals (2nd, 4th, 5th and 9th cirs.). Law clk. US Immigration Ct.; asst. dist. counsel Immigration and Naturalization Svc., NYC; spl. asst. US atty. (ea. dist.) NY US Dept. Justice, trial atty. Office Immigration Litig. Civil Rights Divsn. Washington, spl. coun. for immigration related unfair employment practices, 2007—; chief immigration counsel Judiciary Com. US Senate, Washington; dir. policy & planning, Immigration & Customs Enforcement US Dept. Homeland Security, Washington, 2004; assoc., dir. govt. rels. Fragomen, Del Rey, Bernsen & Loewy, LLP, Washington. Office: US Dept Justice / Civil Rights Divsn Office of Spl Coun 950 Pennsylvania Ave, NW Washington DC 20530 Office Phone: 202-616-5594. Office Fax: 202-616-5509.

SHEN, RONGER, artist, educator; b. Shanghai, Nov. 11, 1942; came to U.S., 1984; d. Jianping and Huijun (Peng) S.; m. Yi Wu, Dec. 31, 1965; 1 child, Yan Wu. BA, Nat. Nanjing Acad. Arts, 1965. Dir. arts and crafts dept. Jiangsu Light Industry Bur., Nanjing, 1965-79; dir. Jiangsu Acad. Arts and Crafts, 1982—. Profl. painter Jiangsu Acad. Traditional Chinese Painting, 1979—; pres. Qigong Ctr., Inc., N.Y., 1989—; Qigong cons. to dept. orthopedics Mt. Sinai Sch. Medicine, N.Y.C., 1991—, N.J. Med. Ctr. Pain Mgmt. Ctr., Newark, 1991; NIH approved rsch. project on Life Info. Pictures, Life Info. Rhythm and Qigong, 1993; dir. Assn. Modern Chinese Arts Inc., 1994—. Mem. Artists Assn. China (Jiangsu br.), Acad. Arts and Crafts China, Eastern Am. Qigong U.S. (chmn. 1991—). Home: 32-05 146th St Flushing NY 11354-3151 Personal E-mail: daan3205@yahoo.com.cn.

SHEN, SHIHUI, research assistant; d. Qiyou Shen and Zhenhua Ma; m. Hai Huang, Jan. 7, 2004; 1 child, Sarah Huang. PhD, U. Ill., Urbana, 2006. Rsch. asst. U. Ill., Urbana, 2001—. Rsch. asst. Jiangsu Transp. Rsch. Inst., Nanjing, Jiangsu Province, China, 2000—01. Recipient 1st prize Student Poster Contest award, FAA Ann. Conf., 2003; fellow, U. Ill., 2003; scholar, SE U., Nanjing, China, 1995—96; Helene M. Overly Meml. Grad. scholar, Chgo. chpt. Women's Transp. Seminar, 2005. Achievements include design of Moisture Permeability Test Equipment For Pavement. Home: 1630 NE Valley Rd Apt 0106 Pullman WA 99163-4408

SHEN, WEI, performing company executive, choreographer; b. Hunan, China, 1968; With Hunan State Xian Opera Co., 1984—89; original mem., dancer & choreographer Guangdong Modern Dance Co., 1991—94; founder & artistic dir. Shen Wei Dance Arts, NYC, 2000—. Work presented Am. Dance Festival, 1995, Nat. Theater Taiwan, 1996, Place Theater, London, 1997, Asia Soc., NYC, 1997, Stockholm Dance House, 1999, Brighten Arts Festival, 2000, Edinburgh Festival Theater, 2000, Germany Millennium Moves Festival, 2000; exhibitions include, Lincoln Ctr. Festival, NYC, 2003, New Vision Festival, Hong Kong, 2006, NY State Theater, 2007. Recipient 1st prize for Choreography & Performance, Inaugural Nat. Modern Dance Competition, China, 1994, Nijinsky award for Emerging Choreographer, 2004, Helpmann award for Best Ballet or Dance Work, 2005, Les Etoiles de Ballet, Palais des Festival, Cannes, France, 2006; fellow, NY Found. for the Arts, 2000, Ben Sommer fellow, Am. Dance Festival, 2000, John Simon Guggenheim fellow, 2001, MacArthur fellow, 2007; scholar, Nikolais/Louis Dance Lab, 1995. Office: Shen Wei Dance Arts Ste 303 520 8th Ave New York NY 10018 Office Phone: 212-962-1113. Office Fax: 212-962-1313.

SHEN, WEIXING, meteorologist; arrived in USA, 1991, naturalized, 2005; m. Grace Furonghe Howe; children: Emily, Kimberly. BS in Meteorology, Hangzhou U., China, 1984; MS in Atmospheric Dynamics, Chinese Acad. Sci., Beijing, 1987; PhD, SUNY, 1995. Rsch. asst. Stony Brook U., NY, 1991—95; from postdoctoral rschr. to asst. marine scientist U. RI, Kingston, 1996—2001; vis. scientist U. Corp. Atmospheric Rsch., Camp Springs, Md., 2001—05; vis. rsch. scientist U. Md., College Park, 2005—. Named Environ. Hero, NOAA, 2002. Mem.: Am. Geophy. Union (assoc.), Am. Meteorol. Soc. (assoc.). Achievements include development of a simple physical model for hurricane intensity research and prediction; discovery of environmental circulation-associated zonal variability of transient atmospherics waves in the tropics; nonlinear responses of stratospheric Quasi-Biennial Oscillation to sea surface temperature changes; modeling of standing surface water's effects on landfall hurricanes. Home: 10627 Alison Dr Burke VA 22015 Personal E-mail: wshenhz@yahoo.com. Business E-Mail: wshen@essic.umd.edu.

SHEN, XIAOPING, geography educator; b. China; 1 child, Jane An. BS, Beijing Normal U., China, 1983, MS; PhD, U. Ottawa, Canada, 1995. Lectr. Beijing Normal U., Beijing, 1986—89; prof. Ctrl. Conn. State U., New Britain, 1995—. Adj. prof. Grad. Sch. Chinese Acad. Scis., Beijing, 2003—06. Contbr. articles various profl. jours., chapters to books. Activity coord. Conn. Chinese Culture Ctr., Hartford, 2000—03. Faculty Rsch. grantee, Conn. State U., 2000—. Mem.: Assn. Am. Geographers (chair, china splty. group 2002—03), Gamma Theta Upsilon Internat. Geog. Honor Soc. (regional councilor for New Eng. - St. Lawrence Valley 2000—06). Office: Ctrl Conn State U 1615 Stanley St New Britain CT 06050

SHEN, YING H., medical educator; d. Yimin Shen and Shuxian Hu; m. Lin Zhang, Aug. 8, 1988; children: Michelle Shen Zhang, Nicholas Shen Zhang. MD, Beijing Med. Sch., 1985; PhD, NSW U., Sydney, 1997. Asst. prof. Baylor Coll. Medicine, Houston, 2004—; profl. staff Tex. Heart Inst., Houston, 2007—. Mem.: Am. Heart Assn. (award 2005—), Assn. Academic Surgery, Am. Diabetes Assn. Achievements include discovery of selective vascular insulin resistance in development of prothrombotic state in obesity and diabetes; PTEN in development of insulin resistance. Office: Baylor Coll Medicine C-1095 Texas Heart Inst 6770 Bert Houston TX 77030 Office Fax: 832-355-9951. Business E-Mail: hyshen@bcm.edu.

SHEN, ZHENG-XUAN, researcher; d. Hong-sheng Shen and Mingjuan Zhang; 1 child, Yan Pu. MD, Capital Med. and Sci. Inst., Beijing, 1983. Contbr. articles. Achievements include discovery of cholinesterases serve central role in the systems or networking biology; causes of gulf war sysndrome. Personal E-mail: zhengxshen@yahoo.com.

SHENEFELT, PHILIP DAVID, dermatologist; b. Colfax, Wash., July 31, 1943; s. Roy David and Florence Vanita (Cagle) S.; m. Debrah A. Levenson; children: Elizabeth, Sara, Shaina. BS with honors, U. Wis. Madison, 1966, MD, 1970, MS in Adminstrv. Medicine, 1984. Diplomate Am. Bd. Dermatology, Am. Bd. Med. Hypnosis. Intern U.S. Naval Hosp., Bethesda, Md., 1970-71; gen. practice Oreg. (Wis.) Clinic, 1975; resident in dermatology U. Wis. Hosp., Madison, 1975-78, mem. staff, 1978-87; asst. prof. dermatology U. South Fla., Tampa, 1987—97, assoc. prof., 1997—. Chief dermatology sect. VA Hosp., Bay Pines, Fla., 1987—89, asst. chief, Tampa, 1988—2002, chief, 2002—07; dermatologist Univ. Health Svc. U. Wis., Madison, 1978—87, VA Hosp., Madison, 1982—85. Served to lt. comdr. USN, 1969-74; capt. USNR (ret.); med. corps officer Submarine and Diving. Kellogg fellow, 1980-82. Mem.: AMA, Fla. Med. Assn., Soc. Clin. Exptl. Hypnosis, Noah Worcester Dermatol. Soc., Fla. West Coast Dermatol. Soc., Fla. Dermatol. Soc., Am. Soc. Clin. Hypnosis, Am. Coll. Physician Execs., Am. Acad. Dermatology. Home: 15919 Notting Hill Dr Lutz FL 33548-6147 Office: U South Fla Dermatol # 79 12901 Bruce Downs Blvd Tampa FL 33612-4742 Office Phone: 813-974-2188. Business E-Mail: pshenefe@health.usf.edu.

SHENG, JINHUA, research scientist; b. Hefei, Anhui, China, May 6, 1965; arrived in United States, 2001; m. Qiao Zhang, Feb. 12, 1991; 1 child, Yutian. BS in Elec. Engring., Hefei U. Tech., China, 1984, MS in Elec. Engring., 1989; PhD in Nuc. Electronics, U. Sci. & Tech. China, Hefei, 1997. Assoc. prof., assoc. dean grad. sch. China Acad. Telecom. Tech., Beijing, 1997—2001; vis. scholar U. Ill., Chgo., 2001—03; rsch. fellow Rush U., Chgo., 2003—05; rsch. assoc. U. Wis., Milw., 2005—. Mem. edn. com. China Acad. Telecomm. Tech., 1997—2000, Info. and Electronics China, 1998—99. Chief editor: Jour. Telecom. Tech., 1998—2001; contbr. papers to more than 40 profl. jours. and confs.; reviewer: to profl. jours. and confs. Mem.: IEEE (sr.). Achievements include patents for methods and apparatus for joint image reconstruction and coil sensitivity estimation in parallel MRI; high-speed parallel magnetic resonance imaging. Avocations: gardening, fishing, stamp collecting/philately. Office Fax: 414-229-2769. Personal E-mail: j.sheng@yahoo.com. Business E-Mail: jsheng@uwm.edu.

SHENG, QIN, mathematics professor; s. Re and Sh Sheng; m. Helen Huang, Jan. 1, 1962; children: Andy, Danny. BS, U. Nanjing, China, 1982, MS, 1985; PhD, U. Cambridge, England, 1990. Prof. U. Dayton, Ohio, 2001—04, Baylor U., Waco, Tex., 2004—. Rsch. fellow, USAF, 2005—. Mem.: Am. Math Soc., Ctr. Astrophysics, Space Physics and Engring. Rsch. Achievements include research in applied mathematics and computer simulation. Avocations: music, paintings, sight-seeing, mountain walks. Office: Dept Math Baylor Univ One Bear Pl Waco TX 76798-7328 Office Phone: 254-710-1241. Office Fax: 254-710-3569. Business E-Mail: qin_sheng@baylor.edu.

SHENG, ZHI (CHIH) YONG, surgeon, educator; b. Shanghai, July 1, 1920; m. Yun Xui Zhang, Oct. 9, 1943; children: Ai-lun, Jia-lun, Pei-lun MD, Shanghai Med. Coll., 1942. Resident dept. surgery Red Cross First Hosp., Shanghai, 1942—45, chief resident, dept. surgery, 1945—46; rsch. fellow Surgical Rsch. Lab., U. Tex. Med. Br., Galveston, 1947—48; vis. surgeon Yangtzepoo Hosp., Shanghai, 1949—50, Chongsan Hosp., Shanghai, 1950—52; assoc. rschr., deputy chief, dept. experimental surgery Acad. Mil. Med. Sci., PLA, China, 1952—61; chief, dept. gen. surgery Surgical Emergency Hosp., Shanghai, 1956—57; chief, faculty of topographical anatomy and operative surgery Second Mil. Med. Coll., Shanghai, 1956—57; chief, dept. trauma and burns Gen. Hosp. of PLA, Beijing, 1961—82; prof. of surgery Postgraduate Med. Coll. of PLA, Beijing, 1978—; dir. trauma ctr. Postgraduate Med. Coll. of PLA, 304th Hosp., Beijing, 1982—96; vice dir. 304th Hosp., Beijing, 1982—88, dir. Burns Inst., 1996—97; hon. dir. Burns Inst. First Affiliated Hosp. to Gen. Hosp. of PLA (formerly 304th Hosp.), Beijing, 1997—; academian Chinese Acad. Engring., 1996—2000, sr. academian, 2000—; hon. prof. Jinan U. Med. Coll., 2002—; prof. of surgery Qinghua U. Med. Coll., 2005; Plastic Surgery Hosp. Gen. Hosp. of PLA, 2006—. Editor-in-chief: Med. Jour. of PLA, hon. chief editor: Chinese Jour. Trauma, Chinese Jour. Burns, mem. editl. bd.: Chinese Jour. Critical Care Medicine, Burns, Jour. of Internat. Soc. Burn Injuries, Chinese Jour. Clinical Nutrition, Academic Jour. of Second Mil. Med. U., mem. adv. bd.: Chinese Hour. Traumatology, Chinese Jour. Emergency Medicine, Modern Rehabilitation, author chpts. to books, monographs in field. Recipient First prize, State Prize of Advances in Sci. and Tech., 1985, 2002, Second prize, 1992, 1993, 2005, 2008, Third prize, 1995, 1998, First Prize, Army Prize of Advances in Sci. and Tech., 1996, 1998, 1999, 2001, 2004, Second Prize, 1988—2001, First Prize, Army Prize of Achievement in Clin. Medicine, 2001, Advances in Sci. and Tech., State Bureau of Seismology, 1978, Merit of Honor, Headquarters of Gen. Staff, Gen. Dept. Politics and Logistics, PLA, 1987, Gen. Dept. Logistics, PLA, 1987, Second-class merit, 1987, Third-class merit, 1989, First-class merit, Military Commn., People's Republic of China, 2000, Ho Leung Ho Lee prize, 1999, award for Important Achievements in Sci. and Tech. of Mil. Svc., 1996, Bo Le prize, Gen. Dept. Logistics, PLA, 2000. Mem.: AAAS (internat. mem.), Burns Soc. of PLA (advisor), Trauma Soc. of PLA (advisor), Med. Assn. of PLA, Chinese Soc. for Trauma, Chinese Surgical Soc., Chinese Med. Assn. (hon. mem. bd. trustees), Chinese Burns Soc. (co-founder 1975, vice chmn. 1986—91, chmn. 1991—94, hon. chmn. 1994—2002), Israel Burn Assn. (hon.), Trauma Assn. Can. (hon.), Am. Assn. for Surgery of Trauma (hon.), Internat. Soc. for Burn Injuries (sr.). Avocation: classical music. Office: Burns Inst First Affiliated Hosp Gen Hosp of PLA formerly 304th Hosp 51 Fucheng Rd Beijing 100048 China Office Phone: 86-10-68989158. Personal E-mail: shengzhy@cae.cn. Business E-Mail: shengzy@public.bta.net.cn.

SHENK, LOIS ELAINE LANDIS, writer; b. Ephrata, Pa., May 30, 1944; BA in English, Eastern Mennonite Coll., 1966; MSc in Edn., Temple U., Phila., 1984. English mistress Githumu Secondary Sch., Thika, Kenya, 1966-68; English tchr. Kraybill's Jr. High, Mount Joy, Pa., 1976-77; freelance writer, 1978—; religious news corr. Gospel Herald, Scottdale, Pa., 1978-82. Observer, corr. The US Senate, Washington, 1987-2001, 2006—. Author: Out of Mighty Waters, 1982 (R.I.M. excellence award 1983), The Story of Ephrata Mennonite School, 1996; (one act play) A House for David in (anthology) Swords into Plowshares, 1983; (study guide for Christian edn.) Hebrews, 1988; contbr. poems, stories & features to jours.; editl. work Mennonite Ctrl. Com., Akron, Pa., 1977. Cmty. living advisor Friendship Cmty., Lititz, Pa., 1997-99; Sunday sch. tchr. Ephrata Mennonite Ch., 1997-99; tutor English as a Second Lang., 2004; US amb., World Forum, 2007; mem. Chancel choir, Lancaster Ch. Brethren, 2004—; hon. dir. gen. The Americas IBC, Eng., 2009. Recipient Rep. Senatorial Medal of Freedom, Lifetime Achievement award, Internat. Biog. Ctr., Eng., 2007, Global Fellowship cert., World Forum, Washington, 2007, Ambassadorship of US cert., 2007; named Hon. Dir. Gen. Americas, IBC, Eng., 2009; Order of Internat. fellowship. Avocations: reading, cooking, music. Home and Office: 821 Hershey Ave Lancaster PA 17603-5862 Personal E-mail: loiseshenk@gmail.com.

SHENK, THOMAS EUGENE, molecular biology educator, academic administrator; b. Bklyn., Jan. 1, 1947; s. Eugene Richard and Helen Marie (Deffenbaugh) S.; m. Susan Mary Hillman, July 4, 1979; children: Christopher Thomas, Gregory Thomas BS in Biology, U. Detroit, 1969; PhD in Microbiology, Rutgers U., 1973. Postdoctoral fellow, molecular biology Stanford Med. Ctr.; asst. prof. molecular biology U. Conn., Farmington, 1975-80; prof. molecular biology SUNY, Stony Brook, 1980-84; Elkins prof., dept. molecular biology Princeton U., 1984—, Am. Cancer Soc. prof., 1986—, chmn. dept. molecular biology, 1996—. Bd. dirs. Merck & Co., Inc., 2001—, CV Therapeutics, Inc., Palo Alto,

Calif., 2001—, Cell Genesys, Inc., 2001—, mem. scientific adv. bd., 1997—, Novalon Pharm. Corp.; investigator Howard Hughes Inst.; mem. pres. adv. group Fox Chase Cancer Ctr.; chair Sloan General Motors prize Selection Com.; spkr. in field; chair NIH Virology Study Sect.; bd. trustee Cold Spring Harbor Lab. Co-editor: Enhancers and Eukaryotic Gene Expression, 1983; contbr. articles to profl. jours.editor, Journal of Virology, 1984-94. Recipient NIH Rowe award. Mem. Am. Soc. Microbiology (Eli Lilly award 1982, pres.), NAS, Inst. Medicine, Am. Soc. for Virology (past pres.); fellow Am. Acad. Arts and Sciences., Am. Acad. Microbiology. Achievements include patents in field. Office: Princeton U Dept Molecular Biology Lewis Thomas Lab 203 Princeton NJ 08544-0001

SHENKAR, ROBERT, science educator, researcher; b. Detroit, Apr. 22, 1953; s. George and Anna Stella (Bogucki) S.; m. Yong S. Kwon, Mar. 22, 1989. BS, U. Mich., Ann Arbor, 1974; PhD, Mich. State U., East Lansing, 1979. Rsch. scientist NorthShore U. Health System, Evanston, Ill., 2003—. Contbr. articles to profl. jours. Mem. AAAS, Am. Physiol. Soc. Achievements include characterization of molecular processes involved in cerebral cavernous malformations sepsis and trauma, aging, meiotic recombination, mutagenesis and DNA repair. Office: NorthShore Univ HealthSystem 2650 Ridge Ave Evanston IL 60201

SHENKER, STEPHEN, physics professor; BA, Harvard U., 1975; PhD, Cornell U., 1980. Faculty U. Chgo., 1981—89; prof. Rutgers U., 1989—98; prof. and dir. Stanford Inst. Theoretical Physics, 1998—; Richard Herschel Weiland prof. Sch. Humanities Stanford U., 2004—. Recipient Young Investigator award, Nat. Sci. Found., 1985; fellow Sloan Found., 1983, MacArthur Found., 1987. Fellow: Am. Acad. Arts and Sciences, Am. Physical Soc. Office: Dept of Physics Stanford U Stanford CA 94306 Office Phone: 650-723-4615. Business E-Mail: sshenker@stanford.edu.

SHENKIR, WILLIAM GARY, business educator; b. Three Rivers, Tex., June 27, 1938; s. William and Lydia (Jancik) S.; m. Missy Smith, Jan 1, 1973. BBA, Tex. A & M U., 1960; postgrad. (Rockefeller Bros. Theol. fellow), Drew U. Sem., 1960-61; MBA, U. Tex., 1962, PhD, 1964. Asst. prof. McIntire Sch. Commerce, U. Va., Charlottesville, 1967-69, assoc. prof., 1969-72, prof., 1972—75, dean, 1977-92, Paul Goodloe McIntire prof. Charlottesville, 1977—82; William Stamps Farish prof. McIntire Sch. Commerce U. Va., 1982—2007, William Stamps Farish prof. emeritus, 2007—. Project dir. Fin. Acctg. Stds. Bd., Stamford, Conn., 1973—76; vis. prof. NYU Grad. Sch. Bus., NYC, 1976—77; bd. dirs. ComSonics Corp., Harrisburg, Va., Children Youth, Charlottesville, Va. Editor: Carman Blough: His Professional Career and Accounting Thought, 1978; co-author: The University of Virginia's McIntire School of Commerce: The First 75 Years, 1921-96, 1996, Open-Book Management: Creating an Ownership Culture, 1998, Making Enterprise Risk Management Pay Off, 2001, Making Enterprise Risk Management Pay Off: How Leading Companies Implement Risk Management, 2002, Enterprise Risk Management: Pulling It All Together, 2002, Enterprise Risk Management, 2007; contbr. articles to profl. jours. Capt. USAF, 1964—67. Mem. AICPA, Am. Acctg. Assn. (former v.p.), Acctg. Edn. Change Commn. (former vice chmn.), Assn. Advance Collegiate Schs. of Bus. (former bd. dirs., pres. 1990-91), Fin. Execs. Inst., Va. Soc. CPAs, Raven Soc., Landfall Club, Farmington Country Club, Phi Delta Kappa, Beta Gamma Sigma, Phi Kappa Phi. Presbyterian. Home: 420 Rookwood Dr Charlottesville VA 22903-4732 Business E-Mail: wgs2Z@virginia.edu.

SHENKMAN, MARK RONALD, investment and finance executive; b. Providence, Aug. 17, 1943; s. George and Florence (Littman) S.; children: Andrew Harris, Gregory Alexander; m. Rosalind Schmidt, Aug. 10, 1997; 1 stepson, Justin Warren Slatky. BA, U. Conn., Storrs, 1965; MBA, George Wash. U., Washington, DC, 1967; LHD (hon.), U Conn., Storrs, 2007. Security analyst New Eng. Mchts. Bank, Boston, 1969-71; fin. analyst Stone & Webster Securities Corp., Boston, 1971-73; rsch. analyst, portfolio mgr. Fidelity Mgmt. & Research Co., Boston, 1973-79; v.p. Lehman Bros. Kuhn Loeb, NYC, 1979-83; pres. First Investors Asset Mgmt. Co., NYC, 1983-85; pres., chief exec. officer Shenkman Capital Mgmt. Inc., NYC, 1985—. Bd. dirs. Mason sch. bus. found. Coll. William & Mary. Vice chmn. bd. trustees Wilbraham, Mass. and Monson Acad.; bd. visitors, trustee George Washington U. Sch. Bus.; bd. govs. Hillel Found; bd. dirs. UConn Found. 1st lt. US Army, 1967-69. Mem. Am. Bankruptcy Inst., NY Soc. Security Analysts, Boston Security Analysts Soc., Am. Statis. Assn., CFA Inst. Home: Gaston Farm Rd Greenwich CT 06831 Office: 461 Fifth Ave New York NY 10017-6234 also: 462 Harbor Dr Stamford CT 06902 Office Phone: 212-867-9090.

SHENON, PHILIP, journalist; b. San Francisco, June 26, 1959; s. Peter and Philippa (Richards) Shenon. BA in English Lit., Brown U., 1981. Reporter N.Y. Times, NYC, 1983—85, corr. Washington, 1985—90, S.E. Asia corr. Bangkok, 1991—95, def. corr. Washington, 1996—97, diplomatic corr., 1997—99, investigative corr., 2000—. Author: (book) The Uncensored History of the 9/11 Commission, 2008. Office: NY Times Washington Bur 1627 I St NW Washington DC 20006-4007

SHENOY, SACHINDEV SHANTARAM, astronomer; s. Shantaram and Supriya Shantaram Shenoy. BSc, PES Coll. Arts & Sci., Farmagudi, Goa, India, 1992; MSc, Goa U., Bambolim, 1994; MS, U. Tex., El Paso, 1998; PhD, Rensselaer Poly. Inst., Troy, NY, 2003. Lectr. dept. physics Govt. Coll. Arts and Sci., Sanquelim, Goa, 1994—95; lectr. Dept. Physics, Rensselaer Poly. Inst., Troy, 2002, postdoc. rsch. assoc., 2003—05, adj. prof., 2004—05; postdoc. rschr. Spitzer Sci. Ctr., Calif. Inst. Tech., Pasadena, 2006—. Vol. World Wildlife Fund Nature, Panajim, Goa, 1989—96; coord. Assn. Friends Astronomy, Panajim, 1990—96. Recipient Walter Eppinstein Tchg. award, Dept. Physics, Rensselaer Poly. Inst., 2001; named Amateur Astronomer of Yr., Assn. Friends Astronomy, 1995. Mem.: Am. Astron. Soc., Sigma Pi Sigma. Avocations: birdwatching, travel.

SHEON, AARON, art historian, educator; b. Toledo, Oct. 7, 1937; s. Benjamin William and Katherine (Rappoport) S.; m. Martine Bruel, Jan. 26, 1963 (div. 1986); children: Sandrine, Nicolas; m. Jill Belasco, Nov. 11, 2000. BA, U. Mich., 1959, MA, 1960; M.F.A. (Wilson fellow), Princeton U., 1962, PhD, 1966; postgrad., U. Paris, 1962-63. Staff officer, dir. gen.'s cabinet UNESCO, Paris, 1963-66; asst. prof. U. Pitts., 1966-69, asso. prof., 1969-78, acting chmn. dept. fine arts, 1969, 79-80, dir. univ. program Rouen, France, 1974-75, prof. art history, 1979—2003, prof. emeritus, 2004; vis. prof. Carnegie-Mellon U., 1981, 2002—03. Vis. exhbn. curator Mus. Art, Carnegie Inst., Pitts., 1977-81; program cons. Nat. Endowment Arts and Humanities, 1978-85; visual arts cons. Pa. Arts Council, 1981; vis. mem. Inst. for Advanced Study, Princeton, 1984-85 Author: The Gosman Collection, 1969, Monticelli, His Contemporaries, His Influence, 1978, Organic Vision, The Architecture of Peter Berndtson, 1980, Monticelli, 1986, Paul Guigou, 1987. Recipient Charles E. Merrill faculty award, 1968; Chancellor Bowman award, 1976; Honor award Pa. Soc. Architects, 1982, Innovation award in tchg. Art History Course for Blind Students U. Pitts., 2001, Bellet Teaching award, 2002, Innovation in Tchg. award, 2003; grantee Ford Found., 1967, NEH, 1979, European Union grantee, 2006; Gould Arts Found. fellow, 1986 Mem. Coll. Art Assn., Société de l'histoire de l'art français, Am. Assn. of Mus. Office: U Pitts Dept History Arts & Arch Pittsburgh PA 15260 Office Phone: 412-648-2400. Business E-Mail: ash2@pitt.edu.

SHEPARD, BEATRICE L., retired microbiologist, historian; b. Hillsdale, Mich., May 15, 1919; d. James Wesley Shepard and Ona Ola Kinney. AB in Zoology., U. Calif., Berkeley, 1940. Regional lab. dir. L.A. County Health Dept., LA, 1945-46; sr. biologist, sr. chemist S.E. Regional Lab., Juneau, Alaska, 1946-67; acting chief of labs. Alaska Dept. Health & Social Svcs., Juneau, 1967-70; microbiologist in charge S.E. Regional Lab., Alaska Dept. Health and Social Svcs., 1967—77; ret., 1977. Chemist L.A. County Health Dept., 1944-45, L.A. County Gen. Hosp., 1943-44; dir. pub. health lab. Health Dept. Riverside (Calif.) County, 1942-43. Author: Praise the Lord and Pass the Penicillin, 1979; co-author: Have Gospel Tent, Will Travel, History of 100 Years of Alaskan Methodism, 1986; editor: (newsletter) Western Cir. Rider, 1998—2005, Eagle River United Meth. Camp, 1998—; contbr. articles to profl. jours., chapters to books. Docent Alaska State Mus., 1992—2004; mem. Juneau Borough Commn. on Aging, 1997—; curator Alaska State Mus., 2003; mem. gen. commn. archives and history United Meth. Ch. Archives Ctr., Madison, NJ, 1988—96; historian Alaska Meth. Ch., Alaska Missionary Conf., Anchorage, 1980—; bd. dirs., advocacy chair Mus. Alaska, 1992—2005; sec. bd. dirs. Eagle River Meth. Camp, 1955—2005; bd. dirs. Western Jurisdictional Commn. on Archives and History, 1984—2005; chair Alaska Missionary Conf. Commn. on Archives and History, 1980—2004. Named Outstanding Lay Person of Yr. award Alaska Missionary Conf. of United Meth. Ch., 1986; recipient Meritorious Health Svc. award Alaska Pub. Health Assn., 1990, Lifetime Achievement award Juneau C. of C., 1997-. Mem.: Friends of Alaska State Mus. (hon.; life), Museums Alaska (hon.; life). Avocation: photography. Home: 12585 Glacier Hwy Juneau AK 99801 E-mail: BShep98308@aol.com.

SHEPARD, CHRISTY J., special education educator; d. William E. and Shirley M. Shepard. BS in Spl. Edn., U. Houston, 1974, MS in Occupl. Edn., 1989. Salesperson/customer svc. Sears, Roebuck & Co., Houston, 1968—93; sec. Preston Exterminating Co., Houston, 1971—74; tchr. Aldine Ind. Sch. Dist., Houston, 1974—76; tchr. of students with visual impairments Cypress-Fairbanks Ind. Sch. Dist., Houston, 1976—. Facilitator Region IV Edn. Svc. Ctr., Houston, 1999—. V.p. Harris County MUD #23, asst. sec./treas., 1989—. Mem.: Assn. Tex. Profl. Educators, Assn. Edn. and Rehab. Blind and Visually Impaired (treas. 2000—, Outstanding Mem. award 2007). Avocations: reading, travel, cross stitch.

SHEPARD, DONALD SLOANE, public policy research educator; b. NYC, Sept. 15, 1947; s. Bertram David Shepard and Marjorie (Haspel) Markley; m. Emily A. Maitin, Aug. 17, 1980; children: Melissa R. Maitin-Shepard, Jeremy B. Maitin-Shepard. BA (magna cum laude) with highest honors, Harvard U., 1969, M in Pub. Policy, 1973, PhD, 1976. Lectr. U. Nairobi, Kenya, 1970—71; sr. economist Mass. Dept. Pub. Health, Boston, 1977—79; dir. econ. rsch. VA, West Roxbury, Mass., 1979—85; lectr. Harvard U., Cambridge, Mass., 1977—80, assoc. prof., 1980—91; prof. Brandeis U., Waltham, Mass., 1991—. Co-developer QALY (Quality Adjusted Life Year), 1976; vis. lectr. Harvard U., 1992-99; adj. faculty Boston U., 1986-2004; affiliated faculty Brown U., Providence, 1995—; dir. cost and value work group Schneider Inst. Health Policy Brandeis U., 2000-; health svcs. rsch. study sects. Nat. Inst. Alcohol Abuse and Alcoholism, 1998-2002, Nat. Inst. Drug Abuse, 2004-06, Behavioral and Social Scis. HIV/AIDS Rsch., 2006-. Author: Assessing Costs for Cost-Effectiveness Analysis, 1988, Analysis of Hospital Costs: A Manual for Managers, 2000; guest editor Adminstrn. and Policy in Mental Health, 2005; contbr. more than 100 articles to profl. jours. Bd. sci. advisors Sabin Vaccine Inst., Washington DC, 1994—; bd. councilors Pediat. Dengue Vaccine Initiative, 2002—2005; mem. alumni coun. Phillips Acad.; mem. sci. & tech. adv. group neglected tropical diseases World Health Orgn., Geneva, 2008-. Grad. fellow NSF, 1971; prin. investigator Nat. Inst. on Drug Abuse and Nat. Inst. on Alcohol Abuse and Alcoholism, 1993—, Ctrs. Medicine & Medicaid Svcs., 2000—, Pediat. Dengue Vaccine Initiative, 2003-07, Commonwealth Fund, 2007-. Mem. APHA, Mass. Pub. Health Assn., Acad. Health, Internat. Health Econs. Assn., Phi Beta Kappa. Avocations: cross country skiing, swimming. Home: 16 Cranmore Rd Wellesley MA 02481-1329 Office: Brandeis U Heller Sch 415 South St Waltham MA 02454-9110 Office Phone: 781-736-3975. Business E-Mail: shepard@brandeis.edu.

SHEPARD, GEOFFREY CARROLL, insurance company executive; b. Santa Barbara, Calif., Nov. 7, 1944; s. James J. and Barbara (Hoose) S.; m. Saundra Gayle Carlton, Jan. 10, 1973; children: Jonathan Pettus, William Dabney. BA, Whittier Coll., 1966; JD, Harvard U., 1969. Bar: D.C. 1972, Pa. 1977, U.S. Supreme Ct. 1973. White House fellow, 1969-70; staff asst. to Pres. White House, 1970-72, assoc. dir. domestic coun., 1972-75; sr. assoc. Steptoe & Johnson, Washington, 1975-77; sr. v.p., assoc. gen. counsel CIGNA Corp., Phila., 1977-91; sr. v.p., gen. counsel, corp. sec. Reliance Ins. Group, Phila., 1991-94; pres. corp. divsn. Karr Barth Corp. Div., Phila., 1994—. Author: (book) The Secret Plot to Make Ted Kennedy President, Inside the Real Watergate Conspiracy, 2008. Trustee Whittier Coll., 2002—. Office: Karr Barth Corp Div 40 Monument Rd Bala Cynwyd PA 19004-1797

SHEPARD, JAMES RUSSELL, literature and language professor; b. Bridgeport, Conn., Dec. 29, 1956; s. Albert and Ida Shepard; m. Karen Glazier, 1994; children: Aidan, Emmett, Lucy. BA, Trinity Coll., Hartford, Conn., 1978; MFA, Brown U., Providence, 1980. Lectr. U. Mich., Ann Arbor, 1980—83; J. Leland Miller prof. English Williams Coll., Mass., 1983—. Vis. disting. professorships U. Mont., Brown U., Western Mich. U. Author: (novel) Flights, Paper Doll, Lights Out in the Reptile House, Kiss of the Wolf, Nosferatu. Mem. Pen US, NYC, 2004—09. Recipient Henfield Found. award, Henfield Found., 1980, Award, John Simon Guggenheim Found., 2005, award, John Simon Guggenheim Meml., ALEX award; Artists' Fellowship, Mass. Cultural Coun., 2000. Home: 45 Forest Rd Williamstown MA 01267 Office: Williams Coll Dept English Williamstown MA 01267 Business E-Mail: jshepard@williams.edu.

SHEPARD, JEAN HECK, retired publishing consultant; b. NYC, Feb. 2, 1930; d. Chester Reed and Anna S. (Charig) Heck; m. Lawrence Vaeth Hastings, Mar. 29, 1950 (div. 1953); 1 child, Lance Clifford Hastings; m. Daniel A. Shepard, July 26, 1954 (div. 1981); 1 child, Bradley Reed. BA, Barnard Coll., 1950; postgrad., Columbia U., 1952. Mem. sch. and libr. svc. Viking Press, NYC, 1956-57; asst. dir. sch. and libr. promotion E.P. Dutton, NYC, 1957-58; dir. advt. publicity and promotion Thomas Y. Crowell Co., NYC, 1958-62; dir. advt. and promotion Charles Scribner's Sons, NYC, 1962-67; cons. Stephen Greene Press, Brattleboro, Vt., 1970-73; mktg. mgr. A&W Publishers, NYC, 1979-80, Franklin Watts Publ., NYC, 1980-82; pub. 2 mags., divsn. advt. & promotion mgr. McGraw Hill Book Co., NYC, 1983-85; cons. Monitor Publ. Co., NYC, 1988-2000. Author: Simple Family Favorites, 1971, Herb and Spice Sampler, 1972, Cook With Wine!, 1973, Earth Watch: Notes on a Restless Planet, 1973, Harvest Home Steak Cookbook, 1974, Fresh Fruits and Vegetables Cookbook, 1974, Yankee Magazine, 1972, Let Them be Sea Captains. Mem.: Authors Guild, Am. Libr. Assn., Women's Nat. Book Assn., Pub. Ad Club. Methodist. Avocations: reading, writing, travel, music, dance. Home: 73 Kingswood Dr Bethel CT 06801-1834 Office Fax: 203-798-2924. E-mail: shepardagcy@mindspring.com.

SHEPARD, LANCE HASTINGS, marketing professional, consultant, newscaster; b. NYC, Dec. 11, 1950; s. Lawrence Vaeth Hastings and Jean Heck Hastings Shepard. Student, Boston U., 1969—70; BS in Psychology, Franklin Pierce Coll., Rindge, NH, 1973. Cert. radio operator NY. Mgmt. tng. Waltham Savs. Bank, Mass., 1974—75; news and sports anchor Ch. 10 Cable TV, Danbury, Conn., 1975—76; guest rels. reception Plaza Hotel, Waldorf Astoria, NYC, 1978—80; owner DJ-on-Call, NYC, 1981—88; v.p., dir. fin. Shepard Agy., Brewster, NY, 1988—2000, exec. v.p., treas. Bethel, Conn., 2000—. Umpire Nat. Assn. Baseball Umpires, NH, 1970, Babe Ruth Baseball, Conn., 1978, Little League, Conn., 1978; referee Accredited NH Basketball Ofcls., 1973. Mem.: Princeton Club. Avocations: French horn, trumpet, reading, sports, films. Home: 73 Kingswood Dr Bethel CT 06801 Office: Shepard Agy M&T Bank Bldg Brewster NY 10509 Office Fax: 203-798-2924. Personal E-mail: shepardagcy@mindspring.com.

SHEPARD, RANDALL TERRY, state supreme court chief justice; b. Lafayette, Ind., Dec. 24, 1946; s. Richard Schilling and Dorothy Ione (Donlen) S.; m. Amy Wynne MacDonell, May 7, 1988; one child, Martha MacDonell. AB cum laude, Princeton U., 1969; JD, Yale U., 1972; LLM, U. Va., 1995; LLD (hon.), U. So. Ind., 1995, U. S.C., 1996. Bar: Ind. 1972, U.S. Dist. Ct. (so. dist.) Ind. 1972. Spl. asst. to under sec. U.S. Dept. Transp., Washington, 1972-74; exec. asst. to mayor City of Evansville, Ind., 1974-79; judge Vanderburgh Superior Ct., Evansville, 1980-85; assoc. justice Ind. Supreme Ct., Indpls., 1985-87, chief justice, 1987—. Instr. U. Evansville, 1975-78, Indiana U., 1995, 99; pres. Nat. Conference of Chief Justices, 2005—. Author: Preservation Rules and Regulations, 1980, Indiana Legal History, 2005; contbr. articles to profl. publs. Bd. advisors Nat. Trust for Hist. Preservation, 1980-87, chmn. bd. advisors, 1983-85, trustee, 1987-96; dir. Hist. Landmarks Found. Ind., 1983—, chmn., 1989-92, hon. chmn., 1992—; chmn. State Student Assistance Commn. Ind., 1981-85; chmn. Ind. Commn. on Bicentennial of U.S. Constn., 1986-91; vice chmn. Vanderburgh County Rep. Ctrl. Com., 1977-80. Recipient Disting. Svc. award Evansville Jaycees, 1982, Herbert Harley award Am. Judicature Soc., 1992, Wickler award Nat. Assn. Women Judges, 2004. Mem. ABA (coun. mem. sect. on legal edn. 1991—, chair sect. on legal edn. 1997-98, chair appellate judges conf. 1996-97), Ind. Bar Assn., Ind. Judges Assn., Princeton Club (N.Y.), Capitol Hill Club (Washington), Columbia Club (Indpls.), Woodstock Club (Indpls.). Republican. Methodist. Home: 3644 Totem Ln Indianapolis IN 46208-4171 Office: Ind Supreme Ct 315 State House Indianapolis IN 46204-2213 Office Phone: 317-232-2550.*

SHEPARD, RICHARD BLOUNT, surgeon, educator; b. Birmingham, Ala., May 9, 1926; m. Winyss Renee Acton, Mar. 26, 1955; children: Winyss Elizabeth, Kathryn Bouchelle, Richard Kesniel, Karen Acton. BS in Physics, Pa. State U., 1949; MD, U. Pa., 1953. Intern, resident in surgery U. Pa. Hosp., Phila., 1953-59; instr., rsch. assoc. in physiology U. Pa., Phila., 1954-56; chief resident Fitkin Hosp. Hahnemann Med. Coll., Neptune, NJ, 1959-60; from instr. to prof. surgery U. Ala., Birmingham, 1960-98, prof. surgery, emeritus, 1998—. Engr. Victoreen Instrument Co., Cleve., 1946; engr. Haller, Raymond & Brown, State College, Pa., 1948; cons. for device implant mfrs. and electronics mfr., 1960-2004; chmn. USRA-NASA biomed. com. for studies selection, shuttle orbital flight tests, 1981-83. Contbr. articles to profl. jours. and chpts. to books. With US Army, 1943—46, spl. engr. detatchment Manhattan Project US Army, 1945—46. Grantee Heart Assn. S.E. Pa., NIH. Fellow ACS, Am. Coll. Cardiology, Soc. for Vascular Surgery (disting.); mem. IEEE (life), Heart Rhythm Soc., Soc. Thoracic Surgeons. Achievements include research in blood flow and energy characteristics, especially as related to cardiopulmonary bypass operations and underlying physiology; one of the first to implant cardiac pacemakers and investigational defibrillators; application of physics and tissue biology to clinical and laboratory implantable device development, teaching and problem solutions.

SHEPARD, ROBERT M., lawyer, investment banker, engineer; b. Amityville, NY, Feb. 15, 1932; s. Sidney M. and Undine L. (Lehmann) Shapiro; m. Barbara S. Stannard, June 25, 1955 (div. 1980); children: Karen Michele Shepard Sweer, Daniel Robert; m. Joanne E. Devlin, May 16, 1981 (div. 1993); m. Martha Kothe, Nov. 24, 1999. B.C.E., Cornell U., 1954; MBA, Hofstra Coll., 1960; LL.B., Yale U., 1963; LLM, NYU, 1988. Bar: NY 1964; registered profl. engr., NY, Conn. Project engr. Lockwood Kessler & Bartlett, Syosset, NY, 1956-60; assoc. atty. Cravath, Swaine & Moore, NYC and Paris, 1963-70; gen. ptnr. Kuhn, Loeb & Co., NYC, 1970-77; sr. v.p. Donaldson, Lufkin & Jenrette, NYC, 1977-83; gen. ptnr. Donovan Leisure Newton & Irvine, NYC, 1983-89, Adler & Shepard, NYC, 1989-91, Shepard & van Essche, NYC, 1991, Ballon Stoll Bader & Nadler, P.C., NYC, 1992—. Note and comment editor: Yale Law Jour., 1962-63. Bd. dirs. NY Grand Opera; bd. govs. Regency Whist Club. Recipient Fuertes Medal Cornell U., 1953 Mem. ABA, Am. NY State Bar Assn., Pub. Power Assn., Nat. Assn. Bond Lawyers, Order of Coif, Union League Club (bd. govs.), Regency Whist Club, Inc., Tau Beta Pi, Chi Epsilon. Home: 750 Park Ave Apt 2C New York NY 10021-4252 Office: Ballon Stoll Bader & Nadler 729 Broadway New York NY 10018-2201 Office Phone: 212-575-7900 ext 3320. Business E-Mail: rshepard@ballonstoll.com.

SHEPARD, SAM (SAMUEL SHEPARD ROGERS), playwright, actor; b. Ft. Sheridan, Ill., Nov. 5, 1943; s. Samuel Shepard and Jane Elaine (Schook) Rogers; m. O-Lan Johnson Dark, Nov. 9, 1969 (div. 1984); 1 child, Jesse Mojo; life ptnr. Jessica Lange; children: Hannah Jane, Samuel Walker. Student, Mt. San Antonio Jr. Coll., Walnut, Calif., 1961-62. Playwright-in-residence Magic Theatre, San Francisco. Author: (plays) 4-H Club, Up to Thursday, Dog, Rocking Chair, 1965, Cowboys, The Rock Garden, 1964, Chicago, 1965 (Obie award, 1966), Icarus's Mother, 1965 (Obie award, 1966), Fourteen Hundred Thousand, 1966, Red Cross, 1966 (Obie award, 1966), Melodrama Play, 1966 (Obie award, 1968), La Turista, 1967 (Obie award, 1967), Cowboys #2, 1967, Forensic and the Navigators, 1967 (Obie award, 1968), The Holy Ghostly, The Unseen Hand, 1969, Operation Sidewinder, Shaved Splits, 1970, Mad Dog Blues, Terminal, (with Patti Smith) Cowboy Mouth, Black Bog Beast Bait, 1971, The Tooth of Crime, 1972 (Obie award, 1973), Blue Bitch, (with Megan Terry and Jean-Claude van Itallie) Nightwalk, 1973, Geography of a Horse Dreamer, Little Ocean, Killer's Head, 1974, Action, 1974 (Obie award, 1975), Starving Class, 1977, Buried Child, 1978 (Obie award, 1977, Pulitzer Prize in drama, 1979, Obie award, 1979), Tongues, Savage/Love, Seduced, 1979, True West, 1981, Fool for Love, 1983 (Obie award, 1984), Superstitions, The Sad Lament of Pecos Bill on the Eve of Killing his Wife, 1983, A Lie of the Mind, 1985 (New York Drama Critics' Circle award, 1986), States of Shock, 1991, Simpatico, 1993, The Late Henry Moss, 2000, The God of Hell, 2004, Kicking a Dead Horse, 2008, (collections of plays) Five

Plays by Sam Shepard, 1967, The Unseen Hand and Other Plays, 1971, 1986, Mad Dog Blues and Other Plays, 1972, The Tooth of Crime and Geography of a Horse Dreamer, 1974, Angel City, Curse of the Starving Class and Other Plays, 1976, Buried Child, Seduced, Suicide in B-Flat, 1979, (collection of plays) Four Two-Act Plays by Sam Shepard, 1980, Chicago and Other Plays, Seven Plays, 1981, Fool for Love and The Sad Lament of Pecos Bill on the Eve of Killing His Wife, 1983, Fool For Love and Other Plays, 1984, 1986, contbr. to Oh! Calcutta, 1976, (with Bob Dylan) Renaldo and Clara, 1978, (collection of plays) Paris, Texas, 1984, (other writings) Rolling Thunder Logbook, 1977, Hawk Moon: A Book of Short Stories, Poems and Monologues, 1981, Motel Chronicles, 1982; dir.(writer): (plays) Fool for Love, 1983, A Lie of the Mind, 1985; (screenplays) Far North, 1988, Silent Tongue, 1993; actor: (plays) A Number, 2004—05; (films) Renaldo and Clara, Days of Heaven, 1978, Resurrection, 1980, Raggedy Man, 1981, Frances, 1982, The Right Stuff, 1983 (Academy award nomination best supporting actor, 1984), Country, 1984, Fool for Love, 1985, Crimes of the Heart, 1986, Baby Boom, 1987, Steel Magnolias, 1989, Hot Spot, 1990, Bright Angel, Defenseless, 1991, Thunderheart, 1992, The Pelican Brief, 1993, Safe Passage, 1994, The Good Old Boys, 1995, Curtain Call, The Only Thrill, 1997, All the Pretty Horses, 2000, The Pledge, 2001, Swordfish, 2001, Black Hawk Down, 2001, Leo, 2002, Blind Horizon, 2003, The Notebook, 2004, Don't Come Knocking, 2005, Stealth, 2005, Bandidas, 2006, Walker Payne, 2006, The Return, 2006, Charlotte's Web, 2006, The Assassination of Jesse James by the Coward Robert Ford, 2007, The Accidental Husband, 2008; (TV films) Streets of Laredo, 1995, Lily Dale, 1996, Purgatory, Dash & Lilly, 2000 (nominated for Golden Globe, Best Actor), After the Harvest, 2001, Shot in the Heart, 2001, Ruffian, 2007. Recipient Nat. Inst. and Am. Acad. Arts and Letters award for lit., 1974, Creative Arts award Brandeis U., 1975; named to Theater Hall of Fame, 1994; grantee Rockefeller Found., 1967, Guggenheim Found., 1968, 1971; Fellow, U. Minn., 1966, Yale U., 1967. Mem.: Am. Acad. and Inst. of Arts and Letters.

SHEPARD, STEPHEN BENJAMIN, journalist, educator, retired editor; b. NYC, July 20, 1939; s. William and Ruth Shepard; m. Lynn Povich, Sept. 16, 1979; children: Sarah, Ned. BS, CCNY, 1961; MS, Columbia U., 1964. Reporter, editor, writer Bus. Week, NYC, 1966—75; asst. prof., dir. Walter Bagehot fellowship program econs. and bus. journalism Columbia U., NYC, 1975—76; sr. editor Newsweek, NYC, 1976—81; editor Saturday Rev., NYC, 1981—82; exec. editor Bus. Week mag., NYC, 1982—84, editor in chief, 1984—2005; dean Grad. Sch. Journalism CUNY, NYC, 2005—. Adj. prof. Columbia Grad Sch. Journalism, 1971—75. Bd. visitors Columbia Grad. Sch. Journalism. Recipient Lifetime Achievement award, Gerald Loeb Found., 1999, Henry Johnson Fisher award, Mag. Publs. Am., 2000, President's award, Overseas Press Club, 2003. Mem.: Coun. Fgn. Rls., Am. Soc. Mag. Editors (v.p. 1990—92, pres. 1992—94, Hall of Fame 1999), Century Assn. Office: CUNY Grad Sch Journalism 219 W 40th St New York NY 10018 Business E-Mail: steve.shepard@journalism.cuny.edu.*

SHEPARD, THOMAS ROCKWELL, III, advertising executive; b. Greenwich, Conn., Apr. 21, 1951; s. Thomas Rockwell Jr. and Nancy (Kruidenier) S.; m. Margaret O'Neal, Sept. 1, 1972; children: Amanda Marie, Thomas Rockwell IV, Brian Dickinson. BA, Amherst Coll., 1973. Salesman Union Carbide Battery Products, NYC, 1974-78; advt. dir. Good Housekeeping mag., 1984—90; pub. Country Living mag., 1990—93, Redbook mag., 1993—97; v.p. network advt. sales Manursing Club, N.Y. Athletic Club; sr. v.p. network advt. sales Hearst HomeArts, 1997—99; pres. King Features Syndicate, NYC, 1999—. Office: King Features Ltd 2nd Fl 300 W 57th St New York NY 10019-3741 E-mail: trshepano@hearst.com.

SHEPARD, WILLIAM SETH, diplomat, writer; b. Boston, June 7, 1935; s. Robinson and Myra Ellen (Foster) S.; m. Lois Rosalie Burke, June 25, 1960; children: Stephanie Lee, Cynthia Robin, Warren Burke (dec.) AB cum laude, Wesleyan U., Middletown, Conn., 1957; JD, Harvard U., Cambridge, Mass., 1961. Bar: NH 1961, US Ct. Mil. Appeals 1962 US Supreme Ct., 1970. Aide to ambs. Henry Cabot Lodge and Ellsworth Bunker, Am. embassy, Saigon, Vietnam, 1966-67; staff officer Exec. Secretariat Dept. of State, Washington, 1967-69; consul, polit. officer Am. Embassy, Budapest, Hungary, 1970-73; desk officer Hungarian and Baltic affairs Dept. State, Washington, 1973—75; desk officer Singapore and Malaysian affairs Dept. of State, Washington, 1975-77; dep. polit. counselor Am. embassy, Athens, Greece, 1978-80; consul gen. Am. Consulate Gen., Bordeaux, France, 1983-85; dir. Office Congl. Affairs, ACDA, Washington, 1987-89; cons. to gen. counsel USDA, Washington, 1991-92. Lectr. internat. law U. Singapore, 1965—66; lectr. Chesapeake Coll., 2006—; CEO The Shepard Internat. Group, Inc., 1994—. Author: Consular Tales, 2001, Murder on the Danube, 2001, Vintage Murder, 2002, Foreign Service Tales, 2002, Shepard's Guide to Mastering French Wines, 2003, Murder in Dordogne, 2005, Diplomatic Tales, 2006; wine editor: Bonjour Paris, 2002—, French Wine Explorers, 2009—. Candidate for Rep. nomination 8th Md. Congl. Dist., 1985—86; Rep. nominee for Gov. of Md., 1990; Rep. candidate for Gov. of Md., 1994; del. Rep. Nat. Conv., 1992; Md. co-chmn. Dole Presdl. Campaign, 1996; apptd. mem. citizens adv. com. Chesapeake Exec. Coun., by Gov. of Md., 2004—07. Recipient Pro Libertate Hungariae Commemorative medallion, 1981, Pub. Svc. Leadership award U.S.-Baltic Found., 1996, George L. Plimpton Pub. Svc. award Tilton Sch., 2003; French Govt. teaching asst. and Fulbright travel grantee, 1957-58; Congl. fellow Am. Polit. Sci. Assn. and fgn. policy legis. asst. to Senator Robert Dole, 1982-83. Mem. Soc. Mayflower Desc., Gov. Bradford Compact, Soc. Desc. Colonial Govs. (chancellor gen. 1993-95), Soc. Desc. Colonial Wars, Montesquieu Acad. France (corr.), City Tavern Club (Washington), Flagon and Trencher (Trencher award 2003), Les Chevaliers de Bretvin, Ordre des Compagnons de Bordeaux, Connetablie de Guyenne, La Jurade de St. Emilion, Bontemps Medoc et des Graves, Tred Avon Players. Republican. Unitarian Universalist. Avocations: reading, vintage Bordeaux wines, gastronomy, cruise lecturing. Home: 28800 Outram St Easton MD 21601 *I remember Himalayan peaks, Asian sunsets, Greek islands and Bordeaux vineyards. Along the way, hard work in a principled cause is its own reward. In the end, family life and friends, a foyer, pets, a book worth reading, and a glass of wine matter most.*

SHEPARDSON, DONALD EUGENE, history professor; b. Port Huron, Mich., May 14, 1936; s. Francis Madison and Florence Margaret Shepardson. BS, Ea. Ill. U., Charleston, 1961; MA, U. Ill., Urbana, 1964, PhD, 1970. Prof. history U. Northern Iowa, Cedar Falls, 1970—. Author: (book) Conflict and Diplomacy from the Great War to the Cold War. Mem.: Soc. Mil. History. Home: 2610 Walnut St Cedar Falls IA 50613-0701 Office: Univ Northern Iowa 1227 W 27th St Cedar Falls IA 50614-0701 Office Fax: 319-273-5846. Business E-Mail: donald.shepardson@uni.edu.

SHEPHARD, BRUCE DENNIS, obstetrician, educator, medical writer; b. San Francisco, Apr. 21, 1944; s. Richard G. and Madelyn (Rogers) S.; children: Christopher, Carleton, Elizabeth. BA in History, U. Calif., Berkeley, 1966; MD, U. Calif., San Francisco, 1970. Diplomate Am. Bd. Ob-Gyn. Intern Jackson Meml. Hosp.-U. Miami (Fla.), 1970-71, resident in ob-gyn., 1971-74; pvt. practice Tampa, 1976—; clin. assoc. prof. obstetrics U. So. Fla. Sch. Medicine, Tampa, 1976—. Bd. dirs. Ctr. of Excellence, Humana Women's Hosp., Tampa, Fla., 1983-90, Gulf Coast Health Systems Agy., 1980-83; mem. midwifery adv. com. Fla. Dept. Health and Human Resources, Tallahassee, 1982-86. Prin. author: The Complete Guide to Women's Health, 1982, 3d rev. edit., 1997; prin., writer, spokesperson (series of TV commls.) The Healthy Woman (Gold Link award 1987); mem. med. adv. bd. Baby Talk mag., 1992-2004; bd. dirs. PBS affiliate WEDU, 1998-2005; contbr. articles to profl. jours. and women's mags. Lectr. Continuing Edn., Inc., 2002—; mem. Agy. Health Care Adminstrn., Dept. Health and Rehab. Svcs., Fla., cert. med. expert Fla., 2001—; mem. Healthier Fla. Provider Adv. Bd., 2007—; med. adv. bd. Welcare HMO, 1996—; pres. coun. AVMED HMO, 1999—2002; bd. dirs. Mus. Sci. and Industry, Tampa, 2007—. Served as maj. USAF, 1974—76. Mem. AMA, Am. Coll. Ob-Gyn. (patient edn. com. 1984-86, John McCain fellow 1981), Hillsborough County Med. Assn. (v.p. 2003-05, pres. elect. 2005-06, pres. 2006-07), Phi Beta Kappa. Democrat. Lutheran. Avocations: tennis, photography, golf, antique glass collecting, running. Home: 14516 Nettle Creek Rd Tampa FL 33624 Office: 4302 N Habana Ave Ste 300 Tampa FL 33607

SHEPHARD, WILLIAM DANKS, physicist, educator; b. Gary, Ind., July 8, 1933; m. Barbara Ann Parker, July 25, 1959 (dec. Apr. 26, 1996); m. Nancy S. Kavadas, May 24, 2003. BA, Wesleyan U., 1954; MS, U. Wis., 1955, PhD, 1962. Asst. prof. U. Ky., Lexington, 1960—63; Fulbright sr. rsch. fellow Max Planck Inst. fur Physik und Astrophysik, Munich, 1962—63; asst. then assoc. prof. U. Notre Dame, Ind., 1963—73, prof., 1973—2004, prof. emeritus, 2004—; guest prof. U. Nijmegen, Netherlands, 1975—76. Vis. scientist Fermilab, Batavia, Ill., 1971—; guest scientist Stanford Linear Accelerator Ctr., Palo Alto, Calif., 1980—; vis. scientist Brookhaven Nat. Lab., Upton, NY, 1960—; guest physicist and cons. Argonne Nat. Lab., Ill., 1963—80; organizer XII Internat. Symposium on Multiparticle Dynamics, Notre Dame, 1981. Editor: Multiparticle Dynamics 1981, 1982; contbr. more than 300 articles to profl. jours. Deacon 1st Presbyn. Ch., South Bend, Ind., 1997—99, v.p., 1999—2000, 2003—05, elder, 2000—, pres., 2001—02, 2006—09. Rsch. grantee, NSF, 1963—2004, Fulbright Sr. Rsch. scholar, U.S. Govt., 1962—63, Predoctoral fellow, NSF, 1954—55, 1956—57. Mem.: AAUP, Am. Phys. Soc., Sigma Xi (pres., Notre Dame chpt. 1977—78), Phi Beta Kappa (pres. Epsilon chpt. Ind. 1991—93), Chi Psi. Office: Univ Notre Dame Dept Physics 225 Nieuwland Notre Dame IN 46556-5670 Business E-Mail: shephard.1@nd.edu.

SHEPHERD, BOBBY E., federal judge; b. Arkadelphia, Ark., Nov. 18, 1951; BA, Ouachita Bapt. U., 1973; JD, U. Ark., 1976. Ptnr. Spencer & Spencer, El Dorado, Ark., 1976—81, Spencer, Spencer & Shepherd, 1981—84, Landers & Shepherd, 1987—90; pvt. law practive, 1984—87; circuit-chancery judge Ark. 13th Jud. Dist., 1991-93; magistrate judge US Dist. Ct. (we. dist.) Ark., El Dorado, Ark., 1993—2006; judge US Ct. Appeals (8th cir.), Little Rock, 2006—. Served with US Army Res., 1976-81.*

SHEPHERD, BRUCE P., lawyer; BA, Harvard U., 1979; MBA, JD, U. Calif., Berkeley, 1983. Bar: Calif. 1984. Mng. ptnr. Latham & Watkins LLP, San Diego, and mem. fin. and real estate dept. Bd. dir. San Diego County Big Brothers and Big Sisters, Coronado Schools Found.; elected sch. bd. mem. (pres. 2001-02) Coronado Sch. Dist., 1998—2002. Mem.: ABA. Office: Latham & Watkins LLP Ste 1800 600 W Broadway San Diego CA 92101-3375 also: Latham And Watkins Llp 12636 High Bluff Dr Ste 400 San Diego CA 92130-2071

SHEPHERD, CYBILL LYNNE, actress, singer; b. Memphis, Feb. 18, 1950; d. William Jennings and Patty Shobe (Micci) S.; m. David Ford, Nov. 19, 1978 (div., 1982); 1 child, Clementine; m. Bruce Oppenheim, March 1, 1987 (div., 1990); children: Molly Ariel and Cyrus Zachariah (twins) Student, Hunter Coll., 1969, Coll. of New Rochelle, 1970, Washington Sq. Coll., NYU, 1971, U. So. Calif., 1972, NYU, 1973. Actor: (films) Last Picture Show, 1971, The Heartbreak Kid, 1973, Daisy Miller, 1974, At Long Last Love, 1975, Taxi Driver, 1976, Special Delivery, 1976, Silver Bears, 1977, The Lady Vanishes, 1978, Earthright, 1980, The Return, 1986, Chances Are, 1988, Texasville, 1990, Alice, 1990, Married to It, 1991, Once Upon a Crime, 1992, The Last Word, 1995, The Muse, 1999, Marine Life, 2000, Open Window, 2006, (TV series) The Yellow Rose, 1983-84, Moonlighting, 1985-89, Cybill, 1994-98 (also prodr.), The L Word, 2007-, (TV films) A Guide for the Married Woman, 1978, Secrets of a Married Man, 1984, Seduced, 1985, The Long Hot Summer, 1985, Which Way Home, 1991, Memphis, 1992 (also co-writer, co-exec. prodr.), Stormy Weathers, 1992, Telling Secrets, 1993, There Was a Little Boy, 1993, Journey of the Heart, 1997, Due East, 2002, Martha, Inc.: The Story of Martha Stewart, 2003, Martha Behind Bars, 2005; record albums include Cybill Does It To Cole Porter, 1974, Cybill and Stan Getz, 1977, Vanilla with Phineas Newborn, Jr, 1978; appeared in stage plays A Shot in the Dark, 1977, Picnic, 1980, Vanities, 1981, The Muse, 1999, Marine Life, 2000; co-author Cybill Disobedience, 2000.

SHEPHERD, GILLIAN MARY, physician; b. Mar. 12, 1948; d. John Thompson and Helen (Johnston) S.; m. Eduardo Goar Mestre, Aug. 4, 1973; children: Laura Elena, Cristina Alicia, Eduardo Goar. BA, Wheaton Coll., Norton, Mass., 1970; postgrad., Tufts U., 1970-73; MD, N.Y. Med. Coll., 1976. Diplomate Am. Bd. Internal Medicine, Am. Bd. Allergy and Immunology. Intern, resident Lenox Hill Hosp., NYC, 1976-79; fellow in allergy and immunology N.Y. Hosp./Cornell Med. Sch., NYC, 1979-81; assoc. prof. medicine Cornell U. Med. Coll., NYC, 1988—, clin. assoc. prof. medicine, 1995—. Assoc. attending physician N.Y. Hosp., N.Y.C.; cons. allergy and immunology dept. medicine Meml. Sloan-Kettering Cancer Ctr., N.Y.C., 1982—. Contbr. articles in field to profl. jours. Fellow ACP, Am. Acad. Asthma, Allergy and Immunology (chair Edn. and Rsch. Trust 1999-2001, bd. dirs. 2000-2003); mem. AAAS, Am. Fedn. for Clin. Rsch., Joint Coun. Allergy and Immunology, N.Y. Allergy Soc. (exec. com. 1982-94, pres. 1991-92), N.Y. County Med. Soc. Office: 235 E 67th St Rm 203 New York NY 10021-6040 Office Phone: 212-288-9300.

SHEPHERD, GORDON GREELEY, space physics educator, researcher; b. Senate, Sask., Can., June 19, 1931; s. George Fredrick and Irene Eleanor (Thompson) S.; m. Marian Margaret Morgenroth, Aug. 15, 1953; children: Theodore Gordon, David Michael, Paul Ronald; m. Marianna Genova Gerdjikova, Dec. 19. 1987. BSc in Engring. Physics, U. Sask., 1952, MSc in Physics, 1953; PhD in Physics, U. Toronto, 1956. Asst. prof. physics U. Sask., 1957-64, assoc. prof., 1964-69; prof. York U., Toronto, 1969—, dir. Ctr. for Rsch. in Earth and Space Sci., 1994—. Author: Spectral Imaging of the Atmosphere, 2002, Canada's Fifty Years in Space, 2008. Recipient John H. Chapman award of excellence, Canadian Space Agy., 2003. Fellow Royal Soc. Can., Can. Aeronautics and Space Inst. (Alouette award 2004), Am. Geophys. Union. Avocations: travel, swimming, skiing. Home: 14 E Humber Dr King City ON Canada L7B 1B6 Office: York Univ/Ctr Rsch E/S Sci 4700 Keele St Toronto ON Canada M3J 1P3 Business E-Mail: gordon@yorku.ca.

SHEPHERD, JAMES LEONARD, biology professor; b. Greensburg, Pa., Jan. 17, 1966; s. James Richard and Janet Theresa Shepherd; m. Heather Ann Shepherd, Apr. 15, 1995; children: Kimberlyn Carla, Andrew James. BS, Ind. U. Pa., 1988; MEd, Ohio U., Athens, 1996. Cert. in secondary sci. edn. Pa., 1993, environ. trainer Nat. Environ. Safety & Health Tng. Assn., 1998. Assoc. chemist Antech Ltd., Export, Pa., 1988—91; prof. Zane State Coll., Zanesville, Ohio, 1993—. V.p. Zanesville-Muskingum County Health Dept., Ohio, 2007—09. Democrat. Avocations: skiing, bicycling, travel. Office: Zane State Coll 1555 Newark Rd Zanesville OH 43701 Office Fax: 1-740-454-0035. Business E-Mail: jshepherd@zanestate.edu.

SHEPHERD, JOHN FREDERIC, lawyer; b. Oak Park, Ill., May 22, 1954; s. James Frederic Shepherd and Margaret Joanne (Crotchett) Woollen; m. Jane Lowell Montgomery; children: Eliza Marion, Justine Catherine, Austin Frederic, Jack Lowell. AB magna cum laude, Dartmouth Coll., Hanover, NH, 1976; JD, U. Denver, 1979. Bar: Colo. 1979, US Dist. Ct. Colo. 1979, DC 1981, Okla. 2005, US Dist. Ct. DC 1981, US Ct. Appeals (10th cir.) 1981, US Ct. Appeals (DC cir.) 1982, US Supreme Ct. 1984, US Ct. Appeals (9th cir.) 1990. Assoc. Holland & Hart, Denver, 1979-81, Washington, 1981-85, ptnr., 1985-87, Denver, 1987—; natural resources disting. practitioner in residence U. Denver Coll. Law, 1998. Reporter Mineral Law Newsletter, 1985-92. Mem. 50 for Colo., Denver, 1989. Mem. ABA (chmn. pub. lands and land use com. 1991-93, mem. coun. sect. of natural resources energy and environ. law 1993-96), Rocky Mountain Mineral Law Found. (mem. long-range planning com. 1988—, trustee 1993-95), Inst. Energy Law (exec. com. 2006-), Dartmouth Alumni Club (pres. Washington chpt. 1985-86, trustee Rocky Mt. chpt., 1998-2001), Denver Athletic Club. Avocations: fly fishing, basketball, bicycling. Home: 320 Clermont St Pky Denver CO 80220-5642 Office: Holland & Hart 555 17th St Ste 3200 Denver CO 80202-3950 Office Phone: 303-295-8309. Business E-Mail: jshepherd@hollandhart.com.

SHEPHERD, JOHN MICHAEL, lawyer; b. St. Louis, Aug. 1, 1955; s. John Calvin and Bernice Florence (Hines) S.; m. Deborah Tremaine Fenton, Oct. 10, 1981; children: Elizabeth White, Katherine Tremaine. BA, Stanford U., 1977; JD, U. Mich., 1980. Bar: Calif. 1981, D.C. 1991, U.S. Dist. Ct. (no. dist.) Calif. 1981. Assoc. McCutchen, Doyle, Brown & Enersen, San Francisco, 1980-82; spl. asst. to asst. atty. gen. U.S. Dept. Justice, Washington, 1982-84, dep. asst. atty gen., 1984-86; assoc. counsel to The President The White House, Washington, 1986-87; sr. dep. comptroller of the currency Dept. Treasury, Washington, 1987-91; spl. counsel Sullivan & Cromwell, NYC, 1991-93, Washington, 1993; exec. v.p., gen. counsel Shawmut Nat. Corp., Boston, 1993-95; ptnr. Brobeck, Phleger & Harrison LLP, San Francisco, 1995-2000; exec. v.p., gen. counsel, sec. Bank of New York Co., Inc., NYC, 2001—04; exec. v.p., gen. counsel, chief risk officer, sec. Bank of the West, San Francisco, 2004—, pres., COO, 2006—07, pres., CEO, 2008—. Bd. dirs. Promontory Interfin. Corp., Pacific Mutual Holding Co., Pacific LifeCorp. Contbr. articles to profl. jours. Asst. dir. policy Reagan-Bush Presdl. Transition Team, Washington, 1980-81; bd. dirs. Reagan Dep. Asst. Secs., Washington, 1985-90, Episc. Charities N.Y., 2001-2004, Episc. Charities Calif., 2005-, Common Good, Presidio Trust, 2008-; trustee New Eng. Aquarium, 1994-96. Named one of Outstanding Young Men Am., U.S. Jaycees, 1984; Wardack Research fellow Washington U., 1976. Mem. ABA (chmn. fin. markets and ins. com., antitrust law sect. 1992-95, banking law com. 1983—, vice chair 1998-2002, chmn. bank holding co. acquisitions subcom. 1995-98, bus. law sect., standing com. on law and nat. security 1984-96), DC Bar Assn., Am. Judicature Soc., Coun. Fgn. Rels., Chevy Chase Club, Met. Club, Olympic Club, Fin. Svcs. Roundtable. Office: Bank of the West 180 Montgomery St San Francisco CA 94104 Business E-Mail: michaelshepherd@bankofthewest.com.

SHEPHERD, JON GLEN, lawyer; b. Des Moines, May 22, 1968; s. Jerry Wayne and Vicki Jean (Clark) S.; m. Stacy Kenna York, May 23, 1992. BA, U. No. Iowa, 1990; JD magna cum laude, U. Mich., 1992. Bar: Tex. 1993, U.S. Ct. Appeals (5th cir.) 1994, U.S. Dist. Ct. (no. dist.) Tex. 1994, U.S. Dist. Ct. (ea. dist.) Tex. 1995. Jud. clk. U.S. Ct. Appeals (5th cir.), San Antonio, 1993-94; assoc. Gibson, Dunn & Crutcher LLP, Dallas, 1994—2003, ptnr., 2003—05; crews Shepherd & McCarty LLP, Dallas, 2006—07, ptnr., 2006—07, Alston & Bird LLP, 2007—. Mem. bd. dirs. Sequoia, Inc., 2005—09, v.p., 2006—07, pres., 2007—09; adj. prof., exec. MBA prog. Tex. Woman's U., 2006—07. Exec editor U. Mich. Law Rev., 1992; sr. editor ABA Antitrust Sec. Antitrust Law Jour., 1997—2006. Mem. Tex. Bar Assn., Dallas Bar Assn., Order of Coif. Avocation: sports. Office: Alston & Bird LLP 2200 Ross Ave Ste 3601 Dallas TX 75201 Office Phone: 214-922-3418. Office Fax: 214-922-3899. Business E-Mail: jon.Shepherd@alston.com.

SHEPHERD, KAREN, former congresswoman; b. Silver City, N.Mex., July 5, 1940; m. Vincent P. Shepherd. BA, U. Utah, 1962; MA, Brigham Young U., 1963. Former instr. Brigham Young U., Am. U., Cairo; former pres. Webster Pub. Co.; former adminstr. David Eccles Sch. Bus., U. Utah; former dir. Salt Lake County Social Svcs., Utah; former dir. continuing edn. Westminster Coll.; former mem. Utah Senate; mem. 103d Congress from 2d Utah dist., Washington, 1993—94; exec. dir., U.S. rep. European Bank for Reconstruction Devel., London, 1996—2002; mem. exec. com., chair East West Trade and Investment Forum Am. C. of C., England, 1998—2002; dir. EMILY's List, 2002. Mem. nat. governing bd. Common Cause, Washington, 1995—96, Internat. Del. to Monitor Elections in West Bank and Gaza, Israel, Nat. Planned Parenthood Action Fund, 2004—; founder Karen Shepherd Fund; founding mem. Utah Women's Polit. Caucus, Project 2000; mem. trustee KeyBank Victory Funds; bd. dirs. UBS Bank, USA, O.C. Tanner; fellow Inst. Politics, Harvard U., 1995. Former mem. United Way, Pvt. Industry Coun.; former mem. adv. bd. U.S. West Grad. Sch. Social Work; trustee Westminster Coll.; bd. dirs. Utah Red Cross, 2003-06; chair Grad. Sch. Social Work, U. Utah, 1986-88, David Eccles Sch. Bus., 1996—. Recipient Women in Bus. award, US Small Bus. Assn., Woman of Achievement award, Pathfinder award, Leadership award, YWCA, 1st pl. award, Nat. Assn. Journalists, Disting. Alumni award, U. Utah Coll. Humanities, Eleanor Roosevelt award, Utah Dem. Party, 2002, Merit of Honor award, U. Utah, 2004. Fellow Inst. Politics Kennedy Sch. Govt., Internat. Women's Forum, Salt Lake Area C. of C. (pub. rels. com.)., Coun. on Fgn. Rels. Home: PO Box 1049 Salt Lake City UT 84110-1049

SHEPHERD, KAREN SCHILLER, biology educator; BS, MEd, N. Tex. State Univ. (now Univ. N. Tex), Denton. Biology tchr. Vines H.S., 1984—96, Plano (Tex.) H.S., 1996—, and sci. dept. chair, 2004—. Recipient Edison Soc. award for promoting rsch., 1994, USAF, US Army Awards for promoting student rsch., 1998—2003, Outstanding H.S. Sci. Tchr., Tex. Jr. Sci., Engring., Humanities Symposium, 1998, 2000; named Region 10 Secondary Tchr. of Yr., 2005, Tex. Tchr. of Yr., 2006. Office: Plano Senior High Sch 2200 Independence Pkwy Plano TX 75075 Business E-Mail: kshephe@pisd.edu.

SHEPHERD, KEVIN L., lawyer; b. Wichita, Kans., Aug. 4, 1957; BA magna cum laude, Frostburg State Coll., 1979; JD magna cum laude, Univ. Balt., 1984. Bar: Md. 1985, DC 1985. Law clk. Judge Harry A.

Cole, Md. Ct. Appeals, 1984—85; ptnr., co-chmn. Real Estate practice group Venable LLP, Baltimore & Washington. Editor (in chief): Balt. Law Rev., Probate & Property; contbr. articles to profl. jours. Recipient Am. Jurisprudence awards. Mem.: Am. Coll. Mortgage Attys., ABA (vice chmn. real property divsn., chair real property, probate and trust law sects.), Anglo-Am. Real Property Inst., Am. Coll. Real Estate Lawyers (bd. gov.), Md. State Bar Assn., Bar Assn. Balt. City, DC Bar Assn., Phi Alpha Theta, Pi Sigma Alpha, Heuslier Honor Soc. Office: Venable LLP 1800 Mercantile Bank & Trust Bldg 2 Hopkins Plz Baltimore MD 21201 also: Venable LLP 575 7th St NW Washington DC 20004 Office Phone: 410-244-7772, 202-344-4881. Office Fax: 410-244-7742. Business E-Mail: klshepherd@venable.com.

SHEPHERD, NICK P., film rental company executive; b. United Kingdom; BS in Hospitality and Bus. Mgmt., Sheffield City Polytechnic, UK. Various positions Grand Metropolitan Plc, Allied Lyons Plc, Kingfisher Plc; joined Blockbuster Inc., 1995—, sr. v.p. internat. bus., 1998—2001, chief concept officer, 2001—03, exec. v.p., chief mktg. and merchandising officer, 2003—04, exec. v.p., pres. U.S. stores, 2004—05, v.p. and mng. dir. UK bus., exec. v.p., pres. N. Am., 2005—07, former exec. v.p., pres. worldwide stores, 2007, COO, sr. exec. v.p., 2007—. Office: Blockbuster Inc 1201 Elm St Dallas TX 75270

SHEPHERD, SEAN, composer; b. Reno, Nev., 1979; MusB, Ind. U., performer diploma in bassoon performance; MFA, Juilliard Sch., 2004. Composer: Ozymandias, 2005, Seagulls on High, 2007, Wanderlust, 2009. Recipient Lutoslawski award, 2005, Benjamin H. Danks award, AAAL, 2009; fellow Am. Acad. in Berlin, 2008. Mailing: 934 Stewart Ave Apt 22 Ithaca NY 14850 E-mail: sean@seanshepherd.com.*

SHEPHERD, TERRY LYNN, special education educator; b. Knox, Ind., Feb. 22, 1958; s. A.B. Shepherd and Verona Darlene Preston; m. Melanie Ann Mullet; children: Jared, Samuel; m. Penny Kaye Price (div. Feb. 12, 1985); children: Shaun, William. EdD, Ball State U., Muncie, Ind., 1998. Social studies tchr. Houston Ind. Sch. Dist., Houston, 1982—85; tchr. Family and Children's Ctr., Mishawaka, Ind., 1985—90; spl. edn. tchr. Joint Svcs. for Spl. Edn., Plymouth, Ind., 1990—98; assoc. prof. spl. edn. Tex. A&M Internat. U., Laredo, Tex., 1998—2007; dept. head spl. edn. Ind. U., South Bend, 2007—, assoc. prof., 2007—. Author: (textbook) Working with Students with Emotional & Behavior Disorders: Characteristics & Teaching Strategies, 2009; contbr. articles to profl. jours. Grantee McCay Sch. of Edn. Rsch. Funds, U. Utah, 2000, Regents' Initiative Collaborative Rsch. Grant, State of Tex., 2001; scholar, Tex. A&M Internat. U., 2003—04; Regents' Initiative Fellowship Grant, State of Tex., 2001. Mem.: Coun. for Exceptional Children, Phi Kappa Phi, Pi Lambda Theta. Republican. Baptist. Achievements include research in over representation of Limited English Proficient students in special education; working conditions of special education teachers in Texas. Avocations: music, genealogy, model building. Office: Ind Univ South Bend Greenlawn Hall 129 1700 Mishawaka Ave South Bend IN 46634-7111 Home: 201 Taylors Way North Liberty IN 46554-9226 Office Phone: 574-520-4867. Office Fax: 574-520-4550. Personal E-mail: terrys2956@aol.com. Business E-Mail: tersheph@iusb.edu.

SHEPHERD, WILLIAM MICHAEL, music educator, musician; b. Ft. Knox, Ky., Mar. 26, 1949; s. Elisha and Zella Shepherd; m. Shelley Alice Jaffe, Feb. 10, 1985; children: Kevin, Marc. Student, Vallejo Jr. Coll., Calif., 1968—70; B in Music Edn., Ea. Ky. U., 1975; postgrad., U. Calif., Davis, 1986; MusM, U. Oreg., 1987. Music tchr. Dayton (Ohio) City Schs., 1975—77; profl. musician Stan Kenton, Les Brown, 1977—80; music tchr. Vallejo Unified Schs., 1980—83, Ukiah (Calif.) Unified Schs., 1983—94, Brookings (Oreg.)-Harbor Schs., 1994—2007, Harlan County Sch. Dist., Ky., 2007—. Dir. Curry Big Band, Brookings; leader Banana Belt Brass Quintet, Brookings. Mem.: Internat. Assn. Jazz Educators, Internat. Trumpet Guild, Phi Mu Alpha. Avocations: shooting, sports, fishing, model aviation. Home: PO Box 612 Cawood KY 40815-0612 Office Phone: 541-469-2108, 606-574-2020. Personal E-mail: shphrdwllm@yahoo.com. Business E-Mail: shepherd@harborside.com.

SHEPLEY, HUGH, architect; b. Boston, Mar. 17, 1928; s. Henry Richardson and Anna Lowell (Gardiner) S.; m. Mary Waters Niles, Dec. 27, 1950; children: Hamilton Niles, Philip Foster. BA, Harvard U., 1951; BArch., Boston Archtl. Ctr., 1958; postgrad., Mass. Inst. Tech., 1958-59. Mem. archtl. firm Shepley, Bulfinch, Richardson & Abbott, Boston, 1955-63, ptnr., 1963-91. Bd. dirs. Greater Boston Red Cross, 1967-73, mem. exec. com., 1968-69; bd. dirs. Cmty. Music Ctr., Boston, 1968-72, Boston Ctr. for Blind Children, 1979-87; trustee New Eng. Conservatory Music, 1978-83, overseer, 1983—; trustee Boston Med. Ctr., 1980-92, mem. exec. com., 1981-92, vice chmn. bd. dirs., 1985-89, chmn. bd. dirs., 1989-92; trustee Am. Coll. of Greece, 1983-92, treas., 1986-88; trustee, sec. Rotch Travelling Scholarship, 1987-93, v.p., 1993-2006; mem. adv. coun. Boston U. Med. Ctr., 1990-96, Corp. Old South Assn., 1993-2002; bd. dirs. Manchester (Mass.) Hist. Soc., 1994-2002; overseer Spaulding Rehab. Hosp., 2003—. Fellow AIA; mem. Mass. Assn. Architects (pres. 1972), Boston Soc. Architects (pres. 1974, Medal Honor award 2007), Boston Archtl. Ctr. (pres. 1969-71, hon. D. Arch.), Tavern Club (Boston), Manchester Yacht Club (commodore 1985-87), Essex County Club. Independent. Episcopalian. Home: 8 Andover Ct Bedford MA 01730 E-mail: hshepley@verizon.net.

SHEPLEY, MAGI D., special education educator; b. Toledo, June 9, 1973; d. Myra G. Shepley. BS, LI U., Greenvale, NY, 1996; MS, Johns Hopkins U., Balt., 2002, student, 2004—, CAGS, 2009. Cert. tchr. students physical and mental disabilities Pa., postgraduate profl. lic. Va., advanced profl. cert. Md. Moderate/severe disabilities tchr. Balt. City Pub. Schs., 1996—97; life skills support tchr. Harrisburg City Pub. Schs., Pa., 1997—2000; mild retardation tchr. Fairfax County Pub. Schs., Falls Church, Va., 2000—02; vocat. tng. tchr. Kennedy-Krieger Inst., Balt., 2002—05; cross-categorical spl. edn. tchr. Loudoun County Pub. Schs., Sterling, Va., 2005—. Assessor Nat. Bd. Profl. Tchg. Stds. Client svcs. mgr. ARC Disaster Svcs. Human Resources Sys., Washington, 1987—2006. Recipient Exceptional Svc. award, ARC, 1993, 2004, Bronze Svc. award for Sch. Clubs, Microsoft Innovative Tchr award, 2007, Best Boy Teach award, 2008. Mem.: Coun. Exceptional Children (assoc.; pres. Pa. divsn. devel. disabilities 1999—2000, sec. Md. state unit 2005—). Avocation: swimming. Office: Loudoun County Pub Schs/Park View 400 W Laurel Ave Sterling VA 20164

SHEPLEY, MARDELLE MCCUSKEY, architect, educator; b. Bethesda, Md., June 28, 1949; d. E. Scott McCuskey (father) & James R. and Yvonne Hudson S.; m. Laurence Berger, 1974 (div. 1978); m. Michael Curtis Blair, 1981 (div., 2004); children: Colin, Ian, Teal. BA, Columbia U., 1971, MArch, 1974; MA, U. Mich., 1979, DArch, 1981. Registered architect Calif. Urban designer NYC Dept. City Planning, 1972—74; planner Min. Planning & Econ. policy, Panama, Panama, 1975—77; lectr., teaching asst. U. Mich., Ann Arbor, 1977—81; assoc. Tai Assocs. Architects, San Francisco, 1981—85, The Design Partnership, San Francisco, 1985—93; asst. prof. Tex. A&M U., College Station, 1993—97, assoc. prof., 1997—2003, prof., 2003—, coord. PhD program, 1999-2001, assoc. dean for students, 2001—05, interim head dept. architecture, 2005—06. Rsch. com. Ctr. Health Design, Martinez, Calif., 1993—; assoc. dir. Ctr. Health Sys. and Design, 1995—2004, interim dir., 2004—05, dir., 2005—, prin. art and sci., 2006—; dir. design rsch. Shepley Bulfinch Archs., 2006—. Co-author: Healthcare Environments for Children and Their Families, 1998, A Practitioner's Guide to Evidence Based Design, 2008. Bd. dirs. Assn. for Care of Children's Health, Mt. Royal, NJ, 1998-2000; mem. parent bd. Oakland Montessori Sch., Calif., 1991-93. Recipient Health Facilities Rsch. award AIA, 1992; Tex. A&M U. scholar, 1998; Tex. A&M U. faculty fellow, 2001-, William Pena Endowed Prof., 2003-. Office: Tex A&M U Dept Architecture College Station TX 77843-3137 Business E-Mail: mardelle@tamu.edu.

SHEPP, BRYAN EUGENE, psychologist, educator; b. Cumberland, Md, Sept. 13, 1932; s. Bryan Evert and Dorothy Lorene (Stell) S.; m. June Lee Langeluttig, Jan. 31, 1953; children: Karen Suzanne, David Bryan. BS, U. Md., 1954, MS, 1956, PhD, 1960; MS with honors, Brown U., 1966. Rsch. prof. U. Conn., 1961-63; asst. prof. psychology George Peabody Coll., Nashville, 1963-64, Brown U., Providence, 1964-66, assoc. prof., 1966-69, prof., 1969-98, prof. emeritus, 1998—, chmn. dept. Providence, 1983-88, assoc. dean faculty, 1988-91, dean faculty, 1991-96. Cons. in field; vis. scientist Oxford (Eng.) U., 1970 Contbr. numerous articles to profl. publ.; ad hoc editor for several psychol. jour. Served with USN, 1955-59. Decorated letter of commendation Sec. of Navy; USPHS postdoctoral fellow, 1959-61; Nat. Inst. Child Health and Human Devel. grantee, 1965—82. Fellow APA, Am. Psychol. Soc. (founding fellow); mem. AAAS, AAUP, Psychonomic Soc., Univ. Club. Home Phone: 207-633-4703. Personal E-mail: beshepp@yahoo.com.

SHEPP, JUDITH ROSSER, retired elementary school educator; b. Dayton, Ohio, Mar. 11, 1942; d. Rollin Labarr and Eloise (Comstock) Rosser; m. John W. Shepp, July 12, 1969; children: David, Edward, Cynthia. BS, Eastern Ky. U., Richmond, 1964. Tchr. 5th grade Audubon Elem. Sch., Merritt Island, Fla., 1964-65, Ocean Breeze Elem. Sch., Indian Harbor Beach, Fla., 1965-66; tchr. 4th, 5th grades Audubon Elem. Sch., Merritt Island, Fla., 1966-69; spl. edn. tchr. Eustis Mid. Sch., Fla., 1988-89; tchr. 2nd, 3rd, 4th, 5th grades Orange County Pub. Sch., 1992—2009; spl. ed. tchr. Lovell Elem. Sch., 2001—06, primary team leader, 2008—09; ret., 2009. Faculty rep. Orange County Classroom Tchrs. Assn., Orlando, Fla., 1994-97, 2001—09; primary team leader Maxey Elem. Sch., Winter Garden, Fla., 1994-95, 97-98, mem. adv. coun., 1996-98; bd. mem. Orange County Reading Counc., 1999-2007; ret. from tchg., 2009. Pres. West Pasco Jr. Woman's Club, New Port Richey, Fla., 1973-75, Magnolia Garden Circle, Mount Dora, Fla., 1984-86, Woman's Commn. of Fine Arts, Mount Dora, Fla., 1986-90. Mem. NEA, Internat. Reading Assn., Fla. Reading Coun., Orange County Reading Coun., Orange County Classroom Tchrs. Assn., Gen. Fedn. of Women's Club Mount Dora (pres. 1990-92, newsletter editor Key Notes 1996—, Clubwoman of Yr. 1992), Exec. Women's Golf Assn. Avocations: reading, golf. Home: 30627 S Round Lake Rd Mount Dora FL 32757-9211 Personal E-mail: booknose@embarqmail.com.

SHEPPARD, ALBERT PARKER, JR., retired computer science educator; b. Griffin, Ga., June 6, 1936; s. Albert Parker and Cornelia (Cooper) S.; m. Judith Prosser, Sept. 9, 1957 (div. 1976); children: Frank Phillip; m. Eleanor C. Davis, Feb. 8, 1978 (dec. Oct. 1994); 1 stepchild, Phillip Hancock; m. Marjory W. Dewell, Nov. 18, 1995; stepchildren: Patti Thompson, Ellen Zamarano, Michael. BS, Oglethorpe U., 1958; MS, Emory U., 1959; PhD, Duke U., 1965. Sr. engr. Orlando (Fla.) rsch. div. Martin Marietta Co., 1960-63; physicist U.S. Army Rsch. Office, Durham, N.C., 1963-65; prin. rsch. engr., head spl. techniques br., electronics div. Ga. Inst. Tech., 1965-71, chief of chem. sci. lab., 1971-72, assoc. dean coll. engring., 1972-74, prof. elec. engring., 1972-89, assoc. v.p. for rsch., 1974-88, acting v.p. rsch., 1979-80, asst. to pres. info. tech., 1986, v.p. for interdisciplinary programs, 1988-89, acting v.p. info. tech., 1988-89; Charles and Mildred Jenkins prof. math. Fla. So. Coll., Lakeland, 1989-2000, dir. acad. computing, 1996—2005; ret., 2005. Evening faculty DeKalb Coll., Clarkston, Ga., 1967-71; pres. APS Enterprises Corp., Lakeland, 1980-2006; cons. scholar IBM So. Area 8, 1990-93. Contbr. articles to profl. jours. Inventor linear downdraft biomass gasifier. Trustee Southeastern Univs. Rsch. Assocs., 1983-86. Recipient Disting. Alumni award Oglethorpe U., 1974; Woodrow Wilson fellow, 1959. Mem. IEEE (sr., life mem.), Univ. Space Rsch. Assn. (vice chmn. coun. instns. 1980-81, chmn. 1981-82, trustee 1985-89, vice chmn. bd. dirs. 1986-87, chmn. 1987-88, chmn. engring. sci. coun. 1989-94), Ga. Tech. Rsch. Corp. (trustee 1989-97), Lone Palm Golf Club, Sigma Xi, Sigma Pi Sigma, Kappa Mu Epsilon. Presbyterian. Home: 884 Summerfield Dr Lakeland FL 33803-1896 Home Phone: 863-701-8308. Personal E-mail: apsent@tampabay.rr.com, apsent2000@gmail.com.

SHEPPARD, APRIL SPRING, school librarian; m. Michael L. Sheppard, Aug. 1, 1997. BA in Philosophy, Ark. State U., BFA in Studio Art; MLS, Tex. Women's U., Denton. Govt. docs. libr. Ark. State U., State University, 2005—.

SHEPPARD, BLAIR H., dean, finance company executive, educator; m. Martha Putallaz; children: Philip, Christopher. BA, MA, U. Western Ont.; PhD, U. Ill., 1980. Asst. prof. orgn. behavior Fuqua Sch. Bus., Duke U., 1981—86, assoc. prof., 1986—93, prof. mgmt., assoc. dean, dir. exec. edn., 1993—97, sr. assoc. dean academic programs, 1997—2000, dean, 2007—; CEO Duke Corp. Edn., 2000—07, chmn., 2007—. Recipient NC NationsBank Outstanding Faculty Award, Outstanding Book Award, Internat. Assn. for Conflict Mgmt.; Can. Coun. Doctoral Fellowship. Office: Duke U Fuqua Sch Bus 1 Towerview Dr Durham NC 27708 Office Phone: 919-660-4090. Office Fax: 919-684-8742. E-mail: blair.sheppard@duke.edu.*

SHEPPARD, JENNIFER MODLIN, genealogist, retired government employee; d. Herbert Raleigh Sheppard and Cleo Virginia Price. Grad. H.S., Newport News, Va. Cert. genealogy, profl. option Brigham Young U., Provo, Utah, 1996. With Naval Air Systems Command, Naval Plant Rep. Office, Burbank, Calif., 1973—75, indsl. property clearance specialist, 1975—81; indsl. property mgmt. specialist Naval Air Systems Command, Arlington, 1981—85, Def. Logistics Agy., Alexandria, Va., 1985—88; ret., 1988. Fed. women's program coord. Naval Air Systems Command, Naval Plant Rep. Office, Burbank, Calif., 1974—80. Author: (books) Price Family (History Book award from NC Soc. Historians, Many); contbr. articles to newspapers and profl. publs. Recipient Hist. Article award, NC Soc. Historians, 1994, Family History Book award, 1995, Robert Bruce Cooke Family History Book award, 1997, Joe M. McLauren Newsletter award, 1997, D. T. Smithwick Newspaper & Mag. Article award, 1997, D. T. Smithwick Newpaper/Mag. Article award, 2004, D. T. Smithwick Newspaper/Mag. Article award, 2005, 2005, 2006, Robert Bruce Cooke Family History Book award, 1998, Willie Parker Peace History Book award, 1999, Paul Green Multimedia award, 2000. Mem.: Friends of Oll Martin County Courthouse (life; grant writer 2004—05), Nat. Soc. DAR, UDC (Manassas, Va. chpt. 175) (life; treas. 1987—88), Martin County Geneal. Soc. (life; v.p. 1993—95, pres. 1995—97, newsletter editor 1995—97, exec. com. mem. 1997), UDC (Theodore Hassell chpt. 437) (life; pres. 1996—2000, registrar 1997—2000), Martin County Hist. Soc. (life). Business E-Mail: shepjr@coastalnet.com.

SHEPPARD, LISA MARIE, psychologist; b. Redding, Calif., Feb. 8, 1963; d. Arthur and LaVonne Brown; m. James Sheppard, July 17, 1999; children: Amanda Fern Rhoads, Megan Elise Pendelton, Gavin Tyler Rhoads. M in Psychology, Calif. State U., 1996. Cert. in pupil pers. credential 1996. Psychologist Yuba City Unified Sch. Dist., Calif., 1996—, specialist, 2000—06. Home: 338 Aleut St Biggs CA 95917 Office: Yuba City Unified Sch Dist 750 Palora Ave Yuba City CA 95991 Home Fax: 530-822-3219. E-mail: lsheppard@ycusd.k12.ca.us.

SHEPPARD, LUVON, art educator; b. Aug. 15, 1940; BFA, Rochester Inst. Tech., NY, 1969, MST, 1970. Cert. tchr. NY. Ednl. curator Meml. Art Gallery U. Rochester, NY, 1970—76; prof. art Rochester Inst. Tech., 1972—; adj. prof. SUNY, Geneseo, 1993—. One-man shows include Skoto Gallery, NYC, 2003; author: My Visual Song, 1995. Recipient Eisenhart Outstanding Tchg. award, Rochester Inst. Tech., 1986, Joseph M. O'Brien Excellence in Tchg. award, SUNY Geneseo, 2003. Mem.: NY State Tchrs. Assn., Restoration Art Guild (founder, dir. 2002—). Office: Rochester Inst Tech 90 Lomb Meml Dr Rochester NY 14623-5604 Home: 551 Genesee St Rochester NY 14611

SHEPPARD, WILLIAM J., lawyer; b. Portland, Oreg., Nov. 4, 1941; BS, Fla. State U., 1963; JD, U. Fla., 1967. Bar: Fla. 1968, U.S. Dist. Ct. Fla. (Middle and No. Dist.) 1968, U.S. Ct. Appeals (5th cir.) 1971, U.S. Supreme Ct. 1973, U.S. Ct. Appeals (11th cir.) 1981, U.S. Ct. Appeals (4th cir.) 1982, U.S. Ct. Appeals (7th cir.) 1991, U.S. Ct. Appeals (Fed. cir.) 1995, U.S. Tax Ct. 1999, bd. cert. criminal trial lawyer: Fla. Bar Bd. Legal and Specialization Edn. Ptnr. Sheppard, White & Thomas, P.A., Jacksonville, Fla. Mem. Gov.'s Adv. Com. on Corrections, 1982—86; chmn. Jud. Nom. Commn. Fourth Jud. Cir., 1992—96; mem. civil justice reform act commn. Middle Dist. Fla., 1996—98. Exec. editor: U. Fla. Law Rev., 1966—67; contbr. articles to profl. jours. 1st lt. U.S. Army, 1963—65. Decorated Commendation Medal U.S. Army; recipient Disting. Svc. award, Nat. Fedn. Blind Fla., 1978, Nelson Poynter Civil Liberties award, 1982, Tobias Simon Pro Bono Svc. award, Fla. Supreme Ct., 1985, Civil and Human Rights award, Internat. Assn. Official Human Rights Agencies, 1990, Nelson Poynter Civil Liberties award, 2000. Mem.: NACDL, Chester Bedell Inn of Ct. (master of the bench), Am. Coll. Trial Lawyers, Fla. Assn. Criminal Def. Lawyers (Steven M. Goldstein Criminal Justice award 2001), Fla. Bar. Assn. (mem. criminal law cert. com. 1986—88, Pres. Pro Bono Svc. award 1984, Selig I. Golden Meml. award 1993), Jacksonville Bar Assn. (mem. 4th jud. cir. professionalism com. 1999—2000), Fla. Bar Found. (life Medal of Honor award 2004), Phi Delta Phi. Office: Sheppard White & Thomas PA 215 Washington St Jacksonville FL 32202 Home Phone: 904-727-7191; Office Phone: 904-356-9661. Office Fax: 904-356-9667. Business E-Mail: sheplaw@att.net.

SHEPPE, JOSEPH ANDREW, surgeon; b. Huntington, W.Va., Sept. 24, 1953; m. Kathy Chapman; children: Sheree Nicole, Natalee Marie, Brittany Lee. BS summa cum laude in Chemistry and Zoology, Marshall U., 1975; MD, W.Va. U., 1979. Diplomate Am. Bd. Surgery, Am. Bd. Colon and Rectal Surgery. Intern in gen. surgery Charleston (W.Va.) Area Med. Ctr., 1979-84; fellow in colon and rectal surgery William Beaumont Army Med. Ctr., Royal Oak, Mich., 1984-85; pvt. practice Columbia, SC, 1985—. Physician Bapt. Med. Ctr., Columbia, Providence Hosp., Columbia, Richland Meml. Hosp., Columbia, Lexington Med. Ctr., West Columbia, S.C.; clin. instr. in gen./colorectal surgery U. S.C. Med. Sch. Fellow ACS, Am. Soc. Colon and Rectal Surgery; mem. S.C. Med. Soc., Columbia Med. Soc. Home: 204 Leaning Tree Rd Columbia SC 29223-3009 Office: 1333 Taylor St Ste 4-a Columbia SC 29201-2949 Office Phone: 803-779-5600.

SHEPROW, MATTHEW WARREN, psychologist; BA, Seton Hall U., South Orange, NJ, 1977, PhD, 1997; MEd, Montclair State Coll., NJ, 1982. Cert. handicapped tchr. NJ, 1980; sch. psychologist 1982, lic. psychologist 1990. Staff psychologist Monmouth Med. Ctr., Long Br., NJ, 1984—90; sch. psychologist Regional Child Study Team, Atlantic Highlands, NJ, 1984—90; psychologist-pvt. practice Matthew W.Sheprow, PhD, LLC, Wall Township, NJ, 1999—. Sch. psychologist Monmouth Regional HS, Tinton Falls, NJ, 1990—. Eucharistic min. St. Catharine Parish, Spring Lake, NJ, 1990—2008. Mem.: APA. Office: Matthew W Sheprow PhD LLC 3350 Rt 138 W Bldg 1 Ste 118 Wall NJ 07719

SHEPSON, PAUL BRADFORD, chemistry professor; b. Elmira, NY, Nov. 29, 1956; s. Bradford G. Shepson and Jean Marilyn Burke; m. Jo Anne Witkop, July 16, 2005; children: Sam, Sarah, Olivia. PhD, Pa. State U., Univ. Pk., 1982. Dir. Purdue climate change rsch. ctr. Purdue U., West Lafayette, Ind., 2004—08, head dept. chemistry, 2008—. Avocation: flying. Office: Purdue Univ 560 Oval Dr West Lafayette IN 47907 Office Phone: 765-494-5207. Office Fax: 765-496-2874. Business E-Mail: pshepson@purdue.edu.

SHER, SIR ANTONY, actor, author, artist; b. Cape Town, South Africa, June 14, 1949; Student, Webber-Douglas Acad. Dramatic Art, 1969—71; LittD (hon.), U. Liverpool, U. Exeter, U. Warwick. Performer (plays): Cloud Nine, Goosepimples, Torch Song Trilogy (Laurence Olivier Best Actor award), assoc. artist Royal Shakespeare Co., King Lear, Moliere, Tartuffe, Maydays, Red Noses, Richard III (London Critics Cir. Theatre award, best actor, 1984, London Evening Standard Theatre award, best actor. 1985), The Merchant of Venice, The Revenger's Tragedy, Hello and Goodbye, Singer, Tambulaine the Great, Travesties, Cyrano de Bergerac, The Winter's Tale, Macbeth, The Roman Actor, The Malcontent, Othello, The Tempest; (nat. theater) True West, The Trial, The Resistible Rise of Arturo Ui, Uncle Vanya, Titus Andronicus (TMA Best Actor award), Stanley (Laurence Olivier Best Actor award, 1997, Theatre World award, Tony award nominee 1997), Primo (Outer Critics' Cir. award, outstanding solo performance, 2006, Drama Desk award, outstanding solo performance, 2006); (TV movie) History Man, Mark Gertler, Moliere, Tartuffe, Collision Course, The Land of Dreams, Genghis Cohen, Macbeth, The Moonstone, Home, Primo, God on Trial; (film) Shadey, Erik the Viking, The Wind in the Willows, Alive and Kicking, Mrs. Brown, Churchill The Hollywood Years; author: Year of the King, Middlepost, Characters; The Indoor Boy, Cheap Lives; (with Gregory Doran) Woza Shakespeare!, The Feast, Beside Myself, I.D., Primo, Primo Time, The Giant; (art exhbns.): Barbican Ctr., 1985, Nat. Theatre, 1995, 2009, London Jewish Cultural Ctr., 2007. Achievements include skill for acting and writing. Mailing: c/o Paul Lyon-Maris ICM Oxford House 76 Oxford St London WIN OAX England

SHER, BARTLETT, theater director; b. 1959; s. Joseph and Aird Sher, Doug Chung (Stepfather); m. Kristin Flanders; 1 child, Lucia. Grad., Holy Cross Coll., Worcester, MA. Tchr. Freehold Studio/Theatre Lab; resident dir. Guthrie Theater, Mpls.; assoc. dir. Ahmanson Theater; assoc. artistic dir. Hartford Stage Co.; artistic dir. Intiman Theatre,

Seattle. Bd. mem. CityClub, Seattle. Dir.: (plays) A Man's a Man, Waste, 2000 (Best Play, Obie award, 2000), Don Juan, Pericles, Cymbeline, 2002 (Callaway award, 2002), Three Sisters, Our Town, Singing Forest, Nickel and Dimed; (Broadway plays) The Light in the Piazza, 2005, Awake and Sing!, 2006, South Pacific, 2008 (Outstanding Dir. of a Musical, Oustanding Musical, Drama Desk Awards, 2008, Best Revival of a Musical & Best Direction of a Musical, Tony Awards, 2008), Joe Turner's Come and Gone, 2009; (Operas) Mourning Becomes Electra, Il Barbiere di Siviglia, 2006. Office: Intiman Theatre PO Box 19760 Seattle WA 98109

SHER, DENISE LINDA, judge; b. Oct. 26, 1954; d. Leonard and Ruth Harvey; m. Robert G. Sher, June 26, 1976; children: Noah(dec.), Sarah, Janelle. BA, Queens Coll., 1975; JD, Hofstra U., 1978. Bar: NY 79, U.S. Supreme Ct., U.S. Dist. Ct. (ea. and so. dists.) NY, U.S. Tax Ct. Pres. Nassau County Dist. Ct., Bd of Judges. Contbr. articles to profl. jours. Bd. dirs. sisterhood Hewlett-East Rockaway Jewish Ctr.; mem. Peninsula Counseling Ctr., Ctrl. Coun. PTA, Hewlett; former bd. dirs. Woodmere Sch. Dist.; mem. Five Towns Cmty. Chest; life mem. Hewlett Hadassah; mem. Yashar, Hewlett-East Rockaway ORT; former pub. works chmn. Village of Hewlett Harbor, Hewlett Harbor; bd. dirs. Family and Children's Assn. L.I.; former bd. dirs. Ctr. for Family Resources, Child Care Coun. Nassau County; former coun. Island Park C. of C., Nassau County Coun. Chambers; former mem. planned giving com. Am. Cancer Soc.; former mem. bd. dirs. Friedberg South Shore YJCC; mem. Tilles Cmty. Com.; mem. bd. judges Nassau County Dist. Ct, 2001—; trustee Theodore Roosevelt Inn of Ct.; former mem. legis. com. L.I. Com. for Soviet Jewry. Recipient Pathfinder award, Town of Hempstead, 1992, Martin Luther King Jr. Living the Dream award, 1994, Woman of Yr. award, Ct. Officers Benevolent Assn. Nassau County, 1999, Pub. Svcs. award, Indian Kerala Ctr., 2000, Woman of Distinction award, Soropotimist of Nassau County Inc., 2001, George Estabrook award, Hofstra Law Sch., 2001, Disting. Alumnus award, 2001, Hofstra Law Women, 2004, award, Italian Ct. Officers Nassau County, 2006, Cmty. Svcs. award, Jewish Law Assn., 2009, Hon. Edward Hart Jr. award, Fraternal Order of Court Officers, 2009; named Woman of Yr., Island Park Jewish Ctr., 1988, Alumnus of Yr., Phi Alpha Delta, 1998; named one of Top 50 Women, L.I. Bus. News, 2002, Top 90 Women, Girl Scouts of Nassau County, 2002; named to L.I. Ctr. Hall of Fame. Mem.: ABA, N.Y. Jud. Com. on Women in Cts. (chair emeritus), L.I. Ctr. for Bus. and Profl. Women (Achievers award), Nassau County Dist. Ct. Judges Assn., N.Y. Dist. Ct. Judge's Assn., Nassau Lawyers' Assn. L.I., Inc., Nat. Assn. Women Judges, Jewish Lawyer's Assn. of Nassau County (award 2006), N.Y. State Bar Assn., N.Y. State Women's Bar Assn., Nassau-Suffolk Women's Bar Assn. (bd. dirs., mem. jud. screening com.), Nassau County Bar Assn. (dir. Acad. of Law, mem. matrimonial com., mem. estates and trusts com., mem. young lawyers com., mem. cmty.edn. and pub. rels. com., mem. mentor program, active mock trial, mock jury selection, moot ct. competition, Vol. Lawyer award 1991), Columbian Lawyers Assn. (assoc.), Kiwanis. Office: NYS Ct Claims Acting Supreme Justice Nassau County Supreme Ct 262 Old Country Rd Mineola NY 11501 Business E-Mail: dsher@courts.state.ny.us.

SHER, GEORGE ALLEN, philosophy educator; b. NYC, Nov. 10, 1942; s. Daniel and Clara (Landesberg) S.; m. Emily Fox Gordon, July 10, 1972; 1 child, Sarah Constantine. BA, Brandeis U., 1964; PhD, Columbia U., 1972. Instr. philosophy Fairleigh Dickinson U., Teaneck, NJ, 1966—72, asst. prof. philosophy, 1972—74; assoc. prof. philosophy U. Vt., Burlington, 1974-80, prof., 1980-91; Herbert S. Autrey prof. philosophy Rice U., Houston, 1991—, chmn. dept. philosophy, 1993-2000. Mem. Inst. for Advanced Study, Princeton, N.J., 1987-88. Author: Desert, 1987, Beyond Neutrality: Perfectionism and Politics, 1997, Approximate Justice: Studies in Non-Ideal Theory, 1997, In Praise of Blame, 2005, Who Knew? Responsibility Without Awareners, 2009; editor: Moral Philosophy: Selected Readings, 1989, 2d edit., 1996; contbr. articles to profl. jours. Named fellow Nat. Humanities Ctr., Rsch. Triangle Park, N.C., 1980-81. Mem. Am. Philos. Assn. Home: 2425 Dryden Rd Houston TX 77030-1001 Office: Rice U Dept Philosophy MS 14 6100 Main St Houston TX 77251-1892 Office Phone: 713-348-2723. Business E-Mail: gsher@rice.edu.

SHER, LEO, psychiatrist; b. Kiev, Ukraine, June 13, 1961; s. Alexander and Ivetta (Iokhved) Sher. MD summa cum laude (hon.), Ukrainian Nat. Med. U., Kiev, 1985. Sr. staff fellow NIMH, Bethesda, Md., 1997—2000; asst. clin. prof. psychiatry and behavioral scis. George Washington U., Washington, 2000—02; rsch. psychiatrist NY State Psychiat. Inst., Columbia U. Med. Ctr., NYC, 2000—; asst. clin. prof. psychiatry Columbia U. Coll. Physicians and Surgeons, NYC, 2001—06, assoc. clin. prof. psychiatry, 2006—; assoc. attending physician NY Presbyn. Hosp., Columbia U. Med. Ctr., NYC, 2007—. Contbr. articles over 300 to profl. jours., chapters to books. Recipient Charlotte Marker Zitrin, M.D. award, Albert Einstein Coll. of Medicine Psychiatry Residency Program at L.I. Jewish Med. Ctr., 1997, Internat. award for Excellence in Pub. Clin. Rsch. in Jour. Clin. Endocrinology and Metabolism, Endocrine Soc. and Pfizer, 2004. Mem.: Soc. Biol. Psychiatry. Jewish. Achievements include patents in field. Personal E-mail: drleosher@aol.com.

SHER, SUSAN S., lawyer, federal official; b. 1948; children: Graham, Evan. BA, George Wash. U., 1970; JD, Loyola U., 1974. Bar: Ill. 1974. Ptnr. Mayer, Brown & Platt; assoc. gen. counsel, dir. labor & litigatoin U. Chgo., 1985—89; asst. corp. counsel City of Chgo., 1989—93, corp. counsel, 1993—97; v.p., gen. counsel U. Chgo. Hospitals, 1997—2001, v.p. legal & govt. affairs, gen. counsel, 2001—09; assoc. counsel to Pres., counsel to First Lady The White House, Washington, 2009, chief of staff to First Lady Michelle Obama, 2009—. Mem. steering com. Ill. Hosp. Assn., 2004; spkr. in field. Mem.: ABA, Fed. Bar Assn. Office: The White House 1600 Pennsylvania Ave NW 2nd Fl Washington DC 20502*

SHERAK, THOMAS MITCHELL (TOM SHERAK), motion picture association executive; b. Bklyn., June 22, 1945; s. Myer and Freida (Rosenthal) S.; m. Madeleine Frankfurter, Nov. 22, 1967; children: Barbra, Melissa, William. AA in Mktg., N.Y. Community Coll., Bklyn., 1965. Salesman Paramount Pictures, NYC, Washington, St. Louis, 1970-74; booker film R/C Theatres, Balt., 1974-77; dist. film buyer Gen. Cinema, Cherry Hill, NJ, 1977-78, v.p. film NYC, 1978-82, v.p. head film buyer Cherry Hill, NJ, 1982-83; pres. domestic distbn. & mktg. 20th Century-Fox Pictures, Beverly Hills, Calif., 1983-85, pres. domestic distbn., 1985—2000; pres. Revolution Studios, Santa Monica, Calif., 2000—07. Vis. asst. prof. UCLA Sch. Theatre Film & Television. Mem. So. Calif. Multiple Sclerosis Soc., Fulfillment Fund So. California, So. California Variety, The Children's Soc. Served in US Army, 1967—69. Recipient Lifetime Achievement award, Variety mag., 2007. Mem. Motion Picture Bookers Club (hon.), Motion Picture Pioneer, Will Rogers Democrat. Office: Acad Motion Picture Arts & Sciences 8949 Wilshire Blvd Beverly Hills CA 90211 Office Phone: 310-247-3000. Office Fax: 310-850-9619.*

SHERALI, ZEADALLY, engineering educator; m. Borrara Saeed; 1 child, Zobia Zeadally. BA in Computer Sci., U. Cambridge, Eng., 1991; PhD, U. Buckingham, Eng., 1996. Cert. CITP Brit. Computer Soc.; chartered engr., Engring. Coun., Eng. Rsch. asst. prof. U. Southern Calif., LA, 1997—99; asst. prof. Wayne State U., Detroit, 1999—2006; assoc. prof. U. DC, Washington, 2006—. Recipient Excellence Tchg. award, Wayne State U., 2001, 2003, Pres.'s award, 2004, Outstanding Faculty award, U. DC, 2008, Boeing Welliver Faculty award, 2008; fellow, Brit. Computer Soc., Instn. Engring. Tech. Office: Univ DC 4200 Conn Ave Washington DC 20008

SHERARD, BRENT D., state agency administrator, physician; b. Wheatland, Wyo. BS, Univ. Wyo., 1973; MD, Creighton Univ., 1979; MPH, Emory Univ., 2003. Cert. internal medicine. Residency St. Joseph's Hosp., Denver; private practice internal medicine Wheatland, Wyo.; Platte County Health Officer Wyo.; interim dir. Wyo. Dept. Health, 2002, 2005, dir. & state health officer, 2005—. Adjunct clinical faculty mem. Coll. Health Sci., Univ. Wyo.; vol. physician Cheyenne Cmty. Clinic; bd. dir., former chmn. First State Bank, Wheatland, Wyo. Office: Dept Health 401 Hathaway Bldg 2300 Capitol Ave Cheyenne WY 82002*

SHERBELL-NA, RHODA, artist, sculptor; b. Bklyn. d. Alexander and Syd (Steinberg) S.; m. Mervin Honig, Apr. 28, 1956 (dec.); 1 child, Susan Honig. Student, Art Students League, 1950—53, Bklyn. Mus. Art Sch., 1959—61; pvt. study art, Italy, France, Eng., 1956; master class in Sculptor, Nat. Acad. Design, NYC, 2009. Tchr. Hofstra U., 1990—91, Art Students League, 1980—2009. Cons., coun. mem. Emily Lowe Gallery, Hofstra U., Hempstead, NY, 1978, pres., 1989-81, instr., 1991—, life mem. bd. friends, pres. bd. trustees; tchr. instr. Mus. Modern Art, NYC, 1959, NAD Art Sch., NYC, 1985—, Art Students League, NYC, 1980—; Nat. Portrait Gallery Mus. rep. to 150th anniversary Smithsonian Instn., Washington, 1996; lectr. Nat. Arts Club, NYC. One-woman shows include Hunting Hartford Mus., NYC, 1965, Art in Embassy Program, Prague, 2002-03, Country Art Gallery, Locust Valley, NY, Bklyn. Mus. Art Sch., 1961, Adelphi Coll., A.C.A. Galleries, NYC, 1960, Capricorn Galleries, Rehn Gallery, Washington, 1968, Huntington Hartford Mus., NYC, 1969, NY Cultural Ctr., 1970, Smithsonian Am. Art Mus., Smithsonian Instn., Washington (formerly Nat. Arts Collection), 1970, Montclair Mus. of Art, 1976, Nat. Art Mus. Sport, 1977, Jewish Mus. NYC, 1980, Morris Mus. Arts and Scis., NJ, 1980, Black History Mus., 1981, Queens Mus., 1981-82, Nat. Portrait Gallery, Smithsonian Inst., Washington, 1981-82, Bergen Mus. Arts and Scis., NJ, 1984, William Benton Mus., Conn., 1985, Palace Theatre of the Arts, Stamford, Conn., Bronx Mus. Arts, 1986, Hofstra Mus. Art, LI, NY, 1989-90, 97-98, County Art Gallery, NYC, 1990, Heckscher Mus., LI, 2000, Bronx Mus., NY, Bklyn. Mus., Mus. Modern Art, NYC, Country Art Gallery, 1990, Port Washington Libr., Nat. Mus. Am. Art, Smithsonian Instn., 1982, NAD, NYC, 1984, 89, Castle Gallery Mus., NYC, 1987, Emily Lowe Mus., NYC, 1987, Heckshire Mus., NYC, 1989, Islip Art Mus., NYC, 1989, Gallery Emanuel, NY, 1993, Sundance Gallery, Bridgehampton, NY, 1995, Artist Equity Exhbn., SoHo, 1995, NAD Exhbn., 1995, Main St. Petile Gallery, 2003, Huntington Arts Coun., 2003, 04, Huntington Twp. Art League, 2002-03, The Art Students League Instructors Exhbn., Salandes O'Reilly Gallery, NYC, 2003; 2 person exhbn. Works on Paper, Hofstra Mus., Hofstra U., 1997-98, pastel exhbn., 2006, 2007; exhibited in numerous group shows including Portrait in bronze of Senator Norman J. Levy for Merrick Train Station, 2000, Aaron Copland's America, Heckscher Mus. Art, 2000, Nat. Art Mus., 2002-, Huntington Arts Coun. Inc., 2003, Petite Gallery, Baseball Hall of Fame & Mus., Cooperstown, NY, 2004, Queens Mus., NY, 2004, Allied Arts of Am., 2003-04 (New Foundry award, 2004), Nat. TiesClub Show, 2004, Nat. Burlington Soc. Art Exhibn., 2004, Salamander OReily Gallery, NY, The Art Students League, 2004, Nat. Acad. Design Exhibitors, 2005, Nat. Portrait Gallery, 2005, 06; represented permanent collections, Stony Brook Hall of Fame, William Benton Mus. Art, Colby Coll. Mus., Oklahoma City Mus., Montclair Mus., NJ, Schonberg Libr. Black Studies, NYC, Albany State Mus., Hofstra U., Bklyn. Mus., Colby Coll. Mus., Nat. Arts Collection, Nat. Portrait Gallery, Smithsonian Instn., Baseball Hall of Fame Cooperstown, NY, Nassau C.C., Hofstra U. Emily Lowe Gallery, Art Students League, Jewish Mus., "The Subway Series: The New York Mets Our National Pastime," Queens Mus., Black History Mus., Nassau County Mus., Stamford Mus. Art and Nature Ctr., Jericho Pub. Libr., NY, African-Am. Mus., Hempstead, NY, Stamford Mus. Art and Scis., Conn., (Monument Work) The Am. Baseball Family Story, The Sea Dogs, 2006, MTA, Pub. Monument for Senator Norman J. Levy Merrik R.R. Sta., NY, Yogi Berra Portrait, Nat. Gallery Smithsonian Inst., Mose Soyer painting, Smithsonian Am. Art Mus., Raphare Soyer Portrait, Dept. State, The Embassy Program, Prague, Czech Republic, 2002-04, Nat. Acad., 2005-06, 07, Nat. Art Club, 2005-06, Nat. Portrait Gallery, 2006, Hofstra Mus., 2006-07; also pvt. collections, TV shows, ABC, 1968, 81; ednl. TV spl. Rhoda Sherbell-Woman in Bronze, 1977; prin. works include Seated Ballerina, portraits of Aaron Copland (Bruce Stevenson Meml. Best Portrait award Nat. Arts Club 1989), Eleanor Roosevelt, Variations on a Theme (36 works of collaged sculpture), 1982-86, Portland Sea Dogs Monument, Lareg Monument, American Baseball Family Group, 2007; appeared several TV shows; guest various radio programs; contbr. articles to newspapers, popular mags. and art jours.; mem. Conservation Art Group Coun. City of NY, 1994-97; exhbns. include: Petite Gallery, Huntington, NY, 2003, The Nat. Acad. Mus., 2003-04, Disegno Exhbn., NAD, 2005—, Nat. Sculpture Soc., 2005—, Nat. Art Club, 2005— (Merit award 2005), Brookgreen Gardens,2005-06, Nat. Portrait Gallery, Smithsonian Inst., 2006, solo pastel exhbn. Looking East En Plein Air, Hofstra Mus., 2007, The Art Students League NY, 2008, Long Island Profl. Artist's Showcase, CW Post Campus, Long Island U., 2008; co-curator (exhbns.) The Nat. Art Mus. Sport, 2008, The Sports Mus. America, NYC, 2008, The Art Studens League NY, 2008, Profl. Art Group, LI, 2008-09, Nat. Acad. Design Art Sculpture, 2008-09. Trustee Nat. Art Mus. of Sport, 1959-; coun. mem. Nassau County Mus., 1978, trustee, 1st v.p. coun.; cons., cmty. liaison WNET Channel 13, cultural coord., 1975-83; host radio show Not for Artists Only, 1978-79; commr. Women's Boxing Fedn., 1978; mem. The Art Commn. The City of NY, 1993; chmn. bd. Hofstra Mus., 1978-89. Recipient Gold medal Allied Artists Am., 1989, Alfred G. B. Steel Meml. award Pa. Acad. Fine Arts, 1963-64; Jersey City Mus. prize for sculpture, 1961, 1st prize sculpture Locust Valley Art Show, 1966, 67, Ann. Sculpture prize Jersey City Mus., Bank for Savs. 1st prize in sculpture, 1950, Ford Found. purchase award, 1964, 2 top sculpture awards Mainstreams 77, Cert. of Merit Salmagundi Club, 1978, prize for sculpture, 1980, 81, award for sculpture Knickerbocker Artists, 1980, 81, top prize for sculpture Hudson Valley Art Assn., 1981, Sawyer award NAD, 1985, Gold medal of honor Audubon Artists, 1985, Silvermine Exhbn. award, Gold medal Allied Artists Am., 1990, medal of honor for Bronze Queen Catherine, Nat. Arts Club, 2004, Pres.' award Nat Arts Club NYC, 2009, The Charlotte Danuddie award for Sculpture Nat. Acad. Design, 2003; MacDowell Colony fellow, 1976, AAAL and Am. Inst. Arts and Letters grantee, 1960, Louis Comfort Tiffany Found. grantee, 1962, Ford Found. grantee, 1964, 67, also award, New Foundry award, Allied Artists Am., 2004; named one of top 5 finalist to do Monument of Queen Catherine of England, 1991, Best in Show Nat. Arts Club, NY; named to represent Nat. Portrait Gallery at Smithsonian Mus., 1996, sculpture selected to represent Nat. Portrait Gallery Mus., 1997; guest at Dept. of State Embassy Program, Prague, Czech Republic, 2003-09; Queen Catherine Bronze, Hofstra Mus. Sculpture Gardens, 1985-, award Portrait Prof. Muhamad Yunis, 2009-. Fellow Nat. Sculpture Soc.; mem. NAD (Helen F. Barnett prize 1965, Leila Gordon Sawyer prize 1989, The Dessle Green prize 1993, Charlotte Deenevidde award 2003, award for Am. baseball founding group, 2003, award 2003), Sculpture Guild (dir.), Nat. Assn. Women Artists (Jeffery Childs Willis Meml. prize 1978), Allied Artists Soc. (dir., Gold medal 1990, The Pietro and Alfrieda Montana Meml. award 2000, award 2001), Audubon Artists (dir., Greta Kempton Walker prize 1965, Chaim Gross award, award disting. contbr. to orgn. 1979, 80, Louis Weskeem award), Woman's Caucus Art, Coll. Art Assn., Am. Inst. Conservation Hist. and Artistic Works, NY Soc. Women Artists, Artists Equity Assn. NY, Nat. Sculpture Soc. (E.N. Richard Meml. prize 1989), Internat. Platform Assn., Profl. Artists Guild LI, Painters and Sculptors Soc. NJ (Bertrum R. Hulmes Meml. award), Am. Watercolor Soc. (award for disting. contbn. to orgn.), Catharine Lorillard Wolfe Club (hon. mention 1968), Nat. Arts Club (NYC, Stevenson Meml. award 1989, Pres. award 1992, Robert Sayford award 2000, Bruce Stevenson Meml. award for Portrait 2000, Siegfort award 2000, award for sculpture 2004, award 2005), Portrait Soc. America (bd. mem. 2008-09, lectr. sculpture Va. 2009-). Personal E-mail: RhodaSherbell@mac.com, rhodasherbell@gmail.com.

SHERBIN, DAVID M., lawyer; b. Detroit, Sept. 6, 1959; m. Abbe H. Sherbin. BA with honors, Oberlin College, 1981; JD, Cornell Law Sch., 1987. Assoc. Katten Muchin & Zavis, Chgo., 1987—91; sr. counsel Heller Fin. Inc., 1992—97; assoc. gen. counsel Fed. Mogul Corp., Southfield, Mich., 1997—2001, sec., 1999—, v.p., dep. gen. counsel, sec., 2001—04, sr. v.p., gen. counsel, sec., 2004—05; v.p., gen. counsel, sec. Pulte Homes, Inc., Bloomfield Hills, Mich., 2005; v.p., gen. counsel, chief compliance officer Delphi Corp., Troy, Mich., 2005—. Mem.: Chgo. Bar Assn., ABA. Office: Delphi Corp 5725 Delphi Dr Troy MI 48098-2815 Office Phone: 248-813-3009. Office Fax: 248-813-2491.*

SHERBURN, REBECCA SUE, voice educator; d. Amy Smith and Joseph Calvin Sherburn; 1 child, Curtis Kathryn Sarah. DMA, U. Southern Calif., LA, 1999. Opera singer Staedtische Buehen Ornabrueck, Germany, 1991—93, Neue Flora Theater - Stella Prodns., Hamburg, Germany, 1993—97; assoc. prof. voice UMKC Conservatory Music and Dance, Kansas City, Mo., 1999—. Contbr. articles to profl. jours. Recipient Excellence in Tchg. award, UMKC Conservatory; Travel grants, U. Mo., 2000—, Faculty Rsch. grants, 2000—. Mem.: NATS (kans. city pres. 2004—06). Office: UMKC Conservatory Music and Dance 4949 Cherry Kansas City MO 64110 Business E-Mail: sherburnre@umkc.edu.

SHERBURNE, JANE C., lawyer, bank executive; b. 1951; BA, U. Minn., 1974, MSW, 1976; JD, Georgetown U. Law Ctr., 1983. Legis. asst. to Congressman Donald Fraser US Congress; chief of staff to commr. Social Security; spl. counsel to Pres. The White House, 1994—97; ptnr. Wilmer, Cutler & Pickering LLP; various positions from sr. dep. gen. counsel to gen. counsel global consumer grp. Citigroup Inc., 2001—08; sr. exec. v.p., gen. counsel Wachovia Corp., 2008—. Bd. trustees Nat. Women's Law Ctr., Lawyers' Com. for Civil Rights Under Law, NYC Bar Justice Ctr. Fellow: Am. Bar. Found. Office: Wachovia Corp 301 S Coll St Ste 4000 Charlotte NC 28288 Office Phone: 704-374-6161. Office Fax: 310-919-3072.*

SHERBY, KATHLEEN REILLY, lawyer; b. St. Louis, Apr. 5, 1947; d. John Victor and Florian Sylvia (Frederick) Reilly; m. James Wilson Sherby, May 17, 1975; children: Michael R.R., William J.R., David J.R. AB magna cum laude, St. Louis U., 1969, JD magna cum laude, 1976. Bar: Mo. 1976. Assoc. Bryan Cave, St. Louis, 1976-85; ptnr. Bryan Cave LLP, St. Louis, 1985—. Contbr. articles to profl. jours. Bd. dirs Jr. League, St. Louis, 1989-90, St. Louis Forum, 1992-99, pres., 1995-97; chmn. Bequest and Gift Coun. of St. Louis U., 1997-99; jr. warden Ch. of St. Michael and St. George, 1998-2000; bd. dirs. Bistate chpt. ARC, 2000-06, v.p. fin.; bd. trustees St. Louis Sci. Ctr., 2000—08; officer Clayton Edn. Found., 2003—. Fellow Am. Coll. Trust and Estate Coun. (regent 1997-2004), Estate Planning Coun. of St. Louis (pres. 1986-87), Bar Assn. Met. St. Louis (chmn. probate sect. 1986-87), Mo. Bar Assn. (chmn. probate and trust com. 1996-98, chmn. probate law revision subcom. 1988-96); Phi Beta Kappa. Episcopalian. Home: 47 Crestwood Dr Saint Louis MO 63105-3032 Office: Bryan Cave LLP 1 Metropolitan Sq Ste 3600 Saint Louis MO 63102-2733 Home Phone: 314-727-0523; Office Phone: 314-259-2224. Business E-Mail: krsherby@bryancave.com.

SHERE, DENNIS, lawyer, writer, retired publishing executive; b. Cleve., Nov. 29, 1940; s. William and Susan (Luskay) S.; m. Maureen Jones, Sept. 4, 1965 (div. Aug. 23, 2005); children: Rebecca Lynn, David Matthew, Stephen Andrew. BS in Journalism, Ohio U., 1963, MS in Journalism, 1964; JD, DePaul U., 2003. Staff writer Dayton (Ohio) Daily News, 1966-69; asst. prof. Sch. Journalism Bowling Green (Ohio) State U., 1969-70; fin. editor Detroit News, 1970-72, city editor, 1973-75; editor Dayton Jour. Herald, 1975-80; pub. Springfield (Ohio) Newspapers Inc., 1980-83, Dayton Newspapers, Inc., 1983-88; gen. mgr. Media Group Moody Bible Inst., 1989—2001; with death penalty trial assistance divsn. Il. State Appellate Defender's Office, 2004—05; asst. pub. defender Kane County Pub. Defender's Office, Ill., 2005—07. Author: Cain's Redemption - A Story of Hope & Transformation in America's Bloodiest Prison, 2005. Served with AUS, 1964-66. Mem. Sigma Alpha Epsilon, Omicron Delta Kappa. Home Phone: 630-879-6335. Business E-Mail: Dennis.Shere@moody.edu.

SHEREMATA, WILLIAM A., neurologist, educator; s. Anthony Sheremata and Gwendolyn R. Payne; m. Leah G. Magel, Dec. 20, 1975; children: Shelley R. Hammond, Summer L. BSc, U. Alta., Edmonton, MD, 1959. Dir. multiple sclerosis ctr. Miller Sch. Medicine, U. Miami, Fla., 1977—2008, prof. neurology, 1977—. Fellow: RS (London), ACP, RCPC. Achievements include research in multiple sclerosis. Office: Miller Sch Medicine PAC Bldg Ste 410 1150 NW 14 St Miami FL 33136 Business E-Mail: wsherema@miami.edu.

SHERER, SAMUEL AYERS, lawyer, urban planner, consultant; b. Warwick, NY, June 17, 1944; s. Ernest Thompson and Helen (Ayers) S.; m. Dewi Sudewinahidah, June 28, 1980 (dec. Dec. 2000). AB magna cum laude, Oberlin Coll., 1966; JD, Harvard U., 1970; M in City Planning, MIT, 1970. Bar: DC 1972, U.S. Supreme Ct. 1979. Atty., advisor HUD, Boston, 1970; sr. cons. McClaughry Assoc., Washington, 1970-71, 74-76; cons. Urban Inst., Washington, 1971-72; atty., urban planner IBRD Jakarta Urban Devel. Study, Indonesia, 1972-74; atty., advisor Office Minority Bus. U.S. Dept. Commerce, Washington, 1976-77; ptnr. Topping & Sherer, Washington, 1977-90; pres. Sherer-Axelrod-Monacelli, Inc., Cambridge, Mass., 1978-99; prin. The Washington Team, Inc., 1991—2000, Richardson & Sherer, LLC, 2000—04. Bd. dirs. The Urban Agr. Network; rep. Internat. Devel. Law Inst., Washington, 1983-90; sr. fellow Climate Inst., 1988—; cons. in field. Co-author: Urban Land Use in Egypt, 1977; editor: Important Laws and Regulations Regarding Land, Housing and Urban Development in the

Arab Republic of Egypt, 1977, Important Laws and Regulations Regarding Land, Housing and Urban Development in the Hashemite Kingdom of Jordan, 1981. Bd. dirs. MIT Enterprise Forum of Washington-Balt., 1980-82; mem. DC Rep. Ctrl. Com., 1984-88; nat. governing bd. Ripon Soc., Washington, 1977-83. Urban Studies fellow HUD, 1969-70. Mem. Phi Beta Kappa. Avocations: tennis, reading. Home: 429 N St SW Apt S204 Washington DC 20024-3714 Office: Climate Inst 900 17th St NW Ste 700 Washington DC 20006 Personal E-mail: samuel.sherer@gmail.com.

SHERESKY, NORMAN M., lawyer; b. Detroit, June 22, 1928; s. Harry and Rose (Lieberman) Sheresky; m. Elaine B. Lewis, Oct. 30, 1977; 1 child from previous marriage, Brooke Hillary. BA, Syracuse U., 1950; LLB, Harvard U., 1953. Bar: NY 1953. Assoc. Gold & Pollack, NYC, 1954—60; sole practice, 1960—72; ptnr. Sheresky & Kalman, 1972—77, Colton, Hartnick, Yamin & Sheresky, 1977—93, Baer, Marks & Upham, 1993—95, Sheresky, Aronson & Mayefsky, 1995—. Adj. prof. matrimonial litig. NY Law Sch., 1979—86; mem. jud. com. NYC Bar Assn.; founding mem. Am. Coll. Family Trial Lawyers. Author: On Trial, 1977; co-author (with Marya Mannes): Uncoupling, 1972; contbr., editor: Fairshare mag. Mem.: Met. Trial Lawyers Assn., Assn. Trial Lawyers Am., NY State Bar Assn., Am. Acad. Matrimonial Lawyers (gov., past pres. NY chpt., pres. elect), Internat. Acad. Matrimonial Lawyers (past treas., gov. NY chpt., bd. govs. 1986—, mem. com. to examine lawyer conduct in matrimonial actions 1992—95). Office: Sheresky Aronson Mayefsky Llp 485 Lexington Ave New York NY 10017-2630 Office Phone: 212-521-3501. Business E-Mail: sheresky@samllp.com.

SHERIDAN, ALICE VIRGINIA, photographer, educator; b. Augusta, Ga., Feb. 17, 1956; d. Alice Dulaney Sheridan; m. Ronald Andrew Gibbons, Oct. 6, 1994. MS in Counseling, SW Mo. State, Springfield, 1983; MA in Art History, Fla. State U., Tallahassee, 1987; MFA in Photography, Ohio U., Athen, 1994. Vis. prof. photography Ohio U., 1993—98; asst. prof. photography Jacksonville U., Fla., 1998—, dir. Paris summer study abroad program, 2000—, dir. Florence summer study abroad programs, 2002—, curator, 2004—. Dir., Prague alternative processes workshop, Prague, Czech Republic, 1994—95; curator, various cities, 1994—. Exhibitions include Multiple Bodies of Work. Mem.: Soc. Photographic Educators, Coll. Art Assn. Office: Jacksonville Univ 222B Phillips 2800 Univ Blvd N Jacksonville FL 32211 Business E-Mail: gsherid@ju.edu.

SHERIDAN, CHRISTOPHER FREDERICK, human resources executive; b. Syracuse, NY, June 7, 1953; s. Frederick John and Patricia Ann S.; m. Diane Marie Harman, Dec. 31, 1977; children: Ryan, Kelly. BS in Indsl. Relations, LeMoyne Coll., 1975. Employee rels. trainee Anaconda Co., Buffalo, 1975-76, employee rels. rep. LA, 1976-78; pers. mgr. HITCO, Gardena, Calif., 1978-80; labor rels. rep. Miller Brewing Co., Fulton, NY, 1980-82, labor rels. mgr. LA, 1982-90; employee rels. mgr. Ryder Distbn. Resources, Anaheim, Calif., 1990-91; dir. human resources Alta-Dena Cert. Dairy Inc., City of Industry, Calif., 1991-99; regional human resources dir. west/southwest Dean Foods Co., 1999—2004; regional human resources dir. Mission Foods, 2004—05; fin. cons. Am. Nat. Fin. Svcs. Corp., Upland, Calif., 2006—08; mgr. regional human rels. Bimbo Bakeries USA, 2008—. Mem. Soc. Human Resources Mgmt. Roman Catholic. Avocations: golf, basketball, reading, music. Office: 366 S Acacia Ave Fullerton CA 92831

SHERIDAN, DONALD CHARLES, orthopedist, hand surgeon; b. Dec. 23, 1962; BA in Chemistry, Ariz. State U., Tempe, Ariz., 1986; MD, U. Ariz., 1990. Cert. Am. Bd. Orthop. Surgeons, Am. Acad. Orthop. Surgeons-Surgery of the Hand. Resident, orthop. Mayo Clinic, Rochester, Minn., 1990—95, hand fellowship, 1995—96; instr., orthop. Mayo med. Sch., 1995; chmn., dept. orthop. Scottsdale Healthcare-Shea Hosp., 1998—2001. Hand surgery cons. Ariz. Diamondbacks Baseball Team, Ariz. State U. Athletic Program, Oakland Athletics, Milw. Brewers, San Francisco Giants, Tex. Rangers. Named one of Top Doctors, Phoenix Monthly. Fellow: Am. Acad. Orthop. Surgeons; mem.: Am. Soc. for Surgery of the Hand, State Orthop. Soc., State Med. Soc. Office: 12013 B 92nd St Ste 101 Scottsdale AZ 85258 Office Phone: 480-860-6005. Office Fax: 480-860-1882.

SHERIDAN, EDWARD PATRICK, college dean; b. Detroit, Dec. 2, 1937; s. Geoffrey Francis and Mary Ann (Beirne) S.; m. Kathleen Gentile, June 3, 1967. BA, Windsor U., Can., 1961; MA, U. Detroit, 1964; PhD, Loyola U., Chgo., 1968. Lic. psychologist, Ill., Fla. Intern clin. psychology Hines (Ill.) VA Hosp., 1963-65, Westside VA Outpatient Clinic, Chgo., 1965-66; asst. prof. U. Windsor, 1966-67; sr. psychologist Oakland County CMHC, Birmingham, Mich., 1967-68; asst. prof., coord. tng. U. Ill., Chgo., 1968-73; assoc. prof. Northwestern U. Med. Sch., Chgo., 1973-81, chief psychiatry outpatient svcs., 1973-81, prof., chmn., 1981-90; dean Coll. Arts & Scis. U. Cen. Fla., Orlando, 1990—. Cons. Ill. Dept. Mental Health, Chgo., 1982-86, First Nat. Bank Chgo., 1987—, State of N.Y. Dept. Higher Edn., N.Y.C., 1988—, Edward Hines Jr. VA Hosp., Hines, 1985-90. Editorial bd. Psychology and Health: An Internat. Jour., 1987—; contbr. articles to profl. jours. Fellow APA (chair accreditation com. 1991, chair bd. ednl. affairs 1994-95).

SHERIDAN, JAMES EDWARD, history professor; b. Wilmington, Del., July 15, 1922; s. Phillip Lambert and Ida Alverna (Green) S.; m. Sonia Landy, Sept. 27, 1947; 1 son, Jamy. BS, U. Ill., 1949, MA, 1950; PhD, U. Calif., Berkeley, 1961. Lectr. Chinese history Stanford U., 1960; mem. faculty Northwestern U., 1961—, prof. history, 1968—, chmn. dept., 1969-74, assoc. dean Coll. Arts and Scis., 1985-89, prof. emeritus, 1992—. Author: Chinese Warlord: The Career of Feng Yu-hsiang, 1966, China: A Culture Area in Perspective, 1970, China in Disintegration: The Republican Era in Chinese History, 1912-1949, 1975, A Community of Caring: An Introduction to Kendal at Hanover, 1998; editor: The Transformation of Modern China series, 1975—. Served to ensign USN, 1941-46. Fulbright fellow, France, 1950-51; Ford Found. fellow, 1958-60; grantee Am. Coun. Learned Socs.-Social Sci. Rsch. Coun., 1966-67, 71-72 Home: 80 Lyme Rd Apt 438 Hanover NH 03755-1236 Office: Northwestern Univ Dept History Evanston IL 60201 E-mail: james.e.sheridan@valley.net.

SHERIDAN, JIM, film director, screenwriter; b. Dublin, 1949; Student, Univ. Coll., Dublin. Artistic dir. Project Arts Theatre, 1976—80, N.Y. Irish Arts Ctr., 1982—87; founder Children's Theatre Co., Dublin. Screenwriter: Into the West, 1993; dir.: My Left Foot, 1989, The Field, 1990, In the Name of the Father, 1993, The Boxer, 1997, In America, 2001, Get Rich or Die Tryin, 2005, Brothers, 2008; prodr., exec. prodr. Some Mother's Son, 1996, Agnes Browne, 1999, On the Edge, 2000, Borstal Boy, 2000, Bloody Sunday, 2001. Office: Hells Kitchen Ltd 21 Mespil Rd Dublin 4 Ireland E-mail: hellskit@iol.ie.

SHERIDAN, JOHN J., musician, educator; s. John J. and Martha S. Sheridan; m. Colleen M. Smith, May 5, 1989; children: Erin Colleen, Kelly Ann. AA, Bucks County C.C., 1985; MusB, Temple U., 1989; MA, NYU, 2000. Freelance performer, Langhorne, Pa., 1985—2003; adj. faculty jazz studies Bucks County C.C., Newtown, 1994—2003, assoc. prof. music, 2003—. Arts tech. com. Bucks County C.C., Newtown, Pa., 2002—03, music tech. coord., 1996—2003. Composer, studio musician: songs Another View Point, studio musician: rec. Purity, Is You Is. Office: Bucks County C C 275 Swamp Rd Newtown PA 18940-4106 Business E-Mail: sheridaj@bucks.edu.

SHERIDAN, JUDSON DEAN, academic executive; b. Greeley, Colo., Nov. 10, 1940; s. Everett Judson and Dorothy Margaret (Patterson) S.; m. Katherine Alice Gallison, Aug. 18, 1963; children: Emily Elise, James Judson. BS, Hamline U., 1961; DPhil, Oxford U., 1965. Rsch. fellow and instr. Harvard Med. Sch., Boston, 1965-68; asst. prof., zoology U. Minn., Mpls., 1968-72, assoc. prof., zoology, 1972—77, prof. genetics and cell biology, 1977—78, prof. cell biology and neuroanatomy Med. Sch., 1978-87, assoc. dean grad sch., 1983-87; vice-provost rsch., dean grad. sch. U. Mo., Columbia, 1987—93, prof. physiology and biol. scis., 1987—93; v.p. acad. affairs U. Maine, Orono, 1993-95, prof. zoology, 1993-95; exec. dir. grad. record exams. program ETS, Princeton, NJ, 1996—99; prof. genetics, cell biology and devel. U. Minn., Mpls., 2000—, assoc. dean rsch. coll. biol. sci., 2000—04, dir. internat. programs coll. biol. sci., 2000—. Interdisciplinary endowed Norwegian centennial co-chair U. Minn., 2006—; council & bd. dirs. Grad. Schs., 1990—93, exec. com., 1991—92, Council Rsch. Policy & Grad. Edn., 1991—93, Assn. Grad. Schs., 1992—93; chair Acad. Affairs Council New Eng., 1995. Contbr. articles to profl. jours., books. Pres. Minn. Scottish Celtic Dance Assn., Mpls., 1981-82; mem. north area adv. com. Mpls. Pub. Schs., 1975-78; mem. bus. adv. coun. Royal Norwegian Consulate Gen., Mpls., 2006-; mem. adv. coun. China Ctr. U. Minn., 2003-; pres., 2008-. Rhodes Scholar, Oxford U., 1962-65; named to Outstanding Young Men of Am., 1970, Athletic Hall of Fame, Hamline U., 1982; recipient NIH-Career Devel. award Nat. Cancer Inst., Mpls., 1972-77. Mem. AAAS. Achievements include demonstration of cell coupling in solid tumors, dye coupling between capillary endothelial cells and endothelial cells in culture, cell coupling in chick embryos and xenopus blastomeres; research on gap junction formation in culture, decreased cell coupling in virally-transformed cells. Office Phone: 612-626-4940. Business E-Mail: sheri012@umn.edu.

SHERIDAN, MARK A., physiologist, educator; m. Nancy Ibsen, Oct. 10, 1981. AB, Humboldt State U., 1980, MA, 1982; PhD, U. Calif., Berkeley, 1985. Asst. prof. ND State U., Fargo, 1985—91, assoc. prof., 1991—97, prof., 1997—, James A. Meier prof., 1999—. Dir. regulatory bioscis. ND State U., Fargo, 1991—2000, dir. exptl program to stimulate competitive rsch., 2001—03; editor Gen. and Comparative Endocrinology, 2001—; assoc. editor Comparative Biochemistry and Physiology; panelist NSF, Arlington, Va., 2005—; editor Internat. Jour. Endocrinology, 2008—. Asst. scoutmaster Boy Scout Troop 214, Fargo, ND, 1999. Recipient Excellence in Rsch. award, ND State U., 1996; grantee, NSF, 2005—; fellow, Brazil Internat. Postgrad. Exch. Program, 1998. Fellow: Japan Soc. for Promotion of Sci.; mem.: Endocrine Soc., Soc. for Integrative and Comparative Biology (program officer divsn. comparative endocrinology 1996—99). Achievements include patents for novel somatostatins and methods. Avocations: camping, hiking, bicycling, reading, travel. Office: ND State Univ Stevens Hall Fargo ND 58105 Office Phone: 701-231-8110. Office Fax: 701-231-7149. Business E-Mail: mark.sheridan@ndsu.edu.

SHERIDAN, MARK WILLIAM, mechanical engineer, financial planner; b. Bryn Mawr, Pa., July 9, 1959; s. Phillip Frederick and Shirley Frazer Sheridan; m. Deborah Sazdanoff Sheridan, Aug. 14, 1999; children: Kristina, Katrina, Marlena. BSME, Lafayette Coll., 1981; MBA, Cornell U., 1987, M. Engring. (Mech.), 1988. Registered profl. engr., Ohio. Project engr. Internat. Paper Co., Mobile, Ala., 1981-83, sr. process engr., 1983-85; assoc. Booz-Allen & Hamilton, Cleve., 1988-90; coord. long range planning appliance motor divsn. Emerson Electric Co., St. Louis, 1990-93, resident engr. Paragould Plant, 1993-96; dir. mfg. Thermodisc, Mansfield, Ohio, 1996—2002, dir. ops. devel., 2002—. Summer intern Saturn Corp., Troy, Mich., 1986, 87. Patentee in field. Bd. dirs. ABC Condominium Assn., St. Louis, 1992-94; chmn. JGSM Student Faculty Com./Quality of Life Com., Ithaca, N.Y., 1985-87; pres. Mobile Soap Box Derby, 1983-85; v.p. ways and means, bd. dirs. Mobile Jaycees, 1984-85; mem. Leadership Unltd., 2003-04; active YMCA; treas. First Presbyn. Ch. of Mansfield, 1998-03. Lester B. Knight scholar Cornell U., 1986-88, J. Stanford Smith scholar Cornell U., 1985-87; named Outstanding Young Man of Am., 1984, 85, 87. Mem. ASME, Inst. Indsl. Engrs., The Planning Forum, Soc. Indsl. Archaeology, World Future Soc., St. Louis Jaycees (bd. dirs. 1992-94), Am. Mensa. Republican. Avocations: golf, reading, computing, weightlifting. Home: 2403 Ranchwood Dr Mansfield OH 44903-9044 Office: Thermodisc 1320 S Main St Mansfield OH 44907-5500 Office Phone: 419-525-8295. Personal E-mail: sheridanmark@excite.com.

SHERIDAN, MICHAEL JOHN, bishop; b. St. Louis, Mar. 4, 1945; Grad., Cardinal Glennon Coll., Kenrick Seminary. Ordained priest Archdiocese of St. Louis, Mo., 1971; prof. theology Kenrick Seminary, St. Louis, 1977-87; assoc. pastor St. Stephen Protomartyr Parish, 1987-88; pastor King Parish, St. Louis, 1988-93, Immacolata Parish, St. Louis, 1993-97; aux. bishop Roman Cath. Ch., St. Louis, 1997—2001; ordained bishop, 1997; coadjutor bishop Diocese of Colorado Springs, 2001—03, bishop, 2003—. Roman Catholic. Office: Diocese of Colorado Springs 228 N Cascade Ave Colorado Springs CO 80903 Office Phone: 719-636-2345. Office Fax: 719-636-1216.

SHERIDAN, NICOLLETTE, actress; b. Worthing, Sussex, Eng., Nov. 21, 1963; d. Sally Sheridan; m. Harry Hamlin, Sept. 7, 1991 (div. 1993). Actor: (films) The Sure Thing, 1985, Noises Off, 1992, Spy Hard, 1996, Beverly Hills Ninja, 1997, I Woke Up Early the Date I Died, 1998, Raw Nerve, 1999, .com for Murder, 2002, Lost Treasure, 2003, Code Name: The Cleaner, 2007, (voice) Fly Me to the Moon, 2008,: (TV series) Knots Landing, 1986—93 (Soap Opera Digest award, 1990, 1991), Paper Dolls, 1984, Desperate Housewives, 2004— (co-recipient, Outstanding Performance by an Ensemble in a Comedy Series, Screen Actors Guild award, 2005, 2006); (TV films) Dead Man's Folly, 1986, Deceptions, 1990, Somebody's Daughter, 1992, A Time to Heal, 1994, Indictment: The McMartin Trial, 1995, Silver Strand, 1995, The People Next Door, 1996, Murder in My Mind, 1997, Dead Husbands, 1998, The Spiral Staircase, 2000, Haven't We Met Before?, 2002, Deadly Betrayal, 2003, Deadly Visions, 2004; (TV miniseries) Lucky/Chances, 1990, Knots Landing: Back to the Cul-de-Sac, 1997; TV appearances include Paradise, 1991, Will & Grace, 2003, Becker, 2003. Office: Desperate Housewives Touchtone Television 100 Universal City Plaza Bldg 212B Ste G Universal City CA 91608

SHERIDAN, PATRICK JOSEPH THOMAS, bishop emeritus; b. NYC, Mar. 10, 1922; BA, St. Joseph Sem., 1943; MA, U. Chgo., 1949. Ordained priest Archdiocese of NY, 1947; ordained bishop, 1990; aux. bishop Archdiocese of NY, 1990—2001, aux. bishop emeritus, 2001—. Roman Catholic. Office: John Cardinal O'Connor Residence 5655 Arlington Ave Bronx NY 10471 Office Phone: 212-371-1000. Office Fax: 212-826-6020.

SHERIDAN, PATRICK MICHAEL, retired finance company executive; b. Grosse Pointe, Mich., Apr. 13, 1940; s. Paul Phillip and Frances Mary (Rohan) S.; m. Diane Lorraine Tressler, Nov. 14, 1986; children: Mary, Patrick, Kelly, Kevin, James. BBA, U. Notre Dame, 1962; MBA, U. Detroit, 1975. Acct. Peat, Marwick, Mitchell & Co., Detroit, 1962-72, audit mgr., 1969-72; exec. v.p. fin. Alexander Hamilton Life Ins. Co., Farmington, Mich., 1973-76; sr. v.p. ops. Sun Life Ins. Co. Am., Balt., 1976-78, exec. v.p., 1978-79; pres. Sun Ins. Services, Inc., 1979-81; pres., chief exec. officer Am. Health & Life Ins. Co., Balt., 1981-85; chief exec. officer Gulf Ins. Co., 1985-86; sr. v.p., chief fin. officer Comml. Credit Co., 1985-86, sr. v.p. audit, 1987; exec. v.p., chief fin. officer Anthem, Inc., Indpls., 1987-99, ret., 1999. Author: (book) Bottle-Cap Sundaes, Beneath The Radar, The Doer, God Gets a Dog, Murphy's Other Law. Rep. candidate for U.S. Congress, 1972; past pres. Charlesbrooke Cmty. Assn.; past. v.p. Jr. Achievement of Met. Balt., 1984-85; bd. dirs. Goodwill Industries of Balt., 1986, bd. govs. 1994; bd. dirs. Family Svcs. Assn., 1994, Goodwill Industries of Indpls., 1994; mem. adv. coun. Clowes Meml. Hall. Capt. AUS, 1963-65. Recipient various Jaycee awards. Fellow Life Mgmt. Inst.; mem. Am. Mgmt. Assn. (pres.'s assn.), AICPAs, Mich. Assn. CPAs, Md. Assn. CPAs, Am. Soc. CLUs, U.S. Jaycees (treas. 1973-74), Mich. Jaycees (pres. 1971-72), Detroit Jaycees (pres. 1968-69), Balt. C. of C. (bd. dirs.), Mensa, Notre Dame Club.

SHERIDAN, SONIA LANDY, artist, retired educator; b. Newark, Ohio, Apr. 10, 1925; d. Avrom Mendel and Goldie Cornelia (Hanon) Landy; m. James Edward Sheridan, Sept. 27, 1947; 1 child, Jamy. AB, Hunter Coll., 1945; postgrad., Columbia U., 1946-48; MFA with high honors, Calif. Coll. Arts and Crafts, 1961. Tchr. art public high schs., Calif., 1951-57; chmn. dept. art Taipei (Taiwan) Am. Sch., 1957-59; instr. Calif. Coll. Arts and Crafts, 1960-61; asst. prof. art Sch. Art Inst. Chgo., 1961-67, assoc. prof., 1968-75, prof., 1976-80, prof. emeritus, 1980—, founder, head generative sys. program, 1970-80. Artist-in-residence 3M Corp., 1970, 76, Xerox Corp., 1981; cons. French Ministry of Culture, 1986; lectr. univs., mus., art schs., workshops, Hungarian Acad. Scis. Symposium Collected Essays & Exhbn., Budapest, 1989, Internat. Soc. Electronic Arts, Liverpool, England; presenter in field. One-woman shows include Rosenberg Gallery, Chgo., 1966, Visual Studies Workshop, Rochester, N.Y., 1973, Iowa Mus. Art, Iowa City, 1976, Mus. Sci. Industry, Chgo., 1978, exhibited in group shows at Print Ann., Boston Mus., 1963, Software, Jewish Mus., N.Y.C., 1969—70, Photography into Art, London, 1972—73, Photokino, Cologne, Germany, 1974, Mus. Modern Art, N.Y.C., 1974, MOMA, San Francisco Mus. Modern Art, 1975, 2006, U. Mich. Mus. Art, 1978, Toledo Mus. Art, 1982—83, Mus. Modern Art, Paris, 1983, Siggraph, 1982, 1983, Reina Sofia Mus., Madrid, 1986, Smithsonian Instn., 1990, Tokyo Met. Mus. Photography, 1991, Madrid City Cultural Ctr., 1992, Karl Ernst Osthaus Mus., Hagen, Germany, 1992, Circulo des Belles Artes, Madrid, 1992, Yale U. Art Gallery, 1995, Tokyo Intercom. Ctr., 1995, U. Montreal, 1995, Internat. Soc. Electronic Arts, Liverpool, 1996, Hungarian Art Mus., 1996, Scirpton Mus., The Netherlands, 1997, Video Gallery, Hungary, 2000—02, Mus. Kommunikation, Frankfurt, Germany, 2001, 2d Biennial Museo Nacional de Belles Artes, Buenos Aires, 2002, Represented in permanent collections Hood Mus. Art, Dartmouth, Langlois Found., Montreal, Art Inst. Chgo., San Francisco Mus. Art, Mus. Sci. and Industry, Chgo., U. Iowa Mus. Art, Nat. Gallery Art, Ottawa, Can., Visual Studios Workshop, Rochester, Tokyo Met. Mus. Photography, Fundacion Arte y Technologia, Madrid, Tweed Mus., U. Minn., Scrypton Mus., Tilburg, The Netherlands; author: Energized Artscience: Sonia Landy Sheridan, 1978; co-editor: Leonardo jour.; hon. editor:, 2000; contbr. articles, essays to profl. jours. Recipient citation, Nat. Assn. Schs. Art and Design, 2006; grantee, NEA, 1974, 1976, 1981, Union Ind. Colls., 1975; fellow, Guggenheim Found., 1973, Andrew Mellon Found., 2005—06. Mem.: Internat. Soc. Electronic Arts, Internat. Soc. Interdisciplinary Study Symmetry, Coll. Art Assn. E-mail: sonia.sheridan@valley.net.

SHERIDAN, THOMAS BROWN, mechanical engineering and applied psychology educator, researcher, consultant; b. Cin., Dec. 23, 1929; s. Mahlon Brinsley and Esther Anna (Brown) S.; m Rachel Briggs Rice, Aug. 1, 1953; children: Paul Rice, Richard Rice, David Rice, Margaret Lenore. BS, Purdue U., 1951; MS, UCLA, 1954; ScD, MIT, 1959; Dr. (hon.), Delft U. Tech., The Netherlands, 1991. Registered profl. engr., Mass. Asst. prof. mech. engring. MIT, Cambridge, 1959-65, assoc. prof., 1965-70, prof., 1970-78, prof. engring. and applied psychology, 1978—, prof. aeronautics and astronautics, 1994—, Ford prof., 1995—, prof. emeritus, 2001; sr. fellow DoT Volpe Ctr., 2001—; chief sys. engr. Human Factors, Fed. Aviation Admin, 2007—. Lectr. U. Calif., Berkeley, Stanford U., 1968; vis. prof. U. Delft, The Netherlands, 1972, Stanford U., 1989, Ben Gurion U., Israel, 1995, chmn. com. human factors, mem. com. aircrew-vehicle interaction, com. on commercially developed space facility, com. on human factors in air traffic control, mem. com. on nat. automated hwy. sys., com. on setting and enforcing speed limits, com. on intelligent vehicle initiative; chmn. com. on NASA aviation safety; mem. com. on electronic voting NRC; mem. adv. com. on applied phys., math. and biol. scis. NSF; mem. life scis. adv. com., study group on robotics, oversight com. flight telerobotic servicer NASA; mem. task force on appropriate tech. U.S. Congress Office Tech. Assessment; mem. study sect. accident prevention and injury control NIH; mem. Def. Sci. Bd. Task Force on Computers, Tng. and Gaming, Nuclear Regulatory Commn. on Nuclear Safety Rsch. Rev. Com. Author: Telerobotics, Automation and Human Supervisory Control, 1992, Humans and Automation, 2002; co-author: Man Machine Systems, 1974; editor: (with others) Monitoring Behavior and Supervisory Control, 1976, Perspectives on the Human Controller, 1997; assoc. editor Automatica, 1982-94; mem. edtl. adv. bd. Tech. Forecasting and Social Change, Computer Aided Design, Advanced Robotics, Robotics and Computer Integrated Mfg.; sr. editor Presence: Telerobots and Virtual Environments, 1991-94. Served to 1st lt. USAF, 1951-53. Recipient Nat. Engring. award Am. Assn. Engring. Socs., 1997, Rufus Oldenburger medal ASME, 1997. Fellow IEEE (pres. Systems, Man and Cybernetics Soc. 1974-76, Centennial medal 1984, Norbert Wiener award 1993, Joseph G. Wohl award 1995, Millenium medal 2000), Human Factors & Ergonomics Soc. (Paul M. Fitts award 1977, Arnold Small award 2000, pres. 1990-91, Pres. Disting. Svc. award 2000), Nat. Acad. Engring., Internat. Ergonomics Assn. Democrat. Mem. United Ch. of Christ. Home: 1010 Walthan St Apt 333 Lexington MA 02421-8063 Home Phone: 781-538-6785. Personal E-mail: sheridan@mit.edu.

SHERIF, S. A., engineering educator; b. Alexandria, Egypt, June 25, 1952; came to US, 1978; s. Ahmed and Ietedal H. (Monib) S.; m. Azza A. Shamseldin, Feb. 6, 1977 (div.); children: Ahmed S., Mohammad S.; m. Vitrell Lynn McNair, May 30, 2003. BSME (hon.), Alexandria U., 1975, MSME, 1978; PhD in Mech. Engring., Iowa State U., 1985. Tchg. asst. mech. engring. Alexandria U., 1975-78; tchg. assoc. mech. and environtl. engring. U. Calif., Santa Barbara, 1978-79; rsch. asst. mech. engring. Iowa State U., Ames, 1979-84; asst. prof. No. Ill. U., Dekalb, 1984-87, U. Miami, Coral Gables, Fla., 1987—91; assoc. prof. mech. engring. U. Fla., Gainesville, 1991-2001, prof. mech. and aerospace engring., 2001—, mem. doctoral rsch. faculty, 1992—, founding dir. Wayne K. and Lyla L. Masur HVAC Lab., 1995—, asst. dir. Indsl.

Assessment Ctr., 2001—, minority mentor, 2004—. ABET coord. for mech. engring., 1997—; coord. for mech. engring. So. Assn. Colls. and Schs., 2001—; affiliate Inst. for Sci. and Health Policy U. Fla., 2001—; cons. Solar Reactor Techs., Inc., Miami, 1988-91, Dade Power Corp., Miami, 1988-91, Ind. Energy Sys., Miami, 1988-91, Carey Dwyer Eckhart Mason Spring Beckham, P.A. Law Offices, Miami, 1988-89, Michael G. Widoff, P.A., Attys. at Law, Ft. Lauderdale, Fla., 1989-93, Law Offices Pomeroy and Betts, Ft. Lauderdale, 1991-92, Ctr. for Indoor Air Rsch., 1994-2000; cons. Fla. Power and Light Co., 1996-98; external examiner U. Roorkee, 1994-95, 98—, Indian Inst. Tech., Delhi, 2002-, Alexandria U., Egypt, 2000-; adj. faculty cons. Kennedy Western U., Thousand Oaks, Calif., 1994-97; resident assoc. Argonne (Ill.) Nat. Lab., Tech. Transfer Ctr., summer 1992; faculty fellow NASA Kennedy Space Ctr., Cape Canaveral, Fla., summer 1993; rsch. assoc. summer faculty rsch. program USAF Office Sci. Rsch., Arnold Engring. Devel. Ctr., Arnold AFB, Tenn., 1994; faculty fellow NASA Marshall Space Flight Ctr., Huntsville, Ala., 1996, 97; ABET coord. for aerospace engring., 2002-; coord. for aerospace engring., So. Assn. Colls. and Schs., 2002-. Co-editor: Industrial and Agricultural Applications of Fluid Mechanics, 1989, The Heuristics of Thermal Anemometry, 1990, Heat and Mass Transfer in Frost and Ice, Packed Beds, and Environmental Discharges, 1990, Industrial Applications of Fluid Mechanics, 1990, rev. edit., 1991, Mixed Convection and Environmental Flows, 1990, Measurement and Modeling of Environmental Flows, 1992, Industrial and Environment Applications of Fluid Mechanics, 1992, rev. edit., 1998, Thermal Anemometry-1993, 1993, Developments in Electrorheological Flows and Measurement Uncertainty-1994, 1994, Heat, Mass and Momentum Transfer in Environmental Flows, 1995, Thermal Anemometry, 1996, Fluid Measurement Uncertainty Applications, 1996, Devices for Flow Measurement and Analysis, 1997, Heat and Mass Transfer in Environmental Flows, 1998, Industrial and Environmental Applications of Fluid Mechanics, 1999, rev. edit., 2001, Measurement and Modeling of Environmental Flows, 2002, Industrial and Environmental Applications of Fluid Mechanics, 2003, Fluid Measurement Uncertainty Applications, 2003; reviewer more than 45 internat. jours., more than 200 conf. procs.; mem. editl. com. SECTAM XXI, 2001-2002; book rev. editor ASME Applied Mech. Revs., 2001—; assoc. tech. editor Solar Energy jour., 2002—; guest editor Solar Energy Jour. Spl. Issue on Hydrogen Prodn., 2003-05; contbr. to 16 book chapters and numerous articles to profl. jours. NASA ambassador, 1996-98, lab. host student sci. tng. program Ctr. for Precollegiate Edn. and Tng., 1997—; mem. environ. awareness adv. com., Dade County Pub. Schs., 1989-91, lab. dir. cmty. lab. rsch. program, 1989-91, also faculty liaison design svcs. dept.; active Com. for Nat. Inst. for Environ., 1992—; mem. senate U. Fla., 1994-95, mem. OUTREACH Spkrs. program, 1996-98. Recipient cert. recognition for rsch. contributions, NASA, 1993, 1996, 1997, E.K. Campbell award of Merit for Outstanding Svc. and Achievement in Tchg., ASHRAE, 1997, Kuwait prize for applied scis., 2002. Fellow ASME (mem. energy resources bd. 2001-03, chmn steering com. internat. energy conversion engring. conf., 2002-03, coord. group fluid measurements, fluids engring. divsn. 1987-03, vice chmn. 1990-92, chmn. 1992-94, fluid measurements and instrumentation tech. com., 2003—, fluids engring. divsn. adv. bd. 1994—, fed. honors and awards com. 1995-01, mem. fluid mechs. tech. com. 1990—, fluid mech. com. 1987-90, K-19 com. on environ. heat transfer 1987—, fluid measurements and instrumentation tech. com., 2003-, chmn. 2003—, mem. K-6 com. on heat transfer in energy systems, 2001—, mem. fluid applications and systems tech. com. 1990—, systems analysis tech. com. advanced energy sys. divsn. 1989—, newsletter editor advanced energy sys. divsn. 1995-98, exec. com., 1999—, mem.-at-large honors awards 1999-00, sec., treas. 2000-01, vice chmn., 2001-02, chmn., 2002-03, sr. mem. and past chmn., 2003-04, fundamentals and theory tech. com. solar energy divsn. 1990-97, chmn. CGFM nominating com. 1992-94, mem. 1994-98, chmn. profl. devel. com. Rock River Valley sect. 1987, tech. activities operating com. Gator sect. 1994-96, MFFCC subcom. 1 on uncertainties in flow measurements 1995-00, certificate of appreciation, 1994, 97. 99, 03), ASHRAE (mem. heat transfer fluid flow com. 1988-92, 93-97, corr. mem. 1992-93, 97—, mem. thermodynamics and psychrometrics com. 1988-92, 96-04, corr. mem. 1992-96, vice chmn. 1990-92, mem. liquid to refrigerant heat exchs. com. 1989-93, 96-97, sec. 1990-92, corr. mem. 1993-96, 97-01, corr. mem. air-to-refrigerant heat transfer com., 2000—, chmn. stds. project com. on measurement of moist air properties 1989-95, corr. mem. refrigeration load calculations com., 1999—, mem. tech. activities com. 2004—, head refrigeration sect., 2004-, E.K. Campbell award of merit for Outstanding Svc. and Achievement in Tchg., 1997, Disting. Svc. award, 2003, certificate of appreciation, 1995), AIAA (assoc., mem. terrestrial energy sys. tech. com. 2001—, certificate of appreciation, 2003); mem. AIChE, Internat. Assn. Hydrogen Energy, Internat. Solar Energy Soc., Am. Soc. for Engring. Edn., Internat. Energy Soc. (mem. sci. coun.), European Assn. Laser Anemometry (ASME/FED rep., mem. steering com.), Internat. Inst. Refrigeration (US nat. com., mem. commn. B1 on thermodynamics and transfer processes), Sigma Xi. Muslim. Achievements include co-inventor two US patents. Avocations: reading, soccer, basketball, history, astronomy. Office: U Fla Dept Mech and Aerospace Engring 232 MAE B 720 Bldg PO Box 116300 Gainesville FL 32611-6300 Home: 3440 NE 41st Pl Ocala FL 34479 Home Phone: 352-629-7410; Office Phone: 352-392-7821. Office Fax: 352-392-1071. Business E-Mail: sasherif@ufl.edu.

SHERIN, EDWIN, theater, film and television director, actor; b. Danville, Pa., Jan. 15, 1930; s. Joseph and Ruth (Berger) S.; m. Jane Alexander, Mar. 29, 1975; children: Anthony J., Geoffrey B. (dec.), Jonathan E.; 1 stepchild, Jason E. AB in History and Polit. Sci., Brown U., 1952. Acting tchr. Am. Theatre Wing, NYC, 1962-64; acting tchr. Am. Theatre Tng. Inst. Southeastern Mass. U., South Dartmouth, 1974; Lucille Lortel Disting. guest artist U. Bridgeport (Conn.), 1980; dir. Sch. Theatre Arts Boston U., 1981; acting tchr. Okla. Summer Arts Inst., 1985-86, One on One, LA, 1989, 90; exec. v.p. Altion Prodns., LA, 1985-93; pres. Pumpkin House Prodns., 1993—. Mem. nat. adv. for Mus. Am. Theatre; instr. Okla. Summer Arts Inst., guest dir. Calif. Inst. Arts; prof. dept. drama Fla. State U. Film Sch., Bennington Coll., Columbia U., Sarah Lawrence Coll. Actor with Houseman's troupe Phoenix Theatre, N.Y.C., 1957-58, N.Y. Shakespeare Festival, 1956-60; appeared as: Octavius Caesar in, Anthony and Cleopatra, 1958; appeared in Broadway plays Come Blow Your Horn, 1960, Desert Incident, 1961, Romulus, 1962, Face of a Hero, 1963; TV films Playhouse 90, 1956-58, Studio One, 1956-58, Omnibus, 1957-60, East Side/West Side, 1960; dir. Broadway plays including The Great White Hope, 1968, Glory Hallelujah, 1969, 6 RMS RIV VU, 1973, Find Your Way Home, Of Mice and Men, 1974, Red Devil Battery Sign, 1975, Sweet Bird of Youth, 1976, Eccentricities of a Nightingale, 1976, The First Monday in October, 1978, Goodbye Fidel, 1980, The Visit, 1992; assoc. producing dir. Washington's Arena Stage, 1964-68; dir. Cosi Fan Tutte, N.Y. City Opera Co., 1972, A Streetcar Named Desire, Piccadilly Theatre, London, 1973, Semmelweiss, Studio Arena Theatre, Buffalo, N.Y., 1978, Outrage, Kennedy Ctr., Washington, 1982; films including Valdez is Coming, 1970, My Old Man's Place, 1971; producing artistic dir. Showdown at Adobe Hotel, Semmelweiss, Hedda Gabler, Night Must Fall, A Streetcar Named Desire, Hartman Theatre, Stamford, Conn., 1980-85; dir. Chelsea Walls, Naked Angels, N.Y.C., 1990, Karla, Long Wharf Theater, 2002, Ghosts, Shakespeare Theater, Washington, 2002, Prymate, B'Way, 2004, TV programs Hill Street Blues, Moonlighting, WIOU, L.A. Law, Tour of Duty, MEN, Medium, The Black Donnellys; co-exec. prodr. Law and Order, 1993-94, exec. prodr., 1994-00, (TV films) The Father Clements Story, Lena, My 100 Children, Daughter of the Streets, Getting Even, A Marriage: Georgia O'Keeffe and Alfred Stieglitz, 1991. With USN, 1952-56, Korea. Recipient Outer Circle award, 1969; New Eng. Theatre award, 1969, N.Y. Drama Critics award, 1969, Drama Desk award, 1969, L.A. Drama Cir. award, 1971, Recipient Tony nomination, 1974, London Evening Std. citation, 1973, Joseph Jefferson award, 1976, Buffalo drama award, 1978, Emmy award, 1997; New Eng. Theatre Conf. award; Ford Found. grantee, 1965-66; Am. Theatre fellow Coll. of Am. Theatre. Mem. AFTRA, SAG, Actors Equity Assn., Dirs. Guild Am. (nat. v.p. 1997—), Dramatists Guild, Soc. Stage Dirs. and Choreographers (v.p. 1970-80), Lincoln Soc., Phi Gamma Delta. Office Phone: 914-729-0072. Personal E-mail: edsherin@gmail.com.

SHERIN, KEITH S., corporate financial executive; BA, U. Notre Dame, 1981; MBA, Columbia U., 1991. With fin. mgmt. program GE, 1981-84, mem. corp. audit staff, 1984, exec. audit mgr., mgr. programs and planning; mgr. fin. comml. engine ops. GE Aircraft Engines, 1992-93; dir. fin. GE Plastics Europe, Bergen op Zoom, Netherlands, 1993-95; mgr. global fin. and fin. svcs. GE Med. Systems, 1995-96, v.p. fin. and fin. svcs. operation, 1996-98; sr. v.p. fin., CFO GE, Fairfield, Conn., 1998—2007, vice-chmn., CFO, 2007—. Office: GE 3135 Easton Tpke Fairfield CT 06431-0002*

SHERK, KENNETH JOHN, lawyer; b. Ida Grove, Iowa, Feb. 27, 1933; s. John and Dorothy (Myers) Sherk; children: Karin Fulton, Katrina, Keith, Kyle. BSc, U. Iowa, 1955; JD, George Washington U., 1961. Bar: Ariz. 1962, U.S. Dist. Ct. Ariz. 1962, U.S. Ct. Appeals (9th cir.) 1966, U.S. Supreme Ct. 1974. Assoc. Moore & Romley, Phoenix, 1962-67, ptnr., 1967-79, Romley & Sherk, Phoenix, 1979-85; dir. Fennemore Craig, Phoenix, 1985—. 1st lt. U.S. Army, 1955-58, Korea. Recipient Profl. Achievement Svcs. award George Washington Law Assn., 1986, Ariz. Judges Assn., 1989, Disting. Svc. award Phoenix Assn. Def. Counsel, 1990; named Mem. of Yr. State Bar of Ariz., 1994. Fellow Am. Coll. Trial Lawyers, Am. Acad. Appellate Lawyers, Am. Bar Found., Ariz. Bar Found. (Walter E. Craig award 1999); mem. ABA (ho. of dels. 1990-93), Ariz. Bar Assn. (pres. 1985-86), Maricopa County Bar Assn. (pres. 1978-79). Republican. Congregationalist. Avocations: fishing, hiking, bicycling. Home: 1554 W Las Palmaritas Dr Phoenix AZ 85021-5429 Office: Fennemore Craig 3003 N Central Ave Ste 2600 Phoenix AZ 85012-2913 Office Phone: 602-916-5383. Business E-Mail: ksherk@fclaw.com. E-mail: ksherk@cox.net.

SHERLOCK, PHYLLIS KRAFFT, psychologist; b. Chgo., Dec. 22, 1936; d. Lee M. and Beatrice Elliott Krafft; m. Hugh Paul Sherlock, June 4, 1960 (dec. Oct. 1991); children: William, John, James BA in Philosophy and Religious Studies, U. N.C., 1958; postgrad., Boston U., 1959—60; PhD in Clin. Psychology, Pacific Grad. Sch. Psychology, 1980. Lic. Psychologist, Marriage, Family and Child Counselor. Social work trainee ARC, Chgo., 1959—60; child welfare worker Santa Clara County Social Svcs., San Jose, Calif., 1961—62; counselor Diabesis, San Francisco, 1973—75; counselor chaplaincy svc. Stanford U. Med. Ctr., Calif., 1977—79; intern North County Cmty. Mental Health Clinic, Palo Alto, Calif., 1977—78; postdoctoral intern counseling and psychol. svcs. Cowell Health Svcs., Stanford U., 1980—81; faculty Pacific Grad. Sch. Psychology, 1989—92; pvt. practice, 1979—; supr., clin. dir. The Transitional Program, 1990—2001. Co-founder Pacific Grad. Sch. Psychology, Palo Alto, 1975-76; group facilitator Grad. Sch. Bus., Stanford U., 1980-82; supr. psychol. assts., 1988-2005, clin. dir. The Transitional Program, 1995-2002; adj. clin. faculty Sch. Edn., U. San Francisco, 1990-97 Author: The Feminine Q Set - Research on Wolf's Feminine Image and Theories, 1980; contbr. articles to profl. jours. Vol. Agnew State Hosp., 1971. Mem. Assn. Psychol. Type, Santa Clara County Psychol. Assn. Democrat. Avocations: reading, gardening, art, travel. Office: 1275 Dana Ave Palo Alto CA 94301-3112 Home Phone: 650-325-1962; Office Phone: 650-325-8131. Personal E-mail: phyllisdec22@earthlink.net.

SHERMAN, ARTHUR, theater educator, writer, actor, composer, sculptor; b. Dec. 5, 1920; s. Herman and Fay (Epstein) S.; m. Margery Frost Sherman, Apr. 15, 1974 (div. Sept. 1989); children: Claudia, Andrew Jay. MusB, Juilliard Sch. Music, NYC, 1955; M in Music Edn., Manhattan Sch. Music, 1957; Doctoral Equivalency, CUNY, 1969. Dir. performing arts N.Y.C. (N.Y.) Tech. Coll., 1964-72; prof. speech and theatre John Jay Coll., NYC, 1990—, Borough Man C.C., NYC, 1990—. Judge Film Award Com., Australia, 1972-89, Acad. Awards, 1990; cons. Min. for Edn., Tasmania, Australia, 1977; presenter in field; faculty senate Coll Criminal Justice, 2008. Author: (screenplays) Thistle and Thorn, 1982, Same Difference, 1983, (book and lyrics) Lenore and the Wonder House, 1964, Prisms in the Looking Glass, 1993, Once Upon a Crime, We the Common Earth, Music and Lyrics, 2008; (musical comedy)No Men Claych, 2009; (short stories) Max the Messiah and Noah's Arc, 2005; (book) Paradise Lagoon, 1989, Picture Book for Young Adults Paintings, Music and Lyrics, 1998, Songwriting Is Easy and Fun, 1996, also short stories; (comedy theater) But Its Not Chekhov, 1999; (comic screenplay) Weaning, 1999; (7-book novel) The Pleiades, Burning in Heaven, Freezing in Hell, Bloody Mooring, Scoring in Limbo, Chasing the Phoenix, The Pleiades and Beyond, Betrayal of Self; (with Edward Mapp) The Road to Mainstream, 1999, Red Herrings No Fishing Allowed, 2005; (play) To Hell with Buffalo Wings-Anyone for Eagle Wings?, 1999, Warsaw Ghetto Uprising, 2001; (music drama) Prisms in the Looking Glass, Paul Robeson Theatre, 2006; actor, dir. films, TV, theater in U.S. and Australia; actor: (films) The Punisher, 1979, Death of a Soldier, 1985, Les Patterson Saves the World, 1988, The Last Bastion, 1987; sculptures displayed YWCA, Hamilton, Ont., Can., 1967, Lincoln Ctr., N.Y.C., 1969, State Bank, Sydney, Australia, 1974; bust of Louis Armstron Meml. Mus. and House, Dame Judith Anderson Australian Consulate N.Y.; contbr. design WTC 9/11 Meml., 2003; (musical comedy) Rality Show Musical Tank Town. Pres. United Fedn. Coll. Tchrs., NYC, 1971. With USN, 1943—46. Grantee, Australian Film Commn., 1981. Mem. ASCAP, Australasian Performing Rights Assn., Actors' Equity U.S. and Australia. Achievements include invention of squeer puzzle. Office: John Jay Coll 58th St 10th Ave New York NY 10019 Office Phone: 212-237-8353.

SHERMAN, BARNET, financial services executive; b. Bklyn., Sept. 27, 1958; s. Meyer and Naomi Gertrude (Ullman) S.; divorced; 1 child, Ryan Alexander. BA with honors, Syracuse U., 1980; M in Pub. Adminstrn., Columbia U., 1982. Legis. aide U.S. Rep. Thomas J. Downey, Washington, 1982-83; mcpl. specialist Prudential-Bache Securities, NYC, 1983-84; sr. analyst mcpl. and fixed income research group Smith, Barney, Harris, Upham & Co., NYC, 1984-89; assoc. portfolio mgr. Colonial Mgmt. Assocs., Boston, 1989-91, asst. v.p., 1991-92, v.p., 1992—, dir. mcpl. rsch., 1993-94; v.p., assoc. portfolio mgr. VanKampen Investments, 1994-2000, portfolio mgr., 2000—08; founder & mng. ptnr. Braintree Capital Ptnrs., 2008—. Contbg. columnist Forbes. Bd. dirs. fin. com. MetroWest Med. Ctr., Framingham, Mass., 1994-96; trustee MetroWest Health Ptnrs., Inc., 1996-. Mem. Boston Mcpl. Analysts Soc., New Eng. Outdoor Writers Assn. (bd. dirs. 2004-06), Pi Sigma Alpha. Avocations: american art, salt/fresh/fly fishing. Home: 22 Whitehall St Apt # 1 Dedham MA 02027 Office: Braintree Capital 145 Wood Rd Braintree MA 02184 Office Phone: 617-799-3576. Business E-Mail: bs492@columbia.edu.

SHERMAN, BEATRICE ETTINGER, hotel executive; b. NYC, May 29, 1919; d. Max and Stella (Schrager) Ettinger; m. Herbert Jacob Howard, Feb. 15, 1942 (dec. 1971); children: Robert David Howard, Carolyn Howard Smith; m. Ernest John Sherman, Dec. 29, 1974 (dec. Oct. 2000). Student, Gulf Park Jr. Coll., Gulfport, Miss., 1934—35, Shimer Jr. Coll., Mt. Carroll, Ill., 1936—38; BA, U. Miami, 1940; postgrad., Harvard U., 1940, Paris-Am. Acad., 1972, Alliance Française, Paris, 1973. Corp. sec., dir. Save Electric Corp., Toledo, 1940—67, Verd-A-Ray Corp., Toledo, 1944—67, Penetray Corp., Toledo, 1962—67; ptnr. Stella Assocs., Newark, 1960—80, BHS Ptnrs., Miami, 1983—; pres. Besman Inc., Miami, 1976—, All Am. Mobile Tel. Co., Coral Gables, 1986—2000; pres., bus. exec. hotelier Besman Hospitality, Gainesville, Fla., 1997—. Vol. worker Jewish Welfare Fedn., Toledo, 1942-69; vol. nurse's aid ARC, 1942-45; nat. spkr. United Jewish Appeal; mem. womens divsn. Greater Miami Jewish Fedn., 1969—, trustee, 1986-95; adv. bd. Miami Bell South; active Miami advertiser adv. bd. Bell South Advt. and Pub. Co.; vol. Nat. Coun. Jewish Women, Toledo, 1946-67, v.p., 1964-67, v.p., Miami, 1970-73; active Toledo chpt. Hadassah, 1943-67. Recipient Lion of Judah award Greater Miami Jewish Fedn., 1986. Mem. Assn. Telemessaging Svcs. Internat., Pioneers of Miami Beach. Home: 5108 SW 72d Ave Miami FL 33155-5530 Office: PO Box 558446 Miami FL 33255

SHERMAN, BRADLEY JAMES, United States Representative from California; b. LA, Oct. 24, 1954; s. Maurice H. and Lane (Moss) Sherman. BA summa cum laude, UCLA, 1974; JD magna cum laude, Harvard U., 1979. CPA Calif.; bar: Calif. 1979. Pvt. practice, LA, 1980-91; mem. Calif. Franchise Tax Bd., 1991-95, US Congress from 27th Calif. dist., 1996—, internat. rels. com., judiciary com., fgn. affairs com., fin. svcs. com. Instr. Harvard Law Sch. Internat. Tax Prog.; mem. Calif. State Bd. Equalization, Sacramento, 1990—97, chmn., 1991—95; mem. Dem. Homeland Security Task Force, New Dem. Coalition. Contbr. articles to profl. jours.; lectr. in field (tax law and policy). Bd. dirs., rep. tax issues Calif. Common Cause, 1985—89. Mem.: Calif. Bar Assn. Democrat. Jewish. Office: US Ho Reps 1030 Longworth HOB Washington DC 20515-0527 Office Phone: 202-225-5911. E-mail: brad.sherman@mail.house.gov.*

SHERMAN, CRAIG, Internet company executive; AB magna cum laude, Princeton U. Joined Cendant Corp., 1991, v.p. internat. divsn., 1994—96; CEO Cendant Japan, 1998—99; regional v.p. Am. Internat. Group (AIG), 1999—2000; exec. v.p., gen. mgr. ThirdAge Media; COO MyFamily.com, 2000—05; entrepreneur in residence Benchmark Capital, 2005—06; CEO Gaia Interactive, 2006—. Spkr. in field. Office: Gaia Interactive, Inc Ste 125 50 Airport Parkway San Jose CA 95110 Office Phone: 408-573-8800. Office Fax: 408-573-9800.

SHERMAN, DANIEL JAMES, art history professor; b. Ann Arbor, Mich., May 20, 1958; s. Stanley Morton and Claire Richter Sherman; life ptnr. Eduardo deJesus Douglas. AB, MA, Harvard U., 1980, Yale U., 1981, MPhil, 1982, PhD, 1985. Lectr. history, lit., social studies Harvard U., Cambridge, Mass., 1985—88; vis. asst. prof. Cath. U. Am., Washington, 1989; vis. asst. prof. history U. Rochester, NY, 1989—90; asst. prof. French studies and history Rice U., Houston, 1990—94, assoc. prof. French studies and history, 1994—99, prof. French studies and history, 1999—2001; prof. history U. Wis., Milw., 2001—08, dir. Ctr. 21st Century Studies, 2001—08; prof. art history U. NC, Chapel Hill, 2008—. Author: Worthy Monuments: Art Museums and the Politics of Culture in Nineteenth-Century France, 1989, The Constuction of Memory in Interwar France, 1999; editor: Museums and Difference, 2007; co-editor: Museum Culture: Histories, Discourses, Spectacles, 1994, Terror Culture, Politics: Rethinking 9/11, 2006; contbr. articles to profl. jours. Recipient History and Lit. Jr. prize, Harvard Coll., 1978, Laurence Wylie prize, 2000, award, Assn. American Publishers, 2000; grantee, Am. Coun. Learned Socs., 1988; fellow, NEH, 1988, 1990—91, Inst. Advanced Study, 1993—94, John Simon Guggenheim Meml. Found., 2001—02; Florence Gould Found. fellowship, Nat. Humanities Ctr., 1999—2000, Paul Mellon fellow, Ctr. Advanced Study Visual Arts, Nat. Gallery Art, 2006—07. Mem.: Soc. French Hist. Studies (mem., editl. bd. 1998—2001), Coll. Art Assn., Am. Hist. Assn. (J. Russell Major prize 2000). Jewish. Avocations: travel, photography, cooking. Office: UNC Chapel Hill Dept Art Hanes Art Ctr Campus Box 3405 Chapel Hill NC 27599-3405 Office Fax: 919-962-0722.

SHERMAN, DEMING ELIOT, lawyer; b. Providence, July 22, 1943; s. Edwin Fisk and Martha Amy (Parkhurst) S.; m. Jane Catherine Bauer, Dec. 20, 1966; children: Melissa Jane, Nicholas Deming. BA, Amherst Coll., Mass., 1965; JD, U. Chgo., 1968. Bar: R.I. 1968, U.S. Dist. Ct. R.I. 1970, U.S. Supreme Ct. 1974, Mass. 1985, U.S. Dist. Ct. Mass. 1985. Mng. ptnr. Edwards Angell Palmer & Dodge LLP, Providence, 1986—94, ptnr., 1969—, gen. counsel, 2005—08. Trustee First Night Providence, 1988-93, 2001-04, pres., 1991-93; bd. dirs. R.I. Philharm. Orch., 1985-2003, 04—, pres., 1993-95; trustee Providence Preservation Soc., 1990-2004, pres. 1996-99; trustee Providence Athenaeum, 2004-, v.p., 2006-, pres. 2009-; mem. R.I. Com. on Jud. Tenure and Discipline, 1992-2000; bd. dirs. Providence YMCA, 1975-85, Blackstone Park Improvement Assn., 1979—, Nope's Island Conservation Assn., 1992-98, New Eng. Legal Found., 1994—, R.I. Legal Edn. Partnership, 2000-03, Grow Smart RI, 1998—, sec., 1998-2006, pres., 2006-09; corporator R.I. Hosp., 1989—; bd. dirs. Blackstone Pk. Conservancy, 2001—, pres., 2001-06; trustee Festival Ballet Providence, 2002—, pres., 2005-07. Fellow R.I. Bar Found.; mem. ABA, R.I. Bar Assn., Amherst Alumni Assn. R.I. (pres. 1980-91), Greater Providence C. of C. (bd. dirs. 1991-94). Home: 254 Irving Ave Providence RI 02906-5544 Office: Edwards Angell Palmer & Dodge LLP 2800 Financial Plz Providence RI 02903 Home Phone: 401-861-3313; Office Phone: 401-274-9200. Business E-Mail: dsherman@eapdlaw.com.

SHERMAN, EUGENE JAY, retired marketing professional, bank executive, economist; b. NYC, Jan. 10, 1935; s. Samuel and Sarah (Lavinsky) S.; m. Mary Eileen Van, Apr. 22, 1966; 1 child, Rebecca. BA, CCNY, 1956; MBA, NYU, 1959, postgrad., 1959-63. Economist Fed. Res. Bank N.Y., 1959-62, Chase Manhattan Bank, NYC, 1962-65; v.p. Bank of N.Y., NYC, 1965-72; sr. v.p., exec. dir., dir. rsch. Merrill Lynch and Co., NYC, 1972-78; v.p., chief economist, mgr.internat. investment Internat. Gold Corp., NYC, 1980-86; sr. v.p., chief economist Fed. Home Loan Bank N.Y., 1986-93; sr. v.p., dir. rsch. M.A. Schapiro & Co., Inc., NYC, 1993-96. Gold cons., N.Y.C., 1986—; adj. prof. Touro Coll., NY., 1997-98, Touro Grad. Sch. Bus., 2009-, Baruch Coll., NYC, 1997—, exec.-in-residence; mem. faculty senate, fellow Weissman Ctr. for Internat. Bus. Author: Gold Investment: Theory and Application, 1986; contbr. articles to profl. jours. Recipient Tchg. Excellence award, Zicklin Sch., 2003. Mem. Money Marketeers (pres. 1971-72, honored fellow 1987), Downtown Economist Club (chmn. 1988-89), Forecasters (winner 1986, 95), Treasury Securities Luncheon (pres. 1995-96), N.Y. Assn. Bus. Econs. Avocations: outdoor activities, performing arts. Home: 115 E 9th St New York NY 10003-5414

SHERMAN, FRED, biochemist, educator; b. Mpls., May 21, 1932; s. Harry and Ann (Kaufman) Sherman; m. Revina Freeman, July 25, 1958 (div.); children: Aaron, Mark, Rhea; m. Elena Rustchenko Bulgac, May 5, 2001. BA, U. Minn., Mpls., 1953; PhD, U. Calif., Berkeley, 1958; PhD (hon.), U. Minn., 2002. Postdoctoral fellow U. Wash., Seattle, 1959—60; 60postdoctoral fellow 61Lab. Genetique Physiol., Gif-sur-Yvette, France, 1960-61; sr. instr. U. Rochester, NY, 1961—62, asst. prof. NY, 1962—66, assoc. prof. NY, 1966—71, prof. dept. biochemistry Sch. Medicine & Dentistry NY, 1971—, chmn. dept. biochemistry NY, 1982—99. Instr. Cold Spring Harbor Lab., NY, 1970—87; Wander Meml. lectr., 1975; Wilson prof. U. Rochester, 1982. Co-author: Cold Spring Harbor Manual on Yeast Genetics and Molecular Biology, 1970—87; assoc. editor: Genetics, 1975—82, Molecular Cell Biology, 1979—88. Grantee NIH, 1963; fellow, 1959—61. Mem.: Am. Soc. Microbiology, Genetic Soc. Am. (bd. dirs. 1983—85), NAS (chmn. genet. sec. 2000—03), AAAS. Home: 69 Westminster Rd Rochester NY 14607-2223 Business E-Mail: fred_sherman@URMC.Rochester.edu.

SHERMAN, GREG, professional sports team executive; b. Scranton, Pa. m. Tamara Sherman; children: Katelyn, Delaney. B in Accountancy, U. San Diego, 1992. Asst. gen. mgr. Colo. Avalanche, 2002—09, gen. mgr., 2009—. Office: Colo Avalanche Hockey Club Pepsi Ctr 1000 Chopper Circle Denver CO 80204*

SHERMAN, HOWARD D., financial consultant; b. Tuscon, May 25, 1961; s. Donald J. and Elaine (Schwartz) S. BA, George Washington U., 1982; MBA, U. Pa., 1986. Rsch. asst. Fed. Res. Bd., Washington, 1982—84; sr. analyst Investor Responsibility Rsch. Ctr., Washington, 1986—88; sr. v.p., dir. Inst. Shareholder Svcs., Washington, 1988—97, pres., CEO, 1997—99; pres. Thomson Fin. Investor Rels., NYC, 1999—2000; COO Governance Metrics Internat. Inc., 2001—06, pres., CEO, 2007—. Spkr. in field. Contbr. articles to profl. jours. Mem. bd. dirs., treas. chmn. Audit Com. IRRC Inst., 2008—. Mem. Phi Beta Kappa.

SHERMAN, IAN MATTHEW, lawyer; b. Chgo., Apr. 30, 1953; s. George and Vivian K. (Soffran) S.; m. Barbara Jan Smiley, Aug. 6, 1978; children: Wendy Joyce, Wesley Jacob, David Scott. AB, U. Ill., 1975; JD, Boston U., 1978. Bar: Ill. 1978, U.S. Dist. Ct. (no. dist.) Ill. 1978, U.S. Dist. Ct. (ea. dist.) Wis. 1995, U.S. Dist. Ct. (no. dist.) Ind. 2000, U.S. Ct. Appeals (7th cir.) 1984. Ptnr. Dykema Gossett PLLC (formerly Rooks, Pitts & Poust), Chgo., 1978—. Lectr. in field. Contbr. articles to profl. jours. Participant Youth Motivation Program Chgo. Pub. H.S., 1982; pro bono Am. Jewish Congress, Chgo., 1992—; vol. Chgo. (Ill.) Vol. Legal Svcs. Inst., 1982—; commr. Winnetka (Ill.) Park Dist., 2001—09, v.p., 2002—03, 2007—09; commr. Winnetka Environ. & Forestry Commn., Ill., 2008—09; bd. dirs. The Vol. Ctr., 1986—90, chmn. fin. com., 1986—87, sec., 1987—88, pres., 1988—89. Recipient Disting. Svc. award, Chgo. (Ill.) Vol. Legal Svcs. Inst., 2003; named Ill. Super Lawyer, Law and Politics, 2005—09, Leading Lawyer, Law Bull. Pub. Co., 2005—09. Mem.: Am. Bd. Trial Advocates, Chgo. Bar Assn. (chmn. med.-legal rels. com. 2001—02, cert. appreciation 1983, 2003), Ill. State Bar Assn., Ill. Assn. Healthcare Attys., Ill. Soc. Trial Lawyers, Phi Kappa Phi, Phi Beta Kappa. Home: 923 Oak St Winnetka IL 60093-2440 Office: Dykema Gossett PLLC 10 S Wacker Dr Ste 2300 Chicago IL 60606-7407 Home Phone: 847-501-4829; Office Phone: 312-876-1700. Business E-Mail: isherman@dykema.com.

SHERMAN, IRWIN WILLIAM, biological sciences educator, academic administrator; b. NYC, Feb. 12, 1933; s. Morris and Anna (Ezaak) S.; m. Vilia Gay Turner, Aug. 25, 1966; children: Jonathan Turner, Alexa Joy. BS, CCNY, 1954; MS, Northwestern U., Evanston, Ill., 1959, PhD, 1960. Asst. prof. U. Calif., Riverside, 1962-67, assoc. prof., 1967-70, prof. biology, 1970—2005, chmn. biology dept., 1974-79, dean Coll. Natural and Agrl. Scis., dir. agrl. expt. sta., 1981-88, exec. vice chancellor, 1993-94, emeritus prof., 2006—; vis. scientist Scripps Rsch. Inst., 2006—. Instr. marine biol. lab., Woods Hole, Mass., 1963-68; mem. study sect. tropical medicine NIH, 1970-73; cons. Agy. Internat. Devel., 1978-90; mem. ad hoc study group U.S. Army, 1975-78. Author: The Invertebrates: Function and Form, 1976, Biology: A Human Approach, 1989, Malaria: Parasite Biology, Pathogenesis, Protection, 1998, Molecular Approaches to Malaria, 2005, The Power of Plagues, 2006, Twelve Diseases That Changed Our World, 2007, Reflections on a Century of Malaria Biochemistry, 2009, The Elusive Malaria Vaccine, 2009. Steering com. World Health Orgn., 1978-87. With U.S. Army, 1954-56. USPHS fellow Rockefeller Inst., 1960-62, Guggenheim fellow, 1967, NIH/Nat. Inst. Med. Rsch. fellow 1973-74, Walter and Eliza Hall Inst. for Med. Rsch. fellow, 1986; Wellcome Trust lectr. Brit. Soc. Parasitology, 1987, Scripps Rsch. Inst. fellow 1991, 2003-. Fellow AAAS, Am. Acad. Microbiology; mem. Am. Soc. Tropical Medicine and Hygiene, Soc. Protozoology, Soc. Parasitology, Sigma Xi. Democrat. Jewish. Avocations: painting, reading. Office: Scripps Research Inst Dept Cell Biology ICND 202 10550 N Torrey Pines La Jolla CA 92037 Office Phone: 858-784-2302. E-mail: isherman@scripps.edu.

SHERMAN, JEFFREY BARRY, retired retail executive; b. Passaic, NJ, June 25, 1948; s. Maxwell and Elinor (Richman) S.; m. Karin Lynn Swann, May 1, 1971; children: Erik, Brett, Peter, Kristin BS in Econs., CCNY, 1971; MBA, NYU, 1975. With Bloomingdale's, NYC, 1971—82, v.p. merchandising, 1982-83, sr. v.p., 1983-85, exec. v.p., 1985—89, pres., COO, 1989—2000; chmn., CEO Federated Department Stores, Inc., 2000—02; CEO Limited Stores, 2002—04; COO Polo Retail Group Polo Ralph Lauren Corp., 2004—08. Avocations: skiing, sailing.

SHERMAN, JEFFREY SCOTT, lawyer; b. Bklyn., Oct. 26, 1955; s. Martin and Beatrice (Matrick) S.; m. Susan Ellen Ganz, Aug. 13, 1981; children: Elisabeth Faye, Andrew Harris. BA cum laude, SUNY, Albany, 1976; JD magna cum laude, Bklyn. Law Sch., 1980. Bar: NY 1980. Assoc. Proskauer, Rose et al, NYC, 1980-83, Shereff, Friedman, Hoffman & Goodman, NYC, 1983-87, ptnr., 1988—90; with Wyeth, 1990—2003, v.p., assoc. gen. counsel, 2001—03; v.p., gen. counsel Becton, Dickinson & Co., Franklin Lakes, NJ, 2004—06, sr. v.p., gen. counsel, 2006—. Mem. ABA, Assn. of the Bar of the City of NY (young lawyers com. 1983-86). Office: Becton Dickinson 1 Becton Dr Franklin Lakes NJ 07417-1880 Office Phone: 201-847-3223. Office Fax: 201-848-9228.*

SHERMAN, JEREMY P., lawyer; b. Chgo., Mar. 8, 1951; BA magna cum laude, Am. U., 1973; JD with honors, George Washington U., 1976. Bar: Ill. 1976. Mem. Seyfarth Shaw LLP, Chgo., 1976, ptnr. Nat. chairperson Labor and Employment Practice Group, Ill. Office: Seyfarth Shaw LLP Ste 2400 131 S Dearborn St Chicago IL 60603 Office Phone: 312-460-5901. Business E-Mail: jsherman@seyfarth.com.

SHERMAN, JIMMIE LEE, mathematician, educator; b. LA, Feb. 15, 1944; s. Harold and Lillie Lee (White) Sherman. Student, Compton Jr. Coll. Bus. mgr., reporter Watts (Calif.) Star Rev. Newspaper, 1965—66; publicity dir. Watts Happening Coffee House, 1965—67; screen writer Universal Studios, Universal City, Calif., 1967—68; creative dir., tchr. Watts Writers Workshop, 1987; cons., tchr. Compton (Calif.) Unified Sch. Dist., 1988—90, Nat. Coun. Negro Women, Pomona, Calif., 1997—98; tchr. math. Motivational Inst., LA, 2002—. Publ. Lesson Book Libr. Publ. Co., LA, 1979—; tchr., tutor Jimmie Shermans Literacy Campaign, LA, 1999—; cons. in field. Author: numerous poems, Principles of Immortality, 2003. With US Army, 1961—64. Recipient Quality of Life award, Sigma Gamma Rho, 1994, Breaking Barriers award, KJLH and LA Dodgers, 1997, Shakespeare Trophy of Excellence award, Famous Poets Soc., 2003; named Worlds' Best Tchr. award, God's Little Angels Pvt. Sch., 2000, Poet of Yr., Famous Poets Soc., 2003; named to Wall of Tolerance, by Rosa Parks and Morris Dees, Nat. Campaign for Tolerance, 2005. Mem.: Shermans Future Tchrs. Assn. (hon.). Avocations: painting, poetry, writing, reading. Home Phone: 323-294-3465; Office Phone: 323-294-3465. E-mail: jimmysherman2003@yahoo.com.

SHERMAN, JOHN ERIC, plastic surgeon; b. NYC, 1951; m. Emily Sherman; 2 children. MD, NY Med. Coll., 1975. Internship & residency Montefiore Hospital Med. Ctr., NYC, 1975—78; chief resident plastic surgery Cornell Med. Ctr., 1978—80; fellowship reconstructive plastic surgery Memorial Sloan Kettering Cancer Ctr., 1979—80; plastic surgeon priv. practice, NYC, 1980—; attending plastic surgeon NY Hospital, Lenox Hill Hospital; clinical assist. prof. surgery Cornell U. Med. Coll. Author: Surgery of Facial Bone Fractures, 1987. Fellow: Am. Coll. of Surgeons; mem.: Am. Soc. of Maxillofacial Surgeons, Am. Soc. of Aesthetic Plastic Surgeons, Am. Soc. of Plastic & Reconstructive Surgeons. Avocation: golf. Office: 1016 5th Ave New York NY 10028

SHERMAN, JOHN FOORD, biomedical consultant; b. Oneonta, NY, Sept. 4, 1919; s. Henry C. and Ruth (Foord) Sherman; m. Betsy Deane Murray, Feb. 8, 1944 (dec.); children: Betsy Deane, Mary Ann. BS, Union U., 1949, DSc, 1970; PhD, Yale U., 1953. With NIH, 1953—74; assoc. dir. extramural programs Nat. Inst. Neurol. Diseases and Blindness, 1961—62, Nat. Inst. Arthritis and Metabolic Disease, 1962—63; assoc. dir. for extramural programs Office Dir. NIH, 1964—68, dep. dir., 1968—74; v.p. Assn. Am. Med. Colls., Washington, 1974—91, exec. v.p., 1987—91, spl. cons., 1991—94. Bd. advisors Am. Bd. Internal Medicine, 1991—98; sr. advisor Rsch!Am., 1994—. Asst. surgeon gen. USPHS, 1964—68; spl. rsch. chemotherapy and neuropharmacology; panel on data and studies NRC, 1976—87; biomed. libr. rev. com. NIH, 1981—98; bd. dirs. Spinal Cord Injury Edn. and Tng. Found., 1986—92, Musculoskeletal Transplant Found., 1987—2003. With US Army, 1941—46. Decorated Bronze Star; recipient Meritorious Svc. award, USPHS, 1965, Disting. Svc. award, HEW, 1971, Sec.'s Spl. Citation award, 1973, Nat. Civil Svc. League award, 1973, Disting. Alumnus award, Union U.-Pharmacy Coll. Coun., 1974, Lifetime Achievement award, Nat. Assn. for Biomed. Rsch., 1990, Spl. Recognition award, Assn. Am. Med. Colls., 1996. Fellow: AAAS; mem.: Inst. Medicine NAS, Cosmos Club, Sigma Xi. Congregationalist. Personal E-mail: johnfsherman@msn.com.

SHERMAN, JONATHAN HENRY, lawyer; b. Washington, Jan. 4, 1963; s. Gerald Howard and Lola (Kay) Sherman; m. Catherine Sara Foot, Nov. 4, 2000; children: Benjamin Ashton, Julia Jean. BA in History magna cum laude, U. Rochester, 1984; MA in History, Yale U., 1989; JD, Stanford U., 1991. Bar: NY 1992, US Dist. Ct. (so. dist.) NY 1992, US Supreme Ct. 1995, US Dist. Ct. (ea. dist.) NY 1996, US Ct. Appeals (11th cir.) 1996, US Dist. Ct. (we. dist.) NY 1998, DC 2000, US Ct. Appeals (3d cir.) 2006. Assoc. Cahill Gordon & Reindel, NYC, 1991-2000; ptnr. Boies, Schiller & Flexner LLP, Washington, 2001—. Lectr. Stanford U., Palo Alto, Calif., 1991, Yale Coll., New Haven, 1993; adj. assoc. prof. law Fordham Law Sch., N.Y.C., 1998-2001. Sponsor, mentor Student-Sponsor Partnership, N.Y.C., 1992-96; contbr. The Cornerstone Sch., Jersey City, 1994; bd. dirs. Greater D.C. chpt. Crohn's and Colitis Found. Am., 2004—. Mem. ABA, N.Y. State Bar Assn. (media law com. 1997-99), Phi Beta Kappa. Office: Boies Schiller & Flexner LLP Ste 800 5301 Wisconsin Ave NW Washington DC 20015-2061 Home Phone: 301-320-5134; Office Phone: 202-237-9605. E-mail: jsherman@bsfllp.com.

SHERMAN, MERRILL W., bank executive; AB, Mt. Holyoke Coll., South Hadley; JD, U. Denver Coll. Law; DBA (hon.), Johnson & Wales U. Atty. Hinckley, Allen & Snyder, Providence, 1974—91; exec. v.p., gen. counsel to chmn., CEO Eastland Fin. Corp., 1991—93; atty. Brown, Rudnick, Freed & Gesmer, 1993—96; pres., CEO Bancorp RI, Inc., Providence, 1996—. Dir. Providence Jour. Co. Co-chair individual gifts com. Women & Infants Hosp. Capital Campaign; co-chair Trinity Repertory Co. Pell Awards, 2007; vice chair, bd. trustees RI Sch. Design, 2004—07, chair, bd. trustees, 2007—, Crossroads RI, 2001—04; exec. com., bd. trustees Providence Found.; bd. trustees Johnson & Wales U.; bd. dirs. RI Pub. Expenditure Coun. Recipient Outstanding Women in Bus. award, City of Providence, Providence Tourism Coun., 2001, Bus. Excellence Award, Providence Bus. News, 2003; named New Eng. Entrepreneur of Yr. in Fin. Services, Ernst & Young, 2001, Humanitarian of Yr., Nat. Jewish Med. and Rsch. Ctr., 2003, Citizen of Yr., March of Dimes, 2007, New Eng. Businesswoman of Yr., Bryant U., 2008; named one of 25 Women to Watch, US Banker, 2007; named to RI Heritage Hall of Fame, 2007. Mem.: RI Commodores. Office: Bankcorp RI Inc PO Box 6848 Providence RI 02940-6848 Office Phone: 401-456-5000. Office Fax: 401-456-5059.

SHERMAN, MICKEY (MICHAEL SHERMAN), lawyer; b. 1946; m. Lis Wiehl, June 23, 2006. AB, U. Conn., JD, 1971. Bar: Conn. 1971. Asst. pub. def. Stamford Superior Ct., 1971—72, asst. pros., 1972—76; asst. town atty. Town of Greenwich, 1976—77; ptnr. Sherman & Richichi, Stamford, Conn., 1977—. Legal analyst CBS News; legal commentator on various networks including Court TV, MSNBC, CNBC, FoxNews, NBC. Mem.: ATLA, Conn. Trial Lawyers Assn., Nat. Assn. Criminal Def. Lawyers, Conn. Criminal Def. Lawyers Assn. (founding mem., bd. mem., lectr., past pres.). Office: Sherman Richichi & Hickley LLC 27 5th St Stamford CT 06905*

SHERMAN, MIKE (MICHAEL FRANCIS SHERMAN), college football coach, former professional football coach; b. Norwood, Mass., Dec. 19, 1954; m. Karen Sherman; children: Sarah, Emily, Matthew, Benjamin. Student, Ctrl. Conn. State U., 1974, 76-77. Part-time coach U. Pitts. Panthers, 1981-82; offensive line coach Tulane U. Green Wave, New Orleans, 1983-84; offensive coord. Coll. Holy Cross Crusaders, Worcester, Mass., 1985-88; offensive line coord. Tex. A&M Aggies, College Station, 1989-93, 95-96, head coach, 2008—; offensive line coord. UCLA Bruins, 1994; offensive coord., tight ends coach Seattle Seahawks, 1999; tight ends/asst. offensive line Green Bay Packers, 1997-98, head coach, 2000—05, exec. v.p., 2001—05, gen. mgr., 2001—04; asst. head coach/offense Houston Texans, 2006—07, asst. head coach, offensive coord., 2007. Office: Athletics Dept Tex A&M U PO Box 30017 College Station TX 77842

SHERMAN, NORMAN MARK, advertising agency executive; b. NYC, June 19, 1948; s. Sol and Rhoda (Kaplan) S.; m. Michelle Petnov, Jan. 8, 1978; 1 child, Michael Isaac. BA, U. Buffalo, 1970; MBA, Columbia U., 1972. Cert. tchr., N.Y. Product mgr. RCA Records, NYC, 1972-73; dir. mktg. Shelter Records, NYC, 1973-74; account exec. Rosenfeld Sirowitz & Lawson, NYC, 1974-76, Benton & Bowles, NYC, 1976-78, v.p. account supr., 1978-81, sr. v.p., mgmt. supr., 1981-84; exec. v.p., dir. account mgmt. Avrett, Free & Ginsberg, NYC, 1984-85; sr. v.p., group account dir. D'arcy, Masius, Benton & Bowles, 1985-93, mng. dir., bd. dirs., 1993-96, corp. exec. v.p., 1996-98; mng. dir. The Sr. Network, Stamford, Conn., 1998-99; pres. N.Am. Gundersen Ptnrs. LLC, NYC, 1999—2001; exec. v.p., dir. healthcare Hill, Holliday, Connors, Cosmopulos, 2002—05; ptnr. Troyanos Group, Irvington, NY, 2006—. Home: 330 W 72nd St New York NY 10023-2641 Office: Troyanos Group 106 N Broadway Irvington NY 10533 Office Phone: 914-479-1802. Business E-Mail: norman@troyanosgroup.com.

SHERMAN, PAUL W., animal behavior educator; b. Akron, Ohio, July 6, 1949; s. Philip S. and Kate P. Sherman; m. Cynthia Kagarise, Sept. 8, 1979; children: Laura Saylor, Peter George. BA, Stanford U., 1971; MS, U. Mich., 1974, PhD, 1976. Asst. prof. U. Calif., Berkeley, 1978-80, Cornell U., Ithaca, N.Y., 1980-84, assoc. prof., 1984-91, prof., 1991—. Editor: Exploring Animal Behavior, 2001. Recipient Astor Lectureship award Oxford (Eng.) U., 2001. Office: Cornell Univ Neurobiology and Behavior Mudd Hall Ithaca NY 14853 E-mail: pws6@cornell.edu.

SHERMAN, RICHARD BEATTY, historian, educator; b. Somerville, Mass., Nov. 16, 1929; s. James Beatty and Hilda Louise (Ford) S.; m. Hanni Fey, June 13, 1952; children: Linda Caroline, Alan Theodore. AB, Harvard U., 1951, PhD, 1959; MA, U. Pa., 1952. Instr. history Pa. State U., State College, 1957-60; asst. prof. Coll. of William and Mary, Williamsburg, Va., 1960-65, assoc. prof., 1965-70, prof., 1970-87, chancellor prof., 1987-92, Pullen prof., 1992-94, prof. emeritus, 1994—. Fulbright prof. Am. history U. Stockholm, 1966-67. Author: The Negro and the City, 1970, The Republican Party and Black America, 1973, The Case of Odell Waller, 1992; co-author: The College of William and Mary: A History, 1993; contbr. articles to profl. jours. Served with U.S. Army, 1952-54. Am. Philos. Soc. grantee, 1964, 66, faculty rsch. grantee Coll. William and Mary, 1962, 63, 65, 80, 87. Mem. ACLU, Phi Beta Kappa. Democrat. Office: Coll William and Mary Dept History Williamsburg VA 23185 Home: Corbridge Course 4201 Williamsburg VA 23188 Personal E-mail: richard.sherman@windsormeade.org.

SHERMAN, RICHARD MORTON, composer, lyricist; b. NYC, June 12, 1928; s. Al and Rosa (Dancis) S.; m. Ursula Gluck, July 6, 1957; children— Linda Sue, Gregory Vincent, Victoria Lynn. Student, U. So. Calif., 1945; BA, Bard Coll., 1949. With Walt Disney Prodns., Burbank, Calif., 1960—. Composer popular songs including: You're Sixteen, 1950-60, Let's Get Together, 1961, It's a Small World, 1964, Winnie the Pooh, 1966; film scores include: The Parent Trap, 1961, The Sword in the Stone, 1962, Summer Magic, 1963, Mary Poppins, 1964 (Acad. award for best score, Acad. award for best song, Grammy award for best film score), That Darn Cat, 1965, Winnie The Pooh, 1965, Follow Me Boys, 1966, Happiest Millionaire, 1967, Jungle Book, 1967, Family Band, 1968, Chitty, Chitty Bang Bang, 1968, Aristocats, 1970, Bedknobs and Broomsticks, 1971, Snoopy Come Home, 1972, Charlotte's Web, 1973; composer songs for films including Tom Sawyer, 1973, Huckleberry Finn, 1974, The Slipper and Rose, 1977, When You're Loved, 1978, The Tigger Movie, 2000; composer songs for Disneyland attractions; composer songs for stage prodns. including Over Here!, 1974, Chitty Chitty Bang Bang, London, 2002 (Musical Theater award, Variety Club of Great Britain, 2003), Broadway, 2005, Mary Poppins, London, 2004, Broadway, 2006. Served with AUS, 1953-55. Recipient Christopher medal, 1965, Mousecar award, Disney, 1985, Disney Legends award, 1990, Winsor McCay award for lifetime achievement and contbn. to animation, Intenat. Animated Film Soc., 2003, Nat. Medal Arts, 2008; named to Hollywood Walk of Fame, 1976, Songwriters Hall of Fame, 2005. Mem. Acad. Motion Picture Arts and Scis., Broadcast Music, Inc. (Pioneer award, 1977, Lifetime Achievement award, 1991), Nat. Acad. Recording Arts and Scis., Composers and Lyricists Guild, Writers Guild Am.*

SHERMAN, ROBERT B(ERNARD), composer, lyricist, screenwriter; b. Dec. 19, 1925; s. Al and Rosa (Dancis) S.; m. Joyce Ruth Sasner, Sept. 27, 1953; children: Laurie Shane, Jeffrey Craig, Andrea Tracy, Robert Jason. Student, UCLA, 1943; BA, Bard Coll., 1949; MusD (hon.), Lincoln U., 1990. Songwriter Walt Disney Prodns., Beverly Hills, Calif.; composer, lyricist United Artist, Beverly Hills; v.p. Musi-Classics, Inc.; founder, CEO, exec. prodr. Music World Corp., Beverly Hills, 1958—. Songs include Tall Paul, Pineapple Princess, You're Sixteen (Gold Record), It's a Small World, Winnie the Pooh, Let's Get Together; songwriter films including The Parent Trap, 1961, Summer Magic, 1963, Mary Poppins, 1964 (Acad. awards for best score, best song, 1964, Grammy award, 1965), That Darn Cat, 1965, Winnie The Pooh, 1965, Jungle Book, 1967, Chitty Chitty Bang Bang, 1969, Bedknobs and Broomsticks, 1971; songs Snoopy, Come Home!, 1972; song scores Charlotte's Web, 1972, Cabbage Patch Kids, 1974, Little Nemo, 1992, The Mighty Kong, 1996, The Tigger Movie, 2000; co-producer NBC-TV spl. Goldilocks, 1970; co-producer, composer, lyricist stage musical Victory Canteen, 1971; composer-lyricist Broadway show Over Here!, 1975, Busker Alley, 1995, stage prodn. Chitty Chitty Bang Bang, London, 2002 (Musical Theater award, Variety Club of Great Britain, 2003), Broadway, 2005, Mary Poppins, London, 2004, Broadway, 2006), screenplay and song score Tom Sawyer, 1972, Huckleberry Finn, 1974, The Slipper and the Rose, 1977, The Magic of Lassie, 1978. Served with inf. AUS, 1943-45 ETO. Decorated Purple Heart. Recipient Mousecar award Disney Studios, Disney Legend award, 1990, Winsor McCay award for lifetime achievement and contbn. to animation, Intenat. Animated Film Soc., 2003, Nat. Medal Arts, 2008; named to Hollywood Walk of Fame, 1976, Songwriters Hall of Fame, 2005. Mem. Acad. Motion Picture Arts and Scis. (exec. bd. music br. 12 yrs.), Broadcast Music, Inc. (Pioneer award, 1977, Lifetime Achievement award, 1991), AFTRA, Nat. Acad. Rec. Arts and Scis., Composers and Lyricists Guild (exec. bd.), Dramatists Guild, Authors League. Office: Music World Corp PO Box 16425 Beverly Hills CA 90209-2425 Office Phone: 310-576-8100. E-mail: info@musicworldcorp.com.*

SHERMAN, RUTH TODD, counseling administrator, educator; b. Memphis, July 3, 1924; d. Robbie M. and Lillie M. (Shreve) Todd. BS, Memphis State U., 1972, MEd, 1975; MA, Western Mich. U., 1986; PhD, Ohio State U., 2001. Cert. tchr., counselor. Youth leader Assembly of God Ch., Memphis, 1962-64, youth dir., 1964-66; counselor Teen Challenge, Memphis, 1973-74; marriage and family therapist Memphis, 1976-77; govt. tng. advisor Def. Logistics Agy., Battle Creek, Mich., 1982-87, advisor Alexandria, Va., 1987-94, ret., 1994; tchr. computer graphics Ohio State U., Columbus, 1998—2001; instrnl. devel. specialist Global U., Springfield, Mo., 2004—06. Agy. to Mil. Svc. cons. Def. Logistics Agy., Oklahoma City, 1990-94. Author: Federal Catalog Training Books/Videos, 1987 (Sustained Superior Performance award 1987). Mem. Internat. Assn. Marriage and Family Counselors, Nat.

Employment Counseling Assn., Am. Mental Health Counseling Assn., Am. Assn. Christian Counselors. Avocations: drawing, creating computer animations, photography. Home: 3223 N Maranatha Ln Springfield MO 65803-6102

SHERMAN, S. MURRAY, neuroscientist, neurobiology educator; b. Pitts., Jan. 4, 1944; s. Julius Louis Sherman and Ida Cohodas; m. Marjorie Jean Ebken, Feb. 1, 1969; children: Erika Kirsten, Benjamin William. BS in Biology, Calif. Inst. Tech., 1965; PhD in Anatomy, U. Pa., 1969; MA, Oxford U., Eng., 1985. Pre-doctoral fellow U. Pa., Phila., 1965-69; postdoctoral fellow Australian Nat. U., Canberra, 1970-72; asst. prof. U. Va., Charlottesville, 1972-75, assoc. prof., 1975-78, prof., 1978-79, SUNY, Stony Brook, 1979—; leading prof., 1990—. Vis. prof. Oxford U., 1985-86. Office: SUNY Dept Neurobiology Stony Brook NY 11794-0001

SHERMAN, SPENCER E., ophthalmologist; AB cum laude, Princeton U., Sigma XI, 1958; MD, Columbia Coll. Physicians & Surgeons, 1962. Diplomate Am. Bd. Ophthalmology. Intern Mt. Sinai Hosp., NYC, 1962-63, attending ophthalmologist, 1968—, resident in ophthalmology, 1965-68; asst. clin. prof. ophthalmology NYU Sch. Medicine, NYC; staff Mt. Sinai Hosp., 1998—. Attending ophthalmologist Manhattan Eye & Ear Hosp., NYC, 1968—, Lenox Hill Hosp., NYC, 1968—, NY Eye and Ear Infirmary, Mt. Sinai Hosp., 1970—. Capt. USAMC, 1963-65. Named one of Best Drs. in NY, Castle Connolly Group, 1980—, Top Drs. in US, Ctr. for Study of Svc. Fellow ACS, Internat. Coll. of Surgeons, Am. Acad. of Ophthalmology (Honor and Svc. award); mem. AMA, Nat. Soc. Prevention Blindness, Found. Children with Learning Disabilities, Am. Soc. Refractive Surgeons, NY Acad. Medicine, NY Ophthalmologic Soc., Internat. Soc. Refractive Surgery, Am. Soc. Cataract & Refractive Surgery, Harmonie Club, Sunningdale Country Club, Maidstone Gun Club, Peconic Sportsman Club, East Hampton Tennis Club. Office: 166 E 63rd St New York NY 10021-7636 Office Phone: 212-753-8300. Fax: (212) 752-4285. E-mail: sesmdpc@aol.com.

SHERMAN, STEVEN I., endocrinologist, educator; b. NYC, Mar. 7, 1959; s. Daniel and Theresa Sherman; m. Janine J. Colaianni, Jan. 2, 1988; children: Julia, Michael, Rose. AB, Harvard Coll., 1981; MD, Johns Hopkins U., 1985. Diplomate Am. Bd. of Internal Medicine. Instr. in medicine Johns Hopkins Sch. of Medicine, Balt., 1991—93; asst. prof. of medicine U. Tex. M.D. Anderson Cancer Ctr., Houston, 1993—99, assoc. prof., 1999—, chmn. ad interim dept. endocrine neoplasia and hormonal disorders, 2000—. Dir. Nat. Thyroid Cancer Treatment Coop. Study Group, Houston, 1998—. Fellow: Am. Coll. of Endocrinology; mem.: Nat. Thyroid Soc. for Edn. and Rsch. (dir. 1998—). Achievements include discovery of effect of RXR agonists to cause central hypothyroidism. Office: U Tex MD Anderson Cancer Ctr Unit 435 1515 Holcombe Blvd Houston TX 77030

SHERMAN, VADIM, surgeon, director; b. Bobruisk, Belarus, Jan. 29, 1976; s. Jack and Rita Sherman; m. Erica Hundorfean Sherman. MD, U. Western Ont., Can., 2000; MS, McGill U., Montreal, Quebec, Can., 2007. Cert. Am. Bd. Surgery, 2006, in Healthcare Mgmt. Rice U., 2008. Dir., comprehensive bariatric surgery ctr. Baylor Coll. Medicine, Houston, 2006—, program dir., minimally invasive surgery fellowship, 2006—. Contbr. chapters to books. Fellow: RCS (Can.); mem.: ACS, Soc. Am. Gastrointestinal and Endoscopic Surgeons, Can. Assn. Gen. Surgeons, Am. Soc. Metabolic and Bariatric Surgery (rsch. com. 2006). Office: Baylor Coll Medicine 1709 Dryden Ste 1500 Houston TX 77030 Office Fax: 713-798-4530. Business E-Mail: vsherman@bcm.edu.

SHERMAN, WENDY RUTH, consulting firm executive, former federal agency administrator; b. Balt., June 7, 1949; m. Bruce Edward Stokes; 1 child, Sarah Renee. BA, Boston U., 1971; MSW, U. Md., 1976. Chief of staff to Senator Barbara Mikulski US Senate; spl. sec. for children & youth State of Md., 1987, dir. Office Child Welfare; dir. Washington ops. Dukakis for Pres., 1987-88; dir. Campaign '88 Dem. Nat. Com., Washington, 1988; polit. & pub. policy cons. Ctr. Nat. Policy Foreman & Heidepriem, Washington, 1988-91; ptnr. Doak, Shrum, Harris, Sherman, Washington, 1991-93; asst. sec. for legis. affairs US Dept. State, Washington, 1993-96; pres., CEO Fannie Mae Found., 1996-97; spl. advisor & policy coord. for North Korea The White House; counselor US Dept. State, 1997—2001; prin. The Albright Group LLC, 2001—, Albright Capital Mgmt. LLC (ACM), 2001—. Mem. Commn. on the Prevention of Weapons of Mass Destruction Proliferation & Terrorism, 2008; bd. dirs. Oxfam America; bd. advisors Ctr. for a New Am. Security. Mem.: US-India Strategic Dialogue, Aspen Strategy Group, Coun. Fgn. Rels. Office: The Albright Group LLC 1101 NY Ave NW Ste 900 Washington DC 20005 Office Phone: 202-842-7222. Office Fax: 202-370-3599.*

SHERMAN, WILLIAM BENJAMIN, research scientist; b. NYC; s. Saul Lawrence and Carol Esberg Sherman, Judith Kofsky Sherman (Stepmother). PhD, U. Pa., Phila., 1999. Postdoc. rschr. NY U., NYC, 2000—05; staff scientist Brookhaven Nat. Lab., Upton, NY, 2006—. Vol., ballroom dance tchr. Dancing Classrooms, Bellport, NY, 2007—08. Mem.: AAAS, Internat. Soc. Nanoscale Sci. Computation and Engring., Am. Phys. Soc., USA Dance, Phi Beta Kappa, Sigma Xi. Achievements include research in architecture of complex molecular structures of DNA nanotechnology; patents for molecular robots that can walk in controlled fassion. Avocation: ballroom dancing. Office: Brookhaven Nat Lab PO Box 5000 Upton NY 11973-5000

SHERMAN, WILLIAM FARRAR, lawyer, former state legislator; b. Little Rock, Sept. 12, 1937; s. Lincoln Farrar and Nancy (Lowe) S.; m. Carole Lynn Williams, Sept. 2, 1967; children: John, Anna, Lucy. BA in History, U. Ark., 1960; LLB, U. Va., 1964. Bar: Ark. 1964, U.S. Supreme Ct. 1970. Assoc. Smith, Williams, Friday & Bowen, Little Rock, 1964-66; asst. U.S. atty. Ea. Dist. Ark., Little Rock, 1966-69, Ark. Securities Commr., Little Rock, 1969-71; ptnr. Jacoway, Sherman & Pence, Little Rock, 1971—2004; pvt. practice William F. Sherman Law Office, Little Rock, 2005—. Mem. Ark. Ho. of Reps., 1974-84; spl. assoc. justice Supreme Ct., 1991; del. Constnl. Conv. Ark., 1979. With U.S. Army, 1960-61, now brig. gen. U.S. Army ret. Fellow Ark. Bar Found.; mem. ABA (substitute mem.), Ark. Bar Assn. (sustaining mem.), Pulaski County Bar Assn. Methodist. Office: 809 North Palm St Little Rock AR 72205 Home Phone: 501-661-1963; Office Phone: 501-372-3148. Personal E-mail: wfsherman@sbcglobal.net.

SHERMAN, ZACHARY, civil engineer, aerospace engineer, consultant; b. NYC, Oct. 26, 1922; s. Harry and Minnie (Schulsinger) Sherman; m. Bertha Leikin, Mar. 23, 1947; children: Gene Victor, Carol Beth. BCE, CCNY, 1943; MCE, Polytech. U. N.Y., Bklyn., 1953, PhD in Civil Engring. & Mechanics, 1969; MME, Stevens Inst. Tech., 1968. Registered profl. engr., N.Y., N.J. Stress analyst Gen. Dynamics, San Diego, 1943-45; sr. stress analyst Republic Aviation, Farmingdale, NY, 1945-47, 59-62; prof. civil engring. U. Miss., Oxford, 1954-59; lectr. Stevens Inst. Tech., Hoboken, NJ, 1962-67, CUNY, 1967-69; assoc. prof. aerospace engring. Pa. State U., State College, 1969-73; prin. Dr. Zachary Sherman Cons. Engrs., Santa Monica, Calif., 1973—; aerospace engr. FAA, NYC, 1980-86. Designated cons. engr. rep. FAA, 1986—. Contr.: articles to profl. jours. including Jour. of Aircraft AIAA. NSF grantee, 1972. Fellow: ASCE; mem.: AIAA (v.p. Western Conn. chpt. 1977—78), N.Y. Acad. Scis., Sigma Xi. Achievements include development of beam/beam-column deck suspension bridge; solutions to pothole problems; prestressed aircraft wing. Home and Office: 2021 California Ave Apt 7 Santa Monica CA 90403-4531 Office Phone: 310-264-5990. Fax: 310-264-5990. Personal E-mail: aerozach@earthlink.net.

SHERN, DAVID L., mental health services professional, former dean; b. Pueblo, Colo., Feb. 23, 1951; BA in Psychology, U. Colo., 1973, MA in Social Psychology, 1977, PhD in Social Psychology, 1980; cert. in advanced epidemiologic methods, NIMH Staff Coll., 1980. Asst. dir. research and evaluation sect. Denver Dept. Health and Hosps. Mental Health Programs, 1981-82; research assoc. evaluation services sect. Colo. div. Mental Health, Denver, 1982-84, mgr. sponsored research program, 1984-88; project dir., investigator estimating residential services for chronically mentally ill Colo. divsn. Mental Health, Denver, 1983-87; investigator validation models for estimating mental health need U. Denver, 1983-88; dir. bur. evaluation and svcs. rsch. NY Office of Mental Health, Albany, 1988-95; dean, prof. Louis de la Parte Fla. Mental Health Inst., U. South Fla., Tampa, 1995—2006; pres., CEO Mental Health America, Alexandria, Va., 2006—. Cons. several health facilities, Denver, 1976—88; chmn. Fla. Commn. Mental Health and Substance Abuse, 1999—2000; prin. investigator Treatment Outcome Study, 1988; prin. investigator rsch. grants NIMH Substance Abuse and Mental Health Svcs. Adminstrn., 1988—2000; dir. NIMH Ctr. for Sudy Issues in Pub. Mental Health, 1993—95; mem. Govs. Suicide Prevention Task Force, 2003—06. Contbr. articles to profl. jours. Bd. dirs. Travelers Aid of Denver, 1981-83, Karis Cmty., 1986-88, pres. 1988; founding mem. Albany County Land Conservancy, 1992-95, pres., 1992-95; treas. USF Charter Sch., 1998-2006;active Crisis Ctr. of Tampa Bay, 2004-06. Mem. APA, APHA (chair mental health sect. 1992-93, governing coun. 1995-97), Orgn. for Program Evaluation in Colo. (pres. 1982-83, assoc. editor bull.), Am. Evaluation Assn. Independent. Avocations: hiking, gardening, travel. Office: Mental Health America 2000 N Beauregard St 6th Fl Alexandria VA 22311 Office Phone: 703-838-7500.*

SHERN, STEPHANIE MARIE, investment company executive, accountant; b. Taylor, Pa., Jan. 7, 1948; d. Joseph and Stephanie (Malodovitch) Andrews; m. George Emil Shern, Sept. 25, 1971. AA, Keystone Jr. Coll., 1967; BS, Pa. State U., 1969. CPA, NY. Staff acct. to ptnr., nat. dir. consumer products industry Ernst & Young, NYC, 1969—2001, ptnr., vice chmn., global and US dir. R&CP markets. Bd. mem. Gamestop Corp., 2003-, Embarq Corp., 2006-. Contbr. articles to profl. jours. Named Keystonian of Yr., Keystone Jr. Coll., 1984. Mem. AICPA, NY State Soc. CPAs (bd. dirs. 1985-87), Beta Alpha Psi (mem. adv. forum 1984-86). Republican. Ukrainian Orthodox. Home: 11 Green Briar Rd Little Falls NJ 07424-2307 Office Phone: 973-785-3271. Personal E-mail: stephanieshern@aol.com.

SHERNOFF, DAVID JORDAN, psychology professor; b. Pomona, Calif., July 9, 1967; s. William Martin and JoAnn Shernoff; m. Elisa Steele, June 28, 1997; 1 child, Spencer Laurence. BS, Cornell U., 1989; EdM, Harvard Grad. Sch. Edn., 1991; PhD, U. Chgo., 2001. Asst. prof. No. Ill. U., DeKalb, 2003—. Domestic and internat. rsch. cons.; reviewer jour. articles and conf. papers; presenter in field. Author: (books) The Individual-Maker; co-author: Good Mentoring, 2009; contbr. jour. articles and chapters to books. Recipient Susan Colver-Rosenberger Meritorious Achievement award, U. Chgo., Dept. Edn., 1997—98, Role Motivation Dem. Life award, John G. Nichols Trust, Motivation Edn. Spl. Interest Group, Am. Ednl. Rsch. Assn., 2000—01; fellow, U. Wis., Madison, 2001—03. Mem.: Soc. Rsch. Child Devel., Soc. Rsch. Adolescence, Am. Ednl. Rsch. Assn. Liberal. Jewish. Avocations: water-skiing, racquetball, bicycling. Home: 315 Bridgeview Cir Geneva IL 60134 Office: No Ill U LEPF Graham Hall Coll Edn Dekalb IL 60115-2854 Business E-Mail: dshernoff@niu.edu.

SHERO, RAY (REJEAN SHERO), professional sports team executive; b. St. Paul, Minn., July 28, 1962; s. Fred and Mariette Shero; m. Karen Shero; children: Christopher, Kyle. Grad., St. Lawrence U., 1984. Player agent NHL; sr. ptnr. Sports Consulting Group, 1986—93; asst. gen. mgr. Ottawa Senators, 1993—98, Nashville Predators, 1998—2006; gen. mgr. Pitts. Penguins, 2006—. Achievements include being the general manager of Stanley Cup Champion Pittsburgh Penguins, 2009. Office: Pittsburgh Penguins Mellon Arena 66 Mario Lemieux Dr Pittsburgh PA 15219*

SHERR, BRIAN J., lawyer; b. Apr. 19, 1944; BA, Rutgers U., NJ, 1967; JD, Boston U., 1970. Bar: Fla., US Supreme Ct. Off counsel Greenberg Traurig, Ft. Lauderdale, Fla., 1991—95, shareholder, 1995—. Founder, chmn. First So. Bank, Boca Raton, Fla., 1987—, bd. dirs.; lectr. in field. Contbr. articles to profl. jours. Past bd. govs. Mus. Art, Ft. Lauderdale; mem. adv. bd. Aish Hatorah Jerusalem; past mem. adv. com. U.U. Miami Law Ctr. Inst. Condo. and Cluster Devel.; past pres. Jewish Fedn. Greater Ft. Lauderdale, Fla.; bd. dirs. Daniel D. Cantor Sr. Ctr.; former bd. dirs. Fla. Atlantic U. Found.; past bd. dirs. Broward Ctr. Performing Arts, Nat. Ben Gamla Charter Sch. Found. Inc., Hallandale, Fla. Recipient Tree of Life award, Jewish Nat. Fund., 2006; named one of South Florida's Heavy Hitters in Real Estate, Bus. Jour., 2004; Brian J. Sherr Appreciation Day proclaimed, Broward County Commn., 2006. Mem.: Broward County Bar Assn., Fla. Bar Assn. (co-chmn. condo. and planned devel. com., mem. exec. coun. real property, probate and trust law sect.). Office: 401 E Los Olas Blvd Ste 2000 Fort Lauderdale FL 33301 Office Phone: 954-768-8247. Business E-Mail: sherrb@gtlaw.com.

SHERR, ELLIOTT HAROLD, neurologist, researcher; s. Walter R. and Karen Sherr; m. Linda M. Rubinstein, July 2, 1989; children: Rachel J., David A., Jessica C. BAS in Biology and Philosophy, Stanford U., Calif., 1984; MD, PhD, Columbia U., NYC, 1995. Diplomate Am. Bd. of Psychiatry and Neurology. Vis. scientist La Catolica U., Santiago, Chile, 1995—96; resident in pediats. U. Calif., San Francisco, 1996—2000, instr. neurology and pediats., 2000—02, asst. prof., 2002—, assoc. prof., 2008—. Mem. exec. com. Nat. Orgn. Dosirders of Corpus Callosum, Calif., 2003—06. Recipient Sci. Award, Child Neurology Found., 2004—06, Philip Dodge Young Investigator award, Child Neurology Soc., 2006. Mem.: Am. Acad. Neurology. Independent. Avocations: travel, cooking, cycling. Office: U Calif San Francisco Dept Neurology 350 Parnassus Ave San Francisco CA 94143-0137

SHERR, EVAN A., biomedical engineer, consultant; b. Norwalk, Conn., Mar. 30, 1965; s. Allan Ellis and Sylvia (Fieldstein) S.; m. Elizabeth Baird, June 8, 1996. BA in Biology, Boston U., 1987, BS in Biomed. Engring., 1991, MS in Biomed. Engring., 1996. Supr. clin. dermatology Mass. Gen. Hosp., Boston, 1986-90; rsch. asst., cons. Boston U.-Neuro Muscular Rsch. Ctr., Boston, 1990-92; scientist Summit Tech., Inc., Waltham, Mass., 1992-96; engr. Cynosure, Inc., Bedford, Mass., 1996—. Lab. technician human biochemistry The Children's Hosp., Boston, 1987-88; tech. devel. mgr. Etonic-Tretorn, Inc., Brockton, Mass., 1988; cons. Ultralife, Inc., Lawrenceville, Ga., 1988-96, Medispectra, Inc., Cambridge, Mass., 1996. Author: Zernike Polynomial Estimation of Induced Error in Refractive Surgery, 1996. Capt. WGBH TV-Auction, Boston, 1984-97; coach Boston U. Gymnastics Club, 1987-89. Recipient Undergrad. Biomed. Rsch. award Whitaker Found., 1991. Mem. IEEE, Order of the Engr. Avocations: triathlons, hiking, gardening, diving, brewing. Home: 50 Raymond Way Ashland MA 01721-2430

SHERR, RICHARD, retail executive; Buyer TJX Cos., Inc., Framingham, Mass., 1992, sr. v.p. merchandising Marmaxx Group, 2001—04, exec. v.p. merchandising Marmaxx Group, 2004—05, exec. v.p., chief merchandising officer Marmaxx Group, 2005—07, sr. exec. v.p., COO Marmaxx Group, 2007—. Office: TJX Cos Inc 770 Cochituate Rd Framingham MA 01701 Office Phone: 508-390-1000. Office Fax: 508-390-2091.

SHERRARD, WILLIAM ROBERT, retired operations management educator; b. Langford, SD, July 16, 1932; s. Earl George and Isabel Ann (Williams) S.; m. Miriam Elaine Murren, June 11, 1960. BBA, U. Wash., 1957, MBA, 1958, PhD, 1965. Indsl. engr. Boeing Airplane Co., Seattle, 1957-59; prof. Idaho State U., Pocatello, 1959-60, U. NC, Chapel Hill, 1965-68, San Diego State U., 1968—2006; ret., 2006. Cons. various orgns., San Diego, 1968—. Author: (textbook) Production Management, 1990; contbr. articles to profl. jours. Mem. Decision Scis. Inst. (program chmn. 1972-79), Acad. Mgmt., Am. Inst. Mgmt. Scis., Am. Prodn. Inventory Control Soc., Ops. Rsch. Soc. Am., Beta Gamma Sigma, Sigma Iota Epsilon. Avocations: golf, hiking, jogging. Office Phone: 858-481-3159. Business E-Mail: sherrard@mail.sdsu.edu.

SHERRELL, JOHN BRADFORD, lawyer; b. Indpls., Jan. 27, 1951; s. Carl and Mary Jean (Bell) S.; m. Sherry Naomi Calhoun, Apr. 28, 1974; children: David Alan, Corinne Elizabeth. BA, Yale U., 1973; JD, U. Mich., 1977. Bar: Calif. 1977. Ptnr. Latham & Watkins, Los Angeles, 1977—. Dep. gen. counsel to Ind. Commn. on L.A. Police Dept. Named an Am.'s Top Black Lawyers, Black Enterprise Mag., 2003. Mem. ABA, Calif. Bar Assn. (co-chair real estate fin. subsect. of real property sec. 1990-92), L.A. County Bar Assn. (barrister's exec. com. 1978-80, bd. trustees 1991-93). Office: Latham Watkins 355 S Grand Ave Los Angeles CA 90071-1560 Home: 11576 Chiquita St Studio City CA 91604-2914 Office Phone: 213-891-8174. E-mail: john.sherrell@lw.com.

SHERREN, ANNE TERRY, chemistry professor; b. Atlanta, July 1, 1936; d. Edward Allison and Annie Ayres (Lewis) Terry; m. William Samuel Sherren, Aug. 13, 1966. BA, Agnes Scott Coll., 1957; PhD, U. Fla., Gainesville, 1961. Grad. tchg. asst. U. Fla., Gainesville, 1957-61; from instr. to asst. prof. Tex. Womans U., Denton, 1961-66; rsch. participant Argonne Nat. Lab., 1973-80, 93-94; assoc. prof. chemistry North Cen. Coll., Naperville, Ill., 1966-76, prof., 1976-2001, prof. emeritus, 2001—. Contbr. articles to profl. jours. Ruling elder Knox Presbyn. Ch., 1971—, clk. of session, 1976-94. Mem. Am. Chem. Soc., Am. Inst. Chemists, Sigma Xi, Delta Kappa Gamma (chpt. pres. 2002-2004), Iota Sigma Pi (nat. pres. 1978-81, nat. dir. 1972-78, nat. historian 1989—). Presbyterian. Office: North Ctrl Coll Dept Chemistry Naperville IL 60566 Business E-Mail: atsherren@noctrl.edu.

SHERRER, CHARLES DAVID, dean, clergyman; b. Marion, Ohio, Sept. 21, 1935; s. Harold D. and Catherine E. (Fye) S. AB, U. Notre Dame, 1958, MA, 1965; S.T.L., Gregorian U., 1962; PhD, U. N.C., 1969; HHD, King's Coll., 1997. Ordained priest Roman Cath. Ch., 1961. Instr. English U. Portland, Oreg., 1963-64, asst. prof. Oreg., 1969-74, prof. Oreg., 1990—2005, prof. emeritus Oreg., 2005—, chmn. dept. Oreg., 1970-74, dean Grad. Sch. Oreg., 1982-87, mem. Bd. Regents Oreg., 1986-87, acad. v.p. Oreg., 1987-96; pres. King's Coll., Wilkes Barre, Pa., 1974-81. Bd. trustees Stonehill Coll., 1992-98; dir. studies Holy Cross Fathers, Ind. Province, 1979-88. Office Phone: 503-943-7596. Business E-Mail: sherrer@up.edu.

SHERRER, CHARLES WILLIAM, lawyer, writer; b. Denton, Kans., July 24, 1922; s. Charles Eric and Pearl Bearl (McClellan) S.; m. Marion Sylva Webb, Aug. 27, 1948; children— Gary L., Carol J. Sherrer Davis. BS, U. Kans., 1948; JD, U. Mo. Kans. City, 1951. Bar: Mo. 1950, Kans. 1958, US Supreme Ct. 1959. Atty., US Army C.E., 1955-88; div. counsel South Pacific div., Lafayette, Calif., 1973-88. Served with AUS, 1942-45; to 1st lt., 1950-52. Mem. ABA, Fed. Bar Assn., Mensa, Soc. Am. Mil. Engrs. Author: (with Sherrer) Ethical and Professional Standards for Academic Psychologists and Counsellors, 1980: contbr. articles to legal jours. Home: 3933 Woodside Ct Lafayette CA 94549-3413

SHERRER, JOHN M., III, cultural organization administrator; BA in Eng., Clemson U., SC; MA in Eng., Clemson U.; MA in Applied History, U. SC, Columbia, grad. cert. in mus. mgmt. Hist. interpreter/edn. guide Nat. Trust Hist. Preservation, Drayton Hall Plantation, Charleston, SC, 1994; weekend hist. interpreter Strawberry Banke Mus., Portsmouth, NH, 1995—96; curatorial vol. Old York Hist. Soc., York, Maine, 1994—96, guest curator, 1997, exhibits preparator, 1998; curatorial asst. Hist. Columbia Found., Columbia, SC, 1996—98, coord. vol. & visitor services, 1998—99, acting asst. exec. dir., 1999—2000, dir. collections, 1999—2001, dir. collections & interpretation, 2001—. Instr. Clemson U., Eng. dept., 1991—92; adj. prof. history U. SC, Columbia, 2006. Contbr. articles. Mem. vestry St. John's Episcopal Ch., Shandon, SC, 2004—, jr. warden, vestry, 2006—; mem. Clemson U. Humanities Advancement Bd., 2006—, SC Dept. Archives & History Found., 2007—. Mem.: Anthropology, Mus., Art & Zoo Educators (v.p. 2002), Teaching Am. History Initiative (steering com. 2002), Southeastern Registrar's Assn. (state rep. 2000), S.E. Museums Conf. (scholarship com. 2001, 2004, programs com. 2004), SC Fall Line Consortium, SC Fedn. Museums (profl. devel. com. 1999—2002, chair profl. devel. com. 2001—02, treas. 2002—04, 1st v.p. 2004—06, pres. 2006—), Am. Assn. State & Local History (profl. mentor 2007—, History News editl. vol. 2007—, educators & interpreters com. 2007—). Office: Hist Columbia Found 1601 Richland St Columbia SC 29201 also: SC Fedn Museums PO Box 100107 Columbia SC 29202-3107 Office Phone: 803-252-1770 ext. 28. E-mail: jsherrer@historiccolumbia.org.

SHERRICK, DANIEL NOAH, real estate broker; b. Greenup, Ill., Mar. 28, 1929; s. Conrad Donovan and Helen Lorene (Neeley) S.; m. Dora Ann Moore, Aug. 11, 1957; children: Renata Ann Sherrick McBride, Sherrie Dee Sherrick Sierra BS in Edn., Ea. Ill. U., Charleston, 1956. Owner Midwest Ins. Agy., Greenup, 1956—60; supt. agys. Midwest Life Ins. Co., Lincoln, Nebr., 1960—62; asst. v.p. Gulf Life Ins. Co., Jacksonville, Fla., 1962—71; pres. Bank of Carbondale, Ill., 1971—74, Prescription Learning Corp., Springfield, Ill., 1974—76; exec. v.p. Imperial Industries, Inc., Miami Lakes, Fla., 1976—88, pres., CEO, 1988—90; broker, salesman Coldwell Banker Residential Real Estate, 1990—91, 1993—; pres., bd. dirs. Palmer State Bank, Taylorville, Ill., 1991—93; broker-salesman Coldwell Banker Highlands Properties, 1993—. Pres. Alderman Park Civic Assn., Jacksonville, Ill., 1968, Heritage Hills Home Owners Assn., Carbondale, 1973. With USAF, 1948—52. Mem.: VFW, Greater Sebring C. of C., Am. Legion, Elks, Masons. Presbyterian. Home: 6228 Aquavista Dr Sebring FL 33876 Office: Coldwell Banker Highlands Properties 2521 US Hwy 27 S Sebring FL 33870-2127 Office Phone: 863-382-3157. Personal E-mail: dandora@strato.net.

SHERRILL, GREGG M., automotive executive; BSME, Tex. A&M; MBA, Ind. U. Plant mgr. Ford Motor Com., Dearborn, Mich., dir., supplier tech. assistance; with Johnson Controls, Inc., 1998—2007, v.p., gen. mgr., North Am. automotive ops., 2000—01, grp. v.p., mng. dir., Europe, South Africa, South Am., automotive systems grp., 2001—03, grp. v.p., mng. dir., Japan and Asia Pacific, grp. v.p., gen. mgr., battery ops., automotive systems grp., 2003—07, v.p., pres., power solutions; chmn., CEO Tenneco Inc., Lake Forest, Ill., 2007—. Office: Tenneco Inc 500 N Field Drive Lake Forest IL 60045 Office Phone: 847-482-5000. Office Fax: 847-482-5940.

SHERRILL, THOMAS BOYKIN, III, retired newspaper publishing executive; b. Tampa, Fla., Nov. 19, 1930; s. Thomas Boykin Jr. and Mary Emma (Addison) S.; m. Sandra Louise Evans, Dec. 27, 1969; children: Thomas Glenn, Stephen Addison. Circulation dir. Tampa (Fla.) Tribune, 1962—67, Sarasota (Fla.) Herald-Tribune, 1967—75; v.p. circulation The Dispatch Printing Co., Columbus, Ohio, 1975—78, v.p. mktg., 1978—97, bd. dirs., 1977—97; v.p., bd. dirs. Ohio Mag., Inc., Columbus, 1979—97; ret., 1997. Bd. dirs., past chmn. bd. dirs. Salvation Army; trustee, past chmn. bd. dirs. Better Bus. Bur. Ctrl. Ohio, Inc.; bd. dirs. Ctrl. Ohio Ctr. Econ. Edn.; v.p., trustee Columbus Dispatch Charities; past pres. Wesley Glen United Meth. Retirement Ctr.; pres.'s adv. bd. Meth. Theol. Sch. With USN, 1951-56. Recipient Disting. Svc. award Editor and Pub. Mag., 1978; named hon. pres. Troy State U., 1979, hon. Ky. Col., 1980, hon. lt. col. aide-to-camp to Gov. State of Ala., 1984. Mem. Internat. Newspaper Mktg. Assn., Ohio Newspaper Assn. (bd. dirs. 1984-97, pres. 1986-88, Pres.'s award 1990), So. Circulation Mgrs. Assn. (life; pres. 1967-68, sec. and treas., 1968-75, C.W. Bevinger Meml. award 1972), Audit Bur. Circulations (bd. dirs. 1980-90), Am. Advt. Fedn., Navy League, Ohio Newspapers Found., Ohio Circulation Mgrs. Assn (life; Pres.' award 1989), Columbus Area C. of C., SAR, Internat. Platform Assn., Athletic Club of Columbus, Muirfield Village Country Club, Kiwanis Club of Columbus (life, pres. 1982, George F. Hixon fellow). Republican. Home: 5215 Hampton Ln Columbus OH 43220-2270 Home Phone: 614-457-4395.

SHERRIS, DAVID ALLAN, surgeon, researcher, educator; b. Buffalo, Feb. 1, 1961; s. Donald Allan Sherris and Doris Mary Jones; m. Lisa Ellen Dubiel, Apr. 11, 1993; children: David Jr., Matthew, Lara. BA, Middlebury Coll., 1984; MD, U. Rochester, 1988. Diplomate Am. Bd. Otolaryngology, Am. Bd. Facial Plastic and Reconstructive Surgery. Resident otolaryngology U. Rochester, NY, 1989—93; fellow facial plastic surgery, clin. instr. U. Wash., Seattle, 1993—94; asst. prof. otolaryngology Mayo Med. Sch., Rochester, Minn., 1994—2000, assoc. prof., 2000—03; cons. surgeon Mayo Clinic, Rochester, 1994—2003, chair facial plastic surgery, 2002—03; chair otolaryngology SUNY, Buffalo, 2003—; chief of svc. otolaryngology Kaleida Health, 2003—; prof. otolaryngology U. Buffalo, 2005—. Author: Basic Surgical Skills, 1999, Essential Surgical Skills, 2004; author, editor: The Principles of Facial Reconstruction, 1995, reviewer: Archives of Facial Plastic Surgery, 2000—, mem. editl. bd.: Rhinology Jour., 2002—; contbr. 70 articles to profl. jours. Fellow: Am. Rhinologic Soc., Am. Acad. Otolaryngology Head and Neck Surgery (home study course faculty 2001—), Am. Acad. Facial Plastic and Reconstructive Surgery (active surgeon Face to Face Domestic Violence Program 1994—, Sir Harold Delf Gilles award 1994); mem.: Am. Bd. Otolaryngology (examiner 1999—). Avocations: running, skiing. Office Phone: 716-884-5102. E-mail: dsherris@buffalo.edu.

SHERROD, DANNY TROY, writer, educator; b. North Richland Hills, Tex., Apr. 27, 1963; s. Yvonne Boatman and Dan Sherrod. AA and Sci., El Centro Coll., 1983—86; B of Humanities, So. Meth. U., 1997—2002. Caseworker Tex. Dept. of Human Services, Dallas, 1991—95; libr. specialist So. Meth. U., 1996—2003; tchr. writing, history L.P. Cowart Sch., 2003—06; tchr. L.V. Stockard Middle Sch., 2006—. Author: (short story) Div. When it Rains - pub. in Primavera; editor: (newsletter) Theatre Hist. Soc. of Am.; contbr. jour. Legacies. Mem.: NEA, Am. Fedn. Tchrs., Nat. Coun. Tchrs. of English, US Humane Soc., Tex. SPCA, People for the Ethical Treatment of Animals, Golden Key Nat. Honor Soc. (life). Democrat.

SHERROD, LLOYD BRUCE, retired nutritionist; b. Goodland, Kans., Mar. 5, 1931; s. Charles and Helen S.; m. Judith Harms Sherrod, Dec. 21, 1963; children: Donna J., Barbara E. BS, S.D. State U., Brookings, 1958; MS, U. Ark., Fayetteville, 1960; PhD, Okla. State U., Stillwater, 1964. Rsch. assoc. Okla. State U., Stillwater, 1963; asst. prof. U. Hawaii, Hilo, 1964-67; from assoc. prof to prof. Tex. Tech. U. Ctr., Pantex, 1967-79; nutrition-chemistry instr. Frank Phillips Coll., Borger, Tex., 1979-88; part-time nutrition instr. Amarillo (Tex.) Coll., 1989-95; ret., 1995. Rschr. in field. Contbr. articles to sci. jours. Served with U.S. Army, 1951-53. Mem. AAAS, Am. Soc. Animal Science, Am. Dairy Science Assn., Am. Soc. Agronomy, Am. Inst. Biol. Scis., Tex. Jr. Coll. Tchrs. Assn., Am. Men and Women of Sci., Plains Nutrition Coun., Sigma Xi., Phi Kappa Phi, Gamma Sigma Delta. Home and Office: PO Box 1017 Panhandle TX 79068-1017 Office Phone: 806-537-3729.

SHERROD, PHILIP LAWRENCE, artist, composer, painter, poet; b. Pauls Valley, Okla., Oct. 12, 1935; s. Jesse Lawrence and Edie Mae (Shumate) S.; m. Peggy Anne Elledge, Jan. 17, 1959 (div. 1959); m. Helena Alicia Decastro, Nov. 18, 1961 (div.); 1 child, Sandro Arentino Mateos. BS, Okla. State U., 1957, BA, 1959; postgrad., Art Students League, NYC, 1961-63, Jacques Seligman Coll., 1968, Carroll Reese Mus., 1968. Tchr. Morristown Art Assn., NJ, 1973-74, NJ Ctr. for Visual Arts, 1977—2003, Art Students League, NYC, 1984—2008, Nat. Acad. Design Sch. of Fine Arts, 1994, 1996, 1998, 2005; master tchr. Bd. Cmty. Ctr., South Orange, NJ, 2004—08. Founder Street Painters, NYC, 1977—. One-man shows include Leonard Hutton Hutschnecker Galleries, 1966, Gallery 9, Chatham, NJ, 1967, Jacques Seligmann Gallery, 1968, Selected Artists Gallery, 1968, East Rockaway Art Exhibition, 1969, Allan Stone Gallery, 1969, 1971, 1973, 1975, 1981, 1996-1997, Sonraed Gallery, 1971, Artemis East Gallery, 1972, Pace U., NYC, 1972, The Humanist Ctr., 1973, 74, Grace Gallery, 1973, Allan Stone Gallery, 1973, 75, 76, 83, 96-97, Tower Art Gallery, Highland Falls, NY, 1975, Gallery 100, Princeton, NJ, 1975, Monique Knowlton Gallery, 1976, Cone Gallery, 1976, Bridgeport U., Conn., 1976 Bayonne Jewish Cmty. Ctr., NJ, 1977, 47 Bond St. Gallery, NYC, 1979, Art Awareness Gallery, Lexington, NY, 1980, Artists Choice Mus., NYC, 1983; exhibited in group shows at Allan Frumkin Gallery, 1973, 75, Boston U. Gallery, 1979, SUNY, 1979, Cork Gallery, Lincoln Ctr., NYC, 1981-2000, Nat. Acad. of Design, NYC, 1966, 75, 76, 78, 82, 88-90, 93-95, 97-99, 2001—, NJ Ctr. for the Arts, 1977-2003, Mus. and Sculpture Garden, Smithsonian Inst., Washington, 1989, New England Fine Arts Inst., Boston, 1993, Rita Dean Gallery, Dan Diego, 1993, Gallerie des Hamptons, Westhampton Beach, 1994, Fordham U., 1996; represented in permanent collections Tulane U. Mus., New Orleans, Mus. of Fine Art, Springfield, Mass., Everhart Mus., Scranton, Pa., Rose Art Mus., Brandeis U., Waltham, Mass., Almsford House, Fine Arts Ctr., Anderson, Ind., Mus. City NY, Hirshorn Mus. & Sculpture Garden, Smithsonian Inst. Mus.& Sculpture Garden, The Phillips Exeter Acad., NH, Worcester Fine Arts Mus., Herbert Johnson Mus., Ithica, NY, RI Sch. Design/Newark Mus., NJ, Nat. Acad. Mus., NYC, Am. Broadcasting Corp., Paramount Pictures Prodns., INA Corp., Montgomery Securities, San Francisco, Boston, NYC, Allan Stone, Steven Paine, Richard Brown Baker, Tom and Mary Paxton, Bill Paxton, others; author: (poems) 30 Mental-Talia, 1980, Black Truck, 1981, Mr. Wigley Cums, 1983, Images Below the Belt, 1984, Sex (I) Con, 1985. Grantee Creative Artists Pub. Svc., 1980, Adolphe/Esther Gottlieb Found., 1981, 88, 96, 06, NEA, 1982, Am. Acad. in Rome, 1985-86, The Pollack-Krasner Found., Inc., 1989; recipient Purchase award Am. Acad. Arts and Letters, 1967, 69, 74, Childe Hassam Purchase award Prixe de Roma, 1985-86. Fellow Am. Acad. in Rome. Home: 41 W 24th St New York NY 10010-3210 Home Phone: 212-989-3174. Personal E-mail: bigdaddiehots@gmail.com.

SHERRY, GEORGE LEON, political science professor; b. Lodz, Poland, Jan. 5, 1924; came to US, 1939, naturalized 1945; s. Leon G. and Henrietta (Mess) S.; m. Doris H. Harf, Mar. 6, 1947; 1 child, Vivien Gail Sherry Greenberg. BA summa cum laude, CCNY, 1944; MA, Columbia U., 1951, MA, cert. Russian Inst., 1955, PhM, 1959; DHL (hon.), Occidental Coll., LA, 2005. Reporter, radio news writer The NY Times, NYC, 1944-46; editor, interpreter, then sr. interpreter UN, NYC, 1946-59, from polit. officer to dir. and dep. to under sec.-gen. for spl. polit. affairs, 1959-84; polit. advisor to missions Congo, Cyprus, India and Pakistan, 1962-66; asst. sec.-gen. for spl. polit. affairs UN (office in charge peacekeeping forces which won Nobel Peace Prize, 1988), NYC, 1984-85; Stuart Chevalier prof. diplomacy and world affairs Occidental Coll., LA, 1985—2004. Dir. Occidental at-the-UN program, NYC, 1986-2002; US del. staff Dartmouth Soviet-Am. confs., 1961-94; assoc. seminar on problem of peace Columbia U., NYC; cons. UN dept. peacekeeping ops., 1992, 93; UN envoy to follow Russian elections, 1993; cons. Internat. Peace Acad., 1993-97. Author: The United Nations Reborn: Conflict Control in the Post-Cold War World, 1990; editorial adv. bd. Polit. Sci. Quar., NYC, 1973-89; contbr. articles and revs. to profl. jours. Recipient Townsend Harris medal CCNY, 1993; UN Inst. for Tng. and Rsch. sr. fellow, 1985-93. Mem. Coun. on Fgn. Rels., UN Assn.-USA. Democrat. Avocations: piano playing, skiing, sailing.

SHERRY, LEE FRANCIS, literature and language professor; b. Marietta, Ohio, Aug. 22, 1954; s. Frank John Sherry and Sophia Anne Tomascin; m. Barbara Robin Millman, Oct. 10, 1992. PhD, Columbia U., NYC, 1991. Adj. asst. prof. Drew U., Madison, NJ, 2005—; chair Latin dept. Buckley Sch., NYC, 2006—. Faculty cons. Latin AP ETS, Princeton, NJ, 2000—. Contbr. articles to profl. jour. Mem.: NY Classical Club, Phi Beta Kappa. Home: 23 North St Summit NJ 07901 Office: Buckley Sch 113 E 73rd St New York NY 10021 Business E-Mail: lsherry@buckleyschool.org.

SHERRY, MARK DOMINIC, educator, researcher; b. Melbourne, Australia, July 3, 1966; s. William Peter and Lorna Grace Sherry. BA in Govt. with honors, U. Queensland, 1987, MA, 1995, PhD, 2002. Post doctoral fellow Oreg. Health and Sciences U., Portland, 2002, U. Calif., Berkeley, 2002—03, U. Ill., Chgo., 2003—04; asst. prof. U. Toledo, 2004—; keynote spkr. 2nd Internat. Conf. Alcohol Induced Brain Injury, Melbourne, Victoria, Australia, 2009. Endowed chair in disability studies U. Toledo, 2004—06; post doctoral fellow in disability studies U. Calif., Berkeley, 2003. Keynote spkr., Disabled People's Assembley of New Zealand, Auckland, 2000; adv. inaugural keynote spkr. Nat. Alliance Young People in Nursing Homes, Melbourne, Victoria, Australia, 2005; pres. Brain Injury Action Group, Brisbane, Queensland, Australia, 1998—2002; bd. mem. Brain Injury Assn. Ohio, Columbus, Ohio, 2004—07; dir. Epilepsy Ctr., Toledo, 2004—06. Recipient New Frontiers award, Brain Injury Assn. Ohio, 2004; grantee, Nat. Inst. Disability Rsch. and Rehab., 2004; fellow, 2003, Germand Academic Exch. Svc. and The Einstein Found., 2004. Achievements include research in disability hate crimes; on brain injury. Office: U Toledo 2801 W Bancroft Toledo OH 43606 Office Fax: 419-530-8406; Home Fax: 419-530-8406. Personal E-mail: markdsherry@yahoo.com. Business E-Mail: mark.sherry@utoledo.edu.

SHERRY, PAUL HENRY, minister, religious organization administrator; b. Tamaqua, Pa., Dec. 25, 1933; s. Paul Edward and Mary Elizabeth (Stein) Sherry; m. Mary Louise Thornburg, June 4, 1957; children: Mary Elizabeth, Paul David. BA, Franklin and Marshall Coll., 1955; ThM, Union Theol. Sem., NYC, 1958, PhD, 1969; D (hon.), Ursinus Coll., 1981, Elmhurst Coll., 1990, Defiance Coll., 1991, Lakeland Coll., Sheboygan, Wis., 1991, Ref. Theol. Acad., Debrecen, Hungary, 1994, United Theol. Sem. Twin Cities, 1995, Eden Theol. Sem., St. Louis, 2000, Chgo. Theol. Sem., 2000. Ordained to ministry United Ch. Christ, 1958. Pastor St. Matthew United Ch. of Christ, Kenhorst, Pa., 1958—61, Com. United Ch. of Christ, Hasbrouck Heights, NJ, 1961—65; mem. staff United Ch. Bd. Homeland Ministry, NYC, 1965—82; exec. dir. Com. Renewal Soc., Chgo., 1983—89; pres. United Ch. of Christ, Cleve., 1989—99, pub. policy cons., 2000—02. Mem. gen. bd. Nat. Coun. Chs., NYC, 1989—99, coord. anti-poverty prog.; cons. Ctr. for Cmty. Change, 2001—05; mem. ctrl. com. World Coun. Chs., 1990—99; del. 8th Assembly, Harare, Zimbabwe, 1998, 7th Assembly, Canberra, Australia, 1991; Coord. NCC Anti Poverty Program, 2003—07. Co-author: A Just Minimum Wage, 2005; editor: The Riverside Preachers, Jour. Current Social Issues, 1968—80; contbr. articles to religious jours.; host (weekly progs. local sta.), 1974—78, (weekly programs local sta.), 1984—85, 1993—97, lect. (Union Theo. Seminar) NYC, 2008. Exec. dir. Let Justice Roll, 2009—; bd. dirs. Nat. Interfaith Com. Worker Justice, 2000—. Democrat. Mem. United Ch. Of Christ. Avocations: reading, hiking, cultural events. Home: 12700 Lake Ave # 1612 Lakewood OH 44107 Home Phone: 216-712-4457; Office Phone: 216-712-4457. Personal E-mail: psher973@aol.com.

SHERRY, THOMAS WARREN, ecologist; b. White Plains, NY, Mar. 26, 1951; AB, Dartmouth Coll., 1973, AM, 1975; PhD, UCLA, 1982. Rsch. assoc. Dartmouth Coll., Hanover, N.H., 1981-88, vis. asst. prof. tropical and avian ecology, 1984-88; asst. prof. avian ecology Tulane U., New Orleans, 1989—. Bd. dirs. Orgn. for Tropical Studies, Durham, N.C. Mem. Am. Ornithologists Union. Office: Tulane U 400 Boggshall New Orleans LA 70118 Office Phone: 504-862-8296. Business E-Mail: tsherry@tulane.edu.

SHERTZ, LAURIE, lawyer; BA, U. Wash., 1992; JD, Seattle U., 1995. Bar: Wash. 1995, Oreg. 1996, U.S. Dist. Ct. (we. dist.) Wash. 1997, U.S. Dist. Ct. Oreg. 2001. Prosecutor, rule 9 legal intern Bremerton (Wash.) City Attorney's Office, 1994—95; criminal appellate atty. Nielsen & Acosta, Seattle, 1995—96; staff atty., sr. staff atty. Met. Pub. Defenders, Hillsboro, Oreg., 1996—2001; pvt. practice Portland, Oreg., 2001—03. Spkr. in field. Co-editor: Major Crimes Manual; editor: OCDLA Criminal Law Formbook. Mem.: Reid Inst., Multnomah County Bar Assn., Oreg. Criminal Def. Lawyers Assn. (mem. edn. com. 1998—2004, chair edn. com. 2004—06), Nat. Assn. Criminal Def. Lawyers. Office: 121 SW Salmon 11th Fl Portland OR 97204 Office Fax: 503-296-5669. Business E-Mail: laurie@lshertzlaw.com.

SHERTZER, BRUCE ELDON, education educator; b. Bloomfield, Ind., Jan. 11, 1928; s. Edwin Franklin and Lois Belle S.; m. Carol Mae Rice, Nov. 24, 1948; children: Sarah Ann, Mark Eldon. BS, Ind. U., Bloomington, 1952, MS, 1953, EdD, 1958. Tchr., counselor Martinsville H.S., Ind., 1952-56; dir. div. guidance Ind. Dept. Pub. Instrn., 1956-58; assoc. dir. project guidance of superior students North Ctrl. Assn. Coll. and Secondary Sch., 1958-60; asst. prof. Purdue U., 1960—, assoc. prof., 1962-65, prof., 1965-95, head dept. ednl. studies, 1989-95, prof. emeritus of counseling, 1995—. Vis. prof. ednl. psychology U. Hawaii, 1967; Fulbright sr. lectr., Reading, Eng., 1967-68; vis. prof. U. So. Calif. Overseas Grad. Program, 1975, 82; chmn. Nat. Adv. Council for Career Edn., 1976 Author: Career Exploration and Planning 1973, 2d edit., 1976, Fundamentals of Counseling, 3d edit., 1980, Fundamentals of Guidance, 4th edit., 1981, Individual Appraisal, 1979, Career Planning, 3d edit., 1985, also articles. Chmn. bd. trustees Found. Am. Assn. of Counseling and Devel., 1986-87. With AUS, 1946-47. Mem. Am. Counseling Assn. (pres. 1973-74, Disting. Profl. Svc. award 1986). Home: 1620 Western Dr West Lafayette IN 47906-2236 Office: Beering Hall Purdue University West Lafayette IN 47907 Home Phone: 765-463-6837.

SHERVA, DENNIS G., retired investment company executive; b. Mpls., Dec. 3, 1942; s. Garfield Theodore and Dorothy Genevive (Oberlander) S.; m. Cathleen Marybeth Tischer, Oct. 15, 1965 (dec. July 31, 2004). BA, U. Minn., 1964; MA, Wayne State U., 1965. Chartered fin. analyst. Fin. analyst 1st Nat. Bank, Mpls., 1965-67; fin. analyst Honeywell, Inc., Mpls., 1967; v.p. Smith, Barney & Co., NYC, 1967-71, Baker, Weeks & Co., NYC, 1971-77; mng. dir. Morgan Stanley & Co., Inc., NYC, 1977—2000. Bd. dirs. Morgan Stanley Ventures, San Francisco, Morgan Stanley Venture Capital, N.Y.C., Morgan Stanley Asset Mgmt. Inc., N.Y.C. Recipient All-Am. Research Team 1st place award Instl. Investor Mag., 1979, 81, 83, 84, 85, 87 Mem.: Nat. Assn. Securities Dealers (instl. com. 1985—90), PGA West Club, Torrington Country Club. Home: 42 Old South Rd PO Box 30 Litchfield CT 06759-0030 Home (Winter): 80715 Weiskopf Way La Quinta CA 92253

SHERWIN, EMILY, law educator; b. Paris, July 23, 1955; d. Thomas and Lillian Badtram Sherwin; m. Kevin M. Clermont, Apr. 25, 2001; children: Adrienne Shane Clermont, Jian Louise Clermont. BA, Lake Forest Coll., Ill., 1977; JD, Boston U., 1981. Prof. U. San Diego Sch. Law, 1990—2003, Cornell Law Sch., Ithaca, NY, 2003—. Adv. com. Am. Law Inst. Restatement 3rd Restitution and Unjust Enrichment, Phila, 1998—. Co-author (with Larry Alexander): (book) The Rule of Rules: Morality, Rules, and the Dilemmas of Law, 2001, Demystifying Legal Reasoning, 2008. Office: Cornell Law Sch Myron Taylor Hall Ithaca NY 14850 Business E-Mail: els36@cornell.edu.

SHERWIN, JAMES TERRY, lawyer; b. NYC, Oct. 25, 1933; s. Oscar and Stella (Zins) S.; m. Judith Johnson, June 21, 1955 (div. Apr. 1984); children: Miranda, Alison, Galen; m. Hiroko Inouye, June 15, 1985. BA, Columbia U., 1953, LLB (Stone scholar), 1956. Bar: N.Y. 1956, U.S. Supreme Ct. 1963. Assoc. Kaye, Scholer, Fierman, Hays & Handler, NYC, 1957-60; with GAF Corp., NYC, 1960-83, 84-90, assoc. counsel, gen. mgr. European ops., 1969-71, group v.p. photography, 1971-74, exec. v.p. fin. and adminstrn., legal and investment svcs., 1974-83, vice chmn., chief adminstrv. officer Wayne, NJ, 1984-90; exec. v.p., CFO Triangle Industries, Inc., 1983-84, Hunter-Douglas N.V., 1991—99, bd. dirs., 1999—. Bd. dirs. Internat. Rescue Com., chmn. exec. com., v.p. to 1990-; mem. coun. U. Bath, 2001-07. Lt. comdr. USCGR, 1956-64. U.S. intercollegiate chess champion, 1951-53, NY State champion, 1951, U.S. speed champion, 1956-57, 59-60, internat. master. Am. Chess Found. (pres., bd. dirs. to 1990), Marshall (NY) Chess Club (pres. 1967-69, gov. to 1990), Phi Beta Kappa, Hon. LLD (U. Bath 2007). Home: The Chase Winsley Nr Bradford BA15 2LX England Office Phone: 44 1225 722113. Business E-Mail: jamestsherwin@btconnect.com.

SHERWOOD, ARTHUR LAWRENCE, lawyer; b. LA, Jan. 25, 1943; s. Allen Joseph and Edith S. Sherwood; m. Frances Merele, May 1, 1970; children: David, Chet. BA magna cum laude, U. Calif., Berkeley, 1964; MS, U. Chgo., 1965; JD cum laude, Harvard U., 1968. Bar: Calif. 1969, U.S. Dist. Ct. (cen. dist.) Calif. 1968, U.S. Dist. Ct. (no. dist.) Calif. 1971, Calif. 1971, U.S. Dist. Ct. (so. and ea. dists.) Calif. 1973, U.S. Ct. Appeals (9th cir.) 1973, U.S. Ct. Appeals (D.C. cir.) 1991, U.S. Supreme Ct. 1980. Instr. UCLA Law Sch., 1968—69; assoc. Gibson, Dunn & Crutcher, LA, 1968—75, ptnr., 1975—98, of counsel, 1998—. Judge pro tem L.A. Mcpl. and Superior Ct., 1980—98; instr. law UCLA, 1968—69; arbitrator N.Y. Stock Exch., Nat. Futures Assn. Co-author: Civil Procedure During Trial, 1995, Civil Procedure Before Trial, 1990; contbr. articles to profl. jours. Chmn. East Asian Art Coun., L.A. County Mus. Art, 1992—97, 2005—06. NASA fellow, U. Chgo., 1964—65. Master: Am. Contract Bridge League (life); mem.: Calif. Bar Assn., Phi Beta Kappa. Republican. Avocations: art, history. Office: 10430 Wilshire Blvd Unit 502 Los Angeles CA 90024

SHERWOOD, GLORIA N., graphics designer, genealogist, small business owner; b. Winfield, Kans. d. Edwin E. Schroeder and Anna Y. McClure; stepmother Vivian J. Schroeder; children: Christina Knueven, J.E. Jurey, Jeannette Thornhill. B CMT cert., foster parent cert. Pvt. home health care nurse, Eufaula, Okla., 1996—2006; ret.; bus. owner Angelic Prints, Inc. Author: The Poetic Works of Gloria Sherwood Book 1 vol. 1, 2000, Poetic Work Book 1, vol. 2, 2002, Just Be 2000, Remember Me, 1999, Spiritual Wings, 2001, Awaited Healing, 2001; visual artist: New Trails, 1998, Deep Is the Soul, 2000, Out of Bondage, 2001. Recipient Award of Excellence in Christian Web sites Joyful Mom's Web site. Mem. NAFE, Nat. Home Gardening Club, Nat. Arbor Day Found., Angelwings, Nat. Audubon Soc., Nat. Wildlife Fedn., World Wildlife Fedn., Enfaula Arts Coun. Democrat. Avocations: performing arts, gardening, playing guitar, writing music, crafts.

SHERWOOD, (KAREN) KEHELA, broadcast executive; Grad., UCLA. Asst. prodr. to Brian Grazer Imagine Entertainment, 1986—87, story editor, 1987, dir. devel., v.p., sr. v.p., pres. prodn., co-chair Imagine Films, 1997—. Named one of The 100 Most Powerful Women in Entertainment, Hollywood Reporter, 2006, 2007. Mailing: Imagine Entertainment 7th Floor 9465 Wilshire Blvd Beverly Hills CA 90212

SHERWOOD, KENNETH W., language educator; b. Melrose, Mass., May 25, 1969; s. Kenneth William and Angela Anne Sherwood; m. Dawn M. Smith-Sherwood, June 20, 1992; children: Clara Alba, Cecilia Marisol. BA, Bates Coll., Lewiston, Maine, 1991; MA, SUNY, Buffalo, 1995, PhD, 2000. Asst. prof. English U. Tex. Permian Basin, Odessa, 2001—03, Ind. U. Pa., 2003—; co-director Ctr. Digital Humanities and Culture, 2009. Chair Indikids, Ind., 2004—. Office: Ind Univ Pa Dept English Leonard Hall Indiana PA 15705

SHERWOOD, MICHAEL S., diversified financial services company executive; Investment mgmt. positions in fixed income divsn. The Goldman Sachs Group, Inc., London, 1986—94, ptnr., 1994—, co-head capital markets group Americas NYC, head corp. bond trading, co-head emerging markets debt, head fixed income, currency & commodities divsn. London, 2001—03, co-head global securities, 2003—08, vice-chmn., 2008—, co-CEO Goldman Sachs Internat. London, 2005—. Office: Goldman Sachs Internat Peterborough Ct 133 Fleet St EC4A 2BB London England*

SHERWOOD, MIDGE, author; b. Ironton, Ohio; d. Roy and Addie (Brace) Winters; m. Jack E. Sherwood, Jan. 19, 1946; children: Margaret Sherwood Simms, Melanie Sherwood. BJ, U. Mo., 1938. Women's editor Ironton Daily Tribune, 1933-38; city editor Ironton Daily News, 1938-40; asst. mgr. West coast news bur. TWA, Los Angeles, 1940-42; pub. relations dir. Western Air Lines, 1942-45; aviation columnist, corr. Skyways, So. Flight, 1945-48; owner, operator Midge Winters Agy., 1945-48; assoc. editor Matrix Mag., Women in Communications, 1950-55; book reviewer LA Times, 1963, Western Hist. Quarterly; free-lance writer, 1958—; columnist Pasadena Star-News, Calif., 1987; lectr. on Gen. George Smith Patton and pioneers of Western frontier. Author: And How it Grew, 1965; San Marino Ranch to City, 1977; Days of Vintage, Years of Vision, Vol. 1, 1982, Vol. II, 1987, Fremont: Eagle of the West, 2002, Days of Vintage, Years of Vision, vol. III, 2006, Western Journal Collection (1900-1995), Western Journal Collection (1995-2000); author (plays): Peace at Last; editor Western Jour.; contbr. columns newspapers. Chmn. Hertrich Meml., 1967; Paul Harris fellow Rotary; recipient Commendation award Gov. Pete Wilson, Calif., 1996. Mem. Soc. Fellows of Huntington Library, 1967; founder, archivist San Marino Hist. Soc. Recipient double award Conf. Calif. Hist. Socs., 1987; named Outstanding Citzen of San Marino, 1988, named one of the top 100 writers of 20 by the Internat. Biographical Ctr., Cambridge, Englnd, chmn. Annual Fremont's Day, 2005. Mem. Huntington Westerners (founder), Live Poet's Soc. Huntington Libr. (founder), Westerners Internat. (bd. dirs.), Phi Mu. Home: PO Box 80241 San Marino CA 91118

SHERWOOD, PETER MILES ANSON, chemistry educator; b. London, July 12, 1945; came to U.S., 1985; s. Denis William and Merlyn E. (Green) S.; m. Gillian Thomson Taylor, Dec. 18, 1982. BSc, St. Andrews U., Scotland, 1967; MA, PhD, Cambridge U., Eng., 1970, ScD, 1995. Fellow Downing Coll., Cambridge U., 1970-72; lectr. dept. chemistry U. Newcastle upon Tyne, Eng., 1972-84, sr. lectr., 1984-85; program officer chemistry div. NSF, Washington, 1990-91; assoc. prof. chemistry Kans. State U., Manhattan, 1985-90, prof., 1991-97, univ. disting. prof., head chemistry, 1997—2004; dean Coll. Arts & Scis., 2004—; regents prof. physics Okla. State U., 2004—. Cons. W.R. Grace Co., 1986, E.I. Du Pont de Nemours & Co., 1988-90. Author: Vibrational Spectroscopy of Solids, 1972; editor: Critical Reviews in Surface Chemistry; also numerous articles. Fellow Salter's Co., London, 1970-72. Fellow Royal Soc. Chemistry, Inst. of Physics, Camridge Philos. Soc., AVS Sci. Tech. Soc.; mem. Am. Chem. Soc., Soc. Applied Spectroscopy, Materials Rsch. Soc., Electrochem. Soc., Sigma Xi. Episcopalian. Avocations: church architecture, hill walking, cartography. Home: 2601 Austin Ct Stillwater OK 74074-1044 Office: Okla State Univ Dean Office 201 Life Scis East Stillwater OK 74078-3015 Office Phone: 405-744-5663. Business E-Mail: peter.sherwood@okstate.edu.

SHERWOOD, ROBERT PETERSEN, retired social sciences educator; b. Black Diamond, Wash., May 17, 1932; s. James Brazier and Zina (Petersen) S.; m. Merlene Burningham, Nov. 21, 1951; children: Robert Lawrence, Richard William, Rolene, RaNae. BS, U. Utah, 1956, MS, 1957; EdD, U. Calif., Berkeley, 1965. Tchr. Arden-Carmichael Sch. Dist., Carmichael, Calif., 1957-59, vice prin. jr. high, 1960-61, prin. jr. high, 1962-65; v.p., prin. San Juan Unified Sch. Dist., Sacramento, 1966-70; assoc. prof. Calif. State U., Sacramento, 1966-71; dir. outreach progs. Am. River Coll., Sacramento, 1971-73, acting assoc. dean of instrn., 1973-74, prof. sociology, 1970-92, chmn. sociology/anthropology dept., 1980-86; ret., 1992. Pres. acad. senate Am. River Coll., 1990-91. With USN, 1953-55. Recipient Merit Recognition award, Boy Scouts Am., 1989. Mem. NEA, Calif. Tchrs. Assn., Faculty Assn. Calif. Community Colls., Western Assn. Schs. and Colls., Calif. Fedn. Coll. Profs., Phi Delta Kappa (life). Mem. Lds Ch. Avocations: reading, writing, woodworking, travel. Home: 4053 Esperanza Dr Sacramento CA 95864-3069

SHERZER, HARVEY GERALD, lawyer; b. Phila., May 19, 1944; s. Leon and Rose (Levin) S.; m. Susan Bell, Mar. 28, 1971; children: Sheri Ann, David Lloyd. BA, Temple U., 1965; JD with honors, George Washington U., 1968. Bar: DC 1970, U.S. Ct. Appeals (DC cir.) 1970, U.S. Ct. Fed. Claims 1970, U.S. Ct. Appeals (fed. cir.) 1970, U.S. Supreme Ct. 1974. Law clk. to trial judges U.S. Ct. Fed. Claims, Washington, 1968-69; law clk. to chief judge U.S. Ct. Appeals for Fed. Cir., Washington, 1969-70; assoc. Sellers, Conner & Cuneo, Washington, 1970-75, ptnr., 1975-80, McKenna, Conner & Cuneo, Washington, 1980-82, Pettit & Martin, Washington, 1982-85, Howrey & Simon, Washington, 1985-2000, Howrey Simon Arnold & White, Washington, 2000—01, Greenberg Traurig, McLean, Va., 2001—03, Dickstein Shapiro LLP, Washington, 2003—. Adv. bd. The Govt. Contractor, 1996-99. Author: (with others) A Complete Guide to the Department of Defense Voluntary Disclosure Program, 1996; contbr. articles to profl. jours. Office: Dickstein Shapiro 1825 Eye St NW Washington DC 20006 Home Phone: 301-469-5464; Office Phone: 202-420-4745. Business E-Mail: sherzerh@dicksteinshapiro.com.

SHESTACK, ALAN, retired museum administrator; b. NYC, June 23, 1938; s. David and Sylvia P. (Saffran) S.; m. Nancy Jane Davidson, Sept. 24, 1967. BA, Wesleyan U., 1961, DFA (hon.), 1978; MA, Harvard U., 1963. Mus. curator graphic art Nat. Gallery Art, Washington, 1965-67; assoc. curator prints and drawings Yale Art Gallery, New Haven, 1967-68, curator prints and drawings, 1968-71, dir., 1971-85; adj. prof. history of art Yale U., 1971-85; dir. Mpls. Inst. Art, 1985-87, Boston Mus. Fine Arts, 1987-93; dep. dir. and chief curator Nat. Gallery of Art, Washington, 1994—2008. Mem. adv. com. Art Mus., Princeton, 1972-75; mem. com. prints and illustrated books Mus. Modern Art, NYC, 1972-2007; mem. mus. panel Nat. Endowment for the Arts, 1974-77; mem. Fed. Arts and Artifacts Indemnification Panel, 1979-83; mem. vis. com. Harvard U. Art Mus., 1990-95, Davis Mus. Wellesley Coll., 1997—. Author: Fifteenth Century Engravings of Northern Europe, 1967, The Engravings of Martin Schongauer, 1968, Master LCZ and Master WB, 1971, Exhibitions Organized and Catalogued: Master E.S, 1967, The Danube School, 1969, Hans Baldung Grien, Prints and Drawings, 1981, (exhbn. catalog) Art for the Nation, 2000; contbr. articles to profl. jours. Woodrow Wilson fellow Harvard U., 1963, David E. Finley fellow, 1963-65. Mem. Print Coun. Am. (bd. dirs., v.p. 1970-71), Coll. Art Assn. (bd. dirs. 1972-76), Am. Assn. Mus., Am. Fedn. Arts (trustee 1981-94), Alpha Delta Phi, Phi Beta Kappa. Home Phone: 202-362-3034. Personal E-mail: njandas@comcast.net.

SHESTACK, JEROME JOSEPH, lawyer; b. Atlantic City, Feb. 11, 1925; s. Isidore and Olga (Shankman) Shestack; m. Marciarose Schleifer, Jan. 28, 1951; children: Jonathan Michael, Jennifer. AB, U. Pa., 1944; LLB, Harvard U., 1949; LLD (hon.), Dickinson Coll. Law, 1997, Stetson Sch. of Law, 1998, Whittier Coll. Law, 1998. Bar: Ill. 1950, Pa. 1952. Tchg. fellow Northwestern U. Law Sch., Chgo., 1949—50; asst. prof. law, faculty editor La. State Law Sch., Baton Rouge, 1950—52; dep. city solicitor City of Phila., 1952, 1st dep. solicitor, 1952—55; ptnr. Schnader, Harrison, Segal & Lewis, Phila. and Washington CD, 1956—91, 2009—, Wolf, Block, Schorr & Solis-Cohen, Phila., 1991—2008. Adj. prof. law U. Pa., 1956; U.S. amb. to UN Human Rights Commn., 1979—80; U.S. del. to ECOSOC, UN, 1980; sr. U.S. del. to Helsinki Accords Conf., 1979—80; mem. U.S. Commn. on Improving Effectiveness of UN, 1989—; chmn. Internat. League Human Rights, 1973—94, hon. chmn., 1994—; U.S. del. to CSCE Conf., Moscow, 1991; founder, chmn. Lawyers Com. Internat. Human Rights, 1978—80, Jacob Blaustein Inst. Human Rights, 1988—92; mem. nat. adv. com. legal svcs. OEO, 1965—72; bd. dirs., exec. com. Lawyers Com. Civil Rights; mem. coun. Holocaust Mus., 1999—2004, exec. com., chair com. on conscience. Editor (with others): (monographs) Rights of Americans, 1971, Human Rights, 1979, International Human Rights, 1985, Bill of Rights: A Bicentennial View, 1991, Understanding Human Rights, 1992, Thomas Jefferson: Lawyer, 1993, Francis Scott Key, 1994, Abraham Lincoln, Circuit Lawyer, 1994, The Holocaust, 1997, Moral Foundations of Human Rights, 1997, The Philosophy of Human Rights, 1997, W.B. Yeats, Poet of Passionate Intensity, 1997, Corporate Social Responsibility, 2004. Mem. exec. com. Nat. Legal Aid and Defender Assn., 1970—80; trustee Eleanor and Franklin Roosevelt Inst., 1986—; bd. govs. Tel Aviv U., 1983—, Hebrew U., 1969—; chmn. bd. dirs. Am. Poetry Ctr., 1976—91; trustee Free Libr. Phila., vice chmn., 1989—96; v.p. Am. Jewish Com., 1984—89. With USNR, 1943—46. Fellow, U. Pa. Law Sch., 1980; Rubin fellow, Columbia U. Law Sch., 1984. Mem.: ABA (ho. of dels. 1971—73, 1977—, jud. com. 1985—90, bd. govs. 1992—95, exec. com. 1994—95, pres.-elect 1996, pres. 1997—98, pres. Am. Law Inst.-ABA 1997—98, bd. dirs. 1999—2003, chair Ctr. Human Rights 2003—05, co-chair, Gold medal), Gruber Found. (Justice award), Nat. Conf. Bar Found. (bd. dirs. 1998—, pres. 2004), Internat. Assn. Jewish Lawyers and Jurists (Am. Soc. pres. 2000—02), Am. Acad. Appellate Lawyers, Am. Coll. Trial Lawyers, Am. Arbitration Assn. (Highest ABA medal 2006), Am. Law Inst., Am. Soc. Internat. Law (exec. com. 1993—, internat. com. jurists exec. com. 1998—2001, commr. 1999—), Internat. Acad. Trial Lawyers, Internat. Bar Assn. (chmn. com. on human rights 1990—94, chmn. com. profl. ethics 2000—04), Order of Coif. Home: Parkway House 2201 Pennsylvania Ave Philadelphia PA 19130-3513 Office: Schnader Harrison Segal & Lewis LLP 1600 Market St Ste 3600 Philadelphia PA 19103 Office Phone: 215-751-2290. Business E-Mail: j.shestack@schnader.com.

SHETH, KEVIN NAVIN, neurologist, researcher; b. Richmond, Va., Jan. 15, 1979; s. Navin Dalichand and Sucheta Navin Sheth; m. Sangini Shah, Nov. 29, 2008. BA, Johns Hopkins U., Balt., 1999; MD, U. Pa. Sch. Medicine, Phila., 2003. Diplomate in neurology Am. Bd. Psychiatry & Neurology, 2008. Fellow Mass. Gen. Hosp., Boston, 2007—; chief academic officer Med. Plexus, Boston, 2008—. Chief resident Harvard Combined Neurology Program, Boston, 2006—07. Intern US Senate, Richmond, 1999. Rsch. grant, AMA, 2006. Mem.: Am. Acad. Neurology, Neuro-Critical Care Soc. Achievements include research in non-invasive intracranial pressure monitoring. Avocations: travel, sports, reading, politics. Office: Mass Gen Hosp 55 Fruit St Blake 12 Neuro ICU Boston MA 02114 Personal E-mail: kshethmd@gmail.com.

SHETTY, JAY K., research and development company executive, researcher; s. Narayana K. and Durgamma K. Shetty; m. Shashikala J. Hegde, May 15, 1972; children: Sujith J., Amith J. PhD, Mysore U., India, 1976. Rsch. fellow, v.p. Genencor-Danisco, Palo Alto, Calif., 1966—; v.p., r & d Solvay Enzymes, Elkhart, Ind., 1988—96. Recipient Rsch. Excellence award, Fuel Ethanol Mag., 2008; named Top 100, R&D Award Com., 2005. Home: 4806 Braxton Place Pleasanton CA 94566 Office: Genencor-Danisco 925 Page Mill Road Palo Alto CA 94304 Personal E-mail: ajshetty@aol.com. E-mail: jay.shetty@danisco.com.

SHETTY, KAUP RAJMOHAN, endocrinologist, educator; came to U.S., 1966; s. Muddanna and Girija M. Shetty; m. Vasanthi R. Shetty; children: Sandeep, Suparna. MB BChir, Mysore Med. Coll., Karnataka, 1965. Diplomate Am. Bd. Internal Medicine, cert. in internal medicine, endocrinology and metabolism, geriatric medicine. Resident in internal medicine VA Med. Ctr., Chgo. and Milw., 1967-70; fellow in endocrinology and metabolism Med. Coll. Wis. and Affiliated Hosps., Milw., 1970-72, attending physician in endocrinology and metabolism, 1972—; attending physician in geriatrics and gerontology VA Med. Coll., Milw., 1991—; assoc. prof. medicine Med. Coll. Wis., Milw., 1991-95, prof. medicine, 1995-2000, prof. medicine emeritus, 2000—. Contbr. articles to profl. jours., chapters to books. Fellow ACP, Royal Coll. Physicians Can., Am. Coll. Endocrinology; mem. Endocrine Soc., N.Y. Acad. Scis. Achievements include research in hormones and aging, post-polio syndrome, metabolic accompaniments of inactivity. Avocation: tennis. Office: VA Med Ctr 5000 W National Ave Milwaukee WI 53295-0001

SHEVACH, ETHAN MENAHEM, physician; b. Bklyn., Mass., Oct. 16, 1943; s. Benjamin Jacques and Anne (Pollack) S.; m. Ruth Schneider, May 30, 1967; children: Matthew, Seth. AB, Boston U., Mass., 1963, MD, 1967. Diplomate Am. Bd. Internat. Medicine, Am. Bd. Allergy/Immunology. Intern, resident medicine Bronx Mcpl. Hosp. Ctr., NY, 1967—69; clin. assoc. Lab Clin. Investigation, NIAID, Bethesda, Md., 1969—72; sr. investigator Lab Immunology, NIAID, Bethesda, 1973—87, sect. chief, 1987—; capt. US Pub. Health Svc., Bethesda, Md., 1973—98. Editor: (book) Current Protocols in Immunology. Capt. USPHS, 1973-98. Recipient Pub. Health Svc. Commendation medal 1978, Pub. Health Svc. Meritorious Svc. medal 1986, Disting. Svc. medal 1993, William B. Coly award for Disting. Rsch. in basic and Tumor Immunology, 2004. Mem.: Assn. Am. Physicians, Am. Soc. Clin. Investigation, Am. Assn. Immunologists. Office: Nat Insts Health Blg 10 Rm 11N315 Bethesda MD 20892 Office Fax: 301-496-0222. Business E-Mail: eshevach@niaid.nih.gov.

SHEVCHUK, NIKOLAI ALEXANDROVICH, biologist; b. Novosibirsk, Russia, Nov. 15, 1973; s. Zinaida Ivanovna Dimitrenko and Alexander Alexandrovich Shevchuk. MS (equivalent) in biology, molecular biology, Novosibirsk State U., 1999; PhD in molecular and cellular oncology, George Wash. U., 2006. Rsch. asst. Novosibirsk Inst. Bioorganic Chemistry, 1997—99, Children's Rsch. Inst., Washington, 2001—06; postdoc. fellow Va. Commonwealth U., Richmond, 2006—07. Contbr. scientific papers to profl. jour. Fellow Presdl. Merit Fellowship, George Wash. U., 1999—2001; Children's Nat. Med. Ctr. Fellowship, 2001—06. Achievements include research in a biological explanation of known positive effects on mood and fatigue, and also immunostimulatory effect of repeated cooling, tranquilizing effect of hot hydrotherapy; a method for creation of long DNA molecules from several fragments using polymerase chain reaction. Avocations: swimming, tennis, reading.

SHEWACH, DONNA S., pharmacologist, educator; PhD, U. Tex., Houston, 1981. Assoc. dir. Upjohn Ctr. Clin. Pharmacology, Ann Arbor, Mich., 1999—; prof. pharmacology U. Mich. Med. Sch., Ann Arbor, 2001—. Office: Univ Mich Med Ctr 1150 W Med Ctr Dr Ann Arbor MI 48109-5633

SHEWMAKER, KENNETH EARL, history professor; b. LA, June 26, 1936; s. James Virgil and Jeanette M. (Greenberg) Shewmaker; m. Elisabeth L. Spalteholz, June 12, 1960; children: Richard Glenn, Nancy Jeanette. BS, Concordia Tchrs. Coll., 1960; MA, U. Calif., Berkeley, 1961; PhD, Northwestern U., 1966. Instr. Northwestern U., Evanston, Ill., 1965-66; asst. prof. Coll. William and Mary, Williamsburg, Va., 1966-67; from asst. prof. to assoc. prof. Dartmouth Coll., Hanover, NH, 1967-78, prof. history, 1978—2005, acting chair dept. history, 1985-86, chmn. dept. history, 1986-89, prof. emeritus, 2005—. Author: Americans and Chinese Communists, 1927-45: A Persuading Encounter, 1971 (Stuart L. Bernath prize, 1972); editor: Papers of Daniel Webster, Diplomatic Papers, Vol. 1, 1841-1843, 1983, Vol. 2, 1850-1852, 1987, Daniel Webster, The Completest Man, 1990; contbr. articles to profl. jours. Recipient Disting. Tchg. awards, Dartmouth Coll., 1986, 1996, 2004. Mem.: Soc. Historians Am. Fgn. Rels., N.H. Hist. Soc. Lutheran. Avocations: fly fishing, fly tying. Office: Dept History Dartmouth Coll Hanover NH 03755 Business E-Mail: shewmaker@dartmouth.edu.

SHEWRY, SANDRA, telehealth company executive; BS, Univ. Calif., Santa Cruz; MS, MPH, Univ. Calif., Berkeley. Asst. sec. Calif. Health & Welfare Agency; exec. dir. Calif. Managed Risk Med. Ins. Bd.; dir. health Ctr. for Best Practices, Nat. Governors Assn.; dir. Calif. Dept. Health Svcs., Sacramento, 2004—07, Calif. Dept. Health Care Services, 2007—08; pres., CEO Calif. Ctr. Connected Health, 2008—. Mem. Commn. on High Performance Health Sys., Commonwealth Fund; bd. mem. Insure the Uninsured Project. Office: Calif Ctr Connected Health 3430 American River Dr Ste 100 Sacramento CA 95864 Office Phone: 916-488-8607. Office Fax: 916-484-7643.*

SHEY, JAMES, military officer; married. BEE, US Naval Acad., Annapolis, Md., 2003; MEE, U. Md., 2008; M in Engring. Mgmt., Old Dominion U., 2008. Officer USN, Annapolis, 1999—. Lt USN, 1999—2003, Annapolis. Home: 12 Phythian Rd Apt E Annapolis MD 21402

SHI, CHAO, research scientist; b. Beijing, Apr. 2, 1981; PhD, U. Calif., Santa Cruz, 2006. Rsch. asst. Peking U., Beijing, 2003—06, U. Calif., 2006—. Regent's fellowship, U. Calif., 2006. Achievements include patents for liquid core photonic crystal fiber biosensor using surface enhanced Raman scattering and methods for their use. Office: Univ Calif Santa Cruz 1156 High St Santa Cruz CA 95064 Business E-Mail: chaoshi@soe.ucsc.edu.

SHI, DAVID E., academic administrator, historian; s. Joseph and Evelyn Shi; m. Susan Thomson, June 1974; children: Jason, Jessica. BA magna cum laude, Furman U., 1973; MA, U. Va., 1975, PhD, 1976; HHD (hon.), Ctr. Coll., 2002. From asst. prof. to Frontis W. Johnston prof., chmn. history dept. Davidson Coll., 1976—93; v.p. acad. affairs Furman U., Greenville, SC, 1993—94, pres., 1994—. Bd. dirs. Nat. Comerce Fin. Corp., Memphis. Author: Facing Facts: Realism in American Thought and Culture 1850-1920, 1995, In Search of the Simple Life: American Voices, Past and Present, 1986, The Simple Life: Plain Living and High Thinking in American Culture, 1985 (Editors Choice award), Matthew Josephson, Bourgeois Bohemian, 1981; author: (with George Tindall) America: A Narrative History, 4th edit., 1996; contbr. articles to profl. jours. Bd. dirs. Urban League, Greenville. Capt. USAR. Recipient Presdl. Leadership award, James L. Knight Found., 1998, Presdl. award, John Templeton Found., 1999; grantee, NEH, 1980, 1986; fellow, Nat. Humanities Ctr., 1982—83, NEH, 1982—83, 1991—92, Huntington Libr., 1986—87; Andrew Mellon Faculty fellow, 1978, Travel grant, NEH, 1988. Mem.: Greenville C. of C. (bd. dirs.), Commerce Club (bd. dirs.), Omicron Delta Kappa, Phi Beta Kappa. Home: 1209 Roe Ford Rd Greenville SC 29617 Office: Furman U 3300 Poinsett Hwy Greenville SC 29613 Office Phone: 864-294-2100. Office Fax: 864-294-3939. E-mail: david.shi@furman.edu.*

SHI, DEXIU, laser and optics scientist; b. Huainan, People's Republic of China, June 8, 1946; came to U.S., 1986; d. Zhuansheng Shi and Qinging Li; m. Xiaozheng Xing, Jan. 11, 1971; children: Yihuai Xing, Yijiang Shi. BSME, Hefei Poly. U., People's Republic of China, 1967, MSME, 1968; MS in Biomed. Engring., Duke U., 1989, postgrad., 1989—. Engr. ShenYang (People's Republic of China) Machine Co., 1969-76; lectr., asst. prof. U. Sci. and Tech. of China, Hefei, 1977-85; researcher Duke U., Durham, N.C., 1986—, rsch. fellow, 1988—. Contbg. author: Physics Problems and Solutions III-Optics, 1986; contbr. articles to profl. jours. Mem. IEEE, Optical Soc. Am., Soc. Applied Spectroscopy, Nat. Soc. Profl. Engrs., Soc. Photo-Optical Instrumentation Engrs.

SHI, HONGJIAN, research scientist; BA in Math. Edn., Henan Normal U., 1984; MS in Math., Peking U., China, 1987; PhD in Math., Simon Fraser U., Can., 1997; MA in Elec. Engring., U. British Columbia, 2001; PhD in Elec. Engring., U. Louisville, Ky., 2007. Asst. prof. Nanjing U. Sci. and Tech., China, 1987—93; adj. asst. prof. U. Wis., Milw., 1998—99; rsch. asst. image processing lab., dept. elec. and computer engring. U. B.C., 1999—2000; sr. engr. Ward Labs., 2000—01; cons. Ward Labs. Vector 12 Reality Commerce, 2001—02; rsch. asst. computer vision and image processing lab., dept. elec. and computer engring. U. Louisville, 2002—05, rsch. assoc. divsn. radiology and imaging scis., Sch. Dentistry, 2004—06; rsch. scientist Imaging Scis. Internat. (subs. Danaher Corp.), Hatfield, Pa., 2006—. Contbr. articles to more than 30 jours. and conf. tech. publs. Mem.: Internat. Assn. Dental Maxillofacial and Radiology (Oral Presentation Appreciation award 2007). Achievements include research in image segmentation, registration, finite element modeling, jaw arch detection and panoramic image creation; creation of automatic panoramic image with superior quality from a stack of 2D slices for dental clinic use. Office: Imaging Scis Internat 1910 North Penn Rd Hatfield PA 19440 Office Phone: 215-997-0240. Personal E-mail: hongjian.shi@imagingsciences.com.

SHI, QIN, lawyer, technologist; m. Richard Bone. BSc in Biochemistry, Wuhan U., China, 1989; MSc in Math. and Computer Scis., Loyola U., Chgo., 1997; PhD in Molecular and Cellular Biology, Loyola U., Maywood, Ill., 1997; JD, Georgetown U. Law Ctr., Washington, 2002. Bar: Calif. 2003, D.C. 2004, U.S. Ct. Appeals (9th cir.), U.S. Ct. Appeals (D.C. circ.). Biotech. engr. Wuhan Biotech R&D Ctr., China; bioinformatics specialist Gene Logic, Montgomery County, Md., Foley & Lardner LLP, Washington; informatics sci. advisor Heller Ehrman LLP; attorney Fenwick & West LLP, Mountain View, Calif., Latham & Watkins LLP, Menlo Park, Howrey LLP, Palo Alto. Spkr. ann. meetings Intelligent Sys. Molecular Biology, 2000, 01; spkr. Congress Internat. Drug Discovery Sci. and Tech., China, 2006. Contbr. legal and bus. analysis, articles to profl. jours. and law revs. Mem.: IEEE, AAAS, ABA, Endocrine Soc., Internat. Soc. Computational Biology, Am.

Intellectual Property Law Assn. (spkr. winter conf. 2006). Avocations: hiking, bicycling, running, travel. Office: Howrey LLP 1950 Univ Ave Palo Alto CA 94303 Home: 944 Regent Dr Los Altos CA 94024-7034 Office Phone: 650-798-3522. Business E-Mail: shiq@howrey.com.

SHI, QUN, engineer; m. Yan Li. PhD, U. Pa., Phila., 1990. Engring. mgr. UTSTARCOM, Eslin, NJ, 2000—04; sr. staff engr. ITT, Clifton, NJ, 2004—. Mem.: IEEE (sr. mem. 2000). Home: 20 Paddock Dr Plainsboro NJ 08536 Office: ITT 77 River Rd Clifton NJ 07014 Personal E-mail: qshi_us@yahoo.com.

SHI, SONGTAO, dentist, educator; DDS, Peking U. Sch. Stomatology, Beijing, 1983, MS in Pediatric Dentistry, 1986; PhD in Craniofacial Biology, U. Southern Calif., 1994. Asst. prof. dept. pediatric dentistry Beijing Med. U., 1986—89; rsch. assoc. Doheny Eye Inst. U. Southern Calif., 1989—94; fellow in Skeletal Biology UCSF, 1994—97; pvt. practice S&S Best Dental Ctr., 1998—99; fellow in craniofacial & skeletal diseases NIDCR-NIH, 1999—2001, clinical fellow supr. craniofacial & skeletal diseases, 2002—03, section chief craniofacial & skeletal diseases, 2003—06; asst. prof. U. Southern Calif. Ctr. for Craniofacial Molecular Biology, 2006—08, assoc. prof., 2008—. Recipient Travel award, NIDCR-NIH, 2000. Office: University of Southern California School of Dentistry CSA 148 HSC 9062 Los Angeles CA 90033 Office Phone: 323-442-3038. Office Fax: 323-442-2981. E-mail: songtaos@usc.edu.*

SHI, TIANCHEN, research scientist; BS, Tsinghua U., Beijing, 2000; MS, Northeastern U., Boston, 2003, attending. Rsch. asst. Northeastern U., 2003—07; sr. imaging algorithm scientist Infraredx, Burlington, Mass., 2007—. Contbr. articles to profl. jours. Mem.: SPIE. Achievements include research in NIR cardiovascular imaging system; invention of multi-modality cardiovascular imaging system.

SHI, WEIBIN, medical educator; b. Caoxian, Shandong, China, Jan. 7, 1963; s. Nianlun Shi and Jinrong Meng; m. Yuhua Li; children: Lena Yu, Lisa Jun. PhD, McGill U., Montreal, Can., 1997. Assoc. prof. U. Va., Charlottesville, 2001—. Contbr. chapters to books. Grantee, RSNA, 2003, NIH, 2003—, AHA Mid-Atlantic, 2005; Victoria Hosp. fellowship, McGill U., 1994—96. Mem.: Am. Heart Assn., Am. Genetics Soc., Am. Physiol. Soc. Achievements include research in heart attack, stroke, aneurysm. Home: 1730 Jumpers Run Charlottesville VA 22911 Office: Univ Va 480 Ray Hunter Charlottesville VA 22908 Office Fax: 434-982-5680. Business E-Mail: ws4v@virginia.edu.

SHI, WEISONG, computer scientist, educator; arrived in US, 2000; m. Wei Wang, Feb. 22, 2000; 1 child, Ivy W. B in Computer Sci., Xidian U., 1995; PhD, Chinese Acad. Scis., 2000. Assoc. rsch. scientist NYU, NY, 2000—02; asst. prof. Wayne State U., Detroit, 2002—. Guest editor Jour. Parallel and Distributed Computing. Recipient Pres. Outstanding Honor award, Chinese Acad. Scis., 2000, 100 Outstanding PhD Rsch. China award, China Ministry Edn., 2002, Best Paper award, ICWE, 2004, Career award, NSF, 2007; grantee, Wayne State U., 2004; fellow, Microsoft, 1999. Mem.: IEEE (Best Paper award 2005), Assn. Computing Machinery. Achievements include research in software distributed shared memory system; an infrastructure for composable adaptive network services; dynamic application-layer protocol adaptation, fractal project; dynamic web content caching and delivery; resource sharing in collaborative high-end computing; data quality mangement and resilient wireless sensor networks; security and privacy in vehicular networks. Office: Wayne State Univ 5143 Cass Ave 420 State Hall Detroit MI 48202 Business E-Mail: weisong@cs.wayne.edu.

SHI, YINING, biotechnologist; b. Qinzhou, Guangxi, China, Oct. 10, 1960; s. Jinyi and Zhiying Shi; m. Minjuan Hua, Jan. 13, 1986; 1 child, Yun. BS, South China U. Tech., Guangzhou, Guangdong, 1982; MS, Northern Ariz. U., Flagstaff, 1994; PhD, U. Cin., 1997. Chem. engr. Yizheng Chem. Fiber Co., Jiangsu, China, 1982—92; rsch. asst. Northern Ariz. U., 1992—94, U. Cin., 1994—97; postdoc. assoc. U. Calif., Berkeley, 1998—2000; rsch. scientist GE Healthcare, Sunnyvale, Calif., 2000; scientist Aclara Bioscis. Inc., Mountain View, Calif., 2000—04, Monogram Bioscis. Inc., South San Francisco, 2004—. Author: (book) Interpreting Engineering Drawings for Chemical Manufacturing Technicians, 1994; contbr. articles to numerous profl. jours. Mem.: Am. Assn. Cancer Rsch. Achievements include patents in field. Office: Monogram Bioscis Inc 345 Oyster Point Blvd South San Francisco CA 94080

SHI, YU, engineer, researcher; b. Xiangtan, Hunan, China, May 11, 1981; s. Deliang Shi and Qingyun Li. MS in Engring., Huazhong U. Sci. and Tech., Wuhan, China, 2005; PhD student, U. Wis. Madison, 2006—09. Rsch. asst. Engine Rsch. Ctr., U. Wis. Madison, 2006—. Contbr. chapters to books. Named Outstanding Tchg. Asst., U. Wis. Madison, Dept. Engring. Profl. Devel., 2007. Mem.: ASME, SAE. Achievements include development of advanced and efficient combustion models for engine simulations. Office: Univ Wis Madison 1500 Engring Dr Rm 1004 Madison WI 53706 Personal E-mail: yushi92@gmail.com. Business E-Mail: shi5@wisc.edu.

SHIAKOLAS, PANOS S., mechanical engineer, educator; s. Stavros and Paraskevi Shiakolas; m. Susan Shiakolas; children: Andrea, Evi. BS in Mech. Engring., U. Tex., Austin, 1986, MS in Mech. Engring., 1988; PhD in Mech. Engring., U. Tex., Arlington, 1992. Diploma Higher Tech. Inst., Nicosia, Cyprus, 1982. Faculty assoc. U. Tex., Arlington, 1993—96, asst. prof., 1996—2003, assoc. prof., 2003—. Contbr. articles to profl. jours. Mem. Holy Trinity Greek Orthodox Ch., Dallas, 1991—. Office: Univ Texas at Austin 500 W First Str Rm 204 Arlington TX 76019 Business E-Mail: shiakolas@uta.edu.

SHIAO, SHYANG-YUN PAMELA K., nursing educator, researcher; d. Fan-Mo Kung and Kuang-Mei Kung-Sun; m. Jeansong Gene Shiao, Dec. 17, 1986; 1 child, Jacqueline Nina. PhD, Case Western Res. U., 1993. RN Bd. Nursing Tex., 1999. Regional RN, U. Ala. Hosp., Birmingham, 1987—88; staff devel. instr. MetroHealth Med. Ctr., Cleve., 1988—90; project dir. Case Western Res. U., Cleve., 1991—93, asst. prof., 1993—98; assoc. prof. Oreg. Health Sci. U., Portland, 1998—99, U. Tex. Health Scis. Ctr., Houston, 1999—2006; prof. U. Houston, Sugarland, 2006—; exec. assoc. chief nurse rsch. VA Med. Ctr., Houston, 2007—. ANCC magnet fellow-appraiser for nursing excellence ANA, Washington, 2006. Leader: rsch. Meta-analysis of acupressure (Shannon Dir.'s award NIH, 1997), prin. program investigator: rsch. Oxygen Saturation Monitoring in Neonates, Vagal tone and Validation of Oxygen Saturation Monitoring in Neonates, Validation of Oxygen Saturation Measurements in Neonates (Rsch. award Am. Assn. Critical Care Nurses, 1995). Mem. award com. Am. Assn. Colls. Nursing, Calif., 2005—06; rsch. award com. Sigma Theta Tau, Ind., 2002—. Fellow: Am. Acad. Nursing (life). Office: MEDVAMC 2002 Holcombe Blvd Houston TX 77030 Personal E-mail: pshiao@msn.com.

SHIARI, BEHROUZ, mechanical engineer, researcher; s. Bahman Shiari and Mahvash N. Sharif; m. Flora Gilanpour; 1 child, Aryan. BSc, AmirKabir U. Tech., Tehran, Iran, 1986, MSc, 1988, PhD, 1999. Cert. profl. engr., Ont., Can. Instr. U. Guilan, Rasht, 1988—2000; rsch. assoc. Queen's U., Kingston, Ont., Canada, 2000—02, Carleton U., Ottawa, Ont., Canada, 2002—04, NRC of Can., Ottawa, 2004—. Head mech. engring. dept. Guilan U., Rasht, 1993—95, asst. dean grad. office faculty engring., 1998—2000. Author: Analytical Dynamics of Discrete Systems Vol.1; contbr. articles to profl. jours. Rsch. fellow, NSERC, 2004. Achievements include patents for Pulp Refiner Sensor. Home: 6886 Edgar Brault St Ottawa ON Canada K1C 1L7 Office: Nat Rsch Coun Can 100 Sussex Ottawa ON Canada K1A 0R6 Office Fax: 613 947 2838. Personal E-mail: shiari@yahoo.ca. Business E-Mail: behrouz.shiari@nrc-cnrc.gc.ca.

SHIBA, WENDY C., lawyer; BA, Mich. State U., 1973; JD cum laude, Temple U. Sch. of Law, 1979. Atty. corp. and securities law O'Melveny & Myers, Los Angeles & NYC; corp. chair Phila. Law Dept., Phila.; v.p., sec., asst. gen. counsel Bowater, Inc., Greenville, SC, 1993—2000; gen. counsel PolyOne Corp., Avon Lake, Ohio, 2000—01, v.p., chief legal officer, sec., 2001—07; exec. v.p., gen. counsel, corp. sec. KB Home, LA, 2007—. Former bd. mem. Legal Services Agency of Western Carolina, S.C. Bd. of Accountancy, Greenville Little Theater, Palmetto Soc. of United Way of Greenville County; former mem. United Way of Greenville County Campaign Cabinet, Palmetto Soc. Women's Leadership Council, Greenville Professional Women's Forum. Office: KB Home 10990 Wilshire Blvd Los Angeles CA 90024

SHIBASAKI, YOSHIO, chemistry professor, researcher; b. Gyoda, Japan, Mar. 21, 1934; s. Reiji and Shige (Kobayashi) S.; m. Teiko Ishizuka Shibasaki, Apr. 15, 1967; children: Hideaki, Miki. BS, Saitama U., Japan, 1959; DSc, U. Tokyo, 1980. Tech. official U. Tokyo, Japan, 1960-63, asst., 1963-67; lectr. Saitama U., Urawa, Japan, 1967-70, assoc. prof., 1970-92, prof., 1992-99, ret., 1999. Inventor: Kobunshi Kagaku, 1964, J. Polymer Science, 1967, 80, 98, 99. Mem. AAAS, Japan Soc. Calorimetry & Thermal Analysis. Home: 1642 Tsutsumine Gyoda 361-0035 Japan

SHIBATA, TADASHI, engineering educator; b. Nishinomiya, Hyogo, Japan, Sept. 30, 1948; s. Toshiomi and Miyoko Shibata; m. Junko Nagamiya, Feb. 9, 1975; children: Natsuko, Megumi, Kenji. BS in Electronic Engring., Osaka U., 1971, MS in Materials Sci., 1973; PhD, U. Tokyo, 1984. Rschr. Toshiba Corp., Japan, 1974—84, prodn. engr., 1984—86; assoc. prof. dept. electronic engring. Tohoku U., Sendai, Japan, 1986-97; prof. dept. info. and communication engring. U. Tokyo, 1997—. Vis. rsch. assoc. Stanford U. Electronics Labs., Calif., 1978-80. Contbr. articles to sci. jours, chpts. to books; Author, editor: (textbook) Introduction to VLSI Technology, 1986; inventor of SALICIDE, neuron MOS. Mem.: Computer Soc., Circuits & Systems Soc., Inst. Elec. Engrs. Japan, Japan Soc. Applied Physics, IEEE Electron Devices Soc. Office: U Tokyo Dept Elec Engring & Info Sys 7-3-1 Hongo Bunkyo-ku Tokyo 113 8656 Japan E-mail: shibata@ee.t.u-tokyo.ac.jp.

SHICK, RICHARD ARLON, finance educator; b. DuBois, Pa., July 17, 1943; s. Arlon Elmer and Melva Elizabeth (Bartell) S.; m. Linda B. Shick; children: Richard Arlon, Charles, Elizabeth. BS, SUNY, Buffalo, 1966, MBA, 1968, PhD, 1972. Asst. prof. banking and fin. U. Ga., Athens, 1970-75; assoc. prof. fin. St. Bonaventure (N.Y.) U., 1975-78, chmn. fin. dept., 1975-78, acting chmn. mktg. dept., 1976-99; assoc. prof. fin. Canisius Coll., Buffalo, 1978-99, prof. fin., 1999—, dean Richard J. Wehle Sch. Bus., 1979—2002, dean emeritus, 2008—. Bd. dirs. Better Bus. Bur., 1990-95, Statler Culinary program Emerson H.S., buffalo, 1992-98; sec., treas., bd. dirs. Chautauqua Brick Co., 1995—. Mem. editl. bd. Jour. Bus. Rsch., 1973-76, Jour. Fin. Rsch., 1977-81, Jour. Econs. and Bus., 1984-88, Fin. Rev., 1976-87, editor, 1981-82; contbr. articles to profl. jours. Chmn. mayor's rev. com. Buffalo Bd. Edn., 1982-83; bd. dirs. Buffalo Alliance Edn., Old Ft. Niagara, 1994-95 chmn. bd. dirs.; chmn. devel. com., bd. dirs. Buffalo Philharm. Orch., 1995-97, treas., 1996-97; mem. NY State Com. to Promote Pub. Trust and Confidence in Legal Sys., 1999; bd. dirs. Studio Arena Theatre, 2001-05, v.p. bd., pres., chmn. NDEA fellow, 1966-68; U.S. Savs. and Loan League grantee, 1974, St. Bonaventure U. grantee, 1976, US Govt. Title III grantee, 1999 Mem. Am. Fin. Assn., Jesuit Colls. and Univs. Deans of Bus. Schs. (treas. 1983-84, v.p. 1985-89, pres. 1987-88), Middle Atlantic Assn. Colls. and Schs. Bus. Adminstrn. (v.p. 1985-86, pres. 1986-87), Automobile Club Western N.Y. (bd. dirs. 1995-99, exec. com. 1998-99, 2001), Moon Brook Country Club, Town Club Jamestown, Beta Gamma Sigma, Alpha Kappa Psi, Di Gamma, Alpha Sigma Lambda, Alpha Signa Nu. Republican. Home: 157 Crestwood Ln Buffalo NY 14221-1508 Office: Canisius Coll 2001 Main St Buffalo NY 14208-1035 Office Phone: 716-888-2660. E-mail: shick@canisius.edu.

SHICK, VICKY, dancer, choreographer; b. Budapest, Hungary, 1951; US, 1956; Student, CUNY: Hunter Coll., 1969—74. Mem. Sara Rudner Performance Ensemble, 1977—80, Trisha Brown Dance Co., 1980—86, Susan Rethorst, 1984—2004; tchr. Trisha Brown Studio, Movement Rsch. and CUNY; Hunter Coll., 1980—. Dancer, choreographer A Little Space of Intermediate Time, P.S. 122, NYC, 1988, Solo with Props, Verbier Music Festival, Switzerland, 1999, Still Lives, The Kitchen, NYC, 2000, Undoing, Dance Theater Workshop, NYC, 2003, Repair, Danspace Project, NYC, 2005. Recipient NY Dance and Performance award for Outstanding Creative Achievement, 1985, 2003; co-recipient Multi-Arts Prodn. Fund collaborative award, 2004; grantee Found. Contemporary Arts, 2005—06; fellow John Simon Guggenheim Meml. Found., 2008. Office: Hunter Coll Dance Program 695 Park Ave 614 Thomas Hunter New York NY 10021*

SHIDELER, ROSS PATRICK, literature and language educator, writer, translator, poet; b. Denver, Apr. 12, 1936; BA, San Francisco State U., 1958; MA, U. Stockholm, 1963; PhD, U. Calif., Berkeley, 1968. Instr. in comparative lit. U. Calif., Berkeley, 1967-68; asst. prof. English Hunter Coll., NYC, 1968-69; asst. prof. Scandinavian lang. and comparative lit. UCLA, 1969-73, assoc. prof., 1973-79, prof., 1979—, chmn. program in comparative lit., 1979-86, 92-96, assoc. dean Grad. Divsn., 2003—. Author: (monograph) Voices Under the Ground: Themes and Images in the Poetry of Gunnar Ekelof, 1973, Per Olov Enquist-A Critical Study, 1984, Questioning the Father: From Darwin to Zola, Ibsen, Strindberg and Hardy, 1999; translator: (plays) The Night of the Tribades (Per Olov Enquist), 1977, The Hour of the Lynx (Per Olov Enquist), 1990; co-editor (with Kathleen L. Komar): Lyrical Symbols and Narrative Transformations, Essays in Honor of Ralph Freedman, 1998; U.S. assoc. editor Swedish Book Rev., 1984—. Fellow, Nat. Defense Fgn. Language, 1964—65; Fulbright-Hays fellow, 1966—67. Mem. MLA (exec. com. divsn. Scandinavian Langs. and Lits. 1993-97), Soc. Advancement Scandinavian Study (exec. coun. 1985-89, v.p. 1997-99, pres. 1999-2001), Internat. Comparative Lit. Assn. (treas. 2004-). Office: UCLA Dept Comparative Lit Los Angeles CA 90095

SHIEH, JOHN TING-CHUNG, economics professor, department chairman; b. 1935; BS, Chunghsing U., Taiwan, 1956; MS, Kans. State U., 1960; MA, U. Calif., Riverside, 1970; DBA, U. So. Calif., 1981. Asst. prof. Northwestern State Coll., Alva, 1964—67; asst. prof. econs. Calif. State Poly. U., Pomona, 1967—70, assoc. prof., 1970—81, prof., chmn. dept. econs., 1982—85, prof., 1981—98, prof. emeritus, 1999—; vis. prof. econs. and mgmt. Xian U., China, 2003—. Prof., dir. Inst. Mainland China Studies, 1994-98, dean student affairs, 1997-99, Nat. Dong-hua U., Hualien, Taiwan, 1994-2001; cons. to small bus., So. Calif., Taiwan, 1975—; vis. prof. Tax Inst., U. So. Calif., L.A., 1977-84, U. Calif., Irvine, 1978-79, U. So. Calif., 1978-81, UCLA, 1983-1998. Contbr. rsch. articles to publs. in field. NSF fellow, 1965, 66, 67, 73, fellow seminars in econs. and math. U. Wyo., summer 1972. Mem. Am. Econ. Assn., Omicron Delta Epsilon, Omega Rho. Home: 10556 Ilona Ave Los Angeles CA 90064-2313 Office Phone: 86-10-6539-8635.

SHIELD, JULIE MARIE KARST, artist, educator; b. St. Louis, Mar. 28, 1933; d. Lansing Peter and Margaret Mary Shield. A, Briarcliff Jr. Coll., NY, 1953; studied at, Nat. Acad. Design, NYC, Art Students League. Oil painting art tchr. Buckingham Coun. Arts, 1995—99, 2008; owner Wooden Boat Art Gallery, River John, NS, Canada, 1997—99; painting art tchr. Longwood Ctr. Visual Arts Farmville, 1997-1998, 2000—01; tchr. multi-media art Holly Manor Nursing Home, Farmville, 2001—04. Mem. coun. Longwood Ctr. Visual Arts, Farmville, Va., 2001—08, tchr. art workshops, 2008—. Set designer: (plays) Ring Around the Moon, 1981; (films) Illegally Yours, 1987; one-woman shows include First Nat. Bank of Palm Beach, Fla., 1984—85, Buckingham Coun. Arts, 1996, 1998, 2008, Cumberland Court House, Va., 1999, Cheese & Co., Farmville, Va., 2000, Cafe Zelia, Farmville, 2002, 2005, Va. Southside C.C., Keysville, Va., 2002, exhibited in group shows at Va. Mus. Fine Arts, Warrenton, 1988, Longwood Ctr. Visual Arts Gala, Farmville, 2005, 2007, Hampden Sydney Music Festival, 1998—2009, Ctrl. Va. Arts, Farmville, Potluck, 2008, Buckingham Arts Coun., 1995—2009 (Best of Show, 2007), Potluck Painters, 2005, Represented in permanent collections ARC, Palm Beach County. V.p. ctrl. Va. arts affiliate Va. Mus. Fine Arts, Richmond, 2004—05, pres., 2006—08. Mem.: DAR (corr. sec. 1971—75, bd. mem. 2009—), John Meml. Episcopal Ch. (register 2009—), Buckingham County Coun. Arts (bd. mem. 2007—), Longwood Garden Club (recording sec. Farmville 2008—), Buckingham Artists Guild (planning com. 1995—2008), Curdsville Cmty. Ctr. (sec. 2006), English Speaking Union, Palm Beach, Fla., Friends of the Libr., Hist. Buckingham Inc., Audubon Artists Inc. (assoc.), Art Students League N.Y.C. (life; corr. sec. 1964—67), Buckingham-Dillwyn Garden Club (sec. 1996—2008). Avocations: museums, gardening, miniature horse. Home: 843 Simpson Rd Prospect VA 23960 Personal E-mail: jshield@kinep.net.

SHIELDS, ALLAN EDWIN, writer, educator, photographer; b. Columbus, Ohio, July 3, 1919; s. Richard Edwin and Eloessa (Smith) S.; m. Bernice Clark, Aug. 2, 1941; children: Allan Oakley, Richard Minter, Larry Michael, Catherine Marie AB, U. Calif.-Berkeley, 1941; MA, U. So. Calif., 1947, PhD, 1951. Prof. philosophy San Diego State U., 1949-68, 70-78; emeritus prof. San Diego State Coll., 1978—; dean Coll. Humanities and Fine Arts U. No. Iowa, 1968-70; owner, pub. Jerseydale Ranch Press, 1992-98. Seasonal ranger naturalist Nat. Park Service, Yosemite Nat. Park, 1955-60; freelance writer, photographer, 1978—; violinist-violist, frequent recitalist; mem., sometime concertmaster Merced Symphony Orch., Calif., 1979-91; founder, with wife, Jerseydale Ranch Press, 1992. Author: Guide to Tuolumne Meadows Trails, 1960, rev. edit., 1973, (with Herbert Searles) A Bibliography of the Works of F.C.S. Schiller, 1969, (with Richard Shields) Tuolumne Profile: Yosemite, 1967, (novella) The Tragedy of Tenaya, 1974, new version 1992, A Bibliography of Bibliographies in Aesthetics, 1974, (poetry) A Horse in the House, 1985, Mariposa Now and Then, 1993, Tuffy, an Angel Hid in a Cloud, 1994, What Animals Taught Me, 1995, (with Bernice Shields) Into the Valley: A Brief History of Jerseydale Ranch, 1995, (with John Sharsmith) Climb Every Mountain: A Portrait of Carl Sharsmith, 1996, The Spirit of Rin-Tin-Tin, 2001, also numerous poems and articles; editor: A Yosemite Adventure in 1863, 1992, Wild Bill Neely and the Pagan Brothers' Golden Goat Winery, 1993, The Song of Sonora, 1993, O.S.S.: One Sad Sack—Pvt. Neely Disciplines the Military, 1994, A Yosemite Naturalist's Odyssey, 1994, Wilderness Treks by Foot, Canoe, and Adobe Rocket, and Father's Far-Flung Fables, 1995, Dream Temple and Other Visions, 1997; pub. various profl. jours. Bd. dirs. San Diego Symphony. Served with USAAF, 1942-45 Mudd fellow in philosophy U. So. Calif., 1948-49 Mem. Am. Soc. for Aesthetics (trustee), Phi Beta Kappa, Phi Kappa Phi, Phi Mu Alpha Sinfonia (hon.). Home: 2444 Beverly Ave Clovis CA 93611-5927 Personal E-mail: ashields@csufresno.edu. *My greatest satisfactions have come with tasks completed to the best of my abilities. Whether raising children, building a building, nurturing a marriage, learning the violin, or writing, all have inherent standards demanding recognition. Though there is always joy in the process of doing, joy can be transformed into satisfaction only in completion evaluated against the standards of worth for that kind of undertaking.*

SHIELDS, ANDREA LYN, psychologist, coach, educator; b. Montgomery, Ala., Aug. 19, 1947; d. Theodore and Alma Lea Shields. BA, U. Ariz., 1969; MA in Psychology, U. of the Pacific, 1971; PhD in Clin. Psychology, Fielding Inst., Santa Barbara, Calif., 1977. Trainer So. Ariz. Mental Health Ctr., Tucson, 1968-69; rsch. asst. Stockton (Calif.) State Hosp., 1970; instr. psychology Modesto (Calif.) Jr. Coll., 1970-71, San Bernardino (Calif.) Valley Coll., 1971-72; instr. for Army recruiters Columbia (Mo.) Coll., 1974; instr., head psychology dept. Crafton Hills Coll., Yucaipa, Calif., 1972-88; adminstrv. dir. U. San Francisco, 1980-82; pvt. practice, Rancho Cucamonga, Calif., 1981—2007; fellow Prescribing Psychologists Register, 1997—; coach, psychologist. Presenter in field. Pres. inland unit Am. Cancer Soc., 1993-96. Mem. Rotary (bd. dirs. 1993-96, 2002-, pres. 2005-06). Avocation: hiking. Home Phone: 909-867-3873.

SHIELDS, BROOKE CHRISTA CAMILLE, actress, model; m. Andre Agassi, Apr. 19, 1997 (annulled 1999); m. Chris Henchy, Apr. 4, 2001; children: Rowan Francis Henchy, Grier Hammond Henchy. BA, Princeton U., 1987. Model for Ivory Soap commls. starting in 1966, later for Calvin Klein jeans and Colgate toothpaste commls.; Actor (films) Alice, Sweet Alice, 1975, Pretty Baby, 1977, King of the Gypsies, 1978, Wanda Nevada, 1978, Just You and Me Kid, 1978, Blue Lagoon, 1979, Endless Love, 1980, Sahara, 1983, Backstreet Strays, 1989, Brenda Starr, 1992, Seventh Floor, 1993, Running Wild, 1993, Freaked, 1993, Freeway, 1996, The Misadventures of Margaret, 1998, The Weekend, 1999, The Bachelor, 1999, Black & White, 1999. After Sex, 2000, Rent-A-Husband, 2004, Bob the Butler, 2005, Bag Boy, 2007, The Midnight Meat Train, 2008; (TV movies) The Prince of Central Park, 1977, After the Fall, Wet Gold, I Can Make You Love Me: The Stalking of Laura Black, 1993, Nothing Lasts Forever, 1995, What Makes a Family, 2001, Miss Spider's Sunny Patch Kids, 2003; (TV mini-series) Widows, 2002; (TV series) Suddenly Susan, 1996-99 (People's Choice award Favorite Female in New Series 1997), Lipstick Jungle, 2008-09; TV appearances include: The Tonight Show, Bob Hope spls., The Diamond Trap, 1988, Friends, 1996, Just Shoot Me, 1997, I'm With Her, 2004, That 70's Show, 2004, Niptuck 2006; appeared on Broadway in Grease, 1994-95 (Theatre World award 1995), Wonderful Town, 2004, Chicago, 2005; Author: Down Came the Rain: My Journey Through Postpartum Depression, 2005 (NY Times Bestseller list, 2005). Recipient People's Choice award Favorite Young Picture Performer, 1981—84; named Time Mag. Face of the '80s.

SHIELDS, CHRISTOPHER ANDREW, website director; b. Oneonta, NY, Aug. 8, 1968; s. Alexander J. Shields and Grace Marie Kathmann. BS, SUNY, New Paltz, 1991; MS, U. Md., Adelphi, 1997. Dir. nasdaq.com The Nasdaq Stock Market, Inc., Rockville, Md., 1996—. Prodr.(on-air personality): (podcast) cIndyCenter.com. Home: 282 M St SW Washington DC 20024 Personal E-mail: ifwagba@hotmail.com.

SHIELDS, CHRISTOPHER BRIAN, neurosurgeon; b. Schumacher, Ont., Can., Nov. 3, 1941; came to U.S., 1974; s. Gordon and Elizabeth (McLaughlin) S.; m. Deborah Irene Dickson, July 17, 1970; children: Lisa, Karen. MD, U. Toronto, Can., 1966. Diplomate Am. Bd. Neurol. Surgery. Intern St. Michael's Hosp., Toronto, 1966-67; resident in neurosurgery U. Manitoba, 1968-73; fellow in microvascular surgery U. Vt., 1973-74; asst. prof. divsn. neurol. surgery U. Louisville, 1974-80, assoc. prof. divsn. neurol. surgery, 1980-85, prof. dept. neurol. surgery, 1985-97, prof., chmn. dept. neurol. surgery, 1997—. Fellow Royal Coll. Surgeons Can. Avocations: reading, running. Home: 2400 Gray Fox Rd Louisville KY 40205-1612 Office: Univ Louisville Dept Neurol Surgery 210 E Gray St Ste 1102 Louisville KY 40202-3907 Fax: 502-629-5512. E-mail: cshields@mainlink.net.

SHIELDS, CHRISTOPHER D., legislative staff member; B in Internat. Politics and Economy, Middlebury Coll., Vt., 2004. Field organizer Senator John Kerry's Presdl. Campaign, 2004; press asst., Senator John Rockefeller US Senate, Washington, 2005—06; press sec., Rep. Lynn Woolsey US House of Reps., Washington, 2006—. Democrat. Office: 2263 Rayburn House Office Bldg Washington DC 20515 Office Phone: 202-225-5161. Office Fax: 202-225-5163.*

SHIELDS, CYNTHIA ROSE, college administrator; b. Monterey, Calif., June 1, 1954; d. William Lawrence and Rose Virdell Jackson; m. Franklin Shields, Sept. 19, 1981; 1 child, Brett. AA, San Francisco City Coll., 1980; BS, U. San Francisco, 1986; MPA, Golden Gate U., 1988; MS, Nat. U., 1994; EdD in Ednl. Leadership, U. Calif., Davis, 1997; cert. in conflict mgmt., U. Calif., Irvine, 2003. Cert. community coll. instr., supr., Calif. Acct. exec. KFSN-TV, Fresno, Calif., 1982-85; instr. Merced County Schs., Calif., 1985-89; gen. mgr., owner Ad Line Advt., Merced, 1986-96; instr. Merced Coll., 1989-90, youth outreach specialist, 1990-91, re-entry coord., 1991-98; counselor Long Beach City Coll., Calif., 2000—03, dir. outreach and pub. rels., 2003—. Sr. assoc. Sch. Leadership Ctr., Calif. Sch. Leadership Acad., 1989-92; ednl. cons. 1998-2000, Merced, Calif. Author curriculum materials. Bd. dirs. Merced Cmty. Med. Ctr. Found., 1991, MUHSD Found., 1992-94; mem. citizens adv. bd. Merced City Sch. Dist., 1985-87; chmn. Merced Conv. and Vis. Bur., 1991; coord. Merced Cmty. Housing Resource Bd., 1988-90; mem. Leaders program Nat. Inst. for Leadership Devel., 1996. Mem. AAUW, Merced City C. of C. (bd. dirs. 1991-93, v.p. fin. and ops. 1993-94), Phi Delta Kappa. Democrat. Avocations: community volunteer, reading, golf, bicycling.

SHIELDS, GERALD W., insurance company executive; BBA in Acctg., Baylor U., Waco, Tex., B in Computer Sci. Chief tech. officer, dir. info. svcs. LifeWay Christian Resources, Nashville; sr. info. tech. positions Electronic Data Systems; v.p. info. tech.-enterprises svcs. AFLAC Inc., Columbus, Ga., 2002, sr. v.p., chief info. officer, info. tech., 2005—. Mem. inaugural governing body Atlanta Chief Info. Officers Exec. Summit. Bd. trustees Brewton-Parker Coll., Mt. Vernon, Ga.; bd. trustees Cmty. Tech. Adv. Coun. Muscogee County Sch. Dist. Named one of 100 Premier Chief Info. Officers, Computerworld, 2006, 100 Premier Info. Tech. Leaders, 2007. Mem.: Life Mgmt. Inst. Office: AFLAC Inc 1932 Wynnton Rd Columbus GA 31999 Office Phone: 706-323-3431.

SHIELDS, JOAN MARIE, microbiologist, parasitologist; b. Macon, Ga., Aug. 9, 1964; d. Charles Augustus Hager and Phyllis Ann Nickerson. PhD, U. Calif., Irvine, 2003. Staff fellow FDA, Laurel, Md., 2009—. Guest rschr. Ctrs. Disease Control and Prevention, Atlanta, 2004—09. Named Mentor of Yr., U. Calif., 1999—2003; fellowship, Environ. Profls. Orgn., 1999, Don Owen Water Sci. and Policy fellowship, UC Irvine Urban Water Rsch. Ctr., 1999. Mem.: Am. Soc. Microbiologists. Avocations: reading, gardening, writing. E-mail: joan.shield@fda.hhs.gov.

SHIELDS, JOHN CHARLES, literature educator; b. Phoenix, Oct. 29, 1944; s. Granville Blaine and Elizabeth Merle (Hartgraves) S. BA, U. Tenn., Knoxville, 1967, MA in Coll. Teaching, 1969, PhD, 1978; EdS, George Peabody Coll., 1975. Tchr. English Sevier County High Sch., Sevierville, Tenn., 1967-68; head dept. English Battle Ground Acad., Franklin, Tenn., 1969-71; dir. academics Brentwood Acad., Nashville, 1971-73, Columbia (Tenn.) Mil. Acad., 1973-74; instr. U. Tenn., Knoxville, 1978-79; asst. prof. Ill. State U., Normal, 1979-86, assoc. prof. English, 1986-93, prof. English, 1993—2005, disting. prof. African Am. Brit. and comparative lit., 2005—, dir. Ctr. for Classicism in Am. Culture, 2007—. Cons. Ency. Britannica, Oxford Companion to African Am. Lit., Norton Anthology African Am. Lit., others; project dir. conf. on Phillis Wheatley NEH, 1983-85; faculty advisor Native Am. Student Soc. Ill. State U., 1990; Coll. of Arts and Sci. Lectr., Ill. State U., 2003—. Assoc. editor Style, DeKalb, Ill., 1988-90, guest editor, 1990—; editor: The Collected Works of Phillis Wheatley, 1988, paperback, 1989; mem. adv. bd. Greenwood Ency. Am. Poetry, (7 vol.) contbr., adv. editor, contbr. Oxford Companion to African Am. Lit., 1997—, Am. Nat. Biography, 24 vol., 1994—; contbr. Oxford Dictionary of Nat. Biography, Great Britain, 1995—; author: The Am. Aeneas: Classical Origins of the American Self, 2001 (Winner Outstanding Acad. Book Choice Mag. 2002, Hon. mention Harry Levin prize Am. Comparative Lit. Assn.), paperback, 2005; contbr. articles to lit. jour. and chpt. to books; manuscript reviewer in field. Spokesperson for Native Am. citizens, 1990—. Ford Found. fellow, 1968-69, Soc. for Humanities fellow Cornell U., 1984-85, NEH fellow, 1983, 84, 89, 93, John C. Hodges Teaching Excellence award, 1969. Mem. MLA, Soc. Early Americanists, Internat. Soc. for 18th-Century Studies, Am. Studies Assn., Melville Soc., Coll. Lang. Assn., Phi Mu Alpha Sinfonia, Alpha Phi Omega, Sigma Nu. Unitarian Universalist. Avocations: piano, singing, native american culture, archaeology, rare book collecting. Home: 1412 Donegal Dr Normal IL 61761-5416

SHIELDS, LAWRENCE THORNTON, orthopaedic surgeon, educator; b. Boston, Oct. 2, 1935; s. George Leo and Catherine Elizabeth (Thornton) S.; m. Karen S. Kraus, Sept. 21, 1968; children: Elizabeth Coulter, Laura Thornton, Sarah Daley, Michael Lawrence. AB, Harvard U., 1957; MD, Johns Hopkins U., 1961. Diplomate Am. Bd. Orthop. Surgery. Intern Barnes Hosp., Washington U., St. Louis, 1961—62, resident, 1962—63; resident orthop. surgeon Children's Hosp. Med. Ctr., Boston, 1966—67, Mass. Gen. Hosp., Boston, 1967—68, Peter Bent Brigham, Robert Breck Brigham Hosps., Boston, 1968—69, Harvard Med. Sch., Boston, 1965—69, instr., 1969—; orthop. surgeon Peter Bent Brigham & Women's Hosp., Children's hosps., 1969—, Waltham (Mass.)-Weston Hosp. and Med. Ctr., 1969—, also chief orthop. surgery, pres. med. staff. Mem. Waltham-Weston Orthop. Assocs.; proprietor Boston Athenaeum; mem. staff Hahnemann Hosp., Boston, Newton-Wellesley (Mass.) Hosp.; cons. orthop. surgeon VA Hosp., Boston; mem. faculty Harvard Med. Sch.; vis. scholar Trinity Hall Cambridge U., 1985; hon. prof. New Eng. Coll., Henniker, NH, Sussex, England, 1995; bd. dirs. Wal-West Health Sys., 1986—; pres. Mass. Bay Investment Trust; dir. Waltham Investment Group. Contbr. articles to med. jours. Bd. dirs. Mass. Acad. Emergency Med. Technicians, Waltham Boys' Club; bd. of overseers Boston Lyric Opera, 1993—; trustee, exec. com. Waltham-Weston Hosp. and Med. Ctr. Lt. M.C. USNR, 1963-65. Fellow: ACS, Mass. Hist. Soc. Libr., Am. Acad. Orthop. Surgeons, Mass. Hist. Soc., Olser Club London (corr.); mem.: Irish Georgian Soc., Irish Georgian Soc., Thomas B. Quigley Sports Medicine Soc. (v.p., pres. 2001—), R. Austen Freeman Soc. (v.p.), Mass. Med. Soc. (v.p. 1982—83, councillor), Mass. Orthop. Assn. (sec. 1986—, bd. dirs.), Royal Soc. Medicine, N.Y. Acad. Scis., Cox & Co., Boston Lyric Opera (bd. overseers 1993), Theodore Roosevelt Assn. New Eng. (founding), USS Wasp CV-19 Assn., English Speaking Union (bd. dirs.), Academie Brillat-Savarin, Confrerie de La Chaine des Rotisseurs (elected 1996), Titanic Hist. Soc., Boston Opera Assn. (bd. dirs.), Harvard Mus. Assn., Thoreau Soc., Emerson Soc., Trollope Soc. (founding mem., bd. dirs., London), Handel and Hayden Soc. (bd. overseers), Waltham Hist. Soc., Les Amis d'Escoffier Soc., Internat. Consular Corps (hon.), Charles River Dist. (pres. 1982—83, treas., exec. com.), L'Ordre Mondial (elected 1999), St. Crisplin's Soc. Boston (pres. 1991—, founding mem.), Osler Club London, East India, Devonshire Sports and Pub. Schs. Club (London), Bull Dog Terries, Union Club Boston, Harvard Club, Boston Orthop. Club, New Eng. Orthop. Club, St. Botolph Club (Boston), Algonquin Club Boston (pres. 1990—, bd. dirs.), Clover Club Boston, Rotary, 33 Touchdown Club/Found. (founding), Pi Eta (Harvard). Home: 9 Beverly Rd Newton MA 02461-1112 Office: 721 Huntington Ave Boston MA 02115-6010 also: Lawrence T Shields Md 9 Beverly Rd Newton Highlands MA 02461-1112 Business E-Mail: ltshields@mcb.harvard.edu.

SHIELDS, PATRICIA ALLENE, retail executive; b. Westminster, Md., June 29, 1968; d. Richard Dean and Joan Elizabeth Munroe Schnably; m. Aidan Hugh Shields, Mar. 20, 2004. BA, Wake Forest U., Winston Salem, NC, 1990. Mgr. divisional mdse. Gap, San Francisco, 2001—05; exec. v.p. Charlotte Russe, San Diego, 2005—08; retail exec. cons. Obama America, 2008—. Alumni admissions vol. Wake Forest U., San Diego, 2001—06. Mem.: Delta Delta Delta (life; collegiate dist. officer 2003—06). Home and Office: 540 Verbena Ct Encinitas CA 92024 Home Phone: 760-230-6692; Office Phone: 415-505-7472. Personal E-mail: pattishields@roadrunner.com.

SHIELDS, PATRICIA LYNN, educational broker, consultant; b. Bklyn. BS in Biology, Bucknell U., 1984; BA in Biology, Rutgers U., 2002; MAT in Biol. Scis., Fairleigh Dickinson U., 2002. Pres. Buttercup's Internat., Inc., Middletown, NJ, 1988—. Office: Buttercups Internat Inc PO Box 148 Middletown NJ 07748-0148

SHIELDS, PATRICIA MARY, political science professor; m. George Phillip Glaser, Sept. 14, 1973; children: Daniel Shields Glaser, Jeffrey Shields Glaser. BS in Economics, U. Md., Coll. Pk., 1973; MA in Economics, Ohio State U., Columbus, 1975, PhD in Pub. Adminstrn., 1977. Grad. rsch. assoc. Ctr. Human Resource Rsch., Ohio State, Columbus, 1973—77; prof., polit. sci. Tex. State U., San Marcos, 1978—. Editor, armed forces & soc. Inter-U. Seminar, Chicago, 2001—. Author: (book) Step by Step: Building a Research Paper; contbr. articles to jours. Mem.: ASPA (Laverne Burchfield award 2007), Nat. Assn. Schs. Pub. Affairs & Adminstrn. (Excellence Tchg. award 2002). D-Conservative. Lutheran. Avocations: travel, reading, walking. Office: Tex State Univ 601 Univ Dr San Marcos TX 78666 Office Fax: 512-245-7815. Personal E-mail: patshields@austin.rr.com. Business E-Mail: ps07@txstate.edu.

SHIELDS, ROBERT EMMET, merchant banker, lawyer; b. Ridley Park, Pa., May 18, 1942; s. Joseph Leonard and Kathryn J. (Walsh) S.; m. Mary Katherine Reid, July 22, 1967; children: Christopher D., David R., Kevin M., Kathleen. AB, Coll. Holy Cross, 1964; LLB cum laude, NYU, 1967. Bar: Pa. 1968. Mem. faculty Boalt Hall Sch. Law U. Calif., Berkeley, 1967-68; assoc. Drinker Biddle & Reath, Phila., 1968-74, ptnr., 1974-94, mng. ptnr., 1979-83, 85-94, head corp. and securities group, 1983-93, CFO, 1993-94; mng. dir., prin., ptnr., COO Questor Gen. Ptnr., L.P., 1995—2003, Questor Ptnrs. Funds, L.P. and Questor Mgmt. Co., 1995—2003; vice chmn. AlixPartner Holdings, Inc., Southfield, Mich., 2003—07, Questor Ptnrs. Holdings, Inc., Birmingham, Mich., 2003—, TK Aluminum, Ltd., Hamilton, Bermuda, 2003—08; pres., CEO Lakeview Capital, Inc., Birmingham, 2007—. Sec. Wallquest Inc., Alixpartners LLP; bd. dirs. Plainfield Direct, Inc., Chef Solutions, Inc., Trailer Holdings Corp.; mem. bd. trustees Archmere Acad., Rosemont Sch. HolyChild. Author: (with Eliot B. Thomas) Federal Securities Act Handbook, 4th edit, 1977; (with Robert H. Strouse) Securities Practice Handbook, 1987. Mem.: ABA, Turnaround Mgmt. Assn., Phila. Bar Assn., Am. Law Inst. (life). Office: Lakeview Capital Inc 151 S Old Woodward Ste 400 Birmingham MI 48009 Office Phone: 248-554-4900. Business E-Mail: rshields@lakeviewcapitalinc.com.

SHIELDS, STEPHANIE, psychology professor; b. Omaha; PhD, Pa. State U., University Pk., 1976. Prof., psychology U. Calif., Davis, 1977—96; prof., psychology & women's studies Pa. State U., 1996—. Author: (book) Speaking From The Heart: Gender And The Social Meaning Of Emotion (Disting. Publ. award, 2004). Grantee, NSF, 1986, 2008—, U. Calif. 4-H Ctr. Youth Devel., 1995—96, Nag's Heart Found., 2000—01.

SHIELDS, THOMAS CHARLES, lawyer; b. Evergreen Park, Ill., Apr. 26, 1941; s. Thomas James and Adelaide (McElligott) Shields; m. Nicoline M. Murphy, Sept. 14, 1974; children: Thomas James II, Nicoline M. E. Shoffer, Suzanne Adelaide Browne, Kerry Anne. AB, Georgetown U., 1963; JD cum laude, Northwestern U., 1966. Bar: Ill. 1966, U.S. Dist. Ct. (no. dist.) Ill. 1966, U.S. Ct. Appeals (7th cir.) 1966, U.S. Tax Ct. 1968, U.S. Supreme Ct. 1977. Assoc. Hopkins & Sutter, Chgo., 1966-73, ptnr., 1973-93, K&L Gates LLP, 2009—; mem., chair health law dept. Bell, Boyd & Lloyd, Chgo., 1994—2009; chief counsel Cath. Health Assn. U.S., St. Louis, 1994—2005. Lectr. Ill. Inst. Continuing Legal Edn., 1973; mem. adv. bd. Health Law Inst. Loyola U. Sch. Law, Chgo., 1984—89, Health Law Inst. DePaul U. Sch. Law, Chgo., 1985—96. Contbr. articles to profl. jours. Trustee Village of Riverside, Ill., 2001—09; mem. Ill. Health Facilities Authority, 2000—03; governing mem. Chgo. Zool. Soc., Chgo., Cath. Charities Chgo.; bd. dirs. Cancer Rsch. Found., Chgo., 1987—, Brother Louie and Fannie Roncoli Found., 1994—2006. Mem.: Chgo. Bar Assn., Ill. Assn. Healthcare Attys. (bd. dir. 1983—89, pres. 1987—88), Ill. Bar Assn., Am. Hosp. Assn. (tax adv. group 1987—90), Am. Health Lawyers Assn. (bd. dir. 1983—91, pres. 1989—90), Chgo. Power Squadron, U.S. Power Squadron (legal officer 2005—06), Mid-Am. Club Chgo. (bd. govs. 2001—06, sec. 2004—06), Order of Coif. Avocations: skiing, bicycling, golf, boating. Office: K&L Gates LLP 3 First Nat Plz 70 W Madison St Ste 3100 Chicago IL 60602 Office Phone: 312-807-4232. Business E-Mail: thomas.shields@klgates.com.

SHIELDS, THOMAS WILLIAM, surgeon, educator; b. Ambridge, Pa., Aug. 17, 1922; s. John Jr. and Elizabeth (Flanagan) S.; m. Dorothea Ann Thomas, June 12, 1948; children: Thomas William, John Leland, Carol Ann. BA, Kenyon Coll., Gambier, Ohio, 1943, DSc (hon.), 1978; MD, Temple U., Phila., 1947. Resident surgery Northwestern U. Med. Sch., Chgo., 1949-55, prof. surgery, 1968-92, prof. Emeritus of surgery, 1992—; practice medicine specializing in surgery Chgo., 1956—; chief of surgery VA Lakeside Hosp., Chgo., 1968-87; chief thoracic surgery VA Lakeside Med. Ctr., Chgo., 1987-90. Editor: General Thoracic Surgery, 1972, 5th edit., 2000, 6th edit 2004, Bronchial Carcinoma, 1974, Mediastinal Surgery, 1991; assoc. editor Surgery, Gynecology and Obstetrics, Annals of Thoracic Surgery, 1993-2002; mem. editl. bd. Annals of Thoracic Surgery, Lung Cancer; contbr. articles to profl. jours. Served with U.S. Army, 1951-53. Mem. ACS, AMA, Am. Assn. for Thoracic Surgery, Soc. Thoracic Surgery, Central, Western Surg. Assns., Société Internationale de Chirurgie, Soc. for Surgery of Alimentary Tract, Internat. Assn. for Study Lung Cancer, Japanese Assn. Thoracic Surgery (hon.), Pa. Assn. Thoracic Surgery (hon.), Pan Pacific Surg. Assn., Phi Beta Kappa, Sigma Xi, Alpha Omega Alpha. Office: Northwestern U Feinberg Sch Medicine Galter 3-150 201 E Huron St Chicago IL 60611 Home: 810 Audubon Way Apt 402 Lincolnshire IL 60069 Home Phone: 847-415-2016; Office Phone: 480-451-8296. Personal E-mail: twshields@comcast.net.

SHIELDS, WILLIAM DONALD, physician, educator; b. Salt Lake City, Oct. 29, 1941; s. F. Alburn and Ruth (Clawson) Shields; m. Virginia Mary Howell, May 19, 1970; children: Stephen Christopher, Justin Michael, Christine Rebecca. BA in chemistry, U. Utah, 1967; MD, U. Utah Sch. Medicine, Salt Lake City, 1967—71. Cert. in neurology with special competence in child neurology Am. Bd. Psychiatry and Neurology, 1977, diplomate Am. Bd. Pediat., 1978. Resident U. So. Calif., LA, 1971—73; fellow U. Utah, Salt Lake City, 1973—76; asst. prof. UCLA Sch. Medicine, 1976—83, assoc. prof., 1983—90, prof., 1990—, Rubin Brown prof., 1999—2005. Chief, divsn. pediatric neurology UCLA Sch. Medicine, 1980—2005. Contbr. chapters to books, articles to profl. jours. Pres., bd. mem. Epilepsy Found. L.A., 1981—88; mem. profl. adv. bd. Epilepsy Found. Am., Landover, Md. Recipient Maxwell J. Schleifer Disting. Svc. Award, Exceptional Parent Found., 2004; named a Top Dr., Am.'s Top Doctors, 2001—09; grantee, Milken Family Found., 1986—2004, NIH, 1992—98. Fellow: Am. Acad. Pediat.; mem.: Nat. Inst. Neurologic Disease and Stroke, L.A. County Epilepsy Soc. (chmn, profl. adv. bd. 1981—86, pres. 1986—89), Am. Acad. Neurology, Profs. Child Neurology, Am. Epilepsy Soc. (Svc. Award 1996), Child Neurology Soc. (counselor 1994—96). Office: David Geffen Sch Medicine UCLA 10833 LeConte Ave Los Angeles CA 90095-1752 Office Phone: 310-825-6196. Office Fax: 310-825-5834.

SHIELDS, WILLIAM MICHAEL, biology professor, consultant; b. Valley Stream, NY, Nov. 23, 1947; s. John Francis Shields and Eileen Natalie Sly; m. Barbara Jeanne Hager, Dec. 16, 1989. PhD, Ohio State U., Columbus, 1979. Prof. SUNY CESF, Syracuse, NY, 1979—. Forensic DNA cons. DNA Consulting, Syracuse, 1989—. Author: (book) Philopatry, Inbreeding and the Evolution of Sex (Colo. Plateau Disting. scholar, 1986); editor (author): Proceedings of Two Symposia on Ecology and Evolution. Treas. Melinda Frey Ardia Environ. Found., Skaneateles, NY, 1996—2009. Recipient, NSF. Fellow: Am. Ornithologists Union; mem.: Sigma Xi (pres. 2000—01). Democrat. Avocation: travel. Office: SUNY Coll Env Sci & Forestry 1 Forestry Dr Syracuse NY 13210 Business E-Mail: wms1@syr.edu.

SHIELY, JOHN STEPHEN, manufacturing executive, lawyer; b. June 19, 1952; s. Vincent Robert and Mary Elizabeth (Hope) Shiely; m. Helen Jane Pauly, Aug. 29, 1981; children: Michael, Erin, Megan. BBA, U. Notre Dame, 1974; JD, Marquette U., 1977; M in Mgmt., Northwestern U., 1990. With Arthur Andersen & Co., Milw., 1977-79, Hughes Hubbard & Reed, Milw., 1979-83, Allen-Bradley Co., Milw., 1983-86, Rockwell Internat. Corp., Milw., 1985-86, Briggs & Stratton Corp., Milw., 1986—, gen. counsel, 1986-90, v.p., gen. counsel, 1990-91, pres., COO, 1994-2001, pres., CEO, 2001—03, chmn., pres., CEO, 2003—08, chmn., CEO, 2008—. Bd. dirs. Briggs & Stratton Corp., Quad/Graphics, Inc., Pewaukee, Wis., 1996—, Marshall & Ilsley Corp., Milw., 1999—, Scotts Miracle-Gro Co., 2007—. Mem. Greater Milw. Com., 2000—; chmn. bd. Children's Hosp. and Health Sys., 2005—09; mem. bd. regents Milw. Sch. Engring., 1995—; trustee Med. Coll. Wis., 2003—; mem. corp. bd. dirs. Rock and Roll Hall of Fame and Mus.; bd. dirs. Outdoor Power Equipment Inst. Mem.: Assn. Corp. Growth (past pres. Wis. chpt. 1988—). Office: Briggs & Stratton Corp PO Box 702 Milwaukee WI 53201-0702

SHIEMBOB, MARK S., lawyer; b. Hartford, Conn., 1956; BA with distinction, Univ. Va., 1978, JD, 1982. Bar: Va. 1982. Ptnr., sect. chief, fin. Troutman Sanders LLP, Richmond, Va., mem. exec. com. Mem.: Va. Bar Assn., Am. Coll. Real Estate Lawyers, Mortgage Bankers Assn. Am. Office: Troutman Sanders LLP PO Box 1122 Richmond VA 23218-1122 also: Troutman Sanders LLP Troutman Sanders Bldg 1001 Haxall Point Richmond VA 23219 Office Fax: 804-697-1455, 804-698-6004. Business E-Mail: mark.shiembob@troutmansanders.com.

SHIENTAG, FLORENCE PERLOW, lawyer; b. NYC; d. David and Ester (Germane) Perlow; m. Bernard L. Shientag, June 8, 1938. BS, NYU, 1940, LLB, 1933, JD, 1940. Bar: Fla. 1976, N.Y. Law aide Thomas E. Dewey, 1937; law sec. Mayor La Guardia, 1939-42; justice Domestic Relations Ct., 1941-42; mem. Tchrs. Retirement Bd., NYC, 1942-46; asst. U.S. atty. So. dist. NY, 1943-53; cir. ct. mediator Fla. Supreme Ct., 1992; pvt. practice NYC, 1960—, Palm Beach, Fla., 1976—. Lectr. on internat. divorce; mem. Nat. Commn. on Wiretapping and Electronic Surveillance, 1973—, Task Force on Women in Cts., 1985-86. Contbr. articles to profl. jours. Candidate NY State Senate, 1954; bd. dirs. UN Devel. Corp., 1972-95, Franklin and Eleanor Roosevelt Inst., 1985—; bd. dirs., assoc. treas. YM and YWHA; hon. commr. commerce, NYC. Mem. ABA, Fed. Bar Assn. (exec. com.), Internat. Bar Assn., NY Women's Bar Assn. (pres., dir., Life Time Achievement award 1994, special award 2002), NY State Bar Assn., NYC Bar Assn. (chmn. law and art sect.), NY County Lawyers Assn. (dir.), Nat. Assn. Women LAwyers (sec.). Home: 737 Park Ave New York NY 10021-4256 Office Phone: 212-861-8800. *Success is a product of self respect and hard work at what you do well.*

SHIER, GLORIA BULAN, mathematics professor; b. The Philippines; came to U.S., 1966. d. Melecio Cauilan and Florentina (Cumagun) Bulan; m. Wayne Thomas Shier; children: John Thomas, Marie Teresita, Anna Christina. BS, U. Santo Tomas; MA, U. Ill., 1968; PhD, U. Minn., 1986. Tchr. Cagayan Valley Coll., Cagayan, Philippines, St. Paul Coll., Manila, Manila Div. City Schs.; asst. prof. U. of East, Manila; rsch. asst. U. Ill., Urbana, 1968—69; instr. Miramar C.C., San Diego, 1974—75, Mesa C.C., San Diego, 1975—80, Lakewood C.C., St. Paul, 1984, U. Minn., Mpls., 1986—87, North Hennepin C.C., Brooklyn Park, Minn., 1987—. Cons. PWS Kent Pub. Co., Boston, 1989—. Chairperson Filipino Am. Edn. Assn., San Diego, 1978-79. Fulbright scholar U.S. State Dept., U. Ill., 1966-70; fellow Nat. Sci. Found., Oberlin Coll., 1967; recipient Excellence in Teaching award UN Ednl. Scientific

Cultural Organ., U. Philippines, Cert. Commendation award The Gov. of Minn., 1990, Outstanding Filipino in the Midwest Edn. Cat. award 1992, Cavite Assn., 1998, Gintong Pamana Found.; Outstanding Filipino-Am. in Edn. Mem.: Am. Statis. Assn., Minn. Math. Assn. of Two Yr. Colls., Minn. Coun. Tchrs. Math., Internat. Group for Psychology of Math. Edn., Am. Math. Assn. for Two Yr. Colls., Nat. Coun. Tchrs. Math., Philippine-Am. Acad. Sci. and Engring., Math. Assn. Am., Am. Math. Soc., Fil-Minnesotan Assn. (bd. dirs. 1991—2004, v.p. 2004—), Cultural Soc. Filipino-Ams. (pres. 2001—), Sigma Xi, Phi Kappa Phi. Roman Catholic. Avocation: piano. Office Phone: 763-424-0834. Business E-Mail: mail@bogason.dk.

SHIER, JULIET MARIE, social studies educator; b. Seattle, Jan. 23, 1967; d. James E. and Martha L. Hall; m. Peter M. Shier, Nov. 29, 1991; children: Katherine L., Emily A., Mary E. MS in Edn., Western Oreg. U., Monmouth, 2000. Cert. tchr. K-8 Alaska, 1991. Tchr. 2d and 6th Cath. Schs. of Fairbanks, Alaska, 1991—95; reading tchr. Hunter Elem., Fairnbanks, 1996—97; kindergarten tchr. Anderson Elem., Eielson AFB, Alaska, 1997—99; tchr. 2d grade Pearl Creek Elem., Fairbanks, 1999; tchr. English and lit. North Pole Mid. Sch., Fairbanks, 2000—03; tchr. English and social studies Tanana Mid. Sch., Fairbanks, 2003—. Mentor tchr. U. Alaska, Fairbanks, 2004—. Religious edn. and youth group Cath. D. of Fairbanks, 2002—. Mem.: NEA (assoc.). Catholic. Avocations: travel, reading, kayaking, theater, skiing. Office: Fairbanks North Star Borough School Dist 520 5th Ave Fairbanks AK 99701 Business E-Mail: jshier@northstar.k12.ak.us.

SHIER, SHELLEY M., production company executive; b. Toronto, Mar. 15, 1957; d. Harry Shier and Rosaline (Cutler) Sonshine; m. Hank O'Neal, May 14, 1985. Student, H.B. Studio, NYC, 1975—76, Stella Adler Conservatory, 1976—80. Company mem., actor Soho Artists Theater, NYC, 1976-81; casting dir. Lawrence Price Prodns., NYC, 1981-82; pres. Hoss, Inc., NYC, 1983—; v.p. Chiaroscuro Records, NYC, 1987—; pres. Broadway Bound, Inc., NYC, 1998—. Cons. Peter Martin Assocs., NYC, 1983, Norwegian Cruise Line, Miami, Fla., 1983-98, Floating Jazz Festival, 1983—,Oslo (Norway) Jazz Festival, 1986—, New Sch. Social Rsch., NYC, 1989—, Big Bands Sea, Rhythm & Blues Cruise, Dixieland Sea, 1991—, Blues Cruise, 1991—, Beacons Jazz Awards Ceremony, Tribute Music Bob Wills Texas Playboys, Mardi Gras Sea. Talent acquisition agt. Save Children, NYC, 1986, Tomorrow's Children, NYC, 1990, Barcelona Olympics, NBC, 1992, Royal Caribbean Internat., Miami, 1994-96, Ultimate Caribbean Jazz Spectacular, Country Music Festival Caribbean, CUNARD NYC, 1994—, Broadway Sea, 1996, Millennium Sea, 1999—, Broadway Bound, 1999—, others. Avocations: Karate, photography, riding, fishing, weightlifting. Office: HOSS Inc 830 Broadway New York NY 10003-4827 Office Phone: 212-674-8631. Personal E-mail: shelleymshier@aol.com. Business E-Mail: broadwayboundinc@aol.com.

SHIER, SUSAN LYNNE, music educator; d. Elmer C. and Clara M. Werning; m. Robert L. Shier, June 4, 1982; children: Robert Matthew, Blake M. MusB in Edn., Ctrl. Mo. State U., Warrensburg, 1977, MA in Edn., 1985. Cert. instrumental and vocal music tchr. K-12 Mo., 1977. Band and vocal tchr. King City Sch. Dist., Mo., 1977—81, Platte County R-III Sch. Dist., Platte City, 1981—2008. V.p. North Ctrl. Mo. Bandmasters, Chillicothe, Mo., 1988—89; bldg. planning com. Platte County R-III Sch. Dist., Platte City, 1988—89, 2004—08, new tchr. mentor, 1992—2008; corr. sec. Platte County Educator Assn., 2005—. Mem. Pk. Hill South Band Parents, Riverside, Mo., PTA, Kansas City, 1981—2005; vol. local recycling ctr.; den mother Cub Scouts, Parkville, 1994—96. Nominee Excellence in Edn., Northland C. of C., 2006. Mem.: NEA, Mo. Music Educators, Mo. Bandmasters Assn., Platte County Edn. Assn. (corr. sec. 2005—06, membership chmn. 2005—08), Mo. Edn. Assn., Kappa Delta Pi, Pi Kappa Lambda, Sigma Alpha Iota (v.p. 1979—80). Democrat. Achievements include directing high school band selected to perform at Missouri Music Educators Conference; directing bands earning I ratings at District and State festivals; directing band selected to play for U.S. president during visit to Kansas City. Avocations: gardening, reading, travel.

SHIFF, ALAN HOWARD WILLIAM, judge; b. New Haven, June 2, 1934; s. Philip Robert and Harriet (Panikoff) S.; m. Carol Sweeterman Brumbaugh; children: Daniel Stuart, Andrew Reuben. BA, Yale U., 1957; LLB, U. Va., 1960. Bar: Conn. 1960, U.S. Dist. Ct. Conn. 1960, U.S. Ct. Appeals (2d cir.) 1969. Ptnr. Shiff, Shiff and Schancupp, New Haven, 1960-81; judge U.S. Bankruptcy Ct., Dist. Conn., Bridgeport, 1981—, chief judge, 1996—2003. Mem. bankruptcy apppellate panel svc., 1996—2003; internat. law rels. com. Nat. Conf. Bankruptcy Judges, 1996—98; spl. counsel Conn. Gen. Assembly Energy and Pub. Utilities Com., 1979—80; lectr. in field. Assoc. fellow Berkeley Coll.-Yale U., 2001—. Mem. Conn. Bar Assn., Adminstrv. Office U.S. Cts. (adv. com. on bankruptcy judges 1991-96, task force ofcl. on forms 1984-88, elected to serve 2d cir. gov. Nat. Conf. Bankruptcy Judges 1995-98). Office: US Bankruptcy Court 915 Lafayette Blvd Bridgeport CT 06604-4706 Office Phone: 203-579-5806.

SHIFFER, JAMES DAVID, retired utilities executive; b. San Diego, Mar. 24, 1938; s. Kenneth Frederick and Thelma Lucille (Good) S.; m. Margaret Edith Rightmyer, Sept. 5, 1959 (div. July 1986); children: James II, Elizabeth, Russell; m. Esther Zamora, Sept. 13, 1986; stepchildren: Bryan Boots, Jeremy Hellier, Marisol Loughead. BS in Chem. Engring., Stanford U., 1960, MS in Chem. Engring., 1962. Registered profl. engr., Calif. Nuc. engr. Pacific Gas & Electric Co., Humboldt Bay Power Plant, Eureka, Calif., 1961-71; tech. mgr. Pacific Gas & Electric Co., Diablo Canyon Power Plant, Avila Beach, Calif., 1971-80; mgr. nuc. ops. Pacific Gas & Electric Co., San Francisco, 1980-84, v.p. nuc. power generation, 1984-90, sr. v.p., gen. mgr. nuc. power generation bus. unit, 1990-91; exec. v.p. Pacific Gas & Electric, San Francisco, 1991-97; ret., 1997; pres., CEO PG&E Enterprises, San Francisco, 1994-95, also bd. dirs. Bd. dirs. Math., Engring., Sci. Achievement, 1992-2002. Mem. AIChE, Am. Nuc. Soc., Commonwealth Club of Calif. (bd. govs. 1992-97). Republican. Episcopalian. Avocations: golf, music, painting. Home: 2550 Royal Oaks Dr Alamo CA 94507-2227 E-mail: jshiffer@msn.com.

SHIFFMAN, BERNARD, mathematician, educator; b. NYC, 1942; s. Max and Bella S.; m. Doris Judith Yaffe, July 11, 1965; children: Jonathan, Daniel. BS, MIT, 1964; PhD, U. Calif., Berkeley, 1968. C.L.E. Moore instr. MIT, 1968-70; asst. prof. math. Yale U., 1970-73; assoc. prof. Johns Hopkins U., Balt., 1973-77, prof., 1977—, chair dept. math., 1990-93. Mem. Inst. Advanced Study, Princeton, NJ, 1975, Math. Scis. Rsch. Inst., Berkeley, Calif., 1996, 99; series lectr. U. Kaiserslautern, West Germany, 1977, Inst. Math., Academia Sinica, Beijing, 1978, U. Paris VI, 1979, Nordic Summer Sch., Joensuu, Finland, 1981, U. Tokyo, 2000; mem. Inst. des Hautes Etudes Scientifiques, Bures-sur-Yvette, France, 1979; vis. prof. U. Paris VI, 1981, 85, U. Grenoble, 1992, 95, 2001, 03. Editor Forum Mathematicum, 1989-95; assoc. editor Am. Jour. Math., 1990-92, 2005—, editor, 1992-93, editor-in-chief, 1993-2005; rschr. publs. in complex analysis. Hon. Woodrow Wilson fellow, 1964, NSF fellow, 1965-68, Alfred P. Sloan rsch. fellow, 1973-75; recipient Woodrow Wilson Faculty Devel. award, 1979. Mem. Am. Math. Soc. Office: Johns Hopkins U Dept Math Baltimore MD 21218

SHIFFMAN, KENNETH, orthopedist, surgeon; MD, Univ. So. Fla. Coll. Medicine, Tampa, Fla. Cert. Am. Bd. Orthopaedic Surgery, added qualification in hand surgery. Intern, resident Loyola Univ. Med. Ctr., assoc. prof., orthopaedic surgery; staff physician Hinsdale Hosp., Good Samaritan Hosp., Hinsdale Surg. Ctr., Salt Creek Surgery Ctr.; ptnr. Hinsdale Orthopaedic Associates, S.C., 1990—. Fellow, hand and upper extremity surgery Princess Margaret Rose Hosp., Edinburgh; fellow, orthopaedic trauma Sunnybrook Med. Ctr., Toronto, Canada. Mem.: Chgo. Soc. Surgery of the Hand, Am. Soc. Surgery of the Hand, Am. Acad. Orthopaedic Surgeons. Office: Hinsdale Orthopaedic Associates SC 550 W Ogden Ave Hinsdale IL 60521*

SHIFFMAN, MICHAEL A., lawyer; b. Newark, July 23, 1941; LLB magna cum laude, Lincoln U., 1973. Bar: Calif. 1973, U.S. Dist. Ct. (no. dist.) Calif. 1973; lic. real estate broker. Atty. Lanahan & Reilley, San Francisco, EVP and GC-New City N. Am. Editor: Lincoln U. Law Rev., 1972-73. Mem. ABA, Internat. Bar Assn., State Bar Calif. Office: 201 The Embarcadero Pier 35 San Francisco CA 94111-2002 Business E-Mail: shifflaw@aol.com.

SHIFFRIN, NANCY, writer, educator; d. Martin and Minna Shiffrin. BA, Calif. State U., 1972; PhD, Union Inst., 1994. Adj. prof. LA Cmty. Coll. Dist., 1990—. Editl. and manuscript cons. Author: What She Could Not Name, 1987, The Holy Letters, 2000, My Jewish Name, 2002, The Vast Unknowing wwaow.com, 2008. Recipient 1st prize, Acad. Am. Poets Coll. Competition, 1972. Jewish. Avocations: yoga, hiking, Jewish culture. Office Phone: 310-302-1107. Personal E-mail: nshiffrin@earthlink.net.

SHIFMAN, MIKHAIL, physicist; b. Riga, Latvia, Apr. 4, 1949; came to U.S., 1990; s. Arkady and Raisa (Yakovich) S.; m. Margarita Pusynya, Apr. 21, 1971; children: Julia, Anya. MA in Theoretical Physics, Moscow Inst. Physics & Tech., Dolgoprudny, Russia, 1972; PhD, Inst. Theoretical Exptl. Phys., Moscow, 1976. From jr. rsch. fellow to sr. rschr. Inst. Theoretical & Exptl. Physics, Moscow, 1976-89; prof. theoretical physics U. Minn., Mpls., 1990—. Lectr. on particle physics and field theory. Author: Vacuum Structure and QCD Sum Rules, 1992, Instantons in Gauge Theories, 1994, ITEP Lectures on Particle Physics and Field Theory, 2 vols., 1999, The Many Faces of the Superworld, 2000, The Supersymmetric World, 2000; At the Frontiers of Particle Physics, 4 Vol., 2001 Recipient Humboldt Rsch. award Alexander-von-Humboldt Stiftung, Bonn, Germany, 1993, Rsch. award Japan Soc. for Promotion Sci., 1993, 96. Fellow Am. Phys. Soc. (Sakurai prize 1999, Lilienfeld prize, 2006). Achievements include invention (with others) invisible axion; rsch. in hadronic physics/quantum chromodynamics, SVZ sum rules, heavy-flavor hadrons based on the heavy quark expansions, supersymmetric guage theories in the strong coupling regime. Office: Theoretical Phys Inst Univ Minn 116 Church St SE Minneapolis MN 55455-0149 E-mail: shifman@umn.edu.

SHIFRIN, DONALD LEE, pediatrician; b. Portland, Oreg., Jan. 10, 1949; m. Barbara Sue Chamberlin, Nov. 3, 2002; children: Max Burton, Alexis Chamberlin. MD, Georgetown U., Washington, 1970. Cert. Am. Bd. Pediatrics, 1981. Physician Pediatric Assocs., Bellevue, Wash., 1978—. Clin. prof. pediat. U. Wash. Sch. Medicine, Seattle. Chair Maimonides Soc. Jewish Fedn. Greater Seattle, 2000—. Fellow: Am. Acad. Pediat. Office: Pedatric Associates 2700 Northup Way Bellevue WA 98004 Office Fax: 425-828-2256; Home Fax: 206-275-3244. Business E-Mail: dshifrin@peds-associates.com.

SHIGEMASA, TERESA, mental health services professional, educator; d. Kermin Joseph Guidry and Melva Gene Bell; m. Greg Uichi Shigemasa, June 29, 1996; children: Emily Guidry-Nguyen, Skye. BFA, So. Meth. U., Dallas, 1977; MSCP, Chaminade U., Honolulu, 2000. Cert. LMHC #1, DCCA Hawaii, 2005, RPT-S, S-874 Assn. Play Therapy, 2006, registered play therapist, supr. play therapist candidates Assn. Play Therapy, 2006. Instr. domestic violence Child & Family Svc., Honolulu, 1998—2001; behavioral specialist Dept. Edn.-Sunset Beach Elem. Sch., Haleiwa, Hawaii, 2001—. Dancer, singer, actress profl. summer stock prodns., Dallas, Brunswick, Maine. Vol. local schs. various musical prodns. Mem.: Hawaii Assn. Play Therapy (pub. rels. 2005—06), Assn. Play Therapy, Hawaii Counseling Assn., Psi Chi Honor Soc., Alpha Lambda Delta. Avocations: dance, music. Office: Dept Edn Sunset Beach Elem Sch 59-360 Kamehameha Hwy Haleiwa HI 96712 Personal E-mail: tshigema21@yahoo.com.

SHIGEMITSU, TOSHIRO, ophthalmologist, researcher; b. Kyoto, Feb. 7, 1953; s. Yoshito and Eiko (Yoshioka) S.; m. Kumiko Nakahori, Oct. 27, 1990. MD, Fujita Health U., Toyoake, Japan, 1982, DMS, 1987. Asst. prof. ophthalmology Fujita Health U., Toyoake, 1988-91, assoc. prof. ophthalmology, 1991—2001, vis. assoc. prof. ophthalmology, 2002—. Dir. ophthalmology Hojinkai Med. Found., Kawade Hosp., Toyota, 1984—99; dir., head Shigemitsu Eye Clinic & Rsch. Found., Inc., 2002—. Patentee in field; contbr. articles to profl. jours. Mem. judging com. Fund Med. Security Sys., Aichi, 1996—2002. Recipient Japan Soc. Clin. Ophthalmology poster prize, 1998, Silver medal, Japan Ophthalmol. Soc., 1990; grantee Eye Bank Assn. Aichi, 1993, 94, 95. Mem.: Am. Acad. Opthalmology, Toikai Med. Assn. (bd. dirs. 1999—2005), Japanese Soc. Pathology (sci. councillor 2001—), Toukai Soc. Glaucoma (bd. dirs. 1998—2002), Asia Pacific Intraocular Implant Assn. (faculty 1997—98), Japanese Ophthalmic Pathology Soc. (councillor 1997—), Am. Aging Assn., European Soc. Cataract and Refractive Surgeons, Am. Soc. Cataract and Refractive Surgery. Avocations: travel, movies, golf, art. Office: Shigemitsu Eye Clin & Rsch Fdn Inc 3-6-23 Kuzuha-Asahi Hirakata 573-1111 Japan Office Phone: 81 72 866 2238.

SHIH, CHIANG, mechanical engineer, educator; b. Taipei, Taiwan, Republic of China, Aug. 30, 1956; came to U.S., 1980; s. Chi-Ling and Tze-Lang (Sen) S.; m. Ya-Li Sandy Chang, June 25, 1980; 1 child, Jonathan. BS, Nat. Tsing-Hua U., Tsin-Tsu, Taiwan, 1978; MS, La. State U., 1982; PhD, U. So. Calif., 1988. Asst. prof. mech. engring. Fla. State U., Tallahassee, 1988—. Mem. AIAA, Am. Phys. Soc. Office: Fla State U Dept Mech Engring 2525 Pottsdamer St Tallahassee FL 32310-6046

SHIHAB, FUAD SAID, medical educator, researcher; s. Said Mohamed Shihab and Sania Atef Olabi; m. Samar Foud Jammal, Sept. 2, 1994; children: Saeed, Omar, Tala. BS in Chemistry, Am. U., Beirut, 1981; MD, Am. U., 1985. Diplomate Am. Bd. Internal Medicine, 1989, Nephrology Am. Bd. Internal Medicine, 1992. Resident/intern Md. Gen. Hosp., Balt., 1986—89, chief resident, 1988; fellow nephrology U. Pa., Phila., 1989—91; fellow transplantation medicine Oreg. Health Scis. U., Portland, 1991—92; asst. prof. medicine U. Utah, Salt Lake City, 1992—97, prof. medicine, 2002—. Med. dir. kidney transplant U. Utah, 1994—. Contbr. scientific papers numerous to profl jour., articles. Fellow: ACP, Am. Soc. Nephrology; mem.: Nat. Kidney Found., Am. Soc. Transplantation (chairperson fellowship tng. com. 2002—).

SHIHABI, ZAK K., lab administrator, director; b. Jerusalem, Nov. 17, 1939; 1 child, Sami Zak. PhD, U. SD, Vermillion, 1970. Lab dir. Wake Forest U. Sch. Med., Winston-Salem, NC, 1972—. Contbr. scientific papers. Business E-Mail: zshihabi@wfubmc.edu.

SHIH-CARDUCCI, JOAN CHIA-MO, food service executive, medical technologist, biochemist, writer, educator; b. Rukuan, Chunghua, Taiwan, Dec. 21, 1933; came to U.S., 1955; d. Luke Chiang-hsi and Lien-chin Shih; m. Kenneth M. Carducci, Sept. 30, 1960 (dec. July 1988); children: Suzanne R., Elizabeth M. BS in Chemistry, St. Mary Coll., Xavier, Kans., 1959; intern in med. tech., St. Mary's Hosp., Rochester, NY, 1960. Med. rschr. Strong Meml. Hosp. U. Rochester, 1960-61; pharm. chemist quality control Strasenburgh Labs., Rochester, 1961-62; cooking tchr. adult edn. Montgomery County Pub. Schs., Rockville, Md., 1973-79; tchr. The Chinese Cookery Inc., Rockville, 1975-86, Silver Spring, Md., 1986—, pres., bd. dirs., 1975—; chemist NIH, Bethesda, 1987-2000; analytical chemist NIH/WRAIR, Rockville, Md., 1994-96. Author: The Chinese Cookery, 1981, Hunan Cuisine, 1984, Vegetarian Cuisine, 2000, The Art of The Chinese Cookery, 2001 (The Cook Book Winner of Pinnacle Book award 2005). Mem. Am. Chem. Soc., Internat. Assn. Cooking Profls. (Woman of Yr. 1994-2004). Republican. Roman Catholic. Avocations: piano, music, dance, gardening. Home and Office: The Chinese Cookery Inc 14209 Sturtevant Rd Silver Spring MD 20905-4448 Office Phone: 301-236-5311. Personal E-mail: chinesecookery@aol.com.

SHIKANOV, SERGEY, urologist; b. St. Petersburg, Russia, Aug. 25, 1970; s. Maria Shikanov; m. Ariella Bookh, Apr. 13, 2000; children: Eve, Ruth. MD, Hebrew U. Hadassah Med. Sch., Jerusalem, 1996. Diplomate ECFMG, 2006. Intern Hadassah Med. Ctr., 1996—97, urology resident, 2001—07; med. officer Israeli Def. Forces, 1997—2001; urology rsch. fellow U. Chgo., 2007—. Mem.: Am. Urol. Assn. Achievements include research in urological oncology and minimally invasive surgery. Home: 1337 E Madison Pk app2 Chicago IL 60615 Office: Univ Chgo 5841 S Maryland Ave MC 6038 Chicago IL 60637 Home Fax: 773-702-1001. Personal E-mail: sergeyshikanov@gmail.com.

SHIKUMA, EUGENE YUJIN, travel company executive; b. Tokyo, Nov. 18, 1948; arrived in U.S., 1957; s. Mitsuo and Yukiko (Kanaoka) Shikuma. BSEE, U. Hawaii at Manoa, Honolulu, 1971, MS in Computer Sci., 1975. Lab. test engr. and scientist McDonnell Douglas Astronautics, Inc., 1971-72; systems engr. Lear Siegler Astronics, 1972-73; jr. coord. Japan Travel Bur. Hawaii, Inc., Honolulu, 1978-83, sr. coord., 1983-84, supr., 1984-89, mgr., 1989—, sr. mgr., 2008—. Bd. dir. Maui United Way, Kahului, Hawaii, 1988—89, Maui Hui Malama, Waiulku, 1989—90; mem. Maui County Visitor Task Force, 1995—; adv. bd. mem. Maui Acad. Travel and Tourism; bd. dir. Maui Visitors Bur., 2003—; mem. Maui Sister Cities Internat. Festival Com., 2005; com. mem. Maui County Sister Cities Festival, 2005, Maui Tourism Strategic Plan Com., 2005—; hon. chmn. bus. adv. coun. Hawaii Nat. Rep. Congl. Com., 2003; mem. Honolulu Festival Found., 2007—; bd. dir., sec. Kamoa Views Apt. Owners Assn., 1991—96. Recipient Ronald Reagan Rep. Hawaii Gold medal, Nat. Rep. Congl. Com., 2004, 2005, Congl. medal of distinction, 2006, Congl. Order Merit, 2006, 2007; named Businessman of Yr., 2004, Rep. of Yr., 2006. Mem.: Maui Japanese C. of C., Maui C. of C. Avocations: swimming, coin collecting/numismatics, art, antique prints. Office Phone: 808-871-6600. Business E-Mail: eshikuma@jtb-hawaii.com.

SHILEPSKY, NANCY SUE, lawyer; b. Westport, Conn., Apr. 25, 1952; d. Morris Jacob and Rose (Pfeffer) S. BA magna cum laude, Tufts U., 1974; JD, Boston U., 1978. Bar: Mass. 1978, U.S. Dist. Ct. Mass. 1978. Dir. Legal Info. Ctr. Bklyn. Coll., 1978-79; staff atty. Western Mass. Legal Svcs., Springfield, 1980-81; ptnr. Northampton (Mass.) Law Collective, 1982-84; assoc. Schreiber & Assocs., Boston, 1984-87, McDonald, Noonan & Kaplan, Newton, Mass., 1987-88; ptnr. Rudavsky & Shilepsky, Boston, 1988, Shilepsky, Messing & Rudavsky, Boston, 1988—2005, Perkins Smith& Cohen, Boston, Shilepsky O'Connell, Boston, 2005—. Speaker Mass. Continuing Legal Edn., Inc., Boston, 1988—. Named one of top Boston lawyers, Boston Mag., 2004. Mem.: Boston Bar Assn. (treas. 2004—05), Mass. Bar Assn.-Labor & Employment Law Sect. (chmn. employee rights & responsibilities com. 1990—91, 1993—94, sect. coun. 1993—96), Boston Bar Assn.-Labor & Employment Law Sect. (co-chmn. 1996—99, sect. coun. 1996—). Office: Shilepsky O'Connell 225 Franklin St Boston MA 02110 Home Phone: 617-484-1779; Office Phone: 617-447-2806. Office Fax: 617-447-2800. Business E-Mail: nshilepsky@sholaw.com.

SHILLER, HELEN, alderwoman; BA in History, U. Wis., Madison, 1969; M in Pub. Policy, De Paul U. Sch. New Learning, Chgo., 2005. Freelance photographer, editor, reporter; exec. organizer Employment Action Coalition, 1979-81; pres., CEO Justice Graphics, 1981-87; alderwoman, 46th ward Chgo. City Coun., 1987—. GED tchr. Stockton Sch., 1981—82; lectr. DePaul U. Sch. New Learning. Mem. Chgo. Pvt. Industry Coun., 1983-87, Mayor Washington's Polit. Edn. Project, 1984, Uplift Cmty. Sch. Adv. Com.; bd. mem. Jewish Coun. on Urban Affairs, Kuumba Lynx Youth Performance Group, Kuumba Lynx Coll. Scholarship Program; former vol. Uptown People's Law Ctr., Uptown Cmty. Learning Ctr., Black Lung Assn.; former pres. Stockton Sch. Adv. Coun., Parent Equalizers Chgo., Uptown Cmty. Health Svc. Corp.; former mem. steering com. Alliance Better Schs.; co-chair Heart of Uptown Coalition, 1983-87; former del. Org. the Northeast. Recipient Cmty. Leadership award, Heart Uptown Coalition, 1979, Cmty. Activism award, Cmty. Renewal Soc., 1980, Friend of the Cmty. award, Midwest Cmty. Coun., 1987, Leadership and Commitment to Justice award, Mozambique Support Network, 1989, Outstanding Cmty. Svc. award, Comite Latino, 1990, Dr. Natalie Stephens' Founders award, Rape Victims Advocates, 1995, Pres. award, Harry S. Truman Coll., 1996, Civic award, Chgo. House, 1996, Courageous Voices award, Jewish Coun., 2003, Courage and Leadership award, Org. the Northeast, 2003, Disting. Legis. Svc. award, Vietnamese Assn. Ill., 2004, Silver Circle award, Sarah's Circle, 2004, 100 Champions Legends award, Gay Games VII, 2006; named to Chgo. Gay and Lesbian Hall of Fame (Friend of the Cmty. Inductee), 2000. Mem. NOW, Cmty. Renewal Soc. Africa Roundtable, Comm. Workers Am. Local 16 Typographical Union, Ind. Voters Ill.-Precinct Orgn., Phi Theta Kappa (hon.). Office: 4544 N Broadway St Chicago IL 60640-5602 also: City Hall 121 N LaSalle St Chicago IL 60602 Office Phone: 773-878-4646, 312-744-6831. Office Fax: 773-878-4920. Business E-Mail: ward46@cityofchicago.org.*

SHILLER, ROBERT JAMES, economist; b. Detroit, Mar. 29, 1946; s. Benjamin P. and Ruth R. (Radzville) S.; m. Virginia M. Faulstich, June 13, 1976; 2 sons. BA, U. Mich., 1967; SM, MIT, 1968, PhD, 1972. Asst. prof. U. Minn., 1972-74; rsch. fellow Nat. Bur. Econ. Rsch., Cambridge, Mass., 1974-75; vis. scholar dept. econs. MIT, Cambridge, 1974-75, vis. prof., 1981-82; assoc. prof. dept. econs. U. Pa., Phila., 1974-81, prof. economics, 1981-82; Arthur M. Okun prof. economics Yale U., New Haven, 1982—; prof. fin. Wharton Sch., 1981-82. Co-founder Case, Shiller, Weiss Inc., 1991-2002; co-founder, chief economist, MacroMarkets, LLC, 1999-; vis. scholar dept. econs. Harvard U., 1980. Fgn. editor

Rev. Econ. Studies, 1981-84; assoc. editor Jour. Econometrics, 1980-83; author: Market Volatility, 1989, Macro Markets: Creating Institutions for Managing Society's Largest Economic Risks, 1993, Irrational Exuberance, 2000, New Financial Order: Risk in the 21st Century, 2003, Subprime Solution: How Today's Global Financial Crisis Happened and What to Do About It, 2008; co-author: (with George Akerlof) Animal Spirits: How Human Psychology Drives the Economy, and Why It Matters for Global Capitalism, 2009 Grantee NSF, 1976—; Guggenheim fellow; recipient: Paul A. Samuelson award, 1996, Commonfund prize, 2001; named to The Power 30, Smart Money, mag., 2008 Fellow Econometric Soc., Am. Acad. Arts and Scis., Am. Philos. Soc., Am. Econ. Assn. (v.p. 2005), Ea. Econ. Assn. (pres. 2006-07). Office: Cowles Found PO Box 208281 New Haven CT 06520-8281 also: MacroMarkets LLC 14 Main Street Madison NJ 07940 Office Phone: 203-432-3708. Business E-Mail: robert.shiller@yale.edu.*

SHILLESTAD, JOHN GARDNER, diversified financial services company executive; b. Oak Park, Ill., Oct. 31, 1934; s. John Nelson and Isabel Blanche (Gardner) Shillestad; m. Astri Cedervall; children: Christine C, Annette. BBA, Northwestern U., 1964, MBA, 1967. CLU, CPCU; ChFC. Mktg. dir. spl. plans CNA Ins., Chgo., 1958-66; asst. v.p. Montgomery Ward Life, Chgo., 1966-69; pres., CEO Fort Dearborn Life Ins. Co., Chgo., 1969-79; sr. v.p. Hartford Life Cos., Conn., 1979-85, also bd. dirs. Conn., 1985-87; pres. JGS Fin. Svcs., Inc., 1987—2007, Columbian Mut. Life Ins. Co., Binghamton, NY, 1987—2007. Chmn. Columbian Life Ins Co, Washington Nat. Life NY; with Golden Eagles Sales Corp., 1997—2007; bd. dirs. Reassure Am, Valley Forge Life Ins. Co., 2004. Mem Bd Educ, Dist 30, Northbrook, Ill., 1976—79; mem adv bd SUNY Sch Mgt, Binghamton, Kellogg Sch Bus, Northwestern Univ; bd dirs Salvation Army, Binghamton, Partnership 2000, Southern Tier Equity Fund. With US Army, 1954—56. Mem.: Broome County CofC (bd dirs), Pelican Marsh Golf Club (Naples, Fla), Sunset Ridge Club (Northfield, Ill). Republican. Congregationalist. Home: 3 Regentwood Rd Northfield IL 60093-2728 also: Unit 304 1600 Clermont Dr Naples FL 34109 E-mail: sjackshil@aol.com.

SHILLING, A. GARY, economist, consultant; b. Fremont, Ohio, May 25, 1937; s. A. Vaughn and Lettie E. (O'Harrow) S.; m. Margaret E. Bloete, Dec. 22, 1962; children: Geoffrey B., Andrew J., Stephen E., Jennifer E. AB in Physics magna cum laude, Amherst Coll., Mass., 1960; MA in Econs., Stanford U., Calif., 1962, PhD in Econs., 1965; LLD (hon.), Tiffin U., 1999; DHL (hon.), Ch. Divinity Sch. Pacific, 2006; LHD (hon.), Berkeley Divinity Sch., Yale, 2008; D in Canon Law (hon.), U. South, 2009. Economist Standard Oil Co. (N.J.), NYC, 1963-67; chief economist Merrill Lynch, Pierce, Fenner & Smith, NYC, 1967-71; rsch. dir. Estabrook & Co., NYC, 1971-72; sr. v.p., chief economist White, Weld & Co., NYC, 1972-78; chmn., pres., dir. A. Gary Shilling & Co., Inc., Springfield, NJ, 1978—; pres. Lakeview Econ. Svcs., Inc., Springfield, 1979—; owner Lakeview Svcs., Inc., Springfield, 1993—. Bd. dirs. Nat. Life Vt., Montpelier, 1989-2007, Palm Harbor Homes, Am. Productivity and Quality Ctr., Houston; adv. dir. Austin (Tex.) Trust Co., 1988—, Nat. Life Vt., Montpelier, 1989-2007; informal econ. advisor Former Pres. George Bush, 1978—; mem. Nat. Com. on Jobs and Small Bus., 1986-87. Author: Is Inflation Ending? Are You Ready?, 1983, The World Has Definitely Changed: New Economic Forces and Their Implications for the Next Decade, 1986, After the Crash: Recession or Depression? Investment and Business Strategies for a Deflationary World, 1988, Deflation: Why it's coming, whether it's good or bad, and how it will affect your investments, business, and personal affairs, 1998, Korean and Chinese edits., 2000, Deflation: How to Survive and Thrive in the Coming Wave of Deflation, 1999, Chinese edit., 2000, Letting Off Steam, 2003; creator bd. game The Deflation Game, 1989; columnist Forbes, 1983—, Nihon Keizai Shimbun Jour. Bd. dirs. Aim Packaging Inc., 1986-89, Episcopal Ch. Found., N.Y.C., N.Y., 1989-97; chmn. Episcopal Preaching Found., Springfield, N.J., 1988—; trustee Bates Coll., Lewiston, Maine, 1988-91, Kent Pl. Sch., Summit, N.J., 1983-89, Henry J. Kessler Found., 1987-95; bd. dirs. The Gen. Theol. Episcopal Sem., N.Y.C., 1988-2001, treas., 1994-2001; chmn. N.J. State Revenue Forecasting Adv. Commn., 1995-2005; bd. dirs. Am. Rep. Ins. Co. N.Y., 1978-81, N.J. Shakespeare Festival, 1987-96, chmn., 1994-96. Named Wall St. Top Econs., Instl. Investor Mag., 1975, 76, Top Commodity Trading Advisor, Futures Mag., 1993, Third best Stockmarker Forecaster in the World, Money Sense Mag., 2003. Mem. Nat. Assn. Bus. Economics, N.Y. Soc. Security Analysts, Short Hills Club, Phi Beta Kappa, Sigma Xi. Republican. Episcopalian. Avocations: tennis, travel, gardening, hunting, fishing. Home: 33 Lakeview Ave Short Hills NJ 07078-2264 Office: A Gary Shilling & Co Inc 500 Morris Ave Springfield NJ 07081-1020 Office Phone: 973-467-0070. Business E-Mail: gary@agaryshilling.com.

SHILLING, KAY MARLENE, psychiatrist; b. July 1, 1953; d. Harrison Gene and Rose Marie (Allen) Herber. BS, U. Nebr., Lincoln, 1976; MD, U. Nebr., Omaha, 1980. Diplomate Nat. Bd. Med. Examiners. Resident in psychiatry U. Nebr. Med. Ctr., Omaha, 1981-84; pvt. practice Omaha, 1984—; med. dir., chief of staff La Plaza (Nebr.) Cmty. Health Ctr., 1999—, also bd. dirs. Encore chair Omaha Symphony Guild, 2000—04, v.p. adminstrn., 2003—04, mem. nominating com., 2002, chair Spring Fundraiser, 2004, exec. bd., 2003—04; mem. Henry Doorly Zoo Guild; mem. bd. Opera Omaha Guild, 2003—, chair Holiday meeting, 2004, chair ann. meetings, 2003—04, 2006—07; mem. Fontenelle Nature assn. Guild, 1999—, Omaha Bot. Gardens Guild, 2001—; chair spring fundraiser Omaha Symphony Music Cir., 2004—, chmn. ann. meeting, 2004—05; bd. trustees, faculty com. Grace U.; bd. dirs. Opera Omaha, 2004—09, Joslyn Castle Trust, 2009—, Indian Chicano Health Ctr., 1983—92; bd. dirs., audience devel. com. Opera Omaha, 2004—; bd. dirs. Omaha Symphony Guild, 1999—2000, Museo Latino Feria, 2004—05; mem. guild bd. Durham Western Heritage Mus., 2005—06; co-chair 1st Lady Luncheon Durham Soc., 2006—. Mem. AMA, Royal Soc. Medicine, Ctrl. Neuro Psychiat. Assn. (bd. dirs., pres. 1996-97), Am. Med. Women's Assn. (pres. Omaha chpt. 1986-88, Nebr. State dir. 1988-94, regional gov. 1993-95, bd. dirs. 1993-95, book reviewer for JAMWA, Outstanding Physician award 1989, 90-93, nat. cmty. svc. award 1990), Am. Psychiat. Assn., Met. Omaha Med. Soc., Nebr. Med. Assn., Durham Soc., Kiwanis Internat., Alpha Xi Delta. Avocations: gardening, travel, gourmet cooking, interior decorating, house renovation. Home: 1103 S 80th St Omaha NE 68124-1419 Office: 7602 Pacific St Ste 302 Omaha NE 68114-5405

SHILLING, LILLESS MCPHERSON, healthcare educator; d. Joseph James and Loue Elizabeth Pendleton McPherson; m. Mackie Delano Na, Feb. 12, 1973; 1 child, Paz McPherson Shilling Began. Degree, Skidmore Coll., Saratoga Springs, NY, 1962; AB in English, Social Studies, U. Mich., Ann Arbor, 1964; MA in Edn., Columbia U. Tchrs. Coll., NY, 1969; MA in Journalism, Ohio State U., Columbus, 1975, PhD, 1983. Cert. in French UN Hdqs., NY, 1969, in Spanish 1972. Tchr., English, ESL, Social Studies NYC Sch. Sys., 1966—69; asst. to assoc. editor Assn. Schs. Allied Health Professions, Washington, 1978—84; faculty mem., biomed. comm. divsn., Sch. Allied Med. Professions Ohio State U., 1979—84, asst. dir., office sponsored program devel., 1984—85; faculty mem. Med. U. SC., Charleston, 1985—. Vis. instr., artists-in-schs. program Greater Columbus Arts Coun., 1983. Co-editor: (book) Dictionary of Quotations in Communications, (textbook) Communicating About Communicable Diseases; co-author: Communicating Comfortably: Your Guide to Overcoming Speaking and Writing Anxieties; author: (poem) Perspective; contbr. articles to profl. jours. Vol., adult cancer survivors Camp Bluebird, Charleston, 1988—2007; docent, tchr., mem., choir, gardening coms. Unitarian Universalist Ch. Charleston, Charleston, 1985—. Recipient Tchr. Appreciation award, Med. Comm. Preceptor Conf., Ohio State U., 1980, Svc. Excellence award, Coll. Health Professions, Med. U. SC., 2001, Outstanding Tchg. award, 2007; fellowship, Charleston Area Writing Project, 1988, Lowcountry Writing Project, SC, 2006, grant, Duke Endowment, 2002—05, NIH, 2002—07, US, HHS. Mem.: Assn. Schs. Allied Health Professions (Editor's award 1983, Disting. Author award 1985, Outstanding Poster award 1992, 1996), Kappa Tau Alpha, Phi Kappa Phi. Independent. Unitarian Universalist. Avocations: walking, swimming, poetry, reading.

SHILLING, ROY BRYANT, JR., academic administrator; s. Roy Bryant and Lila M. (Prestage) S.; m. Margaret Riddle, Oct. 16, 1952; children: Roy Bryant III, Nancy Gale. BA, McMurry U., 1951, HHD, 1982; BD, So. Meth. U., 1957; MS, Ind. U., 1966, PhD, 1967. Presdl. asst. McMurry U., Abilene, Tex., 1959-61; asst. to pres. Tenn. Wesleyan Coll., 1961-64; asst. in devel. Ball State U., 1964-65; rsch. assoc. Ind. U., 1965-67; dir. planning and rsch. Baldwin Wallace Coll., 1967-68; exec. v.p. Southwestern U., 1968-69, pres., 1981-2000, pres. emeritus, 2000—; pres. Hendrix Coll., 1969-81, McMurry Univ., 2002. Mem. Nat. Commn. on United Meth. Higher Edn., 1975-77. Mem. Ark. Arts and Humanities Coun., 1970-76, chmn., 1974-75; bd. dirs. Ark. Children's Hosp., 1981; mem. bd. higher edn. and ministry United Meth. Ch., 1972-80, mem. univ. senate, 1980-88, v.p. 1983-84, pres., 1984-88; chmn. Gulf dist. Rhodes Scholarship Selection Com., 1992, Ark. chmn., 1973-74, Tex. chmn., 1985-91; mem. Young Pres. Orgn., 1975-81; mem. bd. visitors Air U., 1991-94. With U.S. Army, 1952-54. Recipient Disting. Alumnus award McMurry U., 1980, Perkins Disting. Alumnus award So. Meth. U., 1987, Owen B. Sherrill award for leadership in econ. devel. Georgetown, 1988; named one of Top 100 Most Effective Coll. Pres. in Nation, Bowling Green State U./Exxon Edn. Found., 1986. Mem. North Ctrl. Assn. Colls. and Schs. (vice chmn., chmn. elect 1980-81), Nat. Assn Schs. and Colls. of United Meth. Ch. (v.p. 1975-76, pres. 1976-77), Nat. Coun. Ind. Colls. and Univs. (bd. dirs. 1984-88), So. U. Conf. (exec. com. 1974-78), 79-86, sec.-treas. 1979-86, v.p. 1991-92, pres. 1992-93), Am. Coun. Edn. (bd. dirs. 1989-91; mem. commn. on govt. and pub. rels. 1999-2000, spl. counselor to the pres. 2000-01), Inst. for Humanities (bd. dirs. Salado, Tex. chpt. 1985-91, mem. internat. coun. advs. 1994), NCAA Divsn. III Pres.'s Coun., 1998-2000, Philos Soc. Tex., Rotary, Masons, Alpha Chi, Phi Delta Kappa. Office: 1405 Mesa Ridge Ln Austin TX 78735-1639 E-mail: shilling@southwestern.edu.

SHILLINGBURG, CONSTANCE JOANNE, historian, retired history professor; b. Las Vegas, N. Mex., May 10, 1938; d. John Bird and Grace Louise (Guffey) Murphy; m. Herbert Thompson Shillingburg, June 11, 1960; children: Lisa Grace, Leslie Susan, Lara Stephanie. BA Cum Laude, U. N. Mex., Albuquerque, 1960; degree, U. Southern Calif., LA, 1961, Moorpark Coll., Calif., 1972; MEd Summa Cum Laude, U. Ctrl. Okla., Edmond, 1978. Cert. secondary schs. tchr. N. Mex. English, journalism tchr. Woodrow Wilson HS, Long Beach, Calif., 1960—61; english tchr. North HS, Torrance, Calif., 1961, Highland HS, Albuquerque, 1967—68; adj. prof. Okla. City Cmty. Coll., Okla. City, 1978—80; US history tchr. Hefner Jr. HS, Okla. City, 1980—93; US world history tchr. Edmond Meml. HS, Okla., 1993—2000. Hist. interpreter Her Royal Majesties Hist. Interpretations, Edmond, 2001—08. Prodr.(writer): (plays, one act play) When Queens Collide, 2005—06;, author monologues. Young democrats Edmond Meml. HS, 2007—08. Named one of Tchr. of Yr., Hefner Jr. HS, Okla., 1990; grant, Commn. Bicentennial US Constn., Okla., 1985, grant Kids, Putnam City found., Okla., 1989, 1992, grant, Edmond Edn. Com., Okla., 1993—94, grant Advanced Placement Tng., Tex. Christian U., Okla., 1995, U. Tex. Austin, Okla., 1996, grant, Coll. Bd. Advanced Placement Tng., Tulsa U., 1998, grant AP computer equipment, State Okla., 1999. Mem.: Okla. City Chpt. English Speaking Union, Amer Assn. U. Women, (Calif.) (Best Chpt. .Publicity Nat. award 1970—71), Ladies Music Club, (Okla.), Delta Kappa Gamma, (Okla.), Phi Alpha Theta, (N. Mex.) (Best Chpt.Publicity Nat. award 1966—67), Phi Kappa Phi, Mortar Bd. Sr. Women's, (N. Mex.), Theta Sigma Phi, (N. Mex.). Avocations: reading, travel, gardening. Home: Edmond, Okla. Died June 28, 2008.

SHILLINGBURG, HERBERT THOMPSON, JR., dental educator; b. Mar. 21, 1938; s. Herbert Thompson and Stefi Marie (Schuster) Shillingburg; m. Constance Joanne Murphy, June 11, 1960; children: Lisa Grace, Leslie Susan, Lara Stephanie. Student, U. N.Mex., 1955-58, 65-66; DDS, U. So. Calif., 1962; Dr (hon.), U. Medicine and Pharmacy Targu Mures, Romania, 2006. Gen. practice dentistry, Albuquerque, 1964-67; asst. prof. fixed prosthodontics sect. UCLA Sch. Dentistry, 1967-70, chmn., 1970-72; chmn. dept. fixed prosthodontics U. Okla. Coll. Dentistry, Okla. City, 1972—2003, David Ross Boyd Disting. prof., 1983, prof. emeritus, 2003—. Cons. VA Hosp., Muskogee, Okla., 1975—84, Oklahoma City, 1977—93, U.S. Army Dental Activity, Ft. Knox, Ky., 1980—94. Author: (also in Japanese, German, Greek, Spanish, Italian, French, Portuguese, Polish, Korean, Chinese, Russian and Croation) Preparations for Cast Gold Restorations, 1974, Fundamentals of Fixed Prosthodontics, 1976, 3d edit., 1997, Guide to Occlusal Waxing, 1979, 3d edit., 2000, Restoration of the Endodontically Treated Tooth, 1984, Fundamentals of Tooth Preparations for Cast Metal and Porcelain Restorations, 1987; co-editor: Quintessence of Dental Technology, 1984—88; sect. editor: Quintessence Internat., 1988—2001, mem. editl. coun.: Jour. Prosthetic Dentistry, 1996—99. Capt. US Army, 1962—64. Recipient Award for tchg. excellence, UCLA Sch. Dentistry, 1969, 1972, 1973, Okla. Coll. Dentistry, 1976, 1978, 1982, 1987, 1993, 1994, 1997, 1st prize, Am. Med. Writers Assn., 1988, La Mèdaille de la Ville de Paris (èchelon Argent), 1990, Outstanding Profl. Achievement award, O U Coll. Dentristy, 2003, Prof. of Hon., U. Medicine and Pharmacy Targu-Mures, 2004; named Disting. Lectr., O U Assoc., 1989, Herbert T. Shillingburg Endowed Professorship Fixed Prosthodontics, Coll. Dentistry, 2006. Fellow: Am. Coll. Dentists; mem.: ADA, Okla. State Dental Assn., Internat. Assn. Dental Rsch., Am. Coll. Prosthodontists (hon.), Am. Acad. Restorative Dentistry, Am. Acad. Fixed Prosthodontics (George H. Moulton award 1998), Am. Acad. Operative Dentistry, Phi Kappa Phi, Omicron Kappa Upsilon (Stephen H. Leeper award for Tchg. Excellence Supreme Ch. 2000). Independent. Episcopalian. Avocations: travel, photography. Home: 1312 Brixton Rd Edmond OK 73034-3314 Office: U Okla Coll Dentistry PO Box 26901 Oklahoma City OK 73190-0001

SHILLINGLAW, GORDON, retired finance educator; b. Albany, NY, July 26, 1925; s. James McCombe and Margaret Blanche (Stephens) Shillinglaw; m. Barbara Ann Cross, June 24, 1950; children: James McCombe, Laura Cross. AB magna cum laude, Brown U., 1945; MS, U. Rochester, 1948; PhD, Harvard U., 1952. Asst. prof. Hamilton Coll., Clinton, NY, 1951-52; cons. assoc. Joel Dean Assocs., Yonkers, NY, 1952-55; asst. prof. MIT, Cambridge, 1955-61; assoc. prof. Columbia U., NYC, 1961-66, prof. acctg., 1966-90, prof. emeritus, 1991—. Vis. prof. Mgmt. Devel. Inst., Lausanne, Switzerland, 1964—65, Lausanne, 1967—69; mem. U.S. Cost Acctg. Stds. Bd., 1978—80, U.S. R.R. Acctg. Prin. Bd., 1985—87; dir., trustee Scudder Funds, AARP Investment Program Funds, 1979—2000; cons. in field. Author: Managerial Cost Accounting, 1961, 5th edit., 1982, Accounting: A Management Approach, 1964, 9th edit., 1993, Financial Accounting: Concepts and Applications, 1989; contbr. articles to profl. jours. Bd. dirs., treas. Feris Found. Am., Stamford, Conn., 1970—94; mem. bd. advisors Fund Directions, 1990—96. With USN, 1943—46. Recipient Disting. Tchr. award, Columbia U., 1970, Lifetime Achievement award, Instnl. Investor Newsletter, 2002. Mem.: Am. Acctg. Assn. (v.p. 1966—67), Beta Gamma Sigma, Phi Beta Kappa. Avocations: golf, genealogy. Home: 1150 8th Ave SW Apt 401 Largo FL 33770-3175 Personal E-mail: gshillinglaw@tampabay.rr.com.

SHILOH, ALLEN, writer; b. Bastrop, La., May 24, 1947; s. Al and Rosia B (Davis) S.; children: Datoya Moneake Penn. Grad. high sch., Bastrop; student in Illustration, Cal/Arts, 1966—68, student in Illustration, 2007—. Mail handler U.S. Postal Svc., Bell, Calif., 1972—2009. Author: (novels) The Brotherhood, Terror, 1973, Bayou Girl, 1990, (paperback) The Real First United States President, 1983, (short stories pub.) New Cosmic Star, 1968. Sgt. USAF, 1968-72, Vietnam. Avocations: photography, drawing. Office: Office Mgmt Human Resources Lori Shah Svc Ctr PO Box 45 Boyers PA 16017 Home Phone: 310-638-4234; Office Phone: 323-729-4121, 888-767-6738.

SHILS, JAY LAWRENCE, neurologist, researcher; b. Phila., July 18, 1966; s. Alan Jay and Elaine Barrie Shils; life ptnr. Juliane Marie Schneider, Dec. 10, 1998. BS in Elec. Engring., Syracuse U., 1988; PhD in Biomed. Engring., U. Pa., 1995. DABNM Am. Bd. Neurophysiological Monitoring, 2006. Engr. Gen. Dynamics Electric Boat Divsn., Groton, Conn., 1986—89; neurophysiology specialist Grad. Hosp., Phila., 1994—97, Beth Israel Med. Ctr., NYC, 1998—2004; movement disorders neurophysiologist Pa. Hosp., Phila., 1997—98; dir. intraoperative neurophysiology The Lahey Clinic, Burlington, Mass., 2004—. Bd. mem. Am. Soc. Intraoperative Neurophysiological Monitoring, Chgo., 2004—; founding sec. Internat. Soc. Intraoperative Neurophysiology, Rome, 2006—. Editor: (textbook) Neurophysiology in Neurosurgery: A Modern Approach; contbr. articles to profl. jours. Mem.: IEEE. Achievements include patents pending for spinal cord stimulation. Office: The Lahey Clinic 41 Mall Rd Burlington MA 01805 Office Fax: 781-744-2662. Business E-Mail: jay.shils@lahey.org.

SHILS, MAURICE EDWARD, physician, educator, research scientist; b. Atlantic City, Dec. 31, 1914; s. Samuel L. and Sarah (Harris) S.; m. Cylia Finkiel, Feb. 19, 1939 (dec. Sept. 1987); children: Loraine J., Jonathan R.; m. Betty Ann Bell, Sept. 24, 1988. BA, Johns Hopkins U., 1937, ScD, 1940; MD, NYU, 1958. Intern joint program Cornell divsn. Bellevue Hosp. and Meml. Hosp., NYC, 1958-59; fellow in physiology Meml. Hosp., 1959-60; instr., asst. prof. nutrition Sch. Pub. Health Columbia U., NYC, 1946-54; instr. biochemistry Sch. Hygiene Johns Hopkins U., Balt., 1940-42; head Ctrl. Metabolic Lab. Sloan Kettering Inst., NYC, 1960-72; from asst. to assoc. attending physician Meml. Hosp., NYC, 1962-72, attending physician, 1972-85; asst. prof. biochem. Sloan-Kettering divsn. Med. Coll. Cornell U., NYC, 1959-62, from asst. prof. to prof. medicine Med. Coll., 1962-85, prof. emeritus, 1985—. Adj. prof. nutrition dept. pub. health scis. Wake Forest U. Sch. Medicine, Winston-Salem, N.C., 1989-94, cons., 1994-97. Author, sr. editor: Modern Nutrition in Health and Disease, 10th edit., 2005; contbr. more than 200 rsch. and review articles to profl. jours. Fellow Am. Coll. Physicians, N.Y. Acad. Medicine (Acad. Plaque award 1987), Am. Soc. Nutrition; mem. AMA (chmn. nutrition adv. group 1974-77, Goldberger award 1983), Am. Soc. Clin. Nutrition (pres. 1985-86, Excellence in Med. Sch. award 1994), Am. Bd. Physician Nutrition Specialists, Phi Beta Kappa, Alpha Omega Alpha. Office Phone: 336-765-4822. E-mail: mshils@triad.rr.com.

SHIM, CHANGSUB, research scientist; s. Sangdon Shim and Jungsuk Jung. BS in Chemistry, Korea U., Seoul, 1991—97, MS in Chemistry, 1999; MS, Rutgers U., New Brunswick, NJ, 2000—02; PhD, Ga. Inst. Tech., Atlanta, 2006. Rsch. and tchg. asst. Korea U., Seoul, 1997—99; rsch. asst. Rutgers U., New Brunswick, NJ, 2000—02, Ga. Inst. Tech., Atlanta, 2002—06; postdoc fellow Jet Propulsion Lab. NASA, Pasadena, Calif., 2006—. Recipient award, Jour. Geophys. Rsch., 2003, 2005, 2006. Mem.: Am. Meteorol. Soc., Am. Geophys. Union (assoc.). Achievements include research in prove the contributions of global biogenic emissions to tropospheric air quality; constraining global isoprene emissions with GOME HCHO column measurements; pollution manifests the springtime tropospheric ozone at northern mid and high latitudes; source characteristic of oxygenated volatile compounds and HCN; global methyl chloride. Office: Jet Propulsion Lab Oak Grove Dr Pasadena CA 91109 Personal E-mail: marchell@gmail.com. Business E-Mail: cshim@jpl.nasa.gov.

SHIM, JAEHO, physical education educator; b. Seoul, Republic Of Korea, Nov. 6, 1969; s. Taesup Shim and Choonji Kang; m. Jahyun Park, Jan. 19, 2002; children: Eubin, Dahbin. PhD, U. Ill., Urbana-Champaign, 1999. Assoc. prof. Baylor U., Waco, Tex., 1999—. Sponsor coll. group Korean United Meth. Ch., Waco, 2004—09. Mem.: NASPSPA. Office: Baylor Univ 1312 S 5th OBP 97313 Waco TX 76798 Office Fax: 254-710-3527. Business E-Mail: joe_shim@baylor.edu.

SHIM, MINSUK KIM, education educator; d. Jongtaek and Nam-Ok Kim; m. Eunjae Jay Shim, June 24, 1984; children: Michael Sunguk, Eric Sunghoon. BA, Seoul Nat. U., 1982; MA, U. Brit. Columbia, 1991; PhD, U. Ill., Urbana, 1995. Tchr. Gang-Seo Mid. Sch., Seoul, Republic of Korea, 1982—86; rsch. scientist U. Ill., Urbana, 1995—97; asst. prof. (rsch.) U. RI, Kingston, 1997—99, asst. prof., 1999—2005, assoc. prof., 2005—. Assoc. dir. Nat. Ctr. on Pub. Edn. & Social Policy, 1997—2003. Author: High achievers in Korea: Who they are and what they do, 2005, Mathematics education in the middle grades, 2000; contbr. articles pub. to profl. jour. Recipient Publ. (Divsn. H) - 1st Pl. Award, Am. Edn. Rsch. Assn., 1999; grantee Comprehensive accountability sys. for sch. improvement, RI Dept. of Elem. & Secondary Edn., 2000-2003. Mem.: APA, Am. Edn. Rsch. Assn., Kappa Delta Phi, Phi Delta Kappa. Office: U R I 707 Chafee Bldg Kingston RI 02881 Business E-Mail: mshim@uri.edu.

SHIM, SANG EUN, engineering educator; m. Young Ran Cho, May 22, 2005; 1 child, Yoo Hyun. BS in Chem. Engring., Inha U., Incheon, South Korea, 1995, MS in Chem. Engring., 1997; PhD in Polymer Engring., U. Akron, Ohio, 2002. Prof. Inha U., Incheon, Republic of Korea, 2004—. Recipient Signature award, Omnova Solutions Found., 2002. Mem.: Am. Chem. Soc., Internat. Rotary Club (Goodwill Mission Amb. scholar 1997—99). Achievements include 18 patents in field. Office Fax: 82-32-872-0959. Business E-Mail: seshim@inha.ac.kr.

SHIM, SANG KOO, mental health services professional; b. Tokyo, Oct. 1, 1942; arrived in U.S., 1968; s. Sang Taek and Kum Ryon (Bae) Shim; m. Jae Hee Lee, July 12, 1972; children: Tammy, David. BS,

Seoul Nat. U., Republic of Korea, 1967; MBA, No. Ill. U., 1970; MS, U. Wis., Madison, 1975. CPA Ill., cert. valuation analyst. Acct. Vaughn Mfg. Co., Chgo., 1970-72, Stewart-Warner Corp., Chgo., 1972-73; fin. cons. Cen. Acctg. Assn., New Baden, Ill., 1977-79; auditor Ill. Dept. Mental Health, Springfield, 1980-82, CFO, 1983-97; chief bur. gen. acctg. Ill. Dept. Human Svcs., Springfield, 1997—2002. Bd. dirs. Metro City Bank, Doraville, Ga. Treas. Korean Assn. Greater St. Louis, 1982. Mem.: Korean-Am. Assn. St. Louis, Nat. Assn. Cert. Valuation Analysts, Assn. Govt. Accts. (cert. govt. fin. mgr.), Ill. CPA Soc., Korean-Am. C. of C. (v.p. Greater St. Louis chpt. 1994—95). Office: Shim & Co CPA 1600 Lebanon Ave Ste 102 Belleville IL 62221 Home: 1157 Stonewolf Trl Fairview Heights IL 62208-4187 Personal E-mail: skshim@aol.com.

SHIM, WOO SUB, research scientist; b. Seoul, Republic Of Korea, July 20, 1976; s. Sang Kyu Shim and Kyung Ae Kim; m. Tae Kyung Kang; 1 child, Abraham J. PhD, NC State U., Raleigh, 2009. Rsch. assoc. Seoul Nat. U., 2002—04, NC State U., 2005—09. Contbr. articles to profl. sci. jours. Sgt. US Army, 1998—2001, Seoul. Mem.: Am. Assn. Textile Chemists and Colorists, Fiber Soc., Am. Chem. Soc., Textile Soc. Americas, Korean-Am. Scientists and Engring. Assn. Home: 132 Prestonian Pl Morrisville NC 27560 Personal E-mail: jacob0720@gmail.com.

SHIMADA, KATSUNORI, retired electrical engineer; b. Tokyo, Mar. 12, 1922; arrived in U.S., 1950; s. Katsujiro and Mume Shimada; m. Ikuko Ueno, Oct. 30, 1975; m. Kazuko Matsumoto; children: Karl, Keiko Shimada Stearns. BSEE, U. Tokyo, 1945; MSEE, U. Minn., 1954, PhD, 1958. Engr. Toshiba Japan, Kawasaki, Japan, 1945—50; instr. U. Minn., Mpls., 1950—58; asst. prof. engring. U. Wash., Seattle, 1958—64; supr. JPL, G&C Rsch. Group, Pasadena, Calif., 1964—80; mgr., Field Ctr. Integration JPL, Pasadena, 1980—85, supr. Celestrial Sensors, 1985—89; ret., 1989. Cons. Boeing Co., Seattle, 1960—63, NASDA of Japan, LA, 1987—91; invited prof. engring. U. Tokyo, 1973; invited lectr. NEDO of Japan, Tokyo, 1983. Contbr. articles to profl. jours., tech. reports and memoranda. Com. mem. Nat. Parents Day Coalition, LA, 1996—99, RSVP of Pasadena, 1993—95, Assoc. Retirees of Caltech/JPL, Pasadena, 1989. Resident rsch. fellow, JPL, 1963—64. Mem.: AIAA, IEEE (sr.), Sigma Xi, Eta Kappa Nu. Achievements include patents for cavity emitter for thermionics; thermionic diode switch; solid state power converter. Avocations: photography, computers, golf, travel. Home: 3840 Edgeview Dr Pasadena CA 91107 Personal E-mail: kshimmitzy@aol.com.

SHIMER, DANIEL LEWIS, finance company executive; b. San Angelo, Tex., July 30, 1944; s. Lewis V. and Mary A. (Slick) S.; married. BS in Acctg. and Mktg., Ind. U., 1972; postgrad., Loyola U., New Orleans, 1977. CPA. Sr. acct. Peat, Marwick, Mitchell & Co., Indpls., 1973—75; asst. treas. LTV Corp., Dallas, 1975—79; v.p. fin. Stoller Chem. Co., Houston, 1979—81; v.p., CFO Petro-Silver, Inc., Denver, 1981—83; v.p., treas. FoxMeyer Corp., Denver, 1983—86; v.p., treas., sec. CoastAmerica Corp., Denver, 1986—88; exec. v.p. Bard & Co., Denver, 1989—90; pres. nat accounts divsn. I Can't Believe It's Yogurt/Brice Foods, Inc., Dallas, 1991—93; exec. v.p., CFO COREStaff Inc., Houston, 1994—96; venture ptnr. Austin Ventures, Dallas, 1996—2004; pres. Shimer Capital Ptnrs., Inc., Dallas, 1996—2004; gen. ptnr. Teakwood Capital, 2005—. Methodist. Avocations: carpentry, fishing. Home: 7436 Glenshannon Cir Dallas TX 75225-2048

SHIMER, JULIE A., health products executive; BS in Physics, Rensselear Poly. Inst.; MSEE, Lehigh U., Bethlehem, Pa., PhD in Elec. Engring. Exec. positions Bethlehem Steel Co., AT&T Bell Labs., 3Com, Motorola; pres., CEO Vocera Comm., Cupertino, Calif., Welch Allyn, Inc., Skaneateles Falls, NY, 2007—. Bd. dirs. Netgear. Bd. dirs. Engring. Info. Found. Mem.: IEEE, Soc. Women Engrs., Sigma Xi. Office: Welch Allyn Inc Corp Hdqs 4341 State Street Rd Skaneateles Falls NY 13153-0220*

SHIMIZU, KAZUHIKO, education educator; b. Akeno, Japan, Jan. 20, 1952; s. Kazuyoshi and Toyoko S.; m. Tsurumi Tamagawa, March 30, 1979; children: Kazutaka, Kazuma, Kazuki. BA, Tokyo U. Edn., 1974, MA, 1976; PhD, U. Tsukuba, Japan, 1997. Rsch. fellow Japan Soc. for the Promotion of Sci., Tokyo, 1980-81; asst. prof. Seisen Women's Jr. Coll., Nagano, Japan, 1983-86, assoc. prof., 1986-88; asst. prof. U. Tsukuba, 1988-91, assoc. prof., 1991-99, prof., 1999—, asst. pres., 2004—06, vice provost grad. sch., 2004—06, chmn. faculty edn., 2006—07, provost grad. sch., 2007—. Vis. assoc. prof. U. Hiroshima, 1992-96; vis. scholar U. Pa., Phila., 1995-96, U. Minn., Mpls., 2002, U. Mo., 2005; spl. lectr. Yonsei U., Seoul, Korea, 1996; guest lectr. Nat. Edn. Commn., Beijing, 1998, East China Normal U., Shanghai, 2001, Beijing Normal U., 2005. Author: Comparative and Hist. Study of Univ. Credit Sys. Between USA and Japan, 1998, Univ. Reform in Japan, 1999; author and editor: Development of University Evaluation, 2004, A Databook of Edn. Statistics, 2006, Education and Human Rights, 2007. Mem. Coun. for Univ. Chartering and Sch. Judicial Person (Monbusho), 2000-02; mem. Japanese Univ. Accreditation Assn., 1994-2000, 2004—; trustee Assn. for the Advancement of Colls. in Japan, 1994—; mem. Inter-Univ. Seminar House, Tokyo, 1997-2002, Ctrl. Coun. for Edn., Monbusho, 2007-; mem. com. for u. evaluation Japan Assn. Nat. Univs., 2008-. Recipient rsch. fund, Assn. Internat. Edn., Japan, 1990; grantee-in-aid for sci. rsch., Ministry of Edn., Sci., Sport and Culture (Monbusho), Tokyo, 1998, 2000, 2001, Sci. Rsch. grant, 2003—08. Mem.: Japanese Assn. Higher Edn. Rsch. (editor 2000—02, trustee 2003—06), Japan Soc. Ednl. Sys. and Orgn. (office dir. 1999—), Japan Assn. Lifelong Edn. (office dir. 1998—2000), Comparative and Internat. Edn. Soc. Avocation: gardening. Home: 3-709-1 Takezono Tsukuba Japan Office: Faculty of Edn U Tsukuba 1-1-1 Tennodai 305-8572 Tsukuba Japan Business E-Mail: shimizuk@human.tsukuba.ac.jp.

SHIMIZU, YOSHIAKI, art historian; b. Tokyo, Feb. 27, 1936; came to U.S., 1953, naturalized, 1999; s. Mamoru and Michiko (Hayasaka) S.; children: Karen Akiko Marie, Kenneth Cuyler Norio, Katherine Kimie, Kei Robert. BA, Harvard U., 1963; MA, U. Kans., 1968; MFA, Princeton U., 1971, PhD, 1974. Asst. prof. dept. art and archaeology Princeton (N.J.) U., 1973-75, prof., 1984—, chmn. dept. art and archaeology, 1990-92, Marquand prof. art and archaeology, 1992—2009, Marquand prof. art and archaeology emeritus, 2009—, dir. program in Asian art and archaeology, 1992—; asst. prof. U. Calif., Berkeley, 1975-78, assoc. prof., 1978-79; curator Japanese art Freer Gallery, Smithsonian Instn., Washington, 1979-84; guest curator Nat. Gallery Art, Washington, 1982-89; guest prof. U. Heidelberg, 1993. Guest prof. Ritsumeikan U., 1996; vis. fellow dept. art history U. Tokyo, 1996; mem. art adv. com. Japan Soc. Gallery, 1984—, adv. com. Asia Soc. Galleries, N.Y.C., 1992—, chmn. adv. com., 1999—; vis. fellow dept. comparative culture Sophia U., Tokyo, 1993; sr. cons. for exhbn. Japan Soc. Galleries, 2006, 07. Author: (with John M. Rosenfield) Masters of Japanese Calligraphy, 1984; editor: (with Carolyn Wheelwright) Japanese Ink Paintings, 1976; author, editor: Japan: The Shaping of Daimyo Culture 1185-1858, 1988; co-authored in Awakenings: Zen Figure Painting in medieval Japan, Japan Soc. and Yale U. Press, 2007; mem. editorial bd. Archives of Asian Art, 1979-89. Adv. bd. Asian Art, Smithsonian Inst., 1985-93; mem. vis. com. Arthur M. Sackler Gallery, Washington, 1984-94. Smithsonian Inst. fellow, 1967, Social Sci. Rsch. Coun./Am. Coun. Learned Socs. fellow, 1977-78, Asian Cultural Coun. fellow, 1995; J.D. Rockefeller III fellow, 1969-70. Mem. Coll. Art Assn. (bd. dirs. 1987-91), Japan Art History Assn., Japan Soc. NY. Office: Princeton U Dept Art and Archaeology Princeton NJ 08540 Home: 57 College Rd W Princeton NJ 08540-5108 Business E-Mail: shimizu@princeton.edu.

SHIMKUS, JOHN MONDY, United States Representative from Illinois; b. Collinsville, Ill., Feb. 21, 1958; s. Gene Louis and Kathleen (Mondy) Shimkus; m. Karen Kay Muth; children: David, Joshua, Daniel. BS, US Mil. Acad., 1980; MBA, So. Ill. U., Edwardsville, 1997. Advanced through grades to capt. U.S. Army, 1980-86; stationed at U.S. Army Base, Columbus, Ga., 1980-81, 85, served at Bamberg, Germany, 1981-84, stationed at Monterey, Calif, 1985-86; tchr. Metro East Luth. H.S., Edwardsville, Ill., 1986-90; treas. Madison County, Edwardsville, 1990-96; mem. U.S. Congress from 19th Ill. dist., 1997—, mem. energy and commerce com. Liaison officer US Mil. Acad., 1987—96; treas. So. Ill. Law Enforcement Commn., 1990—96. Bd. dirs. Sr. Citizen Companion Prog., Belleville, Ill., 1991; trustee Collinsville Twp., Ill., 1989—93; Rep. precinct committeeman Collinsville, 1988—. Lt. col. USAR, 1985—. Mem.: Ill. County Treas. Assn., Nat. Assn. County Treas. & Fin. Officers (bd. dirs.), Am. Legion Post 365. Republican. Lutheran. Home: 504 Sumner Blvd Collinsville IL 62234-1934 Office: US House Reps 2452 Rayburn House Office Bldg Washington DC 20515-1319 also: Springfield Dist Office Ste C 3130 Chatham Rd Springfield IL 62704 Office Phone: 217-492-5090.*

SHIMODA, JERRY YASUTAKA, retired national historic park manager; b. Haleiwa, Hawaii, Mar. 21, 1930; s. Tamotsu and Sasai Shimoda; m. Clara H. Segawa, Aug. 7, 1954; children: Karen Marie K., Randall T., Shaun T., Teri Ellen H., Jacqueline Y., David Y. BA in Govt., U. Hawaii, 1952, MA in Far Ea. Area Studies, 1957; postgrad., St. Louis U., 1957-59; PhD in Pub. Adminstrn., Kennedy-Western U., 2004. Historian Jefferson Nat. Expansion Meml. Nat. Hist. Site, St. Louis, 1957-60; chief historian, in charge hist. rsch. and visitor svcs. Saratoga Nat. Hist. Park, Stillwater, NY, 1960-66; chief historian Home of Franklin D. Roosevelt Nat. Hist. Site and, Frederick Vanderbilt Nat. Hist. Site, Hyde Park, NY, 1966-69; instr. Nat. Park Svc. Stephen T. Mather Tng. Ctr., Harpers Ferry, W.Va., 1969-72; supt. Pu'uhonua o Honaunau (Hawaii) Nat. Hist. Park, 1972-96, Puukohola Heiau Nat. Hist. Site, Kawaihae, 1972-96, Asian Descent, First Nat. Park; ret., 1996. Lectr. environ. edn. Pa. State U., U. W.Va., Shepard Coll., 1969—72; acting supr. Kaloko-Honokohau Nat. Hist. Pk., 1988—90; instr. environ. edn., interpretive and basic instructing techniques U. Hawaii, Hilo, Kapiolani C.C.; instr. Japanese culture U. Hawaii, Hilo, 1994; U.S. del. and translator U.S.-Japan Panel on Nat. Parks and Equivalent Res., 1968—97, 2nd. World Conf. Nat. Parks, Yellowstone, Okla., 1972, World Conf. on Marine Parks, Tokyo, 1975; mem. internat. bd. dirs. Heritage Interpretation Internat., 1989—98; trainer Japan Pk. Interpreters, 1997—2006; cons., presenter in field. Contbr. articles to profl. jours., popular mags., local newspapers. Bd. dirs. Volcano Art Ctr.; adv. com. Wailoa State Ctr.; active Hawaii Gov.'s Task Force on Ocean and Recreation; chmn. restoration com. St. Benedict's Ch., Honaunau, 1982-95; chmn. bd. dirs. Kahua Na'au 'Ao, 1996-97; vol. training cons. Nat. Pk. Svc., 1996-2005. Recipient Spl. Achievement award Nat. Park Svc., 1964, 68, 70, resolution W.Va. Senate, 1971, Hawaii Ho. of Reps., 1982, sec.'s cert. Dept. Interior, 1971, Exec. of Yr. award West Hawaii chpt. Profl. Secs. Internat., 1981, cert. Govt. of Japan, 1981, staff plaque Pu'uhonua o Honaunau Nat. Hist. Park, Puukohola Heiau Nat. Hist. Site and Kaloko-Honokohau Nat. Hist. Park, 1988, cert. Japan Nat. Parks Assn., 1989, cert. of appreciation South Kona Aloha Lions Club, 1990, Meritorious Svc. award Sec. Interior, 1996, others. Mem.: Hawaii Mus. Assn. (bd. dirs. 1988—92), Kona Hist. Soc. (bd. dirs. 1988—92), Big Island Ocean Recreation and Tourism Assn. (exec. com.), Hawaii Natural History Assn. (bd. dirs. 2007—), Polynesian Voyaging Soc. (life; hon.), Kona Judo Club (pres. 1977—96), Rotary (pres. Kona Mauka 1978—79, co-founder Volcano chpt. 2001, Disting. Svc. award 1992, Paul Harris fellow 1991). Avocations: writing, reading, travel, teaching.

SHIMODA, NICK YOSHINARI, lawyer; b. Dothan, Ala., Sept. 11, 1967; s. Narumi Shimoda and Yoshi Hama; m. Laurie N. Shimoda, Aug. 25, 2001; children: Lacey, Lindsey. BS in Econs., Auburn U., Ala., 1990; JD, U. Ala., Tuscaloosa, 1993, LLM in Taxation, 1999. Bar: Ala. 1993, U.S. Dist. Ct. (mid. dist.) Ala. 1993, U.S. Dist. Ct. (no. dist.) Ala. 1996, U.S. Tax Ct. 2002, U.S. Supreme Ct. 2006. Sole practice, Dothan. Office: PO Box 1765 Dothan AL 36302

SHIMOJO, MASAHITO, science educator; PhD, Nagasaki U., Japan. Asst. prof. U. Ky., Lexington, 2002—. Mem.: SFN, ASBMB. Office: Univ Kentucky 741 South Limestone St BBSRB Lexington KY 40536-0509 Office Fax: 859-257-2283. Business E-Mail: mshim1@uky.edu.

SHIMOMURA, OSAMU, chemistry professor; b. Kyoto, 1928; married; 2 children. BS, Nagasaki Coll. Pharmacology, Japan; PhD in Organic Chemistry, Nagoya U., Japan, 1960. Biology rschr. Princeton U., NJ; prof. chemistry Nagoya U.; prof. organic chemistry Boston U.; adj. prof. physiology Boston U. Med. Sch.; prof. emeritus Marine Biol. Lab., Woods Hole, Mass. Recipient Pearse prize, Royal Microscopical Soc., 2004, Asahi prize, Asahi Shimbun, 2007, Nobel Prize in Chemistry, 2008. Achievements include discovery of green fluorescent protein in jellyfish, 1962. Office: c/o Marine Biol Lab 7 M B L St Woods Hole MA 02543 Office Phone: 508-548-3705.*

SHIMOTSU, RYAN, biomedical engineer; b. Honolulu, Apr. 5, 1982; s. Randy and Susan Shimotsu; life ptnr. Vicky Tran. MS Biomed. Engring., Tufts U., Medford, Mass., 2006. Biomed. engr. Neurobehavioral Rsch., Inc., Honolulu, 2006—. Achievements include development of software to quantify white matter lesions in the brain on MRI. Office: Neurobehavioral Rsch Inc 1585 Kapiolani Blvd Honolulu HI 96814

SHIMP, CHARLES PATTERSON, psychologist, educator; b. Columbus, Ohio, Mar. 7, 1939; s. William Bennett and Frances Kalbfus Shimp; m. Peggy E. Roberson, Aug. 9, 1986; 1 child, Andrew Bennett; m. Linda Alt, 1961 (div. 1970). BSc, Ohio State U., Columbus, 1961; PhD, Brown U., Providence, 1965. Prof. psychology U. Utah, Salt Lake City, 1967—2009. Assoc. editor Jour. Exptl. Analysis Behavior, Bloomington, Ind., 1976—79, Jour. Exptl. Psychology: Animal Behavior Processes, Washington, 1986—97; mem. psychobiology panel NSF, Washington, 1979—82; mem. grant panel Nat. Inst. Drug Abuse, Washington, 1997—99. Fellow, APA, AAAS, Am. Psychol. Soc., grant, Foro Found., 1972—73. Office: Univ Utah Rm 502 Dept Psychology 380 S 1530 E Salt Lake City UT 84112-0251 Business E-Mail: charlie.shimp@psych.utah.edu.

SHIN, DONG-HEE, communication technology educator; b. Seoul, Republic of Korea, Oct. 30, 1970; arrived in US, 1997, permanent resident; s. Hong-Sik Shin and Young-Ja Seo; m. Youn Joo Shin, Jan. 7, 2003. BA in Comm., Sung Kun Kwan U., Seoul, 1997; MA in Telecomm., So. Ill. U., 1998; MS in Info. Mgmt., PhD in Telecomm., Syracuse U., 2004. Rschr. Korea Info. Soc. Rsch., Seoul, 1997; reporter Korea Ctrl. Daily, LA, 1999; lectr. Syracuse (NY) U., 2002—04; asst. prof. Pa. State U., Reading, 2004—. Cons. SK Club, Seoul, 2000; rschr. SK Telecomm., Seoul, 2001; project mgr. Verizon and NY State, Syracuse, NY, 2000—03; spkr. in field. Activist Assn. for Cmty. Networking, Chgo., 2002; advisor NY State Pub. Svc. Commn., Albany, 2003; adv. cons. Consortium of Seoul Digital City, 2004. Recipient Outstanding Rschr. award, Pa. State U., 2007; fellow, Syracuse U., 2002; scholar, So. Ill. U., 1997; rsch. grantee, Pa. State U., 2004. Mem.: Am. Info. Sci. Assn., Internat. Comm. Assn., Internat. Telecomm. Soc. Presbyterian. Avocations: tennis, fishing, touring. Office: Pa State U Tulpehocken Rd PO Box 7009 Reading PA 19610 Home: 31 Chapeltowne Cir Nottingham MD 21236-1238 Office Fax: 610-396-6024. Personal E-mail: dhshin1030@yahoo.com.

SHIN, DUCKHEE, literature and language professor; d. Gui-Hyun Shin and Gui-Rye Lee; m. Myung-Goo Choi, Aug. 24, 1984; 1 child, Jong-Ha Choi. PhD, Ind. U., Bloomington, 1991. Prof. sogang U., Seoul, Republic of Korea, 1997—99, Millersville U., Pa., 1993—. Specialist reader MELUS, Storrs, Conn., 2007—; pres. bd. com. Ta-RI, Harrisburg, Pa., 2007—; editl. bd. mem. Jour. Eighteenth Century English Literature, 2007—; v.p. Ctrl. Pa. Korean Assn., Harrisburg, Pa., 2009—. Pres. Asian Am. Culture Com., Millersville, 1994—2006. Grnts, Pa. State Sys., Millersville U., 2003—09. Mem.: Soc. Eighteen Century Studies, Asian Am. Studies Assn. Office: Millersville Univ Chryst Hall 206 Millersville PA 17601 Business E-Mail: duckhee.shin@millersville.edu.

SHIN, ERNEST EUN-HO, physicist, educator, researcher; b. Chin-do, Republic of Korea, Dec. 31, 1935; came to U.S., 1953; s. Hyung Sik and Ok Bin (Lim) S.; m. Shin-Ai Park, July 27, 1963; children: Irene, Juliet, Mariette, Michelle. BS in Physics, Carnegie Inst. Tech., 1957; AM in Physics, Harvard U., 1959, PhD in Physics, 1961. Rsch. fellow Cyclotron Lab., Harvard U., Cambridge, Mass., 1957-58, tchg. fellow physics dept., 1958-59; rsch. assoc. Arthur D. Little, Inc., Cambridge, 1960-62; rsch. assoc. Francis Bitter Nat. Magnet Lab., MIT, Cambridge, 1962-66; prof. physics U. Miami, Coral Gables, Fla., 1966-72, founder, dir. Solid State Physics Lab., 1969-72; dir. Nieman Inst., Dallas, 1972-73; vis. scientist Korea Atomic Energy Rsch. Inst., Seoul, 1973-74; chmn., chief exec. officer Yulsan Am., Inc., San Francisco, 1974-89; dir. Chestnut Hill Inst., Napa, Calif., 1984—. Co-founder Yulsan Group Cos., Seoul, 1974; prof. Intercultural Inst. Calif., San Francisco, 1996—; chmn. Shinergy, LLC, San Francisco, 2001—. Author: Quantum Theory of Transport, 2007; contbr. articles on biophysics, math. physics and elem. particle physics, superconductivity, optical properties of metals to profl. jours.; patentee in field. Woodrow Wilson fellow Harvard U., 1959. Mem. AAAS, Am. Phys. Soc. (life), N.Y. Acad. Scis. Achievements include patent for bouyancy-driven electric power generator, 2005; development of space-time theory of fundamental particles, 2005. Avocations: ranching, gardening, painting, fishing. Office: Chestnut Hill Inst PO Box 3510 Napa CA 94558-0350 Home: 31 Skipping Rock Way Napa CA 94558-7006 Personal E-mail: eunho@aol.com. Business E-Mail: ernestshin@shinergyusa.com.

SHIN, EUI-CHEOL, medical researcher; b. Seoul, Republic Of Korea, Aug. 29, 1971; s. Hyun-Po Shin and Young-Ja Park; m. Sue Haksoo Kim, June 7, 2003. MD, Yonsei U. Sch. Medicine, Seoul, Republic of Korea, 1996; PhD, Yonsei U., Seoul, Republic of Korea, 2001. Lic. doctor Korean Med. Assn., 1996. Chief med. scientist Armed Forces Rsch. Inst. Medicine, Daejon, Republic of Korea, 1999—2002; rsch. fellow Nat. Inst. Diabetes and Digestive and Kidney Diseases, NIH, Bethesda, Md., 2002—07; asst. prof. Grad. Sch. Med. Sci. and Engring., Korea Advanced Inst. Sci. and Tech., Daejon, Republic of Korea, 2007—. Home: 239 Winter Walk Dr Gaithersburg MD 20878 Office: GSMSE KAIST 373-1 Guseong-dong Yuseong-gu Daejeon 305-701 Republic of Korea Office Fax: 82-42-350-4240. Personal E-mail: ecshin@hotmail.com. Business E-Mail: ecshin@kaist.ac.kr.

SHIN, HIEWON, literature and language professor; d. Ok-hyung Shin and Kyungja Hwang; m. Dongjai Lee, Nov. 24, 1996; children: Brendon Lee, Joseph Shin Lee. PhD in Lit., Pa. State U., 2005. Asst. prof. Northgreenville U., Tigerville, SC, 2006—. Contbr. articles to profl. jour. Mem.: Shakesepare Assn. America. Office: North Greenville Univ PO Box 1892 Tigerville SC 29688 E-mail: hshin@ngu.edu.

SHIN, JAE CHEOL, research scientist; b. Seoul, Republic of Korea, Dec. 17, 1975; s. Chan Young Shin and Jeom Bun Park; m. Alemmnarae Jung Shin; 1 child, Yuna Shin. BS, Kyung Hee U., Kyungki, Korea, 1994—2001; MS, Kyung Hee U., Seoul, Korea, 2001—03; PhD, U. Wis., Madison, 2009. Intern rschr. Korea Inst. of Sci. & Tech., Seoul, 2003—05. Contbr. articles to profl. jours. including Jour. Korean Phys. Soc., Applied Physics Letters. Sgt. Inf., 1996—98, Korea. Recipient Prize of a brave man in the divsn., Divsn. comdr. of Republic of Korea army, 1996. Achievements include patents for Spectral Response Change in a Quantum well Infrared Photodetector by using Quantum Well Intermixing Technique, 10-2001-0088870, 2001, Korea. Avocations: golf, soccer, travel. Office Phone: 716-380-7101, 608-265-5403. Personal E-mail: jchshin@gmail.com.

SHIN, JAEWON, research scientist; s. Chul Woo Shin and Gil Ja Park; m. Jungmin Yu, June 27, 2000; children: Jamie, Bennett. BS in Electronics Engring., Yonsei U., Seoul, 1997; MS in Elec. Engring., Stanford U., Calif., 1999, PhD, 2004. Sr. rsch. engr. Sony Corp., San Jose, Calif., 2004—06; sr. staff scientist Broadcom Corp., Santa Clara, Calif., 2009. Rsch. intern Xerox PARC, Palo Alto, Calif., 2000—03, cons. Recipient Presdl. award, Yonsei U., 1995, 1996. Achievements include patents for numerous inventions in the areas of signal, video processing systems; research in distributed signal processing, estimation, identity management; design of signal processing IPs for Broadcom DTV/STB chipsets.

SHIN, JONG-YEOB, aerospace scientist; married; children: Cassidy, James. PhD, U. Minn., Mpls., 2000. Rsch. scientist ICASE, Hampton, Va., 2000—02; sr. rsch. scientist Nat. Inst. Aerospace, Hampton, 2003—08; tech. specialist ii Gulfstream Aerospace Co., Savannah, Ga., 2008—. Contbr. articles to profl. sci. jours. Mem.: AIAA. Home: 79 Byron Dr Richmond Hill GA 31324 Office: Gulfstream Aerospace Co 500 Gulfstream Roads Savannah GA

SHIN, SHUNG JAE, management educators; s. Yong-il Shin and Young-sook Kim; m. Jee Suk Kim. PhD, Tex. A&M U., Coll. Sta., 2003. Assoc. prof. Wash. State U., Richland, 2003—. Contbr. articles to profl. jours. Mem.: Acad. Mgmt.

SHIN, SUNGJAE, nutritionist; b. Busan, South Korea, Dec. 15, 1968; s. Yonggoo Shin and Boonnam Lee; m. Kyungil Choi, Mar. 9, 1996; children: Minsuk children: Chewon, Cheyoung. Doctorate, Tokyo U. Fisheries, 1998. Cert. food processing Korea Certifying Orgn. Investigator Nat. Inst. Health and Nutrition, Tokyo, 2001—03; rsch. scholar U. Pitts., Pitts., 2003—. Contbr. scientific papers to profl. publs. Recipient

Japanese Inviting Ednl. scholarship, Ministry Edn. In Japan, 1994—98, univ. scholarship, Pukyong U., 1987—94, rsch. grant, Jst Co., 2001. Mem.: JSBBA (assoc.). Achievements include research in Influence of the origin and level of dietary protein on TBI-induced oxidative damage in mice; Different onsets of oxidative damage to DNA and lipids in bone marrow and liver in rats given total body irradiation; Prostaglandin E2 reinforces the activation of Ras signal pathway in lung adenocarcinoma cells via EP3; Relation between oxidative damage and dietary protein: marginal protein level which modulates oxidative damage in mice with total body irradiation; Adequate intakes of vitamin E and protein prevent increases of oxidative damage to DNA, lipids, and protein induced by total body irradiation in mice; Vitamin E modulates radiation-induced oxidative damage in mice fed a high-lipid diet; Severe DNA damage in K-ras gene patterns of PCR products in mice fed a 1% protein diet and exposed to a high dose of radiation; High levels of apoptosis induced by total body irradiation in mice fed a low protein-low vitamin E diet; High levels of apoptosis induced by total body irradiation in mice fed a low protein-low vitamin E diet; High oleic acid oil suppresses lung tumorigenesis in mice through the modulation of extracellular signal-regulated kinase cascade; Induction of apoptosis in a human breast cancer cell overexpressing ErbB-2 receptor by alpha-tocopheryloxybutyric acid; Enhanced oxidative damage induced by total body irradiation in mice fed a low protein diet. Office: U Pitts Pittsburgh PA 15219 Home: 6 Resident Dr Apt C Killeen TX 76549-4136 Personal E-mail: ssjkfrihan@hanmail.net.

SHIN, WOO C., chemical engineer; b. Seoul, Republic of Korea, Aug. 24, 1968; s. Hyuntaek Shin and Hyunja Yoo; m. Jinsook Park, Oct. 26, 1995; 1 child, Soolim. PhD in Chem. Engring., Stevens Inst. Tech., Hoboken, NJ, 2006. Rsch. asst. Samyang Corp., Daejon, Chungnam, 1994—2000; sr. engr. Samsung SDI, Suwon, Kyounggi-do, Republic of Korea, 2006—. Mem.: AIChE. Home: 503-410 Mido apt Banpo4 dong Seocho gu Seoul 137788 Republic of Korea Office: Samsung SDI 575 Shin dong Youngtong gu Suwon Kyounggi do 443-731 Republic of Korea Personal E-mail: shinwoocheol@gmail.com. Business E-Mail: woocheol.shin@samsung.com.

SHIN, YONGSOON, research scientist; b. Checheon, Chungcheong buk-do, Republic of Korea, Mar. 1, 1965; s. Hyeonpill Shin and Hwawall Jeong; m. Sookyoung Kim, Dec. 24, 1994; children: Mickey K., Michelle K. PhD, U. Tenn., Knoxville, 1999. Postdoctoral Pacific NW Nat. Lab., Richland, Wash., 1999—2001, sr. rsch. scientist, 2002—. Contbr. scientific papers to profl. publs. Recipient Korean Leadership scholarship, 1985—88, Rsch. Merit award, U. Tenn., 1998, Outstanding Performance awards, Pacific NW Nat. Lab., 2002—09. Mem.: Materials Rsch. Soc. (life), Am. Chem. Soc. (life). Achievements include discovery of 5 synthesis of SiC ceramics by the carbothermal reduction of mineralized wood with silica; research in metal nanocrystals formed on cotton fiber assembly lines; invention of 6 publs., 7 invited presentations including Am. Chem. Soc. Meeting; patents pending for carbon nanospheres from sugars in a closed system. Home: 1043 Sunstone Court Richland WA 99352 Office: Pacific Northwest Nat Lab 902 Battelle Blvd POBox 999 MSIN K2-44 Richland WA 99354 Home Phone: 509-628-8469; Office Phone: 509-375-2693. Office Fax: 509-375-2186. Business E-Mail: yongsoon.shin@pnl.gov.

SHIN, YUNG CHUL, engineering educator; b. Kyungsan, Korea, Mar. 28, 1953; came to U.S., 1981; s. Hyun-dong and Soon-nam (Bae) S.; m. Hwasoon Lee, Oct. 15, 1980; children: Andrea, Eric. BSME, Seoul U., Republic of, 1976; MSME, Korea Advanced Inst Sci. & Tech., Seoul, 1978; PhD, U. Wis., 1984. Rsch. engr. Korea Inst. Machinery & Metals, 1978-81; sr. project engr. Gen. Motors, Warren, Mich., 1984-88; asst. prof. Pa. State U., State Coll., 1988-90; prof. Purdue U., West Lafayette, Ind., 1990—. Editor: Intelligent Engineering System Through Artificial Neural Networks, Vol. 1, 1991, Vol. 2, 1992; contbr. over 120 articles to profl. jours. Grantee NSF, 1993-00; Faculty fellow Gen. Motors Found., 1993, 94, 95. Mem. ASME, N.Am. Mfg. Rsch. Inst. Office: Purdue U 1288 Mechanical Engineering West Lafayette IN 47907-1288 E-mail: shin@ecn.purdue.edu.

SHINAGAWA, SATORU, language educator; m. Kathleen Marie Grondin. MA, U. Iowa, 1987. Instr. Japanese Macalester Coll., St. Paul, 1986—87; prof. Japanese Miami U., Oxford, Ohio, 1987—88, Minn. State U., Akita Campus, Japan, 1991—96, U. Hawaii, Kapiolani CC, Honolulu, 1996—. Online course evaluator Ga. Inst. of Tech., Atlanta, 2001—05; creator Japanese web-based exercises Houghton Mifflin, Boston, 2007—. Recipient Innovative Excellence award, 2005, Innovation of Yr. award, 2007; grant, Japan Found., 2007, Shoyuu Club, 2007. Mem.: Nat. Coun. Japanese Lang. Tchrs., Hawaii Assn. Lang. Tchrs., Assn. Tchrs. Japanese, Am. Coun. Tchg. Fgn. Lang. Office: Univ Hawaii Kapiolani CC 4303 Diamond Head Rd Honolulu HI 96816 Business E-Mail: satoru@shinagawa.us.

SHINAGEL, MICHAEL, dean, English literature educator; b. Vienna, Apr. 21, 1934; came to U.S., 1941; s. Emanuel and Lilly (Hillel) S.; m. Ann Birdsey Mitchell, Sept. 1, 1956 (div. 1970); children: Mark Mitchell, Victoria Stuart; m. Rosa Joanne Bonanno, Dec. 6, 1973 (div. 1993); m. Marjorie Lee North, May 26, 1995. AB, Oberlin Coll., 1957; AM, Harvard U., 1959, PhD, 1964; Doctorate (hon.), Internat. U. Ecuador, 1997; Doctorate (hon.), U. Argentina Empresa, 2003. Teaching fellow Harvard U., Cambridge, Mass., 1958-59, tutor in English, 1962-64, assoc. dir. career office, 1959-64, dean continuing edn., 1975—, lectr. extension, 1976—, sr. lectr. English, 1983—, master Quincy House, 1986—2001, univ. dean of continuing edn.; asst. prof. English, Cornell U., Ithaca, NY, 1964-67; prof., chmn. dept. English, Union Coll., Schenectady, NY, 1967-75. Bd. dirs. Harvard Coop. Soc., publ. Harvard Rev.; pres. bd. dirs. Ednl. Exch. Boston, 1982-87; editor Continuing Higher Edn. Rev., 1997—. Author: Defoe and Middle-Class Gentility, 1968, The Gates Unbarred: A History of University Extension at Harvard, (1910-2009), 2009; co-author: (handbook) Summer Institutes in English, 1965; editor: Concordance to Poems of Swift, 1972, Critical Edition of Robinson Crusoe, 1975 (revised 1993); co-editor: Harvard Scholars in English (1890-1990), 1991. With US Army, 1952—54, Korea. Woodrow Wilson fellow, 1957; NEH grantee, 1965 Mem. Univ. Continuing Edn. Assn., Assn. Continuing Higher Edn., Mass. Hist. Soc., Old South Meeting House, The Johnsonians, The Saturday Club, Harvard Faculty Club (pres. 1985-87), Phi Beta Kappa. Avocations: reading, cooking, music, tennis. Home: 22 Grozier Rd Cambridge MA 02138 Office: Harvard U Divsn Continuing Edn 51 Brattle St Cambridge MA 02138-3701 Office Phone: 617-495-2930. Business E-Mail: michael_shinagel@harvard.edu.

SHINDER, MARCELLA MARIE, marketing executive; b. Indpls., Jan. 4, 1967; d. Anthony S. and Bernice (Duffy) Lazar; m. Richard Shinder, June 29, 1991; 1 child. BEd, Gonzaga U., 1989; MA, Villanova U., 1992. Joined Am. Express, NYC, 1993, with B2B Corp. Svcs., v.p. strategic planning Global Fin. Svcs., v.p. global mktg. Am. Express Bus. Travel, 2003—05; v.p. brand mktg. and strategy OPEN from Am. Express, NYC, 2005—. Polit. analyst NY for Guiliani, 1993. Named one of Best Marketers, BtoB Mag., 2008. Mem.: Women Pres.'s Orgn. (bd. dirs., adv. coun.). Republican. Roman Catholic. Avocation: running. Office: Am Express 200 Vesey St 50th Fl New York NY 10285 E-mail: OPEN.Advocacy.Team@aexp.com.*

SHINDLE, WILLIAM RICHARD, retired musicologist, educator; b. Van Orin, Ill., Nov. 2, 1930; s. Ira William Shindle and Elsie Virginia Showalter. MusB, Ill. Wesleyan U., Bloomington, 1959; MusM in Musicology, Ind. U., Bloomington, 1963, PhD in Musicology, 1970. Sch. tchr. Calvert County HS, Prince Frederick, Md., 1959—60; rsch. asst. Ind. U., 1962—64; instr., libr. Harpur Coll., Binghamton, 1964—65; prof. musicology Kent State U., Ohio, 1966—91, prof. emeritus, 1991—. Contbr. articles to New Grove Dictionary of Music and Musicians, 1st. edit., 1980, 2nd updated edit., 2001, Ercole Pasquini: Collected Keyboard Works, 1966, Girolamo Frescobaldi: Keyboard Compositions Preserved in Manuscripts, 3 Vol., 1968, Jean de Macque: Sieben Madrigale zu 5 und 6 Stimmen, 1987, and Contbr. articles to Frescobaldi Studies, 1987 and Encyclopedia of Keyboard Instruments, Vol.1, 1994. Rsch. asst. to Willi Apel, Ind. U., 1962-64. 2nd class petty officer USN, 1951—55. Fellow, Ind. U., 1965—66; Summer Rsch. fellow, Kent State U., 1974, 1980, 1983. Mem.: Am. Musicological Soc., Pa. German Soc. Avocation: genealogy.

SHINDLER, STEVEN M., telecommunications industry executive; m. Mary Kay Shindler; 3 children. BA, U. Mich.; MBA, Cornell U. Positions through mng. dir. comm. fin. group Toronto Dominion Bank, 1987—96; exec. v.p., CFO Nextel Comm. (now NII Holdings, Inc.), 1996—2000, CEO, 2000—02; chmn., CEO NII Holdings, Inc., Reston, Va., 2002—08, exec. chmn., 2008—. Bd. dirs. NII Holdings, Inc., 1997—. Recipient Bravo Bus. award as Internat. CEO of the Yr., Latin Trade mag.; named Greater Washington area Entrepreneur of the Yr., Ernst & Young.

SHINDO, KATSUHISA, surgeon; b. Osaka, Japan, Nov. 2, 1939; s. Tomoo and Setsue (Danyasu) Shindo; m. Takako Inoue, June 15, 1968; children: Masahisa, Tokuhisa. MD, Tokyo Med. and Dental U., 1966; PhD, Osaka U., 1974. Intern U.S. Naval Hosp., Yokosuka, Japan, 1966-67; resident in surgery Osaka U. Hosp., 1967-69, Temple U. Hosp., Phila., 1969-71; rsch. fellow Osaka U. Sch. Medicine, 1971-75, asst. in surgery, 1976-84; asst. pathology Heidelberg U., Germany, 1975-76; vice adminstr. Kawachi Gen. Hosp., Higashi-Osaka, 1984-86; assoc. prof. Kinki U. Sch. Medicine, Osaka-Sayama, Japan, 1987-94, prof. surgery, 1994—, chief dept. surgery, 1999—, head Health Affairs Ctr., 2003—. Judge Exam. Bd. Soc. Ins. Fund, Osaka, 1991—; del. Japan ISO TC173/SC3, Stockholm, 1991—; convenor ISO TC173/SC3/WG4&5, Tokyo, 1996—; cons. indsl. hygiene, 1993—. Author: Stoma Rehabilitation, 1974, How to be Free from Piles, 1994, Informed Consent Manual, 1995, Terminology of Stoma-Rehabilitation Science, 1997, Clinical Skills and Practical Materials for Informed Consent, 1999, The Science of Stoma Rehabilitation, 2007; editor-in-chief: STOMA, 1982—, Asian Ostomy, 2002—. Recipient 1st award, Internat. Acad. Proctology, 1972, Hon. award, 1975; grantee Osaka Anticancer Assn. Rsch. grantee, 1980. Mem.: Japan Cytometry Soc. (councillor 2001—), Asian Soc. Stoma Rehab. (founder 1999, dir. gen. 2002—), Asian Fedn. Colo-proctology (founder 1975), Japan Surg. Assn. (councillor 1998—), Japanese Soc. Cancer Colon Rectum (sec. gen. 1992—), Japanese Soc. Surg. Pathology (councillor 1996—), Japanese Soc. Abdominal Emergency Surgery (councillor 1995—), Japanese Soc. Hepato, Biliary and Pancreatic Surgery (councillor 1995—), Japan Soc. Clin. Oncology (councillor 1995—), Japanese Soc. Genetics Aspects Human Malignancy (gov. 1986—2004), Japanese Coll. Surgeons (councillor 1995—), Japanese Soc. Gastroent. Surgery (councillor 1989—), Japanese Soc. Stoma Rehab. (bd. dirs. 1984—, pres. 1998), Japan Soc. Colo-Proctology (v.p. 1991—92, dir. 2001—), Internat. Soc. Univ. Colon and Rectal Surgeons (continental sec. 1978—98, continental v.p. 1998—, congress convenor 2000—02, v.p. 2004—). Achievements include research in new histochemical examination of phosphoamidase and its application to the digestive epithelium; diagnostic pattern of DNA-content in the borderline neoplasm of the large intestine. Avocation: computers. Home: 13-4 Ohnodai 7-chome Osaka Sayama 589-0023 Japan Office: Kinki U Ctr Health Affairs 3-4-1 Kowakae Higashi Osaka 577-8502 Japan

SHINE, JOHN, molecular geneticist, researcher, biochemist; b. Brisbane, Australia, July 3, 1946; arrived in US, 1984; s. Patrick and Molly Gertrude (Hoare) Shine; m. Kathleen Mary Morgan, Feb. 15, 1969; children: Rebecca Kathleen, Michael Patrick. BS with honors, Australian Nat. U., 1972, PhD, 1975; DSc (hon.), U. New South Wales, 2006. Rsch. fellow molecular biology unit Australian Nat. U., Canberra, 1978—80, fellow dept. genetics, 1980—83, sr. fellow, 1983—84, founder Ctr. Recombinant DNA Rsch., 1982; v.p. rsch. & devel. Calif. Biotech., Inc., Mountain View, 1984—86, pres., chief sci. officer, 1986—87; prof. molecular biology U. New South Wales, 1987—, prof. medicine; dep. dir. Garvan Inst. Med. Rsch., Australia, 1987—90, exec. dir., 1990—. Bd. dirs. Biotech. Rsch. Ptnrs., Mountain View, 1984—87, Calif. Biotech., Inc., 1986—90; adj. prof. medicine U. Calif., San Francisco, 1985—87; chmn. bd. dirs. Pacific Biotech. Ltd., 1987—90; chmn. Australian Nat. Health & Med. Rsch. Coun., 2003—06. Editor: Molecular Biology & Medicine, DNA; contbr. articles to profl. jour. Decorated Officer, Gen. Divsn. Order Australia, 1996; recipient Boehringer-Mannheim medal, Australian Biochem. Soc., 1980, Centenary medal, 2001. Fellow: Royal Coll. Pathologists Australasia, Australian Acad. Sci. (Gottschalk medal 1982). Achievements include first to clone a human hormone gene; demonstrate that hormone genes cloned in bacteria could be expressed in a biologically active form; patents in field. Office: Garvan Inst Med Rsch 384 Victoria St Darlinghurst Sydney NSW 2010 Australia E-mail: j.shine@garvan.org.au.*

SHINE, KENNETH IRWIN, academic administrator, cardiologist, educator; b. Worcester, Mass., 1935; Grad., Harvard Coll., 1957; MD, Harvard U., 1961. Diplomate Am. Bd. Internal Medicine. Intern Mass. Gen. Hosp., Boston, 1961—62, resident, 1962—63, 1965—66, fellow in cardiology, 1966—67; surgeon USPHS, 1963—65; instr. Harvard Med. Sch., 1968—; asst. prof. medicine UCLA Sch. Medicine, 1971—73, assoc. prof., 1973—77, prof., 1977—92, prof. emeritus, 1993—, dir. CCU, 1971—75, chief div. cardiology, 1975—79, vice chmn. dept. medicine, 1979—81, exec. chmn., 1981—86, dean, 1986—92, provost for med. scis., 1991—92; clin. prof. medicine Georgetown U. Med. Ctr., Washington, 1993; pres. Inst. of Medicine, Washington, 1992—2002; dir. RAND Center for Domestic and International Health Security, 2003; exec. vice chancellor for health affairs U. Tex. Sys., 2003—, interim chancellor, 2008—09. Master: Am. Coll. Physicians; fellow: Am. Coll. Cardiology; mem.: Inst. Medicine, Assn. Am. Med. Colls. (adminstrv. bd. coun. deans 1989—92, exec. bd. 1990—92, chmn. coun. deans 1991—92), Am. Heart Assn. (pres. 1986—87). Office: U Texas Sys O Henry Hall Room 204 601 Colorado St Austin TX 78701 Office Phone: 512-499-4224. E-mail: kshine@utsystem.edu.

SHINER, JOSETTE SHEERAN (JOSETTE SHEERAN), international organization official, former federal agency administrator; b. Orange, NJ, June 12, 1954; d. James Joseph and Sarah Ann (Gallagher) Sheeran; children: Nicole Munier, Daniel John, Gabrielle. BA, U. Colo., 1976. Nat. desk editor N.Y. News World, 1976-77, Washington bur. chief, 1977-80; corr. The White House, 1980-82; Capital Life and mag. editor Washington Times, 1982-84, asst. mng. editor, 1984-85, dep. mng. editor, 1985-92, mng. editor, 1992-97; pres., CEO Empower Am., 1997-2000; mng. dir. Starpoint Solutions, Reston, Va., 2000—01; assoc. U.S. Trade Rep. Exec. Office of the Pres., Washington, 2001—03, dep. U.S. Trade Rep., 2003—05; under sec. for econ. bus. & agrl. affairs US Dept. State, Washington, 2005—06, US alt. gov. to The World Bank, Inter-Am. Bank, African Devel. Bank, Asian Devel. Bank, European Bank for Reconstruction & Devel., 2005—06; exec. dir., World Food Programme UN, Rome, 2007—. Mem. Leadership Washington Alumni Assn., 1987-88, v.p., 1988-89, alumni chmn., 1989-90. Recipient Atrium award U. Ga., 1984, 100 Most Powerful Women in Washington award Washington Mag., 1998. Mem. White House Corrs. Assn., Am. News Womens Club, Nat. Press Club (newsmaker chmn. 1980-82, Meritorious Svc. award 1981, Vivian award 1981), Am. Soc. Newspaper Editors, Coun. Fgn. Rels. (Washington adv. bd. 1999-2001), Sigma Delta Chi. Episcopalian. Office: UN World Food Programme Via CG Viola 68 00148 Rome Italy

SHINKEL, BERNIE (BERNARD ALBERT SHINKEL), investment advisor; b. 1947; M in Taxation, Walsh Coll. Accountancy and Bus.; M in Mgmt., Purdue U., PhD in Fin. Sr. portfolio mgr., v.p. Huntington Nat. Bank, 1997, portfolio mgr. New Economy Fund, 2001—, lead portfolio mgr. Growth Fund, 2007—. Avocation: skiing. Office: Huntington Nat Bank 7 Easton Oval Columbus OH 43219 Office Phone: 614-331-9452. Office Fax: 614-331-9394. E-mail: bernard.shinkel@huntington.com.

SHINKLE, JOHN THOMAS, lawyer; b. Albany, NY, May 9, 1946; s. Robert Thomas and Margery Joan (Kneip) S.; m. Csilla Elizabeth Bekasy, Sept. 2, 1967; children: Reka, Ildiko. BA, Yale U., 1967; JD, Harvard U., 1970. Bar: D.C. 1971, N.Y. 1983, U.S. Supreme Ct. 1974. Law clk. U.S. Ct. Appeals for D.C. Cir., Washington, 1970—71; assoc. Caplin & Drysdale, Washington, 1971—77, ptnr., 1977—80; assoc. dir. divsn. corp. fin. SEC, Washington, 1980—81, dep. gen. counsel, 1981—82; gen. counsel Salomon Bros. Inc., NY, 1982—94, v.p., 1982—87, dir., 1988—94, head Asia Pacific legal and compliance, 1995—2003; mng. dir. Salomon Bros. Hong Kong, 1996—97, Salomon Smith Barney Hong Kong, 1998—2003; v.p., dep. gen. counsel Bristol-Myers Squibb Co., NY, 2003—04; gen. counsel global transaction svcs. Citigroup, Inc., NYC, 2003, mng. dir., sr. dep. gen. counsel, global corp. & investment bank, 2004—07, mng. dir., gen. counsel Citi pvt. bank, 2007—. Contbr. articles to profl. jours. Mem. ABA, Assn. Bar City N.Y., Securities Industry Assn. (chmn. fed. regulation com. 1989-91), Futures Industry Assn. (dir. 1989-97). Home: 120 Riverside Blvd Apt 10T New York NY 10069 Office: Citigroup 666 5th Ave Fl 12B New York NY 10103

SHINN, GEORGE, professional sports team owner; b. Kannapolis, NC, May 11, 1941; m. Denise Shinn, Mar. 8, 2003; children: Susan, Chad; 1 child, Chris. Student, Evans Bus. Coll., Concord, NC. Ptnr. Evans Bus. Coll.; owner Rutland Edn. Systems, New Orleans/Okla. City (formerly Charlotte) Hornets, 1988—. Author: Miracle of Motivation, The Am. Dream Still Works, You Gotta Believe! The Story of the Charlotte Hornets, Introduction to Professional Selling, Leadership Development. Co-chair fundraising com. Tulane U.; bd. mem. Boy Scouts Am., Nat. D-Day Mus., New Orleans Metrovision Exec. Com., Loyola U. Mem.: Horatio Alger Assn. of Disting. Ams. (Horatio Alger award 1975). Office: New Orleans/Okla City Hornets 1615 Poydras St Fl 20 New Orleans LA 70112*

SHINN, GEORGE LATIMER, investment banker, consultant, finance educator; b. Newark, Ohio, Mar. 12, 1923; s. Leon Powell and Bertha Florence (Latimer) S.; m. Clara LeBaron Sampson, May 21, 1949; children: Deborah, Amy, Martha, Sarah, Andrew. AB, Amherst Coll., 1948; LLD (hon.), Denison U., 1975, Amherst Coll., 1982; MA, Drew U., 1990, PhD, 1992. Trainee Merrill Lynch, Pierce, Fenner & Beane, 1948-49; various exec. positions, 1949-75; pres. Merrill Lynch & Co., Inc., 1973-75; chmn. bd., chief exec. officer 1st Boston Corp., 1975-83; investment banking cons., 1983—2002. Adj. prof. history Drew U., Madison, N.J., 1992—2002; mem. exec. com. President's Pvt. Sector Survey on Cost Control, 1982-84; exec.-in-residence Columbia U. Grad. Sch. Bus., 1983-85; bd. govs. Am. Stock Exch., 1970-74; bd. dirs., trustee Colonial Group Mut. Funds, 1983-98; bd. dirs. Kelso & Co., 1992—, N.Y. Stock Exch., 1975-83, vice chmn., 1979-83; bd. dirs. N.Y. Times Co., 1978-99, Phelps, Dodge Corp., 1983-95, N.Y. Life Ins. Co., 1983-94, Lehigh Press, 1983-91, Superior Oil Co., 1984-87, Congoleum Corp. Gen. chmn. United Hosp. Fund, N.Y.C., 1973-74; trustee Kent Pl. Sch., Summit, N.J., 1966-73, Carnegie Found. for Advancement Teaching, 1976-85, Pingry Sch., 1977-79, Lucille P. Markey Charitable Trust, 1985-97, Rockefeller Family Office Trust, 1989-97, N.J. Coun. for the Humanities, 1994-2000, Arts Coun. Morris Area, 1978-91, Philharmonic Symphony Soc. N.Y., 1983-91, Nat. Humanities Ctr., 1988-94; trustee emeritus Amherst Coll., 1968-82, chmn. bd. trustees, 1973-80; bd. dirs. Rsch. Corp., 1975-86. Capt. USMCR, 1942-52. Fellow Am. Acad. Arts and Scis., N.Y. Acad. Medicine, River Club, Century Assn. Personal E-mail: gshinn1059@aol.com.

SHINN, JAMES JOSEPH (JIM SHINN), former federal agency administrator; b. NJ, 1951; m. Masako Shinn; 3 children. AB, Princeton U., NJ, 1973, PhD, 2001; MBA, Harvard U., Cambridge, Mass., 1981. With East Asia Bur. US Dept. State, 1976—79; with Advanced Micro Devices; co-founder Dialogic; sr. fellow Asia Coun. Fgn. Rels., 1993—96; US pub. del. to 58th session of Gen. Assembly US Reps. to Gen. Assembly of UN US Dept. State, 2002; nat. intelligence officer for East Asia Office Office Nat. Intelligence, 2003—06; prin. dep. asst. sec. for Asian & Pacific security affairs US Dept. Def., 2006—07, asst. sec. for Asian & Pacific security affairs, 2007—09. Vis. prof. Georgetown U. Sch. Fgn. Svc., 2002—03, Princeton U. Woodrow Wilson Sch. Pub. Affairs, 2002—03. Author: Weaving the Net: Conditional Engagement With China, 1996, Fires Across the Water: Transnational Problems in Asia, 1998; co-author (with Peter Gourevitch): Political Power and Corporate Control: the New Global Politics of Corporate Governance, 2005.*

SHINNAR, REUEL, engineering educator, consultant; b. Vienna, Sept. 15, 1923; came to US, 1962; s. Abraham Emil and Rosa (Storch) Bardfeld; m. Miryam Halpern, June 22, 1948; children: Shlomo, Meir Diploma in Chem. Engring., Technion, Haifa, Israel, 1945, M.Sc. in Chem. Engring., 1954; Dr. Engring. Sci., Columbia U., 1957. Various position in chem. engring., Israel, 1945-58; adj. assoc. prof. Technion, Haifa, Israel, 1958-62; visiting research fellow Guggenheim Labs., Princeton (N.J.) U., 1962-64; prof. chem. engring. CCNY, 1964—, disting. prof., 1979—. Pinhas Naor lectr. Technion U., 1974; Wilhelm Meml. lectr. Princeton U., 1985, Kelly lectr. Purdue U., 1991; cons. to various oil and chem. cos. Contbr. numerous articles to profl. jours.; patentee in field. Fellow AICE (Founders award 1992, Alpha Chi Sigma award 1979), N.Y. Acad. Scis.; mem. AIAA, Am. Chem. Soc., Nat. Acad. Engring. Office: City Coll NY Dept Chem Engring 140th St and Convent Ave New York NY 10031 Office Phone: 212-650-6679. Business E-Mail: shinnar@ccny.cuny.edu.

SHINNAR, SHLOMO, pediatric neurologist, educator; b. Haifa, Israel, Nov. 11, 1950; s. Reuel and Miryam (Halpern) S.; m. Shoshana Ellen Cohen, Aug. 11, 1974; children: Ora Rivka, Aviva Batya, Avraham Ever. BA in Physics summa cum laude, Columbia Coll., 1971; PhD, Albert Einstein Coll. Medicine, 1977, MD, 1978. Diplomate Am. Bd. Pediat., Am. Bd. Psychiatry and Neurology, Am. Bd. Child Neurology and Clin. Neurophysiology. Intern, asst. resident in pediatrics, fellow Johns Hopkins Hosp., Balt., 1978-80, asst. resident, resident in neurology, fellow, 1980-83; from asst. prof. to prof. neurology and pediat. Albert Einstein Coll. Medicine, Bronx, 1983—; from asst. attending to attending neurology and pediat. Montefiore Med. Ctr., Bronx Mcpl. & North Ctrl. Bronx Hosps., 1983—; prof. neurology and pediat. Montefiore Med. Ctr., Bronx, Hyman Climenko prof. neurosci. rsch., 2002—. Co-dir. Epilepsy Mgmt. Ctr. Montefiore Med. Ctr. Albert Einstein Coll. Medicine, Bronx, 1983-86, dir., 1986—; mem. adv. bd. Epilepsy Inst., N.Y.C., 1984—, chair 1996—, instnl. rev. bd. protection of human subjects Montefiore Med. Ctr., Bronx, 1985—, vice-chmn., 1989—, prof. of neuroscience rsch., 2002—; adj. sch. scientist Gertrude Sergievsky Ctr. Columbia Coll. Physicians and Surgeons, N.Y.C., 1985—, Sergievsky Scholar, 1986—; cons. in field. Field editor Epilepsy Advances, 1987-93; editl. bd. The Neurologist, 1993—, Epilepsia, 1994-2000, Pediatric Neurology, 1996—; contbr. articles to profl. jours. NY State Regents scholar, 1967-71; Martin and Emily L. Fisher fellow, 1991— Fellow Am. Acad. Pediats., Am. Acad. Neurology; mem. Am. Epilepsy Soc. (chmn. childhood onset epilepsy com. 1993-95, councillor 1992-95, Rsch. Recognition award 1989), Epilepsy Found. America, Child Neurology Soc., Eastern EEG Soc., Internat. Child Neurology Soc., Nat. Assn. Epilepsy Ctrs., Soc. Pediat. Rsch., Am. Neurol. Assn., Epilepsy Inst. Office: Montefiore Med Ctr 111 E 210th St Bronx NY 10467 Business E-Mail: sshinnar@montefiore.org.*

SHINNERS, STANLEY MARVIN, electrical engineer; b. NYC, May 9, 1933; s. Earl and Molly (Planter) Shinners; m. Doris Shinners, Aug. 4, 1956; children: Sharon Rose Cooper, Walter Jay, Daniel Lawrence. BEE, CCNY, 1954; MSEE, Columbia U., 1959. Equipment engr. Western Electric Co., NYC, 1953-54; staff engr. electronics divsn. Otis Elevator Co., Bklyn., 1954-56; project engr. Consol. Avionics Corp., Westbury, NY, 1956-58; program mgr., fed. sys. Lockheed Martin Corp. (formerly Loral Corp., Unisys Corp.), Mitchel Field, NY, 1958-99. Adj. prof. engrng. The Cooper Union, NYC, 1966—, NY Inst. Tech., Old Westbury, NY, 1972-92, Poly. Inst. Bklyn., 1959-72. Author: Control System Design, 1964, Techniques of Systems Engineering, 1967, A Guide to Systems Engineering and Management, 1976, Modern Control System Theory and Application, 1978, Modern Control System Theory and Design, 1992, 2d edit., 1998, Advanced Modern Control System Theory and Design, 1998. Recipient Career Achievement medal, CCNY Alumni Assn., 1980. Fellow IEEE (life); mem. Am. Soc. for Engrng. Edn., Eta Kappa Nu, Tau Beta Pi. Home: 28 Sagamore Way N Jericho NY 11753-2358 Personal E-mail: shinnerssm@optonline.net. *I was very poor financially as a child, but I received an abundance of love and encouragement from parents and family. I have always tried to succeed and to help others succeed. Above all, I have always tried to do what is right whether the decision had to be made in the business world or in private and family matters.*

SHINODA, MICHAEL KENJI, musician, artist; b. Calif., Feb. 11, 1977; m. Anna Shinoda, May 10, 2003. BA, Art Ctr. Coll. Design, 1998. Founding mem., singer, songwriter, rapper, keyboardist, rhythm guitarist and art designer Linkin Park, 1996—; founding mem. Fort Minor, 2004—06; co-founder, prodr. Machine Shop Recordings, LA, 2002—. Musician: (albums) The Rising Tied, 2005, Hybrid Theory, 2000, Meteora, 2003, Live in Texas, 2003, Minutes to Midnight, 2007, Road to Revolution Live at Milton Keynes, 2008, (songs) Crawling, 2000 (Grammy award for Best Hard Rock Performance, 2002), In the End, 2000 (MTV Video Music award for Best Rock Video, 2002, 2003), Somewhere I Belong, 2003, Breaking the Habit, 2003 (MTV Video Music award for Viewer's Choice, 2004), (with Jay-Z) Numb/Encore, 2004 (Grammy award for Best Rap/Sung Collaboration, 2006), What I've Done, 2007 (Top Modern Rock Track, Billboard Year-End Charts, 2007, MTV Video Music award for Best Rock Video, 2008), Shadow of the Day, 2007. Recipient Best-Selling Rock Group award, World Music Awards, 2002, 2003, Favorite Alternative Artist award, Am. Music Awards, 2003, 2004, 2007, 2008; named Top Modern Rock Artist, Billboard Year-End Charts, 2001, 2004, 2007. Office: Linkin Park c/o Machine Shop Records PO Box 36915 Los Angeles CA 90036*

SHINOHARA, MINORU, engineering educator; b. Tokyo; married; 1 child, Elena. PhD, U. Tokyo. Asst. prof. Kyoto Coll. Arts and Design, U. Tokyo; vis. asst. prof. U. Colo., Boulder, sr. rsch. assoc.; rsch. assoc. Pa. State U., Univ. Pk.; assoc. prof. Ga. Inst. Tech., Atlanta. Recipient Rsch. Career Enhancement award, Am. Physiol. Soc., 2004. Office: Ga Inst Tech 281 Ferst Dr Atlanta GA 30332-0356 Business E-Mail: shinohara@gatech.edu.

SHINOZAKI, TAMOTSU, retired physician, anesthesiologist; b. Dairen, Japan, Mar. 18, 1934; s. Yuichi and Shizue Shniozaki; m. Kazuko Sakanaka Shinozaki, Feb. 14, 1940; children: Aritomo, Yuji, Emiko. MD, Okayama U., 1958, D in Med. Scis., 1963. Diplomate Am. Bd. Anesthesiology; cert. spl. qualifications in critical care medicine. Intern St. Luke's Internat. Hosp., Tokyo, 1958—59; resident in anesthesiology Mary Fletcher Hosp., 1964—67; attending anesthesiologist Med. Ctr. Hosp. of Vt., Burlington, 1967—99; asst. prof. Med. Sch. U. Vt., Burlington, 1967—72, assoc. prof., 1972—90, clin. prof., 1990—99, med. co-dir. surg. ICU, 1985—99, prof. emeritus, 2000—; adminstrv. dir. surg. ICU Fletcher Allen Healthcare, Burlington, 1997—99, attending emeritus, 2000—. Cons. med. divsn. Hewlett Packard Co., Waltham, Mass., 1972-77, Intelligent Med. Sys., Carlsbad, Calif., 1987. Recipient Quality Cup award, Excellance in the Quality Movement, 1994. Fellow Am. Coll. Critical Care Medicine; mem. Sigma Xi. Home: 335 Dorset Hts South Burlington VT 05403 Business E-Mail: tshinoza@uvm.edu.

SHINSEKI, ERIC KEN, Secretary of Veterans Affairs, retired military officer; b. Lihue, Hawaii, Nov. 28, 1942; BS, U.S. Mil. Acad., 1965; MA in English, Duke U., 1976; student, U.S. Army Armor Sch., Ft. Knox, Ky., 1968-69, Army Command and Staff Coll., Ft. Leavenworth, Kans., 1978-79, Nat. War Coll., Ft. Lesley McNair, Washington, 1985-86. Commd. 2d lt. US Army, 1965, advanced through grades to gen., 1997, ret., 2003; forward observer B battery 2d battalion, 9th artillery, 3d brigade, 25th Infantry Divsn., U.S. Army, Vietnam, 1965-66; asst. S1 (pers.) base defense command XXIV Corps US Army, Vietnam, 1969-70; comdr. A Troop, 3d squadron, 5th cavalry, 9th infantry divsn attached to 1st brigade, 5th infantry divsn. U.S. Army, Vietnam, 1970; pers. staff officer US Army Pacific, Fort Shafter, Hawaii, 1971-74; instr. dept. English U.S. Mil. Acad., West Point, N.Y., 1976-78; comdr. 3d squadron 7th cavalry, 3d infantry divsn. then asst chief of staff, G-3, U.S. Army Europe and 7th Army, Germany, 1982-85; comdr. 2d brigade, 3d infantry divsn., to asst chief staff G3 VII Corps, U.S. Army Europe and 7th Army, 1987-90; dep. chief of staff adminstrn./logistics Allied Land Forces So. Europe, Germany, 1990-92; asst. divsn. comdr., 3d infantry divsn. U.S. Army & 7th Army Europe, Germany, 1992-93; commanding gen. 1st Cavlry Divsn., Ft. Hood, Tex., 1994-95; asst. dep. chief of staff (ops. and plans) to dep. chief of staff US Army, Washington, 1995-97, comdr. in chief, comdr. Stblzn. Force US Army Europe & 7th Army Bosnia-Herzegovina, 1997-98, vice chief of staff Washington, 1998-99, chief of staff, 1999—2003; sec. US Dept. Veterans Affairs, Washington, 2009—. Decorated Defense Disting. Svc. medal, Disting. Svc. medal, Legion of Merit with oak leaf cluster, Bronze Star medal with V device with 3 oak leaf clusters, Purple Heart with oak leaf cluster, Meritorious Svc. medal with 2 oak leaf clusters, Air medal, Army Commendation medal with oak leaf cluster, Army Achievement medal. Office: US Dept Veterans Affairs 810 Vermont Ave NW Rm 1000 Washington DC 20420*

SHIOTANI, SEIJI, diagnostic radiologist; b. Kyoto, Dec. 22, 1965; s. Kiyoshi and Aichiyo Shiotani; m. Kuniko Oka, Sept. 8, 1991; 1 child, Nobuaki. MD, Shimane Med. U., Izumo, Japan, 1991. Intern Shimane Med. U., 1991—93; resident Kanagawa Cancer Ctr., Yokohama, Japan, 1993—96; fellow Shimane Med. U., 1996—99; chief Tsukuba Med. Ctr., Japan, 1999—2009. Contbr. articles to various profl. jours. Mem.: Japanese Assn. Acute Medicine, Japanese Coll. Radiology, Japan Soc. Legal Medicine, Japan Radiol. Soc. Achievements include research in Postmortem Computed Tomography (PMCT); Establishment of Radiol. Thanatology, contributions to establish PMCT findings in Cardiopulmonary arrest on arrival patients and to evaluate the usefulness at PMCT of detection of the cause of death. Office: Tsukuba Med Ctr Hosp 1-3-1 Amakubo Tsukuba 305-8558 Japan Business E-Mail: shiotani@tmch.or.jp.

SHIOTSU, MASAHIRO, engineering educator; b. Osaka, Japan, June 15, 1942; m. Yoshi Oyama, July 9, 1972. B in Engring., Kyoto U., 1966, D of Engring., 1978. Rsch. assoc. Kyoto U., Uji, 1968-79, assoc. prof., 1979-96, prof., 1996—2006. Mem. ASME (Best Paper award 1990, Melville medal 1991), Japan Soc. Mech. Engrs., Atomic Energy Soc. of Japan, Cryogenic Energy Soc. Japan, Heat Transfer Soc. Japan.

SHIPKO, JANET M., human resources specialist; b. Schenectady, NY, Nov. 3, 1953; d. Frederick J. and Elizabeth Shipko. MSc in Health Care Mgmt., U. Md., 1996. Asst. chief of staff, res. affairs Tripler Army Med. Ctr., Honolulu, 2003—06; chief res. policy Office of Surgeon Gen., Falls Church, Va., 2006—07; program dir. res. affairs Office of Sec. of Def., 2007—08; chief of staff 807th MDSC, Salt Lake City, 2008—. Col. USAR, 1982. Decorated Meritorious Svc. medal US Army, Army Commendation medal, Army Superior Unit award, Armed Forces Res. medal, Army Achievement medal, Nat. Def. Svc. medal, Global War on Terrorism medal, Def. Meritorious Svc. medal. Office: Chief Staff 807th MDSC Salt Lake City UT Home: 3709 S George Mason Dr #1705 E Falls Church VA 22041 Office Phone: 801-656-4073. Business E-Mail: janet.m.shipko@us.army.mil.

SHIPLER, DAVID KARR, journalist, writer; b. Orange, NJ, Dec. 3, 1942; s. Guy Emery Jr. and Eleanor (Karr) Shipler; m. Deborah S. Isaacs, Sept. 17, 1966; children: Jonathan Robert, Laura Karr, Michael Edmund. AB, Dartmouth Coll., 1964; LittD (hon.), Middlebury Coll., 1988, Glassboro State Coll., NJ, 1988; AM (hon.), Dartmouth Coll., 1994; JD (hon.), Birmingham Southern Coll., 2006. News clk. N.Y. Times, 1966—67, news summary writer, 1968, reporter met. staff, 1968—73, fgn. corr. Saigon bur., 1973—75, fgn. corr. Moscow Bur., 1975—, bur. chief Moscow Bur., 1977—79, chief Jerusalem bur., 1979—84, corr. Washington bur., 1985—87, chief diplomatic corr., 1987—88; sr. assoc. Carnegie Endowment for Internat. Peace, Washington, 1988—90. Guest scholar Brookings Instn., 1984—85; adj. prof. Am. U. Sch. Internat. Svc., Washington, 1990; Ferris prof. journalism and pub. affairs Princeton U., 1990—91; Woodrow Wilson vis. fellow, 1990—; writer-in-residence U. So. Calif., 1998; Montgomery fellow, vis. prof. gov. Dartmouth Coll., 2003. Author: Russia: Broken Idols, Solemn Dreams, 1983 (Overseas Press Club award), revised, 1989, Arab and Jew: Wounded Spirits in a Promised Land, 1986 (Pulitzer prize for Gen. Nonfiction, 1987, Pulitzer prize Jury for Gen. Nonfiction, 2009), revised, 2002, A Country of Strangers: Blacks and Whites in America, 1997, The Working Poor: Invisible in America, 2004 (Myers Outstanding Book award Simmons Coll., finalist Nat. Book Critics Cir. award, finalist Helen Bernstein N.Y. Pub. Lib. award); exec. prodr.: (documentaries) from Arab and Jew: Wounded Spirits in a Promised Land, 1989 (Alfred DuPont-Columbia U. award for Broadcast Journalism, 1990), Arab and Jew: Return to the Promised Land, 2002; contbr. articles to nat. mags. Trustee Dartmouth Coll., 1993—2003. With USNR, 1964—66. Recipient award for disting. reporting, Soc. Silurians, 1971, award for disting. pub. affairs reporting, Am. Polit. Sci. Assn., 1971, award, N.Y. chpt. Sigma Delta Chi, 1973, Vento award, Nat. Law Ctr. on Homelessness and Poverty, 2004, Martin Luther King, Jr. Social Justice award, Dartmouth Coll., 2005, Labor Communicator of Yr. award, NY Labor Comms. Coun., 2005, award, DC Employment Justice Ctr., 2005; co-recipient George Polk award, 1982. Office: 4005 Thornapple St Chevy Chase MD 20815-5037 *I have been governed professionally by the conviction that an open society needs open examination of itself to survive. Defining problems, inspecting blemishes, probing wounds, and exposing injustice are the required pastimes of a free people. Nothing intelligent can come from ignorance. If information does not guarantee wisdom, it is at least a prerequisite, for the only wise course is through knowledge. To write about current affairs, then, is to play a small role in a great endeavor. It is to measure one's own performance continually against the highest standards of honesty, fairness, thoroughness, intelligence, to search every day for a bit of truth, then share it. These are the ingredients of happiness, for such a job involves a life of constant learning, perpetual self-education. It keeps a man whole.*

SHIPLEY, SAMUEL LYNN, advertising and public relations executive; b. Marlborough, Mass., Nov. 14, 1929; s. Clifford Lynn and Esther (Jacobs) S.; m. Sue Finucan, Sept. 5, 1955; children: Jeffrey Lynn, Beth Ann, Amy. Student, Charles Morris Price Sch. Advt. and Journalism, U. N.H., 1948-50. Exec. dir. Democratic Party N.H., 1953-56; pres., chmn. Shipley Assos., Inc., Wilmington, Del., 1962—, former chmn.; pres. Cable TV Advt. Inc., 1982—; chmn. emeritus Star Shipley Inc. Dir. Del. Devel. Dept., Dover, 1965-69; mem. bd. overseers Del. Coll. Art and Design. Nominee for U.S. Congress, 1976; pub. relations dir. Del. Democratic Com., 1964-68; chmn. Del. Dem. Com., 1982-90; bd. dirs. Blood Bank of Del., Jobs for Del. Grads., For Children; mem. Del. Heritage Commn.; trustee Grand Opera House; former chair Dem. State Com. With U.S. Army, 1951-53. Recipient Freedoms Found. Honor medal, 1966, Outstanding Grad. award Charles Morris Price Sch., 1974 Mem. Am. Advt. Fedn., Nat. Press Club, Wilmington Advt. Club, Masons. Home: 1196 Paper Mill Rd Newark DE 19711-2924 Office: 135 South West St Wilmington DE 19801 Office Phone: 302-434-8717. Business E-Mail: samshipleyl@comcast.net. *The ingredients for success are good health, average intelligence, a giving spirit, positive thinking, good imagination, self-discipline, hard work, and persistence.*

SHIPLEY, TONY L(EE), investor, software company executive; b. Elizabethton, Tenn., July 19, 1946; s. James A. and Edith J. (Crowder) S.; m. Lynda Anne Jenkins, Nov. 19, 1971; children: Blake Alan, Sarah Robyn. BS in Indsl. Engring., U. Tenn., 1969; MBA, U. Cin., 1975. Indsl. engr. Monsanto Co., Pensacola, Fla., 1969—72; mktg. mgr. SDRC, Cin., 1972—76; v.p. sales and mktg. Anatrol Corp., Cin., 1977—81; pres. Entek Sci. Corp., Cin., 1981—96; pres., CEO Entek IRD Internat. Corp., 1996—2000; founding mem. Queen City Angels, chmn. Bd. dirs. CHMack, The Circuit, U. Cin. E-Ctr., RhinoCyte, Forte Industries, Resource Systems, Global Shelter Systems, U. Cin. Found., Health Found Greater Cin. Named Small Bus. Person of Yr., Greater Cin. C. of C., 1994, Entrepreneur of Yr. in Cin., No. Ky. Region, 1996; recipient Entrepreneurial Excellence award U. Cin., 2001, C.H. Lindner Outstanding Bus. Achievement award U. Cin., 2004; Hamilton County Bus. Ctr., Larry Albice Entrpreneurship award, 2006, E & Y Supporter Entrpreneur, 2007. Mem. ASME, Soc. Automotive Engrs., Greater Cin. Software Assn. (pres. 1996-97, chmn. 1997-99, bd. dirs.), Greater Cin. C. of C., Leadership Class XVIII, Terrace Park (Ohio) Country Club (past pres.). Republican. Avocations: golf, boating. Home: 7825 Calderwood Ln Cincinnati OH 45243-1319

SHIPLEY, WALTER VINCENT, retired bank executive; b. Newark, Nov. 2, 1935; s. L. Parks and Emily (Herzog) S.; m. Judith Ann Lyman, Sept. 14, 1957; children: Barbara, Allison, Pamela, Dorothy, John. Student, Williams Coll., 1954-56; BS, NYU, 1961. With Chem. Bank, NYC, 1956-96; chmn., CEO, chmn. bd. dirs. Chase Manhattan Corp., NYC, 1996-99; ret., 1999. Bd. dirs. Exxon Mobil Corp. Mem. Coun. Fgn. Rels., Augusta Nat. Golf Club, Baltusrol Golf Club (Springfield, N.J.). Office: JPMorgan Chase & Co 270 Park Ave New York NY 10017-2070

SHIPMAN, BARBARA LOWTHER, librarian; d. Malcolm Alfred and Mary Louise Lowther; m. John Lewis Shipman, June 23, 1979; children: Andrew William children: Timothy Michael. BS, U. Mich., Ann Arbor, 1974, AMLS, 1977. Staff assoc., info. svc. Libr. Am. Hosp. Assn., Chgo., 1978—79; head, interlibrary loan and reference, info. svc. libr. U. Mich., Sch. Info. Libr. Studies, Ann Arbor, 1979—82, adj. lectr., 1993; online svc. coord. U. Mich., Alfred Taubman Med. Libr., 1982—89, acting collection devel. officer, 1985—88, coord., health scis. database svc., 1990—91, coord., health scis. electronic info. resources and tech. systems, 1991—95, head, electronic info. systems, 1995—96, head, libr. collections, 1996—2006; liaison libr., Health Scis. Libraries U. Mich., Ann Arbor, 2006—. Contbr. chapters to books, articles to jours. Mem.: Mich. Health Scis. Libr. Assn., Med. Libr. Assn., Beta Phi Mu (dir. 1983—84). Office Fax: 734-763-1473. Business E-Mail: bshipman@umich.edu.

SHIPMAN, JEAN PUGH, medical librarian; b. Chambersburg, Pa., Aug. 6, 1957; d. Andrew Richard and Sara Elizabeth (Bert) Pugh; m. Mark James Shipman, Oct. 8, 1988. BA, Gettysburg Coll., 1979; MSLS, Case Western Res. U., 1980. Reference libr. Johns Hopkins Sch. Medicine, Balt., 1980-81, sr. reference libr., 1981-82, access libr., 1982-84, psychiatry-neuroscis. librarian, 1984-88; mgr. libr. and audiovisual svcs. Greater Balt. Med. Ctr., 1988-90, NN/LM southeastern/atlantic regional coord., 1990—93; outreach info. svcs. libr. Health Scis. Libr., U. Wash., 1993—95, acting head access svcs., 1993—95, assoc. dir. info. resources mgmt., 1995—2000; dir. Tompkins-McCaw Libr. for Health Scis., assoc. Univ. Libr. Va. Commonwealth Univ. Librs., Richmond, Va., 2000—08; dir. Spencer S. Eccles Health Scis. Libr., U. Uttah, Salt Lake, 2008—. Contbr. articles to profl. jours. Mem. Med. Libr. Assn. (bd. dirs. 1999-2002, sec. 2000-02, pres.-elect 2005-06, pres. 2006-2007, immediate past pres., 2007-08), Beta Phi Mu, Beta Beta Beta. Democrat. Lutheran. Avocations: tennis, reading, cooking. Office: Spencer S Eccles Health Scis Libr Univ Utah 10 N 1900 E Bldg 589 Salt Lake City UT 84112-5890 Home: 7909 S Desert Ridge Cove Cottonwood Heights UT 84121-5682

SHIPP, DAN SHACKELFORD, lawyer; b. Yazoo City, Miss., Jan. 6, 1946; m. Carolyn Julie Perry, Nov. 30, 1974; children: Perry Lee, Clay Alexander. AA, Holmes Jr. Coll., 1966; BA, Miss. State U., 1968; JD, U. Miss., 1971. Bar: Miss. 1971, U.S. Dist. Ct. (no. dist.) Miss. 1971, U.S. Dist. Ct. (so. dist.) Miss. 1976, U.S. Ct. Appeals (5th cir.) 1982, Colo. 1986, U.S. Ct. Appeals (10th cir.) 1986, U.S. Dist. Ct. Colo. 1986. Pvt. practice, Yazoo City, 1974-83, Aspen, 1986—2001, Basalt, Colo., 2002—. Spkr. in field. Recipient Master Adv. Cert. award, Nat. Inst. Trial Advocacy Notre Dame Law Sch., 1993; named Superb Lawyer, Colo. AVVO. Mem.: ABA, ATLA, Nat. Coll. DUI Def., Colo. Trial Lawyers Assn. (bd. dirs. 1986—88), Colo. Bar Assn., Toastmasters Internat. Avocations: hunting, archery, travel. Home: 0300 Vagneur Ln Basalt CO 81621-9103 Office Phone: 970-927-2255. Personal E-mail: danshipplaw@comcast.net.

SHIPPEY, SANDRA LEE, lawyer; b. Casper, Wyo., June 24, 1957; d. Virgil Carr and Doris Louise (Conklin) McClintock; m. Ojars Herberts Ozols, Sept. 2, 1978 (div.); children: Michael Ojars, Sara Ann, Brian Christopher; m. James Robert Shippey, Jan. 13, 1991; 1 child, Matthew James. BA with distinction, U. Colo., 1978; JD magna cum laude, Boston U., 1982. Bar: Colo. 1982, U.S. Dist. Ct. Colo. 1985. Assoc. Cohen, Brame & Smith, Denver, 1983-84, Parcel, Meyer, Schwartz, Ruttum & Mauro, Denver, 1984-85, Mayer, Brown & Platt, Denver, 1985-87; counsel western ops. GE Capital Corp., San Diego, 1987-94; assoc. Page, Polin, Busch & Boatwright, San Diego, 1994-95; v.p., gen. counsel First Comml. Corp., San Diego, 1995-96; legal counsel NextWave Telecom Inc., San Diego, 1996-98; ptnr. Procopio, Cory, Hargreaves and Savitch, LLP, 1998—, mgmt. com. Spkr. in field. Contbr. articles to profl. jours. Active Pop Warner football and cheerleading; bd. dirs. Southwestern Christian Schs., Inc., 2002—, San Diego Christian Found., 2001—. Mem. Calif. State Bar (co-chair uniform comml. code com., 2004-05), Phi Beta Kappa, Phi Delta Phi. Republican. Mem. Ch. of Christ. Avocations: tennis, golf, photography. Home: 15839 Big Springs Way San Diego CA 92127-2034 Office: Procopio Cory Et Al 530 B St Ste 2100 San Diego CA 92101-4496 Home Phone: 858-722-6072; Office Phone: 619-515-3226. Business E-Mail: sls@procopio.com.

SHIPTSOVA, RIMMA, economics professor; b. Riga, Latvia, Sept. 13, 1961; d. Oleg Shiptsov and Tatiana Chernauska; m. Alex Blas, Apr. 13, 1984. PhD, Ohio State U., Columubs, 1998. Cert. in level 2 alpine Profl. Ski Instrucotr Assn. UT, 2008. Asst. prof. Utah State U., Logan, 2002—08; on-line facutly U. Phoenix, 2008—. Cons. Aktivist Fin., Washington, 2005—08. Vol. Sundance Inst., Park City, Utah, 2008—; mem. Food Distbn. Rsch. Soc., 2006—08, Oak Crest Gardens, Salt Lake City, 2008. Recipient Nominated bd. mem., Oak Christ Gardens, 2008. Mem.: Profl. Ski Instr. Assn., Food Distbn. Rsch. Soc. Home: 900 Donner Way #206 Salt Lake City UT 84108 Office Phone: 935-363-4330. Personal E-mail: shiptsova@gmail.com.

SHIRAI, SHUN, law educator, lawyer; b. Tokyo, June 18, 1942; s. Kyo and Tomi Shirai; m. Junko Matsushita, Apr. 10, 1969; children: Akiko, Yuko, Jin. LLB, Hitotsubashi U., Tokyo, 1966, LLM, 1969. Pub. prosecutor Tokyo Dist. Pub. Prosecutor's Office, 1973—74; asst. prof. criminal law Kokugakuin U., Tokyo, 1974-81, prof., 1981—, dean Grad. Sch., 1999-2001. Atty. Tokyo 2nd Bar Assn., 1992—. Author: Phenomenology of Crime, 1984, new edit., 2008, Thought on Criminal Law of Ancient India, 1985, Legal History on Criminal Law of Ancient India, 1990, Philosophy of Criminal Law in Ancient India, 1995, Phenomenology and Indian Philosophy for the Study on Ancient Indian Criminal Law, 1997, Prof. Shirai's Lectures on the Law of Criminal Procedure, 1998, Philosophy of Criminal Law in Bhagavad-gītā at Ancient India, 1998, Crime and Sorrowness of Human Being, 1999, Defence Lawyer's Statements in Criminal Court, 2000, Thoughts on Death Penalty in Ancient India, 2000, The Sanskrit, as a Legal Language, appearing in Judicial Documents of British India and Non-Violent Theory of Punishment, originated in Ancient India, 2000, Thought on Righteousness in Criminal Law, handed down by Tradition from Ancient India, 2002, On Basic Principles of Hindu Criminology, derived from Ancient Indian Criminal Law, 2002, Introduction to Study on Practice of Japanese Criminal Jurisdiction, 2003, Philosophy of Crime of Contemporary Indian Thought on Human Being, 2003, Peculiarity in Research Method on Hindu Criminology, 2004, On the Legal Meaning of Yājñavalkyasmṛti, Ancient Indian Legal Script, Book II, Section 1, 2005, Phenomenological Criminology and Transcendental Intersubjectivity, 2006, Thoughts on Sin, Observed in Undercurrent of Indian Legal History and Peculiarity of Method on Treatment for Sinner, 2006, Victimology Without Sense of Victim's Revenge, A Criminological Research to the Dhammapada, 2007, Transcendence for Criminal Nihilism by Dāna of Buddhism in Indian Legal History, 2008, Thought on Criminal Law and Philosophy of Crime, Appearing in Mahabharata Santi-Parvan as Materials of Indian Legal History in Ancient Hindu Society, 2009; contbr. chpts. to books. Mem. Indian History Congress. Buddhist. Home: 703 Kinsen Bldg 2-16-1 Hanakawado Taito-ku Tokyo 111-0033 Japan Office: Kokugakuin U 4-10-28 Higashi Shibuya-Ku Tokyo 150-8440 Japan Office Phone: 03-5466-0111.

SHIRAYANEGI, PETER SEIICHI CARDINAL SEIICHI, cardinal, archbishop; b. Hachioji, Japan, June 17, 1928; PhD in Philosophy, Sophia U, Tokyo; PhD in Canon Law, Pontifical Urbanian Univ., Rome. Ordained priest Roman Cath. Ch., 1954, consecrated bishop Roman Cath. Ch., 1966, created cardinal Roman Cath. Ch., 1994. Ordained priest Archdiocese of Tokyo, 1954, pastor, 1954—66; ordained bishop, 1966; aux. bishop Archdiocese of Tokyo, 1966—69, coadjutor archbishop, 1969—70, archbishop, 1970—2000; elevated to cardinal, 1994; cardinal-priest S. Emerenziana a Tor Fiorenza, 1994—; archbishop emeritus Archdiocese of Tokyo, 2000—. Pres. Japanese Bishops Conf., 1983—92. Roman Catholic. Office: c/o Archdiocese of Tokyo Sekiguchi 3-16-15 Bunkyo 112-0014 Japan

SHIRAZI, EMAN ALI, dentist; b. Shiraz, Iran, Sept. 21, 1975; arrived in US, 1983; s. Mohammad Shirazi and Parvin Asadzadeh; m. Marissa Guzman, Sept. 30, 2006. BA in Biology, U. Iowa, Iowa City, 1996; DDS, NY U., NYC, 2001. Dentist Smile Ctr., Chgo., 2001—04, Brighton Pk. Dental, Chgo., 2002—06, Water Tower Family Dental, Lake in the Hills, Ill., 2005—. Fellow: AGD, ICOI; mem.: ADA (presiding chair 2007), Chgo. Dental Soc. (chairperson 2006—). Avocations: travel, golf, reading, movies. Office: Water Tower Family Dental 2250 W Algonqoin Rd Ste 101 Lake In The Hills IL 60156

SHIRE, DAVID LEE, composer; b. Buffalo, July 3, 1937; s. Irving Daniel and Esther Miriam (Sheinberg) S.; m. Talia Rose Coppola, Mar. 29, 1970 (div.); 1 child, Matthew Orlando; m. Didi Conn. Feb. 11, 1984; 1 child, Daniel Joshua. BA, Yale U., 1959. Film scores include The Conversation, 1974, The Taking of Pelham 1-2-3, 1974, Farewell, My Lovely, 1975, The Hindenburg, 1975, All the President's Men, 1977, Saturday Night Fever (adaptation and additional music), 1977, Norma Rae, 1979 (Acad. award for best original song It Goes Like It Goes), Only When I Laugh, 1981, The World According to Garp, 1982, Max Dugan Returns, 1983, 2010, 1984, Return to Oz, 1985, Short Circuit, 1986, 'Night, Mother, 1986, Vice Versa, 1988, Monkey Shines, 1988, Paris Trout, 1991, Bed and Breakfast, 1992, The Journey Inside (IMAX), 1993, One Night Stand, 1994, Ash Wednesday, 2002, The Tollbooth, 2004, Zodiac, 2007, Beyond A Reasonable Doubt, 2008; TV scores include Raid on Entebbe, 1977 (Emmy nomination), The Defection of Simas Kudirka, 1978 (Emmy nomination), Do You Remember Love?, 1985 (Emmy nomination), Promise, 1986, Echoes in the Darkness, 1987, The Women of Brewster Place, 1989, The Kennedys of Massachusetts, 1990 (Emmy nomination), Common Ground, 1990, Sarah Plain & Tall, 1991, Last Wish, 1992, Broadway Bound, 1992, Skylark, 1993, Remember, 1993, The Companion, 1994, My Brother's Keeper, 1995, Serving in Silence, 1995, The Heidi Chronicles, 1995, My Antonia, 1995, The Streets of Laredo, 1995, Last Stand at Saber River, 1997, Rear Window, 1998 (Emmy nomination), Double Platinum, 1999, Small Vices, 1999, These Old Broads, 2001, Two Against Time, 2001; theatre scores include The Sap of Life, 1961, Graham Crackers, 1962, The Unknown Soldier and His Wife, 1967, How Do You Do, I Love You, 1968, Love Match, 1970, Starting Here, Starting Now, 1977, Baby, 1983 (Tony nominee best mus. and best original score), Urban Blight, 1988, Closer Than Ever, 1989 (Outer Critics Circle award best off-Broadway musical and best score), Big, 1996 (Tony nominee best score), Time for Love, 2006, Take Flight, 2007, Stream of Voices, 2008; composer Sonata for Cocktail Piano, 1965, (Symphonic Suite for Doubler and Orch.) Shades of Blue, 2007; recorded songs include Autumn, 1959, Starting Here, Starting Now, 1965, What About Today?, 1969, Manhattan Skyline, 1977, The Promise, 1978 (Acad. award nomination), It Goes Like It Goes, 1979 (Acad. award), With You I'm Born Again, 1979; albums include Saturday Night Fever, 1977 (Grammy award 1978), Starting Here, Starting Now, 1977 (Grammy nomination 1977), Baby, 1984, Return to Oz, 1985, Closer Than Ever, 1990, David Shire at The Movies, 1991, Big, 1996. With Army N.G., 1960-66. Mem. Composers and Lyricists Guild Am., Am. Fedn. Musicians, Broadcast Music Inc., Acad. Motion Picture Arts and Scis., Nat. Acad. Rec. Arts and Scis., Nat. Acad. TV Arts and Scis., Dramatists Guild Am. (coun. mem.). Jewish. Office: Ste 304 16501 Ventura Blvd Encino CA 91436-2067 Office Phone: 818-971-7300. Personal E-mail: dshire@aol.com.

SHIRE, DONALD THOMAS, retired chemicals executive, lawyer; b. Boston, Jan. 13, 1930; s. Thomas J. and Nellie M. S.; m. Anne Court Bither, Nov 21, 1953; children: Jennifer Anne, Andrew Carter, Daniel Orchard. BS in Bus. Adminstrn, Boston U., 1951, LL.B., 1953; postgrad., Harvard Bus. Sch., 1985; LLD (hon.), Muhlenberg Coll., 1997. Atty. Air Products and Chems., Inc., 1957-64, atty., 1964-75, sec., asst. gen. counsel, 1975-78, v.p. energy and materials, 1978-85, v.p. human resources, 1986-90, sr. v.p. human resources and adminstrn., 1990-91, sr. v.p. adminstrn., 1991-93; ret., 1993; also bd. dirs. Air Products and Chems., Inc. Chmn. Air Products Found., 1991-93; bd. dirs. Lehigh Valley Bus./Edn. Partnership. Trustee Muhlenberg Coll. (life), 1976-95, Lehigh Valley Health Network., 1983-99, Lt. USNR, 1954-57. Mem. Am. Arbitration Assn. Home: 27 Drake Ln Scarborough ME 04074

SHIREMAN, PAULA K., medical educator; d. Paul E. Shireman and Martha L. Drudge-Shireman; m. Patrick T. Conroy, Aug. 17, 2006; children: Paul Eugene Conroy, Patrick T. Conroy, Paul E. Conroy, Aine M. Conroy. MD, Ind. U. Sch. Medicine, Indpls., 1990. Diplomate general and vascular surgery Am. Bd. Surgery, 1998. Assoc. prof. U. Tex. Health Sci. Ctr., San Antonio, 1999—. Achievements include research in R01 HI074236. Office: Univ of Tex Health Sci Ctr 7703 Floyd Curl Dr San Antonio TX 78229

SHIRER, ROBERT LLOYD, clergyman; b. Ouagadougou, W. Africa, Apr. 14, 1929; s. Wilbert Lloyd and Margaret Peoples S.; m. Juanita Shirer, June 1, 1951 (div. 1971); m. Anne Kleier, Sept. 1, 1973; children: Brenda Margaret, Bruce Robert (dec.). AB magna cum laude, Asbury Coll., 1950; MA, U. Pa., 1951; BD, Princeton Theol. Seminary, 1954; postgrad., NYU, 1955-62. Ordained minister Presbyterian Ch.; CPM Inst. of Real Estate, Maine; real estate broker, Fla. Asst. minister White Plains Presbyn. Ch., NY, 1954—55; minister of edn. Huguenot Meml. Ch., Pelham Manor, NY, 1955—57; pastor First Presbyn. Ch., Peekskill, NY, 1957—62, Maximo Presbyn. Ch., St. Petersburg, Fla., 1962-67; exec. dir. Presbyn. Social Ministries, St. Petersburg, 1967-73; pres. Shirer & Assocs., Inc., Seminole, Fla., 1973—; parish assoc. Good Samaritan Ch., Pinellas Park, Fla., 1996—2003. Mem. Suncoast Bd. Realtors, St. Petersburg, 1974—; mem. Inst. Real Estate Mgmt., Chgo., 1975—. Mem. bd. adjustment Indian Rocks Beach, Fla., 1980-81; mem. human rels. adv. com., St. Petersburg, 1965-67; vice-chair Pinellas County Dem. Com., 1996-2002, chmn. grievance com., 2004-06. Named Ky. Col., 1972. Mem. Nat. Assn. Mng. Agts. (bd. dirs. 1974-90), Southeast Assn. of HUD Mng. Agts. (bd. dirs., pres. 1983—), Presbytery of Tampa Bay (pres. trustees 1994-96). Avocation: worldwide travel. Personal E-mail: rlsrascal@tampabay.com.

SHIRES, LINDA M., English educator, writer; b. Providence, July 29, 1950; d. Philip Munroe and Helen English Shires; m. Ulrich C. Knoepflmacher, Aug. 15, 1988; 1 child, Alexander stepchildren: Julie, Paul, Daniel. BA in Classics, Wheaton Coll., Norton, Mass., 1972; MA in Classics, Brown U., 1973; BA in English, Oxford U., Eng., 1977; MA/PhD in English, Princeton U., 1981. From asst. to assoc. prof. Syracuse (N.Y.) U., 1981—96, prof. English, 1996—, dir. grad. studies, 2007—08; prof. English Stern Coll., Yeshiva U., NY, 2008—, chair, 2009—. Referee presses, jours., univs., other orgns.; mem. adv. bd. Victorians Inst. Jour. U. N.C., 1995—; vis. assoc. prof. Princeton U., 1990—92. Author: British Poetry of the Second World War, 1985, Coming Home, 2003, Perspectives, 2009; co-author: Telling Stories, 1988, 5th edit., 2002; editor: Rewriting the Victorians, 1992, The Trumpet Major, 1998, Far From the Madding Crowd, 2002, Tess of the d'Urbervilles, 2005; mem. editl. bd.: Nines, 2004—; mem. editl. bd. Victorians Inst. Jour., 1995—. Recipient directorship, NEH, 1993, 1995; fellow, Guggenheim Found., 1993—94. Mem.: MLA (elections com. 1990—92), N.Am. Victorian Studies Assn., N.E. Victorians Assn., Oxford Alumni Assn. Jewish. Office: 245 Lexington Ave New York NY 10016 Office Phone: 917-326-4801. Business E-Mail: shires@yu.edu.

SHIRILAU, MARK STEVEN, utilities executive; b. Long Beach, Calif., Dec. 13, 1955; s. Kenneth Eugene and Marrjorie Irene (Thorvick) Shirey; m. Jeffery Michael Lau, Nov. 25, 1984 (dec. Aug. 9, 1993). BSEE, U. Calif., Irvine, 1977, MS in Bus. Adminstrn., 1980, PhD, 1988; M in Engring., Calif. Poly. State U., 1978; diploma in theology, Episc. Theol. Sch., Claremont, Calif., 1984; MA in Religion, Sch. Theology at Claremont, 1985. Ordained priest Ecumenical Cath. Ch., 1987, consecrated bishop, 1991; registered profl. engr., Calif., N.Y., Tex.; lic. contractor, Calif. Grad. asst. Electric Power Inst., 1977-78; pres., CEO M.S.E., Santa Ana, Calif., 1977-87; adminstrv. mgr. EECO Inc., Santa Ana, 1979-83; fin. engr. So. Calif. Edison Co., Rosemead, 1983-84, conservation engr., 1984-85, conservation supr., 1985-89; exec. v.p. Aloha Sys., Inc., Villa Grande, Calif., 1989-93, pres., 1993—, also bd. dirs.; lectr. engring. Citrus Coll., Glendora, Calif., 2000—. Bd. dirs. Ewing Consol. Corp., Outrider Trucking, Inc.; part-time instr. Santa Ana Coll., 1982-84, Citrus Coll., Glendora, Calif., 2000-; lectr. engring. West Coast U., Orange, Calif., 1984-91; bd. dirs. Am. Electronics Assn. Credit Union, Sweetwater Springs Water Dist., Heat Pump Coun. So. Calif., AIDS Interfaith Network Sonoma County, Stampede Svcs. Inc., Ewmark Corp. Author: Triune Love: An Insight into God, Creation, and Humanity, 1983, Salvation, Scripture and Sexuality, 1992, History and Overview of the Ecumenical Catholic Church, 1993, Power 101, A Basic Introduction to Electric Utility Power, 1998, The Five Fatal Fears, 2002, (screenplay) Blackout!, 2005. Archbishop, primate Ecumenical Cath. Ch.; chief chaplain svcs. Nolanville (Tex.) Police Dept., 1998-2000; chaplain Jonestown (Tex.) Police Dept., 2001—. Mem. IEEE (sr.), ASHRAE, Internat. Assn. Chiefs Police, Assn. Energy Mgrs. (sr.), Assn. Profl. Energy Mgrs. (bd. dirs.), Am. Soc. Nondestructive Testing, Assn. Energy Svcs. Profls. (bd. dirs., charter mem., exec. v.p.), Am. Soc. Safety Engrs., Nat. Assn. Chiefs Police, Pacific Bears Club (v.p.), Dignity Integrity (life), Eta Kappa Nu. Democrat. Personal E-mail: marks@alohasys.com. Business E-Mail: archbishop@ecchurch.org.

SHIRLEY, CRAIG P., public relations executive, writer; b. Syracuse, NY, Sept. 24, 1956; m. Zorine Shirley; children: Taylor, Andrew, Matthew, Mitchell. BA in History & Polit. Sci., Springfield Coll., 1978. Press sec., staff mem. to US Senator Gordon Humphrey, 1978; dir. ind. expenditure campaign Fund for a Conservative Majority, 1980; advertising account exec. NYC, 1981; comm. advisor Rep. Nat. Com., 1982; dir. comm. Nat. Conservative Polit. Action Com., 1984; founder, pres. Craig Shirley & Assocs., 1984—87, 1992—2000; co-founder, CEO Keene, Shirley & Assocs., 1987—92; pres., CEO Shirley & Banister Pub. Affairs (formerly Craig Shirley & Assocs.), 2000—. Bd. dirs. Am. Conservative Union; bd. govs. Reagan Ranch; adv. bd. Patrick Henry Ctr.; lectr. in field. Author: Reagan's Revolution: The Untold Story of the Campaign That Started It All, 2005, Rendezvous with Destiny: Ronald Reagan and the Campaign That Changed America, 2008; editor: Are You a Conservative or a Liberal?, Coaching Youth Lacrosse; contbr. articles to profl. jours. Bd. mem. United Seniors Assn., No. Va. Youth Lacrosse League, Fort Hunt Youth Athletic Assn. Republican. Avocation: sailing. Office: Shirley & Banister Pub Affairs 122 S Patrick St Alexandria VA 22314 Office Phone: 703-739-5920. Office Fax: 730-739-5924. E-mail: info@sbpublicaffairs.com.

SHIRLEY, DONALD DEAN, appraiser; b. Belle Plaine, Iowa, Dec. 21, 1934; s. Lloyd Leslie and Lulu Ann (Waterman) S.; m. Karin K. Shirley, Nov. 28, 1957; children: Reneé Roze, Kevin Donald. Grad. H.S., Algona, Iowa. Cert. engring. technician. Asst. party chief Iowa Hwy. Commn., Ames, 1952-62, chief estimator, 1962-69, staff appraiser, 1969-79; condemnation hearing officer Iowa Dept. Transp., Ames, 1979-82, chief fiscal agt., 1982-91, chief appraiser, 1991-98, ret., 1998; dir. Mem.'s 1st Cmty. Credit Union, Iowa, 1998—. Active Trinity Luth. Ch., Boone, Iowa, 1961—. Mem. Internat. Right of Way Assn. (sr. mem.). Avocations: fishing, golf, travel. Home: 1104 Country Club Dr Boone IA 50036-5103 Home Phone: 515-432-3506.

SHIRLEY, EDWARD D., consumer products company executive; b. Lynn, Mass., Nov. 7, 1956; BSBA, U. Mass., Amherst, 1977. Inventory acct. safety razor divsn. Gillette, Boston, 1978—79, cost acct. safety razor divsn., 1979—81, fin. analyst safety razor divsn., 1981—83, cost acctg. supr. safety razor divsn., 1983—84, asst. mgr. fin. planning Papermate divsn., 1984—86, info. resource mgr. Papermate divsn., 1986—87, fin. planning mgr. Papermate divsn., 1987—88, v.p. U.S. fin. & adminstrn. Oral-B Labs. Belmont, Calif., 1988—91, dist. sales mgr. Oral-B US, 1991—92, gen. mgr. Oral-B US consumer products divsn., 1992—94, pres. Oral-B N.Am., 1994—97, Kronberg, Germany, 1997—98, pres. Braun global sales Germany, 1998—99, pres. Gillette Europe Isleworth, England, 1999—2002, sr. v.p. Gillette global value chain and global mktg. resources Boston, 2002—04, pres. Gillette internat. comml. ops., 2004—05; pres. Gillette comml. ops. internat The Procter & Gamble Co., Cin., 2005—06, group. pres. N.Am., 2006—08, vice chair global beauty & grooming, 2008—. Mem. bd. and exec. com. GS1; mem. industry affairs coun. GMA; past. mem. bd. dirs. Transora; past mem. exec. bd. ECR Europe, Global Commerce Initiative, AIM Europe; bd. dirs. Time Warner Cable, 2009—. Mem. bus. adv. coun. U. Mass. Isenberg Sch. Mgmt.; past pres. Boys and Girls Club of Am., Salem, Mass.; past mem. bd. dirs. City Yr. Boston. Office: Procter & Gamble PO Box 599 Cincinnati OH 45201-0599*

SHIRLEY, JON ANTHONY, former computer software company executive; b. San Diego, Apr. 12, 1938; s. Joseph Roy and Mercedes (Miller) Shirley; m. Gail Grieg (div. June 1964); 1 child, Erickson; m. E. Mary L. Johanson, July 7, 1964; children: Peter, Mary. Attended, MIT, 1956-57. With Radio Shack divsn. Tandy Corp., Ft. Worth, 1963-72, v.p. computer merchandising, 1972-83; pres., COO Microsoft Corp., Redmond, Wash., 1983—90, bd. dir., 1983—2008. Bd. dir. Manzanita Capital, Seattle. Chmn. bd. trustees Seattle Art Mus.; trustee Mus. Flight, Seattle, Hill Sch., Pottstown, Pa.; mem. chmn. council Mus. Modern Art, NYC. Named one of Top 200 Collectors, ARTnews Mag., 2004—08. Mem.: Assn. Data Processing Service Orgn. (bd. dirs. 1986—), Seattle Yacht. Democrat. Avocations: Collector of Modern & Contemporary Art, Collecting, restoring, showing and racing of Vintage Ferrari Motor Cars.

SHIRLEY, KAHLERT, literature and language professor; d. Benjamin Henry and Anna Rimkus Kahlert; children: Natalie Elizabeth Hall, Nicholas Sean Hall. PhD, U. Calif., LA. Prof. English Merced Coll., Calif., 1994—; lectr. English U. Calif., 2005—08; instr. English U. Hawaii Manoa, Honolulu, 1972—77. Pres. Merced Coll. Faculty Assn., 2004—06. Fellowship, Danforth Found., 1979. Office: Merced Coll 3600 M St Merced CA 95348 Business E-Mail: kahlert.s@mccd.edu.

SHIRLEY-QUIRK, JOHN, singer, educator; b. Liverpool, Eng., Aug. 28, 1931; arrived in US, 1990, naturalized, 2002; s. Joseph Stanley and Amelia (Griffiths) S.-Q.; m. Patricia May Hastie, July 1955 (dec. Feb. 1981); children: Kate, Peter; m. Sara Van Horn Watkins, Dec. 29, 1981 (dec. Dec. 1997); children: Benjamin, Emily (dec.), Julia; m. Teresa May Perez, Mar. 2009. BSc, Liverpool U., 1953, MusD (hon.), 1977; D Univ., Brunel U., 1981. Asst. lectr. Acton Tech. Coll., London, 1956-60; vicar choral St. Paul's Cathedral, London, 1960-61; profl. singer, 1960—; joint artistic dir. Aldeburgh Festival, 1981-84. Mem. voice faculty Peabody Conservatory, Balt., 1991—; vis. artist Carnegie-Mellon U., Pitts., 1994-98. Numerous recs. and 1st performances, especially works of Benjamin Britten. Mem. ct. Brunel U., 1977-81. Flying officer RAF, 1952-55. Decorated comdr. Order of Brit. Empire. Mem. Royal Acad. Music (hon.), Royal Philharmonic Soc. Personal E-mail: jssq@peabody.jhu.edu.

SHIROMA, WAYNE A., engineering educator; s. Charles Y. and Jean A. Shiroma. BS, U. Hawaii, Manoa, 1986; MEng, Cornell U., 1987; PhD, U. Colo., Boulder, 1996. Asst. prof. U. Hawaii, 1996—2001, assoc. prof., 2001—08, co-dir., Hawaii Space Flight Lab., 2007—, prof., 2008—. Founder UH Small-Satellite Program, 2001—; co-founder Pipeline Comm. and Tech., Inc., Honolulu, 2004. Contbr. articles to engring. jours. Recipient UH Hi Chang Chai Excellence Tchg. award, 1998, 2002, 2006, UH Regents Excellence Tchg. medal, 2003, 1st Pl., UH Bus. Plan Competition, 2004. Mem.: IEEE (gen. chair, MTT-S Internat. Microwave Symposium 2007, MTT-S N. Walter Cox award 2009), Am. Soc. Engring. Edn., Eta Kappa Nu (faculty advisor, Delta Omega chpt. 1999—). Achievements include patents for retrodirective antennas. Office: Univ Hawaii 2540 Dole St Holmes 483 Honolulu HI 96822

SHIRTLIFF, BRYAN, retail executive; m. Eve Shirtliff; 4 children. B, U. Mont. Asst. store mgr. to sr. mktg. mgr. health and beauty Am. Stores Co., 1983—96; v.p. health and beauty care and gen. mdse. Bruno's Inc.; dir. health care Rite Aid Corp., Camp Hill, Pa., 1998—99, dir. health care and seasonal, 1999—2000, v.p. seasonal and hardlines, 2000—03, sr. v.p. category mgmt., 2003—. Home: Rite Aid Corp 30 Hunter Ln Camp Hill PA 17011 Office Phone: 717-761-2633.

SHIRVANI, SIR HAMID, architect, educator, philosopher, writer, university president; b. Tehran, Iran, Oct. 20, 1950; arrived in US, 1974, naturalized, 1986; s. Majid and Taji (Granpisheh) Shirvani; m. Fatemeh Shokrollahi, Oct. 4, 2002. Diploma in architecture, Poly. of Cen. London, 1974; MArch, Pratt Inst., 1975; MS, Rensselaer Poly. Inst., 1977; MLA, Harvard U., 1978; MA, Princeton U., 1979, PhD, 1980; LHD (hon.), Soka U., Japan, 2003. Project designer London Borough of Barnet, 1973-74; asst. prof. architecture Pa. State U., 1979-82; prof., dir. grad. studies SUNY, Syracuse, 1982-85; prof., dir. Sch. Urban Planning and Devel., U. Louisville, 1985-86; prof. architecture and urban design U. Colo., Denver, 1986-92, dean Sch. of Architecture and Planning, 1986-91; prof. philosophy, dean Coll. Arts and Scis. U. Mass., Lowell, 1992-95; v.p. grad. studies and rsch., prof. urban studies CUNY Queens Coll., Flushing, 1995-2000; provost, exec. v.p., Martha Masters prof. art/architecture Chapman U., Orange, Calif., 2000—05; pres., prof. art and architecture Calif. State U., Stanislaus, 2005—. Vis. faculty So. Calif. Inst. Architecutre, U. So. Calif.; lectr. in field. Author: Urban Design: A Comprehensive Reference, 1981, Urban Design Review, 1981, Urban Design Process, 1985, Beyond Public Architecture, 1990; editor Urban Design Rev., 1982-85, Urban Design and Preservation Quar., 1985-88; mem. editorial bd. Jour. Archtl. Edn., 1988-94, Avant Garde, 1988-93, Jour. Planning Edn. and Rsch., 1987-93, Art and Architecture, 1974-78, Jour. Am. Planning Assn., 1982-88. Recipient Gold medal in Architecture and Urbanism, 1988, Faculty Honor award, 1990, Acad. Leadership award, Faculty Rsch. award, Commendation award AIA, 2003, Justice award SGI, 2003, 09, Pres. of Yr. award Calif. State U. Student Assn., 2007, 09; Knight of Holy Sepulchre, 2004, Knight of Malta, 2009. Fellow World Acad. Arts and Scis., Am. Soc. Landscape Archs. (recognition award), Royal Geog. Soc., Royal Soc. Arts, World Acad. Arts and Scis.; mem. NCAA (pres. coun.), Am. Inst. Cert. Planners, Am. Planning Assn. (chmn. urban design divsn. 1987-89, Disting. award 1984, Urban Design award 1985), Sigma Xi, Omicron Delta Epsilon, Tau Sigma Delta (Silver medal in archtl. edn. 1988), Tau Beta Pi, Sigma Lambda Alpha, Phi Kappa Phi. Office: Calif State U One University Cir Turlock CA 95382 Office Phone: 209-667-3201. Office Fax: 209-667-3206. Business E-Mail: president@csustan.edu.

SHISHOV, MICHAEL, rheumatologist; b. Leningrad, Russia, Aug. 24, 1973; s. Andrei and Irina Shishov; m. Srisunee Riantongchana, Oct. 7, 2007. BA, Brandeis U., Waltham, MA, 1995. Cert. physician Israel, 2000. Pediat. resident NYU. Med. Ctr., 2000—03; pediat. rheumatology fellow Cin. Children's Hosp. Med. Ctr., 2003—06; divsn. chief, pediat.

rheumatology Phoenix Children's Hosp., 2006—. Vol. Arthritis Found., Phoenix. Mem.: ACR (rsch. fellowship 2006). Office: Phoenix Children's Hosp 1919 E Thomas Rd Rheumatology Phoenix AZ 85016 Office Fax: 602-546-0911.

SHISLER, ARDEN L., insurance and transportation company executive; b. Massillon, Ohio, 1941; COO K&B Transport, Dalton, Ohio, 1986—92, pres., CEO, 1992—2003; chmn. Nationwide Mut. Ins. Co., Columbus, Ohio, 2003—08. Mem. Wayne County Farm Bureau; bd. mem. Ohio 4-H Found.; v.p. Ohio Farm Bur., 1974-84; pres. Ohio Agriculture Mktg. Assn., 1982-84.

SHIUE, YEU-SHENG PAUL, mechanical engineer, educator; married. PhD, U. Memphis, 1992. Prof. Christian Bros. U., Memphis, 1992—. Mem.: ASME. Office: Christian Bros Univ 650 East Pky South Memphis TN 38104

SHIUE, YUNN-SHIN JESSIE, materials scientist, researcher; BS, Nat. Taiwan U., Taipei, 1991; MS, Rutgers U., Piscataway, NJ, 1995, PhD, 1998. Postdoctoral fellow Rutgers U., 1998—2001; rsch. assoc. Academia Sinica, Nankang, Taipei, Taiwan, 2001—04, rsch. scientist, gen. mgr. nanosci. core facility ctr., 2005—. Contbr. articles to profl. jours. Mem.: Materials Rsch. Soc., Am. Phys. Soc. Achievements include research in subcritical crack growth in high strength silica is dominated by entropy effects; development of incorporation of silica nanoparticles in the secondary coating of optical fibers greatly enhances the resistance; focused-ion-beam sputtering microdeposition; nanofabrication of complex oxides. Office: Inst Physics Academia Sinica 128 Sec 2 Academia Rd Taipei Nankang 115 Taiwan Business E-Mail: yshiue@phys.sinica.edu.tw.

SHIVCHARRAN, JAIGOBIN, secondary school educator, consultant; b. Rose Hall, Guyana, Apr. 23, 1941; arrived in U.S., 1980; s. Moochoon and Yawa Shivcharran; m. Kawa Sakhichand-Beckley (div.); children: Sharmila, Rajesh, Ormila; m. Ruby Singh, July 11, 1983. BA in Humanities, Thomas Edison State Coll., 1989; MA in ESL, CUNY, NYC, 1993; BS in Psychology and Sociology, Regents Coll., 1996; PhD in Linguistics, Summit U., 1998. Cert. tchr. N.Y., 1997. Tchr. Dept. Edn., Guyana, 1961—80, 1995—; figure clk. Feature Enterprise, NYC, 1981—89; case mgr. Dept. Social Svcs., NYC, 1989—95. Instr. Coll. St. Rose, NYC, Albany, 2000—, Adelphi U., Garden City, NY, 2001—; staff developer United Fedn. TRS, NYC, 2000—; cons. NY State United Tchrs., NYC, 2000—; trainer of student peer mediator in conflict resolution NYC Dept. Edn. Author: Native Language Transfer in Second Language Learning, 1997, Anthology of Short Stories, 2005. Mem.: Am. Soc. Notaries, Nat. Coun. Social Studies, Nat. Coun. Tchrs. Eng., Acad. Polit. Sci., Nat. Assn. Scholars, NY State Assn. Scholars. Avocations: reading, walking, dance, writing. Home: 132 Freeman St #2D Brooklyn NY 11222-5853 Office: Automotive High Sch 50 Bedford Ave Brooklyn NY 11222 Personal E-mail: jayshivcharran@aol.com.

SHIVE, RICHARD BYRON, architect; b. Cleve., Jan. 16, 1933; s. Roy Allen and Mary Elizabeth (Thompson) S.; m. Patricia Butler, Aug. 28, 1954; children: Lisa Ann, Laura Mary, John Thompson, Nancy Butler. BS, Rensselaer Poly. Inst., Troy, NY, 1954; postgrad., NJ Inst. Tech., 1957, Rutgers U., 1960-63. Registered N.J., N.Y., Pa., Vt.; lic. profl. planner N.J. Field engr. Wigton-Abbott Corp., Plainfield, NJ, 1954-55, The Glenwal Co., Rochelle Park, NJ, 1955; asst. supt. Wigton-Abbott Corp., Plainfield, 1955-57; archtl. draftsman Raymond B. Flatt, Architect, Bloomfield, NJ, 1957-58, chief draftsman, 1958-60; project architect Scrimenti/Swackhamer/Perantoni Architects, Somerville, NJ, 1960-66, assoc., 1966-69; ptnr. Scrimenti, Shive, Spinelli, Perantoni Architects, Somerville, 1969-86, Shive/Spinelli/Perantoni & Assocs., Architects & Planners, Somerville, 1986-97; prin. emeritus SSP Archtl. Group, 1998—2002; pvt. practice Richard B. Shive, AIA, Architect, 2003—. Adv. com. First Fidelity Bank, Bound Brook, N.J., 1989-91; chmn. bd. Somerset Health Care Corp., 1987-91. Contbr. articles to profl. jours. Bd. dirs., exec. com. N.J. Hosp. Assn., Princeton, 1986-92, 93-95; chmn. bd. trustees Somerset Med. Ctr., Somerville, 1973-96; mem. Nat. Trust for Hist. Preservation; bd. dirs. Ctr. for Health Affairs, Inc., 1992-93; mem. Borough of Bound Brook Planning Bd., 2000—; chmn. Borough of Bound Brook Redevel. Adv. Com., 2000-08; mem. Somerset County Econ. Devel. Incentive Adv. Com., 1997—. Recipient award James F. Lincoln Arc Welding Found., 1973, Pres. award Rolling Hills coun. Girl Scouts U.S.A., 1988, Trustee of Yr. award NJ Hosp. Assn., 1993, Outstanding Citizen of Yr. award Somerset County C. of C., 1993, Spirit of Somerset award, 2000, Honor award Bound Brook-Middlesex Rotary Club and Bound Brook Area C. of C. Ball, 2007; Paul Harris fellow Bound Brook-Middlesex Rotary Club, 1993. Mem. AIA, ASTM, ASHRAE, ACI (chpt. bd. dirs. 1978-83), N.J. Soc. Architects, Illuminating Engring. Soc., Nat. Fire Protection Assn., Greater Somerset County C. of C. (v.p. 1985-86, 92-93, Outstanding Citizen of Yr. award 1993), Rotary (pres. 1969-70, Paul Harris fellow 1993), Wash. Campground Assn. (pres. 1975-76, v.p. 1977-78, sec. 1978-97), Chi Phi (sec. 1973). Republican. Congregationalist. Avocations: fishing, photography, skiing, canoeing, backpacking. Home and Office: 1786 Middlebrook Rd Bound Brook NJ 08805-1432 Office Phone: 732-469-2682. Personal E-mail: rshive@verizon.net.

SHIVELY, BONNIE LEE, pastor; b. Dover, Del., Feb. 13, 1961; d. Donald Hudson and Nancy (Durham) Shively. BS, Salisbury U., Md., 1984; MDiv, Wesley Theol. Sem., Washington, 1997. Ordained deacon Meth. Ch., 1995, ordained elder Meth. Ch., 2000. Pastor Church Creek United Meth. Ch., 1993—97, Bethel United Meth. Ch., Dagsboro, Del., 1997—2003, Hurlock-Wesley United Meth. Ch., Md., 2006—; pastor of caring ministries Kent Island United Meth. Ch., Chester, Md., 2003—06. Vol. Cmty. Food Pantry, Selbyville, Del., 1997—2003; mem. Friends of Prince George's Chapel, Dagsboro, 1998—2003, Dover Dist. Hispanic Ministries Com., 1999—2002, Peninsula Del. Conf. Disaster Relief Task Force, 2003—06; mem. adv. bd. Interfaith Vol. Caregivers, Frankford, Del., 1999—2002; bd. dirs. Queen Annes County Cmty. Partnership for Children, 2003—06; chaplain Church Creek Vol. Fire Co., 1993—97; bd. dirs. Del. Ecumenical Coun., Wilmington, 2000—03. Mem.: Commn. on Archives and History (sec. 1998—2004), Dagsboro Century Club. Avocations: genealogy, local history, needlecrafts. Office: Hurlock-Wesley United Meth Church PO Box 298 Hurlock MD 21643 Home Phone: 410-943-4730; Office Phone: 410-943-3222. Personal E-mail: blshively@intercom.net, revshive@aol.com.

SHIVELY, FREDRICK HAROLD, religious studies educator; b. Springfield, Ohio, Aug. 22, 1939; s. Thelma Louise Shively; m. Kay Murphy Shively, Sept. 9, 1961; children: Kevin Fredrick, Mark Jonathan. B.S., MDiv, Fuller Theol. Sem., Pasadena, Calif., 1982, PhD in Ministry, 1982. Registered ordained minister Southern Calif. Ch. God, 1965. Min. music South Bay Ch. God, Torrance, Calif., 1962—65; pastor Inter-Cmty. Ch. God, Covina, Calif., 1967—74; prof. religion Anderson U., Ind., 1974—, dir. ministry edn., 1982—, leader internat. mission experiences TRI-S; pastor Hoodview Ch. God, Woodburn, Oreg., 1978—82; faculty Warner Pacific Coll., Portland, Oreg., 1979—82; pastor Maple Grove Ch. God, Anderson, Ind., 1992—94. Author: (religious books) The Widening Witness; Jesus: Savior and Lord. Mem. and chair Outreach Com., Pk. Pl. Ch. God, Anderson, Ind., 1982; mem. bd. Christian Ctr. and Rescue Ministries, Anderson, 1995—98, Urban League Madison County, Anderson, 1988—96. Mem.: Soc. Bibl. Lit., Am. Acad. Religion. Democrat. Mem. Church Of God. Avocations: travel, music, photography, reading. Home: 809 Westgate Dr Anderson IN 46012 Office: Anderson Univ 1100 East Fifth St Anderson IN 46011 Business E-Mail: fhshively@anderson.edu.

SHIVELY, JOHN TERRY, cruise line executive; b. Middletown, NY, July 1, 1943; s. Marvin Rathfelder and Esther (Manning) Westervelt; adopted child, Harold Eugene Shively. BA, U. N.C., 1965. Vol. worker VISTA, Bethel and Fairbanks, Alaska, 1965-68; health planner Greater Anchorage Area Cmty. Action Agy., 1968-69; health cons. Alaska Fed. Natives, Anchorage, 1969; dep. dir. Rural Alaska Cmty. Action Program, Anchorage, 1971-72; exec. v.p. Alaska Fedn. Natives, Anchorage, 1972-75; v.p. ops. NANA Regional Corp., Kotzebue, Alaska, 1975-77, NANA Devel. Corp., Anchorage, 1977-82; sr. v.p. NANA Regional Corp. Inc., 1986-92; pres. NANA Devel. Corp., 1992-94; commr. DNR, 1995-2000; chmn., CEO United Bar Corp., United Bank Alaska, 1987-88; sr. ptnr. Jade North, 2000—02; v.p. govt. and cmty. rels. Holland Am., 2002—08; CEO Pebble Partnership, 2008—. Dir. Unicorp. Inc., United Bank of Alaska, Resource Devel. Coun., exec. com., 2001—, pres, 2003—; dir. Alaska State C. of C., exec. com., 2003—. Mem. Greater Anchorage Area Comprehensive Health Plan Coun., 1969-75, chmn., 1969-75; founding mem. bd. dirs. Alaska Pub. Interest Rsch. Group, 1974-75, 86-90, chmn. 1987-90; mem. Gov.'s Rural Affairs Coun., 1971-76, Gov.'s Manpower Commn., 1971, Greater Anchorage Health Bd., 1969-75, Alaska Pipeline Edn. Com., 1973-74; bd. regents U. Alaska, 1979-83; bd. trustees Alaska Permanent Fund Bd., 1999-2000. Democrat. Episcopalian. Home and Office: 2301 Loren Cir Anchorage AK 99516 Personal E-mail: jtshively@att.net.

SHIVELY, WILLIAM PHILLIPS, political scientist, educator; b. Altoona, Pa., Mar. 31, 1942; s. Arthur and Ruth Shively; m. Barbara Louise Shank, Aug. 29, 1964; children: Helen, David. BA, Franklin and Marshall Coll., 1963; PhD, U. NC, 1968. Mem. faculty U. Oreg., Eugene, 1967-68, Yale U., 1968-71; mem. faculty U. Minn., Mpls., 1971—, prof. polit. sci., 1979—, provost arts, scis. & engring., 1995-97. Author: Craft of Political Research, 1974, 7th edit., 2008, Research Process in Political Science, 1985, Power and Choice, 1986, rev. edit., 1989, 11th edit., 2008, Comparative Governance, 1995, (with Christopher Achen) Cross-Level Inference, 1995; editor Am. Jour. Polit. Sci., 1977-79; contbr. articles on elections and voting to profl. jours. Home: 1572 Northrop St Saint Paul MN 55108-1322 Office: U Minn Dept Polit Sci 1414 Social Scis Tower Minneapolis MN 55455 Business E-Mail: shively@umn.edu.

SHIVERY, CHARLES W., utilities executive; BA, BS, Johns Hopkins U.; MBA, U. Balt. With Balt. Gas & Electric Co., 1972—80, asst. treas., 1980—88, treas., asst. sec., 1988—89, v.p. corp. fin., 1989—93, v.p., CFO, 1993—97; chmn., pres., CEO Constellation Power Source, Inc., 1997—2002; CEO, pres. Constellation Enterprises, Inc., 1998—2002; pres., CEO Constellation Power Source Holdings, Inc., 2000—02; co-pres. Constellation Energy Group, Inc., 2000—02, 2000—02; pres., CEO NU Enterprises, Inc., 2002—04; interim pres. N.E. Utilities, Berlin, Conn., 2004, chmn., pres., CEO, 2004—. Bd. dirs. Elec. Power Rsch. Inst., Energy Ins. Mut., MetroHartford Alliance, The Bushnell, Webster Fin. Corp., 2009—. Mem.: Edison Elec. Inst. (bd. dirs.), Conn. Children's Med. Ctr. (bd. dirs.), Conn. Sci. Ctr. (bd. dirs.), Conn. Bus. and Industry Assn. (bd. dirs.), Assn. of Edison Illuminating Cos. (bd. dirs.). Office: Webster Financial Corp Webster Plz Waterbury CT 06702 Office Phone: 203-465-4364. Office Fax: 203-465-4364.*

SHIVES, PAULA J., lawyer, food service executive; b. Monongahela, Pa., Sept. 28, 1950; m. William Sutton. BA, Western Ky. U., Bowling Green, 1973; JD, U. Ky., Lexington, 1979. Bar: Ky. 1979. Assoc. gen. counsel Long John Silver Restaurants, Inc., Lexington, Ky., 1985—95, sr. v.p., gen. counsel, sec., 1995—99, Darden Restaurants, Inc., Orlando, Fla., 1999—. Mem.: ABA, Ky. Bar Assn., Fayette County Bar Assn. Office: 5900 Lake Ellenor Dr Orlando FL 32809 Home: 2011 Via Tuscany Winter Park FL 32789-1557 Office Phone: 407-245-6566. Business E-Mail: pshives@darden.com.

SHIVKUMAR, KALYANAM, cardiologist, consultant; b. Madras, Tamilnadu, India, July 8, 1968; came to U.S., 1991; s. Saraswathi (Venkataraman) K. MD, U. Madras, 1991. Bd. cert. diplomate Am. Bd. of Internal Medicine, 1994. Internal medicine intern/resident Henry Ford Hosp., Detroit, 1991-94, chief med. resident, 1994-95; fellow cardiovasc. medicine UCLA Med. Ctr., 1995—; clin. instr. UCLA Sch. of Medicine. Mem. cardiopulmonary resuscitation com. Henry Ford Hosp., 1994-95, DNR com., 1994-95, resident rsch. com., 1994-95, residency selection com., 1994-95, quality improvement team, 1994-95, acute care com. UCLA Med. Ctr., 1996-97; CCU adv. com.UCLA Med. Ctr., 1995—; GSA rep. libr. com. U. Calif. L.A., 1995-96. Lectr. in field; contbr. articles to profl. jours., chpts. to books. Mem. AMA, ACP (com. mem. 1995, Best Rsch. Presentation award 1994, 95), Am. Heart Assn. (Melvin Marcus Young Investigator Award finalist 1997), Am. Coll. Chest Physicians, Am. Med. Physicians Assn., Am. Coll. Cardiology, Osler Club. Avocations: travel, reading. Office: UCLA Sch of Medicine 47-123 10833 Le Conte Los Angeles CA 90024

SHKLAR, GERALD, pathologist, periodontist, educator; b. Montreal, Que., Can., Dec. 2, 1924; came to U.S., 1950, naturalized, 1955; s. Louis and Ann (Schleifstein) S.; m. Judith Nisse, June 16, 1948 (dec. Sept. 18, 1992); children: David, Michael, Ruth; m. Se-Kyung Oh, July 13, 1997. BS, McGill U., 1947, DDS, 1949; MS, Tufts U., 1952; MA (hon.), Harvard U., 1971; D (hon.), U. Athens. Diplomate Am. Bd. Oral Pathology, Am. Bd. Periodontology. Asst. prof. oral pathology Sch. Dental Medicine Tufts U., Boston, 1953—59, assoc. prof. Sch. Dental Medicine, 1960—61, prof. oral pathology, rsch. prof. peridontology Sch. Dental Medicine, 1961—71, lectr. oral pathology Sch. Dental Medicine, 1971—. Head dept. oral medicine and oral pathology Sch. Dental Medicine Harvard U., Boston, 1971-93, Charles A. Brackett prof. oral pathology, 1971-2000, Charles A. Brackett prof. oral pathology emeritus, 2000—; sr. clin. investigator Forsyth Inst., Boston, 1994—2000; cons. oral pathology Children's Hosp. Med. Ctr., Brigham and Women's Hosp., Mass. Gen. Hosp. Author: Oral Cancer, 1984; co-author (with Edmund Cataldo and Henry Goldman): Oral Pathology: An Atlas of Microscopic Pathology, 1975; co-author: (with Philip L. McCarthy) The Oral Manifestations of Systemic Disease, 1976, Diseases of the Oral Mucosa, 2d edit., 1982; co-author: (with David Chernin) Libellus De Dentibus, 1563, of Bartholomaei Eustachii, 1999, A Sourcebook of Dental Medicine, 2002; co-author: (with Fermin Carranza) History of Periodontology, 2003; contbr. over 350 articles to profl. jours., chapters to books. Fellow AAAS, Am. Acad. Dental Sci., Am. Acad. Oral Medicine, Am. Acad. Oral Pathology, Am. Coll. Dentists, Internat. Coll. Dentists; mem. ADA, Internat. Assn. Dental Rsch., Am. Acad. Periodontology, Am. Cancer Soc., Am. Assn. Cancer Rsch., Am. Assn. Cancer Edn., Am. Acad. History Dentistry, History of Sci. Soc., Sigma Xi, Omicron Kappa Upsilon. Avocations: harpsichord, flute. Home: 154 Evelyn Rd Waban MA 02468-1042 Home Phone: 617-332-6452.

SHLAES, JOHN B., foundation administrator; b. LA, Mar. 17, 1942; s. Burton L. and Jacquelyn (Metzger) Kramer; m. Kay Irene Edwards, Feb. 27, 1966; children: Darren, Katie. BS in Bus., U. So. Calif., 1963; MA in Internat. Transactions, George Mason U., 1993; cert. in internat. exec. mgmt., Georgetown U., 1995; adv. studies global trade strategies, Oxford U., 1996. Dir. spl. projects Chgo. Tribune, 1964-66; exec. dir. comms. Bellevue (Wash.) Pub. Schs., 1966-67; advt. mgr. Nixon for Pres. campaign, NYC, 1967-69; cons. to dir. USIA, Washington, 1969; spl. asst. to dir. U.S. Peace Corps, Washington, 1970-72; dir. comms. Pres. Office of Emergency Preparedness, Washington, 1972; staff of counselor, staff asst. to pres., then dir. confs. White House, Washington, 1972-77; pres. John B. Shlaes Assocs., Washington, 1977-79; dir. govt. affairs Edison Electric Inst., Washington, 1979-92; exec. dir. Global Climate Coalition, Washington, 1991-97; cons. EXEC COACN, 1997—2009. Advisor US Del. UN Interwomen's Yr. Conf., 1975; chmn., pres. Nat. Energy Resource Orgn., Washington, 1987-89. Mem. exec. com. Def. Adv. Com. Women in the Svcs., 1988-91; adv. US DEZ UN Internat. Womens Yr. Conf., 1975, bd. dirs. Wash. Campus, 1980—, Internat. Amb. Bd., Variety Clubs Internat., N.Y.C., 1988-92. Sgt. USAR, 1963-69. Recipient Disting. Svc. award, Pres. Office Emergency Preparedness, Internat. Pres. award. Avocations: skiing, scuba. Home: 5629 Lambeth Rd Bethesda MD 20814-1140 Office Phone: 301-656-6002. Personal E-mail: jbsdcmd@gmail.com.

SHLAPENTOKH, DMITRY VLADIMIR, history educator; b. Kiev, USSR, May 31, 1950; came to U.S., 1979; s. Vladimir Emanuilovich and Liubov Raisovna S.; m. Angela Burlako; m. Natalia Mogileva; children: Leon, Anna-Vera. MA, U. Moscow, 1973, Mich. State U., 1980; PhD, U. Chgo., 1988. Asst. prof. SUNY, Oswego, N.Y., 1987-88; fellow Russian Rsch. Ctr., Harvard U., 1990-91, Hoover Instn., Stanford, Calif., summer 1992; assoc. prof. Ind. U., South Bend, 1991—. Vis. scholar Columbia U., N.Y.C., summer 1997. Author: The French Revolution in Russian Intellectual Life, 1996, The French Revolution and the Anti-Democratic Tradition in Russia, 1997, The Counterrevolution in Revolution, 1999; contbr. numerous articles to profl. jours. Office: Ind U PO Box 7111 South Bend IN 46634-7111

SHLAUDEMAN, HARRY WALTER, retired diplomat; b. LA, May 17, 1926; s. Karl Whitman and Florence (Pixley) S.; m. Carol Jean Dickey, Aug. 7, 1948; children: Karl Frederick, Katherine Estelle, Harry Richard. BA, Stanford U., 1952. Joined U.S. Fgn. Svc., 1955; vice consul Barranquilla, Colombia, 1955-56; polit. officer Bogotá, Colombia, 1956-58; assigned lang. tng. Washington, 1958-59; consul Sofia, Bulgaria, 1960-62; chief polit. sect. Santo Domingo, Dominican Republic, 1962-64; officer charge Dominican Affairs State Dept., 1964-66; asst. dir. Office Caribbean Affairs, 1965-66; sr. seminar fgn. policy State Dept., 1966-67, spl. asst. to sec. state, 1967-69; dep. chief of mission Santiago, Chile, 1969-73; dep. asst. sec. state for Inter-Am. affairs Washington, 1973-75; amb. to Venezuela, 1975-76; asst. sec. state for Inter-Am. affairs, 1976-77; amb. to Peru, 1977-80; amb. to Argentina, 1980-83; exec. dir. Nat. Bipartisan Commn. on Central Am., 1983-84; spl. amb. to Cen. Am., 1984-86; amb. to Brazil Brasilia, 1986-89; amb. to Nicaragua, 1990-92; ret., 1992. Served with USMCR, 1944-46. Recipient Disting. Honor award Dept. State, 1966, Pres. Disting. Svc. award, 1988, Brazil's Order of Cruzeiro Benementium, 1989, Pres. Medal Freedom, 1992. Mem. Am. Acad. Diplomacy, San Luis Obispo Golf and Country Club, Phi Gamma Delta. Home: 7006 Pebble Beach Way San Luis Obispo CA 93401-8916 Office Phone: 805-544-7539. Personal E-mail: harrywal@aol.com.

SHLESINGER, MICHAEL F, physicist, educator; b. New York, Aug. 8, 1948; s. David and Elizabeth Shlesinger; m. Nava Pechersky, Dec. 7, 1977; children: Adi, Ben, Dan. BS, SUNY, Stony Brook, NY, 1970; PhD, U. Rochester, NY, 1975. Chief scientist nonlinear sci. Office Naval Rsch., Arlington, Va., 1983—; Kinnear prof. physics US Naval Acad., Annapolis, Md., 2008—. Founding co-editor FRACTALS World Sci. Pub., Singapore, 1993—; divisional assoc. editor Phys. Rev. Letters, Ridge, NY, 2005—. Recipient Superior Civilian Svc. award, Dept. Navy, 1991, Medal Valor, City Rockville, 1991, Michelson Lecture award, US Naval Acad., 1992, Presdl. Rank award, U.S. Sr. Exec. Svc., 2004, Disting. Postdoc Alumni award, U. Md. Coll. Pk., 2004, Saalfeld Outstanding Lifetime Achievement Sci., Office Naval Rsch., 2006; named Regents Lectr., U. Calif. San Diego, 1994. Fellow: Am. Phys. Soc. Jewish. Achievements include patents for algorithmic design of peptides for receptor binding. Home: 412 Green Pasture Dr Rockville MD 20852 Office: Office Naval Rsch Code 30 875 N Randolph St Arlington VA Business E-Mail: mike.shlesinger@navy.mil.

SHLIMOVICH, PAVEL, internist; b. St. Petersburg, Russia, June 9, 1941; came to U.S., 1988; s. Boris and Basia Shlimovich; m. Masha Shlimovich, Aug. 1, 1964 (div. Jan. 1990); children: Katia, Shira, Nira; m. Tamara Shlimovich, Feb. 15, 1991; 1 child, Miriam. MD, Leningrad Med. Sch., St. Petersburg, 1965; PhD, Inst. Physiology, St. Petersburg, 1969. Diplomate Am. Bd. Internal Medicine with subspecialties in endocrinology and geriatrics. Intern Montefiore Med. Ctr., NYC, 1989-90, resident, 1990-92, fellow, 1992-94; asst. prof. medicine 2d Leningrad Med. Sch., 1969-79; attending physician City Hosp. # 4, 1980-88; cons. St. U. Clinic, St. Petersburg; attending physician Montefiore Med. Ctr., NYC, 1994—, Maimonides Med. Ctr., NYC, 1998—; asst. prof. Albert Einstein Coll. Medicine, Bronx, 1995—. Cons. Shorefront Jewish Geriat. Ctr., Bklyn., 1998—. Contbr. more than 65 articles to profl. jours. Fellow ACP; mem. Am. Geriat. Soc., Am. Diabetes Assn., Endocrine Soc. Avocations: reading, tennis. Personal E-mail: p&s1192000@yahoo.com.

SHLOFMITZ, RICHARD ALAN, cardiologist; b. NYC, Jan. 22, 1955; MD, NYU Sch. Medicine, 1980. Cert. Internal Medicine, 1984, Cardiovascular Disease, 1987, Interventional Cardiology. Intern, medicine North Shore U. Hosp., Manhasset, NY, 1980—81, resident, cardiology, 1981—84; fellow Columbia Presbyn. Med. Ctr., NYC, 1984—87; with St. Francis Hosp., Roslyn, NY, 1987—, dir., cardiac catheterization lab and interventional cardiology, attending physician. Prin. investigator in numerous percutaneous interventional trials St. Francis Hosp., Roslyn, NY. Office: 100 Port Washington Blvd Roslyn NY 11576 Office Phone: 516-390-9640. Office Fax: 516-390-9650.

SHMAILO, LARISSA, poet, director; b. Bklyn., May 31, 1956; BA, Barnard Coll., NYC, 1985. Dir. TWIN Poetry, London. Pub. coord. Fulcrum Poetry, Cambridge, Mass. Poet (poetry collection) No-Net World, Exorcism. Home: 253 W 72nd St #715 New York NY 10023 Personal E-mail: slidingsca@aol.com.

SHMAVONIAN, GERALD S., political organization administrator; b. LA, June 26, 1945; s. Sergius Neshan and Berje-Lucia (der Hareutunyan) Shmavonian. Student, U. Calif., Berkeley, 1964-70. Leader archaeol. excavation team, Guatemala, Turkey, 1970-75; pub. City Mags., 1975-80; spl. advisor Bicentennial Commission, Washington, DC, 1975; chmn. Am. Nationalities Coun., Stanford U., 1983-86; pres. Am. Talent, 1986—2000; ptnr. Assembly Plant Ptnrs., 2001—. Founder Tommorw Party, 2000—; pres. emeritus C.A.U.S.E., 2007—. Recipient Intercollegiate Boxing Championship, 1965. Fellow Am. Documentary Film

Acad.; mem. Calif. Scholarship Fedn. (life, pres. 1963), Nat. Forensic League (pres. 1963, degree of honor). Avocation: art. Home: 6219 N Prospect Ave Fresno CA 93711-1658

SHNAYERSON, ROBERT BEAHAN, editor, consultant; b. NYC, Dec. 8, 1925; s. Charles and Madalene (Griffin) Beahan; m. Lydia Conde Todd, Dec. 23, 1950 (dec. Sept. 1973); children: Michael, Kate; m. Laurie Platt Winfrey, June 9, 1980; children: Maggie, Bonnie. AB, Dartmouth, 1950. Reporter N.Y. Daily News, 1946; reporter Life mag., NYC, 1950-54; corr. Time-Life News Svc., 1954-56; contbg. editor Time mag., 1957-59, edn. editor, 1959-64, law editor, 1964-67, sr. editor, 1967-71; editor-in-chief Harper's Mag., NYC, 1971-76; editor, pub. Quest mag., NYC, 1976-81, Technology mag., NYC, 1981-82; editorial dir. Sci. Digest mag., 1986-87. Editl. cons. Lear's mag., 1987-90; cons. in mag. field; sr. advisor Travel Holiday mag., 1989-95. Author: Illustrated History of the Supreme Court, 1986; author, editor: Wordworks, 1995—; contbr. articles to various mags. With USNR, 1943-46. Home: 118 Riverside Dr New York NY 10024-3708 Office Phone: 212-787-4590. E-mail: shnay@aol.com.

SHNEIDERMAN, BEN ABRAHAM, computer science educator, writer; b. NYC, Aug. 21, 1947; s. Samuel Leib and Eileen (Szymin) S.; m. Nancy Helman, Mar. 25, 1973 (div. Dec. 1994); children: Sara Beth, Anna Rose; m. Jennifer Preece, June 17, 2001. BS, CCNY, 1968; MS, SUNY, Stony Brook, 1972, PhD, 1973; DSc (hon.), U. Guelph, Ont., Can., 1995. Asst. prof. computer sci. Ind. U., Bloomington, 1973-76; asst. prof. U. Md., College Park, 1976-82, assoc. prof., 1982-89, prof., 1989—. Cons. Apple Computers, IBM, GE, Microsoft, Intel. Author: Software Psychology, 1980, Designing the User Interface, 1987, 2d edit., 1992, 3rd edit., 1998, 4th edit., 2004, 5th edit, 2009, Leonardo's Laptop, 2002, Hypertext Hands-On, 1989; co-author: Readings in Information Visualization, 1999, The Craft of Information Visualization, 2003; editor: Sparks of Innovation, 1992. Fellow ACM, AAAS. Avocation: skiing. Office: Univ Md Dept Computer Sci College Park MD 20742-0001 Business E-Mail: ben@cs.umd.edu.

SHNEOUR, ELIE ALEXIS, biophysicist, researcher, historian; b. Neuilly-sur-Seine, France, Dec. 11, 1925; came to U.S., 1941, naturalized, 1944; s. Zalman and Salomea (Landau) S.; children, Mark Zalman, Alan Brewster. BA, Columbia U., 1947; DSc (hon.), Bard Coll., 1969; MA, U. Calif., Berkeley, 1955; PhD, UCLA, 1958. Tchr. and rsch. fellow U. Calif., Berkeley, 1953-55, Am. Heart Assn. rsch. fellow, 1958-62, tchg. and rsch. fellow LA, 1958; rsch. fellow Nat. Cancer Inst., 1956-57; Am. Heart Assn. rsch. fellow NYU, 1958-59; rsch. assoc. genetics Stanford U., 1962-65; assoc. prof. biology and neuroscis. U. Utah, 1965-69; rsch. neurochemist City of Hope Nat. Med. Ctr., Duarte, Calif., 1969-71. Dir. rsch. Calbiochem., 1971-75; pres. Biosystems Insts., Inc., 1975—; dir. Biosystems Rsch. Inst., 1979; steering com. Nat. Acad. Sci. Study Group on Biology and the Exploration of Mars, 1964; chmn. Western Regional coun. Rsch. in Basic Bioscis. for Manned Orbiting Missions, Am. Inst. Biol. Scis., NASA, 1966-69; fellow Com. Skeptical Inquiry, 1996—; mem. editl. bd. Skeptic Mag., 1992-2008. Author: Extraterrestrial Life, 1965, (with Eric A. Ottesen) National Academy of Sciences, National Rsch. Coun., 1966, (with S. Moffat) Life Beyond the Earth, 1966, The Malnourished Mind, 1974; contbr. articles to profl. jours. Chmn. citizens adv. coun. San Diego Pub. Schs., 1971-72; adv. coun. Cousteau Soc., 1977-98; bd. dir. Lunar Power System Coalition, 1993-2002; internat. v.p. Transinnova S.A. France, 1990—; chmn. sci. adv. bd. County of San Diego, 1995-2002, 2006-08. With U.S. Army, 1944-45. Recipient William Lockwood prize, Bard Coll. of Columbia U., 1947. Mem. IEEE, AAAS (chmn. So. Calif. Skeptics soc. Pacific divsn. 1988-90), Am. Chem. Soc., N.Y. Acad. Scis., Am. Inst. Biol. Scis., Am. Soc. for Biochemistry and Molecular Biology (chmn. sci. advisors program 1973-75, mem. com. on pub. policy 1974-76, congl. liaison 1992—), Am. Soc. Neurochemistry (mem. coun. 1971-73), Soc. Neurosci., Internat. Soc. Neurochemistry, U.S. C. of C. (bd. dirs. 1993-98), La Jolla Chamber Music Soc. (bd. dirs. 1994-97), Internat. Coun. for Global Health Progress (N.Am. adv. bd. 1996—), Sigma Xi, Phi Sigma. Office: Biosystems Rsch Inst 700 Front St m/s CDM 608 San Diego CA 92101-6085

SHNIDER, BRUCE JAY, lawyer; b. Lansing, Mich., Oct. 16, 1950; s. Harold A. and Raynor (Seidner) Shnider; m. Patricia Lynn Strandness, Dec. 28, 1973; 1 child, Ruth Strandness. AB magna cum laude, Dartmouth Coll., 1972; MPP, JD magna cum laude, Harvard U., 1977. Bar: Minn. 1977, US Dist. Ct. Minn. 1977, US Tax Ct. 1978, US Ct. Appeals (8th cir.) 1980, US Supreme Ct. 1981. Asst. to dir. Mich. Dept. Commerce, Lansing, 1972-73; law clk. United Mineworkers Am. Health/Retirement Funds, 1975; summer assoc. Robins, Davis & Lyon, Mpls., 1976; assoc. Dorsey & Whitney, Mpls., 1977-82, ptnr., 1983—2006, chmn. diversity com., 1990-93, chmn. tax practice group, 1994-98, of counsel, 2007—. Vis. disting. prof. Law. Sch., U. Minn., 2006—. Bd. dirs. Minn. Justice Found., Mpls., 1989—91; v.p. Emergency Food Shelf Network, 2003—05, pres., 2005—07. Mem.: ABA, Hennepin County Bar Assn., Minn. State Bar Assn. Home: 1908 James Ave S Minneapolis MN 55403-2831 Office: Dorsey & Whitney 50 S 6th St Ste 1500 Minneapolis MN 55402-1498 Office Phone: 612-340-2862. Business E-Mail: shnider.bruce@dorsey.com.

SHOAF, FRANK JOSEPH, military officer; b. Biddeford, Maine, Oct. 16, 1975; s. Bernard Joseph and Marilyn Delores Shoaf; m. Tammy Marie Shoaf, June 26, 1999; 1 child, Kylee Marie. BA polit. sci. and pub. admin., Calif. U. Pa., Calif. PA., 1998. Student asst. Mandarino Libr., Calif., Pa., 1994—98; customer svc. Grindstone Foodland, Grindstone, Pa., 1995—97; adminstr. asst. State Farm Ins., Summerville, SC, 1999; customer svc. Lowe's Home Improvement, Summerville, SC, 1999; crew chief USAF, Charleston, SC, 2000—02, dep. missile combat crew comdr. Gt. Falls, Mont., 2003—. Mem. Charleston Airman's Coun., Charleston, SC, 2000—01, Co. Grade Officer's Coun., Gt, Falls, Mont., 2003. 2d. Lt. USAF, 2002—, Gt. Falls, Mont. Recipient Airman of the Quarter, USAF, 2000, Top Performer, 2000, Order of Omega, Order of Omega Leadership Honor Soc., 1997. Mem.: Air Force Assn. (assoc.), Acad. of Polit. Sci. Republican. Roman Catholic. Avocations: reading, volunteering, outdoor activities, sports, family. Home: 3 Woodland Terr Duncansville PA 16635 Home Phone: 814-695-2091. Personal E-mail: fshoaf@atlanticbb.net.

SHOCHAT, STEPHEN JAY, pediatrician, surgeon; b. Balt., Dec. 17, 1938; s. Albert J. and Rose (Blechman) S.; m. Sheila Floam, July 1960 (div. July 1979); children: Francine Lynne, Alisa Joy; m. Carla Ann Centi, Jan. 26, 1980; children: David Robert, Sarah Elizabeth. BS, Randolph Mason Coll., 1959; MD, Med. Coll. Va., 1963. Surg. resident Washington U. Med. Ctr., St. Louis, 1963-68; pediatric surg. resident Boston Children's Hosp., 1968-70; thoracic surg. resident Queen Elizabeth Hosp., Birmingham, Eng., 1970, George Washington Hosp., Washington, 1972; chief pediatric surgery Hershey (Pa.) Med. Ctr., 1973-77, Stanford (Calif.) Med. Ctr., 1977-94; sr. surgeon Children's Hosp. Phila., 1994-96; surgeon-in-chief, chmn. dept. surgery St. Jude Children Rsch. Hosp., Memphis, 1996—2009, mem. dept. surgery, 2009—; prof. pediats. and surgery U. Tenn., Memphis, 1996—. Lt. col. USAF, 1970-72. Office: St Jude Children Rsch Hosp Dept Surgery Memphis TN 38105 Office Phone: 901-595-2911. Business E-Mail: stephen.shochat@stjude.org.

SHOCK, EVERET, biochemist, educator; s. Cleon Virgil and Myrtle Leon Shock; m. Allison Schoenfeld, Oct. 25, 1984. PhD, U. Calif., Berkeley, 1987. Prof. Wash. U., St. Louis, 1987—2002, Ariz. State U., Tempe, 2002—, dir., W.M. Keck Found. Lab. Environ. Bio-Geochemistry, 2002—. Contbr. articles to sci. rsch. jours. Numerous Rsch. grants, NSF, 1988—, Dept. Energy, 1988—2005, NASA, 1990—. Fellow: Am. Geophys. Union. Achievements include discovery of metastable equilibrium among organic compounds in high temperature aqueous solutions. Office: Ariz State Univ Tempe AZ 85287 Office Fax: 480-966-8102. Business E-Mail: eshock@asu.edu.

SHOCKEY, JEREMY CHARLES, professional football player; b. Ada, Okla., Aug. 18, 1980; s. Lucinda. Student, Northeast Okla. A&M Jr. Coll., 1999, U. Miami, 2000—02. Tight end NY Giants, 2002—08, New Orleans Saints, 2008—. Vol. United Way Found. Named NFL Rookie of the Yr., 2002; named to Nat. Football Conf. Pro-Bowl Team, 2002—03, 2005. Achievements include being a member of NCAA Champion Miami Hurricanes, 2001; Super Bowl XLII Champion NY Giants, 2008. Office: New Orleans Saints 5800 Airline Dr Metairie LA 70003*

SHOCKLEY, ANN ALLEN, librarian, writer; b. Louisville, June 21, 1927; d. Henry and Bessie (Lucas) Allen; children: W. Leslie Shockley Jr., Tamara Ann Shockley. BA, Fisk U., 1948; MSL.S., Case Western Reserve U., 1959. Asst. librarian Del. State Coll., Dover, 1959-60; asst. librarian U. Md. Eastern Shore, Princess Anne, 1960-66, assoc. librarian, 1966-69, Fisk U., Nashville, 1969-98. Author: (novels) Loving Her, 1974, Say Jesus and Come to Me, 1982, Celebrating Hotchclaw, 2005,(short stories) The Black & White of It, 1980, (with E. J. Josey) Handbook of Black Librarianship, 1977, (with Sue P. Chandler) Living Black American Authors, 1973; editor: (anthology) Afro-American Women Writers 1746-1933, 1988 (Susan Koppelman Award 1989). Recipient Hatshepsut Award for Lit., N.Y., 1981, Martin Luther King Jr. Black Author award, Nashville, 1982; A Crossroad to Freedom award in Recognition of Outstanding and Profl. Librarianship, Western Br. Louisville KY Libr., 2005, Alice B. Readers Appreciation award, 2006. Mem. Authors Guild, ALA (Black Caucus, Black Caucus award for editing caucus newsletter 1975, Black Caucus award for Extraordinary Achievement in Profl. Activities, 1992). Home: 5975 Post Rd Nashville TN 37205-3232

SHOCKLEY, CAROL FRANCES, psychologist, psychotherapist; b. Atlanta, Nov. 24, 1948; d. Robert Thomas and Frances Lavada (Scrivner) Shockley. BA, Ga. State U., Atlanta, 1974, MEd, 1976; PhD, U. Ga., Athens, 1990. Cert. in gerontology, diplomate Am. Bd. Forensic Examiners. Counselor Rape Crisis Ctr., Atlanta, 1979-80; emergency mental health clinician Gwinnett Med. Ctr., Lawrenceville, Ga., 1980-86; psychotherapist Fla. Mental Health Inst., Tampa, 1987-89, Tampa Bay Acad., Riverview, Fla., 1990-91; sr. psychologist State of Fla. Dept. of Corrections, Bushnell, 1991-92; pvt. practice psychologist Brunswick, Ga., 1992—2000, Griffin, Ga., 2002—. Mem. adv. bd. Mental Health/Mental Retardation, 1992—94. Author (with others): (book) Relapse Prevention with Sex Offenders, 1989. Vol. Ga. Mental Health Inst., Atlanta, 1972; leader Alzheimer's Disease Support Group, Athens, Ga., 1984; vol. therapist Reminiscence Group Elderly, Athens, 1984—85. Recipient Meritorious Svc. award, Beta Gamma Sigma, 1975. Mem.: APA, Ga. Psychol. Assn., Psi Chi, Sigma Phi Omega. Avocations: astronomy, archaeology, music, travel. Office: 315 W Solomon St Ste 210 Griffin GA 30223

SHOCKLEY, EDWARD JULIAN, retired air transportation executive; b. Augusta, Ga., Oct. 31, 1924; s. Julian P. and Margaret (Epps) S.; m. Dorothy Elizabeth Holley, Nov. 24, 1945; children: Edward J., Steven Holley. B.Aero. Engring., Ga. Inst. Tech., 1950; postgrad. (Sloan fellow), Stanford U. Grad. Sch. Bus., 1962-63. Flight test engr. Douglas Aircraft Co., 1950-53; with Lockheed-Ga. Co., 1953-80, dir. quality and safety, 1965-74, dir. mktg., 1974-78, v.p., 1978-80; pres. Lockheed Aircraft Service Co. div. Lockheed Corp., Burbank, Calif., 1980-86, sr. advisor to pres., 1986-87, ret., 1987; pres. Millimeter Wave Tech., Inc., Marietta, Ga., 1988-90, vice chmn. bd. dirs., 1991-92; ret., 1992. Dir. Aerosurge Mgmt. Cons., 1991-92; pres. Lockheed-Ga. Fed. Credit Union, 1971-74 Mem. bus. adv. coun. Ga. So. U.; mem. adv. coun. Sch. Bus. and Econs., Coll. of Charleston. Served with USN, 1941-46. Mem. Cherokee Town and Country Club. Republican. Methodist. Personal E-mail: eshock@charter.net.

SHOCKLEY-ZALABAK, PAMELA SUE, academic administrator; b. May 25, 1944; d. James William and Leatha Pearl (Cartwright) Shockley; m. Charles Zalabak, Dec. 30, 1975. BA in Comm., Okla. State U., 1965, MA in Comm., 1972; PhD in Orgnl. Comm., U. Colo., 1980. Instr. comm. Coll. Letters, Arts and Scis. U. Colo., 1976, from asst. to full prof., 1992, prof. comm. Colorado Springs, 1992—, dir., net and media ctr., 1992, spl. asst. to chancellor, 1994, vice chancellor for student success Colorado Springs, 1998—2001, interim chancellor, 2001—02, chancellor, 2002—. Cons. in field. Author six books; prodr.: (six video documentaries); contbr. articles to profl. jours. Recipient Disting. Svc. award, Colo. Speech Comm. Assn., Telly award; Lew Wentz Tri Delt scholar, 1961—65. Mem.: Internat. Comm. Assn., Speech Comm. Assn., Phi Kappa Phi. Democrat. Avocations: skiing, hiking, fly fishing. Office: Univ Colorado Chancellor's Office 1420 Austin Bluffs Pkwy Colorado Springs CO 80918

SHOEMAKE, ANGELA NICHOLE, nursing educator; b. Pottsville, Pa., Jan. 17, 1976; d. Mary Wagner; m. Nathan Thomas Shoemake; 1 child, Adeline Michelle. MS in Nursing, U. Phoenix, 2004. Instr. Career Tng. Solutions, Fredericksburg, Va., 2001—, adv. bd. mem., 2007—08; asst. prof. Northern Va. CC, Springfield, 2005—. Mem.: Sigma Theta Tau, NLN. Home: 725 Canterbury Dr Ruther Glen VA 22546 Office: Northern Va CC 6699 Springfield Ctr Dr Springfield VA 22150

SHOEMAKER, CAROLYN SPELLMAN, planetary astronomer; b. Gallup, N.Mex., June 24, 1929; d. Leonard Robert and Hazel Adele (Arthur) Spellmann; m. Eugene Merle Shoemaker, Aug. 18, 1951 (dec. July 1997); children: Christine Shoemaker Abanto, Patrick Gene, Linda Shoemaker Salazar. BA cum laude, Chico State Coll., 1949, MA, 1950; ScD, No. Ariz. U., 1990, St. Mary's U., NS, Can., 2003. Vis. scientist Br. astrogeology U.S. Geol. Survey, Flagstaff, Ariz., 1980—; rsch. asst. Calif. Inst. Tech., Pasadena, 1981-85; rsch. prof. astronomy No. Ariz. U., Flagstaff, 1989—; mem. staff Lowell Obs., Flagstaff, 1993—. Guest observer Palomar Obs., Palomar Mountain, Calif., 1982-94; Ruth Northcott Meml. lectr. R.A.S.C., 1995; co-McGovern lectr. Cosmos Club Found., 1995. Co-recipient Rittenhouse medal Rittenhouse Astron. Soc., 1988, Scientist of Yr. award ARCS Found., 1995, James C. Watson medal NAS, 1998; recipient Woman of Distinction award Soroptimists, 1994, 20th Anniversary Internat. Women's Yr. award Zonta and 99s, 1995, NASA Exceptional Scientific Achievement medal, 1996, Woman of Distinction award Nat. Assn. Women in Edn., 1996, Shoemaker award Am. Inst. Profl. Geologists, 1997, plaque Internat. Forest Friendship, Atchison, Kans., 1997, Robert Burnham Jr. award Western Regional Astron. League, 2000, Ariz. Woman of Distinction award Alpha Delta Kappa, 2004; named Disting. Alumna of the Calif. State U., Chico, 1996. Fellow AAAS, Am. Acad. Arts and Scis., Am. Geophys. Union; mem. Meteoritical Soc., Sigma Xi. Achievements include discovery of 32 comets including Periodic Comet Shoemaker-Levy 9 which impacted Jupiter in July 1994, more than 500 asteroids including 44 Earth approachers and approximately 68 Mars crossers, meteorites at Veevers Crater, Australia and impactites at Wolfe Creek Crater, Australia. Home: 5231 Hidden Hollow Rd Flagstaff AZ 86001-3821 Office: Lowell Obs 1400 W Mars Hill Rd Flagstaff AZ 86001-4499 Business E-Mail: cshoemaker@usgs.gov.

SHOEMAKER, CYNTHIA CAVENAUGH JONES, academic dean; b. Washington, Feb. 13, 1938; d. Robert LaTourrette and Herta (Wilson) Cavenaugh; m. Roger H. Jones, July 4, 1958 (div. Dec. 1984); children: Roger, Michael, Steve, Allison; m. Douglas B.G. Shoemaker, Oct. 21, 1989. BS in Human Ecology, Cornell U., 1959; MEd in Edn., U. Md., 1974, PhD in Edn., 1981, postgrad., 1987-91. Sr. v.p. Home and Sch. Inst., 1972-75; exec. dir. Early Childhood Edn. Adminstrn. Inst., 1975—2009; asst. to dean continuing edn. Cath. U., 1982; program dir. continuing edn. Montgomery Coll., 1983-84; assoc. dir. off-campus programs George Washington U., Washington, 1984—2000; acad. dean u. programs So. Md. Higher Edn. Ctr., California, 2002—. Parent-child presch. observation program tchr. Montgomery County (Md.) Pub. Schs., 1972-75; adj. prof. M.A. in Teaching Trinity Coll., Washington, 1974-78, asst. prof., 1978-84; adj. prof. Webster Coll., St. Louis, 1981; adj., assoc. prof. George Mason U., Fairfax, Va., 1989-95; speaker various meetings, confs. and workshops throughout U.S., 1970-94; exec. bd. Md. Coun. Staff Devel., 1987-89; chmn. Tri-County Staff Devel. Consortium, Charles County, St. Mary's County and Calvert Counties, Md.; program chmn. Assn. Fed. Info. Resource Mgmt., 1993-94; conf. chmn. AFFIRM/SIGCAT, 1994, exec. v.p., 1995-96, dir., 1996-2009. Author: Leadership and the Use of Power in ECE Adminstration, 1980, Motivating Staff, Parents and Children, 1981, Home Learning Enablers and Other Helps, 1992, 94, Adminstration and Management of Programs for Young Children, 1994, Leadership in Continuing and Distance Education in Higher Education, 1998, Leadership and Management of Programs for Young Children, 2000, Leadership in Continuing Education in Higher Education, 2007; co-author: (with Dorothy Rich) Success for Children Begins at Home, 1973, The Home New Educational Partnership, 1974, A Family Affair: Education, 1977; contbr. articles to profl. jours. Elder Rockville Presbyn. Ch. Grantee U.S. SBA, Montgomery C.C., 1983, 84, Md. State Dept Edn., Tri-County Staff Devel. Consortium, 1988; recipient nat. award Parent Coop. Preschs. Internat., 1970. Mem. ASCD, Nat. Assn. Edn. Young Children, Assn. Childhood Edn. Internat., Assn. Fed. Info. Resource Mgmt. (exec. bd. dirs., 1991-2009), Am. Soc.of Pub. Adminstr. Episcopalian. Office: So Md Higher Edn Ctr 44219 Airport Rd California MD 20619 Business E-Mail: eceai@erols.com, cshoemaker@smhec.org. *Helping children and adults develop to their full potential and helping east and west understand each other better are two very rewarding goals of my life.*

SHOEMAKER, GRADUS LAWRENCE, chemist, educator; b. Zeeland, Mich., Jan. 18, 1921; s. Corey and Hattie (Lubbers) S.; m. Florence Etta Wright, June 5, 1952; children— Robert Neil, Betty Lynn. AB, Hope Coll., 1944; MS, U. Ill., 1947, PhD, 1949. Mem. faculty U. Louisville, 1949—, prof. chemistry, 1965—88, prof. emeritus, 1988—, chmn. dept., 1963—64, 1965—67, chmn. divsn. natural sci., 1967—79. Mem. exec. bd. Covenant Housing, Inc., 1989-97. Served as ensign USNR, 1944-45. Mem. Am. Chem. Soc. (councillor 1968-80), AAUP, Ky. Acad. Sci., Blue Key, Sigma Xi, Alpha Epsilon Delta, Phi Kappa Phi, Phi Lambda Upsilon Presbyterian. Home: 2815 Meadow Dr Louisville KY 40220-2406

SHOEMAKER, HELEN E. MARTIN ACHOR, civic worker; b. Houston, Mar. 24, 1915; d. Earl L. and Blanche L. (Williams) Martin; m. Harold E. Achor, Oct. 11, 1935; children: Dianne Achor Johnston, Lana Achor Rainville; m. Robert N. Shoemaker, May 19, 1972. AB, Anderson Coll., Ind., 1960, LLD, 1978. Resident dir. Anderson Coll., 1967-69, dir. alumni svcs., 1969-72; legis. counsel Ind. Colls. and Univ. Ind., 1970-72; spl. asst. Ctr. Pub. Svc., Anderson, 1973-77, spl. asst. to dean for acad. devel., 1977-78. Sec.-treas. Ind. State Libr. and Hist. Bldg. Expansion Commn., 1973-78; mem. com. region VII, Girl Scouts U.S.A., 1958-66; adv. coun. fin. aid to students Office Edn. HEW, 1976-78; mem. Ind. Ho. of Reps. from Madison County, 1968-70; v.p. Ind. Fedn. Women's Rep. Clubs, 1945-46; treas. Nat. Fedn. Women's Rep. Clubs, 1947-51; Rep. precinct vice chmn. Madison County, 1946-68, vice chmn., Anderson, 1967-68; bd. dirs. Urban League Madison County, 1969-76; adv. com. Georgetown U. Grad. Sch. Acad. in Pub. Svc., 1976-83; adv. com. on sex discrimination Ind. Civil Rights Commn., 1978-83; bd. dirs. Anderson Symphony Womens Guild, Anderson Symphony Orch. Women's Guild, 1987, hon. mem.; trustee Anderson Coll., 1978-85; bd. dirs. Opportunities Industrialization Ctr., Inc., Madison County, 1980-84, Ind. Acad. Pub. Svc., 1981-83, Women's Alternatives Inc., Anderson, 1982-93 (Elizabeth Howard McMahan award 1987); exec. com. devel. bd. St. John's Med. Ctr., Anderson, 1981-92; bd. dirs. life enrichment Park Place Ch. God, 1989-94 Recipient William B. Harper award Urban League Madison County, 1975; named Sagamore of Wabash, State of Ind., 1979. Mem. LWV (dir. Madison County 1973-76, 78-84, 87), Anderson Coun. Women, Anderson Fine Arts Ctr. (treas.). Mem. Ch. Of God. Home: 8432 Peace Lily Ct Lorton VA 22079

SHOEMAKER, INNIS HOWE, art museum curator; b. Reading, Pa. d. William Erety and Jean (Miller) S. AB, Vassar Coll., 1964; MA, Columbia U., 1968, PhD, 1975. Curator Vassar Coll. Art. Gallery, Poughkeepsie, NY, 1965-68, 73-76; asst. dir. Ackland Art Mus., U. N.C., Chapel Hill, 1976-82, dir., 1983-86; Audrey and William H. Helfand sr. curator prints, drawings and photographs Phila. Mus. Art, 1986—; adj. prof. U. Pa., 2001—. Fellow in art history Am. Acad. in Rome, 1971-73; adj. prof. U. N.C., Chapel Hill, 1983-86. Author: Mad for Modernism: Earl Horter and His Collection, 1999, Jacques Villon and his Cubist Prints, 2001, Adventures in Modern Art:The Charles K.Williams II Collection, 2009; co-author: The Engravings of Marcantonio Raimondi, 1981, Paul Cézanne: Two Sketchbooks, 1989; contbr.: Mexico and Modern Printmaking: A Revolution in the Graphic Arts, 2006. Mem. vis. com. Lehman Loeb Art Ctr., Vassar Coll., 1993-. Mem. Coll. Art Assn. Am., Am. Assn. Mus., Print Coun. Am. (bd. dirs. 1986-89). Office: Phila Mus Art PO Box 7646 Philadelphia PA 19101-7646

SHOEMAKER, LAWRENCE R., pediatrician, educator; MD, Vanderbile U., 1986. Assoc. prof. pediat. U. Louisville, 2001—; pediat. nephrology divsn. chief U. Children's Kidney Specialists, Louisville, 2003—.

SHOEMAKER, ROBERT MORIN, retired military officer, commissioner; b. Almont, Mich., Feb. 18, 1924; s. Uriah Beebe and Pomala (Morin) S.; m. Mary Alice Rickard, July 17, 1948. BS, U.S. Mil. Acad., 1946; postgrad., U.S. Army Command and Gen. Staff Coll., 1959, Army War Coll., 1967. Commd. 2d lt. U.S. Army, 1946, advanced through grades to gen., 1978, platoon leader, bn. staff officer, co. comdr. 18th Inf., Fed. Republic Germany, 1947-50, co. comdr., regtl. S2, S3, 23d Inf. Republic of Korea, 1953-54, staff officer inf. br. DA, 1954-56, student, faculty officer U.S. Army Aviation Sch. Ft. Rucker, Ala., 1959-62, project officer Army Concept Team Vietnam, 1962-63, bn. comdr., asst. chief of staff, G-3, 11th Air Assault Div. Ft. Benning, Ga., 1963-65, bn. cmdr., squadron comdr. 1st Cav. Div., Vietnam, 1965-66, chief plans and programs Army Aviation DA, 1967-69, chief of staff, asst. div. comdr. 1st Cav. Vietnam, 1969-70, dep. comdr., chief. of staff III Corps and Ft. Hood, Tex., 1970, dept. comdr. MASSTER Ft. Hood, Tex., 1971-72, comdr. 1st Cav., 1973-75, comdr. III Corps Ft. Hood, 1975-77, dep. comdr. FORSCOM Ft. McPherson, Ga., 1977-78; comdr. U.S. Army Forces Command, 1978-82; ret., 1982; county commr. Bell County, Tex., 1987-94. Decorated D.S.M., Silver Star medal with oak leaf cluster, Legion of Merit, D.F.C., Bronze Star, Air medal with 48 oak leaf clusters, Army Commendation medal with oak leaf cluster, Croix de Guerre (France), Gallantry Cross with palm (Republic of Vietnam), RVN Honor medal 1st class; Robert M. Shoemaker H.S., Killeen, Tex. named in his honor, Aug. 2001; named Disting. Grad., West Point, 2004. Home: 111 Bluff Ln Belton TX 76513-9804 E-mail: bshoe5@embargmail.com.

SHOEMAKER, SCOTT DAVID, network consultant, educator; b. Milw., Oct. 28, 1958; s. Alan Kent and Barbara Jean (Pepe) S.; m. Glenda Faye Coates, June 8, 1985; children: Brock, Paige, Leah. BA in Secondary Edn., Purdue U., West Lafayette, Ind., 1982; MEd, Ariz. State U., 1987; MS in Computer Sci. Edn., U. Evansville, Ind., 1988. Cisco cert. network assoc., foundation cert. Info. Tech. Infrastructure Libr. Tchr. Monument Valley High Sch., Kayenta, Ariz., 1982-86; instr. computer sci. Grand Canyon U., Phoenix, 1986-90; systems analyst Bull NH Info. Systems, Phoenix, 1990-92; sr. network cons. Honeywell IAC, Phoenix, 1992—99; dir. strategy consulting Insight Enterprises, Phoenix, 1999—. Seminar instr. PCAI mag. Hands-On Seminars, Phoenix, 1985-90. Contbr. articles to profl. mags. Elder, Metro Presbyn. Ch., Glendale, Ariz., 1992-2004; bd. dirs. NEED, Inc., 2001-04; spkr. ch. leadership confs., Uganda, 1998, Japan, 2005. Republican. Presbyterian. Avocations: photography, fishing, shooting. Office: 7500 College Blvd Overland Park KS 66210 Home: 12106 S Acuff LN Olathe KS 66062-6000 Personal E-mail: sdshoemaker@kc.surewest.net.

SHOEMAKER, TROY, hazardous materials response team coordinator, fire captain; b. Alliance, Nebr., July 12, 1971; s. Freddie and Virginia Shoemaker; children: Keaton, Kadin. Cert. firefighter I 1992, apprentice fire protection specialist 1992, fire officer I 1995, airport firefighter 1995, hazardous materials technician 1997, advanced hazardous materials technician 1997, registered nat. emergency med. basic technician 2002. Damage controlman, firefighter USN, San Diego, 1989—94; sr. fire capt. Antarctic Support Assoc., Englewood, Colo., 1994—96; hazmat coord., fire capt. Scottsbluff Fire Dept., Nebr., 1996—. Mem. Scotts Bluff County Local Emergency Planning Com., Nebr., 2002—, Nebr. Hazardous Materials Adv. Coun., Lincoln, 2000—; founding chairperson Nebr. Hazardous Materials Assn., 2005. Contbr. articles to profl. jours. With USN, 1989—94. Mem.: Internat. Assn. Firefighters, Mo. Valley Assn. Fire Chiefs, Internat. Assn. Fire Chiefs. Office: Scottsbluff Fire Dept 1818 Ave A Scottsbluff NE 69361-1779 Office Phone: 308-630-6231.

SHOEMAKER, WILLIAM EDWARD, corporate financial executive; b. Charleston, W.Va., Sept. 17, 1945; s. Robert Edward and Janet Elizabeth (Hoglund) S.; 1 child, Marcus. BBA, U. Notre Dame, 1967. Assoc. buyer Proctor & Gamble, Cin., 1971; gen. mgr. Eastwind Inc., Anchorage, 1972-73; pres., operator Golden Horn Lodge, Inc., Bristol Bay, Alaska, 1973-79; treas. Hawley Resource Group, Inc., Anchorage, 1979-88; treas., chief fin. officer Golden Zone Resources, Inc., Campbell, Calif., 1988-90; ptnr. Resort Mgmt. Corp., Anchorage, 1987-90; pres. Discovery Holdings, Inc., Ft. Lauderdale, Fla., 1991—2005; pres., CEO Foresight Digital Co., 2005—. Bd. dirs. Pacific Art & Design Cons., Inc. Bd. dirs. Anchorage Econ. Devel. Corp., 1988-90, 4 Children's Sake, 1997—; mem. exec. com. Broward Child Welfare Initiative, 2002—; dir. Lovewell Inst. for Creative Arts, 2004-. Served to lt. USN, 1967—71. Republican. Avocations: boating, skiing, fishing. Home: 3271 Seaward Dr Pompano Beach FL 33062-6840 Office: Foresight Digital Co 1000 Corporate Dr Ste 340 Fort Lauderdale FL 33334 Office Phone: 954-491-0180.

SHOEMAKER, WILLIAM JOSEPH, neuroscientist; b. Boston, Sept. 20, 1941; s. William McCune and Clementine Shoemaker; life ptnr. Teena Gravel; children: Monica Yvette Anschel-Geraghty, Benjamin John. BA in Zoology, U. Mass., Amherst, 1964; PhD in Biochemistry and Metabolism, MIT, Cambridge, 1971. Assoc. sect. chief NIMH, Bethesda-Washington, 1972—76; sr. scientist The Salk Inst., La Jolla, Calif., 1976—84; prof. U. Conn. Health Ctr., Farmington, 1985—. Cons. rsch. programs at numerous instns. Contbr. articles to numerous profl. jours., chapters to books. Mem. leadership group Unitarian Soc. Hartford, Conn., 1987. Unitarian. Achievements include life master rating one-star by American Cribbage Congress. Avocations: bicycling, cribbage. Home: 175 Thistle Pond Dr Bloomfield CT 06002 Office: Univ Conn Health Ctr 263 Farmington Ave Farmington CT 06030-1410

SHOEN, EDWARD JOSEPH, transportation and insurance companies executive; s. Leonard and Anna (Carty) S. BA, Coll. Holy Cross, 1971; MBA, Harvard U., 1973; JD, Ariz. State Univ., 1981. With Amerco Corp, 1971—; pres. U-Haul Internat., Inc., 1990—; pres., chmn. Amerco Corp., Reno, 1986—. Office: Amerco 1325 Airmotive Way Reno NV 89502

SHOFFNER, MARTHA ANN, state treasurer; b. July 10, 1944; Attended, U. Memphis, Ark. State U. Lic. real estate agent. With Sink Realty, Newport, Ark.; mem. Dist. 79 Ark. House of Reps., Little Rock, 1997—2003; asst. auditor State of Ark., Little Rock, treas., 2006—. Chmn. State Agencies and Govt. Affairs Com.; mem. Joint Budget Com., Joint Com. on Retirement and Soc. Security. Named Jackson County Woman of Yr., 1996. Mem.: DAR, Newport C. of C., Jackson County Humane Soc., Bus. & Profl. Women's Club. Office: State Treasury 220 State Capitol Little Rock AR 72201*

SHOFFNER, ROBERT L., III, economics professor; s. Robert Shoffner and Linda Alexander; m. Carolina Shoffner, Feb. 26, 2005. MS in Economics, East Carolina U., Greenville, NC, 2003. Instr. economics Ctrl. Piedmont CC., Charlotte, NC, 2004—. Adv. bd. NC State Employees Credit Union, Matthews, 2008. Office: Ctrl Piedmont CC Charlotte NC 28204

SHOGAN, ROBERT, news correspondent; b. NYC, Sept. 12, 1930; s. Albert and Millie (Jacobs) S.; m. Ellen Shrewsbury, May 26, 1959; children: Cynthia Diane, Amelia Ford. BA, Syracuse U., 1951; postgrad., U. Mich. Inst. Pub. Adminstrn., 1951, Columbia U., 1952. Reporter Detroit Free Press, 1956-59; telegraph editor Miami (Fla.) News, 1959-61; asst. editor Wall St. Jour., NYC, 1961-65; evaluation officer Peace Corps, Washington, 1965-66; corr. Newsweek, Washington, 1966-73; nation polit. corr. Los Angeles Times, Washington, 1973-99. Profl.-in-residence Annenberg Sch. Communication, U. Pa., 1993; adj. prof. Johns Hopkins U., Ctr. for Study of Am. Govt., Washington, 1999—. Author: Question of Judgement, 1972, Promises to Keep, 1977, None of the Above, 1982, The Riddle of Power, 1991, Hard Bargain, 1995, Fate of the Union, 1998, The Double-Edged Sword, 1998, Bad News, 2001, War Without End, 2002, The Battle of Blair Mountain, 2004, Backlash, 2006, No Sense of Decency, 2009; co-author: (with Tom Craig) The Detroit Race Riot, 1964. Served with U.S. Army, 1952-54. Recipient 1st prize Feature Writing, Mich. AP, 1959, Disting. Reporting Pub. Affairs award Am. Polit. Sci. Assn., 1969, Scribes Book award, 1972; rsch. grantee Harry S Truman Presdl. Libr., 1989, Lyndon B. Johnson Presdl. Libr., 1989, Gerald R. Ford Presdl. Libr., 1989; McCormick fellow Hoover Presdl. Libr., 1993; fellow Media Studies Ctr., 1998. Mem. Phi Beta Kappa Home: 3513 Raymond St Chevy Chase MD 20815-3227

SHOGE, RUTH CASANDRA, library director; b. Ocho Rios, St Ann, Jamaica, Oct. 11, 1948; d. Reuben A. and Edith M. Henry; m. Simeon Babatunde Shoge, July 2; children: Ruth Y., Richard O., Maryann T., Samuel T. BA, Howard U., Washington, 1973; MLS, Columbia U. Sch. Libr. Svc., New York, 1974, DLS, 1982. Libr. dir. Mico Tchrs. Coll., Kingston, Jamaica, 1975—77; reference instrn. libr. Upsala Coll., East Orange, 1985—90, Wash. Coll., Chestertown, Md., 1990—2000, libr., 2003—. Treas. Kent County Commn. Human Rels., Chestertown; sec. First United Meth. Ch. Bd. Trustees, Chestertown, 2006. Mem.: ALA, MICUA Roundtable, Congress Acad. Libr. Dirs. Md. (pres. 2006—07). Methodist. Avocation: investigating caribbean diaspora. Office: Wash Coll 300 Washington Ave Chestertown MD 21620 E-mail: ruthshoge@gmail.com.

SHOHAM, DAVID A., epidemiologist, educator; s. Daniel and Denise Shoham; married. BA, U. Chgo., 1995; MSPH, Emory U., Atlanta, 2001; PhD, UNC, Chapel Hill, 2005. Asst. prof. Loyola U. Chgo., Maywood, Ill., 2007—; postdoctoral fellow UNC, Chapel Hill, NC, 2005—07. Mem.: APHA, Soc. Epidemiologic Rsch. Office: Loyola Univ Chgo 2160 S First Ave Maywood IL 60153

SHOHET, ZION, bank executive; BA in econ., with high honors, Princeton U.; JD with high honors, Harvard U. With Oliver, Wyman and Co.; sr. mgr. McKinsey & Co., NYC; v.p. efinanceworks; with Citigroup, 2001—, head of strategy and mergers and acquisitions, treas., head of corp. finance, 2007—. Office: Citigroup 399 Park Ave New York NY 10043*

SHOJAEIAN, PARVIN, research scientist, educator; d. Mahnaz Shahrestani. BS, U. Calif., Irvine, 2005. Tchr. McNichols Learning Ctr. & Dyslexia Found., Newport Beach, Calif., 1999—; grad. student rschr. U. Calif., 2006—; intern Network Exptl. Rsch. on Evolution, Irvine, 2006—. Recipient ADRIANA prize, U. Calif., 2005. Mem.: Associated Grad. Students Coun. (rep. sch. of biol. scis. 2008—). Achievements include research in physiology of aging & late life using drosophila melanogaster as a model organism. Office: Univ Calif 321 Steinhaus Hall UC-Irvine Irvine CA 92697-2525

SHOJI, KAKUKO, language educator; d. Toshio and Kikuyo Shoji; m. Mitsunori Shoji; 1 child, Andrew Kiyonori. Degree, Internat. Christian U., Tokyo U., U. Hawaii. Cert. tchr. Flower Arrangement-Sogetsu Sch., Tokyo, 1958, Iida Miyuki Art Flower Sch., 1988. Recipient Faculty award, Ctr. Japan Studies, Honolulu, 1978—79, Commendation award, Govt. Japan, 2000, Outstanding award, Hui PoloKela Chpt. Mortar Bd, 1999—2000, Excellence Tchg. award, U. Hawaii, 2002; Summer grant, Ctr. Japan Studies, Honolulu, 1991—94. Avocations: art, reading, music, flower arranging.

SHOKET, ANN E., editor-in-chief; b. June 16, 1972; BA cum laude, NYU; degree in Media Mgmt., The New School, NYC. With Am. Lawyer; editor React mag.; various positions CosmoGIRL! Hearst Corp., 1999—2003, exec. editor, 2003—07, web editorial dir. Cosmogirl.com, 2000, editor-in-chief Seventeen mag., 2007—. Dir. CosmoGIRL!'s leadership campaign Project 2024. Office: Seventeen 300 W 57Th St New York NY 10019-3741*

SHOMAKER, ANDREA KAY, secondary school educator; d. Leon A. and Diane D. Strickland; m. Paul Clay Shomaker, Aug. 17, 1971; children: Emma Catherine, Paul Carson, Ava Elizabeth. AA in Psychology, Macon State Coll., Ga., 1996; BA in French and Politcal Sci., Ga. Coll. and State U., Milledgeville, 1995; MAT Fgn. Lang. Edn., Ga. Coll. and State U., Macon, 1996, EdS in Social Sci. Edn., 2001; PhD in Ednl. Policy Studies, Ga. State U., Atlanta, 2003. Sales assoc. Belk Matthews, Macon, Ga., 1992—94; resident adviser, sr. resident adviser Ga. Coll. and State U., Milledgeville, 1993—95, distance learning site coord. Macon, 1995—96; instr., head fgn. lang. dept. Bibb County Pub. Schs., 1996—2001; sales assoc. Carlyle & Co. Jewelers, 1997—97; tchr., French, Spanish, social studies Monroe County Bd. Edn., Forsyth, 2001—04; instr., head fgn. lang. dept. First Presbyn. Day Sch., Macon, 2004—. Lang. cons. Evans Clay Kaolin, McIntyre, Ga., 1997—97; editl. cons. Carlyle & Co. Jewelers, Macon, 1997—97; ednl. and rsch. cons. pvt. practice, 1996; polit. campaign cons. Cecil Staton, 2002—02; standardized patient pilot program assessment participant Mercer U., Nat. Bd. Med. Examiners, 1999—2000; instr. continuing edn. Macon State Coll., 1995—97; adj. prof. French Mercer U, Macon, 2004. Coord. blood donor ARC, 2004; mem. Jr. League, Macon, Ga., 2005; sponsor FPD Spanish Club Cmty. Outreach, Macon, 2004, various youth orgns., 1995; artist donating works benefit Macon-Bibb County Citizens Advocacy, 2006; vol. translator Macon-Bibb County Conv. and Visitor's Bur., 1996—97; mem., sponsor Macon Hist. Found., 2005, Mus. Arts and Sciences, 2004; web designer Bibb County Young Reps., Macon, 2002—03; mem. Bibb County Rep. Party Exec. Com., 2002—04; sec. Children's Coun. Mulberry United Meth. Ch., 2005; mem., former treas., current leader Deborah Cir. Mulberry United Meth. Ch., 2003; mem. Meth. Home Aux., 2005; social chair, corr. sec., web site designer Mustard Seed Class Mulberry United Meth. Ch., 2002—04; 2k and 3k sunday sch. tchr. Mulberry United Meth. Ch., 2003, vacation bible sch. tchr., 2004; mem., chair young alumnae com. St. Timothy's Sch., Stevenson, Md., 2003, reunion chair 1991, 2001; site sponsor EF Ednl. Tours Abroad, 2000; organizer, dir., and com. chair pub. rels. Internat. Dinner Festival of Westside H.S., 1997—99. Mem.: Ga. Educators Assn. (assoc.), Tchrs. English as Second Lang. (assoc.), Fgn. Lang. Assn. Ga. (assoc.), Am. Ednl. Rsch. Assn. (assoc.), United Meth. Women (sec. children's coun. 2005), Nat. Soc. DAR (life; chair jr. membership 1995—97), Healy Point Country Club (assoc.), Mensa. Avocations: travel, study of languages and linguistics, distance education and web design. Office: First Presbyterian Day School 5671 Calvin Drive Macon GA 31210

SHOMIN, JANET L., paralegal; d. Walter Frederick and Betty Darlene Redsted; 1 child from previous marriage, Matthew James. Cert. in paralegal, Rockhurst U., Kansas City, Mo., 2006. Legal sec. Shughart, Thomson & Kilroy, Kansas City, 1975—87; paralegal Cochran Oswald & Room, Blue Springs, Mo., 1987—2004, Dodig, Arbuckle & Carey, Lee's Summit, Mo., 2004—05, Thompson Law Office, Kansas City, 2005—06, Wagstaff & Cartmell, Kansas City, 2006—07, Horn Law Firm, 2007—. Active Raytown emergency Assistance Program, Raytown, Mo., 2003—04, Grain Valley Cmty. Svcs., Mo., 2004; neighborhood coord. Night Out Against Crime, Blue Springs, 1990; mem. Celebrate Am. benefit, 2000, 2003, 2004; bd. dirs. First United Meth., Blue Springs, 2000. Mem.: Am. Assn. for Justice, Assn. Trial Lawyers Am. Avocations: singing, volleyball. Home: 609 NE Sunnybrook Dr Blue Springs MO 64014 Office: Horn Law Firm 19049 E Valley View Pky Independence MO 64053

SHONK, ALBERT DAVENPORT, JR., advertising executive; b. LA, May 23, 1932; s. Albert Davenport and Jean Spence (Stannard) S. BS in Bus. Adminstrn., U. So. Calif., 1954. Field rep. mktg. divsn. LA Examiner, 1954-55, asst. mgr. mktg. and field supr. mktg. divsn., 1955-56, mgr. mktg. divsn., 1956-57; account exec. Hearst Advt. Svc., LA, 1957-59; account exec., mgr. Keith H. Evans & Assocs., San Francisco and Los Angeles, 1959-65; owner, pres. Albert D. Shonk Co., LA, 1965-97; gen. ptnr. Shonk Land Co. Ltd., Charleston, W.Va., 1989-00; dir. Shonk, LLC, Del., 2001—. Pres. Signet Cir. Corp., Inc., 1977-81, dir., 1962-81, hon. life dir., 1981—, treas., 1989-2002, pres., 2002—. Founding chmn. Crittenton Assocs.; bd. dirs. Balboa Island Improvement Assn., 2000—07, pres., 2005—07, immediate past pres., 2008—; bd. dirs. Balboa Island Mus. & Hist. Soc., 1999—2008, pres., 2008—; co-chair Centennial com. Florence Crittenton Ctr., 1992, bd. dirs., sec., 1978, 1st v.p., 1978—79, exec. v.p., 1979—81, pres., 1981—83, chmn. bd., 1983—85, hon. life dir., 1986, treas., 1997, pres., 1997—2001, chmn. bd. dirs., 2002—03, pres., 2004—05, pres. emeritus, 2006. Recipient Medallion of Merit Phi Sigma Kappa, 1976, Founders award, 1961, NIC Interfraternal award, 1989. Mem.: LA Rotary Found. (bd. dir. 2006—, sec. 2006—08, vice chair 2009—), Jr. Advt. Club LA (hon. life, dir., treas., 1st v.p.), Nat. Assn. Pubs. Reps. (past v.p. West Coast 1981—83), Pubs. Rep. Assn. of So. Calif., Advt. Club LA, Town Hall, U. So. Calif. Alumni Assn. (bd. govs. 2000—03, 2007—08, Pres.s' award 2008), Marshall Assocs. (bd. dirs. 1999—), U. So. Calif. Assocs., U. So. Calif. Marshall Sch. Bus. Alumni Assn. (nat. bd. 1991—99, treas. 1995—99), World Affairs Coun., U. So. Calif. Half Century Trojans (co-chair 50 yr. reunion 2004, bd. dirs. 2004—, pres.-elect 2006—07, pres. 2007—08, past pres. 2008—), Skull and Dagger (Arnold Eddy Vol. Svc. award 2009), Trojan Club, Rotary (sec. LA Rotary Found. 2006—08, bd. dirs. 2006—, Paul Harris fellow), U. So. Calif. Cardinal and Gold, Alpha Kappa Psi, Phi Sigma Kappa (dir. grand coun. 1962—70, 1977—79, grand pres. 1979—83, v.p. meml. found. 1979—84, chancellor 1983—87, pres. meml. found. 1984, found. trustee pres. 1984—95, chancellor 1990—91, recorder 1995—, found. trustee emeritus 1995—), Inter-Greek Soc. (v.p. 1976—79, pres. 1984—86, co-founder, hon. life, dir.). Home and Office: 225 Sapphire Ave Newport Beach CA 92662-1148 E-mail: adshonk@msn.com.

SHONS, ALAN RANCE, plastic surgeon, surgical oncologist, educator; b. Freeport, Ill., Jan. 10, 1938; s. Ferral Caldwell and Margaret (Zimmerman) S.; children: Lesley, Susan. AB, Dartmouth Coll., 1960; MD, Case Western Res. U., 1965; PhD in Surgery, U. Minn., 1976. Diplomate Am. Bd. Surgery, Am. Bd. Plastic Surgery. Intern U. Hosp., Cleve., 1965-66, resident in surgery, 1966-67; rsch. fellow transplantation immunology U. Minn., Mpls., 1969-72, asst. prof. plastic surgery, 1976-79, assoc. prof., 1979-84, prof., 1984; resident in surgery U. Minn. Hosp., 1972-74; resident plastic surgery NYU, 1974-76; dir. divsn. plastic and reconstructive surgery U. Minn. Hosp., St. Paul Ramsey Hosp., Mpls. VA Hosp., 1976-84; cons. plastic surgery St. Louis Park Med. Ctr., 1980-84; prof. surgery Case Western Res. U., Cleve., 1984-93, dir. divsn. plastic and reconstructive surgery, 1984-92; prof. surgery, assoc. dir. comprehensive breast program, H. Lee Moffitt Cancer Ctr. and Rsch. Inst. U. South Fla., Tampa, 1992—2003; surgeon pvt. practice, Great Neck, NY, 2004—. Examiner Am. Bd. Plastic Surgery, 1987-2000; dir. divsn. plastic surgery Glen Cove Hosp., NY, 2006-. Author: (with G.L. Adams and D. McQuarrie) Head and Neck Cancer, 1986; (with R. Jensen) Plastic Surgery Review, 1993. Capt. USAF, 1967-69. Fellow ACS (chmn. Minn. com. on trauma 1978-84); mem. AMA, Am. Soc. Plastic and Reconstructive Surgeons, Am. Assn. Plastic Surgeons, Minn. Acad. Plastic Surgeons (pres. 1981-82), Soc. Head and Neck Surgeons, Transplantation Soc., Plastic Surgery Rsch. Coun., Am. Soc. Aesthetic Plastic Surgery, Am. Soc. Maxillofacial Surgeons, Am. Assn. Immunologists, Soc. Exptl. Pathology, Am. Cleft Palate Assn., Am. Soc. Craniofacial Surg. Assn., Fla. Soc. Plastic and Reconstructive Surgeons, Sigma Xi. Office: 935 Northern Blvd Great Neck NY 11021 Office Phone: 516-482-6893.

SHOOK, JON, chef; b. Miami, 1981; Grad., Inst. Ft. Lauderdale. Chef The Strand restaurant, South Beach, Mark's, Café Maxx, The River House, Wildflower Restaurant, Vail, Chadwick Restaurant, LA; co-owner, exec. chef Animal Restaurant, LA, 2008—. Co-owner, chef catering bus. Chef (TV series) Two Dudes Catering, The Food Network; co-author: Two Dudes One Pan, 2008 (Top 10 Cookbooks of 2008, Nat. Pub. Radio). Named one of America's Best New Chefs, Food & Wine Mag., 2009. Office: Animal Restaurant 435 N Fairfax Ave Los Angeles CA 90036 Office Phone: 323-782-9225.*

SHOOSHAN, ALYSSA, legislative staff member; 1 child, Kate. Grad., U. NH. Legis. asst. Senator Judd Gregg, Washington, legis. dir., project dir. NH, chief of staff Washington, 2008—. Bd. dirs. Sarah's Circle, Washington; coord. Cure Autism Now 5K race, Washington. Office: Office of Senator Judd Gregg 393 Senate Russell Office Bldg Washington DC 20510-2904 Office Phone: 202-224-3324. E-mail: alyssa_shooshan@gregg.senate.gov.*

SHOOTER, ERIC MANVERS, retired neurobiology professor, consultant; b. Mansfield, Eng., Apr. 18, 1924; arrived in U.S., 1964; s. Fred and Pattie (Johnson) Shooter; m. Elaine Staley Arnold, May 28, 1949; 1 child, Annette Elizabeth. BA, Cambridge U., Eng., 1945, MA, 1949, PhD, 1950, ScD, 1986; DSc, U. London, 1964. Sr. scientist biochemistry Brewing Industry Rsch. Found., 1950—53; biochemistry lectr. Univ. Coll., London, 1953—63; assoc. prof. genetics Stanford U., 1963—68, prof. genetics and biochemistry, 1968—75, prof., chmn. neurobiology dept., 1975—87, prof. neurobiology, 1987—2004, prof. neurobiology emeritus, 2004—, chmn. Neurosci. PhD Program, 1972—82. Assoc. Neurosci. Rsch. Program, NYC, 1979—89; mem. tchg. staff Internat. Sch. Neurosci., Praglia, Italy, 1987—93; sr. cons. Markey Charitable Trust, Miami, Fla., 1985—97; bd. dirs. Regeneron Pharm., Inc., Tarrytown, NY. Assoc. editor (book series) Ann. Rev. Neuroscis., 1984—2001; contbr. articles to profl. jours. Recipient Wakeman award, Duke U., 1988, Award for Disting. Achievement in Neurosci. Rsch., Bristol-Myers-Squibb, 1997; scholar, Josiah Macy Jr. Found., N.Y.C., 1974—75. Fellow: AAAS, Am. Acad. Arts and Scis., Royal Soc. (London); mem.: NAS, Am. Philos. Soc., Internat. Brain Rsch. Orgn., Internat. Soc. Neurochemistry, Am. Soc. Neurochemistry, Am. Assn.

Biol. Chemists, Soc. for Neurosci. (Ralph W. Gerard prize 1995), Inst. Medicine of NAS, Alpha Omega Alpha (hon.). Avocation: travel. Home: 370 Golden Oak Dr Portola Valley CA 94028-7757 Office: Stanford U Sch Medicine Dept Neurobiology 299 Campus Dr Stanford CA 94305-5125 Business E-Mail: eshooter@stanford.edu.

SHOPE, TIMOTHY ROBERT, medical educator; b. Pottstown, Pa., Sept. 30, 1970; MD, Hahnemann U., Phila., 1997. Diplomate Am. Bd. Surgery, 2005. Asst. prof. dept. surgery Penn State Hershey Med. Ctr., Pa., 2003—. Fellow: ACS. Office: Penn State Hershey Med Ctr 500 Univ Dr H149 Hershey PA 17033 Office Fax: 717-531-4729. Business E-Mail: tshope@psu.edu.

SHOPTAUGH, TERRY LEE, historian, archivist; b. St. Louis, Feb. 9, 1952; s. Don C. and Virgalee Shoptaugh; m. Deborah K. Janzen, May 13, 1952; 1 child, Amelia J. BA, Ctrl. Meth. Coll., 1974; PhD in Am. History, U. NH, 1984. Archivist S.E. Mo. State U., Cape Girardeau, 1982—86; prof. history, archivist Minn. State U., Moorhead, 1986—. Author: Roots of Success, 1997 (Red River Valley Heritage award, 1997), Moorhead: Images of America, 2004, You Have Been Kind Enough to Assist Me: Herman Stern and the Jewish Refugee Crisis, 2008. Mem.: Soc. Am. Archivists (life; cert. archivist). Office: Minn State Univ 1104 S Seventh Ave Moorhead MN 56563 Office Fax: 218-477-5924. Business E-Mail: shoptaug@mnstate.edu.

SHORE, AMY ELIZABETH, performing arts educator, director; b. Abington, Pa., Sept. 10, 1971; d. Larry Jerome and Helen Louise Shore; m. Philip Shore, Mar. 13, 1997; 1 child, Maya Heimes. BA in Spanish Lit., U. Del., NY, 1993; MA in Cinema Studies, NY U., 1995, PhD in Cinema Studies, 2003. Sr. program mgr. NYNSR Annenberg Challenge Project, NYC, 1997—98; dir., comm. & grants Fund City NY, 1998—2000; mgr., nat. proposal group KPMG, NYC, 2000—01; dir. comm. Ctr. Ednl. Innovation, NYC, 2001—07; asst. prof. & program dir. Cinema & Screen Studies, SUNY, Oswego, NY, 2005—; co-owner Heimes Comm., Manlius, NY, 2007—. Mem. ARTSwego, Oswego, NY, 2006—09. Curriculum Devel. grant, Can. Embassy, 2007—08, SUNY Oswego, 2007, Tchg. & Rsch. fellowships, NY U., 1996—97. Mem.: Soc. Cinema & Media Studies. Achievements include research in films made by and about the American woman suffrage movement. Office: SUNY Oswego 314 Poucher Hall Oswego NY 13126 Personal E-mail: shoreamy@gmail.com.

SHORE, ELEANOR GOSSARD, retired medical school dean; b. Ottawa, Ill., Aug. 11, 1930; d. Arthur Paul and Mary Catherine (Lineberger) Gossard; m. Miles Frederick Shore, July 4, 1953; children: Miles Paul, Rebecca Shore Lewin, Susanna Shore LeBoutillier. BA magna cum laude, Radcliffe Coll., 1951; MD, Harvard U., 1955, MPH, 1970. Diplomate Am. Bd. Preventive Medicine. Med. intern New Eng. Med. Ctr. Hosp., Boston, 1955-56; resident in occup. medicine Harvard U. Health Svcs., Cambridge, Mass., 1966-68; Macy scholar Radcliffe Inst., Radcliffe Coll., Cambridge, 1966-68; resident in preventive medicine Harvard Sch. Pub. Health, Boston, 1970-71; asst. physician Radcliffe Coll., 1959-61, Harvard U. Health Svcs., 1961—96; rsch. assoc. dept. microbiology Harvard U. Sch. Pub. Health, 1971-76; asst. to pres. Harvard U., 1972-81; assoc. dean for faculty affairs Harvard Med. Sch., 1978-89, mem. faculty, 1978—2004, dean for faculty affairs, 1989—2004, sr. cons. to office acad. and clin. programs, 2005—. Mem. editl. bd. Harvard Med. Alumni Bull., 1976—. Bd. dirs. Mass.-Ukraine Citizens Bridge, Brockton, Mass., 1989-94, pres., 1991-92; bd. dirs. Needham (Mass.) Found. for Pub. Sch. Edn., 1990-94; bd. dirs. Mass. Health Rsch. Inst., Inc., 1990-99, sec., 1995-99; overseer Boston Mus. Sci., 1981—; trustee Schepens Eye Rsch. Inst., Boston, 1993—; mem. acad. coun. Real Colegio Complutense, Harvard U., 1995—; dep. dir. Harvard Med. Sch. Ctr. for Excellence in Women's Health, 1998-2004. Recipient Pres.'s Recognition award Am. Med. Women's Assn., 1996. Fellow Am. Acad. Preventive Medicine; mem. AAAS, APHA, Mass. Pub. Health Assn., Mass. Med. Soc., Aesculapian Club (treas. 1986-89, pres. 1990-91). Business E-Mail: eleanor_shore@hms.harvard.edu.

SHORE, JAMES H(ENRY), psychiatrist; b. Winston-Salem, NC, Apr. 6, 1940; s. James Henry and Ellen Elizabeth (Hayes) S.; m. Christine Lowenbach, Aug. 24, 1963; children— Ellen Ottilie, James Henry. MD, Duke U., 1965. Diplomate Am. Bd. Psychiatry and Neurology. Intern U. Utah Med. Ctr., 1965-66; resident in psychiatry U. Wash., 1966-69; chief mental health office Portland Area Indian Health Svc., Oreg., 1969-73; assoc. prof. psychiatry, dir. cmty. psychiatry tng. program U. Oreg. Health Sci. Ctr., 1973-75, prof., chmn. dept. psychiatry, 1975-85; from chmn. dept. psychiatry Health Sci. Ctr. to chancellor U. Colo., Aurora, 1985—2004, chancellor Health Scis. Ctr., 2004—05, chancellor emeritus Health Scis. Ctr., 2006—. Mem. exptl. and spl. edn. com. NIMH-Internal Rev. Group, 1976-80; dir. Colo. Psychiatry Hosp., 1985-99; interim dir. U. Colo. Hosp., Denver, 1987-88, interim exec. vice chancellor, 1995-97, chancellor, 1998-2005; cons. in field. Contbr. numerous articles to profl. publs. Mem. Various community bds. Served with USPHS, 1969-73. Decorated USPHS Commendation medal; various grants. Fellow Am. Psychiat. Assn., Am. Coll. Psychiatry (pres. 2003-04); mem. Am. Assn. Chmn. Depts. Psychiatry (pres. 1989), Am. Bd. Psychiatry and Neurology (dir. 1987—, pres. 1994), Residency Rev. Com. for Psychiatry (chmn. 1991-92). Office: U Colo Health Scis Ctr Mail Stop F800 PO Box 6508 Aurora CO 80045

SHORE, MILES FREDERICK, psychiatrist, educator; b. Chgo., May 26, 1929; s. Miles Victor and Margaret Elizabeth S.; m. Eleanor M. Gossard, July 4, 1953; children: Miles Paul, Rebecca M. Lewin, Susanna G. LeBoutillier. BA, U. Chgo., 1948; AB, Harvard U., 1950, MD, 1954. Intern U. Ill. Research and Edn. Hosp., Chgo., 1954-55; resident in psychiatry Mass. Mental Health Center, Beth Israel Hosp., Boston, 1956-61; asst. prof. psychiatry Tufts U. Sch. Medicine, Boston, 1964-68, assoc. prof., 1968-71, prof., 1971-75, prof. community health, 1972-75; founder, dir. Tufts Community Mental Health Center, 1968-74, asso. dean community affairs, 1972-75; mem. faculty Boston Psychoanalytic Inst., 1973—; Bullard prof. psychiatry Harvard Med. Sch., Boston, 1975—; supt. Mass. Mental Health Ctr., 1975-93; vis. scholar John F. Kennedy Sch. Govt. Harvard U., 1993—; cons. exec. edn. Harvard Med. Internat., 1999—, sr. cons., 2000—. Dir. program for chronic mental illness Robert Wood Johnson Found., 1985-92. Editl. bd. Psychat. Svcs. Jour., 1990; bd. editors Jour. Interdisciplinary History, 1975, Psycho History Rev., 1978; column editor Harvard Rev. Psychiatry, 1993; contbr. articles to profl. jours. Bd. dirs. Federated Dorchester Neighborhood Houses, Boston, 1975-78, tr. House, Boston, 1995—; bd. dirs. Med. Found., Boston, 1987—, chmn., 1999-2001; mem. Blue Ribbon Commn., Mass. Dept. Mental Health, 1979-80. Capt. U.S. Army, 1956-58. Community Mental Health Center grantee, 1964-75. Fellow Am. Psychiat. Assn. (life, joint commn. on pub. affairs, adminstrv. psychiatry award 1987), Am. Coll. Psychiatrists (chmn. fin. com. 1983-89, bd. regents 1988-90, 1st v.p. 1994, pres. 1996-97, Bowis award for svc. 1990, Arthur P. Noyes award 1994); mem. Assn. Am. Med. Colls. (coun. acad. socs. 1992—), Boston Psychoanalytic Soc. and Inst. (chmn. bd. trustees 1970-73), Mass. Psychiat. Soc. (pres. 1970-71), Mass. Hosp. Assn. (trustee 1980-85), Am. Hosp. Assn. (chmn. governing coun. for psychiat. and substance abuse svcs. 1992-93, ho. of dels. 1996—02, region I policy bd. 1997—2000), Roxbury Clinic Record Club, Aesculapian Club, Mass. Hist. Soc. Office: Harvard Med Internat Ste 902 1135 Tremont St Boston MA 02120 Business E-Mail: miles_shore@harvard.edu.

SHORE, RICHARD ARNOLD, mathematics professor; b. Boston, Aug. 18, 1946; s. Philip M. and Miriam (Krensky) S.; m. Naomi J. Spiller, Aug. 3, 1969; children: Deena A., Aviva R. B in Jewish Edn., Hebrew Coll., 1966; AB, Harvard U., 1968; PhD, MIT, 1972. Instr. U. Chgo., 1972-74; asst. prof. Cornell U., Ithaca, NY, 1974-78, assoc. prof., 1978-83; asst. prof. U. Ill.-Chgo., 1977; prof. math. Cornell U., Ithaca, 1983—. Organizing com. Logic Yr. at MSRI, 1989-90, other internat. meetings; pub. ASL, 2008—; vis. prof. MIT, 2008. Author: (with A. Nerode) Logic for Applications; editor North-Holland, Studies in Logic and the Foundations of Mathematics, 1996-2007; cons. editor Jour. Symbolic Logic, 1980-83, editor, 1984-93, coord. editor, 1989-91; mng. editor: Bull. Symbolic Logic, 1993-2000; contbr. articles to profl. jours. V.p. for edn. Hillel Acad. Broome County, Binghamton, N.Y., 1985-89; treas. Beth David Synagogue, 1993-96; pres. Jewish Fedn. of Broome County, 1998-2000; bd. dirs. Project Euclid, 2002—. Grantee, NSF, 1973—; vis. scholar, MIT, 1997, Harvard U., 1997, 2002. Mem. Am. Math. Soc., Spl. Interest Group in Algorithms and Computation Theory, Assn. for Computing Machinery, Assn. for Symbolic Logic (coun. 1984—, pres. 2001-2004., pub. 2008-) Jewish. Home: 14 Kenwood Ave Newton MA 02459 Office: Cornell U Dept Math Malott Hall Ithaca NY 14853 Office Phone: 607-255-4081. Business E-Mail: shore@math.cornell.edu.

SHORE, RICHARD M., radiologist, educator; b. Chgo., July 27, 1949; s. Lloyd G. and Judith K. Shore; m. Suzanne H. Heindl, May 28, 1977. BS, U. Wis., Madison, 1971; MD, U. Mich. Med. Sch., Ann Arbor, 1975. Diplomate Am. Bd. Pediat., 1980, Am. Bd. Nuc. Medicine, 1981, Am. Bd. Radiology, 1988, added qualifications in pediat. radiology 1995, in pediat. radiology 2004. Sect. head, nuc. medicine Children's Hosp., Columbus, Ohio, 1981—85; attending radiologist Children's Hosp. Mich., Detroit, 1989—90, Children's Meml. Hosp., Chgo., 1990—2001, head, divsn. gen. radiology and nuc. medicine, 2001—; asst. prof., pediat. and radiology Ohio State U., Columbus, 1981—85; asst. prof., radiology Northwestern U. Med. Sch., Chgo., 1990—2002; assoc. prof., radiology Northwestern U. Feinberg Sch. Medicine, 2002—09, prof. radiology, 2009—. Mem.: John Caffey Soc., Am. Coll. Radiology, Am. Roentgen Ray Soc., Radiol. Soc. N.Am., Soc. Nuc. Medicine, Internat. Skeletal Soc., Soc. Pediat. Radiology. Office: Children's Meml Hosp 2300 Children's Plz Chicago IL 60614 Business E-Mail: rshore@northwestern.edu.

SHORE, SHELDON G., chemist, educator; BS in Chemistry, U. Ill., 1951; PhD in Chemistry, U. Mich., 1957. With Ohio State Univ., 1957—, prof. chemistry, math. and physical sci., Charles H. Kimberly Chair Chemistry; asst. prof. Ohio State U., 1957, assoc. prof., 1962, prof., 1965. Contbr. articles to publs. Recipient award in inorganic chemistry, Am. Chem. Soc., 2007. Achievements include patents in field. Office: Ohio State U 2042 Evans Laboratory 88 W 18th Ave Columbus OH 43210 Office Phone: 614-292-6000. Business E-Mail: shore.1@osu.edu.

SHORE, THOMAS SPENCER, JR., retired lawyer; b. Akron, Ohio, Jan. 1, 1939; s. T. Spencer and Harriet G. (Delicate) S.; m. Margaret F. Kudzma, Aug. 12, 1961; children— Thomas Spencer III, John Christopher, Daniel Andrew, Mary Margaret. BA, Brown U., 1961; JD, Northwestern U., 1964. Bar: Ohio 1964. Assoc. Taft, Stettinius and Hollister, Cin., 1964-69, Rendigs, Fry, Kiely & Dennis, Cin., 1969-71, ptnr., 1972—2003; ret., 2003. Adj. asst. prof. Chase Law Sch., U. No. Ky.; adj. Maine Law Sch. Bd. dirs. United Cerebral Palsy of Cin., 1978—; bd. dirs., sec. Boys Club Am., Cin.; trustee emeritus Family Svc. of Cin. Area; past pres. Vis. Nurse Assn. of Cin., hon. trustee; mem. Kennebunkport Zoning Bd. Appeals. Mem. Ohio Bar Assn., Maine Bar Assn., Cin. Country Club, Queen City Club, Webhanet Club, Edgcomb Tennis Club., River Club. Office: 900 4th and Vine Tower 1 W 4th St Cincinnati OH 45202 Home: PO Box 629 Kennebunkport ME 04046 E-mail: t.shore@rendigs.com.

SHORENSTEIN, ROSALIND GREENBERG, internist; b. NYC, Jan. 14, 1947; d. Albert Samuel and Natalie Miriam (Sherman) Greenberg; m. Michael Lewis Shorenstein, June 18, 1967; children: Anna Irene, Claire Beth. BA in Chemistry, Wellesley Coll., 1968; MA in Biochemistry and Molecular Biology, Harvard U., 1970, PhD in Biochemistry and Molecular Biology, 1973; MD, Stanford U., 1976. Diplomate Am. Bd. Internal Medicine. Resident in internal medicine UCLA Med. Ctr., 1976-79; pvt. practice internal medicine Santa Cruz, Calif., 1979—. Mem. dept. internal medicine Dominican Hosp., Santa Cruz, 1979—; co-dir. med. svcs. Health Enhancement & Lifestyle Planning Systems, Santa Cruz, 1983—. Contbr. articles to profl. journals. Dir. Santa Cruz Chamber Players, 1993-94, pres., bd. dirs., 1994—. Recipient Charlie Parkhurst award Santa Cruz Women's Commn., 1989; NSF fellow, 1968-72, Sarah Perry Wood Med. fellow Wellesley Coll., 1972-76. Mem. Am. Soc. Internal Medicine (del. 1994, 95), Calif. Soc. Internal Medicine (trustee 1994—, sec.-treas. 1996-2000), Am. Med. Women's Assn. (Outstanding Svc. award 1987, br. #59 pres. 1986—), Calif. Med. Assn. (com. on women 1987-93), Santa Cruz County Med. Soc. (mem. bd. govs. 1993—, sec. 1997-99, pres. 2000-01, sec. 2002-), Phi Beta Kappa, Sigma Xi. Jewish. Office: 700 Frederick St Ste 103 Santa Cruz CA 95062-2239 Office Phone: 831-458-1002.

SHORENSTEIN, WALTER HERBERT, commercial real estate development company executive; b. Glen Cove, NY, Feb. 23, 1915; m. Phyllis J. Finley, Aug. 8, 1945 (dec.); children: Joan (Dec.), Carole, Douglas. Student, Pa. State U., 1933-34, U. Pa., 1934-36; D in Econs. (hon.), HanYang U., Seoul, Republic of Korea, 1988. With property sales mgmt. depts. Milton Meyer & Co., San Francisco, 1946-51, ptnr., 1951-60, owner, chmn. bd. dirs., 1960—, Shorenstein Group, San Francisco, Shorenstein Co., San Francisco, 1960—. Appt. by Pres. Johnson adv. del. UN Econ. Commn. for Asia and Far East, 1967, Pub. Advisory Com. U.S. Trade Policy; apptd. Pres. Carter Com. for Preservation fo White House; appt. by Pres. Clinton bd. dirs. Corp. Nat. Svc., 1994-96, adv.com. U.S. Commerce Dept. Industry, 1995-96. Past chmn. bd. trustees Hastings Law Ctr., U. Calif., San Francisco; founding mem. exec. adv. com. Hubert H. Humphrey Inst. Pub. Affairs, U. Minn.; bd. visitors; past pres., hon. life bd. dirs. San Francisco Park and Recreation Commn.; chmn. Vietnam Orphans Airlift; bd. dirs. San Francisco Performing Arts Ctr.; trustee Asia Found.; fin. chmn. Dem. Nat. Conv., 1984; founder Joan Shorenstein Ctr. on Press, Politics and Public Policy, Harvard U., 1986; apptd. by Pres. Clinton to Nat. Svc. Commn., 1994, Bd. of Americorp, founding mem. WWII Nat. Monument com., Nat. Endowment Arts, White House Endowment Fund; apptd. by Pres. Carter chair White House Preservation Fund; apptd. by Mayor Frank Jordon chair Save the San Francisco Giants com.; personal advisor Pres. Johnson, Carter, Clinton; chmn. Pacific Rim Econ. Coun., San Francisco; bd. visitors Internat. Studies Bd. Stanford U.; co-founder Orpheum, Curran and Golden Gate Theatres, San Francsico; founder Johnson Presdl. Libr., Carter Ctr.; chmn. San Francisco U. N50 nat. com., 1995, also numerous polit. activities. Maj. USAF, 1940-45. Named Leader of Tomorrow, Time mag., 1953, Calif. Dem. of Yr., 1985; recipient Nat. Brotherhood award NCCJ, 1982, Disting. Svc. award Dem. Nat. Com., 1983, Golden Plate award Am. Acad. Achievement, 1991, Svc. to Youth award Cath. Youth Orgn., 1994, Lifetime Achievement award Dem. Party, 1997; inducted Real Estate Legends Hall of Fame, 1997, Bay Area Coun. Bay Area Bus. Hall of Fame, 1998; Shorenstein award named in his honor Dem. Nat. Com., 1999. Mem. Calif. C. of C. (past bd. dirs.), San Francisco C. of C. (past chmn. bd. dirs., life bd. dirs.). Office: Shorenstein Co 555 California St Ste 4900 San Francisco CA 94104-1714

SHORENSTEIN HAYS, CAROLE, theater producer; b. San Francisco, Sept. 15, 1948; d. Walter and Phyllis Shorenstein; m. Jeffrey Hays; children: Wally, Gracie. Co-owner Curran Theatre, Golden Gate Theatre, Orpheum Theatre, San Francisco. Prodr.: (Broadway plays) Can-Can, 1981, Woman of the Year, 1981—83 (Tony nom. best musical, 1981), Oliver!, 1984, Fences, 1987 (Tony award best play, 1987), A Midsummer Night's Dream, 1996 (Tony nom. best revival of a play, 1996), The Old Neighborhood, 1997—98, The Chairs, 1998 (Tony nom. best revival of a play, 1996), Not About Nightingales, 1999 (Tony nom. best play, 1999), Closer, 1999 (Tony nom. best play, 1999), The Tale of the Allergist's Wife, 2000—02 (Tony nom. best play, 2001), Proof, 2000—03 (Tony award best play, 2001), The Goat, or Who Is Sylvia?, 2002 (Tony award best play, 2002), Topdog / Underdog, 2002 (Tony nom. best play, 2002), Take Me Out, 2003—04 (Tony award best play, 2003), Caroline, or Change, 2004 (Tony nom. best musical, 2004), Gem of the Ocean, 2004—05 (Tony nom. best play, 2005), Doubt, 2005—06 (Tony award best play, 2005, Drama Desk award outstanding new play, 2005), Julius Caesar, 2005; (plays) Well, 2006; (Broadway plays) Rock 'n' Roll, 2007—08. Office: Curran Theatre 445 Geary St San Francisco CA 94102 also: Golden Gate Theatre P O Box 7110 San Francisco CA 94102

SHORRIS, ANTHONY ERNEST, former state agency administrator; b. NYC, Mar. 7, 1957; s. Earl and Sylvia (Sasson) S.; married, 1 child BA with honors, Harvard U., 1977; MA in Pub. Affairs, Princeton U., 1979. Analyst NYC Dept. Gen. Services, 1979-80, dir. mgmt. planning, 1980-82; dep. asst. dir. NYC Office Mgmt. & Budget, 1982-84, asst. dir., 1984-86, dep. dir., 1986-88; commr. NYC Dept. Fin., 1989—91; dep. exec. dir. The Port Authority of NY & NJ, 1991—95; exec. v.p. Healthfirst Inc., 1995—2001; dep. chancellor ops. & policy NYC Dept. Edn., 2001—03; mem. faculty, dir. Policy Rsch. Inst. Woodrow Wilson Sch. Pub. & Internat. Affairs, Princeton U., 2003—07; exec. dir. The Port Authority of NY & NJ, 2007—08. Cons. Dem. Nat. Com., Washington, D.C., 1978-1992; adj. faculty NY U., 1990-98; co-chair Coro Ctr., NY, 1998-2001; chmn. Bd. Ctr. Employment Opportunities, 2000-2001; vis. faculty U. Luigi Bocconi, Milan, 2000, 2002; fellow Century Found., 2008-. Officer Community Planning Bd., N.Y.C., 1979-82; mem. N.Y. Dem. County Com., N.Y.C., 1980-82. Mem. Am. Council Young Political Leaders. Jewish.

SHORT, ALEXANDER CAMPBELL, lawyer; b. Washington, July 26, 1940; s. Joseph Hudson and Beth (Campbell) S.; m. Patricia Graves Thompson, Aug. 24, 1968; children: Joseph Graves, Ashley Campbell, Justin Owen. BA, Amherst Coll., 1963; MA, U. Pa., 1968; JD, U. Va., 1972. Bar: Conn. 1972, Md. 1973. Field and site rep. U.S. Dept. of HUD, Phila., 1963-69; assoc. Reid & Riege P.C., Hartford, Conn., 1972-73, Piper & Marbury, Balt., 1973-79, Miles & Stockbridge, Balt., 1979-81, ptnr., 1981-94; pvt. practice Balt., 1994-95; ptnr. Hooper, Kiefer & Cornell, LLP, Balt., 1995-96, Eastman & Short, LLP, Balt., 1996-2000; asst. atty. gen. State of Md., 2000—. Pres. Handel Soc. adv. bd. to Handel Choir, Balt., 1983-87; bd. dirs. Handel Choir, Balt., 1987-88, 2002-03, pres., 1987-88. Pres. North Balt. Neighborhood Coalition, 1996—2000; bd. dirs. Homeland Assn., Balt., 1984—85, Kernewood Assn., Balt., 1995—, Greater Homewood Cmty. Corp., 1997—2001; mem. bd. mgrs. Camp Dudley YMCA, 1991—96, 1998—2001, 2004—. Mem. Md. Bar Assn. (real property planning and zoning sect., 2004-, coun. 1981-88, 96-98, sec. 1982-84, chmn. elect 1984-86, chmn. 1986-88), Balt. Rotary Found. (bd. dirs. 2004-), Rotary Club Balt. (bd. dirs. 2004-). Democrat. Presbyterian. Avocations: choral singing, gardening. Office: Office of Atty Gen Ednl Affairs Divsn 200 St Paul Pl Baltimore MD 21202 Home Phone: 410-323-6519; Office Phone: 410-576-6967. E-mail: ashort@oag.state.md.us.

SHORT, DEAN C., II, lawyer; b. Akron, Ohio, Mar. 16, 1948; s. Dean C. and Mildred I. (Hahn) S.; m. Carolyn Kay Smith, Jan. 1, 1982; children: Matthew, Emily, Molly, Sadie. BSBA magna cum laude, U. Ariz., 1969; JD cum laude, Harvard U., 1972. Bar: Calif. 1972, U.S. Dist. Ct. (so. dist.) Calif. 1972, Ariz. 1974, U.S. Dist. Ct. Ariz. 1974, U.S. Tax Ct. 1974, U.S. Supreme Ct. 1977. Assoc. Higgs, Fletcher & Mack, San Diego, 1972-74; ptnr. Evans, Kitchel & Jenckes, Phoenix, 1974-85, Jones, Jury, Short & Mast, Phoenix, 1985-88, Gallagher & Kennedy, Phoenix, 1988, also bd. dirs., shareholder. Adj. faculty Ariz. State U. Coll. of Law, 1974—76. Contbr. articles to profl. jours. Pres. Ariz. Friends of Foster Children Found., Phoenix, 1984-85. Recipient Best Lawyers Am., by Woodward/White, Inc., 2007. Mem. Ariz. State Bar (cert. specialist in tax law), State Bar Calif., Whisper Rock Golf Club, Harvard Club Ariz., Sports Lawyers Assn. Avocations: golf, tennis. Office: Gallagher & Kennedy PA 2575 E Camelback Rd Ste 1100 Phoenix AZ 85016 Home: 7525 N 70th St Paradise Valley AZ 85253 Office Phone: 602-530-8308. Office Fax: 602-530-8500. Business E-Mail: dcs@gknet.com.

SHORT, ELIZABETH M., internist, educator, retired federal agency administrator; b. Boston, June 2, 1942; d. James Edward and Arlene Elizabeth (Mitchell) Meehan; m. Michael Allen Friedman, June 21, 1976; children: Lia Gabrielle, Hannah Ariel, Eleanor Elana. BA in Philosophy magna cum laude, Mt. Holyoke Coll., 1963; MD cum laude, Yale U., 1968. Diplomate Am. Bd. Internal Medicine, Am. Bd. Med. Genetics. Resident in internal medicine Yale New Haven Hosp., 1968-70; postdoctoral fellow in human genetics Yale Med. Sch., 1970-72; resident U. Calif., San Francisco, 1972-73; sr. chief resident Stanford (Calif.) Med. Sch., 1973-75, asst. prof. medicine, 1975-83, assoc. dean student affairs, med. edn., 1978-83; dep. dir. acad. affairs, dir. biomed. rsch. Assn. Am. Med. Colls., Washington, 1983-88; dep. assoc. chief med. dir. for acad. affairs VA, Washington, 1988-92, assoc. chief med. dir. for acad. affairs, 1992-96; health policy cons. HHS, 1996—2001; emerita prof. clin. medicine Georgetown U. Sch. Medicine; ret., 2001. Vis. prof. human biology Stanford U., 1983-86; mem. Accreditation Coun. Grad. Med. Edn., 1988-97; mem. White House Task Force on Health Care Reform, 1993. Assoc. editor Clin. Rsch. Jour., 1976-79, editor 1980-84; contbr. articles to profl. jours. Mem. Nat. Child Health Adv. Coun., NIH, 1991-97; com. edn. and tng. Office Sci. and Tech. Policy, White House, Washington, 1991-96, Calif. Philharm., 2003-07; bd. dirs., 2003-07, treas.,06-07, Hillsides Home Children, 2003-, bd. dirs., 2003, exec. com., 2004-, chair program evaluation com., 2006-, search com., 2009, Pacific Asia Mus., 2008-; bd. trustees, 2008-, planning com., 2009-, Mus. Am. West Nat. Adv. Coun., 2008-. Recipient Maclean Zoology award; Munger scholar, Markle scholar, Sara Willis-ton scholar Mt. Holyoke Coll., 1959-63, Yale Men in Medicine scholar,

1964-68; Bardwell Meml. Med. fellow, 1963. Mem. AAAS, Am. Soc. Human Genetics (pub. policy com. 1984-95, chmn. 1986-94), Am. Fedn. Clin. Rsch. (bd. dirs. 1973-83, co-chmn. com. status women 1975-77, editor Clin. Rsch. Jour., 1978-83, nat. coun., exec. com., pub. policy com. 1977-87), Western Soc. Clin. Investigation, Calif. Acad. Medicine, Phi Beta Kappa, Alpha Omega Alpha. Home and Office: 3535 Ranch Top Rd Pasadena CA 91107 Personal E-mail: elizshort@aol.com.

SHORT, MARIANNE DOLORES, lawyer; b. Mpls., Mar. 12, 1951; d. Robert Earl and Marion (McCann) S.; m. Raymond Louis Skowyra Jr., Nov. 1, 1980; 2 children, R. Louis Skowyra III & Nicholas Skowyra. BA in Philos. and Polit. Sci., Newton Coll. of Sacred Heart, 1973; JD, Boston Coll. Law Sch., 1976. Bar: Minn. 1976, Mass. 1977, US Dist. Ct. Minn. 1976, US Dist. Ct. Mass. 1980, US Dist. Ct. ND 2000, US Ct. Appeals (8th cir.) 1980, US Supreme Ct. 1988; civil trial specialist, Minn. State Bar Assn. Spl. asst. atty. gen., St. Paul, 1976-77; assoc. Dorsey & Whitney LLP, Mpls., 1977-82, ptnr., litig. practice, 1983—88, mem. policy com., 1987—88, 2000—, mem. profl. pers. com., 2000—02, mem. capital contbn. com., 2001—03, mem. ptnr. compensation com., 2002—03, mng. ptnr, 2007—; judge Minn. Ct. Appeals, 1988—2000. Chmn. recruiting com. Dorsey & Whitney, Mpls., 1985-87. Trustee Boston Coll., 1985—, Visitation Convent, St. Paul, 1985-91, St. Thomas Acad., 2000—; bd. overseers Boston Coll. Law Sch., 1998—, U. Minn. Law Sch., 2001—. Recipient Corp. Woman of Achievement award, Nat. Assn. Women Bus. Owners, 2004; named Minn. Super Lawyer, Minn. Law & Politics Mag., 2000—07, Women to Watch, Bus. Jour., 2005, Atty. of Yr., Minn. Lawyer, 2005; named one of 15 Top Attys. in Minn., Minn. Lawyers, 2005. Mem. ABA, Mass. Bar Assn., Minn. Bar Assn., Hennepin County Bar Assn. (ethics com.), Ramsey County Bar Assn., Am. Arbitration Assn. (arbitrator), Acad. Cert. Trial Lawyers Minn. Clubs: Town and Country (St. Paul), Mpls. Club (bd. govs.), Am. Acad. Appellate Lawyers, Am. Coll. Trial Lawyers. Avocations: running, skiing. Office: Dorsey & Whitney LLP Ste 1500 50 S Sixth St Minneapolis MN 55402-1498 Home Phone: 651-645-9015; Office Phone: 612-340-2833. Office Fax: 612-340-2807. Business E-Mail: short.marianne@dorsey.com.

SHORT, MARION PRISCILLA, neurogenetics educator; b. Milford, Del., June 12, 1951; d. Raymond Calistus and Barbara Anne (Ferguson) S.; m. Michael Peter Klein; 1 child, Asher Calistus Klein. BA, Bryn Mawr Coll., 1973; diploma, U. Edinburgh, Scotland, 1975; MD, Med. Coll. Pa., 1978. Diplomate Am. Bd. Psychiatry and Neurology, Am. Bd. Internal Medicine. Intern in internal medicine Hahnemann Med. Coll. Hosp., Phila., 1978-79; med. resident in internal medicine St. Lukes-Roosevelt Hosp., NYC, 1979-81; neurology resident U. Pitts. Health Ctr., 1981-84; fellow in med. genetics Mt. Sinai Med. Ctr., NYC, 1984-86; fellow in neurology Mass. Gen. Hosp., Boston, 1986-90, asst. neurologist, 1990-95; asst. prof. dept. neurology Harvard Med. Sch., Boston, 1990-95; asst. prof. dept. neurology, pediat. and pathology U. Chgo., 1995—2000, clin. assoc. pediat. neurosurgery, 2000—, fellow McLean Ctr. for Clin. Med. Ethics, 2002—03, sr. fellow McLean Ctr. for Clin. Med. Ethics, 2003—04; program dir. genetics, transplantation and clin. rsch. AMA, Chgo., 1997—2002. Recipient Clin. Investigator Devel. award, NIH, 1988—93; fellow, Inst. Medicine, Chgo., 1999. Mem. AMA, Am. Acad. Neurology, Am. Soc. for Human Genetics, Am. Coll. Med. Genetics. Office: Pediat Neurosurgery U Chgo MC 4066 5481 S Maryland Ave Chicago IL 60637-4325 Office Phone: 773-702-2475. Business E-Mail: mpshort@surgery.bsd.uchicago.edu.

SHORT, MARTIN, actor, comedian, film critic; b. Hamilton, Ont, Canada, Mar. 26, 1950; s. Charles Patrick and Olive Short; m. Nancy Dolman, 1980; children: Katherine, Oliver, Henry. Degree in social work, McMaster U., 1972. Actor: (films) Three Amigos, 1986, Innerspace, 1987, Cross My Heart, 1987, Three Fugitives, 1989, The Big Picture, 1989, Pure Luck, 1991, Father of the Bride, 1991, Captain Ron, 1992, (voice) We're Back! A Dinosaur's Story, 1993, Clifford, 1994, (voice) The Pebble and the Penguin, 1995, Father of the Bride 2, 1995, Mars Attacks!, 1996, Jungle 2 Jungle, 1997, The Fairy Godmother, 1997, A Simple Wish, 1997, Mumford, 1998, Akbar's Adventure Tours, 1998, (voice) Prince of Egypt, 1998, Get Over It, 2001, (voice) Jimmy Neutron: Boy Genius, 2001, (voice) Treasure Planet, 2001, Cinemagique, 2002, (voice) Treasure Planet, 2002, The Santa Clause 3: The Escape Clause, 2006, The Spiderwick Chronicles, 2008; (TV series) The Associates, 1979, I'm a Big Girl Now, 1980-81, SCTV Network 90, 1982-84 (Emmy award for Outstanding Writing 1983), Saturday Night Live, 1985-86, (voice) The Completely Mental Misadventures of Ed Grimley, 1988-89, The Martin Short Show, 1994, (miniseries) Merlin, 1998; (TV films) The Family Man, 1979, Sunset Limousine, 1983, Alice in Wonderland, 1999, Prince Charming, 2001; writer (TV films) Martin Short's Concert for the North Americas, 1985, I, Martin Short Goes Hollywood, 1989, (TV series) Second City TV, 1981, SCTV Network 90, 1981-82, SCTV Channel, 1983, Saturday Night Live, 1984-85; exec. prodr. (TV series) The Martin Short Show, 1994, 99, Primetime Glick, 2001-03; writer, prodr. (TV films) Martin Short Shorts, 2003; dir. (TV films) Friends of Gilda, 1993; actor, writer, prodr. (films) Jiminy Glick in La La Wood, 2004; also numerous revues and cabaret appearances with Second City comedy troupe; 1977-78, Broadway appearances include The Goodbye Girl, 1993, Little Me, 1999 (Tony award for Best Actor in a Musical); stage appearances Martin Short: Fame Becomes Me, 2006. Office: William Morris Agency care Ames Cushing 1 William Morris Pl Beverly Hills CA 90212-2775

SHORT, MICHAEL J., automotive executive; Grad., US Naval Acad., Annapolis, Md., 1982; MBA, Columbia U., NYC, 1991. Helicopter pilot, tactics instr. USN, Norfolk, Va.; various fin. positions Univeral Orlando, Joseph E. Seagram & Sons, Inc. and IBM Corp., 1992—2000; exec. v.p., CFO Universal City Devel. Ptnrs., Ltd., 2000—07, AutoNation, Inc., Ft. Lauderdale, Fla., 2007—. Office: AutoNation Inc 110 SE 6th St Fort Lauderdale FL 33301 Office Phone: 954-769-7000.

SHORT, STEVE EUGENE, engineer; b. Crockett, Calif., Oct. 17, 1938; s. Roger Milton and Ida Mae (Mills) S.; m. Yumie Sedaka, Feb. 2, 1962; children: Anne Yumie, Justine Yumie, Katherine Yumie. BS in Gen. Engring. with honors, U. Hawaii, 1972, MBA, 1973; MS in Meteorology, U. Md., 1980. Registered profl. engr., Hawaii. With Nat. Weather Svc., NOAA, 1964—; pres. Short & Assocs., Inc., 1994—. Govt. exec. Silver Spring, Md., 1974-81, program mgr. ASOS,1981—, transition dir. 1991—; ind. tech. cons., 1994—; pres. Short & Assocs., Inc.; cons. engring. and mgmt.; cons. SBA. Contbr. articles to profl. jours. With USMC, 1956-60. Recipient Gold Medal award U.S. Dept. Commerce, 1992, Presdl. Meritorious Exec. award, 1992. Mem. VFW, Am. Meteorol. Soc., Japan-Am. Soc., Am. Soc. Pub. Adminstrn. Office: 3307 Rolling Rd Chevy Chase MD 20815-4033 E-mail: sshort@compuserve.com.

SHORTAL, TERENCE MICHAEL, retired systems company executive; b. St. Louis, Oct. 13, 1937; s. Harold Leo and Catherine Margaret S.; m. Linda Margaret Elias, May 29, 1965; children: Jennifer, Bradley Alexander. BSEE, U. Mo., 1961; MS, U.S. Naval Postgrad. Sch., 1966; grad. program execs., Carnegie Mellon U., 1979. Commd. ensign USN, 1961, advanced through grades to capt., 1980, asst. officer in charge Engring. Duty Officer Sch. Vallejo, Calif., 1974-77, ship engring. mgr. AEGIS shipbldg. project Naval Ea. Sys. Command Washington, 1977-79, tech. dir. DDGX project, 1979-81, ret., 1981; sr. v.p., dir. Kastle Sys., LLC, 1981—2006. Trustee Cathedral Choral Soc., Washington, 1983-95, 1997-2006, pres., 1986-88, 2000-2002; mem. vestry St. John's Episcopal Ch., McLean, Va., 1982-85; bd. dirs. Langley Sch., McLean, 1984-94, pres. 1986-88. Decorated Meritorious Svc. medal (2), Navy Commendation medal (2); recipient award of merit Cathedral Choral Soc., 1996. Mem. IEEE (life, br. award 1961), Nat. Press Club (Washington),Gridiron Club (Washington), Sigma Xi, Phi Kappa Theta, Order St. John. Republican. Episcopalian. Home: 858 Canal Dr Mc Lean VA 22102-1408 Personal E-mail: mshortal@verizon.net.

SHORTELL, CYNTHIA K., vascular surgeon; b. NYC, Feb. 17, 1958; d. Alfred Keene and Sylvia Rachlin S.; m. Bruce Theodore Peyser; children: Christopher, Caroline, Timothy. AB, Dartmouth Coll., 1980; MD, Cornell U., 1984. Diplomate in Am. Bd. Surgery. Resident, fellow U. Rochester, N.Y., 1984-93, vascular surgeon N.Y., 1993—. Mem. vascular subcom. Blue Choice, Rochester, 1996—. Contbg. author textbooks in field, 1997; contbr. articles to profl. jours. Mem. Am. Coll. Surgeons, Peripheral Vascular Surgery Soc., Am. Women's Surgeons. Republican. Roman Catholic. Avocations: skiing, tennis, reading. Office: Univ Rochester 601 Elmwood Ave Rochester NY 14642-0001 E-mail: cynthia_shortell@urmc.rochester.edu.

SHORTER, JAMES RUSSELL, JR., lawyer; b. NYC, June 10, 1946; s. James Russell and Helen (Ibert) S. AB, Columbia Coll., 1968; JD, Harvard U., 1975; LLM in Taxation, NYU, 1979. Bar: NY 1976, US Dist. Ct. (so. and ea. dists.) NY 1976, US Tax Ct. 1987. Assoc. Thacher Proffitt & Wood, NYC, 1975-84, ptnr., 1984—2008. Capt. USNR, 1968-98. Mem. ABA (tax, bus. law sect.), N.Y. State Bar Assn. (internat. law and practice sect.), Assn. Bar City N.Y., Internat. Fiscal Assn., Harvard Club (N.Y.C.), Down Town Assn. (N.Y.C). Republican. Office: Two World Financial Ctr 26th Fl New York NY 10281 Home Phone: 212-628-4206. Business E-Mail: jshorter@shorterlaw.net.

SHORTER, WALTER WYATT, paper company executive; b. 1932; married. BS in Chemistry, Va. Mil. Inst., 1953; MS in Pulp and Paper Tech., U. Maine, 1957. With Union Camp Corp., 1957—58, v.p. resident mgr., 1978; pres. MacMillan Bloedel Inc., Pine Hill, Ala., 1978—; sr. v.p. container bd. and packaging MacMillan Bloedel Ltd., 1989—, also bd. dirs. Bd. dirs. First Ala. Bank Montgomery, First Ala. Bancshares, Inc., Jenkins Brick Co., U.K. Corrugated Ltd. Mem. Gov.'s Agrl. Emphasis Com., Ala.; treas. Leadership Ala.; trustee Huntingdon Coll., Inst. Paper Sci. and Tech.; past chmn. Ala. Alliance Bus. and Industry. Capt. USMC, 1953—58. Mem.: Ala. Coun. Econ. Edn., Am. Paper Inst. (bd. dirs.), Bus. Coun. Ala. (bd. dirs.), Paper Industry Mgmt. Assn. (past pres., trustee, chmn. bd. trustees).

SHORTLIFFE, EDWARD HANCE, internist, medical educator, computer scientist; b. Edmonton, Alta., Can., Aug. 28, 1947; s. Ernest Carl and Elizabeth Joan Shortliffe. AB, Harvard U., 1970; PhD, Stanford U., 1975, MD, 1976. Diplomate Am. Bd. Internal Medicine. Trainee NIH, 1971—76; intern Mass. Gen. Hosp., Boston, 1976—77; resident Stanford Hosp., Palo Alto, Calif., 1977—79; asst. prof. medicine Stanford U. Sch. Medicine, Palo Alto, 1979—85, assoc. prof., 1985—90, chief divsn. gen. internal medicine, 1988—95, prof., 1990—2000; assoc. chair medicine Primary Care, 1993—95; assoc. dean info. resources and tech. Stanford U. Sch. Medicine, 1995—2000; prof., chair dept. biomed. informatics Columbia U. Coll. Physicians and Surgeons, NYC, 2000—07, Rolf H. Scholdager prof. biomed. informatics, 2005—07; deputy v.p. Info. Tech., Health Scis., Columbia U., NYC, 2002—07; founding dean U. Ariz. Coll. Medicine, Phoenix, 2007—08, prof. basic med. scis., prof. medicine, 2007—09; prof. biomed. informatics Ariz. State U., 2007—09, U. Tex. Houston, 2009—; pres., CEO Am. Med. Informatics Assn., Bethesda, Md., 2009—. Advisor Nat. Bd. Med. Examiners, Phila., 1987—93; pres. Symposium on Computer Applications in Med. Care, Washington, 1988—89; mem. Nat. Fed. Networking Adv. Coun., NSF, 1991—93; mem. computer sci. and telecomm. bd. NRC, 1991—96; bd. regents ACP, 1996—2002; mem. Pres.'s Info. Tech. Adv. Com., 1997—2002; chmn. com. on healthcare and next generation internet NRC, 1998—2000; mem. Nat. Com. on Vital Health Stats., 2000—03; trustee N.Y. Acad. Medicine, 2005—; bd. dirs. Medco Health Solutions, Inc., 2003—07. Editor: Rule-Based Expert Systems, 1984, Readings in Medical Artificial Intelligence, 1984, Medical Informatics: Computer Applications in Health Care, 1990, Medical Informatics: Computer Applications in Health Care and Biomedicine, 2d edit., 2000, Biomedical Informatics, 3d edit., 2006. Com. sci. engring. and pub. policy NAS, 2001—03, 2005—07. Recipient Grace M. Hopper award, Assn. Computing Machinery, 1976, Young Investigator award, Western Soc. Clin. Investigation, 1987, Rsch. Career award, Nat. Libr. of Medicine, 1979—84; scholar, Kaiser Family Found., 1983—88. Fellow: Am. Coll. Med. Informatics (pres. 1992—94), Am. Assn. Artificial Intelligence; mem.: Am. Clin. and Climatol. Assn., Assn. Am. Physicians, Am. Med. Informatics Assn., Am. Soc. for Clin. Investigation, Inst. Medicine (mem. coun. 2000—03, 2005—07), Soc. for Med. Decisionmaking (pres. 1989—90). Achievements include development of several medical computer programs including MYCIN and ONCOCIN. Avocations: skiing, jazz. Office: Am Med Informatics Assn 4915 St Elmo Ave Ste 401 Bethesda MD 20814-6052 Office Phone: 301-657-1291. Business E-Mail: shortliffe@amia.org.

SHORTLIFFE, LINDA MARIE DAIRIKI, urology educator, researcher; b. Boston, Feb. 28, 1949; d. Setsuo and Norma Masako (Yoshida) Dairiki; children: Lindsay Ann, Lauren Leigh. AB in Hist. and Sci., Harvard U., 1971; MD, Stanford U. Sch. Medicine, Calif., 1975. Diplomate Am. Bd. Urology. Resident gen. surgery Tufts-New Eng. Med. Ctr., Boston, 1976-77; intern Stanford U. Med. Ctr., 1975-76, resident urology, 1977-81, chief pediat. urology, 1991—, chair dept. urology, 1995—; asst. prof. surgery urology Stanford U. Sch. Medicine, 1981-88, assoc. prof., 1988-93, prof., 1993—. Com. mem. spl. grants Nat. Inst. Diabetes, Digestive and Kidney Diseases, Bethesda, Md., 1990—94; pres. elect, trustee Am. Bd. Urology, 2001—07; pres. Soc. Univ. Urologists, 2004—05; bd. dirs. VIVUS, Inc., 1999—; dir. Am. Found. Urol. Disease, Balt., 2004—. Contbr. articles to profl. jours. Named one of Best Dr.'s in America, Woodward and White, Inc., America's Top Dr.'s, Castle Connolly Med. LTD; named to Nat. Libr. Med. Fellow: ACS, Am. Acad. Pediat. (chair-elect urology sect. 2007—08); mem.: Soc. Pediat. Urology, Am. Urol. Assn. Office: Stanford U Med Ctr Dept Urology 300 Pasteur Dr S287 Stanford CA 94305-5118 Office Phone: 650-498-5042. Business E-Mail: lindas@stanford.edu.*

SHORTZ, RICHARD ALAN, lawyer; b. Chgo., Mar. 11, 1945; s. Lyle A. and Wilma Warner (Wildes) S.; m. Jennifer A. Harrell; children: Eric, Heidi. BS, Ind. U., 1967; JD, Harvard U., 1970. Bar: Calif. 1971, U.S. Supreme Ct. 1980. Assoc. Gibson, Dunn & Crutcher, LA, 1970-73; sr. v.p., gen. counsel, sec. Tosco Corp., LA, 1973-83; ptnr. Jones, Day, Reavis & Pogue, LA, 1983-95, Rogers & Wells, LA, 1995-97, Morgan Lewis & Bockius, LA, 1997—. Mem. L.A. World Affairs Inst., 1983—, Town Hall L.A., 1983—. 2nd lt. US Army, 1970—71. Mem.: Calif. Bar Assn., L.A. Bar. Assn., ABA, Valley Club (Santa Barbara, Calif.), Merion Golf Club (Ardmore, Pa.), Loch Lomond Golf Club (Scotland), L.A. Country Club (Bd. Dir.), Beach Club (Santa Monica, Calif.), Calif. Club. Republican. Episcopalian. Home: 1343 Pavia Pl Pacific Palisades CA 90272-4047 Office: Morgan Lewis & Bockius 300 S Grand Ave Ste 2200 Los Angeles CA 90071-3132 Office Phone: 213-612-2526. Office Fax: 213-612-2501. Business E-Mail: rshortz@morganlewis.com.

SHORTZ, WILL, puzzle editor; b. Crawfordsville, Ind., Aug. 26, 1952; s. Lyle A. and Wilma Warner (Wildes) S. AB, Ind. U., 1974; JD, U. Va., 1977. Editor Penny Press, Stamford, Conn., 1977-78; assoc. editor Games Mag., NYC, 1978-82, sr. editor, 1982-89, editor, 1989-93; crossword editor New York Times, NYC, 1993—; dir. Sudoku Nat. Championship Phila., 2007—. Founder, dir. Am. Crossword Puzzle Tournament, Stamford, Conn., 1978-2007, Bklyn., 2008-, World Puzzle Championship, N.Y.C., 1992, Stamford, 2000; puzzlemaster Weekend Edit. Sunday, NPR, Washington, 1987—; U.S. team capt. Internat. Crossword Marathon, 1989-90, World Puzzle Championship, 1993-99; riddle writer Batman Forever, 1995; co-founder, chmn. World Puzzle Fedn., 1999-2004, treas. 2004-; puzzle contb. Reader's Digest, 2002-07. Author: Brain Games, 1979, The American Quiz Book, 1979, Brain Games 2, 1980, The Bantam Great Masters Winning Crossword Puzzles, vol. 1-3, 1980, World Class Championship Crosswords, 1982, Brain Games 3, 1983, Games Mag. Book of Crossword Puzzles, 1985, American Championship Crosswords, 1990, Games Mag. Giant Book of Games, 1991, Will Shortz's Best Brain Busters, 1991, Games Mag. Best Pencil Puzzles, 1992, Brain Twisters from the First World Puzzle Championships, 1993, NY Times Daily Crossword Puzzles, vol. 40-72, 1995-2006, The Puzzlemaster Presents, 1996, vol. 2, 2004, Will Shortz's Tournament Crosswords, 1997, NY Times Sunday Crossword Puzzles, vol. 24-32, 1992-2006, Will Shortz's Favorite Crossword Puzzles, 2002, Will Shortz's Tournament Crosswords, vol. 2, 2005, Sudoku-100 Wordless Crossword Puzzles, vol. 1-3, 2005, Mind Games: 100 Alphabet Riddles, 2008. Named Wordplay documentary subject, 2006. Mem. Am. Antiquarian Soc., Am. Cryptogram Assn., Authors Guild, Nat. Puzzlers' League (pres. 1977, 81, historian 1992—). Avocations: ping pong/table tennis, book collecting. Office: New York TImes 620 8th Ave New York NY 10018-1405 Office Phone: 212-556-7435.

SHOSS, CYNTHIA RENÉE, lawyer; b. Cape Girardeau, Mo., Nov. 29, 1950; d. Milton and Carol Jane (Duncan) S.; m. David Goodwin Watson, Apr. 13, 1986; 1 child, Lucy J. Watson. BA cum laude, Tulane U., 1971, JD, 1974; LLM in Taxation, NYU, 1980. Bar: La. 1974, Mo. 1977, Ill. 1978, N.Y. 1990. Law clk. to assoc. and chief justices La. Supreme Ct., New Orleans, 1974-76; assoc. Stone, Pigman et al, New Orleans, 1976-77, Lewis & Rice, St. Louis, 1977-79, Curtis, Mallet-Prevost, et al, NYC, 1980-82; ptnr. LeBoeuf L.L.P., NYC, 1986—; mng. ptnr. London office LeBoeuf, Lamb, Leiby & MacRae, 1987-89. Assoc. editor Tulane Law Rev., 1972-74; frequent speaker before profl. orgns. and assns. Contbr. articles to profl. jours. Mem. bd. overseers Sch. Risk Mgmt., Ins. and Actuarial Sci., St. John's U. Mem.: Internat. Ins. Soc., The Risk Found. (bd. dirs.), Assn. Life Ins. Counsel (bd. govs.). Office: Dewey & LeBoeuf 1301 Avenue of Americas New York NY 10019-6092 Office Phone: 212-259-8129. Business E-Mail: cshoss@dl.com.

SHOSTAK, LINDA E., lawyer; b. May 9, 1948; BA, Vassar Coll., 1970; JD, Harvard U., 1973. Bar: NY 1974, Calif. 1975. Lawyer Morrison & Foerster, San Francisco, 1974, ptnr., 1979—. Lectr. CEB, Rutter Grp.; taught (advanced pro. of trial advocacy) Nat. Inst. of Trial Advocacy; spkr. in field. Mem. Phi Beta Kappa. Office: Morrison & Foerster 425 Market St San Francisco CA 94105 Office Phone: 415-268-7202. Office Fax: 415-268-7522. Business E-Mail: lshostak@mofo.com.

SHOSTAK, S. RICHARD, lawyer; b. Omaha, July 16, 1931; s. Max Reubin and Reva Ruth (Gross) S.; m. Carole Ruth Blumenthal; children: Stuart Robert, Dennis Alan, Cynthia Robin. AB, U. Calif., Berkeley, 1951, BA, 1953, JD, 1956. Bar: Calif. 1956, U.S. Dist. Ct. (so. and cen. dists.) 1956, U.S. Ct. Appeals (9th cir.), U.S. Supreme Ct. 1960, U.S. Ct. Appeals (fed. cir.) 1960, D.C. 1980, U.S. Ct. Internat. Trade 1981. Assoc. Geary, Spridgen & Moskowitz, Santa Rosa, Calif., 1956-58; dep. dist. atty. Sonoma County Dist. Atty., Santa Rosa, 1958-59; ptnr. Stein and Shostak, LA, 1960-76; v.p. Stein, Shostak, Shostak & O'Hara, Washington, San Diego, 1976—2005, Stein, Shostak, Shostak Pollock and O'Hara LLP; ptnr. Stein, Shostak, Shostak & O'Hara, Washington, San Diego, LA, Shanghai, 2005—. Hearing examiner City of L.A. Police Commn., 1964-79; lectr. UCLA Ext., 1975-92. Author: U.S. Customs Laws and Regulations, 1978, 79, 80; contbr. articles to profl. jours. Chmn. World Trade Week, L.A., 1976; sec. Com. for 807, Washington, 1980-88, Com. for Prodn. Sharing, Washington, 1989-92. Mem. ABA, Wilshire Bar Assn., Fgn. Trade Assn. So. Calif. (pres., chmn. bd. 1976-78), L.A. C. of C. Avocation: golf. Home: 4211 Clear Valley Dr Encino CA 91436-3315 Office: Stein Shostak Shostak Pollack and O'Hara 865 S Figueroa St Ste 1388 Los Angeles CA 90071-3329 Home Phone: 818-784-2757; Office Phone: 213-630-8888. Office Fax: 213-630-8890. E-mail: dshostak@steinshostak.com.

SHOTWELL, MALCOLM GREEN, minister; b. Brookneal, Va., Aug. 14, 1932; s. John Henry and Ada Mildred (Puckett) S.; m. LaVerne Brown, June 19, 1954; children: Donna (dec.), Paula. BA in Sociology, U. Richmond, 1954; MDiv, Colgate Rochester Div. Sch., 1957; D Ministry, Ea. Bapt. Theol. Sem., 1990; DD (hon.), Judson Coll., 1990. Ordained to ministry Am. Bapt. Ch. in U.S.A., 1957. Student asst. Greece Bapt. Ch., Rochester, NY, 1954-57; pastor 1st Bapt. Ch., Cuba, NY, 1957-62, sr. pastor Galesburg, Ill., 1962-71, Olean, NY, 1971-81; area minister Am. Bapt. Chs. of Pa. and Del., 1981-90; regional exec. minister Am. Bapt. Chs. of Great Rivers Region, Ill. and Mo., 1990-96; interim pastor First Bapt. Ch., Jacksonville, Ill., 2002, Galesburg, Ill., 2003, Decatur, Ill., 2005—06. Mem. Midwest Commn. on Ministry Am. Bapt. Chs. U.S.A., 1990—96, mem. task force for So. Bapt. Am. Bapt. Chs. Relationships, 1990—96; cons. for ch. growth and planning. Author: Creative Programs for the Church Year, 1986, Renewing the Baptist Principle of Associations, 1990; contbg. writer Baptists in the Balance, 1997; rschr., writer, performer: (dramatic monologue) Our Neighbors, the Lincolns: A Clergyman Remembers, 1999—. Trustee No. Bapt. Theol. Sem., Lombard, Ill., 1993-96; mem. gen. exec. coun., 1990-96, regional exec. ministers coun., 1990-96; trustee Judson Coll., 1990-2003, trustee emeritus, 2003-, chmn., 1997-00, chmn. presdl. search com., 1997-98; bd. dirs. Ctrl. Bapt. Theol. Sem., Kansas City, Kans., 1990-96, Old State Capitol Found., 2004-; sec. bd. dirs. Shurtleff Fund, Springfield, Ill., 1990-96; tchr., libr. Ctrl. Bapt. Ch., Springfield, 1997-05; mem. Hist. Commn. Am. Bapts. Ill. and Mo., 1998-02; retreat leader in stress mgmt., 1985—; conf., spkr., pulpit supply preacher Bapt. Ch.; mentor ILES Elem. Sch., Old State Capital Reenactment of Lincoln-Douglas Debates, 1999-01, 03-08; tour guide Old State Capital, Springfield, 2003—, Abraham Lincoln Presdl. Libr. and Mus., 2005-. Recipient George Younge Biennal award The Am. Bapt. Hist. Soc., 2006; Walter Pope Binns fellow William Jewell Coll., 1995. Mem. Ministers Coun. Ill. and Mo., Coun. Ret. Execs., Abraham Lincoln Assn., Am. Bapt. Men of Ill. and Mo. (v.p., coord. disaster relief ministries, Man of Yr., 2009).

SHOU, SHARON LOUISE WIKOFF, vocational rehabilitation counselor; b. Mpls., Oct. 23, 1946; d. Wallace S. and Phyllis Wikoff; m. James Kouping Shou, Dec. 27, 1969 (dec. June 4, 1989); children: Michelle, Darren. Student, U. Colo., 1971-72, Chinese U. Hong Kong, 1966-67; BA, Macalester Coll., 1968; MA, U. Denver, 1975. Cert. vocat. rehab. counselor, case manager, employment counselor; lic. clin. profl. counselor. Employment counselor Colo. Dept. of Employment, Denver, 1971-74; acad. advisor U. Ky., Lexington, 1978-81; employment advisor DeVry Inst. Tech., Lombard, Ill., 1985-86; trainee asst. specialist County of DuPage, Wheaton, Ill., 1987; sr. rehab. case mgr. CRA Managed Care (Comprehensive Rehab. Assoc.), Boston, 1987-97; rehab. specialist EVR, Batavia, Ill., 1997—2000; sr. vocat. rehab. counselor Unum, 2000—. Vocat. rehab. expert witness. Fellow: Am. Bd. Vocat. Experts; mem. AAUW (internat. rels. com. 1983), Naperville (Ill.) Chinese Assn. (adminstrv. com. 1984), Internat. Assn. Rehab. Profls. in the Pvt. Sector. Office: Unum 655 North Central Ave Ste 900 Glendale CA 91203

SHOUL, MELVIN I., retired surgeon; b. Newburyport, Mass., 1922; MD, Tufts U., 1947. Diplomate Am. Bd. Surgery. Intern Boston City Hosp., 1947-49, resident in surgery, 1949-52; chief gen. surgery Murphy Army Hosp., 1954; pvt. practice surgery, 1954—94; clin. instr. surgery Harvard Med. Sch., 1954—94; ret., 1994. Contbr. articles to profl. jours. With US Army, 1953—54, Korea. Fellow ACS; mem. AMA, Boston Surg. Soc. Personal E-mail: melvinshoul@comcast.net.

SHOULDERS, PATRICK ALAN, lawyer, educator; b. Mar. 26, 1953; m. Lisa Shoulders; children: Samantha Bucur, Andrew. BA in English, Ind. U., Bloomington, 1975; JD magna cum laude, Ind. U., Indpls., 1978. Bar: Ind. 1978, US Dist. Ct. (so. dist.) Ind. 1978, US Ct. Appeals (7th cir.) 1979, US Supreme Ct. 1985, Ky. 1986, US Dist. Ct. (we dist.) Ky. 1987, US Ct. Appeals (6th cir.) 1997. Assoc. Kahn, Dees, Donovan & Kahn, Evansville, Ind., 1978—81, ptnr., 1981—87, Ziemer, Stayman, Weitzel & Shoulders, Evansville, 1987—. Mem. local rules advisory com. US Dist. Ct. (so. dist.) Ind., mem. Civil Justice Reform Act adv. com.; treas., dir. Vanderburgh County Work Release Jobs Program, Inc., 1983—85; mem. Vanderburgh County Pub. Defender Commn., 2000—; pres. Vanderburgh Law Libr. Found., 1983—84. Co-host (public affairs program) Shively & Shoulders WNIN-TV. Judge nat. finals We The People...The Citizen and the Constitution Competition, Washington, 1997—99; past pres. Ind. U. Coll. Arts and Scis. Alumni Bd., Woodburn Guild; gen. chmn. TV auction WNIN Pub. TV, Evansville, 1985; founder Arts Fest River Run, Evansville, 1987; spkr. law-related edn. Evansville-Vanderburgh Sch. Corp.; chmn. Evansville Bill of Rights Bicentennial Celebration, 1991; mem. Evansville Conv. and Visitors Bur., 1993—96; mem. judges panel Entrepreneur of Yr. Awards INC mag., Evansville, 1993; treas. Ind. Equal Justice Fund, 1996—97; trustee Ind. U., 2002—; mem. Bd. Park Commrs. City of Evansville, 1984—87, Ind. State Recount Commn., 1992, Evansville-Vandeburgh County Unification Study Com., 2005; dir. Well House Soc.; mem. alumni bd. Ind. U. Law Sch. Indpls.; mem. med.-ethics com. St. Mary's Med. Ctr., Evansville, 1980—2002, mem. instnl. rev. bd., 1980—2003; pres. bd. dir. Evansville Parks Found., 1982, 1983; bd. dir. Arts Fest River Run, Evansville, 1987—2001; pres. bd. dir. YMCA Southwestern Ind., Inc., Evansville, 1990—94, Evansville Mus. Arts and Scis., 1991—92; bd. dir. Acodia Bus. Benefits Evansville, Inc., 1992—97; dir. Ind. U. Found., 2002—, Ind. U. Ctr. on Philanthropy, 2002. Recipient William L. Brooks Hospitality award, Evansville Conv. and Visitors Ctr., 1996, Roast in Honor of Patrick Shoulders, Albion Fellows Bacon Ctr., 1996, Maynard K. Hine Outstanding Alumni medal, Ind. U. - Purdue U. Indpls., 2005, Herman B. Wells Leadership award, Sigma Nu, 2005, Disting. Citizen award, Ind. Social Studies Tchr.'s Assn., 2001; named Boss of Yr., Evansville Legal Sec. Assn., 1988, Vol. of Yr., Evansville YMCA, 1989, Vol. Action Ctr., 1989, Evansville Arts Ctr., 1990; named a Sagamore of Wabash, Gov. Evan Bayh, 1996; named one of Top 50 Super Lawyers, Indpls. Monthly, 2005, 2006; named to William Henry Harrison HS Hall of Fame, 1996. Fellow: Am. Bar Found., Ind. Bar Found (chmn. fellows Ind. Bar Found. 1996, Pres.'s award 2000, master fellow), Am. Coll. Trial Lawyers; mem.: ABA (mem. trial practice com. litigation sect.), Ind. Trial Advocacy Coll. (co-chair 1996—), 7th Cir. Bar Assn., Am. Bd. Trial Advocates (assoc.), Ky. Bar Assn., Ind. State Bar Assn. (chmn. spring meeting 1991, chmn. litigation sect. 1991—92, mem. BAR-PAC bd. trustees 1991—95, chmn. legal edn. com. 1996—2000, coun. mem. appellate practice sect. 1997—98, mem. bd. govs. 1998—2000, mem. house del., Presidl. citation 2000), Evansville Bar Assn. (pres. 1985—86, James Bethel Gresham Freedom award 1993), Fedn. Ins. and Corporate Counsel, Friends of Kinsey Inst., Ind. U. Alumni Assn. (pres. 2000—01, chmn. 2000—01), Hoosier Hundred, Golden Key, Ky. Col. Office: Ziemer Stayman Weitzel & Shoulders 20 NW 1st St PO Box 916 Evansville IN 47706

SHOULSON, IRA, neurologist, pharmacologist, educator; b. Erie, Pa., Apr. 4, 1946; BA, U. Pa., 1967; MD, U. Rochester, 1971. Cert. Internal Medicine, 1974, Neurology, 1980. Intern in internal medicine Strong Meml. Hosp., Rochester, NY, 1971—72, resident in neurology, 1972—73, 1975—77; fellow NIH, Bethesda, Md., 1973—75; mem. faculty U. Rochester Med. Ctr., 1977—, prof. neurology, prof. pharmacology and physiology, Louis C. Lasagna prof. in exptl. therapeutics, 2004—; founder Parkinson Study Group, 1985, Huntington Study Group, 1994. Mem.: Inst. Medicine, Movement Disorder Soc. (hon.), Alpha Omega Alpha. Office: U Rochester Sch Medicine and Dentistry 601 Elmwood Ave Box 673 Rochester NY 14642*

SHOUP, ANDREW JAMES, JR., retired oil industry executive; b. Monroe, La., Mar. 26, 1935; s. Andrew James Sr. and Ruth (Landis) S.; m. Sue Cowles, Sept. 12, 1959 (dec. May 1998); children: Catherine Shoup Collins, Andrew James III; m. Julia Conger Galloway, May 6, 2000. BS in Petroleum Engring., La. State U., 1957; M in Indsl. Adminstrn., Yale U., 1959. Registered engr., Tex. Prodn. engr. Continental Oil Co., Houston, 1959-65; v.p. DeGolyer and MacNaughton, Dallas, 1965-74; chmn., CEO Sabine Corp., Dallas, 1974-89; pres. Pacific Enterprises Oil Co. U.S.A, Dallas, 1989-90; pres., CEO The Wiser Oil Co., Dallas, 1991-2000; ret., 2000. 2nd lt. U.S. Army, 1959-60. Mem. Soc. Petroleum Engrs. of AIME, Dallas Petroleum Club, Dallas Country Club. Avocations: skiing, golf.

SHOUP, CHARLES SAMUEL, JR., chemicals and materials executive; b. Nashville, Dec. 10, 1935; s. Charles Samuel and Leola Ruth (Turner) S.; m. Frances Carolyn DiCarlo, June 7, 1958 (dec. Apr. 1999); children: Mark Steven, Elizabeth Ann Shoup Kehoe, Margaret Carol Shoup Meyer; m. Sara Jo Denkmann, May 5, 2001. AB, Princeton U., 1957; MS, U. Tenn., 1961, PhD, 1962. Rsch. chemist Oak Ridge (Tenn.) Natl. Lab., 1962-67; mgr. special projects Union Carbide Corp., NYC, 1967-68; mgr. planning and controls Bell and Howell Co., Lincolnwood, Ill., 1968; v.p. Bell and Howell Sch. Inc., Chgo., 1968-69; mgr. tech. planning Cabot Corp., Boston and Billerica, Mass., 1969-70, dir. corp. rsch., Mass., 1970-73; gen. mgr. Aearo Corp., Westwood, Mass and Indpls., 1973-87; v.p., Indpls. Cabot Corp., Boston and Indpls., 1984-87; pres. Alphaflex Ind. Inc., Indpls, 1987-88, bd. dirs., 1988, Cemkote Corp., Indpls., 1988-91. Chmn. bd. dirs. Blasterz Corp., Carmel, Ind., 1992-2001; mem. adv. bd. Technalysis, Inc., Indpls., 1996-99; bd. dirs. Exec. Svc. Corps, Indpls., 1993—2004, mem. exec. com., 1994-2003, vice chmn., sec., 1997-99, chmn. bd. dirs., 2001-03; mem. bd. visitors Coll. Arts and Scis., U. Tenn., Knoxville, 1994-2000, assoc. bd. visitors, 2000—; bd. dirs Nat. Exec. Svc. Corps, Ind., 2001-04. Contbr. articles to profl. jours. Treas. Oak Ridge Arts Ctr., 1965-67; pres. Sherborn Edn. Found., 1974-76; chmn. Met. Div. United Way, 1982; bd. trustees, Ind. Safety Equipment Assn. 1978-81. Fellow Am. Inst. Chemists; mem. AAAS, Am. Chem. Soc., Noise Control Products and Materials Assn. (trustee 1977-87, pres. 1982-84), Sigma Xi. Presbyterian. Home: 13045 Abraham Run Carmel IN 46033-8618

SHOUPE, DONNA, obstetrician-gynecologist, educator; b. Findlay, Ohio, Mar. 22, 1949; d. Thomas and Wendene (Wilson) S. BS, U. Ky., 1971, MIT, 1974; MD, Ohio U., 1977. Diplomate Am. Coll. Gyn-Ob. Intern, resident U. Southern Calif. Med. Ctr., LA, 1978-81, fellow reproductive endocrinology, 1981-83; staff physician Womnen's Hosp., LA, 1983—. Sect. chief U. So. Calif. U. Hosp. Mem. Am. Coll. of Ob-Gyns., Am. Fertility Soc., Soc. for Gynecol. Investigation, Pacific Coast Fertility Soc.

SHOUSE, AUGUST EDWARD, lawyer; b. Houston, Aug. 12, 1949; s. Earl Edward Shouse and Mary Ann (Myers) Carrico; m. Deborah Lee Symonds; children: William Bundy, Edwrd Booth, Tucker Clayton. BS, Stanford U., 1971; JD, U. Tex., 1974. Bar: Tex. 1974. From assoc. to ptnr. Vinson & Elkins, Houston, 1974—2004; pvt. practice Houston, 2004—. Bd. dirs. Greater Houston area chpt. ARC. Mem. Order of Coif, Phi Beta Kappa, Tau Beta Pi. Episcopalian. Office: 2001 Kirby Dr Ste 906 Houston TX 77019-6042 Business E-Mail: aes@aeshouse.com.

SHOUSE, PETER JOHN, soil scientist, researcher; b. Tacoma, Oct. 26, 1951; s. Robert Harold and Bette Lu Shouse; m. Maureen Richelle Dugan, Nov. 25, 1971; children: Andrew Gregory Daniel, Geoffrey Patrick. PhD, U. Calif., Riverside, 1979. Rsch. soil scientist USDA-ARS, Riverside, 1984—. Achievements include research in soil physical properties. Office: US Salinity Lab 450 W Big Springs Rd Riverside CA 92507 Office Fax: 951-342-4964. Business E-Mail: pete.shouse@ars.usda.gov.

SHOUSHTARI, AMIR H., research scientist; s. Hamid Shoushtari and Zahra Hosseini. PhD, U. Md., Coll. Pk., 2004. Rsch. assoc. U. Md., Coll. Pk., 2004—. Co-dir. Small & Smart Thermal Sys. Lab., U. Md., 2006—. Fellowship, U. Md., 1999—2001, grant-in-aid award, Am. Soc. Heating, Refrigerating & Air-Conditioning Engrs., 2003. Achievements include research in development of small-scale pumps. Office: Univ Md 2181 Glenn L Martin Hall College Park MD 20742 Office Fax: 301-405-5006.

SHOVER, JOAN, retired secondary school educator; b. St. Joseph, Mo., Apr. 7, 1948; d. Jay S. and Clara Lillian (Burkett) Marquis; m. Rolland Craig Shover, May 31, 1975; children: Terra Jayne, Thomas Jay. BS in Edn., Ctrl. Mo. State U., 1971, MS in Edn., 1976, postgrad., 1989-96. Cert. tchr., edn. specialist, Mo. Phys. edn. tchr. Worth County H.S., Grant City, Mo., 1971-73, Blue Springs (Mo.) H.S., 1973—2003, ret., 2003; health educator City of Independence Health Dept. Rev. com. Mo. Dept. Elem. and Secondary Edn., Jefferson City, 1993—; mem. Mo. Quality Health/Phys. Edn. Cadre, 1998—; health educator City of Independence Health Dept. Mem. Mo. Gov.'s Council for Fitness and Health, 2002—. Named Educator of Yr., Am. Cancer Soc., 1989, Top 36 Am. Tchrs. award, Disney Corp., 1992, Mo. State Secondary Physical Educator of Yr., 1996. Mem. Am. Coun. on Exercise, Internat. Dance Exercise Assn., Mo. Assn. Phys. Edn., Health, Recreation and Dance (Kansas City rep. 1988—, pres. elect 1998-99, pres. 1998-99, past pres. 1999-2000, Kansas City Dist. Phys. Educator award 1989, Presdl. award 1988), Mo. State Tchrs. Assn., Delta Kappa Gamma. Avocations: reading, dance, skiing, running. Office: 515 S Liberty Independence MO 64050 Home: 813 NW 12th St Blue Springs MO 64015 Business E-Mail: jshover@indepmo.org. E-mail: jshover50@aol.com.

SHOVKOVY, IGOR ANDRIYOVICH, physicist, researcher; s. Andiy Ivanovich Shovkovy and Lidiya Oleksiyivna Shovkova; m. Oksana Vasylivna Mikhalchenko, Aug. 2, 1971; 1 child, Sophia Igor. PhD, Bogolyubov Inst. Theoretical Physics, Kiev, Ukraine, 1997. Jr. rsch. fellow Bogolyubov Inst. for Theoretical Physics, Kiev, Ukraine, 1997—97; rsch. assoc. U. Cin., Cincinnati, 1997—2000, U. Minn., Minneapolis, 2000—02, J. W. Goethe U., Frankfurt am Main, Germany, 2002—04, 2002—. Rsch. assoc. J. W. Goethe U., Frankfurt am Main, Germany, 2002—04. Scholar V.N. Gribov scholar, Internat. Sch. of Subnuclear Physics, Italy, 1997; grant, Soros Found., 1993, 1995. Achievements include research in Gapless color superconducting phases. Office: Arizona State Univ Wanner 101L 6073 S Backus Mall Mesa AZ 85212 Personal E-mail: shovkovy@yahoo.com.

SHOWALTER, BETSY S., mathematics educator; b. Rockford, Ill., July 25, 1954; d. Donald James and Grace Lutz Curran; children: Thomas, David. BA in Math., U. Okla., Norman, 1976, MA in Math., 1978; PhD in Math. Edn., Okla. State U., Stillwater, 2005. Cert. secondary math. tchr., k-12 library media Okla. Math. tchr. Midwest City HS, Okla., 1978—80, Drumright HS, Okla., 1986—87, Stillwater HS, 1988—91; adj. math. instr. Okla. State U., 1980—86, 1991—93, Southwestern Okla. State U., Weatherford, 1987—88; instr. math. Langston U., Okla., 1993—. Mem.: Math. Assoc. Am., Okla. Coun. Tchrs. Math., Math. Assn. Am., Nat. Coun. Tchrs. Math., Phi Kappa Phi, Kappa Delta Pi. Home: 2402 W 8th Ave Stillwater OK 74074 Office: Langston U Math Dept 202A Jones Hall Langston OK 73050

SHOWALTER, DAVID SCOTT, teaching professor; b. Harrisonburg, Va., May 23, 1953; s. Harold Marvin and Martha (Myers) Showalter; m. Elizabeth Allison, June 1, 1974; children: Braxton, Allison, Mason. AS, Ferrum Coll., 1973; BSBA, U. Richmond, 1975. CPA Ill., 1994, Mo., 1997, Wis., 1995, Ind., 1988, NJ, 2003, NY, 2004; cert. govt. fin. mgr. 1994. Asst. to nat. industry dir. KPMG, NYC, 1981-84, asst. to vice-chmn., 1986-88, ptnr., 1986—, area ptnr. in charge, Indpls., 1993-96; nat. industry dir. state, local govts., Chgo., 1996-98; global mng. ptnr. Assurance & Adv. Svcs. Ctr., Montvale, NJ, 1998—2002, industry sector leader pub. sector, 2002—04, dept. profl. practice, risk mgmt., 2004—08; prof. NC State U., 2008—. Vis. prof. U. Ill.; vis. scholar Ind. U.; trustee KPMG Found., NYC, co-founder Audit Com. Inst., co-founder Assurance Rsch. Inst.; spkr. in field. Co-editor (newsletters) Govt. Acct. and Auditing Update, Current Issues in Auditing. Pres, Indpls. Youth Hockey Assn., 1990—93; pres. coun. Boy Scouts Am., St. Charles, Ill., 1995—97, chmn. bd. dirs., 1997—98, bd. dirs., 1998—; mem. U.S. C. of C. Homeland Security Task Force; bd. dirs. Greater Indpls. Rep. Fin. Com., 1990—94; elder 1st Presbyn. Ch., Ramsey, 2004—08. Recipient Silver Beaver Award, Boy Scouts Am, 1994, Dist Eagle Scout Award, 1998; named Ky Col, State of Ky, 1986, Sagamore of Wabash for Serv to State of Ind, 1990, D Scott Showalter Day named in his honor, City of Indianapolis, 1994; named one of Top 100 Most Influential in Acctg., Acctg. Today, 2001. Mem.: AICPA (mem. com.), Assn. Sch. Bus. Ofcls., Ill. CPA Soc., NJ CPA Soc., Am. Acctg. Assn. (v.p. practice, auditing sect., vice chmn. profl. rels. com., co-editor Current Issues in Auditing jour., chmn. Strategy Mgmt. Team, Outstanding Svc. award 2009), Govt. Fin. Officers Assn. (mem. com.). Presbyterian. Avocations: camping, jogging, backpacking, stamps. Home: 6605 Rest Haven Dr Raleigh NC 27612 Office: NC State Univ Dept Acctg Campus Box 8113 Raleigh NC 27695 Office Phone: 919-513-0526. Business E-Mail: scott_showalter@ncsu.edu.

SHOWALTER, MARK ROBERT, astronomer; b. Abington, Pa., Dec. 5, 1957; s. James Grove Showalter and Sandra Khuen-Kryk; life ptnr. Frank Yellin, June 10, 1990. BA, Oberlin Coll., Ohio, 1979; PhD, Cornell U., Ithaca, NY, 1984. Prin. investigator SETI Inst., Mountain View, Calif., 2005—. Mgr. Rings Node, NASA's Planetary Data Sys., Mountain View, 1989—2006. Mem.: Am. Astron. Soc., Phi Beta Kappa. Achievements include discovery of outer gossamer ring of Jupiter; Pan, 18th moon of Saturn; Mab, 26th moon of Uranus; Cupid, 27th moon of Uranus; mu and nu, outer rings of Uranus. Office: SETI Inst 515 N Whisman Rd Mountain View CA 94043 Office Phone: 650-961-6633. Business E-Mail: mshowalter@seti.org.

SHOWALTER, MICHAEL, marketing executive; Healthcare cons. Marsh & McLennan, Watson Wyatt, eBenX; with UnitedHealth Group; v.p. market solutions Definity Health; v.p. consumerism CIGNA Healthcare, Bloomfield, 2005; chief mktg. officer CIGNA Corp., Phila., 2007—. Founding bd. mem. Inst. Health Care Costs and Solutions Nat. Bus. Group on Health. Named one of Best Marketers, BtoB Mag., 2008. Office: CIGNA Corp 2 Liberty Pl 1601 Chestnut St Philadelphia PA 19192 also: CIGNA Corp 900 Cottage Grove Rd Bloomfield CT 06002*

SHOWALTER, SHIRLEY H., former academic administrator; b. July 30, 1948; BA cum laude in English, Ea. Mennonite U., Harrisonburg, Va., 1970; MA in Am. civilization, U. Tex., Austin, 1974, PhD in Am. civilization, 1981. Tchr. English Harrisonburg HS, Va., 1970—72; tchg. asst. English and Am. Studies depts. U. Tex., Austin, 1973—75, asst. instr. Am. Studies dept., 1976; dir. continuing edn. Goshen Coll., Ind., 1979—82, project dir. Title II tech. and liberal arts devel. grant, 1982—85, project dir. Consortium Advancemet of Pvt. Higher Edn. grant, 1985—86, asst. to prof. English, 1967—, pres., 1997—2004. Coord. Humanities program Harrisonburg (Va.) H.S., 1970—72; co-dir. Study-Svc. Term in Haiti Goshen Coll., 1981—82; rsch. asst. Consortium Advancement of Pvt. Higher Edn., Washington, 1986—87, interim v.p., 1987; chair English dept. Goshen Coll., 1990—93; sr. fellow Lilly Fellows program in Humanities and Arts Valparaiso U., Ind., 1993—94; co-dir. Study-Svc. Term in Ivory Coast Goshen Coll., 1993; lectr. and spkr. in humanities. Contbr. chapters to books, articles to profl. jours. Bd. mem. South Bend Symphony Assn.; mem. blue ribbon adv. group Boys and Girls Club; vice chair and mem. Hist. Com. of Mennonite Ch., 1984—88; co-sponsor Kid's Club No. Va. Mennonite Ch., 1987—88; chair curriculum com. Sojourner's Sunday Sch. class Coll. Mennonite Ch., 1987—88, mem. constn. revision com., 1988—92, tchr. H.S. age class, 1988—91, mem. worship commn., 1994—96; bd. mem. Coun. Christian Coll. and U., 2000—. Ind. Colls. of Ind., 1999—, Lantz Ctr. Christian Vocations, Indpls., 1998—; dir. Coun. Ind. Colls., 1999—; bd. dir. Mennonite Mutual Aid Trust; dir. Elkhart County Cmty. Found. Recipient Tchg. Excellence and Campus Leadership award, Sears Roebuck Found., 1990, Faculty Rsch., Goshen Coll., 1990, Knight Presdl. Leadership award, John S. and James L. Knight Found., 1999, 1999; grantee Faculty Rsch., Goshen Coll., 1977, 1982, Summer Stipend, Lilly Endowment, 1991; fellow, George H. Gallup Rsch. Inst., 1999—2000, Coolidge Fellow, Yale U., Assn. Religion in Intellectual Life, 1996. Mem.: AAUW, Am. Studies Assn., Am. Assn. Higher Edn. (Goshen Coll. rep. Forum on Exemplary Tchg. 1992, bd. dir. 1992—96), No. Ind. Partnership for the Arts, Willa Cather Pioneer Mem., Ind. Hist. Soc., Ellen Glasgow Soc., Blue Sky Assoc. Office: VP Programs Fetzer Inst 9292 West KL Ave Kalamazoo MI 49009-9398

SHOWERS JOHNSON, VIOLET MARY-ANN IYABO, history professor; b. Lagos, Nigeria; arrived in US, 1985, naturalized, 2002; d. Samuel Dandeson and Edna Taiwo Showers; m. Percy Ayomi Johnson; 1 child, Percy Ayomi Johnson, Jr. BA in History with honors, U. Sierra Leone, Freetown, 1979; MA, U. NB, Fredericton, NB, Canada, 1983; PhD, Boston Coll., Chestnut Hill, Mass., 1992. Lectr. dept. modern history Fourah Bay Coll., U. Sierra Leone, Freetown, 1983—85; history prof. Agnes Scott Coll., Decatur, Ga., 1992—, chair dept. history, 2001—, dir. African studies, 1995—2002. Proposals reviewer NEH Summer Seminars and Insts., 2000; grant screener Am. Coun. Learned Scholars, 2000—01; mem. scholars working group Atlanta Regional Consortium for Higher Edn. Civil Rights Virtual Libr. Project, 2001—03; external reviewer dept. history Spelman Coll., 2003. Author: The Other Black Bostonians: West Indians in Boston, 1900-1950, 2006; mem. editl. bd.: Jour. Am. Ethnic History; contbr. articles to profl. jours. Mem. African Am. initiatives bd. Atlanta History Ctr., 2001—05; applications reviewer, scholarship com. Atlanta Caribbean Assn., 2004; spkr. various events Auburn Ave. Rsch. Libr. on African-American Culture and History, Atlanta. Recipient Durham prize for the best result in the Faculty of Arts, Fourah Bay Coll., U. Sierra Leone, 1979, Vulcan Tchg. Excellence award, Vulcan Materials Co., 2002, Outstanding Woman award, Women Multi-Ethnicity and Nationality, 2004, Joseph R. Gladden Pub. Lecture award for noteworthy scholarship, Bd. Trustees, Agnes Scott Coll., 2005; grantee, NEH, 1998; Jr. Fulbright fellow, Fulbright Found., 1985—92. Mem.: Soc. for Multi-Ethnic Studies: Europe and the Americas, Forum for European Contbns. in African Am. Studies (mem. editl. bd.), Am. Hist. Assn., Assn. for the Study of African Am. Life and History, Immigration and Ethnic History Soc., Collegium African Am. Rsch. (exec. bd. mem.). Office: Agnes Scott College 141 East College Ave Decatur GA 30030 Office Fax: 404-471-6369; Home Fax: 404-471-6369. Business E-Mail: vjohnson@agnesscott.edu, vjohnson@agnesscout.edu.

SHPUZA, ERMAL, architecture educator; b. Shkoder, Albania, May 18, 1969; s. Jusuf and Shpresa Shpuza; m. Pegah Zamani, Sept. 30, 2003. Diploma in Arch., Poly. U. Tirana, 1992; MSc, U. Coll. London, Bartlett, 1995; PhD, Ga. Inst. Tech., Atlanta, 2006. Instr. Emory U., Atlanta, 2001—; asst. prof. Southern Poly. State U., Marietta, Ga., 2005—. Contbr. articles to profl. jours. Supplementary grant, Open Soc. Inst., 2002, scholarship, Albanian Govt., UN Devel. Program. Mem.: Albanian Assn. Archs., Internat. Soc. Arts, Math., & Architecture, Internat. Seminar Urban Form. Office: Southern Poly State Univ 1100 S Marietta Pkwy Marietta GA 30060 Office Fax: 678-915-7228. Personal E-mail: ermal@morphostudio.net.

SHR, MINGDR, research scientist; s. Tun Shih and Shiu-Mei Shih-chang; m. Yuchen Liao, June 19, 1995; children: Hsinyu Shih, Hsintung Shih. PhD, Nat. Chung Cheng U., Chia-Yi, 2006. Cert. in sr. civil svc. Taiwan Govt., 1995. Jr. tech. staff Chung Sang Inst. Sci. & Tech., Long-Tang, Taoyung, Taiwan, 1989—95; sr. tech. staff Taipei MCpt. Sung-Shan Vocat. Indsl. Agrl., Taiwan, 1996—97, Nat. Cheng Kung U., Tainan, Taiwan, 1997—99; engr. Taiwan Semiconductor Mfg. Co., Shan-Ha, Tainan, 1999—2003; vis. scholar & rsch. assoc. La. State U., Baton Rouge, 2003—05, postdoc. rschr., 2006—. Mem.: IEEE, ACM. Achievements include research in photo-lithography machine constraint in semiconductor manufacturing. Home: 3650 Nicholson Dr Apt 2169 Baton Rouge LA 70802 Office: La State Univ 298 Coates Hall Baton Rouge LA 70803 Business E-Mail: mshr1@lsu.edu.

SHRADER, CHARLES REGINALD, historian; b. Nashville, July 3, 1943; s. Reginald Woodrow and Freda Olene (Presley) S.; m. Carole Anne Analore, Aug. 17, 1963; children: Peter Reginald, Sheila Lynne Shrader Bixby. BA cum laude, Vanderbilt U., 1964; MA History, Columbia U., 1970, M Phil, 1974, PhD History, 1976; Grad., U.S. Army Command/Gen. Staff, Coll., 1978, U.S. Army War Coll., 1982, NATO Def. Coll., 1984. Commd. 2d lt. U.S. Army, 1964, advanced through grades to lt. col., ret., 1987; asst. prof. history U.S. Mil. Acad., 1971-74; instr. European Divsn. U. Md., Pirmasens and Landstuhl, Germany, 1974-77; instr. U.S. Army Command and Gen. Staff Coll., 1977-80, U.S. Army War Coll., 1980-84; mem. staff NATO Def. Coll., Rome, 1984-85; independent historian, 1987—; exec. dir. Soc. for Mil. History, Carlisle, Pa., 1992-2000. Pres. Nat. Coalition Ind. Scholars, 2000-2002; adj. instr. Elizabethtown Coll., 1988-89, Penn State U.-Harrisburg, 1988-90; lectr. various Army svc. schs., CIA, U. Kans., U. Victoria/B.C., NATO Def. Coll. Mem. Carlisle Mcpl. Authority, 1993-2003, Carlisle Zoning Hearing Bd, 2005-. Mem. Army and Navy Club, Phi Kappa Psi, Phi Beta Kappa. Roman Catholic. Home and Office: 910 Forbes Rd Carlisle PA 17013-1721 Home Phone: 727-249-5625; Office Phone: 717-249-5625. E-mail: heriger@embarqmail.com.

SHRADER, RALPH WILLIAM, consulting firm executive; b. Miami, Fla., Sept. 20, 1944; m. Janice Shrader, 1969. BS in Electrical Engring., U. Pa., 1966; MSEE in Math. & Nuc. Physics, U. Ill., PhD in Elec. Engring. Nat. dir. advanced systems planning Western Union; with Booz Allen & Hamilton, McLean, Va., 1974—78, v.p., 1978—94, pres. worldwide tech. divsn. Mc Lean, Va., 1994—99, chmn., CEO, 1999—. Bd. dirs. ServiceSource Network, 2004—. Bd. dirs. Wolf Trap Found. Nat. Park for Performing Arts, Abilities, Inc.; adv. coun. Character Edn. Partnership; chmn. The Neediest Kids, Inc., Light the Night Walks, Washington, 2004; bd. dirs. Abilities, Inc., ServiceSource, Va. Recipient David Sarnoff award, Armed Forces Communications & Electronics Assn., Cmty. Leadership award, Northern Va. Cmty. Found., 2001; co-recipient Emergence award, Dance Theatre Harlem, 2003. Office: Booz Allen & Hamilton Inc 8283 Greensboro Dr Mc Lean VA 22102 E-mail: shrader_ralph@bah.com.*

SHRADER-FRECHETTE, KRISTIN, science educator; m. Maurice Frechette; children: Danielle, Eric. B in Math. summa cum laude, Edgecliff Coll., Xavier U., 1967; PhD in Philosophy, U. Notre Dame, 1972. Asst. prof., philosophy Edgecliff Coll., 1971—73; prof., philosophy, natural sciences U. Louisville, 1973—82; prof., philosophy of sci., environ. studies U. Calif., Santa Barbara, 1982—84; prof., philosophy, natural sciences U. Fla., 1984—87; disting. rsch. prof., philosophy, environ. scis. U. So. Fla., 1987—98; O'Neill Family prof., dept. biol. sci. and dept. philosophy U. Notre Dame. Vis. philosopher Coun. on Philosophical Studies, 1980, 87; US NAS/NRC coun. del. Internat. Union Hist. & Phil. Sci., 1987; chair, internat. geosphere/biosphere program. Internat. Union Hist. & Phil. Sci. & Internat. Conf. Scientific Unions, 1988—91; chair, sci. and ethics com. Internat. Conf. Scientific Unions, 1990—96; mem. adv. bd. Tech., Risk, and Soc.: An Internat. Series in Risk Analysis, 1983—, Earth Ethics Rsch. Group, 1990—, Integration, Environ. Assessment and Environ. Indicators, EPA, 1992—, Planet Ctrl. TV Cable Network (environ. issues), 1993—, Vision for 2010, PBS TV series on the environment, 1993—, Ont. Soc. for Environ. Ethics, 1994—; panelist referee Nat. Endowment for the Humanities, 1979—, NSF, 1980—, EPA, Atmospheric Rsch. and Exposure Assessment, 1992—; mem. Blue Ribbon Panel US Dept. Energy Performance Evaluation of US Nuclear Facilities, 1994—96, US Dept. Energy Performance Evaluation of Sites for Mixed Nuclear Wastes, 1994—97; mem. adv. bd. Inst. Hydrology and Water Quality, 1995—; chair, sci. ethics com. 10th Congress of Logic, Methodology, Philosophy Sci., 1995; chair World Congress Philosophy Sect. on Philosophy and Tech., 1998; chair com. bioethics EPA, mem. sci. adv. bd., 2003—; prin. investigator grants NSF, Nat. Endowment for the Humanities, Coun. Philosophical Studies, U.S. Dept. Energy; dir., Ctr. for Environmental Justice and Children's Health U. Notre Dame; invited lectr. in field. Author: (books) Nuclear Power and Public Policy, 1983, Environmental Ethics, 1991, Four Methodological Assumptions in Cost Benefit Analysis, 1983, Science, Policy, Ethics, and Economic Methodology, 1984, Risk Analysis and Scientific Method, 1985, Nuclear Energy and Ethics, 1991, Risk and Rationality, 1991, Burying Uncertainty: Risk and the Case Against Geological Disposal of Nuclear Waste, 1993, Method in Ecology, 1993, The Ethics of Scientific Research, 1994, Environmental Justice: Creating Equality, Reclaiming Democracy, 2002, Taking Action, Saving Lives: Our Duties to Protect Environmental and Pub. Health, 2007; co-editor: Technology and Human Values, 1996; co-author: Policy for Land: Law and Ethics, 1992; assoc. editor: Bioscience, 1994—2002, editor-in-chief: Oxford U. Press monograph series Environ. Ethics and Sci. Policy, 1988—; mem. editl. bd. Humanities and Tech., 1980—, Environmental Ethics, 1981—, Philosophy and Tech., 1986—, Jour. Agr. and Environ. Ethics, 1986—, Pub. Affairs Quarterly, 1987—, Jour. Law and Pub. Policy, 1987—, Studies in Religion and the Social Order, 1991—, Risk: Issues in Health and Safety, 1991—, Syntheis: An Internat. Jour. in Logic, Epistemology and Philosophy of Sci., 1993—, Eco Spheres, 1993—, Organization and Environ., 1995—, Ethics and the Environment, 1995—, Environmental Values, 1995—, Encyclopedia of Philosophy Sci., 1996—, Poiesis and Praxis, 1999—, Europaische Akademie, 1999—, Bus. Ethics Quarterly, 2002—, Biological Theory, 2004—, Accountability in Rsch., 2004—; Article Referee Behavioral Science, 1975-, Philosophy Sci., 1977-, Sci., Tech., and Human Values, 1980-, Sci., 1982-, Jour. Bus. Ethics, 1983-, Energy Policy Studies, 1984-, Synthese, 1984-, Environment International, 1985-, Risk Analysis, 1985-,Environmental Management, 1985-, Ethics, 1987-, Hypatia, 1988-, Soc. and Natural Resources, 1989-, Biology and Philosophy, 1993, Economics and Philosophy, 1992-, Conservation Biology, 1993-, Bulletin Ecological Soc. Am., 1995-, Environmental Professional, 1995-, Newsletter on Philosophy and Tech., 1995-, Environ. Sci. and Tech., 1996-, Environ. Health Perspectives, 2005-present; Book Referee MIT Press, 1981-, Reidel Press, 1981-, Macmillan Publishers, 1984-, Prentice-Hall, 1984-, Univ. Calif. Press, 1984-, Oxford Univ. Press, 1987-, Kluwer Academic Publishers, 1988-, Cambridge Univ. Press, 1991-, Rowman and Littlefield, 1991-, Univ. Ariz. Press, 1991-, Temple Univ. Press, 1992-, Univ. Press Kans., 1992-, Univ. Georgia Press, 1994-, Yale Univ. Press, 1994-; contbr. several articles to profl jours. including Ethics, Jour. Philosophy, Philosophy of Sci., Synthese, Trends in Ecology Revolution, others Recipient NEH/NSF Interdisciplinary Incentive award, 1982, NSF Scholar's award in Philosophy of Sci., 1982, World Tech. award in Ethics, 2004; named Kentucky's Outstanding Young Women, 1977; Woodrow Wilson Nat. Fellowship, 1967—68, NSF Fellow, 1968—71, Carnegie Found. Fellowship in Philosophy Sci., 1971. Mem.: NAS ((with NRC) bd. dirs. environ. studies and toxicology 1993—96, (with NRC) oversight com. environ. monitoring and assessment program 1993—96, (with NRC) com. risk characterization 1994—96, (with NRC) com. to evaluate zinc-cadmium-sulfide 1995—96, (with NRC) mem. com. on ecosystems svcs. 2002—03), Humanities and Tech. Assn. (bd. mem. 1980—90), Assn. Internat. de Cyberétique (mem. Am. bd. 1976—78), Internat. Soc. Environ. Ethics (mem. nominating com. 1992—, mem. adv. bd. 1995—, pres. 2000—03), Risk Assessment and Policy Assn. (pres. 1995—98, chair, mtg. program com. 1997), Soc. Philosophy and Tech. (v.p./pres.-elect 1983—85, pres. 1985—87, past pres.), Philosophy Sci. Assn. (mem. nominating com. 1981—82, mem. program com. 1986, mem. mtg. program com. 1986, 1996, mem. program com. 1998, mem. mtg. program com. 1998, mem. program com. 2006), Am. Philosophical Assn. (mem. program com. 1981, mem. adv. com. on ethics 1989—92, mam. adv. bd. Newsletter on Feminism and Philosophy 1992—), DAR. Avocations: scuba diving, canoeing, hiking, volunteer work. Office: Dept Philosophy and Dept Biol Scis 100 Malloy Hall Univ Notre Dame Notre Dame IN 46556-5639 Office Phone: 574-631-2647. Office Fax: 574-631-8209. Business E-Mail: kristin.shrader-frechette.1@nd.edu.

SHRAUNER, BARBARA WAYNE ABRAHAM, electrical engineer, educator; b. Morristown, NJ, June 21, 1934; d. Leonard Gladstone and Ruth Elizabeth (Thrasher) Abraham; m. James Ely Shrauner, 1965; children: Elizabeth Ann, Jay Arthur. BA cum laude, U. Colo., 1956; AM, Harvard U., 1957, PhD, 1962. Postdoc. mrschr. Free U. Brussels, 1962-64, NASA-Ames Rsch. Ctr., Moffett Field, Calif., 1964-65; asst. prof. Washington U., St. Louis, 1966-69, assoc. prof., 1969-77, prof., 1977—2003, sr. prof., 2003—. Sabbatical Los Alamos (N.Mex.) Sci. Lab., 1975-76, Lawrence Berkeley Lab., Berkeley, Calif., 1985-86; cons. Los Alamos Nat. Lab., 1979, 84, NASA, Washington, 1980, Naval Surface Weapons Lab., Silver Spring, Md., 1984. Contbr. articles on transport in semiconductors, hidden symmetries of differential equations, plasma physics to profl. jours. Fellow Am. Phys. Soc. (sr. divsn. plasma physics, exec. com. 1980-82, 96-98); mem. IEEE (sr.; sr. exec. com. of standing tech. com. on plasma sci. and applications 1996-98), AAUP (local sec.-treas. 1980-82), Am. Geophys. Union, Phi Beta Kappa, Sigma Xi, Eta Kappa Nu, Sigma Pi Sigma. Home: 7452 Stratford Ave Saint Louis MO 63130-4044 Office: Washington U Dept Elec and Systems Engring 1 Brookings Dr Saint Louis MO 63130-4899 Home Phone: 314-727-1012; Office Phone: 314-935-6134. Business E-Mail: bas@wustl.edu.

SHREEVE, JEAN'NE MARIE, chemist, educator; b. Deer Lodge, Mont., July 2, 1933; d. Charles William and Maryfrances (Briggeman) Shreeve. BA in Chemistry, U. Mont., 1953, DSc (hon.), 1982; MS in Analytical Chemistry, U. Minn., 1956; PhD in Inorganic Chemistry, U. Wash., 1961. From asst. prof. to assoc. prof. chemistry U. Idaho, Moscow, 1961—67, prof., 1967-73, 2000—, acting chmn. dept. chemistry, 1969-70, 1973, head dept. and prof., 1973-87, v.p. rsch. and grad. studies, prof. chemistry, 1987-99, Jean'ne M. Shreeve chemistry prof., 2004—. Mem. nat. com. Stds. Higher Edn., 1965—67, 1969—73; Lucy W. Pickett lectr. Mt. Holyoke Coll., 1976; George H. Cady lectr. U. Wash., 1993; chmn. com. nat. medal sci. Pres. U.S., 2003—07. Mem. editl. bd. Jour. Fluorine Chemistry, 1970—2003, Jour. Heteroatom Chemistry, 1988—95, Accounts Chem. Rsch., 1973—75, Inorganic Synthesis, 1976—; contbr. articles to sci. jours. Mem. bd. govs. Argonne (Ill.) Nat. Lab., 1992—98. Recipient Disting. Alumni award, U. Mont., 1970, Outstanding Achievement award, U. Minn., 1975, Sr. U.S. Scientist award, Alexander Von Humboldt Found., 1978, Excellence in Tchg. award, Chem. Mfrs. Assn., 1980; named Hon. Alumnus, U. Idaho, 1972; named to Idaho Hall of Fame, 2001; NSF Postdoctoral fellow, U. Cambridge, Eng., 1967—68, U.S. Hon. Ramsay fellow, 1967—68, Alfred P. Sloan fellow, 1970—72. Mem.: AAUW (officer Moscow chpt. 1962—69), AAAS (bd. dirs. 1991—95), Idaho Acad. Sci. (Disting. Scientist 2001), Am. Chem. Soc. (bd. dirs. 1985—93, chmn. fluorine divsn. 1979—81, mem. adv. bd. Petroleum Rsch. Fund 1975—77, mem. women chemists com. 1972—77, Harry and Carol Mosher award Santa Clara Valley sect. 1992, Shirley B. Radding award Santa Clara Valley sect. 2003, Garvan medal 1972, award for creative work in fluorine chemistry 1978), Göttingen (Germany) Acad. Scis. (corr.), Phi Beta Kappa. Avocations: fishing, gardening. Office: U Idaho Dept Chemistry Box 442343 Moscow ID 83844-2343 Office Phone: 208-885-6215. Business E-Mail: jshreeve@uidaho.edu.

SHREM, CHARLES JOSEPH, metals corporation executive; b. Cairo, May 9, 1930; arrived in U.S., 1959; s. Joseph C. and Paula (Cadranel) S.; m. Vivian L. Chalom, Jan. 30, 1955; children: Jeff, Leslie Allen. Degree in bus. and economy, Coll. Français, Cairo, 1951. Export mgr. Stanton Ironworks U.K., Middle East, 1950-57; comml. mgr. Soc. Sovibor, Paris, 1957-59; purchasing dir. Montanore, Inc., NYC, 1959-65; exec. v.p. Commonwealth Metal Corp., Englewood Cliffs, NJ, 1965-85, pres., CEO, 1985-2000, chmn., 2000—02; bus. cons. Pompton Plains, NJ, 2002—. Bd. dirs. Adult Edn., Pequannock, N.J., 1970-80; chmn. bd. govs. Internat. Grad. U., Washington. Mem. U.S. C. of C. (econ. coun., exec. com. U.S. Polish Coun./U.S. C. of C.). Office: 933 Rte 23 Pompton Plains NJ 07444 Office Phone: 973-831-0111. Personal E-mail: charles.shrem@verizon.net.

SHRESTHA, NABIN K., physician, researcher; s. Prachanda and Lila Shrestha; married; m. Rojina Shrestha; children: Priyanka, Nishan. B in Medicine and Surgery, Delhi U., Maulana Azad Med. Coll., 1994; MPH, Cleve. State U., 2006. Diplomate in internal medicine Am. Bd. Internal Medicine, 1999, in infectious diseases Am. Bd. Internal Medicine, 2001, in med. microbiology Am. Bd. Pathology, 2005. Asst. prof. B.P. Koirala Inst. Health Scis., Dharan, Nepal, 2002—04, assoc. prof., 2004; assoc. staff physician Cleve. Clinic, 2004—06, quality rev. officer, dept. infectious disease, 2005—, staff physician, 2006—, program dir., clin. microbiology fellowship program, 2006—; asst. prof. Case Western Res. U., Cleve., 2009—. Contbr. articles to profl. jours. Recipient Joseph Cash Meml. award, Cleve. Clinic, 2002. Fellow: ACP, Coll. Am. Pathologists, Infectious Diseases Soc.; mem.: AAAS, Am. Nepal Med. Found. (bd. dirs. 2008—, sec. 2009—), Soc. for Healthcare Epidemiology Am., Am. Soc. Microbiology, Beta Gamma Sigma (life). Office: Cleveland Clinic 9500 Euclid Ave / S-32 Cleveland OH 44195

SHREVE, ANITA, writer; b. Boston, Oct. 7, 1946; d. Richard H. and Bibiona (Kennedy) Shreve; children: Katherine, Christopher. BA in English, Tufts U., Medford, Mass., 1968. Former HS tchr., journalist, Nairobi, Kenya, creative writing tchr. Amherst Coll., Mass. Author: (fiction) Past the Island, Drifting, 1975 (O. Henry prize, 1975), Eden Close, 1989, Strange Fits of Passion, 1991, Where or When, 1993, Resistance, 1995, The Weight of Water, 1997, The Pilot's Wife, 1998, Fortune's Rocks, 1999, The Last Time They Met, 2001, Sea Glass, 2002, All He Ever Wanted, 2003, Light on Snow, 2004, A Wedding In December, 2005, Body Surfing, 2007, Testimony, 2008 (Publishers Weekly bestseller), (nonfiction) Remaking Motherhood: How Working Mothers are Shaping Our Children's Future, 1987, Women Together, Women Alone: The Legacy of the Consciousness-Raising Movement, 1989. Recipient Page One award, Newspaper Guild NYC, 1984, New Eng. Book award for fiction, 1998. Mem.: PEN (L.L. Winship award 1998), Authors's Guild. Mailing: c/o Hachette Book Group 237 Park Ave New York NY 10017*

SHREVE, GREGORY MONROE, language educator, department chairman; b. Mun, Aug. 3, 1950; 1 child, Justin Gregory. PhD, Ohio State U., Columbus, 1975. Cert. advanced study info. sci. U. Pitts., 1980. Prof., dir. Kent State U., Inst. Applied Linguistics, Kent, Ohio, 1988—2004; prof., chmn. Kent State U., Modern Langs., Kent, 2004—. Chmn. U. Leipzig, 1993. Editor: (book) Cognitive Processes in Translation and Interpreting; author: Translation as Text, The Genesis of Structures in African Narrative. Recipient Governor's award, State Ohio, 2001. D-Liberal. Avocations: travel, martial arts, antiques. Office: Kent State Univ 101 Satterfield Hall Kent OH 44242 Business E-Mail: gshreve@kent.edu.

SHREVE, SUSAN RICHARDS, writer, educator; b. Toledo, May 2, 1939; d. Robert Kenneth and Helen (Greene) Richards; children—Porter, Elizabeth, Caleb, Kate. BA, U. Pa., 1961; MA, U. Va., 1969. Prof. English lit. George Mason U., Fairfax, Va., 1976—. Vis. prof. Columbia U., NYC, 1982—, Princeton U., 1991-93 Author: (novels) A Fortunate Madness, 1974, A Woman Like That, 1977, Children of Power, 1979, Miracle Play, 1981, Dreaming of Heroes, 1984, Queen of Hearts, 1986, A Country of Strangers, 1989, Daughters of the New World, 1992, The Train Home, 1993, Skin Deep: Women & Race, 1995, The Visiting Physician, 1995; (pseudonym Annie Waters) Glimmer, 1997, Plum & Jaggers, 2000, A Student of Living Things, 2006, A Memoir: Warm Springs: Traces of a Childhood, 2007; (children's books) The Nightmares of Geranium Street, 1977, Family Secrets, 1979, Loveletters, 1979, The Masquerade, 1980, The Bad Dreams of a Good Girl, 1981, The Revolution of Mary Leary, 1982, The Flunking of Joshua T. Bates, 1984, How I Saved the World on Purpose, 1985, Lucy Forever and Miss Rosetree, Shrinks, Inc., 1985, Joshua T. Bates In Charge, 1992, The Gift of the Girl Who Couldn't Hear, 1991, Wait for Me, 1992, Amy Dunn Quits School, 1993, Lucy Forever & the Stolen Baby, 1994, The Formerly Great Alexander Family, 1995, Zoe and Columbo, 1995, Warts, 1996, A Goalie, 1996, Joshua Bates in Trouble Again, 1997, Jonah, The Whale, 1997, Ghost Cats, 1999, The End of Amanda, The Good, 2000, Blister, 2002, Trout & Me, 2003, Under the Watson's Porch, 2004, Kiss Me Tomorrow, 2006; The Lovely Shoes, 2009, editor: Dream Me Home Safely, 2003; co-editor: How We Want to Live: Narratives on Progress, 1996, (with Porter Shreve) Outside the Law: Narratives on Justice, 1997, How We Want to Live: Narratives on Progress, 1998, Tales Out of School: Narratives on Education, 1999. Recipient Jenny Moore award George Washington U., 1978; John Simon Guggenheim award in fiction, 1980, Nat. Endowment Arts fiction award, 1982 Mem. PEN/Faulkner Found. (pres.), Phi Beta Kappa. Office Phone: 703-993-1338. Personal E-mail: srshreve@aol.com.

SHRIBMAN, DAVID MARKS, editor; b. Salem, Mass., Mar. 2, 1954; m. Cindy Skrzycki, Sept. 9, 1978; children: Elizabeth, Natalie. AB summa cum laude, Dartmouth Coll., 1976, AM, 1993; LHD, Salem State Coll., 1995. Mem. city staff and Washington bur. Buffalo Evening News, 1977-80; mem. feature and nat. staff The Washington Star, 1980-81; with Washington bur. NY Times, 1981-84; congl. reporter, nat. polit. corr. The Wall St. Jour., 1984-93; chief Washington bur., asst. mng. editor The Boston Globe, 1993—2003; exec. editor, v.p. Pitts. Post-Gazette, 2003—. Bd. visitors Nelson A. Rockefeller Ctr. for Social Scis. Dartmouth Coll.; panelist Washington Week in Rev. PBS; analyst BBC radio; vis. fellow Woodrow Wilson Nat. Fellowship Found., 2007—08; lectr. in field. Author: I Remember My Teacher, 2002. Trustee Dartmouth Coll. James B. Reynolds scholar Jesus Coll.; recipient Pulitzer Prize for beat reporting, 1995. Mem. Phi Beta Kappa. Office: Pittsburgh Post Gazette 34 Blvd of the Allies Pittsburgh PA 15222 Office Phone: 412-263-1890. E-mail: dshribman@post-gazette.com.*

SHRIER, ADAM LOUIS, investment company executive, consultant; b. Warsaw, Mar. 26, 1938; came to U.S., 1943, naturalized, 1949; s. Henry Leon and Mathilda June (Czamanska) S.; m. Diane Kesler, June 10, 1961; children: Jonathan, Lydia, Catherine, David. BS, Columbia U., 1959; MS (Whitney fellow), MIT, 1960; D. Engr. and Applied Sci. NSF fellow, Yale U., 1965; postdoctoral visitor, U. Cambridge, Eng., 1965—66; JD, Fordham U., 1976. With Esso Rsch. & Engring. Co., Florham Park and Linden, NJ, 1963—65, 1966—72, head. environ. scis. rsch. area, 1969—72; coord. pollution abatement activities, tanker dept. Exxon Internat. Co., NYC, 1972—74; project mgr., energy sys. Exxon Enterprises Inc., NYC, 1974—75, gen. mgr. solar energy projects, 1975—77, pres. solar thermal sys. divsn., 1977—81; corp. planning cons., sec. new bus. investments Exxon Corp., NYC, 1981—82; divsn. mgr. supply and transp. Exxon Internat. Co., NYC, 1983—86, mgr. policy and planning, 1986—88; mng. dir. Splty. Tech. Assocs., Washington, 1988—97; pres. Global Devel. Opportunities, LLC, Washington, 1997—. Adj. lectr. chem. engring. Columbia U., NYC, 1967-69, adj. prof. internat. and pub. affairs, 2005—; adj. prof. internat. bus. Am. U., Washington, 2000—; vis. prof. internat. bus. Xiamen U., China, 2006-09; industry adv. bd. Internat. Energy Agy., 1984-88, Energy and Environ. Policy Ctr., Harvard U., 1986-88, Internat. Energy Program, Johns Hopkins U., 1987-88; sr. assoc. Global Bus. Forum, 1988—, Cambridge Energy Rsch. Assocs., 1988-2006, Internat. Exec. Svc. Corps, 2001—, Citizens Devel. Corps, 2006—; course leader CWC Energy, Ltd., 2006—. Contbr. articles to profl. jours. Mem. AIChE, Internat. Assn. Energy Econs., Am. Chem. Soc., U.S. Energy Assn., Mid. East Inst., Acad. Internat. Bus., Cosmos Club, Sigma Xi, Tau Beta Pi, Phi Lambda Upsilon. Achievements include patents in field. Office: 4000 Cathedral Ave NW Washington DC 20016-5249 Personal E-mail: alshrier@comcast.net. Business E-Mail: as2750@columbia.edu.

SHRINER, THOMAS L., JR., lawyer; b. Lafayette, Ind., Dec. 15, 1947; s. Thomas L. Sr. and Margaret (Kamstra); m. Donna L. Galchick, June 5, 1971; children: Thomas L. III, John H., Joseph P., James A. AB, Ind. U., 1969, JD, 1972. Bar: Wis. 1972, US Dist. Ct. (ea. dist.) Wis. 1973, US Dist. Ct. (we. dist.) Wis. 1977, US Dist. Ct. Colo. 2005, US Ct. Appeals (7th cir.) 1972, US Ct. Appeals (8th cir.) 1989, US Ct. Appeals (fed. cir.) 1990, US Supreme Ct. 1978, US tax Ct., 2008. Law clk to Hon. John S. Hastings U.S. Ct. Appeals (7th cir.), Chgo., 1972-73; assoc. Foley & Lardner, Milw., 1973-79, ptnr., 1979—. Adj. prof. Law Sch. Marquette U., Milw., 2005—. Chmn. bd. trustees Cath. Charities of Archdiocese of Milw., 2001—02; mem. bd. trustees Cardinal Stritch U., 2009—. Fellow Am. Coll. Trial Lawyers; mem. 7th Cir. Bar Assn. (pres. 1993-94), Phi Beta Kappa. Republican. Roman Catholic. Office: Foley & Lardner LLP 777 E Wisconsin Ave Ste 3800 Milwaukee WI 53202-5306 Home Phone: 414-964-6315; Office Phone: 414-297-5601. Business E-Mail: tshriner@foley.com.

SHRINSKY, JASON LEE, lawyer; b. Pitts., June 15, 1937; s. Abe and Sylvia S.; children: Jeffrey, Steven, Stacy. BA, U. Pitts., 1959; JD, George Washington U., 1962. Sr. ptnr. Shrinsky, Weitzman & Eisen, Washington, DC, 1971-87; ptnr., chair Telecom. Dept. Kaye, Scholer LLP, Washington, DC, 1987—, mem. exec. com., 1998. Panelist Paul Kagan Seminars on Radio and TV Acquisitions, Inst. Soc. Internat. Rsch.; atty.-advisor Complaints and Compliance Div. Broadcast Bur. FCC, Washington, 1961-64; bd. dirs. U.S. Com. Sports for Israel, Phila., FCC Bar Assn. Contbr. articles to Radio and Records mag., Broadcast Cable Fin. Jour. Presdl. del. Mt. Sinai transfer ceremonies, 1978; U.S. basketball chmn. 12th, 13th and 14th Maccabiah games, Israel; bd. dirs. Washington Hebrew Congregation, 1978-85, Spanish Broadcasting Sys., Inc.; mem. adv. bd. Bi-Wak Digital Music, Inc. Mem. Internat. Radio and TV Soc., Nat. Broadcaster's Club (past pres.), U. Pitts. Alumni Assn. (bd. dirs.). Jewish. Office: Kaye Scholer LLP McPherson Building 901 15th St NW, Ste 1100 Washington DC 20005-2327 Office Phone: 202-682-3500. E-mail: jshrinsky@kayescholer.com.

SHRIVASTAVA, AMITESH, materials engineer; s. Devendra Kumar and Chanda Shrivastava; m. Noopur Shrivastava. BE, Govt. Engring. Coll., Raipur, Madhya Pradesh, India, 2000; MTech, Indian Inst. Tech., Kanpur, India, 2003; PhD, U. SC., Columbia, 2008. Grad. tchg. asst. Indian Inst. Tech., Kanpur, 2001—03, sr. project assoc., 2003—04; grad. rsch. asst. U. SC., 2004—08; process tech. devel. engr. Intel, Hillsboro, Oreg., 2009—. Contbr. scientific papers. Joint sec. Joint Effort Social & Individual Devel., Raipur, 1999—2000. A. F. McKissick Fellowship, Grad. Sch., 2007. Mem.: ASM, IEEE. Achievements include patents pending for developed a process to control morphological defects & lifetime in silicon carbide based epilayers for power devices; research in growth & characterization of 4 degree off 4H-SiC epilayers without step bunching; demonstration high growth-rate by using halide based chemistry for SiC epilayer growth; mechanism of conversion of basal plane dislocation to threading edge dislocation. Personal E-mail: amitesh.shrivastava@gmail.com.

SHRIVER, EDWIN R., psychologist; b. Wheeling, W. Va., Nov. 2, 1980; s. Edwin G. and Barbara S. Shriver. BA in Psychology and Sociology Minor, Kent State U., Ohio, 2004; MA in Psychology, Miami U., Oxford, Ohio, 2006. Grad. asst. Miami U., 2004—. Contbr. articles to profl. jours. Mem.: Midwestern Psychol. Assn., Phi Beta Kappa (Horace A Paige award 2004). Independent. Avocations: politics, reading, running, camping. Home: 301 Brookview Ct Apt 6 Oxford OH 45056 Office: Miami Univ 90 N Patterson Ave Oxford OH 45056 Office Fax: 513-529-2420. Business E-Mail: shriveer@muohio.edu.

SHRIVER, MARIA OWINGS, former news correspondent; b. Chgo., Nov. 6, 1955; d. Robert Sargent and Eunice Mary (Kennedy) S.; m. Arnold Schwarzenegger, Apr. 26, 1986; children: Katherine Eunice, Christina Maria Aurelia, Patrick Arnold, Christopher Sargent BA, Georgetown U. Coll. Am. Studies, Washington, 1977. News producer Sta. KYW-TV, 1977-78; producer Sta. WJZ-TV, 1978-80; nat. reporter PM Mag., 1981-83; news reporter CBS News, Los Angeles, 1983-85; news correspondent, co-anchor CBS Morning News, NYC, 1985-86; co-host Sunday Today, NBC, 1987-90; anchor Main Street, NBC, 1987; co-anchor Yesterday, Today, and Tomorrow, NBC, 1989; anchor NBC Nightly News Weekend Edition, 1989-90, Cutting Edge with Maria Shriver, NBC, 1990, First Person with Maria Shriver, NBC, 1990—2004; First Lady of Calif., 2003—. Co-anchor Summer Olympics, Seoul, Korea, 1988; substitute anchor NBC News at Sunrise, Today, NBC Nightly News with Tom Brokaw; contbg. anchor Dateline, NBC, 1995-2004. Author: What's Heaven, 1999, Ten Things I Wish I'd Known Before I Went Into the Real World, 2000, What's Wrong With Timmy, 2001, What's Happening to Grandpa?, 2003, And One More Thing Before You Go..., 2005, Just Who Will You Be?: Big Question, Little Book, Answer Within, 2008; exec. prodr: (documentary) The Alzheimer's Project, 2009 Recipient Christopher award for "Fatal Addictions", 1990, Exceptional Merit Media award Nat. Women's Political Caucus, first-place Commendation award Am. Women in Radio and TV, 1991, Emmy nomination, George Peabody Award, 1998. Democrat. Roman Catholic. Office: First Lady Maria Shriver State Capitol Bldg Sacramento CA 95814-4906*

SHRIVER, PHILLIP RAYMOND, academic administrator; b. Cleve., Aug. 16, 1922; s. Raymond Scott and Corinna Ruth (Smith) S.; m. Martha Damaris Nye, Apr. 15, 1944; children: Carolyn (Mrs. William Shaul), Susan (Mrs. Lester LaVine), Melinda (Mrs. David Williams), Darcy, Raymond Scott II. BA, Yale U., New Haven, Conn., 1943; MA, Harvard U., Cambridge, Mass., 1946; PhD, Columbia U., NYC, 1954; LittD, U. Cin., 1966; LLD, Heidelberg Coll., Tiffin, Ohio, 1966, Ea. Mich. U., Ypsilanti, 1972, Ohio State U., 1973; DH, McKendree Coll., Lebanon, Ill., 1973; DPS, Albion Coll., Mich., 1974; LHD, Ctrl. State U., Wilberforce, Ohio, 1976, No. Ky. State U., 1980, Miami U., 1984, U. Akron, Ohio, 1988. Mem. faculty Kent (Ohio) State U., 1947-65, prof. Am. history, 1960-65; dean Coll. Arts and Scis., 1963-65; pres. Miami U., Oxford, Ohio, 1965-81, pres. emeritus, prof. Am. history, 1981-99. Pres. Ohio Coll. Assn., 1974-75; chmn. coun. pres.'s Mid-Am. Conf., 1971-77; chmn. Ohio Bicentennial Commn. for NW Ordinance and U.S. Constn., 1985-89, Ohio Tuition Trust Authority, 1989-92; chmn. coun. pres.'s Nat. Assn. State Univs. and Land Grant Colls., 1975-76, mem. exec. coun., 1976-78. Author: The Years of Youth, 1960, George A. Bowman: The Biography of an Educator, 1963, (with D.J. Breen) Ohio's Military Prisons of the Civil War, 1964, A Tour to New Connecticut in 1811: The Narrative of Henry Leavitt Ellsworth, 1985, Miami University: A Personal History, 1998, (with C.E. Wunderlin Jr.) The Documentary Heritage of Ohio, 2000, (with E.F. Puff) The History of Presbyterianism in Oxford, Ohio, 2000. Bd. dirs. Cin. Ctr. Sci. and Industry, 1965-70, Fed. Reserve Bank Cincinnati, 1968-72, chmn. bd. 1971-72; trustee Ohio Coll. Library Center, 1968-74; chmn. bd. Univ. Regional Broadcasting, 1975-76, 78-79. Served to lt. (j.g.) USNR, 1943-46, PTO. Decorated Order of Merit (Grand Duchy of Luxembourg); recipient Disting. Acad. Svc. award AAUP, 1965, Gov.'s award 1969, A.K. Morris award, 1974, Ohioana Career medal, 1987, Converse award, 1990, award of merit Am. Assn. for State and Local History, 1993, Bjornson award Ohio Humanities Coun., 2001, John E. Dolibois History prize, 2003, Statesman award Cin. Soc. Assn. Execs., 2004. Mem. Orgn. Am. Historians, Ohio Acad. History (pres. 1983-84, Disting. Svc. award 1991), Archaeol. Inst. Am., Ohio Hist. Soc. (trustee 1982-91, v.p. 1983-84, pres. 1984-86), Ohio Humanities Coun. (Bjornson award 2001), Am. Studies Assn., Mortar Board, Phi Beta Kappa, Omicron Delta Kappa, Phi Alpha Theta, Alpha Kappa Psi, Kappa Delta Pi, Phi Eta Sigma, Phi Kappa Phi, Kappa Kappa Psi, Alpha Lambda Delta, Beta Gamma Sigma, Sigma Delta Pi, Alpha Phi Omega, Delta Upsilon (Disting. Alumni Achievement award 1985) Clubs: Rotary. Presbyterian. Home: 5115 Bonham Rd Oxford OH 45056-1428 Business E-Mail: shrivepr@muohio.edu.

SHRIVER, ROBERT SARGENT, JR., (SARGENT SHRIVER), lawyer; b. Westminster, Md., Nov. 9, 1915; s. Robert Sargent and Hilda Shriver; m. Eunice Mary Kennedy, May 23, 1953 (dec. Aug. 11, 2009); children: Robert Sargent III, Maria Owings, Timothy Perry, Mark Kennedy, Anthony Paul Kennedy. Student, Canterbury Sch.; BA cum laude, Yale U., 1938, LLB, 1941; LLD, St. Procopius Coll., 1959, Notre Dame U., DePaul U., Seton Hall Coll., 1961, St. Louis U., Kansas State U., Brandeis U., 1962, St. Michael's Coll., Vt., Fordham U., Boston Coll., Yale U., Duquesne U., N.Y.U., Wesleyan U.; DCL, U. Liberia, 1963; HHD, Salem Coll., 1963, Bowling Green State U.; LHD, Springfield Coll., Mass., 1963, U. Scranton, Providence Coll.; D in Polit. Sci., Chulalongkorn U., Bangkok, Thailand, The Am. U. of Paris, 2002. Bar: N.Y. 1941, Ill. 1959, U.S. Supreme Ct. 1969, D.C. 1971. With Winthrop, Stimson, Putnam & Roberts, 1940—41; asst. editor Newsweek, 1945—46; assoc. Joseph P. Kennedy Enterprises, 1947—48; asst. gen. mgr. Merchandise Mart, Chgo., 1948—61; dir. Peace Corps., Washington, 1961—66, Office Econ. Opportunity, Washington, 1964—68; spl. asst. to the Pres. The White House, Washington, 1965—68; U.S. amb. to France US Dept. State, Paris, 1968—70; sr. ptnr. Fried, Frank, Harris, Shriver & Jacobson, NYC, Washington, L.A., London, Eng., 1971—86, of counsel, 1986—; pres. Spl. Olympics, Washington, 1986—90, CEO, 1990—96, chmn. bd. dirs., 1990—2003, chmn. emeritus, 2003—. Mem. Am. Com. on East-West Accord, 1978—, Ams. for SALT, 1979—. Author: Point of the Lance, 1964. Pres. Chgo. Bd. Edn., 1955—60; mem.-at-large Nat. Coun. Boy Scouts Am.; chmn. Internat. Orgn. Patrons on Israel Mus., 1972—75; bd. dirs. The Arms Control Assn., 1983—; Dem. candidate for v.p., 1972; ran for Dem. presdl. election, 1976; pres. Cath. Interracial Coun. Chgo., 1955—60. Lt. comdr. USNR, 1940—45. Recipient Vet. of the Year award, 1956, Yale U. medal, 1957, Chgo. medal of merit, 1957, James H. Hooey award, Cath. Conf. for Interracial Justice Coun. N.Y., 1958, Golden Heart Presdl. award, Philippines, 1964, Nat. Father of the Year award, 1964, Notre Dame Patriotism award, 1965, Nat. Brotherwood award, 1966, Laetare medal, U. Notre Dame, 1968, Hannah G. Solomon award, Nat. Coun. of Jewish Woman, 1972, Franklin D. Roosevelt Freedom from Want award, 1993, Presdl. Medal of Freedom, 1994, Equal Justice award, Nat. Ctr. on Poverty Law, 1999, William O. Douglas award, Pub. Counsel Law Ctr., 1999, Disting. Am. award, John F. Kennedy Library & Found., 2001, Lifetime Achievement award, The Am. Lawyer mag, 2005; named Lay Churchman of Yr., Religious Heritage Am., 1963; named to the Order of the Smile, 1989. Mem.: Chgo. Coun. Fgn. Rels. (dir.), Yale U. Law Sch. Assn. (exec. com., James J. Hooey award N.Y. chpt. 1958), Navy League (life), Yale Club (N.Y.C.), Onwentsia Club (Lake Forest, Ill.), Execs. Club (Chgo.), Econ. Club, Serra Club, Racquet Club, Delta Kappa Epsilon. Roman Catholic. Achievements include extensive world travel to visit Peace Corps projects, 1961-1966.*

SHRIVER, WILLIAM RUSSELL, secondary school educator; b. Garfield Heights, Ohio, Aug. 15, 1950; s. William Washington and Olive Elizabeth (Doutt) S.; m. Karen Ann Wolfe, June 20, 1987; children: Lauren, Matthew. BA, Coll. of Wooster, 1972; MA, U. Chgo., 1973; postgrad., Cleve. State U., 1973-74. Nat. bd. cert. tchr. soc. studies 2002. Summer staff Philmont Scout Ranch, Cimarron, N.Mex., 1968-76; tchr. Mt. Vernon (Ohio) Sr. H.S., 1974—. Tchr. Kenyon Acad. Partnership Kenyon Coll./Mt. Vernon Sr. H.S., 1983—; vice chair state tchr. edn. cert. adv. commn. Ohio Bd. Edn., Columbus, 1991-99, state tchr. cert. standards revision com., 1992-95; bd. examiners Nat. Coun. Accreditation of Tchr. Edn., Washington, 1993-02; mem. Ohio Gov.'s Commn. on Tchg. Success, 2001-03; mem. Ohio Educators Stds. Bd., 2004-, chair, 2004-2006. Bd. of session First Presbyn. Ch., Mt. Vernon, 1980-87, 89-95, 2001—2007, 2009-, clk session, 2009-. Mem. NEA (assembly del. 1983-99), Ohio Edn. Assn. (exec. com. 1987-93, 96-2002), North Ctrl. Ohio Edn. Assn. (pres. 1984-85, exec. sec. 1993-2004), Mt. Vernon Edn. Assn. (pres. 1976-78), Pi Lambda Theta. Presbyterian. Avocations: photography, genealogy. Office: Mt Vernon HS 300 Martinsburg Rd Mount Vernon OH 43050-4246 Business E-Mail: wshriver@mt-vernon.k12.oh.us.

SHROCK, JOEL D., history professor; b. Kendallville, Ind., May 24, 1968; s. James and Judy Shrock; m. Kelly Kirby, Aug. 31, 1991; children: Owen, James, Brenton. PhD, Miami U., Oxford, Ohio, 1996. Assoc. prof. Anderson U., Ind., 2005—. Dir. Ctr. Pub. Svc., Anderson, 2008—. Author: (book) The Gilded Age. At large bd. mem. Ind. Assn. Historians, 2007—. Mem.: Soc. History of Childhood and Youth, Soc. Historians of Gilded Age and Progressive Era. Office: Anderson Univ 1100 E Fifth St Anderson IN 46012 Business E-Mail: jdshrock@anderson.edu.

SHROFF, NESS, medical educator, researcher; PhD, Columbia U., NY, 1994. Prof., sch. elec. Purdue U., West Lafayette, Ind., 1994—2007, prof. computer engring., 1994—2007; eminent scholar Ohio State U., Columbus, 2007—, chaired prof. ECE and CSE, 2007. Contbr. articles to profl. jours. (Best Paper award, 2006, 2008). Fellow: IEEE. Achievements include first to developed a new analytical framework to characterize delay performance in high-speed networks and a new loosely coupled cross-layer architecture to achieve both high throughput with low complexity in emerging multi-hop wireless networks; created the notion of opportunistic scheduling to exploit the channel conditions to substantially improve the performance of wireless cellular networks. Office: Ohio State Univ 2015 Neil Ave Columbus OH 43210 Business E-Mail: shroff@ece.osu.edu.

SHROPSHIRE, DONALD GRAY, hospital executive; b. Winston-Salem, NC, Aug. 6, 1927; s. John Lee and Bess L. (Shouse) S.; m. Mary Ruth Bodenheimer, Aug. 19, 1950; children: Melanie Shropshire David, John Devin. BS, U. NC, 1950; postgrad Erickson fellow, U. Chgo., 1958-59; LLD (hon.), U. Ariz., 1992; PhD (hon.), Tucson U., 1994. Personnel asst. Nat. Biscuit Co., Atlanta, 1950-52, asst. personnel mgr. Chgo., 1952-54; adminstr. Eastern State Hosp., Lexington, Ky., 1954-62; assoc. dir. U. Md. Hosp., Balt., 1962-67; adminstr. Tucson Med. Ctr., 1967-82, pres., 1982-92, pres. emeritus, 1992—; pres. Tucson Hosps. Med. Edn. Program, 1970-71, sec., 1971-86; pres. So. Ariz. Hosp. Council, 1968-69; bd. dirs. Ariz. Blue Cross, 1967-76, chmn. provider standards com., 1972-76; chmn. bd. Healthways, Inc., 1985-92. Mem. bd. La Posada at Park Centre, Inc., Green Valley, Ariz., 1996-2000, chmn., bd. emeritus, 2000—. Bd. dirs. Health Planning Coun. Tucson, mem. exec. com., 1969-74; chmn. profl. divsn. United Way, Tucson, 1969-70, vice chmn. campaign, 1988, Ariz. Health Faciltities Authority, bd. dirs., 1992-2005; chmn. dietary svcs. com., vice chmn., 1988, Md. Hosp. Coun., 1966-67; bd. dirs. Ky. Hosp. Assn., 1961-62, chmn. coun. profl. practice, 1960-61; past pres. Blue Grass Hosp. Coun.; trustee Assn. Western Hosps., 1974-81, pres., 1979-80; mem. accreditation Coun. for Continuing Med. Edn., 1982-87, chair, 1986; bd. govs. Pima C.C., 1970-76, sec., 1973-74, chmn., 1975-76, bd. dirs. Found., 1978-82, Ariz. Bd. Regents, 1982-90, sec., 1983-86, pres., 1987-88; mem. Tucson Airport Authority, 1987—, bd. dirs., 1990-95, pres., 1995; v.p. Tucson Econ. Devel. Corp., 1977-82; founder, dir., bd. dirs. Vol. Hosps. Am., 1977-88, treas., 1979-82; mem. Ariz. Adv. Health Coun. Dirs., 1976-78; bd. dirs. Tucson Tomorrow, 1983-87, Tucson Downtown Devel. Corp., 1988-95, Rincon Inst., 1992-97, Sonoran Inst., 1992-97, Pima County Med. Res. Corps, 2006—, Ariz. Skill Standards Commn., 2007-; dir. Mus. No. Ariz., 1988-2002, dir. emeritus, 2002—; nat. bd. advisors Eller Coll. Mgmt. U. Ariz., 1990-2007, mem. Dean's Bd. Coll. Fine Arts, 1992—, chmn., 1992-96, pres. Ariz. Coun. Econ. Edn., 1993-95; vis. panel Sch. Health Adminstrn. and Policy Ariz. State U., 1990-92; bd. dirs. Cmty. Found. So. Ariz., 1996-2001; mem. adv. bd. Steele Meml. Rsch. Ctr., U. Ariz. Coll. Medicine, 1996-2004; mem. student health adv. com. U. Ariz., 1990-07, Ariz. Skill Stds. Commn., 2007-. Named to Hon. Order Ky. Cols.; named Tucson Man of Yr. 1987, Tucson Father of Yr. 1997, Hon. Alumnus, Coll. Nursing, U. Ariz., 1998; recipient Disting. Svc. award Anti-Defamation League B'nai B'rith, 1989, Sticking-Your-Neck-Out award Pima Coun. on Aging, 1991, Il Magnifico award U. Ariz. Coll. Fine Arts, 1996, Humanitarian award Arthritis Found. S.Am., 2001, Crystal Apple Lifetime Achievement award Tucson Metro Edn. Commn., 2004, Pima Med. Found. award, 2005, Humanitarian Achievement award, Ednl. Enrichment Found., 2005; co-recipient Paloma Family Svcs. Commitment to Children award, 2005; Pima CC Dinner honoree, 1986, 92. Mem. Am. Hosp. Assn. (nominating com. 1983-86, trustee 1975-78, ho. dels. 1972-78, chmn. coun. profl. svc. 1973-74, regional adv. bd. 1969-78, chmn. joint com. with NASW 1963-64, Disting. Svc. award 1989), Ariz. Hosp. Assn. (Salisbury award 1982, bd. dirs. 1967-72, pres. 1970-71), Ariz. C. of C. (bd. dirs. 1988-93), Assn. Am. Med. Colls. (mem. assembly 1974-77), Health Care Execs. Study Soc., 1975-, Tucson C. of C. (bd. dirs. 1968-69, 1974), Nat. League for Nursing, Ariz. Town Hall (bd. dirs. 1982-92, chmn. 1990-92, treas. 1985, Circle of Disting. Svc. award 2002), Pima County Acad. Decathlon Assn. (dir. 1983-85), Rotary Club (Tucson) (pres. 1993-94, McPherson award, 2008), U. Ariz. Alumni Assn. Coll. Nursing (hon. alumnus 1998), Pi Alpha Alpha (hon.). Baptist/Presbyterian (ch. moderator, chmn. finance com., deacon, ch. sch. supt., trustee, bd. dirs. ch. found.) Office: Tucson Med Ctr 5301 E Grant Rd Tucson AZ 85712-2805 *It seems important to put something back into life - for all we take from it.*

SHROPSHIRE, WALTER, JR., biophysicist, pastor; b. Washington, Sept. 4, 1932; s. Walter and Mary Virginia (Anderson) S.; m. Audrey Marie McConkey, June 28, 1958; children: Janet Marie, Susan Lynn, Edward Allen. BS in Physics, George Washington U., 1954, MS in Botany, 1956, PhD in Plant Physiology, 1958; MDiv summa cum laude, Wesley Theol. Sem., 1990; postdoctoral fellow biophysics, Calif. Inst. Tech., 1957-59. Ordained to ministry United Meth. Ch., 1977. Physicist Smithsonian Instn., Washington, 1954—63; asst. dir. Smithsonian Environ. Rsch. Ctr., Washington, 1963-86; Gast prof. U. Freiburg, Germany, 1968-69; biophysicist, dir. Omega Lab., Cabin John, Md., 1986—. Professorial lectr. botany George Washington U., 1960-85; Gast prof. U. Zurich, Switzerland, 1985-86; part-time adj. prof. Practice Min. and Mission Wesley Theol. Sem., 1990-2008. Editor: Phytochrome, 1972, Joys of Research, 1981, Photomorphogenesis, Vol 16A, 16B, 1983, Photobiology, 1984-85, Max Delbrück and New Perception Biology, 1906-1981, 2007; Contbr. 55 articles to profl. jours. Pastor, Foundry United Meth. Ch., Washington, 1991-2003. Recipient Smithsonian Outstanding Performance award, 1967, Smithsonian Research award, 1968, Merit award Soc. John Wesley, 1997, Templeton Sci. and Religion Course prize, 1999, 2002; NSF grantee, 1960-66. Fellow Explorers Club, Am. Solar Energy Soc. Office: Omega Lab PO Box 6130 Silver Spring MD 20916-6130 Home Phone: 301-929-1827; Office Phone: 301-929-3150. E-mail: wshrop@erols.com. *The world is an incredible place, rich with unexplored and unexplained interconnections between the biological and physical domains. I am fortunate to have been born when science has begun to unravel some of the mysteries of these interconnections and especially fortunate to have had teachers who shared their enthusiasm for learning. I also have benefited from mystical religious experiences of others and my own that enable me to work at the interface between science and religion. My belief is that the pursuit of both subjective and objective knowledge of ourselves and the universe we live in is necessary to enable humanity to develop to its fullest potential. This is an exciting pursuit I hope to continue to participate in a long time.*

SHROTRIYA, VISHAL, research scientist; b. Mathura, Uttar Pradesh, India, July 10, 1979; s. Satish Vijay and Manjesh Shrotriya. B of Tech., Indian Inst. Tech., Mumbai, 2002; MS, postgrad., UCLA, 2004—. Rschr. UCLA, 2002—. Fellow, Henry Samueli Sch. Engring. and Applied Sci. Mem.: Am. Phys. Soc., Materials Rsch. Soc. Hindu. Achievements include invention of very efficient plastic solar cells.

SHROYER, KENNETH REED, medical educator, department chairman; b. New Haven, Conn., Jan. 18, 1956; s. Joseph Mark and Nancy Jane Shroyer; m. Annie Laurie Winkley, Jan. 27, 1978; 1 child, Robert Joseph. BA, Colo. Coll., 1978; PhD, U. Colo., Denver, 1983; MD, U. Colo., 1987. Diplomate anatomic and clin. pathology Am. Bd. Pathology, 1991, cytopathology Am. Bd. Pathology, 1995. Prof. and vice chmn., dept. pathology U. Colo. Health Sci. Ctr., 2002—07; prof. and chmn., dept. pathology Stony Brook U. Med. Ctr., 2007—. Contbr. scientific papers to profl. jours. Grant, NIH, 1991—. Mem.: CAP, USCAP, AACR, ASC, ASIP. Achievements include invention of dinitrophenyl (DNP) labeling of nucleic acids & use for mRNA in situ hybridization; patents for method of identifying clonal cell samples; OVR110 antibody compositions & methods of use. Office: Stony Brook Univ Med Ctr Bst9 Rm 140 Stony Brook NY 11794-8691

SHRUM, JOHN, equal rights officer; b. Flora, Ill., Apr. 13, 1953; s. William E. and Agnes M. Shrum; children: Jason E., Jarred W. Laborer Labor Union Local 1375, Flora, 1976—2003, bus. agt., 1981—83; dir. asst. employee Fed. Emergency Mgmt. Agy., Chgo., 1993—; equal rights officer Ill. Dept. Transp., Effingham, 2003—. Mem. Clay County Bd., 2004—; precinct committeeman, vice chmn. Dem. Party Clay County, Ill., 1978—; trustee Faith Luth. Ch., 1990—. Named to Wall of Tolerance, So. Poverty Law Ctr., Montgomery, Ala., 2004. Home: 141 Fox Creek RD Flora IL 62839-4118 Personal E-mail: jwshrum@hotmail.com.

SHRUM, ROBERT MATTHEW (BOB SHRUM), political strategist, educator, journalist; b. Connellsville, Pa., 1943; m. Marylouise Oates; 1 stepchild, Michael Oates Palmer. BA, Georgetown U., 1965; JD, Harvard U., 1968. Prin. speechwriter to Senator George McGovern, 1972; staff dir., chief counsel US Senate Select Com. on Nutrition and Human Needs; press. sec. to Senator Edward M. Kennedy, 1980—84, speechwriter, 1980; polit. advt. prodr., 1985—2005; sr. advisor Gore-Lieberman campaign, 2000, Kerry-Edwards campaign, 2004; sr. fellow, prof. Robert F. Wagner Grad. Sch. Pub. Svc., NYU, 2005—; polit. analyst MSNBC, 2005—. Tchr. Yale U., Boston Coll. Columnist Slate; author: No Excuses: Concessions of a Serial Campaigner, 2007. Mem.: Am. Assn. of Polit. Cons. (Pollie Award 1986, 1994, 1998). Democrat. Office: NYU Wagner The Puck Bldg 2nd Fl 295 Lafayette St New York NY 10012-9604 Office Phone: 212-998-7556. Business E-Mail: robert.shrum@nyu.edu.*

SHU, CHI-WANG, mathematics professor, researcher; b. Beijing, Jan. 2, 1957; arrived in US, 1982, naturalized, 1993; s. Kuang-Yao and Ding-Zhen (Shi) Shu; m. Din-Sui Loh, May 1, 1984; 1 child, Hai-Shuo. BS, U. Sci. and Tech. of China, 1982; PhD, UCLA, 1986. Rsch. assoc. U. Minn., Mpls., 1986—87; asst. prof. applied math. Brown U., Providence, 1987—91, assoc. prof., 1992—96, prof., 1996—, Theodore B. Stowell U. prof. applied math., 2008—, chmn., 1999—2005. Co-chief editor: Jour. Sci. Computing, 2000—09, chief editor:, 2009—; mng. editor Math. of Computation, 2002—, mem. editl. bd. SIAM Jour. Numerical Analysis, 1993—2001, Jour. Computational Math., 1993—, Comm. in Applied Analysis, 1996—, Acta Mathematicae Applicatae Sinica, —; contbr. Recipient Pub. Svc. Group Achievement award for pioneer work in computational fluid dynamics, NASA, 1992, First Feng Kang prize of Sci. Computing, Chinese Acad. Sci., 1995, Highly Cited Author in Math., Inst. Scientific Info. Web Sci., 2004—, Computational Sci. and Engring. prize, Soc. for Indsl. and Applied Math./Assn. for Computer Machinery, 2007, 2009; grantee, NSF, NASA, Army Rsch. Office. Mem.: Soc. for Indsl. and Applied Math., Am. Math. Soc. Achievements include research in numerical solutions for discontinuous problems. Home: 135 Woodbury St Providence RI 02906-3511 Office: Brown U Div Applied Maths 182 George St Providence RI 02912-9056

SHU, FRANK HSIA-SAN, physics professor, research scientist, educator; b. Kunming, China, June 2, 1943; arrived in US, 1949; s. Shien-Siu and Irene I-Jen (Hsia) Shu; m. Helen Chien-Ping Pu, June 22, 1968. BS in Physics, MIT, 1963; PhD in Astronomy, Harvard U., 1968. Asst. prof. SUNY, Stony Brook, 1968-71, assoc. prof., 1971-73, U.

Calif., Berkeley, 1973-76, prof. astronomy, 1976—2002, chmn. Dept. Astronomy, 1984-96, chancellor's prof. astronomy, 1996—98, univ. prof., 1998—2002, faculty rsch. lectr. sci. & engring., 2001; pres. Nat. Tsing Hua U., Taiwan, 2002—06; disting. prof. U. Calif., San Diego, 2006—, univ. prof., 2006—. Rsch. assoc. MIT, Cambridge, 1968, sr. rsch. assoc., 71; vis. scientist Kapteyn Astron. Lab., Groningen, Netherlands, 1973; mem. Inst. Advanced Study, Princeton, NJ, 1982; Oort prof. Leiden U., Netherlands, 1996; served on US Nat. Rsch. Coun. Blue-Ribbon Com., 2001; Thomas Gold lectureship Cornell U., 2002; chmn. selection com. in astronomy The Shaw Prize, Hong Kong, 2003—07, mem. bd. adjudicators, Hong Kong, 2005—07; mem. Sci. & Tech. Adv. Group Advisor on Energy to Premier, Taiwan; Caroline Herschel lectr. Space Telescope Sci. Inst., 2007; Ta-You lectr. U. Mich., 2007. Author: The Physical Universe, 1982; contbr. articles to profl. jours. Pamphlet writer McGovern Campaign, Suffolk County, NY, 1972. Recipient Bok prize, Harvard U., 1972, Warner prize, 1977, Dirk Brouwer award for Dynamical Astronomy, 1996, Heinemann prize, 2000, Centennial Medal, Harvard U., 2008, Shaw prize in Astronomy, The Shaw Prize Found., 2009; Sloan rsch. fellow, 1972—74. Mem.: NAS, AAAS, Am. Philos. Soc., Astron. Soc. of Pacific (bd. dirs. 1985—86, Catherine Wolfe Bruce Gold Medal for a lifetime of achievement in astronomy 2009), Am. Astron. Soc. (councilor 1982—85, pres. 1994—96, Warner prize 1977, Dannie Heineman prize for astrophysics 2006), Internat. Astron. Union, Am. Acad. Arts and Scis., Academia Sinica, Sigma Xi. Democrat. Avocations: chess, poker, bridge, sports, wine, food. Office: U Calif San Diego 9500 Gilman Dr # 0424 La Jolla CA 92093-0424 Office Phone: 858-534-9085, 858-534-3460. Fax: 858-534-2294. E-mail: fhshu@ucsd.edu.*

SHU, JENNIFER A., pediatrician, writer; b. May 21, 1967; MD, Med. Coll. Va., 1992. Cert. Pediat. Resident, pediat. U. Calif., San Francisco, 1992—96; mem. pediat. staff Dartmouth Hitchcock Med. Ctr., Lebanon, NH, 2004—. Cons. in field. Host (blogspot) parentingsense.blogspot.com; author: Heading Home with Your Newborn from Birth to Reality, 2005, Baby and Child Health, 2006, Food Fights, 2007; interviewed by NBC Nightly News, CNN Headline News, MSNBC, Discovery Health Channel, US News and World Report, USA Today, US Weekly and local and nat. TV, newspapers and radio shows and multiple parenting magazines and websites, regular host ReachMD on XM satellite radio. Office: Dartmouth Hitchcock Pediat 1 Medical Center Dr Lebanon NH 03756*

SHUART, JAMES MARTIN, retired academic administrator; b. College Point, NY, May 9, 1931; s. John and Barbara (Schmidt) Shuart; m. Marjorie Strunk, Apr. 5, 1953; children: James Raymond, William Arthur. BA, Hofstra U., 1953, MA, 1962; PhD, NYU, 1966; D (hon.), L.I. U., 2000. Group rep. Home Life Ins. Co., 1955—57, N.Y. Life Ins. Co., 1957—59; adminstr. Hofstra U., Hempstead, NY, 1959—70, asst. dir. admissions, asst. dean faculty, asst. pres., exec. dean student svcs., assoc. dean liberal arts scis., trustee, 1973—75, v.p. adminstrv. svcs., 1975—76, pres., 1976—2001, pres. emeritus, 2001—. Mem. higher edn. adv. com. NY State Senate, 1979—95; trustee Commn. on Ind. Colls. and Univs., NY State, 1982—89, 1992—95, chmn., 1988—89; mem. Am. Coun. on Edn.'s Labor/Higher Edn. Coun., 1983—88, Am. Coun. on Edn.'s Commn. on Leadership Devel., 1987—89, Peat Marwick Higher Edn. Pres.'s Adv. Com., 1988—96; bd. dirs. European Am. Bank, 1990—2001, Travelers-Solomon, Smith Barney World Funds, 1995—2000; chair Nassau County Property Tax Relief Commn., 1990—92; co-chair NY State Temporary Commn. for LI Tax Relief, 1990—93; mem. nominating com. NASDQ, 2000—06. Dep. county exec. Nassau County, 1973—75, commr. social svcs., 1971—73; commr. LI Regional Planning Bd., 1978—83, chmn., 1981—83, Nassau Bd. Social Svcs., 1971—73; mem. Nassau County Charter Revision Commn., 1993—96; pres., bd. dirs. Health Welfare Coun., Nassau County, 1971—80; bd. dirs. LI Assn., 1986—90, Winthrop U. Hosp., 1979—86; trustee Molloy Coll., 1973—77, LI Power Authority, 2004—06, Uniondale Pub. Libr., NY, 1966—68, LI Hosp. Planning Coun., 1971—75; mem. adv. bd. Adelphi U. Sch. Social Work, 1973—84. Decorated officer Order of Orange Nassau (Netherlands); recipient Founders Day award NYU, 1967, Alumnus of Yr. award Hofstra U., 1973, George M. Estabrook Disting. svc. award Alumni Assn., 1974, Leadership in Govt. award C.W. Post Coll., L.I. U., 1978, Man of Yr. award Hempstead C. of C., 1978, award L.I. Pers. and Guidance Assn., 1977, Lincoln Day award Syosset-Woodbury Rep. Club, 1981, Disting. Leadership award L.I. Bus., 1982, 96, Joseph Giacalone award 1986, Medal of Honor L.I. Assn., 1988, Achievement award Pub. Rels. Profls. of L.I., 1995, Award L.I. Bus. Devel. Coun., 1994, 98, Educator of Yr. award WLIW Ch 21, 1999, Lifetime Achievement award L.I. Assn., 2001, award L.I. Software and Tech. Network, 2001; others; named to L.I. Hall of Fame, 1985, Lifetime Achievement award Met. Lacrosse Found., 2001. Home: 111 Cherry Valley Ave # M35 Garden City NY 11530-1570

SHUB, HARVEY ALLEN, surgeon; b. Bklyn., Oct. 28, 1942; s. Irving and Sara (Levin) S.; m. Susan Jayne Smith, Dec. 26, 1970; children: Carolyn, Todd. Student, NYU, 1960-61, 64-65; BS in Zoology, Physics, U. Miami, 1964; MD, U. Rome, Italy, 1971. Diplomate Am. Bd. Colon and Rectal Surgery. Intern Beth Israel Med. Ctr., NYC, 1971-72, resident in surgery, 1972-76; fellow in colon and rectal surgery Muhlenberg Hosp., Plainfield, NJ, 1976-77; practice medicine specializing in colon and rectal surgery Orlando, Fla., 1977—; chmn. dept. surgery Fla. Hosp., 1988-89, dept. colon and rectal surgery, 1999—2001. Pres. med. staff Fla. Hosp., 1992-93; asst. cons. prof. dept. surgery Duke U., 1995; mem. staff Winter Park Meml. Hosp., South Seminole Cmty. Hosp., Fla. Hosp. and Med. Ctr., Orlando Regional Healthcare Sys.; clin. asst. prof. dept. family medicine U. South Fla., Tampa, 1982—; med. dir. Brevard Profl. Network, 2002-2004. Consulting editor Jour. Fla. Med. Assn.; contbr. articles to profl. jours. Chmn. pub. edn. com. Am. Cancer Soc. Orange County, 1982—86. Capt. M.C., USAR, 1971-77. Recipient Physician's Recognition awards AMA. Fellow ACS, Am. Soc. Colon and Rectal Surgeons, Internat. Coll. Surgeons, Southeastern Surg. Congress, Internat. Soc. Univ. Colon and Rectal Surgeons; mem. AMA, So. Med. Assn., Fla. Med. Assn. (sect. splty. medicine), Orange County Med. Assn., Piedmont Soc. Colon and Rectal Surgeons (pres. elect 1997, pres. 1998-2000), Orange County Ostomy Assn. (med. adviser), Fla. Soc. Colon and Rectal Surgeons (sec.-treas. 1980-82, pres. 1983-84, sec.-treas. 1986-98, pres. 1998-2000, treas. 2005—), Am. Soc. Gastrointestinal Endoscopy, Am. Soc. Laser Medicine and Surgery, Soc. Am. Gastrointestinal Endoscopic Surgeons. Home: 5252 Vista Club Run Sanford FL 32771-7153 Personal E-mail: tushmd4@aol.com.

SHUBB, WILLIAM BARNET, judge; b. Oakland, Calif., May 28, 1938; s. Ben and Nellie Bernice (Fruechtenicht) Shubb; m. Sandra Ann Talarico, July 29, 1962; children: Alisa Marie, Carissa Ann, Victoria Ann. AB, U. Calif., Berkeley, 1960, JD, 1963. Bar: Calif. 1964, US Ct. Internat. Trade 1981, US Customs Ct. 1980, US Ct. Appeals (9th cir.) 1964, US Supreme Ct. 1972. Law clk. US Dist. Ct., Sacramento, 1963—65; asst. US atty. US Dist. Ct. Ea. Dist. Calif., 1965—71, chief asst. US atty., 1971—74, chmn. com. drafting of local criminal rules, 1974; assoc. Diepenbrock, Wulff, Plant & Hannegan, Sacramento, 1974—77; mem. speedy trial planning com. US Dist. Ct. Ea. Dist. Calif., 1974—80; ptnr. Diepenbrock, Wulff, Plant & Hannegan, 1977—80; US atty. US Dist. Ct. Ea. Dist. Calif., 1980—81; ptnr. Diepenbrock, Wulff, Plant & Hannegan, 1981—90; judge US Dist. Ct. Ea. Dist. Calif., 1990—, chief judge, 1996—2003; adj. prof. U. The Pacific, McGeorge Sch. Law; vis. prof. law U. Calif., Davis Sch. Law. Instr. McGeorge Sch. Law U. Pacific, 1964—66; lawyer rep. 9th cir. US Jud. Conf., 1975—78; mem. faculty Fed. Practice Inst., 1978—80. Mem.: Fed. Bar Assn. (Sacramento chpt.) (judge liaison), Sacramento Rotary Club.

SHUBERT, JOSEPH FRANCIS, librarian; b. Buffalo, Sept. 17, 1928; s. Joseph Francis and Lena M. (Kohn) Shubert; m. Dorothy Jean Whearty, Feb. 5, 1955 (div. Feb. 1980); children: Julia Ellen, Susan, Alan Joseph. BS, State U. Tchrs. Coll., Geneseo, NY, 1951; MA, U. Denver, 1957. Reference and ext. libr. Nev. State Libr., Carson City, 1951-57, libr. cons., 1957-59, state libr., 1959-61; asst. dir. internat. rels. office ALA, 1962-66; state libr. Ohio, 1966-77; sec., treas. chief officer state Libr. Agys. N.Y. State Edn. Dept., 1973-76, chmn., 1976-78, state libr., asst. commr. librs., 1977-96, state libr. emeritus, 1996—; mem. adv. coun. U.S. Pub. Printer, 1974-77; mem. adv. com. White House Conf. Libr. and Info. Svcs., 1977-79; chmn. steering com. survey state libr. agys. U.S. Nat. Ctr. Edn. Stats., 1992—2003. Trustee Ohio Coll. Libr. Ctr., 1976—78; Disting. Alumnus lectr. U. Denver, 1979; mem. adv. com. Ctr. for Book Libr. of Congress, 1979—82, mem. network adv. coun., 1981—96; mem. adv. coun. Sch. Libr. and Info. Sci., Pratt Inst., 1980—2000; bd. dirs. N.E. Document Conservation Ctr., 1980—82, treas., 1986—89; mem. design task force White House Conf. Libr. and Info. Svcs., 1985; chmn. chief officers State Librs. in N.E., 1987—89; bd. dirs. Capital Dist. Regional Info. Svc. Network State U. Albany, NY, 1994—97. Editor: The Bookmark, 1987—96; contbr. articles to periodicals. Dir. Friends N.Y. State Libr., Inc., 1998—; mem. adv. com. U. Wis. Inst. Edn., Federally Funded Literacy Program, 1992—94; co-chair 50th anniversary com. Coll. Geneseo, 2001. Recipient Exceptional Achievement award, ALA Assn. Specialized and Coop. Libr. Agy. Assn., 1985, Disting. Pub. Svc. award, SUNY-Albany, Nelson A. Rockefeller Coll. Pub. Affairs and Policy, 1987, Hall of Fame award, Ohio Libr. Assn., 1991, Velma K. Moore award, N.Y. State Assn. Libr. Bds., 1996, Minerva award, SUNY-Geneseo & Friends of Milne Libr., 2006; named Disting. Alumnus, SUNY-Geneseo, 1985; named to Alumni Honor Roll, 1997. Mem.: ALA (grass roots adv. 1996), Chief Officers State Libr. Agys. (chmn. 1977—78), N.Y. Libr. Assn. (hon. chair capital campaign 1999—2000, Outstanding Svc. award 1996), Meml. Libr. Assn., North Collins Libr. Assn., Nev. Libr. Assn. (pres.), Assn. Specialized and Coop. Lit. Agys. (pres. 1988—89), Task Force Pub. Libr. Stats. (mem. adv. com. 1990—96, chair steering com. NCES Survey State Libr. Agys. 1993—2003), Nat. Commn. Librs. and Info. Svcs., Nat. Ctr. Ednl. Stats., Nev. Congress Parents and Tchrs., Torch Club Albany. Roman Catholic. Home: 2308 Evergreen Dr Plano TX 75075-7460

SHUBIN, JOANNA, science educator; b. Long Island City, NY, June 24, 1945; d. Vincent and Theresa Spampanato; m. Jonathan Simon Shubin, Mar. 30, 1980; 1 child, David Jonathan. BA, Queens Coll., 1967, MS, 1972. Cert. Teacher N-6 1973, Social Studies Teacher 1972, Biological Science Teacher 1991, Teacher Nat. Sci. Tchrs. Assn., 1987. Sci. tchr. St. Stanislaus Sch., Bklyn., 1969—71, Most Precious Blood Sch., LI City, 1971—81, Garden Sch., Jackson Heights, NY, 1981—85, Sci. Mus. LI, Manhasset, NY, 1985—86, Garden Sch., 1986—90, Great Neck South Mid. Sch., NY, 1992, Roslyn Mid. Sch., Roslyn, NY, 1992—. Contbr. articles to jours. Sci. tchr. Schneider Children's Hosp., Queens. Recipient Educator of Month, Hofstra U. and News 12, 2001, Excellence in Tchg., Sci. Tchrs. Assn. of NY State, 2002. Mem.: LI Sci. Edn. Leadership Assn. Inc., Astronomical Soc. of the Pacific, Sci. Tchrs. Assn. NY State, Nat. Sci. Tchrs. Assn. Avocations: astronomy, travel, reading. Home: 427 Bellmore Rd East Meadow NY 11554 Office: Roslyn Mid Sch Locust Lane Roslyn NY 11576

SHUCHART, EUGENE JOSEPH, retired accountant; b. New Freedom, Pa., May 22, 1924; s. Albert Alan Shuchart and Victoria Ann Ryer-Shuchart; m. Angelita Rodriguez Shuchart, Nov. 24, 1956; children: Eugene Joseph Jr., Michael Albert, Larry Francis, Lisa Marie, David Alan. BS in Econs., Villanova U., Pa., 1950; MBA, U. Pa., 1951. CPA Dept. Energy State Va., Richmond, Va., 1956—80, ret., 1980. With US Gen. Acctg. Office, 1951—68; assoc. prof. George Washington U., 1968—79; commr. Fed. Power Commn./Fed. Energy Regulatory Commn., 1968—80; instr. Edison Coll., 1981—97. With US Army, 1943—46, Pacific. Decorated Purple Heart U.S. Army. Mem.: Nat. Assn. Ret. Fed. Employees (Disting. Career Svc. award 1980), Disabled Am. Vets. (treas. 1996—97). Avocations: organ, piano, swimming, walking. Personal E-mail: eshuchart@comcast.net.

SHUE, ELISABETH, actress; b. Wilmington, Del., Oct. 6, 1963; m. Davis Guggenheim, 1994; children: William, Stella Street, Agnes Charles Student, Wellesley Coll.; BA in Govt., Harvard U., 2000; studied with Sylvie Leigh, Showcase Theater. Appeared in Broadway plays including Some Americans Abroad, Birth and After Birth; Actor (films) The Karate Kid, 1984 (Young Artist award 1984), Link, 1986, Adventures in Babysitting, 1987, Cocktail, 1988, Body Wars, 1989, Back to the Future Part II, 1989, Back to the Future Part III, 1990, Soapdish, 1991, The Marrying Man, 1991, Twenty Bucks, 1993, Heart and Souls, 1993, Radio Inside, 1994, Blind Justice, 1994, The Underneath, 1995, Leaving Las Vegas, 1995 (Oscar nominee for Best Actress), The Trigger Effect, 1996, The Saint, 1996, Palmetto, 1997, Deconstructing Harry, 1997, Cousin Bette, 1997, Molly, 1998, Hollow Man, 2000, Tuck Everlasting, 2002, Leo, 2002, Mysterious Skin, 2004, Hide and Seek, 2005, Dreamer: Inspired by a True Story, 2005, Gracie, 2007, First Born, 2007, Hamlet 2, 2008; (TV movies) Charles and Diana, Double Switch, 1987, Hale the Hero, 1992, Blind Justice; (TV series) Call to Glory, 1984, Amy & Isabelle, 2001. Office: c/o Mgmt 360 9111 Wilshire Blvd Beverly Hills CA 90210

SHUER, LAWRENCE MENDEL, neurosurgery educator, dean; b. Toledo, Apr. 12, 1954; s. Bernard Benjamin and Estelle Rose (Drukker) S.; m. Paula Ann Elliott, Sept. 4, 1976; children: Jenna, Tammy, Nichole. BA with high distinction, U. Mich., 1975, MD cum laude, 1978. Diplomate Am. Bd. Neurol. Surgery, Nat. Bd. Med. Examiners. Fellow in neurology Inst. Neurology, London, 1979; intern in surgery Stanford U. Sch. Medicine, Calif., 1978-79, resident in neuropathology, 1980, resident in neurosurgery, 1980-84, clin. asst. prof. surgery and neurosurgery, 1984-90, assoc. prof., 1990—2002, assoc. dean Grad. Med. Edn., 1996—, assoc. chair neurosurgery, 2004—; chief of staff Stanford U. Hosp. and Clinics, 1996—2008, prof., 2002—. Numerous presentations in field. Contbr. articles and abstracts to med. jours., chpts. to books. Recipient Kaiser tchr. award Stanford U., 1993; James B. Angell scholar. Mem. AMA, Am. Assn. Neurol. Surgeons, Congress Neurol. Surgeons, Western Neurosurg. Soc., Calif. Assn. Neurol. Surgeons (bd. dirs., treas. 1995—98, 2nd v.p. 1998-99, 1st v.p. 1999-2000, pres.-elect 2000-01, pres. 2002-03), Calif. Med. Assn., Am. Heart Assn. (fellow stroke coun.), Santa Clara County Med. Assn., San Francisco Neurol. Soc., Alpha Omega Alpha. Conservative. Jewish. Avocations: skiing, swimming, travel. Office: Stanford U Med Ctr 300 Pasteur Dr R229 Palo Alto CA 94304-5327 Home Phone: 650-222-5433; Office Phone: 650-723-6093. Business E-Mail: lshuer@stanford.edu.*

SHUGAN, STEVEN MARK, finance educator; b. Chgo., Apr. 21, 1952; s. David Lester and Charlotte Rose Shugan; m. Irene H. Shugan, Dec. 16, 1973; children: Adam Joshua, Elliot Hillel, Ross Isaac, Henry Andrew. BS in Chemistry, So. Ill. U., 1973, MBA, 1974; PhD in Managerial Econs. and Decision Scis., Northwestern U., 1978. Lectr. Grad Sch. Mgmt., Northwestern U., Evanston, Ill., 1975—76; asst. prof. bus. adminstrn. Grad Sch. Mgmt., U. Rochester, NY, 1977—79; asst. prof. mktg. Grad. Sch. Bus., U. Chgo., 1979—82, assoc. prof., 1982—87, prof., 1987—92; Russ Berrie eminent scholar, prof. mktg. U. Fla., Gainesville, 1991—. Chmn., organizer sessions numerous nat. confs., 1979—; cons. various cos., 1976—; chmn. Mktg. Sci. Conf., 1963—96. Editor-in-chief Mktg. Sci., 2002; contbr. articles to profl. bus. jours. Recipient numerous awards. Mem.: Am. Statis. Assn., Inst. Mgmt. Scis. (pres. coll. mktg.), Assn. Consumer Rsch., Ops. Rsch. Soc. Am., Am. Mktg. Assn. Office: Univ Fla 209 Bryan Hall Gainesville FL 32611-2014 Business E-Mail: sms@ufl.edu.

SHUGART, HOWARD ALAN, physicist, researcher; b. Orange, Calif., Sept. 21, 1931; s. Howard Ancil and Bertha Elizabeth (Henderson) S.; m. Elizabeth L. Hanson, Feb. 6, 1971. BS, Calif. Inst. Tech., 1953; MA, U. Calif., Berkeley, 1955, PhD, 1957. Tchg. asst. physics U. Calif., Berkeley, 1953-56, assoc., 1957, lectr., 1957-58, acting asst. prof., 1958-59, asst. prof., 1959-63, assoc. prof., 1963-67, prof., 1967-93, prof. emeritus, 1993—, vice chmn., 1968—70, 1979—87, 1989—2001, acting chmn., 1979—81, 1983—84, 1987. Cons. Convair divsn. Gen. Dynamics Corp., 1960-61; mem. com. nuc. constants NRC, 1960-63; atomic beam group leader Lawrence Berkeley (Calif.) Nat. Lab., 1965-79, guest rschr., 1999—. Fellow Am. Phys. Soc. (acting sec. Pacific Coast 1961-64, exec. com. divsn. electron and atomic physics 1972-74), Nat. Speleological Soc. (gov. 1954-56); mem. Sigma Xi. Office: U Calif Dept Physics Berkeley CA 94720-7300

SHUGART, JILL, retired school administrator; b. Dallas, July 15, 1940; d. Claude Ernest and Allie Merle (Hamilton) S. BA, Baylor U., 1962; MA, Tex. Woman's U., 1972, PhD, 1980. Middle sch. English tchr. Garland (Tex.) Ind. Sch. Dist., 1962-63, high sch. social studies tchr., 1963-76, high sch. asst. prin., 1976-79, dir. communications, 1979-82, asst. supt., 1982-85, supt., 1985—99, ret., 1999—; exec. dir. Region X Edn. Svc. Ctr., 2004—07. Mem. legis. coun. U. Interscholastic League, Tex., 1989-99; chmn. Dist. III music com., Tex., 1989-99; adj. prof. Tex. Women's U., Denton, 1983; chmn. Region X ESC Adv. Coun., rep. to commr.'s supt.'s com., 1993-95; cons. Richardson and Carrollton-Farmers Br. Sch. Dists., 2000-04; coord. Region 10 ESC Supr.'s Acad., 2000-04, mem. commrs. cabinet regional svcs., 2004-07. Gen. chmn. Boy Scouts Am. Scouting Night, Dallas, 1988-89; chmn. City of Garland Comty. Action Com., 1995-99; sec. Tex. Sch. Alliance, 1995-96, chmn., 1998-99; life mem. Tex. and nat. PTA; pres. Garland br. Am. Heart Assn., 1990-91; co-chmn. sustaining dr. Garland YMCA, 1995-96; mem. Adv. Com. to Gov. and State Legisture, 1998; mem. steering com. Garland Econ. Devel. Partnership, 1994-99, Tex. Fast Growth Sch. Coalition; chair Tex. Sch. Alliance, 1998—. Recipient Lamar award for excellence Masons, Award of Distinction, Tex. Ret. Tchrs. Assn.; named Top 100 Educators to Watch, Executive Educator mag., 1985, Finalist as Outstanding Tex. Sch. Supt., 1990, Woman of Distinction, Soroptomist Club, Disting. Alumnus, Garland H.S., 2005; Paul Harris fellow. Mem. Quality Tex. Bd. Examiners, Garland Edn. Found. (bd. dirs. 1999—), Baylor Med. Ctr. Garland (bd. dirs. 2001—). Baptist. Avocations: travel, lake activities. Home: 345 Winding Shore Kemp TX 75143 Personal E-mail: jillshugart@aol.com.

SHUGER, DEBORA KULLER, humanities educator; m. Scott Shuger (dec. 2002); 1 child, Dale. PhD, Stanford Univ., 1983. Prof., English UCLA. Co-editor: Religion and Culture in Renaissance England, 1997; author: Sacred Rhetoric, 1988, Habits of Thought in the English Renaissance, 1990, The Renaissance Bible, 1994, Political Theologies in Shakespeare's England, 2001, Censorship and Cultural Sensibility, 2006. Grantee Guggenheim Fellowship, Rockefeller Found. Fellowship. Fellow: Am. Acad. Arts & Scis. Office: Humanities Bldg 297 UCLA PO Box 951417 Los Angeles CA 90095-1417 Office Phone: 310-825-3897. Business E-Mail: shuger@humnet.ucla.edu.

SHUGHART, WILLIAM FRANKLIN, II, economics professor, consultant; b. Harrisburg, Pa., Dec. 3, 1947; s. William Franklin and Mary Lucille Shughart; m. Hilary Celia Kauffman, Dec. 29, 1986; children: William Franklin III, Frank Jefferson. BA, Tex. A&M U., College Station, 1969, MS, 1970, PhD, 1978. Economist FTC, Washington, 1978—83; asst. prof. econs. Clemson (SC) U., 1984—85; assoc. prof. econs. George Mason U., Fairfax, Va., 1985—88; prof. econs. U. Miss., University, 1988—. Pres. Oxford (Miss.) Economics, Inc., 2004—. Author: Antitrust Policy and Interest-Group Politics, 1990, The Organization of Industry, 1990, Modern Managerial Economics, 1994, The Organization of Industry, 2nd ed., 1997, The Political Economy of the New Deal, 1998; editor: The Causes and Consequences of Antitrust, 1995, Taxing Choice, 1997, The Elgar Companion to Public Choice, 2001, The Economics of Budget Deficits, 2002, Policy Challenges and Political Responses, 2005. Petty officer 3rd class USN, 1971—74. Recipient Sir Anthony Fisher Internat. Meml. award, Atlas Econ. Rsch. Found., 1998; named F. A. P. Barnard Disting. prof., U. Miss., 1998—. Mem.: Pub. Choice Soc., Western Econ. Assn., Am. Econ. Assn., So. Econ. Assn. (trustee 1996—98), Am. Political Sci. Assn. (assoc.). Home: 21 County Rd 3024 Oxford MS 38655 Office: Univ Miss Dept of Economics University MS 38677-1848 Office Fax: 662-915-6943. Personal E-mail: wfs2@aggienetwork.com. Business E-Mail: shughart@olemiss.edu.

SHUHY, DAVID E., theater educator, set designer; b. Washington, Sept. 12, 1974; m. Katherine Franzke; children: Lilian, Eli. PhD in Theatrical Design Aesthetics and Theory, Union Inst. and U., Cin., 2004. Residence artist Regent U., Virginia Beach, 2005—08; lectr. Salisbury U., Md., 2000—05, asst. prof., 2008—. Resident scene designer (theatre production) Regent University Main Season (Kennedy Ctr. Am. Coll. Theatre Festvial Meritorious Achievement award, 2006), resident lighting and scene designer Salisbury University Main Season, scene designer Virginia Shakespeare Festival (Taming of the Shrew; Othello; Complete History of America Abridged), The Foreigner, The Crucible, Twelfth Night, Peer Gynt, The Imaginary Invalid, How to Succeed in Business without Really Trying (Kennedy Ctr. Am. Coll. Theatre Festival: Cert. of Merit Faculty Designer, 2006), Noises Off; contbr. articles to profl. jours. Mem.: United Scenic Artists, US Inst. Theatre Tech.(Chesapeake Region).

SHUKLA, DEEPSHIKHA, research scientist; PhD, Ohio U., Athens, 2006. Postdoc. rschr. George Wash. U., Washington, 2006—; postdoc. rsch. assoc. U. NC, Chapel Hill, 2009. Office: George Washington Univ 725 21st St NW Corcoran 105 Washington DC 20052

SHULA, MIKE (MICHAEL JOHN SHULA), professional football coach, former college football coach; b. Balt., June 3, 1965; s. Donald F. and Mary S. Shula. BA in Labor Rels., U. Ala., 1987. Offensive asst. Tampa Bay Buccaneers, 1988—90, quarterbacks coach, 1990—91, offensive coord., 1996—99; coaches asst. Miami Dolphins, 1991—92, quarterbacks coach, 2001—02; asst. coach Chgo. Bears, 1993—95; head coach U. Ala., 2003—06; quarterbacks coach Jacksonville Jaguars, 2007—. Office: Jacksonville Jaguars 1 ALLTEL Stadium Pl Jacksonville FL 32202*

SHULA, ROBERT JOSEPH, lawyer; b. South Bend, Ind., Dec. 10, 1936; s. Joseph Edward and Bertha Mona (Buckner) S.; m. Gaye Ann Martin, Oct. 8, 1978; children: Deirdre Regina, Robert Joseph II, Elizabeth Martin. BS in Mktg., Ind. U., 1958, JD, 1961. Bar: Ind. 1961. Ptnr. Bingham Summers Welsh & Spilman, Indpls., 1965-82, sr. ptnr., 1982-89; ptnr. Price & Shula, Indpls., 1989-91, Lowe Gray Steele & Darko, Indpls., 1991—2003; of counsel Norris Choplin and Schroeder, Indpls., 2003—05; pvt. practice Indpls., 2005—. Mem. faculty Nat. Inst. Trial Advocacy; guest lectr. Brit. Medicine and Law Soc., 1979, Ind. U. Sch. Law; medico-legal lectr. Ind. U. Schs. Medicine, Dentistry, and Nursing. Bd. dirs. Arts Ind., Indpls., 1995-99; founding pres. Oriental Arts Soc., Indpls., 1975-79, Meridian Women's Clinic, Inc., Indpls.; trustee Indpls. Mus. Art, 1975-78, life trustee, 1984—; bd. dirs. Ind. Repertory Theatre, Indpls., 1982-92, chmn. bd. dirs., pres., 1985-89; pres. Repertory Soc., 1993-96; v.p., bd. dirs. Flanner House of Indpls., Inc., 1977-88, chmn., 1988-99; pres. Internat. Ctr. of Indpls., Inc., 1993-96; commr. Indpls. Met. Devel. Commn., 2005-. Maj. JAGC, USAFR, 1961—65. Recipient Gov.'s award of Sagamore of the Wabash, 1998. Master Am. Inns of Ct.; 20th Fighter Wing Assn. (v.p. 2005—); mem. ABA, FBA, Am. Assn. for Justice, Am. Law Inst. (diplomate), Am. Bd. Trial Advs. (pres. 2000), Am. Coll. Legal Medicine, Ind. Bar Assn., Indpls. Bar Assn. Ind. Trial Lawyers Assn. Democrat. Episcopalian. Avocations: flying, art. Home: 7924 Beaumont Green Pl Indianapolis IN 46250-1663 Office: 9333 N Meridian St Ste 105 Indianapolis IN 46260 Home Phone: 317-845-1857; Office Phone: 317-582-0006. Business E-Mail: shulalaw@sprynet.com.

SHULDINER, ALAN RODNEY, endocrinologist, educator; b. Irumagawa, Japan, Feb. 5, 1957; parents Am. citizens; s. Julius and Janet (Gursky) S.; m. Jill Francie Bresman, June 27, 1984; children: Seth David, Scott Ross. AB in Chemistry magna cum laude, Lafayette coll., 1979; MD with honors, Harvard U., 1984. Diplomate Am. Bd. Internal Medicine, Am. Bd. Endocrinology and Metabolism. Intern in medicine Columbia-Presbyn. Hosp., NYC, 1984-85, resident in medicine, 1985-86; med. staff fellow Diabetes Br. Nat. Inst. Diabetes and Digestive and Kidney Diseases NIH, Bethesda, Md., 1986-88, sr. staff fellow, 1988-90; asst. prof. div. geriatric medicine and gerontology Sch. Medicine Johns Hopkins U., Balt., 1990-91, assoc. prof. div. geriatric medicine and gerontology, 1993—97; prof., head division of diabetes, obesity and nutrition U. Maryland Medical Sch., 1997—99, prof., head division of endocrinology, diabetes and nutrition, 1999—, John Whitehurst Professor of Medicine, 2005—, dir., Interdepartmental Program in Genetics and Genomic Medicine, 2005—; core investigator, geriatric rsch. and education clinical ctr. Balt. Veterans Administration Medical Ctr.; network dir., Joslin Diabetes Ctr. U. Maryland. Guest rschr. Nat. Inst. on Aging NIH, Balt., 1991—96; prof., head divsn. diabetes, obesity and nutrition U. Md. Sch. Medicine, 1997—99; dir. Joslin Diabetes Ctr, 1997—, head divsn. endocrinology, diabetes & nutrition, 1999—; lectr. Endocrine Soc. meetings, 1996, 99, Japan Diabetes Soc. meeting, 1996, Am. Heart Assn. meeting, 1996, FASEB meeting, 1997, Am. Diabetes Assn. meeting, 1997, 99, VII Internat. Symposium on Insulin Action, 1998, with, 2000, NAASD, 2001, FASEB, 2002. Co-author: Current Therapy in Endocrinology and Metabolism, 3d edit., 1988, 4th edit., 1991, Handbook of Endocrine Research Techniques, 1993, Diabetes Mellitus: A Fundamental and Clinical text, 1996, 3d edit., 2003; contbr. articles to profl. jours. including Archives Biochem. Biophysics, Jour. Biol. Chemistry, New Eng. Jour. Medicine, Diabetes, Analytical Biochemistry, Endocrinology, Gene, Nucleic Acids Rsch., Procs. NAS, Biotechniques, Jour. Clin. Endocrinology Metabolism, Diabetes. Recipient Paul Beeson Physician Faculty Scholar award Am. Fedn. Aging Rsch., 1996. Fellow: ACP (Betty Stevens award 2003); mem.: AMA, AAAS, Endocrine Soc., Am. Diabetes Assn. Office: Univ Maryland 660 W Redwood St Rm 494 Baltimore MD 21201-1009 E-mail: ashuldin@medicine.umaryland.edu.*

SHULER, CAROLETTA ALEXIS, criminal justice educator; b. Orangeburg, SC, Mar. 17, 1967; d. Tom and Bernadean Shuler. BA, U. SC, Columbia, 1989, BS, 1994, M of Criminal Justice, 1996; EdD, U. SD, Vermillion, 1998. Asst. mgr. Fast Mart Store, Orangeburg, SC, 1990—92; parking enforcement officer SC State U., Orangeburg, 1992—93; resident adv. divsn. student affairs U. SC, Columbia, 1993—94, asst. hall dir. divsn. of student affairs, 1994, grad. asst. coll. criminal justice, 1995—96, tchg. intern coll. criminal justice, 1996; grad. asst. higher edn. program U. SD, Vermillion, 1997—98; vis. asst. prof. SC State U., Orangeburg, 1998—99, asst. prof., 1999—2007; online faculty criminal justice South U., 2007—. Campus dir. SC Tchg. Fellows Program, Orangeburg, 2000—07. Mem.: Am. Study of Higher Edn., SC Coun. for the Social Studies, Philosopy Edn. Soc., Nat. Coun. for History Edn., Nat. Coun. for the Social Studies, Pi Lambda Theta (faculty liaison 1999), Kappa Delta Pi (faculty counselor 1999), Alpha Kappa Alpha. Democrat. Roman Catholic. Business E-Mail: calexisshuler@msn.com.

SHULER, DENNIS W., entertainment company executive; b. NY; married; 2 children. BS in Bus Adminstrn., magna cum laude, SUNY, Oswego; MA in Human Resources Mgmt., summa cum laude, U. Ala. Lectr. Highline CC, Seattle; assoc. Kaiser Aluminum and Chem. Corp.; various position including human resources mgr. and dir. human resources UK/Ireland Procter and Gamble Co., 1984—2002, v.p. human resources, beauty and health & well being, 2002—08; exec. v.p., chief human resources officer Walt Disney Co., 2008—. Vis. prof., bus. adminstrn. Northumbria U., Newcastle, England; vis. prof. Durham U. Mem. Am. C. of C., London; vol. Jr. Achievement; active Greater Cin. Fine Arts Fund; fin. contbr. Cin. Children's Hosp.; bd. governors Woking Coll.; former bd. mem. Coll. Mt. St. Joseph, Cin.; bd. visitors U. Ala., Tuscaloosa; adv. bd. mem. Durham U.; bd. mem. Xavier U. Williams Coll. Bus., Cin. Fellow: Royal Soc. Arts London; mem.: Phi Beta Kappa (Beta Gamma Sigma Chpt. Disting. Alumni award 2007). Office: Walt Disney Co 500 S Buena Vista St Burbank CA 91521*

SHULER, ELLIE GIVAN, JR., retired military officer, museum administrator; b. Raleigh, NC, Dec. 6, 1936; s. Ellie Givan and Berta (Williams) S.; m. Annette Fontaine Maury, Mar. 22, 1961; children: Ellie Givan III, Franklin Maury, Gray Hays. BSCE, The Citadel, 1959; MS in Mgmt., Rensselaer Poly. Inst., 1967; grad., Squadron Officer Sch., Maxwell AFB, Ala., 1964; postgrad., Naval War Coll.; grad. command and staff course, Nat. War Coll., 1976; grad. cen. flight instr. course, Castle AFB, Calif. Engr. in tng., S.C. Commd. 2d lt. U.S. Air Force, 1959, advanced through grades to lt. gen., 1988, various positions and locations, 1959-68, F-4C pilot, asst. flight comdr. 558th Tactical Fighter Squadron Cam Ranh Bay AFB, Republic of Vietnam, 1968-69, indsl. engr., then asst. dep. chief Engring. Mgmt. Div., Hdqrs. 2d Air Force Barksdale AFB, La., 1969-71; asst. exec. officer to comdr. in chief U.S. Air Force in Europe, Lindsey Air Sta., West Germany, 1972-73, base civil engr., comdr. 86th Civil Engring. Squadron Ramstein Air Base, Fed. Republic Germany, 1973-75; dir. ops. 3902d Air Base Wing, comdr. 3902d Ops. Squadron Offutt AFB, Nebr., 1976; dir. programs Office Dep. Chief of Staff for Engring. and Services SAC, Offutt AFB, Nebr., 1976-77, exec. to comdr. in chief, 1977-79; vice comdr., then comdr. 19th Bombardment Wing Robins AFB, Ga., 1979-80; comdr. 42d Bombardment Wing Loring AFB, Maine, 1980-81; comdr. 4th Air Div. F.E. Warren AFB, Wyo., 1981-84; comdr. 3rd Air Div. SAC, Andersen AFB, Guam, 1984-86; asst. dep. then dep. chief of staff, ops. SAC Hqrs., Offutt AFB, Nebr., 1986-88; comdr. 8th Air Force SAC, Barksdale AFB, 1988-91; retired, 1991; chmn. bd., CEO 8th Air Force Heritage Mus., 1992—98. Trustee, Longs Peak coun. Boy Scouts Am., 1983-84, chair bd. trustees, 1992-2004; trustee Falcon Found., USAF Acad., 8th Air Force Heritage Mus., 1992—. Decorated D.S.M. with oak leaf cluster, Legion of Merit with oak leaf cluster, D.F.C., Air medal with five oak leaf clusters, Air Force Commendation medal with oak leaf cluster; recipient medal of Honor DAR, 2005, Disting. Eagle Scout award Boy Scouts Am., 2006; named Disting. Alumnus, The Citadel, 2007. Mem. Soc. Am. Mil. Engrs. (chpt. pres. 1971), Am. Def. Preparedness Assn. (regional bd. dirs. 1981-84), Order of Dadaelians (hon. flight capt. 1981-85), Council on Am.'s Mil. Past, Mil. Order of World Wars, Kiwanis, Tau Beta Pi. Republican. Episcopalian. Avocations: numismatics, golf, hunting, military, history. Home: 5914 Marthas Glen Rd Columbia SC 29209 Home Phone: 803-776-6462. Personal E-mail: egshulerjr@bellsouth.net.

SHULER, HEATH (JOSEPH HEATH SHULER), United States Representative from North Carolina, retired professional football player; b. Swain County, NC, Dec. 21, 1971; s. Joe and Margie Shuler; m. Nikol Shuler, 1998; children: Island, Navy. BA in Psychology, U. Tenn., 2001. Quarterback Wash. Redskins, 1994—96, New Orleans Saints, 1997; co-owner, pres. Heath Shuler Real Estate, LLC, Knoxville, Tenn., 1998—2003; mem. US Congress from 11th Tenn. dist., 2007—. Bd. dirs. United Cmty. Bank; mem. Blue Dog Caucus US Congress, 2007—, mem. small bus. com., transp. and infrastructure com., natural resources com., 2007—. Founder Heath Shuler Found.; charter mem. Friends of Smokies; bd. mem. Knoxville Boys & Girls Club; nat. spokesman Character Counts; mem. scholarship com. NC Assn. Advancement of Teaching. Mem.: Blue Dog Coalition, Fell. Christian Athletes. Democrat. Baptist. Office: 356 Biltmore Ave Ste 400 Asheville NC 28801 also: US House of Reps 422 Cannon House Office Bldg Washington DC 20515 Office Phone: 828-252-1651. Office Fax: 828-252-8734.*

SHULER, KURT EGON, chemist, educator; b. Nuremberg, Germany, July 10, 1922; came to U.S., 1937, naturalized, 1944; s. Louis and Donie (Wald) Schulherr; m. Beatrice Gwyn London, Nov. 11, 1944. BS, Ga. Inst. Tech., 1942; PhD, Cath. U. Am., 1949. Fellow Johns Hopkins U., 1949-51; sr. staff mem., asst. group supr., chem. physics group Applied Physics Lab., Johns Hopkins, 1951-55; supervisory phys. chemist Nat. Bur. Standards, 1955-58, cons. to dir., 1958-61, asst. dir., sr. research fellow, 1963-68; rsch. staff, sci. adviser to v.p. rsch. Gen. Motors Corp., 1958; spl. asst. to dir. rsch. Inst. Def. Analyses, 1961-63; vis. prof. chemistry U. Calif., San Diego, 1966-67, prof. chemistry, 1968-91, prof. emeritus, 1991—, chmn. dept., 1968-70, 84-87. Cons. in field; mem. Solvay Conf., 1962, 78; mem. adv. panel, chemistry div. NSF, 1973-75. Author, editor tech. books; assoc. editor: Jour. Math. Physics, 1963-66; bd. editors: Jour. Statis. Physics, 1968-80; mem. adv. bd.: Chem. Engring. News, 1967-70; contbr. articles to profl. jours. Served with U.S. Army, 1944-46. Recipient Distinguished Service award Nat. Bur. Standards, 1959, Gold medal award Dept. Commerce, 1968; Solvay Found. fellow, 1975 Fellow Am. Inst. Chemists, AAAS, Am. Phys. Soc., Washington Acad. Sci.; mem. Am. Chem. Soc., Washington Philos. Soc. Clubs: Rancho Santa Fe Golf. Achievements include the department of chemistry and biochemistry at the University of California San Diego establishing an endowed chair in his name in 2006. Home: PO Box 1504 Rancho Santa Fe CA 92067-1504 Office: Univ Calif San Diego Dept Chemistry La Jolla CA 92093 Business E-Mail: kshuler@ucsd.edu.

SHULEVITZ, URI, writer, illustrator; b. Warsaw, Feb. 27, 1935; came to U.S., 1959, naturalized, 1965; Student, Tel-Aviv Art Inst., 1953-55; Tchrs. Cert., Tchrs. Coll. Israel, 1956; student, Bklyn. Museum Art Sch., 1959-61. Instr. illustrating and writing children's books The New Sch., 1970-86; dir. illustrating and writing children's books Hartwick Coll., 1974-92. Author, illustrator: The Moon In My Room, 1963, One Monday Morning, 1967, Rain Rain Rivers, 1969, Oh What a Noise, 1971, The Magician, 1973, Dawn, 1974, The Treasure, 1978, (Caldecott honor book 1979), The Strange and Exciting Adventures of Jeremiah Hush, 1986, Toddlecreek Post Office, 1990, The Secret Room, 1993, Snow, 1998 (Caldecott Honor book 1999), What is a Wise Bird like you Doing in a silly tale like this?, 2000, The Travels of Benjamin of Tudela, through three Continents in the Twelfth Century, 2005, So Sleepy Story, 2006; author: Writing with Pictures: How to Write and Illustrate Children's Books, 1985, How I Learned Geography, 2008; illustrator: The Mystery of the Woods, 1964, Charley Sang a Song, 1964, A Rose, A Bridge and A Wild Black Horse, 1964, The Second Witch, 1965, The Carpet of Solomon, 1966, Maximilian's World, 1966, The Silk Spinners, 1967, The Fool of the World and the Flying Ship, 1968 (Caldecott medal 1969), Runaway Jonah and Other Tales, 1968, The Twelve Dancing Princesses, 1966, Oh What A Noise!, 1971, Soldier and Tsar in the Forest, 1972, The Fools of Chelm, 1973, The Touchstone, 1976, Hanukah Money, 1978, The Lost Kingdom of Karnica, 1979, The Golem, 1982, Lilith's Cave: Jewish Tales of the Supernatural, 1988, The Diamond Tree, 1991, The Golden Goose, 1995, Hosni The Dreamer, 1997, others. Served with Israeli Army, 1956-59. Guggenheim fellow, 1999. Mem Authors Guild. Office: Farrar Straus Giroux 18 W 18th St New York NY 10011-4607

SHULKIN, MARTIN B., lawyer; b. Cambridge, Mass., Apr. 24, 1944; BA, Williams Coll., 1966; JD, Boston Coll., 1969. Bar: Mass. 1969, Fla., US Ct. Appeals (5th cir.), US Dist. Ct., Mass., State Cts. of Fla. Jud. clk. to Hon. G. Joseph Tauro Superior Ct. Mass., 1969-70; assoc. Burns & Levinson LLP, Boston, 1970—71, ptnr., 1980—99, mng. ptnr., 1992—96; founding ptnr. Soble, Soble & Shulkin, Boston, 1972—79; ptnr. Sweeney & Franklin, Boston, 1979—80, Duane Morris LLP, Boston, 1999—, mng. ptnr. Boston office, 1999—. Editor Boston Coll. Law Rev., 1968—69; contbr. articles to law jours. Mem.: ABA, Assn. Corp. Growth, Boston Bar Assn., Order of Coif. Office: Duane Morris LLP Ste 500 470 Atlantic Ave Boston MA 02210 Office Phone: 857-488-4210. Office Fax: 857-488-4201. Business E-Mail: mbshulkin@duanemorris.com.*

SHULKINA, TATYANA, botanist, researcher; b. St. Petersburg, Russia, July 16, 1939; arrived in U.S., 1991, naturalized, 1996; d. Vladimir and Elizabeth (Troizky) Borovsky; m. Yuri Shulkin, Mar. 17, 1961; 1 child, Kate Goldenberg. BS with honors, Forest U., St. Petersburg, 1962; MS, Bot. Inst., Acad. Sci., St. Petersburg, 1965, PhD, 1984. Lead rschr. Bot. Inst. Acad. Sci., St. Petersburg, 1962—65, scientist, 1965—84, rschr., 1984—91; asst. prof. Truman Coll., Chgo., 1992—95; asst. curator Mo. Bot. Garden, St. Louis, 1996—99, curator, 2000—. Mem. sci. coun. Bot. Inst. Russia, St. Petersburg, 1985—91, Plant Industry Inst., St. Petersburg, 1986—91; cons. Chgo. Bot. Garden, Glencoe, 1993—; with internat. projects Red Book Cacasus. Author (in Russian): Rock Gardens, 1975; author: (in English) Ornamental Plants from Russia, 2004; Healing Herbs in the USA, 2006; contbr. articles to profl. jours. Tchr. Soc. Knowledge, 1966—91. Recipient medal, Internat. Bot. Congress, 1975, 1999. Mem.: Am. Soc. Plant Taxonomists. Office: Mo Bot Garden 4500 Shaw Rsch Ctr Saint Louis MO 63110 Office Phone: 314-577-0853. Business E-Mail: tatyana.shulkina@mobot.org.

SHULL, JOHNNY THOMAS, finance educator; s. Johnny Stowe Shull and Dorris Watson; m. Ashley Smith, July 20, 2002; 1 child, Kelcey. BA, Campbell U., Buies Creek, NC, 2002; MBA, Campbell U., 2003. Lead instr. bus. & economics Ctrl. Carolina CC, Lillington, NC, 2005—; pres. Surreal, Inc., Coats, NC, 1998—2005. Glaxosmithkline faculty fellow Inst. Emerging Issues NC State U., Raleigh, 2008—. Recipient MO Phillips award, Coats Area Chamber of Commerce; Presdl. Scholar, Campbell U. Mem.: Intercollegiate Studies Inst., Adam Smith Soc., Phi Beta Lambda. Office: Central Carolina CC 1075 East Cornelius Harnett Blvd Lillington NC 27546 Business E-Mail: jshull@cccc.edu.

SHULMAN, ABRAHAM, otolaryngology educator, hospital administrator; b. NYC, Feb. 24, 1929; s. Ben and Libby (Sarnoff) S.; m. Arlene P., Sept. 8, 1957; children: Rachel, Melanie. BS, CCNY, 1950; MD, U. Berne, 1955. Bar:; diplomate Am. Bd. Otolaryngology., 1962. Rotating surg. intern Queens County Gen. Hosp., 1955—56; resident in otolaryngology Kings County Hosp., Bklyn., 1957—60; clin. instr. Downstate Med. Ctr. SUNY, 1962—64, assoc. prof. Downstate Med. Ctr., 1975—89; prof. clin. otolaryngology SUNY Health Sci. Ctr., Bklyn., 1989—92, prof. emeritus clin. otolaryngology, 1992—; clin. instr. Albert Einstein Coll. Medicine, 1966—68, asst. clin. prof. otolaryn. surgery, 1968—75. Asst. surgeon Bklyn. Eye & Ear Hosp., 1966-69; otology cons. College Point chief of otolaryngology Lincoln Hosp., 1967-70, Bklyn. VA Med. Ctr., 1977-85, chief otolaryngology, staff attending otolaryngologist, 1985—, acting chief of otolaryngology, 1990-91; lectr., asst. attending otolaryngologist Mt. Sinai Hosp., 1974; chief otolaryngology Lincoln Hosp., 1967-1970; asst. attending otolaryngology Bronx Mcpl. Hosp., 1967-75; chief Otolaryngologist, asst. attending otolaryngologist, Kings County Hosp., 1962-64, dir. otolaryngology, 1975-92, attending otolaryngologist, 1975—, Brookdale Med. Ctr., 1982-86; chief otolaryngology Cath. Med. Ctr., Bklyn. and Queens, 1969-94, attending otololaryngologist St. John's Queens Hosp., 1969-94; chmn. Internat. Tinnitus Forum, 1982—; Martha Entenmann Tinnitus Rsch. Ctr., Inc., dir. otology neurotology 1994—. Editor (co-chief): Internat. Tinnitus Jour., 1994—; editor: (text) Tinnitus Diagnosis and Treatment, 1991—. Cons. Children's Devel. Ctr., 1975; med. cons. Office Vocat. Rehab., 1974; dir. med. svc. Lexington Sch. of the Deaf, 1972-74. Lt. comdr. USNR, 1960-62. Recipient Cert. of Appreciation, Am. Speech and Hearing Assn., 1989—, Hocks award, Am. Tinnitus Assn., 1990, Honor award, Am. Acad. Otolaryngology, 1994, Myrtle Reed award, Hadassah Zionist Orgn. Am., honoree, Neuro Equilibrimetric Soc., 1998. Fellow ACS, AMA, Am. Acad. Ophthalmology and Otolaryngology, Am. Neurotology Soc., Am. Audiology Soc., Am. Soc. Ophthalmologic and Otolaryngology Allergy, Am. Soc. Facial Plastic Surgery, Internat. Coll. Surgeons, Adam Politzer Soc.; mem. Am. Coun. Otolaryngology, Am. Soc. Contemporary Medicine and Surgery, Pan-Am. Assn. Otorhinolaryngology and Bronchoesophagology, N.Y. Acad. Sci., Soc. for Cryosurgery, Queens County Med. Soc., Soc. Univ. Otolaryngologists, Bklyn. Oncology Soc., Assn. for Rsch. in Otolaryngology, Neuroequilibrimetric Soc., Harvey Soc., Centurion Club, Sigma Xi. Office: SUNY Health Sci Ctr Bklyn Div Otolaryngology 450 Clarkson Ave Brooklyn NY 11203-2056 Office Phone: 718-773-8888.

SHULMAN, ARTHUR, communications executive; b. NYC, Mar. 4, 1927; s. Jacob and Sarah (Hochman) S.; m. Jan. 30, 1958; children: James, Karen. BA, Syracuse U., 1950. Asst. to pub. TV Guide Mag., Radnor, Pa., 1958-72; pub. Seventeen Mag., NYC, 1972-73; dir. regional ops. TV Guide, 1974-82; dir. comm. B'nai B'rith Internat., Washington, 1983-93. Author: How Sweet It Was, 1966, The Television Years, 1972. Dir. Penn Wynne (Pa.) Civic Assn., 1965-66. S/Sgt. US Army, 1945-46, Japan. Mem. Radio & TV Execs. Soc., Nat. Press Club, Overseas Press Club, Nat. Acad. TV Arts & Scis. Jewish. Address: 4017 Jardin Ln Sarasota FL 34238-4504 Personal E-mail: artshulman@comcast.net.

SHULMAN, BERNARD H., psychiatrist, educator; b. Balt., Sept. 14, 1922; s. Harry and Yetta Shulman; m. Phyllis Mann; children: Mark, Robert, Cynthia. AB, Johns Hopkins U., 1943; MD, Chgo. Med. Sch., 1946. Lic. Ill., 1949, cert. Am. Bd. Psych. and Neorology, 1957. Perceptorship for Rudolf Dreikurs, 1949—51; internship Mercer Hosp., Trenton, NJ, 1946, Veterans Hosp., Hines, Ill., 1951—52, 1954—55; chief liason svcs. Va. Hosp., 1955—56; psychiatrist Psychiatric Inst. Mcpl. Ct., 1956—58; faculty dept. psychiatry Northwestern U. Sch. Medicine, 1957—73, 1980—84; chmn. dept. psychiatry St. Joseph Hosp., Chgo., 1964—84; dir. psychiatric svcs. Diamond Headache Clinic., 1986—; chmn. bd. Adler Sch., 2000—05, bd. mem., 2005—08. Dir. resident training cons. Galesburg State Rsch. Hosp., 1960—65; training cons. Ill. State Psychiatric Inst., 1960—65, VA Hosp., Downey, Ill., 1960—76; instr. Adler Sch. Profl. Psychology, 1960—90, bd. trustees, 1962—, disting. prof., 1990, chmn. bd., 2000—; chmn. dept. psychiatry St. Joseph Hosp., Chgo., 1964—84; clin. prof. dept. psychiatry Loyola U. Stritch Sch. Medicine, 1973—80; clin. prof. Northwestern U. Sch. Medicine, 1980—84. Author: Essays in Schizophrenia, 1968, Contributions to Individual Psychology, 1973, Schizophrenia: Causes, Characteristics & Cures, 1974, How to Survive Your Aging Parents, 2d edit., 2002, How to Caring Your Aging Parents, 2009; author: (with R. Forgus) Personality: A Cognitive View, 1979; author: (with H. Mosak) Handbook for the Life Style, 1988; author: (with D. Peven) Who is Sylvia, 2002. Capt. med. corps. AUS, 1952—54, chief Mental Hygiene Consultation Svc., Ft. Belvoir, Va. Recipient Dist. Life Fellow, Am. Psych. Assn., 2003. Fellow: Am. Psychiatric Assn. (life disting. life fellow); mem.: Nat. Headache Found., Internat. Assn. Individual Psychology (pres. 1972—80), N. Am. Soc. Adlerian Psychology (pres. 1962—64), Ill. Med. Soc., Chgo. Med. Soc., Am. Bd. Adminstrv. Psychiatry, Am. Bd. Neurology Psychiatry. Office Phone: 847-679-8000. Personal E-mail: rbshulman@earthlink.net.

SHULMAN, DOUGLAS H., federal agency administrator; b. 1967; m. Susan Shulman; children: Benjamin, Eve. BA, Williams Coll., 1989; MPA, Harvard U., 1996; JD magna cum laude, Georgetown U., 1999. Cons. AT Kearney; sr. policy adv. to chief of staff Nat. Commn. on Restructuring the IRS, 1996—97; v.p. Darby Overseas Investments, Ltd., 1998—2000; co-founder, exec. v.p. FoundryOne, Inc., 2000—01; pres. regulatory services & ops. Nat. Assn. Securities Dealers, Inc. (NASD), Washington, vice chmn., pres. markets, services & info., 2006—07; vice chmn. Fin. Industry Regulatory Authority Inc. (FINRA), Washington, 2007—08; commr. IRS US Dept. Treasury, 2008—. Co-founder Teach for Am.; former mem. bd. dirs. World Fedn. Exchanges; bd. dirs., mem. audit and governance coms. Depository Trust and Clearing Corp. (DTCC). Office: IRS 1111 Constitution Ave NW Rm 3000 Washington DC 20224*

SHULMAN, LAWRENCE EDWARD, biomedical researcher, rheumatologist; b. Boston, July 25, 1919; s. David Herman and Belle (Tishler) S.; m. Pauline K. Flint, July 19, 1946; m. Reni Trudinger, Mar. 20, 1959; children: Kathryn Verena, Barbara Corina. AB, Harvard U., 1941, postgrad., 1941-42; PhD, Yale U., 1945, MD, 1949. Diplomate Nat. Bd. Med. Examiners. Intern Johns Hopkins Hosp., 1949-50, resident and fellow in internal medicine, 1950-53; dir. connective tissue div. Johns Hopkins U., 1955-75, assoc. prof. medicine, 1964—; assoc. dir. div. arthritis, musculoskeletal and skin diseases NIH, Bethesda, Md., 1976-86, dir., 1982-86, dir. Nat. Inst. Arthritis, Musculoskeletal and Skin Diseases, 1986-94, dir. emeritus, 1994—, emissary for clin. rsch., 1995—. Chmn. med. adminstrn. com. Arthritis Found., Atlanta, 1974-75, exec. com., 1972-77; dir. Lupus Found. Am.; med. adv. bd. United. Scleroderma Found., Watsonville, Calif., 1977-88; chmn. sci. group rheumatic diseases WHO, 1989; W.R. Graham meml. lectr., 1973; Cochrane disting. lectr., 1993; vis. prof. Imperial Coll., London, 2002. Discoverer: Eosinophilic Fasciitis, 1974, new med. sign friction rubs in scleroderma, 1961. Recipient Sr. Investigator award Arthritis Found., 1957-62, Disting. Svc. award, 1979, Heberden medal for rsch., London, 1975, Superior Svc. award USPHS, 1985, master Am. Rheumatism Assn., 1986, Spl. Recognition award Nat. Osteoprosis Found., 1991, Spl. award Am. Acad. Orthop. Surgeons, 1992, Presdl. citation for leadership Am. Acad. Dermatology, 1993, Leadership award Lupus Found. Am., 1994, Career Achievement award Am. Coll. Rheumatology, 1994, Outstanding Support Rsch. award Am. Soc. Bone Mineral Rsch., 1994, Gold medal Am. Coll. Rheumatology, 1995, award of Merit, NASA, 1995, Dean's Spl. Recognition award Johns Hopkins Medicine, 2004. Fellow ACP, AAAS; mem. Am. Rheumatism Assn. (pres. 1974-75), Pan-Am. League Against Rheumatism (pres. 1982-86, Morino Gold medal award 2002), Soc. Investigative Dermatology, Am. Soc. Bone Mineral Rsch. Home: Apt 7BC 3900 Watson Pl B NW Washington DC 20016 Office: NIH 9000 Rockville Pike Bethesda MD 20892-0003 Office Phone: 301-496-4574. E-mail: lcshulman@comcast.net.

SHULMAN, LEE S., former educational association administrator; b. Chgo., Sept. 28, 1938; BA, MA, U. Chgo., 1959, PhD, 1963; doctorate (hon.), U. Judaism, 1989, Hebrew Union Coll., 1995, Mich. State U., 1996, Drury Coll., 1999, U. Aveiro Portugal, 1999, So. Ill. U., 2001. Prof. ednl. psychology and med. edn. Mich. State U., 1963—82; prof. edn. and psychology Stanford U., Calif., 1982-98, Charles E. Ducommun prof. edn. emeritus, 1998—; pres. Carnegie Found. for the Advancement of Tchg., Stanford, Calif., 1997—2008, pres. emeritus, 2008—. Co-author: Educating Lawyers: Preparation for the Profession of Law, 2007; author: The Wisdom of Practice: Essays on Teaching, Learning, and Learning to Teach, 2004, Teaching as Community Property: Essays on Higher Education, 2004. Recipient Grawemeyer Prize in Edn., 2006; fellow Ctr. Advanced Study in Behavioral Scis.; vis. scholar Guggenheim Fellow. Fellow: AAAS, Am. Acad. Arts and Scis.; mem.: Am. Psychol. Assn. (E.L. Thorndike Award for Disting. Psychol. Contributions to Edn. 1995), Nat. Acad. Edn., Am. Ednl. Rsch. Assn. (past pres.). Home: 1040 Cathcart Way Stanford CA 94305 Office: Carnegie Found for Advancement of Tchg 51 Vista Lane Stanford CA 94305 Office Phone: 650-566-5110. Office Fax: 650-326-0278. E-mail: shulman@stanford.edu.*

SHULMAN, MICHAEL EBEN, psychoanalyst, psychologist, consultant; s. Kenneth and Jean Carol (Lewit) S., m. Meryl Berlin. PhD, U. Mich., 1987. Cert. Mich. Psychoanalytic Inst., 2006. Psychologist, cons. various, West Palm Beach, Fla., 1990—98, Ann Arbor, Mich., 1998—; ins., psychoanalysis U. Mich., Ann Arbor, Mich., 2006—. Dir., Outpatient Ctr. and Psychology Tng. Oakwood Ctr. of the Palm Beaches, West Palm Beach, Fla., 1990—94; cons., Practice Directorate Am. Psychol. Assn., DC, 1992—94; grad. tchr. Madonna U., Livonia, Mich., 2002—09, U. Toledo, Toledo, 2005—09. Contbr. articles to prof. jours. Chair, Program Com. Mich. Psychoanalytic Soc., Farmington Hills, Mich., 2007—08. Departmental assoc., U. Mich., 1982-84; Nathan Segel Prize, Mich. Psychoanalytic Soc., 2006. Mem. Am. Psychol. Assn., Am. Psychoanalytic Assn., Com. on Psychoanalysis and Undergrad. Edn. (co-chair, 2008-). Avocations: travel, discussion groups. Office: 117 N First St Ste 113 Ann Arbor MI 48104 Personal E-mail: drmichaelshulman@gmail.com.

SHULMAN, MILDRED, artist; b. Perth Amboy, NJ, Aug. 13, 1927; d. Abraham and Estelle Shulman; m. Ben Spina, Feb. 20, 1947 (div. Aug. 1954). Student, Sch. Indsl. Arts, NYC, 1942—45, McDowell Sch. Art, 1946—47, NYU, 1961—62, Art Student's League, 1991—95. Contr. Continental Mdse. Co., Inc., NYC, 1959-65, Famous Fashion Shops, NYC, 1966-69; owner, pres. Luminere Creations, Inc., NYC, 1969-91; self-employed artist NYC, 1991—. Author: Barter "The Silent Giant", 1985, The Talking Mammal, 2006. Mem.: Midtown West Art Assn., Am. Soc. Portrait Artists, Nat. Mus. Women in Arts, Art Students League, New Art Ctr., Nat. Arts Club (NYC) (resident mem.), Salmagundi Club. Achievements include 3 patents flexible screen partitions, electrical lighting design, sculpting method. Avocations: hiking, swimming.

SHULMAN, ROBERT JAY, pediatrician, nutritionist, gastroenterologist, educator; b. Newark; s. Irving Jack and Shirley Shulman; children: David Ian, Hannah Rachel. BA, Emory U., 1972; MD, Chgo. Med. Sch., 1976. Diplomate in pediatrics and pediatric gastroenterology Am. Bd. Pediatrics. Asst. prof. pediat. Baylor Coll. Medicine, Houston, 1982-89, assoc. prof., 1989—96, prof., 1996—2008; dir. nutritional support team Tex. Children's Hosp., Houston, 1982—2008; chair pediatric gastroenterology Tex. Children's Hosp. Found., 2003. Chmn. sub-bd. in pediatric gastroenterology Am. Bd. Pediatrics, 2003—06; chmn., nutrition com. North Am. Soc. Pediat. Gastroenterology, Hepatology and Nutrition, 2007—08. Author: Young Chef's Nutrition Guide and Cookbook, 1990, Keys to Child Nutrition, 1991; author: (with others) Pediatric Gastroenterology and Nutrition in Clinical Practice, 2001, Principles and Practice of Pediatrics, 2006, Pediatric Nutrition Support, 2007; co-editor: Nutrition in Your Pocket, 2002; mem. editl. bd. Jour. Pediat. Gastroenterology and Nutrition, 1994—96. Fellow: Am. Acad. Pediat.; mem.: Soc. Pediat. Rsch., N.Am. Soc. Pediat. Gastoenterology and Nutrition (exec. coun. 1997—99), Am. Inst. Nutrition, Am. Soc. Patenteral and Enteral Nutrition (chmn. pediatric sect. 1997—99, pres. 1997—99), Am. Gastroent. Assn. Avocation: guitar. Office: Baylor Coll Medicine 1100 Bates Ave Houston TX 77030-2600

SHULMAN, STEPHEN NEAL, lawyer; b. New Haven, Apr. 6, 1933; s. Harry and Rea (Karrel) S.; m. Sandra Paula Still, Aug. 14, 1954; children— Harry, Dean, John. BA, Harvard, 1954; LL.B. cum laude, Yale, 1958. Bar: Conn. 1958, D.C. 1960. Indsl. rels. Bendix Aviation Corp., 1954-55; law clk. to Justice Harlan, U.S. Supreme Ct., 1958-59; vis. asst. prof. U. Mich. Law Sch., 1959; assoc. firm Covington & Burling, Washington, 1959-60; asst. U.S. atty. Washington, 1960-61; exec. asst. to sec. labor, 1961-62; dept asst. sec. of def., 1962-65; gen. counsel U.S. Air Force, 1965-66; chmn. Equal Employment Opportunity Commn., 1966-67; mem. Kane, Shulman & Schlei, Washington, 1967-70; mem. firm Cadwalader, Wickersham & Taft, NYC, also Washington, 1971-95, Freedman, Levy, Kroll & Simonds, Washington, 1995-99, O'Connnor & Hannan, L.L.P., Washington, 1999—2005; counsel Ivins, Phillips & Barker, Chartered, Washington, 2005—. Vis. asst. prof. law U. Mich., 1959; vis. prof. mgmt. U. Okla., 1965-66. Co-author: The Law of Equal Employment Opportunity, 1990; editor in chief Yale Law Jour., 1957-58. Recipient Medal for Disting. Public Svc., Dept. Defense, 1966, Exemplary Svc. in Public Adminstrn. award, William A. Jump Meml. Found., 1966. Mem. Book and Gavel, Order of Coif, Cum Laude Soc., Phi Alpha Delta. Home: 1332 Skipwith Rd Mc Lean VA 22101-1841 Office: Ivins Phillips & Barker Chartered 1700 Pennsylvania Ave Washington DC 20006-4723 Office Phone: 202-662-3455. Business E-Mail: sshulman@ipbtax.com.

SHULMAN, YECHIEL, engineering educator; b. Tel Aviv, Jan. 28, 1930; came to the U.S., 1950; s. David and Rachel (Chonowski) S.; m. Ruth Danzig, June 29, 1950; children: Elinor D., Ron E., Orna L. BS in Aero. Engring., MIT, 1954, BS in Bus. and Engring. Adminstrn., 1954, MS in Aero. Engring., 1954, DSc Aero. and Astro., 1959; MBA, U. Chgo., 1973. Assoc. prof. mech. engring. Northwestern U., Evanston, Ill., 1959-67; v.p. adv. engring. Anocut, Inc., Elk Grove Vill., Ill., 1967-72; v.p. corp. devel. Alden Press, Elk Grove Vill., Ill., 1973-84; pres. MMT Environ., Inc., Shoreview, Minn., 1984-87; cons. Shulman Assocs., Mpls., 1987-89; prof. mech. engring. dept. U. Minn., Mpls., 1989-2000, H. W. Sweatt chair in technol. leadership and dir. ctr. for devel. technol. leadership, 1989-2000, dir. grad. studies mgmt. of tech. program, 1990-2000, prof. emeritus mech. engring. dept., 2000—. Mem. ASME, Internat. Assn. for Mgmt. of Tech. Business E-Mail: shulman@umn.edu.

SHULTIS, ROBERT LYNN, finance educator, consultant, retired professional society administrator; b. Kingston, NY, June 30, 1924; s. Albert H. and Dorothy Elizabeth (Jenkins) S.; m. Bernice Elizabeth Johnson, Jan. 20, 1946; 1 son, Robert Lee. BS, Columbia Univ. Sch. Bus., 1949, postgrad., 1949-51. Staff acct. Price Waterhouse, NYC, 1949-52; credit mgr., controller Organon, Inc., West Orange, NJ, 1952-68; v.p., treas., chief fin. officer Arwood Corp., Rockleigh, NJ, 1968-72; v.p., controller Technicon, Tarrytown, NY, 1972-80; exec. dir. Inst. of Mgmt. Accts., Montvale, NJ, 1980-86; faculty, exec. dir. Ctr. for Exec. Devel. Coll. William & Mary, Williamsburg, Va., 1987-91. Instr. Rutgers U., 1964-74, Fairleigh Dickinson U., 1967-68; mem. Fin. Acctg. Standards Adv. Coun., 1981-86; lectr., seminar leader, cons. on controllership, activity-based costing, cost mgmt., cost sys. design Boston U., U. Calif., Berkeley, U. Minn., Michigan State U., So. Meth. U., Baldwin Wallace Coll., George Mason U., James Madison U., U. N.C., Colo. State U., others, 1990—. Editor: Management Accountants' Handbook, and supplements, 1991-94; contbr. feature articles to Va. Gazette, 2001-; contbr. articles to profl. jours. Bd. advs. U. Fla. Sch. Accountancy, James Madison U. Sch. Accountancy; fin. and budget com. Kingsmill Cmty. Svcs. Assn.; interpreter Historic Jamestowne Island, 1997-07; Citizens Budget Advisory Com., Williamsburg, James City, With USAF, 1943-45 Decorated Presdl. Unit Citation, ETO Ribbon, eight battle stars. Mem. AAUP, Am. Legion, Fin. Execs. Internat. (editl. adv. bd.), Inst. Mgmt. Accts., Assn. for Preservation of Va. Antiquities, Kingsmill Club, Beta Alpha Psi (adv. forum).

SHULTS, ANNA, elementary school educator; BA in Elem. Edn., Anderson Univ., 1996; MA in Elem. Edn., Ind. Wesleyan Univ. Recipient Hamilton Southeastern Thank An Educator award (five); named Fall Creek Elem. Tchr. of Yr., 2006, Hamilton Southeastern Tchr. of Yr., 2006, Ind. Tchr. of Yr., 2007; nominee Disney's Am. Tchr. award, 2000. Office: Fall Creek Elem Sch 12130 Olio Rd Fishers IN 46037 Office Phone: 317-594-4180. Business E-Mail: ashults@hse.k12.in.us.

SHULTZ, GEORGE PRATT, economics professor, former United States Secretary of State; b. NYC, Dec. 13, 1920; s. Birl E. and Margaret Lennox (Pratt) S.; children: Margaret Ann Shultz Tilsworth, Kathleen Pratt Shultz Jorgensen, Peter Milton, Barbara Lennox Shultz White, Alexander George; m. Charlotte Mailliard, Aug. 15, 1997. BA in econs., Princeton U., 1942; PhD in indsl. econs., MIT, 1949; Hon. degree, Yeshiva U., U. Tel Aviv, Technion-Israel Inst. Tech., Keio U., Tokyo, Brandeis U., U. Notre Dame, Princeton U., Loyola U., U. Pa., U. Rochester, Carnegie-Mellon U., Baruch Coll., Northwestern U., Tblisi State U.; Hon. degree (hon.), Columbia U.; degree (hon.), Williams Coll. Mem. faculty MIT, 1949-57, assoc. prof. indsl. relations, 1955-57; prof. indsl. relations Grad. Sch. Bus., U. Chgo., 1957-68; dean sch. Grad. Sch. Bus. U. Chgo., 1962-68, fellow Ctr. for Advanced Study in Behavioral Scis., 1968-69; sec. US Dept. Labor, 1969-70; dir. Office Mgmt. & Budget Exec. Office of the Pres., 1970-72; sec. US Dept. Treasury, 1972-74; asst. to the Pres. The White House, 1972—74; chmn. Council on Econ. Policy, East-West Trade Policy com.; exec. v.p. Bechtel Corp., San Francisco, 1974-75, pres., 1975-81, vice chmn., 1977-81; also dir.; pres. Bechtel Group, Inc., 1981-82; prof. mgmt. and pub. policy Stanford U., 1974-82, prof. internat. econs., 1989-91, prof. emeritus, 1991—; chmn. Pres. Reagan's Econ. Policy Adv. Bd., 1981-82; sec. US Dept. State, 1982-89; Thomas W. and Susan B. Ford disting. fellow Hoover Instn., Stanford, 1989—. Bd. dirs. Accretive Health, Fremont Group; mem. adv. coun. Bechtel Inc.; chmn. J.P. Morgan Chase Internat. Coun.; chmn. adv. coun. Inst. Internat. Studies, 2002—07; mem. Calif. Gov.'s Econ. Policy Adv. Bd., 1995—98, 2003—; chmn. Govs. Coun. Econ. Advisors, 2004—. Author: Pressures on Wage Decisions, 1950, (with Charles A. Myers) The Dynamics of a Labor Market, 1951, (with John R. Coleman) Labor Problems: Cases and Readings, 1953, (with T.L. Whisler) Management Organization and the Computer, 1960, (with Arnold R. Weber) Strategies for the Displaced Worker, 1966, (with Robert Z. Aliber) Guidelines, Informal Controls and the Marketplace, 1966, (with Albert Rees) Workers and Wages in the Urban Labor Market, 1970, Leaders and Followers in an Age of Ambiguity, 1975, (with Kenneth W. Dam) Economic Policy Beyond the Headlines, 1977, 2d edition, 1998, Turmoil and Triumph: My Years as Secretary of State, 1993, (with John B. Shoven)Putting Our House in Order: A Guide to Social Security and Health Care Reform, 2008; also articles, chpts. in books, reports, and essays. Served to maj. USMCR, 1942—45. Recipient Medal of Freedom, 1989, Seoul Peace prize, 1992, Eisenhower medal for Leadership and Svc., 2001, Reagan Disting. Am. award, 2002, Ralph Bunche award for diplomatic excellence, 2002, Am. Spirit award, Nat. WWII Mus., 2006, George Marshall award, US Agency Internat. Devel., 2007, Truman medal, 2007, Rumford price, Am. Acad. Arts & Scis., 2008, Comdts. Leadership award, Marine Corps-Law Enforcement Found., 2009. Fellow Am. Econ. Assn. (disting.); mem. Indsl. Rels. Rsch. Assn. (pres. 1968), Nat. Acad. Arbitrators. Republican. Office: Stanford U Hoover Instn Stanford CA 94305-6010 Business E-Mail: susan.schendel@stanford.edu.

SHULTZ, JOHN DAVID, lawyer; b. LA, Oct. 9, 1939; Student, Harvard Coll., Cambridge, Mass., 1960—61; BA, U. Ariz., Tucson, 1964; JD, U. Calif., Berkeley, 1967. Bar: N.Y. 1968, Calif. 1978. Assoc. Cadwalader, Wickersham & Taft, NYC, 1968—77; ptnr. Lawler, Felix & Hall, LA, 1977—83, mem. exec. com., chmn. planning com., co-chmn. recruiting and hiring com.; ptnr. Morgan, Lewis & Bockius, LA, 1983—, chmn. mgmt. com., mem. lateral entry com., chmn. profl. evaluation com., chmn. practice devel. com., chmn. recruiting com. Mem. adv. bd. Internat. and Comparative Law Ctr., Southwestern Legal Found., 1981—; active Practicing Law Inst. Adv. Bd., Corp. and Securities Law, 1992—; Trustee St. Thomas Ch., NYC, 1969—72, Shore Acres Point Corp., Mamaroneck, NY, 1975—77. Mem.: N.Y. State Bar Assn., State Bar Calif., Assn. Bar City of N.Y., ABA. Office: Morgan Lewis & Bockius LLP 300 S Grand Ave Ste 22 Los Angeles CA 90071-3109

SHULTZ, LOIS FRANCES CASHO, nursing supervisor; b. Phila., Apr. 29, 1936; d. Ellwood Francis Casho and Beatrice Mae Gunther Casho; m. Thomas Eugene Shultz, Aug. 15, 1959 (div. June 1983); children: David T., Patricia Shultz Bichefsky, Jeffrey A. Nursing diploma, Temple U. Hosp., 1957; BSN, U. Pa., 1961. RN Pa., 2007, bd. cert. gerontol. nursing, ANCC, 2001. Staff nurse Temple U. Hosp., Phila., 1957, pvt. duty nurse, 1958-59; nursing instr. St. Luke's Hosp. Sch. Nursing, Bethlehem, Pa., 1959-61, Reading (Pa.) Area C.C., 1985-88; asst. DON Reading Nursing Ctr., West Reading, 1988-89; night supr. Berks County Home-BerksHeim, Leesport, Pa., 1989—2004; ret., 2004. Mem. Berks County Bd. Assistance, Reading, 1980—, chmn., 1988-2001, chmn. cmty. rels. com., 2001—; pres., dir. Berks County Med. Soc. Aux.; past bd. dir., chmn., mem. children and youth com. Berks County Mental Health Assn.; organizer, past dir. Reading Is Fun-damental Berks County; past mem., chmn., mem. programs and svcs. sub-com. United Way Home Health Care Study Com.; bd. dir. Berks-Schuylkill unit Arthritis Found., 2005-06, sec., 2006. Mem. Nat. Soc. DAR (1st vice-regent br. Berks County chpt. 1977-80). Republican. Presbyterian. Home: 5 Wendy Rd Reading PA 19601-1031 Personal E-mail: templenurse@1usa.com.

SHUM, HARRY, computer software company executive; b. China, 1969; PhD in Robotics, Carnegie Mellon U. Sr. rsch. scientist Realspace, San Jose, Calif.; rschr. Microsoft Rsch., Redmond, Wash., 1996—99; with Microsoft Rsch. Asia, Beijing, 1999—2007, rsch. mgr., 1999, asst. mng. dir., mng. dir., disting. engr., 2006—07; corp. v.p. Microsoft Corp., Redmond, Wash., 2007—, chief scientist, search & advt. platform group, 2007, dir. Internet Services Rsch. Ctr., 2007, corp. v.p. search product devel., 2008—. Editl. bd. Internat. Jour. Computer Vision; gen. co-chair Internat. Conf. Computer Vision, 2005, program chair, 07; founding mem. Lotus Hill Inst. Computer Vision & Info. Sci., China. Fellow: IEEE, Assn. Computing Machinery; mem.: Soc. Indsl. & Applied Math. (editl. bd. SIAM Jour. on Imaging Sciences). Office: Microsoft Corp Search Product Devel 1 Microsoft Way Redmond WA 98052-6399 E-mail: hshum@microsoft.com.

SHUM, MATTHEW, social sciences educator; b. Houston, Feb. 21, 1970; m. Lerma Angeles, Dec. 10, 2004; children: Zoe Irene, Mark Caleb. PhD, Stanford U., Calif., 1998. Prof. Johns Hopkins U., Balt., 2000—08, Calif. Inst. Tech., Pasadena, 2008—. Office: Calif Inst Tech 1200 E California Blvd Pasadena CA 91125

SHUMAKER, JAROD KYLE, music educator; b. Cape Girardeau, Mo., July 5, 1978; s. Gerald Dale and Linda Christine Shumaker. AA, Shawnee CC, Ullin, Ill., 1998; BS, So. Ill. U., Carbondale, 2000; attending, Murray State U., Ky., 2006—. Cert. tchr. Ill., 2000. Music tchr. New Simpson Hill Sch., Tunnel Hill, Ill., 2000—02, Vienna Grade Sch., Ill., 2000—05, Vienna HS, 2000—; prof. music Shawnee CC, Ullin, 2003—. Condr. So. Ill. Children's Choir., Carbondale, 1998—2000; recruiter music dept. Shawnee CC, 2003—06; condr. Vienna Cmty. Choir, 2004—05; founder, owner Music Studio, Tamms, Ill., 2008. Composer: Boxes, 2000, Counterpoint for Two Horns, 2002. Named Heartland's Best Tchr., KFVS-12 TV, Cape Girardeau, 2005. Mem.: NEA, Am. Choral Dirs. Assn., Ill. Music Educators, Music Educators Nat. Conf., Sierra Club. Independent. Mem. Deist. Avocations: collecting CDs, bicycling, NASCAR racing. Home: 23405 Olive Branch Rd PO Box 442 Olive Branch IL 62969 Office Phone: 618-306-2450, 618-306-3607. Personal E-mail: jks_horn@hotmail.com.

SHUMAN, EARL STANLEY, songwriter, music publisher; b. Boston, Aug. 2, 1923; s. Benjamin Morris and Mildred Judith (Kaplan) S.; m. Margaret Stein, Nov. 25, 1956; children: Cathy Elizabeth, Daniel James, Steven Lewis. BA, Yale U., 1945. Owner, pres. Earl/Peg Music Cos., NYC, 1957—; pub. BMI, ASCAP, NYC, 1977—. Composer (lyric writer) popular songs including Seven Lonely Days, 1953 (Country and Western award 1970), Hey There Lonely Girl, 1970 (Gold record), Banjo's Back in Town, Caterina, Clinging Vine, Close to Cathy, Hotel Happiness, Left Right Out of Your Heart, Most People Get Married, My Shy Violet, The River, Starry-Eyed, Theme For a Dream, Time, Time, Young New Mexican Puppeteer; lyricist (musicals) Secret Life of Walter Mitty, 1964 (award 1965), (country song) Leaves are the Tears of Autumn, 1968 (Country and Western award 1969), (TV themes) Coronet Blue, ABC TV, 1967, Confidence/NFL-CBS, 1967-76, (Movie Title Songs) The Disorderly Orderly, Dondi, Judith, Situation Hopeless But Not Serious, Robinson Crusoe on Mars, Barrabas, Monica (love theme from The Carpetbaggers), Love Me Longer (love theme from Arrivederci Baby); songs in feature films include Seven Lonely Days featured in Shag, Persons Unknown, Traveller, Sweet Dreams, Hey There Lonely Girl featured in Nothing to Lose, Must Love Dogs, Love is a Christmas Rose featured in Serving Sarah, Marriage is for Old Folks featured in Confetti; pub. Bat Out of Hell album, 1977 (platinum award 1979). Capt. USMCR, 1943-46, 50-51. Mem.: ASCAP. Avocations: music, baseball, travel. Home and Office: 111 E 88th St Apt 3B New York NY 10128-1158 Office Phone: 212-289-9036. Personal E-mail: earlsshuman@yahoo.com.

SHUMAN, JOSEPH DUFF, lawyer; b. Pitts., Dec. 27, 1942; s. Joseph and Anna Jane (Phillips) D.; m. Ann Stewart McMillan, Nov. 9, 1969; children: David Stewart, Lauren Forbes. BA, Yale U., 1964; LLB, Harvard U., 1967. Bar: Pa. 1968, U.S. Dist. Ct. (we. dist.) Pa. 1968. Assoc. Thorp, Reed & Armstrong, LLP, Pitts., 1967-73, ptnr., 1974—2004, co-chmn., corp. and bus. law dept., 1990-94, chmn., 1994-97, sr. counsel, 2004—. Republican. Presbyterian. Office: Thorp Reed & Armstrong LLP One Oxford Ctr 301 Grant St 14th Fl Pittsburgh PA 15219-1425 Business E-Mail: jshuman@thorpreed.com.

SHUMAN, R. BAIRD, academic administrator, consultant, language educator, writer; b. Paterson, NJ, June 20, 1929; s. George William and Elizabeth (Evans) Shuman. AB (Trustees scholar), Lehigh U., 1951; M.Ed., Temple U., 1953; PhD (Univ. scholar), U. Pa., 1961; cert. in philology, U. Vienna, Austria, 1954. Tchr. Phila. Pub. Schs., 1953-55; asst. instr. English U. Pa., 1955-57; instr. humanities Drexel U., Phila., 1957-59; asst. prof. English San José (Calif.) State U., 1959-62; asst. prof. English, edn. Duke U., 1962-63, assoc. prof., 1963-66, prof. edn., 1966-77; prof. English, 1977-93, dir. English edn. U. Ill., Urbana-Champaign, 1977-85, dir. freshman rhetoric, 1979-84, coord. Univ. Associates in Rhetoric Program, 1978-84, dir. devel., 1988-93, acting dir. Ctr. for Study of Writing, 1989-90, prof. emeritus, 1993—. Vis. prof. Moore Inst. Art, 1958, Phila. Conservatory Music, 1958—59, Lynchburg Coll., 1965, King Faisal U., Saudi Arabia, 1978, Saudi Arabia, 81, Bread Loaf Sch. English, Middlebury Coll., 1980, E. Tenn. State U., Johnson City, 1980, Olivet Nazarene Coll., 1984, 86, 88, U. Tenn., Knoxville, 1987; com. mem. William Inge Nat. Festival, 1989—95; contbg. cons. Lit. Rsch. Ctr.; cons. in field. Author: Clifford Odets, 1962, Robert E. Sherwood, 1964, William Inge, 1965, Strategies in Teaching Reading: Secondary, 1978, Elements of Early Reading Instruction, 1979, The First R: Strategies in Early Reading Instruction, 1987;: rev. edit., 1989,

Classroom Encounters: Problems, Case Studies, Solutions, 1989, Resources for Writers, 1992, American Drama 1918-1960, 1992, Georgia O'Keeffe, 1993; author: (with Robert J. Krajewski) The Beginning Teacher: A Guide to Problem Solving, 1979; author: (with Eric Hobson) Reading and Writing in High School; author: (with Denny T. Wolfe Jr.) Teaching English Through the Arts, 1990; editor: Nine Black Poets, 1968, An Eye for an Eye, 1969, A Galaxy of Black Writing, 1970, Creative Approaches to the Teaching of English: Secondary, 1974, Questions English Teachers Ask, 1977, Educational Drama for Today's Schools, 1978, Education in the 80's-English, 1980, The Clearing House: A Closer Look, 1984, 70th anniversary issue Clearing House, 1995, Great American Writers: 20th Century, 13 vols., 2002, Cyclopedia of Literary Places, 3 vols., 2003, The Clearing House: A Retrospective, 2004, Ednl. Leadership, 1989—96; exec. editor: Clearing House Jour., 1976—2006, cons. editor: Poet Lore, 1977—90, Cygnus, 1978—2001, Jour. Aesthetic Edn., 1978—82, contbg. editor: Reading Horizons, 1975—85. Active Nat. Trust Hist. Preservation. NEH grantee, Trinity Coll., Dublin, Ireland, 1985. Mem.: MLA, Union Profl. Employees (editor newsletter, mem. exec. com. 1988—92, mem. editl. bd. Poeteka 2005—), Am. Fedn. Tchrs., Nat. Soc. Study Edn., Internat. Assn. Univ. Profs. English, Internat. Reading Assn. (coord. symposium cultural literacy Queensland, Australia 1988), Conf. English Edn. (mem. exec. com. 1976—79), Internat. Fedn. Tchrs. English, Nat. Coun. Tchrs. English (evaluator ERIC Clearing House, mem. com. alt. careers English profs.). Democrat. Home: PO Box 27647 Las Vegas NV 89126-1647 Personal E-mail: rbaird@intermind.net, r2baird@yahoo.com. *An education that does not produce people who are vibrantly alive, intoxicated with the wonder of existence, has fallen short. Joy of learning is the fulcrum upon which the human equation is balanced. I have always believed that emotion prevails over intellect and have led my life accordingly with the inevitable result of being extraordinarily happy for most of my days.*

SHUMAN, SAMUEL IRVING, lawyer, educator; b. Fall River, Mass., Aug. 7, 1925; s. Max and Fannie S.; children: Maxim Erric, Michael A.; m. Gordana Potkonjak, Feb. 21, 2007. AB, U. Pa., 1947, MA, 1948, PhD, 1951; JD, U. Mich., 1954; SJD, Harvard U., 1959. Bar: Mich. 1954, Tex. 1979. Research asst. Legis. Research Center, U. Mich., Ann Arbor, 1953-54, vis. prof. law, 1961; vis. prof. U. Rome, 1963-64; asst. prof. law Wayne State U., Detroit, 1954-55, assoc. prof., 1955-56, prof., 1957-80; prof. dept. psychiatry Wayne State U. Med. Sch. Lectr. Internat. Faculty Comparative Law, Luxembourg, 1964; prof. forensic psychiatry, spl. counsel Lafayette Clinic, Mich. Dept. Mental Health; gen. counsel Mich. Psychiat. Assn., Epilepsy Center Mich. Author: Legal Positivism: Its Scope and Limitations, 1963; (with N.D. West) Introduction to American Law: Cases and Materials, 1971, Psychosurgery and the Medical Control of Violence: Autonomy and Deviance, 1977; mem. editl. bd.: Am. Jour. Jurisprudence, 1969-79. Bd. dirs. Tex. Modern Art Found. Recipient Wayne State U. Bd. Govs. Faculty Recognition award, 1978; Probus Club award Disting. Acad. Achievement in Humanities, 1963; Fulbright fellow Italy, 1961; Rockefeller Found. grantee, 1959, 61; Fulbright travel grantee Germany, 1961; Wayne State U. research grantee, 1960-64; Internat. Research & Exchanges Bd. grantee, 1973 Mem. Am. Law Inst. (life). E-mail: sishuman@sbcglobal.net.

SHUMAN, STANLEY S., investment banker; b. Cambridge, Mass., June 22, 1935; s. Saul A. and Sarah L. (Saxe) S.; m. Ruth H. Lande, 1967 (div. 1979); children: David Lande, Michael Adam; m. Sydney Roberts Gould, 1992. BA, Harvard U., Cambridge, 1956, JD, 1959, MBA, 1961. Bar: Mass. 1959, N.Y. 1991. Mng. dir. Allen & Co., LLC, NYC, 1961—. Bd. dirs. News Corp., 1982—2005, dir. emeritus, 2005—; mem. Pres.'s Fgn. Intelligence Adv. Bd., 1995—2001; bd. dirs. Sesac Inc., 1992—; dir. Ripplewood Holdings LLC, 1995—; chmn. adv. com., bd. advisors Palamon Capital Ptnrs., 1999—. Pres. Wiliwyck Sch., 1971—78; alumni trustee Phillips Acad., Andover, Mass., 1972—84, charter trustee, 1985—; v.p. exec. com. Jewish Guild for the Blind, 1973—80; chmn. Nat. Econ. Devel. and Law Ctr., 1978—83, Marc Haas Found., 1995—; mem. Fin. Control Bd., NYC, 1977—97, Coun. on Fgn. Rels., 1995—, Econ. Club NY; bd. trustees The Dalton Sch., 1977—84, hon. trustee, 1984—; trustee Jewish Publ. Soc., 1986—90, NY Law Sch., 1990—96, Carnegie Hall, 1990—, The Markle Found., 1992—, Vilar Ctr. Arts Found., Vail, Colo., 1999—; trustee emeritus Nat. Pub. Radio Found., 1992—, Paley Ctr. Media, 1996—, Vail Valley Found., 1998—; trustee Channel 13 WNET, 1990—2002, life trustee, 2002—; chmn. adv. bd. Inst. Policy Scis. and Pub. Affairs, Duke U., 1992—96; bd. advisors Harvard Exec. Com. Bd. Overseers Com. U. Resources, 1995—; dir. Lower Manhattan Devl. Corp., 2003—05, Mayors Fund Advance NYC, 2003—. Clubs: Harvard (Boston), Harvard (NYC), Deepdale Golf Club, Atlantic Golf Club, Eagle Springs Golf Club, Quaker Ridge Golf, East Hampton Tennis.

SHUMAN-RILEY, BRENDA, literature and language educator; b. Marietta, Ga. 2 children. BA in English Edn., Ga. So. Univ., Statesboro, specialist degree in Ednl. Adminstrn. and Supervision, PhD in Ednl. Administrn. and Leadership; MA in English Edn., Univ. Ga., Athens. Named Ga. Tchr. of Yr., 2006. Mem.: SPAGE future tchr. org., Profl. Assn. Ga. Educators, Delta Kappa Gamma Soc., Phi Delta Kappa, Kappa Delta Pi. Office: Dublin High Sch 1951 Hillcrest Dr Dublin GA 31021 Office Phone: 478-275-3025. Business E-Mail: bshumanr@doe.k12.ga.us.

SHUMATE, DAVID JOHN, literature and language professor; s. John and Jane Shumate; m. Carol Ann Burns; children: Matthew, David. MA in English, Ind. U., Bloomington, 1987. Tchr. Marian Coll., Indpls. Recipient Agnes Lynch Starrett prize, 2003; fellowship, Nat. Endowment Arts, 2009. Business E-Mail: dshumate@marian.edu.

SHUMWAY, LARRY K., state official, school system administrator; m. Mary Shumway; 6 children. BA, MA, Brigham Young U.; EdD, U. Nev., Las Vegas. Tchr., Ariz., Idaho; vice prin. Pine View HS, St. George, Utah; prin. North Sevier HS, Salina; dir. alternative schs. and programs Davis Sch. Dist.; supt. Tooele Sch. Dist.; dir. educator quality and licensing, coord. Carson Smith Spl. Needs Scholarship Program Utah State Office of Edn., 2005—09, dep. supt., supt. pub. instrn., 2009—. Adj. faculty mem. Brigham Young U. Office: Utah State Office of Edn 250 E 500 S PO Box 144200 Salt Lake City UT 84114-4200*

SHUMWAY, SANDRA ELISABETH, shellfish biologist; b. Taunton, Mass., Mar. 29, 1952; d. Alonzo Harrison and Lois Elisabeth (Tyndal) S. BS summa cum laude, Southampton Coll., 1974; PhD, Univ. Coll. North Wales, 1976; DSc, 1993. Rschr. Marine Sci. Labs., Menai Bridge, Wales, 1974-77, Portobello (New Zealand) Marine Lab., 1978-79; rsch. asst. dept. ecology and evolution SUNY, Stony Brook, 1979-82; scientist Dept. Marine Resources, Boothbay Harbor, Maine, 1983-93, Bigelow Lab., Boothbay Harbor, 1984—; prof. biology and marine scis. Southampton Coll., L.I. U., 1994—2002; rsch. prof. U. Conn., 2002—. Editor: Jour. Shellfish Rsch., 1986—; editor jour. Exptl. Marine Biol. Ecology, 1998—, Harmful Algae; mem. editl. bd. Revs. in Fisheries Scis., Jour. Med. and Applied Malacology, Malacological Revs.; editor 3 books on scallop biology, shellfish safty; contbr. articles to sci. publs. Grantee Marine Aquaculture Innovation Ctr., New Eng. Fisheries Devel. Assn., NOAA/Sea grantee Nat. Marine Fisheries Svc., NSF, EPA. Fellow AAAS (Aldo Leopold fellow), U. Wales (hon.); mem. Marine Biol. Assn. UK, Nat. Shellfisheries Assn. (pres. 1991-92, 2003-05), World Aquaculture Soc. (sec. 1993-95, bd. dirs., v.p. 1996-97), Can. Aquaculture Assn., Am. Malacological Union, Am. Soc. Zoologists, Assn. Women in Sci., Nature Conservancy, Coun. Biology Editors, European Assn. Sci. Editors, Sigma Xi. Home: 17 Jupiter Point Rd Groton CT 06340-6014

SHUN, ZHENMING, statistician, director; PhD, U. Chgo. Dir. Sanofi-Aventis, Bridgewater, NJ, 2000—. Office: sanofi-Aventis 200 Crossing Blvd Bridgewater NJ 08807 Office Fax: 908-231-2151. Business E-Mail: zhenming.shun@sanofi-aventis.com.

SHUPACK, JEROME LEONARD, dermatologist, educator; b. Apr. 3, 1939; AB in Chemistry summa cum laude, Columbia Coll., NYC, 1959; MD, Columbia U., 1963; postgrad. in Dermatology, NYU, 1967-71. Diplomate Am. Bd. Dermatology, Nat. Bd. Med. Examiners. Intern Mt. Sinai Hosp., NYC, 1963-64, resident in internal medicine, 1964-65; resident in Dermatology NYU Med. Ctr., NYC, 1967-71, asst. prof. Dermatology, 1971-78, with head skin and cancer pavilion, 1973-78, assoc. prof. Clin. Dermatology, 1978-89, dir. Dermatopharmacology sect. dept. Dermatology, 1978—, dir. Psoriasis Consultation unit, Skin and Cancer unit, 1985—, prof. Clin. Dermatology, 1990—. Cons. Upjohn Co., 1984-87, Pfizer-Roerig Pharm. Co., 1985-87, Sandoz Labs., 1987, Hoechst Roussel, 1987, 88, Wilderson Group, 1988; sci. advisor Janssen Pharmaceutica, 1988; seminar dir. Ann. Acad. Dermatology, 1976-79; mem. NYU Pharmacy and Therapeutics Com., 1972—. Mem. editorial bd. Jour. of Cutaneous Aging and Cosmetic Dermatology, 1989—; author (book) Dermatologic Formulary, Skin and Cancer Unit, 1989; contbr. chpts. to books, articles to profl. jours. Lt. comdr. USNR, 1965-67. Mem. AMA, N.Y. Dermatol. Soc., Am. Acad. Dermatology (chmn., health industry liaison, 1990, task force on therapeutic agents 1986—, Derm/Pharm task force 1985—), Dermatol. Soc. Greater N.Y., Med. Soc. State of N.Y., Internat. Soc. Tropical Dermatology, Soc. for Investigative Dermatology, N.Y. Acad. Scis. Office: NYU Med Ctr dept Dermatology 562 1st Ave New York NY 10016-6402 Home: 250 E 31 St New York NY 10016 Office Phone: 212-263-7344.

SHUR, MICHAEL, electrical engineer, educator, consultant; b. Kamensk-Uralski, Sverdlovsk, USSR, Nov. 13, 1942; came to US, 1976. s. Saul and Anna (Katz) S.; m. Paulina Gimmelfarb, Sept. 25, 1966; children: Luba, Natasha. MS, Leningrad Elec. Tech. Inst., 1965; PhD, Ioffe Inst., Leningrad, 1967; DSc, Ioffe Inst., St. Petersburg, 1992; Hon. Doctorate, St. Petersburg State Tech. U., 1994. Scientist Ioffe Inst., 1965-75; asst. prof. Wayne State U., Detroit, 1976-77, Oakland U., Rochester, Mich., 1978; prof. U. Minn., Mpls., 1979-92; John Marshall Money prof. U. Va., Charlottesville, Va., 1989-96; Patricia W. and C. Sheldon Roberts prof. Rensselaer Poly. Inst., 1996—; assoc. dir., acting dir., prof. physics. and info. tech. Ctr. Integrated Electronics and Electronics Mfg., 1997—; dir. Ctr. for Broadband Data Transport Sci. and Tech., 2002—; co-dir. NSF Industry/Univ. Coop. Rsch. Ctr. Connection One, 2004—; co-founder, v.p. Sensor Electronic Tech., Inc., 1999. Editor-in-chief Internat. Jour. High Speed Electronics and Systems, mem. hon. editl. bd. Solid State Electronics, Internat. Semiconductor Device Rsch. Symposium; contbr. over 1000 articles to profl. jours., chapters to books; author: Gunn Effect, 1971, Physics of Semiconductor Devices, 1990, GaAs Devices and Circuits, 1991, Introduction to Electronic Devices, 1996, many others; co-author: Ferroelectrics and Antiferroelectrics, 1971, Gunn Effect, 1975, Semiconductor Device Modeling for VLSI, 1993, Introduction to Device Modeling and Circuit Simulation, 1998, Introduction to Solid State Lighting, 2002; co-editor: Semiconductor Technology: Processing and Novel Fabrication Techniques, 1997, Sensitive Skin, 2000, others; regional editor (USA): physicia status solidi. Recipient Van Der Ziel award, Internat. Semiconductor Device Rsch. Symposium, 1999, Humboldt Sr. Rsch. award, 2002, SOE Rsch. award, Rensselaer Poly. Inst., 2003, Compound SEMI Pioneer award, 2003. Fellow: AAAS, IEEE (v.p. pubs. IEEE Sensor Coun., assoc. editor IEEE Trans. 1990—93, Leon Kirchmaier award 2007, Donald Fink award 2007, Best Paper award 2007, Leon Kirchmaier Grad. Tchg. award 2007, MTT Disting. Microwave lectr., EDS Disting. lectr.), Inst. Engring. Tech., World Innovation Found., Electrochemical Soc., Am. Phys. Soc.; mem.: ASEE, Humboldt Soc. Am., Materials Rsch. Soc., Sigma Xi, Tau Beta Pi, Eta Kappa Nu. Achievements include more than 40 patents on solid-state devices. Office: Rensselaer Poly Inst CII 9017 110 8th St Troy NY 12180-3590 Office Phone: 518-276-2201. E-mail: shurm@rpi.edu. *When we were penniless refugees, the United States adopted me and my family with compassion and friendship, gave us work and citizenship. Our debt of gratitude to the American people who accepted us as their own we will never be able to repay.*

SHURE, MYRNA BETH, psychologist, educator; b. Chgo., Sept. 11, 1937; d. Sidney Natkin and Frances (Laufman) Shure. Student, U. Colo., 1955; BS, U. Ill., 1959; MS, Cornell U., Ithaca, NY, 1961, PhD, 1966. Lic. psychologist Pa. Asst. prof. U. RI; head tchr. Nursery Sch., Kingston, 1961-62; asst. prof. Temple U., Phila., 1966-67, assoc. prof., 1967-68; instr. Hahnemann Med. Coll., Phila., 1968-69, sr. instr. psychology, 1969-70, asst. prof., 1970—73, assoc. prof., 1973—80, prof., 1980—2002, Drexel U., Phila., 2002—. Spl. cons. PBS Children's TV Show The Puzzle Place; adv. bd. Parents Mag., 2004—07. Author (with George Spivack): Social Adjustment of Young Children, 1974; author: (with George Spivack and Jerome Platt) The Problem Solving Approach to Adjustment, 1976; author: (with George Spivack) Problem Solving Techniques in Childrearing, 1978; author: (child curricula manual) I Can Problem Solve, 1992; author: (trade book) Raising a Thinking Child, 1994; author: (audiotape, workbook, paperback) Raising a Thinking Preteen, 2000 (Parents' Choice award, 2001, Parent's Guide Classic award, 2001); author: Thinking Parent, Thinking Child, 2004; mem. editl. bd. Jour. Applied Devel. Psychology. Recipient Lela Rowland Prevention award, Nat. Mental Health Assn., 1982, Sarah award, Women in Comm. (Phila. chpt., 1998, Psychology in the Media award, Pa. Psychol. Assn., 1999, award, Ctr. for Substance Abuse Prevention, 2001; rsch. grantee, NIMH, 1971—75, 1977—79, 1982—85, 1987, 1988—93, NJ Gov.'s Juvenile Justice and Delinquency Prevention grantee. Fellow: APA (divsn. clin. psychology, child sect. 1994, Disting. Contbn. award divsn. cmty. psychology 1984, Task Force on Prevention award 1987, Task Force on Model Programs award 1994, U. Utah and Juvenile Justice Dept. of Delinquency Prevention award 1996, US Dept. Edn. award 2001); mem.: Phila. Soc. Clin. Psychologists, Soc. Rsch. in Child Devel., Nat. Assn. Edn. Young Children, Nat. Assn. Sch. Psychologists. Office: Drexel U Dept Psychology 245 N 15th St MS 626 Philadelphia PA 19102 Office Phone: 215-762-7205. Business E-Mail: mshure@drexel.edu.

SHURTLEFF, MARK L., state attorney general; b. Utah, Aug. 9, 1957; m. M'Liss Shurtleff; 5 children. BA in Polit. Sci., Brigham Young U., 1981; JD, U. Utah, 1985. Officer, atty. JAG USN, 1985—90; pvt. practice in law Calif., 1990—93; asst. atty. gen. State of Utah, 1993—97; dep. county atty. Salt Lake County, 1997—98; commr. Salt Lake County Commn., 1999—2000, chmn., 2000; atty. gen. State of Utah, 2001—. Leader Boy Scout troops, 1980—; anti-drug lectr., at-risk youth mentor. Republican. Office: Office of Atty Gen State Capitol Rm 236 Salt Lake City UT 84114-0810 Office Phone: 801-538-9600.*

SHURTLIFF, MARVIN KARL, lawyer; b. Idaho Falls, Nov. 6, 1939; s. Noah Leon and Melba Dorothy (Hunting) S.; m. Peggy J. Griffin, Nov. 23, 1963; 1 dau., Jennifer Karyl. BA, Idaho State Coll., 1962; JD, U. Idaho, 1968. Bar: Idaho 1968. Tchr. pub. schs., Jefferson County, Idaho, 1964-65; atty. U.S. Dept. Justice, Washington, 1968-74; commr. Idaho Pub. Utilities Commn., 1974-75, pres., 1975-76; spl. asst., legal counsel Gov. of Idaho, Boise, 1977; U.S. atty. for Dist. of Idaho, Boise, 1977-81; practice law Boise, 1981—. Mem. Idaho Ho. of Reps., 1962-64 Mem. Idaho State Bd. Edn., 1990—95, Idaho Commn. on Redistricting, 2001. Mem. Idaho Bar Assn. Democrat. Home: 62 Horizon Dr Boise ID 83702-4419 Office: PO Box 1652 Boise ID 83701-1652

SHUSHKEWICH, KENNETH WAYNE, structural engineer; b. Winnipeg, Man., Can., Sept. 22, 1952; m. Valdine Cuffe, Sept. 28, 1980. BSCE, U. Man., Winnipeg, 1974; MS in Structural Engring., U. Calif., Berkeley, 1975; PhD in Structural Engring., U. Alta., Edmonton, Can., 1985. Engr. Wardrop and Assocs., Winnipeg, 1974—78, Preconsult Can., Montreal, Que., 1978—80; prof. U. Alta., 1981—85, U. Man., 1985—87; engr. T.Y. Lin Internat., San Francisco, 1988—90, H.J. Degenkolb Assocs., San Francisco, 1990—92, Ben C. Gerwick, Inc., San Francisco, 1993—94, J. Muller Internat., Chgo., 1994—95, T.Y. Lin Internat., San Francisco, 1995—99, KSI Bridge Engrs., San Francisco, 1999—. Prin. works include design of prestressed concrete segmental bridges; design mgr. for long-span west approach bridge of Northumberland Strait Crossing in Can.; contbr. articles to profl. jours. Recipient award for design of Vierendeel truss bridge, Man. Design Inst., 1977. Fellow ASCE; mem. Am. Concrete Inst., Prestressed Concrete Inst., Internat. Assn. Bridge and Structural Engrs. Achievements include invention of strutted box widening method for long-span bridge widening. Office: PO Box 2590 San Francisco CA 94126-2590

SHUST, DIANE MARIE, educational association administrator, lawyer, educator; b. Binghamton, NY, Aug. 17, 1954; d. Joseph E. and Rose Lillian (Ondrusek) Shust. BA summa cum laude, U. Pa., 1976, MA in Edn.; JD, Georgetown U., 1979. Bar: DC 1980. Law clk. to Hon. David L. Norman DC Superior Ct., Washington, 1979-80; atty. alts. for jailed children project Nat. Ctr. on Insts. and Alts., Washington, 1980-82; atty. human svcs. com. DC Coun., Washington, 1982; sr. supervising atty. juvenile svcs. program Pub. Defender Svc. of DC, Washington, 1982-87; mem. profl. counsel select com. on children, youth and families Ho. of Reps., Washington, 1987-89; legis. asst./counsel to Congressman George Miller, Washington, 1989; adj. faculty mem. Columbus Sch. Law Cath. U. Am., Washington, 1990—; mgr. fed. rels. NEA, Washington, dir. govt. rels., 2002—. Bd. mem. Alliance for Justice. Bd. dirs. Oak Hill Scholarship Club, Washington, 1983-87, sec., 1985-87; bd. dirs. Visitors Svcs. Ctr., Washington, 1982-87, pres., 1984-85, sec., 1986—. Mem. ABA (juvenile justice com.), DC Bar Assn. (panelist Criminal Practice Inst. Manual 1983-87, contbr. manual 1987). Democrat. Roman Catholic. Avocations: cooking, music, running. Office: NEA 1201 16th St, NW Washington DC 20036-3290*

SHUSTER, ALVIN, journalist, reporter; b. Washington, Jan. 25, 1930; s. Fred and Dora (Levy) S.; m. Miriam Schwartz, June 22, 1952; children: Fred, Jessica, Beth. AB, George Washington U., 1951. Reporter Washington Bur. N.Y. Times, 1952-61, asst. news editor, 1961-66, reporter London Bur., 1967-70; bur. chief Saigon, Vietnam, 1970-71, London, 1971-75, Rome, 1975-77; dep. editor editorial pages L.A. Times, 1977-83, fgn. editor, 1983-95, sr. consulting editor, 1995—. Pres. Fgn. Corrs. Assn., London, 1973-74; trustee Monterey (Calif.) Inst. Internat. Studies, 1983-99; chmn. Pulitzer Prize Jury Internat. Reporting, 1999. Editor: The Witnesses, 1964, Washington: The New York Times Guide to the Nations' Capital, 1967, International Press Institute Report, 1995-99; assc. editor Global Journalist, 1999-2004; contbg. author: The Kennedy Years, 1964; contbg. editor Columbia Journalism Rev., 1999-2004. Nieman fellow Harvard U., 1966-67. Mem. Reform Club (London). Office: Los Angeles Times 202 W 1st St Los Angeles CA 90012

SHUSTER, FREDERICK, retired internist, gastroenterologist; b. Newark, Sept. 12, 1933; s. Ralph and Anne (Weinstein) S.; m. Jane A. Block, June 11, 1958; children: Alan R., Robert G. BS, Rutgers U., 1955; MD, U. Chgo., 1959. Diplomate Am. Bd. Internal Medicine, Am. Bd. Gastroenterology. Intern U. Mich. Hosp., Ann Arbor, 1959-60, resident internal medicine, 1960-62; resident gastroenterology VA Hosp. U. Miami, Fla., 1962-63; pvt. practice N. Miami Beach, Fla., 1963-97; from clin. instr. to assoc. prof. medicine U. Miami, Fla., 1963—; pvt. practice Aventura, Fla., 1997-98, North Miami Beach; ret., 1998. Chmn. dept. medicine Parkway Regional Med. Ctr., N. Miami Beach, 1967, 70, chief of staff, 1974-75, chief divsn. gastroenterology, 1976-77, chmn. pharmacy and therapeutics com., 1978-98. Chmn. med. advisory com. Crohn's and Colitis Found., S. Fla. chpt., Miami, 1979-81. Major U.S. Army, 1967-69. Recipient Physician's Recognition award in Continung Edn., AMA, Chgo., 1970—. Fellow Am. Coll. Physicians, Am. Coll. Gastroenterology, Alpha Omega Alpha. Jewish. Avocations: bowling, ballroom dancing, stock market research and investing. E-mail: fred991@att.net.

SHUSTER, KIRK STEVEN, retired primary school educator; b. Ft. Wayne, Ind., Nov. 21, 1949; s. Clayton Alden and Betty Jean Shuster; m. Elizabeth Ann Pflieger, Aug. 17, 1996. B of Edn., Ind. U., Ft. Wayne, MEd, 1996. Elem. edn. endorsement Ind. Tchr. kindergarten Ft. Wayne Cmty. Schs., 1991—2002, tchr. 1st grade, 2002—. Mem. ACRES, Huntertown, Ind., 2003—. Mem.: NEA, Am. Volksport Assn., Ft. Wayne Edn. Assn., Ind. State Tchrs. Assn., Ft. Wayne Edn. Assn. (bldg. rep. 2004—), Rockford Writers' Guild. Avocations: gardening, reading, writing, cooking, hiking. Home: 7117 Country Hill Dr Fort Wayne IN 46835

SHUSTER, ROBERT G., electronics executive, consultant; b. NYC, June 1, 1927; s. Robert Chandler and Therese G. (Giraud); m. Marianne B. Lynski, Apr. 20, 1970 (div. Jan. 1987); m. H. Elizabeth Young, May 20, 1989 (div. Dec. 1995); m. Erika Megas, May 5, 2002. BSEE, CCNY, 1948; MSEE, Columbia U., 1955, postgrad., 1959-64. Test engr. Elec. Testing Labs., NYC, 1948-50; project leader Sperry Gyroscope Co., Great Neck, NY, 1950-59; project mgr. RCA Advanced Communications Lab., NYC, 1959-67; prin. scientist Tracor, Inc., Rockville, Md., 1967-75, v.p. electronics systems div., 1975-87; pres. Tracor Tech. Resources, Inc., Rockville, Md., 1984-90, RGS Assocs., McLean, Va., 1990—; v.p. C-Cubed Corp., Alexandria, Va., 1990-93, pres., 1993-95; sr. cons., 1996—. Mem. IEEE (sr.), N.Y. Acad. Scis. Avocations: photography, hiking.

SHUSTER, WILLIAM (BILL SHUSTER), United States Representative from Pennsylvania; b. McKeesport, Pa., Jan. 10, 1961; s. E.G. "Bud" Shuster; m. Rebecca Shuster; children: Ali, Garrett. BA in Polit. Sci. and Hist., Dickinson Coll., Carlisle, Pa., 1983; MBA, American U.,

Washington. Mgr. retail stores Goodyear Tire and Rubber Corp.; dist. mgr. Bandag Inc.; mem. US Congress from 9th Pa. dist., 2001—. Mem. armed svcs. com. US Congress, mem. transp. and infrastructure com., mem. small bus com., mem. natural resources com. Mem.: Rural Health Care Coalition, Nat. Fedn. Ind. Bus., NRA, Masons. Republican. Lutheran. Office: 310 Penn St Ste 200 Hollidaysburg PA 16648 also: US House of Reps 204 Cannon House Office Bldg Washington DC 20515 Office Phone: 202-225-2431, 814-696-6318. Office Fax: 814-696-6726.*

SHUSTERMAN, NATHAN, underwriter, financial consultant; b. Montreal, Que., Can., Aug. 27, 1927; arrived in US, 1950; s. Aaron and Annie (Nulman) S.; m. Norma Thalblum, Jan. 1950; children: Mark D., Claudia S. Student, Sir George Williams Coll., Montreal, 1944-47; grad., N.Y. Inst. Fin. CLU, chartered fin. cons. Retailing mgr. Jefferson Stores, Miami, Fla., 1950-65; gen. agt. Protective Life Ins. Co., Miami, 1965—. Chmn. emeritus field adv. coun., past pres. Protective Club; pres. Am. Fin. Counseling Corp., Miami; instr. estate and tax planning Am. Coll., Bryn Mawr, Pa., 1972—, U. Miami, Coral Gables, Fla., 1972—; registered rep. Pro Equity Services Inc.; cons. in field. Named Man of Yr., Gen. Agts. and Mgrs. Assn., Miami, 1965-67. Mem. North Dade-South Broward Estate Planning Coun., Million Dollar Round Table (life), Top of Table, Assn. Advanced Life Underwriting, Soc. Fin. Svc. Profls. (past pres. Miami chpt.), Nat. Assn. Ins. and Fin. Advisors (Nat. Sales Achievement award, Nat. Quality award), Fla. Assn. Ins. and Fin. Advisors, Miami Assn. Ins. and Fin. Advisors, Internat. Assn. Fin. Planners, Am. Soc. Pension Actuaries (assoc.), Optimists (pres. North Miami Beach, Fla. chpt. 1971), Masons, Shriners, B'nai B'rith (pres. Miami chpt. 1950). Office: Am Fin Counseling Corp 16121 NE 18th Ave Miami FL 33162-4749 Home: 21050 NE 38th Ave Apt 1701 Miami FL 33180-4078

SHUSTERMAN, NEAL DOUGLAS, writer, scriptwriter; b. NYC, Nov. 12, 1962; s. Milton and Charlotte Ruth (Altman) S.; m. Elaine Gale Jones, Jan. 31, 1987; children: Brendan, Jarrod, Joelle, Erin. BA in Psychology and Drama, U. Calif., Irvine, 1985. Author, screenwriter, 1987—. Author: Guy Talk, 1987, The Shadow Club, 1988 (Children's CHoice award Internat. Reading Assn. 1989), Dissidents, 1989, Speeding Bullet, 1991 (Best Book for Teens award N.Y. Pub. Libr., nominated Calif. Young Reader Medal 1995-96), Kid Heroes, 1991, What Daddy Did, 1991 (Best Book for Young Adults award ALA, Outstanding Work of Fiction award So. Calif. Coun. Lit. for Children and Young People, Children's Choice award and Young Adult Choice award Internat. Reading Assn., Pick of the List award ABA, Best Book for Teens award N.Y. Pub. Libr., Okla. Sequoyah award 1994), The Eyes of Kid Midas, 1992 (ALA Best Book for Reluctant Readers), Darkness Creeping, 1993, Piggyback Ninja, 1994, Scorpion Shards, 1995 (N.Y. Pub. Libr. Best Book for the Teenaged), Darkness Creeping II, 1995, Mindquakes, 1996 (ALA YALSA Quick Pick), Mindstorms, 1996, Mindtwisters, 1997, The Dark Side of Nowhere, 1997 (ALA Best Book, ALA Quick Pick--Top 10 Book), Thief of Souls, 1999, Downsiders, 1999 (ALA Best Book, ALA Quick Pick), MindBenders, 2000, The Shadow Club Rising, 2002, Shattered Sky, 2002, Full Tilt, 2003 (Tex. Lonestar award), The Schwa Was Here, 2004 (Boston Globe Horn Book award, ALA Best Book, ALA Notable, Calif. Young Reader medal 2008), Dread Locks, 2005 (ALA Quick Pick, IRA Young Adult Choice), Red Rider's Hood, 2005 (ALA Quick Pick), Duckling Ugly, 2006 (IRA Young Adult Choice), Everlost, 2006, Unwind, 2007 (ALA Best Book, ALA Top Ten Quick Pick), Antsy Does Time, 2008; screenwriter: Double Dragon, 1992, Evolver, 1993; dir. Heart on a Chain, 1991 (Golden Eagle award CINE), What About the Sisters, 1993 (Golden Eagle award CINE), Games: How to Host a Teen Mystery, Hot Times at Hollywood High, 1994, Barbecue with the Vampire, 1997, Roswell that Ends Well, 1999, How to Host a Murder: Roman Ruins, 1996, The Good, the Bad and the Guilty, 1997, The Tragical Mystery Tour, 1998, The Maiming of the Shrew, 2000, Saturday Night Cleaver, 2000, An Affair to Dismember, 2003, (TV) Goosebumps: The Werewolf of Fever Swamp, 1996, Goosebumps: Night of the Living Dummy III, 1997, Animorphs (staff writer), 1998, Pixel Perfect, 2004. Mem. PEN, Writers Guild Am. West, Soc. Children's Book Writers and Illustrators. Avocations: swimming, tennis, storytelling. Home: P O Box 80093 Rancho Santa Margarita CA 92688 E-mail: NStoryman@aol.com.

SHUSTERMAN, RICHARD MARC, philosophy educator; b. Phila., Dec. 3, 1949; s. Murray H. and Judith Carol (Weiner) S.; m. Rivka Nahmani, Aug. 16, 1970 (div. Oct. 1987); children: Damon, Aelia, Eden; m. Erica Ando, March 14, 2000; 1 child, Talia. BA magna cum laude, Hebrew U., Jerusalem, 1972, MA magna cum laude, 1974; DPhil, Oxford U., 1979. Lectr. Ben-Gurion U., Beer-Sheva, Israel, 1980-82, sr. lectr., 1983-87; lectr. Bezalel Acad. of Art, Jerusalem, 1980-81, Hebrew U., Jerusalem, 1981-83; assoc. prof. Temple U., Phila., 1985-92, prof., 1992—2004, chair dept. philosophy, 1998—2004; Schmidt eminent scholar chair in humanities Fla. Atlantic U., Boca Raton, 2005—. Vis. fellow St. John's Coll. Oxford U., Eng., 1984-85; vis. prof. Coll. Internat. de Philosophie, Paris, 1990-92, program dir., 1995—; vis. prof. New Sch. Social Rsch., NYC, 1992-2002; vis. prof. Hiroshima U., Japan, 2002-03; dir. d'Etudes associés Ecole des hautes etudes en sciences sociales, Paris, 1990; Fulbright prof., Berlin, 1995-96. Author: The Object of Literary Criticism, 1984, T.S. Eliot and the Philosophy of Criticism, 1988, Pragmatist Aesthetics, 1992, 2d edit., 2000, L'art à l'état vif, 1992, Kunst Leben, 1994, Sous l'interpretation, 1994, Practicing Philosophy, 1997, Performing Live, 2000, Philosophie als Lebenspraxis, 2001, Vivre la Philosophie, 2001, Surface and Depth, 2002, Conscience du Corps., 2007, Body Conciousness: A Philosophy of Mindfulness and Somaethetics, 2008; editor: Analytic Aesthetics, 1989, Relativism, Interpretation, and the Metaphysics of Culture, 1999, Bourdieu: A Critical Reader, The Range of Pragmatism and the Limits of Philosophy; mem. editl. bd. Jour. Metaphilosophy, 1993, Yeats-Eliot Rev., 1988, Constellations, 1993, Poetics Today, 1997, Jour. Aesthetics and Art Criticism, 1999, Jour. Speculative Philosophy, 1999. Recipient Rsch. award Israeli Nat. Lottery Found., 1975; grantee NEH, 1988, Am. Coun. Learned Socs., 1988; fellow NEH, 1990, Fulbright Found., 1995-96, Humboldt Transcoop, 2006-09, French Ordre des Palmes Académique. Fellow: Japan Soc. Promotion Sci., mem. Am. Philos. Assn. (advisor to program com. 1989-92), Am. Soc. for Aesthetics (steering com. 1989-92, trustee 2000-2003), Greater Phila. Philosophy Consortium (assoc. dir. 1991-2004), Soc. Advancement Am. Philosophy, Feldenkrais Guild Democrat. Jewish. Avocations: music, hiking, running, t'ai chi. Office: Fla Atlantic U Coll Arts and Letters 777 Glades Rd Boca Raton FL 33431

SHUTRAN, RICHARD, lawyer; b. New Britain, Conn., Mar. 27, 1952; BA, Trinity Coll., 1974; JD cum laude, NYU, 1978. Bar: N.Y. 1979, US Dist. Ct. (ea. & so. dist. N.Y.). Co-chair corp. dept. & chmn. global fin. group Dewey & LeBoeuf LLP, NYC. Mem.: N.Y. State Bar Assn. Office: Dewey & LeBoeuf LLP 1301 Ave of the Americas New York NY 10019-6092 Office Phone: 212-259-6710. Office Fax: 212-259-6333. Business E-Mail: rshutran@dl.com.

SHUTTLEWORTH, ANNE MARGARET, psychiatrist; b. Detroit, Jan. 17, 1931; d. Cornelius Joseph and Alice Catherine (Rice) S.; m. Joel R. Siegel, Apr. 19, 1959; children: Erika, Peter. AB, Cornell U., 1953, MD, 1956. Intern Lenox Hill Hosp., NYC, 1956-57; resident Payne Whitney Clinic-N.Y. Hosp., 1957-60; practice medicine specializing in psychiatry Maplewood, NJ, 1960—. Cons. Maplewood Sch. System, 1960-62; instr. psychiatry Cornell U. Med. Sch., 1960; mem. Com. to Organize New Sch. Psychology, 1970. Mem. AMA (Physicians Recognition award 1975, 78, 81, 84, 87, 90, 93, 96, 99, 02, 05, 08), Am. Psychiat. Assn., Am. Med. Women's Assn., NY Acad. Scis., Acad. Medicine NJ, Phi Beta Kappa, Phi Kappa Phi. Office: 2066 Millburn Ave Maplewood NJ 07040-3715 Office Phone: 973-763-2929.

SHUTTLEWORTH, THOMAS B., II, lawyer; b. Evanston, Ill., Oct. 27, 1945; BS, Fla. Atlantic U., 1967; JD, Washington & Lee U., 1973. Bar: Va. Dist. Ct. 1973, US Dist. Ct. 1973, Ea. Dist. Va. 1973, US Ct. Appeals 4th Cir. 1974, US Supreme Ct. 1976, civil trial advocate: Nat. Bd. Trial Advocacy. Sr. ptnr. personal injury and criminal cases Shuttleworth, Ruloff, Swain, Haddad & Morecock, PC, Va. Beach; prof. William & Mary Law Sch. Named one of Best Lawyers in Am., 1991—; named to The Martindale-Hubell, Legal Elite. Mem.: The Assn. Trial Lawyers Am., Internat. Acad. Trial Lawyers, Fed. Bar Assn. (pres. tidewater chapter 1989), Va. State Bar (chmn. 2nd dist. ethics com. 1980—81), Va. Trial Lawyers Assn. (mem. bd. govs. 1978—84). Achievements include the successful trial of several cases to million dollar verdicts; acquittals in several major felony cases including overturning the wrongful conviction of NBA basketball player Allen Iverson. Office: Shuttleworth Ruloff Swain Haddad & Morecock PC 4525 S Blvd Ste 300 Virginia Beach VA 23452 Office Phone: 757-671-6000. Business E-Mail: tshuttleworth@srgslaw.com.

SHVEDOVA, ANNA ALEXANDROVNA, nutrition research manager, consultant; b. Kaliningrad, Russia, Feb. 22, 1947; came to U.S., 1990; d. Tamara Shvedova; m. Valerian Efimovich Kagan Sr., Mar. 31, 1978; 1 child, Valerian Kagan Jr. MS, Moscow U., 1971, PhD (hon.), 1975; DSc (hon.), Acad. Sci., Moscow, 1987. Rsch. asst. MV Lomonosov, Moscow, 1971-72, Inst. Chem. Physics, Moscow, 1972-78; staff rsch. scientist USSR ACAD. Scis., Moscow, 1978-90; chair rsch. team Inst. Chem. Physics, Moscow, 1984-90; rsch. assoc. antioxidants in medicine U. Calif., Berkeley, 1990-91; pharm. cons. Medicine Inc., Southampton, Pa., 1991-92; rsch. assoc. U. Pitts., 1992-95. Com. mem. Allegheny County-Erie Soc. Toxicology, Pitts., 1990—; nat. expert Sci. Internat. Inc., Alexandria, Va., 1996—. Reviewer: Leukocyte Biology Jour., 1994-95, Viking Penguin Publs., N.Y.C., 1995; contbr. numerous papers to internat. jours.; patentee in field. Rep. Russian-Indian Friendship Soc., Moscow, 1988-90. Recipient Bronze award Nat. Exhbn. in Econs. & Sci., Moscow, 1989, Gold award, 1990; grantee NIHS, 1992-95. Mem. AAAS, Soc. Toxicology, Biochem. Soc. Avocations: classical music, tennis, writing. Home: 131 Berryhill Rd Glenshaw PA 15116-3125 Office: Gen Nutrition Corp 300 6th Ave Pittsburgh PA 15222-2514

SHVO, MICHAEL, real estate broker; b. Tel Aviv, Dec. 29, 1972; s. Hannah Shvo. With Prudential Douglas Elliman, NYC, 1998—2005, v.p., 2002—05; founder, pres. Shvo Group, 2005—. Mem.: Real Estate Bd. NY. Office: Shvo Group 724 Fifth Ave New York NY 10019 Office Phone: 212-380-2100. E-mail: mshvo@shvo.com.*

SHWAYDER, ELIZABETH YANISH, sculptor; b. St. Louis; d. Sam and Fannie May (Weil) Yaffe; m. Nathan Yanish, July 5, 1944 (dec.); children: Ronald, Marilyn Ginsburg, Mindy; m. M.C. Shwayder, 1988 (dec.). Student, Washington U., 1941, Denver U., 1961; pvt. studies. One-woman shows include Woodstock Gallery, London, 1973, Internat. House, Denver, 1963, Colo. Women's Coll., Denver, 1975, Contemporaries Gallery, Santa Fe, 1963, So. Colo. State Coll. Pueblo, 1967, others; group shows include Salt Lake City Mus., 1964, 71, Denver Art Mus., 1961-75, Oklahoma City Mus., 1969, Joslyn Mus., Omaha, 1964-68, Lucca (Italy) Invitational, 1971, Denver Art Mus., Mus. Natural History, Sculpturin Vance Kirkland Mus., 2008, Mizel Mus., Eden Theatrical Workshop, Rose Hosp. Aux., Nat. Mus. Women in the Arts, Colo. Chpt. 8th Air Force Aux., Women's Art Ctr., others; represented in permanent collections Colo. State Bank, Bmh Synagogue, Denver., Colo. Women's Coll., Har Ha Shem Congregation, Boulder, Colo., Faith Bible Chapel, Denver, others; pub. Colo. Abstract Painting and Sculpture, 2009. Chmn. visual arts Colo. Centennial-Bicentennial, 1974-75; pres. Denver Coun. Arts and Humanities, 1973-75; co-chmn. visual arts spree Denver Pub. Schs., 1975; trustee Denver Ctr. Performing Arts, 1973-75; chmn. Concerned Citizens for the Arts, 1976; pres. Beth Israel Hosp. Aux., 1985-87; organizer Coat Drive for the Needy, Denver, N.Y.C., 1982-87, Common Cents penny drive for homeless, 1991-93; active Mayor's Com. on Cultural Affairs, Denver Art Mus., Mus. Natural History, Freedom Found. at Valley Forge, Hospice of Metro. Denver; bd. dirs. Mizel Mus., Srs., Inc., Rainbow Bridge, Diabetes Found., Asian Arts Assn. Denver Art Mus., also pres.; historian Childrens Diabetes Found., Univ. Colo. Found. Inc. Humanities scholar Auraria Librs.-U. Colo.; recipient McCormick award Ball State U., Muncie, Ind., 1964, purchase award color Women's Coll., Denver, 1963, Tyler (Tex.) Mus., 1963, 1st prize in sculpture 1st Nat. Space Art Show, 1971, humanitarian award Milehi Denver Sertoma, 1994, The Gleitsman Found., 1994, svc. to mankind awards Freedom Found. at Valley Forge, Mile Hi Sertoma Club, Minoruyasui Found., Gleitsman Found. Mem. Denver Art Mus., Asian Arts Assn. (pres.). Home: Unit 503 2400 Cherry Creek South Dr Denver CO 80209-3259

SHWAYDER, JAMES MARK, obstetrician-gynecologist; b. Greeley, Colo., Nov. 12, 1951; MD, U. Colo. Cert. ob-gyn. Intern Maricopa Med. Ctr., Phoenix, Ariz., 1978-79, resident in ob-gyn., 1979-82; with Riverside Regional Med. Ctr., Newport News, Va., Mary Immaculate Hosp., 1982—, Sentara Hampton Gen. Hosp., 1994—. Mem. ACOG, Am. Fertility Soc., Am. Assn. Gynecol. Laparoscopists, GLS. Office: James River Gyn-Infertility 12720 Mcmanus Blvd Ste 204 Newport News VA 23602-4414

SHYAMALAN, M. NIGHT (MANOJ NELLIYATTU SHYAMALAN), film director; b. Pondicherry, Tamil-Nadu, India, Aug. 6, 1970; s. Jayalakshmi Shyamalan and Nelliate C; m. Bhavna Vaswani, 1993; 2 children. Grad., NYU, 1992. Actor, dir., prodr., writer: (films) Praying with Anger, 1992, Unbreakable, 2000, Signs, 2002, The Village, 2004, Lady in the Water, 2006, The Happening, 2008; actor, dir., writer: The Sixth Sense, 1999 (Bram Stoker Award for Best Screenplay, 1999, Golden Satellite Award for Best Original Screenplay, 1999, Visionary Award, Palm Springs Internat. Film Festival, 2000, Nebula Award for Best Script, Sci. Fiction and Fantasy Writers Am., 1999, nominated for Best Dir. and Best Original Screenplay, Acad. Awards 2000, Nominated for Best Screenplay, Golden Globes, 2000); dir., writer: Praying Wide Awake, 1998; writer screenplay Stuart Little, 1999; actor (TV appearances) Entourage, 2007 Recipient Samman award, Pravasi Bharatiya Divas, 2005, Padma Shri, India, 2008; named one of 50 Most Powerful People in Hollywood, Premiere mag., 2003—05. Office: Creative Artists Agency 2000 Avenue Of The Stars Los Angeles CA 90067-4700

SHYER, JOHN D., lawyer; b. Nashville, May 4, 1956; s. Michael and Hilda (Wertheim) S.; m. Marsha Anne Gisser, May 7, 1989; children: Allison Parcell, Michael Wertheim. AB, Princeton U., 1978; JD, Stanford U., 1981. Bar: NY 1982, US Ct. Appeals (2d cir.) 1983, US Ct. Appeals (3d cir.) 1992. Assoc. Donovan, Leisure, Newton & Irvine, NYC, 1981-85, Latham & Watkins LLP, NYC, 1985-89, ptnr., 1989—. Trustee Princeton Broadcasting Svc., NJ, 1985—. Mem. Assn. Bar City NY, Employment and Labor Lawcast (bd. editl. advisors 1994—), Employment Law Strategist (editl. bd. mem. 2006-). Avocations: travel, hiking, reading. Office: Latham & Watkins LLP 885 3rd Ave Ste 1000 New York NY 10022-4834 Office Phone: 212-906-1200. Business E-Mail: john.shyer@lw.com.

SI, QIMIAO, physics professor; b. Zhuji, Zhejiang, China, Jan. 18, 1966; BS in Physics, U. Sci. and Tech. China, Hefei, Anhui, 1986; PhD in Physics, U. Chgo., 1991. Harry C. and Olga K. Wiess prof. physics Rice U., Houston, 1995—. Contbr. articles to sci. jours. Fellow: Am. Phys. Soc., Inst. Physics, Eng., Alfred P. Sloan Found. Office: Rice Univ Dept Phys MS61 6100 Main St Houston TX 77005

SIA, KA CHEUNG, application developer; BS in Engring., Chinese U. Hong Kong, 2001, MPhil, 2003; attending, UCLA, 2003—. MCSE Hong Kong, 2000. Rschr. UCLA, 2004—; intern Amgen Inc., Thousand Oaks, Calif., 2005; rsch. intern NEC Labs Am., Cupertino, Calif., 2006—07; software engring. intern Google Inc., Mountain View, Calif., 2008. Author: (book) Efficient Monitoring Algorithm for Fast News Alert, 2007. Achievements include 1st place in 2008 UCSD datamining competition.

SIALM, CLEMENS, finance educator; PhD, Stanford U., Palo Alto, 2001. Asst. prof. fin. U. Mich., Ann Arbor, 2001—07, U. Tex., Austin, 2007—. Office: Univ Tex 1 University Sta B6600 Austin TX 78712 Business E-Mail: clemens.sialm@mccombs.utexas.edu.

SIAWAY, ARTHUR T.G., finance educator, educator; b. Tappita, Liberia, June 3, 1949; s. Greekeah and Monay Z. Siaway; m. Victoria L. Gontaye, June 3, 1995; children: Yeeloe J., Tarmen, Liamon, Tiatay, Tarmen, Dovie L.M., Tiiwon Z; m. Doris Lockett, Mar. 15, 1989 (div. July 11, 1991). BSc, U. Liberia, Monrovia, 1974; MA in Interdisciplinary Studies, Oreg. State U., Corvallis, Oreg, 1978; D, Oreg. State U., 1986. Dir. stats. & rsch. Agri. Ministry, Gov. Liberia, 1975—80; asst. prof. agri. resource economics Tuskegee U., 1977—78, assoc. rsch. prof. agri. & resource econ., 1978—; alt. permanent representative to the fao of the un Govt. Liberia, Monrovia, 1980—82. Project dir. US Agy. Internat. Devel., Morogoro, Tanzania, 1990—2004. Chmn. Kwaplah Internat., Inc., Corvallis, 1993; pres. & ceo African Pvt. Enterprise Devel. Orgn., a Charity Org., Corvallis, 2005. Internat. Devel. Grants, US AID, 1977—78, 1990—2004, Spl. Consultancy on Policy, 2005, SSI Spkr. Grant, US State Dept., 2008. Mem.: Gamma sigma Delta (pres. 2007—08). Achievements include research in international development activities. Home: 448 Planters Rd Montgomery AL 36109 Office: Tuskegee Univ Rm 205 Campbell Hall Tuskegee Institute AL 36088 Home Fax: 334-724-4451. Personal E-mail: arthursiaway@hotmail.com. Business E-Mail: siaway@tuskegee.edu.

SIBBALD, JOHN RISTOW, management consultant; b. Lincoln, Nebr., June 20, 1936; s. Garth E.W. and Rachel (Wright) S.; div.; children: Allison, John, Wright. BA, U. Nev., 1958; MA, U. Ill., 1964. Office mgr. Hewitt Assocs., Libertyville, Ill., 1964-66; coll. rels. mgr. Pfizer Inc., NYC, 1966-69; pres., CEO Re-Con Systems, NYC, 1969-70; v.p. Booz, Allen & Hamilton, NYC, 1970-73, Chgo., 1973-75; pres., founder John Sibbald Assocs., Inc., Chgo., 1975. Mem. Nat. Advisory Coun., Nat. Club Assn. Author: The Career Makers, 1990, 92, The New Career Makers, 1995; pub. Club Leaders Forum, Platinum Clubs of America; contbr. articles to profl. jours. Capt. AUS, 1958-64. Mem. St. Louis Club, Anvil Club. Episcopalian. Office: 7733 Forsyth Blvd Saint Louis MO 63105-1817 Home: 3220 Oleander Way Lauderdale By The Sea FL 33062 Office Phone: 314-727-0227. Business E-Mail: jsibbald@sibbaldassociates.com.

SIBENER, STEVEN JAY, chemistry educator; b. Bklyn., Apr. 3, 1954; s. Daniel Irving and Gerie S.; m. Linda Young, May 29, 1990. BA in Physics, BS in Chemistry, U. Rochester, 1975; MS, U. Calif., Berkeley, 1977, PhD, 1979. Postdoctoral fellow Bell Labs., Murray Hill, N.J., 1979-80; asst. prof. U. Chgo., 1980-85, assoc. prof., 1985-89, prof. chemistry, 1989—, dir. materials rsch. Sci. and Engring. Ctr., 1997—. Vis. fellow Joint Inst. for Lab. Astrophysics, Boulder, Colo., 1992-93; cons. Dow Chem. Co., Midland, Mich., 1982-85, Teltech Resource Network, Chgo., 1985—, Inst. Def. Analyses, Alexandria, Va., 1985—. Contbr. over 75 sci. articles to profl. publs. Alfred P. Sloan Found. fellow, 1983-87; recipient Camille Henry Dreyfus Young Faculty in Chemistry award, Dreyfus Found., 1980, IBM Faculty Devel. award, 1984-86. Fellow Am. Phys. Soc. (chmn. chem. physics divsn. 1996); mem. AAAS, Am. Chem. Soc., Royal Soc. Chemistry (Marlow medal 1988), Sigma Xi, Phi Beta Kappa. Achievements include crossed molecular beam studies on gas-phase oxidation reaction mechanisms; contributions on nature of surface catalytic reactions, gas-surface energy transfer, surface photochemistry, surface metallurgy, dynamics for thin polymer films, and materials growth. Office: Univ Chgo The James Franck Inst 5640 S Ellis Ave Chicago IL 60637-1433

SIBERT, EDWIN L., chemistry professor; b. White Plains, Ny, Oct. 25, 1956; s. Edwin Luther and Margaret Larsen Sibert; m. Catherine A. Jagoe, Aug. 5, 1989; 1 child, Toby Jagoe. BA, Colgate U., Hamilton, Ny, 1978; PhD, U. Colo., Boulder, 1983. Prof. U. Wis., Madison, 1986—. Pres. Telluride Sci. Rsch. Inst., Colo., 1998—2001; vis. prof. Ministerio de Ciencias Education, Madird, 2006—07. Recipient Presdl. Young Investigator, NSF, 1988; Fellowship, NATO, 1984, Miller Rsch. Inst., Berkeley, 1985—86. Mem.: Am. Chem. Soc. (pres. local sect. 2008—). Democrat. Avocations: swimming, tennis, travel, bicycling, literature. Office: University of Wisconsin 1101 University Ave Madison WI 53706

SIBERT, POLLY LOU, conductor, educator; b. Washington, Pa., Sept. 22, 1962; d. Earl Richard and Virginia Gray Sibert. B in Music Edn., James Madison U., Harrisonburg, Va., 1984, MusM in Orchestral Conducting, 1996; D in Music Edn., Shenandoah Conservatory, Shenandoah U., Winchester, Va., 1999. Orch. dir. Chesterfield County Schs., Va., 1985—92, Charlottesville City Schs., Va., 1992—. Self-employed violin maker, restorer, Chester, Va., 1989—92, Charlottesville, 1992—; first violinist Lynchburg Symphony, Va., 2002—; expert panelist mid. sch. music AECT Project Pa. State U. Edn. Sch., 2002—; cons. music publ. Frank J. Hackinson Music Co., Inc., Ft. Lauderdale, 2003—. Bowing editor (music) Nancy's Waltz, 1997, contbr. author (book) Strategies for Teaching: Technology, 2001. Mem.: NEA, Nat. Sch. Orch. Assn., Am. String Tchrs. Assn., Va. Music Educators Assn. Methodist. Achievements include building two stringed instruments: a violin and a viola. Avocations: golf, antiques, crocheting. Home: 3003 Colonial Dr Charlottesville VA 22911-9109 Office: Charlottesville City Schs 1564 Dairy Rd Charlottesville VA 22903 E-mail: PLSibert@aol.com.

SIBITZ, MICHAEL WILLIAM, school system administrator; b. San Francisco, July 22, 1937; s. Michael Jacob and Erna Anna Elsa (Altendorf) S.; m. Marilyn Joyce Pricco, Nov. 19, 1966; children: Elizabeth, Ryan. BA, San Francisco State U., 1959, MA, 1964; EdD, U San Francisco, 1980; postgrad., Notre Dame Coll. of Calif., Stanford U. Tchr., Pacifica, Calif., 1959—64, Dept. Def., 1964—65, Belmont, Calif., 1965—71; adminstr., 1971—80; supr. instrn., prin. Los Altos, Calif., 1980—84; asst. supt. Sylvan Union Sch. Dist., Modesto, Calif., 1983—97; supt., interim program dir. St. Mary's Coll., Moraga, Calif., 1989—2004. Adj. faculty St. Mary's Coll., Moraga, Calif., 2005—, Edn. Dept. Mills Coll., Oakland. Contbr. articles to profl. jours. Bd. dirs. Modesto Symphony, 1993-2002; mem. Stanislaus Arts Commn.; past pres. United Way Stanislaus County, Stanislaus County Industry Edn. Coun. Served with U.S. Army, 1960-66. Mem. NEA (life), ASCD, Assn. Calif. Sch. Adminstrs. (charter-life), Calif. Assn. Supervision and Curriculum Devel. (bd. dirs. 1997, treas. 1999-2001), Phi Delta Kappa. Roman Catholic. Home: 1400 Pinnacle Ct 205 Richmond CA 94801 Home Phone: 510-215-1567. Personal E-mail: m2sibitz@comcast.net.

SIBLEY, JESSICA, publishing executive; BA in English Lit., Hobart & William Smith Colls., Geneva, NY. From fin. advt. dir. to mid-atlantic regional mgr. Forbes Inc.; various positions including v.p. fin. advt. and agy. rels., dir. nat. fin. advt., assoc. regional mgr. NY office to v.p. multimedia sales Wall Street Journal; sr. v.p., worldwide pub. BusinessWeek mag. McGraw-Hill Cos. Inc., 2008—. Office: BusinessWeek Editl Offices 1221 Ave of Americas New York NY 10020 Office Phone: 212-512-2511.*

SIBLEY, WILLIAM ARTHUR, retired academic administrator, physics professor, consultant; b. Ft. Worth, Nov. 22, 1932; s. William Franklin and Sada (Rasor) S.; m. Joyce Elaine Gregory, Dec. 21, 1957; children: William Timothy, Lauren Shawn, Stephen Marshall. BS, U. Okla., Norman, 1956, MS, 1958, PhD, 1960. Tchg., rsch. asst. U. Okla., 1956-60; postdoctoral rsch. in defect solid state Kernforschungsanlage Julich and Tech. U. Aachen, Germany, 1960-61; rsch. solid state divsn. Oak Ridge Nat. Lab., 1961-70; prof., head physics Okla. State U., Stillwater, 1970-76, dir. Sch. Phys. and Earth Scis., 1976-78, asst. v.p. rsch., 1978-88; v.p. acad. affairs U. Ala., Birmingham, 1990-96; program dir. NSF, Washington, 1988-89, acting dir. divsn. materials rsch., 1990, program dir., 1996-99, acting divsn. dir. rsch., evaluation and comm. divsn., 1998-99; pres. Okla. Ctr. for Advancement of Sci. and Tech., 2000—02; CEO, dir. Okla. Sci. and Tech. R & D, 2002—04; ret., 2004. Solid state sci. com. NAS, 1977-83; bd. dirs. Oak Ridge Assoc. Univs., 1982-88, Coun. on Govt. Rels., 1987-93, Okla. Ctr. for Advancement Sci. and Tech., 1987-88; trustee, chmn. materials rsch. counsel Southeastern Univ. Rsch. Assn., 1992-95; vis. scholar Coll. Math. & Sci., U. Ctrl. Okla., cons. in field; vis. scholar U. Ctrl. Okla. Edmond. Author: University Management 2010, 1998; contbr. articles to profl. jours. Pres. Stillwater Indsl. Found., 1985-86. Served to lt. AUS, 1951-53. Maj. USAR, 1953-60, Korea. Fellow Am. Phys. Soc.; mem. Sigma Xi, Sigma Pi Sigma. Baptist. Home: 2517 Thunderwind Cir Edmond OK 73034-6880 Personal E-mail: sibleybill@aol.com.

SIBLEY, WILLIS ELBRIDGE, anthropology educator, consultant; b. Nashville, Feb. 22, 1930; s. Elbridge and Elizabeth Reynolds (LaBarre) S.; m. Barbara Jean Grant, June 9, 1956 (dec.); m. Marjorie Arielle Hegge, July 6, 2002; children: Sheila Katherine, Anthony Grant, Michael David. BA, Reed Coll., 1951; MA, U. Chgo., 1953, PhD, 1958. Instr. sociology and anthropology Miami (Ohio) U., 1956-58; asst. prof. anthropology U. Utah, 1958-60; from asst. prof. to prof. anthropology Wash. State U., 1960-71; prof. anthropology Cleve. State U., 1971—, chmn. dept., 1971-77, Cleve. (City) faculty fellow, 1987, interim chmn., 1989-90, prof. emeritus, 1990—; sr. program analyst EPA, Washington, 1977-78; Govtl. fellow Am. Coun. on Edn., 1978; Rockefeller Found. vis. prof. anthropology U. Philippines, Quezon City, 1968-69; postdoctoral fellow in society and tech. Carnegie-Mellon U., 1981-82. Fulbright grantee, 1954-55, 64; NIMH grantee, 1959-61; NSF grantee, 1964-71; Nat. Acad. Scis.-NRC travel grantee, 1966; Office Edn., HEW research grantee, 1967 Fellow AAAS, Assn. Profl. Anthropologists (pres. Washington chpt. 1999—), Am. Anthropol. Assn. (treas. 1989-91, com. on pub. policy 2000-2002), Soc. Applied Anthropology (sec. 1977-80, pres. 1981-82, Sol Tax Disting. Svc. award 2006); mem. AAUP (treas. Wash. State U. chpt. 1962-63, v.p. 1963-64, pres. 1965-66, pres. Cleve. State U. chpt. 1979-80, treas. 1980-81, interim pres. 1989-90), ACLU (pres. Pullman chpt. 1963, 66), Ctrl. States Anthropol. Soc. (past mem. exec. bd., treas. 1986-89), Wash. Assn. Profl. Anthropologists, Edgewater Yacht Club (Cleve., commodore 1991), Chesapeake Yacht Club (Shady Side, Md.) (gov. 1999, 2000). Democrat. Unitarian Universalist. Avocation: sailing. Home: 1190 Cedar Ave Shady Side MD 20764 Office: Cleve State U Dept Anthropology Cleveland OH 44115 Office Phone: 301-261-9404. Personal E-mail: shadyside1190@comcast.net.

SIBO, ELSA LYNETTE, secondary school educator; d. Lawrence E. and V. Azalee Chapman; m. Richard J. Sibo, Feb. 8, 1964 (dec. Mar. 1, 1986). BA, Blue Mountain Coll., 1962; MEd, U. Nev., 1978. Tchg. cert. Miss., 1962, Tex., 1972, Ga., 1973, Nev., 2002. Tchr. English Greenville H.S., Miss., 1962—64, Schertz-Cibolo Ind. Sch. Dist., Schertz, Tex., 1964—65; tchr. English, speech Randolph Field Ind. Sch. Dist., Universal City, Tex., 1965—72, Clayton County Sch. Dist., Jonesboro, Ga., 1973—74; tchr. English St. Yves H.S., Las Vegas, 1975—76; grad. asst. reading ctr. part time staff U. Nev., 1976—78; tchr. English Clark County Sch. Dist., 1978—2002, C of So. Nev., Henderson, 2003—. Mem., pres., sec., treas., com. mem. Gamma Chpt., Delta Kappa Gamma, Las Vegas, 1972—2008. Fellow Study Stipend, Delta Kappa Gamma, 1982. Mem.: NEA (life), Delta Kappa Gamma (Rose of Recognition 1983), Kappa Delta Pi (assoc.). Independent. Methodist. Avocations: travel, hiking, ballroom dancing. Personal E-mail: lynnsibo@gmail.com.

SIBOLSKI, ELIZABETH HAWLEY, academic administrator; b. Gt. Barrington, Mass., Aug. 18, 1950; d. William Snyder and Frances Harrington (Smith) Gallup; m. John Alfred Sibolski Jr., Aug. 15, 1970. BA, Am. U., Washington, DC, 1973, MPA, 1975, PhD, 1984. Acting dir. acad. adminstrn. Am. U., Washington, 1974, planning analyst, 1974—79, asst. dir. budget and planning, 1980—83, dir. instl. rsch., 1984—85, exec. dir. univ. planning and rsch., 1985—2000; exec. assoc. dir. Middle States Commn. on Higher Edn., Phila., 2000—06, exec. v.p., 2007—. Trustee Mortar Bd. Nat. Found., 1989—95. Recipient Commencement award, Am. U. Women's Club, 1973. Mem. Soc. Coll. and Univ. Planning (bd. dirs. 1995-2000, pres. 1998-99), Mortar Bd. (sect. coord. 1975-82), Pi Alpha Alpha, Phi Kappa Phi (chpt. officer 1986-92), Pi Sigma Alpha, Omicron Delta Kappa. Avocations: breed, raise and show morgan horses. Home: 565 Wayward Dr Annapolis MD 21401-6747 Office: Middle States Commn on Higher Edn 3624 Market St Philadelphia PA 19104-2614 Business E-Mail: esibolski@msche.org.

SICA, FRANK VINCENT, investment company executive; b. Mar. 12, 1951; s. Vincent F. and Patricia Clair Sica; m. Colleen McMahon, May 16, 1981. BA, Wesleyan U., 1973; MBA, Dartmouth Coll., 1979. Investment banker project-fin. group Dean Witter Reynolds Inc.; mng. dir. mergers and acquisitions dept. Morgan Stanley, mng. dir. merchant banking divsn., 1988—98; mng. dir. Soros Pvt. Funds Mgmt., 1998—2000, pres., 2000—03, sr. advisor, 2004—05; mng. ptnr. Tailwind Capital, NYC, 2006—; vice chmn. JetBlue Airways Corp., 2008—. Bd. dirs. CSG Sys. Internat., Inc., Kohl's Corp., 1988—, NorthStar Realty Fin. Corp., JetBlue Airways Corp., 1998—. Bd. mem. Cancer Rsch. Inst., 2003—; trustee Wesleyan U. Lt. USAF, 1974—77. Office: Tailwind Capital 485 Lexington Ave New York NY 10017 Office Phone: 212-271-3800. Office Fax: 212-271-4911.

SICART, PIERRE-ALEXANDRE SERGE HENRY, writer, scholar; b. Toulouse, France, Jan. 27, 1975; s. Pierre Alain Thierry Sicart and Micheline Marie Mauricette Ory. DEUG in English, U. Toulouse II, France, 1997, MA in French Lit., 1998, DEA in French Lit., 1999, LittD with highest honors, 2005; Licentiate in Integrated European Studies, U. St. Andrews, Scotland, 1998; MPhil in French Lit., NYU, NYC, 2001, PhD in French Lit. with honors, 2005. Computer expert trainee Tocqueville Asset Mgmt., NYC, 1996; web designer, asst. forum mgr. and interpreter Leisure On Line, Saint-Orens, France, 1996—98; tchg. asst. French lang. and lit. NYU, 2001—03; freelance voice actor NY Audio Prodns., 2006—; French asst. prof. PLL U., 2007—. Contbr. articles to profl. jours. V.p. Karate Club, 2001—02, pres., 2002; founder Martial Arts Club, 2002, pres., 2003, webmaster, 2003—04; capt. Taekwondo Club, 2003—04. Recipient Pres.'s Svc. Leadership award, NYU, 2003; named Taekwondo Most Valuable Player, NYU Athletics, 2001—02, Graduation Std. Bearer, Grad. Sch. Arts and Scis. NYU, 2005; finalist Dean's Outstanding Grad. Student Tchg. award, GSAS, NYU, 2003; grantee, Grad. Sch. Arts and Scis. NYU, 2002—03, 2004—05, Tech. and Tchg. Mentoring Program, NYU, 2003—04; MacCracken fellow, Grad. Sch. Arts and Scis. NYU, 1999—2003, Dean's Dissertation fellow, 2003—04, Socrates-Erasmus scholar, European Union, 1997—98, Merit scholar, French Govt., 1998—99. Mem.: MLA, Lab. PLH, Poetic Genius Soc., Mensa. Office: Chinese Culture Univ Dept French 55 Hwakang Rd Taipei 11114 Taiwan Personal E-mail: sicart@gmail.com. Business E-Mail: spd@faculty.pccu.edu.tw.

SICH, JEFFREY JOHN, health education analyst; b. Youngstown, Ohio, Oct. 8, 1954; s. John Paul and Frances Louise (Verbnak) S. BS, Davidson Coll., 1977; MS, U. Cin., 1981, PhD, 1983. Asst. prof. microbiology Denison U., Granville, Ohio, 1983-84; asst. prof. U. Tampa, Fla., 1984-86; asst. to assoc. prof. Youngstown State U., 1986-91; asst. dir. for ednl. programs, office of edn. NIH, Bethesda, Md., 1991—. Chair judging com. Ohio Jr. Acad. of Scis., Dist. 15 Sci. Bd., 1989-91; mem. planning com. Pub. Health Svc. conf. on Life Sci. Edn. and Sci. Literacy, 1990-91. Contbr. articles to profl. jours. Shift coord. Tod Children's Hosp. telethon, Youngstown, 1987-90; active Friends of Am. Art, Youngstown, 1987-91; ruling elder Tabernacle Evang. Presbyn. Ch., Youngstown, 1990-91. Grantee rsch. NIH, 1988, equipment NSF, 1988. Mem. Am. Soc. Microbiology (mem. com. ann. meeting planning bd. edn. and tng., Washington, 1989—, chair 1990-91, 91—), Sigma Xi (chpt. sec. 1989-91). Office: NIH Office of Edn Rm 1C 129 Bldg 10 Bethesda MD 20892-0001

SICHERER, SCOTT H., pediatric allergist, researcher; MD, Johns Hopkins U. Sch. Medicine, NY. Diplomate Am. Bd. Pediat., Am. Bd. Allergy & Immunology. Resident pediat. Mt. Sinai Hosp.; fellowship allergy and immunology Johns Hopkins U. Hosp.; assoc. prof. pediat. Mt. Sinai Sch. Medicine; rschr. Jaffe Food Allergy Inst.-Mt. Sinai Hosp. Mem. med. adv. bd. Food & Allergy Anaphylaxis Alliance. Author: (children's book) Maya and Andrew Learn About Food Allergies, 2000, (book) Understanding and Managing Your Child's Food Allergies, 2006; co-author: The Complete Peanut Allergy Handbook, 2005; contbr. chapters to books, articles to profl. jours. Fellow: Am. Acad. Allergy, Asthma, and Immunology; mem.: Am. Acad. Pediat. Achievements include research in allergic diseases caused by specific foods such as peanuts, tree nuts, egg, seafood and milk; the natural history,epidemiology and genetics of food allergy; gastrointestinal manifestations of food allergies; psychosocial issues associated with food allergies. Office: Mt Sinai Sch Medicine Dept Pediat Box 1198 5 E 98th St 10th Fl New York NY 10029 Office Phone: 212-241-5548. Office Fax: 212-426-1902. Business E-Mail: scott.sicherer@mssm.edu.

SICHERMAN, MARVIN ALLEN, lawyer; b. Cleve., Dec. 27, 1934; s. Harry and Malvina (Friedman) S.; m. Sue Kovacs, Aug. 18, 1957; children: Heidi Joyce, Steven Eric. BA, Case Western Res. U., 1957, LLB, 1960, JD, 1968. Bar: Ohio 1960, US Dist. Ct. (no. dist.) Ohio 1961, Ct. Appeals (6th cir.) 1969, US Supreme Ct. 1975. Mng. prin. Dettelbach, Sicherman & Baumgart, Cleve., 1971—. Mem. editl. bd.: Case-Western Res. Law Rev, 1958-60; contbr. articles to legal jours. Mem. Beachwood Civic League, Ohio, 1972-92; mem. Beachwood Bd. Edn., 1978-86, pres., 1981, 85, v.p., 1984; trustee Beachwood Arts Coun., 1977-84. Mem. Ohio Bar Assn. (lectr. truth in lending 1969, lectr. bankruptcy 1972, 81, 84, 99, 2000-06, Meritorious Service awards 1971, 77, 78, 79, 83, 84, 85, 86, 87), Cleve. Met. Bar Assn. (lectr. practice and procedure clinic 1960-80, 82-87, chmn. bankruptcy ct. com. 1971-73; award established in his honor by Bankruptcy & Commercial Law Sect., 2007), Jewish Chautauqua Soc., Tau Epsilon Rho, Zeta Beta Tau. Jewish (trustee Temple brotherhood 1968-76, sec. 1971-73). Jewish. Home: 24500 Albert Ln Cleveland OH 44122-2302 Office: Dettelbach Sicherman & Baumgart 1100 Am Trust Bank Ctr Cleveland OH 44114 Home Phone: 216-464-1244; Office Phone: 216-696-6000. Business E-Mail: msicherman@dsb-law.com.

SICHUK, GEORGE, entrepreneur, creator and builder mental analyst, writer, atomic scientist, biochemist, physiologist, transcendental academic theologian; b. Butler Twp., Pa., May 10, 1933; s. Stephan Nicholas and Eva (Hawranick) Sichuk; m. Georgiana Nadya Stroyen, July 27, 1968. BA, Drew U., 1954; DS, Rutgers U., 1962. Rsch. assoc. Sloan-Kettering Inst. Cancer Rsch., NYC, 1961—71; asst. prof. biology Montclair State Coll., Upper Montclair, NJ, 1972—75, William Paterson Coll., Wayne, NJ, 1975; lectr. interdisciplinary studies Bloomfield (N.J.) Coll., 1976; sci. tchr. Eastside H.S., Paterson, NJ, 1988—93; entrepreneur author Lincoln Park, NJ, 1993—. Author: Gabriel's Voice, 1996, Uriel's Light, 1997, One Man's Testament, 1998, Constitutional Imperatives for Rational Government, 2003, Common Sense Plus, 2004, The Pentian Truth: Thomas Paine, the Mozart of Reason, 2004, Miracles of Evolution, Tragedies of Evolution Voodoo Religions, 2007, Invisible Essentials of the Biosphere, 2007, The Pythagorean Fact: Life is not a Theory, 2008, Miracles of Spring, Evolution Equals Food; contbr. articles to profl. med. jours.; author: Life is a Rohrshach test, 2009. Good will amb. U.S. Govt., Cuba, 1960; coach Police Athletic League, Lincoln Park, 1977—79; CEO NJ Citizens Orgn., 1967—68; exec. and coach Orthodox Citizens' Club, NJ, 1980—90. Achievements include clarification of relationship of the endocrine and immune systems to cancer to direct attention to the nucleic acids (DNA and RNA); clarification of transplantation immunology; proof that "butter yellow" a dibenzanthracene used to give margarine a yellow color is a carcinogen; research in the role of sex hormones in thrombotic disease; dynamic relationship between dietary protein quality and function of adrenal cortex in mammals; nanotechnology and peaceful use of atomic energy; harmonic function of the human brain, denial of monotheism; and proof of origin of viruses, identifying vectors of disease; kidney transplantation; proof that DES can cause thromboembolic disease. Avocations: geo-politics, house maintenance engineering, golf, flying, music. Home: 18 Sewanois Ave Lincoln Park NJ 07035-1710

SICILIANO, ROCCO CARMINE, cultural institute executive; b. Salt Lake City, Mar. 4, 1922; s. Joseph Vincent and Mary (Arnone) S.; m. Marion Stiebel, Nov. 8, 1947; children: Loretta, A. Vincent, Fred R., John C., Maria. BA with honors, U. Utah, 1944; LL.B., Georgetown U., 1948; LHD, Hebrew Union Coll., Gettysburg Coll., 2000, U. Utah, 2001. Bar: D.C. bar 1949. Legal asst. to bd. mem. NLRB, Washington, 1948-50; asst. sec.-treas. Procon Inc., Des Plaines, Ill., 1950-53; asst. sec. for charge employment & manpower US Dept. Labor, Washington, 1953-57; spl. asst. to Pres. for pers. mgmt. The White House, Washington, 1957-59; ptnr. Wilkinson, Cragun & Barker, 1959-69; pres. Pacific Maritime Assn., San Francisco, 1965-69; under sec. US Dept. Commerce, Washington, 1969-71; pres., chmn. bd., chief exec. officer Ticor, Los Angeles, 1971-84, chmn., exec. com., 1984-85; of counsel Jones, Day, Reavis & Pogue, 1984-87; chmn., CEO Am. Health Properties, Inc., 1987-88; chmn. Dwight D. Eisenhower World Affairs Inst., Washington, 1991-2001; mem. Eisenhower Meml. Commn., 2000, chmn., 2001—. Chmn. Ctr. for Govtl. Studies, 1992—; commr. Calif. Citizens Budget Commn.; mem. Fed. Pay Bd., 1971-73; trustee emeritus J. Paul Getty Trust. Author: Walking on Sand, 2004. Past chmn. Calif. Bus. Roundtable; trustee Com. for Econ. Devel.; co-chmn. Calif. Commn. on Campaign Financing. 1st lt. AUS, 1943-46, MTO, ETO. Decorated Bronze Star for Valor, Combat Infantryman's badge; Order of Merit (Italy); named to Hall of Fame, Inf. Sch., Ft. Benning, Ga. Mem. Nat. Acad. Pub. Adminstrn., Met. Club (Washington), L.A. Philharm. Assn. (life dir.), Calif. Club (L.A.). Home: 612 N Rodeo Dr Beverly Hills CA 90210-3208 Office Phone: 310-276-5912.

SICK, WILLIAM NORMAN, JR., technology company executive; b. Houston, Apr. 20, 1935; s. William Norman and Gladys Phylena (Armstrong) S.; m. Stephanie Anne Williams, Sept. 14, 1963; children: Jill Melanie, David Louis. BA, Rice U., Houston, 1957, BSEE, 1958. With Tex. Instruments Inc., various locations, 1958-87; exec. v.p. Tex. Instruments Inc., Dallas, 1982-87; pres. semicondr. products group Tex. Instruments Inc., Dallas, 1982-86; bd. dirs. Tex. Instruments, Inc., 1985-87; CEO Am. Nat. Can Co., Chgo., 1988-89; also bd. dirs. Am. Nat. Can. Co., Chgo., 1988-89; mem. exec. com. Pechiney, Paris, 1989; bd. dirs. Pechiney Internat., 1989; vice chmn., bd. dirs. Triangle Industries, NYC, 1988—89; chmn., CEO, Bus. Resources Internat., Winnetka, Ill., 1989—; co-founder, mng. dir. Signature Capital Mgmt., LLC, Northfield, Ill., 1997—2003. Bd. dirs., former chmn. Acoustic Tech., Mesa, Ariz.; co-founder Metasolv, Dallas; bd. dir., co-founder VIRxSYS, Gaithersburg, Md.; former chmn. Aware, Bedford, Mass., Power Trends, Warrenville, Ill.; guest lectr. Sophia U., Tokyo, 1973. Chmn. Fairhill Sch., Dallas, 1980-91; life trustee, past chmn. Shedd Aquarium, Chgo., 1990—; trustee Rice U., 1996-2006; trustee, Santa Fe Inst., 2000—; bd. dirs. Millennium Park Inc., 2004—; mem. Chgo. Coun. Global Affairs. Mem. Exec. Club Chgo., Glen View Club, Sigma Xi, Tau Beta Pi, Sigma Tau. Episcopalian. Office: Bus Resources Internat 565 Sheridan Rd Winnetka IL 60093-2344

SICKLES, ROBIN C., economics and statistics professor, consultant; b. Pitts., Dec. 24, 1949; s. Walter E. and Georgene N. Sickles; m. Janet C. Meininger, July 3, 1981; children: Danielle L., David C. BS in Econs., Ga. Inst. of Tech., 1972; PhD in Econs., U. of N.C., 1976. Asst. prof. dept. of econs. George Wash. U., Washington, 1976—79; vis. prof. dept. of econs. U. of Pa., Phila., 1979—80, asst. prof. dept. of econs., 1980—85; faculty rsch. fellow Nat. Bur. of Econ. Rsch., Cambridge, 1984—92; assoc. prof. dept. of econs. Rice U., Houston, 1985—87, prof. dept. of econs., 1987—; vis. scholar dept. of econs. U. of Mich., Ann Arbor, 1992; vis. adj. prof. European Inst. of Bus. Adminstrn., Fontainebleau, France, 1992—94; vis. scholar Bd. Govs. Fed. Res. Sys., Washington, 1993; vis. prof. pure and applied math. Inst. of Stats. Univ. Catholique de Louvain, Louvain-la-Neuve, Belgium, 1999. Dir. Rice U. Ctr. for the Study of Institutions and Values, Houston, 1999—2002; dir. grad. program in econs. Rice U., Houston, 2000—; dir. Law and Econ. Cons. Group, Houston, 2002—. Author: (book) The Causes, Correlates and Consequences of Death Among Older Adults: Some Methodological Approaches and Substantive Analysis-Kluwer, Unlocking the Assets: Energy and the Future of Central Asia and the Caucasus: A Political, Economic, and Cultural Analysis-Palgrave, (book chpt.) Handbook of Population and Family Economics-North Holland, Handbook of Applied Economics, Volume II-Microeconometrics-Basil Blackwell, (jour. articles) Internat. Econ. Rev., Rev. of Econs. and Stats., Jour. of Econs., Jour. of Bus. and Econ. Stats., Jour. of Applied Econometrics, Am. Econ. Rev., Jour. of Productivity Analysis, Internat. Jour. of Indsl. Orgn., Econ. Jour.; editor (in chief): (profl. jour.) Jour. of Productivity Analysis; assoc. editor (profl. jour.) Jour. of Applied Econometrics, Comms. in Stats., So. Econ. Jour., Jour. of Bus. and Econ. Stats., Jour. of Econometrics, Empirical Econs., editl. bd. Jour. of Productivity Analysis. Mem. bd. dirs. Afton Oaks Civic Assn., Houston, 1988—94; coach Southwestern YMCA, Houston. Grantee, NSF, 1978—80, 1980—82, 1980—83, 1984—87, Nat. Bur. of Econ. Rsch., 1982, NIH, 1986—89, Baker Inst. for Pub. Policy, 1996—2002. Mem.: Am. Econ. Assn., Econometric Soc. Office: Dept of Econs Rice Univ 6100 S Main St MS-22 Houston TX 77005-1892

SICKMEYER, KENT A., agricultural studies educator; b. Sparta, Ill., Sept. 1, 1958; s. Lou Ann Sickmeyer; married; children: Seth A., Hannah J. MBA, SIUE, Edwardsville, Ill., 2001. Herdsman SIUC, Carbondale, Ill., 1986—91; prof. Rend Lake Coll., Ina, Ill., 1992—2001, Kaskaskia Coll., Centralia, Ill., 2008—. Mem.: Ill. Beef Assn. (bd. govs. 1995—2002). Conservative. Home: 17183 Parrish Rd West Frankfort IL Office: Kaskaskia Coll 27210 College Rd Centralia IL 62801 Business E-Mail: ksickmeyer@kaskaskia.edu.

SICOLI, MARY LOUISE CORBIN, psychologist, educator; b. Delaware County, Pa., Nov. 15, 1944; d. C.M. Lewis and Lucille (Weber) Corbin; m. Thomas Sicoli, Aug. 27, 1967; children: Michael, Kathryn Francesca. BS, West Chester U., Pa., 1966, MS, 1974, U. Wis., Madison, 1967; PhD, Bryn Mawr Coll., Pa., 1977. Tchr. music, supr. Unionville-Chadds Ford (Pa.) Sch. Dist., 1967-70; supr. student tchrs. Rosemont (Pa.) Coll., 1976-78; prof. psychology, campus psychologist, coord. psychol. svcs. Cabrini Coll., Radnor, Pa., 1974—. Cons. Children's Svcs. Southea. Pa., 1974-80; supr. doctoral interns in psychology Bryn Mawr Coll., 1979-86; presenter in field. Contbr. articles to profl. jours., scientific papers at profl. Confs. Founding mem. bd. dirs. Maternal Support Sys. Chester County, 1981—; mem. Citizens Action for Better TV, 1981—; founder, chair Psychol. Aspects Popular Culture, Popular Culture Assn. Recipient Legion of Honor award Chapel of the Four Chaplains, 1980, Christian and Mary Lindback award for Disting. Coll. Tchg., 1984; named hon. alumnus Cabrini Coll., 2005. Fellow Pa. Psychol. Assn. (founder campus psychologist network); mem. AAUP, Am. Psychol. Assn. (reviewer rsch. papers 1980-), Ea. Psychol. Assn., Jean Piaget Soc., Assn. Moral Devel., Kappa Delta Pi, Psi Chi (founding adv., reviewer rsch. papers 1980-, Ea. Region Chptr. award 2005), Delta Epsilon Sigma. Home: 404 Darlington Dr West Chester PA 19382-2139

Office: Cabrini Coll Dept Psychology Radnor PA 19087 Home Phone: 610-696-8116; Office Phone: 610-902-8310. Personal E-mail: mlcorbin@verizon.net. Business E-Mail: mlsicoli@cabrini.edu.

SIDAMON-ERISTOFF, ANNE PHIPPS, not-for-profit developer; b. NYC, Sept. 12, 1932; d. Howard and Harriet Dyer (Price) Phipps; m. Constantine Sidamon-Eristoff, June 29, 1957; children: Simon, Elizabeth, Andrew. BA, Bryn Mawr Coll., 1954. Chairwoman emerita Am. Mus. Natural History, NYC; dir.-at-large Black Rock Forest Consortium; cons. mem. distbn. com. N.Y. Cmty. Trust. Trustee God Bless Am. Fund, Storm King Art Ctr., Mountainville, NY; hon. trustee World Wildlife Fund; bd. dirs. Greenacre Found., Highland Falls (N.Y.) Libr.; past bd. dirs. Scenic Hudson, St. Bernard's Sch., NYC, Mus. Modern Art, NYC, Mus. Hudson Highlands, Hudson River Found. Address: 120 E End Ave New York NY 10028-7552

SIDAMON-ERISTOFF, CONSTANTINE, lawyer; b. NYC, June 28, 1930; s. Simon C. and Anne Huntington (Tracy) Sidamon-E.; m. Anne Phipps, June 29, 1957; children: Simon, Elizabeth, Andrew. BSE in Geol. Engring, Princeton U., 1952; LLB, Columbia U., 1957. Clk., then assoc. firm Kelley Drye Newhall Maginnes & Warren, NYC, 1957-64; individual practice law NYC, 1964-65, 74-77; exec. asst. to Congressman John V. Lindsay, 1964-65; city coord. Lindsay Mayoral Campaign, NYC, 1965; asst. to mayor City of NY, 1966, commr. hwys., 1967-68, transp. adminstr., 1968-73; ptnr. Sidamon-Eristoff, Morrison, Warren, & Ecker, NYC, 1978-83; counsel Morrison & de Roos, 1984-88; pvt. practice NYC, 1988-89; regional adminstr. Region II EPA, NYC, 1989-93; of counsel Patterson, Belknap, Webb & Tyler, NYC, 1993-99, Lacher & Lovell-Taylor, NYC, 1999—. Mem. NY State Met. Transp. Authority Bd., 1974—89; commr. NY State Jud. Commn. on Minorities, 1987—91; mem. Gov.'s Coun. on Hudson River Valley Greenway, 1989; trustee United Mut. Savs. Bank, NYC, 1979—82, Phipps Houses, NYC, 1974—, chmn., 1986—2001, chmn. emeritus, 2001—. Trustee Am. the Beautiful Fund, Washington, 1985—97, Allaverdy Found., NYC, 1962—, Carnegie Hall, NYC, 1967—92, Millbrook Sch., NY, 1971—89, hon. trustee, 1989—; trustee Am. Farm Sch., Thessaloniki, Greece, 1973—79, Orange County Citizens Found., NY, 1974—81, Coun. Mcpl. Performance, 1981—85, vice chmn., 1986—87; bd. dirs. Mid-Hudson Pattern for Progress, Poughkeepsie, NY, 1975—89, chmn., 1981—85, Am. Friends of Ga., Inc., 1995—, Audubon NY, 1999—; dir. Nat. Audubon Soc., 2005—, Citizens Union Found., 1997—2007; NY State Rep. committeeman, 1980—89; mem. Orange County Planning Bd., NY, 1997—; bd. dirs. Tolstoy Found., NYC, 1975—2002, chmn. bd. dirs., 1979—89, 1994—2001; bd. dirs. Caramoor Ctr. Music and Arts, Katonah, NY, 1961—80, Boyce Thompson Inst. for Plant Rsch., Ithaca, NY, 1994—2006. 1st lt. arty. AUS, 1952—54, Korea. Decorated Bronze Star; recipient Honor award, Kings County chpt. NY State Soc. Profl. Engrs., 1969, Greater NY Coun. Girls Scouts US, 1973, Nat. and NY Parks and Conservation Assn., 1992, Bd. Leadership award, Coun. Mcpl. Performance, 1984, Transp. Man of Yr. award, Greater NY March of Dimes, 1985, award of excellence, Pattern for Progress, 1990, Lifetime Achievement award, 2007, Bronze medal, USEPA, 1993; co-recipient Civic Leadership award (with wife), Citizens Union, 1997, Force for Nature award (with wife), Natural Resources Def. Coun., 1999, Environ. Leadership award (with wife), Nat. Audubon Soc., 2001. Mem. ABA, NY State Bar Assn., Assn. Bar of City of NY, NY County Lawyers Assn., Kent Moot Ct., AIME, Phi Delta Phi, Delta Psi, Century Assn. (NYC), Knickerbocker Club (NYC), Racquet and Tennis Club (NYC). Republican. Eastern Orthodox. Office: Lacher & Lovell-Taylor 460 Park Ave New York NY 10022-1906 Office Phone: 212-872-1500. Office Fax: 212-872-1630. Business E-Mail: cseristoff@lltlaw.com. E-mail: ananouri@aol.com.

SIDANIUS, JAMES H., psychology professor; b. Dec. 11, 1945; married; 1 child. BA in Psychology, CUNY, 1968; PhD, Univ. Stockholm, 1977. Academic Diagnostician and Counselor Hunter Coll., NYC, 1969—70; asst. instr., psychology Univ. Stockholm, 1974—77, asst. prof., 1977—78, univ. lektor, 1978—80, assoc. prof., 1987; vis. asst. prof., postdoctoral fellow Carnegie Mellon Univ., Pitts., 1983—84; asst. prof., govt. Univ. Tex., 1984, assoc. prof., 1987, UCLA, 1988—2006; prof. psychology, African Am. studies Harvard Univ., 2006—. Author: Social Dominance, 1999, Racialized Politics, 2000, Key Readings in Political Psychology, 2004; assoc. editor Political Psychology, 1998—, editl. bd. Social Justice Research, 2003—. Recipient Hon. Mention, Gordon Allport Intergroup Rels. Prize, 2004—05. Fellow: Am. Acad. Arts & Scis.; mem.: Internat. Soc. Political Psychology (v.p.). Office: Harvard U William James Hall Rm 1544 33 Kirkland St Cambridge MA 02138 Office Phone: 617-495-3804. Business E-Mail: sidanius@wjh.harvard.edu.

SIDBURY, ROBERT, pediatrician; b. Durham, NC, Sept. 23, 1963; s. James Buren Jr. and Alice Rayle Sidbury; 1 child, Claire Winnie. BS in Psychology, Duke U., 1985, MD, 1993; MPH, Harvard Sch. Pub. Health, 2008. Diplomate Am. Bd. Dermatology, Am. Bd. Pediat. Dermatology. Intern U. Calif., San Francisco, 1993—94, rsch. fellow, 1994—95; resident in dermatology Oreg. Health & Sci. U., Portland, Oreg., 1995—98; fellow pediat. dermatology Childrens Meml. Hosp., Chgo., 1998—2000; asst. prof. pediat. Childrens Hosp., Seattle, 2000—; rsch. fellow Harvad Pediat. Health Svc., 2007—08; asst. prof., dept. dermatology Harvard Med. Sch., Boston Children's Hosp., 2006—09; chief, div. dermatology assoc. prof., dept. pediat. Seattle Children's Hosp., U. Wash. Sch. Medicine, 2009—. Faculty U. Wash. Sch. Medicine, 2004—05; instr. dermatology Bastyr U.; presenter, lectr. in field. Mem. editl. bd.: On The Surface; contbr. articles to profl. jours., chapters to books. Recipient Dermatology Investigator award, Dermatology Found., 1998; named Tchr. of Yr., Providence Family Practice, 2003, Top Doctor, Seattle Mag., 2004. Fellow: Am. Acad. Pediatrics, Am. Acad. Dermatology (edn. slide series task force 2004); mem.: Soc. for Pediat. Dermatology. Democrat. Office: Childrens Hosp Univ Wash Sch Med 4800 Sand Point Way NE Seattle WA 98105 Office Phone: 206-987-2158. Office Fax: 206-987-2217. Business E-Mail: robert.sidbury@seattlechildrens.org.

SIDDEEK, M. S.M., marine biologist, educator; arrived in U.S., 2000; s. M. L.M. Shareef and I. L.M. Zulaiha; m. Fathima Zeena Siddeek, May 21, 1985; children: Hani, Esra Fathima. PhD, U. of East Anglia, Norwich, Eng., 1981; BSc in Math. with honors, U. of Colombo, Sri Lanka, 1972. Med. lab. tech. Med. Rsch. Inst. Med. lab. technologist Gen. Hosp., Colombo, 1967—74; rsch. officer (biometrics) Nat. Aquatic Resources Agy., Colombo, 1974—85; assoc. rsch. scientist Kuwait Inst. for Sci. Rsch., Kuwait, 1985—90; assoc. prof. fisheries Sultan Qaboos U., Muscat, Oman, 1990—2000; shellfish biometrician Alaska Dept. Fish and Game, Juneau, Alaska, 2000—. Crab plan team mem. NPFMC, 2000—; vis. lectr. fisheries U. of Colombo, 1983—85; keynote spkr. Sultan Qaboos U., 2001, 05; invited spkr., Halifax, Canada, 02; independent rev. on snow crab assessment and mgmt. tech. report DFO, Moncton, Canada, 2007—09; invited reviewer internat. jour. articles and tech. reports in fisheries. Contbr. articles and tech. reports to profl. publs. Recipient Assessment and Mgmt. grant, Kuwait Inst. Sci. Rsch., 1986—89, Shrimp Ecology and Assessment grant, Ministry of Fisheries, Muscat, 1995, Kingfish Stock Assessment and Mgmt. grant, 1998, scholarship for PhD study, Colombo Plan, 1978, Crab Biometrics grant, NOAA, 2000—08; named Outstanding Rschr., Sultan Qaboos U., 1997. Mem.: Sri Lanka Assn. for Advancement of Scis., Am. Fisheries Soc. Office: Alaska Dept Fish and Game PO Box 115526 1255 W 8th St Juneau AK 99811-5526 Office Phone: 907-465-6107. Office Fax: 907-465-2604. Business E-Mail: shareef.siddeek@alaska.gov.

SIDDENS, PAUL JACKSON, III, communication educator; b. Indpls., Aug. 14, 1954; s. Paul Jackson Jr. and Marjorie Joan (Thacker) S. BA, Ind. U., 1976; MS, So. Ill. U., 1985, PhD, 1989. Film maker/ video producer Ind. U. Sch. Medicine, Indpls., 1979-84; artistic dir. Indpls. Theatre Co., 1983-86; instr. performance studies U. No. Iowa, Cedar Falls, 1988-91, asst. prof. comm. studies, 1991-96, assoc. prof. comm. studies, 1996—. Contbr. articles to profl. and lit. jours. Mem. Nat. Comm. Assn., Ctrl. States Comm. Assn., Iowa Comm. Assn. (pres. 1996-98, Outstanding Tchr. 1994), Phi Kappa Phi, Sigma Pi Alpha. Avocations: playing guitar, reading, creative writing. Office: Comm Studies Dept Univ Northern Iowa Cedar Falls IA 50614-0139 Office Phone: 317-273-5898. Business E-Mail: paul.siddens@uni.edu.

SIDDIQI, MOHAMMAD A., journalist, educator; s. Mohammad H Siddiqi and Siddiqa Khatoon; m. Tayyeba Muslim, June 28, 1991; children: Shazia A., Kamran A. MS in Physics, Aligarh Muslim U., India, 1973; MS, U. Ill., Chgo., 1983; PhD, Temple U., Phila., 1987. Prof. Western Ill. U., Macomb, Ill., 1987—; v.p., academic affairs Am. Islamic Coll., Chgo., 1988—2002, bd. mem., 1988—2002. Dir. journalism program Western Ill. U., Macomb, 2006—. Author: (book) Islam, Muslims & Media: Myths & Realities (Faculty Excellence award, 1992); editor: Islam: A Contemporary Perspectives; contbr. monograph. Sec. gen. World Coun. Muslims Interfaith Rels, Chgo., 2002—08; pres. Islamic Ctr. Macomb, 2002—06. Recipient King Saud Gold medal, Aligarh Muslim U., 1970. Mem.: Pub. Rels. Soc. Am., Internat. Assn. Media and Comm. Rsch. (chair, islam and media working group 1998—2008), Islamic Soc. North Am. Democrat. Office: Dept Journalism Western Ill 1 University Circle Macomb IL 61455 Office Fax: 309-298-2974.

SIDDIQI, MUNAWAR, anesthesiologist, consultant; b. Karachi, Sindh, Pakistan, June 12, 1959; s. Intikhab Hussain and Nusrat Jehan Siddiqi; m. Samina Munawar Junaid, Apr. 22, 1987; children: Ayesha Anadil, Manahil, Adil. MD, Sindh Med. Coll., Karachi, Pakistan, 1985. Cert. Ednl. Commn. Fgn. Med. Grads., 1995, lic. anesthesiologist Med. Coll. Ohio, 2001. Clin. assoc. Cleve. Clinic Found., Cleve., 2002—04; anesthesiologist So. Ohio Med. Ctr., Portsmouth, 2005—06, Dayton Pain Ctr., Ohio, 2007—. Pain specialist Mercy Hosp. Clermont, Batavia, Ohio, 2006—; fellow med. toxicology Hartford Hosp., 1997. Contbr. articles to profl. jours. Mem.: Am. Soc. Anesthesiologists. Achievements include research in silicone breast implants and induction of heat shock proteins. Home: 3004-Old Field Way Lexington KY 40513 Office: Dayton Pain Ctr One Elizabeth Pl Ste-D Dayton OH 45408 Office Fax: 513-735-8995.

SIDDIQUE, AKHTAR, finance company executive; b. Bangladesh, Jan. 14, 1968; married. PhD, Duke U., Durham, NC, 1995. Asst. prof. Georgetown U., Washington, 1995—2003; lead expert Office Comptroller Currency, Risk Analysis Divsn., Washington, 2004—. Office: Office Comptroller Currency 250 E St SW Washington DC 20219

SIDDIQUI, AFZAL A., medical educator; b. Aligarh, U.P., India, 1958; arrived in U.S., 1986, naturalized, 2004; s. Iqbal Siddiqui and Jamal Nizami; m. Shahana Siddiqui; children: Bilal, Sabrina. MS, Aligarh U., India, 1978, MPhil, 1982; PhD, U. Westen Ont., 1986. Post-doctoral rsch. assoc. Morehouse Coll. and Ctrs. Disease Control, Atlanta, 1986—87, U. Ill., Rockford, Ill., 1987—88; rsch. scientist and coordinator vaccine program U. We. Ont., London, Ontario, Canada, 1988—95; rsch. fellow Sch. Pub. Health Harvard U., Boston, 1995—97; asst. prof., health rsch. scientist East Tenn. State U., Johnson City, Tenn., 1997—2000, Veterans Affairs Med. Ctr., Johnson City, 1997—2000; assoc. prof. medicine Health Scis. Ctr. Tex. Tech U., Amarillo, Tex., 2000—. Grant reveiwer in field; paper reveiwer in field. Contbr. chapters to books, articles to profl. jours. Grantee, NIH, 2001—. Mem.: Am. Soc. Microbiology, Infectious Diseases Soc. Am., Am. Soc. Tropical Medicine and Hygiene, Am. Soc. Parasitologists, Sigma Xi. Achievements include research in vaccines and new therapies for parasitic infections. Office: Texas Tech Univ Health Sciences Center 1400 Wallace Blvd Amarillo TX 79106 E-mail: afzal.siddiqui@ttuhsc.edu.

SIDDIQUI, FOUZIA, neurologist; d. Ajaz Ahmed Siddiqui and Rakhshanda Ajaz. PECHS, Govt. Coll. Women, Karachi, 1988; MBBS, Dow Med. U., Karachi, 1996; FCPS in Medicine, Coll. Physician and Surgeons Pakistan, Karachi, 2001. Internship Cert. Civil Hosp. Karachi, 1997, residency cert. Liaquat Nat. Hosp., 2001. Internship psychiatry Civil Hosp. Karachi, 1996, internship surgery, 1997, internship medicine, 1997; emergency med. officer Liaquat Nat. Hosp., Karachi, 1998, resident medicine; asst. prof. Hamdard U., Karachi, 2002—03; cons. physician PECHS trauma and gen. Hosp., Karachi; externship neurology Regions Hosp., St. Paul, 2001; rsch. fellow NJ Neurosci. Inst. JFK Med. ctr., Edison, NJ, 2003—06, sleep medicine fellow; preliminary medicine U. Toledo Med. Ctr., 2006—07, resident neurology, 2007—. Rsch. fellow NJ Neurosci. Inst. JFK Med. ctr., Edison, NJ, 2003—06. Contbr. articles to profl. med. jours. Vol. worker Patients Welfare Orgn., Karachi, 1991—96; asst. editor Amnesty Internat., Karachi, 1994—98. Recipient Travel award, Internat. Restless legs Group, 2004. Mem.: Internat. Restless Legs Study Group, Am. Acad. Neurology. Avocations: travel, reading. Office: Univ Toledo Medical Ctr 3000 Arlington Ave Toledo OH 43614 Office Fax: 419-383-3093. Personal E-mail: drfsid@yahoo.com.

SIDDIQUI, MUSTAQEEM AHMAD, physician; b. Houston, July 29, 1976; s. Ahmad Abdul Muqeet and Ishrat Sultana Siddiqui; m. Sana Faiz, Apr. 20, 2006. M.B., B.S., Aga Khan U. Med. Coll., Karachi, Pakistan, 2002. Diplomate Am. Bd. Internal Medicine, 2007. Rsch. fellow Beth Israel Med. Ctr., Harvard Med. Sch., 2002—04; resident physician Mayo Clinic, Rochester, Minn., 2004—07, fellow, hematology and oncology, 2007—. Mem.: ACP, AMA, Am. Soc. Hematology, Minn. Med. Assn., BMW Car Club Am. Achievements include research in day 15 natural killer cell recovery predicts progression-free survival after autologous stem cell transplantation in Non-Hodgkin's Lymphoma; absolute lymphocyte count recovery during standard chemotherapy; autologous stem cell transplantation in first remission for patients with Mantle Cell Lymphoma; the utilization of oxygen concentrators in six villages across three provinces in central Java; a prospective study of lymphocyte subset recovery following autologous stem cell transplantation; absolute lymphocyte count at diagnosis; survey of patients with seronegative spondyloarthropathies presenting to the Aga Khan University from 1995-2000. Office: Mayo Clinic 200 First St SW Rochester MN 55905

SIDDIQUI, RAZIA SULTANA, retired psychotherapist, educator; d. Gurcharan Singh and Bhupinder Kaur Sangha; m. Mohammed Sadiq Siddiqui, May 2, 1963; children: Niloufer Siddiqi Dennis, Adeeba Sultana Siddiqi, Khalid Mohammed Siddiqi. BA, Dayanand Mlathradas Coll., Moga, India, 1956; BT, Dayanand Plathradas Coll., Moga, India, 1959; MA in Psychology, Lucknow U., India, 1958; diploma in Med. & Social Psychology, Mysore U., Bangalore, India, 1962; cert. in psychotherapy, Southwestern Med. Sch., Dallas, 1972; PhD in Neuropsychology, Postgrad. Inst. Med. Edn. and Rsch., Chandigarh, India, 1994. Asst. prof. ednl. psychology Saraswati Tng. Coll., Amritsar, India, 1959—60; clin. psychologist Niloufer Pediat. Hosp., Hyderabad, India, 1962—65; asst. prof. med. psychology Nangrahar Med. Sch., Jalalabad, Afghanistan, 1965—80, dir. publs., 1968—80; assoc. prof. psychology Kabul U., Afghanistan, 1980—88, assoc. prof. ednl. psychology Faculty Edn., 1980—88, dir. fgn. rels., 1982—88. Asst. editor Kabul Times, 1967—68. Election officer tech. Registrar of Voters, San Diego, 2006—. Home: 2162 Crystal Clear Dr Spring Valley CA 91978 E-mail: goodie65@hotmail.com.

SIDDONS, JEFFREY G., school librarian; b. Milwaukee, Wis., Dec. 24, 1951; s. James K. and Dolores V. Siddons; m. Martha J. Upton, June 8, 1973; children: Upton G., Jeffrey D. MLIS, Rutgers, New Brunswick, NJ, 1977; BS in Zoology, U. Tulsa, Okla., 1974. Engring. libr. asst. Princeton U., NJ, 1976—77; life sci. libr. Northwestern U., Evanston, Ill., 1977—78; geophys. data technician Amerada Hess Corp., Tulsa, 1980—83; LRC coord. Tulsa CC, 1983—; reference libr. U. Tulsa, 1987—. Chair Okla. Libr. Assn., 2005—. Contbr. articles to profl. jours. Campus chair Tulsa Area United Way, 2008—08. Liberal. Unitarian Universalist. Avocations: travel, motorcycling, boating. Office: Tulsa CC 7505 West 41 St Tulsa OK 74107-8633 Business E-Mail: jsiddons@tulsacc.edu.

SIDDONS, JOY GARBEE, music educator; b. Lynchburg, Va., July 18, 1952; d. Clyde Lewis and Julia Schmitt Garbee; m. James Siddons, July 2, 1977. BS, Liberty U., 1984; MEd, Lynchburg Coll., 1996; MusEdM, Shenandoah U., 1998. Cert. in elem. music edn. Nat. Bd. Profl. Tchg. Standards, 2007. Music educator Bedford County Pub. Schools, Bedford, Va., 1989—2003, Fairfax County Pub. Schools, Va., 2003—. Dir. of music United Meth. & Luth. Chs., 1988—. Dir.: children's choirs and musical theater prodns. United Methodist. Office: Fairhill Elem Sch 3001 Chichester Ln Fairfax VA 22116 Home: 800 Ivy Lake Dr Forest VA 24551

SIDEBOTTOM, CHARLES BENTON, engineering executive; s. Oscar H. and Goldia B. Sidebottom; m. Carolyn Sue Padley, May 25, 1969. BSEE, Iowa State U., Ames, 1968; MSEE, U. Mo., Columbia, 1979. Indsl. engr. Kansas City Power & Light Co., 1968—69, sys. planning engr., 1973—74, mgr. tech. svcs., 1974—80; mgr. software systems Medtronic, Inc., Mpls., 1984—85, engring. project mgr., 1985—87, product planner, 1987—89, mgr. engring. dept., 1989—92, mgr. stds., 1992—2000, dir. corp. stds., 2000—. Sec. com. 62a Internat. Electrotech. Commn., Geneva, 1996—; sec. com. 150/SC 5 Internat. Stds. Orgn. Geneva, 2007—. Author: (reference book) International Labeling Requirements for Medical Devcies, Medical Equipment, and Diagnostic Products; contbr. reference book, articles to profl. jours. Co-chmn. planning bd. USE, Inc., Washington, 1983—84; mem. Colonial Williamsburg Capital Soc., Va., 1987; chmn. USE, Inc., Mpls., 1982—84; active Spirit Hope United Meth. Ch., Golden Valley, Minn., 1984—. With USN, 1969—73. Mem.: ASTM (mem. sec. com. 2002—07, recording sec. com. 2008—, Robert Fairer award 2005—, Patrick Laing award 2009), IEEE, Internat. Stds. Orgn. (sec. com. ISO/TCISO/SC 5 2007—), Assn. Advancement Med. Instrumentation (co-chiar pacemaker com. 1993—2003, dir. 2000—, industry vice chmn. 2004—06, co-chmn. stds. bd. 2005—08, chair elect 2006—08, nominating com. 2006—, bd. chmn. 2008—, Sds. Developer award 2007), Stds Engring. Soc., Regulatory Affairs Profl. Soc. Office: Medtronic Inc 710 Medtronic Pky Minneapolis MN 55432

SIDEK, NAIM, information scientist; married. PhD, Vanderbilt U., Nashville, Tenn., 2008. Rsch. asst. Vanderbilt U., 2003—. Grantee, NSF, 2005—08. Mem.: IEEE. Achievements include research in modeling and control of nonholonomic wheeled mobile robot. Home: 3414 Murphy Rd 15 Nashville TN 37203 Personal E-mail: naim.sidek@gmail.com.

SIDER, RONALD J., theology educator, author; b. Stevensville, Ont., Can., Sept. 17, 1939; m. Arbutus Lichti Sider, Aug. 19, 1961; children: Theodore Ronald, Michael Jay, Sonya Maria. BA with honors, Waterloo Luth. U., Ont., Can., 1962; MA in History, Yale U., New Haven, Conn., 1963, BD, 1967, PhD in History, 1969; D (hon.), Westminster Coll., New Wilmington, Pa., 1998; DHL (hon.), Malone Coll., Canton, Ohio, 2005; DST (hon.), Messiah Coll., 2009. Lectr., asst. prof., then assoc. prof. Messiah Coll., Phila., 1968-78, acting dir., dean, 1971-75; assoc. prof. theology Ea. Bapt. Theol. Sem., Wynnewood, Pa., 1978-84, prof. theology and culture, 1984—2002, Ronald J. Sider prof. theology, holistic ministry and pub. policy, 2002—; dir. Sider Ctr. on Ministry and Pub. Policy Palmer Seminary, Eastern U., 2002—. Coord., chair, convenor workshops in field; coord. Internat. Consultation on Simple Lifestyle, London, 1980; lectr. in field. Author: Christ and Violence, 1979, Japanese edit., 2004, Karlstadt's Battle with Luther: Documents in a Liberal-Radical Debate, 1978, 82, Evangelism, 1985, Rich Christians in an Age of Hunger: A Biblical Study, 1977, rev. edit., 1984, 90, 97, 2005, German edit., 1979, Dutch edit., 1980, Portuguese edit., 1984, Japanese edit., 1989, Chinese edit., 1998, Korean edit., 1998, Polish edit., 2009, Andreas Bodenstein Von Karlstadt, 1974, Genuine Christianity, 1996, (with Richard K. Taylor) Nuclear Holocaust and Christian Hope, 1982, English edit., 1984, (with Oliver O'Donovan) Peace and War: A Debate About Pacifism, 1985, (in Chinese) Evangelical Faith and Social Ethics, 1986, Completely Pro-Life, 1987, (with Michael A. King) Preaching About Life in Threatening World, 1988, (with Kathleen Hayes), JustLife/88: A 1988 Election Study Guide for Justice, Life and Peace, 1988, Testing the Limits of Nonviolence, 1988, One-Sided Christianity? Uniting the Church to Heal a Lost and Broken World, 1993, Chinese edit., 1998, Cup of Water, Bread of Life: Inspiring Stories About Overcoming Lopsided Christianity, 1994, Korean edit., 1999, Good News and Good Works: A Theology for the Whole Gospel, 1999, Living Like Jesus, 1999, Just Generosity: A New Vision for Overcoming Poverty in America, 1999, 2d edit., 2007, (with Philip N. Olson and Heidi Rolland Unruh) Churches That Make a Difference: Reaching Your Community with Good News and Good Works, 2002, Doing Evangelism Jesus' Way, 2003, The Scandal of the Evangelical Conscience, 2005, (with Heidi Rolland Unruh) Saving Souls, Serving Society: Understanding The Faith Factor in Church Based Social Ministry, 2005, I Am Not A Social Activist: Making Jesus The Agenda, 2008, The Scandal of Evangelical Politics: Why Are Christians Missing The Chance To Really Change The World?, 2008; editor: Preaching on Peace, 1982, Lifestyle in the Eighties: An Evangelical Commitment to Simple Life-Style, 1982, Evangelicals and Development: Toward a Theology of Social Change, 1982, Living More Simply, 1980, Cry Justice: The Bible on Hunger and Poverty, 1988, 91, For They Shall Be Fed, 1997, (with Diane Knippers) Toward an Evangelical Public Policy,

2005, (with Heidi Unruh) Hope for Children in Poverty, 2007; co-editor: Transformation mag., 1984-99; editor, contbr.: The Chicago Declaration, 1974; pub. Prism mag., 1993—, Green Cross, 1994-98, Creation Care, 1998-2002; contbr. numerous articles to profl. publs., chpts. to books. Head voter registration drive, New Haven, 1967; pres. Diamond St. Cmty. Ctr., 1986-91; exec. dir. Evangelicals for Social Action, 1987-92, pres., 1992—; exec. dir. Just Life, 1987-91, pres., 1991-94; bd. dirs. Bread for the World, 1978-84, Mennonite Ctrl. Com., 1978-80, Nat. Religious Partnership on the Environ., 1994-, Call to Renewal, 1996-2007, Sojourners, 2007-, Evangel. Environ. Network, 2005—; co-chair Nat. Workshop on Race and Reconciliation, Atlanta, 1975. Malcolm Chase fellow, 1962-63, R.E. Darling fellow, 1963-64, fellow Yale U., 1967-68, Inst. for Advanced Christian Studies, 1976; co-chair Working Group on Human Needs and Faith-Based and Cmty. Initiatives II, 2002-03. Mem. Nat. Assn. Evangelicals (mem. social action commn. 1975—). Mennonite. Home: 312 W Logan St Philadelphia PA 19144-4120 Office: Palmer Sem 6 E Lancaster Ave Wynnewood PA 19096-3430 Office Phone: 484-384-2974. Business E-Mail: rsider@eastern.edu.

SIDEREAS, PANAGIOTIS, physicist; b. Chgo., Jan. 22, 1978; s. Angelos and Lily Sidereas; m. Kathryn Bauer, June 28, 2008. MS in Physics, DePaul U., Chgo., 2003, MS in Computer Sci., 2008. Radiation physicist STERIS Corp., Libertyville, Ill., 2003—. Achievements include research in temperature effects during interruption of irradiation on various dosimeters.

SIDERS, DAVID L., oil industry executive, educator; b. Bowling Green, Ohio, Sept. 15, 1942; s. Walter H. and Dorothy L. Siders; m. Sharon H. Huffman, Aug. 28, 1968. BS, Bowling Green State U., Ohio, 1964, MBA, 1966; JD, Coll. William and Mary, Williamsburg, Va., 1969. Part time instr. Coll. William and Mary, 1967—69; staff tax atty. Reynolds Metals Co., Richmond, Va., 1969—73; mgr. taxes Chase Brass & Copper Co., Shaker Heights, Ohio, 1973—75, M.A. Hanna Co., Cleve., 1975—82; sr. tax counsel Midland Ross Corp., Shaker Heights, 1982—86; dir. minerals taxation BP Am. Inc., Cleve., 1986—88, dir. internat. taxation, 1988—91, dir. corp. taxation, 1991—92; adj. prof. law Case We. Res. U., Cleve., 1992—96; part time lectr. John Carroll U., University Heights, Ohio, 1994—98, vis. prof., 1998—2003; adj. prof. Notre Dame Coll., South Euclid, Ohio, 1996—97, Cleve. State U., 1997—2003, Bridgewater Coll., Va., 2003—. Treas. Tax Exec. Inst., Cleve., 1973—92, bd. dirs., 1973—92; officer Cleve. Tax Club, 1973—2003; chmn. Cleve. Internat. Tax Club, 1977—82. Contbr. articles to profl. jours. Parishioner St. Bedes Cath. Ch., Williamsburg, 1968—69, St. Paul's Cath. Ch., Richmond, 1969—82, St. Dominick's Cath. Ch., Shaker Heights, 1973—82, St. Anne's Cath. Ch., Cleveland Heights, 1982—2003, St. Patricks's Cath. Ch., Lexington, Va., 2003. Named Number one in class, Bowling Green State U. MBA program, 1969. Mem.: Ohio State Bar, Va. State Bar (assoc.). Independent. Roman Catholic. Avocations: reading, golf, football, baseball, hockey. Office: Bridgewater Coll 402 East College St Bridgewater VA 22812 Business E-Mail: dsiders@bridgewater.edu.

SIDES, I. RUTH S., retired music educator; d. John Daniel Donald and I. Ruth Schulmeyer; m. Anthony Fred Sides, May 25, 1972 (dec. Sept. 7, 1997); children: Rebecca Ruth Desenti, Connie Susanne Moore. BA, Baldwin Wallace Coll., 1968. Cert. tchg. Ohio, 1968. Dir. band, choruses Ridgemont Local Schs., Ridgeway, Ohio, 1967—71; dir. choral music Groveland H.S., Fla., 1972—93, South Lake H.S., 1993—2005, chair dept. fine arts and fgn. langs., 2002—05. Cert. judge Fla. BBQ Assn., Fla., 2002—. Recipient Tchr. Of The Yr., Hardin County Schools, 1969-1970, Outstanding Young Women Am., 1973, Teacherific - Judge's Choice, Walt Disney World, 2000; nominee Disney's Am. Tchr., 2001. Mem.: Fla. Vocal Assn., Fla. Music Educators Assn. Avocations: cooking, sewing, travel. Home: 11844 Lake Minneola Shores Clermont FL 34715

SIDHWA, FRANK N., engineering executive; BEE, CUNY, 1980; MBA, Adelphi U., NY, 1984. Cert. project mgmt., U. Calif., 1998. Design engr. Sperry Sys. Mgmt., Great Neck, NY, 1980—83; sys. engr. Harris Corp., Syosset, NY, 1983—85; engring. mgr. Raytheon Corp., Melville, NY, 1985—86; prin. engr. Douglas Aircraft, Long Beach, Calif., 1986—91; sys. engring. mgr. PB/DMJM Metro Rail Projects, LA, 1991—93; sr. mgr. engring. Boeing Co., Long Beach, 1993—. Contbr. scientific papers in field. Recipient Best paper award. Mem.: NSPE, IEEE, Am. Mgmt. Assn. Achievements include research in avionics automated testing. Office: Boeing Co 2401 E Wardlow Rd 52-681 Long Beach CA 90080

SIDLE, DOUGLAS M., medical educator; MD, U. Ill., Chgo. Diplomate Am Bd. Facial Plastic & Reconstructive Surgery, 2008. Asst. prof. Northwestern U., Chgo., 2006—. Office: Northwestern Faculty Found 675 N St Clair St Suite 15-200 Chicago IL 60611

SIDMAN, ROBERT JOHN, lawyer; b. Cleve., Aug. 4, 1943; s. Charles Frances and Louise (Eckert) S.; m. Mary Mato, July 29, 1967; children: Christa Mary, Alicia Mary. BA, Benedictine Coll., 1965; JD, U. Notre Dame, 1968. Bar: Ohio 1968, U.S. Dist. Ct. (so. dist.) Ohio 1970, U.S. Ct. Appeals (6th cir.) 1971, U.S. Supreme Ct. 1971. Law clk. US Dist. Ct. (so. dist.) Ohio, Columbus, 1968—70, judge Bankruptcy Ct., 1975—82; assoc. Mayer, Tingley & Hurd, Columbus, 1970-75; ptnr. Vorys, Sater, Seymour & Pease, Columbus, 1982—. Prof. Ohio State U. Law Sch., Columbus, 1984, 85, 86. Mem. Nat. Conf. Bankruptcy Judges (bd. dirs. 1981-82), Assn. Former Bankruptcy Judges (bd. dirs. 1983-89, treas. 1986-87, pres. 1988-89). Office: Vorys Sater Seymour & Pease PO Box 1008 52 E Gay St Columbus OH 43215-3161 E-mail: rjsidman@vssp.com, rsidman843@aol.com.

SIDNER, ROBERT BROWN, museum director; BA in English, St. Meinrad Coll., Ind.; STB, Gregorian U., Rome; MA in Liturgy, Notre Dame U., Ind. Assoc. pastor, Ohio, 1969—77; asst. prof., dir. formation St. Meinrad Coll., 1977—81; pastor St. John's Ch., Delphos, Ohio, 1981—85, St. Charles Ch., Lima, Ohio, 1985—91; owner, dir. Cable Gallery, San Diego, 1991—92; membership coord. Mingei Internat. Mus., 1993—94, dir., pub. rels., 1994—96, asst. dir., 1996—2005, acting dir., 2005—06, dir., 2006—. Spkr. in field. Bd. dirs. Akaloa Resource Found., 2007—. Mem.: San Diego/Tijuana Japan Soc., Nat. Fedn. Spiritual Dirs. (pres. 1977—81). Office: Mingei Internat Mus 1439 El Prado San Diego CA 92101 Office Phone: 619-239-0003.

SIDORA-ARCOLEO, KIMBERLY JOAN, nursing educator; b. Rochester, NY, Nov. 12, 1955; d. Joan Dorothy and George Meschko (Stepfather); m. Frank Richard Sidora, Aug. 22, 1981 (div. July 31, 1997); children: Tara Lyn Sidora, Amanda Christine Sidora; m. Joseph John Arcoleo, Aug. 14, 2004. BA in Biology, SUNY, Buffalo, 1977; MPH, U. Rochester, 1996, PhD in Health Svcs. Rsch., 2006. Ophthalmic asst. Bausch and Lomb, Inc., 1979—86, quality assurance documentation coord., 1986—87, clin. rsch. monitor, 1987—89; sr. rsch. assoc. U. Rochester Sch. Nursing, 1989—2006; asst. prof. Ariz. Stste U., Coll. Nursing and Healthcare Innovation, Phoenix, 2006—; assoc. dir., ctr. healthcare innovation and clin. trials ASU Coll. Nursing and Healthcare Innovation, 2006—. Contbr. articles to profl. jours. Recipient Health Care Rsch. award, NIH, 1997, 1st Pl. award, Collier Rsch. Day Mental Health Rsch. Poster Session, 2004, Ellen Rudy Clore Excellence in Rsch. Writing award, Jour. Pediatric Healthcare, 2005. Mem.: APHA. Achievements include development of online graduate certificate and masters degree programs in clinical research management in Arizona; research in health disparities in childhood asthma. Avocations: running, golf, hiking, reading, jazz. Office: Ariz State Univ 500 N 3d St Phoenix AZ 85004 Office Fax: 602-496-0986. Business E-Mail: kimberly.arcoleo@asu.edu.

SIDOROV, JAAN ERIK, physician, researcher; b. Weisbaden, Germany, Aug. 22, 1955; came to U.S., 1956; s. Viktor and Esther (Ryssdal) S.; m. Sharon, May 19, 1981; children: Erik, Greg, Kristin. BA, Villanova U., Pa., 1977; MD, Milton Hershey Med. Ctr., Pa., 1981. Assoc. dept. gen. internal medicine Geisinger Med. Ctr., Danville, Pa., 1985-95; asst. med. dir. Gersinger Health Plan, Danville, Pa., 1995. Contbr. articles to profl. jours. Fellow ACP; mem. AMA, Soc. Gen. Internal Medicine, Pa. Med. Soc. Methodist. Avocation: korean martial arts. Home: RR 6 Box 415 Danville PA 17821-8701 Office: Geisinger Health Plan Danville PA 17822-0001

SIDRAN, MIRIAM, retired physicist; b. Washington, May 25, 1920; d. Morris Samson and Theresa Rena (Gottlieb) S. BA, Bklyn. Coll., 1942; MA, Columbia U., NYC, 1949; PhD, NYU, 1956. Rsch. assoc. dept. physics NYU, NYC, 1950-55, postdoctoral fellow, 1955-57; asst. prof. Staten Island Community Coll., Richmond, NY, 1957-59; rsch. scientist Grumman Aerospace Corp., Bethpage, NY, 1959-67; prof. N.Y. Inst. Tech., NYC, 1967-72; NSF rsch. fellow Nat. Marine Fisheries Svc., Miami, Fla., 1971-72; assoc. prof. then prof. physics Baruch Coll., NYC, 1972-89, chmn. dept. natural scis., 1983-89, prof. emerita, 1990—. V.p. Baruch chpt. Profl. Staff Congress, 1983-89. Contbr. numerous articles to profl. and govtl. publs., chpts. to books. N.Y. State Regents scholar, 1937-41; NSF summer fellow, Miami, 1970. Mem. N.Y. Acad. Scis., Am. Assn. Physics Tchrs., Physics Club N.Y., N.Y. Gilbert and Sullivan Soc., Wynmoor Computer Club, Friends of Mozart, Sigma Xi, Sigma Pi Sigma. Avocations: french and hebrew languages, music, bicycling, poetry, opera. Home: 210 W 19th St Apt 5G New York NY 10011-4009

SIDRANSKY, DAVID, molecular biologist; b. El Paso, Tex., June 21, 1960; s. Julia and Amalia Sidransky; m. Lynn R. Clahr, Sept. 26, 1990; children: Elie M., Anina Libi, Yair S. BS in Chemistry, magna cum laude, with highest honors, Brandeis U., 1981; MD, Baylor Coll. Medicine, 1984. Diplomate Am. Bd. Internal Medicine, Am. Bd. Med. Oncology. Intern in internal medicine Baylor Coll. Medicine, Houston, 1984-85, resident in internal medicine, 1985-87, clin. investigator Inst. Molecular Genetics, 1986-87, chief resident in internal medicine, 1987-88; sr. clin. fellow in oncology Johns Hopkins Hosp., Balt., 1988-89, rsch. fellow in oncology, 1989-92, asst. prof. oncology, 1992-94, asst. prof. otolaryngology, head and neck surgery, 1992-94, assoc. prof. oncology, 1994-98, dir. head and neck cancer rsch. divsn., 1994—, prof. otolaryngology, head and neck surgery, 1998—, prof. pathology, 1998—, prof. cellular and molecular medicine, 1998—, prof. urology, 1999—. Mem. external adv. bd. U. Calif., San Diego Cancer Ctr., U. Tex. M.D. Anderson Cancer Ctr., Houston; mem. sci. adv. coun. Israel Cancer Sch. Fund; mem. med. adv. coun. Israel Children's Cancer Found.; mem. devel. diagnostics com. Nat. Cancer Inst., 1996—, mem. cancer prevention and control com., 1996—, bd. sci. counselors, chmn. early detectin rsch. network; bd. dirs. ImClone, 2004-, Alfacell Corp., 2004-; sr. editor Clinical Cancer Research. Contbr. articles to profl. jours. including Sci., Cancer Rsch., Sci., Nature Medicine; chmn., editl. bd. Internat. Jour. Cancer-Predictive Oncology; sr. editor Clin. Cancer Rsch.; assoc. editor Cancer Rsch., Jour. Nat. Cancer Inst., Oral Oncology. Recipient Nat. Rsch. Svc. award, 1989-91, Young Investigators Merit award, 1992, Clinician Scientist award, 1992, award Found. for the Promotion of Cancer Rsch., Japan, 1995, Sarstedt Internat. Rsch. prize German Soc. Clin. Chemistry, 1997, Cheng Suen Man Shook Found. award Hong Kong Cancer Inst., 1998, Walter Hubert award Brit. Assn. Cancer Rsch., 1998, Alton Ochsner award Relating Smoking and Health Am. Coll. Chest Physicians, 1998, Internat. Union Against Cancer Roll of Honour, 1999, Osserman award, Israel Cancer Rsch. Fund, 2001, Richard and Hinda Rosenthal Found. award, Am. Assn. Cancer Rsch., 2004. Mem. AAAS, Am. Soc. for Head and Neck Surgery, Am. Assn. for Cancer Rsch., N.Y. Acad. Scis. Jewish. Avocation: racquetball. Office: Johns Hopkins U Ross Rsch Bldg 720 Rutland Ave Ste 818 Baltimore MD 21205-2109

SIEBEN, J(OHN) KENNETH, retired humanities educator, writer, editor; b. Irvington, NJ, Mar. 10, 1939; s. Oscar August and Dorothy Maude (Burke) S.; m. Regina Marie Monks, June 18, 1960; children: Joseph Richard, Mark Thomas, Ann Karen, Gregory Paul, Laura Jean Jerry. BS, Seton Hall U., 1960, MA, 1962; PhD, NYU, 1971. Tchr. French and English Essex Cath. H.S., Newark, 1960—62; tchr. English Middleton Twp. H.S., NJ, 1962—65; supr. remedial reading ctr. Kilmer Job Corps Ctr., Edison, NJ, 1965—67; curriculum coord. pub. svc. career program CUNY, NYC, 1967—68; dean continuing edn. Essex County Coll., Newark, 1968—70, prof. humanities, 1970—2000, ret., 2000. Spkr., presenter Nat. Coun. Tchrs. English, Coll. English Assn. Author: (textbook) Communication Skills Lab, 1976, 83, Composition Five, 1982, 85; 82 short stories and novel, Joanie M, 2007; fiction editor Northwoods Jour., 1992-2002. Lt. USNR, 1956-74. Summer scholar NEH, 1974. Avocations: sailing, fishing, hiking, cooking. E-mail: kensieben@comcast.net.

SIEBERSMA, DANIEL, state librarian; BA, Morningside Coll., Sioux City, Iowa; MA in Librarianship, U. Denver. Dir. Compell County Pub. Libr., Gillotte, Wyo., 1981—89, Euclid Pub. Libr., Euclid, Ohio, 1989—92, Lakeland Libr. Cooperative, Grand Rapids, Mich., 1999—2006; state libr. SD State Libr., Pierre, 2007—. Mem.: ALA. Office: SD State Libr Mercedes MacKay Bldg 800 Governors Dr Pierre SD 57501 Office Phone: 605-773-3131, 605-773-6962.

SIEBERT, CALVIN D., economist, educator; b. Hillsboro, Kans., Feb. 11, 1934; s. Ira and Margaret (Everett) S.; m. Valerie Dawn Nanninga, Feb. 18, 1960; children: Douglas Erik, Derek Christopher. BA, U. Kans., 1958, MA, 1960; PhD in Econs., U. Calif., Berkeley, 1966. Asst. prof. econs. U. Iowa, 1965-68, assoc. prof., 1968-75, prof., 1975—, chmn. dept., 1969-71, 75-79. Rockefeller Found. vis. asso. prof. U. Philippines, 1971-72 Contbr. articles to profl. jours. With US Army, 1954-56. Ford Found. grantee, 1964-65 Mem. Am. Econ. Assn., Phi Beta Kappa. Home: 341 N 7th Ave Iowa City IA 52245-6003 Office: U Iowa Dept Econs S318 Pbb Iowa City IA 52242 Business E-Mail: calvin_siebert@uiowa.edu.

SIEBERT, DIANE DOLORES, author, poet; m. Robert William Siebert, Sept. 21, 1969. RN. Author: Truck Song, 1984 (Notable Childrens Book award ALA 1984, Sch. Libr. Jour. one of Best Books 1984, Outstanding Childrens Book award NY Times Book Rev. 1984, Reading Rainbow Selection book 1991), Mojave, 1988 (Childrens Editors Choice 1988, Internat. Reading Assn. Tchr. Choice award 1989, others), Heartland, 1989 (award Nat. Coun. for Social Studies/Childrens Book Coun. 1989, on John Burroughs List Nature Book for Young Readers 1989, Ohio Farm Bur. Women award 1991), Train Song, 1990 (Notable Childrens Book award ALA, 1990, Redbook Mag. one of Top Ten Picture Books 1990, one of Best Books award Sch. Libr. Jour. 1990, others), Sierra, 1991 (Outstanding Sci. Trade Book for Children award NSTA 1991, Notable Childrens Trade Book in Field Social Studies award Nat. Coun. Social Studies 1991, Beatty award Calif. Libr. Assn. 1992), Plane Song, 1993 (Outstanding Sci. Trade Book for Children 1994, Reading Rainbow Selection book, Platinum award Oppenheim Toy Portfolio, Tchrs. Choice award Internat. Reading Assn. 1994), Cave, 2000 (Notable children's Book in the english Language Arts, 2001, Nat. Coun. of English Tchr., named to John Burroughs List of Nature Books for Young Readers 2000), Mississippi (named to John Burroughs List 2001), 2001, Motorcycle Song, 2002, Rhyolite, 2003, Tour America, 2006 (Oreg. Book award for children's literature, Eloise Jarvis McGraw award 2006, Lee Bennett Hopkins Honor Book award 2007, Notable Social Studies Trade Books for Young People 2007, Cybils award finalist 2007), Spring, Summer, Autumn, Winter, 2007. Avocations: environmental affairs, running, classical guitar, motorcycle, animals. Home: 9676 SW Jordan Rd Culver OR 97734-9567 Personal E-mail: dsiebert48@msn.com.

SIEBERT, JOHN WESTON, plastic surgeon; b. Madison, Wis., Feb. 8, 1955; MD, U. Wis. Med. Sch., 1981. Cert. Surgery, Plastic Surgery. Resident in surgery Mass. Gen. Hosp., 1981—86; resident in plastic surgery NYU Med. Ctr., 1986—88, clin. fellow in microsurgery, 1988—89, assoc. prof., surgery, 1989, adj. prof. plastic surgery; attending surgeon Manhattan Ear, Eye and Throat Hosp., NYC, 1989—, Bellevue Hosp. Ctr., NYC, 1989—, NY Ear and Eye Infirmary, NYC, 1989—; prof. surgery U. Wis. Med. Sch. Recipient Golf Digest Top 100 Golf Doctors in Am., 2006. Achievements include pioneering microsurgery on facial deformities, aesthetic surgery. Office: NYU Med Ctr Dept Plastic Surgery 550 First Ave New York NY 10016 also: Clin Sci Ctr 600 Highland Ave Madison WI 53792 also: 630 Park Ave New York NY 10065 Office Phone: 212-737-8300, 212-263-5181. Office Fax: 212-737-8340. Business E-Mail: johnwSiebert@minuspring.com.

SIEBERT, MURIEL (MICKIE), brokerage house executive, retired bank executive; b. Cleve., 1932; d. Irwin J. and Margaret Eunice (Roseman) Siebert. Student, Western Res. U., 1949-52; DCS (hon.), St. John's U., St. Bonaventure U., Molloy Coll., Adelphi U., St. Francis Coll., Mercy Coll., Coll. New Rochelle, St. Lawrence U., Manhattan Coll., Seton Hall Coll., Case Western Res. U., Marymount Manhattan Coll., Hofstra U., U. Rochester, U. NC, Asheville, 2004, U. NC, Greensboro, 2005. Security analyst Bache & Co., 1954-57; analyst Utilities & Industries Mgmt. Corp., 1958, Shields & Co., 1959-60; ptnr. Stearns & Co., 1961, Finkle & Co., 1962-65, Brimberg & Co., NYC, 1965-67; individual mem. (first woman mem.) NY Stock Exch., 1967; chmn., pres. Muriel Siebert & Co., Inc., 1969-77; trustee Manhattan Savs. Bank, 1975-77; supt. banks, dept. banking State of NY, 1977-82; dir. Urban Devel. Corp., NYC, 1977-82, Job Devel. Authority, NYC, 1977-82, State of NY Mortgage Agy., 1977-82; chmn., pres. Muriel Siebert & Co., Inc., NYC, 1983—. Former assoc. in mgmt. Simmons Coll.; former mem. adv. com. Fin. Acctg. Stds. Bd., 1981-84; former mem. adv. bd. Minority and Women-Owned Bus. Enterprise; guest lectr. numerous colls. Author: Changing the Rules - Adventures of a Wall Street Maverick, 2002. Ran for Rep. nomination, U.S. Senate, 1982; former mem. women's adv. com. Econ. Devel. Adminstrn., NYC; former trustee Manhattan Coll.; former v.p., current mem. exec. com. Greater NY Area coun. Boy Scouts Am.; former mem. NY State Econ. Devel. Bd., NY Coun. Economy; bd. overseers NYU Sch. Bus., 1984-88; former bd. dirs. United Way of NYC; former trustee Citizens Budget Commn., LI U.; mem. bus. com. Met. Mus., bus. com. of NY State Bus. Coun.; adv. coun. Women's Campaign Fund.; bd. dirs., past pres. NY Women's Agenda; trustee Guild Hall Mus. EH; current appointee Commn. Jud. Nomination; founding mem. The Mus. Women-The Leadership Coun; founder, bd. dirs. The WISH List; bd. dirs. Breast Cancer Rsch. Found., Animal Rescue Fund of the Hamptons; mem. Bretton Woods Com., bd. govs. Friars Club; former Tokyo adv. com. Sister City Program NYC, bd. govs. Friars Club Recipient Spirit of Achievement award Albert Einstein Coll. Medicine, 1977, Women's Equity Action League award, 1978, Outstanding Contbns. to Equal Oppty. for Women award Bus. Coun. UN Decade for Women, 1979, Silver Beaver award Boy Scouts Am., 1981, Elizabeth Cutter Morrow award YWCA, 1983, Emily Roebling award Nat. Women's Hall of Fame, 1984, Entrepreneurial Excellence award White House Conf. on Small Bus., 1986, NOW Legal Def. and Edn. Fund award, 1981, Brotherhood award NCCJ. 1989, Women on the Move award Anti-Defamation League, 1990, Bus. Philanthropist of Yr. award So. Calif. Conf. for Women Bus. Owner's, 1990, award Borough of Manhattan, 1991, Benjamin Botwinick prize Columbia Bus. Sch., 1992, Women in Bus. Making History award Women's Bus. Coun. NY C. of C., 1993, Disting. Woman of Yr. award Greater NY Boy Scouts of Am., 1993, Corning Excellence award NYC Bus. Coun., 1993, Woman of Yr. award Fin. Women's Assn. NY, 1994, Medal of Honor award Ellis Island, 1994, Star award N.Y. Women's Agenda, 1994, NY Urban Coalition's Achievement award, 1994, Women of Distinction award Crohn's and Colitis Found., 1994, Entrepreneurial Leadership award Nat. Found. Tchg. Entrepreneurship, 1994, Athena award, 1997, USO Women of Yr. award, 1998, Sara Lee Frontrunner award, 1998, Mattel/Barbie Ambassador of Dreams award, 1999, Town Hall Friend of Arts award, 2000, Pride of NY (PONY) award, 2001, I.O. Salzberger award, 2001, Friars Found. Applause award, 2003, numerous others; honoree Am Bankers Assn., 2003, Enterprising Women's Mag. Lifetime Achiev. award, 2003, Lifetime Achievement award US China Women Bus. Leaders, 2005; inductee Nat. Woman's Hall of Fame, Seneca Falls, NY, 1994, 2007 - Hadassah - Myrtle Wreath award "Women Who Have Broken the Glass Ceiling," Internat. Women's Forum Hall of Fame, 1994, Ohio Women's Hall Fame, 1994, US Bus. Hall of Fame, 2009; NY Univ.'s Stern Sch. Bus. 1st Woman Stovall fellow, 1992, grant Ctr. Ednl. Innovation-Pub. Pioneering Fin. Lit., 2008; established Siebert Entrepreneurial Philanthropic Program, 1990, named. US Bus. Hall of Fame, 2009, Pioneering Fin. Literacy award Ctr. Ednl. Innovation, Pub. Edn Assn. Mem. Women's Forum (founding mem., pres.), Com. 200, Fin. Women's Assn. (Cmty. Svc. award 1993), Coun. on Fgn. Rels, Nat. Assn. Women Bus. Owners (NAWBO's Veuve Clicquot Bus. Women of Yr. award 1992, Mayor's Lifetime Achievement award for Women Bus. Owners 1993), Econ. Club (exec. com.), Southampton Bath and Tennis Club (founding mem., bd. dirs.), Women's Campaign Fund, Fashion Group Internat., Friars Club, River Club, Doubles Club, Westchester Country Club, Breakers Country Club of Palm Beach. Office: Muriel Siebert & Co Inc 885 3rd Ave Ste 1720 New York NY 10022-4834 Home Phone: 212-758-1904. Personal E-mail: MSiebert@siebertnet.com.

SIEBURTH, RICHARD, literature educator, interpreter; BA, U. Chgo., 1970; PhD, Harvard U., 1976. Prof. French and Comparative Lit. NYU, 1983—. Author: Instigations, 1978; editor: Ezra Pound, A Walking Tour in Southern France, 1992; translator: Walter Benjamin, Moscow Diary, 1986, Friedrich Hölderlin, Hymms & Fragments, 1984, Gerard de

Nerval, Selected Writings, 1999. Decorated chevalier Ordre des palmes academiques (France); recipient Book of the Month-Translation prize PEN USA. Fellow Am. Acad. Arts & Scis.

SIECKERT, KRISTINE ELLEN, school psychologist, consultant; b. Milw., Oct. 25, 1948; d. Jacob George and Leopoldine Christina Schweitzer; m. Dana Jeffery Sieckert, Nov. 11, 1971 (div. June 3, 1992); 1 child, Christopher Jacob. BS, U. Wis., Milw., 1970, MS, 1979; EdS, Pitts. State U., Kansas, 1980. Nationally cert. sch. psychologist NASP, 1986. Sch. psychologist Miami Pub. Schs., Okla., 1980—85, acting dir. spl. edn., 1984—85; sch. psychologist Oconomowoc Area Pub. Schs., Wis., 1986—; coord. English lang. learner svcs. Oconomowoc Area Sch. Dist., 1999—. Crisis response leader Nat. Orgn. Victims Assistance, 1997—; mem. Nat. Emergency Assistance Team, NASP, 1997—; cons. Wis. Govs. Task Force Sch. Safety, Madison, 1999, Wis. Atty. Gen. Task Force Sch. Safety, Madison, 2000, ARC, Milw., 2001—02; adj. prof. Carroll Coll., Waukesha, Wis. Co-author: Active Best Practice on the Aggressive Youth. Crisis response leader NASP, 1997—, Nat. Assn. Victims Assistance, Washington, 1997—. Recipient Educator of Dist. award, Miami Pub. Schs., 1984, Wis. Suicide Prevention Program award, 1992, Wis. Sch. Psychologist of Yr., Wis. Sch. Psychologist Assn., 1999, Nat. Sch. Psychologist of Yr., Nat. Sch. Psychologist Assn., 2000; nominee Woman of Distinction award, YWCA, 2001. Mem.: NASP (nat. emergency assistance team charter mem. 1997—, Nat. Sch. Psychologist of Yr. 2000), Nat. Assn. Sch. Psychologists (retirement chair 2007—), Suburban Sch. Psychologist Assn. (pres. 1993—95), Wis. Sch. Psychologist Assn. (pres. 2001—03, crisis chair 2006—, Wis. Sch. Psychologist of Yr. 1999). Roman Catholic. Avocations: walking, swimming, reading, travel. Office: Oconomowoc Area Sch Dist 7077 Brown St Oconomowoc WI 53066 Personal E-mail: kristine.sieckert@yahoo.com.

SIEDLECKI, PETER ANTHONY, English language and literature educator; b. North Tonawanda, NY, May 19, 1938; s. Anthony Paul and Mary Barbara (Litwin) S.; m. Rose Mary Murphy, June 25, 1960 (div. 1978); children: Christopher, Gregory, Jeffrey, William; m. Lynnette Noreen Mende, Apr. 26, 1980; children: Peter Emmanuel Mende-Siedlecki. BA, Niagara U., 1960, MA, 1966; PhD, SUNY, Buffalo, 1982. Tchr. English Lewiston-Porter Sr. HS, Youngstown, NY, 1960—64, Grand Island Sr. HS, NY, 1964—65; prof. English Rosary Hill Coll., Amherst, NY, 1965—74, Daemen Coll., Amherst, 1974—, dean, divsn. arts and scis., 2001—07, chair divsn. humanities and social scis., 1998—2001, dir. honors program, 2008—; prof. Am. Lit. Jagiellonian U., Cracow, Poland, 1982-84, Friedrich-Schiller U., Jena, 1988-89. Commentator pub. radio, 1995—. Author (poetry) Voyeur; contbr. articles to profl. jours. Bd. dirs., baritone Freudig Singers. Fulbright Sr. lectr., Council for Internat. Exchange of Scholars, 1982-84, 88-89. Mem. MLA, Assn. Am. Colls. and Univs., Coll. English Assn., Fulbright Alumni Assn. Democrat. Avocations: woodworking, racquetball. Home: 249 Winspear Ave Buffalo NY 14215-1035 Office: Daemen College 4380 Main St Buffalo NY 14226-3592 Home Phone: 716-837-2863; Office Phone: 716-839-8304. Business E-Mail: psiedlec@daemen.edu.

SIEG, ALBERT LOUIS, photographic company executive; b. Chgo., Mar. 25, 1930; s. Albert Fredrick and Louise Augusta (Strege) Sieg; m. Irma Alice Spencer, Sept. 3, 1955; children: Karen, Diane, Susan. BS in Chemistry, U. Ill., 1951; PhD in Organic Chemistry, U. Rochester, 1954; P.MD, Harvard Bus. Sch., 1971. Supr. emulsion Eastman Kodak Co., Rochester, NY, 1970-72, corp. mgr. instant, 1972-76, mgr. paper mgmt., 1976-81, v.p., dir., 1981-84; pres. Kodak Japan K.K., Tokyo, 1984-89; pres., rep. dir. Eastman Kodak Japan, Tokyo, 1989-91, also bd. dirs.; pres., rep. dir. Eastman Chems. Japan Ltd., Tokyo, 1989-91; v.p., dir. strategic resources, sec. imaging bd. Eastman Kodak Co., Rochester, 1991-92, ret., 1992; prin., cons. Albert L. Sieg Assocs., Rochester, 1992—. Bd. dirs. Kodak Japan Industries, Ltd., XM Corp.; sr. lectr. U. Rochester, 1960—69; mem. adv. bd. World scape, Inc., 2001—. Co-author: 8th Here's How, 1972; author (with S. Bennett, Oliver Wright): Tokyo Chronicles, 1994; inventor in field. Chmn. corp. gifts Rochester Philharm. Orch., 1982—84; bd. dirs. St. John's Home Found., 2000—08; chmn. corp. gifts Internat. Mus. Photography at George Eastman House, 1993, 1994; bd. dirs. St. John's Home for Aging, 1994—99, vice chmn. bd. dirs., 1997—99, St. John's Nursing Home, 1997—99, bd. dirs., 1994—99, chmn., 1999—2001; bd. dirs. St. John's Sr. Svcs., 1997—2001, chair elect, 1997—99, chair, 1999—2001, pres., 1997—2001; bd. dirs. St. John's Found., 2001—, sec., 2005—06, chmn.-elect, 2006—07; pres. Reformation Luth. Ch., Rochester, 1978—83. With Med. Svc. Corps US Army, 1955—57. Recipient George Eastman medal, Kodak Camera Clubs, 1980; named to Internat. Hall of Fame Photography, 2007; Kiwanis Club Chgo. fellow, U. Ill., 1947—51, Am. Cyanamide fellow, 1953—54. Fellow: Photog. Soc. Am. (v.p. 1969—84, bd. dirs. 1992—, exec. v.p. 1995—99, pres. 1999—2003, Harold Lloyd award 1978, Progress medal 1995), Am. Inst. Chemists; mem.: AAAS, Internat. Photography Hall of Fame (bd. dir. 2007—), Nat. Stereoscopic Assn. (bd. dir. 2007—, mem. bd. dir. 2008—, elected chmn. bd. 2009—), Internat. Stereoscopic Union (pres. 1993, 1994), Soc. Photog. Scientists and Engrs., Am. Chem. Soc., N.Am. Nature Photography Assn. (mem. bd. dir. 2003—07, bd. dirs. 2005—06, pres. 2006—07, 2006—07, past pres. 2007—), Am. C. of C. Japan (bd. govs. 1988—91, v.p. 1989—91), Rochester C. of C., Fgn. Corrs. Club, Am. Club Tokyo. Republican. Avocations: skiing, photography, gardening. Home and Office: 159 Hillhurst Ln Rochester NY 14617-1938 Personal E-mail: albert4182@aol.com.

SIEG, SCOTT FREDERICK, biology educator; b. South Euclid, Ohio, Nov. 8, 1964; s. Frederick and Mildred (Attanasio) S.; m. Francesca Lina Policicchio, June 16, 1990; 1 child, Jessica. BS, La Roche Coll., 1987; MS, Duquesne U., 1989; PhD, Case Western Res. U., 1996. Part-time instr. Allegheny C.C., Pitts., 1989-90; rsch. technician Montefiore U. Hosp., Pitts., 1989-90; rsch. student NIH, Bethesda, Md., 1991-92; postdoctoral fellow Case Western Res. U., Cleve., 1996-98, instr., 1998—. Part-time instr. Lakeland C.C., Cleve., 1997—. Contbr. articles to Jour. Immunology, Jour. Virology, Procs. NAS, Cellular Immunology. Mem. AAAS. Avocations: writing poetry and short stories, weight-lifting, gardening, wine collecting. Home: 4480 Ammon Rd Cleveland OH 44143-2806 Office: Case Western Res Univ 2109 Adelbert Rd Cleveland OH 44106-2624

SIEG, WILFRIED, philosophy educator; b. Lünen, Fed. Republic of Germany, July 1, 1945; came to U.S., 1971; s. Friedrich and Irma (Jesse) S.; m. Gail C. Francis, Aug. 11, 1979; children: Emily Payne, Clara Francis. MS, Münster U., 1971; MA, Stanford U., 1975, PhD, 1977. From asst. to assoc. prof. Columbia U., NYC, 1977-85; vis. asst. prof. Stanford (Calif.) U., 1981-82; assoc. prof. Carnegie-Mellon U., Pitts., 1985—88, prof. dept. philos., 1989—; vis. prof. Ludwig-Maximilians U., Munich, 1987—88. Dir. logic and computation prog. dept. philos. Carnegie Mellon U., 1985—94, head dept. philos., 1994—2005, Patrick Supper prof. philosophy, 2008—. Co-author: Iterated Inductive Definitions, 1981; editor: Acting and Reflecting-The Interdisciplinary Turn in Philosophy, 1990, Logic and Computation, 1990, Reflections on the Foundations of Mathematics, 2002; contbr. articles to profl. jours. Rsch. grantee, Am. Coun. Learned Socs., 1985, Deutsche Forschungsgemeinschaft, Godesberg, Fed. Republic of Germany, 1987, 1990—2000, Buhl Found., Pitts., 1987—90, NSF, 1994, 1998, 2006—, NEH, 2000—02. Fellow: Am. Acad. Arts and Scis.; mem.: Assn. Symbolic Logic, Am. Math. Soc. Avocations: running, violin. Office: Carnegie Mellon U Dept Philosophy Pittsburgh PA 15213 Office Phone: 412-268-8565. Business E-Mail: sieg@cmu.edu.

SIEGAL, ALLAN MARSHALL, journalist, consultant; b. NYC, May 1, 1940; s. Irving and Sylvia Norma (Wrubel) S.; m. Gretchen M-P. Leefmans, May 31, 1977; children: Anna Marianita, Peter Bert Grad., NYU, 1962. With New York Times, 1960—2006, editor Pentagon Papers, 1971, asst. fgn. editor, 1971-76, asst. to exec. editor, 1976-77, news editor, 1977-87, asst. mng. editor, 1987—2006, standards editor, 2003—06, founding editor nat. edit., 1980; tchr. journalism NYU, 1966, Columbia U., 1967-69. Juror Pulitzer Prizes, 1987-89. Co-author: The New York Times Manual of Style and Usage, 1999. Recipient Ethics in Journalism award, Soc. of Profl. Journalists, 2006; Shorenstein fellow in press, politics, and public policy, John F. Kennedy Sch. Govt., Harvard U., 2006. Mem. Century Assn., Am. Soc. Newspaper Editors.

SIEGAL, BURTON LEE, product designer, consultant, inventor; b. Chgo., Sept. 27, 1931; s. Norman A. and Sylvia (Vitz) S.; m. Rita Goran, Apr. 11, 1954; children: Norman, Laurence Scott BS in Mech. Engring., U. Ill., 1953. Torpedo designer U.S. Naval Ordnance, Forest Park, Ill., 1953-54; chief engr. Gen. Aluminum Corp., Chgo., 1954-55; product designer Chgo. Aerial Industries, Melrose Park, Ill., 1955-58; chief designer Emil J. Paidar Co., Chgo., 1958-59; founder, pres. Budd Engring. Corp., Chgo., 1959—. Dir. Dur-A-Case Corp., Chgo.; design cons. to numerous corps. Holder more than 127 patents in more than 40 fields including multimemory for power seats and electrified office panel sys., Piezo ink jet valves; contbr. articles to tech. publs. Mem. math., sci. and English adv. bds. Niles Twp. High Schs., Skokie, Ill., 1975-79; electronic cons. Chgo. Police Dept., 1964. Named Winner, Internat. Extrusion Design Competition, 1975, Inventor of Yr., Patent Law Assn. Chgo., 1986, Disting. Alumni, Coll. Engring., U. Ill., 2005; nominee Presdl. medal Tech., Sen. Paul Simon and Rep. Dan Rostenkowski. 1986. Mem. ASME, Soc. Plastics Engrs., Soc. Mfg. Engrs., Inventors Coun., Soc. Automotive Engrs., Pres.'s Assn. Ill. Office: Skokie IL 60076 *A true professional can perform any time, any place, independent of his mood.*

SIEGAL, GENE PHILIP, pathology educator; b. Bronx, NY, Nov. 16, 1948; s. Murray H. and Evelyne (Philips) S.; m. Sandra Helene Meyerowitz, Aug. 3, 1972; children: Gail Deborah, Rebecca Stacey. BA, Adelphi U., Garden City, NY, 1970; MD, U. Louisville, 1974; PhD, U. Minn., 1979; cert. in hosp. mgmt., U. N.C., 1988. Diplomate Nat. Bd. Med. Examiners, Am. Bd. Pathology. Intern, resident, rsch. fellow Mayo Clinic Found., Rochester, Minn., 1974-79; rsch. assoc. Lab. Pathophysiology, Nat. Cancer Inst., NIH, Bethesda, Md., 1979-81; fellow surg. pathology U. Minn., Mpls., 1981-82; asst. prof. pathology U. N.C., Chapel Hill, 1982-88, assoc. prof. pathology, 1988-90; mem. Lineberger Comprehensive Cancer Ctr., Chapel Hill, 1983-90; prof. pathology U. Ala., Birmingham, 1990—2008, prof. cell biology, prof. surgery, 1991—, sr. scientist, group leader breast, ovary, prostate program, Comprehensive Cancer Ctr., 1993—99, Robert W. Mowry Endowed prof. Pathology, 2008—; exe. vice chair, pathology U. Ala. Health Sys., 2008—. Mem. Children's Cancer Study Group, 1987-90, Pediatric Oncology Group, 1990-2000, Children's Oncology Group, 2001—, mem. osteosarcoma pathology com.; sr. scientist Ctr. for Aging, Cell Adhesion and Matrix Rsch. Ctr., 1995—, Ctr. Metabolic Bone Disease, 1997—, Gene Therapy Ctr., 2000—.; editor-in-chief Lab. Investigation, 2008-. Co-editor: Molecular Antibodies in Diagnostic Immunohistochemistry, 1988, Updates in Diagnostic Pathology, 2003; sr. assoc. editor Am. Jour. Pathology, 2003-08; assoc. editor Archives of Pathology and Lab. Medicine, 1989-90; sect. editor, 2006-; mem. editl. bd. Yearbook of Pathology, 1983-91, Archives of Pathology and Lab. Medicine, 1990-91, Am. Jour. Clin. Pathology, 1990—, Modern Pathology, 1996—, Advances in Anat. Pathology, 1999-, Am. Jour. Surg. Pathology, 2000-, Annals Diagnostic Pathology, 2003—, Skeletal Radiology, 2003—, Lab. Investigation, 2004-08, Jour. Molecular Medicine, 2005-, CAP Today, 2005-, Human Pathology, 2005-, Am. jour. Translocational Res., 2009-, Open Breast Cancer Jour., 2009-, Musculoskeletal and Spinal Diseases, 2009-, Cancer Growth and Metastasis, 2009-, clin. Medicine: Pathology, 2009-. With USPHS, 1979-81. Clin. fellow Am. Cancer Soc., Chapel Hill, 1981-82, jr. faculty fellow, 1983-86, Jefferson-Pilot fellow in acad. medicine, U. N.C., Chapel Hill, 1985-86. Fellow Am. Soc. Clin. Pathologists (bd. dirs. 2005-06, chair fellows coun. 2005-06, mem. ann. meeting com. 2004-, membership com. 2005-), Coll. Am. Pathologists (insp. 1990—, mem. surg. pathol. and vice chair pub. coms. 2005-), Royal Soc. Medicine (London); mem. AMA, AAAS, Internat. Skeletal Soc. (exe. com. 2007-), Am. Soc. for Investigative Pathology (councilor 2002-05, mem. publs. com. 2005-08), U.S. and Can. Acad. Pathology (abstract rev. bd. 1989-91, 2003-05), A.P. Stout Surg. Pathologists (pres. 2005-07, chair exec. com. 2005-09), Metastasis Rsch. Soc., Am. Assn. Cancer Rsch., Assn. Dirs. Anatomic and Surg. Pathology (coun. 2000-05, mem. Castleman award com. 2005-08), Intersoc. Pathology Coun. (sec.-treas. exec. com. 2003-07, chair 2007-09), Sigma Xi (pres. chpt. 1989-90), Alpha Omega Alpha, Phi Beta Delta. Democrat. Jewish. Office: Univ Ala at Birmingham Dept Pathology 506 Kracke Birmingham AL 35233 Home Phone: 205-956-6199; Office Phone: 205-934-6608. Business E-Mail: gsiegal@path.uab.edu.

SIEGAL, JOEL DAVIS, lawyer; b. Plainfield, NJ, Feb. 9, 1937; s. Samuel and Florence (Ravitz) Siegal. BA in Polit. Sci., U. Pa., 1958; JD, Yale U., 1961; MA in Internat. Rels., U. Stockholm, 1963. Bar: NJ 1962, US Dist. Ct. NJ 1962, US Ct. Appeals (3d cir.) 1963, NY 1965, US Supreme Ct. 1969, US Dist. Ct. (so. and ea. dists.) NY 1975. Law clk. to Hon. Arthur S. Lane US Dist. Ct., Newark, 1961—62; law clk. to Hon. Phillip Forman US Ct. Appeals (3d cir.), 1963-64; assoc. Hellring Lindeman Goldstein & Siegal, Newark, 1967-70, ptnr., 1970—. Commr. Nat. Conf. Commrs. Uniform Laws, 1991—98; mem. US Dist. Ct. Adv. Bd., Newark, 1991—92. Fellow: Am. Bar Found.; mem.: ABA, Assn. Fed. Bar NJ (nat. del. NJ 1974, pres. 1990—92, adv. bd. 1993—), Bergen Bar Assn., Essex County Bar Assn., NJ Bar Assn., Harmonie Club NYC. Office: Hellring Lindeman Goldstein Siegal 1 Gateway Ctr Fl 8 Newark NJ 07102-5386 also: 32-40 N Dean St Englewood NJ 07631 Office Phone: 973-621-9020. Business E-Mail: jdsiegal@hlgslaw.com.

SIEGAL, RITA GORAN, engineering company executive; b. Chgo., July 16, 1934; d. Leonard and Anabelle (Soloway) Goran; m. Burton L. Siegal, Apr. 11, 1954; children: Norman, Laurence Scott. Student, U. Ill., 1951-53; BA, DePaul U., 1956. Cert. elem. tchr. Ill. Tchr. Chgo. Public Schs., 1956-58; founder, chief exec. officer Budd Engring. Corp., Skokie, Ill., 1959—; founder, pres. Easy Living Products Co., Skokie, 1960—; pvt. practice in interior design, Chgo., 1968-73; dist. sales mgr. Super Girls, Skokie, 1976. Guest spkr. nat. radio and TV, 1979—; lectr. Northwestern U., 1983. Contbr. articles to profl. jours. Mem. adv. bd. Skokie HS, 1975—79; advisor Cub Scouts Skokie coun. Boy Scouts Am., 1975; leader Great Books Found., 1972; founder Profit Plus Investment, 1970; bus. mgr. Nutrition Optimal Health Assn., Winnetka, Ill., 1980—82, pres., 1982—84, v.p. med./profl., 1985—93; bd. dirs. Noha, Internat. Recipient Cub Scout awards, Boy Scouts Am., 1971—72, Nat. Charlotte Danstrom award, Nat. Women of Achievement, 1988, Corp. Achievement award, 1988, Frannie Award, U. Ill., 1998; named Prominent Alumni, Sullivan HS, 2001. Mem.: Inventors Coun., Pres. Assn. Ill. (bd. dirs. 1990—94, membership chair 1991—93), North Shore Women Mgmt. (pres. 1987—88), Oriental Art Soc. Chgo. (publicity chair). *Believe in yourself, if others can do it so can you. Prioritize so you are not overwhelmed by your responsibilities.*

SIEGEL, BARRY, journalist, writer, literature educator; b. St. Louis, Sept. 7, 1949; m. Marti Devore; 1 child, Alexandra Nicole. BA magna cum laude, Pomona Coll., 1971; MS in Journalism, Columbia U., 1972. Stringer LA bur. Newsweek, 1973; news editor West Coast Women's Wear Daily, 1973—76; writer View sect. LA Times, 1976—78, writer spl. assignment, 1979, corr. Nat., 1980—83, corr./sr. writer, 1983—2003, spl. corr., 2003—; prof. English & comparative lit. U. Calif., Irvine, 2003—, dir. lit. journalism program, 2003—. Vis. lectr. U. So. Calif., 1988. Author: A Death in White Bear Lake, 1990, Shades of Gray, 1992, The Perfect Witness, 1998, Actual Innocence, 1999, Lines of Defense, 2002, Claim of Privilege:A Mysterious Plane Crash, a Landmark Supreme Court Case, and the Rise of State Secrets, 2008; contbr. articles to profl. jours. Recipient USA West Journalism award, PEN Ctr., 1987, USA West Lit. award in Journalism, 2000, Golden Medallion Media award, State Bar Calif., 1984, Silver Gavel award, ABA, 1985, Paul Tobenkin Meml. award, 1997, Pulitzer Prize for Feature Writing, 2002. Office: U Calif Mail Code: 2650 408 Humanities Instructional Bldg Irvine CA 92697 Office Phone: 949-824-3023. Office Fax: 949-824-2916. Personal E-mail: barry@barry-siegel.com. Business E-Mail: bsiegel@uci.edu.

SIEGEL, BARRY ALAN, radiologist; b. Nashville, Dec. 30, 1944; s. Walter G. Siegel and Lillian B. Ivener; m. Pamela M. Mandel, Aug. 18, 1968 (div. Mar. 1981); children: Peter A., William A.; m. Marilyn J. Siegel, Jan. 29, 1983. AB, Washington U., St. Louis, 1966, MD, 1969. Diplomate Am. Bd. Nuc. Medicine, Am. Bd. Radiology. Intern Barnes Hosp., St. Louis, 1969-70; from resident in radiology to prof. Mallinckrodt Inst. Radiology Washington U., 1970—79, prof. radiology Mallinckrodt Inst. Radiology, 1979—, dir. divsn. nuc. medicine Mallinckrodt Inst. Radiology, 1973—, mem. Siteman Cancer Ctr., 1996—. Dir. Am. Bd. Nuc. Medicine, LA, 1985—90, sec., 1990; chmn. adv. com. on med. uses of isotopes NRC, Washington, 1990—96; chmn. radiopharm. drugs adv. com. FDA, Rockville, Md., 1982—85, radiol. devices panel, 1992—95; mem. U.S. Pharmacopeia Adv. Panel on Radiopharms., 1975—2000, Armed Forces Radiobiol. Rsch. Inst., Bethesda; coun. experts, chair radiopharm. expert com. U.S. Pharmacopoeial Conv., 2000—05; co-chair working group Nat. Oncologic PET Registry, 2005—; cons. in field. Author, editor 33 books; contbr. articles to profl. jours., chpts. in books. Maj. USAF, 1974—76. Recipient Commr.'s Spl. citation U.S. FDA, 1988, Honor citation U.S. Pharmacopeial Conv., 1995, 2000. Fellow: ACP, Am. Coll. Nuc. Physicians, Am. Coll. Radiology (vice chmn. commn. nuc. medicine 1981—93, editor-in-chief profl. self evaluation program 1988—2002, chmn. nuc. medicine com. imaging network 1998—2006, med. dir. PET core lab. imaging network 2006—, Gr. Deputy Co-Chair Imaging Network 2008—); mem.: ACS (chmn. diagnostic imaging com. oncology group 1998—2007, mem. exec. com. 2000—07), AMA, Acad. Molecular Imaging (chair inst. Clin. PET coun. 2001—02, bd. dirs. 2004—07, Disting. Clin. Scientist award 2008), Soc. Nuc. Medicine (trustee 1981—85, 1987—91, Georg Charles de Hevesy Nuclear Pioneer award 2003), Radiol. Soc. N.Am., Assn. Univ. Radiologists, Am. Roentgen Ray Soc. Office: Washington U Mallinckrodt Inst Radiology 510 S Kingshighway Blvd Saint Louis MO 63110-1016 Home Phone: 314-367-3650; Office Phone: 314-362-2809. Business E-Mail: siegelb@mir.wustl.edu.

SIEGEL, BERNARD L., lawyer; b. Pitts., Sept. 15, 1938; s. Ralph Robert and Frieda Sara (Stein) S.; m. Marcia Margolis, Sept. 3, 1961 (div. Aug. 1983); children: Jonathan, Sharon; m. Susan Erickson, Aug. 31, 1997 (div. June 2001). BA, Brandeis U., 1960; JD, Harvard U., 1963. Bar: Pa. 1964, US Dist. Ct. (we. dist.) Pa. 1964, US Dist. Ct. (ea. dist.) Pa. 1985, US Ct. Appeals (3d cir.) 1985, US Supreme Ct. 1985. Assoc. Silin, Eckert & Burke, Erie, Pa., 1963-66; ptnr. Silin, Eckert, Burke & Siegel, Erie, 1966-73; 1st asst. dist. atty. Erie County, 1972-76; dep. atty. gen. Pa. Dept. Justice, Phila., 1976-78; dep. dist. atty. Dist. Atty. of Phila., 1978-86; pvt. practice Phila., 1986—. Adj. prof. La Salle U., Phila., 1986—95, 2006, Temple U. Law Sch., Phila., 1996—; lectr. Fed. Law Enforcement Tng. Ctr., Glynco, Ga., 1986—97, Mercyhurst Coll., Erie, 1974—76, Nat. Coll. Dist. Attys., Houston, 1978—85; mem. criminal rules com. Pa. Supreme Ct., Phila., 1976—85; commr. Pa. Crime Commn., Harrisburg, 1976—79. Author: (with others) Pennsylvania Grand Jury Practice, 1983, By No Extraordinary Means, 1986. Mem.: ABA, Phila. Bar Assn. (chmn. criminal justice sect. 1990—91, Justice Thurgood Marshall award 2004), Pa. Bar Assn. (chmn. criminal law sect. 1988—91), Pa. Assn. Criminal Def. Lawyers (bd. dirs. 1988—, treas. 2002—04, v.p. 2004—07, pres. 2007—08, Josel Advocacy award 2005), Nat. Assn. Criminal Def. Lawyers. Democrat. Jewish. Avocations: bicycling, reading, hiking. Office: 1515 Market St Ste 1915 Philadelphia PA 19102-1920 Home Phone: 215-632-2515; Office Phone: 215-751-9830. Personal E-mail: bernardlsiegel@comcast.net.

SIEGEL, BETTY LENTZ, president emeritus; b. Cumberland, Ky., Jan. 24, 1931; d. Carl N. and Vera (Hogg) Lentz; m. Joel H. Siegel, June 6; children: David Jonathan, Michael Jeremy. BA, Wake Forest U., 1952; M in Edn., U. NC, 1953; PhD, Fla. State U., 1961; postgrad., Ind. U., 1964-66; doctorate (hon.), Miami U., 1985, Cumberland Coll., 1985, Ea. Ky. U., 1992, Morehead State U., 2002; degree (hon.), Lynchburg Coll., So. Conn. State U. Asst. prof. Lenoir Rhyne Coll., Hickory, N.C., 1956-59; assoc. prof., 1961-64; asst. prof. U. Fla., Gainesville, 1967-70, assoc. prof., 1970-72, prof., 1973-76, dean acad. affairs for continuing edn., 1972-76; dean Sch. Edn. and Psychology Western Carolina U., Cullowhee, N.C., 1976-81; pres. Kennesaw State U., Marietta, Ga., 1981—2006, chair, leaderships, ethics & character; disting. chair Siegel Inst. Leadership, Ethics, and Character. Bd. dirs. Nat. Services Industries; cons. numerous sch. systems. Author: Problem Situations in Teaching, 1971; co-author: Becoming An Invitational Leadership, 2002; contbr. articles to profl. jours. Bd. dirs. United Way Atlanta, Ga. Partnership for Excellence in Edn., Ga. Coun. Econ. Edn., Northside Hosp. Found., Atlanta Ballet; Ga. rep. so. growth policy bd. Commn. on Future of South, 1998. Recipient Disting. Tchr. of Yr. award U. Fla., 1969; Mortar Bd. Woman of Yr. award U. Fla., 1973, Mortar Bd. Educator of Yr., Ga. State U., 1983, CASE award, 1986, Alumna of Yr. award Wake Forest U., 1987, "Grad Made Good" award Fla. State U. Alumni Assn, Omicron Delta Kappa, 1991, Spirit of Life award City of Hope, 1992, Woman of Achievement award Cobb Chamber YWCA, 1992, First Lifetime Achievement award YWCA, N.W. Ga., Oak award outstanding Alumni Ky., 1998, Adminstrv. Leadership award Assn. Gerontology in Higher Edn., 2001, Women in Bus. Lifetime Achievement award, 2001, Peabody award UNC-Chapel Hill Sch. Edn., 2003, Justice Robert Benham award outstanding leadership, svc. and commitment equality of all citizens Black's United for Youth of Cobb County,

2004, Howard Washington Thurman Ecumenical award Morehouse Coll.'s Martin Luther King, Jr. Internat. Chapel, 2005, Leita Thompson Lifetime Achievement award; named 50 Most Influential Women in Ga., One of 100 Most Influential People in State of Ga., Ga. Trend Mag., Outstanding Alumni, Fla. State U. Coll. Edn. Alumni Assn., 1992, Cobb Citizen of Yr., 1996, Ga. Woman of Yr. Ga. Commn. Women, 1997, Divas for Life Bus. to Bus. Mag., 2001, 100 Most Disting. Alumni Cumberland Coll.; named to Jr. Achievement Hall of Fame, 1999, 20 Women Making a Mark on Atlanta Atlanta mag., 20 Yrs., 20 Leaders Ga. Trend mag., Ga. Author of Yr., One Bank GCAPP, 2006, Longest Woman U. Pres., USA, First U. Pres., Ga. Regents U. Mem. Am. Psychol. Assn., Am. Assn. State Colls. and Univs. (bd. dirs., chmn. 1990), Am. Coun. Edn. (bd. dirs., bd. advisors), Am. Inst. Mng. Diversity (bd. dis.), Soc. Internat. Bus. Fellows, Commn. on Women in Higher Edn., Internat. Alliance Invitational Edn. (co-founder, co-dir.), Nat. Ctr. Study of Freshman Yr. Experience, So. Inst. Bus. and Profl. Ethics (mem. gov. bd.), Am. Cancer Soc. (Cobb chpt.), Cobb Exec. Women (founder), Ga. Exec. Women's Network, Internat. Bus. Forum, State Bar Ga., Found. Freedom, Bus./Higher Edn. Forum, mem. exec. com.), Cobb C. of C. (chair 1996), Kiwanis (Atlanta chpt.), Am. Humaries, Inc., Phi Alpha Theta, Pi Kappa Delta, Alpha Psi Omega, Kappa Delta Pi, Pi Lambda Theta, Phi Delta Kappa, Delta Kappa Gamma. Office: Office of the President Emeritus 1000 Chastain Rd MD 91C Kennesaw GA 30144-5591 Office Phone: 678-797-2222. E-mail: b.siegel@kennesaw.edu.

SIEGEL, EDWARD M., lawyer; b. NYC, Apr. 14, 1934; s. Charles and Rose (Fritzhand) S.; m. Elyse R. Roth, Mar. 9, 1969; children: Eric, Eve-Lynn. BA, Columbia Coll., 1955; MA, Columbia U., 1957, JD, 1960. Bar: NY 1961. Legal asst. to dean Columbia U. Law Sch., NYC, 1960-65; gen. counsel Transp. Displays, Inc., NYC, 1965-75, corp. sec., 1968-75, v.p., 1972-73, sr. v.p., 1973-75; pub. affairs mgr. J.C. Penney Co., NYC, 1975-77; gen. counsel, corp. sec. Electro Audio Dynamics, Inc., Great Neck, N.Y., 1977-85, v.p., 1981-85; v.p. legal affairs East View Co., NYC, 1985-87; ptnr. Bangser Klein Rocca & Blum (formerly Bangser & Weiss), NYC, 1988-92; sr. v.p., gen. coun., corp. sec. Nat. Med. Funding Corp., NYC, 1992-94; atty pvt. practice NYC, 1994—. Mem. N.Y. State Bar Assn., Columbia Law Sch. Alumni Assn. (dir. 1966-70). Home: 1036 Park Ave Apt 6D New York NY 10028-0971

SIEGEL, FREDERIC RICHARD, geology educator; b. Chelsea, Mass., Feb. 8, 1932; s. Louis and Eva (Minsky) S.; m. Felisa Matilde Puszkin, Mar. 3, 1962; children: Gabriela Davina, Galia Dinah. BA, Harvard U., 1954; MS, U. Kans., 1958, PhD, 1961. Prof. titular Universidad Nacional de Tucuman, Argentina, 1961-63; head geochemistry divsn. Kans. Geol. Survey, Lawrence, 1963-65; assoc. prof. geochemistry George Washington U., Washington, 1965-69, prof., 1969-99, prof. emeritus geochemistry, 1999—, dir. geochemistry program, 1965-99, chmn. dept. geology, 1976-86. Tech. cons. UN Devel. program, Havana, Cuba, 1980. Author: Applied Geochemistry, 1974, Geoquimica Aplicada, 1992, Natural and Anthropogenic Hazards in Development Planning, 1996, Environmental Geochemistry of Potentially Toxic Metals, 2001, Demands of Expanding Populations and Development Planning; Clean Air, Safe Water, Fertile Soil, 2008; co-author: Geochimica Ambientale, 2004; editor: Review of Research on Modern Problems in Geochemistry, 1979. With U.S. Army, 1954-56; ETO. Recipient Erasmus Haworth award Dept. Geology, U. Kans., 1958; Fulbright prof., 1970, Best Paper award Energy Minerals divsn. Am. Assn. Petroleum Geologists, 1989. Mem. Assn. Applied Geochemists (councillor 1988-95). Jewish. Home and Office: 4353 Yuma St NW Washington DC 20016-2027 Home Phone: 202-362-2545. Business E-Mail: nzkara@gwu.edu.

SIEGEL, GEORGE HENRY, management consultant; b. Bklyn., Oct. 8, 1926; s. Samuel S. and Sara Siegel; m. Lenore D. Greenberg, Oct. 28, 1951; children: Arthur B., Ellen S. BEE, CCNY, 1948; MS Indsl. Engring, NYU, 1951. Registered profl. engr., N.Y. From engr. to gen. mgr. Gen. Electric Corp., Syracuse, Utica and Binghamton, NY, 1951-74; v.p., gen. mgr. flight systems div. Bendix Corp., 1974-77, chief tech. officer, 1977-79, v.p., gen. mgr. diesel engine controls, 1979-82; v.p., group exec. Bendix Automation Co., Cleve., 1983-84; v.p. tech. Allied-Signal Internat., Morristown, NJ, 1984-90; v.p. Volt Tech. Svcs. Co., NYC, 1991-93; pres. Point North Assocs., Inc., Madison, NJ, 1990—. Invited guest lectr. UCLA, 1960-63. Bd. visitors Oakland U., Rochester, Mich., 1977-83. Served with AUS, 1944-46. Mem. IEEE (sr., life, sect. chmn. 1965-2007), Soc. Automotive Engrs. Personal E-mail: siegelgh@att.net.

SIEGEL, HERBERT BERNARD, management consultant; b. NYC, Mar. 10, 1934; s. Jacob and Clara Dora (Goldgeier) S.; m. Joan Miriam Goodkin, Nov. 6, 1955; children: Jeffrey Roy, Lori Robin, Amy Hope, Jonathan Stuart. Degree, NYU, 1959, postgrad., 1960—63, Harvard U., Cambridge, Mass., 1975; PhD in Internat. Law, Columbia PU., NYC, 1999; postgrad., Coll. of Law of Eng. and Wales, 2003—05. Diplomate Am. Acad. Profl. Cons. and Legal Experts; cert. profl. mgmt. cons.; chartered cons., U.K.; accredited profl. cons. Pres. Emle Industries, Inc., NYC, 1968-72; fed. pres. trustee Toys R Us, NYC, 1973-78; pres. Nat. Silver Co., NYC, 1973-78, F.B. Rogers Silver Co., NYC, 1979-82; pres., chief exec. officer Quaker City Steel Co., 1980-86, Seal-Kap Packaging Co., NYC, 1980-90, J. Ramsey Reese, Inc., Tarrytown, N.Y., 1980-87; pres. Deerhill Devel. Corp., 1980-87, Columbia Profl. Baseball Club, Inc., 1980-87; pres., CEO J.R. Reese Enterprises, Ltd. et al, 1989—2007; prin. officer Whitestone Cons. Group, Ltd., 2007—08; cons.-in-residence Magrill Bros., Inc.; expert witness. Thesis examiner Grad. Sch. Banking, Rutgers U., 1963-64; chmn. Fin-Tec Corp.; lectr. Grad. Sch. Mgmt. and Orgn., Yale U.; bd. dirs. Swissco Industries, Inc., Fin-Tec Svc. Corp., Nat. Coin Entertainment Co. Inc., Motorcycle Malls of Am., Inc., Advanced Rehab. Ctrs., Inc., N.Y. Pacific Exch. Ltd., Silvergull Industries Inc., Havemeyer Equities, Inc., Lionville Packing Co., Coast-to-Coast Mktg. Am., Inc., Tritium Card Svcs., Inc., Topps Discount Stores, Inc., White Front Stores, Inc., Magrill Bros., Inc., Interstate Stores, Inc.; trustee Dime Savs. Bank of Williamsburg, N.Y.C., Neisner Bros. Dept. Stores, United Cerebral Palsey, Nassau; expert witness. Author: A Trustee's View of Chapter Ten, 1981, Tomorrow's America, Made Today in the U.S.A., 1993, The Entropy of Government Deficits, 1995, Corporate Rehabilitation After Bankruptcy, 1995, The Masquerade of Cost Cutting, 1996, Market Economics for Multinational Corporations, 1997, International Trade and the Competitive Environment, 1997, Accounting Strategies for Multinational Corporations, 1998, Statistics That Measure the Wealth of Multinational Companies, 1998, Developments and Organizational Behavior in International Business Environments, 1998, Privatization: A Social Milestone or Millstone?, 1999. Served security agy. US Army, 1955—57. Mem.: ABA, Inst. Bus. Appraisers, Prime Raters Fin. Club (pres.), Soc. Profls. in Dispute Resolutions, Turnaround Mgmt. Assn., Am. Soc. Appraisers, N.Y. Acad. Sci., Nat. Assn. Corp. Dirs., Am. Acad. Profl. Consultants and Experts, Am. Bankruptcy Inst., Am. Mgmt. Assn., Internat. Studies Assn., Am. Lawyers Expert Network, Internat. Bar Assn., Am. Cons. League, Mensa, NYU Alumni Club. Business E-Mail: herbert515@verizon.net.

SIEGEL, HERBERT JAY, communications executive, director; b. Phila., May 7, 1928; s. Jacob and Fritzi (Stern) S.; m. Ann F. Levy, June 29, 1950; children: John C., William D. BA in Journalism, Lehigh U., 1950. Sec., dir. Official Films, Inc., NYC, 1951-54; v.p., dir. Bev-Rich Products, Inc., Phila., 1955-56; chmn. bd. Westley Industries, Inc., Cleve., 1955-58; v.p. Phila. Ice Hockey Club, Inc., 1955-60; chmn. bd. Fort Pitt Industries, Inc., Pitts., 1956-58, Seeburg Corp., 1958-60, Centlivre Brewing Corp., Ft. Wayne, Ind., 1959-61; dir. Baldwin Rubber Co., Pontiac, Mich., Mono-Sol Corp., Gary, Inc., 1959-62; chmn. bd. Baldwin-Montrose Chem. Co., 1960-67; pres., chmn. bd. Gen. Artists Corp., 1960-64, chmn., 1960-62; chmn. bd., pres. Chris-Craft Industries, Inc., 1968—2001; chmn. bd. BHC Comm. Inc., 1977—2001, pres., 1977-96; chmn. bd. dirs. United TV, Inc., 1982—2001, chmn. bd., 1982-96, CEO, 1983-90; bd. dirs. Warner Communications, Inc., 1984-89. Bd. dirs. Piper Aircraft Corp., 1971-77, Paramount Pictures, 1963-64, Harvard-Mahoney Neurosci. Inst., 2000. Bd. dirs. Friends of Israel Defense Forces, 1996—, Research to Prevent Blindness, 2000—, Phoenix House, 1978-81; bd. advisors Vets. Bedside Network, 1980-90; v.p. Friars Nat. Assn. Found., 1980—, Chas. A. Dana Found., Inc., 1996—; trustee Lehigh U., 1989-92, Blair Acad., 1985-92. Named one of Forbes Richest Americans, 2006. Office: 55 E 59th St Fl 22 New York NY 10022-1112

SIEGEL, IRA T., retired publishing executive; b. NYC, Sept. 23, 1944; s. David Aaron and Rose (Minsky) S.; m. Sharon Ruth Sacks, Sept. 5, 1965. BS, NYU, 1965; MBA, L.I. U., 1968. Bus. mgr. Buttenheim Pub. Co., NYC, 1965-72; corp. v.p. rsch. Cahners Pub. Co. divsn. Reed Pub. USA, Boston, 1972-86; pres., COO R.R. Bowker Pub. Co. divsn. Reed Pub. USA, New Providence, NJ, 1986-91; pres. Martindale-Hubbell divsn. Reed Pub. USA, New Providence, NJ, 1990-91; pres., CEO Reed Reference Pub. (includes R.R. Bowker Co., Martindale-Hubbell, Nat. Register Pub. Co., The Salesman's Guide, Marquis Who's Who), New Providence, NJ, 1991-95; CEO Lexis-Nexis, Dayton, Ohio, 1995-97. Bd. dirs. Seisint (formerly eData.com), Boca Raton, Fla., 1999-2004, The World Shoe Assn., 2006-.

SIEGEL, JACK MORTON, retired pharmaceutical executive; b. Sioux City, Iowa, June 11, 1922; s. Harry and Rose (Perlman) S.; m. Betty Virginia Collins, Feb. 22, 1946 (dec. Feb. 1986); children: Jennifer L. Mastricola, Marjorie G., Thomas A.; m. Dolores E. Williams Kinert, Dec. 20, 1991. BS in Chemistry, UCLA, 1944; PhD in Chemistry, Washington U., St. Louis, 1950. Chemist The Clinton Labs., Oak Ridge, Tenn., 1944-46; asst. prof. chemistry U. Ark. Sch. Medicine, Little Rock, 1950-55; chemist, v.p. P-L Biochems. Inc., Milw., 1955-82; v.p., gen. mgr. Pharmacia P-L Biochems. Inc., Milw., 1982-87, pres., 1987-89. Contbr. articles to profl. jours. Mem. AAAS, Am. Chem. Soc. Democrat. Jewish.

SIEGEL, JEANNE HINTON, occupational health nurse practitioner, educator; d. Edward J. and Mary Joanne Hinton; m. Stephen Harold Siegel, June 19, 1982; children: Katherine Anne, Sarah Marie. BSN, Emory U., Atlanta, 1978; MSN, PhD, U. Miami, Coral Gables, Fla., 2007. RN in advanced practice, Stat Fla., 2001. Mgr. edn. HealthSouth Rehab., Miami, 1996—99; asst. prof. U. Miami, 2001—. Pres. Beta Tau Chpt., Sigma Theta Tau, Coral Gables, 2008—. Mem.: Fla. Nurses Assn. Office: Univ Miami Sch Nursing 5030 Brunson Dr Coral Gables FL 33146 Business E-Mail: jsiegel@miami.edu.

SIEGEL, JEFFREY NORTON, lawyer; b. NYC, Nov. 27, 1942; s. George Siegel and Rose (Friedman) Gerber; m. Judith Sharon Chused, June 11, 1966; children: Daniel, Linda. AB, Brown U., 1964; LLB, Harvard U., 1967. Bar: N.Y. 1968. Assoc., ptnr. Golenbock & Barell, NYC, 1967—89; ptnr. Whitman & Ransom, NYC, 1990—93, Shack Siegel Katz & Flaherty, P.C., NYC, 1993—2005, Blank Rome LLP, NYC, 2005—. Mem. ABA, Assn. Bar City N.Y. (com. securities regulation 1987-90, com. profl. responsibility 1979-84), Phi Beta Kappa. Home: 975 Park Ave New York NY 10028-0323 Office: Blank Rome LLP 405 Lexington Ave New York NY 10174-0002 Business E-Mail: jsiegel@blankrome.com.

SIEGEL, JEREMY JAMES, finance educator; b. Chgo., Nov. 14, 1945; s. Bernard G. and Gertrude (Levite) S.; m. Ellen Ruth Schwartz, Jan. 14, 1980; children: Andrew M., Jeffrey Eric. BA, Columbia U., 1967; PhD, MIT, 1971. Asst. prof. bus. econs. Grad. Sch. Bus. U. Chgo., 1972-76; assoc. prof. fin. Wharton Sch. Bus. U. Pa., Phila., 1976—86, prof. fin. Wharton Sch. Bus., 1986—98, Russell E. Palmer Prof. Fin. Wharton Sch. Bus., 1998—. Macroecons. coord. The Morgan Bank, (Now J.P. Morgan) NYC, 1984-99; acad. dir. Securities Industry Inst., 1987-; sr. investment strategy adv. Wisdom Tree Inc., 2004-. Author: Revolution on Wall Street, 1993, Stocks for the Long Run: The Definitive Guide to Financial Market Returns and Long-Term Investment Strategies, 1994, 98, 02, 08, The Future for Investors: Why the Tried and the True Triumph Over the Bold and the New, 2005; contbr. numerous articles to profl. jours. NSF fellow, 1971-72; recipient Graham and Dodd award Assn. Investment Mgmt., 1992, Nicolas Molodovsky award CFI Inst., 2005; voted best bus. sch. prof. Bus. Week mag., 1994. Office: U Pa Wharton Sch Dept Fin Philadelphia PA 19104

SIEGEL, KENNETH S., lawyer; BA, Cornell U., 1977; JD, NYU, 1980. Assoc. Cravath, Swaine & Moore, NYC, 1980—85, O'Sullivan, Graev & Karabell, LLP, NYC, 1985—87, ptnr., 1987—94, Baker & Botts, LLP, NYC, 1994—97; sr. v.p., gen. counsel Cognizant Corp., Westport, Conn., 1997—98, IMS Health, Westport, Conn., 1998—2000, Gartner Grp., Stamford, Conn., 2000; exec. v.p., gen. counsel Starwood Hotels and Resorts Worldwide Inc., White Plains, NY, 2000—, sec., 2001—, chief adminstrv. officer, gen. counsel, 2006—. Office: Starwood Hotels & Resorts Worldwide Inc 1111 Westchester Ave White Plains NY 10604

SIEGEL, LAURIE F., accountant, painter; b. Chgo., Aug. 25, 1959; d. Phil P. and Carol Siegel; life ptnr. Mary Ruth Cadwallader. BA, U. Wis., 1982. CPA Va., 1989. Freelance writer, Chgo., 1982—83; investigative reporter, intern with Jack Anderson Washington, 1983; investigative reporter, intern CNN, Washington, 1984; reporter Washington Times, 1984; acct. various firms, Md., 1984—89; pvt. practice Arlington, Va., 1989—. Contbr. columns in newspapers. Mem.: AICPA, Nat. Assn. Tax Profls., Md. Soc. Accts., Va. Soc. CPAs. Independent. Avocations: running, travel, racquetball. Office: Laurie F Siegel CPA PC 1307 S Monroe St Arlington VA 22204 Business E-Mail: siegel@lsiegelcpa.com.

SIEGEL, LLOYD HARVEY, architect, real estate developer, consultant; b. NYC, Nov. 27, 1928; s. Saul M. and Lillian (Bell) Siegel; m. Margot Kopsidas Phillips, Oct. 25, 1987. BArch, Princeton U., 1949; MArch, MIT, 1953. Registered architect, N.Y., N.J., Conn., Ohio, Ill., Mich., cert. Nat. Coun. Archtl. Registration Bds. Designer Skidmore, Owings & Merrill, then I. M. Pei & Assocs., then Antonin Raymond, NYC, 1955-60; assoc. Kelly & Gruzen, NYC, 1960-66; dep. health svcs. adminstr. City of N.Y., 1966-70; dep. exec. dir. health and hosps. governing commn. Cook County, Chgo., 1970-76; prin. L.H.S. Cons. in Health Planning, Facility Design & Mgmt., Washington, 1976—, Siegel & Schroeder, P.C., Chgo., 1983-87; dir. Office Architecture & Engring. VA, Washington, 1987-94, dir. Facilities Quality Office, 1994-98, dir. Facilities Mgmt. Svc. Delivery Office, 1999-2001; dir. Facilities Strategic Mgmt. Office, 2001—. Prin. Yacht Harbor Devel. Co., South Haven, Mich., 1983—88, Siegel & Schroeder Developers Inc., Chgo., 1983—88; mem. adv. coms. HEW; mem. pub. adv. panels GSA; mem. adv. com. Legislature State of Ill.; mem. fellowship evaluation com. AIA-Am. Hosp. Assn.; mem. tech. adv. com. Northeastern Ill. Planning Commn.; chmn. Com. Architecture for Health, 1984. Author: (book) Hidden Asset? Interstitial Space, A Critical Evaluation, 1987; photography (permanent collections) Met. Mus. Art, N.Y.C., Mus. Modern Art, others; prin. works include N.Y. World's Fair Spanish Pavillion, N.Y.C. (N.Y. chpt. AIA award, 1964), Williams Meml. Residence, Flushing, N.Y. (Queens C. of C. award, 1964), Hebrew Home for Aged, Riverdale, N.Y. (Bronx C. of C. award, 1966). Recipient Presdl. Fed. Design Achievement award, Pres.'s award, Nat. Inst. Bldg. Scis., 2002; Fulbright fellow, Università di Roma, 1954, Politecnico di Milano, 1955, Fellow: AIA; mem.: Urban Land Inst., Univ. Club, Cosmos Club, Arts Club. Avocations: micology, micophagy, oenology. Home: 3133 Connecticut Ave NW 502 Washington DC 20008-5147 Office: VA 810 Vermont Ave NW Washington DC 20420-0001

SIEGEL, LOUIS PENDLETON, retired forest products executive; b. Richmond, Va., Nov. 6, 1942; s. John Boschen Jr. and Francis Beale (Tyler) S.; m. Nancy Dicks Blanton, Apr. 10, 1974 (dec. July 1976); m. Nancy Northon, June 26, 1982; children: Kathryn Tyler. AB in Econs., Dartmouth Coll., 1967. Asst. cashier, security researcher First Nat. Citibank, NYC, 1967-71; v.p. security rsch. Drexel Burnham Lambert, NYC, 1971-79; with Potlatch Corp., San Francisco and Spokane, Wash., 1979—, sr. v.p. fin. and adminstrn. San Francisco, 1989, group v.p. wood products and corp. planning, 1989-92, group v.p. pulp and paperboard and corp. planning, 1992-93, exec. v.p. pulp-based ops. and corp. planning, 1993-94, pres., COO San Francisco and Spokane, Wash., 1994-99, also bd. dirs. Spokane, CEO, 1999—2006, chmn., 1999; ret., 1999. Bd. dirs. San Francisco Fed. Corp., 1985-96. Pres., bd. dirs. Bay Area Sci. Fair, San Francisco, 1989-90; trustee Am. Forest Found., 1999-, chmn. trustees, 2000-; bd. dirs. Nat. Coun. for Air and Stream Improvement, 1999-, chmn. bd., 2003-06; pres. Area One, Boy Scouts Am., 2003-05. With USCG, 1964-65. Mem.: Am. Forest & Paper Assn. (bd. dirs. 1999—). Republican. Episcopalian. Avocations: golf, fishing. Office: Potlatch Corp 601 W First Ave Ste 1600 Spokane WA 99201 Office Phone: 509-835-1565.

SIEGEL, LUCY BOSWELL, public relations executive; b. NYC, July 5, 1950; d. Werner Leiser and Carol (Fleischer) Boswell; m. Henry Winter Siegel, Nov. 11, 1979 (div.); children: David Alan Siegel, Joshua Adam Siegel. BA, Conn. Coll., 1972. Assoc. editor Conn. Western, Litchfield, Conn., 1972-73; assoc. editor, editor United Bus. Publ., NYC, 1974—78; mgr. external communications Equitable Life Assurance Soc., NYC, 1978—86; mgr. internat. affairs Cosmo Pub. Rels. Corp., Tokyo, 1986-87, dir. internat. affairs, 1987-88, pres. NYC, 1988—90, Siegel Assocs. Internat., NYC, 1990—97; sr. v.p. Lobsenz Stevens, NYC, 1997—99; sr. prin., mng. dir. Publicis Dialog, NYC, 1999—2000, exec. v.p., group mng. dir., 2000—04; pres., CEO Bridge Global Strategies LLC, NYC, 2004—. Contbr. articles to jours. and mags. Bd. dirs. NYC chpt. Am. Jewish Com., 1993-2007, sec. 1993-05. Mem. Pub. Rels. Soc. Am. (treas., exec. com. bd., N.Y.C. chpt. 2004-06, exec. bd. internat. sect. 2004, bd. dirs. 2007—), Pub. Rel. Boutiques Internat. (pres. 2008), Women Execs. in Pub. Rels. (bd. dirs. 1997-99), Inst. Pub. Rels. (mktg. com. mem., 2004-06). Democrat. Jewish. Home: 41 W 96th St Apt 12B New York NY 10025-6519 Office: 15th Fl 575 Lexington Ave New York NY 10022

SIEGEL, MARVIN, newspaper editor; b. NYC, June 23, 1935; s. Murray and Belle (Diamond) S.; 1 child, Joshua Murray. BA, U. Mich., 1957. Reporter The Record, Hackensack, NJ, 1957-59; free-lance writer Western Europe, 1960-62; reporter Fairchild Publs., NYC, 1962-63; editor The World Telegram, NYC, 1963-66; copy editor The N.Y. Times, 1966-67, asst. met. editor, 1967-76, founding editor Weekend sect., 1976-82; founding editor World of N.Y., 1982-86; founding editor Edn. Life The N.Y. Times, 1986, dep. editor Week in Rev., 1987, culture news editor, 1988-92, dep. editor Book Rev., 1992-95; asst. to mng. editor, 1995—. Co-author: The World of New York, 1985, The New York Times Great Lives of the 20th Century, 1988; editor: Deadly Sins, 1994, The Last Word: The New York Times Book of Obituaries and Farewells, 1997; Judge Turks and Caicos Internat. Film Festival, 2004, Dubrovnik Internat. Film Festival, 2005. Pfc. U.S. Army. Jewish. Office: NY Times Co 620 Eighth Ave New York NY 10018 Business E-Mail: marvins@nytimes.com.

SIEGEL, MICHAEL ELLIOT, nuclear medicine physician, educator; b. NYC, May 13, 1942; s. Benjamin and Rose (Gilbert) S.; m. Marsha Rose Snower, Mar. 20, 1966; children: Herrick Jove, Meridith Ann. AB, Cornell U., 1964; MD, Chgo. Med. Sch., 1968. Diplomate Nat. Bd. Med. Examiners. Intern Cedars-Sinai Med. Ctr., LA, 1968-69, resident in radiology, 1969-70; NIH fellow in radiology Temple U. Med. Ctr., Phila., 1970-71; NIH fellow in nuclear medicine Johns Hopkins U. Sch. Medicine, Balt., 1971-73, asst. prof. radiology, 1972-76; assoc. prof. radiology and medicine U. So. Calif., LA, 1976—, prof. radiology, 1989—, dir. divsn. nuclear medicine, 1982-99. Dir. Sch. Nuclear Medicine, Los Angeles County-U. So. Calif. Med. Ctr., 1976-99; dir. divsn. nuclear medicine Kenneth Norris Cancer Hosp. and Rsch. Ctr., L.A., 1983-99; dir. dept. nuclear medicine Orthopaedic Hosp., L.A., 1981-2006, Intercmty. Hosp., Covina, Calif., 1981-2006, U. So. Calif. Univ. Hosp., L.A., 1993—; clin. prof. radiology U. Calif., San Diego, 2000—. Author: Textbook of Nuclear Medicine, 1978, Vascular Surgery, 1983, 88, numerous other textbooks; editor: Nuclear Cardiology, 1981, Vascular Disease: Nuclear Medicine, 1983. Mem. Maple Ctr., Beverly Hills. Served as maj. USAF, 1974-76. Recipient Outstanding Alumnus award Chgo. Med. Sch., 1991. Fellow Am. Coll. Nuclear Medicine (sci. investigator 1974, 76, nominations com. 1980, program com. 1983, trustee 1993, disting. fellow, 1993, bd. reps. 1993—, bd. dirs. 1994—, treas. 1996—, chmn. ann. sci. program 1996—, pres.'s award 1997, v.p. 1997-98, pres. 1999—, CEO 2005—); mem. Soc. Nuclear Medicine (sic. exhbn. com. 1978-79, program com. 1979-80, Silver medal 1975), Calif. Med. Assn. (sci. adv. bd. 1987—), Radiol. Soc. N.Am., Soc. Nuclear Magnetic Resonance Imaging, Friars So. Calif., Alpha Omega Alpha. Achievements include research on development of nuclear medicine techniques to treat recurrent joint effusions, evaluate cardiovascular disease and diagnose and treat cancer; clinical utilization of video digital displays in nuclear medicine development; invention of pneumatic radiologic pressure system. Office: U So Calif Med Ctr Rm 5250 1200 N State St Los Angeles CA 90033-1029 Business E-Mail: mesiegel@usc.edu.

SIEGEL, NATHANIEL HAROLD, sociology educator; b. Bklyn., May 17, 1929; s. Victor and Yetta (Kogel) S.; m. Annabelle Replansky, Mar. 3, 1958; children— Anthony, Jennifer. AB, Bklyn. Coll., 1950; A.M., N.Y.U., 1952, PhD, 1956. Asst. prof. sociology Columbia, 1956-59; sociologist Hillside Hosp., Queens, NY, 1958-63; assoc. dir.

behavioral research N.Y.C. Dept. Health, 1963-64; chief social sci. tng. sect. NIMH, 1964-67, cons., 1970-79; prof. sociology Queens Coll., 1967-79, chmn. dept., 1967-70, v.p., dean faculty, 1970-74, provost, 1974-77, acting pres., 1977-78; sr. v.p. acad. affairs SUNY Purchase, 1979-94; prof. sociology SUNY, 1979-2000, prof. emeritus, 2000—. Served with M.C. AUS, 1950-51. Home: 8 Birchfield Rd Larchmont NY 10538-1505

SIEGEL, NEIL GILBERT, computer engineer, consultant; b. Bklyn, Feb. 19, 1954; s. Bernard Siegel and Judith Love Cohen; m. Robyn Christine Friend, July 8, 1979. BA cum laude, U. So. Calif., 1974, MS, 1976, PhD, 1977. Sr. staff mem. TRW Sys., Inc., Redondo Beach, Calif., 1988—, v.p., gen. mgr. tactical sys.; sector v.p. tech. & v.p. and chief engr. Command, Control and Comm. Northrop Grumman Mission Sys., Redondo Beach, Calif., 2002—. Lectr. UCLA, 1973, cons., 1984—. Contbr. articles to profl. jours, Bd. dirs. Inst. Persian Performing Arts, Calif. State Abalone Cove Landslide Abatement Dist.; mem. various U.S. govt. panels including Def. Advanced Rsch. Project Agy. "command, control, comm., computers and intelligence" (C41) review panel, 1994, Def. Sci. Bd. "summer studies", 1996, 98. Inducted into Order of St. Barbara, U.S. Army. Mem.: NAE. Achievements include 5 U.S. patents. Office: Northrop Grumman Mission Sys 1800 Glenn Curtiss St DH6-2265 Carson CA 90746 Home: 19 Golden Spar Pl Rolling Hills Estates CA 90274-2431 Office Phone: 310-764-3003. E-mail: neil.siegel@ngc.com.

SIEGEL, PAUL, judge; b. Troy, NY, May 7, 1938; s. Benjamin and Mary (Silverman) S.; 1 child, Mark Aron; m. Janique Auvertin, Apr. 30, 1994. BS in Physics magna cum laude, U. Miami, 1958, LLB cum laude, 1962. Bar: Fla. 1963, DC 1964, U.S. Supreme Ct. 1967, U.S. Ct. Appeals (5th cir.) 1967, U.S. Ct. Appeals (11th cir.) 1982; cert. civil trial lawyer Fla. Bar. Mem. gen. counsel's office AEC, Washington, 1962-65; ptnr. Sinclair, Louis, Siegel, Heath, Nussbaum & Zavertnik, P.A., Miami, Fla., 1972-91; judge Dade County (Fla.) Cir. Ct., 1991—. Author: Florida Trial Objections, 2004; editor-in-chief, exec. editor: U. Miami Law Rev. Chmn. bd. dirs. Alliance Francaise of Dade County, 1983-87, pres., 1990-92; pres. Pro-Mozart Soc. Greater Miami, 1984-92. Home: 235 E San Marino Dr Miami FL 33139-1151 Office: Lawson E Thomas Courthouse Ctr 175 NW 1st Ave Ste 2815 Miami FL 33128 Office Phone: 305-349-5726. E-mail: psiegel@jud11.flcourts.org.

SIEGEL, PHILIP HARRIS, finance educator; b. Jacksonville, Fla., Oct. 3, 1941; s. Benjiamin I. and Eva Siegel; 1 child, Philip H. PhD, U. Memphis, 1985. CPA Fla., 1967. Prof. acctg. Fla. Atlantic U., Boca Raton, 2004—. Author: (book) Applications of Fuzzy Sets To Accounting. Home: 435 Windsor S West Palm Beach FL 33417 Personal E-mail: phsiegel2@yahoo.com.

SIEGEL, RANDY, publishing executive; BA with honors, Wesleyan U., Conn.; MBA, Yale U., 1988. Pub., editor Cleveland Free Times; mktg. mgr. Washington Post; mktg. dir. Newsweek; pres. Venturion, Ltd; cons. Parade Publs., 1999—2001, sr. v.p., 2001—03, assoc. publ., 2003, exec. v.p., pub., 2003—04, pres., pub., 2004—. Contbr. articles to NY Times, Washington Post, Wall Street Journal, USA Today, Newsweek. Bd. trustees Share Our Strength, Washington, CURE, Chgo. Mem.: Soc. Professional Journalists. Office: Parade Publ Inc 711 3rd Ave New York NY 10017-4014 Office Phone: 212-450-0980. Office Fax: 212-450-7091. Business E-Mail: randolph_siegel@parade.com.*

SIEGEL, REVA B., law educator; BA, Yale Coll., 1978; MPhil in Am. Studies, Yale U., 1982; JD, Yale Law Sch., 1986. Law clk. for Hon. Spottswood W. Robinson, III, US Ct. Appeals, Washington, 1986—87; acting prof. U. Calif., Berkeley, 1988—94, prof. law, Boalt Hall Sch. Law, 1994; vis. prof. Yale Law Sch., New Haven, 1993—94, prof. law, 1994—99, dep. dean intellectual life, 1994—, Nicholas deB. Katzenbach prof. law and prof. Am. Studies, 1999—. Vis. prof. law Harvard Law Sch., 1998—99, Felix Frankfurter Vis. Prof., 2006; vis. prof. law Columbia Law Sch., 2001—02. Editor: Reasoning From the Body: An Historical Perspective on Abortion Regulation and Questions of Equal Protection, 1992, Why Equal Protection No Longer Protects: The Evolving Forms of Status-Enforcing State Action, 1997, She the People: The Nineteenth Amendment, Sex, Equality, Federalism, and the Family, 2002, Equality Talk: Antisubordination and Anticlassification Values in Constitutional Struggles over Brown, 2004, Social Science Research Network (SSRN), Law & Humanities, Legal History, Yale Public Law & Legal Theory; co-editor: Legislative Constitutionalism and Section Five Power: Policentric Interpretation of the Family and Medical Leave Act, 2003, Directions in Sexual Harassment Law, 2004; co-author: Processes of Constitutional Decisionmaking, 2006; contbr. articles to law jours.; editl. bd. mem. Yale Journal of Law and Feminism, 1994—, Law and History Review, 2000—, Harvard Law and Policy Review, 2007—. Bd. dirs. Nat. Constitution Ctr., 1999—, Ctr. for Worklife Law, 2007—. Fellow: Am. Acad. Arts & Scis.; mem.: Am. Constitution Soc. (chair, faculty bd., Yale Chpt.), Women's Faculty Forum (mem. steering com., Yale U.), Am. Soc. for Legal History (bd. dirs. 2005—07). Office: Yale Law Sch PO Box 208215 New Haven CT 06520-8215 Office Phone: 203-432-6791. E-mail: reva.siegel@yale.edu.

SIEGEL, ROBERT, heat transfer engineer; b. Cleve., July 10, 1927; s. Morris and Mollie (Binder) S.; m. Elaine Jane Jaffe, July 19, 1951; children: Stephen, Lawrence. BS, Case Inst. Tech., 1950, MS, 1951; ScD, MIT, 1953. Heat transfer engr. GE, Schenectady, NY, 1953-54; heat transfer analyst Knolls Atomic Power Lab., Schenectady, 1954-55; rsch. scientist NASA Lewis Rsch. Ctr., Cleve., 1955-99; tech. cons., 1999—. Adj. prof. U. Toledo, 1981, 85, 95, adj. prof. mech. engring. U. Akron (Ohio), 1987, adj. prof. mech. engring. Cleve. State U., 1989, 91; mem. adv. coun. U. Akron, 1989-96. Author: Thermal Radiation Heat Transfer, 1972, 4th edit., 2002; tech. editor ASME, 1973-83, AIAA, 1986-98; author numerous sci. papers. With U.S. Army, 1945-47. Recipient Exceptional Sci. Achievement medal NASA, 1986, Space Act award, 1993, ASME-AIChE Max Jakob Meml. award, 1996. Fellow ASME (Heat Transfer Meml. award 1970, Max Jakob Bd. of award 1999-2002), AIAA (Thermophysics award 1993); mem. Sigma Xi, Tau Beta Pi. Jewish. Avocations: ballroom dancing, piano. Home and Office: 3052 Warrington Rd Shaker Heights OH 44120-2425

SIEGEL, ROBERT CHARLES, broadcast journalist; b. NYC, June 26, 1947; s. Joseph and Edith Ruth (Joffe) S.; m. Jane Claudia Schwartz, June 17, 1973; children: Erica Anne, Leah Harriet. BA, Columbia U., 1968, postgrad. sch. journalism, 1969-70. Newscaster Sta. WGLI, Babylon, N.Y., 1968-69; reporter, news dir. Sta. WRVR-FM, NYC, 1971-76; assoc. producer, editor Nat. Pub. Radio, Washington, 1976-78, sr. editor, 1976-79, dir. news and info., 1983-87, host All Things Considered, 1987—, sr. editor London, 1979-83. Host Ea. Europe: Breaking with the Past, The Learning Channel, Washington, 1990, Earth Scope, Arlington, Va., 1990-91. Editor: The NPR Interviews. Recipient duPont-Columbia U. award, 1984, 2009. Jewish. Avocations: reading, golf, baseball. Home: 1340 19th Rd S Arlington VA 22202-1637 Office: Nat Pub Radio All Things Considered 635 Massachusetts Ave NW Washington DC 20001-3753 E-mail: rsiegel@npr.org.*

SIEGEL, ROBERT HAROLD, English literature educator, writer; b. Aug. 18, 1939; married; 3 children. Student, Denison U., 1957-59; BA in English, Wheaton Coll., 1961; MA, Johns Hopkins U., 1962; PhD in English, Harvard U., 1968. Instr. Dartmouth Coll., 1967-68, asst. prof., 1968-75; vis. lectr. Princeton (N.J.) U., 1975-76; poet-in-residence, McManes vis. prof. Wheaton (Ill.) Coll., 1976; asst. prof. U. Wis., Milw., 1976-79, assoc. prof. English, 1979-83, prof., 1983—99, prof. emeritus, 1999—. Poet on faculty Summer Writers' Inst., Wheaton Coll., 1980, Wesleyan U., 1982, 83, New Eng. Young Writers Conf., 2002-2009; vis. prof. J. W. v. Goethe U., Frankfurt, Fed. Republic Germany, 1985; Nick Barker writer in residence, Covenant Coll., 2008; lectr., reader various univs. Author: (fiction) Alpha Centauri, 1980, Whalesong, 1981, The Kingdom of Wundle, 1982, White Whale, 1991, The Ice at the End of the World, 1994; (poetry) The Beasts and the Elders, 1973, In A Pig's Eye, 1980, The Waters Under the Earth, 2005, A Pentecost of Finches: New and Selected Poems, 2006; contbr. poems to Atlantic Monthly, Sewanee Rev., other jours. Recipient Margaret O'Loughlin Foley award Am. mag., 1970, award Cliff Dwellers' Arts Found., 1974, Chgo. Poetry prize Soc. Midland Authors, 1974, Poetry prize Prairie Schooner, 1977, Jacob Glatstein Meml. prize Poetry mag., 1977, award Ingram Merrill Found., 1979, Gold medallion ECPA, 1981, Book of Yr. award Campus Life mag., 1981, 1st Pl. prize for juvenile fiction Coun. for Wis. Writers, 1981, 1st Pl. prize poetry Soc. Midland Authors, 1981, Matson award Friends of Lit., 1982, Golden Archer award Sch. Libr. Sci., U. Wis., Oshkosh, 1986, 1st prize Milton Ctr. Poetry Contest, 1994, EPA 1st place in poetry, 2003; Dartmouth Coll. faculty fellow, 1971; Gilman fellow Johns Hopkins U., 1961-62; tchg. fellow Harvard U., 1965-67, Yaddo Artists' Colony, 1974, 75, Transatlantic Rev. fellow Bread Loaf Writers Conf., 1974, Nat. Endowment for Arts, 1980; grantee U. Wis., 1978, 84, 88-89, 96-97. Office: U Wis English Dept Milwaukee WI 53201 Business E-Mail: grindel@msn.com, siegelrh@uwm.edu.

SIEGEL, ROBERT M., pediatrician, educator; m. Claudia M. Reilly; children: Benjamin, Jeremy, Zachary. MD, NY U. Sch. Medicine, 1984. Diplomate pediat. Am. Bd. Pediat., 1988. Adj. assoc. prof. Cin. Children's Hosp., 1992—, med. staff pres., 2008—; med. dir. St. Luke Pediat. Ctrs., Bellevue, Ky., 1994—. Contbr. scientific papers. Recipient Rsch. award, Dr. Robert C. and Veronica Atkins Found., 2004—08; Rsch. grant, Am. Acad. Pediat., 1999—2000. Democrat. Home: 4055 Clifton Ridge Dr Cincinnati OH 45220 Office: Cin Children's Hosp 3333 Burnet Ave Cincinnati OH 45229 Personal E-mail: rsiegel@zoomtown.com. Business E-Mail: bob.siegel@cchmc.org.

SIEGEL, ROBERT STEVEN, internist, oncologist, educator; b. Phila., Pa., Feb. 5, 1951; MD, George Washington U. Sch. Medicine, 1977. Cert. Internal Medicine, Hematology, Med. Oncology. Intern, internal medicine Duke U. Med. Ctr., Durham, NC, 1977—78, resident, hematology oncology, 1978—80, fellow, 1980—82; hosp. appointment George Washington U. Med. Ctr., Washington, prof. medicine, dir., divsn. hematology and oncology, mem., Med. Faculty Assocs. Named one of Top Doctors, Washingtonian.com, 2005. Office: George Washington U Med Ctr 2150 Pennsylvania Ave NW Ste 3-428 Washington DC 20037 Office Phone: 202-741-2478, 202-741-2210. Office Fax: 202-741-2487.

SIEGEL, SAMUEL, metals company executive; b. Elizabeth, NJ, Oct. 30, 1930; s. Morris and Anna (Fader) S.; m. Raenea Kershenbaum, Mar. 29, 1953; children: Daryl Lynn, Annie Roslyn. BBA, CUNY, 1952. CPA, N.Y. Cost accountant Seaporcel Metals, Inc., Long Island City, NY, 1955-56; asst. to controller Deltown Foods, Inc., Yonkers, NY, 1956-57; sr. accountant Touche Ross, NYC, 1957-61; co-founder, vice chmn., chief fin. officer, treas., sec., dir. Nucor Corp., Charlotte, NC, 1961-99; ret., 2000. Mem. AICPA, Am. Soc. Corp. Secs., Fin. Execs. Inst., Fin. Execes. Intl. Hall Fame. Office: 3421 Windbluff Dr Charlotte NC 28277-9850 Office Phone: 704-542-8000.

SIEGEL, STANLEY, financial executive; b. NYC, Nov. 22, 1935; s. Samuel and Betty (Krinsky) S.; m. Joan G. Lerner, Jan. 26, 1958 (div. Dec. 1988); children: Gregg Mitchell, Holli Beth. BBA, Bernard M. Baruch Coll., 1957. CPA, N.Y. Jr. acct. Henry Rosenberg, NYC, 1957-59; sr. acct., mng. acct. Zvi Levavy & Co. CPA's, NYC, 1959-68; treas. Uniweave Corp., Paterson, N.J., 1968-79; exec. v.p., treas. Chromatex, Inc., Paramus, N.J., 1979-87; also bd. dirs.; v.p., chief fin. officer EPI Internat. Inc., Port Newark, N.J., 1987-90, bd. dirs.; cons. The SXS Group, 1990—; dir. fin. Contingency Planning Rsch., Inc., 1993-96; dir. fin. and devel. Blood Ctr., Paramus, NJ, 1999—; v.p., chief fin. officer Bergen Cmty. Regional Blood Ctr., Paramus, 2002—. Trustee Bergen Cmty. Regional Blood Ctr., Paramus, N.J., 1995-96. Recipient Heritage award. Mem. N.Y. State Soc. CPA's. Jewish. Avocations: golf, reading, puzzles.

SIEGEL, STANLEY, lawyer, educator; b. NYC, Mar. 2, 1941; s. David Aaron and Rose (Minsky) S. BS summa cum laude, NYU, 1960; JD magna cum laude, Harvard U., 1963. Bar: NY 1963, DC 1964, Mich. 1970, Calif. 1976; CPA, Md. Atty. Office Sec. of Air Force, 1963-66; asst. prof. law U. Mich., Ann Arbor, 1966-69, assoc. prof., 1969-71, prof., 1971-74; ptnr. Honigman, Miller, Schwartz & Cohn, Detroit, 1974-76; prof. law UCLA, 1976-86, NYU, 1986—, assoc. dean, 1987-89. Vis. prof. Stanford Law Sch., 1973, Ctrl. European U., Budapest, 1993—2001, U. Konstanz, Germany, 1996, Tel Aviv U., 1998; fellow Max-Planck Inst., Hamburg, 1988; cons. reorgn. US Postal Svc., 1969—71; exec. sec. Mich. Law Revision Commn., 1973; mem. bd. examiners AICPA, 1980—83. Author: (with Schulman and Moscow) Michigan Business Corporations, 1979, (with Conard and Knauss) Enterprise Organization, 4th edit., 1987, (with D. Siegel) Accounting and Financial Disclosure: A Guide to Basic Concepts, 1983, (with others) Swiss Company Law, 1996; mem. editl. bd. Lexis Electronic Author's Press, 1996-98. Served to capt. USAF, 1963-66. Mem. ABA, DC Bar Assn., Calif. Bar Assn., Assn. of Bar of City of NY, Am. Law Inst., AICPA. Office: NYU Law Sch 40 Washington Sq S New York NY 10012-1099

SIEGEL, STEPHANIE S., mathematics professor; d. Marvin and Gerry Siegel. BA in Math. with honors, Herbert H. Lehman Coll., 1977; MS in Quantitative Analysis., NYU Grad. Sch. Bus. Adminstrn., 1980. Adj. instr. math. Herbert H. Lehman Coll., Bronx, NY, 1978—79, 1991; adj. instr. stats. NYU, NYC, 1991—96; instr. math. Touro Coll., Bklyn., 1997—. Mem.: Am. Math. Soc. Avocations: chess, poetry, animal activist. Office: Touro Coll 1602 Ave J Brooklyn NY 11230 Business E-Mail: ssiegel@touro.edu.

SIEGEL, STEVEN L., finance company executive, consultant; b. New Rochelle, NY, Feb. 21, 1962; s. Stuart A. Siegel and Stephanie (Kaplita); m. Elizabeth Ellen Starr, Dec. 12, 1987 (div. Jan. 1993). BS in Fin., Calif. Coast U., MBA in Internat. Fin.; DSc magna cum laude in Internat Fin., So. Calif. U., Santa Ana. Fin. analyst Am. Express, Plantation, Fla., 1982-84; investment banker Kidder Peabody & Co., Ft. Lauderdale, Fla., 1985-87, Shearson Lehman Hutton, Boca Raton, Fla., 1987-89; pres. internat. divsn. Cabe Internat. Cons., Inc., Boca Raton, 1989-92; fin. and adminstv. dir. Ensec, Inc., Boca Raton, 1994-95, Art Collectors Internat., Miami, Fla., 1995-96; CFO, COO Enternet Entertainment Group, Inc., Ft. Lauderdale, 1996—97, S.L. Siegel and Assoc. Consulting Group, 1997—2004, Pan Am., 2004—05, NYAG, 2005—06; mng. dir. Schapiro, Siegel & Co. Capital Ptnrs., 2007—. Mng. dir. Fed. Group Ltd., 2001—02, bd. dir., Bought Deal, Inc.; bd. advisors Howa Telco, 1997—2002; pres., CEO Champion Accessories, 2002—03. Mem. Lambda Alpha Epsilon. Achievements include designed, negotiated and developed licensing, strategic partnerships, profit sharing, and joint ventures involving paten table technology with international companies including AOL, AT&T, Samsung, Deutsche Telekom, MSN, Sumitomo and Motorola; manufacturing and development of a Vanadium Redox Battery (VRB) technology. Avocations: golf, sailing. Address: 2460 Deercreek CC Blvd Suite 209 Deerfield Beach FL 33442 Office Phone: 917-325-0114. Personal E-mail: drsls@earthlink.net.

SIEGEL, STUART ELLIOTT, pediatric oncologist, educator; b. Plainfield, NJ, July 16, 1943; s. Hyman and Charlotte Pearl (Freinberg) S.; m. Linda Wertkin, Jan. 20, 1968 (dec. 2003); 1 child, Joshua; m. Barbara Frankel, May 29, 2005. BA, MD, Boston U., 1967. Diplomate Am. Bd. Pediatrics, Am. Bd. Pediatric Oncology. Intern U. Minn. Hosp., Mpls., 1967-68, resident, 1968-69; clin. assoc. NIH, Bethesda, Md., 1969-72; asst. prof. pediatrics U. So. Calif. Sch. Medicine, LA, 1972-76, assoc. prof., 1976-81, prof., 1981—, vice chmn. dept. pediat., 1994—; head div. hematology-oncology Childrens Hosp. LA, 1976—, dep. physician-in-chief, 1987-90; dir. Childrens Ctr. for Cancer and Blood Diseases, LA, 1996—. Mem. clin. cancer program project com. NIH, Nat. Cancer Inst., HEW, Bethesda, Md., 1978-82; pres. So. Calif. Children's Cancer Services, LA, 1977-95. Bd. dirs. Nat. Leukemia Broadcast Coun., 1987—, Ronald McDonald Children's Charities, 1988-95, Make-A-Wish Found., 1987-95, Children's Hosp. LA Found., 1994-2000, Ronald McDonald House Charities, 1995—, LA Regional Coun. Am. Cancer Soc., 1996—, Nat. Childhood Cancer Found., 1995-2003, 2005—; pres. Ronald McDonald House Charities So. Calif., 1996-2008; bd. trustees, Children's Hosp., LA, 2000—; treas. Padres Contra El Cancer, 2003-04; mem. steering com. Live Strong Young Adult Alliance, 2005—, v.p. Thinkcare Bd. Dirs., 2008-. Surgeon USPHS, 1969-72. Named to NAt. Caring Hall of Fame, 2001. Fellow Am. Acad. Pediatrics. Office: Childrens Hospital Of La PO Box 27980 Los Angeles CA 90027-0980 Home Phone: 310-454-0946; Office Phone: 323-361-2205. Business E-Mail: ssiegel@chla.usc.edu.

SIEGELE, PAUL K., oil industry executive; b. Tokyo, 1959; BSc in Geology, Calif. Luth. U., Thousand Oaks, 1980; MSc in Geology, Calif. State U., Northridge, 1990. Petroleum geologist, LA divsn. to numerous tech. and managerial positions and exploration assignments in North and South America Texaco, 1980—95, upstream coord., corp. planning and econs. group Harrison, NY, 1995—97, regional mgr., internat. exploration divsn., regional mgr., exploration and new ventures divsn. Bellaire, Tex.; exploration mgr. Chevron North America Exploration and Prodn. Co., New Orleans, 2001—05, v.p. deepwater exploration and projects Gulf of Mex., 2005—08; v.p. strategic planning Chevron Corp., 2008. Mem.: Am. Assn. Petroleum Geologists, Geol. Soc. America. Office: Chevron Corp Hdqs 6001 Bollinger Canyon Rd San Ramon CA 94583*

SIEGER, DIANA R., foundation administrator; b. Detroit, Oct. 15, 1951; d. Robert R. and Rosemary F. Sieger; m. Thomas A VanTol, July 21, 1973 (div. Apr. 2, 1982). BA, Western Mich. U., 1973, MSW, 1978; DHL (hon.), Aquinas Coll., 1998, Grand Valley State U., 2000. Asst. program dir., svc. mil. families, vets. and disaster svcs. ARC, Kent County Chpt., Grand Rapids, Mich., 1974—77; student asst. State of Mich., Dept. Labor and Governor's Office, Lansing, 1977—78; assoc. exec. United Way Kent County, 1978—87; pres. Grand Rapids Cmty. Found., 1987—; with Western Mich. U. Found. Bd., 2009—, Mich. Child Welfare Improvement Task Force, 2008—. V.p., cmty. founds. Coun. Mich. Founds., Grand Haven, 1999—, mem.,com. cmty. founds., 1988—; bd. dirs. Mich. Cmty. Founds. Venture Funds; chairperson, com. cmty. founds. Coun. Founds., Washington, 1995—2000. Com. mem. maj. corridor task force ITP, Grand Rapids, 2001—02; bd. chairperson, bd. mem. Leadership Grand Rapids, 1991—97; bd. mem. Butterworth Hosp., 1994—97; mem., regional issues com. Grand Rapids Area C. of C., 1990—2002; v.p. cmty. founds. Coun. Mich. Founds., 1999—2002; bd. mem. Mich. Cmty. Founds. Venture Funds, 1994—2002; mem. Kent County Family and Children's Coordinating Coun., 1995—, chairperson, 2001—03; mem., fellowship selection com. Transatlantic Cmty. Found. Fellowship German Marshall Fund, Washington, 2000—; chairperson, com. cmty. founds. Coun. Founds., 1995—2000, mem. stds. implementation com., 2001—; chmn. Mich. Cmty. Founds. Venture Funds, 1994—. Recipient Tribute award, YWCA, 1995, Galaxy award, Nat. Kidney Found. Mich., 1999; named Grantmaker of Yr., Nat. Soc. Fund Raising Profls., 1996, Disting. Cmty. Trustee, Leadership Grand Rapids, 2001, Outstanding Alumni Acad., Western Mich. U., 2002; named one of Most Influential Women in West Mich., Grand Rapids Bus. Jour., 2004, 2006, 2008; named to Nat. Honor Soc. Pub. Affairs and Adminstrn., Pi Alpha Alpha Soc., 1998; fellow Transatlantic Cmty. Found. fellow, German Marshall Fund, C.S. Mott Found., King Baudoin Found., 2000. Mem.: Grand Rapids C. of C. Avocations: travel, art collecting, running, dancing - tap. Office: Grand Rapids Cmty Found 185 Oakes SW Grand Rapids MI 49503 E-mail: dsieger@grfoundation.org.

SIEGFRIED, CARY ANN, library director; B, U. Iowa; MLS, La. State U. Positions including support svcs. adminstr., asst. dir. tech. svcs. and asst. dir. librs. City of Arlington, Tex., 1992—2004; interim dir. Arlington, Tex. Pub. Libr., 2004, dir. librs., 2004—. Office: Arlington Tex Pub Libr George W Hawkes Ctrl Libr 101 E Abram St Arlington TX 76010-1183 Office Phone: 817-459-6916. Office Fax: 817-459-6902. E-mail: siegfriedc@pub-lib.ci.arlington.tx.us.

SIEGFRIED, CLIFFORD A., museum director; BS in Zoology, U. Calif., Davis, 1969, PhD in Ecology, 1974. Post-doctoral assoc. U. Calif., Davis, 1975—79; environ. scientist, Biol. Survey NY State Mus., Albany, 1979—92, chief, NY State Biol. Survey, 1992—95, dep. dir. rsch. and collections, 1995—98, asst. commr. museums, dir., 1998—. Bd. mem. Natural Sci. Collections Alliance, NY State Biodiversity Rsch. Inst.; mem. NY State Task Force on Invasive Exotics. Bd. mem. Albany County Visitors and Conv. Bur. Office: NY State Mus 3023 Cultural Edn Ctr Albany NY 12230 Office Phone: 518-474-5812. Business E-Mail: csiegfri@mail.nysed.gov.

SIEGFRIED, DAVID CHARLES, retired lawyer; b. NYC, Feb. 15, 1942; s. Charles Albert and Marjorie Claire (Young) S.; m. Meri Stephanie (Smith); children: Karin Elisabeth, Christine Elise. BA, Princeton U., 1964; JD, Harvard U., 1967. Bar: N.Y., 1970. Assoc. Milbank, Tweed, Hadley, and McCloy, NYC, 1968-76, ptnr., 1977—98, resident ptnr. Hong Kong and Singapore, 1979-83, 85-88. Spkr. in field. Adv. Bd. mem. Cmty. Agy. Corp. N.J., Inc., pres. alumni assn.; chmn. Princeton U. Alumni Coun.; 1st lt. USAR, 1967-74, trustee, Crossroads Am. Revolution Assn. Mem.: Crossrds. Am. Revolution Assn. (trustee), Millburn Short Hills Hist. Soc. (bd. advisor, past pres.), Assn. Bar City of N.Y., N.Y. State Bar Assn., Cricket Club, Tanglin Club (Singapore),

Am. Club (Hong Kong and Singapore), Baltrusrol Golf Club, Short Hills (NJ) Club, Princeton Club. Congregationalist. Avocations: running, historic reading. Home: 30 Western Dr Short Hills NJ 07078-3230

SIEGFRIED, JAN BROOKS, music educator, director; d. Shirley Brooks and George Sims (Stepfather); m. William Edward Siegfried, Oct. 29, 1988; children: William Ray, Robert Allen. BS, Ball State U., Muncie, Ind., 1982. Master sgt. USAF, Washington, 1983—2003; instrumental specialist USAF Band, Washington, 1983—2003; orch. dir. St. Stephens Cmty. Orch., Burke, Va., 2004—; instrumental music dir. Paul VI Cath. HS, Fairfax, Va., 2005—. Music dir. Reunion Music Soc., Annandale, Va., 2006—07. Mem.: Music Educators Nat. Conf. Avocations: fishing, travel, gardening. E-mail: jsiegfried@paulvi.net.

SIEGLER, MARK, internist, educator; b. NYC, June 20, 1941; s. Abraham J. and Florence (Sternlieb) S.; m. Anna Elizabeth Hollinger, June 4, 1967; children: Dillan, Alison, Richard, Jessica. AB with honors, Princeton U., 1963; MD, U. Chgo., 1967. Diplomate Am. Bd. Internal Medicine. Resident, chief resident internal medicine U. Chgo., 1967-71; hon. sr. registrar in medicine Royal Postgrad. Med. Sch., London, 1971-72; asst. prof. medicine U. Chgo., 1972-78, assoc. prof. medicine, 1979-85, acting dir. div. gen. internal medicine, 1983-85, dir. MacLean Ctr. Clin. Med. Ethics, 1984—, prof. medicine, 1985—, Lindy Bergman prof., 1997-2000, Lindy Bergman Disting. Svc. prof., 2000—, dir. fellowship tng. program in clin. med. ethics, 1986—. Vis. asst. prof. medicine U. Wis., Madison, 1977; vis. assoc. prof. medicine U. Va., Charlottesville, 1981-82. Co-author: Clinical Ethics, 1981, 6th edit., 2006, An Annotated Bibliography of Medical Ethics, 1988, Institutional Protocols for Decisions About Life-Sustaining Treatment, 1988; co-editor: Changing Values in Medicine, 1985, Medical Innovations and Bad Outcomes, 1987; editl. bd.: Am. Jour. Medicine, 1979—94, 1997—, Archives Internal Medicine, 1979—90, Bibliography of Bioethics, Jour. Med. Philosophy, 1978—89, Jour. Med. Philosophy, 1978—89, Jour. Clin. Ethics, 1989—; contbr. articles to profl. jours. Mem. adv. bd. Bioethics Inst., Madrid, Notre Dame Ctr. for Ethics and Culture; trustee Princeton U., 2006—. Grantee Andrew W. Mellon Found., Henry J. Kaiser Family Found., Pew Charitable Trusts, Field Found. Ill., Ira De Camp Found., Gaylord & Dorothy Donnelley Found., Irving Harris Found.; Phi Beta Kappa vis. scholar, 1991-92, Chirone prize Italian Nat. Acad. Medicine, 1996; mem. NAS Cloning Panel, 2001-02, others. Fellow ACP (human rights com., ethics com. 1985-90), Hastings Ctr.; mem. ACS (ethics com. 1992—), Assn. Am. Physicians, Chgo. Clin. Ethics Program (pres. 1989-90). Office: Univ Chgo MC 6098 MacLean Ctr Clin Med Ethics 5841 S Maryland Ave Chicago IL 60637-1463 Office Phone: 773-702-1453. E-mail: msiegler@medicine.bsd.uchicago.edu.

SIEGLER, RICHARD LOUIS, pediatric nephrologist, educator; b. Vallejo, Calif., May 5, 1939; s. Alfred Charles and Loyola Ann (Wolf) S.; m. Karen Koenig, June 25, 1963; children: Mark, Matthew, Amy. BA in Life Sci., Calif. State U., Sacramento, 1961; MD, Creighton U., 1965. Diplomate Am. Bd. Pediats., Am. Bd. Pediat. Nephrology. Intern in mixed medicine-pediatrics Creighton Meml. - St. Joseph's Hosp., Omaha, 1965-66, resident in pediatrics, 1966-67, U. Utah Med. Ctr., 1969-71; fellowship in nephrology Dept. Medicine, U. Utah Med. Ctr., 1971-72; asst. prof. U. Utah Sch. Medicine, Salt Lake City, 1972—78, chief pediat. nephrology dept. pediats., 1972—2001, assoc. prof., 1978—90, acting chmn. dept. pediats., 1982-83, vice chair clin. affairs, 1983-87, prof., 1990—2005, prof. emeritus, 2005—; prof. affilate pediat. nephrology, sch. medicine San Carlos U., Guatemala City, 2008—. Mem. exec. com. Primary Children's Med. Ctr., Salt Lake City, 1982-83; dir. pediat. renal disease program U. Utah Health Scis. Ctr., Salt Lake City, 1982-86; bd. dirs. Sacramental Children's Home, 2008-. Contbr. articles to profl. jours., book chpts. Bd. trustees Utah Children, Salt Lake City, 1989-90. Capt. U.S. Army, 1967-68, Viet Nam. Decorated Bronze Star; recipient Rsch. awards Southern Ariz. Found., 1990-91, Svc. to Children award Am. Acad. Pediat., Utah Chpt., 2006; Thrasher Rsch. Fund grantee, 1978-79, 82-85, RO1 grantee NIH, 1996-2001, R21 co-grantee NIH, 2006-08. Fellow Am. Acad. Pediats. (mem. exec. com. Utah chpt. 1986-90, pres. Utah chpt. 1988-90, chair legis. com. 1990-92); mem. Am. Soc. Nephrology, Am. Soc. Pediat. Nephrology. Achievements include being honored by the president of Guatemala and by the naming of the first pediatric kidney dialysis clinic in gratitude for pioneering work in helping to bring kidney health services to the children of Guatemala. Avocations: bicycling, violin, photography. Home: 2840 Prado Ln Davis CA 95618 Office: 430 F St Ste E Davis CA 95616 Office Phone: 530-297-7007.

SIEKERT, ROBERT GEORGE, retired neurologist, educator; b. Milw., July 23, 1924; s. Hugo Paul and Elisa (Kraus) S.; m. Mary Jane Evans, Feb. 17, 1951; children: Robert G. Jr., John E., Friedrich A.P. BS, Northwestern U., 1945, MS, 1947, MD, 1948. Diplomate Am. Bd. Psychiatry and Neurology. Instr. anatomy U. Pa., Phila., 1948-49; fellow neurology Mayo Found., Rochester, Minn., 1950-54; cons. Mayo Clinic, Rochester, 1954-91, head neurology sect., 1966-76, bd. govs., 1973-80, prof. neurology med. sch., 1969-91, prof. emeritus neurology, 1991—. Chmn. Internat. Stroke Conf. Am. Heart Assn., 1976-93. Editor Mayo Clinic Procs., 1982-86; cons. editor Jour. Stroke, 1992-2001; contbr. articles to profl. jours.; described transient cerebral ischemic attacks. Trustee Mayo Found., Rochester, 1973-81, chmn. emeritus com., 1997-98. Served to lt. j.g. M.C., USNR, 1950-52. Recipient Disting. Achievement award, Am. Heart Assn., 1984, Merit award, 1989, Robert G. Siekert Young Investigator award Am. Heart Assn., 1986. Fellow Am. Coll. Physicians; mem. Am. Neurol. Assn., Northwestern U. Med. Sch. Alumni Assn. (Service award 1983), Swiss Neurol. Soc. (corr.), Alpha Omega Alpha. Avocation: stamp collecting/philately. Office: Mayo Clinic 200 1st St SW N-10 Rochester MN 55905-0002 Home Phone: 507-282-1290.

SIEKIERSKI, MACIEJ M., curator; b. Poznan, Poland; s. Konrad Siekierski and Helena Buczak-Siekierski; m. Anna Bendisz-Siekierski, Mar. 24, 1979; children: Nicholas, Victoria, Maximilian. BA in History and Russian, San Jose State Coll., 1970; MLS, San Jose State U., 1986; MA in History, U. Calif., Berkeley, 1971, PhD in History, 1984. Curator Hoover Inst., Stanford U., Calif., 1984—. Contbr. articles to profl. jours. Mem.: Polish Inst. Arts and Scis. Am., Am. Assn. Advancement Slavic Studies, Am. Hist. Assn. Home: 1752 Hull Ave Redwood City CA 94061 Office: Hoover Inst Stanford CA Office Phone: 650-725-6955.

SIEKMANN, DONALD CHARLES, accountant; b. St. Louis, July 2, 1938; s. Elmer Charles and Mabel Louise (Blue) S.; m. Linda Lee Knowles, Sept. 10, 1966; 1 child, Brian Charles. BS, Washington U., St. Louis, 1960. CPA, Ohio, Ga. Regional mng. ptnr. Arthur Andersen & Co., Cin., 1960-98. Trustee Touchstone Group Mut. Funds, Riverfront Group Mut. Funds, Constellation Group Mutual Funds; exec. Duro Bag Mfg. Co. Columnist Cin. Enquirer, 1983-86, Gannett News Services, 1983-86; editor "Tax Clinic" column Tax Advisor mag., 1974-75. Mem. bd. Cin. Zool. Soc., 1985-88; officer, bd. dirs. Cin. Found. for Pub. TV, 1984-88, Cin. Symphony Orch., 1973-85, Cin. Ballet Co., 1973-88, Atlanta Symphony Orch., 1988-91, The Atlanta Opera, 1988-91, Cin. Theatrical Assn., Jewish Hosp., 1993—, Cin. Assn. for Performing Arts, 1992—, Cin. United Way, 1992-99, Cin. Pk. Bd. Found., 1995-98; pres. Greater Cin. Arts and Edn. Ctr., 1996-99; mem. Friends of Sch. for Creative and Performing Arts, 1996-99, Cin. Arts Festival, 1992-96, Ronald McDonald House, 1998—. Mem. AICPA, Ohio Soc. CPAs, Cin. Country Club (trustee 1983-88), Optimists Club (pres. Queen City chpt. 1986). Clubs: Cin. Country (trustee 1983-88). Lutheran. Home: 5495 Waring Dr Cincinnati OH 45243-3933 Office Phone: 513-561-9324. Personal E-mail: dsiekmann@aol.com.

SIELAFF, TIMOTHY DAVID, oncologist, department chairman; b. Ohio; BS, U. Wis.-Madison, 1984; MD, Med. Coll. Va., Richmond, 1989; PhD in Surgery, U. Minn., Mpls., 1997; MBA, U. St. Thomas, St. Paul, 2008. Diplomate Am. Bd. Surgery, 2009. Asst. prof. U. Minn. Med. Sch., Mpls., 1998—2004, assoc. prof., 2004; Eugene W. & Elizabeth B. Leonard trusts chair, oncology Va. Piper Cancer Inst., Mpls., 2004—; pres., oncology clin. svc. line Allina Hosps. & Clinics, Mpls., 2009—. Chair ACS Commn. Cancer, Mpls., 2005—; gov. at large ACS Bd. Govs., Minn., 2008—. Hepatopancreatobiliary Surgery & Liver Transplantation fellowship, U. Toronto, 1998. Fellow: Am. Coll. Surgeons; mem.: Soc. Surgery Alimentary Tract, Soc. Am. Gastrointestinal & Endoscopic Surgeons, Am. Soc. Clin. Oncology, Pancreatic Cancer Rsch. Team, Americas Hepato-Pancreato-Biliary Assn. Office: Virginia Piper Cancer Inst 800 E 28th St Minneapolis MN 55407

SIEMENS, REYNOLD (RENE SIEMENS), lawyer; s. Lloyd and Agatha Siemens; m. Carolyn Hull, Dec. 28, 1994; children: Elijah Hull, Alexandria Hull. BA, U. Winnipeg, Man., Can., 1983; PhB, U. Oxford, Eng., 1985, PhD, 1989; JD, Harvard Law Sch., Cambridge, Mass., 1995. Cert.: Spkr. Assembly State Calif. (recognition pro bono activities) 2002, State Bar Calif. (recognition pro bono legal svcs.) 2003. Shareholder Heller Ehrman LLP, LA, 1995—. Dir. Western Ctr. Law & Poverty, LA, 2003—08. Bd. mem. Western Ctr. Law and Poverty, LA, 2003—. Recipient Richard Guggenhime Pro Bono award, Heller Ehrman LLP, 2000; named Pro Bono Vol. Atty. of Yr., Bet Tzedek Legal Svcs., 1999; fellowship, Commonwealth Found., 1985. Mem.: ABA, LA Bar Assn., State Bar Calif. (Wiley W. Manuel award 2003). Office: Proskauer Rose LLP 2049 Century Pk E 32nd Fl Los Angeles CA 90067-3206 Office Phone: 310-284-5676. Business E-Mail: rsiemens@proskauer.com.

SIEMER, DEANNE CLEMENCE, lawyer; d. Edward D. and Dorothy J. (Helsdon) S.; m. Howard P. Willens; 1 child, Jason L. BA, George Washington U., 1962; LLB, Harvard U., 1968. Bar: NY 1968, DC 1969, Md. 1972, Commonwealth of No. Mariana Islands 1976. Economist Office of Mgmt. and Budget, Washington, 1964-67; assoc.; then ptnr. Wilmer, Cutler & Pickering, Washington, 1968-77, 80-90; ptnr. Pillsbury, Madison & Sutro, Washington, 1990-95; mng. dir. Wilsie Co., Washington and Saipan, 1995—; hearing officer, dept. labor CNHI, 2007—. Gen. counsel US Dept. Def., Washington, 1977—79; spl. asst. to sec. US Dept. Energy, Washington, 1979—80. Author: Tangible Evidence, 3d edit., 1996, National Security and Self-Determination: United States Policy in Micronesia, 1999, Corel Presentations for Litigators, 2000, PowerPoint for Litigators, 2000, Effective Use of Courtroom Technology: A Judge's Guide to Pretrial and Trial, 2001, An Honorable Accord: The Covenant Between the Northern Mariana Islands and the United States, 2001, Effective Use of Courtroom Technology: A Lawyer's Guide to Pretrial and Trial, 2002, Easy Tech: Cases and Materials on Courtroom Technology, 2002, The Patronus Technique: A Practical Proposal In Asbestos-Driven Bankruptcies, 2002, Power Point 2002 for Litigators, 2002, Basic Power Point Slides, 2003, Argument Slides, 2003, The Evidence Camera, 2004, Oral Histories of the Northern Mariana Islands: Political Life and Developments 1945-1995, 2004, The Digital Projector and Laptop Computer, 2005, PowerPoint 2003: 50 Great Tips for Better, Easier Slides, 2005, From the White House: Documents on the Northern Mariana Islands and Micronesia (1945-1995) Collected from the Presidential Libraries, 2005, The Secret Guam Study: The Documents, 2005, Asbestos Prepackaged Bankruptcies: Apply the Brakes But Retain Flexibility for Debtors, 2005, The Making of a Constitution: Northern Mariana Islands Conventions (1976-1996), 2006, Teaching Legal Strategy, 2007, Teaching E-Discovery, 2007; contbg. editor: Beyond Fortress America: National Security Controls on Science And Technology in a Globalized World, 2009. Mem. Lawyers Com. Civil Rights, Washington, 1973—; mediator US Ct. Appeals, Washington, 1988—; trustee Nat. Inst. Trial Advocacy, 1989—, Am. Law Inst., 1988—; arbitrator Atty. Client Arbitration Bd., 1990-, NASD, 2001-; mem. com. sci. and nat. security NAS, 2002-. Recipient citation Air Force Assn., 1977, Dist. Pub. Svc. medal Sec. of Def., 1979, Commendation Pres. of US 1981; grantee Nat. Endowment Humanities, Commonwealth of No. Mariana Islands Divsn. Hist. Preservation. No. Mariana Islands Coun. Humanities, Spl. Svcs. award, 2006. Mem. DC Bar Assn. (Disting. Svc. award 2006), No. Marianas Bar Assn. Episcopalian. Business E-Mail: wilsieco@aol.com.

SIEMER, PAUL JENNINGS, public relations executive; b. St. Louis, Jan. 24, 1946; s. Robert Vincent and Pauline Mary (Nece) S.; m. Susan MacDonald Arnott, Aug. 26, 1967 Student, U. Notre Dame, 1964-67. Reporter South Bend Tribune, Ind., 1967-69; reporter St. Louis Globe-Democrat, 1969-76; account exec. Fleishman-Hillard Inc., St. Louis, 1976-79, v.p., sr. ptnr., 1979-84, exec. v.p., sr. ptnr., 1984-95; ptnr. Stolberg & Siemer Inc., St. Louis, 1995—. Mem. Pub. Relations Soc. Am. Roman Catholic. Home: 2961 Hatherly Dr Saint Louis MO 63121-4551 Office: Stolberg & Siemer Inc 818 Lafayette Ave Saint Louis MO 63104-3702 Office Phone: 314-436-6577.

SIEMIONOW, MARIA, microsurgeon; b. Poznan, Poland, May 3, 1950; came to U.S., 1989; d. Bronislaw and Zofia (Jackowska) Kusza; m. Wlodzimierz Siemionow, Apr. 26, 1975; 1 child, Krzysztof. MD, Med. Acad. (Karol Marcinkowski Univ. Faculty of Medicine), Poznan, 1974; degree in Orthopedics, Med. Acad., Poznan, 1981, PhD in Microsurgery, 1985, DSc in Microcirculation, 1992. Fellow Univ. Hosp., Helsinki, Finland, Univ. Louisville Hosp., Ky.; intern Univ. Hosp., Pozan, Poland; resident Inst. for Orthopaedics and Rehabilitation Medicine, Pozan, Poland, Mcpl. Hosp., Piekary Slaskie, Finland; asst. clin. instr. Inst. Orthopedics/Rehab. Medicine, Poznan, 1978-81, sr. asst. lectr., 1982-86, adj. orthopedics, hand and microsurgery, 1990-95; rsch. assoc. prof., rsch. dir. U. Utah, Salt Lake City, 1995—; rsch. dir. Cleve. Clinic Found., 1995—, current sect. head plastic surgery rsch., dir. plastic surgery rsch., head, microsurgery tng., current mem., Transplantation Ctr., current mem., Orthopaedic Surgery, current mem., Immunology. Vis. prof. U. Guadalajara, Mex., 1986, U. Monastir, Tenesia, 1989, Mount Vernon Hosp., London, 1992, Chang Gung Meml. Hosp, Taipei, Taiwan, 1994. Editl. bd. Jour. Investigative Surgery, 1991-93, Jour. Reconstructive Microsurgery; author: Tissue Surgery, 2005, Transplanting a Face: Notes on a Life in Medicine, 2007; contbr. articles to sci. jours. Christine Kleinert Hand Surgery fellow, 1985; recipient: James Barrett Brown award, Am. Assn. Plastic Surgeons, 2007 Mem. Am. Soc. Reconstructive Microsurgery (pres. 1992), Internat. Soc. Reconstructive Microsurgery (pres. 1993), Plastic Surgery Rsch. Coun., Physicians for Peace (pres. 1993), Interplast-Turkey (pres. 1993). Achievements include being the first surgeon to perform a face transplant in the United States, 2008. Avocations: art, skiing, hiking, photography, languages. Office: Dept of Plastic Surgery (A60) Cleve Clinic Found 9500 Euclid Ave Cleveland OH 44195 Office Phone: 216-445-2405.*

SIEPI, CESARE, opera singer; b. Milan, Feb. 10, 1923; Operatic debut in Rigoletto, Schio, 1941, Il Nabucco, LaScala Opera, Milan, 1946, Don Carlo, Met. Opera, N.Y.C., 1950; soloist debut in, Carnegie Hall, N.Y.C., 1951; sang in Mozart and Verdi requiems, Edinburgh Festival, Albert Hall, London; leading bass at, Salzburg Festival, LaScala, Milan; appeared in: play Bravo Giovanni, 1962; appeared: play Vienna Staatsoper; made many opera recordings for, London Records. (Winner Nat. Singing Competition, Florence 1941, recipient Italy's Orfeo award 1956). Home: 12095 Brookfield Club Dr Roswell GA 30075-1261

SIERA, STEVEN G., career planning administrator, educator; b. Detroit, Apr. 19, 1949; s. Lucian F. and Ethel M. Siera; m. Maureen Stern, July 24, 1971; 1 child, Scott G. BS, Maryville Coll., 1970; MS, U. Tenn., 1974; PhD, N.Mex State U., 1984. Dir., career planning and placement No. State Coll., Aberdeen, SD, 1980—83; dir., student svcs. U. Sci. and Arts of Okla., Chickasha, 1984—86; assoc., asst. prof. Northeastern State U., Tahlequah, Okla., 1986—92; assoc. prof. U. of Pacific, Stockton, Calif., 1992—94; dir., rsch. and assessment Kent Sch. Dist., Wash., 1994—2003; assoc. prof., assoc. dean coll. edn. St. Martin's U., Lacey, Wash., 2003—. V.p., bd. dirs. Wolf Haven Internat., Tenino, Wash., 2005—. Recipient Contributions to Survey Rsch. in Edn. award, Am. Ednl. Rsch. Assn., 2005, President's award, Wash. Orgn. for Reading Devel., 2005. Mem.: ASCD, Wash. Ednl. Rsch. Assn., NW Assn. Colleges Tchr. Edn., Am. Assn. Colleges Tchr. Edn., Am. Ednl. Rsch. Assn. (chair 1995—97, program chair 2004—06, chair 2006—). Achievements include multiple research studies in teacher education, survey research, education of young children and the relationship of entry exams to professional performance; research in Comparability of prediction of first grade reading achievement for the Peabody Picture Vocabulary Test and the Test de Vocabulario en Imagenes Peabody; Dental school and undergraduate school performance, aptitude examination, and demographic data as predictors of performance on the California Dental Licensure Examination; Instruction does make a difference: Attitudes and perceptions of young readers in whole language and traditional classrooms; Vocabulary generated by students in whole language and basal first grade classrooms; Emergent literacy, preschool through first grade: Three studies; Validity of a state certification examination with respect to principals' ratings after three years; Reading perceptions and attitudes of kindergarten students. Avocations: travel, golf, gardening. Office: St Martin's U 5300 Pacific Ave SE Lacey WA 98503 E-mail: ssiera@stmartin.edu.

SIERACKI, ERIC P., diversified financial services company executive; BS in Econs., U. Pa. Mgr. Grant Thornton; sr. v.p. Countrywide Asset Mgmt. Corp., 1988—89; exec. v.p. corp. fin. Countrywide Fin. Corp., Calabasas, Calif., 1989—94, mng. dir., 1994—2002, sr. mng. dir. corp. fin., treas., & corp. develop., investor rels., 2002—05, exec. mng. dir., CFO, 2005—. Recipient Best Fin. Exec., Am. Bus. Awards, 2007. Office: Countrywide Fin Corp 4500 Park Granada Calabasas CA 91302-1613

SIERLES, FREDERICK STEPHEN, psychiatrist, educator; b. Bklyn., Nov. 9, 1942; s. Samuel and Elizabeth (Meiselman) S.; m. Laurene Harriet Cohn, Oct. 25, 1970 (div. Aug. 1990); children: Hannah Beth Alterson, Joshua Caleb; m. Terrie Lee Stengel June 28, 2008. AB, Columbia U., 1963; MD, Rosalind Franklin U., 1967. Diplomate Am. Bd. Psychiatry and Neurology. Intern Cook County Hosp., Chgo., 1967-68; resident in psychiatry Mt. Sinai Hosp., NYC, 1968-69, assoc. attending psychiatrist Chgo., 1973-74; resident in psychiatry Rosalind Franklin U., North Chgo., Ill., 1969-71, chief resident, 1970-71, instr. psychiatry, 1973—74, asst. prof., 1974-78, assoc. prof., 1978-88, dir. med. student edn., 1974—94, chair, 1994—2002, residency dir., 1999—2001; inaugural mem. Mater Tchr.'s Guild, 2009—; staff psychiatrist U.S. Reynolds Army Hosp., Ft. Sill, Okla., 1971-73. Cons. psychiatry Cook County Hosp., 1974-79, St. Mary of Nazareth Hosp., 1979-82, Gt. Lakes Naval Hosp., 1987-90, Jackson Park Hosp., 1987-89, Mt. Sinai Hosp., 1988—, Elgin Mental Health Ctr., 1997—; chief mental health clinic, North Chicago VA Hosp., 1982-85, chief psychiatry svc., 1983-85. Author: (wth others) General Hospital Psychiatry, 1985, Behavioral Science for the Boreds, 1987, rev. 2d edit., 1989, rev. 3d edit., 1993, USMLE Behavioral Science Made Ridiculously Simple, 1998; editor: Clinical Behavioral Science, 1982, Behavioral Science for Medical Students, 1993; mem. editl. bd. Acad. Psychiatry, 2000-07; contbr. articles to profl. jours. Coach Glenview (Ill.) Youth Baseball, 1987-89, mgr. 1990 (age 10-12 Glenview World Series winner 1990), Glenview Tennis Club, 1986-90 (3.5 Men's Doubles League winner 1989-90). Maj. M.C., U.S. Army, 1971-73. N.Y.State Regents scholar, 1959-63; NIMH grantee, 1974-83, Chgo. Med. Sch. grantee, 1974-83; recipient Seymour Vestermark award NIMH/Am. Psychiat. Assn., 2003. Fellow Am. Psychiat. Assn. (disting. life fellow, 2006-, coun. edn. and career devel. 1993-95); mem. Ill. Psychiat. Soc. (fellowship com. 1985-89), Columbia Coll. Alumni Secondary Schs. Com., Assn. Dirs. Med. Student Edn. in Psychiatry (exec. coun. 1985-99, chmn. program com. 1987-88, treas. 1989-91, pres-elect 1991-93, pres. 1993-95, immediate past pres. 1995-99), Alliance for Clin. Edn., Am. Assn. Dirs. Psychiat. Residency Tng. (exec. coun. 2000-03, chair workforce coalition 2000-03), Sigma Xi, Alpha Omega Alpha, Phi Epsilon Pi. Office: Rosalind Franklin Univ Chgo Med Sch 3333 Green Bay Rd North Chicago IL 60064-3037 Business E-Mail: frederick.sierles@rosalindfranklin.edu.

SIEROCKI, JOHN STANLEY, oncologist; b. New Haven, 1947; MD, Hahnemann U., 1973. Diplomate Am. Bd. Internal Medicine, Am. Bd. Med. Oncology. Intern Hahnemann U., Phila., 1973—74, resident in medicine, 1974—76; fellow in med. oncology Meml. Sloan-Kettering Cancer Ctr., NYC, 1976—78; attending physician in medicine, hematology and med. oncology Med. Ctr. at Princeton, NJ, 1983—. Assoc. clin. prof. medicine U. Medicine and Dentistry N.J.-R.W. Johnson, 1985—. Named one of Top Drs. in N.Y. Metro Area, Castle Connolly, Top Drs. 2003, N.J. Monthly Mag. Office: Princeton Med Group 419 N Harrison St Princeton NJ 08540-3521 Home Phone: 609-575-4809; Office Phone: 609-924-9300. Business E-Mail: jsierocki@princetonhcs.org.

SIESS, ALFRED ALBERT, JR., engineering executive, management consultant; b. Bklyn., Aug. 16, 1935; s. Alfred Albert and Matilda Helen (Suttmeier) S.; m. Gale Murray Scholes, Dec. 17, 1966; children: Matthew Alan, Daniel Adam. BCE, Ga. Inst. Tech., 1956; postgrad. in bus., Boston Coll., 1968; MBA, Lehigh U., 1972. With fabricated steel constrn. divsn. Bethlehem Steel Corp., Pa., 1958-76, project mgr. Pa., 1969-76, engr. projects and mining divsn. Pa., 1976-86; sr. cons. T.J. Trauner Assocs., Phila., 1986-87; assoc. S.T. Hudson Internat., Phila., 1987-90; dir. mktg. SWIN Resource Sys., Inc., Bloomsburg, Pa., 1989-90; mem. adj. faculty Drexel U., 1976-96. Weekly columnist Economic and Environmental Issues, East Pa. edit. The Free Press, 1981-86; co-patentee suspension bridge erection equipment. Founder

S.A.V.E. Inc., Coopersburg, Pa., 1969, pres., 1970, 75, 81, bd. dirs. 1970—. Served with C.E., USN, 1956-58. Recipient Environ. Action award, S.A.V.E., Inc., 1975. Mem. ASCE (chmn. environ. tech. com. Lehigh Valley sect. 1971-83, life), Lions, Chi Epsilon. Republican. Mem. United Church of Christ. Home: 6460 Blue Church Rd Coopersburg PA 18036-9371 Office: C E Resource Group PO Box 39 Coopersburg PA 18036-0039 Office Phone: 610-965-3263. Business E-Mail: oldmill09@ptd.net.

SIEVERS, DAVID, secondary school educator; s. Dennis and Cathy Sievers; m. Julie Sievers, July 6, 1996; children: Shelby, Sierra. BS, semo, Cape Girardeau, Mo, 1988. Tchr., coach PbHS, Poplar Bluff, Mo., 1988—. Leader Pb Fca, Mo., 1988—2008. Office: Poplar Bluff HS 1300 Victory Ln Poplar Bluff MO 63901

SIEVERT, VICKI LEE, retired music educator; d. Joe Sproul and Ruby Baughman-Sproul; m. Richard Paul Sievert, Mar. 16, 1974; children: Michael William, Cassandra Ruth. MusB, Bowling Green State U., 1970. Profl. tchg. cert. Ohio, cert. Level 1 Am. Orff Schulwerk Assn., cert. Level II Am. Orff Schulwerk Assn. Music specialist pub. sch. Benton/Carroll/Salem Sch. Dist., Oak Harbor, Ohio, 1970—2003; elem. music specialist Genoa (Ohio) Local Sch. Dist., 2003—04; music dir. Oak Harbor United Meth. Ch., 2002—. Music dept. chair Benton/Carroll/Salem Sch. Dist., Oak Harbor, Ohio, 1989—98, co-chair curriculum update com. dept. music, 2001—03, chair curriculum and nat. standards com. music strategic plan, 2002—04. Com. chair Oak Harbor (Ohio) United Meth. Ch., choir dir., 2000—, bd. mem. Mem.: Music Educators Nat. Conf. (assoc.), Ohio Educators Assn. (assoc.; sec. 1996—98), Ohio Music Educators Assn. (life; mentor). Avocations: handcrafts, playing piano. Home: 8845 W State Rt 163 Oak Harbor OH 43449

SIEVERTS, JORGEN FRANCOIS, engineering executive; b. Hellerup, Denmark, Apr. 3, 1933; s. Borge and Grete (Ohrgaard) S.; m. Jytte Alice Berg Kristensen, Apr. 27, 1937; children: Christian, Lene. Engring. degree, Danish Tech. U., 1957. Civil engr. Bornholms Konservesfabrik Ltd., Hvidovre, Denmark, 1959-63, dir., 1963—2000. Mem. maritime and comml. ct., Denmark, 1982—2004. Named Knight of the Dannebrog, 1994. Mem. Assn. Wholesalers in Groceries (chmn. 1985-95), Danish Fish Canners' Assn. (chmn. 1986-2000), Rotary. Business E-Mail: j.sieverts@webspeed.dk.

SIEVING, CHARLES E., energy executive, lawyer; BA, Denison U.; JD, U. Cin. Ptnr., corp. securities & fin. practice group Hogan & Hartson LLP, 1998; exec. v.p., sec. gen. counsel PAETEC Holding Corp., 2007—08; exec. v.p., gen. counsel FPL Group Inc., 2008—. Office: FPL Group Inc 700 Universe Boulevard North Palm Beach FL 33408 Office Phone: 561-694-4000. Office Fax: 561-694-4999.

SIEVING, PAUL A., federal agency administrator, ophthalmologist, educator; BS in Physics and Hist., with honors, Valparaiso U., Ind., 1970, DS (hon.), 2003; MS in Physics, Yale U., New Haven, 1973; MD, U. Ill. Med. Sch., 1978; PhD in Bioengring., U. Ill. Grad. Sch., 1980. Diplomate Nat. Bd. Med. Examiners, Am. Bd. Ophthalmology, lic. Ill., Calif., Mass., Mich. Resident ophthalmology U. Ill. Eye & Ear Infirmary, 1978—82; postdoc. fellow retinal physiology U. Calif., San Francisco, 1982—84; clin. fellow retinal degenerations Harvard Med. Sch., Mass. Eye & Ear Infirmary, 1984—85; asst. prof. ophthalmology U. Mich., Ann Arbor, 1985—89, assoc. prof., 1989—94, prof., 1994—2001, Paul R. Lichter prof. ophthalmic genetics, 1990—2001, founding dir. Ctr. Retinal & Macular Degeneration, Dept. Ophthalmology & Visual Scis., 1990—2001; dir. Nat. Eye Inst. (NEI), NIH, Bethesda, Md., 2001—. Vice-chair clin. rsch. Found. Fighting Blindness, 1996—2001; jury mem., award vision rsch. Champalimaud Found., Portugal. Contbr. articles to profl. jours., chapters to books. Recipient Disting. Alumnus award, Valparaiso U., 1991, Rsch. to Prevent Blindness Sr. Sci. Investigator award, 1998, Alcon award, Alcon Rsch. Inst., 2000, Pisart Vision award, NY Lighthouse Internat. for Blind, 2005; named one of Best Dr.'s in America, 1996—98, 2001, 2005. Mem.: Am. Optometric Assn. (Health Care Leadership award 2007), NAS Inst. Medicine, Internat. Soc. Clinical Electrophysiology of Vision (tres. 1986—94), Am. Ophthal. Soc., Retina Soc. (assoc.), Sigma Xi. Office: NEI NIH Campus 31 Ctr Dr Bethesda MD 20892-2510 Office Phone: 301-496-2234. Business E-Mail: paulsieving@nei.nih.gov.*

SIEWERS, ALFRED KENTIGERN KARLSON, literature educator; s. Karl Loren and Marjorie Lois Fisher Siewers; m. Olesya Konstantinovna Tarasova; children: Nicholas Kentigern Konstantin Karl, Kevin Seraphim Mark Brian. BA, Brown U., Providence RI, 1981; MSJ, Northwestern U., Medill Sch. Journalism, Evanston Ill., 1982; MA, U. Wales, Aberystwyth, 1994; PhD, U. Ill., Urbana Champaign, 2001. Staff & urban affairs writer Chgo. Sun-Times, Chgo., 1989—93; assoc. prof. Bucknell U., Lewisburg, Pa., 2002—. Convenor Susquehanna River Heartland Humanities Coun., Lewisburg, 2005—; nature & human cmtys. coord. Bucknell Environ. Ctr., Lewisburg, 2006—. Co-editor: (book) Tolkien's Modern Middle Ages; author: Strange Beauty: Ecocritical Approaches to Early Medieval Landscape, (chgo. Sun-Times) Lost Horizons (Peter Lisagor award, 1990). Office: Bucknell Univ English Dept Lewisburg PA 17837 Business E-Mail: asiewers@bucknell.edu.

SIEWERT, JAKE (RICHARD L. SIEWERT JR.), communications executive, former White House press secretary; b. NYC, Feb. 1, 1964; s. Richard L. and Patricia (Nicholson) Siewert; m. Christine Lynn Anderson, Dec. 10, 2005. BA in Humanities, Yale U., New Haven, 1986; attended, U. Calif. at Berkeley Law Sch. Comm. dir. Democratic Governors' Assn., Washington; spl. asst. to the pres. econ. affairs Nat. Econ. Coun., Washington; dep. press sec. The White House, Washington, 1998—2000, press sec., 2000—01; v.p. global comm. & pub. strategy Alcoa, Inc., NYC, 2001—05, v.p. environment, health & safety & pub. strategy, 2005—. Office: Alcoa Inc 390 Park Ave New York NY 10022 Office Phone: 212-836-2674.

SIFF, MARLENE IDA, artist, designer; b. NYC; d. Irving Louis and Dorothy Gertrude (Lahn) Marmer; m. Elliott Justin Siff, July 11, 1959; children: Bradford Evan, Brian Douglas. BA, Hunter Coll., 1957. Cert. tchr. elem. edn., NY, NJ. Tchr. Stewart Manor (NY) Sch. Sys., 1957-59, Teaneck (NJ) Sch. Sys., 1959-60; freelance interior designer Westport, Conn., 1966-70; designer Varo Inerteial Products, Trumbull, Conn., 1970; designer signature collections J.P. Stevens & Co. Inc., NY, 1974-78, J.C. Penney Co., NY, 1978, C.R. Gibson Co., Norwalk, Conn., 1980. Corp. sec., treas., bd. dirs. Belmar Corp., Westport, 1972—; chmn. bd. Marlene Designs Inc., Westport, 1973-77; owner Marlene Siff Design Studio, Westport, 1978—; aesthetic cons. Alcide Corp., Norwalk, 1980-88; art adv. coun. Herbert F. Johnson Mus. Art Cornell U., Ithaca, NY. One-person shows include David Segal Gallery, NYC, 1987, Conn. Pub. TV Gallery, Hartford, 1987, Paul Mellon Art Ctr., Choate Rosemary Hall, Wallingford, Conn., 1989, Conn. Nat. Bank Hdqs., Norwalk, 1990, Michael Stone Collection, Washington, 1992, Bergdorf Goodman Men, NYC, 1993, Joel Kessler Fine Art, Miami Beach, Fla., 1994, Park Pl., Stamford, Conn., 1995, Westport Arts Ctr., 1995, Mitchells, Westport, 1998, NIH, Bethesda, Md., 1999, Durst Lobby Gallery, NYC, 1999, Rosenthal Gallery at Rich Forum, Stamford, Conn., 2005, Walter Wickiser Gallery, NYC, 2007, others; exhibitions include Cheesebrough Pond's Gallery, Westport Arts Ctr., Conn., 1984-87, 1991, 1995, Conn. State Cap. Bldg., 1990, Aldrich Mus., Ridgefield, Conn., 1991-92, Galleri Seven, Danbury, Conn., 1991, Funding Ctr., Alexandria, Va., 1992-93, Michael Stone Collection, Washington, DC, 1992-93, Am. Soc. Interior Designers Nat. Hqds., Washington, DC, 1992-93, Joel Kessler Fine Arts, Miami Beach, 1993-94, Wave Gallery, New Caanan, Conn., 1993-94, Galerie Début, Nagoya, Japan, 1993-94, Internat. Cancer Alliance, Nat. Inst. Health, Bethesda, Md., 1993, Boston Corp. Art, 1994, Art Miami Internat. Exposition, 1994, Share Gallery, Funibashi, Japan, 1995, Reece Gallery, NYC, 1995, Whitney Gallery, Westport, Conn., 1996, B'nai B'rith Klutznick Nat. Jewish Mus. Washington, DC, 1998, Studio Tour, Westport Arts Ctr., 2000, Kenneth Raymond Gallery, Boca Raton, Fla., 2001-06, River Rd. Gallery, Wilton, Conn., 2002-05, Hall-Brooke Behavioral Health Services Art Show, Westport, Conn., 2004, Bendheim Gallery, Greenwich, Conn., 2007; represented in permanent collections B'nai B'rith Klutznick Nat. Jewish Mus., Washington, 1997, Toronto Internat. Art Fair, 2007-08, Art Now Fair, Miami Beach, 2007, The Barnum Mus., Bridgeport, CT, 2008, Walter Wickiser Gallery, NYC, 2008,09, The Lichtenstein Ctr. for Arts, Pitts., Mass., 2008, Calvin Charles Gallery, Scottsdale, Ariz., 2008, 09, Katonah Mus. Art Assn., Katonah, 2009, Northern Westchester Hospital, Mt. Kisco, Ny, 2009, Westport Hist. Soc., 2009. Decorator Easter Seal Home Svc. Charity Ball, 1976; bd. dirs. United Jewish Appeal, Westport, 1982-86; com. mem. Levitt Pavillion of the Performing Arts, Westport, 1982-89. Recipient award for creating the most beautiful working environment in an indsl. facility in lower Conn., Lower Conn. Mfrs. Assn., 1970. Mem.: LVW, Am. Israel Pub. Affairs Com., Anti Defamation League, Nat. Coun. Jewish Women, Kappa Pi. Jewish. Avocations: tennis, swimming, race walking, gardening. Home: 15 Broadview Rd Westport CT 06880-2303 Home Phone: 203-227-4270. Office Fax: 203-227-4273. Business E-Mail: marlene@marlenesiff.com.

SIFFEL, CSABA, medical epidemiologist; b. Mór, Hungary, May 29, 1968; s. József Siffel and Rozália Németh; m. Sarolta Tulipán; children: Gábor, Ádám. MD, Semmelweis U. Medicine, Budapest, Hungary, 1992; PhD, Eötvös U., Budapest, 2003. Programme dir. Hungarian congenital abnormality registry, dept. human genetics and teratology WHO Collaborating Ctr., "Bela Johan" Nat. Ctr. Epidermiology, Budapest, 1997—2000; med. epidemiologist Nat. Ctr. Birth Defects & Devel. Disabilities, Atlanta, 2003—. Sec., treas. Internat. Clearinghouse, Rome, 1998—2000; conf. chair Ctrl. & Ea. European Summit, Budapest, 2008. Contbr. articles to public health (Pro Hygiene award, 1999), to profl. jours. Recipient Career Devel. award, Assn. Tchrs. Preventive Medicine, USA, 2000—03; Rsch. grant, European Commn., 1998—2002. Mem.: Internat. Clearinghouse Birth Defects Surveillance & Rsch., Nat. Birth Defects Prevention Network, U.S.A., The Teratology Soc. Office: 1600 Clifton Rd MS E-86 Atlanta GA 30333 Office Phone: 404-498-3821. Business E-Mail: csiffel@cdc.gov.

SIFFERT, JOHN SAND, lawyer, educator, writer; b. NYC, Mar. 26, 1947; s. Robert Spencer and Miriam (Sand) S.; m. Goldie Alfasi-Siffert, June 1, 1975; children: David Alfasi, Matthew Alfasi. BA, Amherst Coll., 1969; JD, Columbia U., 1972. Bar: N.Y. 1973, U.S. Dist. Ct. (so. dist.) N.Y. 1974, (ea. dist.) N.Y. 1974, U.S. Ct. Appeals (2d cir.) 1974, U.S. Supreme Ct. 1979. Law clk. to Hon. Murray I. Gurfein U.S. Dist. Ct. (so. dist.) N.Y., 1972-74; asst. U.S. atty. (so. dist.) N.Y., 1974-79; ptnr. Fulop & Hardee and predecessor firm Barovick, Konecky et al, NYC, 1979-83, Lankler & Siffert, NYC, 1983-84, Lankler Siffert & Wohl LLP, NYC, 1984—. Adj. prof. NYU, 1979—; adv. coun. procurement policy bd. City of NY, 1991-95; spl. master First Dept. Appellate Divsn., 1999-; mem. divsn. first dept. Indigent Def. Orgn. Oversight Com., 2003-2004; mem. appellate divsn. Dept. Disciplinary Com. 1st Jud. Dept., 2005—. Co-author: Business Crime, 1981, Modern Federal Jury Instructions-Criminal, Modern Federal Jury Instructions-Civil. Mem. adv. bd. NY Civil Rights Coalition, 1995—; bd. dirs. NY Lawyers for Pub. Interest, 1998—, sec., 2003—06, chair, 2006—08. Fellow: Am. Bar Found., Am. Coll. Trial Lawyers (chmn. com. on admission to fellowship 2001—04, chmn. N.Y. downstate com. 2004—06, bd. regents 2006—); mem.: ABA, N.Y. Coun. Def. Lawyers (bd. mem. 2004—08), Fed. Bar Coun. (pres. Inns of Ct. 2001—02), Assn. Bar City N.Y. (chmn. fed. legis. com. 2003—06, exec. bd. com. 2006—), N.Y. State Bar Assn. Democrat. Jewish. Office: Lankler Siffert & Wohl LLP 500 5th Ave Fl 33 New York NY 10110-3398 Business E-Mail: jsiffert@lswlaw.com.

SIFFERT, ROBERT SPENCER, orthopedic surgeon; b. NYC, June 16, 1918; s. Oscar and Sadye (Rusoff) Siffert; m. Miriam Sand, June 29, 1941; children: Joan, John. AB in Biology with honors, NYU, 1939, MD, 1943. Diplomate Am. Bd. Orthrop. Surgery, Nat. Bd. Med. Examiners. Intern Kings County Hosp., Bklyn., 1943; resident in orthop. surgery Mt. Sinai Hosp., NYC, 1946-49, fellow in pathology, 1949-52, mem. staff, 1949—, attending orthop. surgeon, 1986—, dir. orthop. surgery, orthop. surgeon in chief, 1960-86, Lasker/Siffert Disting. Svc. prof., 1986—, chmn. emeritus, 1990—; pvt. practice NYC, 1949—. Sr. orthop. cons. N.Y.C. Dept. Health, 1952—60; attending orthop. surgeon Blythedale Children's Hosp., Valhalla, 1960—86, cons., 1986—90; dir. dept. orthops. City Hosp., Elmhurst, 1965—86; prof., chmn. dept. orthrops. Mt. Sinai Sch. Medicine, 1966—86, Dr. Robert K. Lippman prof., 1983—86, acting chmn., 1993—94, emeritus prof. and chair, 1986—. Author (with J. F. Katz): Management of Hip Disorders in Children, 1983; author: See How They Grow, 1985; contbr. articles to profl. jours. Bd. dirs., mem. profl. adv. com. Easter Seal Soc. Crippled Children and Adults, 1st v.p., 1977—79; mem. adv. bd. CARE-MEDICO, 1972—83, bd. dirs., chmn., 1981—83; bd. dirs. CARE, 1983—90; mem. adv. bd. Orthopaedics Overseas, 1981—93. Capt. USAAF, 1944—46, CBI. Decorated 4 Battle Stars; recipient Ann. award in medicine, N.Y. Pub. Health Assn., 1956, N.Y. Philanthropic League, 1959, Richman award for humanism in medicine, Mt. Sinai Sch. Medicine, 1989, Lifetime Achievement award, NY Arthritis Found., 2004. Fellow: APHA, ACS; mem.: N.Y. State Med. Soc. (chmn. orthrop. sect. 1967—68), N.Y. Acad. Medicine (fellow orthop. sect. 1952, sec. 1962—63, chmn. 1963—64), Orthop. Rsch. Soc., Internat. Skeletal Soc., Internat. Soc. Orthop. Surgery and Traumatology, Assn. Bone and Joint Surgeons, Am. Acad. Orthop. Surgery (chmn. com. care handicapped child), Am. Orthop. Assn., Century Assn. (N.Y.C.), Phi Beta Kappa, Alpha Omega Alpha. Office Phone: 212-288-2515. Personal E-mail: rssiffert@aol.com.

SIFFORD, CHARLIE (CHARLES LUTHER SIFFORD), professional golfer; b. Charlotte, NC, June 2, 1922; m. Rose Sifford; children: Charles, Craig. LLD (hon.), U. St. Andrews, Scotland, 2006. Profl. golfer, 1948—; mem. PGA Tour, 1960—80, Sr. PGA Tour, 1980—, Super Sr. Tour, 1991—. With 24th Inf. US Army. Recipient Old Tom Morris award, Golf Course Supts. Assn. America, 2007, Golden Tee award, Met. Golf Writers Assn., 2008; named to World Golf Hall of Fame, 2004. Achievements include breaking the color barrier in professional golf as the first African American to compete on the PGA Tour, 1960; winning PGA Tour events the Greater Hartford Open, 1967, the Los Angeles Open, 1969; winning the PGA Seniors' Championship, 1975; winning the Champions Tour event, the Suntree Classic, 1980; winning other notable events including the UGA National Negro Open, 1952-56, 1960, Long Beach Open, 1957, Puerto Rico Open, 1963, Sea Pines, 1971. Office: World Golf Hall Of Fame 12173 Ripken Cir N Jacksonville FL 32224-4638

SIFRI, ZIAD C., emergency physician, educator; s. Charles and Mari-Louise Sifri. MD, CM, McGill U., Montreal, Can. Asst. prof. surgery UMDNJ, Newark, 2002—, surtical trauma and critial care attending, 2003—, chmn. factor vii utilization sub-com., 2007—. Contbr. scientific papers to profl. jours., chapters to books. Recipient Golden Apple Tchg. award, NJ Med. Sch., 2005—06, 2008. Fellow: ACS; mem.: AMA, Soc. Critical Care Medicine, Sigma XI Sci. Rsch. Soc., Ea. Assn. Surgery of Trauma, Shock Soc., ACS NJ Com. on Trauma, Rush Surg. Soc., Assn. Academic Surgery, Surg. Infection Soc., Johns Hopkins Med. and Surg. Assn. Office: UMDNJ 150 Bergen St Newark NJ 07101 Business E-Mail: sifrizi@umdnj.edu.

SIFTON, DAVID WHITTIER, retired magazine editor; b. NYC, Sept. 12, 1940; s. David William and Dorothy (Whittier) S. BA, Trinity Coll., Hartford, Conn., 1962; MA, Stanford U., 1967. Editor Inside Edn., N.Y. State Edn. Dept., 1968-70; adminstrv. editor Med. Econs., Oradell, NJ, 1970-72; editor Drug Topics, Oradell, 1972-75; editor in chief Current Prescribing, Oradell, 1975-78, RN mag., Oradell, 1978-83; dir. spl. editorial projects Med. Econs. Co., 1983-90; editor PDR Publs., Montvale, 1990—2003; ret., 2003. Founder Physicians' Desk Reference on CD-ROM, PDR's Drug Interactions and Side Effects Index, PDR's Indications Index, Pocket PDR (handheld electronic database), The PDR Family Guide to Prescription Drugs, The PDR Family Guide to Women's Health, The PDR Family Guide to Nutrition and Health, The PDR Family Guide to Lifelong Health, The PDR Family Guide Encyclopedia of Medical Care, The PDR Family Guide to Over-the-Counter Drugs, The PDR Family Guide to Natural Medicines and Healing Therapies, The PDR Family Guide to Common Ailments, The PDR Family Guide to Nutritional Supplements, The PDR Guide to Biological and Chemical Warfare Response, The PDR Drug Guide for Mental Health Professionals. Served to 1st lt. USAF, 1963-66. Decorated Air Force Commendation medal; grantee Ford Found., 1967 Mem. Am. Bus. Press (chmn. editorial com. 1975-76) Republican. Episcopalian.

SIFTON, SAM, editor; AB, Harvard U., 1988. Asst. editor Am. Heritage, 1988—90; media critic NY Press, restaurant critic, mng. editor; founding editor Talk Mag.; dep. dining editor NY Times, NYC, 2001, dep. culture editor, 2004—05, culture editor, 2005—. Tchr. NYC Pub. Schs., 1990—94. Office: Culture Editor NY Times 229 W 43rd St New York NY 10036 Office Phone: 212-556-7411. Office Fax: 212-556-1516.*

SIGAL, ELLIOTT C., pharmaceutical executive; b. 1952; BS in Indsl. Engring., MS in Indsl. Engring., Purdue U., 1973, PhD, 1977; MD, U. Chgo., 1981. V.p., co-founder Pritsker Assocs., 1973—75; clin. fellow, rsch. fellow pulmonary medicine U. Calif., San Francisco, 1984—88, instr. medicine, 1988—89, asst. prof. medicine, 1989—92, asst. dir. Cystic Fibrosis R & D prog., 1990—92; exec. dir. Ctr. Inflammation Rsch. Syntex, 1992—95; v.p. inflammation and immunology rsch. Roche Bioscience, 1995—96; pres., CEO Mercator Genetics, 1996—97; v.p. dept. applied genomics Bristol-Myers Squibb Co., 1997—99, sr. v.p. early discovery & applied tech., 1999—2001, sr. v.p. drug discovery and exploratory devel., 2001—02, sr. v.p. global clin. and pharm. devel., co-chair brand devel. oper. com., 2002—04, exec. v.p., chief sci. officer, pres. R & D, 2004—, mem. exec. com., 2009—. Asst. adj. prof. medicine U. Calif., San Francisco, 1992—94, assoc. adj. prof., 1994. Office: Bristol-Myers Squibb Co 345 Park Ave New York NY 10154-0037*

SIGAL, JILL LEA, nuclear energy industry executive, former federal agency administrator; b. 1961; m. Bob Muth; 1 child. BA, Vermont U.; JD, George Washington U. Pres. Jill Sigal Assocs.; adv. Office Gen. Counsel US Dept. Energy, dep. asst. sec. for environ. & sci., 2003—04, prin. dep. asst. sec., 2004—05, acting asst. sec. for cong. & intergovernmental affairs, 2005, asst. sec., 2005—07; sr. v.p. govt. rels. EnergySolutions, Salt Lake City, 2007—. Office: EnergySolutions 423 W 300 S Ste 200 Salt Lake City UT 84101

SIGAL, LEONARD H., physician; b. NYC, Aug. 26, 1951; s. Morris Lloyd and Theresa (Green) S.; m. Judith Halden, June 6, 1976 (div. May 31, 1981); m. Barbara K. Snyder, June 15, 1986; children: Merissa, Caroline SB, MIT, 1972; MD, Stanford U., 1976. Intern, resident Mt. Sinai Hosp., NYC, 1976-79; chief internal medicine Westchester Community Health Plan, White Plains, NY, 1979-81; fellow rheumatology Yale U. Sch. Medicine, New Haven, 1981-84, fellow immunology, 1982-84; chief rheumatology Syracuse (N.Y.) VA Med. Ctr., 1984-88; asst. prof. medicine and immunology SUNY Health Sci. Ctr., Syracuse, 1984-88; asst. prof. medicine UMDNJ - R.W. Johnson Med. Sch., New Brunswick, NJ, 1988—, asst. prof. molecular genetics and microbiology, 1988—91, prof., chief divsn. rheumatology, dept. medicine, 1991—2003; dir. Immunology Pharm. Rsch. Inst. Bristol-Myers Squibb, Princeton, NJ, 2003—. Speaker in field. Author (editor): Immunology to Inflammation: Basic Mechanisms and Clinical Consequences, 1990. Recipient Research Grant Arthritis Found., 1988, Research Grant Am. Heart Assn., 1989. Fellow ACP, Am. Coll. Rheumatology; mem. Am. Assn. Immunologists, Clin. Immunology Soc., Soc. Exptl. Biology and Medicine, MIT Club. Democrat. Jewish. Avocations: reading, tennis, sailing, photography, kayaking. Home: 26 Hastings Rd Belle Mead NJ 08502 Office: J3100 Pharm Rsch Inst Bristol Myers Squibb Rte 206 and Provinceline Rd PO Box 4000 Princeton NJ 08543-4000 Office Phone: 609-252-6050. Business E-Mail: leonard.sigal@bms.com.

SIGAL, SAMUEL HAROLD, gastroenterologist; b. Indpls., Oct. 24, 1959; s. Max Victor and Stella (Rosenblum) S.; m. Sandra Molinas, Oct. 31, 1963. BS, AB, Ind. U., 1979; MD, U. Chgo., 1983. Resident in pathology U. Pa., Phila., 1983-87; resident in medicine St. Luke's Hosp., NYC, 1987-90; fellow in gastroenterology Albert Einstein Coll. Medicine, Bronx, 1990-93; fellow in liver diseases Mt. Sinai Med. Ctr., NYC, 1993-94; asst. clin. prof. Mt. Sinai Sch. Medicine, NYC, 1994—2004, NY Weill Cornell Med. Ctr., 2004—. Mem. ACP, N.Y. Acad. Scis., Internat. Acad. Pathology, Phi Beta Kappa. Home: 2734 Arlington Ave Bronx NY 10463-4807 Office: 1300 York Ave New York NY 10021 Office Phone: 646-962-5483. Business E-Mail: shs2015@med.cornell.edu.

SIGAL-IBSEN, ROSE, artist; b. Bucharest, Romania, Aug. 22; arrived in U.S., 1957; d. Joseph and Tilly (Eckstein) Cohen; m. Albert D. Sigal, Dec. 25, 1941 (dec. May 1970); 1 child, Daniel M.; m. Joseph Ibsen, Oct. 1973 Diploma, Fashion Inst. Technology, NYC, 1978; Parson, Sch. of Design, NYC, 1985—86; student, Koho Sch. of Sumi-E, NYC, 1979—90, Zhejiang Acad. Fine Arts, China, 1990. Curator Metro N.Y. Chpt. of Sumi-E Soc., 1990—, v.p., 1990—. One-woman shows include

China-Gallery Weizhi Schubert, Hanover, Germany, 1991, Manhattan Savs. Bank, N.Y.C., 1993—94, Chem. Bank, 1993—95, N.Y. Pub. Libr., 1996, Bankers Fed., N.Y.C., 1996, Rep. Bank for Savs., 1996, Roumanian Cultural Found., Bucharest, 1998, World Fine Art Gallery, N.Y.C., 1998, Romanian Embassy, Washington, 2000, Berkeley Coll. Gallery, 2006, Riverrock Health Spa Woodstock, NY, 2007—08, others, numerous group shows including most recently, exhibited in group shows at Beyond the Form, Taipei Gallery & Chinese Am. Art Coun., 1998, Broome St. Gallery, NYC, 2001—02, Art of Ink in America, Newark Mus., 2000, Broome St. Gallery, 2005—06, Sumi-e Soc. Am. Inc. at Courthouse Galleries of Portsmouth Va., 2001 (Hallie Hazen Meml. award, 2001), ASCA, Sarah Lawrence Coll., 2001, Pen and Brush Ann. Mixed Media, 2002, Korean Cultural Ctr., L.A., 2002, Japanese Artists Assn. N.Y., 2002, Blue Hill Art & Cultural Ctr., Pearl River, 2002, JAA NY, Tenri Cultural Inst. and Art of Ink in America, Portland, Oreg., 2002, Nat. Taiwan Art Edn. Inst., Art Ink in Xian, China, 2003, Mobile Mus. Art, 2004, NY Hall of Sci., 2005, Hammond Mus., 2005, Keith and Janet Kelly U. Art Gallery, Calif. State Poly. U., Pomona, 2005, JAA NY, Hammond Mus., 2005, Contemporary Artist Guild, 2006—08, JAA Annuak Exch., Tenri Cultural Inst., NY, 2006—08, Sumi-e Soc. America, Farmington Art Ctr., St. Paul, 2006, Art Ink America, Tenri Inst., Paris & Ulsan-Korea, 2007, Strathmore Art Ctr., Bethesda, Md., 2008, Irvine Art Ctr., Calif., 2008, Courage Card design, 1998. Recipient Manhattan Arts award Cover Art Competition, N.Y.C., 1992, 94, 95, 97, King Point award, Fla., 1991, Tenth Japanese Internat. Calligraphy Exhbn. award, N.Y.C., 1996, Manhattan Arts Internat. Showcase award, Emily N. Hatch Meml. award Pen and Brush, Inc., Spring Watercolor Exhbn., 1998, Hallie Hazen Meml. award Sumi-e Soc. Am., Inc., 2001. Mem. Nat. Mus. of Women in the Arts, Artist Equity of N.Y., Am. Soc. Contemporary Artists, Art of Ink in Am., The Oriental Brushwork Soc. of Am., Sumi-e Soc. (hon.). Avocations: sculptor in clay, dance. Home: One Irving Pl Apt P22B New York NY 10003-9741 Office Phone: 212-979-2459.

SIGALL, HAROLD FRED, psychology professor; b. NYC, June 29, 1943; s. Walter and Regine (Goldenberg) S.; m. Brenda Ann Alpert, Aug. 8, 1965; children: Elana, Jennifer, Emily. BS, CUNY, 1964; PhD, U. Tex., 1968. Asst. prof. psychology U. Rochester, NY, 1968-72; assoc. prof. U. Md., College Park, 1972-78, prof., 1978—, dir. grad. program in social psychology, dir. grad. studies dept. psychology, 2000—06, acting chair dept. psychology, 2006—07; cons. editor Jour. Applied Social Psychology, 1992—. Cons. social rsch. and decision making to numerous orgns., lectr. Smithsonian Inst., Washington, 1984, 85; vis. prof. U. Bologna, 1997, 2002. Editor Personality and Social Psychology Bull., 1977-81. Bd. dirs. Columbia (Md.) Jewish Congregation, 1985-87, Howard County (Md.) Jewish Cmty. Sch., Columbia, 1986-87; mem. Human Rights Commn., Howard County, 1994-99. NDEA fellow, 1967-68, Danforth Found. fellow, 1970-71. Fellow APA, Am. Psychol. Soc.; mem. Soc. Exptl. Social Psychology. Home: 5060 Castle Moor Dr Columbia MD 21044-1871 Office: U of Md Dept Psychology College Park MD 20742-0001 Office Phone: 301-405-0424. Business E-Mail: hsigall@psyc.umd.edu.

SIGEL, JOHN D., lawyer; b. 1953; BA, Middlebury Coll., 1975; JD, Cornell Univ., 1980. Bar: Mass. 1980. Ptnr., chmn. Bankruptcy & Comml. dept. Wilmer Cutler Pickering Hale & Dorr, Boston. Editor (mng.): Cornell Law Rev.; contbr. articles to profl. jours. Fellow: Am. Coll. of Bankruptcy; mem.: Mass. Bar Assn., Boston Bar Assn. Office: Wilmer Cutler Pickering Hale & Dorr 60 State St Boston MA 02109 Office Phone: 617-526-6728. Office Fax: 617-526-5000. Business E-Mail: john.sigel@wilmerhale.com.

SIGEL, MARSHALL ELLIOT, financial consultant; b. Hartford, Conn., Nov. 25, 1941; s. Paul and Bessie (Somer) Sigel; m. Sybil R. Miller, Nov. 23, 1995. BS in Econs., U. Pa., 1963; JD, U. Miami, 1982, LLM in Taxation, 1983. Exec. v.p. Advo-Sys. divsn. KMS Industries, Inc., Hartford, 1963—69, pres., 1969—72, Ad-Type Corp., Hartford, 1963—69, Ad-Lists, Inc., Hartford, 1963—69; fin. cons. Hartford, 1972—83, Boca Raton, Fla., 1987—; pvt. practice law, 1983—87. Bd. dir. Wharton Sch. Club S. Fla. Mem.: World Pres. Orgn., Saratoga Golf and Polo Club, Boca Grove Club, 100 Club So. Palm Beach County. Home and Office: PO Box 273408 Boca Raton FL 33427-3408

SIGETY, CHARLES BIRGE, investment company executive; b. NYC, Sept. 30, 1952; s. Charles Edward and Katharine Kinne (Snell) S.; m. Elizabeth Ross Pennington, Nov. 27, 1976; children: Austin Douglas, Katharine Colyer, Alexander Birge. BA in English Lit., Bates Coll., 1975. Lic. nursing home adminstr. Adminstr. in tng. Florence Nightingale Nursing Home, NYC, 1972, asst. dir. facility ops., 1975, dir. facility ops., 1975-78, assoc. adminstr., 1978-81, exec. dir., 1981-82; pres., CEO Profl. Med. Products, Inc., Greenwood, SC, 1982-96; pres. Upper Savannah Internat. Trade Assn., Greenwood, 1993; CEO Bison Investments, Inc., Tampa, Fla., 1996—, Aerial Machine & Tool Corp., Vesta, Va., 1998—2006, Polyten Plastics, LLC, Washington, 1998-2000, Coeur Acquisition, LLC, Washington, NC, 1999, Polyten, LLC, Washington, NC, 2000—03; mng. ptnr. Bison Mgmt. Solutions LLC, 2008—. Mem. adv. bd. Liberty Mut. Ins. Cos. S.C., 1986—96, NationsBank (Bank of Am.), Greenwood, SC, 1984—96; vice chmn. Upper Savannah Bus. Group on Health Care, 1981—87, S.C. Bus. Roundtable for the Initiative for Work Force Excellence, Columbia, 1988—92; dir. exec. com. Osteo Am., Inc., 1993—96; bd. advisors Capital South Ptnrs., 2004—06; pres. Petersburg Landing Devel., Inc., 2005—, Boonsborough, LLC, 2006—; mem. bd. adv. MD Internat., 1992—2000, 2003—09. Bd. visitors Med. U. S.C., 1988; treas. YPO HealthCare Focus Forum, 1997; bd. dirs. Stewards Found., 2003-07; active Soc. Internat. Fellows 1999-2006, Defense Orientation Conf. Assn. 2004-. Mem. Health Industry Mfrs. Assn. (ofcl. rep. 1982-96, 99-2002), Upper Savannah Internat. Trade Assn. (pres. 1993), Young Pres.'s Orgn., Chief Execs. Orgn., World Pres.' Orgn., Def. Orientation Conf. Assn. Avocations: hunting, sailing. Office: Bison Investments Inc 3225 S Macdill Ave # 129-236 Tampa FL 33629-8171 Office Phone: 813-832-6359.

SIGETY, CHARLES EDWARD, lawyer, financial planner; b. NYC, Oct. 10, 1922; s. Charles and Anna (Toth) S.; m. Katharine K. Snell, July 17, 1948; children: Charles, Katharine, Robert, Cornelius, Elizabeth. BS, Columbia U., 1944; MBA, Harvard U., 1947; LLB, Yale U., 1951; LHD (hon.), Cazenovia Coll., 1994. Bar: NY 1952, DC 1958. With Bankers Trust Co., 1939-42; instr. adminstrv. engring. Pratt Inst., 1948; instr. econs. Yale U., 1948-50; vis. lectr. acctg. Sch. Gen. Studies Columbia U., NYC, 1948-50, 52; rapporteur com. fed. taxation for U.S. coun. Internat. C. of C., 1952-53; asst. to com. fed. taxation Am. Inst. Accts., 1950-53; with Compton Advt. Agy., NYC, 1954; vis. lectr. law Yale U., 1952; pvt. practice law NYC, 1952—; pres., dir. Video Vittles, Inc., NYC, 1953—67; dep. commr. FHA, 1955-57; of counsel Javits and Javits, 1959-60; 1st asst. atty. gen. NY, 1958-59; dir., mem. exec. com. Gotham Bank, NYC, 1961—63; dir. NY State Housing Fin. Agy., 1962—63; chmn. Met. Ski Slopes, Inc., NYC, 1962—65; pres., exec. adminstr. Florence Nightingale Health Ctr., NYC, 1965—85; dir. Schaerer AG, Wabern, Switzerland, 1982-88; chmn. Kenbar Group, NYC, 1997—, Internat. Bioimmune Sys., Inc., Great Neck, NY, 1999—. Professorial lectr. Sch. Architecture, Pratt Inst., NYC, 1962-66; mem. Sigety Assocs., cons. in housing mortgage financing and urban renewal, 1957-67; ho. cons. Govt. of Peru, 1956; mem. missions to Hungary, Poland, Fed. Republic Germany, Malta, Czechoslovakia, Russia, Israel, Overseas Pvt. Investment Corp., 1990-92; owner, operator Peppermill Farms, Pipersville, Pa., 1956—. Bd. dirs., sec., v.p., treas. Nat. Coun. Health Ctrs., 1969-85; bd. dirs. Am.-Hungarian Found., 1974-76, Pritikin Rsch. Found., 1991—, Stratford Arms Condo Assn., 1992-93, 2002-08, Global Leadership Inst., 1993—2008, Hepatitus B Found., Doylestown, 2005-; founding mem., bd. dirs., Natl. Assn. for Continence, 1982, trustee Cazenovia Coll., NY, 1981-2002, Delaware Valley Coll. Sci. and Agr., Doylestown, Pa., 1998-2005; trustee, v.p. Woodmere Art Mus. Phila., 2000-05, Navy Supply Corps Found., Athens, Ga., 2000—; del. White House Conf. on Aging, 1971, White House Conf. on Mgmt. Tng. and Market Econs. Edn. in Ctrl. and Ea. Europe, 1991; bd. visitors Lander Coll., U. SC, Greenwood, 1982-84; mem. fin. com. World Games, Santa Clara, 1981, London, 1985, Karlsruhe, 1989, The Hague, 1993, Confrerie des Chevaliers du Tastevin, Confrerie de la Chaine des Rotisseurs, Wine and Food Soc., Wednesday 10; chmn. Alumni Assn. Townsend Haris HS, NYC, 2005-. Lt. (j.g.) Supply Corps, USNR, 1942-46. Recipient President's medal Cazenovia Coll., 1990, George Washington laureate Am. Hungarian Found., 1996; named Prin. for Day, Townsend Harris HS NYC Bd. Edn., 1997-2001, 2006, Disting. Alumnus US Navy Supply Corps Sch., Athens, Ga., 1998; Baker scholar Harvard U., 1947. Mem. DOCA (Defense Orientation Conf. Assn.). Presbyterian. Office Phone: 212-410-8787. Personal E-mail: sigety@msn.com.

SIGETY, CORNELIUS EDWARD, real estate developer, director; b. NYC, June 6, 1958; s. Charles Edward and Katharine (Snell) Sigety; m. Virginia White, Oct. 28, 1995; children: Charles Edgar, Bradford Earle, Cornelia Ring. BA, U. Rochester, NY, 1980; MBA, Harvard U., Boston, 1985. Asst. adminstr. Florence Nightingale Health Ctr., NYC, 1980-83; v.p. Profl. Med. Products, Greenwood, SC, 1985-88; mng. dir. Kenbar Mgmt., NYC, 1988—. Bd. dirs. Heritage Conservancy. Mem. sch. bd. Buckingham Friends Sch., Lahaska, Pa. Mem. Union Club, Doylestown Country Club, Bay Head Yacht Club, Mantoloking Yacht Club. Presbyterian. Avocations: sailing, golf, skiing. Office: Kenbar Mgmt 1500 Lexington Ave New York NY 10029 Personal E-mail: cesigety@hotmail.com.

SIGETY, ELIZABETH DONNEM, lawyer; b. NYC, Apr. 8, 1964; d. Roland William and Sarah (Lund) Donnem; m. Robert Griswold Sigety; children: Sarah Katharine, William Hall, Elizabeth Brandon, George Lund. BA cum laude, Yale U., New Haven, 1986; JD, U. Chgo., 1989. Bar: Conn. 1989, NY 1990, Pa. 1997. Atty., assoc. Debevoise and Plimpton, NYC, 1989—97; atty. Antheil, Maslow and MacMinn, Doylestown, Pa., 1997—2004; ptnr. Fox Rothschild LLP, Warrington, Pa., 2004—. Mng. dir., co-founder Del. Crossing Investor Group, Warrington, Pa., 2005—; co-chair franchising, distbn. licensing group Fox Rothschild LLP, 2005—, mem. tech. and venture fin. practice group and securities practice group, 2005—. Bd. mem. East Side Ho. Settlement, Bronx, NY, 1991—, exec. v.p., 2000—04; bd. mem., v.p. Child, Home and Cmty., Doylestown, Pa., 1999—2004; bd. mem. Village Improvement Assn., Doylestown, 2000—, Doylestown Hosp., 2004—06; chair ann. fund Buckingham Friends Sch., Pa., 2004—06; bd. mem. Doylestown Health Found., Pa., 2006—. Mem.: Am. Coll. Investment Counsel, Bucks County Bar Assn., Internat. Franchise Assn., NYC Bar Assn., Pa. Bar Assn., Am. Bar Assn. (Forum on Franchising and Bus. Law Sect.), Montgomery County Bar Assn. (assoc.). Avocations: tennis, sailing, cooking, skiing. Office: Fox Rothschild LLP 2700 Kelly Rd Ste300 Warrington PA 18976 also: 100 Park Ave Ste 1500 New York NY 10017 Office Phone: 215-918-3554. Business E-Mail: esigety@foxrothschild.com.

SIGGINS, ROBERT G., legislative staff member; Chief of staff to Rep. Earl Pomeroy US House of Reps., Washington, 2002—. Democrat. Office: 1501 Longworth House Office Bldg Washington DC 20515 Office Phone: 202-225-2611. Office Fax: 202-226-0893.*

SIGH, ROBERT VIRGIL, public health physician; b. Houston, Aug. 9, 1964; s. Odea D. and Rosie L. Sigh; m. Miriam Lynette Sigh, July 21, 1991; 1 child, Caleb Robert. BA, Oakwood Coll., Huntsville, Ala., 1985; MPH, Loma Linda U., Calif., 1992, MD, 1996. Residency in family practice Fla. Hosp., Orlando, 1996—99; residency in preventative medicine, pub. health Loma Linda Univ., Calif., 1999—2000; med. dir. Adventist Whole Health Network, Reading, Pa., 2001—03, Margaret J. Weston Cmty. Health Ctr., Clearwater, SC, 2003—06; clin. dir., ready responder HRSA/NHSC, Rockville, Md., 2003—06; with USPHS, 2003—; staff physician Oakhurst Med. Ctr., 2006—09; regional med. cons., pub. health analyst HRSA Office Performance Review, Atlanta Regional Office, 2009—. Decorated Field Med. Readiness Badge; recipient Crisis Response award, Health Resource Svc. Adminstrn., Rockville, 2005, 2008; named Outstanding Unit Citation; named one of America's Top Family Drs. Mem.: Commd. Officers Assn., Rres. Officer Assn., Delta Sigma Phi. Avocations: saxophone, woodworking, hiking, camping. Home: 140 Barcelona Dr Covington GA 30016-6526

SIGLE, JOHN WALTER, science educator; b. Muskogee, Okla., Aug. 8, 1944; s. Walter Edward and Bessie Cyrene Sigle; m. Deborah Elizabeth Stille, June 30, 1985; m. Kaoru Adachi Kaoru Adachi (dec. Apr. 25, 1985); 1 child, Akiko Lisa. BS in Math Edn., Northeastern State U., Tahlequah, Okla.; MA, U. Okla., Norman; PhD in Computing Sci., Tex. A&M U., Coll. Sta. Asst. prof. computer sci. Trinity U., San Antonio, 1976—81; assoc. prof. computer sci. La. State U., Shreveport, 1981—86, prof. computer sci., 1986—, 2005—08, chair, 2005—08. Pres. Highland Restoration Assn., Shreveport, 1992—93; bd. mem. Highland Area Partmership, Shreveport, 1991—2001. Mem.: Assn. Computing Machinery.

SIGLER, JAMIE-LYNN, actress; b. Jericho, NY, May 15, 1981; d. Steven and Consuela (Lopez) Sigler; m. A.J. DiScala, July 11, 2003 (div. 2006). Student, NYU, 1999. Actor: (films) A Brooklyn State of Mind, 1997, Campfire Stories, 2001, Death of a Dynasty, 2003, Extreme Dating, 2004, Love Wrecked, 2005, Homie Spumoni, 2006, Blinders, 2006, Dark Ride, 2006, New York City Serenade, 2007; (TV films) Call Me: The Rise and Fall of Heidi Fleiss, 2004; (TV series) The Sopranos, 1999—2007 (Outstanding Performance by an Ensemble in a Drama Series, SAG, 2008), (TV appearances) Will & Grace, 2004, Higglytown Heroes, 2005, 2007, Entourage, 2008; (TV miniseries) The Gathering, 2007; (Broadway plays) Beauty and the Beast, 2002—03; author: (autobiography) Wise Girl: What I've Learned About Life, Love, and Loss, 2002; singer: (albums) Here to Heaven, 2001. Achievements include started acting at NY regional theaters; starred in over two dozen theatrical prodns. including Annie, The Wizard of Oz, The Sound of Music, The Wiz, and Gypsy.

SIGLER, JOHN CHARLES, former firearms association executive; BS, U. NC, Wilmington; JD, Widener U. Bar: 1987. With City of Dover (Del.) Police Dept., 1971—91; corp. in-house counsel Del., Md.; pres. NRA, Fairfax, Va., 2007—09. Served in USN, 1967—71. Mem.: NRA (life; bd. dirs. 1996—, chmn. finance com., law enforcement assistance com. 1997—2007, first v.p. 2005—07, pres. 2007—), NRA Heritage Soc. (co-founder, planning chair Nat. Firearms Law seminar 1999—2005).*

SIGLER, PAULETTE TERRY, music educator; d. Wallace Roland Terry, Jr. and Apphia Adele Terry; m. Thomas Burke Sigler, Feb. 28, 1976; children: James Adam, Catherine Adele. MusB in Edn., U. So. Miss., 1976; postgrad., Meredith Coll., 1989—92. Cert. tchr. Ga., 1998. Choir dir. Waynesboro (Miss.) So. Meth. Ch., 1980—88; tchr. Wayne Acad., Waynesboro, 1987—88; music tchr. band, chorus, voice Raleigh (N.C.) Christian Acad., 1989—92; dir. youth music Northside Bapt. Ch., Charlotte, NC, 1993—95; voice tchr. Johnson Ferry Bapt. Music Conservatory, Marietta, Ga., 1996—99; choral dir. Hightower Trail Mid. Sch., Marietta, 1998—2005; choral specialist Mt. Bethel Christian Acad., Marietta, 2005—. Singer and soloist Charlotte Choral Soc., 1994—95; chorus mem. Opera Carolina, Charlotte, 1995—96; founder Cantare Youth Choirs of St., 2005—; ind. cons. Choral Clinician; adj. voice tchr. Dir.: (choral performance-featured choir) Allegro Mixed Chorus Georgia Music Educator's Annual State Conf., Hightower Trail Mid. Sch. (Cert. of Appreciation, 2005), Allegro Treble Chorus Georgia Music Educator's Annual Conf. (Cert. of Appreciation, 2004); singer: (vocal performance) Concerto Performance with the Raleigh Symphony (Winner of Competition-Symphony Performance, 1992). Music provider for elder citizens Sunrise Assisted Living, Marietta, 2000—04; active Mt. Bethel United Meth. Ch., Marietta, 2003—05. Mem.: DAR, Profl. Assn. Ga. Educators, Am. Choral Dirs. Assn., Ga. Music Educator's Assn. (choral chair dist. 12 2002—05, music festival adjudicator and clinician 2004—). Republican. Avocations: swimming, acting, reading, skiing. Office: Mt Bethel Christian Acad 4385 Lower Roswell Rd Marietta GA 30068 Personal E-mail: paulettesigler@yahoo.com.

SIGLER, THERESA JANE, school system administrator; b. Marion, Ohio, Mar. 24, 1951; d. William Howard and Joanna Elizabeth Byrd; m. Timothy Joseph Sigler, July 11, 1981; 1 child, Andrew Joseph. BA summa cum laude, Walsh U., North Canton, Ohio, 1972; MA, U. Mo., Kansas City, 1979. Cert. elem. edn. K-8 Walsh U., 1972, reading edn. K-12 U. Mo., 1979, gifted edn. K-12 Ashland U., 1985, gen. supervision K-12 Ashland U., 1985, elem. prin. Ashland U., 1987, asst. supt. cert. Ashland U., 1988, supt. Ashland U., 1990. Tchr. grade 1 Sandy Valley Local Sch. Dist., Canton, Ohio, 1972—73; tchr. multiage 3/4 Ctr. City Sch., Dayton, Ohio, 1973—74; tchr. grade 6 St. Pius X, Reynoldsburg, Ohio, 1974—76; reading specialist Canton Local Sch. Dist., 1980—84; reading/lang. arts supr. Stark County Bd. Edn., Canton, 1984—86; dir. curriculum and staff devel. Barberton (Ohio) City Sch. Dist., 1986—2000, Woodridge Local Sch. Dist., Peninsula, Ohio, 2000—. Cons. Am. Book Co., NYC, 1976—80; adj. prof. Ashland U., Massillon, Ohio, 1984—; presenter in field. Designed/developed (how to teaching audio visual vhs tape) Implementing and Integrating a New Language Arts Program at Grades K-8. Com. mem. United Way, Barberton, Ohio; mem. Barberton Head Start, 1996—2000, Decker Family Devel. Ctr., Barberton, 1996—2000; sec. Magical Theatre Co., Barberton, 1996—2000. Recipient Title I Program of the Yr. - Barberton City Schools, Ohio Dept. Edn. - Fed. Programs, 1994, Star Partnership award - Decker Family Devel. Ctr., Summit Edn. Initiative Found., 2000; grantee, Ohio Dept. Edn., 1986—2004, Barberton Found., 1996—2000; scholar, Kiwanis, 1970—72. Mem.: ASCD (assoc.), Internat. Reading Assn. (assoc.), Nat. Staff Devel. Coun. (assoc.), Ednl. Rsch. Svc. (assoc.), Delta Kappa Gamma (assoc.), Phi Delta Kappa (assoc.). Avocations: golf, reading, theater, bicycling, music. Home: 6516 Shenandoah Ave NW Canton OH 44718 Office: Woodridge Local Schools 4411 Quick Rd Peninsula OH 44264

SIGMAN, SCOTT P., lawyer; s. Bruce and Marsha Sigman; m. Pamela Errico, Oct. 4, 1996. BA, Am. U., DC, 1998; JD, Temple U. Sch. Law, Phila., 2001. Asst. dist. atty. Phila. Dist. Atty.'s Office, 2001—05; assoc. Bochetto & Lentz, P.C., Phila., 2005—. V.p. U.S. Dept. of Justice North Phila. Weed & Seed Program, 2005—; mem. exec. bd. Temple Law Alumni Assn., Phila., 2003—. Editor-in-chief: Temple Internat. & Comparative Law Jour., 2000—01. Bd. mem. 26th Police Dist. Adv. Coun., Phila., 2001, East Divsn. Crime Victim Svcs., Phila., 2001; mem. Variety Club, Phila., 2003, World Affairs Coun. of Phila., 2005, Young Friends of the ARC, Phila., 2003, Young Am. Polit. Action Com., Phila., 2002. Recipient Outstanding Achievement, Phila. Dist. Atty.'s Office, 1999, Outstanding Svc. award, 2001, Outstanding Svc. in Pub. Safety award, Bracetti Charter Sch. Police Dept., 2004, Citation, Phila. Police Dept., 26th Police Dist., 2005; named Pa. Rising Star Super Lawyer, Phila. Mag.: Law & Politics, 2005, 2006, Lawyer on the Fast Track, The Legal Intelligencer, 2006. Mem.: Phila. Bar Assn. (fin. sec. young lawyers divsn. 2003—04, vice chair young lawyers divsn. 2004—06, chair elect 2007—), Pa. Bar Assn. (zone chair young lawyers divsn. 2003—), Lawyers Club Phila. (treas. 2005—). Home: 1524 Locust St Philadelphia PA 19102 Office: Bochetto & Lentz PC 1524 Locust St Philadelphia PA 19102 Office Fax: 215-735-2455. Business E-Mail: ssigman@bochettoandlentz.com.

SIGMAN, STANLEY T., retired telecommunications industry executive; b. Lubbock, Tex. m. Gerry Lynn Sigman; 2 children. BBA, W. Tex. State U., 1970. Stockman Southwestern Bell Telephone, Hereford, Tex., 1965; exec. v.p. Southwestern Bell Mobile Sys., 1986—91, mng. dir., cellular and paging, SBC Comm., Teléfonos de México Mexico City, 1991—93, v.p., gen. mgr. Okla., 1993—94, exec. v.p., 1994—95, pres., CEO, 1995—99, group pres., SBC opers., 1999; sr. exec. v.p., svcs. Southwestern Bell Telephone Co., CEO, pres.; group pres., COO SBC Communications Inc., 2001—02; pres., CEO Cingular Wireless LLC, Atlanta, 2002—06; pres., CEO mobility AT&T Inc., 2006—08.

SIGMON, J. LEWIS, JR., medical educator; b. Newton, NC, July 8, 1940; MD, U. N.C., 1966. Intern David Grant USAF Hosp., 1966-67; resident Charlotte (N.C.) Meml. Hosp., 1969-71; chmn. dept. family medicine Carolinas Med. Ctr., Charlotte, 1984-95, clin. coord. Charlotte Ofcl Reg. Primary Care Edn., 1995—2001, sr. ind. cons. in grad. med. edn., family and ins. medicine, 2001—, dir. family medicine residency program Monroe, 1997—2001; prof. family medicine U. NC, 1993—2004, prof. emeritus, 2004—. Acad. coun. Nat. Inst. for Program Dir. Devel., Kansas City, Mo., 1999—2003; chair Am. Bd. Family Medicine Found., 2000—; residency rev. com. for family medicine ACGME, 1997—2003, specialist site visitor for residency rev. com., 2004—; step 3 test material devel. com. USMLE/NBME, 2005—09, step 3 test devel. com. scriptor, 2009—; mem. Am. Bd. Family Medicine, 1995—2000. Recipient Disting. Svc. award, U. NC Sch. Medicine, 2005. Mem. AMA, N.C. Acad. Family Physicians, Am. Acad. Ins. Medicine. Office Phone: 704-578-1416. Personal E-mail: sigmonjr@aol.com.

SIGMOND, CAROL ANN, lawyer; d. Irwin and Mary Florence (Vollmer) S. BA, Grinnell Coll., 1972; JD, Cath. U., 1975. Bar: Va. 1975, D.C. 1980, US Dist. Ct. 1982, US Dist. Ct. (DC cir.), 1984, Md. 1988, N.Y. 1990, U.S. Dist. Ct. (ea. dist.) Va. 1975, U.S. Dist. Ct. (so. and ea. dist.) N.Y. 1991, U.S. Ct. Appeals (4th cir.) 1976, US Dist. Ct. DC, 1981, US Dist. Md., 1990, U.S. Ct. Appeals (fed. cir.) 1987, U.S. Ct.

Appeals (2d cir.) 2000, Fed. Claims Ct. 2002, Ct. Internat. Trade 2006. Asst. gen. counsel Washington Met. Area Transit Authority, 1978-85; acting assoc. gen. counsel for appeals and gen. law, 1985-86; assoc. Patterson, Belknap, Webb & Tyler, Washington, 1986-89, Tunstead Schecter & Torre, 1989—91, Berman, Paley, Goldstein & Kannry, NYC, 1991—93; prin. Law Offices of Carol A. Sigmond, NYC, 1993—97; of counsel Pollack & Greene, LLP, NYC, 1998—2000; pvt. practice NYC, 2000—03; ptnr. Kehl, Katzive, & Sigmond, NYC, 2004—05, Dunnington, Bartholow & Miller, LLP, NYC, 2005—. Mem. ABA, DC Bar Assn., NY State Bar Assn. (House of dels. 2007—), Assn. Bar City NY, NY County Lawyers Assn. (bd. dirs. 2007—, chair constrn. law com. 2007-), Women's Nat. Dem. Club. Democrat. Avocations: piano, bridge. Office Phone: 212-682-8811. Business E-Mail: csigmond@dunnington.com.

SIGMUND, CYNTHIA MARIE, elementary school educator; m. Lawrence M. Sigmund. BFA, Pittsburg State U., Kans., 1974. Cert. art tchr. K-12 Kans. Tchr. Unified Sch. Dist. 273, Stockton, Kans., 1974—75, Unified Sch. Dist. 240, Arma, Kans., 1975—81, Unified Sch. Dist. 440, Halstead, Kans., 1983—. Recipient VFW Nat. Citizenship Edn. Tchr. award, 2002—03. Mem.: NEA, Unified Tchrs. Assn. Kans. Avocations: drawing, painting, gardening, reading. Office: Unified Sch Dist 440 520 W 6th Halstead KS 67056 Office Phone: 316-835-2694. Business E-Mail: csigmund@usd440.com.

SIH, ANDREW, biologist, educator; b. NYC, Mar. 10, 1954; s. Peter and Helen (Chiu) S.; m. Marie-Sylvie Baltus, Oct. 14, 1983; children: Loric. BS in Biology, SUNY, Stony Brook, 1974; PhD in Biology, U. Calif., Santa Barbara, 1980. Postdoctoral fellow Ohio State U., Columbus, 1980-81, Mich. State U., Hickory Corners, 1981-82, U. Calif., Berkeley, 1982; asst. prof. U. Ky., Lexington, 1982-87, assoc. prof., 1987-91, prof. biology, 1991—, univ. rsch. prof., 1996-97. Vis. scientist Oxford (England) U., 1990; panel mem. NSF, Washington, 1991, 92, 96. Editor: Predation: Direct and Indirect Impacts on Aquatic Communities, 1987; mem. editl. bd. Am. Naturalist, 1997—; contbr. articles to profl. jours. Rsch. grantee NSF, 1985-88, 88-91, 91-93, 93-96, 96—, Training grantee NSF, 1988-91, 91-94, 94—. Mem. Animal Behavior Soc. (pres.-elect 1998), Am. Soc. Naturalists, Ecol. Soc. Am. (edn. com. 1980-83, eminent ecologist com. 1991-92, Buell award 1980), Internat. Soc. Behavioral Ecology, Soc. for Study of Evolution. Achievements include research on effects of conflicting demands on behavior, population and community dynamics of fresh water organisms, the roles of natural selection, evolutionary history and behavioral genetics. Office: U Ky Sch Biol Scis Lexington KY 40506-0001

SIHLER, WILLIAM WOODING, finance educator; b. Seattle, Nov. 17, 1937; s. William and Helen Alice (Wooding) S.; m. Mary Elizabeth Unwin, Aug. 21, 1963; children: Edward Wooding, Jennifer Sihler Zysman. AB summa cum laude in Govt., Harvard U., 1959, MBA with high distinction, 1962, DBA, 1965. Instr., asst. prof. Harvard U. Bus. Sch., 1964-67; asso. prof. Darden Grad. Bus. Sch., U. Va., Charlottesville, 1967-72, prof., 1972-76, A.J. Morris prof., 1976-84, Ronald E. Trzcinski prof., 1984—, assoc. dean acad. affairs, 1972-77; exec. dir. Bankers Assn. Fgn. Trade/Ctr. for Internat. Banking Studies, 1977-91; dir. Tayloe Murphy Ctr. U. Va., 2006—09. Bd. dirs. Curtiss-Wright Corp.; pres. Southeastern Cons. Group, Ltd. Co-author: Financial Management: Text and Cases, 2d edit., 1991, The Troubled Money Business, 1992, Financial Service Organizations: Cases in Strategic Management, 1993, Cases in Applied Corporate Finance, 1994, Building Value with Capital-Structure Strategies, 1998, Financial Turnarounds--Preserving Value, 2001, Smart Financial Management: The Essential Reference for the Successful Small Business, 2004; editor: Classics in Commercial Bank Lending, vol. 1, 1981, vol. 2, 1985; contbr. articles to profl. jours. Vis. com. Sch. Mgmt., Case Western Res. U., 1976-86, bd. overseers, 1980-86. Recipient DeL. K. Jay prize Harvard U., Disting. Prof. award U. Va. Alumni Assn., 1982; C.J. Bonaparte scholar Harvard U.; Sheldon fellow 1959-60. Mem. Fin. Mgmt. Assn., Am. Econ. Assn., Am. Fin. Assn., Eastern Fin. Assn., Univ. Club (N.Y.C.), Harvard Club (N.Y.C.), Greencroft Club (Charlottesville), Phi Beta Kappa, Beta Gamma Sigma. Home: 3215 Heathcote Ln Keswick VA 22947-9160 Office: PO Box 6550 Charlottesville VA 22906-6550 Office Phone: 434-924-7489.

SIKDAR, SIDDHARTHA, engineering educator; married. PhD, U. Wash., Seattle, 2005. Asst. prof. George Mason U., Fairfax, Va., 2008—; sr. fellow U. Wash., Seattle. Mem.: IEEE. Achievements include patents pending for Ultrasound Doppler Vibrometry. Office: George Mason Univ 4400 University Dr MS 1G5 Fairfax VA 22030

SIKDER, ABDUR R., information technology executive, director; s. Abul Hashem Sikder and Shamsunnesa Begum; m. Khurshida Begum, June 28, 1995; children: Sanam, Subah. PhD, U. Sydney, Australia, 2007. Postdoc. fellow Mich. Tech. U., Hmmughton, Mich., 2007, UC Berkeley, Calif., 2007—08; ceo & founder XDOTCOM, Berkeley, 2008—. Author: (travel story) Sydney Theke Vatican. Founder AALO, Sydney, 2005—08. Recipient Hon. Assoc., U. Sydney, 2008. Mem.: IEEE. Achievements include research in protein domain prediction. Office: Xdotcom 1728 Curtis St Berkeley CA 94702 Business E-Mail: sikder@xdotcom.com.

SIKER, EPHRAIM S., anesthesiologist; b. Port Chester, NY, Mar. 24, 1926; s. Samuel S. and Adele (Weiser) S.; m. m. Eileen Mary Bohnel, Aug. 5, 1951; children— Kathleen Ellen, Jeffrey Stephen, David Alan, Paul William, Richard Francis. Student, Duke U., 1943-45; MD, N.Y.U., 1949. Diplomate: Am. Bd. Anesthesiology (dir. 1971—, sec.-treas. 1974-82, pres. 1982-83) Nat. Bd. Med. Examiners. Intern Grasslands Hosp., Valhalla, N.Y., 1949-50, resident in anesthesia, 1950; resident dept. anesthesiology Mercy Hosp., Pitts., 1952-53, assoc. dir. dept., 1955-62, chmn., 1962-92; practice medicine, specializing in anesthesiology Pitts., 1954—; pres. Pitts. Anesthesia Assocs., Ltd., 1967-89; dir. anesthesia services Central Med. Ctr., Pitts., 1973-89. Courtesy staff St. Clair Meml. Hosp., Pitts., 1954—89; clin. prof. dept. anesthesiology U. Pitts. Sch. Medicine, 1968—; mem. exec. com. Am. Bd. Med. Spltys., 1978—81; Exch. cons. Welsh Nat. Sch. Medicine, Cardiff, 1955—56; mem. Pa. Gov.'s Commn. on Profl. Liability Ins., 1968—70; mem. adv. panel U.S. Pharmacopeia, 1970—76; mem. Am. Acupuncture Anesthesia Study Group NAS to Peoples Republic China, 1974; mem. adv. com. on splty. and geog. distbn. of physicians Inst. Medicine NAS, 1974—76; trustee Ednl. Coun. for Fgn. Med. Grads., 1980—82, Mercy Hosp. Found., 1983—95; bd. dirs., sec. Anesthesia Patient Safety Found., 1985—89, mem. exec. com., 1985—92, exec. dir., 1992—97. Author: (with F.F. Foldes) Narcotics and Narcotic Antagonists, 1964; sect. on narcotic: (with F.F. Foldes) numerous other publs. in med. lit. Ency. Brittanica. Served to lt. M.C. USNR, 1950-52. USPHS postdoctoral research fellow, 1954; hon. fellow faculty anaesthetists Royal Coll. Surgeons, Eng., 1974; hon. fellow faculty anesthetists Coll. Medicine South Africa, 1983; recipient Hippocratic award Mercy Hosp., 1982 Fellow Royal Coll. Surgeons Ireland, Faculty Anaesthetists (hon. 1988); mem. Am. Soc. Anesthesiologists (pres. 1973—, bd. dirs. Disting. Svc. award 1984), AMA (alt. del. 1962), Pa. Med. Soc., Allegheny County Med. Soc., Pa. Soc. Anesthesiologists (pres. 1965, Disting. Svc. award 1986), Royal Soc. Medicine (Eng.), Pitts. Acad. Medicine, Am. Coll. Anesthesiologists (bd. govs. 1969-71), World Fedn. Anesthesiologists (chmn. exec. com. 1980-84, v.p. 1984-88), Assn. Anesthesia Program Dirs. (pres. 1987-89), Japanese Soc. Anesthesiologists (hon.). Achievements include developing Siker Laryngoscope, 1956. Home: 185 Crestvue ManorDr Pittsburgh PA 15228-1814 E-mail: rsiker@msn.com. *If you have to tell someone who you are, then you probably aren't. People are measured by more than their deeds, and such estimations are frequently made on the basis of their inter-personal relationships. While achievement and effort usually bear a linear relationship to each other, the impact that the achiever has on society depends upon the impact he makes on individuals.*

SIKES, CYNTHIA LEE, actress, singer; b. Coffeyville, Kans., Jan. 2, 1954; d. Neil and Pat (Scott) S.; m. Alan Bud Yorkin, June 24, 1989. Student, Am. Conservatory Theater, San Francisco, 1977-79. Actor: (TV series) St. Elsewhere, 1981—83, L.A. Law, 1989, JAG, 2000—01, Arliss, Young and the Restless, 2008, (TV movies) Oceans of Fire, 1986, His Mistress, 1990; prodr., actor: Sins of Silence, 1996; actor: (films) Man Who Loved Women, That's Life, Arthur on the Rocks, Love Hurts, 1988, Possums, 1998, Going Shopping, 2005, (Broadway musical) Into the Woods, 1988—89. Active Hollywood Women's Polit. Com.; apptd. Pres. Clinton's Adv. Com. on Arts John F. Kennedy Ctr. for Performing Arts, 1999; apptd. commr. Calif. Svc. Corps, 2005-08., adv. bd. mem. UCLA Recipient Gov.'s Medal of Merit, Kans., 1986. Democrat. Avocations: hiking, writing, reading.

SIKES, MARY TAGGART, librarian; b. Oceanside, Calif., Aug. 29, 1964; d. Billy Ray and Joycln Ruth Taggart; m. Clay Daniel Sikes, Dec. 17, 1995; children: Victoria Celeste, Zachary Daniel. AA, Weatherford Coll., Tex., 1984; BA, U. N. Tex., 1987, MLS, 1993. Receiving clk. Walden Books, Denton, Tex., 1986, asst. store mgr. Denton, Irving, Tex., 1986-90, store mgr. Sherman, Tex., 1990-93; reference libr. Ft. Worth Pub. Libr., 1993-95, reference asst. mgr., 1995-98, interlibrary loan supr., 1998—2007, periodicals/government docs. supr., 2007—. Big Bros. Big Sisters, Tarrant County; Junior Girl Scouts troop leader. Mem.: ALA, Tex. Libr. Assn. (alt. counselor interlibr. loan roundtable 1999—2000, counselor interlibr. loan roundtable 2001—03, mem. Woll meml. grant com. 2002—07, sec.-treas. 2003—04, vice chair interlibrary loan roundtable 2005—06, chair interlibr. loan roundtable 2006—07, chair PLD scholarship com. 2007), Phi Theta Kappa, Beta Sigma Phi. Republican. Home: 637 Catalpa Rd Fort Worth TX 76131 Office: Fort Worth Pub Libr 500 W 3d St Fort Worth TX 76102 Office Phone: 817-871-7733.

SIKLOS, RICHARD, reporter; Media editor BusinessWeek; editor-in-chief Inside mag.; corp. media reporter NY Times, 2005—07; editor at large Fortune, 2007—. Author: Shades of Black, 1995, Shades of Black: Conrad Black - His Rise and Fall, 2004. Office: Fortune 16th Fl 1271 6th Ave New York NY 10020 Office Phone: 212-556-1474. Office Fax: 212-556-1448.

SIKMA, JACK WAYNE, professional basketball coach, retired professional basketball player; b. Kankakee, Ill., Nov. 14, 1955; m. Shawn Strickland, 1984; children: Jacob, Lucas, Nathan. B, Ill. Wesleyan U., Bloomington, 1977. Ctr. Seattle Supersonics, 1977-86, spl. assignments coach, 2003—04, asst. coach, 2004—08; ctr. Milw. Bucks, 1986—91; asst. coach Houston Rockets, 2008—. Named to All-Rookie Team, NBA, 1978, Western Conf. All-Star Team, 1979—85. Achievements include member of NBA Finals championship winning Seattle Supersonics, 1979; leading the NBA in: defensive rebounds, 1982, 1984; free throw percentage, 1988. Avocation: golf. Office: Houston Rockets 1510 Polk St Houston TX 77002*

SIKORA, DIANA MARIE, elementary school educator; b. St. Louis, June 13, 1945; d. Roy K. and Margaret Anne (Heffner) Hennen; m. Theodore George Sikora, Nov. 12, 1966; children: Christine Ann Fix, Elizabeth Jane Pritchard. BS in Edn., Southern Ill. U., Edwardsville, 1967; MEd in Counseling, U. Mo., St. Louis, 1996. Cert. in counseling Mo. Tchr. grade 1 Commons Lane Sch., Florissant, Mo., 1967—69; tchr. grade 2-3 Graham Sch., Florissant, 1971—74; tchr. St. Ferdinand Cath. Sch., Florissant, 1974—86, Ferguson Mid. Sch., Mo., 1986—92; tchr. Vogt grade 4-5 Ferguson Florissant Sch. Dist., 1992—99; guidance counselor grades k-6 Halls Ferry Sch., Florissant, 1999—2007. Supt. Salem Sunday Sch., 2000—. Named Bldg. Tchr. of Yr., Graham Sch., 1973, Ferguson Mid. Sch., 1989. Mem.: Chi Iota, Alpha Delta Kappa (chaplain 1999). Avocations: singing, nature, reading. Home: 1800 Layven Ave Florissant MO 63031 Office Phone: 314-831-1023.

SIKOROVSKY, EUGENE FRANK, retired lawyer; b. Jackson, Mich., Nov. 27, 1927; s. Frank Joseph and Betty Dorothy (Malik) S.; m. Patricia O'Byrne, July 11, 1953; children: Paul, Charles, Catherine, Elizabeth, Emily. BSEE, U. Mich., 1948; LLB, Harvard U., 1951. Bar: N.Y. 1952, Va. 1970, Ill. 1978. Assoc. predecessor firms Cahill, Gordon & Reindel, 1954-63, ptnr., 1964-68; v.p., gen. counsel, dir. Reynolds Metals Co., Richmond, Va., 1969-76; gen. counsel Gould Inc., Rolling Meadows, Ill., 1977-79, v.p., 1977-81; dep. gen. counsel Bell & Howell Co., Skokie, Ill., 1981-83, v.p., 1983-88, gen. counsel, 1983-92, sec., 1984-92, sr. v.p., dir., 1988-92. Lt. USNR, 1951—54. Mem. Tau Beta Pi, Eta Kappa Nu, Phi Eta Sigma, Phi Delta Theta. Episcopalian. Home: 720 Grandview Ln Lake Forest IL 60045-3953 Personal E-mail: genesikor@gmail.com.

SIKORSKI, GERRY, lobbyist, lawyer, former congressman; b. Breckenridge, Minn., Apr. 26, 1948; s. Elroy and Helen S.; m. Susan Jane Erkel, Aug. 24, 1974; 1 dau., Anne. BA with highest honors, U. Minn., 1970; JD with high honors, U. Minn. Law Sch., 1973. Bar: Minn. 1973, DC 1997. Mem. Minn. Senate, 1976-82, majority whip, 1980-82; mem. US Congress from 6th Minn. dist., 1983—93; freshman whip 98th-99th Congresses; ptnr. Holland & Knight LLP, Washington, gov. sect. leader, former chmn. dirs. com., former chair, pub. law dept. Mem. Energy and Commerce Com., Post Office and Civil Service Com., Select Com. on Children Youth and Families; served with Chmn. John D. Dingell, Subcommittee on Oversight and Investigations; vice chair to Henry Waxman, Health and Environment Subcommittee; sponsor Clean Air Act. Author: Community Right to Know Law, Acid Rain Control Act. Named one of 50 Top Lobbyists, Washingtonian mag., 2007. Mem.: ABA, DC Bar, Phi Beta Kappa. Office: Holland & Knight LLP 2099 Pennsylvania Ave NW Ste 100 Washington DC 20006 Office Phone: 202-828-5007. Business E-Mail: gsikorsk@hklaw.com.*

SIL, SAMIK, geophysicist; b. Kolkata, West Bengal, India, Dec. 15, 1975; s. Narayan Chandra and Krishna Sil. BS, Indian Sch. Mines, Dhanbad; MS, U. Alaska Fairbanks, 2006; PhD, U. Tex. at Austin, 2009. Rsch. asst. U. Tex. at Austin, 2006—09; geophysicist ConocoPhillips, Houston, 2009—. Sr. exec. PCI India Pvt. Ltd., Kolkata, 2000—03. Pres. U. Tex. at Austin Geophys. Soc., 2007—08. Fellowship, Marathon Oil Co., 2009, Chevron Inc., 2007—08. Mem.: AGU, AAPG, SEG. Achievements include research in seismic anisotropy and fracture characterization. Personal E-mail: samiksil@gmail.com.

SILANTIEN, JOHN JOSEPH, music educator; b. Pawtucket, RI, Nov. 20, 1947; s. John and Lucy Helen Silantien; children: John Andrew, Ryan Danek. BA in Music Edn., Hartt Coll. Music, West Hartford, Conn., 1964—68; MusM, Cath. U., DC, 1968—71; MusD, U. Ill., Urbana, 1975—80. Soloist The U. S. Army Band, Washington, DC, 1968—71; choral, gen. music tchr. Andrew Jackson Jr. H.S., Suitland, Md., 1971—72; dir. choral activities Northwood H.S., Silver Spring, Md., 1972—75; asst. prof. Eastman Sch. Music, Rochester, NY, 1977—80; editor The Choral Jour., Lawton, Okla., 1992—98; music dir. San Antonio Symphony Mastersingers, 1983—; dir. choral activities U. Tex., San Antonio, 1980—; dir. choral music U. Presbyn. Ch., San Antonio. Lectr. in field. Contbr. articles to profl. jours. Specialist five US Army, 1968—71, Ft. Myer, Arlington, Va. Recipient, Fulbright-Hays Award, 1978—79; grantee, Rockefeller Found., 1973; scholar, Presser Found., 1964—65. Mem.: Tex. Choral Directors Assn., Tex. Music Educators Assn., Coll. Music Soc., Internat. Fedn. for Choral Music, Chorus Am., Am. Choral Directors Assn., Pi Kappa Lambda, Phi Mu Alpha Sinfonia. Office: Dept Music Univ Texas San Antonio TX 78249 Office Fax: 210-458-4381. Business E-Mail: john.silantien@utsa.edu.

SILAS, CECIL JESSE, retired petroleum company executive; b. Miami, Fla., Apr. 15, 1932; s. David Edward and Hilda Videll (Carver) S.; m. Theodosea Hejda, Nov. 27, 1965; children: Karla, Peter, Michael, James. BSChemE, Ga. Inst. Tech., Atlanta, 1953. With Phillips Petroleum Co., Bartlesville, Okla., 1953-94, pres. Europe-Africa, Brussels and London, 1968-74, mng. dir. natural resource group Europe/Africa London, 1974-76, v.p. gas and gas liquids div. natural resources group Bartlesville, 1976-78, sr. v.p. natural resources group, 1978-80, exec. v.p. exploration and prodn., minerals, gas and gas liquids, 1980-82, pres., chief operating officer, 1982-85, chmn., CEO, 1985-94. Bd. dirs. Boys/Girls Clubs Am., Atlanta, parton councillor Atlantic Coun. of the U.S.; bd. dirs. Okla. Found. for Excellence, Ga. Tech. Found.; trustee Frank Phillips Found. Served to 1st lt. Chem. Corps, AUS, 1954-56. Decorated comdr. Order St. Olaf (Norway); inducted into Ga. Inst. Tech. Athletic Hall of Fame, 1959, recipient Former Scholar-Athlete Total Person award, 1988; inducted into Okla. Bus. Hall of Fame, 1989; named CEO of Yr., Internat. TV Assn., 1987. Mem. Am. Petroleum Inst., U.S. C. of C. (past chmn. bd. dirs.), 25 Yr. Club, Phi Delta Theta. Avocations: fishing, golf, hunting. Office: PO Box 2127 Bartlesville OK 74005-2127

SILAS, PAMALA M., professional society administrator; BS in Econs., DePaul U., Chgo. Regional adminstrv. specialist Four-Phase Systems, Inc.; assoc. dir. Am. Indian Econ. Devel. Assn.; exec. dir. Met. Tenants Orgn., Chgo., Am. Indian Sci. and Engring. Soc., Albuquerque. Mem. Cmty. Devel. Adv. Coun., Chgo., Chgo. Coun. Women, Low Income Housing Trust Fund Bd., Chgo., Menominee Tribal Gaming Commn. Office: Am Indian Sci and Engring Soc PO Box 9828 Albuquerque NM 87119-9828 Office Phone: 505-765-1052 ext. 111. Office Fax: 505-765-5608. E-mail: pam@aises.org.

SILBER, DAVID ELLIOT, clinical psychologist, educator; b. Detroit, Sept. 19, 1935; s. Morris and Ethel (Kraunz) S.; m. Doris J. Kendler, Apr. 29, 1962 (div. Mar. 1987); children: Barry I., Alan M., Daniel J.; m. Eileen Rose, June 1997. BA, Wayne State U., 1958; MA, Ohio U., 1960; PhD, U. Mich., 1965. Lic. clin. psychologist, D.C. Asst. prof. psychology George Washington U., Washington, 1965-70, assoc. prof., 1970-76, prof., 1976—; chair, dept. psychology U. Washington, 1991—96, 1999—2000. Vis. assoc. prof. Hebrew U. of Jerusalem, 1972-73; cons. U.S. Secret Svc., Washington, 1986-94. Co-author: Apperceptive Personality Test, 1989; contbr. articles to profl. jours. Fellow Soc. Personality Assessment; mem. Am. Psychol. Assn. Avocations: collecting pens, folk dancing. Office: George Washington U Dept Of Psychology Washington DC 20052-0001

SILBER, JEFF SCOTT, physician, educator; b. Syosset, NY, Feb. 9, 1964; s. Michael and Rosalie Silber; m. Laurie Beth Musinger, Nov. 23, 1996; children: Jared Samuel, Brett Landon, Dylan Jake. MD, NY Med. Coll., Valhalla, 1995. Assoc. prof., attending physician North Shore-LIJ Health Sys., New Hyde Park, NY. Philanthropic Med. Socs. & Action Coms., NY, 2001. Spine fellowship, Thomas Jefferson U., 2000—09. Office: North Shore-LI Jewish Med 865 Northern Blvd Great Neck NY 11021 Office Fax: 516-918-6363. Business E-Mail: jsilber@nshs.edu.

SILBER, JOHN ROBERT, retired academic administrator, law and philosophy educator; b. San Antonio, Aug. 15, 1926; s. Paul G. and Jewell (Joslin) S.; m. Kathryn Underwood, July 12, 1947 (dec.); children: David Joslin (dec.), Mary Rachel, Judith Karen, Kathryn Alexandra, Martha Claire, Laura Ruth, Caroline Jocasta. Postgrad., Northwestern U., 1944; BA summa cum laude, Trinity U., 1947; postgrad., Yale Div. Sch., 1948, U. Tex. Sch. Law, 1949; MA, Yale, 1952, PhD, 1956; L.H.D., Kalamazoo Coll., 1970; many others. Instr. dept. philosophy Yale U., 1952—55; asst. prof. U. Tex., Austin, 1955—59, assoc. prof., 1959—62, prof. philosophy, 1962—70, chmn. dept. philosophy, 1962—67, Univ. prof. arts and letters, 1967—70, chmn. (Comparative Studies Program), 1967, dean Coll. Arts and Scis., 1967—70; Univ. prof., prof. philosophy and law Boston U., 1971—, pres., 1971-96, prof. internat. rels., 1996—2003, chancellor, 1996—2003, pres. emeritus, 2003—. Vis. prof. Bonn U., 1960; fellow Kings Coll. U. London, 1963-64; bd. dirs. Mut. Am. Inst. Funds, Inc. Author: The Ethical Significance of Kant's Religion, 1960, Straight Shooting: What's Wrong With America and How to Fix It, 1989, Ist Amerika zu retten?, 1992, Architecture Of The Absurd: How 'Genius' Disfigured A Practical Art, 2007; editor: Kant's Religion Within the Limits of Reason Alone, 1960, Works in Continental Philosophy, 1967—; assoc. editor: Kant-Studien, 1968-; contbr. to profl. jours. Chmn. Tex. Soc. to Abolish Capital Punishment, 1960-69; mem. Nat. Commn. United Meth. Higher Edn., 1974-77; exec. bd. Nat. Humanities Inst., 1975-78; trustee Coll. St. Scholastica, 1973-85, U. Denver, 1985-89, WGBH Ednl. Found., 1971-96, Adelphi U., 1989-97; bd. visitors Air U., 1974-80; bd. dirs. Greater Boston coun. Boy Scouts Am., 1981-93, v.p. fin., 1981-93, Silver Beaver award, 1989, Disting. Eagle, 1997; mem. Nat. Humanities Faculty, 1968-73, Nat. Captioning Inst., 1985-94; bd. advisors Matchette Found., 1969-70; mem. Nat. Bipartisan Commn. on Ctrl. Am., 1983-84, U.S. Strategic Inst., 1983-2001; Presdl. Adv. Bd. Radio Broadcasting to Cuba, 1985-92, v.p. 1984-98, vice chmn., 1998-2001; bd. dir. US Strategic Inst., 1983-2001, v.p., 1984-98, vice chmn., 1998-2001; adv. bd. Schurman Libr. of Am. Hist., Ruprecht-Karl U., Heidelberg, 1986—; mem. def. policy bd. U.S. Dept. Def., 1987-90; mem. internat. coun.advisors Inst. for Humanities at Salado, 1988—; bd. dirs. New Eng. Holocaust Meml. Com., 1989-95, Brit. Inst. of U.S., 1989—, Bette Davis Found., 1997—, Boston Police Found., 1997—; Dem. gubernatorial candidate of Mass., 1990; bd. dirs. U.S. Strategic Inst., 1983-2001, vice chmn., 1998-2001; bd. dirs., vice chmn. Americans for Med. Progress, 1992—, chmn., 1994-95, mem. exec. com. 1995—; chmn. Mass. Bd. Edn., 1996-99; bd. advisors Nat. Assn. Scholars. Recipient E. Harris Harbison award for disting. tchg. Danforth Found., 1966, Wilbur Lucius Cross medal Yale Grad. Sch., 1971, Outstanding Civilian Svc. medal U.S. Army, 1985, Disting. Pub. Svc. award Anti-Defamation League of B'nai B'rith, 1989, Horatio Alger award, 1992, Am.-Swiss Friendship award, 1991, Israel Peace medal,

1985, Ehrenmedaille U. Heidelberg, 1986, White House Small Bus. award for entrepreneurial excellence, 1986, Cross of Paideia, Greek Orthodox Archdiocese of North and South Am., 1988, Pro Bene Meritis award U. Tex., Austin, 1997; Fulbright rsch. fellow Germany, 1959-60; Guggenheim fellow Eng., 1963-64; decorated with Knight Comdr.'s Cross with Star of Order of Merit Fed. Republic of Germany, 1983; commandeur Nat. Order of Arts and Letters (France), 1985. Fellow Royal Soc. Arts; mem. Am. Philos. Assn., Am. Soc. Polit. and Legal Philosophy, Royal Inst. Philosophy, Am. Assn. Higher Edn., Nat. Assn. Ind. Colls. and Univs. (dir. 1976-81), Phi Beta Kappa. Office: Boston Univ 73 Bay State Rd Boston MA 02215-1708 Office Phone: 617-353-2208.

SILBER, SHERMAN J., urologist, consultant; b. Chgo., Dec. 18, 1941; BA in English, U. Mich., 1966, MD, 1966. Lic. Alaska, Calif., Mich., Mo., NY, cert. Am. Bd. Urology, 1977, Am. Urologic Assn., 1978. Intern Stanford U., 1966—67; gynecology asst. US Pub. Health Svc., 1967—69; resident in nephrology U. Mich., 1969—70, resident in urology, 1970—73; urologist & reproductive microsurgeon St. Luke's Hosp., dir. Infertility Ctr. of St. Louis; assoc. dir. New Hope Infertility Ctr. Instr. U. Melbourne Med. Sch., 1973—74, U. Calif. Med. Sch., 1974—76; cons. Dutch-Speaking Free U., Tel Hashomer Hosp., Tel Aviv, Kato Ladies Clinic, Tokyo, MIT Whitehead Inst. Author: How to Get Pregnant, 2007. Office: 224 S Woods Mill Rd Ste 730 Chesterfield MO 63017 Office Phone: 314-576-1400. Office Fax: 314-576-1442.*

SILBERBERG, DONALD H., neurologist; b. Washington, Mar. 2, 1934; s. William Aaron and Leslie Frances (Stone) S.; m. Marilyn Alice Damsky, June 7, 1959; children: Mark, Alan. MD, U. Mich., 1958; MA (hon.), U. Pa., 1971. Intern Mt. Sinai Hosp., NYC, 1958-59; clin. assoc. in neurology NIH, Bethesda, Md., 1959-61; Fulbright scholar Nat. Hosp., London, 1961-62; NINDB spl. fellow in neuro-ophthalmology Washington U., St. Louis, 1962-63; assoc. neurology U. Pa., 1963-65, asst. prof., 1965-67, assoc. prof., 1967-71, prof., 1971-73, acting chmn. dept., 1973-74, prof., vice chmn. neurology, 1974-82, chmn., 1982-94, sr. assoc. dean, dir. internat. programs, 1994—2004. Active staff U. Pa. Med. Ctr., Phila.; pres., CEO Betasteron Found., Inc., 1994-2007 Contbr. articles to profl. jours., abstracts, chpts. in books. Recipient grants in study of multiple sclerosis. Mem.: Global Network for Rsch. on Mental and Neurol. Health (founding v.p.), World Fedn. Neurology, Phila. Neurol. Soc. (pres. 1978—79), Assn. Univ. Profs. Neurology (pres.-elect 1993), Nat. Multiple Sclerosis Soc. (trustee 1997—99, 2001—03), Coll. Physicians Phila., Am. Acad. Neurology, Am. Neurol. Assn. (hon.), Alpha Omega Alpha. Office: U Pa Med Ctr Dept Neurology 3400 Spruce St Philadelphia PA 19104-4206

SILBERBERG, RICHARD HOWARD, lawyer; b. NYC, Feb. 20, 1951; BA, U. Wis., 1972; JD, NYU, 1975. Bar: NY 1976, US Dist. Ct. (so. and ea. dists.) NY, 1976, US Ct. Appeals (2d cir.) 1981, US Ct. Internat. Trade 1983, U.S. Ct. Appeals (fed. cir.) 1988, US Ct. Appeals (3d cir.) 1991, US Supreme Ct. 1994, US Ct. Appeals (11th cir.) 1996, US Ct. Appeals (1st cir.) 1997. Assoc. Delson & Gordon, NYC, 1975-83, ptnr., 1983—87; ptnr., trial group Dorsey & Whitney, NYC, 1988—, mng. ptnr., 1994—97, co-chair global trial group, 2004—06, chmn. global advocacy group, 2007—. Mem. panel arbitrators U.S. Dist. Ct. for Ea. Dist. N.Y., 1987-; mem. panel mediators US Dist. Ct. So. Dist. NY, 1992—; trustee Lawyers Com. Civil Rights Under Law, 1992-; dir. Fund Modern Cts., 1999-, High 5 Tickets to the Arts, 1999—, NYU Law Alumni Assn., 2002-06. Mng. editor NYU Jour. Internat. Law and Politics, 1974-75. Mem.: Am. Arbitration Assn. (mem. panel neutrals 1992—). Office: Dorsey & Whitney LLP 250 Park Ave New York NY 10177-0001 Office Phone: 212-415-9231. Office Fax: 212-953-7201. Business E-Mail: silberberg.richard@dorsey.com.

SILBERFARB, PETER MICHAEL, psychiatrist, educator; b. Jersey City, Oct. 28, 1938; m. Anne Wagner, 1962; children: Benjamin, Leah S. BS, Bucknell U., 1960; postgrad., NYU, 1960-61; MD, Hahnemann Coll., 1965; MA (hon.), Dartmouth Coll., 1986. Diplomate Nat. Bd. Med. Examiners, Am. Bd. Psychiatry and Neurology (pres. 1998). Intern Hahnemann Med. Coll. Hosp., Phila., 1965-66; resident in internal medicine Dartmouth Affiliated Hosps., Hanover, NH, 1966-68, resident in internal medicine and psychiatry, 1968-69, psychiatry resident, 1971-72, chief resident in psychiatry, 1972-73; instr. in psychiatry Med. Sch., Dartmouth Coll., Hanover, 1972-73, asst. prof. of psychiatry, 1973-77, dir. tng. and edn., 1976-86, assoc. prof. clin. psychiatry, assoc. prof. clin. medicine, 1977-80, dir. grad. edn. and residency tng., 1978-86, assoc. prof. psychiatry, assoc. prof. medicine, 1980-82, dir. tng. and edn., 1984—2002, prof. psychiatry, prof. medicine, 1986—2002, chmn. dept. psychiatry, 1986—2002, Raymond Sobel prof. psychiatry, 2003, prof. emeritus. Cons. psychiatrist Mary Hitchcock Meml. Hosp., Hanover, 1973—; dir. psychiat. in-patient svc. Dartmouth-Hitchcock Med. Ctr., 1973-75, dir. cancer psychiatry program Norris Cotton Cancer Ctr., 1975-2002, acting dir. psychiatry consultation svc., 1977-79, assoc. dir. cancer control Norris Ctr., 1981-86; sec. psychiatry com. Cancer and Leukemia Group B, 1976-79, vice chmn., 1979-2000; mem. grant rev. com. for cancer control Nat. Cancer Inst., 1979, 80, mem. spl. grant rev. com., 1981, 82, 85, cons. to bd. sci. counselors, 1982, mem. cancer control grant rev. com., 1986-90; vice chmn. adv. com. for psychosocial and behavioral rsch. Am. Cancer Soc., 1982-88, chmn., 1988-89; cons. collaborative ctr. for cancer pain relief WHO, Milan, 1985; mem. accreditation coun. for grad. med. edn. Appeals Bd. for Psychiatry, Chgo., 1983, specialist site visitor, 1985-90, mem. residency rev. com. for psychiatry, 1991-96; dir. Am. Bd. Family Practice, 1996-2000; mem. exec. com. Am. Bd. Med. Specialties, 1996-99. Author chpts. to books; mem. editl. bd. Jour. Psychosocial Oncology, 1983-91, Internat. Jour. Psychiatry in Medicine, 1986-90, Contemporary Psychiatry, 1987-91, Psychooncology, 1991-96; referee numerous manuscripts; contbr. articles to profl. jours. Surgeon USPHS, 1969-71. Fellow Am. Psychiat. Assn. (cons. to task force on treatment if psychiat. disorders 1989), Am. Coll. Psychiatrists; mem. AMA, Am. Soc. Psychiat. Oncology/AIDS, Am. Soc. Clin. Oncology, Am. Assn. Dirs. Psychiat. Residency Tng. (mem. curriculum com. 1979-88, mem. task force on med. students and residents, chmn. com. regional dirs. 1984-88, mem. exec. com. 1984-88), Am. Psychosomatic Soc., N.H. Psychiat. Soc. (chmn. membership com. 1974-76, chmn. continuing edn. com. 1977-79), N.H. Med. Soc., Assn. Rsch. in Nervous and Mental Disease, Assn. Acad. Psychiatry, Benjamin Rush Soc. Home: Bragg Hill Norwich VT 05055 Office: Dartmouth Coll Med Sch Dept Psychiatry Lebanon NH 03756-0001

SILBERGELD, ARTHUR F., lawyer; b. St. Louis, June 1, 1942; s. David and Sabina (Silbergeld) S.; m. Carol Ann Schwartz, May 1, 1970; children: Diana Lauren, Julia Kay. BA, U. Mich., 1968; M in City Planning, U. Pa., 1971; JD, Temple U., 1975. Bar: N.Y. 1976, Calif. 1978, D.C. 1983, U.S. Ct. Appeals (2nd cir.), U.S. Ct. Appeals (9th cir.), U.S. Ct. Appeals (D.C. cir.), U.S. Supreme Ct. 1999. Assoc. Vladeck, Elias, Vladeck & Lewis, NYC, 1975-77; field atty. NLRB, LA, 1977-78; ptnr., head employment law practice group McKenna, Conner & Cuneo, LA, 1978-89; ptnr. Graham & James, LA, 1990-96; labor ptnr. Sonnenschein Nath & Rosenthal, LA, 1996-99; ptnr. Proskauer Rose LLP, LA, 1999—. Instr. extension divsn. UCLA, 1981-89. Author: Doing Business in California: An Employment Law Handbook, 2nd edit., 1997, Advising California Employers, 1990-95 supplements; contbr. articles to profl. jours. Founding mem. L.A. Mus. Contemporary Art; bd. dirs. Bay Cities unit Am. Cancer Soc., Calif., 1981-85, Jewish Family Svc., L.A., 1981-85, So. Calif. Employers Roundtable, Leadership coun., So. Poverty Law Ctr., Leadership Task Force, Drs. Without Borders; pres. Mo. Valley Fedn. of Temple Youth, 1959-60, Exec. Com., Calif. Com. South Human Rights Watch, 2005-; treas. L.A. Child Devel. Ctr., 2001-. Mem. ABA (labor and employment law sect.), L.A. County Bar Assn. (mem. exec. com. 1984-, chmn. labor and employment law sect. 1999-2000, trustee 2000-01), Mus. Modern Art (N.Y.C.), Coll. of Labor and Employment Lawyers. Office: Proskauer Rose LLP 2049 Century Park E Fl 32 Los Angeles CA 90067-3101 Office Phone: 310-557-2900.

SILBERGELD, ELLEN KOVNER, epidemiologist, toxicologist, researcher; b. Washington, July 29, 1945; d. Joseph and Mary (Gion) Kovner; m. Alan Mark Silbergeld, 1969; children: Sophia, Nicholas. AB, Vassar Coll., 1967; PhD, Johns Hopkins U., 1972. Kennedy fellow Johns Hopkins Med. Sch., Balt., 1974—75; scientist NIH, Bethesda, Md., 1975—81; chief toxics scientist Environ. Def. Fund, Washington, 1982—90; prof. epidemiology, toxicology and pharmacology U.Md., Balt., 1990—2001, affil. prof. environ. law, 1990—2001, dir. program in human health and environ., 1996—2000, prof. dept. pathology, 1995—2000, adj. prof. dept. pharmacology and exptl. therapeutics, 1995—2000; prof. environ. health scis. epidemiology, and health policy and mgmt. Bloomberg School Public Health, Johns Hopkins U., Balt., 2001—. Mem. sci. adv. bd. EPA, 1983—89, 1993—99, Dept. Energy, 1994—95; mem. bd. on environ. sci. and toxicology NAS-NRC, 1983—89; mem. Com. Geosci. Environ. and Resources, 1994—98; mem. bd. biotech. and agr., 1999—2004; mem. bd. sci. councellors Nat. Inst. Environ. Health Scis., 1987—93; cons. Oil and Chem. Atomic Workers, 1970, NSF, 1974—75, OECD, 1987—90. Mem. editl. bd.: Neurobehavioral Toxicology, 1979—87, Am. Jour. Medicine, 1980—, Neurotoxicology, 1981—86, Environ. Rsch., 1983—, editor-in-chief:, 1994—. Mem. Homewood Friends Meeting. Recipient Wolman award, Md. Pub. Health Assn., 1991, Barsky award, APHA, 1992, Md. Gov. Excellence citation, 1990, 1993; Fulbright fellow, London, 1967, Woodrow Wilson and Danforth fellow, 1967, NAS Exch. fellow, Yugoslavia, 1976, MacArthur Found. fellow, 1993—98, Baldwin scholar, Coll. Notre Dame. Mem.: APHA, AAAS, Soc. for Neurosci., Soc. Toxicology, Soc. for Occupl. and Environ. Health (sec.-treas. 1983—85, pres. 1987—89), Collegium Ramazzini (councillor), Delta Omega, Phi Beta Kappa. Office: Bloomberg Sch Pub Health 615 N Wolfe St Baltimore MD 21205

SILBERGLEIT, ALEXANDER, physicist, mathematician; b. St. Petersburg, Russia, Mar. 24, 1948; s. Samuil Isaacovich S. and Irina Petrovna Shevyakhova; m. Evgeniya Georgievna Makarova, Feb. 15, 1970; children: Dmitri, Kseniya. Engr., Physicist, Poly. Inst., Leningrad, 1972; PhD in Math. Physics, A.F. Ioffe Phys.-Tech. Inst., Leningrad, 1978, DSc, 1987. Jr. scientist A.F. Ioffe Phys.-Tech. Inst., Acad. Scis. USSR, Leningrad, 1972-78, scientist, 1978-84, lead scientist, 1988-91, lab. head, 1992—94, sr. scientist, 1984-88, GP-B Stanford U., 1994—. Assoc. prof. Leningrad Poly. Inst., 1974-79, prof., 1990-92; reviewer Math. Revs., Ann Arbor, Mich., 1978-2003. Author: Spectral Thoery of Guided Waves, 1996; translator: Hot Rock (Donald Westlake), 1990, Yakov Ilich Frenkel (V. Ya. Frenkel), 1996; mem. editl. bd. Jour. Energy Rsch., 1993-1996; contbr. articles to profl. jours. Mem. Com. Soviet Scientists for Peace Against Nuclear Threat, Leningrad, 1988-94. Mem. Am. Math. Soc., Am. Phys. Soc., Leningrad Phys. Soc. Avocations: literature, music, basketball, chess. Office: Stanford Univ 11 GP-B HEPL Stanford CA 94305-4085 Office Phone: 650-723-1641. Office Fax: 650-725-8312.

SILBERLING, BRADLEY MITCHELL, film director; b. Calif., Sept. 8, 1962; s. Robert Murray and Joyce (Tucker) S.; m. Amy Brenneman Sept. 30, 1995; 1 child. BA, U. Calif., Santa Barbara, 1984; MFA, UCLA, 1987. Dir. Universal Studios, Universal City, Calif., 1987—. Writer, prodr.: Moonlight Mile, 2002; exec. prodr. Bananas, 2004; dir., editor (film) Repairs, 1987 (Eagle award Council on Internat. Nontheatrical Events 1987); dir.: (TV series) Alfred Hitchcock Presents, 1988, Doogie Howser, M.D., 1990-91, L.A. Law, 1991, NYPD Blue, 1993, Judging Amy, 1999, Felicity, 1999, others, (films) Casper, 1995, City of Angels, 1998, Lemony Snicket's A Series of Unfortunate Events, 2004, dir., exec. prodr., writer 10 Items of Less, 2006, dir. Land of the Lost, 2009 Democrat. Avocations: still photography, soccer. Office: Universal Studios 100 Universal City Plz Universal City CA 91608-1002*

SILBERLING, LOUISE STILLMAN, sociologist, writer, editor; d. Edwyn and Margaret Ann Pargellis Silberling. BS, U. Wis., Madison, 1985; MS, Cornell U., Ithaca, NY, 1992, PhD, 2000. Cert. fluent spkr. in Portuguese, Spanish, French, and English NY, 2009. Mem. editl. office Philos. Rev., Cornell U., 2006—; environment and devel. cons.; writer and editor. Vis. fellow Yale U., 1994; sec. bd. Atmosphere Conservancy, Ft. Collins, Colo., 2008—. Contbr. chapters to books, articles to profl. jours. Vol. Kennebunkport Conservation Trust, Kennebunkport, Maine, Carecen, Washington, 1985—88, Paleontol. Rsch. Inst., Ithaca, 2006—08. Fellow, Conservation and Rsch. Found., 1992, 1998, Post-doc. fellowship, Rockefeller Found., 2002—03, Fulbright-Hays Doctoral Rsch. fellow, Fulbright Commn., Writing grant, Polson Inst. Global Devel., 1998, grant, FLAS, 1998—99, Rsch. grant, Cornell Internat. Inst. Food and Agrl. Devel. Mem.: AAA, IASCP, RSS, ASA, LASA, Phi Kappa Phi, Gamma Sigma Delta, Alpha Kappa Delta. Achievements include research in participatory land use planning in the Brazilian Amazon for extractive reserves.

SILBERMAN, JOHN ALAN, lawyer; b. Balt., Sept. 20, 1951; s. Ronnie A. and Dovera (Gogel) S. BA, Northwestern U., 1973; JD, Harvard U., 1976. Bar: N.Y. 1977, U.S. Dist. Ct. (so. and ea. dists.) N.Y. 1977. Assoc. Paul, Weiss, Rifkind, Wharton & Garrison, NYC, 1976-84, ptnr., 1985-96; pvt. practice NYC, 1996—. Mem.: NY Bar Assn., NY City Bar Assn., Phi Beta Kappa. Office: 145 E 57th St New York NY 10022-2141 Office Phone: 212-319-3737. Office Fax: 212-319-8188.

SILBERMAN, LAURENCE HIRSCH, federal judge; b. York, Pa., Oct. 12, 1935; s. William and Anna (Hirsch) S.; m. Rosalie G. Gaull, Apr. 28, 1957 (dec. Feb. 23, 2007); children: Robert Stephen, Katherine DeBoer Balaban, Anne Gaull Otis. BA, Dartmouth Coll., 1957; LLB, Harvard U., 1961. Bar: Hawaii 1962, DC 1973. Assoc. Moore, Torkildson & Rice and Quinn & Moore, Honolulu, 1961-64; ptnr. Moore, Silberman & Schulze, Honolulu, 1964-67; atty. appellate divsn. gen. counsel's office NLRB, Washington, 1967-69; solicitor US Dept. Labor, Washington, 1969-70, under sec., 1970-73; ptnr. Steptoe & Johnson LLP, Washington, 1973-74; dep. atty. gen. US Dept. Justice, Washington, 1974-75; US amb. to Yugoslavia US Dept. State, Belgrade, 1975-77; mng. ptnr. Morrison & Foerster LLP, Washington, 1978-79, 83-85; exec. v.p. Crocker Nat. Bank, San Francisco, 1979-83; judge US Ct. Appeals (DC cir.), Washington, 1985—2000, sr. judge, 2000—. Lectr. labor law and legis. U. Hawaii, 1962—63; adj. prof. adminstrv. law Georgetown U., Washington, 1987—94, 1997, 1999—2001, NYU, 1995, 96, Harvard U., 1998; adj. prof. labor law Georgetown U., Washington, 2001, disting. visitor from the Judiciary tchr. adminstrv. law and labor law, 2002—; Pres.' spl. envoy on ILO affairs, 1976; gen. adv. com. on Arms Control and Disarmament, 1981—85; mem. Def. Policy Bd., 1981—85; vice-chmn. State Dept.'s Commn. on Security and Econ. Assistance, 1983—84. Bd. dirs. Com. on Present Danger, 1978-85, Inst. for Ednl. Affairs, 1981-85; mem US Fgn. Intelligence Surveillance Act. Ct. of Rev., 1996-2003; co-chmn. Commn. on Intelligence Capabilities of the US Regarding Weapons of Mass Destruction, 2004; vice chmn. adv. coun. on gen. govt. Rep. Nat. Com., 1977-80. With AUS, 1957-58. Am. Enterprise Inst. sr. fellow, 1977-78, vis. fellow 1978-85; recipient Presdl. Medal of Freedom, The White House, 2008 Mem. Coun. on Fgn. Rels.*

SILBERMAN, ROBERT A. S., lawyer; b. Lebanon, Pa., Mar. 4, 1945; s. Henry T. and Genevieve (Mensh) S.; m. Nancy D. Netzer, Nov. 10, 1974. BA magna cum laude, Yale U., 1967; JD, Harvard U., 1970. Bar: Mass. 1970, Pa. 1984. Assoc. Csaplar & Bok, Boston, 1970—78, ptnr., 1978—90, Gaston & Snow, Boston, 1990—91, Edwards, Angell, Palmer & Dodge, LLP (formerly Edwards & Angell), Boston, 1991—2000, Israel & Silberman PC, Wellesley, Mass., 2000—. Mem. editl. bd. Managed Care Law Strategist, Am. Lawyer Media newsletter, 1999-2001. Citizens rev. com. United Way Mass. Bay, Boston, 1981-89; bd. dirs. All Newton (Mass.) Music Sch., 1994-96, v.p., 1995-96; bd. overseers Boston Baroque, 1998-2000, bd. dirs., chmn. bd. overseers, 2000-02, chmn. bd. dirs., 2003—. Mem. ABA (vice chmn. health law com. sect. bus. law 1992-95, chmn., 1995-99), Internat. Bar Assn., Boston Bar Assn., Phi Beta Kappa. Office: Israel & Silberman PC 15 Walnut St Ste 100 Wellesley MA 02481 Office Phone: 781-235-1500. Business E-Mail: rsilberman@israelsilberman.com.

SILBERSACK, JOHN WALTER, literary agent; b. NYC, Dec. 8, 1954; s. Walter Roy and Joan Small Silbersack; m. Elionora van Tyen Wilking, June 29, 1985; children: Nichols Clay, Johanna van Tyen, Catryn Center. AB, Brown U., 1977. Pub. dir. Roc Books Penguin Pub. Group, NYC, 1986—92; editor in chief Warner Aspect, Warner Books, NYC, 1992—93; sr. vice pres./pub. dir. Harper Entertainment/Harper Children's Entertainment, Harper Collins Publishers, NYC, 1993—99; exec. v.p. Trident Media Group, 2001—. Author: No Frills Science Fiction, 1983, Rogers Rangers, 1983; editor: The Berkley Showcase: New Writings in Science Fiction and Fantasy, 1980—83. Mem.: Manhasset Bay Sailing Found. (trustee 2008—), Sci. Fiction Writers Am., Thurs. Evening Club, Manhasset Bay Yacht Club (trustee 2006—), Century Assn. Home: 5 Harbor Rd Sands Point NY 11050 Office: Trident Media Group 41 Madison Ave New York NY 11010 Office Phone: 212-333-1513. Office Fax: 646-607-2046. Personal E-mail: quidnetma@aol.com. E-mail: jsilbersack@tridentmediagroup.com.

SILBERSACK, MARK LOUIS, lawyer; b. Cin., Dec. 27, 1946; s. Joseph Leo and Rhoda Marie (Hinkler) S.; m. Ruth Ann Schwallie, Sept. 7, 1985. AB, Boston Coll., 1968; JD, U. Chgo., 1971. Bar: Ohio 1971, U.S. Dist. Ct. (so. dist.) Ohio 1973, U.S. Ct. Appeals (6th cir.) 1974, U.S. Supreme Ct. 1975. Atty. Dinsmore & Shohl LLP, Cin., 1971—. Lectr. Ohio CLE Inst., Columbus, 1981-91. Co-author: Managed Care: The PPO Experience, 1990, Information Sharing Among Health Care Providers, 1994. Bd. dirs. United Way Greater Cin., 1985-89, 2001—08, chmn. pub. policy com., 1998—2008; vice-chmn. Ohio United Way, Columbus, 1989-94, chmn. bd. dir., 1994-96; pres. Hyde Park Neighborhood Coun., Cin., 1989-91, Hyde Park Ctr. for Older Adults, 1989-91; Cin. Bd. Health, 1991-97, chmn., 1995-97; bd. dirs. Cath. Social Svc. of S.W. Ohio, 1998-2003, Children, Inc., 2003-; mem. Cincinnatus Assn., 2000—, Cin. Human Svcs. Adv. Comm., 2009-. Mem. ABA, FBA, Ohio State Bar Assn. (chmn. antitrust sect. 2005-07), Cin. Bar Assn., Hyde Park Golf and Country Club. Republican. Roman Catholic. Avocations: reading, travel, theater. Home: 3465 Forestoak Ct Cincinnati OH 45208-1842 Office: Dinsmore & Shohl LLP 1900 Chemed Ctr 255 E 5th St Cincinnati OH 45202-4700 Home Phone: 513-321-1806; Office Phone: 513-977-8243. Business E-Mail: mark.silbersack@dinslaw.com.

SILBERSCHATZ, ABRAHAM (AVI SILBERSCHATZ), computer scientist, educator, researcher; arrived in US, 1968, naturalized; s. Joseph and Vera (Rosenblum) S.; children: Lemor, Sivan, Aaron. MS, SUNY, Stonybrook, 1973, PhD, 1976. From asst. prof. to assoc. prof. U. Tex., Austin, 1976-84, prof., 1984-96; v.p., Info. Sci. Rsch. Ctr. Bell Labs., Murray Hill, NJ, 1993—2003; Sidney J. Weinberg prof. computer sci. Yale U., 2003—, chair, dept. computer sci. Co-author: Database System Concepts, 1996, 2004 Operating System Concepts, 1998, 2005. Sgt. Israel mil., 1965-68. Recipient Pres. award, Bell Labs., 1998, 1999, 2004. Fellow IEEE (Taylor L. Booth Edn. award 2002), Assn. for Computing Machinery (SIGMOD Contbn. award 1997, Karl V. Karlstrom Outstanding Educator award 1998). Jewish. Achievements include 48 patents. Office: Yale U Dept Computer Sci Rm 214 PO Box 208285 New Haven CT 06520-8285 Office Fax: 203-436-4918.

SILBERSTEIN, EDWARD BERNARD, nuclear medicine educator, oncologist, hematologist, researcher; b. Cin., Sept. 3, 1936; s. Bernard Gumpert and Harriet Louise (Kahn) S.; m. Jacqueline Rose Mervis, Oct. 2, 1988; children: Scott, Lisa. BS magna cum laude, Yale U., 1958; MD, Harvard U., 1962; postgrad. in art history, U. Cin. Bd. cert. in Internal Medicine, Hematology, Nuclear Medicine, Med. Oncology Am. Bd. Internal Medicine. Intern Cin. Gen. Hosp., 1962—63, resident in internal medicine, 1963—64; resident Univ. Hosps. Cleve., 1966—67; NIH fellow in hematology New Eng. Med. Ctr., Boston, 1967—68; asst. prof. radiol. medicine U. Cin. Med. Ctr., 1968—72, assoc. prof. radiol. medicine, 1972—76, prof. radiol. medicine, 1976—, Eugene L. and Sue R. Saenger prof. radiol. scis., 1998—2000, prof. emeritus of radiology and medicine, 2000—. Assoc. dir. E.L. Saenger Radioisotope Lab., 1980—; chmn. Environ. Safety Health Com. Dept. Energy Fernald Facility, 1986-91; mem. U.S. Pharmacopeia Com. of Revision, 1990—; mem. Nat. Coun. on Radiation Protection and Measurement, 1997—; cons. Nuc. Regulatory Commn., 1988—; dir. divsn. nuc. medicine Jewish Hosp., 1976-95; cancer pain panel Agy. for Health Care Planning and Rsch., 1992-93; mem. Am. Nuclear Soc. Com. on Isotope Assurance, 2003-05, Am. Coll. Radiology Appropriateres Panel, vis. prof. various lecturerships; reviewer in field. Author: Differential Diagnosis in Nuclear Medicine, 1984, Bone Scintigraphy, 1984, Diagnostic Patterns in Nuclear Medicine, 1998; contbr. articles to profl. jours., chpts. to books. Active Race Rels. Commn. Greater Cin., 1995—2000; trustee Cin. Opera Assn., 1993—, v.p., 2003—; active Jewish Cmty. Rels. Coun., 1992—2005; trustee Isaac M. Wise Temple, 1992—2000, treas., 1997—2000; bd. dirs. Talbert House, 1969—, Air Pollution Control League, Cin., 1980—95. Capt. US Army Med. Corps, 1964—66. Recipient Pearl S. Gantz award for Cmty. Svc., United Way of Cin., 2002, VIP Volunteerism award, Hamilton County Mental Health Bd., 2005; fellow, Am. Col. Nuc. Physicians. Mem.: Am. Bd. Nuclear Medicine (chmn. 1999), Soc. Nuc. Medicine (sec. 1989—92, 1989—92, bd. dirs. 1989—99, pres. S.E. chpt. 1990—91, chair sci. program 1992—94, spkr. Ho. of Dels. 2002—04, Speaker's award 2004, Marshall Brucer award 2002), Literary Club, Sigma Xi, Phi Beta Kappa. Jewish. Avocations: tennis, history of art, archaeology, travel. Office: U Cin Med Ctr Mont Reid Pavilion G026 234 Goodman St Cincinnati OH 45219-2364 Office Phone: 513-584-9032. Business E-Mail: silbereb@healthall.com.

SILBERSTEIN, STEPHEN DAVID, health facility administrator, neurologist; b. June 6, 1942; MD, U. Pa., 1967. Intern U. Pa., 1967-68; resident in neurology HUP, Phila., 1968-69; rsch. assoc. in pharmacology, toxicology Nat. Inst. Mental Health, Bethesda, MD, 1969-72; resident in neurology HUP, Phila., 1972-75; chief sect. neurology Germantown Hosp. & Med. Ctr., Phila., 1975-97; prof. neurology Thomas Jefferson U. Hosp., Phila., 1997-98; dir. Comprehensive Headache Ctr., Phila., 1982-97, Jefferson Headache Clinic, Phila., 1997—. Fellow: American Academy of Neurology, American Headache Soc., ACP. Office: Jefferson Headache Ctr Ste 8130 Gibbon 111 South 11th St Philadelphia PA 19107*

SILBERSWEIG, DAVID ALAN, physician; b. NYC; MD, Cornell Med. Coll., NYC. Diplomate Am. Bd. Psychiatry and Neurology. Chmn. dept. psychiatry, chmn., Inst. Neuroscis. Brigham and Women's Hosp., Harvard Med. Sch., Boston, 2008—. Vice chmn. rsch., dept. psychiatry, dir. divsn. neuropsychiatry, co-dir., functional neuroimaging lab. Weill Cornell Med. Coll., NYC. Achievements include research in neuropsychiatric functional neuroimaging. Office: Brigham and Women's Hosp 75 Francis St Boston MA 02115

SILBERT, JONATHAN E., judge; b. Stamford, Conn., 1943; m. Bonnie McHale; children: Corey, Jessica. AB cum laude, Dartmouth Coll., 1965; JD, Harvard U., 1968. Bar: 1968. Vice chmn. Guilford Bd. Edn., Conn.; judge Conn. Superior Ct., New Haven, 1991—. Cons. to justice prog. Edna McConnel Clark Found.; co-chmn. Conn. Pskov Rule of Law Proj., 2002—. Recipient Hon. Robert A. Zampano award for Excellence in Mediation, 2005. Mem.: Russian Am. Rule of Law Consortium (treas.), New Haven Inn of Ct. (former pres.), New Haven County Bar Assn. (exec. com.), Conn. Bar Assn. (Henry J. Naruk Judiciary award 2003), Conn. Trial Lawyers Assn. (Judiciary award 2001), Phi Beta Kappa. Office: Judicial Dist Courthouse 235 Church St New Haven CT 06510 Office Phone: 203-503-6830. Office Fax: 203-789-6826.*

SILBERT, JONATHAN E., ophthalmologist, educator; b. St. Louis, Nov. 17, 1967; s. David Frederick and Shirley Wang Silbert; m. Abby Wiggetman, Aug. 22, 1998; children: Jacob David, Carly Rebecca. MD, Wash. U., St. Louis, 1995. Diplomate ophthalmologist Am. Bd. Ophthalmology, 2000. Clin. instr. ophthalmology Wash. U., 1999—2000; oculoplastic fellow Dean McGee Eye Inst., Okla. City, Okla., 2000—02; oculoplastic specialist with multisplty. ophthalmology group Eye Care Group, Waterbury, Conn., 2002—. Clin. instr. Yale Dept. Ophthalmology, New Haven, 2002—; dir. ophthalmology divsn. St. Mary's Hosp., Waterbury, Conn., 2007—. Contbr. scientific papers (Tchr. of Yr., 2000). Fellow: Am. Bd. Ophthalmology; mem.: AMA, Conn. Soc. Eye Physicians. Avocations: travel, baseball, stamp collecting/philately. Office: Eye Care Group 1201 W Main St Waterbury CT 06708 Office Fax: 203-597-1696.

SILBEY, JOEL HENRY, history professor; b. Bklyn., Aug. 16, 1933; s. Sidney and Estelle (Mintzer) S.; m. Rosemary Johnson, Aug. 13, 1959; children: Victoria, David. BA, Bklyn. Coll., 1955; MA, U. Iowa, 1956, PhD, 1963. Asst. prof. San Francisco State Coll., 1960-64, U. Md., College Park, 1965-66; asst. prof. Am. History Cornell U., Ithaca, NY, 1966-67, assoc. prof., 1967-68, prof., 1968-86, Pres. White prof. history, 1986—2002, prof. emeritus, 2002—; Harold V. Harmsworthy prof. Am. history U. Oxford, 2004—05. Vis. asst. prof. history U. Pitts., 1964-65. Author: The Shrine of Party, 1967, The Transformation of American Politics, 1968, A Respectable Minority: The Democratic Party in the Civil War Era, 1977, The Partisan Imperative: The Dynamics of American Politics before the Civil War, 1985, The American Political Nation, 1838-1893, 1991, The American Party Battle, 1828-1876, 1999, Martin Van Buren and the Emergence of American Popular Politics, 2002, Storm Over Texas: The Annexation Controversy and the Road to Civil War, 2005, Party Over Section: the Rough and Ready Presidential Election of 1848, 2009; editor: (with others) Voters, Parties and Elections, 1972, American Political Behavior, 1984, The History of American Electoral Behavior, 1978; editor-in-chief: Encyclopedia of the American Legislative System, 1993; editorial cons. numerous publs.; contbr. numerous articles to profl. jours Am. Philos. Soc. fellow, 1969-70; NSF fellow, 1970-74; NEH fellow, 1980-81; vis. fellow Ctr. for Advanced Study in the Behavioral Scis., 1985-86; vis. scholar Russell Sage Found., 1988-89; John Simon Guggenheim Meml. fellow, 1989-90. Mem. Am. Hist. Assn. (program com. 1977), Orgn. Am. Historians (chmn. program com. 1983), So. Hist. Assn., Social Sci. History Assn. (co-chmn. membership com., mem. exec. com). Home: 105 Judd Falls Rd Ithaca NY 14850-2715 Office: Cornell U 140 Mcgraw Hall Ithaca NY 14853-4601 Office Phone: 607-255-4966. Business E-Mail: jhs3@cornell.edu.

SILBEY, ROBERT JAMES, chemistry professor, researcher, consultant; b. NYC, Oct. 19, 1940; s. Sidney Richard and Estelle (Mintzer) S.; m. Susan Sorkin, June 24, 1962; children: Jessica, Anna. BS, CUNY Bklyn. Coll., 1961; PhD, U. Chgo., 1965; PhD (hon.), Bklyn. Coll., 2004. From asst. prof. to assoc. prof. MIT, Cambridge, 1966-76, prof., 1976—, chmn. dept. chemistry, 1990-95, dir. ctr. for materials sci. and engring., 1998-2000, dean sci., 2000—07. Vis. prof. U. Utrecht, The Netherlands, 1972-73, 97, U. Grenoble, France, 1983, U. groningen, The Netherlands, 2008; cons. Exxon Rsch., Clinton, N.J., 1984-98. Author: Physical Chemistry, 1991, 4th edit., 2004; editor: Conjugated Polymers, 1991; contbr. articles to profl. jours. Recipient Alexander von Humboldt Found. Sr. Scientist award, 1989, Max Planck award, 1992; Alfred P. Sloan fellow, 1968, John S. Guggenheim fellow, 1972; Dreyfus Found. Tchr.-Scholar grantee, 1969. Fellow AAAS, Am. Acad. Arts and Sci., Am. Phys. Soc.; mem. NAS. Avocations: sailing, swimming. Office: MIT Dept Chemistry 77 Mass Ave Cambridge MA 02139-4307 Office Phone: 617-253-1470. Business E-Mail: silbey@mit.edu.

SILBEY, VICTORIA E., lawyer; b. San Francisco; BA, Cornell Univ., 1985; M.Phil., Oxford Univ., 1987; JD, Cornell Univ., 1990. Bar: Pa. 1992. Law clk. Judge John Davies, US Dist. Ct., Ctrl. Dist. Calif., 1990—91; assoc. Morgan, Lewis & Bockius LLP, Phila., 1991—97; joined SunGard Data Sys. Inc., Wayne, Pa., 1997, v.p. legal, asst. gen. counsel, 2004—05, v.p. legal, gen. counsel, 2005—06, sr. v.p. legal, gen. counsel, 2006—. Mem.: ABA, Am. Corp. Counsel Assn. Office: SunGard Data Sys Inc 680 E Swedesford Rd Wayne PA 19087 Office Phone: 484-582-5542. E-mail: victoria.silbey@sungard.com.

SILBIGER, MARTIN L., radiologist, educator, dean; b. Ravenna, Ohio, Mar. 17, 1938; s. Alfred James and Evelyn Norma (Cheswick) Silbiger; m. Ruth Hope Steele, June 4, 1957; children: Martin, Eve, Jonathan, Holly, Wendy. BA, U. Pa., 1958; MD, Western Reserve U., 1962; MBA, U. South Fla., 1989. Diplomate Am. Bd. Radiology, Am. Bd. Nuc. Medicine. Intern Univ. Hosps. Cleve., 1962—63; resident Johns Hopkins Hosp., 1963—66; with NIH, 1966—68; radiologist Tampa (Fla.) Gen. Hosp., 1968—; prof. U. South Fla., Tampa, 1982—; chief of staff Tampa Gen. Hosp., 1978—80; chmn. dept. radiology U. South Fla. Coll. Medicine, 1982—95; dean coll. medicine U. South Fla., 1995—2000, v.p. health scis., 1995—2000. Founder Hillsborough County Med. Assn. Found., Tampa, 1992; treas. Cmty. Found. Tampa, 1993—95; bd. dirs. Moffitt Cancer Ctr., Tampa, 1985—2000, Moffitt Cancer Ctr. Found., 1994—2000. Avocations: reading, rollerblading, golf, tennis. Home: 1827 Bayshore Blvd Tampa FL 33606-3210 Office: 3301 Alumni Dr Tampa FL 33612-9413 also: 1209 Bruce B Downs Blvd PO Box 66 Tampa FL 33601-0066

SILCOX, GORDON BRUCE, executive coach; b. Takoma Park, Md., May 11, 1938; s. Walter Bruce and Ruth May (Davis) S.; m. Judith Andrea Smith, Mar. 7, 1970 (div. Apr. 1998); children: Andrea Davis, Jessica Lyn. AB, Princeton U., 1960; MBA, U. Pa., 1965. Trust investment officer Am. Security Bank, Washington, 1967—69; v.p., trust investment officer, head trust investment divsn. First Am. Bank, N.A., 1969—77; v.p., prin. Paul Stafford Assocs., Ltd., Washington, 1977-83; v.p., mgr. MSL Internat. Ltd., Washington, 1983-86; v.p. Manchester, Inc., Washington, 1987-91, sr. v.p., 1991—2003; prin. Words on Purpose LLC, Fairfax, Va., 2003—. Pres. Wash. Human Resource Forum, 1993-95. Treas. Princeton U. Class of 1960, v.p., 1980-85. Lt. (j.g.) USN, 1962-63. Mem. Univ. Club, Princeton Club (treas. Washington 1972-74, N.Y.C.). Home and Office: 3159 Colchester Brook Ln Fairfax VA 22031-2609 Home Phone: 703-280-1041; Office Phone: 703-280-1041. E-mail: gsilcox@wordsonpurpose.com.

SILEO, NANCY M., special education educator; EdD, U. Northern Colo., Greeley, 1998. Cert. multisubject tchg. credential State of Calif., lic. spl. edn. tchr. State of Hawaii. Prof. early childhood spl. edn. UNLV, 1998—. Contbr. articles to profl. jours. Higher edn. rep. State of Nev. Interagency Coordinating Coun., Carson City. Mem.: Nat. Minority Coun. AIDS, Nat. Assn. Edn. Young Children, Coun. Exceptional Children (tchr. edn. divsn. mem., early childhood dvsn. mem.). Office: Dept Spl Edn UNLV 4505 Maryland Pky PO Box 3014 Las Vegas NV 89154-3014

SILEO, RICHARD NICHOLAS, physics educator; s. Nicholas Francis Sileo and Caroline Barbara Zane; m. Karen Hale, June 5, 1971; 1 child, Laura Michelle. BS, U. Notre Dame, Ind., 1969; MS, Binghamton U., NY, 2004; PhD, Cornell U., Ithaca, NY, 1974. Rsch. scientist McDonnel-Douglas Rsch. Labs., St. Louis, 1974—77; sys. engr., analyst, mktg. rep. IBM, Endicott, NY, 1977—2002; physics instr. Binghamton U., 2004—. Office: Binghamton Univ Physics Dept PO Box 6000 Binghamton NY 13902-6000 Business E-Mail: rsileo@binghamton.edu.

SILER, DENNIS JAMES, literature and language professor; s. James Joseph and Robbie Louan Siler; m. Martha Caroline Davis, June 22, 1985; children: Allyson Emeline, Zachary Gaines, Jacob Deidrich. BA, U. Ctrl. Ark., Conway, 1990; MA, Wake Forest U., Winston, Salem, NC, 1991; PhD in English, U. Ark., Fayetteville, 2006. Adj. instr. Dabney Lancaster CC, Clifton Forge, Va., 1991—92; grad. tchg. asst. U. Tex., Arlington, 1992—93; instr. Petit Jean Coll., Morrilton, Ark., 1993—98; master lectr. U. Ark., 1998—2000, asst. prof. Fort Smith, 2000—. Honors com. chair U. Honors Program, Fort Smith, 2006—. Author: (book) Channeling Ovid: Shakespeare's Meta-Ovidian Tendency. Recipient Magna Cum Laude, Honors Coll. U. Ctrl. Ark., 1990. Mem.: Internat. Marlowe Soc., Shakespeare Assn. Am., Alpha Chi. Avocations: travel, music. Office: Univ Ark 5210 Grand Ave Fort Smith AR 72913-3649 Office Fax: 479-788-7802.

SILER, EUGENE EDWARD, JR., federal judge; b. Williamsburg, Ky., Oct. 19, 1936; s. Eugene Edward and Lowell (Jones) Siler; m. Christy Dyanne Minnich, Oct. 18, 1969; children: Eugene Edward, Adam Troy. BA cum laude, Vanderbilt U., 1958; LLB, U. Va., 1963; LLM, Georgetown U., 1964, U. Va., 1995. Bar: Ky. 1963, Va. 1963, DC 1963. Pvt. practice, Williamsburg, 1964—65; county atty. Whitley County, Ky., 1965—70; US atty. (ea. dist.) Ky. US Dept. Justice, Lexington, 1970—75; judge (ea. & we. dist.) Ky. US Dist. Ct., 1975—91, chief judge (ea. dist.) Ky., 1984—91; judge US Ct. Appeals (6th Cir.), 1991—2001, sr. judge, 2001—. Trustee Cumberland Coll., Williamsburg, 1965—73, 1980—88; campaign co-chmn. Congressman Tim L. Carter, 1966, 5th Congl. Dist., US Senator J.S. Cooper, 1966; 1st v.p. Ky. Bapt. Convention, 1986—87, 2002—03, pres., 2003—04; bd. dirs. Bapt. Healthcare System Inc., 1990—2004, 2006—. With USN, 1958—60, with USNR, 1960—83. Recipient Freedom's Found. medal, 1968; E. Barrett Prettyman fellow, 1963—64. Mem.: Va. State Bar, DC Bar Assn., Ky. Bar Assn. (Judge of Yr. 1992), Fed. Bar Assn. Republican. Baptist. Home: PO Box 129 Williamsburg KY 40769-0129 Office: US Ct Appeals 310 S Main Street Room 333 London KY 40741*

SILET, CHARLES LORING PROVINE, emeritus literature and language professor; b. Chgo., Apr. 25, 1942; s. Charles Leonard and Elizabeth Walker Provine Silet; m. Kay Helen Zickefoose, Feb. 21, 1976; children: Kristin Marie Davis, Scott Andrew, Karin Ann, Emily Elizabeth. Degree, U. Vienna, 1963, Jesus Coll., Cambridge U., Eng., 1971; BA, Butler U., Indpls., 1964; MA, PhD, Ind. U., Bloomington, 1973. Assoc. prof. Iowa State U., Ames, 1979—86, prof. English, 1989—2004. Book rev. editor Hitchcock Ann., NYC, 1996—2001; consulting editor Strand Mag., Birmingham, Mich., 1998—, MysteryNet Website, NYC, 1998. Author: (books) Lindsay Anderson, Paul Rosenfeld, Talking Murder, Transistion, The Critical Response to Chester Himes, Hamlin Garland and Henry Blake Fuller, The Literary Manuscripts of Upton Sinclair; editor: The Films of Woody Allen: Critical Essays, The Worlds Between Two Rivers, Oliver Stone: Interviews, Steven Spielberg: Critical Essays, Images of American Indians on Film. Mem. Iowa Humanities Bd., NEH, Iowa City, 1996—2001; co-host monthly WOI Radio, NPR, Ames, 1996—. Fellowship, NEH, 1978, grant, Iowa State U., 1978—79, 1989, 2002. Mem.: Soc. Cinema Studies, Iowa Film Critics Assn. Liberal. Avocations: travel, gardening. Office: English Dept Iowa State Univ 203 Ross Hall Ames IA 50011 Business E-Mail: csilet@iastate.edu.

SILFIES, SHERI, physical therapist, educator; d. Paul H. and Catherine E. Silfies. BS, U. Scranton, Pa., 1987; MS, Ind. U., Pa., 1994; PhD, MCP Hahnemann U., Phila., 2002. Cert. phys. therapist Pa., 1987. Phys. therapist Alleghany & Chesapeak Phys. Therapist, Johnstown, Pa., 1987—92; asst. prof. Coll. Misericordia, Dallas, Pa., 1992—99, Drexel U., Phila., 2002—, dir. rehab. scies. rsch. labs., 2004—. Recipient Rsch. prize, Internat. Soc. Study Lumbar Spine, 2005; Switzer fellowship, Dept. Edn., 2003—04, Mentored Rsch. Scientist grant, NIH, 2007—. Mem.: Internat. Soc. Posture & Gait Rsch., Am. Soc. Biomechanics, Am. Phys. Therapy Assn. Office: Drexel Univ 245 N 15th St Mail Stop 502 Philadelphia PA 19102 Business E-Mail: silfies@drexel.edu.

SILK, ALVIN JOHN, management educator, consultant; b. Winnipeg, Manitoba, Can., Dec. 31, 1935; came to U.S., 1959, naturalized, 1975; s. John Edward and Bertha Lena (Kirton) S.; m. Diane D. Wilson (dec. 2003); children: Jonathan, Andrea, Stephanie. BA, U. Western Ont., 1959; MBA, Northwestern U., 1960, PhD, 1968. Asst. prof. mgmt. UCLA, 1963-66; asst. prof. U. Chgo., 1966-68; from assoc. prof. to prof. Sloan Sch. Mgmt., MIT, Cambridge, 1968-88; dep. dean MIT Sloan Sch. Mgmt., Cambridge, 1981-87; Lincoln Filene prof. Grad. Sch. Bus. Adminstrn. Harvard U., Boston, 1988—. Vis. rsch. fellow Mktg. Sci. Inst., Cambridge, Mass., 1970-71, trustee, 1984-96, Disting. rsch. assoc., 2001--; Ford Found. vis. prof. European Inst. for Advanced Studies in Mgmt., Brussels, 1975-76, Harvard Bus. Sch., 1987—; bd. dirs. Reed and Barton, Inc., Taunton, Mass. Co-editor: Behavioral and Management Science in Marketing, 1978; assoc. editor: Mgmt. Sci., 1969-77; co-editor: Quantitative Mktg. Absracts, Social Sci. Rsch. Network; mem. editl. bd. Jour. Mktg. Rsch., 1969-73, Jour. Mktg., 1978-81, Mktg. Sci., 1980-93; author, co-author numerous articles to profl. jours. Mem. Am. Mktg. Assn. (O'Dell award 1983), INFORMS (Achievement award 1982, 83), Beta Gamma Sigma, Zeta Psi. Home: 464 Starboard Ln Osterville MA 02655-1432 Office Phone: 617-495-6036. Business E-Mail: asilk@hbs.edu.

SILK, THOMAS, lawyer; b. Beaver, Pa., Dec. 12, 1937; s. Thomas and Alice Genevieve (Beck) S.; m. Arlene Schlaifer, 1959 (div.); 1 child, Nicole Amory; m. Susan Clark, 1979 (div.); m. Suzanne Vinson, 1996. AB, U. Calif., Berkeley, 1959, JD, 1963. Bar: Calif. 1964, U.S. Dist. Ct. (no. dist.) Calif. 1964, U.S. Ct. Appeals (D.C., 2-10th cirs.) 1966-68, U.S. Tax Ct. 1966, U.S. Supreme Ct. 1967. Appellate atty. tax divsn. U.S. Dept. Justice, Washington, 1964-66, spl. asst. to asst. atty. gen. tax divsn., 1966-68; assoc. Brobeck, Phleger & Harrison, San Francisco, 1968-71; founder, chmn. Silk, Adler & Colvin, San Francisco, 1972—2008; founder & prin. Sick Non Profit Law, San Fransisco, 2008—. Lectr., author, advisor in field; advisor project on the principles of law of nonprofit orgns. Am. Law Inst., 2004—. Editor, co-author: Philanthropy and Law in Asia, 1999; author: Corporate Philanthropy and Law: A Guide to Tax Charities and An Introduction to Compliance with Anti-Terrorist Laws, 2003, Good Governance Practices for 501(c) (3) Organizations: Should the IRS Become Further Involved, 2007—. Trustee sec. gen. coun. Hertz Found. Office: Silk Nonprofit Law 1408 Kearny St San Francisco CA 94133 Office Phone: 415-986-6000. Business E-Mail: tom@silknonprofitlaw.net, tom@silklaw.net.

SILKENAT, JAMES ROBERT, lawyer; b. Salina, Kans., Aug. 2, 1947; s. Ernest E. and Mildred R. (Iman) S.; children: David Andrew, Katherine Anne. BA, Drury Coll., 1969; JD, U. Chgo., 1972; LLM, NYU, 1978. Bar: N.Y. 1973, D.C. 1980. Assoc. Cravath, Swaine & Moore, NYC, 1972-80; counsel Internat. Fin. Corp., Washington, 1980-86; ptnr. Morgan, Lewis & Bockius, NYC, 1986-89, Morrison & Foerster, NYC, 1989-92, Pillsbury, Winthrop, NYC, 1992—2002, Arent Fox, NYC, 2002—09, Sullivan & Worcester, NYC, 2009—. Chmn. Council N.Y. Law Assocs., 1978-79, Lawyers Com. Internat. Human Rights, 1978-80. Editor ABA Guide to Fng. Law Firms, Moscow Conf. on Law Bilateral Econ. Rels., ABA Guide to Internat. Bus. Negotiations, The Imperial Presidency and the Consequences of 9/11, The Law of International Insolvencies and Debt Restructurings; contbr. articles to profl. jours. Capt. U.S. Army, 1972-73. Fellow NEH, 1977, U.S. Dept. State, 1981. Fellow Am. Bar Found. (chmn. 2004-05); mem. ABA (chmn. internat. law and practice sect. 1989-90, chmn. sect. officer's conf. 1990-92, mem. ho. of dels. 1989—, bd. govs. 1994-97). Office: Sullivan & Worcester 1290 Ave of the Americas New York NY 10104 Home Phone: 212-245-5815; Office Phone: 212-660-3052. Business E-Mail: j.silkenat@sandw.com.

SILL, MELANIE, editor-in-chief; b. Nebr. m. Bennett Groshong. BA in Journalism, U. NC, Chapel Hill, 1981. With Transylvania Times, Brevard, NC, United Press Internat., News & Observer, Raleigh, NC, 1982—2007, mng. editor, 1998—2002, exec. editor, sr. v.p., 2002—07; editor, sr. v.p. Sacramento Bee, 2007—. Recipient Pulitzer prize for Public Svc. Reporting, 1996; Nieman fellow, Harvard U., 1993—94. Fellow: News Leadership 2009 Knight Media Ctr.; mem.: Investigative Reporters & Editors, Am. Soc. Newspaper Editors. Office: Sacramento Bee PO Box 15779 Sacramento CA 95852 also: 2100 Q St Sacramento CA 95816 Office Phone: 916-321-1002. E-mail: msill@sacbee.com.*

SILLARS, MALCOLM O., communications educator; b. Union City, NJ, Feb. 12, 1928; s. Malcolm Osgood and Dorothy Edna (Browning) S.; m. Charlotte Jane Grimm, June 1, 1948; children: Paul Louis, Bruce Malcolm, Alan Leslie. BA, U. Redlands, 1948, MA, 1949; PhD, U. Iowa, 1955. Asst. prof. comm. Iowa State U., Ames, 1949-53; asst. prof. Calif. State U., LA, 1954-56, prof., 1956—71, dean, 1970-71; pres. Calif. State U. Northridge, 1969-70; prof. U. Mass., Amherst, 1971-74; prof. communication U. Utah, Salt Lake City, 1974-97, dean humanities, 1974-81, ret., 1998. Author: Speech: Content and Communications, 6th edit., 1991, Argumentation and Critical Decision Making, 7th edit., 2009, Communication Criticism, 2d edit., 2001; contbr. articles to profl. jours. Recipient Silver Beaver award Boy Scouts Am. Mem. ACLU, Nat. Comm. Assn. (pres.), We. States Comm. Assn. (pres.). Democrat. Home: 3508 Eastoaks Dr Salt Lake City UT 84124-3811 E-mail: m.sillars@utah.edu.

SILLER, KEITH A., neurologist, psychiatrist; MD, NYU, 1989. Cert. Neurology. Intern in psychiatry NYU Med. Ctr., 1989—90, resident in neurology, 1990—93, clin. fellow in cerebrovascular disease, 1993—95, asst. prof. neurology and psychiatry; med. dir. NYU Comprehensive Stroke Care Ctr. Office: NYU Langone Med Ctr HCC 5 5A 530 1st Ave New York NY 10016 Office Phone: 212-263-1485. Office Fax: 212-263-7871. E-mail: keith.siller@nyumc.org.*

SILLER, STEPHEN I., lawyer; b. May 8, 1949; m. Helen Seewald, June 6, 1971. BA, Bklyn. Coll., 1970, JD cum laude, 1973; LLM, NYU, 1978. Bar: N.Y. 1974, U.S. Dist. Ct. (so. and ea. dists.) N.Y. 1974, U.S. Ct. Appeals (2d cir.) 1974. Assoc. Fried, Frank, Harris, Shriver & Jacobson, NYC, 1973-78, Feit & Ahrens, NYC, 1978-80, ptnr., 1981-87; founder, sr. ptnr. Siller Wilk LLP, NYC, 1987—. Mem. ABA (partnership law com., negotiated acquisitions com.), Internat. Bar Assn., Assn. Bar City of N.Y. (transp. com. 1978, U.S. in global economy com. 1996-97). Office: Siller Wilk LLP 675 3rd Ave Fl 9 New York NY 10017-5704 Office Phone: 212-421-2233. Business E-Mail: ssiller@sillerwilk.com.

SILLERMAN, ROBERT F. X., communications executive, banker; b. NYC, Apr. 12, 1948; s. Michael McKinley and Estelle (Levande) Sillerman; m. Jane Waxenberg, July 13, 1969 (div. Dec. 1970); m. Laura Baudo, Feb. 25, 1974. BS magna cum laude, Brandeis U., 1969. CEO, chmn. bd. Youth Markets Cons., Inc., Boston, 1966-74, Nat. Discount Mktg., Great Neck, NY, 1974-78, Sillerman-Morrow Broadcasting Group, Middletown, NY, 1978-85; co-chmn. bd. Legacy Broadcasting, LA, 1985-89; CEO, chmn. bd. Sillerman-Magee Comm. Mgmt. Corp. (now Sillerman Comm. Mgmt. Corp.), NYC, 1985, TV Programs of Am., Hollywood, Calif., 1985; founder, CEO, chmn. SFX Broadcasting, Inc.(acquired by Hicks, Muse, Tate & Furst), 1992—95, exec. chmn., 1995—98; founder, exec. chmn., mem. of the office of the chmn., dir. SFX Entertainment, Inc. (acquired by Clear Channel Communications), 1997—2000; chmn. FXM, Inc., 2000—05; founder, mng. mem. FXM Asset Mgmt. LLC, 2003—; mng. mem. MJX Asset Mgmt., 2003—; CEO, pres., chmn. bd. CKX, Inc., Las Vegas, Nev., 2005—. Co-chmn. Legacy Broadcasting, Inc., 1986—; chmn. Met. Broadcasting, Inc., 1988-89. Recipient Bearer of the Torch award Anti-Defamation League, N.Y.C., 1982. Mem. Nat. Assn. Broadcasters, Nat. Radio Broadcasters

Assn. Office: CKX Inc 6730 S Las Vegas Blvd Las Vegas NV 89119 also: Southampton College Liu 121 Speonk Riverhead Rd Riverhead NY 11901-3444 Office Phone: 702-798-7777, 631-283-4000. Office Fax: 702-798-6847, 631-283-4081.

SILLERUD, ARLEN ROGER, retired secondary school educator; b. Nov. 28, 1934; BS, Moorhead State U., Minn., 1958; postgrad., Bemidji State U., Minn., 1969-70, U. Minn., 1988-90. Tchr. Ada School Dist., Ada, Minn., 1958-90. Chmn. Norman County Reps., Ada, Minn., 1996—, county, dist., and state del., 1994-2000, 2002—, state ctrl. del., 1997-2001, alt., 2000—07, 09; elder Zion Luth. Ch., Ada, 1994-2005, Gideon spkr., 1971—. Achievements include rsch. in heart fibrillation, that the heart can be restarted by electric shock; creator five solutions to clean up oil spills; inventor wind deflector for trucks. Home: 807 3rd Ave E Ada MN 56510-1120

SILLITOE, ALAN, writer; b. Mar. 4, 1928; s. Christopher and Sabina (Burton) S.; m. Ruth Fainlight, Oct. 19, 1959; 1 child, David Nimrod; 1 adopted child, Susan. Student, Nottingham schs. Radio operator RAF, 1946-50; writer, 1950—. Author: (novels) Saturday Night and Sunday Morning, 1958, The General, 1960, Key to the Door, 1961, The Death of William Posters, 1965, A Tree on Fire, 1967, A Start in Life, 1970, Travels in Nihilon, 1971, Raw Material, 1972, Flame of Life, 1974, The Widower's Son, 1976, The Storyteller, 1979, Her Victory, 1982, The Lost Flying Boat, 1983, Down From the Hill, 1984, Life Goes On, 1985, Out of the Whirlpool, 1988, The Open Door, 1989, Last Loves, 1990, Leonard's War, 1991, Snowstop, 1993, The Broken Chariot, 1998, The German Numbers Woman, 1999, Birthday, 2001, A Man of His Time, 2004, (autobiography) Life Without Armour, 1995, Alligator Playground Stories, 1997, (essays) Mountains and Caverns, 1975, A Flight of Arrows, 2003, (stories) The Loneliness of the Long Distance Runner, 1959, The Ragman's Daughter, 1963, Guzman, Go Home, 1968, Men, Women and Children, 1973, The Second Chance, 1981, Collected Stories, 1995, New and Collected Stories, 2003, (poems) The Rats, 1960, A Falling Out of Love, 1964, Love in the Environs of Voronezh, 1968, Storm and Other Poems, 1974, Snow on the North Side of Lucifer, 1979, Sun Before Departure, 1984, Tides and Stone Walls, 1985, Collected Poems, 1994, Travel: Road to Volgograd, 1964, (with David Sillitoe) Nottinghamshire, 1986, Leading the Blind, 1995, (with Fay Godwin) The Saxon Shore Way, 1983, Gadfly in Russia, 2007, (juvenile) The City Adventures of Marmalade Jim, 1967, Big John and the Stars, 1977, The Incredible Fencing Fleas, 1978, Marmalade Jim on the Farm, 1979, Marmalade Jim and the Fox, 1984, (plays) (with Ruth Fainlight) All Citizens Are Soldiers, 1969, This Foreign Field, 1970, Three Plays, 1978. Address: 14 Ladbroke Ter London W11 England

SILLMAN, ARNOLD JOEL, physiologist, educator; b. NYC, Oct. 10, 1940; s. Philip and Anne L. (Pearlman) S.; m. Jean Fletcher Van Keuren, Sept. 26, 1969; children: Andrea Jose Callaway, Diana Van Keuren Taylor. AB, UCLA, 1963, MA, 1965, PhD, 1968. Asst. prof. UCLA, 1969-73, U. Calif., Davis, 1975-78, assoc. prof., 1978-85, prof., 1985—2007, prof. emeritus, 2007—; asst. prof. U. Pitts., 1973-75, interim dir. aquaculture and fisheries program, 1994—95, vice chair sect. neurobiology, physiology and behavior, 1998—2007, acting chair, 2001. Contbr. articles to profl. jours. USPHS trainee, UCLA, 1966-67; fellow NSF, 1967-68, Fight for Sight, Inc., 1968-69. Recipient Acad. Senate Disting. Tchg. award, 1996. Jewish. Avocations: backpacking, gardening, woodworking. Home: 1140 Los Robles St Davis CA 95618-4927 Office: U Calif Dept Neurobiology Physiology & Behavior Coll Biol Scis Davis CA 95616 Business E-Mail: ajsillman@ucdavis.edu.

SILLS, EDWARD M., pediatric rheumatologist; b. Bklyn., Jan. 8, 1938; MD, NYU Sch. Medicine, 1963. Diplomate Am. Bd. Pediat. Intern pediat. Bronx Mcpl. Hosp. Ctr., 1963—64, resident pediat. rheumatology, 1964—67; dir. pediat. rheumatology Johns Hopkins Children's Ctr., Balt., 1969—; assoc. prof. pediat. Johns Hopkins U. Sch. Medicine, Balt., 1969—. Med. dir. pediat Johns Hopkins Home Health Grp.; prog. dir. pediat continuing edn. Johns Hopkins U. Sch. Medicine. Contbr. articles to profl. jours. Named one of America's Top Dr.'s, Castle Connolly Med. LTD. Mem.: Am. Coll. Rheumatology. Office: Hopkins Childrens Park 321 600 N Wolf St Towson MD 21204 Office Phone: 410-955-6145. Business E-Mail: esills1@jhmi.edu.

SILLS, SCOTT E., nanotechnologist; s. F. Eric and Susan M. Sills; m. Amanda J. Lee. BChE, U. Del., Newark, 1995; MS, PhD, U. Wash., Seattle, 2004. EIT Soc. Profl. Engrs., Del., 1995. Refinery equipment insp. Del. City Refinery, Star Enterprise, Del., 1994; engrng. asst., reaction engrng. dept. EI DuPont Nemours & Co., Wilmington, Del., 1994—95; process engr. II FMC Corp., Kemmerer, Wyo., 1995—99; grad. rsch. asst. chem. engrng. U. Wash., 1999—2004; pre-doctoral fellow IBM Almaden Rsch. Ctr., San Jose, Calif., 2002—03, postdoc. rsch. fellow, Stanford U., 2005—06; devel. engr. Micron Tech., Inc., Boise, 2006—07; technologist Advanced Tech. Group, Micron Tech., Inc., Boise, 2007—. Tech. advisor Montvista Capital, Miami, Fla., 2004—07. Contbr. chapters to books, scientific papers to tech. conf., articles to numerous profl. jours. Mem. Boy Scouts America, 1980—90; asst. wrestling coach Kemmerer HS, Wyo., 1996—99, with; ptnr. edn., rope rescue team mem. FMC Corp., 1997—99; vol. Wash. Kayak Club, Seattle, 2001—02. Mem.: Am. Whitewater. Achievements include patents in field.

SILMAN, ROBERTA KARPEL, fiction writer, critic; b. Bklyn., Dec. 29, 1934; d. Herman and Phoebe Karpel; m. Robert Silman, June 14, 1956; children: Miriam, Joshua, Ruth. BA, Cornell U., 1956; MFA, Sarah Lawrence Coll., 1975. Sec. Saturday Rev. Mag., NYC, 1957, sci. writer, 1958—60; freelance fiction writer Ardsley, NY, 1961—. Author: Somebody Else's Child, 1976 (award Child Study Assn.), Blood Relations, 1977 (Hon. Mention Pen Hemingway prize, Hon. Mention Janet Kafka prize), (novels) Boundaries, 1979 (Hon. Mention Janet Kafka prize), The Dream Dredger, 1986 (Washington Irving award), Beginning The World Again, 1990, short stories; contbr. articles to newspapers (Nat. Magazine award, 1984). Mem. adv. coun. Coll. Arts & Scis. Cornell U. Fellow, Guggenheim Found., 1979—80, Nat. Endowment for Arts, 1982—83. Mem.: PEN (Syndicated Fiction award 1981, 1983), Poets and Writers, Authors Guild, Phi Beta Kappa. Democrat. Jewish. Avocations: piano, classical music, hiking, travel. Home: 18 Larchmont St Ardsley NY 10502 Office Phone: 914-693-2816. Personal E-mail: rsilman@verizon.net.

SILSBY, PAULA D., prosecutor; b. Ellsworth, Maine, 1951; JD, U. Maine, 1976; BA, Mt. Holyoke Coll. Bar: Maine 1976. US atty. dist. Maine US Dept. Justice, Portland, 2001—. Fellow: Maine Bar Found. Office: US Attys Office 100 Middle St Plaza East Tower 6th Fl Portland ME 04101-4182

SILVA, A. R., surgeon, educator; MD, U. Para, Brazil, 1953. Intern Monmouth Med. Ctr., Long Branch, NJ, 1957, resident surgery, 1958—62; intern surgery UCLA, 1963—64; pvt. practice Gen. Surgery and Oncology Corona, Calif., 1965—. Rsch. surgeon, clin. investigator Surgery Dept. UCLA, 1962—65; assoc. clin. prof. U. Calif. Irvine, 1977—; staff mem. Corona Regional Med. Ctr., U. Calif. Irvine Med. Ctr., Orange; chmn. cancer com. Corona Regional Med. Ctr., mem. exec. com. Contbr. articles to profl. jours. Bd. dirs. Corona Regional Med. Ctr. Found.; pres. Inland Empire unit Am. Cancer Soc., bd. dirs. Inland Empire unit. Mem.: AMA, ACS (regional surveyor cancer dept.), Tri-County Surg. Soc. So. Calif. (bd. dirs.), N.Y. Acad. Scis., So. Calif. Acad. Clin. Oncology, Soc. Surg. Oncology, Soc. Lagaroendoscopic Surgeons, Royal Soc. Medicine Eng., Riverside County Med. Assn. (bd. councilors, past pres. 1988, mediation and med. care com., past chmn. credentials com.), Pan Pacific Surg. Assn., Pan Am. Med. Soc., Orange County Surg. Soc., John E. Connelly Surg. Soc., Internat. Coll. Surgeons, Calif. Med. Assn. (alt. del Dist. II), Assn. Clin. Faculty, Am. Soc. Colon and Rectal Surgeons, Am. Soc. Clin. Oncology, Am. Soc. Abdominal Surgeons, Am. Bd. Surgery, Am. Assn. Fgn. Med. Grads. Office: PO Box 515 Corona CA 92878

SILVA, CAROLE, elementary school educator; BS in Bus., Mills Coll., Oakland, Calif., 1954; MEd in Curriculum, U. So. Calif., LA, 1981. Cert. tchr. Calif., reading specialist Calif. Tchr. Santa Monica-Malibu Unified Sch. Dist., Calif., 1972—94. Adj. prof. Calif. State U., LA, 1994—2005; mem. K-12 art com. Santa Monica Unified Sch. Dist., 1996—, founder adult reading lab; presenter in field. Musician: U. So. Calif. Cmty. Orch., 2004—09; contbr. articles to profl. jours. Bd. dirs. Calif. Philharmonic Orch. Mem.: Am. Literacy Corp. (v.p., dir. planning exec. bd. dirs.), UK Reading Lit. Assn., Teach America (mentor), Calif. Reading Assn. (former mem. state exec. bd., pres., chmn. interest groups, mem. Calif. young reader medal state com., Margaret Lynch award 1989), Freedoms Found. Valley Forge (v.p. LA chpt., nat. bd. dirs.). Home: PO Box 261363 Encino CA 91426

SILVA, CESAR ERNESTRO, mathematics educator; b. Lima, Peru, Mar. 29, 1955; came to U.S., 1977; s. Aurelio Ernesto and Maria Luisa (Posada) S; m. Margaret Oxtoby 1993; children: Emily Luise, Rebecca Bryn. BS, Cath. U., 1977; MA, U. Rochester, 1979, PhD, 1984. Asst. prof. math. Williams Coll, Williamstown, Mass., 1984-91; assoc. prof. math. Williams Coll., Williamstown, Mass., 1991—98, math. prof., 1998—2007, Hagey family prof. math., 2007—. Visiting asst. prof. math. U. Md., College Park, 1987-88. Contbr. articles to profl. jours.; co-editor: Measure and Measurable Dynamics, 1989; author: Invitation to ergodic theory, 2008. Mem. Am. Math. Soc., Math. Assn. Am., Sigma Xi. Office: Williams Coll Dept Math Williamstown MA 01267 Business E-Mail: csilva@williams.edu.

SILVA, CLARENCE RICHARD, bishop; b. Honolulu, Aug. 6, 1949; Student, St. Joseph Sem., Mountain View, Calif., St. Patrick Sem., Menlo Pk. Ordained priest Diocese of Oakland, Calif., 1975; parochial vicar St. Bernard Parish, Oakland, St. Bede Parish, Hayward, Calif.; pastor St. Peter Martyr Parish, Pittsburgh, Pa., St. Anthony Parish, Oakland, Calif., St. John the Baptist Parish, El Cerrito, Calif., St. Andrew-St. Joseph Parish, Oakland, Calif., St. Leonard-St. Paul Parish, Fremont, Calif.; vicar gen. & moderator of curia Diocese of Oakland, 2004—05; ordained bishop, 2005; bishop Diocese of Honolulu, Hawaii, 2005—. Roman Catholic. Office: Diocese of Honolulu 1184 Bishop St Honolulu HI 96813-2858 Office Phone: 801-533-1791. Office Fax: 801-521-8428.

SILVA, DANIEL JOSEPH, writer; b. Kalamazoo, Dec. 19, 1960; s. Richard and Carol Ann (Koerber) Silva; m. Jamie Sue Gangel, Oct. 8, 1988; children: Lily Elizabeth, Nicholas Jacob. BA, Calif. State U., Fresno, 1983. Fgn. news editor UPI, Washington, 1985-86; Mideast corr. Cairo, Egypt, 1986-87; exec. prodr. Washington bur. CNN, 1988—97. Apptd. coun. mem. US Holocaust Meml. Mus., Washington, 2009—. Author: (novels) The Unlikely Spy, 1997 (NY Times bestseller), The Mark of the Assassin, 1998 (NY Times bestseller), The Marching Season, 1999 (NY Times bestseller), The Kill Artist, 2000 (NY Times bestseller), The English Assassin, 2002 (NY Times bestseller), The Confessor, 2003 (NY Times bestseller), A Death in Vienna, 2004 (NY Times bestseller), Prince of Fire, 2005 (NY Times bestseller), The Messenger, 2006 (NY Times bestseller, Barry award for Best Thriller, 2006), The Secret Servant, 2007 (Publishers Weekly bestseller, NY Times bestseller), Moscow Rules, 2008 (#1 Publishers Weekly bestseller, #1 NY Times bestseller), The Defector, 2009 (#1 Publishers Weekly bestseller). Office: c/o Marilyn Duckworth Putnam 375 Hudson St New York NY 10014*

SILVA, EUGENE JOSEPH, lawyer; b. Gloucester, Mass., May 23, 1942; s. Edward Joseph and Rose (Lebre) Silva; m. Nancy Blue-Pearson, Jan. 8, 1972; children: Eugene Joseph II, Michael Joseph. BS with honors, Maine Maritime Acad., Castine, 1964; JD, U. Notre Dame, Ind., 1972. Bar: Calif. 1972, US Dist. Ct. (so. and cen. dists.) Calif. 1972, Tex. 1977, US Dist. Ct. (so. and ea. dists.) Tex. 1978, US Ct. Appeals (5th, 9th, 2d and 11th cirs.) 1978, US Supreme Ct. 1981; lic. Master Mariner. Assoc. Luce, Forward, Hamilton & Scripps, San Diego, 1972-77, Vinson & Elkins, Houston, 1977-79, ptnr., 1980—2003. Mem. adv. bd. Admiralty Law Inst. Tulane U., 1999—. Bd. dirs. Cabrillo Festival Inc., San Diego, 1974—77, San Jose Clinic, Inc., 1990—97, pres., 1993—95; bd. dirs. Portuguese Heritage Scholarship Found., 1995—, St. Joseph Hosp. Found., 1995—2000. Decorated Knight Grand Cross Equestrian Order Holy Sepulchre Jerusalem; recipient Outstanding Alumni award, Maine Maritime Acad., 1990; named one of Best Lawyers in Am., 1991—. Mem. Calif. Bar Assn., Tex. Bar Assn., Grays Inn U. Notre Dame Sch. Law (pres. 1970-72), Maritime Law Assn. US (proctor in admiralty 1974-2005), Portuguese Union Calif. (bd. dirs. 1973-74), Portuguese Am. League San Diego (pres. 1974-75), Portuguese Am. Leadership Coun. US, Notre Dame Club (pres. San Diego chpt. 1976-77). Roman Catholic. Home: 8 Smithdale Estates Dr Houston TX 77024-6600 Personal E-mail: ejsilva@swbell.net.

SILVA, JUAN LUIS, food processing engineer, educator; b. Cumana, Sucre, Venezuela, June 24, 1957; came to U.S. 1978; s. Pedro Luis and Olga (Pacheco) S. Technol. degree, Capital Region U. Inst. Tech., Venezuela, 1977; BS, Miss. State U., 1980, MS, 1983, PhD, 1986. Asst. process supr. Indsls. Oleaginosas, Venezuela, 1977; lab. asst. Miss. State U., 1981, rsch. asst., 1983-85, instr./researcher, 1985-87, asst. prof., 1987-91, assoc. prof., 1991—. Author: (book chpt.) Catfish Processing Plant; contbr. to profl. jours. Sec.-treas. Internat. Group of St. Joseph Cath. Ch., Miss., 1991-93. Mem. AIChE, Inst. Food Technologists (mem. indsl. achievement com., mem. com. on diversity 1992—, sec.-treas. Magnolia sect., chairperson so. regional sects.), R & D Assocs. for Mil. Foods and Packaging (chairperson sci. devel.), Sigma Xi, Phi Tau Sigma (exec. sec.), Gamma Sigma Delta. Roman Catholic. Avocations: swimming, tennis, travel. Office: Miss State U PO Box 9805 Mississippi State MS 39762-9805

SILVA, JULIE, social sciences educator; d. Luis Ramos and Carolyn Silva; m. Stewart Duncan, Jan. 6, 2005. PhD, Rutgers U., New Brunswick, NJ, 2005. Asst. prof. U. Fla., Gainesville, 2006—. Office: Univ Fla PO Box 117315 Gainesville FL 32611-7315 Office Fax: 352-392-2435.

SILVA, MARY BARNES, retired elementary school educator; d. Walter Howard and Rosalinda M. Barnes. BEd, Kent State U., 1964; MEd, U. Hawaii, 1976. Provisional Ohio, profl. Hawaii. Tchr. St. Louis Sch., Louisville, Ohio, 1960—62, Elyria Pub. Schs., Ohio, 1962—68, Kailua Elem., Hawaii, 1968—78, tchr. academically gifted and talented, 1978—88; tech. coord. Royal Sch., Honolulu, 1988—2001; ret., 2001. Adviser student coun., newspaper, yearbook Kailua Elem., 1979—88, chair grade level, 1975—78, Royal Sch., Honolulu, 1993—2001, chair sch. cmty.-based mgmt., 1994—99, sch. facilitator, 1995—99, tech. trainer, 1996—2001. Pres., vp., sec., treas. Assn. of Apt. Owners, Honolulu, 1979—2004, 2006—08. Named Tchr. of Yr., Honolulu Dist., 1997. Mem.: NEA (life), Hawaii State Ret. Tchrs. Assn., Hawaii Edn. Assn. (life), Contemporary Mus., Bishop Mus., Acad. Arts. Avocations: travel, the arts. Home: 410 Magellan Ave 808 Honolulu HI 96813 Personal E-mail: malia.aloha@hawaiiantel.net.

SILVA, OMEGA LOGAN, physician; b. Washington, Dec. 14, 1936; d. Louis Jasper and Ruth (Dickerson) Logan; m. C. Francis A. Silva, Oct. 25, 1958 (div. 1981); 1 child, Frances Cecile; m. Harold Bryant Webb, Nov. 28, 1982. BS cum laude with honors in chemistry, Howard U., Washington, 1958, MD, 1967. Bio-chemist NIH, Bethesda, Md., 1958-63; resident in medicine Vets. Affairs Med. Ctr., Washington, 1967—70, fellow in endocrinology, 1970—71, rsch. assoc., 1971—74, clin. investigator, 1974—77, asst. chief endocrinology, 1977-96, dir. diabetes clin., 1977—96; assoc. prof. medicine George Washington U., Washington, 1975-91; physician Mitchell-Trotman Med. Group, P.C., Washington, 1996-97; prof. George Washington U., Washington, 1991-98, prof. emeritus, 1999—; prof. Howard U., Washington, 1977-96. Mem. exec. com. Health Care Coun. Nat. Capital Area, 1995—, bd. dirs.; med. rev. officer Employee Health Programs, Bethesda, 1998-2004; bd. dirs. NRC Women and Children. Author: (with others) Endocrinology, 1990; featured Nat. Libr. Medicine's Changing the Face of Medicine, an Exhibition on America's Women Physicians, 2003; contbr. articles to profl. jours. Charter mem. Nat. Mus. of Women in the Arts, Washington, 1986; trustee Howard U., 1991-97, chair, hon. com. Coll. Medicine, Howard U., 2008. Recipient Disting. Alumni award Howard U. Coll. Medicine, 1997. Master ACP (mem. com. 2003-06, Best Sci. Presentation award 1974); fellow African Am. Inst. 2006; mem. Am. Med. Women's Assn. (br. I v.p. 1986-87, pres. 1987-88, anti-smoking task force 1989-92, chair govtl. affairs, 1992-96, mem. nominations com. 1992, gov. region III 1996-97, v.p. program 1997-99, chmn. leadership com. 1996-97, pres. elect 1999-00, pres. 2000-02, chair policy & advocacy com. 2006-, founder Internat. Women in Medicine Hall of Fame, 2001, AMWA Bertha Van Hoosen award, 2008), Howard U. Med. Alumni (pres. 1983-88, bd. dirs. 1983-), Endocrine Soc. (life), Alpha Omega Alpha, ACS (emeritus mem., 2007), Am. Diabetes Assn. (DC) (cmty. leadership bd. 2009). Avocations: dress and hat design, furniture design, home construction.

SILVA, PETER S., federal agency administrator, civil engineer; b. 1952; m. Ana Silva Silva; 1 child, Diego. BS in Civil Engring., Calif. State Poly. U., Pomona, 1977. Registered civil engr., Calif. With Calif. Regional Water Quality Control Bd., LA, San Diego; resident engr. Internat. Boundary and Water Commn., 1983—87; asst. dep. dir. clean water program City of San Diego, 1987—92, dep. dir. pub. water utility, 1992—97; bd. dirs. Border Environment Cooperation Commn., Juarez, Mexico, 1994, dep. gen. mgr., 1997—2000; mem. to vice chair Calif. Water Resources Control Bd., 2000—06; sr. policy advisor on lower Colo. River issues Met. Water Dist. of Southern Calif.; asst. adminstr. for water EPA, Washington, 2009—. Mem.: Am. Water Works Assn., Am. Soc. Civil Engrs. Democrat. Office: EPA Office of Water 1200 Pennsylvania Ave NW Washington DC 20460*

SILVA, ROBERT OWEN, retired protective service official; b. La Junta, Colo., June 5, 1935; s. Owen Delbert and Gertrude H. (Kerr) Silva; m. Meredith Ann Ginn Silva, Dec. 18, 1953; children: Edward, Andrew, Colleen. Student, Pueblo Jr. Coll., 1953, FBI Nat. Acad., 1975, Police Found. Exec. Program, 1979—80. Cert. peace officer Colo. Police officer Pueblo Police Dept., Colo., 1958—66, sgt., 1966—72, capt., 1972—77, chief of police, 1977—92; ret. dir. Colo. Police Officers Standards & Tng. Bd. dirs. Salvation Army, Pueblo, Easter Seals Soc., Pueblo, Cmty. Corrections Bd.; with gov. Colo. Crim. Justice Comsn., 1990. Served with US Army, 1955—57. Mem.: Rocky Mountain Info. Network (chmn. bd. dirs. 1986—), Colo. Assn. Chiefs Police, Organized Crime Strike Force (pres. 1984—85), Pikes Peak Cmty. Coll. Criminal Justice Program (chmn. adv. bd. 1981), Leadership Pueblo Steering Com., Pueblo Cmty. Coll. Criminal Justice Adv. Bd., Elks, Kiwanis (bd. dirs. 1982—84). Presbyterian.

SILVA, SUSAN See NIKIRK, SUSAN

SILVA-GUZMAN, ANGELICA, literature and language educator; BA in Spanish Tchg., Comm. & Lit., U. Queretaro, Mex., 1995; MA in Hispanic Lit., Western Mich. U., Kalamazoo, 1999; PhD in Hispanic Cultural Studies, Mich. State U., East Lansing, 2006. Mid. sch. Spanish tchr. USEBEQ, Queretaro, 1993—97; spanish tchr. & lang. lab. asst. Gardner Web U., Boiling Spring, NC, 1995—96; Spanish tchr. Evening Coll., Mich. State U., East Lansing, 2000—01; spanish tchr. TELAMON, 2002—07; spanish vis. lectr., Spanish & Portuguese Dept. Mich. State U., 2004—05; spanish & hispanic culture faculty Ctrl. Mich. U., Mt. Pleasant, Mich., 2006—07; spanish lang. & hispanic cultural studies asst. prof. DeSales U., Center Valley, Pa., 2007—. Coord. svc. trips & study abroad programs DeSales U., Center Valley, Pa., 2007—. Translator: Sí se Puede Project, Psychology Dept., Mich. State U. Svc. learning coord. DeSales U., Salesian Sch. Jacareizinho, Rio de Janeiro, 2008; coord. DeSales U., Center Valley, Pa., Peru, 2008; lang. coord. TELAMON Corp. Head Start Migrant Program, East Lansing, Mich., 2002—06. Recipient Dissertation Rsch. award, Dept. Spanish & Portuguese. Mich. State U., 2005; scholar Spanish Tchg. Exch. Program, U. Queretaro, Gardner-Web U. Boiling Springs, 1995—96; Grad. Studies fellowship, Bur. Pub. Edn. Queretaro.,Mex., 1997—2001, Tinker Field Rsch. grant, Ctr. Latin Am. & Caribbean Studies. Mich. State U., 2002, Global Young Scholar grant, Internat. Studies & Programs. Mich. State U., 2002, Rsch. & Travel grant, Grad. Sch. Mich. State U., 2005, Summer Retention fellowship, 2006, Rsch. & Travel grant, Fgn. Lang. Literatures & Cultures Dept. Ctrl. Mich. U., 2007, Travel grant., Humanities Dept. DeSales U., 2008. Mem.: Assn. Female Hispanic Lit., Congreso Internacional de Literatura Hispanica, Instituto Literario y Cultural Hispánico, Ctr. Latin Am. & Caribean Studies,Mich. State U., Mich. Acad. Sci., Arts & Letters, Latin Am. Indian Lits. Assn., Latin Am. Studies Assn., MLA Am., Sigma Delta Pi. Avocations: travel, dance, photography, cooking, films.

SILVEIRA, FERNANDA DE PINHO, infectious diseases physician, educator; d. Orley Bruno and Marina P. Silveira; m. Frederico G. S. de Toledo, Apr. 29, 1999. MD, Fed. U. Rio de Janeiro, 1998. Internal medicine resident U. Miami, Jackson Meml. Hosp., Fla., 2000—03; infectious diseases fellow U. Pitts. Med. Ctr., 2003—05, transplant infectious diseases fellow, 2005—06, instr. medicine, 2006—08, asst.

prof. medicine, 2008. Mem.: Internat. Soc. Heart and Lung Transplantation, Am. Soc. Transplantation, Am. Soc. Microbiology, Infectious Diseases Soc. Am. Office: Univ Pitts Med Ctr 3601 Fifth Ave Ste 3A Pittsburgh PA 15213

SILVER, ADAM, sports association executive; b. 1962; BA in Polit. Sci., Duke U., 1984; JD, U. Chgo., 1988. Legis. aide to Rep. Les AuCoin US Congress, Washington; law clk. to Hon. Kimba Wood US Dist. Ct. (so. dist.) NY, NYC; litig. assoc. Cravath, Swaine & Moore LLP, NYC; spl. asst. to commr. NBA, 1992—93, chief of staff, 1993—95; sr. v.p., COO NBA Entertainment, Secaucus, NJ, 1995—97, pres., 1997—2006, COO, 2000—06; COO, dep. commr. NBA, 2006—. Prodr.: Michael Jordan to the Max, 2000. Mem. Spl. Presdl. Coun. on Campus Life and Culture at Duke U.; mem. vis. com. U. Chgo. Law Sch.; bd. mem. PENCIL, Hands on Network Corp. Svc. Coun., Partnership for a Drug-Free Am., Duke U. Libr., NYC Sports Devel. Corp., 2003—. Named one of The Most Influential People in Sports Bus. Jour., Sports Bus. Jour., The Most Powerful People in Sports, The Sporting News, 2005, The Most Influential People in the World of Sports, Bus. Week, 2007, 2008. Jewish. Office: NBA Olympic Tower 645 5th Ave Fl 10 New York NY 10022-5986*

SILVER, AUDREY WILMA, nurse, educator, writer; b. Nashville, Nov. 29, 1945; d. David and Roslyn Silver; m. Lawrence Claster Falk (div. June 1973); children: Wendy Falk MacGregor, Laurie Falk Fields, PJ MacGregor, Jason Fields; m. Stuart Alan Berney, May 20, 1988; stepchildren: Elizabeth Berney Weiskopf, Joshua Forrest Berney. AS in Nursing, Tenn. State U., Nashville, 1992, BS in Psychology cum laude, 1997. RN Tenn., Fla., cert. case mgr.; lic. real estate broker Tenn., Fla. Consumer health writer, editor Healthy Earth Comms., Nashville, Columbia/Hosp. Corp. Am., Nashville; nurse educator, case mgr., disease mgr. Health Integrated, Tampa, Healthways, Nashville, 1999—. Contbr. articles to profl. publs., ency. Contbr. Feeding America; precinct county chmn. Kerry for Pres., Pinellas County, Fla.; health edn. coord. Hadassah, 2006. Recipient Top Internet Content award, US News and World Report, 1996, Top Health Content award, AOL and Dow Jones, 1997, award, USA Today; grantee Virtual Body feature award, CNN, 1997. Mem.: LWV, Sierra Club, Fla. Assn. Realtors, Nat. Assn. Realtors, Case Mgmt. Soc. Am., Mensa, Planned Parenthood, Habitat for Humanity, So. Poverty Law Ctr. Jewish. Avocations: bicycling, photography, reading, exercise. E-mail: audreys@tampabay.rr.com.

SILVER, BARRY MORRIS, lawyer; b. Mt. Vernon, NY, Nov. 18, 1956; s. Samuel Manuel and Elaine Martha (Shapiro) Silver. BA, Fla. Atlantic U., 1979; JD, Nova U., 1983. Bar: Fla. 1983. Atty. pvt. practice, Boca Raton, 1986—. Tchr. bilingual edn. Palm Beach County Schs., Delray Beach, Fla., 1981—83; faculty Palm Beach Jr. Coll., Boca Raton, 1990—; atty. NOW, South Palm Beach County. Vol. Haitian Refugee Ctr., Miami, 1982; mem. Fla. Ho. Reps., 1997—98; rabbi Congregation L'Dor Va-Dor, Lake Worth, Fla. Mem.: Palm Beach County Bar Assn., Fla. Bar Assn., Sierra Club. Democrat. Jewish. Avocations: languages, tennis, frisbee, chess. Office: 1200 S Rogers Cir Ste 8 Boca Raton FL 33487- Home: 18624 Cape Sable Dr Boca Raton FL 33498-6374 Office Phone: 561-483-6900.

SILVER, DAVID, lawyer; b. NYC, Jan. 27, 1931; s. Sol and Fannie (Stein) S.; m. Meryl Young, Sept. 14, 1952 (dec.); children: Daniel, Matthew, Joshua; m. Ann Schwartz, June 4, 1993. BA, CCNY, 1953; LL.B. cum laude, Harvard U., 1958. Bar: N.Y. 1958, D.C. 1979. Pvt. practice law, NYC, 1960-61; spl. counsel SEC, Washington, 1961-65; gen. counsel Investors Planning Corp., NYC, 1965-66; asst. counsel Investment Co. Inst., Washington, 1966-69, gen. counsel, 1969-77, pres., 1977-91, ICI Mut. Ins. Co., Washington, 1987-2001. Cons. securities regulation Govt. of India, 1964; mutual fund regulation Govt. of China, 1999; lectr. Law Sch. Boston U., 1995—98; mem. individual investor adv. com. N.Y. Stock Exch., 1994—99; dir. PGAM, Milan, 2001—. Served with U.S. Army, 1953-55. Mem. Fed. Bar Assn. (exec. coun. securities com., past chmn. investment co. com.). Home and Office: 9410 Brooke Dr Bethesda MD 20817-2110 Business E-Mail: anndave@verizon.net.

SILVER, DEE EDWARD, physician, neurologist; b. Keystone, Iowa, Dec. 8, 1939; s. Grant Mason and Cora Ann (Larson) S.; m. Penelope Neena Diumenti (div. May 1988); 1 child, Helen Diumenti Silver; m. Marilyn Janet Lyddy, Mar. 8, 1998. BA, Iowa State Tchrs. Coll., Cedar Falls, 1961; MD, U. Iowa, Iowa City, 1967. Diplomate Am. Bd. Neurology. Head dept. electroencephalography and neurophysiology Balboa Naval Hosp., San Diego, 1971—73; physician, ptnr., head dept. neurology Coastal Neurol. Med. Group, La Jolla, Calif., 1973—. Med. dir. San Diego Parkinsons Disease Info. Ctr., 1986—; bd. dirs. Ellen Browning Scripps Soc., San Diego, 1986-94, 1996-2005; mem. exec. cabinet Scripps Inst. Medicine and Sci., San Diego, 1994-2004; head neurology dept. Balboa Naval Hosp., 1972-73 Author and editor publs. in field Lt. comdr. USN, 1971-73 Mem. AMA, Calif. Med. Assn. (del. 1981-84), Am. Acad. Neurology, Movement Disorder Soc., Rotary Internat. (Paul Harris fellow 1986), Purple Key Soc Republican. Avocations: tennis, fly fishing, hunting, golf, trumpet. Home: PO Box 224 Rancho Santa Fe CA 92067-0224 Office: 9850 Genesee Ave Ste 740 La Jolla CA 92037-1218

SILVER, ELAINE TERRY, lawyer; b. Balt., May 11, 1953; Student, Hebrew U., 1972-73; BA with honors, Bucknell U., 1974; JD, NYU, 1977. Bar: Conn. 1977, U.S. Dist. Ct. Conn. 1977, U.S. Ct. Appeals (2d cir.) 1980. Assoc. Glazer, Seelig & Glazer, Stamford, Conn., 1977-81, 82-83; vis. prof. law Beijing U., 1981-82; ptnr. Fleisher, Trow & Silver, Stamford, 1983-87, Silver, Golub & Teitell LLP, Stamford, 1987—2000; founder Law Office of Elaine T. Silver, Lake Mary, Fla., 2005—. Counsel Domestic Violence Service, Stamford, 1983-85; founder Silver Divorce Ctr., 2004-; adj. family law instr., Barry U. Sch. Law, 2007 Pres., bd. dirs. Rape and Sexual Abuse Crisis Ctr., Inc., Stamford, 1985-87. Mem. ABA (family law sect. Fla. Bar) Office: Seminole County Bar Assn Orange County Bar Assn 1515 International Pkwy St 1019 Lake Mary FL 32746 Office Phone: 407-712-6787. E-mail: ESilver@SilverDivorce.com.

SILVER, HARRY R., lawyer; b. Phila., Aug. 8, 1946; s. Jerome Benjamin Silver and Josephine Sandler (Steinberg) Furr; m. Jessica Dunsay, Nov. 23, 1972; children: Gregory, Alexander. BA, Temple U., 1968; JD, Columbia U., 1971. Bar: N.Y. 1972, D.C. 1973, U.S. Dist. Ct. D.C., U.S. Ct. Claims, U.S. Ct. Appeals (1st, 4th, 5th, 7th, 8th, 9th, 10th, fed. and D.C. cirs.), U.S. Supreme Ct. Law clk. to Hon. Harold R. Medina, U.S. Ct. Appeals (2d cir.), NYC, 1971-72; assoc. Arent, Fox, Kintner, Plotkin & Kahn, Washington, 1972-74; atty. U.S. Dept. Justice, Washington, 1974-77, U.S. Dept. Energy, Washington, 1977-78; assoc. Akin, Gump, Strauss, Hauer & Feld, Washington, 1978-81, ptnr., 1981-88, Oppenheimer, Wolff & Donelly, Washington, 1988-91, Davis Wright Tremaine, Washington, 1991-94, Ober, Kaler, Grimes & Shriver, Washington, 1994—2004, Patton Boggs, Washington, 2004—. Mem.: ABA, Fed. Bar Assn. Avocations: running, music, travel. Home: 6829 Wilson Ln Bethesda MD 20817-4948 Office: Patton Boggs 2550 M St NW Washington DC 20037 Home Phone: 301-229-2295; Office Phone: 202-457-6453. E-mail: hsilver@pattonboggs.com.

SILVER, HERBERT, physician; b. Bklyn., Feb. 18, 1932; s. Ben and Sylvia (Weinstock) S.; m. Judith Elaine Miller, Aug. 28, 1966; children: Rand Kenneth, David Jeffrey. BA, Adelphi U., 1953; MD, SUNY, Buffalo, 1957. Diplomate Am. Bd. Pathology. Intern Maimonides Med. Ctr., 1957-58; resident Nassau Univ. Med. Ctr., 1958-60, Hosp. of U. of Pa., 1960-62; assoc. pathologist, dir. blood bank/hematology Barnes-Jewish Hosp., St. Louis, 1964-70; dir. transfusion medicine Hartford (Conn.) Hosp., 1970—2001; assoc. prof. U. Conn. Med. Ctr., Farmington, 1970-90, U. Conn. Sch. of Allied Health, Storrs, 1977—2002. Cons. St. Francis Med. Ctr., Hartford, Conn., 1978-2002, Conn. Children's Med. Ctr., 1980-2002; med. dir. Hartford Med. Lab, 1985-99; adv. coun. Capital Cmty. Coll. Found., Hartford, Conn., 2002—. Author, editor: Probability of Inclusion in Paternity Testing, 1982, Problem Solving in Immunohematology, 1987; guest editor Transfusion Jour., 1992-96; contbr. articles to profl. jours. Bd. dirs. Emanuel Synagogue, West Hartford, Conn. Capt. U.S. Army Med. Corps, 1962-64. Mem.: AMA, Coll. Am. Pathologists, Am. Soc. Clin. Pathology, Am. Assn. Blood Banks (bd. dirs. 1987—92, Disting. Svc. award 1993, John Elliott Meml. award 2000). Democrat. Jewish. Avocations: bicycling, clarinet. Home: 32 Beacon Hill Dr West Hartford CT 06117-1003

SILVER, JOAN MICKLIN, film director, screenwriter; b. Omaha, May 24, 1935; d. Maurice David and Doris (Shoshone) Micklin; m. Raphael D. Silver, June 28, 1956; children: Dina, Marisa, Claudia. BA, Sarah Lawrence Coll., 1956. Writer, dir. (movies) Hester Street, 1975 (Writers Guild best screenplay nomination), Chilly Scenes of Winter, 1981, (TV film PBS) Bernice Bobs Her Hair starring Shelly Du Vall, 1975; dir. (TV films HBO) Finnegan, Begin Again with Robert Preston and Mary Tyler Moore, Parole Board, A Private Matter with Sissy Spacek and Aidan Quinn, (TV film Showtime) In The Presence of Mine Enemies, 1997, (films) Between the Lines, 1976, Crossing Delancey with Amy Irving, 1988, Loverboy, 1989; dir. stage plays and musicals including Album, Maybe I'm Doing It Wrong, Off-Broaday prodn. A...My Name is Alice; prodr. On The Yard, (radio) Great Jewish Stories from Eastern Europe and Beyond, 1995; dir. (feature film) A Fish in the Bathtub, 1998, (TV film Lifetime) Invisible Child, 1999, (TV film Showtime) Charms for the Easy Life, 2001, TV film LifeTime) Hunger Point, 2003. Office: Silverfilm Prodns Inc 510 Park Ave New York NY 10022-1105

SILVER, JOEL, film producer; b. South Orange, NJ, July 14, 1952; m. Karyn Fields, July 10, 1999. Attended, Lafayette Coll. Owner Silver Pictures; co-owner (with Robert Zemenckis) Dark Castle Entertainment. Film producer: The Warriors, 1979, Xanadu, 1980, 48 Hours, 1982, Jekyll & Hyde...Together Again, 1982, Streets of Fire, 1984, Brewster's Millions, 1985, Weird Science, 1985, Commando, 1985, Jumpin' Jack Flash, 1986, Lethal Weapon, 1987, Predator, 1987, Action Jackson, 1988, Die Hard, 1988, Lethal Weapon 2, 1989, Roadhouse, 1989, The Adventures of Ford Fairlane, 1990, Die Hard 2, 1990, Predator 2, 1990, Hudson Hawk, 1991, Ricochet, 1991, The Last Boy Scout, 1991, Lethal Weapon 3, 1992, Demolition Man, 1993, Richie Rich, 1994, Demon Knight, 1995, Assassins, 1995, Fair Game, 1995, Executive Decision, 1996, Bordello of Blood, 1996, Father's Day, 1997, Conspiracy Theory, 1997, Lethal Weapon 4, 1998, Made Men, 1999, The Matrix, 1999, The House on Haunted Hill, 1999, Romeo Must Die, 2000, Dungeons and Dragons, 2000, Exit Wounds, 2001, Proximity, 2001, Swordfish, 2001, Thir13en Ghosts, 2001, Ghost Ship, 2001, Cradle 2 the Grave, 2003, The Matrix Reloaded, 2003, The Matrix Revolutions, 2003, Gothika, 2003, House of Wax, 2005, Kiss Kiss Bang Bang, 2005, V for Vendetta, 2005, The Reaping, 2007; TV prodr.: W.E.I.R.D. World, 1995, Action, 1999, The Strip, 1999, Freedom, 2000, Jane Doe, 2001, Newton, 2003, Next Action Star, 2004, Bet Your Life, 2004, Veronica Mars, 2004, The Studio, 2005. Office: Silver Pictures care Warner Bros Pictures 4000 Warner Blvd Bldg 90 Burbank CA 91522-0001

SILVER, LYNN LESLIE, research scientist, consultant; b. NYC, Sept. 12, 1946; d. Aaron Jack Silver and Shirley Silver Black. BA, Brandeis U., Waltham, Mass., 1968; PhD, Tufts U. Sch. Medicine, Boston, 1974. Rsch. fellow Merck & Co., Rahway, NJ, 1982—87, sr. rsch. fellow, 1987—95, sr. investigator, 1995—2003; prin. LL Silver Consulting, LLC, Springfield, NJ, 2004—. Mem. editl. bd. Antimicrobial Agents and Chemotherapy, Washington, 1997—; mem. sci. adv. bd. Cumbre Pharms., Dallas, 2005—; invited spkr., leader, chmn. and co-chmn. numerous sci. meetings. Author (and co-author): (peer reviewed sci. papers) Jour. Biol. Chemistry; Nature; Science. Mem.: Am. Soc. Microbiology. Achievements include discovery of antibacterial agents; research in mechanism of action and resistance to antibacterial agents.

SILVER, MALCOLM DAVID, pathologist, educator; b. Adelaide, South Australia, Apr. 29, 1933; s. Eric Bertram and Stella Louisa (Riley) S.; m. Meredith May Galloway, Jan. 19, 1957; children: Stuart Faulkner, Claire Eleanor, Caryl Louise. MD, U. Adelaide; PhD, McGill U. Diplomate: Am. Bd. Pathology. Resident med. officer Royal Adelaide Hosp., 1957-58; resident in pathology Royal Victoria Hosp.-Pathol. Inst., McGill U., Montreal, Que., Canada, 1958-63; research fellow dept. exptl. pathology John Curtin Sch. Med. Research, Australian Nat. U., Canberra, 1963-65; asst. prof. pathology U. Toronto, 1965-68, assoc. prof., 1968-74, prof., 1974—79, chmn. dept. pathology, 1985-95, prof. dept. lab. medicine and pathobiology, 1996—98; staff pathologist Toronto Gen. Hosp., 1965-72, sr. staff pathologist, 1972-79; prof., chmn. dept. pathology U. Western Ont., London, Ont., Canada, 1979-85; chief pathology Univ. Hosp., London, 1979-85; pathologist in chief Toronto Gen. Hosp., 1985-89, The Toronto Hosp. (Toronto Gen. and Toronto Western Divs.), 1989-91, sr. staff pathologist, 1991-98. Prof. emeritus U. Toronto, 1998—. Contbr. articles to profl. jours. Fellow Royal Coll. Pathololgists Australasia, Royal Coll. Physicians and Surgeons Can.; mem. Can. Assn. Pathologists, Ont. Assn. Pathologists, Internat. Acad. Pathology, Can. Cardiovasc. Soc., Soc. for Cardiovasc. Pathology. E-mail: md.silver@utoronto.ca.

SILVER, MICHAEL, education educator; b. Landsberg, Germany, Jan. 30, 1948; came to U.S., 1949; s. Norman and Esther Silver; m. Beverley Ann Moss, May 16, 1971; children: Sabina, Joseph. AB, Washington U., 1970, MEd, 1973, PhD, 1982. Cert. supt. Mo., Wash. Tchr. Normandy Sch. Dist., St. Louis, 1970-72, Parkway Sch. Dist., St. Louis, 1972-75, asst. prin., 1976-79, adminstrv. asst., 1979-83, asst. to supt., 1983-84, asst. supt., 1984-86; supt. Tukwila Sch. Dist., Seattle, 1986—2003; asst. prof. edni. adminstrn. Seattle U. Bd. dirs. Cities in Schs., Seattle; mem. adv. bd. Sta. KCTS, Seattle, 1990-2003; vis. exec. Seattle U. Sch. Edn., 1995. Author: Values Education, 1976, Facing Issues of Life and Death, 1976. Pres. SeaTac Task Force, Seattle, 1989; bd. dirs. Anti-Defamation League, Seattle, 1987—; mem. City of Tukwila (Wash.) 2000 Com., 1988-90. Recipient A Plus award Wash. Coun. Econ. Edn., 1992, Excellence in Ednl. Leadership award Univ. Coun. for Ednl. Adminstrn., 1998, Art Tribute award, Wash. Art Edn. Assn., 2001; named Exec. Educator, 100 Exec. Educator Mag., 1985, 1996 Assoc. for Inst. for Ednl. Inquiry Leadership Program; named to Homework Ctrl.; 100 Most Influential People in U.S. Pub. Edn.; I/D/E/A fellow Charles F. Kettering Found., 1978, 88, Title VI fellow Washington U., 1971-73, Svc. Learning Faculty fellow Seattle U., 2005-06; New Prin. grantee Wash. Mutual, 2005; named Supt. of Yr. Wash. Libr. Media Assn., 2000. Mem. ASCD, Am. Assn. Sch. Adminstrs., Wash. Assn. Sch. Adminstrs. (met. chpt., pres. 1989-90), King County Supts. (chmn. adv. com. 1989-90, 95-96), Southcenter Rotary Club (Paul Harris fellow 1994), Southwest King County C. of C., Phi Delta Kappa. Home: 14127 SE 50th St Bellevue WA 98006-3409 Office: Seattle U Sch Edn PO Box 222000 901 12th Ave Seattle WA 98122 Office Phone: 206-296-5798. Personal E-mail: 4silver@gmail.com. Business E-Mail: silverm@seattleu.edu.

SILVER, MORRIS, economist, educator; b. NYC, July 9, 1931; s. Julius and Lilly Silver; m. Sondra P. Hartman, Jan. 26, 1958; children: Gerald David, Ronald Alan. BA, CCNY, 1958; PhD (Earhart Found. fellow, Ford Found. fellow), Columbia U., 1964. Mem. faculty City Coll. CUNY, 1964—, assoc. prof. econs., 1968—, prof., 1972—, chmn. dept., 1969-95. Rsch. assoc. Nat. Bur. Econ. RSch., 1967—71; cons. crime deterrence and offender career Nat. Ctr. Health Svcs. Rsch., 1970—, Hudson Inst., 1974. Author (with r. D. Auster): The State as a Firm, 1979; author: Affluence, Altruism, and Atrophy: The Decline of Welfare States, 1980, Prophets and Markets: The Political Economy of Ancient Israel, 1983, Enterprise and the Scope of the Firm, 1984, Economic Structures of the Ancient Near East, 1985, Foundations of Economic Justice, 1989, Taking Ancient Mythology Economically, 1992, Economic Structures of Antiquity, 1995. With US Army, 1953—55. Mem.: Am. Econ. Assn. Jewish. Office: Dept Econs City Coll 133 D St New York NY 10031 E-mail: msilver12@nyc.rr.com.

SILVER, NATE, statistician, writer; b. East Lansing, Mich., Jan. 13, 1978; BA in Econs., U. Chgo. Econ. cons. KPMG, Chgo., 2000—03; mng. ptnr. Baseball Prospectus, 2003—09; founder, blogger FiveThirtyEight.com, 2008—. Contbr. articles to newspapers, magazines, Web sites; co-author: Baseball Prospectus, 2003—, Mind Game: How the Boston Red Sox Got Smart, Won a World Series, and Created a New Blueprint for Winning, 2005—, Baseball Between the Numbers, 2006, It Ain't Over 'til It's Over: The Baseball Prospectus Pennant Race Book, 2007. Named one of The World's Most Influential People, TIME mag., 2009. Achievements include development of PECOTA (Player Empirical Comparison and Optimization Test Algorithm) a statistical system that projects the future performance of hitters and pitchers. Address: FiveThirtyEight.com New York NY Business E-Mail: 538dotcom@gmail.com.*

SILVER, R. PHILIP, packaging products executive; b. 1942; Grad., U. Mo., 1967. With Amour & Co., Atlanta, 1967—68, Boise Cascade Corp., Idaho, 1968—75; exec. v.p. Fla. Gas Co., Orlando, Fla., 1975—80; pres. Continental Can, Norwalk, Conn., 1980—86; pres., treas. Silgan Holdings Inc., Stamford, Conn., 1987—93, chmn., co-CEO, 1994—2004, co-chmn., co-CEO, 2004—06, co-chmn., 2006—. Office: Silgan Holdings Inc 4 Landmark Sq Stamford CT 06901

SILVER, RALPH DAVID, financial planner; b. Chgo., Apr. 19, 1924; s. Morris J. and Amelia (Abrams) S.; m. Lois Reich, Feb. 4, 1951; children: Jay, Cappy. BS, U. Chgo., 1943; postgrad., Northwestern U., 1946-48; JD, DePaul U., 1952. Bar: Ill. bar 1952. Staff accountant David Himmelblau & Co. (C.P.A.'s), 1946-48; internal revenue agt. U.S. Dept. Treasury, 1948-51; practice in Chgo., 1952-55; atty. Lawrence J. West, 1952-55; exec. v.p.-fin., bd. dirs. Barton Inc., Chgo., 1955-92. Arbitrator N.Y. Stock Exch., Cir. Ct. of Cook County, Ill. Bd. dirs., pres. Ralph and Lois Silver Found. Lt. (j.g.) USNR, 1943-46. Mem. ABA, Chgo. Bar Assn., AICPA. Home: 1124 Old Elm Ln Glencoe IL 60022-1235

SILVER, RICHARD TOBIAS, oncologist, educator, hematologist; b. Jan. 18, 1929; m. Barbara Silver; 1 son, Adam Bennett. BA, Cornell U., 1950, MD, 1953. Diplomate Nat. Bd. Med. Examiners, Am. Bd. Internal Medicine, Am. Bd. Clin. Oncology. Intern N.Y. Hosp.-Cornell Med. Ctr., NYC, 1953-54, asst. resident in medicine, 1956-57, resident in hematology, 1957-58; clin. assoc. gen. medicine br. Nat. Cancer Inst., NIH, Bethesda, Md., 1954-56; asst. in medicine Cornell U. Med. Coll., NYC, 1956-58, instr. medicine, 1958-62, clin. asst. prof., 1962-67, clin. assoc. prof., 1967-73, clin. prof., 1973—2002; asst. attending physician NY Hosp., 1964-67, assoc. attending physician, 1967-73, attending physician, 1973—, dir. clin. oncology and chemotherapy rsch., divsn. Hematology & Med. Oncology, 2000; prof. medicine, med. dir. Leukemia and Myeloproliferative Ctr., Weill Cornell Med. Coll., 2002—. Asst. vis. physician 2d Cornell Med. div. Bellevue Hosp., NYC, 1963-66; vis. Fulbright prof. U. Bahia Sch. Medicine, Brazil, 1958-60; vis. prof. Hershey Hosp.-Pa. State Hosp., 1976, Mayo Clinic, 1977, Upstate Med. Ctr., Binghamton, NY, 1977, Med. Coll. Va., 1979, Med. Sch. Colubia U., 1982, NJ Coll. Medicine, New Brunswick, 1983, Meml. Med. Ctr. U. Ga., 1984, 86; invited lectr. and presenter in field; chair 1st, 2d, 3d, 4th, 5th Internat. Congresses Myelproliferative and Myelodysplastic, 2001, 03, 05, 07, 09; vis. faculty curriculum devel. Annenberg Ctr. Rancho Mirage, Calif., 1994—; mem. rev. bd. NIH, Nat. Cancer Inst.; cons. Cancer Chemotherapy Investigative Rev. Bd., 1980, clin. trials com., 1979-81; mem. Cornell U. Coun., 1987—; spl. site visitor medicine A Roswell Park Meml. Inst., NIH-Nat. Cancer Inst., 1976, mem. combined modality com. divsn. cancer treatment, 1977-79, clin. trials com., 1979-81, cons. cancer chemotherapy rev. bd., 1980, ad hoc site visitor, MD Anderson Hosp., Houston, 2003, prin. investigator Internat. Myeloprolifentive Rsch. Consortium, 2006-, chmn. membership com., 2006-, vice-chmn. Internat. Working Group for Myelofibrosis Rsch. and Treatment, 2006-; vis. Fulbright lectr. Sch. Medicine U. Bahia, Brazil, 1958-59; lectr., presenter in field. Author: Morphology of the Blood and Marrow in Clinical Practice, 1970; co-author: (with R.D. Lauper, C.I. Jarowski) A Synopsis of Cancer Chemotherapy, 1977, 2ndedit., 1986, monographs; editor: Clinical Topics in Cancer: Diagnosis and Treatment, 1982, Myeloproliferative Disorders: Biology and Management, 2008; cons. editor Am. Jour. Medicine, 1974-84, mem. editl. adv. bd., 1984; editor, contbr.: Topics in Cancer, 1982, Myeloproliferative Disorders: Biology and Treatment, 2007; mem. editl. adv. bd. Cancer Investigation, 1983-94; ad-hoc rev. New Eng. Jour. Medicine, Annals of Internal Medicine, Leukemia, European Jour. Haematology, Jour. Clin. Oncology, Mayo Clinic Procs., Blood, Cancer, Am. Jour. Hematology, Med. Rsch. Coun., Eng., Biology and Management of Myeloprowferative Disorder, 2008, others; contbr. chpts. to books and articles to profl. jours. Trustee Frances and Edwin Cummings Meml. Fund, 1985-92, Rectory Sch., Pompret, Conn., 2004-; med. dir. Rsch. for Blood Health, Inc., 1968-85, Arnold K. Krakower Hematology Found., 1966-75, Cancer Rsch. and Treatment Fund, 1985—. Recipient Pasmantier award, Timothy Gee award for outstanding tchr., clinician, inventor and humanist, 2001, Lifetime Achievement award Cancer Rsch. & Treatment, 2008, Invited Plenary Lectr., Internat. Menarini Bologna, Italy, 2007; N.Y. State scholar for profl. study of medicine. Fellow ACP; mem. Cornell U. Med. Coll. Alumni Assn. (pres. 1973-76, sr. advisor 1976—), Am. Soc. Clin. Oncology (mem. com. clin. practice 1976, com. on pub. affairs 1981-83, chmn. program com. 1977), Internat. Soc. Hematology (chmn. bone marrow biopsy wokshop XV congress 1974, internat. adv. com. XX Congress 1984, lectr.), Am. Soc. Hematology (chmn., guidelines com., mem. devel. com. 2003-06, chmn. and covener, Internat.

Congress Myelodysplastic & Myeloproliferative Disease, 2001, 03, 05, 07, 07, 09), Leukemia Soc. Am. (med. dir., v.p. NYC chpt. 1968-78), Chronic Myeloid Leukemia (mem. devel. com., 2003-06), Sass Found Hematologic Rsch. (bd. advs.), NY Soc. Study of Blood, NY County Med. Soc., NY State Med. Soc. Oncologists and Hematologists (pres. 1991-2001, mem. exec. com. 1991—, chmn. nominating com., 2007), Harvey Soc., Am. Fedn. Clin. Rsch., Am. Assn. Cancer Rsch., Explorers Club (bd. dirs., chmn. sci. adv. com. 1987), Sigma Xi, (life) Cornell U. Coun. (life). Office: NY Presby Hosp Weill Cornell Med Ctr 525 E 68th St Box 581 New York NY 10021 Home Phone: 212-746-2541; Office Phone: 212-746-2098. Business E-Mail: rtsilve@med.cornell.edu. E-mail: rtsilvermd@gmail.com.

SILVER, RONALD G., chemical engineer, researcher; s. Howard F. and Alice G. Silver; m. Cindy Hendricks, June 15, 1991; children: Courtney K., Alexander J., Ashley B. BS in Chem. Engring, U. Wyo., Laramie, 1984; MS, U. Tex., Austin, 1986, PhD, 1989. Rsch. engr. ASEC Mfg., Tulsa, Okla., 1989—97; engring. supr. Syntroleum, Tulsa, 1997—98; staff rsch. engr. United Techs. Fuel Cells, South Windsor, Conn., 1999—2003; engring. rsch. specialist Caterpillar Inc., Mossville, Ill., 2004—08, devel. team leader, 2008—. Pres. Tulsa sect. AIChE, 1996, Catalysis Soc. New Eng., Worcester, Mass., 2003—04. Editor: (book) Catalytic Control of Air Pollution, ACS Symposium. Bd. mem. North Prospect Neighborhood Assn., Peoria, Ill., 2007—08. Mem.: Soc. Automotive Engrs., Am. Chem. Soc., Tau Beta Pi. Achievements include seven patents in field of exhaust aftertreatment catalyst applications; development of Pd only three way pollution control catalyst; improved water-gas shift catalyst; improved exhaust aftertreatment catalyst for diesel engines. Home: 5631 N Prospect Rd Peoria IL 61614 Office: Caterpillar Inc Tech Ctr F Mossville IL 61552 Business E-Mail: silver_ron@cat.com.

SILVER, SALLY, minister; b. Farmington, Maine, July 8, 1943; d. Edwin Raymond and Ethel Elizabeth Pearson; children: Gregory, Peter. Spiritual min., Fairfield Spiritual Ch., 1990—92. Tchr. Tangwala Healing Ctr., Oquossoc, Maine, 1973—80; founder, tchr. Western Maine Woman's Meditation Soc., Kingfield, Maine, 1979—85, Crystalmaineia, Eustis, Maine, 1980—86; reader, min. tchr. Light of the Moon, Portland, Maine, 1993—98; min., bd. mem. Ctr. of Eternal Light, Cape Coral, Fla., 1994—97; min., clairvoyant tchr. Planet Earth Book Ctr., Ft. Myers, Fla., 1997—2005; reader Leapin Lizards, Portland, Maine, 2005—08; reader, psychic Sunday New Edge Events, Portland, Maine, 2006, 2007, 2008; tchr., psychic devel. Farmington, Maine. Bd. mem. Ctr. of Eternal Light, Cape Coral, Fla., 1994—97. Min. Universal Brotherhood Movement, 1994—, Fla. Assn. of Spiritual Ministers, 1994. Avocations: reading, painting. Home: 99 W Kingfield Rd Kingfield ME 04947-4252 Office Phone: 239-272-9165.

SILVER, SHELDON, state legislator; b. NYC, Feb. 13, 1944; s. Nathan and Frieda (Bearman) S.; m. Rosa Mandelkern, June 25, 1967; children: Edward, Janine, Michelle, Esther. BA, Yeshiva U., 1965; JD, Bklyn. Coll., 1968. Bar: NY 1969, U.S. Dist. Ct. (so. and ea. dists.) NY 1970. Assoc. Schechter & Schwartz, NYC, 1968-71; law sec. to Judge Francis Pecora NY Civil Ct., NYC, 1971-76; ptnr. Agri, Bilder & Silver, NYC, 1976-81; mem. Dist. 64 NY State Assembly, Albany, 1977—, interim spkr., 1994, spkr. of the house, 1994—, chmn. ways & means com., 1992—94, chmn. rules com., 2001—; of counsel Weitz & Luxenberg, NYC, 2002—. V.P. Bialystoker Synagogue, Young Israel Synagogue. Recipient: United Jewish Appeal Citation for Humanitarian Efforts, Legis. of Yr. award Environ. Planning Lobby, Centennial Citation of Merit for Leadership in Edn. Nat. Arts Club, Friend of SUNY award, Govt. Hero award Downtown Lower Manhattan Assn., Disting. Pub. Svc. award Fed. Jewish Philanthropies, 1982, Chinese Journalist Assn. award, Gouverneur Hosp. Cmty. Svc. award, Disting. Lawmaker of Yr. award, LI Breast Cancer Action Coalition, Margaret Sanger award Family Planning Advocates, Presdl award NY State Nurses Assn., Elizabeth Blackwell, M.D. medal NYU Downtown Hosp.; Named Man of Yr., United Jewish Coun., 1976, Harry S. Truman Dem. Club, 1977 Mem.: Assembly Puerto Rican /Hispanic Task Force. Democrat. Jewish. Avocation: basketball. Office: Dist Office 250 Broadway Ste 2307 New York NY 10007 also: Weitz & Luxenberg 180 Maiden Ln New York NY 10038 also: Capitol Office Legislative Office Bldg 932 Albany NY 12248 Office Phone: 518-455-3791. Business E-Mail: speaker@assembly.state.ny.us.*

SILVER, STEVEN DAVID, science educator; s. Harry Aaron and Adele Sasha Silver. MA, U. Chgo., 1977; PhD, U. Calif., Berkeley, 1984, U. Cambridge, Eng., 1996. Instr. U. Calif., Berkeley, 1982—84, vis. asst. prof. Davis, 1984—86; assoc. prof. Calif. State U., San Jose, 1986—88, prof., 1988—; Lucas fellow, 2006—. Fellow U. Cambridge, 1996—2003; vis. fellow Hoover Instn., Stanford, Calif., 2003—08. Author: (books) Consuming Knowledge, Status Through Consumption: Dynamics of Consuming in Structured Environments; contbr. articles to profl. jours. Mem. adv. bd., state Smogcheck program design State of Calif., Sacramento, 1988—90; mem. adv. and design com. Mayor's Com. Performing Arts, San Jose. Rsch. grant, NSF, 1986—88, Postdoc. fellowship, NIH, 1996. Mem.: IEEE. Office: Lucas Grad Sch Bus Calif State Univ 1 Washington Sq San Jose CA 95192 Personal E-mail: sds1000@gmail.com. Business E-Mail: silver_s@cob.sjsu.edu.

SILVER, TIMOTHY MILTON, physician, educator; s. Charles Earl Frazier (Stepfather); m. Kim Yvette Ferguson, May 9, 1991; children: Timothy Milton Jr., Charles Benjamin Anthony, Rachel Violetta, Katherine Mariah. BS, Va. Union U., Richmond, Va., 1991; MS, Barry U., Miami Shores, Fla., 1993; MD, East Carolina U. Sch. of Medicine (Brody), Greenville, NC, 1997. Board Certified PM&R Amercan Bd. of Phys. Medicine and Rehab., 2003. Med. dir. sah-s Sheltering Arms Hosp., Mechanicsville, Va., 2005—; chief of pm&r svc. McGuire Vets. Med. Ctr., Richmond, Va., 2001—05; asst. prof. Va. Commonwealth U. Sch. of Medicine Dept. of PM&R, Richmond, Va., 2001—, pm&r resident / ho. staff, 1998—2001; internal medicine resident/ housestaff Yale U. Internal Medicine, Norwalk, Conn. Dir. and chief of svc. Sheltering Arms Hosp. -South, Midlothian, Va., 2005—; athletic care physician -Athens 2004 Internat. Olympic com., Athens, Greece, 2004; athletic care physician- Athens 2004 Internat. Paralympic Com., Athens, Greece; team physician/ chmn. med. adv. bd. WKA-USA, Richmond, Va., 1999—. Editor: (regional managing editor) Rehab in Review, (scientific peer reviewer) Veteran Administration Rehabilitation Research annual assenbly; contbr. scientific papers. Vol. med. advisor Nat. Kidney Found., Richmond, Va., 2003—05. Decorated Army Commendation Medal (3), Army Achievement Medal, Nat. Def. Ribbon, Profl. devel. Ribbon, Drill Sgt. ID Badge. US Army; recipient Physician Recognition Award with Commendation, AMA, 2005, Clin. Excellence Award, Va. Commonwealth U. Sch. of Medicine Dept. of PM&R, 2000; scholar Bd. of Govs. Scholar, U. NC Governing Bd., 1994, 1995, 1996, 1997. Fellow: Am. Acad. of PM&R; mem.: Richmond Acad. of Medicine, Am. Coll. of Sports Medicine, Am. Assn. of Ringside Physicians. Avocations: cycling, swimming, golf, tennis. Office: Sheltering Arms Hosp S 8254 Atlee Rd Mechanicsville VA 23116 Personal E-mail: tsilv@comcast.net.

SILVER, VANESSA MARIE, educational therapist, consultant; b. Gary, Ind., Apr. 29, 1957; d. George and Fannie Platis; children: Alexander, Michael. BA, Valparaiso U., Ind., 1982; MS, San Diego State U., 1988. Resource specialist LA Unified Sch. Dist., 2000—03; ednl. therapist Calif. Dir., owner Silver Strand Acad., Calif., 2002—; pres., owner Silver Lining Ednl. Svcs., Inc, Calif., 2000—. Mem.: Learning Disabilities Assn., Internat. Dyslexia Assn., Coun. Learning Disabilities, Coun. Exceptional Children (state student pres. 2001—02), Calif. Assn. Resource Specialists (treas. 2002—04), Assn. Ednl. Therapists (pub. rels. dir. 2003—04). Jewish. Avocations: tennis, photography. Office: Silver Lining Educational Services Inc 12654 Braxton Pl Granada Hills CA 91344-1511 E-mail: vmsbcet@aol.com.

SILVER, WARREN M., state supreme court justice; m. Evelyn Silver. Grad., Tufts U., 1970; JD, Am. U. Wash. Coll. of Law, 1973. Atty., priv. practice, Bangor, 1977—2005; justice Maine Supreme Ct., 2005—. Bd. dir. Bangor Museum and Ctr. History. Mem.: Maine Trial Lawyers Assn. (bd. govs. 1987—97, pres. 2001—05, liaison supreme judicial court civil rules com. 2005—07, liaison bd. bar examiners 2008). Office: Maine Supreme Ct Penobscot Cty Courthouse 97 Hammond St Bangor ME 04401 Office Phone: 207-561-2325.*

SILVERANG, KEVIN J., lawyer; b. Bklyn., Apr. 22, 1955; s. Arthur H. and Sandra Silverang; m. Claudia J. Auer, May 30, 1981; 1 child, Leigh A. BA, Franklin and Marshall Coll., Lancaster, Pa, 1977; JD, Villanova U., Pa., 1980. Bar: US Dist. Ct. (ea. dist.) Pa. 1980, Pa. 1980. Mng. ptnr. Phila. office Buchanan Ingersoll, PC, 1997—2004; gen. counsel O'Neill Properties Group, King of Prussia, Pa., 2004—07; ptnr. Silverang & Donohoe LLC, St. Davids, Pa., 2007—. Bd. dirs. Progress Bank, Blue Bell, Pa., Continental Bank, Plymouth, Pa. Mem.: NJ Bar Assn., Pa. Bar Assn. Avocations: bluegrass guitar, cooking, rugby. Home: 242 Waterloo Ave Berwyn PA 19312 Office: Silverang & Donohoe LLC 595 East Lancaster Ave Ste 203 Saint Davids PA 19087 Office Fax: 215-754-4934; Home Fax: 215-754-4934. Business E-Mail: ksilverang@sanddlawyers.com.

SILVERBERG, ALICE, mathematician, educator; b. NYC, Oct. 6, 1958; d. Al and Shirley Silverberg. AB in Math. summa cum laude, Harvard U., 1979; cert. advanced study in math., U. Cambridge, 1980; MA in Math., Princeton U., 1981, PhD in Math., 1984. Asst. prof. dept. math. Ohio State U., Columbus, 1984-90, assoc. prof., 1990—. Vis. researcher Harvard U., 1990-91, Math. Scis. Rsch. Inst., Berkeley, Calif., 1986-87, rsch. professorship 1992-93. Contbr. articles to Inventiones Mathematicae, Duke Math. Jour., Compositio Mathematica, Am. Jour. Math. Sloan Found. fellow, 1990-91, IBM fellowship, 1988-89, NSF fellowship, 1984-87, 79-82. Mem. Phi Beta Kappa. Research interests include number theory and arithmetical algebraic geometry. Office: Ohio State U Dept Math 231 W 18th Ave Columbus OH 43210-1101

SILVERBERG, KRISTEN LEE, former ambassador; b. Tex., 1970; d. Eric and Rhoda Silverberg; m. Paul V. Lettow, May 24, 2008. BA, Harvard U.; JD, Tex. U., 1996. Law clk. to Hon. David Satelle US Ct. Appeals (DC Cir.), 1996—97; assoc. Williams & Connolly, LLP, 1997—98; law clk. to Justice Clarence Thomas US Supreme Ct., 1998—99; spl. asst. to Pres. for policy The White House, dep. asst. to Pres. for domestic policy, 2003—04, dep. asst. to Pres., adv. to chief of staff, 2004—05; sr. advisor to amb. Paul Bremer US Embassy, Baghdad, 2003; asst. sec. for internat. orgn. affairs US Dept State, Washington, 2005—08, US amb to the European Union Brussels, 2008—09. Bd. dirs. Vorbeck Materials Corp., 2009—. Named a Maverick, Details mag., 2007.*

SILVERBERG, MICHAEL JOEL, lawyer; b. Rochester, NY, Aug. 12, 1932; s. Goodman and Minnie (Krovetz) S.; m. Charlotte Goldman, June 19, 1955; children: Mark (dec. 1999), Daniel. BA, U. Rochester, 1954; JD, Columbia U., 1957. Bar: N.Y. 1958, U.S. Dist. Ct. (so. dist.) N.Y. 1965, U.S. Dist. Ct. (ea. dist.) N.Y. 1990, U.S. Ct. Appeals (2d cir.) 1975, U.S. Supreme Ct. 1967. Instr. Columbia U. Law Sch., NYC, 1957—58; assoc. Phillips Nizer LLP (formerly Phillips, Nizer, Benjamin, Krim & Ballon), NYC, 1960—67, ptnr., 1967—2006, counsel, 2006—08. Vol. civil rights lawyer Miss. Lawyers Com. for Civil Rights Under Law, 1965; cons. sci. program com. Am. Psychiat. Assn., 2000—01. Bd. editors Columbia Law Rev., 1955—57. Bd. dirs. Nat. Alliance on Mental Illness of NY State, 1998-2004, 2005-08, pres., 1999-2004, 2005-06, 1st v.p. 2006-07; pres. Nat. Alliance on Mental Illness NYC, 1997-2003, pres. emeritus, 2006; mem. adv. bd. NYC Vis. Nurse Svc.; mem. nat. adv. coun. Columbia Teen Screen Program; mem. bd. editors Columbia Law Rev., 1955-57. Fulbright scholar U. Strasbourg, France, 1958-59; named one of NY Super Lawyers Gen. Litig., 2006-07. Home: 205 W End Ave New York NY 10023-4804

SILVERMAN, AL, editor; b. Lynn, Mass., Apr. 12, 1926; s. Henry and Minnie (Damsky) S.; m. Rosa Magaro, Sept. 9, 1951; children: Thomas, Brian, Matthew. BS, Boston U., 1949, LittD, 1986. Assoc. editor Sport mag., 1951-52; sports editor True mag., 1952-54; asst. editor Argosy mag., 1954-55; free-lance mag. writer, contbr. Saturday Evening Post, Coronet, Pageant, This Week, Am. Weekly, Am. Heritage, Saturday Review, others, 1955-60; editor-in-chief Saga mag., Impact mag., Sport Library, Sport mag., 1960-72; exec. v.p., editorial dir. Book-of-the-Month Club, 1972—, pres., chief operating officer, 1981—, chmn., chief exec. office, 1985-88; v.p., contbg. editor Viking Penguin, 1989-92, sr. v.p., pub., editor in chief, 1992—, sr. v.p., editor-at-large NYC, 1994-97, editl. advisor, 1998—. Author: Warren Spahn, 1961, Best from Sport, 1961, (with Phil Rizzuto) The Miracle New York Yankees, 1962, The World of Sport, 1962, Mickey Mantle, Master Yankee, 1963, World Series Heroes, 1964, (with Paul Hornung) Football and the Single Man, 1965, The Specialist in Pro Football, 1966, Sports Titans of the 20th Century, 1968, (with Frank Robinson) My Life is Baseball, 1968, More Sport Titans of the 20th Century, 1969, Joe DiMaggio, The Golden Year, 1969, I Am Third, (with Gale Sayers), 1970, Foster and Laurie, 1974; editor: The Book of the Month, 1986; co-editor: The 20th Century Treasury of Sports, 1992, It's Not Over 'Til It's Over, 2002, 2008, The Time Of Their Lives, 2009, Yankee Colors. Mem. Authors Guild. Home: 411 E 53rd St Apt 16H New York NY 10022 E-mail: rsilverman79@nyc.pr.com.

SILVERMAN, ALAN HENRY, lawyer; b. NYC, Feb. 18, 1954; s. Melvin H. and Florence (Green) S.; m. Gretchen E. Freeman, May 25, 1986; children: Willa C.F., Gordon H.F. BA summa cum laude, Hamilton Coll., 1976; MBA, JD, U. Pa., 1980. Bar: N.Y. 1981, U.S. Dist. Ct. (so. and ea. dists.) N.Y. 1981, U.S. Ct. Internat. Trade 1981, D.C. 1986, U.S. Supreme Ct. 1990. Assoc. Hughes, Hubbard & Reed, NYC, 1980-84; asst. counsel Newsweek, Inc., NYC, 1984-86; v.p., gen. counsel, sec., dir. adminstrn. Cable One, Inc., Phoenix, 1986—. Contbr. articles to profl. jours. Mem. prevention adv. com. Gov. Pa. Justice Commn., 1975-79; bd. dirs. Lawyers' Alliance for N.Y., 1982-85, N.Y. Lawyers Pub. Interest, 1983-85, Nat. Assn. JD-MBA Profls., 1983-85, Bus. Vols. for Arts, Inc., Phoenix, 1989-93, Ariz. Vol. Lawyers for the Arts, Inc., 1994-97, First Amendment Coalition Ariz., Inc., 1991—, Phoenix Falcons Fencing Club, Inc., 2003-05; mem. Maricopa County Citizens Jud. Adv. Coun., 1990-93; mem. citizens' bond com. City of Phoenix, 2000. Mem. ABA, Assn. of Bar of City of N.Y., D.C. Bar Assn., Phi Beta Kappa. Home: 5833 N 30th St Phoenix AZ 85016-2401 Office: Cable One Inc 1314 N 3d St Phoenix AZ 85004 Office Phone: 602-364-6190.

SILVERMAN, ALLISON, television producer, scriptwriter; BA, Yale U., 1994. Writer (TV series) Late Night with Conan O'Brien, 1993—94, The Daily Show, 1996—2001 (Primetime Emmy for Outstanding Writing for Variety, Music or Comedy Program, Acad. TV Arts and Scis., 2001), Late Night with Conan O'Brien: 10th Anniversary Special, 2003, The Daily Show with Jon Stewart: Indecision 2006 Election Night, 2006, (video game) You Don't Know Jack!, 1999, You Don't Know Jack!: Mock 2, 2000, co-exec.prodr., co-writer (TV series) The Colbert Report, 2005—07, exec. prodr., 2007— (Primetime Emmy for Outstanding Writing for Variety, Music or Comedy Program, Acad. TV Arts and Scis., 2008, Prodr. of Yr. award in Live Entertainment/Competition, Prodrs. Guild America, 2009). Named one of The 50 Most Powerful Women in NYC, NY Post, 2007. Office: Viacom 1515 Broadway New York NY 10036

SILVERMAN, AMY JOCELYN, psychiatrist; b. Royal Oak, Mich., Apr. 6, 1972; d. Fredrick and Evelyn Simon; m. Stephen Silverman, Sept. 15, 2001; 1 child, Alexandra Joy. BA in Psychology, Brandeis U., Waltham, Mass., 1994; MD, Mt. Sinai, NYC, 1998. Resident Harvard Longwood Psychiatry Residency Tng. Program, Boston, 1998—2001; fellow Ny Presbyn. Hosp.-Payne Whitney, Manhattan, 2001—03; psychiatrist NY Presbyn. Hosp., Weill Cornell Med. Ctr., White Plains, NY, 2003—08; pvt. practice psychiatrist, 2008—. Recipient Physician of Yr., NY Presbyn. Hosp.-Westchester Divsn., 2005. Mem.: Am. Acad. Child and Adolescent Psychiatry, Am. Psychiat. Assn. Office: 600 Mamarneck Ave Ste 400 Harrison NY 10528 Personal E-mail: asilvermanmd@gmail.com.

SILVERMAN, ARNOLD BARRY, lawyer; b. Sept. 1, 1937; s. Frank and Lillian Lena (Linder) S.; m. Susan L. Levin, Aug. 7, 1960; children: Michael Eric, Lee Oren. B of Engring. Sci., Johns Hopkins U., 1959; JD cum laude, U. Pitts., 1962. Bar: US Dist. Ct. (we. dist.) Pa. 1963, Pa. 1964, U.S. Patent and Trademark Office 1965, US Supreme Ct. 1967, Can. Patent Office 1968, US Ct. Claims 1975, US Ct. Appeals (3d cir.) 1982, US Ct. Appeals (fed. cir.) 1985, US Ct. Appeals (4th cir.) 2000. Patent atty. Alcoa, New Kensington, Pa., 1962-67, 68-72, sr. patent atty., 1972-76; ptnr. Price and Silverman, Pitts., 1967-68; v.p., gen. patent counsel Joy Mfg. Co., Pitts., 1976-80; ptnr. Murray Silverman & Keck, Pitts., 1980-81, Buell, Blenko, Ziesenheim & Beck, Pitts., 1981—84, Eckert, Seamans, Cherin & Mellott, Pitts., 1984—2005, chmn. intellectual property dept., 1992—2005; sr. counsel, 2009—; chmn. info. tech. practice group Eckert, Seamans, Cherin & Mellott, Pitts., 1992-97, sr. counsel, 2006—; spl. asst. atty. gen. State of W.Va., 1985—; spl. counsel patents U. Pitts., 1975—. Nat. panel of arbiters Am. Arbitration Assn., 1987—; spkr. in field. Contbr. 90 articles to profl. jours. Mem. Churchill CSC, Pa., 1967-90, chmn., 1975-90; mem. Pitts. law com. Anti-Defamation League, 1981—, regional adv. bd., 1982—, ch-chmn. Pitts. region ann. dinner, 1983, mem. chmn. by-laws com., 1983; bd. govs. Slippery Rock U. Found., 1985-91; Pitts. steering com. MIT Enterprise Forum, 1986-87. With US Army, 1963-64. Recipient Am. Spirit Honor medal, Ft. Knox, 1963; named Pa. Super Lawyer Pa. Law and Politics Mag., 2004, 05, 06, 07, 08, 09. Fellow: Mensa (nat. assoc. counsel patents and trademarks copyrights 1980—82, inventors' spl. interest group 1980—86, chmn. trademark and logo com. 2006—); mem.: ASME, ABA, U. Pitts. Gen. Alumni Assn. (bd. dir. 2008—), Assn. Corp. Patent Counsel (emeritus mem.), Intertel (treas. Pitts. Forum 1983—), Stratford Cmty. Assn. (v.p. 1966—67, gov. 1966—70, pres. 1967—68), Golden Panthers, U. Pitts. Law Alumni Assn. (bd. dirs. 1992—2002, treas. 1997—98, v.p. 1998—99, pres.-elect 1999—2000, pres. 2001—02), Johns Hopkins Soc. Engring. Alumni, Johns Hopkins U. Alumni Assn. (chmn. publicity com. 1963—66, exec. com. 1966—87, v.p. 1969—70, pres. 1971—72, nat. alumni coun. 1989—92, 2003—), Brit. Inst. Chartered Patent Agts. (fgn. mem.), Licensing Execs. Soc. (co-chmn. Pitts. chpt. 1994—96), Am. Chem. Soc. (chemistry and the law sect.), Nat. Assn. Coll. and Univ. Attys., Pa. Bar Assn. (sports/entertainment arts law com. 1999—), DC Bar Assn., US Trademark Assn. (chmn. task force on advt. agys. 1981, membership com. 1987—89), Am. Intellectual Property Law Assn. (membership com. 1985—88, pub. rels. com. 1994—), Pitts. Intellectual Property Law Assn. (chmn. pub. rels. com. 1968—69, chmn. patent laws com. 1970—72, chmn. legis. action com. 1972—75, chmn. nominating com. 1973, bd. mgrs., newsletter editor 1974—88, sec.-treas. 1976—84, v.p. 1984—85, pres. 1985—86, pub. rels. com. 1994—95, program com. 1995—96, co-chmn. 2001—03), U. Pitts. Gen. Alumni Assn. (life; bd. dir. 2001—06, exec. com. 2002—06, bd. dir. 2002—06, sec. 2003—06, strategic planning com. 2003—06, leadership coun. 2006—07, awards com. 2006—, bd. dirs. 2008—), Robert Bruce Assn. Law Fellows (life), Allegheny County Bar Assn. (chmn. pub. rels. com. 1978—80, vice-chmn. intellectual property sect. 1981—83, chmn. 1984—85), Duquesne Club, Order of Coif, Psi Chi, Tau Epsilon Rho. Republican. Jewish. Home: 2019 High Pointe Ct Murrysville PA 15668-8515 Office: 600 Grant St 44th Fl Pittsburgh PA 15219-2703 Office Phone: 412-566-2077. Business E-Mail: abs@escm.com. *Welcome challenge and perform all tasks with enthusiasm, in a moral manner and to the very best of your ability.*

SILVERMAN, ARTHUR CHARLES, lawyer; b. Lewiston, Maine, June 13, 1938; s. Louis A. and Frances Edith (Brownstone) Silverman; m. Donna Linda Zolov, June 18, 1961; children: Leonard Stephen, Daniel Edward. BS in Elec. Engring. and Indsl. Mgmt., MIT, 1961; JD, Columbia U. Sch. Law, NYC, 1964. Bar: NY 1965, US Dist. Ct. (NY), US Supreme Ct. 1971. Engring. asst. GE, Pittsfield, Mass./Phila., 1958—62; assoc. Baer & Marks, NYC, 1965—68, Golenbock & Barell, NYC, 1968—72, ptnr., 1972—89, Thelen LLP, NYC, 1989—2008, Duane Morris LLP, NYC, 2008—. Bd. govs. MIT Hillel Found., 1979—84; mem. exec. com. Nat. Jewish Ctr. Learning & Leadership, 1984—90. Named a NY SuperLawyer, 2008; named one of America's Leading Bus. Lawyers, Chambers USA, 2008, 2009. Mem.: ABA, NY Soc. Profl. Engineers, Construction Specifications Inst. (profl. mem.), Assn. Bar City of NY, Fed. Bar Coun., Nat. Soc. Profl. Engineers (assoc.). Office: Duane Morris LLP 1540 Broadway New York NY 10036-4082 Office Phone: 212-692-1096. Office Fax: 212-401-4729. Business E-Mail: asilverman@duanemorris.com.*

SILVERMAN, BARRY G., federal judge; b. NYC, Oct. 11, 1951; 1 child, Bagel Ann. BA summa cum laude, Ariz. State U., 1973, JD, 1976. Bar: Ariz. 1976, US Dist. Ct. Ariz. 1976, US Ct. Appeals (9th cir.) 1976, US Supreme Ct. 1980. Asst. city prosecutor, Phoenix, 1976—77; dep. atty. Maricopa County, 1977—79; ct. commr., 1979—84; judge Superior Ct. Ariz. Maricopa County, 1984—95; apptd. magistrate judge US Dist. Ct. Ariz., 1995—98; judge US Ct. Appeals (9th cir.), 1998—. Instr. constnl. law Coll. Law, Ariz. State U., 1983, adj. prof. advanced criminal procedure, 89; lectr. cmty. property BAR/BRI Ariz., Idaho and Nev. Bar Rev. Courses, 1989—94. Recipient Exel award, Soc. Nat. Assn. Publs.,

1992. Mem.: ABA, Maricopa County Bar Assn. (Henry Stevens award 1991), State Bar Ariz. Avocations: magic, beagles, baseball, wine tasting. Office: US Ct of Appeals 401 W Washington St SPC 78 Phoenix AZ 85003*

SILVERMAN, BEN, broadcast executive, television producer; b. Pittsfield, Mass., Aug. 15, 1970; BA in Hist., magna cum laude, Tufts U. V.p. New World/Marvel Entertainment; head of internat. packaging divsn. & NY cons. br. William Morris Agy.; founder, CEO, exec. prodr. Reveille Prodns., 2002—07; co-chmn. NBC Entertainment & NBC Universal TV Studio (name changed to Universal Media Studios), 2007—09. Writer (TV series) The Restaurant, 2003—04, co-creator & exec. prodr. Nashville Star, 2003, The Biggest Loser, 2004; exec. prodr.: (TV series) Coupling, 2003, $25 Million Dollar Hoax, 2004, Blow Out, 2004, The Club, 2004—05, 30 Days, 2005, The Office, 2006—09, Ugly Betty, 2006—07, Are You Smarter Than a 5th Grader?, 2007—09; (TV miniseries) The Tudors, 2007; prodr.: (TV films) 9/11, 2002. Active in Seeds of Peace. Named a Maverick, Details mag., 2007, 2008; named one of 40 Under 40, Advt. Age, 2007. Office: c/o Savage Agy 6212 Banner Ave Los Angeles CA 90038*

SILVERMAN, BRUCE GARY, advertising executive, consultant; b. NYC, Feb. 16, 1945; s. Edward E. and Lillian (Brill) S.; children: Jennifer, Matthew; m. Nancy Cole, 1996; children: Christen Cole, Larry Cole. BA, Adelphi U., 1965; JD, Albany Law Sch., 1967. Sr. v.p., exec. creative dir. Ogilvy & Mather Inc., NYC, 1967-80; exec. v.p., exec. creative dir. Bozell & Jacobs Inc., Dallas, 1981-83, Batten, Barton, Durstine & Osborn Inc., LA, 1984-85; exec. v.p., creative dir. Asher/Gould Advt. Inc., LA, 1986-89, pres., chief creative officer, 1989-95, pres., COO, 1996-97; pres. Western Internat. Advocacy Group, LA, 1997-98; exec. v.p., mng. dir. Initiative Media, LA, 1998—; pres., CEO Initiative Ptnrs., USA, 1999—2002; pres. WONGDOODY Advt., LA, 2003—05; chmn., CEO Pocket Billboards, Inc., Studio City, Calif., 2005—; prin. Silverman Consulting, LA, 2005—. V.p., bd. dirs. L.A. Children's Mus., 1984-88; chmn. Resource Devel. com. Starbright Pavillion Found., 1993. Mem. Acad. TV Arts and Scis., Am. Assn. Advt. Agys. (bd. dirs., vice chmn. western region 2002), UCLA Ext. (dean adv. bd.). Home: 3168 Dona Mema Pl Studio City CA 91604-4264 Office: Pocket Billboards Inc 4400 Coldwater Cyn Ave Ste 355 Studio City CA 91604 Personal E-mail: bgsla@roadrunner.com.

SILVERMAN, DEBORA LEAH, history professor; BA, Princeton U., 1975, PhD, 1983. With hist. dept. UCLA, 1981—, prof. history and art history, presdl. chair modern European history, art and culture. Author: Selling Culture: Bloomingdale's, Diana Vreeland, and the New Aristocracy of Taste in Reagan's America, 1986, Art Nouveau in Fin-de-Siecle France: Politics, Psychology and Style, 1989 (Berkshire History prize, 1990), Van Gogh and Gauguin: The Search for Sacred Art, 2000 (PEN Am. Ctr./Archtl. Digest Nat. prize for Arts Writing, 2001, Ralph Waldo Emerson prize, Phi Beta Kappa Soc., 2001, J. Russell Major prize, Am. Hist. Assn., 2001). Fellow John S. Guggenheim Meml. Found., 1992, NEH, 2005—06; Getty scholar, 1998. Fellow: Am. Acad. Arts and Sciences. Office: UCLA Dept History 6265 Bunche Hall Box 951473 Los Angeles CA 90095-1473 Office Phone: 310-825-4601. Office Fax: 310-206-9630. E-mail: silverma@history.ucla.edu.

SILVERMAN, ELAINE ANN, mathematics educator; b. Cin., Aug. 22, 1951; d. Samuel David and Freda Miller; children: Jennifer, Mindy, Brandon. BS magna cum laude, U. Cin., 1973. Cert. tchr. Nev. Math. tchr., dept. chair Quannah McCall Sixth Grade Ctr., Las Vegas, Nev., 1973—75; third grade tchr. Harvey Dondero Elem. Sch., Las Vegas, 1975—78; middle sch. math. tchr., head tchr., master tchr. The Meadows Sch., Las Vegas, 1992—. Pvt. math. tutor, Las Vegas. Bd. dirs., v.p. Jewish Fedn. Women's Divsn., 1979—86; presch. dir. Temple Beth Sholom, 1980—85; bd. dirs. Jewish Family Svcs., 1985—86, Solomon Schechter Day Sch., 2006—08. Recipient Excellence in Leadership, Jewish Fedn. of Las Vegas. Mem.: Math. Assn. Am. (Edyth May Sliffe award for disting. jr. high sch. math. tchg. 2003), Nat. Coun. Tchrs. Math. Avocation: travel. Office: The Meadows Sch 8601 Scholar Ln Las Vegas NV 89128 Business E-Mail: esilverman@themeadowsschool.org.

SILVERMAN, ERIC F., lawyer; b. Phila., Sept. 21, 1954; s. Robert L. and Marilyn L. S.; m. Melenie Silverman, June 4 2005; children: Amy, Laura, Charlie, Wyatt. BA, Middlebury Coll., 1976; JD, Georgetown U., 1982. Bar: N.Y. 1982. Energy/environ. planner Henningson, Durham, Richardson, Washington, 1976-79; mgmt. cons. Booz Allen & Hamilton, Washington, 1980; ptnr. & chmn. global project fin. grp. Milbank Tweed Hadley & McCloy, NYC, 1982—. Author: Resource Recovery - A Plan for Small Communities and Institutions, 1976; editor, Project Finance newsletter. Mem. Fed. Energy Bar Assn., ABA (energy/environ. natural resources div.), N.Y. State Bar Assn., Bar Assn. City of N.Y. Office: Milbank Tweed Hadley McCloy 1 Chase Manhattan Plz Fl 54 New York NY 10005-1401 Office Fax: 212-530-5219. Business E-Mail: esilverman@milbank.com.

SILVERMAN, GORDON, engineering educator; BA, Columbia Coll., NYC, 1955; BSEE, Columbia U. Coll. Engring., NYC, 1956, MSEE, 1957; PhD in Sys. Sci., Poly. U., Bklyn., 1972. Sr. engr. ITT Lab., Nutley, NJ, 1957—61; project engr. Loral Electronics Corp., Bronx, NY, 1961—64; sr. rsch. assoc. Rockefeller U., NYC, 1964—85; prof. elec. engring. Fairleigh Dickinson U., Teaneck, NJ, 1985—91; prof. elec. & computer engring. Manhattan Coll., Riverdale, NY, 1991—. Contbr. articles to sci. jours. Mem.: IEEE (chair, i&m chpt. 2000—08), Eta Kappa Nu. Achievements include patents for computer control of communication signals. Office: Manhattan College Manhattan College Pky Riverdale NY 10471

SILVERMAN, HENRY RICHARD, private equity firm executive; b. NYC, Aug. 1, 1940; s. Herbert Robert and Roslyn (Moskowitz) S.; m. Susan H. Herson, June 13, 1965 (div. Jan. 1977); children: Robin Lynn, Deborah Leigh; m. Nancy Ann Kraner, Jan. 22, 1978; 1 child, Catherine Anne Grad. cum laude, Hackley Sch., Tarrytown, NY, 1957; BA with honors in Art History, Williams Coll., 1961; JD, U. Pa. Law Sch., 1964; postgraduate student in Corp. Fin. and Taxation, NYU, 1965. Bar: NY 1965, US Tax Ct. 1965, US Ct. Appeals (2nd cir.) 1965. Atty., 1965—66; practice lawyer White, Weld & Co., 1965—66; gen. ptnr. Oppenheimer & Co., 1965—66; pres., CEO ITI Corp., 1970—72; founder, pres. Trans-York Securities Corp., 1970—72; exec. v.p., chmn. exec. com. Ladenburg, Thalmann & Co., 1972; pres., CEO Vavasseur Am. Ltd., subs. UK mcht. bank, 1973; gen. ptnr. Brisbane Ptnrs., 1974—75; prin. Silverman Energy Co., NYC, 1977—2004, NBC Channel 20, Springfield, Ill., 1977—83, ABC Channel 9, Syracuse, NY, 1977—81, outdoor advt., music pub., motion picture prodn., radio broadcasting & hardware mfg. companies, 1977—86; prin., dir. Delta Queen Steamboat Co., New Orleans, 1977—81; pres., CEO Reliance Group Holdings, Inc., NYC, 1982, Reliance Capital Group, 1983—89; chmn., CEO Days Inns America, Inc., Atlanta, 1984—89; founder, pres., CEO Telemundo Group, Inc., NYC, 1986—90; gen. ptnr. Blackstone Group, NYC, 1990—91; founder, chmn., pres., CEO Hospitality Franchise Sys. Inc. (HFS, Inc.), NYC, 1990—97; pres. Cendant Corp., NYC, 1997—2004, CEO, 1997—2006, chmn., 1998—2006; chmn., CEO Realogy Corp., Parsippany, NJ, 2004—07, non-exec. chmn., 2007—; COO Apollo Management L.P., NYC, 2009—. Chmn. Bus. Roundtable Fiscal Policy Task Force, 2005—; bd. commr. Port Authority of NY and NJ, 2002—, vice-chmn., 2007—; mem. nat. adv. bd. JP Morgan; mem. G-100. Bd. dirs. NYU Hosp., NYC, 1987; trustee NYU and Sch. Medicine and Med. Ctr., U. Pa.; former trustee Dance Theater of Harlem, Hosp. for Joint Diseases, Whitney Mus. of American Art; dir. NYU Child Study Ctr.; mem. exec. com., World Travel and Tourism Coun.; mem. adv. bd. US Travel and Tourism; philanthropy includes Silverman Hall (new law building, U. Pa.), Silverman-Rodin Scholars and the Silverman Prof. Law at Pa. Law Sch., Silverman Prof. Obstetrics and Gynecology, Silverman Reproductive Choice Found., Silverman Cancer Rsch. Lab. at NYU Sch. Medicine. Officer USNR, 1965—72. Recipient Am. Heritage Award, Anti-Defamation League, 1998, honored for efforts to promote diversity in the workplace, Jackie Robinson Found., 2001, US Hispanic C. of C., 2003. Mem.: Harmonie (NYC). Republican. Jewish. Avocation: tennis. Office: Apollo Management LP 9 W 57th St 43rd Fl New York NY 10022*

SILVERMAN, HUGH J., philosophy educator; b. Boston, Aug. 17, 1945; s. Leslie and Eleanore (Riffin) S.; m. L. Theresa Watkins, June 22, 1968 (div. Apr. 1983); children: Claire Christine, H. Christopher; m. Gertrude Postl, Sept. 1, 1987. BA, Lehigh U., 1966, MA, 1967; postgrad., U. Paris, 1968, 71-72; PhD, Stanford U., 1973. Lectr. Stanford U., Calif., 1973-74; asst. prof. SUNY, Stony Brook, 1974-79, assoc. prof., 1979-83, prof. philosophy and comparative lit., 1983—, affiliated faculty mem. dept. European langs., lits. and cultures, 2004, dept. art, 2005—. Vis. sr. lectr. U. Warwick, Coventry, Eng., 1980, U. Nice, France, 1980, 81; vis. prof. Duquesne U., Pitts., 1978, 2000, NYU, 1978-80, 85-86, U. Leeds, Eng., 1988, U. Torino, Italy, 1989, U. Vienna, Austria, 1993, 94, 97, 2000, U. Nice, France, 1994, U. Helsinki, Finland, 1997, 99, U. Sydney, Australia, 1998, U. Milan, U. Rome II, 2001, U. Trondheim, Norway, 2002, Ul Klagenfurt, Austrlia, 2003, 05; co-dir. Internat. Philos. Seminar, Alto Adige, Italy, 1991—; Fulbright Disting. chair humanities U. Vienna, 2000-01. Author: Inscriptions: Between Phenomenology and Structuralism, 1987, Textualities: Between Hermeneutics and Deconstruction, 1994 (German translation 1997), Inscriptions: After Phenomenology and Structuralism, 1997; editor: Piaget, Philosophy and the Human Sciences, 1980, 97 (Spanish translation 1989), Philosophy and Non-Philosophy since Merleau-Ponty, 1988, 97, Derrida and Deconstruction, 1989, (Korean translation 1999), Postmodernism - Philosophy and the Arts, 1990 (Korean translation 1990), Gadamer and Hermeneutics, 1991, Writing the Politics of Difference, 1991, Questioning Foundations: Truth/Subjectivity/Culture, 1993, Cultural Semiosis: Training the Signifier, 1997, Philosophy and Desire, 2000, Lyotard: Philosophy, Politics and the Sublime, 2002; co-editor: Jean-Paul Sartre: Contemporary Approaches to His Philosophy, 1980, Continental Philosophy in America, 1983, Hermeneutics and Deconstruction, 1985, Descriptions, 1985, Critical and Dialectical Phenomenology, 1987, Horizons of Continental Philosophy, 1987, Postmodernism and Continental Philosophy, 1988, The Textual Sublime: Deconstruction and its Differences, 1990, Merleau-Ponty: Texts and Dialogues: On Philosophy, Politics and Culture, 1992, 96, Textualität der Philosophie-Philosophie und Literatur, 1994, Derrida und Die Politiken der Freundschaft, 2003, co-editor; series editor: Routledge Continental Philosophy series, 1986—; co-editor: Humanities Press Humanity Books Contemporary Studies in Philosophy and the Human Sciences series, 1989—, assoc. editor, 1979-89; editor: Humanities Press Humanity Books Series in Philosophy and Literary Theory, 1989—, SUNY Press Contemporary Studies in Philosophy and Literature, 1988-96, Northwestern U. Press Series in Philosophy, Literature, and Culture, 1996-2001; Bull. for Rsch. in Humanities, 1983-84, Continuum Books Textures: Philosophy/Literature/Culture Series, 2001—; mem. editorial bd. Rsch. in Phenomenology, 1981—, Rev. of Existential Psychology and Psychiatry, 1979—, Symploké, 2000-, Chiasmi: Intz Merleau-Ponty Studies, 2001-; translator: Consciousness and the Acquisition of Language, 1973; contbr. numerous articles to profl. jours., and chpts. in books. Fulbright-French Govt. and Alliance Francaise fellow, Paris, 1971-72; faculty rsch. fellow SUNY-Stony Brook, 1977, 78, 81; rsch. fellow Am. Coun. Learned Socs., 1981-82; Experienced Faculty Travel fellowship SUNY, 1985, 88, 93, 99; Fulbright travel grant, Netherlands and Germany, 2001; recipient MLA travel grant (Brazil), 1993, N.Y. Coun. for Humanities grant, 1976-77, SUNY Chancellor's award for excellence in teaching, 1977, medal U. Helsinki, 1997. Mem. Soc. Phenomenology and Existential Philosophy (exec. co-dir. 1980-86), Internat. Assn. Philosophy and Lit. (exec. com. 1976—, exec. sec. 1979-87, exec. dir. 1987—), Brit. Soc. Phenomenology (exec. com. 1980-95), Merleau-Ponty Circle (chmn. publs. com. 1978-2001), Heidegger Conf., Am. Soc. Aesthetics, Am. Philos. Assn. (program adv. com. 1986-89, 2003-, lectures publs. and rsch. com. 1991-94). Office: Stony Brook U Dept Philosophy Stony Brook NY 11794-3750 Business E-Mail: hugh.silverman@stonybrook.edu.

SILVERMAN, IRA NORTON, news producer; b. Bklyn., May 17, 1935; s. Joseph and Mildred (Axelrod) S.; m. Elizabeth Parsons Aspray, June 16, 1979; children by previous marriage: Gary, Bruce; stepchildren: Elizabeth, Aime, Alison. AB, Columbia U., 1957. Newspaper, mag. and book editor, 1957—67; prodr., writer NBC News, 1967—79; sr. prodr. spl. projects NBC Nightly News, Washington, 1977—95; contbr. The New Yorker, NYC, 1995—, editl. cons., 1995—96; cons. NBC News, 1998, PBS, 1999, 2002. Co-author: The Pleasant Avenue Connection, 1976. Recipient Nat. Headliner award, 1977, 78, 81, 87, Alfred I. DuPont-Columbia U. award, 1983-84, 85-86, Emmy award for news and documentary, 1985, 87, award Overseas Press Club Am., 1987, 90, George Polk award L.I. U., 1988, Excellence in TV award Channels mag., 1990, George Foster Peabody award U. Ga., 1991, Citation for Excellence Overseas Press Club, 1992.

SILVERMAN, JERRY MARK, political science professor, consultant; b. Chgo., May 17, 1942; s. Maury W. and Rose Silverman; m. Andrea Lee Jones, Aug. 17, 1990; children: Martin Harold, Deanna Michelle Ball, Mauri Sami, Mira Sandrine, Milena Luisa. BA in Polit. Sci., Calif. State Coll., Long Beach, Calif., 1963; PhD in Internat. Govt. Rels., Claremont Grad. Sch. & U. Ctr., Calif., 1967. Sr. planning advisor Devel. Alternatives Inc., Gema Gofa, Ethiopia, chief-of-party Jakarta, Indonesia, 1978—81, Cairo, 1981—82, sr. devel. specialist, 1981—83; instr., polit. sci. Ctrl. Wash. State Coll., Ellensburg, 1965—66; fgn. svc. res. officer US AID, Vietnam, 1967—68, cons. intermittent, 2000—06; asst. prof., polit. sci. McMaster U., Ont., Canada, 1968—72; local govt. advisor Inst. Pub. Adminstrn., Saigon, Vietnam, 1972—73; project specialist social scis. Ford Found. SE Asia Regional Office, Saigon, 1973—75, Bangkok, 1975—77; prin. instl. devel. specialist Africa World Bank, 1983—95, unit mgr., east Asia and pacific Jakarta, Indonesia, 1995—99, cons. intermittent, 2000—03; pvt. practice Lima, Peru, 2002—04, Savannah, Ga., 2004—; prof. Savannah State U., 2007—. Vis. fellow Harvard U., 1976, guest spkr., 2000, Duke U., 2002; cons. intermittent Govt. UK & Northern Ireland Dept. Internat. Devel., 2000—03, Asian Devel. Bank, 2000—07. Author: (book) Action-Planning Workshops for Development Management: Guidelines, 1991, Technical Assistance and Aid Agency Staff: Alternative Techniques for Greater Effectiveness; contbr. articles to jours. Named to Alumni Hall of Fame, Claremont Grad. U., 2001. Mem.: Southern Polit. Sci. Assn. Personal E-mail: jmsilverman5@comcast.net.

SILVERMAN, JOSEPH, chemistry professor; b. NYC, Nov. 5, 1922; s. Jakob and Mary (Chechick) S.; m. Joan Aline Jacks, Jan. 14, 1951; children: Joshua Henry, David Avrom. BA, Bklyn. Coll., 1944; A.M., Columbia U., 1948, PhD, 1951. Head research dept. Walter Kidde (nuclear labs.), Garden City, N.Y., 1952-54; v.p., tech. dir. RAI Research Corp., L.I. City, N.Y., 1954-59; assoc. prof. chemistry State U. N.Y., Stony Brook, 1959-60; prof. dept. materials and nuclear engring. U. Md., College Park, 1960-92, dir. Inst. for Phys. Sci. and Tech., 1976—83, prof. emeritus, nuc. engring., 1992—. Cons. Danish AEC, Indsl. Research Inst., Japan, Boris Kidric Inst., Yugoslavia, Bechtel Co., GPU Nuclear Corp., GE, IAEA, Vienna; disting. vis. prof. Tokyo U., 1974; gen. chmn. 2d Internat. Meeting on Radiation Processing, Miami, Fla., 1978, 3d Tokyo, 1980, hon. chmn. 6th, Ottawa, 1987; trustee Washington Inst. Values in Pub. Policy, 1981-87. Editor Internat. Jour. Applied Radiation and Isotopes, 1973-78, Trans. 1st Internat. Meetings on Radiation Processing, 1977, 3d edit., 1981; mem. editorial adv. bd. Radiation Physics and Chemistry, 1978-95. Served with AUS, 1944-46. Recipient Founders award 6th Internat. Meeting on Radiation Processing, 1987, Centennial medal U. Md. Coll. Engring., 1994; grad. rsch. fellow Brookhaven Nat. Lab., 1949-51; Guggenheim fellow, 1966-67. Fellow Nordic Soc. Radiation Chemistry and Tech., Am. Phys. Soc., Am. Nuclear Soc. (Radiation Industry award 1975); mem. Am. Chem. Soc., Sigma Xi. Home: 8101 Connecticut Ave Apt S407 Chevy Chase MD 20815-2839 Office: U Md Dept Materials Sci and Engring College Park MD 20742-2115 Home Phone: 301-951-9009; Office Phone: 301-405-5228. Business E-Mail: jagman@umd.edu.

SILVERMAN, JOSEPH HILLEL, mathematics professor; b. NYC, Mar. 27, 1955; s. Harry and Shirley (Seiner) S.; m. Susan Leslie Greenhaus, June 13, 1976; children: Deborah, Daniel, Jonathan. ScB, Brown U., 1977; MA, Harvard U., 1979, PhD, 1982. Moore instr. MIT, Cambridge, 1982-86; assoc. prof. Boston U., 1986-88; assoc. prof. math. Brown U., Providence, 1988-91, prof., 1991—, chmn., 2001—04. Founder and v.p. rsch., NTRU Cryptosystems, Inc., 1997—. Author: Arithmetic of Elliptic Curves, 1986; editor: Arithmetic Geometry, 1987, Rational Points on Elliptic Curves, 1992, Advanced Topics in Arithmetic of Elliptic Curves, 1995, Diophantine Geometry (with M. Hindry), 2000, Arithmetic of Dynamical Systems, 2007. Fellow NSF, 1983-86, Sloan fellow Sloan Found., 1987, Guggenheim Found. fellow, 1998. Mem. Am. Math. Soc. (Steele prize 1998). Avocation: bridge. Office: Brown U Dept Math PO Box 1917 Providence RI 02912-1917

SILVERMAN, JOSH, communications executive; Grad. magna cum laude, Brown U.; MBA, Stanford Grad. Sch. Bus. Staff mem. to US Senator Bill Bradley; mgmt. positions ADAC Labs; sr. cons. Booz Allen & Hamilton; co-founder, CEO Evite, 1998—2001; gen. mgr. Marktplaats.nl; CEO Shopping.com Ltd. (eBay, Inc. Co.), 2003—08; pres., CEO Skype, Ltd., 2008—. Office: Skype (eBay Inc Co) 2145 Hamilton Ave San Jose CA 95125 Address: Skype Technologies SA 22/24 Boulevard Royal 6e etage L-2449 Luxembourg Germany*

SILVERMAN, KENNETH EUGENE, language educator, writer; b. NYC, Feb. 5, 1936; s. Gustave and Bessie (Goldberg) S.; children: Willa Zahava, Ethan Leigh. BA, Columbia U., 1956, MA, 1958, PhD, 1964. Instr. English U. Wyo., Laramie, 1958-59; preceptor in English Columbia U., NYC, 1962-64; prof. English, co-dir. The Biography Seminar NYU, NYC, 1964-2001. Adv. coun. Inst. Early Am. History and Culture, 1984-87. Author: Timothy Dwight, 1969, A Cultural History of the American Revolution, 1976, The Life and Times of Cotton Mather, 1984, Edgar A. Poe: Mournful and Never-ending Remembrance, 1991, Houdini!!! The Career of Ehrich Weiss, 1996, Lightning Man: The Accursed Life of Samuel F.B. Morse, 2003; editor: anthology Colonial American Poetry, 1968; compiler: Selected Letters of Cotton Mather, 1976; mem. editl. bd. Early Am Lit., 1969-72, 77-80, William and Mary Quar., 1984-87, Am. Lit. 1987-90. Recipient Bancroft prize in Am. history, 1985, Pulitzer Prize for biography, 1985, Edgar Allan Poe award Mystery Writers Am., 1992; grantee Bicentennial award NEH, 1972-74, Am. Philos. Soc., 1986, Am. Coun. Learned Socs., 1986; Guggenheim fellow, 1989-90. Mem. Am. Acad. Arts and Scis., Soc. Am. Historians, Am. Antiquarian Soc., Authors Guild, Soc. Am. Magicians. Jewish. Personal E-mail: ks2@nyu.edu.

SILVERMAN, LOUIS E., information technology executive; BA, Amherst Coll., Mass.; MBA, Harvard U., Cambridge, Mass. Chief ops. officer CorVel Corp., Irvine, Calif.; pres., CEO Quality Systems Inc., Irvine, Calif., 2000—, bd. dirs., 2005—. Office: Quality Systems Inc 18111 Von Karman Ave Ste 600 Irvine CA 92612-7100 Office Phone: 800-888-7955. Office Fax: 949-255-2605.

SILVERMAN, MARTIN ARNOLD, psychiatrist; s. Meyer and Evelyn Silverman; m. Lila Rose Ringel; children: Gail Ellen Farb, Ilene Vakkur, Kenneth Mark. MD, SUNY, Downstate, 1959. Diplomate Am. Bd. Psychiatry & Neurology, 1974, child psychiatry 1976, cert. in psychoanalysis Bd. Profl. Standards, Am. Psychoanalytic Assn., 1974, child and adolescent psychoanalysis 1976. Clin. prof. psychiatry NY U. Coll. Medicine, NYC, 1965—; tng. and supervising analyst IPPNJ/CCAPS, Livingston, NJ, 1986—, Psychoanalytic Inst. NY U., NYC, 1982—, supervising child analyst, 1984—. Contbr. chapters to books, articles to profl. jours.; assoc. editor: Psychoanalytic Quar., 1981—. Capt. US Army, 1963—65, Frankfurt, Germany. Named Best Doctors in America, Best Doctors award, NJ Magazine. Mem.: NJ Coun. Child and Adolescent Psychiatry (pres. 1986—88, Best Child Psychiatry award 2006), Tri-County Chpt. NJ. Psychiat. Assn. (pres. 1980—86), Assn. Child Psychoanalysis (pres. 2000—02), Psychoanalytic Assn. NY, Am. Assn. Child and Adolescent Psychiatry, Am. Psychoanalytic Assn., Am. Psychiat. Assn. Avocation: tennis. Office: Martin A Silverman MD PA 551 Ridgewood Rd Maplewood NJ 07040 Office Fax: 973-762-1387.

SILVERMAN, MICHAEL J., lawyer; b. Chgo., Apr. 16, 1963; BS in Acctg., U. Ill., Urbana-Champaign; JD, Northwestern U. Sch. Law, Evanston, Ill., 1990. CPA Ill., 1985; bar: Ill. 1990, US Dist. Ct. (no. dist.) Ill., Supreme Ct. Ill. Sr. auditor, cons. Laventhol & Horwath, Chgo., 1985—87; cons. Morton Group, Chgo., 1987—88; assoc. Holleb & Coff, Chgo., 1990—98, ptnr., 1998—99, Duane Morris LLP, 1999—. Contbr. articles to profl. jours. Named to All-Star Team for Corp. Transactions, BTI Client Svc., 2007. Mem.: ABA, Assn. Cert. Fraud Examiners, Am. Inst. CPA's, Computer Law Assn., Chgo. Bar Assn., Fed. Trial Bar. Office: Duane Morris LLP 190 S LaSalle St Ste 3700 Chicago IL 60603 Office Phone: 312-499-6707. Office Fax: 312-277-6958. Business E-Mail: MJSilverman@duanemorris.com.*

SILVERMAN, MOSES, lawyer; b. Bklyn., Mar. 3, 1948; s. Bernard and Anne Silverman; m. Betty B. Robbins, Jan. 19, 1980; children: Benjamin, Rachel. AB, Colby Coll., 1969; JD, NYU, 1973. Bar: NY 1974, Washington 1982, US Supreme Ct. 1977, US Dist. Ct. (so. and ea. dists.) N.Y. 1974, US Dist. Ct. D.C. 2001, US Ct. Appeals (2d cir.) 1974,

US Ct. Appeals (D.C. cir.) 1977, US Ct. Appeals (fed. cir.) 1985, US Ct. Appeals (11th cir.) 2001, US Ct. Appeals (9th cir.) 2002, US Ct. Appeals (6th cir.) 2006, US Ct. Appeals (3rd cir.) 2009. Assoc. Paul, Weiss, Rifkind, Wharton & Garrison, NYC, 1973-81, ptnr., 1981—. Vol. U.S. Peace Corps., Istanbul, Turkey, 1969-70; bd. dirs. Legal Aid Soc., 1998-05; overseer Colby Coll., 2002-. Mem. ABA, N.Y. State Bar Assn., Assn. Bar City N.Y. Home: 7 Gracie Sq New York NY 10028-8001 Office: Paul Weiss Rifkind Wharton & Garrison 1285 Ave of Americas New York NY 10019-6064 Office Phone: 212-373-3355. Business E-Mail: msilverman@paulweiss.com.

SILVERMAN, NORMAN HENRY, cardiologist, educator; b. Johannesburg, Sept. 29, 1942; came to U.S., 1972; s. Simon Cecil and Jean (Krawitz) S.; m. Heather Silverman. DSc in Medicine, U. Witwatersrand, Johannesburg, 1985, postgrad. Diplomate Am. Bd. Pediatrics. Prof. pediat. Stanford U. Med. Ctr., Palo Alto, Calif., 1974—75, prof. pediat. cardiology, 2002—; asst. prof. pediatrics U. Calif., San Francisco, 1975—79, assoc. prof. radiology, 1979—85, prof. pediat. in residence, 1985—2002, prof. radiology in residence, 1985—2002. Co-author: Two Dimensional Echocardiography, 1982, Congenital Heart Disease, 1990; author: Pediatric Echocardiography, 1993; co-editor: Fetal Cardiology, 2003. Lt. South African Def. Force, 1968-69. Grantee March Dimes, 1977-79, Am. Heart Assn., 1978-80, 90-92; Roma and Marvin Auerback scholar pediat. cardiology Lucile Packard Children's Hosp. and Stanford U. Med. Ctr. Fellow Am. Coll. Cardiology, Coll. Physicians South Africa, Soc. Pediatric Rsch., Am. Pediatric Soc., Am. Heart Assn., Am. Soc. Echocardiography. Achievements include research in echocardiography of congenital heart disease in infants and children; fetal echocardiography and treatment. Office: Stanford U Med Ctr 750 Welch Rd #305 Palo Alto CA 94304 Office Phone: 650-723-7913. E-mail: norm.silverman@stanford.edu.

SILVERMAN, OZZIE, consulting strategist; b. Montreal, Que., Can., Jan. 30, 1939; s. Louis and Fanny (Black) S.; m. Sheela Marsha Zangwill, Aug. 22, 1962; children: Caroline, Marjorie. BSME, McGill U., 1963, diploma in mgmt., 1968, MBA, 1969. Cert. Que. Order of Engrs. Supr. quality control engring. Pratt and Whitney, Montreal, 1964-68; sr. mktg. rschr. United Aircraft, Montreal, 1969-70; asst. chief internat. Dept. Industry, Trade and Commerce, Ottawa, Ont., Canada, 1972-77; dir. industry projects Ministry of State for Sci. and Tech., Ottawa, 1978-85; dir. strategic techs. policy Industry, Sci. and Tech. Can., Ottawa, 1986-91; dir. gen. sci. strategy and innovation policy Industry Can., Ottawa, 1992-98; cons. ptnr. SECOR Cons., Inc., Ottawa, 1998—. Chmn. com. for sci. and tech. policy Orgn. for Econ. Coop. and Devel., Paris, 1995-98. Avocation: Inuit and Japanese graphic art. Home and Office: 112 Pigeon Terr Ottawa ON Canada K1V 9H7 Office Phone: 613-737-5596. E-mail: osilverman@secor.ca.

SILVERMAN, PATRICIA R., communications educator; d. Patricia B Joyner and William H. Richardson; m. Steven R. Silverman, Mar. 12, 1996; 1 child, Bethany S. PhD in Communication, U. Tenn., Knoxville, 2007. Cert. Pub. Rels. Soc. Am., NY, 1999. Pub. rels. dir. Christian Broadcasting Network, Virginia Beach, Va., 1994—99; assoc. prof. pub. rels. Lee U., Cleve., Tenn., 2000—. Recipient Outstanding Academic Advisor award, Lee U. Communication & Arts Dept., 2002, 2004; fellowship, ACA, 2007. Avocations: camping, gardening, travel. Office: Communication & Arts Lee Univ 1120 N Ocoee St Cleveland TN 37311 Office Fax: 423-614-8348. Business E-Mail: psilverman@leeuniversity.edu.

SILVERMAN, RICHARD BRUCE, chemist, biochemist, educator; b. Phila., May 12, 1946; s. Philip and S. Ruth (Simon) Silverman; m. Barbara Jean Kesner, Jan. 9, 1983; children: Matthew, Margaret, Philip. BS, Pa. State U., 1968; MA, Harvard U., Cambridge, Mass., 1972, PhD, 1974. From asst. prof. to prof. Northwestern U., Evanston, Ill., 1976—86, prof., 1986—, mem. Inst. Neurosci., 1990—. Mem. adv. panel NIH, Bethesda, Md., 1981, 83, 85, 87-91, 2001; expert analyst CHEMTRACTS; scientific adv. bd. Influx, Inc., 1998-2003, Protez Pharml., 2004—, Synchem, 2003—. NIGMS adv. coun., 2002, 2005; mem. Faculty of 1900; cons. in field. Mem. editl. bd.: Jour. Enzyme Inhibition, 1988—2002, Archives Biochem. & Biophys., 1993—, Jour. Medicinal Chemistry, 1995—2000, Enzyme Inhibition and Medicinal Chemistry, 2002—, Letters in Drug Design & Discovery, 2003—, Bioorganic & Medicinal Chemistry, 2003—, Bioorganic & Medicinal Chemistry Letters, 2003—, Current Enzyme Inhibition, 2004—. Mem. adv. bd. Ill. Math. & Scis. Acad., 1988. With U.S. Army, 1969-71. Recipient Career Devel. award USPHS, 1982-87, E. LeRoy Hall award for tchg. excellence, 1999, Northwestern Alumni Tchg. award, 2000; postdoctoral fellow Brandeis U., Waltham, Mass., 1974-76, DuPont Young Faculty fellow, 1976, Alfred P. Sloan Found. fellow, 1981-85, Alumni fellow, Penn. State U., 2008; grantee various govt. and pvt. insts., 1976—. Arthur C. Cope. Sr. scholar ACS, 2003. Fellow: AAAS; mem.: ACS (div. med. chem. mem., Hall of Fame 2009, Perkin medal 2009), Am. Chem. Soc. (nat. elected nominating com. divns. biol. chemistry 1993—96, long-range planning com. divsn. med. chem. 1999—2002), Am. Soc. Biochem. Molecular Biology, Am. Inst. Chemists. Avocations: golf, tennis. Office: Northwestern U Dept Chemistry 2145 Sheridan Rd Evanston IL 60208-3113 Office Phone: 847-491-5653. Business E-Mail: Agman@chem.northwestern.edu.

SILVERMAN, RONALD, plastic surgeon; MD, U. Md., Balt., 1994. Cert. Am. Bd. Plastic Surgery, 2001. Chief plastic surgery U. Md., 2006—. Office: Univ Md Med Ctr 22 S Greene St Baltimore MD 21201 Business E-Mail: rsilverman@smail.umaryland.edu.

SILVERMAN, ROSS O., lawyer; b. Toledo, Aug. 3, 1960; BA, Ohio State U., 1982; JD cum laude, U. Toledo, 1985. Bar: Ga. 1986, DC 1989, Ill. 1995, NY 2003, US Dist. Ct., So. and Ea. Dist. NY, No Dist. Ill., US Ct. Appeals, 7th Cir. Trial atty. Criminal Sect. Tax Div., US Dept. Justice, 1988—90; asst. US atty. No. Dist. Ill., 1990—94; ptnr. Katten Muchin Zavis Rosenman, Chgo. Mem.: DC Bar, State Bar Ga., Ill. State Bar Assn., Chgo. Bar Assn. Office: Katten Muchin Zavis Rosenman 525 W Monroe St Chicago IL 60661 Office Phone: 312-902-5240. Office Fax: 312-577-8989. Business E-Mail: ross.silverman@kattenlaw.com. E-mail: ross.silverman@kmzr.com.

SILVERMAN, SAM MENDEL, physicist, lawyer; b. NYC, Nov. 16, 1925; s. Moshe Aaron and Gitel (Korenbaum) S.; m. Jacqueline Greenberg, Sept. 12, 1948 (div. Apr. 1965); children: Ann, William, Nancy; m. Phyllis Rolfe, June 26, 1966; children: Gila, Aaron. BChE, CCNY, 1945; PhD, Ohio State U., 1952; JD, Suffolk U., Boston, 1982. Bar: Mass. 1982, US Dist. Ct. Mass. 1982, US Ct. Appeals (1st cir.) 1982, NY 1983, US Supreme Ct. 1986, NH, 2007. Assoc. Ohio State U., Columbus, 1952-55; asst. prof. chem. physics U. Toledo, 1955-57; rsch. physicist Air Force Cambridge Rsch. Labs., Bedford, Mass., 1957-80, chief polar atmospheric processes br. and dir. geopole obs., 1963-74, cons., 1980—. Vis. rsch. assoc. Queens U., Belfast, 1963-64; vis. prof. Osmania U., Hyderabad, India, 1965-66; mem. adv. bd. Inst. Space and Atmospheric Studies, U. Sask., Can., 1965-69; sr. rsch. physicist Boston Coll., 1981-97; co-chmn. interdivisional commn. history Internat. Assn. Geomagnetism and Aeronomy, 1987-91; lectr. palliative care courses, Poland, 1993, 94, 2000. Contbr. articles to profl. jours. Mem. Town Meeting Lexington, Mass., 1973-79, 84—; elected mem. Lexington Dem. Town Com., 1996—; legal counsel Internat. Work Group on Death, Dying and Bereavement. With USAAF, 1945-46. Recipient Thurgood Marshall award, com. pub. counsel svcs. Mass. Pub. Defender's Agy., 2002. Fellow Am. Phys. Soc., Explorers Club; mem. Am. Geophys. Union (editor History of Geophysics newsletter 1983-91), Internat. Work Group on Death, Dying and Bereavement. Home: 18 Ingleside Rd Lexington MA 02420-2522 Office Phone: 781-861-0368. Personal E-mail: smpr111@verizon.net.

SILVERMAN, SARAH, comedian, actress; b. Bedford, NH, Dec. 1, 1970; Actor: (TV series) Saturday Night Live, 1993—94, Mr. Show with Bob and David, 1995—97, Greg the Bunny, 2002, The Sarah Silverman Program, 2007—, (voice only) Crank Yankers, 2002,: (TV miniseries) Pilot Season, 2004; (TV films) Mr. Show and the Incredible, Fantastical News Report, 1998, Smog, 1999, Late Last Night, 1999, Rocky Times, 2000, (voice only) Saddle Rush, 2002,: (films) Overnight Delivery, 1998, Bulworth, 1998, There's Something About Mary, 1998, The Bachelor, 1999, The Way of the Gun, 2000, Black Days, 2001, Say It Isn't So, 2001, Heartbreakers, 2001, Evolution, 2001, Run Ronnie Run, 2002, The School of Rock, 2003, Nobody's Perfect, 2004, (voice only) Hair High, 2004, Rent, 2005, I Want Someone to Eat Cheese With, 2005, School for Scoundrels, 2006, Funny People, 2009; actor, co-prodr.: Who's the Caboose?, 1997; writer, actor Sarah Silverman: Jesus is Magic, 2005; actor: (TV appearances) Star Trek: Voyager, 1996, The Larry Sanders Show, 1996, Seinfeld, 1997, Brotherly Love, 1997, JAG, 1997, The Naked Truth, 1997, Futurama, 2000, V.I.P., 2002, Frasier, 2003, Monk, 2004, Entourage, 2004, (voice only) Aqua Teen Hunger Force, 2004, Drawn Together, 2004, American Dad, 2005. Recipient Nightlife award for comic female stand-up, 2007. Office: c/o Thruline Entertainment 9250 Wilshire Blvd Gound Fl Beverly Hills CA 90212*

SILVERMAN, STANLEY WAYNE, chemical company executive; m. Ellen J. Seligsohn, June 7, 1970. BSChemE, Drexel U., 1969, MBA, 1974; AMP, Harvard U., 1989. Process engr. Atlantic Richfield Co., Phila., 1969-71, PQ Corp., Phila., 1971-74, mgr. oper. planning Valley Forge, Pa., 1974-76, product mgr., 1976-80, mktg. mgr., 1980-82, nat. sales mgr., 1982-84, pres. Nat. Silicates Ltd. subs. Toronto, Ont., Can., 1984-87, pres. ind. chem. group Valley Forge, 1987-90, exec. v.p., COO, 1990-99, pres., CEO, bd. dirs., 2000—05; dir. C&D Techs., 2003—. Chmn. adv. coun. Drexel U. Coll. Engring, 1991-93, alumni bd. govs., 1998, bd. trustees, 2000—; bd. dirs. Phila. Acad., Inc., 1999—2004. Named among 100 most accomplished grads. Drexel U., 1993; recipient Alumni Achievement award Drexel U., 1995. Mem. Soap and Detergent Assn. (bd. dirs. 2001-05, chmn bd. 2004-05), Am. Chemistry Coun. (bd. dirs. 2001-05), Femco Machine Co. (bd. dirs. 2007-), A. Schulman Inc. (bd. dirs. 2008-). Business E-Mail: stan.silverman@comcast.net.

SILVERMAN, STEVEN DONALD, lawyer; b. Balt., Oct. 28, 1966; s. Joseph A. and Sydna R. Silverman; m. Paula Bridges Silverman, June 12, 1993; children: Samantha, Ryan. BA, U. Richmond, 1988; JD, U. Balt., 1991. Bar: Md. 1991, U.S. Dist. Ct. Md. 1994, D.C. 2002. Law clk. Md. Atty. Gen.-Civil Litig., Balt., 1989—91; asst. pub. defender felony narcotics Office of Pub. Defender, Balt., 1991—94; pvt. practice, mng. ptnr. Silverman Thompson & White, Balt., 1995—. Lectr. in field. Mem.: ATLA, Md. Commn. Jud. Disabilities, Balt. City Bar (jud. selection com. 2001—02), Md. Criminal Def. Attys. Assn., Md. Bar Assn., Million Dollar Advs. Forum. Office: Silverman Thompson & White 26th Fl 201 N Charles St Baltimore MD 21201 Office Phone: 410-385-2225.

SILVERN, LEONARD CHARLES, retired engineering executive; b. NYC, May 20, 1919; s. Ralph and Augusta (Thaler) S.; m. Gloria Marantz, June 1948 (div. Jan. 1968); 1 child, Ronald; m. Elisabeth Beeny, Aug. 1969 (div. Oct. 1972); m. Gwen Taylor, Nov. 1985. BS in Physics, L.I. U., 1946; MA, Columbia U., 1948, EdD, 1952. registered profl. consulting engr., Calif. Apprenticeship, 1939—42; tng. supr. U.S. Dept. Navy, NYC, 1942—49; tng. dir. exec. dept. N.Y. Divsn. Safety, Albany, 1949-55; resident engring. psychologist Lincoln Lab, MIT for Rand Corp., Lexington, 1955-56; engr., dir. edn., tng., rsch. labs. Hughes Aircraft Co., Culver City, Calif., 1956-62; assisted in establishing Howard Med. Inst., 1985—85; dir. human performance engring. lab., sr. scientist Northrop Norair, Hawthrone, Calif., 1962-64; prin. sci., v.p., pres. Edn. & Tng. Cons. Co., 1964—, Sedona, Ariz., 1980—2009. Pres. Systems Engring. Labs. divsn., 1980—; cons. hdqrs. Air Tng. Command USAF, Randolph AFB Tex., 1964-68, Elec. Industries Assn., Washington, 1963-69, Edn. R and D Ctr., U. Hawaii, 1970-74, Ctr. Vocat. and Tech. Edn., Ohio State U., 1972-73, Coun. Exceptional Children, 1973-74, Canadore Coll. Applied Arts and Tech., Ont., Can., 1974-76, Centro Nacional de Productividad, Mexico City, 1973-75, N.S. Dept. Edn., Halifax, Can., 1975-79, Aeronutronic Ford-Ford Motor Co., 1975-76, Nat. Tng. Systems, Inc., 1976-81, Nfld. Pub. Svc. Commn., 1978, Legis Affairs Office USDA, 1980, Rocky Point Techs., 1966; adj. prof. edn., pub. adminstrn. U. So. Calif. Grad. Sch., 1957-65; vis. prof. computer sci. U. Calif. Extension Divsn., L.A., 1963-72. Contbg. editor Ednl. Tech., 1968-73, 81-85; reviewer ACM Computing Revs., 1962-93 & 1996-2002; contbr. numerous articles to profl. jours. Dist. ops. officer, disaster comm. svc. L.A. County Sheriff's Dept., 1973-75, dist. comm. officer, 1975-76; bd. dirs. SEARCH, 1976—; mem. adv. com. West Sedona Cmty. Plan of Yavapai County, 1986-88; councilman City of Sedona, 1988-92; rep. COCOPAI, 1988-89; vol. earth team Soil Conservation Svc., U.S. Dept. Agr., 1989-92; Verde Resource Assn., 1988-90, Group on Water Logistics, 1989-90; chair publs. com. Ariz. Rural Recycling Conf., 1990. With USN, 1944-46. Mem. IEEE (sr.), APA, Am. Radio Relay League (life), Nat. Soild Waste Mgmt. Symposium (chmn. publs. com. 1988-89), Ariz. Rural Recycling Conf. (chair publs. com. 1990), Friendship Vets. Fire Engine Co. (hon.), Soc. Wireless Pioneers (life), Quarter Century Wireless Assn. (life), Sierra Club (treas. Sedona-Verde Valley Group 1991-93), Assn. Bldg. Coms., Vox Pop (chmn. bd. dirs. Sedona 1983-93, dir. 1993-95), Nat. Parks and Conservation Assn., Wilderness Soc., Ariz. Ctr. Law Pub. Interest, Old Old Timers Club. Office: PO Box 1015 Clarkdale AZ 86324-1015

SILVERS, DAMON ABRAHAM, lawyer; b. 1964; BA summa cum laude, Harvard Coll., Cambridge, Mass., 1986; MBA with high honors, Harvard U. Bus. Sch., Mass., 1995; JD, Harvard U. Law Sch., Mass., 1996; student in history, Kings Coll., Cambridge U. Fellow, enforcement divsn. SEC; with Cravath, Swaine & Moore, Credit Suisse First Boston; rsch. dir. Harvard Union Clerical and Tech. Workers; asst. dir., office corp. and fin. affairs Amalgamated Clothing and Textile Workers Union; law clk., Chancellor William T. Allen and Vice-Chancellor Bernard Balick Del. Ct. Chancery; assoc. gen. counsel AFL-CIO; counsel to the chmn. ULLICO Inc. Mem. standing adv. group Pub. Co. Acctg. Oversight Bd.; mem. Oversight Panel Overseeing Implementation of the Econ. Stabilization Act, 2008—; mem. user adv. coun. Fin. Acctg. Stds. Bd.; mem. corp. governance task force Am. Acad. Arts. Sciences; mem. stock options voting task force NY Stock Exch.; mem. adv. com. on analyst independence US House Reps. Capital Markets Subcom.; mem. subcom. on internat. corp. governance ABA. Author: Challenging Wall Street's Conventional Wisdom: Defining a Worker-Owner View of Value, 2001, The Origins and Goals of the Fight for Proxy Access, 2004. Baker Scholar, Harvard U. Office: AFL-CIO Office the Gen Counsel 815 16th St NW Washington DC 20006*

SILVERS, GERALD THOMAS, retired publishing executive; b. Cin., Aug. 26, 1937; s. Steve Allen and Tina Mae (Roberts) S.; m. Ann Gregory Woodward, July 25, 1964. BA, U. Ky., Lexington, 1960. Asst. rsch. svcs. mgr. Cin. Enquirer, 1963-72, rsch. svcs. dir., 1972-74, rsch. dir., 1974-90, v.p. mktg. svcs., 1990-94, v.p. market devel., 1994—2003; ret., 2003. Active U. Ky. Devel. Coun., Lexington, 1986—; trustee Neediest Kids of All, 1991—; region 5 exec. com. Ohio Sch. to Work, 1997-2000; corps. com. St. Elizabeth Med. Ctr. Found., 1998-2007; bd. overseers Taft Mus. Art, 1999—, treas., bd. govs., 2002—, vice chmn., 2007.; vice chairman UC, 2008, 09; 1st lt. U.S. Army, 1960-62. Recipient Thomas H. Copeland award of merit, 1991. Mem. U. Ky. Alumni Assn. Cin. Chpt. (pres. 1985), Newspaper Rsch. Coun. (pres. 1985-86), Internat. Newspaper Market Assn., Am. Mktg. Assn., Am. Art Soc. Cin. (pres. 1999-2001), Cin. MACDowell Soc. Presbyterian. Home: 229 Watch Hill Rd Fort Mitchell KY 41011-1822

SILVERS, ROBERT B., editor; b. NY, Dec. 31, 1929; s. James J. and Rose (Roden) S. AB, U. Chgo., 1947; cert., Ecole de Sci. Politiques, Paris, 1956; LittD (hon.), Harvard U., 2007. Paris editor Paris Rev., 1954-59; asst. editor Harpers Mag., NYC, 1959-63; co-editor N.Y. Rev. of Books, NYC, 1963—. Editor: Writing in America, 1962, Hidden Histories of Science, 1995, Doing It: Five Performing Arts, 2001; co-editor: The Legacy of Isaiah Berlin, 2001, Striking Terror: America's New War, 2002, The Company They Kept: Writers on Unforgettable Friendships, 2006. Trustee NY Pub. Libr., 1997—, Ditchley Found., 1996—, Am. Acad. in Rome, 1998-, Paris Rev. Found., 2002-. With SHAPE US Army, 1952. Decorated Legion d'Honneur, l'Ordre Nat. du Merite France; recipient Literarian award outstanding svc. to Am. lit. cmty., Am. Book Found., 2006. Mem. Am. Acad. Arts and Scis., Coun. Fgn. Rels., Century Assn., Knickerbocker Club. Office: 435 Hudson St New York NY 10014-3994 Office Phone: 212-757-8070.

SILVERS, SALLY, choreographer, performing company executive; b. Greeneville, Tenn., June 19, 1952; d. Herbert Ralston and Sara Elizabeth (Buchanan) S.; life ptnr. Bruce Erroll Andrews. BA in Dance and Polit. Sci., Antioch Coll., 1975. Artistic dir. Sally Silvers & Dancers, NYC, 1980—. Mem. faculty Leicester Poly., 1986, 87, 89, summer choreography project Bennington Coll., 1988-92, Chisenhale Dance Space, London, 1989, 91, Am. Dance Festival, Durham, N.C., 1990, 92; guest tchr. European Dance Devel. Ctr., Arnhem, The Netherlands, 1992—. Choreographer (performances) Politics of the Body Microscope of Conduct, 1980, Social Movement, 1981, Connective Tissue, 1981, Less Time You Know Praxis, 1981, Don't No Do And This, 1981, Lack of Entrepreneurial Thrift, 1982, Celluoid Sally and Mr. E, 1982, Mutate, 1982, Being Red Enough, 1982, Disgusting, 1982, Bedtime at the Reformatory, 1982, Eat the Rich, 1982, They Can't Get It in the Shopping Cart, 1982, Blazing Forceps, 1982, And Find Out Why, 1983, Choose Your Weapons, 1984, Extend the Wish for Entire, 1985, No Best Better Way, 1985, Every All Which is Not Us, 1986, Swaps Ego Say So, 1986, Be Careful Now, You Know Sugar Melts in Water, 1987, Fact Confected, 1987, Both, Both, 1987, Tizzy boost, 1988, Moebius, 1988, Whatever Ever, 1989, Get Tough, Sports and Divertissement, 1989, Flap, 1989, Swan's Crayon, 1989, Fanfare Tripwire, 1990, Harry Meets Sally, 1990, Along the Skid Mark of Recorded History, 1990, Matinee Double-You, 1991, Grand Guignol, 1991, Dash Dash Slang Plural Plus, 1992, The Bubble Cut, 1992, Vigilant Corsage, 1992, Oops Fact, 1992, Small Room, 1993, Exwhyzee, 1993, Elegy, 1993, Now That It Is Now, 1994, Give Em Enough Rope, Swoon Noir, 1994, Radio Rouge, 1995, Braceletizing, 1995, Hush Comet, 1995, Bite the Pillow, 1995, Pandora's Cake Stain, 1996, Secrets Of, 1997, HUSHHUSH, Sugar Raised, 1998 Capture, Teddy Growl, 1999, Storming Heaven, 2000, Swaphot Trouble, 2001, Strike Me Lightning, 2002, Spaced Out, 2003, Dreams Do Come True, 2004, Dang Me, 2004, Yessified!, 2009, 25th Anniversary Season: RUPT, Puppy Skills, Oven Rack, 2005, dancer Yvonne Rainer, 2006—; video and performance filmmaker: (films) Little Lieutenant, 1993 (Silver); N.Y. Dance on Camera Festival, Mechanics of the Brain, 1997; co-author: (book) Resurgant New Writings By Women, 1992; contbr. articles to profl. jours. Grantee Nat. Endowment Arts, 1987, 89, 90, 91, 98, Jerome Found., 1993, 1996, Meet the Composer N.Y. Found. for the Arts, 1995; Guggenheim Found. fellow, 1988; Found. Contemporary Performance Arts, 2001. Mem. Segue Found. (bd. dirs. Segue Performance Space 1992-2002). Avocations: reading, writing, art events, costume design. Home: 303 E 8th St Apt 4F New York NY 10009-5212

SILVERS, WILLYS KENT, geneticist; b. NYC, Jan. 12, 1929; s. Lewis Julian and Miriam Elizabeth (Rosenzweig) Silvers; m. Abigail M. Adams, Sept. 29, 1956 (dec. June 18, 2005); children: Deborah Elizabeth, Willys Kent. BA, Johns Hopkins U., 1950; PhD, U. Chgo., 1954. Assoc. staff scientist Jackson Lab., Bar Harbor, Maine, 1956-57; assoc. mem. Wistar Inst., Phila., 1957-65; mem. faculty U. Pa. Med. Sch., 1965—, prof. genetics, 1967-98, prof. emeritus, 1998—. Mem. allergy and immunology study sect. NIH, 1962—66, adv. bd. primate rsch. ctrs., 1968—71; mem. com. cancer immunobiology Nat. Cancer Inst., 1974—78; bd. sci. overseers Jackson Lab., Bar Harbor, 1980—89. Author: The Immunobiology of Transplantation, 1971, The Coat Colors of Mice: A Model for Mammalian Gene Action and Interaction, 1979; mem. editl. bd. Transplantation, 1963—71, Jour. Exptl. Zoology, 1965—70, 1981—86, Jour. Immunology, 1973—77, Jour. Reticuloendothelial Soc., 1974—77; contbr. articles to profl. jours. Mem.: Am. Genetic Assn. (coun. 1980—83, pres. 1983). Home: 1500 Monk Rd Gladwyne PA 19035 Personal E-mail: wsilvers@aol.com.

SILVERSTEIN, BARBARA ANN, producer, musician; b. Phila., July 24, 1947; d. Charles and Selma (Brenner) S.; m. Bernard J. Taylor II, Aug. 19, 1978. Student, Bennington Coll., 1965-67; BMus, Phila. Coll. Performing Arts, 1970; MA, U. Del., 1997. Assoc. music dir. Suburban Opera Co., Chester, Pa., 1967-75; asst. condr. Toledo Opera Assn., 1975-76; asst. condr., coach Curtis Inst. Music, Phila., 1973-77; asst. condr. Phila. Lyric Opera, 1971-74, Des Moines Opera Festival, Indianola, Iowa, 1974-78; music dir., condr. Savoy Co., Phila., 1977-80, Miss. Opera, Jackson, 1979-82; artistic dir., condr. Pa. Opera Theater, Phila., 1976-93; guest condr. Opera Del., Wilmington, 1981, 83, Anchorage Opera, 1982, Utah Festival Opera Co., 1993-96, Lyric Opera Kansas City, 1995, Opera Roanoke, Va., 1995, 98, Hollins U., 1999; prof. English U. Del., Ursinus, 1996—2004; mng. editor Epotec Inc., 1999-2000, dir. comm., 2000—01; artistic producer Kimmel Ctr. Festival, Phila., 2007—; freelance writer, translator, 1980—. Recipient alumni award U. of Arts. Mem. Am. Fedn. Musicians, Music Fund Soc., Pa. Coun. on the Arts (adv. panel 1987-90, OPERA Am. (bd. dirs. 1987-93, exec. com. 1988-93). Jewish. Avocations: scuba diving, reading, agility training.

SILVERSTEIN, JANET HOPE, pediatrician, educator; b. Bronx, NY, June 21, 1944; d. Jesse and Beatrice (Zuckerman) Fisher; m. Burton Silverstein, Aug. 18, 1978; children: Craig Darryl, Todd Alan. BS, U. Rochester, 1966; MD, U. Pa., 1970. Diplomate Am. Bd. Pediat. Clin.

assoc., pediat. Duke U. Med. Ctr., Durham, NC, 1977-78; instr. in pediat., cmty. health U. Fla., Gainesville, 1978-80, asst. prof. pediat., cmty. health, 1980-84, assoc. prof., 1984-90, prof. pediat., 1990—, chief divsn. pediat. endocrinology, 1994—, med. dir., Pediatric Clinic, 1998—2004. Med. dir. Fla. Diabetes Camp, Gainesville, 1988—, Diabetes Project Unit, Gainesville, 1979—2002; gov.'s diabetes adv. coun., Tallahassee, 1984—2000, 2004—; sci. adv. bd. Diabetes Action Rsch. and Edn. Found., Washington, 1990—; program dir. U. Fla. Diabetes Rsch., Edn. and Treatment Ctr., 1991—; com. Am. Bd. Pediat.; mem. editl. bd. Jour. Pediat., 2004—. Med. editor Kids Corner, 1994—2005; contbr. articles to profl. jours. Co-creator Diabetes Resdl. Unit for Children Having Trouble Coping with Diabetes; creator Bring a Friend to Camp, After Hours Pediat. Clinic. Named Olympic Torch Bearer, 1996. Mem.: Soc. Pediatric Rsch. (elected), Ambulatory Pediat. Assn., Lawson Wilkins Pediat. Endocrinology Soc. (chair diabetes com. 2000—01, bd. dirs. 2003—07, past chmn. drug, therapeutics com.), Endocrine Soc., Am. Diabetes Assn. (chair coun. on youth 2001—03), Am. Acad. Pediats. (chair exec. com. sect. on endocrinology 2000—04), Am. Pediat. Soc., Nat. Diabetes Edn. Program (chmn. children's work group 2004—). Avocations: jogging, bicycling, art, reading. Home: 1932 NW 24th St Gainesville FL 32605-3848 Office Phone: 352-334-1390.

SILVERSTEIN, JONATHAN CHARLES, surgeon, researcher; s. Gerald Ellis and Mickie Silverstein; m. Tracey Anne Silverstein; children: Jacob Anthony, Jessica Lynn, Joshua Andrew. BS, U. Ill., 1986; MD, Wash. U., 1990; MS, Harvard Sch. Pub. Health, 1998. Cert. Am. Bd. Surgery, 1997. Assoc. dir. Computation Inst., 2001—; assoc. prof. surgery U. Chgo., 2001—. Contbr. articles to profl. jours. Jr. bd. mem. Dystonia Med. Rsch. Found. Grantee, Nat. Libr. Medicine/NIH, 1998—2002, 2000, 2003—, The U. Chgo. Provost's Program for Academic Tech. Innovation, 2002—03. Fellow: ACS (mem. regents com. informatics 2001); mem.: Am. Med. Informatics Assn., Chgo. Surg. Soc., Assn. Surg. Edn., Am. Med. Soc., Ill. Surg. Soc., Biomedical Libr. Informatics Rev. Com. Avocations: skiing, rowing, percussion. Office: Computation Inst Univ Chgo Chicago IL 60637-1470 E-mail: silverstein@post.harvard.edu.

SILVERSTEIN, LARRY A., real estate developer; b. Bklyn., 1932; m. Klara Silverstein, 1956; children: Roger, Lisa, Sharon. BA, NYU, 1952; JD, Brooklyn Law Sch. Bar: N.Y. Pres. Silverstein Properties, Inc., NYC; owner 529 Fifth Ave., 570 Seventh Ave., One River Place, Two River Place, 120 Wall St., 120 Broadway, Seven World Trade Ctr., 529 Fifth Ave., NYC, 520 Seventh Ave., NYC, 575 Lexington Ave., NYC, 1177 Ave. of the Americas, NYC; 99 year leaseholder World Trade Ctr., 2001—. Gov., past chmn. Real Estate Bd. N.Y.; founder, chmn. emeritus NYU Real Estate Inst.; chmn. Realty Found. Trustee NYU, vice chmn. bd. trustees; trustee South St. Seaport Mus., Mus. Jewish Heritage; bd. chmn. United Jewish Appeal, Fedn. Jewish Philanthropies, NY. Avocations: classical music, yachting. Office: Silverstein Properties Inc 120 Broadway Suite 230 New York NY 10271 Office Phone: 212-732-9700. E-mail: rsilverstein@silvprop.com.*

SILVERSTEIN, RICHARD, advertising agency executive; b. 1949; m. Carla Emil Silverstein; children: Aaron, Simone. Grad., Parsons Sch. Design, NYC. Various graphic design positions in San Francisco including art dir. Rolling Stone mag., McCann Erickson, Bozell & Jacobs, Foote, Cone & Belding, Ogilvy & Mather; co-founder, co-chmn., co-creative dir. Goodby, Silverstein & Ptnrs. (formerly Goodby, Berlin, & Silverstein), San Francisco, 1983—. Active Corp. Design Found., Cambridge, Mass.; bd. dirs. USA Cycling Fedn., Golden Gate Nat. Parks Assn. Named Creative Dir. of Yr., Adweek, 1990, 1992, Agy. Exec. of Yr., 1994; named to Hall of Fame, Art Dirs. Club NY, 2002, Creative Hall of Fame, The One Club for Art & Copy, NYC, 2004. Office: Goodby Silverstein & Ptnrs 720 California St San Francisco CA 94108-2404 Office Phone: 415-392-0669.*

SILVERSTEIN, RUSSELL L., physician; m. Judy Silversteinh. MD, U. Tex. Med. Br., Galveston, 1972. Diplomate Am. Bd. Internal Medicine, 1975, Am. Bd. Nephrology, 1977. Sr. ptnr. Dallas Nephrology Assocs., 1977—. Fellow: ACP, Am. Soc. Nephrology. Office: Dallas Nephrology Assocs 13154 Coit Rd Ste #100 Dallas TX 75230 Office Fax: 214-366-6430.

SILVERSTEIN, SAMUEL CHARLES, cellular biology and physiology professor, researcher; b. NYC, Feb. 11, 1937; s. Paul Robert and Jeanette (Kamen) S.; m. Jo Ann Kleinman, Apr. 2, 1967; children: David Paul, Jennifer Kate. AB, Dartmouth Coll., 1958; MD, Albert Einstein Coll. Medicine, 1963. Intern in medicine U. Colo. Med. Center, 1963-64; postdoctoral fellow dept. cell biology Rockefeller U., 1964-67; resident in medicine Mass. Gen. Hosp., 1967—68; asst. prof. cellular physiology and immunology Rockefeller U., 1968-71, assoc. prof., physician, 1972—; John Dalton prof. physiology, prof. medicine Columbia U. Coll. Physicians and Surgeons, NYC, 1983—, chmn. dept., 1983—2003. Founder, dir. Columbia U. Summer Rsch. Program for Secondary Sch. Sci. Tchrs., 1990—; prin. investigator, program dir. Pre and Post-doctoral Tng. Immunology, 1997—2005. Editor: Transport of Macromolecules in Cellular Systems, 1979; chmn. editl. bd. Jour. Cell Biology, 1979-82, editor, 1978-89. Bd. dirs. Arnold P. Gold Found., 1998—, Cancer Rsch. Fund, Damon Runyon Found., 1990—; bd. dirs. Rsch. Am., 1993-2005, mem. exec. com., 1996-2006. Recipient John Oliver LaGorce medal, Nat. Geog. Soc., 1967, Marie Bonazinga Rsch. award, Soc. Leukocyte Biology, 1984, Disting. Alumnus award, Albert Einstein Coll. Medicine, 1987, N.Y.C. Mayor's award Publ. Understanding of Sci. and Tech., 2003, Westy award Contbns. Sci. Edn. N.Y.C. Schs., 2004, Fountain Valley Sch. Trustees 75th Anniversary award, Colorado Springs, 2005, Silverstein Peak, Sentinel Range, Antarctica named in his honor by, US Geol. Survey, 2006; fellow Helen Hay Whitney, 1964—67, John Simon Guggenheim, 2005, Pres. Lasker/Funding First, 2001—04. Fellow: AAAS (chair sect. medicine 1998), N.Y. Acad. Sci. (edn. com.), Am. Soc. Microbiology; mem.: Am. Acad. Arts and Scis., Inst. Medicine Nat. Acad. Scis., Fedn. Am. Socs. for Exptl. Biology (bd. dirs. 1991—96, v.p. 1993—94, pres. 1994—95, chmn. pub. affairs adv. com. 1995—96), Practitioners Soc. N.Y., Assn. Am. Physicians, Am. Physiol. Soc., Am. Soc. Biol. Chemists, Infectious Diseases Soc. Am., Am. Assn. Immunologists, Am. Soc. Clin. Investigation, Am. Soc. Cell Biology (Bruce Alberts award for Excellence in Sci. Edn. 2005), Century Assn., Explorers Club, Am. Alpine Club (dir. 1963—64, 1969—74), Dartmouth Coll. Chpt. Phi Beta Kappa (elected 2008). Achievements include research and numerous publications in field of virology, cell biology, immunology, seconary science education, science policy, and mountaineering. Office: Columbia U Coll Physicians & Surgeons 630 W 168th St New York NY 10032-3795 Office Phone: 212-305-3546. Business E-Mail: scs3@columbia.edu.

SILVERSTEIN, SCOTT A., trading card company executive; b. 1961; m. Amy G. Silverstein. BA, Brandeis U., Waltham, Mass.; JD, U. Pa. Law Sch. Atty. Shea & Gould, Hutton Ingram Yuzek Gainen Carroll & Bertolotti, 1990—93; gen. counsel The Topps Co., NYC, 1993—95, v.p. bus. affairs, gen. counsel, 1995—2000, exec. v.p., head sports and entertainment group, 2000—04, pres., COO, 2004—08, pres., CEO, 2008—. Office: The Topps Co US One Whitehall St New York NY 10004 Office Phone: 212-376-0300. Office Fax: 212-376-0573.

SILVERSTEIN, SUZANNE, art therapist; b. LA, Jan. 14, 1948; d. Lita (Factor) Kilpatrick; m. Andrew Chiaramonte, July 4, 1988; 1 child, Jaysen Pascal. BFA, Calif. Inst. of the Arts, LA, 1971; MA, Immaculate Heart Coll., LA, 1975. Art therapy coord., supr. family and child program Thalians Mental Health Ctr., LA, 1977—; art therapy coord., supr. famil and child program dept. psychiatry Cedars-Sinai Med. Ctr., LA, 1977—; pres., co-founder Psychol. Trauma Ctr., LA, 1981—. Faculty clin. art therapy dept. Immaculate Heart Coll., 1975-81, Loyola Marymount U., 1981-82, leader, group dynamics class, 1975-82; adminstr. Psychol. Trauma Ctr., 1981—, pres. 1981—. Author: (with others) Expanding Mental Health Interventions in Schools, 1988. Fellowship Thalians Mental Health Ctr./Cedars Sinai Med. Ctr., L.A., 1975-76. Mem. Am. Art Therapy Assn., So. Calif. Art Therapy Assn. Office: Psychol Trauma Ctr 8730 Alden Dr Rm C212 Los Angeles CA 90048-3811 Office Phone: 310-423-3541. Business E-Mail: suzanne.silverstein@cshs.org.

SILVERSTONE, LEON MARTIN, neuroscientist, cardiologist, educator, research scientist; b. London, May 21, 1939; came to US, 1976; s. Jack Stanley and Sadie (Osen) S.; children from previous marriage: Samantha, Frances, Mark; m. Deborah Advani, Sept. 13, 1998. Student, U. London, 1958-59; L.D.S., U. Leeds, UK, 1963, B.Ch.D., 1964, D.D.Sc., 1971; L.D.S., Royal Coll. Surgeons, Eng., 1964; PhD, U. Bristol, Eng., 1967; postgrad., U. London, 1969-76. House surgeon Leeds Dental Hosp., England, 1963-64; rsch. fellow med. rsch. coun. unit Bristol Med. and Dental Sch., 1964-67; lectr. dental surgery U. Bristol, 1967-68; sr. lectr. child dental health Med. Coll., Royal London Hosp., 1969-75, reader in preventive and pediat. dentistry, 1975-76; cons. Royal London Hosp., 1973-76; vis. Lasby prof. Dental Sch. U. Minn., Mpls., 1974-75; prof., head divsn. cardiology Dows Inst. Dental Rsch., Coll. Dentistry, U. Iowa, Iowa City, 1976-82; assoc. dean rsch. U. Colo. Health Scis. Ctr., Denver, 1982-89, dir. Oral Scis. Rsch. Inst., 1986-89; biomed. cons., 1990; v.p. R & D Synaptic Corp., La Jolla, Calif., 1990-95; dir. R & D BioSciences Sys. LLC, La Jolla, Calif., 1995—2002; pres., chmn. NeuroMed Devices Inc., 2003—. Vis. Nicholaysen prof. U. Oslo, 1972; cons. Pan Am. Health Orgn., WHO, 1973-85, dental rsch. Va, 1978-85; mem. study sect. and program adv. com. NIH-Nat. Inst. Dental Rsch., 1976-84, chmn. subcom. on dental caries, 1982-83, chmn. program adv. com., 1983-84; pres. Neura Corp., La Jolla, Calif., 1997-98. Mem. editorial bd. Caries Research, 1976-86; contbr. chpts. to books, articles in field to profl. publs. Recipient Nobel-Pharma A.B. Bofors prize, Copenhagen, 1971, ORCA-ROLEX rsch. prize, Zurich, 1973, Disting. award child dental health, 1981; NIH/Nat. Inst. Rsch. grantee, 1976-89. Mem. European Orgn. Caries Rsch.(mem. bd., sci. councillor 1971-83, pres. 1977-79), Internat. Assn. Dental Research (pres. cariology group 1982-83, Disting. Scientist award 1984), Am. Assn. Dental Rsch. (pres. cariology group chpt. 1982-83, chmn. publs. com. 1985-86), Brit. Dental Assn., Internat. Assn. Pedodontics (exec. com. 1972-79, jour. editor 1971-79), AAAS, Soc. Exptl. Biology and Medicine, Space Medicine Com., AAUP, Am. Acad. Pedodontics, Omega Kappa Upsilon, Sigma Xi. Office: Neuro Med Devices PO Box 100 Oakley UT 84055 Home Phone: 435-655-1081; Office Phone: 435-783-6696. Personal E-mail: neuromed@allwest.net.

SILVERTON, NANCY, chef; b. June 20, 1954; m. Mark Peel (div.); 3 children. Student, Calif. State U., Cordon Bleu, London, Ecole Le Notre, France. Asst. pastry chef Michael's Restaurant, Santa Monica, Calif.; 1st exec. pastry chef Spago, West Hollywood, Calif., 1982—85, 1987—89; v.p. product devel., exec. v.p., baker, owner LaBrea Bakery, LA, 1989—2001, Las Vegas, 1998—2001; pastry chef, co-owner Campanile restaurant; chef, co-owner Pizzeria Mozzo, LA, 2006—, Osteria Mozza, LA, 2006—. Author: Desserts, 1991, Nancy Silverton's Breads from the La Brea Bakery, 1996, Nancy Silverton's Pastries from the La Brea Bakery, 2000, Nancy Silverton's Sandwich Book, 2002, Twist of the Wrist, 2007; co-author: Mark Peel and Nancy Silverton At Home: Two Chefs Cook for Family and Friends, 1994, The Food of Campanile, 1997. Involved in Garden Sch. Project, LA, Meals-on-Wheels, Chgo., NYC, LA. Recipient Fine Dining award, Nation's Restaurant News, 1996, RCA Pioneer award, 2003, Internat. Star Diamond award for Outstanding Hospitality, 2004, WCR Golden Bowl award, 2005; named Best Pastry Chef of Yr., James Beard Found., 1990, LA Culinary Master of Yr., 1994, Restaurateur of Yr. and Restaurant of Yr., Southern Calif. Restaurant Writers, 1995, Pastry Chef of Yr., Chocolatier Mag., 1995; named a Who's Who in Am. Cooking, James Beard Found., 1990, Food Artisan, Bon Appetite Best of Food & Entertaining, 1999; named one of America's Best New Chefs, Food & Wine mag., 1990, 50 New Taste Makers, Nation's Restaurant News, 1999; named to The West 100: The most influential people in Southern Calif., LA Times, 2006. Office: Osteria Mozza 6602 Melrose Ave Los Angeles CA 90038 Office Phone: 323-297-0100.

SILVESTRI, CLAUDIO, information technology executive; Positions through v.p. info. tech. Compaq Canada, 1988—2000; dir. small bus. channel org. Microsoft Canada, 2000—04; group v.p. info. tech. Business Objects, 2004—05; chief info. officer Cognos Inc., 2005—. Office: Cognos Inc 3755 Riverside Dr Ottawa ON K1G 4K9 Canada Mailing: Cognos Inc PO Box 9707 Sta T Ottawa ON K1G 4K9 Canada

SILVESTRI, GEORGE JOSEPH, JR., retired thermodynamics engineer; b. Jessup, Pa., Aug. 3, 1927; m. Betty A. Huber, 1961 (dec. July 2002); children: Mary E. Silvestri Philbrick and Janet C. Silvestri Travis. BS, Drexel U., 1953, MS, 1956. Registered profl. engr., Pa. Devel. engr. Westinghouse Elec. Corp., 1953-69, fellow engr., 1969-72, 74, applications engr., 1972-73, adv. engr., 1974-94; project mgr. Elec. Power Rsch. Inst., 1973-74; ret., 1994. 59 patents in field. Mem. ASME (chmn. edn. and rsch. com. power divsn. 1982-85, 90-91, bd. rsch. and technol. devel. 1985-91, lectr. course on steam turbines power divsn. 1989-97, performance test code course on testing 1991-95, rsch. com. properties steam, James Harry Potter Gold medal 1993), Am. Nuclear Soc. Achievements include research in advanced power generation cycles, operation procedures to enhance steam turbine performance, low pressure turbine laboratory testing, improved steam property algorithms, steam turbine performance computer program. Address: 209 Robin Dr Souderton PA 18964-2160 E-mail: gjs803@verizon.net.

SILVESTRI, VITO NICHOLAS, communications educator; b. Vandergrift, Pa., Nov. 23, 1932; s. Vito Antonio Silvestri and Elvira DiVincenzo; 1 child, Marc. Student, Wayne U., Detroit, 1952; BS in Edn., Indiana State Tchrs. Coll., Pa., 1958; MS in Speech, Emerson Coll., Boston, 1959; PhD in Rhetoric and Pub. Address, Ind. U., Bloomington, 1966. Prof. English NY State Coll., Potsdam, 1959—64; prof. comm. studies Emerson Coll., Boston, 1964—96; founder, pres. The Bach Ensemble, Naples, Fla., 2002—. Vis. prof. U. ND, Grand Forks, 1969, Boston U., 1979, Stonehill Coll., Easton, Mass., 2001; cons. Nat. Fire Protection Assn., Quincy, Mass., 1980—86; adj. prof. comm. Fla. Gulf Coast U., Ft. Myers, 2002—05; mediator small claims Quincy Dist. Ct., Mass., 1988—92; cons. St. Lawrence Mental Health Agy., Potsdam, NY, 1960—64. Author: (textbook) Interpersonal Communication, 3d edit., 1991, JFK: Profile in Communication, 2000; contbr. articles to profl. jours. Cpl. US Army, 1952—54. Recipient Pro Arts Pub. Svc. in Arts award, City of Boston, 1992; Theodore Sorenson fellow, Kennedy Libr. Found., 1998—99. Democrat. Avocations: singing, cooking, reading, dance, travel. Home and Office: 3667 Arctic Cir Naples FL 34112

SILVESTRO, CLEMENT MARIO, museum director, historian; b. New Haven, Sept. 7, 1924; s. Joseph and Rose (Griego) S.; m. Betty C. Mack, June 26, 1950; 1 dau., Elizabeth J. Silvestro Casner. BS, Central Conn. State Coll., 1949; MS, U. Wis., 1951; PhD, 1959. Asst. to dir. Wis. Hist. Soc., 1956-57; dir. Am. Assn. State and Local History, 1957-64; editor History News, 1957-64; assoc. dir. Chgo. Hist. Soc., 1964-65, dir., 1965-74, sec., 1970-74; dir. Mus. of Our Nat. Heritage, Lexington, Mass., 1974-92. Mem. exec. com. Am. Assn. Museums, 1965-71, v.p., 1966-71; vis. lectr. Northeastern U., 1983-85 Co-author: A Decade of Collecting: Maps, 1985 Mem. Chgo. Archtl. and Landmark Com., 1968-74; mem. Ill. Historic Sites Adv. Council, 1970-74, U.S. ICOM, Nat. Com., 1970-74; chmn. Pres.'s Adv. Council on Historic Preservation, 1974-77; mem. adv. bd. Eleutherian Mills-Hagley Found., 1973-76; U.S. rep. to UNESCO Internat. Adv. Com. to Safeguard City of Venice, 1975; trustee U.S. Capitol Hist. Soc.; trustee, pres. Fruitlands Mus., 1982-85. Served with USAAF, 1943-45. Decorated Air medal with oak leaf clusters. Mem. Am. Assn. Mus., Orgn. Am Historians (chmn. hist. sites com. 1973-78), Chgo. Hist. Soc., Colonial Soc. Mass., Bostonian Soc., Mass. Hist. Soc. (resident), Union Club Boston, Masons. Home: 200 West Shore Rd Hancock ME 04640 Home Phone: 207-422-3097. Personal E-mail: silvestro@roadrunner.com.

SILVESTRY, RUBEN, philologist, educator; s. Ruben Silvestry and Celia Mercedes Feliciano. PhD, U. Tex., Austin, 1991. Vis. asst. prof. Coll. Charleston; coord. modern langs. SC State U., Oragengeburg, 2006—. Independent. Avocations: travel, reading, gardening. Home: 495 Robinson St Orangeburg SC 29115 Office: SC State Univ 300 College St NE PO Box 7486 Orangeburg SC 29117-0001 Business E-Mail: rsilvest@scsu.edu.

SILVEY, ANITA LYNNE, editor; b. Bridgeport, Conn., Sept. 3, 1947; d. John Oscar and Juanita Lucille (McKitrick) Silvey. BS in Edn., Ind. U., 1969; MA in Comm. Arts, U. Wis., 1970. Editorial asst. children's book dept. Little Brown and Co., Boston, 1970-71; asst. editor Horn Book Mag., Boston, 1971-75; mng. editor, founder New Boston Rev., 1975-76; mktg. mgr. children's books, libr. svcs. mgr. trade divsn. Houghton Mifflin, Boston, 1976-84; editor-in-chief Horn Book Mag., Boston, 1985-95; v.p., pub. Children's Books Houghton Mifflin Co., Boston, 1995—2001. Editor: Children's Books and Their Creators, 1995, Help Wanted: Stories About Young People and Work, 1997, Essential Guide to Children's Books and their Creators, 2002, 100 Best Books for Children, 2004, 500 Great Books for Teens, 2006, I'll Pass for your Comrade, 2008, Everything i Need to Know to Learned from a Children's Book, 2009. Named one of 70 Women Who Have Made a Difference, Women's Nat. Book Assn., 1987. Mem.: ALA (chmn. children's librs., Laura Ingalls Wilder award 1987—89), Assn. Am. Pubs. (mem. libr. com.), Internat. Reading Assn. (mem. IRA Book award com. 1985—87), New Eng. Round Table (chmn. 1978—79). Personal E-mail: anitasilvey@aol.com.

SIM, FRANKLIN H., orthopedic surgery educator; children: Leslie, Sheridan. MD, Dalhousie U. Med. Sch., 1964. Cert. orthopedic surgeon MN, 1972. Prof. orthop. surgery Mayo Clinic, Rochester, Minn., 1983—. Chair, divsn. orthop. oncology Mayo Clinic, 2000—. Physician US Nat. Hockey Team. 2d. lt. Black Watch Rgt., 1961, Germany. Recipient Outstanding Svc award, Canadian Orthop. Assn., 2000, Disting. award, Mayo Clinic, 2003. Fellow: Royal Australian Coll. Surgeons (hon.); mem.: SICOT, AMA, Orthop. Practice Soc., Orthop. Rsch. Soc., Musculoskeletal Tumor Soc., Minn. Orthop. Soc., Mid-Am. Orthop. Assn., Internat. Soc. Limb Salvage, Internat. Soc. Intraoperative Radiation Therapy, Internat. Skeletal Soc., Internat. Orthop. Assn., Canadian Orthop. Found. (bd. dirs.), Am. Orthop. Assn., Am. Orthop. Soc. Sports Medicine, Am. Coll. Sports Medicine, Am. Acad. Orthop. Surgeons, 20th Century Orthop. Soc., Ruth Jackson Orthop. Soc. (hon.), Sigma Xi (sci. rsch. soc.). Office: Mayo Clinic 200 First St SW Rochester MN 55905

SIM, JUDITH, marketing executive; BS, U. Calif., Davis. With Oracle Corp., Redwood Shores, Calif., 1991—, chief mktg. officer, 2003—. Named one of Best Marketers, BtoB Mag., 2008. Office: Oracle Corp 500 Oracle Pkwy Redwood City CA 94065*

SIMA, CHAO, biologist, researcher; s. Zhendong Sima and Funu Li; m. Xiaojia Chen, July 7, 2006. PhD, Tex. A&M U., Coll. Sta., 2006. Postdoc. rsch. assoc., dept. stats. Tax. A&M U., Coll. Sta., 2006—07; assoc. investigator Translational Genomics Rsch. Inst., Phoenix, 2007—. Contbr. articles to engrng. jours. Mem.: IEEE (Phoenix) (sesssion chair, Internat. Workshop Genomic Signal Processing and Stat. 2008, program com. mem. 2008). Achievements include research in revealed a series of phenomena for feature selection in samll sample settings. Office: Translational Genomics Rsch Inst 445 5th St Ste 600 Phoenix AZ 85006

SIMAAN, MARWAN, electrical engineering educator; m. Rita Simaan. MSEE, U. Pitts., 1970; PhDEE, U. Ill., 1972. Registered profl. engr., Pa. Rsch. engr. Shell Devel. Co., Houston, 1974-76; assoc. prof. elec. engrng. U. Pitts., 1976-85, prof., 1985-89, Bell of Pa., Bell Atlantic prof., 1989—2008, chmn. dept. elec. engrng., 1991—2008; interim dean Coll. Engrng. & Computer Sci., U. Ctrl. Fla., 2009—; Fla. 21st Century chair, disting. prof. U. Ctrl. Fla. Cons. Gulf Rsch. and Tech., Pitts., 1979-85, ALCOA, Pitts., 1986-89. Editor: Vertical Seismic Profiles, 1984, Two-dimensional Transforms, 1985, Artificial Intelligence in Petroleum Exploration, 1989, Expert Systems in Exploration, 1991, (series) Advances in Geophysical Signal Processing; co-editor jour. Multidimensional Sys. and Signal Processing; mem. editl. bd. profl. jours., including IEEE Procs., IEEE Transactions on Cirs. and Sys., IEEE Transactions on Geosci. and Remote Sensing, Jour. Optimization Theory and Applications, Integrated Computer-aided Engrng. Jour., Jour. Cirs., Sys. and Computers; contbr. over 300 articles on signal processing and control to profl. publs. Grantee NSF, NIH, ONR, Def. Advance Rsch. Project Adminstrs., Ben Franklin, Westinghouse, Gulf, ALCOA; recipient Outstanding ECE Alumnus U. Ill., 1995, Coll. Engrng., Disting. Svc. award, 2007. Fellow: NAE, AAAS (sec. engrng. sect. M 2003—), IEEE (Best Paper award 1985, 1999), Am. Soc. Engrng. Edn.; mem.: Am. Assn. Artificial Intelligence, Soc. Exploration Geophysics, Sigma Xi (Best Paper award Alcoa chpt. 1988), Eta Kappa Nu. Achievements include patent in application of signal processing technology in aluminum manufacturing. Office: Univ Ctrl Fla Coll Engrng & Computer Sci Orlando FL 32816

SIMANDLE, JEROME B., federal judge; b. Binghamton, NY, 1949; s. Paul R. Sr. and Mary F. Simandle; married; children: Roy C., Liza Jane. BSE magna cum laude, Princeton U., 1971; JD, U. Pa., 1976; diploma in Social Scis., U. Stockholm, 1974-75. Bar: Pa. 1977, N.J. 1978. Law clk. to Hon. John F. Gerry U.S. Dist. Ct., NJ, 1976-78; asst. U.S. atty. Dist. N.J., 1978-83; U.S. magistrate judge U.S. Dist. Ct., NJ, 1983-92, judge NJ, 1992—. Mem. lawyers adv. com. U.S. Dist. Ct., NJ, 1984—95; mem. ct. adminstrn. case mgmt. com. Jud. Conf. U.S., 1991—97; mem. human resources adv. coun. Adminstrv. Office US Cts., 2002—08; mem. CPR Inst. for Dispute Resolution Commn. on Ethics and Stds. in Alternative Dispute Resolution, 1996—2002; chair Third Cir. Com. on Rules of Practice and Procedure, 2003—; mem. Third Cir. Model Civil Jury Instrns. Com., 2004—, Codes Conduct Com. Jud. Conf. US, 2008—; chair Dist. NJ Patent Rules Com., 2008—. Internat. grad. fellow Rotary Found., 1974-75. Master: Camden Inn of Ct. (program chmn. 1990—93, vice chmn. 1996—2004); fellow: Am. Bar Found.; mem.: Camden County Bar Assn., Am. Judicature Soc., Fed. Judges Assn. (bd. dirs. 1997—, treas. 2003—09, co-editor In Camera 2004—08). Office: Mitchell H Cohen US Courthouse Rm 6010 1 John F Gerry Pl Camden NJ 08101-0888

SIMANSKI, CLAIRE DVORAK, art educator; d. George James and Gertrude Louise Dvorak; m. Robert Simanski, June 20, 1970 (div. Sept. 2000); children: Joseph Brian, John Francis. BFA, Md. Inst. Coll. Arts, Balt., 1968. Cert. art tchr. K-12 Va. Dept. Edn. Tchr. Ann Arundle County Bd. Edn., Annapolis, 1969—71; day care provider Landoverimd, Andover, 1973—77; fine arts instr. Bolling AF Base, Md., Md. Nat. Capital Parks, 1981—84; sales Loudon Jewelers, Loudon, 1989—90; vol. coord. Telecom. Exch. for Deaf, Great Falls, Va., 1990; tchr. Fairfax County Schs., Herndon, Va., 1992—. Mem. character counts com. Herndon Mid. Sch., 1999—2001; prodr., writer, bd. dirs. Herndon Cable TV, 1999—2008, sec., 2001, 03, 05; dept. chair Fine & Performing Arts, Herndon, 2000—; mem. P.A.R. com. Johns Hopkins U., Balt., 2003—06, Positive Behavior System Com., 2007. Contbr. articles to profl. publs. Active Art in Pub. Places, Herndon, Reston, 1998—2008; com. mem. Cmty. Arts Ctr., Herndon, 2001—02; bd. dirs. Laura Ratcliff House. Recipient Partnership in Edn. award, Optomists of Herndon, 1998, Fairfax County Police Dept. award, 2001, Outsanding Vol. award, Mayor, Herndon, Va., 2003, 2005, 2007, 2008, Hon. Commn., Congl. Youth Leadership Coun., Outstanding Vol. award, Herndon Cable TV, 2003. Mem.: Va. Edn. Assn., Fairfax Educators Assn. Avocations: antiques, writing. Office: Herndon Mid Sch Herndon VA 20170

SIMBERLOFF, DANIEL, biologist, educator; b. Easton, Pa., Apr. 7, 1942; s. Isaac and Ruth (Koplowitz) Simberloff. AB, Harvard U., 1964, PhD, 1969. Asst. prof. biology Fla. State U., Tallahassee, 1968—73, assoc. prof., 1973—78, prof., 1978—97, Robert O. Lawton Disting. prof., 1986; Nancy Gore Hunger prof. environ. studies dept. ecology and evolutionary biology U. Tenn., 1997—. Vis. prof. U. Mich., 1974, U. Minn., 1980, Hebrew U., Jerusalem, 1984; bd. dirs. Nat. Sci. Bd., 2000—06; mem. species survival commn. Internat. Union Conservation Nature and Natural Resources. Editor: Jour. Biogeography, 1974—, Biodiversity and Conservation; co-editor: Ecological Communities: Conceptual Issues and the Evidence, 1984; co-editor: (with D. Schmitz and T. Brown) Strangers in Paradise: Impact and Management of Nonindigenous Species in Florida, 1997; mem. editl. bd.: Jour. Biogeography, Northeast Gulf. Sci., Environ. and Ecol. Statistics, Raffles Bulletin of Zoology, Ecologia, Oecologia, BioSci., Biol. Invasions; contbr. articles to sci. jours. Recipient Developing Scholar award, Fla. State U., 1977, Rector's medal, U. Helsinki, Finland, 1983, Disting. Statistical Ecologist award, Internat. Assn. Ecology, 1994. Mem.: Soc. for Systematic Zoology, Brit. Ecol. Soc., Soc. for Study Evolution, Am. Soc. Naturalists, Ecol. Soc. Am., Nature Conservancy, Soc. Conservation Biology, Brit. Ecol. Soc., Am. Acad. Arts and Scis. Jewish. Home: 2145 Indian Hills Dr Knoxville TN 37919-8914 Office: Ecology and Evolutionary Biology Univ Tenn 480 Dabney Hall Knoxville TN 37996-1610 Office Phone: 865-974-0849. Office Fax: 865-974-3067. E-mail: dsimberloff@utk.edu.

SIME, DONALD RAE, retired business administration educator; b. Los Angeles, July 20, 1926; s. Chester I. and Gaynal (Ramage) S.; m. Patricia Evelyn Hawes, Sept. 4, 1949; children: Julia, Paul, Jill. BA, Pepperdine Coll., 1949, MA, 1951; BD, Princeton Sem., 1954; PhD, U. Chgo., 1962. Prof. religion Harding Grad. Sch. Harding Coll., 1954-66; prof. dept. religion and psychology Pepperdine Coll., 1966-68, chmn. dept. bus. adminstrn., 1968-69; dean Sch. Bus. and Mgmt. Pepperdine U., 1969—79, v.p., 1979—81, prof., 1978-96. Cons. orgnl. devel., affirmative action programs Webco, Page Group, Los Angeles Cons. Group, Conceptual Consultants. Contbr. articles to bus. and religious publs. Served with USNR, 1944-46. Home: 170 S Main St Apt 345 Mars Hill NC 28754

SIMECKA, BETTY JEAN, marketing executive; b. Topeka, Apr. 15, 1935; d. William Bryan and Regina Marie (Rezac) S.; m. Alex Pappas, Jan. 15, 1956 (div. Apr. 1983); 1 child, Alex William. Student, Butler County C.C., 1983—85. Freelance writer and photographer, L.A., also St. Marys, Kans., 1969-77; co-owner Creative Enterprises, El Dorado, Kans., 1977-83; coord. excursions into history Butler County C.C., El Dorado, 1983-84; dir. Hutchinson Conv. & Visitors Bur., Kans., 1984-85; dir. mktg. divsn. Exec. Mgmt., Inc., Wichita, 1985-87; exec. dir. Topeka Conv. and Visitors Bur., 1987-91, pres., CEO, 1991-96; pres. Internat. Connections, Inc., 1996-97, Simecka and Assoc., 1996-99, Pinnacle Prodns., L.L.C., 1997-99; pres., CEO Cultural Exhbns. and Events, L.L.C., 1999—2003; organizer Czars: 400 Years of Imperial Grandeur exhbn., 2002—04; v.p. mktg. Sunflower Exhbns., LLC, 2003—04; mktg. cons., 2003—06; employment cons. Joblink, Cottonwood, Inc., Lawrence, Kans., 2006—. Dir. promotion El Dorado Thunderboat Races, 1977-78. Contbr. articles to jours. and mags.; columnist St. Marys Star, 1973-79. Pres. El Dorado Art Assn., 1984; chair Santa Fe Trail Bike Assn., Kans., 1988-90; co-dir. St. Marys Summer Track Festival, 1973-81; chair spl. events Mulvane Art Mus., 1990, sec., 1991-92; membership chair, 1993-94, bd. dirs., 1995-96; bd. dirs. Topeka Civic Theater, 1991-96, co-chair spl. events, 1992; Kans. chair Russian Festival Com., 1992-93; vice-chair Kans. Film Commn., 1993-94, chair, 1994; bd. dirs. Kans. Expoctr. Adv. Bd., 1990-96, Brain Injury Assn. Greater Kansas City, Concerned Citizens Topeka, 1998-2000; pres. Kans. Internat. Mus., 1994-96. Recipient Kans. Gov.'s Outstanding Tourism award Kans. Broadcaster's Assn., 1993, Disting. Svc award City of Topeka, 1995, Hist. Ward Meade Disting. award Topeka Parks and Recreation Dept., 1995; named Kansan of Yr., Topeka Capitol-Jour., 1995, Sales and Mktg. Exec. of Yr., 1995, Internat. Soroptomists, Topeka chpt., Woman of Distinction, 1996. Mem. Nat. Tour Assn., Sales and Mktg. execs. (bd. dirs. 1991-92), Internat. Assn. Conv. and Visitors Burs. (co-chair rural tourism com. 1994), Am. Soc. Assn. Execs., Travel Industry Assn. Kans. (membership chair 1988-89, sec. 1990, pres. 1991-92, Outstanding Merit award 1994), St. Marys C. of C. (pres. 1975), I-70 Assn. (v.p. 1989, pres. 1990), Optimists (social sec. Topeka chpt. 1988-89). Independent. Methodist. Holder Nat. AAU record for 100-yard dash, 1974.

SIMEK, JAN F., academic administrator, anthropologist, educator; BA, U. Calif., Santa Cruz, 1976; MA, SUNY, Binghamton, 1978, PhD in Anthropology, 1984. Founder Cave Archaeology Rsch. Team U. Tenn., 1996, disting. prof. sci., 2001—, head Anthropology Dept., interim dir. Sch. Art, interim dean Coll. Architecture and Design, 2003—05, chief of staff to chancellor, 2005—08, interim chancellor, 2008—09; interim pres. U. Tenn. Sys., 2009—. Rsch. assoc., vis. prof. Inst. de Quaternaire, U. Bordeaux, France, 1979—; mem. Commn. 8 on Upper Paleolithic of Europe, Internat. Union of Prehistoric and Protohistoric Scis., 1989; vis. scholar, lectr. Universitat Autonoma de Barcelona, 1991. Contbr. articles to profl. jours. Recipient Certificate of Appreciation for Valuable Svc. to our Nat. Heritage, Tenn. Valley Authority (TVA), 1996. Office: U Tenn Office of Pres 831 Andy Holt Tower Knoxville TN 37996-0180 Office Phone: 865-974-2241. Office Fax: 865-974-3753.*

SIMENDINGER, THEODORE JOHN, writer, publishing executive; b. Phila., Oct. 6, 1954; s. Theodore John and Margaret Smith Simendinger; m. Bonita Ann Kolish; 1 child, Grace. BS, Jacksonville U., 1976. Founder, chmn. Pro Leisure Tour, Inc., Greenwood Village, Colo., 2000—. Career devel. cons. Airplane Reader Pub., Greenwood Village, 2000—. Author: Critters, Fish & Other Troublemakers, 2001, Rich Without Money, 2002, 12 Miles to Paradise, 2003, Searching for Tendulkar, 2004, Jurassic Trout, 2004, The Rise And Fall of Piggy Church, 2006, Tuki Banjo, Superstar, 2007, Maximum Horsepower: How to Strengthen Your Sales Force Quickly, 2008, Highway to Somewhere, 2008, Managing the Worry Circle, 2009. Founder, chmn. No Bats Baseball Club, Global Ambassadors for the Good of the Game, Greenwood Village, Colo., 1991—. Named Alumnae of the Yr., Jacksonville U., 2003. Avocations: reading, writing, comedy, fishing. Office Phone: 877-611-6222.

SIMEONOV, SIMEON, computer scientist; BS in Computer Sci., Economics and Math., Macalester Coll.; MS in Computer Sci., Boston U. V.p. Emerging Technologies; chief arch. Macromedia Corp.; prin. Polaris Ventures, 2002—. Author: Building Web Services with Java, 2001. Named one of Top 100 Young Innovators, MIT Tech. Review, 2004. Office: Polaris Ventures 1000 Winter St Waltham MA 02451

SIMERAL, WILLIAM GOODRICH, retired chemical company executive; b. Portland, Oreg., May 22, 1926; s. Claire Cornelius and Geneva G. Simeral; m. Elizabeth Louise Ross, June 25, 1949; children: Linda Simeral McGregor, Karen Simeral Schousen, William Goodrich Jr., John David; m. Marion Poore Anderson, Nov. 3, 2001. BS in Physics, Franklin and Marshall Coll., Lancaster, Pa., 1948; PhD in Physics, U. Mich., 1953. With E.I. duPont de Nemours and Co., Inc., 1953-87, v.p., gen. mgr. plastics dept. Wilmington, Del., 1974-76, v.p., gen. mgr. plastic products and resins dept., 1976-77, sr. v.p., dir., mem. exec. com., 1977-81, exec. v.p., dir., mem. exec. com., 1981-87; vice chmn. bd., chief operating officer Conoco Inc., 1984-85. Trustee Franklin and Marshall Coll., 1977—, chmn. bd., 1991-94; trustee, bd. dirs. Wilmington Med. Ctr., 1978-93, chmn. bd., 1982-86; bd. dirs. YMCA Wilmington and New Castle County, 1978-81. Mem. Chem. Mfrs. Assn. (vice chmn. bd. 1980-81, chmn. exec. com. 1981-82, chmn. bd. 1982-83), Am. Phys. Soc., Phi Beta Kappa, Sigma Xi, Wilmington Country Club.

SIMES, MICHAEL LOUIS, lawyer; b. Hartsdale, NY, Oct. 8, 1969; s. Irwin M. and Ann L. Simes; m. Deborah Tamara Schaefer, Jan. 21, 2007. BA, SUNY, Albany, 1988—91; JD, U. Ariz., Tuscon, 1991—94; MBA, Ariz. State U., Tempe, 2001—03. Bar: Ariz. 1994, Colo. 1996. Atty. Simes Ptnrs., PLLC, Phoenix, 2000—. Contbr. articles to profl. jours. Sec. Ariz. Coalition for Tomorrow, Phoenix, 1995—99. Recipient Pres. award, Ariz. Coalition for Tomorrow, 1998. Achievements include being a recognized expert in website and electronic services by the state bar of Arizona. Office: Simes Partners PLLC 3219 E Camelback Rd # 816 Phoenix AZ 85018 Business E-Mail: ms@michaelsimes.com.

SIMES, STEPHEN MARK, pharmaceutical executive; b. NYC, Nov. 23, 1951; s. Herbert H. and Mimi (Maurer) S.; m. Anita H. Herzog, Aug. 23, 1975. BS in Chemistry, Bklyn. Coll., 1973; MBA in Mktg., NYU, 1980. Sales rep. G.D. Searle and Co., NYC, 1974-78, supr. sales tng. Chgo., 1978-79, dist. sales mgr. NYC, 1979-81, product mgr. Chgo., 1981-82, sr. product mgr., 1982-83, dir. pub. affairs and communications, 1983-84; v.p. Gynex Inc., Chgo., 1984-88; dir. Gynex Pharms. Inc., Deerfield, 1985-93; pres., dir. Gynex Labs., Chgo., 1985-88; pres., CEO Contracap Inc., 1988-89, Gynex Pharms., Inc., Chgo., 1989-93, chmn., 1992-93; sr. v.p., dir. Bio-Technology Gen. Corp., 1993-94; pres., CEO, dir. Unimed Pharms., Inc., 1994-97; bd. dirs., CEO, pres. Simes Pharm. Cons., 1997-98. Vice chmn., CEO, pres., BioSante Pharms., Inc., Lincolnshire, Ill., 1998—. Mem.: Internat. Soc. For Study of Women's Sexual Health, Drug Info. Assn., iBio, Biotech. Industry Orgn., N.Am. Menopause Soc., Endocrine Soc., Licensing Exec. Soc., Chgo. Coun. Fgn. Rels. Office: 111 Barclay Blvd Lincolnshire IL 60069

SIMIC, CHARLES, language educator, poet; b. Beograd, Yugoslavia, May 9, 1938; arrived in U.S., 1954, naturalized, 1971; s. George and Helen (Matijevich) Simic; m. Helen Dubin, Oct. 1964; children: Anna, Philip. BA, NYU, 1967. Editl. asst. Aperture, Quar. of Photography, NYC, 1966—69; prof. English Calif. State U., Hayward, Calif., 1970—73, U. N.H., Durham, NH, 1973—. Author: What the Grass Says, 1967, Somewhere Among us a Stone is Taking Notes, 1969, Dismantling the Silence, 1971, White, 1972, Return to a Place Lit by a Glass of Milk, 1974, Biography and a Lament, 1976, Charon's Cosmology, 1977, Classic Ballroom Dances, 1980, Austerities, 1982, Weather Forecast for Utopia and Vicinity, 1983, Selected Poems, 1985, rev. edit., 1990, Unending Blues, 1986, The World Doesn't End, 1989 (Pulitzer Prize for poetry, 1990), The Book of Gods and Devils, 1990, Hotel Insomnia, 1992, A Wedding in Hell, 1994, Frightening Toys, 1995, Walking the Black Cat, 1996, Looking for Trouble, 1997, Selected Early Poems, 1999, Jackstraws, 1999, rev. edit., 2000, Night Picnic, 2001, Voice at 3 A.M., 2003, My Noiseless Entourage, 2005, That Little Something: Poems, 2008, (essays) The Uncertain Certainty, 1985, (novels) Wonderful Words, Silent Truth, 1990, Dimestore Alchemy, 1992, The Unemployed Fortune Teller, 1994, Orphan Factory, 1998, A Fly in the Soup, 2000, Metaphysician in the Dark, 2003, Memory Piano, 2005; translator (with C.W. Truesdale): Fire Gardens, 1970; translator: The Little Box, 1970; translator: (with Mark Strand) Another Republic, 1976; translator: Four Modern Yugoslav Poets, 1970, Homage to the Lame Wolf, 1979; translator: (with P. Kastmiler) Atlantis, 1987; translator: Roll Call of Mirrors, 1987, Some Other Wine and Light, 1989, Bandit Wind, 1991, The Horse Has Six Legs, 1992, Night Mail, 1992, Devil's Lunch, 1999, A Wake for the Living, 2002; contbr. Selected Poems of Tomaz Salamun, 1987, RollCall of Mirrors, 1987, poems to mags. and anthologies. With US Army, 1961—63. Recipient PEN Internat. award for transl., 1970, 1980, Edgar Allan Poe award, Am. Acad. Poets, 1975, award, Nat. Inst. Arts and Letters, 1976, AAAL award, 1976, Harriet Monroe poetry award, U. Chgo., 1980, CiCastignola award, Poetry Soc. Am., 1980, Wallance Students prize, Acad. Am. Poets; named US Poet Laureate, Libr. Congress, 2007—; fellow Guggenheim fellow, 1972—73, Nat. Endowment for the Arts, 1974—75, 1979—80, Fulbright Travelling fellow, 1982, Ingram Merrill fellow, 1983—84, Mac Arthur fellow, 1984—89. Mem.: Acad. Arts and Letters. Home: PO Box 192 Strafford NH 03884-0192 Office: U NH Dept English Durham NH 03824

SIMIN, GRIGORY, science educator; b. St. Petersburg, Russia, Nov. 3, 1948; s. Solomon Simin and Nadezhda Simina; m. Marianna Simina, Aug. 20, 1982; children: Kirill, Mikhail. PhD, Giricond, St. Petersburg, 1970. Cert. rsch. scientist, Supreme Com. Academic Degrees, Russia, 1985. Rsch. scientist Giricond Sci. & Rsch. Inst., St. Petersburg, 1971—85, sr. rsch. scientist, 1985—97, A.F. Ioffe Physico Tech. Inst., Russian Acad. Sci., St. Petersburg, 1997—98; rsch. assoc. prof U. SC., Columbia, 1998—2001, assoc. prof., 2001—.

SIMINI, JOSEPH PETER, accountant, financial consultant, writer, former educator; b. Buffalo, Feb. 15, 1921; s. Paul and Ida (Moro) S.; m. Marcelline McDermott, Oct. 4, 1968. BS, St. Bonaventure U., 1940, BBA, 1949; MBA, U. Calif.-Berkeley, 1957; DBA, Western Colo. U., 1981. CPA, Calif. Insp. naval material Bur. Ordnance, Buffalo and Rochester, N.Y., 1941-44; mgr. Paul Simini Bakery, Buffalo, 1946-48; internal auditor DiGiorgio (Fruit) Corp., San Francisco, 1950-51; tax acct. Price Waterhouse & Co., San Francisco, 1953; sr. acct. Richard L. Hanlin C.P.A., San Francisco, 1953-54; prof. acctg. U. San Francisco, 1954-79, emeritus prof., 1983—. Mem. rev. bd. Calif. Bd. Accountancy, 1964-68; host The Bus. Doctor Stas. WALE and KCCF, 1998. Author: Accounting Made Simple, 1967, rev. edit., 1987, Cost Accounting Concepts for Nonfinancial Executives, 1976, Become Wealthy! Using Tax Savings and Real Estate Investments, 1982, Balance Sheet Basics for the Nonfinancial Managers, 1989, Petals of the Rose, 1990, How to Become Financially Independent, 1996, 10 Steps to Financial Independence Guaranteed, 2000, Entwined Lives, 2003; tech. editor Accounting Essentials, 1972; patentee Dial-A-Trig and Verbum Est card game. Mem. coun. com. Boy Scouts Am., Buffalo, San Francisco, 1942-65, Souters Key, San Francisco coun.; bd. dir. Nat. Italian Am. Found., Washington, 1979-85. Lt. j.g. USNR, 1944-46. Recipient Bacon-McLaughlin medal St. Bonaventure U., 1940, Laurel Key, 1940; Outstanding Tchr. award Coll. Bus. Adminstrn., U. San Francisco, 1973, Disting. Tchr. award U. San Francisco, 1975, Joseph Per Simini award, 1977, Crown Zellerbach Found. fellow, 1968-69, Gold Medal Associazione Piemontese nel Mondo, Turin, Italy, 1984; decorated Knight Order of Merit, Republic of Italy, 1982. Mem. AICPA's, MENSA, Calif. Soc. CPAs (past chmn. ednl. stds., student rels. com. San Francisco chpt.), Inst. of Mgmt. Accts. (past pres. San Francisco chpt.), Am. Acctg. Assn., Am. Mgmt. Assn. (lectr. 1968-78), Serra (past pres. Golden Gate chpt.), Il Cenacolo (past pres.), Toastmasters (past pres. Magic Word, treas. Dist. 4, 1996-97), K.C., Rotary (past pres. Daly City), Delta Sigma Pi (past pres. San Francisco alumni club), Beta Gamma Sigma. Roman Catholic. Office: PO Box 31420 San Francisco CA 94131-0420 Home: 5235 Diamond Heights Blvd #209 San Francisco CA 94131 *Personal philosophy: You can succeed! but you must program yourself for success and know what you want.*

SIMINOVITCH, LOUIS, geneticist, educator, scientist; b. Montreal, Que., Can., May 1, 1920; s. Nathan and Goldie (Wachman) S.; m. Elinore Esther Faierman, July 2, 1944 (dec. 1995); children: Harriet Jane, Katherine Anne, Margo Ruth. B.Sc., McGill U., 1941, PhD, 1944; D honoris causa, Meml. U., 1978, McMaster U., 1978, U. Montreal, 1990, McGill U., 1990, U. Western Ont., 1990, U. Toronto, 1995, U. Ottawa, Can., 1999; DSc, U. Guelph, 2001. Mem. staff Nat. Research Council Can., 1944-47; Canadian Royal Soc. fellow Pasteur Inst., Paris, 1947-49; mem. staff Centre Nationale de la Recherche Scientifique, 1949-53; Nat. Cancer Inst. Can. fellow U. Toronto, Ont., Can., 1953-56, asst. prof. dept. med. biophysics, 1956-58, assoc. prof. med. biophysics, 1958-60, prof. med. biophysics, 1960-85, prof. Inst. Med. Sci., 1968-85, prof., chmn. dept. med. cell. biology, 1969-70, prof. dept. med. genetics, 1970-85, chmn. dept. med. genetics, 1970-81, assoc. prof. pediatrics, 1972-78, univ. prof., 1976-85, univ. prof. emeritus, 1985—; dir. rsch. Samuel Lunenfeld Rsch. Inst. Mt. Sinai Hosp., Toronto, 1985-94, dir. emeritus Samuel Lunenfeld Rsch. Inst., 1994—; sr. fellow Massey Coll, U. Toronto, 2009. Scientist divsn. biol. rsch. Ont. Cancer Inst., Toronto, 1956-69, head microbiology sect. divsn. biol. rsch., 1957-63, head divsn. biol. rsch., 1963-69; geneticist-in-chief Hosp. Sick Children, Toronto, 1970-85; mem. virology and rickettsiology sect. NIH, 1966-68; mem. health research com. Ont. Coun. Health, 1966-82; mem. panel sect. Nat. Cancer Inst., Can., 1965-69, mem. rsch. adv. group, 1969-74, chmn., 1970-72, bd. dirs. 1975-85, pres. 1982-84; bd. dirs. Can. Weizmann Inst. Sci., 1972—; mem. adv. bd. Ont. Mental Health Found., 1974-78; chmn. Ont. Health R&D Com., 1974-82; task force on genetic services Ont. Ministry Health, 1974-76; mem. Ont. Task Force On Health Research Requirements, 1974-76; mem. grants com. for cancer, growth and differentiation Med. Rsch. Coun. Can., 1967-70, mem. grants com. for genetics, 1971-74, chmn. com. on guidelines for Recombinant DNA, 1975-77, mem. exec., 1977-83; bd. dirs. Mount Sinai Hosp., Toronto, 1975-82; mem. United Ch. Can. Gen. Coun. Commn. on Genetic Engring., 1974-78; mem Killam selection com. The Can. Coun., 1975-78; bd. advisors Clin. Rsch. Inst. Montreal Center Bioethics, 1976-80; mem. adv. com. on genetic services Ont. Ministry Health, 1976-82; mem. Sci. Coun. Can., 1976-80; mem. Ont. Coun. Health, 1976-82; mem. bd. sci. counsellors Nat. Cancer Inst., NIH, 1978-83; G. Malcolm Brown Meml. lectr. Royal Coll Physicians and Surgeons, 1978; bd. dirs. Cancer Care Ont. (formerly Ont. Cancer Treatment and Rsch. Found.), 1979-93, chmn. rsch. adv. panel, 1986-98, mem. exec. com., bd. dirs., 1991-93; mem. Alfred P. Sloan Jr. selection com. Gen. Motors Cancer Rsch. Found., 1980-81, 83-84; nat. bd. dirs. Canadian Cancer Soc, 1981-84; mem. sci. adv. bd. Huntingtons Soc. Can., 1984-89; adv. com. Coll. Biol. Scis., Guelph, Ont., 1986-90; mem. rsch. coun. Can. Inst. Advanced Rsch., Toronto, 1982-91, chmn. adv. com. evolutionary biology, 1986-93; mem. med. adv. bd. The Gairdner Found., 1983-93; mem. bd. govs. Baycrest Centre Geriatric Care, 1987—, bd. dirs.; chmn. adv. bd. Allelix, Inc., 1987-91; mem. sci. tech. svcs. sub-com. Sci. Coun. Can., 1988-89; chmn. steering com. for evaluation of MRC grants program MRC, Ottawa, 1989-91; chmn. sci. adv. com. Rotman Rsch Inst., Baycrest Centre, 1990—; mem. Can. Inst. Acad. Medicine, 1992—; mem. Montreal Neurol. Inst. adv. bd. Montreal, 1992—; spl. adv. rsch. to dean Sch. Medicine U. Toronto, 1994—, chmn. program adv. com., sci. adv. com. Tanenbaum Chairs, 1995-02; mem. sci. adv. bd. Med. Discoveries Fund, 1994-01; bd. dirs. Glycodesign, Toronto, 1995-96, chmn. sci. adv. com., 1996-01; mem. sci. and med. adv. bd. Hybrisens, Ltd., Toronto, 1995-96; mem. sci. adv. bd. Apoptogen, 1995-99, GeminX, 1997-2003, Genesense Techs., 1998-99, Ottawa Gen. Hosp. Rsch. Inst., 1998-2000; chmn. sci. adv. bd. Lorus Therapeutics, 1999—; mem. rev. panel rsch. resources program med. scholars Howard Hughes Med. Inst., 1995; chmn. external adv. com. Loeb Inst. Med. Rsch., 1987-00; bd. dirs. Ottawa Civic Hosp. Loeb Rsch. Inst., 1996-00; chmn. sci. adv. bd. Bioniche, 1996-98; bd. dirs. U. Med. Discoveries, Inc., 1996-05; mem. neuro adv. coun. Montreal Neurol. Inst. and Hosp., 1997-00; chmn. sci. adv. com. The KLARU, Baycrest Ctr. Geriatric Care, Toronto, 1997—, bd. dirs., 1998—; chmn. sci. adv. com. Phagetech, 1998-2004; bd. dirs. Premier's Rsch. Excellence Awards Program, 1998-05; chmn. sci. adv. bd. Cytochroma Inc., 1999-06; bd. dirs. Viventia Biotech, 1999-2006; mem. sci. adv. bd.

Aurelium Bioplasma, 2002-04; mem. sci. adv. com. Genetic Diagnosis, Inc., 2003-05, chair sci. & rsch. com. Thunder Bay Regional Rsch. Inst., 2007-. Editor Virology, 1960-80, Bacteriological Revs., 1969-72, Jour. Molecular and Cellular Biology, 1980-90; founding mem., pres. editl. bd. Sci. Forum, 1966-79; mem. editl. bd. Cell, 1973-81, Somatic Cell Genetics, 1974-84, Jour. Cytogenetics and Cell Genetics, 1974-80, Mutation Rsch., 1976-82, Jour. de Microscopie et de Biologie Cellulaire, 1976-86, Cancer Genetics and Cytogenetics, 1979-84, Jour. Cancer Surveys, 1980-89; corr. editor Proc. Royal Soc. B, 1989-93; contbr. numerous articles to sci. jours. Recipient Lifetime Achievement award, Toronto Biotech. Initiative, 2005; named to Canadian Med. Hall of Fame, 1997, Canadian Sci. & Engring. Hall of Fame, 2008. Fellow Royal Soc. Can. (mem. AIDS study steering com. 1987-88, mem. adv. com. on evaluation rsch. 1989-92, Centennial medal 1967, Flavelle medal 1978), Royal Soc. London, Nat. Acad. Scis. US (fgn. assoc.). Home: 130 Carlton St # 805 Toronto ON Canada M5A 4K3 Office: Samuel Lunenfeld Rsch Inst Mt Sinai Hosp 600 University Ave Toronto ON Canada M5G 1X5 Home Phone: 416-975-5535; Office Phone: 416-586-4800 8223. Business E-Mail: lsimin@mshri.on.ca.

SIMIS, THEODORE LUCKEY, investment banker, information technology executive; b. NYC, June 17, 1924; s. Theodore William Ernest and Helen (Luckey) S.; m. Laura Cushman Ingraham, Sept. 8, 1946; children— Nancy Simis Ricca, Theodore Steven, Karen Simis Woods, June Simis Sobocinski BS, NYU, 1950, MBA, 1952. With Bell System, 1941-79; various positions to officer level with N.Y. Telephone Co., N.J. Telephone Co., and AT&T; v.p. Warner Amex Cable Co., 1980-81; sr. v.p. E.F. Hutton, Sarasota, Fla., 1982-87; vice chmn., bd. dirs. XMX Corp., Burlington, Mass., 1986-2000, 2005—, OPIX Corp., Burlington, 2000—04; pres. Pvt. Transatlantic Telecommunication System Inc., McLean, Va., 1987-89; chmn. Value Added Network System, Inc., Sarasota, Fla., 1990-91. Dir. Liebenzell Mission, Schooleys Mountain, N.J.; vis. Nieman fellow Harvard U., 1977. Life mem. Republican Nat. Com., 1981—. 1st lt. U.S. Army, 1942-53, ETO Mem. N.Y. Acad. Scis., U.S. C. of C., NYU Club. Lutheran. Home: 6025 Manasota Key Rd Englewood FL 34223-9245 Office Phone: 941-474-8690. Fax: 941-475-1128. Personal E-mail: tlslns@verizon.net.

SIMITIS, SPIROS, legal educator; b. Athens, Greece, Oct. 19, 1934; s. George and Fanny (Christopoulo) S.; m. Ilse Grubrich, Aug. 3, 1963. JD, U. Marburg, Fed. Republic Germany, 1956. Assoc. prof. U. Frankfurt, Germany, 1969—, dir., Advanced Studies Humanties, 2008—; prof. U. Giessen, Fed. Republic Germany, 1964-69; vis. prof. London Sch. Econs., U. Calif. - Berkeley, 1976, U. Pa., 1980, U. Strasbourg, France, 1987-88, Paris, 1990—2001, Yale U., New Haven, 1981—. Sec. gen. Internat. Civil Status Commn., 1966—80; chmn. Data Protection Experts Com. of the Coun. of Europe, Strasbourg, 1982—86; with Hesse Data protect commr., 1975—91; mem. rsch. coun. European Univ. Inst.; chmn. social rights com. European Commn., 1998; chmn. German Nat. Ethic Coun., 2000—05. Contbr. numerous articles to legal publs. Mem.: Athens Acad. Scis., German Coun. Pvt. Internat. Law, German Lawyers Assn. (bd. dirs. 1970—82). Office: Johann Wolfgang Goethe U Senckenberganlage 31 Postfach 111932 60054 Frankfurt Germany Office Phone: 0049-69-79834230. E-mail: simitis@jur.uni-frankfurt.de.

SIMJEE, AISHA, ophthalmologist, educator; b. Surat, India, Jan. 23, 1944; came to U.S., 1970; d. Yusuf Esmail Simjee and Amina Ahmed Badat; m. Sabbir A. Dadabhai, Apr. 28, 1978; children: Alia Dadabhai, Sufia Dadabhai. Intermediate Sci. degree, Rangoon U., Burma, 1963; MB, BS, Inst. Medicine, Rangoon, 1968. Diplomate Am. Bd. Ophthalmology. Intern Rangoon Gen. Hosp., 1968-69, South Balt. Gen. Hosp., 1970-71; rschr. in ophthalmology Johns Hopkins Hosp., Balt., 1971-72; resident in ophthalmology Eye Dept. Howard U. Hosp., D.C. Gen. Hosp., Armed Forces Inst. Pathology, Washington, 1972-75; fellow in cornea external diseases Wills Eye Hosp., Phila., 1975-76; fellow in ophthalmic pathology and med. retina Scheie Eye Inst., Phila., 1976-77; asst. prof. ophthalmology Howard U., Washington, 1977-78; clin. assoc. prof. ophthalmology U. Calif., Irvine, 1978—; pvt. practice Orange, Calif. Mem. med. adv. bd. Orange County Eye & Tissue Bank, 1990—; attending physician St. Joseph Hosp., Orange, 1978—, U. Calif. Irvine Med. Ctr., 1978—. Contbr. articles to profl. jours. Vol. ophthalmologist La Amistad de Jose Clinic, Sponsor Care Program of St. Joseph Hosp., 1988—, Testing 1-2-3 Screening Clinic St. Joseph Hosp., ann. eye screening for local sch. children, Project Orbis, S.E.E. Internat., Santa Barbara, Am. Eye Care Project, Hope World Wide, 2002—, Internat. Asst. Mission, 2002—. Named Woman of Achievement, Rancho Santiago Coll., Santa Ana, 1990; recipient certs. of recognition Calif. state senator John Seymour, Calif. congressman Christopher Cox, Calif., lt. gov. Leo McCarthy; recipient Pride in the Profession award AMA Found., 2005, Woman of Vision award We Give Thanks or Orange County, 2006. Fellow ACS, Am. Acad. Ophthalmology (Nat. Eye Care Project 1986—); mem. AMA (Pride in Profession award 2005), Calif. Med. Assn., Orange County Med. Assn. (bd. dirs. 1995-02), Orange County Soc. Ophthalmology (exec. com. 1992-02). Office: 1310 W Stewart Dr Ste 501 Orange CA 92868-3856 Home Phone: 714-771-2033; Office Phone: 714-771-2020. Personal E-mail: drsimjee@sbcglobal.net.

SIMKANI, MEHRDAD, mathematics professor; b. Shiraz, Fars, Iran, Sept. 20, 1957; s. Hossein Reza Simkani and Mehry Akhlaghian; m. Golara Behboodian; children: Sana, Seena. PhD, U. South Fla., Tampa, 1987. Vis. asst. prof. Oakland U., Rochester, Mich., 1987—88; prof. math. U. Mich., Flint, 1988—, chair math., 2002—06. Contbr. articles to profl. jour. Office: Univ Mich-Flint 303 E Kearsley St Flint MI 48502-1950 Business E-Mail: simkani@umich.edu.

SIMKIN, SUSAN M., retired astronomer; b. Detroit, July 26, 1940; d. Norman and Alice Smith; m. Roger Simkin, Jan. 4, 2002; children: Daniel, Benjamin. PhD, U. Wis., Madison, 1966. Rsch. assoc, adj. prof. Columbia U., NYC, 1966—74; nato fellow Kapteyn Inst., Groningen, Netherlands, 1975—76; sr. rsch. fellow Mt Stromlo Obs., Canberra, Act, Australia, 1977—79; sci. editor Astrophysy. Jour., 2001—08; asst. prof. Mich. State U., East Lansing, 1974—2002, emeritus prof., 2002. Avocations: bicycling, camping, travel. Office: Nrao-Aoc 1003 Lopezville Rd PO Box 0 Socorro NM 87801-0387

SIMKO, JAN, English, foreign language and literature educator; b. Zlaté Moravce, Slovakia, Oct. 30, 1920; arrived in U.S., 1967; s. Simon Simko and Terezia Simkova; m. Libusa Safarikova, Dec. 20, 1950 (div. 1970, dec. 2004); children: Jan, Vladimir (dec.). Diploma in English, U. Bratislava, 1942, Diploma in German, 1943, PhD in English, 1944; MPhil in English, U. London, 1967. Tchr. English and German various bus. schs., 1942-45; asst. depts. English and German U. Bratislava, 1945-46; instr. English Econom U., 1946-47; faculty U. Bratislava, 1950-68, from asst. prof. to prof. English, 1957-68; prof. English Rio Grande Coll., Ohio, 1968-75. Instr. Shakespeare Georgetown U., 1982-84; vis. prof. English, scholar-in-residence W. Va. U., Parkersburg, 1989-90; instr. Slovak Fgn. Svc. Inst., Washington, 1974, 96, fed. govt., 1989, 91-93, IMF & World Bank, 1994-95; examiner critical langs. program Kent (Ohio) State U., 1974-91; feature writer Voice of Am., 1983-94; translator U.S. Dept. State, 1997—2005; bd. linguistics Slovak Acad. of Scis., 1957-67. Author: 3 English textbooks, 2 bilingual dictionaries, 1 linguistic monograph; editor: Lectures in the Circle of Modern Philology, 2 vols., 1965-66; chief consulting editor: textbooks of Slovak and Czech, 1993-96; contbg. writer: The Review, 1995-2002; Am./Can.-Slovak press; contbr. articles to profl. jours. With Czechoslovak infantry, 1946. Grantee Brit. Coun., 1947-49, Folger Shakespeare Libr./U.S. Dept. State, 1967-68; Internat. Rsch. and Exch. Bd., 1982, others; recipient awards W.Va. U., 1990, Bratislava U., 1995, medal Pres. of Slovakia, 2002. Mem. MLA (life), Slovak Studies Assn., Soc. for Scis. and Arts, Met. Opera Guild, Shakespeare Theater Guild, Nat. Symphony Orch. Assn., English-Speaking Union. Roman Catholic. Avocations: classical music, opera, theater, fine arts, swimming. Home: Apt 511 725 24th St NW Washington DC 20037 Office Phone: 202-429-8899. Personal E-mail: jansimko@hotmail.com.

SIMMONDS, ROBERT MAURER, operations research analyst; b. Beaver Falls, Pa., Apr. 16, 1947; m. Deborah Lynne Carawan, June 25, 1977; children: Stephen Maurer, Kent Hayes. BS, Youngstown State U., 1973, MS, 1975; advanced cert. edn., Coll. William and Mary, 1983, EdD, 1985; grad. sr. exec. prog. JFK Sch. Govt., Harvard, 2004; MA, Naval War Coll., 2008. Assoc. prof. St. Leo Coll., Ft. Eustis, Va., 1985—88, 1988—2001; dept. chmn. sys. engring. dept. US Army Logistics Mgmt. Coll., Ft. Lee, 2001—06; sr. ops. rschr., analyst US Army Human Resources Command, Washington, 2006; sr. army fellow, dep. undersec., 2006—09; dep. dir. programs Oepm, Mpp, Osd, 2009—. Contbr. articles to profl. jours. With USN, 1965—68. Avocations: walking, golf. Business E-Mail: robert.simmonds@osd.mil.

SIMMONS, ADELE SMITH, foundation executive, former educator; b. Lake Forest, Ill., June 21, 1941; d. Hermon Dunlap and Ellen T. (Thorne) Smith; m. John L. Simmons; children: Ian, Erica, Kevin BA in Social Studies with honors, Radcliffe Coll., 1963; PhD, Oxford U., Eng., 1969; LHD (hon.), Lake Forest Coll., 1976, Amherst Coll., 1977, Franklin Pierce Coll., 1978, U. Mass., 1978, Alverno Coll., 1982, Marlboro Coll., 1987, Smith Coll., 1988, Mt. Holyoke Coll., 1989, Am. U., 1992, Tufts U., 1994. Asst. prof. Tufts U., Boston, 1969-72; dean Jackson Coll., Medford, Mass., 1970-72; asst. prof. history, dean student affairs Princeton U., NJ, 1972-77; pres. Hampshire Coll., Amherst, Mass., 1977-89, John D. and Catherine T. MacArthur Found., Chgo., 1989—99; vice chair, sr. exec. Chgo. Metropolis 2020, 1999—; sr. assoc. Ctr. for Internat. Studies U. Chgo., 1999—2005. Bd. dirs. Marsh & McLennan Cos., N.Y.C., Shorebank Corp., Chgo., Union Concerned Scientists, Synergos Inst., Environ. Def., bd. mem., Am. Prospect; bd. dirs. Field Mus., Chgo., Mexican Fine Arts Ctr. Mus., Chgo. Coun. on Fgn. Rels., Winning Worlplaces; emeritus mem. bd. dirs. Rocky Mountain Inst.; former corr. in Mauritius and Tunisia for N.Y. Times, The Economist; high level adv. bd. UN, 1993—; mem. adv. com. World Bank Inst.; mem. bd. overseers Harvard U., 1972-78; chair Fair Labor Assn.; sr. advisor World Econ. Forum. Co-author: (with Freeman, Dunkle, Blau) Exploitation from 9 to 5: Twentieth Century Fund Task Force Report on Working Women, 1975; author: Modern Mauritius, 1982; contbr. articles on edn. and pub. policy in The N.Y. Times, Christian Sci. Monitor, The Bulletin of Atomic Scientist, Harper's, The Atlantic Monthly and others. Commr. Pres.'s Commn. on World Hunger, Washington, 1978-80, Pres.'s Commn. on Environ. Quality, 1991-92; mem. Commn. Global Governance; trustee Carnegie Found. for Advancement Teaching, 1978-86; chair Mayor Richard Daley's Youth Devel. Task Force, 1993-95. Named one of Chgos. 100 Most Influential Women, Crain's Chgo. Bus., 2004. Fellow Am. Acad. Arts and Scis.; mem. Phi Beta Kappa. Office: Chgo Metropolis 2020 30 W Monroe St Chicago IL 60603 Home Phone: 773-404-5566; Office Phone: 312-332-8161. Business E-Mail: adele.simmons@cm2020.org.

SIMMONS, ANTHONY, virology educator, physician, researcher; b. Leicestershire, U.K., Mar. 12, 1954; s. Alfred William and Sarah Sylvia Simmons; m. Mary-Jane Potter, June 8, 2002; children: Katie Anne, Matthew James. MD, PhD, Cambridge, UK, 1976—86. FRCPath Royal Coll. Pathologists, 1986. Sr. med. specialist Inst. Med. and Vet. Sci., Adelaide, Australia, 1986—2001; prof. pediat. pathology: microbiology and immunology U. Tex., Galveston, 2001—. Mem. editl. bd. Jour. Virology, Herpes Jour.; contbr. articles to profl. jours. Mem.: Australian Herpes Mgmt. forum (founding mem.), Am. Social Health Assn. (sci. adv. com.), Am. Soc. Virology, Am. Assn. Immunologists. Achievements include patents for compositions and methods for herpes simplex prophylaxis and treatment. Avocations: sailing, rock climbing, snowboarding. Home: 1001 Postoffice St Galveston TX 77550 Office: U Tex Med Br 301 University Blvd Galveston TX 77555-0372 Business E-Mail: ansimmon@utmb.edu.

SIMMONS, BARBARA, nursing educator, director; b. Chgo., Apr. 10, 1949; d. Joseph Szymanski; children: Gregory Waitkoff, Megan Downey. BSN, Loyola U., Chgo., 1971; MS, U. Ill., chgo., 1976; PhD, Loyola U., 2000. Registered nurse, Ill. Dept. Profl. Regulation, 1971. Asst. prof. UIC Coll. Nursing, Chgo., 2000—, U. Ill., 1976—79, Lewis U., Romeoville, 1989—2000; adj. faculty St. Xavier U., Chgo., 1998—2000; staff nurse, clin. educator Good Samaritan Hosp., Downers Grove, Ill., 1980—90. Coord., grad. entry program U. Ill., 1995—, dir., advanced practice forensic nursing program, 2007—. Contbr. columns in newspapers. Recipient Acad. Disting. Tchrs., U. Ill. Coll. Nursing, 2005, Excellence in Tchg. and Learning, Tchg. Recognition Program, U. Ill., 2007; Advanced Practice Forensic Nursing Program, US HHS, 2007—. Mem.: Internat. Assn. Forensic Nurses. Office: Univ IL Chgo 845 S Damen Ave Chicago IL 60612 Office Fax: 312-996-7949. E-mail: simmonsb@uic.edu.

SIMMONS, CHARLES BEDFORD, JR., judge; b. Greenville, SC, Dec. 4, 1956; s. Charles Bedford and Mary Margaret (Mason) S.; children: Charles B. III, Elizabeth S., Mason W. BS magna cum laude, E. Tenn. State U., 1979; JD, U. S.C., 1982. Bar: S.C. 1982, U.S. Dist. Ct. S.C. 1983, U.S. Ct. Appeals (4th cir.) 1986. Law clk. to presiding justice S.C. Cir. Ct., Greenville, 1982-83; with Carter Law Firm, Greenville, 1983-86; ptnr. Wilkins, Nelson, Kittredge & Simmons, Greenville, 1986-89; civil ct. judge Greenville, 1989—; presiding judge 13th Circuit Drug Ct. Mem. bench-bar com. S.C. Supreme Ct., 1992-97; presiding judge 13th cir. Drug Ct; bd. mem. Nat. Assn. Drug Ct. Profls (chmn. bd. 2007-). Mem. adv. com. paralegal program Greenville Tech. Coll., 1989-97, chmn., 1990-91; mem. Friends of 200 Adv. Bd., 1991-99. Named Big Brother of Yr., Big Bros.-Big Sisters, 1988; recipient Svc. to Mankind award Rotary Club, 1989, Outstanding Young Disting. Svc. award Greenville Jaycees, 1990-91. Mem. ATLA, S.C. Bar Assn. (young lawyer liason 1985-89, named Outstanding Young Lawyer of Yr. 1989), Nat. Assn. Drug Ct. Profls. (bd. dirs.), Greenville Bar Assn., S.C. Trial Lawyers Assn., Greenville Young Lawyers (pres. 1988—1990), Gamma Beta Phi, Pi Gamma Mu, Phi Delta Phi. Clubs: Greenville City, Textile (v.p. 1985-87), Revelers (Greenville). Presbyterian. Office: Ste 313 County Courthouse Greenville SC 29601 Office Phone: 864-467-8556. Business E-Mail: csimmons@greenvillecounty.org.

SIMMONS, CLINTON CRAIG, human resources executive; b. Cleve., Nov. 25, 1947; s. Benjamin F. and Catharin (Thornton) R.; m. Cheryl LeRoy, June 16, 1973; 1 child, Eric. BBA, Miami U., Oxford, Ohio, 1969; grad. quality mgmt. course, Winter Park, Fla., 1986. Cert. quality edn. system instr. Specialist employee, cmty. rels. Euclid Lamp Plant, GE, Cleve., 1970-75; employee, indsl. rels. rep. Bailey Controls Co., Wickliffe, Ohio, 1975-78; mgr., coll. recruiting Gen. Tire and Rubber, Akron, Ohio, 1978-81, profl. staffing coord., 1981-82; regional human resource mgr. Gilbane Bldg. Co., Cleve., 1982-86, human resource mgr. Western regions, 1987-88; asst. v.p., dir. human resources St. Alexis Hosp. Med. Ctr. CA Div. Sisters of St. Francis, 1988-90; corp. pers. mgr. MK-Ferguson Co., 1990-94, mgr. human resources, 1993-94; mgr. human resources engring., constrn. and environ. group Washington Group Internat., Cleve., 1994-2001, sr. mgr. human resources, 2001—; human resources cons. Key Source HCI, LLC, 2003—, Highbridge Assoc., 2003—07; chmn. human resource consultors Health, Human Svcs. Secretariat Cath. Diocese Cleve., 2005—; pres. Diversity Leaders, LLC, Cleve., 2005—; diversity practice lead, sr. recruiting cons. Qualigence, Inc., Cleve., 2007—; v.p., exec. Edward Luttner Assocs., 2007—. Author: (with w.J. McBurney Jr.) College Recruitment: Effective Programs and Practices, 1982. Past chmn. orgn. and extension com. Newton D. Baker Dist., Greater Cleve. coun. Boy Scouts Am., 1970-71; mem. Human Resource Com. for Greater Cleve. United Way, NAACP, Urban League of Cleve.; mem. pension and benefit coms. Greater Cleve. Hosp. Assn., 1988-90; Bd. Edn. commr. Villa Angela Acad. (pres., 1986-87, U.S. Edn. Dept. award 1987); founder, advisor Explorer Post, Gilbane Bldg. Co., Cleve., 1984-88; Cleve., 1988—; v.p. adv. bd. Cath. Social Svcs. Cuyahoga County, chmn. coun. advisors, 1992-93; mem. urban regional bd. Cath. Edn. Cleve., 1986; trustee Marotta Montessori Sch. of Cleve., 1993—, pres.-elect, 1993, pres., 1993-2000; founding trustee Harambee Svcs. Orgn. Cleve., 1987—; trustee Cath. Charities Svcs. Corp. N.E. Ohio, 1992—, Laurel Lake Retirement Cmty., 2006—; vice chmn. bd. trustees Benedictine H.S., 2006—; mem. edn. commn. Villa Angela St. Joseph High Sch., 1990—, pres., 1993—; chmn. coun. advisors Cath. Social Svcs. Cuyahoga County, 1992—; bd dirs CSA Health Sys., 2005-. Recipient commendation Nat. Alliance of Bus., Akron, 1979, Cmty. Svc. award WJW-Northwest Orient Airlines, 1975. Mem. Cleve. EEO Assn., Soc. Human Resources Mgmt., Soc. Am. Mil. Engrs., U.S. Naval Inst., Mid-West Coll. Placement Assn. (chmn. rubber industry com. 1979-81), Ctr. for Human Svcs. (v.p., trustee, vice chmn. bd. trustees), Internat. Human Resources Assn., Indsl. Rels. Rsch. Assn., Human Resources Systems Assn., Alpha Phi Alpha. Democrat. Roman Catholic. Home: 24400 Emery Rd Warrensville Heights OH 44128-5614

SIMMONS, DONNA MARIE, neuroscientist, histotechnologist, neuroendocrine anatomist, researcher; b. Hartford, Conn., Oct. 13, 1943; d. John Henry and Ellen Louise (Meehl) Strayer; m. Corvin Gale Simmons, Sept. 17, 1964. Student, U. Wash., We. Wash. State U.; PhD, U. So. Calif., 2005. Histologic technician, instr. Tacoma Gen. Hosp. Sch. Med. Tech., Tacoma, 1963; lab. technician Med. Sch. U. Wash., 1964; histologic technician Northgate Med. Lab., Seattle, 1964—67; rsch. technologist in neuroanatomy Regional Primate Rsch. Ctr. U. Wash., 1967—82; rsch. asst. Devel. Neurobiology Lab. Salk Inst., La Jolla, Calif., 1982—85, sr. technician. lab. mgr. Neural Sys. Lab. Howard Hughes Med. Inst., 1985—90; vis. faculty neurosciences dept. Baylor U. Med. Sch., 1990; rsch. assoc. dept. biol. scis.-neurobiology U. So. Calif., LA, 1990—, Neurosci. Rsch. Inst., 2002—. Cons., lectr. in field; judge Greater San Diego Sci. and Engring. Fair, 1987-89, Calif. Sci. Fair, 1992—; leader sci. del. to People's Rep. of China, 1986; chair China Scientist Exch. Fund, 1986-87; mem. Swiss Histology Meeting Exch., 1990. Author tech. articles, revs. in field; mem. editl. bd. Jour. Histotech, 1982-2002. Recipient Diamond Cover award Jour. Histotech., 1990; various svcs. awards; best non-clin. pub. in field, 1985; Hudson Hoagland USA-Australia Exch. Med. Rsch. fellow Prince Henry's Rsch. Inst. Monash U., 1996. Mem. AAAS, Am. Neuroendocrine Soc., Am. Soc. Clin. Pathologists (affiliate), Am. Physiol. Soc., Wash. State Histology Soc. (past pres., histology liason Am. Soc. Med. Tech.), Nat. Soc. Histotech. (charter, regional dir. 1980-82, jud. chair 1983-86), Calif. Soc. Histotech. (San Diego dir. protem 1985-86), Assn. Women in Sci. (San Diego charter, bd. dirs. 1985-90), Soc. for Neurosci., Women in Neurosci., NY Acad. Sci., J.B. Johnston Club, Cajal Club, Sierra Club, NOW, Am. Alpine Club, Sigma Xi. Office: U So Calif Mc 2520 Los Angeles CA 90089-2520 Business E-Mail: dsimmons@mizar.usc.edu.

SIMMONS, GENE (CHAIM WITZ, GENE KLEIN), musician; b. Haifa, Israel, Aug. 25, 1949; came to U.S., 1958, naturalized, 1963; s. Flora Witz; (children with Shannon Tweed). Nicholas, Sophie BE, SUNY, 1970; BA in Edn., Richmond Coll., CUNY, 1972. Tchr., Spanish Harlem, NY; asst. to editor Glamour and Vogue; asst. to dir. Puerto Rican InterAgeny Coun.; member in bands called Bullfrog Beer, Coffee, Long Island Sounds, Cathedral, and Wicked Lester; co-founder Kiss, 1973—; founder Simmons Records; ptnr. Simmons Abramson Mktg., 2006—; chmn. NGTV (No Good TV), 2006—. Singer: (albums with Kiss): Kiss, 1974, Hotter Than Hell, 1974, Dressed to Kill, 1975, Alive, 1975, Destroyer, 1976, Rock & Roll Over, 1976, Love Gun, 1977, Alive II, 1977, Double Platinum, 1978, Dynasty, 1979, Unmasked, 1980, Music From the Elder, 1981, Killers, 1982, Creatures of the Night, 1982, Lick It Up, 1983, Animalize, 1984, Asylum, 1985, Crazy Nights, 1987, Hot In The Shade, 1989, Smashes, Thrashes and Hits, 1989, Revenge, 1992, Alive III, 1993, Kiss My Ass, 1995, MTV: Kiss Unplugged, 1996, Carnival of Souls, 1997, You Wanted the Best You Got the Best!, 1997, Greatest Kiss, 1997, Psycho Circus, 1998, Kiss: The Box Set, 2001, The Very Best of Kiss, 2002, Kiss Symphony Alive VI, 2003, Kiss Alive 35, 2008, Sonic Boom, 2009; (solo albums) Gene Simmons, 1978, ***Hole, 2004; actor (films) Runaway, 1984, Never Too Young To Die, 1986, Trick or Treat, 1986, Wanted: Dead or Alive, 1987, The Decline of Western Civilization Part II: The Metal Years, 1988, The Return of Bruno, 1988, Red Surf, 1990, Detroit Rock City, 1999, Wish You Were Dead, 2000, The New Guy, 2002; (TV series) My Dad the Rock Star, 2003 Gene Simmons' Rock School, 2005, Gene Simmons Family Jewels, 2005-; (TV appearances) The Paul Lynde Halloween Special, 1976, KISS Meets the Phantom of the Park, 1978, Miami Vice, 1985, Hitchhiker, 1986, Millennium, 1996, Talk to Me, 2000, (voice only) Family Guy, 2001, 2002, 2005, King of the Hill, 2003 Who Wants to Be a Millionaire, 2001, At Any Cost, 2002, (voice only) King of the Hill, 2003, Gene Simmons TV Special '24/7', 2004, Third Watch, 2004; creater (TV) Baby 101, Mr. Romance, The Apprentice 3, 2005; guest judge American Idol: The Search for a Superstar, 2005; composer (films) Reform School Girls, 1986, Less Than Zero, 1987, (TV) Kiss: The Last Kiss, 2000, Kiss: Beyond the Makeup, 2001, (video game) Underground, 2003; prodr. (TV series) Detroit Rock City, 1999, Smash, 2001; writer (video) KISS: eXposed, 1987; author: Kiss and Makeup, 2001, Sex Money Kiss (both NY Times Best Selling Books), 2005; founder Simmons Publishing; published(magazine) Gene Simmons Tongue, 2001-(Sterling/Macfadden), Gene Simmons Game mag.; released (audio visual, CD) Speaking in Tongues; launched fashion label, Gene Simmons-Dragonfly, 2002; perfomer, writer (song) I Am Indy, 2006; TV commericals, shows and advertising associated with KISS include Cannon Camera (Japan), NASCAR, Nat. Hot Rod Assn. (NHRA), Pepsi Cola, Coca Cola, Holiday Inn, VISA cards, KISS/Platinum online comics, KISS Girls; sponsor Worldwide Mktg. and Branding of Indy Racing League, 2006-. Winner 27 Gold Record Albums, 9 Platinum Record Albums, 7 Multi-Platinum Record Albums. Mem. Am. Fedn. Musicians, AFTRA, ASCAP. Discovered Van Halen in 1977 and produced 15 song demo album; inventor of Axe bass guitar in 1980; speaks several languages English, Hungarian, Hebrew, German, learning Japanese and Mandarin Chinese; Kiss has been America's Number One Gold Record award winning group of all time according to RIAA; in honor of Gene Simmons US Postage Stamp; self-titled debut from the group BAG to mark first release from Gene Simmons' Simmons Records in over a decade in 2005. Office: $immons Records PO Box 15097 Beverly Hills CA 90210 *Listen to everyone around you, but do only what you believe.*

SIMMONS, GEORGE FINLAY, retired mathematics professor; b. Austin, Tex., Mar. 3, 1925; s. George Finlay and Armede Victoria (Hatcher) S.; m. Hope Bridgeford, Sept. 11, 1954; 1 child, Nancy Bingham. BS, Caltech, 1946; MS, U. Chgo., 1948; PhD, Yale U., 1957. Instr. U. Chgo., 1947-50, U. Maine, Orono, 1950-52, Yale U., New Haven, 1952-56; asst. prof. U. R.I., Kingston, 1956-58, Williams College, Williamstown, Mass., 1958-62; assoc. prof. math. Colo. Coll., Colorado Springs, 1962-65, prof., 1965-90, prof. emeritus, 1990—. Author: Introduction Topology and Modern Analysis, 1962, Differential Equations, 1972, 3d edit., 2006, Precalculus Mathematics in a Nutshell, 1981, Calculus with Analytic Geometry, 1985, 2nd edit., 1995, Calculus Gems: Brief Lives and Memorable Mathematics, 1992, repub., 2007. Mem. Math. Assn. Am. Avocations: travel, cooking, fishing, billiards. Home: 1401 Wood Ave Colorado Springs CO 80907-7348 Office: Colorado College Dept Math Colorado Springs CO 80903

SIMMONS, HAROLD C., investment and sugar company executive; b. 1931; m. Annette Simmons; 6 children. BA, MA with Phi Beta Kappa key, U. Tex., 1952. Investigator U.S. Civil Service, Dallas, 1952-55; book examiner Fed. Deposit Ins. Corp., Dallas, 1955-56; loan officer Republican Nat. Bank, Dallas, 1956-61; with Amalgamated Sugar Corp., Dallas, 1961—, chmn., chief exec. officer, also bd. dirs. Ogden, Utah; pres., chief exec. officer, dir. Contran Corp., Dallas; chmn., dir. NL Industries Inc., Houston, 1961—; chmn. Nat. City Lines, Dallas; chmn. bd. dir. Valhi, Inc., Dallas. Founder Harold C. Simmons Comprehensive Cancer Ctr., 1988; founder, chmn. Simmons Found., 1988. Named one of Forbes' Richest Americans, 1999—, World's Richest People, Forbes mag., 2001—. Office: Valhi Inc Three Lincoln Centre 5430 Lbj Fwy Ste 1700 Dallas TX 75240-2620 also: NL Industries Inc 300 N Sam Houston Pky E Houston TX 77060-3301 Office: The Amalgamated Sugar Company 3184 Elder St Boise ID 83705-4709

SIMMONS, HARRIS H., bank executive; b. Salt Lake City, June 25, 1954; s. Roy William and Elizabeth (Ellison) S. BA in Econs., U. Utah, 1977; MBA, Harvard U., 1980. Comml. loan officer Allied Bancshares, Houston, 1980-81; asst. v.p. Zions Bancorp, Salt Lake City, 1981, fin. v.p., 1981-82; sr. v.p. fin. Zions Utah Bancorp, Salt Lake City, 1982-83, exec. v.p., sec., treas., 1984-86, pres., 1986—90; pres., CEO Zions 1st Nat. Bank, Salt Lake City, 1990—98, chmn., 1990—; pres., CEO Zions Bancorporation, Salt Lake City, 1990—, chmn., 2002—. Bd. dirs. Questar, Inc., Salt Lake City, Entrada Industries, Inc., Salt Lake City, Keystone Comm., Salt Lake City, Simmons Family, Inc., Salt Lake City, Zions 1st Nat. Bank, Salt Lake City, Nat. Bank Ariz., Tucson, Nev. State Bank, Las Vegas. Bd. dirs. United Way, Salt Lake City, 1983-89; bd. dirs. Utah Symphony, 1986—, vice chmn., 1990-95, chmn., 1995—; trustee Salt Lake City C.C., 1993—; v.p. fin. Great Salt Lake coun. Boy Scouts Am., 1991-95; co-chair Greater Salt Lake Shelter-the-Homeless Com., 1986-89, v.p., 1989—. Pres., dir., past vice-chmn. ABA; mem. Utah Bankers Assn. (bd.dirs. 1987-92, chmn. 1990-91), Salt Lake Area C. of C. (bd. dirs. 1991-94), Phi Beta Kappa. Mem. Lds Ch. Office: Zions Bancorporation 1 S Main St Salt Lake City UT 84111

SIMMONS, JANET BRYANT, writer, publishing executive; b. Oakland, Calif., Apr. 22, 1925; d. Howard Pelton and Janet Horn (McNab) Bryant; m. William Ellis Simmons, May 17, 1944 (div. 1979); children: William Howard, Janet Margaret Simmons McAlpine. BA, San Jose State U., Calif., 1965; MA, U. San Francisco, 1979. Social worker Santa Clara County Social Svcs., San Jose, Calif., 1965-91; editor, pub. Enlightenment Press, Santa Clara, 1994—. Author: The Mystical Child, 1996. Mem. AAUW, Am. Booksellers Assn., Pubs. Mktg. Assn., Bay Area Ind. Pubs. Assn., Audubon Soc., Jacques Cousteau Soc. Avocations: playing piano, swimming, tai chi, travel, gardening. Office: Enlightenment Press PO Box 3314 Santa Clara CA 95055-3314 Office Fax: 408-248-3222.

SIMMONS, JEAN BYERS, academic administrator, director; b. Ft. Worth, July 29, 1956; d. James Clifford and Don Jean Carter; m. Jim Allen Simmons, Sept. 20, 1973; children: Jeffrey Brent, Joshua Allen. B of Arts History magna cum laude, Columbia Coll., Mo., 2002; M of History, Tarleton State U., 2004. DataTel Columbia Coll., 2000. Office mgr. Columbia Coll., 2002—03, acad. advisor, 2003—05; dir. Embry Riddle Aeronautical U., 2005—. Trainer Columbia Coll., Columbia, Mo., 2000—05. Fund raising Little League, White Settlement, Tex., 1984—90; mem. PTA, 1980—93; treas. Brewer Bear Athletic Booster Club, 1990—93. Mem.: Phi Alpha Theta (life), Alpha Sigma Lambda (life). Democrat-Npl. Baptist. Avocations: travel, reading, swimming, researching. Home: 508 Meadow Park Dr White Settlement TX 76108 Office: Embry-Riddle Aeronautical Univ NAS JRB Bldg 1525 Fort Worth TX 76127 Personal E-mail: js114729@sbcglobal.net. Business E-Mail: jean.simmons@erau.edu.

SIMMONS, J.K. (JONATHAN KIMBLE SIMMONS), actor; b. Detroit, Mich., Jan. 9, 1955; s. Donald William and Patricia (Kimble) Simmons; m. Michelle Schumacher, 1996. Student, Ohio U., Athens, Ohio State U., Columbus; BMus, U. Montana, Missoula, 1978; student, HB Studios, NYC. Studied acting with Jacqueline Barton; studied voice with Mario Alch, Esther England and John Mount; mem. of theatre co. Seattle Repertory Theatre, 1984—85. Actor: (plays) The Fantasticks, 1981, Das Barbecu, 1994, (touring musical) Doonesbury, 1984, (Off-Broadway musical) Birds of Paradise, 1987; (Broadway plays) A Change in the Heir, 1990, Guys and Dolls, 1992—95, Laughter on the 23rd Floor, 1993, (Broadway and touring revival) Peter Pan, 1991—92; (TV films) Popeye Doyle, 1986, Face Down, 1997, Homeward Bound, 2002, Path to War, 2002, 3: The Dale Earnhardt Story, 2004, Bury My Heart at Wounded Knee, 2007; (TV series) Law & Order, 1994—2004, Oz, 1997—2003, Law & Order: Special Victims Unit, 2000—01, The Closer, 2005—; (films) The Ref, 1994, The Scout, 1994, The First Wives Club, 1996, Extreme Measures, 1996, Love Walked In, 1997, (voice only) Anastasia, 1997, The Jackal, 1997, Crossing Fields, 1998, Celebrity, 1998, For Love of the Game, 1999, (voice only) I Lost My M in Vegas, 1999, The Cider House Rules, 1999, Above Freezing, 2000, The Gift, 2000, Beautiful Joe, 2000, Autumn in New York, 2000, Hit and Runaway, 2001, The Mexican, 2001, Spider-Man, 2002, Disposal, 2003, Off the Map, 2003, Hidalgo, 2004, The LadyKillers, 2004, Spider-Man 2, 2004, Harsh Times, 2005, Thank You for Smoking, 2006, The Astronaut Farmer, 2006, First Snow, 2007, Spider-Man 3, 2007, Rendition, 2007, Juno, 2007, Postal, 2007, The Way of War, 2008, Burn After Reading, 2008, The Vicious Kind, 2009, New in Town, 2009, Red Sands, 2009, I Love You, Man, 2009, Post Grad, 2009, (TV appearances) New York News, 1995, The Adventures of Pete and Pete, 1995, Swift Justice, 1996, Homicide: Life on the Street, 1996, New York Undercover, 1996, Spin City, 1997, Remember WENN, 1998, Third Watch, 2000, Law & Order: Criminal Intent, 2002, John Doe, 2003, Everwood, 2003, ER, 2004, The D.A., 2004, Without a Trace, 2004, The Jury, 2004, Nip/Tuck, 2004, Justice League (4 episodes), 2004—06, Arrested Development, 2005, Jack & Bobby, 2005, Numb3rs, 2005, The West Wing, 2006, The Simpsons (2 episodes), 2006—07, Queens Supreme, 2007, Kim Possible (3 episodes), 2007, American Dad (2 episodes), 2007—08, Phineas and Ferb, 2008, Ben 10: Alien Force, 2008; appeared in: (documentaries) Guys and Dolls Off the Record, 1992. Recipient Achievement award, U. Mont., 2002. Office: c/o Stephen Hirsh The Gersh Agy 232 N Canon Dr Beverly Hills CA 90210*

SIMMONS, JOHN DEREK, retired financial consultant; b. Essex, Eng., July 17, 1931; arrived in U.S., 1952; s. Simon Leonard and Eve (Smart) Simmons; m. Rosalind Wellish, Mar. 5, 1961; children: Peter Lawrence, Sharon Leslie. BS, Columbia U., 1956; MBA, Rutgers U., 1959; postgrad., NYU, 1959-62. Chief cost acct. Airborne Accessories, Hillside, NJ, 1952-57; sr. cost analyst Curtiss-Wright Corp., Wood Ridge, NJ, 1957; sr. fin. analyst internat. group Ford Motor Co., Jersey City, 1958-60; rsch. assoc. Nat. Assn. Accts. (now Inst. Mgmt. Accts.), NYC, 1960-64; asst. to v.p. fin. Air Reduction Co., Inc., 1965—67; mgr. corp. planning Anaconda Wire & Cable Co., NYC, 1968; assoc. cons. Rogers, Slade & Hill, Inc., NYC, 1969-71; v.p., security analyst, economist Moore & Schley, Cameron & Co. (name now Fourteen Rsch. Corp.), 1972-81; v.p., security analyst Merrill Lynch Capital Markets, NYC, 1981-88; security analyst Arnhold and S. Bleichroeder, Inc., 1988—89; v.p., security analyst, corp. fin. specialist Smith Barney, Harris Upham & Co., Inc. (now Salomon Smith Barney, Inc.), 1989—90; sr. cons. Carl Byoir & Assocs., 1991—94; assoc. mng. dir. Commonwealth Assocs., 1994—95; mng. dir. State St. Capital Markets Corp., 1996; v.p. GKN Securities Corp., 1996—97; dir. instnl. sales Gabelli & Co., Rye, 1997; assoc. Manning, Selvage & Lee, NYC, 1998—2001; ret., 2001. Lectr. fin. bus. Rutgers U., NJ, 1957—64; lectr. Marymount Manhattan Coll., NYC, 2002—. Contbr. articles to profl. jours. Docent Asia Soc. and Mus., NYC, 2002—05. 1st lt. Brit. Army, 1950—52. Grantee personal coat of Arms, by Queen Elizabeth II: manorial Lord of Ash, Suffolk, Eng. Mem.: Knight Templar Sovereign Mil. Order Temple of Jerusalem. Avocations: photography, travel, fishing. Home: 360 E 72d St New York NY 10021-4753 Personal E-mail: johnlordash@aol.com.

SIMMONS, JOSEPH (RUN SIMMONS, REV RUN), musician; b. Hollis, Queens, NY, Nov. 24, 1964; s. Daniel and Mary Simmons; m. Justine Jones Simmons, June 25, 1994; 1 adopted child, Miley children: Daniel, Russell II, Victoria(dec.);children from previous marriage: Angela, Vanessa, Joseph Jr. Founding mem. Run-D.M.C., 1983—2002. Co-owner & pres. Phat Farm Footwear; co-owner & CEO Run Athletics. Musician: (albums) Run-D.M.C., 1984, King of Rock, 1985, Raising Hell, 1986, Tougher Than Leather, 1988, Back from Hell, 1990, Down With the King, 1993, Crown Royal, 1999, (solo albums) Distortion; actor: (films) Krush Groove, 1986, Tougher Than Leather, 1988, Who's the Man?, 1993, Red Dragon, 2002; co-exec. prodr., actor (TV series) Run's House, 2005—; co-author: Take Back Your Family: A Challenge to America's Parents, 2008. Ordained min. Zoe Ministries, NYC. Named to Rock & Roll Hall of Fame as member of Run-D.M.C., 2009. Office: Phat Farm Corp Office 512 Fashion Ave New York NY 10018 also: Zoe Ministries 310 Riverside Dr New York NY 10025*

SIMMONS, KARLA PEAVY, researcher, educator; b. Las Vegas, July 17, 1970; d. John Lester and Patricia Vail Peavy; m. Gill Simmons, Aug. 1, 1998. BS, Auburn U., 1992, MS, 1996; PhD, N.C. State U., 2002. Quality control mgr. Oneita Industries, Andrews, SC, 1992—93; asst. prof. U. Mo., Columbia, 2002—05, Auburn U., Ala., 2005—. Adv. bd. mem. Lori Coulter True Measure, St. Louis, 2002—. Mem. Howard County Christian Women's Orgn., Fayette, Mo., 2004—06, Friends of Mo. Hist. Costume Collection, Columbia, 2005—. Grantee, USDA, 2004—, Nat. Textile Ctr., 2006—. Mem.: DAR, ASTM, Internat. Textile and Apparel Assn., Kappa Alpha Theta (adv. bd. 1994—97). Conservative. Achievements include research in 3D Body Scanning and Site Manager of SizeUSA National Sizing Study. Avocations: sewing, crafts. Office: Auburn U 308 Spidle Hall Auburn University AL 36849 Office Fax: 334-844-1340. E-mail: ksimmons@auburn.edu.

SIMMONS, KEVIN MARK, finance educator; s. Hugh and Anne Simmons; m. Susan Kay Bishop, Apr. 29, 1978; children: Jonathan Andrew, Haley Melissa. PhD, Tex. Tech U., Lubbock, 1999. Prof. economics Austin Coll., Sherman, Tex., 2003—. Mem.: Am. Econ. Assn. Office: Austin Coll 900 N Grand Ste 61591 Sherman TX 75090-4400 Office Fax: 903-813-2477. Business E-Mail: ksimmons@austincollege.edu.

SIMMONS, KIMORA LEE (KIMORA LEE PERKINS), apparel designer, television personality, model; b. St. Louis, May 3, 1975; d. Vernon Whitlock and Joanne Perkins; m. Russell Simmons, 1998 (div. Jan. 2009); children: Ming Lee, Aoki Lee; 1 child, Kenzo Lee Hounsou. Former model Chanel; founder, CEO, creative dir. Baby Phat Clothing (started with Baby Phat Farm runway show in 1991), 1998—. Product line also includes accessories, lingerie, handbags, footwear, beauty line and swimwear.; two limited edition Motorola cell phones; signature fragrance line includes Baby Phat Golden Goddess, Baby Phat Goddess, Baby Phat Fabulosity, 2008. Appearances include (films) Unzipped, 1995, Catwalk, 1996, Brown Sugar, 2002, The Big Tease, 1999, Beauty Shop, 2005, Rebound, 2005, judge (TV series) America's Next Top Model, 2003, co-host Life & Style, 2004—05, appearances include Fashion Week Diaries, 2005, StarTrekking with Kimora Lee Simmons for MSN.com, (TV specials) for VH-1, InsideOut: Kimora Lee Simmons presents NY Fashion Week and Style-Party Fabulous with Kimora Lee Simmons; exec. prodr.: (Broadway plays) Def Poetry Jam, 2003 (Tony award); author: Fabulosity: What It Is and How to Get It, 2006. Established Kimora Lee Simmons Scholarship Fund, Kimora Lee Simmons Found.; active member of youth advocacy organizations including Amfar, The G&P Found., Keep a Child Alive, Hetrick-Martin Inst. and Rush Philanthropic (also bd. dirs.). Named Vibe Vixen, Vibe mag., 2005, Outstanding Stylemaker, Asian Excellence Awards, 2006; named one of The 100 Most Influential Women in NYC Bus., Crain's NY Bus., 2007; named to Power 150, Ebony mag., 2008. Office: Sony Pictures Entertainment 10202 W Washington Blvd Culver City CA 90232

SIMMONS, LYNDA MERRILL MILLS, retired principal; b. Salt Lake City, Aug. 31, 1940; d. Alanson Soper and Madeline Helene (Merrill) Mills; m. Mark Carl Simmons, Nov. 17, 1962; children: Lisa Lynn Simmons Morley, William Mark, Jennifer Louise, Robert Thomas. BS, U. Utah, Salt Lake City, 1961, MS, 1983. Cert. sch. adminstr., Utah. Tchr. Wasatch Jr. H.S./Granite Dist., Salt Lake City, 1961-64, Altamont (Utah) H.S./Duchesne Dist., 1964-66; tchr. spl. edn. Park City (Utah) H.S., 1971-73; resource tchr. Eisenhower Jr. H.S., Salt Lake City, 1979-88; tchr. specialist Granite Sch. Dist., Salt Lake City, 1985-90; asst. prin. Bennion Jr. H.S., Salt Lake City, 1990-93; prin. Hartvigsen Sch., Salt Lake City, 1993—2002; ret., 2002. Adj. prof. spl. edn. U. Utah, Salt Lake City, 1987—, Utah Prin. Acad., 1994-95, co-chair Utah Spl. Educators for Computer Tech., Salt Lake City, 1988-90; adv. com. on handicapped Utah State Office Edn., 1990-93; cons., presenter in field. Author: Setting Up Effective Secondary Resource Program, 1985; contbr. articles to profl. jours. Dist. chmn. Heart Fund, Cancer Dr., Summit Park, Utah, 1970-82; pack leader Park City Area coun. Boy Scouts Am., 1976-80; bd. dirs. Jr. League Salt Lake City, 1977-80, cmty. bd., 1997—; cookie chmn. Park City area Girl Scouts U.S., 1981; dist. chmn. March of Dimes, 1982—. Recipient Amb. award Salt Lake Conv. and Vis. Bur., 1993; named Bus. Woman of Yr., South Salt Lake C. of C., 2001. Mem. Nat. Assn. Secondary Sch. Prins., Park City Young Women's Mut. (pres. 1989-93, family history cons. 1993-95), Women's Athanaeum (v.p. 1990-93, pres. 1994-2001), Gen. Fedn. Women's Clubs (pres. Salt Lake dist. 1998-02, cmty.-improvement chairperson Utah 1996-98, chairperson Woman of Yr. 1998—, state treas. 2006-) Coun. for Exceptional Children (pres. Salt Lake chpt. 1989-90, pres. Utah Fedn. 1991-93, Spl. Educator of Yr. 1995), Granite Assn. Sch. Adminstrs. (sec.-treas. 1992-94); Mission for Ch. of Jesus Christ of Latter Day Saints, Blacksburg, Va., 2003-04. Mem. Lds Ch. Avocations: reading, cooking, writing, sports, handiwork.

SIMMONS, LYNDA TEEL, nurse, healthcare executive; d. A. Stokes. A in Nursing, Columbus Coll., 1969, BA in Psychology, 1973; BSN, Troy State U., 1984, MSN magna cum laude, 1986. RN State Med. Agy., Clin. Nurse Specialist. Head nurse emergency room Columbus Med. Ctr., Ga., 1972—75; hosp. supr. Drs. Hosp. Hosp. Corp. Am., 1975—80; dir. surgical nursing divsn. Columbus Med. Ctr., 1980—82; critical care instr. BSN Program Auburn U., Auburn, Ala., 1985; RN State Med. Agy., Columbus, Ga., 1988—93; CEO Simmons Healthcare Enterprises, 1996—. Lectr. Seminars: Legal Nursing, Nurology, Renal, 2004—08. Mem.: Am. Assn. Critical Care Nurses, Emergency Nurse Assn., Soc. Critical Care Medicine, Am. Assn. Legal Nurse Cons., Sigma Theta Tau. Avocations: horseback riding, fencing, tennis, swimming. Office: Simmons Healthcare Enterprises 1303 Pagoda Dr Columbus GA 31907 Office Phone: 706-563-1891.

SIMMONS, MARVIN GENE, retired geophysics educator; b. Dallas, May 15, 1929; s. Burt H. and Mable (Marshall) S.; m. Dorothy Richter; children by previous marriage: Debra Lynn, Sandra Kay, Pamela Jean. BS, Tex. Agrl. and Mech. Coll., 1949; MS, So. Methodist U., 1958; PhD, Harvard U., 1962. Registered profl. geologist, N.H., Ky. Petroleum engr. Humble Oil Co., 1949-51; propr. gravel business, 1953-58; asst. prof. So. Meth. U., 1962-65; prof. geophysics MIT, 1965-89, prof. emeritus, 1989—; ret., 1989; prin. Hager-Richter Geoscience Inc., 1989—. Cons. NASA, 1965-72; chief scientist NASA (Manned Spacecraft Center), Houston, 1969-71; cons. on siting of nuclear facilities; sec. Internat. Heat Flow Com., 1967-71; chmn. com. drilling for sci. purposes Nat. Acad. Scis., 1965; Mem. geophysics panel NSF. Served with USAF, 1951-53. NSF postdoctoral fellow, 1961-62 Fellow Geol. Soc. Am., Am. Geophys. Union; mem. ASTM (com. C-18 on dimension stone 1986—), Boston Geol. Soc. (pres. 1967-68), Soc. Exploration Geophysicists, Sigma Xi, Tau Beta Pi. Achievements include research on physical properties of materials, lunar exploration, marine geophysics, temperature of earth, regional geophysics, engineering geology and geophysics. Home: 140 Range Rd Windham NH 03087 Office: 8 Industrial Way Unit D10 Salem NH 03079-2837

SIMMONS, MONIKA, microbiologist, researcher; d. Arno Rudi and Maria Kessler. MS, Johns Hopkins U., Balt., 1994. Microbiologist Naval Med. Rsch. Ctr., Silver Spring, Md., 1989—. Contbr. articles to sci. jours. Achievements include patents for recombinant dengue virus envelope protein,maltose-binding protein antigens and subunit vaccine compositions containing said antigens; research in characterization of antibody responses to combinations of a dengue virus type 2 DNA vaccine and two dengue virus type 2 protein vaccines in rhesus macaques; antibody responses of mice immunized with a tetravalent dengue recombinant protein subunit vaccine; evaluation of the protective efficacy of a recombinant dengue envelope B domain fusion protein against dengue 2 virus infection in mice. Avocations: travel, hiking, theater. Office: Naval Med Rsch Ctr 503 Robert Grant Ave Silver Spring MD 20910 Office Fax: 301-319-7451. Business E-Mail: monika.simmons@med.navy.mil.

SIMMONS, PETER A., medical researcher; s. Alan Jay and Mary Marcella Simmons; m. Carolyn Marie Thummel, Apr. 12, 1997; children: A. Jacob Alan, Emily Hope Chrisman. BA, Amherst Coll., Mass., 1975; PhD, Yale U., New Haven, Conn., 1980. Diplomate Am. Acad. Optometry, 2008. Prof. Southern Calif. Coll. Optometry, Fullerton, 1983—99; scientist Allergan, Irvine, Calif., 2000—05, prin. clin. rsch. scientist, 2005—07, rsch. dir., 2007—. Vis. prof. Glasgow Caledonian U., Scotland, 1998. Contbr. articles to profl. sci. jours. Vol. Orange County Performing Arts Ctr., Costa Mesa, Calif., 1998—2008; bd. mem., asst. condr. Placentia Cmty. Chorus, Calif., 2005—08; pastoral coun. St. Joseph Cath. Ch., Placentia, 2006—08. Mem.: Assn. Rsch. Vision and Ophthalmology, Sigma Xi. Roman Catholic. Achievements include patents pending for ophthalmic compositions and methods for treating eyes. Avocations: singing, hiking, backpacking. Office: Allergan 2525 Dupont Dr T2-4D Irvine CA 92612 Office Fax: 714-796-9388. Business E-Mail: simmons_peter@allergan.com.

SIMMONS, PETER LAWRENCE, lawyer; b. NYC, May 1, 1965; s. John Derek and Rosalind (Wellish) S.; m. Corinne Ryan, Apr 7, 2001; children: Mark R., Matthew S. AB magna cum laude, Columbia U., 1985, JD, 1987. Bar: NY 1987, US Dist. Ct. (so. and ea. dists.) NY 1988, US Ct. Internat. Trade 1991, US Spreme Ct. 1991, US Ct. Appeals (2d cir.) 1992, US Ct. Appeals (1st cir.) 1993, US Ct. Appeals (6th cir.) 2001, US Ct. Appeals (9th cir.) 2006. Law clk. to Hon. Lawrence W. Pierce U.S. Ct. Appeals (2d cir.), NYC, 1987-88; assoc. Fried, Frank, Harris, Shriver & Jacobson LLP, NYC, 1988-94, ptnr., 1994—. Treas., sr. editor Columbia Law Rev., 1985-87. Dir., treas. Selfhelp Cmty. Svcs., Inc. Harlan Fiske Stone scholar, 1985-87. Mem.: ABA, Assn. Bar City NY (civil rights com. 1989—92, profl. responsibility com. 1998—2001, fed. cts. com. 2007—), NY Bar Assn., Fed. Bar Coun., Phi Beta Kappa. Home: 91 West Rd Short Hills NJ 07078 Office: Fried Frank Harris Shriver & Jacobson LLP 1 New York Plz Fl 22 New York NY 10004-1980 Office Phone: 212-859-8455. Business E-Mail: peter.simmons@friedfrank.com.

SIMMONS, RICHARD L., surgeon; b. Boston, Feb. 23, 1934; s. Nathanial J. and Anne Dorothy (Levenson) S.; widowed (Feb. 1993); children: Nicole, Janine. AB in Biochem. Scis. magna cum laude, Harvard U., 1955; MD summa cum laude, Boston U., 1959. Diplomate Am. Bd. Surgery. Intern, resident in surgery Columbia Presbyn. Med. Ctr., NYC, 1959-66; clin. and rsch. fellow Mass. Gen. Hosp., Boston, 1965; rsch. fellow in surgery Harvard Med. Sch., Boston, 1965; instr. surgery Columbia U. Coll. P&S, NYC, 1965-68; from asst. prof. to assoc. prof. surgery U. Minn., Mpls., 1968-72, prof. surgery and microbiology, 1972-87; George V. Foster prof. surgery U. Pitts., 1987—98; chmn. dept. surgery U. Pitts. Med. Ctr., 1987-98; chmn. emeritus, 1998—; assoc. dean for clin. affairs Sch. Medicine U. Pitts., 1989-92, prof. molecular genetics and biochemistry, 1992—; med. dir. U. Pitts. Med. Ctr., 1996—. Chief of surgery Presbyn.-Univ. Hosp.,

Pitts., 1987—98. Author/co-author 15 books; contbr. more than 1200 articles to profl. jours. Recipient Disting. Svc. Prof. Surgery, 1994, other awards and grants. Mem. AMA, AAAS, ACS (pres. Southwestern Pa. chpt. 1992), NAS Inst. Medicine, Am. Soc. for Microbiology, Am. Soc. Transplant Surgeons (pres. 1980-81), Am. Assn. Immunologists, Am. Assn. Pathologists, Am. Surg. Assn. (chmn. program com. 1990), Assn. for Acad. Surgery, Ctrl. Surg. Assn., Cell Transplant Soc., Halsted Soc., Infectious Diseases Soc. Am., Midwest Surg. Soc. (hon.), Reticuloendothelial Soc., Soc. for Leukocyte Biology, Soc. for Microbiology, Soc. Clin. Oncologists, Surg. Infection Soc. (pres. 1988), Soc. Surg. Chmn., Soc. Univ. Surgeons (exec. coun. 1973-81, pres. 1977-78), Allegheny County Med. Soc., Transplantation Soc. (councillor 1974-80, Peter Medawar prize 2004—), others. Office: Univ Pittsburgh Med Ctr 200 Lothrop St Pittsburgh PA 15213-2582 Home Phone: 412-767-4642; Office Phone: 412-647-0680. Business E-Mail: simmonsrl@upmc.edu.

SIMMONS, RICHMOND HOGLE, retired obstetrician, gynecologist; b. Novi, Mich., Mar. 31, 1925; s. George Richmond Simmons and Eva Norine Hogle; m. Audrey Irene Hunt, June 21, 1952; children: Audrey Anne, Richmond Hunt, Clark David, Lauren Lucile, Scott Daniel. BS, U. Mich., Ann Arbor, 1951, MD, 1954. Intern, resident ob-gyn. Mt. Carmel Mercy Hosp., Detroit, 1954—58; assoc. Jacksonville Ob-gyn. Assocs., Ill., 1958—85. Med. staff pres. Pssavant Meml. Hosp., Jacksonville, 1964, chmn., ob-gyn. dept.; pres. Morgan-Scott Counties Med. Soc., Jacksonville, 1973. Author: (books) Joshua Simmons III and His Descendants, 1996, rev. edit., 2007. Co.-chmn. United Fund. Dr., Jacksonville, 1968—69; v.p. Elm City Rehab. Ctr., Jacksonville, 1970; treas. St. Matthias Episcopal Ch., Clermont, Fla., 1989—2001, sr. warden, 2002—05; bd. mem. South Lake Cmty. Hosp., Clermont, 1988—95; charter bd. mem. South Lake County Cmty. Found., 1995—2000; bd. dirs. YMCA, Jacksonville, 1972—75; charter mem. Elm City Rehab. Bd., Jacksonville. Recipient Gem of Hills award, South Lake, Fla. C. of C., 2005. Mem.: AMA (life), Am. Coll. Ob-gyn. (life), Ill. State Med. Soc. (life; mem. maternal welfare com. 1980—85), Rotary Club (pres. 1961). Republican. Episcopalian. Avocations: genealogy, history, stamp collecting/philately, numismatics.

SIMMONS, ROBERT RANDOLPH, principal; b. Phila., Aug. 27, 1935; s. Aaron J. Simmons and Lou (Randolph) Higgs; m. Patricia Ann Grace, June 26, 1975; children: Darris, William, Cynthia L., Tricia M., Robby R. BA in History, Mich. State U., 1958; MA in Community Sch. Leadership, Ea. Mich. U., 1967, Specialist of Arts, 1976; EdD, U. Mich., 1978; doctoral postgrad., Marygrove Coll., Detroit, 2004. Cert. tchr., elem. sch. adminstr., Mich., cert. primary and elem. sch. tchr., elem. prin. Flint Cmty. schs., N.Y., primary 8th grade. Tchr. Flint (Mich.) Cmty Schs., 1962-68; African-Am. elem. prin Flint Cmty. Schs., Mich., 1968—70, prin., 1970—2007, elem. liaison prin., 1992—; dir. EDS partnerships for students Stewart Sch., 1991. Adj. prof. edn. Ea. Mich. U., Ypsilanti, 1988-97; NEA Mastery In Learning sch. renewal site-based cons., 1987-92, cons. parent edn. Flint Community Schs., 1970—, cons. sch. improvement, Mich., 1989—; presenter Mich. Dept. Edn., MSU, 1987—; co-sponsor Mentor's for At-Risk Males Program, Stewart Sch., 1989-2005; sch. reform peer reviewer State of Mich., 2002; peer mentor and reviewer Nat. Youth Leadership Coun., 2000-. Author: Job satisfaction of Elementory Principals, U. Mich., 1978, A Pioneer in Home, School Partnership; Contbr. to book: Parents and Schools: From Visitors to Partners, 1993; contbr. articles to profl. jours.; contbg. author in-dist. teaching materials Flint Cmty. Schs; contbr. Nat. Soc. Experiential Edn., 1997-, Quarterly edn., Svc. Learning Elem. Sch. Assessment, 1997, Family Literacy Ctr., 2000. Deacon bd. New Jerusalem Full Gospel Bapt. Ch., security ministry Flint Jr. C. of C., 1965-1968; adv. bd. Cmty. Alliance Resource Environment, Flint, 1989—; bd. dirs., co-sponsor Stewart/Brennan Youth Clubs, Inc., 1987—; active Coalition for Positive Youth Devel., 1990—, dir. Steware Sch. Eds ptnr., 1991, co founder, Quinn Chapel Ame Ch., 1989-2005, Urban League Flint; Leonard Floyd scholarship com. New Jerusalem Full Gospel Bapt. Ch., pres. Inspirational Voice Choir, 1983-85, 90—2007, The Kings men Choir New Jerusalem Full Gospel Bapt. Ch., 1995; Nat. Youth Leadership Coun. Svc. Learning Peer Mentor Nat. 2003—, exec. bd. mem., Dont Oak Pk. Neighbourhood House Unitede Methodist Ch., Flint. Mich., 1970-1978. Recipient Drum Maj. award Mayor Woodrow Stanley, City of Flint, 1992, 96, Staff Devel. Policy Bd. award Mich. State Bd. Edn., 1987, Chpt. 1 Excellence in Edn. scholarship award, 1986, Flint Tchr.'s Golf Champaionship award, 1974, 78, 79, 81, 83, 84, Golf award Greater Flint Olympian-CANUSA Assn., 1981, 83, 84, 88, 96Outstanding Achievement in Edn. cert. Ctrl. Flint Optimist, 1993, Gov. and Mich. Cmty. Svc. Commn. award, 1993, Vol. Action award, Flint Cmty. Schs. Neighborhoods Pride award, 1994, Flint Mich. Debutant Cotillion award, 2004, Pres. Svc. Learning Vol. Action award Bill Clinton, 1994, Dozier Meml. CME Ch. Christian Methodist Episcopal Ch., 1986, grant, Flint Communist Schs., 1974, 79, 80, 2003, African Am. Men of Achievement award, 1996, Nat. Burtley Golf Champion award, 1998, Exec. Declaration Reading award, State of Mich., 2000, Pupil Pers. Golf trophy Flint Cmty. Sch., 2002, Mich. Adaptive Golf McClaren Hosp. award, 2006, 07, 08, Golf Therapist Mich. Adaptive Golf Mich. Hosp., Flint, 2007, Internat. 40 Yr. Mem. award, Phi Delta Kappa, 2007, Martin Luther King Jr. Major award, 1992,1996, Svc. Learning Cmty. award Gov. John Engler Outstanding Mich. Comm., Achievement award, Mayor Woodrow Stanley, Flint City, 1996 and other numerous awards. Mem. NAESP (Presenter award 1988), ASCD, NAACP, Nat. Community Edn. Assn. (Presenter award 1973), Mich. Elem. and Mid. Sch. Prin. Assn. (Presenter awards 1987-91), Flint Assn. Elem. Sch. Prins., Congress Flint Sch. Adminstrs. (pres. 1991—95), Mich. Community Edn. Assn. (Presenter award 1973), Phi Delta Kappa (treas. Flint chpt. 1985-87, 25 Yr. Svc. award 1992, OBE Pioneer award, Flint Cmty. Schs., Named Employer of Month, Grante, 1990-93), Alpha Phi Alpha. Democrat. Baptist. Avocations: golf, jazz, reading, music, sports. Home: PO Box 804 2262 NOLEN DRIVE Flint MI 48501-0804 Personal E-mail: rsimm1002@aol.com.

SIMMONS, ROBERT RUHL, former congressman; b. NYC, Feb. 11, 1943; s. Charles Herbert Jr. and Roxane Page (Ruhl) S.; m. Edith Heidi Paffard, June 22, 1974; children: Jane Adams, Robert Waldo Ruhl. BA, Haverford Coll., 1965; MPA, Harvard U., 1979; LLD (hon.), U. New Haven, 2003; DHL (hon.), U. Bridgeport, 2005. Ops. officer CIA, Washington, 1969-79; legis. asst. to Senator John H. Chafee US Senate, Washington, 1979-81, staff dir. intelligence com., 1981-85; vis. lectr. Yale U., New Haven, 1986—95; tchg. asst. U. Conn., Storrs, 1988—91; mem. Conn. Gen. Assembly, Hartford, 1991—2001, US Congress from 2d Conn. Dist., Washington, 2001—07; bus. adv. State Conn. Office Policy and Mgmt., Hartford, 2007—08. Contbr. articles to profl. jours. Mem. Republican Nat. Com. Col. USAR, 1970-2003. Decorated Bronze Star with 1 oak leaf cluster, Meritorious Svc. medal, Army Commendation medal with 1 oak leaf cluster, Vietnam Svc. medal with four campaign stars, Nat. Def. medal, Army Res. Achievement medal, Vietnam Civilian Svc. medal; named to Infantry Officer Candidate Sch. Hall of Fame, 2003; assoc. fellow Berkeley Coll., Yale U., 1986-2008. Republican. Episcopalian. Avocations: chinese art, forestry. Office: PO Box 268 Stonington CT 06378-0268 Office Phone: 860-535-8378, 860-415-4633. Office Fax: 860-415-4629. Business E-Mail: rob@joinrobsimmons.com.

SIMMONS, RONNIE (ELIAS R. SIMMONS), legislative staff member; Grad., U. Fla., 1990. Chief of staff for Rep. Corrine Brown, US House of Reps., Washington, 2000—. Office: Office on Congresswoman Corrine Brown 2336 Rayburn House Office Bldg Washington DC 20515 Office Phone: 202-225-0123. Office Fax: 202-225-2256. E-mail: ronnie.simmons@mail.house.gov.*

SIMMONS, RUSSELL, recording industry executive; b. Queens, NY, Oct. 4, 1957; s. Daniel and Evelyn Simmons; m. Kimora Lee, Dec. 20, 1998 (div. Jan. 2009); children: Ming, Aoki Lee. Attended, CCNY. Co-founder, owner Def Jam Records, NYC, 1983—; chmn., CEO, pres. Rush Communications, 1990—; owner Rush Artist Mgmt., PHAT Fashion, Rush Prodr. Mgmt.; partner Rush Model Mgmt.; founder GlobalGrind.com. Represents Public Enemy, LL Cool J, others. Co-prodr.: (films) Krush Groove, 1985, The Funeral, 1996; prodr.: Tougher Than Leather, 1988, The Nutty Professor, 1996, How to Be a Player, 1997; exec. prodr.: The Addiction, 1995, Gridlock'd, 1997, Waist Deep, 2006; prodr.: (TV special) Def Comedy Jam Primetime, 1994; (TV series) Def Poetry Jam, 2002; co-author (with Nelson George): Life and Def: Sex, Drugs, Money & God, 2001; co-author: (with Chris Morrow) Do You!: 12 Laws to Access the Power in You to Achieve Happiness and Success, 2007. Founder Rush Philanthropic Arts Found. Recipient 10 gold albums, 6 platinum albums, 2 multiplatinum albums, Étoile award, Savannah Coll. Art and Design, 2009; named one of 100 Most Influential Black Americans, Ebony mag., 2006; named to Power 150, Ebony mag., 2008. Achievements include bringing hip-hop culture into the American mainstream.*

SIMMONS, RUTH J., academic administrator; b. Grapeland, Tex., July 3, 1945; d. Isaac and Fannie Stubblefield; m. Norbert Simmons, 1968 (div. 1989); children: Khari, Maya. Student, Universidad Internacional, Saltillo, Mex., 1965, Wellesley Coll., 1965—66; BA, Dillard U., 1967; postgrad., Universite de Lyon, 1967—68, George Washington U., 1968—69; AM, Harvard U., 1970, PhD in Romance Langs., 1973; LLD (hon.), Amherst Coll., 1995; LHD (hon.), Howard U., 1996, Dillard U., 1996; LLD (hon.), Princeton U., 1996, Lake Forest Coll., 1997; LHD (hon.), U. Mass., 1997; LLD (hon.), Dartmouth Coll., 1997, Mt. Holyoke Coll., 2001, U. Pa., 2001, Harvard U., 2002, George Washington U., 2002, Columbia U., 2002, Washington U., 2002, U. So. Calif., 2003, Boston U., Rensselaer Polytechnic Inst., N.Y. U., Northeastern; D of Women's Studies (hon.), Ewha Woman's U., Rep. of Korea, 2002; LittD (hon.), U. Toronto, 2004; LHD, Jewish Theol. Sem., 2004, Taugaloo Coll., 2004. Interpreter lang. svcs. divsn. U.S. Dept. State, Washington, 1968—69; instr. French George Washington U., 1968—69; admissions officer Radcliffe Coll., 1970—72; asst. prof. French U. New Orleans, 1973—75, asst. dean coll. liberal arts, asst. prof. French, 1975—76; adminstrv. coord. NEH liberal studies project Calif. State U., Northridge, 1977—78, acting dir. internat. programs, vis. assoc. prof. Pan-African studies, 1978—79; asst. dean grad. sch. U. So. Calif., 1979—82, assoc. dean grad. sch., 1982—83; dir. studies Butler Coll. Princeton U., NJ, 1983—85, acting. dir. Afro-Am. studies, 1985—87, asst. dean faculty, 1986—87, assoc. dean faculty, 1986—90, vice provost, 1992—95; provost Spelman Coll., 1990—91; pres. Smith Coll., Northampton, Mass., 1995—2001; pres Brown U., Providence, 2001—, prof. comparative lit. and African studies. Peer reviewer higher edn. divsn. NEH, 1980—83, bd. cons., 1981; mem. grad. adv. bd. Calif. Student Aid Commn., 1981—83; chair com. to visit dept. African-Am. studies Harvard U., 1991; mem. strategic planning task force N.J. Dept. Higher Edn., 1992—93; mem. nat. adv. commn. EQUITY 2000 Coll. Bd., 1992—95; mem. adv. bd. ctrl. N.J. NAACP Legal Def. Fund, 1992—95; mem. Mid. States Assn. Accreditation Team, Johns Hopkins U., 1993; chmn. accreditation team Bryn Mawr Coll., 1999; chair rev. panel for model instns. planning grants NSF, 1993; mem. Conf. Bd., 1995; bd. dirs. MetLife, JSTOR, Pfizer Inc., 1997—, COFHE, Com. Econ. Devel., Goldman Sachs, 1999—, Tex. Instruments, 1999—; mem. adv. coun. dept. Romance Langs. and Lit. Princeton U., 1996; trustee Carnegie Corp., 1999—; presenter, spkr. and panelist in field. Mem. editl. bd.: World Edn. series Am. Assn. Collegiate Registrars and Admissions Officers, 1984—86; contbr. articles to profl. jours. Named mem. Women's Progress Commemoration Commn. by Pres. Bill Clinton, 1999; mem. adv. coun. Bill and Melinda Gates Millennium Scholars Found.; chmn. Congl. Black Caucus Found. Washington, 2004; mem. adv. bd. N.J. Master Faculty Program Woodrow Wilson Nat. Fellowship Found., 1987—90, trustee, 1991—96, Inst. Advances Study, 1995—98, The Clarke Sch. for Deaf, 1995—; chmn. bd. trustees Acad. Music, 1995—98; mem. adv. com. Healthy Steps for Young Children Program, 1996—98; mem. bd. advisors 1st Internat. Conf. on AIDS, Ethiopia, 1998. Recipient Disting. Svc. award, Assn. Black Princeton Alumni, 1989, Dillard U., 1992, Pres.'s Recognition award, Bloomfield Coll., 1993, TWIN award, Princeton Area YWCA, 1993, Women's orgn. Tribute award, Princeton U., 1994, Leadership award, Third World Ctr. Princeton U., 1995, Tex. Excellence award, Leap Program, 1995, Benjamin E. Mays award, A Better Chance, 1995, Centennial medal, Harvard U. Grad. Sch. Arts & Scis., 1997, Achievement award, Nat. Urban League, 1998, Tchr. Coll. Medal for Disting. Svc., Columbia U., 1999, Pres. award, United Negro Coll. Fund, 2001, "Drum Major for Justice" Edn. award, So. Christian Leadership Conf./W.O.M.E.N., 2002, Fulbright Lifetime Achievement Medal, 2002, R.I. History Makers award, 2002, Amelia Earhart award, 2002, ROBIE Humanitarian award, The Jackie Robinson Found., 2004, The Eleanor Roosevelt Val-Kill medal, 2004, fellowship, DAAD, Presdl. Medal of Honor, Dillard U., 2006; named Women of Yr., CBS, 1996, Glamour Mag., 1996, Disting. Fulbright Alumna, Inst. Internat. Edn., 1997, Woman of World, NASA, 1998, Am. Best Coll. Pres., Time mag., 2001, Woman Yr., Ms. mag., 2002; named a Newsweek Person to Watch, 2002; named one of America's Best Leaders, US News & World Report, 2007; fellow, Danforth Found., 1967—73, Sr. Fulbright fellow, 1981; scholar, KYOK, 1963, Worthing Found., 1963—67, Fulbright scholar, U. de Lyon, 1967—68. Fellow: Am. Acad. Arts & Scis.; mem.: AAAS, Coun. Foreign Rels., Am. Philos. Soc. Office: Office of Pres Brown U One Prospect Street, Campus Box 1860 Providence RI 02912 Office Phone: 401-863-2234. Office Fax: 401-863-7737. E-mail: president@brown.edu.*

SIMMONS, SABRINA L., apparel executive; BS in Fin., U. Calif., Berkeley; MBA, UCLA. CPA Calif. Accountant KPMG, Hewlett Packard Co.; asst. treas. Americas Levi Strauss & Co.; dir. fin. planning & analysis PIC Internat. Group PLC, Sygen Internat. PLC, 1999—2000, group fin. dir., bd. dirs., 2000—01; v.p., treas. to sr. v.p. corp. fin. Gap Inc., San Francisco, 2001—07, exec. v.p. fin., acting CFO, 2007—08, mem. exec. leadership team, 2007—, exec. v.p. corp. fin., CFO, 2008—. Bus. adv. coun. mem. U. San Francisco, Sch. Bus. and Mgmt., 2003—. Office: Gap Inc Two Folsom St San Francisco CA 94105 Office Phone: 650-952-4400. Office Fax: 415-427-2553.

SIMMONS, SHARON RITCHEY, counselor; b. Aurora, Ill., Aug. 9, 1949; d. Harold Eugene and Margaret Marion (Eby) Ritchey; children: Shane C., Scott M. BA in Edn., Concordia U., 1972; MS in Counseling and Human Devel., Troy State U., 1996. Cert. elem. tchr., Fla.; cert. occupl. specialist. Tchr. Grace Luth. Sch., Winter Haven, Fla., 1972-75; customer svc. rep. Commonwealth Corp., Tallahassee, 1975-76; tchr. Hartsfield Elem. Sch., Tallahassee, 1976-89; clin. supv. Rose Speech and Acad. Ctr., Tallahassee, 1989-91; alternative edn. tchr. Hartsfield Sch., Tallahassee, 1991-92; occupl. specialist Adult and Cmty. Edn., Tallahassee, 1992—96, counselor, 1996—97. Mem. Tchr. Edn. Ctr., Tallahassee, 1993—95, chairperson com., 1994; coord. Adult Edn. adult Mentor Program, 1992—97; mem. Ltd. English Proficiency Com., 1995—97; counselor Second Chance Sch., Tallahassee, 1997-2003, Fla. State U. Sch., Tallahassee, 2003-05, Wakulla HS, Crawfordville, 2005-; instr. Fla. State U. FYE Program, 2004; tutor and parent coord., TCC-Wakulla Ctr., 2005-08. Editl. columnist I Declare, 1995; guest columnist Wakulla New, Crawfordville, 2005-06. Mem. St. Stephen Luth. Ch., 1985—. Recipient Promising Program award Fla. Dept. Edn., 1993; named Hartsfield Elem. Tchr. of Yr., 1980, Vol. of Yr. Rickards HS, 1986, Educator of Distinction Nobel Family Nat. Soc. HS Scholars, 2007. Mem. ACA, Leon Classroom Tchrs. Assn., Occpl. Specialist Guidance Assn., Fla. Sch. Counselors Assn., Fla. Counseling Assn. Avocations: reading, sewing, writing, crafts. Home: 45A Dispennette Dr Crawfordville FL 32327-2339 Office: TCC-Wakulla Ctr 5 Crescent Way Crawfordville FL 32327 Office Phone: 850-922-7244. Personal E-mail: sharonteacher49@yahoo.com.

SIMMONS, SUE, newscaster; b. NY, May 27, 1943; d. John Simmons. Corr. WTNH-TV, New Haven, 1973-74, WBAL-TV, Balt., 1974, anchor, host Balt. at One, 1975—76; corr./anchor. WRC-TV, Washington, 1976—80; co-anchor News Channel 4/Live at Five/News Channel 4 at 11 p.m WNBC News, NYC, 1980—; host Images: A Year in Review, WNBC, 2002—. Recipient four Emmy awards, award for Outstanding Performance by a News Commentator, Barnabus McHenry, Vice-Chmn. Pres.'s Task Force on Arts and Humanities, 1981; named to the NY State Broadcasters Assn. Hall of Fame, 2005 Office: WNBC-TV 30 Rockefeller Plz New York NY 10112-0002

SIMMONS (NEUMANN), SYLVIA, advertising executive, writer; b. NYC; m. Hans H. Neumann, 1962. BA cum laude, Bklyn. Coll.; MA in English Lit., Columbia U. Dir. sales promotion and direct mail divsn. McCann Erickson, Inc., NYC, 1958-62; v.p., asst. to pres. Young & Rubicam, Inc., NYC, 1962-73; sr. v.p., dir. spl. projects Kenyon & Eckhardt, Inc., NYC, 1975-86; sr. v.p., dir. corp. comms. Bozell, Jacobs, Kenyon & Eckhardt, 1985-86, cons., 1986-88; free-lance speech writer, 1987—. Author: New Speakers Handbook, 1972, The Great Garage Sale Book, 1982, 2d edit. 2000, (with Hans H. Neumann) The Straight Story on VD, 1974, 2d edit., 2000; Dr. Neumann's Guide to the New Sexually Transmitted Diseases, 1983; co-author: (with Thomas D. Rees) More Than Just a Pretty Face, 1987, How to be the Life of the Podium, 1991; contbr. articles to profl. jours., nat. and local newspapers. Recipient Medal of Freedom, 1946, award for best radio comml. NY Radio Broadcasters Assn., 1976-77, Sales Promotion Execs. Assn. award. Mem. Nat. League Am. Pen Women, Authors Guild, Propylaea, Exec. for Peace (founding mem.), Sigma Tau Delta.

SIMMONS, SYLVIA JEANNE QUARLES, academic administrator, educator; b. Boston, May 8, 1935; d. Lorenzo Christopher and Margaret Mary (Thomas) Quarles; m. Herbert G. Simmons, Jr., Oct. 26, 1957; children: Stephen, Alison, Lisa. BA, Manhattanville Coll., 1957; MEd, Boston Coll., 1962, PhD, 1990; DHL (hon.), St. Joseph's Coll., 1994; EdD (hon.), Merrimack Coll., 1999. Montessori tchr. Charles River Park Nursery Sch., Boston, 1970-76; registrar Boston Coll. Sch. Mgmt., Chestnut Hill, 1966-70; dir. fin. aid Radcliffe Coll., Cambridge, Mass., 1970-75, assoc. dean admissions and fin. aid, 1972-75, assoc. dean admissions, fin. aid and women's edn., 1975; assoc. dean admissions and fin. aid Harvard and Radcliffe, from 1975; assoc. v.p. for acad. affairs ctrl. adminstrn. U. Mass., Boston, 1976-79, spl. asst. to chancellor, 1979; v.p. field svcs. Am. Student Assistance, 1982-84, sr. v.p., 1984-93, exec. v.p., 1983-95, pres., 1996; mem. faculty Harvard U., 1970-77, pres. faculty, 1995-96; lectr. Boston U., 1991—. Cons. Mass. Bd. Higher Edn., 1973—77. Co-editor: Student Loans Riches and Realtities, 1987. Past bd. dirs. Rivers Country Day Sch., Weston, Mass., Simons's Rock Coll., Great Barrington, Mass., Wayland (Mass.) Fair Housing, Cambridge Mental Health Assn., Family Svcs. Greater Boston, Concerts in Black and White, Mass., Higher Edn. Assistance Corp.; chmn. bd. dirs. North Shore Cmty. Coll., 1986-88, mem. bd. dirs., 1985—; trustee and alumnae bd. dirs. Manhattanville Coll., 1986—; mem. adv. com. Upward Bound, Chestnut Hill Boston Coll., 1972-74, Women in Politics John McCormick Inst., 1994-2000; Camp Chimney Corners, Becket, Mass., 1971-77; bd. dirs. Am. Cancer Soc. Mass., 1987-89, Boston Coll., 1990-98, Merrimack Coll., 1992-2000, Mass. Found. for Humanities, 1990-92, Mass. Bay United Way, 1990-94, Grimes King Found., 1992—, St. Elizabeta's Hosp., 1991-2005, Anna Stearns Found., 1996—, Regis Coll., 1997-2004, Edn. Resources Inst., 1998—, Supreme Ct. Jud. Hist. Soc., 2001—, Newton Country Day Sch., 2002-2005, Shirley Eustis House, 2002—; trustee Mt. Ida Coll., 1990—, Exec. Svc. Corp., 1997—, Supreme Ct. Judicial Hist. Soc., 2001—, Newton County Day Sch., 2002—; overseer Mus. Fine Arts, Boston, Mass., 2002-2005; chair Coll. Club Scholarship com., 1997. Recipient Educator of Yr. award Boston and Vicinity Club, 1989, Bicentennial medal Boston Coll., 1976, Achievement award Greater Boston YMCA, 1977, Human Rights awsard Mass. Tchrs. Assn., 1988, Pres'. award Mass. Ednl. Opportunity Assn., 1988, Archbishop Timothy Healy award, 1997, Outstanding Alumna award Girl's Latin Sch., 1998; named One of Ten Outstanding Yung Leaders, Boston Jr. C. of C., 1971, Sojourner's Daus.: 25 African women who have made a difference, 1991. Mem. Eastern Assns. Fin. Aid Officers (2st v.p. 1973), Coll. Scholarship Svc. Coun., Links (pres. local chpt. 1967-69), Nat. Inst. Fin. Aid Adminstrs. (dir. 1975-77), Jack and Jill Am. (pres. Newton chpt. 1972-74), Manhattanville Club (pres. Boston 1966-68), Delta Sigma Theta, Delta Kappa Gamma (pres. 1988-90). Home: 19 Clifford St Roxbury MA 02119-2120 Office: 330 Stuart St Boston MA 02116-5237 Personal E-mail: ssimm38414@aol.com.

SIMMONS, TERRY L., lawyer; b. Santa Anna, Tex. BBA cum laude, Baylor U., Waco, Tex., 1977; JD, Baylor Law Sch., 1978; LLM, So. Meth. U. Dedman Sch. Law, Dallas, 1984. Bar: Tex. 1978, Colo. 1998, NY 2006. With Thompson & Knight, LLP, Dallas. Contbr. articles to profl. jours.; pub., co-editor: Charitable Gift Planning News. Past bd. trustees Bapt. Child & Family Svcs.; bd. trustees Tex. Christian U. Brite Divinity Sch., Adv. Coun. of Dallas Found., Dallas Women's Found. Planned Giving Adv. Com.; founding pres. North Tex. Chpt. Nat. Com. Planned Giving, 1988—97, nat. bd. dirs. Indpls., 1990—92; pres., bd. mem. Charitable Accord, 1994—; bd. dirs. Am. Coun. Gift Annuities. Recipient David M. Donaldson Disting. Svc. award, Planned Giving Grp. New Eng., 1996, Disting. Svc. award, Nat. Com. Planned Giving, 1996; named Planned Giving Profl. of Yr., Planned Giving Today, 1994, Exec. of Yr., The NonProfit Times, 1997; named a Tex. Super Lawyer, Tex. Monthly, 2004—06; named one of Top 100 Attys. in Am., Worth mag., 2005—06. Mem.: ABA. Office: Thompson & Knight LLP One Arts Plaza 1722 Routh St Ste 1500 Dallas TX 75201-2533 Office Phone: 214-969-1419. Office Fax: 214-880-3373. Business E-Mail: Terry.Simmons@tklaw.com.

SIMMONS, WILLIAM, retired aerospace engineer, research and development company executive; b. Chgo., Apr. 24, 1932; s. Walter Garfield and Edna Dean (Winch) S.; m. Barbara Millet Haury, Oct. 4, 1954; children: Sheryl Lee, Cynthia Jane, Shelly Jean. BA in Physics, Carleton Coll., 1953; MS in Physics, U. Ill., 1955, PhD in Physics, 1960. Mem. tech. staff Space Tech. Labs., Redondo Beach, Calif., 1960-62; sr. rsch. scientist Gen. Tech., Torrance, Calif., 1962, TRW, Redondo Beach, 1962-71, dir. rsch., 1984-89, chief engr. spl. projects assigned to Lawrence Livermore (Calif.) Labs., 1989-92; engring. mgr. Lawrence Livermore Labs., 1972-84, rsch. reviewer, 1985-89; prof. engring. UCLA, 1968-72. Tech. panel mem. U. Calif., Berkeley, 1985; tech. reviewer Dept. Energy, Washington, 1986—, mem. rev. com., 1987—; cons. in field, 1992-2006. Editor, reviewer 2 books, 1982, 83; contbr. numerous articles to profl. jours. Named Disting. Engring. Prof. of Yr. UCLA, 1972, one of Top 100 Innovators in U.S.A, Sci. Digest, 1986; George F. Baker Found. scholar Carleton Coll., 1949-53; Disting. Alum. Engring Svcs. award, engring U. Ill., 2009. Mem. IEEE (sr., life, gen. chmn. symposia 1988, 89, Simon Ramo Major medal 1987), Laser Engring. and Optical Soc., Am. Phys. Soc., Soc. of Photographic and Instrumentation Engrs., U.S. Chess Club, Phi Beta Kappa, Sigma Xi. Republican. Achievements include 11 patents for electro-optics devices. Avocations: chess, ping pong/table tennis, bridge. Office: Sys Solutions 1621 W 25th St Ste 231 San Pedro CA 90732-4300 Office Phone: 310-541-4140. Business E-Mail: wwsimmons@cox.net.

SIMMONS, WILLIAM SKIP BRUCE, JR, science educator; s. William and Polly Simmons; m. Karen L. Webber, Dec. 7, 1990; children: Lane Demos, Trey. PhD, U. Mich., Ann Arbor, 1973. Prof. U. New Orleans, 1972—, Rsch. Prof., 2000—; adj. prof. U. Mich., Ann Arbor, 1985—. Dir. MP2 Rsch. Group, New Orleans, 1980—. Contbr. scientific papers to publs. Bd. dirs. Friends Mineralogy, National City, 2002—. Recipient Charles A. Salotti Earth Sci. Edn. award, Seaman Mineral Mus. Soc., 2005. Fellow: Mineral. Soc. Am. Achievements include patents for apatite-forming systems: methods & products, & products apatite-forming systems. Office: UNO Dept Earth & Environ Sci 2000 Lakeshore Dr New Orleans LA 70148

SIMMONS-WELBURN, JANICE, dean, library director; BA, Bishop Coll.; MA in Am. History, Atlanta U., MLS, 1978. Libr. Bishop Coll., Dallas, Indpls.-Marian County Pub. Libr., NYU, Ga. Inst. Tech.; interim head Med. Scis. Libr. Ind. U.; head Psychology Libr. Princeton U.; head info. and instrnl. svcs. U. Iowa Librs., 1990—95, dir. human resources and ctrl. processing, 1995—2000, dir. ctrl. pub. librs., 2000—03; assoc. dean U. Ariz. Librs., 2003—06; dean univ. libr. Marquette U., Milw., 2006—. Spkr. in field. Contbr. articles to profl. jours. Office: Marquette U Raynor Meml Librs 1355 W Wisconsin Ave Milwaukee WI 53233 Office Phone: 414-288-7214. Business E-Mail: janice.simmons-welburn@marquette.edu.

SIMMS, LOIS AVERETTA, retired secondary school educator; b. Charleston, SC, May 27, 1919; d. Jasper Simeon and Anna Inez (Ferguson) Simms. BA, Johnson C. Smith U., 1941; MA, Howard U., 1954. Cert. English and social studies educator SC. Directive tchr. Avery Normal Inst., Charleston, 1941-42; tchr. English and French Laing H.S., Mt. Pleasant, SC, 1942-44; tchr. English and math. Henry P. Archer Sch., Charleston, 1944-45; tchr. social studies and English Burke H.S., Charleston, 1945-52; tchr. English Avery H.S., Charleston, 1952-54, Burke H.S., Charleston, 1954-73; tchr. English and history Charleston H.S., 1973-76; ret., 1976. Co-advisor Dramatic Club Burke HS, Charleston, 1945—46, trainer sect. chorus, 1945—47, chief advisor Bulldog Yearbook, 1960—61; advisor Crochet Club Avery HS, 1952—54, Charleston HS, 1973—76. Author: Growing Up Presbyterian: Life in Presbyterian Colleges and Churches, 1991, Profiels of African American Females in Low Country of South Carolina, 1992, A Chalk and Chalkboard Career in Carolina, 1995, A History of Zion, Olivet, and Zion-Olivet Churches 1850-1885, 1989; editor: The Scroll newsletter, 1984—94. Sec. exec. bd. YWCA Greater Charleston, 1950; active YWCA, SC Hist. Soc., SC ETV Endowment; chmn. Super Grandchild Contest fundraiser Barber-Scotia Coll., 2007; vol. Avery Rsch. Ctr., 2009. Recipient plaque, Zion-Olivet Presbyn. Ch., 1987, 2007, Plant, 2007, plaque, Staff Scroll, 1990, C.L. Campbell award, Presbyn. Ch., 1988, Educator's award, Moja Arts Festival, 2003, award for Standing on the Shoulders of our Elders, 2008, Fraternity award, Alpha Phi Alpha, 2008, Recognition, Women's Rsch. Project Inc., 2006; named Svc. in Educator, Alpha Phi Alpha; Honoree, Women's Resource Project, Inc., 2007, Centenniel Celebration of YWCA of Greater Charleston, 2007. Mem.: NAACP (Silver life, Trailblazer award 2002), Presbyn. Women's Assn. (chair com. quar. birthday celebration and grad. ceremony 1999—2003), Barber-Scotia Coll. Alumni, Johnson C. Smith U. Alumni Assn., Assn. Study African-Am. Life and History, SC Soc., Avery Inst. Afro-Am. History and Culture (editor The Bull. 1990—2000, cert.), Charleston County Ret. Educators Assn. Unit 2, Pres.'s Club (plaque 1991). Avocations: reading, music, Scrabble, gardening, creative writing. Home: 28 Jasper St Charleston SC 29403-6006

SIMMS, MARIA KAY, small business owner, writer, artist, publisher; b. Princeton, Ill., Nov. 18, 1940; d. Frank B. and Anna (Haurberg) S.; m. Neil F. Michelsen, Oct. 2, 1987 (dec. 1990); children: Shannon Sullivan Stillings, Molly A. Sullivan, Elizabeth Maria Jossick; m. James L. Jossick, July 12, 1998. BFA, Ill. Wesleyan U., 1962. Cert. cons. profl. astrologer; ordained min. L.A. Cmty. Ch. of Religious Sci. Elder priestess Covenant of the Goddess; tchr. art Dundee, Northbrook, Ill., 1962-65; tchr. H.S. art Danbury, Conn., 1975-76; freelance artist, 1966—75; owner Mystic Arts and Cafe Boheme, New Milford, Conn., 1976—79; prin., owner Gallery, Conn., 1976-79; art dir. ACS Pubs., Inc., San Diego, 1987-90; pres. Astro Comm. Svcs., Inc. (formerly ACS Pubs.), San Diego, 1990-98, dir., 1990-2000, acquisitions editor, 1998—2000; owner, mgr. Starcrafts Publishing, Starcrafts LLC, 2008—. Bd. dirs. Omni Techs. Corp. 1998-2007; lectr., cons. in field. Author: Twelve Wings of the Eagle, 1988, Dial Detective, 1989, 2d edit., 2001, Circle of the Cosmic Muse, 1994, Your Magical Child, 1994, Future Signs, 1996, The Witch's Circle, 1996, A Time for Magick, 2001, Moon Tides, Soul Passages, 2004, 2006; contbr. articles to popular mags.; co-author: Millenium: Fears, Fantasies and Facts, 1998, Search for the Christmas Star, 1989; contr. author The Asteroid Ephemeris 1900-2050, 2008. High priestess Cir. of the Cosmic Muse; elder priestess Covenant of the Goddess, 2d officer Calafia Local Coun., 1995-96, pub. info. officer, 1996-98; mem. adv. bd. Kepler Coll., 1998—. Recipient numerous art awards. Mem. Nat. Coun. Geocosmic Rsch. Inc. (dir., pubs. dir. 1981-92, editor jour. 1984-92, chmn. bd. 1999-2004, mem. advt. bd. 2005—, chair adv. bd., 2005-06), Am. Fedn. Astrologers, Internat. Soc. Astrol. Rsch., New Age Pubs. Assn., Assn. for Profl. Astrologers Internat., Seacoast Art Assn., Alpha Gamma Delta. Office Phone: 603-734-4300. Personal E-mail: maria@starcraftspublishing.com.

SIMOKAITIS, FRANK JOSEPH, military officer, lawyer; b. St. Louis, Dec. 12, 1922; s. Frank and Constance (Ladish) S.; m. Mary Jane Feeny; children: Peggy, Mary, Frank (dec.). Student, Washington U., St. Louis, 1945-47; LL.B., St. Louis U., 1950, JD, 1970. Bar: U.S. Supreme Ct. U.S 1950, Mo. 1950, also other fed. cts. 1950. Commd. 2d lt. USAAF, 1943; advanced through grades to maj. gen. USAF, 1973; plans and ops. officer Hdqrs. Pacific Air Force, 1960-63; staff officer Hdqrs. USAF, Washington, 1963-69, exec. asst. to sec. air force, 1969-73; comdt. Air Force Inst. Tech., 1973-78, Def. Inst. Security Assistance Mgmt.; dir. Dept. Def. affairs Hdqrs. NASA, Washington, 1978-83, cons., 1983—. Bd. dirs. Dayton chpt. ARC, Greater Miami chpt., arbitrator Better Bus. Bur. Decorated D.S.M. with oak leaf cluster, Legion of Merit, Air medal with 4 oak leaf clusters, Air Force Commendation medal, Alumni award, St. Louis U. Mem. Miami Air Force Assn. (bd. dirs.), Navy League (v.p. U.S. Miami coun.), Univ. Club of Washington D.C., Patrick AFB Officers Club. Home: 1594 Frontier Dr Melbourne FL 32940

SIMON, ADAM F., political science professor; s. David Adam and Shirley Simon; m. Stephanie Denmark; children: David Denmark, Helena Denmark. PhD, U. Calif., LA, 1997. Lectr. polit. sci. Yale U., New Haven, 2001—08. Author: (book) The Winning Message: Candidate Behavior, Campaign Discourse and Democracy, Mass Informed Consent: Evidence on Improving Democracy with Polls and New Media. Grad. fellow, NSF, 1992—95. Mem.: Am. Assn. Pub. Opinion Rsch., Internat. Communcation Assn., Am. Polit. Sci. Assn.

SIMON, ALBERT, retired physicist, engineer, educator; b. NYC, Dec. 27, 1924; s. Emanuel D. and Sarah (Leitner) S.; m. Harriet E. Rubinstein, Aug. 17, 1947 (dec. June 1970); children: Richard, Janet, David; m. Rita Shiffman, June 11, 1972. BS, CCNY, 1947; PhD, U. Rochester, 1950. Registered profl. engr., N.Y. State. Physicist Oak Ridge Nat. Lab., 1950-54, assoc. dir. neutron physics divsn., 1954-61; head plasma physics divsn. Gen. Atomic Co., San Diego, 1961-66; prof. dept. mech. engring. U. Rochester, NY, 1966—2005, prof. physics, 1968—2005; prof. emeritus, 2005; chmn. dept. mech. engring. U. Rochester, 1977-84. Mem. Inst. for Advanced Study, Princeton, 1974-75; sr. vis. fellow U.K. Sci. Rsch. Coun., Oxford U., 1975 Author: An Introduction to Thermonuclear Research, 1959; contbr. to: Ency. Americana, 1964, 74; editor Advances in Plasma Physics, 1967—. With USN, 1944—46. Recipient Univ. Mentor award, 1988-89; John Simon Guggenheim fellow, 1964-65. Fellow Am. Phys. Soc. (chmn. plasma physics divsn. 1963-64); mem. ASME, ASEE (chmn. nuc. engring. divsn. 1985-86). Home: 7340 Amberly Ln #309 Delray Beach FL 33446 Office Phone: 585-275-4431. Business E-Mail: simo@me.rochester.edu.

SIMON, BERNECE KERN, retired social worker; b. Denver, Nov. 27, 1914; d. Maurice Meyer and Jennie (Bloch) Kern; m. Marvin L. Simon, Feb. 26, 1939 (dec.); 1 child, Anne Elizabeth. BA, U. Chgo., 1936, MA, 1942. Social worker Jewish Children's Bur. Chgo., 1938-40, U. Chgo. Hosps. and Clinics, 1940-44; mem. faculty U. Chgo., 1944-81, instr., 1944-48, asst. prof., 1948-60, prof. social casework, 1960—81, prof. emeritus, 1981—, Samuel Deutsch prof. Sch. Social Service Adminstrn., 1960—. Mem. bd. editors 17th Edit. Ency. Social Work, 1975—77, Social Svc. Rev., 1975—99, Social Work, 1978—82; book rev. editor: Social Work, 1982—87, cons. editor: Jour. Social Work Edn.; contbr. articles to profl. jours., chapters to books. Mem.: NASW, Nat. Acads. Practice Social Work, Acad. Cert. Social Workers, Coun. Social Work Edn. (mem. nat. bd. dirs., sec. 1972—74). Home Phone: 773-753-4603.

SIMON, CARMON SERENA, biology educator; b. Knoxville, Tenn., Apr. 7, 1976; d. David and Barbara Long; m. Duane Steven Simon, July 22, 2006; 1 child, Lydia Angelle. BS in Biology, U. Ala., Tuscaloosa, 1999. Cert. Tchg. La. Dept Edn., 2008. Husbandry staff aquarist Ripley's Aquarium Smokies, Gatlinburg, Tenn., 2000—04; biology tchr. Lafayette HS, 2006—. Singer: (performance) Chorale Acadienne. Mem.: NABT. Office: Lafayette HS 3000 W Congress Rd Lafayette LA 70506

SIMON, CLIFF, design educator; b. The Bronx, NY, Apr. 6, 1951; s. Murray and Lillian Simon; life ptnr. Julian Maxie Hazlett. BA, Queens Coll., NY, 1974; MFA, U. Tex., Austin, 2002. Graphic designer United Jewish Appeal, NYC, 1984—93; cake designer Cakes Cliff, NYC, Santa Fe, Birmingham, 1984—2008; assoc. prof. UAB, Ala., 2002—08; pvt. practice. Author: (book) They Ate My Cake; cake designer (wedding cake) Diana Ross' Wedding Cake, set designer (scenic design) Present Laughter (Austin Critics award Best Scenic Design, 2007), cake designer (painted cakes) Cakes designed for Liberace, Madonna, James Taylor, Willie Nelson, Malcolm Forbes, etc. Nat. Faculty award, Kennedy Ctr., 2006. Office: UAB 1200 10th Ave S ASC 255 Birmingham AL 35294 Personal E-mail: cliffcakes@earthlink.net. Business E-Mail: csimon@uab.edu.

SIMON, DAVID, real estate company officer; BS, Ind. U.; MBA, Columbia U. Assoc. First Boston Corp., NYC; CFO, COO Melvin Simon & Assocs., Inc.; v.p. Wasserstein Perella & Co., NYC, til 1990; pres., CEO Simon Property Group, 1990-96, CEO, 1996—. 2d. vice-chmn. Nat. Assn. Real Estate Investment Trusts, Inc.; trustee Internat. Coun. Shopping Ctrs.; dir. 1st Health Corp. Mem. urban Land Inst. Office: Simon Property Group Inc 115 W Washington St Ste 1465 Indianapolis IN 46204-3464

SIMON, DAVID FREDERICK, lawyer; b. El Paso, Tex., Apr. 14, 1953; s. Maurice and Susan S.; m. Deborah H., Mar. 1, 1980; children: Alison, Joshua, Rebecca, Nathaniel. BS magna cum laude, U. Buffalo, 1974; JD cum laude, U. Pa., 1977. Bar: Pa. 1977, N.J. 1978. Law clk. to presiding judge Phila. Ct. Common Pleas, 1977-79; assoc. Wolf, Block, Schorr & Solis-Cohen, Phila., 1979-85, ptnr., 1985—90; sr. v.p., gen. counsel US Healthcare Inc., Blue Bell, 1990—2006; chief legal officer Aetna US Healthcare, Inc., Hartford, 1996—2000; chief counsel Pa. Ins. Dept., Harrisburg, 2001—03; sr. v.p., gen. coun. Jefferson Health Sys., Inc., Radnor, Pa., 2003—; gen. counsel Mountain Laurel Risk Retention Group, Inc., 2003—09. Adv. coun. Pa. Dept. Conservation and Natural Resources, 1996-97, Pa. MCare Commn., 2006; bd. mgrs. U. Pa. Law Sch. Alumni, 1997-2003; dean's adv. coun. SUNY Buffalo Sch. Mgmt., 1999—, chmn., 2003-2005. Author: Computer Law Handbook, Philadelphia Court of Common Pleas Civil Practice Manual. Bd. dirs. Phila. Orchestra Assn., 2007—, chair audit com., 2008—09. Recipient Alumni award for svc., U. Buffalo Sch. Management, 2007. Mem. Phila. Bar Assn. (exec. com. young lawyers sect. 1983-85, chmn. computer law com. 1984-85), Pa. Bar Assn. (chmn. in-house counsel com. 1993-94), Pa. Bar Inst. (bd. dirs. 1992-96). Avocations: photography, electronics, music. Home: PO Box 551 Gwynedd Valley PA 19437-0551 Office: Jefferson Health Sys Inc 259 N Radnor-Chester Rd Radnor PA 19087-5288 Home Phone: 215-646-6528; Office Phone: 610-225-6298. Business E-Mail: simond@jhsmail.org.

SIMON, DAVID L., art historian; s. Abe M. and Thelma D. Simon; m. Sonia Chalif Simon, June 11, 1971; 1 child, David L. Jr. BA, Boston U., 1969, MA, 1971; PhD, U. London, 1977. Instr. Boston U., 1973—74; from asst. to assoc. prof. SUNY, Cortland, 1974—81; prof. Colby Coll., Waterville, Maine, 1981—. Author: La Condesa Dona Sancha, 1995; editor: (jour.) Gesta, 1998; co-author: Janson's History of Art, 2006. Recipient award, Am. Coun. Learned Societies, 1978, Basset Tchg. award, Colby Coll., 2005;, Met. Mus. Art fellow, 1980—81. Mem.: Internat. Ctr. Medieval Art, Coll. Art Assn. Office: Colby Coll 5640 Mayflower Hill Waterville ME 04901 Business E-Mail: dlsimon@colby.edu.

SIMON, DOLORES DALY, copy editor; b. San Francisco, Nov. 18, 1928; d. Francis Edward and Jeannette (Cooke) Daly; m. Sidney Blair Simon, Aug. 24, 1952 (div. Nov. 1955); children: John Roderick, Douglas Brian. BA in Journalism, Pa. State U., 1950. County editor Centre Daily Times, State College, Pa., 1950-51; soc. editor Bradford (Pa.) Era, 1951-52; copy editor Harper & Bros., Pubs., NYC, 1955-60; copy chief Harper & Row, Pubs., NYC, 1960-88; freelance editor, copy editor Warwick, NY, 1988—. Co-author: Recipes into Type, 1993 (Best Food Reference 1994). Mem. James Beard Found., Phi Mu., Albert Wisner Pub. Libr. (bd. govs.), Warwick Hist. Soc. (bd. dirs.). Democrat. Avocation: book collecting. Office: Editl Svcs 63 Blooms Corners Rd Warwick NY 10990-2403 Office Phone: 845-986-4442.

SIMON, DONALD JOHN, financial planner, theta healer, small business owner; b. Chgo., July 16, 1947; s. Nicholas J. and Alice R. (Vaughn) S.; 1 child, Joshua K. BSBA, Oglethorpe U., 1969. CFP, CLU, ChFC. Sales rep. D. W. Shaw, Inc., Berlin, NJ, 1969-74; owner Simon Fin. Co., Vero Beach, Fla., 1975—. Avocations: music, bicycling, boating.

SIMON, ECKEHARD (PETER), foreign language educator; b. Schneidemühl, Germany, Jan. 5, 1939; came to U.S., 1955, naturalized, 1960; s. Herbert and Doris (Keiler) S.; m. Eileen Higginbottom, Dec. 19, 1959; children: Anders, Conrad (dec.), Matthew, Frederick. AB, Columbia U., 1960; A.M., Harvard U., 1961, PhD, 1964. Instr., German Harvard U., Cambridge, Mass., 1964-65, asst. prof., 1965-69, assoc. prof., 1969-71, prof., 1971—, Victor S. Thomas prof. Germanic langs. and lit., 1996—2007, Victor S. Thomas rsch. prof. German, 2007—, head tutor and lang. coordinator, 1965-76, chmn. dept. German, 1976—82, 1996—99, chmn. com. on medieval studies, 1992—95, 2001—02. Author: Neidhart von Reuental: Geschichte der Forschung und Bibliographie, 1968, Neidhart von Reuental, 1975, The Türkenkalender (1454) Attributed to Gutenberg and the Strasbourg Lunation Tracts, 1988, Die Anfänge des weltlichen deutschen Schaupiels, 1370-1530, 2003; editor: The Theatre of Medieval Europe, New Research in Early Drama, 1991; mem. editl. bd.: Dictionary of the Middle Ages, 1982-89; contbr. articles to profl. jours. Woodrow Wilson fellow, 1960-61, NEH Younger Scholar fellow, 1968-69, Rsch fellow, 1977-78, Guggenheim fellow, 1968-69, Fulbright fellow U. Cologne, 1983, Sr. Exchange fellow Dumbarton Oaks, Washington, 2001. Mem. MLA, Am. Assn. Tchrs. German, Medieval Acad. Am. (asst. editor Speculum 1981-94, book review editor 1994-2000). Home: 11 Hayes Ave Lexington MA 02420-3521 Home Phone: 781-862-5326; Office Phone: 617-496-9359. Business E-Mail: simon2@fas.harvard.edu.

SIMON, ERIC JACOB, neuroscientist, educator; b. Wiesbaden, Germany, June 2, 1924; came to U.S., 1938, naturalized, 1945; s. Joseph and Paula (Meyer) S.; m. Irene M. Ronis, Aug. 9, 1947; children: Martin A., Faye Ruth, Lawrence D. BS, Case Inst. Tech., Cleve., 1944; MS, U. Chgo., 1947, PhD, 1951; doctorate (hon.), U. René Descartes Sorbonne, Paris, 1982. Postdoctoral trainee in biochemistry Columbia U. Coll. Physicians and Surgeons, 1951-53; lectr. in chemistry CCNY, 1952-59; research assoc. Cornell U. Med. Coll., 1953-59; asst. prof. medicine NYU Med. Center, 1959-64, assoc. prof. exptl. medicine, 1964-72, prof. exptl. medicine, 1972-80, prof. psychiatry and pharmacology, 1980—. Harry Williams Meml. lectr. Dept. Pharmacology Emory U., Atlanta, 1986; mem. initial rev. com. Nat. Inst. Drug Abuse, 1976-80, chmn. 1979-80, mem. Nat. Adv. Coun. on Drug Abuse, 1989-92; Sterling-Winthrop lectr. Albany Med. Coll., 1977; vis. prof. Coll. de France, Paris, 1990; vis. lectr. Shanghai and Beijing, 1985. Trustee Teaneck (N.J.) Bd. Edn., 1975-79. Served with U.S. Army, 1944-46. Recipient Rsch. Pace Setter award Nat. Inst. Drug Abuse, 1977, Louis and Bert Freedman Found. award N.Y. Acad. Scis., 1980, Nathan B. Eddy Meml. award Coll. on Problems of Drug Dependence, Lexington, Ky., 1983, Alumni Profl. Achievement award U. Chgo., 1986, Founder's Lectr. award Internat. NArcotics Rsch. Conf., 1999; Health Rsch. Coun. NYC career scientist, 1959-75. Fellow AAAS, N.Y. Acad. Scis. (trustee 1986-89); mem. Am. Soc. Biol. Chemists, Am. Soc. Neurochemistry, Am. Soc. Pharmacology, Internat. Soc. Neurochemistry, Am. Chem. Soc., Sigma Xi. Lodges: B'nai B'rith. Research, publs. on opiate receptors, endorphins, biochemistry of analgesic action, vitamin E metabolism, acyl-coenzyme A synthesis. Office: 550 1st Ave New York NY 10016-6402 Home: 245 Prospect Ave Apt 6A Hackensack NJ 07601-2571 Office Phone: 212-263-5637. Business E-Mail: eric.simon@nyu.edu.

SIMON, EVELYN, lawyer; b. NYC, May 13, 1943; d. Joseph and Adele (Holzschlag) Berkman; m. Fredrick Simon, Aug. 18, 1963; children: Amy Jocelyn, Marcie Ann. AB in Physics, Barnard Coll., 1963; MS in Physics, U. Pitts., 1964; JD, Wayne State U., 1978; LLB, Monash U., Melbourne, Australia, 1980. Bar: Mich. 1980, Victoria (Australia) 1981. Supr. engring. Chrysler Corp., Detroit, 1964-72; edn. and profl. mgr. Engring. Soc. Detroit, 1972-78; solicitor Arthur Robinson & Co., Melbourne, 1980-81; sr. atty. Ford Motor Co., Detroit, 1981-89; assoc. gen. counsel Sheller-Globe Corp., Detroit, 1989-90; v.p. planning, gen. counsel United Techs. Automotive Inc., Dearborn, Mich., 1991-94, v.p. bus. devel. and legal affairs, 1995-96, v.p. Asian bus. devel., 1997-98; pvt. practice, 1999—. Cons. internat. bus. devel., 1998—. Mem.: Mich. Bar Assn. Office: 1787 Alexander Dr Bloomfield Hills MI 48302-1204 Home Phone: 248-855-5664; Office Phone: 248-539-0969. E-mail: evelynsimon@prodigy.net.

SIMON, GARY LEONARD, internist, educator; b. Bklyn., Dec. 18, 1946; s. Bernard and Dorothy (Ligeti) Simon; m. Vicki Thiessen, Aug. 29, 1970; children: Jason, Jessica. BS, U. Md., 1968, MD, 1975; PhD, U. Wis., 1972. Diplomate Am. Bd. Internal Medicine, Am. Bd. Infectious Diseases. Resident in internal medicine U. Md. Hosp., Balt., 1975—78; fellow infectious diseases Tufts-New Eng. Med. Ctr., Boston, 1978—80; asst. prof. dept. medicine George Washington U., Washington, 1980-84, assoc. prof., 1984-89, assoc. chmn. medicine, 1984-97, prof., 1989—, dir. divsn. infectious diseases, 1993—, vice chmn. medicine, 1997—, Walter G. Ross Prof. Medicine, 2006. Cons. on AIDS Assn. Am. Med. Coll., Washington, 1990—. Contbr. articles to profl. jours. Recipient Outstanding Attending Physician award, George Washington U., 1981, Disting. Rschr. award, 2002, Oscar and Shoshana Trachtenburg award, 2005; named Walter G. Ross Prof. in Clinical Rsch., 2006; named one of Best Doctors in Am., 2004—. Master: ACP (Laureate award 2000); fellow: Infectious Disease Soc.; mem.: Internat. AIDS Soc., Assn. Subspecialty Profs., Am. Soc. Microbiology, Alpha Omega Alpha. Office: George Washington U 2150 Pennsylvania Ave NW Washington DC 20037-3201 Home Phone: 301-983-2873; Office Phone: 202-741-2234. Business E-Mail: gsimon@mfa.gwu.edu.

SIMON, GREGORY E., psychiatrist, researcher; MD, U. N.C., 1982; MPH, U. Wash., 1990. Diplomate Am. Bd. Internal Medicine 1985, Am. Bd. Adult Psychiatry 1990. Scientific investigator Ctr. for Health

Studies, Group Health Coop., Seattle, 1990—2000, staff psychiatrist, 1990—, sr. scientific investigator Seattle, 2000—; rsch. prof. psychiatry and behavioral sciences U. Wash., Seattle, 2005—. Named one of Best Doctors, Seattle Met. mag., 2006, Puget Sound Consumers' Checkbook, 2007. Mem.: Am. Psychiatric Assn. (Eli Lilly "Welcome Back" award 2002, sr. scholar health services rsch. award 2002), Depression and Bipolar Support Alliance (sci. adv. bd., Gerald R. Klerman sr. investigator award 2005). Office: Group Health Coop 1730 MInor Ave #1600 Seattle WA 98112 Business E-Mail: simon.g@ghc.org.*

SIMON, HAROLD, radiologist; b. Trenton, NJ, May 13, 1930; s. John and Rae B. Simon; m. Jane L. Ludwig, Feb. 25, 1956; children: Steven Gregg, John Gregory. MD, Duke U., Durham, NC, 1955. Diplomate Am. Bd. Radiology, Am. Bd. Nuc. Medicine. Intern U.S. Naval Hosp., Chelsea, Mass., 1955-56; resident in radiology Mass. Gen. Hosp., Boston, 1958-61, Oak Ridge Inst. Nuc. Medicine, 1959; instr. radiology Med. Sch., Tufts U., Boston, 1961-63, clin. asst. prof., 1965, assoc. clin. prof., 1971-77, clin. prof., 1977-98; pvt. practice Newton Lower Falls, Mass., 1963-95; mem. staff Newton Wellesley Hosp., Mass., assoc. chief radiology, 1977—, radiologist-in-chief, 1987-95; cons. VA Med. Sys., 1997—. Dir. Sch. Nuc. Med. Tech.; bd. dirs., mem. CRC com., mem. audit com. Grove Bank, chmn. audit com., 1995—96; bd. dirs., treas. Newell Physicians, Inc., 1986—93; mem. staff Intracoastal Med. Sys., West Palm Beach, Fla., 1997—2001; bd. overseers Newell Health Corp.; cons. VA Hosp., Boston, 1999—, Charitas Norwood Hosp., Mass., 1998—2002, Beth Israel Deaconess Hosp., 2007. Contbr. articles to profl. jours. With USNR, 1955—58, med. officer USN, 1956—58 USNR, 1956—58. Fellow: Am. Coll. Radiology; mem.: Palm Beach Civic Assn. (asst. chmn. CPHC 2009), CPAC Jewish Fedn., Palm Beach (sub com. chmn. 2007—09), Mass. Radiology Soc., Mass. Med. Soc. (mem. ins. com. 1992—95), New Eng. Roentgen Ray Soc., Am. Roentgen Ray Soc., Radiol. Soc. N.Am., Banyon Country Club, Belmont Country Club, Pinebrook Country Club (pres. 1982—85), Phi Beta Kappa, Phi Eta Sigma. Home: 252 Atlantic Ave Palm Beach FL 33480-3709

SIMON, HERBERT, real estate developer, professional sports team owner; b. Bklyn., Oct. 23, 1934; s. Max and Mae Simon; m. Bui Simon; children: Jennifer, Stephen, Sarah, Rachel, Asher, Sean. Grad., CCNY. With Albert Frankel Co., Indpls., 1959; co-founder Melvin Simon and Assocs., Inc., Indpls., 1959—; co-owner Pacers Sports and Entertainment, Indpls., 1983—, chmn., CEO, 2008—; went pub. and became Simon Property Group, 1993; CEO Simon Property Group, Inc., 1993—95; merged with DeBartolo Realty Corp. and became Simon DeBartolo Group, 1996; name changed back to Simon Property Group, 1998; co-chmn. bd. Simon Property Group, Inc., 1995—. Named one of Forbes' Richest Ams., 2006. Office: Ind Pacers 125 S Pennsylvania St Indianapolis IN 46204 also: Simon Property Group Inc 225 W Washington St Indianapolis IN 46204*

SIMON, HORST D., computer scientist; b. Aug. 8, 1953; married; 2 children. Diploma in Math., Technische U. Berlin, 1978; PhD, U. Calif., 1982. Asst. prof. SUNY, Stony Brook, NY, 1982—83; with Boeing Computer Svcs., 1983—89, coord. engring. and tech. applications divsn., 1983—86, mgr. computational math. group, 1986—87; mgr. rsch. dept. computer sci. corp. NASA Ames Rsch. Ctr., Moffett Field, Calif., 1989—94; rsch. market devel. mgr. advanced sys. divsn. Silicon Graphics, 1994—96; dir. Nat. Energy Rsch. Sci. Computing Ctr. Lawrence Berkeley Nat. Libr., 1996—, dir. Computational Rsch. Divsn., 2002—, assoc. lab. dir. computing scis., 2004—. Spkr. in field; mem. indsl. adv. bd. dept. computer sci. U. Calif., Davis; mem. internat. adv. panel Inst. HPC, Singapore. Editor: (books) Scientific Applications of the Connection Machine, 1989, Parallel Computational Fluid Dynamics, 1992, Parallel Processing for Scientific Computing, 1995, Solving Irregularly Structured Problems in Parallel, 1998; contbr. articles to profl. jours., chapters to books; mng. editor: Internat. Jour. High Speed Computing, 1989—97, mem. editl. bd.: SIAM Jour. Sci. and Statistical Computing, 1989—95, Jour. Sci. Programming, NHSE Review, Advances in Engineering Software (formerly Computing Systems Engineering), others. Recipient (with NAS Parallel Benchmarks Team) H. Julian Allen award, 1995, (with group from Cray and Boeing) Gordon Bell Prize, 1988. Office: NERSC Divn Dir Berkeley Lab MS 50B-4230 One Cyclotron Rd Berkeley CA 94720-8150 Office Phone: 510-486-7377. Office Fax: 510-486-4300. E-mail: hdsimon@lbl.gov.

SIMON, H(UEY) PAUL, lawyer; b. Lafayette, La., Oct. 19, 1923; s. Jules and Ida (Rogére) S.; m. Carolyn Perkins, Aug. 6, 1949 (dec. Dec. 1999); 1 child, John Clark. BS, U. Southwestern La., 1943; JD, Tulane U., 1947. CPA La., 1947; bar: La. 1947. Pvt. practice, New Orleans, 1947—; asst. prof. advanced acctg. and taxation U. Southwestern La., 1944-45; staff acct. Haskins & Sells (now Deloitte & Touche), New Orleans, 1945-53, prin., 1953-57; ptnr. Deutsch, Kerrigan & Stiles, 1957-79; sr. founding ptnr. Simon, Peragine, Smith & Redfearn, 1979—. Mem. New Orleans Bd. Trade. Author: Community Property and Liability for Funeral Expenses of Deceased Spouse, 1946, Income Tax Deductibility of Attorney's Fees in Action in Boundary, 1946, Fair Labor Standards Act and Employee's Waiver of Liquidated Damages, 1946, Louisiana Income Tax Law, 1956, Changes Effected by the Louisiana Trust Code, 1965, Gifts to Minors and the Parent's Obligation of Support, 1968; co-author: Deductions—Business or Hobby, 1975, Role of Attorney in IRS Tax Return Examination, 1978; assoc. editor: The Louisiana CPA, 1956-60; mem. bd. editors Tulane Law Rev., 1945-46, adv. bd. editors, 1992—; estates, gifts and trusts editor The Tax Times, 1986-87. Bd. dirs., mem. fin. com. World Trade Ctr., 1985-86; mem. New Orleans Met. Crime Commn., Coun. for a Better La., New Orleans Met. Area Com., Bur. Govtl. Rsch., Pub. Affairs Rsch. Coun.; co-chmn. NYU Tax Conf., New Orleans, 1976; mem. dean's coun. Tulane U. Law Sch. Named one of Best Lawyers in Am., 1985—. Fellow Am. Coll. Tax Counsel; mem. ABA (com. ct. procedure tax sect. 1958—), AICPA, La. Bar Assn. (com. on legis. and adminstrv. practice 1966-70, bd. cert. tax atty.), New Orleans Bar Assn., Internat. Bar Assn. (com. on securities issues and trading 1970-88), Am. Judicature Soc., Soc. La. CPAs, New Orleans Assn. Notaries, Tulane U. Alumni Assn., New Orleans C. of C. (coun. 1952-66), Tulane Tax Inst. (program com. 1960-96, emeritus 1997--), Internat. House (bd. dirs. 1976-79, 82-85), Internat. Platform Assn., City Energy Club, Press Club, New Orleans Country Club, Phi Delta Phi (past pres. New Orleans chpt.), Sigma Pi Alpha. Roman Catholic. Achievements include becoming the 11th attorney-CPA in Louisiana history. Office: 30th Fl Energy Ctr New Orleans LA 70163 Mailing: PO Box 2759 Covington LA 70434 Home: 323 Kirkwood Dr Covington LA 70433 Office Phone: 504-258-9177. Personal E-mail: hpsimon@aol.com. Business E-Mail: hpsimon@spsr-law.com. *Words to live by: developing and maintaining consistency and constancy in feeling and showing genuine respect towards others, nourish and stimulate an individual to day by day become a better person. Whether alone or in the presence of others, one who abides by the guidance and rules he would advocate to others invariably finds the greatest reward of all--true respect for one's self.*

SIMON, J. STEPHEN, retired oil industry executive; b. Columbia, Mo., 1943; s. B.D. and Joan Simon; m. Susan Simon; 3 children. BS in Civil Engring., Duke U., 1965; MBA, Northwestern U., Evanston, Ill., 1967. With Exxon USA, 1967, mgr. refinery Baton Rouge; supply and transp. mgr. Esso Europe, London, Esso USA; exec. asst. to the pres. Exxon Corp.; gen. mgr. Esso Caribbean and Ctrl. Am., Coral Gables, Fla.; pres. Esso Italiana, Rome; exec. v.p. Exxon Co. Internat., 1997—99; pres. ExxonMobil Refining and Supply Co., 1999—2004; v.p. ExxonMobil Corp., 1999—2004, sr. v.p., 2004—08. Bd. dirs. ExxonMobil Corp., 2006—08, Am. Petroleum Inst.; mem. Kellogg adv. bd. Northwestern U.; bd. visitors, pres. coun. Duke U. Sch. Engring.; past bd. dir. NAM. Vol. United Way; mem. governance com. Nat. Action Council for Minorities in Engring.; bd. dir. US-China Bus. Council. Served in US Army. Mem.: Sigma Chi Fraternity, Phi Beta Kappa Soc.

SIMON, JACOB MATTHEW, lawyer; b. Pitts., June 22, 1979; s. J. Matthew and Janet DiPasquale Simon. BA, Allegheny Coll., Meadville, Pa., 2001; M in Pub. and Internat. Affairs, U. Pitts., 2005, JD, 2005. Bar: Pa. 2006. Office asst. Western Pa. Sch. for Blind Children, Pitts., 1995—2004; rschr. Goldberg, Persky and White, PC, Pitts., 2004; project asst. Eckert, Seamans, Cherin and Mellot LLC (Choice Counsel, Inc.), Pitts., 2005; law clk. and assoc. Morton B. DeBroff and Assoc., PC, Pitts., 2005—06; assoc. Lieber and Hammer, PC, Pitts., 2006—. Legal extern Edn. Law Ctr. Pa., Pitts., 2002; project intern Pitts. Coun. for Internat. Visitors, 2003; mem. U. Pitts. Niagara Internat. Moot Ct. Team, 2005. Mem. Am. Civil Liberties Union, Pitts., 2001—, Young Dem. Allegheny County, Pitts., 2004—, World Affairs Coun. Pitts., 2004—. Mem.: ABA, U. Pitts. Law Sch. Alumni Assn., U. Pitts. Alumni Assn., Citizens Global Solutions, Pa. Bar Assn., Allegheny County Bar Assn. Home: 114 Yorkshire Dr Pittsburgh PA 15208 Office: Lieber and Hammer PC 5528 Walnut St 2d Flr Pittsburgh PA 15232 Office Phone: 412-687-2231 ext. 12. Business E-Mail: jacob.simon@worldnet.att.net.

SIMON, JACQUELINE ALBERT, political scientist, writer; d. Louis and Rose (Axelroad) Albert; m. Pierre Simon; children: Lisette, Orville. BA cum laude, NYU, MA, 1972, PhD, 1977. Adj. assoc. prof. Southampton Coll., 1977-79; mng. editor Point of Contact, NYC, 1975-76; assoc. editor, US bur. chief Politique Internationale, Paris, 1979—. Sr. fellow Inst. French Studies, NYU, 1980—, adj. assoc. prof., 1982-85, assoc. prof. govt., 1982-83; frequent appearances French TV and radio. Author: A Century of Artists' Letters: Delacroix to Leger, 2004; contbg. editor: Harper's mag., 1984—92; contbr. numerous articles to French mag., revs., books on internat. affairs. Bd. dirs. Fresh Air Fund, 1984—, Overseas Press Club Found. Mem. Overseas Press Club of Am. (bd. dirs., treas. 2000-04, sec. 2006-08, treas., 2008-, Press Club Found. (overseas bd.), Phi Beta Kappa. Home: 988 5th Ave New York NY 10675 Personal E-mail: jasimon@verizon.net.

SIMON, J(ENNINGS) RICHARD, psychologist, educator; s. Leonard Robert and Sophie Sip (Cohn); m. Betty Ethel Pearl, Aug. 26, 1954; children: Alissa, Susan. BBA, U. Wis., 1951, MS, 1953, PhD, 1955. Fulbright rsch. fellow U. Cambridge, Eng., 1955-56; assoc. rsch. scientist Am. Inst. Rsch., Pitts., 1956-57; from asst. prof. to prof. psychology, indsl. engring. U. Iowa, Iowa City, 1957-99, prof. emeritus, 1999—. Vis. prof. U. Sheffield, Eng., 1971-72, U. Warwick, Eng., 1981; hon. rsch. fellow Univ. Coll. London, 1987, 93; vis. prof. Birkbeck Coll., U. London, 1997-99; reviewer for profl. jours., govt. agys. Cons. editor: Jour. Exptl. Psychology, 1970-74, Jour. Exptl. Psychology: Human Learning and Memory, 1975, Jour. Motor Behavior, 1976-88; contbr. articles to profl. jours. NIH fellow, 1971. Fellow APA, Assn. Psychol. Sci. (charter); mem. Inst. Indsl. Engrs., Am. Soc. Engring. Edn., Human Factors Soc., Psychonomic Soc., Midwestern Psychol. Assn., Sigma Xi, Phi Beta Kappa, Phi Kappa Phi, Phi Eta Sigma. Achievements include discovery of Simon effect; research in human info. processing and performance changes accompanying aging. Office: Univ Iowa Dept Psychology Seashore Hall Iowa City IA 52242 E-mail: j-simon@uiowa.edu.

SIMON, JIMMY LOUIS, pediatrician, educator; b. San Francisco, Dec. 27, 1930; s. Sylvain L. and Hilda H. (Netter) S.; m. Marilyn S. Wachter, June 21, 1953; children: Kent, Nancy. AB, U. Calif.-Berkeley, 1952; MD, U. Calif.-Berkeley, San Francisco, 1955. Diplomate Am. Bd. Pediats. Intern U. Calif., San Francisco, 1955-56; resident Grace-New Haven Hosp., 1956-57; sr. asst. resident Boston Children's Hosp., 1957-58; instr., asst. prof. pediats. U. Okla., Oklahoma City, 1960-64; asso. prof. U. Tex. Med. Br., Galveston, 1966-72, prof. pediatrics, 1972-74; prof., chmn. pediats. Bowman Gray Sch. Medicine, Wake Forest U., Winston-Salem, NC, 1974-96; prof., chmn. emeritus Wake Forest U. Sch. Medicine, Winston-Salem, NC, 1996—. With USAF, 1958-60. Mem. Am. Pediat. Soc., Am. Acad. Pediats., Am. Bd. Pediats., Ambulatory Pediat. Assn., Alpha Omega Alpha. Office: Wake Forest U Sch Medicine Dept Pediatrics Medical Center Blvd Winston Salem NC 27157-0001

SIMON, JOHN ANDREW, United States Ambassador to the African Union; b. 1968; m. Laura Jane Simon; 4 children. BA, Princeton U.; M in Pub. Policy, Harvard U. Various positions including dep. dir. rsch. and devel. Exec. Office Adminstrn. Commonwealth of Mass.; dir. bus. fin. and strategic planning Harvard Pilgrim Health Care; dep. asst. adminstr. US Agy. Internat. Devel. (USAID), 2002—03; dir. devel. issues NSC, 2003—05, spl. asst. to Pres., sr. dir. for relief, stabilization and devel., 2005—06; exec. v.p. Overseas Pvt. Investment Corp. (OPIC), 2006—08; US amb. to Africa Union US Dept. State, 2008—. Office: African Union Hdqs Roosvelt St Old Airport Area W21K19 Addis Ababa Ethiopia*

SIMON, JOHN BERN, lawyer; b. Cleve., Aug. 8, 1942; s. Seymour Frank and Roslyn (Schultz) S.; children: Lindsey Helaine Ciral, Douglas Banning. BS, U. Wis., 1964; JD, DePaul U., 1967. Bar: Ill. 1967. Asst. US atty. US Dept. Justice, Chgo., 1967-70, dep. chief civil divsn., 1970-71, chief civil divsn., 1971-74; spl. counsel to dir. Ill. Dept. Pub. Aid, Chgo., 1974-75; legal cons. to Commn. on Rev. of Nat. Policy Toward Gambling, Chgo., 1975-76; ptnr. Friedman & Koven, 1975-85, mem. exec. com., 1983-85; ptnr. Jenner & Block LLP, 1986—; justice US Supreme Ct. Spl. cons. to adminstr. DEA Dept. Justice, 1976-77; special counsel to Gov.'s Revenue Study Commn. on Legalized Gambling, 1977-78; spl. counsel Ill. Racing Bd., 1979-80; lectr. tng. seminars and confs.; instr. U.S. Atty. Gen.'s Advocacy Inst., Washington, 1974; lectr. Nat. Conf. Organized Crime, Washington, 1975, Dade County Inst. Organized Crime, Ft. Lauderdale, Fla., 1976; faculty Cornell Inst. Organized Crime, Ithaca, N.Y., 1976, judge Miner Moot Ct. competition Northwestern U., 1971-73; mem. law coun. DePaul U., 1974-83, mem. alumni assn., 1984-85, chmn., 1975-79; adj. prof. DePaul U. Coll. Law, 1977, 81, 2008-; faculty Practising Law Inst., Chgo., 1984. Contbr. articles to profl. jours. Bd. dirs. Lawyer's Trust Fund of Ill., 1998-2004, treas., 2000-01, v.p., 2002-03, pres., 2003-04, Cmty. Film Workshop of Chgo., 1977-90, Friends of Glencoe Parks, 1977-78, sec., 1978-79; mem. nominating com. Glencoe Sch. Bd., 1978-81, chmn. rules com., 1980-81; pres. Glencoe Hist. Soc., 1979-82; mem. Glencoe Zoning Bd. Appeals, Zoning Commn., Sign Bd. Appeals, 1981-86, chmn., 1984-86; mem. Ill. Inaugural Com., 1979, 83, 87, 95; bd. dirs., mem. exec. com. Chgo. World's Fair 1992 Authority, 1983-85; mem. Chancery divsn. task force Spl. Commn. on Adminstrn. of Justice in Cook County, 1985-87; trustee De Paul U., 1990-, chair phys. plant and property com., 1992-94, vice chair, 1995-2004, chair, 2004-08; commr. Ill. Racing Bd., 1990—2006; gen. trustee Lincoln Acad. Ill., 1993—, regent, 1999—, chancellor, 2001—; mem. Ill. Supreme Ct. Planning and Oversight Com. for Jud. Performance Evaluation Program, 1997-98, 2000-05, Ill. Supreme Ct. Rules Com., 2004—, vice chair, 2008-. Recipient Bancroft-Whitney Am. Jurisprudence award, 1965, 66, Judge Learned Hand Human Rels. award Am. Jewish Com., 1994, award for outstanding svc. to legal profession DePaul U. Coll. Law, 1996, Am. ORT Jurisprudence award, 1999, US Supreme Ct. John Paul Stevens award Chgo. Bar Found., 2008. Mem. ABA (com. on liaison with the judiciary 1983-95), Fed. Bar Assn., Chgo. Bar Assn. (fed. civil procedure com. 1979-85, chmn. 1985-86, bd. mgrs. 1987-89, chmn. house com. 1989-90, treas. 1990-91, 2d v.p. 1991-92, 1st v.p. 1992-93, pres. 1993-94), Ill. State Bar Assn., Women's Bar Assn., Ill. Police Assn., Ill. Sheriffs Assn., U.S. Treasury Agts. Assn., DePaul U. Alumni Assn. (pres. 1985-87, chmn. spl. gifts com. campaign, chmn. Simon Commn. 1989-91, nat. chair for ann. giving 1991-94), Chgo. Bar Found, US Supreme Ct. (Justice John Paul Stevens award, 2008), Std. Club. Office: Jenner & Block LLP 330 N Wabash Ave 43rd Fl Chicago IL 60611

SIMON, JOHN GERALD, law educator; b. NYC, Sept. 19, 1928; s. Robert Alfred and Madeleine (Marshall) S.; m. Claire Aloise Bising, June 14, 1958; 1 son, John Kirby (dec.). Grad., Ethical Culture Schs., 1946; AB, Harvard U., 1950; LLB, Yale U., 1953; LLD (hon.), Ind. U., 1989. Bar: N.Y. 1953. Asst. to gen. counsel Office Sec. Army, 1956-58; with firm Paul, Weiss, Rifkind, Wharton & Garrison, NYC, 1958-62; mem. faculty Yale Law Sch., 1962—, prof. law, 1967-76, Augustus Lines prof. law, 1976—2003, Augustus Lines prof. emeritus law, 2003—, dep. dean, 1985-90, acting dean, 1991, Yale U., 1977—88. Author: (with Powers and Gunnemann) The Ethical Investor, 1972. Pres. Taconic Found., 1967—; trustee, sec. Potomac Inst., 1961-93; mem. grad. bd. Harvard Crimson, 1950—; chmn. bd. dirs. Coop. Assistance Fund, 1970-76, vice chmn., 1977—; mem. governing coun. Rockefeller Archives Ctr., 1982-86; trustee The Found. Ctr., 1983-92, Open Soc. Inst.-N.Y., 1996-2007. 1st lt. U.S. Army, 1953-5 6. Recipient Certificate of Achievement Dept. Army, 1956 Mem. Phi Beta Kappa. Office: Yale U Law Sch PO Box 208215 New Haven CT 06520-8215 Office Phone: 203-432-2698. Business E-Mail: john.simon@yale.edu.

SIMON, JOHN R., utilities executive; B, Colo. Coll., Colo. Springs; law degree, Georgetown U., Washington. Ptnr. Hallenbeck, Lascell, LLP, Rochester, NY; exec. v.p. global human capital TeleTech Holdings, Inc., Denver; sr. v.p. human resources PG&E Corp., San Francisco, sr. v.p. human resources Pacific Gas & Electric Co. subs. Office: PG&E Corp One Market Spear Tower Ste 2400 San Francisco CA 94105-1126 Office Phone: 415-267-7070. Office Fax: 415-267-7268.

SIMON, KEITH R., safety engineer, petroleum engineer, radio personality; b. Lafayette, La., July 2, 1955; s. Jean Raymond and Ranelle T. (Touchet) S.; m. Martha Simon, Oct. 16, 1976 (div. Oct. 1979); 1 child, Jamie. BSN, BS, postgrad., U. La., 1980, student, 1981. Cert. nurse, nursing instr.; crane operator, first aid, offshore orientation lead abatement 1991, API thread inspector 1985, safety profl. 1991. Ops. mgr. Boco of Lafayette, 1980-82, exec. v.p., 1982-84, sr. project supr. La., 1980—82, exec. v.p., 1982—84; safety dir., corp. security Petro-Drive, Inc., 1989—91; divsnl. mgr. Petro-Drive/Boco of Lafayette, Inc., La., 1984—86, v.p., 1991—; offshore internat. sector mgr. Sigma Coatings USA, 1998—; ofshore internat. project mgr. Sigmakalon, Houston, 2000—03; v.p. ops. Chavez Svc. Cos., 2004—. Pres. and owner Silver Bullet Prodns. Inc., 1983—, Silver Bullet Limousine, 1983—. Mem. ARC, 1986—. Named Coors Lite Nat. Disc Jockey, 1984, named in Men Achievement, 1991, 2000 Notable Am. Men, 1992, Personalities Am., 1993; recipient Silver Shield of Valor award, 1992, Lifetime Achievement award, 1993. Mem.: ARC, Assn. Gen. Contractors, Am. Bldg. Contractors, Ind. Am. Drilling Contractors, Nat. Safety Coun., Acadiana Safety Assn., Nat. Assn. of Corrosion Engrs., Steel Structure Painting Coun., Lafayette Soc. Tng. and Devel., Am. Soc. Safety Engrs. Achievements include engineered, developed new techs., methodologies for offshore oil drilling. Avocations: skiing, softball, football, disc jockey. Office: 1401 Destrehan Ave Harvey LA 70058-2436 Home: 104 Pomerol Pl Lafayette LA 70503-6527 E-mail: ksimon007@bellsouth.net.

SIMON, KINDRA LEE, language educator, translator; b. Cheraw, SC, Jan. 09; d. Lee N. and Dianne Crawford Simon. BA in English & Psychology, Clemson U., SC, 1993—97. Cert. English tchr. SC Dept. Edn., 2005, ESOL SC Dept. Edn., 2005. Sales rep., trainer ALLTEL Comm., Charlotte, NC, 2000—02; ESOL tchr. Chesterfield County Sch. Dist., SC, 2002—. Translator Chesterfield County Sch. Dist., 2002—. Singer ch. choir, Pageland, SC, 2004. Grantee, Office English Lang. Acquisition, 2003—05. Mem.; Golden Key Honor Soc. (life). Avocations: photography, singing, travel, reading, writing. Home: 1742 Sam Rittenberg Blvd Apt 1e Charleston SC 29407-4905 Office Fax: 843-623-5513. Personal E-mail: kindrasimon@yahoo.com.

SIMON, LISA, travel association executive; b. Lexington, Ky. BA in Pub. Rels., Eastern Ky. U. Cert. tour profl., in fundraising Ind. U. Various positions Nat. Tour Assn., 1985—98, sr. v.p., 1998—2004, pres., 2006—; exec. dir. Internat. Coach Fedn., 2005—06; sr. v.p. IMG Assns., 2007—. Contbr. articles to profl. jours. Mem.: Tourism Cares US Travel Assn. (bd. mem.), Assn. Mgmt. Companies Inst., Assn. Travel Mktg. Execs., Travel Inst., Am. Soc. Assn. Execs. Office: Nat Tour Assn 546 E Main St Lexington KY 40508 Office Phone: 859-226-4249. Office Fax: 859-226-4404. Business E-Mail: lisa.simon@ntastaff.com.

SIMON, LOTHAR, publishing executive; b. Wuppertal, Germany, Sept. 17, 1938; arrived in U.S., 1961, naturalized, 1973; s. Fritz and Erna (Backhaus) S.; m. Jeannine Rechtman, Oct. 30, 1964; 1 child, Charles. Mgr. book dept. Franz Bader Book Shop and Globe Book Shop, Washington, 1961-66; sales mgr. Humanities Press Inc., NYC, 1966-73; pres. Longman Inc., NYC, 1973-81; pub. cons., 1981-82; pres., CEO Sheridan House, Inc., Dobbs Ferry, NY, 1982—. Mem. Assn. Am. Pubs., Town Club (Scarsdale, N.Y.). Democrat. Office: Sheridan House Inc 145 Palisade St Dobbs Ferry NY 10522-1617 Office Phone: 914-693-2410. Business E-Mail: lothars@sheridanhouse.com.

SIMON, LOU ANNA KIMSEY, academic administrator; BA in Math., Ind. State U., 1969, MS in Student Personnel and Counseling, 1970; PhD in Higher Edn., Mich. State U., 1974. Faculty mem. Mich. State U., asst. dir. Office Instl. Rsch., 1974—78, asst. provost gen. academic adminstrn., 1981—87, assoc. provost, 1987—92, v.p. acad. affairs, 1993—2004, interim pres., 2003, pres., 2005—. Office: Mich State U 450 Administration Bldg East Lansing MI 48824-1046 Office Phone: 517-355-6560. Business E-Mail: presmail@msu.edu.*

SIMON, MARTIN STANLEY, economist, consultant; b. St. Louis, Sept. 6, 1926; s. Elmer Ellis and Bee Marion (Werner) S.; m. Rita Edith Scheinhorn, June 18, 1950; children: Deborah, Richard. BBA, CCNY, 1949; MA, NYU, 1953. Econ. statistician Indsl. Commodity Corp,

NYC, 1949-52; agrl. econ. statistician Dept. Agr., Washington, 1952-58; commodity analyst Connell Rice & Sugar Co., Inc., Westfield, NJ, 1958-62, asst. to pres., 1962-67, v.p., 1967-74; sr. v.p. Connell Rice & Sugar Co., Inc. (now The Connell Co.), Berkeley Heights, NJ, 1974-99; pres. Eureka Group, LLC, Westfield, NJ, 1999—, The Rice Econs. Group, LLC, Westfield, NJ, 1999—; cons. AID, Jamaica, 1963; mem. Rice Insp. Industry Adv. Com., Washington, 1971-72; adv. U.S. Del. to UN FAO Intergovtl. Meetings on Rice, 1981; export dir., bd. dirs. Assn. Administrn. Rice Quotas, Inc., 1997-99. Served with U.S. Army, 1944-46, ETO. Recipient Class of 1920 award for merit in econ. stats. CCNY, 1949 Mem. Am. Econ. Assn., Rice Millers Assn. (chmn. legis. options working group 1984-86, govt. programs com. 1986-87, chmn. PL480 subcom. 1988-90), Nat. Economists Club. Office: The Rice Econs Group LLC PO Box 2446 Westfield NJ 07091-2446 Home: 9 Smithfield Ct Basking Ridge NJ 07920 E-mail: rice.economics@prodigy.net.

SIMON, MELVIN, real estate developer, professional sports team owner; b. Oct. 21, 1926; s. Max and Mae Simon; m. Bren Burns, Sept. 14, 1972; children: Deborah, Cynthia, Tamme, David, Max. BS in Acctg., CCNY, 1949, MBA in Real Estate, 1983; PhD (hon.), Butler U., 1986, Ind. U., 1991. Leasing agt. Albert Frankel Co., Indpls., 1955-60; co-founder Melvin Simon & Assocs., Indpls., 1959—, pres., 1960-73, co-chmn. bd., 1973; co-owner NBA Ind. Pacers, Indpls., 1983—; went pub. becoming Simon Property Group, 1993; chmn. bd. Simon Property Group, Inc., Indpls., 1993—95, co-chmn. bd. dirs., 1995—; merged with DeBartolo Realty Corp. to become Simon DeBartolo Group, 1996; reverted to Simon Property Group, 1998. Adv. bd. Wharton's Real Estate, Phila., 1986—. Prodr.: (films) Porky's. Adv. bd. dean's coun. Ind. U., Bloomington; bd. dirs. United Cerebral Palsy, Indpls., Muscular Dystrophy Assn., Indpls., Jewish Welfare Found., Indpls.; trustee Urban Land Inst., Internat. Coun. Shopping Ctrs. Served in US Army. Recipient Horatio Alger award Boy's Club Indpls., 1986; named Man of Yr., Jewish Welfare Found., 1980; named one of Forbes' Richest Ams., 1999—, World's Richest People, 2005—. Democrat. Jewish. Office: Simon Property Group Inc 225 W Washington St Indianapolis IN 46204 also: Indiana Pacers 125 S Pennsylvania St Indianapolis IN 46204*

SIMON, NANCY LYNN, performing arts educator, director; b. Chgo., June 20, 1942; d. Otis Benjamin Simon and Virginia Ruth Gilliland. BA, Whitman Coll., Walla Walla, Wash., 1959—63; MA, Tufts U., Somerville, Mass., 1963—65; PhD, U. Wash., Seattle, 1965—75. Paul Garrett prof. dramatic arts Whitman Coll., 1967—, dir. Harper Joy Theatre, 1992—. Freelance theatre/opera dir. Tacoma Opera, 1983—, Seattle Opera Cmty. Outreach, 1983—, Bellevue Civic Theatre, 1983—, Walla Walla Opera, 1983—, Juneau Lyric Opera, Alaska, 1983—, Shepherd Sch. Music Rice U., Houston, 1983—. Recipient George Ball Advising Excellence award, Whitman Coll., 1997, Thomas D. Howells award for disting. tchg. in humanities and arts, 2005, Paul Garrett Endowed Professorship award, 2006, Faculty award, Whitman Alumni Assn., 2007. Mem.: Artists Trust, Theatre Comm. Group, US Inst. Theater Tech., Actors' Equity Assn. Office: Whitman Coll 345 Boyer Ave Walla Walla WA 99362

SIMON, NORMA PLAVNICK, psychologist; d. Mark and Mary Plavnick; m. Robert G. Simon, Dec. 18, 1949; children: Mark Allan, Susan. BA, NYU, 1952, cert. in psychoanalysis, 1977; MA, Columbia U., 1953, EdD, 1968. Diplomate Am. Bd. Profl. Psychology, Am. Bd. Counseling Psychology, Am. Bd. Psychoanalysis. Psychologist Queens Coll. Counseling Ctr., Flushing, NY, 1968-70, asst. dir., 1970-76, dir., 1976; gen. practice psychology NYC, 1970—. Faculty, supr. New Hope Guild, Bklyn., 1976—, dir. child and adolescent tng. prog., 1988-98; adj. prof. clin. psychology Columbia U., N.Y.C., 1986-2002; supr. NYU Postdoctoral Prog. in Psychoanalysis, 1988—; mem. com. on profl. practice and ethics Nat. Register Health Svc. Providers, 1998-2003. Author: (with Robert G. Simon): Choosing a College Major: Social Science, 1981; co-author 3 book chpts. on licensure and ethics in psychology; mem. editl. bd. The Counseling Psychologist jour., 1986-89, Profl. Practice and Rsch. in Psychology, 1994-99, Jour. Infant, Child and Adolescent Psych Therapy, 1999—. Vice chair N.Y. State Bd. for Psychology State Edn. Dept., Albany, 1978-82, chair, 1982-88; bd. dirs. Pelham (N.Y.) Guidance Coun., 1980-83; pres.-elect Assn. State and Provincial Psychology Bds., 1990, pres., 1991. Recipient Morton Berger award, Assn. State and Provincial Psychology Bds., 1998, Outstanding Psychologist award, Acad. Counseling Psychology, 2003. Fellow: APA (mem. bd. profl. affairs 1987—89, chair bd. profl. affairs 1988—89, policy and planning bd. 1991—93, mem. ethics com. 1995—97, vice chair ethics com. 1996—97, chair ethics com. 1997, workgroup on telehealth 1998—2000, mem. accreditation com. 2004—, non-govtl. orgnl. UN assoc. team mem. 2006—, Karl Heiser award 1993, John Black award 1994, Disting. Psychologist of Yr., Divsn. Ind. Practice 2004), Am. Bd. Counseling Psychology (bd. dirs. 1992—2000, pres.-elect 1999, pres. 2001—03), Nat. Acads. of Practice (elected disting. practitioner), Am. Bd. Profl. Psychology (trustee 1998—2001, pres.-elect 2001—, pres. 2004—05); mem.: ABPP (Russell Bent award 2009), Internat. Assoc. Applied Psychology (non-govtl. orgnl. UN team mem.).

SIMON, PETER E., publishing executive; b. Bklyn., July 29, 1953; BA in English, CCNY, 1971; MA in Libr. Sci., Columbia U., 1980. Database mgr. R.R. Bowker, NYC, 1982-84; v.p. R.R. Bowker/Reed Reference Pubs., 1984-93; sr. v.p. Reed Reference Pub., New Providence, N.J., 1993-95, exec. v.p., 1995-97; v.p. bus. devel. Nat. Info. Svcs./Lexis-Nexis, Horsham, Pa., 1997-98; v.p. new product planning and devel. The Gale Group, Farmington Hills, Mich., 1998—, v.p. product mgmt., 1999, v.p. bus. devel., 1999-2000; dir. content lic. The Deal, LLC, NYC, 2000-2001; v.p. strategic devel. Digital Owl, Orlando, Fla., 2001—02; dir. new bus. devel. Nstein Techs. Corp., 2002—03; v.p. product mgmt. NewsBank, Inc., Naples, Fla., 2003—. Mem. Info. Industry Assn. (chmn. content divsn., bd. dirs.), Phi Beta Kappa.

SIMON, ROBERT, language educator; m. Helena Makohin; 1 child, Sophia. BA, MA, Boston U., 2000; PhD, U. Tex., Austin, 2006. Superior diploma Min. Edn. España, 1994, cert. in nível superior U. Lisboa, Lisbon, Portugal, 2003, in Portuguese superior level ACTFL, 2007. Asst. instr. U. Tex., 2000—06; asst. prof. Kennesaw State U., Ga., 2006—. Author: (acad. book) Understanding the Portuguese Poet Joaguim Pessoa, (poetry books) New Poems from the Airplane and Graveyard (KSU Founders award, 2007), Nao Tirei Fotos, 2009, Osophiadas, 2009; contbr. articles to profl. jours. V.p. Ga. Poetry Soc., Columbus, Ga., 2008—. Recipient Profl. Devel. award, U. Tex., 2005, Casis Dissertation award, 2006; Coll. Humanities and Social Sci. grant, Kennesaw State U., 2007, Inst. Global Initiatives grant, 2007. Mem.: MLA. Independent. Jewish. Achievements include research in post-colonial theory applied to Portuguese fado. Avocations: poetry, travel. Office: Kennesaw State Univ 1000 Chastain Rd MB 1804 Kennesaw GA 30144

SIMON, ROBERT G., lawyer; b. NYC, Feb. 21, 1927; s. Monroe and Claire S. S.; m. Norma Plavnick, Dec. 18, 1949; children: Mark A., Susan. BA, Cornell U., 1947; LLB, JD, Georgetown U., 1950; LLM, NYU, 1961. Bar: D.C. 1950, N.Y. 1951, U.S. Supreme Ct. 1955. Assoc. firms in, NYC, 1950-52; legal sec. to judge U.S. Dist. Ct. So. Dist. N.Y., 1953-58; assoc. Jaffe & Wachtell, NYC, 1958-61; legal adv. TV series The Verdict Is Yours, 1958-60; successively dir. bus. affairs, v.p., sr. v.p., mgr. bus. affairs dept. McCann-Erickson, Inc., NYC, 1961-80; sr. broadcast atty. The Interpublic Group of Cos., NYC, 1980-95. Adj. faculty Manhattan Community Coll., 1967, Baruch Coll., 1968, CCNY, 1968, New Sch. Social Research, 1972-73; speaker in field. Author: (with Norma Simon) Choosing a College Major: The Social Sciences, 1981; contbr. articles to profl. jours. Dem.-Liberal candidate for county clk. Westchester County, N.Y., 1952; chmn. Narcotics Guidance Coun., Pelham, N.Y., 1973; mem. Nat. Media Coun. on Disability, 1986-90; bd. dirs., gen. counsel Nat. Challenge Com. on Disability, 1986-88; mem. adv. bd. The Caption Ctr. WGBH Found., 1987—; mem. state bd. for podiatry N.Y. State Dept. Edn., 2000—. With USAAF, 1944-46, USNR, 1949-59 Mem.: NATAS (chpt. gov. 1972—85, treas. 1976—81, 1st v.p. 1981—83, nat. trustee 1981—85, pres. 1983—85, chpt. gov. 1996—97, nat. trustee 1996—98), Am. Assn. Advt. Agys. (com. on broadcast adminstrn. policy 1985—93), NY County Lawyers Assn. (com. on comms. and entertainment law 1990—2008, not-for-profit orgns., alternate dispute resolution com. 1998—2008), Hemlock Soc. NY (bd. dirs. 2000—05, final exit network NY legal advisor 2005—).

SIMON, RONALD CHARLES, curator, educator; b. Phila., Feb. 23, 1951; s. Samuel Charles and Emily (Luzenberg) Simon. BA, Dickinson Coll., 1973; postgrad., Brit. Film and TV Inst., Stirling, Scotland, 1973, Columbia U., 1973-75. Researcher NBC, NYC, 1976—77; mgr. media prodn. 1st Boston Corp., NYC, 1979; curator TV and Radio Palcy Ctr. for Media, NYC, 1979—. Adj. prof. Hunter Coll., CUNY, 1987—, Columbia U., NYC, 1991—; cons., lectr. to mus. and colls. including Smithsonian Instn., Whitney Mus. Am. Art, NYU, Cooper Hewitt Mus., 1985—. Exhbns. curated include The Television of Dennis Potter, 1992, Witness to History, Jack Benny: The Radio and Television Work, 1991, contbg. author Encyclopedia of TV, 1997, Encyclopedia of Radio, 2002, creative cons., host CD-ROM Total TV, 1997; author: Worlds Without End: The Art and History of Soap Opera, 1997; advisor, contbg. author St. James Ency. Popular Culture, 1999, Violence in America: An Encyclopedia, 1999; author: The Television of Dennis Potter, 1992. Mem. George Foster Peabody Awards Bd., 2003—, chair, 2008—; mem. consultative coun. IETV, Brazil; bd. dirs. United Action for Animals, 2004—07. Decorated chevalier of Art and Sci. Ministry of French Culture; Metzger Conway Fellow, Dickinson Coll., 2002, Cogan Alumni fellow, 2006. Mem.: NATAS (panelist and juror for numerous awards 1985—, mem. editl. bd. TV Quar. 1987—), TV Ltd. (bd. dirs. 2000—). Home: 141 E 17th St New York NY 10003-3402 Office: Television & Radio 25 W 52nd St New York NY 10019-6104 Office Phone: 212-621-6680. Personal E-mail: ronsimonnyc@yahoo.com, ronsimonnyc@gmail.com. Business E-Mail: rsimon@paleycentor.org.

SIMON, RONALD ISAAC, financial executive; b. Cairo, Nov. 4, 1938; came to U.S., 1942; s. David and Helene (Zilkha) S.; m. Anne Faith Hartman, June 19, 1960; children: Cheryl, Eric, Daniel. BA, Harvard U., 1960; MA, Columbia U., 1962, PhD. Mng. dir., chief fin. officer The Henley Group Inc., La Jolla, 1986-90; pvt. practice fin. cons. La Jolla, 1990—2000. Vice-chmn. bd. dirs. Softnet Corp., San Francisco, 1998—2002, acting chmn. and CEO, 2001; CFO WingCast LLC, San Diego, 2001—02; bd. dirs. Collateral Therapeutics, Inc., San Diego, 1999—2002; exec. v.p., CFO/bd. dirs. Western Water Co., San Diego, 1997—2000; bd. dirs. Am. Independence Corp., NY, 2002—, WFS Fin., Inc., Irvine, Calif., 2003—06, BDI Investments, San Diego, 2003—05, Cardium Therapeutics, 2006—09, Ellington Fin. LLC, 2007—. Bd. dirs. San Diego Opera Co., 1988-90, Univ. Art Gallery U. Calif., San Diego, 1991-95; bd. dirs., treas. Lyric Opera, San Diego, 2003-2005; audit com. San Diego Zool. Soc. Ford Found. fellow, 1963-65.

SIMON, SANDRA RUTH WALDMAN, retired state agency administrator; b. NYC, May 11, 1943; d. Jacob S. and Ann Waldman; m. Sanford R. Simon, Aug. 23, 1964 (div.); m. F. Jerry Lucia, Apr. 30, 1989; children: Hilary G., Taylor M., Pamela Lucia, David Lucia. BA, Barnard Coll., 1965; PhD, Rockefeller U., 1972; MSW, SUNY, Stony Brook, 1985. Postdoctoral rsch. assoc. Brookhaven (N.Y.) Nat. Lab., 1972; rsch. assoc. SUNY, Stony Brook, 1972, Developed and Directed Health Edn. Programs, Islip Town, NY, 1977-81; coord. Suffolk County creative learning program L.I. Regional Adv. Coun. Higher Edn., 1979-80; mng. dir. Pandion Stony Brook Assocs., 1984-87; evaluation and planning specialist Tex. Dept. Human Svcs., Austin, 1987-91, supr. planning and evaluation, 1991-93, dir. policy analysis and program evaluation, 1993—2001. Lectr., conf. coord. Women's Health Alliance L.I., St. James, N.Y., 1975-77; field instr. U. Tex. Sch. Social Work, 1989, 2000-01. Welfare Reform Evaluation grantee, 1997-2001. Mem. Nat. Coun. Jewish Women, Story Cir. Network Avocations: walking, opera, writing, acting.

SIMON, SCOTT, neurosurgeon, director; married. Dir. neurosurgical trauma Stamford Hosp., neurosurgical dir. stamford cyberknife; neurosurgical cons. Shriners Hosp. children, Phila., 2005—. Grantee Rsch. grant, Synthes Spine, LP, 2002—03. Office: Orthop and Neurosurgery Specialists 32 Strawberry Hill Ct Tully Ctr Stamford CT 06902 Office Fax: 203-487-0308. Business E-Mail: simon@onsmd.com.

SIMON, SHELDON WEISS, political science professor; b. St. Paul, Jan. 31, 1937; s. Blair S. and Jennie M. (Dim) S.; m. Charlann Lilwin Scheid, Apr. 27, 1962; 1 child, Alex Russell BA summa cum laude, U. Minn., 1958, PhD, 1964; MPA, Princeton U., 1960; postgrad., U. Geneva, 1962—63. Asst. prof., then prof. U. Ky., 1966-75; prof. polit. sci. Ariz. State U., 1975—, chmn. dept., 1975-79, dir. Ctr. Asian Studies, 1980-88. Vis. prof. George Washington U., 1965, U. B.C., Can., 1972-73, 79-80, Carleton U., 1976, Monterey Inst. Internat. Studies, 1991, 96, Am. Grad. Sch. Internat. Mgmt., 1991-92; cons. USIA Rsch. Analysis Corp., Am. Enterprise Inst. Pub. Policy Rsch., Hoover Instn., Orkand Corp.; cons., dir. S.E. Asian Projects, Nat. Bur. Asian Rsch., 1998—; Smithsonian Instn. lectr. internat. politics Crystal and Regent Cruise Lines, 2000—; vis. Asia-Pacific mentor prof. US Naval War Coll., 2008-09. Author: Asian Neutralism and U.S. Policy, 1975, The ASEAN States and Regional Security, 1982, The Future of Asian-Pacific Security Collaboration, 1988; editor: The Military and Security in the Third World, 1978, East Asian Security in the Post-Cold War Era, 1993, Southeast Asian Security in the New Millenium, 1996, The Many Faces of Asian Security, 2001, Disrupting Violence: Religion and Conflict in South and Southeast Asia, 2007, China, the United States and Southeast Asia, Contending Perspectives on Politics, Economics and Security, 2008, others; contbr. articles to profl. jours., chpts. to books. Mem. Com. Fgn. Relations, Phoenix, 1976—; bd. dirs. Phoenix Little Theater, 1976-79 Grantee Am. Enterprise Inst., 1974, Earhart Found., 1979, 81, 92, 84, 88, U.S. Inst. Peace, 1994-96, 2000-01, Nat. Bur. Asian Rsch., 1998, W. Alton Jones Found., 2000, U.S. Pacific Command, 2002-03; Hoover Instn. fellow, 1980, 85; named Outstanding Alumni Notable Achievement, U. Minn., 2007. Mem. Am. Polit. Sci. Assn., Assn. Asian Studies, Internat. Studies Assn. (profl. ethics com. 1987-91, v.p. 1991-93), Asia Soc. (contemporary affairs com. 1987-92), U.S. Coun. for Asia-Pacific Security (exec. bd. 1998-2003), Phi Beta Kappa. Democrat. Jewish. Avocations: acting, singing, tennis. Home: 5630 S Rocky Point Rd Tempe AZ 85283-2134 Office: Ariz State U Polit Sci Dept Tempe AZ 85287-3902 Office Phone: 480-965-1317. Business E-Mail: shells@asu.edu.

SIMON, TED, toxicologist; b. Johannesburg, Nov. 12, 1948; s. Stuart Levine and Beatrice Wix Simon; m. Elizabeth Britton Legg, May 6, 1979; children: Rebecca Kathryn, Adam Creed. PhD, Ga. State U., Atlanta, 1989. Diplomate Am. Bd. Toxicology, 1994. Toxicologist US EPA, Atlanta, 1994—2006; prin. Ted Simon LLC, Winston, Ga., 2006—. Contbr. scientific papers. Mem.: Soc. Toxicology. Avocations: music, photography. Home and Office: Ted Simon LLC 4184 Johnston Rd Winston GA 30187 Business E-Mail: ted@tedsimon-toxicology.com.

SIMON, WILLIAM LEONARD, scriptwriter, television and film producer, writer; b. Washington, Dec. 3, 1930; s. Isaac B. and Marjorie (Felsteiner) Simon; m. Arynne Lucy Abeles, Sept. 18, 1966; 1 child, Victoria Marie 1 stepchild, Sheldon M. Bermont. BEE, Cornell U., 1954; MA in Ednl. Psychology, Golden State U., 1982, PhD in Comm., 1983. Writer features and TV movies, documentary and indsl. films, TV programs, 1958—; lectr. George Washington U., Washington, 1968-70. Juror Coun. Nontheatrical Events Film Festival, 1975—90, Cindy Festival Blue Ribbon Panel, 1985—; jury chmn., bd. dirs. CINE Film Festival, 1988—. Author: more than 600 produced works for motion pictures and TV; author: (screenplays) Fair Woman Without Discretion, Majorca, Swindle, A Touch of Love, Relative Denial; author: (teleplays and documentaries) From Information to Wisdom, Flight of Freedom II, Missing You; author: (TV series) It's Your Turn, TV Syndicated, From Information to Wisdom, Smithsonian World Series, PBS; author: (writer/prodr.) The Star of India; writer, prodr. The Star of India: Setting Sail; co-author: Profit from Experience-The Story of Transformation Management, 1995; author: Beyond the Numbers, 1996; co-author: Lasting Change, 1997, On the Firing Line, My 500 Days at Apple Computer, 1998, High Velocity Leadership--The Mars Pathfinder Approach to Faster, Better, Cheaper, 1999, Driving Digital--What Microsoft is Learning from its Customers about Thriving in the Digital Revolution, 2000, The Afterlife Experiments--Breakthrough Scientific Evidence of Life After Death, 2002, The Art of Deception, 2002, In Search of Business Value, 2004, The Art of Intrusion: The Real Stories Behind the Exploits of Hackers, Intruders and Decievers, 2005, iCon: Steve Jobs - The Greatest Second Act in the History of Business, 2005, The Truth About Medium-Extraordinary Experiments with the Real Allison Du Bois of NBC's Medium, 2005, The G.O.D. Experiments, 2006, Gorgeous Disaster--The Tragic Story of Debra LaFave, 2006, The Healing Energy Experiments -- Science Reveals Our Natural Power to Heal, 2007, A Cat by the Tail, 2007, Think India--The Rise of the Next Superpower and What it Means for Every American, 2007, Act Now, 2009. Pres. Foggy Bottom Citizens Assn., 1963—65, mem. exec. bd., 1965—69; v.p. Shakespeare Summer Festival, 1966—67, trustee, 1965—70; mem. interview com. Cornell U., 1987—88. Lt. USN, 1954—58. Recipient 12 Golden Eagle awards, Cine Film Festival, Gold medal, N.Y. Internat. Festival, Freedoms Found., Gold Cindy, IFPA, awards, Berlin, Belgrade and Venice Film Festivals, others; named 30 Best Bus. Books of 1997, Exec. Book Summaries. Mem.: NATAS (gov. DC chpt. 1970—73, gov. San Diego chpt. 1998—2002), Writers Guild Am., Silver Cir., Rotary (bd. dirs., program chmn.), Tau Beta Pi, Eta Kappa Nu (chpt. pres. 1953—54). Republican. Avocations: crew member square-rigged brig Pilgrim, San Diego Museum ship Star of India, tennis. E-mail: bill@simon1.com.

SIMON, WILLIAM S., retail executive; 2 children. B. in Economics, U. Conn., MBA. Various mktg. and devel. positions Cadbury-Schweppes, Pepsico, RJR-Nabisco; v.p. consumer mktg. Diageo PLC, 1998, pres. Southeast region; sec. Fl. Dept. Mgmt. Services, 2003—05; senior v.p. global bus. devel. Brinker Internat., Dallas, 2005—06; exec. v.p. specialty divsn. Wal-Mart Stores Inc., Bentonville, Ark., 2006—07, exec. v.p., COO US, 2007—. Served USN, served USNR. Office: Wal-Mart Stores Inc 702 SW Eighth St Bentonville AR 72716*

SIMON-CAMPBELL, E'LORIA, nursing educator; d. Frank E. and Hattie E. Simon; m. Louis P. Campbell; 1 child, Veronica Simon. MS in Nursing Edn. Track, U. Tex., Tyler, 2005. Dir. vocat. nursing program Angelina Coll., Crockett, Tex., 2000—05; clin. asst. prof. Prairie View A&M U., Houston, 2005—. Choir Covenent Glen Meth. Ch., Stafford, Tex., 2006. Mem.: Sigma Theta Tau. Office: Prairie View A&M Univ 6436 Fannin Houston TX 77030

SIMONCINI, MATTHEW J., manufacturing executive; BA in Acctg., Wayne State U., Detroit, 1985. With United Technologies Automotive; v.p. fin. Europe Lear Corp., 2001—04, v.p. operational fin., 2004—06, v.p. global fin., chief acctg. officer, 2006, sr. v.p. operational fin., 2006—07, sr. v.p., CFO, 2007—. Office: Lear Corp 21557 Telegraph Rd PO Box 5008 Southfield MI 48086 Office Phone: 248-447-1500. Office Fax: 248-447-1722.

SIMONDS, JOHN EDWARD, retired newspaper editor; b. Boston, July 4, 1935; s. Alvin E. and Ruth Angeline (Rankin) S.; m. Rose B. Muller, Nov. 16, 1968; children— Maximillian P., Malia G.; children by previous marriage— Rachel F. Cobb, John B. BA, Bowdoin Coll., 1957. Reporter Daily Tribune, Seymour, Ind., 1957-58, UPI, Columbus, Ohio, 1958-60; reporter, asst. city editor Providence Jour. Bull., 1960-65, Washington Evening Star, 1965-66; corr. Gannett News Svc., Washington, 1966-75; mng. editor Honolulu Star Bull., 1975-80, exec. editor, 1980-87, sr. editor, editl. page editor, 1987-93; exec. Hawaii Newspaper Agy., Honolulu, 1993-99; reader rep. The Honolulu Advertiser, Honolulu, 1999—2002; ret., 2002. Served with U.S. Army, 1958. Mem. Am. Soc. Newspaper Editors, AP Mng. Editors, Soc. Profl. Journalists, Nat. Conf. Editl. Writers, Orgn. News Ombudsmen, Hawaii Lit. Arts Coun. Home: 5316 Nehu Pl Honolulu HI 96821-1941 Office: The Honolulu Advertiser 605 Kapiolani Blvd Honolulu HI 96813-5195 Home Phone: 808-373-3609; Office Phone: 808-383-7984. Personal E-mail: simondsj001@hawaii.rr.com.

SIMONE, JOSEPH R., lawyer; b. NYC, Jan. 7, 1949; m. Virginia E. Simone, May 29, 1971; children: Jacquelyn, Robert. BA cum laude, Queens Coll., 1971; LLM in Taxation, NYU, 1977; JD cum laude, Fordham U., 1974. Bar: N.Y. 1975, U.S. Dist. Ct. (so. dist.) N.Y. 1975, U.S. Ct. Appeals (2d cir.) 1975. Ptnr. Patterson, Belknap, Webb & Tyler, NYC, 1982-88, Schulte, Roth & Zabel, NYC, 1988—2002; spl. prof. law Hofstra U. Sch. Law, 1998—2006; of counsel Pitney Hardin LLP, NYC, 2003—, ptnr., 2004—06, Day Pitney LLP, NYC, 2007—. Author: (textbooks) Pension Answer Book, 5th edit., 1990, Essential Facts: Pension and Profit-sharing Plans, 1999; editl. advisor Jour. of Pension Planning, associative editor Chief Jour. of Retirement Planning. Mem. PLI Program (chmn.), "Understanding ERISA", P4 Program "ERISA Litigation", Am. Coll. Employee Benefits (counsel 2003—), Phi Beta Kappa. Office: Day Pitney LLP 7 Times Sq New York NY 10036 Office Phone: 212-297-5859. Business E-Mail: jsimone@daypitney.com.

SIMONELLI, LORENZO, manufacturing executive; Degree in Bus. and Economics, Cardiff U. With internat. & corp. fin. Mitsubishi Bank; joined GE, 1994, with internat., with shared svcs., with Nuovo Pignone, with consolidated fin. insurance, joined corp. audit staff, 1997, exec. audit mgr. European Indsl. Bus., 2001, fin. planning and analysis mgr. consumer products, 2002—04, CFO Americas consumer & indsl., 2004—05, gen. mgr. product mgmt. appliances, lighting, electrical distbn. and motors, 2005—07, pres., CEO consumer & indsl. Budapest, Hungary, 2007—08, pres., CEO transp., 2008—.*

SIMONS, ALBERT, III, lawyer; b. Charleston, SC, Nov. 22, 1950; s. Albert Jr. and Caroline Pinckney (Mitchell) S.; m. Theodora Bonnell Wilbur, Jan. 28, 1970; children: Albert IV, Charles A., Theodora B. BA, U. Va., 1972, JD, 1976. Bar: S.C. 1977, N.Y. 1978. Ptnr. Orrick, Herrington & Sutcliffe, NYC, 1984—. Mem. S.C. Bar Assn., N.Y. State Bar Assn. Office: Orrick Herrington & Sutcliffe 666 5th Ave Rm 203 New York NY 10103-1798 Business E-Mail: asimons@orrick.com.

SIMONS, ANNEKE PRINS, artist, educator; b. Amsterdam, The Netherlands, Feb. 15, 1930; arrived in U.S., 1940; d. Raphael Hugo and Charlotte Prins. BA, Vassar Coll., Poughkeepsie, NY, 1952; MAT, Harvard-Radcliffe, Cambridge, Mass., 1953; PhD, Pa. State U., Univ. Park, Pa., 1968; MA in Social Sci., Jersey City State Coll., Jersey City, NJ, 1975. Tchr., originator adult art edn. South End House, Boston, 1953—54; part-time asst. tchr. Boston Mus. Children's Rm., Boston, 1954—56; with Met. Mus. Art, NYC, 1957—61; tchr., art dir. Twin Pines, Oakland, Calif., 1961—62; grad. rsch. asst. tchr. art edn. Pa. State. U., Univ. Park, Pa., 1962—64; prof. N.J. City U., 1967—2000; prof. emeritus. Senator-at-large Jersey City State Coll., mem. personnel com. art dept., dir. art program gifted H.S. students. One-woman shows include The Courtney Gallery, Jersey City State Coll., 1979, The Gallery, Jersey City, NJ, 1981, Stevens Inst. Tech., Hoboken, NJ, 1984, Jersey City Mus., 1996, exhibited in group shows at Gallery Stendhal, NYC, 1991, Jersey City State Coll., 1992, juried show, C.A.S.E. Mus., Jersey City, NJ, 1982, exhibitions include Lemmerman Gallery, NJ City U., 1999, City Spirit Cultural Arts Festival, Jersey City, NJ, 1981 (Best in Show, 1981), Visceglia Art Ctr. Caldwell Coll., Caldwell, NJ, 1994, The Rotunda Gallery, City Hall, Jersey City, NJ, 1995, Viridian Gallery, NYC, 1997, numerous others; contbr. articles to profl. jours. Co-founder Genesis Project, Jersey City, 1986—2004. Recipient Martin Luther King, Jr. Cmty. Svc. award, Jersey City U., 1999; grantee Chinese Art Hist. Coll. Tchrs. summer seminar, Nat. Endowment Humanities, 1975; grad. sch. fellowship, Pa. State U., 1964—65. Mem.: Harvard Club NY, NJ.

SIMONS, BARBARA, retired elementary school educator; b. NYC, May 25, 1947; d. Abraham William and Gertrude (Monash) Cohn; m. Bernard Louis Simons, Dec. 23, 1972. BA, Bklyn. Coll., 1969; MS, Syracuse U., 1970. Lic. tchr., N.Y. Tchr. Pub. Sch. 209K, Bklyn., 1970-71, Pub. Sch. 177K, Bklyn., 1971-75, Pub. Sch. 95K, Bklyn., 1975-92, Pub. Sch. 215K, Bklyn., 1993—2002; ret., 2002. Mem. Am. Fedn. Tchrs., United Fedn. Tchrs. (del. 1976-90), N.Y. United Tchrs., N.Y. Edn. Guild. Avocations: tennis, travel, bowling, golf. Home: 2428 E 27th St Brooklyn NY 11235-2004

SIMONS, BARRY THOMAS, lawyer; b. Lynn, Mass., Dec. 14, 1946; s. Emanuel Isador and Betty (Darish) S.; m. Laurie Jean Louder, May 5, 1985; children: Britton Eugene, Brett Jacob. BS in Govt., Am. Univ., 1968; JD, NYU, 1971. Bar: Calif. 1971, U.S. Dist. Ct. (ctrl. dist.) Calif. 1972, U.S. Ct. Appeals (9th cir.) 1972, U.S. Supreme Ct. 1978, U.S. Dist. Ct. (so. and no. dists.) Calif. 1979. Pvt. practice, Laguna Beach, Calif., 1971—. Co-author: California Drunk Driving Law, 2005; editor (law rev.) N.Y. Law Forum, 1971. Apptd. mem. gen. plan revision com. and local coastal task force City of Laguna Beach, 1980. Mem. Orange County Bar Assn. (bd. dirs. 1981), Newport/Harbor Bar Assn. (bd. dirs. 1979), South Orange County Bar Assn. (pres. 1986, bd. dirs. 1980-95, 2009), Calif. Attys. for Criminal Justice (chair misdemeanor com. 1995), Nat. Assn. Criminal Def. Attys. (vice chair D.U.I. com.), Nat. Coll. D.U.I. Def. (founding mem., dean), Assn. Calif. D.U.I. Defenders (bd. dirs.), Deuce Defenders Assn. (specialist mem.). Office: 260 Saint Anns Dr Laguna Beach CA 92651-2737 Office Phone: 949-497-1729. Fax: 949-497-3971. E-mail: info@simonslaw.com.

SIMONS, CAROL LENORE, magazine editor; b. Bklyn., Feb. 2, 1942; d. Paul and Grace (Rotwein) Seiderman; m. Lewis M. Simons, Feb. 7, 1965; children: Justine, Rebecca, Adam. BA, Tufts U., 1963; MS, Columbia U., 1964. Rschr. Newsweek mag., NYC, 1964-65, CBS News, NYC and Saigon, Vietnam, 1967-68; reporter Denver Post, 1965-67; editor Pres. Commn. on Marijuana and Drug Abuse, Washington, 1971-72; assoc. editor Smithsonian mag., Washington, 1978-82; dir. publs. Am. C. of C. in Japan, Tokyo, 1991-96; exec. editor AARP The Mag., Washington, 2003—, AARP Bull., Washington, 2005—. Office: AARP The Bulletin 601 E St NW Washington DC 20049-0001 Business E-Mail: csimons@aarp.org.

SIMONS, D. BRENTON, not-for-profit executive; b. New Haven, Oct. 24, 1965; s. Elwyn L. Simons and Mary Hoyt Fitch. BS, Boston U., 1988, MEd, 1994. Dir. of edn. New Eng. Hist. Geneal. Soc., Boston, 1993—96, editor of publications, 1996—2000, asst. exec. dir., 2000—04, COO, 2004—05, pres. and CEO, 2005—. Fellow Mass. Hist. Soc., Boston, 2005—; mem. Boston History Consortium, 2006—; standing com. Soc. of Cin. in State of Conn., Conn., 2007—; coun. mem. Colonial Soc. of Mass., Boston, 2008; mem. Am. Antiquarian Soc., Worcester, 2008. Author: (books) Boston Beheld: Antique Town and Country Views, Witches, Rakes, and Rogues: True Stories of Scam, Scandal, Murder, and Mayhem in Boston, 1630-1775 (Award of Merit, Am. Assn. for State and Local History, 2006), The Langhornes of Langhorne Park; co-editor: book The Art of Family: Genealogical Artifacts in New England; guest narrator (audio walking tour cd) The Boston Audissey: See the Sites - Hear the Legends; contbr. articles to publs. Former bd. mem. Friends of Childe Hassam Pk., Boston; trustee Shirley Lusiis House Mus., 2009—; v.p. Simons Family Found., Houston, 1997—2008. Mem.: Partnership Hist. Bostons (mem., adv. bd. 2008—), Union Club, Pi Lamda Theta. Episcopalian. Avocations: fundraising, genealogy, gardening, historic preservation, antiques. Office: New Eng Historic Genealogical Soc 101 Newbury St Boston MA 02116-3007 Office Fax: 617-536-7307. Personal E-mail: brentsimons@aol.com.

SIMONS, DOLPH COLLINS, JR., publishing executive, editor; b. Lawrence, Kans., Mar. 11, 1930; s. Dolph Collins and Marie (Nelson) S.; m. Pamela Counseller, Feb. 7, 1952; children: Pamela, Linda, Dolph Collins, Dan. AB, U. Kans., 1951; LLD (hon.), Colby Coll., 1972. Reporter Lawrence Jour.-World, 1953, asso. pub., 1957, pub., 1962—2004, editor, 1978—, pres., 1969—2004; reporter The Times, London, 1956, Johannesburg (South Africa) Star, 1958; chmn. World Co. Mem. Pulitzer Awards Jury, 1977, 78, 80, 81. Trustee, past pres. William Allen White Found.; trustee Midwest Rsch. Inst.; former trustee Menninger Found., Nat. Parks Conservation Assn.; former mem. governing bd. Children's Mercy Hosp., Kansas City, Mo.; former trustee, former chmn. U. Kans. Endowment Assn.; past bd. dirs. Greater Kansas City Cmty. Found., Commerce Bancshares, Kansas City, Mo.; former trustee The Freedom Forum, Kans. Nature Conservancy; former mem. Kans. Biosci. Authority Bd. Served to capt. USMRC, 1951—53. Recipient Elijah Parish Lovejoy award, 1972; Fred Ellsworth award for significant service to U. Kans., 1976; Disting. Service citation, 1980 Mem. Newspaper Advt. Bur. (past dir.), Am. Soc. Newspaper Editors, Inland Daily Press Assn. (past dir.), Kans. Press Assn. (past pres., dir.), AP (past dir.), Am. Newspaper Pubs. Assn. (past dir., past nat. sec.), Lawrence C. of C. (past pres., dir.), U. Kans. Alumni Assn. (past pres., dir.), Lawrence Country Club, Kansas City Country Club, Kansas City River Club, Masons, Rotary, Sigma Delta Chi, Phi Delta Theta. Republican. Episcopalian. Home: 2425 Vermont St Lawrence KS 66046-4761 Office: 609 New Hampshire St Lawrence KS 66044-2243 Personal E-mail: dsimonsjr@ljworld.com.

SIMONS, DOREEN LEE, language educator, researcher; children: Andre Lee Marques, Jenilee Lea Marques. MA, NY U., 1982. Cert. in tchg. NY, 1984. Am. sign lang. rschr. Haskins Rsch. Ctr., New Haven, 1986—; staff instr. U. Conn., Storrs, 2003—. Parent advisor com. mem. Am. Sch. for Deaf, West Hartford, Conn., 2000, edn. com. mem., 2006. Home: 86 Helm Dr Farmington CT 06032-202 Office: Univ Conn 337 Mansfield Rd Storrs Mansfield CT 06269-1145 Office Fax: 860-231-8746; Home Fax: 860-409-9195. Personal E-mail: jenand43@comcast.net. Business E-Mail: doreen.simons@uconn.edu.

SIMONS, ELIZABETH R(EIMAN), biochemist, educator; b. Vienna, Sept. 1, 1929; came to U.S., 1941, naturalized, 1948; d. William and Erna Engle (Weisselberg) Reiman; m. Harold Lee Simons, Aug. 12, 1951; children: Leslie Ann Mulert, Robert David. BChemE, Cooper Union, NYC, 1950; MS, Yale U., 1951, PhD, 1954. Rsch. chemist Tech. Ops., Arlington, Mass., 1953-54; instr. chemistry Wellesley Coll., Mass., 1954-57; rsch. asst. Children's Hosp. Med. Ctr. and Cancer Rsch. Found., Boston, 1957-59, rsch. assoc. pathology, 1959-62; rsch. assoc. Harvard Med. Sch., 1962-66, lectr. biol. chemistry, 1966-72; tutor biochem. scis. Harvard Coll., 1971-94; assoc. prof. biochemistry Boston U., 1972-78, prof., 1978—, asst. dir. Office Med. Edn., 2000—06. Contbr. articles to profl. jours. Grantee in field. Mem.: AAAS, Soc. for Neurosci., Biophys. Soc., Am. Soc. Hematology, Am. Soc. Cell Biology, Am. Soc. Biol. Chemists, Am. Chem. Soc. Office: Boston U Sch Medicine 80 E Concord St Roxbury MA 02118-2307 Office Phone: 617-638-4332. Business E-Mail: esimons@bu.edu.

SIMONS, ELWYN LAVERNE, physical anthropologist, primatologist, paleontologist, educator; b. Lawrence, Kans., July 14, 1930; s. Verne Franklin and Verna Irene (Cuddeback) S.; m. Friderun Annursel Ankel, Dec. 2, 1972; children: Cornelia Verna Mathilde, Verne Franklin Herbert; 1 child by previous marriage: David Brenton; 1 adopted child Katherine Egan. BS in Biology, Rice U., 1953; MA, Princeton U., 1955, PhD in Paleobiology, 1956; D.Phil., Oxford U., Eng., 1959; MA (hon.), Yale U., 1967; DSc, Oxford U., 1995. Demonstrator, exhibitor Oxford U., 1956-58; lectr. geology Princeton (N.J.) U., 1958-59; asst. prof. zoology U. Pa., Phila., 1959-61; vis. assoc. prof. geology, curator vertebrate paleontology Yale U., New Haven, 1960-61, head divsn. vert. paleontology, 1961-77, prof. paleontology, 1967; prof. geology, curator charge div. vertebrate paleontology Peabody Mus., 1965-77; prof. biol. anthropology, anatomy Duke U., Durham, NC, 1977-82, 1982, prof. zoology, dir. Duke Primate Center, 1977-91, sci. dir., 1991—2001, head, div. fossil primates, 2001—06, dir., div. fossil primates, 2006—. Dir. Paleontol. Expdns., Egypt, 1961—68, Egypt, 1977—2007, India, 1968—69, India, 1996, India, 98, India, 1999—2000; rsch. expdns. for fossil mammals, Wyo., 1960—96, Wyo., 1998—99, Iran, 1970, Spain, 71, Madagascar, 1983—2005; Barbour-Schramm Meml. lectr. U. Nebr., 1974; David French lectr. Claremont Coll., 1974; traveling lectr. French Bur. Fgn. Affairs, 1976. Author: Primate Evolution: An Introduction To Man's Place In Nature, 1972; co-editor: Macmillan Series in Physical Anthropology; A Simons Family History in England and America, 1975, Candebec in France and England, 2005, Tarsiers: Past, Present, and Future; contbr. numerous articles to profl. publs. Decorated chevalier Ordre Nat., Madagascar; recipient Annadale Meml. medal, Asiatic Soc. Bengal, 1973, Sr. U.S. Scientist award, Alexander von Humboldt Found., 1975; named hon. citizen, Fayum Province of Egypt, 1981. Mem. AAAS, Am. Philos. Soc., Nat. Acad. Scis., Soc. Vertebrate Paleontology, Inst. Human Paleontology, Am. Assn. Zool. Parks and Aquariums (primate specialist group, advisor prosimian taxon group), Assn. Phys. Anthropology (Charles R. Darwin award 2000), Madagascar Fauna Group (bd. dirs.), Internat. Assn. Human Biologists, Sigma Xi. Democrat. Achievements include research in on early mammals, prosimians and primate and human evolution, with special interest in living prosimians, higher primate and human origin and evolution; discovery of 1st tarsiers and 1st marsupials in Africa; naming of earliest known ape Aegyptopithecus in Oligocene of Africa; discovery of Gigantopithecus in India, 1968; naming of earliest anthropoids Oligopithecus, 1962, Qatrania, 1983, Serapia and Arsinoea, 1992; discovery of and naming of new species of Propithecus: Golden Crowned Sifaka in Madagascar, 1989; conservation of lemurs and rain forest of Madagascar. Office: Duke Lemur Ctr Divsn Fossil Primates 1013 Broad St Durham NC 27705 Office Phone: 919-416-8420 Ext. 27. Office Fax: 919-416-8584. Business E-Mail: esimons@duke.edu.

SIMONS, GALE GENE, nuclear and electrical engineer, educator; b. Kingman, Kans., Sept. 25, 1939; s. Robert Earl and Laura V. (Swartz) S.; m. Barbara Irene Rinkel, July 2, 1966; 1 child, Curtis Dean. BS, Kans. State U., 1962, MS, 1964, PhD, 1968. Engr. Argonne Nat. Lab., Idaho Falls, Idaho, 1968-77, mgr. fast source reactor, head exptl. support group, 1972-77; prof. nuc. engring. Kans. State U., Manhattan, 1977—2001, assoc. dean for rsch., dir. rsch. coun. Coll. Engring., 1988-97, emeritus prof., 2001—, bd. dirs. Rsch. Found., 1988-97, Presdl. lectr., 1983-96, career counselor, 1984-96. Bd. dirs. Kans. Tech. Enterprise Corp., Topeka; com. mem. Kans. Gov.'s Energy Policy Com., Topeka, 1992-97; presenter, cons. in field Contbr. over 100 articles to sci. jours.; patentee radiation dosimeter. Expert witness State of Kans., Topeka, 1986. Fellow AEC, 1964-67; recipient numerous rsch. grants Mem. AAAS, IEEE, Am. Nuclear Soc., Health Physics Soc., Am. Soc. for Engring. Edn., Masons, Rotary, Phi Kappa Phi, Tau Beta Pi, Pi Mu Epsilon. Home: 2395 Grandview Ter Manhattan KS 66502-3729

SIMONS, HELEN, school psychologist, psychotherapist, educator; b. Chgo., Feb. 13, 1930; d. Leo and Sarah (Shrayer) Pomper; m. Broudy Simons, May 20, 1956 (div. May 1972); children: Larry, Sheri. BA in Biol., Lake Forest Coll., 1951; MA in Clin. Psychology, Roosevelt U., 1972; D of Psychology, Ill. Sch. Profl. Psychology, 1980. Intern Cook County Hosp., Chgo., 1979-80; pvt. practice psychotherapist Chgo., 1980—; sch. psychologist Chgo. Bd. Edn., 1974-79, 80—. Faculty Internat. Soc. for Prevention of Child Abuse and Neglect; lectr., presenter at workshops. Contbr. articles to profl. jours. Mem.: APA, Internat. Sch. Psychologists Assn., Internat. Soc. for Prevention of Child Abuse and Neglect, Chgo. Sch. Psychol. Assn., Ill. Sch. Psychologists Assn., Nat. Sch. Psychologists Assn. Avocations: music, dance, reading. Home: 6145 N Sheridan Rd Apt 29D Chicago IL 60660-6855 Office: Brennemann Sch 4251 N Clarendon Chicago IL 60613 Personal E-mail: hpompers@aol.com.

SIMONS, JAMES HARRIS, hedge fund manager; b. Apr. 25, 1938; m. Barbara Simons (div.); children: Paul(dec.), Nick(dec.); m. Marilyn Hawrys Simons; 3 children. BS in Math., MIT, 1958; PhD in Math., U. Calif., Berkeley, 1961. Math. tchr. MIT, Harvard U., 1961—64; staff mem. comm. rsch. divsn. Inst. Def. Analysis, Alexandria, Va., 1964—68; chmn. math. dept. SUNY, Stony Brook, 1968—78; founder, pres. Renaissance Technologies Corp., East Setauket, NY, 1982—2008, chmn. bd. dirs., 1997—2005, CEO, 2008—. Bd. dirs. Franklin Electronic Pubs. Inc., 1983—; founder Renaissance Institutional Equity Fund, 2005. Co-author (with Shiing-Shen Chern): Characteristic Forms and Geometric Invariants, 1974. Founder Math for America, NYC, 2004; co-founder John Simons Found.; trustee Math. Scis. Rsch. Inst., Berkeley, Brookhaven Nat. Lab., Upton, NY, Rockefeller U., NYC, Inst. Advanced Study, Princeton, NJ; bd. dirs. MIT Corp. Recipient Oswald Veblen prize in Geometry, Am. Mathematical Society, 1976; named Fin. Engr. of Yr., Internat. Assn. Fin. Engineers, 2006; named one of Forbes' Richest Americans, 2005—, World's Richest People, Forbes mag., 2005—. Fellow: Am. Acad. Arts & Scis. Office: Renaissance Techs Corp 600 Route 25A East Setauket NY 11733-2841 also: 800 3rd Ave Fl 33 New York NY 10022-7604*

SIMONS, JOHN NELSON, surgeon, consultant; b. Lawrence, Kans., Sept. 19, 1932; s. Dolph Collins and Marie Nelson Simons; children: John Jr., Andrea, James, Suzanne, Melissa. BA, U. Kans., 1954; MD, U. Pa., 1958; M in Surgery, U. Minn., 1963. Cert. Am. Bd. Surgery, 1965, Am. Bd. Plastic Surgery, 1967. Cons. plastic surgery Mayo Clinic, Rochester, Minn., 1965—66, asst. prof. plastic surgery, 1965—72, head sect. plastic surgery, 1967—73, assoc. prof. plastic surgery, 1972—73. Founder, CEO Health Campus Internat. Consultants in Health Care Delivery, East Gulf Lake, Minn., 1995—. Republican. Home: 10999 Pine Beach Rd East Gull Lake MN 56401

SIMONS, KATHLEEN A., accountant, educator; d. William V. and Gloria D. Robinson. BS in Edn., Edinboro State U., Pa., 1970; MS in Edn., Ea. Ct. U., Willimantic, 1976; MST, Bryant U., Smithfield, RI, 1982; DBA, Boston U., 1990. Cert. in pub. acctg., RI, 1983. Elem. sch. tchr. Putnam Sch. Dist., Conn., 1971—83; pvt. practise Smithfield, 1980—2000; acct. Piccerelli, Gilstein and Co., Providence, 1982—84; prof. acctg. Bryant U., 1984—. Bd. dir. Acad. Bus. Edn., 2007—; assoc. editor Acctg. Edn.: An Internat. Jour., Oxfordshire, England, 2007—. Recipient Best Paper award, Am. Acctg. Assn., Ethics Divsn., 2006, Alumni Disting. Faculty award, Bryant U., 2008. Mem.: Am. Inst. CPAs (exam. content com. 2008—), RI Soc. CPAs (pres. 1994). Avocation: travel. Office: Bryant Univ Route 7 Faculty Ste B Smithfield RI 02917 Business E-Mail: ksimons@bryant.edu.

SIMONS, LAWRENCE BROOK, lawyer; b. NYC, Oct. 19, 1924; s. Harry A. and Marion B. (Brook) Simons; m. Annalou Kadin, Aug. 24, 1947; children: Barbara Flexner, Kenneth. Student, Duke U., 1941-43, 46-47; JD, Columbia U., 1949. Bar: N.Y. 1949, U.S. Dist. Ct. (so. dist.) N.Y. 1949, DC 1984, U.S. Supreme Ct. 1987. Assoc. Spring & Eastman, NYC, 1949-53; v.p., gen. mgr. Caribe Knitting Mills, San Juan, 1953-58; pres. LBS Constrn. Co. Inc., SI, NY, 1958-77; asst. sec. housing FHA commn. HUD, Washington, 1977-81; ptnr. Powell, Goldstein, Frazier & Murphy, Washington, 1981—. Mem. task force quality life Dept. of Def., 1995. Mem. Nat. Housing Task Force, 1988, Nat. Housing Trust, 1990—; chmn. bd. dirs. NY State Urban Devel. Corp., 1975—77, Pa. Ave. Devel. Corp., 1981—87; trustee Bayley Seton Hosp., SI, 1981—90, NHP Found., Inc., 1991—2003, Affordable Housing Found., 1990—92, Ctr. Democracy, 1990—96; pres. Ctr. Housing Policy, 1992—96, bd. dirs., 1996—; commr. Beaufort (S.C.) Housing Authority, 1997—, Affordable Housing Commn., Hilton Head, SC, 1997—99. With US Army, 1943—46, ETO. Named Man of the Yr., Nat. Housing Conf., 1985. Mem.: ABA, Nat. Assn. Home Builders (named to Housing Hall of Fame 2002), Sea Pines Country Club, Lambda Alpha. Democrat. Jewish. Avocation: golf. Home: 40 Plantation Dr Hilton Head Island SC 29928-4402 Personal E-mail: simonshhi1@roadrunner.com.

SIMONS, LYNN OSBORN, educator; b. Havre, Mont., June 1, 1934; d. Robert Blair and Dorothy (Briggs) Osborn; m. John Powell Simons, Jan. 19, 1957; children: Clayton Osborn, William Blair. BA, U. Colo., 1956. Tchr. Midvale (Utah) Jr. H.S., 1956-57, Sweetwater county Sch. Dist. 1, Rock Springs, Wyo., 1957-58, U. Wyo., 1959-61, Natrona County Sch. Dist. 1, Casper, Wyo., 1963-64; credit mgr. Gallery 323, Casper, 1972-77; Wyo. state supt. pub. instrn. Cheyenne, 1979-91; sec.'s regional rep. region VIII U.S. Dept. Edn., Denver, 1993—2001; mem. Denver Fed. Exec. Bd., 1995-2001; mem. exec. bd. combined Fed. campaign, 1994—2001; ednl. cons., 2001—03; state planning coord. Capitol Bldg., Cheyenne, Wyo., 2003; adj. instr. Laramie County CC, 2008—. Mem. State Bds. Charities and Reform, Land Commrs., Farm Loan, 1979-91; mem. State Commns. Capitol Bldg., Liquor, 1979-91; Ex-officio mem. bd. trustees U. Wyo., 1979-91; ex-officio mem. Wyo. Community Coll. Commn., 1979-91; adjunct English instr. Laramine County Cmty. Coll., Cheymne, Wyo; mem. steering com. Edn. Commn. of the States, 1988-90; mem. State Bd. Edn., 1971-77, chmn., 1976-77; advisor Nat. Trust for Hist. Preservation, 1980-86; bd. visitors coll. arts and scis. U. Wyo., 1998—. Bd. dirs. Cheyenne Bot. Gardens Found., 2004—. Mem. LWV (pres. 1970-71). Democrat. Episcopalian.

SIMONS, MICHAEL A., dean, law educator; b. Nov. 22, 1964; m. Karen Moritz; 5 children. BA, Coll. of the Holy Cross, 1986; JD magna cum laude, Harvard U., 1989. Bar: NY, US Ct. Appeals (2nd cir.), US Ct. Appeals, DC, US Dist. Ct. (so. dist.) NY, US Dist. Ct. (ea. dist.) NY. Law clk. to Hon. Louis F. Oberdorfer US Dist Ct., DC, 1989—90; staff atty. The Washington Post, Washington, 1990—91; assoc. Stillman, Friedman & Shaw, NYC, 1991—95; asst. US atty. (so. dist.) NY US Dept. Justice, 1995—98; asst. prof. law St. John's U. Sch. Law, Queens, NY, 1998—2001, assoc. prof., 2001—03, prof. law, 2003—, assoc. dean faculty scholarship, 2005—08, dean, 2009—. Fellow Vincentian Ctr. for Ch. and Soc., St. John's U., 2001—03, sr. fellow, 2003—; vis. adj. prof. Benjamin N. Cardoza Sch. Law, Yeshiva U., NYC, 2003, NYC, 08, vis. prof., 09; lectr. evidence and criminal law BAR/BRI Bar Review, 2003—. Contbr. articles to law jours. Mem.: ABA, Nassau County Bar Assn., Fed. Bar Coun. Office: St John's U Sch Law Office of Dean 800 Utopia Parkway Jamaica NY 11439 Office Phone: 718-990-6013. Office Fax: 718-990-8600. E-mail: simonsm@stjohns.edu.*

SIMONS, PAUL E., United States Ambassador to Chile; BA, Yale U., New Haven; MBA in Fin., NYU Stern Sch. Bus., 1982. Former asst. v.p./banker, NYC; internat. economist US Dept. Treasury; lead economist policy planning staff US Dept. State, joined Fgn. Svc., svc. at US Embassies in Malawi and Colombia, econ. coun. Quito, Ecuador, 1992—96, dep. chief of mission Tel Aviv, acting asst. sec. Internat. Narcotics and Law Enforcement Affairs, dep. asst. sec. Energy, Sanctions, and Commodities, US amb. to Chile, 2007—. Office: DOS Amb 3460 Santiago Pl Washington DC 20521-3460

SIMONS, RICHARD DUNCAN, lawyer, retired judge; b. Niagara Falls, NY, Mar. 23, 1927; s. William Taylor and Sybil Irene (Swick) S.; m. Muriel (Penny) E. Genung, June 9, 1951 (dec. 1992); m. Esther (Esi) Turkington Tremblay, May 21, 1994; children: Ross T., Scott R.,

Kathryn E., Linda A, stepchildren: Cindy Tremblay, Mark Tremblay. AB, Colgate U., 1949; LLB, U. Mich., 1952; LLD (hon.), Albany Law Sch., 1983. Bar: N.Y. 1952. Pvt. practice, Rome, NY, 1952-63; asst. corp. counsel City of Rome, 1955-58, corp. counsel, 1960-63; justice 5th jud. dist. N.Y. Supreme Ct., 1964-83, assoc. justice appellate divsn. 3d dept., 1971-72, assoc. justice appellate divsn. 4th dept., 1973-82; assoc. judge N.Y. Ct. Appeals, 1983—97, acting chief judge, 1992-93; counsel McMahon & Grow, Rome, NY, 1997—; dir. N.Y. State Capital Defender Office, 1997-2000; chief judge Oneida Indian Nation, 1997—. Jurist in residence Syracuse U. Law Sch., 1998; mem. Law Sch. Admission Svcs., Bar Passage Study Com.; mem. chief judges commn. Future of NY Ct.; mem. 4 Cts. on the Judiciary. Editorial staff: N.Y. Pattern Jury Instructions, 1979-83. Chmn. Republican City Com., 1958-62; vice chmn. Oneida County Rep. Com., 1958-62; bd. mgrs. Rome Hosp. and Murphy Meml. Hosp., 1953; trustee Rome Arts and Cmty. Ctr., 2003-2004, mem. chief judge's commn. fidiciary appointments, chief judge's com. promote trust and confidence in legal sys., chair jud. election qualification commn. 5th Jud. Dist., N.Y. Fair Elections Project, Inc., Campaign for Effective Justice; trustee First Presbyn. Ch. Rome. Served with USN, World War II. NEH fellow U. Va. Law Sch., 1979. Fellow Am. Bar Found., N.Y. State Bar Found. (chmn. 1997-98); mem. ABA, N.Y. State Bar Assn. (chair task force on ct. reorgn. 1999-2003, chair spl. com. ct. structure and jud. selection 2004-05, Disting. Svc. award 2000), Oneida County Bar Assn., Rome Bar Assn., Am. Law Inst., Inst. Jud. Adminstrn. Home: 6520 Pillmore Cir Rome NY 13440-7337 Office: McMahon & Grow 301 N Washington St Rome NY 13440-5152

SIMONS, ROBERT EDWARD, mechanical engineer, consultant; s. Stanley and Mary Simons; m. Miriam Freda Andros, Apr. 23, 1940; children: Anthony Robert, Gina Marie DaLatri, Lisa Marie Luber, Mark Edward. AAS, Dutchess C.C., Poughkeepsie, 1960; BSME, Pa. Mil. Coll., Chester, 1962; MS in Ops. Rsch. and Applied Stats., Union Coll., Schenectady, NY, 1985. Engr. GE Corp., Phila., 1962—66, IBM Corp., Poughkleepsie, 1966—69, project/devel. engr. Poughkeepsie, 1969—79, sr. engr., 1979—87, sr. tech. staff mem., 1987—93; cons. Electronics Cooling Applications, Poughkeepsie, 1993—97, IBM Corp., Poughkeepsie, 1997—. Guest editor IEEE Transactions (CHMT/CPT), NYC, 1992—2002. Assoc. editor: Electronics Cooling Mag., 2002—; contbr. chpts. to 9 books. Recipient Best Paper award, IEEE Semiconductor Thermal Measurement and Mgmt. Symposium, 1984, 2000, 1984, 2000, Semi-Therm Significant Contbr. award, IEEE Semiconductor Thermal Measurement and Mgmt. Symposium, 1995, EDN Award for Excellence, EDN Mag., 1969, Outstanding Reviewer award, ASME Jour. Heat Transfer, 2006. Achievements include co-invention of Thermal Conduction Module concept used to cool 3 generations of IBM mainframe computers; 100 patents for cooling electronic packages and equipment; research in liquid cooling techniques for electronic equipment. Home: 16 Shamrock Cir Poughkeepsie NY 12603

SIMONS, STEPHEN, mathematics professor, researcher; b. London, Aug. 11, 1938; came to U.S., 1965; s. Jack Isidore Simons and Ethel Esther (Littman) Harris; m. Jacqueline Mania Berchadsky, Aug. 13, 1963; 1 son, Mark. BA, Cambridge U., Eng., 1959, PhD, 1962. Instr. U. B.C., Vancouver, Can., 1962-63; asst. prof. U. BC., Vancouver, Can., 1964-65, U. Calif., Santa Barbara, 1965-67, assoc. prof., 1967-73, prof., 1973—2002, prof. emeritus, 2002—, chmn. dept., 1975-77, 88-89. Trustee Math. Scis. Rsch. Inst., Berkeley, Calif., 1988-94. Peterhouse rsch. fellow, Cambridge U., 1963-64. Mem. Am. Math. Soc. Office: Univ Calif Dept Math Santa Barbara CA 93106

SIMONS-MORTON, DENISE G., medical researcher; MD, U. Md. Sch. Medicine, Balt., 1979; MPH, Johns Hopkins U. Sch. Hygiene and Pub. Health, Balt., 1982; PhD, U. Tex. Sch. Pub. Health, Houston, 1991. Asst. prof. U. Tex. Med. Br., Galveston, 1984—87, Baylor Coll. Medicine, Houston, 1989—92; rsch. med. officer and leader, prevention sci. rsch. group Nat. Heart, Lung, and Blood Inst., Bethesda, Md., 1992—2002, dir., clin. applications and prevention program, 2002—07, sr. sci. advisor, divsn. prevention and population scis., 2007—. Office: Nat Heart Lung & Blood Inst 6701 Rockledge Dr MSC 7936 Bethesda MD 20892 Business E-Mail: simonsd@nhlbi.nih.gov.

SIMONSON, DAVID C., retired newspaper association executive; b. NYC, May 9, 1927; s. Simon and Rebecca (Coolman) S.; m. Lois E. Sneider, Nov. 1, 1952; children: Peter, Eric, John Frederick. BA, Hamilton Coll., 1948; postgrad., U. Vt., 1949, Art Student League of N.Y., 1949. Copywriter Forwell & Mart Advt., NYC, 1949-50; reporter, editor Croton-Cortlandt News, Croton, N.Y., 1950-52; gen. mgr. Colony Publs., NYC, 1952-54; editor, mgr. County Press Newspapers, Croton, 1955-59; promotion dir. Amcrete Corp., Peekskill, N.Y., 1959-60; various positions in mgmt. Patent Trader, Mt. Kisco, N.Y., 1960-72, pub., 1972-77; pres./pub. Pioneer Press Newspapers, Wilmette, Ill., 1977-86; exec. v.p., chief exec. officer Nat. Newspaper Assn., Washington, 1987-92; retired, 1992. Bd. dirs. Christian Herald Assn., NYC, 1978—2007; lectr. Medill Sch. Journalism, Meridian House, U.S.A., numerous state press assns.; media cons.; seminar leader Ea. Europe for World Pres Freedom Com.; cons. to Slovenian publs. for U.S. Info. Agy., 1993—94; cons. to Slovakian publs. for USIA, 1995; cons. to African publs. for UNESCO, 95; cons. to Bulgarian Publs. for USIA, 96, 97; cons. to U.S. State dept. World Freedom Com., 2002—; cons. to Bulgarian Publs. for USIA Croatian Publs. for USIA, 1999; seminar leader Voice of Am. for Bulgarian Publs., 1997, Bosnian pubs., 2000, Albanian publs., 2000; U.S. rep. Media Conf., Prague, 2001; DVTV U.S. rep. with Chinese journalists, 01; participant Freedom Forum Roundtables; media panel cons. U.S. Dept. of State, 2003. Author: What a Free Press Means to Me, 2004, Global Issues, 2005. Chmn. planning bd. Town of Croton-on-Hudson, N.Y., 1962-67, trustee, 1967, mayor, 1969. With USNR, 1945-46. Recipient Lesher award Suburban Newspapers of Am., 1998. Mem. Suburban Newspapers Am. (pres. 1984-85, bd. dirs. 1980-84), Ill. Press Assn (bd. dirs. 1980-84, 1st v.p. 1986), N.Y. Press Assn. (bd. dirs. 1966-76, 1st v.p. 1976), Nat. Newspaper Assn. (bd. dirs. 1985-86), Cook County Pubs. Assn. (pres. 1983-84). Avocations: painting, cartooning. Home: 1805 28th St S Arlington VA 22202-1536 Personal E-mail: simonsona6@aol.com.

SIMONSON, JAMES S., lawyer; b. Madison, Wis. BA, U. Wis., 1956; LLB, Harvard U., 1959. Bar: Minn. 1959. Ptnr., comml. litigation, chmn. trial dept. Gray Plant Mooty, Mpls. Fellow: Am. Coll. Trial Lawyers; mem.: Fed. Bar Assn., Eighth Cir. Ct. Appeals Bar Assn., Minn. State Bar Assn. Office: Gray Plant Mooty 500 IDS Ctr 80 S 8th St Minneapolis MN 55402 Office Phone: 612-632-3300. Office Fax: 612-632-4300. Business E-Mail: james.simonson@gpmlaw.com.

SIMONSON, LEE STUART, broadcast executive; b. Balt., July 3, 1948; s. Theodore and Sara (Silver) S.; m. Nancy Paula Levin, Mar. 25, 1973; children: Laura Todd, Michael Theodore. BA, U. Md., 1970. Acct. exec. WGMS-AM-FM (subs. RKO Gen.), Washington, 1971-73, retail sales mgr., 1973-76; sales mgr. WFYR-FM (subs. RKO Gen.), Chgo., 1976-80; v.p., gen. mgr. WRKS-FM (subs. RKO Gen.), NYC, 1980-84, WOR-AM (subs. RKO Gen.), NYC, 1984-88; vice chmn., COO, owner radio stas. Broadcasting Ptnrs., Inc., NYC, 1988-95; chmn., CEO Broadcasting Ptnrs. Holdings, LP, NYC, 1997-2000; pres. Simonson Assocs., 2000—. Bd. dirs. TheaterMania.com, MIVA, Inc. Bd. dirs. NY state chpt. March of Dimes, 1982—; bd. mgrs. Border Media Ptnrs., 2007—. With US Army, 1970—76. Jewish. Office Phone: 201-767-9551. Personal E-mail: SIMONSONLS@aol.com.

SIMONT, MARC, artist; b. Paris, Nov. 23, 1915; arrived in US, 1927, naturalized, 1936; s. Josep and Dolors (Basté) Simont; m. Sara Dalton, Apr. 7, 1945; 1 child, Marc Dalton. Attended, Academie Julian, Academie Ranson; asst., André Lhote Sch., all Paris, 1932—35; attended, NAD, NYC, 1936. Jefferson Wing mural Libr. Congress, 1940, 80 books, —; author, illustrator: 9 children's books, 1939—, Opera Soufflé, 1950, Polly's Oats, 1951, The Lovely Summer, 1952, Mimi, 1955, The Plumber Out of the Sea, 1955, The Contest at Paca, 1959, How Come Elephants?, 1965, Afternoon in Spain, 1965, A Child's Eye View of the World, 1972, The Goose That Almost Got Cooked, 1997, author, illustrator (with Red Smith): How to Get to First Base, 1952, translator, illustrator: The Lieutenant Colonel and The Gypsy, 1971, The Stray Dog, 2001 (Caldecott honor, NEBA award, 2005), translator: Ibrahim, 1989. Recipient Caldecott honor, 1950, Caldecott award, 1957, citation merit, Soc. Illustrators, 1965, Il-lustrad'Or, Profl. Assn. Illustrators Catalonia, 1997, Horn Book award, Boston Globe, 2001; Tiffany Found. fellow, 1937. Mem.: Authors Guild. Home: 336 Town St West Cornwall CT 06796-1304

SIMONTON, DEAN KEITH, psychology professor; b. Glendale, Calif., Jan. 27, 1948; s. Dean Clair Simonton and Laverne (Merkobrad) Williams; m. Susan Youel, June 21, 1971 (div. 1982); m. Melody Boyer, Dec. 29, 1984 (div. 2004); m. Karen Horobin, Mar. 20, 2005. BA in Psychology magna cum laude, Occidental Coll., 1970; MA in Social Psychology, Harvard U., 1973, PhD with distinction, 1975. Asst. prof. psychology U. Ark., Fayetteville, 1974-76; from asst. prof. to prof. U. Calif., Davis, 1976—2004, disting. prof., 2004—. Cons. Wissenschaftzentrun, Berlin, 1979, Ctr. for Creative Leadership, Greensboro, N.C., 1983, NATO, Brussels, Belgium, 1980-81, Dept. Def., Washington, 1983, Creative Problem Solving Inst., 1984, Arvin Perlmutter, Inc., 1992, Milken Family Found., 1994, Templeton Found., 2002. Author: Genius, Creativity and Leadership, 1984, Why Presidents Succeed, 1987, Scientific Genius, 1988, Psychology, Science, and History, 1990, Greatness, 1994, Genius and Creativity, 1997, Origins of Genius, 1999, Great Psychologists and Their Times, 2002, Creativity in Science, 2004, Genius 101, 2009; editor Jour. Creative Behavior, 1993-99; assoc. editor jour. psychology of sci. and tech., 2007-; contbr. numerous articles to profl. jours. Recipient Excellence award Mensa Adn. and Rsch. Found., 1986, 2009, Francis Galton award Internat. Assn. Empirical Aesthetics, 1996. Theatrical Innovation prize, Soc. Personality and Soc. Psychology, 2004, Pres. award Nat. Assn. for Gifted Children, 2007. Fellow AAAS, Am. Psychol. Soc., Am. Assn. Applied and Preventive Psychology, Am. Psychol. Assn. (mem.-at-large 1979-82, pres. psychology and the arts divsn. 1985-86, Rudolf Arnheim award Outstanding Contbn. to Psychology and the Arts, 1996, George A. Miller award 1997, William James Book award, 2000, Robert S. Daniel Four Yr. Coll./Univ. Tchg. award, 2006, matter lectr., 2009); mem. Phi Beta Kappa, Sigma Xi. Home: 1331 Arena Dr Davis CA 95616-0274 Office: U Calif Dept Psychology Davis CA 95616 Office Phone: 530-752-1677. Business E-Mail: dksimonton@ucdavis.edu.

SIMONYI, CHARLES, software engineer; b. Budapest, Hungary, Sept. 10, 1948; m. Lisa Persdotter. BS in Engring. Math., U. Calif., Berkeley, 1972; PhD in Computer Sci., Stanford U., 1976; PhD (hon.), U. Pecs, Hungary, 2001. Developer Xerox Palo Alto Rsch. Ctr. (PARC), Calif., 1972-80; dir. application develop., chief architect, and disting. engr. Microsoft Rsch. Corp., Redmond, Wash., 1981—2002; co-founder, pres., CEO Intentional Software Corp., Bellevue, Wash., 2002—. Trustee Inst. for Advanced Study, Princeton, NJ, 1997—, pres. of the corp., 2003—, elected chmn. bd. trustees, 2008—. Recipient Wharton Infosys Bus. Transformaton award, 2004; named one of 400 Richest Americans, Forbes mag., 2006. Mem. NAE, Hungarian Acad. Sci. (corres. mem.); fellow Am. Acad. Arts & Scis. Achievements include development of new approaches in programming technology; program representation where new abstraction mechanisms can be introduced without invalidating legacy code; created the first WYSIWYG (what you see is what you get) text editor called Bravo; endowed a chair for the Public Understanding of Science at Oxford University (1995) and a Charles Simonyi Professorship for Theoretical Physics at the Institute for Advanced Study, Princeton, NJ (1997), among many other educational and charitable contributions through the Charles Simonyi Fund for Arts and Sciences; fulfilled a lifelong dream and became the fifth space tourist for $25 million to take a trip to the International Space Station with Russian cosmonauts on the Russian Soyuz TMA-10 mission in April, 2007. The trip lasted a total of 13 days. Returned to Earth on April 21, 2007; paid $35 million for second trip on the Russian Soyuz TMA-14 mission to the International Space Station in March, 2009. The trip will last 13 days. This trip that makes him the first two-time space tourist. Office: Charles Simonyi Fund For Arts And Scienc PO Box 85900 Seattle WA 98145-1900 Office Phone: 425-467-6600. Office Fax: 425-467-6601. E-mail: charles@intentsoft.com.

SIMOS, NIKOLAOS, engineer, researcher; b. Drosopigi, Konitsa, Greece, Jan. 16, 1958; s. Alexios and Zoe Simos; m. Kathryn Zarcadoolas; 1 child, Anna Zoe. PhD, CUNY, 1988. Cert. engr., NY State, 2000. Scientist Brookhaven Nat. Lab., Upton, NY, 1989—. Adj. prof. City Coll. NY, 1989—95, Poly. U. NY, 1990—94; propr. Matrix Engring. Consulting, Shoreham, NY, 2005—. Achievements include research in radiation damage to materials. Office: Brookhaven Nat Lab Bldg 130 Upton NY 11973 Business E-Mail: simos@bnl.gov.

SIMPKINS, CUTHBERT ORMOND, surgeon, educator, writer; b. Chgo., Aug. 20, 1947; s. Cuthbert Ormond and Dorothy Mary (Herndon) S.; m. Ruby Mae Carroll (div.); m. Carol Jean Garrett (div. Dec. 1982); m. Diane Phipps, June 23, 1983. BS, Amherst Coll., Mass., 1969; MD, Harvard U., 1974. Diplomate Am. Coll. of Surgeons. Chief resident Downstate Med. Ctr., Bklyn., 1980; rsch. assoc. dept. biophysics and physiology Rutgers U., Piscataway, N.J., 1981-82; rsch. fellow dept. surgery Boston U., 1982-83; rsch. fellow Naval Med. Rsch. Inst., Bethesda, Md., 1983-84, prin. investigator, 1984-87, acting br. dir., 1987; chief surg. rsch. D.C. Gen. Hosp., Washington, 1987-91; asst. prof. dept. surgery Howard U., Washington, 1987—, U. Md., Balt., 1991—. Peer reviewer Life Sciences, Tucson, 1988—. Author: Coltrane: A Biography, 1975; contbr. articles to profl. jours. Chairman planning com. D.C. Govt. Task Force on Violence and Victimization, Washington, 1987; judge sci. fair NAACP, Washington, 1991—. Comdr. USN, 1983-87. John Woodruff Simpson fellow Amherst Coll., 1969, Harold Wade fellow, 1982-84; recipient Community Svc. award Charles Gallery, 1976, Outstanding Rsch. Commendation USN, 1983, 87. Mem. AAAS, Assn. Acad. Surgeons, N.Y. Acad. Scis., African-Am. Writers Guild (co-founder, past v.p. Washington chpt.), Orgn. Black Scientist. Democrat. Baptist. Achievements include first demonstration of opioid peptide interactions with neutrophils, interaction between peptides and cytochrome C. Office: U Md Med Ctr Dept Surgery 22 S Greene St Dept Surgery Baltimore MD 21201-1544 also: Erie Co Med Ctr 464 Grider St Buffalo NY 14215-3021 Home: 3060 Nottingham Dr Shreveport LA 71115-9530

SIMPKINS, NEIL P., investment and automotive company executive; Grad. with honors, Oxford U.; MBA, Harvard Bus. Sch. Consultant Bain & Co., London; principal Bain Capital, 1993—99; sr. mng. dir., private equity group Blackstone Group L.P., 1999—; chmn. TRW Automotive, Livonia, Mich., 2003—. Bd. dirs. Vanguard Health Systems Inc. Office: Blackstone Group 345 Park Ave New York NY 10154 also: TRW Automotive 12001 Tech Ctr Dr Livonia MI 48150

SIMPLOT, TOM, Councilman; Bar: Ariz.; lic. realtor. Former sr. adv. Gov. Fife Symington; former adv. Maricopa County Supr. Betsey Bayless; councilman, Dist. 4 Phoenix City Coun., 2003—; vice mayor City of Phoenix. Former pres. Maricopa County Bd. Health, Maricopa County Indsl. Devel. Authority; mem. Fed. Comm. Commn. Intergovernmental Adv. Com., Housing & Neighborhoods, Seniors, Families & Youth, Transp. & Infrastructure Coms. Chmn. METRO Bd. Dirs.; vice chmn. Phoenix Encanto Village Planning Com.; former chmn. Phoenix Hist. Preservation Commn.; bd. mem. Valle del Sol; mem. Phoenix Housing Commn. Mem.: Arizona Multi-housing Assn. (pres.). Office: 200 W Washington St 11th Fl Phoenix AZ 85003 Office Phone: 602-262-7447. Office Fax: 602-534-5438. Business E-Mail: council.district.4@phoenix.gov.*

SIMPSON, ALAN KOOI, lawyer, former senator; b. Cody, Wyo., Sept. 2, 1931; s. Milward Lee and Lorna (Kooi) S.; m. Ann Schroll, June 21, 1954; children: William Lloyd, Colin Mackenzie, Susan Lorna Simpson Gallagher. BS, U. Wyo., 1954, JD, 1958; LLD (hon.), Calif. Western Sch. of Law, San Diego, 1983, Colo. Coll., Colo. Springs, 1986, Notre Dame U., South Bend, Ind., 1987, Am. U., DC, 1989, Rocky Mountain Coll., Billings, Mont., 1996, U. Wyo., Laramie, 1999. Bar: Wyo. 1958, U.S. Supreme Ct. 1964. Asst. atty. gen. State of Wyo., 1959; city atty. City of Cody, 1959-69; ptnr. Simpson, Kepler, and Simpson, Cody, Wyo., 1959-78; mem. Wyo. Ho. of Reps., 1964-77, majority whip, 1973-75, majority floor leader, 1975-77, speaker pro tem, 1977; US Senator from Wyo., 1979—97; asst. majority leader, 1985—87; asst. mimority leader, 1987—95; chmn. vets. affairs com., 1980—84; chmn. fin. subcom. on Social Security and Family Policy; chmn. subcom. on Immigration and Refugee Policy; mem. Spec. Com. on Aging; dir. Inst. Politics Kennedy Sch. Govt. Harvard U., 1999—2000; ptnr. & shareholder Burg Simpson Eldredge Hersh Jardine and Simpson Kepler & Edwards PC, Cody, Wyo. Guest lectr. London exchange program Regent's Coll., London, 1987; vis. lectr. Lombard chair Shorenstein Ctr. for Press, Politics and Pub. Policy, Kennedy Sch. Govt., Harvard U., 1997-2000; mem. Presdl. Debate Commn.; former commr., Am. Battle Monuments Commn., co-chair Continuity in Govt. Commn., 2002-; mem. Iraq Study Group, 2006; mem. external adv. bd. BP Am.; bd. visitors Kennedy Sch. Govt.; co-chmn. Americans for Campaign Reform, adv. com. The Common Good. Author: Right in the Old Gazoo: A Lifetime of Scrapping with the Press, 1997. Chmn. bd. trustees Buffalo Bill Hist. Ctr., Cody; trustee emeritus, Grand Teton Music Festival; former regent Smithsonian Inst., Washington; past adv. bd. Folger Shakespeare Libr., Washington, past bd. mem. Kennedy Ctr. for Performing Arts, Washington. Recipient Nat. Assn. Land Grant Colls. Centennial Alumni award U. Wyo., 1987, Disting. Alumnus award, 1985, Lifetime Svc. award Vietnam Vets. Am., 1993, Thomas Jefferson award in Law U. Va., 1998. Mem. Wyo. Bar Assn., Park County Bar Assn., U. Wyo Alumni Assn. (pres. 1962, 63, Disting. Alumnus award 1985), VFW (life), Am. Legion, Amvets. (Silver Helmet award). Lodges: Eagles, Elks, Masons (33 deg., Order of Grand Cross), Shriners, Rotary. Republican. Office: Burg Simpson Eldredge Hersh & Jardine 1135 14th St PO Box 490 Cody WY 82414 also: 1220 Sunshine Ave Ste B Cody WY 82414

SIMPSON, ANDREA LYNN, communications executive; b. Altadena, Calif., Feb. 10, 1948; d. Kenneth and Barbara Simpson; 1 child, Christopher Ryan Myrdal. BA, U. So. Calif., 1969, MS, 1983; postgrad., U. Colo., Boulder Sch. Bank Mktg., 1977. Mktg. officer United Calif. Bank, LA, 1969-73; asst. v.p. mktg. 1st Hawaiian Bank, Honolulu, 1973-78; v.p. corp. comms. Pacific Resources Inc., Honolulu, 1978-89, BHP Hawaii, Inc., 1989-98; v.p. corp. rels. Tesoro Petroleum Corp., San Antonio, 1998-2000; v.p. corp. comms. Edison Internat., Rosemead, Calif., 2000—01; pres. Simpson Comm., 2001—. Bd. dirs. Arts Coun., Hawaii, 1977-81, Hawaii Heart Assn., 1978-83, Coun. Pacific Girls Scouts USA, 1982-85, Child and Family Svcs., 1984-86, Honolulu Symphony Soc., 1985-91, Sta. KHPR Hawaii Pub. Radio, 1988-92, Kapiolani Found., 1990-95, Hanahauoli Sch., 1991-98, Hawaii Strategic Devel. Corp., 1991-98, Children's Discovery Ctr., 1994-98, Pacific Asian Affairs Coun., 1994-96, Hawaii MADD, 1992-96, Girl Scout Coun. Mt. Wilson Dist., 2005—; adv. dir. Hawaii Kids at Work, 1991-98; bd. dirs., 2d v.p. Girl Scout Coun. Hawaii, 1994-96, adv. bd., 1996-98; trustee Hawaii Loa Coll., 1984-86, Kapiolani Women's and Children's Hosp., 1988-97, Hawaii Sch. for Girls at LaPietra, 1989-91, Kapiolani Med. Ctr. at Pali Momi, 1994-98; bd. dirs. Aloha coun. Boy Scouts Am., 1998, Alamo coun., 1998-2000; found. bd. dirs. Hawaii Pub. TV, 1998, bd. dirs., San Pedro Playhouse, 1999-2000; bd. dirs. Red Cross of San Antonio, 1999-2000; commr. Hawaii State Commn. on Status of Women, 1985-87, State Sesquecentennial of Pub. Schs. Commn., 1990-91. Named Advt. Woman of Yr., Honolulu Advt. Fedn., 1982, Pub. Rels. Profl. of Yr., Honolulu Pub. Rels. Soc., 1993, Communicator of Yr., Utilities Communicators Internat., 1983. Mem. Internat. Pub. Rels. Assn. (Golden World award 1997), Am. Mktg. Assn., Pub. Rels. Soc. America (bd. dirs. Honolulu chpt. 1984-86, Silver Anvil award 1984, Pub. Rels. Profl. Yr. 1991), U. So. Calif. Alumni Assn. (bd. dirs. Hawaii 1981-83), Outrigger Canoe Club, Rotary (pub. rels. chmn. 1988-97, Honolulu chpt., bd. dirs. 1998), Alpha Phi (past pres., dir. Hawaii), Hawaii Jaycees (Outstanding Young Person of Hawaii 1978), San Marino Rotary Club, Hist. Novel Soc.

SIMPSON, ANDREW J.G., molecular biologist, researcher; b. Newcastle Under-Lyme, Eng. s. Hubert G. and Barbara M.C. Simpson; m. Catarina B.C. Simpson, Aug. 26, 1993; children: Victoria, William, Leila. PhD, Nat. Inst. Med. Rsch., London, 1980. Postdoc. fellow NIH, Bethesda, Md.; faculty Nat. Inst. Med. Rsch., 1983—89; vis. scientist Centro de Pesquisas René Rachou, Belo Horizonte, Brazil, 1989—95; head lab. cancer genetics Ludwig Inst. Cancer Rsch., São Paulo, Brazil, 1995—2002, dir. James R. Kerr prog., spl. asst. to dir. NYC, 2002, now sci. dir. Office: Ludwig Inst Cancer Rsch 605 Third Ave 33rd Fl New York NY 10158 Office Phone: 212-450-1500. Office Fax: 212-450-1555.*

SIMPSON, A.W. BRIAN, law educator; b. 1931; Degree (hon.), Dalhousie Law Sch., Can., 2003, U. Kent at Canterbury, Eng., 2003. Fellow Oxford U., Eng., 1955-72; prof. U. Kent, Canterbury, Eng., 1972-84, U. Chgo., 1984-87, U. Mich. Law Sch., Ann Arbor, 1987—, Charles F. and Edith J. Clyne Prof. of Law. Lectr. Centre for Human Rights, London Sch. Econs., 2003. Author: Human Rights and the End of Empire: Britain and the Genesis of the European Convention, History of the Common Law of Contract, Biographical Dictionary of the Common Law, Cannibalism and the Common Law, A History of the Land, Law, Legal Theory and Legal History, In the Highest Degree Odious: Detention Without Trial in Wartime Britain, Leading Cases in the Common Law; contbr. articles to law jours. Named Hon. Queen's Coun., 2001. Fellow: Am. Acad. Arts and Scis., Lincoln Coll., Oxford (hon.); mem.: British Acad. Office: U Mich Law Sch 409 Hutchins Hall 625 S State St Ann Arbor MI 48109-1215 Office Phone: 734-763-0413. Business E-Mail: bsimpson@umich.edu.

SIMPSON, BOB R., energy executive; BS Acctg. with honors, Baylor U., MBA. Tax mgr. Southland Royalty Co., 1976—79, v.p. Fin. & Corp. Devel., 1979—86; co-founder, CEO XTO Energy Inc., Fort Worth, Tex., 1986—96, chmn., CEO, 1996—2008, chmn., 2008—. Mem. Nat. Petroleum Council; bd. dirs. XTO Energy Inc., 1990—. Office: XTO Energy Inc 810 Houston St Fort Worth TX 76102-6298*

SIMPSON, CAROL MANN, librarian, editor, educator, attorney; b. Aberdeen, Md., Nov. 28, 1949; d. Joey Mathew and Grace Winifred (Fielman) Pirrung; m. Robert Smith Mann, Jan. 4, 1969 (div. May 1986); children: Stephen, David (dec.), Sarah; m. Douglas Michael Simpson, Jan. 18, 1992; stepchildren, Brian, Kevin. BS in Edn., Southwestern U., 1971; MA, U. Tex., 1975, MLS, 1977; EdD, East Tex. State U., 1987; JD, Southern Methodist U., 2008. Cert. art and French tchr., libr., learning resources specialist, supr., Tex. Tchr. Round Rock (Tex.) Ind. Sch. Dist., 1970-74; libr. Mesquite (Tex.) Ind. Sch. Dist., 1977-90, coord. libr. and media svcs., 1990-92, facilitator libr. tech., 1992—98; assoc. prof. U. North Tex. Sch. Libr. and Info. Scis., Denton, 1998—2006. Adj. prof. Tex. Women's U., 1992-93; fellow Tex. Ctr. for Digital Knowledge, 2000-06; cons. Orex Petroleum, Dallas, 1988, Mesquite Pub. Libr., 1989-90, HBW Assocs., Dallas, 1988-89; reviewer Booklist, 1984-95, Sch. Libr. Jour., 1984-95, Video Rating Guide for Libr., 1989-92. Author: Copyright for School Libraries, 1994, Internet for Library Media Specialists, 1995, Copyright for Schools, 1997, 2005, Copyright Catechism, 2005, Copyright Administr., 2006, Internet for Schools, 1997, 2003, Ethics for School Librarianship, 2003; editor: Technology Connection, 1995—99, The Book Report, 1999—2003, Library Talk, 1999—2003, Library Media Connection, 2003—08; contbr. articles to profl. jours. Mem. ALA, Tex. Libr. Assn., Am. Assn. Sch. Librs., Tex. Assn. Sch. Librs, Am. Bar Assn. Methodist. Avocations: genealogy, computers, gardening. Home: 1086 Holly Ln Lewisville TX 75067-5710

SIMPSON, CARTER B., lawyer; b. Pitts., July 19, 1950; s. John W. Simpson; m. Paulette Peters, May 1, 1982; children: Christina B., Carter B. Jr. BSE in Elec. Engring., Princeton U., 1972; JD, U. Mich., 1976. Assoc. Cadwalader, Wickersham & Taft, NYC, 1976—86, counsel, 1986—88; counsel, antitrust and litig. Mobil Corp., Fairfax, Va., 1988—91, sr. counsel, antitrust, 1991—96, sr. counsel, antitrust and trade regulation, 1996—99; downstream antitrust counsel Exxon Mobil Corp., Fairfax, 2000—06; sr. counsel antitrust and trade regulation Downstream Cos., 2006—. Adv. bd. mem.: Antitrust Counselor, Bus. Laws Inc., 1995—. Dir. Overlook Condo Assn., Wintergreen, Va., 2005—06. Mem.: ABA Antitrust Sect. (vice chair Clayton Act com. 1995—99, vice chmn. teleseminars com. 2007—). Home: 10007 Thompson Ridge Ct Great Falls VA 22066 Office: Exxon Mobil Corp 3225 Gallows Rd Fairfax VA 22037 E-mail: carter.b.simpson@exxonmobil.com.

SIMPSON, COLLEEN HEALY, lawyer; married. BA, Villanova U., Pa., 1996; JD, Villanova Sch. Law, 1999. Admission to pratice law: Pa. 1999. Assoc. Harkins Cunningham LLP, Phila., 2001—09, ptnr., 2009—. Recipient Rising Star, Law & Politics, 2007—08. Mem.: Profl. Women's Roundtable. Office: Harkins Cunningham LLP 2800 One Commerce Sq 2005 Market St Philadelphia PA 19103

SIMPSON, DANIEL H., ambassador; b. Wheeling, W.Va., July 9, 1939; married; 4 children. BA, Yale U., 1961; cert. in African studies, Northwestern U., 1973. Joined Fgn. Svc., U.S. Dept. State, Washington, 1966—, staff asst. Bur. Security and Consular Affairs, 1966-67, speech writer for asst. sec. state for African affairs, 1968, desk officer for Rhodesia, Botswana, Lesotho, and Swaziland, 1973-74; tng. officer USIA, Washington, 1967-68; polit., econ. and consular officer Am. Embassy, Bujumbura, Burundi, 1968-70, polit. officer Pretoria, Republic South Africa, 1970-72, dep. chief mission Beirut, until 1989; amb. to Ctrl. African Republic, Bangui, 1989-92; dep. comdr. Army War Coll., Carlisle, Pa., 1993-94; ambassador to Somalia Mogadishu, 1994-95; ambassador to Congo Kinshasa, 1995-98; v.p. Nat. Def. U., Washington, 1998-2000; regional dir. OSCE, Bosnia-Herzegovina, 2000—01; assoc. editor Pitts. Post-Gazette and Toledo Blade, 2001—. Address: Pitts Post-Gazette 34 Blvd of the Allies Pittsburgh PA 15222 Home: 112 Washington Pl #20A Pittsburgh PA 15219 Office Phone: 412-263-1976. E-mail: dsimpson@post-gazette.com.

SIMPSON, DANIEL REID, lawyer, mediator; b. Glen Alpine, NC, Feb. 20, 1927; s. James R. and Margaret Ethel (Newton) S.; m. Mary Alice Leonard, Feb. 25, 1930; children: Mary Simpson Beyer, Ethel B. Simpson Todd, James R., II. BS, Wake Forest U., 1949, LLB, 1951. Bar: N.C. 1951, U.S. Dist. Ct. (we. dist.) N.C. 1951, U.S. Ct. Appeals (4th and 5th cirs.) 1980; cert. mediator. Former ptnr. Simpson Aycock PA, Morganton, NC; of counsel Simpson, Kuehnert, Vinay & Jones, P.A., Morganton. Author: American Angels, 2001. Mem. N.C. Ho. of Reps., 1959-65; mem. N.C. Senate, 1984-96; del. Rep. Nat. Conv., 1968, 76; mem. N.C. Rep. Exec. Com. Served with AUS, 1943-45, PTO. Recipient Guardian Small Bus. award Order of Longleaf Pine; named to NRA Legion of Honor; sports complex named in his honor by Town of Glen Alpine, N.C. Mem. N.C. Bar Assn., Burke County Bar Assn., Masons (past master). Baptist. Home: 2358 E Point Rd Nebo NC 28761-9694 Office: Simpson Kuehnert Vinay & Jones PA 216 N Sterling St Morganton NC 28655 also: PO Box 1329 Morganton NC 28680-1329 Office Phone: 828-437-9744. E-mail: jrs@hci.net.

SIMPSON, DAVID WILLIAM, artist, educator; b. Pasadena, Calif., Jan. 20, 1928; s. Frederick and Mary Adeline (White) S.; m. Dolores D. Debus, July 30, 1954; 1 stepchild, Gregory C. Vose; 1 child, Lisa C. B.F.A., Calif. Sch. Fine Arts, 1956; MA, San Francisco State Coll., 1958. Instr. art Am. River Jr. Coll., Sacramento, 1958-60, Contra Costa Jr. Coll., San Pablo, Calif., 1960-65; prof. art U. Calif., Berkeley, 1967-91, prof. emeritus, 1991—. One-man shows include Robert Elkon Gallery, NYC, 1961, 63-64, San Francisco Mus. Art, 1967, Henri Gallery, Washington, 1968, Oakland Mus., 1978, Modernism, San Francisco, 1980-81, 84, 86, 2001, 09, Sheldon Meml. Art Gallery, Lincoln, Nebr., 1990, Mincher/Wilcox Gallery, San Francisco, 1991-93, Angles Gallery, Santa Monica, Calif., 1991-92, 94, 99, Bemis Found., Omaha, 1991, Anthony Ralph Gallery, NYC, 1992, John Berggruen Gallery, San Francisco, 1994, Charlotte Jackson Fine Art, Santa Fe, 1995, 2005, 2007-, Laguna Art Mus., Laguna Beach, Calif., 1995 Haines Gallery, San Francisco, 1997, 99, 2004, 07, Studio La Citta, Verona, Italy, 1998, 2002, 08, Renate Schröder Gallery, Cologne, Germany, 2000-02, Artothek, Cologne, 2002, James Kelly Contemporary, Santa Fe, 2003, Studio G-7, Bologna, Italy, Sonja Roesch Gallery, Houston, 2005, 07, 09; exhibited in group shows at Mus. Modern Art, NYC, 1963, Carnegie Internat., Pitts., 1961-62, 66-67, LA Mus. Art, 1964, U. Ill., 1969, Expo '70, Osaka, Japan, 1970, Josly Art Mus., Omaha, 1970, John Berggruen Gallery, San Francisco, 1979, 93, Angles Gallery, Santa Monica, 1988, 90, John Good Gallery, NY, 1992, Cheryl Haines Gallery, San Francisco, 1996, Mus. di Arte Moderna e Contemporanea, Trento, Italy, 1996, Studio La Citta, Verona, Italy, 1996-2005, Llonja, Palma De Majorca, Spain, 1997, Mus. Cantonale d'Arte, Lugano, Switzerland, 1997, Haines Gallery, San Francisco, 1997, 2008, Palazzo Ducale, Gubbio, Italy, 1999, Palazzo Ducale, Panza Della Gran Guardia, Verona, 2002, Albright-Knox Gallery, Buffalo, NY, 2005, 2007-, Fondazione Marenostrum Porto Venere, Italy, Kunstverein Lingen Kuntshauz, Germany, 2005, Lausberg Gallery, Toronto, Can., 2007, Dusseldorf, Germany, 2007, Dorsky Gallery, Long Island City, NY, 2009, Museo Fortuny Venice, Italy, 2009, others; represented in permanent collections including Phila. Mus. Art, Nat. Collection Fine Arts, Wash., Seattle Art Mus., La Jolla (Calif.) Mus. Art, Mus. Modern Art, NYC, San Francisco Mus. Art, Oakland (Calif.) Mus., Panza Collection, Italy, Laguna Art Mus., Laguna Beach, Calif., U. Art Mus., Berkeley, Calif., Mus. Cantonale d'Arte Lugano, Switzerland, Mus. Di Arte Moderna e Contemporanea Di Trento e Roverato, Sassuolo, Panza Collection, Italy, Albright Knox Gallery, Buffalo, San Jose Mus., Calif. Home: 565 Vistamont Ave Berkeley CA 94708-1244 Office: U Calif Dept Art Berkeley CA 94720

SIMPSON, DENNIS DWAYNE, psychologist, educator; b. Lubbock, Tex., Nov. 9, 1943; s. Homer Arnold and Georgie Lee (Barrett) S.; m. Sherry Ann Johnson, Aug. 20, 1965; children: Jason Renn, Jeffrey Todd, Jennifer Lynn. BA, U. Tex., 1966; PhD, Tex. Christian U., 1970. Asst. prof. psychology Tex. Christian U., Ft. Worth, 1970-74, assoc. prof., 1974-79, prof., 1979-82, dir., prof., 1989—, S.B. Sells prof. psychology, 1992—; dir., prof. Tex. A&M U., College Station, 1982-89. Mem. sci. adv. bd. NICA Rsch. Ctrs., Washington, 1992—; mem. adv. bd. Nat. Drug Treatment Evaluation Studies, Washington, 1992—; cons. WHO, fgn. govts. regarding drug rsch. Mem. editl. bd. Am. Jour. Drug and Alcohol Abuse, Substance Abuse Treatment, Substance Use and Misuse; contbr. over 250 articles to profl. jours.; author: 9 books. Recipient Disting. Rsch. Achievement award Tex. Commn. on Alcohol and Drug Abuse, 1987; recipient numerous grants. Mem.: APA, Southwestern Psychol. Assn., Acad. for Health Svcs. Rsch. and Health Policy, The Coll. on Problems of Drug Dependence. Achievements include research emphasis on the process of treatment service delivery in relation to client attributes and how they related to retention rates, relapse and posttreatment outcomes; research in drug use in the workplace; organizational behavior and its role in transferring evidence-based innovations into practice in community-based treatment agencies as well as criminal justice settings; other areas. Office: Tex Christian U Inst Behavioral Rsch PO Box 298740 Fort Worth TX 76129-0001 Business E-Mail: ibr@tcu.edu.

SIMPSON, DICK WELDON, political science educator; b. Houston, Nov. 8, 1940; s. Warren Weldon and Ola Ela (Felts) S.; m. Sarajane Avidon, Mar. 22, 1987 (dec. March 29, 2006); children: Kate Donley, August Donley. BA, U. Tex., 1963; MA, Ind. U., 1964, PhD, 1968; MDiv, McCormick Theol. Sem., 1984. Ordained to ministry United Ch. of Christ, 1985. Rsch. asst. Ind. U., Bloomington, 1965; fgn. area fellow Ford Found., Africa, 1966-67; instr. U. Ill., Chgo., 1967-68, asst. prof., 1968-71, assoc. prof. polit. sci., 1972-96, prof., 1996—, head dept., 2006—. Exec. dir. Inst. on Ch., Chgo., 1984-86, Clergy and Laity Concerned, Chgo., 1987-89. Author: Winning Elections, 1972, 74, 81, 96, Strategies for Change, 1976, Politics of Compassion, 1989; editor: Chicago's Future, 1976, 80, 83, 88, 93, Rogues, Rebels, and Rubber Stamps, 2001, Inside Urban Politics, 2004, Struggle for Power in Cities and States, 2009; prodr., polit. advisor 8 documentary films including By the People, 1970, Teaching Politics, 2006. Alderman Chgo. City Coun., 1971-79; campaign mgr. McCarthy for Pres., Ill., 1967-68; transition team Mayors Washington and Byrne, 1979, 83, State's Atty. O'Malley and County Clk. Orr, 1990, 91, Ill. Atty. Gen. Lisa Madigan, 2003, Cook County Bd. Pres. Todd Stroger, 2006-07; congl. candidate, 1992, 94. Humanities Inst. fellow U. Ill., Chgo., 1985-86, Great Cities fellow, 1997-98, 2005-06; rsch grantee Joyce, Amoco, Woods, McArthur, Crossroads, Carnegie, Wieboldt Founds., 1972-2009; recipient award Clarence Darrow Cmty. Ctr., Clergy and Laity Concerned, IVI-IPO, Excellence in Tchg. award, U. Ill., Chgo., 1971, 97, 2002, 04. Mem. Am. Polit. Sci. Assn. (mem. tchg. and learning com. 2008-; Excellence in Tchg. award, 2002), Midwest Polit. Sci. Assn., Ill. Polit. Sci. Assn. (past pres.), City Club Chgo. (v.p., award), Soc. Midland Authors. Office: Dept Polit Sci U Ill M/C 276 1007 W Harrison St Chicago IL 60607-7137 Home Phone: 773-728-1110; Office Phone: 312-413-3780. Business E-Mail: simpson@uic.edu.

SIMPSON, DOROTHY AUDREY, retired speech educator; b. Las Vegas, N.Mex., Feb. 29, 1944; d. Clyde Joseph and Audrey Shirley (Clements) Simpson; m. Gary Alan Beimer, May 13, 1972 (div. Apr. 1986); children: Laura Lea Beimer Mitchell, Rose; m. Ian B. Croxton, Dec. 27, 1992 (div. Oct. 1993); m. Doyle W. Hauschulz, Feb. 23, 2001 (div. June 2003). BA, N.Mex. Highlands U., 1965; MS, U. Utah, 1968; EdD, U. N.Mex., 1989. Cert. secondary edn., N.Mex. Tchr. West Las Vegas (N.Mex.) H.S., 1966-67, Santa Rosa (N.Mex.) H.S., 1968-71, Questa (N.Mex.) Consol. Schs., 1972-73; prof. speech comm., assoc. dean coll. arts and scis. N.Mex. Highlands U., Las Vegas, 1975—2003, prof. emeritus, 2003—. Ednl. cons. Rancho Valmora, 2003—07. Author: Hovels, Haciendas, and House Calls: The Life of Carl H. Gellenthien, M.D., 1986, Speaking for Life: A Speech Communication Guide for Adults, 1990, Wreck of the Destiny Train, 1993, From Pajarito to Lungchow, 2003, Audrey of the Mountains: The Story of a Twentieth Century Pioneer Woman, 2008. Active Calvary Bapt. Ch., Las Vegas, 1959—. Recipient Educator of Yr. award Pub. Svc. Co. of N.Mex., Albuquerque, 1990. Mem. P.E.O. Republican. Avocation: writing. Home: PO Box 778 Las Vegas NM 87701-0778 Personal E-mail: dcroxton@cybermesa.com.

SIMPSON, ELBERT C., utilities executive; BS in Elec. Engring. and Nuc. Engring., U. Fla., Gainesville. Various managerial positions including dir. nuc. ops. engring. and projects, dir. nuc. ops. site support and dir. nuc. ops. engring. and licensing Fla. Power Corp.; v.p. nuc. engring. Ariz. Pub. Svc. Co., 1990—93, v.p. nuc. support, 1993; sr. v.p. nuc. engring. PSEG Nuc., sr. v.p., chief adminstrv. officer; sr. v.p. info. tech., chief info. officer PSEG Svcs. Corp., pres., COO, 2006—. Office: PSEG Svcs Corp PO Box 570 Newark NJ 07101 Office Phone: 973-430-7000.

SIMPSON, ELIZABETH B., medical association administrator, management consultant; m. Theron Simpson. BA in English and French, Paine Coll., Augusta, Ga.; MA in Mgmt. and Supervision, Ctrl. Mich. U., Mount Pleasant. Exec. dir. United Svc. Orgn., Europe, Asia; sr. mgmt. The Travelers Companies; v.p. human resources, corp. staff Aetna, Inc., Hartford, Conn.; sr. v.p. human resources Baystate Health Sys., Springfield, Mass.; ptnr. Bentley Simpson Consulting, LLC; acting pres., COO Sickle Cell Disease Assn. America, Balt., 2009—. Mem.: Alpha Kappa Alpha, Eta Alpha Omega. Avocations: painting, gardening, gourmet cooking. Office: Sickle Cell Disease Assn America 231 E Baltimore St Ste 800 Baltimore MD 21202 Office Phone: 410-528-1555. Office Fax: 410-528-1495. Business E-Mail: esimpson@sicklecelldisease.org.*

SIMPSON, EUGENE THAMON, music educator, singer; b. North Wilkesboro, NC, Apr. 10, 1932; s. Eugene Tyra and Roxie Johnson Simpson; m. Ingres La Verne Hill, June 9, 1973 (div.); children: Eugene Tyra II, Adrienne Adele. MusB, Howard U., 1951, Yale U., 1953, MusM, 1954; EdD, Columbia U., 1968. Tchr. music Chelsea High Sch., NYC, 1956; asst. choral dir. Second Army Chorus, Ft. Meade, Md., 1956—58; tchr. music N.Y.C. High Schs., 1959—68; chmn. voice and choral Va. State U., Petersburg, 1968—70; chmn. music dept. Bowie State U., Md., 1970—75; prof. music Rowan U., Glassboro, NJ, 1980—2000, chmn. dept. music, 1980—2000. Author: Analysis and Performance of Schwanengesang of Schubert, 1968, Hall Johnson: Nis Life, His Spirit, and His Music, 2008; composer: Hold On, 1973, Steal Away, Sinnuh Please Don't Let Dis Harvest Pass, Nobody Knows De Trouble I've Seen, True Religion, Too Late Sinnuh, Sistuh Mary Had-a-But One Child, Let Us Break Bread Together; singer: (albums) Danse Calinda, Swing Low Sweet Chariot, Born to Sing the Blues, Life, I Love You Because, 18 Yellow Roses, St. Martin De Porres Mass, The Cascading Voices with Brass, I Hear America Singing, Just A Closer Walk, Melodies of the World, The Wonderful World of Folk, Belefonte at the Greek Theater, Special for Young Lovers, Great Movie Themes, James Brown Showtime, An Evening with Belafonte/Mouskouri, Belafonte, Ballads, Blues and Boasters, King of the Gospel Singers, Porgy and Bess, Mother Nature, Father Time, On the Country Side, Tell Me Why, It's Magic, The Dinah Washington Years, Simon Estes, Singin' Through the Storm, (TV series) The Night They Saved Christmas, The Ed Sullivan Show, Those Ragtime Years, Camera Three. Founding chair Nat. Com. Ethnic Com., 1979—86; mem. adv. bd. Nat. Choral Coun., 1980—85; choral panelist NEA, 1987—88. With US Army, 1956—59. Fellow, Ford Found.; scholar, Howard U., Washington, 1947—51, Yale U., 1951—54; Tanglewood fellow. Mem.: SAG, Am. Coun. Edn., Am. Soc. Composers, Authors and Pubs., Am. Guild Musical Artists, Am. Fedn. Tchrs., Nat. Assn. Tchrs. Singing (gov. 1978—82, mem. com. 1982—87), N.J. Choral Dirs. Assn. (pres. 1977—79), Am. Choral Dirs. Assn. (life; chair ethic music com. 1977—79), Alpha Phi Alpha, Phi Mu Alpha, Pi Kappa Lambda, Kappa Delta Pi, Phi Delta Kappa, Pi Lambda Kappa. Home: 10 Aspen Rd Sicklerville NJ 08081 E-mail: thamspx1@verizon.net.

SIMPSON, FREDERICK JAMES, retired science administrator; b. Regina, Sask., Can., June 8, 1922; s. Ralph James and Lillian Mary (Anderson) S.; m. Margaret Christine Simpson, May 28, 1947 (dec. Apr. 2003); children: Christine Louise, Steven James, Leslie Coleen, Ralph Edwin, David Glen. B.Sc., U. Alta., Can., 1944, M.Sc. in Agr., 1946; PhD in Bacteriology, U. Wis., 1952. With Nat. Research Council Can., 1946-84; asst. dir. Atlantic Research Lab., Halifax, N.S., 1970-73, dir., 1973-84; sci. cons., 1985-90. Vis. scientist U. Ill., Urbana, 1955-56, vis. prof., 1964; mem. exec. council Atlantic Provinces Interuniv. Com. on Scis., 1976-79, chmn., 1981-84; pres. Fed. Inst. Mgmt., Halifax, 1981-82 Contbr. numerous articles to profl. jours. Treas. Lunburg Condominium Corp. No. 1, 1998-2008. Decorated Queen's Silver Anniversary medal. Fellow Royal Soc. of Arts (London); mem. Can. Soc. Microbiologists (hon., sec.-treas. 1969-70, v.p. 1971-72, pres. 1972-73), Nova Scotian Inst. Sci. (v.p. 1975-76, pres. 1977-78), Internat. Phycological Soc., Aquaculture Assn. Can., Sigma Xi. Mem. United Ch. of Canada.

SIMPSON, GEORGE TRUE, II, surgeon, educator; b. Aurora, Colo., Apr. 29, 1943; s. George True and Meryle Flora (Moore) S.; m. Sharon Louise Mason, Mar. 9, 1944; children: Amber-Louise Elizabeth, George True III. BA in History, LaSierra U., 1969; MD, Loma Linda U., 1973, MPH, 1975. Diplomate Am. Bd. Otolaryngology, Am. Bd. Laser Surgery, Nat. Bd. Med. Examiners. Surgery resident U. Ala. Hosp. & Clinics, Birmingham, 1973-75; surgeon Kalabo Hosp., Zambia, 1975; otolaryngology resident UCLA Head/Neck Surgery, LA, 1975-78; pediatric otolaryngology fellow Children's Hosp, Boston, 1978-79; assoc. prof., acting chair Boston (Mass.) U., 1979-90; dir. dept. otolaryngology Boston (Mass.) City Hosp., 1979-90; otolaryngologist-in-chief U. Hosp., Boston, 1984-90; chmn. dept. otolaryngology SUNY, Buffalo, 1991-97, prof. otolaryngology, 1991—; chmn. dept. otolaryngology Sisters of Charity Hosp., Buffalo, 1991—96; pres. U. Head/Neck Surgery, Buffalo, 1991—96; chief head and neck surgery Buffalo VA Med. Ctr., 1995—. Cons. MIT, Cambridge, 1979—, Gillette Corp., Boston, 1984-90, Ministry Pub. Health, State of Kuwait, 1986; pres. Boston City Hosp. Med. Staff, 1983, 85; bd. dirs. Voice Found. Sci. Adv., Phila.; chmn. otolaryngology sect. 10 Internat. Congress on Lasers in medicine and Surgery, Taipei, Taiwan, 1989; examiner Am. Bd. Otolaryngology, Chgo., 1992, 93, 94. Author: Lasers in Otolaryngology, 1985; author, editor: Textbook of General Medicine, 1987; editor: Lasers in Otolaryngology: OTOL Clinics of N.Am., 1990; contbr. articles to profl. jours. Bd. trustees St. Mary's Sch. for Deaf, 1992-2001. With US Army, 1964—66. Recipient Caring Physician award Mass. Nursing Assn., Mass. Med. Assn., 1989. Fellow ACS, Am. Acad. Otolaryngology-Head/Neck Surgery (Honor award 1987), Am. Acad. Pediatrics, Am. Soc. Head/Neck Surgery, Am. Broncheosophagological, Am. Acad. Facial Plastic and Reconstructive Surgery, Am. Acad. Cosmetic Surgery, Royal Soc. Medicine, Am. Bd. Laser Surgery; mem. Am. Assn. Acad. Depts. Otolaryngology, Assn. for Rsch. in Otolaryngology, Soc. Univ. Otolaryngologist, Internat. Soc. for History Otolaryngology (sec./treas. 1984-87, v.p. 1987-89), Buffalo Otolaryngology Soc., Buffalo Canoe Club, Buffalo Club, Orchard Park Country Club, Alpha Omega Alpha. Avocations: medical history, personal computing, music, running, boating. Office: SUNY Buffalo-VA Med Ctr Dept Otolaryngology 3495 Bailey Ave Buffalo NY 14215-1129

SIMPSON, GREG B., psychology professor, department chairman; PhD, U. Kansas, Lawrence, 1979. Prof. cognitive psychology U. Kans., chmn. dept. psychology. Contbr. articles to profl. jours. Office: Univ Kans Dept Psychology 1415 Jayhawk Blvd Rm 426 Lawrence KS 66045-7556 Office Phone: 785-864-4131. Office Fax: 785-864-5696. Business E-Mail: gsimpson@ku.edu.*

SIMPSON, H. RICHARD (DICK SIMPSON), retail merchandiser; b. Oct. 10, 1928; s. Bert M. and Violet K. (Mathias) S.; m. Marion Welty, 1950; children: Carla Sue, Barry Nelson, Richard Drew, Catherine Irene; m. Joan Rose Marshall, March 22, 1970; m. Charlotte S. Fox, Dec. 12, 1999. Student, U. Akron, 1949-50; BS, U. Md., 1955. Mgr. Tex. GMC, Detroit, 1959-62. Pres. Friendly Pontiac, Friendly Toyota, Derrick Chrysler, Simpson Oil Corp., Corp. S., Dick Tiger Homes, Austin, 1962-85, Simpson Hill Country Realty and Builders, 1989-2003, 05, 07. Served to lt. col. USAF, 1953-75; Korea. Decorated D.F.C., Air Medal. Mem. Soc. Automotive Engrs., Res. Officers Assn., Horseshoe Bay Yacht Club, Horseshoe Bay Country Club, Rotary Internat., Masons. Methodist. Office: PO Box 8186 Horseshoe Bay TX 78657-8186 Personal E-mail: dicksimpson_hsb@yahoo.com.

SIMPSON, HUGH L., news correspondent, newswriter; b. Kingston, Jamaica, Jan. 17, 1942; s. Melville Herbert (Stepfather) and Aldina Poulton (Willis) Simpson; m. Stephanie Anna Harcken, Jan. 7, 1988; children: Star, Susan, Andrew(dec.). AA, Maui Cmnty. Coll. Radio stringer WWRL, NYC, 1964; radio news reporter WMCA, NYC, 1964—68; press sec. for black media Robert F. Kennedy Presdl. Campaign, 1968; news writer WABC-TV, NYC, 1968; on-camera news reporter WCBS-TV, NYC, 1968—72; freelance Minn., SD and ND, 1973—. Recipient John B. Russwurm award, Nat. Urban League. Mem.: AFTRA, Profl. Assn. Photographers, Phi Theta Kappa. Personal E-mail: blake19060@aol.com.

SIMPSON, JACK BENJAMIN, medical technologist, business executive; b. Tompkinsville, Ky., Oct. 30, 1937; s. Benjamin Harrison and Verda Mae (Woods) S.; m. Winona Clara Walden, Mar. 21, 1957; children: Janet Lazann, Richard Benjamin, Randall Walden, Angela Elizabeth. Student, Western Ky. U., 1954-57; grad., Norton Infirmary Sch. Med. Tech., 1958. Asst. chief med. technologist Jackson County Hosp., Seymour, Ind., 1958-61; chief med. technologist, bus. mgr. Mershon Med. Labs., Indpls., 1962-66; founder, dir., officer Am. Monitor Corp., Indpls., 1966-77; founder, pres., dir. Global Data, Inc., Ft. Lauderdale, Fla., 1986—. Mng. ptnr. Astroland Enterprises, Indpls., 1968—, 106th St. Assocs., Indpls., 1969-72, Keystones Ltd., Indpls., 1970-82, Delray Rd. Assoc. Ltd., Indpls., 1970-71, Allisonville Assocs. Ltd., Indpls., 1970-82, Grandview Assocs. Ltd., 1977—, Rucker Assocs. Ltd., Indpls., 1974—; mng. ptnr. Raintree Assocs. Ltd., Indpls., 1978—, Westgate Assocs. Ltd., Indpls., 1978—; pres., dir. Topps Constrn. Co., Inc., Bradenton, Fla., 1973-91, Acrovest Corp., Asheville, N.C., 1980—; dir. Indpls. Broadcasting, Inc.; founder, bd. dirs. Bank of Bradenton, 1986-92; founder, CFO Biomass Processing Tech., Inc., West Palm Beach, Fla., 1996—; also bd. dirs. Mem. Am. Soc. Med. Technologists (cert.), Indpls. Soc. Med. Technologists, Fla. Soc. Med. Technologists, Am. Soc. Clin. Pathologists, Am. Assn. Clin. Chemistry, Royal Soc. Health (London), Internat. Platform Assn., Am. Mus. Natural History, Columbia of Indpls. Club, Harbor Beach Surf Club, Fishing of Am. Club, Marina Bay Club (Ft. Lauderdale), Elks. Republican. E-mail: jack_simpson@msn.com.

SIMPSON, JESSICA ANN, singer, actress; b. Abilene, Tex., July 10, 1980; d. Joe and Tina Simpson; m. Nick Lachey, Oct. 26, 2002 (div. June 30, 2006). Launched edible fragrance, cosmetic and body care line, Dessert Beauty, 2004; co-creator and launched, edible fragrance, cosmetic, and body care line, Taste, 04; nat. spokesperson for Operation Smile; designer swimwear line, 2007. Singer: (albums) Sweet Kisses, 1999, Irresistible, 2001, In This Skin, 2004, Rejoyce: The Christmas Album, 2004, A Public Affair, 2006, Do You Know, 2008, (songs) These Boots are Made for Walkin', 2005 (People's Choice award for Favorite Song from a Movie (The Dukes of Hazzard), 2006); actor: (films) The Dukes of Hazzard, 2005, Employee of the Month, 2006, The Love Guru, 2008; (TV series) Newlyweds: Nick and Jessica, 2003—05, (TV) Nick & Jessica's Variety Hour, 2004, Nick & Jessica's Family Christmas, 2004, Nick & Jessica's Tour of Duty, 2005; co-author: I Do: Achieving Your Dream Wedding, 2003; co-host with husband: Saturday Night Live, 2004; co-host with Dane Cook Teen Choice Awards, 2006, guest appearances (TV series) MadTV, 2000, 2001, That '70s Show, 2002, 2003, Punk'd, 2003, Twilight Zone, 2003, Top of the Pops, 2004, Ashlee Simpson Show, 2004, The Apprentice, 2004. Recipient Movies-Choice Breakout (Female), Teen Choice Awards, 2006. Office: Epic Records 550 Madison Ave New York NY 10022-3211

SIMPSON, JOANNE MALKUS, meteorologist; b. Boston, Mar. 23, 1923; d. Russell and Virginia (Vaughan) Gerould; m. Robert H. Simpson, Jan. 6, 1965; children by previous marriage: David Starr Malkus, Steven Willem Malkus, Karen Elizabeth Malkus. BS, U. Chgo., 1943, MS, 1945, PhD, 1949; DSc (hon.), SUNY, Albany, 1991. Instr. physics and meteorology Ill. Inst. Tech., 1946-49, asst. prof., 1949-51; meteorologist Woods Hole Oceanographic Instn., 1951-61; prof. meteorology UCLA, 1961-65; dir. exptl. meteorology lab. NOAA, Dept. Commerce, Washington, 1965-74; prof. environ. scis. U. Va., Charlottesville, 1974—79, W.W. Corcoran prof. environ. scis., 1974—79; head Severe Storms br. Goddard Lab. Atmospheres, NASA, Greenbelt, Md., 1979—88; chief scientist for meteorology Goddard Space Flight Ctr., NASA, 1988—2004, chief scientist emeritus for meteorology, 2004—; project scientist tropical rainfall measuring mission, 1986—98. Mem. Bd. on Atmospheric Scis. and Climate, NRC/NAS, 1990-93, 97-2000, Bd. on Geophys. and Environ. Data, 1993-96, com. on climate, ecosystems, infectious diseases and human health, 1998-2000; mem. sr. adv. bd. NOAA, 1998-2003. Author: (with Herbert Riehl) Cloud Structure and Distributions Over the Tropical Pacific Ocean; assoc. editor: Revs. Geophysics and Space Physics, 1964-72, 75-77; contbr. articles to profl. jours. Mem. Fla. Gov.'s Environ. Coordinating Coun., 1971-74. Recipient Disting. Authorship award NOAA, 1969, Silver medal Dept. Commerce, 1967, Gold medal, 1972, Vincent J. Schaefer award Weather Modification Assn., 1979, Cmty. Headliner award Women in Comm., 1973, Profl. Achievement award U. Chgo. Alumni Assn., 1975, 92, Lifetime Achievement award Women in Sci. Engring., 1990, Exceptional Sci. Achievement award NASA, 1982, William Nordberg award NASA, 1994, NASA Medal Outstanding Leadership, 1998, I.M.O. prize World Meteorol. Orgn., 2002, Presdl. Rank award for Civil Svc., 2003, 04; named Woman of Yr., L.A. Times, 1963; Guggenheim fellow, 1954-55, Goddard Sr. fellow, 1988-2004. Fellow Am. Geophys. Union, Am. Meterol. Soc. (mem. coun. 1975-77, 79-81, mem. exec. com. 1977, 79-81, commr. sci. and tech. activities 1982-88, pres.-elect 1988, pres. 1989, publs. commr. 1992-98, hon. mem. 1995, Meisinger award 1962, Rossby Rsch. medal 1983, Charles Franklin Brooks award 1992, Charles E. Anderson award 2001), World Meterol. Orgn. (IMO prize 2002), Explorers Club, Nat. Acad. Engring., Am. Acad. Arts & Sciences; mem. Royal Meteorol. Soc. (hon.), Cosmos Club, Phi Beta Kappa, Sigma Xi. Personal E-mail: nasajoanne@earthlink.net.

SIMPSON, JOHN BARCLAY, academic administrator; b. Oakland, Calif., June 8, 1947; s. Barclay and Joan (Devine) S.; children: Matthew, Melissa. BA, U. Calif., Santa Barbar, 1969; MA, Northwestern U., 1972, PhD, 1973. Research assoc. U. Pa., Phila., 1973-75; from asst. prof. to prof. psychology U. Wash., Seattle, 1975—98, dir. physiology-psychology program, 1984-88, head of the physiological psychology area, 1986—90, assoc. dean for computing, rsch. and facilities, 1991—94, dean of College of Arts and Sciences, 1994—98; exec. vice chancellor, provost U. Calif., Santa Cruz, 1998—2003; president U. at Buffalo, SUNY, 2004—. Vis. researcher U. Calif., San Francisco, 1976-80; vis. prof. Howard Florey Inst. U. Melbourne, Australia, 1983. Contbr. articles to profl. jours. Grantee NIH. Mem. AAAS, Soc. for Neurosci., Soc. Study Ingestive Behavior. Avocations: skiing, sailing, bicycling. Office: U at Buffalo 501 Capen Hall Buffalo NY 14260-1600 Office Phone: 716-645-2901. Office Fax: 716-645-3728. Business E-Mail: simpson@buffalo.edu.

SIMPSON, LARRY DEAN, lawyer; b. Jacksonville, Fla., June 10, 1949; s. Rufus McCord and Louise Smith Simpson; m. Linda Vaughan, Apr. 17, 1970; children: Louis Martin, Dean McCord. BS, Fla. State U., Tallahassee, 1971, JD, 1973. Bar: Fla. (Criminal Trial Lawyer) 1988. Asst. state atty. State Attorney's Office, Tallahassee, 1974—80; ptnr. Davis, Judkins & Simpson, Tallahassee, 1980—93, Kitchen, Judkins, Simpson & High, Tallahassee, 1993—2004, Judkins, Simpson & High, Tallahassee, 2004—. Master: Tallahassee Am. Inns of Ct. (charter mem. and master of the bench 1994—96); mem.: Fla. Assn. Criminal Def. Attys. (pres., tallahassee chpt. 1994—95), Am. Acad. Forensic Scis., Tallahassee Bar Assn. (pres. 1987—88), Fla. Bar (chair; grievance com. 1982—85, chair: judicial qualifications comn. 1995—98). Office: Judkins Simpson et al 1102 North Gadsden St Tallahassee FL 32303 Business E-Mail: lsimpson@readyfortrial.com.

SIMPSON, LOUIS ASTON MARANTZ, language educator, writer; b. Jamaica, W.I., Mar. 27, 1923; s. Aston and Rosalind (Marantz) S.; m. Jeanne Claire Rogers, 1949 (div. 1954); 1 child, Louis Matthew; m. Dorothy Mildred Roochvarg, 1955 (div. 1979); children: Anne Borovoi, Anthony Rolf; m. Miriam Butensky Bachner, 1985 (div. 1998). Higher schs. certificate, Munro Coll., Jamaica, 1939; BS, Columbia U., 1948, A.M., 1950, PhD, 1959; D.H.L., Eastern Mich. U., 1977; DLitt, Hampden Sydney Coll., 1990. Editor Bobbs-Merrill Pub. Co., NYC, 1950-55; instr. Columbia U., 1955-59; prof. English U. Calif., Berkeley, 1959-67, SUNY, Stony Brook, 1967-91, Disting. prof., 1991—. Author: (poems) The Arrivistes, 1949, Good News of Death, 1955, A Dream of Governors, 1959, At the End of the Open Road, 1963 (Pulitzer prize for poetry 1964), Selected Poems, 1965, Adventures of the Letter I, 1971, Searching for the Ox, 1976, Caviare at the Funeral, 1980, The Best Hour of the Night, 1983, People Live Here: Selected Poems 1949-83, 1983, Collected Poems, 1988, In the Room We Share, 1990, Jamaica Poems, 1993, There You Are, 1995, The Owner of the House, New Collected Poems, 1940-2000, (transl.) Nombres et poussière, 1996, Modern Poets of France, 1997, Kaviar pä begravningen, 1998, François Villon: The Legacy and The Testament, (prose) Riverside Drive, 1962, James Hogg: A Critical Study, 1962, North of Jamaica, 1972, Three on the Tower: The Lives and Works of Ezra Pound, T.S. Eliot and William Carlos Williams, 1975, A Revolution in Taste: Studies of Dylan Thomas, Allen Ginsberg, Sylvia Plath and Robert Lowell, 1978, A Company of Poets, 1981, The Character of the Poet, 1986, Selected Prose, 1989, Ships Going into the Blue, 1994, The King My Father's Wreck, 1995; editor: The New Poets of England and America, 1957, An Introduction to Poetry, 1967. Served with AUS, 1943-45. Decorated Purple Heart, Bronze Star with oak leaf cluster; Hudson Rev. fellow, 1957, Guggenheim fellow, 1962, 70; Am. Coun. Learned Socs. grantee, 1963; recipient Prix de Rome, 1957, Millay award, 1960, Distinguished Alumnus award Columbia U., 1960, medal for excellence Columbia U., 1965; American Acad. of Arts and Letters award in literature, 1976; Centenary medal Inst. of Jamaica, 1980, Jewish Book Coun. award for poetry, 1981, Elmer Holmes Bobst award, 1987, Harold Morton Landon award for translation, 1997. Fellow Am. Acad. in Rome. Home: 7 Stony Rd Stony Brook NY 11790 Office Phone: 631-689-0498. Personal E-mail: louissimpson1@yahoo.com.

SIMPSON, LYLE LEE, lawyer; b. Des Moines, Oct. 15, 1937; s. R. Clair and Martha B. Simpson; m. Janet Pepper Simpson. BA, Drake U., 1960, JD, 1963. Bar: Iowa 1963, U.S. Dist. Ct. (so. and no. dists.) Iowa 1963, U.S. Ct. Appeals (8th cir.) 1963, U.S. Tax Ct. 1963, U.S. Supreme Ct. 1970, U.S. Ct. Mil. Appeals 1972. Pvt. practice, Des Moines, 1963—; mem. Beving and Swanson, Des Moines, 1964-68; sr. ptnr. Peddicord, Simpson & Sutphin, Des Moines, 1968-83; pres. Dreher, Simpson & Jensen, PC, 1984—. Gen. counsel campaign com. Gov. Iowa, 1978-98. Contbr. articles to profl. jours. Chmn. bd. trustees Broadlawns Med. Ctr., 1974-80; mem. Iowa Inaugural Com., 1983, 87, 89, 91, 95; bd. dirs. YMCA Boys Camp, 1967-86, Home, Inc., 1981-85, Project H.E.L.P.E.R., 1983-87, Batten Found.; pres., bd. dirs. Polk County Health Svcs., 1972-88; chmn. Iowa Health Facilities Coun., 1988-93; pres. First Unitarian Ch., 1958-70, Iowa Humanities Bd., 1988-94, Humanist Found., 1980—, East High Alumni Found., 1992-2000; treas. Iowa Humanities Found., 1994-99; chmn. Iowa Health Found., 1993—; mem. investment com., fin. com. Iowa Health Sys., 2000—; bd. Iowa Health System, Des Moines, 2005—. Recipient Oren E. Scott award, Class of 1915 award in liberal arts Drake U., 1960. Mem. ABA, Iowa Bar Assn., Polk County Bar Assn., Am. Arbitration Assn., Am. Humanist Assn. (pres. 1979-84), Prairie Club (pres. 1992), Morning Club (pres. 1965), Le Chevaliers de vin Club (pres. 1976-85), YMCA Heritage Club (pres.), Masons, Scottish Rite, Shriner 33 degree, Rotary. Republican. Congregationalist. Address: 222 Equitable Bldg 604 Locust St Des Moines IA 50309-3723 Office Phone: 515-288-5000. Business E-Mail: lsimpson@dreherlaw.com.

SIMPSON, MELISSA M., federal agency administrator; B, Colo. State Univ.; JD, Creighton Univ. Sr. legis. asst. to US Rep. Scott McInnis, Washington, 2001—03; dep. dir. external & intergovernmental affairs to US Interior Sec. Gale Norton, Washington, 2003—05; counselor to USDA Undersecretary for Nat. Resources & Environ., Washington, 2005—07; dep. undersecretary for Nat. Resources & Environ. USDA, Washington, 2007—. Office: USDA 1400 Independence Ave SW Washington DC 20250*

SIMPSON, MICHAEL, retired metals service center executive; b. Albany, NY, Dec. 10, 1938; s. John McLaren Simpson and Constance (Hasler) Ames; m. Barbara Ann Bodtke, Jan. 5, 1963; children: Leslie Ann, Elizabeth S. Wessel. BA, U. Mich., 1965, MBA, 1966. Product mgr. Armour & Co., Chgo., 1966-68; with A.M. Castle & Co., Franklin Park, Ill., 1968—, pres. Hy-Alloy Steels Co. divsn., 1974-79, v.p. Midwestern region, 1977-79, chmn. bd., 1979—2004, also bd. dirs.; chmn. emeritus, 2004—. Trustee Rush U. Med. Ctr., Chgo., 1978—, mem. exec. com., 1980—, vice chmn., 1991-2009; trustee Oldfields Sch., Glencoe, Md., 1982-87, 95-2003, chmn. bd., 1998-2000; bd. dirs. Lake Forest Hosp. Found. and Lake Forest Hosp., Ill., 1998-2008; chmn. bd. overseers Rush U., Chgo., 1996-2009. Office: AM Castle & Co 3400 N Wolf Rd Franklin Park IL 60131-1319 Office Phone: 847-349-2500.

SIMPSON, MICHAEL K., United States Representative from Idaho; b. Burley, Idaho, Sept. 8, 1950; m. Kathy Johnson, 1971. Student, Utah State U.; DDS, Washington U., St. Louis, 1978. Dentist, Blackfoot, Idaho, 1978—; councilmember Blackfoot City Coun., 1980—84; mem. Idaho Ho. Reps., 1985—99, asst. majority leader, 1989, speaker, 1991—99; mem. US Congress from 2nd Idaho dist., Washington, 1999—, ho. appropriations com., agr., resources, transp. & infrastructure com., vet. affairs com. Former spkr. majority caucus chmn. and asst. majority leader Idaho Ho. Reps. Recipient Boyd A. Martin award, Assn. Idaho Cities, Friend of Edn. award, 1994, Citizen of Yr. award, Idaho Family Forum, 1996; named to Idaho's Rep. Party Hall of Fame. Mem.: Am. Legis. Exch. Coun. (state chmn., nat. bd. dirs., Jefferson award 1994), Idaho State Dental Assn. (Pres.'s award 1998). Republican. Avocations: golf, chess, painting. Office: US Ho Reps 1339 Longworth Ho Office Bldg Washington DC 20515-1202 Office Phone: 202-225-5531. Office Fax: 202-225-8216.*

SIMPSON, MICHAEL KEVIN, academic administrator, political science professor; b. Bellafonte, Pa., Apr. 22, 1949; s. Robert Paul and Helen Elisabeth (Popso) S.; m. Carol Anne Martin, June 27, 1970; children: Jennifer Lyn, Robert Manton. BA, Fordham Coll., 1970; MA, Tufts U., 1974, MA in Law and Diplomacy, 1976, PhD, 1976; MBA, Syracuse U., 1983. Instr. Newbury Jr. Coll., Boston, 1976-77; asst. prof. then prof. polit. sci. Utica (N.Y.) Coll. of Syracuse U., 1976-97, v.p., 1987-88, pres., 1988-97, 1998—2002, Am. U. Paris, 1998—, prof. internat. affairs, 1998—2005; pres. Internat. Space U., Strasbourg, France, 2004—, prof. pub. policy, 2005—. Fulbright lectr. U. Nancy II, France, 1981-82; vis. prof. Syracuse U. Program in Strasbourg, 1981-82, 85-87; resident dir. Internat. Programs, Strasbourg, 1985-87; trustee Savs. Bank of Utica, 1988-2002. Contbr. articles to profl. jours. Bd. dirs. Health and Hosp. Coun., 1989-90; mem. joint hosp. bd. Mohawk Valley Network, 1991-97; dir. ministers and missionaries benefit bd. Am. Bapt. Chs., 1995-2003. Decorated Def. Meritorious Svc. medal; recipient Grad. Alumni award Syracuse U. Sch. Mgmt., 1983, Disting. Tchg. award Utica Coll., 1983, Hon. Alumnus award, 1998; Silver Beaver award Boy Scouts Am.; Paul Harris fellow Rotary Internat. Mem. Internat. Studies Assn., Naval Res. Assn., Rotary (bd. dirs. Utica 1988-97, v.p. 1991-92, pres., 1992), Club of Utica, Phi Beta Kappa, Nat. Space Soc. (bd. govs. 2004-), World Space Week (bd. dirs. 2004-), UN Com. (representative 2004-), Internat. Acad. Astronautics (corr.). Democrat. Home: 4 Blvd de la Victoire Strasbourg France Office: Internat Space Univ Parc d'Innovation 1 rue Jean-Dominique Cassini 67400 Illkirch-Graffenstaden France Home Phone: 33 3 88 245043; Office Phone: 33 3 88 655452. E-mail: simpson@isu.isunet.edu.

SIMPSON, MICHAEL MARCIAL, science and technology specialist, consultant; b. Honolulu, Sept. 24, 1954; s. Marcial and Beatrice S. AB in Biol. Scis., U. Calif., Berkeley, 1976; MS in Biol. Scis., U. San Francisco, 1977; MS in Energy and Resources, U. Calif., Berkeley, 1979; PhD in Environ. Scis. and Engring., UCLA, 1986. Assoc. researcher NASA, Moffett Field, Calif., 1973; radio program host, producer Sta. KUSF-FM, San Francisco, 1976-78; rsch. asst. Lawrence Berkeley Lab., Berkeley, Calif., 1977-79; rsch. assoc. UCLA/U.S. Dept. Energy, 1979-81; congl. fellow, environ. health U.S. Congress, Washington, 1981-82; specialist in environ. techs., life scis., and terrorism U.S. Congl. Rsch. Svc., Washington, 1982—2006, sci. policy advisor on Homeland Security issues, 2006—; sr. prin. leader CSC Inc. Adv. bd. Banbury Ctr., Cold Spring Harbor, N.Y., 1985—; adj. faculty The Washington Ctr., 1992—. Contbr. articles to profl. jours., chapters to books. Fellow AAAS (Named Congl. Sci. fellow 1981-82); mem. Washington Acad. Sci., Library of Congress Profl. Assn., UCLA in Washington (exec. steering com. 1986-92). Avocations: photography, bicycle touring, short story writing, travel. Home Phone: 703-239-8050; Office Phone: 703-461-2011. Business E-Mail: msimpson8@csc.com, DrMichaelMSimpson22015@yahoo.com.

SIMPSON, MILDRED KATHLEEN, health facility administrator; b. Balt., Jan. 4, 1950; d. John Green and Mildred Elizabeth Green-Bieard; children: Sabrina, David, Derek. AA, C.C. of Balt., 1989, cert. of gerontology, 1991; BA, Towson State U., 1998. Program dir. Balt. City Health Dept., 1974—99, acting dir., 1999—2000, project coord., 2000—02, program dir., 2002—. Mem. morale com. Balt. City Health Dept., 2003—; adviser Police Athletic League, Balt., 2002—. Vol. Habitat for Humanity, Balt., 2003—04; booster 4-H Club, Balt., 1999—2003; sponsor So. Law Ctr. Nat. Campaign for Tolerance. Recipient Outstanding Contbn. to Sandtown Comty., 2002, Outstanding Support to Rosemont Comty., 2003. Mem.: NAACP, Towson State U. Active Alumni (adviser to students 2000—02), Madison Ave. Head Start (comty. organizer 2001—03, Outstanding Svc. award 2003). Avocations: travel, reading, community activist, star gazing. Home: 540 Wyanoke Ave Baltimore MD 21218

SIMPSON, MINNIE PEACH, interior designer; b. Kinston, NC, Apr. 8, 1949; d. Michael Joseph and Margie (Philips) Peach; m. John Wimberly Simpson, Aug. 1974 (div. Dec. 1980). BFA in Interior Design, U. Ga., 1973. Interior designer Hinson Galleries, Columbus, Ga., 1974-79; interior designer, sales rep. Crabapple, 1980-81; interior designer kitchen and bath design Larry Bussey, Inc., 1981-85; mem. staff sales/designer dept. Mansours, 1985-86; mgr. interior design/space planning AFLAC, 1986—2004; interior design cons., 2004—. Coord. March of Dimes, Columbus, 1993-96, Salisbury Fair, Columbus, 1996, Volunteers for Corta, Vol. for Allied Cats of Columbus, 2003. Mem. Am. Soc. Interior Designers, Internat. Interior Design Assn., Columbus Regional Tennis Assn. (corta bd., 1999-2001). Avocations: tennis, crafts, antiques, gardening. Home: 7157 Village Loop Columbus GA 31904 Office Phone: 706-596-5883. Personal E-mail: msimpson@bellsouth.net. E-mail: msimpson@aflac.com.

SIMPSON, MURRAY, electrical engineer, consultant; b. NYC, July 27, 1921; s. George and Sonia (Vernov) Simpson; m. Ethel Gladstein, June 29, 1947; children: David, Mindy, Jonathan. BEE, CCNY, 1942; MEE, Polytech. Inst. of NY, 1952. Engr. ITT, NYC, 1942-44; sr. engr. Raytheon Co., Waltham, Mass., 1946-48; sect. mgr. Fairchild Guided Missles div., Farmingdale, NY, 1948-50; v.p. Maxson Elec. Co., NYC, 1950-62; pres. SEDCO Sys. Inc. subs. Raytheon Co., Melville, NY, 1963-86; cons. M. Simpson Assocs., Ft. Lauderdale, Fla., 1986—. Former chmn. bd. dirs. Radyne Corp. Contbr. articles to profl. jours. Former bd. dirs. United Way, LI. Served to lt. (j.g.) USNR, 1944—46, PTO. Fellow: IEEE (chmn. L.I. sect. 1963—64). Avocations: boating, skiing, golf, tennis. *Don't be afraid to take risk in the hope of great reward and satisfaction. The worst that could happen is that you may fail. A much greater loss is that you never tried and perhaps missed the great opportunity of your life.*

SIMPSON, ROBERT G., waste management executive; BS in Acctg., Ind. U.; JD, U. Ill. Dir. fed. taxes Kraft Gen. Foods divsn. Phillip Morris; v.p. tax, gen mgr. Tenneco Bus. Svcs., 1997—98; v.p. taxation Waste Mgmt. Inc., Houston, 1998—2002, v.p., chief acctg. officer, 2002—03, sr. v.p., chief acctg. officer, 2003—04, sr. v.p., CFO, 2004—. Office: Waste Mgmt Inc 1001 Fannin St Ste 4000 Houston TX 77002 Office Phone: 713-512-6200.

SIMPSON, ROBERT GLENN, lawyer; b. Seattle, June 27, 1932; s. Harold Vernon and Anna Rondeau (McCabe) S.; m. Josephine Anne Heald, June 7, 1959; children: Jenifer Jane, Thomas Glenn, Mary Elizabeth. BS, U. Oreg., 1954; LLB, Willamette U., 1959. Bar: Oreg. 1959. Assoc. William B. Adams Law Office, Portland, Oreg., 1959-67; ptnr. Adams McLaughlin & Simpson, Portland, 1967-70, Schwabe Williamson & Wyatt, P.C., Portland, 1970—. Trustee, sec. Legacy Good Samaritan Hosp. and Med. Ctr., Portland, 1983-89, mem. cmty. bd., 1989-98; trustee, chancellor Episcopal Diocese of Oreg., Portland, 1988-2007. Mem. Oreg. State Bar (exec. com. health law sect. 1987-90), Am. Health Lawyers Assn. (program com. 1987-88), Oreg. Health Lawyers Assn.(pres. 1977-78, legis. com. 1989). Home: 13345 SW Iron Mountain Blvd Portland OR 97219-9306 Office: Schwabe Williamson & Wyatt, PC 1211 SW 5th Ave Ste 1800 Portland OR 97204-3795

SIMPSON, ROBERT HOMER, meteorologist, consultant; b. Corpus Christi, Tex., Nov. 19, 1912; s. Clyde Robert and Annie Laurie (Rainey) S.; m. Mazie Houston, Dec. 22, 1935 (div. Dec. 1949); m. Joanne Gerould Malkus, Jan. 6, 1965; children: Peggy A., Lynn S.; stepchildren: David Malkus, Steven Malkus, Karen Malkus. BS, Southwestern U.,

Tex., 1932, DSc (hon.), 1963; MS, Emory U., 1935; PhD, U. Chgo., 1962. Cert. cons. meteorologist. Observer U.s. Weather Bur., Brownsville, Tex., 1940-42, forecaster New Orleans and Miami, Fla., 1942-45, exec. asst. to dep. chief Washington, 1946-48; established Pacific Region of U.S. Weather Bur., Honolulu, 1948-52; rsch. scientist U.S. Weather Bur., Washington, 1952-56, founding dir. Nat. Hurricane Rsch. Project West Palm Beach, Fla., 1956-61, dep. dir. rsch. severe storms Washington, 1961-64; assoc. dir. ops. Nat. Weather Svc., NOAA, Washington, 1964-67, dir. Nat. Hurricane Ctr. Miami, 1967-74; founding dir. Simpson Weather Assoc., Inc., Charlottesville, Va., 1974—; rsch. prof. environ. sci. U. Va., Charlottesville, 1974-80. Helped established Mauna Loa Summit Obs., Hawaii, 1951. Author: (with Herbert Riehl) The Hurricane and Its Impact, 1981; chief editor: Hurricane: Coping with Disaster, 2002; contbr. articles to profl. jours. Recipient Gold medal Dept. Commerce, 1962, Profl. Achievement award U. Chgo. D.C. Alumni Group, 1998, Nona Longtime Acehievement award, 2008. Fellow Am. Meteorol. Soc. (hon. mem., Cleveland Abbe award 1991), Explorers Club NY; mem. (bd. dir. 2008) Wash. Group. Achievements include (with Herbert Saffir) development and implementation of the Saffir-Simpson scale for hurricane damage potential; pioneering research flight in hurricane, Caribbean Sea, W. Pacific Ocean, first over-the-top flight in hurricane, Atlantic Ocean, 1947; many research penetrations of hurricane eyes. Home Phone: 202-479-0052.

SIMPSON, ROBERT LEE, academic administrator, department chairman, biologist, educator; b. San Francisco, Apr. 3, 1942; s. Robert Lee and Valerie Brinley (Serrick) S.; m. Penelope Sue Flint, June 12, 1970; children: Robert Lee III, Elizabeth Jean. BA in Zoology, Fresno State Coll., 1965, MA in Biology, 1967; PhD in Limnology, Cornell U., 1971. Instr. Cornell U., Ithaca, N.Y., 1970; from asst. prof. to prof. biology Rider Coll., Lawrenceville, N.J., 1970-85, chairperson biology dept., 1972-80; acting dean sch. health professions and nursing William Paterson Coll., Wayne, N.J., 1986-87, prof. biology, 1985-91, dean sch. sci. and maths., 1985-91; provost, vice chancellor acad. affairs U. Mich., Dearborn, 1991—2006, prof. biology, 1991—; program dir. MS Environ. Sci., 2008—. Adj. grad. prof. Rutgers U., Camden, N.J., 1976-91; vis. scientist Smithsonian Environ. Rsch. Ctr., Edgewater, N.J., 1977; mem. grad. degree adv. com. N.J. Dept. Higher Edn., Trenton, 1989-91; interim provost, v.p. academic affairs Kettering U., Flint, Mich, 2006-07. Editor: (with D. Whigham, R. Good) Freshwater Wetlands: Ecological Processes & Management Potential, 1978, (with M. Leck, V.T. Parker) Ecology of Soil Seed Banks, 1989, Seedling Ecology and Evolution, 2008; contbr. articles to profl. jours. Mem. N.J. Wetlands Mitigation Coun., Trenton, 1988-91; trustee Chilton Meml. Hosp., Pompton Plains, N.J., 1989-91; bd. dirs. Granville Acad., Detroit, 1991-93; chair acad. affairs affairs subcom. Pres. Coun. of State Univs. of Mich., 1997-2007. Rsch. grantee Office Water Rsch. & Tech., 1975, 79, U.S. EPA, 1976, 78, NSF, 1975, 80, U.S. Geol. Survey, 1983, Challenge to Excellence grantee N.J. Dept. Higher Edn., 1987. Mem. N.J. Acad. Sci. (pres. 1983-85, Outstanding Svc. award 1989), Ecol. Soc. Am., Brit. Ecol. Soc., Soc. Wetland Scientists, Am. Soc. Limnology and Oceanography, Sigma Xi. Home: 2470 Harness Dr West Bloomfield MI 48324-3733 Office Phone: 313-593-5678. Business E-Mail: rlsumd@umich.edu.

SIMPSON, ROBERT LOUIS, music educator; b. Orange, NJ, Apr. 17, 1948; s. Robert Gage and Frances Dean Simpson; m. Marianna Parnas, May 29, 1994; children: Laura Helen, Robert Kirkpatrick. AB, Brown U., 1970; M Sacred Music, Union Theol. Sem., Sch. Sacred Music, 1972. Cert. Assoc. Am. Guild of Organists, NY, 1989, Choirmaster Am. Guild of Organists, NY, 1989. Organist-choirmaster Cathedral Ch. St. Luke, Orlando, Fla., 1974—79, Cathedral St. Philip, Atlanta, 1979—93, Christ Ch. Cathedral, Houston, 1993—; founder and artistic dir. Houston Chamber Choir, 1995—; lectr. ch. music Shepherd Sch. Music, Rice U., Houston, 2003—. Musician (conductor): (choral performances) The Blue Estuaries; musician: (CD) Ravishingly Russian: Secular Choral Music of the 19th and 20th Centuries. Recipient S. Lewis Elmer Award, Am. Guild of Organists, 1988. Mem.: Chorus Am. (bd. mem. 2000—06), Assn. Anglican Musicians, Am. Choral Dirs. Assn. Office: Houston Chamber Choir PO Box 53388 Houston TX 77052-3388 Office Fax: 713-222-2412. E-mail: robertsimpson@houstonchamberchoir.org.

SIMPSON, SANDRA KAY, logistics specialist; b. Rutland, Vt., Feb. 26, 1949; d. Freeman Edward and Ruth Gail (Smith) Campbell. BA, U. Vt., Burlington, 1971; MPA, Troy State U., Europe, 1988, MSc in Internat. Rels., 1991. Isntr., trainer US Govt., Ft. McClellan, Ala., 1975-79, asst. logistics officer Kitzingen, Germany, 1979-82, property acctg. officer Ft. Hood, Tex., 1982-86, Wiesbaden, Germany, 1986-93, maintenance mgmt. coord., 1994—, dep. dir. internal logistics, 1999—2002, theater level logistics mgr., 2002—03, 2005—07, def. logistics agy., 2003—05, 2007—. Cons. U.S. Govt., Kaiserslautern, Germany, 1994—. With US Army, 1973—93. Mem. Women in Mil. Svc. to Am. Found. (charter mem.), USAREUR Retiree Coun., Wiesbaden/Mainz Retiree Coun. (sec. 1994—), Oxford Club. Avocations: photography, marathons. Home: CMR 467 Box 1505 APO AE 09096-1505 Office: DSCPE Unit 23152 APO AE 09227 Business E-Mail: sandy.simpson@us.army.mil.

SIMPSON, SEAN, mathematics professor; b. NY; BA, Canisius Coll., Buffalo, 1999; MA, Pa. State U., State Coll., 2001; MS, Baruch Coll., NYC, 2007. Instr. math. Rutgers U., New Brunswick, NJ, 2001—02; assoc. prof. Westchester CC, Valhalla, NY, 2002—. Mem.: Am. Statis. Assn., Math. Assn. Am., AMATYC, NYSMATYC (curriculum chair 2004—06). Office: Westchester CC 75 Grasslands Rd Valhalla NY 10595

SIMPSON, STEPHEN GEORGE, mathematician; b. Allentown, Pa., Sept. 8, 1945; BA, MS, Lehigh U., 1966; PhD, MIT, 1971. Gibbs instr. Yale U., New Haven, 1971-72; lectr. U. calif., Berkeley, 1972-74; rsch. fellow Oxford (Eng.) U., 1974-75; from asst. prof. to prof. math. Pa. State U., State College, 1975—, Shibley prof., 1987—92. Author Subsystems of Second Order Arithmetic, 1999; contbr. 75 articles to profl. jours. Faculty scholar Pa. State U., 1986. Mem. Assn. Symbolic Logic (exec. bd. 1987-90). Achievements include contributions to Reverse Mathematics, a research program in the foundations of mathematics. Office: Pa State U Mcallister Bldg State College PA 16802 Home Phone: 814-238-2274; Office Phone: 814-865-7527. Business E-Mail: simpson@math.psu.edu.

SIMPSON, STEVEN DREXELL, lawyer; b. Sturgis, Mich., Sept. 20, 1953; s. Rex and Lorraine Simpson; m. Peggy Deibert, Apr. 28, 1979; children: Andrew Drexell, Christine Elizabeth, Marianne Tyner. BA, Hillsdale Coll., Mich., 1975; JD, Wake Forest U., 1978; LLM in Taxation, Georgetown U., 1981. Bar: Fla. 1978, D.C. 1980, N.C. 1984. Assoc. Bradford, Williams et al, Miami, Fla., 1978-80, Webster & Chamberlain, Washington, 1980-82, Fisher, Wayland et al, Washington, 1982-84, Maupin, Taylor & Ellis, P.A., Raleigh, NC, 1984-98; pvt. practice, 1998—2006; counsel Wyrick Robbin Yates & Ponton, LLP, 2007—. Author: Tax-Exempt Organizations: Organizational and Operational Requirements, 2000, Tax-Exempt Organizations: Reporting, Disclosure and Other Procedural Aspects, 2000, Taxable Expenditures, 2000, Tax Compliance for Tax-Exempt Organizations, 2009, Multistate Guides to Regulation and Taxation of Nonprofits, 2009; contbr. articles to profl. jours. Mem. ABA (exempt orgns. com.). Republican. Methodist. Avocations: golf, running. Home: 409 Hillandale Dr Raleigh NC 27609-7036 Office: PO Drawer 17803 4101 Lake Boone Trail Ste 300 Raleigh NC 27619 Home Phone: 919-786-4588; Office Phone: 919-781-4000. Business E-Mail: ssimpson@wyrick.com.

SIMPSON, STEVEN VINCENT, social sciences educator; b. Merrill, Wis., May 29, 1954; s. David Norbert and Barbara Ann Simpson; m. Manyu Hsieh Simpson, Feb. 19, 1993; 1 child, Clare Huei-yu. PhD, U. Minn., Mpls., 1986. Asst. prof. recreation Iowa State U., Ames, 1986—91; assoc. prof. geography Nat. Taiwan U., Taipei, 1991—93; prof. recreation U. Wis., La Crosse, 1993—; prof. environ. edn. Nat. Taiwan Normal U., Taipei, 2008—. Editor Jour. Experiential Edn., 1998—2000. Author: (book) Leader Who is Hardly Known; co-author (with Dan Miller and Buzz Bocher): The Processing Pinnacle. Office: Univ Wis 136 Wittich Hall La Crosse WI 54601 Business E-Mail: simpson.stev@uwlax.edu.

SIMPSON, W. JAMES, literature and language professor; b. Melbourne, Australia, Mar. 16, 1954; s. Ronald C. and Margaret Anne Simpson; m. Luisella M. Brunetti, Mar. 27, 1982; children: Emile V., G. Olivier, Clelia M. MPhil, U. Oxford, Eng., 1980; MPhil (hon.), U. Cambridge, Eng., 1989, PhD, 1996; AM (hon.), Harvard U., Cambridge, Mass., 2004. Lectr. Westfield Coll., U. London, 1982—89, U. Cambridge, 1989—99, prof. medieval and renaissance English, 1999—2003; prof. English Harvard U., 2004—. Contbr. articles to profl. jours. Recipient Paget Toynbee Dante prize, U. Oxford, 1980, John Hurt Fisher prize, Gower Soc., 2003, Sir Israel Gollancz prize, Brit. Acad., 2007, Silver medal, Ind. Pub. Book Awards, 2008. Fellow: Australian Acad. Humanities (hon.). Office: Harvard Univ 12 Quincy St Cambridge MA 02138 Business E-Mail: jsimpson@fas.harvard.edu.

SIMPSON, W(ILBURN) DWAIN, physicist, communications executive; b. Long Grove, Okla., Oct. 4, 1937; s. Joseph Charles and Wilma Ruby (Smith) S.; m. Ann Marie Coratello, Aug. 27, 1967; children: Ketah Marie, Rebecca Elizabeth. BS, U. Miss., 1959, MS, 1961; MA, Rice U., 1963, PhD, 1965. Rsch. assoc. Rice U., Houston, 1965-67; asst. physicist Brookhaven Nat. Lab., Upton, N.Y., 1967-69; v.p., sec., founder Periphonics Corp., Bohemia, N.Y., 1969-80, dir. R&D, 1972-78; v.p., sec., founder, dir. R&D Alta Tech. Inc., Stamford, Conn., 1980-85; pres., founder W.D. Simpson Tech., Inc., Wilton, Conn., 1985-91; v.p., founder Saber Equipment Corp., Fairfield, Conn., 1989-97; pres., founder Synergetic Techs. Inc., Wilton, Conn., 1996—. Cons. Ayentka Cons. Corp., Bay Shore, N.Y., 1980-81; founder, mgr. Saber Techs., LLC, Austin, Tex., 1997—2004, adj. prof. U. Southern Miss., 2006-. Author: New Techniques in Software Project Management, 1987; patentee in computers and electronically controlled advanced fueling systems; over 15 patents issued. Fellow NSF, 1961; NASA, 1963; named Inventor of Yr., U.S. Patent Office, 1973. Mem. AAAS, IEEE, Am. Phys. Soc., N.Y. Acad. Scis., Lions Club Internat. Roman Catholic. Avocations: robotics, computer controlled system, satellite communications. Home: 87122 Golf Club Dr Diamondhead MS 39525-3707 E-mail: dwainsimpson@aol.com.

SIMPSON, WILLIAM, information technology manager, consultant; b. Escondido, Calif., 1953; m. Deborah Simpson. BA in Social Sci., San Diego State U., 1976; MA in Ednl. Tech., U.S. Internat. U., San Diego, 1993. Profl. adminstr. credential Calif. Commn. Tchr. Credentialing, 2003, preliminary adminstrv. svcs. credential Calif. Commn. Tchr. Credentialing, 1993, secondary tchr. credential Calif. Commn. Tchr. Credentialing, 1977. Tchr. Escondido Union Sch. Dist., Calif., 1979—92, coord. tech. and media svcs., 1992—99; dir. staff devel. svcs. San Diego County Office Edn., 1999—. Edn. adv. bd. mem. Apple Computer, Inc., San Diego, 1997—99; co-founder and dir. Innovative Video in Edn., 2001—; dir. Innovative Video in Edn. Adv. Bd.; project dir. techsets San Diego County Office Edn., 2004—; mem. product adv. bd. Learning Frameworks, Inc. Developer: Innovative Video in Education Program (iVIE). Bd. dir. Classroom of the Future Found., San Diego, 1999—2001; mem. program com. San Diego Natural History Mus., 2002—04; edn. com. co-chair Pacific Southwest chpt. NATAS, 2004—. Named Apple Disting. Educator, Apple Computer, Inc., 2003; grantee, Calif. Tech. Assistance Project Region 9 Calif. Dept. Edn., 2003—05, 2005—. Mem.: ISTE, ASCD, Calif. Computer Using Educators (membership chair 1996—97, Tech. Learning Leadership award 2004), Internat. Soc. Tech. in Edn. (Outstanding Leadership 2004). Office: San Diego County Office Edn 6401 Linda Vista Rd San Diego CA 92111

SIMPSON, WILLIAM ARTHUR, insurance company executive; b. Oakland, Calif., Feb. 2, 1939; s. Arthur Earl and Pauline (Mikalasic) S.; m. Nancy Dougery Simpson, Mar. 31, 1962; children: Sharon Elizabeth, Shelley Pauline BS, U. Calif.-Berkeley, 1961; postgrad. Exec. Mgmt. Program, Columbia U. CLU. V.p. mktg. Countrywide Life, LA, 1973-76; v.p. agy. Occidental Life of Calif., LA, 1976-79; pres., CEO Vol. State Life, Chattanooga, 1979-83; exec. v.p. Transam. Occidental Life Ins. Co., LA, 1983-86, pres., 1986-88, pres., CEO, COO, 1988-90, also bd. dirs.; dir. USLIFE Corp., NYC, 1990—; pres., CEO All Am. Life Ins. Co., Pasadena, Calif., 1990-94, USLIFE Life Ins. div. USLIFE Corp., 1994, USLIFE Corp., 1995-97. Chmn. Franklin Life Ins. Co. Pres. Chattanooga coun. Boy Scouts Am., 1982, bd. dirs., LA, 1983, v.p., 1983-85, vice-chmn LA area, 1989, chmn., 1989; pres. bd. councillors LA County Am. Cancer Soc.; trustee Verdugo Hills Hosp. Found., Ill. Symphony Orch.; bd. dirs. Abraham Lincoln coun. Boy Scouts Am., Meml. Medical Ctr., Springfield, Ill. 1st lt. US Army, 1961—64. Mem. Am. Soc. CLUs, Life Ins. Mktg. and Rsch. Assn. (bd. dirs. 1986-89), Ctl. Ill. Ins. Co. (bd. dirs.), Rotary. Republican. Presbyterian. Avocations: golf, skiing. Office: Franklin Life Ins Co 1 Franklin Sq Springfield IL 62713-0002 Office Phone: 217-836-7674. Personal E-mail: neswas@aol.com.

SIMPSON, WILLIAM KELLY, curator, Egyptologist, educator; b. NYC, Jan. 3, 1928; s. Kenneth Farrand and Helen L.K. (Porter) S.; m. Marilyn E. Milton, June 19, 1953; children: Laura Knickerbacker Simpson Thorn, Abby Rockefeller Simpson Mydland. BA, Yale U., 1947, MA, 1948, PhD, 1954; DHL (hon.), Am. U. in Cairo, 2001. Asst. in Egyptian art Met. Mus. Art, 1948-54; rsch. fellow Center Middle East Studies, Harvard U., 1957-58; faculty Yale U., New Haven, 1958—65, prof. Egyptology, 1965—2004, chmn. dept. Near Eastern langs., 1966-69; curator Egyptian and ancient Near Eastern art Mus. Fine Arts, Boston, 1970-86; ltd. partner Kin and Co., 1967-69; ltd. ptnr. Venrock, 1970—. Dir. editor of papers Penn-Yale Archaeol. Expdn. to Egypt, 1960—; mem. adv. council fgn. currency program Smithsonian Instn., 1966-69 Author: Papyrus Reisner I-Records of a Building Project, 1963, Hekanefer and the Dynastic Material from Toshka, 1963, Papyrus Reisner II-Accounts of the Dockyard Workshop, 1965, Papyrus Reisner III: Records of a Building Project in the Early Twelfth Dynasty, 1969, The Terrace of the Great God at Abydos, 1974, The Mastabas of Qar and Idu, 1976, The Offering Chapel of Sekhem-ankh-ptah, 1976, The Offering Chapel of Kayemnofnet in the Museum of Fine Arts Boston, 1992, Papyrus Reisner IV: Personnel Reports, 1986, The Inscribed Material from the Pennsylvania-Yale Excavations at Abydos, 1995, (with others) The Ancient Near East, A History, 2d edit., 1998, The Literature of Ancient Egypt, 1972, The Mastaba of Queen Mersyankh III, 1994. Trustee Am. Sch. Classical Studies, Athens, Am. U. in Cairo, Katonah Mus. Art; mem. internat. council Mus. Modern Art, N.Y.C.; pres. Wrexham Found., 1965-67. Fulbright fellow Egypt, 1955-57; Guggenheim fellow, 1965 Mem. Am. Oriental Soc., Am. Philos. Soc., Archaeol. Inst. Am., Internat. Assn. Egyptologists, Egypt Exploration Soc., Soc. française d'egyptologie, German Archaeol. Inst., Foundation egyptologique Reine Elisabeth. Clubs: Century (N.Y.C.), Met. Opera (N.Y.C.), University (N.Y.C.), Union (N.Y.C.), River (N.Y.C.); Bedford (N.Y.); Golf and Tennis. Home: 129 Katonah Woods Rd Katonah NY 10536-3846 Personal E-mail: william.simpson@yale.edu.

SIMPSON-WENTZ, ASHLEE NICOLE, singer; b. Dallas, Oct. 3, 1984; d. Joe and Tina Simpson; m. Pete Wentz, May 17, 2008; 1 child, Bronx Mowgli Wentz. Studied, Sch. of Am. Ballet. Singer: (albums) Autobiography, 2004, I Am Me, 2005, Bittersweet World, 2008; actor: (films) The Hot Chick, 2002, Raise Your Voice, 2004, Undiscovered, 2005; (TV series) 7th Heaven, 2002—04, The Ashlee Simpson Show, 2004—05; musical guest appearance Saturday Night Live, 2004, guest appearance Saved By the Bell: The New Class, 1993, The View, 1997, Malcom in the Middle, 2001, 60 Minutes, 2004, Newlyweds: Nick & Jessica, 2003, 2004; actor: (plays) Chicago, 2006. Recipient Female New Artist of Yr., Billboard Music Awards, 2004. Avocations: vintage shopping, writing and recording music. Office: c/o Wilhelmina Artist Mgmt 7257 Beverly Blvd, 2nd Fl Los Angeles CA 90036*

SIMS, DALE, former state treasurer; b. Charlotte, NC; m. Debbie Davis; 1 child. BS, We. Carolina Univ., 1978; grad. work, Murray (Ky.) State Univ. Program auditor Comptroller of Treas., 1980—82; staff asst. Dept. Treas., 1982—87, exec. asst., treas, 1987—2003; state treas. State of Tenn., 2003—09; interim vice chancellor, bus. and fin. Tenn. Bd. Regents, 2009—. Mem.: Nat. Assn. State Auditors, Comptrollers and Treas. (exec. com.), Nat. Assn. State Treas. (So. Regional v.p. 2006). Methodist. Office Phone: 615-532-9910. Business E-Mail: sims6884@bellsouth.net.*

SIMS, DALE BENJAMIN, engineering educator; s. Jim and Marlene Sims; m. Debora K. Sims, June 12, 1976. PhD, U. North Tex., Denton, 2002. Sys. network mgr. Conoco, Houston, 1980—88; tech. rep. Info. Builders Inc., Houston, 1988—89; sys. analyst Am. Gen. Corp., Houston, 1989—90; sr. elec. engr. Downhole Seismic Svcs., Houston, 1990; prof. Dallas Bapt. U., 1990—. Cons. Am. Trial Mgmt., Dallas, 1999—2008. Fundraiser Baltic Pastors Inst., Riga, Latvia, 2007—08. Fellow, DBU Svc. Learning Inst., 2004; Fulbright, 2006. Mem.: IEEE, Assn. Computing Machinery, Phi Beta Delta (faculty sponsor of Epsilon Phi chpt. 2008—). Independent. Achievements include invention of fractal search algorithm for nonlinear relational data. Office: Dallas Bapt Univ 3000 Mountain Creek Pky Dallas TX 75211

SIMS, DAVE, sportscaster; b. Phila. s. Ulysses Sims; m. Abby Corsun; 2 children. Degree in mass comm. and English, Bethany Coll., W.Va. Intern Phila. Inquirer; sports reporter NY Daily News; news broadcaster NYC; local sports anchor/reporter Phila.; host, Sports Night with Dave Sims WNBC, MSG Network, NYC; talk radio host WFAN Radio, NYC; Summer Olympics announcer, track & field events NBC Sports, Seoul, Republic of Korea, 1988; radio play-by-play announcer, football Temple U. Owls, Phila.; Maj. League Baseball play-by-play announcer ESPN, coll. basketball announcer, 1991—, ESPN Regional, announcer, Big East Conf. basketball and football, 1997—2001, host, Inside the Big East, 2004—07; sports anchor, reporter, host WCBS-TV, NYC, 1992; announcer, NCAA men's basketball tournament CBS Sports; announcer, Sunday Night Football Westwood One Radio, 1994—; play-by-play announcer, pre-season games Tampa Bay Buccaneers, 1997—2003; host, Phillies Weekly Phila. Phillies, 1999—2001; host, GameFace Metro Guide Channel, NYC, 2000—01; host, Eagles Game Day Live Phila. Eagles, play-by-play announcer, pre-season games, 2004; Internet radio host, The Early Show mlb.com; co-host (with Mike Krzyzewski), Basketball and Beyond with Coach K Sirius-XM Satellite Radio; founder AthletiSense; radio color analyst & TV play-by play announcer, Seattle Mariners Fox Sports Northwest, 2006—. Bd. trustees Chestnut Hill Acad., Phila. Recipient New Eng. Sports Emmy award, football, 1993, Media award, Met. Intercollegiate Basketball Assn., 1995, Phila. Sports Emmy award, basketball, 1997, Asthma Achievement award, Children's Air Ctr. NY Hosp./Cornell U. Med. Ctr., 1998, Lindsey Nelson Outstanding Sportscaster award, Am. Football Found., 2003, Media award, Big East Conf., 2005; named Man of Yr., Tomorrows Children's Fund, Hackensack, NJ, 1987, Media Person of 1988, NY Pro Baseball Scouts; named to Chestnut Hill Acad. Sports Hall of Fame, Phila., 2006. Office: Fox Sports Northwest 3626 156th Ave SE Bellevue WA 98006*

SIMS, DAVID LLOYD, lawyer; b. Pine Bluff, Ark., Dec. 31, 1960; s. Lloyd H. Sims Jr. and Betty S. (Wilson) Sims; m. Joan M. Bennett, Aug. 17, 1985; 1 child, Wilson D. BA cum laude, Ouachita Bapt. U., 1983; JD with honors, U. Ark. Sch. Law, 1986. Bar: Ark. 1986, US Dist. Ct., Ea. Dist. Ark. 1987, US Claims Ct. 1989, US Ct. Appeals 8th Circuit 1989, U.S. Supreme Ct. 2005. Assoc. Bridges, Young, Matthews, Holmes & Drake, Pine Bluff, Ark., 1986—91; mem. Bridges, Young, Matthews & Drake PLC, 1991—. Chmn. Am. Cancer Soc. Relay for Life, Pine Bluff, Ark., 1999—2000; adv. bd. Student Cmty. Svc. Project, 1991—94; dir. United Way of SE Ark., 1992—98, Youth Ptnrs. of Pine Bluff/Jefferson County, 2002—07; asst. scoutmaster Boy Scouts of Am., 2002—. Mem.: ABA, Ark. Bar Assn. (ho. of delegates 1997—2004), Jefferson County Bar Assn., Greater Pine Bluff C. of C., Rotary Club of West Pine Bluff (pres. 1995—96, Paul Harris Fellow 1998). Methodist. Avocations: tennis, hiking, reading, music. Office: Bridges Young Matthews & Drake PLC 315 East 8th Ave Pine Bluff AR 71601 Business E-Mail: davidsims@bridgesplc.com.

SIMS, DELORIS, bank executive; m. Isaiah Sims; 2 children. Attended, Milw. Area Tech. Coll., 1961—62; program grad., U. SC Moore Sch. Bus., 2003, U. SC Grad. Sch. Bank Investment and Fin. Mgmt. Curriculum, 2004. Cert. entrepreneurship owner-mgr. program Marquette U. Part-time teller to positions of increasing responsibility including v.p. and bus. banker Firstar Bank, Milw., 1964—98; founder, pres., CEO Legacy Bancorp, Milw., 1999—. Past chair, vice chair bd. dirs. Legacy Banks; bd. dirs. Legacy Redevel. Corp. Mem. adv. bd. Zilber Found.; bd. dirs. Legacy Found., Nat. Bankers Assn., Milw. Art Mus., Wis. State Investment Bd., Wis. African Am. Women, Ltd., 1290 Scholarship Fund, Bus. Coun. MMAC, Milw. Boarding Sch. Partnership, Gen. Growth Capital, Inc., Great Lakes Scholarship Fund. Named Entrepreneur of Yr. in fin. services, Ernst & Young, 2003; named one of 25 Women to Watch, US Banker, 2008. Mem.: Wis. Urban Bankers Assn. (founder, past pres.). Office: Legacy Bancorp 2102 W Fond Du Lac Ave Milwaukee WI 53206-1533*

SIMS, EDWARD HOWELL, editor, writer; b. Orangeburg, SC, May 29, 1923; s. Hugo Sheridan and Jesse Lucile (Howell) S.; m. Frances Dell Hartt, Jan. 5, 1946; m. Martha Lurene Bass, July 18, 1960; children:

Edward H., Robert; m. Bente Thorlund Christensen, Oct. 4, 1969; children: Edward Christian, Frederik. AB, Wofford Coll., 1943; postgrad., Emory U., 1946-47. Mng. editor Orangeburg Times and Democrat, 1946, editor, 1952—; Washington corr., founder Washington bur. for number S.C. dailies, 1947. Dir. Sims Pub. Co., Orangeburg. Columnist: Looking South From Washington, 1948—; Washington Bur. chief: Editor's Copy syndicate, 1950-52; editor-pub., 1952—; radio news analyst: The News of The Week In Washington, 1951—; Author: American Aces, 1958, Greatest Fighter Missions, 1962, The Fighter Pilots, 1967, Fighter Tactics 1914-70, 1972, Aces Over the Oceans, 1987 The German American Tragedy, 2004, The Life & Times of Eduard H. Sims, 2005; contbr. articles to publs. White House corr. covering Pres.''s confs., 1948—; mem. Senate and House press galleries, 1947—; Am. consul Munich, Germany, 1963-65; cons. Exec. Office of White House, 1966-67; consul gen. Zurich, 1992; apptd. mem. Commn. to Preserve Am. Heritage Abroad, 1987. Served to 1st lt. USAF, World War II. Recipient Young Man of the Year award S.C. Jr. C. of C., 1959 Mem. White House Corrs. Assn., Am. Legion, V.F.W. Clubs: Rotary, Nat. Press; Metropolitan (Washington); R.A.F. (London). Methodist. Home: 3803 Pin Oaks St Sarasota FL 34232-1241 also: PO Box 400 Fairview NC 28730-0400 Office: PO Box 1574 Orangeburg SC 29116-0532 Home Phone: 921-366-2169. Business E-Mail: mail@editorscopy.com.

SIMS, EZRA, composer; b. Birmingham, Ala., Jan. 16, 1928; s. Ezra G. and Kathryn W. (Wallace) S. BA, Birmingham So. Coll., 1947; postgrad., Birmingham Conservatory Music, 1945-48; MusB in Composition, Yale U. Sch. Music, 1952; MA in Composition, Mills Coll., 1956. Librarian Harvard Music Library, Cambridge, Mass., 1958-62, 65-74; music dir. New Eng. Dinosaur Dance Theatre, Boston, 1968-78; instr. theory New Eng. Conservatory Music, Boston, 1976-78; instr. microtonal theory Mozarteum, Salzburg, 1992-93; freelance composer Cambridge, 1974—. Dir. Dinosaur Annex Music Ensemble, Cambridge, pres. 1977-2003; guest composer 23d Ann. Contemporary Music Festival, Ill. Wesleyan U., 1977; lectr. various colls. including Warwick U., Cleve. Inst. Music, Internat. Christian U., Westport Friends of Music, Schlumberger-Doll Rsch., Webster U., Mozarteum, Northwestern U., Hochschule für Musik, Hamburg. Composer over 100 works, predominantly microtonal music for various mediums including Chamber Cantata on Chinese Poems, 1954, Mass, 1955, Two Folk Songs, 1958, String Quartet, 1959, Sieben-Spencer Lieder, 1960, Sonate Concertanti, 1961, Third Quartet, 1962, Buchlein for Lyon, 1962, Cantata III, 1963, Octet for Strings, 1964, In Memoriam Alice Hawthorne, 1967, Antimatter: Three Dances for Toby, 1968, A Frank Overture: Four Dented Interludes and Coda, 1969, Pastorale, 1970, Clement Wenceslaus Lothaire Nepomucene, Prince Metternich (1773-1859), In Memoriam, 1970, Real Toads, 1970, Interlope, 1971, Tango Variations, 1971, Museum Piece, 1972, Where the Wild Things Are, 1973, String Quartet #2 (1962), 1974, After Lyle or Untitled, 1975, When the Angels Blow Their Trumpets, 1976, Celebration of Dead Ladies, 1976, Elegie-nach Rilke, 1976, Collage XIII, 1977, Aeneas on the Saxophone, 1977, Come Away, 1978, Midorigaoka, 1978, 5 Songs, 1979, -And, As I Was Saying..., 1979, Two for One, 1980, Sextet, 1981, All Done From Memory, 1980, Phenomena, 1981, Solo After Sextet, 1981, Quartet, 1982, Pictures for an Institution, 1983, Tune and Variations, 1983, Brief Elegies, 1983, String Quartet #4, 1984, The Conversions, 1985, Wedding Winds, 1986, Quintet, 1987, Chase, 1987, Solo in four movements, 1987, AEDM in memoriam, 1988, Flight, 1989, Night Piece: I.C. Girum Imus nocte et Consuminur Igni, 1989, Concert Piece, 1990, Duo, 1992, Invocation, 1992, Stanzas, 1995, If I Told Him, 1996, Duo, 1996, 97, Encores: Three Parlor Songs, 2000, String Quartet #5, 2000, Musing and Recollection, 2003, -furthermore..., 2004, Concert Piece, 2005, im Mirabell, 2006-08,Landscapes; contbr. articles to profl. jours. Served as pvt. U.S. Army, 1952-54. Recipient Composers Forum award, 1959, Koussevitzky Found. commn., 1983, Am. Acad. Arts and Letters award, 1985; grantee Cambridge Arts Coun., 1975, 76, Martha Baird Rockefeller Found., 1977; fellow Guggenheim Found., 1962, McDowell Colony, 1966, Nat. Endowment for Arts, 1976, 78, Mass. Artists Found., 1979, Djerassi Found., 1990, Fulbright Sr. Scholar, 1992, Wurlitzer Found., 1998, Camargo Found., 2000, Disting. Achievement award, Am. Music Rsch. Ctr. U. Colo Boulder, 2009. Mem. Broadcast Music, Inc. Home and Office: 229 Hurley St Cambridge MA 02141-2133 Address: Rosalie Calabrese Mgmt Box 20580 Park West St New York NY 10025-1521 Office Phone: 617-864-8781. Personal E-mail: ezrsims@aol.com.

SIMS, FRANCIS HARDING, retired medical researcher; b. Auckland, New Zealand, Jan. 27, 1913; s. Robert James and Nannie Emmeline (Entrican) S.; m. Gertrude Jean Miller, Mar. 23, 1946 (div. May 1972); m. Philippa Ethel Anderson, Apr. 5, 1973; children: David John, Helen Mary. MSc, U. New Zealand, 1934, MB ChB, 1941; PhD, U. Edinburgh, 1951; MD, U. Otago, 1991. Resident Auckland Hosp., New Zealand, 1941—43; asst. pathologist Wellington Hosp., New Zealand, 1946—47; med. rschr. U. Edinburgh, 1948—51; chem. pathologist Auckland Group Hosps., 1951—64; pathologist in charge Green Lane Hosp., Auckland, 1964—70; head clin. chemistry, assoc. prof. Women's Coll. Hosp. U. Toronto, Ont., Canada, 1970—78; ret., 1978; tutor pathology Ctrl. Med. Sch., Suva, Fiji, 1979—81; hon. rsch. fellow Sch. Medicine, Auckland, 1981—2008. Chmn. Adv. Com. Pathologists, Auckland, 1968-70; coord. postgrad. tng. clin. chemistry U. Toronto, 1976-78; mem. coun. Ctrl. Med. Sch., Fiji, 1979-81. Contbr. articles to profl. jours. M.O. for Repatriation of New Zealand Prisoners of War, Singapore, 1945. With Royal New Zealand Air Force, 1943-46. Fellow Coll. Pathologists Australasia, Australasian Assn. Clin. Biochemists; mem. Shelly Park Cruising Club (life, commodore 1966-68), Bucklands Beach Yacht Club. Avocations: sailing, music. Home: Bucklands Beach 13 Endymion Pl Auckland New Zealand E-mail: k.sionc@auckland.ac.nz.

SIMS, JANETTE ELIZABETH LOWMAN, retired educational director; b. Lincolnton, NC, July 21, 1934; d. Lee Hobson and Myrtle Elizabeth (Travis) Lowman; m. Mickey Ray Sims, Feb. 2, 1951; children: Carol Lee, Rickey Ray. BS, Lenoir-Rhyne Coll., 1968; MAT, U. N.C., 1973; EdD, U. N.C., Greensboro, 1989. N.C. "G" tchg. cert; cert. devel. edn. specialist. Quality control supr. Kiser Roth Hosiery, Inc., Maiden, N.C., 1959-63; 9th grade phys. sci. and math. tchr. Cherryville Jr. H.S., NC, 1968; phys. sci., chemistry and astronomy tchr. Maiden HS, NC, 1968-75; dir. studies lab. coord. Catawba Valley CC, Hickory, NC, 1975-79, physics, chemistry, math. and computer sci. instr., 1979-90, dir. devel. studies and learning assistance ctr., 1990-2001; ret., 2001. Apprentice program instr. Meredith/Burda Corp., Newton, NC, 1979—88; part-time instr. math. and physics Catawba Valley CC, 2001—03; coord. disability svcs. Peer Acad. Support Svcs. Lenoir-Rhyne U., Hickory, NC, 2004—09. Mem. Conover Planning Bd., 2001—; trustee Catawba County Assn. for Spl. Edn., Conover, 1978—79, Catawba Valley Found., Hickory, 1993—96, chair, 1996; mem. mayor's com. for persons with disabilities Catawba County; tchr., mem. choir Faith Luth. Ch., Conover, 1980—, mem. ch. coun., 1995—97, 2008—, pres. congregation and ch. coun., 1997—98, v.p. congregation and ch. coun., 2001—03, 2008—09. Mem. AHEAD, NCAHEAD, Coll. Reading and Learning Assn., N.C. Assn. Educators (local unit pres.), Nat. Assn. Developmental Educators, N.C. Assn. Developmental Educators (regional chair 1990), Atlantic Assn. Physics Tchrs. (chair nominations com. 1992), N.C. Math. Assn. Two-Yr. Colls. (chairperson devel. math. com. 1991-93, sec. 1996-2000), Coll. Reading and Learning Assn., Am. Legion Aux., Delta Kappa Gamma. Avocations: sewing, cooking. Home: 300 Parlier Ave NE Conover NC 28613-9312 Office: Lenoir Rhyne Univ PO Box 7470 Hickory NC 28603 E-mail: simsJ@lr.edu.

SIMS, JOE, lawyer; b. Phoenix, Sept. 29, 1944; s. Joe and Pauline Jane (Saunders) S.; m. Robin Ann Reed, Jan. 30, 1965; 1 child, Shannon Dane. BS in Fin., Ariz. State U., 1967, JD, 1970. Bar: Ariz. 1970, U.S. Supreme Ct. 1975, D.C 1978. Trial atty. antitrust div. Dept. Justice, Washington, 1970-73; spl. asst. to asst. atty. gen., 1973-75; dep. asst. atty. gen. for policy planning and legislation, 1975-77, dep. asst. atty. gen. for regulatory matters and fgn. commerce, 1977-78; mem. firm Jones, Day, Washington, 1978-79, ptnr., 1979—. Resident fellow Am. Enterprise Inst. for Pub. Policy Rsch., Washington, 1978-79, vis. fellow, 1979-81; prin. Coun. for Excellence in Govt. Contbr. articles to profl. jours. Co-recipient US Antitrust award, Chambers Awards for Excellence Ceremony, 2006; named one of 15 Dealmakers of the Yr., Am. Lawyer mag., 2000, World's Top 10 Antitrust Lawyers, Global Counsel mag., 2001. Mem. ABA (chmn. antitrust law sect. one com. 1987-90, bus. law sect. antitrust law com. 1988-91, antitrust law civil practice and procedure com. 1990-91), Am. Law Inst., D.C. Bar Assn., Firestone Country Club (Akron, Ohio), Mirabel Club (Scottsdale, Ariz.), Talking Rock Club (Prescott, Ariz.). Republican. Office: Jones Day 51 Louisiana Ave NW Washington DC 20001-2113 Office Phone: 202-879-3863. Office Fax: 202-626-1747. Business E-Mail: jsims@jonesday.com.

SIMS, JOHN R., lawyer; b. 1950; B, U. Mo., 1972, JD, 1975. Various legal positions to v.p., dep. gen. counsel Federated Dept. Stores, Inc., Cin., 1980—2002; exec. v.p., gen. counsel Albertson's Inc., Boise, Idaho, 2002—. Mem.: Law Review, Phi Beta Kappa.

SIMS, KENT OTWAY, economist; b. Chickasha, Okla., Nov. 2, 1940; s. Jesse Otway and Mable Vela (Bear) S.; m. Jeanette McCollum, June 9, 1961; children: Marketa, Adam. BA, U. Colo., 1963, PhD, 1966. Registered investment advisor. Economist Urban Renewal Authority, Denver, 1965-66, U.S. Dept. State mission to Pakistan, 1966-69, Fed. Res. Bank of San Francisco, 1969-71, asst. v.p., 1971-72, v.p., dir. research, 1972-74, sr. v.p., 1974-82, exec. v.p., chief fin. officer, 1982-85; fin. advisor, investment mgr., mgmt. cons. Theodore R. Seton, 1985-86; ptnr. C&K Partnership, 1987-89. Pres. Her Equal Share, Inc., 1986-89, San Francisco Econ. Devel. Corp., 1988-91; dir. econ. planning and devel. Mayor's Office, San Francisco, 1992-93, San Francisco Redevel. Agy., 1993-96; dir. spl. projects City Mgr.'s Office, Oakland, Calif., 1997; dep. dir. Com. Econ. Devel., Oakland, 1997-98; cons. Bay Area Life Scis. Alliance, 1999, San Francisco Planning and Urban Rsch. Assn., 2000, Golden Gate Restaurant Assn., 2001-05, San Francisco Small Property Owners, 2003, San Francisco Small Bus. Alliance, 2003, Burnham & Brown, Attys., 2003-05, Calif. Restaurant Assn., San Diego, 2008, petrolerial real estate devel. Baton Rouge, LA, 2009. Bd. govs. Econ. Lit. Coun. Calif., Long Beach, 1983-88; trustee Strybing Arboretum Soc. Golden Gate Park, San Francisco, 1983-96; bd. dirs. Jewish Community Mus., San Francisco, 1986-93, Design Coun. San Francisco Bay Area, 1989-90, Career Resources Devel. Ctr., 1991-92; adv. bd. St. Lukes Hosp., San Francisco, 1988-96. Mem.: Am. Econs. Assn., Audubon Soc. Am., Sierra Club. Personal E-mail: kentsims@pacbell.net.

SIMS, LOWERY STOKES, museum curator, administrator, writer, educator; b. Washington, Feb. 13, 1949; d. John Jacob and Bernice Marion (Banks) S. BA in Art History, Queens Coll., 1970, MPhil, 1989; PhD in Art History, CUNY, 1995; MA in Art History, Johns Hopkins U., 1972; LHD (hon.), Md. Coll. Art, Balt., 1988; ArtsD (hon.), Moore Coll. Art, Phila., 1990; ArtsD, Brown U., Providence, 2003. Mus. edn. assoc. Met. Mus. Art, NYC, 1972-75, asst. curator, 1975-79, assoc. curator, 1979-95, curator, 1995—99; exec. dir. Studio Mus. in Harlem, NYC, 1999—2005, pres., 2005—06, adj. curator, 2006—07; curator Museum Arts and Design, 2007—. Prin. author: (catalogue) Stuart Davis, American Painting, 1991; co-author: (book) Wifredo Lam and the International Avant Guide, 1923, 1982, (catalogue) Wifredo Lam and His Contemporaries, 1992, (catalogue) Challenge of the Modern: African American Arts, 1925-1945, 2002-03, Persistence of Geometry, Cleve. Mus. Art, 2006. Bd. dirs. Tiffany Found., N.Y.C., 2005—, Met. Mus. Art, 2005-07, Art 21, 2006-07. Mem. Internat. Assn. Art Critics, Coll. Art Assn. (bd. dirs. 1993-97, Mather award for art criticism 1991). Democrat. Avocations: needlepoint, collecting black memorabilia. Office Phone: 212-956-3535. Personal E-mail: lsimssmh@aol.com. E-mail: lowevy.sims@madmuseum.org.

SIMS, PAMELA JAN (CERUSSI), writer, minister; b. Little Rock, Sept. 10, 1933; 2 children. Attended, Mt. St. Mary's Acad., St. Scholastica's Coll., Sydney, Delgado Coll., Nola, Tulane U., 1951; DD (hon.). Lic. rev. in Christian ministry specialized svcs. Fla., 2006. Past pres. Ikebana Internat., Le Gals, Inc., 1979—89; pres. Titanic Bead Co.; journalist, notary pub. Fla., 1986—. Tchr. legal secretarial classes, Nola; support writer Pres. George W. Bush, 1999—. Author: Pensacola Today mag., Climate mag., introduction to Bonsai & Basic Ikebana; featured on local TV Guide mag. cover Anskebara Design; prin. works include Bonsai and Ikebana design articles; contbr. articles in mags. and newspapers. Vol. Pensacola Art Mus.; team leader Bush/Cheney Inc., 2002—08; mem. Rep. Nat. Com., Rep. Nat. Woman's Club, Pensacola Christian Women's Club, United Intercessors Inc. Recipient Cert. of Recognition, Rep. Nat. Party, 2002, 2006, Congl. Award of Merit, 2004, 8 Blue ribbons and 3 Tri-Color ribbons, Fla. Fedn. Garden Clubs, 2004, Cert. of Appreciation, Rep. Nat. Com., 2005. Mem.: Coxes of FFGC Claneder, Facdar Club, Sweet Bay GC, Dogwood Club, Pensacola Camellia Club & WRL. Achievements include patents pending for AIDS cure other medical discourses. Office Phone: 850-512-3927. Office Fax: 850-457-1022.

SIMS, RICHARD LEE, retired hospital administrator; b. Columbus, Ohio, Jan. 6, 1929; s. Dorwin Delos and Christine Anna (Hanstein) Sims; m. Marilyn Lou Atkinson, June 2, 1951 (dec. July 2005); children: John Christopher, Steven Paul; m. Norma W. Shilliday, Nov. 17, 2006. BS, Ohio State U., Columbus, 1951. Pres. Doctors Hosp. Found., Columbus, 1977-95; preceptor faculty Ohio State U. Coll. Health Care Adminstrn.; past chmn. Hosp. Coun. Franklin County; ret., 1995. Past chmn. Hosp. Shared Svc. Inc. Past chmn. 1st Cmty. Village Bd.; past chmn. governing bd. 1st Cmty. Ch.; pres. Scioto Valley Health Systems Agy., 1999-2002; pres. Employment for Srs., 1999-2000, Probus, 2003; past chair Columbus area chpt. ARC, emeritus bd. dirs.; mem. 1st Cmty. Found., Drs. Hosp. Devel. Found. Recipient Disting. Svc. award Columbus Jr. C. of C., 1960-63. Fellow Am. Coll. Healthcare Execs. (life), Am. Coll. Osteo. Healthcare Execs. (life); mem. Am. Osteo. Healthcare Assn. (chmn. 1988), Ohio Soc. of Assn. Execs. (past pres.), Ohio Hosp. Assn. (past chmn. bd.), Ohio Osteo. Hosp. Assn. (past pres.), Am. Legion (past post comdr.), Rotary (pres. 1978-79), Columbus Club, Sigma Chi (named Significant Sig 2003). Home: 4848 Slate Run Ct Columbus OH 43220

SIMS, ROBERT JOHN, financial planner; b. Phila., Mar. 18, 1926; s. Stanley Joseph and Marie (Kendrick) S.; m. Gloria MacCarter, Nov. 27, 1965 (dec. June 21, 2005); children: Lisa Byrne, Dana Hospodar, Ernest, William, Peter, Moira. Student, Temple U., 1947-51; MSFS, CLU, ChFC, Am. Coll., Bryn Mawr, Pa., 1957; CFP, Coll. Fin. Planning, Denver. With Provident Mut. Life Ins., Phila., 1947-56, Aetna Life Ins., Phila., 1956-58, Mut. of N.Y., Phila., 1958-68; chmn. Fin-Plan Investments, Inc., Wayne, Pa., 1960—; pres. Fin-Plan Cons., Inc., Wayne, 1960—, Fin-Plan, Inc., Wayne, 1960—; chmn. Sims Fin. Svcs. LLC. Mem. fin. com. Archdiocese of Phila., investment com., trustee Lay Employees Pension Plan. Past trustee Notre Dame Acad. Bd., Radnor, Pa., United Fund; past pres. Phila. Jaycees, past nat. dir. U.S. Jaycees; bd. dirs. Gwynedd Mercy Coll., Phila.; active Big Bros.; mem. adv. bd. St. Charles Borremmeo Sem.; past pres., active Cath. Philopatrian Lit. Inst. With U.S. mil., 1944-46. Mem. Internat. Assn. Fin. Planners (founding pres. Delaware Valley chpt.), Inst. CFPs, Am. Soc. CLU, Phila. Estate Planning Coun., Phila. Assn. Life Underwriters, Golden Key Soc., Union League Phila., Phila. Country Club, Ocean Reef Club, Sky 700 Club. Republican. Roman Catholic. Avocation: golf. Home: 219 Orchard Way Saint Davids PA 19087-4805 Office: Sims Fin Svcs LLC 531 E Lancaster Ave Wayne PA 19087-5112

SIMS, ROGER W., lawyer; b. Cleve., Aug. 3, 1950; BA with high honors, U. Fla., 1972, JD, 1974. Bar: Fla. 1975. Mem. Holland & Knight, Orlando, Fla. Mem. Moot Ct. U. Fla.; contbr. to profl mag. and jour. Mem. ABA (mem. standing com. on environ. law 2000-2003), Fla. Bar Assn. (chmn. environ., land use law sect. 1988-89), Fla. Assn. Water Quality Control (pres. 2006-07), Phi Beta Kappa, Phi Kappa Phi, Omicron Delta Kappa, Phi Alpha Delta, Fla. Blue Key. Office: Holland & Knight PO Box 1526 200 S Orange Ave Ste 2600 Orlando FL 32801-3453 Office Phone: 407-425-8500. Business E-Mail: roger.sims@hklaw.com.

SIMS, RONALD CORDELL, federal agency administrator; b. Spokane, Wash., July 5, 1948; s. James Sr. C. and Lydia T. (Ramsey) Sims; m. Cayan Topacio; children: Douglas, Daniel, Aaron. BA in Psychology, Ctrl. Wash. U., Ellensburg, 1971. Ordained Bapt. min. Investigator consumer-protection divsn. Wash. State Office Atty. Gen.; formerly with FTC; mgr. youth svcs. Seattle Dept. Human Resources, 1979; dir. SE Effective Devel., Seattle; mem. Dist. 5 King County Coun., Wash., 1985—97, King County Exec., 1997—2009; dep. sec. US Dept. Housing & Urban Devel. (HUD), Washington, 2009—. Candidate US Senate, 1994, Gov. of Wash., 2004. Democrat. Office: US Dept Housing & Urban Devel (HUD) 451 7th St SW Washington DC 20410 Office Phone: 202-708-1112.*

SIMS, WILSON, lawyer; b. Nashville, Dec. 24, 1924; s. Cecil and Grace (Wilson) S.; m. Linda Bell, Aug. 12, 1948; children: Linda Rickman, Suzanne, Wilson. BA, U. N.C., 1946; JD, Vanderbilt U., 1948. Bar: Tenn. 1948. Since practiced in, Nashville; ptnr. Bass, Berry & Sims; gen. counsel, dir. of pub. and private rels. Baird Ward Printing Co., Southeastern Capital Corp., Martha White Foods, Synercon Corp., Forrest Life Ins. Co., Charter Co., The Bailey Co., Kenworth of Tenn., Inc. Chmn. Tenn. Commn. for Human Devel., Tenn. Commn. on Continuing Legal Edn.; mem. Tenn. Gen. Assembly, 1959-60; bd. dirs. Nashville YMCA, founder Camp Wigawager, United Cerebal Palsy, Kidney Found., Matthew 25, McKendree Village; trustee Meharry Med. Coll., Webb Sch., Bell Buckle, Tenn.; adv. bd. Jr. League; mem. bd. visitors U. N.C. 1st lt. USMCR, 1942-45, 50-52. Fellow Am. Bar Found. (life), Nashville Bar Found.; mem. ABA, Tenn. Bar Assn. (past spkr. ho. of dels., past pres.), Nashville Bar Assn. (past pres., dir., Pub. Svc. award), Tenn. Bar Found. (past chmn.), Am. Judicature Soc., Am. Acad. Polit. Sci., Vanderbilt U. Law Alumni Assn. (past pres., Disting. Svc. award), Nashville C. of C. (2 terms bd. govs.), Belle Meade Country Club (bd. dirs.), High Hampton Colony Club (bd. dirs., pres.), Hampton Choral Scramble Soc. (pres.), Hillwood Country Club(bd. dirs.) Methodist. Home: 22 Foxhall Close Nashville TN 37215-1862 Office: Bass Berry & Sims Ste 2700 315 Deaderick St Nashville TN 37238-3001 Business E-Mail: wsims@bassberry.com.

SIMSON, GARY JOSEPH, law educator; b. Newark, Mar. 18, 1950; s. Marvin and Mildred (Silberg) S.; m. Rosalind Slivka, Aug. 15, 1971; children: Nathaniel, Jennie Anne. BA summa cum laude, Yale Coll., 1971; JD, Yale U., 1974. Bar: Conn. 1974, N.Y. 1980. Law clk. to judge U.S. Ct. Appeals 2d Cir., 1974-75; asst. prof. law U. Tex., 1975—77, prof. law, 1977—80, Cornell U., Ithaca, NY, 1980—2006, assoc. dean faculty devel., 1997—2000, assoc. dean acad. affairs Ithaca, NY, 2000—04; dean Case Western Reserve U. Sch. Law, 2006—08, Hostetler-Baker & Hostetler prof. law Cleve., 2006—. Vis. prof. law Cornell U., Ithaca, 1979-80, U. Calif., Berkeley, 1986; chmn. adv. bd. law casebook series Carolina Acad. Press. Author: Issues and Perspectives in Conflict of Laws, 1985, 4th edit., 2005; contbr. articles to profl. jours. Mem. ABA, ACLU, Am. Law Inst., Phi Beta Kappa. Office: Case Western Reserve U Sch Law 11075 E Blvd Cleveland OH 44106 Office Phone: 216-368-6351. Business E-Mail: gary.simson@case.edu.*

SIMSON, JO ANNE, retired anatomy and cell biology educator; b. Chgo., Nov. 19, 1936; d. Kenneth Brown and Helen Marjorie (Pascoe) Valentine; m. Arnold Simson, June 1961 (div.); 1 child, Maria; m. Michael Smith, Nov. 10, 1971 (div.); children: Elisabeth Smith, Briana Smith. BA, Kalamazoo Coll., 1959; MS, U. Mich., 1961; PhD, SUNY, Syracuse, 1969. Fellow Temple U. Health Sci. Ctr., Phila., 1968-70; asst. prof. Med. U. S.C., Charleston, 1970-76, assoc. prof., 1976-83, prof. anatomy and cell biology, 1983-96, prof. emerita, 1996—. With overseas program UMUC, 1999—2004; featured in Smithsonian exhibit Sci. in Am. Life, 1994—. Contbr. articles to profl. jours.; author short stories and poems. Grantee NSF, 1959-60, NIH, 1966-67, 72-87, 91-95. Mem. Am. Assn. Anatomists, Am. Soc. Cell Biology, Histochem. Soc. (sec. 1979-82, exec. com. 1985-89), Fogarty Internat. Fellowship Bioctr. (Basel, Switzerland, 1987-88), Amnesty Internat. (newsletter editor Group 168 1982-86), Phi Beta Kappa. *In the end, it is only what a person has created and given to the rest of the world that endures.*

SIN, MO-KYUNG, nurse; d. Yong-Bum Sin and Bok-Su Park. DSc in Nursing, U. Ala., Birmingham, 2001. RN Wash. State Dept. Health, 1993. RN St. Joseph's Med. Ctr., Tampa, Fla., 1995—97, UAB Health Care Sys., Birmingham, 1999—2001, NW Hosp., Seattle, 2003. Contbr. articles to sci. jours. Grant, Nat. Inst. Nursing Rsch., 2001—03, Intramural grant, Seattle U., 2007, Summer faculty fellowship, 2009. Fellow: Hope Heart Inst.; mem.: Sigma Theta Tau (Nu chpt. 1999, Psi chpt. 2002). Office: Seattle Univ Coll Nursing 901 12th Ave PO Box 222000 Seattle WA 98125 Office Phone: 206-296-5667. Business E-Mail: sinm@seattle.edu.

SIN, YONG WOOK, researcher, educator; PhD, Ariz. State U., Tempe, 1991—96. Postdoctoral fellowship Ariz. State U., 1997—99; rsch. prof. U. Mo.-Rolla, 1999—2008; engring. mgr. Protonex Tech., 2008—09; rsch. prof. Colo. Sch. Mines, 2009—. Mem.: Electrochemical Soc., Am. Ceramic Soc., Phi Kappa Phi. Achievements include development of new electrode materials for solid fuel cell, solid oxide fuel-fed electrolyzer cell and oxygen transport membranes; using polymeric precursor, liquid mix, colloidal, composite technology, Pechini method, and glycine-nitrate process to prepare anode, cathode and electrolytes; nano-sized ceramic powders, ceramic inks formulation, and thin and thick films by CVD, PVD, screen printing or tape casting process, and characterized them; research in solid oxide fuel cell-synthesis, processing, stack design, preparation of ceramic materials and characterization using high temperature electrochemistry testers; such as Impedance spectroscopy, potentiostat and galvanostat to fabricate intermediate temperature solid oxide fuel cell. Office: Univ Missouri Rolla 303 Material Research Ctr 1870 Miner Cir Rolla MO 65409 Business E-Mail: ysin@mines.edu.

SINAGRA, JACK G., former state senator; b. Queens, NY, Mar. 18, 1950; m. Eileen Cook, 1978; children: Jacklyn, Alexandra, Patrick. BA, Emporia Coll., 1972. Mayor Town of East Brunswick, NJ, 1989—91; mem. NJ State Senate from Dist. 18, Trenton, 1992—2002; chmn. bd. The Port Authority of NY & NJ, 2001—07. V.p. Turtle & Hughes, Linden, N.J. Mem. Assn. for a Better Middlesex County.

SINAI, ALLEN LEO, economist, educator; b. Detroit, Apr. 4, 1939; s. Joseph and Betty Paula (Feinberg) Sinai; m. Lee Davis Etsten, June 23, 1963; children: Lauren Beth, Todd Michael. AB, U. Mich., 1961; MA, Northwestern U., 1966, PhD, 1969. From asst. prof. to prof. econs. U. Ill., Chgo., 1966-75; sr. v.p., chmn. fin. info. group, chief fin. economist Data Resources, Lexington, Mass., 1971-83; chief economist, mng. dir. Lehman Brothers and Shearson Lehman Brothers Inc., NYC, 1983—88; chief economist, exec. v.p. The Boston Co. Inc., 1988-93; pres., CEO Boston Co. Econ. Advisors Inc., Boston, NYC, 1988-93; mng. dir., chief global economist, dir. global economics Lehman Brothers Inc., NYC, 1993-96; pres., chief global economist, strategist Decision Economics, Inc., Boston, NYC, London, 1996—; chief global economist, vice-chmn. WEFA Group, 1997-2000; global chief economist, exec. v.p. Global Insight, Inc., Lexington, Mass., 2001—03. Cons. Laural Cons., Lexington, Mass.; vis. assoc. prof. econs. and fin. MIT, Cambridge, 1975—77, vis. faculty Sloan Sch., 1989—91; adj. prof. econs. Boston U., 1977—78, 1981—83, NYU, NYC, 1984—88; adj. prof. econs. and fin. Lemberg Sch., Brandeis U., 1988—95; bd. economists Time Mag., 1991—2003; bd. dirs. Boston Pvt. Fin. Holdings, Inc., 1997—; spkr. in field. Contbr. articles to profl. jours., chapters to books. Mem. reducing fed. budget deficit task force Roosevelt Ctr., Washington, 1984; econ. policy adviser Rep. and Dem. Adminstrns., Washington, 1975—; bd. govs. Com. Developing Am. Capitalism, 1984—96, chmn., 1990—95. Recipient Alumnus Merit award, Northwestern U., 1985, Otto Eckstein prize, 1988; named Top Forecaster, Bus. Week, 1997, USA Today, 2003, 2005, Wall St. Jour., 2006, Market Watch, 2004—; named one of Ten Smartest Men in Boston, Boston Mag., 1993. Mem.: Am. Econ. Assn., Econometric Soc., Western Econ. Assn. (bd. dirs. 1995—97), Ea. Econs. Assn. (v.p. 1988—89, pres. 1990—91), N.Am. Econ. Fin. Assn. (pres. 2004—05, v.p. 2003—04). Jewish. Avocations: tennis, skiing, golf, bicycling. Home Phone: 781-861-0950, 617-686-7954; Office Phone: 617-994-0503. Office Fax: 212-884-9451. Business E-Mail: asinai@decisioneconomicsinc.com.

SINAI, YAKOV G., theoretical mathematician, educator; b. Moscow, Sept. 21, 1935; BS, Moscow State U., 1957, PhD in Math., 1960, Doctor Degree, 1963; D Honoris Causa, Warsaw U., 1993, Budapest U. Sci. and Tech., 2002, Hebrew U., Jerusalem, 2005. Sci. rschr. lab. probabilistic and statis. methods Moscow State U., 1960-71; sr. rschr. Landau Inst. Theoretical Physics Acad. Scis., Moscow, USSR, 1971—; prof. math. Moscow State U., 1971-93; prof. math. dept. Princeton (N.J.) U., 1993—. Loeb lectr. Harvard U., 1978; plenary speaker Internat. Congresses Math. Physics, Berlin, 1981, Marseille, 1986, Internat. Congress Math., Kyoto, 1990; disting. lectr., Israel, 1989; S. Lefshetz lectr., Mex., 1990. Recipient Boltzman Gold medal, 1986, Heineman prize, 1989, Markov prize, 1990, Paul Adrian Maurice Dirac medal Internat. Centre for Theoretical Physics, 1992, Wolf prize in math. Wolf Found., Israel, 1997, Moser Prize, 2001, Nemmers Prize in Mathematics, 2002. Mem. Am. Acad. Arts and Sci. (fgn. hon.), Russian Acad. Scis., Hungarian Acad. Scis. (fgn.), London Math. Soc. (hon.), Nat. Acad. Scis. of USA (fgn. assoc.), Brazilian Acad. Scis. (fgn.). Office: Princeton University Dept of Mathematics 708 Fine Hall Washington Rd Princeton NJ 08544-0001 Home Phone: 609-924-6094; Office Phone: 609-258-4199.

SINAY, JOSEPH, retail executive; b. Chgo., Dec. 5, 1920; s. Hyman and Ella S.; m. Ruth Milman, Mar. 7, 1961; 1 dau., Elise Sinay Spilker. Student, Herzl Jr. Coll., 1939. Gen. mgr. Fanchon & Marco Theatres, LA, 1943-54; v.p., founder Interstate United, Chgo., 1953-56; ptnr. Josam Investment Co., LA, 1956-97, Sinay Co. L.L.C., LA, 1997—; pres., CEO R B Industries Inc., LA, 1956-89, also chmn. bd. dirs., cons.; chmn. bd. dirs. Gorian Sinay Land Co., Inc., LA, 1997—. Bd. dirs. Am. Acad. Dramatic Arts; pres. Variety Clubs Internat., 1985-87; gen. chmn. United Jewish Welfare L.A., 1976; pres. We. region Am. Friends Hebrew U., 1980; Calif. fin. chmn. Muskie for Pres., 1972; trustee Idyllwild Arts Found., 1968-73; bd. dirs. Constl. Rights Found., 1973-78. Mem. Nat. Home Furnishing Assn. Jewish. Office: Sinay Co LLC 1801 Century Park E Los Angeles CA 90067-2302 Home Phone: 310-553-2340. Business E-Mail: joe@sinaycompany.com.

SINBAD, (DAVID ADKINS), actor, comedian; b. Benton Harbor, Mich., Nov. 10, 1956; m. Meredith, 1985 (div. 1992); children: Paige, Royce. Student, U. Denver. Stand-up comedian various comedy clubs and concerts nationwide; regular on TV series A Different World, NBC, 1987-91, The Sinbad Show, 1993, (host) Vibe, 1997-98, Hollywood Squares, 1998, other TV appearances include Starch Search (winner stand-up comedian competition 1984), The Cosby Show, Keep on Cruisin, The Redd Foxx Show, Cosby, 1998, 99, Moesha, 2000; occasional co-host Showtime at the Apollo; toured with The Pointer Sisters, Anita Baker, Luther Vandross, Smokey Robinson; appeared in films including That's Adequate, 1989, Necessary Roughness, 1991, Meteor Man, 1993, Coneheads, 1993, Houseguest, 1994, Jingle All The Way, 1996, (voice) Homeward Bound II: Lost in San Francisco, 1996, First Kid, 1996, Good Burger, 1997, Crazy as Hell, 2002, (voice) Hansel & Gretel, 2002, Treading Water, 2002, Cuttin Da Mustard, 2006, Leila, 2006, Stompin', 2007; TV movies: Ready to Run, 2000; author: Sinbad's Guide to Life. Active USAF, to 1983. Address: 12031 Ventura Blvd #3 Studio City CA 91604-2636 Office: Creative Artists Agency 2000 Avenue Of The Stars Los Angeles CA 90067-4700

SINCLAIR, ALASTAIR JAMES, geology educator; b. Hamilton, Ont., Can., Aug. 1, 1935; s. Burton Leslie and Grace (Isherwood) S.; m. Elizabeth Mary Sylvia Hill, June 13, 1964; children: Alison Trevena, Fiona Tamsin. BS, U. Toronto, Can., 1957, MS, 1958; PhD, U. B.C., Can., 1964. Asst. prof. U. Wash., Seattle, 1962-64, U. B.C., Vancouver, 1964-68, assoc. prof., 1968-74, prof., 1974-98, prof. emeritus, 1999—, head dept. geol. scis., 1985-90, dir. Geol. Engring., 1979-80, 81-82, 92-98. Pres. Sinclair Cons. Ltd., Vancouver, 1980—, Internat. Croesus Venture Corp. (now Zinco Mining Corp.), 2004—07; dir. Deal Capital, 2006—07, Eureka Resources, 2006—, Zinco Mining, 2007—, Waverly Biotech Inc., 2008—. Author: Applied Mineral Inventory Estimation, 2002, Applied Ore Microscopy and Minerolography, 2003, Quality Control of Assay Data, 2004, Empirical Methods of Resource/Reserve Estimation, 2006; contbr. articles to profl. jours. Recipient Spl. Tribute Information of Mineral Deposit Research Unit, U. BC, 2008, Selwyn G Blaylock medal, Canadian Inst. Mining Metallurgy & Petroleum, 2009, Frank Woodside Disting Svc. award, Assn. Mineral Exploration British Columbia, 2008; Killam Sr. fellow, 1990—91. Fellow Geol. Assn. Can. (treas. mineral deposits divsn. 1978-89, Disting. Svc. award 2001), Soc. Econ. Geologists; mem. Assn. Profl. Engrs. B.C., Assn. Exploration Geochemists (councillor 1992-96), Can. Inst. Mining, Metallurgy and Petroleum (life, disting. lectr. 1999-2000, Robert Elver award 1991), Geol. Soc. Brazil (hon. mem. sci.-tech. commn. geochemistry 1982), Brazilian Geochem. Soc. (hon.), Assn. Mineral Exploration BC (life Frank Woodside award 2008). Avocations: classical music, skiing, golf. Home: 2972 W 44th Ave Vancouver BC Canada V6N 3K4 Office: U BC Dept Earth and Ocean Scis Vancouver BC Canada V6T 1Z4 Home Phone: 604-261-8477; Office Phone: 604-822-3086. E-mail: asinclai@eos.ubc.ca, ajsincon@shaw.ca.

SINCLAIR, ALISTAIR, science educator, researcher; married. PhD, U. Edinburgh, 1988. Prof. computer sci. U. Calif., Berkeley, 1994—. Contbr. articles to rsch. jours. (Fulkerson prize, 2006, Goedel prize, 1996). Mem.: Assn. Computing Machinery. Office: Univ Calif Soda Hall Berkeley CA 94720-1776 Office Phone: 510-643-8144.

SINCLAIR, CAROLE, publishing executive, editor; b. Haddonfield, NJ, May 13, 1942; d. Earl Walter and Ruth (Sinclair) Dunham; 1 child, Wendy. Student, U. Florence, Italy, 1963; BA in Polit. Sci., Bucknell U, 1964. Advt. copywriter BBD&O Advertising, NYC, 1966-67; sales promotion mgr. Macmillan Pub. Co., NYC, 1967-71; mktg. mgr. Doubleday & Co., Inc., NYC, 1972-74, promotion dir., 1974-76, advt. mgr., sales and promotion, chmn. mktg. com., 1976-80; v.p. mktg., editorial dir. Davis Pubs., NYC, 1980-83; founder, pub., editorial dir., sr. v.p. Sylvia Porter's Personal Fin. Mag., NYC, 1983-90; pres. The Sylvia Porter Orgn., Inc., NYC, 1980—; founder, pres. Sinclair Media Inc., NYC, 1990—. Mktg. dir. Denver Pub. Inst., summers 1975-78; lectr. Columbia U. Bus. Sch. and Sch. of Journalism, 1976; host nationally syndicated TV show, Sylvia Porter's Money Tips, syndicated daily radio show, Sylvia Porter's Personal Fin. Report, audio cassette series on fin. topics. Author: Keys for Women Starting and Owning a Business, 1991, Keys to Women's Basic Professional Needs, 1991, When Women Retire, 1992; contbg. editor Pushcart Prize, 1977; contbr. The Business of Publishing, 1980. Renaissance Art Program fellow, Florence, Italy, 1963; White House intern, 1962. Mem. Women's Forum, Intercorp. Communications Group, Mag. Pubs.' Assn., Advt. Women in N.Y., Spence Sch. Parent's League. Clubs: Pubs. Lunch. Presbyterian. Avocation: boating.

SINCLAIR, DAISY, communications executive; b. Perth Amboy, NJ, Mar. 22, 1941; d. James Patrick and Margaret Mary (McAniff) Nieland; m. James Pratt Sinclair, May 25, 1978; children: Duncan, Gibbons. BA, Caldwell Coll., 1962. Jr. copywriter Young & Rubican, NYC, 1962-64; various positions in casting dept. Ogilvy & Mather, NYC, 1964-90, sr. v.p., dir. casting, 1990—. Mem.: Drama League N.Y. (3d v.p. 1982—), Am. Assn. Advt. (talent agt. com. 1972—), N.Y. Yacht Club, Union Club, Tuxedo Club, Chapaquoit Yacht Club, Edgartown Yacht Club, Knickerbocker Greys (pres.). Republican. Episcopalian. Avocations: opera, theater, sailing, skiing. Home: 4 E 95th St New York NY 10128-0705 Office: 636 11th Ave New York NY 10036

SINCLAIR, FRANCES TERESA, music educator, musician; d. Joe Neal Sinclair, Jr. and Ruth Spears Smith; m. John Jay Galland, July 31, 1999; 1 stepchild, Hill Autumn Galland. MusB with distinction, U. N.C., Chapel Hill, 1986; MusM, Fla. State U., Talahassee, 1989; DMA, U. N.C., Greensboro, 1997. Choral dir. Pinecrest HS, Southern Pines, NC, 1989—93; asst. prof. and asst. dir. choral activities Clemson U., SC, 1998—2000; instr. music applied and class piano Sandhill's CC, Pinehurst, NC, 2000—03; asst. prof., interim dir choral activities U. NC, Charlotte, 2003—04, dir. choral music, coord. vocal studies Asheville, 2005; asst. prof., dir. choral activities Coastal Carolina U., Conway, SC, 2005—. Guest condr.; clinician; adjudicator local to regional festivals, competitions and clinics. Contbr. articles to profl. jours. Mem. Moore County Choral Soc., Pinehurst, NC, 1989—91, Moore County Music Soc., 1989—93, So. Pines Bus. and Profl. Women, 2000—02; dir. music Cmty. Presbyn. Ch., Pinehurst, 1991—; mem. bd. dir. Moore County chpt. N.C. Symphony, So. Pines, 1989—93. Recipient Outstanding Young Musician of Yr., Moore County Music Soc., 1991; finalist Tchr. of Yr., Pinecrest H.S., 1991, Prof. of Yr., Coastal Carolina U., 2006. Mem.: Am. Choral Dir. Assn. (exec. bd. N.C. and S.C. chpt. 1998—), Coll. Music Soc., Music Educators Nat. Conf. (sec. jr. high exec. bd. 1991—93). Home: 5 Wampanoag Ln Pinehurst NC 28374 Office: Coastal Carolina U Conway SC 29528

SINCLAIR, JACK L., retail executive; BA in Econs. and Mktg., U. Strathclyde. Trainee Shoppers' Paradise, England, 1982; with Tesco Stores Ltd.; bd. dirs. Safeway PLC; European devel. dir. SB Capital; with McCurrach; exec. v.p. grocery divsn. Walmart US Wal-Mart Stores, Inc., 2008—. Office: Wal-Mart Stores, Inc 702 SW 8th St Bentonville AR 72716-8611*

SINCLAIR, JAMES BURTON, retired plant pathology educator, consultant; b. Chgo., Dec. 21, 1927; s. James Lawrence Sinclair and Helen Marie (Thompson) Owens. BSc, Lawrence U., 1951; PhD, U. Wis., 1955. Grad. rsch. asst. U. Wis., Madison, 1951-55, grad. rsch. assoc., 1955-56; from asst. prof. to assoc. prof. La. State U., Baton Rouge, 1956-65, prof., 1965-68, adminstrv. asst. to chancellor, 1966-68; prof. U. Ill., Urbana, 1968-96, dir. nat. soybean rsch. lab., 1992-96; ret. Co-author: Basic Plant Pathology Methods, 1985, 1995, Principles of Seed Pathology, 1987, 1997, Anatomy and Physiology of Diseased Plants, 1991; contbr. articles to profl. jours. Pres. bd. dirs. W.R. and C.V. Spurlock Mus., Urbana, 1998-00; sec., editor Greater Cmty. AIDS Project, 1996-00; sec. Econ. Devel. Commn., Savoy, 2004-; fin. planning com. Carle Hospice, 2001-02; mem. (docent), dir bd. Spurloch Mus. World Culture, 1998-, mem. pub. com., 2005—; mem., chmn. catalogue collection com. Choir Krannert Art Mus. and Kincaid Pavilion, 1998-2009, docent; active Village Savoy Econ. Devel. Com., 2004-. Sgt. US Army, 1946-47. Recipient Soybean Rsch. Recognition award, Am. Soybean Assn., 1983, Prodn. Rsch. award, 1989, Paul A. Funk award, 1984, Sr. Faculty award for Excellence Rsch., Coll. Agrl. Consumer and Environ. Svc., 1988, Disting. Svc. award, USDA, 1988, Devel. Diagnostic Guide for Soybean Disease award, Am. Soybean Assn., 1899, Disting. Svc. award, Phytopathol. Soc. (north ctrl. divsn.), 1991, Rsch. award, Land of Lincoln Soybean Assn., 1992, Lucia R. Briggs Disting. Achievement award, Lawrence U., 2001. Fellow Am. Phytopathol. Soc., Nat. Acad. Scis. (India); mem. Ill. Crop Improvement Assn. (hon.), Am. Soc. Agronomy (hon.), Rotary (chmn. internat. com. Savoy chpt. 1990-91, v.p. 1991-93, pres. 1993-94, chmn. club svc. conf. 2003-04). Home: 408 Arbours Dr Savoy IL 61874-9752 Personal E-mail: jsinclai@uiuc.edu.

SINCLAIR, MICHAEL DAVID, mathematics and science educator; b. Leon, Iowa, Apr. 30, 1955; s. Melvin and Teresa Sinclair; m. Karen Lynn Doucette, Aug. 22, 1981; children: Kimberly, Christopher. BS in Psychology, Mont. State U., Bozeman, 1977, BS in Edn., 1983; MA in Math., Ohio State U., Columbus, 1987. Mich. profl. cert. Mich. Dept. Edn., 1992, cert. in AYAI sci. Nat. Bd., 2007. Math. and sci. tchr. Mountain View H.S., Wyo., 1983—86, Mattawan H.S., Mich., 1987—88, Kalamazoo Area Math and Sci. Ctr., 1988—. Kalamazoo Area Math. and Sci. Ctr. rep. Heyl Scholarship Com., Kalamazoo, 1996—. Author: (novels) The Hammer of God, 2004. Capt. US Army, 1977—81. Decorated Army Commendation medal US Army; recipient Significant Educator award, Kalamazoo County Excellence in Edn., 1990—2006, Tandy Tech. award, Tandy/Radio Shack Corp., 1997, Edn. award, Nat. Bd. Ctr, 2007, EDn. Excellence award, 1990—2008; Grad. fellow, Ohio State U., 1986. Mem.: Am. Assn. Physics Tchrs., Mich. Sci. Tchrs. Assn. (Mich. H.S. Sci. Tchr. of Yr. 2006), Ohio State U. Alumni Assn. (life Outstanding Alumni award West Mich. chpt. 2006), Nat. Speleological Soc., Kalamazoo Astron. Soc. (pres. 1996—2001, Hans Baldauf Meml. award Gt. Lakes chpt. 1996). Avocations: reading, writing, exercise. Home: 3704 Alamo Ave Kalamazoo MI 49006 Office: Kalamazoo Mathematics & Science Center 600 W Vine Suite 400 Kalamazoo MI 49008 Office Phone: 269-337-0023. Office Fax: 269-337-0049. Business E-Mail: msinclair@kamsc.k12.mi.us.

SINCLAIR, PATRICIA WHITE, language educator; b. Selma, Ala., Feb. 26, 1963; d. Lorenzo Vaughn and Elizabeth Morrison Sinclair. BA, U. of N. Tex., Denton, 1991. Lic. tchr. English, ESL(PreK-12), Gifted, and Earth/Space Science Va., 2006, cert. tchr. secondary edn., ESL and gifted edn. Tex., 2005. Tchr. English 9-12, TAAS remediation, creative and practical writing and reading Lewisville Ind. Sch. Dist., Colony HS, 1995—99; tchr. English, SAT prep., TAKS remediation and creative writing Lewisville Ind. Sch. Dist., Hebron HS, Carrollton, Tex., 1999—2006; tchr., dept. chair ESL Park View HS, Sterling, Va., 2006—. Co-author, collaborator on English curriculum, grades 9-12 and creative writing Lewisville Ind. Sch. Dist., 1997—2003, presenter, English/lang. arts tchr. inservices on state testing strategies, incorportating media to meet the teks, & questioning strategies, 1997—2003; acad. decathlon coach Hebron HS, 2001—05. Author: (short story) Death by Natural Causes (Second Pl., Fiction, U. of North Tex. Green Fuse Lit. Competition, 1988), Drink Entire Against the World (Publ. in The Green Fuse, 1987), Briar Patch (Publ. in The Elk River Rev., 1991), (poem) Heroes for Breakfast (Publ. in The Elk River Rev., 1991). Mem.: ASCD, Nat. Coun. Tchrs. English (state leader Tex. program to recognize excellence in student lit. mags), Va. Tchrs. ESOL, Delta Kappa Gamma, Va. Edn. Assn. Democrat-Npl. Humanistic-Methodist. Avocations: writing, photography, horseback riding, reading, films. Business E-Mail: patricia.sinclair@loudoun.k12.va.us.

SINCLAIR, ROBERT EWALD, retired physician; b. Columbus, Jan. 19, 1924; s. George Albert and Bertha Florence (Ewald) S.; m. Mary Almira Underwood, Mar. 31, 1945; children: Marcia Ann, Bonnie Sue. BA, Ohio State U., Columbus, 1948, MD, 1952. Lic. physician, Ohio, Colo., Ala., Kans. Intern Mt. Carmel Hosp., Columbus, 1952—53; resident neurology and psychiatry Columbus State Hosp., 1964—66, chief psychiat. resident adolescent unit, 1965—66; pvt. practice medicine Columbus, 1953—57, Granville, Ohio, 1957—64; dir. student health svc., prof. health edn., team physician Denison U., 1957—64; dir. student health svc., team physician U. Cin., 1966—70; dir. Lafene Student Health Ctr. and U. Hosp.; team physician Kans. State U., Manhattan, 1970—80; dir. Russell Student Health Ctr. and Hosp.; prof. medicine U. Ala., University, 1980—88, ret., 1988. Physician Westinghouse Electric Corp., Columbus, 1953-57; asst. zone chief Civilian Def., Columbus, 1954-57; mem. Licking County Bd. Health, Ohio, 1958-59. Bd. dirs. social health com. Cin. and Hamilton County, Ohio, 1967-70, drug abuse and edn. com., 1968-70. With USNR, 1943-46. Named Hall of Fame, West High Alumni Assn., Columbus, Ohio, 2004. Mem. AMA, Ohio Med. Soc., Kans. Med. Soc., Ala. Med. Soc., Columbus Acad. Medicine, Licking County Med. Soc., Riley County Med. Soc. (Kans.), Tuscaloosa County Med. Soc., Nat. Athletic Trainers Assn., Ohio Coll. Health Assn. (editor Newsletter 1968-70, pres. 1970-71), Central Coll. Health Assn. (pres. 1972-73), So. Coll. Health Assn. (pres. 1986), St. Andrews Soc., So. Medicine Assn., Delta Tau Delta (faculty advisor), Nu Sigma Nu, Nu Sigma Nu Ohio State Alumni Assn. (pres. 1953-54), Kiwanis, Rotary. Home: 1 Rollingwood Tuscaloosa AL 35406-2261 Personal E-mail: unsink2@comcast.net.

SINCLAIR, ROLF MALCOLM, retired physicist; b. NYC, Aug. 15, 1929; s. Nathan and Elizabeth S.; m. Margaret Lee Andrews, June 13, 1959 (div. 1978); children: Elizabeth Ann, Andrew Caisley; m. Allyn J. Miner, July 29, 1991 (div. 1998); m. Sarah Richards, Mar. 18, 2004. BS, Calif. Inst. Tech., 1949; MA (Reade scholar), Rice U., 1951, PhD (Inst. fellow), 1954. Physicist Westinghouse Rsch. Labs., 1953—56; vis. scientist U. Hamburg, Germany, 1956—57, U. Paris, 1957—58, U.K. Atomic Energy Authority, Culham Lab., England, 1965—66; rsch. physicist Princeton U., 1958—69; program dir. NSF, Washington, 1969—98; ret., 1998. Mem. Solstice Project, 1978-91; NSF rep. U.S. Solar Eclipse Expdn. to Can., 1979, to India, 1980, Amundsen-Scott South Pole Sta., 1995, 96; Disting. vis. prof. N.Mex. State U., 1985; vis. prof. No. Ariz. U., 1986; vis. scientist Los Alamos Nat. Lab., 1988-89, guest scientist, 1989—; cons. to industry, 1960-69, 98—; sr. advisor Centro de Estudios Cientificos, Valdivia, Chile, 1999—. Fellow Am. Phys. Soc. (panel pub. affairs 1976-77, nominating com. 1988-90), AAAS (sec. physics sect. 1972-2000, 2007-, chair 2005-2006, ret. chair 2006-2007, sec 2007-, coun. 1972-73, nominating com. 1982-83); mem. Soc. Am. Archaeology, Sigma Xi. Achievements include research and publs. on physics, archaeoastronomy, tech. and instrumentation. Home: 7508 Tarrytown Rd Chevy Chase MD 20815-6027 E-mail: rolf@santafe.edu.

SINCLAIR, VIRGIL LEE, JR., judge, writer; b. Canton, Ohio, Nov. 10, 1951; s. Virgil Lee and Thelma Irene S.; children: Kelly, Shannon; m. Janet Brahler Sinclair. BA, Kent State U., 1973; JD, U. Akron, 1976; postgrad., Case Western Res. U., 1939. Adminstr. Stark County Prosecutor's Office, Canton, 1974-76; mem. faculty Walsh Coll., Canton, 1976-78; asst. pros. atty. Stark County, Canton, 1976-77; ptnr. Amerman Burt Jones Co. LPA, Canton, 1976-91, Buckingham, Doolittle and Burroughs Co., L.P.A., Canton, 1991-95; judge Stark County Common Pleas Ct., 1995—, adminstrv. judge, 1996, presiding judge, 1999; faculty Nat. Judicial Coll., U. Nevada, Reno, 1998—. Mem. faculty Ohio Jud. Coll., 1991—, lead faculty, 1998—; mem. legal adviser Mayor's Office, City of North Canton, Ohio, 1978-79; referee Stark County Family Ct., Canton, 1981, Canton Mcpl. Ct., 1991—; spl. referee Canton Mcpl. Ct., 1985-86. Author: Law Enforcement Officers' Guide to Juvenile Law, 1975, Lawy Manual of Juvenile Law, 1976, Handling Capital Punishment Cases, 1998, Ohio Jury Institutions, Capital Punishment Approved, Jury Instructions, 2000; editor: U. Akron Law Rev.; contbr. to Ohio Family Law, 1983, also articles to profl. jours. Mem. North Canton Planning Comm., 1979-82; bd. mgrs. North Canton YMCA, 1976—, Camp Tippecanoe, Ohio, 1981—; spl. sep. Stark County Sheriff Dept., 1983-1995; trustee Palace Theatre Assn., Canton, 1983—. Recipient Disting. Service award U.S. Jaycees, 1984; named to Hall of Distinction, Plain Local Schs., 1999, Jud. Hall of Fame, U. Akron Sch. Law, 2000. Mem. ABA, Ohio Bar Assn., Stark County Bar Assn. (lects. 1984), Ohio Trial Lawyers Assn., Assn. Trial Lawyers Am., Nat. Dist. Attys. Assn.,

Akron Law Sch. Alumni Assn. (trustee), Jaycees, Elks, Eagles, Masons, Delta Theta Phi (bailiff 1976, nat. key winner 1975-76). Republican. Methodist. Office Phone: 330-451-7789.

SINCOFF, MICHAEL Z., human resources and marketing executive, educator; b. Washington, June 28, 1943; s. Murray P. and Anna F. (Jaffe) S. m. Kathleen M. Dunham, Oct. 9, 1983. BA, U. Md., 1964, MA, 1966; PhD, Purdue U., 1969. Instr. U. Tenn., Knoxville, 1968; asst. prof. Ohio U., Athens, 1969-74, dir. Ctr. for Comm. Studies, 1969-76, assoc. prof., 1974-76; vis. prof. U. Minn., St. Paul, 1974; dir. personnel devel. Celanese Corp., NYC, 1976-79; dir. employee comm. The Mead Corp., Dayton, Ohio, 1979-81, dir. edn. and tng., 1981-83; assoc. dean Sch. of Bus. Adminstrn., Georgetown U., Washington, 1983-84; v.p. human resources ADVO-Sys., Hartford, Conn., 1984—87; v.p. human resources, corp. officer DIMAC Direct Inc., St. Louis, 1987-88; sr. v.p. human resources and adminstrn., sr. corp. officer DIMAC Mktg. Corp. (parent of DIMAC Direct Inc.), St. Louis, 1988-97, also sec., asst. treas., exec. com., 1988-97; sr. v.p. human resources, exec. corp. officer Brooks Fiber Properties, Inc., St. Louis, 1997-98; pres., CEO Michaelson Group Ptnrs., Dayton, Ohio, 1969—. Vis. prof. Wright State U., Dayton, Ohio, 1999-2001, assoc. prof., 2001-07, prof., 2007-;chair WSU Athletics Coun., 2006-09, mem. WSU Faculty Senate, 2007-09, assoc. grad. faculty mem. Ctrl. Mich. U., Mt. Pleasant, 1999—, 2007-09. Author, editor human resources sect. Am. Mgmt. Assn. Mgmt. Handbook, 3d edit.; author approximately 60 books and articles; mem. edtl. adv. bd. Jour. Applied Comm. Rsch., 1991-97; sr. adv. dir., sr. editor Franklin Pub. Co., 2007-. Life mem. Internat. Comm. Assn. (bus. mgr.-exec. sec. 1969-73, fin. com. 1982-85); mem. Am. Mgmt. Assn. (human resources coun. 1990-2000), Printing Industries of Am. (employer resources group 1989-97).

SINDING, STEVEN WILLIAM, political scientist; b. Orange, NJ, June 29, 1943; s. Steven Walter and Brigitte (Osterman) S.; m. Monica Katherine Knorr, June 19, 1965; children: Katherine Anne, Jennifer Sarah. AB, Oberlin Coll., 1965; PhD, U. N.C., 1970. From population officer to dir. mission to Kenya U.S. Agy. for Internat. Devel., Washington, 1971-90; sr. population advisor The World Bank, Washington, 1990-91; dir. population scis. Rockefeller Found., NYC, 1991-99; prof. pub. health and internat. affairs Columbia U., 1999—. Advisor The Packard Found., Los Altos, Calif., 1996-99; bd. dirs. Pathfinder Internat., Watertown, Mass., 1990—, Population Resource Ctr., Princeton, N.J., 1990—; U.S. Com. for UNFPA. Del. U.S. Delegation to Internat. Conf. Population & Devel., Cairo, 1993-94. Mem. Coun. Fgn. Rels., Population Assn. Am., Yale Club. Avocations: skiing, hiking, amateur theater. Office: Ctr for Population and Family Health 60 Haven Ave New York NY 10032-2604

SINDLER, BRIAN PAUL, artist; b. Chgo., Jan. 19, 1957; s. Leonard and Beverly Sindler; m. Giulia Parazzoli, Oct. 27, 1990; children: Adam Michael, Elenna Maria. BA, Columbia Coll., Mo., 1979. Prin. works include painter (Utrecht award excellence, 2007).

SINDT, CHRISTINE W., medical educator; d. Frances Wiles; m. Steven J. Sindt, June 24, 1994; children: Benjamin, Matthew. OD, Ohio State U., Columbus, 1994. Dir. contact lens clinic U. Iowa, Iowa City, 1995—, assoc. prof. clin. ophthalmology, 2006—. Fellow: Am. Acad. Optometry; mem.: Am. Optometric Assn. (coun. mem. 2004—08, vice chair 2007—, Kame award 2005). Office: Univ Iowa 200 Hawkins Dr Iowa City IA 52242

SINEATH, TIMOTHY WAYNE, librarian, educator, dean; b. Jacksonville, Fla., May 21, 1940; s. Holcombe Asbury and Christine Marcel (Cook) S.; m. Patricia Ann Greenwood, June 8, 1962; children: Philip Greenwood, Paul Byron. BA, Fla. State U., 1962, MS, 1963; PhD (Higher Edn. Act fellow), U. Ill., 1970. Reference librarian U. Ga., 1963-64, catalog librarian, 1964-66; acad. coordinator continuing edn. in library sci. U. Ill., 1966-68; asst. prof. library sci. Simmons Coll., 1970-74, coordinator doctoral program, 1974-77; prof., dean Coll. Libr. Sci. and Info. Sci. U. Ky., Lexington, 1977-87, prof., 1987-97, dir. sch. Libr. and Info. Sci., 1997—2008. Cons. to libraries, schs., chs., industry; mem. Lexington (Ky.) Public Library Bd., 1978— Author profl. reports; contbr. articles on library and info. sci., gen. info. mgmt., organizational and small group behavior to profl. jours. Mem. ALA, Am. Soc. Info. Sci. and Tech., Assn. for Libr. and Info. Sci. Edn. (pres. 1993). Episcopalian. Office: U Ky M King Bldg Lexington KY 40506-0039 Office Phone: 859-257-8100. E-mail: tsineath@uky.edu.

SINEGAL, JAMES D. (JIM SINEGAL), wholesale distribution executive; b. Pitts., Jan. 1, 1936; m. Janet Sinegal, 1961; 3 children. BA, San Diego State U., 1959. With Fed-Mart Corp., 1954-77, exec. v.p.; v.p. Builders Emporium, 1977-78; exec. v.p. Price Co., 1978-79; with Sinegal/Chamberlin & Assocs., 1979-83; pres., COO Costco Wholesale Corp., Issaguah, Wash., 1983—93, pres., CEO, 1993—. Bd. dirs. Costco Wholesale Corp., 1983—. Named one of The 100 Most Influential People in the World, TIME mag., 2006. Address: Costco Wholesale PO Box 34331 999 Lake Dr Ste 200 Issaquah WA 98027-8982*

SINEL, NORMAN MARK, lawyer; b. New Haven, Dec. 8, 1941; s. Nathan and Mona S.; m. Ellen Winnick, June 16, 1963; children: Joshua, Natasha. BA, Yale U., 1963; LL.B., Stanford U., 1966. Bar: Calif. 1967, D.C. 1968. Law clk. to Judge Weigel, Dist. Ct. No. Dist., Calif., 1966-67; assoc. firm Wilmer, Cutler & Pickering, Washington, 1967-71; gen. counsel Public Broadcasting Service, Washington, 1971-73, v.p., gen. counsel, 1973-76, sr. v.p. for corp. mgmt., gen. counsel, 1976-79; ptnr., Telecom. Practice Group Arnold & Porter, Washington, 1979—. Mem. Calif. Bar Assn., D.C. Bar Assn. Office: Arnold & Porter 555 12th St NW Washington DC 20004-1206 Office Phone: 202-942-5222. Office Fax: 202-942-5999. Business E-Mail: norman.sinel@aporter.com.

SINES, RANDY D., retail executive; b. Spokane, Jan. 16, 1948; s. Myron Jones and Paula Inez (Walls) S.; m. Irene Cheng, Mar. 18, 1981. Student, Wash. State U., 1966—67, U. Wash., 1968—69. Lic. water well contractor, Wash., Mont. With Boeing Co., 1967, Winchell's Donut House, Inc., Seattle, 1968—71; owner, mgr. bakeries Wash. and Mont., 1972—78; owner, mgr. Sonsine Inc., Great Falls, Mont., 1976—79; pres. Gardian Port Corp., Oxnard, Calif., 1980—82; pres., chmn. SNS Motor Imports, Inc., Oxnard, 1982—86; chmn. Karakal Corp. of Ams., Ventura, Calif., 1986—89; CEO, chmn. Steel Stix, U.S.A., 1990—; chmn. MITT U.S.A.-Corp., 1991—; mng. ptnr. Sharps Internat., 1999—. CEO Casinovations Inc., 1995-96; founder, CEO Inven Corp., Spokane, 1996-97; chmn. Digideal Corp., Las Vegas, 1998-2005; chmn. eCardless Bancorp., Spokane, 2000-; CEO CodeCard, Inc., Spokane, 2000-09. Holder more than 75 utility patents. Recipient alumni grant Wash. State U., 1967. Home: 4056 S Madelia St Spokane WA 99203-4227

SINFELT, JOHN HENRY, chemist; b. Munson, Pa., Feb. 18, 1931; s. Henry Gustave and June Lillian (McDonald) Sinfelt; m. Muriel Jean Vadersen, July 14, 1956; 1 child, Klaus Herbert. BS, Pa. State U., 1951; PhD, U. Ill., 1954, DSc (hon.), 1981. Research engr. Exxon Research Engrng. Co., Linden, NJ, 1954—57, sr. research engr., 1957—62, research assoc., 1962—68, sr. research assoc., 1968—72, sci. advisor, 1972—79, sr. sci. advisor, 1979—96, sr. sci. advisor emeritus, 1996—. Vis. prof. chem. engring. U. Minn., 1969; Lacey lectr. Calif. Inst. Tech., 1973; Reilly lectr. U. Notre Dame, 1974; Frontiers in Chemistry lectr. Case Western Res. U., Cleve., 1978; Matthew Van Winkle lectr. U. Tex., 1979, disting. vis. lectr. in chemistry, 81; Francois Gault lectr. catalysis Coun. Europe Rsch. Group Catalysis, 1980; Mobay lectr. in chemistry U. Pitts., 1980; Robert Welch Found. lectr. Confs. on Chem. Rsch., 1981; Camille and Henry Dreyfus lectr. UCLA, 1982; Edward Clark Lee Meml. lectr. U. Chgo., 1983; Dow disting. lectr. in chemistry Mich. State U., 1984; Arthur D. Little lectr. Northeastern U., 1985; Vollmer W. Fries lectr. Rensselaer Poly. Inst., 1986; disting. lectr. Ctr. Chem. Physics U. Fla., 1988; David M. Mason lectr. Stanford U., 1995, cons. prof. dept. chem. engring., 1996—. Contbr. articles to profl. jours. Recipient Dickson prize, Carnegie-Mellon U., 1977, Internat. prize for new materials, Am. Phys. Soc., 1978, Nat. medal of sci., 1979, Perkin medal in chemistry, Soc. Chem. Industry, 1984, Disting. Alumnus award, Pa. State U., 1985; named to N.J. Inventors Hall of Fame, 1991. Fellow: AIChE (Alpha Chi Sigma award 1971, Profl. Progress award 1975), Am. Inst. Chemists (Chem. Pioneer award 1981, Gold medal 1984), Am. Acad. Arts and Scis.; mem.: NAE, NAS (award for indsl. application of sci. 1996), Am. Philos. Soc., Catalysis Soc. (Emmett award 1973), Am. Chem. Soc. (Carothers lectr. Del. sect. 1982, Petroleum Chemistry award 1976, Murphree award 1986). Methodist. Achievements include development of bimetallic clusters as catalysts; invention of polymetallic cluster catalysts used commercially in petroleum reforming. Home: PO Box 364 Oldwick NJ 08858

SING, ROBERT FONG, physician; b. Camden, NJ, May 29, 1953; s. William Fong and Elizabeth (Maxwell) S.; m. Lauren McNamee, May 11, 1991. BS in Biology, Ursinus Coll., 1975; DO, Coll. Osteo. Medicine and Surgery, 1978. Intern Met. Hosp., Phila., 1978-79, resident in family practice, 1979-80; dir. emergency dept. Springfield (Pa.) Hosp., 1984—2000; dir. sports medicine Sports Sci. Ctr., 1987—; med. dir. Emergency Ambulance Svcs., Inc., 1994-95, Universal Ambulance Svcs., 2005—; owner J. Enright Jewelers, Inc., Swarthmore, Pa., 1995-97; owner, pres. Springfield Sports Emergency Med. Corp., 1999—. Owner, pres. Finish Line Sports, Inc., Phila., 1988-94; sch. and team physician Springfield Sch. Dist., 1989—, Rose Tree-Media (Pa.) Sch. Dist., 1987—; chief med. officer Kent Profl. Bicycling Tour of China, 1995, U.S. Olympic Cycling Trials, 1996. Author: Dynamics of the Javelin Throw, 1984. Med. dir. Springfield Ambulance Corp., 1988—, med. dir. Springfield Fire Co., 2006-. Named to Ursinus Coll. Athletic Hall of Fame, 1985. Fellow Am. Coll. Sports Medicine, Am. Osteo. Acad. Sports Medicine; mem. Am. Coll. Osteo. Emergency Physicians, Am. Coll. Emergency Physicians., NFL Players Assn. (physician, 1995-), Internat Javelin Competition (Finland) (chief med. officer, 2008) Avocations: track and field, classical music, bicycling. Home: 1274 Gradyville Rd Glen Mills PA 19342-9614 Office: Sports Sci Ctr 166 Saxer Ave Springfield PA 19064-2335 Office Phone: 610-328-7262. Personal E-mail: sing3035@aol.com.

SING, WILLIAM BENDER, lawyer; b. Houston, Oct. 16, 1947; s. William Bender, Sr. and Alice Irene Sing; m. Doris Anne Sing, Sept. 1, 1967; children: Erin Elaine, Emily Elizabeth. BS cum laude, U. Houston, 1968, JD magna cum laude, 1971; MLA, U. St. Thomas, 1995. Bar: Tex. 1971. Assoc. Fulbright & Jaworski, LLP, Houston, 1973-80, ptnr., 1980—. Past pres., bd. dirs. St. Andrew's Presbyn. Sch., Houston; past pres. Houston CC Place civic Assn.; elder, trustee St. Andrew's Presbyn. Ch., Houston. 1st lt. US Army, 1971—77. Mem.: ABA, Houston Bar Assn., Tex. Bar Assn., U. Houston Alumni Orgn. (life), Order of Barons Law Honor Soc., Omicron Delta Epsilon, Phi Kappa Phi, Phi Delta Phi (life). Avocations: history, literature. Office: Fulbright and Jaworski LLP 1301 Mckinney St Houston TX 77010-3095 Office Phone: 713-651-3709.

SINGER, ALAN DANIEL, artist; b. NYC, June 19, 1950; s. Arthur B. and Edith (Goulfine) S.; m. Anna K. Sears, Sept. 1, 1979; 1 child, Nathaniel. BFA, Cooper Union, 1972; MFA, Cornell U., 1975; student, Yale U., 1971; postgrad., Pratt Inst., 1976-77. Artist, painter, freelance writer, educator, designer, illustrator and curator, 1974—; prof. dept. fine art Rochester Inst. Tech., 1987—; adult edn. instr. N.Y. Bot. Garden, 1985-88; instr. Asa Wright Nature Ctr., Trinidad, W.I., 1978-80. Designer program Franklin Mint Graphics for TDK/Impressions Illustration and Design Exhibits, Bklyn. Bot. Garden, 1987, designs and mechanicals for L.I. U. Brochures/N.C. Zool. Assn., 1986, others; designer, illustrator stamps U.S. Postal Svc., 1980-81; illustrator for Levaquin (Johnson & Johnson), 2006; vis. lectr. and artist Syracuse U., 2006. One-man shows include arts & cultural coun., Rochester, NY, 2008, Redhouse Gallery Syracuse, NY, 2007, Hobart William and Smith Coll., Geneva, NY, 2001, The Mill Art Ctr., Honeoye Falls, NY, 2001, Century Club, Rochester, 1999, Upstairs Gallery: Gallery Arabesque, Ithaca, NY, 1998, Germanow-Coffey Gallery, 1997, Angel Fire Gallery, Rochester, 1993, 55 Mercer St. Gallery, NYC, 1985, 92, Haenah-Kent Gallery, NYC, 1991, Bali Miller Gallery, NYC, 1988, Smithsonian Mus. of Natural History, Washington, 1987, Dyer Art Gallery, R.I.T., Rochester, 2004, Art and Cultural Coun., 2005, Red House Gallery, Syracuse, 2007, others; group shows include Everson Mus., Syracuse, NY, 1999, 06, Norman Rockwell Mus., Stockbridge, Mass., 2000, Sonnenberg Gardens, Canandaigua, NY, 2000, Kew Gardens, Eng., 1997, Buffalo Mus. Sci., 1997, Monroe C.C., 1997, Meml. Art Gallery, Rochester, 1991, 93, Angel Fire Gallery, 1992, Rochester Inst. Tech., 1988, Nat. Acad. Design, NYC, 1986, Cmty. Gallery, Bklyn. Mus., 1985, Coffey Germanow Gallery, 1995, Mill Art Ctr., Honeyoye Falls, NY, 2003, Nat. Postal Svc. Mus., 2003, Bausch & Lomb Hdqrs., Rochester, Mercer Gallery Monroe CC, Rochester, Art & Cultural Council, Rochester, 2008, Botnicals- Hunt Libr. Bot. Documentation, Pitts., 2009-; others; author: Wildlife Art, 1999, Botanica 2000, 2000—, Traveling the Erie Canal by Watercolor, 2001, Alan Singer, Selections 2007; author essays in mus. catalogs, newspapers and jours. Recipient cert. Merit Soc. Illustrators, 1985, Best of Yr. award Postal Commemorative Soc., 1983, Purchase award Nassau C.C., 1976, Pres.'s award Nat. Arts Club, N.Y.C., 1975; Rochester Inst. Tech. grantee, 1991, Faculty Devel. grantee, 1997. Mem. Rochester Print Club (pres.). Avocations: gardening, guitar, hiking. Office: Rochester Inst Tech One Lomb Memorial Dr Rochester NY 14623 E-mail: alan@singerarts.com.

SINGER, ALFRED, immunologist, researcher; MD, Columbia U. Clin. training Columbia-Presbyn. Med. Ctr.; fellow in immunology Rockefeller U.; now chief Exptl. Immunology Br. Ctr. Cancer Rsch., Nat. Cancer Inst., NIH, Bethesda, Md., also head Lymphatic Devel. Sect. Office: Exptl Immunology Br Ct Cancer Rsch 10 Center Dr Bldg 10 Rm 4B36 Bethesda MD 20892 Office Phone: 301-496-5461. Office Fax: 301-496-0887. E-mail: singera@nih.gov.*

SINGER, ALLEN MORRIS, lawyer; b. Mpls., Dec. 30, 1923; s. William and Ida (Simenstein) S. JD, U. Chgo., 1948; LLM, Harvard U., Cambridge, Mass., 1958. Bar: Ill. 1948, Calif. 1949. Pvt. practice, 1950-55, 59—; v.p., sec., gen. counsel ABM Industries, San Francisco, 1969-85. Assoc. prof. law U. Oreg., 1955-59; lectr. law Stanford (Calif.) U., 1960-62; of counsel Cooper, White & Cooper, San Francisco, 1970-97. Contbr. articles to profl. jours. Mem. U. Chgo. Nat. Alumni Cabinet, 1978-80. 2nd lt., USAAF, 1943-45. Mem. ABA, San Francisco Bar Assn., Calif. Bar Assn. Office: 1070 Green St Ste 703 San Francisco CA 94133-5414 Home Phone: 415-447-5495; Office Phone: 415-673-9149.

SINGER, BEVERLY R., social sciences educator, film producer; d. James and Bertha M. Singer. PhD, U. N.Mex, Albuquerque, 1987. Program coord. Am. Mus. Natural History, NYC, 1998—2000; assoc. prof. anthropology and native Am. studies U. N.Mex, Albuquerque, 2000—. Rsch. officer Columbia U., NYC, 1990—96. Prodr.: (video documentary) The Answer Lies Within: Institute of American Indian Arts in Southern Africa; assoc. prodr. (museum film exhibition) Who We Are: Smithsonian National Museum of the American Indian film about America Indigenous Peoples; dir.: (video) A Video Book (Dreamspeakers Film and Video Festival, Alta., Can., 1995); video, Rainwater Harvesting: A Garden Project; author: (book) Wiping the War Paint Off the Lens: Native American Film and Video, Rising Voices: Writings by Young Native Americans. Exec. mem. Ind. TV Svc., San Francisco, 2002—09. Recipient Lincoln Ethics Scholar, Ariz. State U., Coll. Architecture and Environ. Design, 2004. Avocations: meditation, travel, cooking, gardening, exercise. Home: P O Box 444 Espanola NM 87532 Office: Univ New Mex Deppt Anthropology MSCO1-1040 Albuquerque NM 87131 Office Phone: 505-277-3027. Home Fax: 505-747-0056. Business E-Mail: mesa@unm.edu.

SINGER, CECILE DORIS, bank executive, former state legislator; BA, Queens Coll.; DHL (hon.), Pace U., 1997. Past rep. Spl. Svcs. for Children, NYC; past exec. dir. N.Y. State Assembly Social Svcs. and Judiciary Coms., Joint Legis. Com. on Corps., Authorities and Commns.; past pub. rep. Yonkers (N.Y.) Emergency Control Bd.; past coord. Westchester County Assembly Dels.; past chief of staff for dep. minority leader; mem. N.Y. State Assembly, Albany, 1988—94, leadership sec. Rep. Conf., mem. assembly children & families com., mem. various other coms.; prin. Cecile D. Singer Cons. Past rep. Temp. Commn. to Revise Social Svcs. Law; mem. Presdl. Commn. on Privacy Conf., NY State Senate Transp. Conf.; task force on substance abuse Am. Legis. Exch. Coun., task force on econ. devel., crime victims' rights, hosp. crisis, women's issues, com. on mass transit; sec. Rep. Conf. Nat. Adv. Panel Child Care Action Campaign; chmn. Westchester County Commn. on Pub. Financing of Campaigns; chmn. Lower Hudson Valley Adv. Com. NY State Divsn. for Women.; past dir. commn. on poverty and pregnancy, dir. Yonkers IDA, NY; treas. Riverside Corp.; chair, NY State Hudson Valley Coun.; pres. Women's Enterprise Devel. Ctr.; mem. Westchester County Women's advisory bd.; bd. dirs. Hudson Valley Holding Corp., Hudson Valley Bank, NY; exec. com. and HOAN com. Audit Compensation and Benefits Hung; prin. Cecile D. Singer Cons. Chair adv. com. Westchester C.C. Found., chair audit com., Westchester 2000 Rsch., Womens Adv. Bd. Westchester County; task force on certiorari Westchester County Sch. Bds. Assn.; sch. and cmty. chmn. Yonkers PTA; bd. dirs. Yonkers chpt. United Jewish Appeal; v.p. Westchester Sr. Housing; chair Women's Networking, Women in Bus. and the Professions award, 2005; v.p. Westchester Srs. Housing; trustee, treas. St. John Hosp. Recipient Jenkins Meml. award, Nat. PTA award, 1990, Bus. and Profl. award Yonkers C. of C., 1996, Yonkers Fedn. Tchrs. Friend Edn. award, 2000, Lillian Vernon award West Chester Assn., 2005, Women Bus. Owners, 2002, Star award Mental Health Assoc., 2008, Yonkers Woman Valor award, 2007, Trustee award St. Johns Hosp., 2006, Disting. Svc. award, Women's Enterprise Devel. Corp., 2009, Svc. award, WSCS, 2009; inducted into Women's Hall of Fame, 1999, Sr. Citizens Hall of Fame, 1996, Westchester County Cert. Svc., 2008, WACS Cert. of Svc. 2009. Mem. Rotary. Office: 21 Scarsdale Rd Yonkers NY 10707-3204 Home: 1 Scarsdale Rd Tuckahoe NY 10707-3215 E-mail: ceds@optonline.net.

SINGER, CRAIG, entrepreneur, inventor, executive; b. NYC, Aug. 13, 1947; s. Albert and Dorothy (Blackman) Singer; m. Ellen Rappaport, Aug. 31, 1969 (div. Oct. 26, 2006); children: Chad Adam, Cara Danielle. BS, Cornell U., 1969; JD, Columbia U., 1972. Bar: N.Y. 1973. Exec. Continental Wingage Co., Inc., NYC, 1972-74, Integrated Resources, Inc., NYC, 1974-87; pres. Westminster Fin. Group, Inc., Bedford Corners, NY, 1989—2006; mng. dir. Richman Mortgage Assets Mgr. LLC, 2007—. Chmn. bd. dirs. Integrated Resources Funding Corp., AIM Capital Mgmt. Corp., 1983—87; entrepreneur; inventor; bus. exec., 2007—. Former mem. editl. adv. bd. Bur. Nat. Affairs Housing and Devel.; former dir. Assn. Govt. Assisted Housing, Inc., 1976—84; former mem. exec. com. Coalition Low and Moderate Income Housing. Home: 148 Meeting House Rd Bedford Corners NY 10549-4241

SINGER, DALE, reporter, editor; s. Philip and Alicia Singer; m. Merle Silverman; children: Emily Beth, Jill Susan. BA, Wash. U., St. Louis, 1971. Reporter, editor St. Louis Post-Dispatch, 1980—2008, St. Louis Beacon, 2008—. Mem.: Phi Beta Kappa.

SINGER, DANIEL MORRIS, lawyer; b. Bklyn., Oct. 10, 1930; s. Samuel W. and Fannie G. (Sabloff) S.; m. Maxine Frank, June 15, 1952; children: Amy E., Ellen R., David B., Stephanie F. BA with honors, Swarthmore Coll., 1951; LLB, Yale U., 1954. Bar: N.Y. 1956, U.S. Dist. Ct. D.C. 1957, U.S. Ct. Appeals (D.C. cir.) 1957, U.S. Supreme Ct. 1959. Motions clk. U.S. Ct. Appeals for D.C. Circuit, Washington, 1956-57, law clk. to Judge George T. Washington, 1957-58; assoc. Fried, Frank, Harris, Shriver & Jacobson, Washington, 1958-64, ptnr., 1965-87, counsel, 1987—. Arbitrator complex comml. case and constrn. nat. panels; mediator US Dist. Ct., Washington; vol. atty. Lawyers Com. for Civil Rights Under Law, 1965, 66; mem. exec. com. Washington Lawyers Com. for Civil Rights Under Law, 1973—; spl. asst. corp. counsel, D.C., 1995-2000. Bd. mgrs. Swarthmore Coll., 1987—91; dir., sec.-treas. Coun. for a Livable World, 1962—64; dir. Am. Soc. for Protection of Nature in Israel, 1986—; mem. governing coun., mem. exec. com. Am. Jewish Congress, 1986—96, v.p., 1988—92; bd. dirs., sec.-treas. Nat. Com. Tithing in Investment, 1964—65; bd. dirs. D.C. Developing Families Ctr., 1999—, D.C. Appleseed Ctr., 1996—, chmn. bd., 2000—04. With Signal Corps US Army, 1954—56. Mem.: ABA, D.C. Bar. Home: 5410 39th St NW Washington DC 20015-2902 Office: Fried Frank Harris Shriver & Jacobson 1001 Pennsylvania Ave NW Washington DC 20004-2596 Office Phone: 202-639-7222.

SINGER, DAVID MICHAEL, marketing and public relations executive; b. Bklyn., Feb. 11, 1957; s. Seymour Allen and Ellen Sybil (Pavnick) S.; m. Pamela Rae Silton, July 20, 1986; children, Max!, Bobby. BA in History, NYU, 1978; MA in Comms., Syracuse U., 1979; MA in Media, New Sch. Social Rsch., 1983; JD, Yeshiva U., 1981. Cons. pub. rels. Burson-Marsteller, NYC, 1979-81, The Haas Group, NYC, 1981-84, Braff & Co., NYC, 1987-89; pub., editor-in-chief Lodestone Pub., NYC, 1984-87; chief oper. officer Pentagon Ltd., NYC, 1989-91; v.p. pub. rels. Braff & Co., NYC, 1991-92; v.p. G.S. Schwartz & Co., NYC, 1993-97; v.p. mktg. comm. Imedia, Morristown, NJ, 1998-99; pres. S&S Mktg. Comms. Inc. Lectr. evening div. NYU, 1982-96; dir. media rels. Braff & Co. Contbr. articles and poems to profl. and consumer jours. and mags. Pres. Jewish Cultural Found., N.Y.C., 1976. Named to Outstanding Young Man of Am., Jaycees, 1977; recipient

Cert. Recognition Am. Film Inst., 1982, ANDY Design award Advt. Club N.Y., 1983, Proclamation Bklyn. Borough Pres., 1987. Mem. Alpha Epsilon Pi (Bro. of Yr. 1976). Avocations: baseball, politics, ping pong/table tennis, films, theater. Personal E-mail: singer2389@aol.com.

SINGER, DINAH S., federal agency administrator, immunologist, researcher; Grad., MIT, 1969; MPhil, PhD, Columbia U. Post-doctoral fellow Lab. Biochemistry Nat. Cancer Inst., sr. investigator Immunology Branch; sr. scientific officer Howard Hughes Med. Inst., 1998—99; dir. Divsn. Cancer Biology Nat. Cancer Inst., 1999—, also chief Molecular Regulation Sect. of Exptl. Immunology Branch. Mem.: Am. Assn. Immunologists. Office: Nat Cancer Inst Divsn Cancer Biology 6130 Executive Blvd, EPN 5044 Bethesda MD 20892-7390 Office Phone: 301-496-8636. E-mail: ds13j@nih.gov.*

SINGER, DONNA LEA, writer, editor, educator; b. Wilmington, Del., Oct. 6, 1944; d. Marshall Richard and Sara Emma (Eppihimer) S. BA in English cum laude, Gettysburg Coll., 1966; postgrad., Montclair State Coll., 1972-73, U. Birmingham, Eng., 1977; M of Letters, Drew U., 1985. Asst. to dir. student activities Fairleigh Dickinson U., Madison, crw., 1966-68; tchr., drama coach Morris Hills High Sch., Rockaway, N.J., 1968-84; free-lance editor Basic Books, Inc., NYC, 1983-86; adj. instr. Fairleigh Dickinson U., Madison, 1986-87; free-lance writer, editor Visual Edn. Corp., Princeton, N.J., 1988—, Fact's on File, Bantam, Random House, Fodor's Travel Books, NYC, 1990—, John Wiley & Sons, NYC, 1990—; tchr. Sylvan Learning and Tech. Ctr., Sarasota, Fla., 1999—. Co-founder, co-dir. Traveling Hist. Troupe, Rockaway, 1976-78; tour leader Am. Leadership Study Groups, 1976, 78, 82; theatre studies participant Royal Shakespeare Co., Stratford, Eng., 1978-79, 81; docent, lectr. acting co. Hist. Spanish Point, Osprey, Fla., 1989-2001; grant facilitator NEA, Sarasota, Fla. Author: numerous poems; contbr. chapters to books, articles to profl. jours. Big sister Big Bros./Big Sisters, Sarasota, Fla., 1990-98; NEA grant facilitator Asolo Theater, Sarosota, Fla. Mem. Internat. Women's Writing Guild, West Coast Writers, Met. Mus. Art, Royal Shakespeare Company Assocs., Emerald Coast Writers, Travel Writers Internat. Network. Avocations: dance, theater, travel, antiques. E-mail: shakesds@aol.com.

SINGER, ERIC T., investment banker; b. NYC, 1952; s. Roger M. and Meredith Singer; m. Aet Paaro, Aug. 10, 1974; children: Brett A., Jamison P. BA, SUNY, Stony Brook, 1974; JD, Cornell U., 1977. Assoc. Barrett, Smith et al, NYC, 1977-80; v.p. Smith Barney, NYC, 1980-84; sr. v.p. PaineWebber, NYC, 1984-88; exec. v.p. Metromedia Hotels, NYC, 1988-90; exec. v.p., dir. corp. fin. Gerard Klauer Mattison, NYC, 1990-99; mng. dir., pres. H.C. Wainwright & Co., Inc., NYC, 1999—2003; mng. dir. Pali Capital, Inc., NYC, 2003—; mng. ptnr. Singer Congl. Fund Singer Funds, 2004—. Mem. Cornell Law Rev. Mem. U.S. Maccabiah Squash Team, 1997, 2001, 2005. Mem. Heights Casino Club, Yale Club, Phi Beta Kappa. Home: 72 Hicks St Brooklyn NY 11201-1709 Home Phone: 718-522-6893.

SINGER, FREDERICK RAPHAEL, medical researcher; b. St. Louis, June 27, 1939; s. Meyer and Lee (Minkle) S.; m. Sandra Joy Barnes, Aug. 16, 1964; children: Stefanie, Jeffrey. Student, UCLA, 1956—59; BS, U. Calif., Berkeley, 1960; MD, U. Calif., San Francisco, 1963. Diplomate Am. Bd. Internal Medicine, Am. Bd. Endocrinology and Metabolism. Intern UCLA Affiliated Hosp., 1963-64; resident VA Hosp., LA, 1964-65, 68-69; instr. in medicine Harvard U., Boston, 1971-72; asst. prof. medicine UCLA, 1972-73, U. So. Calif., LA, 1973-74, assoc. prof., 1974-78, prof., 1978-89, prof. orthop. surgery, 1980-89; dir. Bone Ctr. Cedars-Sinai Med. Ctr., LA, 1989-92, clin. prof. medicine, 1993—. Dir. Osteoporosis/Metabolic Bone Disease program St. Johns Hosp. and Health Ctr., Santa Monica, Calif., 1992—; dir. Skeletal Biology Lab. John Wayne Cancer Inst., Santa Monica, 1992—; mem. endocrine and metabolic drug adv. com. FDA, USPHS, Bethesda, Md., 1983-87. Author: Paget's Disease of Bone, 1977; contbr. numerous articles, revs. to profl. jours. Vice chmn. cmty. adv. com. Univ. H.S., L.A., 1984. Capt. USAF, 1965-67. Calif. State scholar, 1956-60; clin. investigator VA, 1971-73. Mem. Endocrine Soc., Am. Soc. Clin. Investigation, Am. Soc. Bone and Mineral Rsch. (chmn. pub. affairs 1981-86, coun. 1987, pres.-elect 1989, pres. 1990), Paget's Disease Found. (chmn. bd. dirs. 1990—2006), Fibrosis Dysplasia Found. (bd. dirs. 2006—). Office: John Wayne Cancer Inst 2200 Santa Monica Blvd Santa Monica CA 90404-2302 Personal E-mail: singerf@yahoo.com.

SINGER, JACK WOLFE, medical educator; b. NYC, Nov. 9, 1942; s. Leon Eugene and Sarah Betty (White) S.; m. Celestia S. Higano, Dec. 15, 1984; children: Constantine Jeremiah, Emily Savoye, Anna Taylor. BA, Columbia U., NYC, 1964; MD, SUNY, Bklyn., 1968. Diplomate Am. Bd. Internal Medicine, Am. Bd. Hematology, Am. Bd. Oncology. Intern then resident U. Chgo., 1968-70; fellow in hematology and oncology U. Wash., Seattle, 1972-75, asst. prof. medicine, 1975-78, assoc. prof., 1979-85, prof., 1986—. Chief med. oncology VA Med. Ctr., Seattle, 1975—; mem. Fred Hutchinson Cancer Ctr., Seattle, 1975-92; chief med. officer, founder Cell Therapeutics Inc. Author: Cancer Care-A Personal Guide, 1979; contbr. articles to profl. jours. Mem. bd. dirs Cell Therapeudics Inc., Diakine. Served to lt. comdr. USPHS, 1970—72. Mem. Am. Soc. Clin. Investigation, Am. Soc. Hematology, Am. Soc. Clin. Oncology, Western Assn. Physicians, Western Soc. Clin. Investigation, Internat. Soc. Exptl. Hematology Avocation: classical piano. Home Phone: 206-329-7316; Office Phone: 206-272-4405. Business E-Mail: jsinger@ctiseattle.com.

SINGER, JANE BESS, communications educator; b. NY, 1955; d. Malvin and Anne Fleischer Singer. ABJ in Liberal Studies, U. Ga., Athens, 1976; MA in Liberal Studies, NY U., 1990; PhD in Journalism, U. Mo., Columbia, 1996. Newspaper reporter & editor Daily Newspapers Fla., Va., Pa., 1977—82; news mgr. Prodigy Svcs. Co., White Plains, NY, 1982—92; grad. instr. Sch. Journalism, U. Mo., 1992—95; asst. prof. dept. tech. journalism Colo. State U., Fort Collins, 1996—99; assoc. prof. sch. journalism & mass communication U. Iowa, 1999—; Johnston press chair digital journalism U. Ctrl. Lancashire, Preston, England, 2007—. Recipient Dean's Scholar award, Coll. Liberal Arts & Scis., U. Iowa, 2005, Clifford G. Christians Ethics Rsch. award, Carl Couch Ctr. Social & Internet Rsch., 2007. Mem.: Online News Assn., Soc. Profl. Journalists, Internat. Communication Assn., Assn. Edn. Journalism & Mass Communication (divsn. chair 1997—2002), Phi Beta Kappa (pres., alpha Iowa chpt. 2005—06), Kappa Tau Alpha (pres., v.p. 2006—). Office: Univ Iowa W 341 Adler Journalism Bldg Iowa City IA 52242

SINGER, JOY DANIELS, journalist, consultant; b. NYC, Feb. 22, 1928; d. Maurice Blumberg and Anna S. (Kleegman) Daniels; m. Jack Singer, July 30, 1955; children: Meriamne B., Daniel C., Richard K. BA, Cornell U., 1948; postgrad., The Sorbonne, Paris, 1949. Advt. copywriter Franklin Spier, George Knoerr & Assocs., Parents Mag., Diener & Dorskind, March Advt., NYC, 1950-68; CEO J.D. Singer, NYC, 1968—. Scriptwriter Can. TV show, Magistrate's Court, 1968-69; syndicated columnist with Marlies Wolf, Women at Work, Feature Assocs., San Rafael, Calif., 1979—. Author: My Mother, The Doctor, 1970. Dem. County committeewoman, 1960-61. Mem. Direct Mktg. Creative Guild (v.p., corp. sec.), Friends Com., Gen. Soc. Libr. (chmn.), NATAS. Home and Office: 1725 York Ave Apt 19F New York NY 10128-7811 Office Phone: 212-348-0881. E-mail: imrejoysing@aol.com.

SINGER, MARKUS MORTON, retired trade association administrator; b. NYC, Dec. 20, 1917; s. Isadore and Nettie (Stromer) S.; m. Phyllis Berger, June 26, 1945; children: Fredric L., Robert B. B.C.S., NYU, 1939; postgrad., George Washington U., 1951-55. With Nat. Food Brokers Assn., Washington, 1946—, v.p., 1961-65, exec. v.p., 1965-71, pres., 1972-83, pres. emeritus, 1983—, acting pres., chief exec. officer, 1987-88. Lifetime hon. trustee Nat. Food Brokers Assn. Edn. and Tng. Found. Served with AUS, 1942-45. Recipient Pres.'s award as Man of Yr. Can. Food Brokers Assn., 1976 Mem. European Food Brokers Assn. (hon. life), Frozen Food Industry Disting. Order of Zerocrats. Jewish.

SINGER, MARTIN DORI, lawyer; b. Bklyn., Apr. 25, 1952; BA, CCNY, 1974; JD, Bklyn. Law Sch., 1977. Bar: Calif. 1977, US Dist. Ct., DC 1978, US Ct. Appeals (9th Cir) 1990. Ptnr. Lavely & Singer Profl. Corp., 1982—. Calif. labor commr. Author: (Law Handbook) Regulation of Talent Agent, 1983. Named to The Top 100 Attorneys in California, Daily Jour., 2005, 2006. Mem.: Beverly Hills, Century City and LA County Bar Associations. Office: Lavely & Singer 2049 Century Pk E Ste 2400 Los Angeles CA 90067 Office Phone: 310-556-3501. Office Fax: 310-556-3615. E-mail: msinger@lavelysinger.com.

SINGER, MAXINE FRANK, retired biochemist, science association director; b. NYC, Feb. 15, 1931; d. Hyman S. and Henrietta (Perlowitz) Frank; m. Daniel Morris Singer, June 15, 1952; children: Amy Elizabeth, Ellen Ruth, David Byrd, Stephanie Frank. AB, Swarthmore Coll., 1952, DSc (hon.), 1978; PhD, Yale U., 1957, DSc (hon.), 1994, Wesleyan U., 1977, U. Md.-Baltimore County, 1985, Cedar Crest Coll., 1986, CUNY, 1988, Brandeis U., 1988, Radcliffe Coll., 2000, Williams Coll., 1990, Franklin and Marshall Coll., 1991, George Washington U., 1991, NYU, 1992, Lehigh U., 1992, Dartmouth Coll., 1993, Harvard U., 1994, Yale U., 1994, U. Nebr., 2004; PhD honoris causa (hon.), Weizmann Inst. Sci., 1995. USPHS postdoctoral fellow NIH, Bethesda, Md., 1956—58, rsch. chemist biochemistry, 1958—74; head sect. on nucleic acid enzymology Nat. Cancer Inst., 1974—79; chief Lab. of Biochemistry, Nat. Cancer Inst., 1979—87, rsch. chemist, 1987—88; pres. Carnegie Inst. Washington, 1988—2002, pres. emeritus, 2002—. Regents vis. lectr. U. Calif., Berkeley, 1981. Mem. editl. bd.: Jour. Biol. Chemistry, 1968—74, Sci. mag, 1972—82, chmn. editl. bd.: Procs. of NAS, 1985—88; co-author (with Paul Berg): 3 books on molecular biology and a sci. biog.; contbr. articles to scholarly jours. Chmn. Smithsonian Coun., 1992—93; trustee Wesleyan U., Middletown, Conn., 1972—75, Yale Corp., New Haven, 1975—90, Carnegie Inst. Wash., 2002—; bd. govs. Weizmann Inst. Sci., Rehovot, Israel, 1978—; bd. dirs. Whitehead Inst., 1985—94, chmn. bd., 2003—04. Recipient award for achievement in biol. scis., Washington Acad. Scis., 1969, award for rsch. in biol. scis., Yale Sci. and Engring. Assn., 1974, Superior Svc. Honor award, HEW, 1975, Dirs. award, NIH, 1977, DSM, HHS, 1983, Presdl. Disting. Exec. Rank award, 1987, U.S. Disting. Exec. Rank award, 1987, Mory's Cup, Bd. Govs. Mory's Assn., 1991, Wilbur Lucius Cross Medal for Honor, Yale Grad. Sch. Assn., 1991, Nat. Medal Sci., NSF, 1992, Pub. Svc. award, NIH Alumni Assn., 1995, Vannevar Bush award, Nat. Sci. Bd., 1999, Pub. Welfare award, NAS, 2007; named to Washington D.C. Hall of Fame, 2000. Fellow: Am. Acad. Arts and Scis.; mem.: AAAS (Sci. Freedom and Responsibility award 1982, Philip Hauge Abelson prize 2004), NAS (coun. 1982—85, com. sci., engring. and pub. policy 1989—91, chmn. 1999—2005, Pub. Welfare medal 2007), Am. Soc. Cell Biology, Pontifical Acad. of Scis., Inst. Medicine of NAS, Am. Philos. Soc., Am. Chem. Soc., Am. Soc. Microbiologists, Am. Soc. Biol. Chemists. Home: 5410 39th St NW Washington DC 20015-2902 Office: Carnegie Inst Washington 1530 P St NW Washington DC 20005-1933

SINGER, MYER R(ICHARD), lawyer; b. Everett, Mass., Oct. 24, 1938; s. Nathan and Celia (Rudin) Singer; m. Elaine Doris Ginesky, June 17, 1962; children: Andrew L., Stephen D., Jocelyn G. BSBA, Boston U., 1960, LLB, 1963. Bar: Mass. 1963. Atty. Boston Legal Aid Soc., 1963—64; pvt. practice Dennis Port, Mass., 1965—2001; ptnr. Singer & Singer, LLC, 2001—, Martindale Hubbell AV Rated. Corporator Cape Cod Five Cents Savs. Bank, Harwich Port, Mass., 1977—, trustee, 1980—, mem. bd. investment, 1989—, vice chmn., bd. trustee, bd. investment, 2009—; trustee Cape Cod Mus. of Natural History, 2001—; faculty Mass. Continuing Legal Edn., Inc., 1985, 1990—98; mem. & trustee exec. com. Cape Cod Five Cents Savs. Bank Charitable Found. Trust, 2006—, Work Force Housing Task Force Land VJE Sub Com., 2006—07; program chmn. Real Estate Devel. Cape Cod-Mass. Bar Inst., 1999; corporator Heritage Mus. and Gardens, 2003—06; spkr. in field. Co-author: (book) Creation and Care of Condominiums, 1985, Everything You Need to Know about the Cape Cod Commission Act, 1990. Pres. Dennis Yarmouth Band Parents, 1986—87; mem. adv. bd. Cape Mus. Fine Arts, Dennis, 1988—96; former trustee Cape Cod Synagogue; mem., clk. Yarmouth (Mass.) Zoning Bd. Appeals, 1980—86; former bd. dirs. Cape Cod and Island chpt. of Mass. Heart Assn.; former pres. Legal Svcs. of Cape Cod and Island, Inc. Mem.: ABA, Barnstable County Bar Assn. (mem. exec. com. 1999—2003), Mass. Bar Assn. (chmn. bar assn. program real estate devel. Cape Cod 1999). Achievements include Martindale Hubbell peer review rating AV. Avocations: boating, photography. Home: 238 Greenland Circle East Dennis MA 02641-1302 Office: PO Box 67 26 Upper County Rd Dennis Port MA 02639-0067 Office Phone: 508-398-2221. Business E-Mail: mrsinger@singer-law.com.

SINGER, NIKI, media consultant; b. Rochester, NY, Sept. 10, 1937; d. Goodman A. and Evelyn (Simon) Sarachan; m. Michael J. Sheets, 1973; children: Romaine Kitty, Nicholas Simon Feramorz. BA cum laude, U. Mich., 1959. Mgr. advt. sales promotion Fairchild Publ., NYC, 1959-67; acct. exec., acct. supr. Vernon Pope Co., NYC, 1967-69, v.p., 1969-71; pres. Niki Singer, Inc., NYC, 1971-93; sr. v.p. M. Shanken Comm., Cigar Aficionado, Wine Spectator, 1994—2002; founder Niki Singer, LLC, 2003—. Mem.: Les Dames d'Escoffier (bd. dirs.), Am. Inst. Wine and Food (bd. dirs.). Office: 1035 5th Ave New York NY 10028-0135 E-mail: sheets@nyc.rr.com.

SINGER, PAUL RICHARD, retired ophthalmologist; b. NYC, Feb. 1, 1947; m. Katherine W. Singer, June 13, 1970; children: Amy E., Evan P. BA with honors, U. Rochester, NYC, 1969, MD, 1973. Diplomate Am. Bd. Ophthalmology. Internal medicine intern U. N.C., Chapel Hill, 1973-74, resident in neurology, 1974-75; resident in ophthalmology Washington U. Sch. Medicine, St. Louis, 1975-78, Fight for Sight postdoctoral rsch. fellow dept ophthalmology, 1978-79; pres. Hartford (Conn.) Eye Physicians, 1980—; sr. staff dept. ophthalmology Hartford Hosp., 1980—2008; ret., 2008. Chmn. bd. dirs. Prevent Blindness Conn., Middletown, 1990-92, Combined Health Appeal, Hartford, 1993-95. Recipient Cmty. Svc. award Hartford County Med. Assn., 1993, Robert Polk award for outstanding vol. svc. Prevent Blindness Conn., 1993. Office: Hartford Eye Physicians 55 Nye Rd Ste 103 Glastonbury CT 06033-4394

SINGER, ROBERT, plastic surgeon; b. Buffalo, Oct. 22, 1942; s. Murray and Fay Singer; m. Judith Harris. Student, SUNY, Buffalo, 1960-63; MD, SUNY, 1967. Lic. physician, Calif.; diplomate Am. Bd. Plastic and Reconstructive Surgery. Resident in gen. surgery Stanford Med. Ctr., Palo Alto, Calif., 1967-69, Santa Barbara Cottage and Gen. Hosp., 1972-74; resident in plastic surgery Vanderbilt U., 1974-76; pvt. practice specializing in emergency and trauma San Diego, 1971-72; pvt. practice plastic, reconstructive and aesthetic surgery La Jolla, Calif., 1976—. Clin. prof. plastic surgery U. Calif., San Diego; sr. staff, chief plastic surgery Scripps Meml. Hosp., La Jolla, 1980-86, vice chmn. dept. surgery, 1989-91; co-chmn. editl. adv. bd. NewBeauty Mag. Contbr. articles to profl. jours. Active San Diego Opera, San Diego Mus. of Man, La Jolla Playhouse, Voices for Children, San Diego Zoo, Mus. Photog. Arts, KPBS, others. Served, Vietnam, ret. lt. comdr. USNR, served in emergency dept., Balboa Naval Hosp., San Diego. Named one of Best Cosmetic Surgeons in Country, Town & Country Mag.; named to Best Doctors in America. Fellow ACS; mem. AMA, Calif. Med. Assn., San Diego County Med. Soc. (named to Best Plastic Surgeons in San Diego), San Diego Internat. Soc. Plastic Surgery (pres. 1988-89), Calif. Soc. Plastic Surgeons (pres. 1995-96), Am. Soc. Aesthetic Plastic Surgeons (pres. 1994-95, traveling vis. prof., Plastic Surgery Leadership award), Internat. Soc. Clin. Plastic Surgeons, Am. Soc. Plastic and Reconstructive Surgeons (trustee 1996—, chmn. bd. trustees 1998-99), J.B. Lynch Soc., Royal Soc. Medicine, Am. Assn. for Accreditation of Ambulatory Surgery Facilities (pres. 1991-2000), San Diego Plastic Surgery Soc. (pres. 1989-90), Aesthetic Surgery Edn. and Rsch. Found. (pres., 2000—) Avocations: tennis, travel, pre-columbian art. Office: 9834 Genesee Ave Ste 100 La Jolla CA 92037-1214 Office Phone: 866-660-0206, 858-455-0240.

SINGER, ROBERT H., biology professor; Prof. neuroscience Yeshiva U. Albert Einstein Coll. Medicine, prof. cell biology, prof. & co-chair anatomy & structural biology. Contbr. articles to profl. jours. Mem.: Am. Acad. Arts & Sciences. Achievements include patents in field. Office: Yeshiva Univ ASB AECOM Golding 601 1300 Morris Park Ave Bronx NY 10461 Office Phone: 718-430-8646 ext. 8647. Office Fax: 718-430-8697. Business E-Mail: rhsinger@aecom.yu.edu.*

SINGER, STEVEN D., lawyer; b. 1954; BA summa cum laude, Tufts U., 1976; JD magna cum laude, Harvard U., 1979. Bar: Mass. 1979. Ptnr., vice chmn. Corp. dept., co-chmn. Life Sci. dept. Wilmer Cutler Pickering Hale & Dorr, Boston. Mem. bd. overseers Beth Israel Deaconess Med. Ctr.; bd. dir. Beelzebubs Found.; past pres. Temple Beth Shalom, Needham, Mass. Named a Mass. Super Lawyer, Boston Mag., 2004. Mem.: ABA, Mass. Biotechnology Council, Biotechnology Ind. Org. Jewish. Office: Wilmer Cutler Pickering Hale & Dorr 60 State St Boston MA 02109 Office Phone: 617-526-6410. Office Fax: 617-526-5000. Business E-Mail: steven.singer@wilmerhale.com.

SINGH, ABHAY KUMAR, psychiatrist, department chairman; b. Gaya, Bihar, India, Jan. 1, 1960; arrived in US, 1997; MD, A.N. Magadh Med. Coll., Gaya, 1988. Lic. Am. Bd. Psychiatry and Neurology, 2005, Am. Soc. Addiction Medicine, 2006. Intern Fletcher-Allen Health Care, U. Vt., 2000—01; resident in psychiatry U. Vt., 2003—04, chief resident, dept. psychiatry, 2003—04, clin. faculty, dept. psychiatry, UVM Coll. Medicine, 2004—; attending psychiatrist St. Mary's Regional Med. Ctr., Lewiston, Maine, 2004—, chmn. dept. psychiatry, 2006—; med. dir. Cmty. Clin. Svcs., Lewiston, 2007—. Contbr. articles to profl. jours.; co-author: Comprehensive Review of Psychiatry. Vol. Manhattan Psychiat. Ctr., NYC, 1998—2000. Recipient Spl. Appreciation award, NY Office Mental Health, 1999. Mem.: Am. Soc. Addiction Medicine, Am. Psychiat. Assn. Achievements include research in the nicotinic receptor system; atypical antipsychotic induced hyperglycemia; dopamine receptor agonist induced mania and mecamylamine. Office: Cmty Clin Svcs 100 Campus Ave Ste 208 Lewiston ME 04240 Office Phone: 207-777-8974. Business E-Mail: abhay.singh@uvm.edu.

SINGH, AJAY KUMAR, nephrologist, educator; b. New Delhi, June 2, 1960; s. Jasbir Jawand and Gita Singh; m. Ritu Rai, Sept. 4, 1989; 1 child, Anika. BSc, U. Coll., London, 1980, MB BS, 1984; MBA, Boston U., 2001. Med., surg. intern Stafford Gen. Infirmary Stoke Mandeville Hosp., England, 1984—85; med. resident Southend Hosp., England, 1985—87; renal fellow New Eng. Med. Ctr., Boston, 1987—89, renal rsch. fellow, 1989—92, assoc. prof. medicine, 1992—98, Harvard Med. Sch., Boston, 1998—; clin. dir. renal divsn. Brigham and Women's Hosp., Boston, 1998—. Dir. inpatient nephrology New Eng. Med. Ctr., Boston, 1996—98; dir. dialysis svcs. Brigham and Women's Hosp., Boston, 1998—; med. dir. KIDNE Renal Disease Mgmt., 1998—. Editor: (CD-Rom) Images in Internal Medicine from the IRIM, 1999, Intensive Review of Internal Medicine, 2000; co-author: Harrison's Principles of Internal Medicine. Chairperson New Eng. Renal Disease Initiative, 2000—; spkr. Kidney-Dialysis-Transplantation Assn., 2001. Recipient Excellence in Clin. Tchg. award, Tufts U. Med. Sch., 1997. Mem.: Royal Coll. Physicians (London). Office: Brigham & Women's Hosp Renal Divsn 75 Francis St Boston MA 02115

SINGH, AMANDEEP, emergency physician; Asst. clin. prof. medicine UC San Francisco, 2003—; co dir. resident edn., dept. emergency medicine Highland Gen. Hosp., Oakland, Calif., 2006—. Office: Highland Gen Hosp 1411 E 31st St Oakland CA 94602

SINGH, AMRIK, literature and language professor; s. Sewa Singh and Jagir Kaur; m. Surinder Kaur, May 25, 1986; children: Aabneet Kaur, Inayat Kaur. PhD, Panjab U., Chandigarh, 2000. Cert. tchr Edn. Nat. U. Calif., 2008. Adj. faculty Calif. State U., Sacramento, 2006—; adj. prof. Sacramento City Coll., 2007—. Pres. Punjabi Sahit Sabha, Sacramento, 2005—07. Contbr. articles to profl. jours. (Best Columnist Writing award, 2006). Chief advisor lit. activities Punjabi Sahit Sabha, 2006. Rsch. grant, Indo Am. Ctr. Internat. Studies, 1998, Tchr. fellowship, U. Grant Commn. India, 1998. Mem.: Toni Morrison Soc. Home: 8339 Holly Jill Way Sacramento CA 95823 Office Phone: 916-212-8550. Personal E-mail: drsinghamrik@gmail.com, amriksaini@yahoo.com.

SINGH, AVINASH, mechanical engineer; s. Ravindra Prasad and Krishna Singh; m. Manisha Roy; 1 child, Atishay. B. Tech. in Mech. Engg., IIT, Varanasi, India, 1990; MS in Mech. Engg., Oh. State U., Columbus, 1992, PhD, 1997. Sr. project engr. Gen. Motors Powertrain, 1995—2002, sr. staff engr., 2002—08, engring. group mgr., 2008—. Vice chair, power transmission com. ASME, 2006—, program chair, Nev., 2006—07, San Diego, 2008—, assoc. editor, jour. mech. design, 2007—. Contbr. scientific papers. Mem.: ASME. Office: GM Powertrain Global Hdqs 895 Joslyn Ave Bldg C Pontiac MI 48340

SINGH, BEDI AJAY, film company executive; b. Palwal, Haryana, India, Aug. 20, 1959; came to the U.S., 1995; s. Bedi Joginder and Mohini (Mahna) S.; m. Bharathi G. Singh, Oct. 4, 1984; children: Nisha, Arjun. BSc in Econs. with honors, London Sch. Econs., 1980. Audit staff Arthur Andersen & Co., London, 1980-86, experienced sr., 1986-87, sr. mgr. Lagos, Nigeria, 1987-90, London, 1990-91; fin. contr. News Internat. plc, London, 1992-94; sr. v.p. News Corp., L.A., 1995-96; sr.

v.p. strategic planning, dep. CFO Fox Filmed Entertainment, L.A., 1997—99; exec. v.p., CFO Sony Pictures Entertainment, L.A., 1999—2003; chief adminstrv. officer, CFO Novartis Pharma A.G., Basel, Switzerland, 2004—06; exec. v.p., CFO Gemstar-TV Guide Internat., L.A., 2006—08; pres. fin. & adminstn., CFO Metro-Goldwyn-Mayer Inc., L.A., 2008—, mem. Office of CEO, 2009—. Bd. dirs. Children's Inst. Internat., L.A., 1997—, L.A. Youth, 1997—. Fellow Inst. Chartered Accts. Eng. and Wales; mem. Inst. Chartered Accts. India, Royal Overseas League U.K., Royal Commonwealth Club U.K., Inst. Dirs. U.K., Gymkhana Club New Delhi, Harvard Alumnae Assn., Arthur Andersen Alumnae Assn. Avocations: bicycling, racquetball, fishing, clay pigeon and field shooting, swimming. Office: Metro-Goldwyn-Mayer Inc 10250 Constellation Blvd Los Angeles CA 90067*

SINGH, CHITRANJAN K., electronics engineer; s. Brajnandan Prasad and Subhadra Singh; m. Sarita Singh. BS, Indian Inst. Tech., Kanpur, 1998; PhD, U. Tex., Dallas, Richardson, 2008. Rsch. engr. C-DOT, New Delhi, 2001; sr. ASIC design engr. Adaptec Inc., Milpitas, Calif., 2001—03; intern Intel, Santa Clara, Calif., 2007; staff engr., project mgr. NextWave Wireless, San Diego, 2008—. Vol. non-govtl. orgn. Asha, Chatra, Bihar, 1994—97. Mem.: IEEE (Young Student award 2004). Achievements include patents pending for technique to reduce PAPR in OFDM system; research in high throughput VLSI architecture for MIMO detection.

SINGH, HARJIT, medical educator, artist; b. Shimla, Himachal Pradesh, India, Sept. 26, 1936; s. Achal Singh and Sunder Kaur; m. Cecilia Sepulveda, July 17, 1993; children: Namrita, Arshdeep. MB, BS, Govt. Med. Coll., Patiala, India, 1958; MD, Punjabi U., Patiala, 1964. Lic. Punjab Med. Coun., Ludhiana, India, 1958, cert. Ednl. Coun. for Fgn. Med. Grads., 1962, lic. pediat. specialist Dept. Health, Dubai, UAE, 1990. Sr. lectr. in pediat. Govt. Med. Coll., Patiala, Punjab, India, 1965—66, Med. Coll., Rohtak, Haryana, India, 1966—70, asst. prof. pediat., 1970—75, reader in pediat., 1975—76, assoc. prof. pediat., 1976—77, 1978—82, prof. pediat., 1977—78, 1982—84, Arab Med. U., Benghazi, Libya, 1984—88; cmty. pediatrician Am. Hosp., Dubai, United Arab Emirates, 1997—2000; CME program dir. Hackettstown Regional Med. Ctr., NJ, 2002—. Examiner in pediat. Arab Med. U., Benghazi, 1985—88; vis. prof. Sch. Tropical Medicine, Liverpool, 1986—95. Exhibitions include Dubai Internat. Art Ctr., 1991—99, Yolo County Art Coun., 2001, Sussex County Art & Heritage Coun., 2002, Warren County Art Coun., 2002, Triveni Art Gllery, New Delhi, 1970, Represented in permanent collections, India, Can., UK, UAE, US; contbr. scientific papers to profl. publs. Grantee, Indian Coun. Med. Rsch., New Delhi, 1975—88; fellowship in pediat. hematology, WHO, 1974-75. Mem.: Alliance of CME (corr.), Indian Assn. Advancement Med. Edn. (life), Perinatology Forum (life). Office: Hackettstown Regional Med Ctr 651 Willow Grove St Hackettstown NJ 07840 Office Fax: 908-950-6815. E-mail: hsingh@hrmend.org.

SINGH, HARPAL, research scientist; b. Saharanpur, Uttar Pradesh, India, Dec. 4, 1964; m. Monika Singh, May 24, 2002; 1 child, Yuvraj. BSc, Meerut U., Uttar Pradesh, 1986, MSc, 1988; PhD, Indian Inst. Tech., Roorkee, Uttarakhand, India, 2007. Cert. Microsoft Office Indian Inst. Tech., 1997, C++ Indian Inst. Tech., 1997, in software devel. Indian Inst. Tech., 1998. Rsch. fellow NISCAIR, New Delhi, 1989—90; sr. scientist Ctrl. Bldg. Rsch. Inst., Roorkee, 1990—. Contbr. articles to numerous sci. rsch. papers. Mem.: Material Rsch. Soc. India (Life membership 1992), Loss Prevention Assn. India (Life membership 1990). Hindu. Avocations: cricket, tennis. Office: Savannah State Univ 3219 College St Savannah GA 31404 Office Fax: 911332272272, 912-353-5134; Home Fax: 911332272272. Business E-Mail: singhh@savstate.edu. E-mail: harpal26@yahoo.com.

SINGH, JATINDER PAL, research scientist, consultant; b. Moga, Punjab, India, Sept. 6, 1978; s. Surinder Singh and Jasbir Kaur. BS, Indian Inst. Tech., Delhi, 2000; MS, Stanford U., Calif., 2002, PhD, 2005. Intern IBM India Rsch. Lab., New Delhi, 1999, Intel Corp., San Jose, Calif., 2001; mobile networks intern Robert Bosch Corp., Palo Alto, Calif., 2002; intern IBM T.J. Watson Rsch. Ctr., Hawthorne, NY, 2003; cons. Deutsche Telekom, Berlin, 2005; sr. rsch. scientist Deutsche Telekom Labs., Berlin, 2006—; rschr. Tech. U. Berlin, 2006—; cons. asst. prof. Stanford U., 2007—; cons. Airtemis Networks, Sunnyvale, Calif., 2007—. Cons. Deutsche Telekom, Berlin, 2005; ind. tech. cons. Airtemis Networks, Sunnyvale, Calif., 2007—. Contbr. articles to profl. jours. Vol. Nat. Svc. Scheme, New Delhi, 1996—2000. Recipient Inst. Merit awards, Indian Inst. Tech., 1996—2000, Inst. Silver medal, 2000; grad. fellow, Stanford U., 2000—04, Deutsche Telekom fellow, Stanford Networking Rsch. Ctr., Stanford U., 2005. Mem.: IEEE. Achievements include patents for method and System to model TCP throughput, assess power control measures, and compensate for fading and path loss, for highly mobile broadband systems; patents pending for method and communication system for optimizing the throughput of a TCP flow in a wireless network; method and communication system for channel state awareness based transmission power adaptation for the optimization of TCP throughput in a wireless network; method and system for peer-to-peer content dissemination; method and communication system for dynamical traffic flow assignment to a plurality of access networks; method and multi-homed communication device for dynamic transmission rate control; method and IEEE 802.11e capable access point for centralized scheduling of traffic streams in a WLAN. Avocations: meditation, writing, sports.

SINGH, KULDEV, medical educator; b. Washington, Feb. 20, 1961; s. Mandev and Kulwanti M. Singh. BS, McGill U., Montreal, Can., 1982; MD, Johns Hopkins U., Balt., 1986; MPH, 1987. Diplomate Am. Bd. Ophthalmology, 1992. Prof. ophthalmology Stanford U. Sch. Medicine, Calif., 1992—. Exec. v.p. World Glaucoma Assn., 2008—. Office: Stanford Univ 900 Blake Wilbur Dr Menlo Park CA 94025

SINGH, KUNWAR PAL, manufacturing executive, researcher; b. Bharatpur, Rajasthan, India, July 20, 1973; PhD, Delhi U., India, 2004. Dir. Simutech, Gainesville, Fla., 2007—. Contbr. scientific papers.

SINGH, KUSHAL PAL (K.P.), real estate developer; b. Bulandshahar, Uttar Pradesh, India, Aug. 15, 1931; married; 3 children. Attended, Meerut Coll., India, Indian Mil. Acad., Dehradun. Mgmt. positions Am. Universal Elec. Co., 1960—71; positions through mng. dir. Willard India Ltd., 1971—79; mng. dir through chmn. DLF Group, New Delhi, 1979—. Nat. adv. India GE, 1989—93, mem. nat. adv. bd., 1993—; dir. ctrl. bd. Reserve Bank India; mem. exec. com. Fedn. Indian C. of C. & Ind.; past. pres. ASSOCHAM; bd. gov. Nat. Inst. Tech., Durgapur, India; mem. econ. policy council Rajasthan Govt.; council mem. Ea. Regional Org. Planning & Housing, India. Officer Deccan Horse, Indian Army. Recipient Delhi Ratna award; named one of India's 40 Richest, Forbes Mag., 2005, World's Richest People, 2005—. Office: DLF Group DLF Centre Sansad Marg New Delhi 110001 India

SINGH, MADHU, social sciences educator; d. Jai Rattan J. and Savitri Kathuria; life ptnr. Abhai Singh, Dec. 13, 1978; 1 child, Samai Suhani. PhD, U. Rajasthan, Jaipur, India, 1975. Rsch. assoc. Sri Ram Ctr. Rsch., New Delhi, 1969—70; asst. prof. Sophia Coll., Ajmer, Rajasthan, 1970—75, Jesus & Mary Coll., New Delhi, 1975—79; assoc. prof. Tougaloo Coll., Miss., 2001—. Orgnl. bd. mem. Consortium Rsch. Ednl. Accountability and Tchr. Evaluation, Louisville, 2006—08, Miss. Acad. Sci., Jackson, 2007—08. Recipient Tchg. award, Tougaloo Coll. Nat. Alumni Assn., 2007; grant, NSF, 2001—04, fellow, Fulbright, 2005. Mem.: Miss. Psychol. Assn., South Eastern Psychol. Assn. Avocations: travel, reading, music.

SINGH, NARENDRA, cardiologist, researcher, medical educator; b. Saraiya, Uttar Pradesh, India, June 10, 1963; Can., US; s. Rudra Prasad and Manorma Singh; m. Mitra Kumari Kandhal, June 26, 1993; children: Shailin Raj, Ishaan Vivek, Vrushali Kumari. BS in Biochemistry, Dalhousie U., Halifax, Can., 1983, MD, 1987. Diplomate Am. Bd. Internal Medicine, Am. Bd. Cardiovascular Disease, Cert. Bd. Nuclear Cardiology, NASPE Testamur. Rotating intern St. Michael's Hosp., U. Toronto, 1987—88, resident in internal medicine, 1988—91, cardiology fellow, 1991—93; cardiologist Centenary Cardiology Assocs., Toronto, Ont., Canada, 1994—2002; dir. Scarborough Cardiology Rsch., Toronto, 1996—2002; cardiologist Northside Cardiology P.C., Atlanta, 2002—, dir. rsch., 2003—; cardiology sect. chair Northside Hosp., Atlanta, 2003—06. Lectr. U. Toronto, 1994—2002; med. dir. Pacemaker/ICD Programme, 1995—2002, Cardiac Cath Lab., 1999—2001; co-founder Greater Toronto Area Cmty. Cardiologists, 1995—2001; clin. asst. prof. Emory U. Sch. Medicine, Atlanta, 2002—; mem. regional lipid adv. bd. Merck, Canada; mem. nat. adv. bd. Pfizer, Canada; regional spkrs. bur. Pfizer, GSK, Novartis; heart failure adv. bd. Saint Joseph's Hosp.; vice chair Saint Joseph's Rsch. Inst.; CME chairperson GG Am. Coll. Cardiology. Contbr. articles to profl. jours. Bd. dirs. Hosp. Found., Toronto, 1998—2002. Recipient award plaque in recognition for contbns., Greater Toronto Area Cmty. Cardiologists, Leadership award, Northside Hosp., 2006; scholar, Dalhousie U., 1981, 1983, 1985; Rsch. fellow, U. Toronto, 1993. Fellow: Am. Coll. Cardiology (councillor, Atlanta region, Ga. chpt. 2008—, mem. nat. needs assessment working group), Royal Coll. Physicians and Surgeons Can. (cert. in cardiology/internal medicine), Am. Heart Assn. (bd. dirs. Atlanta 2008—); mem.: Am. Soc. Nuc. Cardiology, Med. Assn. Ga., Can. Med. Assn., Med. Staff Soc. (bd. govs., mem. med. adv. com. 1995—97, pres. Centenary site, mem. strategic planning com. 1996), Can. Cardiovasc. Soc. (coun. mem. 1999—2002, nat. sec. 2000—02, sec., mem. exec. com., chairperson membership com. 2000—02). Avocations: travel, golf, theater. Office: Northside Cardiology PC 5670 Peachtree-Dunwoody Rd Ste 880 Atlanta GA 30342 Office Phone: 404-256-2525. Office Fax: 404-256-2535. Business E-Mail: nsingh@nscatl.com.

SINGH, NARSINGH BAHADUR, chemist, researcher; b. Newada, India, July 12, 1949; s. Chhabi Raj and Jayarajee Singh; m. Kusum Singh, June 30, 1971; children: Manisha, Manish, Mamata. BSc, Gorakhpur U., India, 1969, MSc, 1971, PhD, 1977. Asst. prof. T.D. Post Grad. Coll., Jaunpur, India, 1971-79; rsch. assoc. Rensellaer Poly. Inst., Troy, N.Y., 1979-84; sr. engr. Westinghouse R&D, Pitts., 1984-86, fellow engr., 1986-88, adv. engr., 1988-89; program mgr. Westinghouse/Northrop, Balt., 1989—. Patentee in field; editor; assoc. editor Program Grystal Growth, 19990—. Baseball/softball coach FAAA, Murrysville, Pa., 1985-98. Fellow Am. Soc. Materials Internat., SPIE-Internat. Soc. Optics and Photonics; mem. TMS, Am. Assn. for Crystal Growth, Sigma Xi. Home: 5106 Crystal View Ct Ellicott City MD 21043 E-mail: narsingh_b_singh@md.northgrum.com.

SINGH, OM V., biotechnologist, researcher; b. Chandosi, Uttar Pradesh, India, Jan. 8, 1972; s. Uday V Singh and Indu B Devi; m. Rashmi Singh; 1 child, Manav V. BS in Biol. Science, Meerut U., 1992; MS in Zoology, CCS U., 1994; PhD, Indian Inst. Tech., India, 2000. Rsch. scholar Indian Inst. Tech., Roorkee, Uttaranchal, India, 1995—2000; rsch. assoc. Inst. Microbial Tech., Chandigarh, Punjab, India, 2000—02; postdoctoral rsch. assoc. U. Mo., Rolla, 2002—03; postdoctoral rsch. fellow U. Louisville, 2003, Johns Hopkins Sch. Medicine, Balt., 2003—. Mem. editl. bd.: World Jour. Microbiol. Biotech., Optics: A Jour. of Integrative Biology, Jour. Jnd. Microbiol. Biotech., Proteome Sci. Post-doctoral Rsch. Assoc. fellowship, Monsanto Inc. St. Louis, 2002, Post-doctoral Rsch. fellowship, Nat. Inst. Aging, NIH, 2003, Eudowood Divsn. Pediatric Respiratory Scis., Johns Hopkins U. Sch. Medicine, 2003. Mem.: Soc. Applied Microbiology (assoc.), Water Environment Fedn. (assoc.), Internat. Soc. for Computational Biology (assoc.), Internat. Proteome Soc. (assoc.), Am. Soc. Cell Biology (assoc.), Assn. Environ. Engring. and Sci. Profs. (assoc.), Am. Soc. Microbiology (assoc.), Indian Sci. Congress Assn. (life), Assn. Microbiologist of India (life). Achievements include discovery of novel fermentation techniques and microorganism; novel therapeutic targets for cystic fibrosis using 2D gel electrophoresis and mass spectrometry; pharmacoproteomics for cystic fibrosis. Avocations: billiards, chess, horseback riding, reading. Office: Johns Hopkins Sch Medicine 600 N Wolfe St Pk 316 Baltimore MD 21287 Personal E-mail: ovs11@yahoo.com.

SINGH, PRAMIL NAND, epidemiologist, educator; s. Bramah Nand and Mother Singh; m. Sharda Kalla, Aug. 15, 2003; children: Anusha, Ankit Vyas. PhD, Sch. Pub. Health, 1999. Asst. prof. epidemiology Loma Linda U., Calif., 1999—, assoc. prof. epidemiology, 2004. Jour. reviewer Jour. AMA, Balt. Author: Vegetarian Nutrition. Recipient Chancellors award, Loma Linda U., 1999, New Investigator award, North Am. Menopause Soc., 2001; named Alumni Scholar, U. Calif. Bd. Regents, 1987. Mem.: Delta Tau Omega. Achievements include conducted the first study to show the independent associations of several animal products on risk of colon cancer that may in part be mediated through insulin levels; conducted the first research to implicate estrogen levels in the higher mortality risk of lean older women; conducted the first research showing protective effects of moderate weight gain in lean postmenopausal women; conducted the first research to show 4 extra years of life expectancy for long term vegetarians. Office: Loma Linda Univ Nichol Hall Sch Public Health Loma Linda CA 92350 Personal E-mail: pramilnsingh@yahoo.com.

SINGH, RAJENDRA, mechanical engineering educator, director; b. Dhampur, India, Feb. 13, 1950; came to U.S., 1973; s. Raghubir and Ishwar (Kali) S.; m. Veena Ghungesh, June 24, 1979; children: Rohit, Arun. BS with honors, Birla Inst., 1971; MS, Indian Inst. Tech., 1973; PhD, Purdue U., 1975. Grad. instr. Purdue U., West Layfayette, Ind., 1973-75; sr. engr. Carrier Corp., Syracuse, NY, 1975-79; asst. prof. Ohio State U., Columbus, 1979-83, assoc. prof., 1983-87, prof., 1987—, Donald D. Glower chair in engring., 2001—, dir. Smart Vehicle Concepts Ctr., 2006—, sr. fellow Ctr. Automotive Rsch., 2006—. Adj. lectr. Syracuse (N.Y.) U., 1977-79; bd. dirs. Inst. of Noise Control Engring., 1994-96, 99-04, v.p., 2009-, v.p. tech. activities, 2000-02, pres., 2003; gen. chmn. Nat. Noise Conf., Columbus, 1985; leader U.S. delegation to India-U.S.A. Symposium on Vibration and Noise Engring., 1996; vis. prof. U. Calif., Berkeley, 1987-88; pres. Inter-Noise 2002 Congress; chmn. India-USA Symposium on Vibration and Noise, 2001; cons., lectr. in field. Author: Emerging Trends in Vibration and Noise Engineering, 1996; contbr. more than 375 articles to profl. jours.; guest editor jours. Recipient Gold medal IIT Roorkee, 1973, R. H. Kohr Rsch. award Purdue U., 1975, Excellence in Tchg. award Inst. Noise Control Engring., 1989, Rsch. award Ohio State U., 1983, 87, 91, 96, 01, 06, Educator of Yr. award GM Tech. Edn. Program, 1998. Fellow ASME, Acoustical Soc. Am., Soc. Auto Engring.; mem. Inst. Noise Control Engring.(cert.), Am. Soc. Engring. Edn. (George Westinghouse award 1993). Achievements include patent for rolling door; development of new analytical and experimental techniques in machine dynamics, acoustics, vibration. Home: 4772 Belfield Ct Dublin OH 43017-2592 Office: Ohio State U Mech Engring Dept 201 W 19th Ave Columbus OH 43210 Office Phone: 614-292-9044. Business E-Mail: singh.3@osu.edu.

SINGH, SAHJENDRA NARAIN, electrical engineering educator, researcher; b. Patna, India, Jan. 7, 1943; came to U.S., 1969; s. Shyam N. and Yashoda Singh; m. Sobha Sinha, June 25, 1973; children: Himanshu Kumar, Manish Kumar. ME, Indian Inst. Sci., Bangalore, 1968; PhD, Johns Hopkins U., 1972. Asst. lectr. Regional Inst. Tech., Jamshedpur, India, 1965-66; rsch. scientist Indian Space Rsch. Orgn., Trivandrum, 1973-77; rsch. assoc. NASA Langley Rsch. Ctr., Hampton, Va., 1977-78; vis. prof. Fed. U. Santa Maria, Brazil, 1978-79; prof. Fed. U. Santa Catarina, Florianopolis, Brazil, 1980-83; sr. scientist Vigyan Rshc. Assocs., Hampton, 1983-86; prof. U. Nev., Las Vegas, 1986—. Rsch. assoc. AFOSR Summer Faculty, Edwards AFB, Calif., 1991, disting. summer faculty Naval Air Warfare Ctr., Pa., 1994-95, Naval Undersea Warfare Ctr., R.I., 1996-97, Naval Air Warfare Ctr., Md., 1998. Contbr. articles to profl. jours. NASA-NRC resident assoc. NRC, Hampton, 1977. Fellow AIAA (assoc.); mem. IEEE (sr.), IEEE Aerospace & Electronic Systems Soc. (control systems panel). Achievements include research on nonlinear systems and control theory, stability and control of aerospace vehicles & robotics. Office: U Nev Las Vegas 4505 S Maryland Pky Las Vegas NV 89154-9900

SINGH, SANDEEP, research scientist; s. Ram Bilash and Rita Singh; m. Roli Singh, Nov. 22, 2004. PhD, U. Cin., 2006. Sr. rsch. fellow I.I.T.Kanpur, Uttar Pradesh, India, 2002—05; rschr. U. Cin., 2006—. Achievements include research in fuel cell materials. Home: 579 Martin luther King Dr W Apt # 215 Cincinnati OH 45220

SINGH, SARABJEET, cardiologist; arrived in US, 2004; s. Jaswant Singh and Gurmit Kaur; m. Jasleen Duggal, Jan. 15, 2005. MB, Calcutta U. NRS Med. Coll. and affliated Hosps., India, 1999; MD, Lala Rajpat Rai Meml. Med. Coll. and Saradar Vallbh Bhai Patel Hosps., India, 2007; MD in Internal Medicine, Chgo. Med. Sch., 2007. Diplomate Am. Bd. Internal Medicine, 2007; cert. Ednl. Commn. Fgn. Med. Grads. 2003. Housestaff LLRM Med. Coll., Meerut, 2001—04, Chgo. Med. Sch. and affiliated Hosps., 2004—07, cardiology fellow, 2007—. Instr., Am. Heart Assn. advance cardiac life support Mt. Sinai Hosp., Chgo., 2007—. Contbr. articles to profl. jours. Souvenir com. Hypertension Soc. India, Delhi, 2002—03. Recipient Presdl. Poster award, 2005, 1st prize, World Congress Gastroenterology, 2002, Best of Best Sessions, Am. Heart Assn., 2007; Travel grants, Chgo. Med. Sch., 2004—07. Mem.: ACP, Internat. Med. Sci. Acad., Am. Soc. Nuc. Cardiology, Am. Heart Assn., Am. Coll. Cardiology, Sigma Xi. Sikh. Achievements include clinical cardiovascular research. Avocations: bicycling, billiards. Office: Chgo Med Sch 3333 Green Bay Rd North Chicago IL 60064 Personal E-mail: sarabjeetsingh_2000@yahoo.com.

SINGH, SATINDER P., medical educator, director; m. Lorraine. MBBS, U. Coll. Med. Sci., Shahdara, Delhi, 1984. Cert. in TB & chest diseases V.B. Patel Chest Rsch. Inst., 1988. Dir., cardiac ct UAB Health Sys., 2005—, dir., cardiothoracic abdominal imaging, 2005—, chief, cardiopulmonary radiology, 2007; assoc. prof. U. Ala. Health Sys., Birmingham, 2009—. Mem.: Radiol. Soc. N.Am. Office: Univ Ala Health Sys 619 S 19th St Birmingham AL 35233 Office Fax: 205-934-5688. Business E-Mail: ssingh@uabmc.edu.

SINGH, VIJAY, professional golfer; b. Lautoka, Fiji, Feb. 22, 1963; m. Andrea Seth Singh; 1 child, Qass Seth. Profl. golfer, 1993—. Player The President's Cup, 1994, 96, 98, 2000, 03, 05, World Cup, 2002. Hon. chairperson Nat. Golf Day, 1999. Recipient Samman award, Pravasi Bharatiya Divas, 2005, Byron Nelson award, PGA of America, 2004, Vardon Trophy, 2004; named Rookie of Yr., PGA Tour, 1993, Player of Yr., PGA European Tour, 2004, PGA of America, 2004, PGA Tour, 2004; named to World Golf Hall of Fame, 2006. Achievements include having 34 career PGA Tour victories and 23 international victories; winning PGA Tour Major Championships: PGA Championship, 1998, 2004, Masters Tournament, 2002; winning World Golf Championships: Buick Classic, 1993, 1995, Phoenix Open, 1995, 2000, Meml. Tournament, 1997, Buick Open, 1997, 2004, 2005, Spirit Internat., 1998, Honda Classic, 1999; Shell Houston Open, 2000, 2004, 2005, The Tour Championship, 2000, EDS Byron Nelson Championship, 2003, John Deere Classic, 2003, FUNAI Classic, 2003, AT&T Pebble Beach Nat. Pro-Am, 2004; HP Classic, 2004, Deutscche Bank Championship, 2004, 2008, Bell Canadian Open, 2004, 84 Lumber Classic, 2004, Chrysler Championship, 2004, Sony Open, 2005, Wachovia Championship, 2005; Barclays Classic, 2006, Mercedes Championships, 2007, Arnold Palmer Invitational, 2007, Bridgestone Invitational, 2008, The Barclays, 2008; set single season record for earnings, ranked No. 1 in the world, 2004; holds record for: most wins on PGA Tour after the age of 40, most wins by an international player. Avocations: snooker, cricket, rugby, soccer. Office: PGA Tour 112 TPC Blvd Ponte Vedra Beach FL 32802

SINGH, VIJAY PAL, civil engineer; b. Agra, India, July 15, 1946; came to U.S., 1970; s. Gurdayal and Bhagwan (Kuwari) S.; m. Anita Singh, Jan. 14, 1976; children: Vinay, Arti. BSE, U.P. Agrl. U., Pantnagar, India, 1967; MS, Guelph U., Can., 1970; PhD, Colo. State U., 1974; DSc, U. Witwatersrand, South Africa, 1998. Registered profl. engr., La.; registered profl. hydrologist Am. Inst. Hydrology. Asst. prof. N.Mex. Tech., Soccoro, 1974-77; assoc. rsch. prof. George Washington U., Washington, 1977-78; assoc. prof. Miss. State U., 1978-81, La. State U., Baton Rouge, 1981-83, prof. civil engring., 1983—, dir. water resources rsch. inst., 1984-86, Arthur K. Barton endowed prof., 1999—. Vis. prof. U. Wollongong, Australia, 1982, Vrije U., Brussels, 1982, 84, 85, 86, dept. water resources engring. Lund (Sweden) U., 1990, 92, 94, 95, U. Basilicata (Italy), 1990, 94, EPFL and ETH, Switzerland, 1990, 92, 95, U. Roorkee, India, 1997, Nanyang Tech. U., Singapore, 2000-2001; sr. rsch. engr. U.S. Army Corps Engrs., 1983, 86; cons. to nat. and internat. orgns.; internat. lectr.; keynote spkr. and chmn. numerous confs. sessions; dir. confs. and symposia. Author: Hydrologic Systems: vol. 1 Rainfall Runoff Modeling, 1988, vol. 2 Watershed Modeling, 1989, Elementary Hydrology, 1992, Dam-Breach Modeling Technology, 1996, Kinematic-Wave Modeling in Water Resources: Surface-Water Hydrology, 1996, Kinematic Wave Modeling in Water Resources: Environmental Hydrology, 1997, Entropy-Based Parameter Estimation in Hydrology, 1998, Design of Water Quality Monitoring Networks, 1999, Snow and Glacer Hydrology, 2000, SCS-CN Methodology, 2003, Water Resources Systems Planning and Management, 2003; contbr. chpts. to 50 books; editor 41 books; contbr. numerous articles to profl. jours. Founder G.B. Sch., Agra, 1994, FARA, Inc., 1998. Recipient 40 awards and numerous honors; grantee NSF, USDA, USDI, among others. Fellow ASCE, Am. Water Resources Assn., Indian Assn. Hydrologists, Instn. Engrs. India, Indian Water Resources Soc., Indian Soc. Agrl. Engrs.; mem. Am. Geophys. Union, Internat. Assn. Hydraulic Rsch., Internat. Assn. Hydrological Scis., Brit. Hyerological Soc., Mex. Acad. Sci., Mex. Acad. Engring., Ga. Acad. Sci., Ga. Fazisi Acad., Russian Acad. Water Mgmt. & Scis., Engring. Acad. Czech Rep., Hazard Forum, Indian Assn. Soil and Water Conservationists, Polish Acad. Sci, U. Guelph Alumni Assn., Colo. State U. Alumni Assn., Sigma Xi. Office: Dept Civil/Environ Engring La State U Baton Rouge LA 70803-0001 Home: 5100 Inverness Dr Bryan TX 77802-6095 Office Phone: 225-578-6697. Business E-Mail: ceing@lsu.edu.

SINGHAL, AVINASH CHANDRA, engineering administrator, educator; b. Aligarh, India, Nov. 4, 1939; s. Shiam Sunder and Pushpa Lata (Jindal) S.; m. Uma Rani Sharma, Sept. 5, 1967; children: Ritu Chanchal, Anita, Neil Raj. BSc, Agra U., India, 1957; BSc in Engring., St. Andrews U., Dundee, Scotland, 1959, degree (hon.) in engring., 1960; MS, MIT, 1961, CE, 1962, ScD, 1964; certificate in bus. mgmt., UCLA, 1971; postgrad., 2005. Registered profl. engr., N.Y., Que., Ariz. Rsch. engr. Kaman Aircraft, Burlington, Mass., 1964-65; prof. Laval U., Quebec, Can., 1965-69; asst. program mgr. TRW, Redondo Beach, Calif., 1969-71; mgr. GE, Phila., 1971-72; mgr. tech. svcs. Engrs. India Ltd., New Delhi, 1972-74; project engr. Weidlinger Assocs., NYC, 1974-77; prof. Ariz. State U., Tempe, 1977—; dir. Cen. Bldg. Rsch. Inst., 1992-93. Dir. Earthquake Rsch. Lab., Ariz. State U., Tempe, 1978—89, grad. coord. structural engring., 1991—92, senator acad. senate, 1995—98, chmn. governance grievance, 1995—96, faculty ombudsman, 1996—97, coord. Computer Aided Design and Modeling, 1997—98, com. acad. freedom and tenure, 1998—99, com. promotion and tenure; cons. McDonnel Aircraft Corp., St. Louis, 1977—78, Sperry Corp., 1979—80, McDonnell Douglas Helicopter Co., 1990—91, Ariz. Nuc. Power Plant, 1991—92; U.S. del. U.S./China Workshop on Arch Dams, Beijing, 1987; Can. del. Shell Structures, USSR, Ukraine, 1964; session chmn. Internat. Conf. on Soil Dynamics and Earthquake Engring., Karlsruhe, Germany, 1991; rsch. prof. Nat. Ctrl. U. Taiwan, 1990; vis. prof. U. Melbourne, Australia, 1983—84, U. Auckland, New Zealand, 1983—84; nodal dir. wood substitute rsch. program, India, 1992—93; instr. Indian Inst. Tech., Madras, 1997—98, Indian Inst. Sci., Bangalore, 1997—98. Mem. editl. bd. Soil Dynamics and Earthquake Engring., 1991—, Advances in Earthquake Engring., 1995—; reviewer Jour. Psychol. Reports, Perceptual and Motor Skills; contbr. Nuclear Waste Storage, 1986, (proc. publ.) Earthquake Behavior of Buried Pipelines, 1989, Wood Substitute: A National Priority, 1992, System Flexibility and Reflected Pressures, 1993, Simulation of Blast Pressures on Flexible Panels, 1994, Dynamic Analysis of Dams with Nonlinear Slip Joints, 1998, Performance of Retrofit Arch Dams, 1998, Ariz. Emergency Ctr. Retrofit, 1998, others; editor: Seismic Performance of Pipelines & Storage Tanks, 1985, Recent Advances in Lifeline Earthquake Engineering, 1987, Seismic Ground Motions Response, Repair and Instrumentation of Pipes and Bridges, 1992; contbr. articles to Jour. Performance of Constructed Facilities, ASCE, Jour. Computers and Structures, Jour. ASME, Jour. Aerospace Engring. ASCE; reviewer, bd. editors Jour. Earthquake Engring. and Structural Dynamics, Structural Engring. Papers Jour. ASCE. Bd. dirs., pres. Las Estadas Homeowner's Assn., Tempe, 1996-97; chmn. bd. dirs. India Assn. Greater Phoenix, 1985-86; pres. India Assn. Greater Boston, 1964-65; v.p., treas. Dobson Ranch Homeowners Assn., Mesa, Ariz., 1988-91; founding mem. Asian Am. Assn. Ariz., Phoenix, 1987-89; founding mem., pres. Asian Am. Faculty Assn., Ariz. State U., Tempe, 1986-88; cons. UN Devel. Program New Delhi, 1991-92. McLintock fellow MIT, 1960, Carnegie fellow MIT, 1960-63, fellow Royal Astron. Soc., London, 1961-64, rsch. fellow Kobe U., Japan, 1990; Denninson scholar Instn. Civil Engrs., London, 1959; Henry Adams Rsch. medal Structural Engrs., London, 1972; grantee Can. Def. Rsch. Bd., 1966-69, NSF, 1978-82, Engring. Found., 1978-79, U.S. Army Corps Engrs., 1984-86, U.S. Dept. Interior, 1986-88, Office Naval Rsch., 1994. Ariz. Dept. Emergency Mgmt., 1997-98; recipient 1st prize bridge bldg. Instn. Strucural Engrs., Merit award Inst. Engrs., India. Fellow ASCE, Ctrl. Bldg. Rsch. Inst. (chmn. mgmt. coun., chmn. APEX com.), Sigma Xi, Tau Beta Pi, Chi Epsilon. Achievements include research in computer modeling, blast effects on structures, in lifeline engineering, earthquake strengthening of deteriorated dams, steel and concrete buildings, bridges, materials, and non-linear finite element dynamics. Home: 2258 W Monterey Ave Mesa AZ 85202-7330 Office: Ariz State U Dept Civil Engring 2258 W Monterey Cir Mesa AZ 85202-7330 Personal E-mail: univprof579@cox.net. Business E-Mail: singhal@asu.edu. *Service to mankind and love for the family and friends is the key to success and happiness.*

SINGHAL, SUBHASH C., engineer; BE, Indian Inst. Sci., 1965; BS, Agra U., 1963; PhD in Materials Sci. and Engring., U. Pa., 1969; MBA, U. Pitts., 1977. Mgr. fuel cell technology Siemens Westinghouse Power Corp.; Battelle fellow, dir. fuel cells rsch. Pacific N.W. Nat. Lab., US Dept. Energy, Richland, Wash., 2000—. Contbr. articles to profl. jours. Fellow: AAAS, ASM Internat., Electrochem. Soc., Am. Ceramic Soc.; mem.: NAE, Mineral, Metals and Materials Soc. Office: Pacific NW Nat Lab PO Box 999 Richland WA 99352 Home Phone: 509-628-2365; Office Phone: 509-375-6738. E-mail: singhal@pnl.gov.

SINGHVI, SURENDRA SINGH, financial consultant; b. Jodhpur, Rajasthan, India, Jan. 16, 1942; arrived in US, 1962, naturalized, 1986; s. Rang Raj and Ugam Kanwar (Surana) Singhvi; m. Sushila Bhandari, July 7, 1965; children: Seema, Sandeep. B in Commerce, Rajasthan U., 1961; MBA, Atlanta U., 1963; PhD, Columbia U., NYC, 1967. CPA, cert. mgmt. acct. Asst. prof. fin. Miami U., Oxford, Ohio, 1967-69, assoc. prof. fin., 1969-70; adj. prof. fin., 1970-95; fin. mgr. ARMCO Inc., Middletown, Ohio, 1970-79, asst. treas., 1979-83, gen. fin. mgr., 1983-86; v.p. and treas. Edison Bros. Stores, Inc., St. Louis, 1986-90; pres. Singhvi & Assocs., Inc., Dayton, Ohio, 1990—. Bd. dirs. Columbia Indsl. Sales Corp., Hauer Music Co., Oasis Property Inc., Om Hospitality, Inc. Author: Planning for Capital Investment, 1980; co-editor: Frontiers fo Financial Management, 4th edit., 1984, Global Finance 2000 - A Handbook of Strategy and Organization (The Conference Board), 1996; contbr. articles to profl. jours. Trustee South Ctrl. Ohio Minority Bus. Coun., 2000—. Recipient Chancellor's Gold medal, Rajasthan U., Ahimsa (Non-Violence) award, Fedn. Jaina Assns. N.Am., 1999. Mem.: Dayton Minority Supplier Devel. Coun. (dir. 1997—, chmn. 2000), Fin. Mgmt. Assn., Fin. Execs. Inst., Inst. Mgmt. Accts. (Bayer Silver medal 1978), India Club (pres. Dayton chpt. 1980), Rotary (dir. internat. program Middletown chpt. 1973—86, Dayton chpt. 1995—, treas., dir. 2001—02). Achievements include established two endowment fund at Columbia University in NY in 1970 and at Miami University in 1975. Avocations: swimming, kanasta, travel, writing. Home and Office: Singhvi and Assocs Inc 439 Ridge Line Ct Dayton OH 45458-9546 Office Phone: 937-885-7414. Personal E-mail: ssinghvi@yahoo.com.

SINGLA, DINENDER K., science educator, consultant; s. Lal Chand and Maya Rani Singla; m. Reetu D. Bansal; children: Reetish K., Danush. PhD, Postgrad. Inst. Chandigarh, Punjab, India, 1996. Asst. prof. U. Vt., Burlington, 2004—07; assoc. prof. U. Ctrl. Fla., Orlando, 2007—. None. Grantee, NIH. Fellow: Am. Heart Assn. Home: 3019 Lake Jean Dr Orlando FL 32817 Office: Univ Ctrl Fla # 2O 4000 Central Blvd Orlando FL 32816 Business E-Mail: dsingla@mail.ucf.edu.

SINGLETARY, ALVIN D., lawyer; b. Sept. 27, 1942; s. Alvin E. and Alice (Pastoret) Singletary; m. Judy Louise Singletary, Dec. 3, 1983; children: Kimberly Dawn, Shane David, Kelly Diane. BA, La. State U., 1964; JD, Loyola U., New Orleans, 1969. Bar: La. 1969, U.S. Dist. Ct. (ea. dist.) La. 1972, U.S. Ct. Appeals (5th cir.) 1972, U.S. Ct. Appeals (11 cir.) 1981, U.S. Ct. Internat. Trade 1981, U.S. Ct. Customs and Patent Appeals 1982, U.S. Supreme Ct. 1978. Instr. Delgado Coll., New Orleans, 1976—77; sole practice Slidell, La., 1970—. Spl. asst. dist. atty 22d Judicial Dist. Ct., Parish of St. Tammany, La.; sec., treas. St. Tammany Pub. Trust Fin. Authority, 1978—2002. Chmn. sustaining membership enrollment Cypress dist. Boy Scouts Am., 1989—; treas. Slidell Centennial commn.; councilman-at-large City of Slidell, 1978—2002, interim mayor, 1985; mem. Dem. State Ctrl. Com., 1978—82; mem. Rep. State Ctrl. Com. Dist. 76, La., 1996—2000; del. La.Constl. Conv., 1972—73; chmn. Together We Build Program First Baptist Ch. of Slidell, La.; bd. dir. St. Tammany Coun. on Aging. Mem.: Lions, Delta Theta Phi. Baptist. Office: PO Box 1158 Slidell LA 70459-1158

SINGLETARY, DEJUAN THERESA, child and adolescent psychiatrist; b. Berkeley, Calif., Apr. 7, 1965; d. Wilbert Paul and Frances Mahala Thomas; m. Craig Singletary, Jan. 31, 2003. AA in Gen. Edn., Chalot Coll., Hayward, Calif., 1986; BS in Physiology, U. Calif., Davis, 1989; MD, U. So. Calif., LA, 1995. Diplomate Am. Bd. Psychiatry and Neurology. Intern LAC/USC Med. Ctr., LA, 1995—96; resident U. Calif.-Davis Dept. Psychiatry, 1996—98; fellow U. Ariz. Health Sci. Ctr., Tucson, 1998—2000; child and adolescent psychiatrist Carmel Psychiat. Assocs., Charlotte, NC, 2001—03, N.E. Psychiat. and Psychol. Inst., Concord/Harrisburg, NC, 2003—05; Elon Homes for Children, 2005, The Keys of the Carolinas, Charlotte, 2005, DeJuan T. Singletary LLC/St. Charles Med. Ctr., Bend, Oreg., 2005—. Cons. Best Care Treatment Svcs., Madras, Oreg., 2006—, Luth. Family Svcs., 2006—. Mem.: AMA (polit. action com. 2000—), Am. Acad. Child and Adolescent Psychiatrists, Am. Psychiat. Assn. (Psychiatry Resident of the Yr. 1999), Golden Key (life). Avocations: gourmet cooking, antiques, travel. Office: 2100 NE Wyatt Ct Ste 202 Bend OR 97701

SINGLETARY, ELOISE, business educator; b. Lake City, SC, Aug. 21, 1942; d. Otto and Lillie (Barr) S. BS, Fayetteville State U., 1969; postgrad., Winthrop U., 1973, U. Va., 1974; EdM in Cmty. and Occup. Programs in Edn., U. SC, Columbia, 1978, EdM in Sch. Adminstrn., 1982; postgrad., SC State U., Orangeburg, 1995. Nat. bd. cert. tchr., 2002. Bus. tchr. Lake View (S.C.) High Sch., 1969-76, Hemingway (S.C.) High Sch., 1976-83, Florence (S.C.) Career Ctr., 1983—. Advisor Hemingway High Sch. Newspaper, 1976-83, Future Bus. Leaders Am., Hemingway, 1976-79. Pres. Dem. Caucus, Lake City, 1984-85, Dem. precinct 2, Lake City, 1984-90; del. State and Local Convs., Columbia and Florence, S.C., 1984-85. Named Lifetime Dep. Gov., 1989, Two Thousand Notable Am. Women Hall of Fame, 1989, Most Admired Decade, Am. Biog. Inst., 1992. Mem. NEA, ASCD, NAFE, NAACP (life), Nat. Bus. Edn. Assn. (Merit award 1969), So. Bus. Edn. Assn., S.C. Bus. Edn. Assn., Fayetteville State U. Alumni Assn., U. S.C. Alumni Assn. (life), Joint Stock Lodge #151 (sec. 1972—), Alpha Kappa Alpha. Baptist. Avocations: reading, spectator sports, tennis, sewing and collecting patterns. Home: PO Box 208 Lake City SC 29560-0208 Office: Florence Career Ctr 126 E Howe Springs Rd Florence SC 29505-5004

SINGLETARY, MIKE, professional football coach, retired professional football player; b. Houston, Oct. 9, 1958; m. Kim Singletary; children: Kristen, Matthew, Jill, Jackie, Brooke, Becky, John. BA in Mgmt., Baylor U., 1981. Middle linebacker Chgo. Bears, 1981-93; linebackers coach Balt. Ravens, 2003—04; asst. head coach, linebackers coach San Francisco 49ers, 2005—08, head coach, 2008—. Motivational spkr. Wash. Speakers Bur. Author: Calling the Shots, 1986; co-author (with Jerry B. Jenkins): Singletary on Singletary, 1991; co-author: (with Russ Pate) Daddy's Home at Last: What it Takes for Dads to Put Families First, 1999; co-author: (with Jay Carty) Mike Singletary One-on-One: The Determination That Inspired Him to Give God His Very Best, 2005. Named NFL Defensive Player of Yr., AP, 1985, 88, Walter Payton Man of Yr., 1990; named to Sporting News Coll. All-Am. team, 1980, NFL Pro Bowl team, 1983-92, Sporting News All-Pro team, 1984-89, 91, College Football Hall of Fame, 1995, Pro Football Hall of Fame, 1998. Achievements include being a member of Super Bowl XX Championship winning Chicago Bears, 1985. Office: San Francisco 49ers 4949 Centennial Blvd Santa Clara CA 95054*

SINGLETON, DAVID MICHAEL, chemist, researcher; b. Upton, Poole, Dorset, Eng., Nov. 3, 1939; came to U.S., 1965; s. Hubert Frederick and Marjorie Clare (Clutterbuck) S.; m. Elizabeth Ann Sloan, Sept. 14, 1962; children: David Arthur, Katherine Ann. BSc, U. London, 1960; PhD, McMaster U., Hamilton, Ont., Can., 1965. Postdoctoral fellow Case Inst. Tech., Cleve., 1965-67; rsch. chemist Shell Devel. Co., Emeryville, Calif., 1967-72, Houston, 1972-74, sr. rsch. chemist, 1974-75, 76-92; exch. scientist Shell Rsch. BV, Amsterdam, The Netherlands, 1975-76; sr. rsch. chemist Shell Chem. Co., Houston, 1992-99, ret., 1999. Adj. prof. U. Houston, 1985-91; mem. adv. bd. Tex. State Tech. Coll., Waco, 1994—; chmn. organometallic chemistry Gordon Conf., Newport, R.I., 1987; lectr. McMaster U., Queen's U., RWTH Aachen, Tulane U., U. Houston. Contbr. articles to profl. jours. Fellow Royal Soc. Chemistry; mem. Am. Chem. Soc. (chair Greater Houston sect. 1998, councilor 2003—, SW Regional Indsl. Innovation award, 2003), S.W. Catalysis Soc. (sec. 1978, chair 1982), Archaeol. Inst. Am., Coun. on Brit. Archaeology, N.Y. Acad. Scis. (mem. adv. bd. Catalysis Conf. 1978), Curling Club Houston (treas. 1995-2007). Achievements include 24 U.S. patents and 2 British patents. Personal E-mail: dsingleton5@comcast.net.

SINGLETON, DONALD EDWARD, retired journalist; b. Morristown, NJ, Nov. 8, 1936; s. Edward Leslie and Charlotte (Angerbauer) S.; m. Maureen Ann McNiff, Aug. 8, 1959 (div. 1977); children: Nancy Ann, Mark Aram, Jill Susan. Student, Fairleigh Dickinson U., 1955-58. Reporter Dover (N.J.) Advance, 1959-61, Morristown Daily Record, 1961-63, Newark Eve. News, 1963-64; feature reporter-writer N.Y. Daily News, 1964—2007; ret., 2007. Organizer Com. to Save Church Sq. Park, Hoboken, N.J.; vice chmn. Hoboken Environment Com.; mem. due process com. ACLU., Mem. bd. edn., City of Hoboken, 1974-77. Recipient Pub. Service award N.Y. Council Civic Affairs, 1967; President's Distinguished Service award N.Y.C. Council, 1969; Newspaper award merit Women's Press Club N.Y.C., 1970, 79; citation VFW, 1970; Heywood Broun Meml. award Am. Newspaper Guild, 1970; Silver medal for pub. service journalism N.Y. chpt. Pub. Relations Soc. Am., 1970; certificate merit Am. Bar Assn., 1971; Page One award Newspaper Guild N.Y., 1970; Feature award Newspaper Reporters Assn. N.Y., 1972; Consistent Excellence award Uniformed Firefighters Assn., 1991. Mem. Am. Newspaper Guild. Clubs: Press (N.Y.C.). Home: 366 Ogden Ave Jersey City NJ 07307-1115 Office: 220 E 42nd St New York NY 10017-5806 Personal E-mail: donaldnj@comcast.net. *In reporting, I try very hard to avoid gathering facts in such a way as to fulfill a preconception. I also attempt to force myself to review constantly my opinions about my subjects, and to keep my mind as open as possible. In writing, I try to ask myself the following questions regularly: "Is this what I really believe? Or am I simply writing this way because I believe that this is what some other person or group would like me to write?" Unless I can answer the first question in the affirmative, and the second in the negative, I am not satisfied with a particular story.*

SINGLETON, HARRY MICHAEL, lawyer; b. Meadville, Pa., Apr. 10, 1949; s. Getdins T. and Rose Ann Singleton; children: Harry M. Jr., Leah Rose. BA, Johns Hopkins U., 1971; JD, Yale U., 1974. Bar: D.C. 1975, Pa. 1976, Calif. 1999, Md. 1999, U.S. Dist. Ct. D.C. 1975, U.S. Dist. Ct. Md. 2001, U.S. Ct. Appeals (D.C. cir.) 1975, U.S. Ct. Mil. Appeals 1975; lic. realtor Va., 2004, D.C., 2004. Assoc. Houston & Gardner, Washington, 1974-75, Covington & Burling, Washington, 1976-77; atty. FTC, Washington, 1975-76; dep. minority counsel Com. on D.C./U.S. Ho. of Reps., Washington, 1977-79, minority chief counsel, staff dir., 1979-81; dep. asst. sec. U.S. Dept. Commerce, Washington, 1981-82; asst. sec. U.S. Dept. Edn., Washington, 1982-86; pres. Harry M. Singleton & Assocs., Washington, 1986-91; pvt. practice law Washington, 1991—; pres. Singleton Entertainment, LLC, Washington, 1999-2000; pres., gen. counsel Single Source Tech. Solutions, LLC, Washington, 2001—03; realtor DC, 2004—, Va. Assn. Realtors, 2004—, Nat. Assn. Realtors, 2004—, Md., 2008—. Legis. cons. Am. Enterprise Inst., Washington, 1975. Pres. bd. trustees Barney Neighborhood House, Washington, 1978-80; corp. bd. dirs. Children's Hosp. Nat. Med. Ctr., Washington, 1984-88; mem. crime com. Boys and Girls Clubs of Greater Washington, 1994-97; mem. D.C. Rep. State Com., 1991—2004, Rep. Nat. Com., 1992-2000, R.N.C. exec. coun., 1993-95, resolutions com., 1997-2000; mem. Rep. Nat. Hispanic Assembly Washington, 1991-92. Mem. Rep. Nat. Lawyers Assn. (bd. dirs. D.C. chpt. 1990-91), Coun. of 100 Black Reps. (bd. dirs. 1991-92), D.C. Black Rep. Coun. (chmn. 1992-93), Rep. Nat. African-Am. Coun. (nat. chmn. 1993-2001), D.C. Rep. Nat. African-Am. Coun. (chmn. 1993-2001). Republican. Presbyterian. Office: 1250 Connecticut Ave NW Ste 200 Washington DC 20036

SINGLETON, JONETTA WILLIAMS, poet, retired special education educator; b. Bunkie, La., June 9, 1920; d. Josephus and Carrie Smith Williams; m. Jonetta W. Singleton; children: Carrie Elizabeth, Lafayette Jr. AA, Balt. Jr. Coll., 1971; BS in Biology and English, Coppins State Coll., 1973, Master's in Spl. Edn., 1974, Master's in Counseling, 1975. Tchr. Balt. Pub. Sch., Baltimore City, Md., 1974—94; ret., 1994. Poet: Poems from the Heart, 2004. Active ARC. Mem.: AAUW, ACLU. Democrat. Methodist.

SINGLETON, KEN, sportscaster, retired professional baseball player; b. NYC, June 10, 1947; m. Suzanne Molino; 4 children. Attended, Hofstra U., Hempstead, NY. Outfielder NY Mets, 1970—71, Montreal Expos, 1972—74, Balt. Orioles, 1975—84; ret., 1984; analyst, Montreal Expos broadcasts The Sports Network, 1985—86; analyst, play-by-play announcer CIQC Radio, Montreal, 1991—96; lead analyst FOX Sports, 1996, 1997; analyst Major League Baseball Internat., 1997, 1998; analyst, play-by-play announcer, NY Yankees broadcasts Madison Sq. Garden Network, NY, 1997—2002, Yankees Entertainment and Sports Network, NY, 2002—. Recipient Roberto Clemente award, 1982; named Most Valuable Oriole, 1975, 1977, 1979; named to Am. League All-Star Team, Maj. League Baseball, 1977, 1979, 1981. Achievements include leading the National League in: on-base percentage, 1973; leading the American League in: plate appearances, 1975; member of the World Series championship winning Baltimore Orioles, 1983. Office: Yankees Entertainment and Sports Network LLC The Chrysler Bldg 405 Lexington Ave 36th Fl New York NY 10174-3699*

SINGLETON, MARVIN AYERS, state legislator, otolaryngologist; b. Baytown, Tex., Oct. 7, 1939; s. Henry Marvin and Mary Ruth Singleton. BA, U. of the South, 1962; MD, U. Tenn., 1966. Diplomate Am. Bd. Otolaryngology. Intern City of Memphis Hosps., 1966-67; resident in surgery Highland Alameda City Hosp., Oakland, Calif., 1967-68; resident in otolaryngology U. Tenn. Hosp., Memphis, 1968-71; fellow in otolaryngic pathology Armed Forces Inst. Pathology, Washington, 1971; fellow in otologic surgery U. Colo. at Gallup (N.Mex.) Indian Med. Ctr., 1972; practice medicine specializing in otolaryngology/allergies Joplin, Mo., 1972—. Founder, operator Home and Farm Investments, Joplin, 1975—, staff mem. Freeman Hosp., Dameron Hosp. Stockton, St. John's Hosp., Joplin; cons. in otolaryngology Mo. Crippled Children's Service; pres. Ozark Mfg. Co., Inc., Joplin; mem. St. Joaquin Commn. on Aging, 2005—; dir. St. Mary's Interfaith Svcs., Stockton, 2007—; med. dir. Health Choice NW Mo. Mem. Internat. Arabian Racing Bd., 1983-88; mem. Mo. State Senate, 1990-2003; del. Rep. Nat. Conv., 1988, 92. Served with USNG, 1966-72. Fellow Am. Coll. Surgeons, Am. Acad. Otolaryngologic Allergy (past pres.), Am. Assn. Acad. Asthma, Allergy and Immunology; mem. AMA (Mo. del.), Mo. State Med. Assn., So. Med. Assn., Mo. State Allergy Assn., Ear Nose & Throat Soc. Mo. (past. pres.), Calif. Med. Assn. (trustee 2005—), San Joaquin Med. Soc. (pres. 2006-07), Masons (32d degree), Sigma Alpha Epsilon, Phi Theta Kappa, Phi Chi. Republican. Episcopalian. Home: 1637 W Swain Rd Stockton CA 95207-4172 Office: 7373 W Ln Stockton CA 95210 Home Phone: 209-951-7273; Office Phone: 209-476-5623. Personal E-mail: senatorsingleton@hotmail.com.

SINGLETON, TANYA, nursing educator; b. Tuscaloosa, Ala., July 23, 1958; d. Crimpton and Inez Virginia (Powe) Singleton; children: David, Edward, Brittany Summerhill; m. Michael B. Brown, Nov. 2003. BS in Nursing, U. Ala., 1982; MPH in Maternal-Child Health, George Washington U., 1997. Cert. high risk perinatal nurse, childbirth educator Lamaze; cert. lactation cons. Commd. 2d lt. U.S. Army, 1986, advanced through grades to capt., 1988; staff nurse labor and delivery Druid City Hosp., Tuscaloosa, 1982—83, Huntsville (Ala.) Hosp., 1983—86; perinatal counselor Cen. North Ala. Health Svcs. Inc., Huntsville, 1984—86; staff nurse Tripler Army Med. Ctr., Honolulu, 1986—90; asst. head nurse newborn nursery, staff nurse labor and delivery, childbirth counselor and inpatient lactation cons. DeWitt Army Hosp., Ft. Belvoir, Va., 1990—92; maternal infant health educator Providence Hosp., Washington, 1992—95; instr. Montgomery Coll. Sch. of Nursing, 1994; founder Sacred Conceptions Childbirth and Parenting Svcs., 1996—; exec. dir. Women's Wellness Ctr., Fredericksburg, Va., 1999—2000; tobacco cessation coord. MediCorp Health Sys., Fredericksburg, 2001—03; perinatal bereavement coord. Prince William Health Sys., 2002—04, nurse recruiter, 2004—, 2004—. Mem. low risk neonatal test com. Nat. Certification Corp., 1994—95; rsch. assoc. NIH-DC Initiative to Decrease Infant Mortality in D.C. Pride in Parenting Study, 1995—; pres. Rappahannock Teen Abstinence Program; organizer Rappahannock Healthy Families Initiative Planning Bd., Ptnrs. in Prevention VA Planning Dist. XVI. Chair health com. Stafford County br. NAACP. Maj. USAR, 1995—2000, instr. 91C program 80th Tng. Divsn. USAR, res. comp. cmdr. 91W transition program USAR, 2001—04, Ft. Lee. Mem. ANA, Assn. Women's Health, Obstetric and Neonatal Nurses, Internat. Childbirth Edn. Assn.,

Sigma Theta Tau., Lamaze Internat. Home: 6917 Smith Station Rd Spotsylvania VA 22553-1808 Home Phone: 540-898-0560. Personal E-mail: singmo40@aol.com. Business E-Mail: tanya.singleton@medicorp.org.

SINGLETON, TERESA, engineering educator; b. High Point, NC, Nov. 29, 1964; d. Betty Ann McDuffie; 1 child, Shakyrah Lynnette. PhD, U. Md., Balt., 1996. Postdoc. fellow NIH, Bethesda, Md., 1996—99; asst. to assoc. prof. Del. State U., Dover, 1999—2005; assoc. prof. Winston-Salem State U., NC, 2005—, prin. investigator, 2005—. Mem.: NIH (grant 2007—), Am. Soc. Microbiology, Alpha Kappa Alpha Sorority Inc. (Winston-Salem) (grad. mem., Phi Omega Chpt. 2005). Democrat. Baptist. Office: Winston-Salem State Univ 601 Martin Luther King Jr Dr Winston Salem NC 27110 Office Fax: 336-750-3094. Business E-Mail: singletont@wssu.edu.

SINGLETON, WILLIAM DEAN, publishing executive; b. Graham, Tex., Aug. 1, 1951; s. William Hyde and Florence E. (Myrick) S.; m. Adrienne Casale, Dec. 31, 1983; children: William Dean II, Paige, Adam Nicholas. Student, Tyler Jr. Coll., Tex., El Centro Coll., Dallas; BS, U. Tex., Arlington. Vice chmn., CEO MediaNews Group Inc., Denver, 1983—. Chmn. and pub. Denver Post; chmn. bd. Denver Newspaper Agency; pub. Salt Lake City Tribune; bd. dir. Associated Press, chmn. bd. dir., 2006—; former chmn. Newspaper Assn. Am. Mem. Salvation Army, Am. Heart Assn. of Ft. Bend County. Recipient Cmty. Cultural Enhancement award, Mizel Mus., 2009. Mem. Newspaper Assn. Am. (bd. govs.), So. Newspapers Assn., New Eng. Newspaper Assn., NJ Press Assn., Tex. Daily Newspaper Assn., Greater Houston Partnership Assn. Baptist. Office: Denver Post 101 W Colfax Ave Denver CO 80202*

SINGLETON-WOOD, ALLAN JAMES, communications executive; b. Newport, Monmouthshire, Eng., Feb. 13, 1933; arrived in Can., 1968; s. Charles James and Violet Anne (Bond) S.-W.; m. Joan Davies, June 23, 1956; children: Ceri, Glendon. Student, London U., 1949-51. TV and radio musical dir., 1953-57; TV producer, 1957-61; freelance producer for BBC, 1962-64; indsl. advt. mgr. Western Mail, Cardiff, Wales, 1964; advt. dir. Voice of Brit. Industry Mags., London, 1966; mktg. svcs. exec. The Sun and The People, I.P.C. Newspapers, London, 1966-68; mktg. svcs. mgr. Fin. Post, Toronto, Ont., Can., 1969-71, rsch. mgr., 1971-76, nat. sales mgr., 1976-77; pub. Fin. Post Mag., 1978-79, dir. advt. sales Fin. Post divsn., 1980-83; pub. Small Bus. Mag., 1983-87; v.p. pub. Bedford House Ltd., Toronto, 1987-88; pub. Small Bus. mag., v.p. CB Media Ltd., Toronto, 1988—; v.p. pub. Can. Bus. and Small Bus. mags., Who's Who in Can. Bus., Who's Who in Can. Fin., 1989—; corp. pub., gen. mgr. Sentry Comm., Willowdale, Ont., 1991-92; sr. group pub. Bus. Publs. divsn. MacLean Hunter Ltd., Toronto, 1992-93; pres. Can. Productivity divsn. CB Media Ltd., Toronto, 1994-96; pres., CEO Singleton-Wood Comm. Inc., Victoria, B.C., Canada, 1996—. Pres., CEO, founder Can. Info. Productivity Awards, 1994—2001; lectr., cons. in field. Composer: contemporary music including title theme of Swing High, BBC nat. network series, 1953-57. Mem. Anglican Catholic Ch. Achievements include development of first computer media evaluation program for Canadian advertising industry. Home and Office: 12-14 Erskine Ln Victoria BC V82 757 Canada Office Phone: 250-383-8562. E-mail: asingleton-wood@shaw.ca.

SINGLEY, JOHN EDWARD, JR., retired environmental scientist, consultant; b. Wildwood, NJ, July 31, 1924; s. John Edward Singley and Dorothy Mae (Pfrommer) S.; children: Gladys, Ann, Margaret, Patricia; m. June Walden Calohan, Apr. 28, 2001; stepchildren: Daniel, Christopher Calohan. BS, Ga. Inst. Tech, 1950; MS, Ga. Inst. Tech., 1952; PhD, U. Fla., 1966. Chemist Redstone Arsenal, Huntsville, Ala., 1950-51; dir. tech. svs. Tenn. Corp., College Park, Ga., 1951-64; lectr. chemistry Ga. State U., Atlanta, 1954-64, assoc. prof., 1964-67; prof. environ. engring. sci. U. Fla., Gainesville, 1967-90, prof. emeritus, 1990—; dir. TREEO Ctr., Gainesville, 1978-86; v.p. James M. Montgomery, Cons. Engrs., Inc., Gainesville, 1984-93, Montgomery Watson Cons. Engrs. Inc., Gainesville, 1993-96; sr. v.p. Environ. Scis. Engring. Inc., Gainesville, 1977-84; prin. Water and Air Rsch., Gainesville, 1970-77; v.p. Metcalf & Eddy, Gainesville, 1996-99; ret., 1999. Cons. Carollo Engrs., Sarasota, Fla., Jones, Edmunds Assocs., Gainesville. Patentee in field of polymers. Mem. Fulton County Rep. Exec. Com., 1962-64; mem. founding bd. Water for People, 1990-92. With USN, 1943-45. Recipient Donald R. Boyd award Met. Water Agys., 1992. Fellow Am. Inst. Chemists, Inst. Water and Environ. Mgmt.; mem. Am. Water Works Assn. (hon., life, bd. dirs. 1984-87, exec. com. 1986-87, 89-93, v.p. 1989-90, pres.-elect 1990-91, pres. 1991-92, Fuller award 1974, rsch. award 1983, Abel Wolman Excellence award 1995, Disting. Pub. Svc. award 1995, Water Industry Hall of Fame 2000), Fla. Water and Pollution Control Operators Assn. (Flanigan award 1979), Nat. Lime Assn. (Recognition award), Internat. Water Supply Assn., Nat. Assn. Corrosion Engrs., Internat. Ozone Assn. (bd. dirs. 1985-93). Clubs: Gainesville, Civitan (pres. 1972, lt. gov. Fla. dist. 1973-76). Presbyterian. Office: 1719 NW 23rd Ave PHE Gainesville FL 32605-3027 Home and Office: 2474 NW 77th Blvd #4007 Gainesville FL 32606 E-mail: h2odoceds@aol.com.

SINHA, AUM C., language educator; m. Corazon C. Sinha. BA in English with honors, Bhagalpur U., India, 1966; MA in English, Patna U., India, 1969; MA in Linguistics, U. Poona, India, 1971; MA in English, Eastern N.Mex. U., 1975; PhD in English-Linguistics, Okla. State U., Stillwater, 1980. Assoc. prof. English U. Tex., Brownsville, 2003—. Mem.: TESOL Internat., Linguistics Soc. India (life), Linguistics Soc. of Philippines (life), Pi Gamma Mu. Office: U Tex 80 Fort Brown Brownsville TX 78520

SINHA, BIKASH KUMAR, mechanical engineer, researcher; b. Patna, Bihar, India, Dec. 14, 1947; came to U.S., 1970; s. Kedar Nath and Shanti S.; m. Asha Sinha, Jan. 14, 1976; children— Monica, Seema. B.Sc. with honors, St. Xavier's Coll., 1965; B.Tech. with honors, Indian Inst. Tech., Kharagpur, 1968; M.A. Sci., U. Toronto, 1970; Ph.D., Rensselaer Poly. Inst., Troy, N.Y., 1973. Postdoctoral fellow McGill U., Montreal, 1973-74; vis. asst. prof., sr. research assoc. Rensselaer Poly. Inst., 1975-79; mem. profl. staff, program leader Schlumberger-Doll Research, Ridgefield, Conn., 1979—. Contbr. articles to profl. jours. Patentee stress compensated quartz resonators, surface acoustic wave sensors. Mem. IEEE, Tau Beta Pi. Current work: Research interests include wave propagation in piezoelectric solids, electroacoustic devices for applications in the design of resonators, transducers, pressure and temperature sensors. Subspecialties: Theoretical and applied mechanics; Acoustics. Home: 39 Topledge Rd West Redding CT 06896-1807

SINHA, NEETI, biophysicist, researcher; married; 1 child. PhD, U. Oxford, England, 1998. Postdoctoral rschr. NIH, Frederick, Md., 1998—2003; assoc. rsch. scientist Johns Hopkins U., Balt., 2003—. Asst. dir. Ctrl. Drug Rsch. Inst., Lucknow, India, 2004. Author: (book) Absolute: Multidimensional Beingness, 2006; mem. editl. bd.: Protein and Peptide Letters, Current Protein and Peptide Science, Open Biochemistry Journal, International Reviewers Panel Medical Science Monitor; contbr. articles to profl. jours. Office: Johns Hopkins U Mudd Hall 3400 N Charles St Baltimore MD 21218

SINHA, PAWAN, research scientist, educator, entrepreneur; B Tech, Indian Inst. Tech., New Delhi, 1988, MS, 1992; PhD in Computer Sci., MIT, 1995. Co-founder Imagen, Inc.; rsch. fellow Max Planck Inst.; asst. prof., psychology U. Wis., Madison; assoc. prof., vision and computational neuroscience, dept. brain and cognitive sciences MIT, 1999—. Vis. scientist Mass. Gen. Hosp.; affiliated faculty mem. Athinoula A. Martinos Ctr. for Biomedical Imaging. Contbr. articles to profl. jours. Recipient AT&T Rsch. award, NEC Rsch. award, John Merck Scholars Program award in Biology Develop. Disabilities in Children, Wade award for Creative Rsch.; co-recipient Troland Rsch. award, NAS, 2007. Contributions towards understanding of how the brain interprets and encodes visual information to perform complex tasks such as face recognition; launched Project Prakash, combines social, humanitarian, and scientific relevance. It focuses on the large population of blind children in India. This project will improve the lives of several children by helping them with treatment and rehabilitation, and answering some of the basic questions of neuroscience regarding brain plasticity and cognitive development; creator of the world's smallest book in the Guinness Book of World Records. Office: Dept Brain and Cognitve Sciences Bldg 46-4077 Sinha Lab Mass Inst Tech 77 Massachusetts Ave Cambridge MA 02139-4307 Office Phone: 617-253-1434. Office Fax: 617-253-2964. Business E-Mail: psinha@mit.edu.

SINHA, RAKESH KUMAR, computer scientist, researcher; s. RamKrishna and Sanyukta Sinha. PhD in Computer Sci., U. Wash., Seattle, 1995. Asst. prof. Sch. Computer Sci., Miami, Fla., 1995—98; mem. tech. staff Bell Labs., Murray Hill, NJ, 1998—2000; prin. engr. Ciena Core Switching Divsn., Cupertino, Calif., 2000—01; tech. cons. AT&T Labs Rsch., Middletown, NJ, 2001—. Contbr. articles to profl. jours. Mem.: IEEE, Assn. Computing Machinery. Achievements include patents in field. Personal E-mail: rakesh_sinha100@yahoo.com. Business E-Mail: sinha@research.att.com.

SINHA, SUNIL K., aerospace engineer, consultant; b. Patna, Bihar, India, Aug. 19, 1949; arrived in US, 1973; s. Awadh Bihari and Sumitra Kumari Sinha; m. Suman Sinha, Apr. 23, 1978 (dec. July 2006); children: Neena P., Anjuli M. BS, Patna U., India, 1968; MS, So. Ill. U., 1974; PhD, U. Ill., Urbana-Champaign, 1977—77; MTech., Indian Inst. of Tech., Bombay, 1973. Sr. rsch. asst. Indian Inst. of Tech., Bombay, 1969—73; grad. tchg. asst. U. of Ill., Urbana-Champaign, 1974—77; stress and vibration analyst Foster Wheeler Energy Corp., Livingston, NJ, 1977—79; sr. tech. analyst Westinghouse Electric Corp., Boston, 1979—83; sr. engr. GE Appliances, Louisville, 1983—89; sr. staff engr. GE Aircraft Engines, Evendale, Ohio, 1989—2001; prin. engr. GE Aviation, Evendale, 2002—. Mem. LS-Dyna Aerospace Working Group, Livermore, 2000—. Contbr. articles to profl. jours. Mem. Elfun Soc., Cin., 1989—2006. Mem.: ASME. Non-Partisan. Achievements include research in Pioneering transient dynamics work in the area of rotordynamics such as blade-out and tip-rub, contained and uncontained failure of rotating components; Missile Impact on a Commercial Jet engine; Dynamic Stability of Airfoils; High-speed impact dynamics. Home: 11025 Woodlands Way Cincinnati OH 45241 Office: Imapct Dynamics 1 Neumann Way Cincinnati OH 45215

SINIAWER, EIKO MARUKO, history professor; b. Fresno, Calif. BA, Williams Coll., Mass., 1997; MA, Harvard U., Cambridge, Mass., 1999, PhD, 2003. Asst. prof. history Williams Coll., 2003—. Author: (book) Ruffians, Yakuza, Nationalists: The Violent Politics of Modern Japan, 1860-1960. Office: Dept History Williams Coll 85 Mission Park Dr Williamstown MA 01267 Home: 259 Hancock Rd Williamstown MA 01267 Home Phone: 617-388-0492. Business E-Mail: eiko.maruko@williams.edu.

SINISCALCO, GARY RICHARD, lawyer; b. NYC, Aug. 14, 1943; BA in Econs., Le Moyne Coll., 1965; JD, Georgetown U., 1969. Bar: Calif. Regional counsel, sr. trial atty. EEOC, San Francisco, 1969-78; ptnr. Orrick, Herrington & Sutcliffe, San Francisco, 1978—, past co-chair employment law dept. Mem. adv. bd. Nat. Employment Law Inst.; fellow, Coll. of Labor and Employment Lawyers; lectr. in field. Co-author: Manager's Guide to Lawful Terminations, 1991; author: (with others) Employment Discrimination Law, 1979, 3rd edit., 1996; contbr. articles to profl. jours. Mem. ABA (mem. com. on internat. labor rels. and equal employment opportunity, mgmt. co-chair equal employment opportunity com. 1996-98, co-chair internat. labor law com. 2006—), State Bar Calif., Am. Employment Law Coun. (founder and mem. of the bd.). Office: Orrick Herrington 405 Howard St San Francisco CA 94105 Office Phone: 415-773-5833. E-mail: grsiniscalo@orrick.com.

SINISE, GARY, actor; b. Blue Island, Ill., Mar. 17, 1955; s. Robert L. Sinise; m. Moira Harris, 1981; children: Sophie, McCanna, Ella. Ph.D (hon.), Amherst Coll., 2003. Co-founder, artistic dir. Steppenwolf Theatre, 1974-, Chgo. Appeared in (plays) The Indian Wants The Bronx, 1977, Getting Out, 1980 (Joseph Jefferson award), Of Mice And Men, 1980, Loose Ends, 1982, True West, 1983 (also dir., Obie award best dir. 1982-83), Balm in Gilead, 1984, Streamers, 1985, The Caretaker, 1986, Grapes of Wrath, 1990 (Tony award and Drama Desk), Buried Child, 1996 (Tony award nominee, Joseph Jefferson award, 1996), One Flew Over the Cuckoos Nest, 2001; film appearances include A Midnight Clear, 1991, Jack The Bear, 1991, Forrest Gump, 1994 (Acad. award nomination for Best Supporing Actor, 1994, Disabled Am. Veterans Nat. Commanders award, 1994), The Quick and the Dead, 1995, Apollo 13, 1995, Ransom 1996, Albino Alligator, 1996, Snake Eyes, 1998, That Championship Season, 1999, Being John Malkovich, 1999, Reindeer Games, 1999, Mission to Mars, 1999, Bruno, 1999, All the Rage, 1999, The Green Mile, 1999, A Gentleman's Game, 2001, Made-Up, 2002, Mission: Space, 2003, The Human Stain, 2003, The Big Bounce, 2003, This Old Cub, 2004, The Forgotten, 2004, (voice) Open Season, 2006; (TV films) True West, 1984, Family Secrets, 1984, The Final Days, 1989, The Grapes of Wrath, 1991, The Witness, 1992, My Name is Bill W., 1989, The Stand, 1994, Truman, 1995 (Cable Ace award 1996, Golden Globe, 1996, Screen Actors Guild Award, 1996), Wallace, 1997 (Emmy award, 1998, Screen Actors Guild award, 1998, Cable ACE Award), That Championship Season, 1999, Path to War, 2002, Fallen Angel, 2003; (TV series) CSI: NY, 2004-; (TV appearances) Knots Landing, 1980, Crime Story, 1986, 1987, Hunter, 1990, Frasier, 1995, CSI: Miami, 2004, 2005; actor, dir. prodr., (films) Of Mice and Men, 1991; actor, prodr. Impostor, 2002; dir., Miles from Home, 1988; dir. (plays) Frank's Wild Years, Action, The Miss Firecracker Contest, Waiting for the Parade, Tracers, Orphans, Landscape of the Body, 1984 Office: care Creative Artists Agy 9830 Wilshire Blvd Beverly Hills CA 90212-1804 also: Licker & Ozurovich 2029 Century Park E Ste 1060 Los Angeles CA 90067-2919*

SINISI, KYLE SCOTT, history professor; b. New Orleans; s. Rocco and Judith Sinisi; m. Christina Zimmerman; children: Scott, Lindsey. BA, Va. Mil. Inst., Lexington, 1984; MA, PhD, Kans. State U., Manhattan. Prof. history Citadel, Charleston, SC, 1994—. Author: (book) Sacred Debts; co-editor: Warm Ashes. 1st lt. US Army, 1984—88. Conservative. Lutheran. Office: Citadel 171 Moultrie St Charleston SC 29409 Business E-Mail: sinisik@citadel.edu.

SINK, ADELAIDE ALEXANDER, state official; b. Mt. Airy, NC, June 5, 1948; d. Kester Andrew and Adelaide (Bunker) S.; m. William Howard McBride, Jr., July 10, 1986; children: William Albert (Bert), Cheryle Alexander (Lexie). BS, Wake Forest U., 1970. Tchr. Meth. Girls High Sch., Freetown, Sierra Leone, 1970-71, Am. Sch. of Liberia, Monrovia, 1971-72; v.p. NCNB, Charlotte, N.C., 1974-81, sr. v.p. NYC, 1981-84, Miami, Fla., 1984-89; exec. v.p. Nations Bank, Tampa, Fla., 1989-93; pres., Fla. Banking Divsn. Nations Bank (now Bank of America), Fla., 1993—2000; CFO, dept. financial services State of Fla., 2007. Appointed to Commn. on Govt. Accountability to the People; vice chair Fla. TaxWatch. Campaign chair United Way of Hillsborough County, Tampa, 1993; trustee Wake Forest U., 1992—; chair Hillsborough Edn. Found., 1994-96, bd. dir.; chair Take Stock in Children; svc. with Fla. Chpt. Nature Conservancy, Jr. Achievement of West Ctrl. Fla., Beth El Farm Workers Ministry, Redlands Christian Migrant Assn. Recipient Disting. Alumnus award Wake Forest U., 1993. So. Growth Policies Bd., Fla. Taxwatch, Bus./Higher Edn. Partnership. Democrat. Presbyterian. Avocations: fishing, politics. Home: PO Box 219 Thonotosassa FL 33592-0219 Office: Fla Dept Financial Services 200 E Gaines St Tallahassee FL 32399-0300 Office Phone: 850-413-3100.

SINK, ALEX, state treasurer; b. NC, June 4, 1948; m. Bill McBride; children: Bert, Lexi. Grad., Wake Forest U. Pres. Bank of America, Fla.; mem. Commn. on Govt. Accountability to the People, Fla., Commn. on Edn., Fla.; vice-chmn. Fla. TaxWatch; CFO State of Fla., Tallahassee, 2007—. Office: Dept Financial Services 200 E Gaines St Tallahassee FL 32399 Office Phone: 850-413-3100.*

SINK, HARRY LEE, transportation executive; b. Va. married. PhD, U. Tenn., Knoxville, 1995. Corp. mgmt. Dan River Inc., Danville, Va., 1996—2004, Air Products & Chemicals, Inc., Allentown, Pa., 1978—90. Office: NC A & T State Univ 1601 E Market St Greensboro NC 27411 Business E-Mail: hlsink@ncat.edu.

SINKFIELD, CAROLIN LADELL, agricultural studies educator; d. Oughtly and Maggie Denmon; m. Ralph Ricks Sinkfield, July 27, 1974; children: Terence Andwele, Dell Von, Trey Ricks-Denmon. BS in Edn., Tex. State U., San Marcos, 1971; MEd, Tex. Tech U., Lubbock, 2001; PhD, Uni. Incarnate Word, San Antonio, 2006. Cert. tchr. State Bd. Educator, 1971, in visual impairment & blindness State Bd. Tchr., 1990. Tchr. Edgewood ISD, San Antonio, 1972—74, Northside ISD, San Antonio, 1974—76, Houston County ISD, Warner Robins, Ga., 1978—79, Randolph Field ISD, Universal City, Tex., 1980—84, 1986—92; vision specialist Mil. ISD Coop., San Antonio, 1992—2005; u. prof. U. Tex. San Antonio, 2007, Tex. A & M U. San Antonio Sys., 2007—. Cons. Mil. Coop., San Antonio, 2008—. Bd. mem. Women's Global Connection, San Antonio, 2008—. Recipient Excellence award, U. Tex., 1992. Mem.: Assn.Edu. & Rehab.Blind & Visually Impaired, AERA, PDK Internat., Coun. Exceptional Children. Office: Tex A & M Univ San Antonio Ctr 1450 Gillette Blvd San Antonio TX 78224

SINKFORD, JEANNE CRAIG, dental association administrator, retired dentist, dean, educator; b. Washington, Jan. 30, 1933; d. Richard E. and Geneva (Jefferson) Craig; m. Stanley M. Sinkford, Dec. 8, 1951; children: Dianne Sylvia, Janet Lynn, Stanley M. III. BS, Howard U., 1953, MS, 1962, DDS, 1958, PhD, 1963; DSc (hon.), Georgetown U., 1978, U. Med. and Dentistry of N.J., 1992, Detroit Mercy Med. Coll., 1996, Meharry Med. Coll., 2008. Instr. prosthodontics Sch. Dentistry Howard U., Washington, 1958—60, faculty dentistry, 1964—, rsch. coord., co-chmn. dept. restorative dentistry, assoc. dean, 1968—75, dean, 1975—91, prof. Prosthodontics Grad. Sch., 1977—91, dean emeritus, prof., 1991—; spl. asst. Am. Assn. Dental Schs., 1991—93, dir. office women and minority affairs, 1993—97, assoc. exec. dir., 1998—. Instr. rsch. and crown and bridge Northwestern U. Sch. Dentistry, 1963—64; cons. prosthodontics and rsch. VA Hosp., Washington, 1965—; resident Children's Hosp. Nat. Med. Ctr., 1974—75; cons. St. Elizabeth's Hosp.; mem. attending staff Freedman's Hosp., Washington, 1964—; adv. bd. DC Gen. Hosp., 1975—; mem. nat. adv. dental rsch. coun. Nat. Bd. Dental Examiners; mem. ad hoc adv. panel Tuskegee Syphilis Study for HEW; sponsor DC Pub. Health Apprentice Program; mem. adv. coun. to dir. NIH; adv. com. NIH/NIDR/NIA Aging Rsch. Coun.; rschr. Advisory Com. Womans Health; mem. dental devices classification panel FDA; mem. select panel for promotion child health, 1979—80; mem. spl. med. adv. group VA; bd. overseers U. Pa. Dental Sch., Boston U. Dental Sch.; bd. advisors U. Pitts. Dental Sch.; mem. bd. visitors Temple U. Sch. Dentistry, Howard U Coll. Dentistry, Ind. U. Sch. Dentistry, W.Va. U. Health Ctr.; mem. anat. rev. bd. DC NRC Governing Bd.; cons. FDA; mem. Nat. Adv. Dental Rsch. Coun., 1993—96; active NRC Governing Bd. Mem. Mayor's Block Grant Adv. Com., 1982; mem. parents' coun. Sidwell Friends, 1983; adv. bd. United Negro Coll. Fund, Robert Wood Johnson Health Policy Fellowships; mem. women's health task force NIH; bd. dirs. Girl Scouts U.S.A., 1993—95; pres. NY Adv. Coun. NIH Office Rsch. Women's Health, 2008—; bd. visitors Temple U. Sch. Dentistry, W.Va. U. health Scis. Ctr., Howard U. Coll. Dentistry. Fellow Louise C. Ball fellow grad. tng., 1960—63. Fellow: Internat. Coll. Dentists (Merit award), Am. Coll. Dentists (mem. editl. bd. 1988—2006, sec.-treas. Wash. met. sect.); mem.: ADA (chmn. appeal bd. coun. on dental edn. 1975—82), Nat. Adv. Coun. Rsch. Women's Health, Children's Dental Health Found. (mem. adv. bd.), Fedn. Dentistry Internat., Links Inc., Dean's Coun. (chair), Smithsonian Assocs., NY Acad. Scis., Am. Soc. Dentistry for Children, Inst. Medicine of NAS (coun.), Nat. Dental Assn., Fed. Prosthodontic Orgn., Am. Prosthodontic Soc., Am. Pedodontic Soc., Leadership in Acad. Medicine (adv. bd.), Health Professions Partnership Initiative (adv. bd.), Assn. Am. Women Dentists, Wash. Coun. Adminstrv. Women, So. Conf. Dental Deans (chmn.), Inst. Grad. Dentists (trustee), Am. Inst. Oral Biology, Dist. Dental Soc., Internat. Assn. Dental Rsch., Am. Soc. for Geriatric Dentistry (bd. dirs.), North Portal Civic League, Golden Key, Beta Kappa Chi, Psi Chi, Omicron Kappa Upsilon, Phi Beta Kappa, Sigma Xi (pres.). Achievements include first female dental dean at Howard U., and in the U.S.A.

SINNAMON, WALTER BRUCE, college administrator, biology educator; b. Phila., Dec. 27, 1947; m. Carol Sinnamon; 1 child, Michel. BS in Zoology, Houghton Coll., 1969; postgrad., SUNY, Geneseo, 1975-77; PhD in Zoology, Clemson U., 1985. Cert. tchr. biology, chemistry, phys. sci., gen. sci., N.Y. Sci. instr. Houghton Acad., NY, 1969-77, bus. mgr., 1973-77; grad. teaching asst. dept. zoology Clemson U., SC, 1977-82; asst. prof. So. Wesleyan U., 1982-85, assoc. prof., 1985-90, prof. biology, 1990—, spl. asst. to the pres., 1993—2003, dean Coll. Arts Sci., 2005—, dept. chair, 2003—. Grant writer US Dept. Edn., Washington, 1990, Cannon Found., Kannapolis, N.C., 1991, JanIrve Found., Asheville, N.C., 1991, NSF, Washington, 1991, Consortium for Advancement of Pvt. Higher Edn; mem. advisory com., Tri County Tech. Coll., 2002-; coun. mem., Coll. Arts & Scis.; mem. instl. biosafety com., Clemson U. Contbr. articles to profl. jours. Recipient Gov.'s Distinguished Prof. award, So. Wesleyan U., 2007, Prof. of the Yr., 2008, Excellence in Tchg. award, SI Ind. Coll., U., 2008. Mem. Am. Assn. Advancement of Sci., History of Sci. Soc., Nat. Assn. Advisors for Health Profls., Affiliation Christian Biologists, Human Anatomy and Physiology Soc., Am. Sci. Affiliation, Soc. Integrative Comparitive Biology, S.C. Acad. Sci., Gideons Internat., Wycliff Assocs., Sigma Xi. Home: 423 Pin Du Lac Dr Central SC 29630-9435 Office: So Wesleyan U PO Box 1817 Central SC 29630-0407 Office Phone: 864-644-5265. Business E-Mail: wsinnamon@swu.edu.

SINNARD, ELAINE JANICE, painter, sculptor; b. Fort Collins, Colo., Feb. 14, 1926; d. Elven Orestes and Catherine (Bennet) S. Student, Art Students League, 1948, NYU, 1953, Sculpture Ctr., NYC, 1954, Academie Grande Chaumiere, Paris, 1956. Painter, sculptor. Works exhibited Riverside Mus., NYC, 1955, City Ctr., NYC, 1954-56, Nat. Arts Club, NYC, 1959-90, Lord & Taylor, NYC, 1963-78, Bergdorf Goodman, NYC, 1980-90, Zantman Art Galleries, Carmel-by-the-Sea, Calif., 1970-73, Chevy Chase Gallery, Washington, 1981-88; one woman shows and group exhbns. include: Bergdorf Goodman Nena's Choice Gallery, Sinnard Art Studios; tchr. open workshop for artists, (murals) Trinity Assembly of GOD, Middletown, NY. Mem. Nat. Arts Club NYC. Home and Studio: PO Box 304 New Hampton NY 10958-0304 Home Phone: 845-374-8128. Personal E-mail: sinnard@warwick.net.

SINNO, R. RALPH, civil engineer, educator; BS in Civil Engring., U. Fla., Gainesville, 1962; MS, La. State U., Baton Rouge, 1964; PhD, U. Tex., Coll. Sta., 1968. Registered civil engr. Miss., La. Prof. dept. civil & environ. engring. Miss. State U. Contbr. articles to profl. jours. Fellow: Am. Soc. Civil Engring. (T.Y. Lin award). Achievements include research in structural systems using full scale testing of real life hurricane wind loadings on metal buildings. Business E-Mail: sinno@cfe.msstate.edu.

SINNOTT, JOHN PATRICK, lawyer, educator; b. Bklyn., Aug. 17, 1931; s. John Patrick and Elizabeth Muriel (Zinkand) Sinnott; m. Rose Marie Yuppa, May 30, 1959; children: James Alexander, Jessica Michelle. BS, US Naval Acad., 1953; MS, USAF Inst. Tech., 1956; JD, No. Ky. U., Highland Heights, 1960. Bar: Ohio 1961, NY 1963, NJ 1970, Ga 2000, US Patent Office 1963, US Supreme Ct 1977. Assoc. Brumbaugh, Graves, Donohue & Raymond, NYC, 1961-63; patent atty. Bell Tel. Labs., Murray Hill, NJ, 1963-64, Schlumberger Ltd., NYC, 1964-71; asst. chief patent counsel Babcock & Wilcox, NYC, 1971-79; chief patent and trademark counsel Am. Std. Inc., NYC, 1979-92; of counsel Morgan & Finnegan, NYC, 1992-99, Langdale Vallotton, LLP, Valdosta, Ga., 2000—. Adj lectr NJ Inst Technology, Newark, 1974—89; adj prof Seton Hall Univ Sch Law, Newark, 1989—98. Author: Counterfeit Goods Suppression, 1998, World Patent Law and Practice, 1999; co-author: To Paris! August, 1914 and Now-Belgian and Northern French Battlefields, 2006, Document Authentication, 2009; contbr. articles to profl. jours. Mem. local Selective Serv Bd., Plainfield, NJ, 1971; bd dirs New Providence Community Swimming Pool, NJ, 1970. Capt. USAF, 1953—61, col. AUS ret., 1977—91. Decorated Legion of Merit, others. Mem.: Ga. State Bar Assn., Squadron A Assn., Valdosta Country Club, Cosmos Club. Republican. Roman Catholic. Home: 2517 Rolling Rd Valdosta GA 31602-1244 Office: Langdale Vallotton LLP 1007 N Patterson St PO Box 1547 Valdosta GA 31603 Office Phone: 229-244-5400.

SINNOTT, STEPHEN P., former prosecutor; b. May 7, 1955; JD, Loyola U., 1979. 1st asst. US atty. (we. dist.) Wis. US Dept. Justice, Madison, interim US atty., 2005—06, acting US atty. (we. dist.), 2009—. Office: US Atty PO Box 1585 Madison WI 53701-1585 Office Phone: 608-264-5158.*

SINNOTT, WILLIAM F., lawyer; b. 1957; BA, Holy Cross Coll., Worcester, Mass.; JD, Suffolk Univ. Law Sch. Former asst. dist. atty.; former asst. US atty. Office US Atty.; corporation counsel Boston Law Dept., 2006—. Colonel USMC, reserve mem. USAR, 2005, Iraq. Office: Boston City Law Dept Rm 615 One City Hall Plz Boston MA 02201 Office Phone: 617-635-4034. Office Fax: 617-635-3150. Business E-Mail: e-mail.william.sinnott@cityofboston.gov.

SINOFSKY, STEVEN J., computer software company executive; BA with hon., Cornell U., 1987; MS in Computer Sci., U. Mass., 1989. With Microsoft Corp., Redmond, Wash., 1989—, software design engr., project lead, develop. tools group, 1989—94, dir., program mgmt., Microsoft Office, 1994—98, v.p., Microsoft Office, 1998—99, sr. v.p. Microsoft Office, 1999—2006, sr. v.p. Windows and Windows Live Engring. group, 2006—09, pres. Windows divsn., 2009—. Vis. scholar Harvard U. Bus. Sch., Cambridge, Mass., 1998. Office: One Microsoft Way Redmond WA 98052-6399*

SINOR, DENIS, history professor, linguist; b. Kolozsvar, Hungary, Apr. 17, 1916; s. Miklos and Marguerite (Weitzenfeld) S.; m. Eugenia Trinajstic (dec.); children: Christophe (dec.), Sophie. BA, U. Budapest, 1938; MA, Cambridge U., Eng., 1948; Doctorate (hon.), U. Szeged, Hungary, 1971, U. Humanities, Kazan, Russia, 2007. Attache Centre National de la Recherche Scientifique, Paris, 1939-48; univ. lectr. Altaic studies Cambridge U., 1948-62; prof. Uralic and Altaic studies and history Ind. U., Bloomington, 1962-81, disting. prof. Uralic and Altaic studies and history, 1975-86, disting. prof. emeritus Uralic and Altaic studies and history, 1986—, chmn. dept. Uralic and Altaic studies, 1963-1981, dir. Lang. and Area Ctr., 1963-88, dir. Asian studies program, 1965-67, dir. Asian Studies Rsch. Inst., 1967-79, dir. Rsch. Inst. for Inner Asian Studies (renamed Denis Sinor Inst. for Inner Asian Studies), 1979-1981, 85-86. Sec. gen. Permanent Internat. Altaistic Conf., 1961-2007; rsch. project dir. U.S. Office Edn., 1969-70; sec. Internat. Union Orientalists, 1954-64; vis. prof. Inst. Nat. des Langues et Civilisations Orientales, Paris, spring 1974; scholar-in-residence Rockefeller Found. Study Ctr., Bellagio, 1975; vice chmn. UNESCO Commn. for History Civilization Cen. Asia, 1981-2005, consultative com. UNESCO Silk Rd. Project, 1990-97; summer seminar dir. NEH, 1988, 2005; hon. prof. Inst. Oriental Studies, Russian Acad. Scis. Author: Orientalism and History, 1954, History of Hungary, 1959, Introduction à lètude de l'Eurasie Centrale, 1963, Aspects of Altaic Civilization, 1963, Inner Asia, 1968, Inner Asia and Its Contacts with Medieval Europe, 1977, Tanulmányok, 1982, Essays in Comparative Altaic Linguistics, 1990, Studies in Medieval Inner Asia, 1997; editor, contbr.: Modern Hungary, 1977, Studies in Finno-Ugric Linguistics, 1977, Uralic Languages, 1988, Essays on Uzbek History, Culture and Languages, 1993, Cambridge History of Early Inner Asia, Handbook of Uralic Studies, Jour. Asian History, Ind. U. Uralic and Altaic Series; mem. editl. bd. Britannica-Hungarica. Served with Forces Françaises de l'Intérieur, 1943-44. With Free French Army, 1944—45. Rsch. grantee Am. Coun. Learned Soc., 1962, Am. Philos. Soc., 1963, NEH grant, 1981, 87-88; Guggenheim fellow, 1968-69, 1981-82; recipient Jubilee prize U. Budapest, 1938, Barczi Geza Meml. medal, 1981, Gold medal Permanent Internat. Altaistic Conf., 1982, 1996, Arminius Vambery Meml. medal, 1983, Thomas Hart Benton Mural medal Hungarian Order of Star, 1986, UNESCO Avicenna medal, 1998, medal for outstanding svcs. U. Szeged, 2002, UNESCO 60th Anniversary medal, 2005, Middle Cross Hungarian Order of Merit, 2006, John W. Ryan award, Ind. U., 2006, Pres.'s medal, 2008; named Denis Sinor Inst. for Inner Asian Studies in his honor, 2006. Fellow Körösi Csoma Soc. (hon.); mem. Royal Asiatic Soc. (hon. sec. 1954-64, Denis Sinor medal for Inner Asian Studies named in his honor 1992), Am. Oriental Soc. (pres. Midwest br. 1968-70, nat. pres. 1975-76, medal of honor 1999), Assn. Asian Studies, Am. Hist. Soc., Soc. Asiatique (hon.), Tibet Soc. (pres. 1969-74), Mongolia Soc. (pres. 1987-94), Correspondant de l'Académie des inscriptions et belles lettres (Paris), Hungarian Acad. Scis. (hon.), Acad. Europaea (fgn.), Deutsche Morgenlandische Gesellschaft, Suomalais-Ugrilaisen Seura (hon.), Soc. Uralo-Altaica (v.p. 1964-94, hon.), Internat. Union Oriental and Asian Studies (v.p. 1993—), Cosmos Club Washington, Explorers Club NYC, United Oxford and Cambridge Club London. Achievements include reached the North Pole on a Russian icebreaker, 2004. Home: 5581 E Lampkins Ridge Rd Bloomington IN 47401-8674 Office: Indiana U Dept Ctrl Eurasian Studies Goodbody Hall Bloomington IN 47405 E-mail: sinord@indiana.edu.

SINOR, HOWARD EARL, JR., lawyer; b. New Orleans, Sept. 6, 1949; s. Howard E. and Beverly M. (Bourgeois) S.; m. Katy K. Sinor; children: Sally, Vera Sue, Sarah, Sadie. BA with honors, U. New Orleans, 1971; JD cum laude, Harvard U., 1975. Bar: La. 1975, U.S. Supreme Ct. 1983, U.S. Ct. Appeals (3rd, 5th and 11th cir.), U.S. Dist. Ct. (Ea., Middle, We.) Dist. La. Ptnr. Jones, Walker, Waechter, Poitevent, Carrere & Denegre, 1975-98, Gordon Arata, New Orleans, 1999—. Contbg. author: La. Appellate Practice Handbook, 1990, 97; editor: CLE Manual of Recent Developments, 1985; contbr. articles to profl. jours. Recipient Pres.'s award, La. State Bar Assn., 1987. Fellow La. Bar Found.; mem. ABA, FBA, La. State Bar Assn. (chmn. antitrust sect. 1987-89). Avocations: golf, hiking.

SINSHEIMER, ROBERT LOUIS, retired academic administrator, educator; b. Washington, Feb. 5, 1920; s. Allen S. and Rose (Davidson) S.; m. Flora Joan Hirsch, Aug. 8, 1943 (div. 1972); children: Lois June (Mrs. Wickstrom), Kathy Jean (Mrs. Vandagriff), Roger Allen; m. Kathleen Mae Reynolds, Sept. 10, 1972 (div. 1980); m. Karen Current, Aug. 1, 1981. S.B., MIT, 1941, MS, 1942, PhD, 1948. Staff mem. radiation lab. MIT, Cambridge, 1942-46; assoc. prof. biophysics, physics dept. Iowa State Coll., Ames, 1949-55, prof., 1955-57; prof. biophysics Calif. Inst. Tech., Pasadena, 1957-77, chmn. div. biology, 1968-77; chancellor U. Calif., Santa Cruz, 1977-87, chancellor emeritus, 1987—, prof. Santa Barbara, 1988-90, prof. emeritus, 1990—. Editor: Jour. Molecular Biology, 1959-67, Ann. Rev. Biochemistry, 1966-72. Named Calif. Scientist of Year, 1968; recipient N.W. Beijerinck-Virologie medal Netherlands Acad. Sci., 1969 Fellow Am. Acad. Arts and Scis.; mem. Am. Soc. Biol. Chemists, Biophys. soc. (pres. 1970), AAAS, Nat. Acad. Scis. (mem. council 1970-73, chmn. bd. editors Proc. 1972-80), Inst. Medicine. Achievements include discovery of single-stranded DNA, circular DNA; research in first in vitro replication of infective DNA. Avocations: photography, travel. Office: U Calif MCD Biology Santa Barbara CA 93106 Home Phone: 805-683-2247; Office Phone: 805-893-8038. Business E-Mail: sinsheim@lifesci.ucsb.edu.

SINSHEIMER, WARREN JACK, lawyer; b. NYC, May 22, 1927; s. Jerome William and Elizabeth (Berch) S.; m. Florence Dubin, Mar. 30, 1950; children: Linda Ruth, Ralph David, Alan Jay, Michael Neal. Student, Ind. U., 1943-47; JD cum laude, NY Law Sch., 1950; LLM, NYU, 1957; MPhil, Columbia U., 1977; HLD (hon.), Drew U., 2002. Bar: NY bar 1950. Ptnr. Sinsheimer, Sinsheimer & Dubin, NYC, 1950-78, Satterlee & Stephens, NYC, 1978-86, Patterson, Belknap, Webb & Tyler, NYC, 1986-91; counsel Patterson Belknap Webb & Tyler, NYC, 1991-96; pres., bd. dirs. Neighborhood Bagel Corp., 1994—. Pres. Plessey, Inc., NYC, 1956-70, chmn., CEO, 1970-89; dir. oversees ops. devel. Plessey Co., Ltd., Illford, Essex, Eng., 1969-70, dep. chief exec., dir., 1976-89; dir. Plessey, Inc.; trustee NYU Sch. Law, 1996—; pres., bd. dirs. Partnership for Children's Rights, 1998—. Chmn. Com. of 68, 1964-67; Mem. Westchester County Rep. Com., 1956-73; chmn. Nat. Scranton Pres. Com., 1964; mem. NY State Assembly, 1965-66; Bd. visitors Wassaic State Sch., 1962-64; trustee Sch. Law, NYU, 1996—, bd. dirs. Shalom Hartman Inst., Jerusalem, 1991—, treas., 1996—; trustee Citi Bar Fund, 1998-2004. Served with USNR, 1944-45; with USAF, 1950-52. Mem. ABA, Assn. Bar City NY, Torch and Scroll, Century Club (Purchase, NY, gov., treas. 1997—), Century Assn. NYC, Univ. Club, Zeta Beta Tau. Jewish. Home: 22 Murray Hill Rd Scarsdale NY 10583-2828 Office: 271 Madison Ave New York NY 10016-1001 Office Phone: 212-683-7999. Business E-Mail: Sinsheimer@kidslaw.org.

SINTZ, EDWARD FRANCIS, librarian; b. New Trenton, Ind., Feb. 6, 1924; s. John and Edith E. (Rudicil) S.; m. Donna Norris, Apr. 12, 1952; children: Ann Kristin, Lesley Elizabeth, Julie Melinda. BA, U. Kans., 1950; MA in L.S, U. Denver, 1954; MS in Pub. Adminstrn, U. Mo., 1965. With Kansas City (Mo.) Pub. Library, 1954-66, asst. dir., 1964-66; asso. librarian St. Louis Pub. Library, 1966-68; dir. pub. libraries Miami-Dade Pub. Libr., 1968—89, ret. Instr. Washington U., St. Louis, 1966-67; library surveys for Mo. State Library, 1967-68; library bldg. cons., 1965—. Editor: Mo. Library Assn. Quar., 1956—58. Served with USAAF, 1942-45. Mem. ALA, Fla. Library Assn. (pres. 1975-76), Southeastern Library Assn. Clubs: Kiwanian. Home: 7105 Lakeside Dr Charlotte NC 28215 Personal E-mail: edanddonna9@bellsouth.net.

SIO, JIMMY ONG, embryologist; b. Manila, Philippines, Mar. 9, 1954; arrived in U.S., 1973; s. Vicente and SiokBee (Ong) Sio. Biology major, U. Philippines, 1971—73; BS in Biology, Calif. State Coll. Bakersfield, 1976; PhD of Cell Biology, U. Tex. Health Sci. Ctr., Dallas, 1985; MD, Emory U., 1985. Diplomate Nat. Bd. Med. Examiners, Am. Bd. Hosp. Physicians, Am. Coll. Ethical Physicians. Resident in anat. pathology Emory U., Atlanta, 1985—86; resident in internal medicine Kern Med. Ctr., Bakersfield, Calif., 1990—93; physician Kaiser So. Calif. Permanente Med. Group, Bakersfield, 1993—, asst. area med. dir., 2006—. Pvt. Philippine Armed Forces, 1971—73. Recipient Businessman of Yr., NRCC, 2003, Man of Yr., IBC and ABI, 2004. Fellow: Am. Biog. Inst.; mem.: Internat. Biog. Assn., NY Acad. Scis., Order of Internat. Fellowship, InterNet Assocs. Avocation: reading. Home: 8604 Dinard Pl Bakersfield CA 93311 Office: Kaiser So Calif Permanente Med Group 8800 Ming Ave Bakersfield CA 93311 Office Phone: 661-664-3706. Personal E-mail: doctorsio@aol.com.

SION, MAURICE, mathematics professor; b. Skopje, Yugoslavia, Oct. 17, 1928; came to Can., 1960; s. Max and Sarah (Alalouf) S.; m. Emilie Grace Chisholm, Sept. 15, 1957; children: Crispin, Sarah, Dirk. BA, NYU, 1947, MA, 1948; PhD, U. Calif., Berkeley, 1951. Mathematician Nat. Bur. Stds., Washington, 1951-52; instr. U. Calif., 1952-53; asst. prof. U. Calif., 1957-60; mem. Inst. for Advanced Study, Princeton, NJ, 1955-57, 62; asst. prof. U. B.C., Vancouver, Canada, 1960, assoc. prof., 1961, prof., 1964-89, prof. emeritus, 1989—, head math. dept., 1984-86, dir. Quadra Inst. Math., 1970-89. Author: Introduction to Methods of Real Analysis, 1969, Theory Semi Group Valued Measures, 1973; contbr. articles to profl. jours. With U.S. Army, 1953-55. Mem. Am. Math. Soc., Can. Math. Soc. (v.p. 1972-74). Office: U BC Dept Math Vancouver BC Canada V6T 1Z2

SIPIERA, PAUL P., JR., foundation administrator, retired geology and astronomy professor; b. Chgo., Nov. 30, 1948; s. Paul P. and Frances A.; m. Diane M. Vidmar, May 22, 1993; children: Paula Frances, Caroline Antarctica. BA in History, Northeastern Ill. U., 1971, MS in Earth Sci., 1975; PhD in Natural Sci., U. Innsbruck, Austria, 2004. Prof. geology and astronomy Harper Coll., Palatine, Ill., 1976—2006, prof. emeritus, 2006—. Rsch assoc. Field Mus. Natural History, Chgo., 1976—92; exec. bd. Ill. State Acad. Sci., Springfield, 1978—83; rsch. sci. Antarctic search for meteorites NSF, Washington, 1983—84; pres. and CEO Planetary Studies Found., Algonquin, Ill., 1989—. Author: Gerald Ford, 1989, Amundsen & Scott: Race to the South Pole, 1990, Ernest Shackleton: A Life of Antarctic Exploration, 2002; contbr. chapters to books, to profl. publ. Adv. bd. mem. X-Prize Found., St. Louis, 1996—. Recipient Nininger Meteorite Rsch. award, Ariz. State U., 1975—76, Antarctic Svc medal, U.S.A, 1984, Disting. Faculty award, Harper Coll., 1996. Fellow: Ill. State Acad. Sci.; mem.: New Zealand Antarctic Soc., Geol. Soc. New Zealand, Meteoritical Soc. Achievements include asteroid 31931 named in his honor. Avocations: photography, farming. Home and Office: 10 Winterwood Ln Galena IL 61036 Home Phone: 815-858-3362; Office Phone: 847-854-0468. Business E-Mail: psipiera@planets.org.

SIPIORA, LEONARD PAUL, retired museum director, art appraiser; b. Lawrence, Mass., Sept. 1, 1934; s. Walter and Agnes S.; m. Sandra Joyce Coon, 1962; children— Alexandra, Erika. AB cum laude, U. Mich., 1955, MA, 1956. Dir. museums, City of El Paso, Tex., 1967-90; ret. Co-founder, pres. El Paso Arts Coun., 1969-71; sec.-treas. El Paso Coun. Internat. Visitors, 1968-71; trustee El Paso Mus. Art; bd. dirs. Tex. Com. Humanities, Assn. Southwestern Humanities Coun.; adv. bd. S.W. Arts Found.; expert Antiques Roadshow-U.S.A. Bd. dirs. Cmty. Concert Assn. El Paso, El Paso Symphony Orch., El Paso Hist. Soc. Mem. Assn. Mus. Dirs., Mountain Plains Mus. Assn. (pres. 1978-79), Tex. Assn. Museums (pres. 1977-79), Appraisers Assn. Am., Knights of Malta (decorated Grand Cross), Prior of Tex., Kappa Pi. Republican. Lutheran. Home: 1012 Blanchard Ave El Paso TX 79902-2727

SIPOWICZ, SHARIE, pharmaceutical executive, researcher; d. Kenneth W. and Linda L. Schneeman; 1 child, Mykaila H. Degree in Bus. - Computer Info. Sys., Ind. U., Indpls., 2002. Publ. specialist Eli Lilly & Co., Indpls., 2000—05, genomic specialist, 2005—. Personal E-mail: sipo1337@comcast.net.

SIPPEL, SERRA, advocate; MA in religion. Internat. prog. dir. Catholics for a Free Choice; dep. dir. Ctr. Health and Gender Equity, Washington, 2006, pres. Office: Ctr Health and Gender Equity Ste 400 1317 F St NW Washington DC 20004 Office Phone: 202-393-5930. Office Fax: 202-393-5937. E-mail: change@genderhealth.org.*

SIPPEL, WILLIAM LEROY, lawyer; b. Fond du Lac, Wis., Aug. 14, 1948; m. Barbara Jean Brost, Aug. 23, 1970; children: Katharine Jean, David William. BA, JD, U. Wis. Bar: Wis. 1974, U.S. Dist. Ct. (we. dist.) Wis. 1974, Minn. 1981, U.S. Dist. Ct. Minn. 1981, U.S. Ct. Appeals (10th cir.) 1984, U.S. Ct. Appeals (8th cir.) 1985. Research assoc. dept. agrl. econs. U. Wis., Madison, 1974-75; counsel monopolies and comml. law subcom. Ho. Judiciary Com., Washington, 1975-80; spl. asst. to asst. gen. antitrust div. U.S. Dept. of Justice, Washington, 1980-81; from assoc. to ptnr. Doherty, Rumble & Butler, Mpls. and St. Paul, Minn., 1981-99; ptnr. Oppenheimer, Wolff & Donnelly, LLP, Mpls., 1999—2007, of counsel, 2008—. Bd. dirs. Music in the Park, Inc.; adj. faculty antitrust William Mitchell Coll. Law, 2000-01; adj. faculty grad. program U. Minn. Carlson Sch. Mgmt., 2007. Co-author: The Antitrust Health Care Handbook, 1988; contbg. author: ABA Energy Antitrust Handbook, 2002. Mem. program com. Minn. World Trade Assn., Mpls., St. Paul, 1985-86, bd. dirs., 1986, Minn.; former dir. Music in the Park, Mpls.; former dir. Person to Person Inc.; chmn. antitrust mktg. orders com. Nat. Coun. Farmer Coops., 2001—. With USAR, 1971-77. Mem. ABA (vice chmn. ins. industry com. 1990-91, contbr. ABA Joint Ventures in Health Care), Minn. Bar Assn. (co-chmn. antitrust sect. 1986-88, internat. law sect. coun. 1986-89, treas. 1989-90, sec. 1990-91, vice chmn. 1995-96, chmn. 1996-97), Minn. Med. Alley Assn. (co-chmn. internat. bus. com. 1990-95, Hennepin County Office Internat. Trade (bd. dirs. 1988-93), Phi Beta Kappa. Roman Catholic. Avocations: reading, photography, computers. Home: 2151 Commonwealth Ave Saint Paul MN 55108-1730 Office: Oppenheimer Wolff Donnelly LLP Plaza VII 45 S Seventh St Ste 3400 Minneapolis MN 55402-1609 Home Phone: 651-645-3630; Office Phone: 612-607-7251. Business E-Mail: bsippel@oppenheimer.com.

SIPPEL-WETMORE, FRANCES MARIE, microbiologist, retired business owner; b. Phila., Apr. 17, 1930; d. Jacob Harry Jr. and Catharine Seachrist (Hershey) Pickle; m. Roy Joseph Sippel, Feb. 8, 1958 (div. June 1979); m. Orville Chase Wetmore, June 14, 1997. BA Biology and Chemistry with honors, Hood Coll., 1952; postgrad., Women's Med. Coll., Pa., 1952—54; MS Microbiology, U. Pitts., 1956. Rsch. asst. to Dr. Jonas Salk U. Pitts., 1955; rsch. asst. to Dr. T.S. Danowski Children's Hosp., Pitts., 1956; bacteriologist Shadyside Hosp., Pitts., 1956—57; rsch. asst. to Dr. Leonard Hayflick Wistar Inst., Phila., 1958—59; asst. editor Biol. Abstracts, Phila., 1959—60; lit. chemist E.I. du Pont de Nemours & Co., Wilmington, Del., 1960—66; sec.-treas. Can-Am Sales Corp., West Chester, Pa., 1972—73; sales rep. Quick Courier Svc., Phila., 1977—82; owner Color Profile, West Chester, 1982—97. Bd. dirs. Chester County Emergency Med. Svcs., Pa., 1980-97; co-chair Holiday House Tour, 1989-93, chair House Acquisitions, 1995; vol. YWCA. Mem. AAUW (Outstanding Woman from West Chester br. 1991), LWV (chmn. Chester County coun. 1993-95), Am. Soc. Microbiologists, Phila. Hood Coll. Club (past pres.), Chester County Hist. Soc. (antiques show com.), Wilmington Country Club, Sigma Xi Republican. Unitarian Universalist. Avocations: art, music, downhill skiing, travel. Home: 1007 Oriente Ave Wilmington DE 19807-2260

SIRAGUSA, CHARLES J., judge; b. Rochester, NY, 1947; BA, Lemoyne Coll., 1969; JD, Albany Law Sch., 1976. Asst. dist. atty. Monroe County Dist. Atty.'s Office, NY, 1977—92; state supreme ct. justice (dist. 7) NY State Supreme Ct., 1993—97; judge US Dist. Ct. (we. dist.) NY, 1997—. Office: 1360 US Courthouse 100 State St Rochester NY 14614-1350 Office Phone: 585-613-4050.

SIRAGUSA, DANIEL, radiologist, educator; BS in Chemistry, U. Fla., Gainesville, 1991; MD, U. South Fla., Tampa, 1995. Diplomate diagnostic radiologist Am. Bd. Radiology, 1999, vascular & interventional radiologist Am. Bd. Radiology, 2001. Asst. prof. radiology U. Fla. COM, Jacksonville, 2000—, program dir., vir fellowship, 2003—. Office: Univ Fla COM Jacksonville 655 W 8 th St Box C90 Jacksonville FL 32209 Office Fax: 904-244-5845. Business E-Mail: daniel.siragusa@jax.ufl.edu.

SIRAGUSA, TONY (ANTHONY SIRAGUSA), sportscaster, retired professional football player; b. Kenilworth, NJ, May 14, 1967; m. Kathy Giacalone, Apr. 22, 1995; 3 children. Grad., U. Pitts. Tackle Indpls. Colts, 1990—96, Balt. Ravens, 1997—2001; co-owner Tiffany's Restaurants; founder Goose's BBQ Products; sideline reporter NFL on FOX. Actor: 25th Hour, 2002, The Sopranos, 2004; host: (TV series) Man Caves; Mega Machines. Founder Tony Siragusa Found. Achievements include being a member of Super Bowl XXXV Championship winning Baltimore Ravens, 2001. Office: c/o FOX Sports PO Box 900 Beverly Hills CA 90213-0900 also: Goose's BBQ Products 9 Business Pk Unit 2-3 Branford CT 06405*

SIRAISI, NANCY GILLIAN, historian, writer, educator; b. July 1932; BA, U. Oxford, 1953, MA, 1958; PhD, CUNY, 1970. Prof. history Hunter Coll., NYC, 1970—2003, disting. prof. emeritus, 2003—; prof. history CUNY Grad. Ctr., NYC, 1976—2003. Disting. lectr. renaissance studies Ariz. Ctr. Medieval and Renaissance Studies, Ariz. State U., 1999. Author: Taddeo Alderotti and His Pupils, 1981 (William H. Welch Medal, Am. Assn. for the History of Medicine), Avicenna in Renaissance Italy, 1987, Medieval and Early Renaissance Medicine, 1990 (Watson Davis and Helen Miles Davis Prize, History of Sci. Soc.), The Clock and the Mirror, 1997, History, Medicine, and the Traditions of Renaissance Learning, 2007. Recipient George Sarton Medal, History of Sci. Soc., 2003, Paul Oskar Kristellar Award for Lifetime Achievement, Renaissance Soc. America, 2004, Am. Hist. Assn. Award for Scholarly Distinction, 2005; named a MacArthur Fellow, The John D. and Catherine T. MacArthur Found., 2008. Office: Hunter Coll 695 Park Ave New York NY 10065

SIRANGELO, MARK N., aerospace transportation executive; BS, Seton Hall U., South Orange, NJ; M in Bus., Seton Hall U., JD. Prin. founder, chmn., CEO PGI, Inc.; mng. mem. QS Advisors, LLC, 1998—2005; sr. officer Natexis Bleichroeder, Inc., 2001—03; founder, mng. mem., CEO Quanstar Group, LLC, 2003—05; vice chmn., CEO SpaceDev, Poway, Calif., 2005—06, CEO, chmn. bd., 2006—. Dir. Adam Aircraft Industries. Dir. Nat. Ctr. Missing and Exploited Children; dir., treas. Internat. Ctr. Missing and Exploited Children. Named one of Space Tech. Hall of Fame. Office: SpaceDev 13855 Stowe Dr Poway CA 92064 Office Phone: 858-375-2000. Office Fax: 858-375-1000.

SIRBU, MARVIN ALAN, engineering educator; b. Dayton, Ohio, July 15, 1945; s. Marvin Alan and Beatrice Friedlander Sirbu; m. Barbara Beth Lazarus, Jan. 9, 1979 (dec. July 15, 2003); children: Margaret Ann, Benjamin James. SB, MIT, Cambridge, Mass., 1966, SM, 1968, SCD, 1973. Rsch. assoc. MIT, 1973—78, prin. rsch. assoc., 1979—83, asst. prof., 1984—85; assoc. prof. Carnegie Mellon U., Pitts., 1985—90, prof., 1990—. Sr. cons. Hammer & Co., Cambridge, 1981—83, Comm. Studies and Planning, Cambridge, 1983—85; dir. Telelogic Corp., Somerville, Mass., 1984—88, Comav Corp., Framingham, Mass., 1998—99; mem. FCC Technol. Adv. Com., Washington, 1999—2001; founder Carnegie Mellon Info. Networking Inst. Co-author: (book) Microprocessor Applications; contbr. articles to profl. jours. (Best Paper award, 1976), chapters to books. Recipient Karl Compton award, MIT, 1966, Benjamin Teare Outstanding Tchg. award, Carnegie Mellon U., 1991; fellowship, NSF, 1966—71. Mem.: IEEE, Telecom. Policy Rsch. Conf. (co-chmn. 1980, bd. dirs. v.p. 1994), Sigma Xi, Eta Kappa Nu, Tau Beta Pi. Jewish. Achievements include patents for method and apparatus for purchasing and delivering digital goods over a network; method for certifying delivery of secure electronic transactions. Avocations: jogging, tennis, travel. Office: Carnegie Mellon Univ 5000 Forbes Ave Pittsburgh PA 15213-3890 Office Fax: 412-268-3757. Business E-Mail: sirbu@cmu.edu.

SIRES, ALBIO, United States Representative from New Jersey, former state legislator; b. Bejucal, Cuba, Jan. 26, 1951; arrived in USA, 1962; m. Adrienne Sires; 1 stepchild, Tara Kole. BA in Spanish & Mktg., St. Peter's Coll., Englewood Cliffs, NJ, 1974; MA in Spanish, Middlebury Coll., Vt., 1985. Dir Hispanic Outreach Dept. Cmty. Affairs, State of NJ, 1987—88; owner A.M. Title Agy., Inc.; mayor Town West NY, NJ, 1995—2006; mem. NJ Gen. Assembly from Dist. 33, 2000—06, spkr., 2002—06; acting gov. State of NJ, 2002, 2005; mem. US Congress from 13th NJ Dist., 2006—, US House Fgn. Affairs Com., US House Transp. & InfrastructureCom.; vice chmn. Democratic Congressional Campaign Com. (DCCC), 2009—. Recipient Cmty. That Works award, NJ State, William J. Brennan Citation for Justice, NJ Bar Assn., 2005; named Mayor of Yr., NJ Conf. Mayors, 2004. Mem.: Legis. Svcs. Commn. Democrat. Roman Catholic. Office: US Congress 1024 Longworth House Office Bldg Washington DC 20515 also: 5500 Palisade Ave Ste A West New York NJ 07093 Office Phone: 201-558-0800. Office Fax: 201-617-2809.*

SIRICA, ALPHONSE EUGENE, pathology educator; b. Waterbury, Conn., Jan. 16, 1944; s. Alphonse Eugene and Elena Virginia (Mascolo) S.; m. Annette Marie Murray, June 9, 1984; children: Gabrielle Theresa, Nicholas Steven. MS, Fordham U., 1968; PhD in Biomed. Sci., U. Conn., 1977. Asst. prof. U. Wis., Madison, 1979-84; assoc. prof. Med. Coll. Va., Va. Commonwealth U., Richmond, 1984-90, prof. of pathology, 1990—, divsn. chair exptl. pathology, 1992-99, divsn. chair cellular and molecular pathogenesis, 1999—. Vis. prof. Pa. State U. Coll. Medicine, 2000; regular mem. sci. adv. com. on carcinogenesis and nutrition Am. Cancer Soc., Atlanta, 1989—92; metabolic pathology study sect. NIH, Bethesda, 1991—95, ad hoc mem. study sect., 1997—2006, 2008. Editor, author: The Pathobiology of Neoplasia, 1989, The Role of Cell Types in Hepatocarcinogenesis, 1992, Cellular and Molecular Pathogenesis, 1996; co-editor, author: Biliary and Pancreatic Ductal Epithelia: Pathobiology and Pathophysiology, 1997; mem. editl. bd. Pathobiology, 1990-99, Hepatology, 1991-94; rev. bd. In Vitro Cellular and Devel. Biology-Animal, 1987—, Exptl. and Molecular Pathology, 1999—, World Jour. Gastroenterology, 2006-09; contbr. articles to profl. jours. including Am. Jour. Pathology, Cancer Rsch., Hepatology, and other. Recipient Rsch. Recognition award, Va. Commonwealth U. Sch. Medicine, 2002, 2007. Fellow: Am. Gastroent. Assn.; mem.: AAAS, Soc. Toxicology, Han. Popper Hepatopathology Soc., Soc. Exptl. Biology and Medicine, NY Acad. Scis., Am. Assn. Study Liver Diseases (chair conf. pathobiology of biliary epithelia and cholangiocarcinoma), Am. Soc. Investigative Pathology (chair program com. 1994—96), Assn. Clin. Scientists, Soc. for In Vitro Biology, Am. Assn. Cancer Rsch. (chmn. Va. state legis. com. 1992—95), Am. Soc. Cell Biology. Achievements include development of collagen gel-nylon mesh system for culturing hepatocytes; first establishment and characterization of hyperplastic bile ductular epithelial cells in culture; research in hepato- and biliary carcinogenesis, pathobiology of hepatocyte and biliary epithelial cells and molecular pathogenesis and experimental therapeutics of biliary cancer. Office: Med Coll Va Va Commonwealth U PO Box 980297 Richmond VA 23298-0297 Home Phone: 804-346-9210; Office Phone: 804-828-9549. Business E-Mail: asirica@mcvh-vcu.edu.

SIRIGNANO, WILLIAM ALFONSO, aerospace and mechanical engineer, educator; b. Bronx, NY, Apr. 14, 1938; s. Anthony P. and Lucy (Caruso) S.; m. Lynn Haisfield, Nov. 26, 1977; children: Monica Ann, Jacqueline Hope, Justin Anthony. B.Aero.Engring., Rensselaer Poly. Inst., 1959; PhD, Princeton U., 1964. Mem. research staff Guggenheim Labs., aerospace, mech. scis. dept. Princeton U., 1964-67, asst. prof. aerospace and mech. scis., 1967-69, assoc. prof., 1969-73, prof., 1973-79, dept. dir. grad. studies, 1974-78; George Tallman Ladd prof., head dept. mech. engring. Carnegie-Mellon U., 1979-85; dean Sch. Engring., U. Calif.-Irvine, 1985-94, prof., 1994—. Cons. industry and govt., 1966—; lectr., cons. NATO adv. group on aero. rsch. and devel., 1967, 75, 80; chmn. nat. and internat. tech. congs.; chmn. acad. adv. coun. Indsl. Rsch. Inst., 1985-88; mem. space sci. applications adv. com. NASA, 1985-90, chmn. combustion sci. microgravity disciplinary working group, 1987-90; chmn. com. on microgravity rsch. space studies bd. NRC, 1991-94, Henry Samueli endowed chair in engring., 2004-. Spl. issues editor: Combustion Sci. and Tech., 1969-70, 2000-06; assoc. tech. editor Jour. Heat Transfer, 1986-92; contbr. articles to profl. jours. Recipient Disting. Alumni Rsch. award U. Calif. Irvine, 1992, Recognition award Am. Electronics Assn., 1994, Excellence award Orange County Engring. Coun., 1994; United Aircraft rsch. fellow, 1973-74. Fellow: AAAS, ASME (Freeman scholar 1992), AIAA (Pendray Aerospace Lit. award 1991, Propellants and Combustion award 1992, Energy Systems award 2004, Sustained Svc. award 2006, Wyld Propulsion award 2009), Soc. Indsl. & Applied Math., Am. Phys. Soc.; mem.: NAE, Combustion Inst. (treas. internat. orgn., chmn. ea. sect., Alfred C. Egerton Gold medal 1996), Inst. Dynamics Explosives and Reactive Sys. (v.p. 1991—95, pres. 1995—99, Oppenheim award 1993). Office: U Calif Irvine Sch Engring S3202 Engring Gtwy Irvine CA 92697-3975

SIRILLA, GEORGE M., lawyer; b. Perryopolis, Pa., May 1, 1929; s. Michael and Helen Sirilla; m. Floranne Zalewski Sirilla, Nov. 23, 1968; children: Michael George, Joseph David. BSME, Rensselaer Poly. Inst., Troy, NY, 1952; LLB, Georgetown Law Sch., Washington, JD, 1956. Bar: Va. 1956, DC 1956. Assoc. Cushman, Darby & Cushman, Washington, 1955—59, ptnr., 1960, 1968—96, Pillsbury, Madison & Sutro, 1996—, Pillsbury Winthrop, McLean, Va., 2001—05, Pillsbury Winthrop Shaw Pittman, 2005—. Adj. prof. George Washington Law Sch., Washington, 1982—83; mem. mng. bd. Cushman, Darby & Cushman, 1988—89, Pillsbury, Madison & Sutro, 1999—2000. Contbr. articles to law revs. Sgt. US Army, 1946—47, Korea. Named Master, Giles S. Rich Inn of Ct., 1992—2001. Fellow: Am. Coll. Trial Lawyers. Office: Pillsbury Winthrop Shaw 1650 Tysons Blvd Mc Lean VA 22102 Office Phone: 703-770-7784.

SIRIWARDANE, HEMA J., science educator; b. Sri Lanka; BSc with honors, U. Ceylon, Peradeniya, Sri Lanka, 1975; PhD, Va. Tech, Blacksburg, 1980. Cert. in PE, W.Va., 1996. Prof. W.Va. U., Morgantown, 1981—. Co-author: (book) Constitutive Laws for Engring. Materials; editor: Computer Methods and Advances in Geomechanics; contbr. over 100 tech. papers and reports. Recipient Over 20 Tchg. Awards, 1990—2008. Mem.: Internat. Assn. Computer Methods and Advances in Geomechanics. Office: West Virginia Univ Dept Civil & Environmental Engineering Morgantown WV 26506-6103

SIRKEN, MONROE GILBERT, statistician; b. NYC, Jan. 11, 1921; s. Irving and Henrietta (Oram) S.; m. Blanche Skalak Hurwitz (div. 1960); children: Robert, Philip. BA, UCLA, 1946, MA, 1947; PhD, U. Wash., 1950. Lectr. Med. Sch. U. Wash., Seattle, 1949; fellow Stats. Lab. U. Calif., Berkeley, 1950; statistician Census Bur., Suitland, Md., 1951-54, Pub. Health Svc., Washington, 1954-60, Nat. Ctr. Health Stats., Hyattsville, Md., 1961—. Cons. NIH, 1980-85, Nat. Inst. Drug Addiction, 1976-80, NSF, 1986—, Health Care Fin. Adminstrn., 1989-90. Contbr. articles to Jour. Am. Statis. Assn., Biometrics, Demography, Jour. APHA, Pub. Health Reports, also others. Home: 3114 Gracefield Rd Apt 405 Silver Spring MD 20904 Office Phone: 301-458-4505. Personal E-mail: mgsirken@aol.com. Business E-Mail: mgs2@cdc.gov.

SIRKIN, JOEL H., lawyer; b. Pitts., Jan. 7, 1946; s. Sidney and Marion (Wolkin) S.; m. Karen Sargent, Aug. 7, 1977; children: Alex S., Jacob O. BA magna cum laude, Johns Hopkins U., 1967; JD cum laude, Harvard U., 1972. Bar: Mass. 1972. Prin. Cambridge (Mass.) Pilot Sch., 1970-71; staff atty. Cambridge-Somerville Legal Services, 1972-74; sr. ptnr., chmn. Real Estate dept. Hale & Dorr, Boston, 1974—2004; ptnr., chmn. Real Estate dept., mem. exec. com. Wilmer Cutler Pickering Hale & Dorr, Boston, 2004—. Author: Public School Law. Dir. Mass. Children's Lobby, Boston, 1980-84; mem. fin. com. Town of Wayland, Mass., 1993-96. Named a Mass. Super Lawyer, Boston Mag., 2004—08; named one of Best Lawyers America, America's Leading Lawyers for Bus., Chambers USA, Band ONC, 2006—08. Mem. Phi Beta Kappa. Avocations: gardening, tennis, golf. Home: 10 Wildwood Rd Wayland MA 01778-2122 Office: Wilmer Cutler Pickering Hale & Dorr 60 State St Boston MA 02109-1816 Office Phone: 617-526-6279. Office Fax: 617-526-5000. Business E-Mail: joel.sirkin@wilmerhale.com.

SIRKIN, MICHAEL S., lawyer; b. Newark, Feb. 21, 1947; BS in industl. engring., Rutgers U., 1969; JD, Columbia U., 1972. Bar: N.Y. 1973. Mem. Proskauer Rose LLP, NYC, 1989—. Office: Proskauer Rose LLP 1585 Broadway Fl 27 New York NY 10036-8299 Home Phone: 212-734-1947; Office Phone: 212-969-3840. E-mail: msirkin@proskauer.com.

SIRLIN, ALBERTO, physics professor; b. Buenos Aires, Nov. 25, 1930; s. Bernardo and Raquel Sirlin; m. Sonia Klin, Aug. 17, 1963; children: Claude Bernard, Diana Karina Glatzer. PhD, Cornell U., Ithaca, NY, 1957. Rsch. assoc. Columbia U., NYC, 1957—59; asst. prof., physics NY U., NYC, 1959—61, assoc. prof., physics, 1961—68, prof., physics, 1968—2008, prof. emeritus physics, 2008—. Mem., com. selection Guggenheim Found., NYC, 1986—2002. Contbr. scientific papers (J.J. Sakurai prize, 2002). Recipient award, Alexander von Humboldt Found., 1997. Office: NYU Dept Physics 4 Washington Pl New York NY 10003-6621 Office Fax: 212-995-4016. Business E-Mail: alberto.sirlin@nyu.edu.

SIRMANS, BARBARA C., library director; Dir. Birmingham Pub. Libr., Ala., 2002—. Mem. exec. coun. Ala. Libr. Assn., 1999, conv. chair, 2004; bd. dirs. Workshops, Inc., 2004. Office: Birmingham Pub Libr 2100 Park Pl Birmingham AL 35203 Office Phone: 205-226-3614. Office Fax: 205-226-3731. Business E-Mail: barbara@bham.lib.al.us.

SIRNA, GAIL CAROLYN, artist, educator, writer; b. Detroit, Apr. 7, 1943; d. John Arthur and Viola Rose McKeown; m. Robert G. Sirna, May 28, 1966; children: Michele Lee Grace, Cheryl Lynn, Anthony McKeown. AB, St. Louis U., 1965; MA, U. Mich., 1969. Tchr., counselor Hazel Park (Mich.) Pub. Schs., 1972—82; tchr. Nat. Needlework, 1980—; shopowner The Fancyworks, Sterling Heights, Mich., 1982—85. Contbr. bi-monthly column; author: In Praise of the Needlewoman: Embroiderers, Knitters, Lacemakers, & Weavers in Art, 2007. Named a Notable Needlewomen Mich., Mich. Women's Hist. Mus. Mem.: Am. Needlepoint Guild (master tchr. 1988, nominating com. 2000—03, Best of Show 1999), Nat. Embroidery Tchrs. Assn. (pres. 1985—88, sec. 2002—07), Embroiderers' Guild Am. (mastercraftsman in canvas 1980, region dir. 1990—92, cert. grad. tchr. 1997, chmn. cert. grad. tchr. program 2001—04), Nat. Acad. Needlearts (cert. tchr. needlearts 1982, cert. judge 1988, dir. 1990—2009, treas. 2000—, Lifetime Achievement award 2004, honors 2002), Mensa, Phi Kappa Phi. Roman Catholic. Avocations: needlecrafts, reading, travel, bird-watching, automobiles.

SIROKY, ALLEN JAMES, history professor; b. Lewistown, Mont., July 25, 1947; s. James and Ruth Siroky; m. Helen Frances Loftin, Nov. 23, 1986; 1 child, Jeanne Frances. PhD, Grad. Ctr. CUNY, NYC, 1996. Tchr. St. Cornelius Sch., Richmond, Calif., 1973—75, St. Joseph Sch., Pinole, Calif., 1975—76; tchr. & coach Wasatch Acad., Mt. Pleasant, Utah, 1978—88, Tabor Acad., Marion, Mass., 1997—99; prof., history Fresno City Coll., Calif., 1999—. Contbr. scientific papers. E-4 Res. US Army, 1970—76, Billings, Mont., Ft. Ord US Army, San Rafael, Calif. Mem.: Faculty Assn. Calif. Cmty. Colls., Orgn. Am. Historians, Am. Hist. Assoc. Liberal. Methodist. Avocations: weightlifting, walking, hiking. Office: Fresno City Coll 1101 E University Ave Fresno CA 93741 Personal E-mail: drsiroky@yahoo.com. Business E-Mail: allen.siroky@fresnocitycollege.edu.

SIROTA, WILBERT H., lawyer; b. Balt., 1937; BA, Johns Hopkins U., 1958; JD, U. Md., 1961; LLM, Georgetown U., 1964. Bar: Md. 1961. Law clk. Md. Ct. Appeals, 1961—62; atty., office of chief counsel IRS, 1963; assoc. Frank Bernstein Conaway & Goldman, 1966—68, ptnr., 1968—92, DLA Piper, Balt., 1992—2006; of counsel, chair Balt. office Duane Morris LLP, 2006—. Lectr. Georgetown Univ. Sch. Law, Univ. Md. Sch. Law, Loyola Coll. Bd. dir. & treas. World Trade Ctr. Inst., Balt.; bd. dirs. & counsel Econ. Alliance Greater Balt.; mem. bd. vis. Univ. Md. Balt. County; mem. bd. Lifebridge Health Care; bd. trustees Balt. Coun. on Foreign Affairs. Office: Duane Morris LLP 111 S Calvert St Ste 2000 Baltimore MD 21202

SIROTIN, NICOLE ASHLEY, physician; b. Pk. Ridge, Ill., Aug. 9, 1976; d. Nick and Barbara Wirth Sirotin. BA, Rutgers Coll., New Brunswick, 1999; MD, UMDNJ-NJMS, Newark, 2005. Diplomate Am. Bd. Internal Medicine, 2008. Resident physician U. Calif., San Francisco, 2005—08; assoc. physician U. Calif., San Diego, La Jolla, 2008—. Ethics com. mem. Nat. Physicians Alliance, Reston, Va., 2009—. Recipient award, Arnold P. Gold Found. Honors Soc., 2004, Exceptional Physician Award, UCSF Med. Ctr., 2008, Reza Gandjei Humanism award, UCSF Dept. Medicine, 2008. Mem.: Soc. Gen. Internal Medicine, Delta Phi Alpha, Phi Beta Kappa Soc. Avocations: reading, soccer, travel. Office: Univ Calif San Diego 10111 N Torrey Pines Rd La Jolla CA 92093

SIROTY, WILLIAM CHARLES, physician; b. NYC, June 9, 1951; s. Daniel Hirsch and Eileen (Gusman) S. BS, SUNY, Stony Brook, 1973; MD, Georgetown U., Washington, DC, 1977. Diplomate Am. Bd. Internal Medicine, Am. Bd. Allergy-Immunology. Intern in internal medicine Beth Israel Med. Ctr., NYC, 1977-78, resident in internal medicine, 1977-78; fellow allergy and immunology NY Hosp.-Cornell U. Med. Ctr., 1980-82; pvt. practice NYC, 1982-94; staff physician Nashua (NH) Med. Group, 1994—. Editor: NH News Links, 2000—08. Co-founder, first co-chair Gay People in Medicine Caucus Am. Med. Student Assn., 1976—77; active NH State Dem. Com., 1998—2006, Hillsborough County Dem. Com., NH, 1998—2006, vice-chmn., 2004—06; del. Dem. Nat. Conv., 2000, 2004; chair Dems. Amherst, 2002—06; bd. dirs. Democracy for NH, 2006—, Elizabeth Streb Ringside, Inc., NH Civil Liberties Union. Mem. Am. Acad. Allergy, Asthma and Immunology, NH Med. Soc. Office: Nashua Med Group 173 Daniel Webster Hwy Nashua NH 03060-5224

SIRVÉN, JOSÉ E., lawyer; b. Camaguey, Cuba, Aug. 28, 1956; AA with honors, Miami-Dade CC, 1976; BBA in Acctg. with honors, Fla. Internat. U., 1978; JD cum laude, U. Miami, 1981. Ptnr. Holland & Knight LLP, Miami, Fla., mem. dir. com. Articles and comment editor U. Miami Law Review, 1980—81. Mem.: Cuban Am. Bar Assn., Fla. Bar, Dade County Bar Assn. Office: Holland & Knight LLP 701 Brickell Ave Ste 3000 Miami FL 33131 Office Phone: 305-789-7784. Business E-Mail: jsirven@hklaw.com.

SIRY, JOSEPH VINCENT, environmentalist, educator; s. Vincent John Siry and Irene Marie Wadowicz; m. Barbara Louise MacMorrow, Oct. 10, 1983. PHD in History, U. Calif., Santa Barbara, 1978. Instr. Santa Rosa Jr. Coll., Calif., 1978—78, Sonoma State U., Cotati, Calif., 1984. Instr. Solano CC, Suisun City, Calif., 1978—83; assoc. prof. Rollins Coll., Winter Pk., Fla., 1984—; dir. Fla. Climate Alliance, Winter Pk., 1999—2001; treas. Save the Manatee Club, Maitland, Fla., 2003—. Author: (environmental history, sci. & policy) Marshes the Ocean Shore. Exec. com. Fla. Defenders Environment, Gainesville, Fla., 1985—2009. Recipient Cypress award, Sierra Club Fla. Chpt., 2001. Mem.: Assn. Environ. Studies and Scis. Buddhist. Achievements include research in global warming and climate change. Avocations: travel, hiking, kayaking, snorkeling, swimming. Office: Rollins Coll 1000 Holt Ave Winter Park FL 32789

SISCHO, LACEY, social studies educator; d. Dennis and Mary Jo Sischo; m. Stephen G. Morris, June 14, 2007; 1 child, Zoe Morris. PhD, Fla. State U., Tallahassee, 2008. Grad. asst. Fla. State U., 2002—08; instr. Ctrl. Mich. U., Mt. Pleasant, 2009—. Contbr. articles to jour. Mem.: Am. Sociol. Assn. Home: 2306 Univ Ave Saint Joseph MO 64503 Personal E-mail: lsischo@gmail.com.

SISCHY, INGRID BARBARA, editor, art critic; b. Johannesburg, Republic of South Africa, Mar. 2, 1952; came to U.S., 1967; d. Benjamin and Claire S.; with Sandra J. Brant. BS, Sarah Lawrence Coll., 1973; PhD (hon.), Moore Coll. Art, 1987. Assoc. editor Print Collector's Newsletter, NYC, 1974-77; dir. Printed Matter, NYC, 1977-78; curatorial intern Mus. Modern Art, NYC, 1978-79; editor ArtForum Mag., NYC, 1979-88; editor-in-chief Interview, NYC, 1989—2008; internat. editor Vanity Fair Italy, Vanity Fair Spain, Vogue Germany & Vogue Russia Conde Nast, 2008—.

SISIOPIKU, VIRGINIA P., civil engineer; b. Thessaloniki, Greece, July 16, 1965; d. Poulios and Paraskevi (Rammou) S.; m. Yiannis Argyropoulos, Sept. 12, 1993; 2 children. BSCE, Aristotelian U. Thessaloniki, 1988; MS in Civil Engring., U. Ill., Chgo., 1991, PhD in Civil Engring., 1994. Registered profl. engr., Greece. Rsch. and tchg. asst. U. Ill., Chgo., 1989-93; rsch. fellow Fed. Hwy Adminstrn., McLean, Va., 1992-93; transp. cons. P/R Michaels Assocs., Ltd., Chgo., 1994-95; assoc. rsch. scientist U. Ill./IVHS Lab., Chgo., 1994-95; adj. asst. prof. Ill. Inst. Tech., Chgo., 1994-95; asst. prof. Mich. State U., East Lansing, Mich., 1995—2002; assoc. prof. U. Ala., Birmingham, 2002—. Faculty advisor UABITE Student Chpt., 2002—. Recipient Grant Shaw Meml. award Ill. Assn. Hwy. Engrs., Palatine, Ill., 1992, Faculty Fellowship award Fed. Hwy. Adminstrn., Washington, 1995, 98, 2003, Pres.'s Tchg. Excellence award U. Alabama, Birmingham, 2007; Helen Overly scholarship Women Transp. Seminar, Seattle, 1991, scholar NSF ADVANCE, 2005, 06, 07. Mem. Transp. Rsch. Bd., Inst. Transp. Engrs.

(pres. 1993-94, Outstanding Student Paper Nat. award 1991), Intelligent Transp. Soc. Mich., Safety Mgmt. Systems. Avocations: travel, baking, stamp collecting/philately. Office: U Ala Birmingham 1075 13th St S Birmingham AL 35294

SISK, DANIEL ARTHUR, lawyer; b. Albuquerque, July 12, 1927; s. Arthur Henry and Myrl (Hope) S.; m. Katharine Banning, Nov. 27, 1954; children: John, Sarah, Thomas. BA, Stanford U., 1950, JD, 1954. Bar: N.Mex. 1955, Calif. 1954. Ptnr. firm Modrall, Sperling, Roehl, Harris & Sisk, Albuquerque, 1954-70, 71—; justice N.Mex. Supreme Ct., Santa Fe, 1970. Chmn. bd. Sunwest Fin. Svcs., Inc., Albuquerque, 1975-90. Pres. Legal Aid Soc., Albuquerque, 1960-61; trustee Sandia Sch., 1968-72, Albuquerque Acad., 1971-73, A.T. & S.F. Meml. Hosps., Topeka, 1966-82; bd. dirs. N.Mex. Sch. Banking Found., 1981-85. Served with USNR, 1945-46, PTO; to capt. USMCR, 1951-52, Korea. Mem. N.Mex. Bar Assn., Albuquerque Bar Assn. (dir. 1962-63), ABA, State Bar Calif. Presbyn. (elder). Office: 500 4th St NW Albuquerque NM 87102-5324

SISK, EILEEN VICTORIA, writer, journalist; b. Henderson, Nev., Nov. 8, 1952; d. Hugh Albert and Susan Apathy (Kuyrkendall) S.; m. Richard James Adams, Dec. 28, 1974 (div. Mar. 1979); m. Stephan Rudolph Tetreault, Aug. 29, 1981 (div. Oct. 1993); children: Jeffrey Hugh Tetreault, Douglas Gerard Tetreault; m. Samuel Ragan Mellar, Apr. 14, 1995 (div. June 2001). BA in Comm., Calif. State U., Fullerton, 1979. Feature writing intern L.A. Times, 1977-78; pub. info. asst. Orange County Transit Dist., Garden Grove, Calif., 1978; copy editor Las Vegas Rev. Jour., 1978-79, Sunday editor, 1979-81; copy editor U.S. C. of C., Washington, 1981-83, The Washington Post, 1982-86, design editor, 1987-92; copy editor II The Tennessean, Nashville, 2000—09. Freelance journalist various media outlets including sirius XM Satellite Radio, Continuum Ency., Popular Music of the World, Am. Cowboy, Nev., others. Author: Honky-Tonks: Guide to Country Dancin' and Romancin', 1995. Vol. NOW, Washington, 1981, Gloucester County Pub. Schs., 1992-99. Recipient 4 Merit awards Calif. Photographers Pro Show, 1978. Mem.: Investigative Reporters and Editors, Soc. Newspaper Design (4 awards of excellence 1990, 1992), Soc. Profl. Journalists (profl. devel. com. 1986—92). Avocations: walking, reading, cooking, dance.

SISK, FRED DEAN, retired cartographer; b. Johnson City, Tenn., May 26, 1940; s. Aubrey Mackenzie and Violet Mae (McCartt) S.; m. Martha Lynn Robinson, Aug. 25, 1963. BS, East Tenn. State U., 1962; MS, George Mason U., 1984. Cert. State Va. Cartographer Def. Mapping Agy., Brookmont, Md., 1965—79, sr. cartographer, sr. instr., master instr. Ft. Belvior, Va., 1979—88, course mgr., 1981—88, dep. divsn. chief, 1983—88, new employees tng. coord. Bethesda, Md., 1988—89; tng. coord. Def. Mapping Agy. Reston Ctr., Va., 1989—90, security analyst, 1990—95; ret., 1995. Mem. scholarship com. George Mason U. Alumni Assn., Fairfax, 1990; mem. Rep. Nat. Com., Rep. Presdl. Task Force, Washington, 1990—, adv. com. House of Dels., 54th Dist., 1995-2002; officer of election City of Fredericksburg, 1995—, mem. pub. transit adv. bd., 1996—, chmn. memls. adv. commn., 2000-03; notary public, 1996—, security officer, 1996—; pres. Fox Run Homeowners Assn., 1996—. 1st lt. battery commdr. U.S. Army, 1962-64. Fellow: Internat. Biog. Assn. (Cambridge, Eng.) (life; dep. dir. gen.); mem.: Internat. Freelance Photographers Orgn. (master photographer 2004—, Lifetime Achievement award in Photography, Master Photographer Regnant, Hon. Degree of Distinction, Hall of Fame), Civil War Round Table (v.p. to pres. 2007—09, past pres.), NRA (life). Baptist. Home: 18 Devonshire Dr Fredericksburg VA 22401-2100

SISK, GREGORY CHARLES, lawyer, educator; b. Des Moines, May 29, 1960; s. James Anderson and Roberta Jean (Thornburg) S.; m. Melinda Fay Gilchrist, June 14, 1981; 1 child, Caitlin Anne. Student, Western Mont. Coll., 1978; BA in Polit. Sci., Mont. State U., 1981; JD, U. Wash., 1984. Bar: Wash. 1985, Iowa 1992, US Ct. Appeals (3d cir. and 9th cir.) 1986, US Ct. Appeals (2d, 5th, 11th and DC cir.) 1987, US Ct. Appeals (4th, 8th and fed. cir.) 1988, US Ct. Appeals (1st cir.) 1989, US Supreme Ct. 1988. Legis. asst. US Senate, Washington, 1984-85; jud. clk. US Ct. Appeals (9th cir.), Seattle, 1985-86; appellate staff atty. civil div. US Dept. Justice, Washington, 1986-89; assoc. Karr, Tuttle & Campbell, Seattle, 1989-91; asst. prof. Drake U., Des Moines, 1991-94, assoc. prof., 1994-97, prof., 1997—2003, Richard M. and Anita Calkins disting. prof., 1999—2003; Ovestes A. Brownson prof. U. St. Thomas, Mpls., 2003—. Mem. ABA, Am. Law Inst., Fed. Bar Assn., Christian Legal Soc., Order of Coif, Nat. Order of Barristers, Law and Soc. Assn., Am. Polit. Sci. Assn. Republican. Roman Catholic. Office: Univ St Thomas Sch Law 1000 La Salle Ave Minneapolis MN 55403-2005 Office Phone: 651-962-4923. Business E-Mail: gcsisk@stthomas.edu.

SISK, JANE ELIZABETH, economist, educator; b. West Reading, Pa., Sept. 23, 1942; 2 children. BA with honors, Brown U., 1963; MA, George Washington U., 1965; PhD, McGill U., Montreal, Que., Can., 1976. Cons. Nat. Planning Assn., Washington, 1976; scholar VA, Washington, 1978-81; rsch. dir. Office Tech. Assessment, U.S. Congress, Washington, 1976-78, sr. analyst, 1981-84, sr. assoc., 1984-91. Vis. prof. Columbia U. Sch. Pub. Health, N.Y.C., 1990-91, prof., 1992—99; prof. Mt. Sinai Sch. Medicine, N.Y.C., 1999—, dir. divsn. health care stats. Nat. Ctr. for Health Stats., Ctrs. for Disease Control, Hyattsville, Md., 2004—. Co-author: Toward Rational Technology in Medicine, 1981; mem. editl. bd. Internat. Jour. Tech. Assessment in Health Care, 1987—, vol. editor, 1990, 98; asst. editor Am. Jour. Pub. Health, 1990-91; mem. editl. bd. Health Svcs. Rsch., 1994—; contbr. articles to profl. jours. Pres. Internat Soc. Tech. Assessment in Health Care, 1991-93, bd. dirs., 1987-95; mem. N.Y. State Task Force on Clin. Guidelines & Med. Tech. Assessment, 1994-96; mem. study sect. on health care quality and effectiveness rsch. U.S. Agy. for Health Care Policy and Rsch., 1997-2001. Elisah Benjamin Andrews scholar Brown U., 1961, 63; Bronfman fellow McGill U., 1971. Fellow Assn. for Health Svcs. Rsch.; mem. Inst. of Medicine, NAS (mem. cancer policy bd. 1997-2000, inst. medicine, 2001—), Phi Beta Kappa. Office Phone: 301-458-4157.

SISKE, REGINA, artist; b. Varen Muritz, Germany, Oct. 11, 1944; d. Peter Paul and Olga Vanda Markunas; m. Roger Charles Siske, May 31, 1969 (dec.); children: Kelly, Jennifer, Kimberly. BSN, U. Ill., 1966; postgrad. in MSN program, U. Mich., 1968—69; ind. fine art studies, North Shore Art League, Winnetka, Ill., 1970s, Alain Gavin, Art Inst. Chgo., 1980s, Tom James, Wilmette, Ill., 2000—; Degree, Sumi-e-Studies Kay Thomas; Asian brush painting and calligraphy studies Lampo Leong, U. Mo., 1998—; Asian brush painting and Chinese calligraphy studies Moon Yan Huen, City Coll., San Francisco, 1999—2002; Asian brush painting and Chinese calligraphy studies, Charles Liu, Westmont, Ill., 1999—, numerous workshops, NYC and Chgo. RN Ill., 1966. Staff med.-surg. nurse Presbyn.-St. Luke's Hosp., Chgo., 1966—67, Mass. Gen. Hosp., Boston, 1967—68; nursing staff devel. VA Rsch. Hosp., Chgo., 1969—70, Evanston/Northwestern Hosp., Evanston, Ill., 1971, St. Francis Hosp., Evanston, Ill., 1971—73; nursing cons. Evanston Hosp., 1971; rsch. and quality control studies VA Hosp., Chgo., 1969—70; cmty. outreach and edn. Evanston and St. Francis Hosps., 1971—73. Chair Asian art exhibit and workshop Suburban Fine Arts Ctr., 2004. Exhibitions include Mobile Mus. Art, Ala., 1998, Bayard Cutting Arboretum, LI, NY, 1999, Suburban Fine Arts Ctr., Highland Park, Ill., 1999—2009 (award, 2001), Alliance Gallery, Indpls. Mus. Art, 2000—01, Strathmore Hall of Arts, Bethesda, Md., 2000 (award, 2000), 2003 (award, 2003), 2009, Courthouse Gallery, Norfolk, Va., 2001, Nat. Juried Virtual Exhbn., Internet, 2002, 2004, Chinese Fine Arts Soc., Westmont, Ill., 2001, Chgo. Bot. Gardens, Art League Alliance, 2004, J. Harrison Smith Fine Art Gallery, Clearwater, Fla., 2005, Bloomington Art Ctr., Minn., 2006, Represented in permanent collections, exhibitions include Wilmette Library Juries Exhibition, 2009 (award, 2008). Vol. Kellogg Cancer Rsch. Ctr., Evanston Hosp., 1988—89; bd. dir. St. Elizabeth Nursery Sch., Glencoe, Ill., 1981—82, Josselyn Ctr. for Mental Health, Northfield, Ill., 1989—93, devel. chmn., 1992—93. Recipient Cert. & Achievement award, Women Devel. North; named hon. lifetime trustee, Josselyn Ctr. Mental Health, 1993—, Honoree, Josselyn Ctr. Ann. Benefit, 2006. Mem.: Nat. Sumi-e Soc. Am., Midwest Sumi-e Soc. (program dir. 2000—09, juiried mem. gallery 659, Gleneoe 2008, pres. 2008—09). Avocations: piano, jewelry design, skiing, swimming, tennis. Home and Studio: 248 Hawthorn Ave Glencoe IL 60022 Fax: 847-835-2836. E-mail: sisker@aol.com.

SISKIN, EDWARD JOSEPH, engineering and construction company executive; b. Bklyn., Apr. 30, 1941; s. Haskell and Sylvia (Steckler) S.; m. Patricia Ann Moore, June 26, 1965 (div. Apr. 1990); children: Candice P. Howard, Cristin Jo Blackman; m. Jean Elizabeth Bowen, Dec. 17, 1994. BSEE, U. Pa., 1963; cert., Bettis Reactor Engring. Sch., West Mifflin, Pa., 1965; postgrad., George Washington U., 1963—67. Registered profl. engr., Pa., Mass., N.Y., N.J., Ill., Mich., Fla., W.Va., Ind., S.C., Tex., La., Nebr., Calif., Ala. Engr. U.S. Atomic Energy Commn., Washington, 1963-67, field office mgr. Pitts., 1967-70, Groton, Conn., 1970-77; project mgr. Stone & Webster Engring. Corp., Boston, 1977-78, asst. engring. mgr., 1978-79, engring. mgr. NYC, 1979-83, v.p., mgr., 1984-86, sr. v.p., mgr. Cherry Hill, NJ, 1987-88, exec. v.p., 1988-90, also bd. dirs. Boston; gen. mgr. Superconducting Supercollider Lab., Dallas, 1990-94; pres. Enerjoin Svcs., Inc., 1994—, 2005—; dir. office fissile materials disposition US Nat. Nuc. Security Adminstrn., 2000—05. Mem. adv. com. Inst. of Nuc. Power Ops., Atlanta, 1987-90, adv. bd. Ctr. for Chem. Plant Safety, N.Y.C., 1988-90. Bd. dirs. PenJerDel Coun., Phila., 1987-90. Lt. USN, 1963-69. Office: PO Box 445 Voorhees NJ 08043

SISKIND, ARTHUR MICHAEL, lawyer; b. NY, Oct. 11, 1938; s. William and Sylvia (Schuman) S.; m. Mary Ann Silverman, Nov. 10, 1962; children: Laura, Julie, Kenneth. BA in Liberal Arts, Cornell U., 1960, LLB with distinction, 1962. Ptnr. Squadron, Ellenoff, Plesent & Lehrer, NYC, 1970-91; group gen. counsel News Corp., NYC, 1991—2004, exec. v.p., 1991—96, sr. exec. v.p., 1996—2004, sr. advisor to chmn., 2005—, bd. dirs.; sr. exec. v.p., gen. counsel Fox Entertainment Group. Inc., 1998—2004. Adj. prof. Georgetown Law Ctr., Washington, 2005—07, Cornell Law Sch., Ithaca, 2007—09; bd. dirs. Brit. Sky Broadcasting Group, PLC, PLC; adv. coun. sch. journalism CUNY, 2005. Active Cornell Law Sch. Adv. Coun., 1996—; nat. chmn. Cornell Law Sch. Alumni Fund, 1998-01, Citizens Budget Commn. NYC. Capt. U.S. Army, 1963-65. Mem. ABA, City Bar Assn., Cornell Club, Stockbridge Golf Club. Office: News Corp 1211 Avenue Of The Americas New York NY 10036-8795 Business E-Mail: asiskind@newscorp.com.

SISKIND, DONALD HENRY, lawyer; b. Providence, Dec. 25, 1937; s. Samuel and Sadie (Wasserman) S.; m. Beth Mohel, July 15, 1962; children: Steven M., Edward M. BS, U. Pa., 1959; LLB, Columbia U., 1962. Bar: Mass. 1962, N.Y. 1963. Assoc. Marshall Bratter Greene Allison & Tucker, NYC, 1962-69, ptnr., 1969-82, Katten Muchin Rosenman, 1982—99, of counsel, 1999—. Mem. adv. bd. Chgo. Title Ins. Co.; chmn. various seminars Practicing Law Inst., 1974—; vis. lectr. Columbia U. Sch. Law, 1993-95; mem. adv. bd. Wharton Real Estate Ctr. Contbr. articles to profl. jours. Pres. Greenville Community Coun., 1974-76; pres. bd. edn. Union Free Sch. Dist., Scarsdale, N.Y., 1980-81 Mem.: Am. Coll. Real Estate Lawyers (past pres.), Anglo Am. Real Property Inst. (past chmn.), Assn. of Bar of City of N.Y., Phi Alpha Psi. Home: 876 Park Ave New York NY 10075-1832 Office: Katten Muchin Rosenman 575 Madison Ave Fl 15 New York NY 10022-2585 Home Phone: 212-772-9061; Office Phone: 212-940-8610. Business E-Mail: donald.siskind@kattenlaw.com.

SISKO, DIANE, film producer; BA, Purdue U., W. Lafayette, Ind., 1969. Cert. lifetime credential Calif., 1976. Prof. LA City Coll. Theatre Acad., 1973—; prodr. writer BS Prodns., LA, 2008—. Fashion, lifestyle historian, cons., LA, 2003—. Mem.: Kennedy Ctr. Am. Coll. Theatre Festival (design respondent 2000—08). Office: BS Prodns 7250 Franklin Ave 301 Los Angeles CA 90046 Office Fax: 818-762-9176. Business E-Mail: diane.sisko@gmail.com.

SISLEY, NINA MAE, physician, public health service officer; b. Jacksonville, Fla., Aug. 19, 1924; d. Leonard Percy and Verna (Martin) S.; m. George W. Fischer, May 16, 1962 (dec. 1990). BA, Tex. State Coll. for Women, 1944; MD, U. Tex., Galveston, 1950; MPH, U. Mich., 1963. Intern City of Detroit Receiving Hosp., 1950-51; resident in gen. practice St. Mary's Infirmary, Galveston, Tex., 1951-52; sch. physician Galveston Ind. Sch. Dist., 1953-56; dir. med. svcs. San Antonio Health Dept., 1960-63, acting dir., 1963-64; resident in pub. health Tex. Dept. Pub. Health, San Antonio, 1963-65; dir. cmty. health svcs. Corpus Christi-Nueces County Dept. Health, Tex., 1964-67; dir. Tb control region 5 Tex. Dept. Health, Corpus Christi, 1967-73; chief chronic illness control City of Houston Health Dept., 1973-78; dir. pub. health region 11 Tex. Dept. Health, Rosenberg, 1978-87; dir. Corpus Christi-Nueces County Dept. Pub. Health, 1987—2002. Lectr. Incarnate Word Coll., San Antonio, 1963-64; adj. prof. U. Tex. Sch. Pub. Health, Houston, 1980—2002; adj. prof. Tex. A&M U., Corpus Christi, 1997—2002; pvt. practice Galveston, Stockdale, Hereford and Borger, Tex., 1952-59; mem. adv. bd. Cmty. Adv. Coun.; clin. instr. U. Tex. Health Sci. Ctr., San Antonio, 1997-2002 Mem. Nueces County Child Fatality REv. Com.; mem. adv. com. Nueces County Hosp. Dist.; mem. adv. bd. Alzheimers Assn.; mem. health adv. bd. Corpus Christi Ind. Sch. Dist.; bd. dirs. Coastal Bend chpt. ARC, Corpus Christi, 1990—94, 2003—07, pres., 1990—91; bd. dirs. United Way-Coastal Bend, Coastal Bend Coalition on AIDS, 1988—94, Charlie's Place Alcohol and Drug Rehab. Ctr. Fellow Am. Coll. Preventive Medicine; mem. Tex. Med. Assn., Nueces County Med. Soc. (pres. 1997-98), Tex. Assn. Pub. Health Physicians, Tex. Pub. Health Assn. (pres. 1991-92), Local Emergency Planning Assn., Long Term Health Assn., Asthma Coalition. Episcopalian. Avocations: fishing, crossword puzzles, raising african violets. Home: 62 Rock Creek Dr Corpus Christi TX 78412-4214 E-mail: nsisley@sbcglobal.org.

SISNEY, NED, education educator; b. Kansas City, Mo., Feb. 9, 1947; s. Dwight E. and Jeann A. Sisney; m. Mary A. Petersen, Sept. 9, 1988; 1 child, Kaitlyn J. Master's, Concordia U., Mequon, Wis., 2003. Cert. tchr. Wis., 2006. Prof. Concordia U., 1988—. Actor(and dir.): ednl. and profl. theatre. Mem.: Pi Kappa Delta (life), Actor's Equity Assn. (life), Phi Delta Kappa (life), Alpha Psi Omega (life; chpt. pres. 1968—69). Home: 7808 W Rolling Field Dr Mequon WI 53097

SISNEY, SHERLEEN SUE, secondary education educator; b. Stillwater, Okla., Oct. 19, 1946; m. Lee Sisney, June 11, 1969; 1 child, Shara Lee. B.S. in Secondary Edn., Okla. State U., 1968; M.Ed., U. Louisville, 1975. Tchr. Merrill Jr. High Sch., Denver, 1968-69, Monterey High Sch., Calif., 1969-71, Ballard High Sch., Louisville, 1971—92; exec. dir., Ky. Gov.'s Scholars Program, dir., Career Acad., Louisville; mem. pub.'s adv. council Quantum Communications, Inc.; dir. New Foundations in Edn., 1984—; mem. adv. council tchr. and edn. div. Met. Life Found.; mem. Gov.'s Council on Edn. Reform, Joint Council Econ. Edn.; mem. task force social studies Ky. Dept. Edn. Mem. Okla. State U. Centennial Adv. Commn., Jr. League Louisville. Named Nat. Tchr. of Yr., 1984. Recipient Chris Mattingly award for Outstanding Leadership in Ky., Univ. Louisville, 1999. Mem. Ky. Edn. Assn. (Outstanding Tchr. 1979-80), Phi Delta Kappa, others. Home: 8002 Montero Ct Prospect KY 40059-9424 Office: Gov Scholars Program Ste 210 1024 Capital Ctr Dr Frankfort KY 40601

SISON, MICHELE JEANNE, United States Ambassador to Lebanon; b. Arlington, Va., May 27, 1959; d. Pablo B. and Veronica Sison; m. Jeffrey Jones Hawkins (separated); children: Jessica, Alexandra. BA in Polit. Sci., Wellesley Coll., 1981; studied at, London Sch. Econs. Joined Fgn. Svc., US Dept. State, assigned to US missions Port-au-Prince, Haiti, 1982—84, Lome, Togo, 1984—88, Cotonou, Benin, 1988—91, US Dept. State, Douala, Cameroon, 1991—93, Abidjan, Cote d'Ivoire, 1993—96, consul gen. US Consulate Gen. Chennai, India, 1996—99; dep. chief of mission, chargé d'affairs US Embassy, Islamabad, Pakistan, 1999—2002; prin. dep. asst. sec. Bur. South Asian Affairs US Dept. State, Washington, 2002—04, US amb. to United Arab Emirates Abu Dhabi, 2004—08, US amb. to Lebanon Beirut, 2008—. Recipient Presdl. Meritorious Svc. award. Roman Catholic. Office: DOS Amb 6070 Beirut Pl Washington DC 20521-6070*

SISSMAN, LIRON, artist, painter; d. Arie and Atara Sissman. BSc magna cum laude, The Hebrew U., Jerusalem, 1987; attended, Avni Fine Art Inst., Tel Aviv, 1988, NY Acad. Art, 1999; MBA, NYU, 1991. One-man shows include Taro Pharms., Hawthorne, NY, 2002 (Purchase award, 2002), Sound Fed. Savs., Cos., Cob, Conn., 2004, Patriot Bank, Old Greenwich, Ct., 2004, Waltuch Gallery, Tenafly, NJ, 2004, Block Gallery, Montclair, NJ, 2005, Shimon and Sara Birnbaum Gallery, Bridgewater, NJ, 2005, The Synaptic Art Gallery, Paramus, NJ, 2005, ADP Hdqrs., 2005, Watchung Arts Ctr., NJ, 2005, Johnson & Johnson World Hdqrs. Gallery, New Brunswick, NJ, 2006, The Pk. Ave Club, Florham Pk., NJ, 2006, Walter Skulski Art Gallery, Clark, NJ, 2007, The Donald B. Palmer Museum, Springfield, NJ, 2007, The Atrium Gallery, YJCC, Washington Township, NJ, 2007, 08, two person show, Synagogue for the Arts, NYC, 2006, 2007, Pomona Cultural Center, Pomona, NY, 2007, three person show, Best Little Art Gallery, Mahwah, NJ, 2005, Perkins Gallery, Stoughton, Mass., 2005, Euro Art Gallery, Montclair, NJ, 2006, commd. oil painting, Bar Scene, 2002, Donna, 2003, Donna II, 2004, Hanna, 2004, Sea Scape, 2004, Leaving the Nest, 2004, Steve Finley, 2005, Coupling, 2006, Aviv, 2007, Princeton Golf, 2007, Asaf, 2008, Shai, 2008, Pelican on a Seashore, 2008, Yuval, 2009, Pelican on a Seashore, 2009, Aviv, 2009, exhibitions include Cmty. Arts Assn., Ridgewood Art Inst., 2002, Salmagundi Club, NYC, 2002, 2003, Westminster Gallery, 2003, St. John on the Mountain, Bernardville, NJ, 2004, Audobon Artists, 2004, Gallery 214, Montclair, NJ, 2005, Am. Artists Profl. League, Salmagundi Club, NYC, 2005, 07, Hudson Valley Art Assn., Newington-Cropsey Mus., Hastings-on-Hudson, NY, 2005, The Art Center of Northern NJ, New Milford, NJ, 2007, The Four Seasons, Hudson Guild, New York, NY, 2008, Chelsea 32 Art Group, NYC, 2008-09, Unusual Still Lifes, Hudson Guild Gallery II, NYC, 2009, exhibited in group shows at Madison Gallery, NYC, 2000, Limner Gallery, NYC, 2000, The Artist Gallery, Ridgewood, 2001, Midday Gallery, Englewood, NJ, 2004, Montclair State U. Art Galleries, Montclair, NJ, 2004, Port of Call Gallery, Warwick, NY, 2004, Geneva Gallery, Morristown, NJ, 2004, Galleria Nuova, Warwick, NY, 2005, C. Magor Gallery, Ridgewood, NJ, 2005, Geary Gallery, Darien, Conn., 2007 (ongoing representation), Peter McPhee Fine Arts, Stone Harbor, NJ, 2007-08, Courtyard Gallery, Mystic, Conn. (ongoing representation), 2008, Oceanside Gallery, Belmar, NJ, 2008, Burt Mills Galleries, Bernardsville, NJ, 2008, William Ris Gallery, Stone Harbor, NJ, 2009, Also represented by JSO Art Assoc., Westport, Conn., Sheldon FineArt, Newport, RI, 2008, Beacon Fine Arts, Red Bank, NJ, 2009, Jack Leustig Imaging, Arroyo Seco, NM, Helene Forbes Fine Art, NYC, Represented in permanent collections PeproTech, Inc., NJ, Taro Pharms., NY, Sq. Bus. Products, Inc., NJ, Potomac Homes, NJ, Lounge Zen, NJ, AtlantiCare Med. Ctr., NJ, Wex Trust Capital, NY, Glendale Adventist Med. Ctr., Calif, Jesta Group, NYC, Mont Sinai Med. Ctr., NYC, Ridgewood Oral & Maxillofacial Surgery, Data Recovery NJ, pvt. collections, Can., US, UK, and Israel; contbr. articles to varoius publs. featuring artist work; featured guest: PKRG-TV. Recipient Cert. of Achievement, 2004, 1st Pl. Oil award, Bergenfield Arts Festival Collection, 2005, Best of Art, Edgewater Arts Festival, 2006, hon. mention, Renewal Interpreted, Art Ctr. Northern NJ, 2007, 1st prize, Oil and Acrylic Painting, Trees, Waltuch Gallery, 2007; named Best in Show, Mid Rockland Arts Festival, Nanuet Hebrew Ctr., 2004. Mem.: Landscape Artists Internat., Studio Montclair (assoc.), Audubon Artists (assoc.), Allied Artists Am. (assoc.), Am. Artists Profl. League (assoc.). Business E-Mail: liron@liron.com.

SISSOM, LEIGHTON ESTEN, engineering educator, dean, consultant; b. Manchester, Tenn., Aug. 26, 1934; s. Willie Esten and Bertha Sarah (Davis) S.; m. Evelyn Janelle Lee, June 13, 1953; children: Terry Lee, Denny Leighton. BS, Middle Tenn. State Coll., 1956; BS in Mech. Engring., Tenn. Technol. U., 1962; MS in Mech. Engring., Ga. Inst. Tech., 1964, PhD, 1965. Diplomate Nat. Acad. Forensic Engrs.; registered profl. engr., Tenn. Draftsman Westinghouse Electric Corp., Tullahoma, 1953-57; mech. designer ARO, Inc., Tullahoma, 1957-58; instr. mech. engring. Tenn. Technol. U., Cookeville, 1958-62, chmn. dept. mech. engring., 1965-79, dean engring., 1979-88, dean of engring. emeritus, 1988—; prin. cons. Sissom & Assocs., Cookeville, Tenn., 1962—. Bd. dirs. Accreditation Bd. Engring. and Tech., N.Y.C., 1978-86, treas., 1982-86. Author: (with Donald R. Pitts) Elements of Transport Phenomena, 1972, Heat Transfer, 1977, 1,000 Solved Problems in Heat Transfer, 1991; contbr. An Attorney's Guide to Engineering, 1986; contbr. articles to various publs. Fellow ASME (sr. v.p. 1982-86, gov. 1986-88, Golden medallion), Am. Soc. Engring. Edn. (bd. dirs. 1984-87, pres. 1991-92), Accreditation Bd. Engring. and Tech.; mem. NSPE, Soc. Automotive Engrs., Nat. Engring. Deans Coun. (chmn. 1984-87), Order of the Engr. (chmn. bd. govs. 1994-96), Tau Beta Pi (v.p. 1986-89, councillor 1986-89). Home and Office: 1151 Shipley Church Rd Cookeville TN 38501-7730 Office Phone: 931-526-9123. Business E-Mail: sissom@frontiernet.net.

SISSON, BERNICE BELAIR, advocate; b. St. Paul, Oct. 25, 1922; d. Kenneth Theodore Belair and Bernadette Josephine Cormier; m. John McCormick Sisson, May 8, 1948 (dec. Feb. 12, 2005); children: Hilde,

Lydwine, John, Catherine, Angela, Paul, Kenneth, David, Marie, Joseph. BA, Minn. Met. State U., St. Paul, 1986. LPN. Maternity nurse Miller Hosp./United Hosp., St. Paul, 1966—80; dir. Region XI Battered Women's Consortium, St. Paul, 1980—84; coord., legal adv. older battered women's program St. Paul Intervention Project, 1989—; co-founder, first chair Minn. Network on Abuse in Later Life, St. Paul, 2002, also bd. dirs. Co-founder, early pres. Women's Advocate Shelter, St. Paul, 1974—84; facilitator Home Free Shelter Support Groups, Plymouth, Golden Valley, Minn., 1984—87. Co-author: Old Women: Breaking the Silence, 1987. Tutor reading East Side Literacy, St. Paul, 2001—03. Recipient Sunshine Peace award, Nat. Coalition Against Domestic Violence, 1998, Disting. Svc. award, Office of Justice, Dept. Pub. Safety, 2005; named Marvelous Minn. Woman, Minn. Gov., Minn. Women's Consortium, 1993, Woman of Vision and Courage award, Minn. Met. State U., 2001. Mem.: Minn. Women's Consortium, Minn. Coalition Against Domestic Violence. Avocations: reading, music, Sudoku, card and board games, theater. Office: St Paul Intervention Project 1509 Marshall Ave Saint Paul MN 55104 Home: 8583 Granada Ave S Cottage Grove MN 55016-2702 Office Phone: 651-645-2824. Personal E-mail: bernicesisson@comcast.net.

SISSON, KATHY B., chef; b. Asmara, Ethiopia, May 28, 1962; d. Elbert W. and Lois O. Bruce; m. Kelly D. Cross, June 25, 2005. BA, U. Calif., Berkeley, 1984; MA, San Francisco State U., Calif., 2002. Cert. profl. chef Calif. Culinary Acad., 1986. Program co-chair Soc. Sci. Study Of Sexuality, San Francisco, 2005, western region rep., 2005—07, program chair Redondo Beach, Calif., 2006. Contbr. articles to profl. jours. Recipient Disting. Achievement award, San Francisco State U., 2001—02. Home: 640 Fathom Dr San Mateo CA 94404 Office Phone: 650-703-1029. Business E-Mail: kisson@comcast.net.

SISSON, LAURENCE P., artist; b. Boston, Apr. 27, 1928; s. Arthur Foster and Gertrude Davis Sisson; m. Judy Haslee Zimmermann, May 17, 1990; m. Beatrice Bachelder Sisson (div.); children: Mark D., Kerry, David B., Derek Phoenix. Student, Yale U., 1948—49; grad., Worcester Mus. Sch., Mass., 1949; DFA, Maine Coll. Art (formerly Portland Sch. Art), 1992. Artist-in-residence Publick House, Sturbridge, Mass., 1950; guest lectr. Cin. Mus., 1954; instr., dir. Portland Sch. Art, Maine, 1954—58; corporator Worcester Art Mus., Mass., 1972. Artist (cover) Fortune Mag., 1951, artist, actor (film) Maine Harvestors of the Sea, 1969; author: (book) Along Time River, 1975; Represented in permanent collections inclusing Boston U., Berkshire Mus., Bowdin Coll., Clark U., Columbia Mus. Fine Art, Boston Mus. Fine Arts, DeCordova Mus., Darthmouth Coll., and others. With US Army, 1946—47. Recipient 4th Am. prize, Hallmark Internat. Show, 1949, 1st prize, Boston Arts Festival, 1956, 1964, Boston Watercolor Soc., 1957. Avocations: golf, croquet. Home: 1408 Camino Amparo NW Albuquerque NM 87107 E-mail: LPSisson@comcast.net.

SISSON, RAY L., retired dean, author; b. Pueblo, Colo., Apr. 24, 1934; s. William Franklin and Lillie Mae (Hall) S.; m. Dixie Lee McConnell, Oct. 5, 1952; children: Mark Lynn, Bryan Keith, Tammy Sue Ann. AA, Pueblo Coll., 1958; BSEE, U. Colo., 1960; MSEE, Colo. State U., 1966; EdD, U. No. Colo., 1973. Electronic technician TV Svcs. Co., Pueblo, 1958, Sid's Appliance Ctr., Tucson; from instr. engring. to asst. prof. So. Colo. State Coll., Pueblo, 1960-63, assoc. prof., 1963-76, engring., electronics dept. head, 1968-70; dean Sch. Applied Sci. and Engring. Tech. U. So. Colo., Pueblo, 1973-84, prof., 1976—, interim dean Coll. Engring. and Sci., 1984-85, dean Coll. Applied Sci. and Engring. Tech., 1985-96, dean, prof. emeritus, 1996—; curator Pueblo Weisbrod Aircraft Mus. Cons. Escuela Superior Politecnica del Litoral, Ecuador, 1979-82, SUNY, Alfred, Farmingdale, 1982, Moorhead U., 1985, N.Mex. Highlands U., 1985, 90, Kans. State U., Salina, 1994, Ministry Edn., Republic of Yemen, 1996, Min. Edn., State of Kuwait, 1998. Author: Pueblo Army Air Base 1942-46 A Chronological History, 2001. Bd. dirs. Colo. Transp. Inst., 1993-96; exec. dir. So. Colo. Bus. and Tech. Ctr., 1994-96. With USN, 1952-56. Recipient James H. McGraw award Am. Soc. Engring. Edn., 1990; NSF grantee, 1964, 65, 67, 68, 80-83. Mem. IEEE, ABET (tech. accreditation commn. 1990-96, chmn. definition com. 1991, vice chmn. tech. accreditation commn., 1993-96), Am. Soc. Engring. Edn. (active, spectrum com. 1989-90, chmn. definition com. 1991, fellow 1993), Engring. Tech. Leadership Inst. (founding mem., bd. dirs. 1983-88, chmn. 1984-85), Profl. Engrs. Colo. (So. chpt., assoc. mem., chair young engrs. 1969, scholarship, edn. com. 1969, chair state scholarship com. 1968), Pueblo Pachyderm Club (pres. 1986, 89, 98), Pueblo Hist. Aircraft Soc. (historian 1999—, curator 2003—), Retirees Assn. (pres. 1998, 99), Phi Delta Kappa, Eta Kappa Nu, Tau Alpha Pi. Home: 403 Starlite Dr Pueblo CO 81005-2685 Office Phone: 719-948-9219. Personal E-mail: sisson@email.com. Business E-Mail: Ray.Sisson@colostate-pueblo.edu.

SISULU, SHEILA VIOLET MAKATE, international organization official, diplomat; m. Lungi Sisulu. BA, U. Lesotho; BE, Witwatersrand U. Various sr. positions South African Com. for Higher Edn., 1978-88; edn. coord. African Bursary Fund South African Coun. Chs., 1988-91; dir. Joint Enrichment Project, 1991-94; spl. advisor Min. Edn., 1994-97; consul-gen. South African Consulate-Gen., NY, 1997-99; amb. extraordinary and plenipotentiary to the U.S. South African Govt., 1999—2002; deputy exec. dir. U.N. World Food Programme, 2003—. Organizer, coord. several confs., workshops and seminars on youth and edn.; presenter in field. Mem. ANC Nat. Edn. Com., U.S.A./South Africa Leadership Tng. Program, Cmty. Bank Found.; coun. mem. U. Witwatersrand; trustee Equal Opportunity Found., Women's Devel. Found., Women's Devel. Bank, South African Broadcasting Cooperation. Office: via CG Viola 68 Parco Dei Medici 00148 Rome Italy Fax: 202-265-1607. E-mail: wfpinfo@wfp.org.

SIT, ARTHUR J., ophthalmologist, researcher; s. John and Helen Sit; m. Vinita Phord-Toy; children: William, Catherine. BS in Applied Sci., U. Toronto, 1990, MD, 1999; MME, MIT, Cambridge, 1995. Cert. Profl. Engrs. Ont., 1993; diplomate Am. Bd. Ophthalmology, 2006, lic. Med. Coun. Can., 2000. Sr. cons. Andersen Consulting, Toronto, 1990—93; grad. rsch. asst. MIT, 1993—95; ophthalmology resident U. Toronto, 1999—2004; glaucoma fellow, clin. instr. U. Calif. San Diego, La Jolla, 2004—05; sr. assoc. cons., Coll. Medicine Mayo Clinic, Rochester, Minn., 2005—08, asst. prof. ophthalmology, 2006—, cons. ophthalmologist, 2008—. Assoc. adv. bd. mem. World Glaucoma Assn., Amsterdam, 2006—; editl. bd. mem. Internat. Glaucoma Rev., Geneva, 2007—; reviewer Exptl. Eye Rsch., Ophthalmology, Investigative Ophthalmology and Visual Sci., Eye, Brit. Jour. Ophthalmology. Contbr. chapters to books, articles to profl. jours. Recipient Samuel Castrilli award, U. Toronto, 1996—99, Alumni award, 2002, Dr. Michael Shea award, 2004, Dr. Sigmund Vaile award, 2004, Clinician Scientist award, Am. Glaucoma Soc., 2007, Young Physician Scientist award, 2008; named fellow of year award; fellow, Dept. Ophthalmology, U. Calif., 2005. Fellow: Royal Coll. Surgeons Can., Am. Acad. of Ophthalmology; mem.: Minn. Med. Assn., Assn. Rsch. in Vision and Ophthalmology, Am. Glaucoma Soc. Achievements include patents for pressure regulating glaucoma shunt; research in circadian variations in aqueous humor dynamics; measurement of episcleral venous pressure; hydrodynamics of aqueous humor outflow. Office: Mayo Clinic 200 First St SW Rochester MN 55905

SIT, PING-FAI, research scientist; b. Hong Kong, Nov. 6, 1967; came to U.S., 1992; PhD, Case Western Res. U., 2001. Rsch. asst. dept. biomed. engring. Johns Hopkins U., Balt., 1992-94, Case Western Res. U., Cleve., 1994—2001; asst. rsch. prof., dept. chemistry NJ Ctr. for Biomaterials Rutgers U., Piscataway, NJ, 2001—. Recipient Best Grad. Student Rsch. award Biomed. Engring. Soc., 1998. Mem. AAAS, ACS, Biophys. Soc., Soc. for Biomaterials. Office: Rutgers U Dept Chemistry 610 Taylor Rd Piscataway NJ 08904

SITA, MICHAEL JOHN, pharmacy educator; b. Apr. 28, 1953; s. Julianne Gail; m. Nora Ann Dillon, June 1, 1974 (div. 1996); children: Michael John III, Paul Thomas, Julianne Joyce; m. Christine Elizabeth Nordmann, Aug. 22, 1997; children: Mary Elizabeth, April Christine. BS, St. Louis Coll. Pharmacy, 1976; MBA, So. Ill. U., 1983. Registered pharmacist Mo., Ill. Staff pharmacist Luth. Med. Ctr., St. Louis, 1976-78, asst. chief pharmacist, 1978-81, adminstrv. coord. pharmacy svcs., 1981-85; dir. pharmacy svcs. Jefferson Meml. Hosp., 1985-98; pharmacist Mo. Bapt. Hosp., 1998-2000, Walgreen's, 2000—. Instr. St. Louis Coll. Health Careers, 1983-86; adj. instr. pharmacy practice St. Louis Coll. Pharmacy, 1980-98; relief pharmacist Dolgins Apothecary, St. Louis, 1976-86, Best Pharmacy, 1986-88, Carraige Drugs, 1989-93, Medicine Shoppe, Festus, Mo., 1990-97, Otto (Mo.) Drug, 1997-2000. Author, editor: Pharmacy Capsule quar., 1977-85. Mem. St. Louis Soc. Hosp. Pharmacists (treas. 1985-87, pres. 1988-89, sec. 1990-92, Pharmacist of Yr. 1994-95), Mo. Soc. Hosp. Pharmacists, Hosp. Assn. Met. St. Louis (chmn. pharmacy tech. adv. com. 1985-86). Avocations: carpentry, rehabbing. Office: Walgreens 7339 Gravois Saint Louis MO 63116 Office Phone: 314-752-0722.

SITARZ, ANNELIESE LOTTE, pediatrician, educator; b. Medellin, Colombia, Aug. 31, 1928; arrived in US, 1935; d. Hans and Elisabeth (Noll) Sitarz. BA cum laude, Bryn Mawr Coll., Pa., 1950; MD, Columbia U., 1954. Diplomate Nat. Bd. Med. Examiners, Am. Bd. Pediatrics, Am. Bd. Pediatric Hematology and Oncology. Intern Children's Med. Ctr., Boston, 1954—55; resident in pediat. Babies Hosp.-Columbia-Presbyn. Med. Ctr., NYC, 1955—57; mem. faculty Columbia U., NYC, 1957—74, assoc. prof. clin. pediat., 1974—83, prof., 1983—2000, prof. emerita, spl. lectr. in pediat., 2000—; attending in pediat. Babies and Children's Hosp., NYC, 1983—2007. Cons. pediatrics, hematology and oncology Harlem Hosp., NYC, 1967—72, Overlook Hosp., Summit, NJ, 1975—2001. Contbr. articles to profl. jours. Pres. Mt. Prospect Assn., Summit, 1987—. Fellow: Am. Acad. Pediat.; mem.: Internat. Soc. Hematology, Am. Soc. Hematology, Am. Soc. Clin. Oncology, Am. Assn. Cancer Rsch., Harvey Soc. Republican. Episcopalian. Avocations: gardening, sewing, hiking, stamp collecting/philately, photography. Office: Childrens Hosp of NY Presbyn Irving Pavilion 161 Ft Washington Ave New York NY 10032-3710 Office Phone: 212-305-5808. Business E-Mail: als4@columbia.edu.

SITES, JAMES PHILIP, lawyer; b. Detroit, Sept. 17, 1948; s. James Neil and Inger Marie (Krogh) Sites; m. Barbara Teresa Mazurek, Apr. 9, 1978; children: Philip Erling, Teresa Elizabeth. Student, U. Oslo, Norway, 1968-69; BA, Haverford Coll., 1970; JD, Georgetown U., 1973, ML in Taxation, 1979. Bar: Md. 1973, DC 1974, U.S. Supreme Ct. 1978, Mont. 1984, U.S. Dist. Ct. Mont. 1984, U.S. Tax Ct. 1984, U.S. Ct. Appeals (9th cir.) 1988. Law clk. to Hon. James C. Morton, Jr. Ct. Spl. Appeals Md., Annapolis, 1974-75; law clk. to Hon. Orman W. Ketcham Superior Ct. DC, Washington, 1975-76; gen. atty. U.S. Immigration & Naturalization Svc., Washington, 1976-77; trial atty. tax divsn. U.S. Dept. Justice, Washington, 1977-84; ptnr. Crowley Fleck PLLP, Billings, Mont., 1984—; consul for Govt. of Norway State of Mont., Billings, 1987—. Instr. Norwegian Eastern Mont. Coll., 1987—88, Sons of Norway, 1989—; instr. polit. sci. Mont. State U., Billings, 1997—; v.p. Scandinavian Studies Found., 1989—; bd. dirs. Billings Com. Fgn. Rels., Festival Cultures; mem. Mont. Coun Internat. Visitors, Norsemen's Fedn. Chmn. local exec. bd. Mont. State U., Billings, 1993—. Decorated knight 1st class Royal Norwegian Order Merit; scholar, U. Oslo, 1969. Mem.: Am. Imigration Lawyers Assn., DC Bar Assn., Mont. State Bar (co-chmn. com. income and property taxes 1987—91, chair tax and probate sect. 1991—92), Md. Bar Assn., Billings C. of C. (bd. dirs. 1998—, chair), Norwegian-Am. C. of C., Kenwood Golf and Country Club, Hilands Golf Club. Avocations: hiking, Nordic skiing. Office: Crowley Fleck PLLP Consulate for Norway 490 N 31st St Billings MT 59101-1256 Office Phone: 406-252-3441. Business E-Mail: jsites@crowleylaw.com.

SITES, JERRY, agricultural studies educator; Asst. prof. agr. Ark. State U., Beebe, 2002—. Home: 204 N Hickory Beebe AR 72012 Office: Ark State Univ-Beebe 1507 W Ctr Beebe AR 72012

SITES, KEVIN, news correspondent, journalist, web blogger; Masters Degree, Medill Sch. Journalism, Northwestern U. Corr. covering wars and disasters for nat. networks (Iraq, Afghanistan, Columbia and Kosovo, Indonesia 2004 Tsumami, Katrina Hurricane, New Orleans), 2000—; freelance solo journalist NBC News in Asia, 2004, NBC and MSNBC News (Northern and Eastern Alliance forces prior to fall and after fall of Taliban); corr. CNN; war news corr., online news svc., Kevin Sites in the Hot Zone Yahoo! News, 2005—. Covered US Anti-Drug effort in Columbia, 2000—01; broadcast lectr. in journalism dept. Calif. Polytechnic State, San Luis Obispo, 2000—01. Prodr.: NBC News (Edward R. Murrow award for coverage of the war in Kosovo, nominated for nat. Emmy award for contributions to a series on landmines); worked in local, cable, and network news, including (ABC) This Week with David Brinkley & (NBC) Nightly News with Tom Brokaw, published numerous articles in newspapers and magazines, author of monthly media column NY Times alternative weekly. Recipient Payne award for Ethics, RAVE award (Blogs), WIRED mag., 2005, Daniel Pearl award for Courage and Integrity in Journalism, LA Press Club, 2006; named Disting. Lectr. 2000-2001 Academic Yr., Calif. Faculty Assn., Best News Site (Hot Zone) in Online Film & Video Cat., Webby awards, 2007; named one of Top 25 Web Celebs, Forbes mag., 2006. Travels to major hotspots of the world and reports on various armed conflicts occurring to date; while covering initial invasion of Iraq in 2003 for CNN, was captured and briefly held by Saddam Hussein's militia. Business E-Mail: kevin@kevinsites.net.

SITES, RICHARD LOREN, lawyer, educator; b. Feb. 16, 1948; s. Loren Richard and Frances Mary (Tellaro) Sites; m. Karen Ann Heazlit, Oct. 6, 1979; children: Brian, David. BA, Coll. Wooster, 1970; JD, U. Denver, 1973, MS, 1975. Bar: Colo. 1973, Ohio 1975, U.S. Dist. Ct. 1973, U.S. Supreme Ct. 1977; cert. health care fin. mgmt. Ohio State U., 1984. Sole practice, Columbus, Ohio, 1973—; atty. HHS, Columbus, 1975—85, Ohio Hosp. Assn., Columbus, 1985—. Academic adv. Ctrl. Mich. U., 1992—2005, adj. faculty, 1992—; faculty Franklin U., Ohio, 1999—2001, Wittenberg U., Ohio, 2002—; exec. dir. OHA Purchasing Solutions, 2004—07; trustee eHealth Ohio, Inc., 2002—; mem. newborn genetic screening adv. coun. and others Ohio Dept. Health; co-founder Ohio Bleeding Disorders Coun., 2004—. Co-editor: OHA Hosp. Law Handbook, 2005—; contbr. articles to profl. jours. Trustee Ctrl. Ohio Chpt. Nat. Hemophilia Found., 2008—; co-founder FAMOHIO, Inc., 1992, pres., 1996—98, v.p. legal, 1992—95, 2001—; leader Boy Scouts Am., 1992—2002; alumni admissions rep. Coll. Wooster, Ohio, 1979—85, fund raiser, 1984; v.p. Sycamore Hills Residents Assn., Columbus, 1983, pres., 1984; chair hemophilia adv. coun. Ohio Dept. Health, 1995—2000. Recipient Spl. Contbn. award, Ohio Soc. for Hosp. Engring., 1988, 1993, Ira Gaffin Meml. award, Famohio, Inc., 1999, Rosie Haas Adv. award, NW Ohio Hemophilia Found., 2002. Mem.: Am. Health Lawyers Assn. Office: Ohio Hosp Assn 155 E Broad St Fl 15 Columbus OH 43215-3609 Home Phone: 614-457-0027; Office Phone: 614-221-7614.

SITHARAMAN, BALAJI, biomedical engineer, educator; s. Balasubramanian and Kalyani Sitharaman; m. Juee Vinayak, Oct. 25, 2006. BS, Indian Inst. Tech., Kharagpur; PhD, Rice U., Houston, Tex., 2005. J. Evans Attwell Welch postdoc. fellow Richard E Smalley Inst. Nanoscale Sci. and Tech., Rice U., Houston, 2005—07; asst. prof. Stony Brook U., NY, 2007—, project mem., Inst. Chem. Engr. & Drug Discovery, 2007—. Cons. Bridges Sustainability, Golder Assocs., Houston, 2005—06; reviewer Jour. Tissue Engring., Jour. Biomed. Nanotech., Jour. Biomaterials. Contbr. scientific papers to profl. jours. Recipient Rsch. award, Carol M Baldwin Breast Cancer Fund, 2008, Harry B. Weiser Rsch. award, Rice U. Mem.: Soc. Biomaterials, Soc. Molecular Imaging, Internat. Soc. Magnetic Resonance Medicine, Tissue Engring. and Regenerative Medicine Soc., Biomed. Engring. Soc. Achievements include research in novel nanocomposites scaffolds for bone tissue engineering applications; carbon nanomaterials as molecular imaging agents for MRI; conducted studies with carbon nanomaterials to test their efficacy as new non-viral vectors for gene therapy; discovery of nanoparticles such as gold nanoparticles and carbon nanotube facilitate the photoacoustic and thermoacoustic stimulation of stem cells and differntiate them into bone cells; gadonanotubes as high performance contrast agents for magnetic resonance imaging; single-walled carbon nanotube and biodegradable polymer as scaffolds for bone tissue engineering; patents pending for carbon nanotubes-based nanocomposites; metal encapsulated carbon nanotubes; bone cell regeneration utilizing the photoacoustic effect and carbon nanotubes. Office: Dept Biomed Engiring Pyschology A Rm 348 Stony Brook NY 11794-2580 Office Fax: 631-632-8577.

SITKEI, GYÖRGY, engineer, educator; b. Orosháza, Hungary, Feb. 13, 1931; s. Lajos Sitkei and Erzsébet Szabó; m. Emilia Bereczky, Aug. 18, 1959 (dec. 1993); 1 child, Zsuzsanna. MS, Tech. U., Budapest, Hungary, 1954, PhD, 1960; D Engring. Sci., Hungarian Acad. Scis., Budapest, 1964; D (hon.), U. Gödöllo, 1999, U. Sopron, 2000. Doctorant U. Agr., Moscow, 1954-57; rschr. Tech. U., Budapest, 1957-75; head dept. Agrl. Machinery Trust, Budaörs, Hungary, 1975-80; prof., head U. Sopron, Hungary, 1980-97, prof. emeritus, 1997—. Mem. State Sci. Accreditation Com., Budapest, 1993—. Author: Mixture Formation and Combustion in Diesel Engines, 1964, Heat Transfer and Thermal Loading in IC Engines, 1974, Soil Mechanics Problems of Agricultural Machines, 1976, Mechanics of Agricultural Materials, 1986 (Acad. award 1988), Theory of Mechanical Wood Processing, 1994. Recipient Szent-Györgyi Albert award Ministry of Edn., 1993, Pattantyus Á. Géza award Sci. Soc. Mech. Engring. Budapest, 1994. Mem. N.Y. Acad. Scis., Hungarian Acad. Scis. (mem. com. for agrl. mechanization 1975—, com. for thermal engines 1978—), Internat. Soc. for Terrain Vehicle Sys. Avocation: ornamental trees and shrubs. Home: Széher ut 19 H-1021 Budapest Hungary Office: U Sopron Ady E u 5 H-9401 Sopron Hungary E-mail: dwoodma@fmk.nyme.hu.

SITOMER, ALAN LAWRENCE, literature and language educator; m. Tracy Sitomer; 1 child, Sienna. Lang. arts tchr. Lynwood (Calif.) H.S.; and instr., grad. sch. edn. Loyola Marymount Univ. Co-author (with Michael Cirelli): Hip-Hop Poetry and the Classics, 2004; author: The Hoopster, 2005, Hip-Hop High School, 2006, Homeboyz, 2007. Recipient Classroom Excellence award, So. Calif. Tchrs. of English, 2006; named Tchr. of Yr., Calif. Literacy, 2003, Calif. Tchr. of Yr., 2007. Office: Lynwood High Sch 4050 E Imperial Hwy Lynwood CA 90262 Address: Milk Mug Pub-- Ste #253 9190 W Olympic Blvd Beverly Hills CA 90212 E-mail: alanlawrencesitomer@yahoo.com.

SITOMER, RICHARD ALLEN (RICKY SITOMER), air transportation executive; b. 1968; s. Geoffrey and Behera Sitomer; m. Lori Levy, Aug. 28, 1994; children: Jordan Mark, Taylor Nicole. BBA, Emory U., 1990. Chief exec. TRS Trading Co., NYC; founder, CEO Millenium Securities, NYC; co-founder, CEO Blue Star Jets Inc., NYC, 2001—. Mem.: Beta Kappa Alumni Assn.

SITOMER, SHEILA MARIE, television producer and director; b. Hartford, Conn., Aug. 25, 1951; d. George W. and Mary E. (Chaponis) Bowe; m. Daniel J. Sitomer, Aug. 25, 1985. BA, Smith Coll., 1973. Field producer, dir. Good Morning Am., ABC-TV, NYC, 1981-86; field producer Evening Magazine, WWOR-TV, KDKA-TV, Pitts. and Secaucus, NJ, 1978-79, 88; supervising producer The Reporters, Fox Broadcasting, NYC, 1988; producer Inside Edition, King World Prodns., NYC, 1988-95; co-exec. prodr. Inside Edition and Am. Jour., 1995-98; exec. prodr. Extra, 1998-2000; exec. prodr. program devel. ABC News, NYC, 2000—. Recipient Peabody award, Columbia Dupont award, AWRT Gracie award, 3 Emmys, New England chpt. TV Acad. Arts & Scis., 1975-78, 2 Emmys, N.Y. chpt. TV Acad. Arts & Scis., 1979, 89, recipient first prize Internat. Film & TV Festival N.Y., 1988, No. N.J. Press Club award, 1988, George Polk award, Sigma Delta Chi award, IRE award Nat. Headliners, Columbus Film Festival. Mem. Dirs. Guild Am., Actors Equity Assn. Office: ABC News 47 W 66th St New York NY 10023 E-mail: sheila.sitomer@abc.com.

SITRICK, MICHAEL STEVEN, public relations executive; b. Davenport, Iowa, June 8, 1947; s. J. Herman and Marcia B. (Bofman) S.; m. Nancy Elaine Eiseman, July 1, 1969; children: Julie, Sheri, Alison. BS in Bus. Adminstrn. and Journalism, U. Md., 1969. Coord. press services Western Elec., Chgo., 1969-70; asst. dir. program services City of Chgo., 1970-72; asst. v.p. Selz, Seabolt & Assocs., Chgo., 1972-74; dir. comm. and pub. affairs Nat. Can Corp., Chgo., 1974-81; dir. comm. Wickes Cos., Inc., San Diego, 1981-82, v.p. comm. Santa Monica, Calif., 1982-84, sr. v.p. comm., 1984-89; chmn., CEO Sitrick & Co., LA and NYC, 1989—. Mem. adv. bd. The 1939 Club. Author: Spin--How to Turn the Power of the Press to Your Advantage, 1998. Office: Sitrick and Co 1840 Century Pk E Ste 800 Los Angeles CA 90067 Office Phone: 310-788-2850.

SITTENFELD, CURTIS, writer; b. Cin., Aug. 23, 1975; Student, Vassar Coll., Poughkeepsie, NY; BA in Creative Writing, Stanford U., Palo Alto, Calif., 1997; MFA, U. Iowa Writers' Workshop, 2001. Writer Charlotte Observer, NC, Fast Co. mag., Boston. Writer in residence St. Albans Sch., Washington, 2002—03, English tchr., 2003—05. Author: (novels) Prep, 2005 (One of NY Times 10 Best Books of 2005, Named a Best Book of 2005, Washington Post, Chgo. Tribune,), The Man of My

Dreams, 2007, American Wife, 2008 (Publishers Weekly bestseller); contbr. numerous short stories to mags. Mailing: c/o Random House Inc Hdqs 1745 Broadway New York NY 10019*

SITTIG, JAMES CHRISTOPHER, art dealer, painter, sculptor, landscape artist, poet; b. East Stroudsburg, Pa., Mar. 9, 1954; s. Edgar Hans and Charlotte Frances Sittig. Pres., ex. dir. Worthington Ave. Gallery, Shawnee-on Del., Pa., 1992—2001; owner James C. Sittig Fine Arts Am. Paintings, Waverly, 1989—. Juror many art exhbns., pvt. art dealer, collector, rschr. and restorer early 19th to early 20th century Am. paintings. Prin. biographer Strauser on Strauser Video Biography, 1994, Sterling Strauser Sterling Strauser: A Modernist Revisited, 1999; author: Salvage Style for the Garden, Found Object Sculptures, 2003. Appraiser paintings Monroe County Hist. Soc., Stroudsburg, 1999—2003, Western Pocono Libr., Bradheaderville, Pa., 1999—2006, WYOU TV, Scranton, Pa., 2001. Recipient Albert Handell Stewart Klonis award, Art Student League, NY, 1977. Mem.: Nat. Trust Hist. Preservation, Pocono Arts Coun., Am. Mus. Britain, Mus. Am. Folk Art, Allentown Art Mus., Smithsonian Instn., Phila. Mus. Art, Reading Pub. Mus. Avocations: tennis, skiing, hiking, bicycling.

SITTON, CLAUDE FOX, newspaper editor; b. Atlanta, Dec. 4, 1925; s. Claude B. and Pauline (Fox) S.; m. Eva McLaurin Whetstone, June 5, 1953; children: Lea Sitton Stanley, Clinton, Suzanna Sitton Greene, McLaurin. AB, Emory U., 1949, L.H.D., 1984. Reporter Internat. News Service, 1949-50; with U.P., 1950-55, writer-editor NYC, 1952-55; information officer USIA, 1955-57; mem. staff N.Y. Times, 1957-68, nat. news dir., 1964-68; editorial dir. The News and Observer Pub. Co., Raleigh, NC, 1968-90, dir., 1969-90, v.p., 1970-90; editor News and Observer, 1970-90; sr. lectr. Emory U., Atlanta, 1991-94. Active Pulitzer Prize Bd., 1985-94, chmn., 1992-93; bd. counselors Oxford Coll. Emory U., 1993-2001. Lay mem. Commn. on Evaluation of Disciplinary Enforcement, Ga. Supreme Ct., 1995-96; mem. Ga. First Amendment Found. Bd., 1994-97. With USNR, 1943-46, PTO. Recipient Pulitzer prize for commentary, 1983. Home: PO Box 1326 Oxford GA 30054-1326

SIU, WANG-NGAI, solicitor; b. Hong Kong, Feb. 14, 1938; s. Man-Wan and Wai-Ying (Cheung) S.; m. Yuen-Ling April Lee. Grad., St. Francis Xavier's Coll., 1959, Coll. Law, London, 1967. Solicitor T.S. Tong & Co., Hong Kong, 1971-73, Chan & Ho, Hong Kong, 1973-77; solicitor, ptnr. Gallant Y.T. Ho & Co., Hong Kong, 1977—97; ret., 1998. Chmn. Fedn. Hong Kong-Macau Photographic Assns., Hong Kong; co. photographer Hong Kong Ballet, 1994—. Author: Chinese Opera: Images and Stories, 1997, Hong Kong Ballet, 2003. Royal Photographic Soc. Gt. Britain fellow, Bath, 1985, 89. Mem. Law Soc. Hong Kong, Soc. Notaries, Photographic Soc. Am. Avocations: photography, classical music, Go.

SIV, SICHAN AUN, former ambassador; b. Phnom Penh, Cambodia, Mar. 1, 1948; came to U.S., 1976; s. Chham and Aun (Chea) S.; m. Martha Pattillo, Dec. 24, 1983. Diplome du Professorat, U. Phnom Penh, Cambodia, 1972; B. en Droit, U. Phnom Penh, 1974, Lic. es Lettres, 1975; M. Internat. Affairs, Columbia U., 1981. Flight attendant Royal Air Cambodge, 1969-70; tchr. high sch. Phnom Penh, 1972-74; program assoc. Care-Cambodia, Phonm Penh, 1974-75; statistician Lower East-side Svc. Ctr., NYC, 1977-78; staff asst. Lutheran Immigration & Refugee Svc., NYC, 1978-80; mgmt. assoc. Marine Midland Bank, NYC, 1981-82; adminstr., fin. officer Episcopal Ch., NYC, 1982-83; UN rep. Cambodian Non Communist Resistance, NYC, 1983-87; Asia-Pacific mgr. Inst. Internat. Edn., NYC, 1987-89; dep. asst. to The Pres. for pub. liaison The White House, Washington, 1989—93; U.S. rep. to econ. and social coun. of U.N. U.S. Dept. State, Washington, 2001—06.

SIVACOLUNDHU, RAMESH KUMAR, veterinarian; b. Colombo, Sri Lanka, Oct. 20, 1968; s. Sinnappu and Prakash Sivacolundhu; m. Renata Louise Bryce, July 13, 2002; 1 child, Kira Mireya. BSc, Murdoch U., Perth, Australia, BVMS, 1990; MVS, U. Melbourne, Victoria, Australia, 1997. Veterinarian Ridgehaven Vet. Hosp., Adelaide, 1991—94; intern, small animal medicine & surgery U. Melbourne Vet. Clinic & Hosp., 1994, resident, 1994—97, Murdoch U. Vet. Hosp., 1998—2000; registrar U. Queensland Sch. Vet. Sci., Brisbane, Queensland, Vet. Specialist Ctr., Sydney, NSW, 2000—01; dir. Melbourne Vet. Surg. Svcs., 2001—03; staff surgeon Animal Med. Ctr., NYC, 2004—; staff surgeon, surg. oncology Colo. State U., Fort Collins, 2009—. Reviewer Vet. Surgery Jour., 2009—, Jour. Small Animal Practice, 2008—; exec. com. Australian Coll. Vet. Scientists, Surgery Chpt., Australia, 2000—02, examiner, membership level, 2003; seminar organizer Pfizer, Melbourne, 2002—03; guest editor Clin. Techniques Small Animal Practice Jour., 2008. Contbr. articles to profl. jours. Fellow: Australian Coll. Vet. Scientists; mem.: AVMA, Ea. Comparative Oncology Group, European Soc. Vet. Oncology, Vet. Soc. Surg. Oncologists, Vet. Cancer Soc., NYC Vet. Med. Assn. Avocations: travel, languages, magic.

SIVAK-CALLCOTT, JENNIFER A., ophthalmologist; MD, Ohio State U., Columbus, 1996. Diplomate Am. Bd. Ophthalmology, 2002. Assoc. prof. W.Va. U., Morgantown, 2001—.

SIVANESAN, SIVARUBAN, mechanical engineer; s. Sinniah and Meenalogani Sivanesan; m. Nishiya Das, Feb. 1, 1998; children: Maathanggi Maijuu Sivaruban, Eashwar Arya Sivaruban. BSc in Mech. Engring., Ryerson U., Toronto Can., 1994; MBA, U. Nebr., Kearney, 2002. Auditor corp. quality systems C.R. Bard, Murray Hill, NJ, 2002—05; sr. supplier quality engr. Ethicon Inc., Somerville, NJ, 2005—. Contbr. articles to profl. jours. Site coord. SAI Orgn., Easton, Pa., 2005—07. Mem.: Am. Soc. Quality (assoc. cert. quality auditor), Profl. Engs. Ont. (assoc. cert.). Avocation: yoga. Office: Ethicon Inc a Johnson and Johnso Co Rt 22W Somerville NJ 08876 Home: 14310 75TH Ave NE Bothell WA 98011-4929 Personal E-mail: rsivanesan@hotmail.com.

SIVAPALAN, MURUGESU, engineer educator, consultant; b. Puttur, Sri Lanka, Apr. 19, 1953; arrived in Australia, 1988; s. Sangarapillai Murugesu and Umadevi (Kanagasabai) M.; m. Banumathy Rajadurai Sivapalan, July 11, 1981; children: Mayuran, Kavin. BS in Engring. (hon.), U. Ceylon, Peradeniya, Sri Lanka, 1975; M in Engring., Asian Inst. Tech., Bangkok, Thailand, 1977; MA, Princeton U., 1983, PhD, 1986. Rsch. assoc. Asian Inst. Tech., Bangkok, Thailand, 1977; sr. cons. Rocks & Stones Ltd., Ibadan, Nigeria, 1978-81; rsch. assoc. Princeton U., 1986-88; lectr. U. Western Australia, Perth, 1988-92, sr. lectr., 1992-95, assoc. prof., 1995-99, prof., 1999—. Head dept. environ. engring. U. Western Australia, Perth, 1996—97; Lise Meitner fellow Austrian Sci. Found., Vienna, 1995—96; vis. prof. Delft Tech. U., Netherlands, 2000—01; assoc. editor Jour. of Hydrology, Amsterdam, 1996—, Hydrological Processes, London, 1996—, Environmental Modeling of Software, London, 1997—, Advances in Water Resources, Amsterdam, 2000—. Editor: Scale Issues in Hydrological Modelling, 1995; contbr. articles of profl. jours. Fellow: Modeling and Simulation Soc. of Australia and New Zealand, Australian Acad. Technol. Scis. and Engring.; mem.: New Zealand Hydrological Soc., Internat. Water Acad. Oslo (life), Internat. Assn. Hydrological Scis., Am. Geophys. Union. Avocations: cricket, current affairs. Office: Univ of Illinois 220 Davenport Hall 607 S Mathews Ave Urbana IL 61801 Home: 2502 Branch Rd Champaign IL 61822 Office Fax: 217-244-1785. Business E-Mail: sivapala@illinois.edu.

SIVASUBRAMANIAM, KIRUBA HARAN, engineer; s. Sabapathy and Luxmi Sivasubramaniam; m. Vidya Iyer; 1 child, Priya Amuthini. BS, Obafemi Awolowo U., Ile-Ife, Nigeria, 1994; MS, PhD, Rensselaer Poly. Inst., Troy, NY, 2000. Adj. asst. prof. Rensselaer Poly. Inst., 2003—05; sr. engr. GE Global Rsch., Niskayuna, NY, 2000—. Mem.: IEEE. Achievements include patents in field; patents pending in field; development of advanced drivetrains for next generation wind turbines; research in superconducting devices for energy and healthcare industry. Office: Gen Electric Global Rsch Ctr 1 Rsch Cir Niskayuna NY 12309

SIVASUBRAMANIAN, KOLINJAVADI NAGARAJAN, neonatologist, educator; b. Coimbatore, Madras, India, May 9, 1945; came to U.S., 1971; s. Kolinjavadi Ramaswamy and Sukanthi (Subramanian) Nagarajan; m. Kalyani Hariharier, Feb. 5, 1975; children: Ramya, Rajeev, Ranjan. BSc, Madras U., 1964, MBBS, 1969. Diplomate Am. Bd. Pediatrics and Neonatal-Perinatal Medicine. Intern in pediat. Jewish Hosp. and Med. Ctr., Bklyn., 1971-72; resident in pediat. U. Md. Hosp., Balt., 1972-74; fellow in neonatology Georgetown U. Hosp., Washington, 1974-76, attending neonatologist, 1976—, dir. nurseries, chief neonatology, 1981—, vice chair pediat., 1988-98, prof. pediat. and ob-gyn. Co-chair rsch. com. Georgetown U. Med. Ctr., 2005—, co-chair children's health and devel., 2005—. Editor: Trace Elements/Mineral Metablolism During Development, 1993; editor pub. SIDS Series, 1985; editor jour. Current Concepts in Neonatology, India, 1990—; internat. editor Indian Jour. Pediat., India, 1988—. Chmn. Siva Vishnu Temple, Lanham, Md., 1981-91; mem. Fetus and New Born Com., Washington, 1988; founder, bd. dirs. Coun. of Hindu Temples U.S.A.; founder, coord. United Hindu Temples of Met. Washington; 1st v.p. Interfaith Conf., Washington; mem. D.C. bd. dirs. Nat. Youth Leadership Forum. Recipient "Preemies" cover article Newsweek, 1988, Interfaith Bridge Builder award, 2006, MAGIS Master Tchr. award, 2007, Clin. Tchr. of Yr. award, 2007; featured in "Washingtonian" jour., 1996, 2005, Georgetown U. Med. Ctr. Web Mag., 2003, 2007. Fellow Am. Coll. Nutrition, Am. Acad. Pediat.; mem. AAAS, N.Y. Acad. Scis., Internat. Soc. for Trace Element Rsch. in Humans, Soc. for Bioethics Consultation, Am. Soc. Law, Medicine and Ethics. Hindu. Achievements include research in neonatology, trace elements kinetics, reduction in infant mortality, neonatal immunology, and bioethics. Office: Georgetown U Hosp 3 South Hospital 3800 Reservoir Rd NW Washington DC 20007-2113 Office Phone: 202-444-8709. Business E-Mail: sivasubk@georgetown.edu.

SIVE, REBECCA ANNE, public relations executive; b. Jan. 29, 1950; d. David and Mary (Robinson) S.; m. Clark Steven Tomashefsky. BA, Carleton Coll., 1972; MA in Am. History, U. Ill., Chgo., 1975. Asst. to chmn. of pres.' task force on vocations Carleton Coll., Northfield, Minn., 1972; rsch. asst. Jane Addams Hull House, Chgo., 1974; instr. Loop Coll., Chgo., 1975, Columbia Coll., Chgo., 1975-76; dir. Ill. Women's History Project, 1975-76; founder, exec. dir. Midwest Women's Ctr., Chgo., 1977-81; exec. dir. Playboy Found., 1981-84; v.p. pub. affairs/pub. rels. Playboy Video Corp., 1985—85; v.p. pub. affairs Playboy Enterprises, Inc., Chgo., 1985-86; pres. The Sive Group, Inc., Chgo., 1986—. Instr. Roosevelt U., Chgo., 1977-78; dir. spl. projects Inst. on Pluralism and Group Identity, Am. Jewish Com.; trainer Midwest Acad. Contbr. articles to profl. jours. Commr. Chgo. Park Dist., 1986-88; del.-at-large Nat. Women's conf., 1977; mem. Ill. Human Rights Commn., 1980-87, Ill. coordinating com., Internat Womens Yr.; coord. Ill. Bicentennial Photog. Exhbn., 1977; mem. Ill. Employment and Tng. Coun.; bd dirs. Nat. Abortion Rights Action League and NARAL Found., Ill. div. ACLU, Midwest Women's Ctr. Recipient award for outstanding cmty. leadership YWCA Met. Chgo., 1979, award for outstanding cmty. leadership Chgo. Jaycees, 1988. Office: The Sive Group Inc 1235 N Astor St Chicago IL 60610-5213 Office Phone: 312-397-9857. Business E-Mail: rebecca@rebeccasive.com.

SIVERD, ROBERT JOSEPH, lawyer; b. July 27, 1948; s. Clifford David and Elizabeth Ann (Klink) S.; m. Bonita Marie Shulock, Jan. 8, 1972; children: Robert J. Jr., Veronica Leigh. AB in French, Georgetown U., 1970, JD, 1973; postgrad., The Sorbonne, Paris, 1969. Bar: N.Y. 1974, U.S. Dist. Ct. (so. and ea. dists.) N.Y. 1974, U.S. Ct. Appeals (2d cir.) 1974, U.S. Supreme Ct. 1980, U.S. Dist. Ct. (ea. dist.) Pa. 1984, U.S. Ct. Appeals (3d cir.) 1984, U.S. Ct. Appeals (6th cir.) 1985, Ohio 1991, Ky. 1992. Assoc. Donovan Leisure Newton & Irvine, NYC, 1973-83; staff v.p., litigation counsel Am. Fin. Group, Inc., Greenwich, Conn., 1983-85, v.p. litigation counsel, 1986-87, v.p. assoc. gen. counsel Cin., 1987-92; sr. v.p., gen. counsel and sec. Gen. Cable Corp., 1992-94, exec. v.p., gen. counsel and sec., 1994—. Mem. Ky. Bar Assn. Republican. Office: Gen Cable Corp 4 Tesseneer Dr Newport KY 41076-9167 Business E-Mail: rsiverd@generalcable.com.

SIVORI, JOHN P., health and medical products executive; BBA, Calif. State U., Chico. CPA. Audit mgr. KPMG Peat Marwick; various fin. positions Sutter Health, Sacramento; various sr. mgmt. positions Found. Health Corp., 1994—98; sr. v.p., CFO Health Net Pharm. Svcs. (formerly Integrated Pharm. Svcs.), 1998—2001, pres., 2001; sr. v.p. Health Net, Inc. Office: Health Net Inc 21650 Oxnard St Woodland Hills CA 91367 Office Phone: 818-676-6000.

SIX, STEPHEN N., state attorney general, former judge; b. Dec. 11, 1965; s. Frederick N. Six; m. Betsy Six; children: Emily, Sam, Henry, Will. B, Carleton Coll., Northfield, Minn., 1988; JD, U. Kans. Sch. Law, Lawrence, 1993. Law clk. to Hon. Deanell R. Tacha US Ct. Appeals (10th Cir.), 1993—94; ptnr. Shamberg, Johnson & Bergman, Kansas City, Mo., 1994—2005; dist. judge Kans. Jud. Dist., Douglas County, 2005—08; atty. gen. State of Kans., Topeka, 2008—. Contbg. editor: Kans. Law Rev., 1993. Bench-bar com. US Dist. Ct. Kansas; bd. trustees Kans. Bar Found. Mem.: Kans. Bar Assn. (bd. govs., bench-bar com., chmn. mandatory malpractice disclosure com.), Order of the Coif. Democrat. Office: Office Atty Gen Memorial Hall Fl 2 120 SW 10th St Topeka KS 66612*

SIZEMORE, GLEN WILLIAM, medical educator; b. Fort Dodge, Iowa, Jan. 16, 1937; s. Earl Lloyd and Wilma Cleo (Thompson) S.; m. Juliet Ann Whitten, Oct. 29, 1977; children: Andrea, Christopher. BA in Chemistry and Zoology, Carleton Coll., 1959; MD, U. Rochester, 1963. Diplomate Am. Bd. Internal Medicine, Am. Bd. Internal Medicine (Endocrinology). Intern, med. resident, chief med. resident, endocrine fellow U. Ky. Coll. Medicine, Lexington, 1963—67; USPHS grad. trainee endocrinology Mayo Grad. Sch. Medicine, Rochester, Minn., 1969-72; asst. prof. medicine Mayo Med. Sch. U. Minn., Rochester, 1973-77, assoc. prof. medicine, 1977-82, prof. medicine, 1982—; chmn. dept. medicine St. Francis Hosp., Evanston, Ill., 1983-87; prof. medicine Loyola U. Stritch Sch. Medicine, Maywood, Ill., 1984—. Acting chief sect. endocrinolgoy Loyola U. Stritch Sch. Medicine, Maywood, Ill., 1991-93. Contbr. articles to profl. jours. Capt. USAF, 1967-69. Recipient Disting. Achievement award, Carleton Coll., 2009. Fellow Am. Assn. Clin. Endocrinology; mem. Alpha Omega Alpha, Am. Soc. Bone and Mineral Research, Am. Thyroid Assn., Cen. Soc. Clin. Rsch., Endocrine Soc., Sigma Xi. Republican. Office: Loyola U Med Ctr 54 137 2160 S 1st Ave Maywood IL 60153-3304 Office Phone: 708-216-6015.

SIZEMORE, MICHAEL MAYNARD, architectural firm executive; b. Detroit, July 20, 1943; s. Arthur Logan and Evelyn (Willer) S.; m. Christine Wick, June 1, 1968; children: Christine Corsaut, James Gawne. BArch, Ga. Inst. Tech., 1966; MArch in Urban Design, Carnegie-Mellon U., 1968. Registered arch. Owner Sizemore & Assocs., Atlanta, 1974-76; v.p. CRS, Sizemore/CRS, Houston and Atlanta, 1976-78; sr. prin. Sizemore Floyd (now Sizemore Group), Atlanta, 1973—. Mem. bd. advisors dist. coun. Urban Land Inst.; trustee The Ga. Conservancy. Author: Energy Planning in Buildings, 1979; prin. works include redesign of hqrs. AIA, Washington, Emory U. Clinic, Hale Ctr. Theatre, Salt Lake City, Atlanta C. of C., master plan of Centennial Olympics, Atlanta, 1996, master plan, feasibility Centennial Olympic Park, hqrs. Atlanta Com. Olympic Games, Smyrna Town Ctr. Design and Devel. (Nat. award Urban Land Inst. 1997). Fellow AIA; mem. Atlanta C. of C. (bd. advisors). Office: 1700 Commerce Dr NW Atlanta GA 30318-3123 Home Phone: 404-355-0839; Office Phone: 404-605-0690.

SIZEMORE, NICKY LEE, computer scientist; b. NYC, Feb. 13, 1946; s. Ralph Lee and Edith Ann (Wangler) S.; m. Frauke Julika Hoffmann, Oct. 31, 1974; 1 child, Jennifer Lee Sizemore; 1 stepchild, Mark Anthony Miracle. BS in Computer Sci., SUNY, 1989. Sgt. first class U.S. Army, 1964-68, 70-86; computer operator UNIVAC, Washington, 1968-69, programmer, 1969-70; programmer/analyst Ultra Systems, Inc., Sierra Vista, Ariz., 1986-87; computer scientist Comarco, Inc., Sierra Vista, 1987-92, ARC, Profl. Svcs. Group, Sierra Vista, 1992-93, Computer Scis. Corp., Ft. Huachuca, Ariz., 1994; sr. cons. Inference Corp., 1995; subject matter expert Northrop Corp., Sierra Vista, Ariz., 1995—; sr. info. sys. engr. Harris Corp., Sierra Vista, Ariz., 1996—2001; sys. analyst EWA Svcs., Inc., Ft. Huachaca, 2002—08, Mantech Inc., 2009—. Speaker numerous confs., seminars, symposia; tech. columnist Sierra vista Herald. Mem.: IEEE, Internat. Coun. Sys. Engring., IEEE Computer Soc., Assn. Computing Machinery, Am. Assn. Artificial Intelligence (validation and test of knowledge-based sys. 1988, co-dir. workshop on verification). Avocations: chess, jogging, tai chi. Home: 880 E Charles Dr Sierra Vista AZ 85635-1611 Office Phone: 520-538-2527. Personal E-mail: sizemorn@fhu.disa.mil.

SIZEMORE, WILLIAM CHRISTIAN, retired academic administrator, county official; b. South Boston, Va., June 19, 1938; s. Herman Mason and Hazel (Johnson) S.; m. Anne Catherine Mills, June 24, 1961; children: Robert C., Richard M., Edward S. BA, U. Richmond, 1960; BD, Southeastern Bapt. Theol. Sem., Wake Forest, NC, 1963; MLS, U. N.C., 1964; MLS (advanced), Fla. State U., 1971, PhD, 1973; postgrad., Harvard U., 1989. Library asst. U. N.C., Chapel Hill, 1963-64; assoc. librarian, instr. grad. research Southeastern Bapt. Theol. Sem., 1964-66; librarian, assoc. prof. South Ga. Coll., Douglas, 1966-71, acad. dean, prof., 1971-80, dean coll., prof., 1980-83, acting pres., 1982-83; pres. Alderson-Broaddus Coll., Philippi, W.Va., 1983-94, William Jewell Coll., Liberty, Mo., 1994-2000, chancellor, 2000—02; dir. bus. expansion Clay County Econ. Devel. Coun., Kansas City, Mo., 2003—. Cons. Continental R&D, Shawnee Mission, Kans., 1987-92, So. Assn. Colls. and Schs., Atlanta, 1977, S.C. Commn. on Higher Edn., Columbia, 1975-76, State Coun. Higher Edn. for Va., Richmond, 1969-70, Software Valley Corp., 1989-94; adv. bd. Software Valley Found., 1991-94. Contbr. articles to profl. jours. Active Barbour County Devel. Authority, Philippi, 1984-94, Barbour County Emergency Food and Shelter Bd., 1985-94, Barbour County Extension Com., 1990-94; mem. exec. coun. Yellow Pine area Boy Scouts Am., Valdosta, 1974-76; pres. Satilla Librarians Ednl. Coun., Douglas, 1969-71; lectr., workshop leader on Bible studies various orgns., 1966—; bd. advisors Swatow Kakwang Profl. Acad., Peoples Republic China; pres. bd. dirs. W.Va. Intercollegiate Athletic Conf., 1985-86, coun. of pres. Nat. Assn. Intercollegiate Athletics; bd. dirs., mem. exec. com. Broaddus Hosp., Philippi, 1983-94; chmn. W.Va. Productive Industry Efforts Found., 1989-92; mktg. com. W.Va. Life Scis. Park Found., 1989-94, Gov.'s Partnership for Progress, 1989-94; mem. adv. panel W.Va. Rural Health Initiative, 1991-94; gov. bd., bd. dirs. W.Va. Alliance of Hosps., 1991-94; bd. dirs. Clay-Platte Econ. Devel. Coun., 1996—; bd. dirs. ARC, Kansas City, 1996-02, exec.com. 2000-02; adv. com. Mo. Conservation Heritage Found. Discovery Ctr. Campaign, 1998-2002; mem. Clay County Millennium Hist. Bd., 2002-; mem. Liberty HIstory Book Steering Com., 2001-04; bd. dirs., v.p. Immaculata Manor, 2003-; adv. bd. North Kansas City Schs., 2003-; mem. steering com., co-chair Freedom House, 2004-, bd. dir. Joseph Ruzicka scholar N.C. Library Assn., 1963; recipient Douglas Pilot Club Edn. award, 1981, Good Citizenship Silver medal Nat. Soc. Sons of Am. Revolution, 1999. Mem. ALA, Am. Assn. for Higher Edn., Am. Assn. Univ. Adminstrs., Nat. Coun. Instrnl. Adminstrs., W.Va. Assn. Coll. and Univ. Pres. (exec. com., v.p., pres. 1992), Mountain State Assn. Colls., W.Va. Found. for Ind. Colls. (dir. 1983-84, v.p. 1988-92), Mo. Colls. Fund (exec. com. 1997-98), Barbour County C. of C. (bd. dirs. 1988-94, v.p. 1988-90, pres. 1990-92, chmn. bd. 1992-94), Liberty Area C. of C. (bd. dirs. 1995-97), Clay County Hist. Soc. (life), SAR (pres, William C. Corum Chpt., 2008-), Gen. Soc. Sons Revolution, Pi Kappa Alpha, Gen. Soc. Mayflower Descs. Democrat. Baptist. Avocations: woodworking, gardening. Home: 1417 Woodbury Dr Liberty MO 64068-1266 Office: Clay County Econ Devel Coun Office 110 NW Barry Rd Kansas City MO 64155

SIZEMORE, WILLIAM HOWARD, JR., journalist; b. South Boston, Va., Dec. 18, 1948; s. W. Howard and Genevieve T. (Walton) S.; m. Mary K. Lamont, Jan. 29, 1972; children: Justin, Jennifer, Julie. BA in Philosophy, Coll. William and Mary, 1971. Editor The Clarksville (Va.) Times, 1972-75; reporter The Roanoke (Va.) Times, 1975-76, The Times-Herald, Newport News, Va., 1976-81; editor, pub. The York Town Crier, Yorktown, Va., 1981-88; copy editor The Ledger-Star, Norfolk, Va., 1982-89, news editor, 1989-95; writer, editor The Virginian-Pilot, Norfolk, Va., 1995—. Recipient various Journalism awards Va. Press Assn., 1972-2007. Avocations: tennis, music, bicycling, camping. Home: 4704 Yarrow Ct Williamsburg VA 23188-2427 Office: Virginian-Pilot 150 W Brambleton Ave Norfolk VA 23510-2075 Office Phone: 757-446-2276. Business E-Mail: bill.sizemore@pilotonline.com.

SIZER, PHILLIP SPELMAN, retired oil and gas industry executive; b. Whittier, Calif., Apr. 11, 1926; s. Frank Milton and Helen Louise (Saylor) S.; m. Evelyn Sue Jones, Aug. 16, 1952; children: Phillip Spelman Jr., Ves Warner. BSME, So. Meth. U., 1948. Registered profl. engr., Tex. With Otis Engring. Corp., Dallas, 1948-91, project engr., 1958-62, chief devel. engr., 1962-70, v.p. R & D, 1970-73, v.p. engring. and rsch., 1973-76, sr. v.p., tech. dir., 1977-91, bd. dirs., 1975-91; pres. Sizer Engring. Inc., 1992—; prin. Crawford-Sizer Devel. Co., 1996—. Cons. in field; mem. exec. com. Offshore Tech. Conf., 1976-79. Patentee in field Mem. vis. com. dept. mech. engring. U. Tex., 1977-83. Named to Hall of Achievement Coll. Engring., U. Tex., Arlington, 1983 Fellow ASME (chmn. 1972, exec. com. petroleum divsn. 1974-75, SPPE-1 chmn. main com. 1981-88, Engr. of Yr. award North Tex. sect. 1971, centennial medal 1980, OILDROP award petroleum divsn. 1982, Dedicated Svc. award 1985, Silver Patent award 1990, region x Clifford H. Shumaker award 1993); mem. Soc. Petroleum Engrs., S.W. Rsch. Inst. (trustee 1981—), Petroleum Engrs. Club of Dallas, Rotary Internat., Kappa Sigma, Tau Beta Pi, Kappa Mu Epsilon. Home: 14127 Tanglewood Dr Dallas TX 75234-3851 Office Phone: 972-247-6087. Personal E-mail: sizer26@tx.rr.com.

SIZER, THEODORE R., education educator; b. New Haven, June 23, 1932; m. Nancy Faust; 4 children. BA in English Lit., Yale U., 1953; MAT in Social Studies, Harvard U., 1957, Phd in Am. History and Edn., 1961; PedD (hon.), Lawrence U., 1969; LittD (hon.), Union Coll., 1972; LLD (hon.), Conn. Coll., 1984; LHD (hon.), Williams Coll., 1984; MA ad eundem, Brown U., 1985; LHD (hon.), U Mass., Lowell, 1985, Dartmouth Coll., 1985, Lafayette Coll., 1991, Webster U., 1992, Ind. U., 1993, Mt. Holyoke Coll., 1993, U. Maine, 1993, Iona Coll., 1995, L.I. U., 1996, Bridgewater State Coll., 1996. English and math. tchr. Roxbury Latin Sch., Boston, 1955-56; history and geography tchr. Melbourne (Australia) Grammar Sch., 1958; asst. prof. edn., dir. MA in tchrs. program Harvard U., Cambridge, Mass., 1961-64, dean grad. sch. edn., 1964-72; headmaster, instr. in history Phillips Acad., Andover, Mass., 1972-81; chmn. A Study of High Schs., 1981-84; prof. edn. Brown U., Providence, 1984-96, chmn. edn. dept., 1984-89, Walter H. Annenberg prof. edn., 1993-94, dir. Annenberg Inst. Sch. Reform, 1994-96, univ. prof. emeritus, 1997—. Chmn. Coalition of Essential Schs., 1984—97, chmn. emeritus, 1997—; vis. prof. U. Bristol, England, 1971, Brown U., Providence, 1983; vis. prof. edn. Brandeis U., 2001—. Author: Secondary Schools at the Turn of the Century, 1964, The Age of the Academies, 1964, Religion and Public Education, 1967; author: (with Nancy F. Sizer) Moral Education: Five Lectures, 1970; author: Places for Learning, Places for Joy: Speculations on American School Reform, 1972, Horace's Compromise: The Dilemma of the American High School, 1984, rev. edit., 2004, Horace's School: Redesigning the American High School, 1992, Horace's Hope: What Works for the American High School, 1996; author: (with Nancy Faust Sizer) The Students Are Watching: Schools and the Moral Contract, 1999; author: (with Deborah Meier & Nancy F. Sizer) Keeping School: Letters to Families from Principals of Two Small Schools, 2004; author: The Red Pencil: Convictions from Experience in Education, 2004. Capt. U.S. Army, 1953-55. Named Guggenheim fellow, 1971; recipient citations Am. Fedn. Tchrs., Nat. Assn. Secondary Sch. Prins., Phillips Exeter Acad., Boston C. of C., Andover C. of C., Lehigh U. Edn. Alumni, 1991, Nat. Assn. Coll. Admissions Counsellors, 1991, Anthony Wayne award Wayne State U., 1981, Gold medal for excellence in undergrad. teaching CASE, 1988, Tchrs. Coll. medal Tchrs. Coll., Columbia U., 1991, Harold W. McGraw prize in edn., 1991, James Bryant Conant award Edn. Commn. States, 1992, Disting. Svc. award Coun. Chief State Sch. Officers, 1992, Coun. Am. Private Edn., 1993, Nat. award of Distinction U. Pa., 1993, Alumni award Harvard Grad. Sch. Edn., 1994. Fellow Am. Acad. Arts and Scis., Am. Philos. Soc.; mem. Nat. Acad. Edn. Office: FW Parker Charter Essential Sch Tchrs Ctr 49 Antietam St Ayer MA 01432

SIZYUK, VALERYI, physicist; b. Kobrin, Brest, Belarus, Sept. 25, 1966; m. Tatyana Sizyuk, Nov. 19, 1988; 1 child, Yuriy. MS in Physics, Belarus State U., Minsk, 1990, PhD, 1997. Rsch. scientist Phys.-Engring. Inst., Acad. Sci. Belarus, Minsk, 1990—2000; sr. rsch. scientist Inst. Heat and Mass Transfer, Acad. Sci. Belarus, Minsk, 2000—02; vis. scientist Argonne Nat. Lab., Ill., 2002—04, computational physicist, 2004—. Co-chief coun. young scientists Acad. Sci. Belarus, Minsk, 2000—02. Grantee, Byelorussian-Russian Found., 2000. Achievements include invention of method of optical coating deposition on the selenide zinc element. Avocation: fishing. Office: Argonne Nat Lab 9700 S Cass Ave Bldg 308 Argonne IL 60439-4825 Office Fax: 630-252-3250. Business E-Mail: sizyuk@anl.gov.

SJOBLOM, THOMAS V., lawyer; BA summa cum laude, U. Minn., 1974; JD, William Mitchell Coll. Law, 1978; LLM, Georgetown U., 1982. Bar: Minn. 1978, DC 1978, Pa. 2000, NY 2003. Branch chief Divsn. Market Regulation, Securities & Exchange Commn. (SEC), 1980—82, spl. counsel, 1982—87, asst. chief litig. counsel, 1987—99; spl. asst. US atty. (ctrl. dist.) Calif. US Dept Justice, 1990—92, spl. asst. US atty. (we. dist.) NY, 1991—92, spl. asst. US atty. (ea. dist.) Pa. Pa., 1996—98; litig. ptnr., chair securities practice grp. Dilworth Paxson LLP, Phila., 1999—2002; ptnr. Chadbourne & Parker LLP, NYC, 2002—06, Proskauer Rose LLP, Washington, 2006—. Named to NY Super Lawyers, 2006. Mem.: ABA (mem. litig. sect. & bus. law sect.), Swedish-Am. Chamber Commerce, Assn. Trial Lawyers of Am., Washington DC Bar Assn., NY Bar Assn., Fed. Bar Counsel NY, Am. Conf. Inst. (co-chair "The Corporate Counsel's Guide to Internal Investigations" 2003), Phi Beta Kappa. Office: Proskauer Rose LLP 1001 Pennsylvania Ave NW Ste 400 S Washington DC 20004 also: 30 Rockefeller Plaza New York NY 10112 Office Phone: 202-416-5805, 212-969-3110. Office Fax: 202-416-6899, 212-969-2900. E-mail: tsjoblom@proskauer.com.*

SJOERDSMA, ALBERT, research and development company executive; b. Lansing, Ill., Aug. 31, 1924; s. Sam and Agnes S.; m. Fern E. MacAllister, Dec. 2, 1950; children— Leslie, Ann, Albert, Britt. Ph.B., U. Chgo., 1944, BS, 1945, PhD, 1948, MD, 1949. Research asst. U. Chgo., 1947-49, NIH postdoctoral research fellow, 1950; intern U. Mich. Hosp., Ann Arbor, 1949-50; resident physician Michael Reese Hosp., Chgo., 1951; resident in internal medicine USPHS Hosp., Balt., 1951-53; sr. investigator, chief exptl. therapeutics br. Nat. Heart and Lung Inst., Bethesda, Md., 1953-71; v.p. Merrell Internat. Co., Strasbourg, France, 1971-78; v.p. pharm. research and devel. Richardson-Merrell Inc., 1978-81; v.p. pharm. research Merrell Dow Pharms., Cin., 1981-83; pres. Merrell Dow Research Inst., Cin., 1983-89, pres. emeritus, 1989-94; med. scis. cons., 1994—. Vis. spl. fellow Gen. Hosp., Malmo, Sweden, 1959-60; spl. lectr. George Washington U., 1959-71; Anton Julius Carlson lectr. U. Chgo., 1984; hon. chmn. 2d World Conf. on Clin. Pharmacology and Therapeutics, Washington, 1983; clin. prof. medicine U. Cin. Med. Ctr., 1986-91. Mem. AAAS (Theobold Smith award med. scis. 1958), Am. Soc. Pharm. and Exptl. Therapeutics (Harry Gold award in clin. pharmacology 1977, Exptl. Therapeutics award 1990), Am. Soc. Clin. Pharmacology and Therapeutics (Oscar B. Hunter Meml. award in therapeutics 1981, 50 Yr. Membership cert. 2007), Internat. Soc. Hypertension, Coun. High Blood Pressure Rsch., Am. Heart Assn., Am. Fedn. Clin. Rsch., Am. Soc. Clin. Investigation, Am. Soc. Exptl. Biology and Medicine, Assn. Am. Physicians, Am. Coll. Neuropsychopharmacology. Home and Office: 263 N Dogwood Trail Kitty Hawk NC 27949-3138

SJOSTRAND, FRITIOF STIG, biologist, educator; b. Stockholm, Nov. 5, 1912; s. Nils Johan and Dagmar (Hansen) S.; m. Marta Bruhn-Fahraeus, Mar. 24, 1941 (dec. June 1954); 1 child, Rutger; m. Ebba Gyllenkrok, Mar. 28, 1955; 1 child, Johan; m. Birgitta Petterson, Jan. 23, 1969; 1 child, Peter. MD, Karolinska Institutet, Stockholm, 1941, PhD, 1945; PhD (hon.), U. Siena, 1974, North-East Hill U., Shillon, India, 1989. Asst. prof. anatomy Karolinska Institutet, 1945-48, assoc. prof., 1949-59, prof. histology, 1960-61; research assoc. MIT, 1947-48; vis. prof. UCLA, 1959, prof. zoology, 1960-82, prof. emeritus molecular biology, 1982—. Author: Über die Eigenfluoreszenz Tierischer Gewebe Mit Besonderer Berücksichtigung der Säugetierniere, 1944, Electron Microscopy of Cells and Tissues, Vol. I, 1967, Deducing Function from Structure, Vols. I and II, 1990; also numerous articles. Decorated North Star Orden Sweden; recipient Jubilee award Swedish Med. Soc., 1959, Anders Retzius gold medal, 1967; Paul Ehrlich-Ludwig Darmstaedter prize, 1971 Fellow Royal Micros. Soc. (hon., London), Am. Acad. Arts and Scis.; mem. Electron Microscopy Soc. Am. (hon., Disting. Scientist award 1992), Japan Electron Microscopy Soc. (hon.), Scandinavian Electron Microscopy Soc. (hon.). Achievements include development technique for high resolution electron microscopy of cells, fluorescence microspectrography; inventor ultramicrotome. E-mail: fsjostra@ucla.edu.

SKAFF, JOSEPH JOHN, state agency administrator, retired military officer; b. Charleston, W.Va., June 13, 1930; s. Michael Joseph and Zahia S.; m. Maree A. Fleming, Aug. 4, 1957; children: Joseph M., Lynn M. Johnson, Gregory M., Nancy E. Kochman. BS, U.S. Mil. Acad., 1955; MS, George Wash. U., 1968. Commissional 2d. lt. U.S. Army, 1955, commd. 1/27 FA bn. Vietnam, 1968-69; mem. staff and faculty U.S. Mil. Acad., 1972-76; advance through grades to maj. gen.; dep. dir. internat. negotiations U.S. Army Joint Chiefs of Staff, Washington, 1979-81; also dep. commr. U.S. Del. Standing Consultative Commn., Geneva, 1979-81; dep. dir. ops. readiness and moblzn. hdqrs. U.S. Army, Washington, 1981-83, dep. commdg. gen., chief staff Japan, 1982—84; dep. comdg. gen. 1st U.S. Army, Fort Devens, Mass., 1985-89; cabinet sec. mil. affairs and pub. safety W.Va., 1989-97. Assoc. mem. Luth. Ch. Decorated DSM U.S. Army, Def. Superior Svc. medal, Legion of Merit, Bronze Star, Air medal, others; recipient Disting. W. Va. award. Mem. Assn. Grads. US Mil. Acad., Assn. US Army, Adj. Gens. Assn. US, N.G. Assn. U.S., Fellowship Christian Athletes (regional bd.), Union Mission Ministries (mem. bd.). Eastern Orthodox. Avocations: golf, travel.

SKAGEN, SUSAN K., biologist; PhD, U. Wis., Madison, 1986. Rsch. wildlife biologist US Geol. Survey, Fort Collins, Colo., 1988—. Office: US Geol Survey 2150 Ctr Ave Bldg C Fort Collins CO 80526 Business E-Mail: skagens@usgs.gov.

SKAGGS, DAVID EVANS, state official, former congressman; b. Cin., Feb. 22, 1943; s. Charles and Juanita Skaggs; m. Laura Locher, Jan. 3, 1987; 1 child, Matthew; stepchildren: Clare, Will. BA in Philosophy, Wesleyan U., 1964; student law, U. Va., 1964-65; LLB, Yale U., 1967. Bar: NY 1968, Colo. 1971, DC 1999. Assoc. Patterson, Belknap & Webb, NYC, 1967-68, Newcomer & Douglass, Boulder, Colo., 1971-74, 77-78; chief of staff to Rep. Tim Wirth US Congress, Washington, 1974-77; ptnr. Skaggs, Stone & Sheehy, Boulder, 1978-86; mem. Colo. Ho. of Reps., 1980—86, minority leader, 1982—85; mem. US Congress from 2nd Colo. dist., Washington, 1987-99, appropriations com., 1991-98, select. com. on intelligence, 1993—94, 1996—98; exec. dir. Democracy and Citizenship program The Aspen Inst., Washington, 1999—2001; of counsel Hogan & Hartson LLP, 1999—2007; exec. dir. Center for Dem. & Citizenship Council for Excellence in Govt., Washington, 2001—07; exec. dir. Colo. Dept. Higher Edn., 2007—. Del., Dem. Nat. Convention, 1984, '88, '92, '96; mem. Task Force on Nonproliferation Programs in Russia, 1999-2000, Overseas Presence Advisory Panel, 1999; adj. prof. U. Colo., 1999-2002; vice chair US Pub. Interest Declassification Bd.; steering com., East West Parliamentary Project Former bd. dirs. Rocky Mountain Planned Parenthood, Mental Health Assn. Colo., Boulder County United Way, Boulder Civic Opera; bd. trustees Wesleyan U., 1991-94 Capt. USMC, 1968—71, South Vietnam, major USMC Res., 1971—77. Decorated Navy Commendation medal, Navy Achievement medal with Combat V. Mem. Colo. Bar Assn., Boulder County Bar Assn., Boulder C. of C., US Capitol Historical Soc., US Assn. Former Members of Congress Democrat. Congregationalist. Office: Colo Dept Higher Edn 1560 Broadway Ste 1600 Denver CO 80202 Office Phone: 303-866-2723.

SKAGGS, DAVID L., orthopedist, educator; BA in Neurosci. and Psychology, Amherst Coll., Mass., 1985; MD, Columbia U. Coll. of Physicians and Surgeons, NYC, 1989; Masters of Med. Mgmt., Marshal Sch. Bus., U. So. Calif., 2005—06. Diplomate Am. Bd. of Orthop. Surgery, 1998. Intern Columbia-Presbyterian Med. Ctr., NY, 1989—90, resident, 1990—94; Frank E. Stinchfield orthop. rsch. fellowship Columbia U., NY, 1991—92; pediatric orthop. fellowship U. So. Calif., Children's Hosp., LA, 1994—95; asst. prof., divsn. orthop. surgery U. Ala. Sch. Medicine, 1995—96; asst. prof. orthop. surgery U. of So. Calif.-Keck Sch. of Medicine, 1996—2002, assoc. prof. of orthop. surgery, 2002—; assoc. dir. Children's Orthop. Ctr., Children's Hosp. LA, endowed chair, pediatric spinal disorders. Cons. Stryker Spine, Allendale, NJ; instr. Am. Acad. of Orthop. Surgeons, Rosemont, Ill.; cons. Medtronics Sofamor Danek, Memphis; instr., rschr. Stryker Spine, Westchester, Pa. Author: (textbook) Staying Out of Trouble in Pediatric Orthopaedics; contbr. articles to profl. jours.; featured on Miracle Workers (ABC), 2006. Recipient Young Investigator Award, Pediatric Orthopaedic Soc. of N.Am., 2000, Sandoz award, Columbia U. of Coll. of Physicians and Surgeons, 1989; fellow Am., Brit., Can. Traveling Fellow, Am. Orthop. Assn., 2003, Traveling fellow, Pediatric Orthop. Soc. of N.Am., 2002. Mem.: Am. Acad. of Pediat., Sect. of Orthopedics (exec. com.), Am. Acad. of Orthop. Surgeons, Pediatric Orthop.Soc. of N.Am. (bd. of directors, Young Investigators Award, Traveling Fellos 2000, 2002), Scoliosis Rsch. Soc. (program com.), LA Tennis Club, Salt Air Club. Achievements include design of Pediatric spinal instrumentation. Avocations: meditation, tennis, weightlifting, boogie boarding, yoga. Office: Childrens Hospital Los Angeles 4650 Sunset Blvd #69 Los Angeles CA 90027 Office Fax: 323-666-4409.

SKAGGS, RICKY, country musician; b. Ky., July 18, 1954; s. Hobert and Dorothy Skaggs; m. Sharon White, 1981; 4 children. Mandolin player Ralph Stanley's Clinch Mountain Boys, 1969; with Country Gentlemen, J.D. Crowe & New South, Emmylou Harris' Hot Band, 1977, The Whites; founder Boone Creek; joined Grand Ole Opry, 1982. Musician: (albums) Waitin' for the Sun to Shine, 1981, Highways and Heartaches, Don't Cheat in Our Hometown, Country Boy, 1984, Favorite Country Songs, Live in London, Love's Gonna Get Ya!, Comin' Home To Stay, 1988, Kentucky Thunder, 1989, My Father's Son, 1991, Super Hits, 1993, Solid Ground, 1998, Ricky Skaggs Portrait, 1992, Life Is a Journey, 1997, Bluegrass Rules, 1998 (Grammy award for Best Bluegrass Album, 1999), Ancient Tones, 1999 (Grammy award for Best Bluegrass Album), Soldier of the Cross, 2000 (Grammy award for Best Bluegrass Gospel Album), Big Mon-The Songs of Bill Monroe, 2000, The Essential Ricky Skaggs, 2003, Brand New Strings, 2004, Instrumentals, 2006 (Grammy award for Best Bluegrass Album, 2007), Ricky Skaggs & Bruce Hornsby, 2007, Salt of the Earth, 2007 (Grammy award for Best Bluegrass Gospel Album, 2008), Honoring the Fathers of Bluegrass: Tribute to 1946 & 1947, 2008 (Grammy award for Best Bluegrass Album, 2009), The High Notes, 2008, (songs) Wheel Hoss, 1984 (Grammy award for Best Country Instrumental Performance), Raisin' the Dickens, 1986 (Grammy award for Best Country Instrumental Performance), Restless, 1991 (Grammy award for Best Country Collaboration with Vocals), Same Old Train, 1998 (Grammy award for Best Country Collaboration with Vocals), A Simple Life, 2003 (Grammy award for Best Country Group Vocal Performance). Recipient Horizon award for best newcomer Country Music Assn., 1982, male vocalist of yr. award, 1982, best instrumental group award, 1983, 1984, 1985, 6 Country Music Assn. awards including Entertainer of Yr. award, 1985, Vocal Event of Yr. award, 1991, 6 Acad. of Country Music awards, MusicDove award, Gospel Music Assn., Edison award, 1987, 50th Anniversary award, USO, 1989, various awards Music City News, Cash Box, Radio and Records, Musician of Yr. award, Christian Country Music Assn., 1994, Instrumental Group of Yr. award (with Kentucky Thunder, Internat. Bluegrass Music Awards, 1998—2006; named Playboy Reader's Poll Best Country Instrumental Performance, 1989, Eng.'s Country Music Round Up Most Popualr Internat. Male, 1986—87, Christian Country Artist of Yr., Gospel Voice Mag., 1993. Address: Skaggs Family Records 329 Rockland Rd Hendersonville TN 37075-3423*

SKAGGS, ROBERT C., JR., utilities executive, lawyer; BA, Davidson Coll.; JD, W. Va. Univ.; MBA, Tulane Univ. With Columbia Energy Group, 1981—2000, law dept., 1981—96, pres., Columbia Gas Ohio & Ky., 1996—2000; pres. Bay State Gas, No. Utilities, other Columbia cos. NiSource Inc., 2000—03, exec. v.p., 2003—04, pres., 2004—, CEO, 2005—. Bd. dir. Southeastern Gas Assn.; mem. Midwest Energy Assn.; mem. leadership council Am. Gas Assn. Mem.: ABA, Energy Bar Assn., W. Va. Bar Assn. Office: NiSource Inc 801 E 86th Ave Merrillville IN 46410

SKAGGS, SANFORD MERLE, lawyer; b. Berkeley, Calif., Oct. 24, 1939; s. Sherman G. and Barbara Jewell (Stinson) Skaggs; m. Sharon Ann Barnes, Sept. 3, 1976; children: Stephen, Paula Ferry, Barbara Gallagher, Darren Peterson. BA, U. Calif., Berkeley, 1961; JD, U. Calif., 1964. Bar: Calif. 1965. Atty. Pacific Gas and Electric Co., San Francisco, 1964-73; gen. counsel Pacific Gas Transmission Co., San Francisco, 1973-75; ptnr. Van Voorhis & Skaggs, Walnut Creek, Calif., 1975-85, McCutchen, Doyle, Brown & Enersen, San Francisco and Walnut Creek, 1985—2002, Bingham McCutchen LLP, 2002—; dir. John Muir Mt. Diablo Health Sys., 1997—2005. Mem. Calif. Law Revision Commn., 1990—2001, chmn., 1993. Councilman City of Walnut Creek, 1972-78, mayor 1974-75, 76-77; bd. dirs. East Bay Mcpl. Utility Dist., 1978-90, pres., 1982-90; dir. Episcopal Sr. Cmtys., 2005-. Mem.: San Fransisco & Contra Costa County Bar Assns., Calif. State Bar Assn., Phi Delta Phi, Alpha Delta Phi, Lambda Alpha. Episcopalian. Office: Bingham McCutchen LLP Three Embarcadero Ctr San Francisco CA 94111-4067 Office Phone: 415-393-2528. Office Fax: 415-262-9233. Business E-Mail: s.skaggs@bingham.com.

SKAGGS, STACY L., elementary school educator; b. Greensburg, Ky., Nov. 19, 1974; d. Winfred and Glenda Simpson; m. Tony W. Skaggs, Sept. 27, 2003. BS in Elem. Edn., Western Ky.U., Bowling Green, 1998; MA in Secondary Guidance, Western Ky. U., Bowling Green, 2002. Tchr. Green County HS, Greensburg, Ky. Mem.: Ky. Assn. Tchrs. Family and Consumer Sci. (pres. 2006—).

SKAGGS, WAYNE GERARD, retired diversified financial services company executive; b. Bonneterre, Mo., Dec. 12, 1929; s. Jasper Pinkney and Lattie May (Duren) S.; m. Hana Kaneko, June 1, 1952; children: Robert Kenneth, Melody Jane, Joy Elizabeth. Student, Mo. Inst. Acctg. and Law, 1947-48, U. Mo., Columbia, 1954-55. With Advantage Capital Corp. (formerly Am. Capital Corp.), Houston, 1955-96, ret., 1996; pres., COO Mktg. Group of Cos., Houston, 1976-80, corp. v.p., cons., 1972-90. Served with USAF, 1950-54, Korea. Mem. Nat. Assn. Securities Dealers (nat. vice-chmn. 1977, dist. chmn. 1972), Nat. Bus. Conduct (gov., chmn. 1976), Investment Co. Inst., Am. Legion (life), VFW (life), Optimists (life, pres. 1966). Home: PO Box 726 Wimberley TX 78676-0726 Personal E-mail: hanawayn@vownet.net.

SKAINE, JAMES C., retired communications educator; b. Monongahela, Pa., Jan. 3, 1936; s. James Skaine, Jr. and Ruth Stamper Skaine; m. Rosemarie Keller, June 4, 1957; children: James Keller, Forrest Todd. BA, Sioux Falls Coll., SD, 1957; MA, U. SD, Vermillion, 1958; Doctoral study, Cornell U., Ithaca, NY, 1958—66, U. Iowa, Iowa City, 1968—78. Lic. to preach Ctrl. Pk. Bapt. Ch., Buffalo, NY, 1954. Grad. asst. U. SD, 1957—58, Cornell U., 1958—60; tchr. George Jr. Republic, Freeville, NY, 1960; prof., comm. Ithaca Coll., Ithaca, NY, 1960—63; asst. prof., comm. Mid. Tenn. State Coll., Murfreesboro, 1963—65, U. No. Iowa, Cedar Falls, 1965—99. Faculty advisor, UNI chpt., Iowa pub. interest rsch. group U. No. Iowa, Cedar Falls, 1976—78, presenter, ofcl. guest, exch. program with China at universities: Beijing Normal, Hebei tchrs., Shaanxi, & Guangxi tchrs., 1991, founders days presdl. com., 1988—90, coll. of humanities & fine arts senator, 1982—83, sec., United Faculty, 1978—79, academic freedom & profl. rights chair, United Faculty, 1980—86, treas., United Faculty, 1986—89, pres., United Faculty, 1989—94; exec. sec. NY State Debate Assn., Ithaca, 1962—63; mem. Speech Comm. Assn., Des Moines, 1965—72, Iowa Comm. Assn., Des Moines, 1972—85; cons., pub. speaking and voice improvement, Cedar Falls - Waterloo, Iowa. Co-author: (book) A Man of the Twentieth Century: Recollections of Warren V. Keller, A Nebraskan; contbr. chapters to books, articles to profl. pubs. Pres. Friends of the Accused, Waterloo, Iowa, 1974—76; parliamentarian Iowa LWV, Des Moines, 1979—81; host in our home Zhu Qizhen, the amb. extraordinary & plenipotentiary of the People's Republic of China to the USA and his wife, Wang Yude Iowa US Senator Charles Grassley's Iowa Internat. Trade Symposium III, 1990; candidate US Congress, Iowa, Dem. Primary Election, Third District, 1972—74; min. Presbyn. Ch., Rockvale, Tenn., 1964—65, Bapt. Ch., Turkey Valley, Enfield, NY, 1960—62, Viborg, SD, 1957—58; with Presdl. Campaign, Obama-Biden, 2008. Mem.: NEA, Iowa State Edn. Assn., Pi Kappa Delta (life). Democrat. Baptist. Avocations: travel, gardening. Home: 2215 Clay St Cedar Falls IA 50613 Office: Author's Castle Publisher 2215 Clay St Cedar Falls IA 50613 Office Fax: 319-266-1406; Home Fax: 319-266-1406. Business E-Mail: jskaine@cfu.net.

SKAINE, ROSEMARIE KELLER, writer, publisher, consultant; d. Warren V. Keller and Marie W. Kuehner Keller; m. James Cole Skaine, June 4, 1957; children: James Keller, Forrest Todd. BA, U. SD, Vermillion, 1958; MA, U. No. Iowa, Cedar Falls, 1977. Cert. secondary edn. tchr. NY, 1959, SD, 1958. English tchr. Ovid Ctrl. Sch., NY, 1958—60; adminstrv. and legislative asst. Pres. Kennedy's Consumer Adv. Coun. Chairperson, Ithaca, NY, 1963; adj. instr., sociology Wartburg Coll., Waverly, Iowa, 1979—80; adj. instr., composition Hawkeye C.C., Waterloo, Iowa, 1998—98. Cons., institutes on sexual harassment Adult Edn. Bd. YWCA, Waterloo, Iowa, 1992; cons., sexual harassment KCET Pub. TV, Los Angeles, Calif., 1991—94; ct. testimony, sexual harassment Dist. Ct., Waterloo, Iowa, 1989—99; US del. XII Internat. Congress on Family Law, Havana, Cuba, 2002; speaking tour, women of Afghanistan under the Taliban SD Ctr. for the Book's three day program, Maintaining Democracy in an Unstable World, Aberdeen, Brookings, Mitchell and Sioux Falls, SD, 2002; presenter, Am. family, Guilin, Shijiazhuang, Xian, China U. No. Iowa, Cedar Falls, 1993; featured author 4th anniversary hostage-taking Radio Free Europe, Moscow Dubrovka House of Culture, 2006. Co-author (with Warren V. Keller and James C. Skaine): (book) A Man of the Twentieth Century: Recollections of Warren V. Keller, A Nebraskan, 1999; author: Women at War: Gender Issues of Americans in Combat, 1999, Power and Gender: Issues in Sexual Dominance and Harassment, 1996 (Gustavus Myers Ctr. award for the study of human rights in N.Am. for the outstanding work on intolerance in N.Am., 1997), Sexual Harassment: Questions and Answers, 2d revised edit., 1990, (nonfiction book) Female Genital Mutilation: Legal, Cultural and Medical Issues, 2005, (short stories) Lessons in Love and Life, (book) The Cuban Family: Custom and Change in an Era of Hardship, 2004, Questions and Answers about Sexual Harassment, 1980, Paternity and American Law, 2003, The Women of Afghanistan Under the Taliban, 2002, Women College Basketball Coaches, 2001, Female Suicide Bombers, 2006, Women Polit. Leaders in Africa, 2008, Women of Afganistan in the Post Taliban Era: How Lives Have Changed and Where They Stand Today, 2008; contbr. articles to profl. jours. Panel mem., women in Afghanistan Cable TV Here and There, Cedar Falls, Iowa, 2001; voters svc. chair, pres. LWV of Waterloo-Cedar Falls, Cedar Falls, Iowa, 1964—69; with Obama-Biden Presdl. Compaign, 2008; nat. steering com., hon. mem. Gore 2000 Presdl. Campaign, 2000, Clinton-Gore Presdl. Campaign, 1996; campaign mgr. James Skaine for U.S. Congress, Cedar Falls, Iowa, 1972—74; precint chairperson for Ohama presdl. Primary Campaign, 2007—08. Recipient award, Women's Studies Undergraduate and Grad. Programs, U. of No. Iowa, Cedar Falls, 1998, So. Poverty Law Ctr., Montgomery, Ala., 2003—, Hall of Honor Inductee, Grand Island NE Sr. High Sch., 2008. Mem.: Alpha Kappa Delta, Pi Kappa Delta (life). Office: Author's Castle Publishing PO Box 1044 Cedar Falls IA 50613 Office Fax: 319-266-1406; Home Fax: 319-266-1406. Personal E-mail: rskaine@cfu.net.

SKAINS, THOMAS E., gas industry executive; BBA, Sam Houston State Univ.; JD, Univ. Houston. Sr. atty. Trans-Continental Gas Pipeline Corp., 1981—86, v.p., 1986—89, sr. v.p. transp. & customer svc., 1989—95; sr. v.p. mktg. & supply svc. Piedmont Natural Gas, Charlotte, NC, 1995—2002, pres., COO, 2002—03, chmn., pres., CEO, 2003—. Bd. dir., mem. exec. com. Am. Gas Assn.; chmn. So. Gas Assn.; regional bd. adv. Wachovia Bank. Bd. dir., mem. exec. com. Charlotte C. of C.; bd. mem. United Way Ctrl. Carolinas; chmn. bd. trustees Providence Day Sch. Mem.: State Bar Tex. Office: Piedmont Natural Gas 4720 Piedmont Row Dr Charlotte NC 28210 Mailing: Piedmont Natural Gas PO Box 33068 Charlotte NC 28233

SKALAGARD, HANS MARTIN, artist; b. Skuko, Faroe Islands, Feb. 7, 1924; came to U.S., 1942, naturalized, 1955. s. Ole Johannes and Hanna Elisa (Fredriksen) S.; m. Mignon Diana Haack Haegland, Mar. 31, 1955; 1 child, Karen Solveig Sikes. Pupil, Anton Otto Fisher, 1947. Joined U.S. Mcht. Marine, 1942, advanced through grades to chief mate, 1945; ret., 1965; owner, operator Skalagard Sq. Rigger Art Gallery, Carmel, Calif., 1966—; libr. Mayo Hays O'Donnel Libr., Monterey, Calif., 1971-73; painter U.S. Naval Heritage series, 1973—. Lectr., bd. dirs. Allen Knight Maritime Mus., 1973—, mem. adv. and acquisitions coms., 1973-77; spkr. in field. One-man shows include Palace Legion of Honor, San Francisco, 1960, J.F. Howland, 1963-65, Fairmont Hotel, San Francisco, 1963, Galerie de Tours, 1969, 72-73, Pebble Beach (Calif.) Gallery, 1963, Laguna Beach (Calif.) Gallery, 1969, Arden Gallery, Atlanta, 1970, Gilbert Gallery, San Francisco, Maritime Mus. of Monterey, 1993, 97, Rigger Art Gallery, Carmel, Stanton Ctr., Monterey, 1993, Monterey Maritime Mus., 1993, 1997, St. Francis Yacht Club, San Francisco, 1995, Ventura County Maritime Mus., Oxnard, Calif., 1998, Monterey Maritime Mus., 2006, Santa Barbara Maritime Mus., 2007, Petaluma Carnegie Mus., 2007; exhibited in group shows at Am. Artists, Eugene, Oreg., Robert Louis Stevenson Exhibit, Carmel Valley Gallery, Biarritz and Paris, David Findley Galleries, N.Y.C. and Faroe Island, Maritime Mus., Calif., 1993, 94, 95, Pacific Coast Lumber Schooners, 1994, San Francisco Art Expo, 2000, Herrschoff Marine Mus., Bristol, R.I., 2002, numerous others; represented in permanent collections Naval Post Grad. Sch. and Libr., Allen Knight Maritime Mus., Monterey, Robert Louis Stevenson Sch., Pebble Beach, Carmel Art Gallery; work represented in numerous books including Modern Masters of Marine Art, 1993; featured artist KTEH-TV On-Air Art Auction, 1998; profiled in profl. jours.; subject of cover and article Palette Talk, 1980, Compass mag., 1980; artist (series of paintings) American Revolutionary War at Sea, 2003, Life Under Sail Art Retrospective Hans Skalagred Monetory Maritime Museum, 2007, 2008, Designed Speed America Cup Defenders, 2009, Aurora Colors Gallery, Petaluma, Petaluma's Historic Opera House Ky. St. Chairperson Mayor's Choice Exhibit, Carmel, 1993-95; co-founder Carmel Gallery Alliance, 2000--. Recipient Silver medal Tommaso Campanella Internat. Acad. Arts, Letters and Scis., Rome, 1970, Gold medal, 1972, Gold medal and hon. life membership Acad. Italia dell Arti e del Honoro, 1980, Gold medal for artistic merit Acad. d'Italia, Statue of Victory award Acad. d'Italia, 2003. Mem. Navy League (bd. dirs. Monterey), Internat. Platform Assn., Sons of Norway (cultural dir. 1974-75, 76-77), Am. Mcht. Marine Vets. Assn. (Goden Gate chpt.), Combat Mcht. Marine WWII Assn. (coun.), Mariners (San Francisco Bay area chpt.). Home: 602 Stony Point Rd Petaluma CA 94952-1048 Home Phone: 707-769-9340. Personal E-mail: skalagard@aol.com.

SKALSKY, ASKOLD, retired literature and language professor; b. Czernivtsi, Ukraine, Aug. 14, 1940; s. Ostap Skalsky and Irene Horda; children: Sviatoslav, Boris, Roman. BA, U. Pa., Phila., 1964; MA, City Coll. NY, 1966. Prof. English and German Hagerstown CC, Hagerstown, Md., 1968—2008, editor hedge apple, 1999—2006. Author: Introduction The Mummery Book; contbr. articles to profl. jours. Writer and editor newsletter News Ukraine, Frederick, Md., 1968—87.

SKAMANGAS, ANNA LYNN, manufacturing executive, educator; d. Emmanuel Skamangas and Skamangas Despina; m. Constantinos Scaros, May 30, 2009. Degree in Elem. Edn., Pa. State U., State Coll., 1992, degree in Greek History and Archaeology, 1992; MS in Sci. Edn., Lebanon Valley Coll., Annville, Pa., 2000. Cert. tchr. Pa., 1992, in spl. edn. Lebanon Valley Coll., 2002. Dir. Children's Sch. Lebanon County, Pa., 1992—98; pres. Baklava Goddess, Inc., Schaefferstown, Pa., 1999—; instr. Harrisburg Area CC, Lebanon, Pa., 2000—, PCLE, Lebanon, 2000—. Child adv. and cons. Pvt., Schaeffestown, Pa., 1999—. Adv. and co-chair Taxpayers Opposed Over Regulation, Annville, Pa., 2006—09. Greek Orthodox. Avocations: travel, cooking, reading, exercise, chess. Home and Office: Baklava Goddess Inc 100 S Mkt St Schaefferstown PA 17088 Office Fax: 717-949-3368. Personal E-mail: baklavagoddess@yahoo.com.

SKAMBIS, CHRISTOPHER CHARLES, JR., lawyer; b. Painesville, Ohio, Jan. 21, 1953; s. Christopher Charles and Anne (Haritos) S.; m. Susan Elaine Adrianson, Dec. 18, 1976 (div. Mar. 1997); m. Kathleen Louise Maloney, Feb. 1999; children: Adrianne Elaine, Christopher Roy. Student, U. Pa., 1970-72; BA, U. Conn., 1972-74; JD, Ohio State U. Coll. Law, Columbus, 1975-78. Bar: Fla. 1978, US Dist. Ct. (mid. dist.), 1979, US Dist. Ct. (no. and so. dists.) 1997, US Ct. Appeals (5th and 11th cir.) 1981, US Supreme Ct. 1989. Assoc. VandenBerg, Gay & Burke, Orlando, Fla., 1978-81, ptnr., 1982, VandenBerg, Gay, Burke, Wilson & Arkin, Orlando, Fla., 1982-85, Foley & Lardner, Orlando, Fla., 1985—95, Moran & Shams PA, Orlando, Fla., 1996-99, The Skambis Law Firm, Orlando, 2000—. Mem. Orange County Bar Assn., Orlando, Fla., 1978, Fla. Bar 9D Grievance Commn., Orlando, Fla., 1989; arbitrator Fla. Bar 9th Cir. Fee Arbitration Commn., Orlando, 1987; co-chair Federal and State Trial Practice Co., Orlando, 1992-93. Mem. Am. Judicature Soc., ABA. Avocation: amateur ham radio operator. Office: The Skambis Law Firm 715 Vassar St Orlando FL 32804-4920 Office Phone: 407-649-0090. Office Fax: 407-649-0191. Business E-Mail: cskambis@skambislaw.com.

SKANCKE, NANCY J., lawyer; b. Mar. 24, 1950; d. Frank and LaVerne Hubbard; m. Steven Lynn Skancke, Nov. 29, 1975; children: Matthew David, Carolyn Elizabeth. BS in Math. (hon.), Purdue U., West Lafayette, Ind., 1972; JD (hon.), George Washington U., DC, 1975. Bar: Va. 1975, D.C. 1975, U.S. Ct. Appeals (5th, D.C. 11th cirs.), U.S. Supreme Ct. Ptnr. Ross, Marsh & Foster, Washington, 1980—92, Baller Hammett, Washington, 1992-93, Grammer, Kissel, Robbins & Skancke, Washington, 1993-96, Grammer, Kissel, Robbins, Skancke & Edwards, Washington, 1996—2000, GKRSE, 2000—. Bd. dirs. Found. of Energy Law Jour., 1986—89, 1998—2001. Contbr. articles to profl. jours. Master, Prettyman-Leventhal Am. Inns of Ct., 1988—2001, pres., 1992—93. Named Disting. Sci. Alumnus, Purdue U., 2006. Fellow: Am. Bar Found. (life); mem.: ABA (sect. natural resources energy law, sect. adminstrv./regulatory law), Nat. Pk. Performing Arts Assocs. (bd. dirs. 1989—93), Wolf Trap, Gleaning For World (bd. dirs. 2008—09), Orgn. Mgmt. Comm. (chmn. 2006—08), U.Va.Families Bd., Ctr. Christian Study, Parents Coun. (chair 2006—09), Internat. Mcpl. Lawyers' Assn. (chmn. mcpl. contracts and franchises tech. sects. 2005—07, program planning com., Pres. award 2003), Nat. Hydropower Assn. (bd. dirs. 2002—05, treas. 2003—05, chair, regional meeting com. 2005—09, chair Small Hydra coun. 2009—), Energy Bar Assn. (bd. dirs. 1985—88), George Mason U. Century Club (founding mem. 1992—93). Home: 833 Nethercliffe Hall Rd Great Falls VA 22066-2717 Office: Law Offices of GKRSE Ste 330 1500 K St NW Washington DC 20005 Home Phone: 703-759-4927; Office Phone: 202-408-5400. Business E-Mail: njskancke@gkrse-law.com.

SKANDERA TROMBLEY, LAURA ELISE, academic administrator, literature educator; b. LA, Nov. 1, 1960; d. John and Mary Ruth (Chaney) S.; m. Nelson Edmund Trombley, July 13, 1991. BA, Pepperdine U., 1981, MA summa cum laude, 1993; PhD in English Lit., U. So. Calif., 1989. Asst. prof. Dept. English SUNY, Potsdam, 1990—92, assoc. prof., 1993—97, spl. asst. to pres., 1994—97, dir. Tchg., Tenure and Promotion Assistance Program, 1994—97, asst. provost, 1995—97; v.p. academic affairs, dean faculty Coe Coll., Cedar Rapids, Iowa, 1997—2002; pres. Pitzer Coll., Claremont, Calif., 2002—. Asst. lectr. writing program U. So. Calif., 1983—85, 1987; vis. prof. Am. studies U. Eichstaett, Bavaria, Germany, 1985—86, Bavaria, 1987—88; vis. asst. prof. Dept. English Pepperdine U., 1988—90. Author: Epistemology: Turning Points in the History of Poetic Knowledge, 1986, Mark Twain's Literary Marriage, 1992, Mark Twain in the Company of Women, 1994; editor: Critical Essays on Maxine Hong Kingston, 1998; co-editor: Constructing Mark Twain: New Directions in Scholarship, 2001; contbr. articles to profl. jours. Named Quarry Farm fellow Ctr. for Mark Twain Studies, 1988, Finklestein fellow U. Soc. Calif., 1988. Mem.: Internat. Assn. Univ. Prof. English, Internat. Assn. Univ. Pres., Am. Assn. Univ. Women, Mark Twain Circle of Am. Office: Office of Pres Pitzer Coll 1050 N Mills Ave Claremont CA 91711 Office Phone: 909-621-8198. E-mail: president@pitzer.edu.*

SKARBEK, DENISE MARIE, music educator; d. Albert William and Lillian Rose Skarbek; m. James Frederick Hendricks, Jan. 5, 2005; children: Melissa Rose Dickey, Michelle Marie. BSc in Spl. Edn., Ind. U., South Bend, 1988, MSc, 1993; PhD, U. South Fla., Tampa, 2000. Lic. in tchg. Ind., 1989. Tchr. South Bend Cmty. Sch. Corp., 1989—93; assoc. prof. Ind. U., 2000—. Editor: (novel) Bulletproof Vests vs. The ethic of Care: Which Strategy is Your School Using ?, The Passion of Teaching: Dispositions in the School; co-author: What You Don't Know will Hurt You: Sexual Abuse in Schools. Sch. bd. mem. Trinity Luth. Sch., Elkhart, Ind., 2008—. Recipient Disting. Alumni award, Ind. U. Mem.: WCCI. Achievements include research in special education and violence. Office: Ind Univ South Bend 1700 Mishawaka Ave South Bend IN 46634-7111 Business E-Mail: dskarbek@iusb.edu.

SKARECKY, DOUGLAS WILLIAM, lab administrator; s. Jerry and Violet Lucille Skarecky; m. Pamela Lynn Flodman, Sept. 24, 1994; children: Dale, Dara. BS, Ariz. State U., Tempe, 1972. Sr. clin. coord. U. Calif., Irvine, Orange, 1978—. Contbr. chapters to books, articles to profl. jours. Treas. U. Cmty. Assn., Irvine, 2003—04. Recipient 1st Prize Poster, Western Sect. Am. Urol. Assn., 2005, Best Poster award, Am. Urol. Assn., 2008. Achievements include research in human genetics, huntington disease evolutionary biology, robotic-assisted laparoscopic radical prostatectomy, prostate cancer. Avocations: bicycling, sailing, art.

SKARIE, DAVID P., food products executive; BBS, Minn. State Univ. Mgmt. positions through v.p. field sales Ralcorp Holdings Inc., St. Louis, 1986—93, v.p., dir. sales human foods, 1993—94, corp v.p., dir. customer devel. group, 1994—2000, corp. v.p., 2000—03, pres. Ralston Foods, 2000—, pres. Carriage House Co., 2002—, co-CEO, pres., 2003—. Chmn. Private Label Mfr. Assn. Office: Ralcorp Holdings Inc 800 Market St Saint Louis MO 63101

SKEAN, MARK EDGAR, finance educator, consultant; b. Knoxville, Tenn., Nov. 02; s. James Dan Skean and Nellie Ann Sherrill; m. Diane Gail Ouse, June 15, 1991. AB, Western Ky. U., Bowling Green, 1982; MBA, Ind. U., Bloomington, 1984; PhD, U. N.D., Grand Forks, 1993. CPA Ohio, CMA, Inst. Mgmt. Acctg., CFM, Inst. Mgmt. Acctg., CSA, Inst. Internal Auditors. Sr. fin. analyst Union Underwear, Bowling Green, Ky., 1984—86; sr. field auditor Ky. Revenue Cabinet, Ft. Mitchell, 1986—88; asst. prof. Lees Coll., Jackson, 1988—89, Mayville State U., ND, 1990—93, assoc. prof., 1994—98, prof., 1999—. Rep. N.D. Coun. Coll. Faculties, 1994—96; pres. Assn. N.D. Acctg. Instrs., 2003; presenter in field. Recipient Tchr. of Yr., Mayville State U. Student Senate, 2006; grantee, Bush Found., Mpls., 1998—. Office: Mayville State Univ 330 3rd St NE Mayville ND 58257

SKEEN, DAVID RAY, systems engineer, consultant, engineering executive, educator; b. Bucklin, Kans., July 12, 1942; s. Claude E. and Velma A. (Birney) S.; m. Carol J. Stimpert, Aug. 23, 1964; children: Jeffrey Kent, Timothy Sean, Kimberly Dawn. BA in Math., Emporia State U., Kans., 1964; MS, Am. U., DC, 1972; grad., Fed. Exec. Inst., 1983, Naval War Coll., 1984; DSc in Engring. Mgmt., George Washington U., DC, 1998. Cert. office automation profl. Computer sys. analyst to comdr.-in-chief U.S. Naval Forces-Europe, London, 1967-70; computer sys. analyst Naval Command Sys. Support Activity, Washington, 1970-73; dir. data processing Office Naval Rsch., U.S. Navy Dept., Arlington, Va., 1973-78; dir. mgmt. info. sys. Naval Civilian Pers. Command, Washington, 1978-80; dep. dir. manpower, pers. tng. automated sys. Dept. Naval Mil. Pers. Command, Washington, 1980-85; dir. manpower, pers. tng. info. resource mgmt. Chief Naval Ops., Washington, 1985-91; assoc. dir. Office of IRM, USDA, Washington, 1992-96; dir. modernization of adminstrn. processes program, 1996-98; dep. dir. office of ops. USDA, Washington, 1998; sr. engring. mgr., cons. Lockheed Martin, Washington, 1998—2004; sys. engr., cons. GCI, 2004—07; cons. Enterprise Bus. Solutions, 2008—. Lectr. Inst. Sci. and Pub. Affairs, 1973-76; cons. Electronic Data Processing Career Devel. Programs, 1975—; detailed to Pres.'s Reorgn. Project for Automated Data Processing, 1978, spl. Navy IRM studies, SECNAV, 1991, USDA/Office of Mgmt. and Budget IRM, 1993, spl. USDA Field Structure Studies, 1997; adj. prof. Sch. Engring. and Applied Sci. George Washington U., 1985—, Dept. Pub. Adminstrn. George Mason U., 2005—; mem. Pres.'s Fed. Automated Data Processing Users Group, Washington, 1978-80 Contbr. articles to profl. jours. Capt. USNR, 1960-91. Recipient Outstanding Performance award Interagy. Com. Data Processing, 1976, Adminstrv. Staff Performance award, 1998, Sec.'s cert. Appreciation, 1998. Mem. Internat. Coun. on Sys. Engring., Sr. Exec. Assn., Assn. Fed. IRM, Naval Res. Assn., Pres. Fed. Automated Data Processing Users Group. Avocations: travel, photography, reading. Personal E-mail: docskeen@embarqmail.com.

SKEENS, LEE ROY, psychology professor; b. Davenport, Iowa, July 22, 1952; s. Betty Joe Skeens; m. Ruth Nell Kelly, Mar. 18, 1995; children: Tiffany Anne Frye, Brandi L. Chapman, Jeremy Lee, Melissa Derr, Jeremy Derr, Meranda Anderson children: Eric Derr. MA, Webster U., St. Louis, Mo, 1986. Capt. USAF, 1974—90; prof. Southeastern Cmty. Coll., West Burlington, Iowa, 1990—. Author: (textbook) Understanding Psychology. Chmn. Higher Edn. Com. Iowa State Edn. Assn., Des Moines, 2007—09. Decorated Bronze Star Valor Dept. Def., Def. Meritorious Svc. Medal; recipient Vol. Svc. award, Gov. Iowa, 1991. Mem.: KC (faithful navigator 2008—09). Democrat-Npl. Roman Catholic. Office: Southeastern Cmty Coll 1500 W Agy Rd West Burlington IA 52655

SKEES, WILLIAM LEONARD, JR., lawyer; b. Indpls., Jan. 26, 1947; s. William Leonard and Marian Catherine (Fagan) S.; m. Cindy Lee Keeton; children: Kristina Suzanne Carlsen, Elizabeth Ann Garrison, Catherine Fagan, William Leonard III (dec.), Samuel Jackson. BA, Ball State U., 1969; JD magna cum laude, Ind. U., 1971. Bar: Ind. 1971, Ky. 1981. Law clk. U.S. Dist. Ct. (no. dist.), Fort Wayne, Ind., 1971-72; mem. Frost Brown Todd, LLC, Louisville, 1981—. Contbr. articles to jours. in field. Mem. bd. visitors Ind. U. Sch. Law, 1975-91; bd. dirs., past pres. Louisville Housing Partnership, 1978—; bd. dirs. Stage One, Louisville Children's Theatre, pres., 1990-91; bd. dirs. Ky. chpt. Nat. SIDS Found.; grad. Leadership Ky., 1996. Mem. ABA, Ky. Bar Assn., Ind. Bar Assn., Louisville Bar Assn., Nat. Assn. Bond Lawyers. Office: Frost Brown Todd LLC 400 W Market St Fl 32D Louisville KY 40202-3346 Office Phone: 502-568-0301. Business E-Mail: bskees@FBTLaw.com.

SKELLAND, ANTHONY HAROLD PETER, chemical engineering professor; b. Birmingham, Eng., Feb. 21, 1928; came to U.S., 1959; s. Harold and Hilda Skelland. BSChemE, U. Birmingham, 1948, PhD in Chem. Engring., 1952. Mgr. Procter and Gamble, Eng., 1954-56, R&D engr., 1956-59; asst. prof. Ill. Inst. Tech., Chgo., 1959-62; assoc. prof. U. Notre Dame, South Bend, Ind., 1962-66, prof., 1966-69; Ashland prof. U. Ky., Lexington, 1969-79; prof. Ga. Inst. Tech., Atlanta, 1979—. Cons. Monsanto, Babcock and Wilcox, Union Carbide, E.I. duPont de Nemours, FMC Corp., Westinghouse and others. Author: Non-Newtonian Flow and Heat Transfer, 1967, Diffusional Mass Transfer, 1974; contbr. over 90 articles to profl. jours. Fellow AIChE, Inst. Petroleum; mem. Royal Soc. Chemistry (Eng.), Inst. Chem. Engrs. (Eng.). Avocations: tennis, theater, dining out.

SKELLEY, DEAN SUTHERLAND, clinical laboratory administrator; b. Melrose, Mass., Mar. 27, 1938; s. Robert Henry and Roberta Jane (Morse) S.; m. Eleanor Bachofen, Dec. 21, 1966; children: Caroline, Rachel, Jonathan, Susanna. BS, Bates Coll., 1960; MS, Ohio State U., 1966, PhD, 1968. Asst. prof. Coll. Vet. Medicine Ohio State U., Columbus, 1968-70; asst. prof. ob-gyn. Baylor Coll. Medicine, Houston, 1970-76; clin. biochemist Meml. Hosp., Houston, 1976-83; dir. ops. Severance Reference Lab., San Antonio, 1983-84; v.p. ops. Cone Biotech., Inc., Seguin, Tex., 1984-86; dir. product devel. MCLAS Techs. Inc., San Antonio, 1986-87; tech. dir. Lab Corp Am. (formerly, Nat. Health Labs., Inc.), San Antonio, 1989-99. Pres. Tech. and Profl. Svcs., Inc., San Antonio, 1973—; lab.-tech. dir. BioCom Clin. Labs., Weslaco. Tex. and Monterrey, Mex., 1999-2000; dir. lab. svcs. South Texas Blood and Tissue Ctr., San Antonio, 2000—04; med. dir. Ctr. Disease Detection, San Antonio, 2004-; lab. dir. McKenna Health Sys., New Braunfels, Tex., 2005-. Editor (newsletter) Internat. Bonhoeffer Soc., 2002—. Moderator Spirit of Peace Ch., San Antonio, 2001-05, United Ch. of Christ; mem. admissions com. Bates Coll., Lewiston, Maine, 1990—, mem. Bates Alumni Fund com., 1998—. Coalition Co-Chmn., New Tech. for Newborn Screening, Tex.; Mem. Safety Com., U. of Tex., Health Sci. Ctr., San Antonio, Tex.; chairperson Bexar Area Harm Reduction Coalition, 2006—; pres. Pleasure Hill Assn., 2006-. With U.S. Army, 1961-63. Mem.: Am. Med. Writers Assn., New England Hist. Geneal. Soc., Internat. Bonhoeffer Soc. (English lang. sect.), Nat. Geog. Soc., Am. Acad. Religion, Am. Congrl. Assn. (bd. dirs. 2003—). Democrat. Mem. United Ch. of Christ. Avocations: reading, hiking, music, theology, photography. Home: 16330 Hidden View St San Antonio TX 78232-2812 Home Phone: 210-496-0367; Office Phone: 830-606-9111 3231. Personal E-mail: dskelley@satx.rr.com.

SKELLY, MICHAEL, energy executive; b. Oct. 19, 1961; m. Anne Skelly; 3 children. Degree, U. Notre Dame, Harvard Bus. Sch. Owner Horizon Wind Energy, Houston. Mem. Peace Corps. Mem. Mayor White's green bldg. adv. com. Mem.: Am. Wind Energy Assn. (bd. mem.). Democrat. Cath. Office: Horizon Wind Energy 808 Travis Ste 700 Houston TX 77002*

SKELLY, MICHAEL JOHN, environmental engineer, consultant; b. NYC, Apr. 5, 1941; s. Patrick J. and Mary (Marron) S.; m. Georgerte T. Katra, Sept. 11, 1965; children: Michael T., Julie A., Lisa A. BCE, Manhattan Coll., 1963, M Engring., 1964; PhD, Cornell U., 1968. Registered profl. engr., N.Y., N.J., Md., Calif., Ill., Mass., Ind., Pa.; cert. NCEE. Project engr. Quirk, Lawler & Matusky Engrs., NYC, 1968-71, group mgr. Tappan, N.Y., 1971-73, ptnr., 1973-74; gen. mgr. Lawler, Matusky & Skelly Engrs. LLP, Pearl River, 1974—85, mng. ptnr., 1986—98, CEO, 1998—2005; sr. v.p. HDR/LMS (formerly Lawler, Matusky & Skelly Engrs. LLP), 2005—. Mem. Accreditation Bd. Engring. and Tech., Inc., 1997-2003; GECAB adv. bd. of DPIC Cos., Inc., Monterey, Calif. Pres. Jr. Achievement Rockland County, 1982-85, Rockland Ptnrs. Ams., 1989-91; bd. dir. Rockland County coun. Boy Scouts Am., 1989-93; pres. Rockland Children Psychiat. Found., Inc., 1991—; mem. Small Bus. Adv. Bd. NY. Mem. ASCE (bd. dirs. 1992-95), N.Y. Water Environ. Fedn. (bd. dirs. Met. sect. 1983-86). Roman Catholic. Avocations: tennis, antiques, clock collecting. Office: HDR/ LMS One Blue Hill Plz Pearl River NY 10965 Office Phone: 845-735-8300.

SKELLY, THOMAS P., federal agency administrator; b. Washington, Jan. 19, 1952; BA in Govt., Coll. William and Mary, 1974; MA in Govt., U. Va., 1975. Budget analyst US Dept. Edn., Washington, 1975-76, budget analyst Nat. Inst. Edn., 1977-79, budget analyst Office of Planning, Budget and Evaluation, 1979-80, dir. budget sys. divsn., 1982-96, dir. budget svc., 1996—, acting CFO, 1999—2001, 2008—. Treas. Lyon Village Cmty. House, 1989-91; dir. vol. Cherry Blossom 10 Mile Race, 1978-91; bd. dirs. Arlington Havens, Inc., 1993—. Recipient Meritorious Presdl. Rank award, 1989, Dist. Presdl. Rank award, 1992. Mem. Assn. Budget and Program Analysis (bd. dirs. 1988-89). Office: US Dept Edn Budget Svc 400 Maryland Ave SW Washington DC 20202-0001*

SKELOS, DEAN GEORGE, state legislator; b. Rockville Center, NY, Feb. 16, 1948; m. Gail Bernhardt, 1990; 1 child, Adam. BA in History, Washington Coll., 1970; JD, Forham U., 1975. Of counsel Ruskin Moscou Faltischek P.C.; mem. Dist. 19 NY State Assembly, Albany, 1981-82; mem. Dist. 9 NY State Senate, Albany, 1984—, dep. majority leader, 1995—2008, majority leader, 2008, 2009—, minority leader, 2009; acting lt. gov. State of NY, 2008. Chmn. Standing Com. on Aging, 1985-94, Majority Task Force on Aging in 21st Century, 1989-92, co-chmn. legis. task force on dem. rsch. and reapportionment, 1989-, mem. majority task force on religious desecration and bigotry, mem. legis. commn. on sci. and tech., mem. majority task force on def. spending, chmn. task force on econ. recovery and job devel., mem. numerous coms. Mem. fact-finding mission to Israel Jewish Cmty. Rels. Coun.; former mem. Coun. of Nat. Inst. on Aging. Recipient Torch of Liberty award B'nai B'rith. Mem. State Legis. Leaders Found., 1998, Elks, Sons of Italy, Kiwanis, Order of AHEPA, State Legis. Leaders Found., Nat. Conf. of State Legislators, Phi Sigma Kappa Republican. Office: Dist Office 55 Front St Rockville Centre NY 11570-4040 also: Ruskin Moscou Faltischek PC East Tower 15th Fl 1425 RexCorp Pl Uniondale NY 11556 also: Capitol Office 907 Legislative Office Bldg Albany NY 12247 E-mail: skelos@senate.state.ny.us, dskelos@rmfpc.com.*

SKELTON, IKE (ISAAC NEWTON SKELTON IV), United States Representative from Missouri; b. Lexington, Mo., Dec. 20, 1931; s. Isaac Newton and Carolyn (Boone) Skelton; m. Susan B. Anding, June 22, 1961 (dec. Aug. 23, 2005); children: Ike, Jim, Page. AA, Wentworth Mil. Acad., 1951; student, U. Edinburgh, Scotland, 1953; AB in Hist., U. Mo., Columbia, 1953, LLB, 1956. Bar: Mo. 1956. Atty. pvt. practice, Lexington, Mo.; pros. atty. Lafayette County, Mo., 1957-60; spl. asst. atty. gen. State of Mo., 1961-63; mem. Mo. State Senate from 28th dist., 1971—76, US Congress from 4th Mo. Dist., 1977—; chmn. US House Armed Services Com., 2007—. Vice chmn. bd. trustees Harry S. Truman Scholarship Found. Recipient W. Stuart Symington award, Air Force Assn., 1994, Henry M. Jackson Disting. Svc. award, Jewish Inst. Nat. Security Affairs, 1999, Hon. Commandant award, Indsl. Coll. Armed Forces, 2005, Mil. Order of Iron Mike award, Marine Corps League; named Minuteman of Yr., Res. Officers Assn. US, 1995. Mem.: Sigma Chi, Mo. Bar Assn., Shriners Club, Elks Club, Masons Lodge, Phi Beta Kappa. Democrat. Office: US Congress 2206 Rayburn House Office Bldg Washington DC 20515-2504 also: 219 N Adams St Lebanon MO 65536 Office Phone: 202-225-2876.*

SKENDERIAN, JESSICA JOSEPHINE, psychologist; b. Glendale, Calif., Aug. 2, 1976; d. Joseph Richard and Susan Niles Skenderian; m. Ryan Joshua Eckardt, Aug. 25, 2007. BA in Psychology, U. Calif., La., 1998; MS in Kinesiology & Phys. Edn., Calif. State U., Long Beach, 2003; MA in Applied Social Psychology & Evaluation, Claremont Grad. U., Calif., 2005. Tchg. assoc., rsch. asst. Calif. State U., 2002—03; rsch. asst. Claremont Grad. U., Calif., 2004—08; rsch. asst., project mgr. Pomona Coll., Claremont, Calif., 2006—07; rsch. analyst Calif. State U., Office Chancellor, 2007—. Psychology intern Orange County Health Care Agy., Calif., 2005—06. Contbr. articles to profl. jour., chapters to books. Mem.: Western Psychol. Assn., Western Soc. Phys. Edn. Coll. Women, Sigma Xi, Phi Delta Gamma, Phi Kappa Phi.

SKERIS, ROBERT ALEXANDER, theology and church music educator; b. Sheboygan, Wis., May 11, 1935; s. Alex F. and Eugenia Teresa (Cizauskas) S. ThD, U. Bonn, Germany, 1975. Ordained Roman Catholic priest, 1961. Dir. hymnology sect. Internat. Inst. for Hymnol. and Ethnomusicol. Studies, Maria Laach, Germany, 1978-86; prefetto della casa Pontifical Inst. Sacred Music, Rome, 1986-90; prof. chmn. theology dept. Christendom Coll., Front Royal, Va., 1990—99; dir. Ward Ctr., B.T. Rome Sch. Music Cath. Univ. Am., Washington, 2000—. Author: Chroma Theou, 1976, Divini Cultus Studium, 1990; editor: Crux et Cithara, 1983, Cum Angelis Canere, 1990. Decorated Ordem Nacional dos Bandeirantes, Ordem Mater (Brazil); knight Republic of Austria; knight comdr. Holy Sepulchre. Mem. Consociatio Internat. Musical Sacrae (counselor 1978-90), Am. Musicol. Soc., Ch. Music Assn. Am. (gen. sec. 1970-72, v.p. 1972-76, dir. 1977—86, pres., 1986-2004, chmn. Dom Mocquerau Fund, 2001-), Cath. Ch. Music Assocs. (pres. 1976—). Office: Cath Univ Am Sch Music 135 Ward Hall Washington DC 20064 Office Phone: 202-319-5420. Business E-Mail: skeris@cua.edu. E-mail: rskeris@sbcglobal.net.

SKERLOS, STEVEN JOHN, engineering educator; b. Chgo., Sept. 2, 1972; m. Laura Ann Thill, Aug. 5, 2000. PhD in Indsl. Engring., U. Ill., Urbana-Champaign, 2000. Assoc. prof. mech. engring., civil and environ. engring. U. Mich., Ann Arbor, 2000—. Office: Univ Mich 2250 GG Brown Bldg Ann Arbor MI 48109-2125 Business E-Mail: skerlos@umich.edu.

SKERPAN-WHEELER, ELIZABETH PENLEY, English language educator; b. Ravenna, Ohio, Oct. 11, 1955; d. Alfred Andrew and Ruth Elizabeth (Penley) S.; m. Kenneth John Winkle, July 24, 1976 (div. June 1987); m. Charles Anthony Wheeler, May 17, 1997 (div. Feb. 02, 2008). AB magna cum laude, Miami U., 1976; MA, U. Wis., 1977, PhD, 1983. Substitute instr. Madison Area Tech. Coll., 1983; asst. prof. English S.W. Tex. State U., 1983-90, assoc. prof. English, 1990-97, prof. English, 1997—. Asst. to curator of rare books Meml. Libr., U. Wis., Madison, 1979; lectr. in field. Editor South-Ctrl. Renaissance Assn. newsletter, 1990-92; contbg. editor Renaissance and Renascences in Western Lit., 1979-81; author: The Rhetoric of Politics in the English Revolution, 1642-1660, 1992; contbr. articles to profl. jours. Mem. MLA, Nat. Coun. Tchrs. English, Renaissance Soc. Am., South-Ctrl. Renaissance Assn. (exec. bd. 1987-90), Tex. AAUP (del. spring conv. 1985), Tex. State Tchrs. Assn. (del. to state convs.), Tex. Faculty Assn. (exec. com. 1993-97), Phi Beta Kappa, Phi Kappa Phi. Democrat. Office: English Dept SW Tex State U 601 University Dr San Marcos TX 78666-4685 Business E-Mail: es10@txstate.edu.

SKERRETT, I. MARTHA, cell physiology professor; b. Port Colborne, Ont., Can., Nov. 27, 1965; d. Anna Margareta and Philip Garry Skerrett; m. Derek Beahm; children: Anna Evanthea Beahm, Megan Louise Sunners, Samuel James Sunners, Ryan Philip Carson Beahm. PhD, Flinders U., Adelaide, Australia, 1996. Postdoc. fellow SUNY, Buffalo, 1997—2002; asst. prof. Brock U., St. Catharines, Ontario, Canada, 2003—04, Buffalo State Coll., 2005—, honors and undergraduate rsch., Biology Dept., 2005—. Contbr. articles profl. jours. Recipient Thennie Baddams Bursary, Australian Fedn. U. Women, 1994, Australian Postgrad. Rsch. award, Grad. Rsch. Edn. Com., 1996; fellow Internat. Agy. Rsch. Cancer, WHO, 1997; Scientist Devel. Grant, Am. Heart Assn. Nat. Affiliate, 2008, Postdoctoral fellowship, Am. Heart Assn., N.E. Affiliate. Mem.: Am. Soc. Cell Biology, Shorewalk Assn., Biophysical Soc. Office: Buffalo State Coll 1300 Elmwood Ave Buffalo NY 14222 Business E-Mail: skerreim@buffalostate.edu.

SKERRETT, SHAWN JOSEPH, physician; b. LA, Sept. 21, 1953; s. Joseph Francis S. and Bronwen Olga (Williams) Weiss. BA with distinction, Stanford U., 1974; MD, NYU, 1978. Diplomate Am. Bd Internal Medicine. Intern Yale-New Haven Hosp., New Haven, 1978-79, resident, 1979-81; fellow U. Wash., Seattle, 1983-89, instr., 1986—, asst. prof., 1991—97, assoc. prof., 1997—, prof., 2009—. With USPHS, 1981-83. Mem. ACP, Am. Thoracic Soc., Am. Coll. Chest Physicians, Am. Soc. Microbiology, Am. Fedn. Clin. Rsch. Avocations: music, literature, gymnastics, bicycling, swimming. Office: Harborview Med Ctr 325 Ninth Ave Seattle WA 98104

SKEWIS, CHARLES ARTHUR, librarian; b. Emmetsburg, Iowa, Jan. 21, 1955; s. Robert M. and Ruth M. Skewis. AS, Iowa Lakes CC, Emmetsburg, 1975; BS, U. Wis., Platteville, 1977; MLS, George Peabody Coll. Tchrs., Vanderbilt U., Nashville, 1978. LTA II Southern Ill. U., Carbondale, 1979—81; asst. acquisitions libr. Baylor U., Waco, Tex., 1981—85; acquisitions libr. SUNY, Morrisville, 1985—87, U. Ala., Tuscaloosa, 1987—93; electronic acquisitions and serials libr. U. Tex., San Antonio, 1993—96; head collection and resource svcs. dept. Henderson Libr., Ga. Southern U., Statesboro, 1996—. Mem.: Beta Phi Mu. Office: Georgia Southern Univ 1 Lake Dr Statesboro GA 30460-8074 Office Fax: 912-478-0289. Business E-Mail: cskewis@georgiasouthern.edu.

SKIDD, THOMAS PATRICK, JR., lawyer; s. Thomas Patrick and Anna Skidd; m. Judith Chase Roberts, Sept. 10, 1960; children: Suanne C., Sherry E., Thomas Patrick III, Jody E. BA in Econs. cum laude, Georgetown U., 1958; LLB, Yale U., 1961. Bar: Conn. 1961, U.S. Supreme Ct. 1963. Ptnr., prin. Cummings & Lockwood LLC, Stamford, Conn., 1961—. Mem.: Regional Bar Assn., Conn. Bar Assn. (real estate sect. and land use sect.). Office: Cummings & Lockwood LLC 6 Landmark Sq 9th Fl Stamford CT 06904-0120 Office Phone: 203-327-1700. Business E-Mail: tskidd@cl-law.com.

SKIDMORE, MICHELLE MARIE, elementary school educator, principal; b. Newport Beach, Calif., Oct. 11, 1969; d. Rene and Jan Sommer; m. James Jonathan Skidmore, June 28, 2002. BA in Psychology, U. Calif., Davis, 1991; MS in Edn., Calif. State U., Fullerton, 2002. Tchr. 4th & 5th grade, tchg. asst. prin. Capistrano Unified Sch. Dist., San Juan Capistrano, Calif., 1996—; faculty reading dept. Calif. State U., Coll. Edn., Fullerton, 2003—. Coord. Ladera Ranch Sch. Improvement Coun., Calif., 2003—; beginning tchr. support & assistance support provider Calif. Commn. for Tchr. Credentialing, 2003—; asst. dir. CSUF Coll. Kids Reading Clinic, Mission Viejo, 2002—02. Keynote spkr. conf. Contitutional Rights Found., Irvine, Calif., 2006—06; vol. Ladera Ranch Ednl. Found., Ladera Ranch, 2003—06; dir. Change Change Program, 2004—06. Recipient Tchr. Yr., Capistrano Unified Sch. Dist., 2005, Orange County Dept. Edn., 2006, award, Hines Found., 2006; grantee, Capistrano Unified Sch. Dist., 2005, Ladera Ranch Edn. Found., 2006; Japan Fulbright Meml. scholar, 2005. Mem.: Calif. Assn. Gifted, Computer Using Educators, Internat. Reading Assn., Calif. Tchrs. Assn., Golden Key, Phi Beta Kappa, Pi Beta Phi. Home: 112 Sellas Road South Ladera Ranch CA 92694 Office: Ladera Ranch School 29551 Sienna Parkway Ladera Ranch CA 92694 Home Fax: 949-218-4795. Personal E-mail: mmskidmore@capousd.org.

SKIDMORE, TYLER LEE, music educator; b. Medina, Ohio, May 26, 1982; s. Lee and Brenda Skidmore. BA in Music Edn., Mt. Vernon Nazarene U., Ohio, 2004; postgrad., Kent State U., Ohio, 2005—. Music tchr. North Royalton City Sch. Dist., Ohio, 2004—07, Medina City Sch. Dist., 2007—. Singer: Cleve. Orch. Chorus, Blossom Festival Chorus, Kent State Opera, Apollo's Fire, 2007—, Quire Cleveland, 2009—; freelance singer:. Ch. musician Wadsworth Ch. of the Nazarene, Ohio, 2004—, bd. dirs., 2005—. Mem.: Nat. Assn. Music Edn. (collegiate chpt. pres. 2003—04), Am. Choral Dirs. Assn., Barbershop Harmony Soc. Home: 1045 N Jefferson St Unit C Medina OH 44256-1296 Office: Medina HS 777 E Union St Medina OH 44256 Office Phone: 330-636-3200.

SKIFF, FREDERICK NORMAN, physics educator, researcher; b. Albany, NY, Jan. 22, 1957; s. John Victor Jr. and Florence Louise (Schelleng) S.; m. Janet Faith Bell, July 25, 1981; children: Steven, Christen, David. BSc, Cornell U., 1979; MA, PhD, Princeton U., 1985. Rsch. physicist Ecole Poly. Federale, Lausanne, Switzerland, 1985-89; asst. prof. physics U. Md., College Park, 1989—. Contbr. articles to sci. jours. Recipient Presdl. Young Investigator award NSF, 1990; fellow Fannie and John Hertz Found., 1979, Alfred P. Sloan Found., 1990. Mem. Am. Phys. Soc. Achievements include first to demonstrate the role of chaos in plasma wave-particle experiments, first to discover plasma waves through measurements of dielectric motion.

SKIGEN, PATRICIA SUE, lawyer; d. David P. and Gertrude H. (Hirschhaut) Skigen; m. Irwin J. Sugarman, May 1973 (div. Nov. 1994); 1 child, Alexander David Sugarman; m. Gary W. Guttman, May 2001. BA with distinction, Cornell U., 1964; LLB, Yale U., 1968. Bar: NY 1968, US Dist. Ct. (so. dist.) NY 1969. Law clk. Anderson, Mori & Rabinowitz, Tokyo, 1966-67; assoc. Rosenman Colin Kaye Petschek Freund & Emil, NYC, 1968-70, Willkie Farr & Gallagher, NYC, 1970-75, ptnr., 1977-95, J.P. Morgan Chase & Co., NYC, 1995—2002, mng. dir., assoc. gen. counsel, 2002—04; gen. coun. fin. svcs. Am. Internat. Group, Inc., 2005—. Dep. supt., gen. counsel NY State Banking Dept., NYC, 1975-77, first dep. supt. banks, 1977; adj. prof. Benjamin Cardozo Law Sch. Yeshiva U., 1979. Contbr. articles to profl. jours. Cornell U. Dean's scholar, 1960-64, Regent's scholar, 1960-64, Yale Law Sch. scholar, 1964-68. Mem.: ABA (corp. banking and bus. law sect.), Assn. of Bar of City of N.Y. (chmn. com. banking 1991—94, long range planning com. 1994—96, audit com. 1994—2001), Phi Kappa Phi, Phi Beta Kappa. Office Phone: 212-770-8805. Business E-Mail: patricia.skigen@aig.com.

SKIKO, MARLA, communications executive; BS, U. Ill., Urbana-Champaign. Formerly with Leo Burnett, 1993, Starcom Hispanic; various positions including v.p., dir. digital innovation Tapestry, Chgo.; v.p., dir. digital investment SMG Multicultural, Chgo., 2007—08, sr. v.p., dir. digital innovation, 2008—. Mem. adv. bd. AOL Inc. Recipient Los Pioneros award, Interactive Advt. Bur., 2005; named a Woman to Watch, Advt. Age, 2009; named an All-Star for Interactive, Marketing y Medios mag., 2006. Office: SMG Multicultural 35 W Wacker Dr Chicago IL 60601 Office Phone: 312-220-5300. Office Fax: 312-220-6561.*

SKILES, SCOTT ALLEN, professional basketball coach; b. LaPorte, Ind., Mar. 5, 1964; m. Kim Skiles; children: Scott Jr., Sean, Shelby. Grad., Mich. State U. Profl. basketball player Milw. Bucks, 1986—87, Ind. Pacers, 1987—89, Orlando Magic, 1989—94, Washington Bullets, 1994—95, Phila. 76ers, 1995—96; head coach PAOK Thessaloniki BC, Greece, 1996—97; asst. coach Phoenix Suns, 1997-99, head coach, 1999—2002, Chgo. Bulls, 2003—07, Milw. Bucks, 2008—. Named NBA Most Improved Player, 1991. Achievements include holding the NBA record for assists in a game (30), Dec. 30, 1990. Office: Milw Bucks 1001 N Fourth St Milwaukee WI 53203*

SKILLERN, GWENDOLYN D., accountant; 2 children. BS in Acctg., U. Calif., Berkeley; MBA, Stanford U. CPA. Audit mgr. Deloitte & Touche, LLP; acct. corp. fin. and internal audit Kaiser Found. Health Plan, Bass Hotels & Resorts; current sr. v.p. and gen. auditor CareFirst BlueCross BlueShield. Named one of Top 100 Women, Md. Daily Record, 2006, Top 100 Most Influential People in Acctg., 2006, 2007, 25 Most Influential Black Women in Bus., Network Jour., 2007; named to Power 150, Ebony mag., 2008. Mem.: Inst. Internal Auditors, Am. Inst. CPA's, Nat. Assn. Black Accountants (life; nat. pres., Nat. Outstanding mem. award, Presdl. Svc. award). Office: Nat Assn Black Accts Inc 7249 A Hanover Pky Greenbelt MD 20770 Office Phone: 301-474-6222. Office Fax: 301-474-3114.

SKILLERN, MICHAEL PHILLIP, museum administrator; b. Long Beach, Calif., Aug. 30, 1940; s. Robert Earl and Ruby Page Skillern; m. Tracey Lynn Tate, Jan. 10, 2002; children: James, Deborah, Angela, Shauna, Dana, Stephen, Allen. ASEE, Portland CC, Oreg., 1994. Elec. engr. Wyo. Hwy. Dept., Cheyenne, 1979—84; design engr., prodn. supr. Internat. Game Tech., Reno, 1984—87; contract elec. engr. Christiansen Motoryacht Corp., 1988—94, West State Inc., Portland, Oreg., 1988—94; v.p. S.W. Wash. Vets. Meml. Mus., Vancouver, 1994—. Dir. H. J. Kaiser Ships Victory Hist. Preservation Project; N.W. coord. APA Hist. Preservation Project, Vancouver, 1999—2004, Save the USS Gage Hist. Preservation Project, Vancouver, 1999—2004. Vol. Walk for Life March of Dimes, Vancouver, 1999—2001, vol. Jail and Bail Project, 1999—2001; bd. dirs. Adonaiś Haven and Christian Bookstore. Chief petty officer USN, 1957—78. Named Instr. of the Yr., USN, 1969. Mem.: NRA (life), VFW (life; bd. dirs., officer 1999—2002), Fleet Res. Assn., Destroyer Escort Sailors Assn. (life), Naval Inst. (life), N.Am. Hunting Club (life), Masons. Republican. Avocations: fishing, painting, architecture. Home: PO Box 1336 Goldendale WA 98620 Office: SW Wash Vets Meml Mus PO Box 1336 Goldendale WA 98620 Office Phone: 509-250-2573.

SKILLINGSTAD, CONSTANCE YVONNE, social services administrator, educator; b. Portland, Oreg., Nov. 18, 1944; d. Irving Elmer and Beulah Ruby (Aleckson) Erickson; m. David W. Skillingstad, Jan. 12, 1968 (div. Mar. 1981); children: Michael, Brian. BA in Sociology, U. Minn., Mpls., 1966; MBA, U. St. Thomas, St. Paul, 1982. Cert. lay spkr. United Meth. Ch.; lic. social worker; cert. vol. adminstr., lic. real estate agt. Social worker Rock County Welfare Dept., Luverne, Minn., 1966-68, Hennepin County Social Svc., Mpls., 1968-70, vol. coord., 1970-78, St. Joseph's Home for Children, Mpls., 1978-89, mgr. cmty. resources, 1989-94; exec. dir. Mpls. Crisis Nursery, 1994-97; mem. cmty. faculty Met. State U., St. Paul and Mpls., 1980-97; faculty U. St. Thomas Ctr. Non Profit Mgmt., 1990—2001; asst. adminstr. St. Joseph's Home Children, Mpls., 1997-98; asst. dir. Cath. Charities Archdiocese of St. Paul and Mpls., 1998-2000; dir. mem. svc. Minn. Coun. Founds., 2001—02; pres. Golden Girl Homes, Inc., 2001—; exec. dir. Prevent Child Abuse Minn., St. Paul, 2002—. Trainer, mem. adv. commn. Mpls. Vol. Ctr., 1978—90, cons., 1980—, chmn. Contbr. articles to profl. jours. Mem. adv. bd. MADD, Minn., 1986—88, Congregations Concerned for Children, 2002—, Stop It Now!, Minn., 2003—, Grandkids and Me; bd. dirs. Survivors Network Minn., 2005—, Authentic Voices Internat., Ctr. Grief, Loss and Transition, U. Minn. Children Youth and Family Consortium; vice chmn., chmn. adminstrv. coun., lay leader Hobart United Meth. Ch.; lay rep. ann. conf. fin. chair Spencer Brook United Meth. Ch., 1989—92; chmn. social concerns commn. Park Ave. United Meth. Ch., 1992—; bd. dirs. NATLL Assn. Prevention Sexual Abuse Children, 2006—. Named Woman of Distinction, Mpls. St. Paul Mag./Sta. KARE-TV, 1995; named one of Outstanding Young Women in Am., 1974. Mem.: Minn. Social Svcs. Assn. (pres. 1981, 1998—99, bd. dirs. 1996—2001, mem. legis. com., Disting. Svc. award 1987), Assn. Vol. Adminstrn. (v.p. regional affairs 1985—87, mem. assessment panel 1986—94, coord. nat. tng. team, cert. process vol. adminstr. 1986—92, profl. devel. chair 1990—92), Minn. Assn. Vol. Dirs. (pres. 1975, sec., ethics chmn. 1987—). Dfl. Avocations: bridge, volleyball, travel, reading, accordion. Office: Prevent Child Abuse Minn Ste 202 S 1821 University Ave Saint Paul MN 55104 Home: 28544 Lakewood Dr NW Isanti MN 55040 Office Phone: 651-523-0099. Business E-Mail: cskillingstad@pcamn.org.

SKILLMAN, BECKY SUE, Lieutenant Governor of Indiana, former state legislator; b. Bedford, Ind., Sept. 26, 1950; d. Jack Delmar and Catherine Louise (Flinn) Foddrill; m. Stephen E. Skillman, 1969; 1 child, Aaron. Dep. recorder Lawrence County, 1971-76, county recorder, 1977-84; clk. Lawrence County Cir. Ct., 1985—92; mem. Ind. State Senate from 44th dist., 1992—2005; lt. gov. State of Ind., Indpls., 2005—. Co-dir. Lawrence County Young Reps., 1973-78; co-chmn. State Young Reps. Conv., 1975, 77; vice chmn. Lawrence County Rep. Ctrl. Com. Recipient "Champion of Small Bus." award, Small Bus. Coun, 1995, Disting. Pub. Policy award, Ind. Rural Health Policy award, 2003; named The Outstanding Elected Official of 2000, Ind. Assn. Area Agencies, "Legislator of the Year", Ind. Library Found., 2002. Republican. Office: Office Lt Governor State Capitol Rm 333 Indianapolis IN 46204 Office Phone: 317-232-4545. Office Fax: 317-232-4788.

SKILLMAN, WILLIAM ALFRED, consulting engineering executive; b. Lakehurst, NJ, Jan. 22, 1928; s. Wilbur Newton and Greta Alfreda (Ekman) S.; m. Anne Marie Cavender, Sept. 19, 1948; children: Thomas R., Gregory A., Karen L. BS in Engring. Physics, Lehigh U., 1952; MS in Physics, U. Rochester, 1954. Assoc. engr. Westinghouse Electric Corp., Balt., 1954-56, engr., 1956-58, sr. engr., 1958-61, supervisory engr., 1961-64, adv. engr., 1964-73, sr. adv. engr., 1973-85, cons. engr., 1986-93, cons. electronic systems group, 1993—. Author: Radar Calculations Using the TI-59 Programmable Calculator, 1983; author: (with others) Radar Handbook, 2d edit., 1990; patentee in field Served with USN, 1946-48. Fellow IEEE (life, Dennis J. Picard medal for radar technologies and applications 2003); mem. Aerospace and Electronic Sys. Soc. (Pioneer award 1995), Phi Beta Kappa. Republican. Methodist. Avocations: photography, travel, genealogy, programming. Home and Office: 605 Forest View Rd Linthicum Heights MD 21090-2819 Personal E-mail: wskillman@aol.com.

SKILLRUD, HAROLD CLAYTON, minister, retired bishop; b. St. Cloud, Minn., June 29, 1928; s. Harold and Amanda Skillrud; m. Lois Dickhart, June 8, 1951; children: David, Janet, John. BA magna cum laude, Gustavus Adolphus Coll., 1950; MDiv magna cum laude, Augustana Theol. Sem., Rock Island, Ill., 1954; STM, Luth. Sch. Theology, Chgo., 1969; DD (hon.), Augustana Coll., 1978, Newberry

Coll., 1988. Ordained to ministry Evang. Luth. Ch. in Am., 1954. Supply pastor Saron Luth. Ch., Big Lake, Minn., 1950-51; mem. staff 1st Luth. Ch., Rock Island, Ill., 1951-52; intern, organizer new mission Faith Luth. Ch., Syosset, NY, 1952-53; sr. pastor St. John's Luth. Ch., Bloomington, Ill., 1954-79, Luth. Ch. of the Redeemer, Atlanta, 1979-87; bishop Southeastern Synod Evang. Luth. Ch. in Am., Atlanta, 1987-95, regional rep. bd. pensions, 1995—2007. Del. to various convs. Luth. Ch. in Am., Luth. World Fedn. in Helsinki, 1963, mem. bd. publ., 1976-84, pastor-evangelist Evang. Outreach Emphasis program, 1977-79, mem. exec. bd. Ill. synod, 1977-79, pres. bd. publ., 1980-84, leader stewardship cluster Southeastern synod, 1983, mem. exec. bd. Southeastern synod, 1984-87; mem. exec. coun., Luth. Ch. in Am., 1984-87; mem. task force on new ch. design Commn. on New Luth. Ch., task force on ch. pub. house, 1985; del. constituting conv. Evang. Luth. Ch. in Am., 1987, del. assemblies Evang. Luth. Ch. in Am., 1989, 91, 93, 95; mem. commn. on clergy confidentiality Luth. Coun. in USA, 1987; co-chair USA Luth.- Roman Cath. Dialogue, 1990-97; mem. Task Force on Theol. Edn. Author: LSTC: Decade of Decision, 1969; co-editor Scripture and Tradition, Lutherans and Catholics in Dialogue, 1995; mem. edtl. bd. Partners mag., 1978-80; contbr. articles and sermons to religious jours. Former bd. dirs. Augustana Theol. Sem.; bd. dirs. Augustana Coll., 1969-77, chmn. bd., 1976-77; bd. dirs. Kessler Reformation Collection, Newberry Coll., Luth. World Relief, Augsburg Fortress; chmn. bd. dirs. Luth. Sch. Theology, Chgo., 1962-69; mem. Leadership Atlanta, 1980-81, United Way, Atlanta, 1980-81; mem. Bishop's Commn. on Econ. Justice, 1985-86; pres. bd. dirs. Atlanta Samaritan House, 1986-87. Recipient Alumni award Luth. Sch. Theology, Chgo., 1976, award Leadership Atlanta, 1981, The Rev. John Bachman award, Luth. Theol. Sem., Columbia, S.C., 1996. Mem. Luth. Sch. Theology Alumni Assn. (pres. 1975-77), Conf. of Bishops, Kiwanis (pres. Midtown chpt. 1984-85). Lutheran. Avocations: travel, photography. Home: 104 Hawthorne Lake Dr Bloomington IL 61704

SKILTON, JOHN SINGLETON, lawyer; b. Washington, Apr. 13, 1944; s. Robert Henry and Margaret (Neisser) S.; m. Carmen Fisher, Jan. 28, 1967; children: Laura Anne, Susan Elizabeth, Robert John. BA, U. Wis., 1966, JD, 1969. Bar: Wis. Supreme Ct. 1969, U.S. Dist. Ct. (ea. and we. dists.) Wis. 1969, U.S. Ct. Appeals (7th cir.) 1969, U.S. Supreme Ct. 1989, U.S. Ct. Appeals (Fed. cir.) 1991. Law clk. 7th Cir. Ct. Appeals, Chgo., 1969-70; assoc. Foley & Lardner, Milw., 1970-77, ptnr. Madison, Wis., 1977-2000, Perkins Coie LLP, Madison, Wis., 2008—; shareholder Heller, Ehrman, White & McAuliffe, Washington, 2000—08. Bd. visitors U. Wis. Law Sch., Madison, 1982-90, chmn., 1988-89; chair Wis. Fed. Nominating Commn., 1992; mem. Gov.'s Task Force on Bus. Ct., 1994-95. Recipient Eisenberg Lifetime Achievement award, Equal Justice Fund, 2003, Lifetime Pro Bono Achievement, Dane County Bar, 2005. Fellow Am. Bar Found., Am. Coll. Trial Lawyers, Internat. Acad. Trial Lawyers, ABA (chmn. standing com. on delivery of legal svcs. 1996-2000, chmn. consortium legal svcs. and pub. 2000-02); mem. Am. Law Inst., Am. Acad. Appellate Lawyers, 7th Cir. Bar Assn. (pres. 1985-86, chmn. 7th cir. adv. com. on rules 1994-2000), State Bar Wis. (pres. 1995-96, Pres.'s award of excellence 1989, 2004, 2006, Sinykin award for publ svc. 1996), Western Dist. Wis. Bar Assn. (pres. 1992-93), Western Dist. Adv. Group (chmn. 1991), Wis. Law Found. (pres. 2000-02), James E. Doyle Am. Inn Ct. (coun. 1992-94), Am. Inns Ct. Found. (trustee 1995-98), U. Wis. Law Alumni Assn. (bd. dirs. 1991-97, pres. 1993-95), Lawyers Com. Civil Rights (co-chair 2003-05, Whitney North Seymour award, 2007), Wis. Internat. Trade Coun., Wis. Lincoln Bicentennial Commn. (chair 2008-). Home: 917 Woodward Dr Madison WI 53704 Office: 1 E Main St Madison WI 53703-5118 Office Phone: 608-663-7474.

SKINNER, BRIAN JOHN, geologist, educator; b. Wallaroo, South Australia, Dec. 15, 1928; came to U.S., 1958, naturalized, 1963; s. Joshua Henry and Joyce Barbara Lloyd (Prince) S.; m. Helen Catherine Wild, Oct. 9, 1954; children: Adrienne Wild, Stephanie Wild, Thalassa Wild. B.Sc., U. Adelaide, Australia, 1950; A.M., Harvard U., 1952, PhD, 1955; D Engring. (hon.), Colo. Sch. Mines, 1998; DSc (hon.), U. Toronto, 1998. Lectr. U. Adelaide, 1955-58; research geologist U.S. Geol. Survey, 1958-62, chief br. exptl. geochemistry and mineralogy, 1962-66; prof. geology and geophysics, chmn. dept. Yale U., New Haven, 1966-73, Eugene Higgins prof., 1972—. Hugh Exton McKinstry Meml. lectr. Harvard U., 1978; Alex L. du Toit lectr. Combined Socs. South Africa, 1979; Cecil H. and Ida Green lectr. U. B.C., 1983; Thayer Lindsley Meml. lectr. Soc. Econ. Geologists, 1983; Soc. Econ. Geologists Overseas lectr., 1985; Hoffman lectr. Harvard U., 1986, Joubin-James lectr. U. Toronto, 1987; mem. exec. com. divsn. earth scis. NRC, 1966-69; chmn. com. mineral resources and the environ. Nat. Acad. Scis.-NRC, 1973-75; mem. Lunar Sample Analysis Planning Team, 1968-70, Lunar Sci. Rev. Bd., 1971-72, U.S. Nat. Com. for Geochemistry, 1966-67, U.S. Nat. Com. for Geology, 1973-77, 85-93, chmn., 1987-93, chmn. bd. earth scis. NRC, 1987-88, earth scis. and resources, 1989-90; mem. bd. Internat. Geol. Correlation Program, UNESCO-IUGS, 1985-89, 90-96, chmn., 1986-89; cons. Office Sci. and Tech. Policy, 1977-80, NSF, 1977-82; dir. Econ. Geology Pub. Co.; chmn. governing bd. Am. Jour. Sci., 1972-2004; pres. Econ. Geology Pub. Co., 1996-2000. Author: Earth Resources, 1969, 77, 86, Man and the Ocean, 1973, Physical Geology, 1974, 77, 87, Rocks and Rock Minerals, 1979, The New Iron Age Ahead, 1987, Resources and World Development, 1987, The Dynamic Earth, 1989, 92, 95, 2000, 03, The Blue Planet, 1995, 99, 2000, Environmental Geology, 1996, Geology Today, 1999, Oxford Companion to the Earth, 2000, Visualizing Geology, 2007, 09, Visualizing Earth Science, 2009; editor: Econ. Geology, 1969-96, Oxford Univ. Press Monographs in Geological Sciences, 1979-2005, Internat. Geology Rev., 1995-2008; mem. edtl. bd. Am. Scientist, 1974-90, chmn., 1987-90. Trustee Hopkins Grammar Sch., 1978-83. Recipient Disting. Contbns. award, Assn. Earth Sci. Editors, 1979, medal, Geol. Assn. Can., 1998, Futer's medal, Inst. of Mining and Metallurgy, London, 2002; fellow, Guggenheim fellow, 1970. Fellow Geol. Soc. Am. (councillor 1976-78, chmn. spl. publs. com. 1980-81, chmn. com. on coms. 1983, pres. 1985); mem. Geochem. Soc. (pres. 1972-73), Conn. Acad. Sci. and Engring. (div. chmn. 1978-80, coun. 1982-87), Soc. Econ. Geologists (pres. 1995, Silver medal 1981, Marsden medal 2003, Penrose medal 2005, Hon. Fellow 2008). Home: PO Box 894 Woodbury CT 06798-0894 Personal E-mail: brian.skinner@yale.edu.

SKINNER, CATHY JOANN, school system administrator; d. Orvin and Dorothy Alice Clarice Akre; m. David Allen Skinner, July 22; children: Ginger Cathleen Landmeier, Timothy Eric, Brett Thomas. BEd, Nat. Coll. Edn., Wheeling, Ill., 1990; MEd, Nat. Louis U., Wheeling, Ill., 1992; AA, Elgin C.C., Ill., 1998; EdD, Nat. Louis U., Wheeling, Ill., 2008. Cert. supt. Ill., 2002. Dir. human resources Sch. Dist. U-46, Elgin, 1981—2004; asst. supt. pers. Woodridge Sch. Dist. 68, Ill., 2004—. Mem. tchr. edn. adv. bd. Benedictine U., Lisle, Ill., 2004—; mem. career planning and placement adv. bd. No. Ill. U., Dekalb, Ill., 2002—. Named Woman of Yr., Am. Biog. Inst. Bd. Internat. Rsch., 2006. Mem.: Am. Assn. Pers. Adminstrs. (rep. exec. bd. region 2 1996—), Ill. Assn. Sch. Coll. U. Staffing (state pres. 1992—2006), Ill. Assn. Sch. Pers. Administrs. (mem. state bd. 2006—), Am. Assn. Sch. Pers. Adminstrs. (exec. bd. 2006).

SKINNER, FREDERICK WILLIAM, retired history professor; s. Donald Theodore Skinner and Mary French; m. Lynda Jean Scovill, Mar. 18, 1990; 1 child, Conor Cameron Smith stepchildren: Erin Elizabeth Yonce, Megan Maureen Sturm; m. Joan Marie Jirsa, June 22, 1968 (div. July 30, 1987); 1 child, Hadley Elizabeth Ferguson. BA magna cum laude, U. Colo., Boulder, 1964; MA in History, Russian Inst. Cert., Columbia U., NYC, 1968; PhD in History, Princeton U., NJ, 1973. Intern Bur. Intelligence & Rsch. Ea. Europe, US Dept. State, Washington, 1963; assoc. fgn. affairs editor Facts on File, Inc., NYC, 1966—68; asst. prof. history U. Mont., Missoula, 1973—77, assoc. prof. history, 1977—2005, prof. history, 2005—06, prof. emeritus history, 2006—. Chair Mont. Com. Humanities, Missoula, 1996—99. Petty officer, comm. tech. USN, 1956—60. Recipient Internat. Rsch. and Exchanges Bd. award, 1971—72, Senate Svc. award, U. Mont. Exec. Com., 1991, Merit award, U. Mont., 1998—99, Tchg. Abroad award, 2002; Nat. fellowship, Woodrow Wilson Found., 1964—65, Summer fellowship, Carnegie Found., 1965, Russian Inst. fellowship, Columbia U., 1965—66, Regional Studies fellowship, Princeton U., 1968—70, Fgn. Area fellowship, Ford Found., 1970—71, Fulbright Grad. fellowship, 1970—71. Mem.: Am. Assn. Advancement of Slavic Studies, Am. Beethoven Soc. Liberal. Avocations: music, travel, fishing, hiking, reading.

SKINNER, JAMES A., food products executive; b. Davenport, Iowa; m. Kathleen Skinner; 1 child. Grad, Roosevelt U. Restaurant mgr. trainee to numerous positions within the US Co. McDonald's Corp., 1971—, US zone v.p., 1987—92; sr. v.p., relationship ptnr., 1992—95; exec. v.p., internat. relationship ptnr. McDonald's Ctrl. Europe, Middle East, Africa, India, 1995—97; pres. McDonald's Europe, 1997—2001; pres., COO McDonald's Europe/Asia/Pacific and Middle East, 2001—02, McDonald's Restaurant Group, 2002—03; vice chmn. McDonald's Corp., 2003—04, vice-chmn., CEO, 2004—. Adv. dir. bd. dirs. (twice) McDonald's Corp.; bd. dirs. Walgreen Co., 2005—. Bd. mem. Ronald McDonald House Charities. Office: McDonald's Corp McDonald's Plz 2111 McDonalds Dr Oak Brook IL 60523

SKINNER, JAMES E., retail executive; Grad., Tex. Tech U. CPA. Ptnr. Ernst & Young, 1987—91; chief acctg. officer CompUSA, Dallas, 1991—94, CFO, exec. v.p., treas., 1994—2000; sr. v.p., CFO CapRock Comms. Corp., Dallas, 2000—01; CFO, sr. v.p. The Neiman Marcus Group, Inc., Dallas, 2001—07, exec. v.p., CFO, 2007—. Office: The Neiman Marcus Group Inc 1618 Main St Dallas TX 75201

SKINNER, JAMES LAURISTON, chemist, educator; b. Ithaca, NY, Aug. 17, 1953; s. G. William and Carol (Bagger) S.; m. Wendy Moore, May 31, 1986; children: Colin Andrew, Duncan Geoffrey. AB in Chemistry and Physics with highest honors, U. Calif., Santa Cruz, 1975; AM in Physics, Harvard U., 1977, PhD in Chem. Physics, 1979. Postdoctoral rsch. assoc. Stanford U., Calif., 1980-81; from asst. prof. to prof. chemistry Columbia U., NYC, 1981-90; Joseph O. Hirschfelder prof. chemistry U. Wis., Madison, 1990—, dir. Theoretical Chemistry Inst., 1990—, chair dept. chemistry, 2004—07. Vis. scientist Inst. Theol. Physics U. Calif., Santa Barbara, 1987; vis. prof. physics U. Jos. Fourier, Grenoble, France, 1987, U. Bordeaux, France, 1995. Mem. editl. bd.: Jour. Chem. Physics, 1999—2001, Single Molecules, 2000—03, Jour. Phys. Chemistry, 2004—06, Chem. Physics, 2005—; mem. editl. bd. mol. Physics, 2008—; contbr. articles to profl. jours. Recipient Fresenius award Phi Lambda Upsilon, 1989, Camille and Henry Dreyfus Tchr.-Scholar award, 1984, Presdl. Young Investigator award NSF, 1984-89, Kellett Mid-Career award U. Wis., 1995, Pharmacia Tchg. award, 2000, Chancellor's Disting. Tchg. award, 2003; named Sr. Scientist Humboldt Found., 1993-97; NSF grad fellow, 1975, NSF postdoctoral fellow, 1980, Alfred P. Sloan Found. fellow, 1984, Guggenheim fellow, 1993-94. Fellow: AAAS, Am. Acad. Arts & Sciences, Am. Phys. Soc. Achievements include fundamental research in condensed phase theoretical chemistry. Office: U Wis Dept Chemistry Theoretical Chem Inst 1101 University Ave Madison WI 53706-1322

SKINNER, JAMES LISTER, III, retired language educator; b. Emory, Ga., Sept. 24, 1938; s. James Lister and Josephine Norvell (Fry) S.; m. Ramona Ann York Skinner, Apr. 2, 1961; 1 child, James Lister Skinner IV. AB in English, N. Ga. Coll., Dahlonega, 1960; MA in English, U. Ark., Fayetteville, 1962, PhD in English, 1965. Comdr. Headquarters and Headquarters Battery 28th Artillery Group, Selfridge AFB, Mich., 1964-65; assoc. prof. English Presbyn. Coll., Clinton, SC, 1965-70, prof. English, 1970-92, Charles A. Dana prof. English, 1992—2003, chmn. The Russell Program, 1986-98, co-chmn. English dept., 1996-99, sr. faculty coun., 1995-98, chair sr. faculty coun., 1997-98, chair English dept., 1999-2001, Charles A. Dana prof. English emeritus, 2003—. NDEA fellow U. Ark., Fayetteville, 1960-63; NEH summer fellow Yale U., New Haven, Conn., 1976; hon. vis. fellow Leicester (Eng.) U., 1983; sec. Presbyterian Coll. Faculty, Clinton, S.C., 1995-98. Author: Boys Farm: A History, 2002; editor: The Autobiography of Henry Merrell: Industrial Missionary to the South, 1991, The Refugees: Roswell, 2004; co-editor: The Death of a Confederate, 1996. 1st lt. U.S. Army, 1963-65. Recipient Commendation medal U.S. Army, 1965; named Presbyterian Prof. of Yr. Presbyterian Coll., Clinton, S.C., 1991, State Prof. of Yr. Coun. for Advancement and Support of Edn., 1991, Gov's. Prof. of Yr., Gov. of S.C., Columbia, 1991, DAR History Award medal, 1998, Alumni Hall of Fame award No. Ga. Coll. and State U., 2004. Mem. Phi Beta Kappa, Omicron Delta Kappa, Alpha Psi Omega, Phi Alpha Theta, Sigma Tau Delta. Democrat. Presbyterian. Home: 108 E Maple St Clinton SC 29325-2836

SKINNER, JAUNETH, graphic artist, educator; b. Waco, Tex., Mar. 19, 1958; d. Owen George and Patricia Ann Skinner; 1 child, Miriam Reneé Kessler. AS in Comml. Art Tech., Ind. U., Ft. Wayne, 1990, BFA, 1991; MFA, Bowling Green State U., 1993. Cert. Italian lang. and culture tchr. Università per Stranieri, Perugia, Italy, 2004. Vis. prof., interim chair visual comm. and design, dept. art Ind. U. Purdue U., Ft. Wayne, Ind., 2007—08; curator Lillie M. Kleven print collection dept. visual arts Bemidji State U., Minn., 1994—2007, asst. prof. visual arts, 1994—99, assoc. prof. visual arts, 1999—2004, prof. visual arts, 2004—08, chair visual arts dept., 2005—06; prof., head dept. art Jacksonville State U., Ala., 2008—. Creative dir. Endion Studio, 1986—, Jax Printmakers Ink, 2009; assoc. editor, sr. designer Mid Am. Print Coun. Jour., Chgo., 1994—97; creative dir., master printer The Quiet Crow Press, 2000—. Exhibited in group shows at Lessedra World Art Print Annual, Sofia, Bulgaria., 4th Annual Mini Print International Exhibition 2000, Delta Nat. Small Prints, 2009, 1st Biennial International Miniature Print Exhibition, 31st and 33rd Bradley Internat., The World's Women On-Line!, Acm Siggraph, The Solarplate Revolution, Women's Work, Traditional and Contemporary: 100 Years of Etchings and Woodblock Prints, APA Memorial Print Project, Minnesota Journal Project 2000, The Foot in the Door Show, Border to Border, Ada: Women and Information Technology, Contemporary Prints - National Invitational, Hare of the Dog Press: Printed Works, Ohio Women's Caucus for Art Exhibition, Chicago Printmakers Collaborative: Paradise Lost, Holograms and Computer Prints, From Greenware to Software, The Little Prints Exhibit, The 21st National Print Exhibition, 23rd National Small Works Exhibition, Vital Signs:Drawing as Inquiry, Counterpoint 2000: 32nd Annual National Printmaking, Drawing, and Photography Exhibition, Outside Impressions: A Showcase of Contemporary Printmaking, Annual National Small Works Competition, Innovations in Printmaking, Paperworks '99, Community Visual Art Association, Jackson Hole, Wyoming, 12th Annual Parkside National Small Print Exhibition, Hand-Pulled Prints IV, National Works on Paper, Printwork '95, Americanism: Breaking the Mold, Positive/Negative IV, Regional '93, 16th Annual Proscenium 1992, Concepts and Dimensions, Issues of Color and Gender, Reverent/Irreverent, Women's Caucus for Art Third Annual Juried Exhibit, Digital Images 1990, 54th Annual Tri Kappa Regional Artists Exhibition, Indiana: Works on Paper, Women's Self Image, solo exhibitions include Imprints: Works on Paper, The Illustrated Jour., Impressions: The Graphic Art of Jauneth Skinner, Away: Sabbatical Exhibition, Landscape and Memory, Imprimere: Imprinted on Memory, The Extraordinary in the Prosaic (Works on Paper), All Labels Female, Naked Singularity, print portfolios, Catch Phrase, Women's Self Image, Woman, Sheep, Water, print with Gendron Jensen, Umingmaq, broadside print portfolio, Italia, Lake Songs, Horizon Club Print: Out of the Woods, print published with John Hitchcock, Isolation, with Gendron Jensen, Mandan, print portfolio, Memorial, Women's Work, Past-Tense, A Half Mile From Home, nat. juried exhbm/, The Payne Gallery Print Exhibition, Hunterdon Art Center 32nd National Print Exhibition, North Arlington Library Print Exhibition, Gadsden Mus. Art. Recipient Best of Drawing, Beck Ctr., 1992, First and Second Pl., Preble County Art Assn., 1991, Merit Award, Drawing, Wassenburg Art Ctr., 1991, Third Pl. and Merit Award, Studio Mag. Computer Art Competition, 1989, Merit Award, Third Ann. Liquitex Art Awards Program, 1989, Artist in Residence, Scuola Internazionale di Grafica, Venice, Italy, 2005, Vis. Artist, Kelliher Pub. Sch., Mpls., 2003, Sch. of Art, U. of SD, Vermilion, SD, 2002, 2001, ND State Coll., Wahpeton, ND, 2002, Artist in Residence, Santa Reparata Stamperia d'Arte Grafica, Florence, Italy, 2001, 2000, Am. U., Corciano, Italy, 2001, Voyageurs Nat. Pk., Internat. Falls, MN, 1999, Vis. Artist, Valley City State U., Valley City, ND, 1997, Ctrl. Lakes Coll., Brainerd, MN, 1997, Disting. Artist Award, McKnight Found. and Region 2 Arts Coun., 1996, Manhattan Arts Internat. Merit Award, 1995, Someone Spl. Vol., United Way, 1995, Charles F. Wassenburg Award, Drawing, Wassenburg Art Ctr., 1993, Best of Show Purchase Award, East Tenn. State U., 1993; grantee McKnight Found. Grant with Dust & Fire: Women's Stories, Region 2 Arts Coun., 1999, Individual Artist Grant with poet CarolAnn Russell, McKnight Found. and Region 2 Arts Coun., 1999, McKnight Found. Grant with Loonfeather Press, 1997, Q-7 Ventures Grant, Minn. State Colleges and Universities, 1996, 1995; scholar Paralyzed Veterans of Am., Paralyzed Veterans of Am., 1989, Fine Arts Scholarship, Dept. of Fine Art, Ind. U., 1986, 1987, 1988, 1989, 1990, 1991, Grad. Tchg. Assoc., Sch. of Art, Bowling Green State U., 1992, Fellowship in Graphic Arts, 1992, 1993, Ely Lilly Scholarship, Ely Lilly Found., 1991. Mem.: Coll. Art Assn., No. Printmakers Alliance, Am. Print Alliance, MidAmerica Print Coun., So. Graphics Print Coun. Achievements include Art work in Cradle Oak Press Collection, Bradley University, Peoria, Illinois; Scuola Internazionale di Grafica collection, Venice, Italy; Rossi Library Archives collection, American Academy in Rome; St. Cloud State University collection, Minnesota; University Print Library collection, Università di Palermo, Italy; University of Montana collection, Bozman; Lillie M. Kleven Print Collection, Bemidji State University, Minnesota; University Print Society Collection, Iowa State University, Ames; University of Nebraska, Omaha; Fogg Art Museum collection, Harvard, Cambridge, Massachusetts; Harwood Museum of Art collection, University of New Mexico, Santa Fe; Jerome Library Archives collection, School of Art Print Collection, Bowling Green State University, Ohio; Kennarahásköli Íslands University Print Collection, Stakkahlíð, Reykjavík, Iceland; Arizona State University Print Collection, Tempe; King Jigme Singhe Wangchuk of Bhutan Palace Art Collection; Anoka Ramsey Foundation collection, Anoka Ramsey Community College, Minnesota; Bodleian Library, Oxford University, UK, Beijing University, China. Avocations: travel, reading, gardening. Office: Jacksonville State Univ Dept Art 700 Pelham Rd N Jacksonville AL 36265-1602 Home: PO Box 575 Jacksonville AL 36265 Office Phone: 256-782-5626. Business E-Mail: jauneths@jsu.edu.

SKINNER, JON, rehabilitation hospital administrator; BBA, Hardin-Simmons U.; MBA, U. Colo. CPA. Dir. physician compensation and benefits Health Tex. Provider Network; exec. dir. Baylor Medical Ctr., Southwest Fort Worth; pres. Baylor Inst. Rehab.; interim pres. Baylor Specialty Health Centers and Our Children's House at Baylor. Mem.: Tex. State Soc. CPAs, Am. Inst. CPAs, Healthcare Financial Mgmt. Assn., American Coll. Healthcare Executives. Office: Baylor Inst Rehab 909 N Washington Dallas TX 75246*

SKINNER, JONATHAN SNOWDEN, economics educator; b. Boston, Aug. 29, 1955; s. Walter Jay and Sylvia (H.) S.; m. Martha Amy McLafferty, Oct. 17, 1987; children: Owen, Lucy. BA, U. Rochester, 1977; MA, UCLA, 1978, PhD, 1983. Asst. prof. to prof. economics U. Va., Charlottesville, 1981—95; prof. economics Dartmouth Coll., Hanover, NH, 1995—, chair economics dept., 2004—06, John Sloan Dickey Third Century chair of economics, 2007—; prof. family and cmty. medicine Dartmouth Med. Sch., 1999—, Dartmouth Inst. Health Policy and Clin. Practice, 2007—. Rsch. assoc. Nat. Bur. Econ. Rsch., Cambridge, Mass., 1989—, rsch. fellow, 1991—93; health adv. panel Congl. Budget Office, 2007—. Mem.: Inst. Medicine, NAS. Office: Dartmouth Inst Health Policy & Clin Practice 35 Centerra Pkwy Lebanon NH 03766

SKINNER, MARILYNN KEARNES, finance educator; b. Ft. Benning, Ga., Sept. 30, 1948; d. Robert Arnold and Mary Budd Kearnes; m. John William Skinner, Nov. 1, 1973; children: John William Jr., Ernest Robert, Anna Rebecca. BBA, Ga. Coll., Milledgeville, 1990; MS in Accountancy, U. Ga., Athens, 1991, EdD, 1997. Cert. in bus. edn. 9-12 Ga., 2003, in economics 9-12 2008. Acctg. instr. dept. chair Ctrl. Ga. Tech. Coll., Macon, 1991—2001; acctg. instr. Ga. Coll., 2001—03; tchr. CTAE dept. head Baldwin HS, Milledgeville, 2003—; tech. developer Ga. Virtual Sch., Atlanta, 2008—. Mem.: Assn. Career & Tech. Edn., Nat. Bus. Edn. Assn. Home: 640 Hwy 49 W Milledgeville GA 31061 Personal E-mail: mskinner@alltel.net. Business E-Mail: marilyn.skinner@baldwin.k12.ga.us.

SKINNER, MICHAEL DAVID, lawyer, lobbyist, consultant; b. Shreveport, LA, Jan. 5, 1950; s. Roger Gilman and Jerry Ann (Sneed) S.; m. Janet Louise Horaist, Jan. 7, 1978. JD, La. State U., 1976. Bar: La. 1977, U.S. Dist. Ct. (we. dist.) La. 1978, U.S. Ct. Appeals (5th and 11th cirs.) 1978, U.S. Dist. Ct. (mid. dist.) La. 1982, U.S. Supreme Ct. 1982, U.S. Dist. Ct. (so. dist.) Tex. 1983. Pvt. practice, Lafayette, La., 1976-84; asst. dist. atty. Lafayette Parish, 1983—84; ptnr. Guilliot, Skinner & Everett, 1984-86; asst. parish atty. Lafayette Parish, 1988—93; ptnr. Goode, Skinner & Hawkland, 1986-93; U.S. atty. West Dist. La., 1993-2000; atty. Onebane Law Firm, Lafayette, La., 2001—07, Skinner Law Firm, 2007—. Chmn. La. Democratic Party, 2003—05. Mem. La. State Bar Assn. (mem. ho. of dels.). Democrat. Office: 600 Jefferson St Ste 810 Lafayette LA 70501 Office Phone: 337-354-3030. Business E-Mail: mike@law.glacoxmail.com.

SKINNER, PATRICIA MORAG, state legislator; b. Glasgow, Scotland, Dec. 3, 1932; d. John Stuart and Frances Charlotte (Swann) Robertson; m. Robert A. Skinner, Dec. 28, 1957; children: Robin Ann, Pamela. BA, NYU, 1953. Mdse. trainee Lord & Taylor, NYC; adminstrv. asst. Atlantic Products, NYC; newspaper corr. Salem Observer, NH, 1964-84; mem. N.H. Ho. of Reps., 1972-94, chmn. labor, human resources, and rehab. com., 1975-86, mem. House edn. com., 1987, chmn., 1989-94, exec. com. Nat. Conf. State Legislatures, 1987-90; chmn. N.H. Adv. Coun. Unemployment Compensation, 1984-94. Mem. State Libr. Adv. Coun., 2001—, gov.'s appointee, NH, 2004-09. Bd. dirs. Castle Jr. Coll., 1975, chmn. bd., 1988-96; v.p. bd. Swift Water coun. Girl Scouts U.S., v.p., 1987-92; N.H. Voc-Tech. Coll., Nashua, 1978-83; trustee Nesmith Libr., Windham, N.H., 1982—2008, chmn. bd. trustees, 1994-99; pres. N.H. Fedn. Rep. Women's Clubs, parliamentarian, legis. chmn., 1984-86, 94-96. Mem. Windham Woman's Club (pres. 1981-83), Order Ea. Star. Christian Scientist.

SKINNER, RICHARD L., federal agency administrator; BS, Fairmount State U.; MPA, George Washington U. Asst. inspector gen. audits Fed. Emergency Mgmt. Agency Dept. Homeland Security, Washington, 1991—96, dep. inspector gen., 1996, acting inspector gen., 2002—03; dep. inspector gen. US Dept. Homeland Security, Washington, 2003—05, acting inspector gen., 2004—05, inspector gen., 2005—. Office: Dept Homeland Security Naval Security Station Nebraska and Massachusetts Avenues NW Washington DC 20528 Office Phone: 202-254-4100. Office Fax: 202-254-4285. Personal E-mail: rlskinner2@verizon.net.*

SKINNER, ROBERT EARLE, JR., civil engineer, engineering executive; b. Washington, Aug. 10, 1946; s. Robert Earle and Dorothy Inez (Ballance) S.; m. Dianne Lynette Sands; children: Martha, Jeffrey. BSCE, U. Va., 1969; MS in Civil Engring., MIT, 1971. Registered profl. engr., Va. Sr. assoc. PRC Voorhees, McLean, Va., 1971-79, v.p., 1979-83; sr. staff officer Transp. Rsch. Bd., Washington, 1983-86, dir. studies and info. svc., 1986-94, exec. dir., 1994—. Exec. com. Hwy. Innovative Tech. Evaluation Ctr., Washington, 1994-2000; adv. com. Ctr. for Transp. and the Environment, Raleigh, N.C., 1995-2003, Dept. Civil, Archltl. and Eviron. Engring. U. Tex., 2000-2007; bd. dirs. Innovation Pavement Rsch. Found., Washington, 1999-2002; mem. adv. bd. Ctr. for Urban Transp. Rsch., U. South Fla., 2003—; mem. vis. com. engirng. sys. divsn. MIT, 2004-06; govs. adv. com. Safety Rev. Boston Ctrl. Artery/Tunnel Project, 2007-08. Contbr. articles to profl. jours.; mem. editorial bd. Jour. Trans. and Stats., 1996. Mem. adv. coun. U. Va., 1995—2005. With US Army N.G., 1970-76. Mem.: ASCE. Methodist. Avocations: woodworking, tennis. Office: Transportation Research Bd of the Nat Acads 500 5th St NW Washington DC 20001-

SKINNER, SAMUEL KNOX, lawyer, retired transportation executive, former United States Secretary of Transportation; b. Springfield, Ill., June 10, 1938; m. Mary Skinner. BS in Acctg., U. Ill., 1960; JD, DePaul U., 1966; numerous hon. degrees. Bar: Ill.; cert. jet pilot. Various sales and mgmt. positions IBM Corp., 1960-68; asst. US atty. (no. dist.) Ill. US Dept. Justice, 1968-75; US atty. US Dept. of Justice, 1975—77; sr. litig. & regulatory ptnr. Sidley & Austin, Chgo., 1977-89; chmn. Regional Transp. Authority, 1985-89; sec. US Dept. Transp., 1989—91; chief of staff to Pres. The White House, Washington, 1991-92; pres. Commonwealth Edison Co., 1993—98, Unicom Corp., 1993—98; co-chmn. Hopkins & Sutter, 1998—2000; pres., CEO US Freightways Corp., Chgo., 2000; chmn., pres., CEO USF Corp. (formerly US Freightways Corp.), 2001—03; of counsel Greenberg Traurig, LLP, Chgo., 2004—. Former adj. prof. John Marshall Law Sch., U. Chgo. Harris Sch. Pub. Policy; adj. prof. mgmt. and strategy Kellogg Sch. Mgmt., Northwestern U.; bd. dirs. Chgo. Bd. Options Exch., Navigant Consulting, Inc., Diamond Mgmt. & Tech. Consultants, Inc., Express Scripts, Inc., 2004—; mem. Dept. Def. Base Realignment and Closure (BRAC) Commn., 2005—; chmn. bd. dirs. Echo Global Logistics, Inc.; vice chmn. bd. dirs. Virgin America, APAC customer svcs. Active Northwestern Meml. Hosp., Ill. Econ. Devel. Bd., George Bush Presdl. Libr. Found. Lt. US Army, 1960-61. Recipient Disting. Eagle Scout award, Boy Scouts America, Silver Buffalo award; named Outstanding Salesmen of Yr., Nationwide, IBM, 1967. Mem.: ABA, Comml. Club, Econ. Club. Republican. Presbyterian. Office: Greenberg Traurig LLP 77 W Wacker Dr Ste 2500 Chicago IL 60601 Office Phone: 312-476-5138. Office Fax: 312-456-8435. Business E-Mail: skinners@gtlaw.com.

SKINNER, SARAH JACKSON, economics professor; b. Warcester, Mass., Mar. 10, 1976; d. John Douglas and Martha Gale Jackson; m. Eric Wolfe Skinner, July 13, 2002; children: Sydney Grace, Jackson Wolfe. B, Auburn U., Ala., 1998, M, 2000, PhD, 2003. Instr. Macon State Coll., Ga., 2000—01; grad. tchg. asst. Auburn U., 2001—03; asst. prof. U. La., Laffayette, 2003—. Contbr. articles to profl. jours. Mem.: Southern Econ. Assn., Am. Econ. Assn. Home: 903 Rosedown Ln Lafayette LA 70503 Office: Univ La PO Box 44570 Lafayette LA 70504 Business E-Mail: sskinner@louisiana.edu.

SKINNER, SUE DOSSETT, retired vocational director; b. Geneva, Ky., Dec. 4, 1928; d. Ural Morrison and Nellie Susan (Long) Dossett; m. William Thomas Skinner III, Sept. 7, 1952 (dec.); children: William Thomas IV, John Little Clay. BS, U. Ky., Lexington, 1951; EdM, NC State U., Raleigh, 1972. Asst. home demonstration agt. NC Ext. Svc., Warren County, 1952—60; food svcs. dir. Warren County Schs., 1968—72, tchr. home econ., 1972—88, dir. vocat. edn., 1988—92; ret., 1992. Past chair and vice chair Region III Home Econ. Leadership Coun.; v.p. NC Assn. Educators, Warren County, NC, sec., past pres. home econ. tchrs. sect.; Warren County del. NC Vocat. Assn.; past state sec. NC Home Econ. Assn., past state scholarship chair; mem. state scholarship com. NC Sch. Food Svc. Assn.; past advisor Region III Future Homemakers Am. Contbr. articles to periodicals. Participant Internat. Farm Youth Exch., Finland; local club leader 4-H; past dist. pres. Fedn. Woman's Clubs; past pres., com. chair Warrenton Woman's Club; v.p. Valley Investors; past pres. Littleton Womans Club; elder, choir dir. Presbyn. Ch. Recipient state poetry prizes (4), Fedn. Woman's Clubs; named county and state winner, 4-H Alumni Recognition Program; finalist runner-up, Mrs. NC Contest. Mem.: DAR (state chaplain 1997—2000, pres. 2004—06, chpt. regent 1976—78, 1983—85, 1988—93, 2007—), Gavel Soc., Am. Assn. Career and Tech. Edn., Order of the Merovingian Dynasty, Sons and Daus. Pilgrims, Elder Order Ancient Planters (nat. pres. 2004—05, nat. sec. 2005—07), Jamestowne Soc. (hon. gov. 1st NC chpt. 2005—), Dau. Colonial Wars (state chaplain 2005—06, state pres. 2007—), Dames Ct. Honor (state sec. 2006, state chaplain 2006—), Charlemagne Soc., Colonial Dames Am., Little Garden Club, Delta Kappa Gamma (past pres.). Presbyterian. Avocations: knitting, antiques. Home: PO Drawer 520 Littleton NC 27850-0520

SKINNER, THOMAS E., physics professor; b. Frostburg, Md., July 2, 1952; s. Roger Deforest and Emily Harrington Skinner; m. Mary F. Gibbons; children: John Luke, Emma Christ, Micah Brandlee, Thomas Lee. PhD, Johns Hopkins U., Balt., 1984. Prof. physics Wright State U., Dayton, Ohio, 1993—. Grantee, NASA, 1984—99, NIH, 2000, NSF, 2004—08. Achievements include patents in field. Avocations: piano, travel, yoga, guitar, skiing. Office: Wright State Univ Physics Dept Dayton OH 45435 Office Fax: 937-775-2222.

SKINNER, TIMOTHY JOSEPH, educator; Bachelor, SUNY, Cortland, 2002; Associate degree, Broome CC, Binghamton, NY, 1999. Promotions dir. air talent Citadel Broadcasting, Binghamton, 2002—06; adj. instr. Broome CC, 2006—; youth leader New Life Ministries, Endicott, NY, 2005—08, drama team dir., 2006, svc. prodn. supr., 2007—. Dir.: (informational DVD) Experience Community. Mem. spiedie fest planning com. Citadel Broadcasting, Cath. Charities, Binghamton, 2002—07; co-chmn. comm. com. Citadel Broadcasting, Am. Diabetes Assn., Binghamton, 2005—06; asst. coach Endwell Youth Softball, NY, 2006. Recipient Outstanding Achievement cert., SUNY, 2003. Mem.: Phi Theta Kappa (Named to Nat. Dean's List 1998—99). Office: Broome CC PO Box 1017 Binghamton NY 13901

SKINNER, WILLIAM PHILIP, JR., manufacturing executive; b. Youngstown, Ohio, June 24, 1957; s. William Philip Skinner and Lois Jean Brauninger. Student, Youngstown State U., Ohio, 1982, Palm Beach C.C., Lake Worth, Fla., 1990; cert. in clay modeling, Ctr. Creative Studies, Detroit, 1993. Owner Youngstown Reconditioning, 1982—85; with Nat. Water Svc., Rivera Beach, Fla., 1990—92; treas., head ops. Skinner Interiors, Bklyn., 1992—93; contract employee Modern Engring., Detroit, 1993—2001; owner, pres. Complete Coating Inc., Youngstown, 2001—. Founding mem. Lowellville Hist. Soc., 2005. Mem.: Am. Wine Soc. (mem. Cleve. chpt.), Internat. High IQ Soc., Youngstown Club, Phi Theta Kappa. Avocations: reading, travel. Home: 7100 Lockwood Blvd #405 Boardman OH 44512 Office Phone: 330-233-7384. Business E-Mail: bskinner@completecoatings.com.

SKINSTAD, ANNE HELENE, psychologist, researcher; b. Bergen, Hordaland, Norway, July 8, 1949; d. Alfhild (Hektoen) and Leif Sigurd Skinstad; 1 child, Siri Ødegaard. D in Psychology, U.of Bergen, Norway, 1977; PhD, U.of Bergen, 2001. Diplomate in Clin. Psychology Coll. Problems of Drug Dependence, 1985. Staff psychologist Hjellestad Clinic and Dr. Martens Clinic, Bergen, Norway, Hordaland, Norway, 1977—79; leading psychologist Blå-Kors Social Ctr., Bergen, Norway, 1979—83; facullty mem. U. Iowa, Iowa City, 1990—2001, asst. prof. Coll. Pub. Health, 2001—. Rsch. fellow The U. of Bergen, Norway, 1983—87; leading psychologist treatment ctr. substance abusing women Hjellestad Clinic, Bergen, Norway, 1987—90; program dir. Prairielands Addiction Tech. Transfer Ctr., Iowa City, 1995—2005. Contbr. articles to profl. jours. Recipient numerous grants, Norway, U.S. Mem.: APA, Am. Public Health Assn., Rsch. Soc. Alcoholism, European Roschach Assn. (founding mem. 1989), Nat. ATTC (chmn. liaison com., mem. curriculum com.), Norwegian Psychol. Assn. Avocations: owning Australian sheppards, piano. Office: U Iowa Coll Pub Health E239GH Iowa City IA 52242 Business E-Mail: anne-skinstad@uiowa.edu.

SKIRBOLL, STEPHEN LANCE, neurosurgeon; b. New Brunswick, NJ, June 4, 1961; s. Morton Jay and Bernice Weiss Skirboll; m. Lauren Elizabeth Perlov, Sept. 5, 2004; children: Isabella Rose, Ben Edward. BA, Case Western U., Cleve., 1983; MD, U. Pa., 1989. Cert. Am. Bd. Neurol. Surgery, 2002. Intern, gen. surgery U. Wash. Sch. Medicine, Seattle, 1989—90, resident, neurosurgery, 1990—97, postdoc. fellow, dept. physiology and biophysics, 1992—94; asst. prof. Divsn. Neurosurgery, U. N.Mex. Sch. Medicine, Albuquerque, 1997—2001, Stanford U. Sch. Medicine, Dept. Neurosurgery, Calif., 2001—; chief, neurosurgery sect. Va. Palo Alto Health Care Sys., Calif., 2001—. Registrar, neurol. surgery Atkinson Morley's Hosp., Wimbledon, England, 1995—96. Recipient Mary Ellis Bell prize, U. Pa. Sch. Medicine, 1989, Dr. Edward J. Sachar prize, 1989; Rsch. grant, Nat. Brain Tumor Found. and AANS, CNS Sect., 2007—08, Rsch. fellowship, Karolinska Inst., Stockholm, Am. Heart Assn., 1986—87, Bio-X Interdisciplinary Initiative grant, Stanford U., 2008—, Transnational Seed grant, Stanford U. Cancer Ctr., 2007—08, Glioblastoma Multiform grant, Nat. Brain Tumor Found., 2006—08. Mem.: Soc. Neuro-Oncology, Congress of Neurol. Surgeons, Am. Assn. Neurol. Surgeons (Rsch. fellowship 1992—94). Achievements include development of novel techniques to identify and characterize cancer stem cells and neural stem cells in human brain tumors. Office: Stanford Univ 300 Pasteur Dr R200 Stanford CA 94305 Business E-Mail: skirboll@stanford.edu.

SKIVER, STEPHEN ALLEN, lawyer, physician; b. Toledo, Feb. 14, 1949; s. Arnold Leroy and Elizabeth Jane (Boyer) S.; m. Catherine Ann Reynolds, June 26, 1971; children: Tonia, Justin, Ryan, Laura, Elyssa. BS, Ohio U., 1971; MD, Med. Coll. Ohio, 1974; JD, U. Toledo, 1988. Bar: Ohio 1989, U.S. Dist. Ct. (no. dist.) Ohio 1991; Cert. Am. Bd. Internal Medicine. Physician, Maumee, Ohio, 1977-89; clin. asst. prof. medicine Med. Coll. Ohio, Toledo, 1983-89; physician Toledo, 1989—; assoc. Jacobson, Maynard, Tuschman, Toledo, 1990-97; ptnr. Buckley, King & Bluso, Toledo, 1997—2000. Office: Law Offices Stephen A Skiver Assoc 28350 Kensington Ln Ste 200 Perrysburg OH 43551 Home: 30025 E River Rd Perrysburg OH 43551-3430 Office Phone: 419-931-0067. Business E-Mail: saskiver@skiverlaw.com.

SKJERVOLD, GERALDINE REID See REID, GERALDINE

SKLANSKY, JACK, electrical and computer engineering educator, researcher; b. NYC, Nov. 15, 1928; s. Abraham and Clara S.; m. Gloria Joy Weiss, Dec. 24, 1957; children: David Alan, Mark Steven, Jeffrey Paul. BEE, CCNY, 1950; MSEE, Purdue U., 1952; D in Engring. Sci., Columbia U., 1955. Research engr. RCA Labs., Princeton, NJ, 1955-65; mgr. Nat. Cash Register Co., Dayton, Ohio, 1965-66; prof. elec. and computer engring. U. Calif., Irvine, 1966—94; pres. Scanicon Corp., Irvine, 1980-89; prof. radiology Charles R. Drew U. of Medicine and Sci., LA, 1995—2004. Author: (with others) Pattern Classifiers and Trainable Machines, 1981; editor: Pattern Recognition, 1973, (with others) Biomedical Images and Computers, 1982; editor-in-chief: Machine Vision and Applications, 1987. Recipient best paper award Jour. Pattern Recognition, 1977, 2000; rsch. grantee NIH, 1971-84, Army Rsch. Office, 1984-91, NSF, 1992-96, Office of Naval Rsch., 1995-97, Naval Air Warfare Ctr., 1997-98, Calif. Breast Cancer Rsch. Program, 1997-99, US Army Med. Rsch. and Materiel Command, 1999-2004, Calif. Telehealth and Telemedicine Ctr., 2000-02. Fellow IEEE, Internat. Assn. for Pattern Recognition; mem. ACM. Office: U Calif Dept Elec Engring & Computer Sci MSTB 211 Irvine CA 92697 E-mail: sklansky@uci.edu.

SKLAR, KATHRYN KISH, historian, educator; b. Columbus, Ohio, Dec. 26, 1939; d. William Edward and Elizabeth Sue (Rhodes) Kish; m. Robert A. Sklar, 1958 (div. 1978); children: Leonard Scott, Susan Rebecca Sklar Friedman; m. Thomas L. Dublin, Apr. 30, 1988. BA magna cum laude, Radcliffe Coll., 1965; PhD, U. Mich., 1969. Asst. prof., lectr. U. Mich., Ann Arbor, 1969-74; assoc. prof. history UCLA, 1974-81, chmn. com. to administer program in women's studies Coll. Letters and Sci., 1974-81, prof., 1981-88; Disting. prof. history SUNY, Binghamton, 1988—, co-dir. Ctr. Hist. Study of Women and Gender, 1998—; Harmsworth prof. U.S. history U. Oxford, 2005—. Pulitzer juror in history, 1976; fellow Newberry Libr. Family and Community History Seminar, 1973; active Calif. Coun. for Humanities, 1981-85, N.Y. Coun. for Humanities, 1992—; Harmsworth prof. Am. history Oxford U., 2005—. Author: Catharine Beecher: A Study in American Domesticity, 1973 (Berkshire pri e 1974); editor: Catharine Beecher: A Treatise on Domestic Economy, 1977, Harriet Beecher Stowe: Uncle Tom's Cabin, or Life Among the Lowly: The Minister's Wooing, Oldtown Folks, 1981, Notes of Sixty Years: The Autobiography of Florence Kelley, 1849-1926, 1984, (with Thomas Dublin) Women and Power in American History: A Reader (2 vols.), 1991, (with Linda Kerber and Alice Kessler-Harris) U.S. History as Women's History: New Feminist Essays, 1995, Women's Rights Emerges within the Antislavery Movement: A Short History with Documents, 1830-1870, 2000; co-editor: The Social Survey Movement in Historical Perspective, 1992, Florence Kelley and the Nation's Work: The Rise of Women's Political Culture, 1830-1900, 1995 (Berkshire prize 1996). Social Justice Feminists in the United States and Germany: A Dialogue in Documents, 1885-1933, 1998, Women's Rights Emerges within the Anti-Slavery Movement: A Short History with Documents 1830-1870, 2000, (with James Brewer Stewart) Women's Rights and Transatlantic Anti-Slavery in the Era of Emancipation, 2007, co-editor: The Selected Letters of Florence Kelley, 1869-1931; mem. editl. bd. Jour. Women's History, 1987—, Women's History Rev., 1990—, Jour. Am. History, 1978-81; contbr. chpts. to books; co-dir. Women and Social Movements in the U.S. 1600-2000: An Online Jour. and Datebase, 1997—. Fellow Woodrow Wilson Found., 1965-67, Danforth Found., 1967-69, Radcliffe Inst., 1973-74, Nat. Humanities Inst., 1975-76, Rockefeller Found. Humanities, 1981-82, Woodrow Wilson Internat. Ctr. for Scholars, 1982, 1992-93, Guggenheim Found., 1984, Ctr. Advanced Study Behavioral and Social Scis., Stanford U., 1987-88, AAUW, 1990-91; Daniels fellow Am. Antiquarian Soc., 1976, NEH fellow Newberry Library, 1982-83; Ford Found. faculty rsch. grantee, 1973-74; grantee NEH, 1976-78, UCLA Coun. for Internat. and Comparative Studies, 1983. Mem. Am. Hist. Assn. (chmn. com. on women historians 1980-83, v.p. Pacific Coast br. 1986-87, pres. 1987-88), Orgn. Am. Historians (exec. bd. 1983-86, Merle Curti award com. 1978-79, lectr. 1982—), Am. Studies Assn. (coun. mem.-at-large 1978-80), Berkshire Conf. Women Historians, Am. Antiquarian Soc., Phi Beta Kappa. Avocation: photography. Office: SUNY Dept History Binghamton NY 13902

SKLAR, RICHARD LAWRENCE, political science professor; b. NYC, Mar. 22, 1930; s. Kalman and Sophie (Laub) S.; m. Eva Molineux, July 14, 1962; children: Judith Anne, Katherine Elizabeth. AB, U. Utah, 1952; MA, Princeton U., 1957, PhD, 1961. Mem. faculty Brandeis U., U. Ibadan, Nigeria, U. Zambia, SUNY-Stony Brook, UCLA; now prof. emeritus polit. sci. UCLA. Mem. fgn. area fellowship program Africa Nat. Com., 1970-73; Simon vis. prof. U. Manchester, Eng., 1975, Fulbright vis. prof. U. Zimbabwe, 1984; Lester Martin fellow Harry S. Truman Rsch. Inst., Hebrew U. Jerusalem, 1979; fellow Africa Inst. of South Africa, 1994—. Author: Nigerian Political Parties: Power in an Emergent African Nation, 1963, Corporate Power in an African State, 1975, African Politics in Postimperial Times, 2002; co-author: Postimperialism: International Capitalism and Development, 1987, African Politics and Problems in Development, 1991; co-editor: Postimperialism and World Politics, 1999; contbr. articles to profl. jours. Served with U.S. Army, 1952-54. Rockefeller Found. grantee, 1967 Mem. Am. Polit. Sci. Assn., African Studies Assn. (dir. 1976-78, 80-83, v.p. 1980-81, pres. 1981-82), AAUP (pres. Calif. Conf. 1980-81) Home: 1951 Holmby Ave Los Angeles CA 90025-5905 E-mail: sklar@polisci.ucla.edu.

SKLAREW, ROBERT JAY, biomedical research educator, consultant; b. NYC, Nov. 25, 1941; s. Arthur and Jeanette (Laven) S.; m. Toby Willner, July 15, 1970; children: David Michael, Gary Richard. BA in Zoology, Cornell U., 1963; MS, NYU, 1965, PhD in Biology, 1970. Assoc. rsch. scientist NYU Sch. Medicine, NYC, 1965-70, rsch. scientist, 1971-73, sr. rsch. scientist, 1973-79; rsch. asst. prof. pathology Goldwater Meml. Hosp. Sch. Medicine, NYC, 1979-87, rsch. assoc. prof. pathology, 1987-88; dir. cytokinetics and imaging lab. NYU rsch. svc. Goldwater Meml. Hosp., NYC, 1980-88; prof. cell biology, anatomy and medicine N.Y. Med. Coll., Valhalla, 1988-98. Rsch. assoc. dept. pathology Lenox Hill Hosp., N.Y.C., 1981-88; pres., CEO R.J. Sklarew Imaging Assoc., Inc., Larchmont, N.Y., 1990—2003; chmn. consensus panel for diagnostic cancer imaging Nat. Cancer Inst., 1994. Author: Microscopic Imaging of Steroid Receptors, 1990; sr. author: Cytometry, Jour. Histochem. Cytochem., Cancer, Exptl. Cell Rsch. Group leader Boy Scouts Am., Larchmont, 1978—80; bd. dir. Pinelake Park Coop, 1998—2001, 2006—09, pres., 2007—09. Grantee Am. Cancer Soc., Nat. Cancer Inst./NIH Conc. for Tobacco Rsch., R.J. Reynolds Industries Found., NYU; recipient Shannon award Nat. Cancer Inst., 1991. Mem. AAAS, Cell Kinetics Soc. (sec. 1983-85, 85-87, v.p. 1987-88, pres. 1988-89, chmn. nominations 1991, 93), N.Y. Acad. Sci., Soc. for Analytic Cytology, Soc. for Cell Biology, Tissue Culture Assn., Union Concerned Scientists, Kappa Delta Rho. Democrat. Achievements include development of methodology, algorithms and Receptogram analytic software for application of microscopic imaging in medical research and in pathodiagnosis of cancer, imaging methods for simultaneous densitometry and autoradiographic analysis; research in diagnostic imaging of steroid receptors, oncogenes and DNA ploidy in cancer, proliferative patterns and cell cycle kinetics of human solid tumors. Home: 8 Vine Rd Larchmont NY 10538-1247 Office: RJ Sklarew Imaging Assoc Inc 8 Vine Rd Larchmont NY 10538-1247 Personal E-mail: rjsklarew@aol.com.

SKLARSKY, FRANK S., manufacturing executive; b. Buffalo; married; 2 children. B in Acctg., Rochester Inst. Tech., 1978; MBA, Harvard Bus. Sch., 1983. CPA. Sr. acct. Ernst and Young, Rochester, NY, 1978—81; analyst DaimlerChrysler Corp., Auburn Hills, Mich., 1983, v.p. corp. fin. activities, v.p. product fin., asst. contr. prod. quality, cost mgmt. and procurement, 2001—04, v.p. corp. fin. control, 2004; v.p. fin. consumer divsn. Dell Computer Corp., Austin, Tex., 2000—01; exec. v.p., CFO ConAgra Foods, Omaha, 2004—06; exec. v.p. Eastman Kodak Co., Rochester, NY, 2006—, CFO, 2006—. Avocations: piano, swimming. Office: Eastman Kodak Co 343 State St Rochester NY 14650 Office Phone: 585-724-4000.*

SKLBA, RICHARD JOHN, bishop; b. Racine, Wis., Sept. 11, 1935; Attneded, Old St. Francis Minor Sem., Milw., Pontifical Bibl. Inst., Rome. Ordained priest Archdiocese of Milw., Wis., 1959; ordained bishop, 1979; aux. bishop Archdiocese of Milw., 1979—. Roman Catholic. Office: Archdiocese of Milwaukee PO Box 07912 3501 S Lake Dr Milwaukee WI 53207-0912 Office Phone: 414-769-3300. Office Fax: 414-769-3300.

SKLENAR, HERBERT ANTHONY, industrial products manufacturing company executive; b. Omaha, June 7, 1931; s. Michael Joseph and Alice Madeline (Spicka) S.; m. Eleanor Lydia Vincenz, Sept. 15, 1956; children: Susan A., Patricia I BSBA summa cum laude, U. Omaha, 1952; MBA, Harvard U., 1954; LLD (hon.), Birmingham-So. Coll., 1996. CPA W.Va. V.p., comptr. Parkersburg-Aetna Corp., W.Va., 1956—63; v.p., dir. Marmac Corp, Parkersburg, 1963-66; mgr. fin. control Boise-Cascade Corp., Idaho, 1966-67; exec. v.p. fin. and adminstrn., sec. Cudahy Co.,

Phoenix, 1967-72; chmn. emeritus Vulcan Materials Co., Birmingham, Ala., 1972-97, chmn. bd. dirs. emeritus, 1997—. Author (with others): The Automatic Factory: A Critical Examination, 1955. Trustee Leadership Birmingham, Birmingham-So. Coll Recipient Alumni Achievement award U. Nebr.-Omaha, 1977, cert. merit W.Va. Soc. CPAs, Elizah Watts Sells award AICPA, 1965, Brotherhood award NCCJ, 1993; inductee Ala. Acad. Honor, 1997 Mem.: Rotary Club Birmingham (chmn.), Birmingham Country Club, Shoal Creek Club, Phi Eta Sigma, Phi Kappa Phi, Omicron Delta Kappa, Delta Sigma Pi. Republican. Presbyterian. Home: 2809 Shook Hill Cir Birmingham AL 35223-2618

SKLOVSKY, ROBERT J., naturopathic physician, pharmacist, educator; b. NY; BS summa cum laude, Bklyn. Coll., 1975; MA in Sci. Edn., Columbia U., 1976; PharmD, U. Pacific, 1977; D in Naturopathic Medicine, Nat. Coll. Naturopathic Medicine, 1983. Intern Tripler Army Med. Ctr., Honolulu, 1977; pvt. practice Milwaukie, Oreg., 1983—. Recipient Bristol Labs. award Bklyn. Coll. Pharmacy, 1975, Coll. Gold medal, 1975, NYC Sci. Tchg. award Chemist's Club NY, 1976. Mem.: NY Acad. Sci. Avocations: classical and jazz music, art, gardening, painting. Office: 6910 SE Lake Rd Milwaukie OR 97267-2101 Office Phone: 503-654-3938.

SKLUTE, ADAM, performing company executive, dancer; b. Waterville, Maine; Scholarship student, The Joffrey Ballet Sch., NYC. Dancer Ballet Am. Concert Dancers, 1985-86, Joffrey II Dancers, NYC, 1986-88, The Joffrey Ballet, NYC, 1988, schedule coord., asst. ballet master, 1995—98, ballet master, artistic coord., 1998—2004, asst. artistic dir., 2004—05, assoc. artistic dir., 2005—07; artistic dir. Ballet West, Salt Lake City, 2007—. Guest tchr., coach dance workshops U. Cin., U. Iowa, Joffrey Ballet Sch., Joffrey Workshop Tex., Brigham Young U.; lectr. Chgo. Art Inst.; adj. prof. U. Utah. Named one of 25 Movers and Shakers of Utah Arts Scene, 2007. Office: Ballet West 50 W 200 South Salt Lake City UT 84101 Office Phone: 801-323-6908. Office Fax: 801-359-3504.*

SKLYAR, ADELINA M., lawyer; d. Joseph and Klafira Sklar. BA, NYU, NYC, 1993, JD, 1998. Bar: US Dist. Ct. (ea. dist.) NY 2001. Assoc. Ferro & Kuba, P.C., NYC, 1998—2001, Ferro, Kuba, Bloom, Mangano, Gacovino & Lake, P.C., NYC, 2001—05; ptnr. Ferro, Kuba, Mangano, Sklyar, Gacovino & Lake, P.C., NYC, 2005—. Mem.: ACLU, ATLA, NY State Bar Assn., NY County Lawyers' Assn. (assoc.). Office: Ferro Kuba Mangano Sklyar Ste 1100 360 West 31st St New York NY 10001 Office Fax: 212-244-9393. Business E-Mail: asklyar@ferrokuba.com.

SKOGLUND, MARILYN, state supreme court justice; b. Chgo., Aug. 28, 1946; BA, So. Ill. U., 1971; clerkship, 1977-81. Bar: Vt. 1981, U.S. Dist. Ct. Vt. 1981, U.S. Ct. Appeals (2d cir.) 1983. Asst. atty. gen. Civil Law Divsn., 1981—89, chief, 1988—93, Pub. Protection Divsn., 1993-94; judge Vt. Dist. Ct., 1994-97; assoc. justice Vt. Supreme Ct., 1997—. Office: Vt Supreme Ct 109 State St Montpelier VT 05609-0001*

SKOGSTAD, PHILIPP LEO, engineering company executive, director; b. Starnberg, Germany, Nov. 27, 1980; s. Robert Paul and Annette Margarete Skogstad; life ptnr. Nicole Anne Willmering. BS in Mech. Engring., St. Louis U., 2003; MS in Mech. Engring., Stanford U., Calif., 2005; MBA, U. St. Gallen, Switzerland, 2006. Exec. dir. Stanford U., 2006—08, ICED conf. mgr., 2008—. Contbr. articles to profl. jours. Recipient Nat. Coll. Engring. award, US Achievement Academy; Rsch. grant, Hasso Plattner Found., 2008—. Office: Stanford Univ Design Rsch 424 Panama Mall Bldg 560 Stanford CA 94305 Office Fax: 650-725-8475. Business E-Mail: skogstad@cdr.stanford.edu.

SKOKAN, CATHERINE, engineering educator; b. Cin., Oct. 21, 1948; d. John Anthony and Helene King; m. Jacob Jerome Skokan, Jan. 20, 1973; children: Margaret Christine, Jacob John, Paul Matthew, Mary Catherine, Thomas Andrew. BSc, Colo. Sch. Mines, Golden, 1970, MSc, 1972, PhD, 1975. Assoc. prof. geophysics Colo. Sch. Mines, 1991—96, assoc. prof. engring., 1996—. Chair student com. Environmental & Engring. Geophysics Soc., Denver, 2003—08; program chair, v.p., multidisciplinary engring. divsn. Am. Assn. Eng. Ed., 2007—; violinist Evergreen Chamber Orch., Colo., 1996—. Mem.: Tau Beta Pi, Sigma Xi Rsch. Soc. Am. (regional co-dir., chpt. treas. 2007—). Achievements include design of energy curriculum for tribal colleges and electrical engineering curriculum for petroleum institute, Abu Dhabi. Office: CO Sch Mines Engring 1500 Illinois St Golden CO 80401 Office Fax: 303-273-3602. Business E-Mail: cskokan@mines.edu.

SKOL, ARMAND GEORGE, lawyer; b. NYC, Aug. 26, 1943; s. Joseph and Doris (Karp) S.; m. Gloria Skol, Sept. 18, 1993; children: Edward Van Huysen, Caroline Golda. AB with honors, Clark U., 1964; JD, Georgetown U., 1967. Bar: DC 1968, Calif. 1974, US Supreme Ct. 1971, US Ct. Appeals (DC cir.) 1968, US Dist. Ct. DC 1968, US Dist. Ct. (no. dist.) Calif. 1977. Atty. fgn. commerce sect., antitrust div. US Dept. Justice, Washington, 1967-72; counsel boiling water reactor ops. GE, San Jose, Calif., 1973-78; sr. atty., assoc. gen. counsel Crown Zellerbach Corp., San Francisco, 1978-85; assoc. gen. counsel, v.p., dep. gen. counsel E&J Gallo Winery, 1986—2007, sr. counsel Curtis and Aratu, Modesto Calif., 2007-; commr. Stanislas County Children and Families Commn., 2002-, chair 2004-05. With USAR, 1969. Mem. ABA, DC Bar, State Bar Calif. (chmn. antitrust and trade regulation law sect. 1984-85, sec. 1981-84). Jewish. Office Phone: 209-985-4523.

SKOL, MICHAEL, counter-money laundering consultant; b. Chgo., Oct. 15, 1942; s. Ted and Rebecca (Williams) S.; m. Claudia Serwer, Sept. 29, 1973. BA, Yale U., 1964. U.S. fgn. svc. officer Dept. State, 1965-96; polit. officer U.S. Embassy, Buenos Aires, 1966-67, Saigon, Viet Nam, 1968-70; desk officer Dept. State, Washington, 1970-72; comml. attache U.S. Embassy, Santo Domingo, Dominican Republic, 1972-75; econ. comml. officer U.S. Consulate Gen., Naples, Italy, 1975-76; comml. attache U.S. Embassy, Rome, 1976-78, polit. counselor San Jose, Costa Rica, 1978-82; dep. dir. policy planning Inter-Am. Affairs Bur. Dept. State, Washington, 1982-85; dep. chief of mission U.S. Embassy, Bogota, Colombia, 1985-87; dir. Andean affairs Dept. State, Washington, 1987-88; dep. asst. sec. state for S.Am. U.S. Dept. of State, Washington, 1988-90; amb. U.S. Embassy, Caracas, Venezuela, 1990-93; prin. dep. asst. sec. for Latin Am./Caribbean Dept. State, Washington, 1993-96; sr. v.p. Diplomatic Resolutions, Inc., Washington, 1996-97; pres. Skol & Assoc. Inc., NY, Washington, Bogota, 1998—; chmn. US Colombian Bus. Partnership, 1996-99; mng. dir. L.Am. Decision Strategies, NYC, 1998—2005. Pres. Skol, Ospina & Serna, NYC, Washington and Bogota, 2001—03; prin. Skol & Serna, Washington, Bogota, 2003—. Mem.: Coun. on Fgn. Rels., Yale Club of N.Y. Office: 1710 Rhode Island Ave NW Ste 300 Washington DC 20036 Home: PO Box 596 Dennis MA 02638 Office Phone: 917-843-9753. Personal E-mail: mikeskol@aol.com.

SKOLDBERG, PHYLLIS LINNEA, musician, educator; d. August Theodore Skoldberg and Esther Amanda Carlson. MusB with honors, New Eng. Conservatory, 1955, MusM, 1957; M in Music Edn. with high distinction, Ind. U., 1964, Mus D in Performance, 1967. Violinist Houston Symphony Orch., 1957—59, Cin. Symphony Orch., 1959—62; assoc. instr. Ind. U., Bloomington, 1962—64; prof. music SUNY, Oswego, 1964—77; asst. dean fine arts Ariz. State U., Tempe, 1977—84, prof. music, 1977—2001, prof. emeritus, 2001—. Vis. artist Paris Conservatoire, 1973; vis. prof., cons. Australian String Tchrs. Assn., Brisbane and Sydney, 1984, Shanghai Conservatory Music, 1984; artist-in-residence U. Hong Kong, 1984; adj. prof., coord. string dept. Mesa (Ariz.) CC, 2001—. Author: The Strings: A Comparative View, Vol. I, 1981, Vol. 2, 1982; performer: (solos) Reston (Va.) Music Festival, 1972, 1973, Charles Ives Music Festival, 1975, 1976, Western Music Festival, 1980, (1st violin) Concert Quartet, 2003; soloist Philharmonic. Recipient Boston Civic Music award, 1954; named winner performance competition, Seattle Philharm. Orch., 1952. Mem.: The Phoenix Inst. of Music (founding dir. 2005), Red Rock Music Festival (bd. dirs. 2002—), Music Tchrs. Nat. Assn., Am. String Tchrs. Assn. (adv. bds. 1970—84, Ariz. pres. 1984—86). Home: 12002 S Tuzigoot Ct Phoenix AZ 85044-3467 Office: Mesa CC 1833 W Southern Ave Mesa AZ 85202 Office Phone: 480-461-7575. Office Fax: 480-461-7422. Business E-Mail: phyllis.skoldberg@asu.edu.

SKOLL, JEFFREY S., philanthropist, former Internet company executive; b. Montreal, Jan. 16, 1965; BSEE, U. Toronto, 1987; MBA, Stanford U., 1995; LLD (hon.), U. Toronto, 2003. Founder Skoll Engring., 1987, Micros on the Move Ltd., 1990; mgr. distbn. channels online news info. Knight-Ridder Info.; co-founder, pres., v.p. strategic analysis and planning eBay Inc., San Jose, Calif., 1995—99; founder, CEO Participant Productions, LA, 2004—. Exec. prodr.: (films) Good Night, and Good Luck, North Country, Syriana, American Gun, An Inconvenient Truth, The World According to Sesame Street, Fast Food Nation. Bd. dirs. e-Bay Found., 1998—; founder, chmn. Skoll Found., 1999—; bd. dirs. Cmty. Found. Silicon Valley; mem. advisory bd. Stanford Grad. Sch. Bus. Recipient Leafy award, 1999, Visionary award, Software Development Forum, 2001, Outstanding Philanthropist award, Silicon Valley chapter Assn. Fundraising Professionals, 2002, Internat. Assn. Fundraising Professionals, 2003, Nat. Leadership Award, Commonwealth Club Silicon Valley, 2004, Visionary award, Prodrs. Guild America, 2009; named a WIRED Renegade, WIRED Rave Awards, 2006; named one of the most innovative philanthropists of the past decade, BusinessWeek, 2002, 2003, 50 Most Generous Philanthropists, Fortune Mag., 2005, World's Richest People, Forbes, 1999—, 100 Most Influential People, Time Mag., 2006, 50 Smartest People in Hollywood, Entertainment Weekly, 2007. Office: Skoll Foundation 250 University Ave Ste 200 Palo Alto CA 94301 Office Phone: 650-331-1031. Office Fax: 650-331-1033.*

SKOLNICK, HERBERT, geologist; b. Bklyn., Jan. 15, 1919; s. Samuel Robert and Anna Ethel Skolnick; m. Marilyn Kassel, Aug. 2, 1948; 1 child, Tamara. BS, Bklyn. Coll., 1947; MA, U. Okla., Norman, 1949; PhD, U. Iowa, 1952. Sedimentologist Gulf Rsch. Devel. Co., 1952—53, chief adminstr., 1980—82; stratigrapher Western Gulf Oil Co., Ventura, 1953—59; divsnl. stratigrapher Western Gulf Bakersfield, Calif., 1959—60; chief stratigrapher & paleontologist Spanish Gulf Las Palmas, 1960—63. Sch. bd. treas. Nigerial Am. Sch., Lagos, 1963—67; pres. Spanish Am. Sch., Las Palmas, 1960—63. Capt. US Army, 1941—46. Fellow: Geol. Soc. America; mem.: Am. Assoc. Petrol Geol., Soc. Sigma Xi. Home: 109 S Ridge Dr Monroeville PA 15146

SKOLNICK, MARILYN, civic worker; b. NYC, Jan. 17, 1925; d. Max and Annie Ruth (Stern) Kassel; n. Herbert Skolnick, Aug. 2, 1948; 1 child, Tamara. BA, Bklyn. Coll., 1946; MA, U. Okla., 1948; postgrad., State U. Iowa, 1948-52. Host, prodr. cable TV program Focus on Issues, 1983—; chair citizen participation com. Transp. Rsch. Bd., Nat. Acad. Sci., 1987-94; sec. local transp. fin. com., 1987—. Bd. dirs. Port Authority of Allegheny County, 1982-95; pres. Allegheny County Transp. Coun., 1997-99, v.p., 1999-2000; mem. Pa. Small Bus. Compliance Adv. Com., 1992-2007, Penndot Mobility Plan for Pa., 2004-06. Chair Monroeville Planning Commn., 1983-85, Monroeville Redevelopment Authority, 2008-; bd. dirs. Pa. Planning Assn., 1983-85, Group Against Smog and Pllution; mem. Pa. Transp. Adv. Com., 1983-86; mem. air pollution ctrl. adv. com. Allegheny County Health Dept., 1985—, pollution prevention com. chair, 2004—; mem. Allegheny County Local Emergency Planning Com., 1987—, Allegheny County Comprehensive Plancomm. Pub. Participation Team. Mem. LWV (former bd. dirs.), N.Y. Acad. Scis., Pa. Acad. Scis., Sierra Club (bd. dirs. Pa. chpt. 1986—, chair Allegheny Group 1988-91), Sigma Xi. Home: 109 South Ridge Dr Monroeville PA 15146-4739

SKOLNICK, S. HAROLD, lawyer; b. Woonsocket, RI, June 17, 1915; s. David and Elsie (Silberman) S.; m. Shirley Marshall. AB cum laude, Amherst Coll., Mass., 1936; JD, Boston U., 1940. Bar: RI 1940, US Supreme Ct. 1946, DC 1947, Fla. 1952, US Dist. Ct. (so. dist.) Fla. 1953, US Ct. Appeals (5th cir.) 1960, US Ct. Appeals (11th cir.) 1981. Atty. Dept. of War, Washington, 1940-42; asst. gen. counsel, asst. chief legal dept. Office Chief Ordnance, Dept. of Army, Washington, 1947-50; assoc. Francis I. McCanna, Providence, 1951-52; ptnr. French & Skolnick, Miami, Fla., 1953-60; sole practice Miami, Fla., 1961—. Served to lt. col. US Army, 1942—47. Mem. ABA, Am. Judicature Soc., Nat. Def. Indsl. Assn. (life), RI Bar Assn., DC Bar Assn., Dade County Bar Assn., Estate Planning Coun. Greater Miami, Masons, Shriners. Home and Office: 6521 SW 122d St Miami FL 33156-5550

SKOLNIK, BARNET DAVID, retired lawyer; b. NYC, Feb. 8, 1941; s. Jack and Edythe (Savitz) S.; m. Patricia L. Krohn; children: Sarah, Deborah, Daniel, Joseph, Benjamin, Rebecca, Zachary. AB in Am. Govt. cum laude, Harvard U., 1962, LLB, 1965. Bar: D.C. 1966, Md. 1984, Maine 1991. Atty. criminal div. U.S. Dept. Justice, Washington, 1966-68; asst. U.S. atty. for Dist. Md., Balt., 1968-78; chief public corruption unit U.S. Atty.'s Office, Balt., 1973-78; pvt. practice law Balt. and Washington, 1978—91, Portland, Maine, 1991—94; ret. Tchr., lectr. on trial practice, white collar criminality, pub. corruption. Recipient Spl. Achievement award Dept. Justice, 1972, 74, Spl. Commendation for Outstanding Svc., Dept. Justice, 1978, Younger Fed. Lawyer award Fed. Bar Assn., 1974, Atty. Gen.'s Disting. Service award, 1974, Legal award Assn. Fed. Investigators, 1977 E-mail: bskolnik@gwi.net.

SKOLNIK, MERRILL I., electrical engineer; b. Balt., Nov. 6, 1927; s. Samuel and Mary (Baker) S.; m. Judith Magid, June 4, 1950; children: Nachama, Martin Allen, Julia Anne, Ellen Charlotte. BEng, Johns Hopkins U., 1947, MSEng, 1949, DEng, 1951. Research scientist Johns Hopkins U., Balt., 1947-54, vis. prof., 1973-74; engring. specialist Sylvania Electric, Boston, 1954; staff mem. MIT Lincoln Lab., Lexington, Mass., 1954-59; research mgr. Electronic Communications, Timonium, Md., 1959-64, Inst. Def. Analyses, Arlington, Va., 1964-65; supr. radar divsn. Naval Research Lab., Washington, 1965-96, radar sys. cons., 1996—. Mem. bd. visitors Duke U. Engring. Sch., Durham, N.C., 1976-93; disting. vis. sci. Jet Propulsion Lab., 1990-92; mem. Md. Gov.'s Exec. Adv. Com., 1993-95. Author: Introduction to Radar Systems, 1962, 3d edit., 2001, Radar Handbook, 1970, 3d edit., 2008; editor: Radar Applications, 1988. Recipient Heinrich Hertz premium Instn. Electronic and Radio Engrs., London, 1964, Disting. Alumnus award Johns Hopkins U., 1979, Disting. Civilian Svc. award USN, 1982, Meritorious Exec. award Sr. Exec. Svc., 1986, Johns Hopkins Engring. and Applied Sci. Excellence in Tchg. award, 1998; named to Soc. of Scholars, Johns Hopkins U., 1975. Fellow IEEE (editor Proceedings 1986-89, Harry Diamond award 1983, Centennial medal 1984, Dennis J. Picard medal for radar technologies and applications 2000); mem. Nat. Acad. Engring. Home: 8123 McDonogh Rd Baltimore MD 21208-1005 Office: Naval Rsch Lab Washington DC 20375-5320 E-mail: merrill.skolnik@nrl.navy.mil.

SKOLNIK, RICHARD ALAN, plastic surgeon; b. NYC, Jan. 7, 1951; BA in Biology summa cum laude, C.W. Post Coll., 1972; MD, Cornell U., 1976. Diplomate Am. Bd. Plastic Surgery. Resident gen. surgery Mt. Sinai Med. Ctr., NYC, 1976-79, resident plastic surgery, 1979-82, assoc. attending, 1982—; clin. instr. Mt. Sinai Sch. Medicine, NYC, 1982-84, asst. clin. prof., 1985—2005, assoc. clin. prof., 2005—; assoc. attending Beth Israel Med. Ctr., NYC, 1984—; courtesy staff Beth Israel North (Doctor's Hosp.), NYC, 1987—; plastic surgeon Madison Ave. Plastic Surgery, NYC. Fellow cleft lip and palate Children's Hosp., Lima, Peru, 1982; vis. prof. Reconstructive Surgery Found., Maceo, Brazil, 1990, Pune, India, 1994, Beijing, China, 1998; TV appearances Today Show, The View, Good Morning America, CNN, ABC, CBS, FOX News. Cons. editor: Breast Cancer the Complete Guide, Good Housekeeping's Illustrated Guide to Women's Health. Named one of Top 100 Doctors in NY, 1998—, The Best Beauty Docs, NY Mag., 2003. Fellow ACS; mem. AMA, Am. Soc. Plastic Surgeons, Am. Soc. Anesthetic Plastic Surgery, Med. Soc. State of NY, NY Regional Soc. Plastic and Reconstructive Surgeons, Barsky Soc. Avocations: ceramics, cooking, golf, tennis. Office: Madison Ave Plastic Surgery 21 E 87th St New York NY 10128-0506 Office Phone: 212-722-1977. Office Fax: 212-722-2283.*

SKOLNIKOFF, EUGENE B., political science professor; b. Phila., Aug. 29, 1928; s. Benjamin H. and Betty (Turoff) S.; m. Winifred S. Weinstein, Sept. 15, 1957; children: Matthew, Jessica. BS, MS, MIT, 1950, PhD, 1965; BA, Oxford U., Eng., 1952, MA, 1955. Registered profl. engr. Rsch. asst. in elec. engring. Uppsala U., Sweden, 1950; prof. polit. sci. emeritus M.I.T., 1965—, chmn. polit. sci. dept., 1970-74; dir. Center for Internat. Studies, 1972-87. Vis. rsch. prof. Carnegie Endowment Internat. Peace, Geneva, 1969-70; vis. fellow Balliol Coll., U. Oxford, 1989; vis. scholar Yale U., 1997; sys. analyst Inst. Def. Analyses, Washington, 1957-58; mem. White House staff Office Spl. Asst. to Pres. Sci. and Tech., Washington, 1958-63; adj. prof. Fletcher Sch. Law and Diplomacy, Tufts U., Medford, Mass., 1965-72; sr. cons. White House Office Sci. and Tech. Policy, 1977-81, vice chmn. adv. com. on sci., tech. and devel.; mem. policy rev. com. on nat. low-level nuclear waste mgmt., 1980-86; cons. Dept. State, Office of Tech. Assessment, AID, OECD, MacArthur Found., Resources Future, Am. Soc. Internat. Law, Ford Found., Inst. Def. Analyses; chmn., pres. Sci. and Public Policy Studies Group, 1967-73; mem. Internat. Council Sci. Policy Studies; Montague Burton vis. prof. U. Edinburgh, 1977, mem. NRC coms.; chmn. bd. UN U. Inst. New Tech. (INTECH), Maastricht, Holland, 1998-2005; Michael Dukakis vis. prof. pub. policy Am. Coll. Thessaloniki, Greece, 2000. Author: Science, Technology and American Foreign Policy, 1967, International Imperatives of Technology, 1972, The Elusive Transformation: Science, Technology, and the Evolution of International Politics, 1993; co-editor: World Eco-Crisis, 1972, Visions of Apocalypse, End or Rebirth?, 1985, The Implementation and Effectiveness of International Environmental Commitments, 1998; contbr. articles to publs.; chmn. editorial bd. Pub. Sci., 1971-75; mem. editorial bd. Tech. Rev., 1976-78, Social Studies of Sci., 1970-75, Internat. Orgn., 1974-80, Internat. Rels. of Asia Pacific, 2000-; mem. MIT Press Editl. Bd., 2005-07; patentee hybrid circuits. Trustee German Marshall Fund, 1979-87, chmn., 1980-86; trustee UN Rsch. Inst. for Social Devel., 1979-85; bd. dirs. Saco Def., 1984-86; mem. Overseas Devel. Coun.; mem. U.S. del. UN Commn. for Social Devel., 1979; mem. State Dept. Adv. Com. on Sci. and Tech., 1987-90. Served with U.S. Army Security Agy., 1955-57. Decorated Comdr.'s Cross Fed. Republic Germany, Order of Rising Sun, Golden Rays, Neck Ribbon, Japan; Rhodes scholar, 1950—52, Rockefeller Found. fellow, 1963—65. Fellow Am. Acad. Arts and Scis. (councillor 1973-77), AAAS (sec. sect. K 1967-69, mem. com. on sci. and pub. policy 1973-74, com. on sci., engring. and pub. policy 1984-89); mem. UN Assn., Fedn. Am. Scientists, (coun. 1981-85), Coun. Fgn. Rels., Am. Assn. Rhodes Scholars, Soc. for Social Studies of Sci., Sigma Xi, Tau Beta Pi, Eta Kappa Nu. Home: 3 Chandler St Lexington MA 02420-3601 Office: MIT E53-373 77 Massachusetts Ave Cambridge MA 02139-4307 Home Phone: 781-862-5561; Office Phone: 617-253-3140. Business E-Mail: ebskol@mit.edu.

SKOMAL, EDWARD NELSON, aerospace company executive, electromagnetic environments consultant; b. Kans. City, Mo., Apr. 15, 1926; s. Edward Albert and Ruth (Bangs) Skomal; m. Elizabeth Birkbeck Skomal, Mar. 4, 1951 (dec. June 1987); children: Susan Beth, Catherine Anne, Margaret Elaine; m. Joan Kerner Skomal, Apr. 9, 1988. BA, Rice U., Houston, 1947; MA, Rice U., 1949. Engr. Socony Rsch. Labs., Dallas, 1949—51; asst. sect. head Nat. Bur. Standards, Wash., 1951—56; project engr. Sylvania Microwave Rsch. Lab., Palo Alto, Calif., 1956—59; mgr. solid state sys., components applications engring., chief applications engr. Motorola Solid State Sys. Divsn., Phoenix, 1959—63; dir. comms. engring. dept. Aerospace Corp., El Segundo, Calif., 1959—86; ret., 1986; mem. Presdl. Joint Tech. Adv. Com. Electromagnetic Compatibility, Washington, 1965—75. Author: Man Made Radio Noise, 1978, Automatic Vehicle Locating Systems, 1980, Measuring the Radio Frequency Environment, 1985; contbr. articles to profl. jours. Elder Riverside Presbytery. With USN, 1944—46. Fellow: IEEE (asst. editor Trans. Electromatic Compatibility 1978—86, chmn. tech. adv. com. 1982—86, chmn. tech. com. electromagnetic environments 1976—82, standards com. mem. 1980—86, fellow nominating com. 1980—83, nat. com. standards coordinating com. on definitions 1986—, Richard A. Stoddart award 1980, Cert. of Achievement award 1971, Paper of Yr. award 1970); mem.: Am. Leghion, Friends A.H. Smiley Pub. Libr., Internat. Union Radio Scientists, Am. Phys. Soc., IEEE Electromagnetic Soc. (life), Sigma Xi. Republican. Presbyterian. Achievements include patents in field of radio systems, solid state devices, radar cross sect. reduction of ballistic rentry vehicles and sold state microwave components; research in theory of man-made radio noise; development of solid state microwave components, the application of stochastic processes to man-made radio noise analysis. Home: 1802 Morning Dove Ln Redlands CA 92373 Home Phone: 909-792-1808. Personal E-mail: ejskomal@verizon.net.

SKOOG, DONALD PAUL, retired pathologist, educator; b. Sioux City, Iowa, Sept. 29, 1931; m. Mary Ann Bunn, 1955; children: Robert Eugene, David Alan (dec.), Kristin Marie. BA magna cum laude, Midland Lutheran Coll., Fremont, Nebr., 1953; MD cum laude, U. Nebr., 1958; DSci (hon.), Midland Luth. Coll., 1993. Diplomate Am. Bd. Pathology. Intern, then resident in pathology Bishop Clarkson Meml. Hosp., Omaha, 1958-62; resident in pathology Parkland Meml. Hosp., Dallas, 1962-63; fellow in pathology U. Tex. Southwestern Med. Sch., Dallas, 1962-63; practice medicine specializing in pathology Omaha, 1963-92. Pathologist Bishop Carlson Meml. Hosp., 1963-88, chmn. dept. pathology, 1978-80, chmn. med. edn. com., 1978-83, sec.-treas.

med. staff, 1982-87, dir. dept., 1986-87; prof. pathology and microbiology U. Nebr. Coll. Med., 1977-93, mem. dean's faculty adv. coun., 1977-79, mem. grad. and continuing edn. com., 1980-85, mem. coun. affilitated instns., 1981-83, mem. admissions com., 1986-91, sr. cons. pathology and microbiology, 1993—; assoc. med. dir. ARC Blood Svcs., Midwest Region, Omaha, 1988, med. dir./dir. 1989-91, dir./prin. officer, 1991-92; mem. computer sys. selection com., 1991, ARC Blood Svcs., Washington, 1981-, mem. med. affairs com., 1991-92; mem. exec. com. Nebr. Med. Edn. Fund, 1981-, bd. dirs., 1981-, chmn. loan com., 1983-91, sec.-treas., 1984-91; mem. comm. com. Pvt. Practice Assocs., Omaha, 1998-03, mem. credentials and quality improvement com., 1998-03; chmn. com. Clarkson Legends, Nebr. Med. Ctr., 2005 (Clarkson Legends award, 2007); vol. cons. dept. devel. Nebr. Med. Ctr., 2005-. Mem. editl. bd. Lab. Medicine, 1979—03; editor, lead author: Swedes, Danes, and Norwegians: Oral Histories from Nebraska, 2000; contbr. articles to med. jours. Councilman Luther Meml. Luth. Ch., Omaha, 1966-72, 87-91, vice chmn., 1969-72; trustee Midland Luth. Coll., 1968-87, chmn., 1973-75; mem. Swedish Cultural Com., Omaha, 1975—. Recipient Alumni Achievement award Midland Luth. Coll., 1972, Disting. Svc. award Sch. of Allied Health Program, U. Nebr. Med. Ctr., 1990, Disting. Alumnus award U. Nebr. Coll. Medicine Alumni Assn., 1998. Fellow Am. Soc. Clin. Pathologists (hematology profl. self-assessment com. 1972, 75,78, adv. coun. 1972-78, chmn. coun. hematology 1978-81, editor Hematology Check Sample 1983-88, Disting. Svc. award Commn. on Continuing Edn. 1985, mem. bd. censors 1987-89, mem. nat. meeting activities com. 1989-92, chmn. 1990-92, Israel Davidsohn disting. svc. award 1993), Coll. Am. Pathologists (hematology resource com. 1981-86, vice chmn. 1982-85); mem. AMA, Nebr. Assn. Pathologists, Nebr. Med. Assn., Met. Omaha Med. Soc. (coun. on grievances and profl. ethics 1983-91), Midland Luth. Coll. Alumni Assn. (pres. 1969-70), Alpha Omega Alpha (pres. U. Nebr. chpt. 1976-77, counsellor 1984-90). Republican. Lutheran. Home: 706 S 96th St Omaha NE 68114 Personal E-mail: dpsmd@cox.net.

SKOOG, GERALD DUANE, science educator; b. Sioux City, Iowa, Feb. 27, 1936; s. Paul and Mary Ann Skoog; m. Elizabeth Ann Lee, Dec. 28, 1962; children: Jeffrey, John, Sarah. BS, U. Nebr., 1958. Tchr. various schs., Nebr., Ill., 1958-69; instr. U. Nebr., Lincoln, summer 1969; asst. prof. curriculum and instrn. Tex. Tech U., Lubbock, 1969-72, assoc. prof., coordinator program, 1972-74, assoc. prof., chmn. secondary edn., 1976-80, prof., chmn. secondary edn., 1980-90, prof., chmn. curriculum and instrn., 1990-97, Helen DeVitt Jones prof., 1997-2001, pres. faculty senate, 1986-87, dean Coll. Edn., 2002—03, Paul Whitfield Horn prof., 2000—04, prof. emeritus, 2005; dir. Ctr. Integration Sci. and Edn. Rsch., 2004—. Vis. prof. We. Ill. U., summer 1972; lectr. in field; participant, facilitator numerous workshops; cons. Contbr. numerous articles to profl. jours., also reviewer articles and papers; co-author secondary sch. science textbooks. Bd. dirs. Gloria Dei Luth. Ch., Lubbock, 1971-74, 92-93; bd. dirs. Luth. Coun. Cmty. Action, 1970-71, Good Neighbor Ministry, 1982-84; leader Boy Scouts Am., 1978-79; foster parent Luth. Social Svcs. Tex.; bd. dirs. Triangle Coalition for Sci. and Tech., 1986-95. Recipient Pres.'s Faculty Achievement award Tex. Tech. U., 1986, Disting. Leadership award, 1996, Award of Excellence, U. Nebr., Lincoln Tchrs. Coll. Alumni Assn., 2003; named Notable Alumnus, U. Nebr., Lincoln, Tchrs. Coll., 1998; named to Tex. Sci. Hall of Fame, 2000. Fellow AAAS, AERA (inaugral fellow 2009); mem. ASCD, NSTA (life, bd. dirs. 1977-79, pres. 1985-86, various coms., Disting. Svc. to Sci. Edn. award 1994, Robert H. Carleton award 2004), Nat. Assn. Rsch., Sci. Tchrs. Assn. Tex. (hon., past pres., Skoog Cup award), Nat. Assn. Biology Tchrs., Soc. Study Edn. Lutheran. Office: Tex Tech U Coll Edn Lubbock TX 79409 Home: 4709 116th St Lubbock TX 79424 Office Phone: 806-742-1997 x 259. E-mail: gerald.skoog@ttu.edu.

SKOOG, WILLIAM ARTHUR, retired oncologist; b. Culver City, Calif., Apr. 10, 1925; s. John Lundeen and Allis Rose (Gatz) Skoog; m. Ann Douglas, Sept. 17, 1949; children: Karen, William Arthur, James Douglas, Allison. AA, UCLA, 1944; BA with great distinction, Stanford U., 1946, MD, 1949. Intern in medicine Stanford Hosp., San Francisco, 1948-49, asst. resident in medicine, 1949-50, N.Y. Hosp., NYC, 1950-51; sr. resident in medicine Wadsworth VA Hosp., LA, 1951, attending specialist in internal medicine, 1962-68; pvt. practice internal medicine Los Altos, Calif., 1959-61; pvt. practice hematology and oncology, Santa Monica, Calif., 1971-72; pvt. practice med. oncology, San Bernardino, Calif., 1972-94; ret. Assoc. staff Palo Alto-Stanford Med. Ctr., 1959-61, U. Calif. Med. Ctr., San francisco, 1959-61; assoc. attending physician UCLA Hosp. and Clinics, 1961-78; vis. physician in internal medicine Harbor Gen. Hosp., Torrance, Calif., 1962-65, attending physician, 1965-71; cons. in chemistry Clin. Lab., UCLA Hosp., 1963-68; affiliate cons. staff St. John's Hosp., Santa Monica, 1967-71, courtesy staff, 1971-72; courtesy attending med. staff Santa Monica Hosp., 1967-72; staff physician St. Bernardine (Calif.) Hosp., 1972-94, hon. staff, 1994—; staff physician San Bernardino Cmty. Hosp., 1972-90, courtesy staff, 1990-94; chief sect. oncology San Bernardino County Hosp., 1972-76; cons. staff Redlands(Calf.) Cmty. Hosp., 1972-83, courtesy staff, 1983-94, hon. staff, 1994—; asst. in medicine Cornell U. Med. Coll., N.Y.C., 1950-51; jr. rsch. physician UCLA Atomic Energy Project, 1954-55; instr. medicine, asst. rsch. physician dept. medicine UCLA Med. Ctr., 1955-56, asst. prof. medicine, asst. rsch. physician, 1956-59; clin. assoc. in hematology VA Ctr., L.A., 1956-59; co-dir. metabolic rsch. unit UCLA Ctr. for Health Scis., 1955-59, 61-65; co-dir. Health Scis. Clin. Rsch. Ctr., 1965-68, dir., 1968-72; clin. instr. medicine Stanford U., 1959-61; asst. clin. prof. medicine, assoc. rsch. physician U. Calif. Med. Ctr., San Francisco, 1959-61; lectr. medicine UCLA Sch. Medicine, 1961-62, assoc. prof., 1962-72, assoc. clin. prof., 1973—. Contbr. articles to med. jours. Active duty USNR, 1943—46, lt. M.C. USNR, 1951—53. Fellow: ACP, Am Soc. Internal Medicine; mem.: AMA, San Bernardino County Med. Soc., Am. Soc Clin. Oncology, L.A. Acad. Medicine, Am. Fedn. Clin. Rsch., Western Soc. Clin. Rsch., So. Calif. Acad. Clin. Oncology, Calif. Med. Assn., Redlands Country Club, Alpha Omega Alpha, Sigma Xi, Phi Beta Kappa, Alpha Kappa Kappa. Episcopalian (vestryman 1965-70). Home: 1119 Kimberly Pl Redlands CA 92373-6786 Home Phone: 909-798-7380. Home Fax: 909-798-5016. Personal E-mail: adssredarrow@aol.com.

SKOPIL, OTTO RICHARD, JR., federal judge; b. Portland, Oreg., June 3, 1919; s. Otto Richard and Freda Martha (Boetticher) Skopil; m. Janet Rae Lundy, July 27, 1956; children: Otto Richard III, Casey Robert, Shannon Ida, Molly Jo. BA in Econs., Willamette U., 1941, LLB, 1946, LLD (hon.), 1983. Bar: Oreg. 1946, US Dist. Ct. Oreg., US Ct. Appeals (9th cir.), US Supreme Ct. 1946. Assoc. Skopil & Skopil, 1946—51; ptnr. Williams, Skopil, Miller & Beck (and predecessors), Salem, Oreg., 1951—72; judge US Dist. Ct., Portland, 1972—79, chief judge, 1976—79; judge US Ct. Appeals (9th cir.), Portland, 1979—85, sr. judge, 1986—. Chmn. com. adminstrn. of fed. magistrate sys. US Jud. Conf., 1980—86; co-founder Oreg. chpt. Am. Leadership Forum; chmn. 9th cir. Jud. Coun. Magistrates Adv. Com., 1988—91; chmn. US Jud. Conf. Long Range Planning Com., 1990—95. Hi-Y adviser Salem YMCA, 1951—52; appeal agt. SSS Marion County (Oreg.) Draft Bd., 1953—66; master of ceremonies 1st Gov.'s Prayer Breakfast for State Oreg., 1959; citizens adv. com. City of Salem, 1970—71; Gov.'s Com. on Staffing Mental Instns., 1969—70; pres., bd. dirs. Marion County Tb and Health Assn., 1958—61; bd. dirs. Willamette U., 1969—71; elder Mt. Park Ch., 1979—81; bd. dirs. Willamette Valley Camp Fire Girls, 1946—56, Internat. Christian Leadership, 1959, Fed. Jud. Ctr., 1979. Lt. USNR, 1942—46. Recipient Oreg. Legal Citizen of Yr. award, 1986, Disting. Alumni award, Willamette U. Sch. Law, 1988. Mem.: ABA, Internat. Soc. Barristers, Assn. Ins. Attys. U.S. and Can. (Oreg. rep. 1970), Def. Rsch. Inst., Oreg. Assn. Def. Counsel (bd. dirs.), Am. Judicature Soc., Marion County Bar Assn., Oreg. Bar Assn. (bd. dirs.), Prayer Breakfast Movement (fellowship coun.), Illahe Hills Country Club (pres., bd. dirs. 1964—67), Exchange Club (pres. 1947), Salem Club. Office: Sr Circuit Judge 827 US Courthouse 1000 SW 3rd Ave Portland OR 97204-2930*

SKORTON, DAVID JAN, academic administrator; b. Milw., Nov. 22, 1949; s. Samuel and Pauline (Millstein) Skorton; 1 child, Joshua Samuel. BA, Northwestern U., 1970; MD, Northwestern U., Chgo., 1974. Diplomate Nat. Bd. Med. Examiners, Am. Bd. Internal Medicine, Am. Bd. Cardiovascular Disease. Resident UCLA, 1974—77, fellow in cardiology, 1977—79, chief resident in medicine, 1978—79, adj. asst. prof., 1978—80; instr. medicine U. Iowa, Iowa City, 1980—81, asst. prof., 1981—84, asst. prof. elec. and computer engring., 1982—84, assoc. prof. medicine and elec. and computer engring., 1984—88, prof. medicine, elec. and computer engring., 1988—2006; acting dir., then dir. div. gen. internal medicine U. Iowa Coll. Medicine, Iowa City, 1985—89, assoc. chmn. for clinical programs, 1989—92, v.p. rsch., 1992—2002, v.p. external rels., 2000—03; pres. U. Iowa, 2003—06; pres., prof. medicine, pediat., and biomed. engring. Cornell U., Ithaca, NY, 2006—. Dir. echocardiology lab. VA Med. Ctr., Iowa City, 1980—89; mem. internat. and coop. projects Fogerty Ctr. study sect. NIH, 1988—92, chmn., 1990—92; lectr. in field numerous sci. sessions, nat. and internat. meetings; manuscript reviewer maj. jours. in field. Editor: (book) Cardiac Imaging and Image Processing, 1986, Cardiac Imaging, 1991, Cardiac Imaging, 2d edit., 1996; contbr. articles and abstracts to profl. jours., chapters to books. Chair Task Force on Diversifying NYS Economy Through Industry Higher Edn. Partnerships. Recipient Rsch. Assoc. Career Devel. award, VA, 1981—84, Rsch. Career Devel. award, Nat. Heart Lung & Blood Inst., 1984—89; named Intern-of-Yr., UCLA, 1975; Regents' scholar, 1967—68. Fellow: ACP, Am. Physiol. Soc., Am. Heart Assn., Am. Coll. Cardiology; mem.: AAAS, Nat. Inst. Biomed. Imaging and Bioengring. (mem. adv. coun.), Coun. Fgn. Rels., Bus. Higher Edn. (chair 2008), Internat. Soc. Adult Congenital Cardiac Disease, Assn. Univ. Cardiologists. Jewish. Office: Cornell Univ Office of Pres - Attn Congtance Kitner 300 Day Hall Ithaca NY 14853 Office Phone: 607-255-5201. Office Fax: 607-255-9924. E-mail: president@cornell.edu.

SKOTHEIM, ROBERT ALLEN, retired academic administrator, educator; b. Seattle, Jan. 31, 1933; s. Sivert O. and Marjorie F. (Allen) S.; m. Nadine Vail, June 14, 1953; children: Marjorie, Kris, Julia. BA, U. Wash., 1955, MA, 1958, PhD, 1962; LLD (hon.), Hobart and William Smith Colls., Geneva, NY, 1975; LittD (hon.), Whitman Coll., 1988; LHD (hon.), Coll. Idaho, 1988, Occidental Coll., 1989, Ill. Wesleyan U., 1990; DFA (hon.), Willamette U., 1989; DFA (hon.), Whittier Coll., 2000, Gustavus Adolphus Coll., 2000. Prof. history U. Wash., 1962-63, Wayne State U., Detroit, 1963-66; prof. UCLA, 1966-67, U. Colo., Boulder, 1967-72; provost, dean faculty Hobart and William Smith Colls., 1972-75; pres. Whitman Coll., Walla Walla, Wash., 1975-88, Huntington Libr., Art Collections & Bot. Gardens, San Marino, Calif., 1988-2001, Occidental Coll., LA, 2008—09. Author: American Intellectual Histories and Historians, 1966, Totalitarianism and American Social Thought, 1971; Editor: The Historian and the Climate of Opinion, 1969; co-editor: American Social Thought: Sources and Interpretations, 2 vols, 1972. Guggenheim fellow, 1967-68 Mem. Phi Beta Kappa (hon.) Home: 1852 Campus Rd Los Angeles CA 90041 Home Phone: 206-780-3440; Office Phone: 323-259-2691. Office Fax: 323-259-2907.

SKOV, ARLIE MASON, petroleum engineer, consultant; b. Perry, Okla., Sept. 21, 1928; s. Arnold and Mary (Mason) S.; m. Luella Luticia Sloan, July 31, 1951; children: Gregory Morgan, Jeffrey Markham, Tamara Kay. BS in Petroleum Engring., U. Okla., 1956; postgrad., U. Va., 1966. Engr., Sohio Petroleum Co., Pauls Valley, Oklahoma City, Okla., 1958-66, mgr. spl. projects Oklahoma City, 1966—76; mgr. prodn. planning BP Alaska Inc., San Francisco, 1977-80; project advisor Sohio Gas Pipeline Co., San Francisco, 1980-81; mgr. new tech. devel. Sohio Petroleum Co., San Francisco, 1981-83; dir. prodn. tech. Sohio Petroleum Co. and Standard Oil Prodn., Dallas, 1983-88; sr. cons. BP Exploration, Inc., Houston, 1989-92; owner Arlie M. Skov, Inc. Petroleum Consulting, Houston, 1993—2001. Chair Santa Barbara City Water Commn., 2003—04. Recipient Disting. Svc. award Okla. Petroleum Coun. 1973. Mem. AIME (bd. dirs. 1977-79, trustee 1990-92, 95-97, 2007-) Soc. Petroleum Engrs. (hon.; bd. dirs. 1972-74, exec. com. 1990-92, pres. 1991, pres. Found. 2003-04, Disting. Mem.), Santa Barbara Club, Cosmopolitan Club of Santa Barbara. Avocations: reading, travel. Office Phone: 805-965-5101.

SKOV, LEIF, performing arts association administrator, entrepreneur; b. Helsinge, Denmark, Dec. 30, 1946; s. Frede and Hilda Marie (Pedersen) S.; 1 child, Kamilla Skov Larsen; m. Anne Larsen (dec. Aug. 18, 2005). Grad., Tchrs. Coll., Holbaek Seminarium, 1969. Tchr. Ramsø Kommune, Denmark, 1969-75, careers advisor, 1975-91; founding mem., exec. com. Yourope, Denmark, 1991—2001; gen. mgr. VIP Booking, 2003—04. Chmn., founder Sealand Music Agy., 1974-80; facility dir. Roskilde Festival, 1973-78, artistic dir., 1975-2002; chmn. CAP Rock Ltd., STV Ltd., Bongorama Prodns. Ltd., Global Copenhagen. Bd. dirs. Roskilde Charity Soc., 1975-83, Eurovenue, 1993-97, Montmartre, 1994-95, Vega, 1996-97, Midtfyns Festival, 2002—04, Danish Pop & Rock Acad., 2002-, Ars Nova Ensemble, 2001-02, Jagtvej 69 Found, 2007-, Copenhagen Opera Festival, 2008-, Hove Republic Ltd., 2008-, Living Libr. Internat., 2009-; founder, bd. dirs. Venue Found., 1992-; founder, chmn. Musicon Valley Found., 2001-04; chmn. Danish Sch. Athletics Com., 1977-81; mem. Danish Rock City Com., 2000-04, Danish Govt. Music Coun., 2007-; founder, gen. mgr. byLife, 2002-; founder, chmn. Global Care, 2002-07; chmn. Bjorn Afzelius Internat. Found., 2003-07. Created knight (Denmark), 1998; recipient Music Creativity award DR-TV, 1985, award Danish Contractors Assn., 1995, Cultural Entrepreneur, 1995, Nordic Coun. Cultural prize, 1995, Cultural award Roskilde Fedn. Trade Unions, 2001; apptd. Amb. of City of Roskilde, 1999. Mem.: Rhythmic Roskilde Soc. (chmn. 2000—02). Avocations: running, cross country skiing. Home: Duebrodrevej 16 4000 Roskilde Denmark Personal E-mail: life.s@mail.dk.

SKOWRONEK, STEPHEN LEE, political scientist, educator; b. Somerville, NJ, Mar. 8, 1951; s. Sidney Daniel and Esther (Gordon) S.; m. Susan Jacobs, Dec. 5, 1982; children: Michael, Samuel. AB, Oberlin Coll., Ohio, 1973; MA, Cornell U., Ithaca, NY, 1976, PhD, 1979. From asst. to assoc. prof. UCLA, 1978-85; Pelatiah Perit prof. polit. & social sci. Yale U., New Haven, 1986—. Chair in Am. civilization École des Hautes Études en Sciences Sociales, Paris. Author: Building A New American State: The Expansion of National Administrative Capacities 1888-1920, 1982, The Politics Presidents Make: Leadership From John Adams to George Bush, 1993, rev. ed. The Politics Presidents Make: Leadership from John Adams to Bill Clinton, 1997, (with K. Orren) The Search for American Political Development, 2004, Presidential Leadership in Political Time: Reprise and Reappraisal, 2008; founding mng. editor Studies in Am. Polit. Devel., 1986-2007. Woodrow Wilson Internat. Ctr. Scholars fellow, Washington, 1985-86. Fellow Am. Acad. Arts & Sci.; mem. Am. Political Sci. Assn., Am. Hist. Assn., Social Sci. History Assn., Phi Beta Kappa, Phi Kappa Phi. Office: Yale Univ Dept Polit Sci PO Box 208301 New Haven CT 06520-8301 Business E-Mail: stephen.skowronek@yale.edu.*

SKOWRONSKI, NANCY, library director; m. Dennis Skowronski. Grad., Wayne State U., Detroit, 1975. Acting dir. Detroit Pub. Libr., 2001—02, interim dir., 2002—03, dir., CEO, 2003—. Bd. dirs. ProLiteracy Detroit, 2006—. Mem.: ALA, Univ. Cultural Ctr. Assn. (bd. mem.), Mich. Libr. Assn. Office: Detroit Pub Libr 5201 Woodward Ave Detroit MI 48202 Office Phone: 313-833-3997. Office Fax: 313-833-2327. E-mail: nskowro@detroit.lib.mi.us.

SKOWRONSKI, VINCENT PAUL, musician, recording industry executive; b. Kenosha, Wis., Jan. 22, 1944; MusB, Northwestern U., 1966, MusM, 1968. V.p. Eberley-Skowronski, Inc., Evanston, Ill., 1973-92; internat. dir. mktg. and pub. rels. Vincent Skowronski: Producer of Classical Recordings, Evanston, 1993—. Internat. broker rare instruments Strings & Things, Evanston, 1973-92; owner Vincent Skowronski: Fine Violins, Evanston, 1993—; internat. dir. mktg. and pub. rels. EB-SKO Prodns., Evanston, 1978-92; dir. media comm. E-S Mgmt., Evanston, 1985-92; instr. violin Northwestern U., 1969-71; asst. prof. violin U. Wyo., 1971-72; pvt. violin tchr., chamber music coach, lectr., master classes. Solo violinist debut Chgo. Youth Orch., 1959; soloist Chgo. Civic Orch., 1968, guest solo artist Am. Artist Gala, Nat. Puerto Rican TV, 1960, guest solo artist Peninsula Music Festival, Fish Creek, Wis., 1965, 66; guest solo artist Young Am. Musicians Sta. WKAR-TV Mich. State U., 1966, N.Am. premiere R. Nanes' Rhapsody Pathetique for violin and orch., Chgo. Cultural Ctr., 1994, Beijing, 1994, DePaul U. Ctr., Chgo., 1994, Skowronski in Recital: 20 Years Remembered, Northwestern U., Evanston, Ill., 1994, IV Internat. Tchaikovsky Competition Commemorative Recital-Moscow Remembered: 1970-95, Evanston, Ill., 1995, J.L. Kellogg Sch. Mgmt. Recital Northwestern U., Ill., 1996; featured soloist Artist Showcase, Sta. WGN-TV Chgo., 1966-71, Honors Concert-Northwestern U., 1966, guest solo artist A.M. Am., Sta. ABC-TV, 1977—, Continental Bank Concerts Sta. WFMT-FM Chgo., 1983, 85-86, 88, 90, United Airlines Presents, Live! Sta. WFMT-FM Chgo., Schumann, 1986, Szymanowski, 1987, Bloch, 1988, Saint-Saens, 1989, Grieg, 1991, Excursions in Music: The Artistry of Vincent P. Skowronski, Sta. KQED-FM San Francisco, 1979, Skowronski: Musical Giant, Interlake Profiles, Sta. WFMT-FM Chgo., 1980, Skowronski at 50: A Birthday Celebration Sta. WNIB-FM, Chgo., 1994, Chgo. Musicians Sta. WNIB-FM, 1996-97, Skowronski at 55: A Birthday Celebration Sta. WNIB-FM, Chgo., 1999; guest solo artist, prodr., annotator for LPs Separate But Equal, 1976, All Brahms, 1977; solo artist, exec. prodr., annotator for LPs Gentleman Gypsy, 1978, Strauss and Szymanowski, 1979, Franck and Szymanowski, 1982; exec. prodr., prodr. CDs Skowronski Alone, 1996, Skowronski Plays, Strauss and Szymanowski, 1998, Skowronski Plays, Live in Concert, 2000, Skowronski Plays! Franck, Szymanowski, Bacewicz and Saint-Saens, 2002, Skowronski Plays! Gentleman Gypsy, 2003, Skowronski Plays Beethoven, Live in Concert, 2003 (Top Ten Best Classical CD award, Chgo. Daily Herald, 2003), Skowronski Plays, Avec et Sans, Live in Concert, 2004 (Top Ten Best Classical CD award Chgo. Daily Herald), Skowronski Plays! Avec et Sans, Vol. II, Honegger, Milhaud, Engel, Bloch & Szymanowski, Live in Concert, 2006 (Top Ten Best Classical CD award Chgo. Daily Herald), Skowronski Plays! Schumann and Strauss, Live in Concert, 2007; prodr., annotator for LPs Opera Lady I, 1978, Eberley Sings Strauss, 1980, American Girl, 1983, Opera Lady II, 1984; guest performances numerous TV stas. Bd. dirs. Chgo. Youth Orch., 1973-77, v.p., 1974-77; artistic cons. Classical and Protege Symphony Orchs., Chgo., 1994—; spl. cons. Beck Inst. for Arts, Schaumburg, Ill., 1998-2000; adjudicator ice skating shows and competitions Wilmette (Ill.) Park Dist., 1985-89; guest panelist classical performance-career forum Sch. of Music, Northwestern U., Evanston, 1994, 92; guest cons. career symposium Edwin G. Foreman High Sch., Chgo., 1989; mem. mayor's founding com. Evanston Arts Coun., 1974-75; pres. Vincent Skowronski Music Found., Evanston, 1997—. Recipient Excellence in Performance award Northwestern U., 1958, 59, 60, Nat. H.S. Inst., 1958-60, Roy Harris award Inter-Am. U., San German, P.R., 1960, award Am. Fedn. Musicians, 1961, award Soc. Am. Musicians, 1961, McCormick Found. award Chgo. Tribune, 1965, Wade Fetzer award for excellence in performance Northwestern U., 1966, award Crescendo Musical Club, 1967; selected as one of 7 violinists to represent U.S. in IV Internat. Tchaikovsky Competition, Moscow, 1970; Grammy award entry list Best Chamber Music Performance, 2001, 04—; guest dignitary Papal Audience, The Vatican, 1995. Mem. Internat. Platform Assn. (voting mem.), Nat. Acad. Arts and Scis., Sigma Nu Home Phone: 847-491-9155; Office Phone: 847-491-9155. Personal E-mail: skowronskirecordings@ameritech.net.

SKRAINKA, ALAN FREDERICK, securities analyst; b. St. Louis, May 8, 1961; s. Frederick Ralph and Yvonne M. (Oelawder) S.; m. Julie Lynn Wussler, Jan. 24, 1987. BBA in Acctg. and Fin., U. Mo., 1983; MBA, Washington U., 1990. Chartered fin. analyst. Utility analyst Edward D. Jones & Co., St. Louis, 1983—, ltd. ptnr. Maryland Heights, Mo., 1986-88, gen. ptnr., 1988—, chief market strategist, Investment Policy Adv. Com., 1996—. Mem. Fin. Analysts Fedn. Office: Edward D Jones & Co PO Box 190489 Saint Louis MO 63119-6489

SKRAMSTAD, HAROLD KENNETH, JR., museum consultant; b. Washington, June 3, 1941; s. Harold K. and Sarah (Shroat) S.; m. Susan Chappelear, Dec. 28, 1963; children: Robert, Elizabeth. AB, George Washington U., 1963, PhD, 1971. Asst. dir. Am. studies program Smithsonian Instn., Washington, 1969-71, spl. asst. to dir. Nat. Mus. Am. History, 1971, chief spl. projects Nat. Mus. Am. History, chief exhibit programs Nat. Mus. Am. History, 1971-74; dir. Chgo. Hist. Soc., 1974-80; pres. Henry Ford Mus. and Greenfield Village, Dearborn, Mich., 1981—96; mus. cons., 1996—. Mem. Nat. Coun. on Humanities, 1994-2000; mem. mus. mgmt. adv. com. J. Paul Getty Trust, L.A., 1984-90; mem. presdl. commn., action plan, Nat. Mus. African Am. Hsitory and Culture, 2003. Chmn. bd. Met. Detroit Conv. and Visitors Bur., 1993, chmn., mem. exec. com., 1985—; trustee Coll. Art and Design, Detroit, 1981—; mem. Mich. Travel Commn., 1989—. Recipient Charles Frankel prize Nat. Endowment for the Humanities, 1992; named to Centennial Honor Roll Am. Assn. Museums, 2006. Mem. Am. Assn. Mus. (v.p. 1984-88, accreditation commn. 1982, ethics commn. 1992-93), Smithsonian Instn. Nat. Air and Space Mus. (pub. programming adv. com. 1990—), Smithsonian Coun.

SKRETNY, WILLIAM MARION, federal judge; b. Buffalo, Mar. 8, 1945; s. William S. and Rita E. Skretny; m. Carol Ann Skretny; 3 children. AB, Canisius Coll., 1966; JD, Howard U., 1969; LLM, Northwestern U., 1972. Bar: Ill. 1969, U.S. Dist. Ct. (no. dist) Ill. 1969, N.Y. 1972, U.S. Ct. Appeals (7th cir.) 1972, U.S. Dist. Ct. (we. dist.)

N.Y. 1973, U.S. Ct. Appeals (2d cir.) 1976, U.S. Supreme Ct. 1980. Asst. U.S. atty. Office of U.S. Atty. No. Dist. Ill., Chgo., 1971-73, Office of U.S. Atty. We. Dist. N.Y., Buffalo, 1973-81, 1st asst., 1975-81; gen. ptnr. Duke, Holzman, Yaeger & Radlin, Buffalo, 1981-83; 1st dep. dist. atty. Office Dist. Atty Erie County, Buffalo, 1983-88; with Gross, Shuman, Brizdle and Gillfillan, PC, Buffalo, 1988, Cox, Barrell, Buffalo, 1989-90; judge U.S. Dist. Ct. (we. dist.) N.Y., Buffalo, 1990—. Mem. jud. conf. com. on security and facilities, 1994; chair subcom. on planning and space mgmt.; com. liaison for long range planning; spl. counsel U.S. Atty. Gen.'s Advocacy Inst., 1979; staff atty., Office of Spl. Prosecutor U.S. Dept. Justice, 1980. Mem. ABA, Fed. Judges Assn., Bar Assn. of Erie County, Di Gamma, Phi Alpha Delta, Alpha Sigma Nu. Republican. Roman Catholic. Office: US District Court 68 Court St Rm 507 Buffalo NY 14202-3405 Office Phone: 716-332-7820.

SKRINSKY, ALEXANDER NIKOLAEVICH, physicist, researcher; b. Orenburg, Russia, Jan. 15, 1936; s. Nikolai Alexandrovich Skrinsky and Galina Stepanova Skrinskaya; m. Lidiya Borisovna Golovanova, Sept. 12, 1961; children: Yulia, Nikolai. D in Phys. Math. Sci., Russian Acad. Scis., Inst. Nuc. Physics, Novosibirsk, 1965. Corr. mem. Russian Acad. Sci., Moscow, 1968-70, mem., academician, 1970—, dir. Inst. Nuclear Physics, Siberian divsn., 1978—, chmn., academician-sec. Nuclear Physics Sec., 1988—. Mem. sci. policy com. European Orgn. Nuclear Rsch., Geneva, 1986-92; mem. internat. com. future accelerators Internat. Com. Future Accelerators, 1981-88, chmn., 1989-92; mem. extended sci. coun. Deutches Elektronen Synchrotron, Hamburg, 1995-2002. Contbr. more than 300 articles to profl. publs. Recipient Lenin prize, State Com. in L. Prizes Soviet Union, 1967, State prize, State Com. of Soviet Union, 1989, Veksaler Golden medal, Russian Acad. Sci., 1991, Kapitsa Golden medal, 2004, Wilson prize, Am. Phys. Soc., 2002, State prize, Russian Fedn., 2005, Karpinsky prize, A. Toepfer Stiftung, 2003. Fellow: Am. Phys. Soc.; mem.: Royal Swedish Acad. Sci. Home: Zolotodolinskaya Str 81 Novosibirsk 630090 Russia Office: Inst Nuclear Physics Ac Lavrentiev Av 11 Novosibirsk 630090 Russia Home Phone: 7 383 330-2202; Office Phone: 7 383 330-6031.

SKRIP, CATHY LEE, psychologist; b. Berwyn, Ill., July 19, 1948; d. Raymond Joseph and Gladys Catherine (Mazanec) Jirsa; m. Paul Joseph Skrip, Aug. 29, 1970; children: Carrie Anne, Christie Ellen, Jonathan Paul. AB in English, Miami U., Ohio, 1969; MS in Counseling, Calif. State U., LA, 1971. Cert. counselor, Calif.; lic. psychologist Minn. 1990. Counselor, instr. Rio Hondo Coll., Whittier, Calif., 1971-73; instr. N. Shore C.C., Beverly, Mass., 1974-75, counselor, dir. of placement, 1973-75; instr. Western Wis. Tech. Inst., La Crosse, Wis., 1975; asst. dir. Cmty. Care Orgn. of La Crosse County, Inc., Wis., 1976-79; planning analyst Dept. Health and Social Svcs., Madison, Wis., 1979-80; vol. co-facilitator battered women's support group Alexandra House, Circle Pines, Minn., 1985-88; pvt. practice Hugo, Minn., 1992—98, Crystal, Minn., 1993—98, New Hope, Minn., 1998—2003, Forest Lake, Minn., 1998—. Charter trustee 621 Found., Shoreview, Minn., 1988-91, co-chair, 1990-91, chair, 1991-92, mem. 20th anniversary com.; sec. Rio Hondo Coll. Faculty Assn., Whittier Calif., 1972-73. Author: (with Kristin Kunzman) Women With Secrets: Dealing With Domestic Abuse and Childhood Sexual Abuse in Treatment, 1991. Treas. LWV, La Crosse, 1978-81; mem. Ramsey County Cmty. Initiative to End Family Violence, 1990—94, Family Violence Tng. Task Force, St. Paul, 1991, Mounds View Violence Prevention Coun., 1993—97, Anoka County Domestic Violence Coun., 1994—97, Forest Lake C. of C., 2003-; chair sch. adv. com. Chippewa Elem. Ctr., St. Paul, 1986-87; bd. dirs. YWCA, La Crosse, 1980-81; adv. com. Social Work Dept. U. Wis., La Crosse, 1981-82; bd. dirs. Ret. Sr. Vol. Program, La Crosse, 1980-82; founder, exec. dir. Abuse Resource Ctr., St. Paul, 1988-92; exec. dir. Abuse Resource Ctr. Hugo, 1992-93. Recipient Bertha Provine Oxford Coll. scholarship, Miami U., Oxford, Ohio, 1968, Alumni Assn. Departmental Honors award Calif. State U., LA, 1971. Mem. Minn. Women in Psychology (social action chair 1992-94, Greater Minn. co-chair 1993-94, steering com. 1992-98, vice-chair 1994-95, chair 1995-97, Founding Mother's award 2007, Profl. Devel.-Mentoring Com. 2008-), Minn. Psychol. Assn., Minn. Soc. Clin. Hypnosis, Alpha Omicron Pi. Roman Catholic. Avocations: sewing, bicycling, crafts, running, canoeing. Office: 20 North Lake St Ste 308 Forest Lake MN 55025 Office Phone: 651-464-8918.

SKROBELA, KATHERINE CREELMAN, music producer, data processing executive; b. NYC, Jan. 18, 1941; d. George Douglas and Marjorie Ethel (Broer) Creelman; m. Paul John Skrobela, May 23, 1970 (dec. Feb. 1999). AB, Vassar Coll., 1962; MLS, Columbia U., 1964. Music cataloger Bklyn. Coll., 1964-71; music libr. Middlebury (Vt.) Coll., 1971-80; programmer ADT Co., NYC, 1981-83; sr. cons. Marathon Software & Svcs. Inc., 1983-90; sr. programmer analyst Chase Manhattan Bank, 1990-2000; dir. tech. info., agt. support Brown Harris Stevens, 2003—. Pres. Miranda Music, Inc., 1995—. Editor Music Cataloging bull., 1970-75; prodr. Blame It On My Youth: Berri Blair Sings Ballads, 1999, Karen Oberlin: My Standards, 2000, Christopher Gines: The Way It Goes, 2001, Karen Oberlin: Secret Love: the Music of Doris Day, 2002, John Wallowitch & Bertram Ross: Wallowitch & Ross, 2002, Marcus Simeone: At Last, 2007; author:(dance) I care not for these ladies; composer Magnificat. Treas., bd. dirs. Middlebury Farmers Market, 1979; dir. St. Stephen's Motet Choir, Middlebury, 1975-78; membership chair Bklyn. Bot. Garden Aux, 2003-2007, mem. com. 2008-; treas. Vassar Class of 1962, 2002-05. Recipient Chase Manhattan Bank Excalibur award, 1992. Mem. ALA, Music Libr. Assn. (chmn. com. on cataloging, rep. to ALA catalog code revision com.), Music OCLC Users Group, UFO-Cobol/XE Internat. Users Group (v.p. 1989-91), Country Dance and Song Soc. Am., Manhattan Assn. Cabarets and Clubs, Grace Ch. Bklyn. Choir, NY Sheet Music Soc. Democrat. Episcopalian. Avocations: music, cabaret, singing, dance, needlepoint. Home: 234 Lincoln Rd Brooklyn NY 11225-3432 Office: Brown Harris Stevens 129 Montague St Brooklyn NY 11201 Office Phone: 718-858-5736. Personal E-mail: ceo@mirandamusic.com. Business E-Mail: kskrobela@bhsusa.com.

SKROMME, BRIAN J., engineering educator; b. Giffnock, Scotland, May 16, 1957; came to U.S., 1962; s. Austin G. and Jane I. (Brisben) S.; m. Kathryn K. Katzan, Dec. 5, 1987 (div. May 15, 2006); children: Sara, Daniel, Leah, Matthew. BS with high honors, U. Wis., 1978; MS, U. Ill., 1980, PhD, 1985. Rsch. asst. U. Ill., 1978-84; mem. tech. staff Bellcore, Red Bank, N.J., 1985-89; assoc. prof. Ariz. State U., 1989—2006, prof., 2006—. Proposal reviewer NSF, 1992—, Israeli Basic Rsch. Found., 1991; jour. referee Phys. Rev. B, Phys. Rev. Letters, Applied Physics Letters, others, 1984—. Contbr. 5 chpts. to books; over 75 articles to profl. jours.; over 42 papers to conf. procs. Rsch. grantee NSF, 1991—, Motorola, Inc., 1994-95, DARPA, 1994-97, 2003-04, Office of Naval Rsch., Def. Advanced Rsch. Projects Agy., 2001-06, 08-09. Mem. IEEE (sr.), Am. Phys. Soc., Materials Rsch. Soc. Achievements include discovery of doping-induced structural transformation in SIC, investigations of effects of structural defects on SIC devices, determination of electronic properties of ALN and dopant impurities in several important compound semiconductor materials using optical spectroscopy. Office: Ariz State U Dept Elec Engring Tempe AZ 85287-5706

SKROMME, LAWRENCE H., consulting agricultural engineer; b. Roland, Iowa, Aug. 26, 1913; s. Austin G. and Ingeborg B. (Holmedal) S.; m. Margaret Elizabeth Gleason, June 24, 1939; children: Cherlyn Sue Granrose, Inga Jean Hill, Karen Ann Sequino. BS with honors, Iowa State U., Ames, 1937. Registered profl. engr., Pa. Design and test engr. Goodyear Tire and Rubber Co., Akron, Ohio, 1937-41; project engr., asst. chief engr. Harry Ferguson Inc., Detroit, 1941-51; chief engr. Sperry New Holland div. Sperry Corp., New Holland, Pa., 1951-61, v.p. engring., 1961-78; cons. agrl. engr. Lancaster, Pa., 1978—. Mem. adv. bd. U.S. Congresss Com. on Sci. and Tech., 1989—93; cons. AID, World Bank, others, 1978—85, Saudi Arabia, 1985—86. Patentee; contbr. articles to profl. jours. Dir., pres. Farm and Home Found., Lancaster County, 1968—90, Lancaster County Agrl. Land Preservation Bd., 1978—2002, sec.-treas., 1989—99, dir. emeritus, 2002—; rsch. adv. com. U.S. Dept. Agr., Washington, 1964—68; gov.'s com. agr. and land preservation Gov. of Pa., 1969; bd. dirs. awards com. Engrs. Joint Coun., NYC, 1967—75. Fellow: Am. Soc. Agrl. Engrs. (v.p. 1952—55, pres. 1959—60, Gold medal 1974); mem.: NAE (peer and membership com. 1978—82), Am. Soc. Engring. Edn., Internat. Assn. Agrl. Engrs. (v.p. 1974—79, pres. farm machine divsn.), Nat. Soc. Profl. Engrs., Tau Beta Pi, Alpha Zeta, Phi Kappa Phi. Republican. Methodist. Avocations: collecting old tools and antiques, farm machinery history.

SKROWACZEWSKI, STANISLAW, conductor, composer; b. Lwow, Poland, Oct. 3, 1923; came to U.S., 1960; s. Pawel and Zofia (Karszniewicz) S.; m. Krystyna Jarosz, Sept. 6, 1956; children: Anna, Paul, Nicholas. Diploma faculty philosophy, U. Lwow, 1945; diploma faculties composition and conducting, Acad. Music Lwow, 1945, Conservatory at Krakow, Poland, 1946; L.H.D., Hamline U., 1963, Macalester Coll., 1972; L.H.D. hon. doctorate, U. Minn.; Doctorate (hon.), U. Wroclaw, Poland, 2003. Guest condr. in, Europe, S.A., U.S., 1947—; Composer, 1931—; pianist, 1928—; violinist, 1934—; condr., 1939—; permanent condr., music dir. Wroclaw (Poland) Philharmonic, 1946-47, Katowice (Poland) Nat. Philharmonic, 1949-54, Krakow Philharmonic, 1955-56, Warsaw Nat. Philharmonic Orch., 1957-59, Minnesota Orch., 1960-79; prin. condr., mus. adviser Halle Orch., Manchester, Eng., 1984-91; musical advisor St. Paul Chamber Orchestra, 1986—87, Milw. Symphony, 1995—97; prin. condr. Yominri Nippon Symphony Orch., Tokyo, 2007—; prin. conductor Nippon Symphony Orch., Tokyo, 2007—. First symphony and overture for orch. written at age 8, played by Lwow Philharm. Orch., 1931; adv. music Milw. Symphony, 1994-97. Composer: 4 symphonies Prelude and Fugue for Orchestra (conducted first performance Paris), 1948, Overture, 1947 (2d prize Szymanowski Concours, Warsaw 1947); Cantiques des Cantiques, 1951, String Quartet, 1953 (2d Prize Internat. Concours Composers, Belgium 1953), Suite Symphonique, 1954 (first prize, gold medal Composers Competition Moscow 1957), Music at Night, 1954, Ricercari Notturni, 1978 (3d prize Kennedy Center Friedheim Competition, Washington), Concerti for Clarinet and Orch., 1980, Violin Concerto, 1985, Concerto for Orch., 1985, Fanfare for Orch., 1987, Sextett for Oboe, Violin, Viola, Orchestra, 1980, String Trio for Violin, Viola, 1990, Triple Concerto for Violin, Clarinet, Piano, Orchestra, 1992, Fantasie per Tre (Flute, Oboe, Cello), 1993, Chamber Concerto, 1993, Passacaglia Immaginaria for Orch., 1995, Musica a Quattro for Clarinet, Violin, Viola, Cello, 1998, Concerto for Orch., 1998, Symphony, 2003; also music for theatre, motion pictures, songs and piano sonatas, English horn concerto; rec. by Mercury, Columbia, RCA, Albany, Victor, Vox, EMI, Angel. Decorated comdrs. cross Polonia Restituta, Highest Polish award Gold medal, Gloria Artist, 2007; recipient nat. prize for artistic activity Poland, 1953, 1st prize Santa Cecilia Internat. Concours for Condrs., Rome, 1956, Cannes Festival award for best rec. of 19th century symphonic music, 2002, Disting. Artist award McKnight Found., 2004. Mem. Union Polish Composers, Internat. Soc. Modern hon. doctorate at New England Consenatory Boston 2008 Music, Nat. Assn. Am. Composers-Condrs., Am. Music Center. Office: PO Box 700 Wayzata MN 55391

SKRUPKY, ELAINE CHARLOTTE, art educator; b. Amery, Wis., Nov. 11, 1927; d. Herbert Roy Peterson and Nina Louise Olson; m. Hartford Gay Elaine Charlotte Peterson, June 24, 1950 (dec. Aug. 2, 1982); children: Lynn, Jenene, Van(dec.), Renée, Shawndel(dec.). BSc in Art and English, River Falls U., 1949. Art supr. Rice Lake (Wis.) Schs., 1949—50; art tchr. U. Wis. Ctr., Rice Lake, 1968—69, VIII Pk., Jensen Beach, Fla., 1993—. Author: Poetry Guild Anthology, 1996 (Editors Choice award, 1996), The Best Poems of the 90's, 1997 (named Internat. Poet of Merit, Internat. Soc. Poetry, 1997), Of Moonlight and Wishes, 1997, A Celebration of Poets, 1998, sound of Poetry, 1998; Extra Burt Reynold's B.L. T V Show, 1991. Chmn. and organizer Aquafest Art Show, Rice Lake, 1960—75; chmn. state fine arts Wis. Fedn. Women's Clubs, 1972—74, state drama chmn., 1974—76, dist. art chmn., 1976; pres. Daubers Guild, Rice Lake, 1976—77; chmn. Am. Cancer Dr., Rice Lake, 1979—80, Heart Drive, Rice Lake, 1980; organizer The Red Barn Theatre, Rice Lake; ch. choir Densen Beach Fla., 1989—2009. Recipient State Art award, Rural Artists Wis., 1979, 4th runner-up, Ms. Nat. Sr Queen Contest, 1998, State Achievement award, Wis. Federated Woman's Club, 2000, 2001; named Outstanding Woman in Arts, 2000; named to Internat. Hall of Fame, Internat. Soc. Poetry, 2000. Mem.: Art League, Alpha Psi Omega, Art Gallery Coop, Poetry Club. Avocations: painting, writing, piano, singing, acting. Home (Winter): 10701 S Ocean Dr Jensen Beach FL 34957 Home Phone: 772-229-9502.

SKRUTSKIE, MICHAEL F., science educator; PhD, Cornell U., 1987. Prof. U. Mass., Amherst, 1987—2001; prof. astronomy U. Va., Charlottesville, Va., 2001—. Contbr. articles to profl. jours. Co-recipient James Craig Watson medal, NAS, 2007. Achievements include being the Principal Investigator of the Two Micron All Sky Survey (2MASS) and the developer of several astronomical, near-infrared cameras and spectrographs. Office: Dept Astronomy U Va 262 Astronomy Bldg PO Box 400325 Charlottesville VA 22904-4325 Office Phone: 434-924-4328. Office Fax: 434-924-3104. Business E-Mail: skrutskie@virginia.edu.

SKULINA, THOMAS RAYMOND, lawyer; b. Cleve., Sept. 14, 1933; s. John J. and Mary B. (Vesely) S. AB, John Carroll U., 1955; JD, Case Western Res. U., 1959, LLM, 1962. Bar: Ohio 1959, U.S. Supreme Ct. 1964, ICC 1965. Ptnr. Skulina & Stringer, Cleve., 1967-72, Riemer Oberdank & Skulina, Cleve., 1978-81, Skulina, Fillo, Walters & Negrelli, 1981-86, Skulina & McKeon, Cleve., 1986-90, Skulina & Hill, Cleve., 1990-97; atty. Penn Ctrl. Transp. Co., Cleve., 1960-65, asst. gen. atty., 1965-78, trial counsel, 1965-76; with Consol. Rail Corp., 1976-78; pvt. practice Cleve., 1997—. Tchr. comml. law Practicing Law Inst., N.Y.C., 1970; practicing labor arbitrator Fed. Mediation and Conciliation Svc., 1990—; arbitrator Mcpl. Securities Rulemaking Bd., 1994-98, N.Y. Stock Exch., 1995—, NASD, 1996—; mediator NASD, 1997—, AAA Comml., 1997—; mediator vol. panel EEOC, 1997-99, contract panel, 1999-2000; arbitrator Better Bus. Bur., 2000—. Contbr. articles to legal jours. Income tax and fed. fund coord. City of Warrensville Heights, Ohio, 1970—77; spl. counsel City of North Olmstead, Ohio, 1971—75; spl. counsel to Ohio Atty. Gen., 1983—93, Cleve. Charter Rev. Commn., 1988, referee, 1986—; fact-finder State Employees Rels. Bd., Ohio, 1986—; hearing officer Human Resource Commn., Summit County, Ohio, 2000—03. With US Army, 1959. Mem. ABA (R.R. and motor carrier com. 1988-96, jr. chmn. 1989-96, alt. dispute resolution com. 1999—), FBA, Assn. Conflict Resolution, Cleve. Bar Assn. (grievance com. 1987-93, chmn. 1997-98, trustee 1993-96, ADR com. 1997—), Ohio Bar Assn. (bd. govs. litigation sect. 1986-98, negligence law com. 1989-96, ethics and profl. responsibility com. 1990-91, alt. dispute resolution com. 1996—), Am. Arbitration Assn. (practicing labor arbitrator 1987—), Nat. Acad. Arbitrators, Nat. Assn. R.R. Trial Counsel (emeritus), Internat. Assn. Law and Sci., Pub. Sector Labor Rels. Assn., Internat. Indsl. Rels. Rsch. Assn., Soc. Fed. Labor and Employee Rels. Profls. Democrat. Roman Catholic. Home: 3162 W 165th St Cleveland OH 44111-1016 Office: 24803 Detroit Rd Westlake OH 44145 Home Phone: 216-221-4910; Office Phone: 440-899-1911. E-mail: tskulina@sbcglobal.net.

SKURLA, WILLIAM CHARLES, bishop; b. Duluth, Minn., June 1, 1956; BA in Philosophy, Columbia U., 1981; MDiv, Mary Immaculate Sem., Northampton, Pa., 1986, ThM, 1987. Professed mem. Franciscan Order, 1985; ordained priest Holy Dormitions Monastery, Sybertsville, Pa., 1987; ordained bishop, 2002; bishop Eparchy of Van Nuys (Ruthenian), Calif., 2002—07, Eparchy of Passaic (Ruthenian), NJ, 2007—. Roman Catholic. Office: Eparchy of Passaic 445 Lackawanna Ave West Paterson NJ 07424-7175

SKUTNIK, BOLESH J., optics scientist, lay worker, lawyer; b. Passaic, NJ, Aug. 19, 1941; s. Boleslaw Stanley and Helen Marie (Dzierzynska) S.; m. Phyllis Victoria Wojciechowski, Sept. 2, 1967 (div. July 1991); m. Anita Marie Bacon, Aug. 2, 1997; children: Pam, Janeen, Todd, Darren. BS, Seton Hall U., 1962; MS, Yale U., 1964, PhD, 1967; JD, U. Conn., 1995. Bar: N.Y. 1996, Conn. 1996, U.S. Patent and Trademark Office 1992. Chief scientist Ensign Bickford Coating Co., Simsbury, Conn., 1979-91; prin. B.J. Assocs., New Britain, Conn., 1991-97, West Hartford, Conn., 1997—; patent atty., rsch. scientist Fiberoptic Fabrications, Inc., East Longmeadow, Mass., 1995-97; dir. rsch., dir. patents and licensing Sci. Fiberoptic Fabrications, Inc., East Longmeadow, Mass., 1997—2002; corp. counsel, dir. rsch. CeramOptec Industries, Inc., East Longmeadow, Mass., 2003—. Lector, mem. parish coun. St. Catherine of Siena, West Simsbury, Conn., 1980-85, St. Maurice, New Britain, Conn., 1985-2000, St. Thomas Apostle, West Hartford, 2000-06; chmn., del. synod Archdiocese of Hartford, Conn., 1990-96; chmn. parish Holy Family Retreat League, New Britain, 1989-2000; pres. Enbic Employees Credit Union, Simsbury, 1988-91; asst. prof. chemistry Fairfield U., Conn., 1973-79. Contbr. articles to profl. jours. Interviewer Yale Alumni Schs. Com., L.I. and Hartford, Conn., 1969—; rep. New Britain Club, 1997-2000; mem. New Britain Mus. Am. Art, Hillstead Mus., Wadsworth Mus., Smithsonian, Ctr. Polish Culture, DC, Bushnell Soc. Mem. ABA (subcom. chair 1993, 94, 96), Conn. Bar Assn., N.Y. State Bar Assn., Conn. Intellectual Property Lawyers Assn., Am. Intellectual Property Lawyers Assn., Soc. Photo-optical Engrs. (conf. co-chair, 1987-90, 2006), Optical Soc. Am., Am. Ceramic Soc., (coord. symposium 1991), Materials Rsch. Soc. (chair symposium 1987-89), Am. Chem. Soc. (alt. coun. 1988-90. sect. chair 1994, vice chair 1993, bd. dirs. 1985-2002), Porsche Club Am. (various positions Conn. Valley region), Yale Club New Britain (dir. 1994-2000), Yale Club Hartford, Yale Alumni Assn. Roman Catholic. Achievements include patents in field. Home: 51 Banbury Ln West Hartford CT 06107-1102 Office: CeramOptec Industries Inc 515 Shaker Rd East Longmeadow MA 01028-3126 Office Phone: 413-525-8222. Personal E-mail: boleshsj@aol.com. Business E-Mail: bolesh.skutnik@ceramoptec.com. *The human spirit is stronger than anything that can happen to it.*

SKVORETZ, JOHN VINCENT, sociologist, educator; b. Allentown, Pa., Sept. 8, 1947; s. John Vincent and Ruth Elizabeth (Heffelfinger) S.; m. Sharon Louise Anthony, Aug. 31, 1968 (div. Oct. 1998), Gretchen Elizabeth Koehler, May 15, 1999; children Jonathan, Christopher, Matthew. B.A. in Sociology, Lehigh U., 1969, B.A. in Math., 1969; Ph.D. in Sociology, U. Pitts., 1976. Prof. sociology U. S.C., Columbia, 1986-2005, Coll. Arts and Sci. USF, 2005-08, dean, chmn. dept. sociology, 1984—94. Assoc. editor Social Forces, 1984-87. Contbr. articles to profl. jours. NSF fellow, 1970-73. Mem. Am. Sociol. Assn., So. Sociol. Soc., Phi Beta Kappa. Democrat. Office: USF Dept Sociology 4202 E Fowler Ave CPR 107 Tampa FL 33620-5550 Office Phone: 813-974-7288.

SKWARA, ERICH WOLFGANG, writer, poet, critic, literature educator; b. Salzburg, Austria, Nov. 4, 1948; came to U.S., 1975, naturalized, 1981. s. Alois Gaigg and Hermine Maria Skwara; m. Victoria Anne Dufresne, July 10, 1974 (div. Mar. 1978); m. Gloria Elaine Winniski, June 8, 1978; children: Gabriella Maria, Alexandra Felicitas. BA, U. Paris VII, 1970; MA, Salzburg U., 1972; PhD, SUNY, Albany, 1985. Instr. U. Md., Balt., 1975-77; freelance author Balt. and Paris, 1977-82; vis. lectr. Georgetown U., Washington, D.C., 1982-84; freelance author Salzburg, 1984-86; prof. humanities, comparative lit. and German San Diego State U., 1986—. Dep. editor-in-chief for cultural affairs Die Welt, Berlin, 1993; cultural and lit. corr. for a number of German and Austrian newspapers and media, 1979—; worldwide readings and lecture tours. Author: (novels) Black Sails, 1979, 99, The Cool Million, 1990, Tristan Island, 1992, Die Heimlichen Könige, 1995, Plague in Siena, 1994, 95, Ice on the Bridge, 1997, Versuch einer Heimkehr, 1998, Nach dem Norden, 1998, The Angel of Death, 1998, Anruf aus Rom, 1999, Pest in Siena, 2001, Zerbrechlichkeit, 2002, Träumeerzählen, 2002; Entwurf einer Wste, 2008, Iun Facial Fall, 2010, translated (from English and French to German) works by T. Williams, Thomas Wolfe, J.J. Rousseau, Gustave Flaubert; own works translated into English, French, Japanese, Arabic, Latvian. Recipient Hermann-Lenz-Preis, Germany, 2002; named Hon. citizen, City of Trois-Rivières, Que., Can., 2004; awarded title of prof., Republic of Austria, 2003. Mem. Internat. PEN Club (Austria, France ctrs). Roman Catholic. Avocations: fine wines, travel, walking. Office: San Diego State U Dept Classics Humanities San Diego CA 92182 also: Suhrkamp Verlag Linden Str 29-35 D60325 Frankfurt am Main Germany E-mail: poetskwara@aol.com.

SKWERES, THOMAS W., sales executive, advertising executive, public relations executive, investor, entrepreneur; b. Chgo., May 11, 1929; s. Marion and Sophie R. (Rataiczyk) Skweres; m. Charmaine Liska, 1950 (dec. 2000); m. Carol Lynn Conlon, 2004; children: Thomas Allan, Pamela Charmaine Hulten, Patricia Ann Jacobs. Degree, Wright City Coll., 1949. Attended Northwestern U., Chgo. Campus, 1949—51, 1953—56; prodn. art dept. asst. Hamilton Advt. Agy., 1949—51; prodn. and art dept. Reincke, Meyer & Finn Advt. Agy., Chgo., 1953—55; art dir., prodn. mgr. Hanson & Stevens Advt. Agy. (formerly Hanson & Hanson Advt. Agy.), 1955—58, v.p., account exec., 1958—61; v.p. sales, gen. mgr. Ross & White, Wheeling, Ill., 1961—84; sales mgr. Graphics Plus, Lisle, Ill., 1984—89, Essig Printing, Lisle, Ill., 1989—91; founder Tomco Enterprises, 1991, pres. sr. Sentinels Tomco Printing; ptnr. and CEO Lucky Touch Enterprise. Treas., dir. ABC Property Mgmt.; maj. Adv., Mktg. and Journalism. Mem. various C. of Cs. Wright Coll. SSgt US Army, 1951—53, Eurorean Theatre, artillery instr. 1st divsn. NCO Acad. 30th F.A. Battalion T.I.&E. officer US Army, attended Army Sch. US Army, Inactive reserves, 1953—58. Mem.: Troop Info. and Edn.,

Am. Legion, Men's Club (pres.), ETA-IOTA-PSI. Avocations: travel, writing, poetry. Office: PO Box 475 Lisle IL 60532 Office Phone: 630-964-1453. Business E-Mail: ctskw116@yahoo.com.

SKYLER, EDWARD GABRIEL, city official; b. NYC, Apr. 11, 1973; s. Martin and Rita Skyler. BA in History, U. Pa., 1995; JD, Fordham U. Sch. Law, 2000. Dep. chief of staff, pub. info. dir. NYC Dept. Parks & Recreation, 1995—99; dep. press sec. to Mayor Rudolph W. Giuliani NYC, NYC, 1999—2000; with corp. comm. dept. Bloomberg L.P., NYC, 2000—01; press. sec. Michael Bloomberg's Mayoral Campaign, 2001; press sec., then comm. dir. to Mayor Michael Bloomberg NYC, 2002—06, dep. mayor for adminstrn., 2006—07, dep. mayor for ops., 2007—. Mem.: NY State Bar. Office: City Hall Office of Mayor New York NY 10007 Office Phone: 212-788-3191. Office Fax: 212-788-3229.

SKYLER, JAY S., medical educator, consultant; b. Phila., Feb. 14, 1947; m. Mercedes Armas Bach, Aug. 9, 2003; children: Jennifer Anne, Alexandra Regina Bach, Marcus Richard Bach. BS, Pa. State U., 1967; MD, Jefferson Med. Coll., 1969. Diplomate in internal medicine, also endocrinology, diabetes and metabolism Am. Bd. Internal Medicine. Intern, resident in internal medicine, fellow in endocrinology and metabolism Duke U., Durham, NC, 1969—73, assoc. then asst. prof., 1972—76; assoc. prof. then prof., medicine, pediatrics and psychology, divsn. endocrinology, diabetes, and metabolism, dept. medicine U. Miami, Fla., 1976—. Pres. Am. Diabetes Assn., Alexandria, Va., 1991—92; v.p. Internat. Diabetes Fedn., Brussels, 1994—2000; bd. dirs. Amylin Pharms., San Diego, DexCom, Inc, San Diego. Founding editor-in-chief (med. jour.) Diabetes Care, 1978—82, scientific editor Internat. Diabetes Monitor, 1989—, assoc. editor Diabetes Technology & Therapeutics, 2006—. With USPHS, 1973—75. Master: ACP (mem. bd. regents 1996—99, chmn., coun. of subspecialty societies); mem.: Internat. Diabetes Fedn. (past v.p.), So. Soc. for Clin. Investigation, Internat. Diabetes Immunotherapy Group, Am. Diabetes Assn. (past pres.). Independent. Achievements include research in multiple developments for treatment of diabetes. Office: Univ of Miami Diabetes Research Institut Ste 3054 1450 NW 10th Ave Miami FL 33136 Office Fax: 305-243-4484. Business E-Mail: jskyler@miami.edu.

SKYLSTAD, WILLIAM STEPHEN, bishop; b. Omak, Wash., Mar. 2, 1934; s. Stephen Martin and Reneldes Elizzbeth (Danzl) Skylstad. Student, Pontifical Coll.Josephinium, Worthington, Ohio, 1948—60; student Wash. State U., 1960—61; MA in Edn., Gonzaga U., 1966. Ordained priest Diocese of Spokane, Wash., 1960; asst. pastor Pullman, Wash., 1960-62; tchr. Mater Cleri Sem., 1961-68, rector, 1968-74; pastor Assumption Parish, Spokane, 1974-76; chancellor Diocese of Spokane, 1976-77; ordained bishop, 1977; bishop Diocese of Yakima, Wash., 1977-90, Diocese of Spokane, Wash., 1990—. V.p. US Conf. of Catholic Bishops, 2001—04, pres., 2004—. Roman Catholic. Office: Diocese of Spokane PO Box 1453 1023 W Riverside Ave Spokane WA 99210-1453 E-mail: bishop@dioceseofspokane.org.

SLAATTE, HOWARD ALEXANDER, minister, philosophy educator; b. Evanston, Ill., Oct. 18, 1919; s. Iver T. and Esther (Larsen) S.; m. Mildred Gegenheimer, June 20, 1951; children: Elaine Slaatte, Mark, Paul. AA, Kendall Coll., 1940; BA cum laude, U. ND, 1942; B.D. cum laude, Drew U., 1945, PhD, 1956; Drew fellow, Mansfield Coll., Oxford U., Eng., 1949-50. Ordained to ministry Meth. Ch. as elder, 1943. Pastor Detroit Conf. United Meth. Ch., 1950-65; assoc. prof. systematic theology Temple U., 1956-60; vis. prof., prof. philosophy and religion McMurry Coll. (now named McMurry U.), 1960-65; prof. dept. philosophy Marshall U., Huntington, W.Va., 1965-89, prof. emeritus, 1989—, chmn. dept., 1966-81, mem. grad. council, 1970-73, mem. research bd., 1974-76, mem. acad. standards and policy com., 1975-77, research grantee, 1976, 77; mem. bd. Campus Christian Center, 1973-75; prof. ethics St. Leo (Fla.) Coll., 1993. Lectr. Traverse City (Mich.) State Hosp., 1966-71, Am. Ontoanalytical Assn. internat. conf., Acapulco, Mex., 1970, World Congress Logotherapy, San Diego, 1980, other orgns. Author: Time and Its End, 1962, Fire in the Brand, 1963, The Pertinence of the Paradox, 1968, The Paradox of Existentialist Theology, 1971, Modern Science and the Human Condition, 1974, The Arminian Arm of Theology, 1977, The Dogma of Immaculate Perception, 1979, Discovering Your Real Self, 1980, The Seven Ecumenical Councils, 1980, The Creativity of Consciousness, 1983, Contemporary Philosophies of Religion, 1986, Time, Existence and Destiny, 1988, Critical Survey of Ethics, 1988; co-author: The Philosophy of Martin Heidegger, 1983, Religious Issues in Contemporary Philosophy, 1988, Our Cultural Cancer and Its Cure, 1995, A Re-Appraisal of Kierkegaard, 1995, Plato's Dialogues and Ethics, 1999, A Purview of Wesley's Theology, 2000; contbr. Analecta Frankliana, 1981; gen. editor: (series) Contemporary Existentialism; contbr. to theol. and philos. jours. Mem. W.Va. Conf. United Meth. Ch., 1966-87, ret., 1987; bd. dirs. Inst. for Advanced Philos. Research, 1979-90; chmn. bd. dirs. Salvation Army of Huntington, W. Va.; courtesy prof. U. South Fla., 1993-99. Recipient Outstanding Educators of Am. award, 1975, Profl. Excellence award Faculty Merit Found., State of W.Va., 1986, U. N.D. Found. award, 2000; named to Honorable Order of Ky. Colonels, W.Va. Ambassador of Good Will; named Internat. Man of Yr., 1993; NSF fellow, 1965, Benedum Found. rsch. grantee, 1970, NSF rsch.-grantee, 1965, 71. Mem. W.Va. Philos. Assn. (pres., 1966-67, 83-84), Am. Philos. Assn., AAUP, Am. Acad. Religion. Home: 10820 Penny Rd Apt 119 Cary NC 27518 *Most knowledge is relative, a balanced existential position with empirical implications, except for the divine Absolute encountered by faith in existence. The revealed principles opened up thereby, especially the ultimacy of sacrifical love (Agape), give basis and motivation for vital morality and a healthy culture. True freedom springs from commitment to these principles.*

SLACHTA, GREGORY ANDREW, urologist; b. Paterson, NJ, Mar. 17, 1946; s. Andrew Gregory and Mary Catherine (Shimko) S.; children: Gregory Andrew, Lara Ann, Andrea; m. Patricia A. Albano, Nov. 7, 1981. BS, Pa. State U., 1966; MD, Jefferson Med. Coll., 1968. Diplomate Am. Bd. Urology. Intern Lankenan Hosp., Phila., 1968—69; resident urology Temple U. Hosp., Phila., 1969—70, 1973—75; pvt. practice, Springfield, Mass., 1975—97, Hilton Head Med. Group, SC, 1997—99. Author: Inflammatory Diseases of the Male Genital Tract, 1982. Mem. City Coun. Com. for Health Ins., Springfield, 1984, Springfield Planning Bd., 1991; vice-chmn. UROPAC, 2003-08. Maj. US Army, 1971—73. Fellow ACS; mem. AMA, Am. Urol. Assn. (chmn. socioecon. com. 1986-91, del. to AMA 1991-2008), Mass. Med. Soc. (alt. del. to AMA 1986-91, vice chmn. legis. and nat. legis. affairs com. 1987-89), Hampden Dist. Med. Soc. (pres. 1986-88), Mass. Assn. Practicing Urologists (pres. 1985-87), Beaufort County Med. Soc. (pres. 1998-2001). Republican. Roman Catholic.

SLACIK, CLAUDIA, bank executive; b. 1957; AB, Smith Coll.; MBA, NYU; grad., French Culinary Inst., NYC. V.p., strategic planning World Color Press, 1992; head, asset based fin. group, global fixed income group Citigroup, NYC, sr. credit officer, global head, trade services, fin., 2004—. Bd. dirs. Jonathan Woodner Co., Wickes Co.; founding dir. North Fork Women's Health Fund, LI; co-chair, bd. dirs. Callen-Lorde Cmty. Health Ctr., NYC. Named one of 25 Women to Watch, US Banker, 2006, 25 Most Powerful Women in Banking, 2007. Avocation: golf. Office: Citigroup Inc 399 Park Ave New York NY 10043

SLACK, DONALD CARL, agricultural engineer, educator; b. Cody, Wyo., June 25, 1942; s. Clarence Ralbon and Clara May (Beightol) S.; m. Marion Arline Kimball, Dec. 19, 1964; children: Jonel Marie, Jennifer Michelle. BS in Agrl. Engring., U. Wyo., 1965; MS in Agrl. Engring., U. Ky., 1968, PhD in Agrl. Engring., 1975. Registered profl. engr., Ky., Ariz. Asst. civil engr. City of LA, 1965; research specialist U. Ky., Lexington, 1966—70, agrl. engring. advisor Tha Phra, Thailand, 1970—73, rsch. asst. Lexington, 1973—75; from asst. prof. to assoc. prof. agrl. engring. U. Minn., St. Paul, 1975—84; prof. U. Ariz., Tucson, 1984—, head dept. agrl. and biosys. engring., 1991—2009, prof. watershed mgmt., Cecil H. Miller endowed chair, 2006—; co-dir. Arid Lands Sustainable Bioenergy Inst., 2008—. Mem. Mid. East and Mediterranean Desert Devel. Program, 1997—; vis. prof. dept. atmospheric sci. Fed. U. Paraiba, Campina Grande, Brazil, 1997; vis. prof. dept. irrigation Chapingo Autonomous U., Mexico, 2000; tech. adv. Ariz. Dept. Water Resources, Phoenix, 1985—, Tucson active mgmt. area, 1996—; cons. Winrock Internat., Morrilton, Ark., 1984, Water Mgmt. Synthesis II, Logan, Utah, 1985, Desert Agrl. Tech. Sys., Tucson, 1985—, Portek Hermosillo, Mexico, 1989—, World Bank, Washington, 1992—, Malawi Environ. Monitoring Project, 1996, Mex. Inst. for Water Tech., 1997, Nat. Agrl. Rsch. Inst., La Serema, Chile, 1997; cons. F.J. Hansen Inst. for World Peace San Diego State U., 1997—; dep. program support mgr. Rsch. Irrigation Support Project for Asia and the Near East, Arlington, Va., 1987—94; mem. adv. team Cearan Found. for Meteorology and Hydrology, Fortaleza, Brazil, 1995—; mem. internat. adv. panel Matrou Resources Mgmt. Project, World Bank, Egypt, 1996—2000; cons. Internat. Ctr. for Agrl. Rsch. in Dry Areas, 2005; vis. prof., fulbright fellow Khon Kaen U., Thailand, 2009; bd. dirs. Sonoita Vineyards, Ltd., Watershed Mgmt. Group, Inc. Contbr. articles to profl. jours. Named Adminstr. of Yr., Coll. Agrl. & Life Scis., 2004—05. Fellow ASCE (Outstanding Jour. Paper award 1988), Am. Soc. Agrl. Engrs. (Ariz. sect. Engr. of Yr. 1993); mem. US Com. on Irrigation and Drainage (life), Am. Soc. Engring. Edn. (program evaluator accreditation bd. for enring. and tech., 2001—), SAR, Brotherhood of Knights of the Vine (master knight), Rocky Mountain Elk Found. (life), Wyo. Wildlife Fedn. (life); Sigma Xi, Tau Beta Pi, Alpha Epsilon, Gamma Sigma Delta. Democrat. Lutheran. Achievements include patents pending in field; development of infrared based irrigation scheduling device. Avocations: hunting, camping, hiking, model railroading, fishing. Home: 9230 E Visco Pl Tucson AZ 85710-3167 Office: U Ariz Agrl Biosystems Engring Tucson AZ 85721-0038 Home Phone: 520-722-2162; Office Phone: 520-621-7230. Business E-Mail: slackd@email.arizona.edu. *Personal philosophy: Don't take yourself too seriously and don't take anyone else too seriously either.*

SLACK, MOLLY JOHANNA, theater educator; b. Baytown, Tex., Dec. 1, 1951; d. Thomas Edward and Bonnie Burkman Slack. AA, Lon Morris Coll., Jacksonville, Tex., 1972; BA, Trinity U., San Antonio, 1975; M in Liberal Arts, Houston Bapt. U., 1994. Asst. program dir. Houston Bapt. U., 1994—96; tchr. theatre arts Lamar Consol. Sch. Dist., Rosenberg, 1996—. Supts. secondary adv. com. Lamar Consol. Ind. Sch. Dist., Rosenberg, Tex., 1999—2001; site-based mgmt. com. Wessendorff Mid. Sch., 1997—2001, chair dept. fine arts, 2003—, campus coord. U. Interscholastic League, 1996—, bd. mem. PTO, dist. coord. U. Interscholastic League, 2005—. Dir.(designer): Beauty & the Beast, The Pirates of Penzance, Cinderella, H.M.S. Pinafore, Reynard the Fox (Superior One Act Play Festival, 1999), The Adventures of Tom Sawyer, Peter Pan, You're A Good Man, Charlie Brown; set designer Annie, Once Upon a Mattress, Bye, Bye Birdie, Rodger's and Hammerstein's Cinderella, Guys and Dolls. Coord. fine arts related activities Wessendorff Parent/Tchr. Orgn., 2003—06. Recipient Tchr. Yr., Wessendorff Faculty and Staff, 2001; grantee, Lamar Ednl. Found., 2001—02. Mem.: Tex. Ednl. Theatre Assn., Tex. Assn. Gifted and Talented. Avocations: travel, reading, painting, orchids. Home: 14207 Whitecross Drive Houston TX 77083 Office: Wessendorff Middle Sch 5201 Mustang Rosenberg TX 77471 E-mail: mslack@lcisd.org.

SLACK, WARNER VINCENT, medical educator, researcher; b. East Orange, NJ, June 10, 1933; s. Charles Morse Slack and Evelyn Francis Slack; m. Carolyn Paxton Slack, June 23, 1956; children: Alison Townsend, Charles Warner, Jennifer Cora. AB, Princeton U., NJ, 1955; MD, Columbia U., NYC, 1959; MS (hon.), Harvard U., Cambridge, Mass. Lic. physician Mass., 1970. Intern then resident in neurology U. Wis., Madison, 1959—61; mem. divsn. clin. computing dept. medicine Beth Israel Deaconess Med. Ctr., Boston, 1970—; prof. of medicine Harvard Med. Sch., 1999—. Co-pres. Ctr. Clin. Computing Beth Israel Med. Ctr., Boston; editor-in-chief MDComputing, 1989—99. Author: Cybermedicine, 2001; contbr. articles to profl. jours. Mem. Med. Com. for Human Rights, Chgo., 1964—70; bd. dirs. Com. of Responsibility, Boston, 1968—73, Princeton Project 55, Princeton, NJ, 1993—99; physician doing primary care medicine in Honduras Cape Cares, Cape Cod, Mass. Capt. Med. Corp USAF, 1962—64. Recipient Outstanding Contributions to Soc. award, Princeton U. Class of 1955, 1995, Morris F. Collen award for Excellence, Am. Coll. of Med. Informatics, 2001. Fellow: Am. Coll. of Medial Informatics (life; one of 50 founding fellows 1986). Achievements include ealy contributor to study of uses of computers in medicine; one of first to offer the idea of patient power that patients who want to should be helped and encouraged to particpate as co-equals with their doctors in medical decisions; research in patient-computer dialogue-the use of a computer to interview patients about their medical histories and to help patients help themselves with medical problems; use and misuse of the SAT and other tests of mental ability; psychology of interviewing. Home: 75 Homer St Newton Centre MA 02459 Office: Beth Israel Deaconess Med Ctr 330 Brookline Ave Boston MA 02215 Office Fax: 617-667-1518. Business E-Mail: wslack@bidmc.harvard.edu.

SLADE, BERNARD, playwright; b. St. Catharines, Ont., Can., May 2, 1930; s. Frederick and Bessie (Walbourne) Newbound; m. Jill Florence Hancock, July 25, 1953; children: Laurel, Christopher. Actor: Garden Ctr. Theatre, Vineland, Ont., Crest Theatre, Toronto, CBC-TV, Citadel Theatre, Edmonton, Alta.; screenwriter of over 20 hour TV plays for CBC, CBS, ABC, NBC, 1957—; writer/creator (TV series) Love on a Rooftop, The Partridge Family, The Flying Nun, The Girl with Something Extra, Bridget Loves Bernie; story editor, writer 15 episodes of TV series Bewitched; writer/creator (plays) A Very Close Family, 1962, Same Time Next Year (Drama Desk award 1975, Tony award nomination 1975), Tribute, 1978, Romantic Comedy, 1979, Special Occasions, 1981, Fatal Attraction, 1984, Return Engagements, 1986, Sweet William, 1987, An Act of the Imagination, 1987, I Remember You, 1991, You Say Tomatoes, 1993, Everytime I See You, 1994, Same Time, Another Year, Fling!, 2000, Les Grande Occasions, Paris, 2007; feature films: Same Time, Next Year, 1977, Tribute, 1978, Romantic Comedy, 1979, Shared Laughter-a memoir, 2000, Moving Day, 2005, (film biography) Comedic Genius of Bernard Slade, 2003. Recipient Acad. award nomination Motion Picture Arts and Scis., 1978. Mem. Dramatists Guild Am., Writers Guild Am. (award nomination), Acad. Motion Picture Arts and Scis. (Acad. award nomination 1978), Soc. Authors and Artists (France). Avocation: tennis. Home: 261 S Reeves Dr # 102 Beverly Hills CA 90212-4004 Personal E-mail: bernslade@aol.com. *I am a prisoner of a childhood dream: to write for the theatre. The fulfillment of that dream has lived up to all my expectations. I believe the theatre should be a celebration of the human condition and that the artist's job is to remind us of all that is good about ourselves. I feel privileged to be given a platform for my particular vision of life, and, whether my plays succeed or fail, I am always grateful for the use of the hall.*

SLADE, BERNARD NEWTON, electronics executive; b. Sioux City, Iowa, Dec. 21, 1923; s. William Charles and Katherine Gertrude Slotsky; m. Margot Friedlein, Aug. 18, 1946; children: Steven P., Eric J. BSEE, U. Wis., Madison, 1948; MS, Stevens Inst. Tech., Hoboken, NJ, 1954. Devel. engr. tube divsn. RCA, Harrison, NJ, 1948-55; devel. engr. RCA Labs., Princeton, NJ, 1955-56; mgr. tech. program IBM, Poughkeepsie, NY, 1956-60, mgr. product ops. Hopewell Junction, NY, 1960-64; mgr. mfg. tech. IBM World Trade Corp., Armonk, NY, 1964-65; corp. dir. of mfg. tech. IBM Corp., Armonk, 1965-84; sr. cons. Arthur D. Little, Inc., Cambridge, Mass., 1984-86, Gemini Cons., Morristown, NJ, 1986-93; founder, v.p., bd. dirs. Yieldup Internat. Corp., 1993-97; bd. dirs. V3 Semiconductors, 1996—2003, Anon, Inc. Guest lectr. in field. Co-author: Winning the Productivity Race, 1985; author: Compressing the Product Develop. Cycle, 1992; contbr. articles to profl. jours.; patentee in field; contbg. author: Transistors, 1956, Handbook of Semiconductor Electronics, guest lectr., U. Harvard, Stanford, Chgo., Pa., Cornell, Brigham Young, RPI Grad. Schs. Bus., 1962. 2nd lt. AUS, 1943-46. Mem.: IEEE (sr.), Sigma Xi. Home: 12 Merry Hill Rd Poughkeepsie NY 12603-3214

SLADE, LYNN, lawyer; b. Santa Fe, Jan. 29, 1948; m. Susan Zimmerman, 1 child, Benjamin, 1 child from a previous marriage, Jessica. BA in Econs., U. N.Mex., 1973, JD, 1976. Bar: N.Mex. 1976, US Dist. Ct. N.Mex. 1976, US Ct. Appeals (10th cir.) 1978, US Ct. Appeals (DC cir.) 1984, US Supreme Ct. 1984, US Ct. Appeals (9th cir.) 2007. Ptnr. Modrall, Sperling, Roehl, Harris & Sisk, PA, Albuquerque, 1976—. Adj. prof. U. N.Mex. Sch. Law, Albuquerque, 1990. Editor N.Mex. Law Rev., 1975-76; contbr. articles to profl. jours. Bd. dirs. N.Mex. First, 1999—, chair, 2005—06; trustee-at-large Rocky Mountain Min. L. Found., 1995—97, 2005—; mem. bd. adv. Utton Ctr. for Transboundary Resources, 2005—. Mem. ABA (sect. environ., energy and resources, membership officer 1998-00, chair com. on Native Am. natural resources 1991-94, 2002-, coun. mem. 1995-98, mem. sects. litig., dispute resolution, pub. utilities and comm., and transp. law), N.Mex. State Bar (chair, bd. dirs. sect. natural resources 1983-87, bd. dirs. Indian law sect. 2002-04). Home: 143 Olguin Rd Corrales NM 87048-6930 Office: Modrall Sperling Roehl Harris & Sisk PA 500 4th St NW Ste 1000 Albuquerque NM 87102-2186 Office Phone: 505-848-1800, 505-848-1828. Business E-Mail: lynn.slade@modrall.com.

SLADE, R. ANDREW, literature and language professor; b. St. Petersburg, Fla., Apr. 30, 1973; s. Richard Schubert and Susan Patricia Slade; m. Danielle M Poe, Dec. 29, 1996; children: Tess Leonie Poe-Slade, Lola Marguerite Poe-Slade, Asher Emile Poe-Slade. PhD, SUNY, Stony Brook, 2003. Vis. asst. prof. philosophy U. Dayton, Ohio, 2003—07, asst. prof. English, 2007—. Home: 355 Pk Dr Dayton OH 45410 Office: Univ Dayton 300 College Pk Dayton OH 45469-1520 Personal E-mail: andrew.slade@notes.udayton.edu.

SLADE, ROY, artist, college president, museum director; b. Cardiff, U.K., July 14, 1933; came to U.S., 1967, naturalized, 1975; s. David Trevor and Millicent (Stone) S. N.D.D., Cardiff Coll. Art, 1954; A.T.D., U. Wales, 1954; D of Arts, Art Inst. So. Calif., 1994. Tchr. art and crafts Heolgam High Sch., Wales, 1956-60; lectr. art Clarendon Coll., Nottingham, Eng., 1960-64; sr. lectr. fine art Leeds Coll. Art, Eng., 1964-67; prof. painting Corcoran Sch. Art, Washington, 1967-68, assoc. dean, 1969-70, dean, 1970-77; dir. Corcoran Gallery of Art, Washington, 1972-77; pres., dir. Cranbrook Acad. Art, Bloomfield Hills, Mich., 1977-94, now dir. emeritus. Sr. lectr. Leeds Coll. Art, England, 1968—69; vis. Boston Mus. Fine Arts, 1970; dir. emeritus Cranbrook Art Mus., 2000—. Exhibited one-man shows Howard Roberts Gallery, Cardiff, Wales, 1958, New Art Ctr., London, 1960, U. Birmingham, 1964, 69, Herbert Art Gallery and Mus., Coventry, 1964, Va. State Art League, 1967, Mus. of Arts and Crafts, Columbus, Ga., 1968, Jefferson Place Gallery, Washington, 1968, 70, 72, 73, Park Sq. Gallery, Leeds, 1969, St. Mary's Coll., Md., 1971, Guelph U., Ont., Can., 1971, Hood Coll., 1974, Pyramid Gallery, Washington, 1976, Robert Kidd Gallery, 1981, 92, Herman Miller, Inc., Mich., 1985; group shows in U.K., Washington, Can.; represented in permanent collections Arts Council Gt. Brit., Contemporary Art Soc., Nuffield Found., Ministry of Works, Eng., Brit. Embassy, Washington, Brit. Overseas Airways Corp., U. Birmingham, Wakefield City Art Gallery, Clarendon Coll., Cadbury Bros., Ltd., Eng., Lord Ogmore, Local Edn. Authorities. Mem. D.C. Commn. on Arts.; bd. dirs. Artists for Environment Found., Nat. Assn. Schs. Art; chmn. Nat. Council Art Adminstrs., 1981. Served with Brit. Army, 1954-56. Decorated knight 1st class Order of White Rose (Finland), Royal Order of Polar Star (Sweden); recipient award Welsh Soc., Phila., 1974, Gov.'s Arts Orgn. award, 1988; Fulbright scholar, 1967-68. Mem. Nat. Soc. Lit. and Arts, AIA (hon. Detroit chpt.), Assn. Art Mus. Dirs. (hon.). Home: 31 Island Way Apt 801 Clearwater FL 33767-2206 Personal E-mail: royslade@verizon.net.

SLADEK, RONALD JOHN, physics professor; b. Chgo., Sept. 19, 1926; s. James Joseph and Rose (Vachulka) S.; m. Jeanne T. McFadden, Sept. 19, 1953; children: Linda, James, Frances, Stephen, Rosemarie, Edward. PhB, U. Chgo., 1947, SB, 1949, SM, 1950, PhD, 1954. Rsch. physicist Westinghouse Rsch. Labs., Pitts., 1953-60, fellow scientist, 1960-61; assoc. prof. physics Purdue U., West Lafayette, Ind., 1961-66, prof., 1966-91, prof. physics emeritus, 1992—, acting head dept. physics, 1969-71, assoc. dean sci., 1974-87. Vis. scientist Sci. Center, N.Am. Rockwell Corp., Thousand Oaks, Calif., summer 1967; sabbatical scientist Xerox Rsch. Ctr., Palo Alto, Calif., 1976-77 Contbr. articles to profl. jours. With USNR, 1945-46. AEC fellow U. Chgo., 1952-53. Fellow Am. Phys. Soc. Home: 3504 Flint St Apt 0313 Greensboro NC 27405-3283

SLADKUS, HARVEY IRA, lawyer; b. Mar. 5, 1929; s. Samuel Harold and Charlotte Dorothy Sladkus; m. Harriet Marcia Barske, Nov. 26, 1967 (div.); children: Steven David, Jeffrey Brandon; m. Roberta Frances Pope, Oct. 24, 1986. AB, Syracuse U., 1950; JD, NYU, 1961. Bar: NY 1962, U.S. Supreme Ct. 1967, Conn. 1981. Assoc. Morris Ploscowe, NYC, 1961—67; pvt. practice NYC, 1968—95; ptnr. Dweck & Sladkus and Feiden, Dweck & Sladkus, NYC, 1968-95, Dweck & Sladkus, LLP, NYC, 1996; pres. Harvey I. Sladkus, P.C., 1997—. Small claims arbitrator Civil Ct. City of NY, 1977—; adj. prof. law Benjamin N. Cardozo Sch. Law, 1994—95; lectr. family and matrimonial law. Co-author: (book) Practice Under New York's Matrimonial Law, 1971—79; editor-in-chief: Family Law Practice, 1982, contbg. columnist: It's the Law, Suffolk Times, 1999—2002, Bottom Line, 2000—; contbr. articles to profl. jours. 1st lt. US Army, 1952—53, Korea.

Decorated Bronze Star, War Svc. medal Korean Govt.; recipient George Washington Honor medal, Freedoms Found., Valley Forge, 1953, Empire State Pro Bono award, 2007; named Arbitrator of Yr., NY Civil Small Claims Ct., 2002, Civil Ct. NY County, 2002. Mem.: Suffolk County Bar Assn., Am. Arbitration Assn. (nat. panel arbitrators), Internat. Acad. Matrimonial Lawyers, Am. Acad. Matrimonial Lawyers, Assn. Bar City of NY, NY State Bar Assn. Jewish. Office: 425 Park Ave New York NY 10022-3506 Office Phone: 212-754-9400. E-mail: hisatty@nyc.rr.com. *Notable cases include: Burns vs. Burns, first to constitute a tenant in occupancy to subscribe to shares of an apt. corp. going coop.; Brown vs. Brown, case of first impression reclause in agreement of ex-wife living with another man.*

SLAFF, ALLAN PAUL, military officer, academic administrator, educator, entrepreneur; b. Mt. Vernon, NY, Feb. 2, 1923; s. Frank Alfred and Augusta Raye (Scher) S.; m. Mary Lee Schaeffer; children: Randolph Elliott, Valerie Anne. BS, U.S. Naval Acad., 1944; postgrad., U.S. Naval Post Grad Sch., 1949-50, U.S. Naval War Coll., Newport, RI, 1959-60, Harvard U., 1967. Commd. ensign USN, 1944, advanced through grades to capt., 1965, WWII Battleship Mass. Fast Carrier TF, 1944-46, personal aide to CNO Adm. Arleigh Burke, 1950-51, spl. security officer commd. in Korean War Navy, comdr. USS Lester, Davis, Luce, Albany, 1957-70, sr. naval advisor to Vietnam Navy, 1967-68, ret., 1970; dean, mem. faculty Bus. Sch. Harvard U., Boston, 1970-80; chmn. Luzerne Co. News Co., Wilkes Barre, Pa., 1980-86, LABSPHERE, Inc., N. Sutton, N.H., 1983-94. Cons. Harvard Bus. Sch., 1980-84. Author (autobiography): A Sailor's Story, 2004; contbr. articles to profl. jours. and mags. Decorated Legion of Merit, Bronze Star, Nat. Order of Vietnam, numerous other decorations U.S. Navy, 1941-70; recipient Disting. Grad. award Wyoming Sem., Kingston, Pa., 1990. Mem. Port Royal Club (sec. bd. dirs.), Naples Yacht Club (treas., bd. dirs.), Royal Poinciana Golf Club, Port Royal Property Owners Assn. (bd. dirs.). Republican. Episcopalian. Avocations: golf, travel, photography, gardening. Home: 4151 Gulf Shore Blvd N 601 Naples FL 34103-2292 Personal E-mail: allanslaff@aol.com.

SLAGER, DONALD W., waste management executive; Various mgmt. positions Gen. Waste Svcs., 1985—90, gen. mgr., 1990—92; dist. mgr. Chgo. metro dist. Allied Waste Industries, Scottsdale, Ariz., 1992—96, regional v.p. west region, 1996—97, asst. v.p. ops., 1997—98, v.p. ops., 1998—2001, sr. v.p. ops., 2001—03, exec. v.p., COO, 2003—04, pres., COO, 2005—. Office: Allied Waste Industries 18500 N Allied Way Phoenix AZ 85054

SLAGLE, WILLIAM F., dental educator, dean; b. Alpena Pass, Ark., Feb. 3, 1929; s. William Floyd and Jannie Lou (Watts) S.; m. Shannon Penrod Bartgis, Aug. 15, 1971. BS, Cen. State U., Edmond, Okla., 1950; DDS, U. Mo., Kansas City, 1957; MS, Memphis State U., 1975. Instr. dentistry U. Mo., Kansas City, 1957-59; asst. prof. Coll. Medicine U. Okla., Oklahoma City, 1963-75; pvt. practice Oklahoma City, 1959-72; dept. chmn., coordinator U. Memphis Coll. Dentistry, 1972-74, asst. dean, dept. chmn., 1974-76, assoc. dean, dept. chmn., 1976-78, exec. assoc. dean., 1978-81, acting dean, 1981-82, dean, prof., 1982—. Mem. exec. com. William Bowld Hosp., Memphis, 1982—; cons. VA Hosp., Memphis, 1975—. Sect. editor Craniomandibular Practice; contbr. articles to profl. jours. Staff sgt. USAF, 1950-52. Recipient Outstanding Former Student award Cen. State U., 1983; named Man of Yr. in Dentistry Okla. Dental Assn., 1969. Fellow Am. Coll. Dentists, Internat. Coll. Dentists; mem. ADA (Presdl. citation), Tenn. Dental Assn. (award for Excellence 1988, Fellowship award, Jack Wells award), Memphis Dental Assn., Pierre Fauschard Acad., Omicron Kappa Upsilon. Avocations: flying, golf, boating, reading. Office: U Tenn Coll Dentistry 875 Union Ave Memphis TN 38103-3513

SLAMA, JAMES T., chemistry professor, researcher; PhD, U. Calif., Berkeley, 1977. Asst. prof. biochemsitry U. Tex. Health Sci. Ctr., San Antonio, 1982—91; assoc. prof., medicinal and biol. chemistry U. Toledo, 1991—2005, prof. medicinal and biol. chemistry and chemistry, 2005—, dir., bsps program, Coll. Pharmacy, 2006—. Mem.: Royal Soc. Chemistry (London), Am. Chem. Soc., Am. Soc. Biochemistry and Molecular Biology. Office: Univ Toledo Coll Pharmacy 2801 West Bancroft St Toledo OH 43606-3390 Office Fax: 419-530-7946. Business E-Mail: james.slama@utoledo.edu.

SLAMON, DENNIS JOSEPH, research scientist; b. New Castle, Pa., Aug. 6, 1948; married; 2 children. BA, Washington & Jefferson Coll.; MD, U. Chgo. Pritzker Sch. Medicine, 1975, PhD in Cell Biology, 1975. Intern, medicine U. Chgo. Hosp., Ill., 1975—76, resident Ill., 1976—78; fellow, divsn. hematology-oncology, dept. medicine UCLA Sch. Medicine, 1979—81, assoc. chief divsn. hematology-oncology, 1989—91, chief divsn. hematology-oncology, 1991—, prof., dept. medicine, 1993—, exec. vice chair for rsch. Jonsson Comprehensive Cancer Ctr., 1994—, dir. clin./translational rsch.; dir., Revlon/UCLA Women's Cancer Rsch. Program Jonsson Comprehensive Cancer Ctr., UCLA Sch. Medicine, dir., Revlon/UCLA Women's Health Rsch. Program. Mem. sci. adv. bd. Coastview Capital Inc., New Biotics Inc.; named to Pres. Clinton's Cancer Panel, 2000; dir., med. adv. bd. Nat. Colorectal Cancer Rsch. Alliance. Contbr. articles to profl. jours. Recipient Outstanding Young Investigator award, Western Soc. Clin. Investigation, 1988, Salk Translational award, U. Calif., San Diego, 2000, Bristol-Myers Squibb Oncology Millennium award, 2000, Wadsworth Center's Brown-Hazen award for Excellence in the Basic Scis., 2001, Jeffrey A Gottlieb Meml. award, M.D. Anderson Cancer Ctr., Tex., 2002, Dorothy P. Landon Am. Assn. Cancer Rsch. prize for Translational Cancer Rsch., 2003, Medal of Honor for Clin. Rsch., Am. Cancer Soc., 2004, David A. Karnofsky Meml. award, Am. Soc. Clin. Oncology, 2006, European Inst. Oncology Breast Cancer award, Milan, Italy, 2006, Gairdner Found. Internat. award, 2007; named one of five Men for the Cure, GQ mag. and Concept:Cure, 1999. Achievements include development of the drug Herceptin for treating breast cancer. Office: UCLA Sch Medicine Divsn Hematology Oncology Factor Building 11-244 10833 Le Conte Los Angeles CA 90095 Address: UCLA Sch Medicine Jonsson Comprehensive Cancer Ctr 8-684 Factor Building Box 951781 Los Angeles CA 90095-1781 Office Phone: 310-825-5193. Business E-Mail: dslamon@mednet.ucla.edu.*

SLANSKY, JERRY WILLIAM, investment company executive; b. Chgo., Mar. 8, 1947; s. Elmer Edward and Florence Anna (Kosobud) S.; m. Marlene Jean Cannella, Jan. 29, 1950; children: Brett Matthew, Blake Adam. BA, Elmhurst Coll., 1969; MA, No. Ill. U., 1971. Mktg. rep. Bantam Book Co., Chgo., 1972-73, Charles Levy Circulating Co., Chgo., 1973-76; account exec. Merrill Lynch, Chgo., 1976-77, Oppenheimer & Co., Inc., Chgo., 1977—, asst. v.p., 1978, v.p., 1979, sr. v.p., 1981, mng. dir., 1986, ptnr., 1986—. Bd. dirs. Lake Geneva (Wis.) Beach Assn., 1987-02, Glen Ellyn Youth Ctr., Glenbard West H.S., pres., 1998-99, Booster Club; bd. dirs. Buttonwood Cove, Longboat Key, Fla., 2006-08; mem. bus. affairs com. Presbytery of Chgo., 1999-04. Mem. Nat. Assn. Securities Dealers (arbitrator 1988—), N.Y. Stock Exch., Chgo. Bd. Options, Am. Arbitration. Assn, Omaha C. of C. Presbyterian. Avocations: swimming, water-skiing, golf, skiing, kayaking. Office: Oppenheimer & Co Ste 4000 500 W Madison St Chicago IL 60661 Office Phone: 312-360-5553. Personal E-mail: jerry.slansky@opco.com.

SLARK, MARTIN P., electronics executive; BSE, Reading Univ., England, 1977; MBA, Ea. London Univ. Mgmt. positions Molex Inc., Lisle, Ill., 1976—99, exec. v.p., 1999—2001, pres., COO, 2001—05, vice-chmn., CEO, 2005—. Bd. dir. Hub Group Inc. Office: Molex Inc 2222 Wellington Ct Lisle IL 60532

SLATE, DANIEL MICHAEL, economics professor; b. LA, Feb. 6, 1930; s. Robin Hill and Madeline Carolyn (Burchard) Slate; m. Mary Lou Eagan, June 14, 1952; children: Gregory S., Laurie D., Mary C.; m. Margie Ruth Earnest, June 6, 1969. BS in Psychology, U. Wash., 1952, MA in Econ. Analysis, 1956, PhD in Polit. Economy, 1961. Statis. clk. U.S. Rubber Co., Seattle, 1949; psychiat. aide, psychologist Pinel Psychiat. Hosp., 1951—52; asst. exec. sec., mgr. Distbrs. Assn. Seattle, Inc., 1954—56; labor., rsch. economist Wash. Employers, Inc., Seattle, 1956—57; asst. prof. dept. econs. and bus. U. Hawaii, Honolulu, 1957—61, assoc. prof. Coll. Bus. Adminstrn., 1962—63, dir. Econ. Rsch. Ctr., 1959—60, dir. Bur. Bus. Rsch., 1962—63; assoc. dir. exec. devel. programs in mass mktg. mgmt., asst. prof. Grad. Sch. Bus. Adminstrn. Mich. State U., East Lansing, 1961—63; rschr. Bur. Econ. and Bus. Rsch. U. Ill., Urbana, 1963—64, assoc. prof. Grad. Sch. Bus. Adminstrn., 1963—67, acting dir., 1965—67, assoc. prof. mktg., head dept., 1964—67, acting head dept. indsl. adminstrn., 1966—67; prof., dir. Small Bus. Inst., Robert O. Anderson Grad. Mgmt. U. N.Mex., Albuquerque, 1967—. Staff economist mgmt. scis. divsn. Arthur D. Little, Inc., Cambridge, Mass., 1969; cons. to various state agys., mfg. fin., profl. orgns. and rsch. corps.; cons. Dept. Energy, Los Alamos Nat. Lab. Co-author (with S.M. Mark): Economics in Action, 1959, 1962; author: various reports and articles in field. Lt. (j.g.) USNR, 1952—54, Korea. Fellow Rsch. fellow, Inst. Labor Econs., 1955—56, Ford Found., 1960. Mem.: Am. Econ. Assn., Pi Sigma Epsilon. Home: 6136 Purple Aster Ln NE Albuquerque NM 87111-8083

SLATE, JOE HUTSON, psychologist, educator; b. Hartselle, Ala., Sept. 21, 1930; s. Murphy Edmund and Marie (Hutson) S.; m. Rachel Holladay, July 1, 1950; children: Marc Allan, John David, James Daryl. BS, Athens Coll., 1960; MA, U. Ala., 1965, PhD, 1970. Mem. faculty Athens (Ala.) State Coll., 1965-92, prof. psychology, 1974-92, chmn. behavioral scis., 1974-92; pvt. practice psychology Athens, 1970-92, Hartselle, 1992—; v.p. Slate Security Systems, Hartselle, Ala., 1984—. Author: Psychic Phenomena, 1988, Self-Empowerment, 1991, Psychic Empowerment, 1995, Psychic Empowerment for Health and Fitness, 1996, Astral Projection, 1998, Aura Energy for Health Healing, and Balance, 1999, Rejevenation: Strategies for Living Younger, Longer and Better, 2001, Psychic Vampires, 2002, Beyond Reincarnation, 2005, Connecting to the Power Nature, 2009, Self-empowerment for Everyone, 2009. Named hon. prof. U. Montevallo, 1973, prof. emeritus Athens State U., 1992. Mem. APA, Am. Soc. Clin. Hypnosis, Inst. Parapsychol. Rsch. (founder), Coun. for Nat. Register Health Svc. Providers in Psychology, NEA, Ala. Edn. Assn., Delta Tau Delta, Phi Delta Kappa, Kappa Delta Pi. Home: 210 Main St West Hartselle AL 35640-4442 Office: 110 Sparkman St S Hartselle AL 35640 Personal E-mail: joehslate@aol.com.

SLATER, BRUCE, small business owner; m. Jacquie Slater; children: Aaron, Amelia. Owner Slater Constrn., Pa. Com. person Democratic Party. 3rd class petty officer USN, 1976—79. Democrat. Office: Slater Constrn 5418 Old Philadelphia Pike Gap PA 17527 Office Phone: 717-355-0669.

SLATER, C. STEWART, chemical engineering educator; b. Feb. 24, 1957; s. Clarence S. and Elizabeth Slater. BS, Rutgers U., Piscataway, NJ, 1979, MS, 1981, MPh, 1982, PhD, 1983. Process devel. engr. Procter & Gamble Co., Cin., 1979-81; teaching asst., project mgr. Rutgers U., 1981-83; prof. chem. engring. Manhattan Coll., Riverdale, NY, 1983-95; prof. chem. engring. dept. Rowan U., Glassboro, NJ, 1995—. Cons. to major U.S. corps. Contbr. over 100 articles to profl. publs., several chpts. to books. Recipient Environ. Quality award US Environ. Protection Agy., 2009 Fellow Am. Soc. for Engring. Edn. (divsn. chmn. 2003, program chmn. 1990, New Engring. Educator Excellence award 1987, Dow Outstanding Faculty award 1989, John Fluke award 1992, George Westinghouse award 1996, Chester Carlson award 1999, Joseph J. Martin award 1998, 99), Mem. Am. Chem. Soc., Am. Inst. Chem. Engrs., N. Am. membrance Soc., Sigma Xi, Tau Beta Pi, Omega Chi Epsilon. Achievements include research in membrane technology. Office: Rowan Univ Dept Chem Engring 201 Mullica Hill Rd Glassboro NJ 08028-1702 Office Phone: 856-256-5310. Business E-Mail: slater@rowan.edu.

SLATER, CHARLES JAMES, construction company executive; b. Munich, Feb. 16, 1949; s. Robert Marsh and Mary Elizabeth (James) S.; m. Pamela S. Senning, Sept. 17, 1974 (div. Apr. 1992); children: Mary Katherine, Robert Charles; m. Kristie J. Alexander, May 11, 1992 (dec.). BA in Polit. Sci., U. Tenn., 1974. Cert. safety and health mgr; cert. for profl. safety mgmt. Safety mgr. Daniel Internat. Co., Kingsport, Tenn., 1981-83, safety and med. mgr. Georgetown, S.C., 1983-84; risk mgmt. mgr. Yeargin Inc., Kingsport, 1985-88, Omaha, 1990, resident engr. Frankfort, Ind., 1991, Florence, S.C., 1991; safety and risk mgmt. dir. Harbert-Yeargin Inc., Greenville, S.C., 1992-96; sr. safety mgr. Fluor Corp., Seaford, Del., 1996—2003, sr. HSE mgr. Johannesburg, 2003—06; regional safety mgr. Shaw Group, Inc., 2006—. Bd. advisors Assoc. Bldrs. and Contractors/Nat. Safety Coun., Washington, 1993—. Pres. Tenn. Vol. Firefighters Assn., Sullivan County, 1987-89, Kingsport Area Safety Coun., 1989. Mem. Am. Inst. Constructors (chpt. pres. 1993-94), Am. Soc. Safety Engrs., Nat. Safety Mgmt. Soc., Constrn. Industry Coop. Alliance (instr. 1992), Safety Dirs. League (charter), Constrn. Specifications Inst. Episcopalian. Avocations: golf, chess, reading, cinematography. Office: Shaw Group 128 S Tryon St Ste 600 Charlotte NC 28202-5004 Business E-Mail: charles.slater@shawgrp.com, cjslater@utalum.org.

SLATER, CHRISTIAN, actor; b. NYC, Aug. 18, 1969; s. Michael Hawkins and Mary Jo Slater; m. Ryan Haddon, Feb. 12, 2000; children: Jaden Zach Haddon-Slater, Eliana Sophia Haddon-Slater. Actor: (films) The Legend of Billie Jean, 1985, The Name of the Rose, 1986, Twisted, 1986, Tucker: The Man and His Dream, 1988, Gleaming the Cube, 1989, Heathers, 1989, Beyond the Stars, 1989, The Wizard, 1989, Tales from the Darkside: The Movie, 1990, Young Guns II, 1990, Pump Up the Volume, 1990, Robin Hood: Prince of Thieves, 1991, Mobsters, 1991, Star Trek VI: The Undiscovered Country, 1991, Kuffs, 1992, (voice only) FernGully: The Last Rainforest, 1992, Where the Day Takes You, 1992, Untamed Heart, 1993, True Romance, 1993, Jimmy Hollywood, 1994, Interview with the Vampire: Vampire Chronicles, 1994, Murder in the First, 1995, Bed of Roses, 1995, Broken Arrow, 1996, Austin Powers: Internat. Man of Mystery, 1997, The Tears of Julian Po, 1997, Love Stinks, 1999, White Lies, 1999, The Contender, 2000, 3000 Miles to Graceland, 2001, Who Is Cletis Tout?, 2001, Windtalkers, 2002, Run for the Money, 2002, Masked & Anonymous, 2003, Mindhunters, 2004, The Good Shepherd, 2004, Pursued, 2004, Churchill: The Hollywood Years, 2004, Alone in the Dark, 2005, A License to Steal, 2005, Bobby, 2006, (voice only) Igor, 2008; dir.: Museum of Love, 1996; actor, exec. prodr. (films) The Deal, 2004, Very Bad Things, 1998, actor, co-prodr. Hard Rain, 1998, actor, exec. prodr. Basil, 1998; actor: (TV films) Sherlock Holmes: The Strange Case of Alice Faulkner, 1981, The Hunted Mansion Mystery, 1983, Living Proof: The Hank Williams Jr. Story, 1983, Secrets, 1986, Desperate for Love, 1989, Merry Christmas, George Bailey, 1997, (TV appearances) One Life to Live, 1977, Ryan's Hope, 1985, L.A. Law, 1988, Prehistoric Planet, 2002, The West Wing, 2002, (voice only) Adventures of Jimmy Neutron: Boy Genius, 2003, Alias, 2003, My Name Is Earl, 2006; (TV series) My Own Worst Enemy, 2008; (plays) Music Man, 1980, Between Daylight & Boonville, 1980, Copperfield, 1981, Macbeth, 1982, Merlin, 1983, Landscape of the Body, 1984, Dry Land, 1986, One Flew Over the Cuckoo's Nest, 2004—05, The Glass Menagerie, 2005. Named one of 100 Sexiest Stars in Film History, Empire Mag., 1995.

SLATER, JAMES MUNRO, radiation oncologist; b. Salt Lake City, Jan. 7, 1929; s. Donald Munro and Leone Forestine (Fehr) S.; m. JoAnn Strout, Dec. 28, 1948; children: James, Julie, Jan, Jerry, Jon. BS in Physics, U. Utah, Utah State U., 1954; MD, Loma Linda U., 1963; PhD (hon.), Andrews U., Berrien Springs, Mich., 1996. Diplomate Am. Bd. Radiology. Intern Latter Day Saints Hosp., Salt Lake City, 1963-64, resident in radiology, 1964-65; resident in radiotherapy Loma Linda U. Med. Ctr., White Meml. Med. Center, LA, fellow in radiotherapy, 1967-68, U. Tex.-M.D. Anderson Hosp. and Tumor Inst., Houston, 1968-69; dir. radiation oncology sect. Loma Linda U. Med. Ctr., Calif., 1970—79, dir. radiation sect. Calif., 1975—79, chmn. dept. radiation scis. Calif., 1978—90, chmn. dept. radiation medicine Calif., 1990—2001, dir. Cancer Inst., 1993—97, treas. Calif., 1995-96, exec. v.p. Calif., 1994—95; founder, dir. Loma Linda U./NASA Radiation Biology Lab., Calif., 1997—; vice chair radiation medicine Loma Linda U. Med. Ctr., 2003—. Co-dir. cmty. radiology oncology program L.A. County-U. So. Calif. Comprehensive Cancer Ctr., 1978-83; mem. cancer adv. coun. State of Calif., 1980-85; clin. prof. U. So. Calif., 1982—; founding mem. Proton Therapy Coop. Group, 1985—, chmn. 1987-91; cons. charged particle therapy program Lawrence Berkeley Lab., 1986-94; cons. R&D monoclonal antibodies Hybritech Inc., 1985-94, bd. dirs., 1985-94; cons. Berkeley lab., 1986-94; mem. panel cons. Internat. Atomic Energy Agy. UN, 1994-98; cons. Sci. Applications Internat. Corp., 1979, 89-91. Bd. dirs. Am. Cancer Soc., San Bernardino/Riverside, 1976-84, exec. com., 1976—; pres. Inland Empire chpt., 1981-83. NIH fellow, 1968-69; recipient exhbn. awards Radiol. Soc. N.Am., 1973, exhbn. awards European Assn. Radiology, 1975, exhbn. awards Am. Soc. Therapeutic Radiologists, 1978, Alumnus of Yr. award, 1993-94. Fellow Am. Coll. Radiology; mem. AAAS, AMA, ACS (liaison mem. to commn. on cancer 1976-84), Am. Radium Soc., Am. Soc. Clin. Oncology, Am. Soc. Therapeutics Radiologists, Assn. Univ. Radiologists, Soc. for Clinical Trials, N.Y. Acad. Scis., Calif. Med. Assn., Calif. Radiol. Soc., Gilbert H. Fletcher Soc. (pres. 1981-82), Loma Linda U. Med. Sch. Alumni Assn., Radiol. Soc. N.Am., Bernardino County Med Soc., Soc. Chairmen Of Acad. Radiation Oncology Programs, Alpha Omega Alpha. Achievements include development of proton accelerator system for treating patients with cancer and some benign diseases in a hospital environment; development of computer assisted radiation treatment planning system utilizing patient's digitized anatomic images with overlying radiation distribution images, Loma Linda U. Proton Facility renamed James M. Slater Proton Treatment and Rsch. Ctr., 2007. Office: Loma Linda Univ Med Ctr 25590 Prospect Ave Apt 27c Loma Linda CA 92354-3150 Business E-Mail: jmslater@dominion.llumc.edu.

SLATER, NEIL, music educator, composer; s. Kenneth W. and Violet Elizabeth Slater; m. Andrea Slater, May 8, 1985; children from previous marriage: Kimberly Roy, Elizabeth, Jonathan. MusB, Mansfield U., Pa., 1952; MA, Duquesne U., Pa., 1954. Assoc. prof. music Bridgeport U., Bridgeport, Conn.; prof. jazz studies, chair U. North Tex., Denton. Ret. dir. composer, chair, divsn. jazz studies One O'Clock Lab Band; artistic dir. North Tex. Jazz Festival, 2001—08. Contbr. articles to profl. publs. With US Army, 1952—54, St. Sill. Recipient Jazz Legend, U. North Tex., 2008, Alumnus award, 2000, Presdl. award, 1998, Congl. Record citation, US House of Representatives, 2008; named Jazz Artist of Yr., Sammons Ctr. Arts, Dallas, 2006; fellowship, NEA, 1995. Mem.: ASCAP (Std. award 1987—), Am. Fed. Musicians, Tex. Music Educators Assn., Internat. Assn. Jazz Educators, Nat. Acad. Recording Arts and Scis. (Grammy award 1993). Avocations: tennis, chess, reading. Home: 1921 Willowwood St Denton TX 76205 Office Fax: 940-369-7227. Personal E-mail: neilandrea@verizon.net. Business E-Mail: neil.slater@unt.edu.

SLATER, RODNEY EARL, lobbyist, lawyer, former United States Secretary of Transportation; b. Tutwyler, Miss., Feb. 23, 1955; m. Cassandra Wilkins; 1 child. BS, Ea. Mich. U., 1977; JD, U. Ark., 1980. Asst. atty. gen. State of Ark., 1980-82; spl. asst. for community and minority affairs Gov. of Ark., 1983-85, exec. asst. for econ. and community programs, 1985-87; dir. intergovernmental rels. Ark. State U., 1987-93; adminstr. fed. hwy. adminstrn. US Dept. Transp., Washington, 1993-97, sec., 1997-2001; ptnr. Patton Boggs LLP, Washington, 2001—; vice chair & sr. advisor James Lee Witt Associates, LLC, Washington, 2004—. Mem. Ark. State Hwy. and Transp. Commn., 1987-93, chair, 1992-93; dep. campaign mgr., sr. traveling advisor Clinton for Pres. Campaign, 1992; dep. to chair Clinton/Gore Transition Team, 1992-93; bd. dirs. Africare, 2001—, Joint Ctr Polit. and Econ. Studies, 2001— Ark. liaison Martin Luther King, Jr. Fed. Holiday Commn., 1983-87; mem. Ark. Sesquicentennial Commn., 1986. Recipient Ark. Pub. Transp. Award, Lawyer-Citizen Award, W. Harold Flowers Law Soc., Pres.'s Award, Nat. Bar Assn., Ark. Hero, Ark. Times, 100 Most Influential Black Ams., Ebony mag., Headliner of Yr., Ark. Press Assn., 1997, George Collins Award, Congl. Black Caucus, 1998; named one of Ten Outstanding Young Arkansans, Ark. Jaycees, 50 Top Lobbyists, Washingtonian mag., 2007. Mem. Ark. Bar Assn. (sec.-treas. 1989-93), W. Harold Flowers Law Soc. (pres. 1985-92). Democrat. Office: Patton Boggs LLP 2550 M St NW Washington DC 20037 also: James Lee Witt Assocs 1501 M St NW Washington DC 20005 Office Phone: 202-457-5265. Office Fax: 202-457-6315. E-mail: rslater@pattonboggs.com, rslater@wittassociates.com.*

SLATER, THOMAS GLASCOCK, JR., lawyer; b. Washington, Mar. 15, 1944; s. Thomas G. and Hylton R. Slater; m. Scott Newell Brent, Aug. 31, 1996; children: Thomas Glascock, Tacie Holden Norris, Andrew Fletcher. BA, Va. Mil. Inst., 1966; LLB, U. Va., 1969. Bar: Va. 1969, US Dist. Ct. (ea. dist.) Va. 1970, US Ct. Appeals (4th cir.) 1975, DC 1980, US Ct. Appeals (5th cir.), US Ct. Appeals DC 1980, US Supreme Ct. 1981. Assoc. Hunton & Williams LLP, Richmond, Va., 1969-76, ptnr., 1976—. Group head litig., intellectual property competition and labor group Hunton & Williams LLP; bd. dirs. Tredegar Industries. Pres. VMI Found., 1995—97; with VMI Bd. Visitors, 2003—, pres., 2008—; bd. trustees Va. Hist. Soc.; bd. dirs. Central Va. Legal Aid Soc. Fellow: Va. Law Found., Am. Coll. Trial Lawyers, Am. Bar Found.; mem.: Richmond Bar Assn. (pres. 1989—90), DC Bar

Assn., Va. State Bar Coun. (exec. com.), 4th Cir. Jud. Conf., Va. Mil. Inst. Alumni Assn. (past pres.). Office: Hunton & Williams LLP Riverfront Plz East Tower 951 E Byrd St Richmond VA 23219-4074 Office Phone: 804-788-8475. Business E-Mail: tslater@hunton.com.

SLATER, VALERIE A., lawyer; b. Passaic, NJ, Oct. 13, 1952; BA magna cum laude, Allegheny Coll., 1974; JD, Cath. U. Am., 1977. Bar: DC 1977, US Ct. Appeals (DC cir.) 1978, US Dist. Ct. (DC dist.) 1982, US Ct. Internat. Trade 1984, US Ct. Appeals (fed. cir.) 1984. Ptnr. Akin Gump Strauss Hauer & Feld LLP, Washington, 1990—2003, ptnr., chair internat. trade practice group, 2003—. Mem.: Phi Beta Kappa. Office: Akin Gump Strauss Hauer & Feld LLP 1333 New Hampshire Ave NW Washington DC 20036-1564 Office Phone: 202-887-4112. Office Fax: 202-887-4288. Business E-Mail: vslater@akingump.com.

SLATKIN, LEONARD EDWARD, music director, conductor; b. LA, Sept. 1, 1944; s. Felix and Eleanor (Aller) Slatkin; m. Linda Hohenfeld, Mar. 29, 1986; 1 child, Daniel. Piano study with Victor Aller and Selma Cramer, viola study with Sol Schoenbach, conducting study with Felix Slatkin, Amerigo Marino, Ingolf Dahl; student, Ind. U., LA City Coll.; studied conducting with Jean Paul Morel, Juilliard Sch., NYC; doctorate (hon.), Juliard Sch. Artistic dir., condr. NY Youth Symphony, 1966; asst. condr. St. Louis Symphony Orch., 1968—77, music dir., 1979—96, condr. laureate, 1996—; music adv. New Orleans Symphony/La. Philharm. Orch., 1977—79; music dir. Nat. Symphony Orch., Washington, 1996—2008; prin. guest condr. Philharmonia Orch., London, 1997—2000; chief condr. BBC Symphony Orch., 2000—04; prin. guest condr. LA Philharm., 2004—07, Pitts. Symphony Orch., 2008—, Royal Philharm. Orch., London, 2005—; music dir. Detroit Symphony Orch., 2008—. Founder St. Louis Symphony Youth Orch., 1969; music adv. Nashville Symphony Orch., 2006—09; disting. artist in residence Am. U., Washington, 2007—08; founder, dir. Nat. Conducting Inst.; Arthur R. Metz Found. condr. Ind. U. Jacobs Sch. Music. Conducting debut as asst. condr. Youth Symphony of N.Y., Carnegie Hall, 1966, asst. condr. Juilliard Opera Theater and Dance Dept., 1967, St. Louis Symphony Orch., 1968—71, assoc. condr., 1971—74, guest condr. Concertgebouw, Royal Danish Orch., Tivoli, English Chamber Orch., BBC Manchester, London Philharm., London Symphony Orch., Royal Philmarm. Orch., 1974, Nat. Orch. Paris, Scottish Nat. Orch., NHK Tokyo, 1986, Vienna State Opera, Lyric Opera Chgo., Stuttgart Opera, Stockholm, Oslo, Israel, Goteborg, Berlin, debut Chgo. Symphony Orch., 1974, NY Philharm., 1974, Phila. Orch., 1974, USSR Orchs., 1976—77, Met. Opera, 1991, prin. guest condr. Minn. Orch., 1974—, summer artistic dir., 1979—89, music dir. New Orleans Philharm. Symphony Orch., 1977—78, artistic dir. Great Woods, 1990, artistic adminstr. Blossom, 1991; composer: The Raven, Dialogue for Two Cellos and Orchestra, Ext. 1, 2, 3, 4; rec. artist RCA, Angel EMI, Vox, Telarc, Philips, Warner Bros.; condr.: Arthur R. Metz Found., Ind. U. Decorated Chevalier Legion of Honor, France; recipient Declaration of Honor in Silver, Austrian Govt., 1986, Nat. Medal of Arts, US Congress, 2003, Gold Baton for svc. to Am. music, Am. Symphony Orch. League, Lifetime Achievement award, Washington DC Mayor's Arts Awards, 7 Grammy awards. Mem.: NARAS (bd. govs, Chgo. chpt.). Office: Detroit Symphony Orch 3711 Woodward Ave Detroit MI 48201 Mailing: c/o R. Douglas Sheldon or Sheila E. Pineau Columbia Artists Mgmt LLC 1790 Broadway New York NY 10019*

SLATNER, THOMAS ALLEN, bookseller; b. Marple, Cheshire, Eng., May 1, 1940; arrived in U.S., 1947; s. Hugo and Edith (Elsner) S.; m. Eve Naomi Silberberg, Aug. 11, 1961; children: Nicole, Claude, Genevieve. BA, CCNY, 1961. Mgr. Richard Abel & Co., London, 1968-73; dir. Thomas Slatner & Co., London and N.J., 1978—. Home: 2 Wellfield Ave London N10 2EA England Office: 151 Pritchard Dr Palm Coast FL 32164 E-mail: tslatnerco@blueyonder.co.uk.

SLATON, JOSEPH GUILFORD, social worker; b. NYC, Sept. 29, 1951; s. Joseph Slachta and Hilda Elizabeth (Sims) S.; 1 child, Nicholas Michael. BS, E. Carolina U., 1974; MSW, U. N.C., 1977. Cert. pub. mgr. Cottage parent supr. N.C. Div. Youth Svcs., Rocky Mount, 1974-75, juvenile evaluation counselor Rocky Mount and Butner, N.C., 1975-77; social worker Murdoch Ctr., N.C. Dept. Human Resources, Butner, 1977-78; facility survey cons., mental retardation profl. N.C. Div. Facility Svcs., Raleigh, 1978-81, facility survey cons. long-term care programs, 1981-83, program mgr. health care facilities br., 1983-87, human svcs. planner cert. of need program, 1987-94; sr. analyst, 1994-98; planning coord. divsn. budget planning and analysis N.C. Dept. Health and Human Svcs., Raleigh, 1998—2001, edn. dir., office emergency med. svc., 2001—02, sr. program, budget analyst, office of sec., 2002—; adminstr. Pullen Meml. Baptist Ch., 2005—. Pres. Triangle Rsch. & Planning, Ltd., 1999—; spkr. in field. Author: Guide for the Newly Active Democrat, 1996. Asst. scoutmaster troop 300 Boy Scouts Am.; field officer, NC State Emergency Response Team, 1999-2002, NC Human Svcs. Transp. Coun., 2002-2005, Children's Svcs. Adv. Coun., 2002-; mem. N.C. Rehab. Task Force, Raleigh, 1988-90; chmn. subcom. N.C. Mental Retardation Task Force, Raleigh, 1982-83; active N.C. Regional Strategic Planning Task Force, Raleigh, 1982-83; active N.C. Regional Strategic Planning Task Force on Mental Retardation, 1982; mem. allocations panel Wake County United Way, Raleigh, 1984-95, Health Issues Panel, 2000-2003; mem. planning com. Wake County Ptnrs. Program Sta. WRAL-TV, Raleigh, 1980, coord. Auction Day, 1981, mem. exec. planning com., 1982; campaign mgr., vol. coord., treas. rep. for N.C. Ho. Reps.; treas. Wake County Dem. Party, 1997-2003, Dem. State Exec. Com., 2002-2004; charter pres. Cary Civitan Club, 1997-98, bd. dirs. 2000-02, lt. gov. N.C. dist. East Area V, 1998-99 Mem. NASW (legis. policy com.), Acad. Cert. Social Workers, Triangle Health Execs.' Forum, Am. Health Planning Assn. Episcopalian. Avocations: sailing, woodworking, golf. Office: 2002 Mail Service Ctr Raleigh NC 27699-2002 Home Phone: 919-859-4059; Office Phone: 919-733-1464. E-mail: joseph.slaton@ncmail.net, jslaton@nc.rr.com.

SLATOR, BRIAN M., computer scientist, educator; b. Winnipeg, Manitoba, Can., Oct. 29, 1952; s. Michael and Isabel Vera Slator; m. Rita L. Haney, Jan. 7, 1984; children: Adam Paul Miller, Audrey Ruth, Megan Elizabeth. PhD, New Mex State U., Las Cruces, 1988. Assoc. prof. ND State U., Fargo, 1996—; rsch. asst. prof. Northwestern U., Evanston, Ill., 1990—96. Pres. and founder WoWie Instrn. Co., Fargo, 2002—. Contbr. articles to profl. jours. (Outstanding Paper award, 1999). Recipient Ernest L. Boyer Internat. award, 11th Internat. Conf. Coll. Tchg. and Learning, Jacksonville, Fla., 2000. Mem.: Assn. Computing Machinery. Avocations: motorcycling, reading. Office: Computer Sci Dept IACC # 258 ND State Univ Fargo ND 58105 Personal E-mail: bslator@cableone.net. Business E-Mail: brian.slator@ndsu.edu.

SLATTERY, EDWARD JAMES, bishop; b. Chgo., Aug. 11, 1940; Student, St. Mary of the Lake Sem., Mundelein, Ill., Loyola U., Chgo. Ordained priest Archdiocese of Chgo., Ill., 1966; v.p. Cath. Ch. Ext. Soc., 1971-76, pres., 1976-94; ordained bishop, 1994; bishop Diocese of Tulsa, 1994—. Roman Catholic. Office Phone: 918-294-1904. Office Fax: 918-252-1168.

SLATTERY, MICHAEL G., humanities educator; s. CDR John and Anne Slattery; married. BS, U.S. Naval Acad., Annapolis, 1968; MA Polit. Sci., U. South Fla., Tampa, 1990. Lt.- UDT Det Cmdr & SEAL advisor Vietnam & U.S. Navy, Coronado, Calif., 1970—73; Capt. U.S. Navy, 1963—94; chief staff Joint Spl. Ops. Command, Fort Bragg, NC, 1990—94; adj. prof. Campbell U., Buies Creek, NC, 1995—. Contbr. articles. Decorated DSSM, LOM, Bronze Star DOD & U.S. Navy. Office: Campbell Univ Dept of Hist & Gov PO Box 356 Raleigh NC 27606 Business E-Mail: slatterym@campbell.edu.

SLAUGH, LYNN H., retired chemist; BS, Bringham Young U., 1952; PhD, U. Wash., 1956. With Shell Devel. Co., Houston, 1956—98; ret., 1998. Contbr. articles to profl. jours. Recipient Indsl. Chemistry award Am. Chem. Soc., 1995. Achievements include 162 patents; development of two indsl. processes.

SLAUGHTER, ALEXANDER HOKE, lawyer; b. Charlottesville, Va., Nov. 24, 1937; s. Edward Ratliff and Mary (Hoke) S.; m. Virginia Borah, 1964 (div.); 1 child, David A.; m. Mary Peeples, 1971. BA, Yale U., 1960; LLB, U. Va., 1963. Ptnr. McGuire, Woods, Richmond, Va., 1969—. Episcopalian. Home: 3016 Rugby Rd Richmond VA 23221-3936 Office: McGuire Woods One James Ctr 901 E Cary St Richmond VA 23219-4030 Home Phone: 804-353-1405; Office Phone: 804-775-4346. E-mail: aslaughter@mcguirewoods.com.

SLAUGHTER, ANNE-MARIE, federal agency administrator, former dean; b. Sept. 27, 1958; m. Andrew Moravcsik; children: Edward, Alexander. AB magna cum laude, Princeton U., 1980; JD cum laude, Harvard U., 1985; MPhil, Oxford U., 1982, DPhil, 1992. Tchr. law U. Chgo.; rschr. Harvard U., J. Sinclair Armstrong prof. internat., fgn., and comparative law, dir. internat. legal studies program; Bert G. Kerstetter '66 univ. prof. politics & internat. affairs Princeton U., dean Woodrow Wilson Sch. Pub. and Internat. Affairs, 2002—09; dir. policy planning staff US Dept. State, 2009—. Bd. dirs. Coun. Fgn. Rels., New Am. Found., Can. Inst. Internat. Governace Innovation; spkr. in field. Author: A New World Order, 2004, The Idea That is America: Keeping Faith with Our Values in a Dangerous World, 2007; contbr. articles to profl. jours. Covener, acad. co-chair Princeton Project on Nat. Security. Recipient Francis Deak Prize, Am. Jour. Internat. Law, 1990, 1994. Fellow: Am. Acad. Arts and Scis.; mem.: Am. Soc. Internat. Law (pres. 2002—04). Office: US Dept State 2201 C St NW Washington DC 20520*

SLAUGHTER, EDWARD RATLIFF, JR., lawyer; b. Raleigh, NC, Sept. 15, 1931; s. Edward Ratliff and Mary McBee (Hoke) S.; m. Anne Limbosch, July 25, 1957; children: Anne-Marie, Hoke, Bryan. AB, Princeton U., 1953; postgrad. (Rotary Found. fellow), U. Brussels, 1955-56; LLB, U. Va., 1959. Bar: Va. 1959, D.C. 1981. Assoc. firm McGuire, Woods & Battle (now McGuire Woods) and predecessors, Charlottesville, Va., 1959-64; ptnr. McGuire, Woods & Battle and predecessors, 1964-79, head dept. litig., 1964-79, spl. asst. for litig. to atty. gen. U.S., 1979-81; ptnr. firm Whitman & Ransom, Washington, 1981-84; prin. Slaughter & Redinger, P.C., Charlottesville, 1984-95, Slaughter, Izakowitz, Clarke & Nunley, P.C., 1995-96, Woods, Rogers & Hazlegrove, P.L.C., 1996—2002, of counsel, 2002—03, Michie, Hamlett, Lowry, Rasmussen, & Tweel, PLLC, 2003—. Vis. lectr. trial advocacy U. Va., 1970-77, Va. procedure, 1986-91; disting. lectr. U. Tunis, 1996; mem. standing com. on commrs. of accounts Jud. Coun. of Va., 1993—, chmn., 1995-2001. Chmn. Albemarle County (Va.) Dem. Com., 1969-73; pres. Charlottesville-Albemarle United Way, 1972; commr. accounts Albemarle County, 1986—; trustee Lime Kiln Arts, Inc., 1992-98. Served with USNR, 1953-55. Recipient William J. Brennan award U. Va. Trial Advocacy Inst., 1996. Fellow Am. Bar Found., Am. Coll. Trial Lawyers; mem. D.C. Bar, Charlottesville-Albemarle Bar Assn. (pres. 1976-77), Va. Bar Assn. (pres. 1978), Va. State Bar (bd. govs. internat. practice sect. 1992-2000, bd. govs. sr. lawyers conf. 2004—08), Thomas Jefferson Inn Ct. (pres. 1995-96), Farmington Country Club. Home: 200 Tuckahoe Farm Ln Charlottesville VA 22901-5531 Office: Michie Hamlett Lowry Rasmussen & Tweel PLLC 500 Court Sq Ste 300 PO Box 298 Charlottesville VA 22902-0298 Home Phone: 434-975-3079; Office Phone: 434-295-8310. Business E-Mail: eslaughter@mhlrt.com.

SLAUGHTER, FREEMAN CLUFF, retired dentist; b. Estes, Miss., Dec. 30, 1926; s. William Cluff and Vay (Fox) S.; m. Genevieve Anne Parks, July 30, 1948; children: Mary Anne, Thomas Freeman, James Hugh. Student, Wake Forest U., 1944, Emory U., 1946-47; DDS, Emory U. Sch. of Dentistry, 1951. Lic. real estate broker. Practice gen. dentistry, Kannapolis, N.C., 1951-89; ret. Mem. N.C. State Bd. Dental Examiners, 1966-75, pres., 1968-69, sec.-treas., 1971-74; chief dental staff Cabarrus Meml. Hosp. (now Carolinas Med. Ctr. NE), Concord, N.C., 1965-66, 75; mem. N.C. Adv. Com. for Edn. Dental Aux. Pers.-N.C. State Bd. Edn., 1967-70; advisor dental asst. program Rowan Cabarrus C.C., 1974-76; Duke Med. Ctr. Davison Century Club. Trustee N.C. Symphony Soc., 1962-68, pres. Kannapolis chpt., 1961; mem. Cabarrus County Bd. Health, 1977-83, chmn., 1981-83, acting health dir., 1981; vice chmn. Kannapolis Charter Commn., 1983-84; mem. City Coun. Kannapolis, 1984-85; Mayor protem, Kannapolis, 1984-85; past active Boy Scouts Am., Eagle scout with silver palm. QM2C asst. navigator on USS Xenia AKA 51, co-navigator on USS Gen. George O. Squier AP 130 with USN, 1944-46, WW II, ETO, MTO. Recipient Kannapolis Citizen of Yr. award, 1982. Fellow Am. Coll. Dentists (life); mem. ADA (life), Am. Legion, Kannapolis Jr. C. of C. (v.p. 1952), Toastmasters Internat. (pres. Kannapolis chpt. 1963-64), Am. Assn. Dental Examiners (Dentist Citizen of Yr. 1975, v.p. 1977-79, Recognition plaque, 1980), So. Conf. Dental Deans and Examiners (v.p. 1969), N.C. Dental Soc. (resolution of commendation 1975), N.C. Dental Soc. Anesthesiology (pres. 1964), Southeastern Acad. Prosthodontics, So. Acad. Oral Surgery, Am. Soc. Dentistry for Children (pres. N.C. unit 1957), Internat. Assn. Dental Rsch., Cabarrus County Dental Soc. (pres. 1953-54, 63-64, 69), N.C. Assn. Professions (dir. 1976-80), Kannapolis Music Club (pres. 1962-63), Emory U. Corpus Cordis Aureum (Emory U. disting. alumnus award 2006), Masons, Shriners, Rotary (dir. 1977-80), Omicron Kappa Upsilon, Alpha Epsilon Upsilon.

SLAUGHTER, GYMAMA, engineering educator; married. PhD, Va. Commonwealth U., Richmond, 2005. Asst. prof. Va. State U., Petersburg, 2005—. Contbr. articles to profl. jours. Exec. dir. RAPME, Petersburg, 2005. Grantee Rsch. grant, NSF, 2008—. Mem.: IEEE, ASEE, NSBE. Achievements include research in biosystems & engineering. Office: Va State Univ Po Box 9212 Petersburg VA 23806

SLAUGHTER, JAMES H., lawyer; b. Concord, NC, July 29, 1964; s. Freeman C. and Genevieve A. (Parks) S.; m. Tamara A. Vincent, Oct. 1, 1988; children: Freeman J., McKinley J., Wyatt T. BA with highest honors, U. N.C., 1986, JD, 1989. Bar: N.C., 1989, U.S. Dist. Ct. (mid. and we. dists.) N.C., 1989, U.S. Ct. Appeals (fed. cir.) 1992, Supreme Ct. US; cert. profl. parliamentarian; profl. reg. parliamentarian. Assoc. Henson, Henson, Bayliss & Sue, Greensboro, NC, 1989—91, Floyd & Jacobs, LLP, Greensboro, NC, 1991—96; ptnr. Floyd & Jacobs, Greensboro, NC, 1996—2001, Forman Rossabi Black, Pa., 2001—, pres. Pa., 2003—. Mem. of faculty Williamsburg Practicum of the Am. Inst. of Parliamentarians, 1994-2002. Tech, editor: The Complete Idiot's Guide to Robert's Rules, 2004; contbg. author: Labor Union Law and Regulation, 2005; legal guest columnist News & Record, Greensboro, 1991-95. Pres. Young Dems. of N.C., 1992-93; chmn. State Dem. Coun. of Rev., N.C., 1994-96, 2001—; chmn. Triad chpt. Nat. Conf. Com. Justice, 2004-06; mem. Gov.'s Crime Commn., N.C., 1982-85; mem. N.C. Progress Bd., 1996-98; bd. dirs. Greensboro chpt. ARC, 1996-99, sec., 1997-98; bd. dirs. Greensboro chpt. NCCJ, 1996-99; trustee Greensboro Hist. Mus., 1996-99, pres.-elect, 2006—; elder First Presbyn. Ch., 2000-03, clk. of session, 2001-02. U.S. Truman Scholar, 1984. Master Am. Inns Court; mem. Rotary (Greensboro Crescent club 1993—, Paul Harris fellow), Greensboro Bar Assn. (treas. 1991-92), Nat. Assn. Parliamentarians Ethics (chmn., 2005-), Am. Inst. Parliamentarians (chmn., 2005-), Coll. Cmty. Assn. Lawyers, Am. Coll. Parlimentary Lawyers (pres. 2007-), Phi Beta Kappa. Presbyterian. Home: 2206 Granville Rd Greensboro NC 27408-5012 Office: Forman Rossabi Black PA PO Box 41027 Greensboro NC 27404

SLAUGHTER, JOHN BROOKS, professional society administrator; b. Topeka, Mar. 16, 1934; s. Reuben Brooks and Dora (Reeves) S.; m. Ida Bernice Johnson, Aug. 31, 1956; children: John Brooks, Jacqueline Michelle. Student, Washburn U., 1951-53; BSEE, Kans. State U., 1956, DSc (hon.), 1988; MS in Engring., UCLA, 1961; PhD in Engring. Scis, U. Calif., San Diego, 1971; D Engring. (hon.), Rensselaer Poly. Inst., 1981; DSc (hon.), U. So. Calif., 1981, Tuskegee Inst., 1981, U. Md., 1982, U. Notre Dame, 1982, U. Miami, 1983, U. Mass., 1983, Tex. So. U., 1984, U. Toledo, 1985, U. Ill., 1986, SUNY, 1986; LHD (hon.), Bowie State Coll., 1987; DSc (hon.), Morehouse Coll., 1988, Kans. State U., 1988; LLD (hon.), U. Pacific, 1989; DSc (hon.), Pomona Coll., 1989; LHD (hon.), Alfred U., 1991, Calif. Luth. U., 1991, Washburn U., 1992. Registered profl. engr., Wash. Electronics engr. Gen. Dynamics Convair, San Diego, 1956-60; with Naval Electronics Lab. Center, San Diego, 1960-75, div. head, 1965-71, dept. head, 1971-75; dir. applied physics lab. U. Wash., 1975-77; asst. dir. NSF, Washington, 1977-79, dir., 1980-82; acad. v.p., provost Wash. State U., 1979-80; chancellor U. Md., College Park, 1982-88; pres. Occidental Coll., Los Angeles, 1988-99; co-chair Calif. Citizens Commn. on Higher Edn., 1996-99; ret., 1999. Res., pres, CEO NACME, Inc., N.Y.C.; bd. dirs., vice chmn. San Diego Transit Corp., 1968-75; mem. com. on minorities in engring. Nat. Rsch. Coun., 1976-79; mem. Commn. on Pre-Coll. Edn. in Math., Sci. and Tech. Nat. Sci. Bd., 1982-83; bd. dirs. Solutia, Inc., ARCO, Avery Dennison Corp., IBM, Northrop Grumman Corp.; chmn. advancement com. Music Ctr. of L.A. County, 1989-93. Editor: Jour. Computers and Elec. Engring., 1972—. Bd. dirs. San Diego Urban League, 1962-66, pres., 1964-66; mem. Pres.'s Com. on Nat. Medal Sci., 1979-80; trustee Rensselaer Poly. Inst., 1982; chmn. Pres.'s Com. Nat. Collegiate Athletic Assn., 1986-88; bd. govs. Town Hall of Calif., 1990; bd. dirs. L.A. World Affairs Coun., 1990. Recipient Engring. Disting. Alumnus of Yr. award UCLA, 1978, UCLA medal, 1989, Roger Revelle award U. Calif.-San Diego, 1991, Disting. Svc. award NSF, 1979, Svc. in Engring. award Kans. State U., 1981, Disting. Alumnus of Yr. award U. Calif.-San Diego, 1982, Martin Luther King Jr. Nat. award, 1997; Naval Electronics Lab. Ctr. fellow, 1969-70; elected to Topeka High Sch. Hall of Fame, 1983, Hall of Fame of Am. Soc. Engring. Edn., 1993; named Kansan of Yr. by Kans. Native Sons and Daus., 1994. Fellow IEEE (chmn. com. on minority affairs 1976-80), Am. Acad. Arts and Scis.; mem. NAE (councillor 2003-), Nat. Collegiate Athletic Assn. (chmn. pres. commn.), Am. Soc. for Engring. Edn. (inducted into Hall of Fame 1993), Phi Beta Kappa (hon.), Tau Beta Pi, Eta Kappa Nu. Office: NACME Inc 440 Hamilton Ave White Plains NY 10601-1813

SLAUGHTER, LOUISE MCINTOSH, United States Representative from New York; b. Lynch, Ky., Aug. 14, 1929; d. Oscar Lewis and Grace (Byers) McIntosh; m. Robert Slaughter, 1956; children: Megan Rae, Amy Louise, Emily Robin. BS in Microbiol., U. Ky., Lexington, 1951, MPH, 1953; D (hon.), U. Ky., 2006. Bacteriologist Ky. Dept. Health, Louisville, 1951-52, U. Ky., 1952-53; market rschr. Procter & Gamble Co., Cin., 1953-56; mem. Monroe County Legislature, NY, 1976—79; regional coord. to sec. Mario Cuomo State of NY, Albany, NY, 1976—78, regional coord. to lt. gov. Mario Cuomo, 1979—82; mem. NY State Assembly, 1982—86, US Congress from 30th NY Dist., 1987—93, US Congress from 28th NY Dist., 1993—; chair US House Rules Com., 2007—. Del. Dem. Nat. Conv., 1972, 1976, 1980, 1988, 1992, 1996; mem. adv. bd. Nat. Ctr. Policy Alternatives; mem. Nat. Women's Polit. Caucus. Recipient Disting. Pub. Health Legislator award, Pub. Health Assn., 1997, Award for Outstanding Arts Leadership in the US Ho. Reps., US Conf. Mayors and Am. Assn. for the Arts, 1998, Humane Legislator of Yr., Am. Humane Assn., 2003, Woman of Vision award, Women in Film and Vision, 2004, Sidney R. Yates Nat. Arts Advocacy award, Nat. Assembly State Arts Agencies; named Lay Educator of Yr., Phi Delta Kappa Internat., Rochester chpt., 1999. Mem.: League of Women Voters. Democrat. Episcopalian. Office: US Congress 2469 Rayburn House Office Bldg Washington DC 20515-3228 also: 3120 Fed Bldg 100 State St Rochester NY 14614 Office Phone: 202-225-3615, 585-232-4850. Office Fax: 202-225-7822, 585-232-1954.*

SLAUGHTER, MATTHEW J., economics professor, former federal official; b. 1969; BA in Econ., Notre Dame, 1990; PhD in Econ., MIT, 1994. Asst. prof. econ. Dartmouth Coll., Hanover, NH, 1994—2001, assoc. prof. econ., 2001—02, assoc. prof. bus. adminstrn. Tuck Sch. Bus., 2002—; mem. Coun. Econ. Advisers Exec. Office of the Pres., Washington, 2005—07. Faculty rsch. fellow Nat. Bur. Econ. Rsch., 1995—2002; vis. fellow Inst. for Internat. Economics, 1997—; mem. Coun. Fgn. Rels., 2000—05, sr. fellow for bus. & globalization, 2007; vis. scholar Fed. Reserve Bank, 1998, 2002, IMF, 1996, 97; panel mem. NAS, 2004—; bd. acad. advisors Internat. Tax Policy Forum, 2005—; bd. economists Time mag., 2004; cons. The World Bank, 1995—97, 2000, 02, Emergency Com. for Am. Trade, 1996—2003, Nat. Fgn. Trade Coun., 2003, Com. for Fair Internat. Taxation, 2004, Org. for Internat. Investment, 2004. Recipient Bronze award, AMEX Bank Review Essay Competition, 1994, John M. Manley Huntington Teacher award, Dartmouth Coll., 2001; grantee MIT Industrial Performance Ctr. Doctoral Fellowship, Sloan Found., 1993—94, Nat. Fellowship, Nat. Bur. Econ., 2000—01, Elizabeth R. & Roland A. Jeffe Fellowship, Dartmouth Coll., 2001—02; fellow, NSF, 1990—93. Office: Tuck Sch Bus Dartmouth Coll 100 Tuck Hall Hanover NH 03755 E-mail: matthew.j.slaughter@dartmouth.edu.*

SLAUGHTER, RALPH, academic administrator; BS in Acctg. and Fin., MPA, PhD in Pub. Policy. CPA. V.p. Southern U. System. Chmn. bd. dirs. LA Cap. Fed. Credit Union. Mem. Mount Zion First Bapt. Ch. Named to Power 150, Ebony mag., 2008. Mem.: Treasury Mgmt. Assn., Soc. La. Cert. Pub. Accountants, Am. Inst. Cert. Pub. Accountants, Am. Soc. Pub. Administrators (pres. La. chpt.), Prince Hall Masons La. (grand master, CEO, imperial potentate Prince Hall Shriners, grand chancellor United Supreme Coun., Southern Juristriction). Office: Southern U System PO Box 10878 Baton Rouge LA 70813

SLAUGHTER, RICHARD ARTHUR, political scientist, economist, educator; b. Twin Falls, Idaho, Nov. 20, 1943; s. Walter Arthur and Mary Viola Slaughter; m. Susan Kay Clark, Aug. 17, 1966; children: Scott, Ryan. BA in Polit. Sci., U. Idaho, 1966; MA in Internat. Rels., U. Denver, 1968, PhD in Internat. Politics, 1974. Asst. prof. polit. sci. West Ga. Coll., Carrollton, 1972-76; economist divsn. fin. mgmt. State of Idaho, Boise, 1976-80, chief economist, 1980-84; pres. Richard Slaughter Assocs., Boise, 1984—; dir. Martin Inst. for Peace Studies U. Idaho, 1996—2000; internat. economist Cen. Asia, 1998—2001; cons. economist Climate Impacts Group, U. Wash., 2000—. Vol. exec. dir. Boise Com. on Fgn. Rels., 1989-; mem. adv. bd. Martin Inst., U. Idaho, 1990-96, 2005—; co-founder Am. Coms. on Fgn. Rels., treas. 1995-2001, v.p., 2005-09. Editor Idaho Econ. Forecast jour., 1977-84; author articles on Third World econ. devel. and nation-bldg., global climate change policy. Bd. dirs. Capitol Youth Soccer Assn., Boise, 1980-89, soccer commr., 1983-86. Mem. Coun. Fgn. Rels. Home and Office: 907 Harrison Blvd Boise ID 83702-4052 Home Phone: 208-345-9633; Office Phone: 208-850-1223. Business E-Mail: richard@rsaboise.com.

SLAUGHTER, ROCHELLE DENISE, elementary school educator; b. Kansas City, Kans., Jan. 3, 1956; d. Theodore and Barbara Jean (Williams) Hall; m. Eddie Slaughter, Nov. 1, 1997. AA, Penn Valley C.C., Kansas City, Mo., 1976; BA, U. Mo., Kansas City, 1978, MA, 1985; Edn. Specialist Degree, U. Mo., 1992. Cert. specialist in reading, Mo. Tchr. Kansas City Sch. Dist., 1979-85, reading resource tchr., 1985-95, tchr. 1st grade, 1995—2000, tchr. 3d grade, 2000—; S.T.A.R.R. tchr., 2002—04; instrnl. coach James Accelerated Sch., 2005—; literacy coach James Elem. Sch., 2006—. Supt. Sunday sch. Emmanuel Bapt. Ch., 1992—; del. lang. arts & literacy delegation People to People Citizen Amb. Progra, China, 1995; vol. for adult basic edn. program; tutor Laubach Literacy Coun. Kansas City, 1996-97. Recipient IMPACT Reading award Kansas City Reading dept., 1990. Mem. ASCD, NAACP, Internat. Reading Assn. (chpt. v.p. 1994-95, pres.-elect 1995-97, pres. 1997-99), Phi Delta Kappa (youth advisor 1993-99). Democrat. Baptist. Avocations: reading, computer work, sewing. Office: James Accelerated Sch Kansas City MO 64110 Office Phone: 816-418-3700, 816-418-3722. Personal E-mail: r547cpb@sbcglobal.net. Business E-Mail: rslaughter@kcmsd.net.

SLAUGHTER, SANDRA ANN, management educator; BA, Carroll Coll., Waukesha, Wis., 1980; MBA, Ind. U., Bloomington, 1987; PhD, U. Minn., Mpls., 1995. IT analyst Rockwell Internat., Milw., 1982—85; project leader Hewlett Packard, Mountain View, Calif., 1987—90; rsch. and tchg. asst. U. Minn., 1991—95; asst. prof. Carnegie Mellon U., Pitts., 1995—2001, assoc. prof., 2001—07; prof. Ga. Inst. Tech., Atlanta, 2007—, chair, 2007—. Contbr. articles to profl. jour. Recipient Impact award, Hewlett Packard, 1987, Best Dissertation award, ICIS, 1995, Best Paper award, Acad. of Mgmt., 1999, Best Conf. Paper award, 2004; finalist Best Pub. Paper, 2007; Nat. Doctoral Fellowship, AACSB, 1991, Rsch. Grant, NSF, 2000—02, 2006—08. Mem.: Soc. for Info. Sys., INFORMS, Assn. for Computing Machinery, Assn. for Info. Sys., Acad. of Mgmt. Achievements include being included in the 1993 edition of the Guinness Book of World Records for tandem bicycling 18,077.5 miles around the world from 1989 to 1991. Avocations: swimming, hiking, travel, reading. Office: Georgia Institute of Tech 800 W Peachtree St NW Atlanta GA 30308 Office Fax: 404-894-6030. Business E-Mail: sandra.slaughter@mgt.gatech.edu.

SLAUGHTER, THOMAS FREEMAN, anesthesiologist, educator, physician; s. Freeman Cluff and Genevieve Parks Slaughter; m. Janie C. Thomas, Aug. 3, 1996. Attended, Wake Forest U., Winston-Salem, NC, 1980—83; MD, Duke U. Sch. Medicine, Durham, NC, 1987. Diplomate Nat. Bd. Med. Examiners, 1988, lic. NC Med. Bd., 1991, diplomate Am. Bd. Anesthesiology, 1992, testamur Nat. Bd. Echocardiography, 2002, lic. Va. Bd. Medicine, 2002. Intern Emory U., Atlanta, 1987—88; resident Duke U. Health Sys., 1988—91, fellow cardiothoracic anesthesiology, 1990—92, assoc. in anesthesiology, 1992—93, asst. prof. anesthesiology, 1993—2000, assoc. prof. anesthesiology, 2000—02; attending anesthesiologist Durham VA Med. Ctr., 1992—2002; prof. anesthesiology, dir. cardiothoracic anesthesiology Va. Commonwealth U. Health Sys., Richmond, 2002—04; prof. anesthesiology Wake Forest U. Sch. Medicine, 2004, sect. head cardiothoracic anesthesia, 2006—, dir. cardiothoracic anesthesia fellowship tng. program, 2006—. Chmn. transfusion rev. com. Durham VA Med. Ctr., Durham, NC, 1996—2002, inst. med. rsch., 1996—2002; diagnostic techs. com. Duke U. Health Sys., 1998—2002, human studies instl. rev. com., 1999—2002; sci. program com. Soc. Cardiovascular Anesthesiology, 1996—2000; dir. cardiothoracic anesthesia and fellowship tng. program Va. Commonwealth U. Health Sys., 2002—04, sci. program dir. anesthesiology grand rounds, 2002—04; dir. cardiothoracic anesthesiology Wake Forest U. Sch. of Medicine, Winston-Salem, NC, 2006. Contbr. chapters to books. Recipient Rsch. Career Devel. award, Found. Anesthesia Edn. and Rsch., 1992—94, Individual Clin. Investigator Devel. award, NIH, 1997—2002, Rsch. in Blood Conservation award, Bayer Pharm., 1998, 1999, Elected Hon. Mem., Assn. U. Anesthesiologists, 2001—; nominee Faculty 1000 Medicine, 2009—. Mem.: AMA, Internat. Soc. on Thrombosis and Hemostasis, Soc. Cardiovasc. Anesthesiologists, Internat. Anesthesia Rsch. Soc., NC Soc. Anesthesiologists, Am. Soc. Anesthesiology, Assn. Univ. Anesthesiologists (hon.), Nat. Eagle Scout Assn. (Eagle Scout award 1979), Alpha Epsilon Delta Premed. Honor Soc., Beta Beta Beta Biol. Honor Soc. Achievements include patents for transglutaminase cell line and clones; research in perioperative hemostasis and thrombosis; perioperative blood conservation; transglutaminase biology. Office: Wake Forest Univ Sch Medicine Medical Center Blvd Winston Salem NC 27157-1009

SLAUGHTER-DEFOE, DIANA TRESA, education educator, psychologist; b. Chgo., Oct. 28, 1941; d. John Ison and Gwendolyn Malva (Armstead) S.; m. Michael Defoe (div.). BA, U. Chgo., 1962, MA, 1964, PhD, 1968. Instr. dept. psychiatry Howard U., Washington, 1967-68; rsch. assoc., asst. prof. Yale U. Child Study Ctr., New Haven, 1968-70; asst. prof. dept. behavioral scis. and edn. U. Chgo., 1970-77; asst. to assoc. prof. edn. and African Am. studies and Ctr. for Urban Affairs and Policy Rsch. (now Inst. for Policy Rsch.) Northwestern U., Evanston, Ill., 1977-90, prof., 1990-97; Constance E. Clayton prof. urban edn. Grad. Sch. Edn. U. Pa., 1998—. Nat. adv. bd. Fed. Ctr. for Child Abuse & Neglect, 1979-82, coord. Human Devel. and Social Policy Program, 1994-97; nat. adv. bd. Learning Rsch. and Devel. Ctr. U. Pitts., Ednl. Rsch. & Devel. Ctr., U. Tex., Austin; formerly chmn., dir. public policy program com. Chgo. Black Child Devel. Inst., 1982-84; dir. Ill. Infant Mental Health Com., 1982-83; res. adv. bd. Chgo. Urban League, 1986-97. Mem. editl. bd.: Ednl. Rschr., 2004—06, NHSA Dialog, 2004—, Human Development, 2006—; contbr. articles to profl. jours. Fellow APA (mem. divsn. ethnic and minority affairs, com. on children, youth and families, devel. psychology, bd. sci. affairs 1995-97, bd. advancement psychology pub. interest 2003-06, assoc. editor, mem. editl. bd. Child Devel. 1995-98, Disting. Contbn. to Rsch. in Pub. Policy award 1993); mem. Soc. for Rsch. in Child Devel. (governing coun. 1981-87), Am. Ednl. Rsch. Assn. (editl. bds. Rev. Ednl. Rsch., ednl. rschr.), Nat. Assn. Edn. Young Children, Assn. Study African Am. and History (life), Nat. Head Start (past Rsch. and edn. adv. bd.), Nat. Acad. Scis. (com. on child devel. and publ. policy 1987-93), Lifetime Prof. Achievement award Alumni Assn. U. Chicago, 2007, Pi Lamda Theta (Excellence Edn. award, 2009), Delta Sigma Theta. Office: U Pa Grad Sch Edn 3700 Walnut St Philadelphia PA 19104-6216 Office Phone: 215-573-3947. Business E-Mail: dianasd@gse.upenn.edu.

SLAVENS, THOMAS PAUL, library science educator; b. Cincinnati, Iowa, Nov. 12, 1928; s. William Blaine and Rhoda (Bowen) S.; m. Cora Hart, July 9, 1950; 1 son, Mark Thomas. BA, Phillips U., 1951; MDiv, Union Theol. Sem., 1954; MA, U. Minn., 1962; PhD, U. Mich., 1965. Ordained to ministry Christian Ch., 1953. Pastor First Christian Ch., Sac City, Iowa, 1953-56, Sioux Falls, SD, 1956-60; librarian Divinity Sch., Drake U., Des Moines, 1960-64; teaching fellow Sch. Info., U. Mich., Ann Arbor, 1964-65; instr. U. Mich., Ann Arbor, 1965-66, asst. prof., 1966-69, assoc. prof., 1969-77, prof., 1977—2003, prof. emeritus, 2003—. Vis. prof. U. Minn., 1967, U. Coll. of Wales, 1978, 80, 93; vis. scholar U. Oxford, Eng., 1980; cons. Nutrition Planning Abstracts-UN, N.Y.C., 1977-79. Author-editor: Library Problems in the Humanities, 1981, (with John F. Wilson) Research Guide to Religious Studies, 1982, (with W. Eugene Kleinbaur) Research Guide to the History of Western Art, 1982, (with Terrence Tice) Research Guide to Philosophy, 1983, Theological Libraries at Oxford, 1984, (with James Pruett) Research Guide to Musicology, 1985, The Literary Adviser, 1985, A Great Library through Gifts, 1986, The Retrieval of Information, 1989, Number One in the U.S.A.: Records and Wins in Sports, Entertainment, Business, and Science, 1988, Doors to God, 1990, Sources of Information for Historical Research, 1994, Introduction to Systematic Theology, 1992, Reference Interviews Questions and Materials, 3d edit., 1994, Using the Financial and Business Literature, 2004. Served with U.S. Army, 1946-48. Recipient Warner Rice Faculty award U. Mich., 1975; H.W. Wilson fellow, 1960; Lilly Endowment fellow Am. Theol. Libr. Assn., 1963. Mem. Assn. Libr. and Info. Sci. Edn. (pres. 1972), Beta Phi Mu.

SLAVICK, ANN LILLIAN, retired art educator; b. Chgo., Sept. 29, 1933; d. Irving and Goldie (Bernstein) Friedman; m. Lester Irwin Slavick, Nov. 21, 1954 (div. Mar. 1987); children: Jack, Rachel. BFA, Sch. of Art Inst. of Chgo., 1973, MA in Art History, Theory, Criticism, 1991. Dir. art gallery South Shore Commn., Chgo., 1963-67; tchr. painting, drawing, crafts Halfway House, Chgo., 1972-73; tchr. studio art Conant H.S., Hoffman Estates, Ill., 1973-74; tchr. art history and studio arts New Trier H.S., Winnetka and Northfield, Ill., 1974-80; tchr. 20th century art history New Trier Adult Edn. Program, Winnetka, 1980-81; tchr. art adult edn. program H.S. Dist. 113, Highland Park, Ill., 1980-81; rschr., writer Art History Notes McDougall-Littel Pub., Evanston, Ill., 1984-85; tchr. art and art history Highland Park and Deerfield (Ill.) H.S., 1980-2000; tchr. art history Coll. of Lake County, Grayslake, Ill., 1986-88; ret., 2000. Faculty chair for visual arts Focus on the Arts, Highland Park H.S., 1981-85, faculty coord. Focus on the Arts, 1987-2005; panelist Ill. Arts Coun. Arts Tour, 1999, Evanston Arts Coun., 2000-02, Ill. Arts Coun. Multidisciplinary Grant Awards, 2001-03; reader advanced placement art history exams, 2003, 04, 06; bd. mem. Theatre MIR. One woman show Bernal Gallery, 1979, U. Ill., Chgo., 1983, Ann Brierly Gallery, Winnetka, 1984; exhibited paintings, drawings, prints and constrns. throughout Chgo. area; work represented by Art Rental and Sales Gallery, Art Inst. Chgo., 1960-87, Bernal Gallery, 1978-82; group shows at Bernal Gallery; work in pvt. collections in Ill., N.Y., Calif., Ariz., Ohio; author: Hour Chicago, 25 One Hour Tours Art and Architecture in Chicago. Recipient Outstanding Svc. in Art Edn. award Ea. Ill. U., 1992, Mayors award for contbn. to the arts, Highland Park, 1995. Mem.: Ill. Art Edn. Assn., Nat. Art Edn. Assn. Avocations: cooking, reading, theater. Home: 5057 N Sheridan Rd Chicago IL 60640-3127 Office: Highland Park High Sch 433 Vine Ave Highland Park IL 60035-2099 E-mail: annlslavick@aol.com.

SLAVICKAS, RIMAS ANTHONY, electrical engineer, educator, researcher; s. Silvestras Kasimeras and Sofija (Koncavicius) Slavickas; m. Wilma Johanna Van Sinderen, Sept. 13, 1969; 1 child, Paul Anthony. Diploma Elec.Engring., Gordon Inst. Tech., Geelong, Victoria, Australia, 1962; BSc in Math. & Physics magna cum laude, Laurentian U., Sudbury, Ont., Can., 1969; BSc in Elec. Engring. with honours, Queens U., Kingston, Ont., Can., 1971; MSc in Applied Sci., U. Toronto, Can., 1974; PhD, McMaster U., Can., 1998. Profl. Engr., Ont., 1972. Pres., CEO Welland Hydro-Electric Sys. Corp., Ont., Canada, 1974—2003; prof. industry U. Fla., Gainesville, 2004—. Adv. bd. mem. Savo Tech Inc., Toronto, 2003—; cons. W&E Internat. Corp., Markham, Ont., Canada. Assoc. editor: Internat. Jour. Power and Energy Sys., 1998—; contbr. articles to profl. jours. Recipient Best Paper award, Internat. Conf., 2000. Mem.: IEEE (life), Assn. Profl. Engrs. Australia, Profl. Engrs. Ont. (licentiate; chmn. Niagara chpt. 1985—86). Achievements include arranging a meeting of Chinese delegation from Shanghai Municipal Electric Power Company, with Ontario's Minister of Energy to foster business opportunities between Canada and China. Home: 76 Bridlewood Drive Ontario Welland Canada L3C 6K8 Office: University Florida 320 Benton Hall Gainesville FL 32611-6200 Personal E-mail: lpa@collaborative-research.com. E-mail: ras@ece.ufl.edu.

SLAVIN, PETER L., hospital administrator; AB, Harvard U., 1979, MD, 1984, MBA, 1990. Sr. v.p., chief med. officer Mass. Gen. Hosp., Boston, 1994—97; pres. Barnes-Jewish Hosp., St. Louis, 1997-99; med. dir. Mass. Gen. Physicians Orgn., Boston, chair., CEO, 1999—2003; pres. Mass. Gen. Hosp., Boston, 2003—. Office: Mass Gen Hosp 55 Fruit St Boston MA 02114-2622 Office Phone: 617-724-9300.

SLAVIN, ROSANNE SINGER, textile converter; b. NYC, Mar. 24, 1930; d. Lee H. and Rose (Winkler) Singer; divorced; children: Laurie Jo, Sharon Lee. Grad. student, U. Ill. Prodn. converter Doucet Fabrics, silk prints, NYC, 1953-57; sales mgr., mdse. mgr. print divsn. Crown Fabrics, NYC, 1957-65; owner Matisse Fabrics, Inc. printed fabrics (now Hottmomma Inc.), NYC, 1965—. Recipient Tommy award Am. Printed Fabrics Coun., 1978, 93; designated ofcl. printed fabric supplier for U.S. Olympic swimteam, 1984. Office: 1040 Ave of Americas Ste 2411 New York NY 10018 Office Phone: 212-354-9118.

SLAVIN, SUMNER ANDREW, plastic surgeon; b. Boston, Aug. 19, 1947; MD, Univ. Vt. Coll. Med., 1973. Cert. Am. Bd. Plastic Surgery, 1983. Intern Beth Israel Deaconess Med. Ctr., Boston, 1973—74, resident in surgery, 1974—78; resident in plastic surgery NYU Med. Ctr., NYC, 1978—80, fellow in hand micro surgery, 1980—81; assoc. clin. prof. surgery Harvard Med. Sch., 1996; mem. Harvard Med. Faculty Physicians Beth Israel Deaconess Med. Ctr., Boston, chief Div. of Plastic & Reconstructive Surgery. Contbr. articles to profl. jours. Office: Beth Israel Deaconess Med Ctr 1101 Beacon St Brookline MA 02446 Office Phone: 617-277-7010. Office Fax: 617-734-5223.

SLAVINE, NIKOLAI V., science educator; s. Valentin N. and Olga P. Slavin; m. Irina A. Fokin; children: Valentine N. Slavin, Alexander N. Slavin. PhD, Joint Inst. Nuc. Rsch., Dubna, Russia, 1996. Cert. in theoretical physiscs JINR, Russia, 1996. Sr. rsch. scientist Joint Inst. Nuc. Rsch., Dubna, 1979—99; asst. prof., advanced radiol. scis. UT Southwestern Med. Ctr., Dallas, 1999—. Parishioner St. Nicholas Orthodox Ch., Dallas, Tex., 2001—09. Recipient Best Scientist, JINR, 1991, 1998. Mem.: Am. Assn. Physicists Medicine. Avocations: canoeing, hiking. Office: UT Southwestern Med Ctr Dallas Dept Radiology 5323 Harry Hines Blvd Dallas TX 75390-9058

SLAVIT, DAVID HAL, otolaryngologist; b. NYC, Sept. 5, 1960; s. Leonard S. and Barbara H. (Levine) S.; m. Robin E. Feldman, July 31, 1983; children: Danielle, Evan, Roni. BS, Cornell U., 1982; MD, Mt. Sinai U., 1986. Cert. in otolaryngology. Intern Mayo Clinic, Rochester, Minn., 1986-87, resident in otolaryngology, 1987-91; with Lenox Hill Hosp., NYC. Asst. prof. Health Sci. Ctr.-SUNY Downstate; cons. Juilliard Sch. Music, N.Y.C., 1994-99; dir. Ames Vocal Dynamics Lab., N.Y.C., 1998-2001. Author, editor: (book) Essentials of Otolaryngology, 1993; author: (books) Voice Disorders, 1995, Rhinologic Diagnosis and Treatment, 1996, Systemic Disease of the Nasal Airway, 1993; contbr. articles to profl. jours. Fellow ACS; mem. AMA, Am. Acad. Otolaryngology-Head and Neck Surgery, Am. Acad. Facial Plastic and Reconstructive Surgery, Am. Rhinologic Soc. Office Phone: 212-517-9177.

SLAVITT, DAVID WALTON, retired lawyer; b. Chgo., Mar. 15, 1931; s. Isaac and Fay (Goldstein) S.; m. Roberta Chelnek, July 26, 1953; children: Steven, Denise, Howard. BS, UCLA, 1952, JD, 1955. Bar: Calif. 1956; C.P.A., Calif. Since practiced in Los Angeles; pres. Slavitt & Borofsky (P.C.), 1969-87. Moderator continuing edn. programs. Author articles in field. Served with USNR, 1955. Mem. Am. Assn. Atty.-C.P.A.s (pres. 1964), ABA, State Bar Calif., Calif. Assn. Atty.-C.P.A.s (pres. 1963), Beverly Hills Bar Assn. (vice chmn. continuing edn. of bar 1970, asst. chmn. law practice mgmt. com. 1973).

SLAVSKY, DAVID BRUCE, academic administrator, educator; b. Newark, Sept. 18, 1951; s. Max and Lillian Slavsky; m. Debra Lynne Venckus; children: Jean Gitel, Max Vladas. BS, Brown U., Providence, 1973; MS, Harvard U., Cambridge, Mass., 1975; PhD, U. Tex., Austin, 1984. Acting dean coll. arts and scis. Loyola U. Chgo., 2001—02, dir. ctr. sci. and math edn., 2002—. Polit. action chair Ind. Voters Ill. Ind. Precinct Orgn., Chgo., 1986—88. Earth and Space Sci. Edn. fellowship, ESSEA, 2007—, numerous grants. Liberal. Jewish. Achievements include development of educational programs to enhance teaching skills of Chicago area K-12 science and math teachers. Office: Loyola Univ Chgo 6525 N Sheridan Rd Highland Park IL 60035 Business E-Mail: dslavsk@luc.edu.

SLAY, FRANCIS G., Mayor, St. Louis; b. St. Louis, Missouri, Mar. 15, 1955; s. Francis R. and Anna Slay; m. Kim Slay; children: Francis Jr., Katherine. Law, Saint Louis U. Sch. Law, 1980; postgrad in political sci., Quincy Coll., Ill., 1977. Law clerk Judge Paul J. Simon, Mo. Court Appeals, 1981; pvt. practice Guilfoil, Petzall & Shoemake, ptnr.; alderman City of St. Louis from Dist. 23, Mo., 1985—95; pres. City of St. Louis Bd. of Alderman, Mo., 1995—2001; mayor City of St. Louis, Mo., 2001—. Mem. Mayors Against Illegal Guns Coalition, St. Louis Bd. Alderman, 1985, elected pres., 1995—2001. Democrat. Achievements include development of the CityView program. Office: Mayors Office City Hall Rm 200 1200 Market St Saint Louis MO 63103 Address: Slay for Mayor PO Box 23039 Saint Louis MO 63156 Office Phone: 314-622-3201. Fax: 314-534-2007; Office Fax: 314-622-4061. E-mail: mayorslay@mayorslay.com.*

SLAYBAUGH, DOUGLAS PAUL, history educator; b. Carroll, Iowa, July 6, 1948; s. Paul and Donna Mozena Slaybaugh; m. Nancy Ann Hayes; children: Brooks Christopher, Matthew Clark. BS in History, Iowa State U., Ames, 1970; PhD in Am. History, Cornell U., Ithaca, NY, 1981. Vis. asst. prof. history Tex. Tech U., 1981—83, Wells Coll., Aurora, NY, 1984—85; rschr. Cornell U., 1985—86; asst. prof. history St. Michael's Coll., Colchester, Vt., 1986—93, assoc. prof. history, 1993—2002, prof. history, 2002—. Author: (biography) William I. Myers and the Modernization of American Agriculture. Office: St Michael's Coll Winooski Pk Colchester VT 05439 Business E-Mail: dslaybaugh@smcvt.edu.

SLAYDEN, JAMES BRAGDON, retired retail executive; b. Seattle, Sept. 28, 1924; s. Philip Lee and Ruth Alwin (Bragdon) Slayden; m. Barbara Marie McBride, May 7, 1955; children: Tracy Anne, James Bragdon. BA, U. Wash., 1948; MBA, U. So. Calif., 1949. Buyer Frederick & Nelson, Seattle, 1949-59, div. mdse. mgr., 1959-65; gen. mgr. Bullocks Westwood, Los Angeles, 1965-69; exec. v.p., gen. mdse. mgr. May D&F Co. dept. store, Denver, 1969—72; exec. v.p. Robinson dept. store, LA, 1972—73; pres. J.W. Robinson dept. store, 1974—78; exec. v.p. ops. Marshall Field & Co., Chgo., 1978—80; gen. mgr. Bullocks Del Amo, 1980—85; lectr. mktg. U. So. Calif., 1985—93. Active United Crusade United Way, LA, 1973—78, Chgo. Heart Assn., Chgo., 1978—79; chmn. Pvt. Industry Coun., 1982—95; cons. Internat. Exec. Svc. Corps., 1987—; mem. traffic com. Rancho Palos Verdes, 1994—97; mem. planning commn., 1997—2000; mem. view restoration com., 2000—04. With US Army, 1943—45. Mem.: Phi Kappa Psi. Republican. Christian Scientist. Home: 37 Mela Ln Palos Verdes Peninsula CA 90275-5086

SLAYMAKER, GENE ARTHUR, public relations executive; b. Kenton, Ohio, Sept. 15, 1928; s. Edwin Paul and Anna Elizabeth (Grable) S.; divorced; children: Jill Brook, Scott Wood, Leslie Beth; m. Julie Ann Graff, Feb. 3, 1979; 1 adopted child, Peter Fredric Bannon II; stepchildren: Jennifer Elizabeth Nash, David Frank Nash. BA in Radio Journalism, Ohio State U. Announcer, reporter WLWC-TV, Columbus, Ohio, 1951-52; anchor, reporter WKBN-AM-FM-TV, Youngstown, Ohio, 1952-56, KYW-TV, Cleve., 1956-60; editor news Sta. WFBM-AM-FM-TV, Indpls., 1960-68; pres., founder Slaymaker & Assocs. Pub. Rels., 1969—; dir. news, sports, pub. affairs WTLC-FM and WTUX-AM, Indpls., 1976-92; community rels. liaison Marion County Pros. Atty. Office, Indpls., 1993. Pres., founder Slaymaker and Assocs., Indpls., 1969—. Mambo dancer (movie) Going All the Way, 1996. Past bd. dirs. Park-Tudor Father's Assn.; mem. Meridian Kessler Neighborhood Assn., pres., 1968-69. Recipient Disting. Service award (2). Mem. Ind. AP Broadcasters Assn. (awards), UPI (awards), Nat. Fedn. Press Women, Soc. Profl. Journalists (awards Ind. chpt., bd. dirs., chpt. pres. 1991-92, Radio-TV News Dirs. Assn. (region bd. dirs. 1987-91), Indpls. Press Club, Woman's Press Club Ind., Players Club, Lambs Club (pres. 2000—). Clubs: Nat. Headliners, Unity, Ind. Broadcasting Assn. (inducted, Ind. Broadcast Hall of Fame). Democrat. Avocations: writing, painting, singing, gardening, tennis. Home: 5161 N Washington Blvd Indianapolis IN 46205-1071 Office: Slaymaker Assoc 5161 N Washington Blvd Indianapolis IN 46205-1071 Personal E-mail: slaymakers@aol.com.

SLAYMAN, CAROLYN WALCH, geneticist, educator; b. Portland, Maine, Mar. 11, 1937; d. John Weston and Ruth Dyer (Sanborn) Walch; m. Clifford L. Slayman; children: Andrew, Rachel BA with highest honors, Swarthmore Coll., Pa., 1958; PhD, Rockefeller U., NYC, 1963; DSc (hon.), Bowdoin Coll., Brunswick, Maine, 1985. Instr., then asst. prof. Case Western Res. U., Cleve., 1967; from asst. prof. to prof. genetics Yale U. Sch. Medicine, New Haven, 1967—, Sterling prof.

genetics, 1991—, chmn. dept. genetics, 1984-95, dep. dean acad. and sci. affairs, 1995—. Chmn. genetic basis of disease rev. commn. NIH, 1981—85, nat. adv. gen. med. scis. coun., 1989—93; bd. dirs. J. Weston Walch Pub., Portland, Maine, Applera Corp., 1995—2008; mem. sci. rev. bd. Howard Hughes Med. Inst., 1992—97. Mem. editl. bd. Jour. Biol. Chemistry, 1989-94; contbr. articles to sci. jours. Trustee Foote Sch., New Haven, 1983—89, Hopkins Sch., New Haven, 1988—93; bd. overseers Dartmouth Med. Sch., 1997—2003, Woods Hole Oceanographic Instn., Mass., 1997—2007, Bowdoin Coll., 1976—88, trustee, 1988—2001. Recipient Deborah Morton award Westbrook Coll., 1986. Mem. Am. Soc. Biol. Chemists, Genetics Soc. Am., Soc. Gen. Physiologists, Am. Soc. Microbiology, Inst. Medicine, Phi Beta Kappa Office Phone: 203-737-1770.

SLECHTA, JIRI, theoretical physicist; b. Havlickuv Brod, Bohemia, Czechoslovakia, Apr. 26, 1939; came to Eng., 1969; s. Josef and Marie (Posikova) S.; m. Miriam Vydrarova, July 17, 1971; children: Vera, Martin. Dr rer. nat., Charles U., Prague, Czechoslovakia, 1962. Sr. lectr. dept. theoretical physics Charles U., Prague, 1964-69; rsch. fellow dept. physics U. Warwick, Conventry, Eng., 1969-71; sr. rsch. assoc. Sch. Math. and Physics U. East Anglia, Norwich, Eng., 1971-74; rsch. fellow dept. physics U. Leeds, England, 1976-77. Chair 3 Symposiums 13th Internat. Congress on Cybernetics, Namur, Belgium, 1992; co-chmn. symposium 17th World Congress SVU, Prague, 1994, chair symposium 14th Internat. Congress on Cybernetics, Namur, 1995, Knowledge Transfer 96, London; rschr. and presented in field. Author 67 papers and 42 contbns. at nonpub. confs.; editor Informatica; patentee in field 2d lt. Czechoslovakia mil., 1962-64. Benevolent Fund Inst. of Physics ann. grantee, London, 1979—; recipient Gold Coins Genius 21st Century Am. Biog. Inst., 1994, 95, 96. Assoc. fellow Inst. Math. and Applications; mem. Am. Phys. Soc., Internat. Acad. Scis. San Marino, Inst. Physics, European Phys. Soc., Brit. Cybernetic Soc., Internat. Assn. Cybernetics, Internat. Cybernetics Acad., NY Acad. Scis., Czechoslovak Math. Phys. Union, Czech Soc. Arts and Sci. Mem. Conservative party. Achievements include theory of disordered materials and self-organizing systems (brain, economy, society) and cybernetics; mathematical theory of Darwinism. Home and Office: 5 Beckhill Chase Leeds LS7 2RQ England Office Phone: 44 113 216 5654. Office Fax: 44 113 216 5654. E-mail: jirislechta@hotmail.com, jiri_slechta@yahoo.co.uk.

SLEDD, ROBERT C., food products executive; Dir. Taylor & Sledd Industries, 1974—87, pres. & CEO, 1984—87; dir. Performance Food Group, 1987—, pres., 1987-95, CEO, 1987—2001, 2004—06, chmn., 1995—2008; mng. ptnr. Pinnacle Ventures, LLC, Sledd Properties, LLC. Bd. dir. SCP Pool Corp., Internat. Foodservice Distributor Assn.; bd. dirs. Owens & Minor, Inc., SCP Pool Corp., Universal Corp., 2009. Vice chmn. Homeward, 2000—; bd. dir. Better Housing Coalition, 2000—, Va. Found. for Performing Arts; trustee Va. Found. of Independent Colleges; chmn. bus. adv. bd. Hilliard House. Office: Pinnacle Ventures Ste 110 130 Lytton Ave Palo Alto CA 94301 Office Phone: 650-926-7800. Office Fax: 650-926-7801.

SLEDGE, CHARLES M., oil industry executive; BS in Accounting, La. State U.; grad., Advanced Mgmt. Program, Harvard Bus. Sch. CPA. With Price Waterhouse LLP, 1989—96; v.p., controller Stage Stores Inc., 1996—99, sr. v.p. fin., treas., 1999—2001; corp. controller Cameron Internat. Corp., Houston, 2001—08, v.p., CFO, 2008, sr. v.p., CFO, 2008—. Office: Cameron Internat Corp 1333 W Loop S, Ste 1700 Houston TX 77027*

SLEED, JOEL, columnist; b. NYC, Jan. 29, 1929; m. MaryLou Kalwara, Nov. 15, 1983; children: Jodie, Jill, Jeffrey, Kristin Kalwara, Karen Hepler. Former travel editor The Star-Ledger, Newark, Newhouse News Svc., Washington; columnist travel sect. Sunday Rep., Springfield, Mass.; travel editor Palm Beach Soc. mag. Office: Newhouse Newspapers 711 Third Ave New York NY 10017 E-mail: joelsleed@msn.com.

SLEEP, NORMAN H., geophysics educator; BS in Math., Mich. State U., 1967; MS in Geophysics, MIT, 1969, PhD in Geophysics, 1973. Postdoc. rsch. assoc. Mass. Inst. Tech., Cambridge, 1973; asst. prof. Geophysics Northwestern U., Evanston, Ill., 1973-79; from assoc. prof. to prof. Geophysics Stanford U., Palo Alto, Calif., 1979—. Contbr. articles to profl. jours. including Earth Planetary Sci., J. Geophysical Rsch., Nature. Recipient James B. Macelwane award, 1980, George P. Woollard award, 1991. Fellow Am. Geophysical Union (Walter H. Bucher medal 1998), Geological Soc. Am., AAAS. Office: Stanford U Dept Geophysics Mitchell Bldg Rm 373A Palo Alto CA 94305-2215

SLEEPER, NANCY JOANN, mental health services professional; d. John Harold and Helen Amelia Sagdahl; m. John Edward Tracy (div.); children: Christopher Tracy, Heidi Thorley, Jeffrey Tracy, Scott Tracy; m. Richard Edwin Sleeper, Jan. 26. BS in Psychology, Wash. State U., Pullman, 1977; MA in Clin. Psychology, John F. Kennedy U., Orinda, Calif., 1985. LCSW Wis.; lic. profl. counselor Ill., mental health counselor Wash. Nat. Bd. Addiction Examiners, nat. cert. counselor. Mental health profl. KTSAP Mental Health Svcs., Bremerton, 1988—90; exceptional family mem. program coord. Army Comty. Svc., Schofield Barracks, Hawaii, 1991—93; new parent support team counselor Navy Family Svc. Ctr., Great Lakes, Ill., 1993—95; therapist Luth. Social Svcs., Bremerton, 1995—96; MICA specialist, older adults therapist KTSAP Mental Health Svcs., Bremerton, 1996—2000; substance abuse counselor Dept. Army, 104th ASG, Germany, 2000—03, Dept. Army, Ft. Huachuca, Ariz., 2003—07. Mem. Comty. Emergency Response Team, Sierra Vista, Ariz., 2004—. Fellow: Am. Psychotherapy Assn. (diplomate & fellow); mem.: ACA. Mem. Lds Ch. Office: Behavioral Health Svcs RW Bliss Army Health Ctr Fort Huachuca AZ 85613 Business E-Mail: nancy.sleeper@us.army.mil.

SLEETER, CHRISTINE ELAINE, education educator; b. Medford, Oreg., Sept. 5, 1948; d. Robert W. and Pearl E. (Fawcett) S. BA in Polit. Sci., Willamette U., 1970; BA in Secondary Edn., Cen. Wash. State U., 1972; MA in Curriculum and Instrn., Seattle U., 1977; PhD in Curriculum and Instrn., U. Wis., 1981. Substitute tchr. Seattle Pub. Schs., 1972-73; tchr. learning disabilities program Roosevelt High Sch., Seattle, 1973-77; project asst. tchr. corps asssocs. program U. Wis., Madison, 1978-80, teaching asst. dept. curriculum and instrn., 1977-78, 80-81, rsch. specialist Wis. Ctr. for Edn. Rsch., 1981-82; asst. prof. dept. edn. Ripon (Wis.) Coll., 1982-85; asst. prof. div. edn. U. Wis.-Parkside, Kenosha, 1985-87, assoc. prof., 1987-92, prof., 1992—. Lectr. dept. curriculum and instrn. Seattle U., summer 1979; lectr. dept. ednl. policy studies U. Wis.-Madison, summer 1982, vis. asst. prof., summer 1983; vis. assoc. prof. dept. curricuum and instrn. U. Wash., Seattle, summer 1987; cons., presenter, speaker in field. Author: Keepers of the American Dream, 1992; co-editor: Adolescent Development and Secondary Schooling, 1982, Empowerment Through Multicultural Education, 1991; co-author: After the School Bell Rings, 1986, Making Choices for Multicultural Education: Five Approaches to Race, Class and Gender, 1988, Turning on Learning, 1989; contbr. articles to profl. jours., chpts. to books. Grantee Joyce Found., 1987-91, U. Wis. System Inst. on Race and Ethnicity, 1989. Mem. Midwest Human Rels. Assn. (pres. 1988-91), Wis. State Human Rels. Assn. (pres. exec. bd. 1985-86), Coun. for Exceptional Children, Am. Anthropol. Assn. (coun. on anthropology and edn. 1980—), Am. Ednl. Rsch. Assn. Democrat. Unitarian-Universalist. Avocations: reading, clarinet, sewing, pets, travel. Office: U Wis-Parkside Dept Edn PO Box 2000 Kenosha WI 53141-2000

SLEIGH, SYLVIA, artist, educator; b. Llandudno, North Wales, 1916; came to U.S., 1961; d. John Harold and Katherine Amy (Miller) S.; m. Lawrence Alloway, June 28, 1954. Student, Sch. Art, Brighton, Sussex, Eng., 1932-36; diploma, U. London Extra-Mural Dept., 1947. Vis. asst. prof. SUNY-Stony Brook, 1978; instr. New Sch. Social Research, NYC, 1974-77, 78-80; Edith Kreeger Wolf disting. prof. Northwestern U., Evanston, Ill., 1977; vis. artist Baldwin Seminar Oberlin Coll., Ohio, 1982, New Sch. Social Rsch., NYC. One person shows include Bennington (Vt.) Coll., 1963, Soho 20 Art Gallery, NYC, 1974, 76, 80, 82, 85, 99, 2004, A.I.R. Gallery, NYC, 1974, 76, 78, Ohio State U., Columbus, 1976, Matrix, Wadsworth Atheneum, Hartford, Conn., 1976, Marianne Deson Gallery, Chgo., 1990, G.W. Einstein, Inc., NYC., 1980, 83, 85, U. Mo., Saint Louis, 1981, Zaks Gallery, Chgo., 1985, 95, Milw. Art Mus., Butler Inst., Youngstown, Ohio, 1990, Stiebel Modern, NYC, 1992, 94, Gallery 609, Denver, Canton (Ohio) Art Inst., Deven Golden Fine Arts, NYC, 1999, Phila. Art Alliance, Phila., 2001, Snug Harbor Cultural Ctr., Newhouse Ctr. Contemporary Art, S.I., NY, 2005, Hudson River Mus., Yonkers, NY, 2006, I-20 Gallery, NYC, 2007; exhibited in group shows Newhouse Gallery, S.I., NY, Stamford (Conn.) Mus., 1985, Albany Inst. Art, Cin. Art Mus., New Orleans Mus. Art, Denver Art Mus., Pa. Acad. Fine Arts, 1989, Carlsten Art Gallery, Stevens Point, Wis., 1993, Stiebel Modern, NYC, 1994, Soho 20, NYC, 1993, 96, Katzen Brown Gallery, NYC, 1989, Zaks Gallery, Chgo., 1986, Steinbaum Krauss Gallery, 1997, Deven Golden Fine Arts, Ltd., NYC, 1997, Rutgers U., New Brunswick, NJ, 1984, 86, RioArriba Gallery, Abiquiu, N.Mex., 1996, Milw. Art Mus., 1996, Steinbaum Krauss Gallery, 1997, NY Mus. exhbn. traveling until 2001, David and Alfred Smart Mus., Chgo., Broome St. Gallery, NYC, Deven Golden Fine Arts, NYC, A.I.R. Gallery, NYC, Apex Art Co., NYC, 1998, McKee Gallery, NYC, 1998, Royal Coll. Art, London, 1998, Heckscher Mus. Art, Huntington, N.Y., 1999, Printworks Gallery, 2000, SoHo 20, NYC, 2004, Mason Gross at Rutgers U., NJ, 2005, Mus. Contemp. Art, LA, 2006, I-20 Gallery, NYC, 2006, A+D Gallery, Chgo., 2007. Panelist Creative Artists Pub. Service Program, NYC, 1976. Nat. Endowment for Arts grantee, 1982, Pollock-Krasner Found. grantee, 1985. Mem. Women's Caucus for Art, Coll. Art Assn. (Lifetime Achievement in Art award, 2007). Home: 330 W 20th St New York NY 10011-3302 Personal E-mail: ssallway@verizon.net.*

SLEIK, THOMAS SCOTT, lawyer; b. La Crosse, Wis., Feb. 24, 1947; s. John Thomas and Marion Gladys (Johnson) S.; m. Judith Mattson, Aug. 24, 1968; children: Jennifer, Julia, Joanna. BS, Marquette U., 1969, JD, 1971. Bar: Wis. 1971, U.S. Dist. Ct. (we. dist.) Wis. 1971. Assoc. Hale Skemp Hanson Skemp & Sleik, La Crosse, 1971-74, ptnr., 1975—. Bd. mem. Wis. Lawyer Mut. Ins. Co., 1999—. State pres. Boy Scouts Am., 1981—83, bd. dirs. Gateway Area Con., 1973—99, pres., 1980—81; trustee La Crosse Pub. Libr., 1981—, chair, bd. trustees, 2006—; bd. dirs. Children's Mus. of La Crosse, 1997—2002, Greater La Crosse Area United Way, 1985—92, campaign chmn., 1986, pres., 1987; mem. Sch. Dist. La Crosse Bd. Edn., 1973—77, v.p., 1977; festmaster Oktoberfest (LaCross Festivals Inc.), 2001, trustee, 2001—; bd. mem. Franciscan Skemp Healthcare, 2003—. Fellow Am. Acad. Matrimonial Lawyers (pres. Wis. chpt. 1999-2000); mem. ABA, State Bar Wis. (bd. govs. 1987-94, pres. 1992-93). Roman Catholic. Home: 4082 Glenhaven Dr La Crosse WI 54601-7503 Office: Hale Skemp Hanson Skemp & Sleik 505 King St Ste 300 La Crosse WI 54602-1927

SLEMON, GORDON RICHARD, electrical engineering educator; b. Bowmanville, Ont., Can., Aug. 15, 1924; s. Milton Everitt and Selena (Johns) S.; m. Margaret Jean Matheson, July 9, 1949; children: Sally, Stephen, Mark, Jane. BASc., U. Toronto, 1946, MASc., 1948; D.I.C., Imperial Coll. Sci., London U., Eng., 1951, PhD, 1952; D of Engring. (hon.), Meml. U. Nfld., 1994. Asst. prof. elec. engring. N.S. Tech. Coll., Can., 1953-55; assoc. prof. U. Toronto, Ont., Can., 1955-63, prof. Ont., 1964-90, chmn. dept. elec. engring. Ont., 1966-76, dean of faculty of applied sci. and engring. Ont., 1979-86, prof. emeritus Ont., 1990—. Colombo plan adviser, India, 1963-64; pres. Elec. Engring. Consociates, 1976-79; bd. dirs. Inverpower Controls Ltd., Innovations Found. Author: (with J.M. Ham) Scientific Basis of Electrical Engineering, Magnetoelectric Devices, (with A. Straughen) Electric Machinery; (with S.B. Dewan, A. Straughen) Power Semiconductor Drives, Electric Machines and Drives; contbr. articles to profl. jours. Chmn. Innovations Found., 1980-93, vice chmn., 1993—97; chmn. Microelectronics Devel. Ctr., 1983-88. Decorated officer Order of Can.; recipient excellence in tchg. award Western Electric, 1965, Can. Centennial medal, 1967, Ross medal, 1978, 83, Gold medal Jugoslav Union of Nikola Tesla Socs., Engring. Alumni medal, Educator of Yr. award Can. Engrs., 1992, Hall of Distinction award U. Toronto, 1992, Achievement award IEEE Magnetics Soc., 1997, Arbor award U. Toronto, 1997. Fellow Can. Acad. Engring. (pres. 1998-99), Engring. Inst. Can., Instn. Elec. Engrs. (hon. fellow 1995), IEEE (Centennial medal 1984, Nikola Tesla award, Millennium medal 2000, Prof. Engrs. Engring. Excellence award 2005); mem. Am. Soc. Engring. Edn., others. Achievements include patents in field. Home: 40 Chatfield Dr Don Mills ON Canada M3B 1K5 Office: U Toronto Fac Applied Sci and Engring Toronto ON M5S 3G4 Canada Business E-Mail: g.slemon@utoronto.ca.

SLESNICK, TIMOTHY, cardiologist, educator; MD, Baylor Coll. Medicine, Houston, 2001. Diplomate in pediat. cardiology Am. Bd. Pediat., 2009. Asst. prof. pediatric cardiology Baylor Coll. Medicine, Houston, 2007—08, 2008—. Mem.: Am. Heart Assn. (mem. of the early career and mentoring subcommittee 2006—09).

SLETTEHAUGH, THOMAS CHESTER, retired art educator; b. Mpls., May 8, 1925; s. Melvin Joseph and Gertrude Mary (Henry) Slettehaugh; m. Mary Madonna Rude, June 18, 1946; children: Mary Lee, John Thomas, MaryPaul Karen, Joan Diane, Peter Ford. Diploma naval air fighter pilot and aero. engring., Williams Coll., U. SC and U. Ga., 1943—45; BS, U. Minn., 1949, MEd, 1950; student, Syracuse U., 1954; EdD, Pa. State U., 1956. Grad. tchg. asst. U. Minn., 1949—50; art educator Mpls. Pub. Schs., 1950, Albert Lea H.S., Minn., 1950—52; prof., head art dept. State Tchrs. U., Springfield, SD, 1952—54; art instr., ednl. TV artist Pa. State U., University Park, 1954—56; prof. art State Coll. at Slippery Rock, Pa., 1956—62; vis. prof. art edn. Ctr. for Syracuse U., Chautauqua, NY, 1957—58; prof. art, head art and art edn. Frostburg State Coll., Md., 1962—68; prof. art, head fine arts, dir. gallery and mus. Miss. U. for Women, 1968—70; assoc. prof. art edn., full mem. grad. sch. Coll. Edn. and Human Devel. U. Minn., Mpls., 1970—87, prof. emeritus, 1987—. Vis. prof. art Cambridge U., 1976—77, Leicester Poly., 1976—77, Heidelburg U., Germany, 1976—77, Fine Arts Ctr., Almeria, Spain, 1976—77, Cultural Ctr., Zagreb, Croatia, 1976—77, Pedagogy Inst., Budapest, Hungary, 1976—77, Fine Art Sch., Vienna, 1976—77, Friendship Ctr., Moscow, 1976—77; vis. scholar Ednl. Bur., Xian, China, 1981, Cath. U., Montevideo, Uruguay, 1984, Centro Artistico Artesanai, Buenos Aires, 1984, Kenyatta U., Nairobi, 1986—88, Casa Strobele, Borgo/Valsugana, Italy, 1991, Museu de Arte Contemproanea da Univ., São Paulo, 1991, Internat. Creativita Arte Sella, 1992, Humboldt U., Germany, 1993, U. Lisbon, 2004. Numerous articles to profl. jours., exhibitions include Minn. State Fine Arts Exhbn., Mpls. Inst. Fine Arts, Washington County Mus. Fine Art, Md., Mpls. Pub. Libr., numerous others, Walker Art Ctr., Mpls., The Woman IKKONN photo montage, Lisbon, 2004, Art of Life Sci., Photo Montage, Avignon U., France, 2006, prin. works include outdoor sculptures Shrine St. Anthony, Forrestville, Pa., 1958, Symbol of Excellence at MSCW campus, Columbus, Miss., 1969, prin. works include Apollo 14 Moon Art, 1971; author: Mexico Visto Por Sus Ninos, 1981, Art in Education: An International Perspective, 1984. Aviation cadet USN, 1943—45. Recipient 50 Yr. Artistic Participation award, 2003, Minn. Fine Arts Pinnacle of Achievement award, Cambridge, Eng., 2006, 100 Disting Alumni Centennial award, U. Minn. Coll. Edn. and Human Devel., 2006, Minn.'s Greatest Generation award, Minn. Hist. Soc., 2006; named Hon. Emeritus Artist, Coffman Gallery, St. Paul, Minn., 2009;, Pa. State U. scholar, 1954—56. Mem.: Scottish Soc. Art and Psychopathology, Internat. Union Archs., Internat. Coun. on Edn. for Tchg., Internat. Assn. Empirical Aesthetics, Internat. Soc. Aesthetics, Internat. Congress Art Historians, Internat. Soc. Edn. through Art (U.S. rep. on world coun.), U.S. Soc. for Edn. through Art, Nat. Art Edn. Assn., Ptnrs. of Ams., Minn./Uruguay, U. Minn. Woman's Club (quasi-mem. art sect. 2004). Home: 49 Williams Ave SE Minneapolis MN 55414-3449 Office: Slettehaugh-Studio Gallery 49 WIlliams Ave SE Minneapolis MN 55414-3449 Personal E-mail: slett001@tc.umn.edu.

SLEVIN, EILEEN T., insurance company executive; b. Feb. 10, 1954; B, Lehman Coll., CUNY. Various mgmt. positions NY Life Ins. Co., NYC, 1977—88, asst. v.p., 1988—91, corp. v.p., 1991—93, v.p., 1993—99, sr. v.p., 1999—2007, sr. v.p., chief info. officer, 2007—. Mem.: Health Ins. Assn. Am., Acad. Women Leaders, YWCA NYC. Office: New York Life 51 Madison Ave New York NY 10010*

SLEZAK, SHERI, plastic surgeon; b. Fort Riley, Kans., Dec. 30, 1953; MD, Harvard U., 1980. Cert. Gen. Surgery, Plastic and Reconstructive Surgery. Resident, gen. surgery Columbia-Presbyterian Med. Ctr., NYC, 1980—85; fellow, plastic surgery John Hopkins Hosp., Balt., 1986—89; assoc. prof., plastic surgery U. Md. Sch. Medicine; dir., breast reconstruction U. Md. Med. Ctr. Office: U Md Med Ctr 22 S Greene St Baltimore MD 21201

SLEZKINE, YURI, history professor; b. Moscow, Feb. 7, 1956; came to US, 1983; s. Lev Y. and Karma M. (Goldstein) S.; m. Lisa C. Little, Nov. 21, 1984; 1 child, Peter A. BA, MA, Moscow State U., 1978; PhD, U. Tex., 1989. Transl., Port Beira, Mozambique, 1978-79; editor Progress Pub., Moscow, 1980-82; instr. Linguacoop Lang. Inst., Lisbon, Portugal, 1982-83; instr. Slavic Studies U. Tex., 1983-86; asst. prof. history Wake Forest U., Winston-Salem, NC, 1989—92, Univ. Calif., Berkeley, 1992—94, assoc. prof. history, 1994—98, prof. of history, 1998—, dir. Inst. Slavic, East European & Eurasian studies. Bd. trustees Nat. Coun. Soviet and East European Rsch., 1995—2001; disting. vis. prof. Vassar Coll., Poughkeepsie, NY, 2002; spl. prof. U. Nottingham, England, 2006—09. Author: Arctic Mirrors: Russia and the Small Peoples of the North, 1994 (Book of Yr. award, Am. Hist. Assn., 1995), The Jewish Century, 2004 (Best Scholarly Book in Religion, Assn. Am. Publishers, 2004, Wayne S. Vucinich book prize, Am. Assn. Advancement Slavic Studies, 2005, Nat. Jewish Book award, 2005, Ronald S. Lauder award, 2005); co-author: Speak Russian, 1990; asst. editor Slavic Rev., 1985-87; co-editor: In the Shadow of Revolution: Life Stories of Russian Women from 1917 to the Second World War, 2000, Between Heaven and Hell: The Myth of Siberia in Russian Culture, 1993. Pew grantee Wake Forest U., 1990; Postdoctoral fellow Social Sci. Rsch. Coun., 1990, Fgn. Lang. and Area Studies fellow U. Tex., 1988-89, Univ. fellow U. Tex., 1987-88. Fellow Am. Acad. Arts and Sciences; mem. Am. Hist. Assn. (prog. com., 1995), Am. Assn. Advancement Slavic Studies (bd. dirs.). Office: UC Berkeley History Dept 2220 Dwindle Hall Berkeley CA 94720 also: UC Berkeley ISEES 260 Stephens Hall 2304 Berkeley CA 94720-2304 Office Phone: 510-642-3230, 510-642-2224. Office Fax: 510-643-5045. E-mail: isees@berkeley.edu, slezkine@berkeley.edu.

SLICE, KIMBO (KEVIN FERGUSON), mixed martial arts fighter; b. Nassau, Bahamas, Feb. 8, 1974; s. Rosemary Clarke; 6 children. Attended, Bethune-Cookman Coll., Daytona Beach, Fla., U. Miami, Coral Gables, Fla. Bodyguard RK Netmedia, Miami; underground street fighter Miami; mixed martial arts fighter EliteXC, 2007—08. Winner by submission vs. Bo Cantrell EliteXC: Renegade, 2007; winner by knockout vs. Tank Abbott EliteXC: Street Certified, 2008; winner by tech. knockout vs. James Thompson EliteXC: Primetime, 2008; loser by tech. knockout vs. Seth Petruzelli EliteXC: Heat, 2008. Office: Team Kimbo 1031 N Miami Beach Blvd Miami FL 33162*

SLICHTER, CHARLES PENCE, physicist, researcher; b. Ithaca, NY, Jan. 21, 1924; s. Sumner Huber and Ada (Pence) S.; m. Gertrude Thayer Almy, Aug. 23, 1952 (div. Sept. 1977); children: Sumner Pence, William Almy, Jacob Huber, Ann Thayer; m. Anne FitzGerald, June 7, 1980; children: Daniel Huber, David Pence AB in Physics, Harvard U., 1946, MA in Physics, 1947, PhD in Physics, 1949; DSc (hon.), U. Waterloo, 1993; LLD (hon.), Harvard U., 1996. Rsch. asst. Underwater Explosives Rsch. Lab., Woods Hole, Mass., 1943-46; faculty U. Ill., Urbana-Champaign, 1949—, asst. prof. physics, 1951—54, assoc. prof. physics, 1954—55, prof. physics, 1955, prof. Ctr. for Advanced Study, 1968-97, prof. chemistry, 1986—96, rsch. prof. physics, 1996—, prof. emeritus, 1996—. Morris Loeb lectr. Harvard U., 1961; mem. Pres.'s Sci. Adv. Com., 1964-69, Com. on Nat. Medal Sci., 1969-74, Nat. Sci. Bd., 1975-84, Pres.'s Com. Sci. and Tech., 1976 Author: Principles of Magnetic Resonance, 1963, 3d edit., 1989; Contbr. articles to profl. jours. Former trustee, mem. corp. Woods Hole Oceanog. Instn.; mem. Harvard Corp., 1970-95. Recipient Tau Beta Pi Daniel C. Drucker award, 1989, 2007 Nat. Medal Sci.; Alfred P. Sloan fellow, 1955-61. Fellow AAAS, Am. Phys. Soc.(mem. chem. physics divsn. condensed matter divsn., former councillor, Langmuir prize in chem. physics, 1969, Oliver E. Buckley prize in condensed matter physics, 1996), Internat. Electron Paramagnetic Resonance Soc.; mem. NAS (Comstock prize 1993), Am. Acad. Arts and Scis., Am. Philos. Soc., Internat. Soc. Magnetic Resonance (vp 1983-86, pres. 1987-90, Triennial prize 1986), Phi Beta Kappa, Sigma Xi. Office Phone: 217-333-3834. Office Fax: 217-244-7559. Business E-Mail: cslichte@illinois.edu.

SLIESORAITIS, SARUNAS, pharmacist, educator; s. Vytautas Sliesoraitis and Lazauskiene; m. Indira Malave; children: Mantas, Eva. PharmD, U. Conn., Storrs, 2001; grad., LECOM, Erie, Pa., 2009, DO in Osteopathic Medicine. Cert. oncology pharmacist Bd. Pharmacy Specialties, 2003. Medic Army N.G., Waterburry, Conn., 1995—2001; gen. practice pharmacy resident Froedtert Hosp., Milw., 2001—02; oncology pharmacy practice resident Moffitt Cancer Ctr., Tampa, Fla., 2002—03; asst. prof. pharmacy practice LECOM, 2003—. Contbr. articles to profl. jours. Sgt. US Army. Decorated Army Res. Achievement award Army N.G.; named Tchr. of Yr., 2007—09. Mem.: Sigma Sigma Phi.

SLIETY, MAZIN K., engineering educator; 1 child, Layla Mazin. PhD in Sys. Engring., Oakland U., Rochester, Mich., 2007. Cert. profl. engr., Mich., 2006. Project engr. OnStar, Detroit, 2001—05; principle sys. engr. Harman Internat., Farmington Hills, Mich., 2005—07; asst. prof. Lawrence Tech. U., Southfield, Mich., 2007—. Author: (book) The Performance of GPS Antennas and Receivers in Telematics; contbr. articles to profl. publs. Mem.: IEEE (sr. mem.), Am. Scholars Nat. Honor Soc., Soc. Industry Leaders, Am. Soc. Engring. Educators, Eta Kappa Nu. Achievements include patents in field. Office: Lawrence Tech Univ 21000 West Ten Mile Rd Southfield MI 48075 Business E-Mail: msliety@ieee.org.

SLIFKA, ERIC, oil industry executive; s. Alfred A. Slifka. With Global Cos. LLC, 1987—, various sr. positions in acctg., supply, distbn. and mktg. to predecessor cos., COO, dir., 1998—2004, pres., CEO, dir., 2004, Global Ptnrs., 2005—. Office: Global Ptnrs PO Box 9161 Waltham MA 02454-9161 Office Phone: 781-894-8800.

SLIGAR, STEPHEN GARY, molecular biologist, educator; b. Inglewood, Calif., Mar. 19, 1948; BS, Drexel U., Phila., 1970; MS, U. Ill., Urbana-Champaign, 1971, PhD, 1975. Postdoctoral rsch. assoc. dept. biochemistry U. Ill., Urbana-Champaign, 1975—77, assoc. prof. dept. biochemistry, 1982—86, prof. depts. biochemistry, chemistry and biophysics and Ctr. Biophysics, 1986—, Beckman Inst. prof., 1988—, dir. Sch. Chem. Scis., 1994—97, prof. Coll. Medicine, 1995—, I.C. Gunsalus endowed chair biochemistry, 2005—, dir. Sch. Molecular and Cellular Biology, 2007—; asst. prof. dept. molecular biophysics and biochemistry Yale U., New Haven, 1977—82; pres., CEO Nanodisc, Inc., 2003—06. Mem. sci. bd. Frontier Rsch. Program RIKEN, Wako, Japan, 1997—99. Contbr. articles to sci. jours., chapters to books. Recipient Protein Soc. Ann. Eli Lilly award, 2003; grantee Japan Soc. for Promotion of Sci. Sr. fellowship, 1999. Fellow: AAAS; mem.: Sigma Xi, Phi Kappa Phi, Pi Mu Epsilon, Sigma Pi Sigma. Office: Sch Molecular and Cellular Biology U Ill 393 Morrill Hall 505 S Goodwin Urbana IL 61801 Office Phone: 217-244-7395. Office Fax: 217-265-4073. E-mail: s-sligar@uiuc.edu.

SLIGER, HERBERT JACQUEMIN, JR., lawyer; b. Urbana, Ill., Nov. 21, 1948; s. Herbert Jacquemin and Marina (Mantia) Sliger; children: Lauren Christine, Matthew Ryan, Nicholas Adam, Claire Nicole, Adam Gregory; m. Ann Marceil Short, Nov. 8, 2008. BS in Fin., U. Ill., 1970; JD, U. Ariz., 1974. CPA Okla.; bar: Ariz. 1974, Ill. 1975, US Supreme Ct. 1983, Okla. 1984, US Ct. Appeals (7th cir.) 1980, US Tax Ct. 1980. Lawyer Charles W. Phillips Law Offices, Harrisburg, Ill., 1974—75; trust counsel Magna Trust Co., F/K/A Millikin Nat. Bank, Decatur, Ill., 1976—80, First of America Trust Co., Springfield, Ill., 1980—83; trust counsel personal fin. svcs. group First Interstate Bank Okla. NA, Oklahoma City, 1983—86; mgr. employee benefits trust dept. First Interstate Bank of Okla., NA, Oklahoma City, 1986—89; v.p., pension counsel Star Bank, NA, Cin., Cin., 1989—90; asst. gen. counsel Bank One Ariz. Corp., Phoenix, 1990—95; asst. gen. counsel, nat. practice group head Banc One Corp., Columbus, Ohio, 1995—98, state gen. counsel Phoenix, 1996—97; sec. of bd. and cashier Bank One, Ariz. NA, 1996—97; sec. of bd. and statutory agt. Banc One Ariz. Corp., 1996—97; sec. bd. Bank One Trust Co. N.A., Columbus, 1996—2006; asst. gen. counsel, trust counsel practice group head law dept. Bank One Corp., 1999—2003, sr. counsel, 2003—04, J.P. Morgan Chase & Co., Phoenix, 2004—05, v.p., asst. gen. counsel, 2005—. Co-chmn. Nat. Conf. Lawyers and Corp. Fiduciaries, 1992—94, 2006—; instr. Chaminade U., Hawaii, Hawaii Tax Inst., 1999. Contbr. articles to profl. jours. With USMCR, 1970—76. Mem.: ABA (sect. real property, probate and trust law 1974—, banking law com. 1991—99, sect. taxation, employee benefits com. 1991—2001, fiduciary environ. problems com. 1993—99, sect. bus. law), Am. Corp. Counsel Assn., Am. Bankers Assn. (chmn. trust counsel com. 1992—94, trust and investment divsn. exec. com. 1992—94, mem., head fiduciary dept. Nat./Grad. Trust Sch. Bd. Faculty Advisors 1994—95, spokesman environ. risk task force 1994—95, faculty mem. under ERISA Nat. Employee Benefit Trust Sch. 1994—96, mini-adv. bd. chmn. trusts and estates 1995—99, trust counsel com. 2006—), Okla. Bar Assn., State Bar Ariz. (chmn. ethics com. 2002—05, exec. com. probate and trust sect.). Roman Catholic. Office Phone: 480-333-4472. Business E-Mail: herb.j.sliger@jpmchase.com.

SLIGER, REBECCA NORTH, mechanical engineer; b. Coventry, England, Sept. 23, 1967; came to U.S., 1967; d. Paul and Margaret Ann (Horner) North; m. David Matthew Sliger, Mar. 23, 1991. BS, U. Utah, 1991; MS, U. Wash., 1995, postgrad., 1995—. Analyst Tenera, Idaho Falls, Idaho, 1991-93. Diamond scholar, U. Utah, 1990-91. Mem. ASME, Am. Nuclear Soc., Tau Beta Pi, Pi Tau Sigma.

SLIM, MICHEL S., surgeon, educator, health facility administrator; b. Nov. 18, 1929; s. Saliba and Julia Slim; m. Norma Gebara, Sept. 4, 1958; children: Julie, Lina, Nayla. MD, Am. U., Beirut, Lebanon, 1954. Diplomate Am. Bd. Surgery, Am. Bd. Pediatric Surgery, Am. Bd. Thoracic Surgery. Prof. surgery Am. U., Beirut, 1963-86, N.Y. Med. Coll., 1986—2006, prof. emeritus NY, 2006—; attending Westchester Med. Ctr., Valhalla, 1986—, chief pediatric trauma, 1991—2006, chief pediatric surgery, 1994—2002. Editl. cons. Pediatric Surg. Internat., 1985-2004; reviewer Ann. Thoracic Surgery, Jordan Med. Jour. Jour. Jordan Royal Med. Svcs.; contbr. articles to profl. jours Evarts Graham Traveling fellow Am. Assn. Thoracic Surgery, 1970-71. Fellow ACS, Am. Acad. Pediat., Am. Coll. Chest Physicians, Soc. Critical Care Medicine; mem. Am. Pediatric Surgery Assn., Brit. Assn. Pediatric Surgery, Internat. Soc. Surgery, Eastern Assn. for Surgery of Trauma. Office Phone: 914-493-7620. Personal E-mail: normichslim@gmail.com. E-mail: mslimpedsurg@hotmail.com.

SLIMMER, DAVID ALLEN, physics educator; b. Reading, Pa., Dec. 15, 1964; s. Richard William and Marla Bernice Slimmer; m. Margret Waller, June 1, 1991. MS, Lehigh U., 1988, PhD, 1992. Instr. Muhlenberg Coll., Allentown, Pa., 1992—. Democrat. Lutheran. Home: 1035 Oldstone Rd Allentown PA 18103-4684 Office: Muhlenberg Coll 24th & Chow Sts Allentown PA 18104

SLINGER, MICHAEL JEFFERY, law librarian, director; b. Pitts., Apr. 12, 1956; s. Maurice and Mary Helen (Kengerski) S.; m. Cheryl Blaney, Apr. 19, 1980; children: Rebecca, Sarah. BA, U. Pitts., 1978; M Librianship, U. S.C., 1979; JD, Duquesne U., 1984. Reference libr. Duquesne U. Sch. Law, Pitts., 1983-84; rsch. libr. U. Notre Dame Sch. Law, Ind., 1984-85, head rsch. svcs., 1985-86, assoc. dir. pub. svcs., 1986-90; law libr. dir., assoc. prof. law Suffolk U. Sch. Law, Boston, 1990-93, law libr. dir., prof. law, 1994-95; law libr. dir., prof. law, assoc. dean Cleve. State U., 1995—2008; assoc. dean info. svcs. Widener U. Law Sch., 2008—. Contbr. articles to profl. jours., chpt. to book. Mem.: ALA, ABA, Ohio Regional Assn. Law Librs. (v.p. 1987—88, pres. 1988—89, Pres. award 1989), New Eng. Law Libr. Consortium (treas. 1992—95), Am. Assn. Law Schs. (exec. bd. sect. on law librs. 1993—94), Am. Assn. Law Librs. (chair acad. law libr. spl. interest sect. 2005—). Avocations: reading, sports. Office Phone: 302-477-2111. Business E-Mail: mislinger@widener.edu.

SLIPSAGER, HENRIK C., building services company executive; CFO ISS Internat. Svc. Sys., Inc., 1984-85, exec. v.p., COO, 1985-88, pres., CEO, 1988-94; exec. v.p. janitorial svcs. ABM Industries Inc., San Francisco, 1994-99, sr. v.p., 1997-99, pres. Am. Bldg. Maintenance Co., 1999-2000, CEO, pres., 2000—. Office: Abm Industries Inc 420 Taylor St # 200 San Francisco CA 94102-1702

SLIVE, MICHAEL LAWRENCE, sports association executive, lawyer; b. Utica, NY, July 26, 1940; m. Elizabeth Slive; 1 child, Anna. BA, Dartmouth Coll., 1962; JD, U. Va. Sch. Law, 1965; LLM, Georgetown U. Law Ctr., 1966. Asst. dir. athletics Dartmouth Coll., 1966—69; ptnr. Stebbins & Bradley, Hanover, NH, 1969—77, Coffield Ungaretti & Harris, Chgo., 1986—91; jud. master, clerk Grafton County Superior Ct., NH, 1977—79; asst. exec. dir. Pacific-10 Conf., 1979—81; dir. athletics Cornell U., 1981—83; pvt. practice, 1983—86; commr. Great Midwest Conf., 1991—95, Conf. USA, 1995—2002, Southeastern Conf., 2002—. Judge Hanover Dist. Ct., 1972—77; sr. ptnr., founder Slive-Glazier Sports Group, 1990—91; coord. Bowl Championship Series, 2007—. Named one of Most Influential People in the World of Sports, Bus. Week, 2008; E. Barrett Prettyman fellowship in trial advocacy. Mem.: Nat. Assn. Collegiate Dirs. of Athletics (mem. exec. com.), Collegiate Commrs. Assn. (pres. 2001—03), Sports Lawyers Assn. (bd. dirs. 1997—2001). Office: Southeastern Conf 2201 Richard Arrington Blvd N Birmingham AL 35203 Office Phone: 205-458-3000. Office Fax: 205-458-3031.

SLIVE, SEYMOUR, museum director, art educator; b. Chgo., Sept. 15, 1920; s. Daniel and Sonia (Rapoport) S.; m. Zoya Gregorevna Sandomirsky, June 29, 1946; children: Katherine, Alexander, Sarah. AB, U. Chgo., 1943, PhD, 1952; MA (hon.), Harvard U., 1958, Oxford U., Eng., 1972. Instr. fine arts Oberlin (Ohio) Coll., 1950-51; chmn. art dept. Pomona (Calif.) Coll., 1952-54; mem. faculty Harvard U., Cambridge, Mass., 1954—, prof. fine arts, 1961—, Gleason prof. fine arts, 1973-91, Gleason prof. fine arts emeritus, 1991—, chmn. dept. fine arts, 1968-71, dir. Fogg Art Mus., 1975-82; Elizabeth and John Moors Cabot dir. emeritus Harvard art museums, 1982. Exchange prof. Leningrad (USSR) U., 1961; Ryerson lectr. Yale U., 1962; Slade prof. Oxford (Eng.) U., 1972-73 Author: Rembrandt and His Critics, 1630-1730, 1953, The Rembrandt Bible, 1959, Catalogue of the Paintings of Frans Hals, 1962, Drawings of Rembrandt, 1965, (with Jakob Rosenberg and E.H. ter Kuile) Dutch Art and Architecture 1600-1800, 2nd edit., 1978, Rembrandt's Drawings, 1965, 2009, Frans Hals, 3 vols., 1970-74, Jacob van Ruisdael, 1981, Frans Hals, 1989, Dutch Painting: 1600-1800, 1995, 2d edit., 1998, Jacob van Ruisdael: A Complete Catalogue of His Paintings, Drawings and Etchings, 2001, Jacob Van Ruisdael: Master of Landscape, 2005, Rembrandt Drawings, 2009. Trustee Solomon R. Guggenheim Found., 1978-2008, Norton Simon Mus., 1989-91; bd. dirs. Burlington mag. Found., 1987—. Lt. (j.g.) USNR, 1943-46, PTO. Decorated officer Order Orange Nassau Netherlands, 1962; Fulbright fellow Netherlands, 1951-52; Guggenheim fellow, 1956-57, 78-79; Fulbright research scholar Utrecht (Netherlands) U., 1959-60 Fellow Am. Acad. Arts and Scis.; mem. Karel van Mander Soc. (hon.), Coll. Art Assn. (dir. 1958-62, 65-69), Renaissance Soc., Dutch Soc. Scis. (fgn. mem.), Brit. Acad. (corr. fellow). Office: Harvard U Sackler Art Museum Cambridge MA 02138 Office Phone: 617-495-9151.

SLIVINSKE, ALEC JOSEPH, JR., economics professor; b. Charlottesville, Va., Sept. 22, 1946; m. Kimberly Hanks; children: Alexander Daniel, Shannon Rae. BA, Pa. State U., State Coll., 1970; PhD, U. Tex., Austin, 1995. Prof. economics Austin CC, 1981—2008. Prof. Minnie Stevens Piper Found., 1997. Recipient NISOD Tchg. Excellence awards, U. Tex. Mem.: Phi Theta Katta, Kappa Delta Pi. Home: 10601 Hastings Ln Austin TX 78750 Office: 11928 Stonehollow Dr Austin TX 78758-3101 Business E-Mail: aslivin@austincc.edu.

SLIVKA, ADAM, medical educator; s. William and Helen Slivka; m. Carrie Saratore, June 25, 1983; children: Alexandra, Daniel. MD, Mt. Sinai & City U., NY, PhD, 1988. FASGE and FAGA ASGE and AGA, 2007. Editl. bd. ASGE, Oak Brook, Ill., 2004—08; prof. medicine U. Pitts., 2007—. Office: UPMC 200 Lothrop St Pittsburgh PA 15213 Personal E-mail: cslivka77@comcast.net.

SLJIVIC-SIMSIC, BILJANA B., retired Slavic and Baltic languages educator; b. Belgrade, Yugoslavia, Jan. 20, 1933; arrived in US, 1962; d. Branko M. and Radoyka (Pesic) S.; m. Branislav S. Simsic, Jan. 21, 1953 (div. 1963); 1 child, Violet Ljubica. Diploma, U. Belgrade, 1955; MA, Harvard U., 1963, PhD, 1966. Asst. U. Belgrade, 1957-62; lectr. U. Clermont-Ferrand, France, 1959-61; vis. lectr. UCLA, 1964—65, vis. asst. prof., 1965-66; asst. prof. U. Ky., Lexington, 1966-67, U. Pa., Phila., 1967-73; vis. lectr. Princeton (N.J.) U., 1967-69; assoc. prof. U. Ill., Chgo., 1973-86, head of dept., 1981—96, prof. dept. Slavic and Baltic langs. and lit., 1986—2009. Exch. prof. U. London and Cambridge (Eng.) U., 1989—90, U. Amsterdam, 2000, 02; cons., panelist U.S. Dept. Edn., Fulbright Fellowship, Washington; sr. writer Ohio State U., summers, 1983, 84, 85, 86, 88. Co-author: Serbo-Croatian-English Dictionary, 1972 (grant), Judeo-Spanish Ballads from Bosnia, 1972 (grant); author: Serbo-Croatian, Just For You, 1985 (grant 1983-84); major author 8 vols. of Serbo-Croatian Textbooks for Individualized Studies, 1983-88. Grantee, U. Pa., Phila., 1972; scholar, Radcliffe Coll., 1962—63, Harvard U., 1963—64. Mem.: Am. Assn. for Advancement of Slavic Studies, N.Am. Soc. Serbian Studies (sec.-treas. 1978—84, pres. 1984—86, mem. exec. bd. 1986—88), Assn. Serbian Writers Belgrade, Chgo. Hort. Soc., Harvard and Radcliffe Clubs Chgo. Serbian Orthodox. Avocations: photography, travel, gardening. Personal E-mail: simsic711@comcast.net.

SLOAN, ALLAN HERBERT, journalist; b. Bklyn., Nov. 27, 1944; s. Samuel and Doris (Shanblott) Sloan; m. Nancy Nolan, June 29, 1969; children: Sharon R., Susan M., Dena A. BA, Bklyn. Coll., 1966; MS, Columbia U., 1967. Reporter, sports writer Charlotte Observer, NC, 1968-72; reporter Detroit Free Press, 1972-79; assoc. editor, staff writer Forbes Mag., NYC, 1979-81, sr. editor, 1984-88; staff writer Money Mag., NYC, 1982-84; columnist NY Newsday, NYC, 1989-95; Wall St. editor Newsweek Mag., NYC, 1995—2007; sr. editor-at-large Fortune Mag., NYC, 2007—. Contbr., Marketplace Pub. Radio Internat.; frequent commentator, Nightly Bus. Report PBS TV. Author: Three Plus One Equals Billions: The Bendix-Martin Marietta War, 1982. Recipient Hancock award for fin. journalism, Hancock Found., 1992, Loeb award for fin. journalism, Loeb Found., UCLA Anderson Sch. Mgmt., 1974, 1984, 1991, 1993, 1998, 2007, Lifetime Achievement award, 2001, Disting. Achievement award, Am. Bus. Editors and Writers, 2001, Lifetime Achievement award, NY Fin. Writers Assn., 2009; named Alumnus of Yr., Columbia Grad. Sch. Journalism, 1999. Office: Fortune Time & Life Bldg 1271 6th Ave New York NY 10020

SLOAN, ANNE ELIZABETH, food scientist, writer; d. Thomas and Anne Sloan; m. James Murtland, June 14, 2003. BS, Rutgers U., 1973; PhD, U. Minn., 1976. Mgr. nutrition comm. Gen. Mills, Mpls., 1976—78; dir. Good Housekeeping Inst., NYC, 1978—85; editor-in-chief McCall's Mag., NYC, 1985—92; pres. Sloan Trends and Solution, Stuart, Fla., 1993—2003, Sloan Trends, Escondido, Calif., 2004—. Author: Food For Thoughts, 1977, Contemporary Nutrition Controversies, 1979; contbr. articles to numerous profl. jours. and mag. Recipient Pub. Rels. award, John W. Hill Found.; George Cook scholar, Rutgers U., 1973.

SLOAN, CAROLYN, music educator, composer, lyricist; d. Myron and Susanne Sloan; m. Stuart Zagnit; 1 child, Sam Zagnit. BA, N.Y. U., NYC, 1982. Cert. Orff instr. N.J., 2004. K-12 music chair Berkeley Carroll Sch., Bklyn., 2005—. Author: (book) Finding Your Voice-A Practical and Spiritual Approach to Singing and Living, Hyperion, 1999; composer (lyricist): (theatrical) I Have Found Home, 1986, My Name is Still Alice, 1992—, Pets, 1992—93, That's Life, 1993—94. Recipient Founder's Day Acad. Excellence award, N.Y. U., 1981, 1982. Mem.: ASCAP (assoc.). Achievements include development of new voice technique for singers and actors; two volumes of children's songs currently being used around the country. Avocations: cooking, travel, swimming, bicycling. Personal E-mail: sloantone@aol.com.

SLOAN, CLIFFORD M., lawyer, former publishing executive; b. 1957; m. Mary Lou Hartman; children: Sarah, Annie, Nick. BA, Harvard U., 1979; JD, Harvard Law Sch., 1984. Bar: Ill. 1986, DC 1992. Law clk. to Hon. J. Skelly Wright US Ct. Appeals (DC Cir.), 1984—85; law clk. to Justice Paul Stevens US Supreme Ct., 1985—86; assoc. counsel Office of Ind. Counsel Investigating the Iran-Contra affair, 1987—88; assoc. Onek, Klein & Farr, Washington, 1988—89; asst. to solicitor gen. US Dept. Justice, 1989—91; assoc. then ptnr. Mayer, Brown & Platt, 1991—93; assoc. counsel to Pres. The White House, Washington, 1993—95; ptnr., co-chair Internet Practice Group Wiley, Rein & Fielding LLP, Washington, 1995—2000; v.p. bus. devel., gen. counsel Washingtonpost.Newsweek Interactive, 2000—08; pub. Slate mag., 2005—08; ptnr. Skadden, Arps, Slate, Meagher, & Flom LLP, Washington, 2008—. Adjunct prof. cyberspace and internet law Georgetown U. Law Sch., George Wash. U. Law Sch., Am. U. Wash. Law Ctr.; mem. adv. bd. Corp. Pro Bono, 2002—08. Mem.: ABA. Office: Skadden Arps Slate Meagher & Flom LLP 1440 NY Ave NW Washington DC 20005

SLOAN, DAUPHINE DE MONTLAUR, literature and language professor; d. Guy de Villardi de Montlaur and Adelaide Piper Oates; m. Robert Daniel Sloan, Mar. 2, 1984; children: Alexandra Julia, Caroline Ellen, Edward Guy. M in Russian and English, U. de Paris IV Sorbonne, France, 1980; postgrad. in Soviet and East European Studies, Institut d'Etudes Politiques, Paris, 1981; PhD in Sociology, U. de Paris V Rene Descartes, France, 1984. Asst. dir., Russian and Eurasian studies program Ctr. Strategic and Internat. Studies, Washington, 1989—93; dep. program mgr., ACE Cartermill Internat. Ltd., Brussels, 1994—97, program mgr., action cooperation economics, 1998—99; vis. asst. prof., dept. French and Italian Tulane U., New Orleans, 2004—05, adj. asst. prof. internat. devel., Payson Ctr. Internat. Devel., 2004—, dir. French lang. program, 2006—. Adj. fellow Ctr. Strategic and Internat. Studies, Washington, 1993—94. Editor: (publication) Dictionary of Political Parties and Organizations in Russia; contbr. articles to profl. jours. ESL tchr. Jewish Family Svc., West Hartford, Conn., 2000—03; newsletter editor, fundraiser Wadsworth Atheneum, Hartford, 2000—03. Mem.: MLA, Am. Assn. Advancement Slavic Studies. Roman Catholic. Avocations: travel, tennis, jogging, swimming, singing. Office: Tulane Univ 311 Newcomb Hall 1229 Broadway New Orleans LA 70118 Business E-Mail: dsloan@tulane.edu.

SLOAN, DAVID B., lawyer; b. Martin, Ky., Sept. 20, 1950; BA, Berea Coll., 1972; JD, No. Ky. Univ., 1976. Bar: Ky. 1976, US Dist. Ct. (Ea. Dist. Ky.) 1977, US Ct. Appeals (6th Cir.) 1979. Atty. Stephens, Combs, and Page, Pikeville, Ky., 1976; assoc. O'Harra, Ruberg, Taylor, Sloan & Sergent, Covington, Ky., 1978—82, ptnr., 1982—. Mem.: Am. Bar Assn., Ky. Bar Assn. (pres.-elect 2004, pres.), No. Ky. Bar Assn. (bd. dir.). Office: O'Hara Ruberg Taylor Sloan & Sergent Ste 201 25 Crewstview Hills Mall Rd Covington KY 41017-0411 Office Phone: 859-331-2000. Office Fax: 859-578-3365. Business E-Mail: dsloan@ortlaw.com.

SLOAN, DONNIE ROBERT, JR., lawyer; b. Nashville, July 24, 1946; s. Donnie R. Sr. and Mary Catharine (Willis) S. BS in Indsl. Engring., Ga. Inst. Tech, 1968; JD cum laude, U. Ga., 1971; LLM, Harvard U., 1975. Bar: Ga. 1971, US Dist. Ct. (no. dist.) Ga. 1971, US Ct. Appeals (11th cir.), US Supreme Ct. Atty. Southwire Co., Carrollton, Ga., 1971-74; assoc., ptnr. Hyatt & Rhoads, P.C., Atlanta, 1975-89; pvt. practice, 1989-96; ptnr. Davidson, Fuller & Sloan, LLP, 1996—. Instr. legal rsch. U. Ga., Athens, 1970-71; instr. music law Ga. State U., Atlanta, 1976. Mem. editl. bd. Ga. Law Rev., 1969-71. Treas. Ga. Wheelchair Athletic Assn., Atlanta, 1981-84; pres., treas. Dixie Wheelchair Athletic Assn., Atlanta, 1984-87. Recipient Appreciation award Ga. Wheelchair Sports and Recreation Assn., 1979; named one of Outstanding Young Men of Am., 1981; named to Dixie Wheelchair Athletic Assn. Hall of Fame, 1990. Mem. Am. Judicature Soc., Phi Kappa Phi, Alpha Phi Mu, Ga. Tech. Club, Harvard Club. Methodist. Avocations: skiing, jogging, swimming. Home: 820 Saddlehill Rd Roswell GA 30075 Office: 10475 Medlock Bridge Rd Ste 820 Duluth GA 30097 Business E-Mail: drsloan@dfslaw.com.

SLOAN, EARLE DENDY, JR., chemical engineering educator; b. Seneca, SC, Apr. 23, 1944; s. Earle Dendy and Sarah (Bellotte) S.; m. Marjorie Nilson, Sept. 7, 1968; children: Earle Dendy III, John Mark. BSChemE, Clemson U., 1965, MSChemE, 1972, PhD in Chem. Engring., 1974. Engr. Du Pont, Chattanooga, 1965-66, Seaford, Del., 1966-67, cons. Parkersburg, W.Va., 1967-68, sr. engr. Camden, S.C., 1968-70; postdoctoral fellow Rice U., 1975; prof. chem. engring. Colo. Sch. Mines, Golden, 1976—, dir. Ctr. for Rsch. on Hydrates and Other Solids, 1990—, Gaylord and Phyllis Weaver dist. prof. chem. engring., 1992—. Inaugural pres. faculty senate Colo. Sch. Mines, 1989-90, disting. lectr., 1997-98, appointed senator, 1998; Tokyo Electric Power Co. chair Keio U., Japan, 1996; Erskine fellow U. Canterbury, Christchurch, N.Z., 2002; chmn. Codata Corps Hydrate Database Task Force Group, 2005-, Fed. Methane Hydrate Adv. Com., USA Hydrate Database Com. Author: Clathrate Hydrates of Natural Gases, 1990, 2nd edit., 1998, 3rd edit., 2008, Hydrate Engineering, 2000; chmn. pub. bd. Chem. Engring. Edn., 1990-2006. Scoutmaster local Cub Scouts, 1978-81; elder Presbyn. Ch., Golden, Colo., 1977-79, 92-94; elder Ctrl. Presbyn. Ch., Denver, 1999—07. Recipient Donald L. Katz award for rsch., Gas Processors Assn. Fellow AIChE (chmn. area 1a thermodynamics and transport 1990-93); mem. Am. Soc. for Engring. Edn. (chmn. ednl. rsch. methods divsn. 1983-85, chmn. chem. engring. divsn. 1984), Am. Chem. Soc., Soc. Petroleum Engrs. (Disting. Lectr. 1996-97). Avocations: bicycling, cello, philosophy. Office: Colo Sch of Mines Ctr for Hydrate Rsch Golden CO 80401 Business E-Mail: esloan@mines.edu.

SLOAN, ELAINE FRANK, librarian; b. Pitts., May 20, 1938; d. Maurice and Sarah (Blecher) Frank; m. Howard R. Sloan, Aug. 30, 1959; children: Michael, Stephen, Eric. BA, Chatham Coll., Pitts., 1959; MA, U. Pitts., 1962; M.L.S. (Smithsonian Instn. fellow 1970-72, Outstanding Grad. award), U. Md., 1972, PhD, 1974. Research asst. Johns Hopkins U., 1962-66; asst. to dir. for planning and research, asst.

dir. mgmt. and devel. Smithsonian Instn. Libraries, 1973-76; asso. univ. librarian public services, lectr. Sch. Librarianship, U. Calif., Berkeley, 1977-80; dean univ. librarians Ind. U., Bloomington, 1980-88; v.p., info. services, univ. librarian Columbia U., 1988—. Bd. mem. Commn. on Preservation and Access, 1995—. Mem. Assn. Research Libraries (pres. 1987-88), ALA (chmn. pub. com. 1980-81), Beta Phi Mu (pres. 1987-89). Office: Columbia U Butler Library 535 W 114th St Rm 313 New York NY 10027-7035

SLOAN, F(RANK) BLAINE, retired law educator; b. Geneva, Nebr., Jan. 3, 1920; s. Charles Porter and Lillian Josephine (Stiefer) S.; m. Patricia Sand, Sept. 2, 1944; children: DeAnne Sloan Riddle, Michael Blaine, Charles Porter. AB with high distinction, U. Nebr., 1942, LLB cum laude, 1946; LLM in Internat. Law, Columbia U., 1947. Bar: Nebr. 1946, N.Y. 1947. Asst. to spl. counsel Intergovtl. Com. for Refugees, 1947; mem. Office Legal Affairs UN Secretariat, NYC, 1948—78; gen. counsel Relief and Works Agy. Palestine Refugees, Beirut, 1958—60; dir. gen. legal divsn., dep. to legal counsel UN Legal Office, NYC, 1966—78, rep. of Sec. Gen. to UN Commn. Internat. Trade Law, 1969—78, rep. to Legal Sub-com. on Outer Space, 1966—78; rep. UN Del. Vietnam Conf., Paris, 1973, UN Conf. on Carriage of Goods by Sea, Hamburg, 1978; prof. internat. law orgn. and water law Pace U., 1978—87, prof. emeritus, 1987—. Law lectr. Blaine Sloan Internat., 1988—. Author: United Nations General Assembly Resolutions in Our Changing World, 1991, United Nations Memories, 2005, (with Kathryn Sloan Ashby) A History of the Sloan, Porter, Fournell and Stiefer Families, 2005; contbr. articles to legal jours. Cons. UN Office of Legal Affairs, 1983-84, UN Water Resources Br., 1983; supervisory com., Pace Peace Ctr.; legal advisor Korean Missions, 1951, 53, UNTSO, Jerusalem, 1952, UNEF I, Gaza, 1957-58; prin. sec.UN Commn. to investigate Sec.-Gen. Hammarskjold's crash, 1961-62. Navigator AC, U.S. Army, 1943-46 Decorated Air medal. Mem. Am. Soc. Internat. Law, Am. Acad. Polit. and Social Sci., Am. Arbitration Assn., Order of Coif, Phi Beta Kappa, Phi Alpha Delta (hon.). Republican. Roman Catholic. Office: 78 N Broadway White Plains NY 10603-3710 also: 375 Soubry Pl Forbes Park Fort Garland CO 81133 Home: Foxwind-Forbes Pk 375 Soubry Pl Fort Garland CO 81133

SLOAN, HARRY EVANS, film company executive; b. 1949; BA, UCLA, 1971; JD, Loyola Law Sch., 1976. Founder, entertainment lawyer Sloan, Kuppin and Ament, LA, 1976—83; co-chmn. New World Entertainment Ltd., Los Angeles, 1983—89; chmn. SBS Broadcasting S.A., Luxembourg, 1990—2002, CEO, 1993—2001, exec. chmn., 2002—05; chmn., CEO Metro-Goldwyn-Mayer Inc., 2005—09, chmn., 2009—. Dir. ZeniMax Media Inc. Office: Metro Goldwyn Mayer Inc 10250 Constellation Blvd Los Angeles CA 90067*

SLOAN, HERBERT ELIAS, physician, surgeon; b. Clarksburg, W.Va., Oct. 10, 1914; s. Herbert Elias and Luella (Dye) S.; m. Doris Edwards, May 3, 1943; children: Herbert, Ann, Elizabeth, John, Robert. AB, Washington and Lee U., 1936; MD, Johns Hopkins U., 1940. Diplomate Am. Bd. Surgery, Am. Bd. Thoracic Surgery (bd. dirs. 1966-86, v.p. 1971-73, sec.-treas. 1973-86). Resident in surgery Johns Hopkins Hosp., 1941-44; instr. dept. surgery Johns Hopkins U., 1943-44; resident in thoracic surgery U. Mich. Hosp., Ann Arbor, 1947-49, instr. thoracic surgery, 1949-50; asst. prof. U. Mich., Ann Arbor, 1950-53, assoc. prof., 1953-62, prof. surgery, 1962-87, head sect. thoracic surgery, 1970-85; chief clin. affairs U. Mich. Hosps., Ann Arbor, 1982-86, med. dir. operating room, 1986-87, prof. emeritus surgery, 1987—; med. dir. managed health care U. Mich., Ann Arbor, 1989-96, Herbert Sloan Collegiate Professorship in cardiac surgery, 2003. Mem. staff VA Hosp., Ann Arbor, 1953—, cons., 1968—. Author: The American Board of Thoracic Surgery: A Fifty Year Perspective, 1998, (with Marvin M. Kirsh) Blunt Chest Trauma, General Principles of Management, 1977; editor Annals of Thoracic Surgery, 1969-85; contbr. (with Marvin M. Kirsh) chpts. to books, articles to profl. jours. Served to maj. M.C. U.S. Army, 1944-47. Recipient Bruce Douglas award in thoracic diseases, 1974, Med. Alumni Svc. award Johns Hopkins Sch. Medicine, 1973, Disting. Svc. award Johns Hopkins U. Sch. Medicine, 1983, Disting. Svc. award Mich. Med. Ctr. Alumni Soc., 1988, Herbert Sloan Collegiate Prof. Cardiac Surgery award, 2003; named to Hall of Honor, U. Mich. Med. Sch., 2006. Mem. ACS, Am. Surg. Assn., Am. Heart Assn., Am. Assn. Thoracic Surgery (pres. 1979-80), Soc. Thoracic Surgeons (pres. 1974-75, Disting. Svc. award 1981), Central Surg. Assn., Soc. Univ. Surgeons, So. Thoracic Surgery Assn. (hon.), Thoracic Soc. Gt. Britain (hon.), John Alexander Soc., Western Thoracic Surg. Assn. (hon.), Cardiovascular Surgeons Club, Detroit Heart Club, Am. Trudeau Soc., Mich. Heart Assn., Mich. Trudeau Soc., Am. Acad. Pediatrics, Soc. Vascular Surgery, Frederick A. Coller Surg. Soc., U. Mich. Med. Alumni Soc. (Disting. Svc. award 1988), U. Mich. James Angell Soc., Rsch. Club, Phi Beta Kappa, Alpha Omega Alpha, Omicron Delta Kappa, Sigma Xi. Clubs: Ann Arbor Figure Skating (pres. 1965-66). Home: 471 Barton North Dr Ann Arbor MI 48105-1017 Office: 1500 E Medical Center Dr Ann Arbor MI 48109 Business E-Mail: hsloan@umich.edu.

SLOAN, HUGH WALTER, JR., automotive executive; b. Princeton, NJ, Nov. 1, 1940; s. Hugh Walter and Elizabeth (Johnson) Sloan; m. Deborah Louise Murray, Feb. 20, 1971; children: Melissa, Peter, Jennifer, William. AB in History with honors, Princeton U., 1963. Staff asst. to Pres. U.S. White House, Washington, 1969-71; treas. Pres. Nixon's Re-election Campaign, Washington, 1971; spl. asst. to pres. Budd Co., Troy, Mich., 1973-74, exec. asst. internat., 1974-77, mgr. corp. mktg., 1977-79; pres., gen. mgr. Budd Can. Inc., Kitchener, Ont., Canada, 1979-85; pres. automotive Woodbridge Group, Troy, 1985-98, dep. chmn., 1998—2008. Bd. dirs. Woodbridge Foam Corp., Mfrs. Life Ins. Co., Wescast Industries, Spartan Motors, Inc. Trustee Beaumont Hosp. Lt. USNR, 1963—65. Recipient Outstanding Bus. Leader award, Wilfrid Laurier U., 1987. Republican.

SLOAN, JEANETTE PASIN, artist; b. Chgo., Mar. 18, 1946; d. Antonio and Anna (Baggio) Pasin; children: Eugene Blakely, Anna Jeanette. BFA, Marymount Coll., Tarrytown, NY, 1967; MFA, U. Chgo., 1969. One-woman shows include G.W. Einstein Gallery, NYC, 1977—85, Landfall Press Gallery, Chgo., NYC, 1978, 1987, Roger Ramsay Gallery, Chgo., 1987, 1989, 1992, Tatischeff Gallery, Santa Monica, Calif., 1989, Steven Scott Gallery, Balt., 1989, Butters Gallery, Portland, Oreg., 1989, 1991, 1994, 1996, 1999, Tatistcheff & Co. Inc., 1995, 1997, 1999, Ouartet Editions, NYC, 1995, Elliot Smith Gallery, St. Louis, 1994, Peltz Gallery, Milw., 1994—95, 1999, 2006, 2009, Gerhard Wurzer Gallery, Houston, 1997, 2001, Cline Fine Arts Gallery, Santa Fe, 1998, 2001, LewAllen Contemporary, Santa Fe, N.Am., 2008, J. Cacciola Gallery, NYC, 2004—05, Amarillo Mus. Art, Tex., 2006, William Havu Gallery, Denver, 2007, Landfall Press Gallery, Santa Fe, 2007, Klaudia Marr Gallery, 2007, Represented in permanent collections Art Mus. Chgo., Cleve. Mus. Art, Ill. State Mus., Indpls. Mus. Art, Canton Art Inst., Ohio, Ball State Bus., Mpls. Inst. Art, Fogg Mus. Harvard U., Yale U. Art Gallery, Snite Mus. U. Notre Dame, Met. Mus. Art, NYC, Herbert F. Johnson Mus. Cornell U., Ithaca, NY, Valpariaso Mus. Art, Ind., Nat. Gallery Art, Washington, exhibited in group shows; subject of book by Gerritt Henry Jeanette Pasin Sloan, 2000, subject of book by James Yood The Prints of Jeanette Pasin Sloan, 2003. Studio: 301 Loma Arisco Santa Fe NM 87501 Home Phone: 505-989-9660; Office Phone: 505-699-9234. Personal E-mail: jeanettepasin@aol.com.

SLOAN, JERRY (GERALD EUGENE SLOAN), professional basketball coach; b. McLeansboro, Ill., Mar. 28, 1942; m. Bobbye (dec. 2004); 3 children: Kathy, Brian, Holly. Student, Evansville Coll., Ind., 1965. Player Balt. Bullets, 1965—66, Chgo. Bulls, 1966—76, scout, 1976—77, asst. coach, 1977—79, head coach, 1979—82; scout Utah Jazz, Salt Lake City, 1983—84, asst. coach, 1984—88, head coach, 1988—. Named NBA Coach of Yr., The Sporting News, 2004; named to NBA All-Star Team, 1967, 1969, NBA All-Def. First Team, 1969, 1972, 1974, 1975, Naismith Meml. Basketball Hall of Fame, 2009. Office: Utah Jazz EnergySolutions Arena 301 W South Temple Salt Lake City UT 84101*

SLOAN, KATHERINE (KAY SLOAN), college president; DArts in English, Carnegie Mellon U. Pres. Greenfield C.C., 1988—94, North Hennepin C.C., Mpls., 1994—96, Mass. Coll. Art, Boston, 1998—. Office: Office of President Mass College of Art 621 Huntington Ave Boston MA 02115 Office Phone: 617-879-7100.

SLOAN, MARY JEAN, retired media specialist; b. Lakeland, Fla., Nov. 29, 1927; d. Marion Wilder and Elba (Jinks) Sloan. BS, Peabody Coll., Nashville, 1949; MLS, Atlanta U., 1978, SLS, 1980. Cert. libr. media specialist. Music dir. Pinecrest Sch., Tampa, Fla., 1949-50, Polk County Schs., Bartow, Fla., 1950-54; pvt. music tchr. Lakeland, 1954-58; tchr. Clayton County Schs., Jonesboro, Ga., 1958-59; media specialist Eastualley Sch., Marietta, Ga., 1959-89; ret., 1989. Coord. conf. Ga. Libr. Media Dept., Jekyll Island, 1982-83, sec., Atlanta, 1982-83, com. chmn. ethnic conf., Atlanta, 1978, pres., 1984-85, state pres., 1985-86; program chmn. Ga. Media Orgns. Conf. Jekyll Island, 1988. Contbr. to bibliographies. Recipient Walter Bell award Ga. Assn. Instrnl. Tech., 1988, Disting. Svc. award, 1991. Mem. ALA (del. 1984, 85, 90), NEA, Southeastern Libr. Assn., Am. Assn. Sch. Librs., Soc. for Sch. Librs., Internat., Ga. Assn. Educators (polit. action com. 1983), Beta Phi Mu, Phi Delta Kappa. Republican. Methodist. Home: 797 Yorkshire Rd NE Atlanta GA 30306-3264

SLOAN, MELANIE TOGMAN, lawyer, former prosecutor; b. Washington, Dec. 16, 1965; d. Leonard Seymour and Barbara (Kaufman) T. BA in English, U. Chgo., 1987, JD, 1991. Bar: Calif. 1991, D.C. 1992. Student atty. Mandel Legal Aid Clinic, Chgo., 1988-91; assoc. Sonnenschein, Nath & Rosenthal, LA, 1991-92, Howrey & Simon, Washington, 1992-93; nominations counsel com. on judiciary U.S. Senate, Washington, 1993-94; counsel U.S. Ho. Subcom. on Crime and Criminal Justice, Washington, 1994-95; minority counsel Ho. Jud. Com., Washington, 1995—98; asst. US atty. DC dist. US Dept. Justice, 1998—2003; exec. dir. Citizens for Responsibility & Ethics in Washington, Washington, 2003—. Named one of The 100 Agents of Change, Rolling Stone mag., 2009. Office: Citizens for Responsibility & Ethics in Washington 1400 Eye St NW Ste 450 Washington DC 20005 Office Phone: 202-408-5565.*

SLOAN, MICHAEL ALLAN, neurologist; b. Detroit, July 26, 1954; s. Eugene and Mildred Jody Sloan (Stepmother); children: Jessica Barry, Brittany Erin. MD, Wayne State U., 1980; MS, Rush U., 2003. Diplomate internal medicine Am. Bd. Internal Medicine, 1984, neurology Am. Bd. Psychiatry and Neurology, 1988, vascular neurology Am. Bd. Psychiatry and Neurology, 2005. Assoc. prof. neurology U. Md. Med. Ctr., Balt., 1993—97; neurologist Harbin Clinic, Rome, Ga., 1998—2000; assoc. prof. neurology U. Rush, Chgo., 2000—05; dir. stroke ctr. Carolinas Med. Ctr., Charlotte, NC, 2005—07; adj. prof. neurology U. NC, Chapel Hill, 2005—07; prof. neurology U. South Fla., Tampa, 2007—. AMA del. Am. Soc. Neuroimaging, 2001. Fellow: Am. Heart Assn., Am. Coll. Physicians, Am. Coll. Cardiology, Am. Acad. Neurology. Avocations: politics, music, performing arts, travel, sports. Business E-Mail: msloan@health.usf.edu.

SLOAN, MICHAEL DANA, information systems specialist, management consultant; b. Santa Monica, Calif., Sept. 30, 1960; s. Avery and Beverly Rae (Krantz) S.; m. Barbara Rogers; 1 child, Ashley Harrison. BS in Bus. Adminstrn., Calif. State U., Northridge, 1983; MBA, Pepperdine U., 1987. Programmer/analyst TICOR, Inc., LA, 1979-80; data processing analyst Deluxe Check Printers, Inc., Chatsworth, Calif., 1980-83; fin. systems analyst Wismer & Assocs., Inc., Canoga Park, Calif., 1983-84; sr. systems analyst Coast Savs. & Loan, Granada Hills, Calif., 1984-86; microcomputer systems specialist Litton Industries, Woodland Hills, Calif., 1986-87; systems mgr., info. resources mgr. TRW, Inc.- Space and Def., Redondo Beach, Calif., 1987-93; project mgr. Health Net, Woodland Hills, 1993-95; mgr. fin. and sales systems Merisel Ams. Inc., El Segundo, Calif., 1995-97; sr. mgr. web tech. & devel. Ingram Micro Inc., Santa Ana, Calif., 2000—01; with Ptnrs. Cons. Svcs., Inc., Laguna Beach, Calif., 2001—02, Consulting Solutions, Inc., Calabasas, Calif., 2002—05; sr. mgr. IT ops. DirecTV, 2006—09; program mgr., enterprise architecture Kaiser Permanente, 2009—. Cons. Data Most, Inc., Chatsworth, 1982—83, Home Savs. & Loan, North Hollywood, Calif., 1987, Micro Tech., LA, 1987, TRW, Inc.-Space and Def., Redondo Beach, Calif., 1993—2000, Pacificare Health Sys., Inc., 1997, Nissan N.Am. (formerly Nissan Motor Corp., USA), 1998—99, Prosum Info. Techs., Inc., 2000—01, Am. Honda Motors, Inc., 1999—2000, Toyota Fin. Svcs., 2001—02, Warner Bros. Studios, 2002—05, Oakwood Worldwide, 2005—06; mgmt. cons. Strategic Cons. Solutions, Ltd., Redondo Beach, Calif., 2005—, Kaiser Permanente, 2009—. Mem. IEEE Computer Soc., Salle Gascon Fencing Club, U.S. Fencing Assn., Delta Sigma Pi. Republican. Avocations: fencing, comedy improvisation, tennis, volleyball, travel, sailing. Office: Strategic Consulting Solutions Ltd Ste 1 2607 Vanderbilt Ln Redondo Beach CA 90278

SLOAN, NINA, language educator; b. Volcheyarovka, Lugansk region, Ukraine, Mar. 18, 1956; d. Ivan and Praskovya Borisovich; m. Paul M. Sloan, Jan. 29, 1999; children: Olena Sambucci, Tanya. MA, Kharkov State U., Ukraine, 1981. Cert. ESL K-12; bilingual edn. K-12; English grades 6-12 Idaho State Dept. Edn., 2002. Tchr. English and French Sch. 146, Kharkov; tchr. English as fgn. lang., Am. studies Sch. 169, Kharkov, 1992—98; instr. English prep program Internat. Christian U., Kiev, Ukraine, 1999—2001; tchr. Frontier Elem. Sch., Boise, 2001—02, Centennial H.S., Boise, 2002—. Chair English lang. and country studies Sch. 169, 1992—98, vice prin. fgn. langs., 1996—97; chair English lang. prep program Internat. Christian U., Kiev, 1999—2001. Recipient Excellence in Tchg., Ukraine Ministry Edn. and USAID, 1997, Nat. Winner-Excellence in Tchg. English and Am. Studies, 1998. Mem.: NEA, Meridian Edn1. Assn. Home: 903 W Highland View Dr Boise ID 83702 Office: Centennial HS 12400 W Macmillan Rd Boise ID 83713 Personal E-mail: pnsloan@aol.com.

SLOAN, O. TEMPLE, JR., (TEMPLE SLOAN), automotive equipment executive; b. Sanford, NC, Feb. 21, 1939; s. Orris Temple and Thelma (Hamilton) S.; m. Carol Carson; children: C. Carson Henline, O. Temple Sloan III, Mark H. Sloan. BA in Bus. Adminstrn., Duke U., 1961; LLD (hon.), Northwood U., Midland, Mich., 2007. Founder, chmn., CEO Gen. Parts Internat. Inc., Raleigh, NC, 1961—. Chmn. Highwoods Properties Inc., 1994-, bd. dirs. CARQUEST Corp., Bank of America Corp., 1996-2008, Lowe's Companies, Inc., 2004-, Golden Corral, Global Transpark Found. Trustee Boys and Girls Homes N.C., Lake Waccamaw, 1973; campaign chmn. Wake County United Way, 2001; mem. Centennial Authority, 1995—2005, trustee, former chmn. fin. com.; elder Presbyn. Ch.; exec. bd. Occoneechee coun. Boy Scouts Am., capital campaign chmn. Occoneechee coun., 2004—05, past v.p.Occoneechee coun., past treas. Occoneechee coun.; bd. visitors Peace Coll., Raleigh, 1985—87, trustee, 1987—97, vice chmn. bd. trustees. Recipient Silver Beaver award Boy Scouts Am., Disting. Eagle Scout award Boy Scouts Am., Disting. Svc. citation Automotive Hall of Fame, 1997; named Northwood U. Outstanding Bus. Leader, 1999. Mem. Automotive Warehouse Distbrs. Assn. Inc. (dir. 1969—, chmn. 1976-77, Scholarship award 1977, Automotive Man of Yr. award 1989), The Fifty Group (past pres.), Carolina Country Club (Raleigh). Avocations: fishing, hunting, ranching. Home: 3026 Randolph Dr Raleigh NC 27609-6942 Office: Gen Parts Internat Inc PO Box 26006 Raleigh NC 27611 Business E-Mail: licanipe@gpi.com.*

SLOAN, PHILLIP REID, liberal studies educator; b. Salt Lake City, Jan. 28, 1938; s. Reid John and MaRee Celia Sloan; m. Sharon Lee Borg, Sept. 2, 1958 (dec. Jan. 28, 2009); children: Laura Theresa Mabry, Mary Elizabeth, Kathleen Marie, Sheila Anne Sloan-Evans. BS, U. Utah, Salt Lake City, 1960; MS, Scripps Instn. Oceanography, La Jolla, Calif., 1964; PhD, U. Calif., San Diego, 1970. Asst. prof., biology and medicine U. Wash. Sch. Medicine, Seattle, 1969—74; asst. to assoc. prof. program liberal study U. Notre Dame, 1974—, chmn., program liberal studies Ind., 1985—93, 2002—04, dir., program in history & philosophy sci., 1994—97, dir., reilly ctr. sci., tech. and values, 1997—2000. Lay cons., com. Sci. and human values Nat. Conf. Cath. Bishops, 1998—2006; pres. Assn. Core Texts and Courses, 2002—08. Regional dir. internat. network Sci. Theology & Ontological Quest Project, 2008—09. Recipient medal, Paris Muséum Nat. d'histoire Naturelle, 1994; grant, NSF, 2007—. Fellow: AAAS (sect. L & chair 2003—05). Democrat. Roman Catholic. Home: 1844 Kessler Blvd South Bend IN 46616 Office: Univ Notre Dame 215 O'Shaughnessy Hall Notre Dame IN 46556 Office Fax: 574-631-8209; Home Fax: 574-631-8209.

SLOAN, ROBERT BRYAN, JR., academic administrator; b. Coleman, Tex., 1949; m. Sue Collier; children: Charissa, Bryan, Eraina, Michael, Alathea, Sophia, Paul. BA cum laude, Baylor U., 1970; MDiv magna cum laude, Princeton Theol. Sem., 1973; doktor der theologie insigni cum laude, U. Basel, 1978. Faculty Hardin-Simmons U., Abilene, Southwestern Bapt. Theol. Sem., Fort Worth, 1980—83; faculty, religion Baylor U., Waco, Tex., 1983, George W. Truett chair in Evangelism, 1990—95, dean Truett Sem., 1993—95, pres., CEO, 1995—2005, chancellor, 2005—06; pres. Houston Baptist U., 2006—. Mem. Cooper Found. Bd., Compass Bank Adv. Bd.; pastor, interim pastor over 20 chs., Tex., Okla., N.J., Germany; mem., treas. Big 12 Exec. Com.; bd. dirs. Salado Inst. for the Humanities. Inducted Little League Hall of Excellence. Mem. Studiorum Novi Testamenti Societas, Soc. of Bib. Lit., Inst. for Bib. Rsch. Office: Houston Baptist U 7502 Fondren Rd Houston TX 77074-3298 Office Phone: 281-649-3450.

SLOAN, ROBERT D., energy executive, lawyer; b. Ill., Oct. 27, 1947; m. Dauphine de Montlaur Sloan; children: Alexandra, Caroline, Edward. BA, U. Mich.; JD, Harvard U. Gen. counsel to Minority U.S. Senate Permanent Subcommittee on Investigations; asst. legal adviser, worked on nuclear non-proliferation and politico-military matters U.S. State Dept.'s Office of Legal Adviser; gen. counsel Multinational Force and Observers, Rome, 1981—84; v.p., dir. Sovereign Credit Mgmt. Divsn. 1st Nat. Bank Chgo., 1985—92; ptnr. Pepper, Hamilton and Sheetz Law Firm, Washington, Sloan, Lehner & Ruiz; mng. ptnr. Brussels office McKenna and Cuneo LLP, 1993—98; v.p., gen. counsel GE Indsl. Sys., Plainville, Conn., 1998—2003; sr. v.p., gen. counsel, sec. Entergy Corp., New Orleans, 2003—. Adj. prof. law Georgetown Law Ctr., Washington. Bd. dir. Ctr. for Internat. Bus. Edn., U. Mich., New Orleans Ballet Theatre. Office: Entergy Corp PO Box 61000 New Orleans LA 70160

SLOAN, ROBERT HAL, computer science educator; b. Buffalo, Apr. 1, 1961; s. George and Helen (Cohen) S.; m. Maurine Jo Neiberg, June 27, 1993; children: Rose, Emma. BS, Yale U., 1983; MS, MIT, 1986, PhD, 1989. Postdoctoral fellow Harvard U., Cambridge, Mass., 1989-90; asst. prof. U. Ill., Chgo., 1990-96; prog. dir. Nat. Sci. Found., 2001—02; assoc. prof. U. Ill., Chgo., 1996—2006, prof., 2006—, acting dept. head, 2007—09, dept. head, 2009—. Contbr. articles to profl. publs. Recipient Rsch. Initiation award NSF, 1990; NSF grantee, 1994, 98, 2001, 04, 08 Mem.: IEEE Computer Soc. (bd. govs. 2006—08), Assn. for Computing Machinery. Democrat. Avocations: tournament bridge, cooking, running. Office: U Ill Chgo Computer Sci Dept MC 152 851 S Morgan St Rm 1120 Chicago IL 60607-7053 Office Phone: 312-996-2369.

SLOAN, SHELDON HAROLD, lawyer; b. Mpls., Dec. 25, 1935; s. Leonard Norman Sloan and Mary (Wasserman); m. Loraine Bayer, Nov. 28, 1964; children: Stephen Howard, Jennifer Blair; m. Shelby Jean Sloan. BSBA, UCLA, 1958; JD, U. So. Calif., 1961. Bar: Calif. 1962, US Dist. Ct. (so. and cen. dists.) Calif. 1962, US Claims Ct. 1962, US Supreme Ct. 1962. Atty. US Dept. Justice, Washington, 1962-63; assoc. Brown & Brown, LA, 1963-73, ptnr., 1976-79; judge LA Mcpl. Ct., 1973-76; sole practice, 1980—; of counsel Lewis, Brisbois Bisgaard & Smith LLP. Bd. dirs. ACA JOE, San Francisco, Pioneer Magnetics Inc., Santa Monica, Calif. Trustee, treas. Westlake Sch. for Girls, Los Angeles, 1980; pres., chmn. Coro Found., LA, 1980-81, Frater Friends Music Ctr., LA, 1981-85; chmn. Senator Pete Wilson's Jud. Selection Com., 1982-84, 85—; pres. Guardians Jewish Homes for the Aged, LA, 1986, LA Meml. Coliseum Commn., 1999-2000. Mem.: State Bar Calif. (pres. 2006—07), LA County Bar Assn. (chmn. Jud. Appointments Com. 1984, pres. 1996—97). Republican. Avocation: golf. Office: Lewis, Brisbois Bisgaard & Smith LLP Ste 1200 221 N Figueroa St Los Angeles CA 90012-2601 also: 11111 Santa Monica Blvd Ste 230 Los Angeles CA 90025-3347 Office Phone: 310-268-0622. Personal E-mail: ssloanlaw@aol.com. E-mail: Sloan@lbbslaw.com.

SLOANE, BEVERLY LEBOV, writer, instructor, consultant; b. NYC, May 26, 1936; d. Benjamin S. and Anne (Weinberg) LeBov; m. Robert Malcolm Sloane, Sept. 27, 1959 (dec. May 16, 2002); 1 child, Alison Lori Sloane Gaylin. AB, Vassar Coll., 1958; MA, Claremont Grad. U., 1975, postgrad., 1975—76; grad. exec. mgmt. program, UCLA Grad. Sch. Mgmt., 1982, grad. advanced exec. mgmt. program, 1995; grad. profl. pub. course, Stanford U., 1982, grad. exec. refresher course in profl. pub., 1994; grad. intensive bioethics course Kennedy Inst. Ethics, Georgetown U., 1987, advanced bioethics course, 1988; grad. seminar in health care ethics, U. Wash. Sch. Medicine, Seattle., 1988—90, grad. seminar in health care ethics, 1994; grad. Summer Bioethics Inst., Loyola Marymount U., 1990; grad. Ann. Summer Inst. on Tchg. of Writing, Columbia U. Tchrs. Coll., 1990; grad. Ann. Summer Inst. on Advanced Tchg. of Writing, Columbia Tchrs. Coll., 1993; grad. Ann.

Inst. Pub. Health and Human Rights, Harvard U. Sch. Pub. Health, 1994; grad. women's campaign sch., Yale U., 1998; grad. numerous courses, Inst. Writing and Thinking, Bard Coll., 2005—; grad. memoir writing, Omega Inst., Rhinebeck, NY, 2006, grad. memoir writing, 2009. Cert. in exec. mgmt. UCLA Grad. Sch. Mgmt., 1982, in advanced exec. mgmt. UCLA Grad. Sch. Mgmt., 1995, in transformative mediation tng. Mediation Ctr. Dutchess County, Poughkeepsie, NY, 2006, in initial cmty. mediation tng., in initial connectivity meditation tng. Dispute Resolution Ctr., Ulster County, 2008. Circulation libr. Harvard Med. Libr., Boston, 1958-59; social worker Conn. State Welfare, New Haven, 1960-61; tchr. English Hebrew Day Sch., New Haven, 1961-64; instr. creative writing and English lit. Monmouth Coll., West Long Branch, NJ, 1967-69; writer, cons., 1970—. V.p. coun. grad. students, Claremont Grad. U., 1971-72, adj. dir. Writing Ctr. Speaker Series, 1993-2000, spkr., 1996-98, Claremont Grad. U.; mem. Strategic Planning Task Force Com. Campaign Pre-eminence. 1986-87, Alumni Coun., bd. dirs. Alumni Assn., 1993-96; mem. Vol. Devel. Com., 1994-96, Alumni Awards Com., 1993-96; bd. visitors Claremont Grad. U. Ctrs. for Arts and Humanities, 2001—; adv. coun. tech. and profl. writing Dept. English, Calif. State U., Long Beach, 1980-82; adv. bd. Calif. Health Rev., 1982-83; mem. Foothill Health Dist. Adv. Coun. LA County Dept. Health Svcs., 1987-93, pres., 1989-91; vis. scholar Hastings Ctr., 1996; adj. instr. English composition Marist Coll., Poughkeepsie, NY, 2005-06; instr. memoir writing Lifetime Learning Inst. Bard Coll., Annandale-on-Hudson, NY, 2006-; ethical wills, spkr. in field, 2007—. Author: From Vassar to Kitchen, 1967, A Guide to Health Facilities: Personnel and Management, 1971, 2nd edit., 1977, 3d edit., 1992, Introduction to Healthcare Delivery Organization: Functions and Management, 4th edit., 1999. Co-chmn. Vassar Christmas Showcase Vassar Club, New Haven, 1965—66; pub. rels. bd. Monmouth County Mental Health Assn., 1968—69; co-chmn. Vassar Club So. Calif. Annual Book Fair Vassar Coll., 1970—71; chmn. creative writing group Calif. Inst. Tech. Woman's Club, 1975—79; mem. task force edn. and cultural activities City of Duarte, 1987—88; class rep. Vassar Coll. Alumnae Assn., 1989; chmn. creative writing group Yale U. Newcomers, 1965—66; dir. creative writing group Yale U. Women's Orgn., 1966—67; mem. Exec. Program Network UCLA Grad. Sch. Mgmt., 1987—2000; trustee Ctr. Improvement Child Caring, 1981—83; mem. League Crippled Children, 1982—, treas. for gen. meetings, 1990—91, chmn. hostesses com., 1988—89, pub. rels. com., 1990—91; del. Task Force on Minorities in Newspaper Bus., 1987—89; rep. cmty. County Health Network Tobacco Control Program, 1991; mem. NY Citizens Com. Health Care Decisions, bd. dirs., 2005—; mem. Vassar Coll. Class Gift Com., 1998; bd. mem. com. on aging Town of Rhineback, NY, 2007—; chmn. 1st ann. Rabbi Camillus Angel Interfaith Svc. Temple Beth David, 1978, v.p., 1983—86; cmty. rels. com. Jewish Fedn. Coun. Greater LA, 1985—87; bd. dirs. League Crippled Children, 1988—91; ethics com., human subjects protection com. Jewish Home for Aging, Reseda, Calif., 1994—97; various positions and coms. Claremont Grad. U., 1986—; bd. visitors Claremont Grad. U. Ctr. Arts and Humanities, 2001—; bd. dirs. LA Commn. Assaults Against Women, 1983—84; trustee Rhineback Hist. Soc., 2007—; class corr. Vassar Coll. Quar. Alumnae Mag., 1993—98; class of 1958 coms. Vassar Coll., class v.p., 1998—2000, class co-pres., 2000—01, class pres., 2001—03, program chmn. 40th reunion, 1998, program com. 50th reunion 2008, 2007—08; bd. dirs. Hospice Inc. Dutchess & Ulster Counties, NY, 2008—. Recipient cert. of appreciation City of Duarte, 1988, County of LA, 1988, Ann. Key Mem. award LA Dept. Health Svcs., 1990, cert. of appreciation Alumni Coun. Claremont Grad Sch., 1996; Coro Found. fellow, 1979, Ethics fellow Loma Linda U. Med. Ctr., 1989; named Calif. Communicator of Achievement, Woman of Yr. Calif. Press Women, 1992. Fellow: Am. Med. Writers Assn. (Pacific SW del. to nat. bd. 1980—87, dir. 1980—93, chmn. nat. book awards trade category 1982—83, chmn. Nat. Networking Luncheon 1983—84, nat. chmn. freelance sect. 1984—85, workshop leader, Nat. Ann. Conf. 1984—92, gen. chmn. Asilomar Western Regional Conf. 1985, workshop leader, Asilomar Western Regional Conf. 1985, nat. exec. bd. dirs. 1985—86, nat. adminr. sects. 1985—86, pres.-elect Pacific Southwest chpt. 1985—87, chmn. gen. session nat. conf. 1986—87, chmn. Walter C. Alvarez Mem. Found award 1986—87, program co-chmn. 1987, program chmn. nat. conf. 1987, moderator gen. session. nat. conf. 1987, pres. Pacific S.W. chap. 1987—89, workshop leader, Asilomar Western Nat. Conf. 1988, spkr. Pacific S.W. chpt. 1988—89, program co-chmn. 1989, workshop leader, Asilomar Western Nat. Conf. 1989, Pacific Southwest deleg. to nat. bd. 1989—91, immediate past pres. 1989—91, workshop leader, Nat. Ann. Conf. 1990—92, bd. dirs. 1991—93, workshop leader, Nat. Ann. Conf. 1995, chmn. conv. coms., workshop leader, Nat. Ann. Conf. 1995, Appreciation award for outstanding leadership 1989, named to Workshop Leaders Honor Roll 1991); mem.: AAUP, APHA, AAUW (creative writing chmn. 1969—70, books and plays chmn. Arcadia Br. 1973—74, 1st v.p. program dir. 1975—76, legis. chmn. Arcadia Br. 1976—77, networking chmn. 1981—82, spkr. 1987, chmn. task force promoting individual liberties 1987—88, pres.-elect 1998—99, educ. equity chmn. 1998—99, chmn. deleg. to national conv. 1999, chmn. Technical Trek Sci. Camp Scholarship for Girls 1999, Career Day 1999, pres. Arcadia br. 1999—2000, writer in res Calif. State Am. Assn. Univ. Women 1999—2000, diversity chmn. Arcadia br. 2000—01, LA Interbr. Coun. Arcadia br. repr. 2000—02, Calif. State diversity com. 2000—02, program vice-chmn. LA County Interbr. Coun. 2000—02, Woman of Achievement Arcadia br. 1986, cert. of appreciation 1987), Calif. State AAUW (program co-v.p. 2002), Town Hall Calif. (vice chmn. cmty. affairs sect. 1982—87, faculty-instr. Exec. Breakfast Inst. 1985—86, Exec. Breakfast Inst. spkr. 1986), Pasadena Athletic, Claremont Cols. Faculty House, Women's City (Pasadena), Nat. Writer's Union, Authors Guild, Assn. Writing Programs, NY Acad. Medicine (met. NY Ethics Network), Soc. Health and Human Values, Kennedy Inst. Ethics, Nat. Fedn. Press Women (chmn. state women of achievement comt. 1986—87, nat. co-chmn. task force recruitment minorities 1987—89, del. 1987—89, bd. dirs. 1987—93, nat. dir. spkrs. bur. 1989—93, Plenary past pres. state 1989—, workshop leader, spkr. annual nat. conf. 1990, editor spkrs. bur. directory 1991—92, editor spkrs. bur. addendum dir. 1992, cert. of appreciation 1991, 1st runner up, Nat. Communicator of Achievement 1992, cert. of appreciation 1993), Hastings Cent. (vis. scholar 1996), Ind. Writers So. Calif. (bd. dirs. corp. 1988—89, bd. dirs. 1989—90, dir. at large 1989—90, dir. specialized groups 1989—90, dir. speech writing group 1991—92), NY Acad. Scis., Calif. Press Women (v.p. programs L.A. chpt. 1982—85, pres. 1985—87, state pres. 1987—89, immediate past state pres. 1989—91, chmn. state speakers bur. 1989—95, deleg. nat. bd. 1989—95, dir. family literacy day Calif. 1990, moderator, ann. spring conv. 1990, chmn. nominating comt. 1990—91, Calif. literacy dir. 1990—92, dir. state literacy com. 1990—92, moderator, ann. spring conv. 1992, Cert. of Appreciation 1991, Calif. Communicator of Achievement 1992), Am. Soc. Law, Medicine, Ethics, AAUW Calif. State Comns. Comt. (writer in residence 1999—2000), Coro Nat. Alumni Assn. (bd. dirs. 1999—, continuing edn. com. 2003—), Am. Assn. Higher Edn., Women in Comm. Inc. (NE area rep. 1980—81, bd. dirs. 1980—82, v.p. cmty. affairs 1981—82, chmn. awards banquet 1982, chmn. LA chpt. Agnes Underwood Freedom Info. Awards banquet 1982, nominating com. 1982—83, seminar leader, spkr., ann. nat. profl. conf. 1985, program adv. com. LA chpt. 1987, com. Women of the Press awards luncheon 1988, bd. dirs. 1989—90, v.p. activities 1989—90, Recognition award 1983), Duarte Rotary Club. Home and Office: 22 East Knoll Rhinebeck NY 12572 Office Phone: 845-876-0738.

SLOANE, BONNIE FIEDOREK, pharmacology and cancer biology educator, researcher; b. Pitts., Aug. 12, 1944; d. Leo Anthony and Bettie Thorburn (Findlay) Fiedorek; m. David E. E. Sloane, June 18, 1966 (div. 1976); m. Douglas Roy Yingst, Aug. 21, 1987. BS, Duke U., 1966, MA, 1968; PhD, Rutgers U., 1976. NIH fellow U. Pa., Phila., 1976-78, asst. prof. rsch., 1979; asst. prof. Mich. State U., East Lansing, 1979-80; asst. prof. sch. medicine Wayne State U., Detroit, 1980-84, assoc. prof., 1984-89, prof., 1989—2005, disting. prof., 2005—, interim chair Detroit, 1994-95, chair, 1995—. Mem. pathology B study sect. NIH, 1987-91, 92-94; exec. bd. Internat. Com. on Proteolysis, 1990-99, liason Nat. Inst. Cancer Imaging & Tumor Biol. Programs, 2005-06. Mem. editorial bd. Cancer and Metastasis Revs., Molecular and Cellular Differentiation, Pathology and Oncology Rsch., Internat. Jour. Oncology; contbr. articles to profl. jours. Recipient Acad. Achievement award Probus Club, 1984, Outstanding Grad. Mentor award Wayne State U., 1994; Busch fellow Rutgers U., 1974-75, Nat. Rsch. Svc. postdoctoral fellow, 1977-79, NIH-Nat. Cancer Inst. fellow, 1984-89, Gershenson Dising. Faculty fellow Wayne State U., 1991-93, Jozet Stefans Days plaque Jazet Stefans Inst. Ljubljana Slovenia, 2004, Gold medal Cairo U., 2009. Mem. AAAS, Am. Soc. Cell Biology, Am. Physiol. Soc., Am. Assn. Cancer Rsch. (chair membership com., Clowes award com. 1995), Internat. Proteolysis Soc. (pres. 1999—2001), Am. Soc. Pharmacol Exptl. Therapists, Am. Soc. Biochem. Molecular Biol. Soc. Imaging, Assn. Med. Scx=h. Pharm. (chairs, pres. 2009-) Achievements include research on role of cysteine proteases, cysteine protease inhibitors in malignant progression, functionall imaging of proteolysis. Office: Wayne State U Sch Med 540 E Canfield St Detroit MI 48201-1928 Business E-Mail: bslcane@med.wayne.edu.

SLOANE, CARL STUART, corporate executive, educator, management consultant; b. NYC, Feb. 9, 1937; s. George and Dorothy (Cohen) S.; m. Toby Tattlebaum, Dec. 27, 1958; children: Lisa Beth, Amy Rachel, Todd Cowan. BA, Harvard U., 1958, MBA, 1960. Asst. to pres. Revlon, Inc., NYC, 1960-62; mgmt. cons. Harbridge House, Inc., Boston, 1962-69; pres., CEO, chmn. Temple, Barker & Sloane, Inc., Lexington, Mass., 1970—91; prof. bus. adminstrn. Harvard Grad. Sch. Bus. Adminstrn., Cambridge, Mass., 1991—2001; co-chair Alex Ptnrs. and Questor Funds, 2005—06. Policyholders' examining com. N.W. Mut. Life Ins. Co.; bus. adv. com. Transp. Ctr., Northwestern U., 1984-91; adv. com. Ctr. for Sci. and Internat. Affairs, Kennedy Sch. Govt., Harvard U., 1984-94; dir. Harvard med. faculty physicians at Beth Israel Deaconess Med. Ctr., 2007-; bd. dirs. Rayonier, Inc., Brinks Home Security, Inc. Bd. dirs. Harvard-Radcliffe Hillel, Cambridge, Mass., 1987-98, chmn., 1994-98; bd. dirs., trustee Beth Israel Deaconess Med. Ctr., Boston, 1993—, vice-chmn., 1996-2002, chmn. 2002-05; nat. fund chmn. Harvard. Bus. Sch., 1987-89, vis. com. Mem. Assn. Mgmt. Cons. Firms (chmn. 1984-86), Harvard U. Bus. Sch. Alumni Assn. (v.p. 1989, pres. 1989-91), Boston Yacht Club (Marblehead), Kernwood County Club (Salem), Harvard Club NYC. Office: Harvard Bus Sch Soldiers Fld Boston MA 02163-1317 Home: 402 Paradise Rd Apt 2G Swampscott MA 01907 Business E-Mail: csloane@hbs.edu.

SLOANE, JEREMY STANTON, lawyer; s. Stanton D. Sloane and Cathy B. Kent; m. Tara A. Gordon, Aug. 16, 2003; children: Jackson S., Delaney H. BSBA with Honors, U. Fla. Warrington Coll. Bus. Adminstrn., Gainesville, 1996; JD, U. Fla. Coll. Law, 2000; LLM, U. Miami Grad. Program Taxation, Coral Gables, Fla., 2004. Assoc. atty. Lockheed Martin Global Telecom., Inc., Norristown, Pa., 2000—02, Rice Rose & Snell, Daytona Beach, Fla., 2002—03, DLA Piper, Balt., 2004—06; shareholder Zimmerman Kiser & Sutcliffe, Orlando, Fla., 2006—08; counsel Akerman Senterfitt, Orlando, 2008—. Bd. dir. Avalon Pk. & Blanchard Pk. YMCA, Orlando, 2007—; gen. counsel, exec. com. & bd. dir. South Daytona, Port Orange C of C, Fla., 2003—04; fin. subcom. chmn. United Way Volusia, Daytona Beach, Fla., 2002—03; exec. com. Exec. Adv. Bd. Exch., Orlando, 2006—08; pro bono vol. Fla. Bar YLD Disaster Legal Svcs. Team, Balt., 2004—07. Contbr. articles to profl. pubs. Named Best Attorneys, Fla. Trend, 2008. Mem.: Assn. Corp. Growth (bd. dir. 2008—), Legal Aid Soc., Md. Vol. Lawyers Assn. (vol.), Md. Bar, Fla. Bar, Golden Key Nat. Honor Soc., Phi Kappa Phi, Sigma Phi Epsilon (co-chmn. 2001—02). Conservative. Office: Akerman Senterfitt 420 S Orange Ave Ste 1200 Orlando FL 32801 Office Fax: 407-254-4238. Business E-Mail: jeremy.sloane@akerman.com.

SLOANE, KATHY, real estate broker; b. Pitts., Apr. 22, 1945; m. Harry I. Sloane. BA in Philosophy, Wheaton Coll. With Brown Harris Stevens, NYC, 1986—, sr. v.p., mng. dir. Mem. Com. to Build the Louis Kahn FDR Meml. on Roosevelt Island. Mem.: Real Estate Bd. of NY. Democrat. Office: Brown Harris Stevens 445 Park Ave New York NY 10022 Office Phone: 212-906-9258. Office Fax: 212-303-5408. E-mail: ksloane@bhsusa.com.*

SLOANE, NEIL JAMES ALEXANDER, mathematician, researcher; b. Beaumaris, Wales, Oct. 10, 1939; came to U.S., 1961; s. Charles Ronald and Jessie (Robinson) S.; m. Susanna Stevens Cuyler, Mar. 8, 1980. BA with honors, U. Melbourne, Australia, 1959, BEE, 1960; MS, Cornell U., 1964, PhD, 1967. Asst. prof. Cornell U., Ithaca, NY, 1967-69; mem. tech. staff AT&T Bell Labs., Murray Hill, NJ, 1969-96; prin. mem. tech. staff AT&T Rsch. Labs, 1996—, fellow, 1998. Author: Handbook of Integer Sequences, 1973; co-author: (with F.J. MacWilliams) Theory of Error-Correcting Codes, 1977, (with J.H. Conway) Sphere-Packings, Lattices and Groups, 1988, 32d edit., 1998, (with A.D. Wyner) Claude Elwood Shannon:Collected Papers, 1993, (with S. Plouffe) Encyclopedia of Integer Sequences, 1995, (with A.S. Hedayat and J. Stufken) Orthogonal Arrays, 1999, (with P. Nick) Rock Climbing New Jersey, 2000, (with G. Nebe and E.M. Rains) Self-Dual Codes and Invariant Theory, 2006. Fellow IEEE (editor in chief Trans. Info. Theory jour. 1978-80, Hamming medal 2005); mem. NAE, Math. Assn. Am. (Chauvenet prize 1979, Earle Raymond Hedrick lectr. 1984, David Robbins prize), Am. Math. Soc., Am. Stat. Assn. Avocation: rock climbing. Office Phone: 973-360-8415. E-mail: njas@research.att.com.

SLOAT, RICHARD JOEL, artist; b. Easton, Pa., Sept. 18, 1945; s. Samuel Michael and Florence Elizabeth (Cohen) S.; m. Su-Li Hung, Aug. 18, 1972; 1 child, Benjamin Hung-Hur. BA, U. Pa., 1969; postgrad., Art Students League, NYC, 1971-72. One-man shows include Moon St., Westport, Conn., 1974, Spring Gallery, Taipei, 1979, Martin Summers, N.Y.C., 1987, Wood and Stone Gallery, Taipei, 1990, F.D.R. Gallery, N.Y.C., 1993, The Old Print Shop, N.Y.C., 1995, The Ottendorfer Libr., N.Y.C., 1996, Sonnenshein, Nath & Rosenthal, N.Y.C., 1998, Paul McCarron, N.Y.C., 2001, Howard Salon, Taiwan, 2001, Old Print Shop, 2004, Safe-T-Gallery, N.Y.C., 2005; two-person show Falkenstern Fine Art, N.Y.C., 1990, solo show Port Washington Pub. Libr., 1998, Michael Ingbar Gallery, N.Y.C., 2005; exhibited in group shows at NAD, 1974, 86, 88, 94, 1999, 2000, 03, 04, 05, 07, 09, Taipei Mus., 1976, Terry/Chassman, N.Y.C., 1990, Blum Helman Warehouse, N.Y.C., 1989, Fine Arts Assn., Hanoi, 1991, Curtiba Print Mus., Brazil, 1992, Michael Ingbar Gallery, N.Y.C., 1993, 94, 96, 97, 98, 2000, 01, 05, 06, 08, Duxbury (Mass.) Mus., 1994, 97, 2004, Paul McCarron Gallery, N.Y.C., 1994, 2004, Child's Gallery, Boston, 1994, Br. Consulate, N.Y.C., 1995, Mus. Fine Art, Springfield, Mass., 1995, Kanagawa Prefectural Gallery, Japan, 1995, 97, Roopankar Mus. Fine Arts, India, 1995, Kala Inst., Calif., 1996, Frederick Baker, Chgo., 1996, Fed. Hall, N.Y.C., 1996, N.Y. Transit Mus., N.Y.C., 1997, 2003, Mass. Coll. Art, Boston, 1997, Boston U., 2001, 03, 07, Newark Pub. Libr., 1997, 2000, Daniel Peretz Gallery, N.Y.C., 1997, The Old Print Shop, 1998, 2001, 03, 04, 05, 07, Krasdale Gallery, N.Y.C., 1998, Housatonic Mus. Art, Conn., 1998, Macau Mus. Art, 2000, Albrecht-Kemper Mus. Art, Mo., 2000, Springfield Art Mus., 2001, 05, 08, Mus. Modern Art, N.Y.C., 2002, Mus. City N.Y., 1982, 2002, N.Y. Hist. Soc., N.Y.C., 2002, 04, Susan Teller Gallery, 2004, UBS Paine Weber Art Gallery, 2002, Noble Maritime Collection, 2006, Hollar Soc., Prague, 2006, Graphic Studio Gallery, Dublin, 2006; group shows inlcude AFP Gallery, N.Y.C., 2006, Terrain Gallery, NYC, 2001, 05, 06, 07, 08, Noble Maritime Collection, S.I., N.Y., 2006, ICPNY, Boston U., 2007, Internat. Print Ctr., NYC, 2007, 2008; represented in permanent collections Mus. City of N.Y., N.Y. Pub. Libr., Taipei Mus., Printmaking Workshop, N.Y.C., Fogg Mus., Cambridge, Mass., Nat. Mus. Fine Art, Hanoi, Boston Pub. Libr., Davison Art Ctr., Middletown, Conn., Israel Mus., Jerusalem, Brit. Mus., London, Libr. of Congress, Washington, Portland (Oreg.) Art Mus., Nat. Gallery Art, Washington; author: Journey of Faces, 1985, Mythic City and Friends. Recipient lst Presbyn. Ch. award Washington Square Art Show, N.Y.C., 1976, Leo Meissner prize NAD, l986, 94, Annual prize Audubon Artists, 1974, 96, 97, 98, 99, 2001, 02, 07, Cash award Springfield Mus., 2005, 2007, Additional award, 2007. Mem. Alliance Figurative Artists (program dir. 1982-85), Print Consortium, Printmaking Workshop, Boston Printmakers, Soc. Am. Graphic Artists (coun. 1995—2007, v.p. 1999-2002, pres. 2003-06), Fedn. Modern Painters and Sculptors, Nat. Acad. Design (coun. 2006—, rec. sec. 2006—). Jewish. Avocations: bird watching, travel. Home: 170 2nd Ave 7B New York NY 10003-5754 Studio: 27 Essex St Apt 5A New York NY 10002-4662

SLOBOZHANIN, LEV ARKADIEVICH, fluid mechanics engineer, researcher; b. Nylga, Russia, Sept. 1, 1941; arrived in US, 1995; s. Arkadii Alexandrovich and Iraida Stepanovna (Vlasova) S.; divorced; children: Andrei L., Darya L. Degree in mech. engring. with honors, Kharkov Aviation Inst., Ukraine, 1963; PhD in Physics and Math., Inst. for Low Temperature Physics and Engring., Kharkov, 1968; cert. sr. rsch. scientist, Acad. Scis. of Ukraine, 1975; DSc in Physics and Math., Lavrentyev Inst. Hydrodynamics, Novosibirsk, Russia, 1989. Engr. B. Verkin Inst. Low Temperature Physics and Engring. Nat. Acad. Scis. of Ukraine, Kharkov, 1963-66, sr. engr., 1966-69, jr. scientist, 1969-71, sr. scientist, 1971-89, leading scientist, 1989-98. Sr. tchr. Kharkov Aviation Inst., 1969—71, prof., 1989—90; vis. prof. Madrid Poly. U., 1993—94; vis. scholar U. Ala., Huntsville, 1995—2002; vis. rschr. Case Western Res. U., Cleve., 1999—2002, prin. rschr., 2002—. Co-author: Fluid Mechanics of Weightlessness, 1976, Low-Gravity Fluid Mechanics, 1987, Solution Methods for Fluid Mechanics Problems Under Weightlessness Conditions, 1992; contbr. articles to profl. jours. Chmn. trade union com. B. Verkin Inst. for Low Temperature Physics and Engring., 1986-89. Mem.: Am. Phys. Soc. Office: Case Western Res U 305 Olin Bldg 10900 Euclid Ave Cleveland OH 44106-7222 Office Phone: 216-368-2984. Business E-Mail: lion@case.edu.

SLOCKETT, DEENA, medical educator; d. Gary and Marilyn Marmo; m. David Slockett; children: Brecken, Evan. MBA, Webster U., Orlando, Fla., 2000. Cert. radiologic technologist ARRT & Fla. State, 1994, mammographer 2000. Asst. prof. Fla. Hosp. Coll. Health Scis., Orlando, 2001—07, assoc. prof., 2007—. Grantee, Fla. State, 2006. Mem.: Am. Soc. Radiologic Technologists. Business E-Mail: deena_slockett@fhchs.edu.

SLOCOMBE, WALTER BECKER, lawyer, former federal official; b. Albuquerque, Sept. 23, 1941; m. Ellen Seidman; children: Sarah Cody, Merrin Hayes, Benjamin William. BA, Princeton U., 1963; Rhodes scholar, Balliol Coll., Oxford U., 1963-65; LL.B., Harvard U., 1968. Bar: D.C. 1970. Law clk. to Justice Abe Fortas, US Supreme Ct., Washington, 1968-69; mem. staff Nat. Security Coun., 1969-70; rsch. assoc. Internat. Inst. Strategic Studies, London, 1970-71; assoc. Caplin & Drysdale, Washington, 1971—74, mem., 1974-76, 81-93, 2001—03, 2003—04; prin. dep. asst. sec. for internat. security affairs US Dept Def., Washington, 1977—79, dep. under-sec. for policy planning, 1979-81, prin. dep. under-sec. for policy, 1993-94, under-sec. for policy, 1994—2001; sr. advisor for nat. def. Coalition Provisional Authority, Baghdad, Iraq, 2003. Dir. US Dept. Def. Task Force on Strategic Arms Limitation Talks II (SALT II), 1977—81; mem. Commn. on the Intelligence Capabilities of the US Regarding Weapons of Mass Destruction, 2004. Rhodes scholar, 1963-65; recipient Defense Disting. Pub. Svc. medal, 1981, 85, 97, 2001, 04, Joseph Kruzel award for Disting. Svc. in the Pursuit of Peace, 2000. Mem. Atlantic Coun. US, ACLU, Coun. Fgn. Rels., Internat. Inst. Strategic Studies. Democrat. Office: Caplin & Drysdale 1 Thomas Cir Washington DC 20005 Office Phone: 202-862-5060. Business E-Mail: wbs@capdale.com.

SLOCUM, DONALD WARREN, chemist, educator, researcher; m. Laurel Hopper, 1990 (dec. May 1997); children from previous marriage: Warren, Matthew. BS in Chemistry, U. Rochester, NY, 1956, BA in English, 1956; PhD in Chemistry, NYU, 1963. Postdoctoral rsch. assoc. Duke U., Durham, NC, 1963—64; asst. prof. chemistry Carnegie Inst. Tech., Pitts., 1964—65; from asst. to assoc. prof. chemistry So. Ill. U., Carbondale, 1965—72, prof., 1972—81, adj. prof., 1981—84; program dir. chem. dynamics sect., chemistry divsn. NSF, Washington, 1984—85; program leader divsn. ednl. programs, sr. scientist chem. tech. divsn. Argonne Nat. Lab., Ill., 1985—90; head dept. chemistry We. Ky. U., Bowling Green, 1990—95, prof. chemistry, 1995—2005, rsch. prof. chemistry emeritus, 2005—. Sr. scientist Gulf R&D Co., Pitts., 1980-82; vis. prof. U. Ill., 1970, U. Bristol, Eng., 1973, U. Cin., 1976; vis. fellow U. Bristol, 1972; vis. lectr. Carnegie-Mellon U., 1983-84, U. Pitts., 1983-84; organizer symposia on organometallic chemistry and catalysis; bd. dir. Ctrl. States Univs., Inc., 1986-88, Arts at Argonne, 1988-90; mem. nat. organizing com. XV Internat. Conf. on Organometallic Chemistry Wayne State U., Detroit, 1990; mem. internat. adv. bd. XV Internat. Conf. on Organometallic Chemistry, Warsaw, 1992; mem. NSF/EPSCoR subcom., Ky., 1993-94; mem. coun. on undergrad. rsch. Instnl. Liaison Rep. to We. Ky. U., 1995-2005; cons. in field. Co-editor: Advances in Chemistry Series of Am. Chem. Soc., Vol. 230, 1992, Methane and Alkane Activation (Plenum), 1995; mem. editl. bd. Synthesis and Reactivity in Inorganic, Metal-Organic and Nano-Metal Chemistry, 1971—, Natural Product Rsch., 2006—; regional editor Letters in Organic Chemistry, 2004-05, mem. editl. bd., 2005—; contbr. over 80 articles to profl. jours., chpts. to books Recipient Rsch./Creativity award Ogden Coll. of Sci., Tech. and Health, We. Ky. U., 1996, Sci. award honoring Brian Andreen, Cottrell Coll. Sci., 1999. Mem. Am. Chem. Soc. (sec. gen. elect catalysis and surface sci. secretariat 1992, sec. gen. 1993, organic divsn. rep. to catalysis and surface sci. secretariat, 1993-98, co-chmn. symposium, San Diego, 1994), Chem. Soc. Gt. Britain, Catalysis Soc., Bowling Green Chamber

Singers, Sigma Xi. Avocations: music, literature, sports. Office: Western Ky U Dept Chemistry Bowling Green KY 42101 Office Phone: 270-745-5239. Business E-Mail: donald.slocum@wku.edu.

SLOCUM, JUDITH ANN, retired elementary school educator; b. Kimberly, Wis., Apr. 11, 1942; d. Julius Lawrence and Adele Van Handel; m. Richard Eugene Slocum, June 20, 1964; children: Catherine Jean Wolfla, Susan Marie. BS, U. Wis., LaCrosse, 1964; MS, Ind. U., Bloomington, 1983. Cert. English and speech tchr. Ind. Bd. Edn., 1966, reading and mid. sch. specialist Ind. Bd. Edn., 1983. English tchr. Northmont Schs., Englewood, Ohio, 1964—66, Ellettsville Schs., Ind., 1966—68, Martinsville Schs., Ind., 1974—80; reading specialist Wash. Twp. Schs., Indpls., 1980—94, English tchr., dept. chair, 1994—2004. Grant writer Martinsville Schs., 1978—80; in-service presenter on reading across the curriculum Washington Twp. Schs., Indpls., 1980—2004, co-authored curriculum document, 2000—04. Author: McGrammar, 2003. Mem.: Nat. Coun. Tchrs. of English (assoc.). Achievements include development of system of teaching grammar and writing in McGrammar. Avocations: sailing, swimming, reading. Home: 8876 Crystal River Dr Indianapolis IN 46240 Personal E-mail: jas9149@comcast.net.

SLOCUM, KAY BRAINERD, history professor, musician; d. David Stuart Brainerd and Kathleen Dodd Grant; m. Dieter Droste, July 17, 2003; children: Melissa Kay, James Goodsell. PhD, Kent State U., Ohio, 1987. Gerhold prof. humanities Capital U., Columbus, Ohio, 1988—; violist ProMusica Chamber Orch., Columbus, 1992—. Author: (textbook) Medieval Civilization, Liturgies in Honour of Thomas Becket, 2004. Recipient Praestantia award, Capital U., 1997. Mem.: Am. Musicological Soc., Medieval Acad. America.

SLOMANSKI, REV. PATRICIA PARKER, minister; b. Wilmington, NC, Mar. 6, 1951; d. Robert Homer and Annie Grace Parker; m. Henry Slomanski (dec.); children: Randall Edward, Patricia Grace. BA in Music, U. NC, Wilmington, 1992; MA in Christian Edn., Presbyn. Sch. Christian Edn., Richmond, Va., 1995; MDiv, Union Theol. Sem., Richmond, 1998; postgrad., Columbia Theol. Sem., Decatur, Ga., 2006—. Ordained min. Presbyn. Ch., 2002. Tchr. New Hanover HS, Wilmington, NC, 1993—94; dir. adult ministries St. Giles' Presbyn. Ch., Richmond, 1998—2000; supply pastor Louisa Presbyn. Ch., Va., 2000, Westminster Presbyn. Ch., Richmond, 2001, Milford Presbyn. Ch., Va., 2002, Genito Presbyn. Ch., Powhatan, Va., 2005—06; mem. small ch., new ch. devel. com. Salem Presbytery, 2007; pastor Ashland Presbyn. Ch., Va., 2002—04; min. Hill and Pine Ridge Presbyn. Chs., 2006—07; assoc. pastor Eastminster Presbyn. Ch., Marietta, Ga., 2007—. Chaplain Hermitage United Meth. Retirement Home, 2005; supply ch. organist, pianist; mem. nurturing congregations com. Presbytery of James, 2002, 05. Sunday sch. tchr. Gayton Kirk, Richmond, 1996; organist, choirmaster Grace United Meth. Ch., Wilmington, 1973—74; Sunday sch. tchr. Westminster Presbyn. Ch., Richmond, 1993, Three Chopt Presbyn. Ch., Richmond, 1997; pianist, organist Winter Pk. Bapt. Ch., Wilmington, NC, 1993. A.J. Fletcher Music scholar, U. NC, 1990—92. Mem.: Union/PSCE Alumni Assn., Presbyn. Older Adult Ministry Network, Am. Assn. Christian Counselors. Office: Eastminster Presbyn Ch 3125 Sewell Mill Rd Marietta GA 30062 Home: 2981 Ebenezer Church RD Coats NC 27521-9694

SLOMANSON, LLOYD HOWARD, architect, musician, photographer; b. NYC, July 31, 1928; s. Albert Jerome and Dorothea (Jacobson) S.; m. Joan Barbara Kanel; children: Peter, Eric. BArch, Syracuse U., 1949. Registered architect, 18 states including N.Y. and N.J.; NCARB; registered profl. planner, N.J. Archtl. draftsman Rich & Conn Architects, Bklyn., 1949-50; project architect Fordyce & Hamby/Raymond Loewy, NYC, 1951-53; project architect, assoc. ptnr. Serge P. Petroff, Architect, NYC, 1953-58; project dir. Robert W. Hegardt, Architect, NYC, 1959-60; project architect, ptnr. Fordyce & Hamby Assocs., NYC, 1960-67; ptnr. Fordyce, Hamby & Kennerly, NYC, 1967-69, Hamby, Kennerly & Slomanson, NYC, 1969-72, Kennerly, Slomanson & Smith, NYC, 1972-81; mng. ptnr. Slomanson, Smith & Barresi, NYC, 1981-99; pvt. practice, 1999—. Arbitrator Am. Arbitration Assn. and NASD Dispute Resolution, N.Y.C. Author articles. Served with U.S. Army, 1950-51. Recipient 1st prize for design S.I. C. of C., 1967, 84. Mem. AIA, N.Y. Soc. Architects (Store of Yr. award 1985, Design award 1993), N.Y. State Assn. Architects, Bldg. Ofcls. Conf. Am., Univ. Club, The Players. Avocations: music, photography. Office: 137 W 78th St New York NY 10024-6702 Home Phone: 212-724-8451; Office Phone: 917-441-0067. Personal E-mail: woodpics@aol.com. E-mail: woodpics@msn.com.

SLOMINSKI, ELENA GREGORYEVNA, mathematics educator; b. Vilnius, Lithuania, Feb. 25, 1959; arrived in U.S., 1989, naturalized, 1996; d. Gregory Andreyevich and Irina Andreyevna Maciura; m. Alexander Nicholas Slominski, July 26, 1980; children: Etalia, Elina, Emily, Zachary, Samuel, Elizabetta. MS in Math., Vilnius U., 1981. Cert. tchr. Ariz. Tchr. math. H.S. # 10, Vilnius, 1980—81; substitute tchr. math. Painted Pony Ranch Charter Sch., Prescott, Ariz., 1999—2001; part-time tchr. math. Prep H.S. Tri-City Coll., Prescott, 2001—03, tchr. math. Prep H.S., 2003—. Adj. instr. math. Graceland U., Lamoni, 2003—, Embry Riddle Aero. U., Prescott, 2006—08, adj. math faculty Upward Bound and Math Sci. Regional Ctr., 2006—08; chair dept. math. and sci. Prep H.S. Tri-City Coll., Prescott, 2004—. Named Yarapai County H.S. Tchr. of Yr., Yarapai County Ednl. Found., 2006; nominee Presdl. Math. award, USA Today Math. Team, 2005, Yarapai County Tchr. of Yr., 2005. Mem.: North Ctrl. Ariz. math. and Sci. Consortium (adv. bd. mem.), Ariz. Assn. Tchrs. Math., Math. Assn. Am., Nat. Coun. Tchrs. Math. Avocations: languages, dance, vegetarian cooking. Office: Tri-City Coll Prep HS 5522 Side Rd Prescott AZ 86301 Office Phone: 928-777-0403. Office Fax: 928-777-0402.

SLOMSKY, JOEL HARVEY, federal judge; b. Bklyn., 1946; BA, Bklyn. Coll., CUNY, 1967; JD, NY Law Sch., 1970. Bar: NY 1971, Pa. 1973. Spl. atty. Criminal Divsn., Phila. Strike Force US Dept. Justice, 1971—73; atty. Lipschitz & Danella, 1973—74; pvt. practice, 1974—82, 1990—2008; ptnr. DiGiacomo and Slomsky, 1982—90; judge US Dist. Ct. (ea. dist.) Pa., 2008—. Office: US Dist Ct James A Byrne Fed Courthouse 601 Mkt St Rm 5614 Philadelphia PA 19106 Office Phone: 267-299-7340.

SLONAKER, NORMAN DALE, lawyer; b. Havre, Mont., Sept. 16, 1940; s. Frederick and Agnes (Monson) S.; m. Helen Bogumil, Aug. 29, 1964. BS, U. Wash., Seattle, 1962; LLM, Harvard U., 1965. Bar: NY 1966. Assoc. Sidley Austin LLP, NYC, 1965—72, ptnr., 1973—. Office Phone: 212-839-5356. Business E-Mail: nslonaker@sidley.com.

SLONE, SANDI, artist; b. Boston, Oct. 1, 1939; d. Louis and Ida (Spind) Sudikoff; children: Erric Solomon, Jon Solomon. Student, Boston Mus. Fine Arts Sch., 1970-73; BA magna cum laude, Wellesley Coll., 1974. Sr., grad. painting faculty Boston Mus. Fine Arts Sch./Tufts U., 1975—; instr. grad. program Sch. Visual Art, NYC, 1989-90; lectr. painting Harvard U., Cambridge, Mass., 1982; artist-in-residence City Hall, Barcelona, 1987, 1989; NY Artists resident Santa Fe Art Inst., 2002. Vis. artist Triangle Artists Workshop, NY, 1982, 87, 90; co-founder, dir. Art/Omi Internat. Artists Found., NYC, 1992—; bd. dirs. The Fields Sculpture Pk. and ART OMI, 1991-. One-woman shows include ICA, Boston, 1977, Harcus Krakow Gallery, Boston, 1978, 79, 80, 82, 84, 86, Acquavella Contemporary Art, N.Y., 1977, 79, 80, 82, 84, Stephen Rosenberg Gallery, N.Y., 1988, Levinson Kane Gallery, Boston, 1989, Smith Jariwala Gallery, London, 1990, Jersey City Mus., 1996, The Artists Mus., Lodz, Poland, 1997, Cristinerose Gallery, N.Y.C., 1999, Savage Gallery, Portland, Oreg., 2001, Art Resources Transfer, NYC, 2002, The Santa Fe Art Inst., N.Mex., 2002, The Tower Gallery, Hong Kong, 2004; exhibited in group shows at Mus. Fine Arts, Boston, 1977, Corcoran Gallery of Art 35th Biennial, Washington, 1977, Edmonton Art Mus., 1977, 85, Hayden Gallery MIT, Cambridge, Mass., 1978, New Generation Andre Emmerich Gallery, N.Y., 1980-81, Am. Ctr., Paris, 1980-81, Amerika Haus, Berlin, 1980-81, Carpenter Ctr., Harvard U., Ctr. de la Cultura Contemporania, Barcelona, 1987, Federated Union of Black Artists, Johannesburg, South Africa, 1989, Jan Weiss Gallery, N.Y., 1990, Olympia Internat. Art Fairs, London, 1991, Gallery Korea, N.Y., 1992, Klarfeld Perry Gallery, N.Y., 1994, Out of the Blue Gallery, Edinburgh, Scotland, 1994, Gallery One, Toronto, 1996, Fine Arts Ctr., U. R.I., Kingston, 1996, Crieger Dane Gallery, Boston, 1996, Visual Arts Gallery, N.Y., 1997, TransHudson Gallery, N.Y., 1997, Butler Inst. of Am. Art, Youngstown, Ohio, 1998, 45th Biennial Corcoran Mus. Art, Washington, 1998, Lombard-Freid Fine Arts, N.Y., 1999, 00, Cyclorama, Boston, 2000, Cristinerose Gallery, N.Y., 2001, Queens U., Toronto, 2001, Art Resources Transfer, 2002, U. Cambridge, Eng., 2003, Art in Gen., NYC, 2004, Savage Gallery, Portland, Oreg., 2004, The Transformer Rm. Queens U. Belfast, Ireland, 2006, Dashanzi Int. Art Festival, Beijing, 2006, Queen's U. Art Festival, Belfast, Ireland, 2006, others; represented in permanent collections Mus. Modern Art, N.Y.C., Mus. Contemporary Art, Barcelona, Mus. Fine Arts, Boston, Hirshhorn Mus., Washington, Corcoran Gallery & Mus. Art, Washington. Mus. Fine Arts Boston fellow, Portland Art Mus., Oreg.; Fitzwilliam Mus., Cambridge U., UK; Miami Art Mus.; Hope Mus., Tokyo, 1977, 81; Ford Found. grantee, 1979. Studio: 13 Worth St New York NY 10013-2922 E-mail: sslone@rcn.com.

SLOOTWEG, CAROLINE, marketing executive; b. South Africa, 1975; MA in Bus. With Ogilvy & Mather Worldwide, NYC; freelance account mgr. 180 Amsterdam BV; with Unilever, Rotterdam, Netherlands, 2004—05; dir. digital mktg. and new media Unilever London, 2005—08; head new media Unilever Asia, 2008—. Named a Woman to Watch, Advt. Age, 2008. Office: Unilever House 100 Victoria Embankment EC4Y 0DY London England Office Phone: 44 20 7822 5252. Office Fax: 44 20 7822 5951.*

SLOSBERG, MIKE, advertising executive; b. Phila., Aug. 29, 1934; s. Sam. M. and Florence (Frank) S.; m. Joan Shidler, Aug. 29, 1957 (div. 1984); children: Sydney Ellen (dec.), Robert Morton; m. Janet Cohn, June 10, 1987. BSBA, U. Denver, 1960. With Young & Rubicam, Inc., NYC, 1960-78; pres. Wunderman, Rocotta & Kline, NYC, 1978-83; exec. v.p., exec. creative dir. Marsteller, Inc., NYC, 1983-84, Bozell Jacobs, Kenyon & Eckhardt, NYC, 1984-86, pres. direct mktg. div., 1986-87; exec. creative dir. Bronner Slosberg Humphrey, Boston, 1987-96; vice chmn., chief creative officer Digitas (formerly Bronner Slosberg Humphrey), Boston, 1996-2000; co-founder Digitas, Inc.; ret., 2003. Author: (books) The August Strangers, 1978, The Hitler Error, 2006, Pimp My Walker. Bd. dirs. Keen Co. Theater, The Atlantic Theater Co. Avocation: writing novels. Personal E-mail: mslosberg@digitas.com.

SLOSBURG-ACKERMAN, JILL ROSE, artist, educator; b. Omaha, Aug. 28, 1948; d. Harold Walter and Marion (Gill) Slosburg; m. James Sloss Ackerman, Aug. 8, 1987; 1 child, Jesse August Ackerman. Diploma, Boston Mus. Sch., 1971; BFA, Tufts U., 1971, MFA, 1983. Prof. art Mass. Coll. Art, Boston, 1973—; vis. artist Cranbrook Acad. Art, Bloomfield, Mich., 1993. One-woman shows include Harcus-Krakow-Rosen-Sonnabend Gallery, Boston, 1978, 1980, Helen Shlien Gallery, 1980, 1982, Cohen Arts Ctr., Tufts U., Medford, Mass., 1982, Van Buren/Brazellon/Cutting Gallery, Cambridge, Mass., 1985, Genovese Gallery, Boston, 1995, Manwaring Gallery Cumings Art Ctr., Conn. Coll., New London, 1995, Rose Art Mus., Brandeis U., Waltham, Mass., 1996, Atrium Gallery, U. Mass., Dartmouth, 1999, Judy Ann Goldman Fine Art, Boston, 1999, 2004, exhibited in group shows at Naga Gallery, 1980, DeCordova Mus., Lincoln, Mass., 1980, Jewett Art Ctr., Wellesley, Mass., 1982, Helen Shlien Gallery, Boston, 1982, Cherry Stone Gallery, Wellfleet, Mass., 1984, Quadrum Gallery, Chestnut Hill, Mass., 1985, Fed. Res. Gallery, Boston, 1986, Danforth Mus., 1986, Conseil de la Sculpture, Montreal, 1986, North Hall Gallery, Boston, 1987, Artists Found. Gallery, 1990, Mus. Decorative Arts, Prague, 1991, Nancy Margolis Gallery, N.Y.C., 1991, Bellevue (Wash.) Art Mus., 1992, Artwear, N.Y., 1992, Genovese Gallery, Albany, N.Y., 1992, Judy Ann Goldman Fine Art, Boston, 1997, 2002, 2007, Mills Gallery, 1997—98, 2004, Boston Mus. Fine Arts, 1999, DeCordova Mus., Lincoln, 2000, Nat. Art Mus. China, Beijing, 2001, Forest Hills Cemetery, Boston, 2002, 2004, Coll. Holy Cross, Worcester, Mass., 2003, Concord Art Assn., Mass., 2003, Fuller Craft Mus., 2005, AASpace Gallery, Maynard, Mass., 2007, N.Am. Costa Rica Cultural Ctr., San Jose, 2007, Trustman Gallery, Simmons Coll., Boston, 2007, Paul Kotula Projects, Ferndale, Mich., 2007, Art & History, Nightingale Program House, Brown U., Providence, 2009, Drawings that Work Mills Gallery, Boston, 2009, Represented in permanent collections J. L. Brandeis & Sons, Omaha, Mass. Coll. Art, Boston, Boston Pub. Libr., City of Cambridge, Forest Hills Cemetery, Jamaica Plain, Mass., Boston Mus. Fine Arts, Met. Mus. Art, NY, Worcester Art Mus., Mas.; contbr. articles to profl. jours. Founder, mem. Boston Women's Action Coalition; bd. dirs. Cambridge (Mass.) Multi-Cultural Ctr., Gallery at Green St., 1993—2006. Recipient Patricia Jellinek Hallowell prize for Jewelry, 1984, Disting. Svc. award, Mass. Coll. Art, 1980, 4th prize sterling silver design competition, Nat. Guild Sterling Silversmiths, 1970, Traveling Scholar's award, Sch. Boston Mus. Fine Arts, 1998; grantee, Artist's Resource Trust, 2001, New Eng. Art Critics Assn., 2004, 2006, Anonymous was a Woman, 2007; fellow, Haystack Mountain Sch. Crafts, 1972, 1976, Nat. Endowment Arts, 1974, 1986, The Artists Found., 1984, Mary Ingraham Bunting Inst., 1985—86; Profl. Devel. grantee, Mass. Coll. Art, 1987, Polaroid Corp. Photography grantee, 1988, New Eng. Found. Arts fellow, 1998, Mass. Cultural Coun. Artist's grantee, 1999, 2006. Jewish. Home: 12 Coolidge Hill Rd Cambridge MA 02138-5510 Studio: One Fitchburg St Apt C415 Somerville MA 02143-2128 Home Phone: 617-868-6824; Office Phone: 617-625-4056, 617-694-4410. Personal E-mail: jsackerman44@comcast.net.

SLOTKIN, RICHARD SIDNEY, literature educator; b. Bklyn., Nov. 8, 1942; s. Herman and Roselyn B. (Seplowitz) S.; m. Iris F. Shupack, June 23, 1963; 1 child, Joel Elliot. BA, Bklyn. Coll., 1963; PhD, Brown U., 1967; MA (hon.), Wesleyan U., Middletown, Conn., 1976. Mem. faculty Wesleyan U., 1966—, prof. English, 1976—93, Olin prof., 1982—2008, Olin prof. emeritus, 2008—, chmn. dept. Am. studies, 1976—95. Author: Regeneration Through Violence: The Mythology of the American Frontier, 1600-1860, 1973 (Albert Beveridge award Am. Hist. Assn.), (with J.K. Folsom) So Dreadfull a Judgement: Puritan Responses to King Philip's War, 1675-1677, 1978, The Crater: A Novel of the Civil War, 1980, The Fatal Environment: The Myth of the Frontier in the Age of Industrialization, 1800-1890, The Return of Henry Starr, 1988, Gunfighter Nation: The Myth of the Frontier in Twentieth Century America, 1992 (National Book award nominee, 1993), Abe: A Novel of the Young Lincoln, 2000 (Michael Shaara Civil War Fiction award, 2000), Lost Battalions: The Great War and the Crisis of American Nationality, 2005; and articles. Fellow Center Humanities; fellow Wesleyan U., 1969-70, 74-75, 80—; fellow NEH, 1973-74, Rockefeller Found., 1976-77; recipient Don D. Walker prize AQ; lit. award Little Big Horn Assocs., 1986 Fellow Soc. Am. Historians; mem. AAUP, PEN, Am. Film Inst., Am. Studies Assn. (Mary Turpie prize for tchg. and program-bldg. 1995), Am. Hist. Assn., Orgn. Am. Historians, Authors Guild. Jewish. Office: Wesleyan U Ctr For The Americas Middletown CT 06459-0001

SLOTKIN, TODD, diversified financial services company executive; b. Detroit, Mar. 19, 1953; s. Hugo and Babette Slotkin; m. Judy Scavone, Jan. 30, 1988; children: Matthew, William, Thomas, Peter. BS, Cornell U., 1974, MBA, 1975. With Citicorp, 1975-92, sr. credit officer, 1984-92, head divsn. corp. fin., 1988-90, sr. mng. dir., 1990-92; with MacAndrews & Forbes Holdings, Inc., NYC, 1992—2006, sr. v.p., 1992-98, exec. v.p., 1998—2006, CFO, 1999—2006; mng. dir., co-head Natixis Capital Markets, NYC, 2006—07. Bd. dirs. CBIZ, Inc., Martha Stewart Living Omnimedia, Inc.; sr. mng. dir. Irving Pl. Capital, 2008—. Found. mem., dir., chmn. Food Allergy Initiative, 1999—.

SLOTNICK, BARRY IVAN, lawyer; b. NYC, June 18, 1939; s. Meyer and Rose Ann (Hurwitz) S.; m. Donna Miriam Auerbach, July 12, 1968; children: Stuart Philip, Melissa Lynne, Deborah Anne-Shoshana, Melanie Judith-Chani. BA, CCNY, 1959; JD, NYU, 1961. Bar: N.Y. 1961, U.S. Ct. Appeals (2d cir.), U.S. Dist. Ct. (ea. dist., so. dist.) N.Y., U.S. Supreme Ct., 1966. Pvt. practice, NYC, 1966-68; sr. ptnr. Slotnick & Baker, NYC, 1986-94, Slotnick, Shapiro, & Crocker LLP, NYC, 1994—2005; ptnr. Buchanan Ingersoll & Rooney PC, NYC, 2005—. Adj. prof. in trial practice Cardozo Law Sch., N.Y.C.; judge moot ct. competition NYU and Bklyn. Law Sch. Contbr. articles to profl. jours. Recipient Anti-defamation and Anti-discrimination award Italian Am. Civil Rights League, 1970, Honor plaque Jewish Def. League, 1973, Champion of Youth award B'nai B'rith, 1973, Masada award Jewish Identity Ctr., 1978, AMMY award for best criminal lawyer Am. Lawyer, 1981, Humanitarian award Crime Victims' Polit. Platform, 1982, Award on Behalf of Crime Victims N.Y. Supreme Ct. Officers Assn., 1983, Israel Leadership Peace award Greater Westchester Div., 1984; named Man of Yr. Young Israel Scarsdale, 1982. Mem. N.Y. State Bar Assn. (criminal justice sect.-Outstanding Practitioner award 1987, fed. judiciary com.), Fed. Bar Assn., Inter-Am. Bar Assn., Assn. of Bar of City of N.Y., N.Y. County Lawyer's Assn., Bronx County Bar Assn., P.R. Bar Assn. (assoc. selective svc. examiner 1968-70, spl. dep. atty. gen. 1972). Clubs: Atrium, Downtown Athletic (N.Y.). Republican. Avocation: boating. Office: Buchanan Ingersoll & Rooney PC 620 Eighth Ave 23rd Fl New York NY 10018-1699 Office Phone: 212-444-4444. Office Fax: 212-440-4401. Business E-Mail: barry.slotnick@bipc.com.*

SLOTSVE, GEORGE AARON, economist, educator, consultant; b. Estevan, Saskatchewan, Can., Sept. 5, 1959; s. Stanley and Mary Elizabeth Slotsve. BA honors, Queen's U., Kingston, 1981; MA in Econ., U. We. Ont., 1982; MS in Econ., U. Wis., 1985, PhD in Econ., 1989. Prof. Vanderbilt U., Nashville, 1988—96, No. Ill. U., DeKlab, 1996—. Vis. prof. Queen's U., Kingston, Ont., Canada, 1992, U. Philippines, Quezon City, 1999. Author: (book) Are We Becoming Two Societies?: Income Polarization and the Myth of the Declining Middle Class in Canada. Office: Northern Ill Univ Dept Econ Zulauf Hall Dekalb IL 60115 Business E-Mail: gslotsve@niu.edu.

SLOTTA, OLIVEANN DAVIS, mathematics educator, consultant; m. James G. Slotta; children: Lizann, James D., Jon, Karen Larson. BA, Hiram Coll., Ohio, 1963; MA, U. Colo., Denver, 1992, PhD, 1999. Lic. profl. tchr. Colo., 1991, cert. tchr. Ohio, 1963, Ohio, 1991. Tchr. secondary math Painesville City Schs., Ohio, 1965—69; facilitator Montreal Cath. Sch. Commn., Montreal, Quebec, 1976—79, Inst. Cultural Affairs, Denver, 1979—83; exec. dir. Cornerstone Ctr., Denver, 1983—85; tchr. math. Denver Pub. Schs., 1986—94, 1998—, math. program specialist, 1994—98. Mem. selection com. Am. Tchr. awards, 1993—2005; charter mem. Internat. Assn. Facilitators, 1988—2000; facilitator town meeting program US and Canada, 1975—80. Recipient Am. Tchr. award, Disney Co., 1991, Alumni award, U. Colo. Denver, 1993, Mayor's award, City of Denver, 2005; named Outstanding Math Tchr., Colo. Coun. Tchrs. Math, 1992; named one of Mirabella's 1000, 1994; fellow, U. Colo. Denver, 1997. Mem.: NEA, Nat. Coun. Tchrs. Math., Colo. Edn. Assn. Avocations: knitting, skiing. Home: 1685 Steele St Denver CO 80206-1780 Office Phone: 303-478-8961. Personal E-mail: oslotta@earthlink.net.

SLOTTA, TRACEY, biology professor; m. Douglas J. Slotta; 1 child, Theodore M. PhD, Va. Tech, Blacksburg, 2004. Plant geneticist USDA-ARS, Fargo, ND, 2004; adj. faculty Montgomery Coll., Rockville, Md., 2008—. Systematics editor Castanea-Southern Appalachian Bot. Soc., Newberry, SC, 2008—. Mem.: AAAS, AWIS, Am. Soc. Plant Taxonomists, Bot. Soc. Am. Office: Montgomery Coll Biology 51 Mannakee St Rockville MD 20850 Personal E-mail: tslotta@comcast.net. Business E-Mail: tracey.slotta@montgomerycollege.edu.

SLOUJITEL, JACOB BEN, mathematics professor, researcher; b. Moscow, Nov. 1, 1945; arrived in U.S., 1994; s. Ben Leo Sloujitel and Bertha Gilel Sloujitel-Shamis; m. Mira Noah Rudaya, Aug. 31, 1968; children: Kate, Lev. BS, Inst. Elecs. and Mining Mechanics, 1966; MS, Moscow Mining U., 1968; PhD, State Rsch. Inst., 1976. Cons. Acad. Natural Sci., Moscow, 1993—95; prof., chairperson math. Globe Inst. Tech., NYC, 1997—. Adj. prof. physics CUNY, NYC, 1995—98; vis. prof. math. Ramapo Coll., Mahwah, NJ, 1997—, Fairleigh Dickinson U., Madison, 2002—; pres. J and M Smartel Cons. Ctr., Fair Lawn, 1999—. Author: Underground Melting of Sulphur, 1981. Mgr. Soccer Club, Fair Lawn, 1994—. Fellow, State Rsch. Inst., Moscow, 1968—94. Mem.: Math. Assn. Am. Avocations: soccer, ping pong/table tennis, chess. Home: 38 Beverly Ct Fair Lawn NJ 07410 Office: Globe Inst Tech 500 7th Ave New York NY 10018 Office Phone: 212-624-1806. Business E-Mail: jsloujit@globe.edu.

SLOVER, WILLIAM LEWIS, lawyer; b. Aug. 15, 1937; AB, Yale U., New Haven, 1959; JD, Columbia U., NY, 1962. Bar: DC 1962. Assoc. Pope, Ballard & Loos, Washington, 1962—65, Hogan & Hartson, Washington, 1966; ptnr. Slover & Loftus, Washington, 1967—. Recipient award, Law Profls., Disting. Svc. award, Assn. Transp., Washington, 1996.

SLOVITER, DOLORES KORMAN, federal judge; b. Phila., Sept. 5, 1932; d. David and Tillie Korman; m. Henry A. Sloviter, Apr. 3, 1969 (dec. May 2003); 1 child, Vikki Amanda. AB in Econs. with distinction, Temple U., 1953, LHD (hon.), 1986; LLB magna cum laude, U. Pa.,

1956; LLD (hon.), Dickinson Sch. Law, 1984, U. Richmond, 1992, Widener U., 1994. Bar: Pa. 1957. From assoc. to ptnr. Dilworth, Paxson, Kalish, Kohn & Levy, Phila., 1956—69; mem. Harold E. Kohn PA, Phila., 1969—72; assoc. prof. Temple U. Law Sch., Phila., 1972—74, prof., 1974—79; judge US Ct. Appeals (3rd cir.), Phila., 1979—, chief judge, 1991—98. Bd. overseers U. Pa. Law Sch., 1993—99; bd. trustees Nat. Constitution Ctr., 1998—2007; mem. Jud. Conf. of US, 1991—98. Chair Pa. Rhodes Scholarship Selection Com., 2003—04; mem. Dist. IV Selection Com., Rhodes Scholarship Competitions, 2005—, chair, 2006—; mem. Pa. Women's Forum, 1996—, SE Region Pa. Gov.'s Conf. on Aging, 1976—79, Com. of 70, 1976—79; US com. Bicentennial Constn., 1987—90; com. on Rules of Practice and Procedure, 1990—93; com. on judicial conduct and disability, 2004—; trustee Jewish Publ. Soc. Am., 1983—89; mem. Am. Soc. Internat. Law Jud. Adv. Bd., 2007—. Recipient Juliette Low medal, Girl Scouts Greater Phila., Inc., 1990, Honor award, Girls High Alumnae Assn., 1991, Jud. award, Pa. Bar Assn., 1994, James Wilson award, U. Pa., 1996, Cert. of Honor award, Temple U., 1996; Disting. Fulbright scholar, Chile, 1990. Mem.: ABA, Phila. Bar Assn. (gov. 1976—78, Sandra Day O'Connor award 1997), Am. Judicature Soc. (bd. dirs. 1990—95), Nat. Assn. Women Judges, Am. Law Inst., Fed. Judges Assn., Fed. Bar Assn., Order of Coif (pres. U. Pa. chpt. 1975—77), Phi Beta Kappa. Office: US Ct Appeals 18614 US Courthouse 601 Market St Philadelphia PA 19106-1713*

SLOWIK, RICHARD ANDREW, air force officer; b. Detroit, Sept. 9, 1939; s. Louis Stanley ad Mary Jean (Zaucha) S.; 1 stepchild, Amber Dawn Evans. BS, U.S. Air Force Acad., 1963; BS in Bus. Adminstrn., No. Mich. U., 1967; LLB, LaSalle Extension U., 1969; MBA, Fla. Tech. U., 1972; MS in Adminstrn., Ga. Coll., 1979; MA, Georgetown U., 1983; postgrad. cert., Va. Poly. Inst. and State U., 1986. Commd. 1st lt. U.S. Air Force, 1963, advanced through grades to lt. col; pilot Craig AFB, Ala., 1963-64, Sawyer AFB, Mich., 1964-68; forward air contr. Pacific Air Forces, South Vietnam, 1968-69; pilot SAC, McCoy AFB, Fla., 1969-71; asst. prof. aerospace studies Va. Poly. Inst. and State U., Blacksburg, 1972-76; br. chief current ops. br. Robins AFB, Ga., 1976-80; asst. dep. chief ops. group Hdqrs Air Force, Pentagon, Washignton, 1980-82; Western Hemisphere and Pacific Area desk officer Nat. Mi. Command Ctr., Pentagon, Washignton, 1982-83; mil. rep Ops. Ctr., Dept. State, Washignton, 1983-85; ops. officer 97th Bombardment Wing, Blytheville AFB, Ark., 1985-87; chief base ops. and tng. divsn. 97th Combat Support Group, Blytheville AFB, Ark., 1987-88; chief airfield mgmt. divsn. Eaker AFB, Ark., 1988-91; freelance writer, 1991—. Contbr. articles to profl. jours. Group ops. officer CAP, Marquette, Mich., 1967-67, Orlando, Fla., 1970-72, sr. programs officer, Blacksburg, 1972-76, Warner Robins, Ga., 1976-80, wing plans and programs officer, Washington, 1980—. Decorated Def. Meritorious Svc. medal, 10 Air medals, 3 Air Force Meritorious Svc. medals, 2 Commendation medals, Corss of Gallantry with palm, Presdl. Legion of Merit, Presdl. Medal of Merit (3), Presdl. Achievement award (3), others; recipient Bill Baker Short Story award Miss. County Writers Guild, 1995. Mem. Acad. of Mgmt., Air Force Assn., Cato Inst., Heritage Found., Mil. Order World Wars, Am. Def. Preparedness Assn., Am. Security Coun., Order of Daedalians. Roman Catholic. Home and Office: 1708 N Broadway St Blytheville AR 72315-1320 E-mail: slowik@blyonline.com, ras6@georgetown.edu.

SLOYAN, GERARD STEPHEN, theology studies educator, priest; b. NYC, Dec. 13, 1919; s. Jerome James and Marie (Kelley) S. AB, Seton Hall U., 1940; S.T.L., Cath. U. Am., 1944, PhD, 1948; DLitt, Seton Hall U., 1984; HHD, St. Ambrose U., 1995. Ordained priest Roman Cath. Ch., 1944. Asst. pastor in, Trenton, Maple Shade, N.J., 1947-50; mem. faculty Cath. U. Am., Washington, 1950-67, chmn. dept. religion, 1957-67; prof. N.T. studies Temple U., Phila., 1967-90, chmn. dept. religion, 1970-74, 84-86. Disting. profl. lectr. Georgetown U., 1997—; dist. prof. Cath. U. Am., Washington, 1992—, Iowa State U., 1995. English editor: N.T., The New American Bible, 1970; author: Jesus on Trial: A Study of the Gospels, 2d edit., 2006, Historical Atlas of the Religions of the World, 1974, Is Christ the End of the Law?, 1978, Jesus in Focus, 1983, 2d edit., 1993, The Jesus Tradition, 1986, John: "Interpretation" Commentary, 1988, Jesus, Redeemer and Divine Word, 1989, What Are They Saying About John?, 1991, rev. edit., 2006, Walking in the Truth: 1, 2, and 3 John, 1995, The Crucifixion of Jesus, History, Myth, Faith, 1995, Open Catholicism, The Tradition at Its Best, 1997, Holy Week and Easter, 1999, What Men Owe to Women, Men's Voices from World Religions, 2001, Preaching from the Lectionary: An Exegetical Commentary, 2005, Why Jesus Died, 2004, Jesus Word Made Flesh, 2008. Recipient Pro Ecclesia et Pontifice medal, 1970, Johannes Quasten medal Cath U. Am., 1985, Michael Mathis award Notre Dame Ctr. Pastoral Liturgy, 1994. Mem. AAUP, Cath. Bibl. Assn., Am. Theol. Soc., Cath. Theol. Soc. Am. (John Courtney Murray award 1981, pres. 1993-94), Coll. Theology Soc. (pres. 1964-66), Liturg. Conf. (pres. 1962-64, v.p. 1970-71, 75-88, chmn. bd. dirs. 1980-88), N.Am. Acad. Liturgy (Berakah award 1986). Democrat. Personal E-mail: gerard.sloyan@juno.com.

SLOYAN, PATRICK JOSEPH, journalist; b. Stamford, Conn., Jan. 11, 1937; s. James Joseph and Annamae (O'Brien) Sloyan; m. Phyllis Hampton, Nov. 19, 1960; children: Nora, Amy, Patrick, John. BS, U. Md., 1963. Reporter Albany (N.Y.) Times-Union, 1957—58, Balt. News Post, 1958—60, UPI, Washington, 1960—69, Hearst News Svc., Washington, 1969—74, Newsday, Washington, 1974—81, bur. chief London, 1981—86, Washington, 1986—88, sr. corr., 1988—2001; assoc. editor Digital Journalist.org, 2002—. Dir. Fund for Investigative Journalism, Washington, 1987—. With US Army, 1955—57. Recipient Best Writing award, Am. Soc. Newspaper Editors, 1982, War Reporting award, George Polk Awards, 1992, Pulitzer Prize for internat. reporting, 1992, Raymond Clapper award, 1996; Alicia Patterson Found. fellow, 2000. Mem.: Gridiron Club. Roman Catholic. Avocations: gardening, swimming, tennis. Home: 17115 Simpson Cir Paeonian Springs VA 20129-1735 Personal E-mail: pjs338@yahoo.com.

SLUDIKOFF, STANLEY ROBERT, publisher, writer; b. Bronx, NY, July 17, 1935; s. Harry and Lillie (Elberger) S.; m. Ann Paula Blumberg, June 30, 1972; children: Lisa Beth, Jaime Dawn, Bonnie Joy. B.Arch., Pratt Inst., 1957; grad. student, U. So. Calif., 1960-62. Cert. planner Am. Inst. Cert. Planners. Project planner Robert E. Alexander, F.A.I.A. & Assos., Los Angeles, 1965-66, Daniel, Mann, Johnson & Mendenhall (City and Regional Planning Cons.), Los Angeles, 1967-70; pres., editor, pub. Gambling Times Inc., also Two Worlds Mgmt., Inc., Los Angeles, 1971—2003; v.p. Prima Quality Farms, Inc., PR; chmn. Creative Games, Inc., 1992—. Pres. Las Vegas TV Weekly, also Postal West, Las Vegas, 1975-79; founder Stanley Roberts Sch. Winning Blackjack, 1976; instr. city and regional planning program U. So. Calif., 1960-63; founding mem. Mfrs. Direct, 1996. Author: (under pen name Stanley Roberts) Winning Blackjack, 1971, How to Win at Weekend Blackjack, 1973, Gambling Times Guide to Blackjack, 1983; author: The Beginner's Guide to Winning Blackjack, 1983, Begin to Win at Blackjack, 1997, Begin to Win at Video Poker, 1997, Begin to Win at Craps, 1997; also monthly column, 1977—; creator & tournament dir. The World Casino Games; editor/pub. Poker Player Newspaper, 1982-88, 2003—; inventor Daily Digit lottery game, Straight Out casino game; founder www.gamblingtimes.com, www.pokerplayernewspaper.com; patentee in field. Mem. Destination 90 Forum, Citizens Planning Group, San Fernando Valley, Calif., 1966-67, Rebuild L.A. land use com., 1992-94; pres. Sludikoff Gaming Tournaments, chmn., 2007-. Served to lt. col. US Army, served to lt. col. Aus., ret. Recipient commendation from mayor Los Angeles for work on model cities funding, 1968 Mem. AIA, Am. Planning Assn., Am. Inst. Cert. Planners, Internat. Casino Assn. (sec. 1980-85), Res. Officers Assn. (life), Mensa (life) Achievements include invention of Straight Out gambling game. Avocation: poker. Office: 3883 W Century Blvd Inglewood CA 90303-1003 Office Phone: 310-674-3365. Business E-Mail: sludikoff@yahoo.com. *The challenge of being alive lies in the development of one's maximum potential. To do less is to fly in the face of the gifts of creation, to shorten the aspect of one's life and to deny the fullness of existence. "The weakness of the flesh" prevents anyone's full development from reaching fruition but the personal and societal loss lies in giving up too soon, before we have fully tested our limits.*

SLUPIANEK, ARTUR, medical educator; m. Grazyna Slupianek, Apr. 17, 1993; children: Weronika, Helena. PhD, Poznan U. Med. Scis., Poland. Postdoc. fellow Temple U., Phila., 1999—2001, asst. prof., 2001—. Mem. Del. County Down Syndrome Interest Group, Springfield, Pa., 2000—. Recipient Young Investigator award, Found. Polish Sci., 1997; fellowship, Leukemia Rsch. Found., 1999, 2000, Rsch. grant, Elsa U. Pardee Found., 2001, Lauri Strauss Leukemia Found., 2003, New Investigator grant, Leukemia Rsch. Found., 2003. Mem.: Am. Soc. Hematology (Travel award 1998, 2000). Office: Temple Univ 3400 N Broad St MRB528 Philadelphia PA 19140

SLUSAR, LINDA, library and information scientist; MLS, Northern Ill. Univ., 1985. Prof., coord. libr. & info. tech. prog. Coll. of DuPage, Glen Ellyn, Ill., co-founder Soaring to Excellence teleconference prog. Author: (Book & DVD) Creating Your Professional Portfolio; co-author: (Book & VHS prog.) Ranganathan's Five Laws of Library Science. Recipient Outstanding Supporter of Support Staff award, Libr. Mosaics, 2000; named one of the Movers & Shakers, Libr. Jour., 2007. Office: Coll DuPage 425 Fawell Blvd Glen Ellyn IL 60137 Office Phone: 630-942-2597. Office Fax: 630-858-8757. Business E-Mail: slusar@cdnet.cod.edu.

SLUSSER, ROBERT WYMAN, aerospace transportation executive; b. Mineola, NY, May 10, 1938; s. John Leonard and Margaret McKenzie (Wyman) S.; m. Linda Killeas, Aug. 3, 1968. BS, MIT, 1960; MBA, U. Pa., 1962; ERC, Ft. Belvior Def. Sys. Mgmt. Sch., 1977; AMP, Claremont, 1982. Assoc. adminstr.'s staff NASA Hdqrs., Washington, 1962-65; with Northrop Corp., Hawthorne, Calif., 1965-96; adminstr. Space Labs., 1965-68; mgr. bus. and fin. Warnecke Electron Tubes Co. divsn., Chgo., 1968-71; mgr. bus. adminstrn. YF-17 Program Aircraft Divsn., 1971-75, mgr. adminstrn. F-18/Cobra programs, also mgr. F-18 design to cost program, 1975-79, mgr. engring. adminstrn., 1980-82, acting v.p. engring., 1982, v.p. info. resources, 1983-91, mgr. long range planning, 1991-93, program mgr.-bus. F/A-18E/F program, 1994-96, cons., 1996—. Bd. dirs., CFO So. Calif. Hist. Aviation Found., 1987-90, chmn. bd., pres., 1990-97; treas. Flight Path Learning Ctr. So. Calif., 1996-2001; contracting officer, PDES, 1988-91; dirs. adv. bd. SC Rsch. Authority, 1991-95. Grumman Aircraft Engring. scholar, 1956—60. Fellow AIAA (assoc., membership chmn. L.A. sect. 1996-98); mem. So. Calif. Soc. Info. Mgmt. (mem. exec. com. 1987-91), Northrop Mgmt. Club (bd. dirs. 1992-93, Man of Yr. 1991-92). Avocation: private pilot. Home and Office: 7270 Berry Hill Dr Palos Verdes Peninsula CA 90275-4402

SLUSSER, WILLIAM PETER, investment banker; b. June 20, 1929; s. Eugene and Thelma (Donovan) S.; m. Joanne Eleanor Briggs, June 20, 1953; children: Kathleen E., Martin E., Wendelin M., Caroline E., Sarah A. BA cum laude, Stanford U., 1951; MBA, Harvard U., 1953. Mgr. spl. situations dept. Dean Witter & Co., NYC, 1955-60; ptnr., sr. v.p., mgr. corp. fin. dept. Shields & Co., NYC, 1960—75; sr. v.p. Paine Webber, Inc., NYC, 1975-80; mng. dir., head merger and acquisitions dept., mem. mgmt. com. Blyth Eastman Paine Webber, Inc., NYC, 1980—88; pres. Slusser Assocs., Inc., NYC, 1988—. Bd. dirs. Sparton Corp., Magellan Group Ltd., Unigene Labs., Inc. Contbr. articles to profl. jours. Founding stockholder Assoc. Mortgage Cos., Cap Gemini Sogetti; bd. fin. advisors Columbia U. Bus. Sch.; mem. Calif. Senate Commn. on Local Govt. Investments; mem. Calif. Senate Commn. Corp. Governance, 1985-95. 1st lt. USAF, 1953—55. Mem. Soc. Calif. Pioneers, Knickerbocker Club, Stanford Assoc., Harvard (NYC) Club, Lawrence Beach Club, Alpha Delta Phi (exec. coun. 1956-62, treas. 1961). Home: 901 Lexington Ave New York NY 10065 also: Slusser Ranch Windsor CA 95492 Office: Slusser Assoc Inc 300 Park Ave New York NY 10022-4611

SLUTSKY, LORIE A(NN), foundation executive; b. NYC, Jan. 5, 1953; d. Edward and Adele (Moskowitz) S. BA, Colgate U., 1975; MA in Urban Policy Analysis, New Sch. Social Rsch., NYC, 1977. Program officer NY Cmty. Trust, NYC, 1977-83, v.p., 1983-87, exec. v.p., 1987-89, pres., CEO, 1990—. Former mem. and chmn. bd. Coun. on Founds., Inc., Washington, 1986-95. Trustee emerita, former chmn. budget com. Colgate U., Hamilton, N.Y., 1989-98, BroadSource; former mem. bd. dirs. Found. Ctr., Inc., N.Y.C., L.A. Wallace Fund for Met. Mus. Art, N.Y.C., D. Wallace Fund for Meml. Sloan Kettering, United Way of N.Y.C.; bd. dirs. Alliance Bernstein, AXA Fin. Office: NY Community Trust 22d Fl 909 3d Ave New York NY 10022

SLUTZ, PAMELA JO HOWELL, former ambassador; b. Chgo., 1949; d. Robert and Rose Slutz; m. Ronald Deutch; 2 children. B in Politics, Hollins U., 1970; M in Asian Studies and Polit. Sci., U. Hawaii, 1972. Office of Korean Affairs Bur. East Asian and Pacific Affairs US Dept. of State (FSO), 1981—82, Office of China and Mongolia Affairs Bur. East Asian and Pacific Affairs, 1995—97, Office of East Asian and Pacific Regional Security and Policy Planning Bur. East Asian and Pacific Affairs, 1997—99, amb., fgn. svc. officer Shanghai, 1991—94, Am. Inst. Taiwan, 2001—03; US amb. to Mongolia Dept. State, 2003—06. Mem. U.S. Del. to Nuc. and Space Talks with Russia, Geneva, 1987—89. Fellow, East West Ctr., 1970—72.*

SLY, RIDGE MICHAEL, pediatrician, allergist, immunologist, educator; b. Seattle, Nov. 3, 1933; s. Ridge Joseph and Eva Jean (Ruddell) S.; m. Ann Turner Jennings, June 12, 1957; children: Teresa Ann Perper, Cynthia Marie Schattenfield. AB, Kenyon Coll., Gambier, Ohio, 1956; MD, Washington U., St. Louis, 1960. Diplomate Am. Bd. Pediat., Am. Sub-Bd. Pediat. Allergy, Am. Bd. Allergy and Immunology. Intern, resident in pediat. St. Louis Children's Hosp, 1960—62; chief resident in pediat. U. Ky. Med. Ctr., Lexington, 1962—63; fellow in allergy and immunology UCLA Med. Ctr., 1965—67; from asst. prof. to prof. pediat. La. State U. Med. Ctr., New Orleans, 1967—78; head sect. allergy and immunology Children's Nat. Med. Ctr., Washington, 1978—; prof. pediat. George Washington U., Washington, 1978—. Author: Textbook of Pediatric Allergy, 1985; mem. editl. bd. Annals of Allergy, Asthma, & Immunology, 1982-98, 99-2002, Jour. Asthma, 1982-93, Clin. Revs. in Allergy, 1982-2001, Pediat. Asthma, Allergy, & Immunology, 1987—; assoc. editor Annals of Allergy, Asthma, & Immunology, 1989-90, editor, 1990-98; contbr. articles to profl. jours. Served to capt. USAF, 1963-65 Recipient La. plaque Am. Lung Assn. of La., 1978 Fellow Am. Acad. Allergy, Asthma & Immunology (chmn. com. on drugs 1981-87), Am. Acad. Pediats. (sect. on allergy com. 1972-75), Am. Coll. Allergy, Asthma, and Immunology (Disting. Fellow award 1993, Bela Schick award 1997, chmn. ethics com. 1997-99); mem. Am. Thoracic Soc., Assn. for Care of Asthma (pres. 1980-81, dir. postgrad. courses 1980—, Peshkin Meml. award 1983), Ctr. for Bioethics and Human Dignity, Phi Beta Kappa. Republican. Baptist. Avocations: music, piano, organ. Office: Children's Nat Med Ctr 111 Michigan Ave NW Washington DC 20010-2970

SLYM, KARL, automotive executive; b. Derby, England, Feb. 9, 1962; Grad. in production engring., Derby Univ., England, 1984; MS, Stanford Univ., 2002. Gen. assembly mgr. Toyota UK; mfg. adv. & gen. assembly mgr. Opel Eisenach plant GM Corp., 1995—97, dir. mfg. Opel Polska plant Gliwice, Poland, 1997—99, asst. plant mgr. Oshawa plant Ontario, Canada, 1999—2001, plant mgr. Oshawa plants 1 & 2, 2001—02; pres. CAMI Automotive (GM & Suzuki Motor joint venture), 2002—06; v.p. quality GM Asia Pacific & GM Daewoo GM Corp., 2006—07, pres. & mng. dir. GM India, 2007—. Sloan Fellow. Office: GM Corp 300 Renaissance Ctr Detroit MI 48265*

SMABY, MARY ELLEN, elementary school educator; d. Anthony Edward and Mary Agnes Kroeger; m. Michael William Smaby, July 29, 1989; children: Megan, Heather, Sarah, Rachel. BS, Northern Mich. U., Marquette, 1983; EdM, Viterbo U., LaCrosse, Wis., 2006. 5th-8th grade tchr. Holy Spirit Sch., Norway, Mich., 1983—84, Cornwall Consolidated Sch., West Cornwall, Conn., 1984—87; 6th grade tchr. Gillett Elem. Sch., Gillett, Wis., 1987—88; 4th-8th grade tchr. Omro Pub. Schs., Wis., 1988—93; reading tchr. Little Chute Elem., Wis., 2003—. Sch. coord. Fox River area Girl Scouts USA, Neenah, Wis., 1995—2001; adv. bd. First Books Fox Valley; vol. St. Gabriel Ch., Neenah, Wis., 1989—2006. Mem.: Wis. State Reading Assn., Internat. Reading Assn., Phi Delta Kappa. Avocations: camping, cooking, reading. Home: 1024 Stuart Dr Neenah WI 54956

SMAGALSKI, CAROLYN M., publishing executive, webmaster, director; b. Phila., Aug. 28, 1952; d. Raymond L and Mary K Hanisco; children: Michael M, Tyler A. BA Cum Laude, Temple U., Philadelphia, 1971—75. Lic. private pilot SEL with IFR rating and Complex Aircraft Rating US Dept. of Transp./Fed. Aviation Adminstrn., 1996. Sales svc. rep. Brown Printing Co., East Greenville, Pa., 1996—; exec. dir., author, webmaster, internetwork marketer CQ Web Wide LLC, Harleysville, Pa., 2002—. Beer and brewing advisor Gluten Free Beer Festival U.K., 2006—. Author (editor): (website mag.) Beer and Brewing, 2004—; creator Beer Fox, 2004, guest appearance Beer Fox/Beer Chef, Beer Radio, internat. bear writer Beer Connoisseur Mag., 2009—; author: Bear Hunter, Whiskey Chaser, 2009. Co-founder Philly Beer Geek Finals Competition, 2008; beer and brewing advisor Gluten Free Beer Festival, England, 2006—. Mem.: Better Internet Bur., Internat. Assn. Home Bus. Entrepreneurs, Aircraft Owners & Pilot's Assn. Avocations: information technology, aviation, psychology of brain & socio-emotional challenges, gourmet cooking, public relations & travel. Home: 805 Continental Drive Harleysville PA 19438 Office: CQ Web Wide LLC 805 Continental Drive Harleysville PA 19438 Personal E-mail: carolsmagalski@comcast.net. E-mail: cs1@cqwebwide.com.

SMAGORINSKY, PETER, education educator; b. Princeton, NJ, Oct. 24, 1952; s. Joseph and Margaret (Knoepfel) Smagorinsky; m. Anne O'Gorman, July 10, 1982 (dec. Aug. 1982); m. Jane E. Farrell, Oct. 12, 1985; children: Alysha, David. BA, Kenyon Coll., 1974; MA in Tchg., U. Chgo., 1977, PhD, 1989. English tchr. Westmont (Ill.) H.S., 1977-78, Barrington (Ill.) H.S., 1978-85, Oak Park (Ill.) and River Forest H.S., 1985-90; asst. prof. U. Okla., Norman, 1990-95, assoc. prof., 1995-98, U. Ga., Athens, 1998-2001, prof., 2001—. Author: Standards in Practice, 1996, Tchg. English by Design, Handbook on Adolescent Rsch., 2008, The Discourse of Character Edn., 2005, Rsch. on Composition, Reflective Tchg., Reflective Learning, 2005; co-author: How English Teachers Get Taught, 1995, The Language of Interpretation, 1995; co-editor: Rsch. Tchg. English, 1996—2003, Reading Rsch. Quar. Rev. Ednl. Rsch., Am. Jour. Edn., Written Comm., Reading and Writing Quar. Recipient Steve Cahir award for Rsch. in Writing, Am. Ednl. Rsch. Assn., 1991, Raymond B. Cattell award for Disting. Programmatic Rsch., 1999, ATE Disting. award for rsch. in tchr. edn., 2008. Mem.: Nat. Coun. Tchrs. English (chair standing com. rsch. 1995—96, co-chair assembly rsch. 1996, trustee rsch. found. 1997—2003, chair 2000—03, pres. nat. conf. rsch. lang. and literacy 2001, English Jour. Writing award 1989, Edwin M. Hopkins award 2000, Janet Emig award 2003). Home: 121 Inverness Rd Athens GA 30606 Office: U Ga 0125 Aderhold Hall Athens GA 30602 Office Phone: 706-542-4507. Business E-Mail: smago@uga.edu.

SMAL, LUBA DMITRIEVNA, lawyer; b. Grodno, Belarus; arrived in US, 1999; d. Dmitrij and Elena Smal. JD in Belarussian Law, Grodno U., 1994, PhD, 1997; JD, Creighton U., Omaha, 2004. Bar: Republic of Belarus 1994, Nebr. 2004. Pvt. practice, Omaha, 2004—. Ind. dispute resolution atty. Vol. 24-hour hotline YWCA, Omaha, 2004—. Mem.: ABA, Am. Immigration Lawyers Assn., Nebr. Bar Assn. Office: PO Box 540531 Omaha NE 68154 Office Phone: 402-210-2040. Office Fax: 530-698-5578. Personal E-mail: lubasmal@gmail.com. Business E-Mail: attorney@law-visa-usa.com.

SMALE, STEPHEN, mathematics professor; b. Flint, Mich., July 15, 1930; BS, U. Mich., 1952, MS, 1953, PhD, 1957; PhD (hon.), U. Warwick, 1974, Queens U., Kingston, Ontario, 1987; DSc (hon.), U. Mich., 1996; Doctor Honoris Causa, Universite Pierre et Marie Curie Paris, 1997; DSc (hon.), City U. Hong Kong, 1997; PhD (hon.), Rostov State U., 1999. Assoc. prof. math. U. Calif., Berkeley, 1960—61, prof. math., 1964—94, prof. emeritus math. and economics, 1994—; prof. math. Columbia U., 1961—64; disting. univ. prof. City U. Hong Kong, 1995—2001; prof. Toyota Technological Inst. at Chgo., 2002—. Instr. U. Chgo., 1956—68; mem. Inst. for Advanced Study Princeton, 1958—60, 1966; vis. prof. Coll. of France, Paris, 1962, Yale U., 1974, Inst. de Matematica Pura e Aplicado Rio de Janeiro, 1976, 94, 98, Columbia U., 1987; rsch. prof. Miller Inst. for Basic Rsch. in Sci., Berkeley, 1967—68, Berkeley, 1978—80; vis. mem. Inst. des Hautes Etudes Scientiques, 1969—70, 1972—73, vis. prof., 1976; vis. mem. U. Paris, Orsay, 1972—73; vis. scientist IBM Corp., Yorktown Heights, 1987; fellow Japan Soc. for the Promotion Sci., 1994; hon. prof. U. Yunnan, Kunming, 1997; spkr. in field. Contbr. articles to profl. jours. Recipient U. Mich. Sesquicentennial Award, 1967, Chauvenet prize, Math Assn. Am., 1988, Von Neumann award, Soc. Industry and Applied Math., 1989, Jurgen Moser prize, Soc. Industry and Applied Math., Dynamics Group, 2005, Nat. medal of Sci., NSF, 1996; co-recipient 2006/2007 Wolf Found. prize in Math., Israel; fellow Alfred P. Sloan rsch. fellow, 1960—62. Mem.: NAS, Brazilian Acad. Scis. (foreign mem.), Econometric Soc., Am. Math. Soc. (Veblen prize for geometry 1965), Internat. Union of Math. (Fields medal 1966), Am. Acad. Arts and Scis., Moscow

Math. Soc. (hon.), London Math. Soc. (hon.), Trinity Math. Soc. (hon.), Instituto de Matematica Pura e Aplicada (IMPA) (hon.), Brazilian Nat. Order of Scientific Merit (Class of Grand Cross). Office: Toyota Technological Inst Chgo 5801 S Ellis Ave Chicago IL 60637 Address: Toyota Technological Inst University Press Bldg 1427 E 60th St Second Fl Chicago IL 60637

SMALL, CLARENCE MERILTON, JR., lawyer; b. Birmingham, Ala., July 24, 1934; s. Clarence Merilton and Elva (Roberts) S.; m. Gnetchen Reeves, Sept. 23, 1935; children: William Stephen, Elizabeth Ann, Laura Carol. BS, Auburn U., 1956; LLB, U. Ala., 1961. Founding ptnr. Christian & Small, Birmingham, 1961—. Served to 1st lt., arty. AUS, to capt. JAGC. Fellow Am. Bar Found., Internat. Acad. Trial Lawyers, Am. Coll. Trial Lawyers, Ala. Law Found.; mem. ABA (ho. of dels. 1984-86), Ala. Bar Assn. (pres. 1992-93), Birmingham Bar Assn. (pres. 1979), Ala. Def. Lawyers Assn., Internat. Assn. Def. Counsel. Office: 1800 Financial Ctr Birmingham AL 35203-4611 Home Phone: 205-871-5994; Office Phone: 205-795-6588. Business E-Mail: cmsmall@csattorneys.com.

SMALL, ELISABETH CHAN, psychiatrist, educator; b. Beijing, July 11, 1934; came to U.S., 1937; d. Stanley Hong and Lily Luella (Lum) Chan; m. Donald M. Small, July 8, 1957 (div. 1980); children Geoffrey Brooks, Philip Willard Stanley; m. H. Sidney Robinson, Jan. 12, 1991 (div. 2001). Student, Immaculate Heart Coll., LA, 1951-52; BA in Polit. Sci., UCLA, 1955, MD, 1960. Intern Newton-Wellesley Hosp., Mass., 1960-61; asst. dir. for venereal diseases Mass. Dept. Pub. Health, 1961-63; resident in psychiatry Boston State Hosp., Mattapan, Mass., 1965-66, Tufts New Eng. Med. Ctr. Hosps., 1966-69, psychiat. cons. dept. gynecology, 1973-75; asst. clin. prof. psychiatry Sch. Medicine Tufts U., 1973-75, assoc. clin. prof., 1975-82, asst. clin. prof. ob-gyn, 1977-80, assoc. clin. prof. ob-gyn, 1980-82; from assoc. prof. to prof. psychiatry U. Nev. Sch. Med., Reno, 1982-95; practice psychiatry specializing in psychological effects of bodily changes on women, 1969—; emeritus prof. psychiatry and behavioral scis. U. Nev. Sch. Medicine, Reno, 1995—, from assoc. prof. to clin. assoc. prof. ob-gyn, 1982-88; mem. staff Tufts New Eng. Med. Ctr. Hosps., 1977-82, St. Margaret's Hosps., Boston, 1977-82, Washoe Med. Ctr., Reno, 1983—2006, St. Mary's Regional Med. Ctr., Reno, Truckee Meadows Hosp., Reno, St. Mary's Hosp., Reno; chief psychiatry svc. Reno VA Med. Ctr., 1989-94. Lectr., cons. in field; mem. psychiatry adv. panel Hosp. Satellite Network; mem. office external peer rev. NIMH, HEW; psychiat. cons. to Boston Redevelopment Authority on Relocation of Chinese Families of South Cove Area, 1968-70; mem. New Eng. Med. Ctr. Hosps. Cancer Ctr. Com., 1979-80, Pain Control Com., 1981-82; reproductive sys. curriculum com. Tufts Univ. Sch. Medicine, 1975-82. Mem. editorial bd. Psychiat. Update Am. (Psychiat. Assn. ann. rev.), 1983-85; reviewer Psychosomatics and Hosp. Community Psychiatry, New Eng. Jour. of Medicine, Am. Jour. of Psychiatry Psychosomatic Medicine; contbr. articles to profl. jours. Fellow, Radcliffe Inst., 1967—70; Immaculate Heart Coll. scholar, 1951—52, Mira Hershey scholar, UCLA, 1955. Fellow Am. Coll. Psychiatrists (sci. program com. 1989-98); mem. AMA, Am. Psychiat. Assn. (life, rep. to sect. com. AAAS, chmn. ad hoc com. Asian-Am. Psychiatrists 1975, task force 1975-77, task force cost effectiveness in consultation 1984—, caucus chmn. 1981-82, sci. program com. 1982-88, courses subcom. chmn. sci. program com. 1986-88), Nev. Psychiat. Assn., Assn. for Acad. Psychiatry (fellowship com. 1982), Washoe County Med. Assn., Nev. Med. Soc. Avocations: skiing, cooking. Home and Office: 825 Caughlin Crossing Reno NV 89519-0647

SMALL, GEORGE LEROY, geographer, educator; b. Malden, Mass., Mar. 27, 1924; s. George Arthur and Alice Mildred (Weston) S.; m. Geraldine H. Koepke, July 4, 1970; 1 dau., Elizabeth Mary. BA, Brown U., 1950; M.I.A., Columbia U., 1952, PhD, 1968. French tchr. pvt. schs., Ariz., 1955-62; instr. geography Hunter Coll., 1964-68; asso. prof. geography Coll. S.I., CUNY, 1968—. Cons. in field. Author: The Blue Whale, 1971. Served with U.S. Army, 1942-46. Recipient Nat. Book award, 1972; Rotary Found. fellow, 1952-53 Mem. Assn. Am. Geographers. Office: CUNY Coll Staten Is New York NY 10314

SMALL, HAMISH, chemist; b. Newtown Crommelin, No. Ireland, Oct. 5, 1929; s. Johnston and Jean (Wilson) S.; m. Beryl Maureen Burley, Mar. 27, 1954; children: Deborah Jane, Claire Leslie. BS, Queens U., Belfast, Northern Ireland, 1949, MS, 1953. Chemist U.S. Atomic Energy Authority, Harwell, England, 1949-55; rsch. scientist Dow Chem. Co., Midland, Mich., 1955-83; chemist Rsch. and Invention, 1983—. Author: Ion Chromatography, 1990; contbr. articles to profl. jours. Recipient Albert F. Sperry award Instrument Soc. Am., 1978, A.O. Beckman award, 1983, Herbert H. Dow Gold Medal Dow Chem. Co., 1983, Stephen Dal Nogare award, 1984, Am. Chem. Soc. award in Chromatography, 1991. Mem. Am. Chem. Soc. Achievements include 46 patents in field. Avocations: painting, sketching. Home: 4176 Oxford Dr Leland MI 49654-9716 Personal E-mail: hamish_small@yahoo.com.

SMALL, JONATHAN ANDREW, lawyer, consultant; b. NYC, Dec. 26, 1942; s. Milton and Teresa Markell (Joseph) S.; m. Cornelia Mendenhall, June 8, 1969; children: Anne, Katherine. BA, Brown U., 1964; student, U. Paris, 1962-63; LLB, Harvard U., 1967; MA, Fletcher Sch. of Law and Diplomacy, 1968; LLM, NYU, 1974. Bar: NY 1967. VISTA vol., Washington and Cambridge, Mass., 1968; law clk. to judge US Ct. Appeals (2d cir.), 1968-69; assoc. Debevoise & Plimpton, NYC, 1969-75, ptnr., 1976-99; pres. Nonprofit Coord. Com. NY, 2000—05; spl. cons. Govt. Rels., 2005—. Cons. Spl. Task Force of NY State Taxation, 1976; bd. overseers Fletcher Sch. Law and Diplomacy Tufts U., 2003—. Trustee Brearley Sch., 1985-95; bd. dirs. Nonprofit Coordinating Com. of NY, 1985-2005, Muscular Dystrophy Assn., 1986-88, Human Svcs. Coun. NYC, Inc., 2000-05, Investor Responsibility Rsch. Ctr., Inc., 2000-2006, Lawyers Alliance for NY, 2000-2007, Americans for the UN Population Fund, 2000-09, Pub. Interest Law Inst., 2008-. Mem. ABA, Am. Law Inst., NY State Bar Assn. (chmn. tax sect. com. exempt orgns. 1980-82, co-chmn., 1995), Assn. Bar City NY, Nonprofit Forum, Phi Beta Kappa. Home: 60 E End Ave New York NY 10028-7907 Office: Debevoise & Plimpton 919 Third Ave New York NY 10022 Office Phone: 212-909-6461.

SMALL, LAWRENCE M., former museum executive; b. NYC, Sept. 14, 1941; m. Sandra Small; 2 children. BA in Spanish Lit. with highest honors, Brown U., 1963; LLD (hon.), Morehouse Coll.; LHD (hon.), Brown U.; D Pub. Svc. (hon.), Am. U., 2002; D Arts & Sciences (hon.), Dickinson Coll., 2004; LHD (hon.), Coll. St. Rose, Albany. Mgmt. trainee Citibank, Chile, 1964, sr. exec. in charge comml. banking, info. tech., human resources and worldwide corp. banking, vice chmn., chmn. exec. com., 1964-91; pres., COO Fannie Mae, Washington, 1991-2000; sec. Smithsonian Instn., Washington, 2000—07. Creator Nat. Air and Space Mus. Smithsonian Instn., creator Nat. Mus. Am. Indians; bd. dirs. Chubb Corp., Marriott Internat., Paramount Comm. Inc. Bd. trustees Spanish Repertory Theatre, John F. Kennedy Ctr. Performing Arts, Washington, Nat. Gallery Art, Washington, Woodrow Wilson Internat. Ctr. for Scholars; trustee emeritus Brown U., 1984—90, Morehouse Coll., Atlanta, 1973—99, Collegiate Sch., Mt. Sinai-NYU Med. Ctr. and Health Sys., Joffrey Ballet, Am. Women's Econ. Devel. Corp., Internat. Exec. Svc. Corps, Inst. de Estudios Superiores de la Empresa, Barcelona, Greater NY Councils of Boy Scouts of Am.; mem. Com. for Preservation of the White House, Washington. Avocations: collecting and restoring masks and tribal art, flamenco guitar playing.

SMALL, MELVIN, historian, educator; b. NYC, Mar. 14, 1939; s. Herman Z. and Ann (Ashkinazy) S.; m. Sarajane Miller, Oct. 23, 1958; children: Michael, Mark. BA, Dartmouth Coll., 1960; MA, U. Mich., 1961, PhD, 1965. Asst. prof. history Wayne State U., Detroit, 1965-68, assoc. prof., 1968-76, prof., 1976—, chmn. dept. history, 1979-86, disting. prof., 2004—. Vis. prof. U. Mich., Ann Arbor, 1968, Marygrove Coll., Detroit, 1971, Aarhus (Denmark) U., 1972—74, 1983, Windsor (Ont., Can.) U., 1977—78; Fulbright sr. specialist Coynac Internat. Exch. Scholars, 2007—. Author: Was War Necessary, 1980, Johnson, Nixon and the Doves, 1988, Covering Dissent, 1994, Democracy and Diplomacy, 1996, The Presidency of Richard Nixon, 1999, Antiwarriors, 2002, At The Water's Edge, 2005; co-author: Wages of War, 1972, Resort to Arms, 1982; editor: Public Opinion and Historians, 1970; co-editor: International War, 1986, Appeasing Fascism, 1991, Give Peace a Chance, 1992, The Good Fight Continues, 2006; mem. editl. bd. Internat. Interactions, 1987-91, Peace and Change, 1989—; restaurant critic Detroit Metro Times, 1982-95, 2006—; reviewer Detroit Free Press, 1988-95. Hon. bd. Swords into Plowshares Mus., 1992—; bd. dirs. Abraham Lincoln Brigade Archives, 1998—, Ctr. on Peace and Liberty, 2003-, David S. Wyman Inst. for Holocaust Studies, 2003-. Recipient Disting. Faculty award Mich. Assn. Governing Bds., 1993; Am. Coun. Learned Socs. fellow, 1969; Stanford Ctr. for Advanced Study fellow, 1969-70, Rsch. fellow NATO, 1996; grantee Am. Coun. Learned Socs., 1983, Johnson Libr., 1982, 88, Can. Govt., 1987; named to Hewlett-Woodmere Alumni Hall of Fame, 2005. Mem. Coun. on Peace Rsch. in History (nat. coun. 1986-90, pres. 1990-92), Am. Hist. Assn., Atlantic Coun. (acad. assoc.), Orgn. Am. Historians, Soc. Historians of Am. Fgn. Rels. (Warren Kuehl prize 1989). Home: 1815 Northwood Blvd Royal Oak MI 48073-3919 Office: Wayne State U Dept History 3119 Fab Detroit MI 48202 Office Phone: 313-577-6138. Business E-Mail: M.Small@Wayne.edu.

SMALL, PARKER ADAMS, JR., pediatrician, educator; b. Cin., July 5, 1932; s. Parker Adams and Grace (McMichael) S.; m. Natalie Settimelli, Aug. 26, 1956; children: Parker Adams, Peter McMichael, Carla Edmea. Student, Tufts U., 1950-53; MD, U. Cin., 1957; BS extraordinem, 1986. Med. intern Pa. Hosp., Phila., 1957-58; rsch. assoc. Nat. Heart Inst. NIH, Washington, 1958-60; rsch. fellow St. Mary's Hosp., London, 1960-61; sr. surgeon NIMH, Washington, 1961-66; prof. immunology and med. microbiology U. Fla., 1966-95, chmn. dept., 1966-75, prof. pediat., 1979—2003, prof. emeritus, 2003—, prof. pathology, 1995—2003, prof. emeritus, 2003—, adj. clin. prof. large animal sci., 1999—2003; pres. PigVax Inc., 2000—01. Dir. Ctr. for Coop. Learning for Health Sci. Edn., U. Fla., 1988-2003; vis. prof. U. Lausanne, Switzerland, 1972, U. Lagos, Nigeria, 1982, Al Hada Hosp., Saudi Arabia, 1983; vis. scholar Assn. Am. Med. Colls., Washington, 1973; assoc. life scis. panel Nat. Acad. Scis., 1981-88, co-chmn., 1982-83; bd. dirs. Biol. Sci. Curriculum Study, 1984-90, exec. bd., 1987-90; mem. edn. adv. com. Nat. Fund Med. Edn., 1984-87; mem. study com. Nat. Bd. Med. Examiners, 1983-85, mem. nat. vaccine adv. com., 1987-91, chmn. subcom. on new vaccines, 1987-91; v.p. smallgroupconsultants.com, 2003-; mem. Truro Shellfish Advisory Com.; cons. in field. Creator patient oriented problem solving system/POPS, for tchg. immunology and coop. learning to med. students and Team Packs for tchg. K-12 & coll. students health edn. and coop. learning; co-dir. Fla. Ptnrs. in Prevention of Substance Abuse, 1997-2003; editor: The Secretory Immunologic System, 1971; mem. editl. bd. Infection and Immunity, 1974-76, Jour. Med. Edn., 1978-80; cons. editor Microbios, Cytobios; patentee in field; contbr. more than 150 articles to profl. jours. Sec., treas. Oakmont, Md., 1964-65, mayor, 1965-66; chmn. Citizens for Pub. Schs. Gainesville, Fla., 1969-70; mem. Teen Pregnancy Prevention Action Com., 1998-2000, Truro Shellfish Adv. Com., 2004-. With USPHS, 1958-60, 61-66. Named Tchr. of Yr. U. Fla. Coll. Medicine, 1978-79, Disting. Lectr. AMA, 1986; recipient Presdl. medallion U. Fla., 1987, Nat. Basic Sci. Disting. Tchg. award Alpha Omega Alpha, 1993, Jacob Ehrenzeller award, 1995, Pres.'s Faculty Humanitarian award U. Fla., 1996, Pep award U. Fla., 1998, Lifetime Achievement award U. Fla. Coll. Medicine, 2003; NIH spl. fellow, 1960-61, rsch. grantee, 1966-91, U. Fla. Tchr./Scholar and commencement spkr., 1987; invited lectr. Assn. Am. Med. Colls., 1992. Mem. AAAS, Am. Assn. Immunologists (edn. com. 1983-86), Physicians for Social Responsibility, Fla. Med. Assn., Phi Beta Kappa, Sigma Xi, Alpha Omega Alpha, Theta Delta Chi. Office: U Fla Coll Med PO Box 100275 Gainesville FL 32610-0275 Personal E-mail: smallgroup2@aol.com. Business E-Mail: small@pathology.ufl.edu.

SMALL, RICHARD DONALD, travel company executive; b. West Orange, NJ, May 24, 1929; s. Joseph George and Elizabeth (McGarry) S.; m. Arlene P. Small; children: Colleen P., Richard Donald, Joseph W., Mark G., Brian P. AB cum laude, U. Notre Dame, 1951. With Union-Camp Corp., NYC, 1952-62, Chgo., 1952—62; chmn. Alumni Holidays, Inc., 1962—, Alumni Holidays Internat. Corp., 1962—2003; pres. All Horizons, Inc., 1982—2000; travel industry cons., 2003—. Chmn. AHI, Inc., 1982-89; bd. dirs. French Cruise Lines, Des Plaines, Ill., Russian Cruise Lines, Alumni Campus Abroad, 1994—. Recipient Munich Ptnr. award, 1989. Mem.: Carlton Club (Chgo.), Univ. Club Chgo. Home: Water Tower Pl 180 E Pearson St # 3306 Chicago IL 60611-6730 also: Wailea Golf Estates 3954 Waakaula Pl Wailea HI 96753-5415 Personal E-mail: richarddsmall@gmail.com.

SMALL, SARAH MAE, volunteer; b. Salisbury, NC, Nov. 16, 1923; d. Clint and Lillie Mae (Wilbourn) Evans; m. Jesse Small Sr., May 4, 1941; children: Jesse Jr., Jean Carol Small Bell. Cert., Cortez Bus. Sch., 1948. File clk. gen. acctg. office Fed. Govt., Washington, 1941—47; sec., stenographer CIA, Washington, 1948—52, adminstrv. asst. McLean, Va., 1952—65, ret., 1965. Pres. Energetic Crusaders, Inc., 1993; bd. dirs. ARC, Washington, 1986-87, Children's Edn. Found., Inc., 1989—. Recipient Outstanding and Dedicated Vol. Svc. award Kiwanis Club of Capital Centre, 1985, Plaque in Recognition of Dedicated and Outstanding Vol. Svc. to the Corps and Washington D.C., Cmty. Jr. Citizen's Corps., 1989, Appreciation award for Outstanding and Dedicated Vol. Svc. to Corps, Jr. Citizens Corps., Inc., 1990, Appreciation award Jr. Citizens Corp., Inc., 1990, Cmty. Svc. award for leadership and youth advocacy Bus. and Profl. Women's League, Inc., 1991, Vol. award achievement excellence svc. youths of Jr. Citizens Corps., Inc., 1992, others. Mem. Jr. Citizens Corps (life, pres. 1985—, Dedicated Cmty. Svc. award 1983, Bus. and Cmty. Svc. award 1986), Bus. and Profl. Women's League (treas. 1982-86), Women in Arts (chartered, pres. 1984—), Nat. Coun. Negro Women, World Affairs Coun. Washington, Agrl. Coun. Am. Democrat. Baptist. Avocations: travel, photography, walking, swimming.

SMALL, STACY H., luxury travel company executive, former magazine editor; b. Rochester, NY, 1969; BS in Mag. Journalism, Syracuse U. Samuel Irving Newhouse Sch. Pub. Comm., NY, 1991. With Caribbean Travel & Life mag., Washington; sr. editor Travel Agent Mag., NYC, LA, 1994—2000; founder, pres., chief content provider TheWriteCrowd, LLC, Marina del Rey, Calif., 2000—01; editl. dir. Elite Traveler Mag., 2001—03; contbg. editor Ocean Home Mag., NY Family Mag., Agent@Home Mag., 2004—; founder, pres. Elite Travel International, Brentwood, Calif., 2005—. Contbr. Breast Cancer Rsch. Found. Named Nat. Woman of Yr., Leukemia & Lymphoma Soc., 2006. Mem.: Beverly Hills C. of C., Ladies Who Launch, Travel Tourism & Hospitality Grp., Luxury & Lifestyle Profls., Travel Industry Profls. Worldwide, Travel Industry Exec. Womens Network, World Luxury Travelers Soc., St. Barts Network, Luxury Industry Profls., Women in Tech. Internat. Office: Elite Travel Internat 1011 S Barrington Ave Los Angeles CA 90049 Office Phone: 310-979-9036. Business E-Mail: stacy@elitetravelinternational.com.*

SMALL, WILLIAM EDWIN, JR., association and recreation executive; b. Jackson, Mich., Jan. 18, 1937; s. William Edwin and Lena Louisa (Hunt) S.; m. Ruth Ann Toombs, Mar. 28, 1959; children: Suzanne Marie, William Edwin III, Bryan Anthony. AS, Jackson C.C., 1959; BS in Geology, Mich. State U., 1961, MA in Journalism, 1964. Reporter Sci. Svc., Washington, 1961-62; writer sci. U. Chgo., 1963-64; sci. info. officer Pa. State U., State College, 1964-66; corr. McGraw-Hill, Washington, 1966-69; staff com. pub. works U.S. Senate, 1969—71; founding editor Biomed. News, 1969-71; dir. pub. info. Nat. Bur. Standards, Washington, 1972-76; editor Am. Pharmacy Jour., 1979-82; dir. media and info. svcs. AMA, Washington, 1982-86; exec. dir. Nat. Found. Infectious Diseases, Washington, 1986-91, Assn. Biotech. Cos., 1991-93; CEO, Bioconfs. Internat., Bethesda, Md., 1993-95; exec. dir. Va. Biotech. Assn., 1996—2000, Va. Campground Assn., 2001—03; CEO, WESmall & Assocs., Assn. Execs., Louisa, Va., 1976—. Owner recreation resort Small Country Campground, Louisa, 1976—; developer Weswood Estates properties, Louisa, 2004-. Author: Third Pollution, 1971. With Security Agy., AUS, 1955-59. Recipient Superior Accomplishment award U.S. Dept. Commerce, 1974. Fellow AAAS; life mem. Nat. Assn. Sci. Writers. Office: PO Box 343 Louisa VA 23093-0343

SMALLEY, DONNA WESSON, lawyer, educator; b. Ft. Sill, Okla., Oct. 8, 1955; d. Robert Eugene and Frances Marie (Yates) Wesson; m. Jack Smalley Jr., July 31, 1978 (div. Jan. 1987); 1 child, Jack Smalley III. BA in Journalism, U. Ala., 1975, JD, 1978; cert. instr. Nat. Inst. Trial Advocacy, U. Calif. Berkeley, San Francisco, 1994. Bar: Ala. 1978. State lobbyist U. Ala., Tuscaloosa, 1974-75; personal injury claims adjuster State Farm Mutual Auto Ins., Birmingham, 1978-82; assoc. Williams & Pradat, Tuscaloosa, 1982-83; legal clk., adminstrv. asst. Tuscaloosa County Dist. Ct., 1983-84; assoc. atty., ptnr. Gibson & Smalley, P.C., Tuscaloosa, 1984-88; pvt. practice Tuscaloosa, 1988-95; ptnr., gen. practitioner Smalley & Carr, L.L.C., Tuscaloosa, 1996—2005; sr. assoc. Ivey & Ragsdale, Jasper, Ala., 2005—. Adj. English instr. U. Ala., Tuscaloosa, 1988-91, adj. trial advocacy instr., 1991—; bd. mem. Ala. Lawyers for Children, Montgomery, 1993-96, Ala. Children's Trust Fund Bd., Montgomery, 1994—; cir. judge pro-tem Ala. Adminstrv. Office of Cts., Tuscaloosa, 1995; chair citizen's edn. Ala. State Bar Assn., Montgomery, 1995-96; spkr. in field. Paintings exhibited Jr. League, 1990 (3d place), Lawyers for Children Charitable Auction, 1996. Chair mediation com. Tuscaloosa County Bar, 1989-91; task force mem. Lt. Gov.'s Task Force-Juvenile Crime, Montgomery, 1993-96; exec. com. Ala. State Dem. Party, Birmingham, 1994—; parent-bd. liason Tuscaloosa Acad., 1994-95. Named Outstanding Young Businesswoman, Jaycees, Tuscaloosa, 1984, Outstanding Young Careerist, Bus. and Profl. Women, Tuscaloosa, 1985; recipient Outstanding Achievement-CLE award Ala. State Bar, Montgomery, 1994, 95, Pro Bono award Ala. State Bar, 1997. Fellow Am. Acad. Matrimonial Lawyers; mem. Ala. Trial Lawyers (exec. bd. 1994—). Methodist. Avocations: reading, walking, computers. Office: Smalley & Carr LLC Attys 601 Greensboro Ave Tuscaloosa AL 35401-1730 also: Ivey & Ragsdale Attys 315 W 19th St Jasper AL 35501 Home Phone: 205-799-6078; Office Phone: 205-221-4644.

SMALLEY, ROBERT MANNING, retired diplomat; b. Los Angeles, Nov. 14, 1925; s. William Denny and Helen (McConnell) S.; m. Lois Louisa Williamson, Nov. 28, 1948 (div.) m. Rosemary Sumner, Jan. 4, 1957 (dec. June 18, 2004); children: Leslie Estelle, David Christian. Student, UCLA, 1946-48. Radio news editor Mut. Radio Broadcasting System, Los Angeles, 1950-55; mgr. Agrl. Info. Inc., Sacramento, 1957-59; with Whitaker & Baxter, San Francisco, 1956-57, 59-61; sec. Mayor George Christopher, San Francisco, 1961-63; asst. dir. pub. relations Republican Nat. Com., 1964; press sec. Republican vice presdl. candidate William E. Miller, 1964; dir. pub. relations Republican Nat. Com., 1965; v.p. Whitaker & Baxter, San Francisco, 1966-68; asst. press sec. Republican vice presdl. candidate Spiro Agnew, 1968; spl. asst. Sec. Commerce, Washington, 1969-72; adminstrv. asst. U.S. Senator Robert P. Griffin, Washington, 1972-73; dir. corp. affairs Potomac Electric Power Co., Washington, 1973-75; U.S. rep. devel. assistance com. O.E.C.D., Paris, 1975-77; spl. asst. U.S. Senator Robert P. Griffin, Washington, 1977-78; asst. to campaign mgr. Reagan for Pres. Com., Washington, 1979; sr. advisor mgmt. communications IBM, 1979-82; dep. asst. sec. of state pub. affairs Dept. of State, Washington, 1982-87, U.S. amb. to Kingdom of Lesotho, 1987-89; lectr. in U.S. politics and pub. policy; ret., 1989. Author: (book) The Admiralities at War 1944-45, 2002. Campaign mgr. Senator Robert P. Griffin, MIch., 1966, 72. Served with USN, 1944-46, PTO. Republican. Episcopalian. Home: 3131 Connecticut Ave NW Apt 2302 Washington DC 20008

SMALLWOOD, ARWIN DOREMUS, history professor; b. Windsor, NC, July 19, 1965; s. Bart Fearing and Lois Marie Smallwood; m. Alisa Mayfield, July 17, 1993; children: Justin Emory, Raina Marie. PhD, Ohio State U., Columbus, 1997. Asst. prof. history NC A&T State U., Greensboro, 1993—94; dir. African-American studies and assoc. prof. history Bradley U., Peoria, Ill., 1995—2003; assoc. prof. history U. Memphis, 2003—. Contbr. articles to profl. jours. (GilderLehrman Fellowship, 2003). Edn. bd. mem. Hist. Hope Found., Windsor, NC, 2006—08. Fellowship, NC Soc., Gilder Lehrman Inst. Am. History, Libr. Co. Phila., Virgina Hist. Soc., UNC, 2003. Mem.: Assn. Study African-Am. Life and History, Southern Hist. Assn. Office: Univ Memphis 100 Mitchell Hall Memphis TN 38152-3450 Business E-Mail: asmallwd@memphis.edu.

SMALLWOOD, CAROL, writer; b. Cheboygan, Mich., May 3, 1939; d. Lloyd Gouine and Lucille Drozdowska; m. T.M. Smallwood, 1963 (div. 1976); children: Michael, Ann. BS, Ea. Mich. U., Ypsilanti, 1961, M in History, 1963; MLS, We. Mich. U., Kalamazoo, 1976. Tchr. Mich. Pub. Sch., 1961—64; grad. asst. Western Mich. U., Kalamazoo, 1975-76; Title I libr. cons. Northland, Grand Traverse Library Systems, Mich., 1976-77; head media dir. Pellston Pub. Schs., Mich., 1977—97; writer, libr. cons. classes Mt. Pleasant, 1998—. Asst. dir. Northland Libr. System, Alpena, Mich., 1977; developer, operator ednl. materials clearinghouse, 1981-83; adult edn. tchr. Cheboygan Area Schs., 1985-86. Author: Free Michigan Materials for Educators, 1980, 2nd edit., 1986,

Free Materials Resource Disk, 1983, Exceptional Free Library Resource Materials, 1984, Free Resource Builder, 1985, 2d edit., 1992, A Guide to Selected Federal Agency Programs and Publications for Librarians and Teachers, 1986, Health Resource Builder, 1988, An Educational Guide to the National Park System, 1989, Current Issues Builder, 1989, Library Puzzles and Word Games, for Grades 7-12, 1990, Reference Puzzles and Word Games for Grades 7-12, 1991, Michigan Authors, 1993, Helpful Hints for the School Library, 1993, Recycling Tips for Teachers and Librarians, 1995, An Insider's Guide to Libraries, 1997, Free or Low-Cost Health Information, 1998; (with S. McElmeel) WWW Almanac, 1999; (with B. Hudson, A. Riedling, J. Rotole) Internet Sources on Each U.S. State, 2005, Educators as Writers: Publishing for Personal and Professional Development, 2006; author On The Way To Wendy's, 2008, Thinking Outside the Book, 2008, Librarians as Community Partners: An Outreach Handbook, 2009, poems in English Jour., Poesia, Mich. Feminist Studies, The Writers Chronicle, others; contbr; columnist Detroit News; others. Charter bd. mem., Cheboygan Area Arts Coun.; founder, pres. Cheboygan County Humane Soc.; co-founder Humane Animal Treatment Soc. Mem.: Doris Day Animal Found. Mailing: PO Box 1485 Mount Pleasant MI 48804 E-mail: smallwood@tm.net.

SMALLWOOD, GLENN WALTER, JR., utility marketing management executive; b. Jeffersonville, Ind., Oct. 12, 1956; s. Glenn Walter and Darlene Ruth (Zeller) S. BSBA, SE Mo. State U., 1978, BS in Engring. Tech., 2006; MA in Bus., Webster U., 1992, MBA, 1993, MA in Bus., 1997; MS in Engring and Tech., Okla. State U., 2008. Cert. econ. developer Inst. Econ. Devel., 2006, mgr. Internat. Econ. Devel. Coun., energy mgr. Assn. Energy Engrs., demand side energy profl. Assn. Energy Engrs., mfg. technologist Soc. Mfg. Engrs., econ. devel. fin. profl. Nat. Devel. Coun. Customer svc. advisor Union Electric Co., Mexico, Mo., 1979—95, Cape Girardeau, Mo., 1995—97; cmty. devel. exec. Ameren Svcs., Cape Girardeau, 1997—98, bus. devel. exec., 1998—. Coord. local United Way, 1984; mem., chair Gt. Rivers coun. Boy Scouts Am., chair Shawnee dist. Eagle Scout advancement com., 1999-2001, chair Shawnee Dist. com., 2002--; panelist Mo. Freedmon Forum, 1990; charter mem. class Mo. Leadership; chmn. Leadership Mexico Program; coordinating advisor Jr. Achievement, Mexico H.S.; committeeman, chmn. Republican Party of Audrain County; bd. dirs. Mo. Rep. Grassroots Caucus, S.E. Mo. Univ. Found., 1998— chmn. Cape Girardeau Planning and Zoning Commn., 2004-06; adv. coun. Cape Girardeau County Jr. Achievement, 2005-06. Recipient Disting. Svc. award, Mexico, Mo. Jaycees, 1993; named Commd. Ky. Col., Commonwealth of Ky., 1995, Commd. Disting. Hoosier, State of Ind., 1999; named one of Ten Outstanding Young Missourians, Mo. Jaycees, 1993. Mem. Nat. Eagle Scout Assn. (bd. dirs. St. Louis coun.), Boy Scouts Am., Greater St. Louis Coun., Shawnee Dist. (chair 2002-05), Cape West Rotary Club (pres. 2006-07); SE Mo. U. Found. (bd. dirs. 1998-2004), Mexico Area C. of C. (bd. dirs. 1993-95), Cape Girardeau C. of C. (bd. dirs. 1998-2001, treas., 2000), Inst. Cert. Profl. Mgrs. (cert. mgr.), Assn. Energy Engrs. (cert. energy mgr.), Adminstrv. Mgmt. Soc., Optimists (Youth Appreciation award 1974), Kiwanis (cert. appreciation 1984), Mexico Noon (bd. dirs. 1990, treas. 1990-91, v.p. 1991-92, pres. 1993-94), Audrain County Pachyderm Club (bd. dirs., 2d v.p. 1990-92, pres. 1993), S.E. Mo. Univ. Found. (bd. dirs.), S.E. Mo. Pachyderm Club (founder, pres. 1997-98), Mo. Fedn. Pachyderm Clubs (bd. dirs.), Honorable Order Ky. Cols. (commd. Ky. col. 1995), Sons of Confederate Vets., 1889er Soc., Jr. Achievement Cape Girardeau County (pres. 2005-07). Republican. Avocations: music, sports, baseball, basketball, tennis. Office: Ameren Svcs 2222 Kent Dr Cape Girardeau MO 63701 Business E-Mail: gsmallwood@ameren.com.

SMALLWOOD, ROBERT ALBIAN, JR., retired secondary education educator; b. Phila., Oct. 3, 1946; s. Robert Albian and Mildred May (Miller) S.; m. Geraldine Ann Boozan, May 27, 1972; children: Amy Lynn, Daniel James. BS in Commerce, Bus. Adminstrn., Rider Coll., Lawrenceville, NJ, 1969, MA in Sch. Adminstrn. and Supervision, 1976; EdS in Ednl. Adminstrn. and Supervision, Rutgers U., New Brunswick, NJ, 1983. Cert. social studies tchr., secondary sch. prin., supr. curriculum and instrn., Pa.; cert. social studies and gen. bus. tchr., prin., supr., sch. bus. adminstr., asst. supt. bus., sch. adminstr. (supt.) NJ. Tchr. social studies Trenton Bd. Edn., 1973-76, tchr. bus. edn., 1975-76, sch. disciplinaerian, 1976-84, 94-97; acting asst. prin. Jr. High Sch. 2, 1980-83, tchr. U.S. history, 1983-87, chmn. social studies dept., 1984-85; acting asst. prin. Carroll Robbins Elem. Sch., Jr. High Schs. #1 and #5, 1987-88; tchr. gifted and talented social studies Dunn Jr. High Sch., 1989-93, social studies tchr., 1997-99, whole sch. reform site facilitator, 1999—2005; ret., 2005. Mem. Dist.'s Affirmative Action Adv. Council; mem. Nat. Tchr. Corps Project, Trenton Area; fin. advisor M.S. Prin., 1998-2005. Asst. ops. officer Trenton CD Unit, 1974-76, asst. disaster analysis officer, 1976, disaster analysis officer, 1976-79; trustee N.J. Coun. for Alcohol/Drug Edn., 1983-99, mem. exec. com., 1985-95, 96-99, chmn. nominating com., 1985, 86, treas., 1987-95, acting exec. dir., 1994-95, v.p., 1996-98, pres. 1998-99. With U.S. Army, 1969-72. With US Army, 1969—72. Decorated Bronze Star, Army Commendation medal with oak leaf cluster, Joint Svc. Commendation medal, Good Conduct medal, Nat. Defense Svc. medal, Vietnam Svc. medal, Vietnam Campaign medal with 2 campaign stars. Mem. NEA Ret., Vietnam Vets. Am. (life), Va. Geneal. Soc. (life), Md. Geneal. Soc., Md. Hist. Soc., Geneal. Soc. Pa. (life), Nat. Geneal. Soc., Assn. Profl. Genealogists, Franklin County Hist. Soc., Adams County Hist. Soc., Pa., Assn., Colonial Williamsburg Found., Va. Republican. Baptist. Avocations: genealogy, history. Home: 2 Leese Ave Trenton NJ 08609-1828 Home Phone: 609-587-2364. Personal E-mail: RASteach@aol.com.

SMALLWOOD, SANDRA DENISE, pastor, daycare administrator; b. Buffalo, Feb. 28, 1953; d. Harl and Dorothy Mae Smallwood; children: Samuel Hayes II, Dorinda Hayes, Deana Hayes, Aaron Hayes, Eric Hayes. Student, Erie C.C., 1992—94, Child Devel. Assoc., 2001—02. Ordained pastor 1993. Evangelist prison ministry Eric County Holding Ctr., Buffalo, 1977—80; tchr., evangelist Concerned Citizens Against Violence and Crime, 1990—92; chaplain Shoreline Apts. Block Club, 1995—98; pastor, founder Kingdom of Heaven Light House Growth Min. Ch., 1995—; mem. Buffalo Pub. Access Media, 1995—; dir., owner Kingdom of Heaven Little Ones Day Care, 2003—; chaplain svcs. Mary Agnes & Conerstone Manor, 2003—. Founder TV ministry Bibical Morals & Truth, Buffalo, 1995—; tchr. daycare Cmty. Action Orgn., 1999—2002; dist. parent coord. McKinley High Sch., 2002—04; mem. Child Care Coalition, 2003—06; residential coord. Cornerstone Manor, 2006—08; with Coalition Homeless, 2009—, Homeless Alliance, 2009—, United Oatreach Ministry, 2009—. Mem. Coalition of Homeless, 2009—, Homeless Alliance, 2009—, United Outreach Ministry, 2009—. Avocations: story telling, swimming, reading, singing. Home: 117 Virgil Ave Buffalo NY 14216 Office: Kingdom of Heaven Light House Growth Ministry 117 Virgil Ave Buffalo NY 14216 Office Phone: 716-871-0957. Personal E-mail: rev.sdsmallwood@yahoo.com.

SMALLY, DONALD JAY, consulting engineering executive; b. Cleve., 1922; s. Daniel James and Alice (Rohrheimer) S.; m. Ruth Janet Glasser, July 8, 1944; children: Alan Jon, Leonard Arthur. BME, U. Cin., 1949. Prodn. engr. N. Ransohoff, Inc., Cin., 1949-50; chief engr. Mosby Engring. Assocs., Sarasota, Fla., 1952-55; prin. Smally, Wellford & Nalven, Inc., Sarasota, 1956-91. Mem. tech. adv. com. Manatee Community Coll., Sarasota, 1965-90; mem. adv. com. Vocat.-Tech. High Sch., Sarasota, 1968-80 V.p. Sarasota YMCA, 1968-71, Sarasota Opera Assn., 1975-88, pres., 1988-89; chmn. Sarasota Vol. Talent Pool, 1973-76; sec.-treas. Civitan Found., 1965-79; bd. dirs. Suncoast Heart Assn., 1976; mem. Fla. Coordinating Coun. for Vocat. and Adult Edn., 1984-95, chmn., 1987-88; chmn. Sarasota Hist. Preservation Bd., 1988-91; pres. Sarasota County Rd. Improvement Task Force, 1990-93; mem. Sarasota County Pub. Sch. Found., 1990-95, chmn., 1990-91; v.p. Hist. Soc. Sarasota, 1990-91, Children's Haven and Adult Cmty. Svcs., 1983-99, pres., 1991-94; pres. John Ringling Ctr. Found., 1991-98; mem. Plymouth Harbor Bd., 1994-99; bd. dirs. Sarasota Alliance for Hist. Preservation, 2004—, pres. 2008-. Recipient Good Citizenship award SAR, 1975, Disting. Alumni award U. Cin. Engring. Coll., 1985, Outstanding Svc. award Myakica Chpt. Fla. Engring. Soc., 1993; named Citizen of Yr. Sarasota Civitan Club, 1975, Engr. of Yr. Sarasota-Manatee Engrs. Soc., 1976. Fellow Am. Coun. Engring. Cos. (treas. 1980-82), Fla. Engring. Soc. (pres. Sarasota-Manatee chpt. 1956-58); mem. Sarasota County C. of C. (past dir., v.p. 1983), Cons. Engrs. Council Fla. (pres. 1968), Fla. Soc. Profl. Land Surveyors (chpt. pres. 1973), Am. Water Works Resources Assn. (pres. Fla. Soc. 1981), Sarasota-Manatee Engring. Soc. Personal E-mail: donandjansmally@verizon.net.

SMARDON, RICHARD CLAY, landscape architect, environmental studies professor; b. Burlington, Vt., May 13, 1948; s. Philip Albert and Louise Gertrude (Peters) Smardon; m. Anne Marie Graveline, Aug. 19, 1973; children: Regina Elizabeth, Andrea May. BS cum laude, U. Mass., 1970, MLA, 1973; PhD in Environ. Planning, U. Calif., Berkeley, 1982. Environ. planner, landscape architect Wallace, Floyd, Ellenzweig, Inc., Cambridge, Mass., 1972-73; assoc. planner Exec. Office Environ. Affairs, State of Mass., Boston, 1973-75; environ. impact assessment specialist USDA extension svc. Oreg. State U., Corvallis, 1975-76; landscape architect USDA Pacific S.W. Forest and Range Expt. Sta., Berkeley, 1977; rsch. landscape architect U. Calif., Berkeley, 1977-79; prof. landscape architecture, sr. rsch. assoc. SUNY Coll. Environ. Sci. and Forestry, Syracuse, 1979-86, prof. environ. studies, 1987—, dir. Inst. for Environ. Policy and Planning, 1987-95, chair faculty of environ. studies, 1996—2007. Co-dir. Gt. Lakes Rsch. Consortium, Syracuse, 1986—2007; guest lectr. numerous univs.; adj. asst. prof. U. Mass., Amherst; dir. R. G. Pack Environment Inst., 1996—2007; Sea Grant trainee Inst. Urban and Regional Devel., Berkeley, 1976; condr., presenter numerous seminars and workshops; cons. numerous orgns.; mem. com. environ. design and landscape Transp. Rsch. Bd.-NAS, 1985—95; mem. tech. adv. bd. Wetlands Rsch., Inc., Chgo., 1985; mem. adv. bd. Wetlands Fund, NY, 1985; v.p. Integrated Site, Syracuse, 1990—2002. Co-editor: Our National Landscape, 1979, (spl. issue) Coastal Zone Mgmt. Jour., 1982, The Future of Wetlands, 1983, Foundations for Visual Project Analysis, 1986, The Legal Landscape, 1993, Protecting Floodplain Resources, 1995, Adirondacks and Beyond, 1998, Environmental Knowledge, 2001, (spl. issue) Landscape and Urban Planning, 2005, Sustaining the Worlds Wetlands, 2009; mem. editl. bd. Northeastern Environ. Sci. Jour., 1981—85, Landscape and Urban Planning, 1991—, Environ. Sci. and Policy, 1999—, The Sci. World, 2001—, Internat. Jour. Environ. Scis., 2005; contbr. articles to profl. jours. Pres. Save the County, Inc., Fayetteville, NY, 1986—88, 2002—04; apptd. to Gt. Lakes Adv. Commn., NY, chmn. NY, 1993—98, Gt. Lakes Legal Found., 1999—, NY State Wetlands Forum Bd., 2000—07; bd. dirs. Sackets Harbor Area Hist. Preservation Found., Watertown, NY, 1984—90. Recipient Beatrice Farrand award, U. Calif., 1979, Am. Soc. Landscape Archs. award, 1972, Pub. Svc. award in edn., 1990, Progressive Architecture mag. award, 1992, Pres.'s Pub. Svc. award, 1994. Mem.: NAEP, AAAS, Coastal Soc., Internat. Assn. Impact Assessment, Land Resource Assn. (charter), NY Acad. Sci., Sigma Lambda Alpha, Alpha Zeta (life). Avocations: folk guitar, hiking, skiing, travel. Office: SUNY Faculty Environ Studies Syracuse NY 13210 Office Phone: 315-470-6576. Business E-Mail: rsmardon@esf.edu.

SMARELLI, DAVID JOHN, music educator, musician; b. Springfield, Ohio, Sept. 7, 1959; s. John and Margaret Ann Smarelli; m. Brenda Faye Widmark, Aug. 10, 1985; children: Laura, Marissa, Julia. MusB in Performance and Edn., Bowling Green State U., 1982; MusM in Edn., Miami U., Oxford, Ohio, 1996. Profl. tchg. cert. Ohio Dept. Edn. Orch. tchr. Lima (Ohio) City Schs., 1982—89, Sycamore Cmty. Schs., Cin., 1989—. Lectr. Ohio No. U., Ada, Ohio, 1984—85; dir. Sycamore Electric Ensemble, 2004—. Musician (violinist): Springfield Symphony Orch., 1975—, Blue Ash/Montgemery (Ohio) Symphony Orch., 1997; co-concertmaster: Lima (Ohio) Symphony Orch., 1982—89, concertmaster: Clermont Philharm. Orch., 1999—2004, condr.:, 2004—07. Mem.: Ohio String Tchrs. Assn. (bd. mem. 2008—, named Pub. Sch. Orch. Tchr. of Yr. 2007), Am. Fedn. Musicians, Ohio Orch. String Tchrs. Assn. (summer camp mid. sch. orch. dir. 1994—2004, S.W. regional rep. 1998—2000), Ohio Music Edn. Assn. (S.W. region chair 1993—94). Avocations: computers, coin collecting/numismatics, gardening, genealogy. Home: 1522 Laval Dr Cincinnati OH 45255 Office: Sycamore HS 7400 Cornell Rd Cincinnati OH 45242 Home Phone: 513-374-9028; Office Phone: 513-686-1770. Personal E-mail: smarelli@fuse.net.

SMARKOLA, CLAUDIA, education educator; BBA, Drexel U., Phila.; MEd., Holy Family U., Phila., 1998; PhD in Ednl. Psychology, Temple U., Phila., 2005. Postdoc. fellow Temple U., 2004—05, rschr., 2005—, prof., 2008—. Contbr. articles to peer reviewed pubs. Bd. dir. Assn. Retarded Citizens, Burlington, NJ, 2007—09. Mem.: APA, Am. Ednl. Rsch. Assn. Achievements include research in educational technology. Office: Temple Univ 1803 Broad St 1200 Carnell Hall Philadelphia PA 19122

SMARR, JOSEPH, Internet company executive; m. Michelle Smarr, June 2005. BS in Symbolic Sys., Stanford U., Calif., 2002, MS in Symbolic Sys., 2003. Web arch. Plaxo Inc., Mountain View, Calif., chief platform arch., chief tech. officer. Spkr. in field. Avocations: guitar, soccer, rollerblading. Office: Plaxo Inc 203 Ravendale Dr Mountain View CA 94043 Office Phone: 650-254-5406. Office Fax: 650-254-1435. E-mail: joseph@plaxo.com, jsmarr@plaxo.com.

SMARR, LARRY LEE, science administrator, astrophysicist, educator; b. Columbia, Mo., Oct. 16, 1948; s. Robert L. Jr. and Jane (Crampton) S.; m. Janet Levarie, June 3, 1973; children: Joseph Robert, Benjamin Lee. BA, MS, U. Mo., 1970; MS, Stanford U., 1972; PhD, U. Tex., 1975. Rsch. asst. in physics U. Tex., Austin, 1972-74; lectr. dept. astrophys. sci. Princeton U., 1974-75; rsch. assoc. Princeton U. Obs., 1975-76; rsch. affiliate dept. physics Yale U., New Haven, 1978-79; asst. prof. astronomy dept. U. Ill., Urbana, 1979-81, asst. prof. physics dept., 1980-81, assoc. prof. astronomy and physics dept., 1981-85, prof. astronomy and physics dept., 1985—2000; dir. Nat. Ctr. for Supercomputing Applications, Champaign, Ill., 1985—2000, Nat. Computational Sci. Alliance, 1997—2000, Calif. Inst. for Telecom. and Info. Tech., 2000—; prof. Computer Sci. and Engring. UC San Diego, 2000—. Cons. Lawrence Livermore Nat. Lab., Calif., 1976-1990, Los Alamos (New Nex.) Nat. Lab., 1983—; mem. Commn. on Phys. Sci., Math. and Resources, NRC, Washington, 1987-90, commn. on Geoscience, Environ. and Resources, 1990-1994, adv. panel on Basic Rsch. in the 90's Office Tech. Assesment, 1990—, Adv. Com. to Dir. NIH, 1998-2005, NASA Adv. Coun., 2001-2005, Policy and Globel Affairs Divsn., NRC. Editor: Sources of Gravitational Radiation, 1979; mem. editoral bd. Science mag., 1986-90; contbr. over 50 sci. articles to jours. in field. Co-founder, co-dir. Ill. Alliance to Prevent Nuclear War, Champaign, 1981-84. Recipient Fahrney medal Franklin Inst., Phila., 1990; NSF fellow Stanford U., 1970-73, Woodrow Wilson fellow, 1970-71, Lane Scholar U. Tex., Austin, 1972-73, jr. fellow Harvard U., 1976-79, Alfred P. Sloan fellow, 1980-84. Fellow Am. Phys. Soc.; mem. NAE, AAAS, Am. Astron. Soc., Govt. Rsch. Roundtable U. Ind. Avocations: marine aquarium, gardening.

SMART, AMY, actress; b. Topanga Canyon, Calif., Mar. 26, 1976; d. John and Judy Smart. Actress (films) A & P, 1996, High Voltage, 1997, Campfire Tales, 1997, The Last Time I Committed Suicide, 1997, Starship Troopers, 1997, How to Make the Cruelest Month, 1998, Circles, 1998, Starstruck, 1998, Strangeland, 1998, Varsity Blues, 1999, Outside Providence, 1999, Road Trip, 2000, Scotland, Pa., 2001, Rat Race, 2001, Interstate 60: Episodes of the Road, 2002, After School Special, 2003, The Battle of Shaker Heights, 2003, Blind Horizon, 2003, The Butterfly Effect, 2004, Win a Date with Tad Hamilton!, 2004, Willowbee, 2004, Starsky & Hutch, 2004, Bigger Than the Sky, 2005, The Best Man, 2005, Just Friends, 2005, Peaceful Warrior, 2006, Crank, 2006, Mirrors, 2008, Life in Flight, 2008, Crank: High Voltage, 2009, (TV films) Seduced by Madness: The Diane Borchardt Story, 1996, Her Costly Affair, 1996, Brookfield, 1999, The '70s, 2000, (TV series) Felicity, 1999—2001, Smith, 2006—07, voice Robot Chicken, 2005—07. Spokesperson Heal the Bay, Environ. Media Assn., Human Soc. Named to Women with Organic Style, Organic Style mag., 2004. Office: c/o Untitled Entertainment 1801 Century Park E Los Angeles CA 90067

SMART, EDITH MERRILL, civic worker; b. Sept. 10, 1929; d. Edwin Katte and Helen Phelps (Stokes) Merrill; m. S. Bruce Smart, Jr., Sept. 10, 1949; children: Edith Minturn Smart Moore, William Candler, Charlotte Merrill Smart Rogan, Priscilla Smart Schwarzenbach. Student, Smith Coll., 1947—49, Barnard Coll., 1949—50. Tchr. elem. schs., Gibson Island, Md., 1959—60; guide, instr. Mill River Wetlands Com., Fairfield, Conn., 1967—85; treas. Near and Far Aid Assn., Fairfield, 1970—75, v.p., 1975—77, pres., 1977—79, Nature Ctr. of Environ. Activities, Westport, Conn., chmn., 1981—85; trustee Fairfield U., 1987—93; leader No. Cook County coun. Girl Scouts Am., Kenilworth, Ill., 1962—64; chmn. Southport-Westport Antiques Show, 1974—76; trustee Conn. chpt. Nature Conservancy, 1981—91, Va. chpt. Nature Conservancy, 1992—. Guide Nat. Aquarium, 1985—90; dir. Piedmont Child Devel. Ctr., 1991—97, Land Trust of Va., 2002—. Bd. mem. Land Trust Va.; vestryman St. Timothy's Ch., Fairfield, 1976—79. Mem.: MFH The Fairfax Hunt Club, Upperville Garden Club. Republican. Episcopalian. Home: 20561 Trappe Rd Upperville VA 20184-3021

SMART, FRANK WILSON, physician; b. New Orleans, Apr. 12, 1956; s. Foch Mahlon and Laura Gladys Smart; m. Jaclyn Cutrone, Nov. 16, 1996; children: Daniel, Katherine, Michael. BS in Zoology, So. La. U., 1978; MD, La. State U., New Orleans, 1985. Diplomate Am. Bd. Internal Medicine, Am. Bd. Cardiovascular Disease. Intern Ochsner Found. Hosp., New Orleans, 1985-86, resident, 1986-88; fellow Baylor Coll. Medicine, Houston, 1988-90, fellow in transplant rsch., 1990-91; co-sect. head heart failure and cardiac transplantation Ochsner Med. Instn., New Orleans, 1991-97, dir. med. transplant svcs., multi-organ transplant ctr., 1994-97; dir. transplant Ochsner Clinic, New Orleans, 1991-97; prof. medicine, co-dir. to dir. cardiac transplant program Tulane U. Med. Ctr., New Orleans, 1997; med. dir., adv. heart failure, cardiac transplantation, Tex. Heart Inst. St. Luke's Episcopal Hosp., Houston; dir. cardiology Morristown (NJ) Meml. Hosp., 2006—, chmn., cardiology, vice chmn., cardiovascular medicine, 2006—. V.p., cofounder Rsch. Congestive Heart Failure, New Orleans, 1998—; rep. region 3 United Network Organ Sharing, Richmond, Va., 1999—; mem. adv. bd. Action Heart Failure, Parsippany, N.Y. Mem. editl. bd. Cardiology Today, 1996, Congestive Heart Failure, Jour. Heart & Lung Transplantation; author: The Transplantation & Replacement of Thoracic Organs, 1997, Primer on Transplantation, 1998; reviewer Am. Jour. Cardiology. Recipient Richard Van Reet award Baylor Coll. Medicine, Houston, 1991. Fellow ACP, Am. Coll. Cardiology (Syntex award 1990); mem. AMA, Internat. Soc. Heart or Lung Transplantation, Am. Soc. Transplantation, So. Med. Assn., Alpha Omega Alpha. Office: Morristown Meml Hosp 100 Madison Ave Morristown NJ 07962 Office Phone: 973-290-7316.

SMART, GEORGE M., energy executive, former packaging company executive; BS, Defiance Coll.; MBA, Wharton Sch., U. Penn. With Central States Can Co. (div. of Van Dorn Co.), 1970—78, pres., CEO, 1978—93; chmn., pres. Phoenix Packaging Corp., 1993—2001; pres. Sonoco- Phoenix, Inc., 2001—03; bd. dirs. FirstEnergy Corp., Akron, Ohio, 1997—, chmn., 2004—. Bd. dirs. Ohio Edison Co., 1988—, Ball Corp., 2005—. Office: FirstEnergy Corp 76 S Main St Akron OH 44308

SMART, JAMES ANTHONY, music educator; b. Marietta, Ga., July 21, 1959; s. James Bryant Smart and Patricia Morgan Williams; m. Robin Arlene McDaniel, May 26, 1990; children: Laurel Morgan, Andrew Forrest. MusB, Jacksonville State U., 1982; MusM, Ga. State U., 1985; student in Music Edn., Boston U., 2006—. Adj. prof. U. West Ga., Carrollton, 1995—2001; dir. of bands Cobb County Schs., Mableton, Ga., 2000—; tchg. asst. Auburn U., 1994—96. Orch. dir. First Bapt. Ch., Powder Springs, Ga., 1995—2005. Personal E-mail: james.smart@cobbk12.org.

SMART, JEAN, actress; b. Seattle, Sept. 13, 1951; m. Richard Gilliland, June 7, 1987; 1 child, Connor Douglas. Actor: (films) Gangsters, 1979, Flashpoint, 1984, Protocol, 1984, Fire with Fire, 1986, Project X, 1987, Baby Talk, 1992, Mistress, 1992, Homeward Bound: The Incredible Journey, 1993, The Brady Bunch Movie, 1995, The Odd Couple II, 1998, Guinevere, 1999, Forever Fabulous, 1999, Snow Day, 2000, The Kid, 2000, Sweet Home Alabama, 2002, Bringing Down the House, 2003, Garden State, 2004, I Heart Huckabees, 2004, Lucky You, 2007, Hero Wanted, 2008; (TV films) Before and After, 1979, Piaf, 1984, Single Bars, Single Women, 1984, A Fight for Jenny, 1986, Place at the Table, 1987, A Seduction in Travis County, 1991, Locked Up: A Mother's Rage, 1991, Overkill: The Aileen Wuornos Story, 1992, Just My Imagination, 1992, The Yarn Princess, 1994, The Yearling, 1994, A Stranger in Town, 1995, Undue Influence, 1996, A Change of Heart, 1998, The Man Who Came to Dinner, 2000, Audrey's Rain, 2003, Killer Instinct: From the Files of Agent Candice DeLong, 2003, Kim Possible: A Sitch in Time, 2003, A Very Married Christmas, 2004, Kim Possible: So the Drama, 2005; (TV series) Maximum Security, 1984, Designing Women, 1986—91, High Society, 1995—96, Style and Substance, 1998, Frasier, 2000—01 (Primetime Emmy Outstanding Guest Actress in a Comedy Series, Acad. TV Arts and Scis., 2000, 2001), The District, 2000—04, The Oblongs, 2001, In-Laws, 2002—03, Kim Possible, 2002—07, Center of the Universe, 2004—05, 24, 2006—07, Samantha

Who?, 2007—09 (Primetime Emmy for Outstanding Supporting Actress in a Comedy Series, Acad. TV Arts and Scis., 2008). Office: CBS Studio Ctr Bungalow 15 4024 Radford Ave Studio City CA 91604 also: c/o Untitled Entertainment 1801 Century Park E, Ste 700 Los Angeles CA 90067*

SMART, LEONARD JAMES, JR., science educator; b. Windham, Conn., May 19, 1970; s. Leonard James and Deborah Lynn Smart; m. Tonya Shante Anderson; children: Cameron Avery, Kyler Deante. BS, Trinity Coll., Hartford, Conn., 1992; MS, U. La., Monroe, 1995; PhD, U. Cin., 2000. Instr. Miami U., Oxford, Ohio, 1998—2000, asst. prof., 2000—. Contbr. articles to profl. jour. Mem.: Internat. Soc. for Ecol. Psychology, Human Factors & Ergonomics Soc., Sigma Xi (miami chpt. pres. 2006—08). Achievements include discovery of changes in postural movement precede and are predictive of motion sickness in real and virtual environments. Office: Miami Univ 90 N Patterson Ln Oxford OH 45056 Office Fax: 513-529-2420. Business E-Mail: smartlj@muohio.edu.

SMART, MARY-LEIGH CALL, civic worker; b. Springfield, Ill., Feb. 27, 1917; d. S(amuel) Leigh and Mary (Bradish) Call; m. J. Scott Smart, Sept. 11, 1951 (dec. 1960). Diploma, Monticello Coll., 1934; student, Oxford U., 1935; BA, Wellesley Coll., 1937; MA, Columbia U., 1939, postgrad., 1940—41, NYU, 1940—41; painting student, with Bernard Karfiol, 1937—38. Dir. mgmt. Cen. Ill. Grain Farms, Logan County, 1939—; owner Lowtrek Kennel, Ogunquit, Maine, 1957-73, Cove Studio Art Gallery, Ogunquit, 1961-68; art collector, patron, publicist, 1954—. Cons. in field. Editor: Hamilton Easter Field Art Found. Collection Catalog, 1966; originator, dir. show, compiler of catalog Art: Ogunquit, 1967; Peggy Bacon-A Celebration, Barn Gallery, Ogunquit, 1979. Program dir., sec. bd. Barn Gallery Assoc., Inc., 1958-69, pres., 1969-70, 82-87, asst. treas., 1987-92, hon. dir., 1970-78, adv. trustee, 1992-94, v.p., 1994-2003; curator Hamilton Easter Field Art Found. Collection, 1978-79, curator exhbn., 1979-86, chair exhbn. com., 1987-94; acquisition com. DeCordova Mus., Lincoln, Mass., 1966-78; chancellor's coun. U. Tex., 1972—; pres. coun. U. NH, 1978—; bd. dir. Ogunquit C. of C., 1966, treas., 1966-67, hon. life mem., 1968—; bd. overseers Strawbery Banke, Inc., Portsmouth, NH, 1972-75, 3d vice chmn., 1973, 2d vice-chmn., 1974; bd. advisors U. Art Galleries, U. NH, 1973-89; pres., 1981-89; bd. dir. Old York Hist. and Improvement Soc., York, Maine, 1979-81, v.p., 1981-82; adv. com. Bowdoin Coll. Mus. Art Invitational exhibit, 1975, '76 Maine Artists Invitational Exhbn., Maine State Mus., Maine Coast Artists, Rockport, 1975-78, All Maine Biennial '79, Bowdoin Coll. Mus. Art juried exhbn.; mem. jury for scholarship awards Maine com. Skowhegan Sch. Painting & Sculpture, 1982-84; nat. com. Wellesley Coll. Friends of Art, 1983—; adv. trustee Portland Mus. Art, 1983-85, fellow, 1985—; mus. panel Maine State Commn. on Arts and Humanities, 1983-86; adv. com. Maine Biennial, Colby Coll. Mus. Art, 1983; coun. advisors Farnsworth Art Mus., Rockland, Maine, 1986-98; collections com. Payson Gallery, Westbrook Coll., Portland, 1987-91; dir. Greater Piscataqua Cmty. Found., NH Charitable Fund, 1991-97; com. to establish artist's advancement grant, 2001; mem. corp. Ogunquit Mus. Am. Art, 1988-90, 95-2000; active Maine Women's Forum, 1993—; mem. art com. York Pub. Libr., 2002—07; pres. Class of 1937, Wellesley Coll., 2001-07. Lt. (j.g.) WAVES, 1942-45. Recipient Deborah Morton award Westbrook Coll., 1988, Friend of the Arts award Maine Art Dealers Assn., 1993. Mem. Springfield Art Assn., Jr. League Springfield Ill., Western Maine Wellesley Club. Episcopalian. Address: 30 Surf Point Rd York ME 03909-5053

SMARTSCHAN, GLENN FRED, educational consultant; b. Allentown, Pa., Dec. 11, 1946; s. Fred Gotfred and Joyce Isabel (Hensinger) S.; m. Linda Susan Bastinelli, Mar. 18, 1972; children: Erin Joy, Lauren Nicole. BS in Edn., Kutztown U., 1968; MS in Edn., Temple U., 1972; EdD in Ednl. Adminstrn., Lehigh U., 1979. Cert. NISL instr., tchr. history and comprehensive social studies, secondary prin., supt., Pa. Tchr. 8th grade social studies South Mountain Jr. H.S., 1968-76; adminstrv. asst. to prin. to prin. Raub Jr. H.S., 1976-80, dist. dir. curriculum, 1980-84, asst. to supt. for curriculum and cmty. svcs., 1984-86; supt. schs. Brandywine Hts. Area Sch. Dist., Topton, Pa., 1986-90, Mt. Lebanon Sch. Dist., Pitts., 1990—2003. Adj. prof. Cedar Crest Coll., 1986-88, Duquesne U., 1997, 2005, 06, U. Pitts., 2001, Gannon U., 2007; CEO Ednl. Dynamics Cons.; spkr. and cons. Multiple Client Feedback (MCF), Stakeholder Surveys, Match of Written, Taught and Tested Curriculum, Criterion Referenced Testing, Strategic Planning; educator dir. Adelphoi Village; ednl. planner Burt Hill, 2003—; cons. Tri-State area study coun. U. Pitts for planning and accountability, 2003-07. Bd. dirs. Alternative House, Inc., Bethlehem, Pa., 1976-81, chmn. program com., 1977-78, v.p., 1979, pres., 1980; adv. com. Lehigh County (Pa.) Hist. Mus., 1980-86; bd. dirs. Girls Club Allentown, 1983-86, v.p., 1985. Named Pa. Superintendent of Yr., 1999. Mem. ASCD, Pa. Assn. Supervision and Curriculum Devel. (exec. com., registrar ea. regional meeting, v.p. Ea. region, pres. 1988), Am. Assn. Sch. Adminstrs. (Pa. State Supt. of Yr. 1999), Pa. Assn. Sch. Adminstrs. (pres. 1996), Pa. Sch. Bds. Assn., Juvenile Diabetes Assn. (bd. dirs.), Alumni Coun. Lehigh U. (pres. 1986), Phi Delta Kappa, Fleetwood Club, Rotary (charter mem. Allentown club, exec. com. 1985). Roman Catholic. Home: One Spalding Cir Pittsburgh PA 15228 Office Phone: 412-344-8663. Business E-Mail: edcsmartschan@comcast.net.

SMARTT, RICHARD A., museum director; married. BS, MS, U. Tex., El Paso; PhD in Zoology and Botany, U. N.Mex. Prof. U. Tex., El Paso; dir., chmn. sci. divsn., curator zoology and collections N.Mex. Mus. Natural History, Albuquerque; now exec. dir. The Wildlife Experience, Parker, Colo. Contbr. articles to profl. jours. Office: The Wildlife Experience 10035 S Peoria Parker CO 80134 Office Phone: 720-488-3301. Office Fax: 720-488-3399.

SMATHERS, JAMES BURTON, medical physicist, educator; b. Prairie du Chien, Wis., Aug. 26, 1935; s. James Levi and Irma Marie (Stindt) S.; m. Sylvia Lee Rath, Apr. 20, 1957; children: Kristine Kay, Kathryn Ann, James Scott, Ernest Kent. B.Nuclear Engring., N.C. State Coll., 1957, MS, 1959; PhD, U. Md., 1967. Diplomate Am. Bd. Radiology, Am. Bd. Health Physics, Am. Bd. Medical Physics; cert. in radiation oncology physics; registered profl. engr., D.C., Tex., Calif. Research engr. Atomics Internat., Canoga Park, Calif., 1959, Walter Reed Army Inst. Research, Washington, 1961-67; prof. nuclear engring. Tex. A. and M. U., College Station, 1967-80, prof., head bioengring., 1976-80; prof., head med. physics, dept. radiation oncology UCLA, 1980-2001, prof. emeritus, 2001—. Cons. U.S. Army, Dept. Energy, also pvt.; industry. Served with U.S. Army, 1959-61. Recipient Excellence in Teaching award Gen. Dynamics, 1971; Excellence in Research award Tex. A. and M. U. Former Students Assn., 1976 Mem. Health Physics Soc., Am. Assn. Physcists in Medicine, Am. Coll. Med. Physics, Am. Soc. Therapeutic Radiation Oncology, Am. Coll. Radiology. Home: 18229 Minnehaha St Northridge CA 91326-3427 E-mail: smathers@ucla.edu.

SMEAL, KEMP LESLIE, psychotherapist, musician; s. Ronald Leslie and Patricia Ann Smeal. MusB, Westminister Choir Coll., Princeton, NJ, 1981; MA in Clin. Psychology, Azusa Pacific U., Calif., 1994. Lic. marital and family therapist Bd. Behavioral Scis., Calif., 2000. Min. music Cmty. Presbyn. Ch., Danville, Calif., 1982—92; organist/pianist Glendale Presbyn. Ch., Calif., 1992—99, Glendale City Seventh-day Adventist Ch., 1997—, La Canada Presbyn. Ch., Calif., 1999—; assoc. prof. of accompanying Vanguard U., Costa Mesa, Calif., 2001—03; pvt. practice psychotherapy Long Beach, Calif., 2000—. Organist Welsh Choir So. Calif., North Hollywood, 2001—02; organist for the glory of easter Crystal Cathedral, Garden Grove, 2002—03, interim assoc. organist, 2003; recitalist Cathedral of Our Lady of the Angels, LA, 2003—07. Musician: (CD) Beside Still Waters, Hearts Afire, (featured pianist on time-life video) A Walk With Jesus: A Holy Land Journey With Hymns and Scripture. William and Mary Renneckar scholar, Westminster Choir Coll., 1978—79. Mem.: Calif. Assn. Marriage and Family Therapists (assoc.), Am. Guild Organists Orange County Chpt. (assoc.), Am. Guild Organists LA Chpt. (assoc.). Home: 525E Seaside Way Long Beach CA 90802 Office: 5855 Naples Plz Ste 109 Long Beach CA 90802 Personal E-mail: ksmeal@aol.com. Business E-Mail: kempsmeal@aol.com.

SMEDINGHOFF, THOMAS J., lawyer; b. Chgo., July 15, 1951; s. John A. and Dorothy M. Smedinghoff; m. Mary Beth Smedinghoff. BA in Math., cum laude, Knox Coll., 1973; JD cum laude, U. Mich., 1978. Bar: Ill. 1978, U.S. Dist. Ct. (no. dist.) Ill. 1978. Assoc. McBride, Baker & Coles and predecessor McBride & Baker, Chgo., 1978—84, ptnr., 1985—99, Baker & McKenzie, Chgo., 1999—2006, Wildman, Harrold, Allen & Dixon LLP, Chgo., 2006—. Adj. prof. info. tech. & privacy law John Marshall Law Sch., Chgo., 1985-; adj. prof. bus. law Brennan Grad. Sch. Bus. Dominican U., Chgo., 2004—; chair Ill. Commn. on Electronic Commerce and Crime, 1996—; mem. US Del. to UN Commn. on Internat. Trade Law; mem. legal working group, UN Ctr. For Trade Facilitation and Elec. Bus., 2004-. Author: The Legal Guide to Developing, Protecting & Marketing Software, 1986, Multimedia Law Handbook, 1995, Online Law, 1996, Information Security Law: The Emerging Standard For Corporate Compliance. Fellow: Am. Bar Found.; mem.: ABA (chair electronic commerce divsn. 1995—2003, chair sect. Sci. and Tech. Law 1999—2000, chair Internat. Policy Com. 2003—). Office: Wildman Harrold Allen & Dixon LLP 225 W Wacker Dr Ste 3000 Chicago IL 60606 Home Phone: 708-366-2329; Office Phone: 312-201-2021. Business E-Mail: smedinghoff@wildman.com.

SMEDLEY, LAWRENCE THOMAS, retired organization executive; b. Lorain, Ohio, Sept. 2, 1929; s. Robert E. and Gerda Sofia (Johnson) S.; m. Carmen Nancy Suarez, June 29, 1962; children: Lorraine, Robert, Lawrence, Richard. BA, Bowling Green State U., 1952; MA, U. Mich., 1957; PhD, Am. U., 1972. Analyst Social Security dept. AFL-CIO, Washington, 1962-65, asst. dir. dept., 1965-73, assoc. dir. dept. occupation safety-health-social security, 1973-88; exec. dir. Nat. Coun. Sr. Citizens, Inc., Washington, 1988-96. Former mem. numerous presdl. task forces and coms. on older Ams. and disabled; planning and adv. coms. White House Conf. on Aging, 1971, 81; former adv. coun. on employee welfare and pension plans Dept. Labor, former spl. task force examining policies relating to asset reversions from over-funded pension plans; bd. dirs. Nat. Coun. Sr. Citizens. Co-chmn. Leadership Coun. Aging Orgns., Washington, 1988-95; exec. bd. Com. for Nat. Health Ins., WAshington, 1989—; mem. policy conv. White House Conf. on Aging, 1995; chair Montgomery County Com. Aging. With M.I., U.S. Army, 1952-55, Korea. Recipient Svc. award Commn. on Accreditation of Facilities of Rehab., 1975, Dedicated Svc. award White House Conf. on Handicapped, 1977, award of honor Industry-Labor Coun., 1981, Outstanding Svc. award Pres.'s Com. on Employment of Handicapped, 1987. Democrat. Lutheran. Home: 3154 Grace Field Rd Apt 217 Silver Spring MD 20904 Home Phone: 301-890-4115. Personal E-mail: ltsmed@comcast.net, ltsmed@verizon.net.

SMEDS, EDWARD WILLIAM, retired food company executive; b. Chgo., Feb. 15, 1936; s. Sigvard A. and Ida S.; m. Alice J. Lawler, Jan. 26, 1957; children: Ellen R., Brad W. BS, Carthage Coll., 1957; MS, U. Ill., 1959; grad. advanced mgmt. program, Harvard U., 1977. With Borg Warner Corp., 1958-61, Kraft Foods div. Kraft Inc., 1961-75, v.p., dir. personnel, ops. group, 1976-78, v.p. human resources, 1978-79, sr. v.p. human resources, 1979-80, sr. v.p. fin. and adminstrn., 1980-84; pres. Kraft Asia Pacific, 1984-88; chmn. Kraft Foods Ltd., Australia, 1984-88; pres. Kraft Ltd. Can., 1988-89; sr. v.p. ops. and logistics Kraft Gen. Foods, Glenview, Ill., 1990-94; pres. customer svc. and ops. Kraft, Northfield, Ill., 1993-94, ret., 1994. Chmn. bd. Thrivent Mut. Funds. Chmn. bd. trustees Carthage Coll. Mem. Sunset Ridge Country Club, Club at Pelican Bay, Olde Fla. Home: 10 Regentwood Rd Northfield IL 60093-2728 also: 7575 Pelican Bay Blvd Naples FL 34108-8218 E-mail: eosmeos@gmail.com.

SMEETON, THOMAS ROONEY, government affairs consultant; b. Evanston, Ill., Sept. 26, 1934; s. Cecil Brooks, Jr. and Florence Mary (Rooney).; m. Susan Diane Tollefson, Feb. 23, 1963; children: Sean, Timothy, Shannon, Brendan, Colin. BS in History, Marquette U., 1958; postgrad., U. Notre Dame, 1958-59; grad., Armed Forces Staff Coll., 1972. Intelligence officer U.S. CIA, Langley, Va., 1962-73; vp., gen. mgr. Nowicki Fla. Devel. Corp., Ft. Lauderdale, 1973-75; cons. spl. projects com. on fgn. affairs U.S. House Reps., Washington, 1975-86, minority counsel permanent select com. on intelligence, 1986-92, minority staff dir. Iran/Contra com., 1987-88, exec. dir. Rep. policy com., 1993-94; adminstr., chief investigator House Judiciary Com., Washington, 1995-96; govtl. affairs cons., 1996—. Contbg. author: (with Hyde) For Every Idle Silence, 1985. Bd. dirs. Sylvan Beach Found. With U.S. Army, 1959-62. Recipient Agy. Seal medallion CIA, 1993. Mem. Assn. Former Intelligence Officers, Ctrl. Intelligence Retirees Assn., Am. Legion, Amelia Island Club, Capitol Hill Club, The Notre Dame Club of North Fla. Republican. Roman Catholic. Avocation: golf. Home and Office: PO Box 8029 Fernandina Beach FL 32035-8029

SMEGAL, THOMAS FRANK, JR., lawyer; b. Eveleth, Minn., June 15, 1935; s. Thomas Frank and Genevieve (Andreachi) S.; m. Susan Jane Stanton, May 28, 1966; children: Thomas Frank, Elizabeth Jane. BS in Chem. Engring., Mich. Technol. U., 1957; JD, George Washington U., 1961. Bar: Va. 1961, D.C. 1961, Calif. 1964, U.S. Supreme Ct. 1976. Patent examiner U.S. Patent Office, Washington, 1957-61; staff patent atty. Shell Devel. Co., San Francisco, 1962-65; patent atty. Townsend and Townsend, San Francisco, 1965-91, mng. ptnr., 1974-89; sr. ptnr. Graham and James, San Francisco, 1992-97; ptnr. Knobbe, Martens, Olson & Bear, San Francisco, 1997—2005, Law Offices Thomas F. Smegal, Jr., 2006—. Mem. U.S. del. to Paris Conv. for Protection of Indsl. Property; mem. adv. com. Ct. of Appeals for Fed. Cir., 1992-96. Contbr. articles to profl. jours. Pres. bd. dirs. Legal Aid Soc. San Francisco, 1982-84, Youth Law Ctr., 1973-84; bd. dirs. Nat. Ctr. for Youth Law, 1978-84, San Francisco Lawyers Com. for Urban Affairs, 1972—, Legal Svcs. for Children, 1980-88; bd. dirs., presdl. nominee Legal Svcs. Corp., 1984-90, 1993-2003. Capt. Chem. Corps, U.S. Army, 1961-62. Recipient St. Thomas More award, 1982. Mem. ABA (chmn. PTC sect. 1990-91, ho. of dels. 1988-2000,2006, mem. standing com. Legal Aid and Indigent Defendants 1991-94, 2004—07, chair sect. officer conf. 1992-94, bd. govs. 1994-97, standing com. on Pro Bono and Pub. Svc. 1997-2001, standing com. on Gavel awards 2001-04), Intellectual Property Law Assn. (chmn. nat. coun. 1989), Nat. Inventors Hall of Fame (pres. 1988), Calif. Bar Assn. (v.p. bd. dirs. 1986-87), Am. Patent Law Assn. (pres. 1986), Internat. Assn. Intellectual Property Lawyers (pres. 1995-2001), Bar Assn. San Francisco (pres. 1979), Patent Law Assn. San Francisco (pres. 1974), Olympic Club, Golden Gate Breakfast Club, Claremont Country Club (Oakland). Republican. Roman Catholic. Office: One Sansome Ste 3500 San Francisco CA 94104 Home: 107 King Ave Piedmont CA 94610 Office Phone: 415-217-8383. Business E-Mail: tomsmegal@smegallaw.com.

SMELSER, JUNE, librarian; b. Portland, Oreg., June 1, 1919; d. George and Kathryn Ellen (Reynolds) England; m. Richard O. Williams Jan. 30, 1942 (wid. 1944); m. Lawrence C. Smelser, June 30, 1950 (wid. 1987); children: Jean, Kenneth, Gail, Rosanne, Marianne, Duane, Michael. BA, U. Oreg., 1941; BLS, Columbia U., 1946. Children's librarian Oregon City Pub. Library, 1946-51; librarian David Douglas High Sch., Portland, 1957-69, Lake Oswego (Oreg.) Jr. High Sch., 1969-71; mgr. Food for Thought (Food Coop), Oregon City; cons., distbr. Golden Neo-Life Diamite Internat., Milw., 1976—. Editor newsletter Weedy Acres Gazette, 1988—. Mem. Am. Assn. Ret. Persons (Oreg. state coord. ret. tchrs. 1988-91, dist. dir. Oreg. 1992—), Toastmasters Internat. (pres. club 1988), Trails Club of Oreg. Avocations: hiking, backpacking, cross-country, skiing, reading.

SMELSER, NEIL JOSEPH, sociologist; b. Kahoka, Mo., July 22, 1930; s. Joseph Nelson and Susie Marie (Hess) S.; m. Helen Thelma Margolis, June 10, 1954 (div. 1965); children: Eric Jonathan, Tina Rachel; m. Sharin Fateley, Dec. 20, 1967; children: Joseph Neil, Sarah Joanne. BA, Harvard U., 1952, PhD, 1958; BA, Oxford U., Eng., 1954, MA, 1959; grad., San Francisco Psychoanalytic Inst., 1971. Mem. faculty U. Calif., Berkeley, 1958-94, prof. sociology, 1962—, asst. chancellor ednl. devel., 1966-68; assoc. dir. Inst. of Internat. Studies, Berkeley, 1969-73, 80-89; prof. sociology U. Calif., Berkeley, 1972-94; prof. emeritus, 1994—; dir. edn. abroad program for U. Calif., Berkeley, 1977-79, spl. advisor Office of Pres., 1993-94, dir. Ctr. for Advanced Study in Behavioral Scis., 1994-2001. Bd. dirs. Social Sci. Rsch. Coun., chmn., 1971-73, com. econ. growth, 1961-65; trustee Ctr. for Advanced Study in Behavioral Scis., 1980-93, 1994-2007, chmn., 1984-86; trustee Russell Sage Found., 1990-2000; subcom. humanism Am. Bd. Internal Medicine, 1981-85, 89-90, adv. com., 1992-99, chmn. adv. com., 1995-99; chmn. sociology panel Behavioral and Social Scis. survey NAS and Social Sci. Rsch. Coun., 1967-69; com. on basic rsch. in behavioral and social scis. NRC, 1980-89, chmn., 1984-86, co-chmn., 1986-89; chmn. com. of selection Guggenheim Found., 1996-; chmn. Commn. for Behavioral and Social Scis. and Edn. (NAS/NRC), 1996-2003, German-Am. Acad. Coun., 1999-2000. Author: (with T. Parsons) Economy and Society, 1956, Social Change in the Industrial Revolution, 1959, Theory of Collective Behavior, 1962, The Sociology of Economic Life, 1963, 2d edit., 1975, Essays in Sociological Explanation, 1968, Sociological Theory: A Contemporary View, 1971, Comparative Methods in the Social Sciences, 1976, (with Robin Content) The Changing Academic Market, 1980, Sociology, 1981, 2d edit., 1984, 3d edit., 1987, 4th edit., 1991, 5th edit., 1995, Social Paralysis and Social Change, 1991, Effective Committee Service, 1993, Sociology, 1994, Problematics of Sociology, 1997, The Social Edges of Psychoanalysis, 1999, The Faces of Terrorism, 2007; editor: (with W.T. Smelser) Personality and Social Systems, 1963, 2d edit., 1971, (with S.M. Lipset) Social Structure and Mobility in Economic Development, 1966, Sociology, 1967, 2d edit., 1973, (with James Davis) Sociology: A Survey Report, 1969, Karl Marx on Society and Social Change, 1973, (with Gabriel Almond) Public Higher Education in California, 1974, (with Erik Erikson) Themes of Work and Love in Adulthood, 1980, (with Jeffrey Alexander et al) The Micro-Macro Link, 1987, Handbook of Sociology, 1988, (with Hans Haferkamp) Social Change and Modernity, 1992; (with Richard Munch) Theory of Culture, 1992; (with Richard Swedberg) The Handbook of Economic Sociology, 1994, 2d. edit. 2005; (with Jeffrey Alexander) Diversity and Its Discontents, 1999; (with William Julius Wilson and Faith Mitchell) American Becoming: Racial Trends and their Consequences, 2001, (with Paul B. Baltes) International Encyclopedia of the Social and Behavioral Sciences, 2001; editor Am. Sociol. Rev., 1962-65; adv. editor Am. Jour. Sociology, 1960-62. Rhodes scholar, 1952-54; Jr. fellow Soc. Fellows, Harvard U., 1955-58, fellow Russell Sage Found., 1989-90. Mem. Am. Sociol. Assn. (coun. 1962-65, 67-70, exec. com. 1963-65, pres. elect 1995-96, pres. 1996-97), Pacific Sociol. Assn., Internat. Sociol. Assn. (exec. com. 1986-94, v.p. 1990-94), Am. Acad. Arts and Scis. (hon.), Fedn. State Med. Bds. (bd. dirs. 2006-), (Am. Philos. Soc. (hon.), Nat. Acad. of Scis. (hon.). Business E-Mail: nsmelser@berkeley.edu.

SMELSER, PHILIP SIDNEY, history educator; b. Phoenix, Jan. 18, 1934; s. Joseph Nelson and Susie Marie Smelser; m. Jo Ann Stone, June 25, 1955; children: Stephen Joseph, Mark Eugene, Karin Lee Nowell, Jeffery Lincoln. AA, Phoenix Jr. Coll., 1954; BA, U. Calif., Berkeley, 1956; MA in History, Ariz. State Coll., Tempe, 1960. Tchr. Maricpa CC, Tempe, 1962—. Office: Glendale CC 6000 West Olive Glendale AZ 85302

SMELTZER, DEBRA JEAN, botanist; b. Camden, Ark., Oct. 13, 1953; d. William Dewey and Frankie Jean (Braswell) S.; m. James Richard Ziesler, Sept. 1, 1984. Cert. in interior design, Bauder Fashion Coll., Arlington, Tex., 1973; BA in Botany, U. Tex., 1985. Biol. rsch. asst. U.S. Dept. Interior, Everglades Nat. Park, Fla., 1980; biologist, surveyor Great Lakes Dredge and Dock, Miami Beach, Fla., 1981-82, 1984, biologist, surveyor, drafter Port Everglades, Fla., 1984; biologist, lab. tech. J.B. Reark and Assocs., Miami, 1982-84; fisheries biologist Kathryn Chandler and Assocs., Alexandria, Va., 1981-84; pres. Greensleeves, Inc., Miami and San Juan, P.R., 1985—, San Juan, P.R., 1991-95. Bd. govs. Nat. Coun. for Interior Hort. Cert., Columbus, Ohio, 1989-92; licensee Interior Landscape Internat. Corp., Dade, Monroe, Caribbean, 1990-92. Eucharistic min. St. Timothy Cath. Ch. Recipient Best Project award Interiorscape Mag., 1989, 1996, State Award of Excellence Fla. Nurserymen and Growers Assn., 1989, award of recognition, 1999. Mem. Associated Landscape Contractors Am. (award of Distinction 1989, 91, 92, Grand award 1990, 2001), South Fla. Interior Landscape Assn. (ednl. com. 1987-89, bd. dirs. 1986-87, author newsletter articles 1986-89, founder 1986), Coral Gables C. of C. (trustee coun.), Calif. Interior Plantscape Assn. (judges award, 2001, Distinction award 2001, 02). Republican. Avocations: water-skiing, skiing, scuba diving, photography. Office: Greensleeves Inc The Village at Beacon Lakes 1970 NW 129th Ave Unit 101 Miami FL 33182

SMEMO, IRWIN KENNETH, history professor; b. Brookings, SD, Nov. 23, 1930; s. AlFred and Elizabeth Smemo; m. Nancy O'Brien Smemo; children: Kristoffer, Molly;children from previous marriage: Elizabeth, Margaret, Eric. BS in History, U. Wis., Eau Claire, 1957; MA in History, U. Minn., Mpls., 1959, PhD in History, 1967. Instr. Osseo HS, Wis., 1957—61; asst. prof. to prof. Minn. State U., Moorhead, 1961—2009, dean, grad. studies, 1967—69, chair. dept. history, 1968—69, dir. Scandinavian studies program, 1972—95, dir. Northwest Minn. Hist. Archive, 1972—80, chair. dept. history, 1971—73. Vis. prof. Amerikansk Inst. U. Oslo, 1976. Author: (book) Against the Tide, 1986;

contbr. articles to profl. publs. Sgt. US Army, 1952—54, Korea. Recipient Burlington Northern award, BNRR, 1986, America-Norway Heritage award, Norsemen's Fed. Oslo, 1988; Danforth fellowship, Ralston Purina Inc., 1966—67, Rsch. grant, Kingdom of Norway, Norwegian Ministry of Fgn. Affairs, Oslo, 1972, Minn. State U. Sys., 1969—70, 1974, 1976, 1980. Mem.: Nordmanns-Forbundet, Norwegian-Am. Hist. Assn., Soc. Advancement of Scandinanvian Studies, Orgn. Am. Historians. Office: Minn State Univ Moorhead 1104 7th Ave S Moorhead MN 56563 Business E-Mail: kensmemo@mnstate.edu.

SMERDON, ERNEST THOMAS, engineering educator; b. Ritchey, Mo., Jan. 19, 1930; s. John Erle and Ada (Davidson) Smerdon; m. Joanne Duck, June 9, 1951; children: Thomas, Katherine, Gary. BS in Engring., U. Mo., 1951, MS in Engring., 1956, PhD in Engring., 1959, DSc (hon.), 2003. Registered profl. engr., Ariz. Chmn. dept. agrl. engring. U. Fla., Gainesville, 1968-74, asst. dean for rsch., 1974-76; vice chancellor for acad. affairs U. Tex. System, Austin, 1976-82; dir. Ctr. for Rsch. in Water Resources U. Tex., 1982-88; dean Coll. Engring. and Mines U. Ariz., Tucson, 1988-92, vice provost, dean Engring, 1992-97; sr. edn. assoc. NSF, Arlington, Va., 1997-00; prof. civil engring. and hydrology U. Ariz., Tucson, 1988—2001, dean emeritus, 2001—. Mem. bd. sci. and tech. internat. devel. NRC, 1990—94, mem. com. planning and remediation irrigation-induced water quality problems, 1990—96, chair com. Yucca Mountian peer rev., 1995, mem. com. study rsch.-doctorate programs U.S., 1991—95, mem. com. Mo. River Ecosys. Sci., 1999—2001; chair com. Water Resources Mgmt. Instream Flow and Salmon Survival in Columbia River, 2002—04, Sci. Bases Colorado River Water Mgmt., 2005—07, others. Editor: Managing Water Related Conflicts: The Engineer's Role, 1989. Mem. Ariz. Gov.'s Sci. and Tech. Coun., Tucson, 1989—96; bd. dirs. Greater Tucson Econ. Coun., 1990—95. Recipient Disting. Svc. in Engring. award, U. Mo., 1982, Lifetime Achievement award, Environ. and Water Resources Inst., 2002. Fellow: NAE (acad. adv. bd. 1989—95, tech. policy options com. 1990—91, chair com. career-long edn. engrs. 1997—2000, acad. adv. bd. 1998—99, peer com. 2002—05, chmn. sect. 12 2003—04, com. capacity U.S. Engr. Rsch. Enterprise 2004, peer com. 1986—90, 2002—, steering com. engr. 2020, policy com. Engr. 2020), ASCE (hon. Outstanding Svc. award irrigation and drainage divsn. 1988, Royce Tipton award 1989, Robert C. Park Outstanding Civil Engr. award 2005); mem.: Ariz. Soc. Profl. Engrs. (Engr. of Yr. award 1990), Univ. Coun. Water Resources, Am. Geophys. Union, Am. Soc. Engring. Edn. (chmn., bd. dirs. engring. dean's coun. 1995—97, pres. 1998—99, Outstanding Projects and Leaders award 2008, Benjamin Garver Lamme award 2008), Am. Water Resources Assn. (Icko Iben award 1989), Am. Soc. Agrl. Engrs., Pi Mu Epsilon, Tau Beta Pi, Phi Kappa Phi, Sigma Xi. Avocations: hiking, golf, scuba diving, painting. Office: U Ariz AME Bldg Rm N521 Tucson AZ 85721-0001

SMETANA, FREDERICK O., aerospace engineer, educator, consultant; b. Phila., Nov. 29, 1928; s. Otto Frederick and Emily Edna (Gera) S.; m. Adelaide Virginia Sigmon, Dec. 27, 1952 (dec. 2005); children: Daniel Frederick, Martha Elaine, Andrew Otto, Paul Howard; m. Zenaida Rivera, Dec. 16, 2006. BSME, N.C. State U., 1950, MME, 1953; PhD in Engring., U. So. Calif., LA, 1961. V.p. Philcord Co., Inc., Monroe, N.C., 1950-51; flight test analyst B Douglas Aircraft Co., Santa Monica, Calif., 1951; teaching asst. N.C. State U., Raleigh, 1952-53, prof., 1962-94, prof. emeritus, 1994—; rsch. scientist U. So. Calif., 1955-62. Author: Fortran Codes for Classical Methods in Linear Dynamics, 1982, Computer-Assisted Analysis of Aircraft Performance Stability and Control, 1984, Aircraft Performance Stability and Control, 1988, An Introduction to the Control of Dynamic Systems, 1994, Introductory Aerodynamics and Hygrodynamics of Wings and Bodies: A Software-Based Approach, 1997, Flight Vehicle Performance and Aerodynamic Control, 2001. 1st lt. USAF, 1953-55. Recipient Tech. Svc. award NASA, 1973, 78. Mem. AIAA (sect. chair NC 1970-72, 89-92, gen. aviation systems tech. com. 1984-2004). Republican. Lutheran. Avocation: desktop publishing. Home: 5425 Parkwood Dr Raleigh NC 27612-6228

SMETANA, PAVEL AMOS, religious organization administrator; b. July 14, 1937; s. Jan K. and Vera (Kozáková) Smetana; m. Zdenka Adámková, July 2, 1960; children: Ester, Magdalena, Pavla. MgrTh, Theol. Faculty, Prague, Czechoslovakia, 1956-61; postgrad., New Coll., Edinburgh, Scotland, 1969-70. Min., pastor Ch. of Czech Brethren, Hošťálková, 1964-79, Prague-Libeň, 1979-90, dep. moderator, 1987—90; pres. Ecumenical Coun. of Chs. in Czech Republic, 1990—91; moderator Ch. of Czech Brethren, 1991—2003, mem. evang. com. Prague, 1970—. Chmn. Ecumenical Coun. Czech Republic, 1991—95, pres., 1995—2000. Translator (from Hebrew): Old Testament, 1961—79. Avocations: poetry, music, swimming. E-mail: mgr.smetana@volny.cz.

SMETANKA, SALLY S., small business owner; b. Athens, NY, Aug. 26, 1944; AS, Valencia C.C., Orlando, Fla., 1981; BA, Rollins Coll., Winter Park, Fla., 1991. With labor rels. Walt Disney World, Orlando, Fla., 1978—81, asst. to pres.; owner Carriage House Antiques, Winter Park, Fla., 1983—. Home and Office: Carriage House Antiques 937 Aragon Ave Winter Park FL 32789 Office Phone: 321-217-1687.

SMETHURST, E(DWARD) WILLIAM, JR., investment banker; b. Newark, Apr. 15, 1930; s. Edward William and Helen Lea (Wiener) S.; m. Ludlow Bixby, June 30, 953; children: James, Andrew, Katherine. AB, Amherst Coll., 1952; MBA, Harvard U., 1958. Credit analyst Chase Manhattan Bank, NYC, 1958-60; mgr. securities Irwin Mgmt. Co., Columbus, Ind., 1961-64; ptnr. Wertheim & Co., NYC, 1965-79; sr. v.p. Cyrus J. Lawrence Inc., NYC, 1980-87; mng. dir. Wertheim Schroder & Co. Inc., NYC, 1988-95; pres., chief investment officer Schroder Wertheim Investment Svcs., NYC, 1990-96; chmn., trustee Wertheim Series Trust, NYC; retired, 1996; mng. dir. Byram Capital Mgmt., Greenwich, Conn., 2002—09. Trustee Mount Holyoke Coll., South Hadley, Mass., 1982—98. Lt. USN, 1952—55. Episcopalian. Home: 861 Bingham Rd Ridgewood NJ 07450-2111 Personal E-mail: wsmeth@optonline.net.

SMIALEK, JAMES L., research scientist; b. Cleve. s. Albin A. and Marie A. Smialek; m. Constance M. Habermann, July 14, 1972; children: Craig A., David J., Laurel B., Amy B. BS, Case Inst. Tech., Cleve., 1968, MS, 1971; PhD, Case Western Res. U., Cleve., 1981. Rsch. scientist NASA Glenn Rsch. Ctr., Cleve., 1968—. Contbr. articles to numerous profl. jours. Recipient Exceptional Sci. Achievement award, NASA, 1995—, Distinction award, Cleve. Chpt. ASM, 2007. Fellow: Am. Soc. Metals, Am. Ceramic Soc.; mem.: Oxidation Metals (assoc. editor 1988—2008), Jour. Am. Ceramic Soc. (assoc. editor 1988—2008). Achievements include research in advanced materials and science of high temperature oxidation; patents in field. Office: NASA Glenn Rsch Ctr 21000 Brookpark Rd Cleveland OH 44135 Business E-Mail: james.l.smialek@nasa.gov.

SMIALOWSKI, JOSEPH A., former mortgage company executive; b. 1949; BA in Philosophy, Merrimack Coll., Andover, MA; MS in Computer Systems Mgmt., Rochester Inst. Tech., NY. Mgr. Xerox Corp., 1974—83, Dennison Mfg., 1983—84; ptnr. Price Waterhouse, 1984—93; v.p., chief info. officer Sears, Roebuck & Co., 1993—95, sr. v.p., chief info. officer, 1995—98; exec. v.p. BankBoston, 1998—99; vice chmn., tech. and ops. FleetBoston Fin. Corp., Boston, 1999—2002, exec. v.p., 2002—04; exec. v.p. ops. and tech. Freddie Mac Fed. Home Loan Mortgage Corp., 2004—07, spl. advisor to the chmn. and CEO, 2007; adv. bd. NewVantage Ptnrs., 2008—. Mem. Rochester Inst. Tech. Presdl. Roundtable, Banking Info. Tech. Secretariat, Pvt. Sector Coun. Active mem. United Way of Mass. Bay. Named a Premier 100 IT Leader, Computerworld Mag., 2000; named one of Top 25 People To Watch, 1998. Office: NewVantage Ptnrs 71 Eliot Rd Arlington MA 02474

SMIDA, BESMA, engineering educator, researcher; d. Tahar Smida and Souad Monastiri; m. Belhassen Soltana, May 3, 1999; 1 child, Rayan Soltana. PhD, INRS Telecom., Montreal, Que., Can., 2006. Cert. OIQ, 2004. Rsch. engr. Microcell Inc., Montreal, 1999—2002; lectr. Harvard U., Cambridge, Mass., 2006—, rschr., 2006—. Contbr. scientific papers (Academic Gold medal, 2006). Recipient Nat. Math. Competition award, Tunisian Govt., 1987, Excellence award, Can. Internat. Devel. Agy., 1996—98, Academic Excellence award, INRS, 2006; Postdoc. fellowship, FQRNT, 2006—08, NSERC, 2008—. Office: Harvard Univ 33 Oxford St MD 117 Cambridge MA 02138 Office Phone: 617-496-2942. Business E-Mail: bsmida@seas.harvard.edu.

SMIDDY, JOSEPH CHARLES, retired academic administrator; b. Jellico, Tenn., June 20, 1920; s. Joseph F. and Sara Nan (Tye) Smiddy; m. Reba Graham, Sept. 6, 1985; children: Joseph F., Elizabeth Lee. BA, Lincoln Meml. U., 1948, LHD (hon.), 1970; MA, Peabody Coll., 1952; LLD, U. Richmond, 1975; LHD (hon.), Coll. William and Mary, 1986; DAm (hon.), Cumberland Coll., 1993. Tchr. Jonesville HS, 1948—51, prin., 1951—52; sec.-treas. Powell Valley Oil Co., Big Stone Gap, Va., 1952—53; prof. biology Clinch Valley Coll., U. Va., Wise, 1956—57, dean, 1957—68, dir., 1968—85, chancellor, 1968—85, chancellor emeritus, 1985—. Mem. Charter Day Award Emory and Henry Coll., 1980; mem. Commonwealth Day Award James Madison U., 1985. Musician, singer. Trustee Lincoln Meml. U. With US Army, 1942—45, PTO. Recipient Laurel Leaves award, Appalachian Consortium, 1995, Kanto Ednl. award, Wise County, 1995. Mem.: Bapt. Gen. Assn. Va. (pres. 1974—), Kiwanis, Shriners, Masons. Home: Ridgefield Acres Wise VA 24293 Office: PO Box 3160 Wise VA 24293-3160

SMIDDY, WILLIAM EARL, ophthalmologist; b. Boston, Dec. 4, 1957; s. Earl Raymond Jr. and Helen Maye (Putkisto) S.; m. Julie Therese Fradel, Dec. 27, 1978; children: Robert, Matthew, Rebecca, Susan, Andrew, Samuel, Clara. BS, Johns Hopkins U., 1980, MD, 1983. Diplomate Am. Bd. Ophthalmology. Intern Mercy Hosp., Balt., 1983-84; resident Johns Hopkins U., Balt., 1984-87, fellow, 1987, asst., 1987-88, instr., 1988-89; assoc. prof. ophthalmology U. Miami, Fla., 1989—. Author 1 book, 8 book chpts. and 110 articles. Served to capt. M.C., U.S. Army, 1984-92. Home: 9840 SW 60th Ct Miami FL 33156-1908 Office: Bascom Palmer/U Miami PO Box 016880 Miami FL 33101-6880

SMIDTS, CAROL, mechanical engineer, educator; d. Freddy and Julienne Smidts. PhD, U. Libre, Brussels, 1991. Faculty rsch. assoc. Ecole Poly. U. Libre, Brussels, 1991—92; faculty rsch. assoc. dept. materials and nuc. engring. U. Md., College Park, 1992—94, asst. prof. dept. materials and nuc. engring., 1994—2000, assoc. prof. dept. materials and nuc. engring., 2000—03; assoc. dir. rsch. Nat. Ctr. Sci. Rsch., Toulouse, France, 2000; assoc. prof. dept. mech. engring. U. Md., College Park, 2003—07, prof. dept. mech. engring., 2008—. Assoc. chair reliability engring. program U. Md., College Park, 2000—01; CEO TestSolvers, Bethesda, Md., 2005—08; vis. scientist Inst. for Systems Engring. & Informatics, Italy, 1992, JRC, Italy, 1992, European Communities Commn., Italy, 1992. Organizing com. Jeunesses Scientifiques Belgique, Brussels, 1987—91. Recipient award, Belgian Nuc. Soc., 1986, Flight Safety award, NASA, 1998, Rotary Nat. award, 1998, Achievement award, 1998, Software Assurance Symposium award, 2003; grantee, TEDCO, 2005; fellow, Inst. pour l=Encouragement de la Rsch. Sci. dans l'Industrie Agr., Belgium, 1986—88, Fonds Nat. de la Rsch. Sci., Belgium, 1989. Mem.: AIAA, ANS (Best Paper award 1991), IEEE (sr.). Achievements include patents for QRAS 1.0 software; method and apparatus for a common-cause failure module for probabilistic risk assessment tools; patents pending for domain specific test design automation, domain specific test design automation. Home: 2642 York Rd Columbus OH 43221-3239 Office: E 418 Scott Lab 201 W 19th Ave Columbus OH 43210 Business E-Mail: smidts.1@osu.edu.

SMIETANA, WALTER, educational research director; b. New Bedford, Mass., Nov. 8, 1922; s. Stanislaw and Frances (Wojtal) S.; m. Adele A. Asamowski, April 19, 1955. AB in Edn., U. Mich., 1948; MS, Boston U., 1956, EdD, 1965; ScD (hon.), U. Mass., Dartmouth, 1975. Cert. tchr., Mich. Tchr. sci. and math. Somerset (Mass.) Pub. Schs., 1948-65; prof. edn. Elmhurst (Ill.) Coll., 1965-69, Alliance Coll., Cambridge Springs, Pa., 1969-87, chmn. divsn. social sci., pres., 1971-72; dir. rsch. SYLLAGENES, New Bedford, 1987—. Liaison Study of Undergrad. Experience in Am., Carnegie Found. for Advancement of Teaching, Alliance Coll., 1984; participant Pa. Dept. Edn. ETS, Tchr. Cert. Test Devel., 1986-87; develop and accredite new tchr. edn. programs, state, regional and nat. levels, 1965-87; develop and evaluate year abroad and exch. programs Alliance Coll./Jagiellonian U., Cracow, Poland in coop. with U.S. Office Edn., 1969-85. Chmn. city com. Rep. Party, New Bedford, 1953-58; mem. citizens adv. com. Heritage State Park, New Bedford, 1989-93; chmn. bd. trustees Inst. Tech., New Bedford, 1963-64; chmn. adv. com. The Rsch. Found., New Bedford, 1962-64. Recipient Cert. of Merit for non-English Lang. Resources Rsch., Yeshiva U., 1981; U.S. Office Edn./ERIC grantee, 1969. Mem. World Future Soc., Inst. for Global Ethics, Nat. Space Soc., Inst. Noetic Scis., Libr. of Congress Assocs. (charter mem.). Avocations: astronomy, photography. Home and Office: 84 Ellen St New Bedford MA 02744-1521

SMIGEL, IRWIN, dentist; b. NYC, Oct. 9, 1924; m. Lucia Shvetz, Sept. 30, 1956; children: Bellanca Smigel Rutter, Robert. WSC, DDS, NYU, 1950. Diplomate Am. Bd. Aesthetic Dentistry. Dentist pvt. practice, NYC, 1950—. Vis. prof. Pitts. Dental Sch., 1980-83, Case Western U., 1990—; lectr. SUNY Buffalo, U. Mo., Kansas City, U. Minn.; cons., lectr. in field. Author: Dental Health, Dental Beauty, 1978; contbr. editor Dentistry Today, 1980-, dental adv. bd.; contbr. articles to dental jours. With INF., 1943-45. Irwin Smigel Chair in Aesthetic Dentistry established NYU Sch. Dentistry, 1996, Smigel Prize; recipient Outstanding Contbrn. to Aesthetic Dentistry award, Am. Acad. Cosmetic Dentistry, 1994 Fellow Am. Soc. Dental Aesthetics (founder, pres. 1976-2006); mem. Am. Dental Assn., Acad. Gen. Dentistry, Fedn. Dentaire, First Dist. Dental Soc. Achievements include invention of the Supersmile Whitening brand mouthrinse, toothpaste, floss and brush, tooth bonding technique, supersmile complete oral careline of products. Avocations: reading, tennis, racewalking, art, music. Office: 635 Madison Ave New York NY 10022-1009

SMILEY, CAROL ANNE, health facility administrator, sculptor; b. Cedar Rapids, Iowa, Sept. 11, 1937; d. Ralph Derold and Mary C. Miller; m. Donald Victor Smiley, June 29, 1956 (div. Aug. 1970); children: Donald Victor Jr., Julie Ann, Joseph Charles, Thomas Wayne; m. Douglas Brewster Reed, Aug. 6, 1976 (div. Jan. 1988); 1 child, Brook (dec.). Co-founder, v.p., sec., treas. Anvic Enterprise, Cedar Rapids, 1963-70; co-founder, dir. Yankee Horse Trader, Bennington, Vt., 1974; organic farmer Solon, Iowa, Argyle, NY, 1970-86; fiber sculptor, 1970-86; tchr. Solon H.S., 1973-74; caregiver, coord. Home Health Care and Hospice, Brattleboro, Vt., 1986—; cons. in grassroots home health. Sculpture shows include Green Mt. Collaborative, Bennington, 1974-78, Woman Art Gallery, N.Y.C., 1977-78, Lincoln Ctr. Group Show, N.Y.C., 1978; exhbns. various group shows. Mem. GOP ctrl. com. for Johnson County, Iowa, 1971-72. Mem.: ACLU. Office: Home Health Care Hospice 142 Green St Brattleboro VT 05301-6054

SMILEY, JANE GRAVES, author, educator; b. LA, Sept. 26, 1949; d. James La Verne and Frances Nuelle (Graves) Smiley; m. John Whiston, Sept. 4, 1970 (div.); m. William Silag, May 1, 1978 (div.); children: Phoebe, Lucy; m. Stephen Mark Mortensen, July 25, 1987; 1 child, Axel James. BA, Vassar Coll., Poughkeepsie, NY, 1971; MFA, U. Iowa, 1976, MA, PhD, U. Iowa, 1978. Asst. prof. Iowa State U., Ames, 1981-84, assoc. prof., 1984-89, prof., 1989-90, Disting. prof., 1992-96. Author: (novels) Barn Blind, 1980, At Paradise Gate, 1981 (Friends of Am. Writers prize, 1981), Duplicate Keys, 1984, The Greenlanders, 1988, Ordinary Love & Good Will, 1989, A Thousand Acres, 1991 (Pulitzer Prize for fiction, 1992, Nat. Book Critics Cirle award, 1992, Midland Authors award, 1992, Heartland prize, 1992), Moo, 1995, The All-True Travels and Adventures of Lidie Newton, 1998, Horse Heaven, 2000, Good Faith, 2003, Ten Days in the Hills, 2007; author: (story collections) The Age of Grief, 1987; author: (non-fiction) Charles Dickens, 2003, A Year at the Races: Reflections on Horses, Humans, Love, Money, and Luck, 2004, Thirteen Ways of Looking at the Novel, 2005; contbr. articles and short stories to mags. Recipient O. Henry Award for short stories, 1985. Mem.: AAAL, Screenwriters Guild, Author's Guild. Avocations: cooking, swimming, playing piano, quilting.

SMILEY, MARILYNN JEAN, musicologist; b. Columbia City, Ind., June 5, 1932; d. Orla Raymond and Mary Jane (Bailey) S. BS (State scholar), Ball State U., 1954; MusM, Northwestern U., 1958; cert., Ecoles d'Art Americaines, Fontainebleau, France, 1959; PhD (Grad. scholar, Delta Kampa Gamma scholar), U. Ill., 1970. Public sch. music tchr., Logansport, Ind., 1954-61; faculty music dept. SUNY-Oswego, 1961—, Disting. Teaching prof., 1974—, chmn. dept., 1976-81. Presenter papers at confs. Contbr. articles to profl. jours. Bd. dirs. Oswego Opera Theatre, 1978—, Oswego Orch. Soc., 1978—, Penfield Libr. Assocs., 1985—. Recipient Chancellor's award for Excellence in Tchg., 1973; SUNY Rsch. Found. fellow, summers, 1971, 1972, 1974, NEH grantee, 1990—91. Mem.: AAUW (grantee 1984, pres. Oswego br. 1984—86, br. coun. rep. dist. III, N.Y. State divsn. 1986—88, br. coun. coord. N.Y. State divsn. 1988—90, N.Y. divsn. area intererst rep. cultural interests 1990—92, N.Y. divsn. diversity dir. 1993—96, Oswego br. diversity chair 1995—, N.Y. state unofcl. historian 2000—04, N.Y. state historian 2004—, co-pres. Oswego br. 2007—), NOW, Oswego County Hist. Soc., Early Music Am., Am. Recorder Soc., Soc. Am. Music (membership chair 1998—2003, mem. membership com. 2003—), Renaissance Soc. Am., Coll. Music Soc., Music Libr. Assn., Medieval Acad. Am., Am. Musicol. Soc. (chmn. N.Y. chpt. 1975—77, chpt. rep. to AMS coun. 1993—96, bd. dirs. N.Y. State-St. Lawrence chpt. 1993—96, mem. status of women com. 1997—2000), Oswego Recorder Consort, Ontario Singers, Heritage Found. of Oswego, Phi Kappa Phi, Kappa Delta Pi, Sigma Tau Delta, Sigma Alpha Iota, Pi Kappa Lambda, Delta Phi Alpha, Phi Delta Kappa, Delta Kappa Gamma (music chair State of Ind. 1961, music chair State of N.Y. 1968). Methodist. Office: SUNY Dept Music Oswego NY 13126 Home Phone: 315-343-4803; Office Phone: 315-312-3054. Business E-Mail: marilynn.smiley@oswego.edu.

SMILEY, RICHARD WAYNE, researcher; b. Paso Robles, Calif., Aug. 17, 1943; s. Cecil Wallace and Elenore Louise (Hamm) S.; m. Marilyn Lois Wenning, June 24, 1967; 1 child, Shawn Elizabeth. BSc in Soil Sci., Calif. State Poly. U., San Luis Obispo, 1965; MSc in Soils, Wash. State U., 1969, PhD in Plant Pathology, 1972. Asst. soil scientist Agrl. Rsch. Svc., USDA, Pullman, Wash., 1966-69; rsch. asst. dept. plant pathology Wash. State U., Pullman, 1969-72; soil microbiologist Commonwealth Sci. and Indsl. Rsch. Orgn., Adelaide, Australia, 1972-73; rsch. assoc. dept. plant pathology Cornell U., Ithaca, NY, 1973-74, asst. prof., 1975-80, assoc. prof., 1980-85; supt. Columbia Basin Agr. Rsch. Ctr., 1985-2000; prof. Oreg. State U., 1985—. Vis. scientist Plant Rsch. Inst., Victoria Dept. Agr., Melbourne, Australia, 1982-83. Author: Compendium of Turfgrass Diseases, 1983, 3d edit., 2005; contbr. more than 200 articles to profl. jours. Postdoctoral fellow NATO, 1972. Fellow Am. Phytopath. Soc. (sr. editor APS Press 1984-87, editor-in-chief 1987-91); mem. Coun. Agrl. Sci. and Tech., Rotary (pres. Pendleton chpt. 1991-92, Paul Harris fellow 1993). Achievements include discovery of the etiology of a serious disease of turfgrasses, which led to a redefinition of studies and disease processes in turfgrasses. Office: Oreg State U Columbia Basin Agr Rsch Ctr PO Box 370 Pendleton OR 97801-0370 Business E-Mail: richard.smiley@oregonstate.edu.

SMILEY, ROBERT WILLIAM, JR., investment banker; b. Lansing, Mich., Nov. 17, 1943; s. Robert William Sr. and Rebecca Lee (Flint) S. AB in Econs., Stanford U., 1970; postgrad., San Fernando Valley Coll. Law, 1973—75; MBA in Corp. Fin., City U. L.A., 1979; LLB, LaSalle U., 1982. Bar: Calif. 1984. Sr. v.p. mktg. Actuarial Systems Inc., San Jose, Calif., 1972-73; founder, chmn. Benefit Systems Inc., L.A. and S.E. Nev., 1973-84, Brentwood Sq. Savs. and Loan, LA, 1982-84; chmn., CEO The Benefit Capital Cos. Inc., L.A. and S.E. Nev., 1984—. Lectr. U. Calif. Ext., L.A. and Berkeley, 1977—; instr. Am. Coll. Life Underwriters. Editor, contbg. author: Employee Stock Ownership Plans: ESOP Planning, Implementation, Law and Taxation, 1989, 3d edit. 2006; contbg. author: The Handbook of Employee Benefits, 1984, 7th edit., 2005; contbr. articles to profl. jours. Mem. nat. adv. coun., trustee Reason Found., L.A., 1983-91; bd. dirs. Nat. Ctr. for Employee Ownership, Oakland, Calif.; former trustee The Employee Ownership Found., Washington, 2000-04. With USN, 1961-64, Vietnam. Recipient Spl. Achievement award Pres.' Commn. on Pension Policy, 1984. Fellow Life Mgmt. Inst.; mem. Employee Stock Ownership Plan Assn. (founder, pres., bd. dirs., lifetime dir.), Assn. for Corp. Growth, Western and SW Pension Confs., Nat. Assn. Bus. Economists, ABA, Calif. Bar Assn. Office: The Benefit Capital Cos Inc PO Box 542 Logandale NV 89021-0542 Office Phone: 702-398-3222.

SMILEY, TAVIS, television talk show host, writer; b. Biloxi, Miss., Sept. 13, 1964; s. Emory G. and Joyce M. Smiley. Grad., Ind. U., 1986, D (hon.). Asst. to Mayor Tomilea Allison, LA, 1984—85; coun. aide, 1987; spl. asst. to exec. dir., 1978—88; adminstrv. aide to Mayor Tom Bradley, 1988—90; commentator The Smiley Report, 1990—2001; contbr. CNN, 2001—, HuffingtonPost.com; spl. correspondent ABC-TV, 2001—; commentator Tom Joyner Morning Show; pres., CEO Smiley Group, Inc. Host (TV series) BET Tonight with Tavis Smiley, 1998—2001, supervisory prodr. Tavis Smiley, 2004— (Outstanding TV News, Talk or Information (Series or Spl.), NAACP Image award, 2006), TV appearances include For Your Love, 1999, The Parkers, 2000,

Any Day Now, 2001, American Dreams, 2004; author: Hard Left: Straight Talk about the Wrongs of the Right, 1996, Doing What's Right: How to Fight for What You Believe and Make a Difference, 2000, How to Make Black America Better: Leading African Americans Speak Out, 2002, Keeping the Faith: Stories of Love, Courage, Healing and Hope from Black America, 2002; co-author (with David Ritz): What I Know for Sure: My Story of Growing up in America, 2006; editor: The Covenant with Black America, 2006; host TavisTalks.com. Founder Tavis Smiley Found.; bd. dirs. Challengers Boys and Girls Club, Black Coll. Tour, LA; mem. adv. bd. Martin Luther King Jr. Ctr. Non-Violent Social Change, 1992—93, Inner City Found. Excellence in Edn., 1989—91, After Class Scouting, Scouting USA, 1991; chmn. ops. com. Young Black Profls., LA, 1988—90; mem. steering com. United Way Greater L.A., 1989—90. Recipient Outstanding Bus. Profl. award, Dollars & Sense Mag., 1992, Image award, NAACP, 2000, Mickey Leland Humanitarian award, Nat. Assn. Minorities in Communications, NAACP Image award for News, Talk or Information, Series or Spl. for Katrina-One Year Later, 2007, NAACP Image award for Outstanding Talk-Crisis in Darfur, 2008, NAACP Image award for Outstanding Literary Work-Instructional, The Covenant in Action, 2008; named one of 50 Most Promising Young Leaders, Time Mag., 100 Most Influential Black Americans, Ebony mag., 2006, The World's Most Influential People, TIME mag., 2009; named to Hall of Fame, Vanity Fair, 1996, Power 150, Ebony mag., 2008. Office: Travis Smiley Foundation 4434 Crenshaw BLVD Los Angeles CA 90043-1208*

SMIRNAKIS, STELIOS MANOLIS, medical educator; s. Emmanuel (Manolis) Stylianou Smyrnakis and Akrivi Emmanuel Fragiadaki; m. Karen Vossen Smirnakis, June 2, 2000; children: Emmanuel (Manolis) Stylianou, Ioannis (Yiannis) Stylianou. BA summa cum lauda, Harvard Coll., Cambridge, Mass., 1987; MA, PhD, Harvard Physics GSAS, Cambridge, Mass.; MD magna cum lauda, Harvard Med. Sch., Boston, 1997. Diplomate Am. Bd. Psychiatry and Neurology, 2002. Chief resident neurology Brigham and Women's Hosp., Boston, Mass. Gen. Hosp., Boston, 2000—01, Partners Neurology Program, Harvard Med. Sch; clin. fellow neurocritical care Mass. Gen. Hosp., 2001—03; instr. neurology Harvard Med. Sch., Boston, 2003—06, asst. prof. neurology, 2006—07; postdoc. fellow Howard Hughes Med. Inst., 2001—02; rsch. scientist Max Planck Inst. Biol. Cybernetics, Tuebingen, Germany, 2001—04; asst. prof. neurosci., neurology Baylor Coll. Medicine, Houston, 2007—. Recipient First prize, Greek Math. Assn., 1981, 1982, Detur prize, Harvard Coll., 1984, Robbins prize, Harvard Physics GSAS, 1993, Leon Reznick Meml. prize, Harvard Med. Sch., 1997, Rsch. award, Mass. Gen. Hosp., 2005—06, Early Career award, Howard Hughes Med. Inst., 2006—, Dana Neuroimaging award, Dana Found., 2006—; Paul Dudley White fellowship, Harvard Med. Sch., 1990, Rsch. fellow, Howard Hughes Med. Inst., 1990—91, K08 fellowship, Nat. Eye Inst., 2002—07. Mem.: Am. phys. soc., AAAS, Mass. Med. Assn., Am. Acad. Neurology, Soc. neuroscience, Phi Beta Kappa. Office: Baylor Coll Medicine One Baylor Plaza Rm S517-MS: BCM295 Houston TX 77030 Business E-Mail: ssmirnakis@cns.bcm.edu.

SMISEK, JEFFERY A., air transportation executive; b. Washington, Aug. 17, 1954; married; 2 children. AB, Princeton U., 1976; JD, Harvard U., 1982. Bar: Mass., 1982, Tex. 1983. Ptnr., exec. v.p. Vinson & Elkins LLP, Houston, 1983-95; sr. v.p., gen. counsel Continental Airlines, Inc., Houston, 1995—96, exec. v.p., gen. counsel, sec., 1996—2001, exec. v.p., corp., sec., 2001—03, exec. v.p., 2003—04, pres., 2004—08, pres., COO, 2008—. Bd. dirs. Orbitz, Inc., 2003—, Continental Airlines, Inc., 2004—, Nat. Oilwell Varco, 2005—. Office: Continental Airlines Inc PO Box 4607 Houston TX 77210*

SMISKO, NICHOLAS RICHARD, bishop, educator; b. Perth Amboy, NJ, Feb. 23, 1936; s. Andrew and Anna (Totin) S. BTh, Christ the Saviour Sem., 1959; BA, U. Youngstown, 1961; Lic. in Theology, Halki (Greece) Sch. Theology, 1965. Ordained priest Carpatho-Russian Orthodox Greek Cath. Ch., 1959; elevated to rank of met. bishop, 1997. Pastorate Sts. Peter and Paul Ch., Windber, Pa., 1959-62; prefect of discipline Christ the Saviour Sem., Johnstown, Pa., 1963-65; pastor Sts. Peter and Paul Ch., Homer City, Pa., 1965-71, St. Michael's Ch., Clymer, Pa., 1971-72; pastorate St. Nicholas Ch., NYC, 1972-77; abbot Monastery of the Annunciation, Tuxedo Park, NY, 1978-83; bishop of Amissos Carpatho-Russian Orthodox Diocese, 1983—. Mem. del. Ecumenical Patriarchate World Coun. Chs. 6th Gen. Assembly, Vancouver, B.C., Can.; mem. standing conf. Canonical Orthodox Bishops in Ams.; active Orthodox-Cath. Consultation of Hierarchs. Mem. Halki Alumni Assn. Am., Christ the Saviour Sem. Alumni Assn., Am. Soc. Constantinople. Carpatho-Russian Orthodox. Home and Office: 312 Garfield St Johnstown PA 15906-2122

SMIT, NEIL, telecommunications industry executive; BS, Duke U.; M in internat. bus., Tufts U. Mgmt. positions Pillsbury Co.; regional v.p. Nabisco; with Am. Online, Inc., 2000—05, COO Mapquest.com, COO AOL Local, sr. v.p. product and programming team, exec. v.p. mem. services, 2002—03, exec. v.p. mem. devel., 2003—04, pres. access bus., 2004—05; pres., CEO Charter Comm., Inc., St. Louis, 2005—, also dir., 2005—. Served to lt. comdr. Navy SEALS USN. Office: Charter Comm Inc Ste 1000 12405 Powerscourt Dr Saint Louis MO 63131-3660

SMITH, A. ROBERT, editor, author; b. York, Pa., Feb. 13, 1925; s. Arthur R. and Inez (Dunnick) S.; m. Yvonne Franklin, 1945 (div. 1965); 1 child, Dana C.; m. Elizabeth McDowell Morgan, 1967 (div. 1988); children: Philip S. Morgan IV, Edward A. M. Morgan, Elizabeth A. Morgan; m. Jane Dreifus, 1993 (dec. 1999). BS, Juniata Coll., 1950; postgrad., George Washington U., 1950. Reporter Huntingdon (Pa.) Daily News, 1947, Evening Star, Washington, 1950; Washington corr. Eugene (Oreg.) Register-Guard, 1951-78, Portland Oregonian, 1952-72, King Broadcasting, 1976-78; assoc. editor Virginian-Pilot, Norfolk, 1978-83; editor Venture Inward, Assn. Rsch. and Enlightenment mag., Virginia Beach, Va., 1984—2003. Author: The Tiger in the Senate, 1962, Hugh Lynn Cayce: About My Father's Business, 1988, The Lost Memoirs of Edgar Cayce, 1997, Misdiagnosed: Was My Wife a Casualty of America's Medical Cold War?, 2001, No Soul Left Behind, 2005; co-author: (with Eric Sevareid and Fred J. Maroon) Washington: Magnificent Capital, 1965; (with James V. Giles) An American Rape, 1975 With USNR, 1943-46, PTO. E-mail: abob@cox.net.

SMITH, ABBIE OLIVER, college administrator, educator; b. Augusta, Ga., Jan. 31, 1931; d. Rowland Sheppard and Abigail Seabrook (Hanahan) Oliver; m. William Parkhurst Smith, Jr., July 2, 1953; children: William Parkhurst Smith, III, Oliver Hamilton. BS, George Washington U., 1953, MEd, 1958, EdDin Higher Edn., 1986. Tchr. St. Mary's Acad., Monroe, Mich., 1954-55; tchr., coach Washington-Lee H.S., Arlington, Va., 1955-58; homemaker, cmty. vol. Bethesda, Md., 1959-64; asst. professorial lectr. George Washington U., Washington, 1965-69, adminstr. continuing edn., 1969-80, asst. dean, dir., 1981-89, acting dean divsn. continuing edn., 1989-93, asst. v.p., asst. to dean institutional advancement, 1993—. Panelist TV series WETA, Washington; mem. exec. bd., newsletter editor Tng. Officers Conf., 1989—, chair charter expansion 1992—. Co-author: (workbook) Developing New Horizons for Women, 1975, Manual for Counselors for Developing New Horizons for Women, 1975. Mem. adv. bd. Washington Bd. Trade, 1975-77, women's branch adv. bd. State Nat. Bank, Bethesda, Md., 1978-81; collegiate adv. bd. Episcopal Diocese of Washington, 1977-79. Recipient Leadership in Adult Edn. award, 1976, GW award for outstanding contbn. to univ. life Office of GW Pres., 1991, Washington Women of Achievement, Washington Edn. TV Assn., 1980. Mem. Nat. U. Continuing Edn. Assn. (awards chair divsn. women's edn. 1977-78, nat. chair 1977-78, chair-elect divsn. part-time students program 1984-86, nat. chair 1984-86, chair coun. human resources 1985-86, nat. spl. com. on couns. and divsn. 1984-86, nat. exec. bd. 1984-86, nat. bd. dirs. 1984-98, nat. charters and bylaws coms. 1987-89, sec.-elect divsn. cert. and nontraditional degree programs 1987-89, chair-elect 1989-90, nat. chair 1990-91, nat. ann. planning coms. 1987, 92, sec. region II 1989-90, chair-elect, ann. conf. chair, single host instn. ann. conf. region II 1990-91, chair region II 1991-92, awards com. chair 1992, Walton S. Bittner Svc. Citation 1994, hon. mention for program catalog nat. divsn. mktg. 1988, Floyd B. Fisher Leadership award 1996), Phi Delta Kappa Internat. (G.W. chpt., v.p. for programs 1995-96, pres. 1996-97, newsletter editor 1977—. Newsletter Award Merit 1998-99, Outstanding Newsletter award 1999-2000, 2000-01). Democrat. Episcopalian. Avocations: writing, painting, swimming, dance, travel. Home: 3751 Jocelyn St NW Washington DC 20015-1836 Office: George Washington U 2134 G St NW Washington DC 20037-2797 E-mail: asmith@gwu.edu.

SMITH, ADA LAVERNE, state legislator; b. Amherst County, Va. d. Thomas and Lillian Smith. Grad., CUNY. Dep. clk. N.Y.C.; state senator N.Y. Legislature, Albany, 1988—, mem. various coms., ranking corp. commn. and authorities, 1994, minority whip, 1994—2003, chair Senate Dem. Conf., 2003—05, asst. Dem. leader, policy and adminstrn., 2005—. Mem. Senate Minority Puerto Rican and Hispanic Task Force. Trustee, life dir. Coll. Fund Baruch Coll. Recipient Outstanding Alumni award Baruch Coll. Mem. NY Assn. State Black and Puerto Rican Legislators, Baruch Coll. Alumni Assn. (pres., Disting. Svc. award, Outstanding Achievement award), Nat. Black Caucus of State Legislators (bd. dirs., vice chair telecomms. com.), Women in Govt. (state bd. dirs.). Office: NY State Senate Rm 808 Legis Office Bldg Albany NY 12247 Home: 1600 Weeping Willow Dr Apt H Lynchburg VA 24501-3963 Office Phone: 518-455-3531. E-mail: smith@senate.state.ny.us.

SMITH, ADAM See GOODMAN, GEORGE

SMITH, ADAM, United States Representative from Washington; b. Washington, June 15, 1965; s. Ben Smith; m. Sara Bickle-Eldridge, Aug. 1993; 2 children. BA, Fordham U., NY, 1987; JD, U. Wash., 1990. Driver United Parcel Svc., 1985-87; mem. Wash. State Senate, 1990-96; atty. Cromwell, Mendoza and Belur, 1991—92; asst. pros. atty. Seattle, 1993—95; pro tem judge, 1996; mem. US Congress from 9th Wash. dist., 1997—, mem. armed svcs. com., mem. internat. rels. com. Mem. Kent Drinking Driver Task Force, Highline Citizens for Schs., Kent Meridian HS Site-Based Coun.; bd. mem. Judson Pk. Retirement Home. Mem.: Kiwanis Internat. Democrat. Office: US House of Reps 2402 Rayburn House Office Bldg Washington DC 20515 Office Phone: 202-225-8901. Office Fax: 202-225-5893.*

SMITH, ADRIAN DEVAUN, architect; b. Chgo., Ill., Aug. 19, 1944; s. Alfred D. and Hazel (Davis) S.; m. Nancy L. Smith, Aug. 17, 1968; children: Katherine, Jason. Student, Tex. A&M U., 1962-66; BArch, U. Ill., Chgo., 1969. Registered architect, Ill., Mass., Fla. Design ptnr. Skidmore, Owings, & Merrill, Chgo., 1980—2003, cons. ptnr., 2003—06; founding ptnr. CEO Adrian Smith + Gordon Gill Arch., 2006—. Vis. faculty Sch. Architecture, U. Ill., Chgo., 1984; chmn. U. Ill. Sch. Archtl. Alumni Assn., AIA Jury on Inst. Honors; adv. jury AIA gold metal and architecture firm award, 2004; chmn. nat. AIA awards jury for architecture and 25 yr. award, 2004; chmn. Skidmore Owings Merrill Found., 1989-95; pres. Chgo. Ctrl. Area, 1997-99; bd. dirs. Greater State Street Coun. trustee; bd. govs. Sch. Art Inst. Chgo., 1999—; repr., RIBA British Archtl. Libr. Trust, British Schs. and Univ. Found.; dir., U. Ill. Alumni Found., 88-89. Designer numerous projects including 919 North Michigan Ave, Chgo., 1982, Chgo. Ctrl. Area Plan, 1984, 1992 Chgo. World's Fair, 1980-85, Olympia Ctr., Chgo., 1986, 222 N. LaSalle, Chgo., 1986, Art Inst. Chgo. 2nd Fl. Galleries, 1987, Arthur Anderson Tng. Ctr., St. Charles, Ill., 1987, Rowes Wharf, Boston, 1988 (Nat. AIA Honor award, 1994), AT&T Corp. Ctr., Chgo., 1989, NBC Tower at Cityfront Ctr., Chgo., 1989, 75 State St., Boston, 1989, Continental Bank First Fl. Renovation, Chgo., 1990, USG Hdqs., Chgo., 1991, Washington Univ. Psychology Bldg., Lab., & Animal Facility, St. Louis, 1996, Chgo. Transit Authority, Green Line Rehabilitation, Chgo., 1995, Heller Internat. Tower, Chgo., 1992, State St. Renovation, 1997 (AIA honor award urban design, 1998), Washington Univ. Arts & Scis. Bldg., St. Louis, Mo., 2000, Campus Crusade for Christ Internat., Orlando, Fla., 2000, Millennium Park, Chgo., 2002 (AIA Honor award, 2006), 7 South Dearborn Tower, Chgo., 2002, Manulife Fin., Boston, 2003, GM Global Hdqrs. at Resaissance Ctr., Detroit, 2003, Lakeshore East, Chgo., 2004 (AIA Honor award, 2004), Trump Internat. Hotel & Tower, Chgo., 2006, Bally of Switzerland, 1982, Hdqs. Canary Wharf Fin. Ctr., London, Eng., 1988, United Gulf Bank, Manama, Bahrain, 1986, 10 Fleet Place, Ludgate Office Bldg., London, 1992, Aramco Hdqrs., Dhahran, Saudi Arabia, 1993, Xiamen Posts & Telecommunications Bldg., China, 1994, Frankfurter Allee, 1991, Tower Palace III, Seoul, Korea, 1996, Kowloon MTR Tower, Feasibility, Hong Kong, 1997, Pidemco GSCP MSCP Towers, Singapore, 1997, McGraw Hill European Headquarters, Canary Wharf (FC-2), London, 1990, Canary Wharf, London, 1991, Canary Wharf (DS4), 2002, CSFB European Headquarters, Canary Wharf (DSI), 2002, Morgan Stanley Headquarters for Europe (HQI), Canary Wharf, 2002, Burj Dubai Tower (World's Tallest Bldg., 2009), United Arab Emirates, Jin Mao Tower (World's Tallest Mixed-Use Project), Shanghai, China (Nat. AIA award for interior architecture 2000), 1998, BankBoston Hdqrs., Sao Paulo, Brazil, 2000, 201 Broadgate, London, Eng., 2008, Nanjing Guozi Greenland Fin. Ctr., Nanjing, China, Chemsunny Office Bldg., Beijing, 2008, Shanghai Grand Office Tower, 2008, Shanghai, Pearl River Zero Energy Tower, Guanghou, China, Masdar Hdqs., Dubai, 2008; author: Monograph of Adrian P. Smith, 2002, The Architecture of Adrian Smith 1980-2006: Toward a Sustainable Future, contbr. articles to profl. jours.; subject numerous pubs. in architecture. Mem. com. Task Force for New City Plan, Chgo., Light Up Chgo., Ctrl. Area Com. Task Force Chgo.; chmn. Senator Richard A. Newhouse Bldg. Competition Jury, 1982, Progressive Architecture Design Jury, 1985; bd. dirs. State St. Coun.; lifetime gov., Urban Land Inst. Found.; trustee, Chgo. Architecture Found., 93-99, Bldg. Experiences Trust, 91-95. Recipient silver award, Ill. Ctr. Masonry Coun., 1981, Gold award, 1982, Urban Design and Planning First award, 32nd Annual Progressive Architecture Mag., 1986, Energy award program, Am. Refrigerating & Air Conditioning Engrs., NBC 1988, AT&T 1988, Build Am. award, Assoc. General Contractors of Am. and Motorola, 1989, Excellence on the Waterfront Honor award, 1990, Civic Trust award, Ludgate Office Complex, 1994, Alumni Achievement award, U. Ill., 1995, First Prize, European Commercial Property Development Awards, 1995, Excellence in Engring., ASHRAE, 1995, spl. achievement award, Internat. Downtown Assn., 1997, Best Structure award, Structural Engineers Assn. Ill. 1998, Architect Creation award, World Architect Conf., 2001, Merit award, Illuminating Engring. Soc. N. Am., 2001, award of excellence, ULI, 2004, Pres. award, Korea Inst. Architects, 2005, Am. Architecture award, Chgo. Athenaeum; named Best of Competition, Inst. Bus. Designers, Interior Design Mag., Bally Switzerland, Chgo., 1982. Fellow AIA, chmn. nat. jury arch. and 25 yr. award 2004, Banco de Occidente, 1980, 81, Interior Architecture Award, Citation of Merit, 1984, Interior Architecture award, 1989, Disting. Bldg. award 1981, 87, 90, 91, 92, 94, 97, 98, 2003, 04, 06, Nat. Honor award, 1988, 94, 98, 2004), Royal Inst. Brit. Architects, Archtl. Registration Coun., U.K., Nat. Coun. Archtl. Registration Bds., Architecture Soc. of Art Inst. Chgo., Chgo. Arch. Found., Chgo. Archtl. Club, Urban Found. (bd. trustees) University Club, Arts Club; Am. Acad. Rome (Midwest dir., 85-86); mem. Economic Club Chgo. Office: Adrian Smith & Gordon Gill Architecture 111 W Monroe St #2300 Chicago IL 60603 Office Phone: 312-920-1888. Office Fax: 312-920-1775.

SMITH, ADRIAN M., United States Representative from Nebraska, real estate agent; b. Scottsbluff, Nebr., Dec. 19, 1970; BS in Mktg. Edn., U. Nebr., 1993; student, Portland State U. Legis. page Nebr. Legislature, 1992; mem. Nebr. Legislature from 48th dist., Lincoln, 1998—; staff internat., mktg. specialist Nebrs. Gov.'s Office, 1992; rsch. asst. U. Nebr. Found., 1992-93; educator, staff devel. project mgr. Ednl. Svc. Unit 13, 1994-97; real estate agt., mktg. specialist Buyers Realty, 1997—; mem. US Congress from 3rd Nebr. dist., 2007—, asst. whip, 2007—. Mem. We. Nebr. Regional Airport Ops. Bd., Wyo-Braska Mus. Natural Hist., Scotts Bluff County Visitors Adv. Com., 1995—96, Gering City Coun., 1994—98; chmn. land use task force Vision 2020; bd. dirs. Twin Cities Devel.; mem. Calvary Meml. Evang. Free Ch. Mem.: Farm & Ranch Mus. Assn., Riverside Zool. Soc., N. Platte Valley Hist. Soc., Scotts Bluff County Bd. Realtors, Scotts Bluff Kiwanis Club (bd. dirs. Camp Kiwanis). Republican. Office: US House Reps 503 Cannon House Office Bldg Washington DC 20515 Office Phone: 202-225-6435. Office Fax: 202-225-0207.*

SMITH, A.J., professional sports team executive; b. Feb. 28, 1949; m. Susan Smith; children: Andrea, Kyle. Grad. in Health and Phys. Edn., Ky. Wesleyan Coll., Owensboro, 1971. Tchr. health and phys. edn. Providence Jr. HS Sys., 1971—85; asst. coach Cranston West HS, RI, 1971—76, U. RI, 1978; wide receiver Ea. Football League Attleboro Kings, Mass., 1972—74; head coach Ea. Football League RI Kings, 1976; vol. part-time scout NFL NY Giants, 1977; part-time scout NFL New Eng. Patriots, 1978—80, NFL Houston Oilers, 1981; scouting position US Football League Chgo. Blitz., 1982—83, US Football League Pitts. Maulers, 1984; dir. pro pers. NFL San Diego Chargers, 1985—86, asst. gen. mgr., dir. pro pers., 2001—03, exec. v.p., gen. mgr., 2003—; area scout NFL Buffalo Bills, 1987—89, asst. dir. coll. scouting, 1989—93, dir. pro pers., 1993—2000. Named NFL Exec. of Yr., Pro Football Weekly, 2004, Profl. Football Writers of Am., 2004, FoxSports-.com, 2004, CBSSportsline.com, 2004; named to Am. Football Assn. Minor/Semi-Pro Football Hall of Fame, 1990. Office: San Diego Chargers PO Box 609609 San Diego CA 92160-9609*

SMITH, ALAN DAVID, quantitative and natural sciences educator; b. Orrville, Ohio, May 25, 1952; s. Donald H. and Joy C. (Collins) S.; m. Peggy A. Cole, Feb. 4, 1978; children: Angela C., Amber A. BA, BS, U. Akron, 1975, MS in Tech. Edn., 1978, MS, 1980; BBA, Eastern Ky. U., 1983; MS in Engring., U. Ky., 1983; PhD, U. Akron, 1980, MS in Engring., 1981; MBA, MSBA, Robert Morris Coll., 1991-90. Cert. profl. geol. scientist. Sci. tchr. Hudson (Ohio) Sch. Dist., 1970-77; geotech. engr. cons. ind., Akron, Ohio, 1977-80; asst. prof. geosci. Eastern Ky. U., Richmond, 1980-83, asst. prof. bus. adminstrn., 1983-85, dir. coal mining adminstrn, 1983-85; assoc. prof. quantitative and natural scis. Robert Morris Coll., Pitts., 1985-94, prof. quantitative and natural scis., 1994—. Contbr. over 600 articles to profl. jours. and 250 presentations. High sch. wrestling coach OHSAA, Western Res. Wrestling Assn., 1972—; surface mining reclamation trainer U.S. Bur. of Mines, Frankfort, Ky., 1980-85; Island Creek Coal Rock mech. engr. Island Creek Coacl Co., Lexington, Ky., 1983-84; asst. geologist Ky. Geol. Survey, Lexington, 1983-85; geotech. cons. San Rose Mineral, Inc., Lake City, Tenn., 1984; asst. wrestling coach St. Thomas Aquinas H.S., Louisville, Ohio, 1996-97; mem. Alliance (Ohio) Jr. Chamber chpt., 1986—. Fellow Mining Engrs. of Am. Inst. Mining Engrs.; mem. Ohio Acad. of Sci., Ky. Acad. Sci., W.Va. Acad. of Sci., Collegiate Assn. Mining Educators, S.W. Decision Scis. Inst., S.E. Inst. for Ops. Rsch. & Mgmt. Sci., Sigma Xi, Gamma Theta Upsilon, Sigma Gamma Epsilon, Sigma Beta Delta. Democrat. Home: 756 Vincent Blvd Alliance OH 44601-3958 Office: Robert Morris Coll Dept Quantitative Scis Pittsburgh PA 15219-3099

SMITH, ALAN JAY, computer science educator, consultant; b. NYC, Apr. 10, 1949; s. Harry and Elsie Smith. SB, MIT, 1971; MS, Stanford U., Calif., 1973, PhD in Computer Sci., 1974. From asst. prof. to full prof. U. Calif., Berkeley, 1974—; assoc. editor ACM Trans. on Computers Systems, 1982-93. Vice-chmn. elec. engring. and computer sci. dept. U. Calif., Berkeley, 1982-84; nat. lectr. ACM, 1985-86; mem. editl. bd. Jour. Microprocessors and Microsystems, 1988—2005, Microprocessor Report, 2005-07; subject area editor Jour. Parallel and Distbn. Computing, 1989—; mem. IFIP working group 7.3; program chmn. Sigmetrics 89, Performance 1989, Hot Chips Symposium, 1990, 94, 97. 2005. Recipient AA Michaelson award, Comp. Measurement Group, 2003, Harry Goode award, IEEE computer Soc., 2006. Fellow: AAAS, IEEE (disting. visitor 1986—87, Reynold Johnson Info. Storage Sys. award 2008), Assn. for Computing Machinery (chmn. spl. interest group on ops. sys. 1983—87, nat. lectr. 1985—86, bd. dirs. spl. interest group on performance evaluation 1989—89, chmn. spl. interest group on computer architecture 1991—93, bd. dirs. spl. interest group on computer architecture 1993—2003); mem.: Computer Measurement Group. Office: U Calif Dept Computer Sci Berkeley CA 94720-1776

SMITH, ALAN WADE, music educator; b. Elizabeth City, NC, Oct. 8, 1964; s. Gilbert Richard and Marilyn Kay Smith. AA in Music Edn., St. Petersburg Jr. Coll., Fla., 1986; BS, U. South Fla., 1990. Cert. Secondary Social Studies Edn. S.C., 2005, Fla., 2004. Social studies tchr. Seminole (Fla.) Mid. Sch., 1993—2004; global studies tchr. Dorman HS Freshman Campus, Roebuck, SC, 2004—06; assoc. marching band dir. Dorman HS, Roebuck, SC, 2004—06. Visual designer (marching band competitive field shows) Marching Band Competitive Field Show (Bands of Am. Regional Champions/Nat. Finalists). Recipient Tchr. of the Yr., Seminole Mid. Sch., 1997. Mem.: Music Educator's Nat. Conf., Nat. Coun. for Social Studies (assoc.). Office: Dorman HS Freshman Campus 1225 Cavalier Way Roebuck SC 29376 Home: 13511 Hacienda Dr Largo FL 33774-4610 Personal E-mail: alan88888@aol.com. Business E-Mail: smithaw@spart6.org.

SMITH, ALBERT CROMWELL, JR., investment company executive, writer; b. Norfolk, Va., Dec. 6, 1925; s. Albert Cromwell and Georgie (Foreman) Smith; m. Laura Thaxton, Oct. 25, 1952; children: Albert, Elizabeth, Laura. BSCE, Va. Mil. Inst., 1949; MS in Govtl. Adminstrn., George Washington U., 1965; MBA, Pepperdine U., 1975; PhD in Bus. Adminstrn., LaSalle U., 1994. Enlisted USMC, 1944, advanced through grades to col., 1970, comdr. inf. platoons, cos., landing force; assigned to staffs, U.K. Joint Force, U.S. Sec. Navy, Brit. Staff Coll., Marine Staff Coll., U.K. Staff Coll. and Latimer Staff Coll.;

advisor, analyst amphibious sys. USMC; ret., 1974; pres. A. Cromwell-Smith, Ltd., Charlottesville, Va., 1973; head broker, cons. A. Cromwell Smith, Investments, La Jolla and Coronado, Calif., 1975—. Author: The Individual Investor in Tomorrow's Stock Market, 1977, The Little Guy's Stock Market Survival Guide, 1979, rev. edit., 2000, Wake Up Detroit: The EVs are Coming, 1982, The Little Guy's Tax Survival Guide, 1984, Little Guy's Real Estate Success Guide, 1990, Little Guy's Stock Market Success Guide, 1992, Little Guy's Stock Market Future Effectiveness, 1994, The Little Guy's Sailboat Success, 1996, The Little Guy's Business Success, 1997, Business Success, 1997, Stock Market Success, 1998, Semper Fidelis in Peace and War, 1999, revised edit., 2003, Sailboat Success, 1999, Tax Survival Guide, 1999, The EVs are Coming, 1999, Real Estate Success, 2000, The EVs and Hybrids Are Here, 2005; contbr. articles to profl. jours. Bd. dirs. La Jolla Reps., 1975—76; vestryman St. Martin's Episcopal Ch., 1971—73. Decorated Legion of Merit with oak leaf cluster with V device, Bronze Star with V device with oak leaf cluster, Air medal with two oak leav clusters, Purple Heart, Vietnamese Galantry Cross with gold star. Mem.: VFW, SAR, ASCE, So. Calif. Options Soc., Stockbrokers Soc., Coronado Bd. Realtors, San Diego Bd. Realtors, Calif. Assn. Realtors, Nat. Assn. Realtors, Mil. Order Purple Heart. Address: 1810 Ave del Mundo # 106 Coronado CA 92118 Office Phone: 619-435-0079.

SMITH, ALEX (ALEXANDER DOUG SMITH), professional football player; b. Seattle, Wash., May 7, 1984; s. Douglas D. and Pam Smith. BS in Econ., Utah U., 2003. Quarterback San Francisco 49ers, 2005—. Founder Alex Smith Found., 2005—. Named Nat. Player Yr., The Sporting News, 2004, Mountain West Conf. Player of Yr., 2004. Achievements include being the first overall selection in the 2005 NFL Draft. Office: San Francisco 49ers Marie P DeBartolo Sports Ctr 4949 Centennial Blvd Santa Clara CA 95054

SMITH, ALEXANDRA HELENA, microbiologist, director; d. Frenk Wiederhold and Ineke Wiederhold-Ris; m. Johann C. Smith, Apr. 8, 1995; children: Jared Chad, Taryn Jade. PhD, U. Ill., Urbana Champaign, 2003. Rsch. microbiologist Agrl. Rsch. Coun., Pretoria, South Africa, 1991—2002; rsch. asst. U. Ill., 1997—2002; postdoc. rschr. Southwestern Med. Ctr., Dallas, 2002—06; dir. ruminant rsch. Danisco (formerly Agtech Products Inc.), Waukesha, Wis., 2006—. Mem.: Am. Soc. Microbiology. Office: Danisco W227 N752 Westmound Dr Waukesha WI 53186 Business E-Mail: xandra.smith@danisco.com.

SMITH, ALISON LEIGH, lawyer; b. Brownsville, Tex., Sept. 24, 1952; d. Arthur Lee and June (Allen) Smith; m. Dean A. Burkhardt, Apr. 24, 1981. B in Journalism summa cum laude, U. Tex., 1974, JD cum laude, 1977. Bar: Tex. 1977, US Dist. Ct. (so. dist.) Tex. 1978, US Ct. Appeals (5th cir.) 1981, US Dist. Ct. (no. dist.) Tex. 1987, US Ct. Appeals (DC cir.) 1989. Assoc. Vinson & Elkins LLP, Houston, 1977-84, ptnr., 1984—89, 1991—2004; dep. asst. atty. gen. antitrust divsn. U.S. Dept. Justice, Washington, 1989-91; ptnr. Dewey Ballantine LLP, Houston, 2004—05, Haynes and Boone, LLP, Houston, 2005—. Adj. prof. law U. Tex., Austin, 1992-93. Alternate del. Rep. Nat. Conv., New Orleans, 1988; mem. ethics com. City of Houston, 1988-89; chair Mayor's Animal Protection Task Force, 2005. Mem. ABA (antitrust law sect., chair transp. industry com., 1992-95, co-chmn. pvt. antitrust litig. com. 2001-04, long range planning task force, 2002, vice chmn. Sherman Act sect. one com. 2004-05, econ. evidence task force 2005-06, editl. bd. State Antitrust Practice and Statutes, 2006-, litig. sect. chair, 1999-2000, animal law sect. chair 2008-09), Am. Law Inst., Tex. Bar Found., Houston Bar Assn. Home: 2125 Bolsover St Houston TX 77005-1617 Office: Haynes and Boone LLP 1221 McKinney Ste 2100 Houston TX 77010 Home Phone: 713-520-1979; Office Phone: 713-547-2673. Business E-Mail: alison.smith@haynesboone.com.

SMITH, ALLIE MAITLAND, retired engineering educator; b. Lumberton, NC, June 9, 1934; s. Allie McCoy and Emma Hattie (Wright) S.; m. Sarah Louise Whitlock, June 16, 1957; children: Sara Leianne, Hollis Duval, Meredith Lorren. BME with honors, N.C. State U., Raleigh, 1956, MS, 1961, PhD, 1966. Assoc. engr. Martin Co., Balt., 1956-57; devel. engr. Western Electric Co., 1957-60; mem. tech. staff Bell Tel. Labs., Burlington, NC, 1960-62; instr., then asst. prof. extension N.C. State U., 1958-62; rsch. project engr. Rsch. Triangle Inst., Durham, NC, 1962-66; rsch. supr. Sverdrup/ARO, Inc., Arnold Air Force Sta., Tenn., 1966-79; adj. prof. U. Tenn., Tullahoma, 1967-79; prof. mech. engring. U. Miss., University, 1979—2008, dean Sch. Engring., 1979—2000. Bd. dirs., scholarship bd. Miss. Mineral Resources Inst.; exec. chmn. 14th conf. Southeastern Conf. on Theoretical and Applied Mechanics, exec. com. 13th-16th confs., ops. com. and policy com., 1990-99, session chair, 1994; organizing com., internat. sci. adv. bd., plenary session presiding officer Internat. Conf. on Hydrosci. and Engring., 1993, 95; organizing com., plenary session chair Conf. on Mgmt. of Landscapes Disturbed by Channel Incision, 1997; keynote lecture and plenary sessions chair, 3rd Internat. Conf. on Hydrosci. and Engring., Berlin, 1998 Author: Fundamentals of Silicon Integrated Device Technology, Vol. I: Oxidation, Diffusion and Epitaxy, 1967, also articles, revs.; editor: Radiative Transfer and Thermal Control, 1976, Thermophysics of Spacecraft and Outer Planet Entry Probes, 1977, Fundamentals and Applications of Radiation Heat Transfer, 1987, Developments in Theoretical and Applied Mechanics, Vol. XIV, 1988, Radiation Heat Transfer: Fundamentals and Applications, 1990, Fundamentals of Radiation Heat Transfer, 1991, Radiative Heat Transfer: Theory and Applications, 1993, Solution Methods for Radiative Heat Transfer in Participating Media, 1996, Radiative Heat Transfer, 1997. Fellow AIAA (chmn. thermophysics tech. com. 1975-77, ASME (aerospace heat transfer com. 1975-2007; chmn. radiative heat transfer I and II sessions, Pitts. 2000, chmn. radiation heat transfer II session, St. Louis, 2002, chmn. terrestrial energy sys. tech. com. 1979-81, chmn. confs. 1975, 79, assoc. editor jour. 1975-77, 1986-2007, nat. publ. com. 1979-83, Nat. Thermophysics award 1978, Hermann Oberth award 1984-85, Space Shuttle Flag Challenger plaque 1984, supernumerary dir. Ala.-Miss. sect. 1994-2000); mem. AAUP, NSPE (pres. N.E. Miss. chpt. 1990-91), Am. Soc. Engring. Edn. (host Nat. Engring. Deans' Inst. 1991), NY Acad. Scis., Sigma Xi, Phi Kappa Phi, Tau Beta Pi, Pi Tau Sigma, Upsilon Pi Epsilon, Sigma Pi (scholar 1955), Order of the Engr., Notable. Achievements include discovery of anomalous refraction maxima phenomenon. Home: 305 South Bald Head Wyhd PO Box 3319 Bald Head Island NC 28461-7003 Home Phone: 910-454-9554.

SMITH, AMY B., mechanical engineer, educator; b. Lexington, Mass. BSc, MIT, 1984, MSE, 1995. Vol. Peace Corps, Botswana, 1986—90; inventor, instr. MIT Edgerton Ctr., Cambridge, Mass., 2000—. Founder Designs for Developing Countries Project, MIT; co-founder MIT IDEAS competition (Innovation, Devel., Enterprise, Action, Svc.), Internat. Devel. Initiative. Recipient JFK Peace Corps Volunteer of the Yr. Award, 1988, Carroll Wilson Award, 1994, BF Goodrich Collegiate Inventor's Award, 1999, Lemelson-MIT Student prize, 2000; named a MacArthur Fellow, 2004. Office: MIT Edgerton Ctr Rm 4-405 77 Mass Ave Cambridge MA 02139 Business E-Mail: abs@mit.edu.

SMITH, AMY D., legislative staff member; b. Kans. MBA, Emporia, Kans. Staff mem., Senator Bob Dole US Senate, Washington; legis. asst., Rep. Pat Toomey US House of Reps., Washington, legis. dir., Rep. Brian Bilbray, 2006—08, chief of staff to Rep. Scott Garrett, 2008—; dep. asst. sec. US Treasury Dept., Washington, 2001—03; lobbyist Bartlett, Bendall and Kadesh, LLC, 2003—04. Republican. Office: 137 Cannon House Office Bldg Washington DC 20515 Office Phone: 202-225-4465. Office Fax: 202-225-9048.*

SMITH, ANNE DAY, writer; b. Bath, Maine, Oct. 14, 1937; d. Harry L. Day; m. Gerald H. Smith, Dec. 21, 1957; children: David, Frederick, Stephen. AA, Lasell Coll., Auburndale, Mass., 1957. Contbg. editor Nutshell News Mag., 1979-96; freelance writer various newspapers and mags., 1979—. Author: Interior Design in Miniature, 1986, Masters in Miniature, 1987, The Andrews Collection, 1988, The Period Rooms of Ruth McChesney, 1997; contbg. editor Dollhouse Miniatures mag., 1996—; contbr. articles to publs. Mem. Nat. Assn. Miniature Enthusiasts, Acad. Honor (chmn. 1996-2000), Internat. Guild Miniature Artisans. Avocations: reading, research, travel, antique collecting.

SMITH, ANNE MARIE SCHOEFER, application developer; d. Walter Hellmann Schoefer and Helen MacNeil Fox; children: Jonathan Michael, Jessica Lauren, Matthew Andrew. BA, LaSalle U., Phila., 1980. Cert. artificial intelligence DARPA, Wash. D.C., 1986; programming and macro, Sas Inst., Cary NC, 1995, software engring., GE, Valley Forge, PA, 1984. Software engr. cons. Rainbow Comm. and Software, Palm Beach, Fla., 1986—. Book, Poetry for Lovers and Romanticists: Art in Poetry and Photography. Tour guide MacAuthor Pk., Palm Beach Gardens, Fla., 2003—04. Recipient Alumni Honor Soc. Kappa Mu Epsilon, LaSalle Coll., 1979—80. Mem.: PhilaSUG (assoc.; bd. mem., sec. 1995—2000). R-Conservative. Achievements include development of webpages with poems, art and music. Avocations: travel, swimming, writing, sports. Personal E-mail: rainbowangel@myway.com. Business E-Mail: rainbow_softwr@geocities.com.

SMITH, ANNE SISSON, private school educator; d. Howard and Margaret Sisson; m. Robert Herschel Smith; children: Margaret, Katherine, Claire Taylor. BA, Birmingham-So. Coll., 1966; MA, U. Mobile, Ala., 1989. Cert. tchr. Ala. Dept. chair UMS-Wright Prep. Sch., Mobile, 1990—. Former pres. Mobile Opera Guild, 1987—88. Named Nobel Tchr. of Distinction, Nat. Soc. H.S. Scholars, 2004. Mem.: Nat. Sci. Tchrs. Assn. (assoc.), Am. Chem. Soc. (assoc.), Mortar Bd. (assoc.), Kappa Delta Epsilon (assoc.). Office: UMS-Wright Prep Sch 65 N Mobile St Mobile AL 36607

SMITH, ANNICK, writer; b. Paris, May 11, 1936; came to U.S., 1937; d. Stephen and Helene Deutch; m. David James Smith (dec. 1974); children: Eric, Stephen, Alex, Andrew. Student, Cornell Univ., 1954-55, U. Chgo., 1955-57; BA, U. Wash., 1961. Editor U. Wash. Press, Seattle, 1961-64, Montana Bus. Quarterly, U. Montana, Missoula, 1971-72; founding bd. mem. Sundance Film Inst., Sundance, Utah, 1981-85; founding mem. Ind. Film Project, NYC, 1981-84; acting dir. Montana Com. for the Humanities, Missoula, 1983-84; devel. dir. Hellgate Writers, Inc., Missoula, 1986-96; creative dir. Yellow Bay Writers Workshop, U. Montana Continuing Edn. Dept, Missoula, 1987-98. Freelance filmmaker, producer, arts administrator, writer, Mont., 1974—; past H.S. tchr., cmty. organizer, environ. worker. Exec. prodr. Heartland, 1981; co-prodr. A River Runs Through It, 1992; co-editor: (with William Kittredge) The Last Best Place, (Susan O'Connor) The Wide Open; author: Homestead, 1994, Big BlueStem A Journey into the Tall Grass, 1996, In This We Are Native, 2001; contbr. to anthologies including Best Am. Short Stories, 1992. Recipient Western Heritage award Cowboy Hall of Fame, 1981; Mont. Humanites award Mont. Com. for Humanities, 1988, Okla. Book award, 1997, Bancroft Prize Denver Pub. Libr., 1998. Mem. Trout Unlimited, Blackfoot Challenge. Democrat. Office: 898 Bear Creek Rd Bonner MT 59823

SMITH, ARLAN ROBERT, plastic and reconstructive surgeon; b. Surabaja, Indonesia, Aug. 3, 1948; arrived in Holland, 1954; m. Paulina Jacoba de Jong, May 25, 1990; children: Darryl Nathaniël, Beau Aurora Fabiana, Chloé Aphrodite Zoë. Student, St. Ignatius Coll., Amsterdam, The Netherlands, 1961-66; PhD, U. Amsterdam, The Netherlands, 1972, MD, 1974. Cert. plastic and reconstructive surgeon. Gen. surgery tng. dept gen. surgery U. Maastricht, The Netherlands, 1975-79; clin. and rsch. fellow Mass. Gen. Hosp., Harvard Med. Sch., Boston, 1977-79; specialist in plastic and reconstructive surgery dept. plastic surgery U. Hosp. Dijkzigt Rotterdam, The Netherlands, 1979-82, chef de clinique in microsurgery and hand surgery dept. plastic and reconstructive surgery, 1979-86; head dept. plastic and reconstructive surgery Holy Hosp. Vlaardingen, The Netherlands, 1985-96; vis. prof. plastic and reconstructive surgery U. Kristen Idonesia Jakarta, Indonesia, 1989-91; dir. and owner Clinic Holystaete Vlaardingen, Netherlands, 1991—. Contbr. articles to profl. jours. Mem. Dutch Soc. for Hand Surgery, Dutch Soc. Esthetic Surgery, Dutch Soc. Plastic and Reconstructive Surgery, Internat. Microsurg. Soc., Found. Moshe Yemin clinic Holystaete (chmn. bd.), the Netherlands. Avocations: gardening, pre-Columbian art, modern art, Egyptian and African art. Office: Clinic Holystaete Churchillsingel 480 3137XB Vlaardingen Netherlands Business E-Mail: info@kliniekholystaete.nl. E-mail: abr.smith@planet.nl.

SMITH, ARTHUR B., JR., lawyer; b. Abilene, Tex., Sept. 11, 1944; s. Arthur B. and Florence B. (Baker) S.; m. Marya Argetsinger, 1968 (div. 1996); children: Arthur C., Sarah R.; m. Tracey L. Truesdale, 1999; children: Thomas A. BS, Cornell U., 1966; JD, U. Chgo., 1969. Bar: Ill. 1969, N.Y. 1976. Assoc. Vedder, Price, Kaufman & Kammholz, Chgo., 1969-74; asst. prof. labor law N.Y. State Sch. Indls. and Labor Rels., Cornell U., 1975-77; ptnr. Vedder, Price, Kaufman & Kammholz, Chgo., 1977-86; founding mem. Murphy, Smith & Polk, Chgo., 1986-98; shareholder Ogletree, Deakins, Chgo., 1999—. Guest. lectr. Northwestern U. Grad. Sch. Mgmt., 1979, Sch. Law, spring 1980; chmn. hearing bd. Ill. Atty. Registration and Disciplinary Commn. Author: Employment Discrimination Law Cases and Materials, 6th edit., 2006, Construction Labor Relations, 1984, supplement, 1993; co-editor-in-chief: 1976 Annual Supplement to Morris, The Developing Labor Law, 1977; chpt. editor: The Developing Labor Law, 5th edit.; contbr. articles to profl. jours. Recipient award for highest degree of dedication and excellence in tchg. N.Y. State Sch. Indsl. and Labor Rels., Cornell U., 1977; listed in The Best Lawyers in Am., Leading Lawyers, Chambers USA. Fellow Coll. Labor and Employment Lawyers; mem. ABA (co-chmn. com. on devel. law under Nat. Labor Rels. Act, Sect. Labor Rels. Law 1976-77), N.Y. State Bar Assn., Phi Eta Sigma, Phi Kappa Phi, Union League Club Chgo. Presbyterian. Office: Ogletree Deakins et al 2 First National Plz Fl 25 Chicago IL 60603 Office Phone: 312-558-1230. Business E-Mail: Arthur.Smith@odnss.com.

SMITH, ARTHUR EDWARD, JR., lawyer; b. Oct. 8, 1949; s. Arthur and Audre Smith; m. Janis O'Hara; children: Gregory, Jeffrey. BA in Biology, Columbia U., 1971, MA in Environ. Sci., 1972, MS in Environ. Sci., 1973; JD with distinction, U. Puget Sound, 1976. Bar: Wash. 1976. Assoc. regional counsel Region V, EPA, Chgo., 1976-91; spl. asst. US Atty. (no. dist.) Ill., 1989; environ. officer, counsel NIPSCO Industries (now NiSource), Merrillville, Ind., 1991—2000; sr. v.p., environ. counsel NiSource Inc., Merrillville, Ind., 2000—08; pres. Sustainable Futures LLC. Recipient bronze medal EPA, 1985, 91, Silver medal Am. Gas Assn., 2007; environ. fellow Columbia U. 1972; scholar U. Puget Sound. Home: 300 S Ashland Ave La Grange IL 60525-6308 Office Phone: 708-822-3982. Business E-Mail: sustainable_futures@mac.com.

SMITH, ARTHUR JOHN STEWART, physicist, researcher; b. Victoria, BC, Can., June 28, 1938; s. James Stewart and Lillian May (Geernaert) S.; m. Norma Ruth Askeland, May 20, 1966; children: Peter James, Ian Alexander. BA, U. B.C., 1959, MSc., 1961; PhD, Princeton U., 1966. Postdoctoral fellow Deutsches Electronen-Synchrotron, Hamburg, Germany, 1966—67; mem. faculty dept. physics Princeton U., 1967—, prof., 1978—, Class of 1909 prof., 1992—, assoc. chmn. dept., 1979—83, chmn. dept. physics, 1990—98, chair Rsch. Bd., 2005—, dean rsch., 2006—. Vis. scientist Brookhaven Nat. Lab., 1967—, chair sci. and tech. steering com. Brookhaven Sci. Assocs., 1997—2005, bd. dirs., 2005—; vis. scientist Fermilab, 1974—, Stanford Linear Accelerator Ctr., 1996—, vis. prof., 2000—02, spokesperson BaBar experiment, 2000—02. Assoc. editor Phys. Rev. Letters, 1986-89; contbr. articles to profl. jours. Fellow Am. Phys. Soc. (chmn. divsn. of particles and fields 1991). Achievements include research on experimental high-energy particle physics; kaon decays, physics of the B particles and quark structure of hadrons. Home: 4 Ober Rd Princeton NJ 08540-4918 Office: PO Box 708 Princeton NJ 08544-0001

SMITH, ARTHUR KITTREDGE, JR., academic administrator, political scientist, educator; b. Derry, NH, Aug. 15, 1937; s. Arthur Kittredge and Rena Belle (Roberts) S.; m. June Mary Dahar, Nov. 28, 1959; children: Arthur, Valerie, Meredith. BS, U.S. Naval Acad., 1959; MA, U. N.H., 1966; PhD, Cornell U., 1970. Vis. prof. El Colegio de Mexico, Mexico City, 1968-69; asst. prof. polit. sci. SUNY-Binghamton, 1970-74, assoc. prof., 1974-84, prof., 1984-88, provost for grad. studies and research, 1976-83, v.p. for adminstrn., 1982-88; prof. govt. and internat. studies U. S.C., Columbia, 1988-91, exec. v.p. for acad. affairs, provost, 1988-90, 91, interim pres., 1990-91; pres., prof. polit. sci. U. Utah, Salt Lake City, 1991-97; chancellor U. Houston Sys., 1997—2003; pres. U. Houston, 1997—2003, prof., 2003—. Author: (with Claude E. Welch, Jr.) Military Role and Rule: Perspectives on Civil-Military Relations, 1975; contbr. articles to profl. jours. Officer USN, 1959—65. Lehman fellow, 1966-69, NDEA fellow, 1969-70 Mem. Am. Polit. Sci. Assn., L.Am. Studies Assn., Inter-Univ. Sem. on Armed Forces and Soc., Am. Coun. on Edn., World Affairs Coun. (pres. Binghamton chpt. 1976-76), Bus.-Higher Edn. Forum, Phi Beta Kappa, Pi Sigma Alpha, Omicron Delta Kappa, Phi Delta Kappa, Beta Gamma Sigma, Phi Kappa Phi. Office: Univ Houston 4500 University Dr Rm 2000K Houston TX 77204-6056 Office Phone: 832-443-3008.

SMITH, ARTHUR LEE, lawyer; b. Davenport, Iowa, Dec. 19, 1941; s. Harry Arthur Smith and Ethel (Hoffman) Duerre; m. Georgia Mills, June 12, 1965 (dec. Jan. 1984); m. Jean Bowler, Aug. 4, 1984; children: Juliana, Christopher, Andrew, Wendy. BA, Augustana Coll., Rock Island, Ill., 1964; MA, Am. U., 1968; JD, Washington U., St. Louis, 1971. Bar: Mo 1971, DC 1983. Telegraph editor Davenport Morning Democrat, 1962-64; ptnr. Peper Martin Jensen Maichel & Hetlage, 1971-95, Husch & Eppenberger, St. Louis, 1995—2008, Husch Blackwell Sanders LLP, 2008—. Arbitrator Nat Asn Security Dealers, 1980—, Am Arbitration Assn, 1980—2004; dir. St. Louis Bar Found., 2005—09, v.p., 2005—09. Columnist: St Louis Lawyer, syndicated columnist: Technolawyer.com and other publications. Dir. P. Buckley Moss Found. for Children's Edn., 2001—03; mem. Sedona Conf. Working Group on Electronic Document Prodn.; mem. electronic discovery and ethics com. DRI, Inc., 2007—09. Lt USN, 1964—68. Named Mo.-Kans. Superlawyer, 2006, 2007—09; named one of Best Lawyers in Am., 2005, 2006—09, Best Lawyers in Info.-Tech. in Am., 2006. Mem.: ABA (co-chair electronic discovery subcom.), Bar Assn. Met. St. Louis (chmn law mgt comt 1993—96, chair technology comt 1996—99, Pres.'s award Exceptional Service 1995, 1997), P. Buckley Moss Soc. (dir 1994—2006, v.p 1998—2000, exec vpres 2001—02, pres. 2002—06), Mo. Bar Assn. (vice-chair ins programs comt 1981—83, vice-chair antitrust comt 1981—83, chair admin law comt 1995—97), D.C. Bar Assn. (chmn law practice mgt 1990—91), Order of Coif. Office: Husch Blackwell Sanders LLP Ste 600 190 Carondelet Plz Saint Louis MO 63105-3441 Office Phone: 813-634-2576. Business E-Mail: arthur_smith@verizon.net.

SMITH, B. SCOTT, automotive executive; Grad., Rollins Coll., 1991. Gen. mgr. Town & Country Ford, Charlotte, NC, 1992—97; pres., COO Sonic Automotive Inc., Charlotte, NC, 1997—2002, vice chmn., chief strategic officer, 2002—07, pres., chief strategy officer, 2007—. Office: Sonic Automotive Inc 5401 Independence Blvd Charlotte NC 28212

SMITH, BAKER ARMSTRONG, management executive, lawyer; b. Oct. 3, 1947; s. William Armstrong and Priscilla (Baker) S.; m. Deborah Elizabeth Ellis, Nov. 13, 1982; children: Ellis Armstrong, Elizabeth Anne, Everett Baker, Emery Manning. BS, U.S. Naval Acad., 1969; MBA, Northeastern U., 1975; JD cum laude, Suffolk U., 1977; LLM in Labor, Georgetown U., 1981. Bar: Ga. 1977, D.C. 1978, U.S. Supreme Ct. 1980; cert. turnaround profl., 1994; fellow Family Firm Inst. Commd. ensign USN, 1969, advanced through grades to lt., 1974; exec. dir., founder Ctr. on Nat. Labor Policy, Inc., North Springfield, Va., 1977-81; asst. to sec., dir. labor rels. U.S. Dept. HUD, Washington, 1981-83; exec. v.p. U.S. Bus. and Indsl. Coun., Nashville, 1983-84; pres. Am. Quality Builders, Inc., Nashville, 1984-86; v.p. Hopeman Bros., Inc., Waynesboro, Va., 1986-88, Morris, Anderson, Atlanta, 1988—2008, BDO Consulting Corp. Advisors, LLC, Atlanta, 2008—. Sec., founder U.S. Constnl. Rights Legal Def. Fund, Inc., Atlanta, 1983—; trustee Leadership Inst., Springfield, Va., 1978—; v.p., 1998—; v.p. Turnaround Mgmt. Assn., Chgo., 1998-99; pres. Assn. Cert. Turnaround Profls., Chgo., 1997-98; mem. Coun. for Nat. Policy, Washington, 1981—, Civil Rights Reviewing Authority U.S. Dept. Edn., Washington, 1984-88; transition team leader Office of the Pres.-Elect of the U.S., NLRB, Occupl. Safety and Health Rev. Commn., Fed. Mediation and Conciliation Svc., Nat. Mediation Bd., Fed. Labor Rels. Authority, Washington, 1980-81; instr. law, faculty sec. No. Va. Law Sch., Alexandria, Va., 1980-83; instr. law D.C. Law Sch., Washington, 1978-80. Contbg. author: Mandate for Leadership, 1981; contbr. articles to profl. jours. Bd. dirs. Atlanta Opera, 2006—. Recipient Outstanding Contbn. to the Turnaround Profession award, 1999. Fellow Family Firm Inst.; mem. ABA (Nat. Law Day chmn. 1976-77, Silver Key award 1977), St. George's House, Windsor Castle (assoc.), Phila. Soc., U.S. Supreme Ct. Hist. Soc., Federalist Soc., Beta Gamma Sigma, Phi Delta Phi (pres. 1989-91), Capitol Hill Club (Washington), Piedmont Club (Winston-Salem). Republican. Presbyterian. Home: 3360 E Terrell Branch Ct Marietta GA 30067-5164 Business E-Mail: bsmith@bdocca.com.

SMITH, BARBARA, bank executive; b. Bryan County, Ga. m. Gary Smith. Teller The Heritage Bank, Hinesville, Ga., 1972, sr. v.p. Vol. fundraiser United Way, Am. Cancer Soc., Am. Heart Assn., Am.

Diabetes Assn. Named one of 25 Most Powerful Women in Banking, US Banker, 2006. Mem.: Independent Cmty. Bankers Am. Avocation: quilting. Mailing: The Heritage Bank PO Box 1009 Hinesville GA 31310 Office Phone: 912-408-6102. Office Fax: 912-369-9397. E-mail: bsmith@the-heritage-bank.com.

SMITH, BARBARA BARNARD, music educator; b. Ventura, Calif., June 10, 1920; d. Fred W. and Grace (Hobson) S. BA, Pomona Coll., Claremont, Calif., 1942, DMus (hon.), 2001; MusM, U. Rochester, NY, 1943, performer's cert., 1945. Mem. faculty piano and theory Eastman Sch. Music, U. Rochester, 1943-49; mem. faculty U. Hawaii, Honolulu, 1949—, assoc. prof. music, 1953-62, prof., 1962-82, prof. emeritus, 1982—; sr. fellow East-West Center, 1973. Lectr., recitals in Hawaiian and Asian music, US, Europe and Asia, 1956—; field rschr. Asia, 1956, 60, 66, 71, 80, Micronesia, 1963, 70, 87-88, 90-91, Solomon Islands, 1976. Contbr. articles to profl. jours. Mem. Soc. Ethnomusicology, Internat. Coun. for Traditional Music, Am. Mus. Instrument Soc., Coll. Music Soc., Soc. for Asian Music, Pacific Sci. Assn., Phi Beta Kappa, Mu Phi Epsilon.

SMITH, BARBARA JANE, computer scientist, educator; d. Kenneth O. and Jane Louise Campbell; m. Douglas Brian Smith, Dec. 29, 1984; children: Michael Douglas, James Kenneth. MS in Math., Purdue U., 1981. Assoc. prof. Purdue U., Ft. Wayne, Ind., 1979—84; pres. Software Profls., Inc., Ft. Wayne, 1980—84; sr. sys. analyst Burroughs Corp., Camarillo, Calif., 1984—86, W. L. Gore, Flagstaff, Ariz., 1986—89; instr. Cochise Coll., Sierra Vista, Ariz., 1989—, U. Ariz. South, Sierra Vista, 1996—. Author: Programming Logic and Design. Mem. White Cross, Ft. Wayne, 2005—. Office: Cochise Coll 901 N Colombo Sierra Vista AZ 85635 Personal E-mail: barbaraj@email.arizona.edu.

SMITH, BARBARA JEANNE, retired librarian; b. Jersey Shore, Pa., Apr. 14, 1939; d. Moyer Emmerson and Mary Kathryn (Ebner) S. BS in Edn. (Biology), Pa. State U., 1961, DEd in Higher Edn., 1981; MS in Edn. (English), SUNY, Oswego, NY, 1967; MLS, U. Pitts., 1970. Reference libr. Pa. State U. Librs., University Park, 1970-75, commonwealth campus coord., 1975-82, asst. dean librs., head commonwealth campus librs. divsn., 1982-89; dir. Smithsonian Instn. Librs., Washington, 1989-98. Gen. sci. tchr., Binghampton (N.Y.) City Schs., 1961-62; English tchr., North Syracuse (N.Y.) Ctrl. Schs., 1970-75; mem. Smithsonian Instn. Rsch. Info. Svc. (chair 1993-95), Planning Adv. Group, 1989-93; chair Internet Implementation Com., Smithsonian Instn. Librs. User Adv. Com., 1989-97; founding dir. Chesapeake Info. and Rsch. Libr. Alliance, 1996-98. Contbr. articles to profl. jours.; speaker in field. UCLA Grad. Sch. of Libr. and Info. Sci. Sr. fellow, 1982. Mem. AAUW, ALA (mem. coun. 1987-91), Centre County (Pa.) Hist. Soc. (life), U. Pitts. Alumni Assn. (bd. dirs. 1991-94), Beta Phi Mu. E-mail: bsmith5598@verizon.net.

SMITH, BARNARD ELLIOT, management educator; b. Mpls., May 6, 1926; s. Sheldon Strong and Jessie (Gould) S.; m. Betty Lou Strohschein, Aug. 28, 1949; children: Carolyn Louise, Eileen Elizabeth. BS in Mech. Engring. with distinction, U. Minn., 1949, MS, 1950; PhD, Stanford U., Calif., 1961; MA (hon.), Dartmouth Coll., Hanover, NH, 1971. Asst. prof. mech. engring. U. ND, 1950-51; mfg. specialist A.O. Smith Co., Milw., 1951-54; asst. prof. indsl. engring. Oreg. State Coll., 1954-58, Stanford U., 1958-61; asso. prof. mgmt. Sloan Sch. Mgmt., MIT, 1961-68; prof. mgmt. Indian Inst. Mgmt., Calcutta, 1965-68; prof. engring. Thayer Sch. Engring. Dartmouth Coll., 1968-71; dean Stuart Sch. Mgmt. and Finance, Ill. Inst. Tech., 1971-75, prof. mgmt., 1975-80; David M. French disting. prof. mgmt. U. Mich., Flint, 1980-89, emeritus, 1989; pres. Vineyards of the Acad., 1989, The Acad. of Wine of Oreg. Inc., 1993—. Cons. in field. Served with USNR, 1944-46. Mem. Phi Tau Sigma, Beta Gamma Sigma. Home: 18200 Highway 238 Grants Pass OR 97527-8631 Office Phone: 541-846-6817.

SMITH, BARRY HAMILTON, foundation administrator, physician; b. Orange, NJ, Oct. 6, 1943; s. Kenneth Wright and Harriet (Barr) S.; m. Carley Eldredge, Dec. 13, 1969; children: Christopher, Sara. BA, Harvard U., 1965; PhD, MIT, 1968; MD, Cornell U., 1972. Intern, resident N.Y. Hosp., NYC, 1971—75; resident Mass. Gen. Hosp., Boston, 1975—78; program dir. Neuroscis. Rsch. Program MIT, Boston, 1975—78; dep. dir. Surg. Neurology Br. NIH, Bethesda, Md., 1978—83; dir. sci. & med. Dreyfus Med. Found., NYC, 1983—88; dir. Dreyfus Health Found., NYC, 1988—. Sr. v.p. Rogosin Inst., 1998-2008, dir. 2008-; prof. surgery Cornell U., Peking U. Med. Coll.; bd. dirs. pub. health sys. rsch. panel US Dept. Health and Human Svcs., 2007-08 Editor Ency. Neurosci., 1995-2005; contbr. articles to profl. jours. Bd. dirs. Desmond Tutu Peace Found., Kornfeld Found., N.Y.C. Rescue Mission, Global Health Action Comdr. USPHS, 1978—83. Recipient Commendation Medal award, USPHS, 1982, EEO award, 1983. Mem. AMA, AAAS, Soc. Neurosci., Am. Pain Soc. (audit com. 1983-85), Nat. Coun. Internat. Health (governing bd. 1990-95, chair 1993-95), Global Health Coun. Soc. Critical Care Medicine, Phi Beta Kappa, Sigma Xi, Alpha Omega Alpha Avocations: sailing, writing. Home: 1192 Park Ave Apt 10B New York NY 10128-1314 Office: The Rogosin Inst 505 E 70th St New York NY 10021 Office Phone: 212-746-1551. Personal E-mail: bsmith@dhfglobal.org. Business E-Mail: bas2005@nyp.org.

SMITH, BERNALD STEPHEN, retired pilot; b. Long Beach, Calif., Dec. 24, 1926; s. Donald Albert and Bernice Merrill (Stephens) Smith; m. Marilyn Mae Spence, July 22, 1949; children: Lorraine Ann Smith Foute, Evelyn Donice Smith DeRoos, Mark Stephen, Diane April(dec.). Student, U. Calif., Berkeley, 1944-45, 50-51. Cert. airline transport pilot, flight engr. FAA. Capt. Transocean Airline, Oakland, Calif., Transocean Air Lines, Tokyo, 1951-53, Hartford, Conn., 1954-55; 1st officer United Air Lines, Seattle, 1955, San Francisco, 1956-68, tng. capt. Denver, San Francisco, 1961—68, capt., 1968-86, 2d officer, 1986-93; ret., 1993. Founder, v.p. Avia Am., Palo Alto, Calif., 1970—72, Avia Internat., Palo Alto, 1972—74; founder, trustee AirSailing, Inc., 1970—, Soaring Safety Found., 1985—; cons. Caproni Vizzola, Milan, 1972—84; instr. aviation Ohlone Coll., Fremont, 1976; prin., cons. Internat. Aviation Cons. and Investments, Fremont, Calif., 1985—; founder Pacific Soaring Coun. Author, editor: American Soaring Handbook, 1975, 1980, pub.: Technical Soaring, 2004—08; contbr. articles to profl. jours. Trustee Nat. Soaring Mus., 1975—2001, pres., 1975—78; active RTCA; SSA del., 1992—; FAI del., 1996—. Comdr. USNR. Recipient Gold medal, Nat. Soaring Mus., 2002; named Barnaby Lectr., 2003. Fellow: Internat. GNSS Svc. Geodynamics (observer UN Office Outer Space Affairs); mem.: AIAA (pub. bd. 1977—94), Civil GPS Svc. Interface Com., Inst. Navigation, Commn. de Vol A Voile (US del. 1981—97, v.p. 1988—96), Fedn. Aeronatique Internat. (environ. commn. v.p., U.S. del. 1995—, del. environ. commn. 2002—, del. airspace and navigation commn. 2008—, Paul Tissandier diploma 1992, Lilienthal medal 1993, Bronze medal 2003, Compagnon d'Honneur 2007), Seaplane Pilots Assn., Orgn. Scientifique et Technique Internat. du Vol a Voile (hon.; bd. dirs., U.S. del. 1981—97, pub. Tech. Soaring 2004—08), Airline Pilots Assn., Exptl. Aircraft Assn., Nat. Aero. Assn., Soaring Soc. Am. (bd. dirs. 1963—97, pres. 1969—70, chmn. pub. bd. 1971—84, chmn. ins. com. 1975—93, hon. vice-chmn. bd. dirs. 2000—, Exceptional Svc. award 1970, 1975, Warren Eaton Meml. trophy 1977, Exceptional Svc. award 1982, named to Hall of Fame 1984, Exceptional Svc. award 1988, 1991, Exceptional Achievement award 1996, Warren Eaton Meml. trophy 1997, Schweizer Lifetime Svc. award 2003), Aircraft Owners and Pilots Assn., U. Calif. Alumni Assn. (life). Democrat. Methodist. Office: Internat Aviation Cons Investments PO Box 3075 Fremont CA 94539-0307

SMITH, BERNARD JOSEPH CONNOLLY, retired civil engineer; b. Elizabeth, NJ, Mar. 11, 1930; s. Bernard Joseph and Julia Susan (Connolly) Smith; m. Josephine Kerley, Dec. 20, 1971; children: Julia Susan Alice Birmingham, Teresa Mary Josephine Going, Anne Marie Kathleen Olson. BS, U. Notre Dame, 1951; BSCE, Tex. A&M U., 1957; MBA in Fin., U. Calif.-Berkeley, 1976. Registered profl. engr., Calif., Mo.; lic. real estate broker Calif. Asst. Bernard J. Smith, cons. engr. office, Dallas, 1947-57; hydraulic engr. CE, U.S. Army, San Francisco, 1957-59, St. Paul, 1959-60, Kansas City, Mo., 1960-63, Sacramento, 1963-65; civil engr. Fed. Energy Regulatory Commn., San Francisco, 1965—99; ret., 1999. With US Army, 1952—54, lt. col. CE USAR. Mem.: ASCE, Soc. Am. Mil. Engrs., Res. Officers Assn. (chpt. pres. 1973), Commonwealth Club Calif. Home: 247 28th Ave San Francisco CA 94121-1001 Personal E-mail: bernardojsmith@sbcglobal.net.

SMITH, BETTY, writer, not-for-profit developer; b. Bonham, Tex., Sept. 16; d. Sim and Gertrude (Dearing) S. Student, Stephens Coll.; BJ, U. Tex. Women's editor Daily Texan; pres. Hope Assocs. Corp., NYC; pres., owner Betty Smith Assocs., NYC. Author: A Matter of Heart, 1969, Journey to Valhalla: The Life of Lauritz Melchior, 2007. Bd. dirs. Melchior Heldentenor Found., N.Y.C., 1968—, pres., 1987-97; pres., CEO Gerda Lissner Found., 1994-2006; bd. dirs. Herman Lissner Found., 1990—, CEO, 2004—. Mem. Author's Guild. Home Phone: 212-759-1622. Personal E-mail: bettysmith5@gmail.com.

SMITH, BETTY DENNY, county official, administrator, fashion executive; b. Centralia, Ill., Nov. 12, 1932; d. Otto and Ferne Elizabeth (Beier) Hasenfuss; m. Peter S. Smith, Dec. 5, 1964; children: Carla Kip, Bruce Kimball. Student, U. Ill., 1950-52; student, L.A. City Coll., 1953-57, UCLA, 1965, U. San Francisco, 1982-84. Freelance fashion coordinator, L.A., NYC, 1953-58; tchr. fashion Rita LeRoy Internat. Studios, 1959-60; mgr. Mo Nadler Fashion, LA, 1961-64; showroom dir. Jean of Calif. Fashions, LA, 1965—. Freelance polit. book reviewer for community newspapers, 1961-62; staff writer Valley Citizen News, 1963. Bd. dirs. Pet Assistance Found., 1969-76; founder, pres., dir. Vol. Services to Animals L.A., 1972-76; mem. County Com. To Discuss Animals in Rsch., 1973-74; mem. blue ribbon com. on animal control L.A. County, 1973-74; dir. L.A. County Animal Care and Control, 1976-82; mem. Calif. Animal Health Technician Exam. Com., 1975-82, chmn., 1979; bd. dirs. L.A. Soc. for Prevention Cruelty to Animals, 1984-94, Calif. Coun. Companion Animal Advocates, 1993-97; dir. West Coast Regional Office, Am. Humane Assn., 1988-97; mem. adv. com. Moorepark Coll., 1988-97; CFO Coalition for Pet Population Control, 1987-92; trustee Gladys W. Sargent Found., 1997—, Coalition to End Pet Overpopulation, 1998—, Voice for Animals, 2009-; cons. Jungle Book II, Disney Studios, 1997; mem. adv. com. Wishbone Prodn., 1995-97; mem. govt. rels. and pub. affairs com. Motion Picture & TV Industry Assn., 1992-97; mem. Coalition to Protect Calif. Wildlife, 1996-97, Spl. Commn. Spay/Neuter City L.A., 1998-99; adv. com. La. Dept. of Animal Reg. 2000; mem. adv. com. Calif. Dept. Fish & Game Animal Care, 2003-; trustee Beverly Edne Johnson Estate, 2004-, Voice for Animals,2009-; pres., bd. dirs. Fauna Found., 2004-; mem. Calif. Rep. Cen. Com., 1964-72, mem. exec. com., 1971-73; mem. L.A. County Rep. Cen. Com., 1964-70, mem. exec. com., 1966-70; chmn. 29th Congl. Cen. Com., 1969-70; sec. 28th Senatorial Cen. Com., 1967-68; mem. speakers bur. George Murphy for U.S. Senate, 1970; campaign mgr. Los Angeles County for Spencer Williams for Atty. Gen., 1966; mem. L.A. County Art Mus., L.A. Libr. Assn. Mem. Internat. Platform Assn., LA Conservancy, Mannequins Assn. (bd. dirs. 1967-68), Lawyer's Wives San Gabriel Valley (bd. dirs. 1971-74, pres. 1972-73), L.A. Athletic Club, Town Hall. Home: 1766 Bluffhill Dr Monterey Park CA 91754-4533

SMITH, BETTY L., small business owner, educator; b. Trinidad, Colo., Oct. 17, 1932; d. Howard Melvin and Annabelle (Eastwood) Wade; m. Earl Gilbert Smith, Nov. 26, 1950; children: Wayne David, Christine Ella, Clifford Todd. Student, CalistogaCalif.) Coll., 1961-63. Owner, founder Gilbert's Gallery Frame Shop, Santa Rosa, 1964-84; ind. rep., regional sales dir. Simplex, Santa Rosa, 1984-91; owner, transformation coach Betty Smith Results Coaching, Santa Rosa, 1992—. Facilitator EMC2 Ind., 2003—. Author: Secrets of Living Life Abundantly, 1995, The Power to Change The Shadow Side of Idealism, 2009, (poetry biography) Here I Am, There I Went, 1968; contbr. articles to profl. jours. Art commr. City of Santa Rosa, 1967-68; mem. steering coun. Earth Elders, treas., 1999-2001; mem. Sustainable Sonoma County. Democrat. Avocation: environmental education. Home and Office: 2319 Olympia Dr Santa Rosa CA 95405-8119 Office Phone: 800-975-7726. Personal E-mail: bsetnow@sonic.net.

SMITH, BETTY ROBINSON, retired elementary school educator; b. Athens, Ga., Jan. 31, 1941; d. Willie Martin and Leila Mary Robinson; m. Freddie Smith; children: Natalie Yvonne, Rewa Patrice. BSEd, Tuskegee Inst., Ala., 1964; MS in Early Childhood Edn., Nova U., Ft. Lauderdale, Fla., 1979; cert. early childhood, U. S. Fla. Head tchr. in headstart program Perkins Elem. Sch., St. Petersburg, Fla., 1965; tchr. Orange Grove Elem. Sch., Tampa, Fla., 1967-68, Largo (Fla.) Ctrl. Elem. Sch., 1970-71, North Shore Elem. Sch., St. Petersburg, Fla., 1971-99, Gulfport Elem. Montessori Acad., 2000—06; ret., 2006. Resource cons., bd. dirs. Mt. Zion Christian Acad., 1999—; head tchr. Early Success Program; active Appreciate Cultures Program for sch. improvement plan Pinellas County; chair Multicultural Club; organizer ann. Elem. workshop; network trainer, Gulfport Elem., 2000—; head mutlicultural com., acad network trainer Gulfport Elem. Montessori Acad., 2002-2004; head multicultural liason, 2000-05. Dir. youth choir, active community and religious roles; mem. mass choir Mt. Zion Progressive Baptist Ch.; organizer 55+ Club; head multicultural com. North Shore Elem. Sch. Mem. PCTA, Am. Montessori Soc., Zeta Gamma Zta, PREP (rep. for Pinellas County, Fla.). Home: 4301 Cortez Way S Saint Petersburg FL 33712-4024

SMITH, BETTY W., librarian; b. Lincoln, Nebr., June 29, 1919; d. Clem and Edith Margaret (Stanley) Wilder; m. Dulaney Dale Smith, Mar. 20, 1946; children: Douglas D., Diane E., Richard W. BA, Wayne U., 1940; BS, U. Minn., 1941; MA, Mich. State U., 1955. Cert. libr. Br. libr. Pub. Libr., Park Ridge, Ill., 1941-42, reference libr. Dearborn, Mich., 1942-44; U.S.C.G. SPAR, libr. asst. U.S.C.G. Acad., New London, Conn., 1945-46; reference libr. Libr. Hawaii, Honolulu, 1946-47; libr. Hawaiian Econ. Found., Honolulu, 1947-49; reference libr. Lansing Pub. Libr., Mich., 1967-86, substitute libr., 1986-98. Mem. Citizens for Actions in Mental Health, 1980—86; steering com. Long-Range Planning Mich. Dept. Mental Health, 1986—90; bd. dirs. Tri-Co. Cmty. Mental Health, Lansing, 1992—98; founding and exec. com. mem. Alliance for Mentally Ill, Mich., 1985—2003, now v.p.; adv. coun. Mich. Forensic Ctr., 1988—, Lafayette Clinic, Detroit, 1986—92. Mem. LWV, Mental Health Assn., Mich. Assn. Emotionally Disturbed Children (bd. dirs. 1963-68), Mich. Mental Health (adv. coun. 1986-90), Phi Alpha Theta. Home: 1782 Eifert Rd Holt MI 48842-1976

SMITH, BILL, professional sports team executive; b. North Hampton, NH; m. Becky Smith; children: Allison, Amy, Jennifer. Grad. in French, Hamilton Coll., Clinton, NY. Asst. dir., minor leagues and scouting Chgo. White Sox, 1981—83, gen. mgr. Class A affiliate Appleton, Wis., 1983—86; asst. dir., minor leagues and scouting Minn. Twins, 1986—89, dir., baseball adminstrn., 1989—91, v.p., asst. gen. mgr., 1992—2007, sr. v.p., gen. mgr., 2008—. Bd. trustees Minor League Baseball. Achievements include being one of the first participants in the Major League Baseball executive development program, 1980. Office: Minn Twins Metrodome 34 Kirby Puckett Pl Minneapolis MN 55415

SMITH, BOB, state legislator, lawyer; b. Scranton, Pa., Mar. 25, 1947; s. Philip and Ruth; m. Ellen Smith; 2 children. BA in History, U. Scranton, 1969, MS in Chemistry, 1970; MS in Environ. Sci., Rutgers U., 1973; JD, Seton Hall U., 1981. Bar: NJ 1983. Tchr. Lourdesmont High Sch., Clark Summit, Pa., 1968-70; instr. Middlesex County Coll., 1970—81; law clk. N.J. Dept. Environ. Protection, Trenton, 1980; councilman Piscataway Town Coun., 1977—80; atty. Smith & Schechter, 1981—95; mayor Town of Piscataway, 1981—86; mem. NJ State Assembly, 1986—2001, parliamentarian, 1988—89, dep. minority leader, 1994—95; atty. Bob Smith and Assocs., Piscataway, NJ, 1996—; mem. Dist. 17 NJ State Senate, 2002—. Chmn. senate environ. com., 2004-, mem. jud. com. and environment com.; parliamentarian Assembly Dem. Caucus, 1988-90, chmn. task force on environment, 1987; chmn. Piscataway Dem. Orgn., 1981-90; counsel N.J. State Dem. Platform Com., 1987, 89; chmn. Middlesex County Dem. Orgn., 1991-92; mem. Middlesex County Transp. Coordinating Com., 1980-86; chmn. Piscataway Planning Bd, 1981-86, sec., 1975, chmn., 1976; bd. dirs. N.J. Conf. Mayors, 1984-86; mem. tech. adv. com. air pollution Middlesex County Planning Bd., 1973-74; mem. Greenbrook Basin com. Area 208 Mgmt. Planning Program, 1975-76; mem. commr.'s adv. com. N.J. Dept. Environ. Protection, 1972-86. Recipient Disting. Citizen award Piscataway Jewish Congregation B'nai Shalom, 1982; named Legis. of Yr. Eden Inst., N.J. State VFW, 1998, Environ. Legislator of Yr., N.J. Environ. Fedn., 1990, Environ. Legislator of Yr., N.J. Environ. Lobby, 2005; Presdl. scholar U. Scranton, 1965-69. Mem. Middlesex County Bar Assn., NJ State Bar Assn Democrat. Roman Catholic. Office: 216 Stelton Rd E-5 Piscataway NJ 08854-2600 also: NJ Senate PO Box 099 Trenton NJ 08625-0099 Office Phone: 732-752-0770. Office Fax: 752-752-1590.

SMITH, BRADFORD LEE, computer software company executive, lawyer; b. Milw., Jan. 17, 1959; m. Kathy Surace-Smith; 2 children. AB. summa cum laude, Princeton U., 1981; JD, Columbia U., 1985; student, U. Geneva Grad. Inst. Internat. Studies, Geneva, Switzerland, 1984. Ptnr. Covington & Burling LLP, Washington; mgr., European Law & Corp. Affairs group, Microsoft Corp., Paris, 1993—96, dep. gen. counsel for worldwide sales Redmond, Wash., 1996—2001, sr. v.p., gen. counsel, chief compliance officer, corp. sec. legal & corp. affairs, 2002—. Lectr. Hague Acad. Internat. Law. Contbr. articles. Office: Microsoft One Microsoft Way Redmond WA 98052-6399 Office Fax: 425-706-7329.*

SMITH, BRADLEY E., anesthesiologist; b. Cedar Vale, Kans., Jan. 4, 1933; MD, U. Okla., Norman, 1957. Diplomate Am. Bd. Anesthesiologists. Resident U.S. Naval Hosp., NYC, 1957-60; fellow Columbia Presbyn. Hosp., NYC, 1960—61; faculty Yale U., 1962-63, U. Miami, 1963-69; chmn., prof. dept. anesthesiology Vanderbilt U., Nashville, 1969-93, prof., 1993—, prof. emeritus, 2004—, prof. clin. anesthesiology, 2005—08; trustee Wood Libr. Mus. Anesthesiology, 2008—. Mem.: AMA, ACOG (assoc.), Am. Soc. Anesthesiologists. Office: Vandy Med Ctr Rm 209 Oxford House Nashville TN 37232-4125 Office Phone: 615-936-0718.

SMITH, BRADLEY W., legislative staff member; Chief of staff to Rep. David Dreier US House of Reps., Washington, assoc. staff, rules com. Republican. Office: 233 Cannon House Office Bldg Washington DC 20515 Office Phone: 202-225-2305. Office Fax: 202-225-7018.*

SMITH, BRIAN D., lawyer; AB, Brown U., 1972; JD, U. Va. Law Sch., 1977; PhD, Cambridge U., 1986. Bar: Calif., NY, Am. Bar Assn. Atty., real estate, ptnr. Goodwin Procter LLP, 1991—. Mem.: Lambda Alpha Internat. Office: Goodwin Procter LLP 620 Eighth Ave New York NY 10018 also: Goodwin Procter LLP 16 Saint Martin's Le Grand London England Office Phone: 272-813-8800. Business E-Mail: bdsmith@goodwinprocter.com.

SMITH, BRIAN RICHARD, hematologist, oncologist, pathologist; b. Glen Cove, NY, May 7, 1952; s. Frank C. and Gloria R. S.; m. Keiren Donovan, Apr. 17, 1993. AB in Chemistry summa cum laude, Princeton U., 1972; MD, Harvard U., 1976; MA (hon.), Yale U., 1997. Diplomate Am. Bd. Internal Medicine, Hematology and Med. Oncology, Am. Bd. Pathology Hematopathology. Resident/fellow Harvard U., Brigham and Women's Hosp., 1976-80; instr. medicine Harvard Med. Sch., 1981—84; assoc. physician Brigham & Women's Hosp., Children's Hosp., Dana-Farber Cancer Ins, Boston, 1981-88; asst. prof. medicine Harvard Med. Sch., 1985-88; assoc. prof. medicine, lab. medicine & pediatrics sch. med. Yale U., New Haven, 1988-96, prof. medicine, lab medicine & pediatrics, 1996—, dir. immunohematology; vice chmn. dept. lab. medicine Yale Med. Sch.-Yale New Haven Hosp., 1997—2005, chmn. dept. lab. medicine, 2006—; DeCamp lectr. biomed. ethics Princeton U., NJ, 1992. Contbr. over 150 articles to med. publs. Trustee Richard D. Frisbee III Found.; chair study sect. Am. Heart Assn. Recipient George A. Howe prize Princeton U., 1976; Am. Cancer Soc. fellow, 1981-84, Leukemia Soc. fellow, 1982-88; Leukemia Soc. Am. scholar, 1989, Stohlman scholar, 1993, Nat. Blood Found. scholar, 1996. Fellow ACP, Coll. Am. Pathologists; mem. NIH (recombinant DNA adv. com. 1992-97), Acad. Clin. Lab. Physicians and Scientists (pres. 2006-), Phi Beta Kappa, Sigma Xi, Alpha Omega Alpha. Roman Catholic. Office: Yale U Sch Med PO Box 208035 333 Cedar St New Haven CT 06520-8035

SMITH, BRUCE, real estate company executive, retired professional football player; b. Norfolk, Va., June 18, 1963; m. Carmen Smith; 1 child, Alston. Student, Va. Tech. U. Defensive end Buffalo Bills, 1985-99, Washington Redskins, 2000—03; ret., 2003; founder Bruce Smith Enterprise, LLC, Virginia Beach, Va., 2004—, Bruce Smith Devel., LLC; co-developer Smith's Landing, Blacksburg, Va. Bd. visitors Va. Tech. U.; bd. mem. St. Jude's Children's Hosp., Operation Smile. Recipient Outland trophy, 1984; named First Team All-Pro, 1987, 88, 90, 93-97, AP NFL Defensive Player of Yr., 1990, 96; named to Am. Football Conf. Pro-Bowl, 1987-90, 92-98, Coll. Football Hall of Fame, 2006, Pro Football Hall of Fame, 2009. Achievements include starting in Super Bowls: XXV, 1990, XXVI, 1991, XXVII, 1992, XXVIII, 1993;

setting the National Football League all-time record for career sacks (200), 2003. Office: Bruce Smith Enterprise LLC Virginia Beach VA 23452 Office Phone: 757-413-2800.*

SMITH, BRUCE ALFRED, oil industry executive; b. Coffeyville, Kans., Oct. 12, 1943; s. George Alfred and Isabel (Andrews) S.; m. Cynthia Denton Doughat, Aug. 7, 1969 (div. Jan. 1987); children: Denton Todd, Bruce Chandler, John Paul, Joseph Willimas, Charles Pinson Smith; m. Gail Hutchison, Nov. 10, 1990. BA, Westminster Coll., 1965; MBA, U. Kans., 1967; postgraduate student, U. Chgo., 1971. With Ford Motor Co., Dearborn, Mich., 1967-69; banking officer met. divsn. Continental Ill. Nat. Bank and Trust Co. Chgo., Chgo., 1971-73, 2nd v.p. multinational divsn., 1973-75, v.p. mining divsn., 1975-77, v.p., sect. mgr. Chgo. and London, 1977-80, v.p., mgr. internat. energy divsn. Chgo., 1980-82, v.p., mgr. SW group, comml. banking Houston, 1983-86; corp. v.p., treas. Valero Energy Corp. and Valero Natural Gas Ptnrs., San Antonio, 1986-92; v.p. Tesoro Petroleum Corp., San Antonio, 1992-93, CFO, 1992-95, exec. v.p., 1993-95, exec. v.p. Tesoro Exploration and Prodn. Co., 1993-95, exec. v.p., COO, dir., 1995, pres., CEO, 1995-96, chmn., CEO, pres., 1996—. Bd. dirs. Noble Energy, Inc., Nat. Petrochemical & Refiners Assn. Bd. dirs. San Antonio Sports Found. Served in US Army, 1969—71. Mem. Fin. Execs. Inst. (past pres. San Antonio chpt.). Office: Tesoro Petroleum Corp 300 Concord Plz San Antonio TX 78216-6999

SMITH, BRUCE P., dean, law educator; BA summa cum laude, Williams Coll., 1986; BA, U. Cambridge, 1988, MA in History, 1992; JD with honors, Yale U., 1992. Bar: Pa. 1994, Mass. 1994, DC 1995. Assoc. litig. group Covington & Burling, Washington, 1996—2001; asst. prof. law U. Ill. Coll. Law, Champaign, 2001—04, assoc. prof. law, Corman scholar, 2004—06, co-dir. Ill. Legal History Program, 2004—, prof. law, 2006—, dean, Guy Raymond Jones faculty scholar, 2009—. Vis. prof. George Washington U. Law Sch., Washington, 2007; spkr. in field. Contbr. articles to profl. jours. Mem.: ABA, N.Am. Conf. on British Studies, Law and Soc. Assn., Am. Soc. Legal History, Selden Soc. Office: U Ill Coll Law Office of Dean 504 E Pennsylvania Ave Champaign IL 61820 Office Phone: 217-244-8446. E-mail: smithb@law.uiuc.edu.*

SMITH, BRUCE VAUGHN, electrical engineer; b. Kingsville, Tex., July 28, 1953; s. Robert Vaughn and June Estelle (Link) S.; m. Astrid Marie Ryerson, July 17, 1976; 1 child, Leslie Michelle. BSEE, Iowa State U., 1975, MSEE, 1980, PhD, 1991. Prof. engr., Iowa. Sr. prin. sys. engr. Rockwell-Collins Avionics, Cedar Rapids, Iowa, 1975—2008, prin. engring. mgr., 2008—. Owner Cottonwood Sys. Design, Co., 2001—; adj. prof. Iowa State U., Ames, 1991—, grad. faculty, 1999—; program evaluator, engr. commr., exec. com. Accreditation Bd. Engring. & Tech., Balt., 1995—, mem. exec. com.; state problem capt. Odyssey of the Mind, 1996-2000. Bd. dirs. North Linn Sch. Dist., Troy Mills, Iowa, 1993-95. Mem. IEEE (com. on engring. accreditation activities), Internat. Coun. Sys. Engring. (sec.-treas. Heartland chpt. 2000-), Sigma Xi. Achievements include patents for a pressure sensor. Avocations: target shooting, auto racing. Office: Rockwell Collins Inc 400 Collins Rd NE Cedar Rapids IA 52498-0001

SMITH, (OLLEN) BRUTON, sports association executive; b. Oakboro, NC, 1927; divorced; 4 children. Founder, exec. officer, dir. Lowe's Motor Speedway (formerly Charlotte Motor Speedway), Concord, NC, 1959—61, CEO, dir., 1975—; chmn., CEO Atlanta Motor Speedway, 1990—, Speedway Motorsports, Inc., 1994—, Tex. Motor Speedway, 1995—, Bristol Motor Speedway, 1996—, Infineon Raceway (formerly Sears Point Raceway), 1996—. Owner, operator Sonic Fin. Corp.; chmn., CEO, dir., controlling stockholder Sonic Automotive, Inc. Founder Speedway Children's Charities, 1982—. Named one of Forbes' Richest Americans, 2006, The Most Influential People in the World of Sports, Bus. Week, 2007. Office: Speedway Motorsports 5555 Concorde Pkwy S Concord NC 28027

SMITH, BURTON JORDAN, computer designer; b. Durham, NC, Mar. 21, 1941; s. Sherman Everett and Rebecca Frances (Jordan) S.; m. Dorothy Nan Duncan, Dec. 28, 1966; children: Katherine Page, Julia Jordan. BSEE, U. N.Mex., Albuquerque, 1967; SM, MIT, Cambridge, 1968, Elec. Engring. Diploma, 1969, ScD, 1972. Asst. prof. U. Colo., Denver, 1972-78, assoc. prof., 1978-79; v.p. R&D Denelcor, Inc., Denver, 1979-85; fellow Supercomputing Rsch. Ctr., Lanham, Md., 1985-88; co-founder, chief scientist Tera Computer Co. (purchased Cray Rsch. from Silicon Graphics, Inc. in 2000, renamed Cray, Inc.), Seattle, 1988—2005; chmn. Cray, Inc., Seattle, 1988—99, also bd. dir., 1988—2005; tech. fellow Microsoft Corp., Redmond, Wash., 2005—. Adv. com. on computer rsch. NSF, Washington, 1984-87; fellow, Supercomputing Rsch. Ctr. (now Ctr. for Computing Sciences), divsn. Inst. for Def. Analysis, 1985-88; sci. coun. Universities Space Rsch. Assn., Washington, 1987-91; blue ribbon panel on high performance computing NSF, Washington, 1993, presdl. faculty fellows final selection panel, Washington, 1992-93, Computer Sci. Telecom. Bd. Nat. Rsch. Coun., Washington, 1999-2004. Editor: (book) Multithreaded Computer Architecture, 1994. Precinct committeeman Dem. Party, Denver, 1980-84. With USN, 1960-64. Recipient Eckert-Marchly award, 1990, awarded jointly by IEEE Computer Soc. and Assn. for Computer Machinery, Seymour Cray award IEEE Computer Soc., 2003. Fellow IEEE, Assn. for Computing Machinery; mem. NAE, Eta Kappa Nu, Sigma Xi. Democrat. Avocation: choral singing. Office: Microsoft Corp 1 Microsoft Way Redmond WA 98052-6399

SMITH, C. LEMOYNE, retired publishing executive; b. Atkins, Ark., Sept. 15, 1934; s. Cecil Garland and Salena Bell (Wilson) S.; m. Selma Jean Tucker, May 23, 1964; 1 child, Jennifer Lee BS, Ark. Tech. U., 1956; M.Ed., U. Ark., 1958. Tchr. pub. schs., Little Rock, 1956-58; instr. bus. adminstrn. Ark. Tech. U., Russellville, 1958-60; sales rep. South-Western Pub. Co., Cin., 1960-67, editorial staff, 1967-82, pres., chief exec. officer, 1982-90, chmn., 1990-91, ret., 1991. Bd. dirs. Cin. Council on World Affairs, 1983-95. Mem.: Nat. Bus. Edn. Assn., Delta Pi Epsilon. Republican. Presbyterian. Avocations: bridge, travel, golf. Office: South-Western Pub Co 5191 Natorp Blvd Mason OH 45040-7980 Home Phone: 501-821-2401. Personal E-mail: lemselm@comcast.net.

SMITH, CANDY, economics professor; b. Marysville, Calif., Dec. 14, 1956; d. William Edgar and Betty Jo Vickrey; m. Stephen Doyle Smith; children: Madeline Jeanette, Gina Christine. MA, Nat. U., Fresno, Calif., 1988. Cons. Candy Smith Consulting, Gilroy, Calif., 1991—2000; prof. bus. and economics Folsom Lake Coll., Calif., 2000—. Facilitator Leadership Porterville, Calif., 1996—97, Leadership Gilroy Morgan Hill, Calif., 1998—2000. Pres. Panhellenic Coun., Tulare County, Calif., 1995—96; advisor Students in Free Enterprise. Recipient Highest award Nat. 2nd Pl. Mem.: Alpha Phi Alumnae, Alpha Phi (pres. 1977—78). Democrat. Achievements include development of online programs for Folsom Lake College. Avocations: reading, snow shoeing, cooking. Office: Folsom Lake Coll 10 College Pky Folsom CA 95630

SMITH, CARL BERNARD, education educator; b. Feb. 29, 1932; s. Carl R. and Elizabeth Ann (Lefeld) S.; m. Virginia Lee Cope, Aug. 30, 1958; children: Madonna, Anthony, Regina, Marla. BA, U. Dayton, 1954; MA, Miami U., Oxford, Ohio, 1961; PhD, Case Western Res. U., 1967. Tchr. Cathedral Latin H.S., Cleve., 1954-57; customer corr. E.F. MacDonald Co., Dayton, 1958-59; tchr. Kettering (Ohio) H.S., 1959-61; editor Reardon Baer Pub. Co., Cleve., 1961-62; tchr., rschr. Case Western Res. U., Cleve., 1962-65, Cleve. Pub. Schs., 1966-67; asst. prof. edn. Ind. U., Bloomington, 1967-69, assoc. prof., 1970-72, prof., 1973—99, prof. emeritus, 1999—. Dir. ERIC Ctr., 1988-2004, Family Literacy Ctr., 1990—; pres. Grayson Bernard Pub. Co., 1988—, Am. Family Learning Corp., 1996—. Author: Reading Instruction through Diagnostic Teaching (Pi Lambda Theta Best Book in Edn. award 1972), Getting People to Read, 1978; sr. author: Series r, 1983, New View, 1993, Teaching Reading and Writing Together, 1984, Connect! Getting Your Kids to Talk to You, 1994, Word History A Resource Book, 1995, Self-Directed Learner Curriculum, 1998, (videotape) Make a Difference, 1996, Improving Your Child's Writing Skills, 1999, Gotcha Grandpa, 2000, Talk to Your Children About Books, 2001, Teaching Children to Learn, 2002, Reading to Learn, 2003, Parents Guide to Character Development, 2003, The Spiritual Family, 2005, Teaching Parents How To Listen and Learn, 2007. Pres. Bd. Edn., St. Charles Sch., Bloomington, 1976-80. Recipient Sch. Bell award NEA, 1967, Literacy award Ind. State Reading Assn., 1997. Mem. ASCD, Internat. Reading Assn., Nat. Coun. Tchrs. of English, Am. Ednl. Rsch. Assn., Phi Delta Kappa. Republican. Roman Catholic. Home: 4915 E Cedarcrest Dr Bloomington IN 47401 Office: Reading and English Clearinghouse Smith Rsch Ctr Bloomington IN 47405 Home Phone: 812-336-1800; Office Phone: 812-345-0985. Business E-Mail: smith2@indiana.edu.

SMITH, CARL BRENT, retired chemist; b. Raleigh, NC, Mar. 5, 1944; s. Carl B. and Mary Ellen Smith; m. Nella Webb Smith, Apr. 23, 1967; children: Cevin Brent, Marcus Carl. BS in Chemistry, NC State U., Raleigh, 1966; PhD in Chem. Physics, U. Fla., Gainesville, 1970. Chemist United Merchants, Old Fort, NC, 1970—76; techncial dir. Alamac Divsn. West Point Pepperell, Lumberton, NC, 1976—81; rsch. mgr. Cotton Inc., Raleigh, 1981—84; disting cone mills chair prof. textile chemistry NC State U., 1984—2007. Contbr. scientific papers. Mem.: Am. Assn. Textile Chemists Colorists (Olney medal 2007). Achievements include patents for dyeing and finishing of textile materials. Avocation: music.

SMITH, CARLA ANNE, music educator; b. Albany, NY, Feb. 1, 1955; d. William Anthony and Florence Emma Africano; m. Gil Raymond Smith, Aug. 18, 1974; children: Alycia Erin(dec.), Turner Anthony. Student Ithaca Coll., Eastman Prep. Dept. Grad. Piano, NY, 1974; student, Potsdam State U., NY, 1975; grad., Eastman Sch. Music, Prepatory Dept. Piano and Oboe; BS magna cum laude, Pa. State U., 1977, MEd, 1983; postgrad., Ea. Ky. U., 2001—. Music tchr. Park Forest Jr. HS, State College, Pa., 1978; chorus and music tchr. Bellefonte Mid. Sch., Pa., 1978—82; piano tchr. Muncie, Ind., 1985—95; choir dir. United Meth. Ch., Cammack, Ind., 1986—95; elem. music tchr. Model Lab Sch., Richmond, Ky., 1997—98; piano/oboe tchr. Richmond, Ky., 1995—; band dir., music and humanities tchr. Madison Bd. of Edn., Richmond, Ky., 1998—. Accompanist Madison Bd. Edn., Richmond, 1996—; keyboardist St. Mark's Ch., Richmond, 1995—. Mem. Friend of the Fine Arts, Richmond, 1996—; sch. counselor 4H Talent Show Club, Richmond, 2000—; founding mem. Wall of Tolerance, 2003. Recipient Arts in Edn. award, Richmond Area Arts Coun., 1999, Achievement award, Muncie Matinee Musicals, 1995, Vivian Conley award, AAUW, 1994, Madison County Internat. Artist Exch. Japan, 2003; named an Outstanding Am. Tchr., Nat. Honor Roll, 2005—06; grantee Fine Arts Mini grantee, Madison Bd. Edn., 1998—2001. Mem.: NEA (Madison County Edn. Assn. rep.), Jr. Nat. Young Leaders Conf. (nominating com. mem. 2009), Ky. Edn. Assn., Ky. Fedn. of Music Clubs (jr. counselor 1996—), Ky. Music Educators Assn., Madison Music Makers Club (founder, counselor 1996—), Cecilian Music Club (jr. counselor 1996—), Mortar Bd., Phi Kappa Phi. Avocations: attending art galleries, reading. Home: 1104 Valley Run Dr Richmond KY 40475 Office: Clark-Moores Middle Sch 1143 Berea Rd Richmond KY 40475

SMITH, CARNICE, music educator, director; b. Jackson, Mississippi, Miss., June 8, 1954; d. James Edward and Mary Lee Smith. B in Music Edn., Jackson State U., 1976, M in Music Edn., 1979; Orff cert., Miss. State U., 1993. Nat. bd. cert. tchr. Music tchr. Morrison Elem. Sch. Jackson Pub. Sch., Miss., 1987—95; choral dir. Blackburn Mid. Sch. Jackson Pub. Schools, Miss., 1995—. Dir., sponsor Miss. Songfest Jackson Pub. Schools, 1998—2005. Music scholar, Jackson State U., 1972—76. Mem.: Delta Sigma Theta (life). Democrat. Baptist. Home: 3627 Fontaine Ave Jackson MS 39213 Office: Blackburn Mid Sch 1311 W Pearl St Jackson MS 39203 Personal E-mail: csharp54@yahoo.com.

SMITH, CAROL A., publishing executive; Salesperson Wall St. Jour., NYC, 1973; founding pub. Parenting mag., 1986; grp. pub. Parenting mag. Time Inc., 1990—93, pres., CEO Parenting Grp. San Francisco, 1993—98; v.p., grp. pub. sports divsn. Miller Pub. Grp. LLC, 1998—99; v.p. content eStyle Inc.; sr. v.p., pub. ELLE Grp. Hachette Filipacchi Media US Inc., 2002—. Founding pub. VIBE mag., Martha Stewart Living. Named Exec. of Yr., Advt. Age mag., 2008. Office: ELLE mag Hachette Filipacchi Media 1633 Broadway New York NY 10019 Office Phone: 212-767-6000.*

SMITH, CAROLE, school system administrator; Student, Lewis and Clark Coll., Portland, Oreg., 1972—74; BA in Urban Studies, Oberlin Coll., Ohio, 1976; EdM in Adminstrn. and Counseling, Harvard U., Cambridge, Mass., 1981. Lic. basic adminstrv. license in ednl. adminstrn. Lewis and Clark Coll., 1990, advanced adminstrv. license in ednl. adminstrn. Lewis and Clark Coll., 1995, std. adminstrs. license Oreg. Instr., counselor Thompson Island Edn. Ctr., Boston, 1977, Boston Pub. Schs. liaison, 1977, dir. Thompson Island HS program, 1977—78, ednl. program adminstr., 1979—80; exec. dir. Open Meadow Schs., Portland, Oreg., 1982—2005; dir. Office of Ednl. Options Portland Pub. Schs., 2005—06, interim dir. Office of Student, Family, and Sch. Support, 2006, chief of staff for Supt. Vicki Phillips, 2006—07, supt., 2007—. Founder, chair Coalition of Met. Area Cmty.-Based Schs., Portland, 2000—05; mem. steering com. Connected by 25, Portland, 2004—. Recipient Disting. Svc. Award, NW Assn. Accredited Schs., 2003. Mem.: Confederation of Oreg. Sch. Adminstrs. Office: Portland Pub Schs 501 N Dixon St Portland OR 97227-1807 Office Phone: 503-916-2000.*

SMITH, CAROLE DIANNE, retired lawyer, editor, writer, product developer; b. Seattle, June 12, 1945; d. Glaude Francis and Elaine Claire (Finkenstein) S.; m. Stephen Bruce Presser, June 18, 1968 (div. June 1987); children: David Carter, Elisabeth Catherine. AB cum laude, Harvard U., Radcliffe Coll., 1968; JD, Georgetown U., 1974. Bar: Pa. 1974. Law clk. Hon. Judith Jamison, Phila., 1974—75; assoc. Gratz, Tate, Spiegel, Ervin & Ruthrouff, Phila., 1975—76; freelance editor, writer Evanston, Ill., 1983—87; editor Ill. Inst. Tech., Chgo., 1987—88; mng. editor LawLetters, Inc., Chgo., 1988—89; editor ABA, Chgo., 1989—95; product devel. dir. Gt. Lakes divsn. Lawyers Coop. Pub., Deerfield, Ill., 1995—96; product devel. mgr. Midwest Market Ctr. West Group, Deerfield, Ill., 1996—97; mgr acquisitions, bus. and fin. group CCH, Inc., Riverwoods, Ill., 1997—2002; ret. Author Jour. of Legal Medicine, 1975, Selling and the Law: Advertising and Promotion, 1987; (under pseudonym Sarah Toast) 79 children's books and stories, 1994-2002; editor The Brief, 1990-95, Criminal Justice, 1989-90, 92-95 (Gen. Excellence award Soc. Nat. Assn. Pubs. 1990, Feature Article award-bronze Soc. Nat. Assn. Pubs. 1994), Franchise Law Jour., 1995. Dir. Radcliffe Club of Chgo., 1990-93; mem. parents coun. Latin Sch. Chgo., 1995-96; trustee Winnetka-Northfield Libr. Dist., 2003—09, pres. trustees, 2005-08; mem. Winnetka Plan Commn. 2003-05, Winnetka Forestry Commn., 2004-05 Mem. ABA (editor-in-chief The Brief 1998-2000, mem. publs. editl. bd. tort trial and ins. practice sect. 2003-05, chair 2005—09, coun. mem, Tort Trial and Insurance Sect. 2008-).

SMITH, CAROLYN J(ANE) HOSTETTER, psychologist, educator; b. Indpls., Mar. 29, 1938; d. John Daniel and Louise Margaret (Reiber) Hostetter; m. Thomas Tomasian, June 18, 1988. BA, DePauw U., 1959; MS in Teaching-Guidance & Counseling, U. Chgo., 1962, PhD, 1981. Lic. psychologist, Mass. Guidance counselor Blue Island (Ill.) High Sch., 1962-63, Univ. Chgo. (Ill.) Lab. Schs., 1963-66; counseling dir. Upward Bound, Mundeline Coll., Chgo., 1966-68; assoc. prof. counseling Kennedy-King Coll., Chgo., 1968-82; psychotherapist Worcester County Counseling Assocs., Bolton, Mass., 1982-87; clin. supr. Valley Adult Counseling Svc., Bellingham, Mass., 1982-84; cons. psychologist Mass. Dept. Edn., Bur. of Instnl. Schs., Boston, 1984-90; dir., psychotherapist Ea. Shore Assocs., Shrewsbury, Mass., 1987—. Psychologist Dept. Pediatrics and Psychiatry, St. Vincent's Hosp., Worcester, 1986—; cons., educator various schs. and orgns., Mass., Ill., 1962—; workshop presenter. Bd. mem., chair children's com. Worcester (Mass.) Area Mental Health & Retardation Bd., 1984-87; bd. alumni affairs DePauw U., 2003-; coord. Ctrl. Mass. disaster response network Mass. Psych Assoc., 1999-2005; mem. Local CISM Team, comm. on ministry Dioceses Western Mass., 1995-2005. Recipient Improvement Edn. grant Ford Found., Univ. Chgo., 1962. Fellow Am. Assn. Orthopsychiatry; mem. APA, Eye Movement Desensitization Reprocessing Internat. Assn., Mass. Psychol. Assn., New Eng. Soc. for Study Dissociative Disorders, Pi Lambda Theta, Psi Chi, Delta theta Chi. Episcopalian. Avocations: attending plays, jazz, swimming, travel. Office: Ea Shore Assocs 586 Main St Shrewsbury MA 01545-2920 Office Phone: 508-842-3100 14.

SMITH, CATHERINE H., bank executive; b. 1953; 2 children. BA, Hampshire Coll.; M in pub. and pvt. mgmt., Yale Sch. Orgn. and Mgmt. Sr. positions in investment and healthcare, 1983—98; CFO Aetna Fin. Services; pres., healthcare, edn., govt. distbn. ING US Worksite Fin. Services, COO, broker dealer ops., customer svc., USFS retail and worksite bus. groups; pres. US retail fin. services ING Group, CEO US ins. bus., CEO US retirement services, 2009—. Bd. mem. Outward Bound USA, Conn. Fund for Environment; adv. Conn. Trust for Pub. Land. Named one of 25 Women to Watch, US Banker, 2006, 2008. Avocations: hiking, skiing.*

SMITH, CATHERINE JEAN, artist, educator; b. Washington, Oct. 19, 1950; d. Albert Eugene and Catherine Virginia Smith. MFA, Sch. of the Art Inst. of Chgo., 1990. Prof. of art Mott C.C., Flint, Mich., 1991—. Bd. dirs. Buckham Fine Arts Gallery, Flint, Mich., 1992—. Author: Women in Pants: Manly Maidens, Cowgirls and Other Renegades, 2003 (Amelia Bloomer List, ALA, 2004); curator and author (art exhbn. and book) Witness and Warriors: The 1936-1937 Flint Sitdown Strike, 1999; one-woman shows include Flint Inst. Art, 1977. Recipient Jurors award, Mich. Outdoor Sculpture 5, Southfield, 1995; scholarship, Sch. of the Art Inst. of Chgo., 1989, Creative Artist grant, Arts Found. of Mich., 1993-4, Animating Democracy Initiative grant, C.S. Mott Found., 2001. Mem.: Coll. Art Assn. (assoc.). Democrat. Home: 824 S Leroy St Fenton MI 48430 Office: Mott CC 1401 E Court St Flint MI 48503 E-mail: womeninpants1@sbcglobal.net.

SMITH, CATHERINE MARIE, science educator; b. Bridgeport, Conn., Dec. 28, 1958; d. Arthur Vincent Giles, Sr. and Lila Catherine (Auger) Giles; m. Roger K. Smith, July 16, 1982. BS, U. Bridgeport, 1980; MBA, Sacred Heart U., 1994. Cert. Med. Technologist Am. Soc. Clin. Pathologists, 1981, lic. provisional Conn. educator. Medical technician Bridgeport Hosp., Conn., 1980—88; med. technologist St. Joseph Med. Ctr., Stamford, Conn., 1988—94; lab. mgr. Stamford Medical Group, Stamford, 1994—99; chemistry and biology tchr. Wilbur Cross HS, New Haven, 1999—2003, New Canaan HS, Conn., 2003—. Donor Am. Red Cross, Conn., 1984—; tchr. participant Jr. Sci. & Humanities Symposium, U. Conn., 2000—03; youth min. Our Lady of Assumption, Fairfield, Conn., 1989—2004; emmaus team mem. Holy Family, Fairfield, Conn., 2000—, St. Aloysius, New Canaan, Conn., 2004—. Mem.: NSTA, So. Poverty Law, Am. Soc. Clin. Pathologists, Conn. Nat. Sci. Tchrs. Assn., Pi Lambda Theta, Delta Mu Delta. Roman Catholic. Avocations: car racing, dog training. Personal E-mail: cmbgs@aol.com.

SMITH, CATHERINE R., computer software company executive; BS in Bus. Economics, U. Calif., Santa Barbara; MBA, U. So. Calif. Various fin. positions including v.p., CFO intelligence & info. systems bus. Raytheon Co., 1986—2003; exec. v.p., CFO Bell Systems Textron, Inc., 2003—05; exec. v.p., CFO Kennametal, Inc., 2005—06, Centex Corp., Dallas, 2006—09, GameStop Corp., Grapevine, Tex., 2009—. Bd. dirs. Dick's Sporting Goods, Inc., 2009—. Office: GameStop Corp 625 Westport Pky Grapevine TX 76051 Office Phone: 214-981-5000.*

SMITH, CHARLES ANTHONY, foundation administrator, director; b. Santa Fe, Sept. 16, 1939; s. Frances (Mier) Vigil; m. Paula Ann Thomas, June 26, 1965; 1 child, Charlene Danielle. Student various adminstrv. & law courses. Circulation mgr. Daily Alaska Empire, 1960-63; agt. Mut. of N.Y. Life Ins. Co., Juneau, Alaska, 1964-65; mng. ptnr. Future Investors in Alaska and Cinema Alaska, Juneau, 1961-62; SE Alaska rep. K & L Distbrs., 1966-68; mgr. SE Alaska Alaska Airlines Newspapers, 1969; dep. Alaska Retirement Sys., Juneau, 1970-71; apptd. dir. hwy. safety, gov.'s hwy. safety rep. Juneau, 1971-83; pres. Valley Svc. Ctr., I Nc., 1984-94; chmn. S.E. Alaska Employee Support of the Guard and Reserve, 1992—; pres. 3-S Corp., 1995—. Apptd. chmn. S.E. Alaska for ESGR, 1995; apptd. Alaska state dir. Selective Svc., 1996—. Author various hwy. safety manuals and plans. Alaska pres. Muscular Dystrophy Assn. Am.; pres. SE Alaska Emergency Med. Svcs. Coun., 1965-72; state dir. Selective Svc., 1996. Served to maj. Army N.G., 1964-88. Named Alaska Safety Man of Yr., 1977. Mem. Am. Assn. Motor Vehicle Adminstrs., Alaska Peace Officers Assn., Nat. Assn. Gov.'s Hwy. Safety Reps., N.G. Assn., Internat. Platform Assn., Elks (Juneau). Roman Catholic. Home: PO Box 32856 Juneau AK 99803-2856

SMITH, CHARLES DENNIS, neurologist, researcher; b. Boston, Feb. 17, 1948; s. Charles and Margaret Smith; m. Barbara Hausman-Smith, Aug. 26, 1972; children: Gabriel, Zachary. MD, Tulane Med. Sch., New Orleans, 1979. Diplomate neurology Am. Bd. Psychiatry and Neurology,

1986. Robert p. and mildred moores prof. alzheimer's rsch. Sanders-Brown Ctr. Aging, Lexington, Ky., 2006—; prof. neurology U. Ky. Med. Coll., Lexington, 2001—. Office: Rm 62 MRISC Davis-Mills Building UKMC 800 Rose St Lexington KY 40536-0098 Office Fax: 859-323-1068. Business E-Mail: csmith@mri.uky.edu.

SMITH, CHARLES EDWIN, computer science educator; b. Columbia, Mo., Apr. 15, 1950; s. William Walter and Nelletha Pearl (Lavendar) S.; m. Mary L. Davis, July 27, 1991. AA, Edison C.C., Ft. Myers, Fla., 1971; BS, Troy State U., 1979; MA, Webster U., St. Louis, 1989. Adj. instr. Manatee C.C., Venice, Fla., 1989-90, Edison Coll., Punta Gorda, Fla., 1989-92, prof. computer sci., 1992—, Charles O'Neill endowed chair astronomy, 1997—2001. Cons. Charles E. Smith Consulting, North Port, Fla., 1989-91. Served to maj. USAF, 1975-79, USAFR, 1979-96. Mem. Fla. Assn. C.C.s, Mil. Officers Assn. Am., Air Force Assn., Am. Legion, USGA, Elks. Avocations: reading, fishing, boating, astronomy, golf. Office: Edison C C 26300 Airport Rd Punta Gorda FL 33950-5748

SMITH, CHARLES HADDON, geologist, consultant, retired federal agency administrator; b. Dartmouth, NS, Can., Sept. 3, 1926; s. Albion Benson and Dora Pauline (McGill) S.; m. Mary Gertrude Saint, Sept. 5, 1949; children: Charles Douglas, Richard David, Alan Michael, Timothy McGill. B.Sc. and Diploma in Engring, Dalhousie U., Can., 1946, M.Sc. in Geology, 1948; MS, Yale U., 1951, PhD in Econ. Geology, 1952. Instr. Dalhousie U., Halifax, N.S., 1946-48; geologist Cerro de Pasco Copper Corp., Morococha, Peru, 1949, Geol. Survey of Can., Ottawa, Ont., 1952-64, chief petrological scis. div., 1964-67, chief crustal geology div., 1967-68; sci. adviser Sci. Council Can., Ottawa, 1968-70; dir. planning Dept. Energy Mines and Resources, Ottawa, 1970-71, asst. dep. minister sci. and tech., 1971-75, sr. asst. dep. minister, 1975-81; pres. Charles H. Smith Cons., 1982-94. Mem. adv. coun. dept. geology and geophysics Princeton U., 1967-76; sci. advisor Can. Commn. for UNESCO, 1983-89; exec. dir. Can. Nat. Com./World Energy Conf., 1983-90; bd. govs. Can. Inst. Radiation Safety, 1983-86; hon. mem. Energy Coun. Can., 1991—; coord. 150th anniversary Geol. Survey Can., 1990-93. Mem. editl. bd. Am. Jour. Sci., 1967-72, Mineralium Deposita, 1968-83, Jour. Petrology, 1966-70, Econ. Geology, 1966-70; contbr. articles to profl. jours. Fellow Royal Soc. Can. (fgn. sec. 1986-90), Canadian Acad. Engring., Mineral. Soc. Am., Soc. Econ. Geologists (v.p. N.Am. 1968-70); mem. Can. Inst. Mining and Metallurgy (life mem., v.p. 1982-84), Assn. Profl. Engrs. Ont., Geol. Assn. Can., Can. Geosci. Coun. (pres. 1984), Rotary.

SMITH, CHARLES ISAAC, geology educator; b. Hearne, Tex., Feb. 9, 1931; s. Walter Lee and Nellie Lucille (Clearwater) S.; m. Anita Lou Howell, Aug. 22, 1961; children: Lanita Maylene, James Emmett, Timothy Stephen, Sheila Nell. BS, Baylor U., 1952; MA, La. State U., 1955; PhD, U. Mich., 1966. Geologist Shell Devel. Co., Houston, 1955-60, 62-65; prof. geology U. Mich., Ann Arbor, 1965-77, chmn. dept., 1970-77; prof. geology U. Tex., Arlington, 1977-93, prof. emeritus, 1994—, chmn. dept., 1977-89, cons. geologist, 1993—. Contbr. articles to profl. jours. Home: 3814 Tridens Trl San Angelo TX 76904-7223 Office: Univ Tex Dept Geology Arlington TX 76019-0001

SMITH, CHARLES JOE, SR., music educator; b. Tuskegee, Ala., Aug. 24, 1951; s. Jim Smith and Mattie (Burrell) Wilson; m. Susie Marie Jones, May 9, 1970; children: Charles J., Jr., Yashica C. Profl. diploma, Am. Sch. Photography, Chgo., 1972; B in Music Edn., Jackson State U., Miss., 1973; M in Music Edn., Vandercook Coll. Music, 1982; PhD, Kennedy-Western U., Augoura Hills, Calif., 1988. Cert. music educator, Ga. Dir. bands D.C. Wolfe High Sch., Shorter, Ala., 1973-77, T.W. Josey Comprehensive High Sch., Augusta, Ga., 1977—; adminstrv. asst. Richmond County Band Programs, 1977. Guest condr. Amos Alonzo Stagg Bowl, 1979-81; coord. Cen. Savannah River Area Jazz Fest, 1980-85; adjudicator Alcorn State U. Jazz Fest, 1982-85; asst. dir. John Phillip Sousa Nat. High Sch. Hon. Band, 1985; cons. Ga. Dept. Edn. Tchr. Cert. Test Revision; chmn. Richmond County Bd. Edn. Spring Fling; other activities. Recipient award Augusta Black History Com., badge of merit John Phillip Sousa Found., 1985, Bridge Builders award Upsilon Gamma Gamma chpt. Omega Psi Phi, 2006, Pres.'s award Ga. State Conf. NAACP, 2007; named with D.C. Wolfe High Sch. Band as Ala.'s Bicentennial Band State of Ala., 1976, Hon. Lt. Col. Aide-de-Camp, 1976, one of Outstanding Young Men of Am., 1977, 83, 85, 87, 88, 90, Tchr. of Yr. Augusta, Ga.-Richmond County, 1988-89, Educator of Yr. Augusta Jaycees, 1989, State Citizen of Yr. Omega Psi Phi, 1989, Local Citizen of Yr., 7th Dist. Citizen of Yr., Citizen of Yr. local Psi Omega chpt. Omega Psi Phi, 2006. Mem. NAACP, Nat. Assn. Jazz Educators (chmn. jazz 10th dist. Ga. 1985—, cert. 1986—), Nat. Band Assn., Music Educators Nat. Conf., Richmond County Band Dirs. Assn. (chmn. budget, all-county coms. 1985—), Inst. Cert. Photographers, Inc. (life), Profl. Photographers Am., Ga. Music Educators Assn., 100 Black Men Am., Inc., 100 Black Men Augusta, Omega Psi Phi (chmn. talent hunt, scholarship coms. 1985— Local Citizen of Yr. 1989, State Citizen of Yr. 1989, 7th Dist. Citizen of Yr. Ala., Ga., Fla., Miss., 1989). Clubs: Band Boosters (Augusta) (chmn. budget com. 1977—). Democrat. Baptist. Avocations: music, basketball, tennis, football, golf. Home: 2910 Inwood Dr Hephzibah GA 30815-4158

SMITH, CHARLES WILLIAM, social sciences educator; b. Providence; s. Joseph and Clara (Loitman) S.; m. Rita Cope, Sept. 3, 1963; children: Abigail Cope Saguy, Jonathan Cope. AB, Wesleyan U., 1960; MA, Brandeis U., 1966, PhD in Sociology, 1966. Instr. sociology Simmons Coll., Boston, 1964-65; from lectr. to assoc. prof. Queens Coll., Flushing, NY, 1965-71, from assoc. to prof. sociology, 1979—; grad. faculty Grad. Ctr. CUNY, 1986—. Vis. scholar Nuffield Coll., Oxford, Eng., 1979-80, Wesleyan U., Middletown, Conn., 1987-88; chair dept. sociology Queens Coll., Flushing, 1988-91, 97-00, acting dean of faculty social sci., 1991-92, dean faculty social sci., 1992-97; cons. auctions, 1986—. Author: Critique of Sociological Reasoning: An Essay in Philosophic Sociology, 1979, Auctions: The Social Construction of Values, 1989, Success and Survival on Wall Street: Understanding the Mind of the Market, 1999, Market Values Im American Higher Education, 2000; editor Jour. for Theory of Social Behavior, 1983—. Bd. dirs., pres. Cmty. Action Program of White Plains, N.Y., 1974-79; bd. trustees, v.p. Temple Israel Ctr. of White Plains, 1975-94; class agt., alumni activities Wesleyan U., Middletown, Conn., 1960—. Recipient FIPSE award, Dept. Edn., 1993—96, Ford Found. Diversity grant, 1990—93, 1996—98. Office: Queens Coll CUNY 65-30 Kissena Blvd Flushing NY 11367-1575 Office Phone: 718-997-2840. Business E-Mail: charles.smith@qc.cuny.edu.

SMITH, CHARLES Z., retired state supreme court justice; b. Lakeland, Fla., Feb. 23, 1927; s. John R. and Eva (Love) S.; m. Eleanor Jane Martinez, Aug. 20, 1955; children: Carlos M., Michael O., Stephen P., Felica L. BS, Temple U., 1952; JD, U. Wash., 1955. Bar: Wash. 1955. Law clk. Wash. Supreme Ct., Olympia, 1955-56; dep. pros. atty., asst. chief criminal div. King County, 1956-60; ptnr. Bianchi, Smith & Tobin, Seattle, 1960-61; spl. asst. to atty. gen. criminal div. U.S. Dept. Justice, Washington, 1961-64; judge criminal dept. Seattle Mcpl. Ct., 1965-66; judge Superior Ct. King County, 1966-73; former assoc. dean, prof. law U. Wash., 1973—83; justice Wash. Supreme Ct., Olympia, until 2002. Mem. adv. bd. NAACP, Seattle Urban League, Wash. State Literacy Coun., Boys Club, Wash. Citizens for Migrant Affairs, Medina Children's Svc., Children's Home Soc. Wash., Seattle Better Bus. Bur., Seattle Foundation, Seattle Symphony Orch., Seattle Opera Assn., Community Svc. Ctr. for Deaf and Hard of Hearing, Seattle U., Seattle Sexual Assault Ctr., Seattle Psychoanalytic Inst., The Little Sch., Linfield Coll., Japanese Am. Citizens League, Kawabe Meml. Hous, Puget Counseling Ctr, Am. Cancer Soc., Hutchinson Cancer Rsch. Ctr., Robert Chinn Found.; pres. Am. Bapt. Chs. U.S.A., 1976-77, U.S. Commn. on Internat. Religious Freedom, 1999-2000. lt. col. ret. USMCR Mem. ABA, Am. Judicature Soc., Washington Bar Assn., Seattle-King County Bar Assn., Order of Coif., Phi Alpha Delta, Alpha Phi Alpha. Mailing: PO Box 146 Olympia WA 98507-0146 Home Phone: 206-324-0776; Office Phone: 360-273-0964. Business E-Mail: czsmith@usa.net.

SMITH, CHARLOTTE REED, retired music educator; b. Eubank, Ky., Sept. 15, 1921; d. Joseph Lumpkin and Cornelia Elizabeth (Spenser) Reed; m. Walter Lindsay Smith, Aug. 24, 1949; children: Walter Lindsay IV, Elizabeth Reed. BA in Music, Tift Coll., 1941; MA in Mus. Theory, Eastman Sch. of Music, 1946; postgrad. Juilliard Sch., 1949. Asst. prof. theory Okla. Bapt. U., 1944-45, Washburn U., 1946-48; prof. music Furman U., Greenville, S.C., 1948-92; chmn. dept. music, 1987-92. Editor: Seven Penitential Psalms with Two Laudate Psalms, 1983; author: Manual of Sixteenth-Century Contrapuntal Style, 1989. Mem. Internat. Musicological Soc., Am. Musicological Soc., Soc. for Music Theory, AAUP (sec.-treas. Furman chpt. 1984-85), Nat. Fedn. Music Clubs, Pi Kappa Lambda. Republican. Baptist.

SMITH, CHRISTOPHER ALLEN, operations executive, financial executive; b. Rockford, Ill., Nov. 16, 1961; s. Robert Lee and Martha Ann (Moody) S.; m. Mary G. Meany, Apr. 13, 1991. BA, postgrad., Ind. U., 1983, Golden Gate U., San Francisco, 1986—87; MA, U. Phoenix, Ariz., 2003. Rates analyst North American Van Lines, Ft. Wayne, Ind., 1984-85; mgr., investor rels. BRAE Corp., San Francisco, 1985-87; fin. analyst CIS Corp., San Francisco, 1987-89; dir., corp. devel. Affiliated Computer Systems, Inc., San Francisco, 1989-96; v.p. Sci. Applications Internat. Corp., San Francisco, 1996—. Alumni Dept. of Def. Joint Civilian Orientation Conf. Contbr. articles to profl. jours. Vol. Rep. Party, Foster City, Calif., 1988; apptd. dir. Pvt. Industry Coun. Contra Costa County; apptd. bd. mem. St. Perpetua Sch., 2005-06. With USMCR, 1982-83. Mem. Equipment Leasing Assn. Am. (Jour. award 1991), Ind. U. Alumni Assn. Republican. Roman Catholic. Avocations: writing, photography, gardening. Office: Sci Applications Internat Corp 1000 Broadway Ste 675 Oakland CA 94607 Office Phone: 510-466-7174. Business E-Mail: christopher.a.smith-2@saic.com.

SMITH, CHRISTOPHER HENRY, United States Representative from New Jersey; b. Rahway, NJ, Mar. 4, 1953; s. Bernard Henry and Katherine Joan (Hall) Smith; m. Marie Hahn, July 2, 1977; children: Melissa, Christopher, Michael, Elyse. Student, Worcester Coll., Eng., 1973-74; BA in Bus. Adminstrn., Trenton State Coll., NJ, 1975. Exec. dir. NJ Right to Life Com., Inc., 1976-78; dir. instl. sales Leisure Unlimited Inc., Woodbridge, NJ, 1978-80; legis. agt. NJ Gen. Assembly, 1979; mem. US Congress from 4th NJ dist., 1981—, mem. fgn. affairs and internat. rels. com., ranking mem. security and cooperation in Europe commn., co-chair Pro-Life Caucus. US rep. to UN Internat. Conf. on immunizing world's children. Co-chair Coalition for Autism Rsch. and Edn.; past chair., mem. Commn. on Security and Cooperation in Europe; active in human rights movements Romania, China, Vietnam, former Soviet Union. Recipient William Wilberforce award, 2002, Leader for Peace award, Peace Corps, George (Buck) Gillispie Congl. award, Meritorious Svc. Blinded Am. Vets. Found., 2003; named Legislator of Yr., Internat. Assn. Chiropractors, JWV of America, 1996, Leader of Yr., NJ State Postal Workers Union, 2002. Mem.: Nat. Fedn. Ind. Bus. Republican. Roman Catholic. Office: US House Reps 2373 Rayburn House Office Bldg Washington DC 20515-3004 Office Phone: 202-225-3765. Office Fax: 202-225-7768.*

SMITH, CLYDE RAY, dean; b. Bassett, Va, Apr. 21, 1935; s. William Henry and Ava I. (Roberson) S.; m. Phyllis Jane Watkins, Mar. 25, 1959; children: Anthony William, Cheryl Ann, Theresa Jane. BA, Bridgewater Coll., 1956; MBA, U. Va., 1958; D in Bus. Adminstrn. (hon.), Bridgewater Coll., 2004. Instr. U. Va. - Darden, Charlottesville, Va., 1961-64, asst. prof., 1964-67, assoc. prof., 1967-72, prof., 1972—, assoc. dean MBA prog., 1972-94, assoc. dean exec. edn., 1994-97, interim dean, 1997-98; exec. dir. Darden Sch. Found., 1998—2003; prof. emeritus U. Va. - Darden, Charlottesville, Va., 2003—. Adminstrv. dir. Inst. Chartered Fin. Analysts, Charlottesville, 1962-69; bd. trustees Bridgewater Coll. Co-author: (books) Executive's Guide to Mgmt. Accounting and Control Sys., 1998, Fin. Accounting for Mgmt., 1981. Capt. (res.) US Army, 1958-68. Named Disting. Alumnus Bridgewater Coll., Va., 1991. Mem. AICPA, Colonade Club, Farmington Country Club, Raven Soc., Beta Gamma Sigma, Omicron Delta Kappa. Home: 39 Canterbury Rd Charlottesville VA 22903-4700 Office: Univ Va - Darden Sch PO Box 6550 Charlottesville VA 22906-6550 Office Phone: 434-924-4799. E-mail: crs6n@virginia.edu.

SMITH, CORA ADELE, author; b. Bklyn., Oct. 14, 1939; d. Gabriel and Gemma (DeMartino) Garofalo; m. Mel Warren Smith, July 22, 1967; children— Charles Edward, Dorothy Rose. B.S. in Elem. Edn., Fordham U., 1967; postgrad. N.Y. Inst. Tech., 1979-81, U. Mass., Amherst, 1982. Tchr. pvt. and parochial schs., 1960-72; data processor IRS, Holtsville, N.Y., 1984-87; staff writer monthly Our Voice, Holbrook, N.Y. Author serialized stories for Organian Quest mag. including: Emotions Double Edge, 1979; Contemptable Struggle, 1980; By Appearances Deceiving, 1980; Sweetness in the Air, 1981; Shuttle Ark, 1982; Sweet Times, 1983; A Child Fantasy-Freckles Mother's Day Surprise, 1984. Mem. com. Boy Scouts Am., 1980-85; asst. Girl Scouts U.S.A., 1983-85. Mem. Am. Film Inst., Air Force Sgts. Assn. Aux. Democrat.

SMITH, CORI ELIZABETH, legislative staff member; B, Rhodes Coll., Memphis, 1999. Spl. projects dir., Rep. Mike Ross US House of Reps., Washington, appropriations, grants coord., Rep. Mike Ross, 2003, chief of staff to Rep. Mike Ross, 2003—06, chief of staff to Rep. Brad Ellsworth, 2007—. Democrat. Office: 513 Cannon House Office Bldg Washington DC 20515 Office Phone: 202-225-4636. Office Fax: 202-225-3284. Business E-Mail: cori.smith@mail.house.gov.*

SMITH, CORINNE ROTH, psychologist; b. Reading, Pa., May 22, 1945; d. Zoltan and Elizabeth (Foldes) Roth; m. Lynn Helden Smith, June 9, 1968; children: Juliette Sarah, Rachael Eliza. BA in Psychology cum laude, Syracuse U., 1967, PhD, 1973; MA, Temple U., Phila., 1969. Lic. psychologist, NY. Psychologist experimental presch. program Syracuse City Schs., 1970-71; psychologist reading clinic Syracuse U., 1969-70, coordinator lab. sch. and clinic, 1971-72, asst. prof., 1971—84, founder, dir. psychoednl. teaching lab., 1971—, founder, dir. comprehensive assessment ctr., 1981-83, psychologist Devel. Evaluation Ctr., 1984—96, assoc. dean edn., 1992—2000, prof., 1997—, dean, 2000—02, chair inclusive elem. and spl. edn. program, 2005—, chair inclusive spl. edn. 1-6 MS program, 2005—, chair tchg. and leadership programs, 2006—, chair inclusive presch. spl. edn., 2008—, chair, 1992—, with sexual harassment policies, 2005—, senate agenda com. mem., 2005—08. Mem. Coun. for Exceptional Children; reviewer Aspen, Ablex, Mc Graw Hill, Little Brown & Co., NY, Allyn & Bacon, Pergammon, 1985—; apptd. mem. Gov. NY Coun. for Youth, Albany, 1984-91; chair hon. degrees com., Meredith selection com., sexual harassment com., human svcs. and health professions formation com., Syracuse U., 1993-2009; spkr. in field. Author: Learning Disabilities: The Interaction of Learner, Task and Setting, 1983, 2d edit., 1991, 3rd edit, 1994, 4th edit., 1998, 5th edit., 2004, (retitled) Learning Disabilities: The Interaction of Students and Their Environments, The People's Guide to Drug Education, 1992, Learning Disabilities A to Z: The Complete Parent Guide to Learning Disabiltities from Preschool to Adulthood, 1997, reprinted in Portuguese, Latvian, Korean; contbr. articles to profl. jours. and chpts. to books. Bd. dirs. Ctrl. NY United Way, 1987-93, leadership giving chair, 2003-06; pres. Jewish Comm. Ctr., Syracuse, 1978-81; bd. dirs., chair career womens network Syracuse Jewish Fedn., 1985-87, womens campaign chair, 1987-89, gen. campaign chair, 1990-92, Cmty. Found. of Ctrl., NY, 2009-, Literacy Vol. Greater Syracuse, 2009-. Recipient Disting. Svc. award Jewish Comm. Ctr., 1976, Comm. Leadership award Syracuse Jewish Fedn., 1986, 89, Jewish Family Svc. Humanitarian award, 1991, Roth Humanitarian award, 1992, Citizen of Yr. award, 2000; named Woman of Yr. Post Std., 1990; grantee NY State Office Mental Retardation and Devel. Disabilities, 1985-93; Leadership award Coun. Jewish Women, 1999. Mem. Am. Psych. Assn., Nat. Assn. Sch. Psychologists, NY State Learning Disabilities Assn., Learning Disability Assn. Am., Winnick Hillel (pres. nat. bd. 2003-06, treas. 2007-), Parents Mag. (adv. bd. 2002-07). Avocations: tennis, gardening. Office: Syracuse U 136 Huntington Hl Syracuse NY 13244-0001 Office Phone: 315-443-1468.

SMITH, CRAIG R., health products executive; m. Cynthia Smith; 2 children. BA, Univ. So. Calif. With Owens & Minor, Glen Allen, Va., 1989—, divsn. v.p., group v.p., sr. v.p. distbn. and info. sys., 1989—95, exec. v.p., COO, 1995—99, pres., COO, 1999—2005, pres., CEO, 2005—. Bd. mem. Inst. for Diversity in Health Mgmt., Health Ind. Dist. Assn.; mem. bd. vis. St. Gertrude High Sch., Richmond; mem. bus. council Va. Mus. Fine Arts; bd. dir. Greater Richmond YMCA. Office: Owens & Minor Inc 9120 Lockwood Blvd Mechanicsville VA 23116*

SMITH, CRAIG R., lawyer; BS in Civil Engring., Manhattan Coll., 1992; MS in Environmental Engring., U. Ill., 1994; JD, NYU, 1997. Bar: Mass. 1997. Principal Fish & Richardson, Boston. Mem. bd. dirs. Greater Boston Legal Svcs. Recipient Norman S. Ostrow Moot Ct. award, 1996; named Up and Coming Lawyer, Mass. Lawyers Weekly, 2006; named a Super Lawyer-Rising Star, Boston Mag., 2005. Mem.: ABA. Office: Fish & Richardson 225 Franklin St Boston MA 02110-2804 Office Phone: 617-542-5070. Office Fax: 617-542-8906.

SMITH, CRAIG RICHEY, cardiothoracic surgeon; b. Cleve., Nov. 17, 1948; m. Patricia M. Smith; 1 child, Emily Van Gorder. BA, Williams Coll., Williamstown, Mass., 1970; MD, Case Western Res. U. Sch. Med., Cleve., 1977. Diplomate Am. Bd. Thoracic Surgery, Am. Bd. Surgery, lic. NJ, NY. Intern U. Rochester Hosp., NY, 1977-78, resident, gen. surgery, 1978-82; fellow cardiothoracic surgery Columbia Presbyn. Med. Ctr., NYC, 1982-84, chief, divsn. cardiothoracic surgery, 1996—. Prof. surgery Columbia U. Coll. Physicians & Surgeons, 2001—, interim chmn., dept. surgery, 2007—; adjunct prof. cardiothoracic surgery Columbia Presbyn. Med. Ctr. Contbr. articles to profl. jours. Mem.: ACS, AMA, Internat. Soc. Heart Transplantation, NY Soc. Thoracic Surgery, Am. Coll. Cardiology, Am. Surgical Assn., Am. Heart Assn., Soc. Thoracic Surgeons, Internat. Soc. Minimally Invasive Cardiothoracic Surgery, Cardiothoracic Surgery Network, Am. Assn. Thoracic Surgery (officer, cons., edn. com.). Office: Columbia Presbyn Med Ctr Milstein Bldg 7GN 435 177 Fort Wash Ave New York NY 10032-3713 Office Phone: 212-305-8312. Office Fax: 212-305-0905. Business E-Mail: crs2@columbia.edu.

SMITH, CULLEN, lawyer; b. Waco, Tex., May 31, 1925; s. Curtis Cullen and Elizabeth (Brient) S.; m. Laura Risher Dossett, Mar. 6, 1948 (dec.); children: Sallie Smith Wright, Alethea Risher Smith Gilbert, Elizabeth Brient Smith; m. Ann Brown Parsons, Jan. 3, 2009. Student, Emory U., 1943-44, Duke U., 1944; BBA, Baylor U., 1948, JD, 1950. Bar: Tex. 1950. Ptnr. firm Smith, McIlheran & Smith, Weslaco, Tex., 1950-53, Naman, Howell, Smith & Lee LLP, Waco, 1953—. Lectr. law Baylor U. Sch. Law, 1964-72 Contbr. articles to legal publs. Mem. standing com. Episcopal Diocese of Tex., 1960-63, 74-75; trustee Episcopal Theol. Sem. of S.W., 1962-67; mem. Waco City Coun., 1983-86; chmn. bd. Vanguard Sch., 1975; bd. dirs. G.H. Pape Found., 1993-94; bd. dirs., vice chmn. Tex. Ctr. for Legal Ethics and Professionalism, 1994-99; mem. adv. coun. Baylor U. Coll. Arts and Scis., 1998-2003. 1st lt. USMCR, 1943—46, inactive, 1946—58. Named one of 5 Outstanding Young Texans Tex. Jr. C. of C., 1957, Baylor Lawyer of Yr., 1980; recipient Disting. Alumnus award Waco Ind. Sch. Dist. Edn. Found., 2002; named Outstanding Mentor of Tex., Tex. Young Lawyers Assn., 2007. Fellow Am. Bar Found., Tex. Bar Found. (chmn. bd. 1973-74, 50 Yr. Lawyer award 2000), fellow Coll. of Law Practice Mgmt.; mem. ABA (chmn. standing com. econs. law practice 1965-69, chmn. spl. com. on law book pub. practices 1970-72, chmn. gen. practice sect. 1973-74, mem. house of dels. 1974-81), Am. Law Firm Assn. (chmn. 1989-90), Waco-McLennan County Bar Assn. (pres. 1956-57), Mont. Bar Assn. (hon.), State Bar Tex. (pres. jr. bar 1957-58, chmn. profl. econs. com. 1959-61, chmn. spl. com. on revision Tex. Canons Ethics 1969-71, dir. 1971-74, pres. 1978-79), Philos. Soc. Tex., Baylor U. Law Alumni Assn. (pres. 1962-63), Order of Coif, Delta Sigma Phi, Phi Delta Phi, Am. Inns Ct. (master), Ridgewood Country Club (pres. 1965), Hedonia Club (pres. 1957), Rotary. Avocation: photography. Home: Oak Grove Farm 447 Meandering Way China Spring TX 76633-2905 Office: Naman Howell Smith & Lee LLP Tex Ctr PO Box 1470 Waco TX 76703-1470 Office Phone: 254-755-4100.

SMITH, CURT, think tank executive, journalist; b. Richmond, Ind., May 11, 1957; s. John Robert and Rena Carolyn Smith; m. Debra Diane Sutter, Aug. 21, 1980; children: Stephen, Julie, Andrew, Kimberly. BA, Ind. U., 1978. Press sec. Rep. Dan Coats, Washington, 1983-88, campaign mgr. Fort Wayne, Ind., 1988; comms. dir. U.S. Senator Dan Coats, Washington, 1989-91, state dir., comms. dir., 1991-95; chief of staff U.S. Rep. John Hostettler, Washington, 1995-98; v.p. external affairs Hudson Inst., Indpls., 1998-99, v.p., COO, 1999—2001; pres. Ind. Family Inst., 2001—06. Acting city editor Fort Wayne Jour. Gazette, 1983, staff writer, 1980-83; staff writer Palladium-Item, Richmond, Ind., 1979-80. Stringer for N.Y. Times, 1982-83. Vice chmn., bd. elders, Traders Point Christian Ch., Indpls., 1999, past chmn., elder, 1996—; led UN sanction Election Observer Team, 1999. Named Outstanding Environtl. reporter Izack Walton League of Am., 1983; recipient Voice of Dem. Ind. winner VFW, 1975. Republican. Office: Indiana Family Inst 155 East Market Suite 307 Indianapolis IN 46204 Office Phone: 317-713-3500. E-mail: curt@hoosierfamily.org.

SMITH, CYNTHIA M., bank executive; married; 3 children. MBA, Lansbridge U., Can.; M in Mgmt., Am. Grad. Sch. Mgmt. With US Bank; exec. v.p. ops. ProPay USA, Inc.; sr. v.p. product devel. and bus. planning JP Morgan Chase; sr. v.p. client rels. and program consulting First USA Fin. Services, Inc. - Paymentech, Inc.; sr. v.p., dir. bankcard products and services Zions Bancorporation, Salt Lake City, 2004—. V.p. MABA Bd.; sr. industry cons. Dual Currency Systems, Mpls. Active Global Volunteers. Named one of 25 Most Powerful Women in Banking, US Banker, 2008. Office: Zions Bancorporation One S Main St Salt Lake City UT 84133-1109 Office Phone: 801-524-4787.*

SMITH, D. BROOKS, federal judge; b. 1951; BA, Franklin and Marshall Coll., 1973; JD, Dickinson Sch. Law, 1976. Pvt. practice Jubelirer, Carothers, Krier, Halpern & Smith, Altoona, Pa., 1976-84, mng. ptnr., 1981—83; judge Ct. Common Pleas of Blair County, Pa., 1984-88, US Dist. Ct. (we. dist.) Pa., 1988—2002, chief judge, 2001—02; judge US Ct. Appeals (3d cir.), 2002—. Asst. dist. atty. Blair County, part-time, 1977-79, spl. prosecutor, 1981-83, dist. atty. part-time, 1983-84; adv. com. on criminal rules U.S. Jud. Conf., 1993-99; com. space and facilities, US Jud. Conf., 2006-. Trustee St. Francis Coll., 1992—2004, Phila. U., 2005—06, Mt. Aloysius Coll., 2006—. Mem. Am. Law Inst., Pa. Bar Assn., Am. Judicature Soc., Pa. Soc., Amen Corner, Blair County Game, Fish and Forestry Assn., Fed. Judges Assn. (bd. dirs. 1993-97, 2002—), Inns of Ct., Allegheny County Bar Assn., Pi Gamma Mu. Office: Allegheny Profl Ctr 1798 Old Rte 220 N Ste 203 Duncansville PA 16635*

SMITH, DAN F., chemicals executive; With Atlantic Richfield Co, Los Angeles, Calif., 1967—88; exec. v.p., CFO Lyondell Chem. Co., Houston, dir., 1988—, COO, 1993—96, pres., 1994—, CEO, 1996—. Bd. dir. Cooper Industries. Office: Lyondell Chemical Co 1221 McKinney St Ste 700 Houston TX 77010

SMITH, DANIEL B., federal official; BA, Univ. Colo.; MA, PhD, Stanford Univ. Joined Fgn. Svc. US State Dept., 1983, various Fgn. Svc. positions Bern, Istanbul, Ottawa & Stockholm, exec. asst. to undersecretary for glob. affairs Washington, spl. asst. to asst. sec. for European & Canadian affairs, country officer for Czechoslovakia, prin. dep. asst. sec. for consular affairs, 2002—05, exec. asst. to undersecretary for pub. diplomacy & pub. affairs, 2005—07, exec. sec., exec. secretariat, 2007—. Recipient various State Dept. awards. Office: US State Dept 2201 C St NW Washington DC 20520*

SMITH, DANIEL C., dean, finance educator; BBA, U. Toledo, 1980, MBA, 1982; PhD in bus. adminstrn., U. Pitts., 1988. Asst. prof. U. Wis. Sch. Bus., Madison; asst. to assoc. prof. U. Pitts. Joesph M. Katz Grad. Sch. Bus.; joined faculty Kelley Sch. Bus., Ind. U., 1996, MBA program chair, 1998—2001, chair mktg. dept., 2002—03, Clare W. Barker chair mktg., 2002—, assoc. dean academics, 2003—04, interim dean, 2004—05, dean, 2005—. Mem. editl. rev. bd. Jour. Mktg., Jour. Acad. Mktg. Sci., Jour. Competitive Intelligence, Jour. Personal Selling and Sales Mgmt., Jour. Market Focused Mgmt. Avocations: fly fishing, food and wine. Office: Indiana Univ Kelley Sch Business 1575 E 10 St Ste 2010 Bloomington IN 47405 Office Phone: 812-855-8489. Business E-Mail: dansmith@indiana.edu.*

SMITH, DANIEL CLIFFORD, lawyer; b. Cin., Aug. 9, 1936; s. Clifford John and Vivian Aileen (Stone) S.; m. Carroll Cunningham; children: Edward, Andrew, Scott. BS, Ariz. State U., 1960; postgrad., George Washington U., 1961—62; JD, Am. U., 1965. Bar: D.C. 1965, U.S. Ct. Appeals (D.C. cir.) 1966, U.S. Ct. Appeals (Fed. cir.), U.S. Dist. Ct. D.C. 1966, Va. 1967, U.S. Supreme Ct. 1969, U.S. Ct. Appeals (4th, 5th, 6th, 7th, 9th and 11th cirs.), U.S. Ct. Claims, U.S. Ct. Customs and Patent Appeals, U.S. Tax Ct. Assoc. Alpern & Feissner, Washington, 1963-66; atty. FTC, Washington, 1966-70; ptnr. Arent, Fox, Kintner, Plotkin & Kahn, Washington, 1970-93, Canfield & Smith, Washington, 1993—. Pres., dir. Country Pl. Citizens Assn., Inc., 1974-77; bd. dirs. Sea Watch Condominium, Ocean City, Md., 1978—, treas., 1982-86, pres. 1986—; active Supreme Ct. Hist. Soc., The Federalist Soc., Smithsonian Inst. Assocs., Ariz. State Soc. Served with USMC. Mem. D.C. Bar Assn. (bd. dirs. 1974-76, chmn. consumer protection com. 1972-74, chmn. D.C. affairs sect. 1975-76), Va. State Bar Assn., Fed. Bar Assn., Assn. Trial Lawyers Am., Nat. Field Selling Assn. (gen. counsel), Ariz. State U. Alumni Assn., Rotary Club (pres. 1987-88, 96-97), Optimist (pres. 1972-73), Internat. Town and Country Club (dir. 1969-73), Masons, Delta Theta Phi. Office: Canfield & Smith Ste 800 910 17th St NW Washington DC 20006-2606

SMITH, DANIEL T., retail executive; B in Economics, U. Mich.; M in Human Resources, Washington U., St. Louis. Various positions in merchandising, store ops. and human resources May Department Stores Co., 1984—95; dir. compensation/benefits Borders Group, Inc., 1995, various positions including v.p. human resources Waldenbooks, then v.p. human resources Borders Group, 2001—03, sr. v.p. human resources, 2003—08, exec. v.p. human resources, 2008, chief adminstrv. officer, 2009—. Chmn. adv. coun. Human Resources Forum; chmn. adv. client coun. Merrill Lynch & Co. Inc. Office: Borders Group Inc 100 Phoenix Dr Ann Arbor MI 48108 Office Phone: 734-477-1798. Business E-Mail: dsmith@bordersgroupinc.com.*

SMITH, DARVIN SCOTT, internist; b. Houston, Jan. 4, 1963; MS, Harvard U., 1987; MD, U. Colo. Sch. Medicine, 1992. Diplomate Am. Bd. Internal Medicine. Intern U. Colo., Denver, 1992-93; resident in internal medicine Stanford (Calif.) U., 1993-95, fellow in infectious disease, 1996—. Mem. AMA, Am. Coll. Physicians.

SMITH, DAVID A., medical services executive; BS, U. No. Fla. CPA. Public acctg., 1983—87; regional mgr., gen. mgr., sales mgr. and opers. mgr. PSS/World Medical Inc., Jacksonville, Fla., 1987—93, v.p., 1992—96, CFO, 1992—2002, bd. dirs., 1993—, exec. v.p., 1996—2000, pres., 2000—, CEO, 2002—, chmn., 2007—. Mem. exec. bd. Health Industry Distributors Assn. Office: PSS World Med Inc 4345 Southpoint Blvd Jacksonville FL 32216*

SMITH, DAVID A., museum director; B, MA, Clark U., Worcester, Mass.; PhD in Econ. Geography, U. Pitts. Founder, ptnr. Lane, Nolan, Smith & Co., Inc., Pitts., Pentrust Real Estate Adv. Svcs., Inc.; dir. Powdermill Nature Res., Rector, Pa., 2003—; interim co-dir. Carnegie Mus. Natural History, Pitts., 2007—. Bd. dirs. Forbes Reinsurance Co. Ltd. Bd. chmn. Magee-Womens Hosp.; chmn. Magee-Womens Health Corp.; bd. dirs. U. Pitts. Med. Ctr. Office: Powdermill Nature Res 1847 Rt 381 Rector PA 15677 also: Carnegie Mus Natural History 4400 Forbes Ave Pittsburgh PA 15213 Office Phone: 724-593-4555. Office Fax: 724-593-4554. Business E-Mail: smithd@carnegiemnh.org.

SMITH, DAVID B., geochemist, researcher; s. Burl M. Smith and Louise McDaniel. BA, MS, Vanderbilt U., Nashville, 1972; PhD, Colo. Sch. Mines, Golden, 1979. Rsch. geochemist US Geol. Survey, Denver, 1975—. Chief, geochemistry US Geol. Survey, Denver, 1990—95; co-leader Internat. Union Geol. Scis. Task Group Global Geochem. Baselines, 1997—. Fellow: Applied Geochemists Assn. (sec. 1998—, Past Pres.s' medal 2009); mem.: Soc. Environ. Geochemistry & Health, Internat. Assn. GeoChemistry, The Nature Conservancy. Avocation: travel. Office: US Geol Survey Denver Fed Ctr MS 973 Denver CO 80225 Business E-Mail: dsmith@usgs.gov.

SMITH, DAVID BURNELL, lawyer, state legislator; b. Charleston, W.Va., Apr. 8, 1941; s. Ernest Dayton and Nellie Dale (Tyler) S.; m. Rita J. Hughes, Sept. 25, 1967. BA, U. Charleston, 1967; JD, U. Balt., 1972; MJS, U. Nev., 1995. Bar: Colo. 1972, Md. 1972, U.S. Supreme Ct. 1980, Ariz. 1983, U.S. Dist. Ct. Md. 1972, U.S. Dist. Ct. Colo. 1972, U.S. Ct. Appeals (4th Cir.) 1972, U.S. Ct. Appeals (9th cir. 1972, U.S. Ct. Appeals (10th cir.) 1983. Sales rep. Gulf Oil, Washington, 1967-72; pvt. practice Littleton, Colo., 1972-83, Glendale, Ariz., 1983-86, Phoenix, 1986-88, Scottsdale, Ariz., 1988—; mem. Ariz. Ho. of Reps., 2005—, vice-chmn. judiciary com., 2005—. Pro-tempore judge Wickenburg Mcpl. Ct., 1986—; presiding judge Peoria (Ariz.) Mcpl. Ct., 1987-94, Cave Creek Mcpl. Ct., 1995-98. Appeared as actor in movie Dead Girls Don't Tango, 1990. V.p. South Jefferson County Reps., Lakewood, Colo., 1979, pres., 1990; candidate Dist. 6 for Congress; 2nd vice-chmn. Dist. 7 Rep. Party, pres. Ariz. Rep. Assembly Dist. 28, bd. dirs. Scottsdale (Ariz.) Constitution Commemorative Com., 1995-2003, pres., 2002-; elected Ariz. Ho. of Reps., Dist. 7, 2005-06. With USCG, 1959-66. Mem. ATLA, ABA (vice-chmn. family law 1983), Nat. Assn. Criminal Lawyers, Am. Judicature Soc., Nat. Assn. Criminal Def. Attys., Ariz. Magistrates Assn., Colo. Bar Assn., Ariz. Bar Assn., Scottsdale (Ariz.) Bar Assn. (sec. 2001-2002, v.p. 2002-2003, pres., 2003-2004), Md. Bar Assn., Colo. Trial Lawyers Assn., Maricopa County Bar Assn., Scottsdale Bar Assn. (bd. dirs., sec. 1996—, pres.), Masons, Shriners, Elks. Home: PO Box 5145 36418 N Wildflower Rd Carefree AZ 85377-5145 Office: 4310 N 75th St Scottsdale AZ 85251-3578 Office Phone: 480-990-7500. Personal E-mail: dbsdbsatty@yahoo.com.

SMITH, DAVID CLARK, research scientist; b. Owensboro, Ky., Feb. 8, 1937; s. Robert Emmitt and Mary Margaret (Flaherty) S.; m. Kathleen Sue Kohne, June 27, 1964; children: Christine, Jennifer, Paula. BSME, U. Dayton, 1959; MS, Northwestern U., 1961, PhD, postgrad., Northwestern U., 1964. Rsch. scientist United Techs. Rsch. Ctr., East Hartford, Conn., 1965-67, sr. rsch. scientist, 1967-68, prin. scientist, 1968-80, mgr. exptl. optics, 1980-82, mgr. optical physics, 1982-91; cons. DCS Assoc., Inc., 1992-99, Conn. Tech. Assocs., 1992—, DCS Lasers/Optics LLC, 1997—. Author: (with G. Bekefi) Principles of Laser Plasmas, 1976; contbr. articles to profl. jours. Chmn. Youth and Family Resource Ctr. Commn., 1979-84; bd. dirs. Glastonbury A Better Chance, Conn., 1970-78; mem. Glastonbury Energy Com., 1979-83; tutor YMCA Read to Succeed Literacy; vol. Habitat for Humanity. Recipient Outstanding Svc. award, 1985, Glastonbury, Conn., United Techs. Outstanding Svc. award, 1987; named Man of Yr., Friends of Glastonbury Youth, 1984. Fellow: Am. Soc. Laser Medicine and Surgery; mem.: SPIE, IEEE, AIAA, AAAS, Am. Phys. Soc., Sigma Xi. Democrat. Roman Catholic. Achievements include patentee in field. Home: 514 Main St Old Saybrook CT 06475 Office: DCS Lasers & Optics LLC 514 Main St Old Saybrook CT 06475 Office Phone: 860-214-9322. E-mail: dcslasers@gmail.com.

SMITH, DAVID ELVIN, physician; b. Bakersfield, Calif., Feb. 7, 1939; s. Elvin W. and Dorothy (McGinnis) S.; m. Millicent Buxton; children: Julia, Suzanne, Christopher Buxton-Smith, Sabree Hill-Smith. BS, U. Calif., Berkeley; MS in Pharmacology, U. Calif., San Francisco, 1964, MD, 1967. Intern San Francisco Gen. Hosp., 1965; fellow pharmacology and toxicology U. Calif., San Francisco, 1965-67; clin. prof. U. Calif., San Francisco Med. Ctr., 1967—, dir. psychopharmacology study group, dir. Inst. of Health, 1966-70, assoc. clin. prof., rsch. physician Med. Sch.; clin. prof. U. Calif., San Francisco; practice specializing in toxicology/addiction medicine San Francisco, 1965—. Physician Presbyn. Alcoholic Clinic, 1965—67, Contra Cost Alcoholic Clinic, 1965—67; dir. alcohol and drug abuse screening unit San Francisco Gen. Hosp., 1967—68; co-dir. Calif. drug abuse info. project U. Calif. Med. Ctr., 1967—72; founder, pres., stct med. dir. Haight-Ashbury Free Med. Clinic, San Francisco, 1967—2006; rsch. dir. Merritt Peralta Chem. Dependency Hosp., Oakland, Calif., 1984—2003; med. dir. Drug Abuse Scis., 1999—2003, Calif. Alcohol and Drug Programs, U. Calif. San Francisco Substance Abuse Policy Ctr., 1999; exec. med. dir. Prometa Ctr., Santa Monica and San Francisco, Calif.; assoc. med. dir., med. rev. officer Betty Ford Ctr. Profl. Recovery Program; chmn. Nat. Drug Abuse Conf., 1996—2006, Calif. Gov.'s Commn. on Narcotics and Drug Abuse, 1977—; nat. health adviser to former U.S. Pres. Jimmy Carter; mem. Pres. Clinton's Health Care Task Force on Addiction and Nat. Health Reform, 1993; with Office Drug Abuse Policy, White House Task Force Physicians for Drug Abuse Prevention; dir. Benzodiazepine Rsch. and Tng. Project, Substance Abuse and Sexual Concerns Project, PCP Rsch. and Tng. Project; med. editor AlcoholMD.com, OpiateMD.org, Alcohol MD (CD-ROM); vis. assoc. prof. U. Nev. Med. Sch., 1975—; clin. prof. U. Calif. San Francisco Med. Ctr.; v.p. corp. med affairs Hythiam; cons. in field; chief Addiction Medicine Svcs. Bayside Marin, San Rafael, 2006—; med. dir. Centerpoint, 1996—. Author: Love Needs Care, 1970, The New Social Drug: Cultural, Medical and Legal Perspectives on Marijuana, 1971, The Free Clnic: Community Approaches to Health Care and Drug Abuse, 1971, Treating the Cocaine Abuser, 1985, The Benzodiazepines: Current Standard Medical Practice, 1986, Physicians' Guide to Drug Abuse, 1987; co-author: It's So Good, Don't Even Try it Once: Heroin in Perspective, 1972, Uppers and Downers, 1973, Drugs in the Classroom, 1973, Barbiturate Use and Abuse, 1977, A Multicultural View of Drug Abuse, 1978, Amphetamine Use, Misuse and Abuse, 1979, PCP: Problems and Prevention, 1981, Sexological Aspects of Substance Use and Abuse, Treatment of the Cocaine Abuser, 1985, The Haight Ashbury Free Medical Clinic: Still Free After All These Years, Drug Free: Alternatives to Drug Abuse, 1987, Treatment of Opiate Dependence, Designer Drugs, 1988, Treatment of Cocaine Dependence, 1988, Treatment of Opiate Dependence, 1988, The New Drugs, 1989, Crack and Ice in the Era of Smokeable Drugs, 1992, Clinical Guide to Substance Abuse, 2001, others; also drug edn. films; founder, editor Jour. Psychedelic Drugs (now Jour. Psychoactive Drugs), 1967—; co-author: Clinical Guide to Substance Abuse; contbr. over 300 articles to profl. jours. Mem. Physicians for Prevention White House Office Drug Abuse Policy, 1995; pres. Youth Projects, Inc.; founder, chmn. bd., pres. Nat. Free Clin. Coun., 1968-72; med. dir. Calif. Alcohol and Drug Programs, 1998, U. Calif. Drug Policy Ctr., San Francisco, 1998—99. Recipient Rsch. award, Borden Found., 1964, AMA Rsch. award, 1977, Cmty. Svc. award U. Calif., San Francisco, 1974, Calif. State Drug Abuse Treatment award, 1984, Vernelle Fox Drug Abuse Treatment award, 1985, UCLA Sidney Cohen Addiction Medicine award, 1989, U. Calif. San Francisco medal of honor, 1995, Lifetime Achievement award for sr. workers, Gov. of Calif., 2003; named one of Best Drs. in US, 1995, 1996, 1997, 2002. Mem. AMA (alt. del.), Calif. Med. Assn. (alt. del.), Am. Soc. on Addiction Medicine (bd. dirs., pres. 1995), San Francisco Med. Soc., APHA, Calif. Soc. on Addiction Medicine (pres., bd. dirs.), Am. Soc. Addiction Medicine, Cosmos Club, 2006-, Sigma Xi, Phi Beta Kappa. Methodist. Home and Office: David E Smith MD and Assocs 856 Stanyan St San Francisco CA 94117 Office Phone: 415-933-8759, 415-933-8759. Business E-Mail: drsmith@drdave.org.

SMITH, DAVID ENGLISH, pathologist, educator; b. San Francisco, June 9, 1920; s. David English and Myrtle (Goodin) S.; m. Margaret Elizabeth Bronson, June 9, 1948; children: Ann English Smith Elbert, David Bronson, Mary Margaret. AB, Central Coll. Mo., 1941; MD cum laude, Washington U., St. Louis, 1944. Intern, resident pathology Barnes Hosp., St. Louis, 1944-46; instr. pathology Washington U. Med. Sch., 1948-51, asst. prof., 1951-54, asst. head dept., 1953-54, assoc. prof., 1954-55; prof. pathology U. Va. Sch. Medicine, 1955-73, chmn. dept., 1958-73; dir. div. U. Va. Sch. Medicine (Cancer Studies), 1972-73; prof. pathology Northwestern U. Sch. Medicine, 1974-75, U. Pa. Sch. Medicine, 1976-80, Tulane U. Sch. Medicine, 1980-85, assoc. dean, 1980-85; prof. pathology U. Tex. Med. Br., 1986—. Assoc. dir. Am. Bd. Med. Spltys., 1974-75; v.p., sec., dir. undergrad. evaluation Nat. Bd. Med. Examiners, 1975-80; trustee Am. Bd. Pathology, 1966-73, v.p., 1973; mem. Nat. Bd. Med. Examiners, chmn. pathology test com., 1966-72; chmn. test com. Ednl. Commn. for Fgn. Med. Grads., 1979-91; eligibility & due process com. Nat. Commn. Cert. Physician Assts., 1990-2001. Editor: Survey of Pathology in Medicine and Surgery, 1966-70; contbr. articles to profl. publs. Pres. Va. div. Am. Cancer Soc., 1967-69. Served from 1st lt. to capt. M.C. AUS, 1946-48. Recipient Preclin. Tchr. award, U. Tex. Med. Br., 1999; named Disting. Alumnus, Wash. U. Med. Sch., 2004; Paul Brindley Disting. scholar, U. Tex. Med. Br., 1997. Mem. Va. Soc. Pathology (pres. 1960), Am. Assn. Pathologists, Internat. Acad. Pathology (council 1956-59, pres. 1964-65), Am. Soc. Clin. Pathologists (co-dir. self assessment program 1970-75, Path Educator award 2000), AMA, Am. Assn. Neuropathologists, AAAS, Sigma Xi, Alpha Omega Alpha, Phi Beta Pi, Alpha Epsilon Delta. Home: 59 Colony Park Cir Galveston TX 77551-1737 E-mail: descolpkga@aol.com.

SMITH, DAVID HORTON, social science researcher-theorist, writer, consultant, nonprofit organization founder, internet business founder; b. LA, May 2, 1939; s. Paul Roosevelt Smith and Helen Ethel (Frechem) Mitchell; divorced; children: Gregory David, Laura Ghislaine. Student (hon.), Calif. Inst. Tech., 1957—58; AB magna cum laude, U. Southern Calif., 1960; AB in Philosophy, AB in Psychology, AB in Sociology; MA in Sociology, Harvard U., 1962, PhD in Sociology with distinction, 1965. Asst. prof. sociology U. Southern Calif., LA, 1966—68, co-dir., Lab. for Orgnl. Rsch.; assoc. rsch. prof., dir., Program on Voluntary Participation in Urban World, Inst. Human Scis. Boston Coll.; Chestnut Hill, Mass., 1968—73, assoc. prof. sociology, 1968—76, prof. sociology, 1976—2004, emeritus prof. sociology, 2007—, rsch. prof. sociology, 2009—; founder, mgr., CEO David Horton Smith Internat. LLC, Blue Stone Infinity LLC, 2008—; founder. pres., CEO Miracle Club Internat. Inc., 2008—, Proven Truth Inc., 2009—. Rsch. fellow, lectr. Harvard U., 1965-66; dir. rsch., Ctr. Voluntary Soc., 1970-74; cons. Nat. Ctr. for Voluntary Action, Brit. Nat. Vol. Ctr., Ctr. for Voluntary Soc., Filer Commn. on Pvt. Philanthropy and Pub. Needs, Donee Group, 1974-75; Union of Internat. Assns.; keynote spkr. 7th World Leisure Congress, Kuala Lumpur, Malyasia, 2002; founder Assn. Rsch. Nonprofit Orgns. & Vol. Action, Nonprofit & Vol. Sector Quarterly jour., Sects. on Cmty. & Grassroots Assns. & Values, Religion, Altruism & Drawbacks. Author: Latin American Student Activism: Participation in Formal Volunteer Organizations by University Students in Six Latin Cultures, 1973, Grassroots Associations, 2000, The Dark Side of Goodness: Deviance, Dissent and Incivility in the Angelic Nonprofit Sector, 2009; co-author: Becoming Modern: Individual Change in Six Developing Countries, 1974 (Nat. award 1975; Chinese translation edition, 1992), Voluntary Sector Policy Research Needs: Report of a Participative Inquiry, 1974, Participation in Social and Political Activities: A Comprehensive Analysis of Political Involvement, Expressive Leisure Time, and Helping Behavior, 1980, Why People Recreate: An Overview of Research, 1987, A Dictionary of Nonprofit Terms and Concepts, 2006; editor: Voluntary Action and Social Problems: What Voluntary Action Scholars Can Do to Help, 1971, Voluntary Action Research: 1972, Voluntary Action Research: 1973, Voluntary Action Research: 1974, The Nature of Voluntary Action Around the World, Voluntary Transnational Cultural Exchange Organizations of the US: A Selected List, 1974, Role of US NGOs in International Development Co-Operation, 1978, Volunteerism, Voluntary Assns. and Devel., 1981, Internat. Perspectives on Voluntary Action Rsch., 1983; founding editor-in-chief: Urban and Social Change Review, 1969-73, Jour. Voluntary Action Rsch. (now Nonprofit and Voluntary Sector Quar.), 1971-76, assoc. editor, 1976-1982, cons. editor: 1983-1993, listed past editor, 1994-; adv. editor, Vol. Adminstr., 1972-75, cons. editor, 1976-79; assoc. editor: Sociology and Social Rsch., 1966-68; contbr. articles to profl. jours., chpts. to books, entries to encycs. Mem. Ad Hoc Adv. Coun. Mass. Gov.'s Office Citizens' Participation, 1974-75, Planning Com. for Nat. Forum on Commn. on Volunteerism, 1979-80, mem., bd. dirs. Voluntary Action Ctr. Greater Boston, 1974-79, Fathers United for Equal Justice, 1975-77; founding bd. dirs., Assn. Rsch. Non-Profit Orgns. and Voluntary Action, 1971-78, Nat. Com. for Responsive Philanthropy, 1976-78, Alliance for Volunteerism, 1975-78, Nat. Assn. Pub. Svc. Exec., 1977-80, founder, sec. gen., founding bd. dirs. chair Internat. Voluntary Action and Voluntary Assns. Rsch. Orgn., 1978-1983; dir. rsch. Ctr. for Voluntary Soc., Washington, DC, 1970-74. Woodrow Wilson Hon. fellow, 1960; NSF grad. fellow, 1960-63; named to Internat. Ency. Civil Soc., 2009. Mem. Assn. Rsch. on Non-Profit Orgns. and Voluntary Action (founder, pres. 1971-73, exec. officer 1973-75, rsch. v.p 1975-78, Lifetime Achievement award 1993), Internat. Soc. for Third Sector Rsch. (charter founding mem.), Am. Soc. Assn. Execs., Am. Sociol. Assn., Am. Psych. Assn., Am. Acad. Religion, Soc. Sci. Study Religion, Religious Rsch. Assn., Soc. Study Christian Spirituality, Authors Guild, Am. Assn. for Advancement of Sci., Am. Assn. Retired Persons, NAMI, Wilderness Soc., Nature Conservancy, Rainforest Action Network, World Wildlife Fund., Natural Resources Defense Coun., Harvard Club Sarasota, Freemasons, Shriners of North America, Harvard Alumni Assn., Phi Beta Kappa, Phi Kappa Phi, Alpha Kappa Delta, Pi Epsilon Theta, Alpha Mu Gamma, Sarasota-Manatee Phi Beta Kappa Assn., Nat. Phi Beta Kappa Soc, Miracle Club #1, Congregational United Ch. Christ, Sarasota Film Soc., Manatee County Ministries Assn., Miracle Club Internat. Achievements include invention of interdisciplinary, professional, national and international associations for researchers focused on the voluntary nonprofit sector and voluntary action as a field of study (the "nonprofit sector studies" field); inclusion in the first International Encyclopedia of Civil Society (Springer, 2009) as one of 137 outstanding contributors to civil society worldwide from all of human history; development of first extensive, general theories of the functioning of grassroots associations, paid-staff nonprofit organizations and fundamentally deviant nonprofit groups. Avocations: reading, movies, classical music, writing, photography. Personal E-mail: dhortonsmith@hotmail.com.

SMITH, DAVID JAMES, lawyer; b. 1955; BS, Western Ill. U.; JD, John Marshall Law Sch. Asst. sec. Archer Daniels Midland, Decatur, Ill., 1988-97, asst. gen. counsel, 1995-97, v.p., sec., gen. counsel,

1997—2001, sr. v.p., sec., gen. counsel, 2002—03, exec. v.p., sec. and gen. counsel, 2003—. Office: Archer Daniels Midland Co 4666 E Faries Pkwy Decatur IL 62526-5666 Office Phone: 217-424-5200.*

SMITH, DAVID JOHN, JR., plastic surgeon; b. Indpls., Feb. 20, 1947; s. David John and Carolyn (Culp) S.; m. Nancy Loonsten, June 7, 1975; children: Matthew, Peter, Hadley. BA, Wesleyan U., 1969; MD, Ind. U., 1973. Diplomate Am. Bd. Plastic Surgery. Resident Emory U.-Grady Hosp., Atlanta, 1973-78; resident Ind. U. Med. Ctr., Indpls., 1978-80; Christine Kleinert fellow in hand surgery, 1979; asst. prof. surgery Ind. U. Sch. Medicine, 1980-84; assoc. prof. of surgery Wayne State U. Sch. Medicine, 1984-87; assoc. prof. plastic surgery, surgery sect. head U. Mich. Med. Ctr., Ann Arbor, 1987-92, prof. surgery sect. head, 1992—2001; prof. surgery Coll. Medicine U. South Fla., 2004—, Juan Bolivar chair in surg. oncology, dir. divsn. plastic and reconstructive surgery, 2004—; interim chair, dept. surgery USF. Mem. Residency Rev. Com. for Plastic Surgery, 1992-2000, vice chmn., 1994, chmn. 1996-99; vis. prof. Ctr. Cutaneous Rsch. Queen Mary U., London, Eng., 2004—, Anglia Polytech. U., Cambrige, Eng., 2004—. Mem. editl. bd. Jour. of Surg. Rsch., 1989-95, Annals of Plastic Surgery, 1992-2002, assoc. editor, 1994-2002, Yearbook of Hand Surgery, 1989—; guest reviewer Surgery, 1988—, Plastic and Reconstructive Surgery, 1988—; contbr. articles to profl. jours. Recipient numerous grants. Fellow ACS (com. mem.), Am. Assn. Plastic Surgeons, Am. Surg. Assn., Am. Bd. Plastic Surgeons (vice chmn. 1997-98, chair-elect 1998-99, chmn. oral exam 1995-97, chmn. 1999-2000), Ctrl. Surg. Assn., Am. Soc. for Surgery of the Hand, Am. Soc. Plastic Surgeons, Plastic Surgery Ednl. Found. (bd. dirs. 1988-99, treas. 1994, v.p., pres.-elec., pres., chair nominating com. 1997-98), Plastic Surgery Rsch. Coun., Am. Burn Assn. (chmn. com. on organization and delivery of burn care 1995-98), Am. Burn Life Support Nat. Faculty, Am. Assn. for Hand Surgeons (pres. 1994), Assn. Acad. Chmn. Plastic Surgery (pres.-elect 1997, pres. 1998-99, chmn. nominating com. 1999-2000). Home: 3107 Prospect Rd Tampa FL 33629 Office: Divsn Plastic Surgery 4 Columbia Dr Ste 650 Tampa FL 33606 Home Phone: 813-250-9160. Business E-Mail: dsmith3@health.usf.edu.

SMITH, DAVID JULIAN, educational consultant; b. Boston, Apr. 24, 1944; s. Julian John and Anita Regina (Goldman) S.; m. Suzanne Marilla Shaw, June 18, 1966. AB, Harvard U., 1966; MAT, Reed Coll., 1967. Cert. elem. tchr., Mass., Hawaii, Oreg. 10th grade tchr. Punahou Sch., Honolulu, 1967-69; 7th, 9th grades tchr. U. Hawaii Lab. Sch., Honolulu, 1969-70; 7th grade head tchr. Shady Hill Sch., Cambridge, Mass., 1970-92; pvt. practice ednl. cons. Cambridge, Mass., 1992—. Author: Mapping the World By Heart, 1992, CEESA Web-Site Manual, 1998, If the World Were a Village, 2002, If America Were a Village, 2009, Emergency Procedures Manual for Overseas Schools, 2004; contbr. articles to profl. jours. Bd. dirs. Cambridge Mental Health Assn., 1991-96, Cambridge Ctr. for Adult Edn., 1988-98; active Cambridge Civic Assn. Recipient Breaking the Mold award US Dept. Edn., 1992. Mem. Nat. Coun. Social Studies, Nat. Coun. Geog. Edn., Assn. Am. Geographers (chair cartographic splty. group 1997). Personal E-mail: djsmapping@gmail.com.

SMITH, DAVID LEE, retired editor; b. Shelby, Ohio, Apr. 4, 1939; s. Ferris Francis and Rita Ann (Metzger) Smith; m. Betty Stewart Walker, Sept. 10, 1960; children: Stacie Lynn, Stefanie Linn, David Lee II(dec.). Student, Pontifical Coll. Josephinum, Worthington, Ohio, 1953-56, Ohio State U., Mansfield, 1961. Sports writer Mansfield News-Jour., 1960-61; sports editor Ashland Times-Gazette, Ohio, 1961-63, Miami News, Fla., 1963-67, Ft. Lauderdale News, Fla., 1967-70, Boston Globe, 1970-78, Washington Star, 1978-81; dep. mng. editor, exec. sports editor Dallas Morning News, 1981—2005, sports dir. AH Belo pub. and new media divsns., 1998—2003, v.p., 2003—05; ret., 2005. Condr. seminars. Mem. adv. bd. Dallas Stars Found., Dallas Alliance for the Mentally Ill, SMU Athletics, Jesuit Sch. Found.; bd. govs. Bethesda Home Boys, Savannah, Ga.; bd. dirs. Field Scovell Scholarship Found., Doak Walker Nat. Running Back Award, GTE-SMU Athletic Forum. With USMC, 1957—60. Mem.: Golf Writers Assn., Football Writers Assn., Baseball Writers Assn. (Red Smith award for major contbns. to sports journalism 1990), AP Sports Editors Assn. (1st pres. 1974—75), SMU Athletic Forum (bd. dirs.), Salesmanship Club Dallas, Bent Tree Country Club. Roman Catholic. Home: 16 Mad Turkey Crossing Savannah GA 31411 Personal E-mail: studie.dave@comcast.net.

SMITH, DAVID LYLE, artist, educator; b. Harpersfield, NY, June 6, 1926; s. Thomas Howard and Grace Louisa Smith; m. Alyce Louise Oosterhouse, June 6, 1952; children: C Matthew, Markalan, Elizabeth, Leigh, Stuart. BD in Design, U. Mich., 1951, MA in Edn., 1953; DPhil, Mich. State U., 1966. Graphic artist Ednl. TV Program U. Mich., Ann Arbor, 1952-53; tchr. art C.W. Otto Jr. H.S., Lansing, Mich., 1955-63; tchr. elem. art. Lansing Pub. Schs., 1963-67; assoc. prof. Dept. Art and Design U. Wis., Stevens Point, 1967-96, assoc. prof. emeritus, 1996—; CEO Scarabocchio Art, Stevens Point; founder, mem. Scarabocchio Art Found., Stevens Point. Dir. Stevens Point Program, 1975-86; site adminstr., semester abroad tchr., Poland, 1978, 83; chmn. State Art Edn. Cert. Stds., 1981-83. Exhbns. include U. Wis. Stevens Point Faculty Show, 1974-76, 87, 90-93, 95, 97, Packages-Carlsten Art Gallery, 1978, 79, New Visions Gallery, Marshfield, Wis., 1989, 92, 95, Milw. Art Mus., 1992, U. Colo. Mountainside Art Guild & Fiske Planetarium, 1992-96, N.Mex., Art League, 1993, 94, 96, Alexander House, Port Edwards, Wis., 1993, 95, Sacramento FAC, 1993, 94, 97, 98, Laredo Art League, Tex., 1994, 95, 96, L.I. Arts Coun., Freeport, N.Y., 1994, Green Bay Neville Pub. Mus., 1995, 96, 97, 98, An Art Pl., Chgo., 1995, 97, Akron Soc. Artists, 1994, 96, 98, Mable (Ga.) Cultural Ctr., 1994, 95, 96, 98, Wis. Painters-Sculptors, 1996, 97, 98, 99, Mac Rostie Art Ctr., 1996, 97, 98, Coastal Ctr. Arts, Ga., 1996, 97, 98, Ridgewood Art Inst., N.J., 1997, 98, 99, Salmagundi Club, 1999, Period Gallery, 1998, 99, Glen Eure's Ghost Fleet Gallery, 1998, 99, Eleven East Ashland, 1997, 98, Wis. Edn. Assn. Art Showcase, 1996, 98, Internat. Registry of Artists and Art calendar, 1998, Studio 107, Ridge Art Assn., 1998, 99, others; accepted in nat. juried art competitions, 15 in 1993, 49 in 1994, 22 in 1995, 26 in 1996, 21 in 1997, 20 in 1998, 25 in 1999; one-man shows include Lincoln Ctr., Stevens Point, Wis., 1989, 93, 95, Charles M. White Libr., Stevens Point, Northeast C.C., Whiteville, N.C., 1998, others.; two-man shows (with Richard Schneider) Alexander House 1993; also Ctr. for Visual Arts 1996, Wausau, Wis.; three person show Brown County Libr., Green Bay, Wis., 1996. Style judge State Odyssey of the Mind, 1990-99; dist. dir. ctrl. divsn. Very Spl. Arts Wis., 1985-88. Mem. Nat. Art Edn. Assn., Wis. Art Edn. Assn. (bd. dirs., higher edn. rep. 1978-82), NEA (life), Wis. Edn. Assn. Coun., Assn. U. Wis. Profls. (sec. 1993-96), Wis. Alliance for Arts Edn., Res. Officers Assn. U.S., Ret. Officers, Nat. Assn. Uniformed Svcs., Air Force Assn., Consumers Union. Republican. Presbyterian. Avocations: sketching, gardening, travel. Home: 4242 Janick Cir N Stevens Point WI 54481-2511 Fax: (715) 342-5688. E-mail: d3smith@uswp.edu.

SMITH, DAVID MICHAEL, financial planner; b. Fresno, Calif., Dec. 29, 1944; s. Ralph S. and Verla Fern Smith; m. Barbara J. Bryson, June 27, 1964; children: Brandon, Eric. AA, Fresno City Coll., 1964; AB, Calif. State U., Fresno, 1966. Tchr. English Fresno Unified Sch. Dist., 1967-79; registered rep. TMI Equities, Inc., Fresno, 1979-82, regional mgr. Camarillo, Calif., 1982-85; fin. planner Associated Planners Securities Corp., Camarillo, 1985-89, David M. Smith & Assocs., Camarillo, 1989—2002, Lifetime Planning, Inc., 2003—. Coun. mem. City of Camarillo, 1988—96, mayor, 1991, 1996. Mem.: Fin. Planners Assn. Ventura County (pres. 2004), Fin. Planning Assn., Camarillo Noontime Optimists Club. Office: Lifetime Planning Inc 1200 Paseo Camarillo Ste 190 Camarillo CA 93010-6085 Home Phone: 805-987-5919; Office Phone: 805-987-8938. Personal E-mail: dms.planners@verizon.net.

SMITH, DAVID THORNTON, lawyer, educator; b. Pawtucket, RI, Dec. 11, 1935; s. Herbert Jeffers and Harriet Amelia (Thornton) S.; m. Sandra June Gustavson, Dec. 20, 1958; children: David T., Douglas A., Daniel H. BA, Yale U., 1957; JD cum laude, Boston U., 1960. Bar: Mass. 1961, U.S. Supreme Ct. 1964. Instr. law Ind. U., Bloomington, 1960-62; asst. prof. law Duquesne U., Pitts., 1962-63, Case Western Res. U., Cleve., 1963-65, assoc. prof., 1965-68; assoc. prof. law U. Fla., Gainesville, 1968-69, prof., 1969—2003, prof. emeritus, 2003—. Vis. prof. law U. Ga., 2004, Wake Forest U., 2006, Stetson U., 2007. Author: (with M. Sussman and J. Cates) The Family and Inheritance, 1970, Florida Probate Code Manual, 1975. Mem. Am. Bar Assn., Mass. Bar Assn., Am. Law Inst., Am. Judicature Soc., AAUP (past pres. U. Fla. chpt.), Fla. Blue Key, Selden Soc., Omicron Delta Kappa, Phi Alpha Delta. Lutheran. Office: Univ Fla Coll Law Gainesville FL 32611

SMITH, DAVID WAYNE, retired psychologist, educator; b. Ind., Apr. 16, 1927; s. Lowell Wayne and Ruth Elizabeth (Westphal) S.; m. Marcene B. Leever, Oct. 20, 1948; children: David Wayne, Laurreen Lea. BS, Purdue U., 1949; MS, Ind. U., 1953, PhD, 1955. Diplomate Am. Bd. Psychol. Specialities. Prof. rehab., dir. Rehab. Ctr.; assoc. dean, later asst. v.p. acad. affairs Ariz. Health Scis. Ctr., U. Ariz., Tucson, 1955-80; rsch. prof. rehab., adj. prof. medicine, cons. in rsch. S.W. Arthritis Ctr., Coll. Medicine, 1980-87; prof. rehab. and rheumatology, dept. medicine U. Ariz., Tucson, 1987—, dir. disability assessment program, Ariz. Arthritis Ctr., Coll Medicine, 2007—. Pres. allied health professions sect. Nat. Arthritis Found.; bd. dirs. Nat. Arthritis Found. (S.W. chpt.); nat. vice chmn. bd. dirs.; mem. NIH Nat. Arthritis Adv. Bd., 1977-84; also chmn. subcom. community programs and rehab.; mem. staff Ariz. Legislature Health Welfare, 1972-73; Mem. Gov.'s Council Dept. Econ. Security, 1978-85; pres., bd. dirs. Tucson Assn. for Blind, 1974-86; chmn. Gov.'s Council on Blind and Visually Impaired, 1987—; active Gov.'s Coun. on Arthritis and Musculoskeletal Disease, 1987—, Gov.'s State wide Coun. on Rehab., 1998—, Am. Bd. Forensic Examiners, 1997—. Author: Worksamples; contbr. chpts. to books and articles to profl. jours. Mem. Gov.'s State Rehab. Coun., 1998—, commr. Commn. on Civil Rights, Az., 2002. Recipient Gov.'s awards for leadership in rehab., 1966, 69, 72, 73; awards for sci. and vol. services Nat. Arthritis Found., 1973, 75; 1st nat. Addie Thomas award Nat. Arthritis Found., 1983, Benson award, 1989, Govt. Affairs award, 1989; Arthritis Found. fellow, 1983. Fellow Am. Coll. Forensics; mem. Am. Psychol. Assn. (div. 17 counseling psychology), Assn. Schs. Allied Health Professions, Nat. Rehab. Assn., Ariz. Psychol. Assn. Home: 5765 N Camino Real Tucson AZ 85718-4213 Office: Univ Ariz 1501 N Campbell Ave PO Box 245093 Tucson AZ 85724-5093 Personal E-mail: davesfolly@earthlink.net.

SMITH, DAVID YOUNG, physics professor; b. Schenectady, NY, July 24, 1934; s. William Henry and Cicely Young Smith; m. Barbara Jean Brown, Aug. 7, 1963; children: Sarah Christine, Stephanie Anne Forsland. BS, Rensselaer Poly. Inst., Troy, NY, 1956; PhD, U. Rochester, NY, 1962. Engrng. asst. GE Engrng. Lab., Schenectady, 1955; sci. asst. GE Rsch. Lab., 1957—57; tchg. & rsch. asst. dept. Physics U. Rochester, 1960—62; rsch. asst. prof. dept. Physics U. Ill., Urbana, 1963—66; vis. prof. U. Stuttgart, Wurttemberg, Germany, 1966—67; physicist & asst. divsn. dir. Argonne Nat. Lab., Solid State Sci. Divsn., Ill., 1967—86; prof. emeritus dept. Physics U. Vt., Burlington, 1968—. Cons. US Naval Rsch. Lab., Washington, 1993—93; resident assoc. Argonne Nat. Lab., Physics Divsn., 1999—. Contbr. chapters to books, scientific papers. Pre & Postdoc. fellowships, NSF, 1956—60, 1966, Exch. fellowship, Deutsche Acads. Austauch Dienst, 1975. Mem.: Am. Phys. Soc., Sigma Xi Rsch. Soc. Office: Univ Vermont Dept Physics 82 Univ Place Burlington VT 05405 Office Fax: 802-656-0817.

SMITH, DAWN MERCEDES, assistant dean; d. Harold Jude and Sylvia Morris Smith. BS, Fla. A & M U., Tallahassee, 1990; MA in Libr. & Info. Sci., U. South Fla., Tampa, 1995. Bar: Fla. Atlantic U. (Legal Asst.) 1993; cert. in labor relations Fla. A & M U., 1990. Govt. document reference libr. Fla. Atlantic U., Boca Raton, Fla., 1996—99, govt. docs., dept. head, 1999—2001, dept. head, reference & instrnl. svcs., 2004—07, asst. dean pub. svcs., 2006—. Contbr. articles to profl. jours. (award). Webmaster St. Nicholas Episcopal Ch., Pompano Beach, Fla., 2004—; sr. co-coord. Order Daughters King, Pompano Beach, Fla., 2006—. Recipient Admission award, Nat. Gold Key Honor Soc., 1995. Mem.: ALA, Assn. Coll. & Rsch. Libraries, Beta Phi Mu Internat. Libr., Phi Kappa Phi, Delta Sigma Theta Sorority. Office: FL Atlantic Univ 777 Glades Rd Bldg 3 Ly 132B Boca Raton FL 33431 Office Fax: 561-297-2105. Business E-Mail: dsmith@fau.edu.

SMITH, DEAN, communications advisor, arbitrator; b. NYC, Aug. 10, 1925; s. Franklin Grant and Anna Lucille (Kranebell) S.; m. Andree Marie Praileur, Aug. 9, 1947; children: David F., Christopher P. Student, NYU, 1945-46, Columbia U., 1946-47, N.Y. Sch. Printing, 1946-47. Editor ShowBill Mag., NYC, 1945-47; news editor Boulder City (Nev.) Daily News, 1947-49; owner, pub., editor Tucson Sun-News, NYC, 1949-51; dir. radio and TV news Sta. WBEN/WBEN-TV, Buffalo, 1951-53; dir. pub. svc. and promotion Indpls. Times, Buffalo, 1953-56; v.p., gen. mgr Kendall Assocs., Inc., NYC, 1956-60; dir. Office Publs. and Info., Commerce Dept., Washington, 1961-70, dir. publs. div., 1970; asst. dir. Nat. Tech. Info. Svc., Springfield, Va., 1971-81, dir. office of market devel., 1982-83; assoc. dir. NTIS, Springfield, Va., 1984-85, self-employed communications advisor, 1986—. Chmn. for fed. mail list policy Vice Pres.'s Com. on Right of Privacy; chmn. presdl. domestic policy rev. work group on fed. acquisition of fgn. tech., 1979; bd. dirs. Commerce Fed. Credit Union. Served with AUS, 1943-45 Sgt. 1st divsn., 1943—45. Decorated Silver Star with oak leaf cluster, Bronze Star, Purple Heart with oak leaf cluster; recipient award Ariz. Newspaper Assn., 1950, Ind. Photo Journalism award, 1954 Mem. Am. Arbitration Assn. (panelist), Washington Book Pubs., Soc. Mayflower Descs., Sons of Revolution (treas.), Flagon and Trencher, Soc. for the Descs.of the Colonial Clergy, Soc. Descs. of Founders of Hartford, Oldest Inhabitants of DC., St. Nicholas Soc. of N.Y.C. Democrat. Home and Office: 2325 49th St NW Washington DC 20007-1002 Personal E-mail: dc49@comcast.net.

SMITH, DEAN EDWARDS, retired men's college basketball coach; b. Emporia, Kans., Feb. 28, 1931; s. Alfred Dillon and Vesta Marie (Edwards) S.; m. Linnea Weblemoe, May 21, 1976; children: Sharon, Sandy, Scott, Kristen, Kelly. BS in Math. and Phys. Edn., U. Kans., 1953. Asst. basketball coach USAF Acad., 1955-58; asst. basketball coach U. N.C., 1958-61, head basketball coach, 1961-97, now cons. basketball and athletic dept. Mem. U.S. and Canadian Basketball Rules Com., 1967-73; U.S. basketball coach Olympics, Montreal, Que., Can., 1976; lectr. basketball clinics, Germany, Italy. With USAF, 1954-58. Recipient Joe Lapchick Character award, 2008; named Coach of Yr., Atlantic Coast Conf., 1967, 68, 71, 76, 77, 79, Nat. Basketball Coach of Yr., 1977, Nat. Coach of Yr., US Basketball Writers, 1979, one of Top 5 Coaches of the 20th Century, ABC-TV and ESPN; named to Naismith Basketball Hall of Fame, 1982, Nat. Collegiate Basketball Hall of Fame, 2006. Mem. Nat. Assn. Basketball Coaches (Nat. Basketball Coach of Yr. 1976, dir. 1972—, pres. 1981-82), Fellowship Christian Athletes (dir. 1965-70) Baptist. Office: U NC Basketball Office PO Box 2126 Chapel Hill NC 27515-2126*

SMITH, DEMAURICE FITZGERALD, sports association executive, lawyer; b. Anacostia, Washington, 1964; BA, Cedarville Coll., 1985; JD with honors, U. Va., 1989. Bar: DC, Md. Asst. U.S. atty. DC dist. US Dept. Justice, 1991—98; counsel to dep. atty. gen. DC, 1999—2001; with US Secret Svc. Multi-Agy. Command Ctr., 2001; ptnr. Latham & Watkins LLP, Washington, 2001—06, Patton Boggs LLP, Washington, 2006—09; exec. dir. NFL Players Assn. (NFLPA), Washington, 2009—. Commentator MSNBC, CNN, NBC, Court-TV, Fox TV; tchr. U. Va., George Washington U., Am. U.; bd. governors DC Bar Assn.; bd. dirs. Good Samaritan Found.; faculty mem. Nat. Trial Advocacy Coll., Nat. Inst. Trial Advocacy. Recipient U.S. Atty. Gen. Dir. award, US Dept. Justice, 2000, John Evans Trial Advocacy award, U.S. Atty.'s Assn., Leadership Team award, U.S. atty.'s office, commendation, U.S. Secret Svc., DEA, U.S. Marshal's Svc., Met. Police Dept., others; named one of Young Guns Washingtonian's Top 40 Lawyers Under 40. Office: NFL Players Association (NFLPA) 2021 L St NW Fl 6 Washington DC 20036*

SMITH, DENA MICHELE, physical education educator; d. Edward I. Smith and Beverly M. Metz. BS, U. Wis., La Crosse, 1992. Tchr. phys. edn. and health Shell Lake Schs., Wis., 1993—2000, Sch. Dist. Jefferson, Jefferson, Wis., 2000—. Head coach girls basketball Shell Lake Schs., 1993—2000, head coach girls softball, 1994—2000; head coach girls basketball Sch. Dist. Jefferson, 2000—. Mem.: Wis. Basketball Coaches Assn. Office: Sch Dist Jefferson 700 W Milwaukee St Jefferson WI 53549 Office Phone: 920-675-1185.

SMITH, DENIS JOSEPH, mathematics professor; b. Boston, Mar. 19, 1949; s. Joseph P. and Margaret L. (Stapleton) S.; m. Mary P. MacDougall, Aug. 26, 1972; children: Brandon Edward, Shane F. AB in math. edn., Boston Coll., 1971; MEd, Cambridge Coll., Mass., 1990. Tchr. Xaverian Bros. High Sch., Westwood, Mass., 1971—; math. instr. Dean Coll., Franklin, Mass., 2000—05. Advisor Xaverian Math. Team/New Eng. Math. League, Westwood, Mass.1980—, chmn. Math. Dept. Xaverian Bros High Sch., Westwood, 1982-84, 86-88, 95—; math instr. Dean Coll., 2000—05; bd. dirs. Greater Boston Math. League, Canton, Mass., 1989—, advisor, 1980—; ednl. cons. St. Catherine of Sienna, Norwood, Mass., 1990-92; in house coord. Nat. High Sch. Math. Exam., 1980—, supr. Math Olympiad Level I Exam. Eucharistic min. St. Mary's Ch., 1984—; coach Dedham Youth Soccer, 1985-92; pres. St. Catherine's Homes and Sch. Assn., 1989-91; vice chmn. Cardinal Parish Planning Coun., 1990—2002. Grantee NSF, 1993. Mem. Nat. Coun. Tchrs., Nat. Cath. Ednl. Assn. Roman Catholic. Home: 23 Charles St Dedham MA 02026-3049 Office: Xaverian Bros High Sch 800 Clapboardtree St Westwood MA 02090-1718 Business E-Mail: dsmith@xbhs.com.

SMITH, DENNIS B., neurologist, educator; b. Albany, NY, Sept. 6, 1939; s. Bernard Y. and Virginia Shultes Smith; m. Bonnie Wimburn Smith, July 6, 1984; children: Kimberly, Kendall, Jennifer. BA, Wesleyan U., 1961; MD, Albany U., 1965. Cert. neurology, Am. Bd. Clinical Neurophysiology (CNP). Resident, instr. Yale U., 1965—70; asst. prof. U. Vt., Burlington, 1970—74; assoc. prof. to prof. Med. Coll. Ga., Augusta, 1974—84; chief staff VA Hosp., Hampton, Va., 1984—86; assoc. dean Ea. Va. Med. Sch., Norfolk, 1984—86; dir. Oreg. Epilepsy Program Legacy Health Sys., Portland, 1986—91; assoc. undersec. for health Dept. VA, Washington, 1991—94; prof. neurology Oreg. Health Scis. U., Portland, 1994—. Dir. Office of Stds. in Human Studies Rsch. Dept. VA, Washington, 1994—2000; cons., adv. bd. Oreg. Mus. Sci. and Industry, Portland, 2000—; cons. Nat. Ctr. Auditory Rsch. Dept. VA, Portland, 1997—. Editor: (books) Undergraduate Neurol Education, 1974, Epilepsy, Dx and Rx, 1990, Neurobehavioral Problems in Epilepsy, 1991. Mem. profl. adv. bd. exec. com. Epilepsy Found. Am., Washington, 1987—90; cons., advisor Exec. Office of the Pres., Washington, 1994; bd. dirs. Epilepsy Assn. Oreg., Portland, 1990, 1991. Fellow: Am. Acad. Neurology (edn. chair 1985—90); mem.: So. EEG Soc. (pres. 1984—85), Am. Neurol. Assn., Am. Epilepsy Soc. (exec. bd. 1991—94), Am. Coll. Healthcare Execs. Democrat. Avocations: sailing, painting. Home: 827 NW 25th Ave Portland OR 97210 Office: Oreg Health Scis U Sam Jackson Rd Portland OR 97201 Office Phone: 503-224-3077. Personal E-mail: smithden1@comcast.net. Business E-Mail: smithden@ohsu.edu.

SMITH, DEREK ARMAND, information technology executive; b. Hamilton, Ont., Can., Sept. 2, 1953; came to U.S., 1981; s. Alastair A.G. and Jessie Mead (Maben) S.; m. Rebecca Oldfield, Oct. 10, 1981; 1 child, Alastair Maben Oldfield. BCom., U. Toronto, 1976. Chartered acct.; CPA, Mass. Staff acct. Office of Auditor Gen., Ottawa, 1976-78; chartered acct. Peat Marwick Thorne, Ottawa, 1978-79; v.p. fin. adminstrn. Can. Dry Bottling Ltd., Kingston, Ont., 1979-81; supervising sr. Peat Marwick, Boston, 1981-82; mgr. corp. reporting Warren, Gorham & Lamont, Inc., Boston, 1981-82, asst. contr. NYC, 1982-84, sr. v.p., CFO, 1988-90, Penguin Books USA Inc., NYC, 1990-96; exec. v.p., 1995-96; exec. v.p., CFO Addison Wesley Longman Inc., Reading, Mass., 1996-98; v.p., chief adminstrv. officer Orgnl. Dynamics, Inc., Burlington, Mass., 1998-2000; CFO First Knowledge Ptnrs. Inc., Boston, 2000—02; CFO, v.p. adminstrn. Castel, Inc., Beverly, 2002—08, exec. v.p. adminstrn., CFO, 2008. Pres. Trinity Coll. Sch. Fund, Beverly, Mass., 1992; bd. govs. Trinity Coll. Sch., Port Hope, Ont., 1992-2003, trustee, 2003—. Trustee John Hart Hunter Ednl. Found., N.Y.C., 1992; treas. Trinity Coll. Sch. Found., 2007-, Essex County Youth Soccer Assoc., 2007-. Mem. AICPA (bd. examiners 1998-2003), Assn. Chartered Accts. U.S. Ltd. (treas. 1990-93, dir. 1989-94, hon. dir. 1994—), Kappa Alpha Soc. (exec. com., v.p. 1991-93, pres. 1993-95). Episcopalian. Avocations: skiing, sailing, tennis, paddle tennis, golf. Office: Castel Inc 100 Cummings Ctr Ste 152F Beverly MA 01915 Office Phone: 978-232-7612. Personal E-mail: derekasmith@comcast.net.

SMITH, DIANA MARIE, business educator; b. Des Moines, Oct. 25, 1940; d. Nathan Henry and Helen (Hall) Kitchen; m. Robert Nelson Smith, Jan. 26, 1971 (dec. 12-7-2004); 1 child, Stephen BA, Drake U., Des Moines, Iowa, 1968, MA, 1971. Cert. tchr., Iowa. Stenographer Polk County Welfare Dept., Des Moines, 1960—67; typist Polk County Auditor, Des Moines, 1968, Ctrl. Life Assurance Co., Des Moines, 1976—79; computer oper. IRS, Des Moines, 1988; lead specialist II Norwest Bank, Des Moines, 1978—2002; sec. Shive-Hattery Engrs., Des Moines, 1976—90; instr. adult edn. Des Moines Ind. Dist., 1969—2001; tchr. bus., computers Des Moines Pub. Schs., 1968—2000; instr. computers St. Paul Ch. and Saks Inc., Des Moines, 2000—06. Ind. computer cons.; instr.-authorized tng. assoc. program for WordPerfect,

1994; Mary Kay beauty cons., 1993— Chair meml. com. Burns United Meth. Ch., Des Moines, 1988—, Sunday sch. tchr., 1961-83, 92-98, 2006—, sec. adminstrv. bd., 1983-2004 Democrat. Avocations: reading, computers. Office: Chim Cherie Fireplaces 534 35th St Des Moines IA 50312 Personal E-mail: dsmith1034@aol.com.

SMITH, DONALD ARCHIE, religious business executive, consultant; b. Dayton, Ohio, Feb. 23, 1934; s. Archie Ford and Catherine Rosella (Rabold) S.; m. Joan Sandra Speedie, May 18, 1955; children: Douglas Alan, Keith Cameron, Deirdre Lynn, Neal Ramsey. BA in Sci. and Math., Harvard U., 1956; cert., Indsl. Coll. of Armed Forces, 1971. Mgmt. Acct., 1977, Enrolled Agt., 1996. Nuclear rsch. and project engr. N.Am. Aviation Co., 1956-62; fin. software specialist Nat. Cash Register, 1962-63; mgr. sys. engring. N.Am. Aviation, 1963-67; mgr. bus. planning, mktg. svcs. and pub. rels. N.Am. Rockwell, Columbus, Ohio, 1967-72, mgr. internat. sales and mktg., 1968-73; mgr. strategic planning Rockwell Internat. Corp., Columbus, 1973-76, program mgr. Condor weapons sys., 1976-77, dir. guided bomb programs, 1977-78, dir. bus. devel. and legis. liaison, 1978-80; v.p. fin. applied tech. group Arvin Industries, Columbus, Ind., 1980-84; v.p. fin. Calspan Corp., Columbus, Ind., 1980-82, v.p. fin. and adminstrn., 1982-84, CFO, treas., dir., 1983-84; bus. dir. Franklin United Meth. Home, 1984-86; dir. fin. and adminstrn. North Ind. Conf. of the United Meth. Ch., 1986-92; sr. assoc. gen. sec. health benefits/gen. bd. of pensions United Meth. Ch., 1992-96; staff devel. cons. logal ednl. software, 1996-2000; pres. Kid Solve, Inc., 1999—. Ops. rsch. cons., 1962-64; instr. math. Sinclair Coll., Dayton, Ohio, 1961-63; mem. U.S.-U.K. Bipartite Com. on Nuclear Weapons, 1958-61; industry chmn. Mil. Specifications and Stds. Rev. Com., 1972-79; mgmt. cons., 1984—. Author: Financial Recordkeeping Handbook for Local Churches. Past pres., treas., trustee Players Theatre of Columbus, 1975—80; v.p. Ohio Assn. U.S. Army, 1979—80; dist. commr. Boy Scouts Am., 1970—73, cubmaster, 1965—70; squadron comdr. CAP, 1976; treas., dir. Franklin United Meth. Home, 1982—84; auditor First United Meth. Ch., 1981—84; ch. adminstr. Greenwood United Meth. Ch., 1997—2002; dir., treas. South Ind. United Meth. Found., 2002—; treas., trustee Columbus Arts Guild, 1980—83; mem. audit and rev. com. Gen. Coun. on Fin. and Adminstrn., 1988—92; chmn. Commn. on Racism in Columbus Pub. Schs., 1972; trustee Indpls. East Dist. United Meth. Ch., 2002—. Recipient Nat. award Jr. Achievement, Inc., 1954; Letters of Commendation govt. agys., Am. Def. Preparedness Assn., Boy Scouts Am., 1958-78; Leadership award Nat. Mgmt. Assn., 1979. Mem.: NAEA, NAA, NRA, SAR, AIA (nat. chmn. soc. and aerospace tech. com. 1980—83, nat. pub. policy com.), AARP (state chmn. Ill. 1993—95, mem. nat. tech. com. 1996—98, state adminstr. Ind. 1996—2003), Royal Inst. Nav., Nat. Mgmt. Assn. (v.p., trustee), Nat. Tng. Com. (chmn. 1998—2003, Gt. Lakes regional coord. 2003—), Army and Navy Club, Harvard Club (Ind.), Palatines to Am., Shriners, Masons. Home and Office: 7 E Hill Valley Dr Indianapolis IN 46227-2624 Office Phone: 319-889-0771.

SMITH, DONALD CAMERON, retired preventive medicine physician; b. Peterborough, Ont., Can., Feb. 2, 1922; arrived in U.S., 1952, naturalized, 1960; m. Jean Morningstar, Sept. 11, 1946. MD, Queen's U., 1945; MSc in Medicine, U. Toronto, Ont., 1948, DPH, 1949. Diplomate Am. Bd. Preventive Medicine, Am. Bd. Pediatrics. Intern Victoria Hosp., London, Ont., Canada, 1945-46; fellow in physiology U. Toronto, 1947—49; med. officer health Kent County (Ont.) Health Unit, 1950—52; Commonwealth Fund fellow in pediat. U. Mich. Hosp., 1952-55; prof. maternal and child health Sch. Pub. Health U. Mich., prof. pediat. Med. Sch., chmn. dept. health and human devel., 1961-79; prof. psychiatry and behavioral scis. Northwestern U. Med. Sch., Chgo., 1979-85; ret., 1985. Chmn. Medicaid Adv. Coun., 1969—72; vis. prof. maternal and child health Harvard U., 1969—72; prin. advisor health and med. affairs to gov., Mich., 1972—78; dir. Mich. Dept. Mental Health, 1974—78; chmn. State Pub. Health Adv. Coun., 1982—90; chmn. health care policy bd. Mich. Dept. Corrections, 1986—91; med. dir. Sisters Mercy Health Corp., 1981—91. Surgeon lt. Royal Can. Navy, 1946—47. Address: # 408 807 Asa Gray Dr Ann Arbor MI 48105 Business E-Mail: leelo@umich.edu.

SMITH, DONALD FREDERICK, psychologist, pharmacologist; b. Chgo., Jan. 30, 1945; s. Leonard and Gertrude (Sankstone) S.; m. Helle Birgitte Knudsen; children: Martin Smith, Bo (Smith) Stork. BSc in Psychology, Duke U., Durham, NC, 1967; MA in Physiological Psychology, McMaster U., Ontario, Canada, 1968; PhD in Biopsychology, U. Chgo., 1971; Lic. Medicine, Aarhus U., Denmark, 1974; DSc in Med. Sci., Copenhagen U., 1980. Sr. lectr. psychobiology and health psychology U. East London; with dept biol. psychiatry, postgrad. studies Ctr. Psychiat. Rsch.; med. faculty Aarhus U. Lectr. prins. of sci. rsch. and sci. writing. Editor: Handbook of Stereoisomers: Psychotropic Drugs, Handbook of Stereoisomers: Therapeutic Drugs; contbr. numerous scientific rsch. reports to profl. jours. Office: Psychiat Hosp Aarhus U Skovagervej 2 8240 Risskov Denmark Home: Skaering Sandager 56 8240 Egaa Denmark Personal E-mail: dfsmithdfsmith@gmail.com.

SMITH, DONNIE KAY, state agency administrator, retired military officer; b. Franklin, Ky., Dec. 4, 1947; s. Norris Justin and Ruby Evelyn Smith; m. Rhonda Joan Cowan; children: Haley Ann, Jennifer Leigh, Justin Patrick, Heather Marie. BA, Western Ky. U., Bowling Green, 1970. Deliveryman Nashville Surg. Supply, 1965—66; radio announcer WPHC Radio, Waverly, Tenn., 1966—67; music dir., announcer WBGN Radio, Bowling Green, 1967—70; 2d lt. US Army, Augusta, Ga., 1970—71; music dir., announcer WBGN Radio, 1971—72; music dir., radio announcer WSM Radio and TV, Inc., Nashville, 1972—75; capt., adminstrv. asst. HQ, Office of the Adj. Gen., Dept. of Mil., Tenn., Nashville, 1975—79; tchr. Trevecca Nazarene Coll., Nashville, 1978—79; capt., state recruiting and retention mgr. HQ, Tenn. Army NG, Nashville, 1979—80; maj., tng. officer 130th Rear Area Ops. Ctr., Smyrna, Tenn., 1980—85; lt. col., plans, ops. and mil. support officer HQ, Tenn. Army NG, 1985—88, lt. col., tng. adminstr., 1988—90; lt. col., pers. mgmt. officer HQ, Tenn. Army and Air NG, Nashville, 1990—91; col., dep. chief of staff for pers. HQ, Tenn. Army NG, 1991—2000; col., dep. chief of staff for human resources Joint Forces HQ, Tenn. Army and Air NG, Nashville, 2000—03; exec. adminstrn. officer Tenn. Emergency Mgmt. Agy., Nashville, 2004—. Assoc. editor Volstate Guardsman Newspaper, Nashville, 1974—75. Decorated Legion of Merit US Army, Meritorious Svc. medal (3), Army Commendation medal (4), Army Achievement medal, Commendation medal USAF, Fla. Meritorious Svc. medal Fla. N.G., Iowa Meritorious Svc. medal Iowa N.G., Pa. DSM Pa. N.G., Tex. Lone Star Medal Tex. N.G., Wis. NG Commendation medal Wis. N.G., Commendation Ribbon (3) Tenn. N.G., Individual Achievement Ribbon (5), Tenn. DSM (2), Ala. DSM Ala. N.G., Ky. DSM Ky. N.G., Miss. Magnolia medal Miss. N.G.; recipient Eagle Trophy, Nat. Mil. Pers. Adv. Com., NG Bur., Washington, 1997—2000, plaque, Bulgarian Army Gen. Staff, 2000, Minuteman Trophy, N.G. Assn. Tenn., 2000. Democrat. Presbyterian. Home: 116 Deer Rd Smyrna TN 37167-9743 Office: Tenn Emergency Mgmt Agy 3041 Sidco Dr Nashville TN 37204-1502 Office Fax: 615-741-0006. Personal E-mail: donnieksmith@yahoo.com. Business E-Mail: dsmith@tnema.org.

SMITH, DWIGHT MORRELL, chemistry professor, academic administrator; b. Hudson, NY, Oct. 10, 1931; s. Elliott Monroe and Edith Helen (Hall) S.; m. Alice Beverly Bond, Aug. 27, 1955 (dec. 1990); children— Karen Elizabeth, Susan Allison, Jonathan Aaron; m. Elfi Nelson, Dec. 28, 1991. BA, Ctrl. Coll., Pella, Iowa, 1953; PhD, Pa. State U., 1957; ScD (hon.), Ctrl. Coll., 1986; LittD (hon.), U. Denver, 1990. Postdoctoral fellow, instr. Calif. Inst. Tech., 1957—59; sr. chemist Texaco Rsch. Ctr., Beacon, NY, 1959—61; asst. prof. chemistry Wesleyan U., Middletown, Conn., 1961—66; assoc. prof. Hope Coll., Holland, Mich., 1966—69, prof., 1969—72; prof. chemistry U. Denver, 1972—, chmn. dept., 1972—83, 1999—2001, vice chancellor for acad. affairs, 1983—84, chancellor, 1984—89; pres., bd. trustees Hawaii Loa Coll., Kaneohe, 1990—92. Mem. Registry for Interim Coll. and Univ. Pres.; mem. adv. bd. Solar Energy Rsch. Inst., 1989—91; mem. vis. com. Zettlemoyer Ctr. for Surface Studies Lehigh U., 1990—96; dept. chemistry and geochemistry Colo. Sch. Mines; mem. sci. adv. bd. Denver Rsch. Inst.; sr. advisor Rocky Mountain Ctr. Homeland Def. Editor Revs. on Petroleum Chemistry, 1975-78; editl. adv. bd. Recent Rsch. Devels. in Applied Spectroscopy, 1998—; contbr. articles to profl. jours. Chmn. Chs. United for Social Action, Holland, 1968-69; mem. adv. com. Holland Sch. Bd., 1969-70; bd. commrs. Colo. Adv. Tech. Inst., 1984-88, Univ. Senate, United Meth. Ch., Nashville, 1987-88, 91-93; mem. adv. bd. United Way, Inst. Internat. Edn., Japan Am. Soc. Colo., Denver Winter Games Olympics Com.; mem. ch. bds. or consistories Ref. Ch. Am., N.Y., Conn., Mich., United Meth. Ch., Colo. DuPont fellow, 1956-57, NSF fellow Scripps Inst., 1971-72; recipient grants Rsch. Corp., Petroleum Rsch. Fund, NSF, Solar Energy Rsch. Inst., Camille & Henry Dreyfus Found., Inc. Mem. AAAS, Am. Assn. Aerosol Rsch., Am. Chem. Soc. (chmn. Colo. 1976, sec. we. Mich. 1970-71, joint coun. and bd. com. on sci. 1997-98, award Colo. sect. 1986), Soc. Applied Spectroscopy, Mile High Club, Sigma Xi. Achievements include patents for selective hydrogenation and fuel, lubricant additives. Home: 1931 W Sanibel Ct Littleton CO 80120-8133 Office: U Denver Dept Chem & Biochem Denver CO 80208-0001 Office Phone: 303-871-2938. Personal E-mail: elfidwight@comcast.net. Business E-Mail: dwismith@du.edu.

SMITH, E. ASHLEY, lawyer, insurance company executive; LLM, U. Houston; JD, U. Tex., Austin. Gen. counsel, v.p. Southwestern Group Fin.; pres., CEO Inst. for Rehab. and Rsch. (TIRR); vice chancellor govtl. rels. and policy U. Tex. Sys.; exec. v.p., chief legal officer Stewart Info. Svcs. Corp., 2006—. Mem. Tex. Ho. of Reps., Harris County. Office: Stewart Info Svcs Corp 1980 Post Oak Blvd Houston TX 77056 Office Phone: 713-625-8309. Business E-Mail: easmith@stewart.com.

SMITH, EARL CHARLES, nephrologist, educator; b. Pitts., Mar. 1, 1936; s. Mose and Irene Smith. BS, Tufts U., 1957; MD, U. Pitts., 1961. Diplomate in internal medicine and nephrology Am. Bd. Internal Medicine. Intern UPMC Montefiore Hosp., Pitts., 1961—62; resident, fellow Cleve. Clinic, 1964-68; physician Cook County Hosp., Chgo., 1968-71; chief nephrology divsn. Mt. Sinai Hosp., Chgo., 1971—, pres. med. staff, 1985-87, vice chair medicine, 1987—, interim chair medicine, 1994—95, 2005—06; chief nephrology divsn. Chgo. Med. Sch., 1994—, prof. medicine, 1995—, interim program dir., 2007—08. Cons. Internat. Jour. Artificial Organs, Milan, 1986—; med. adv. bd. Kidney Found. Ill., Chgo., 1980—; bd. dirs. Hektoen Inst. Medicine. Co-author: Medical Exam Book-Nephrology, 1976, Self Assessment in Internal Medicine, 1980; assoc. editor Kidney jour., 1991—; contbr. articles to profl. jours. Chair hypertension com. Chgo. Heart Assn., 1973-75. Capt. USAF, 1962-64. Recipient Meritorious Svc. award, Chgo. Heart Assn., 1975. Fellow Am. Coll. Physicians, Am. Soc. Nephrology; mem. Am. Soc. Artificial Internal Organs, Am. Soc. Hypertension Specialist in Clin. Hypertension, Internat. Soc. Nephrology, Phi Beta Kappa, Alpha Omega Alpha, Sigma Xi. Office: Mount Sinai Hosp 15th and California Ave Chicago IL 60608 Business E-Mail: smie@sinai.org.

SMITH, ED H., alderman; b. Roxie, Miss., 1945; s. Robert Smith and Elvia Witherspoon; m. Carolyn Reed; children: Javante, Kevia. BS, Alcorn State U., Miss.; MA, Northeastern Ill. U., Chgo. Mem. US Peace Corps, India, 1967—69; v.p. mktg. Chgo. Econ. Devel. Corp., 1969—76; alderman, 28th ward Chgo. City Coun., 1983—. Committeeman Democratic Ward, Chgo., 1984—, 7th Congl. Dist., Chgo., 1988—. Mem. Hawthorne Sch. Parent Coun., Operation PUSH, Midwest Cmty. Coun., Westside People for Progress, Chgo. Black United Communities, Boy Scouts America. Recipient Spl. Recognition, Peace Corps Svc., The White House, Outstanding Leadership award, Lawndale Art Fair, 1971, Leadership Motivation award, Tilton Sch., 1983, Cmty. Svc. award, Chgo. Police Dept., 1986. Democrat. Office: 259 N Pulaski Chicago IL 60624 also: City Hall 121 N LaSalle St Rm 203 Chicago IL 60602 Office Phone: 773-533-0900. Office Fax: 312-744-3066. Business E-Mail: ehsmith@cityofchicago.org.*

SMITH, EDMUND JOHNSTON, middle school educator; b. New London, Conn., June 18, 1956; s. Salem Virgil Smith and Florence Eugenia Hurlbutt; m. Pauline Marie Hayes, June 26, 1997; children: Ruby Florence Hayes, Sagan Ruth Hayes, Sam Huckleberry Hayes. BS in Natural Resources and Conservation, 1981; MEd, U. Conn., Storrs, 2000; BA, U. Conn. Cert. tchr. Conn. Bd. Edn., 1998. Vocat. agr. tchr. Suffield HS, Conn., 1990—92; mid. sch. sci. tchr. Windham Bd. of Edn., Willimantic, Conn., 1992—96; agr. edn. tchr. Rockville HS, Vernon, Conn., 1994—95; sci. tchr. Edwin O. Smith HS, Storrs, 1996—2003; exploratory sci. tchr. Two Rivers Magnet Mid. Sch., East Hartford, Conn., 2003—. Camp dir. Hartford County 4-H Camp, Marlborough, Conn., 1995—98; camp coord. East Conn. Camp Exploration, Hampton, 1999—2001; camp dir. Windham Tolland 4-H Camp, Pomfret Center, Conn., 2006—07; coord. for New Eng. Nat. Sci. Bowl, US Dept. Energy, 2006—. Commr. Windham Water Commn., Willimantic, 1992—2002. Recipient Conn. BioBlitz Educator award, U. Conn., 2007; named Conservation Tchr. of Yr., Tolland County Soil and Water Conservation Dist., 1995. Mem.: NEA (assoc.), Conn. Edn. Assn. (assoc.). Secular Humanist. Avocations: swimming, bicycling, canoeing, landscaping. Home: 166 Storrs Rd Mansfield Center CT 06250 Office: Two Rivers Magnet Mid Sch 337 E River Dr East Hartford CT 06108 Office Fax: 860-290-5330. Personal E-mail: esmith18b@sbcglobal.net. Business E-Mail: esmith@crec.org.

SMITH, EDWARD KENDRICK, lawyer; b. Atlanta, Dec. 9, 1956; s. Alexander Wyly and Elizabeth (Haverty) Smith; m. Caryl Greenberg Smith, Oct. 16, 1983; children: Gina Leigh, Jacob Ryan. BA, U. NC, Chapel Hill, 1974—78; JD, U. Ga., Athens, 1978—81. Bar: Ga. 1981, US Ct. Appeals (4th and 11th cirs.), US Dist. Ct. (no., mid. & so. dist.), US Supreme Ct. Ptnr. Smith Gambrell & Russell, LLP, Atlanta, 1981—2005, Jones Day, Atlanta, 2005—. Instr. Lorman Bus. Inst. 1989—, Inst. Continuing Legal Edn., Nat. Bus. Inst., Inc., Tax Exec. Inst., Faculty for Advanced Tax Sch., Leadership Atlanta, 1997. Chmn. Rsch. Atlanta, 1993—97; program chair Leadership Ga., Atlanta, 1997—98; chmn. Servants Relief for Incurable Cancer, Atlanta, 2000—; mem. exec. com. Atlanta Downtown Partnership, 1990—92; pres. The Bridge, Atlanta, 1991—99; trustee SW Hosp. & Med. Ctr., Atlanta, 1991—2002; bd. dirs. Ctrl. Atlanta Progress, Atlanta, 1994—, Zoo Atlanta, Atlanta, 2004—; mem. bd. visitors U. Ga. Law Sch., Athens, 2004—07; co-chmn. Fernbank Soc., 2005—06; pres. Tate Mt. Assocs., 2005—06; trustee John & Mary Franklin Found., 2002—. Recipient Ga. Legal Elite, Ga. Trend Mag., 2003, 2004, 2005, 2006, Ga. Super Lawyer, Atlanta Mag., 2003—, Ga. Legal Leader, James Mag., 2005, 2006, Top Ga. Lawyer, 2007, Leaders in the Field, Chambers USA, 2008—09, Best Lawyers America, 2009. Mem.: ABA, Inst. Profls. Taxation, Ctrl. Atlanta Progress, Piedmont Driving Club. Avocations: squash, hiking, piano, bicycling. Office: Jones Day 1420 Peachtree St Ste 800 Atlanta GA 30309 Office Fax: 404-581-8330. Business E-Mail: eksmith@jonesday.com.

SMITH, EDWARD M., labor union administrator; m. Betty Smith; children: Jordan, Matt. AA, Shawnee Coll.; B, Nat. Labor Coll.; grad. trade union program, Harvard U., Cambridge, Mass. Regional leader Laborers' Internat. Union North America, local bus. mgr., internat. v.p., midwest regional mgr., asst. to the pres.; exec. v.p. Union Labor Life Ins. Co., Inc., pres., 2008—. Leadership position Ill. State Bd. Investment, Ill. Dept. Labor Adv. Bd., Dem. Nat. Com., Nat. Alliance Fair Contracting. Benefactor Therapy Ctr., Carterville, Ill.; bd. mem. I Can Read Program. Recipient Outstanding Alumni award, Shawnee Coll., 1992. Democrat. Office: ULLICO Inc 1625 Eye St NW Washington DC 20006*

SMITH, EDWARD PAUL, JR., lawyer; b. Westbury, NY, Jan. 13, 1939; s. Edward Paul Sr. and Margaret (Eisenhauer) S.; m. Mary Elizabeth Neagle, Mar. 29, 1980; children: Nora, Edward, Brian, Thomas, Brendan. BA, Coll. of the Holy Cross, 1960; LLB, Columbia U., 1963. Bar: NY 1964, Fla. 1966. Assoc. Chadbourne & Parke LLP, NYC, 1964-75, prin., 1975—, ptnr. corp. dept., employment dept. Corp. sec. Am. Bur. Metal Statis., NYC, 1978—. Contbr. articles to profl. jour. Capt. USAF, 1964-67. Mem. NY State Bar Assn., Fla. Bar Assn. Roman Catholic. Office: Chadbourne & Parke LLP 30 Rockefeller Plz Fl 31 New York NY 10112-0129 Home Phone: 914-787-8350; Office Phone: 212-408-5100. Office Fax: 212-541-5369. Business E-Mail: esmith@chadbourne.com.

SMITH, EDWIN ERIC, lawyer; b. Louisville, Sept. 29, 1946; s. Lester Henry and Nancy Joy (Heyman) S.; m. Katharine Case Thomson, Aug. 16, 1969; children: Benjamin Clark, George Louis, Andrew Laurence. BA, Yale U., 1968; JD, Harvard Law Sch., 1974. Bar: Mass. 1974, NY, 2005, US Dist. Ct. Mass. 1974. Assoc. Bingham McCutchen LLP, Boston, 1974—81, ptnr., 1981—, co-chmn. fin. instn. practice group. Lectr. in field; Mass. commr. on uniform state laws; articles 5 and 9 drafting com. Uniform Comml. Code, chmn. payments article divsn. drafting com., editl. bd., 2005—; chmn. Article 9 Joint Review Com., 2008—; U.S. del. to receivables assignment working group UN Commn. on Internat. Trade Law Trustee Uniform Law Found. Lt. USNR, 1969-71. Recipient Achievement Medal USN, 1971. Mem. ABA (chmn. uniform comml. code com. bus. law sect. 1995-99, permanent editl. bd. uniform comml. code 1999-), Am. Law Inst. (Uniform Comml. Code article 9 study com.), Am. Coll. Comml. Fin. Lawyers (pres. 2002-03), Assn. Comml. Fin. Attys., Nat. Bankruptcy Conf., Am. Coll. Bankruptcy. Office: Bingham McCutchen LLP One Federal St Boston MA 02110-1713 Office Phone: 617-951-8615. Office Fax: 617-951-8736. Business E-Mail: edwin.smith@bingham.com.

SMITH, ELAINE DIANA, foreign service officer; b. Glencoe, Ill., Sept. 15, 1924; d. John Raymond and Elsie (Gelbard) S. BA, Grinnell Coll., 1946; MA, Johns Hopkins U., 1947; PhD, Am. U., 1959. Commd. fgn. svc. officer U.S. Dept. State, 1947; assigned to Brussels, 1947-50, Tehran, Iran, 1951-53, Wellington, New Zealand, 1954-56, Dept. State, Washington, 1956-60, Ankara, Turkey, 1960-69, Istanbul, Turkey, 1969-72, Dept. Commerce Exch., 1972-73; dep. examiner Fgn. Svc. Bd. Examiners, 1974-75; Turkish desk officer Dept. State, Washington, 1975-78. Consul gen., Izmir, Turkey, 1978—. Author: Origins of the Kemalist Movement, 1919-1923, 1959. Recipient Alumni award Grinnell Coll., 1957. Mem. U.S. Fgn. Svc. Assn., Phi Beta Kappa. Office: Lynn House 4400 braddock Rd Alexandria VA 22304-1010

SMITH, ELBERT BENJAMIN, historian, educator; b. Benham, Ky., May 1, 1920; s. Elbert Benjamin and Margaret Gladys (Huffaker) S.; m. Jean Frances Smith, Dec. 26, 1944; children: Randall, Stephen, Amy, Scott, Robert. AB, Maryville Coll., 1940; AM, U. Chgo., 1947, PhD, 1949. Assoc. prof. Youngstown (Ohio) U., 1949-57; assoc. prof., then prof. Iowa State U., Ames, 1957-67; prof. U. Md., College Park, 1968-90, prof. emeritus, 1990—. Vis. prof. U. Wis., Madison, 1967-68; vis. Fulbright prof. U. Tokyo, 1954-55, Moscow State U., 1976, 82, Leningrad (USSR) U., 1991; exch. prof. Beijing U., 1983, 88; lectr. cruise ships, 1989-2005. Author: Magnificent Missourian: Life of Thomas Hart Benton, 1958, 71, The Death of Slavery, 1967, 71, 73, The Presidency of James Buchanan, 1975 (Phi Alpha Theta award), Francis Preston Blair, 1980 (Phi Alpha Theta award), The Presidencies of Zachary Taylor and Millard Fillmore, 1988, Zachary Taylor: The Hero President, 2007; contbr. articles to profl. jours. Dem. candidate U.S. Senate, 1962, 66; mem. U.S. Bd. Fgn. Scholarships, Washington, 1979-81; founding pres. DC chpt. Fulbright Assn., 1984, nat. pres., 1989-90. Lt. (j.g.) USNR, 1942-45. Recipient Disting. Alumni citation, Maryville Coll., 1981. Mem. Am. Assn. UN (chmn. Iowa Spkr. Bur. 1961-65), Am. Hist. Assn., Orgn. Am. Historians. Presbyterian. Avocations: sailing, travel, athletics, lecturing on cruise ships. Home: 6647 Chesapeake Ter Tracys Landing MD 20779-2521 E-mail: ebs@wam.umd.edu.

SMITH, ELDEN LEROY, recreational vehicle and manufactured housing company executive; b. Berwyn, Ill., June 1, 1940; s. Frederick M. and Margaret I. (Larson) Smith; m. Barbara G. Whaley, Apr. 4, 1963; children: Jill Marie, David Elden. BA in Bus. Adminstrn., Whittier Coll., Calif., 1962. Mkt. analyst autonetics divsn. N.Am. Aviation, Anaheim, Calif., 1963—66; sales mgr. Pendleton Tool Industries, LA, 1966—68; plant gen. mgr. Fleetwood Enterprises, Inc., Hancock, Md., 1969—71, v.p. recreational vehicle group Riverside, Calif., 1972—88, sr. v.p., 1988—97, pres., dir., CEO, 2005—. Trustee Whittier Coll., 1991—99. Served with USNR, 1962—63. Mem.: Recreation Vehicle Industry Assn. (chmn. 1980—82, dir. 1975—97). Office: Fleetwood Enterprises 3125 Myers St Riverside CA 92503

SMITH, ELDON, cardiologist, physiologist, educator; MD, Dalhousie U., Halifax, NS, Can., 1967. From asst. prof. to assoc. prof. medicine and physiology Dalhousie U., 1973—80; prof. medicine and physiology and biophysics U. Calgary, Canada, 1980—2004, prof. emeritus, 2004—, chief divsn. cardiology, 1980—86, chair dept. medicine, 1985—90, assoc. dean clin. affairs, 1990—92, dean faculty of medicine, 1992—97. Corp. dir. Can. Natural Resources, Ltd., 1997—, Vasogen, Inc., 1998—, Sernova Corp., 2000—09, Aston Hill Fin., Inc., 2005—. Editor-in-chief: Can. Jour. Cardiology, 1997—2009. Bd. dirs., pres. Peter Lougheed Med. Rsch. Found., 1999—2007, Premier's adv. coun. health, 2000—02, health professions adv. bd., 2002—07; trustee Alta. Heritage Found. for Med. Rsch., Canada, 2000—07. Recipient officer Order of Can. Fellow: Can. Acad. Health Scis., Am. Heart Assn., Internat. Acad. Cardiovasc. Scis., Am. Coll. Cardiology, Royal Coll.

Physicians and Surgeons Can. Office: U Calgary Faculty Medicine 3330 Hosp Dr Calgary AB Canada T2N 4N1 Home Phone: 403-286-6800; Office Phone: 403-220-5500. Business E-Mail: esmith@ucalgary.ca.

SMITH, ELISE FIBER, international non-profit development agency administrator; b. Detroit, June 14, 1932; d. Guy and Mildred Geneva (Johnson) Fiber; m. James Frederick Smith, Aug. 11, 1956 (div. 1983); children: Gregory Douglas, Guy Charles; life ptnr. Jac Smit, 1990. BA, U. Mich., 1954; postgrad., U. Strasbourg, France, 1954-55; MA, Case Western Res. U., 1956. Tchr. US Binat. Ctr., Caracas, Venezuela, 1964-66; instr. English Am. U., 1966-68; prof. lang. faculty Catholic U., Lima, Peru, 1968-70; coord. English lang. culture program, lang. faculty El Rosario U., Bogota, Colombia, 1971-73; lang. specialist, mem. faculty Am. U., English Lang. Inst., 1975-78; exec. dir. OEF Internat. (name formerly Overseas Edn. Fund), Washington, 1978-89, bd. dirs.; dir. Global Women's Leadership Program Winrock Internat., 1989-98, sr. policy advisor on gender, 1998—. Co-founder, founding chair Women Thrive Worldwide (formerly Women's EDGE Coalition), 1997—2009, ex officio bd. mem. 2005—09, co-founder, 2008-; v.p. Pvt. Agys. Collaborating Together, NYC, 1983-89; trustee Internat. Devel. Conf., Washington, 1983-2001, exec. com., 1985-90; hon. com. for Global Crossroads Nat. Assembly, Global Perspectives in Edn., Inc., NYC, 1984, Washington, 1984-92, gen. assembly, 1992; nat. com. Focus on Hunger '84, LA; ofcl. observer UN Conf. on Status Women, 1980, UN 3rd World Conf. on Women, 1985, del. NGO Forum, UN 4th World Conf. on Women, del. NGO Forum, 1995; mental health adv. com. Dept. State, 1974-76; US del. planning seminar integration women in devel. OAS, 1978; participant Women, Law and Devel. Forum; exec. com., chair commn. advancement women interaction Am. Coun. for Vol. Internat. Action, 1994-97, co-founder, 1985-88, Interaction Adv. Com. to Commn. Advancement Women, 2006-, chmn. bd., 1985-88; adv. bd. Global Links Devel. Edn., Washington, 1985-86; adv. coun. Global Fund for Women, 1988-93; US del. Vital Voices Conf. Women and Democracy, Iceland, 1999, Women in Democracy Conf., Lithuania, 2000, Baltic Women in Democracy Conf., Estonia, 2003. Co-editor: Toward Internationalism: Readings in Cross-cultural Communication, 1979, 2d edit. 1986; author: (book chpt.) Developing Power: How Women Transformed International Development, 2004. Mem. USAID Adv. Com. on Vol. Fgn. Aid, 1994—2009, Women, Faith & Devel. Adv. Coun., 2008—; mem. women and conservation adv. com. World Wildlife Fund, 1998—2002; mem. State Dept. Adv. Com. US Internat. Econ. Policy, 2000—; bd. dirs. Internat. Ctr. Rsch. on Women, 1992—2001, Sudan-Am. Found. Rotary Internat. ambassadorial scholar Strasbourg, France, 1954-55; grantee Dept. State, 1975. Mem. Assn. Women in Devel., UNIFEM, Coalition Women in Internat. Devel. (co-founder 1979, chair 1993-96),pvt. Agys. in Internat. Devel. (co-chmn. 1980-82, pres. 1982-85), Nat. Assn. Fgn. Student Affairs (grantee 1975), U. Mich. Alumni Assn., Women's Fgn. Policy Group, Rotary Internat. (mem. global com. Women in Future Soc. 1996). Unitarian Universalist. Home Phone: 202-362-6234.

SMITH, ELIZABETH A. (LIZ SMITH), cosmetics company executive; BA, U. Va., Charlottesville, 1985; MBA, Stanford U. Grad. Sch. Bus., Calif. Fin. analyst in pvt. placement Paine Webber, Inc., 1986; gen. mgr., category bus. mgr. Callard and Bowser-Suchard; asst. brand mgr. Kraft Foods Inc., 1990, gen. mgr. beverage divsn., exec. v.p., 2000—02; group v.p. Kraft Foods N.Am.; pres. Kraft Beverages, Desserts and Cereals, 2002—04, group v.p., pres. US Beverages and Grocery Sectors, 2004; pres. global brands Avon Products, Inc., 2005—07, pres. N.Am., exec. v.p. NYC, 2005—07, pres., 2007—. Bd. dirs. Carter's Inc., 2004—08, Staples, Inc., 2008—, The Cosmetic, Toiletry and Fragrance Assn., Personal Care Products Coun. Named one of Top Marketers, Advt. Age, 1996, 50 Most Powerful Women in Bus., Fortune mag., 2007, 2008, 25 Leaders Reshaping NY, Crain's NY mag., 2008, 100 Most Powerful Women, Forbes mag., 2009. Mem.: Phi Beta Kappa. Office: Avon Products Inc 1345 Ave of the Americas New York NY 10020*

SMITH, ELIZABETH MACKEY, retired financial consultant; b. Phila., Mar. 23, 1941; d. William Norman and Celeste (Parvin) Mackey; m. George Van Riper Smith, Aug. 15, 1964; children: Douglas George, Todd Mackey. BA, Gettysburg Coll., 1963; MAT in French, Ga. State U., 1978. ChFC. Tchr. fgn. lang. Haverford (Pa.) H.S., 1963-65; registered rep. Am. Express Fin. Advisors, Inc., Macon and Savannah, Ga., 1979-2000, br. mgr. Tybee Island, Ga., 2000—05, ret., 2005. Reader Atlanta Serv for the Blind, 1968; hostess Atlanta Coun Int Visitors, 1972—74; foreign exchange student coord Loisirs Culturels a l'Etranger, 1990; staff protocol vol sailing venue Olympic Games, Savannah, 1996. Mem.: Delta Gamma, Delta Phi Alpha, Phi Sigma Iota. Avocations: tennis, swimming. Home: 104 Landings Way North Savannah GA 31411-1512 Personal E-mail: islandwoman64@earthlink.net.

SMITH, ELLEN LOUISE, retired language educator; b. Tulsa, Feb. 25, 1935; d. Joe D. and Laura Betty (McBrien) Hurt; m. Robert Lester Smith. BA, Ctrl. State Coll., Edmond, Okla., 1955; MA, U. Okla., Norman, 1958; PhD, U. Oreg., Eugene, 1964. Acting dir. publs. Ctrl. State Coll., Edmond, Okla., 1956-57; tchg. asst. U. Okla., Norman, 1957-59; instr. English U. Oreg., Eugene, 1959-64; asst. prof. English U. Calif. Santa Barbara, 1964-66; instr. English U. Granada, Spain, 1967-70; Fulbright lectr. English U. Valladolid, Spain, 1973-74; dep. dir. Spanish Fulbright Commn., Madrid, 1974-75; prof. English Stetson U., DeLand, Fla., 1977—2003. Contbr. articles to profl. jours. Mem. Delta Kappa Gamma. Democrat.

SMITH, ELLIS CARLTON, history educator, consultant; b. Quantico, Va., Nov. 15, 1937; s. Ellis Carlton Smith and Eunice Wells; children from previous marriage: Catherine, Caron. BGS, Chaminade U., Honolulu, 1972; MA, Pepperdine U., Malibu, Calif., 1973. Chief master sgt. U.S. Air Force, 1955—81; tchr. social studies Bastrop Mid. Sch., Tex., 1981—83, Dripping Springs H.S., Tex., 1983—. Advanced placement cons. Coll. Bd. Southwest Region, Austin, Tex. Recipient Spl. Recognition award, Coll. Bd. Southwest Region, 1997, Excellence in Tchg. award, Dripping Springs Ind. Sch. Dist. Edn. Found. Bd., 2003; named Top Tex. Tchr., Republic of Tex. Press, 2002. Mem.: Tex. Fedn. Tchrs., U.S. Tennis Assn., Phi Delta Kappa. Methodist. Avocation: tennis. Office: Dripping Springs HS Hwy 290 and Tiger Ln Dripping Springs TX 78620-0479 Home: Apt B 357 Fantail Loop Lakeway TX 78734-4191 E-mail: smithellis@sbcglobal.net.

SMITH, ELMER, telecommunications industry executive; Grad., Tulane U. Various positions Berry Co. (now Bellsouth Corp.), pres., CEO, pres. advt., pub. Atlanta, 2001—. Mem.: Assn. Directory Mktg. (bd. dirs.), Yellow Pages Integrated Media Assn. (chmn. 2003—04).

SMITH, EMMITT (EMMITT JAMES SMITH III), sportscaster, retired professional football player; b. Pensacola, Fla., May 15, 1969; s. Emmit Jr. and Mary Smith; m. Patricia Southall, Apr. 22, 2000; 4 children. BA in Pub. Recreation, U. Fla., 1996. Running back Dallas Cowboys, 1990—2003, Ariz. Cardinals, 2003—04; football analyst ESPN, 2007—. Recipient NFL MVP award, 1993, Super Bowl XXVIII MVP, 1993; named NFL Offensive Rookie of Yr., 1990, NFL All-Pro, Sporting News, 1992, 1993, NFL Player of Yr., 1993; named to NFC Pro-Bowl Team, 1990—95, 1998—99, Coll. Football Hall of Fame, 2006. Achievements include recognized as NFL's all-time leading rusher, 2002; leading NFL in rushing, 1991-93, 95; leading NFL running backs in scoring, 1992, 95; leading NFL in rushing touchdowns, 1992, 1994-95; being a member of Super Bowl Champion Dallas Cowboys, 1992, 1993, 1995; winner, Dancing With the Stars, 2006. Office: ESPN Plz 935 Middle St Bristol CT 06010

SMITH, EPHRAIM PHILIP, academic administrator; b. Fall River, Mass., Sept. 19, 1942; s. Jacob Max and Bertha (Horvitz) S.; m. Linda Sue Katz, Sept. 3, 1967; children: Benjamin, Rachel, Leah. BS, Providence Coll., 1964; MS, U. Mass., 1965; PhD, U. Ill., 1968. Chmn. dept. acctg. U. R.I., Kingston, 1972-73; dean Sch. Bus. Shippensburg State Coll., Pa., 1973-75; dean Coll. Bus. Adminstrn. Cleve. State U., 1975-90; dean Sch. Bus. Adminstrn. and Econ. Calif. State U., Fullerton, 1990-98, v.p. acad. affairs, 1998—. Co-author: Principles of Supervision: First and Second Level Management, 1984, Federal Taxation-Advanced Topics, 1995, Federal Taxation-Basic Principles, 2009, Federal Taxation Comprehensive Topics, 2009; contbr. articles to profl. jours. Mem. Am. Acctg. Assn., Am. Taxation Assn., Am. Inst. Decision Scis., Fin. Execs. Inst., Beta Gamma Sigma, Beta Alpha Psi. Office: Calif State Univ - Fullerton VPAA Office MH-133 800 N State College Blvd Fullerton CA 92831-3599 Office Phone: 657-278-2614. Business E-Mail: esmith@fullerton.edu.

SMITH, ERIC J., state official, school system administrator; b. Ga., 1956; BA, Colo. State U.; MA in Sch. Adminstrn., U. Ctrl. Fla.; PhD in Curriculum and Instruction, U. Fla., Gainesville. Supt. Newport News Pub. Sch., 1992, NC Sch. Sys., NC, 1995—2002, Charlotte-Mecklenberg Sch. Sys., 1996—2001, Danville Pub. Sch. Sys., Anne Arundel County Pub. Sch. Sys., Annapolis, Md., 2002; sr. v.p. coll. readiness, head EXCELerator project Coll. Bd.; commr. edn. Fla. Dept. Edn., Tallahassee, 2007—. Recipient McGraw prize in Edn., 2002; named Urban Educator of Yr., Coun. of Great City Sch., 2000. Office: Fla Dept Edn / Office of Commr Turlington Bldg, Ste 1514 325 W Gaines St Tallahassee FL 32399 Office Phone: 850-245-0505. Office Fax: 850-245-9667. E-mail: Commissioner@fldoe.org.*

SMITH, ERIC LEDELL, historian; b. Detroit, Oct. 9, 1949; s. Warren Cornelius and Henrietta Volena Smith. BA in Humanities, Mich. State U., 1971, MA in Philosophy, 1973, student, 1973—78; MLS, U. Mich., 1980; MA in Performance Studies, NYU, 1985. Sales clk. Dawn Treader Bookshop, Ann Arbor, Mich., 1980—90; asst. Libr. U. Mich., Ann Arbor, 1980—90; curator jr. edn. Detroit (Mich.) Hist. Mus., 1990—92; curator African Am. Mus., Phila., 1992—93; historian Pa. State Archives, Harrisburg, Pa., 1993—2001, State Mus. Pa., Harrisburg, 2001—. Archivist R.E. Olds Mus., Lansing, Mich., 1985; curator jr. edn. Dossin Great Lakes Mus., Detroit, 1989; curator exhbns. Author: Bert Williams: A Biography of the Pioneer Black Comedian, 1992 (nominee Pulitzer prize in biography, 1992), Blacks in Opera: A Biographical Dictionary of People and Companies, 1873-1993, 1995, African Americans in Pennsylvania: Shifting Historical Perspectives, 1997, Commemorating African American History in Pennsylvania: The First Twenty-five Years of the Conference on Black History in Pennsylvania, 2002, African American Theater Buildings, 2003 (Ray and Pat Browne Book award, 2003), The State Museum of Pennsylvania: A Centennial History, 2005; co-author: The African Americans in Pennsylvania, 1997, African Americans of Harrisburg, 2005; mem. editl. bd.: Pa. History, 1999—2001, Pa. Mag. History and Biography, 2004—; author: (plays) African Americans at the Capital Making Jazz History, 1999, When Lincoln Came to Harrisburg, 2000, The Liberation of Jim Phillips, 2001; contbr. articles to profl. jours. and mags. Bd. dirs. U.S. Colored Troops Inst., Harrisburg, Pa., 2002—03, African Am. Mus., Harrisburg, 1994—97; dir. exec. bd. Fedn. State Cultural Ednl. Profls., 2005—. Recipient Contbn. award, Pa. Dept. Edn., 1999, Individual Achievement award, Pa. Fedn. Mus. and Hist. Socs., 2003; finalist Excellence Hist. Recorded Sound Rsch. award, Assn. Recorded Sound Collections, 1993. Mem.: Hist. Harrisburg Assn., Dauphin County Hist. Soc. (bd. dirs. 1994—97), African Am. Mus. Phila., Assn. Study African Am. History, Pa. Hist. Assn. (Philip S. Klein award 1999), Org. Am. Historians. Democrat. Roman Cath. Office: The State Mus of Pa 300 North St Harrisburg PA 17120 Home: 660 Boas St Apt 512 Harrisburg PA 17102 Office Phone: 717-787-7179. Business E-Mail: ersmith@state.pa.us.

SMITH, ERIN ANN, science educator; b. Midland, Mich., Jan. 5, 1970; d. Jennifer Jenson and John Adams Smith. BA, BS, Mich. State U., East Lansing, 1991; PhD, Duke U., Durham, NC, 1997. Assoc. prof. U. Tex., Richardson, 1997—. Contbr. articles to profl. jours. (Anthony award Nominee, 2001). Mellon fellowship, Woodrow Wilson Found., 1991—97, Nat. Humanities Ctr. fellowship, Lilly Found., 2002—03, Summer Stipend fellowship, Nat. Endowment Humanities, 2002, Louisville Inst., 2002.

SMITH, ERNEST KETCHAM, electrical engineer; b. Peking, China, May 31, 1922; (parents Am. citizens); s. Ernest Ketcham and Grace (Goodrich) S.; m. Mary Louise Standish, June 23, 1950; children: Priscilla Varland, Nancy Smith Johnson, Cynthia Jackson. BA in Physics, Swarthmore Coll., 1944; MSEE, Cornell U., 1951, PhD, 1956. With Mut. Broadcasting Sys., 1946-49, chief plans and allocations engr., 1949; with radio propagation lab. Nat. Bur. Stds., Boulder, Colo., 1951-65, chief ionosphere rsch. sect., 1957-60, divsn. chief, 1960-65; dir. aeronomy lab. Environ. Sci. Svcs. Adminstrn., Boulder, 1965-67; dir. Inst. Telecom. Scis., 1968, dir. univ. rels., 1968-70; assoc. dir. Inst. Telecom. Scis. Office of Telecom., Boulder, 1970-72, cons., 1972-76; tech. staff Jet Propulsion Lab. Calif. Inst. Tech., Pasadena, 1976-87; adj. prof. dept. elec. and computer engring. U. Colo., Boulder, 1987—. Vis. fellow Coop. Inst. Rsch. on Environ. Scis., 1968; assoc. Harvard Coll. Obs., 1965-75; adj. prof. U. Colo., 1969-76; internat. vice-chmn. study group 6, Internat. Radio Consultative Com., 1958-70, chmn. U.S. study group, 1970-76; mem.-at-large U.S. nat. com. Internat. Sci. Radio Union, 1985-88; convenor Boulder Gatekeepers to the Future, 1990—. Author: Worldwide Occurrence of Sporadic E, 1957; (with S. Matsushita) Ionospheric Sporadic E, 1962. Contbr. numerous articles to profl. jours. Editor: Electromagnetic Probing of the Upper Atmosphere, 1969; assoc. editor for propagation IEEE Antennas and Propagation Mag., 1989—. Mem. 1st Congl. Ch., moderator, 1995-97. Recipient Diplôme d'Honneur, Internat. Radio Consultative Com., Internat. Telecom. Union, 1978; named to Gallery of Disting. Scientists, Engrs. and Adminstrs., Nat. Bur. Stds., Nat. Inst. Stds. and Tech., Gaithersburg, Md., 2003, USNC - URSI Special Recognition award, 2008. Fellow: IEEE (com. mem. 1993-1995, AAAS, Electromagnetics Acad.; mem. Am. Geophys. Union, Athenaeum (Pasadena), UN Assn. of US (convenor Boulder chpt., treas. 1994-2005), Sigma Xi (pres. U. Colo. chpt. 1994-95, v.p. 95-98). Home: 4900 Thunderbird Dr Apt 605 Boulder CO 80303-3835 Home Phone: 720-562-8175. Business E-Mail: ernest.smith@colorado.edu, ernestksmith@comcast.net. *A weakness of many large organizations is that it is difficult for senior administrators to step down after peaking in their 40s. I'm grateful for a crisis at age 50 which resulted in my taking early retirement at age 54 and then accepting a more modest job until age 65.*

SMITH, ESTHER THOMAS, communications executive; b. Jesup, Ga., Mar. 13, 1939; d. Joseph H. and Leslie Thomas; m. James D. Smith, June 2, 1962; children: Leslie, Amy, James Thomas. BA, Agnes Scott Coll., 1962. Staff writer Sunday women's editor Atlanta Jour.-Constn., 1961-62; mng. editor Bull. of U. Miami Sch. Medicine, 1965-66; corr. Atlanta Jour.-Constn. and Fla. Times-Union, 1964, 67-68; founding editor Bus. Rev. of Washington, 1978-81; founding editor, gen. mgr. Washington Bus. Jour., 1982; pres., bd. dirs. TechNews, Inc., 1986-96, CEO, 1995-96; founder, editor-at-large Washington Tech., 1986-97, Tech. Transfer Bus. Mag., 1992-95; co-chair editl. bd. TechCapital Mag., 1997-99; prin. Poretz Group Investor Rels., McLean, Va., 1998—2000; ptnr. Qorvis Comm. LLC (successor to Poretz Group), McLean, 2000—. Bd. dirs. Provant Inc., Women Connect.com, telezoo inc., World Affairs Coun. Washington, Atlantic Coun., Netpreneur Program Morino Inst., 1996—2002; mem. internat. adv. bd. Kilby Awards Found.; mem. MIT Enterprise Forum of Washington/Balt., 1981—82, Internat. Women's Forum, 1981—, No. Va. Bus. Round Table, exec. com., 1993—98; mem. adv. bd. Va. Math Coalition, 1991—94; commr. NACD Blue Ribbon Commn., 2001; trustee Ctr. for Excellence in Edn., 1993—96; bd. dirs., trustee Capital Region Technology Investors Conf.; bd. advisors George Washington U., Va., 1996—99; trustee George Mason U. Found., 2004—. Recipient Lifetime Achievement award, Women in Tech., 2000; named to, Washington Bus. Hall of Fame, 2002. Mem.: Md. High Tech. Coun., No. Va. Tech. Coun. (sr. adv. bd. 1998—2000, exec. com., bd. dirs., Earle C. Williams Leadership award 1999), Assn. Tech. Bus. Couns. (chmn. bd. advisors 1989—94), Econ. Club Washington. Office: Qorvis Comm LLC 1201 Connecticut Ave NW Ste 600 Washington DC 20036 Home Phone: 703-893-2195; Office Phone: 202-683-3212. Business E-Mail: esmith@qorvis.com.

SMITH, EUGENE WILSON, retired academic administrator, education educator; b. Forrest City, Ark., June 10, 1930; s. Milton Saumel and Frank Leslie (Wilson) S.; m. Rebecca Ann Slaughter, May 27, 1956; children: Lucinda Anne, Bradley Eugene. BA, Ark. State U., 1952; M.Ed., U. Miss., 1955, Ed.D., 1958. Mem. faculty Ark. State U., State University, 1958-92, prof. edn., 1971-92, v.p. adminstrn., 1968-71, dean Grad. Sch., 1971-84, interim pres., 1980, sr. v.p., 1980-84, pres., 1984-92, 94-95, pres. emeritus, 1992—, interim pres., 1994-95. Pres. Jonesboro Indsl. Devel. Corp., 1983-94; mem. exec. com. Conf. So. Grad. Schs., 1973-74, Ark. State Coun. on Econ. Edn., 1987-90; pres. Am. South Athletic Conf., 1987-89; dir. Mercantile Bank of Jonesboro, Union Planters Bank of Northeast Ark., Regions Bank of N.E. Ark. Alderman, City of Jonesboro, 1982-84, dir., pres. The Kays Found. Served to 1st lt. AUS, 1952-54, Korea. W.K. Kellogg Found. rsch. fellow, 1954-58 Mem. Ark. Adv. Coun. Elem. and Secondary Edn., Jonesboro C. of C. (dir. 1967-69, 80-85, v.p. 1981-82, pres. 1982-83), Phi Kappa Phi, Phi Delta Kappa, Kappa Delta Pi. Clubs: Rotary (pres. 1974-75). Home: 407 Lynne Ct Jonesboro AR 72401-8807

SMITH, EVA JOYCE, retired counselor, social worker; b. Coleman, Tex., Feb. 7, 1939; d. Thomas Charles and Donnie Mae (Herring) Bomar; children: George William, Melissa Jo Means. BS, Sam Houston U., Huntsville, Tex., 1961; M, Sul Ross U., Alpine, Tex., 1988. Cert. Teaching Tarleton State, 1977. Juvenile probation officer Bexan County Jud. Dept., San Antonio, 1961—62; social worker McKnight State Hosp., Carlsbad, Tex., 1965—66; elem. tchr. S.H.A.P.E. Elem. Dept. Def., Belgium, 1973—76; social studies tchr. Lampases Jr. H.S., Tex., 1976—84; secondary social studies tchr. Seoul Am. Sch., Republic of Korea, 1984—86; social studies tchr. Uvalde Jr. H.S., Tex., 1986—88; counselor k-8 Coleman Intermed. Sch. Dist., Tex., 1988—92; itinerant rural counselor Yukon Koyukok Sch. Dist., Fairbanks, Alaska, 1992—93; elem. sch. counselor Northwest Elem. Sch., Brownwood, Tex., 1993—95, Ballinger Elem., Tex., 1995—2001; ret., 2001. Editor: (plays) Little Bit of History Never Hurt Anyone, 1990. Adv. Girl Scouts of Am., San Angelo, 1963—66; missionary to various countries; med. records Operation Smile, Norfolk, Va., 2002—08, vol. Cambodia, China, Belgium, Jordan, Nicaragua; spring ho.chmn. Lampasas C. of C., Tex., 1979—82; cancer dr. chmn. United Fund, Lampasas, 1978; ct. apptd. spl. adv., 2002—; sponsor C.A.S.A. Recipient History Fair award, Hist. Assn. of Tex., 1976—80, Ms. Congeniality, Tex. Sr. Am. Pageant, 2002, for Outstanding Work, State Legislator in History, 1978. Mem.: Kiwanis Club. Presbyn. Avocations: horseback riding, travel, gardening. Home: 1251 County Rd 411 Coleman TX 76834 Personal E-mail: lilranch@web-access.net.

SMITH, FLOYD LESLIE, insurance company executive; b. Silver Creek, NY, Nov. 12, 1931; s. Harry Lee and Fanny Diem (Arnold) S.; m. Jane Kathryn Elters, Feb. 18, 1956; children: Keith Arnold, Bruce Erik. AB, Oberlin Coll., (Ohio), 1953; MBA, NYU, 1962. Investment analyst Mut. of N.Y., NYC, 1953-64, dir. investments, 1964-66; asst. v.p. securities investment Mut. of N.Y., NYC, 1966-69; 2d v.p. securities investment Mut. of N.Y., NYC, 1969-74, v.p. securities investment, 1974-78, sr. v.p., 1978-81, chief investment officer, 1981-83, exec. v.p., chief investment officer, 1983-89, vice chmn., chief investment officer, 1989-91; trustee The Mut. Life Ins. Co. of N.Y., 1988-91; dir. MONY Series Fund, 1983—2005, Empire Fidelity Investments Life Ins. Co., 1994—. Trustee MONY Real Estate Investors, N.Y.C., 1981-90; bd. dirs., chmn. exec. com. Ins. Systems Am., Atlanta, 1974-82. Trustee chmn. fin. com. Friends Sem., N.Y.C., 1975-84; trustee dep. major Village of Saltaire, 1984-87; dir. St. Maarten Condo. Assn., Naples, Fla., 1993—; mem. Saltaire (N.Y.) Zoning Bd. Appeals, 1982-84; mem. fin. com. N.Y. Quarterly Meeting Soc. of Friends, 2004-07. With Signal Corps, U.S. Army, 1954-56. Mem. Ft. Worth Boat Club, Skytop Club.

SMITH, FRANK EARL, retired trade association administrator; b. Fremont Ctr., NY, Feb. 4, 1931; s. Earl A. and Hazel (Knack) S.; m. Caroline R. Gillin, Aug. 14, 1954; children: Stephen F., David S., Daniel E. BS, Syracuse U., 1952. With Mellor Advt. Agy., Elmira, NY, 1954-55; asst. mgr. Elmira Assn. of Commerce, 1955-56; retail dept. mgr. C. of C., Binghamton, NY; mgr. Better Bus. Bur., Broome County, NY, 1956-60; exec. v.p. C. of C., Chemung County, Elmira, 1960-65, Schenectady County (N.Y.) C. of C., 1965-69, Greater Cin. C. of C., 1969-78; pres. Greater Detroit C. of C., 1978-95; ret., 1995. Bd. dirs., sec. Presbyn. Devel. Corp. of Detroit, Inc., 1995-2006. 1st lt. USAF, 1952-54. Named Young Man of Yr. Jr. C. of C. Elmira, 1964. Mem. C. of C. Execs. Mich., Am. C. of C. Execs. (past chmn.), NY State C. of C. Execs. (past pres.), Ohio C. of C. Execs. (past pres.), C. of C. of US (past bd. dirs. Ctr. Internatl Pvt. Enterprise, past chmn. nat. bd. regents, Inst. for Orgn. Mgmt.). Presbyterian. Home: 1626 Shallow Shores Dr Gaylord MI 49735

SMITH, FRANK TUPPER, lawyer; b. May 21, 1929; s. Frank T. and Mary Elizabeth Smith; m. Jill A. Jacobsen, Mar. 9, 1957; children: Delia, Lisa Noel, Kathryn. BA, Columbia Coll., 1951; JD, Columbia U., 1954; MBA, NYU, 1963. Bar: N.Y. 1956, Calif. 1966, Tex. 1974, U.S. Supreme Ct. 1963; cert. estate planning and probate law specialist, Tex. Assoc. Vaughn & Lyons, NYC, 1956-60, Edward R. Peckerman, NYC, 1960-63; v.p. Bank of Calif., San Francisco, 1963-69; assoc. Paul Hastings Janofsky & Walker, LA, 1969-72; v.p., trust officer Republic Nat. Bank, Dallas, 1972-74; ptnr. Smith, Miller & Carlton, Dallas, 1975-87; sr. ptnr. Frank Tupper Smith & Assocs. PC, 1987—. Lectr.

estate and tax planning U. Tex., Dallas, Dallas Community Coll. Dist. Bd. dirs. Am. Heart Assn., 1979-82, Tex. chmn. planned giving com., 1980-82, nat. chmn. planned giving com., 1983-86; bd. dirs., v.p. fund raising Brain/Behavior Ctr., 1992-98; bd. dirs. Planned Living Assistance Network North Tex., Inc., 1996-2000. With AUS, 1954-56. Mem. ABA, Calif. State Bar Assn., Tex. State Bar Assn., Dallas Bar Assn., Columbia U. North Tex. Club (pres. 1980-86), Univ. Club, Rush Creek Yacht Club. Home: 3975 High Summit Dr Dallas TX 75244-6623 Office: 3860 W Northwest Hwy Dallas TX 75220-5183 Office Phone: 972-241-2122. Personal E-mail: tuppertalk@tx.rr.com.

SMITH, FREDERICK AUGUSTUS, librarian; b. Bklyn., Aug. 1, 1952; s. Frederick Smith and Virginia Brady; m. Kathleen Stein Smith, May 5, 1984; children: Frederick Andrew, Sean Daniel, Patrick Edward. BA with honors, NYU, 1974, MA with honors, 1976; MS with honors, Columbia U., NY, 1978; Student, CUNY Bklyn.,Summer Latin Inst., 1975, Student, 1976. Periodicals libr. Coll. New Rochelle, NY, 1978—86; head periodicals libr. Jersey City State Coll., 1986—93, libr. director, 1993—94; head reference libr. NJ City U., 1994—. Recipient Merit award, Jersey City State Coll., 1989, award, NEH, 1976. Mem.: Orgn. Am. Historians, Am. Hist. Assn., Beta Phi Mu, Pk. History Honor Soc., Red Dragon Soc. Office: New Jersey City Univ 2039 Kennedy Boulevard Jersey City NJ 07305

SMITH, FREDERICK COE, retired manufacturing executive; b. Ridgewood, NJ, June 3, 1916; s. Frederick Coe and Mary (Steffee) S.; m. Ruth Pfeiffer, Oct. 5, 1940; children: Frederick Coe, Geoffrey, Roger, William, Bart. BS, Cornell U., 1938; MBA, Harvard U., 1940. With Armstrong Cork Co., Lancaster, Pa., 1940-41; with Huffy Corp., Dayton, Ohio, 1946-86, pres., chief exec. officer, 1961-72, chmn., chief exec. officer, 1972-76, chmn., 1976-78, chmn. exec. com., 1979-86. Past chmn. Sinclair C.C. Found.; past chmn. nat. bd. dirs. Planned Parenthoo Fedn.; past dir. Internat. Parenthood Fedn.; past chmn. Dayton Found.; trustee emeritus Alan Gutmacher Inst., Ohio United Way; past chmn. employment and tng. com. Gov.'s Human Investment Coun. Lt. col. USAAF, 1941-46. Decorated Legion of Merit. Office Phone: 937-228-7998. Office Fax: 937-223-1441. Personal E-mail: dotti8@att.net.

SMITH, FREDERICK M., religious studies educator; life ptnr. Tonja Robins. MA in Sanskrit, Pune U., India, 1976; PhD, U. Pa., Phila., 1984. Prof. U. Iowa, Iowa City, 1991—. Author: (book) The Self Possessed: Deity and Spirit Possession in South Asian Literature and Civilization; translator: The Vedic Sacrifice in Transition. Sr. Rsch. grant, Fulbright, 1995, 2006. Mem.: Assn. Asian Studies, Am. Acad. Religion, Am. Oriental Soc. Office: Univ Iowa 314 Gilmore Hall Iowa City IA 52242 Business E-Mail: frederick-smith@uiowa.edu.

SMITH, FREDERICK ORVILLE, II, agricultural products executive, retired military officer; b. Cambridge, Mass., July 17, 1934; s. Harry Francis and Dorothy Spaulding (Zeller) S.; m. Mabel Roxy Moore, June 6, 1965; children: Sarah Zeller, Jennifer Joy, Erika Hildred. BA, Bowdoin Coll., 1956; MA in Polit. Sci., U. Vt., 2000. Deck officer, 1st lt. USS The Sullivans USN, 1957-59; officer US Naval Sta., Adak, Alaska, 1959-60; clk. & exec. Fred O. Smith Mfg. Co., New Vineyard, Maine, 1960-71, pres., treas., 1971—; res. officer Naval Res. Tng. Ctr., Augusta, Maine, 1960-69, Bangor, Maine, 1970-79 (ret.). Co-owner Sugarwood Gallery, Inc., Farmington, Maine, 2000—08, corp. sec., 2007—08. Editor: New Vineyard, Maine 1802-2002, Its Settlement, Its People, Its History, A New Vineyard Historical Society Document, 2002, 2nd edit., 2008. Notary pub., 1978—; chair, mem. nat. com. Young Reps., Maine, 1960—68, pres. New Eng. coun., 1962—64; chmn. Franklin County (Maine) Rep. Com., 1976—80, v.p. state conv., 1994; mem. Maine Rep. State Com., 1980—86, 1992—94, 1998—2002, 2006—, Maine Rep. Platform Com., 2008; mem. state com. ASCO, 1998—2002; town chmn. Rep. Com., New Vineyard, 1972—86, Farmington, Maine, 1992—2008; ecumenical rep. Old South Congl. Ch., 2007—, moderator, 2008—, mem. Paul Harris fellow Farmington Rotary Club, 1996. Mem.: Farmington Zoning Bd., Porter Lake Assn. (bd. dirs. 2005—), Up Country Artists (bd. dirs. 1996—2003, v.p. 1997, pres. 1998—2000, bd. dirs. 2000—03, v.p., bd. dirs. 2005—06), Franklin County Arts and Crafts (v.p. 2002—05, pres. 2006—), Shriners, Am. Legion, Masons, Kora Temple Shrine. Avocations: photography, cabinet making & design, skiing, hiking, writing. Home: 127 Anson St Farmington ME 04938-5734 Office: The Fred O Smith Mfg Co PO Box 248 New Vineyard ME 04956-0248 Office Phone: 207-778-4177. Fax: 207-779-0716. E-mail: fosmith@somtel.com.

SMITH, FREDERICK WALLACE, delivery service executive; b. Marks, Miss., Aug. 11, 1944; s. Frederick C. Smith & Sally (Wallace) S.; m. Linda Black Grisham, 1969 (div. 1977), 2 children; m. Diane Avis; 8 children BS in Econs., Yale U., 1966. Cert. comml. pilot. Owner Ark Aviation, 1969-71; founder FedEx Express Corp., Memphis, 1971—, pres., 1971—75, CEO, 1977—98, chmn. bd., 1975—; chmn. bd., pres., CEO FedEx Corp., 1998—. Served with USMC, 1966-70, co-chmn. WWII Meml. Campaign. Decorated Silver Star, Bronze Star, Purple Heart; recipient Peter F. Drucker Strategic Leadership award, 1997, Eagle of Aviation award, Embry-Riddle Aero. award, 2001, Champion of Workplace Learning and Performance award, Amer. Soc. Tng. and Devel., 2002, Bower award for Bus. Leadership, Franklin Inst., 2008; named CEO of Yr., Chief Executive Mag., 2004, Person of Yr., French-Am. C. of C., 2006; named one of 400 Richest Ams., Forbes mag., 2006. Office: FedEx Corp 942 S Shady Grove Rd Memphis TN 38120-4117*

SMITH, FREDRICA EMRICH, rheumatologist, internist; b. Princeton, NJ, Apr. 28, 1945; d. Raymond Jay and Carolyn Sarah (Schleicher) Emrich; m. Paul David Smith, June 10, 1967. AB, Bryn Mawr Coll., Pa., 1967; MD, Duke U., Durham, NC, 1971. Intern, resident U. N.Mex. Affiliated Hosps., 1971-73; fellow U. Va. Hosp., Charlottesville, 1974-75; pvt. practice, Los Alamos, N.Mex., 1975—. Chmn. credentials com. Los Alamos Med. Ctr., 1983—, chief staff, 1990, 2003; bd. dirs. N.Mex. Physicians Mut. Liability Ins. Co., Albuquerque, 1988-97; regional adv. bd. Am. Physicians Assurance, 1997-; cons. PPAC, 2008-. Contbr. articles to med. jours. Mem. bass sect. Los Alamos Symphony, 1975—; active Los Alamos County Parks and Recreation Bd., 1984-88, 92-96, 2007-, Los Alamos County Med. Indigent Health Care Task Force, 1989—2003; ops. subcom. Aquatic Ctr., Los Alamos County, 1988—,Los Alamos Country Pk. Recreation Bd., 2009-. Fellow ACP, Am. Coll. Rheumatology; mem. N.Mex. Soc. Internal Medicine (pres. 1993-96), Friends of Bandelier. Democrat. Avocations: swimming, music, reading, hiking. Office: Los Alamos Med Ctr 3917 West Rd Los Alamos NM 87544-2275 Office Phone: 505-662-9400.

SMITH, G. RICHARD, psychiatry educator; BS in Chem.-Biology, Rhodes Coll., Memphis, Tenn., 1973; MD, U. Ark. Coll. Medicine, Little Rock, 1977. Intern, resident psychiatry U. Hosp., Little Rock, 1977—80; fellow, instr., psychiatry and med., med./psych liaison group U. Rochester, NY, 1980—81; asst. prof., psychiatry and medicine U. Ark. Med. Sch., Little Rock, 1981—85, dir., residency tng., dept. psychiatry and behavioral sciences, 1982—86, assoc. prof., medicine, 1985—97, assoc. prof., psych, dept. psychiatry and behavioral sciences, 1985—2001, vice-chmn., dept. psychiatry and behavioral sciences, 1985—2001, prof., psychiatry, dept. psychiatry and behavioral sciences, 1991—2001, prof. medicine, 1997—, Marie Wilson Howells prof. & chair, dept. psychiatry and behavioral sciences, 2001—, dir., Ctrs. for Mental Healthcare Rsch., dept. psychiatry and behavioral sciences, 1989—2001, prof., dept. health policy and mgmt., Coll. Pub. Health, 2001—; vis. scholar LBJ Sch. Pub. Affairs, U. Tex., Austin, 1997—98; CEO Psychiatric Assessment Systems, 2004—. Mem. NIMH Initial Review Group Services Rsch., 1989—93, chair, 1991—93; mem. NIMH Nat. Mental Health Adv. Coun., 1995—98, coordinating mem., 1996—98. Contbr. several articles to profl. jours. Office: U Ark Coll Pub Health 4301 WMarkham # 820 Little Rock AR 72205*

SMITH, GARVIN, economics professor; b. Bothel, Wash., Aug. 30, 1953; m. Deborah Peterson, Nov. 17, 1979; children: Joshua Joseph, Caleb Cannon, Jennifer Joy Joslyn, Sarah Serene Heiner, Rebekah Rejoice, Abraham Ammon, Angel Anna Day; 1 child, Hyrum Harrison. M in Economics, U. Ctrl. Fla., Orlando, 1997. Asst. prof. economics Daytona State Coll., Daytona Beach, Fla., 1998—. Home: 172 Ibis Rd Longwood FL 32779 Office: Daytona State Coll 1200 W Intl Speedway Blvd Daytona Beach FL 32120 Business E-Mail: smithg@daytonastate.edu.

SMITH, GARY RICHARD, technology educator; b. Little Rock, Ark., Jan. 21, 1929; s. C. Ray and Maureen (Martin) S.; m. Mary Clare Beacom, June 16, 1956; children: Raymond, Timothy, Daniel, Laura, Carolyn. BA, Cornell Coll., 1952; MEd, Nat. Coll. Edn., Evanston, Ill., 1954; PhD, Northwestern U., 1960. Asst. editor Chem. Processing Mag., Chgo., 1952-53; tchr. various elem. schs. Evanston, Ill., 1954-58; instr. Northwestern U., Evanston, 1958-60; asst. prof. Wayne State U., Detroit, 1960-63, assoc. prof., 1964-69, prof., 1970—. Edn. rsch. cons. Mich. Senate Edn. Com., Lansing, 1973-74, Mich. Com. to Redistrict Detroit Pub. Schs., 1981. Contbr. articles to profl. jours. With U.S. Army, 1948-49. Mem. Internat. Soc. for Technology in Edn. Home: 3514 Arrowvale St Orchard Lake MI 48324-1506 Office: Wayne State U Rm 227 Edn Bldg Detroit MI 48202

SMITH, GENE, athletic director; m. Sheila Smith; children: Matt, Lindsay, Nicole, Summer. BA, U. Notre Dame, 1977. Asst. football coach U. Notre Dame, 1977—81; mktg. rep. IBM; athletic dir. Ea. Mich. U., 1983—93, Iowa State U., 1993—2000, Ariz. State U., 2000—05, Ohio State U., 2005—, assoc. v.p., 2007—. Recipient John L. Toner award, Nat. Football Found., 2008; named one of 50 Most Powerful Blacks in Sports, Black Enterprise mag., 2005. Mem.: NCAA (chmn. divsn. I men's basketball com. 2010—, mem. football rules com., mem. com. on infractions). Office: Ohio State Univ 224 St John Arena 410 Woody Hayes Dr Columbus OH 43210 Office Phone: 614-292-7572. Office Fax: 614-292-0506.*

SMITH, GENE See SMITH, LINDA

SMITH, GENE, professional sports team executive; b. Dec. 31, 1963; married; 2 children. BEd, Heidelberg Coll., Tiffin, Ohio, 1986; M in Athletic Adminstrn., Ohio U., 1987; attended NFL managers program, Stanford U., Calif., 2008. Grad. asst., asst. coach Ohio U. Bobcats, 1986—88; asst. coach., recruiting coord., strength and conditioning coord. Edinboro U. Fighting Scots, Pa., 1989—94; scouting rep., BLESTO combine, coll. scout Jacksonville Jaguars, 1994—2000, dir. coll. scouting, exec. dir. coll. and pro pers., 2000—08, v.p. player pers., 2008—09, sr. v.p. player pers., gen. mgr., 2009—. Mem. coll. adv. com. NFL, mem. Nat. Invitational Camp selection com. Named to Monroeville HS Hall of Fame, Ohio. Office: Jacksonville Jaguars One Stadium Pl Jacksonville FL 32202*

SMITH, GEORGE CURTIS, judge; b. Columbus, Ohio, Aug. 8, 1935; s. George B. and Dorothy R. Smith; m. Barbara Jean Wood, July 10, 1963; children: Curtis, Geoffrey, Elizabeth Ann. BA, Ohio State U., 1957, JD, 1959. Bar: Ohio 1959, U.S. Dist. Ct. (so. dist.) Ohio 2002. Asst. city atty. City of Columbus, 1959-62; exec. asst. to Mayor of Columbus, 1962-63; asst. atty. gen. State of Ohio, 1964; chief counsel to pros. atty. Franklin County, Ohio, 1965-70; pros. atty., 1971-80; judge Franklin County Mcpl. Ct., Columbus, 1980-85, Franklin County Common Pleas Ct., 1985-87; sr. judge U.S. Dist. Ct., 2002—. Mem. 2003 Ohio Bicentennial Com.; mem. Historical Marker com., 2003; mem. Ohio Supreme Ct. Coun. on Victims Rights; judge in residence Law Sch. U. Cin.; chair Fed. Ct. Case Settlement Seminar; faculty Ohio Jud. Coll., Litig. Practice Inst.; chmn., Fed. Bench-Bar Conf.; lectr. ABA Anti-Trust Sec.; alumni spkr. law graduation Moritz Coll. Law, Ohio State U.; pres. Young Rep. Club; chmn. Perry Group, 2005; exec. com. Franklin County Rep. Party, 1971-80 Elder Presbyn. Ch. Recipient Superior Jud. Svc. award Supreme Ct. Ohio, Outstanding Pub. Svc. award Fr. Co. Rep. Orgn., 2001, Judge W.K. Thomas award Ohio State U. Law Alumni, Disting. Jurist, 2006, Ohio Pros. of Yr. award Ohio Pros. Attys. Assn., 1976, Hon. Leadership award, 1977. Mem. Columbus Bar Assn., Columbus Bar Found., Columbus Athletic Club (pres. 1980, dir.), Lawyers Club of Columbus (pres. 1975), Masons (pres. 33rd assn.), Shriners, Gyro Club (pres. 2003), Putin Bay Yacht Club (commodore 2007). Office: 85 Marconi Blvd Columbus OH 43215-2823 Office Phone: 614-719-3220.

SMITH, GEORGE DRURY, publishing executive; b. Dayton, Ohio, Mar. 10, 1927; s. Martin Jefferson and Viola (Haas) Smith; m. Anne Llard Jennings, Apr. 1967 (div. 1977); life ptnr. Leston Chandler Buell, 1996. AB cum laude, Marietta Coll., 1953; Diplome de Phonetique, U. Grenoble, 1950; student, U. Madrid, 1950-51, Heidelberg U., 1951-52, U. Minn., 1953-55, U. Calif.-Berkeley, 1965, UCLA, 1968. CFO Argonaut newspaper, 1972—. Editor: Beyond Baroque, 1968—80, NewLetters, 1969—75, NewBooks, 1976—78. Founder Beyond Baroque Found., Venice, Calif., 1968, chmn., 1968—80, chmn. emeritus, 1980—; active Mcpl. Arts Adv. Bd., LA, 1980—82; chmn. Save Westminster Auditorium Com., Venice, 1977—80. With US Army, 1945—47. Grantee, Nat. Endowment Arts, 1973—80, Calif. Arts coun., 1977—80, Mcpl. Arts Commn., 1977—80, Coordinating Coun. Lit. Mags., 1974—80. Home Fax: 323-443-3808. Personal E-mail: georgedrurysmith@yahoo.com. *I believe that if we have faith we can live without fear; that the universe is benevolent if we can love unconditionally; that we can live righteously and prosper if we are honest and seek divine guidance; and that our mission is to enjoy life and strive for beauty.*

SMITH, GEORGE PATRICK, II, lawyer, educator; b. Wabash, Ind., Sept. 1, 1939; s. George Patrick and Marie Louise (Barrett) S. BS, Ind. U., 1961, JD, 1964; certificate, Hague Acad. Internat. Law, 1965; LLM, Columbia U., 1975; LLD, Ind. U., 1998. Bar: Ind. 1964, U.S. Supreme Ct. 1968. Kannert teaching fellow Ind. U. Sch. Law, 1964-65; instr. law U. Mich. Sch. Law, 1965-66; practiced in Ind. and Washington, 1965—; legal adviser Fgn. Claims Settlement Commn., Dept. State, Washington, 1966; asst. prof., asst. dean State U. N.Y. at Buffalo Law Sch., 1967-69; vis. asst. prof. law George Washington U., Nat. Law Center, summer 1968; assoc. prof. law U. Ark., 1969-71; spl. counsel EPA, Washington, 1971-74; adj. prof. law Cath. U. Law Sch., Washington, 1973-74, prof., 1977—. Spl. counselor environl. affairs Gov. Ark., 1969—71; mem. Ark. Waterway Commn., 1970—71; mem. com. hwy. rsch. NRC, NAS, 1971—81; adj. prof. law Georgetown U., 1971—75; assoc. prof. law U. Pitts., 1975—78; vis. prof. U. New South Wales, Australia, 2001, U. Sydney, Australia, 2003, others; disting. vis. prof. Macquarie U., Sydney, 2005; cons., lectr. in field; vis. scholar, Ctr. Ethics & Culture Notre Dame U., 2009; vis. fellow Ctr. Biomed. Ethics & Humanities, U. Va., Charlottesville, 2009. Author: Restricting the Concept of Free Seas, 1980, Legal, Ethical and Social Issues of the Brave New World, 1980, Genetics, Ethics and the Law, 1981, Medical-Legal Aspects of Cryonics, 1983, The New Biology, 1989, Final Choices: Autonomy in Health Care Decisions, 1989, Bioethics and the Law, 1993, Legal and Healthcare Ethics for the Elderly, 1996, Family Values and the New Society: Dilemmas of the 21st Century, 1998; Human Rights and BioMedicine, 2000, The Christian Religion and Biotechnology, 2005 (nominated Pulitzer prize, 2005), Distributive Justice and The New Medicine, 2008; contbr. articles to profl. jours. U. Ark. del. Pacem In Maribus Conf., Malta, 1970. Recipient Disting. Alumni award Ind. U. Bd. Trustees, 1985, citation for Path-Breaking Work; vis. fellow Law Sch. Fordham U., 1999, fellow Emmanuel Coll. Cambridge (England) U., 1999, vis. fellow Program Law and Pub. Health Johns Hopkins U., Washington, 2001—2002; vis. fellow Australian Inst. Ethics and Professions U. Queensland, Brisbane, Australia, 2003, vis. fellow Inst. Health Law Loyola U., Chgo., 2004, vis. fellow Ctr. Interdisciplinary Study Religion Emory U., Atlanta, 2005, vis. fellow U. Ctr. Law, Ethics and Health, U. Mich., Ann Arbor, 2007; vis. scholar Ctr. Clin. Bioethics Georgetown U., Washington, 1998—1999, vis. scholar Ctr. Theology and Natural Scis. U. Calif., Berkeley, 1999, vis. scholar Ctr. Study Sci. and Religion Columbia U., 2002, vis. scholar Reilly Ctr. Sci., Tech. and Values Notre Dame U., 2002, vis. scholar Law Sch. Cardiff (Wales) U., 2002, vis. scholar Ctr. Ethics in Culture, 2003, vis. scholar Inst. Spirituality and Health George Washington U., 2006, vis. scholar Ctr. for the Study of Religion and Politics U. St. Andrews, Scotland, 2006, vis. fellow Rothermere Am. Inst. Oxford U., England, 2006, St. Edmund's Coll., U. Cambridge, 2008, Australian Nat. U. Law Faculty, 2008, Ctr. Health Governance, Law and Ethics U. Sydney Law Sch., Australia, 2008, vis. scholar The Hastings Ctr., NY, 2006, vis. scholar Inst. Ethics, AMA, 2006; establishment of George P. Smith II Disting. Professorship of Law, Ind. U., Bloomington, 1986; inducted Ind. U. Acad. Law Alumni Fellows, 2007. Mem. ABA (rep. UN Conf. on Human Environ., Stockholm 1972, rep. Law of Sea Conf., UN, N.Y.C. 1976, Switzerland 1979, cons. UNESCO Declaration on the Protection of the Human Genome, Paris 1995-97), Am. Law Inst., Soc. Ind. Pioneers, Am. Friends of Cambridge U., Order of St. John Hospitaller, Alpha Kappa Psi, Phi Alpha Delta, Sigma Alpha Epsilon, Order of Omega. Clubs: Cosmos (Washington). Republican. Office Phone: 202-319-5162, 202-319-5160, 202-319-5140. *Think big, work hard and, above all, have a dream: these are the simple guideposts for a fulfilling life.*

SMITH, GEORGE THORNEWELL, retired state supreme court justice; b. Camilla, Ga., Oct. 15, 1916; s. George C. and Rosa (Gray) S.; m. Eloise Taylor, Sept. 1, 1943 (dec.). Grad., Abraham Baldwin Agrl. Coll., 1940; LLB, U. Ga., 1948. Bar: Ga. 1947. Assoc. Cain & Smith, Cairo, Ga., 1947-71; city atty. Cairo, 1949-58; atty. Grady County, 1950-59; solicitor Cairo City Ct., 1951-59; mem. Ga. Ho. of Reps., 1959-67, speaker of the house, 1963-67; lt. gov. State of Ga., 1967-71; city atty. East Point, Ga., 1973-76; judge Ga. Ct. Appeals, 1976-81; justice Ga. Supreme Ct., Atlanta, 1981-91, presiding justice, 1990-91; of counsel Browning & Smith LLC, Marietta, Ga., 1992—. Past mem. exec. com. Nat. Conf. Appellate Judges; vice chmn. Nat. Conf. Lt. Govs. Trustee Nat. Arthritis Found. Lt. comdr. USN, 1940-45. Only person in the state's history to serve in an elective capacity in all 3 brs. of govt.; recipient Guardian of Justice award, Ga. Trial Lawyers, Regent's Hall of Fame award, U. Ga. Found., 2007, Disting. Svc. award, Abraham Baldwin Agrl. Coll., 2007. Mem. State Bar Ga., Cobb County Bar Assn., Lawyers Club Atlanta, Am. Legion, VFW, Moose, Kiwanis. Avocations: hunting, golf. Office: Browning & Smith 31 Atlanta St Ste 201 Marietta GA 30060 Home Phone: 770-516-7074; Office Phone: 770-424-1500.

SMITH, GEORGE VINAL, librarian; b. Chgo., May 14, 1943; s. Earl Wesley and Frances (Kenney) S.; m. Chrystal Jean Stillings, Jan. 29, 1966; children: Rebecca Tyson, Morgen Elizabeth. BA, Whitman Coll., 1965; MA, Wash. State U., 1967; PhD, No. Ill. U., 1974; MS, U. Ill., 1975. Reference libr. Illinet/U. Ill., Urbana, 1975-76; info. svcs. cons. Lincoln Trail Libr. System, Champaign, Ill., 1977-79; circulation and network svcs. supr. Oreg. State Libr., Salem, 1979-81, adminstr. of libr. devel., 1983-85; dir. Canby (Oreg.) Pub. Libr., 1981-82, Woodburn (Oreg.) Pub. Libr., 1982-83; dep. dir. Alaska State Div. of Librs., Archives and Mus., Juneau, Alaska, 1985—2002, acting dir., 2002—05; assoc. dep. dir. state programs Inst. of Mus. and Libr. Svcs., Washington, 2005—. Vol. Peace Corps, Thailand, 1967-69; vis. asst. prof. Grad. Sch. Libr. Sci., U. Ill., 1977-78; instr. Chemekata C.C., Salem, 1980-83, Marylhurst Coll., Lake Oswego, Oreg., 1982; course mentor Grad. Sch. Libr. Sci., U. Ariz., Juneau, Alaska, 1992-94; mem. State of Alaska Personnel Reinvention Com., 1996; Library Fellow to Bulgaria, US State Dept., 2000. Author: The Dutch in 17th-Century Thailand, 1977; co-editor and author: Contributions to Asian Studies, 15, 1980. Pres., bd. dirs., coach Juneau Soccer Club, 1992-94; dir., adminstrv. staff Arctic Winter Games/Team Alaska, Fairbanks, 1992-2005; coach, referee, referee trainer, Juneau Parks and Recreation Dept., 1986-2005; vol., patron Alaska Folk Festival, 1986—. NDEA fellow No. Ill. U., 1972-73; recipient Gov.'s Mgmt. Recognition award, Gov. Oreg., 1985. Mem. ALA (Libr. fellow to Nat. Libr. Cambodia 1994-95), Pacific N.W. Libr. Assn. (pres., v.p. 1987-89), Alaska Libr. Assn., Oreg. Libr. Assn. (pres., v.p. 1984-85). Avocations: fishing, hiking, backpacking, soccer coaching and refereeing. Office: Inst of Mus and Libr Svcs 1800 M St NW Washington DC 20036 Office Phone: 202-653-4650. E-mail: vinal2@verizon.net.

SMITH, GEORGE WOLFRAM, physicist, researcher; b. Des Plaines, Ill., Sept. 19, 1932; s. Murray Sawyer and Alice Lucile (Wolfram) S.; m. Mary Lee Sackett, Sept. 7, 1956; children: Dean, Grant. BA, Knox Coll., 1954; MA, Rice U., 1956, PhD, 1958. Welch Found. fellow Rice U., 1958-59; sr. rsch. physicist GM, Warren, Mich., 1959-76, dept. rsch. scientist, 1976-81, sr. staff rsch. scientist, 1981-87, prin. rsch. scientist, 1987-99; retired, 1999. Lectr. physics and astronomy Cranbrook Inst. Sci., Bloomfield Hills, Mich., 1963-87, mem. sci. adv. com., 1989-; instr. Lawrence Inst. Tech., 1963-65; vice chmn. Gordon Rsch. Conf. on Orientational Disorder in Crystals, 1976, chmn., 1978; co-chmn. Internat. Symposium on Particulate Carbon, 1980; mem. rev. com. Liquid Crystal Inst., Kent (Ohio) State U., 1984-85; mem. adv. com. Conf. on Electrorheological Fluids, 1991, 93; mem. adv. bd. NSF Sci. and Tech. Ctr. for Advanced Liquid Crystalline Optical Materials, 1996-00; physics co-chair Internat. Sci. and Engring. Fair, 2000; invited spkr. Ill. Assn. Physics Tchrs., 2003. Co-editor: Particulate Carbon: Formation During Combustion, 1981; editl. cons. Ency. Applied Physics, 1988-00; contbr. Handbook of Chemistry and Physics; contbr. 100 articles to sci. and tech. jours.; patentee on temperature measuring device, liquid crystal device tech., dielectric heating, graphite fiber growth, polymer-dispersed liquid crystals. Mem. Mich. Regtl. Civil War Roundtable, 1965—, pres.,

1971-72. Recipient Knox Coll. Achievement award 1977, John M. Campbell Research award, 1980, Charles L. McCuen Achievement award, Gen. Motors, 1985. Fellow Am. Phys. Soc. (com. on applications of physics 1988-91, chmn. 1991, chmn. com. on tutorials 1991, mem. Pake Prize Com. 1993-94); mem. Soc. Info. Display (program com. 1990-93), Detroit Zool. Inst. (docent 2001-03, sr. docent 2003-07), Phi Beta Kappa, Sigma Xi (chpt. pres. 1980-81), Phi Delta Theta, Alpha Delta. Home: 41140 Fox Run Rd Apt 519 Novi MI 48377

SMITH, GERARD PETER, neuroscientist; b. Phila., Mar. 24, 1935; s. Stanley Alward and Agnes Marie (McLarney) S.; m. Barbara McInnis, May 12, 1962; children: Christopher, Mark, Hilary, Maura. BS, St. Joseph's U., Phila., 1956; MD, U. Pa., 1960; ScD (hon.), U. Camerino, Italy, 2002. Intern, resident N.Y. Hosp., 1960-62; with dept. neuroendocrinology Walter Reed Army Inst. Rsch., 1962—64; asst. prof. physiology U. Pa. Sch. Medicine, Phila., 1964-68; from asst. to assoc. prof. Cornell U., NYC, 1968—, prof. psychiatry (behavioral neurosci.), 1973—. Vis. prof. MIT, 1973—74, Rockefeller U., 1979—80, adj. prof., 1982—86; cons. NIH; Curt Richter lectr. Johns Hopkins U., 1976; Leon lectr. U. Pa., 1990, Stellar lectr., 93; Rushton lectr. Fla. State U., 1992; Merck, Sharpe, and Dohm prof. neurosci. U. Flinder, Australia, 1992; Loucks lectr. U. Wash., 1995; dir. Eating Disorders Inst. N.Y. Hosp.-Cornell Med. Ctr., 1984—88. Recipient Rsch. Scientist, USPHS, 1982; grantee, NIH. Mem. AAAS, Am. Physiol. Soc., Soc. for Study Ingestive Behavior (pres., Disting. Career award 2004), Internat. Behavioral Neurosci. Soc. (pres., Myers Lifetime Achievement award 2001), Alpha Omega Alpha, Alpha Sigma Nu. Office: NY Presbyn Hosp Westchester Divsn 21 Bloomingdale Rd White Plains NY 10605-1504 Office Phone: 914-682-9100 x 2666. Business E-Mail: gpsmith@med.cornell.edu.

SMITH, GLENN A., lawyer; b. Oakland, Calif., July 11, 1946; BA, Pomona Coll., 1968; JD, U. Calif., Berkeley, 1971; LLM in Taxation, NYU, 1973. Bar: Calif. 1972, D.C. 1975. Law clerk to Hon. William M. Drennen U.S. Tax Ct., 1973-75; ptnr. Heller, Ehrman, White & McAuliffe, Palo Alto, San Francisco, Calif., 1981—2001; KPMG Mountain View, san Fransisco, 2001—04; pvt. practice Palo Alto, Calif., 1985—. Office: Ste 205 459 Hamilton Ave Palo Alto CA 94301 Office Phone: 650-473-1000. Office Fax: 650-473-9550.

SMITH, G(ODFREY) T(AYLOR), college president; b. Newton, Miss., Nov. 12, 1935; s. Taylor and Edna (Blanton) S.; m. Joni Eaton, Sept. 1, 1956; children: Paul Brian, Sherry Lynn. BA, Coll. of Wooster, 1956; MPA with distinction, Cornell U., 1960; LLD (hon.), Bethany Coll., 1979. Assoc. dir. devel. Cornell U., Ithaca, NY, 1960-62; dir. devel. Coll. Wooster, Ohio, 1962-66, v.p., 1966-77; pres. Chapman U., Orange, Calif., 1977-88, pres. emeritus, 1988—; exec. dir. Talaris Rsch. Inst., Seattle, 2001—03; pres. Bethany Coll., Bethany, W.Va., 2004—. Lectr. in field. Contbr. numerous articles to profl. publs. Bd. dirs. Wayne County (Ohio) Indsl. Devel. Corp., 1966-72, World Affairs Coun. Orange Coun., Calif., 1978-89, Orange County chpt. NCCJ, 1979-86, Orange County coun. Boy Scouts Am., 1980-85, Coun. Ind. Colls., 1985-87; bd. dirs. div. higher edn. Christian Ch. (Disciples of Christ), 1980-86, chmn., 1984-86; bd. dirs., mem. exec. com. Ind. Colls. So. Calif., 1979-88, pres., 1981-82; mem. exec. com. Assn. Ind. Calif. Colls. and Univs., 1980-88, treas., 1982-87. Recipient William A. Galpin prize The Coll. Wooster, 1956, Steuben Apple award for tchg. excellence Coun. for Advancement and Support Edn., 1984, Disting. Alumnus award Coll. of Wooster, 1991, Faith and Reason award Christian Ch. (Disciples of Christ), 1993, Laureate award for Lifetime Achievement Inst. for Charitable Giving, 1997; Smith Hall dedicated at Chapman U., 1988; Alfred P. Sloan fellow Cornell U., 1960. Presbyn. Office: G T Buck Smith Center Global Inst Bethany Coll 110 Old Main Bethany WV 26032 Home: 345 Harpertown Rd Elkins WV 26241-9657 Office Phone: 304-830-3900. Business E-Mail: buck@bethanywv.edu. *If we treat people as they are, they will stay as they are. But if we treat them for what they might be and might become, they will become those better selves.*

SMITH, GORDON A., diversified financial services company executive; b. United Kingdom; MA in Internat. Mgmt., Am. Grad. Sch. Internat. Mgmt. Mgmt. positions through sr. v.p. American Express Co., 1978—2000, exec. v.p. svc. del., 2000—01; pres. consumer card services American Express Travel Related Services, Inc., 2001—05, pres., global comml. card group, 2005—07; CEO credit card services J.P. Morgan Chase & Co., NYC, 2007—. Bd. dirs. Choice Hotels Internat., 2004—. Office: JP Morgan Chase & Co 270 Park Ave New York NY 10017-2070*

SMITH, GORDON HAROLD, lobbyist, former United States Senator from Oregon; b. Pendleton, Oreg., May 25, 1952; s. Milan Dale and Jessica (Udall) S.; m. Sharon Lankford; children: Brittany, Garrett (dec.), Morgan. BA in History, Brigham Young U., 1976; LLB, Southwestern U., 1979. Law clk. to Justice H. Vernon Payne N.Mex. Supreme Ct.; pvt. practice Ariz., 1979—80; pres., CEO Smith Frozen Foods, 1981—97; mem. Oreg. State Senate from Dist. 29, 1992-95, pres., 1995-96; US Senator from Oreg., 1997—2009; sr. advisor govt. affairs & internat. trade practice Covington & Burling LLP, Washington, 2009—. Mem. com. Indian affairs US Senate, com. fin., com. energy and natural resources, com. commerce, sci. and transp., commn. security and cooperation in Europe; mem. Presdl. Adv. Commn. Holocaust Assets in US. Author: Remembering Garrett: One Family's Battle with a Child's Depression, 2006. Recipient Torch of Liberty award, Nat. Conf. Soviet Jewry, 2001, Cmty. Health Defender award, Nat. Assn. Cmty. Health Centers, 2003, Homeownership Hero award, Homeownership Alliance, 2004. Republican. Lds Ch. Office: Covington & Burling LLP 1201 Pennsylvania Ave NW Washington DC 20004 Office Phone: 202-662-5051. Office Fax: 202-778-5051. E-mail: gsmith@cov.com.*

SMITH, GORDON PAUL, management consultant; b. Salem, Mass., Dec. 25, 1916; s. Gordon and May (Vaughan) S.; m. Daphne Miller, Nov. 23, 1943 (div. 1968); m. Ramona Chamberlain, Sept. 27, 1969; children: Randall B., Roderick F. BS in Mgmt., U. Mass., 1947; MS in Govt. Mgmt., U. Denver, 1948; postgrad. in polit. sci, NYU, 1948-50; DHL (hon.), Monterey Inst. Internat. Studies, Middlebury Coll., 1994. Mem. Calif. State Bds. & Commrs.; with Econ. Rsch. Tax Found., Inc., NYC, 1948—51, Booz, Allen & Hamilton, 1951-70, partner San Francisco, 1959-62, v.p., 1962-67, mng. pntr. Western U.S., 1968-70; ptnr. Harrod, Williams and Smith, San Francisco, 1962—69; dir. fin. State of Calif., Calif., 1967—68; pres. Gordon Paul Smith & Co., Mgmt. Cons., 1968—; pres., CEO Golconda Corp., 1972—74, chmn. bd., 1974-85. Pres. Cermetek Corp., 1978-80; adviser task force def. procurement and contracting Hoover Commn., 1954-55; spl. asst. to pres. Republic Aviation Corp., 1954-55; cons., Hawaii, 1960-61, Alaska, 1963; cons. Wash. Hwy. Adminstrn., 1964, Am. Baseball League and Calif. Angels, 1960-62, others; bd. dirs. Monterey Coll. Law; chmn. Ft. Ord Econ. Devel. Adv. Group, 1991; chmn. Coalition on Rsch. and Edn., 1993—97; spkr. in field. Contbr. articles to profl. jours. Mem. Calif. Select Com. on Master Plan for Edn., 1971—73; mem. alumni coun. U. Mass., 1950—54, bd. dirs. alumni ass., 1964—70; chmn. West Coast Cancer Found., 1976—87, Coalition Rsch. and Edn., 1993—, Jim Tunney Youth Found., 1994—; trustee, chmn. Monterey Inst. Internat. Studies, 1978—92, trustee emeritus, 1995—; trustee Northfield Mt. Hermon Sch., 1983—93, Robert Louis Stevenson Sch., 1993—; mem. devel. coun. Cmty. Hosp. of Monterey Peninsula, 1983—84; sr. advisor Pres. Calif. State U., Monterey, Calif., 1998—; mem. 15 bds. and commns. State of Calif., 1967—72; bd. dirs. Alumni Assn. Mt. Hermon Prep. Sch., 1963; bd. dirs. Stanford Med. Ctr., 1960—62, pres., chmn., 1962—66; bd. dirs. Friends of the Performing Arts, 1985—, Monterey County Symphony Orch., 1991—96, Monterey Bay Futures Project, 1992—, Ctr. for Nonproliferation of Weapons of Mass Destruction, 1998—, Calif. Inst. for Local Self Govt., 2000—. Recipient spl. commendation Hoover Commn., 1955, Alumni of Yr. award U. Mass., 1963, Trustee of Yr. award Monterey-Peninsula, 1991, Monterey-Peninsula Outstanding Citizen of Yr. award, 1992, Laura Bride Powers Heritage award, 1991, U.S. Congl. award, 1992, Calif. Senate and Assembly Outstanding Citizen award, 1992, Wisdom award of honor Wisdom Soc., 1992; named Global Citizen of Yr., Internat. Sch. Monterey, Calif, 2005; permanent Gordon Paul Smith Disting. Chair for Internat. Studies established at Monterey Inst. Internat. Studies; named Gordon Paul Smith Scholarship Fund in his honor Northfield Mt. Hermon Sch.and Robert Louis Stevenson Sch.; named to Honorable Order of Ky. Cols. Mem. Monterey History and Art Assn. (bd. dirs. 1987-92, pres. 1985-87, chmn. 1987-92, hon. lifetime dir. 1992—), The Stanton Heritage Ctr. (chmn. 1987-92, chmn. emeritus 1992—), Salvation Army (bd. dirs., chmn. hon. cabinet), Monterey Peninsula Mus. Art, Carmel Valley (Calif.) Country Club, Monterey Peninsula Country Club, Old Capitol Club, San Francisco Stock Exch. Club. Home: 253 Del Mesa Carmel CA 93923 Home Phone: 415-831-8119, 891-624-8119. Personal E-mail: gp1225@aol.com. *If the quest for personal success is only for an accumulation of prestige, power or wealth, then personal failure will be assured. Genuine personal success can surely be found, however, through a significant and lasting contribution toward helping the progress of others and raising the human worth. This is the true mark of leadership.*

SMITH, GRANT WILLIAM, language educator, volunteer; b. Bellingham, Wash., July 26, 1937; s. George Whitfield and Hazel (Speirs) S.; m. Lelia Dickinson, June 9, 1961; children: Kathryn, Gavin. BA, Reed Coll., 1964; MA, U. Nev., 1966; PhD, U. Del., 1975. Asst. prof. Eastern Wash. U., Cheney, 1968-76, assoc. prof., 1976-79, prof., 1979—. Faculty pres. Eastern Wash. U., Cheney, 1976-77, chair English dept., 1978-84, acting vice provost, 1987-88, coord. humanities, 1979—, dir. cultural outreach, 1995-97; host Pub. TV, Here's Shakespeare, 1980, 81; mem. Wash. Bd. Geog. Names, 1987—; guest editor: NAMES, 1989, ONOMA, 2005; dissertation rsch. advisor Mukogawa Women's U., Japan, 2007-08. Editor Procs. of Am. Name Soc., 1997, 98, 99; contbr. articles to profl. jours. and conf. procs. Chair devel. Spokane Symphony, 2000—01; program chair Coun. Geo. Names Authorities, 1999; moderator Cheney United Ch. of Christ, 1982—84. With US Army, 1957—60. Grantee U.S. Geol. Survey, State Humanities Commn., NEH; Fulbright faculty assoc., 2005-06, 09. Mem. MLA, AAUP, Placename Survey U.S. (chair 1990—), Connoisseur Concerts Assn. (pres. 1992-95), Am. Dialect Soc. (regional sec. 1982-98), Rocky Mountain MLA (program chair 1987, 95), Internat. Coun. Onomastic Scientists (exec. bd. dirs. 1999—, v.p. 2002-05, editl. bd. ONOMA 2000—), Internat. Soc. Dialectology and Geolinguistics, Am. Name Soc. (v.p. 1996-98, pres. 1999-2001), CenterStage (pres. 2003-07), Spokane Dinner Club (v.p. 2008-). Avocations: jogging, reading, singing, dance. Home: 905 Gary St Cheney WA 99004-1341 Address: Eastern Wash Univ 250 Patterson Hall Dept of English Cheney WA 99004-2430 Office Phone: 509-359-6023. E-mail: gsmith@ewu.edu.

SMITH, GREGORY ARNOLD, dean; b. Mo., 1972; s. James Arnold and Sharon Smith; m. Nicole Ray Manweiler; children: Isaac, Levi. BA Missions and Bible, Bapt. Bible Coll., Springfield, MO, 1994; MA in Info. Sci. and Learning Techs, U. Mo., Columbia, 1998; Additional grad. study, Liberty U., Lynchburg, VA, 2003—. Assoc. dean libr. svcs & instl. rsch. Bapt. Bible Coll., 2008—, libr. dir., 1995—2003; adminstrv. svcs libr. Liberty U., 2006—08, dean, integrated learning resource ctr., 2003—06. Digital content mgr. Assn. Christian Libr, Cedarville, Ohio, 2006—08. Contbr. articles. Mem.: Assn. Christian Libr. (Vol. of Yr. 2007). Baptist. Office: Baptist Bible Coll 628 E Kearney St Springfield MO 65803 Business E-Mail: gsmith@gobbc.edu.

SMITH, GREGORY BUTLER, lawyer; b. Muncie, Ind., June 20, 1946; AB, Ind. U., 1968, JD, 1971. Bar: Ind. 1971, Ind. (US Dist. Ct. (so. dist.)) 1971, Ill. 1978. Ptnr. Smith & Smith, Muncie, 1971—2003; dep. prosecutor Delaware County, Muncie, 1971—72; pvt. practice Muncie, 2004—. Adj. instr. Ball State U. Contbr. articles to profl. jours. Mem. East Ctrl. Ind. Estate Planning Coun., Muncie, 1980—88; pres. Muncie Common Coun., 1981; bd. dirs. Muncie Transit Sys., 1983—96; vol. Meals Wheels. Mem.: Ind. State Bar Assn., Soc. Profl. Dispute Resolution (pres. Ind. chpt. 1994—95), Am. Pub. Transit Assn. (legal affairs com.), Muncie Bar Assn. (pres. 1980—81), Ind. Bar Assn. (mem. unauthorized Practive of law com.), Kiwanis, Sigma Iota Epsilon, Phi Alpha Delta. Office: Smith Law Office PC 425 N High St Ste 3 Muncie IN 47305 Business E-Mail: attorney_gsmith@onecommail.com.

SMITH, GREGORY DALE, lawyer, judge; b. Knoxville, Feb. 1, 1963; s. James C. and Essie Pearl (Norman) S.; m. Cynthia Luckett, Oct. 15, 1988; children: Leora, Philip. BS, Middle Tenn. State U., 1985; JD, Cumberland Law Sch., 1988. Bar: Tenn., U.S. Supreme Ct., U.S. Ct. Appeals (fed. crct.), U.S. Ct. Mil. Appeals, U.S. Dist. Ct. (mid., ea. and we. dists.) Tenn., Army Ct. of Mil. Rev., U.S. Ct. Vet. Appeals. Mcpl. magistrate City of Birmingham, Ala., 1987-88; assoc. Marks, Marks & Shell, Clarksville, Tenn., 1988-89; juvenile referee Montgomery County Juvenile Ct., Clarksville, Tenn., 1992-95; assoc. Richardson & Richardson, Clarksville, Tenn., 1989-93; pvt. practice Clarksville, 1993—; mcpl. judge Pegram, Tenn., 2004—06. Adj. prof. Austin Peay State U., Clarksville, 1989-93; lectr. in field; hearing officer Tenn. Bd. Profl., 1993-2001; mcpl. judge, Pleasant View, Tenn., 1997-2001. Author: The TACDL Guide to Defending Juvenile Cases in Tennessee, 1993; co-author: Juvenile Courts in Tennessee, 1998; contbr. articles to profl. jours. Bd. dirs. Treehouse Daycare Ctr., 1991-95, sec., 1992, v.p., 1993, pres. 1994; Leadership Clarksville; participant UN conf. juvenile drug prevention, 1994. Named Internat. Man of the Yr. Internat. Biog. Ctr., Cambridge, Eng., 1992, Outstanding Young Alumnus, Middle Tenn. State U., 1999. Mem. ABA (juvenile justice com. nat. chmn. 1990-92, nat. vice chmn. litigation 1992-93), Tenn. Assn. Criminal Def. Lawyers (chmn. juvenile justice com. 1991-95, chmn. ethics com. 1995-97), Montgomery County Young Lawyers (pres. 1991-92), Tenn. Bar Assn. (assoc. gen. counsel 1995-2001, Pro Bono Atty. of Yr. 2001), Tenn. Young Lawyers Conf. (bd. dirs. 1992-94), Tenn. Mcpl. Judges Assn. (pres. 2002-04, 05-09), Tenn. Ct. of the Judiciary. Office: 331 Franklin St Ste 1 Clarksville TN 37040-3448 Office Phone: 931-647-1299. Personal E-mail: gregorydsmith@prodigy.net.

SMITH, GREGORY WHITE, writer; b. Ithaca, NY, Oct. 4, 1951; s. William R. and Kathryn (White) S. BA, Colby Coll., 1973; JD, Harvard U., 1977, MEd, 1980. Bar: Mass., 1980. Fellow Thomas J. Watson, 1973-74; co-founder & editor Woodward/White, Inc. (publishers of Best Lawyers in Am., Best Doctors in Am., Best Dentists in Am.), 1981—. Author: (with Steven Naifeh) Moving Up in Style, 1980, Gene Davis, 1981, How to Make Love to a Woman, 1982, What Every Client Needs to Know About Using a Lawyer, 1982, The Bargain Hunter's Guide to Art Collecting, 1982, Why Can't Men Open Up?: Overcoming Men's Fear of Intimacy, 1984, The Mormon Murders: A True Story of Greed, Forgery, Deceit, and Death, 1988, Jackson Pollock: An American Saga, 1989 (Nat. Book award nomination for nonfiction 1990, Pulitzer Prize for biography 1991), Final Justice: The True Story of the Richest Man Ever Tried for Murder, 1993, A Stranger in the Family: A True Story of Murder, Madness, and Unconditional Love, 1995, On a Street Called Easy, In a Cottage Called Joye: A Restoration Comedy, 1996, Making Miracles Happen, 1997; editor: (with Naifeh) The Best Lawyers in America series, The Best Doctors in America series, The Best Dentists in America series. Chmn. Aiken Historic Preservation Commn. Office: Woodward/White 129 First Ave SW Aiken SC 29801 E-mail: gsmith@bestlawyers.com.

SMITH, GREIG LOUIS, councilman; b. South Pasadena, Calif., Nov. 26, 1948; s. John Harold and Gloria Mae (Pitre) S.; m. Christine Marie Crippen, Apr. 14, 1973; children: Krista Lynn, Matthew John. AA, Pierce Coll., 1978; cert. advt., UCLA, 1988. Area dir. Rep. Ctrl. Com., 1969-70; youth dir. Re-elect Senator Murphy, LA, 1970-71; mktg. dir. V.I.V.A., LA, 1971-72; exec. dir. Ams. for Agnew, Washington, 1972-73; owner Greig's Formal Wear, Northridge, Calif., 1973-81; chief dep. for Councilman Bernson LA City Coun., 1979; reserve police officer, Valley's Devonshire divsn. LA Police Dept., 1992, reserve police officer, detective hdqs. robbery homicide divsn.; councilman, Dist. 12 LA City Coun., 2003—. Govt. rels. officer L.A. Olympic Organizing Com., 1984. Vice chmn. San Fernando Valley Breakfast Forum, 1975-78, C.I.V-.I.C.C., San Fernando Valley, 1976-78; pres. North Hills Jaycees, Granada Hills, Calif., 1976-77; chmn. bd. North Valley YMCA, Mission Hills, Calif., 1979-80, 92—; founding mem. North Valley Rep. Assembly, 1992., founding mem. SOLID Foundation, bd. mem. U. Southern Calif. Sch. Pub. Policy Planning and Devel. Named Citizen of Yr. Granada Hills C. of C., 1977, Vol. of Yr. North Valley YMCA, 1988, Citizen of Yr. Internat. Order of Foresters, 1990, Reserve Officer of Yr., LA Police Dept., 1996. Mem. Jr. Chamber Internat. (senator, life), Alpha Sigma Gamma. Office: City Hall 200 North Spring St Rm 405 Los Angeles CA 90012 Office Phone: 213-473-7012. Office Fax: 213-473-6925. Business E-Mail: councilmember.smith@lacity.org.*

SMITH, GRIFFIN, executive editor; b. Fayetteville, Ark., June 29, 1941; s. Griffin and Mildred Smith; m. Mary Elizabeth Routh, Sept. 1, 1979. BA in History, Rice U., 1963; MA in Polit. Sci., Columbia U., 1965; postgrad. in philosophy, Oxford U., 1966; JD, U. Tex., 1969. Bar: Tex. 1969, US Dist. Ct. (ea., we., no. and so. dists.) Tex. 1969, Ark. 1981, US Dist. Ct. (ea. and we. dists.) Ark. 1981. Spl. asst. to Senator Fulbright US Senate, Washington, 1968-69; atty. estate and gift tax div. IRS, Houston, 1970; rsch. dir. Tex. gubernatorial campaign Paul Eggers, 1970; chief counsel constl. amendments com. Tex. Senate, 1971, chief counsel drug law reform com., 1971-73; editor natural areas survey Lyndon B. Johnson Sch. Pub. Affairs U. Tex., Austin, 1973-77; sr. editor Tex. Monthly mag., 1973—77; speech writer Pres. of US, 1977-78; ptnr. Smith & Nixon (formerly Smith, Smith, Nixon & Duke), Little Rock, 1984-92; exec. editor Ark. Democrat-Gazette, Little Rock, 1992—. Author: (book) A Consumer Viewpoint on Taxation, 1971, Marijuana in Texas, 1972, The Best of Texas Monthly, 1978, Texas Monthly's Political Reader, 1978, 1980, Journey into China, 1982, Forgotten Texas: A Wilderness Portfolio, 1983, The Great State of Texas, 1985. Recipient Disting. Alumni award, Rice U., 1999; fellow Woodrow Wilson, 1964. Mem.: Tex. Inst. Letters (award for best work of journalism in Tex. 1974, 1976), State Bar Tex. Episcopalian-Reformed. Office: Ark Democrat-Gazette 121 E Capitol Ave Little Rock AR 72201-3819 also: Ark Democrat-Gazette PO Box 2221 Little Rock AR 72203

SMITH, GROVER C(LEVELAND), language educator; b. Atlanta, Sept. 6, 1923; s. Grover C. and Lillian Julia (McDaniel) S.; m. Phyllis Jean Snyder, June 19, 1948 (div. 1965); children: Alice Elizabeth, Charles Grover; m. Dulcie Barbara Soper, Dec. 29, 1965; children: Stephen Kenneth, Julia Margaret. BA with honors, Columbia U., 1944, MA, 1945, PhD, 1950. Instr. English Rutgers U., 1946-48, Yale U., 1948-52, Duke U., 1952-55, asst. prof., 1955-61, assoc. prof., 1961-66, prof., 1966-93, prof. emeritus, 1993—. Mem. summer faculty CUNY, 1946, 47, 48, Columbia U., 1963, 64, NYU, 1963, Wake Forest U., 1966, vis. lectr., 1963, 64; instr. coll. entrance exam bd. Summer Inst. Comm. on English, 1962. Author: The Poems of T.S. Eliot 1909-1928: A Study in Symbols and Sources, 1950, T.S. Eliot's Poetry and Plays: A Study in Sources and Meaning, 1956 (Poetry Chapbook award) rev. edit., 1974, Archibald MacLeish, 1971, Ford Madox Ford, 1972, The Waste Land, 1983, T.S. Eliot and the Use of Memory, 1996; editor: Josiah Royce's Seminar, 1913-1914: As Recorded in the Notebooks of Harry T. Costello, 1963, Letters of Aldous Huxley, 1969. Mem. Christian Gauss Award com., 1973-75; mem. com. of sponsors Sir Julian Huxley Tribute, NY Soc. for Ethical Culture, 1975. With U.S. Army, 1943. Alexander M. Proudfit fellow Columbia U., 1945-46; Guggenheim fellow, 1958; Am. Philos. Soc. grantee, 1965; Am. Learned Socs. grantee, 1965; NEH grantee, 1979, fellow, 1980. Mem. T.S. Eliot Soc. (hon., Eliot Meml. Lectr. 1986, bd. dirs. 1986-94, 96-99, v.p. 1986-88, editor News and Notes, 1987-88, 90-91, pres. 1989-91, supr. elections 1992-94, sec. 1996-99), Am. Lit. Assn. (rep. to coun.of Am. Author Socs. 1990-91), Nat. Assn. Scholars. Home: 2 Silver Maple Ct Durham NC 27705-5642

SMITH, HAMILTON OTHANEL, molecular biologist, educator; b. NYC, Aug. 23, 1931; s. Bunnie Othanel and Tommie Harkey S.; m. Elizabeth Anne Bolton, May 25, 1957; children: Joel, Barry, Dirk, Bryan, Kirsten. Student, U. Ill., 1948-50; AB in Math, U. Calif., Berkeley, 1952; MD, Johns Hopkins U., 1956. Intern Barnes Hosp., St. Louis, 1956-57; resident in medicine Henry Ford Hosp., Detroit, 1959-62; USPHS fellow dept. human genetics U. Mich., Ann Arbor, 1962-64, rsch. assoc., 1964-67; asst. prof. molecular biology and genetics Sch. Medicine Johns Hopkins U., Balt., 1967-69, assoc. prof., 1969-73, prof., 1973—, emeritus prof. molecular biology and genetics; scientist Celera Genomics (bus. unit Applera Corp.), Rockville, Md., 1998—. Asso. Inst. für Molekularbologie der U. Zurich, Switzerland, 1975-76; assoc. Rsch. Inst. Molecular Pathology, Vienna, 1990-91; trustee The Inst. for Genomic Rsch. Contbr. articles to profl. jours. Served to lt. M.C. USNR, 1957-59. Recipient Nobel prize in physiology or medicine, 1978; Guggenheim fellow, 1975-76. Mem. Am. Soc. Microbiology, AAAS, Am. Soc. Biol. Chemists, Nat. Acad. Sci. Office: Celera Genomics 45 West Gude Dr Rockville MD 20850 Home: 5430 Park Heights Ave Baltimore MD 21215-4699*

SMITH, HAROLD CHARLES, pension fund administrator; b. NYC, Jan. 11, 1934; s. Harold Elmore and Hedwig Agnes (Gronke) S. BA cum laude with honors, Ursinus Coll., 1955; MBA, NYU, 1958; M in Div., Union Theol. Sem., NYC, 1958; DD (hon.), 1993; DD (hon.), Ursinus Coll., 1997; DHum (hon.), Springfield Coll., 1998. CFA; ordained minister United Ch. Christ, 1959. V.p. YMCA Retirement Fund, Inc., NYC, 1958-69, portfolio mgr., 1960—, assoc. sec., 1969-77, v.p., 1977-80, exec. v.p., 1980-82, pres. elect, 1982-83, pres., 1983-2000; assoc. prof. bus. and fin. L.I. U., 1969-71. Trustee Bank Mart, Bridgeport, Conn., 1983-91; bd. dirs. Y Mut. Ins. Co., treas. 1988—. Author: Getting It All Together in Retirement, 1977. Trustee YWCA Greater Bridgeport, 1975—79, Pension Funds United Ch. of Christ, 1968—2007, Springfield Coll., Mass., 1983—2009, United Ch. Found., 1968—, vice chmn., 1995—98, chmn., 1998—99; chmn. bd. trustees NY State YMCA; bd. dirs. Springfield Coll., Mass., 1983—; pastor 1st E&R Ch., Bridgeport, Conn., 1958—88, Unity Hill United Ch. of Christ, 1988—2000, 1st Congl. Ch., Union, NJ, 2001—02, River Edge, NJ, 2002—03, 2008—09, Lordship Cmty. Ch., Stratford, Conn., 2006—08, 1st Congregational Ch., River Edge, NJ, 2008—; treas. United H. Homes of N.J. Inc., 2001—; exec. coun. UCC, 2000—07; bd. dirs. United Ch. Residencies, 1962—65, YMCA Greater N.Y., 2002—04, 1983—97, Bridgeport Area Found., 1989—2000, Ursinus Coll., Pa., 1994—, Coun. of Chs. Greater Bridgeport, 1995—96, Silver Bay Christian Conf. Ctr., 1997—2003. Mem. Am. Econs. Assn., N.Y. Soc. Security Analysts, Fin. Analysts Fedn., Masons, Order Ea. Star.

SMITH, HAROLD HASKEN, university administrator; b. Cin., Mar. 16, 1942; s. Harold C. and Ruth V. (Hasken) S.; m. Karen A. Willis, Dec. 20, 1969; children: Amy Elizabeth, Andrew David, Anne Cameron. AB, Centre Coll., 1964; MBA, Am. U., 1968; LLD (hon.), Cumberland Coll., 2003. Admissions counselor Centre Coll., Danville, Ky., 1964-66, assoc. dir. admissions, 1968-70, dir. admissions, 1970-73, dean admissions, 1973-80, v.p., den students, 1980-83, lectr. econs. mgmt., 1973-80; v.p. devel. Muskingum Coll., New Concord, Ohio, 1983-97; pres. Pikeville Coll. and Coll. Osteo. Med., Ky., 1997—2009, pres. emeritus, 2009—. Cons. in edn. Dir. Boyle-Mercer County YMCA, Ky., 1979-83; mem. bd. trustees Southeast Ohio Regional Med. Ctr., 1987-97; bd. dirs. Southeast Ohio Symphony Orch., 1983-97, Renew Environment of New Concord, 1983-97, Leadership Ky., 2002—. Recipient Disting. Chmn. award Rotary Found., 1981-82; named Bus. Person of Yr. Pike County C. of C., 2001, Disting. Alumnus Centre Coll., 2006; named to Pikeville Coll. Athletic Hall of Fame, Akeville Coll., 2009. Mem. Ctr. Coll. Athletic Hall of Fame, 1994, Assn. Ind. Ky. Colls. and Univs. (exec. com. 2004—), Nat. Assn. Student Personnel Adminstrs., Am. Coll. Personnel Assn., Nat. Assn. Intercollegiate Athletics (coun. pres. 2004—), Cambridge C. of C. (bd. dirs. 1984-97), Nat. Assn. Coll. Admissions Counselors, So. Assn. Colls. and Schs. (commr. coll. commn. 2005—), Rotary (pres. 1979-80, dist. gov.'s rep. 1981-82), Zanesville Country Club, Green Meadow Country Club, Cardinal Club Office: Pres's Office Pikeville Coll Pikeville KY 41501 Home Phone: 502-896-6740. Business E-Mail: halsmith64@gmail.com.

SMITH, H(AROLD) LAWRENCE, lawyer; b. Evergreen Pk., Ill., June 27, 1932; s. Harold Lawrence and Lorna Catherine (White) Smith; m. Madonna Jeanne Koehl, June 9, 1956 (div. 1968); children: Lawrence Kirby, Sandra Michele, Madonna Clare Galloway; m. Nancy Leigh Baum, May 2, 1970 (dec. 1983); m. Louise Fredericka Jeffrey, Nov. 2, 1984 (div. 1994); m. Marianne Lorraine Laug, Apr. 19, 1997. BS, US Naval Acad., 1956; JD, John Marshall Law Sch., 1965. Bar: Ill. 1965, Mich. 1986, U.S. Dist. Ct. (no. dist.) Ill. 1965, U.S. Ct. Appeals (7th cir.) 1967, U.S. Ct. of Customs and Patent Appeals, 1976, U.S. Ct. Appeals (fed. cir.) 1982, U.S. Patent and Trademark Office 1968. Asst. prof. naval sci. U. Notre Dame, 1960-61; tech. asst. Langner, Parry, Card & Langner, Chgo., 1961-65, assoc., 1965-69; patent atty. Borg-Warner Corp., Chgo., 1970-74; sr. patent atty. Continental Can Co., Inc., Chgo. and Oak Brook, Ill., 1974-82, asst. gen. counsel Stamford and Norwalk, Conn., 1982-86; ptnr. Varnum, Riddering, Schmidt & Howlett, Grand Rapids, Mich., 1986-96, counsel, 1996-97; ptnr. Rader, Fishman, Grauer & McGarry, Grand Rapids, 1997—2001; of counsel McGarry Bair LLP, Grand Rapids, 2001—03; intellectual property counselor, 2003—. Adj. prof. patent law Cooley Law Sch., 1991—. Served to lt. USN, 1956-61. Life Fellow Mich. State Bar Found.; mem. Intellectual Property Law Assn. Chgo., Chartered Inst. Patent Agts. (London 1971-2003), World Affairs Coun. Western Mich. (bd. dirs. 1996-2002, treas. 1998-2000). Office: 39533 Woodward Ave Ste 140 Bloomfield Hills MI 48304

SMITH, HARVEY ALVIN, mathematics professor, consultant; b. Easton, Pa., Jan. 30, 1932; s. William Augustus and Ruth Carolyn (Krauth) S.; m. Ruth Wismer Kolb, Aug. 27, 1955; children: Deirdre Lynn, Kirsten Nadine, Brinton Averil. BS, Lehigh U., 1952; MS, U. Pa., 1955, AM, 1958, PhD, 1964. Asst. prof. math Drexel U., 1960-65; mem. tech. staff Inst. Def. Analyses, Arlington, Va., 1965-66; assoc. prof. math Oakland U., 1966-68; ops. rsch. scientist Exec. Office of Pres., Washington, 1968-70; prof. math. Oakland U., 1970-77; prof. Ariz. State U., Tempe, 1977—2003, prof. emeritus, 2003—. Cons. U.S. Army Security Agy., 1967—68, Inst. Def. Analyses, 1967—69, Exec. Office Pres., 1967—73, U.S. Arms Control and Disarmament Agy., 1973—79, Los Alamos Nat. Lab., 1980—93. Author: Mathematical Foundations of Systems Analysis, 1969. NSF fellow, 1964-65; recipient Meritorious Service award Exec. Office of Pres., 1970 Mem. Soc. Indsl. and Applied Math., Am. Math. Soc., AAAS, Sigma Xi Home: 18 E Concorda Dr Tempe AZ 85282-3517 Office: Ariz State U Dept Math Tempe AZ 85287-1804 Office Phone: 480-968-6813. Business E-Mail: hsmith@math.asu.edu.

SMITH, HAYWOOD CLARK, JR., astronomer, educator; s. Haywood Clark Sr. and Anne Tremont (Burr) S.; m. Sylvia Ann Mullis, June 14, 1969; children: Lisa, Christopher. AB in Physics, U. NC, Chapel Hill, 1967; MA in Astronomy, U. Va., Charlottesville, 1969, PhD in Astronomy, 1972. Vis. asst. prof. astronomy U. South Fla., Tampa, 1972—77, asst. prof. astronomy, 1977—79; assoc. prof. astronomy U. Fla., Gainesville, 1979—, assoc. chair astronomy, 2004—. Exec. com. Divsn. Dynamical Astronomy, AAS, Washington, 1979—81, 1984—86. Contbr. articles to Astron. Jour., Astrophys. Jour. Mem. Internat. Astron. Union, Am. Astron. Soc. (exec. com. Dynamical Astronomy divsn. 1979-81, 84-86). Conservative. Anglican. Achievements include elucidation of bias in analysis of parallax data, establishing that unavoidable integration errors of N-body calculations do not seem to invalidate statistical (macroscopic) results and that, the masses of clusters of galaxies can be systematically under- or overestimated, depending on central concentration of background (unseen) mass relative to visible matter (Limber effect). Office: Astronomy Dept Univ Fla PO Box 112055 Gainesville FL 32611 Office Fax: 352-392-5089. Business E-Mail: hsmith@astro.ufl.edu.

SMITH, HEDRICK LAURENCE, journalist, television producer; b. Kilmacolm, Scotland, July 9, 1933; s. Sterling L. and Phebe (Hedrick) S.; m. Ann Bickford, June 29, 1957 (div. Dec. 1985); children: Laurel Ann, Jennifer Laurence, Sterling Scott, Lesley Roberts; m. Susan Zox, Mar. 7, 1987. BA, Williams Coll., 1955, LittD (hon.), 1975; postgrad. (Fulbright scholar), Balliol Coll., Oxford, Eng., 1955-56; LittD (hon.), Wittenburg U., 1985, N.H. Coll., 1991; LHD (hon.), Columbia Coll., 1992; LittD (hon.), Amherst Coll., 1992; LHD (hon.), U. S.C., 1992; LittD (hon.), Furman U., 1996. With U.P.I., Memphis, Nashville, Atlanta, 1959-62; with NY Times, 1962-88, Washington and S.E., 1962-63, Vietnam, 1963-64; Middle East corr. NY Times, Cairo, U.A.R., 1964-66, diplomatic news corr. Washington, 1962-64, 66-71, Moscow Bur. chief, 1971-74, dep. nat. editor, 1975-76, Washington Bur. chief, 1976-79, chief Washington corr., 1980-85; Washington correspondent NY Times mag., 1987-88. Vis. journalist Am. Enterprise Inst., 1985-87; fellow Fgn. Policy Inst., Johns Hopkins U. Sch Advanced Internat. Studies, 1989-97; panelist Washington Week in Rev., PBS, 1969-95. Author: The Russians, 1975 (Overseas Press Club award, 1976), The Power Game: How Washington Works, 1988, The New Russians, 1990 (Overseas Press Club citation, 1991), Rethinking America, 1995; co-author: The Pentagon Papers, 1972, Reagan the Man, the President, 1981, Beyond Reagan: The Politics of Upheaval, 1986, Seven Days That Shook the World, 1991, (TV documentaries) Star Wars, 1985, Moscow Jews, 1986, Space Bridge, Chernobyl: Three Mile Island, 1987, 4-part Power Game series, PBS, 1989, Countdown to White House: The Bush Transition, 1989, 4-part series Inside Gorbachev's USSR, 1990 (George Polk award, Gold Baton award Columbia-DuPont), Guns, Tanks and Gorbachev (Frontline), 1991, Soviets, 1991 (George Peabody award), After Gorbachev's USSR (Frontline), 1992, 4-part series PBS, Challenge to America, 1994 (Cine Golden Eagle award, Rias award), Across the River, PBS, 1995 (Hillman award), The People and the Power Game, 1996 (Silver award Houston Film Festival), Surviving the Bottom Line, 1998 (Cine Golden Eagle award), Seeking Solutions, 1999 (nat. award for pub. svc. Sigma Delta Chi, spl. gold medal Houston Film Festival), Duke Ellington's Washington, 2000 (NY Film Festival Bronze prize), Critical Condition, 2000 (Emmy nomination), Dr. Solomon's Dilemma (Frontline), 2000 (Chris award), Juggling Work and Family, 2001, Rediscovering Dave Brubeck, 2001, Inside the Terror Network (Frontline), 2002 (co-winner Columbia-Dupont Gold Baton), Bigger Than Enron (Frontline), 2002 (Cine Gold Eagle), The Wall Street Fix (Frontline), 2003 (Emmy award, Cine Gold Eagle, Chris award), Tax Me If You Can (Frontline), 2004 (Emmy nomination), Is Walmart Good for America?, 2004 (Writer's Guild award nomination), Making Schools Work With Hedrick Smith, 2005, Can You Afford to Retire, 2006 (Emmy), Spying on the Home Front, 2007 (Writers Guild nomination), Poisoned Waters Frontline, 2009. Trustee Williams Coll., 1982-97, Nat. Ctr. for Humanities, 2005-2007; mem. Aspen Inst. Domestic Strategy Group, 1997-2002; bd. dirs. New American Schs., 1996-2004; mem. steering com. Concerned Journalists, 2001—. With USAF, 1956-59. Recipient Pulitzer prize for pub. svc. Pentagon Papers Series, 1972, for internat. reporting from Soviet Union and Ea. Europe, 1974, William Allen White award U. Kans., 1996; Nieman fellow Harvard U., 1969-70. Mem. Gridiron Club, Phi Beta Kappa. Office: Hedrick Smith Prodns Inc 6935 S Wisconsin Ave Chevy Chase MD 20815 Office Phone: 301-654-9848. E-mail: hsmithprod@aol.com.

SMITH, HENRY CHARLES, III, symphony orchestra conductor; b. Phila., Jan. 31, 1931; s. Henry Charles Jr. and Gertrude Ruth (Downs) S.; m. Mary Jane Dressner, Sept. 3, 1955; children: Katherine Anne, Pamela Jane, Henry Charles IV. BA, U. Pa., 1952; artist diploma, Curtis Inst. Music, Phila., 1955. Solo trombonist Phila. Orch., 1955-67; condr. Rochester (Minn.) Symphony Orch., 1967-68; assoc. prof. music Ind. U., Bloomington, 1968-71; resident condr., ednl. dir. Minn. Orch., Mpls., 1971-88; prof. music U. Tex., Austin, 1988-89, Frank C. Erwin Centennial Prof. of Opera, 1988-89; music dir. S.D. Symphony, Sioux Falls, 1989-2001; prof. Ariz. State U., Tempe, 1989-93, prof. emeritus, 1993—. Vis. prof. U. Tex., Austin, 1987-88; founding mem. Phila. Brass Ensemble, 1956—; music dir. World Youth Symphony Orch., Interlochen, Mich., 1981-96; artistic advisor, prin. guest conductor Cedar Rapids Symphony, Iowa, 2004-. Composer 5 books of solos for trombone including Solos for the Trombone Player, 1963, Hear Us As We Pray, 1963, First Solos for the Trombone Player, 1972, Easy Duets for Winds, 1972; editor 14 books 20th century symphonies lit. Served to 1st lt. AUS, 1952-54. Recipient 3 Grammy nominations, 1967, 76, 1 Grammy award for best chamber music rec. with Phila. Brass Ensemble, 1969. Mem. Internat. Trombone Assn. (dir.), Am. Symphony Orch. League, Music Educators Nat. Conf., Am. Guild Organists, Am. Fedn. Musicians, Tubist Universal Brotherhood Assn., Acacia Fraternity. Republican. Congregationalist. Home: 8032 Pennsylvania Rd S Bloomington MN 55438-1135

SMITH, HENRY IGNATIUS, engineering educator; b. Jersey City, May 26, 1937; m. Mary Anne Smith; children: Elizabeth, Timothy, Eileen. BS, Holy Cross Coll.; PhD, Boston Coll., 1966. Asst. prof. physics Boston Coll., 1966—68; engr. MIT Lincoln Lab., 1968-77, engrng. mgr., 1977-80; prof. elec. engrng. MIT, Cambridge, Mass., 1980—, founder, dir. NanoStructures Lab., 1980—, Joseph F. and Nancy P. Keithley chair elec. engring. Cambridge, Mass., 1990—2005. Founder, pres. LumArray, Inc., 2004-; chmn. Principia Tech. Group; vis. scientist U. Coll., London, 1972, Thompson CSF, Paris, Norwegian Inst. Tech., Trondheim, 1976, Nippon Telephone and Telegraph Corp., Atsugi, Japan, 1990, U. Glasgow, Scotland, 1990, U. Goettingen, Germany, 1999; adj. prof. Submicoron Structure Lab., MIT, 1977-80; internat. adv. bd. MacDiarmid Inst., New Zealand; adv. com. Internat. Conf. Electron, Ion and Photon Beam Tech.; sci. adv. bd. Nantero, Inc., NanoNex, NM2. Officer USAF, 1960—63. Recipient Alexander von Humboldt award, 1999, Baccus award, SPIE, Robert H. Hill meml. award, Electrochem. Soc. Fellow IEEE (Cledo Brunetti award, 1995), Am. Acad. Arts and Scis.; mem. NAE, Am. Phys. Soc., Am. Vacuum Soc., Materials Rsch. Soc., Optical Soc. America, Sigma Xi. Achievements include research to bring new knowledge of submicron structures, nanofabrication, methods for preparing semiconductor-on-insulator films, electonic devices and quantum effects in sub-100 nm structures. Office: MIT 77 Massachusetts Ave Rm 39-427 Cambridge MA 02139-4307

SMITH, HILARY CRANWELL BOWEN, investment banker; b. Balt., Nov. 1, 1937; s. Henry Bowen and Clayton (Cranwell) S.; m. Janet Simmons, June 9, 1962; children: Kent C.B., Kendall S., Hillary E. BA, Colgate U., 1960; MBA, U. Va., 1967. V.p. Merc. Safe Deposit & Trust, 1967—69, Goldman, Sachs & Co., NYC, 1969-74, E. F. Hutton & Co., NYC, 1974-77; sr. v.p. Blyth Eastman Dillon, NYC, 1977—79; mng. dir. Salomon Bros., NYC, 1979—2004, UBS, NYC, 1990—2004; sr. advisor Greenhill & Co., NYC, 2004—08, Houlihan Lokey, 2009—. Trustee Wheaton Coll., 1997-2003, Chesapeake Maritime Mus., 1998-2004, Greenwich Acad., 1988-94, Mystic Seaport, 2005, Nat. Maritime Hist. Soc., 2006—; treas. Riverside Theater, 2007; bd. dirs. Forest 2 Market, 2000-. Lt. USN, 1960-63. Office: Houlihan Lokey 245 Park Ave New York NY 10126

SMITH, HOWARD RUSSELL, manufacturing executive, director; b. Clark County, Ohio, Aug. 15, 1914; s. Lewis Hoskins and Eula (Elder) S.; m. Jeanne Rogers, June 27, 1942 (dec. Apr. 04, 2009); children: Stewart Russell, Douglas Howard, Jeanne Ellen Smith James. AB, Pomona Coll., 1936. Security analyst Kidder, Peabody & Co., NYC, 1936-37; economist ILO, Geneva, 1937-40; asst. to pres. Blue Diamond Corp., Los Angeles, 1940—; v.p., gen. mgr., dir. Avery Dennison Corp., Pasadena, Calif., 1946-56, pres., 1956-75, chmn. bd., 1975-84, chmn. exec. com., 1984-95; dir. emeritus, 1995—; chmn. bd. Kinsmith Fin. Corp., San Marino, Calif., 1979—. Bd. dirs., past pres., chmn. Los Angeles Philharm. Assn.; chmn. emeritus, bd. trustees Pomona Coll., Claremont, Calif.; past chmn. bd. Children's Hosp. Los Angeles, Community TV of So. Calif. (Sta. KCET), Los Angeles. Lt. USNR, 1943-46. Home: 1458 Hillcrest Ave Pasadena CA 91106-4503 Office: Avery Dennison Corp 150 N Orange Grove Blvd Pasadena CA 91103-3534 Office Phone: 626-304-2153.

SMITH, HOWARD WELLINGTON, education educator, retired dean; b. Granby, Mo., Jan. 19, 1929; s. Howard W. and Margaret L. (Sanderson) S.; m. Margaret E. Bell, Mar. 1, 1953; 1 child, Christopher Alan. BS, S.W. Mo. State U., 1954; MEd, U. Mo., 1955, EdD, 1959. Tchr. Newton County (Mo.) Pub. Schs., 1948-51; instr. U. Mo., Columbia, 1955-59; asst. prof. So. Meth. U., Dallas, 1959-61; from asst. to full prof. U. North Tex., Denton, 1961-97, dean emeritus. Assoc. dean Coll. Edn. U. North Tex., 1972-76, assoc. v.p. acad. affairs, 1976-79, v.p. acad. affairs, 1979-82, interim dean, 1994-97; interim chancellor U. North Tex. Coll. Osteo. Medicine, Denton and Ft. Worth, 1981; sr. cons. Am. Assn. State Colls. and Univs., Washington, 1982; cons. Srinakharinwirot U., Thailand, 1986, Tex. Internat. Edn. Consortium, Austin, 1992, sr. author Operation Manual Al Akhawayn U., 1993; vis. prof. Shanxi Ednl. Coll. Taiyuan, China, 1993. Contbr. articles to ednl. jours. Prin. investigator Micro Tchg. Lab., 1967—69; chair Ret. Instrs., Pers. and Spouses U. North Tex., 2001; accreditation cons. Art Inst. Dallas, 2001—; chair Denton County Hist. Soc., 1999—2004; exec. coun. U. North Tex. Friends of Libr., 2005—; trustee Art Inst. Dallas, 2005—; adv. bd. Coll. Edn. U. North Tex., 1997—2005, adv. bd. Bill J. Priest Ctr. for C.C. Edn., 1999—2002, Coll. of Edn. devel. bd., 1999—2002, devel. bd. Coll. Edn., 2006—; pres. bd. dirs. Tex. Lakes Trail, 2002—04; bd. dirs. HOPE, Inc., 2007—. With USAF, 1951—53. Democrat. Presbyterian. Avocations: travel, reading. Office: U North Tex Coll Edn PO Box 311337 Denton TX 76203-1337

SMITH, IAN CORMACK PALMER, biophysicist; b. Winnipeg, Man., Can., Sept. 23, 1939; s. Cormack and Grace Mary Smith; m. Eva Gunilla Landvik, Mar. 27, 1965; children: Brittmarie, Cormack, Duncan, Roderick. BS, U. Man., 1961, MS, 1962; PhD, Cambridge U., Eng., 1965; PhD (hon.), U. Stockholm, 1986; DSc (hon.), U. Winnipeg, 1990, Brandon U., 2001, Cracow Polish Acad. Sci., 2006; diploma in tech. (hon.), Red River Coll., 1996. Fellow Stanford U., 1965-66; mem. rsch. staff Bell Tel. Labs., Murray Hill, NJ, 1966-67; rsch. officer divsn. biol. scis. NRC, Ottawa, Canada, 1967-87, dir. gen., 1987-91, Inst. Biodiagnostics, Winnipeg, Canada, 1992—. Adj. prof. chemistry and biochemistry Carleton U., 1973—90, U. Ottawa, 1976—92; adj. prof. biophysics U. Ill., Chgo., 1974—80; adj. prof. chemistry, radiology, physics and anatomy U. Man., 1992—; allied scientist Ottawa Civic Hosp., 1985—98, Ottawa Gen. Hosp., 1989—98, Ont. Cancer Found., 1989—91, St. Boniface Hosp., 1992—, Health Scis. Ctr., 1993—; exec. com. Man. Health Rsch. Coun., 1996—98, Econ. Tech. Innovation Coun., Man., 1994—98; chmn. Man. Health Rsch. Coun., 1998—2002, mem. exec. bd., 2007—; mem. adv. bd. Loeb Inst., Ottawa, 1999—2001, Keystone Ventures, 1999—2002, Western LIfe Scis. Fund, 2002—08, Novadaq, 2004—06, St. Boniface Hosp. Rsch. Enterprise, 2006—, Cancer Care Man., 2007—; bd. govs. U. Manitoba, Canada, 2000—06; bd. dirs. ENSIS Growth Fund, DIASPEC Holdings, IMRIS Inc., Magnetic Resonance Vets., Photonics Rsch. Ont., Spectex Pty., Biomed. Commercialization Can., Ontario Centres of Excellence, Genome Prairie, Man. Inst. Cell Biology. Contbr. chapters to books, articles to profl. jours. Mem. adv. bd. Smart Winnipeg, 2000—03; mem. Premier's Econ. Adv. Bd., Man., 2001—, exec. com. Man., 2004—. Decorated Order of the Star of Romania; recipient Barringer award, Can. Spectroscopy Soc., 1979, Herzberg award, 1986, Organon Teknika award, Can. Soc. Clin. Chemists, 1987, Sr. Scientist award, Sigma Xi, 1995, Queen's Jubilee medal, 2003, Paul Harris award, Rotary Club, 2006, Distingushed Alumni award, U. Manitoba, 2007, Outstanding Achievement award, 2008, Order of Can., 2009. Fellow: Soc. Magnetic Resonance Medicine (mem. exec. com. 1989—94), Royal Soc. Can. (Flavelle medal 1996), Chem. Inst. Can. (Merck award 1978, Labatt award 1984); mem.: Ont. Ctr. Photonics (chmn. bd. mgmt. 2002—), Internat. Union Pure and Applied Biophysics (mem. coun. 1993—, v.p. 1996—99, 2002—05, pres. 2005—08), Biophys. Soc. Can. (pres. 1992—94), Can. Biochem. Soc., Biophysical Soc., Internat. Coun. Sci. Unions (mem. gen. com. 1989—94), U. Man. Alumni Assn. (bd. dirs. 1994—2000, v.p. 1997—98, pres. 1998—99). Office: Inst Biodiagnostics Winnipeg MB Canada R3B 1Y6 Home Phone: 204-897-0650; Office Phone: 204-983-7526. Business E-Mail: ian.smith@nrc-cnrc.gc.ca.

SMITH, IAN K., writer, columnist, physician; b. July 15, 1969; AB, Harvard U., 1992; MA, Columbia U., 1993; attended, Dartmouth Coll., Hanover, NH; MD, U. Chgo. Pritzker Sch. Medicine, 1997. Med. corr. NBC Nightly News, Today Show, The View, Men's Health Mag., Celebrity Fit Club, VH1. Host Meet the Faith, Black Entertainment TV, HealthWatch; author: Dr. Ian Smith's Guide to Medical Websites, 2001, The Blackbird Papers, 2004 (Black Caucus ALA fiction Hon. Book award, 2005), The Take-Control Diet, 2005, The Fat Smash Diet, 2006, The Extreme Fat Smash Diet, 2007, The 4 Day Diet, 2009. Bd. mem. NYC Mission Soc., Cancer Rsch. Found. Am., Am. Coun. on Exercise, North Shore-Long Island Jewish Rsch. Inst., Henry H. Kessler Found., Bldg. with Books. Office: PO Box 765 FDR Station New York NY 10150 Business E-Mail: ian@doctoriansmith.com.*

SMITH, ISABEL FRANCIS, financial planner; b. Detroit, May 21, 1935; d. Edward Hugh and Isabel (Winegar) Francis; m. Lawrence Smith, June 7, 1958; children: Mark, Hugh, Claire. Student, Newton Coll., 1953—54; BA, U. Mich., 1957, MA, 1958, postgrad., 1975—76. Registered investment adviser. Tchr. Edison Sch., Hazel Park, Mich., 1958—61, Warren Valley Sch., Dearborn Heights, Mich., 1958—61; counselor Riverside HS, Dearborn Heights, 1961—62; former pres. Isabel Francis Smith Ltd., Farmington Hills, Mich., 1980—2004, Integrated Fin. Strategies Ltd., Farmington Hills, 1980—. Registered rep., dist. mgr. Investors Diversified Svcs., Oak Park, Mich., 1978—80; instr. Oakland CC, 1979—; cons. to women's orgns.; dir. pres. Oakland County Fin. and Estate Planning Coun., 1988—94; writer, profl. radio and TV personality. Lectr., trustee Bloomfield Twp. Libr., 1978—99, Interlochen Ctr. Arts, 1989—; founder Interlochen Friends, life trustee, 2007; founder Vol. Network for Women. Recipient Heart of Gold award, United Found., 1976, Outstanding New Rep. award, Investors Diversified Svcs., 1979, Bravo award, Interlochu Alumni Assn., 2005. Mem.: AAUW, Inst. Cert. Fin. Planners (nat. dir. 1980—86, dean retreat 1987, 1989, past regional dir., leadership devel. com., cert. fin. planner), Internat. Assn. Fin. Planners (past pres. S.E. Mich. chpt.), U. Mich. Alumni Assn., Interlochen Alumni Founder Assn. (past pres., award), Village Club, Mut. Svcs. Corp. (pres. club 1992—2002, Outstanding Rep. award 1981—90), Phi Beta Kappa (nat. chmn., past pres., exec. com. Pres. award Detroit assn.). Home: 7110 Paterese Dr Bloomfield Hills MI 48301-3764 Office: 31884 Northwestern Hwy Farmington Hills MI 48334-1628 Office Phone: 248-932-9329. Business E-Mail: isabel@ifs-ltd.com.

SMITH, ISHMAEL WADADA LEO (WADADA LEO SMITH), musician, composer; b. Leland, Miss. Student, US military band prog., 1963, Sherwood Sch. Music, 1967—69, Wesleyan U., 1975—76. Tchr. U. New Haven, 1975—76, Creative Music Studio, Woodstock, NY, 1975—78, Bard Coll., 1987—93; Dizzy Gillespie chair music Calif. Inst. Arts, 1993, coord. African-Am. improvisational music. Author: Notes (8 Pieces), Source of a New World Music: Creative Music, 1973; musician: (albums) Creative Music, 1972, Reflectativity, 1974, Song of Humanity, 1976, Mass on the World, 1978, Divine Love, 1978, Budding of a Rose, 1979, Go in Numbers, 1980, Spirit Catcher, 1980, Akhreanvention, 1981, Human Rights, 1982, Procession of the Great Ancestry, 1983, Rastafari, 1983, If You Want the Kernels, You Have to Break the Shells, 1985, Kulture Jazz, 1995, Tao-Njia, 1996, Prataksis, 1997, Golden Hearts Remembrance, 1997, Condor, Autumn Wind, 1998, Light Upon Light, 1999, Reflectativity, 2000, Golden Quartet, 2000, Red Sulphur Sky, 2001, The Year of the Elephant, 2002, Luminous Axis, 2002, Organic Resonance, 2003, Saturn, Conjunct the Grand Canyon in a Sweet Embrace, 2004, Lake Biwa, 2004, Snakish, 2005, Compassion, 2006, Wisdom in Time, 2007, Freedom Now!, 2008, Tabligh, 2008, America, 2009. Grantee Asian Cultural Coun., 1993, Nat. Endowment for the Arts, 1972, 1974, 1981; fellow NY Found. Arts, 1990, John Simon Guggenheim Meml. Found., 2009. Mem.: Assn. for the Advancement of Creative Musicians, Broadcast Music, Inc. Office: Herb Alpert Sch Music Calif Inst Arts 24700 McBean Pkwy Valencia CA 91355 E-mail: wlsmith@calarts.edu.*

SMITH, J. KELLUM, JR., foundation administrator, lawyer; b. NYC, July 18, 1927; s. James Kellum and Elizabeth Dexter (Walker) S.; m. Sarah Tod Lohmann, July 22, 1950 (div. 1993); children: Alison Andrews, Timothy Kellum, Jennifer Harlow, Christopher Lohmann; m. Angela Marina Brown, Feb. 3, 1995. Grad., Phillips Exeter Acad., 1945; AB magna cum laude, Amherst Coll., 1950; LL.B., Harvard, 1953. Bar: N.Y. 1955. Assoc. Lord, Day & Lord, NYC, 1953-59; asst. sec. John Simon Guggenheim Meml. Found., 1960-62; mem. staff Rockefeller Found., 1962-74, asst. sec., 1963-64, sec., 1964—74; v.p., sec. Andrew W. Mellon Found., NYC, 1974—89, sr. fellow, 1989-92; sr. advisor, 1992-98; pres. Hill and Hollow Music, Inc., 1995—; pvt. practice cons. and writer. Trustee Nat. Sculpture Soc., 1955-71, Nat. Ins. Archtl. Edn., 1961-69, St. Bernard's Sch., N.Y.C., 1968-78, Found. for Child Devel., 1968-74; trustee Brearley Sch., N.Y.C., 1964-80, pres., 1973-78; trustee Am. Acad. in Rome, 1964-95, treas., 1965-66, 2d v.p., 1968-72, 84-88, sec., 1973-84, 89-95. With USAAF, 1945-46. Mem. Phi Beta Kappa. Clubs: Century Association (N.Y.C.).

SMITH, J. ROY, museum director, education educator; b. Washington, Ga., Sept. 13, 1936; s. James Roy and Nellie Irene (Mansfield) S. BA, Mercer U., 1956; postgrad., Brown U., 1957; cert., Oxford U., Eng., 1963. Tchr. City of Cranston, RI, 1957-59; with Charleston County, Charleston, SC, 1962-64, 76-79; tchr. Fulton County, Fairburn, Ga., 1965-76, Berkeley County, Moncks Corner, SC, 1979-94; assoc. dir. Karpeles Manuscript Mus., Charleston, 2005—. Lt. (j.g.) USN, 1959-62. Lowcountry Writing Project fellow, Newspaper Fund of the Wall Street Jour. fellow; English Speaking Union scholar Oxford U., 1963 Mem. SAR (sec.-treas. S.C. Soc. 1977-78), Ga. S.R., Soc. Second War with Great Britain, Sons and Daus. of Pilgrims (gov. Ga. br. 1976, hon. gov. 1976—), S.C. Hist. Soc., Ga. Hist. Soc., Kappa Phi Kappa (registered tour guide, lectr.). Home and Office: 110 Coming St Charleston SC 29403-6103

SMITH, JACK DAVID, lawyer; b. Honolulu, Jan. 4, 1946; s. Jack David and Gloria June (Slater) S.; m. Alexa Drubay, June 12, 2006; children: Amy Elizabeth, Amanda Marie. BA in Polit. Sci., George Washington U., 1968, JD, 1971. Bar: Va. 1971, U.S. Ct. Mil. Appeals 1971, U.S. Ct. Appeals (1st and D.C. cirs.) 1975, U.S. Ct. Appeals (2d and 7th cirs.) 1976, U.S. Supreme Ct. 1976, D.C. 1986. Atty. litig. div. FCC, Washington, 1974-81, dept. chief common carrier bur., 1981-83, chief common carrier bur., 1983-84, gen. counsel, 1984-86; dep. gen. counsel Fed. Home Loan Bank Bd., Washington, 1986-89, Fed. Deposit Ins. Corp., Washington, 1989—2006; dir. Internat. Ctr. Asset Recovery, Basel, Switzerland, 2006—07, anti corruption cons., 2007—09; dir. Internat. Repatriation Fund, 2009—. Served to capt. USMC, 1971-74. Mem. Va. Bar Assn., D.C. Bar Assn. Avocations: tennis, running, skiing. Office Phone: 610-566-3815. Personal E-mail: jackdsmith@gmail.com.

SMITH, JACK N., secondary school educator; b. Carson City, Nev., Feb. 3, 1960; s. Donold E. Smith and Marge Anderson; married. BS, Navada-Reno, 1992. Sch. tchr. Sch. Dist., Revo, NY, 1993—2006, Winnemucca, Nev., 2007—. Head girls basketball coach, Nev. Recipient 3A Coach of Yr., 2008; named Coach of Yr., 2001—03, All Nevada Prep. Coach Yr., 2001. Home: 4850 Raw Bow RD Winnemucca NV 89445

SMITH, JACLYN, actress; b. Houston, Oct. 26, 1947; d. Jack and Margaret Ellen S.; m. Dennis Cole (div. 1981); m. Tony Richmond, Aug. 4, 1981; 1 dau., Spencer Margaret. Student, Trinity U., San Antonio. Worked as model. Motion picture appearances include The Adventurers, 1970, Bootleggers, Deja Vu; TV film appearances include Bogen County, 1977, The Users, 1978, Rage of Angels, 1980, Nightkill, 1980, Jacqueline Bouvier Kennedy, 1981, Sentimental Journey, 1984, George Washington (miniseries), 1984, Florence Nightingale, 1985, The Night They Saved Christmas, 1986, Wind Mills of the Gods (miniseries), 1988, The Bourne Identity, 1988, Settle the Score, 1989, Danielle Steele's Kaleidoscope, 1990, Lies Before Kisses, 1991, The Rape of Dr. Willis, 1991, In The Arms Of A Killer, 1992, Love Can Be Murder, 1992, Family Album, 1994, Cries Unheard: The Donna Yaklich Story, 1994, My Very Best Friend, 1996, Married to a Stranger, 1997, Before He Wakes, 1998, Three Secrets, 1999, Freefall, 1999; one of prin. roles TV series Charlie's Angels, 1976-80, (ABC Saturday Night Movie) Christine Cromwell, 1989-90; other TV appearances include Get Christy Love, McCloud, The Rookies, Love Boat, Switch, Navigating the Heart, 2000, The District, 2000; appeared in numerous TV commls. Mem. AFTRA. Office: ICM 8942 Wilshire Blvd Beverly Hills CA 90211-1934

SMITH, JAMES A., lawyer; b. Akron, Ohio, June 11, 1930; s. Barton H. and Myrna S. (Young) S.; m. Melda I. Perry, Jan. 17, 1959; children: Hugh, Sarah Louise. AB, Western Res. U., 1952; postgrad., Columbia U., 1954-56, LLB, 1961; postgrad., Yale U., 1956-58. Bar: Ohio 1961, U.S. Dist. Ct. (no. dist.) Ohio 1963, U.S. Ct. Appeals (6th cir.) 1973, U.S. Supreme Ct. 1974, U.S. Ct. Appeals (11th cir.) 1983, U.S. Ct. Appeals (D.C. cir.) 1984. Assoc. Squire, Sanders and Dempsey, Cleve., 1961-70, ptnr., 1970-91, counsel, 1991-96; adj. prof. Case Western Res. U. Sch. Law, 1997-98, ret., 1996. Mem. spl. adv. com. Nat. Conf. Commrs. on Uniform State Laws, 1972-74. Trustee Chagrin Falls Park Cmty. Ctr., 1968-78, Greater Cleve. Neighborhood Ctrs. Assn., 1973-78, Legal Aid Soc. Cleve., 1977-80, Cleve. Inst. Music, 1994—96; mem. Charter Rev. Commn., Chagrin Falls, 1966. Lt. (j.g.) USNR, 1952-54. Fellow Am. Coll. Trial Lawyers; mem. ABA, Ohio Bar Assn., Cleve. Bar Assn. (trustee 1988-92), U.S. Ct. Appeals for 6th Cir. Jud. Conf. (life), Ohio Ct. Appeals for 8th Jud. Dist. Conf. (life), Ct. of Nisi Prius (clk. 1975-76, judge 1994-95), Appalachee Vill. Assn. (pres. 2004-05), Phi Beta Kappa, Omicron Delta Kappa, Delta Sigma Rho. Democrat. Personal E-mail: jasasmith1@aol.com.

SMITH, JAMES FINLEY, economist, educator; b. Dallas, Nov. 4, 1938; s. Emerson Russell and Achsah Elizabeth (Foster) S.; children: Carter Emerson, Jade, Curtis Noel, Marshall Edward; m. Linda M. Topp, Aug. 5, 2001. BA, So. Meth. U., 1961, MA, 1964, PhD, 1971. Math. analyst Sears, Roebuck & Co., Oak Brook, Ill., 1965-68, adminstrv. asst. to v.p. and treas. Chgo., 1968-69, dir. econometric rsch., 1969-75; sr. economist Bd. Govs. FRS, Washington, 1975-77; dir. credit rsch. Sears, Roebuck & Co., Chgo., 1977-80; chief economist Union Carbide Corp., Danbury, Conn., 1980-85; dir. regional svcs. and U.S. cons. Wharton Econometric Forecasting Assocs., Phila., 1986; dir., chief economist Bur. Bus. Rsch. U. Tex., Austin, 1987-88; prof. fin. U. NC, Chapel Hill, 1988—, sr. fellow Kenan Inst. Pvt. Enterprise, 2002—; chief economist Nat. Assn. Realtors, Washington, 1999—2000; dir. Ctr. for Bus. Forecasting, U. N.C., 2002—; chief economist Soc. Indsl. and Office Realtors, Washington, 2002—06, Parsec Fin., Asheville, NC, 2006—; prof., practice Inst. Economy and Future, Western Carolina U., Cullowhee, NC, 2006—09. Econ. adv. bd. U.S. Dept. Commerce, 1977-80, 83-93; cons. Pres.'s Coun. of Econ. Advisers, Washington, 1978-83; dir. Nat. Bur. Econ. Rsch., Cambridge, Mass., 1992-95; bd. advisors Thurston Arthritis Rsch. Ctr., Chapel Hill, N.C., 1994-99; dir. Am. Fin. Svcs. Assn. Edn. Found., 1997—. Author: (quarterly) UNC Business Forecast, 1988-2005, Jim Smith's Econ. Outlook, 2005—; (with others) Economic Growth and Investment in Higher Education, 1987, The New Texas Economy, 1988; (with Elsie Echeverri-Carroll) The Economic Impact of Travel on Texas Counties: 1986, 1988; contbr. articles to profl. jours. Served to lt. U.S. Army, 1961-62. Fellow NDEA, 1962—65. Fellow Nat. Assn. Bus. Econ. (v.p. 1988-89, pres. 1989-90, dir. 1980-84, 85-92); Nat. Economists Club (bd. govs. 1984-87), Am. Econ. Assn., Economists Group Switzerland, European Coun. Econ.(co chair 2001-03), Fin. Mgmt. Assn., Bus. Economists UK, Nat. Bus. Econ. Issues Coun. (pres. 1981-83). Methodist. Office: Parsec Fin 6 Wall St Asheville NC 28802 Business E-Mail: j_smith@unc.edu.

SMITH, JAMES FITZPATRICK, literature educator; m. Hester Westley, June 14, 2008. PhD in Brit. and Am. Lit., Wash. U., St. Louis, 2002. Asst. prof. Calif. State U., Chico, 2002—05, Wittenberg U., Springfield, Ohio, 2005—. Pres. Phi Beta Kappa, Omicron Chpt., Springfield, 2007—09. Recipient Tchr. of Yr., Panhellenic Coun., Wittenberg U., 2007. Mem.: Phi Beta Kappa (Omicron Chpt. Springfield) (pres. 2007—). Office: Wittenberg Univ PO Box 720 Springfield OH 45501 Business E-Mail: jfsmith@wittenberg.edu.

SMITH, JAMES LAWRENCE, research physicist; b. Detroit, Sept. 3, 1943; s. William Leo and Marjorie Marie (Underwood) S.; m. Carol Ann Adam, Mar. 27, 1965; children: David Adam, William Leo. BS, Wayne State U., 1965; PhD, Brown U., 1974. Mem. staff Los Alamos Nat. Lab., N.Mex., 1973—82, fellow, 1982—86, 1987—, dir. Ctr. Materials Sci., 1986—87; chief scientist Superconductivity Tech. Ctr., 1988—99. Sci. editor: Los Alamos Rsch. Quar., 2002-03; N.Am. editor: Philos. mag., 1990-95, 03-06; editor: Philos. mag. B, 1995-02, Philos. Mag., 2003-06; contbr. articles to profl. jours. Recipient E.O. Lawrence award, 1986, Disting. Alumni award Wayne State U., 1993. Fellow Am. Phys. Soc. (internat. prize for new materials 1990); mem. AAAS, Materials Rsch. Soc., Minerals Metals Materials Soc., Am. Crystallographic Assn., Brown Alumni Assn. (bd. govs. 1998-2000), Phi Beta Kappa. Achievements include patents for design of magnetic field and high-strength conductors. Office: Los Alamos Nat Lab Mail Stop G770 Los Alamos NM 87545-0001 Office Phone: 505-667-4476. Business E-Mail: jlsmith@lanl.gov.

SMITH, JAMES ORMAL, engineering educator; b. South Bend, Ind., Oct. 7, 1949; s. George Ormal and Sylvia R. Smith; children: Laurie Ann Larime, Jamie Susanne. Student, Buchanan Trade Sch., Mich., 1969—73. Mgr. chem. engrng. support svcs. U. Notre Dame, Ind., 1999—. Blood donor South Bend Med. Found. Ctrl. Blood Bank, Ind., 1982—2007; youth vol. Camp Evergreen Hospice and Palliative Care, South Bend, 1995—2007, patient care vol., 2003—07; team capt. Relay for Life Am. Cancer Soc., Notre Dame, 2002—07. Named Outstanding Ski Patrol Dir., Royal Valley Ski Patrol, 1982. Mem.: ASME, Soc. Mfg. Engrs. (sr.). Achievements include development of automation of electronics assembly lines; design of Nano CNC Milling Machine; adjustable volume adjustable flow acid re-action vessals; vacuum hood variable speed sample spinner; blood filtration/seperation research equipment. Home: 50911 Rothbury Dr Granger IN 46530 Office: University Notre Dame B-01 Fitzpatrick Hall Notre Dame IN 46556 Office Fax: 574-631-8366. Business E-Mail: jsmith1@nd.edu.

SMITH, JAMES PATRICK, economist; b. Aug. 3, 1943; s. James P. and Winefred (Harrison) S.; m. Sandra Berry, Oct. 25, 1983; children: Gillian Clare, Lauren Theresa. BS, Fordham U., 1965; PhD, U. Chgo., 1972. Rsch. assoc. Nat. Bur. Econ. Rsch., NYC, 1972-74; sr. economist Rand Corp., Santa Monica, Calif., 1974—, dir. of rsch. labor and population, 1977-93. Bd. dirs. Occupl. Safety and Health Standards State Calif. Editor: Female Labor Supply, 1980, Black Economic progress After Myrdal, The New Americans, 1997, The Immigration Debate, 1998, Healthy Bodies and Thick Wallets, 2006, Disease Disadvantage in United States and England; bd. editors: Am. Econ. Rev., 1980-83; contbr. articles to profl. jours. Recipient Merit award NIH, 1995-2005 Mem. NIA (monitoring com., health and retirement survey, chair NAS panel on immigration, chair adv. com. Korean HRS KLOSA, Chinese HRS CHARLES and Indian HRS LASI), Am. Econ. Assn., Phi Beta Kappa. Office: RAND PO Box 2138 Santa Monica CA 90407-2138 Business E-Mail: smith@rand.org.

SMITH, JAMES WARREN, pathologist, educator, microbiologist, parasitologist; b. Logan, Utah, July 5, 1934; s. Kenneth Warren and Nina Lou (Sykes) S.; m. Nancy Chesterman, July 19, 1958; children: Warren, Scott. BS, U. Iowa, 1956, MD, 1959. Diplomate Am. Bd. Pathology. Intern Colo. Gen. Hosp., Denver, 1959—60; resident U. Iowa Hosps., Iowa City, 1960—65; asst. prof. pathology U. Vt., Burlington, 1967—70; prof. pathology Ind. U., Indpls., 1970—98, chmn. dept. pathology and lab. medicine, 1992—98, Nordshow prof. of lab. medicine, 1997—98, prof. emeritus, 1998—. Contbr. articles to profl. jours. Served to lt. comdr. USN, 1965-67. Recipient Outstanding Contbn. to Clin. Microbiology award South Ctrl. Assn. Clin. Microbiology, 1977. Fellow Coll. Am. Pathologists (chmn. microbiology resource com. 1981-85); mem. AMA, Infectious Disease Soc. Am., Am. Soc. Investigative Pathology, Royal Soc. Tropical Medicine and Hygiene, Am. Soc. Clin. Pathology, Am. Soc. Microbiology, Am. Soc. Tropical Medicine and Hygiene, U.S.-Can. Acad. Pathology, Assn. Pathology Chairs, Binford Dammin Soc. Infectious Disease Pathologists, Soc. Protozoologists. Home: 4375 Cold Spring Rd Indianapolis IN 46228-3327 Office: Ind U Med Ctr 635 Barnhill Dr Rm A128 Indianapolis IN 46202-5126

SMITH, JANE SCHNEBERGER, retired city administrator; b. Chgo., Aug. 9, 1928; d. Frank R. and Marion (Durante) Schneberger; m. Z. Erol Smith Jr., Oct. 28, 1950 (div. 1974); children: Suzan MacKenzie Smith, Tracy Smith Cawley, Cameron Farley, Z. Erol III, Kimberly Van Den Elzen, Scott. BA in Chemistry, U. Colo., 1950; MA in Comm., Mich. State U., East Lansing, 1978, PhD in Ednl. Adminstrn., 1987. Chemist Kellogg Switchboard, Chgo., 1950-51; v.p. South Cook County Girl Scouts, Harvey, Ill., 1967-69, staff advisor, 1970-72; tchr. Crab Orchard Sch., Palos Heights, Ill., 1969-70; program and tng. dir. Mich. Capitol. Coun. Girl Scouts, Lansing, Mich., 1972-75; dir. svc. learning ctr. Mich. State U., East Lansing, 1975-81; city clk. City of Ashland, Wis., 1981-89, interim city adminstr., 1989-90; ret., 1990; acting city clk. City of Ashland, 2003, 2006. Cons. vol. adminstrn., Mich., Wis., 1975—. Co-editor: Looking Backward Moving Forward, 1987, Roots and Wings, 2002; contbr. articles to profl. jours. V.p. Mich. Capitol Girl Scout Coun., Lansing, 1976-78; bd. dirs. Lansing RSVP, 1976-81, Ashland Mus., 1985-87, Ptnrs. in Recovery, 1985-87; v.p. Friends of the Libr., 1992-97, pres., 1997-99; sec. New Horizons, 1985-90, New Day Shelter, 1990-99, v.p., 1993-95, pres., 1995-97, sec., 1997-99; pres. LWV of Ashland Bayfield County, 1992-93, 96-98; sec. No. Wis. History Ctr., 1992-94; commr. Ashland Water and Wastewater Utility, 1993-96; mem. Ashland Beautification Com., 1993-2007, Big Top Chautauqua, 1996-2003, vice chair Alliance for Sustainability, 1994-99; v.p. GFWC/Ashland Monday Club, 1994-98, pres., 1998-2000, 1st v.p. 10th Dist. GFWC-WI, 2000-02; mem. Ashland County Human Svcs. Bd., 1998—, vice chair, 2003-04, Restore the Depot Com., 2001—; co-chair comprehensive plan update com., 2002—05. co-chair comprehensive plan implementation com., 2006-08; mem. tree bd. City of Ashland, 2002-08, planning commn., 2004—. Recipient cert. appreciation Mich. Capitol Girl Scout Coun., 1975, Thanks Badge, 1972, Tribute to Excellence award LWV of Wis., 1999. Mem. Internat. Assn. Mcpl. Clks., Wis. Mcpl. Clks. Assn. (dist. dir. 1984-86), Am. Bus. Women's Assn. (scholarship chmn. 1985), Zonta (pres. 1979-81), Ashland Hist. Soc. (bd. dirs.). Roman Catholic. Avocations: stained glass, gardening, stamp collecting/philately, genealogy. Home: 700 MacArthur Ave Ashland WI 54806-2903 Personal E-mail: jsmith023@centurytel.net.

SMITH, JANET SUE, systems process specialist; b. Chgo., Jan. 15, 1945; d. Curtis Edwin and Margaret Louise (Yost) Smith. BA, Ind. U., 1967. Sales mgr. Marshall Field & Co., Chgo., 1968-70, programmer, 1970-72; sr. programmer, analyst Trailer Train Co., Chgo., 1972-75; mgr. data base and systems devel. Railinc-Assn. Am. R.R., Washington, 1975-85, asst. v.p., corp. sec., 1985-93, asst. v.p. strategic systems, 1994-98; exec. dir. Interline Svc., 1998-99, asst. v.p. bus. svc., 1999—2001; owner JSSmith Consulting LLC, Chapel Hill, NC, 2002—05, Bloomington, Ind., 2005—. Nat. student v.p. YWCA, 1966-67; bd. dir., v.p. planning and fin. Guide Internat.; advisor Jr. Achievement; pres. alumni bd. dir. Coll. Arts and Scis. Ind. U., co-chair colloquium for women, mem. internat. studies adv. coun. Mem.: Woodburn Guild, Ind. U. Alumni Assn. (life). Home and Office: JSSmith Cons LLC 3141 E Wyndam Ct Bloomington IN 47401-4495

SMITH, JANET SUSANNAH, literature and language educator, department chairman; b. Waynesville, NC, Aug. 1, 1956; d. Jerry Liner, Jr. and Patricia Ruth Cooper; m. Fletcher Wade Smith, Apr. 23, 1996; children from previous marriage: Jessica Music Tripp, Allysen Alexis, Aimee Ruth Tripp. BS summa cum laude, Fla. State U., Tallahassee, 1992; EdM, State U. Ga., Carrollton, 1994; EdS, Lincoln Meml. U., Knoxville, Tenn., 1999. Cert. gifted edn. Internat. Baccalaureate Tng., 2001, tchr. English grades 7-12, adminstrn. and supervision, nat. bd. cert. adolescent young adult in English and lang. arts 2003, cert. Advanced Placement Tng., 2001. Instr. English S.E. Whitfield HS, Dalton, Ga., 1992—, dept. chair lang. arts, 2006. Mem. content adv. com. Profl. Stds. Commn., Atlanta; chair Ann. Yearly Progress Com.; region literary sponsor, 2004—; polit. speechwriter. Recipient Golden Apple award, 1995, 1998; nominee Tchr. of Yr., Southeast Whitfield H.S., 1992—2006; scholar, So. Scholarship Found. Mem.: NEA, Nat. Coun. Tchrs. English, Ga. Assn. Educators, Golden Key, Phi Kappa Phi, Phi Theta Kappa. Office: Southeast Whitfield HS 1954 Riverbend Rd Dalton GA 30721-5547

SMITH, JANICE YODER, biology professor; PhD in Molecular Biology, Tex. Woman's U., Denton. Prof., biology Tarrant County Coll. NW Campus, Fort Worth, Tex., 1989—, faculty assn. pres., 1997—98. Recipient Chancellor's award. Business E-Mail: janice.smith@tccd.edu.

SMITH, JASON, retired professional hockey player; b. Calgary, Alta., Can., Nov. 2, 1973; married. Defenseman Albany River Rats (Am. Hockey League), 1993—95, NJ Devils, 1995—97, Toronto Maple Leafs, 1997—99, Edmonton Oilers, 1999—2007, capt., 2001—07; defenseman Phila. Flyers, 2007—08, capt., 2007—08; defenseman Ottawa Senators, 2008—09. Achievements include being a member of Calder Cup Champion Albany River Rats, 1995.

SMITH, JASON A. B., lawyer; b. Washington, Aug. 21, 1971; BA, Columbia Univ., 1993; JD, NYU, 1996. Bar: NY 1998. Ptnr., structured fin. and derivatives practice Weil Gotshal & Manges, NYC. Mem.: ABA, NY State Bar Assn. Office: Weil Gotshal & Manges 767 Fifth Ave New York NY 10153 Office Phone: 212-310-8914. Office Fax: 212-310-8007. Business E-Mail: jason.smith@weil.com.

SMITH, JASON KEMMITT, communications educator; b. Balt., Dec. 26; s. James Joseph and Suzanne Patricia Smith. BA in Comm., U. RI, Kingston, 1999; MA, U. Hartford, Conn., 2002; PhD in Mass Comm., Fla. State U., Tallahassee, 2007. Asst. mgr. Casarella Painting, Ashford, Conn., 1996—2006; asst. audio visual tech. Presentation Svcs., New Orleans, 1999—2000; asst. prof. Western Carolina U., Cullowhee, 2006—07; lectr. U. RI, Kingston, 2007—; adj. prof. U. Conn., Storrs, 2008—. Tel. recovery support Conn. Ctr. Addiction Recovery, Willimantic, 2008. Mem.: Broadcasting and Musicians Inc., PADI (lic. scuba diver 1994), Chi Phi. Liberal. Roman Catholic. Avocations: guitar, scuba diving, writing. Office: Univ RI Dept Comm Davis Bldg Kingston RI 02881

SMITH, JAY LAWRENCE, financial planning company executive; b. Detroit, June 10, 1954; s. Paul Edward Smith and Gloria D. Lawrence; m. Janice Irene Acheson, May 21, 1978; children: Kevin Hamilton, Travis Jay. Student, Oakland U., 1972-75. CFP. Asst. tng. dir. Equitable Cos., Troy, Mich., 1978-81; pres. JLS Fin. Planning Corp., Oxford, Mich., 1978—. Adj. faculty Oakland U., Rochester, Mich., 1986-87; commentator TV show Your Money and You, 1987. Cons. Practicing Fin. Planning, 1990; contbr. articles to profl. jours. Mem. Internat. Assn. Fin. Planning (v.p. 1985-87, bd. dirs. 1987-89), Inst. Cert. Fin. Planners (bd. dirs. 1988-90), Inst. Cert. Fin. Planners-Mich. (pres. 1992-93), Fin. Profl. Adv. Panel, Internat. Bd. Cert. Fin. Planners, Rotary (bd. dirs. 1984-86, treas. 1985-87, pres. Oxford 1992-93). Republican. Methodist. Avocations: skiing, music, raquetball. Office: Investment Mgmt & Rsch Inc PO Box 4 28 S Washington St Oxford MI 48371-4985

SMITH, JAY S., museum director; BA in Pop Culture, Bowling Green State U., Ohio, 1990, MA in Am. Culture Studies, 1992; MA prog. Hist. with emphasis in Pub. Hist., Mus. Studies Track, Middle Tenn. State U., Murfreesboro, 1993—95. Intern Wood County Hist. Ctr., Inc., Bowling Green, Ohio, 1990—92, Rutherford B. Hayes Presdl. Ctr., Fremont, Ohio, 1992, Nat. Park Svc., Wash., DC, 1994, The Carter House, Franklin, Tenn., 1994; grad. rsch. asst. Bowling Green State U., 1992; intern Ft. Meigs State Meml., Perrysburg, Ohio, 1992, hist. interpreter, 1992—93; grad. tchg. asst. Middle Tenn. State U., 1993—94, 1994—95; archeol. staff asst. Republic Conservation, Restoration, Anthropology, Nashville, 1994; hist. interpreter The Homeplace-1850, Golden Pond, Ky., 1995; exec. dir. Reno County Mus., Hutchinson, Kans., 1995—2005; project dir. Kans. Underground Salt Mus., Hutchinson, 1999—2005; site mgr. Kans. City Mus., 2005, dir., 2005, Hubbard Mus. of Am. West, Ruidoso Downs, N.Mex., 2005—. Grant reviewer IMLS Museums for Am. Prog., 2003—04, 2008. Editor, writer, interviewer

Legacy: The Journal of the Reno County Historical Society; contbr. columns in newspapers Hutchingson News; co-author: The Hutchinson Spirit, 2004. Vol. United Way Reno County, Hutchinson, 1996—2000, Old Northeast Fall Festival, 2005; landmarks commr. Hutchinson Landmarks Commn., 1996—98; judge State of Kans. Hist. Day competition, 1996—2005; task force chmn. Mayor's Task Force on Downtown Revitalization, Hutchinson, 1999—2000; coord. Dist. 7 Hist. Day, 2001—04; Hist. Day judge Ruidoso Regional and State Competition, 2006—; adv. bd. mem. Greater Hutchinson Conv. and Visitor's Bur., 1996—99, 2004—05; bd. pres. Downtown Hutchinson, Inc., 1997—99, 2001—02, bd. mem., 1999—2000, Emancipation Day Com., Hutchinson, 1998—99; adv. bd. mem. Kans. Dept. Commerce & Housing, 1999—2003; vice chmn. Downtown Hutchinson Revitalization Partnership, Inc., 2002; chmn. World Trade Ctr. Meml. Com., 2002—05; bd. mem. Northeast Kans. City Coun. Arts Commn., 2005, Econ. Devel. Coun., Ruidoso Downs, 2006—; bd. mem., com. mem. Ruidoso Downs C. of C., 2006—; com. mem. Lincoln County Cowboy Symposium, 2006. Recipient Pub. Svc. award, Kans. Dept. Commerce and Housing, 2001, Cmty. Leadership award, Altrusa Internat. of Hutchinson, 2001, 2002; named Vol. of Yr., Kans. Dept. Commerce and Housing, 2000. Mem.: Hutchinson Exec. Assn., Assn. Grad. Students in Hist. (pres., co-founder 1995), Kans. State Hist. Soc. (mem. bd. dirs. 2000—05, chmn. James W. Ripley Award Com. 2001—04), Kans. Mus. Assn. (membership chmn. 1997—99, Award of Excellence 1999), Am. Assn. State and Local Hist., Nat. Trust for Hist. Preservation, Mountain Plains Mus. Assn. (co-chmn. mktg. com. 2006—, bd. mem. 2007), AAM, Hutchinson Rotary Club. Office: Hubbard Mus of the Am West 841 Hwy 70 W PO Box 40 Ruidoso Downs NM 88346 Office Phone: 575-378-4142 ext. 228. Office Fax: 575-378-4166. Business E-Mail: jaysmith@hubbardmuseum.org.

SMITH, JEFF M., secondary school educator; b. Dec. 8, 1980; adopted s. David Nickalus and Prudence Smith; 1 child, Rachael E. Hall. BS, Spring Arbor U., Mich., 2003. Tchr. Western Sch. Dist., Jackson, Mich., 2004—. Coord. Lansing Parks and Recreation, Mich., 2002—08. Advisor, Lansing. Conservative. Avocation: sports. Office: Western Sch Dist 3950 Catherine St Jackson MI 49203 Business E-Mail: smithje@westernschools.org.

SMITH, JEFFREY A., lawyer; b. Trenton, Tenn., Sept. 27, 1963; s. Nathan L. and Mary Jane (Ledsinger) S. BS in Acctg., U. Tenn. at Martin, 1985; JD, MBA, Memphis State U., 1991. Cost acct. Goodyear Tire & Rubber, Union City, Tenn., 1986-88; atty. Bill Barron, Atty., Trenton, Tenn., 1991-93, Kizer, Bonds, Crocker & Hughes, Milan, Tenn., 1993-95, Jeffrey A. Smith, Trenton, Tenn., 1995—. City atty. City of Dyer, Tenn., 1993-95, City of Kenton, Tenn., 1996—; bd. dirs. United Way of West Tenn., Jackson, 1997—. Elected mem.-alderman Bd. of Mayor & Aldermen, Rutherford, Tenn., 1993-00; elected mem.-commr. Gibson County Bd. County Commrs., 1994-02. Office: Jeffrey A Smith Atty PO Box 126 Trenton TN 38382 Home: 16 Mcwherter Ln Rutherford TN 38369-9605

SMITH, JEFFREY CHIPPS, art educator; MA, Columbia U., 1975, MPhil, 1977, PhD, 1979. Kay Fortson chair in European art U. Tex., Austin, 1979—; pres. Interdisciplinary Internat. Acad. Group, 2008—. Co-editor Jour. Historians Wetherlandish Art, 2009—. Author: Nuremberg, A Renaissance City, 1500-1618, 1983, German Sculpture of the Later Renaissance, c. 1520-1580: Art in an Age of Uncertainty, 1994, Sensuous Worship: Jesuits and the Art of Early Catholic Reformation in Germany, 2002, The Northern Renaissance, 2004, The Art of the Goldsmith in Late Fifteenth Century Germany: The Virgin and Her Bishop, 2006; editor: New Perspectives on the Art of Renaissance Nuremberg: Five Essays, 1985; editor: (introduction to) E. Panofsky, The Life and Art of Albrecht Durer, 1943—2005; co-editor: The Essential Dürer, 2009; reviewer in field, —; contbr. articles to profl. jours. Alexander von Humboldt-Stiftung fellow, Bonn, Germany, ACLS grantee, NEH grantee, Getty Found. grantee, Guggenheim Found. grantee, Kimbell Art Found. grantee, Zentralinstitut Kunstgeschicht fellow. Mem.: Sixteenth Century Soc. and Conf. (bd. dir. 2004—07), Renaissance Soc. Am. (bd. dirs. 2000—, editor Renaissance Quarterly 2003—06), Coll. Art Assn. (bd. dir. 1996—2000). Office: U Tex Dept Art and Art History Austin TX 78712 Home Phone: 512-451-0097; Office Phone: 512-232-2609. Business E-Mail: chipps@mail.utexas.edu.

SMITH, JEFFREY GREENWOOD, retired military officer; b. Ft. Sam Houston, Tex., Oct. 14, 1921; s. Henry Joseph Moody and Gladys Adrienne (Haile) S.; m. Dorothy Jane Holland, June 2, 1948; children: Meredith B. Exnicios, Jennifer H. Smith, Jeffrey Greenwood, Tracy E. McDonald, Melissa A. Deutsch, Ashley A. Pollock. BS in Civil Engring, Va. Mil. Inst., 1943; MS in Mech. Engring, Johns Hopkins U., 1949; MA in Internat. Affairs, George Washington U., 1964. Commd. 2d lt. U.S. Army, 1944, advanced through grades to lt. gen., 1975; service in CBI, Korea, Germany and Vietnam; comdr. 2d Inf. Div., Korea, 1971-73; dep. chief staff ops. Hdqrs. Army Forces Command, Ft. McPherson, Ga., 1973-74, chief staff, 1974-75; comdr. 1st U.S. Army, Ft. Meade, Md., 1975-79; ret., 1979; dir. govt. rels. Ethyl Corp., Washington, 1980—, v.p. govt. rels., 1992—, ret., 1994. Dir. Army Hist. Found. Decorated D.S.M., Silver Star, Legion of Merit with 3 oak leaf clusters, D.F.C., Bronze Star with V device and 2 oak leaf clusters, Air medal with 12 oak leaf clusters, Army Commendation medal with oak leaf cluster, Purple Heart with oak leaf cluster, Combat Inf. badge (2); breast Order Yun Hui Republic China; Order Security Merit Korea; Gallantry Cross with silver and gold stars (Vietnam) Army Distinguished Service Order Mem. Assn. U.S. Army, Mil. Order Carabao, U.S. Cavalry Assn., Kappa Alpha, Tau Beta Pi. Clubs: Army and Navy. Home: 3000 Sevor Ln Alexandria VA 22309-2221 E-mail: genjeffrey@aol.com.

SMITH, JEFFREY HARTMAN, lawyer; b. Salina, Kans., Oct. 24, 1944; s. Robert B. and Alice Mae (Williams) S.; m. Claudia Jean Chyle, June 18, 1966; children: Amy Elisabeth, Katherine Ann. BS, U.S. Mil Acad., 1966; JD, U. Mich., 1971. Bar: Mich. 1971, D.C. 1989. Asst. legal advisor Office of Legal Advisor Dept. of State, Washington, 1975-84; minority counsel Senate Armed Svcs. Com., Washington, 1984—86, gen. counsel, 1986-88; ptnr. Arnold & Porter, Washington, 1988—95; gen. counsel CIA, 1995—96; ptnr., Govt. Contracts Practice Group & Public Policy/Legislative Practice Group Arnold & Porter, Washington, 1996—. Mem. bd. dirs. The Henry L. Stimson Ctr., Washington, 1990-; mem. Commn. to Review Roles & Missions of Armed Svcs. & chmn., Joint Security Commn., US Dept. Def.; chief, Clinton Transition team, US Dept. Def., 1992-1993. Mem. Bd. Vis., US Mil. Acad., 1993-97; bd. vis., Univ. Mich. Law Sch.; gen. counsel The Goldwater Found., Washington, 1988—; trustee Aerospace Corp., El Segundo, Calif., 1990—; dir. Edn. for Employment Found., 2003-. Atty. JAG Corps US Army, 1971—75. Mem. Am. Soc. Internat. Law, Coun. Fgn. Rels. Office: Arnold & Porter 555 12th St NW Washington DC 20004-1206 Office Phone: 202-942-5115. Office Fax: 202-942-5999. Business E-Mail: jeffrey.smith@aporter.com.

SMITH, JEFFREY MICHAEL, lawyer; b. Mpls., July 9, 1947; s. Philip and Gertrude E. (Miller) S.; 1 son, Brandon Michael. Student, U. Malaya, Kuala Lumpur, 1967—68; BA summa cum laude, U. Minn., Mpls., 1970, JD magna cum laude, 1973. Bar: Ga. 1973. Assoc. Powell, Goldstein, Frazier & Murphy, 1973-76; ptnr. Rogers & Hardin, 1976-79, Bondurant, Stephenson & Smith, 1979-85, Arnall, Golden & Gregory, 1985-92, Katz, Smith & Cohen, 1992-98; prin. shareholder Greenberg Traurig LLP, 1998—. Hon. prof., Ctrl. U. Fin. and Economics, Beijing, 2008-; vis. lectr. Duke U., 1976-77, 79-80, 89-93; adj. prof. Emory U., 1976-79, 81-82; lectr. Vanderbilt U., 1977-82. Editor, reviewer Accountant's Legal Liability, 1981; co-author: Preventing Legal Malpractice, 1999, Legal Malpractice, 2009, Legal Opinions in Business Transactions, 2009. Bd. dirs. Atlanta Cmty. Food Bank, 2007-; bd. trustees UNICEF, USA, 2007-09; Bd. visitors Law Sch. U. Minn., 1976-82. Mem. ABA (vice-chmn. com. profl. liability 1980-82, mem. standing com. lawyers's profl. liability 1981-85, chmn. 1985-87, standing com. lawyer competency 1993-95), State Bar Ga. (chmn. profl. liability and ins. com. 1978-89, trustee Inst. Cont. Legal Edn. in Ga. 1979-80), Order of the Coif, Phi Beta Kappa. Home: 145 15th St NE Unit 811 Atlanta GA 30309-3559 Office Phone: 678-553-2333. Business E-Mail: smithj@gtlaw.com.

SMITH, JEROME, not-for-profit developer, film producer, writer; b. Birmingham, Ala., Sept. 10, 1956; s. Herny Horace and Susie Govan Smith. BS in Edn., Daniel Payne Coll., Birmingham, Ala., 1979. Cert. tchr. Ala., Ohio. Tchr. Birmingham Bd. of Edn., Ala., 1979—84, Cleve. Bd. of Edn., 1984—95; CEO Poise Entertainment Edn., Cleve., 1999—. Ednl. prodr. Urban League, Cleve., 2001—03, United Black Fund, Cleve., 2000—03, Rock and Roll Hall of Fame, Cleve., 1999—, dir. cmty. svc., 2003—; songwriter Hilltop Records, Hollywood, Calif., 2004—; TV host You Can Do It Program. Author: Greatest You Can Do It Program, 2004; host, prodr. Poise Entertainment Edn. Co.'s "You Can Do It Program" Hall of Fame and Mus. Recipient Best Song honors, Hilltop Records, Best Songwriter honors, Americord, Cmty. Svc. award, Help Educate for Svc.; named to Nat. Dean's List; grantee, Urban League, 2002, United Black Fund, 2003, Ward 7 City of Cleve., 2004. Baptist. Avocations: songwriting, horseback riding. Office: Poise Entertainment Edn Co 15115 Elm Ave Cleveland OH 44112 Office Phone: 216-561-0277. Personal E-mail: poiseed@aol.com, jeromesmith5238@sbcglobal.net.

SMITH, JERRY EDWIN, federal judge; b. Del Rio, Tex., Nov. 7, 1946; s. Lemuel Edwin and Ruth Irene (Henderson) Smith; m. Mary Jane Blackburn, June 4, 1977; children: Clark, Ruth Ann, J.J. BA, Yale U., 1969, JD, 1972. Bar: Tex. 1972. Law clk. to judge US Dist. Ct. (no. dist.) Tex., Lubbock, 1972—73; assoc. then ptnr. Fulbright & Jaworski, Houston, 1973—84; dir. Harris County housing auth., Tex., 1978—80; special asst. office of atty. gen., Tex., 1981—82; Chmn. Houston Civ. Svc. Comm., 1982—84; city atty. City of Houston, 1984—87; judge US Ct. Appeals (5th cir.), Houston, 1988—. Chmn. Harris County Rep. Party, Houston, 1977—78; committeeman State Rep. Exec. Com., Tex., 1976—88. Mem.: Houston Bar Assn., State Bar Tex. Methodist. Office: US Ct Appeals Bob Casey US Courthouse 515 Rusk St Rm 12621 Houston TX 77002-2698*

SMITH, JESSE GRAHAM, JR., dermatologist, educator; b. Winston-Salem, NC, Nov. 22, 1928; s. Jesse Graham and Pauline Field (Griffith) S.; m. Dorothy Jean Butler, Dec. 28, 1950; children: Jesse Graham, Cynthia Lynn, Grant Butler. BSM, Duke U., 1962, MD, 1951. Diplomate: Am. Bd. Dermatology (dir. 1974-83, pres. 1980-81). Intern VA Hosp., Chamblee, Ga., 1951—52; resident in dermatology Duke U., 1954—56, assoc. prof. dermatology, 1960—62, prof., 1962—67; resident U. Miami, 1956—57, asst. prof., 1956—60; prof. dermatology Med. Coll. Ga., 1967—91, chmn. dept. dermatology, 1967—91, acting chmn. dept. pathology, 1973—75, acting v.p. devel., 1984—85; chief staff Talmadge Meml. Hosp., Augusta, Ga., 1970—72; chief divsn. of dermatology U. South Ala., Mobile, 1991—98, prof. dermatology, 1991—99, prof. emeritus, 1999—. Mem. adv. coun. Nat. Inst. Arthritis, 1975-79 Mem. editl. bd. Archives of Dermatology, 1963-72, Jour. Investigative Dermatology, 1966-67, Jour. AMA, 1974-80; mem. editl. bd. So. Med. Jour., 1976-2000, assoc. editor, 1991-92, editor, 1992-2000; editor Jour. Am. Acad. Dermatology, 1978-88; contbr. chpts. to books, articles to profl. jours. Served with USPHS, 1952-54. Recipient Disting. Alumnus award Duke U. 1981 Fellow ACP, Royal Soc. Medicine; mem. Am. Acad. Dermatology (hon., dir. 1971-74, 78-88, pres.-elect 1988-89, pres. 1989-90, master 2003), Can. Dermatol. Assn. (hon.), Am. Dermatol. Assn. (hon. sec. 1976-81, pres. 1981-82), Soc. Investigative Dermatology (dir. 1964-69, pres. 1979-80), S.E. Dermatol. Assn. (sec. 1970-71, pres. 1975-76), Ga. Soc. Dermatology (pres. 1979-80), So. Med. Assn. (chmn. sect. dermatology 1973-74, Disting. Svc. award 2005), Assn. Profs. Dermatology (dir. 1976-77, 80-82, pres. 1984-86), Med. Rsch. Found. Ga. (bd. dir. 1967-91, pres. 1974-75), Alpha Omega Alpha Home: 4272 Bit and Spur # 4 Mobile AL 36608 Office: Diagnostic and Med Clinic 1700 Spring Hill Ave Mobile AL 36604-1407 Office Phone: 251-435-1200. E-mail: skeesmith@mindspring.com.

SMITH, JESSIE P. DOWLING, retired social services administrator; b. Sturgills, NC, June 15, 1918; d. Rohe V. and Stella Pennington (Eller) Smith; m. F. P. Smith, July 22, 1983. AB, Berea Coll., 1939; MSW, Columbia U., 1945. Social work assignments WPA, Ky., 1939—43; social worker ARC, New Orleans, 1943—45, Bklyn., 1943—45, Huntington, W.Va., 1946—56, Washington, 1946—56; instr. Sch. Social Work W.Va. U., Morgantown, 1953—54; cons. W.Va. Dept. Mental Health, Charleston, 1954—55; program supr. USPHS Clin. Ctr., Bethesda, Md., 1956—62; cons., social work NIMH, Chgo., 1962—66, NYC, 1962—66; assoc. regional health dir. Mental Health Programs, NYC, 1966—81; ret., 1981; v.p. adv. bd. Mental Retardation Substance Abuse Programs Davidson County Mental Health, NC, 1987—89, pres., 1988—89. Pres. resident coun. Thomas House Sr. Residence, Washington, 1999—2001, 2009—. Mem.: NASW (exec. bd. 1968—70, pioneer steering com. 1999—, pres. Washington Met. Area chpt., pioneer 1998—), Columbia U. Alumni Fedn. Bd., Columbia U. Sch. Social Work Alumni Assn. (pres. 1979—81), Columbia U. Sch. Social Work (adv. coun.), Social Casework (editl. adv. bd. 1968—70), NC Coun. of Cmty. Mental Health Programs (adv. bd. 1987—92). Home: Apt 703 1330 Massachusetts Ave NW Washington DC 20005-4154 Home Phone: 202-737-4578.

SMITH, JIMMIE DEE, lawyer; BBA, No. Ariz. U.; JD, Ariz. State U., 1970. Solo law practice, Yuma, Ariz., 1970—. Mem.: State Bar Ariz. Bd. Govs. (sec.-treas., 2nd v.p., 1st v.p., pres.-elect 2005—06, pres. 2006—07), Yuma County Bar Assn. (former pres.). Office: Atty at Law 221 S 2nd Ave Yuma AZ 85364-2265 Office Phone: 928-783-7809. Office Fax: 928-783-7800. E-mail: jimmiedeesmith@azbar.org.

SMITH, JIMMY WAYNE, SR., forensic specialist; s. William Moody Smith and Virginia M. Howard, Robert D. Howard (Stepfather); m. Kathleen B. Chandler; children: Tonya N., Jimmy Jr. W. BS in Acctg., U. Sci. and Arts of Okla., 1984, BS in Sociology, 1984. Cert. Am. Bd. Forensic Document Examiners. Lt. Chickasha (Okla.) Police Dept., 1969—85; investigator, forensic document examiner Okla. Insp. Gen., Oklahoma City, 1985—95; forensic document examiner Las Vegas (Nev.) Met. Police Dept., 1995—. Author: (research) Using an Alternative light Source to Restore Writing (Publ. JFS). Fellow: Am. Acad. Forensic Scis. (sec. 2005—); mem.: Assn. Cert. Fraud Examiners, Southwestern Assn. Forensic Document Examiners (new letter editor 1994—98, bd. dirs. 1995—99). Achievements include research in using an alternative light source to restore writing. Office: Las Vegas Metropolitan Police Department 5605 W Badura Ave Ste 120B Las Vegas NV 89118 Personal E-mail: cherokee48@cox.net. Business E-Mail: j4927s@lvmpd.com.

SMITH, JOAN H., retired women's health nurse, educator; b. Akron, Ohio; d. Joseph A. and Troynette M. (Lower) McDonald; m. William G. Smith; children: Sue Ann, Priscilla, Timothy. Diploma, Akron City Hosp., 1948; BSN in Edn., U. Akron, 1972, MA in Family Devel., 1980. Cert. in inpatient obstetric nursing. Mem. faculty Akron Gen. Med. Ctr. Sch. Nursing, 1964; former dir. obstet. spl. procedures Speakers Bur., Women's Health Ctrs. Akron Gen. Med. Ctr., 1988; ret., 1990. Cons., speaker women's health care. Mem. Assn. Women's Health, Obstet. and Neonatal Nursing (charter, past sec.-treas., past vice chmn. Ohio sect., chmn. program various confs.). Home: 873 Kirkwall Dr Copley OH 44321-1751

SMITH, JOANN CARROLL, library and information scientist; m. Michael Smith; children: Jenifer Jeané Wilkinson, Jonna Jarie Hawkins. BS, U. Ala., Tuscaloosa, 1972; MA, U. of Ala., Tuscaloosa, 1974; EdS, U. Ala., 1979; M in Libr. Svc., U. of Ala., Tuscaloosa, 1984, EdS level in Libr. Svc., 1993. Cert. Tchr. Tenn., 1997, Ala., 1972. Libr. media specialist Sullivan East HS, Bluff City, Tenn., 1997—2001, Sullivan South HS, Kingsport, Tenn., 2001—. Mem. bd. examiners Nat. Coun. Accreditation Tchr. Edn., bd. dirs. Treas. PACE Polit., North Johnson City Bapt., Johnson City, Tenn., 2004—06; dist. 1 dir. Tenn. Edn. Assn., Nashville, 2002—05. Recipient Oustanding Svc. to Ala. Librs., Libr. and Media Profls., 1996—97. Mem.: NEA, Tenn. Edn. Assn. (chair nea concerns com. 2002—04, bd. dirs. 2002—05, chair human rels. com. 2004—05), Sullivan County Edn. Assn. (pres. 1999—2001, treas. 2001—06, pres. 2006—), Tenn. Assn. Sch. Librs. (chair constn. and bylaws 2006—), Delta Kappa Gamma. Baptist. Avocations: reading, singing, travel. Home: 141 Bentley Parc Johnson City TN 37615 Office: Sullivan South HS Libr 1236 Moreland Dr Kingsport TN 37664 Home Fax: 423-283-9037. Personal E-mail: joannsmi@yahoo.com.

SMITH, JOANNE, marketing executive; Mgr. aviation mktg. & cargo sales DHL, v.p. mktg. planning; v.p. mktg. customers Song Airlines, 2003—05, pres., 2005—06; v.p. mktg. Delta Air Lines Inc., 2006—07, sr. v.p. flight services & global product devel., 2007—. Named a Woman to Watch, Advt. Age, 2007; named one of 50 Women to Watch, The Wall St. Jour., 2008. Office: Delta Air Lines Inc PO Box 20706 Atlanta GA 30320-6001 Office Phone: 404-715-2600.*

SMITH, JOANNE C., health facility administrator; b. 1962; m. Rory Repicky; 2 children. BS, Oakland U.; MD, Michigan State U.; MBA, U. Of Chgo. Grad. Sch. Of Bus. Cert. Physical Medicine and Rehabilitation. Chief residency Northwestern U. Med. Sch.; attending physician Rehabilitation Inst. of Chgo., 1992—94, med. dir. Day Rehabilitation Centers program, 1994—95, sr. v.p., COO Corp. Partnerships, 1995—97, sr. v.p. Corp. Strategy and Bus. Devel., 1997—2002, pres. nat. divsn., 2005—06, pres. CEO, 2006—. Asst. prof. Physical Medicine and Rehabilitation at Northwestern U. Feinberg Sch. of Medicine; founder Women's Health Rehabilitation program, Rehabilitation Inst. of Chgo.; vice-chmn. Hillenbrand Industries Inc., mem. bd. dirs., Aptar-Group Inc. Named a Woman to Watch, Crain's Chgo. Bus., 2007; named one of Chicago's 'Top Doctors', Chgo. Mag., 2004, 2005, 2006. Mem.: The Chgo. Network. Office: Rehabilitation Inst of Chgo 345 E Superior St Chicago IL 60611 Office Phone: 312-238-6044.*

SMITH, JOANNE GENEVIEVE, nursing educator; d. Robert S. and Patricia A. Walters; m. Ronald E. Smith, Apr. 14, 1982; children: Jennifer L. Ledden, Christina M., Robert M., Richard A. ADN, Kankakee CC, Ill., 1996; BSN, U. Phoenix, Ariz., 2004, MSN, 2005. RN Ill., 1996. Surg. RN Provena St. Mary's Hosp., Kankakee, 1996—2005; prof. nursing Kankakee CC, 2005—. Mem.: Sigma Theta Tau Internat. Achievements include research in DHA. Office: Kakakee CC 100 College Dr Kankakee IL 60901

SMITH, JOBETH, elementary school educator; b. Houston, Sept. 3, 1955; d. Fred Tillman and JoBeth Lambert; m. Norman Kendall Smith, June 15, 1979; children: Amy Leeanne Hancock Smith, Kelli Elizabeth. AA, Lon Morris Coll., Jacksonville, Tex., 1975; BS, Tex. Wesleyan Coll., Ft. Worth, 1978. Cert. Provisional Elem. and Music Tex., 1978. Tchr. Aldine Ind. Sch. Dist., Houston, 1978—79, Everman Ind. Sch. Dist., Ft.Worth, 1979—80, Kate Burgess Elem. Sch., Wichita Falls, Tex., 1980—82; music specialist Austin Elem. Sch., Wichita Falls, 1982—87, Jefferson Elem. Sch., Wichita Falls, 1987—97, Maedgen Elem. Sch., Lubbock, Tex., 1997—2006, Rockenbaugh Elem. Sch., Southlake, Tex., 2006—. Dir. elem. choral Jefferson Honor Choir, Wichita Falls, 1987—97, Maedgen Elem., Lubbock, 1997—2006, dir. elem. chimes & boomwhacker ensemble, 1997—2006; dir. all city elem. choir Lubbock Ind. Sch. Dist., 1998—2000, Wichita Falls Ind. Sch. Dist., 1990—97. Composer: (elem. music composition) Parting Song (Music K-8 Mag. Contbr., 2000). Musician City Of Lubbock Newcomers & Christmas Tour, 2000—01, Sweet Adelines, Wichita Falls, 1980—82; dir. Miracle on 34th St. Parade, Tex., 2004—05; musician Civic Chorus, Wichita Falls, 1980—82, Wesley United Meth. Ch., Wichita Falls, 1983—97, St. Luke's United Meth. Ch., Lubbock, 1997—2006. Recipient Lubbock Avalanche- Jour., Best Elem. Music Tchr., City of Lubbock, 2004, Extra Mile Award, United Meth. Ch., 1982, Lubbock Ind. Sch. Dist. Tchr. Spotlight, Glen Teal, Prin. Maedgen Elem., 2006, West Found. Excellence in Tchg. award, Wichita Falls Ind. Sch. Dist., 1990, Wichita Falls. Ind. Sch. Dist., 1994, Tchr. of Yr., Ladies Aux. VFW, 1992, KLUR Tchr. of Yr., Wichita Falls, 1987; named Tchr. of Yr., Wichita Fall Ind. Sch. Dist., 1991, KLUR Tchr. of Week, Wichita Falls, 1996, 1987, 1988; named to Who's Who Among Am. Tchrs., Former Students, 1996, 1994, 1998, 2006; scholar Harvard U. Grad. Sch. of Edn. Assessment, Wichita Falls Ind. Sch. Dist., 1991. Mem.: Tex. Music Educators Assn. (assoc.), Tex. Congress Parent and Tchr. (life). R-Consevative. Methodist. Avocations: travel, music. Home: 10220 Renwick Cove Keller TX 76248 Office: Rockenbaugh Elem Sch 301 Byron Nelson Pkwy Southlake TX 76092

SMITH, JOE (JOSEPH LEYNARD SMITH), professional basketball player; b. Norfolk, Va., July 26, 1975; Grad., U. Md., 1995. Forward Golden State Warriors, 1995-97, Phila. 76ers, 1997—98, 2006—07, Minn. Timberwolves, 1998—2000, 2001—03, Detroit Pistons, 2000—01, Milw. Bucks, 2003—06, Denver Nuggets, 2006—07, Chgo. Bulls, 2007—08, Cleve. Cavaliers, 2008, 2009, Oklahoma City Thunder, 2008—09, Atlanta Hawks, 2009—. Actor: (films) Rebound, 1996. Named 1st Team All-Am., AP, 1995, NCAA Player of Yr., 1995, Naismith Coll. Player of Yr., 1995; named to NBA All-Rookie Team, 1996. Achievements include being the first overall pick in the NBA Draft, 1995. Office: Atlanta Hawks 101 Marietta St NW Ste 1900 Atlanta GA 30303*

SMITH, JOELLEN, dean, literature and language educator; b. Johnstown, Pa., May 1, 1957; d. Joseph J. and Ellen I. Piskura; m. Edward Smith, July 18, 1981 (div. Apr. 1, 2005); 1 child, Matthew Edward. BS in Elem. Edn., U. Pitts., 1981; MEd in Instrnl. Tech., Am. Intercontinental U., 2004. Cert. tchr. Tex., 1988, user specialist Microsoft Office, 2005. Tchr. St. Thomas More Parish Sch., Houston, 1986—, dean of students, lang. arts coord., 1993—. Mem. critical thinking curriculum Diocese of Galveston-Houston, 1988—89, accreditation team mem., 1996—2004, mem. lang. arts curriculum, 1996—2003; trainer, presenter Profile Approach to Writing Evaluation, College Station, Tex., 1998—99. Grantee Tech. Grant, U. St. Thomas, Houston Endowment, 2004-2005. Mem.: ASCD, Am. Classical League, Internat. Reading Assn., Nat. Mid. Sch. Assn., Nat. Coun. Teachers English. Home: 2210 Mustang Springs Dr Missouri City TX 77459 Office: St Thomas More Parish Sch 5927 Wigton St Houston TX 77096 Business E-Mail: jsmith@stmorenews.com.

SMITH, JOHN B., publishing executive; b. LaGrange, Ga. s. John Watson and Pressarene Whitfield Smith; m. Frances M. Evans; children: Pamela, Lori, John B. Jr. BS, Morehouse Coll.; MA, Atlanta U. Tchr. Price High Sch., Atlanta; part-time advt. salesman Atlanta Inquirer, 1961, pub., CEO, pres. Bd. dirs. Atlanta Fair & Exposition, Grade Homes Boys' Club, Boy Scouts of Am. Named Young Man of Yr.; named one of Most Influential Black Americans, Ebony mag., 2006, 25 City Shapers, Atlanta Mag.; named to Power 150, Ebony mag., 2008. Mem.: Nat. Newspaper Publishers Assn. (mem. bd. dirs., 2nd vice chair, 1st vice chair 2003, Publisher of Yr. Award). Office: Nat Newspaper Pub Assn 3200 13th St, NW Washington DC 20010

SMITH, JOHN BREWSTER, library administrator; b. Bryan, Tex., June 26, 1937; s. Elmer Gillam and Sara Roland (Lull) S.; m. Ida Hawa, Dec. 28, 1963; children: Susan Helen, Rona Esther. BA, Tex. A & M U., 1960; MS, Columbia U., 1963, cert. advanced librarianship, 1984, DLS, 1991. Asst. law librarian Columbia U., NYC, 1963-66; asst. library dir. for pub. services Tex. A & M U., College Station, 1966-69, dir. libraries, 1969-74; dir. libraries, dean library scis. SUNY, Stony Brook, 1974-96, dir. library and info. sci. tchg. program, 1996-97; chief libr. Bronx Cmty. Coll., CUNY, 1997-2000, cons. on libr. mgmt., 2000—. Named Librarian of Year Tex. Library Assn., 1972 Mem. ALA. Home: 6505 Bramber Ln Austin TX 78754-5784 Office Phone: 512-863-2835. Personal E-mail: jscounterpoint@yahoo.com.

SMITH, JOHN EDWIN, philosophy educator; b. Bklyn., May 27, 1921; s. Joseph Robert and Florence Grace (Dunn) S.; m. Marilyn Blanche Schulhof, Aug. 25, 1951; children: Robin Dunn, Diana Edwards. AB, Columbia U., 1942, PhD, 1948; BD, Union Theol. Sem., NYC, 1945; MA, Yale U., 1959; LL.D., U. Notre Dame, 1964. Instr. religion and philosophy Vassar Coll., 1945-46; instr., then asst. prof. Barnard Coll., 1946-52; mem. faculty Yale U., 1952—, prof. philosophy, 1959—, chmn. dept., 1961—, Clark prof. philosophy, 1972-91, Clark prof. philosophy emeritus, 1991—. Vis. prof. Union Theol. Sem., 1959, U. Mich., 1958; guest prof. U. Heidelberg, Germany, 1955-56; Fagothey chair of philosophy U. Santa Clara, 1984, vis. prof. Boston Coll., 1992; Dudleian lectr. Harvard, 1960; lectr. Am. Week, U. Munich, Germany, 1961; Suarez lectr. Fordham U., 1963; pub. lectr. King's College, Univ. London, 1965; Aquinas lectr. Marquette U., 1967; Warfield lectr. Princeton Theol. Sem., 1970; Fulbright lectr. Kyoto U., Japan, 1971; Sprunt lectr. Union Theol. Sem., Va., 1973; Mead-Swing lectr. Oberlin Coll., 1975; H. Richard Niebuhr lectr. Elmhurst Coll., Ill., 1977; Merrick lectr. Ohio Wesleyan U., 1977; Roy Wood Sellars lectr. Bucknell U., 1978; O'Hara lectr. U. Notre Dame, 1984; Winston Churchill lectr. Bristol (Eng.) U., 1985; Hooker disting. vis. prof. Mc Master U., 1985; mem. adv. com. Nat. Humanities Inst., New Haven, 1974, dir., 1977-80; Winston Churchill lectr. Bristol U., Eng., 1985. Author: Royce's Social Infinite, 1950, Value Convictions and Higher Education, 1958, Reason and God, 1961, The Spirit of American Philosophy, 1963, 2d edit., 1983, The Philosophy of Religion, 1965, Religion and Empiricism, 1967, Experience and God, 1968, revised edit., 1995, Themes in American Philosophy, 1970, Contemporary American Philosophy, 1970, The Analogy of Experience, 1973, Purpose and Thought: The Meaning of Pragmatism, 1978, America's Philosophical Vision, 1992, Jonathan Edwards, Puritan, Preacher, Philosopher, 1992, Quasi-Religions: Humanism, Marxism, Nationalism, 1994, Reason, Experience, and God, 1997; translator: (R. Kroner): Kant's Weltanschauung, 1956; editor: (Jonathan Edwards): Religious Affections, Vol. 2, 1959, An Edwards Reader, 1995; gen. editor, Yale edit.: Works of Jonathan Edwards, 1965-91, gen. editor emeritus, 1992—; Editorial bd.: Monist, 1962—, Jour. Religious Studies, Philosophy East and West, Jour. Chinese Philosophy, The Personalist Forum, Jour. Faith and Philosophy, Jour. Speculative Philosophy. Named Hon. Alumnus, Harvard Div. Sch., 1960; recipient Herbert W. Schneider award Soc. for Advancement of Am. Philosophy, 1990, Founder's medal Metaphys. Soc. Am., 1996; Am. Coun. Learned Socs. fellow, 1964-65. Mem. Culinary Inst. Am. (dir. New Haven affiliate), Am. Philos. Assn. (v.p. 1980, pres. 1981), Am. Theol. Soc. (pres. 1967-68), Metaphys. Soc. Am. (pres. 1970-71, founder's medal, 1996), Hegel Soc. Am. (pres. 1971), Charles S. Peirce Soc. (pres. 1992). Home: 300 Ridgewood Ave Hamden CT 06517-1428 Office: PO Box 201562 New Haven CT 06520-1562 E-mail: john.smith@yale.edu.

SMITH, JOHN F., automotive executive; b. Kansas City, Mo. Grad. in engring., Gen. Motors Inst. (now Kettering U.), Flint, Mich., 1973; M in Bus., Harvard U. Bus. Sch., Mass., 1976. Joined Chevrolet-Kansas City assembly plant Gen. Motors Corp., 1968, various analytical and exec. positions, treasurer's office NYC, 1976—82, mem. comptroller's staff, 1982—83, asst. comptr., Pontiac, 1983—84, asst. comptr., Buick-Oldsmobile-Cadillac group, 1984—85, mem. internat. joint venture programs, Chevrolet-Pontiac-Gen. Motors Can. group, 1985—87, dir. planning, Buick-Oldsmobile-Cadillac group, 1987—89, v.p. planning, Europe, 1989—94, pres., Allison Transmission Indpls., 1994—97, v.p., gen. mgr., Cadillac Motor Car divsn., 1997—2000, v.p., gen. mgr., svc. parts ops., 2000—02, v.p., gen. mgr., field sales, svc. and parts, 2002—03, group v.p., No. America vehicle sales, svc. and mktg., 2003—05, group v.p., global product planning, 2005—. Past chair, mem. bd. dirs., Detroit Area Coun. Boy Scouts America, nat. exec. bd. dirs.; gen. chair United Way Torch Dr., 2001, 2002; bd. mem. United Way, Detroit, Detroit Inst. Art, St. John Health. Recipient Sagamore and Wabash award, State of Ind., Disting. Eagle Scout award, Boy Scouts America. Office: Gen Motors Corp PO Box 33170 Detroit MI 48232-5170*

SMITH, JOHN FRANCIS, JR., (JACK SMITH), retired automotive executive; b. Worcester, Mass., Apr. 6, 1938; s. John Francis and Eleanor C. (Sullivan) S.; children: Brian, Kevin; m. Lydia G. Sigrist, Aug. 27, 1988; 1 stepchild, Nicola. BBA, U. Mass., 1960; MBA, Boston U., 1965. Fisher Body divsn. mgr. GM, Framingham, Mass., 1961-73, asst. treas. NYC, 1973-80, comptr. Detroit, 1980-81, dir. worldwide product planning, 1981-84, pres., gen. mgr. Oshawa, Ont., Canada, 1984-85, exec. v.p. internat. ops. Detroit, 1988-90, vice chmn. internat. ops., 1990, bd. dirs., mem. fin. com., 1990-98, COO, 1992, CEO, 1992—2000, pres., 1992—98, chmn. bd., 1996—2003; exec. v.p. GM Europe, Glattbrugg, Switzerland, 1986-87, pres., 1987-88. Mem. US Japan Bus. Coun.; bus. coun. Meml. Sloan-Kettering Cancer Ctr.; bd. dirs. Procter & Gamble Co., 1995-2008, Delta Air Lines Inc., 2000-2007, non-exec. chmn., 2004-2007; chmn. adv. bd. Alix Ptnrs. LLC/Questor Ptnrs. Funds. Mem. chancellor's exec. com. U. Mass., dir.; trustee United Way SE Mich., New Am. Revolution, Boston U.; bd. dirs. The Nature Conservancy. Mem. Am. Soc. Corp. Execs., Am. Auto Mfrs. Assn. (bd. dirs.), Econ. Club Detroit (bd. dirs.), The Bus. Coun., Beta Gamma Sigma (pres.), Dirs. Table. Roman Catholic.

SMITH, JOHN FRANCIS, III, lawyer; b. White Plains, N.Y., Sept. 24, 1941; s. John Francis and Mary Dake (Mairs) S.; m. Susan Brown; children: John, Stephen, Peter. AB, Princeton U., 1963; LLB, Yale U., 1970. Bar: Pa. 1970, U.S. Supreme Ct. 1985. Assoc. Dilworth, Paxson, Kalish & Kauffman, Phila., 1970-75, ptnr., 1975-86, sr. ptnr., 1986-91; sr. litigation ptnr. Reed Smith LLP, Phila., 1991—, mem. exec. com., 1993-04; chancellor Reed Smith U., 2004—. Mem. exec. com. Employment Discrimination Referral Project, 1971-74; pres. Society Hill Civic Assn., 1975-76, Phila. Chamber Ensemble, 1977-80; bd. govs. Economy League Greater Phila., 1983—, sec. 1995-97; vice chair, 2008, chair, 2009; bd. dirs. World Affairs Council Phila., 1983-87, chmn. program com., 1986-87; Burn Found., 1987-95, Internat. House Phila., bd. trustees, 2004-, chmn., 2005-09; moderator Main Line Unitarian Ch., 1986-89, 2000—; founder and pres. Found. for Individual Responsibility and Social Trust (FIRST), 1995-2000. Served to lt. (j.g.) USNR, 1963-67; Vietnam. Fellow Am. Bar Found.; mem. ABA, Unitarian Universalist Assn. (pres.'s coun.), Yale Law Sch. Alumni Assn. (exec. com. 1982-88, sec. 1987-88). Office: Reed Smith LLP 2500 One Liberty Pl Philadelphia PA 19103 Home Phone: 610-527-3320; Office Phone: 215-241-7920. E-mail: jfsmith@reedsmith.com.

SMITH, JOHN MORTIMER FOURETTE, bishop; b. Orange, NJ, June 23, 1935; Student, Immaculate Conception Sem., Darlington, NJ, South Orange, NJ, Cath. U., Washington. Ordained priest Archdiocese of Newark, NJ, 1961, aux. bishop, 1987—91; ordained bishop, 1988; coadjutor bishop Diocese of Trenton, 1995—97, bishop, 1997—. Roman Catholic. Office Phone: 609-406-7400. Office Fax: 609-406-7412.

SMITH, JOHN POWELL, entomologist, educator; b. Lenoir, Nc., July 24, 1952; s. John Henry and Rebecca Caroline Smith; m. Catherine Anne Santos, Mar. 22, 1980; children: Sarah Emily, Rebecca Marie Haynie, Meagan Blair, John William. BS in Agr. - Microbiology, U. Ga., Athens, 1979, MS in Plant Protection and Pest Mgmt., 1984; PhD in Entomology, Clemson U., SC, 2003. Cert. crop advisor Am. Soc. Agronomy, 1996. Crop rsch. supt. A. Duda & Sons, Oveido, Fla., 1984—86; tech. svcs. rep. So. Agrl. Insecticides, Hendersonville, NC, 1986—87; plant health specialist Van Wingerden Internat., Fletcher, NC, 1987—88; ext. educator Clemson Coop. Ext. Svc., Lexington, SC, 1988—. Agrl. cons. USAID-CRSP, Tamale, Ghana, 1997. Hosp. corpsman 2nd class US Navy, 1972—76, Camp Lejeune, NC. Recipient Superior Performance award, Clemson U. Coop. Ext. Svc., 1998, Achievement award, Nat. Assn. County Agrl. Agents, 1996; finalist, 2006. Mem.: Entomol. Soc. America, Am. Phytopathological Soc., SC Nat. Assn. County Agrl. Agents. Home: 158 Thedo Bush Rd Gilbert SC 29054 Office: CUCES-Lexington County 605 W Main St Ste 109 Lexington SC 29072 Business E-Mail: jpsmth@clemson.edu.

SMITH, JOHN W(ESLEY), JR., data processing executive, consultant; b. Bklyn., Jan. 6, 1946; s. John Wesley and Eunice (Davis) S.; m. Carolyn Ferrebbee, Aug. 19, 1971 (div. 1980); children: John Wesley III, Janine Carol. Student, NYU, 1989—. Supr. computer ops. Shearson Lehman Stone, Inc., NYC, 1967—70; sr. ops. analyst Fin. Data Svcs., Inc., NYC, 1970—77; coord. tng. program Chem. Bank, NYC, 1977—78; sr. hardware analyst ADP, Clifton, NJ, 1978—79; adminstr. data base Depository Trust Co., NYC, 1979—81; mgr. data ctr. ops. Leviton Mfg. Co., Littleneck, NY, 1981—83; dir. corp. info. svcs. Reed Robert's Assocs., Inc., Uniondale, 1983—86; dir. prodn. planning and control Human Resource Adminstrn., NYC, 1986—87; mgmt. cons. Asbach/Sci., Inc., NYC, 1987—. Mem. Data Processing Mgmt. Assn., Am. Soc. Notaries, Am. Mgmt. Assn., Am. Arbitration Assn. (comml. panel 1983—), Inst. Certification Computer Profls. (cert systems profl.). Avocation: real estate.

SMITH, JOHN WILLIAM HUGH, civil engineer; b. Port Arthur, Ont., Can., Oct. 16, 1937; s. George Edward and Nina Edith Smith; m. Anne Patten; children: Scott, Steven, Richard. AA with honors, Lakehead U., Thunder Bay, Ont., 1959; BSCE with honors, Mich. Tech. U., 1962. Proposal engr. Surface Combustion Div. Midland-Ross Corp., Toledo, 1962-65, sr. project engr. Toronto, 1965-70; div. mgr. Holcroft & Co. (Can.) Ltd., London, Ont., 1970-76; mgr. engring. Holcroft, Livonia, Mich., 1976-81, tech. dir., mgr., sales and mktg., v.p., tech. dir., 1981-93; pres. Sterling Systems, Royal Oak, Mich., 1993—2004, John W. Smith Engring Svcs., LLC, Waldport, Oreg., 2004—. Contbr. chpts. to books; patentee in field. Mem. Am. Soc. Metals Internat. Office: JWSES 691 NW Legion Rd PO Box 665 Waldport OR 97394 Office Phone: 541-961-3784. Business E-Mail: john.smith@jwses.com.

SMITH, JONATHAN CHARLES, dancer, educator; b. Port Arthur, Tex., Nov. 27, 1948; s. June Rose Smith; 1 child, Jordan O'Hara. BA in Dance, U. Houston, Clear Lake, Tex., 1993; MFA in Dance, Sam Houston State U., Tex., 2000. Prin. dancer Kans. City Ballet, Mo., 1974—79; choreographer Theatre Under Stars, Houston, 1980—95, Miss Tex. Scholarship Orgn., Font Worthj, 2000—08; tchr. Theatre Under Stars, dancer. (musical) A Chorus Line. Mem.: Actor Equity Assn. (assoc.). Democrat. Office: Sam Houston State Univ PO Box: 2269 Huntsville TX 77340 Office Fax: 936-294-3954. Business E-Mail: dnc_jcs@shsu.edu.

SMITH, JOSEPH A., JR., state banking agency administrator; b. Charleston, W.Va., Nov. 9, 1949; m. Elizabeth Marion; children: Joseph A. III, Matthew M. BA in Hist., Davidson Coll., 1971; JD, U. Va., 1975. Bar: NY 1975, NC 1989. Assoc. atty. pub. fin. Brown, Wood, Ivey, Mitchell & Petty (now Sidley, Austin, Brown & Wood), NYC, 1975—79; corp. counsel PepsiCo, Inc., Purchase, NY, 1979—84; asst. gen. counsel Emery Air Freight Corp., Wilton, Conn., 1984—88; ptnr. Poyner & Spruill, Raleigh, NC, 1988—91; gen. counsel, sec. Centura Banks, Inc., Rocky Mount, NC, 1991—2000; counsel Thacher, Proffitt & Wood, Washington, 2000—02; commr. of banks NC Banking Commn., 2002—. Contbr. articles to profl. publs. Mem. steering com. UNC Law Sch. Ctr. Banking & Fin. Office: Commr Banks 4309 Mail Svc Ctr Raleigh NC 27699-4309 Office Phone: 919-733-3016. Office Fax: 919-733-6918. E-mail: jsmith@nccob.org.*

SMITH, JOSEPH PHELAN, film company executive; b. NYC, 1911; s. John William and Margaret Mary (Phelan) S.; m. Madelyn Eleanor Davis, Jan. 17, 1942; children: Kevin, Karen, Margaret, Lisa. BS, Columbia U. Former salesman Van Alstyne Noel & Co., NYC, RKO Radio Pictures, Inc., Boston, Omaha, div. mgr., Los Angeles, Portland, Oreg., San Francisco, 1938-47; former exec. v.p. Lippert Prodns., Hollywood, Calif.; former v.p., gen. mgr. sales Telepictures, NYC; founding pres. Cinema Vue Corp.; now chmn. Pathe News Inc., NYC, 1995—, Pathe Pictures Inc., NYC, 1995—. Served with U.S. Army. Mem. Motion Picture Pioneers, Am. Film Inst., Elks. Republican. Office: Pathe News Inc 300 W 43rd St Rm 604 New York NY 10036-6404

SMITH, JUANITA BÉRARD, lawyer, artist; b. St. Martinsville, La., Oct. 23, 1947; d. Zachary Joseph and Lucille Bourque Bérard; m. Mark Christian Smith III, Mar. 16 (dec. 2003); children: Mark IV, Brett, Robyn, Tara. BA in History, Loyola U., La., 1979, JD, 1982. Bar: La. 1982. Pvt. practice, New Orleans, 1982—; pres. Marie Antoinette Hotel, 2003, owner, 2004; pres. 730 Bienville Inc., 2003—, TSL Properties Inc., 2003—, Century Hotels Inc., 2003—; owner, pres. St. Louis Hotel, 2003—, St. Ann Hotel, 2003—, Louis XVI Restaurant, 2003—, La Louisiane Restaurant, 2003—, Woodstone Subdivsn., Mandeville, 2003—, McCrory's, 2003—, Mark Smith Enterprises, 2004. Exhibited in group shows at Alexander and Victor Gallery Fine Art, New Orleans, Alexander and Victor Gallery, Coral Gables, Fla., Palma Gallery, New Orleans, one-woman shows include Louis XVI Gallery, 1987, La Louisiana Gallery, New Orleans, 2004—07. Named one of Women of Yr., New Orleans City Bus., 2004. Mem.: La. State Bar Assn., New Orleans Bar Assn. Avocations: skiing, theology. Office: 730 Bienville Partners Ltd 1000 Iberville St New Orleans LA 70130 Studio: 106 Mariners Island Mandeville LA 70448 Mailing: PO Box 57929 New Orleans LA 70157 Personal E-mail: smith_jb@bellsouth.net.

SMITH, JULIAN CLEVELAND, JR., chemical engineering professor; b. Westmount, Que., Can., Mar. 10, 1919; s. Julian Cleveland and Bertha (Alexander) S.; m. Joan Elsen, June 1, 1946; children: Robert Elsen, Diane Louise Smith Brook, Brian Richard. B.Chemistry, Cornell U., 1941, Chem. Engr., 1942. Chem. engr. E. I. duPont de Nemours and Co., Inc., 1942-46; mem. faculty Cornell U., 1946—, prof. chem. engring., 1953-86, prof. emeritus, 1986—, dir. continuing engring. edn., 1965-71; assoc. dir. Cornell U. (Sch. Chem. Engring.), 1973-75, dir., 1975-83. Vis. lectr. U. Edinburgh, 1971-72; cons. to govt. and industry, 1947-2001; UNESCO cons. Universidad de Oriente, Venezuela, 1975 Author: (with W. L. McCabe and P. Harriott) Unit Operations of Chemical Engineering, 1956, 7th edit., 2005, also articles; sect. editor: Perry's Chemical Engineers' Handbook, 1963. Recipient Warren K. Lewis award, AIChE, 2008. Fellow Am. Inst. Chem. Engrs.; mem. Am. Chem. Soc., Paleontologic Rsch. Instn., Ithaca Country Club, Savage Club, Sigma Xi, Tau Beta Pi, Phi Kappa Phi, Alpha Delta Phi. Home: 208 Savage Farm Dr Ithaca NY 14850-6501 Business E-Mail: jcs29@cornell.edu.

SMITH, JULIE ANN, pharmaceutical executive; BS, Cornell Univ. Mktg. div. Bristol-Myers Squibb; comml. team Novazyme Pharmaceutical Corp.; v.p. product strategy and devel. Genzyme Corp., v.p. global mktg.; v.p., mktg. Jazz Pharmaceuticals, 2006—. Clinical rschr. neuroendocrinology Mass. Gen. Hosp. Named one of 40 Under 40, Boston Bus. Jour., 2005. Office: Jazz Pahrmaceuticals 3180 Porter Dr Palo Alto CA 94304

SMITH, JULIOUS PERRY, JR., lawyer; b. Richmond, Va., Jan. 10, 1943; s. Julious Perry and Mary Inez (Whitlow) S.; m. Sherrill Marie Poehler, July 28, 1967; children: Julious P. III, S. Hayes, Sarah Graham. BS, Hampden-Sydney Coll., Va., 1965; LLB, U. Va., 1968. Bar: Va. 1968, U.S. Dist. Ct. (ea. dist.) Va. 1969. Assoc. Williams Mullen, Richmond, 1968-73, shareholder, 1973—, pres., 1983—99, chmn., CEO, 1999—. Bd. dirs. LandAm. Fin. Group, Inc., 2000—08, Hilb Rogal and Hobbs Co., 2000—08; chmn. Hilb Rogal and Hobbs Co., Nat. Assn. Soc., Va., 2008—; spkr. Joel A. Rose Conf. on Law Firm Mgmt., 1995, 98, 2000, 04, 09; chmn. Mut. Assurance Soc. Va., 2009—. Chmn. profl. divsn. United Way, 1990—92, campaign chmn., 1994—95, de Tocqueville Chair, 2000; Va. state chair U.S. Olympic Com., 1996—2000; trustee Hampden-Sydney Coll., 1996—2005, vice chmn., 2004—06; bd. dirs. Theater Va., pres., 2001—02; chair Multiple Sclerosis Dinner, 2002, CCA-Fin.-Am. Cancer Soc. Golf Championship, 2004; mem. sch. bd. St. Bridget's Cath. Ch., Richmond, 1981—88, chmn. capital fund raising campaign, 1991. Recipient Micheli award Richmond Touchdown Club, 1981, Patrick Henry award Hampden-Sydney Coll., 2003; named to Salvation Army Boys and Girls Club Hall of Fame, 1997 Fellow: Va. Law Found., Am. Coll. Trust and Estate Coun.; mem.: ABA, Va. Found. Independent Coll. (trustee), Chambers Internat. Lawyers, Va. Super 50 Lawyers, Best Lawyers in Am., Va. Legal Elite, Richmond Mgmt. Round Table, Soc. Internat. Bus. Fellows (Va. chair 1996—97), Richmond Bar Assn. (chmn. young lawyers sect. 1973—74, bd. dirs. 1985—87, 1989—92, pres. 1995—96, Hill-Tucker Pub. Svc. award 2005), Va. Bar Assn., Kinloch Golf Club, Farmington Country Club, Forum Club, Country Club Va., Commonwealth Club (bd. govs. 1997—2000, v.p. 2005—07, pres. 2007—09). Roman Catholic. Avocations: reading, sports, travel. Office Phone: 804-783-6408. Business E-Mail: jsmith@williamsmullen.com.

SMITH, KAREN ANN, nutritionist; m. Jerry Thomas Smith, Jan. 2, 1992; children: Nicolina Marie, Rachael Nicole. MS, U. Memphis, Tenn., 1996. Registered dietitian Am. Dietetic Assn., 1987. Clin. coord. St. Jude Children's Rsch. Hosp., Memphis, 2002—; rsch. and edn. coord. Office: Saint Jude Children's Rsch Hosp 332 N Lauderdale St MS 732 Memphis TN 38105-3678 Office Fax: 901-595-3202. Business E-Mail: karen.smith@stjude.org.

SMITH, KAREN L., elementary school educator; b. Shreveport, La., Feb. 18, 1978; d. Willie J. and Carol L. Smith; children: Khalil R. children: Kahlis J. BA in Elem. Edn., La. State U., Shreveport, 2001; MS in Curriculum & Instrn., La. Tech. U. Tchr. Edward Livingston Mid. Sch., New Orleans, 2002—04, Sunset Acres Elem. Sch., Shreveport, 2004—. Asst. tchr. Teach Am., Bronx, 2002. Young women's ministry Bright Star Bapt. Ch., Shreveport, 2008—09. Mem.: Nat. Coun. Tchrs. Math. (assoc.). Conservative. Baptist. Avocations: reading, travel. Office: Sunset Acres Elementary School 6514 W Canal Blvd Shreveport LA 71108 E-mail: klsmith@caddo.k12.la.us.

SMITH, KATHRYN LEE, artist, educator; b. Washington, Aug. 31, 1953; d. Jay Lloyd and Sibyl (Warthen) Smith; m. Joseph Thayer Papaleo (div.); 1 child, Liana Angele. BFA, U. Md., College Park, 1975; coursework, Md. Inst. Art, Balt., 1976, Colo. State U., Ft. Collins, 1984, U. Colo., Boulder, 1984. Ednl. coord. Provincetown Art Assn., Mass., 1998—99; program designer PIAI, Mass., 1998—99; mem. faculty Herman and Mary Robinson Mus. Sch., Provincetown, 1998—; coord. dept continuing edn. Cape Cod C.C., Provincetown, 1999—2000; coord. Dept Acad. Affairs, Provincetown, 2000—01; printmaking instr. Herman and Mary Robinson Mus. Sch., Provincetown, 1991—; instr. prints and drawing Cape Cod CC, Provincetown, 2006—08; current rep. William Carl Fine Prints. Trustee PAAM, Provincetown, 1996—2000, chmn. Mus. Sch., 1999—2001. Exhibited in group shows at Cape Mus. Fine Arts, Dennis, Mass., 1999, exhibitions include Schoolhouse Ctr., Silas Kenyon Gallery, Provincetown, Mass., 1998—2007, Fitzwilliam Mus., Cambridge, Eng., 1999, Comenos Fine Arts, Boston, 1999—2009, Lamia, Inc., NYC, 1999, C3TV Gallery, Yarmouthport, Mass., 2000, Davis Gallery, Wellfleet, Mass., 2000, 2004, Schoolhouse Ctr., Provincetown, Mass., 1998—2007, SAGA, NYC, 2002—06, Harmony, Lamia

Ink and Handmade Culture Club, KamiGori, Japan, 2003, DNA Gallery, Provincetown, Mass., 2003, Corcoran Gallery Art, Washington, 2004, Silas Kenyon Gallery, Provincetown, 2004, 2006, 29 Newbury St., Boston, 2005, Represented in permanent collections Provincetown Art Assn. and Mus., Fitzwilliam Mus., Cambridge, Eng., Boston Pub. Libr., one-man shows include New Bedford Art Mus., 2008. Recipient First recipient Art Bridge Workshop Residency, Lamia Ink, N.Y.C., Kami Gori, Japan, 2003, award, Nat. Soc. Arts and Letters, Washington, 1972; grantee, Provincetown Cultural Coun., Mass. Cultural Coun., 1994. Mem.: Provincetown Arts Assn. and Mus., Washington Print Club.

SMITH, KATHRYN NALLY, history educator; d. Rupert Edward and Frances Michael Nally; 1 child, Jay Lloyd. MA, U. Del., Newark, 2003. Cert. tchr. U. Del. Secondary sch. history tchr. Ctrl. York Sch. Dist., Pa., 2005—06, mid. sch. lang. arts tchr., 2006—08, HS history tchr., 2008—. Adj. history prof. York Coll. Pa., Pa., 2003—. Campaign, elect rep. to congress, Pa., 2006—06. Business E-Mail: ksmith@ycp.edu.

SMITH, KATIE (KATHERINE MAY SMITH), professional basketball player; b. Logan, Ohio, June 4, 1974; d. Don Smith. Degree in zoology, Ohio State U., 1996. Guard Columbus Quest, ABL, 1997—98, Minn. Lynx, 1999—2005, Lotos VBW Clima, EuroLeague, Gdynia, Poland, 2001—02, Detroit Shock, 2005—. Mem. USA Basketball Women's Sr. Nat. Team, Sydney, 2000, Athens, Greece, 04, Beijing, 08. Recipient Gold Medal, FIBA World Championships, 1998, 2002, Gold medal, women's basketball, Sydney Olympic Games, 2000, Athens Olympic Games, 2004, Beijing Olympic Games, 2008; named Ohio State Female Athlete of the Century, Columbus Touchdown Club, 2002, WNBA Finals MVP, 2008; named to ABL All-Star Team, 1997—98, All-ABL First Team, 1998, WNBA All-Star Team, 2000—06, All-WNBA First Team, 2001, 2003. Achievements include being a member of ABL Championship winning Columbus Quest, 1997, 1998; first female in history of Ohio State University to have number retired, 2001; being a member of WNBA Championship winning Detroit Shock, 2006, 2008. Office: Detroit Shock 5 Championship Dr Auburn Hills MI 48326

SMITH, KAYE TRAIN, artist; b. Camden, NJ, July 15, 1927; d. William Matthew Biddle and Jennie May Leibensperger; m. Robert L. Smith, Aug. 18, 1995; m. John Martin Train, June 3, 1945 (dec. Jan. 2, 1993); children: Jeanne Carole Train, Suzanne Kathryn Coffee, Kurt Robert Train. Airbrush artist Norcross Greetings Corp., NYC, 1945—46; profl. in-house model Jo Collins Sportswear Corp., St. Louis, 1947—48; freelance artist Fremont, Calif., 1967—, Roseville, Calif., 1967—. Exhibit coord. Placerville Art Assn., 1971—72. Recipient Nat. Design award, Am. Greetings Corp., 1966. Mem.: Roseville Arts, Sun City Roseville Art Club (pres. 1996—97, various coms., signature painting, 8th ann. show 2003). Home: 7260 Timberrose Way Roseville CA 95747 Personal E-mail: bobnk@surewest.net.

SMITH, KEITH E., hotel and gaming company executive; b. 1960; Corp. controller Boyd Gaming Corp., 1990, sr. v.p., controller, exec. v.p., ops., 1998—2001, COO, 2001—05, pres., COO, 2005—07, pres., CEO, 2008—. Dir., bd. of dirs. Boyd Gaming Corp.; vice-chmn., bd. of dirs. NV Resort Assn., Las Vegas Convention and Visitors Authority. Office: Boyd Gaming Corp 3883 Howard Hughes Pkwy Ninth Fl Las Vegas NV 89118 Office Phone: 702-792-7200. Office Fax: 702-792-7263.

SMITH, KENNETH ALAN, chemical engineer, educator; b. Winthrop, Mass., Nov. 28, 1936; s. James Edward and Alice Gertrude (Walters) S.; m. Ambia Marie Olsson, Oct. 14, 1961; children: Kirsten Heather, Edward Eric, Andrew Ian Beaumont, Thurston Garrett. BS, MIT, 1958, MS, 1959, DSc, 1962; postgrad., Cambridge U., Eng., 1964-65. Asst. prof. chem. engring. MIT, 1961-67, assoc. prof., 1967-71, prof., 1971—, Edwin R. Gilliland prof. chem. engring., 1989—, acting head dept., 1976-77, assoc. provost, 1980-81, assoc. provost, v.p. rsch., 1981-91, dir. Whitaker Coll. Health Sci. and Tech., 1989-91. Cons. chem. and oil cos. NSF fellow, 1964-65, Overseas fellow, Churchill Coll., (Eng.), 1993, 01,08. Mem. Am. Inst. Chem. Engrs., Nat. Acad. Engring., Am. Chem. Soc., AAAS, Sigma Xi, Phi Lambda Upsilon, Tau Beta Pi. Episcopalian. Home: 32 School St Manchester MA 01944-1336 Office: MIT Bldg 66-540 Cambridge MA 02139 Home Phone: 978-526-1743; Office Phone: 617-253-1973. E-mail: kas@mit.edu.

SMITH, KENNETH J., medical educator, researcher; b. Phila., Aug. 29, 1955; s. Harry Logan and Frances Smith; m. Christine Falco, June 16, 1979; children: Caitlan Elizabeth, Alison Frances. MD, Jefferson Med. Coll., Phila., 1979; MS, U. Pitts., 2005. Diplomate Am. Bd. Internal Medicine, 1982. Assoc. dir., internal medicine and transitional residency programs Mercy Hosp. Pitts., 1993—2001; asst. prof., medicine U. Pitts., 2001—07, assoc. prof., medicine, 2007—. Recipient W.W.G. MacLachlan award, Mercy Hosp. Pitts., 1999, K23 Rsch. Career Devel. award, Nat. Inst. Allergy and Infectious Diseases, 2004—08; R01 grant, 2008—, fellow, ACP, 1995. Office: Univ Pitts 200 Meyran Ave Ste 200 Pittsburgh PA 15213 Office Fax: 412-246-6954. Business E-Mail: smithkj2@upmc.edu.

SMITH, KENNETH JUDSON, JR., chemistry professor; b. Raleigh, NC, Sept. 4, 1930; s. Kenneth Judson and Irene (Strickland) S.; m. Dorothy Margaret Ratcliffe, Mar. 6, 1953; children: Patricia Lynne Smith Pittman, Pamela Jean. AB, East Carolina U., 1957; MA, Duke U., 1959, PhD, 1961. Research chemist Chemstrand Research Center, Durham, N.C., 1961-65, sr. research chemist, 1965-68; asst. prof. polymer research SUNY Coll. Environ. Sci. and Forestry, Syracuse, 1968-70, assoc. prof., 1970-73, prof., 1973-95, emeritus prof., 1995—, asst. dir. Polymer Research Center, 1971-79, acting dir., 1979-83, dir. Organic Materials Sci. Program, 1971-75, chmn. dept. chemistry, 1972-84. Vis. prof. Instituto di Chimica Industriale, U. Genoa, Italy, 1979; cons. U.S. Army Materials and Mechanics Rsch. Ctr., Watertown, Mass., 1973-75, cert. of appreciation 1973, NRC, Washington, 1980-87; mem. adv. coun. Syracuse Met. Transp. Coun., 1975-84; mem. adv. bd. confs. in polymer sci. and tech. SUNY, New Paltz, 1977-85; mem. rsch. found. joint com. on procedures SUNY, Albany, 1974-81; cons. Hong Kong Rsch. Coun., 1995—. Contbr. articles to profl. jours. Served with USMC, 1951-54. Recipient cert. Appreciation U.S. Army Materials and Mechanics Rsch. Ctr., 1973. Mem. AAAS, Am. Chem. Soc. (dir. Syracuse sect. 1977-79, chmn. 1978, councilor 1979-82), Am. Phys. Soc. (com. on internat. freedom of scientists, small coms.), Am. Inst. Chemists, Soc. Plastics Engrs., Math. Assn. Am., N.Y. Acad. Scis., Sigma Xi, Phi Lambda Upsilon, Kappa Delta Pi. Achievements include research on statistical mechanics, mechanical properties and theoretical studies of polymers; rubber elasticity and thermoelasticity; crystallization of networks; structure-property relationships; ultimate properties of fibers; thermodynamic theory of polymer fiber properties; thermodyanic theory of fiber strength. Office: Coll Environ Sci and Forestry Suny Syracuse NY 13210

SMITH, KENNETH RUPERT, JR., neurosurgeon, educator; b. St. Louis, Sept. 23, 1932; s. Kenneth R. and Jocelyn (Ulmet) S.; m. Marjorie R. Sandin, 1956; children: Sue, Sally, Kenneth III, Nancy, Carol, Joanne, Patricia. Student, Greenville Coll., Ill., 1950-53; MD, Washington U., St. Louis, 1957. Diplomate Am. Bd. Neurol. Surgery. Intern in medicine Johns Hopkins Hosp., Balt., 1957-58; asst. resident surgery Washington U., St. Louis, 1958-59, resident neurosurgery, 1960-63, instr. neurosurgery and anatomy, 1964-66; asst. prof. surgery St. Louis U., 1966-67, assoc. prof., 1967-71, prof., 1971—2008, prof. emeritus, 2009. Contbr. articles to profl. jours. Cons. Bd. Police Commrs., St. Louis, 1967; chmn. Mayor's Health Task Force, St. Louis, 1977-81; mem. bd. commrs. St. Louis Mus. Sci. and Natural History, 1979-85. Named Disting. Alumnus Greenville (Ill.) Coll., 1983. Mem. AAAS, Am. Assn. Anatomists, Soc. Neurosci., Am. Assn. Neurol. Surgeons (nominating com. 1992-94), Soc. Univ. Neurosurgeons (pres. 1986), Soc. Neurol. Neurosurgeons (pres. 1986), Soc. Neurol. Surgeons (pres. 1995-96), St. Louis Med. Soc. (pres. 1983), St. Louis Soc. Neurol. Scis. (pres. 1975-77), Alpha Omega Alpha. Democrat. Avocations: hunting, music. Office: St Louis U Sch Medicine 3635 Vista Ave Saint Louis MO 63110-2539 Office Phone: 314-577-8796.

SMITH, KENNETH T., retail executive; BS acctg., Wake Forest Univ. CPA. Acctg. positions Ernst & Young LLP; mgmt. positions Beall's Dept. Stores; mgmt. positions through sr. v.p. fin. Family Dollar Stores, Charlotte, NC, 1990—2007, sr. v.p., CFO, 2007—. Mailing: Family Dollar Stores PO Box 1017 Charlotte NC 28201-1017

SMITH, KENT ASHTON, information scientist, consultant; b. Boston, Sept. 3, 1938; s. Kent Wooliscroft and Dorothy Patten Smith; m. Mary Margaret Gaffney; children: Holly L. Smith, Kent W. BA, Hobart Coll., 1960; MBA, Cornell U., 1962; postgrad., Am. U., 1978-79. Mgmt. analyst Office of Sec., HEW, Washington, 1962-65; adminstrv. officer divsn. rsch. facilities and resources NIH, Bethesda, Md., 1965-67, asst. exec. officer divsn. rsch. facilities and resources, 1967-68, exec. officer divsn. rsch. resources, 1968-71, asst. dir. adminstrn. Nat. Libr. Medicine, 1971-78, dep. dir., 1978—2004, PHS spl. expert-info. scientist, 2000—02; cons. Nat. Ctr. for Biotechnology Info., 2004—, Computercraft Corp., 2004—, Office Sci. and tech. Info. Dept. Energy, 2005—. Mem. exec. bd. and bur. Internat. Coun. Sci. and Tech. Info., Paris, 1983—2001; v.p. U.S. Nat. Com. of UNESCO-PGI, Washington, 1983—85; mem. exec. adv. bd. Fed. Libr. and Info. Ctr. Com., Washington, 1984—89; exec. com. CENDI-Info. Consortia, Washington, 1985—; treas. Internat. Coun. Sci. and Tech. Info., Paris, 1986—89; pres. Nat. Fed. Abstracting and Info. Sci., Phila., 1988—89, v.p., 1987—88; chmn. Info. Policy Com., 1988—89, CENDI-Info. Consortia, Washington, 2001—04; mem. US Nat. Commn. for CODATA, 1990—2001, Science.gov Alliance, 2002—04, NISO Blue Ribbon Panel, 2004; pres. Internat. Coun. Sci. and Tech. Info., Paris, 1990—94; mem. panel US Dept. Energy info. infrastructure NAS, 2000, 07; reviewer study digital strategy for Libr. Congress NRC, 2000; mem. panel on Nat. Tech. Info. Svc. Nat. Commn. Libr. and Info. Sci., 2000; long-range planning panel mem. Nat. Libr. Medicine, 2005—07; bd. mem. Nat. Tech. Info. Svc. Adv. Bd., 2006—; mem. Dept. Energy panel on accelerating knowledge diffusion NAS, 2007. Contbr. articles to profl. jours., chpt. to book: Management of Federally Sponsored Libraries, 1995. Mem. Citizens Com. for Pub. Libr. Montgomery County, Bethesda, 1981-82; fin. dir. Christ Ch., Rockville, Md., 1990-91. Recipient Asst. Sec. for Health Exceptional Achievement award USPHS, 1978, Sr. Exec. Svc. award, 1996, 97, 98, 99, HEW Superior Svc. medal 1974, Nat. Fedn. Abstracting Info. Sci., 1998, Miles Conrad hon. lectureship, Hammer award V.P. US, 1999, MLA Govt. Rels. award, 2009 Fellow Nat. Fedn. Abstracting and Info. Svcs.; mem. ASPA (vice chmn. 1971-72), AAAS, Int. Assn. Sci. Tech. and Med. Pubs., Am. Mgmt. Assn., Am. Soc. Info. Svc., Med. Libr. Assn. (hon.; Pres. award 1997, ICSTI Disting. Svc. award 2001, Joseph Leiter Hon. Lecturship, 2007, sponsor, Fun award for Govtl. Relations), Assn. Rsch. Librs. (Alfred Zipf fellow com. chair 2001-04), Cosmos Club. Episcopalian. Avocations: golf, baseball, genealogy, theater, birdwatching, antiques. Home and Office: 17517 Hidden Garden Ln Ashton MD 20861 Office Phone: 301-496-5359.

SMITH, KENT B., councilman; Councillor-at-large Indpls.-Marion County City-County Coun., 2008—. Chmn. cmty. affairs com. Indpls.-Marion County City-County Coun. Sch. bd. mem. Fall Creek Acad., Indpls. Republican. Office: Indpls Marion County City County Coun 241 City County Bldg 200 E Washington St Indianapolis IN 46204 Office Phone: 317-327-4242. Business E-Mail: ksmith4ccc@gmail.com.*

SMITH, K(ERMIT) WAYNE, computer company executive; b. Newton, NC, Sept. 15, 1938; s. Harold Robert and Hazel K. (Smith) S.; m. Audrey M. Kennedy, Dec. 19, 1958; 1 son, Stuart W. BA, Wake Forest U., 1960; MA, Princeton U., 1962, PhD, 1964; postgrad., U. So. Calif., 1965; LLD (hon.), Ohio U., 1992; LHD (hon.), Ohio State U., 1998. Instr. Princeton U., 1963; asst. prof. econs. and polit. sci. U.S. Mil. Acad., 1963-66; spl. asst. to asst. sec. def. for sys. analysis Washington, 1966-69; program mgr. def. studies RAND Corp., Santa Monica, Calif., 1969-70; dir. program analysis NSC, Washington, 1970-72; group v.p. planning Dart Industries, LA, 1972-73, group pres. resort devel. group, 1973-76; exec. v.p. Washington Group, Inc., 1976-77; mng. ptnr. Coopers & Lybrand, Washington, 1977-80, group mng. ptnr., 1980-83; chmn., CEO World Book, Inc., 1983-86; prof. Wake Forest U., 1986—88, 2001—04; CEO OCLC Online Computer Libr. Ctr., Inc., Dublin, Ohio, 1989-98, pres. emeritus, 1998—. Sr. cons. Dept. Def., Dept. State, NSC, NASA, Dept. Energy, OMB, GAO; con. prof. (hon.) Tsinghua U., Beijing, 1996; chmn. Rainbow Care For Kids Found., 1999-2000. Author: How Much is Enough? Shaping the Defense Program, 1961-69, 1971, reprinted as RAND classic, 2005; editor: OCLC 1967-97: Thirty Years of Furthering Access to the World's Information, 1998; contbr. articles to profl. jours. Mem. vis. com. Brookings Instn., Washington, 1971-79; mem. bd. visitors Wake Forest U., 1974-78, 82-90, chmn. bd. visitors, 1976-78, trustee, 1991-95, 96-00, 01-05, 06-, vice chmn., 2006-07, chmn., 2007—; mem. bd. visitors Def. Sys. Mgmt. Coll., 1982-85, Lenoir Rhyne Coll., 1988-94, Mershon Ctr. Ohio State U., 1990-92, Columbus Assn. for Performing Arts, 1991-95, U. Pitts. Sch. Libr. and Info. Sci., 1992-95; mem. bd. visitors Bowman Gray Bapt. Hosp. Med. Ctr., 1992-95, chmn. bd. visitors, 1993-95; bd. dirs. Wake Forest U. Bapt. Med. Ctr., 2007—. Danforth fellow, Woodrow Wilson fellow Princeton U., 1962-64. Mem. ALA (hon., life), Coun. Fgn. Rels., Internat. Inst. Strategic Studies, Inst. Internat. Edn., Coun. Higher Edn., Am. Assn. Higher Edn., Chgo. Club, Phi Beta Kappa, Omicron Delta Kappa, Kappa Sigma. Methodist. Home: 2606 Sigmon Dairy Rd Newton NC 28658-7609 Office: Online Computer Libr Ctr Inc 6565 Frantz Rd Dublin OH 43017-5308

SMITH, KERRY CLARK, lawyer; b. Phoenix, July 12, 1935; s. Clark and Fay S.; m. Michael Waterman, 1958; children: Kevin, Ian. AB, Stanford U., 1957, JD, 1962. Bar: Calif. 1963, U.S. Supreme Ct. 1980. Assoc. Chickering & Gregory, San Francisco, 1962-70, ptnr., 1970-81, Pettit & Martin, San Francisco, 1981-95, Hovis, Smith, San Francisco, 1995-99; pvt. practice San Francisco, 1999—. Mem. editl. bd. Stanford Law Rev., 1961-62. Lt. USN, 1957-60. Mem. Calif. Bar Assn., Orinda County Club, La Quinta Citrus Golf Club.

SMITH, KEVIN, film director, writer, actor; b. Red Bank, NJ, Aug. 2, 1970; s. Donald Smith and Grace Smnith; m. Jennifer Schwalbach, Apr. 25, 1999; 1 child, Harley Quinn. LHD (hon.), Illinois Wesleyan U., 2000. Owner Jay and Silent Bob's Secret Stash Comic Book Store, Red Bank, NJ, 1997—, L.A., 2007—, View Askew Productions, 1996—. Dir., writer, actor (films) Clerks, 1994, Mall Rats, 1996, Chasing Amy, 1997, Dogma, 1999, Jay and Silent Bob Strike Back, 2001; dir., prodr., writer: Jersey Girl, 2004, Clerks II, 2006: writer, dir. (films) Zack and Miri Make a Porno, 2008; exec. prodr. Good Will Hunting, 1997, Vulgar, 2000, Reel Paradise, 2005, Small Town Gay Bar, 2006: screenwriter: (TV movies) Roadside Attractions, 2002, dir., screenwriter: (TV movies) The Flying Car, 2002; writer, actor, exec. prodr. (TV series) Clerks, 2000; actor: (films) Scream 3, 1999, Daredevil, 2003, Bottom's Up, 2006, Southland Tales, 2006, Catch and Release, 2006, (voice only) Doogal, 2006, TMNT, 2007, Live Free or Die Hard, 2007; (TV movies) Manchild, 2007; (TV appearances) Law & Order, 2000, Duck Dodgers, 2003, Veronica Mars, 2005, Reaper, 2007; performer: (one man shows) Silent Bob Speaks: An Evening With Kevin Smith, 2009; Author: Silent Bob Speaks: The Collected Writings of Kevin Smith, 2005, My Boring-Ass Life: The Uncomfortably Candid Diary of Kevin Smith, 2007 Office: View Askew Productions Inc 116 Broad St Red Bank NJ 07701*

SMITH, KIKI, artist; b. Nuremberg, Germany, Jan. 18, 1954; d. Tony Smith. One-woman shows include The Kitchen, NYC, 1982, Fawbush Gallery, 1988, 1992, 1993, Galerie René Blouin, Montreal, 1989, 1991—92, 1994, Dallas Mus. Art, 1989, Ezra and Cecile Zilkha Gallery Ctr. for the Arts Wesleyan U., Middletown, Conn., 1989, Tyler Gallery Tyler Sch. Art Temple U., Phila., 1990, Ctr. d'Arte Contemporaine, Geneva, 1990, Inst. Art and Urban Resources The Clocktower, Long Island, NY, 1990, Inst. Contemporary Art, Amsterdam, 1990, Mus. Modern Art, NYC, 1990—91, Shoshana Wayne Gallery, Santa Monica, Calif., 1991, 1992, 1992—93, MAK Galerie, Vienna, 1991, U. Art Mus., Berkeley, Calif., 1991, Art Awareness, Inc., Lexington, N.Y., 1991, Corcoran Gallery Art, Washington, 1991, Greg Kucera Gallery, Seattle, 1991, Rose Art Mus. Brandeis U., Waltham, Mass., 1992, Österreichisches Mus. angewandte Kunst, Vienna, 1992, Moderna Mus., Stockholm, 1992, Bonner Kunstverein, Bonn, 1992, Galerie M & R Fricke, Düsseldorf, Germany, 1992—93, Williams Coll. Mus. Art, Williamstown, Mass., 1992—93, Ohio State U., Columbus, 1992—93, Anthony d'Offay Gallery, London, 1993, 1995, Phoenix Art Mus., 1993, U. Art Mus., Santa Barbara, Calif., 1994, La. Mus. Modern Art, Humlebaek, Denmark, 1994, The Israel Mus., Jerusalem, 1994, Barbara Gross Galerie, Munich, 1994, Laura Carpenter Fine Art, Santa Fe, 1994, Pace Wildenstein, NY, 1994, Royal LePage Gallery, Toronto, 1994—95, Barbara Krakow Gallery, Boston, 1994—96, Whitechapel Art Gallery, London, 1995, San Francisco Mus. Modern Art, 2005, Contemporary Art Mus., Houston, 2006, numerous others, exhibited in group shows at Brooke Alexander Gallery, NY, 1980, 1991, White Columns, NY, 1981, 1983, 1990, Artists Space, 1981, 1990, Barbara Gladstone Gallery, 1982, Hallwalls, Buffalo, NY, 1983, Whitney Mus. Am. Art, NYC, 1984, Susan Caldwell Gallery, NY, 1984, 1987, Galerie Engstrom, Stockholm, 1984, Art City, NY, 1985, Moderna Mus., Stockholm, 1985, Cin. Art Mus., 1985, Bklyn. Mus., 1986, 1989, Curt Marcus Gallery, NY, 1986, Fawbush Gallery, 1987, 1989, 1990, Mus. Modern Art, NYC, 1988, 1992, 1998, IBM Gallery, NY, 1988, Arch Gallery, Amsterdam, 1988, Tom Cugliani Gallery, 1989, Simon Watson Gallery, NY, 1990, Corcoran Gallery, Wash, DC, 1990, Mus. Fine Arts, Boston, 1990, 1995—96, Hunter Coll. Art Gallery, 1991, New Mus. Contemporary Arts, NY, 1991, Milw. Art Mus., 1992, Whitney Biennial, Whitney Mus Am Art, 1992, 1993, 2002, Paula Cooper Gallery, 1993, Serpentine Gallery, London, 1994, Guggenheim Mus. SoHo, 1995—96, Mus. Nat. D'Art Mod. Ctr., Georges Pompidou, Paris, 1995—96, PaceWildenstein, NY, 1995, 1997, 1998, Ace Gallery, Mex., 1997, Am. Acad. Arts & Letters, 1997, Hayward Gallery, London, 1997—98, Nat. Gallery Victoria, Melbourne, Australia, 1998, Yale U. Art Gallery, New Haven, Conn., 1998, Mus. Contemporary Art, San Diego, 1998, Fabric Workshop & Mus., Phila., 1999, St Louis Art Mus., 1999, John Berggruen Gallery, San Francisco, 2005, numerous others. Recipient Urban Glass award, 1996, Skowhegan Medal for Sculpture, 2000; named one of 100 Most Influential People, Time Mag., 2006. Mem.: Nat Acad Design, AAAL. Office: c/o Pace Wildenstein 32 E 57th St New York NY 10022-2513

SMITH, KIMBERLY M., assistant principal, educational consultant; b. NY, Sept. 1, 1970; d. Donald Hill and Maurine Wofford; m. Isaac Smith, May 26, 1970; children: Allan Pereira, Isaiah. EdD, Argosy U., Sarasota, Fla., 2007. Cert. ednl. leadership Ga., 2000. Classroom tchr. Gwinnett County Pub. Schs., Lawrenceville, Ga., 2000—04; asst. prin. Level Creek Elem. Sch., Suwanee, Ga., 2004—07; prin. Suwanee Elem. Sch., 2007—. Mem.: Alpha Kappa Alpha. Home: 294 Azalea Chase Dr Suwanee GA 30024-3906

SMITH, KIMMIE CHRISTINE, small business owner; b. Redding, Calif., Apr. 28, 1971; d. Steven Burton Tyler and Kim Kassina Hern; m. Kenneth Thomas Smith, Nov. 12, 1988; 1 foster child, Savannah children: Stephanie, Shannon, Steven, Shelby, Danika. AAS, U. Alaska, Sitka, 2003, AA, 2004, BLA, 2005; postgrad. in Psychology, Walden U. Owner, adminstr. Krissy's Playland Childcare Ctr., Wrangell, Alaska, 1995—. Facilitator Wrangell Spl. Needs Team, 2003—; mem. elem. advisory com., 2007—; early childhood cmty. liaison Assn. for Edn. of Young Children-S.E. Alaska. V.p. Emblem Club #87, 2006—. Named Family Childcare Provider of Year, AEYC-SEA, 2005. Avocations: hunting, scrapbooks, fishing. Home: PO Box 615 Wrangell AK 99929 Office: Krissy's Playland PO Box 615 Wrangell AK 99929 Office Phone: 907-874-4307. Business E-Mail: krissysplayland@aptalaska.net. E-mail: shelby@aptalaska.net.

SMITH, KINGSTON EARL, lawyer; b. Newport News, Va., Apr. 11, 1946; s. John Howard and Jane Elizabeth (Fawcett) S.; m. Juliana Parker, June 10, 1978; children: Andrew Earl, Christina Louise. BA, Duke U., 1968; JD, U. Richmond, 1977. Bar: Va. 1977, U.S. Ct. Appeals (4th cir.) 1977, U.S. Dist. Ct. (we. dist.) Va. 1979, U.S. Supreme Ct. 1981, Air Force Mil. Rev. 1992. Tchr., coach Poquoson (Va.) Pub. Schs., 1973-74; assoc. atty. May, Miller & Parsons, Richmond, 1977-80; gen. atty. Office Gen. Counsel, Vets. Adminstrn., Washington, 1980-84; minority counsel & dep. staff dir., 1985—94; gen. counsel & dep. staff dir. Com. Vet. Affairs, U.S. Ho. Rep., Washington, 1995—96; staff dir., Subcommittee on Oversight & Investigations, 1997—2003; dep. chief counsel; chief counsel, 2001—06; rep. chief counsel, 2007—; Com. Vet. Affairs U.S. Ho. Rep., Washington. Sr. advisor for vets. and nat. security,Bush-Quayle campaign, 1988, sr. advisor for vets. and nat. security, Bush-Quayle campaign, 1992, vets. adv. bd.; vol. Dole-Kemp campaign, 1996. USAF, 1968-72, pilot Vietnam, reserve JAG, air staff 1981-97, Lt. col. USAFR (ret.). Decorated DFC, Air medal with 1st oak leaf cluster. Mem.: Duke Club Washington (bd. mem.). Republican. Office: Committee on Veterans' Affairs Room 333 Cannon House Office Building Washington DC 20515-6335

SMITH, L. DOUGLAS, business educator; s. William and Dixie Smith; m. Ruth Agar, 1944; children: Alison, Jeffrey, Janice, Colin. BSc, McMaster U., Hamilton, Can., 1966, MBA, 1968; PhD, U. Minn., Mpls.,

1972. Asst.-assoc prof. U. Sask., Saskatoon, Canada, 1971—73. Prof., dir. Ctr. Bus. and Indsl. Studies, U. Mo., St. Louis, 1985—. Contbr. articles to profl. jours. Recipient Mgmt. Innovation award to Bi-State Transit Agy., Am. Pub. Transp. Assn., 1987, Best Paper awards, Decision Scis. Inst., WDSI, 1994, 1997, 2001, HICSS, 2007. Achievements include development of analytical models and computer-based systems for the solution of managerial problems. Office: Univ Mo Saint Louis One University Blvd Saint Louis MO 63121

SMITH, LAMAR SEELIGSON, United States Representative from Texas; b. San Antonio, Nov. 19, 1947; s. Campbell and Eloise Keith (Seeligson) Smith; m. Elizabeth Schaefer, Mar. 20, 1992; children: Nell Seligson, Tobin Wells. BA, Yale U., 1969; JD, So. Meth. U. Sch. Law, 1975. Mgmt. intern SBA, Washington, 1969-70; bus. writer Christian Sci. Monitor, Boston, 1970-72; assoc. Maebius & Duncan, Inc., San Antonio, 1975-76; chmn. Rep. Party of Bexar County, San Antonio, 1978—82; mem. Tex. State House Reps. from Dist. 57-F, San Antonio, 1981-82; commr. Bexar County Precinct 3, Tex., 1982—85; mem. US Congress from 21st Tex. dist., 1987—, ranking mem. judiciary com., former chmn. ethics com., mem. sci. com., mem. homeland security com. Ptnr. Lamar Seeligson Ranch, Premont, Tex., 1975—. Office: US Ho Reps 2409 Rayburn Ho Office Bldg Washington DC 20515-4321 Office Phone: 202-225-4236.*

SMITH, LANTY LLOYD, bank executive, lawyer; b. Sherrodsville, Ohio, Dec. 11, 1942; s. Lloyd H. and Ellen Ruth (Newell) S.; m. Margaret Hays Chandler, June 11, 1966; children: Abigail Lamoreaux Presson, Margaret Ellen Smith-Rhee, Amanda Prescott Lacoff. BS in Math. with honors, Wittenberg U., Springfield, Ohio, 1964; LLB with honors, Duke U., 1967. Bar: Ohio 1967. Assoc. Jones, Day, Cockley & Reavis, Cleve., 1967-73; ptnr. Jones, Day, Reavis & Pogue, Cleve., 1974-77; exec. v.p., sr. gen. counsel Burlington Industries, Inc., Greensboro, NC, 1977-86, pres., 1986-88; chmn. Precision Fabrics Group Inc., Greensboro, NC, 1988—, Wachovia Corp., Charlotte, NC, 2008, interim CEO, 2008. Bd. dirs. Nat. Humanities Ctr.; pres., CEO MediWave Star Tech. Inc., 1999—; chmn. to CEO Tippet Capital, 2007—, Scion Neurostim, 2007—. Mem. bd. visitors Duke U. Sch. Law; vice chmn. exec. com. Duke U. Mgmt. Co. Mem.: NC Inst. Medicine. Home: 3150 Cone Manor Ln Raleigh NC 27613-6606

SMITH, LARRY GLENN, retired state judge; b. Montgomery, Ala., Aug. 6, 1924; s. Alonzo Nathan and Louise (Norman) S.; m. Mary Emmalyn Murphree, Feb. 28, 1948; children: Cynthia Lynn Smith, Larry Glenn Jr., Celia Dell Smith Rudolph. Student, U. Ala., Tuscaloosa, 1942-43, 46-48; LLB, U. Fla., 1949. Bar: Fla. 1949. Pvt. practice, Panama City, Fla., 1949-53; assoc. Mathis & Mathis, Panama City, 1953-57; asst. state atty. Office State Atty. (14th cir.), Panama City, 1953-57; rsch. asst. Fla. Supreme Ct., Tallahassee, 1958-60; ptnr. Baker, Baker & Smith, Orlando, Fla., 1960-64, Isler, Welch, Smith, Higby & Brown, Panama City, 1964-72; judge cir. ct. Fla. 14th Jud. Cir., Panama City, 1973-79; judge Fla. 1st Dist. Ct. Appeal, Tallahassee, 1979-94; ret., 1994; chief judge Fla. 1st Dist. Ct. Appeal, Tallahassee, 1987-89; ret., 1994; sr. judge State of Fla., 1994—2005. Mem. Fla. Bd. Bar Examiners, Tallahassee, 1967-72, Fla. Ct. Edn. Coun., Tallahassee, 1979-81, 86-91, Fla. Bench and Bar Commn., Tallahassee, 1990-91; pres. Fla. Conf. of Dist. Ct. Appeals Judges, Tallahassee, 1986-87; instr. We the People: the Citizen and the Constitution, Gulf Coast C.C., Panama City, 2001-. Mem. Panama City Airport Authority, 1952-55; past pres. Bay County Libr. Assn., Panama City. Lt. (j.g.) USNR, 1943-45. Fellow Am. bar Found.; mem. ABA, Fla. Bar, Tallahassee Bar Assn., Am. Judicature Soc., Bay County Bar Assn., St. Andrews Bay Am. Inn of Ct. (pres. 2001-2002). Avocations: hiking, biking, skiing, photography, reading. Home: 109 Bunkers Cove Rd Panama City FL 32401 Personal E-mail: s.larry1@worldnet.att.net.

SMITH, LAUREN ASHLEY, lawyer, clergyman, physicist, journalist; b. Clinton, Iowa, Nov. 30, 1924; s. William Thomas Roy and Ethel (Cook) S.; m. Barbara Ann Mills, Aug. 22, 1947; children: Christopher A., Laura Nan Smith Pringle, William Thomas Roy II. BS, U. Minn., 1946, JD, 1949; postgrad., U. Chgo., 1943-49; MDiv, McCormick Theol. Sem., 1950; postgrad., U. Iowa, 1992. Bar: Colo. 1957, Iowa 1959, Ill. 1963, Minn. 1983, U.S. Supreme Ct. 1967; ordained to ministry Presbyn. Ch., 1950. Pastor Presbyn. Ch., Fredonia, Kans., 1950-52, Lamar, Colo., 1952-57, Congl. Ch., Clinton, 1975-80; editor The Comml., Pine Bluff, Ark., 1957-58; ptnr. Schoenauer Smith & Fullerton ASP, Clinton, 1995—. CEO LASCO Pub. Group, Clinton, 1995—; CEO, founder Interlink for the Internet Generation; internat. conferee Stanley Found., Warrenton, Va., 1963—72; legal observer, USSR, 1978; co-sponsor All India Renewable Energy Conf., Bangalore, 1981; law sch. conferee U. Minn., China, 1983; lectr. law, religion, physics, nat. policy U. Wis., 2001, Spl. lectr. contemporary physics and religion, 01. Author: (jurisprudence treatise) Forma Dat Esse Rel, 1975; co-author: India On to New Horizons, 1989; columnist Crow Call, 1968—; co-editor Press and News of India, 1978-82; pub. Crow Call; pseudonym Christopher Crow, 1981—; writer BBC World Svc., London; editor Asian Econ. Cmty. Jour.; contbr. articles to religious publs. Assoc. Westar Inst. (The Jesus Seminar), Santa Rose, Calif.; active Quad City Estate Planning Coun.; minister-at-large Presbyn. Ch. U.S.A., Iowa, 1987—; bd. dirs. Iowa divsn. UN Assn. U.S.A., Iowa City, 1970—85; fellow Molecular Nanotechnology Foresight Inst., Palo Alto, Calif., Franciscans UN Non Govt. Orgn.; founder, CEO Interlink relating quantum mechanics and religion, Clinton, Iowa, 1998—; founding dir. Project 67/74, Clinton, 2002—. Recipient World Wide Essay Contest award, Radio China Internat., 2003—04. Mem. ABA, Iowa Bar Assn., Ill. Bar Assn., St. Andrews Soc., Clinton County Bar Assn. (pres. 1968, Best in Iowa citation), Clinton Ministerial Assn., Samaritan Health Systems Chaplain Corps. (pres.), European Soc. for Study of Sci. and Religion, Quad City Estate Planning Coun., Quaker Internat. Yokefellow, Nat. Network for New Spiritual Formation Presbyn. Ch. USA, Franciscans Internat., Parish Without Walls (founding dir.), City Club of Quad Cities (bd. dirs.), Cath. Order St. Francis (assoc., founder project 67/74), New Rd. Map for Am. (founder). Office: 230 4th Ave S Clinton IA 52732-4311

SMITH, LAURENCE, social sciences educator; b. Chgo. married. PhD, Cornell U., Ithaca, NY, 1996. Prof., dept. geography UCLA, 1996—. Author: (nonfiction book) The New North (under contract for 2010). Recipient Bellagio Residency award, Rockefeller Found., 2007; Guggenheim fellowship, John S. Guggenheim Found., NY, 2006. Mem.: Am. Geophys. Union. Achievements include research in climate change research. Office: UCLA Dept Geography Box 951524 Los Angeles CA 90095-1524

SMITH, LAVENSKI ROY, federal judge; b. Hope, Ark., Oct. 31, 1958; m. Trendle Smith; 2 children. BA, U. Ark., 1981, JD, 1987. Law clerk Hall, Wright & Morris, 1985—87; staff lawyer Ozark Legal Svcs., 1987-91; pvt. practice Springdale, 1991-94; asst. prof. John Brown U., 1994-96; regulatory liaison to Gov. State of Ark., Little Rock, 1996—97; chmn. Ark. Pub. Svc. Commn., 1997—99, commr., 2001—02; interim assoc. justice Ark. State Supreme Ct., 1999—2000; judge US Ct. Appeals (8th cir.), 2002—. Bd. dirs. N.W. Ark. Christian Justice Ctr.; trainer Ptnrs. for Family Tng., 1993-96; chmn. Ark. Pub. Svc. Commn., 1996-98. Republican. Office: Fed Bldg Rm 316 35 E Mountain St Fayetteville AR 72702*

SMITH, LAWRENCE GERARD, dean, medical educator, health facility administrator; b. NYC, Nov. 2, 1949; s. Gerald Joseph and Marion Margaret (Pfeiffer) Smith; m. Deborah Anne Smith, June 26, 1971; children: Kristofer, Kevin, Matthew, Patrick. BS in Physics, Fordham Sch. U., 1971; MD, NYU, 1976. Diplomate Am. Bd. Med. Examiners, Am. Bd. Internal Medicine and Critical Care. Resident physician U. Rochester, NY, 1976-79; staff physician Fitzsimmons Army Med. Ctr., Denver, 1979-81; gen. internist Northshore Med. Group, Huntington, NY, 1981-89; dir. edn., program dir. residency program internal medicine Stony Brook U. Hosp., SUNY, asst. prof. medicine, 1982—89, assoc. prof. medicine, 1989—93; vice chmn. Dept. Medicine, residency program dir. Mount Sinai Sch. of Medicine, NYC, 1994, prof. medicine, 1993—2005, dean med. edn., 2002—05; chief academic officer, sr. v.p. academic affairs North Shore-LI Jewish Health Sys. (North Shore-LIJ), 2005—06, chief med. officer, 2006—; founding dean Hofstra U. Sch. Med., 2008—. Team physician NY Islanders, Uniondale, 1982—90; adv. bd. Hazelton Found., NYC, 1994; profl. cons. Women's First Healthcare, NYC, 1997. Editor: International Medical Graduates in US Hospitals-A Guide for Program Directors and Applicants, 1995; contbr. articles to profl. jours. Capt. US Army, 1979—81. Fellow: ACP; mem.: Orgn. Program Dirs. Assn. (exec. com. mem.), Assn. Program Dir. in Internal Med. (former pres.), Soc. of Med. Decision Making, Soc. of Gen. Internal Medicine, Phi Beta Kappa. Avocations: reading, wine-tasting, golf. Office: North Shore U Hosp 300 Community Dr Manhasset NY 11030

SMITH, LEE ELTON, surgery educator, retired military officer; b. Ventura, Calif., July 19, 1937; s. Raymond Elroy and Edith Irene (Jordan) S.; m. Carole Sue Smith; children: Justine Diane, Alexander Loren. BS, U. Calif., Berkeley, 1959; MD, U. Calif., San Francisco, 1962. Diplomate Am. Bd. Surgery, Am. Bd. Colon and Rectal Surgery (pres. 1992-93). Commd. ens. USN, 1960, advanced through grades to capt., 1977; intern U. Utah, Salt Lake City, 1962-63; resident USN, San Diego, 1966-70, staff surgeon Bremerton, Wash., 1970-72; resident colorectal surgery U. Minn., Mpls., 1972-73; dir. colorectal surgery Nat. Naval Med. Ctr. USN, Bethesda, Md., 1973-82, ret., 1983, Seattle, 1982; clin. prof. surgery Uniformed Svcs. U., Bethesda, 1976—; prof. surgery George Washington U., Washington, 1983-96, Georgetown U., Washington, 2001—; dir. sect. of colon and rectal surgery Washington Hosp. Ctr., 1996—. Pres. Am. Bd. Colon and Rectal Surgery, 1993-94. Editor: Practical Guide to Anorectal Physiology, 1990, 2d edit., 1995; assoc. editor Diseases of the Colon and Rectum, 1984-96, Perspectives in Colon and Rectal Surgery, 1989-2000. Mem. ACS (pres. Met. Washington chpt. 1993-94), Soc. Am. Gastrointestinal Endoscopic Surgeons (pres. 1989-90), Am. Cancer Soc. (v.p. D.C. chpt. 1985-93), Am. Soc. Colon & Rectal Surgeons (pres. 1998-99). Home: 7512 16th St NW Washington DC 20012 Office: Washington Hosp Ctr 106 Irving St NW Washington DC 20010-2975 Office Phone: 202-877-8484. E-mail: lee.e.smith@medstar.net.

SMITH, LEO W., II, museum director; b. Omaha, Nebr., Mar. 13, 1936; BS in Mil. Engring., US Mil. Acad., 1958; MS in Govt., Southern Ill. U., 1971. Mil. asst. to dep. dir. for def. rsch. and engring., strategic and space systems Office Sec. Def., Wash., DC, 1973; exec. dir. Durham Western Heritage Mus., Omaha. B-52G co-pilot USAF, Loring Air Force Base, Maine, dep. missile combat crew comdr. squadron level USAF, 1962, Malmstrom Air Force Base, Mont., dep. missile combat crew comdr. wing Standardization Divsn. USAF, Malmstrom Air Force Base, Mont., with 15th Air Force Missile Tng. and Standardization Divsn. USAF, 1965, March Air Force Base, Calif., co-pilot 314th Tactical Airlift Wing USAF, Ching Chuan Kang Air Base, Taiwan, aircraft comdr. 314 Tactical Airlift Wing USAF, Ching Chuan Kang Air Base, Taiwan, ops. planner airborne command post USAF, 1967, Strategic Air Command Hdqs., air ops. staff officer Future Concepts Aircraft Br. USAF, Strategic Air Command Hdqs., chief Future Concepts Missile Br. USAF, Strategic Air Command Hdqs., chief Strategic Offensive Forces Divsn. USAF, 1977, US Air Force Hdqs., Wash., DC, asst. dep. dir. strategy, doctrine, long-range planning USAF, 1978, Air Force Hdqs., Wash., DC, chief Planning and Integration Divsn. USAF, Air Force Hdqs., Wash., DC, vice comdr. 93rd Bombardment Wing USAF, 1979, Castle Air Force Base, Calif., comdr. 93rd Bombardment Wing USAF, 1980, Castle Air Force Base, Calif., comdr. Strategic Air Command 57th Air Divsn. USAF, 1981, Minot Air Force Base, ND, asst. dep. chief of staff for plans USAF, 1982, Strategic Air Command Hdqs., dir. budget USAF, 1985, US Air Force Hdqs., dep. comptroller, budget USAF, 1987, Office of Sec. Air Force, asst. dep. chief of staff for plans and ops. USAF, 1988, US Air Force Hdqs., prin. dep. asst. sec. fin. mgmt. USAF, 1989, Wash., DC, lt. gen. USAF, 1989, vice comdr. in chief Hdqs. Strategic Command USAF, 1991, Offutt Air Force Base, Nebr. Decorated Disting. Svc. medal, Legion of Merit with two oak leaf clusters, Meritorious Svc. medal with oak leaf cluster, Air medal with oak leaf cluster, Air Force Commendation medal, Air Force Outstanding Unit award, Air Force Organizational Excellence award, Combat Readiness medal, Nat. Def. Svc. medal with two svc. stars, Vietnam Svc. medal with two service stars, Air Force Overseas Ribbon-Short, Air Force Longevity Svc. award ribbon with seven oak leaf clusters, Air Force Tng. ribbon, Republic Vietnam Campaign medal. Office: Durham Western Heritage Mus 801 S 10th St Omaha NE 68108 Office Phone: 402-444-5071. Business E-Mail: lsmith@dwhm.org.

SMITH, LEONARD R., information technology executive, educator; m. Judith A. Smith, July 11, 1969; children: Joseph M., Jill E. MS in Computer Higher Edn., Nova U., Ft. Lauderdale, FL, 1984. Chairperson Aquinas Coll., Grand Rapids, Mich., 1982—. Fin. elder Oakhill Ch., Grand Rapids, 2001—04. Sp4 US Army, 1966—68, Vietnam. Personal E-mail: ilovewood@hotmail.com. Business E-Mail: len.smith@aquinas.edu.

SMITH, LEONORE RAE, artist; b. Chgo. d. Leon and Rose (Hershfield) Goodman; m. Paul Carl Smith, Apr. 17, 1943; children: Jill Henderson, Laurie Christman. Student, Chgo. Art Inst., 1935-40, U. Chgo., 1939—. Performer in many Broadway shows, with Met. Opera Quartet, Carnegie Hall, nat. concerts; portrait, landscape painter; signature artist Oil Painters of Am., Chgo., 1992-2006, Am. Acad. of Women Artists, 1997-98; ofcl. artist U.S. Coast Guard, Washington, 1989-2000; cert. artist Am. Portrait Soc., Huntington Harbor, Calif., 1985; nat. adv. bd. The Portrait Club, N.Y.C., 1983. Pres. Pacific Palisades Rep. Women, Calif. Recipient Best of Show awards, Salamagundi U.S. Coast Guard, 1989, Pacific Palisades Art Assn., 1987, 1st prize in oils, Greater L.A. Art Competition, Santa Monica, Calif., 1995, prize, The Artist's Mag., 1995, Internat. Soc. Artists, 1977, 1st pl. award, Dream Studio competition, 1996, 1st pl. in portrait, O.P.A. Nat. Show, 2001, award, Northlight Art Mag., 2002, Internat. Artist Mag., 2002, several awards, Calif. Art Club, shown at Nat. Mus. Naval Aviation, Carnegie Mus., Frederick Weisman Mus., Malibu, Calif.; named one of Master Artists of the World, Internat. Artist Mag., 1996. Mem. Am. Acad. Women Artists (signature), Salmagundi Club, Pacific Palisades Art Assn. (past pres.), Oil Painters Am. (signature, 1st Pl. 2001), Am. Portrait Soc. (cert.). Achievements include completing over 50 oil paintings of fallen military in Iraq and Afghanistan. Avocations: singing, acting, poetry. Office Phone: 310-454-4096, 310-454-4223. Personal E-mail: leonorpaul@aol.com.

SMITH, LEROY HARRINGTON, JR., mechanical engineer, consultant; b. Balt., Nov. 3, 1928; s. Leroy Harrington and Edna (Marsh) S.; m. Barbara Ann Williams, July 7, 1951; children: Glenn Harrington, Bruce Lyttleton, Cynthia Ann. BS in Engring., Johns Hopkins U., 1949, MS, 1951, Dr. Engring., 1954. Compressor aerodynamacist Gen. Electric Co., Cin., 1954-61, mgr. turbomachinery devel., 1961-68, mgr. compressor & fan design tech., 1968-75, mgr. turbomachinery aerodynamics tech., 1975-92, cons. technologist Turbomachinery Aerodynamics, 1992-94, cons., 1994—. Contbr. articles to ASME Trans. Recipient Perry T. Egbert Jr. awards, 1969, 83, Charles P. Steinmetz award, 1987 Gen. Electric Co. Fellow ASME (Gas Turbine award 1981, 87, R. Tom Sawyer award 1987, Aircraft Engine Tech. award 1993); mem. NAE, Internat. Soc. Air Breathing Engines (award 2001), Ohio River Launch Club. Achievements include patents in field. Office: GE Aviation 30 Merchant St Princeton Hill P20 Cincinnati OH 45246 Office Phone: 513-552-5702. E-mail: leroy.smith@ae.ge.com.

SMITH, LESLIE EDGAR, vocational school administrator; b. Pitts., Dec. 28, 1950; s. Joel David and Margaret Elizabeth Smith; m. Pamela S. Ghost, June 17, 1994; children: Bethani E. Thomas, Kylene D. Clickner, Andrew J. Clickner. BA, Calif. U. Pa., 1972, MEd, 2006. Vocat. instr. Steel Ctr. AVTS, Jefferson Hills, Pa., 1989—99, vocat. adminstr., 1999—. Baptist. Home: 400 Bunola River Rd PO Box 251 Bunola PA 15020 Office: Steel Center AVTS 565 Lewis Run Rd Jefferson Hills PA 15025 Personal E-mail: lps50@msn.com. Business E-Mail: leslie.smith@aiu3.net.

SMITH, LEWIS J., medical educator, researcher; b. NYC, Oct. 17, 1948; m. Ellen J. Jarrow; children: Laura M.Lang, Deborah S. Wood. BA, CCNY, 1969; MD, U. Rochester, 1973. Diplomate in internal medicine and pulmonary medicine Am. Bd. Internal Medicine. Intern, resident Strong Meml. Hosp., Rochester, NY, 1973—76; pulmonary fellow Boston U., 1976—79; prof. medicine Northwestern U. Feinberg Sch. Medicine, Chgo., 1991—. Office: Northwestern Univ 750 N Lake Shore Dr Ste 707 Chicago IL 60611 Office Phone: 312-503-0501. Business E-Mail: ljsmith@northwestern.edu.

SMITH, LEWIS MOTTER, JR., retired advertising and direct marketing executive; b. Kansas City, Mo., Nov. 4, 1932; s. Lewis Motter and Virginia (Smith) S.; m. Alice Allen, June 28, 1975; children: Katherine Allen, Patience Allen. Student, Kenyon Coll., 1951-53, Columbia U., 1956-58. Copywriter mail order divsn. Grolier Soc., Inc., NYC, 1957-59; free lance copywriter Santa Fe, 1960-61; v.p. creative svcs. Grolier Enterprises Inc., NYC, 1962-67; v.p., creative planning dir. Wunderman, Ricotta & Kline, Inc., NYC, 1968-72; exec. v.p., creative dir., 1972-79; exec. v.p. Young & Rubicam Direct Mktg. Group, 1980; sr. v.p., dir. mktg. Book-of-the-Month Club, Inc., 1980-84, dir., 1981-84; exec. v.p., creative dir. SSC&B: Vos Direct Inc., NYC, 1985-87; pres., dir. creative services Lintas: Direct Inc. (formerly SSC&B: Vos Direct Inc.), NYC, 1987-89; pres. Lew Smith & Assocs., Inc., Hyde Park, NY, 1989—2001. Bd. dirs. Young Concert Artists, Inc., N.Y.C., 1966-67, Harlem Sch. Arts, 1967-68. Served with U.S. Army, 1953-56. Mem. Delta Phi. Episcopalian. Home: 215 East Dr Hurley NY 12443 Personal E-mail: alsmith75@verizon.net.

SMITH, LINDA B., psychology professor, department chairman; BS, Univ. Wis., Madison, 1973; PhD, Univ. Pa., 1977. Asst. prof., psychology Univ. Ind., Bloomington, 1977—81, assoc. prof., 1981—85, prof., 1985—97, chancellor's prof., 1997—, chair, dept. psychol. and brain sciences. Contbr. articles to profl. jours. Recipient Rsch. Career Devel. award, NIH, 1984—89, Award for Early Career Contribution, APA, 1985, James McKeen Cattell Sabbatical award, 1985. Fellow: Am. Acad. Arts & Scis.; mem.: Soc. Exptl. Psychologists, Cognitive Sci. Soc. (governing bd.), Phi Beta Kappa. Office: Psychological & Brain Sci Indiana Univ 1101 E Tenth St Bloomington IN 47405 Office Phone: 812-855-6052. Business E-Mail: Smith4@indiana.edu.*

SMITH, LINDA GENE (GENE SMITH), former legislative staff member; BA, Brigham Young U., 1964, MA, 1966. TV script writer, prodr., on-camera tchr. WETA, 1974; press. sec., legis. asst. Office of Rep. Allan Howe US House of Reps., 1975—76, spl. asst. Office of Rep. Teno Roncalio, 1977—78, press sec. Office of Rep. Gillis Long, 1978—85, press sec. House Dem. Caucus, 1981—85, chief of staff Office of Rep. Tim Wirth, 1985—86, chief of staff Office of Rep. Howard Berman, 1986—2008. Bd. dirs. House Adminstrv. Assts. Assn., Calif. State Soc.*

SMITH, LISA COLEMAN, autism and neurological disabilities special educator; d. Sherman and Ann (Justice) Smith; m. Byron J. Hare, Oct. 14, 1995 (div. 2001); 1 child, Emma Ann; m. Jason Bennett Thatcher, May 25, 2003; 1 child, Olivia Mae. BA in Psychology with honors, U. South Fla., Tampa, 1992; M in Spl. Edn. with honors, Converse Coll., Spartanburg, SC, 2002. Cert. mild mental disabilities disabled SC Dept. Edn., 2003, moderate mental disabilities SC Dept. Edn., 2005, learning disabilities SC Dept. Edn., 2006. Dist. mgr. Nine West Group Inc., Charlotte, NC, 1993—2000; spl. educator resource Pickens County Sch. Dist., Easley, SC, 2002—03; spl. educator, 2003—04; spl. educator neurol. and autism spectrum disorders Greenville County Sch. Dist., Mauldin HS, 2005—. Coach occupl. diploma program Mauldin HS, 2005—, mem. refresh com. tech. support and instrnl. integration, Greenville County. Vol. Country Santa Children's Charity, Pickens County, SC, 2002—, Nat. Health Care Nursing Home, Mauldin, 2005—07, Washington Ctr., Greenville County, 2006—, Briarwood Nursing Home, Simpsonville, 2007—; vol. pre-sch. music instr. Goddard Sch., Simpsonville, SC, 2007—; team leader Strides for Autism Rsch. and Awareness, Greenville County, 2008—. Recipient Pres.'s award, Nine West Group, Divsn. Jones NY, 1997—99; named Dist. Mgr. of Yr., 1997, 1998; grantee, B. Calhoun Hipp Fund for Special Edn., Greenville County, 2008. Mem.: SC Autism Soc. (adv., instr. 2007—, Bravo award 2007), Parent Tchr. Student Assn., Bethel Elem. PTA. Unitarian Universalist. Avocations: gardening, community advocacy for those with disabilities, home improvement projects, history. Office: Mauldin HS 701 E Butler Rd Mauldin SC 29662 Business E-Mail: licsmith@greenville.k12.sc.us.

SMITH, LISA J., lawyer; d. Thomas F. and Carol M. (Severson) Smith. BS, Towson State U.; MA, Auburn U.; JD, U. Md. Jud. clk. Hon. Carol E. Smith Cir. Ct. Balt. City, 1999—2000; assoc. atty. Saul E. Kerpelman & Assocs., P.A., Balt., 2000—06, Schochor, Federico & Staton, P.A., Balt., 2006—. Recipient Adv. for Justice award, Md. Trial Lawyers Assn., 2006. Mem.: Md. Trial Lawyers Assn. Office: Schochor Federico & Staton PA 1211 Saint Paul St Baltimore MD 21202

SMITH, LIZ (MARY ELIZABETH SMITH), columnist, newscaster; b. Ft. Worth, Feb. 2, 1923; d. Sloan and Sarah Elizabeth (McCall) S.; m. George Edward Beeman (div.) BA in Journalism, U. Tex., Austin, 1948. Editor Dell Publns., NYC, 1950-53; assoc. producer CBS Radio, 1953-55, NBC-TV, 1955-59; assoc. Cholly Knickerbocker newspaper column, NYC, 1959-64; film critic Cosmpolitan mag., 1966; columnist Chgo. Tribune-N.Y. Daily News Syndicate (now Tribune Media Services), 1976-91; TV commentator, Live at Five WNBC-TV, NYC, 1978-91; commentator Fox-TV, NYC, 1991—; columnist Newsday, L.A. Times Syndicate, 1991—2005, Family Circle mag., 1993—; freelance mag. writer; commentator Gossip Show E! Entertainment; columnist N.Y. Post, NYC, 1995—2009; publishes column in Daily Variety; contbg. editor Parade Mag., 2009—; co-founder wowOwow-.com (Women on the Web), 2008, columnist, 2009—. Author: The Mother Book, 1978, Natural Blonde, 2000, Munich at Your Door, 2003, Dishing:Great Dish—and Dishes—From America's Most Beloved Gossip Columnist, 2005. Recipient Emmy award for reporting, 1995; named one of The 50 Most Powerful Women in NYC, NY Post, 2007, 2008. *A career in Journalism? Any career at all? I say learn to type. Read a lot. Keep on keeping on. Work is its own reward and success is loving your work. And remember, never give up. After the Middle Ages comes the Renaissance.**

SMITH, L.J., professional football player; b. Highland Park, NJ, May 13, 1980; s. John, Kathy. BA in Labor Studies, Rutgers U., 2003. Tight end Phila. Eagles, 2003—09, Balt. Ravens, 2009—. Sideline reporter NY-NJ All Star Classic, 2008. Founder L.J. Smith Scholarship Fund. Named to All Big-East Team, 2002—03. Achievements include ranking second among tight ends in Rutgers University history with 122 receptions for 1,458 yards and 10 touchdowns. Office: Balt Ravens 1101 Russell St Baltimore MD 21230 Office Phone: 215-632-4495.*

SMITH, LLOYD, musician; b. Cleve., Dec. 1, 1941; s. Thomas George Russell and Anita May (Speer) S.; m. Rheta R. Naylor, Mar. 30, 1967 (div. Nov. 1994); 1 child, Peter Eldon; m. Nancy R. Bean, June 6, 1995. MusB, Curtis Inst. Music, 1965. Tchr. Settlement Music Sch., 1970-72, 92—. Cellist Pitts. Symphony, 1965-67, Phila. Orch., 1967—, asst. prin. cello, 1988-2002, acting assoc. prin. cello, 2002-2003, ret., 2003; soloist Indpls. Symphony, 1958, 68, Garden State Philharm., 1964, Lansdowne Symphony, 1965, West Jersey Chamber Orch., 1991, Haverford-Bryn Mawr Symphony, 1992, The Phila. Orch., 1994, Ocean City Symphony, 2001, The Brn Athym Orch., 2003, The Everett Symphony, 2004; mem. Huntingdon Trio, 1974-93, Wister quartet, 1988—; composer Sonata for cello and piano, Op. 1, 1997, Quintet, Op. 2 for Saratoga Chamber Music Festival, 1998, duet for cello Four Hands, 1999, "You're Invited" for string quartet and violin, 1999, Suite for accordion and strings, Op. 4, 2000, String Quartet Op. 3, 2000, Full Circle for cello Op. 5, 2003, Ceremonial, Op. 6 for 8 cellos, 2004, Trio for cellos, Op. 7, 2004, Cherry Blossoms for Double Quartet, Op. 8, 2006, Zephyr for Double Quartet, Op. 9, 2007, Memorial Op. 10, Cherish the Life, Op. 11, 2007.,Zephyrs op.12, caprice op.13, Quartet 2, Op. 14, 2009, Cherish, Op. 15, 2009, Arches, Op. 16, 2009. Alumni rep. Curtis Inst. Music Bd. Trustees, chmn. Parents' Com., 1989-90; bd. dirs. Phila. Youth Orch., 1987-91, Cmty. Out Reach Partnership, 1988-90, Musical Fund Soc. Phila., 2005—. Recipient C. Hartman Kuhn award for outstanding achievement, Phila. Orch., 2002. Mem. Am. Soc. Ancient Instruments (asst. artistic dir. 1975-77, music dir. 1977-80), Curtis Inst. Music Nat. Alumni Assn. (treas., bd. dirs. 1989-90), 1807 & Friends (bd. dirs. 1994—). Home and Office: 5639 E Wister St Philadelphia PA 19144-1522 E-mail: frnd1807@verizon.net.

SMITH, LLOYD FRANKLIN, political organization administrator; Chief of staff to Rep. Jo An Emerson US House of Reps., Washington; exec. dir. Mo. Rep. Party, 2009—. Republican. Office: Mo Rep Party 204 East Dunklin Jefferson City MO 65101*

SMITH, LLOYD HOLLINGSWORTH, physician; b. Easley, SC, Mar. 27, 1924; s. Lloyd H. and Phyllis (Page) S.; m. Margaret Constance Avery, Feb. 27, 1954; children— Virginia Constance, Christopher Avery, Rebecca Anne, Charlotte Page, Elizabeth Hollingsworth, Jeffrey Hollingsworth. AB, Washington and Lee U., 1944, D.Sc., 1969; MD, Harvard, 1948. Intern, then resident Mass. Gen. Hosp., Boston, 1948-50, chief resident physician, 1955-56; mem. Harvard Soc. Fellows, 1952-54; asst. prof. Harvard Soc. Fellows (Med. Sch.), 1956-63; vis. investigator Karolinska Inst., Stockholm, 1954-55, Oxford (Eng.) U., 1963-64; prof. medicine, chmn. dept. U. Calif. Med. Sch., San Francisco, 1964-85, assoc dean, 1985-2000. Mem. Pres.'s Sci. Adv. Com., 1970-73 Bd. overseers Harvard, 1974-80. Served to capt., M.C. AUS, 1950-52. Mem. Am. Acad. Arts and Scis., Am. Soc. Clin. Investigation (pres. 1969-70), Western Soc. Clin. Rsch. (pres. 1969-70), Assn. Am. Physicians (pres. 1974-75), Am. Fedn. Clin. Rsch. Achievements include special research genetic and metabolic diseases. Home: 309 Evergreen Dr Kentfield CA 94904-2709 Office: U Calif San Francisco Med Ctr San Francisco CA 94143-0001 E-mail: lloydhsmith@aol.com.

SMITH, LOIS ARLENE, actress, writer; b. Topeka, Nov. 3, 1930; d. William Oren and Carrie D. (Gottshalk) Humbert; m. Wesley Dale Smith, Nov. 5, 1948 (div. 1973); 1 child, Moon Elizabeth. Student, U. Wash., Seattle, 1948-50; studied with Lee Strasberg, Actor's Studio, NYC, 1955—. Guest dir. Juilliard Sch., 1987; Clarence Ross fellow Am. Theater Wing at Eugene O'Neill Theater Ctr., 1983; mem. adv. panel program fund Pub. Broadcasting Service, 1981-82; hon. founder Harold Clurman Theatre Artists Fund, Ctr. for Arts, SUNY-Purchase, 1981 Author: play All There Is, 1982; debut in Time Out for Ginger, Biway 1952; actress Broadway and off-Broadway prodns., 1952—; stage appearances include Theater of the Living Arts, Mark Taper Forum, Long Wharf Theater, Balt. Centerstage and Steppenwolf Theater Co.; appears on network and pub. TV programs; stage appearances include, The Young and the Beautiful, 1955, The Glass Menagerie, 1956, Blues for Mr. Charlie, 1964, Orpheus Descending, 1957, Miss Julie, 1966, Uncle Vanya, 1965, 69, The Iceman Cometh, 1973, Harry Outside, 1975, Hillbilly Women, 1979, 81, the Vienna Notes, 1985, The Stick Wife, April Snow, 1987, The Grapes of Wrath, 1988-89, 90, Measure for Measure, Beside Herself, 1989, Escape from Happiness, 1993, Buried Child, 1995-96, Defying Gravity, 1997, Impossible Marriage, 1998, Mrs. Warren's Profession, 1999, Give Me Your Answer, Do, 1999, Mother Courage, 2001, The Trip to Bountiful, 2005, 2008 (Lucille Lortel award, outstanding actress 2006, Outer Critics' Cir. award outstanding actress in a play 2006, OBIE award Village Voice 2006, Drama Desk award outstanding actress in a play, 2006, Kingsley-Evans award, 2006, Jeff award, Chgo., 2008), Surface to Air, 2007; 100 Saints You Should Know, 2007, The Tempest, 2009, Dividing The Estate, 2009, films include East of Eden, 1955, Five Easy Pieces, 1970, Next Stop Greenwich Village, 1975, Resurrection, 1980, Four Friends, 1981, Green Card, 1990, Fried Green Tomatoes, 1991, Falling Down, 1993, How to Make an American Quilt, 1995, Dead Man Walking, 1995, Larger than Life, 1996, Twister, 1996, Tumbleweeds, 1998, Minority Report, 2002, The Laramie Project, 2002, Iron-Jawed Angels, 2004, Best Thief in the World, 2004, P.S., 2004, Sweet Land, 2005, Hollywoodland, 2006, Kill Shot, 2006, Diminished Capacity, 2008, TV True Blood, 2008. Recipient Tony nominations, for Grapes of Wrath, 1990, Buried Child, 1996, Steppenwolf Ensemble Nat. Medal of Arts, 1998, Theatre Hall of Fame, 2007; named Best Supporting Actress for Five Easy Pieces, Nat. Soc. Film Critics, 1971; named to named to Filmdom's Famous Fives for East of Eden, Failm Daily mag., 1955. Mem. SAG, AFTRA, Actors Equity Assn., Dramatists Guild, Actors Studio, Ensemble Studio Theater, Steppenwolf Theatre Co. Ensemble, Acad. Motion Picture Arts and Scis.

SMITH, LORAN BRADFORD, political science professor; b. Medford, Mass., July 23, 1946; s. Gordon T. and Edith A. S. BA, Salem State Coll., 1968; MA, Okla. State U., 1971; PhD, U. Nebr., 1980. Instr. Black Hills State Coll., Spearfish, S.D., 1971-74, Augustana Coll., Sioux Falls, S.D., 1974-77; asst. prof. Mo. So. State Coll., Joplin, 1980-82, Washburn U., Topeka, Kans., 1982-86, assoc. prof., 1988-92; grad. faculty U. Kans., Lawrence, 1988-89; prof. Washburn U., 1992—. Election analyst KSNT-TV, Topeka, 1984-92, KTKA-TV, Topeka, 2008-. Contbr. articles to profl. jours. Chair pilot task force City of Topeka, 1983-84, mem. charter rev. com., 1999; chair Univ. Coun., 2003-2005; mem. coll. faculty coun., chair CAS curriculum com., social sci. divsn. Mem. Am. Polit. Sci. Assn., Am. Soc. Pub. Adminstrs. (Kans. chpt. v.p. 1985-87, pres. 1987-88), Urban Affairs Assn., Kansas Delta Alumni Corp., Sigma Phi Epsilon (Disting. Alumnus award 1997, vol. Yr. 2008). Home: 4301 SW 15th St apt 309 Topeka KS 66604-4311 Office: Washburn U 1700 SW College Ave Topeka KS 66621-0001 Office Phone: 785-670-2026.

SMITH, LOREN ALLAN, federal judge; b. Chgo., Dec. 22, 1944; m. Catherine Yore; children: Loren Jr., Adam (dec.). BA in Polit. Sci., Northwestern U., Evanston, Ill., 1966, JD, 1969; LLD (hon.), John Marshall Law Sch., 1995, Capitol U. Law Sch., 1996, Campbell U., Buies Creek, NC, 1997. Bar: Ill. 1970, US Ct. Mil. Appeals 1973, US Ct. Appeals (DC circuit) 1974, US Supreme Ct. 1974, US Ct. Claims, 1985, US Ct. Appeals (fed. circuit) 1986, US Ct. Fed. Claims. Host nightly radio talk show What's Best for America?, 1972; cons. Sidney & Austin, Chgo., 1972-73; gen. atty. FCC, 1973; asst. to spl. counsel to the pres. The White House, Washington, 1973-74; spl. asst. US atty US Dept. Justice, Washington, 1974-75; chief counsel Reagan for Pres. campaigns, 1976, 80; prof. Delaware Law Sch., 1976-84; dep. dir. Office Exec. Br. Mgmt. Presdl. Transition, 1980-81; chmn. Adminstrv. Conf. US, 1981-85; judge US Ct. Fed. Claims, Washington, 1985—2000, chief judge, 1986-2000, sr. judge, 2000—. Disting. lectr. Columbus Sch. Law, Cath. U. America, 1996—; Disting. adj. prof. law George Mason U. Sch. Law, 1998—; past mem. President's Cabinet Coun. Legal Policy, Presidents' Cabinet Coun. on Mgmt. and Adminstrn.; chmn. Coun. Ind. Regulatory Agys.; served as disting. jurist in residence U. Denver; Allen chair U. Richmond Sch. Law, 1995, internat. elections observer Chile and Serbia; internat. speaker in field; internat. appearances on TV and radio. Co-author: Black America and Organized Labor: A Fair Deal?, 1979; contbr. articles to profl. jours. Advisory bd. mem. WETA Public Radio Cmty. Advisory Bd. Recipient Presdl. medal Cath. U. America Law Sch., 1993, Romanian medal of justice Romanian Ministry Justice, 1995, Ronald Reagan Public Svc. award Nat. Property Rights Conf., 1997. Mem. Bar Assn. DC (honoray mem., jud. honoree award 1997), U. Club (Washington, named club mem. of yr. 1991, chmn. entertainment com., centennial com.). Republican. Jewish. Office: US Ct of Fed Claims 717 Madison Pl NW Washington DC 20005*

SMITH, LOUIS JOHN, historian; b. Harvey, Ill., Mar. 6, 1940; s. Louis and Agnes Smith; m. Sharon Ann Moeller, June 13, 1965; children: David Louis, Deborah Ann Tully. BA in History, Carthage Coll., Kenosha, Wis., 1963; MA in History, Ill. State U., Normal, 1967; PhD in History, Mich. State U., East Lansing, 1977. Asst. prof. Ill. State U., Normal, 1969—70; sr. editor, chief European and gen. divsn. historian's office US Dept. State, Washington, 1971—2005; dir. oral history program Hist. Office, Office of Sec. of Def., Washington, 2006—08. Author: Yorktown: Cornerstone of Independence, 1981; editor: The Foreign Relations of the United States, 20 vols., 1974—2005; contbg. editor: American Foreign Relations: Current Documents, 10 vols., 1980—90. Sec. Chapel Sq. West Civic Assn., Annandale, Va., 1985—2005; pres. bd. dirs. Queen of Peace Ch., Arlington, Va., 1975—80. Recipient Superior Honor and Franklin awards, US Dept. State, 1980—2004, Sec. of State's Lifetime Achievement award, 2005; named to Hall of Fame, Coll. Arts and Scis., Ill. State U., 2005. Mem.: Soc. Historians of Am. Fgn. Rels., Orgn. Am. Historians, Am. Hist. Assn. Avocations: opera, gardening, golf, youth athletics. Home: 8327 Epinard Ct Annandale VA 22003 Office: Hist Office Office of Sec of Defense 1777 Kent St Arlington VA 22209 Home Phone: 703-425-9063; Office Phone: 703-688-7575.

SMITH, LOVIE, professional football coach; b. Gladewater, Tex., May 8, 1958; m. MaryAnne Smith; children: Mikal, Matthew, Miles. BA, U. Tulsa, 1979. Head coach Big Sandy HS Football Team, 1980, Cascia Hall Prep, Tulsa, 1981, U. Tulsa, 1983—86, U. Wis., 1987, Ariz. State U., 1988—91, U. Ky, 1992, U. Tenn., 1993—94, Ohio State U., 1995, Chgo. Bears, 2004—; linebacker coach Tampa Bay Buccaneers, 1996—2001; defensive coord. St. Louis Rams, 2001—03. Named NFL Coach of Yr., AP, 2005. Achievements include being one (of two) African-American head coaches to lead a NFL team to the Super Bowl, 2007. Office: Chgo Bears 1000 Football Dr Lake Forest IL 60045*

SMITH, MABEL HARGIS, retired secondary school educator, musician; b. Ruby, La., Sept. 29, 1917; d. Ildephonso Albinos Hargis and Stella Gertrude Baker; m. Thomas Leonard Smith, Jr., Dec. 29, 1950; 1 child, Susan Claire Smith McLaughlin. BA, La. Coll., 1938; MusM, Northwestern U., 1952. Tchr. Tioga H.S., La., 1938—75; pianist-organist children's choir Tioga First Bapt. Ch., Tioga, 1941—2002. Recipient Cmty. Svc. award, Matinee Music Club, 1953—54, Recognition for musical contbns., Curtis T. Hines Masonic Lodge, 1997; named Sr. Adult of Yr., First Bapt. Ch., 1989, Disting. Alumna, La. Coll., 1977; named one of Women of Century, Daily Town Talk, Alexandria, La., 1999. Mem.: La. Music Educators (Hall of Fame 1999), Music Educator's.Nat. Conf., Delta Omicron Internat., Delta Kappa Gamma. Baptist. Avocations: sewing, cooking, reading, gardening. Home: 415 McMahon St Deridder LA 70634

SMITH, DAME MAGGIE (MARGARET NATALIE SMITH CROSS), actress; b. Ilford, Eng., Dec. 28, 1934; d. Nathaniel and Margaret Hutton (Little) S.; m. Robert Stephens, 1967 (div. 1974), 2 children; m. Beverley Cross, 1974 (dec. 1998). Grad., Oxford High Sch. Girls; D.Litt. (hon.), St. Andrews, 1971; DLitt (hon.), Oxford U., 1994. Asst. stage mgr., actor Oxford Playhouse, 1951—53. Stage and film actress, 1952—, stage appearances include New Faces, debut N.Y.C, 1956, Share My Lettuce, 1957, The Stepmother, 1958, Rhinoceros, 1960, Strip the Willow, 1960, The Rehearsal, 1961, The Private Ear and the Public Eye, 1962 (Evening Standard award for best actress, 1962), Mary, Mary, 1963 (Variety Club award named actress of yr., 1963), Othello, 1964, Twelfth Night, 1952, Hay Fever, 1964, 1977, Master Builder, 1964, Much Ado About Nothing, 1965, 1980, Miss Julie, 1965, Black Comedy, 1965, Hedda Gabler, 1970 (Evening Standard award, 1970), Three Sisters, 1970, 1976, Private Lives, 1972, 1974 (Variety Club award, 1972), 1978, Cleopatra, 1976, Way of the World, 1976, 1984—85 (Evening Standard award for best actress, 1984), A Midsummer Night's Dream, 1977, Richard III, 1977, As You Like It, 1977, Macbeth, 1978, Night and Day, 1979—80, Virginia, 1980 (Evening Standard award for best actress, 1982), Interpreters, 1985—86, Lettice and Lovage, 1987—88 (Tony Award for best actress, 1990), 1990, The Importance of Being Earnest, 1993, Three Tall Women, 1994—95 (Evening Standard award for best actress, 1994, Variety Club award for best actress, 1994), Talking Heads, 2004, Bed Among the Lentils, 1996, A Delicate Balance, 1997—98, Lady in the Van, 1999—2000, Breath of Life, 2002—03, The Lady from Dubuque, 2007, appearances at Old Vic, 1959—60, charter mem. Royal Nat. Theatre, London, 1963—; actor: (films) Child in the House, 1956, Nowhere to Go, 1958, Go to Blazes, 1962, The VIPs, 1963, The Pumpkin Eater, 1964, Young Cassidy, 1965, Othello, 1965, The Honey Pot, 1967, Oh What a Lovely War, 1968, Hot Millions, 1968, The Prime of Miss Jean Brodie, 1969 (Brit. Acad. of Film & TV Arts for best actress, 1969, Film Critic's Guild for best actress, 1969, Acad. award for best actress, 1970, Variety Club for film actress of yr., 1988), Travels with My Aunt, 1973, Love and Pain and the Whole Damn Thing, 1973, Murder by Death, 1976, Death on the Nile, 1978, California Suite, 1978 (Golden Globe for best supporting actress, 1979, Acad. award for best supporting actress, 1979), Quartet, 1981 (Evening Standard award for best actress, 1981), Clash of the Titans, 1981, Evil under the Sun, 1981, Better Late Than Never, 1982, The Missionary, 1983, A Private Function, 1984 (Brit. Acad. of Film & TV Arts for best actress, 1984), A Room with a View, 1986 (Brit. Acad. of Film & TV Arts for best supporting actress, 1986, Golden Globe for best supporting actress, 1986), The Lonely Passion of Judith Hearn, 1988 (Brit. Acad. of Film & TV Arts for best actress, 1989), Paris by Night, 1988, Hook, 1991, Sister Act, 1992, The Secret Garden, 1993, Sister Act 2: Back in the Habit, 1993, Richard III, 1995, The First Wives Club, 1996, Washington Square, 1997, Tea with Mussolini, 1999 (Brit. Acad. of Film & TV Arts for best supporting actress, 2000), The Last September, 2000, Harry Potter and the Sorcerer's Stone, 2001 (Golden Satelite (Internat. Press Assn.) for best supporting actress, 2002), Gosford Park, 2001 (NY Critics Online for best supporting actress, 2002, SAG award for best ensemble in a motion picture, 2002), Divine Secrets of Ya-Ya Sisterhood, 2002, Harry Potter and the Chamber of Secrets, 2002, Harry Potter and the Prisoner of Azkaban, 2004, Ladies in Lavender, 2004, Harry Potter and the Goblet of Fire, 2005, Keeping Mum, 2005, Harry Potter and the Order of the Phoenix, 2007, Becoming Jane, 2007; (TV films) Night of the Plague, 1957, Boy Meets Girl, 1957, The Widower, 1958, The Curious Savage, 1958, Sunday Out of Season, 1958, A Phoenix Too Frequent, 1959, For Services Rendered, 1959, Guardian Angel, 1960, The Savages, 1961, Hay Fever, 1965, Penelope, 1965, Much Ado About Nothing, 1967, Home and Beauty, 1967, On Approval, 1968, Man and Superman, 1968, The Merchant of Venice, 1972, The Millionairess, 1972, Mrs. Silly, 1983, Lily in Love, 1983, Bed Among the Lentils, 1988 (Brit. Acad. of Film & TV Arts for best actress, 1987, Baniff (Can.) for best actress, 1987), Memento Mori, 1992, Suddenly Last Summer, 1993, Curtain Call, 1998, David Copperfield, 1999, All the King's Men, 1999, My House in Umbria, 2003 (Emmy award for best actress miniseries or movie, 2003), Capturing Mary, 2007;, performer albums and tapes. Recipient Best Film Actress award Soc. Film and TV Arts U.K., 1968, Best Actress LA Critics, 1970, Taomina Gold award, 1985, Hanbury Shakespeare prize, FVS Found. 1991, Lifetime Achievement award, Brit. Acad. of Film & TV Arts, 1992, William Shakespeare award for Classical Theatre, Wahington, DC's Shakespeare Theatre, 1999; decorated Commdr. British Empire, 1970, Dame of the British Empire, 1990; named to Theater Hall of Fame, 1994. Fellow: British Film Inst., British Acad. Film & Television Arts. Office: 41 Warbeck Rd London W12 8NS England*

SMITH, M(AHLON) BREWSTER, retired psychologist, educator; b. Syracuse, NY, June 26, 1919; s. Mahlon Ellwood and Blanche Alice (Hinman) S.; m. Jean Dresden Schwartz, June 1942 (div. 1945); m. Deborah Anderson, June, 1947; children: Joshua H., T. Daniel, Rebecca M., J. Torquil. Student, Reed Coll., Portland, Oreg., 1935-38; AB, Stanford U., 1939, AM, 1940; PhD, Harvard U., 1947. Jr. analyst Office Coordinator of Info., U.S. Govt., 1941; Rantoul scholar Harvard U., 1940-41, Social Sci. Research Council fellow, 1946-47, asst. prof. social psychology, dept. social rels., 1947-49; prof. psychology, chmn. dept. Vassar Coll., 1949-52; staff Social Sci. Rsch. Coun., 1952-56; prof. psychology NYU, 1956-59, U. Calif. at Berkeley, 1959-68, dir. Inst. Human Devel., 1965-68; prof., chmn. dept. psychology U. Chgo., 1968-70; prof. psychology U. Calif. at Santa Cruz, 1970-88, prof. emeritus, 1988—, vice chancellor social scis., 1970-75, ret., 1988. Fellow Ctr. Advanced Studies Behavioral Scis., 1964-65; v.p. Joint Commn. Mental Illness and Health, 1955-61. Author: Social Psychology and Human Values, 1969, Humanizing Social Psychology, 1974, Values, Self and Society, 1991, For a Significant Social Psychology, 2003; co-author: The American Soldier, vol. 2, 1949, Opinions and Personality, 1956; editor: Jour. Social Issues, 1951-55, Jour. Abnormal Soc. Psychology, 1956-61; contbr. articles to profl. jours. Rsch. officer Info. and Edn. divsn. War Dept., 1943-46; rsch. assoc. spl. com. on soldier attitudes Social Sci. Rsch. Coun. 1946. Maj. AUS, 1942-46 Decorated Bronze Star medal; NIMH fellow, 1964-65, NEH fellow, 1975-76; Belding scholar Found. for Child Devel., 1982-83; Gold medal award Am. Psychol. Found., 1992 Fellow AAAS, APA (pres. 1978, Disting. Contbn. to Pub. Interest award 1988, Henry A. Murray award 1993); mem. Soc. Psychol. Study Social Issues (pres. 1959, Kurt Lewin Meml. award 1986, Presdl. citation 2004), Western Psychol. Assn. (pres. 1986, Lifetime Contbn. award 1996), Psychologists for Social Responsibility (pres. 1987-90), Internat. Soc. Polit. Psychology (Harold Lasswell award 1993), Internat. Assn. Applied Psychology (pres. divsn. polit. psychology 1994-98), Soc. Peace, Conflict and Violence (Lifetime Contbn. to Peace Psychology award 1999), Cosmos Club (Washington), Phi Beta Kappa, Sigma Xi. Democrat. Home: Dominican Oaks Apt B-203 3400 Paul Sweet Rd Santa Cruz CA 95065

SMITH, MALCOLM A., state legislator; b. Queens, NY, Aug. 9, 1956; m. Michele Lisby; children: Julian, Amanda. BS in Bus. Adminstrn., Fordham U., Bronx, NY, 1978; MBA in Fin., Ops. Mgmt., Adelphi U., Garden City, NY; postgraduate, NYU, NYC, 1985. Procurement mgr., Office Econ. Devel. NYC, 1985—86; sr. aide to Rep. Floyd H. Flake US House of Reps., Washington, 1986—91; chief of staff to Councilman Archie Spigner NY City Coun.; City Hall asst. to Mayor Ed Koch Office of the Mayor, NYC; founder Smith Devel. Corp., 1991; pres. Smith Darmon Group-Developers, 1991—99; mem. Dist. 14 NY State Senate, 2000—, majority leader, 2009, pres. pro tempore, 2009, temporary pres., acting lt. gov., 2009—. Founder Operation Everybody Works, Peninsula Preparatory Acad.; mem. Southeast Queens Housing Devel. Corp., Urban League. Trustee Greater Allen Cathedral, Merrick Acad.-Queens Pub. Charter Sch.; pres. Neighborhood Housing Services. Mem.: NAACP, Kiwanis, Delta Mu Delta. Democrat. Office: 909 Legislative Office Bldg Albany NY 12247 also: 205-19 Linden Blvd Saint Albans NY 11412 Office Phone: 518-455-2701, 718-528-4290. Business E-Mail: masmith@senate.state.ny.us.*

SMITH, MALCOLM BERNARD, investment company executive; b. Lynn, Mass., May 27, 1923; s. Philip and Ida (Zenis) S.; m. Betty Booth, June 20, 1948; children: Eric, Daniel. BA summa cum laude, Dartmouth Coll., 1944; MA in Econs., Harvard U., 1948; degree (hon.), New Sch.

Social Rsch., 1995. Sec. Gen. Am. Investors Co., NYC, 1956-57, treas., 1957-59, v.p., 1958-61, pres., 1961-89, vice chmn., 1989-97; sr. cons., 1997—. Chmn. fin. com. N.Y. Found., 1973—82, treas., 1979—82, trustee, 1973—89; chmn. N.Y. Found., 1982—85; chmn. New Sch. for Social Rsch., NYC, 1985—95, trustee, 1982—, treas., 1982—84, chmn. ednl. policy com., 1984—85, chmn. exec. com., 1985—95; mem. investment com. Phi Beta Kappa Found., 1987—96; bd. dirs. Learning Smith, Inc., 1992—93, Cybersmith, Inc., 1994—97; mem. investment com. Fedn. Jewish Philantrophies, NY, 1975—96; bd. dirs. Human Rights Watch, 1993—2001, emeritus, 2001—; trustee John Simon Guggenheim Meml. Found., 1982—95, chmn. fin. com., 1985—95; mng. trustee Permanent Fund of MLA, 1987—. With US Army, 1943—46. Mem. AAAS (chmn. investment and fin. com. 1975—), Investment Co. Inst. (bd. govs. 1987-95), Assn. Publicly Traded Investment Funds (bd. dirs. 1970-87, chmn. 1971-79, Coun. on Fgn. Rels., N.Y. Soc. Security Analysts, Harvard Club (bd. mgrs. 1984-86), Century Assn. N.Y.c. (treas., bd. mgrs. 1999-2003), Phi Beta Kappa Fellows (adv. com. 1984-93, bd. dirs. 1993—), Phi Beta Kappa. Home: PO Box 358 Pound Ridge NY 10576-0358 Office: 1150 Park Ave New York NY 10128-1244

SMITH, MALCOLM SOMMERVILLE, bass vocalist; b. Rockville Centre, NY, June 22, 1933; s. Carlton Newell and Margaret (Sommerville) S.; m. Margaret Yauger, Oct. 4, 1975. B.Music Edn., Oberlin Coll., 1957, B.Mus., 1960; MA in Ednl. Adminstrn, Columbia Tchrs. Coll., 1958; student, Ind. U. Sch. Music, 1960-62. Dir. choral music Ramapo Regional H.S., Wyckoff, NJ, 1958—60; artist, faculty U. So. Maine, 2003—09. Mem. artist faculty U. So. Maine, 2003—07. Bass: Lyric Opera, bass soloist: Russian tour, Robert Shaw Choral, 1962; leading bass N.Y.C. Opera, 1965—70, Deutsche Oper Am Rhein, Dusseldorf, Germany, 1971—, Vienna State Opea, 1973—74, 86 Met. Opera, Japan tour, 1975, Met. Opera, N.Y.C., 1975—77, Paris Opera, 1978, Barcelona Opera, 1978, Sao Paulo, Brazil, 1978, Mexico City, 1979, 80, Berlin Opera, 1979, 80, Montreal Symphony, 1979, 80, 81, 82, Hamburg Opera, 1981, Koln Opera, 1980, Stuttgart Opera, 1980, Frankfurt Opera, 1980, Rome Opera, 1980, Trieste (Italy) Opera, 1981, Berlin Staatsoper, 1982, 85, Lyric Opera Phila., 1982, L.A. Philharm. at Hollywood Bowl, 1984, Mannheim Opera, Germany, 1986, Turin Opera, Italy, 1986, 88, Bordeaux, France, 1987, Dresden Opera, Germany, 1987, Staats Opera Berlin Japan tour, 1987, Polish TV, 1989, Oslo Opera, 1987, Paris Radio, 1988-89, Orange Festival, France, 1988, Penderecki Festival, Krakow, Poland, 1988, maj. soloist Schleswig Holstein Festival, Germany, 1989, Krakow Philharmonic, Poland, 1988, Maggio Musicale, Florence, Italy, 1988, Boston Symphony, Minn., Cin., Houston, Utah, Seattle, Chgo., Phila., Balt. Symphony, 1993, Mex. Nat. Symphony, 1993, nat. symphonies, also Cin. Summer Opera, Central City (Colo.), Summer Opera, Festival of Two Worlds, Spoleto, Italy, Saratoga Festival, 1985, debut La Scala, Milan, Italy, 1982, Salzburg Festival, 1986, Athens Festival, 1987, Bordeaux (France) Opera, 1987, Ft. Worth Opera, 1988, Orange Festival, France, 1988, Staatsoper Munich, 1990, Bastille Opera, Paris, 1991, Heidelberg Summer Festival, 1991, 92, Brussels Opera, 1992, 93, 94, 97, Opera Nice, France, 1992, Opera Montpelier, France, 1992, Cin. Opera, 1994, 2000, Dusseldorf Opera, 1994, Japan tour, 1994, Bregenz (Austria) Festival, 1996, Honolulu Opera, 1996, 98, Balt. Opera, 1996, Prague Autumn Festival, 1997, Cin. Opera, 1998, 2000, Grand Rapids Opera, 2000, Dusseldorf Opera, 2001, 2002, Portland Opera, 2001, Portland Symphony, 2002, recorded War and Peace, 1986, Penderecki Requiem, 1990, Aspen Music Festival, 1997; musician: Portland Symphony Orch., 2002—05, Schwerin Opera Festival, 2003, Opera Orch. NY, 2005, Springfield Festival, 2006, Spoleto Festival, 2006, Port Opera, 2006, 2008, Helena Mont. Symphony, 2007, Longleaf Opera, NC, 2008, Dusseldorf Opera, 2008—; U. So. Maine, 2003—08. Served with AUS, 1954-56. Recipient Kämmersanger title Dusseldorf (Germany) Opera, 1996. Congregationalist. Office: care Thea Dispeker Artists Rep 59 E 54th St New York NY 10022-4211 Business E-Mail: malcolms.smith@maine.edu. *Hard work and a sense of humor.*

SMITH, MARGARET TAYLOR, volunteer; b. Roanoke Rapids, NC, May 31, 1925; d. George Napoleon and Sarah Luella (Waller) T.; m. Sidney William Smith Jr., Aug. 15, 1947; children: Sarah Smith, Sidney William Smith III, Susan Smith, Amy Smith. BA in Sociology, Duke U., 1947. Chair emeritus bd. trustees Kresge Found., Troy, Mich., 1985—; chmn. Nat. Coun. for Women's Studies Duke U., NC, 1986—, chmn. Trinity Bd. Visitors NC, 1988-98; chair emeritus. Chmn. bd. visitors Wayne State U. Med. Sch., 1993; bd. dirs., mem. exec. com. Detroit Med. Ctr.; mem. bd. govs. Detroit Med. Ctr. Recipient the Merrill-Palmer award Wayne State U., Detroit, 1987, Zimmerman award Gtr. Detroit Health Coun., Athena award C. of C., 1998, Women of Achievement award Mich. Women's Fedn., 1999, disting. svc. award Wayne State U., 1999; named disting. alumna award Duke U. Mem. The Village Club, Internat. Women's Forum, Pi Beta Phi, Phi Beta Kappa. Methodist. E-mail: sidmyth@aol.com.

SMITH, MARGUERITE IRENE, gifted and talented educator; b. Duryea, Pa., Aug. 10, 1950; d. John Sylvester and Irene Anne Morris; m. James Michael Smith, June 9, 1973; children: Jennifer Lynn Smith Ruth, Kimberly Ann Smith Ikeler. BS in Secondary Edn., Bloomsburg U., 1972, EdM in Reading, 1995. Tchr. head start, home visitor Ctrl. Susquehanna Intermediate Unit 16, Montandon, Pa., 1987—91, intervention specialist, 1993; tchr. Spanish H.S. Lewisburg Area Sch. Dist., 1991—92, aide, 1992—94; tchr. reading Lewisburg Area Sch. Dist., Donald H. Eichhorn Mid. Sch., 1994—98, specialist reading, coord. gifted, 1998—. Mem. Am. Legion Post #841 Marching Band, Montandon; sec., treas. No. Deanery Coun. of Cath. Women, Sacred Heart Coun. of Cath. Women, Lewisburg, 1984—88; pres. Parish Coun. Sacred Heart, 1988—89; eucharistic min. Sacred Heart Jesus Ch., 1989—2003; asst. to Cath. chaplain Geisinger Med. Ctr., Danville, 1988—91. Mem.: AAUW (v.p. membership 1988—89), ASCD, Keystone State Reading Assn., Susquehanna Valley Reading Coun., Internat. Reading Assn., Buffalo Valley Singers (pres. 2001—02), Mifflinburg Buggy Mus. Roman Catholic. Avocations: French horn, singing, reading, needlecrafts, gardening. Office: Donald H Eichhorn Mid Sch 2057 Washington Ave Lewisburg PA 17837

SMITH, MARIE EDMONDS, real estate agent, property manager; b. Quapaw, Okla., Oct. 5, 1927; d. Thomas Joseph and Maud Ethel Edmonds; m. Robert Lee Smith, Aug. l4, 1966 (dec. 1983). Grad. vocat. nurse, Hoag Hosp., Costa Mesa, Calif., 1953; BA, Vanguard U., 1955; MS, U. Alaska, 1963. Lic. vocat. nurse, Calif.; cert. sci. tchr., Alaska. Nurse Calif. Dept. Nurses, Costa Mesa, 1952-60; tchr. Alaska Dept. Edn., Aniak and Anchorage, 1955-60; tchr. sci. Garden Grove Sch. Dist., Calif., 1960-87; property mgr. Huntington Beach, Calif., 1970—; agent Sterling Realtors, Huntington Beach, 1988—. Author: Ocean Biology, l969. Bd. dirs., tchr. Newport Mesa Christian Ctr., Costa Mesa, 1983-2001; com. chmn. Garden Grove Unified Sch. Dist. PTA, 1977. NSF grantee, 1960-62. Mem. AAUW, Vanguard U. Alumnae Assn. Republican. Avocations: skin diving, travel. Home: 83ll Reilly Dr Huntington Beach CA 92646 Office: L8l53 Brookhurst St Fountain Valley CA 92708

SMITH, MARIE F., lobbyist, former association executive; b. East St. Louis, Ill., Mar. 12, 1939; d. David and Christina Ford; m. Richard Stanley Smith, Dec. 13, 1986; stepchildren: Jeffrey, Reginald, Laurie Debrotz. BA, Fisk U., Nashville, 1961. Dir. manpower mgmt. & orgn. planning Social Security Adminstrn.; commr. Status of Women; chair Nat. Legis. Coun., Am. Assn. Retired Persons (AARP), Washington, spokesperson Women's Initiative Prog., mem. audit & fin. com., exec. dir. search com., 2000—02, treas. found. bd. dirs., 2000—02, pres. elect, 2002—04, pres., 2004—08. Active Interfaith Vol. Caregivers; sec. bd. dirs. Maui Adult Day Care Ctr.; pres. bd. dirs. Maui Vol. Ctr. Recipient Woman of Excellence award, Commn. Status of Women, Circle of Women award, County Commn. Status of Women; named one of America's 100 Most Influential African Am. Leaders, Ebony mag. Mem.: Nat. Assn. Ret. Fed. Employees (pres.), African Am. Heritage Found. Maui (pres.), Zonta Internat. Avocations: writing, travel, golf.*

SMITH, MARION PAFFORD, retired avionics company executive; b. Waycross, Ga., Dec. 12, 1925; s. Rossa Elbert and Lillian Solee (Pafford) S.; m. Esther Pat Davis, Nov. 23, 1952; children: Bryan P., Danton D., Patricia Anne. Student, Okla. State U., 1944, Yale U., 1945; BS in EE, La. State U., 1949; postgrad., U. So. Fla., 1966-70. Engr. Bell Telephone Co., Baton Rouge, 1949-51; mgr. engring. Vitro Labs., Silver Spring, Md., 1952-57; design engring. mgr. dept. design and constrn. flight hand contrs. Space Shuttle and Space Sta. Honeywell Avionics Div., Clearwater, Fla., 1957-98. Vice chmn., bd. dirs. First Union, Largo, Fla., 1985-93; cons. U.S. Army Mgmt. Engring. Tng. Agy., 1975-79; U.S. Del. Internat. Elec. Tech. Commn., 1965-85, chmn. chief U.S. tech. adviser com. on reliability and maintainability, 1975-85, v.p., exec. com. U.S. nat. com., 1975-84; U.S. del. NATO Quality Conf., 1973; mem. White House Summit Conf. on Inflation, 1975; del. White House Conf. on Handicapped, 1977; mem. nat. adv. coun. on devel. disabilities HEW, 1974-78, Fla. Devel. Disabilities Coun., 1974-78; pres. Fla. Advocacy Ctr. for Persons with Disabilities, Inc., 1997-2000; commr. State of Fla. Occupl. Access Commn., 2000-2002; mem. devel. coun. Morton Plant Hosp., Clearwater, 1971-74. 1st lt. Signal Corps, AUS, 1944-45, 51-52. Served to 1st lt. Signal Corps AUS, 1944-45, 51-52. Recipient McDonald award Fla. Rehab. Assn., 1968; Bilgore award Citizen of Year Clearwater, Fla., 1969; Outstanding Svc. award Am. Soc. Quality Control, 1968-69; United Comml. Travelers award Most Outstanding Svc. Retarded Fla., 1970; named Engr. of Year Fla. W. Coast, 1970; Svc. to Mankind award Sertoma Clubs, 1977 Fellow IEEE (dir., Nat. Reliability award 1979); mem. Assn. Retarded Citizens USA (pres. 1973-75, nat. govt. affairs chmn. 1975-83), Am. Assn. Mental Deficiency, Nat. Symposium Reliability Quality Control (gen. chmn.), Sigma Chi. Presbyterian elder. Club: Kiwanis (Marion P. Smith award established in his honor). Home: 1884 Oakdale Ln N Clearwater FL 33764-6441 Personal E-mail: m.paffordmps2@aol.com. *True turning points in life are sometimes difficult to recognize, but for those who have become parents of a handicapped child, particularly a mentally retarded child, then that turning point is easy to recognize. After the difficult period of adjustment, one becomes aware of a realization that all persons have human dignity and worth and can make a contribution to humanity and to society.*

SMITH, MARK ANTHONY, neuroscientist, educator; b. Leicester, Eng., Aug. 15, 1965; came to U.S., 1992; s. John and Rita Joyce (Haywood) S. BSc with honors, Durham U., Eng., 1986; PhD, Nottingham U., Eng., 1990. Postdoctoral biochemist Sandoz Forschungsinstitut, Vienna, 1990-91, Karl Landsteiner rsch. fellow, 1991-92; rsch. assoc. Case Western Res. U., Cleve., 1992-94, instr. pathology, 1994-95, asst. prof., 1995—99, assoc. prof., 1999—2002, prof., 2002—. Cons. Stress-Gen Biotechs. Corp., Victoria, BC, 1999, Panacea Pharms, Potomac, 2000—05, Prion Devel. Labs, Vernon Hills, 2001—04, Voyager Pharmacies, Raleigh, NC, 2001—07, Neuropharm, England, 2006—. Author: (peer-reviewed publication) Science, Nature, Journal of Biological Chemistry, Journal of Neurochemistry, 2001 (Jordi Folch-Pi Award, American Society of Neurochemistry, 2000); editor-in-chief: Jour. Alzheimer's Disease, mem. editl. bd., Ddep. chief editor reviews: Jour. Neurochemistry; contbr. articles to profl. jours. Dalland fellow Am. Philos. Soc., 1995; recipient Ruth Salta Investigator award, 1995, Young Scientist Lectr. award Internat. Soc. Neurochem., Nathan Shock New Investigator award Gerontol. Soc. Am., Hermann-Esteibauer award, 2002, fellowship HNE Soc., 2005, Denham Harmen Rsch. award Am. Aging Assn., 2008. Mem. AAAS, Am. Assn. Neuropathology, Microscopic Soc. Northeast Ohio (pres. elect 1997—), N.Y. Acad. Scis., Internat. Soc. Neurochemistry, Am. Agency Assn.(exec. dir. 2009); fellow. Royal Coll. Pathologist. Avocations: golf, soccer, music, current affairs. Office: Case Western Res U Dept Pathology 2103 Cornell Rd Cleveland OH 44106 Home: 7416 Chagrin Rd Chagrin Falls OH 44023-4435 Office Phone: 216-368-3670. Business E-Mail: mark.smith@case.edu.

SMITH, MARK ARTHUR, information scientist, educator; s. Marvin (Mark) Ira and Cora S. Smith. AAS in Music, Nassau CC, 1977; MusB in Music Edn., SUNY, Fredonia, 1980; MS in Edn., Elmira Coll., Fredonia, 1987; MLS, U. Buffalo, 1992. Cert. music edn. tchr. NY, 1980, sch. libr. media specialist NY Dept. Edn., 1992. Vocal music tchr. Canisteo Ctrl. Sch., NY, 1981—91; info. sys. libr. NY State Coll. Ceramics, Alfred U., 1994—, full prof., 2007—. Provost adv. com., liaison SUNY Librs., Albany, 1998—. Musician (choral condr.): Hornell Cmty. Choir; musician: (choir) Orpheus Chorale; contbr. articles to profl. jours. Adv. bd. New Media Consortium Horizon Report, 2008; actor, dir. Hornell Rotary Club, NY, 1992; dir. Orpheus Chorale Hornell; bd. dirs. Hornell Area Arts Coun., NY, 2004—06; bd. mem. ARTS of Southern Finger Lakes, 2008—. Recipient Chancellors Award for Excellence in Librarianship, SUNY, 2004. Mem.: ALA, South Ctrl. Rsch. Libr. Coun. (mem. adv. com. on info. techs. 2002—, chair adv. com. on info. techs. 2005), Libr. and Info. Tech. Assn., Assn. of Coll. and Rsch. Librs., Am. Choral Dirs. Assn., SUNY Librs. Assn. (pres. 1999—2000), Phi Beta Mu, Phi Kappa Phi. Avocations: music performance, theatrical performance, choral directing. Office: NYS Coll of Ceramics Alfred Univ 2 Pine St Alfred NY 14802 Personal E-mail: mark@opus57.com. Business E-Mail: msmith@alfred.edu.

SMITH, MARK EUGENE, nuclear engineering service company executive; b. Wareham, Mass., Apr. 1, 1951; s. Mark Alvin and Evelyn Marie (Somers) S.; m. Brigid Ann Murray, Oct. 17, 1979; children: Hugh Talmidge, Patrick Morgan. AS, New England Inst. Tech., 1981. Owner Marks Motor Co., Wareham, 1965-69; chief designer HF Scientific Instrument, Ft. Myers, Fla., 1981-83; chief designer HVE Keltron Corp., Waltham, Mass., 1984-85; CEO Home Svcs., Ft. Myers, 1985-90, Gen. Capitol, Mocksville, N.C., 1990—. Cons. Underwood & Assocs., Cape Coral, Fla., 1981-89, Shaban Mfg. Co., Ft. Myers, 1982-83; chief designer Keltron Corp., Waltham, 1984-85; sr. designer Proctor & Schwartz, Lexington, NC, 1990-99; lead discipline designer Mixed Oxide Fabrication Facility (MOX-MFFF), Shaw, Ariva Mox Svcs., Aiken, SC, 2003—. Co-author: The Art of Custom Painting, 1978. With USMC, 1969-72. Named Advanced Designer, Metalflake Design Group, Springfield, Mass., 1977. Mem. Soc. Mech. Engrs., Soc. Automotive Engrs., Am. Inst. Design and Drafting (nat. drafting award 1981), Am. Nuc. Soc. Republican. Avocations: antiquarian, numismatics. Home: PO Box 906 Jackson SC 29831-0906 Office Phone: 803-819-8600. Personal E-mail: markussmithium@email.com. Business E-Mail: mesmith@moxproject.com.

SMITH, MARK LEE, architect; b. LA, Nov. 16, 1957; s. Selma (Moidel) Smith. BA in History of Architecture, UCLA, 1978, MA in Architecture, 1980, MA in History, 2006, CPhil in History, 2008. Registered architect Calif., Nev., Oreg., Wash., Tenn., Colo., NY, Ohio. Designer, drafter John B. Ferguson and Assocs., LA, 1976-83, architect, 1983; pvt. practice architecture LA, 1984—. Mem. LA County Archtl. Evaluation Bd., 1990-2004; spkr. Western Pool and Spa Show, 1997—2001. Author: A Bridge Across the Continents, 2003; essay columnist AIA/SFV monthly, 1997—; founding editor ARCHimpressions.org mag., 2003-2005, When Stones Could Speak, 2005; contbr. articles to profl. jours Bd. govs. UCLA John Wooden Ctr., 1978-80; judge Bank Am. Achievement Awards, 1998—2000, chair, 1999-2000. Regents scholar, U. Calif., Berkeley, UCLA, 1975-78; UCLA Grad. Sch. Architecture Rsch. fellow, 1979-80. Mem. AIA (treas. San Fernando Valley chpt. 1986, bd. dirs. 1986—, v.p. 1987, pres. 1988, Design award 1988, 89, 90, 91, 99, chmn. Design awards 1994, 2007, bd. dirs. Calif. coun. 1989-94, v.p. 1991-94, chmn. continuing edn. 1991-93, chmn. 1992 conf.), Phi Beta Kappa. Office: 18340 Ventura Blvd Ste 225 Tarzana CA 91356-4278

SMITH, MARSCHALL IMBODEN, lawyer; b. San Antonio, Oct. 3, 1944; s. Lowell B. and Jacqueline I. Smith; m. Elizabeth Braswell (div. 1973); m. Ann McNamara, June 3, 1976; children: Catherine, Elizabeth, Margaret, Austin, Lillian. AB in Hist. cum laude, Princeton U., NJ, 1966; JD, U. Va., 1973; MBA, U. Chgo., 1987. Bar: NY 1974, US Ct. Appeals (2nd cir.) 1974, US Dist. Ct. (so. dist. NY) 1974, Ill. 1980. Assoc. Debevoise & Plimpton, NYC, 1973-75, Paul, Weiss, Rifkind, Wharton & Garrison, NYC, 1975-81; atty. Baxter Travenol Labs., Deerfield, Ill., 1980-82, Baxter Internat. Inc., Deerfield, Ill., 1982-83, 1983-85, asst. gen. counsel, 1985-87, assoc. gen. counsel, 1987—92; v.p., gen. counsel Am. Med. Holdings Inc., 1992—93; sr. v.p., gen. counsel, sec. IMC Global Inc. (formerly IMC Fertilizer Group Inc.), Northbrook, Ill., 1993—99; exec. v.p., gen. counsel Digitas Inc., Boston, 1999—2001; v.p., gen. counsel, corp. sec. Brunswick Corp., Lake Forest, Ill., 2001—07; sr. v.p. legal affairs, gen. counsel 3M Co., St. Paul, 2007—. Adj. faculty Lake Forest Grad. Sch. Mgmt., 1985—88. Maj. USMC, 1966—73, Vietnam. Mem.: Assn. Corp. Counsel, Christian Legal Soc., Chgo. Bar Assn. Office: 3M Co 3M Corp HQ 3m Ctr Saint Paul MN 55144-1000 Office Phone: 847-735-4430.*

SMITH, MARSHALL SAVIDGE, foundation executive; b. East Orange, NJ, Sept. 16, 1937; s. Marshall Parsons and Ann Eileen (Zulauf) S.; m. Carol Goodspeed, June 25, 1960 (div. Aug. 1962); m. Louise Nixon Claiborn, Aug. 1964; children: Adam, Jennifer, Matthew, Megan. AB, Harvard U., 1960, EdM, 1963, EdD, 1970. Systems analyst and computer programmer Raytheon Corp., Andover, Mass., 1959-62; instr., assoc. prof. Harvard U., Cambridge, Mass., 1966-76; asst., assoc. dir. Nat. Inst. Edn., Washington, 1973-76; asst. commr. edn. HEW, Washington, 1976-79, chief of staff to U.S. Dept. Edn. sec., 1980; prof. U. Wis., Madison, 1980-86, Stanford (Calif.) U., 1986—2003, dean Sch. Edn., 1986—94; under-sec. edn. U.S. Dept. Edn., 1993-2000, acting dep. sec. edn., 1996-2000; program dir. Hewlett Found., 2001—09; sr. counselor to sec. US Dept. Election, 2009—. Task force, chmn. Clinton Presdl. Transition Team, 1992-93; chmn. PEW Forum on Ednl. Reform; chmn. bd. internat. com. studies in edn. NAS, 1992-93. Author: The General Inquirer, 1967, Inequality, 1972; contbr. articles to profl. jours, chpts. to books. Pres. Madison West Hockey Assn., 1982-84. Mem. Am. Ednl. Rsch. Assn. (chmn. orgn. instl. affiliates 1985-86), Nat. Acad. Edn. Democrat. Avocations: environmental issues, philanthropy. Home: 1256 Forest Ave Palo Alto CA 94301 Office: Wm & Flora Hewlett Found Menlo Park CA Personal E-mail: mike.marshallsmith@gmail.com. Business E-Mail: marshall.smith@ed.gov.

SMITH, MARTHA C., college librarian; b. Lansing, Mich., July 24, 1961; d. William K. and Margaret L. Smith; m. Steven E. Robinson, Aug. 5, 2000. BA in Studio Art, Wellesley Coll., Mass., 1982; MA in Art History, Ind. U., Bloomington, 1990; MLS, Rutgers U., New Brunswick, NJ, 1996. Cert. tchr. ACRL Inst. Info. Literacy, Kingston, RI, 2003. Art & humanities libr. Purchase Coll. SUNY, 1996—2001; rsch. & instrn. libr. Gannett-Tripp Libr. Elmira Coll., NY, 2001—. Adminstrv. sec., festival coord. Free Spirit Alliance, Lambertville, NJ, 2006—08. Mem.: ALA, Assn. Coll. and Rsch. Librs., NY Libr. Assn. Avocations: gardening, music, art. Office: Gannett-Tripp Libr Elmira Coll One Park Pl Elmira NY 14901 Business E-Mail: msmith@elmira.edu.

SMITH, MARTHA VIRGINIA BARNES, retired elementary school educator; b. Camden, Ark., Oct. 12, 1940; d. William Victor and Lillian Louise (Givens) Barnes; m. Basil Loren Smith, Oct. 11, 1975; children: Jennifer Frost, Sean Barnes. BS in Edn., Ouachita Bapt. U., 1963; postgrad., Auburn U., 1974, Henderson State U., 1975. Cert. tchr., Mo. 2d and 1st grade tchr. Brevard County Schs., Titusville and Cocoa, Fla., 1963-65, 69-70; 1st grade tchr. Lakeside Sch. Dist., Hot Springs, Ark., 1965-66, Harmony Grove Sch., Camden, 1972-76; 1st and 5th grade tchr. Cumberland County Schs., Fayetteville, NC, 1966-69; kindergarten tchr. Pulaski County Schs., Ft. Leonard Wood, Mo., 1970-72; 3d grade tchr. Mountain Grove (Mo.) Schs., 1976-99; ret., 1999. Chmn. career ladder com. Mountain Grove Dist., 1991-99. Children's pastor 1st Bapt. Ch., Vanzant, Mo., 1984-88. Mem. NEA (pres.-elect Mountain Grove chpt. 1995-97, pres. Mountain Grove chpt. 1997-99), Kappa Kappa Iota. Avocation: antique and classic cars.

SMITH, MARTIN BERNHARD, retired journalist; b. San Francisco, Apr. 20, 1930; s. John Edgar and Anna Sophie (Thorsen) S.; m. Joan Lovat Muller, Apr. 25, 1953; children: Catherine Joan, Karen Anne. AB, U. Calif., Berkeley, 1952, M Journalism, 1968. Reporter, city editor Modesto (Calif.) Bee, 1957-64; reporter, mng. editor Sacramento Bee, 1964-75; polit. editor, columnist McClatchy Newspapers, Sacramento, 1975-92; ret., 1992. Episcopalian. Personal E-mail: Joan_and_Marty@msn.com.

SMITH, MARTIN HENRY, retired pediatrician; b. Gainesville, Ga., Nov. 3, 1921; s. Charles E. and Mamie Mae (Emmett) S.; m. Mary Gillis, Feb. 25, 1950; children: Susan, Margaret, Mary MD, Emory U., 1945. Diplomate Am. Bd. Pediatrics. Intern City Hosp. System, Winston-Salem, NC, 1945-46; fellow in infectious diseases Grady Meml. Hosp., Atlanta, 1948-49; resident Henrietta Egleston Hosp., Atlanta, 1949-50, Children's Hosp., Washington, 1950-51; practice medicine, specializing in pediatrics Gainesville, Ga.; ret., 1988; clin. asst. prof. Emory U. Hosp., Atlanta; chief of staff Hall County Hosp., Gainesville, 1965-66. Mem. Nat. Vaccine Adv. Commn., 1990—, chmn., 1991. Contbr. articles to profl. jours. Chmn. Nat. Vaccine Adv. Com., 1991—. Capt. M.C., U.S. Army, 1946-48 Fellow Am. Acad. Pediatrics (chpt. chmn. 1966-69, dist. chmn. 1977-83, pres.-elect 1984-85, pres. 1985-86); mem. Hall County Med. Soc. (pres. 1960), Ga. Pediatric Soc.

(pres. 1965-66), Med. Assn. Ga., AMA, Alpha Omega Alpha Clubs: Chattahoochee Country (Gainesville); Piedmont Driving (Atlanta). Episcopalian. Personal E-mail: drmsmith@earthlink.net, martinhsmith@att.net.

SMITH, MARY ANN, alderwoman; m. Ronald S. Smith; children: Michael, Andrew. Aide, chief of staff to Alderwoman Kathy Osterman Chgo. City Coun., alderwoman, 48th ward, 1991—; adminstrv. asst. Lake Mich. Fedn.; coord. pub. participation Ill. Ho. Rep. Com. on Lake Mich.; pub. rels. cons. Chmn. parks com. Chgo. City Coun. Mem. adv. coun. on green devel. City of Chgo. Recipient Cmty. Svc. award, Mundelein Coll., Earth's 500 award, UN Environ. Program, Soles and Spokes award, Chicago Area Transportation Study, Chgo. Civic Fedn. award; grantee, Environ. Def. Fund. Office: 5533 N Broadway St Chicago IL 60640-1405 also: City Hall 121 N Lasalle St Rm 300 Chicago IL 60602 Office Phone: 773-784-5277, 312-744-6860. Office Fax: 773-784-5033. Business E-Mail: maryann@masmith48.org.*

SMITH, MARY ELLEN, educational program facilitator; b. Provo, Utah, Aug. 2, 1954; d. Lloyd Coltrin McEwan and Barbara Jean Saxey; m. Samuel Adam Smith, Oct. 4, 1988; children: Brandy Lee Wilbur, Jeremy Mark Penrod. BS in Elem. Edn., So. Utah U., 1987; MA in Elem. Edn. Diverse Learners, U. Phoenix, Provo, Utah, 1998. Spl. edn./resource tchr. Jordan Sch. Dist., Eastmont Mid. Sch., Sandy, Utah, 1987—90; 6th grade tchr. Jordan Sch. Dist., Sprucewood Elem., Sandy, 1990—95, kindergarten tchr., 1995—98; clin. faculty assoc. Brigham Young U., Provo, Utah, 1998—2002; partnership facilitator Brigham Young U./Jordan Sch. Dist., Midvale, Utah, 2002—. Conf. co-chair Univ. Partnership, Sandy, 2005—. Judge State Geography Bee, Lehi, Utah, 1999—. Named Tchr. of Month, Jordan Edn. Assn., 1995; grantee, Jordan Edn. Found., 2005. Mem.: ASCD (assoc.), Internat. Reading Assn. (assoc.), Assn. Childhood Edn. Internat. (assoc.), Phi Delta Kappa (assoc.; constl. conv. rep. 2002—03). Mem. Lds Ch. Avocations: reading, travel, children and youth activities. Home: 675 N 1150 E Lehi UT 84043 Office: Copperview Elem 8449 S 150 W Midvale UT 84047 Office Fax: 801-302-4912. Personal E-mail: marysunshine73@hotmail.com. Business E-Mail: mary.smith@jordan.k12.ut.us.

SMITH, MARY L., lawyer; b. Aug. 28, 1962; BS magna cum laude in Math. and Computer Sci., Loyola U. Chgo., 1984; JD cum laude, U. Chgo., 1991. Law clk. to Hon. R. Lanier Anderson III US Ct. Appeals (11th cir.); atty. Ross & Hardles, 1992—94; trial atty. civil divsn. comml. litig. br. US Dept. Justice, 1994—96, nominee for asst. atty. gen. Tax divsn., 2009; assoc. dir. policy planning Domestic Policy Coun. White House, 1997—2000, assoc. counsel to Pres. Clinton, 2000—01; sr. assoc. Skadden, Arps, Slate, Meagher & Flom LLP, Washington, 2001—05; sr. litig. counsel Tyco Internat. Inc.; ptnr. Schoeman Updike & Kaufman LLP, Chgo. Tchr. trial advocacy Nat. Inst. Trial Advocacy; sr. advisor Native Am. policy Kerry-Edwards Presdl. Campaign, 2004; bd. mem. Chgo. Bar Found. Mem. Cherokee Nation. Fellow: Am. Bar Found.; mem.: ABA (bd. govs. 2009—, vice chair civil rights and equal opportunity com. 2005—06, coun. mem. Sect. Individual Rights and Responsibilities, mem. commn. on women in profession), Native Am. Bar Assn. DC, Native Am. Bar Assn., DC Bar Assn., Chgo. Bar Found., Chgo. Bar Assn. Office: Schoman Updike & Kaufman LLP 333 W Wacker Dr Chicago IL 60606 Office Phone: 312-726-6000. Office Fax: 312-726-6045. E-mail: msmith@schoeman.com.

SMITH, MARY LOUISE, former real estate broker; b. Eldorado, Ill., May 29, 1935; d. Joseph Henry Smith and Opal Marie (Smith) Hungerford; m. David Lee Smith, June 18, 1961; children: Rick, Brenda Sue Smith Millsap. Student, So. Ill. U., 1954-56, 57-58. Cert. substitute tchr., Mo.; cert. inactive real estate broker, Mo. With acctg. dept. Cen. Hardware Co., St. Louis, 1958-61; mgr. income tax office Tax Teller Inc., St. Louis, 1967-69; substitute tchr. Mo., 1967—; mgr. income tax office H&R Block Co., St. Louis, 1970—76, tax preparer, 1992—2001; with acctg. dept. Weis Neumann Co., St. Louis, 1976-79; broker/salesperson Century 21 Neubauer Realty Inc., St. Louis, 1980-83, 88-90; sales assoc. John R. Green Realtor, Inc., St. Louis, 1983-85, Century 21 Action Properties, St. Louis, 1985-88, real estate broker/salesperson, 1986-88, Century 21 Neubauer Realty, Inc., St. Louis, 1988-90, L.K. Wood Realtors, 1992-96; security officer Reliance Security, 1995-97; tax preparer H&R Block Co., St. Louis, 1983, 1992—2001. Younger children's dir. Lafayette Park Bapt. Ch., St. Louis, 1981-95; children dir. Kingshwy. Bapt. Ch., 1999-01; vol. tax preparer for UAW Local 136 retirees, 1982-86. Mem. Am. Fedn. Tchrs., St. Louis Real Estate Bd. (equal rights com. 1986-88). Baptist. Avocation: writing children's stories.

SMITH, MATTHEW DENMAN, ecologist; b. 1974; BA in Biology, Earlham Coll., Richmond, Ind., 1997; MS in Wildlife Sci., U. Ariz., Tucson, 2004; attending, U. Fla., Gainesville, 2005—. Rsch. asst. Tufts U., Medford, Mass., 1998; project coord. burrowing owl conservation rsch. Wash. State U., Richland, 2000; project coord., burrowing owl demography rsch. U. Ariz., 2000, grad. tchg. asst., 2000—04; vis. instr. dept. biology Earlham Coll., 2004—05; grad. tchg. assoc. U. Fla., 2005—08, grad. rsch. asst., 2008—. Contbr. scientific papers to profl. jours., chapters to books. Recipient John Olowo Meml. award, U. Fla., 2006; Grinter fellowship, 2005—08, grant, Sigma Xi, 2006, Lerner-Grey grant, Am. Mus. Natural History, 2008. Mem.: Soc. Integrative and Comparative Biology, Animal Behaviour Soc. Office: Univ Fla Dept Biology 316 Bartram Hall Gainesville FL 32611 Business E-Mail: madsmith@ufl.edu.

SMITH, MATTHEW JOSEPH, literature and language professor; s. Robert Lee and Martha Anne Smith; m. Kari Vos, June 15, 2002; children: Cassandra Frances, Madelyn Ann. BA, DePauw U., Greencastle, Ind., 1990; MA, Purdue U., West Lafayette, Ind., 1992, PhD, 1997. Assoc. prof., english U. St. Francis, Ft. Wayne, Ind., 2002—, dir., gen. edn., 2008—. Office: Univ Saint Francis 2701 Spring St Fort Wayne IN 46808

SMITH, MAURA ABELN, chief legal officer, paper company executive; b. Reading, Pa., Oct. 3, 1955; d. Henry Joseph and Lynn (Blashe) Abeln; children: Gwendolyn Casebeer, Karl Casebeer; m. Steven A. Smith, Dec. 18, 1999. AB, Vassar Coll., 1977; M Philosophy, Oxford U., 1979; JD, U. Miami, 1982. Bar: Fla. 1982, Tenn. 2007. Assoc. Steel, Hector & Davis, Miami, 1982—87; ptnr. Baker & McKenzie, Miami, 1987-91; gen. counsel GE Co./Plastics, Pittsfield, Mass., 1991—93, v.p., gen. counsel, 1993—98; sr. v.p., gen. counsel, sec. Owens Corning, Toledo, 1998-2000, chief restructuring officer, sr. v.p., gen. counsel, sec., 2000—03, bd. dirs.; sr. v.p., gen. counsel, sec., global govt. relations Internat. Paper, Memphis, 2003—; commr. Tenn. Access Justice Commn. Rhodes scholar, Oxford, Eng., 1977-79; John M. Olin fellow in law and econs., Olin Found., 1979-82. Mem.: Phi Beta Kappa. Avocations: tennis, golf, horseback riding. Office: 6400 Poplar Ave Memphis TN 38197 Office Phone: 901-419-3829. E-mail: maura.abelnsmith@ipaper.com.

SMITH, MEREDITH WOOD, political organization administrator; b. Attleboro, Mass. m. Joe Smith; 4 children. BA in Edn., U. Ky. Small bus. owner, pres. of a local bus. assn., sales rep. for a mid-sized nat. corp.; dir. Clackamas County Juvenile Svc. Commn.; western states vice chair rep. Assn. State Dem. Chairs Exec. Com.; vice chair Dem. Party of Oreg., chairwoman, 2008—. Active John F. Kennedy Presdl. Campaign, Ky., 1961. Democrat. Office: Dem Party of Oreg 232 NE 9th Ave Portland OR 97232-2915 Office Phone: 503-224-8200. E-mail: chair@dpo.org.*

SMITH, MEREDYTH HULL, real estate broker; BA in Art History and English with honors, Amherst Coll. With Christie's Internat., NYC; sales agent Sotheby's Internat. Realty-East Side Manhattan Brokerage, NYC, now assoc. broker, sr. v.p. Office: Sotheby's International Realty East Side Manhattan Brokerage 38 E 61St St New York NY 10065 Office Fax: 212-909-8163, 212-606-7683. E-mail: Meredyth.Smith@sothebysrealty.com.*

SMITH, MERRITT ROE, history professor; b. Waverly, NY, Nov. 14, 1940; s. Wilson Niles and Mary Eleanor (Fitzgerald) S.; m. Bronwyn M. Mellquist, Aug. 24, 1974. AB, Georgetown U., 1963; MA, Pa. State U., 1965, PhD, 1971; LHD (hon.), Rensselaer Poly. Inst., 1997. Asst. prof. history Ohio State U., Columbus, 1970-74, assoc. prof., 1974-78; vis. prof. history and sociology of sci. U. Pa., Phila., 1976; prof. history tech. program in sci., tech. and society M.I.T., Cambridge, 1978—, Metcalfe prof. engring. and liberal arts, 1989-92, dir. progam in sci., tech. and society, 1992—96, 2000—02, Leverett and William King Cutten prof., 1993—. Author: Harpers Ferry Armory and the New Technology, 1977, Military Enterprise and Technological Change, 1985, Science, Technology and the Military, 2 vols., 1988, Does Technology Drive History?, 1994, Major Problems in the History of American Technology, 1998, Inventing America, 2002, 2d edit., 2006; mem. editl. bd. Tech. and Culture, 1973-91, Bus. History Rev., 1978-85, MIT Press, 1986-91, Archimedes, 1995—2001. Mem. Mass. Hist. Soc.; bd. advisors MIT Mus. Recipient Cert. of Commendation Am. Assn. State and Local History, 1978, Disting. Tchg. award Ohio State U., 1978, Founders Day award Charles River Mus. Industry, 2003, Arthur C. Smith award MIT, 2006; grantee Ohio State U., 1972, Am. Philos. Soc., 1974, Harvard Bus. Sch., 1974-75, Eleutherian Mills-Hagley Found., 1978-79, Alfred P. Sloan Found., 1994-2002; Guggenheim fellow, 1983-84, Regents fellow Smithsonian Instn., 1984-85. Mem. AAAS, Am. Acad. Arts and Scis., Soc. History Tech. (mem. exec. coun., Dexter Prize com., Da Vinci medal 1994, mus. com., v.p., pres. 1989-91), Orgn. Am. Historians (Frederick Jackson Turner award 1977, Disting. lectr. 2004—), Bus. History Conf., Am. Antiquarian Soc., Newcomen Soc. N.Am., Soc. Indsl. Archeology, History Sci. Soc. (Pfizer award 1978), Phi Kappa Phi, Phi Alpha Theta. Office: STS Program MIT 77 Massachusetts Ave Rm E51-185 Cambridge MA 02139 Office Phone: 617-253-4008. Business E-Mail: roesmith@mit.edu.

SMITH, (CARL) MICHAEL, lawyer, former federal agency administrator; b. Oklahoma City, Oct. 11, 1944; s. Carl W. Jr. and Nina (Furr) S.; m. Sharon Kay Lewis, June 5, 1971. BA, U. Okla., 1966, JD, 1969. Bar: Okla. 1969, U.S. Dist. Ct. (we., no. and ea. dists.) Okla. 1971, U.S. Ct. Appeals (10th cir.) 1976, U.S. Supreme Ct. 1976. Mem. firm Lawrence, Smith & Harmon, Oklahoma City, 1977-80; pres. Red Rock Exploration, Inc., Oklahoma City, 1980-83; mem. firm Lawrence & Ellis, P.A., Oklahoma City, 1983—95; sec. Okla. Dept. Energy, Oklahoma City, 1995—2002; asst. sec. for fossil energy US Dept. Energy, Washington, 2002—04; of counsel Dunlap, Codding & Rogers, Washington, 2004—. Mem. Blue Ribbon Commn. on Natural Gas, Oklahoma City, 1982; chmn. Okla. Polit. Action Com., Oklahoma City, 1986-90; mem. Okla. Legis. Interim Task Force on Environ. Regulation, Oklahoma City, 1991-92; sec. Okla. Energy Resources Bd., 1992-94; Capt. U.S. Army, 1969-71, Vietnam. Mem. Okla. Ind. Petroleum Assn. (pres. 1994-95). Office: Dunlap Codding & Rogers PC 1601 NW Expressway Ste 1000 Oklahoma City OK 73118 Office Phone: 202-327-5495, 405-607-8600. E-mail: cmike_smith@okpatents.com.

SMITH, MICHAEL BRYAN, civil engineer; b. Bethesda, Md., Oct. 9, 1958; s. Peggy Ann and Guy Raymond Smith; m. Margaret Ann Statzer, Oct. 15, 1994; 1 child, Logan Carlos. BS, U. Md., Coll. Pk., MS, 1984; PhD, U. Ljubljana, Slovenia, 1992. Registered profl. engr., Md., 1987. Agrl. engr. USDA Soil Conservation Svc., Westminster, Md., 1980, planning engr. Coll. Pk., 1980—82, asst. area engr. Easton, Md., 1984—85; rsch. asst. dept. civil engring. U. Md., 1982—84, U. Ljubljana, 1987—92; rsch. hydrologist NOAA Nat. Weather Svc., Silver Spring, Md., 1994—. Contbr. articles to profl. jours. Provide repair and constrn. asst. Prince of Peace Home Girls, Guatemala City, 2007; small group leader Grace Cmty. Ch., Fulton, Md., 1993—2008. Hydraulic engr. corps engrs. USAR, 1985—87, Balt. Recipient NOAA Bronze medal. Mem.: Am. Geophys. Union. Conservative. Avocations: woodworking, running. Office: NOAA Nat Weather Svc 1325 E West Hwy SSMC 2 Silver Spring MD 20910 Business E-Mail: michael.smith@noaa.gov.

SMITH, MICHAEL CREMIN, neurologist, director; s. Francis Edward and Jeanne Catherine Smith; m. Deirdrte Neenan; children: Hannah Grace, Liam Thomas, Patrick Malley, Griffin Marie, Michael Francis; m. Ann Goddeyne (div.); 1 child, Brenna Colleen Garrett. MD, Rush Med. Coll., Chgo., 1979. Dir., Rush epilepsy ctr. Rush U. Med. Ctr., 1996—, prof., dept. neurol. scis., 2008. Bd. mem. Epilepsy Found. Greater Chgo., 1995—2008. Office: Rush Univ Medical Ctr 1653 W Congress Pky Chicago IL 60612

SMITH, MICHAEL D., dean, electrical engineering and computer science professor; m. Chris K. Smith; 2 children. BS, Princeton U., 1983; MS in Elec. Engring., Worcester Polytechnic Inst., 1985; PhD in Elec. Engring., Stanford U., 1993. Rsch. asst. Stanford U., 1986—92; instr. Harvard U., Cambridge, Mass., 1992—93, asst. prof., 1993—97, dir. undergraduate studies engring. scis., 1994—97, assoc. prof., 1997—2000, Gordon McKay prof. computer sci. and elec. engring., 2000—, assoc. dean computer sci. and engring. Sch. Engring. and Applied Scis., 2005—07, dean Faculty Arts and Scis., 2007—. Rschr. Ctr. Rsch. on Computation and Soc.; founder, chief scientist, chmn. Liquid Machines, Lexington, Mass., 2001—. Contbr. articles to profl. jours. Recipient Young Investigator Award, NSF, 1994, Phi Beta Kappa teaching prize. Mem.: IEEE, Assn. Computing Machinery. Office: Harvard U Dean FAS University Hall 2 South Cambridge MA 02138 also: FAS Dean's Office Univ Hall Cambridge MA 02138 Office Phone: 617-495-1566. Office Fax: 617-495-8208. Business E-Mail: milan_smith@harvard.edu.

SMITH, MICHAEL PETER, social sciences educator, researcher; b. Dunkirk, NY, Aug. 2, 1942; s. Peter Joseph and Rosalie Barbara (Lipka) S.; m. Patricia Anne Lendway, Aug. 21, 1965. BA magna cum laude, St. Michael's Coll., 1964; MA in Polit. Sci., U. Mass., 1966, PhD in Polit. Sci., 1971. Instr., asst. prof. dept. govt. Dartmouth Coll., Hanover, NH, 1968—71; asst. prof. dept. polit. sci. Boston U., 1971—74; assoc. prof., prof. dept. polit. sci. Tulane U., New Orleans, 1974—86; prof. cmty. studies U. Calif., Davis, 1986—2008, disting. prof. cmty. studies, 2008—, chmn. dept. applied behavioral scis., 1986—91, chmn. cmty. studies and devel. program, 2001—. Vis. prof. pub. policy U. Calif., Berkeley, 1981, city planning U. N.C., Chapel Hill, 1982, city planning U. Calif., Berkeley, 1985, 2009; vis. scholar in govt. U. Essex, Eng., 1979; vis. scholar polit. and social sci. U. Cambridge, Eng., 1982; vis. scholar Inst. Urban and Regional Devel., U. Calif., Berkeley, 1990, 94 Internat. Ctr. for Advanced Studies, NYU, 1998, Ctr. Migration, Policy and Soc., Oxford U., 2005. Author: The City & Social Theory, 1979, City, State and Market, 1988, Transnational Urbanism, 2001; co-author: Restructuring the City, 1983, California's Changing Faces, 1993, Citizenship Across Borders, 2008; editor: Cities in Transformation, 1984, Breaking Chains, 1991, After Modernism, 1992, Marginal Spaces, 1995, Comparative Urban & Community Research, 1986—; co-editor: The Capitalist City, 1987—, The Bubbling Cauldron, 1995, Transnationalism from Below, 1998, City and Nation: Rethinking Place and Identity, 2001, The Human Face of Global Mobility, 2006, Transnational Ties, 2008; mem. editl. bd. Global Networks., 1999—. Office: Dept Human & Cmty Devel Univ Calif Davis CA 95616 Office Phone: 530-752-2243. Business E-Mail: mpsmith@ucdavis.edu.

SMITH, MICHAEL R., dean, academic administrator; BA, U. Mich., 1975; JD, U. NC, Chapel Hill, 1978. Faculty mem. Inst. Govt. U. NC, Chapel Hill, 1978, dir. Inst. Govt., 1992—2001, dean Sch. Govt., 2001—, vice chancellor pub. svc. and engagement, 2006—. Recipient C. Knox Massey Disting. Svc. Award, 1999. Office: U NC Sch Govt CB#3330, Knapp Bldg Chapel Hill NC 27599-3330 Office Phone: 919-966-5381. Office Fax: 919-962-0654. E-mail: msmith@sog.unc.edu.*

SMITH, MICHAEL ROBERT, electro-optical engineer, physicist; b. Tela, Honduras, Aug. 24, 1937; s. Ike Morgan and Edith Helen (Hudson) S.; m., div., remarried Lorraine L. Smith, Apr. 26, 2002; children: Stephen, Monica, Meryl. BME, Ga. Inst. Tech., 1959, MS in Nuclear Engring., 1961; PhD, Case Inst. Tech., 1965. Mem. tech. staff Hughes Rsch. Labs., Malibu, Calif., 1965-68; v.p., dir. rsch. Britt Corp., LA, 1968-73; sr. staff engr. Singer/Librascope divsn., Glendale, Calif., 1973-78; pres. Exocor Tech., Newbury Park, Calif., 1978-95; asst. prof., head physics program Calif. Luth. U., Thousand Oaks, 1990-96; design leader LIGO project Calif. Inst. Tech., Pasadena, 1996—. Contbr. articles to profl. jours.; inventor emergency vehicle warning and traffic control sys., emergency vehicle warning sign, flat electro-optic display panel, high power mirror, laser recording film with opaque coating, pulsed gas laser with radiation cooling, infrared laser photocautery device; 8 U.S. patents; 9 fgn. patents. Greek folk dance tchr. Arts Coun., Thousand Oaks, Calif., 1991-97. Mem. IEEE, Laser Electro-Optic Soc. (chair 1995-97), Sigma Xi, Pi Tau Sigma. Republican. Home: 1611 N Roosevelt Ave Pasadena CA 91104-1927 Business E-Mail: smith@ligo.caltech.edu.

SMITH, MICHAEL S., interior designer, furniture designer; b. Newport Beach, Calif. Grad., Otis Coll. Art and Design, LA. With Gep Durenberger, John Saladino, NYC; opened home furnishings store, Calif.; owner, designer Michael S. Smith Inc., Santa Monica, 1990—; designer fabric and leather collection Cowtan and Tout, 1997; designer lines for Kallista brand and Anna Sacks Tile Kohler, 1999; design partnerships with Visual Comfort Lighting, Mansour Modern Rugs, Patterson, Flynn and Martin Carpeting, Samuel and Sons Passementrie, Agaria Home Fragrances. Mem. bd. trustees Otis Coll. Art and Design; co-chair Am. Friends of Olympia Internat. Fine Art and Antique Fair; family quarters decorator The White House, 2009. Author: (books) Elements of Style, 2007, Houses, 2008; featured in Elle Decor Mag., Archtl. Digest, House Beautiful, Town and Country, Domino mag., Metro. Home, Interior Design, W. Named Designer of Yr., Elle Decor, 2003; named one of The AD 100, Archtl. Digest, 2002, 2004, Stars of Design, LA Pacific Design Ctr., 2004. Achievements include winning the commission to redecorate The White House, 2009. Office: Michael S Smith Inc 1646 19th St Santa Monica CA 90404 Office Phone: 310-315-3018. Office Fax: 310-315-3059. Business E-Mail: info@michaelsmithinc.com.*

SMITH, MICHAEL W., physician, medical editor; MD, Mercer U. Sch. Medicine, Macon, Ga., 1994. Cert. Am. Bd. Internal Medicine. Intern Med. Ctr. Central Ga.; chief resident Ga. Baptist Med. Ctr.; chief med. editor WebMD Health; pvt. practice. Mem.: AMA, Am. Coll. Physicians. Office: 111 8th Ave 7th Fl New York NY 10011 Office Phone: 212-624-3700.*

SMITH, MIKE (MICHAEL A. SMITH), former professional sports team executive; b. Potsdam, NY, Aug. 1945; m. Judith Smith (dec. 2000); 1 child, Jason. BS in Social Scis., Clarkson U.; PhD in Polit. Sci. and Russian Studies, Syracuse U. Head coach Christian Brothers Acad., Syracuse, NY; asst. coach NY Rangers, 1976—77; with Winnipeg Jets, 1979—94, gen. mgr., 1988—94; cons. Chgo. Blackhawks, 1995—97, mgr. hockey ops., 1999—2000, gen. mgr., 2000—03; assoc. gen. mgr. Toronto Maple Leafs, 1997—99. Gen. mgr. Team USA, IIHF World Championship, 1981, 94, 95; blogger The Hockey News, 2007—. Named NHL Exec. of Yr., Sporting News, 2002; named to NY State HS Hockey- Hall of Fame, 2002. Office: c/o The Hockey News 25 Sheppard Ave, Ste 100 Toronto ON M2N 6S7 Canada*

SMITH, MIKE, professional football coach; b. Chgo., June 13, 1959; m. Julie Smith; 1 child, Logan. Student, East Tenn. U., 1977—81. Linebacker Winnipeg Blue Bombers, 1982; part-time asst. coach San Diego State U. Aztecs, 1982, linebackers coach, 1983—85; def. line coach, recruiting coord. Morehead State U. Eagles, 1986; def. line coach Tenn. Tech U. Golden Eagles, 1987, spl. teams coord., 1988—95, def. coord., linebackers coach, 1996—98; def. asst., def. line coach Balt. Ravens, 1999—2001, linebackers coach, 2002; def. coord. Jacksonville Jaguars, 2003—07; head coach Atlanta Falcons, 2008—. Named NFL Coach of Yr., AP, 2008. Achievements include being a member of Super Bowl XXXV winning Baltimore Ravens, 2001. Office: Atlanta Falcons 4400 Falcon Pky Flowery Branch GA 30542 Office Phone: 770-965-3115.*

SMITH, MILAN DALE, JR., federal judge; b. Pendleton, Oreg., May 19, 1942; BA cum laude, Brigham Young U., 1966; JD, U. Chgo., 1969. Bar: Calif. 1970, DC 1972, US Supreme Ct. 1977, US Tax Ct. 1978. Assoc. O'Melveny & Myers LLP, L.A., 1969-72; ptnr. Smith Crane Robinson & Parker LLP (formerly Smith & Hilbig LLP), Torrance, Calif., 1972—2006; judge US Ct. Appeals (9th cir.), 2006—. Pres. Los Angeles State Office Bldg. Authority, 1983-92, Informed Voters League, Torrance, 1975-77; vice chmn. bd. Ettie Lee Homes for Youth, 1973-82, Calif. Fair Employment and Housing Commn., 1987-91; mem. Cabinet of the Interfaith Coalition to Heal L.A., head econ. devel. subcom., 1992-94; bd. trustees Deseret Trust Co. Calif., 2000-06; sec.-treas. Criminal Justice Legal Found., 1996-2005; chair, bd. visitors Sch. Religion, Claremont U., 2005-06. Nat. Honor scholar, 1966-69, U. Chgo. Mem. Brigham Young U. Alumni Assn. (bd. dirs. 1982-86). Office: US Ct Appeals 222 N Sepulveda Blvd El Segundo CA 90245-5648 Office Phone: 310-607-4020. Business E-Mail: judge_m_smith_jr@ca9.uscourts.9o.*

SMITH, MONICA, chiropractor, researcher; DC, Logan Coll. Chiropractic, St. Louis, 1986; PhD, St. Louis U., 1997. Health sci. specialist DVA Med. Ctr., St. Louis, 1987—96; assoc. prof. Palmer Chiropractic U. Sys., Davenport, Iowa, 1996—.

SMITH, MORTON EDWARD, ophthalmology educator, dean; b. Balt., Oct. 17, 1934; m. Paula Smith; 3 children. BS, U. Md., 1956, MD, 1960. Bd. cert. Ophthalmology Bd.; lic. physician Mo., Md., Wis. Rotating intern Denver Gen. Hosp., 1960-61; resident, nat. inst. of neorol. diseases and blindness fellow in ophthalmology Washington U. Sch. Medicine-Barnes Hosp., 1961-63; NIH spl. fellow in ophthalmic pathology Armed Forces Inst. of Pathology, Washington, 1964; chief resident, instr. ophthalmology Washington U. Sch. Medicine, St. Louis, 1965-66, instr. ophthalmology, 1966-67, asst. prof. ophthalmology and pathology, 1967-69, assoc. prof. ophthalmology and pathology, 1969-75, prof. ophthalmology and pathology, 1975—, asst. dean, 1978-91, assoc. dean, 1991-96, prof. emeritus, assoc. dean emeritus, 1996—; prof. ophthalmology U. Wis., Madison, 1995-2001. Vis. scholar Eye Inst., Columbia Presbyn. Med. Ctr., N.Y.C., 1966; prof./lectr. Montefiore Hosp., Pitts., 1969, U. Ark., 1970, 77, 80, 82, 84, 86, 88, U. Fla., 1972, 81, U. Tex. and Lackland AFB, San Antonio, 1973, U. Colo., 1974, 82, U. Mo., 1974, 79, 80, 88, So. Ill. U., Springfield, 1974, U. Md., 1975, Montreal (Can.) Gen. Hosp., 1975, U. Wis., 1976, 87, 93, U. Pitts., 1977, 83, 87, U. Iowa, 1977, 87, Cleve. Clinic, 1978, Colo. Ophthalmol. Soc., 1978, Brooke Army Hosp., San Antonio, 1979, Wills Eye Hosp., Phila., 1980, USPHS Hosp., San Francisco, 1981, U. Calif., Davis, 1981, Sinai Hosp., Balt., 1985, 89, 94, U. Calif., San Diego, 1985, Tufts U., Boston, 1985, Cornell U., N.Y.C., 1988, U. Wash., Seattle, 1990, Brown U., Providence, 1990, Vanderbilt U., Nashville, 1991, Duke U., Durham, N.C., 1992; Chandler lectr. Harvard U., 1988; The Lois A. Young-Thomas Meml. lectr. U. Md., 1991; Braley lectr. U. Iowa, 1993; Havener Meml. lectr. Ohio State, 1994. Editor pathology sect.: Perspectives in Ophthalmology, 1977; mem. editl. bd. Ophthalmic Plastic & Reconstructive Surgery, 1986-90; contbr. articles to profl. jours. With USAR M.C., 1958-66. Scholar U. Md., 1958, 59; Founder's Day award Wash. U., St. Louis; Grand Marshall Wash. U., 2007. Fellow Am. Acad. Ophthalmology (ophthalmic pathology com. 1977-83, chmn. ophthalmic com. 1979-83, Honor award for svc. 1981, Sr. Honor award 1992); mem. AMA, Am. Bd. Ophthalmology (diplomate, bd. dirs. 1992—), Assn. for Rsch. in Vision and Ophthalmology (chmn. sect. pathology ann. meeting 1971), Am. Assn. Ophthalmic Pathologists (pres. 1977-80), Assn. Am. Med. Colls. (group med. edn. 1985—), Mo. Med. Assn., Mo. Ophthalmol. Soc., Verhoeff Soc., Theobald Soc., St. Louis Med. Soc., St. Louis Ophthalmol. Soc., Soc. Med. Coll. Dirs. for Continuing Med. Edn., Alpha Omega Alpha (sec.-treas. chpt. 1993-95, councillor 2003—). Home: 1275 Castle Gate Dr Saint Louis MO 63132 Office: Campus Box 8096 660 S Euclid Ave Saint Louis MO 63110-1093 Office Phone: 314-747-5559. Business E-Mail: smithm@vision.wustl.edu.

SMITH, MORTON HOWISON, religious organization administrator, educator; b. Roanoke, Va., Dec. 11, 1923; s. James Brookes and Margaret Morton (Howison) S.; m. Lois Virginia Knopf, July 7, 1925; children: Samuel Warfield, Susanne Rochet Margaret. BA, U. Mich., 1947; BD, Columbia Theol. Sem., 1953; ThM, ThD, Free U., Amsterdam, The Netherlands, 1962. Ordained to ministry Presbyn. Ch., 1954. Pastor Springfield-Roller Presbyn. Chs., Carroll County, Md., 1954; prof. bible Belhaven Coll., Jackson, Miss., 1954-63; guest lectr. Westminster Theol. Sem., Phila., 1963-64; prof. Reformed Theol. Sem., Jackson, 1964-79; stated clk. gen. assembly Presbyn. Ch. in Am., Decatur, Ga., 1973-88; prof. systematic theology Greenville Presbyn. Theol. Sem., 1987—, dean faculty, 1987-98. Moderator gen. assembly Presbyn. Ch. Am., 2000-01; advisor to bd. dirs. Greenville (S.C.) Presbyn. Theol. Sem., 1986-98, bd. dirs.; mem. bd. dirs. Presbyn. Jour., Asheville, N.C., 1965-87; lectr. on theology Republic of So. Africa, June-July, 1988, Riga, Latvia, 1992, Budapest, Hungary, 1994, Prague, Czech Republic, 1994, 95, Trinidad and Tobago, 1995, Zlin, Czech Republic, 1998, 99, on missions, Republic of Korea, June-July, 1989, Munkton, Can., 1998, 99, Recife, Brazil, 1998, 2002, Reformed Sem., St. Petersburg, Russia, New Zealand, 2003. Author: Studies in Southern Presbyterian Theology, 1962, 2d edit. 1987, How Is the Gold Become Dim, 1973, republished 1998, (pamphlet) Reformed Evangelism, 1970, Testimony, 1986, Commentary on the Book of Church Order of the Presbyterian Church in America, 1990, Harmony of the Westminster Confession and Catechisms, 1990, Systematic Theology, 1994; contbr. articles to profl. jours. Trustee Covenant Coll., Lookout Mountain, Tenn., 1982-90. 1st lt. USAAF, 1942-45. Fulbright fellow U.S. Govt., 1958. Mem. N.Am. Presbyn. and Reformed Coun. of Chs. (sec. 1977-92). Presbyterian. Avocations: flying, travel, genealogy. Office: Greenville Presbyn Theol Sem PO Box 690 Taylors SC 29687-0014 Office Phone: 864-322-2717. Personal E-mail: wcflcsc@mtnisp.com.

SMITH, MYRON JOHN, JR., librarian, author; b. Toledo, May 3, 1944; s. Myron John and Marion Oliva (Herbert) S.; 1 son, Myron John III. Student, Coll. Steubenville, 1962; AB, Ashland Coll., 1966; MLS, Western Mich. U., 1967; MA, Shippensburg U., 1969; postgrad., U. Wis., Purdue U.; LittD, Cardinal Newman Coll., 1982. Rsch. librarian G.W. Blunt White Libr., Mystic Seaport, Conn., 1967-68; asst. librarian Western Md. Coll., Westminster, 1969-72; libr. dir. Huntington (Ind.) Pub. Libr., 1972-76; prof. history and libr. sci., dir. librs. Benedum Libr. Salem-Teikyo U.; dir., then assoc. dir. aviation program Salem (W.Va.) Coll., 1976-90; prof. history and libr. sci., libr. dir. Tusculum Coll., Greeneville, Tenn., 1990—. Mem. Am. Com. on History 2d World War, Assn. for Bibliography of History Author: American Naval Bibliography Series, 1972-74, Huntington Centennial Handbook, 1973, The Sophisticated Lady: The Battleship Indiana in World War II, 1973, World War II at Sea: A Bibliography of Sources in English, 1976, (with Robert Webber) Sea Fiction Guide, 1976, The Cloak and Dagger Bibliography, 1976, World War I in the Air, 1977, Air War Chronology 1939-45, 1977, Air War Bibliography Series, 1977—, The Mountain State Battleship: USS West Virginia, 1979, Air War Southeast Asia, 1979, The Soviet Navy, 1941-1978, 1979, The Secret Wars Series, 1980-81, The Soviet Air and Strategic Rocket Forces, 1941-1980, 1981, The Soviet Army, 1941-1980, 1981, Equestrian Studies: The Salem College Guide, 1981, The Cloak and Dagger Fiction Guide: An Annotated Guide to Spy Thrillers, 1981, (with Terry White) 3d edit., 1994, The Mountaineer Battlewagon: USS West Virginia, 1982, The Keystone Battlewagon: USS Pennsylvania, 1983, The Golden State Battlewagon: USS California, 1983, Watergate: A Bibliography, 1983 World War II: Mediterranean and European Theaters, 1984, The United States Navy and Coast Guard, 1946-1983: A Bibliography of English Language Works and 16mm Films, 1984, U.S. Television Network News: A Guide to Sources in English, 1984, Battleships and Battlecruisers, 1884-1984: A Bibliography and Chronology, 1985, Baseball: A Comprehensive Bibliography, 1986, 99th Infantry Division Bibliography, 1986, The Airline Bibliography: The Salem College Guide to Sources on Commercial Aviation, Vol. I, The United States, 1986, Vol. II, Airliners and Foreign Carriers, 1987, Passenger Airliners of the United States, 1926-86: A Pictorial Guide, 1987, rev. edit. through 1991, 1991, 3d rev. edit. through 1995, 4th revised edit., 2002, Brooklyn/Los Angeles Dodgers: A Bibliography, 1987, American Warplane Bibliography, 1989, Volunteer Battlewagon: The U.S.S. Tennessee (BB-43), 1989; editor: Sports Teams and Players Bibliography Series, 1987, Battle and Leaders Bibliography Series, 1988, 100 Years of Opportunity: A Pictorial History of Salem College, 1888-1988, 1988, Pro Football Bio-Bibliography, 1920-1988, 1989, Pearl Harbor, December 7, 1941: An Annotated Bibliography, 1991, Battles of the Coral Sea and Midway, 1942: A Bibliography, 1991, World War II at Sea, 1974-1989: A Bibliography, 1990, Professional Football: The Official Pro Football Hall of Fame Bibliography, 1993, Baseball: A Comprehensive Bibliography-1st Supplement: 1985-1991, 93, The College Football Bibliography, 1994, Glimpses of Tusculum College: A Pictorial History, 1794-1994, 1994, Baseball: A Comprehensive Bibliography-2d Supplement: 1992-1997, 1998, The Airline Encyclopedia, 1909-2000, 2002, The Baseball Bibliography, 2d edit., 2006, Le Roy Fitch: The Civil War Career of a Union River Gunboat Commander, 2007, The Timberlands in the Civil War: The Lexington, Tyler and Comestog on the Western waters, 2008, Tinclads in the Civil War: Union Light-Draught Gunboat Operations on Western Waters 1862-1865, 2009; contbr. articles to various jours. Recipient Nelson Ross award Profl. Football Rsch. Assn., 1993; 1st Am. recipient Richard Franck Gold medal Bibliothek für Zeitgeschichte, Stuttgart, Fed. Rep. Germany, 1981. Mem. ALA, U.S. Naval Inst., U.S. Mil. Inst., U.S. Air Force Found., Assn. Bibliog. of History (pres. 1981-82), Alliance of Librs. in Northeast Tenn. (pres. 1997—), Beta Phi Mu, Phi Alpha Theta. Clubs: Optimist. Office: Tusculum Coll PO Box 5005 60 Shiloh Rd Greeneville TN 37743-0001 Home Phone: 423-639-7364; Office Phone: 423-636-7320.

SMITH, NEAL EDWARD, former congressman, lawyer; b. Hedrick, Iowa, Mar. 23, 1920; s. James N. and Margaret M. (Walling) S.; m. Beatrix Havens, Mar. 23, 1946; children: Douglas, Sharon. Student, U. Mo., 1945-46, Syracuse U., 1946-47; JD, Drake U., 1950. Bar: Iowa 1950. Farmer, Iowa, 1937—; sole practice Des Moines, 1950-58; atty. 50 sch. bds. in Iowa, 1951-58; asst. county atty. Polk County, Iowa, 1951; mem. from 4th Dist. Iowa US Ho. of Reps, 1959—94; ptnr. Davis, Hockenberg, Wine, Brown, Koehn & Shors, 1994, of counsel, 1995—. Chmn. Polk County Bd. Social Welfare, 1954-56; pres. Young Democratic Clubs Am., 1953-55. Served with AUS, World War II. Decorated Air medal with 4 oak leaf clusters, Purple Heart, nine battle stars. Mem. Am. Bar Assn., Farm Bur., Farmers Union, DAV. Clubs: Masons. Home: Plaza Box 90 300 Walnut Des Moines IA 50309 Office: Davis Brown Koehn Shors The Financial Ctr 215-10th St Ste 1300 Des Moines IA 50309 Office Fax: 515-243-0654.

SMITH, NICK H., former congressman, archivist, farmer; b. Addison, Mich., Nov. 5, 1934; s. LeGrand John and Blanche (Nichols) S.; m. Bonnalyn Belle Atwood, Jan. 1, 1960; children: Julianna, Bradley, Elizabeth, Stacia. BA, Mich. State U., 1957; MS, U. Del., 1959. Radio & TV farm editor Sta. WDEL, Wilmington, Del., 1957-59; radio editor Sta. KSWD, Wichita Falls, Tex., 1959-60; capt. intelligence USAF, 1959-61; mem. twp. bd. Somerset Twp., Addison, 1962-68; asst. dep. adminstr. USDA, Washington, 1971—74; state rep. Mich. Ho. of Reps., Lansing, 1978-82; state senator, pres. pro-tem Mich. State Senate, Lansing, 1982-92; mem. U.S. Congress from 7th Mich. dist, 1993—2005, mem. agr., sci., and internat. rels. coms. Mem. budget com. Mich. State Senate, 1993—99, chmn. sci. rsch. com., 1999—2005. Del. Am. Assembly on World Population & Hunger, Washington, 1973; nat. del. on U.S.-Soviet Cooperation and Trade, 1991; deacon Somerset Congl. Ch. Capt. USAF, 1959-61. Fellow Kellogg Found., 1965; named Hon. FFA State Star Farmer, 1987, SCF Conservator of Yr. Hillsdale County, 1988. Mem. Mich. Farm Bur. (bd. dirs.), Jackson C. of C., Mich. State U. Varsity Club, Masons. Republican.

SMITH, NORMAN OBED, retired physical chemist, educator; b. Winnipeg, Man., Can., Jan. 23, 1914; came to U.S., 1950, naturalized, 1958; s. Ernest and Ruth (Kilpatrick) S.; m. Anna Marie O'Connor, July 1, 1944; children: Richard Obed, Graham Michael, Stephen Housley. B.Sc., U. Man., 1935, M.Sc., 1936; PhD, NYU, 1939. Teaching fellow NYU, 1936-39; mem. faculty dept. chemistry U. Man., Winnipeg, 1939-50, asst. prof., 1946-49, assoc. prof., 1949-50, Fordham U., NYC, 1950-65, prof. chemistry, 1965-84, prof. emeritus, 1984—, chmn. dept., 1974-78; ret., 1984. Sr. phys. chemist Arthur D. Little, Inc., Cambridge, Mass., 1957; indsl. cons. Author: (with others) The Phase Rule and Its Applications, 1951, Chemical Thermodynamics, A Problems Approach, 1967, Elementary Statistical Thermodynamics, A Problems Approach, 1982; contbr. to: Ency. Brit, 1974. Fellow Chem. Inst. Can.; mem. Am. Chem. Soc., Asso. Can. Coll. Organists, Am. Guild Organists (dir. chpt. 1964-66, 79-82, 91-92), Sigma Xi, Phi Lambda Upsilon. Home: 811 E Central Rd Apt 112 Arlington Heights IL 60005-3293

SMITH, NORMAN RANDY, federal judge; b. Logan, Utah, Aug. 11, 1949; s. Norman Busby and Patricia (Mendenhall) S.; m. La Dean Egbert, Jan. 3, 1984. BS magna cum laude, Brigham Young U., 1974, JD, 1977. Bar: Idaho 1977, U.S. Dist. Ct. Idaho 1977, U.S. Ct. Claims 1979, U.S. Tax Ct. 1978, U.S. Ct. Appeals (9th cir.) 1979, U.S. Supreme Ct. 1981. Asst. gen. counsel J.R. Simplot Co., Boise, Idaho, 1977-82; assoc. Merrill & Merrill, Pocatello, Idaho, 1982—84, ptnr., 1984—95; dist. judge Idaho 6th Judicial Dist., 1995—2007, adminstrv. dist. judge, 2004—07; judge US Ct. Appeals (9th cir.), 2007—. Adj. prof., Boise St. U., 1979-81, Idaho State U., 1984- Party chmn. Idaho Rep. Party, 1993-96; county chmn. Bannock County Rep. Party, Pocatello, 1991-93; pres. Idaho State Civic Symphony, Pocatello, 1992-95, 98-99. Recipient George G. Granada award, Outstanding judge in Idaho, 2004; named Idaho Statesman of Yr., 2005; named a Tchr. of Yr., Coll. Bus., 2005. Mem. Idaho Dist. Judges Assn. (pres. 1998-2000), Idaho Def. Counsel (pres. 1992-93), Def. Rsch. Inst. (del. Idaho state 1992-94, Exceptional Performance Citation 1993), 6th Dist. Bar Assn. (pres. 1994-95), Rotary (Gate City pres. 1993-94). Avocations: golf, gardening, work. Office: US Courthouse 801 E Sherman Pocatello ID 83201 Office Phone: 208-478-4140.*

SMITH, NUMA LAMAR, JR., lawyer; b. Rock Hill, SC, Nov. 22, 1915; s. Numa Lamar and Grace (Hanes) S.; m. Mary Catherine Gray, Mar. 24, 1941; children: Patricia Gray (dec.), Elizabeth Hanes, Lamar Douglas. AB summa cum laude, Furman U., 1938; LLB with distinction, Duke U., 1941. Bar: N.Y. 1942, D.C. 1946. Assoc. firm White & Case, NYC, 1941-42, Miller & Chevalier, Washington, 1946-49, partner, 1949-83, counsel, 1983—; bd. visitors, 1973-83. Sr. fellow Duke U. Law Sch., 1979-80 Assoc. editor: Duke Law Jour, 1940-41. Served with U.S. Army, 1942-46; with Judge Adv. Gen. Corps 1944-46. Recipient Gen. Excellence award Furman U., 1938 Fellow Am. Bar Found.; mem. ABA, D.C. Bar Assn., Am. Law Inst., Duke Law Alumni Assn. (pres. 1967-69), Order of Coif, Met. Club (Washington), Burning Tree Club (Bethesda, Md.), Washington Golf Club (Arlington, Va.), The Club at Pelican Bay, Sigma Alpha Epsilon. Baptist. Home: 7515 Pelican Bay Blvd Naples FL 34108-6520

SMITH, O. BRUTON, automotive company executive; Founder Charlotte Motor Speedway, 1959, CEO & dir., 1975—; chmn., CEO Sonic Automotive, Inc., Charlotte, NC, 1997—, Speedway Motor Sports, Inc., Charlotte, 1994—; owner operator Town and Country Ford and various other pvt. bus., Charlotte, NC. Founder Speedway Children's Charities, 1984. Recipient Award of Excellence, NASCAR, 1997; named to, Greater Charlotte Sports Hall of Fame, 2005. Office: Sonic Automotive Inc 6415 Idlewild Rd Ste 109 Charlotte NC 28212

SMITH, ORIN ROBERT, chemical company executive; b. Newark, Aug. 13, 1935; s. Sydney R. and Gladys Emmett (DeGroff) S.; m. Stephanie M. Bennett-Smith; children: Lindsay, Robin; 1 stepchild, Brendan. BA in Econometrics, Brown U., 1957; MBA in Mgmt., Seton Hall U., 1964; PhD in Econs. (hon.), Centenary Coll., 1991; LLD (hon.), Monmouth Coll., 1994. Various sales and mktg. mgmt. positions Allied Chem. Corp., Morristown, NJ, 1959-69; dir. sales and mktg. Richardson-Merrell Co., Phillipsburg, NJ, 1969-72; with M&T Chems., Greenwich, Conn., 1972-77, pres., 1975-77; with Engelhard Minerals & Chems. Corp., Menlo Park, Edison, NJ, 1977-81, corp. sr. v.p., 1978-81, pres. div. minerals and chems., 1978-81, also bd. dirs., 1979-81, pres., dir. various U.S. subs., 1979-81; exec. v.p., pres. div. minerals and chems. Engelhard Corp., Menlo Park, Edison, 1981-84, bd. dirs., 1981—, pres., CEO, Iselin, NJ, 1984-95, chmn., CEO, 1995—; also bd. dirs. Bd. dirs. Summit Bank Co., The Summit Bancorp, Vulcan Materials Co., PE Corp., Ingersoll-Rand Corp., Engelhard Corp., Mfrs. Alliance. Trustee N.J. State C. of C., Inst. for Tech. Advancement; mem. bd. overseers N.J. Inst. Tech.; trustee Plimoth Plantation; 1st vice chmn. bd. trustees Centenary Coll.; past dir. Minorco, La. Land and Exploration Co.; past trustee Henry R. Kessler Found., Inc.; past chmn. Ind. Coll. Fund N.J.; past dir.-at-large U. Maine Pulp and Paper Found. Lt. (j.g.) USN, 1957-59. Mem. Chem. Mfrs. Assn. (past bd. dirs.), Econ. Club (N.Y.C.), Union League Club (N.Y.C.), Duxbury Yacht Club, New Bedford Yacht Club, N.Y. Yacht Club.

SMITH, OTIS FITZGERALD, professional sports team executive, retired professional basketball player; b. Jacksonville, Fla., Jan. 30, 1964; Grad., Jacksonville U., 1986. Player Denver Nuggets, 1986—87, Golden State Warriors, 1987—89, dir. cmty. rels./Warriors Found., 2000—02, exec. dir. basketball ops., 2002—03; player Orlando Magic, 1989—92, cmty. rels. mgr., 1992—94, dir. player devel., 2003—05, asst. gen. mgr., 2005—06, gen. mgr., 2006—. Founder, bd. dirs. Otis Smith Kids Found., 1989—; v.p. mktg. and cmty. rels. Boys and Girls Club Ctrl. Fla. Office: Orlando Magic 8701 Maitland Summit Blvd Orlando FL 32810*

SMITH, OTTO J. M., electrical engineering educator; b. Urbana, Ill., Aug. 6, 1917; s. Otto Mitchell and Mary Catherine (Carr) S.; m. Phyllis P. Sterling, Sept. 3, 1941; children: Candace B., Otto J.A., Sterling M., Stanford D. BS in Chemistry, Okla. State U., 1938; BSEE, U. Okla., 1938; PhDEE, Stanford U., 1941. Registered profl. engr., Calif. Instr. elec. engring. Tufts U., Medford, Mass., 1941-43; asst. prof. elec. engring. Denver U., 1943-44; rsch. engr. Westinghouse Rsch. Labs., Forest Hills, Pa., 1944-46; sr. rsch. fellow econs. and engring. Monash U., Melbourne, Australia, 1966-67; prof. elec. engr. U. Calif., Berkeley, 1947—. Chief engr. Smith and Sun, Berkeley, 1976—; mem. coop. sci. program NSF, Romania, 1973; chief energy efficiency EPA, Poland, 1992. Author: Feedback Control Systems, 1958; contbr. articles to profl. jours.; patentee in field. Dist. commr. Boy Scouts Am., Berkeley, 1949-53; trustee South Campus Community Ministry, Berkeley, 1968-70, Wesley Found., Berkeley, 1969-72; vol. Natural Resources Conservation Svc., U.S. Dept. Agr., 1996—. Guggenheim fellow, 1960. Fellow AAAS, IEEE; mem. Am. Solar Energy Soc., Internat. Solar Energy Soc., Am. Wind Energy Assn., Calif. Writer's Club. Clubs: Berkeley City Commons (pres. 1963). Democrat. Methodist. Avocations: photography, travel, guitar, violin, chorus. Home: 612 Euclid Ave Berkeley CA 94708-1332 Office: U Calif Dept Elec Engring & Computer Scis Berkeley CA 94720-0001 Office Phone: 510-525-9126. Business E-Mail: otto.enabler@olympus.net.

SMITH, OZZIE (OSBORNE EARL SMITH), retired professional baseball player; b. Mobile, Ala., Dec. 26, 1954; m. Denise Jackson, Nov. 1, 1980; children: Osborne Earl Jr., Dustin Cameron. Grad., Calif. State Poly. U., San Luis Obispo. Shortstop San Diego Padres Baseball Club, Nat. League, 1977—82, St. Louis Cardinals Baseball Club, Nat. League, 1982—96; baseball analyst St. Louis Cardinals Sta. KPLR, St. Louis, 1997—. Mgr. US nat. team Maj. League Baseball Futures Game, 2009. Recipient Most Valuable Player award, Nat. League Championship Series, 1985, Golden Glove award, 1980—92, Silver Slugger award, 1987; named to All-Star Team, Nat. League, 1981—92, 1994, Sporting News, 1982, 1984—87, Baseball Hall of Fame, 2002. Achievements include member of World Series championship winning St. Louis Cardinals, 1982. Avocations: jazz, word puzzles, backgammon.*

SMITH, PAMELA LATRICE, school psychologist; b. Monroe, La., Jan. 11, 1975; d. Tommy Lee Smith and Lovely Marie Bams. BA, N.E. La. U., Monroe, 1997, MS, 1999. Cert. specialist in sch. psychology 2000, supr. sch. psychol. svcs. 2004, trainer CPI's Non-Violent Phys. Crisis Intervention. Sch. psychologist Westside Alternative Sch., Tallulah, La., 1999—2000; sch. psychologist, divsn. student support svcs. Monroe City Schs., 2000—. Instr. psychology U. La., Monroe, 2002—. Founding mem. Wall of Tolerance, Montgomery, Ala., 2002—; mem. Southern Poverty Law Ctr., 2005—. Recipient Outstanding Academic Achievement, 1992—93; scholar La. Honor's Scholarship award, 1993. Mem.: AAUW, La. Sch. Psychol. Assn., So. Property Law Ctr., Cooking Club of Am. (life), Mortar Bd. Honor Soc., Phi Kappa Phi, Psi Chi Nat. Honor Soc., Delta Sigma Theta Sorority Inc. Democrat. Avocations: travel, reading, music, shopping. Office: Divsn Student Support Svcs PO Box 4180 Monroe LA 71211 Home: 98 Nelson Rd Monroe LA 71203 Home Phone: 318-342-8340; Office Phone: 318-388-3747 ext. 5230. Personal E-mail: psmith2002@bellsouth.net. Business E-Mail: pamela.smith@mcschools.net.

SMITH, PAMELA ROSEVEAR, air transportation executive; b. Corvallis, Oreg., Nov. 26, 1953; BS, U. Oreg., 1977; MBA, valedictorian, C.W. Post Coll., L.I. U., 2003. V.p. inflight customer svc. Air America, LA, 1984—90, MGM Grand Air, LA, 1990—95; dir. sales Ogden Aviation, New York, 1995—; pres., owner Sader-Smith Mktg., Inc., 1995—; v.p. sales the Am's. Pourshins P/C, NYC, 1998—; v.p. sales, mem. mgmt. bd. Pourshins Inc., NYC, 2004—, bd. dir., corp. sec. Bd. dirs. Pourshins Mgmt., 2004—. Recipient Dean's Award for acad. Excellence, L.I. U., 2003. Mem.: Internat. Flight Svcs. (exec. bd. 1999—), Greater L.I. Running Club, Kappa Alpha Theta (v.p. 1998—99). Avocation: sports, travel, education, cooking, Japanese language. Home and Office: 63 Tooker Ave Oyster Bay NY 11771 Home Phone: 516-624-7083. Personal E-mail: pampplc@verizon.net.

SMITH, PATRICIA ANN (PAT SMITH), elementary school educator; b. Wichita, Kans., Dec. 30, 1947; d. Orville Stark Kildow and Jean Robison, Ann Stine Kildow (Stepmother); m. Wilton Ray Smith, Aug. 26, 1967; children: Kevin Ray, Lee Clayton. BA in Edn., Wichita State U., Kans., 1969. Elem. tchr. Derby Pub. Sch., Kans., 1969—70, Broken Arrow Pub. Sch., Okla., 1978—2003. Edn. cons. Houghton Mifflin Pub. Co., Dallas, 2004—. Adv. com. mem. Journey Through the Universe Challenger Ctr., Alexandria, Va., 1998—2005; vol. Tulsa Air and Space Mus., 1997—2006. Recipient Using Heroes award, Reliastar/No. Life, 2001, Golden Apple award, Broken Arrow Sch. Bd., 2004; named Tchr.

of Yr., WalMart, Ea. Okla., 2001; named to book Teachers, by John Yow, 2001, Udvar-Hazy Wall of Honor, Washington, DC, 2005; grantee, Nat. Geog., 2003; Christa McAuliffe fellow, Okla., 1995, 1998. Mem.: Okla. Ret. Tchrs. Assn., Alpha Delta Kappa (pres. 2006—08). Achievements include Teacher in Space; Ambassador on the Governor's Education Team, OASIS. Personal E-mail: patsmithba@yahoo.com.

SMITH, PATRICIA CRAWFORD, elementary school educator; d. Billy Monroe and Jewel Ann Crawford; m. John William Smith, June 16, 1978; children: Stephanie D'Ann, Whitney Lauren. Degree in elem. edn., Athens State Coll., Ala., 1994; M in elem. edn., U. N.Ala., Florence, 2000, degree in adminstrv. leadership, 2006. Cert. elem. edn. K-6 Ala., 1994. Tchr. Athens City Sch., Ala., 1989—2006, amsti trainer, 2004—06. Named Tchr. of Yr., 2000—01. Mem.: Adminstrv. Leadership. Office: Athens Intermediate Sch 1916 Hwy 72 W Athens AL 35611

SMITH, PATRICIA GRACE, federal official; b. Nov. 10, 1947; d. Douglas and Wilhelmina (Griffin) Jones; m. J. Clay Smith, Jr., June 25, 1983; children: Eugene Douglas, Stager Clay, Michelle L., Michael L. BA in English, Tuskegee Inst., 1968; postgrad., Auburn U., 1969-71, Harvard U., 1974, George Washington U., 1983, Fed. Exec. Inst., 1997. Cert. exec. mgmt. tng. devel. assignments Dept. Def., 1986, U.S. Senate Commerce Com., 1987. Instr. Tuskegee Inst., Ala., 1969-71; program mgr. Curber Assocs., Washington, 1971-73; dir. placement Nat. Assn. Broadcasters, Washington, 1973-74, dir. pub. affairs, 1974-77; assoc. prodr. Group W Broadcasting, Balt., 1977, prodr., 1977-78; dir. affiliate rels. and programming Sheridan Broadcasting Network, Crystal City, Va., 1978-80; dep. dir. policy, assoc. mng. dir. pub. info./reference svc. FCC, Washington, 1992-94, acting assoc. mng. dir., pub. info. and reference svcs., 1994—. Chief of staff office assoc. adminstr. for comml. space transp. FAA, U.S. Dept. Transp., 1994-96, dep. assoc. adminstr. for comml. space transp., 1996-97, acting assoc. adminstr., 1997, assoc. adminstr., 1998—. Vice-chmn. Nat. Conf. Black Lawyers Task Force on Comms., Washington, 1975-87; trustee, mem. exec. com., nominating com., youth adv. com. Nat. Urban League, 1976-81; mem. comms. com. Cancer Coordinating Coun., 1977-84; mem. Braintrust Subcom. on Children's Programming, Congl. Black Caucus, 1976—; mem. adv. bd. Black Arts Celebration, 1978-83; mem. NAACP; mem. journalism and comms. adv. coun. Auburn U., 1976-78; mem. Washington Urban League, 1985—; bd. dirs. Black Film Rev., 1989-91; mem. D.C. Commn. on Human Rights, 1986-88, chmn., 1988-91; mem. adv. coun. NIH, 1992-96; mem. bd. advisors The Salvation Army, 1993-2000. Named Outstanding Young Woman of Yr., Washington, 1975, 78; recipient Sustained Superior Performance award FCC, Washington, 1982-95, Disting. Alumnus award Tuskegee U., 1996, C. Alfred Anderson award, 2002. Mem. Women in Comms., Inc. (mem. nat. adv. com.), Broadcasters Club (bd. dirs. 1976-77), Lambda Iota Tau. Democrat. Baptist. Avocations: writing, swimming. Office: DOT/AST 800 Independence Ave SW Rm 331 Washington DC 20591-0001 Office Phone: 202-267-7793.

SMITH, PATRICIA H., library association director; B, Austin Coll., Sherman, Tex.; MLS, U. Tex., Austin. Exec. dir. Tex. Libr. Assn. Mem.: Austin Conv. and Visitors Bur. (bd. dirs. 2007—), Tex. Soc. Assn. (execs. ex bd. vice chmn. 2002—06, 2007—09), Com on Legislation (chmn. 2000—01), Coun. for 6 Terms (budget chmn. 2001—05), Tex. Libr. Assn. (Libr. of Yr. 1989, Disting. Svc. award 1994), ALA (mem. exec. bd. 1995—99, 2005—08). Office: Tex Libr Assn 3355 Bee Cave Rd Ste 401 Austin TX 78746-6763 Office Phone: 512-328-1518. Office Fax: 512-328-8852. Business E-Mail: pats@txla.org.

SMITH, PATRICIA LYNNE, artist; b. Camden, NJ, Nov. 3, 1955; d. Thomas Patrick Connelly and Elizabeth Jean (Swope) Shober; m. William Clarence Smith, Nov. 30, 1973 (div. June 1980); children: Travis, Taryn. BA, Rutgers U., Camden, NJ, 1980; MFA, Rutgers U., New Brunswick, NJ, 1984. Adj. instr. Rutgers U., New Brunswick, 1983-84, Trenton State Coll., 1989-90. One-woman shows include Piezo Electric Gallery, NYC, 1996, SOMA Gallery, Berlin, 1994, AIR Gallery, NYC, 1994, St. Peter's Ch., 1994, Croxhapox Gallery, Belgium, 1995, Black and Herron Gallery, N.Y.C., 1996, Studio Five Beekman, 1997, Front Room Gallery, Bklyn., 2006, 2008, others, exhibited in group shows at Art Exch. Fair, NYC, 1996—97, Bklyn. Mus. Art, 1997, Cornerhouse, Manchester, Eng., 1997, Gas Works, London, 1997, Gramercy Art Fair, 1997, Rotunda Gallery, 1997, Kunstlerhause, Vienna, 1998, Vassar Coll., Poughkeepsie, N.Y., 1998, Bard Coll., Rheinbeck, N.Y., 1998, Eyewash Gallery, Bklyn., 1994, 1999—2000, Project Space, Toronto, Can., 2001, Sideshow Gallery, Bklyn., 2001, 2008, Exit Art, NYC, 2002, Voorkamer, Lier, Belgium, 2002, 2006, Art Ctr. Coll. Design, Pasadena, Calif., 2002, U. Md., College Park, 2003, Solway Jones Gallery, LA, 2003, Carlsbad Mus., N.Mex, 2003, Krasdale Gallery, NY, 2004, Stadt Mus., Lier, Belgium, 2004, Stedelijk Mus., Aalst, Belgium, 2004, 2006, Ill. State U., 2004, Gallery 32, London, 2004, Shore Inst. Contemporary Art, Long Branch, N.J., 2005, Pierogi, NY, 2005, Galerie In Situ, Aalst, Belgium, 2006, Weatherspoon Art Mus., Greensboro, NC, 2006, Tex. Tech. U., Lubbock, 2007, Ruth Bachofner Gallery, LA, 2007, Housatonic Mus., Bridgeport, Conn., 2007, Rupert Ravens Contemporary, Newark, 2007, Istanbul Biennial, 2007, Front Room Gallery, Bklyn., 2008, Gallery Joe, Phila., 2008, Galerie Jan Colle, Ghent, Belgium, 2008, Jancar Gallery, LA, 2009, John Michael Kohler Arts Ctr., Sheboygan, Wis., 2009, Dorsch Gallery, Miami, Fla., 2009. Recipient Stedman Purchase prize, Rutgers U., 1980; Garden State fellow, 1982—84, Exhbn. grantee, Artist's Space, 1988, 1990. Home Phone: 917-282-2042. Personal E-mail: smithpl@frontiernet.net.

SMITH, PATRICIA M. (PATTI SMITH), state supreme court justice; married; 2 children. BA, Troy State U., 1973; JD, Jones Sch. of Law, 1976. Atty. Bell, Johnson and Medaris; asst. dist. atty. Shelby County, Ala., 1976—80, dist. judge Ala., 1980—2004; assoc. justice Ala. Supreme Ct., 2005—. Organized Shelby County's Children's Policy Council; mem. Governor's Commn. on Crime, Commn. on Future of Juvenile Justice System, Ala. Jud. System Study Commn. on Sentencing; chmn. Task Force on Dependency, Interagency Conference on Youth. Named Judge of the Yr., Nat. Ct. Appointed Special Advocates, 2001. Mem.: Ala. State Bar Assn., Shelby County Bar Assn., Ala. Assn. of Juvenile and Family Ct. Judges, Ala. Assn. of Dist. Ct. Judges. Office: Ala Supreme Ct 300 Dexter Ave Montgomery AL 36104 Office Phone: 205-670-6400.*

SMITH, PATRICK (PATRICK SANTOSUOSSO), columnist, pilot; b. 1966; Airline pilot; air travel columnist salon.com, 2001—. Author: Ask the Pilot: Everything You Need To Know About Air Travel, 2004. Office: c/o Salon Media Group Inc 101 Spear St Ste 203 San Francisco CA 94105 Office Phone: 415-645-9200. Office Fax: 415-645-9204. Personal E-mail: aviateur@askthepilot.com. Business E-Mail: PatrickSmith@salon.com.

SMITH, PATRICK JOHN, editor, writer; b. NYC, Dec. 11, 1932; s. H. Ben and Geraldine (Wilson) S.; m. Elisabeth Munro, Nov. 27, 1964; children: Douglass Munro, Matthew Wilson. Student, Phillips Exeter, 1951; AB, Princeton U., 1955. Freelance writer and critic, 1958-70; editor, pub. The Mus. Newsletter, NYC, 1970-77; pres. Music Critics Assn., Washington, 1977-81; dir. opera mus. theater program NEA, Washington, 1985-89; editor Opera News, NYC, 1989-98, editor-at large, 1998—. Author: The Tenth Muse: A History of the Opera Libretto, 1970, A Year at the Met, 1983. Office: Opera News 70 Lincoln Center Plz New York NY 10023-6548

SMITH, PATSY JUANITA, retired financial executive; b. Dallas, Aug. 3, 1939; d. Roland Murl and Ruby Esther (Whiteside) Stephens; m. Jerry Arlin Kerby, June 7, 1957 (div. Nov. 1971); children: Timmy Wayne, Pamela Anita; m. Charles Albert Smith, June 17, 1977. Student, Ins. Inst., Dale Carnegie Sch. Claims adjuster Crum & Forster, Dallas, 1967—77, Atlantic Mut. Co., Dallas, 1978—79, Am. States Ins. Co., Dallas, 1979—81, Trinity Adjusting Co., Dallas, 1981—83; beauty cons. Mary Kay Cosmetics, Dallas, 1980—83, sales dir., 1983—84; loan officer Westco Fin. Svcs., Dallas, 1984—2009. Precinct chmn. Dem. Party, Dallas, 1981, election judge, 1981, 1982. Recipient Claims Profl. of Yr. award, Ins. Women Dallas, 1998, Ins. Woman of Yr. award, 1999; named Queen of Recruiting, 1982. Mem.: Nat. Assn. Ins. Women, Am. Bus. Womans Assn., Dallas (Tex.) Claims Assn. (pres. 2002—03), Women's Coun. Realtors (state pub. rels. com.), Greater Dallas Bd. Realtors, Mortgage Bankers Assn., Am. Bus. Women Assn. (sec. 1980), Ins. Women of Dallas (pres. 1981—82, 2000—02, Claimswoman of Yr. 1979, 1980, Ins. Woman of Year 1998), Order Blue Goose. Home: 8488 County Rd 2400 Quinlan TX 75474-7612

SMITH, PAUL LETTON, JR., geophysicist; b. Columbia, Mo., Dec. 16, 1932; s. Paul Letton and Helen Marie (Doersam) S.; m. Mary Barbara Noel; children: Patrick, Melody, Timothy, Christopher, Anne. BS in Physics, Carnegie Inst. Tech., 1955, MSEE, 1957, PhD in Elec. Engring., 1960. From instr. to asst. prof. Carnegie Inst. Tech., Pitts., 1955-63; sr. engr. Midwest Rsch. Inst., Kansas City, Mo., 1963-66; from rsch. engr. to sr. scientist and group head Inst. Atmospheric Scis., S.D. Sch. Mines and Tech., Rapid City, 1966-81; vis. prof. McGill U., Montreal, Que., Canada, 1969-70; chief scientist Air Weather Svc. USAF, Scott AFB, Ill., 1974-75; dir. Inst. Atmospheric Scis., S.D. Sch. Mines and Tech., Rapid City, 1981-96, prof. emeritus, 1996—. Lectr. Tech. Svc. Corp., Silver Spring, Md., 1972-91; vis. scientist Alberta Rsch. Coun., Edmonton, Can., 1984-85; dir. S.D. Space Grant Consortium, Rapid City, 1991-96; Fulbright lectr. U. Helsinki, 1986; nat. assoc. Nat. Acads., 2004—. Contbr. over 70 articles to profl. jours. Fellow Am. Meteorol. Soc. (Editor's award 1992, Remote Sensing lectr. 2006); mem. IEEE (life, sr.), NRC (assoc.), Weather Modification Assn. (Thunderbird award 1995), Sigma Xi. Home: 2107 9th St Rapid City SD 57701-5315 Office Phone: 605-394-2291. Business E-Mail: paul.smith@sdsmt.edu.

SMITH, PAUL VERGON, JR., retired gas industry executive; b. Lima, Ohio, Apr. 25, 1921; s. Paul Vergon and Aleta Rose (Bowers) S.; m. Alta Fern Chipps, Mar. 2, 1945; children: Douglas, Marsha, Jeffrey, Alison AB, Miami U., Oxford, Ohio, 1942; MS, U. Ill., 1943, PhD, 1945. With Exxon Rsch. & Engring. Co., 1946—66; with Exxon Rsch & Engring Co., 1972—86, mgr. pub. affairs, 1972—86, mgr. ednl. and profl. soc. rels. Florham Park, NJ, 1981—86; asst. dir. chem. rsch. Esso Petroleum Co., Abingdon, England, 1966—67; dir. chem. rsch. Esso Rsch. S.A., Brussels, 1967—71; mem. adv. bd. Cache, Inc., Austin, Tex., 1979—86; pres. APS Assocs., Westfield, NJ, 1986—90. Bd. dirs., treas. Jets, Inc., Alexandria, Va.; dir. CENTCOM, Ltd.; mem. exec. bd. N.J. Bus./Industry/Sci. Edn. Consortium Patentee in field; contbr. numerous articles to profl. jours., chpts. to books Bd. dirs. United Way Union County, N.J., 1980-86; chmn. rsch. adv. coun. Miami U., 1980-84 Recipient Pres.'s award Am. Assn. Petroleum Geologists, 1955; Spl. award N.J. Sci. Tchrs. Assn., 1985 Mem. AAAS, Am. Chem. Soc. (dir. 1978-86, chmn. bd. 1984-86; Belden award 1984), Am. Soc. Engring. Edn. (dir. 1980-86, v.p. 1980-86), Country Club Naples, Phi Beta Kappa, Sigma Xi, Omicron Delta Kappa, Phi Eta Sigma, Alpha Chi Sigma, Pi Mu Epsilon, Sigma Pi Sigma, Phi Lambda Upsilon Republican. Methodist. Home Phone: 239-262-4901.

SMITH, PAULETTE WEATHERWAX, secondary school educator; d. Robert and Irene M. Weatherwax; m. Michael C. Smith; children: Ellen Elizabeth, Deborah Lindsay, Stephen Michael. BS, SUNY, Oneonta, 1970; MEd, Pa. State U., State College, 1972. Dale Carnegie instr. Ralph Nichols Group, Livonia, Mich., 1987—; social studies tchr. Clawson Pub. Sch., Mich., 1989—; mem. bias and sensitivity com., content com., rangefinding com. Mich. Dept. Edn., Lansing, 2004—. Inspirational workshop leader, spkr.; presenter in field; mem. Mich. Coun. Social Studies, 2007—. Author: (travel guide) Las Vegas on the Cheap!, 2001. Speech contest coach Clawson- Troy Optimist Club, Clawson, Mich., 1994—2004; recycling coord. Abitibi Recycling, Clawson, 2004—. Mem.: NEA, Mich. Assn. Mid. Sch. Educators (conf. presenter), Mich. Edn. Assn., Clawson Edn. Assn. (rep. NEA 2001—, Mich. Edn. Assn. rep.), Pa. State Alumni Assn. (life). Avocation: travel. Home: 31072 Pickwick Ln Franklin MI 48025 Office: Clawson Pub Schs 150 John M Clawson MI 48017

SMITH, PETER GUY, neuroscience educator, researcher; b. Boston, July 22, 1950; s. Harvey James and Susan Alta (Muto) S.; m. Ellen Penny Averett, Feb. 22, 1986; 1 child, Harrison Jesse. BA, U. N.H., 1973; PhD, Duke U., 1978. Rsch. assoc. dept. pharmacology Duke U., Durham, N.C., 1978-82, asst. med. rsch. prof., 1982-87; assoc. prof. dept. physiology U. Kans. Med. Ctr., Kansas City, 1987-93, prof. dept. physiology, 1993-95, dir. grad. studies in physiology, 1995-97. Mem. neurology B2 study sect. NIH, 1991-95, chmn. 1993-95; mem. rsch. adv. com. Kans. affiliate Am. Heart Assn., Topeka, 1991-96. Contbr. articles to Brain Rsch., Neurosci., Hypertension, Jour. Comparative Neurology, Exptl. Neurology. Recipient Excellence in Edn. award Student Voice, U. Kans. Sch. Medicine, 1991, 92, investigator rsch. award, 1996; fellow Pharm. Mfrs. Assn. Found., 1978-80, W.T. Kemper Found., 1997; grantee NIH, 1986—, Marrion Merrel Dow Found., 1991-93. Mem. Soc. for Neurosci., World Fedn. Neurology (rsch. group on autonomic nervous system), Am. Heart Assn. (high blood pressure rsch. coun., established investigator 1983-88), Internat. Soc. for Autonomic Neurosci. Achievements include contributions to fields of development plasticity of the autonomic nervous system. Office: U Kans Med Ctr Physiology Dept 3901 Rainbow Blvd Kansas City KS 66160-0001

SMITH, PETER J., engineering software company executive; BSEE, Northeastern U., Boston; MBA, U. Notre Dame, Ind. Mgr. worldwide applications devel. and mktg. activities Digital Equipment Corp., v.p. European ops., 1991—94; pres. Ansys Inc., Canonsburg, Pa., 1995—99, CEO, 1995—2000, chmn., 1995—. Former chmn. Neartek Inc.; chmn. Bluesocket Inc.; dir. Accellos Inc. Office: Ansys Inc Southpointe 275 Technology Dr Canonsburg PA 15317 Office Phone: 724-746-3304. Office Fax: 724-514-9494.

SMITH, PETER K., cardiothoracic surgeon; b. Cleve., Ohio, Aug. 20, 1951; MD, Duke U. Sch. Medicine, 1977. Cert. Am. Bd. Thoracic Surgery, Am. Bd. Surgery. Intern Duke U. Med. Ctr., Durham, NC, resident, cardiovascular rsch., 1987, divsn. chief; asst. prof., surgery Duke U., Durham, NC, 1987, prof. surgery, thoracic and cardiovascular surgery. Contbr. several articles to profl. jours. Tchg. Scholar, Am. Heart Assn. Clinician Scientist Awardee, Duke U. Med. Ctr., NC, 1980—83. Office: Duke U Med Ctr Box 3442 Durham NC 27710 Office Phone: 910-684-2890. Office Fax: 919-681-7905.

SMITH, PETER WILLIAM EBBLEWHITE, electrical engineer, educator, research scientist, physicist; b. London, Nov. 3, 1937; m. Jacqueline Marie Mankiewicz, June 18, 1966; children: Christal, Dawn N. BSc, McGill U., Montreal, Que., Can., 1958, MSc, 1961, PhD, 1964. Profl. physicist. Mem. of staff Can. Marconi Co., Mont., 1958-59; mem. tech. staff Bell Labs., Holmdel, NJ, 1963-83; dist. mgr. Bellcore, Red Bank, NJ, 1984-88, div. mgr., 1988-92; prof. elec. and computer engring. U. Toronto, 1992—2003, prof. emeritus, 2003—; exec. dir. Ont. Laser and Lightwave Rsch. Ctr., 1992-95; dir. Nortel Inst. Telecom., 1999—2003. Editor-in-chief IEEE Press Progress in Lasers and Electro-Optics Series, 1987—92, Optics Letters, 1989—95; contbr. over 340 refered publs. Bd. dirs. Monmouth Arts Found., Red Bank, 1965-82; pres. The Circle for Children Found., 2003—. Recipient Sr. Scientist award NATO, 1979. Fellow IEEE (life, Quantum Electronics award 1986, Third Millennium medal 2000), Optical Soc. Am. (bd. dirs., chmn. bd. editors), Inst. Physics U.K.; mem. IEEE Lasers and Electro-Optics Soc. (pres. 1984). Achievements include first demonstration of waveguide gas laser, non-linear optical interface; development of hybrid bistable optical devices; 34 patents in field. Office: U Toronto Dept Elec & Computer Engring Toronto ON Canada M5S 3G4 E-mail: peter.smith@utoronto.ca.

SMITH, PETER WOLFGANG, physicist, artist; b. Rostock, Germany, May 16, 1929; s. Hans Schmidt-Isserstedt and Gertrude Calo; m. Marie Smith, Sept. 8, 1954; children: Nicholas, Lydia, Caroline. Scholar, King's Coll. Choir Sch., Cambridge, Eng., 1940—43, Felsted Sch., Essex, Eng., 1943—48; student, Cambridge Art Coll., Eng., 1950; BS with 1st honors in natural philosophy, St. Andrews U., 1952; postgrad., Edinburgh U., 1952—54. Sci. officer Admiralty Signal and Radar Establishment, Portsmouth, England, 1954—60; scientist Plessey Co., Hampshire, England, 1960—67; supr. Norden Sys., Norwalk, Conn., 1967—89; cons. Peter Smith, Westport, Conn., 1989—94; artist Pierre Cochon, Westport, 1993—. Patentee in field; contbr. articles to profl. jours.; artist exhibiting in Wessex shows, U.K., 1956-60, various Conn. shows, 1996—. Mem. Inst. of Physics of London. Avocations: music, art history, golf. Home and Office: 7 Darbrook Rd Westport CT 06880-3611 Office Phone: 203-226-5162.

SMITH, PHIL, medical educator, director; b. Conn., 1955; s. Robert and Louise Smith; 1 child, Marilla Hewitt. BA in Lit. and Writing, Franconia Coll., NH; MEd in Intensive Spl. Edn., U. Vt., Burlington, EdD in Ednl. Leadership and Policy Studies. Exec. dir. Vt. Devel. Disabilities Coun., Waterbury, 2001—03; dir. Vt. Self-Determination Project, Waterbury, 1999—2001; prof. Eastern Mich. U., Ypsilanti, 2004—. Chair Assn. Cmty. Advocacy, Ann Arbor, Mich., 2007—09. Mem.: Am. Assn. Intellectual and Devel. Disabilities (bd. mem. Mich. Chpt.). Office: Eastern Michigan Univ 110 Porter Ypsilanti MI 48197 Business E-Mail: psmith16@emich.edu.

SMITH, PHILIP DANIEL, academic administrator, education educator; b. Dayton, Ohio, Dec. 25, 1933; s. Hubert Edgar and Edith (Parker) S.; m. Marilyn Brown, Nov. 25, 1953; children: Carolyn Smith Valentine, Norman Daniel, Stanley Nathan. BS cum laude, Bob Jones U., 1955; MEd, Miami U., Oxford, Ohio, 1956; EdD, Pa. State U., 1964. Dean coll. arts and sci. Bob Jones U., Greenville, SC, 1961-65, registrar, 1965-81, prof. edn., 1956—2005, provost, 1981—2005, provost emeritus, 2005—. Mem. edn. adv. bd. One Touch Systems, Inc., 1995-96; ednl. analyst Bible Colls., Gospel Fellowship Missions Assn., 2007—. Cons. for BJ Help Network, BJ Linc, and BJU Press books Beginnings for Christian Schools, English Skills for Christian Schools, Handwriting for Christian Schools. Pres. Bob Jones U. Alumni Assn., Greenville, 1970-71; mem. coll. parallel adv. com. Tri-County Tech. Coll., Pendleton, S.C., 1973-86. Mem. Assn. Ednl. Communications and Tech. (life mem.; membership coord. profl. assns. 1969-72, vice chair nat. membership com. 1972-73, chair nat. membership com. 1973-75, council del. S.C. chpt. 1972-73, audiovisual instrn. editorial adv. com. 1974-75, del. to Lake Okoboji ednl. media leadership conf. 1972, 74), Assn. Ednl. Communications and Tech. of S.C. (bd. dirs. 1970-75, pres. 1972-73, award for outstanding contbns. and service 1971), Am. Assn. Collegiate Registrars and Admissions Officers, Phi Delta Kappa. Republican. Baptist. Office: Bob Jones U Office Provost Greenville SC 29614-0001 Office Phone: 864-242-5100. Business E-Mail: psmith@bju.edu.

SMITH, PHILIP J., performing arts organization administrator; b. 1931; m. Tricia Walsh-Smith, Oct. 1999 (div. July 2008). Ticket seller Imperial Theater, 1957; box office treas.; v.p. The Shubert Orgn., Inc., NYC, exec. v.p., pres., 1996—2008, chmn., co-CEO, 2008—; chmn. The Shubert Found., 2008—. Mem. Tony Awards Adminstrn. com. Broadway League; mem. exec. com. Bd. Govs.; bd. mem. The Actors' Fund, Broadway Cares/Equity Fights AIDS. Recipient Ellis Island Medal of Honor, NECO. Mem.: Knights of Malta. Office: The Shubert Orgn 234 W 44th St Fl 6 New York NY 10036*

SMITH, PHILIP JOHN, industrial and systems engineering educator; b. Bradenton, Fla., July 11, 1953; s. John Fredrick and Valerie Eline (Polk) S. BA in Psychology, U. Mich., 1975, MS in Indsl. and Ops. Engring., 1976, PhD in Psychology and Indsl. Engring., 1979. Lectr. dept. indsl. engring. U. Mich., Ann Arbor, 1979-80, rsch. scientist Ctr. for Ergonomics, 1979-80; asst. prof. dept. indsl. engring. Ohio State U., Columbus, 1980-86, assoc. prof., 1986-92, prof. indsl. and sys. engring., 1992—, dir. Inst. for Ergonomics, 1998—. Cons. Metron, Washington, 1998—, BAE Systems, 2006—, Lockhood, 2007- Co-editor: Challenges in Indexing Electronic Text and Images, 1994; contbr. articles, paper to profl. publs. Fellow Human Factors Soc.; mem. IEEE Sys., Man and Cybernetics, Am. Soc. for Info. Sci., Assn. Computing Machinery. Avocation: dressage. Home: 7197 Calhoun Rd Ostrander OH 43061-9335 Office: Ohio State U Engring Dept 1971 Neil Ave Columbus OH 43210-1210 Business E-Mail: smith.131@osu.edu.

SMITH, PHILIP JONES, lawyer; b. York, Pa., May 14, 1941; s. Clark S. and Margaret Ann (Jones) S.; m. Ann F. Johnson, Apr. 21, 1973; 1 child, James M. BA cum laude, Williams Coll., 1963; LLB, U. Va., 1966. Bar: Mass. 1967. Assoc. Ropes & Gray, Boston, 1967-76, ptnr., 1976—2007, sr. counsel, 2008—. Lectr. Boston U. Sch. of Law, 1984—98. Contbr. chapters to books, articles to profl. jours. Bd. dirs., pres. Greater Boston Youth Symphony Orch., Boston, 1978-2000; bd. dirs., v.p., pres., treas. Keewaydin Found., Salisbury, Vt., 1980—2008; bd. dirs., past treas. Project STEP, Boston, 1987-95; overseer, chair facilities com. New Eng. Conservatory, Boston, 1989-95. Fulbright scholar, U. Madrid, 1966—67. Mem.: Essex County Club, N.Y. Yacht Club, Eastern Yacht Club (sec. 1977—83, planning com.chair 2001—05, bd. dirs. 2001—, rear commodore 2006—07, vice commander 2008—), Order of Coif. Home: 35 Harbor Ave Marblehead MA 01945-3636 Office: Ropes & Gray One Internat Pl Boston MA 02110-2624 Office Phone: 617-951-7744. Business E-Mail: psmith@ropesgray.com.

SMITH, PHILIP MEEK, science administrator, consultant; b. Springfield, Ohio, May 18, 1932; s. Clarence Mitchell S. and Lois Ellen (Meek) Dudley. BS, Ohio State U., 1954, MA, 1955; DSc (hon.), NC State U., 1986. Mem. staff U.S. Nat. Com. for Internat. Geophys. Yr., NAS, 1957-58; program dir. NSF, 1958-63, dir. ops. U.S. Antarctic Rsch. program, 1964-69, dep. head divsn. polar programs, 1970-73, exec. asst. to dir. and sci. advisor to pres., 1974-76; chief gen. sci. br. Office Mgmt. and Budget Exec. Office of Pres., 1973-74; assoc. dir. Office Sci. and Tech. Policy, Exec. Office of Pres., 1976-81; exec. officer NRC-NAS, Washington, 1981-94; ptnr. McGeary and Smith, Washington, 1995—2004; chmn. external adv. com. Nat. Computational Sci. Alliance, 1997—2001, mem., 2002—03; prin. Smith Sci. Policy and Mgmt., Santa Fe, 2004—. Bd. dirs. Aurora Flight Scis. Corp.; adv. cons. bd. U. Ala. Geophys. Inst., 1994—98; adv. bd. Sci.'s Next Wave, 1998—2002; advisor Com. for Econ. Devel., 1997; com. on sci., tech. and health aspects fgn. policy agenda US NRC, 1998—2000, com. on sci. and tech. counter terrorism, 2001—02, mem. com. sci. bases Colo. River Basin water mgmr., 2005—07, mem. com. sci. basis decision making internat. sustainable devel. orgns., 2002—05; chair com. orgn. & strategy Sci. Com. Antarctic Rsch., 1999—2000; co-chair adv. bd. Calif. Inst. Telecom. & Info. Tech., 2000—; mem. US Nat. Com. Internat. Polar Yr., 2003—05; history of geophysics com. Am. Geophys. Union, 2004—; bd. dirs. found. Los Alamos Nat. Lab., 2006—07; advisor Lapides Found., 2007—; chair Review Group Sci. Com. Antarctic Rsch., 2008—09. Author: (with others) The Frozen Future, a Prophetic Report from Antarctica, 1973; contbr. articles to profl. jours. Bd. dirs. Washington Project for Arts, 1983-84, Washington Sculptors Group, 1983-84; mem. N.Mex. First., 2008-. 1st lt. U.S. Army, 1955-57. Fellow AAAS, Antarctican Soc.; mem. Cosmos Club (Washington), Am. Alpine Club (Golden, Colo.), Sigma Xi, Grand Canyon River Guides. Office: Smith Sci Policy & Mgmt 767 Acequia Madre 2 Santa Fe NM 87505-2868 Personal E-mail: smithphil767@gmail.com.

SMITH, PHILLIP H., biology professor, educational association administrator; PhD, Pa. State U., 1973. Prof. cell and devel. biology SUNY Upstate Med. U., Syracuse. Co-founder Nat. Inst. of Health Diabetes Rsch. and Edn. Ctr., U. Wash., Seattle; prin. investigator on grants for NIH, NSF, VA; scientific advisor Am. Diabetes Assn., Juvenile Diabetes Found. Contbr. articles to porfl. jours. Mem.: NY State United Tchrs. (Higher Edn. Mem. of Yr. 2006), United Univ. Professions (pres. 2008—, v.p. academics, chief negotiator 2003—07, Nina Mitchell Disting. Svc. Award 2005). Office: Upstate Med U 750 E Adams St Syracuse NY 13210 also: United Univ Professions PO Box 15143 Albany NY 12211-5143 Office Phone: 315-464-8571. E-mail: smith@upstate.edu.

SMITH, PHILLIP WALTON, retired surgeon; b. Alton, Ill., Oct. 5, 1929; MD, Yale U., 1955. Cert. in surgery. Intern Grace-New Haven Hosp., 1955-56, resident in surgery, 1959-62, West Haven VA Hosp., 1963; fellow in thoracic surgery Grace-New Haven Hosp., 1958-59; with Charlton-St. Annes Hosp., Fall River, Mass., 1959-95; ret., 1995. Fellow ACS; mem. AMA, New Eng. Surg. Soc., Mass. Med. Soc.

SMITH, PHILLIPS GUY, banker; b. Orange, NJ, Sept. 15, 1946; s. Phillips Upham and Helen Ottilie (Voderberg) S.; m. Ann Dixon Schickhaus, Dec. 29, 1973; children: Guy Dixon, William Schickhaus, Louisa Upham. B in Engring., Stevens Inst. Tech., Hoboken, NJ; MBA, U. Pa., 1975. Comml. banking rep. The Bank of N.Y., NYC, 1976-78, asst. treas., 1978-79, asst. v.p., 1979-80, v.p., 1980-85, sr. v.p., 1985-93; mng. dir. Internat. Strategy Svcs., Inc., NYC, 1993-2000; prin. Sippican Group LLC, Greenwich, Conn., 2000—08; mng. dir. Nat. Securities Corp., NYC, 2008—. Vestryman Ch. of The Heavenly Rest, N.Y.C., 1983-88, treas., 1985-87; trustee Tabor Acad., Marion, Mass., 1987—, treas., 1991—. Lt. USN, 1970-74, Vietnam. Mem. Racquet and Tennis Club, Down Town Assn., Rockaway Hunting Club, Nantucket Yacht Club. Episcopalian. Home: 9 E 94th St New York NY 10128-0611 Office: Nat Securities Corp 330 Madison Ave New York NY 10017 Business E-Mail: psmith@nationalsecuritiesib.com.

SMITH, PHYLLIS, actress; b. Lemay, Mo., July 10, 1951; Studied ballet and tap with Majorie Mendolia; B in Elementary Edn., U. Mo., St. Louis. Former St. Louis Cardinals Cheerleader; ballet dancer St. Louis Civic Ballet, The St. Louis Dance Theater; profl. jazz dancer under Raoul Appel; toured the country as a dancer with Able's Baggy Pants Burlesque; toured the country as a dancer and comic skit performer with Mercer Brother's show, Giggles Galore; pre-school tchr. Casting asst. (TV films) A Taste for Killing, 1992, casting assoc. (TV series) Dr. Quinn, Medicine Women, 1993, Spin City, 1996; actor: (TV series) The Office, 2005— (Outstanding Performance by an Ensemble in a Comedy Series, SAG, 2007, 2008); (films) I Want Someone to Eat Cheese With, 2006; guest appearances Arrested Development, 2005, Curb Your Enthusiasm, 2005. Mem.: SAG.

SMITH, PRESTON, retired minister, small business owner; s. Arthur W. and Syble M. Smith; children: Cynthia Ann Smith Jones, Carey R. BS, Little Rock U., 1959; BA in Religion, Campbell Coll., 1973; MDiv in Pastoral Care, S.E. Sem., 1978; postgrad., East Carolina U., 1994; D of Ministry, Grad. Theol. Found., 1997. Cert. chaplain, ordained to ministry Free Will Bapt. Ch., 1968. Pastor Welcome Home Ch., Beaufort, N.C., 1968-71, Rains Crossroads, Princeton, N.C., 1972-76, Piney Grove, Kenly, N.C., 1976-78; res. chaplain U. N.C. Hosp., Chapel Hill, 1978-80, fellow in pastoral care, 1980-81; dir. of pastoral care Nash Gen. Hosp., Rocky Mount, NC, 1981—2003; owner Walker Enterprises and Silver Dollar Press, Inc., Hot Springs Village, Ark., 2003—. Cons. for ch. conflict Presbyn. Chs., Rocky Mount, N.C., 1984-87, N.C. Chaplains Assn., 1986-2003; bioethics bd. Nash Health Care Sys., 1994-2003; bd. dirs. Down East Christian Ins., 1996; mem. sci. textbook selection com. Ark. Coun. Tchrs. Math., Little Rock, Ark., 1983. Author, pub.: Free E-Book About Free E-Books, 2004, How to Adjust and Repair Your Sewing Machine, 2005. Bd. dirs. Kiwanis, Rocky Mount, 1988-90; mem. United Way, Rocky Mount. Mem. N.C. Chaplains Assn. (pres. v.p., sec. exec. com. 1986-94, Outstanding Leadership award 1994), Coll. of Chaplains (state rep. 1991-96, chair mem. svc. coun., bd. dirs. 1996), Order of De Molay (master councillor). Democrat. Avocations: woodworking, candle making. Office: PO Box 8394 Hot Springs Village AR 71910

SMITH, R. GORDON, lawyer; b. Roanoke, Va., May 28, 1938; BA with highest honors, U. Va., 1960; LLB magna cum laude, Harvard U., 1964. Bar: Va. 1964. Law clk. to judge U.S. Ct. Appeals (5th cir.), 1964-65; ptnr. McGuire, Woods, Battle & Boothe, Richmond, Va., 1969—. Exec., legislation editor Harvard Law Rev., 1963-64; bd. dirs. Scott & Stringfellow Fin., Inc., Trigon Healthcare, Inc., Va. C. of C., mem. coun., Virginia Inst. Marine Sci. Fellow Am. Bar Found.; mem. Va. Bar Assn. (pres. 1987-88), Am. Law Inst., Phi Beta Kappa, Omicron Delta Kappa. Office: McGuire Woods 901 E Cary St Richmond VA 23219-4057 Office Phone: 804-775-4347.

SMITH, R. JEFFREY, national investigative correspondent; b. Milw. s. Robert J. and Eileen Smith; m. Lola Pavlovic Smith, 2003. With Sarasota Herald-Tribune, NY, Des Moines Register, Iowa, Milw. Jour., Science mag., Washington, 1979—86; nat. security corr. Washington Post, 1986—98, bur. chief Rome, 1998—2001, nat. investigative corr. Washington, 2001—07, nat. investigative editor, 2007—. Recipient Sci.-in-Soc. Journalism award, Nat. Assn. Sci. Writers, 1982, Nat. Mag. award, 1986, Pulitzer Prize for investigative reporting, 2006. Office: Washington Post 1150 15th St NW Washington DC 20071 Office Phone: 202-334-7334.

SMITH, RALPH HARRISON, II, lawyer; b. Albuquerque, Nov. 2, 1951; s. Robert Tatum and Harriet Smith; m. Helen Elizabeth Oakley, July 13, 1974; children: Harrison, William, Robert BA, Washington and Lee U., 1973; MA, Oxford U., 1976; JD, Yale U., 1979. Bar: D.C. 1979, Ala. 1982. Assoc. Convington & Burling, Washington, 1979—82, Cabaniss, Johnston, Gardner, Dumas & O'Neal, Birmingham, Ala., 1982—84; ptnr. Johnston, Barton, Proctor & Powell LLP, Birmingham, 1984—2004; gen. counsel U. Ala. Sys., 2004—. Disting. lectr. law U. Ala. Law Sch., 2005—; pres.'s adv. coun. Birmingham So. Coll., 1987-88; leadership coun. U. Ala., Birmingham, 1988-91, Med. Clinics Bd., Birmingham, 1997; dir. Comm. on Fgn. Rels., Birmingham, 1996-2002; selection com. Rhodes Scholarship, 1982-87, 98—; Ala. sec. Rhodes Scholarship Trust, 2003-04, dist. sec., 2005—; dir. Assn. Am. Rhodes Scholars, 2006—; mem. Am. Bar. Assn. Ctr. for Racial & Ethnic Diversity, 2008-; adminstr. Am. Trust for Oxford U., 2008-. Trustee Highland's Day Sch., Birmingham, 1985-89; pres. bd. St. Martin's in the Pines Nursing Home, Birmingham, 1990; dir. Ala. Sch. Fine Arts Found., Birmingham, 1993-98, Farrah Law Soc., U. Ala. Law Sch. Found., 2008-; mem. Leadership Birmingham, 1988, membership coun., 1998-2001; chancellor Episcopal Diocese of Ala., 2000-200, Rhodes scholar, 1973. Mem. Birmingham Bar Assn., Tuscaloosa Bar Assn., D.C. Bar Assn., Birmingham C. of C. (trustee 1993-2004), Am. Assn. Rhodes Scholars (dir. 2006—), Rotary Club Birmingham (dir., v.p. 1989-91, 90-91, 2001-02, Paul Harris fellow 2001), Fellow Ala. Bar Found. Episcopalian. Home: 3519 Country Club Rd Birmingham AL 35213-2826 Office: 401 Queen City Ave Tuscaloosa AL 35401 Office Phone: 205-348-8345. Business E-Mail: rsmith@uasystem.ua.edu.

SMITH, RALPH LEE, writer, musician; b. Phila., Nov. 6, 1927; s. Hugh Harold and Barbara (Schatkin) S.; m. Betty H. Smith, Sept. 1954 (div. Jan. 1963); children: David Bruce, Robert Hugh; m. Mary Louise Hollowell, 1971 (div. 1977); m. Shizuko Maruyama, 1977; 1 child, Lisa Koyuki. BA, Swarthmore Coll., Pa., 1951; MEd, U. Va., Charlottesville, 1987. Folk musician on Appalachian dulcimer; recs. include Dulcimer: Old Time and Traditional Music, 1973, Tunes of the Blue Ridge and Great Smoky Mountains, 1983, Across the Blue Ridge, 2005; author: The Story of the Dulcimer, 1986, Appalachian Dulcimer Traditions, 1997, Songs and Tunes of the Wilderness Road, 1999, Folk Songs of Old Kentucky, 2003, Greenwich Village: The Happy Folksinging Days, 2008. Recipient writing awards Columbia U. Grad. Sch. Journalism, U. Mo. Grad. Sch. Journalism, AMA. Home: 1662 Chimney House Rd Reston VA 20190-4302 E-mail: ralphleesmith@comcast.net.

SMITH, RALPH WESLEY, JR., retired federal judge; b. Ghent, NY, July 16, 1936; s. Ralph Wesley and Kathleen S. (Callahan) S.; m. Nancy Ann Fetzer, Dec. 30, 1961 (div. 1981); children: Mark Owen, Tara Denise, Todd Kendall; m. Barbara Anne Milian, Nov. 8, 1982; stepchildren: Kim Highter, Jeffrey Highter, Eric Highter. Student, Sorbonne, U. Paris, Paris, 1954-55; BA, Yale U., 1956; LLB, Albany Law Sch., 1966. Bar: N.Y. 1966, U.S. Dist. Ct. (no. dist.) N.Y. 1966. Assoc. Hinman, Straub Law Firm, Albany, N.Y., 1966-69; chief asst. dist. atty. Albany County, N.Y., 1969-73, dist. atty. N.Y., 1974; regional dir. state nursing home investigation Asst. Atty. Gen., Albany, 1975-77; dir. State Organized Crime Task Force, 1978-82; U.S. magistrate judge U.S. Dist. Ct. (no. dist.) N.Y., Albany, 1982-2001. Judge moot ct. Albany Law Sch., 1983-2001; lectr. N.Y. State Bar Assn., 1985—, Am. Inns of Ct., 1994-99. Capt. USNR, 1957-82, ret. Mem. Fed. Magistrate Judges Assn. (dir. 2d cir. 1992-99), Columbia County Magistrates Assn. Independent. Roman Catholic. Avocations: fishing, bicycling, skiing, sailing, camping. Home: 40 Wequasset Rd Harwich Port MA 02646

SMITH, RAOUL NORMAND, computer science educator; b. West Warwick, RI, May 15, 1938; s. Luke Joseph and Lucienne (Anchambault) S.; m. Mary Frances Hand, Nov. 12, 1966; children: Stephen Edward, Timothy Luke. AB, Brown U., 1963, AM, 1964, PhD, 1968. Instr. Northwestern U., Evanston, Ill., 1967—68, asst. prof., 1968—73, assoc. prof., 1973—80; sr. mem. tech. staff GTE Labs., Waltham, Mass., 1981—83, prin. mem. tech. staff, 1983; prof. Northeastern U., Boston, 1983—2000, dir. grad. schs., 1984—85, dir. rsch., 1985—86, prof. emeritus, 2000—; vis. prof. Jilin U. Tech., Changchun, China, 1985; v.p. China Edn. Corp., 2000—02. Chmn. bd. dirs. Cognitive Computers, Newton, Mass., 1985-87; prin. Raoul N. Smith and Assocs., Cons. Author: Dictionary of Artificial Intelligence, 1989, The Language of Jonathan Fisher, 1985, Probabilistic Performance Models of Language, 1973; co-author: Lexical-Semantic Relations, 1980. Trustee Acton (Mass.) Hist. Soc., 1988-90, dir., 2002-04; mem. AIDS action com., 1985-88. With USAF, 1957-61. Grantee NSF, 1966, 66-67, 71, Am. Philos. Soc., 1974, Am. Coun. of Learned Socs., 1974, Nat. Endowment for the Humanities, 1975, 76-79. Mem. Assn. for Computing Machinery (co-chair spl. interest group on computer and human interaction 1981-85), Union Club. Avocations: antique porcelain, silver and jewelry. Home: 206 Nagog Hill Rd Acton MA 01720-3228 Personal E-mail: raouls500@verizon.net.

SMITH, RAYMOND LEIGH, plastic surgeon; b. Norristown, Pa., Sept. 27, 1940; s. Walter Joseph and Pauline C. (Wolfskill) S.; m. Coralynn Elder, Jan. 8, 1966; children: Susan, Elizabeth, Christine. BS, Ursinus Coll., 1962; MD, Temple U., 1966. Diplomate Nat. Bd. Med. Examiners, Am. Bd. Plastic Surgery. Active staff Reading Hosp., Pa., 1976—2005, chief sect. of plastic surgery, 1994-2000, ret. 2005, assoc. physician Reading Hosp. Med. Ctr. Wound Care & Hyperbaric Ctr., Mem. Republican Majority Found. Mem. ACS, Am. Soc. Plastic Surgeons, Robert H. Ivy Soc., Am. Assn. Hand Surgery, Northeastern Soc. Plastic Surgeons, Pa. Med. Soc., Lipoplasty Soc. N.Am., Berks County Med. Soc. Lutheran. Office Phone: 610-568-3949.

SMITH, RAYMOND LLOYD, former university president, consultant; b. Vanceboro, Maine, Jan. 25, 1917; s. Ivan and Genevieve (Gatcomb) S.; m. Beatrice Bennett, Dec. 4, 1943 (dec. Apr. 16, 1998); children: Bennett Charles, Martin Lloyd; m. Rachel Malcolm, March 10, 2002. BS in Mining Engring. cum laude, U. Alaska, 1943; MS in Metall. Engring, U. Pa., 1951, PhD in Metall. Engring, 1953; D.Sc. (hon.), Western Mich. U.; LL.D., No. Mich. U.; D.Eng. (hon.), Mich. Technol. U., S.D. Sch. Mines and Tech. Instr. math. U. Alaska, 1946-47, asst. prof. metallurgy, 1948-49; rsch. assoc. dept. metallurgy U. Pa., 1949-53; sr. rsch. metallurgist Franklin Inst. Labs., Phila., 1953, sect. chief metallurgy, 1954-56, head solid state physics, 1957, tech. dir., 1958-59; prof., head metall. dept. Mich. Technol. U., Houghton, 1959-64, coord. rsch., 1960-64, pres., 1965-79, Am. Soc. Metals, 1979-80, Houghton (Mich.) Daily Mining Gazette, 1979-81, R. L. Smith, Inc. Am. Soc. Metals/The Metallurgical Soc. joint disting. lectr. in materials; lectr. in field. Contbr. articles to sci. jours. With AUS, 1943—46. Recipient Distinguished Alumnus award U. Alaska, Clair M. Donovan award Mich. Tech. U., D. Robert Yarnall award U. Pa. Engring. Sch.; Outstanding Service award Air Force ROTC; Rotary Paul Harris fellow. Fellow Metall. Soc., AIME (Henry Krumb meml. lectr. 1981), Am. Soc. for Metals (hon.); mem. Scabbard and Blade, Blue Key, Tau Beta Pi, Alpha Sigma Mu (hon. lectr. 1982), Alpha Phi Omega, Phi Kappa Phi, Theta Tau. Achievements include patents in field. Home: PO Box 726 Green Valley AZ 85622-0726 Personal E-mail: raysmith726@cox.net. *A sense of humor is one of the important building blocks for that firm sense of balance so necessary to meet the challenges of life. It's like the seasoning of a chef's masterpiece.*

SMITH, RAYMOND THOMAS, anthropology educator; b. Oldham, Lancashire, Eng., Jan. 12, 1925; s. Harry and Margaret (Mulchrone) S.; m. Flora Alexandrina Tong, June 30, 1954; children: Fenela, Colin, Anthony. BA, Cambridge U., Eng., 1950, MA, 1951, PhD, 1954. Sociol. research officer govt., Brit. Guiana, 1951-54; research fellow U. West Indies, 1954-59, sr. lectr. sociology, prof. anthropology, 1962-66; prof. sociology U. Ghana, 1959-62; prof. anthropology U. Chgo., 1966-95, prof. emeritus, 1995—, chmn. dept. anthropology, 1975-81, 84-85, 94-95. Vis. prof. U. Calif.-Berkeley, 1957-58, McGill U., Montreal, 1964-65; mem. com. on child devel. rsch. and pub. policy NRC, 1977-80; dir. Caribbean Consortium Grad. Sch., 1985-86. Author: The Negro Family in British Guiana, 1956, British Guiana, 1962, 2d edit., 1980, Kinship and Class In The West Indies, 1988, The Matrifocal Family, 1996; co-author: Class Differences in American Kinship, 1978; editor: Kinship Ideology and Practice in Latin America, 1984; contbr. articles to profl. jours. Co-investigator urban family life project U. Chgo., 1986-90. Served with RAF, 1943-48. Guggenheim fellow, 1983-84 Fellow Am. Anthrop. Assn.; mem. Assn. Social Anthropologists. Office: Univ Chicago Dept Anthropology 1126 E 59th St Chicago IL 60637-1580 Office Phone: 831-471-0471. Business E-Mail: r-smith@uchicago.edu.

SMITH, RAYMOND W., investment banking executive; b. Pitts., 1937; BS, Carnegie-Mellon U., 1959; MBA, U. Pitts., 1969. Budget dir. AT&T, 1976-77; v.p.-regulatory Bell of Pa. and Diamond State Tel., Phila., 1981-83; pres., CEO Bell of Pa. and Diamond State Tel., Phila., 1983-85; vice chmn., CFO, dir. parent co. Bell Atlantic Corp., Phila., 1985-88, pres., COO, 1988, chmn., CEO Phila., 1989-98, Rothschild North America, Inc., NYC, 1999—; founding ptnr., chmn. exec. com. Arlington Capital Partners, 1998—. Bd. dirs., US Airways, CBS Corp., Banneker Technologies; mem. Bus. Roundtable, 1990; mem. nat. adv. bd. Pvt. Sector Coun., 1990; mem. James Madison nat. coun. Libr. of Congress, 1990. Pub. playwright. Mem. Lincoln Ctr., Pres. Commn.-Arts and Humanities, WETA, Carnegie Corp., Carnegie Mellon, Rockham Ventures; trustee, Rockefeller Found., 2006-; With Signal Corps, US Army, 1959-60. Fellow: Am. Acad. Arts and Sciences. Office: Rothschild North Am Inc 1251 Avenue Of The Americas New York NY 10020-1104 also: Arlington Capital Ptnrs Ste 660 600 New Hampshire Ave NW Washington DC 20037

SMITH, REBECCA ANSTINE, harpist, educator; b. York, Pa., Dec. 5, 1955; d. Ruth Elizabeth (Fitzpatrick) Anstine; m. Jeffrey Alan Smith, Sept. 20, 1986; children: Amelia Helen, Neal William. BA, Dickinson Coll., 1977; MM, Peabody Conservatory, 1979. Prin. harpist Kennedy Ctr. Orch., Washington, 1980-90, Filene Ctr. Orch., Wolf Trap, Va., 1980—, N.Y.C. Opera at Wolf Trap, Vienna, Va., 1980-87, Nat. Gallery Art Orch., Washington, 1982—. Performed with Nat. Symphony Orch., Balt. Symphony Orch.; instr. U. Md., College Park, 1983, Shenandoah Conservatory, Winchester, Va., 1988-92, Howard U., Washington, 1987-88; faculty mem. The George Washington U., 1997. Harp soloist Kennedy Ctr., Dickinson Coll.; recitalist Jolivet Trio. Fellow Am. Harp Soc., Am. String Tchrs. Assn. Republican. Episcopalian. Avocations: crafts, gardening. Home: 1796 Reading St Crofton MD 21114-2606

SMITH, REBECCA L., musician; b. Atlanta, July 14, 1961; d. Lowell E. and Lil R. Smith. EdS, Piedmont Coll., Demorest, Ga., 2006; B Music Edn., Brenau Coll., 1983; MA, U. Phoenix, 2004. Cert. tchr. Ga., 2006. Band dir. Towns County, 1984—86, Lumpkin County, 1986—87, Banks Co. Sch. Sys., Homer, Ga., 1987—2001; tchr. Buford (Ga.) H.S., 2001—. Mem.: NEA, Ga. Assn. Educators. Home: 5194 Clarks Br Rd Gainesville GA 30506 Office: Buford High School 2750 Sawnee Ave Buford GA 30518 Personal E-mail: beckysmith7@bellsouth.net.

SMITH, REGINALD BRIAN FURNESS, retired anesthesiologist, educator; b. Warrington, Eng., Feb. 7, 1931; s. Reginald and Betty (Bell) S.; m. Margarete Groppe, July 18, 1963; children: Corinne, Malcolm. MB, BS, U. London, 1955; DTM and H, Liverpool Sch. Tropical Medicine, 1959. Intern Poole Gen. Hosp., Dorset, England, 1955-56, Wilson Meml. Hosp., Johnson City, NY, 1962-63; resident in anesthesiology Med. Coll. Va., Richmond, 1963-64, U. Pitts., 1964-65, from clin. instr. to prof., 1965-78, acting chmn. dept. anesthesiology, 1977-78; anesthesiologist in chief Presbyn. Univ. Hosp., Pitts., 1976-78; dir. anesthesiology Eye and Ear Hosp., Pitts., 1971-76; prof., chmn. dept. U. Tex. Health Sci. Ctr., San Antonio, 1978-98, anesthesiologist in chief hosps., 1978-98, clin. prof. anesthesiology, 1999—2007, clin. prof. rehab. medicine, 2003—07, med. dir. hyperbaric medicine and wound-care unit Univ. Hosp., 1993-2000, mem. med. staff Univ. Hosp., 2003—07; ret., 2000. Contbg. editor: Internat. Ophthalmology Clinics, 1973, Internat. Anesthesiology Clinics, 1983; contbr. articles to profl. jours. Served to capt. Brit. Army, 1957—59. Fellow ACP, Am. Coll. Anesthesiologists, Am. Coll. Chest Physicians; mem. AMA, Internat. Anesthesia Rsch. Soc., Am. Soc. Anesthesiologists (pres. Western Pa. 1974-75), Tex. Soc. Anesthesiologists, San Antonio Soc. Anesthesiologists (pres. 1990), Tex. Med. Assn., Bexar County Med. Soc. Home: 9 Bristol Green San Antonio TX 78209-1104

SMITH, REX WILLIAM, journalist; b. Danville, Ill., Oct. 19, 1952; s. Ralph William and Lillian Grace (Hart) S.; m. Marion Roach, July 15, 1989. BA cum laude, Trinity U., San Antonio, 1974; MS with highest honors, Columbia U., NYC, 1980. Mng. editor Rensselaer (Ind.) Rep. newspaper, 1974-75; legis. asst. U.S. Rep. Floyd J. Fithian, Washington, 1975-79; reporter, spl. writer Newsday, LI, NY, 1980-87, chief Albany (N.Y.) bur., 1987-91; editor The Record, Troy, NY, 1991-95; mng. editor Times Union, Albany, NY, 1995—2002, editor, v.p., 2002—. Vice chair NY Fair Trial Free Press Conf., 2002—. Contbr. numerous articles to newspapers and mags. Recipient Cmty. Svc. award Rensselaer C. of C., 1975, Media award World Hunger Fund, 1983, Disting. Svc. medal Soc. Profl. Journalists, 1987, Editl. award Common Cause, 1992, Disting. Cmty. Svc. award N.Y. State Pubs. Assn., 1994; Rotary fellow, 1979, Pulitzer Travel fellow Columbia U., 1982; named Citizen of Yr. N.Y. State LWV, 1999. Mem. N.Y. State Assoc. Press Assn. (pres. 1998), Am. Soc. Newspaper Editors, ASNE Com. Edn. (chair 2008-). Home: 3 Middle Hill Rd Troy NY 12180-6827 Office: Times Union PO Box 15000 Albany NY 12212-5000 Home Phone: 518-266-9424; Office Phone: 518-454-5040. Business E-Mail: rsmith@timesunion.com.

SMITH, RICHARD A., real estate company executive; BS, Columbus State U., Ga.; MS, Troy State U. Various mgmt. positions including corp. dir. risk mgmt., v.p. pers., sr. v.p. human resources, sr. v.p. adminstrn. and mem. oper. com. Days Inns of Am.; exec. v.p. ops. Cendant (formerly HFS Inc.), 1992—96, chmn., CEO real estate svcs. divsn., 1996—2006; vice chmn., pres. Realogy Corp., Parsippany, NJ, 2006—07, pres., CEO, 2007—. Mem. policy adv. bd. Joint Ctr. Housing Studies of Harvard U.; bd. trustees Columbus State U. Found.; hon. mem. nat. bd. dirs. Easter Seals. Recipient Ellis Island Medal of Honor, Nat. Ethnic Coalition of Orgns. Found., Inc., 2000; named one of Real Estate's 25 Most Influential Thought Leaders, Realtor Mag., 2006. Office: Realogy Corp 1 Campus Dr Parsippany NJ 07054 Office Phone: 973-407-2000.

SMITH, RICHARD ALAN, publishing and specialty retailing executive; b. Boston, 1924; married. BS, Harvard U., 1946; LLD (hon.), Boston Coll., 1988. With Smith Mgmt. Co., 1947-61; chmn. bd., CEO Gen. Cinema Corp. (name changed to Harcourt Gen., Inc. 1993), Chestnut Hill, Mass., 1961-91; chmn., CEO Harcourt Gen. Inc., Chestnut Hill, Mass., 1993—2007; chmn. bd., CEO Neiman Marcus, Chestnut Hill, Mass., 1987—2007; chmn., CEO, pres. GC Cos., Inc., Chestnut Hill, Mass., 1993-95, chmn., CEO, 1995—.

SMITH, RICHARD BOWEN, retired national park superintendent; b. Grandville, Mich., Mar. 8, 1938; s. William Jr. and Mary Elizabeth (Bowen) S.; m. Katherine Theresa Short, Sept. 21, 1980. BA in History, Albion Coll., 1960; MA in English, Mich. State U., 1967. Tchr. Grand Rapids (Mich.) Jr. H.S., 1960-66; vol. Peace Corps, Asuncion, Paraguay, 1968-70; ranger Nat. Pk. Svc., Yosemite, Calif., 1971-76, ranger. instr. Grand Canyon, Ariz., 1976-78, ranger, legis. specialist Washington, 1978-80, asst. supt. Everglades, Fla., 1980-83, assoc. regional dir. ops. Phila., 1984-86, supt. Carlsbad Caverns, N.Mex., 1986-88, assoc. regional dir. ops. Santa Fe, 1988-89; assoc. regional dir. resources mgmt. Nat. Park Service, Santa Fe, 1990-94; cons. on protected area mgmt. in L.Am., 1994—; temp. supt. Yellowstone Nat. Pk., 1994—; owner R & K Internat., 1994—2000; assoc. Orgnl. Quality Assocs., 2000—. Pres. Assn. Nat. Park Rangers, 1977-78; coord. Congress of Internat. Ranger Fedn., San Jose, Costa Rica, 1997, v.p., 1998-2000, pres., 2000-03; bd. dirs. Paso Pacifico, 2007-. Bd. dirs. Yellowstone Assn., 1995-97, Ptnrs. in Parks, 1998-2000. Recipient Meritorious Svc. award Dept. Interior, 1992, Disting. Alumnus award Albion Coll., 2006. Mem. Assn. Nat. Park Rangers (chmn. internat. com. 1997-2000), George Wright Soc. (bd. dirs. 1998—2004), Coalition of Nat. Park Svc. Retirees (exec. coun. 2004-08). Home: 2 Roadrunner Trl Placitas NM 87043-9424 Business E-Mail: rsmith0921@earthlink.net.

SMITH, RICHARD F., financial services company executive; BS, Purdue Univ., 1983. Sales rep. Owens Corning, Kans. City, Kans., 1981—83; various mgmt. positions GE, 1983—2005; sales rep. GE Plastics Bus. Group, Itasca, Ill., mktg. mgr., gen. mgr.; pres., CEO GE Capital Modular Space, Malvern, Pa., GE Capital Fleet Services, Eden Prairie, Minn., GE Global Property & Casualty Reinsurance, Overland Park, Kans.; COO GE Ins. Solutions, Overland Park, Kans.; pres., CEO Equifax Inc., Atlanta, 2005, chmn., CEO, 2006—. Office: Equifax Inc 1550 Peachtree St NW Atlanta GA 30309 Mailing: Equifax Inc PO Box 4081 Atlanta GA 30302

SMITH, RICHARD HOWARD, banker; b. Tulare, Calif., Aug. 27, 1927; s. Howard Charles and Sue Elizabeth (Cheyne) Smith; m. Patricia Ann Howery Smith, Mar. 12, 1950 (dec. Sept. 2001); children: Jeffrey Howard, Holly Lee, Gregory Scott, Deborah Elaine; m. Charlene Burruel Smith, Mar. 27, 2004. BA, Principia Coll., 1958; LLB, LaSalle U., 1975; postgrad., Sch. Banking U. Wash., 1972. Prin. Aurora Elementary Sch., Tulare, 1951—53, Desert Sun Sch., Idyllwild, Calif., 1953—55; trust adminstr. trainee Bank Am., San Diego, 1955—58; asst. trust officer Ventura, Redlands, Riverside, LA, 1958—65, Security Pacific Bank, Fresno, Calif., 1965—68, trust officer, 1968—72, v.p., mgr., 1972—88, Security Pacific Bank, Pasadena, 1988—94; v.p. Bank America, LA, 1994—95, ret., 1995; pres. Fiduciary Svcs., Fresno, 1995—; instr. San Bernardino Valley Coll., 1962—, Fresno City Coll., 1977—. With USN, 1945—46. Home: 3222 W Dovewood Ln Fresno CA 93711-2125 Office: Smith Fiduciary Svc 163 7081 N Marks Ave #104 Fresno CA 93711-0232 Office Phone: 559-432-6573.

SMITH, RICHARD J., energy executive; BS in Acctg., Ind. U. and Purdue U.; MBA, U. Indpls. V.p. fin. Energy Svcs. bus. unit Cinergy Corp., Cin., 1996—99, v.p. energy svcs., 1999, pres. Cinergy Resources, Inc., 1999; sr. v.p. transition mgmt. Entergy Corp., 1999—2000, pres. Retail, 2000, group pres. Utility Ops., pres., COO, 2007—. Office: Engery Corp 1340 Echelon Pkwy Ste 100 Jackson MS 39213-8210 Office Phone: 504-576-4000.

SMITH, RICHARD JAMES, retired music educator; b. Baton Rouge, Nov. 28, 1950; s. Jimmie P. and Agnes Mae Smith; m. Lenora Faye McMillon, Mar. 3, 1981 (div. Feb. 28, 1988); m. Dewanna Ann Davis, July 3, 1992 (div. May 2003); m. Elissa Sisk Parks, Oct. 14, 2003; 1 child, James. MusB Edn., La. State U., Baton Rouge, 1972, MusM Edn., 1977, PhD, 1986. Cert. tchr. La. State Dept. Edn., 1972. Band dir. Northside H.S., Atlanta, 1972—73, Redemptorist H.S., Baton Rouge, 1973—74, East Beauregard H.S., DeRidder, La., 1974—77, Hammond H.S., Hammond, La., 1977—78, Silliman Inst., La., 1978—81, Mansfield H.S., Mansfield, La., 1981—83; dir. band and choir Breaux Bridge H.S., Breaux Bridge, La., 1984—85; band dir. Raynaud Mid. Sch., Lake Charles, La., 1985—86, Tallulah H.S., Tallulah, La., 1988—91, Pointe Coupee Ctrl. H.S., LaBarre, La., 1991—94, Glen Oaks H.S., Baton Rouge, 1994—95, Claiborne Acad., Haynesville, La., 1995—97, Jonesboro-Hodge H.S., Jonesboro, La., 1997—98; piano instr. Recreation and Parks Commn., Baton Rouge, 1998—99; band dir. East Iberville H.S., St. Gabriel, La., 1999—2000; piano instr. Recreation and Pks. Commn., Baton Rouge, 2000—. Composer: Symphonic Essay for Band, 1973, March Triumphe, 1974, Go, Ye Trojans, 1975, Adagio for unaccomanpied flute, 1975, Serenade for Unaccomanpied Flute, 1975, Noble Knights, 1976, In Memoriom, 1976, Requiem Mass in D minor, 1977, Fight On!, 1978, Sillman Inst. Alma Mater, 1978, Elegy, 1980, The Silver Star, 1980, Freedom Express, 1982, Marche Royale, 1984, Hail to Liberty, 1986, Hall of Justice, 1986, Freedom and Unity, 1988, InGod We Trust, 1988, Th Blue and the Gold, 1989, River City Grand March, 1989, Beyou-Fest, 1990, A Touch of Tenderness, 1999, The National Game, 2005, The Bride Elect, 2005, Yorktown Centennial March, 2005, The Diplomat, 2005, America First, 2005, The Aviators, 2005, The White Rose, 2005, The Wolverine March, 2005, others; contbr. articles to profl. jour. Mem. Baton Rouge Concert Band, Baton Rouge, 1977—81, Lafayette Concert Band, Lafayette, La., 1984—85, Lake Charles Cmty. Band, Lake Charles, La., 1986—88, North La. Cmty. Band, Monroe, La., 1989—91, Baton Rouge Concert Band, 2001—. Recipient Mem. of All-American Coll. TV Band - La. State U. Marching Band, Chevrolet Corp., 1970, Superior Rating at Dist. Band Festival - Tallulah H.S. Band, La. Music Educators Assn., 1991, Superior Rating at Dist. Choir Festival - Breaux Bridge H.S. Choir, 1985, First Pl. in Mansfield Christmas Parade - Mansfield H.S. Band, Mansfield, LA, Chamber of Commerce, 1981. Mem.: NEA (life), U.S. Achievement Acad. (nat. adv. bd. 1983—2002), La. Bandmasters Assn., La. Music Educators Assn., Music Educators Nat. Conf., La. Educators Assn. (life), Pi Kappa Lambda, Kappa Kappa Psi (life Outstanding pledge 1969). Avocations: travel, reading, music, building 3-d puzzles, miniature golf. Home: 10515 Tallowwood Ave Baker LA 70714 Office: Recreation and Parks Commission 3140 N Sherwood Forest Dr Baton Rouge LA 70814 Personal E-mail: rjsmith56@bellsouth.net.

SMITH, RICHARD JAY, anthropologist, educator, dean; b. Aug. 10, 1948; s. Benjamn and Miriam Smith; m. Linda Sharon Harris, Aug. 22, 1970; children: Jason Andrew, Owen Harris, Hilary Rachele. BA, CUNY, 1969; MS in Anatomy, Tufts U., 1973, DMD, 1973; PhD in Anthropology, Yale U., 1980. Asst. clin. prof. orthodontics U. Conn., Farmington, 1976—79; asst. prof. U. Md., Balt., 1979—81, assoc. prof., 1981—84; prof. orthodontics, biomed. sci., chmn. dept. orthodontics, adj. prof. anthropology Washington U., St. Louis, 1984—91, assoc. dean, 1987—89, dean Sch. Dental Medicine, 1989—91, cons. orthodontics Cleft Palate and Craniofacial Anomalies Team, 1984—91, prof. anthropology, 1991—2001, chmn. dept. anthropology, 1993—2008, Ralph E. Morrow disting. univ. prof., 2001—, dir. program in applied statistics, 2002—04, dean Grad. Sch. Arts & Scis., 2008—. Vis. assoc. prof. cell biology Sch. Medicine Johns Hopkins U., Balt., 1980—84; orthodontic cons. St. Louis VA Med. Ctr., 1986—91; mem. staff Barnes Hosp., 1986—91, St. Louis Children's Hosp., 1985—91. Editor-in-chief: Jour. Balt. Coll. Dental Surgery, 1981—84, contbr.: numerous articles in orthodontics, anthropology, comparative biology to profl. jours. Am. Fund for Dental Health dental tchr. tng. fellow, 1977—78, postdoctoral fellow, NIH, 1978—79. Fellow: Am. Coll. Dentists, Internat. Coll. Dentists; mem.: ADA, Internat. Primatological Soc., Am. Assn. Phys. Anthropologists, Am. Assn. Orthodontists, Alumni Assn. Student Clinicians (bd. govs. 1984—90, pres. 1988—89, Alan J. Davis award 1983). Office: Washington Univ Grad Sch One Brookings Dr Campus Box 1187 Saint Louis MO 63130 Home: 8025 Maryland Ave # 8F Saint Louis MO 63105 Office Phone: 314-935-4843. Office Fax: 314-935-4887. Business E-Mail: rjsmith@wustl.edu.

SMITH, RICHARD MILLS (RICK), former publishing executive; b. Detroit, Jan. 12, 1946; s. William Steele Smith and Janet (Mills) Morrison; m. Lee Ann Vanderstoep (div.); children: Scott William, Anna Mills; m. Soon-Young Yoon, Oct. 20, 1978; 1 child, Song-Mee. BA summa cum laude, Albion Coll., 1968; MS, Columbia U., 1970; LLD (hon.), Albion Coll., 1993. Reporter Associated Press, NY, 1969; assoc. editor foreign dept. Newsweek, NY, 1970—73, gen. editor nat. affairs dept. NY, 1973—74, editor Asian region, bur. chief Hong Kong Hong Kong, 1974—77; mng. editor Newsweek Internat., NY, 1977—81; asst. mng. editor Newsweek, NYC, 1982, exec. editor, 1983, pres., 1991—98, CEO, 1991—2007, editor in chief, 1984—2007, chmn., 1998—. Trustee Albion Coll; bd. dirs. Cooper-Hewitt Nat. Design Mus., Smithsonian Instn., Harvard AIDS Inst., Temple Inland, Inc., Forestar Real Estate Group, TalkMarket.com. Recipient Disting. Alumni award, Albion Coll., 1974. Mem.: Mag. Pubs. America (chmn 1996—97, Henry Johnson Fisher award 2001), Century Assn., Coun. Fgn. Rels., Mag. Pubs. Assn. (chmn.), Am. Soc. Mag. Editors (mem. exec. com. 1985—88), Phi Beta Kappa. Office: Newsweek Inc 251 W 57th St New York NY 10019-1802 Office Phone: 212-445-4469.

SMITH, RICHARD NORTON, historian, former library director; b. Leominster, Mass., Oct. 2, 1953; s. Frank Chandler and Ruth Adeline (Richards) S. BA in Govt. magna cum laude, Harvard Coll., 1975. Intern The White House, Washington, 1975; freelance writer Washington Post, The Real Paper, and other publs., various cities, 1975-77; speechwriter Sen. Edward Brooke, Boston, 1977-78, Sen. Robert Dole, Washington, 1979-85; biographer, rschr. book on Thomas E. Dewey Rochester, N.Y., 1980; speechwriter, cons. various fed. officials, Washington, 1981-87; staff speechwriter Sen. Pete Wilson, Washington, 1984-87; dir. various presdl. libraries and foundations, including Herbert Hoover Libr., Dwight D. Eisenhower Ctr., Ronald Reagan Libr., Gerald R. Ford Mus. and Libr., 1987—2001; speechwriter Pres. Ronald Reagan, V.P. and Mrs. Dan Quayle, and others, Washington, 1989; dir. Robert J. Dole Inst. of Politics, Lawrence, Kans., 2001—03; exec. dir. Abraham Lincoln Presdl. Libr. and Mus., Springfield, Ill., 2003—06; scholar-in-residence of history & pub. policy George Mason U., Washington, 2006—. Cons. Nixon and Reagan Librs., 1989-91. Author: Thomas E. Dewey and His Times, 1982, An Uncommon Man: The Triumph of Herbert Hoover, 1984, The Harvard Century, 1986, Patriarch: George Washington and the New American Nation, 1992, The Colonel: The Life and Legend of Robert R. McCormick, 2003; co-author: (with Robert and Elizabeth Dole) Unlimited Partners, 1988. Mem. White House bicentennial planning com., Washington, 1990—; mem. World War II 50th anniversary planning com. Nat. Archives, Washington, 1991—. Republican. Christian Scientist. Avocations: reading, travel. Office: George Mason U Robinson B 359 4400 University Dr MSN 3G1 Fairfax VA 22030 Office Phone: 703-993-9822. E-mail: rsmit2@gmu.edu.*

SMITH, RICHARD P., dairy product company executive, lawyer; b. LI, NY; BA cum laude, U. Mass., 1974; JD, St. John's U., 1979. Bar: NY 1979. Tchr. Smithtown Ctrl. Sch. Dist., NY, 1974-76; assoc. Bond, Schoeneck & King, Syracuse, NY, 1979-82; v.p., gen. counsel Dairylea Coop., Inc., Syracuse, 1982-88, CEO, 1988—2005; pres., bd. dirs. DCI Holding Corp., Syracuse; mgmt. positions including pres., COO Dairy Farmers of America, Kans. City, Mo., 2001—05, pres., CEO, 2006—. Bd. dirs. Agri-Svc. Agys., Inc., Syracuse, Nat. Milk Producers Fedn., Washington, Nat. Livestock Producers Assn. Mem. ABA, NY State Bar Assn., Onondaga County Bar Assn. Office: Dairy Farmers of America 10220 NW Ambassador Dr Kansas City MO 64153 Office Phone: 816-801-6410. Office Fax: 816-801-6411. Business E-Mail: rsmith@dfamilk.com.

SMITH, RICHEY, manufacturing executive; b. Akron, Ohio, Nov. 11, 1933; s. Thomas William and Martha (Richey) S.; m. Sandra Cosgrave Roe, Nov. 25, 1961; children: Mason Roe, Parker Richey. Grad., Hotchkiss Sch.; BS, U. Va., Charlottesville, 1956. Asst. to pres. Sun Products Corp., Barberton, Ohio, 1960-64, v.p., 1964-67, gen. mgr., dir., 1967-69, chmn., CEO, 1969-76; prin. A.T. Kearney Co., Cleve., 1977-87; chmn., CEO Richey Industries, Inc., Medina, Ohio, 1987—. Bd. dirs. Jaite Packaging, Inc. Exec. com. Gt. Trail coun. Boy Scouts Am.; chmn. capital funds dr. Summit County Planned Parenthood; trustee, found. pres. Old Trail Sch., Barberton Citizens Hosp., Medina County Arts Coun., Akron Regional Devel. Bd.; treas. Friends of Metro Park; found. trustee, vestryman St. Paul's Episcopal Ch.; corp. bd. Cleve. Mus. of Art; bd. govs. The Hotchkiss Sch. Lt. USN, 1957—60, lt. comdr. USNR, 1961—69. Mem. Ohio Commodores, Bluecoats (trustee), Navy League (pres. Akron coun. 1972-73), Young Pres. Orgn., Portage Country Club (bd. dirs.), Mayflower Club, Sawgrass Country Club (Fla.) Farmington Country Club (Charlottesville, Va.), Rotary (trustee Akron 1974-75), Yale Club (NYC), Rockwell Springs Trout Club, Chi Psi (pres.), Turkey Foot Island Club. Office: 910 Lake Rd Medina OH 44256-2453 Home: 333 N Portage Path Aspen 18 Akron OH 44303 Office Phone: 330-725-4997 x 304. Personal E-mail: rsmith@richeyind.com.

SMITH, RICK, professional sports team executive; b. Petersburg, Va., Sept. 3, 1969; m. Tiffany Smith; children: Robert LaMar, Avery Jordan. BA, Purdue U., Ind., 1992. Asst. strength and conditioning coord. Purdue U. Boilermakers, 1992—93, tight ends coach, 1993—94, secondary coach, 1994—96; asst. defensive backs coach Denver Broncos, 1996—99, head, pro pers. ops., 1999—2005, asst. gen. mgr., 2006; gen. mgr. Houston Texans, 2006—. Mem. NFL Gen. Mgrs. Adv. Com., NFL Competition Com., 2008—. Recipient Tank Younger award, Fritz Pollard Alliance, 2008. Mem.: Fellowship Christian Athletes. Office: Houston Texans Two Reliant Park Houston TX 77054 Office Phone: 832-667-2000.*

SMITH, RICK, foundation administrator; 1 child. Grad. in recreation adminstrn., U. N.Mex., Albuquerque, 1975. Dir. programs and phys. edn. North Side YMCA, Witchita, Kans.; exec. dir. Am. Cancer Soc., Md., Am. Diabetes Assn., N.Mex., regional v.p., western US, pres. & CEO, Calif. affiliate; area v.p., western US Nat. Multiple Sclerosis Soc., pres., Ariz. chpt., pres., Md. chpt.; pres., CEO Am. Liver Found., NYC, 2007—. Mem. nat. mgmt. team Nat. Multiple Sclerosis Soc., mem. Blue Ribbon Panel on orgnl. structure. Active Albuquerque Pub. Schools, Camp Fire Girls N.Mex., Greater Balt. Com., Ariz. Voluntary Health Agencies. Office: Nat Liver Found 75 Maiden Ln Ste 603 New York NY 10038 Office Phone: 212-668-1000. Office Fax: 212-483-8179.*

SMITH, RITA REX, mechanical engineer; b. Akron, Ohio, Dec. 11, 1954; d. Marvin George and Mabel (Howell) Rex. BSME, U. Akron, 1979; MSME, U. N.Mex., 1989, postgrad. in Nuclear Engring., 1990—. Asst. stress engr. nuclear equip. div. Babcock & Wilcox, Barberton, Ohio, 1979-81; application engr. McKenzie-Ris Mfg. Div. Ecodyne Corp., Massillon, Ohio, 1981; assoc. stress engr. nuclear equip. div. Babcock & Wilcox, Barberton, 1982; rsch. scientist bureau of engring. rsch. U. N.Mex., Albuquerque, 1987-88, teaching asst. dept. math., 1990; grad. rsch. assistantship Los Alamos (N.Mex.) Nat. Lab., 1990; rsch. asst. nuclear engring. U. N.Mex., 1993-94. Tchg. asst. dept. physics U. N.Mex., Los Alamos, summers 1993, 94, 95; grad. rsch. asst. Los Alamos Nat. Lab., 1994-96; owner, mng. dir. SofTalk Engring., 1997—. Adult trainer Girl Scouts Am., Akron, Ohio, 1981-86. Recipient rsch. grant Air Force Weapons Lab., 1987-88, instructional grant Ohio Bd. Regents, 1973-74, fellowship Air Force Office of Sci. Rsch., 1987. Mem. Kappa Mu Epsilon. Achievements include research in optical propagation through turbulence; addition of an empirical correction for compressibility effects to the turbulence model; furthering the understanding of how turbulence and optics equations are coupled, development of smoothed particle hydrodynamics algorith for modeling turbulence analyses; writing of a parallel SPH code to run on the CM-5 using CM Fortran; theoretical and computational modeling of optical imaging of brain tissue; assessment of scientific lab equipment for Y2K problems. Personal E-mail: rrs@nmia.com.

SMITH, ROBERT A., medical association administrator; Dir. breast cancer screening Am. Cancer Soc. Office: 250 Williams St NW Atlanta GA 30303*

SMITH, ROBERT B., geophysicist, educator; BS, Utah State U., 1960; MS, Utah State U., 1965; PhD, U. Utah, 1967. Emeritus rsch. prof. geology & geophysics U. Utah. Office: University of Utah Dept Geology & Geophysics 135 S 1460 E Rm 719 Salt Lake City UT 84112-0111 Office Phone: 801-581-7129. E-mail: robert.b.smith@utah.edu.*

SMITH, ROBERT BOULWARE, III, vascular surgeon, educator; b. Atlanta, June 15, 1933; s. Robert Boulware Jr. Smith and Mary Eva (Black) Fanning; m. Florence Chance Limehouse, Aug. 22, 1953; children: Victoria Joanne Smith Harkins, Robert Boulware IV, Brian Scott. MD, Emory U., 1957. Diplomate Am. Bd. Surgery. Intern in surgery Columbia Presbyn. Hosp., NYC, 1957-58, resident in surgery, 1960-65; asst. prof. surgery Emory U. Sch. Medicine, Atlanta, 1966-69, assoc. prof., 1969-77, prof., 1977—, head gen. vascular surgery, 1984-98. Chief surg. svc. VA Med. Ctr., Atlanta, 1969-88; assoc. med. dir. Emory U. Hosp., 1993-95, med. dir., 1995-2006. Co-editor: Trauma to the Thorax and Abdomen, 1969, Medical Management of the Surgical Patient, 1982, 4th edit., 2006; contbr. articles to profl. jours.; chpts. to books. Capt. M.C., U.S. Army, 1958-60. Mem. ACS, Am. Surg. Assn., So. Assn. Vascular Surgery (sec. 1986-91, pres. 1992-93), Soc. Vascular Surgery, Assn. VA Surgeons (pres. 1983-84, Disting. Svc. award 1988), Ga. Surg. Soc. (pres. 1992-93), Atlanta Vascular Soc. (pres. 1986-88), Internat. Soc. for Cardiovasc. Surg. (pres. 1996-97). Phi Beta Kappa, Alpha Omega Alpha. Republican. United Methodist. Avocations: music, travel. Office: Emory Univ Hosp 1364 Clifton Rd NE B206 Atlanta GA 30322-1013 Home: 6205 Springhouse Cir Stone Mountain GA 30087-6739 Office Phone: 404-727-3573. Business E-Mail: rsmit06@emory.edu.

SMITH, ROBERT CARLISLE, retired department administrator, retired welding educator; b. St. Albans, W.Va., Sept. 2, 1939; s. Clarence Mack (stepfather) and Artimitia (Blake) Smith Fowler; m. Janet Lee Koehn, Dec. 28, 1958; children: Teresa Lynn, Stephen Carlisle. BA, Glenville State U., 1984; MSc, Marshall U., 1994. Cert. welding inspector, non-destructive tester. Br. mgr. Va. Welding, Charleston, W.Va., 1963—76; prin. Weld Inspection and Cons., St. Albans, 1976—94; mgr. quality assurance Kanawha Mfg., Charleston, 1988—2003; dept. head, instr. welding W.Va. U., Parkersburg, 1981—2003; prof. emeritus WVU Parkersburg Campus. Chair edn., adv. com. Mt. Olive Correctional Ctr., W.Va. Contbr. articles. Lt. ROTC 1957-71; committeeman Rep. Party, Kanawha County, 1968-69; former Sun. sch. tchr. Highlawn Baptist Ch.; presenter Nat. Educators Workshop NASA, Langley Space Flight Ctr., 1993. Recipient Disting. West Virginian award Gov. W.Va., 1968, Tchr. of Excellence award Nat. Inst. for Staff and Orgnl. Devel.; named Outstanding Prof. of Yr. W.Va. U. Parkersburg campus, 2005. Mem. Am. Welding Soc. (chmn. 1971-72, program chairperson 1989-90, educator of yr. 1990, 92, 2003-04), Am. Soc. Non-Destructive Testing (membership recruiter 1988), W.Va. Edn. Assn., W.Va. C.C. Assn. Protestant. Avocations: autos, trucks, writing, fishing, banjo. Home: 2302 S Walnut Dr Saint Albans WV 25177-3947 Business E-Mail: carlsmith@mail.wvu.edu.

SMITH, ROBERT EARL, space scientist; b. Indpls., Sept. 13, 1923; s. Harold Bennett and Bernice (McCaslin) S.; m. Elizabeth Lee Usak, Jan. 3, 1947 (dec. 1984); children: Stephanie Lee, Robert Michael, Cynthia Ann, Kelly Andrew; m. Lyla Lee Lewellen, July 1, 1988. BS, Fla. State U., 1959, MS, 1960, U. Mich., 1969, PhD, 1974. Enlisted U.S. Army Air Force, 1943-44; advanced through grades to maj. U.S. Air Force, 1955; airway traffic controller Berlin, 1945; staff weather reconnaissance officer 9th Air Force, 1956; ret., 1963; project scientist Atmospheric Cloud Physics Lab.; dep. chief atmospheric scis. div. NASA/Marshall Space Flight Ctr., Ala., 1963-86; sr. scientific cons. Univs. Space Rsch. Assn., Huntsville, Ala., 1986-87; sr. computer cons. Computer Scis. Corp., Huntsville, 1987-89; chief space sci. and applications div. FWG Assocs., Inc., Huntsville, 1989-92; NASA program mgr. Physitron, Inc., Huntsville, 1992-96; sr. computer scientist Computer Scis. Corp., Huntsville, 1996—2002. Mem. AIAA, Pi Mu Epsilon, Sigma Phi Epsilon. Avocation: golf. Home: 125 Westbury Dr SW Huntsville AL 35802-1619 Personal E-mail: r01913smith@bellsouth.net.

SMITH, ROBERT EVERETT, lawyer; b. NYC, Mar. 15, 1936; s. Arthur L. and Augusta (Cohen) S.; m. Emily Lucille Lehman, July 17, 1960; children: Amy, Karen, Victoria. BA, Dartmouth Coll., 1957; LLB, Harvard U., 1960. Bar: N.Y. 1960, U.S. Dist. Ct. (so. dist.) N.Y. 1962, U.S. Ct. Appeals (2d cir.) 1963, U.S. Supreme Ct. 1967, U.S. Dist. Ct. (ea. dist.) N.Y. 1969, U.S. Ct. Appeals (3d cir.) 1982, U.S. Ct. Appeals (9th cir.) 1988. Assoc. Paul, Weiss, Rifkind, Wharton & Garrison, NYC, 1960-65; from assoc. to ptnr. Baar, Bennett & Fullen, NYC, 1965-74; ptnr. Guggenheimer & Untermyer, NYC, 1974-85, Rosenman & Colin LLP, NYC, 1985-98, chmn., 1994-97, counsel, 1998—2002, Katten Muchin Rosenman LLP, NYC, 2002—. With U.S. Army, 1961-64. Mem. ABA, N.Y. State Bar Assn., Assn. of Bar of City of N.Y., Fed. Bar Coun., N.Y. County Lawyers Assn., Internat. Bar Assn., Am. Arbitration Assn. (nat. panel arbitrators), Am. Law Inst. Office: Katten Muchin Rosenman LLP 575 Madison Ave Fl 26 New York NY 10022-2585 Home Phone: 212-744-1208; Office Phone: 212-940-8850. Business E-Mail: robert.smith@kattenlaw.com.

SMITH, ROBERT HUGH, retired engineering construction company executive; b. Wichita, Kans., Dec. 29, 1936; s. Richard Lyon and E. Eileen (O'Neal) S.; m. Melinda Louise Fitch, Sept. 26, 1959 (div. Dec. 1969); children: Robert Blake, Thomas Hugh; m. Margaret Anne Moseley, Dec. 11, 1971; 1 child, Steven Richard. BS, Kans. State U., 1959; MS, U. Kans., 1964, PhD, 1970. Sr. process engr. FMC Corp., Lawrence, Kans., 1959-64; rsch. engr. Phillips Petroleum Co., Bartlesville, Okla., 1964-66; group leader Standard Oil of Ohio, Warrenville Heights, Ohio, 1966-67; sr. rsch. assoc., group leader Atlantic Richfield, Plano, Tex., 1970-80; regional mgr., sr. mgr., sales mgr. Fluor Daniel, Houston and Marlton, NJ, 1980-90; v.p., gen. mgr. Badger Design & Construction, Tampa, Fla., 1990-93; exec. v.p., COO Process divsn. Black & Veatch, Overland Park, 1993-2000; ret., 2000. Patentee in the field; contbr. to profl. jours. Adv. bd. dept. chem. engring, coll. of engring. U. Kans., Lawrence, 1993—; mem. adv. bd. coll. engring. Kans. State U., 1998-2005. Recipient Disting. Svc. award Kans. State U., 1998; named to Engring. Hall of Fame Kans. State U., Chem. and Petroleum Engring. Hall of Fame, U. Kans., 2000. Fellow AIChE (chmn., vice chmn., sec. Dallas chpt. 1962—, exec. bd. Engr. and Cons. Contracting divsn., 1995-97, bd. dirs. 2002-04, career and edn. ops. coun. 2002-03, bd. trustees 2007—, Engr. of Yr. award Dallas chpt. 1980), Phi Lambda Upsilon, Sigma Xi. Avocations: tennis, sailing, skiing, reading. Personal E-mail: bobsmith29@everstkc.net.

SMITH, ROBERT JOHN, anthropology educator; b. Essex, Mo., June 27, 1927; s. Will Dan and Fern (Jones) S.; m. Kazuko Sasaki, Aug. 22, 1955. BA summa cum laude, U. Minn., 1949; MA, Cornell U., 1951, PhD, 1953. Engaged in cultural anthrop. field research, N.S., Canada, 1950, Japan, 1951-52, 55, 57-58, Brazil, 1966-67; mem. faculty Cornell U., 1953—, prof. anthropology, 1963-74, Goldwin Smith prof. anthropology, 1974-97, prof. emeritus, 1997—, chmn. dept. Asian studies, 1961-66, chmn. dept. antropology, 1967-71, 76-82, prof. emeritus, 1997—. Vis. prof. anthropology U. Ariz., 1971, U. Hawaii, 1978, Nat. Mus. Ethnology, Osaka, Japan, 1982 Author: (with Cornell) Two Japanese Villages, 1956, (with Cornell, Saito and Maeyama) Japanese and Their Descendants in Brazil, 1967; editor: (with Beardsley) Japanese Culture: Its Development and Characteristics, 1962, Social Organization and the Applications of Anthropology, 1974, Ancestor Worship in Contemporary Japan, 1974, Kurusu: The Price of Progress in a Japanese Village, 1951-75, 1978, (with Wiswell) Women of Suye Mura, 1982, Japanese Society: Tradition, Self and the Social Order, 1983, (with K. Smith) Diary of a Japanese Innkeeper's Daughter, 1984 Served with AUS, 1944-46. Tng. grantee Social Sci. Rsch. Coun., Japan, 1951-52; recipient Individual Exch. award to Japan Inst. Internat. Edn., 1957-58; Fulbright lectr. Tokyo Met. U., 1962-63; NSF rsch. grantee, 1965-67; Japan Found. grantee, 1979; awarded Order of the Rising Sun, Govt. of Japan, 1993. Fellow Assn. Asian Studies (v.p. 1987-88, pres. 1988-89), Soc. Applied Anthropology (editor jour. Human Orgn. 1961-66). Home: 322 Savage Farm Dr Ithaca NY 14850

SMITH, ROBERT LEONARD, pastor, religious studies educator; b. San Antonio, Dec. 23, 1924; s. Leonard and Alice Jewel (Horton) S.; m. Ethelyn Hughes, Feb. 8, 1945; children: Robert Leonard, Judy Claire Smith Bynum. BS, Centenary Coll., Shreveport, La., 1947; BDiv, Southwestern Seminary, 1953, MDiv, 1987; DD (hon.), Ouachita U., 1961. Ordained to ministry, Bapt. Ch., 1953. Pastor First Bapt. Ch., Crossett, Ark., 1953-55, Pine Bluff, Ark., 1955-65, Houston, 1965-69, Pompano Beach, Fla., 1969-84; disting. prof. preaching and ch. adminstrn., dean Howard Payne U., Brownwood, Tex., 1984-94, dean emeritus, sch. ch. studies, 2007, adj. prof. old & new testament, 2009—. Mem. Bapt. Sunday Sch. Bd., Nashville, 1957-65; presented Sermons in Art in 38 states. Author: Successful Chalk-Talk, 1972; author, prodr. (TV series) The Art of Living, 1960-67; contbr. articles to religious jours.; oil and watercolor artist; one man shows include Stetson U., Deland, Fla., 1984, Lighthouse Point Nat. Bank, Fla., 1975, First Nat. Bank, Pompano Beach, Fla., 1976, Citizens Nat. Bank, Brownwood, Tex., 1991, Howard Payne U., Brownwood, 1994; exhibited at Jefferson County Fair, Pine Bluff, Ark., 1964, First Meth. Ch., Pompano Beach, 1974. Mem. Ark. Exec. Bd., Little Rock, 1954-62, Tex. Exec. Bd., Dallas, 1966-80, Fla. Exec. Bd., Jacksonville, 1966-80; trustee Pine Bluff (Ark.) Mental Health Ctr., 1959, Henderson Mental Health Clinic, Ft. Lauderdale, Fla., 1971-75, Stetson U., DeLand, Fla., 1978-82. Named Artist of the Yr., 2007. Mem. Rotary Internat. Avocations: oil and watercolor painting, flying, golf. Home: 3 Quail Creek Rd Brownwood TX 76801-6309 Office: Howard Payne U 1000 Fisk Ave Brownwood TX 76801-2794

SMITH, ROBERT LOUIS, construction company executive; b. Parkersburg, W.Va., Apr. 19, 1922; s. Everett Clerc and Janet (Morrison) S.; m. June Irene Odbert, Oct. 25, 1948; children: Peter Clerc, Morrison James, Edna Louise. BS in Civil Engring., Lehigh U., 1944. Design engr. Chrysler Corp., 1944-46; engr. Harrison Constrn. Co., Charleston, W.Va., 1946-47; sr. engr. Creole Petroleum Co., Las Piedras, Venezuela, 1947-55; v.p. Rea Constrn. Co., Charlotte, N.C., 1955-64; exec. v.p. Warren Bros. Co., Cambridge, Mass., 1964-68, pres., 1968-79; also dir.; sr. v.p. Ashland Oil, Inc., Ky., 1974-79; pres. Robert L. Smith & Assos., Lexington, 1979—; pres., dir. Tree Farm Devel. Corp., Cambridge, 1979—. Dir. Panastalto (S.A.), Wilder Constrn. Co., Inc., J.H. Shears Sons, Inc. Fellow ASCE; mem. Nat. Asphalt Pavement Assn. (dir.), Phi Beta Kappa, Tau Beta Pi, Sigma Chi. Republican. Unitarian Universalist. Home and Office: 1010 Waltham St Apt A412 Lexington MA 02421-8065 Home Phone: 781-861-0489; Office Phone: 781-861-0489. Personal E-mail: rlouissmith@comcast.net.

SMITH, ROBERT MICHAEL, sculptor, educator; s. Walter Alfred and Virginia Paula Smith; children: Fonda Yoshimoto, Amorette Brygene. MFA, U. Hawaii Manoa, Honolulu, 1982. Assoc. prof. NY Inst. Tech., NYC, 1999—. Pres. emeritus Sculptors Guild, NYC, 1998—; bd. dir. SIGGRAPH, Manhattan, NYC, 1999—2003, Internat. Sculpture Ctr., Hamilton, NJ, 2003—05; founding bd. dir. Digital Stone Project, Hamilton, NJ, 2003—. Exhibitions include Digital Stone, Beijing, Shanghai, Chongqing, Digital and Beyond, Rockland Ctr. Arts, Nycak, NY, Art Cologne, Germany, Sculpture Numerique et Biomorphisme, Nancy, Frane, Alien Beauty-A Universal Form, Foresight Art Ctr., Amman, Jordan, Archival to Contemporary: Six Decades of Sculptors Guild, Hillwood Art Mus., Brookville, NY, Sculpture on the Plaza, White Plains, NY, internat. RP sculpture exhbn. Exhbn. grant, Cultural Sect. US Embassy in Amman, 2006, Faculty ISRC grant, NY Inst. Tech., 2007. Home: 954 Lexington Ave #269 New York NY 10021 Office: NY Inst Tech 1855 Broadway New York NY 10023-7692 Personal E-mail: sculpt3d@yahoo.com. Business E-Mail: rmsmith@nyit.edu.

SMITH, ROBERT POWELL, former ambassador, retired foundation administrator; b. Joplin, Mo., Mar. 5, 1929; s. Powell Augusta and Estella (Farris) S.; m. Alice Irene Rountree, Aug. 22, 1953; children: Michael Bryan, Steven Powell, Karen Louise, David Robert. BA, Tex. Christian U., 1954, MA, 1955. Fgn. svc. officer Dept. State, 1955-81; press officer Washington, 1955; vice-consul Lahore, Pakistan, 1956—58; 2d sec. Beirut, 1959-61; consul and prin. officer Enugu, Nigeria, 1962-65; officer-in-charge Ghanaian Affairs, 1966; officer-in-charge Nigerian Affairs, dep. dir. Office West African Affairs, 1967-69; dep. chief of mission, counselor of embassy Pretoria, South Africa, 1970-74; amb. to Malta, 1974-76; amb. to Ghana, 1976-79; amb. to Liberia, 1979-81. Pres. Africa Wildlife Leadership Found., 1981-85. Served with USMCR, 1946-49, 50-52. Decorated Air medal.; recipient Meritorious Honor award State Dept., 1967 Mem. Am. Fgn. Service Assn. Baptist.

SMITH, ROBERT SHERLOCK, state appeals court judge; b. NYC, Aug. 31, 1944; s. Robert and Janet W. (Welt) S.; m. Dian Goldston Smith, Aug. 31, 1969; children: Benjamin Eli, Emlen Matthew, Rosemary Friedman. BA with great distinction, Stanford U., 1965; LLB magna cum laude, Columbia U., 1968. Bar: N.Y. 1968, U.S. Dist. Ct. (so. dist.) N.Y. 1969, U.S. Dist. Ct. (ea. dist.) N.Y. 1977, U.S. Ct. Appeals (2d cir.) 1970, U.S. Ct. Appeals (4th cir.) 1986, U.S. Ct. Appeals (1st cir.) 1988, U.S. Ct. Appeals (7th cir.) 1989, U.S. Ct. Appeals (6th cir.) 1995, U.S. Ct. Appeals (D.C. and 8th cirs.) 1997, U.S. Ct. Appeals (5th cir.) 1999, U.S. Tax Ct. 1974, U.S. Supreme Ct. 1979. Assoc. Paul, Weiss, Rifkind, Wharton & Garrison, NYC, 1968-76, ptnr., 1976—2003; individual practitioner, spl. counsel Kornstein, Veisz, Wexler & Pollard, NYC, 2003—04; assoc. judge NY State Ct. Appeals, NYC, 2004—. Vis. prof. Columbia Law Sch., N.Y.C., 1980-81, lectr. law, 1981-90; adj. Benjamin N. Cardozo Sch. Law, 2006—. Editor-in-chief Columbia Law Review. Mem. ABA, N.Y. State Bar Assn. (vice chair com. ct. adminstrn. 2001-04), Assn. Bar City N.Y. (com. fed. legis. 1981-84, com. on judiciary 1984-87, com. on bicentennial of U.S. Constitution 1988-91), Federalist Soc. N.Y. (pres. lawyers chpt. 1994-2003). Republican. Mem. Reformed Ch. Office: State NY Ct Appeals 20 Eagle St Albany NY 12207-1095 also: 780 Third Ave 18th Fl New York NY 10017 Office Phone: 646-386-3824. Business E-Mail: rssmith@courts.state.ny.us.*

SMITH, ROBERT VICTOR, academic administrator, educator; b. Glendale, NY, Feb. 16, 1942; s. Robert Arthur and Marie Marlene (Florence) S. BS in Pharm. Sci., St. John's U., Jamaica, NY, 1963; MS in Pharm. Chemistry, U. Mich., 1964, PhD in Pharm. Chemistry, 1968. Asst. prof., then assoc. prof. U. Iowa, Iowa City, 1968-74; assoc. prof., asst. dir. U. Tex., Austin, 1974-77, area coordinator basic pharmaceutics, 1975-76, assoc. dir. Drug Dynamics Inst., 1977-78, dir. Drug Dynamics Inst., Coll. Pharmacy, 1979-85, James E. Bauerle Centennial prof. Coll. Pharmacy, 1983-85; prof., dean Coll. Pharmacy, Wash. State U., Pullman, 1985-86, vice provost for rsch., dean Grad. Sch., 1987-97; vice provost for rsch. and grad. edn., dean Grad. Sch., U. Conn., Storrs, 1997-2000; provost, vice chancellor acad. affairs U. Ark., Fayetteville, 2000—08, provost, vice chancellor emeritus and prof., chemistry, 2008—09; provost, sr. v.p. Tex. Team U. Lubbock, 2009—. Cons. E.R. Squibb, New Brunswick, N.J., 1979-82, Upjohn Co., Kalamazoo, 1982-85; external examiner U. Malaysia, Penang, 1981-82; mem. sci. adv. bd. Biodecision Labs., Pitts., 1985-86; Wash. Exposition Sci. Tech. Found., 1989-90; mem. noms. com. Coun. Grad. Schs., Washington, 1990-91, 96-97; accreditation evaluator Northwest Assn. Schs. and Colls., Seattle, 1991-97; mem. exec. com. grad. deans African-Am. Inst., N.Y., 1992-2000; bd. dirs. Coun. Grad. Schs., 1998, Grad. Record Exam, 1999-2003; exec. sec. U. Ark. 2010 Commn., 2000—; chair Southeastern Conf. Provosts Group, 2003-04. Author: Textbook of Biopharmaceutic Analysis, 1981, Graduate Research: A Guide for Students in the Sciences, 1998, Development and Management of University Research Groups, 1986, The Elements of Great Speechmaking: Adding Drama and Intrigue, 2004, Pedestals, Parapets and Pits: The Joys, Challenges and Failures of Professional Life, 2005, Where You Stand is Where You Sit: An Academic Administrator's Handbook, 2006. Bd. dirs. Wash. Tech. Ctr., 1990-92; exec. sec. 2010 Commn. Grantee NIH, 1974-83; fellow Acad. Pharm. Scis., 1981, Am. Assn. Pharm. Scientists, 1987; recipient Disting. Alumnus award Coll. Pharmacy U. Mich., 1990, Outstanding Svc. award Wash. State U., Grad. and Profl. Student Assn., 1993, 95. Mem. Am. Assn. Colls. Pharmacy (chmn. research and grad. affairs com. 1983-84), U.S. Pharmacopeia (revision com. 1985-90), Acad. Pharm. Scis. (chmn., vice chmn. 1983-85, 90, Presdl. citation 1985), Wash. Rsch. Found. (bd. dirs. 1989-97). Unitarian Universalist. Office: CHEM 119 Fayetteville AR 72701 Home: 10501 Utica Ave Lubbock TX 79424-7305 Office Phone: 806-742-2184. Business E-Mail: bobsmith@ttu.edu.

SMITH, ROBERT W., JR., (JAY), lawyer; b. Balt., Aug. 1, 1951; BS magna cum laude, Univ. Pa., 1973; JD with honors, Univ. Md., 1977. Bar: Md. 1977. Ptnr., chair corp. and securities practice group, mem. exec. com. DLA Piper US LLP, Balt. Bd. trustees McDaniel Coll., Center Stage. Mem.: ABA, Md. State Bar Assn., Order of Coif. Office: DLA Piper US LLP 6225 Smith Ave Baltimore MD 21209-3600 Office Phone: 410-580-4266. Office Fax: 410-580-3266. Business E-Mail: jay.smith@dlapiper.com.

SMITH, ROBIN, political organization administrator; b. Ga., 1963; m. Scott Smith; children: Callie, Caleb. Grad., U. Tenn., 1985. Chmn. Hamilton County Rep. Party, 1998—2002, Tenn. Rep. Party, 2007—; commr. Tenn. Human Rights. Del. Rep. Nat. Conv., 2004; mem. women's adv. com. Rep. Nat. Com.; mem. Stanford Adv. Project Mgmt. Mem. Hixson Ctrl. Baptist. Republican. Office: Tenn Rep Party 2424 21st Ave Ste 200 Nashville TN 37212 Office Phone: 615-269-4260. Office Fax: 615-269-4261. Business E-Mail: robin@tngop.org.

SMITH, ROBIN DEBRA, primary school educator; b. Harrisburg, Pa., Aug. 9, 1969; d. Robert DuBois and Gertrude Elizabeth Aud; m. Stephen Mark Smith, Dec. 22, 1990; children: Caleb, Stephen, Mikayla, Emily. BA in Elem. Edn., Messiah Coll., Grantham, Pa., 1990. Cert. elem. tchr. Fla. Presch. tchr. Piermont Cmty. Playgroup, NY, 1991—92; 3d grade tchr. Hawthorne Christian Acad., NJ, 1992—94; 2d grade tchr. Boca Raton Christian Sch., Fla., 1993—97, kindergarten tchr., 2002—; tchr., dir. A Child's Pl., Boca Raton, Fla., 2000—02. Home: 5267 Inwood Dr Delray Beach FL 33484

SMITH, ROBIN L., television personality, psychologist, writer; d. Warren and Rosa Lee Smith; B, La Salle U., Phila., 1983; M, Eastern Bapt. Theol. Sem.; PhD in Counseling Psychology, Temple U., Phila. Lic. psychologist. Segment host, With An Eye On Life Ask Dr. Robin Sta. KYW-TV3, Phila.; host, XM Satellite Radio The Dr. Robin Show on Oprah & Friends; TV contbr. The Oprah Winfrey Show, The Today Show, Good Morning America, The Early Show, MSNBC, The Fox News Channel; founder, pres. Ordered Steps Internat., Inc. Adj. prof. Palmer Theol. Sem.; with psychol. services Swarthmore Coll. Author: Inspirational Vitamins: A Guide To Personal Empowerment, 2004, Lies at the Altar: The Truth About Great Marriages, 2006 (nat. best-seller). Bd. dirs. Albert Einstein Med. Ctr., Belmont Hosp., Eagleville Hosp.; adv. bd. Barristers' Assn., Phila. Office: The Dr Robin Show on Oprah & Friends c/o XM Radio 1500 Eckington Pl NE Washington DC 20002

SMITH, ROD, retired professional football player; b. May 15, 1970; Postgrad in econ. & fin., Mo. So. State Coll., postgrad in gen. bus., postgrad in mktg. & mgmt. Wide receiver Denver Broncos, 1994—2008; ret. Named to NFL Pro-Bowl, 2000—01, 2005. Achievements include being a member of Super Bowl Champion Denver Broncos, 1997, 1998; being the only undrafted NFL reciever to catch more than 10,000 yards; holding Denver Broncos franchise records for career receptions (849), receiving yards (11,389), touchdown catches (68), touchdowns (71) and 100-yard games (31).

SMITH, RODGER FIELD, financial executive; b. Milw., Jan. 23, 1941; s. Millard Beale and Alice Catherine (Field) S.; m. Sarah Godfrey, June 19, 1964 (dec. Dec. 1999); children: Rodger F. Jr., Scott G., Reid W. BSChemE, U. Wis., 1964, MBA in Fin. with distinction, 1965. V.p. Allis Chalmers, Milw., 1966-76; mng. dir. Greenwich (Conn.) Assocs., 1976—. Trustee Harbor Funds, Chgo., 1987—; bd. dir. Arlington Capital, London, 1992—09; chair dean's adv. bd. U. Wis. Sch. Bus., 2006-08; mem. Tokeneke Tax Dist. Author articles and spkr. on investing pension funds. Fund raiser United Way, Milw., 1966—76. Mem.: Wis. Sch. Bus. (chair dean's adv. bd. 2006—08), Tokeneke Tax Dist. 2, Bascom Hill Soc., U. Wis. Alumni Assn. (nat. bd. dir. 1994—2000), Wee Burn Country Club (fin. com.), Beta Gamma Sigma, Tau Beta Pi (chmn. trust adv. com. 1986—). Avocations: travel, golf, tennis, coin collecting/numismatics. Office: Greenwich Assocs 6 High Ridge Park Stamford CT 06905 Home Phone: 203-655-8977; Office Phone: 203-625-5069. Personal E-mail: rodger.home@gmail.com. Business E-Mail: rodger@greenwich.com.

SMITH, ROGER WINSTON, retired political theory educator; b. Birmingham, Ala., July 9, 1936; s. Buford Houston and Sarah Louise (Trucks) S.; m. Martha Christin Daniels, Jan. 16, 1960; children: Louisa, David AB magna cum laude, Harvard U., 1958, postgrad. in law, 1958—59; MA in Polit. Sci., U. Calif., Berkeley, 1963, PhD in Polit. Sci., 1971. Teaching assoc. U. Calif.-Berkeley, 1965-66; asst. prof. govt. Coll. William and Mary, Williamsburg, Va., 1967-72, assoc. prof., 1972-80, prof, 1980-2001, prof. emeritus, 2001—. Sr. lectr. politics Glasgow U., 1977-78; lectr. NEH, 1988; cons. Nelson-Hall Pubs., Chgo.; mem. coun. Inst. Internat. Conf. on the Holocaust and Genocide, Jerusalem; chair acad. adv. bd., dir. genocide and human rights univ. program Zoryan Inst., Toronto; v.p. Inst. Study of Genocide, NY. Co-author, editor: Guilt: Man and Society, 1971; co-author: Genocide and the Modern Age, 1987, Genocide, vol. 2, 1991, Bearing Witness to the Holocaust, 1939-89, 1987, The Coming Age of Scarcity, 1998, Pioneers of Genocide Studies, 2002, When Will Genocide Ever End?, 2002, On the Edge of Scarcity, 2002, Race and Ethnic Relations, 15th ann. edit., 2005, Encyclopedia of Genocide and Crimes Against Humanity, 2004; editor: Genocide, 1999; contbg. editor Internet on the Holocaust and Genocide; contbr. articles to profl. jours. Served to 1st lt. U.S. Army, 1960-62, Japan Fellow NSF, 1966, College of William and Mary, 1977; recipient: award, 2008. Mem. Am. Polit. Sci. Assn., Internat. Assn. Genocide Scholars (co-founder, v.p., past pres.), Human Rights Watch, PETA. Democrat. Avocations: gardening, walking, opera. Home: 102 Lake Dr Williamsburg VA 23185-3113 Office: Coll William and Mary Dept Govt Williamsburg VA 23187 Office Phone: 757-229-8843. Personal E-mail: theseus51@msn.com, theseus510@msn.com.

SMITH, ROGERS MOOD, political scientist, educator; b. Sept. 20, 1953; s. Henry Dale and Betty (Mood) Smith. BA in Polit. Sci., Mich. State U., 1974; MA, Harvard U., 1978, PhD, 1980. Asst. prof. polit. sci. Yale U., New Haven, 1980—85, assoc. prof., 1985—89, Alfred Cowles prof. govt, 1989—2001; Browne Disting. prof. polit. sci. U. Pa., Phila., 2001—. Author: Liberalism and American Constitutional Law, 1985, Citizenship Without Consent, 1985, Stories of Peoplehood, 2003, The Unsteady March, 1999, Civic Ideals, 1997; contbr. articles to profl. jours. Fellow: Am. Acad. Arts & Sci.; mem.: New Eng. Polit. Sci. Assn. (Pres.'s award 1982), Social Sci. History Assn. (Sharlin award), Orgn. Am. Historians (Curie prize), Am. Polit. Sci. Assn. (Greenstone prize, Bunche prize, Easton prize). Avocation: baseball. Office: Univ Pa Dept Political Science 208 S 37th St Philadelphia PA 19104-6215 Home Phone: 610-660-8509; Office Phone: 215-898-7662. E-mail: rogerss@sas.upenn.edu.

SMITH, ROLAND BLAIR, JR., university administrator; b. Washington, Mar. 21, 1946; s. Roland Blair and Annie Louise S.; m. Valerie Peyton, June 16, 1969; children: Rovelle Louise, Roland Blair III. BA, Bowie State U., 1969; MPA, Ind. U., 1976; EdD, Harvard U., 1988. Dir. upward bound Notre Dame (Ind.) U., 1973-83, 86-88, dir. Ctr. for Edn. Opportunity, 1980-83, assoc. prof., 1991-96, dir. urban inst., 1992-96; assoc. provost, adj. prof. edn. and sociology Rice U., Houston, 1996—. Tchg. fellow and grad. asst. Harvard U., 1983-86; exec. asst. to pres. U. Notre Dame, Notre Dame, Ind., 1988-96; 1st v.p., treas. Pvt. Industry Coun., St. Joseph Coun., Ind., 1987-91; cons. Lilly Endowment, Indpls., 1990-91; outside reviewer Nat. Ctr. Ednl. Stats, Washington, 1991-92; chmn. bd. dirs. Nat. Assn. Presidential Assts. in Higher Edn., Washington, 1993-94. Contbg. author: (ency.) African- American Education, 1996. Commr. Martin Luther King Fed. Holiday Commn., Washington, 1993-94; trustee YMCA of Michiana, St. Joseph County, Ind.; bd. dirs. NRTS Corp., City of South Bend, Ind., 1993-96, Harvard Alumni Assn. Bd., Cambridge, Mass., 1995—, LifeGift Organ Donation Ctr., 2000—; bd. visitors Bowie State U., 1998-2002; mem. South Bend Elkhart Camp United Negro Coll. Fund; bd. pres. Ctr. faith and Health, 2004—. Recipient Outstanding Achievement award Bowie (Md.) State U., 1985; Named Disting. Alumnus Ind. U., South Bend, Ind., 1983, Nat. Assn. for Equal Opportunity in Higher Edn. (Bowie State U.), 1998. Mem. Am. Assn. Higher Edn. (Black caucus vice chair 1995-97, chair 1997-99, Service award 1998), Am. Conf. Acad. Deans, Phi Delta Kappa, Kappa Alpha Psi (Achievement award 1986). Democrat. Methodist. Office: Rice U PO Box 1892 - MS #3 Houston TX 77251-1892 Home Phone: 281-997-2778; Office Phone: 713-348-5688. Business E-Mail: rbsmith@rice.edu.

SMITH, ROLAND C., food service company executive; BS in Engring., US Mil. Acad., West Point, NY. Various mgmt. positions KFC Internat., Schering-Plough Corp., Pepsi Cola Internat., Procter & Gamble Co.; pres., CEO Arby's, Inc., 1997—99, AMF Bowling Worldwide, Inc., 1999—2003, Am. Golf Corp. & Nat. Golf Properties, 2003—05, Arby's Restaurant Group, Inc., 2006—08, Wendy's/Arby's Group, Inc., 2007—. Bd. dirs. Carmike Cinemas, Inc., 2002—, Dave Thomas Found., Wendy's/Arby's Group, Inc., 2007—. Platoon leader transp. and aviation corps, dep. dir. Army progs., aide-de-camp, maintenance officer, pilot US Army. Office: Wendy's Arby's Grp Inc 1155 Perimeter Ctr W Atlanta GA 30338 Office Phone: 678-514-4500.*

SMITH, RONALD EDWARD, ophthalmologist; b. Walkersville, Md., Oct. 7, 1942; s. Harry Otto and Marjorie Lee Smith; m. Sara Gutelius Watt, Sept. 4, 1965 (div. Oct. 1977); children: Kelly, Matt; m. Suzette Edith Le Blanc, Sept. 6, 1980. BA, Johns Hopkins U., 1964, MD, 1967. Diplomate Am. Bd. Ophthalmology. Intern Johns Hopkins Hosp., Baltimore, Md., 1967—68; resident opthalmology Johns Hopkin's Hosp., Baltimore, Md., 1968—72; asst. prof. U. So. Calif., LA, 1975—78, assoc. prof., 1978—81, prof., 1981—95, prof., chmn. dept. ophthalmology, 1995—. Co-author: Intraocular Inflammation, 1980, Vitrectomy Techniques, 1983, Uveitis: A Clinical Approach, 1986. Lt. comdr. USPHS, 1973—78. Recipient gold medal, Internat. Uveitis Study Group, 1998, Light award, Braille Inst., 1998. Mem.: Am. Acad. Ophthalmology (pres. 1994—95, 1998—, chmn. found. 1998—99). Avocations: golf, skiing, tennis. Office: USC Dept Ophthalmology 2617 E Chapman No 301 Orange CA 92829

SMITH, RONALD LYNN, health system executive; b. Algona, Iowa, Sept. 22, 1940; s. Russell Malcom and Helen Lucille (Gridley) S.; m. Jacqueline Sue Yarger, Dec. 23, 1962 (div. Aug. 1981); children: Sheri Rene, Gregory Mark, Brenton Alan; m. Sylvia Jo Grotjan, Dec. 31, 1982; 1 child, Russell Lynn. BS, Iowa State U., 1962; postgrad., U. S.D., 1963; MA, U. Iowa, 1965. With Harris Hosp.-Methodist, Ft. Worth, 1967-82, assoc. exec. dir., 1974-76, exec. dir., 1977-82; pres., CEO Harris Meth. Health System, Ft. Worth, 1982—; sr. exec. v.p. Tex. Health Resources, 1997-98. Mem. Premier, Inc., Nat. Com. for Quality Health Care; mem. adv. coun. Hill-Rom Co., 1991; mem. healthcare exec. adv. coun. IBM, 1991; mem. bd. Tex. Commerce Bank. Trustee Tarrant County United Way, 1977-79, campaign chmn., 1992, chmn. bd. trustees 1993, chmn. bd. dirs., 1994, area-wide svcs. chair, 1988-91, self-sufficiency task force; bd. mem. Tex. Rsch. League, 1990-95, nat. bd. visitors Tex. Christian U., 1990—; bd. visitors Tex. Wesleyan U., 1995—. Fellow Am. Coll. Hosp. Execs.; mem. Tex. Hosp. Assn. (trustee 1983-87, chmn. 1986-87), Tex. Healthcare Coun., Healthcare Leadership Coun., Dallas-Ft. Worth Hosp. Coun. (pres. 1981), Ft. Worth C. of C. (bd. dirs. 1992), Rotary. Methodist.

SMITH, ROSEMARY J., biology educator, researcher; b. Washington, Oct. 9, 1962; BA, Pomona Coll., 1984; MS, U. Ariz., 1988, PhD, 1991. Grad. teaching asst. U. Ariz., 1984-90; asst. prof. biology Nebr. Wesleyan U., Lincoln, 1991—. Trustee Rocky Mt. Biol. Lab. Crested Butte, Colo., 1994—. Contbr. articles to profl. jours. including: Oecologia, Jour. of Mammalogy, Southwestern Naturalist, Am. Biology Tchr.; presenter at numerous nat. sci. meetings. Advisor Nature Conservancy, Omaha, 1993-94. Grantee: Am. Mus. Natural History, 1989, Nebr. Wesleyan U., HHMI, 1994. Mem. AAAS, Ecol. Soc. Am., Am. Soc. Naturalists, Am. Soc. Mammalogists, Sigma Xi (grantee 1990). Avocations: outdoor recreation, reading. Office: Nebr Wesleyan Univ Biology Dept 5000 Saint Paul Ave Lincoln NE 68504-2760

SMITH, ROY (R. SMITH), lawyer; b. 1958; m. Donna Lee Shira, Sept. 9, 1989. AB cum laude, Princeton U., 1980; JD, Columbia U., 1983. Bar: NY 1984. Assoc. Cahill, Gordon & Reindell, 1983—92; atty. Am. Cyanamid Co., 1992—94; sr. atty. Cytec Industries, Inc., West Paterson, NJ, 1994—98, asst. gen. counsel, 1998—2001, v.p., gen. counsel, sec., 2002—. Editor: Columbia Law Review. Office: Cytec Industries Inc Five Garret Mountain Plz West Paterson NJ 07424 Office Phone: 973-357-3100. Office Fax: 973-357-3058.

SMITH, ROY PHILIP, judge; b. SI, NY, Dec. 29, 1933; s. Philip Aloysius and Virginia (Collins) S.; m. Elizabeth Helen Wink, Jan. 23, 1965; children: Matthew P., Jean E. BA, St. Joseph's Coll., Yonkers, NY, 1956; JD, Fordham U., 1965. Bar: NY. Asst. reg. counsel FAA, NYC, 1966-79; adminstrv. law judge U.S. Dept. Labor, Washington, 1979-83; adminstrv. appeals judge Benefits Rev. Bd., Washington, 1983—, chmn., chief adminstrv. appeals judge, 1988-90. Adj. prof. aviation law Dowling Coll., Oakdale, N.Y., 1972-79; adj. prof. transp. law Adelphi U., Garden City, N.Y., 1975-79; vis. prof. Georgetown U. Law Sch., 1989—. With US Army, 1957—59. Mem.: Fed. Adminstrv. Law Judges Conf. (treas. 1983—84, exec. com. 1982—83), Assn. Bar of City of N.Y. (sec.-treas. aeronautics com. 1978—79), Georgetown U. Libr. Assocs., Friendly Sons of St. Patrick, Edgemoor Club. Avocation: tennis. Home: 6700 Pawtucket Rd Bethesda MD 20817-4836 Office: Benefits Rev Bd 200 Constitution Ave NW Washington DC 20210-0001 Business E-Mail: smith-roy@dol.gov.

SMITH, RUSSELL B., surgeon; MD, U. Mo., Columbia, 1995. Cert. in otolaryngology Am. Bd. Otolaryngology, 2001. Asst. prof. U. Iowa, Iowa City, 2001—07; assoc. prof. U. Nebr. Med. Ctr., Omaha, 2007—.

SMITH, RUSSELL LOUIS, lawyer; b. Atlanta, Sept. 9, 1946; s. Nathan Harry and Edith (Carfield); m. Judith Beth Lavine, June 20, 1971; 1 child, Harris Charles Smith. BA, Vanderbilt U., 1968; JD, U. Ga., 1972. Bar: D.C., 1973, U.S. Supreme Ct., 1977, U.S. Ct. Appeals, (D.C. cir.), 1978. Atty.-advisor U.S. Dept. Treasury, 1972-76; Washington counsel Consol. Rail Corp., Washington, 1976—82; dir. Office of Automotive Industry Affairs U.S. Dept. Commerce, Washington, 1982-84; minority counsel Com. on Energy and Commerce U.S. Ho. Reps., Washington, 1984-88; assoc. McNair Law Firm, Washington, 1988-89; spl. counsel Govt. Rels. Dept. Willkie Farr & Gallagher LLP, Washington, 1989—. Adj. prof. Georgetown Pub. Policy Inst., Georgetown U., 2005—06. Pres. Adas Israel Hebrew Congregation, Washington, 2005—07. Mem.: Met. Club. Republican. Jewish. Office: Willkie Farr & Gallagher LLP 1875 K Street, NW Washington DC 20006 Home Phone: 202-332-3020; Office Phone: 202-303-1116. Business E-Mail: rsmith@willkie.com.

SMITH, S. KINNIE, JR., lawyer; BA in Econs., Yale U., New Haven, Conn., 1953; JD, U. Wisc. Law Sch., 1956. Ptnr. Sidley & Austin, Chgo., 1964—75; gen. counsel through vice chmn., Am. Natural Resources Company; sr. v.p. and dir. Coastal Corp., 1975—87; pres., vice chair, gen. counsel CMS Energy, Jackson, Mich., 1988—96; counsel Skadden, Arps, Slate, Meagher & Flom, 1996—2002; vice chmn., gen. counsel CMS Energy, Jackson, Mich., 2002—06; sr. counsel Miller, Canfield, Paddock & Stone, P.L.C., Detroit, 2006—. Mem. bd. vis. Univ. Wis. Law Sch. Mem.: ABA, Mich. Bar Assn., Chgo. Bar Assn. Office: Miller Canfield Paddock & Stone Ste 2500 150 W Jefferson Detroit MI 48226-4415 Office Phone: 313-496-8477. Business E-Mail: smithsk@millercanfield.com.

SMITH, SAM, columnist, writer; b. Bklyn., Jan. 24, 1948; s. Leon and Betty (Pritzker) S.; m. Kathleen Ellen Rood, Jan. 24, 1976; children: Connor, Hannah-Li. BBA in Acctg., Pace U., NYC, 1970; MA in Journalism, Ball State U., Muncie, Ind., 1974. Acct. Arthur Young & Co., NYC, 1970-72; reporter Ft. Wayne (Ind.) News Sentinal, Ft. Wayne, 1973-76, States News Svc., Washington, 1976-79; press sec. U.S. Senator Lowell Weicker Jr., 1979; writer/reporter Chgo. Tribune, 1979-90, columnist, 1991—. Commentator ESPN Radio. Author: The Jordan Rules, 1991, Second Coming, 1995; co-author: Total Basketball Encyclopedia, 2004, The Perfect Team, 2006; columnist: Hoop Japan nbcsmc.com; contbr. to publs. With USAR, 1970-76. Recipient Journalism awards, AP, UPI, Sigma Delta Chi, Sports Local Emmy award, WGN-TV; named Ball State U. Journalism Alumnus of Yr.; named to Ball State U. Journalism Hall of Fame, 2002. Mem.: Basketball Writers Assn. (pres. 1998—2005). Office: Chicago Tribune 435 N Michigan Ave Chicago IL 60611-4066 Office Phone: 312-222-5445. Business E-Mail: sasmith@tribune.com.

SMITH, SAMUEL HOWARD, academic administrator, plant pathologist; b. Salinas, Calif., Feb. 4, 1940; s. Adrian Reed and Elsa (Jacop) Smith; m. Patricia Ann Walter, July 8, 1960; children: Samuel, Linda Kjelgaard. BS in Plant Pathology, U. Calif., Berkeley, 1961, PhD in Plant Pathology, 1964; D (hon.), Nihon U., Tokyo, 1989, Far Eastern State U., Vladivostok, Russia, 1997. NATO fellow Glasshouse Crops Research Inst., Sussex, England, 1964-65; asst. prof. plant pathology U. Calif., Berkeley, 1965-69; assoc. prof. Pa. State U., University Park, 1969—74, prof., 1974—85, head dept. plant pathology, 1976—81, dean Coll. Agr., dir. Pa. Agrl. Expt. Sta. and Coop. Extension Service, 1981—85; pres. Wash. State U., Pullman, 1985—2000, pres. emeritus, 2000—. Bd. dirs. Blethen Corp., 1994—, Met. Mortgage & Securities, 2000—04, Nat. Assn. State Univs. & Land-Grant Colls., 1994—, chair, bd. dirs., 1999—2000, exec. dir., W.K. Kellogg Found., Food & Soc. Project, 2000—04, mem. Audit & Fin. Com., 1999—2000, chair, Coun. Pres.', 1998—99, exec. dir., Com. Food & Soc., 2000—04, mem. Ad-Hoc Com. Fed. Support Agrl. Sci., Ext., & Edn., 1998—2000, mem. Commn. Info. Tech., 1994—2000, chair, Commn. Info. Tech., 1994—96, mem. Pres.' Policy Bd. Info. Tech., 1997—2000, mem. Kellogg Commn. Twenty-First Century State & Land-Grant Univs., 1995—2000; chair, exec. com. NCAA, 1997—99, Div. I bd. dirs., 1997—99, mem. Pres.' Commn., 1994—97, chair, Pres.' Commn., 1996—97, div. I chair, Pres.' Commn., 1995; bd. dirs. The Tech. Alliance, 1996—2000, Assn. Western Univs., 1993—2000; mem. adv. com. Wash. Sch. Employees Credit Union, 1993—95, Battelle Pacific N.W. Lab., 1993—2000; mem. Wash. Coun. Internat. Trade; chair of pres.' and chancellors Pacific-10 Conf. CEOs, 1993—94; bd. dirs. Norman Borlaug U., 2000—02, Seattle Times, 1998—; pres., bd. dirs. Talaris Rsch. Inst., 2000—; bd. trustees Western Gov.'s U., 1997—, spl. adv. to pres., 2000—05, chair, pres. adv. coun., 1996—2005, exec. com., 1997—, chair, acad. policy com., 1997—, mem., nominating com., 1997—. Founding bd. mem. Coll. Success Found., Washington, 1997—; bd. trustees Pilchuck Glass Sch., 2000—04, Wash. State Hist. Soc., 2000—04, highly edn. coordinating bd., 2007—, exec. com., 2007—, chair, edn. com. Mem.: Am. Phytopath Soc., Pi Kappa Alpha (hon.). Business E-Mail: smithsh@wsuwest.edu.

SMITH, SCOTT, Mayor, Mesa, Arizona, business, financial and legal consultant; m. Kim Smith. BS in Acctg., Brigham Young U., Utah, 1980; MBA, Ariz. State U., Tempe, 1985; JD, Ariz. State U. Coll. Law, 1996. Mgr. NWL&O, 1985; fin. and bus. cons. ExecuShare, Ltd., 1986—; acctg. and fin. instr. U. Phoenix, 1988—93; pres. Great Western Homes, 1994—2003; regional pres. K. Hovnanian Homes, 2003—07; mayor City of Mesa, Ariz., 2008—. Chmn. Phoenix-Mesa Gateway Airport Authority, 2008—. Mem. Superstition Vistas Steering Com., Mesa Bldg. Bd. Appeals; pres. Mesa Cmty. Found.; bd. dirs., campaign chmn. Mesa United Way; bd. dirs. East Valley Partnership, Esperanza, Inc., Southwest Shakespeare Co. Address: Office of the Mayor City of Mesa PO Box 1466 Mesa AZ 85211 Office Phone: 480-644-2388. Business E-Mail: mayor.smith@cityofmesa.org.*

SMITH, SCOTT A., lawyer; b. Grand Forks, ND, July 17, 1957; married. BA, Stanford U., 1978; JD, U. Calif., Berkeley, 1981. Bar: Wash. 1981, U.S. Ct. Appeals (9th cir) 1982, U.S. Dist. Ct. (Ea. and We. dists.) Wash. Law clk. to Hon. Jerome Farris 9th Cir. U.S. Ct. of Appeals, 1981—82; assoc. Preston, Gates & Ellis, Seattle, 1982—88; ptnr. Short, Cressman & Burgess, Seattle, 1988—2004; prin. Riddell Williams, Seattle, 2004—. Chair Wash. State Access to Justice Bd., Seattle, 2002—04. Recipient Pro Bono award, Wash. State Bar Assn., Allies for Justice award, LEGALS of Wash. Fellow: Am. Bar Found.; mem.: King County Bar Assn. (pres. 1996—97, trustee 1991—97, Helen Geisness award Exemplary Svc.). Office: Riddell Williams Ste 4500 1001 Fourth Ave Seattle WA 98154 Business E-Mail: SSmith@riddellwilliams.com.

SMITH, SCOTT CLYBOURN, retired publishing executive; b. Evanston, Ill., Sept. 13, 1950; s. E. Sawyer and Jerolanne (Jones) S.; m. Martha Reilly, June 22, 1974; children: Carolyn Baldwin, Thomas Clybourn. BA, Yale U., 1973; M.Mgmt., Northwestern U., 1976. With Northern Trust Co., Chgo., 1973-77, Tribune Co., Chgo., 1977—93, sr. v.p., chief fin. officer, 1989-91, sr. v.p. for devel., 1991-93; pres., pub., CEO Sun Sentinel Co., Ft. Lauderdale, Fla., 1993-97, Chgo. Tribune Co., 1997—2004, interim pres., pub., CEO, 2006—08; pres. Tribune Publishing, 2005—08. Bd. dirs. McCormick Tribune Found., Chgo. Pub. Edn. Fund, Northwestern Meml. Healthcare, Chgo. Symphony Orch., Nat.-Louis U. Mem.: Newspaper Assn. Am. (chmn. pub. policy com.). Episcopalian.

SMITH, SELMA MOIDEL, lawyer, composer; b. Warren, Ohio, Apr. 3, 1919; d. Louis and Mary (Oyer) Moidel; 1 child, Mark Lee. Student, UCLA, 1936-39, U. So. Calif. Law School, 1939-41; JD, Pacific Coast U., 1942. Bar: Calif. 1943, U.S. Dist. Ct. 1943, U.S. Supreme Ct. 1958. Gen. practice law; mem. firm Moidel, Moidel, Moidel & Smith, 1943—. Field dir. civilian adv. com. WAC, 1943—45; charter mem. nat. bd. Med. Coll. Pa. (formerly Woman's Med. Coll. Pa.), 1953—, mem. exec. bd., 1976—80, pres., 1980—82, chmn, past pres. com., 1990—92, spkr., honoree 50th anniversary gala, 2003. Author: A Century of Achievement: The National Association of Women Lawyers, 1998, The First Women Members of the ABA, 1999; composer: Espressivo-Four Piano Pieces (orchestral premiere, 1987, performance Nat. Mus. Women in the Arts, 1989), numerous works. Decorated La Orden del Merito Juan Pablo Duarte (Dominican Republic), 1956. Fellow Am. Bar Found. (life); mem. ASCAP, ABA (jr. bar. conf., 1946-52, activities com., 1948-49), Sr. Lawyers divsn. ABA (vice-chair editl. bd. Experience mag. 1997-99,2008-, chair arts com. 1998-99, chair editl. bd. Experience Mag. 1999-2001, exec. coun. 1999-2003, Experience mag. adv. bd. 2001-08, nominating com. 2003-04, co-chair newsletter 2003-04, chair newsletter 2004-05, asst. sec., 2005-07, Dist. Svc. award 2003, 07), Calif. Supreme Ct. Hist. Soc. (bd. dirs. 2001-, programs and pubs. com., 2004-, State Bar program coord., 2006, founding chair writing competition, 2007-, chair. publs., 2008-, editor in chief Calif. Legal Hist. 2009), Assn. Learning in Retirement Orgns. in West (pres. 1993-94, exec. com. 1994-95, Disting. Svc. award 1995), Plato Soc. UCLA (discussion leader Constitution Bicentennial Project 1985-87, moderator extension lecture series 1990, Toga editor 1990-93, sec. 1991-92, chmn. colloquium com. 1992-93, Exceptional Leadership award 1994), Euterpe Opera Club (chair auditions 1972, chair awards 1973-75, v.p. 1974-75), Docents L.A. Philharm. (press and pub. rels. 1972-75, cons. coord. 1973-75, v.p. 1973-83, chair Latin Am. Cmty. Rels., Recognition and Honor award, 1978), Calif. Fedn. Music Clubs (chair Am. music 1971-75, conv. chair 1972), Nat. Fedn. Music Clubs (vice-chair Western region 1973-78), Nat. Assn. Composers USA (dir. 1974-79, luncheon chair 1975), Calif. Pres. Coun. (1st v.p.), L.A. Bus. Women's Coun. (pres. 1952), Calif. Bus. Women's Coun. (dir. 1951), Coun. Bar Assns. L.A. County (charter sec. 1950), Inter-Am. Bar Assn., League of Ams. (dir.), Nat. Assn. Women Lawyers (regional dir. western states, Hawaii 1949-51, jud. adminstrn. com. 1960, nat. chair world peace through law com. 1966-67, liaison to ABA Sr. Lawyers Divsn. 1996, chair bd. elections 1997-98, centennial com. 1997-99, chair com. unauthorized practice of law, social commn. UN, Lifetime Svc. award 1999, honoree annual Selma Moidel Smith law student writing competition 2005-), L.A. Lawyers Club (pub. defenders com. 1951), L.A. Bar Assn. (servicemen's legal aid com. 1944-45, psychopathic ct. com. 1948-53, Outstanding Svc. award 1993), State Bar Calif. (conf. com. on unauthorized practice of medicine 1964, Disting. Svc. award 1993), Women Lawyers Assn. LA (formerly So. Calif. Women Lawyers Assn.)(hon life; pres., 1947, 48, chair law day com. 1966, subject of oral hist. project 1986, 2001), Iota Tau Tau Legal Scholastic Soc. (1st prize 1942, dean L.A. 1947, supreme treas. 1959-62). Home: 5272 Lindley Ave Encino CA 91316-3518

SMITH, SETH AARON, medical educator; b. Huntington, W.Va., Jan. 2, 1979; s. William Barry and Brenda Susan Smith; m. Tiffany Davis, Sept. 6, 2003. BS in Physics, Va. Tech., Blacksburg, 2001, BS in Math., 2001; PhD in Biophysics, Johns Hopkins U., Balt., 2006. Rsch. assoc. F.M. Kirby Ctr. Kennedy Krieger Inst., Balt., 2006—09; asst. prof. radiology Johns Hopkins U., 2009—. Contbr. articles to profl. jours. Grantee, NIBIB, Nat. Insts. Health, 2009—. Mem.: Am. Acad. Neurology, Internat. Soc. Magnetic Resonance Medicine (1st prize 2007). Achievements include patents for alternative reference standard for magnetization transfer imaging of the spinal cord. Office: FM Kirby Ctr Kennedy Krieger Inst 707 N Broadway Baltimore MD 21205 Business E-Mail: smith@mri.jhu.edu.

SMITH, SHARINA, marketing executive, writer; b. Chgo., Feb. 10, 1964; d. George and Sharon Chalupnik Alongi; m. Charles Smith, Mar. 21, 2003; m. David Adkins, May 8, 1993 (div. Dec. 4, 2002); children: Laura Adkins, Daniel Adkins. BA, Bryn Mawr Coll., Pa., 1986; MS in Adminstrn., West Chester U. Sch. Bus. and Pub. Affairs, Pa., 1993. Asst. dir., pub. rels. Ct. & Plz. Shopping Ctrs., King of Prussia, Pa., 1986—87, dir., mktg., 1988—89; advt. coord. Eagle's Eye Co., Malvern, Pa., 1987—88, mktg. asst. to v.p., 1987—88; dir., pub. rels. Sullivan Assocs. Inc., Phila., 1989—91; asst. dir., regional campaigns Bryn Mawr Coll., Pa., 1991—92; reporter, photographer West Plains Daily Quill, Mo., 1995; adj. instr. Mo. State U., West Plains, 1999—2000; worship pastor's asst. Ridgecrest Bapt. Ch., Springfield, Mo., 2003—06; sr. dir., mktg., comm. SW Bapt. U., Bolivar, Mo., 2006—. Owner Gentle People Co., West Plains, 1995—2000, Intentional Life Inc., West Plains, 2000—02; coach, cons., Springfield, 2002—. Author: (book) Shout for Joy: Poems from the Journey. Recipient Outstanding Grad., West Chester U. Sch. Bus. & Pub. Affairs, 1993. Mem.: Pub. Rels. Soc. America (exec. bd., SWMO, comm. chair 2008—), Assn. Women in Comm. (exec. bd., student chpt. liaison 2007—08), Bolivar C. of C. (exec. bd., seminar chair 2007—), Christian Coaches Network. Office: SW Baptist Univ 1600 University Ave Bolivar MO 65613 Business E-Mail: scsmith@sbuniv.edu.

SMITH, SHARMAN BRIDGES, state librarian; b. Lambert, Miss. BS, Miss. U. for Women, Columbus, 1972; MLS, George Peabody Coll., Nashville, 1975. Head libr. Clinton (Miss.) Pub. Libr., 1972-74; asst. dir. Lincoln-Lawrence-Franklin Regional Libr., Brookhaven, Miss., 1975-77, dir., 1977-78; info. svcs. mgr. Miss. Libr. Commn., Jackson, 1978-87, asst. dir. libr. ops., 1987-89, dir. libr. svcs. div., 1989-92; state libr. State Libr. Iowa, Des Moines, 1992—2001; exec. dir. Miss. Libr. Commn., Jackson, Miss., 2001—. Recipient Friend of Edn. award, Iowa Computer Using Educators, 1995, Mem. of Yr. award, Iowa Libr. Assn., 1996. Office: Miss Libr Commn 3881 Eastwood Dr Jackson MS 39211 Office Phone: 601-432-4039. Business E-Mail: sharman@mlc.lib.ms.us.

SMITH, SHARON A., museum administrator; BA in History and Govt., Arcadia U.; M in Polit. Sci., Temple U. Cert. in higher edn. mgmt. Harvard U. With Hahnemann U., Springside Sch., CC Phila.; dean coll. advancement Delaware County CC; CEO Girl Scouts Southeastern Pa., Inc., 1997—2007; pres., CEO Civil War and Underground Railroad Mus., Phila., 2007—. Exec. dir. Delaware County CC Edn. Found. Bd. dirs. Sch. Dist. Phila. Campaign for Human Capital, Mayor's Scholarship Commn., Women's Way, Coun. for Advancement and Support of Edn. Mem.: Forum of Exec. Women (past pres., bd. dirs.), Sunday Breakfast Soc., Pa. Soc. Office: Civil War & Underground Railroad Mus 1805 Pine St Philadelphia PA 19103 Office Phone: 215-735-8196. Office Fax: 215-735-3812. Business E-Mail: ssmith@cwurmuseum.org.

SMITH, SHAWN, language educator; s. Kenneth and Carol Smith; m. Hwayoung Heather Cho, June 29, 1996; 1 child, Tristan Taeyoung. BA in English, Boston U., 1990; MA in Comparative Lit., Purdue U., West Lafayette, Ind., 1993; PhD, Yale U., New Haven, 2001. Asst. prof. English Ga. Southern U., Statesboro, 2001—03; assoc. prof. English Longwood U., Farmville, Va., 2003—. Office: Longwood Univ 201 High St Farmville VA 23909 Business E-Mail: smithsb@longwood.edu.

SMITH, SHEPARD (DAVID SHEPARD SMITH JR.), newscaster; b. Holly Springs, Miss., Jan. 14, 1964; s. David Shepard and Dora Ellen (Anderson) Smith. BA Journalism, U. Miss. Reporter A Current Affair, 1995, FNC, NY, 1996—; anchor FNC The FOX Report, 1999—; host FNC FOX News Live; sr. correspondent FNC; correspondent Fox News Edge, LA. Office: FOX News 1200 Ave Am New York NY 10036-*

SMITH, SHERWOOD HUBBARD, JR., retired electric utilities executive; b. Jacksonville, Fla., Sept. 1, 1934; s. Sherwood Hubbard and Catherine Gertrude (Milliken) S.; m. Eva Hackney Hargrave, July 20, 1957; children: Marlin Hamilton Dohlman, Cameron Hargrave Callaway, Eva Hackney Davis. AB, U. N.C., 1956, JD, 1960; D civil laws, St. Augustine's Coll., 1988; LDD, Campbell U., 1990; HHD, Francis Marion Coll., 1990. Bar: N.C. 1960. Assoc. Lassiter, Moore & Van Allen, Charlotte, 1960-62; ptnr. Joyner & Howison, Raleigh, 1962-65; assoc. gen. counsel Carolina Power & Light Co., Raleigh, 1965-70, sr. v.p., gen. counsel, 1971-74, exec. v.p., 1974-76, pres., 1976-92, CEO, 1979-96, chmn. bd., 1980-99, chmn. emeritus, 1999—; with Progress Energy Co., 2005—. Former dir. NorTel Network, Northwestern Mut. Life Ins. Co., Wachovia Corp., Durham Corp., Springs, Ind. Trustee Z Smith Reynolds Found., 1978-96, Nat. Humanities Ctr., 1990-93; bd. dirs. NC Citizens Bus. and Industry, chmn., 1985-86; bd. dirs. Rsch. Triangle Found. NC, NC Inst. Medicine; mem. bd. govs. Ctr. Creative Leadership; mem., chmn. Triangle Univs. Ctr. Advanced Studies, 1986—; dir. Franklin St. Ptnrs.; former chmn. bd. trustees, chmn. Rex Hosp.; gov. Boys and Girls Clubs Am. Recipient Nat. Humanitarian award Am. Lung Assn., 1993, Outstanding Leadership award in Mgmt. scis. Am. Soc. Mech. Engrs., 1983, A.E. Finley Disting. Svc. award Greater Raleigh C. of C., 1985, Disting. Citizenship award N.C. Citizens Bus. and Industry, 1997; named to N.C. Bus. Hall of Fame, 1999. Mem.: Greater Raleigh C. of C. (pres. 1979), Phi Beta Kappa. Home: 408 Drummond Dr Raleigh NC 27609-7006 Office: Progress Energy Co PO Box 1551 Raleigh NC 27602-1551

SMITH, SHIRLEY, artist; b. Wichita, Kans., Apr. 17, 1929; d. Harold Marvin and Blanche Carrie (Alexander) S. BFA, Kans. State U., Manhattan, 1951; postgrad., Provincetown Workshop, Mass., 1962-66. One-woman shows include 55 Mercer St. Gallery, NYC, 1973, Wichita Art Mus., Kanas, 1978, Stamford Mus. and Nature Ctr., Conn., 1987, Aaron Gallery, Washington, 1987, 1988, Joan Hodgell Gallery, Sarasota, Fla., 1987, Marianna Kistler Beach Mus. 38 Yr. Retrospective, Kans. State U., 1999—2000, John Jay Gallery, NYC, 2000, Represented in permanent collections Whitney Mus. Am. Art, Phoenix Art Mus., The Aldrich Mus. Contemporary Art, Ridgefield, Conn., Ulrich Mus., Wichita State U., Kans., Everson Mus., Syracuse, NY, U. Calif. Berkeley Art Mus., Marianna Kistler Beach Mus., Kans. State U., Manhattan, Telfair Mus. of Art, Savannah, Ga. Recipient Grumbacher Cash award for mixed media New Eng. Exhbn., Silvermine, Conn., 1967, Acad. Inst. award Am. Acad. Arts and Letters, NYC, 1991, Richard Florsheim Art Funds grantee, 1998, Retrospective Opening grantee, 1999. Mem. Artist Equity. Democrat. Presbyterian. Home: 141 Wooster St New York NY 10012-3163

SMITH, SIBLEY JUDSON, JR., historic site administrator, educator; b. Alexandria, La., June 26, 1955; s. Sibley Judson and Eunice Lee (Raulins) S.; children: Jacob Lee, Casey Raulins. Student, N.E. La. U., 1973-76; BA in History magna cum laude, Christopher Newport Coll., 1985; MA in Am. Studies, Coll. of William and Mary, 1992. Mus. interpreter Colonial Williamsburg (Va.) Found., 1979-87; coord. of interpretation Hist. Hudson Valley, Inc., Tarrytown, NY, 1987-88; historic site mgr. Philipse Manor Hall State Hist. Site, Yonkers, NY, 1988-91; exec. dir. Hist. Allaire (N.J.) Village, Inc., 1991-97; dir. edn. Vietnam Era Ednl. Ctr., N.J. Vietnam Vets. Meml. N.J. Dept. Mil. and Vet. Affairs, Holmdel, 1997—. Mem. Alpha Chi, Alpha Psi Omega. Avocations: gardening, theater, movies, mus. Office: Vietnam Era Ednl Ctr 1 Memorial Ln PO Box 648 Holmdel NJ 07733-0648 Office Phone: 800-648-8387. Business E-Mail: sjsmith2@njvvmf.org.

SMITH, SIDNEY CRAWLE, JR., cardiologist, educator; b. Wilmington, Del., 1941; MD, Yale U., 1967. Diplomate Nat. Bd. Med. Examiners, 1969, Am. Bd. Internal Medicine, 1972, Cardiovascular Disease, 1973. Intern Peter Bent Brigham Hosp., Boston, 1967—68, resident cardiology, 1968—69, fellowship, 1969—71, Harvard Med. Sch., Boston, 1969—71; dir. cardiovascular labs. U. Colo. Health Sci. Ctr., 1973—77; dir. San Diego Cardiac Ctr. at Sharp Healthcare, 1977—94; chief cardiology U. NC, Chapel Hill, 1994—2001, dir. Ctr. Cardiovascular Sci. and Medicine, 1996—. Asst. prof. U. Colo., Denver, 1973—77; asst. clin. prof. medicine U. San Diego, 1977—85, assoc. clin. prof., 1985—90, clin. prof., 1990—94; prof. U. NC Sch. Medicine, 1994—. Contbr. articles to med. jours. Recipient Eugene Drake Award, 2003, Award Spl. Recognition, Nat. Heart, Lung, and Blood Inst., NIH, 2003. Mem.: Am. Coll. Cardiology, Am. Heart Assn. (chief sci. officer 2001—03, nat. pres. 1995—96, Physician of Yr. Award 1993, Disting. Nat. Leadership Award 1996, Gold Heart Award 2000), Inter Am. Soc. Cardiology (v.p.), World Heart Fedn. (exec. com. mem.), World Heart Forum (chmn.). Office: U NC / Divsn Cardiology CB #7075, Bioinformatics Bldg 130 Mason Farm Rd, 4th Fl Chapel Hill NC 27599-7075 Office Phone: 919-966-0732. Office Fax: 919-843-9654. E-mail: scs@med.unc.edu.

SMITH, SIDNEY OSLIN, JR., lawyer; b. Gainesville, Ga., Dec. 30, 1923; s. Sidney Oslin and Isabelle Caroline (Charters) S.; m. Patricia Irwin Horkan, Aug. 4, 1944 (dec. Oct. 19, 2001); children— Charters Smith Wilson, Ellen Smith Andersen, Sidney Oslin III; m. Carolyn S. Reed, Nov. 29, 2004. AB cum laude, Harvard Coll., 1947; LL.B. summa cum laude, U. Ga., 1949. Bar: Ga. 1948. Ptnr. Telford, Wayne & Smith, Gainesville, Ga., 1949-62; asst. solicitor Superior Cts., Northeastern Jud. Cir. Ga., 1951-61, judge, 1962-65, U.S. Dist. Ct. (no. dist.) Ga., 1965-68, chief judge, 1968-74; ptnr. Alston, Miller & Gaines, Atlanta, 1974-82, Alston & Bird, Atlanta, 1982-94, of counsel, 1994—. Chmn. Gainesville Bd. Edn., 1959-62; trustee Brenau Coll., Gainesville, 1974—, chmn., 1976-84; mem. state bd. regents Univ. System of Ga., 1980-87, chmn., 1984-85. Served to capt. U.S. Army, 1943-46, ETO. Fellow ABA, Am. Coll. Trial Lawyers; mem. Am. Law Inst., Am. Judicature Soc., Chattahoochee Club, Phi Beta Kappa, Phi Kappa Phi, Phi Delta Phi, Phi Delta Theta. Republican. Episcopalian. Home: 3206 Club Pointe Way Gainesville GA 30506-1638 Office: Alston & Bird 1 Atlantic Ctr Atlanta GA 30309-3400 E-mail: smit977@bellsouth.net.

SMITH, SPENCER BAILEY, engineering and business educator; b. Ottawa, Ont., Can., Jan. 31, 1927; s. Sidney B. and Etta (Bailey) S.; m. Mildred E. Spidell, Dec. 31, 1954 B in Engring., McGill U., 1949; MS, Columbia U., 1950, DSc in Engring., 1958. Adminstrv. engr. Mergenthaler Linotype Co., NYC, 1953-58; ops. research mgr. Raytheon Co., Newton, Mass., 1958-61; ops research mgr. Montgomery Ward & Co., Chgo., 1961-66; assoc. prof., then prof. Ill. Inst. Tech., 1966-96, prof. emeritus, 1996—, chmn. dept. indsl. and systems engring., 1971-77, dir. Stuart Sch. Office of Research, 1977-82. Tchr. TV courses Nat. Tech. U. Author: Computer-Based Production and Inventory Control, 1989; contbr. articles to profl. jours.; patentee on order quantity calculator, 1964. Vol. cons. on sch. redistricting Elem. Sch. Dist., Evanston, Ill., 1972-74 Research grantee Harris Trust and Savs. Bank, 1968-70, Ill. Law Enforcement Commn., 1972-74, U.S. Army C.E., 1981, Am. Prodn. and Inventory Control Soc., 1980 Mem. INFORMS, ASME, Inst. Indsl. Engrs., Univ. Club (Chgo.). Presbyterian. Home: 2530 Lawndale Ave Evanston IL 60201-1158 E-mail: montrosemillennium@comcast.net.

SMITH, STACY J., computer company executive; BBA, Univ. Tex., Austin, MBA, 1988. IT mgr. Matt David Corp.; mgmt. positions Intel Corp., Santa Clara, Calif., 1988—96, group contr. assembly test mfg. group, 1996—99, group contr. worldwide sales & mktg., 1999—2001, gen. mgr. Europe, Asia & Middle East, 2001—04, v.p. sales & mktg., 2002—04, v.p., CIO, 2004—06, v.p., asst. CFO, 2006—07, v.p., CFO, 2007—. Mem. advisory bd. McCombs Sch. Bus., Univ. Tex., Austin. Office: Intel Corp 2200 Mission Coll Blvd Santa Clara CA 95054-1549*

SMITH, STAN VLADIMIR, economist, finance company executive; b. Rhinelander, Wis., Nov. 16, 1946; s. Valy Zdenek and Sylvia Smith; children: Cara, David. BS in Ops. Research, Cornell U., 1968; MBA, U. Chgo., 1972, PhD in Econs., 1997. Diplomate Am. Bd. Disability Analysts. Lectr. U. Chgo., 1973; economist bd. govs. Fed. Res. System, Washington, 1973-74; staff economist First Nat. Bank of Chgo., 1974; assoc. December Group, Chgo., 1974-77; founding pres. Seaquest Internat., Chgo., 1977-85; mgr., ptnr. Ibbotson Assocs., Chgo., 1981-85; pres. Smith Econ. Group Ltd. divsn. Corp. Fin. Group, Chgo., 1985—. Expert econ. witness in field; adj. prof. DePaul U. Coll. Law, Chgo., 1990. Author: Economic/Hedonic Damages, 1990; founding editor Stocks, Bonds, Bills and Inflation yearbook, 1983-01; editor Jour. Forensic Econs., 1990-01; contbr. articles in field. Founder, exec. dir. Inst. for Value of Life, 1996. Fellow Allied Chem., 1967, John McMullen Trust, 1969; grantee Ford Found., 1972, U.S. Fed. Res., 1973. Fellow: Am. Coll. Forensic Examiners (bd. cert. 1996—); mem.: Soc. Litig. Economists (bd. govs. 1999—), Acad. Econ. and Fin. Experts, Am. Bd. Forensic Examiners, Nat. Future Assn. (arbitrator), Am. Arbitration Assn. (arbitrator 1994—96), Nat. Acad. Econ. Arbitrators (founder 1989—), Nat. Assn. Forensic Econs. (v.p. 2000—03), Am. Fin. Assn., Am. Econ. Assn., Alpha Delta Phi. Office: Smith Econ Group Ltd Ste 600 1165 N Clark St Chicago IL 60610-7861 Office Phone: 312-943-1551. Business E-Mail: stan@smitheconomics.com.

SMITH, STANLEY BERTRAM, clinical and anatomic pathologist, allergist, immunologist; b. Phila., 1929; MD, Washington U., St. Louis, 1956. Diplomate Am. Bd. Clin. Pathology, Am. Bd. Allergy and Immunology, Am. Bd. Anatomic Pathology. Intern Barnes Hosp., St. Louis, 1956—57; resident in pathology Jackson Meml. Hosp., 1957—62; fellow in immunology Sch. Medicine Yale U., New Haven, 1963—65; pathologist Miami (Fla.) Children's Hosp., 1966—. Mem. AAAS, AMA, Internat. Acad. Pathology, Am. Soc. Clin. Pathology, Coll. Am. Pathologists, Am. Soc. Hematology. Office: Miami Children's Hosp 3100 SW 62nd Ave Miami FL 33155-3009 E-mail: Stanley.Smith@mch.com.

SMITH, STEPHANIE RENAE, middle school educator; b. Atlanta, Apr. 25, 1969; d. Jasper and Dianna H. Smith; 1 child, Kare K. Greene. BS, Tuskegee U., Ala., 1993; MA, Ctrl. Mich. U., Mount Pleasant, 2002; EdS, Argosy U., Sarasota, Fla., 2003, EdD, 2006. Cert. tchr., gifted edn. and reading tchr. Ga. Tchr. grad. sci. lab. Atlanta Pub. Sch. Sys., 1997—99, 8th grade phys. sci. tchr., 1999—2004, after sch. tutor, 2000—, 8th grade earth sci. tchr., 2003—04, tutor 21st century aftersch. program, 2004—07, gifted/challenged tchr. L. Judson Price Mid. Sch., 2004—08, Sylvan Hills Middle Sch., 2008—, sci. facilitater, 2008—. Adj. prof. Ctrl. Mich. U., 2007—. Active sci. instr. Antioch Bapt. Ch. North, Atlanta, tchr. Adult Christian Class. Named Tchr. of Yr., W. L. Parks Mid. Sch., Atlanta, 2001—02. Mem.: NSTA, Ga. Assn. Gifted, Argosy U. Alumni Assn., Central Mich. Alumni Assn., Tuskegee Alumni Assn., Hall of Tolerance, Stopping Hate, Sheriff Assn. Home: 2805 Amber Forest Dr Douglasville GA 30135-7306 Office Phone: 770-842-2291. Personal E-mail: ksrs69@aol.com, stephaniesmith100@comcast.net.

SMITH, STEPHEN F., food service executive; b. El Dorado, Ark. m. Jan Smith; 6 children. Student, South Ark. U. Mgr. Sysco Corp., Jackson, Minn., 1980—81, v.p. wholesale co. El Paso, Tex., 1981—83, pres., CEO Atlanta, 1983—87, Little Rock, 1987—95, Orlando, 1995—2002, sr. v.p. food svc. ops. Ocoee, Fla., 2002—08, exec. v.p. So. & We. food service ops. Houston, 2008—. Office: Sysco Corp 1390 Enclave Pkwy Houston TX 77077*

SMITH, STEPHEN GRANT, journalist; b. NYC, Mar. 6, 1949; s. John J. and Nora O.S.; m. Sarah Rowbotham Bedell, May 22, 1982; children: R. Kirk Bedell, Elisabeth DeCou Bedell, David Branson Smith. Student, Deerfield Acad.; BA, U. Pa., 1971. City Hall reporter Daily Hampshire Gazette, Northampton, Mass., 1971-73; spl. assignment reporter Albany Times-Union, 1973-74; dep. regional editor Phila. Inquirer, 1974-76; asst. met. editor Boston Globe, 1976-78; sr. editor Horizon Mag., 1978; staff writer Time Mag., 1978-80, sr. editor, 1980-82, Nation editor, 1982-85, acting asst. mng. editor, 1985-86; exec. editor Newsweek Mag., 1986-91; Washington news editor Knight Ridder newspapers, 1991-94; founding editor Civilization Mag., Washington, 1994-96; editor Nat. Jour., 1996-98, U.S. News and World Report, 1998-2001; exec. v.p. Winner & Assocs., 2001—02; v.p., dir. comm. Brookings Instn., 2003—04; Wash. bur. chief Houston Chronicle, 2004—07; editor Washington Examiner, 2007—. Mem. bd. Nat. Press Found., 2005—. Mem. bd. overseers U. Pa., 2001—07; mem. bd. U. Pa. Press, 2005—07. Mem.: Overseas Press Club, Nat. Press Club, U. Pa. Alumni Soc. (exec. com. 1994—2000), World Affairs Coun. Washington, Coun. on Fgn. Rels., Royal St. George's Golf Club, Sakonnet Golf Club, Fourth Estate Golf Soc., White's Club, Beefsteak Club, Chevy Chase Club, Met. Club, Century Club, Brook Club. Office: Washington Examiner 1015 15th St NW Washington DC 20005 Personal E-mail: sgrasmith@gmail.com.

SMITH, STEPHEN MARK, lawyer; b. Newport News, Va., July 1, 1948; s. Joseph and Marian (Sturman) Smith; children: Ryan David, Miles Stephen. BA in Psychology, William & Mary, 1971, JD, 1974. Bar: Va. 1974, N.Y. 1975, D.C. 1975, U.S. Supreme Ct., U.S. Ct. Appeals (2d, D.C., 4th cirs.). Lawyer Rothblatt, Rothblatt, et al., NYC, 1974-76, Joseph Smith Ltd., Hampton, Va., 1976-99; founding mem. Brain Injury Law Ctr. P.C. Mem. com. Va. Beach Dems., 1990—; bd. dirs., coord. Va. state Trial Lawyers Pub. Justice. Mem. AAJ, Am. Bd. Trial Advocates (diplomate), Va. Trial Lawyers Assn. (bd. dirs. 1978—), Brain Injury Assn. Va. (pres. 2007). Avocations: fishing, reading, boating, jogging, golf. Office: Brain Injury Law Center 2100 Kecoughtan Rd Hampton VA 23661 Home: PO Box 829 Virginia Beach VA 23451-0829 Home Phone: 757-362-3266; Office Phone: 757-244-7000. Business E-Mail: ssmith@braininjurylawcenter.com.

SMITH, STEPHEN P., utilities executive; BS in Petroleum Engring., Colo. Sch. Mines; MBA, U. Chgo. Grad. Sch. Bus. Sr. v.p., CFO Columbia Gas Transmission Corp., 1996—99; sr. v.p., dep. CFO Columbia Energy Group, 1999—2000; pres., COO NiSource Corp. Svcs. Co., 2000—03; sr. v.p., treas. Am. Electric Power Co., 2003—07, sr. v.p. shared svcs., 2008; exec. v.p., CFO NiSource Inc., 2008—. Bd. dirs., mem. audit com. Natural Resource Ptnrs., L.P., 2004—. Office: NiSource Inc Corp Hdqs 801 E 86th Ave Merrillville IN 46410*

SMITH, STEPHEN PUNTENNEY, plastic surgeon, educator; b. Rochester, NY, Aug. 18, 1970; s. Stephen P. Smith and Mackey Smith Jane Rae; m. Nevada Smith, July 29, 1995; children: Charlotte, Averill, Blaine. BA, U. Pa., Phila., 1992; MD, Ohio State U. Coll. Medicine, Columbus, 2001. Cert. State Med. Bd. Ohio, 2002, diplomate Am. Bd. Otolaryngology, 2007, Am. Bd. Facial Plastic and Reconstructive Surgery, 2009. Dir., divsn. facial plastic and reconstructive surgery Ohio State U. Med. Ctr., 2007—; asst. prof., dept. otolaryngology-head and neck surgery Ohio State U. Coll. Medicine, 2007—. Office: Ohio State Univ Divsn Facial Plastic Surgery 565 Metro Pl Ste 400A Dublin OH 43017 Office Fax: 614-760-1693.

SMITH, STEPHEN RANDOLPH, aerospace executive; b. Des Moines, Apr. 17, 1928; s. Norvin Ellis and Helen (Heberling) S.; m. Margaret Anne Graves, Dec. 20, 1950; children: Stephen Randolph Jr., Susan Canning, Sara Kutler, Anne Yee, Julia Carroll. BSME, Stanford U., 1951, MSME, 1952; MBA Advanced Mgmt. Program, Harvard U., 1974. Registered profl. engr., Calif. Sr. analyst, preliminary design engr. Northrop & Garrett Corps., L.A. and Hawthorne, Calif., 1952-55; propulsion lead design engr. Northrop Corp., Hawthorne, 1955-59, engring. rep. ea. dist. Washington, 1959-60, T-38/F-5/F-5X program mgr. Hawthorne, 1960-75, v.p. Iran ops. Tehran, 1975-78, v.p. advanced stealth projects Hawthorne, 1978-83, v.p. engring. and advanced devel., 1983-86, v.p., program mgr. F-20/YF-23A, 1986-88, corp. v.p., gen. mgr. aircraft divsn., 1988-92; cons. tech. mgmt. Palos Verdes, Calif., 1992—. Bd. mem. Quarterdeck Ptnrs., Inc., L.A. and Washington, 1992—; NASA Advanced Aeronautics Com., 1984-86; invited lectr. aircraft design USAF Acad., 1983. Author, designer, patentee in field. Bd. dirs. Boy Scouts Am., L.A. coun., 1986—, explorer exec. com., 1943—; pres. Penn Srs., Palos Verdes, Calif., 1996; trustee Western Mus. Flight; sr. warden St. Francis Ch. Sgt. U.S. Army, 1946-48. Recipient Disting. Civilian Svc. medal for Tacit Blue, U.S. Dept. Def., Washington, 1983. Fellow AIAA (chmn. L.A. sect. 1985-86, adv. bd. 1988—, Spl. Citation 1994), Inst. Advancement Engring.; mem. Soc. Automotive Engrs. (chmn. aerotech. 1986-87, honors 1987), Sierra Club, Trailfinders Conservation Coun. (life, coun. chief 1940), Redondo Beach Yacht Club (charter), King Harbor Yacht Club (charter). Republican. Episcopalian. Avocations: competitive sailing, tennis, backpacking, skiing, running. Home and Office: 2249 Via Guadalana Palos Verdes Estates CA 90274 Home Phone: 310-375-1039; Office Phone: 310-375-1039.

SMITH, STEVE, pharmaceutical executive; s. Robert and Evelyn Smith. Pres., CEO Tec Labs., Albany, Oreg., 1998—. Speaker Oregon State U. Entrepreneurship Soc. Meeting. Mem. Portland Bus. Alliance. Office: Tec Laboratories Inc 7100 Tec Labs Way SW Albany OR 97321*

SMITH, STEVEN RAY, law educator; b. Spirit Lake, Iowa, July 8, 1946; s. Byrnard L. and Dorothy V. (Fischbeck) Smith; m. Lera Baker Smith, June 15, 1975. BA, Buena Vista Coll., 1968; JD, MA, U. Iowa, 1971. Bar: Iowa 1971, Ky. 1987, Ohio 1992. Asst. to assoc. dean Sch. Law U. Louisville, 1974—81, acting dean, 1974—76, prof. law, 1971—88; assoc. medicine Med. Sch., 1983—88; dep. dir Assn. Am. Law Schs., 1987—88; dean, prof. law Cleve. State U., 1988—96; pres., dean and prof. Calif. Western Sch. Law, 1996—. Trustee U. Louisville, 1980—82, SCRIBES, 1993—; pres. Ky. Congress Senate Faculty Leaders, 1982—84; bd. trustees Am. Bd. Profl. Psychology, 1994—2001; bd. dirs. Nat. Register Health Svc. Providers Psychology, 2002—, San Diego Vol. Lawyers Program, 1998—, Nat. Conflict Resolution Ctr., 2003—; sec., bd. dirs. Assn. Accreditation of Human Rsch. Protection Programs, 2001—. Author: Law, Behavior and Mental Health: Policy and Practice, 1987; contbr. chapters to books, articles to profl. jours. Recipient Grawemeyer award, Metroversity Consortium, 1983. Fellow: Ohio State Bar Found. (coun. of dels. 1992—96); mem.: APA (pub. mem. ethics com., chmn. librs. com., dep. dir. 1987—88, accreditation com. mem. 1993—96, chair accreditation com. 1994—96), ABA (stds. rev. com. 1991—95, govt. rels. com. 1993—95, joint commn. ABA/Assn. Am. Law Schs. financing of legal edn. 1993—94, 1997—98, coun. sect. legal edn. and admission to the bar 1997—, chmn.-elect sect. on legal edn. and admission to the bar 2004—05, chmn. sect. of legal edn. and admissions to the bar 2005—06, bd. govs. San Diego Found. 2006—), Order of Coif, Ohio State Bar Assn., Assn. Am. Law Schs., Am. Econs. Assn., City Club Cleve. (pres. 1994—95). Office: Calif Western Sch Law Office of Dean 225 Cedar St San Diego CA 92101-3046

SMITH, STEVEN SIDNEY, molecular biologist; b. Idaho Falls, Idaho, Feb. 11, 1946; s. Sidney Ervin and Hermie Phyllis (Robertson) Smith; m. Nancy Louise Turner, Dec. 20, 1974. BS, U. Idaho, 1968; PhD, UCLA, 1974. Asst. rsch. scientist Beckman Rsch. Inst. City of Hope Nat. Med. Ctr., Duarte, Calif., 1982-84, staff Cancer Ctr., 1983—, asst. rsch. scientist depts. Thoracic Surgery and Molecular Biology, 1985-87, assoc. rsch. scientist, 1987-95; rsch. scientist City of Hope Nat. Med. Ctr., Duarte, 1995-00, prof. molecular sci., 2000—; dir. dept. cell and tumor biology City of Hope, Duarte, Calif., 1990—2002, assoc. dir. rsch. Prostate Cancer Program, 2003—. Vis. prof. in basic med. scis. Okla. State U., 1995—96; cons. Molecular Biosystems Inc., San Diego, 1981—84, Am. Inst. Biol. Scis., Washington, 1994, Okla. Ctr. for Advancement of Sci. and Tech., 2001—. Editl. bd. mem. Analytical Biochemistry, 1997—2000, exec. editor, 2000—, editl. bd. mem. Inscight Acad. Press., 1998—, Cancer Genomics and Proteomics, 2003; contbr. articles to profl. jours. Named Honors Laureate, Computer World, 2001; fellow Swiss Nat. Sci. Found. fellow, U. Bern, 1974—77, fellow, Scripps Clinic and Rsch. Found., 1978—82, NIH, 1979—81. Mem.: IEEE Computer Soc., Am. Urological Assn., Am. Math. Soc., Am. Chem. Soc., Am. Assn. Cancer Rsch., Am. Soc. Cell Biology, Phi Beta Kappa. Achievements include 5 U.S. patents. Avocations: backpacking, fishing, weightlifting. Office: Familian Science Bldg Rm 1102 City of Hope 1500 E Duarte Rd Duarte CA 91010-3011 Home Phone: 323-913-0418; Office Phone: 626-301-8316. Business E-Mail: ssmith@coh.org.

SMITH, STEVONNE LATRALL (STEVE SMITH), professional football player; b. LA, May 12, 1979; Attended, U. Utah. Wide receiver Carolina Panthers, 2001—. Active Athletes United for Youth. Named First Team All-Pro, AP, 2001, 2005, NFL Comeback Player of Yr., 2005; named to Nat. Football Conf. Pro Bowl Team, NFL, 2001, 2005, 2006, 2008. Achievements include leading the NFL in: non-offensive/punt return touchdowns, yards per touch, 2001; punt returns, 2002; receptions, receiving yards, receiving touchdowns, 2005. Office: Carolina Panthers 800 So Mint St Charlotte NC 28202*

SMITH, STUART LEWIS, community volunteer; b. Richmond, Va., Mar. 28, 1936; d. John Minor Botts Lewis Jr. and Elise Davis Deyerle; m. Isaac Noyes Smith IV, Apr. 30, 1960; children: Isaac Noyes V, Minor Botts, Lyle Davis, Lisa Lewis. BA in Sociology, Hollins Coll., 1958. Home svc. caseworker ARC, Richmond, 1958—60; kindergarten tchr. First Presbyn. Ch. Sch., Charleston, W.Va., 1960—61; W.Va. sales assoc. Stanmar Homes, Sudbury, Mass., 1974—81; sales assoc., clothes cons. The Worth Collection, Charleston, 1992—2002. Mem. devel. com. Hollins Coll., Roanoke, Va., 1985—88; mem. legis. adv. com. Charleston Meml. Hosp., 1975—76; mem. budget and adv. coms. United Way, Charleston, 1965—77, resdl. chair, trustee, 1977—92; mem. legis. adv. com. Cmty. Coun., Children's Svcs., Charleston, 1985—92; master gardener vol. pks. and hosp. planting Wonderful W.Va. Mag.; chairperson cmty. opportunity for study book and author series U. Charleston; contbr., local documentor Smithsonian Archive Am. Gardens; pks. commr., chair long range planning com. Kanawha County Pks. Sys., 1986—; mem. steering com. Kanawha County Cares for Youth, 2004—07; charter mem. Nat. Mus. Women in Arts; mem. collectors club Avanpata Mus.; mem. com. YWCA High Hopes, 2004—07; elder Kanawha United Presbyn. Ch., Charleston, 1968; past pres., bd. dirs. U. Charleston Builders, 1973, Kanawha Garden Club, Charleston, 1973, Briar Hills Garden Club, Charleston, 1969; bd. dirs. Sunrise Mus., 1973—80. Recipient award, W.Va. State Garden Club, 1985, 20 Yrs. of Bd. Svc. award, Ronald McDonald Ho., 2002. Mem.: Robert E. Lee Meml. Assn. (W.Va. dir., sec. to bd. 1975, v.p. 2005—), Garden Club Am. (nat. vice-chair scholarship com. 1990, Outstanding Cmty. Leadership award 2000). Avocations: tennis, travel, gardening, fishing, reading. Home: 153 Abney Cir Charleston WV 25314

SMITH, STUART LYON, psychiatrist, corporate financial executive; b. Montreal, Que., Can., May 7, 1938; s. Moe Samuel and Nettie (Krainer) S.; m. Patricia Ann Springate, Jan. 2, 1964; children: Tanya, Craig. BSc, McGill U., 1958, MD, CM, 1962, diploma in psychiatry, 1967; LLD (hon.), Mt. Allison U., 1992, Royal Rds. U., 2000; B.Ap.Sc. (hon.), Humber Coll., 2005. Intern. Montreal Gen. Hosp., 1962-63, resident in psychiatry, 1963-67; from asst. prof. to assoc. prof. medicine McMaster U., Hamilton, Ont., Canada, 1967-75; leader Ont. Liberal Party Ont. Legislature, 1976-82, leader of the opposition, 1977-82; chmn. Sci. Coun. Can., Ottawa, 1982-87; pres. RockCliffe Rsch. and

Tech., Inc., 1987—, Philip Utilities Mgmt. Corp., Toronto, Ont., 1994-97. Chmn. com. inquiry Can. U. Edn., 1989—91; chmn. Ensyn Tech. Inc., 1990—; sr. adv. ICF Cons., 2002; chmn. Nat. Round Table on Environment and Economy, Ottawa, 1995—2002; chmn. bd. dirs. Humber Coll., 2002—04, Esna Tech., Inc., 2004—. Decorated knight Nat. Order of Merit (France); McLaughlin travel fellow, 1964-65. Fellow Royal Coll. Physicians and Surgeons of Can. Personal E-mail: smithstuart@rogers.com.

SMITH, SUE FRANCES, newspaper editor; b. Lockhart, Tex., July 4, 1940; d. Monroe John Baylor and Myrtle (Krause) Mueck; m. Michael Vogtel Smith, Apr. 20, 1963 (div. July 1977); 1 child, Jordan Meredith; m. Kirkland Gideon Smith, Apr. 17, 1999. B of Journalism, U. Tex., 1962. Feature writer, photographer Corpus Christi Caller Times, 1962-64; feature writer, editor Chgo. Tribune, 1964-76; features editor Dallas Times Herald, 1976-82; sales assoc. Bumpas Assocs., Dallas, 1982-83; asst. mng. editor for features Denver Post, 1983-84, assoc. editor, 1984-91; asst. mng. editor in charge of Sunday paper Dallas Morning News, 1991-94, asst. mng. editor Lifestyles, 1994-96, dep. mng. editor Lifestyles, 1996—2001, dep. mng. editor recruiting/devel., 2001—07. Active Coun. Pres., 1993; juror Pulitzer Prize, 2002, 03. Mem. Am. Assn. Sunday and Feature Editors (pres. 1993), Newspaper Features Coun. (pres. 2002), Tex. AP Mng. Editors (pres. 1999-00, Jack Douglas award disting. svc. 2005, adv. bd. conf. 2005, 06), Delta Gamma, Mayborn Literacy Nonfiction Writers Conf., 2005, 06. Home: 6241 Park Meadow Ln Plano TX 75093-8863 Office: 508 Young St Dallas TX 75202-4893 E-mail: ssmith@dallasnews.com.

SMITH, SURVILLA MARIE, social services administrator, artist, poet; b. Chattanooga, Oct. 17, 1933; d. Charlie and LeGusta (Robinson) Prater; children: Charles, Calvin, Robin. Student, Mass. Bay C.C., Boston, 1965—66; student in English Lit., Northeastern U., 1967—73; student, Mus. Sch. Fine Arts, 1989—91, U. Mass., 1989—96, Simmons Grad. Sch. Mgmt., 1995—97. Exec. sec. The Ecumenical Ctr., Roxbury, Mass., 1965-67, Roxbury Fedn. of Neighborhoods, 1965-68; bus. mgr. Coun. of Elders, Inc., Boston, 1969-72; exec. sec., asst. bookkeeper Edn. Renewal, Inc., Boston, 1972-73; asst. dir. METCO Inter-Dist. Transfer Inc., Roxbury, 1973-75; pupil pers. coord. Met. Coun. for Ednl. Opportunity, Roxbury, 1975-78; with Vis. Nurse Assn. of Boston, 1978-79; sec. Bay State Banner Newspaper, Roxbury, 1980; sr. outreach coord. Mattahunt Community Sch Sr. Outreach, Mattapan, Mass., 1989-95. Founder, chmn., CEO Studio for the Promotion of Arts, Culture, and Excellence, An Artistic Comty., Inc.; founder., chmn., CEO LED, 1995—. Steppin Out, Boston, 1993, Treasured Legacy Gallery, 1995, Dorchester Hist. Soc., 1996, 1997, 1998, Dorchester Art Assn., Boston, 1996, 1997, 1998, New Art N.Eng. Libr. Arts Ctr., Newport, N.H., 1997, Urban League Ea. Mass., Roxbury, 1997—98, Open Studios, South End, Mass., 1998, Roxbury Cmty. Coll. Media Arts Ctr., 1998, Reggie Lewis Ctr., Roxbury, 1998, Rothschild Gallery, Radcliffe Coll., Cambridge, Mass., 1998, Boston City Hall Scollay Sq. Gallery, Boston, 1998, 1999, 2000, Pan African Historical Mus., Springfield, Mass., 1999, Macy's Windows, 1999, 2000, Grove Hall Br. Libr., Roxbury, 2000, Egleston Br. Libr., Mass., 2000, Parker Hill Br. Libr., Roxbury, 2000, South End Open Studios, Mass., 2000, CVS Windows-The Mall at Grove Hall, Roxbury, 2002, CVS Window Porter Sq., Cambridge, 2002—09, Codman Sq. Br. Libr., Dorchester, Mass., 2003—, Boston Bus. Assistance Ctr., Roxbury, Mass., 2005—, North River Cmty. Ch., 2006—08; author: (poetry book) Days, Years to Remember: A Collection of Poems, 2003; Represented in permanent collections N.Eng. Zoo, pvt. collections, artwork published, Art New Eng., Art News, ArtsMedia, Art & Antiques. Active Women's Caucus Art, Boston chpt., Coalition of 100 Black Women, Nat. Coun. Negro Women; chmn. health campaign Grove Hall/Franklin Park AARP, Boston, 1990—; vol. Experiment in Internat. Living, Mass., Mattapan/Franklin Park Jubilee Task Force, WGBH, Am. Cancer Soc.; artwork auction donor various orgns. Recipient award, Nat. Mus. Women Arts, Washington; grantee, New Eng. Found. for the Arts; scholar, U. Mass., Amherst, 1999; Americans for the Arts scholar, 1999. Mem.: PEN N.E., NAACP, Acad. Am. Poets, Nat. Coun. of Negro Women, Greater Boston Chapt., Boston Afro-Am. Artists, Nat. Poetry Soc., South End Artists, Mass. Advocates for the Arts, Scis. & Humanities, Dorchester Art Assn., Am. for the Arts, Nat. Writer's Assn., Poetry Soc. Am. Democrat. Roman Catholic. Avocations: writing, painting, reading, bowling, jazz. Home: 4 Wentworth St Dorchester MA 02124-3517 Office Fax: 617-436-3808. Personal E-mail: someouo@verizon.net. Business E-Mail: 1space@verizon.net.

SMITH, SUSAN, bank executive; b. 1961; married; 2 children. Exec. Boatmen's Ark. Bank (now Regions Bank); sr. exec. v.p., COO Met. Nat. Bank. Chmn. Ark. Commitment Scholarship Program. Named one of 25 Most Powerful Women in Banking, Fortune Mag., 2004, 25 Women to Watch, US Banking, 2007. Office: Metropolitan National Bank 425 W Capitol Little Rock AR 72201 Office Phone: 501-377-7600. Office Fax: 501-377-7608.

SMITH (CAVANAGH), SUSAN CARLTON, artist, illustrator, sculptor; b. Athens, Ga., June 30, 1923; d. Edward Inglis and Hart Wylie Smith; m. George Stanley Terence Cavanagh, Oct. 25, 1977. BS in Zoology, U. Ga., 1947, MFA in Drama, 1961. Sci. illustrator US Pub. Health Communicable Disease Ctr., Atlanta, 1952; artist archeology dept. U. Ga., 1953—, costume designer, speech tchr., drama dept, 1956—61, sci. illustrator biology dept., 1964—65; conservator, asst. curator Med. Ctr. Libr., Duke U., Durham, NC, 1967—90; biological and botanical illustrator Duke U., 1967—90; botanical illustrator U. NC, 1967—90. Lectr. in field. Illustrator Jack & Jill Magazine, 1960—62, (book) Plant Variations and Classification, 1967, Wildflowers of NC, 1968, A Child's Book of Flowers, 1976, A Book of Flowers, 1987, illustrator, text contr. (book) Lady Bug, Lady Bug, 1969 (Top 50 Best Children's Books of Yr., 1969), (Book) Hey Bug!, and Other Poems About Little Things, 1972 (Printers Industries of Am. award), author, illustrator 3 Famous Artists-Naturalists of the Colonial Period, John Abbot, William Bartram, Mark Catesby- A Coloring Book for all Ages, 2002; contbr. to profl. jours.jours.; exhibitions include eleventh Internat. Botanical Congress, Seattle, 1969, Internat. Exhbn. Botanical Art, Johannesburg, South Africa, Second Internat. Exhbn. Twentieth Cent. Botanical Art and Illustration, Carnegie-Mellon U., 1968—69, Duke U. Mus. Art, U. Ga. Mus. Art, Represented in permanent collections Nature Sculptures and Watercolor Miniatures, State Botanical Garden, Ga. Vol. U. NC Botanical Gardens, 1967—89, State Botanical Gardens, Ga., 1989—. Mem.: Trent Soc. History of Med., Duke U., Am. Assn. History of Med., Nat. Soc. Colonial Dames, Jr. Ladies Garden Club, Garden Club Am. (Eloise Payne Lequer medal 1989), Puppeteers of Am., Chi Omega, Phi Kappa Phi. Episcopalian. Avocation: sculpting. Home: 755 Epps Bridge Pkwy #404 Athens GA 30606 Personal E-mail: cavanaghs@bellsouth.net.

SMITH, T. DEWITT, JR., religious organization administrator; b. Chgo. s. T. DeWitt and Ernestine Smith; m. Aretta A. Amith; children: Darin, Derrick, Tonya, Tamara. BA, Judson Coll., Elgin, Ill.; MDiv, Ashland Theol. Sem., Ohio; D in Ministry, Ashland Theol. Sem. Pastor New Hope Bapt. Ch., Akron, Ohio, Prog. Bapt. Ch., Elgin, West Hunter St. Bapt. Ch., Atlanta, 1992—2003; sr. pastor Trinity Bapt. Ch., Atlanta, 2003—; instr. Congress Christian Edn. Prog. Nat. Bapt. Conv., Inc., chmn. bd. edn. and pub., dean Congress Christian Edn., 2nd v.p. of parent body, 1st v.p., pres., 2006—. Mem. World Coun. Chs., mem. decade to overcome violence com.; mem. Bapt. World Alliance, Exec. Com. of Bapt. Joint Com.; bd. mem. Morehouse Sch. Religion of Interdenominational Theol. Ctr.; chair constitutional ministry New Era Missionary Bapt. State Conv. Ga., Inc.; moderator Atlanta ecumenical planning com. World Coun. Chs. US Conf. Decade to Overcome Violence, 2004; pres. Ohio Prog. State Conv. Author: Deacons In The Black Baptist Church, Putting Laypeople To Work, Membership Orientation Handbook, New Testament Deacons In African-American Churches, Training Trustees For Baptist Churches, Deaconess On Duty, Spiritual Gifts For Godly People. Named to Martin Luther King, Jr. Morehouse Coll. Bd. Disting. Preachers, Power 150, Ebony mag., 2008. Office: Prog Nat Bapt Conv Inc 601 50th St NE Washington DC 20019

SMITH, TEFFT WELDON, lawyer; b. Evanston, Ill., Nov. 18, 1946; s. Edward W. and Margery T. (Weldon) S.; m. Nancy Jo Smith, Feb. 25, 1967; children: Lara Andrea, Tefft Weldon II. BA, Brown U., 1968; JD, U. Chgo., 1971. Bar: Ill. 1971, D.C. 2000, U.S. Supreme Ct. 1977. Sr. litigation ptnr. Kirkland & Ellis LLP, Chgo., 1971—, chair, competition and antitrust practice group. Mem. adv. bd. Bur. Nat. Affairs Antitrust and Trade Regulation Reporter; instr. trial advocacy. Contbr. numerous articles on trial practice and antitrust issues to law jours. Mem. ABA (litigation sect., antitrust law sect.), Econ. Club., Univ. Club, Mid-Am. Club, Sea Pines Country Club (Hilton Head, S.C.). Avocations: squash, ferraris, sculpture. Office: 655 15th St NW Washington DC 20005-5701 also: Kirkland & Ellis 200 E Randolph St Fl 54 Chicago IL 60601-6636 Home: 700 New Hampshire Ave NW Washington DC 20037 Office Phone: 202-879-5212. Business E-Mail: tsmith@kirkland.com.

SMITH, TERRI C., accountant, educator; d. James D. and Aud S. Blunt; m. Eddie A. Smith, June 29, 1991. BSBA, SE Mo. State U., Cape Girardeau, 1990; MBA, Ark. State U., Jonesboro, 1994. Cert. specialist Ark. State U., 2001. Staff acct. UARCO, Inc., Kennett, Mo., 1990—92; contr. Twin Rivers Regional Med. Ctr., Kennett, 1992—95; chief acctg. asst. Vis. Nurse Assn. SE Mo., Kennett, 1995—98; instr. info. sys. and acctg. Three Rivers CC, Poplar Bluff, Mo., 1998—. Bd. dirs. Mo. Assn. Acctg. Educators, 2007—. Mem.: Phi Beta Lambda, Alpha Kappa Psi. Office: Three Rivers CC 2080 Three Rivers Blvd Poplar Bluff MO 63901 Office Fax: 573-840-9796. Business E-Mail: tsmith@trcc.edu.

SMITH, THELMA CHERYL, principal, minister; d. Junius Edmund and Mildred Celestine Cromartie; m. Pierce Alexander Smith, Apr. 6, 1974; children: Cheri Nicole, Dawn Alexandra, Pierce Alexander II. BS in Premedicine, U. Dayton, Ohio, 1975; MS in Ednl. Leadership, Hood Coll., Frederick, Md., 1996. Cert. adminstrn. and supervision 1995. Sci. tchr. Seneca Valley H.S., Germantown, Md., 1983—95; resource tchr. Roberto Clemente, Germantown, 1995; asst. prin. Dr. M.L. King Middle Sch., Germantown, 1995—98, N.W. H.S., Germantown, 1998—2000; prin. Gaithersburg Middle Sch., Md., 2000—05, Coastal Christian Acad., 2006—. Assoc. pastor New Life Bapt. Ch., Gaithersburg, 2000—05. Mem.: Nat. Assn. Secondary Sch. Prins. Home: 3041 Egyptian Ln Virginia Beach VA 23456

SMITH, THEODORE GLENN, technology educator, researcher; b. Willowbrook, Calif., Oct. 19, 1957; s. Thomas Eugene and Marilyn Glenna Smith; m. Kathleen Ione, May 27, 1978; children: Melissa Lauren, Melanie Kelly. AAS in Electronic Engring., Clark County CC, North Las Vegas, Nev., 1984; BBA magna cum laude, Nat. U., San Diego, 1987; MEd, U. Nev., Las Vegas, 2001; postgrad., Capella, Mpls. Lic. educator Nev., Tex. Electronic technician E.G.& G. Inc. Nev. Test Site, Mercury, 1978—90; tech. instr. Garside Jr. High Sch., Las Vegas, 1992—99; bus., acctg. instr. Clark High Sch., Las Vegas, 1999—2001; computer instr. Bob Miller Mid. Sch., Las Vegas, 2001—02; cons., tutor Nev. Edn. Cons., Las Vegas, 2002—03; online facilitator Clark County Team Acad., Las Vegas, 2003—06; ednl. technologist Trinity Charter Sch., 2006—. Mem. Internat. Surfing Mus., Huntington Beach, Calif., 1972—, Friends of Sea Otter, Monterrey, Calif., 1995—. Mem.: Tex. Computer Educator's Assn., Internat. Soc. Tech. Edn. (cons. 2001—), Tex. State Hist. Assn., Alpha Kappa Phi. Republican. Home: 1702 Earl Of Dunmore Ln Katy TX 77449-3027

SMITH, THERESA JOANNE, research scientist, educator; b. Corona, NY, Aug. 22, 1959; d. Felix Adolph and Norma Alberta Smith. BA, CUNY, Flushing, NY, 1982; MS, Tex. Woman's U., Denton, Tex., 1984, PhD, 1988. Lic. practical nurse, NY, 1978. Postdoctoral rsch. assoc. Rutgers, The State U. N.J., Piscataway, 1988—92, rsch. assoc., 1992—96, rsch. asst. prof., 1996—99; asst. prof. U. S.C., Columbia, 1999—2005, assoc. prof., 2005—. Cons. NIH, Ctr. for Sci. Rev., Bethesda, Md., 2001—. Contbr. chapters to books, articles to profl. jours. Named Rschr. of Yr., Coll. Pharmacy, U. S.C., 2002; grantee, Am. Cancer Soc., 1998—2002, NIH, 2002—, 2003—06. Mem.: AAAS, Women in Cancer Rsch., S.C. Alliance for Cancer Chemoprevention, Soc. for Nutrition Edn., Am. Assn. for Cancer Rsch. Democrat. Roman Catholic. Avocations: gardening, travel, fishing. Office: University of South Carolina College of Pharmacy 700 Sumter St Columbia SC 29208 Office Fax: 803-777-8356. Personal E-mail: tjsmith822@aol.com. Business E-Mail: smithtj@cop.sc.edu.

SMITH, THOMAS F., immunologist; b. July 14, 1949; s. Oney Percy and Evelyn Fugate Smith; m. Jane S. Snoddy, May 24, 1975; children: Thomas Bryan, Amanda Catherine, Christopher Evan. BA, U. Va., Charlottesville, 1971, MD, 1974. Diplomate Am. Bd. Pediat., Sub-Bd. Pediatric Pulmonology, 1975, Nat. Bd. Med. Examiners, 1975, Am. Bd. Pediat., 1979, Am. Bd. Allergy & Immunology, 1979, Am. Bd. Med. Lab. Immunology, 1983, Amer Bd. Allergy & Immunology, Diagnostic Lab. Immunology, 1990. Intern and resident in pediat. Vanderbilt U. Hosp., Nashville, 1974—77; fellow in pediatric allergy & clin. immunology Nat. Jewish Hosp. & Rsch. Ctr., Denver, 1977—80; instr. pediat. U. Colo. Sch. Medicine, Denver, 1979; assoc. prof. pediat., asst. prof. medicine, asst. prof. microbiology & immunology Emory U. Sch. Medicine, Atlanta, 1980—93, dir. allergy & immunology tng. program, 1986—93; prof. pediat. Wash. U. Sch. Medicine, St. Louis, 1993—98; chief allergy sect. Austin Diagnostic Clinic, Tex., 1998—. Ctrl. region bd. mem. Am. Lung Assn. Tex. Mem. editl. bd. Jour. Allergy and Immunology, 1997—2002; contbr. 67 articles to profl. jours. With Boy Scouts Am., 1967—2007. Recipient Hal M. Davidson Meml. award, Southeastern Allergy Assn., 1982, Cross & Flame award, United Meth. Ch., 1986, Scoutmaster's Merit award, Boy Scouts Am., 1988, Dist. Merit award, 1989; named Tex. Super Dr., Key Profl. Media, Inc., 2005—08; named one of Best Doctors in Am., Best Doctors, Inc., 1992—2008; grantee Rsch. grants, NIH, 1983—89, 1991—98. Mem.: Am. Acad. Pediat., Joint Coun. Allergy, Asthma and Immunology, Am. Coll. Allerg, Asthma and Immunology, Am. Acad. Allergy, Asthma and Immunology, Tex. Allergy and Immunology Soc., Tex. Med. Assn., Sigma Xi, Alpha Phi Omega, Phi Beta Kappa. Episcopalian. Avocations: photography, art, camping, hiking, reading.

SMITH, TIMOTHY W., musician, educator; b. Louisville, Feb. 3, 1969; s. Glendol Lewis and Linda Kay Smith. B Music Edn., Murray State U., 1995; MusM, U. of Cinn. Coll. Conservatory of Music, 2003. Cert. State of Ohio Dept. of Edn. Tchg. Cert. 2001, State of Ky. Dept. of Edn. Tchg. Cert. 1995. Music tchr./band dir. Calloway County Schs., Murray, 1995—2001; instrumental music tchr. Princeton City Schs., Cin., 2001—. Recipient Mid. Sch. Music Educator of The Yr., First Dist. Ky. Music Educators Assn., 2000—01. Mem.: NEA, Ohio Music Edn. Assn., Ky. Music Educators Assn., Music Educators Nat. Conf., Internat. Assn. of Jazz Educators, Internat. Trumpet Guild, Phi Mu Alpha Sinfonia. Avocation: music, travel, golf, fishing. Office: 11080 Chester Rd Cincinnati OH 45246

SMITH, TODD D., museum director; BA, Duke U.; MA, Ind. U. With Dayton Art Inst., Ohio, Mint Mus., Charlotte, NC; pres., CEO Plains Art Mus., Fargo, ND; dir. Knoxville Mus. Art, Tenn., 2002—06, Gibbs Mus. Art, Charleston, 2006—. Office: Gibbes Mus Art 135 Meeting St Charleston SC 29401 Office Phone: 843-722-2706. Office Fax: 843-720-1682. E-mail: tsmith@gibbesmuseum.org.

SMITH, TODD MALCOLM, political consultant; b. Hallettsville, Tex., Aug. 7, 1961; s. Jerome Malcolm and Mary Eugenia (Devall) S. BS in Criminal Justice, S.W. Tex. State U., 1983; postgrad. in Criminal Justice Adminstrn., Sam Houston State U.; cert., Fed. Law Enforce. Tng. Acad., 1987. Juvenile probation officer 25th Jud. Dist. Tex., 1983-84; field coord. Mac Sweeney for Congress, Victoria, Tex., 1984; dist. coord. U.S. Congress-14th Congl. Dist. Tex., 1984-85; chief dep. sheriff Lavaca County Sheriff's Dept. Tex., 1985-88; dir. ops. Clayton Williams for Gov. Com., Austin, Tex., 1988-90; pres. Property Valuation Advisors, San Marcos, Tex., 1991-93; gen. ptnr. Wm. A. Tryon and Todd M. Smith Polit. Cons. Group, Austin, 1991-93; prin. Todd Smith & Assoc., Inc., Austin, 1993—; gen. ptnr. Impact Tex. LLC, 2003—. Coord. Lavaca County Crime Stoppers, Hallettsville, 1985-88; apptd. by Tex. Gov. to Tex. Crime Stoppers Commn. Regulatory Agy., 1986-90; mem., appointee Golden Crescent Regional Planning Commn., Victoria, 1986-88; exec. v.p. E-Comm. Advantage, Inc., Austin, 2000-2004; pres. Demografx, Inc., Austin, 2000-2004; ptr. Impact Tex. Comm., 2004-, Impact US, 2005-. Rep. senatorial dist. 18 State Rep. Exec. Com., 1992-94. 2d lt. Tex. State N.G., 1990-92. Recipient Outstanding Svc. award Tex. Crime Stoppers Adv. Coun., 1990, Outstanding Coord. award Lavaca County Crime Stoppers, 1988. Mem. Am. Assn. Polit. Cons., Masons, Descendents Confederance Veterans (bd. dirs., 2008-), Military Order of Stars & Bars, Shriners, 32° Scottish Rite Mason. Republican. Episcopalian. Avocation: politics. Home: 2204 Hazeltine Ln Austin TX 78723

SMITH, TRACEY, real estate broker; b. Ft. Worth, June 23, 1948; married; 4 stepchildren. BA in Economics, U. Tex. Austin, 1970; MA in Journalism, Ohio State U., 1974. Journalist KDFW-TV, 1978—80; comml. real estate broker, 1984—. Precinct chmn. Dem. Party. Democrat. Office: 1100 Miller Ave Fort Worth TX 76105*

SMITH, TRINA, academic administrator; b. Rogersville, Ala., Sept. 18, 1971; d. Will Buford and Margaret Cannon Smith. BS, Athens State U., 1993; MS, U. Ala., Huntsville, 2000; M of Accountancy, U. Ala., 2001. Cert. Notary Pub. Br. ops. supr. Union Planters Bank, Athens, Ala., 1994—2000; acct. Calhoun Coll., Decatur, Ala., 2000—. Dir. Habitat for Humanity, Athens, 1994—2000; mem. adv. bd. Dogwood Festival Com., Athens, 1999. Vol. Jr. Achievement, Decatur, Ala., 1997—2000, Care Assurance Sys. for Aging and Homebound, Athens, 1995—99, Found. of Aging, Athens, 1999—2008. Recipient Outstanding Support award, Habitat for Humanity, 1996. Mem.: NAFE, NAACP, Am. Inst. of Cert. Pub. Accts., Nat. Assn. Black Accts., Am. Acctg. Assn., Am. Soc. Women Accts., Nat. Notary Assn., Inst. Mgmt. Accts. Baptist. Avocations: gardening, photography, collecting antiques, investments, outdoor activities. Home: 13708 Dart Cir Athens AL 35611 Office: Calhoun Cmty Coll Hwy 31 S Decatur AL 35609 Personal E-mail: TSmith3671@aol.com.

SMITH, TROY, professional football player; b. Cleve., July 20, 1984; s. Tracy Smith and Kenneth Delaney. BA in Comm., Ohio State U., 2006. Quarterback Balt. Ravens, 2007—. Recipient Davey O'Brien award, Davey O'Brien Found., 2006, Walter Camp Player Yr. award, Walter Camp Football Found., 2006, Heisman Meml. Trophy, Heisman Trophy Trust, 2006; named First Team All-American, AP, 2006, Fiesta Bowl MVP, 2006, Big Ten Player Yr., 2006; named to All Big-Ten Conference, 2005—06. Office: Balt Ravens 1 Winning Dr Owings Mills MD 21117

SMITH, TROY ALVIN, aerospace research engineer; b. Sylvatus, Va., July 4, 1922; s. Wade Hampton and Augusta Mabel (Lindsey) S.; m. Grace Marie (Peacock) Dees, Nov. 24, 1990. BCE, U. Va., 1948; MS in Engring., U. Mich., 1952, PhD, 1970. Registered profl. engr., Va., Ala. Structural engr. U.S. Army C.E., Norfolk, Va., Wilmington, NC, Washington, 1948-59; chief structural engr. Brown Engring. Co., Inc., Huntsville, Ala., 1959-60; structural rsch. engr. U.S. Army Missile Command, Redstone Arsenal, Ala., 1960-63, aerospace engr., 1963-80, aerospace rsch. engr., 1980-96; engr. emeritus U.S. Army Aviation and Missile Command, Redstone Arsenal, Ala., 1996—2003, U.S. Army Rsch., Devel., and Engring. Command, Aviation and Missile Rsch., Devel., and Engring. Ctr., Redstone Arsenal, Ala., 2003—. Contbr. articles to profl. jours.; author: 18 major U.S. Army tech. reports on analysis of shells and other structures. With USNR, 1942-46, PTO. Recipient award, Leading Engrs. World, 2006, Lifetime Achievement award, 2008, Disting. Svc. Engring. award, 2008; Fellow, Dept. Army, 1969. Mem. NY Acad. Scis., Assn. US Army, Elks, Sigma Xi. Achievements include research in procedures for analysis of structures. Avocations: ballroom dancing, bowling, travel, classic automobiles. Home: 2202 Yorkshire SE Decatur AL 35601-3470

SMITH, TUBBY, men's college basketball coach; b. Scotland, Md., June 30, 1951; s. Guffrie & Parthenia Smith; m. Donna Smith; children: Orlando, Shannon, Saul, Brian. BS in Health & Phys. Edn., High Point Coll., 1973; HD (hon.), U. Ky., Lexington, 2008. Head basketball coach Gt. Mills (Md.) H.S., 1973-77; head coach Hoke County H.S., Raeford, 1977-79; asst. coach Va. Commonwealth U., 1979-86, U. S.C., 1986-89, Ky. U., 1989-91; head coach U. Tulsa, 1991-95, U. Ga., Athens, 1995-97, U. Ky., Lexington, 1997—2007, U. Minn., Mpls., 2007—. Asst. basketball coach US Men's Nat. Basketball Team, 1999; head coach US Olympic Basketball Team, Sydney, 2000; bd. dirs. Nat. Assn. Basketball Coaches. Founder The Tubby Smith Found., 1987—. Recipient Henry Iba award, 2003; named Jim Phelan Coach of Yr., 2005, Naismith Coll. Coach of Yr., 2003. Coached the U. Ky. to five Southeastern Conf. Titles, 1998-2001, 2003-2004 & 1 NCAA Men's Divsn. I Basketball Championship, 1998. Office: U Minn 205 BFAB 516 15th Ave SE Minneapolis MN 55455

SMITH, V. KERRY, economics professor; b. Jersey City, Mar. 11, 1945; s. Vincent C. and Dorothy E. S.; m. Pauline Anne Taylor, May 10, 1969; children: Timothy, Shelley. AB, Rutgers U., 1966, PhD, 1970.

Asst. prof. Bowling Green State U., Ohio, 1969—72; rsch. assoc. Resources for Future, Washington, 1971-73; assoc. prof. SUNY, Binghamton, 1973-75, prof., 1975-78; sr. fellow Resources for Future, Washington, 1976-79; prof. U. NC, Chapel Hill, 1979-83; Centennial prof. Vanderbilt U., Nashville, 1983-87; univ. disting. prof. NC State U., 1987-94, univ. disting. prof., dir. Ctr. Environ. and Resource Econ. Policy, 1999—; Arts and Scis. prof. environ. econs. Duke U., 1994-99; W.P. Carey prof. econs. Ariz. State U., Tempe, 2006—; rsch. assoc. Nat. Bureau Econ. Rsch., 2007—. Adviser energy div. Oak Ridge Nat. Lab., 1978-80, U. NC Inst. Environ. Studies, 1980-83; mem. panel NSF, 1981-83, sci. adv. bd. EPA. Author: Monte Carlo Methods, 1973, Technical Change, Relative Prices and Environmental Resource Evaluation, 1974, The Costs of Congestion: An Econometric Analysis of Wilderness Recreation, 1976, Structure and Properties of a Wilderness Travel Simulator: An Application to the Spanish Peaks Area, 1976, The Economic Consequences of Air Pollution, 1976, Scarcity and Growth Reconsidered, 1979, (with others) Explorations in Natural Resource Economics, 1982, (with others) Environmental Policy Under Reagan's Executive Order, 1984, (with W.H. Desvousges) Measuring Water Quality Benefits, 1986, (with others) Environmental Resources and Applied Welfare Economics, 1988, (with R.J. Kopp) Valuing Natural Assets: The Economics of Natural Resource Damage Assessment, Resources for the Future, 1993, Estimating Economic Values for Nature, 1996, (with others) The Smoking Puzzle: Information, Perception and Choices, 2003; editor Advances in Applied Micro Econs. series; contbr. numerous articles to profl. jours. Guggenheim fellow, 1976; grantee Resources for Future, 1970, 73, 74, 86, Fed. Energy Adminstrn. 1975, NY Sea Grant Inst., 1975, Ford Found., 1976, NSF, 1977, 79, 83, Electric Power Rsch. Inst., 1978, Nat. Oceanic and Atmospheric Adminstrn., 1980, Sloan Found., 1981, 86, EPA, 1983-88, NC Sea Grant Program, 1987-93. Russell Sage Found., 1989-91; recipient Frederick V. Waugh medal Am. Agrl. Econ. Assn., 1992. Fellow Am. Agrl. and Econ. Assn., Assn. Environ. and Resource Economists (bd. dirs. 1975-79, v.p. 1979-80, chmn. com. 1982-83, pres. 1985-86, Disting. Svc. award 1989); mem. NAS, Am. Econ. Assn., Econometric Soc., So. Econ. Assn. (exec. com. 1981-83, 1st v.p. 1987, pres.-elect 1988, pres. 1989). Office: Ariz State U PO Box 873806 Tempe AZ 85287-3806 Home: PO Box 7437 Cave Creek AZ 85327

SMITH, VALENE LUCY, anthropologist, educator; b. Spokane, Wash., Feb. 14, 1926; d. Ernest Frank and Lucy (Blachly) S.; m. Edwin Chesteen Golay, June 7, 1970 (dec. June 1980); m. Stanley George McIntyre, Nov. 26, 1983 (dec. Oct. 2000); m. George Addison Posey, Oct. 5, 2005 (dec. May 2009). BA in Geography, U. Calif., 1946, MA in Geography, 1950; PhD in Anthropology, U. Utah, Salt Lake City, 1966. Cert. travel counselor. Prof. earth sci. LA City Coll., 1947-67; prof. anthropology Calif. State U., Chico, 1967—. Cons. World Tourism Orgn., Madrid, 1987. Editor: Hosts and Guests: The Anthrop, 1989, Tourism Alternatives: Potentials and Problems in the Development of Tourism, 1992, Hosts and Guests Revisited, 2001. Mem. Soroptimist Internat., Chico, 1968—; founding pres. Chico Mus. Assn., 1978. Recipient Athena award, US C. of C., 1988; named Fulbright prof., Peshawar, Pakistan, 1953—54. Mem. Internat. Acad. for Study Tourism, Cert. Travel Counselors, Am. Anthrop. Assn., AAUW, Soroptimists. Republican. Avocations: travel, aviation, photography. Office: U Calif Dept Anthropology Chico CA 95929-0004 Office Phone: 530-891-1155. Business E-Mail: vsmith@csuchico.edu.

SMITH, VERNON G., education educator, Indiana State Representative; b. Gary, Ind., Apr. 11, 1944; BS, Ind. U., 1966, MS, 1969, EdD, 1978; postgrad., Ind.U.-Purdue U., 1986-90. Tchr. Gary Cmty. Schs., 1966—72; resource tchr. Gary Pub. Schs. Systems, 1971-72; asst. prin. Ivanhoe Sch., Gary, 1972-78; mem. Gary City Coun., 1972—90; prin. Nobel Sch., Gary, 1978-85, Williams Sch., Gary, 1985—91; part-time counselor edn. div. Ind. U. N.W., Gary, 1967-69, adj. lectr., 1987-92, asst. prof., 1991—; mem. Dist. 14 Ind. House of Reps., Indpls., 1990—; assoc. prof. P. U. Northeast, 1992—2009; prof. edn., 2009. Columnist Gary Crusader, 1969-71; speaker Devel. Tng. Inst., 1986—. Author: (with D. McClam) Building Bridges Instead of Walls—History of I.U. Dons, Inc., 1979; also articles. Mem. Gary City Coun., 1972-90; precinct committeeman Gary Dem. Com., 1972-92; founder, chmn. Gary Citywide Festival Com.; bd. dirs. N.W. Ind. Urban League; founder, pres. I.U. Dons, Inc.; past pres. Gary Cmty. Mental Health Bd.; v.p. Gary Common Coun., 1982, 85-87, pres., 1976, 83-84, 88; past mem. bd. dirs. Little League World series; founder, past sponsor Youth Ensuring Solidarity, Young Citizens' League; chmn. Ind. Commn. on Status of Black Males, 1992—; mem. Gov.'s Commn. for Drug-Free Ind., 1990—. Recipient citation in edn. Gary NAACP, 1970, Good Govt. award Gary Jaycees, 1977, Outstanding Svc. award Gary Young Dems., 1979, Businessman of Yr. award Gary Downtown Mchts., 1979, Bd. Dirs. Svcs. award Gary Cmty. Health Ctr., 1982, G.O.I.C. Dr. Leon H. Sullivan award, 1982, Gary Jaycees Youth award, 1983, Info Newspaper Outstanding Citizen of N.W. Ind. and Info. Newspaper's Outstanding Educator award, 1984, Post Tribune Blaine Marz Tap award, 1984, Gary Cmty. Sch. Corp. Speech Dept. Recognition award, 1984, Gary Cmty. Mental Health Ctr.'s 10th Yr. Svc. award, 1985, Roosevelt H.S. Exemplary Svc. award, 1985, Gary Crusader 25th Anniversary award, 1986, Purdue U. Ednl. Opportunity Programs Black History Svc. award, 1986, Educator Par Excellence award Williams Sch., 1987, Black Woman Hall of Fame Found. Success award, 1987, Black Women Hall of Fame Bethune-Tubman-Truth award, 1987, Our Lady of Perpetual Help Ch. Hon. Mem. award, 1987, Gary Educator of Christ Adminstr. Leadership award, 1988, NBC-LEO Appreciation award, 1988, Gary Cmty. Schs. Presenters award, 1991, Mr. G.'s Svc. award, 1991, Appreciation award Ind. Assn. Chiefs Police, 1992, Meth. Hosp., 1992, Bros. Keeper, 1992, Svc. award Ind. Assn. Elem. and Mid. Sch. Prins., 1992, N.W. Ind. Black Expo's Sen. Carolyn Mosby Above and Beyond award, 1995, In the Bethune Tradition award Nat. Coun. Negro Women, 1996, Citizen Yr. award NASW (Ind. chpt.), 1997, 98, Appreciation award Ind. chpt., 1997, Presenters award, Gary Cmty. Sch. Corp. Parent Involvement Program, 1996, Appreciation award, Pitman Square Sch., 1997, 98, 99, Alumni Appreciation award, Froebel High Sch., 1997, 98, 2002, Svc. award, Ind. League Municipal Clerks and Treas., 1998, Facet Excellence in Tchg. award, 1998, Brothers Keeper Appreciation award, 1999, Appreciation award, Lake County Assn. for the Retarded, 1999, New Hope award, 1999, New Hope Men's Day award, 2000; featured cover story Big Brothers Big Sisters Am. Newsletter for Diversity, 2000, Appreciation award, Hoosier Boys Town, 2000, Appreciation award, Gary Reading Coun., 2000, Outstanding Commitment award, Nat. Assn. Social Workers Region I, 2000, Svc. award, Ivanhoe Sch., 2002, Drum Major award, Gary Frontiers, 2002, Majestic Star award, 2002, Appreciation award, City of Lake Station, 2002, New Hope African Am.-Frederic Douglas award, 2003, Chief's award, Lake Station, 2004, Ind. U. Welsh-Bowen award, 2005, E. Chgo. NAACP's Achievment award, 2006, Mental Health Am. Hoosie Idol award, 2007, George Pinnell Svc. award, 2008; numerous other awards. Mem.: NAACP (life Ovington award 1999), No. Ind. Assn. Black Sch. Educators (founder), Ind. Assn. Sch. Prins., Ind. U. N.W. Alumni Assn. (life Disting. Educator award 1992), Phi Delta Kappa (25 Yr. award (N.W. Ind. chpt.) 1996), Omega Psi Phi (life Omega Man Yr. award 1974, Citizen Yr. award 10th dist. 1989, appreciation award Omicron Rho chpt. 1991, Citizen Yr. award (Alpha Kappa Kappa chpt.) 2003, Man Yr. award (Alpha Kappa Kappa chpt.) 2003). Democrat. Baptist. Home: PO Box 64622 Gary IN 46401-0622 Office: Ind U NW 3400 Broadway # 339 Gary IN 46408-1101 also: Indiana House of Representatives 200 West Washington St Indianapolis IN 46204-2786 Office Phone: 219-980-7120, 317-232-9731, 317-232-9600, 800-382-9842 (toll free). Office Fax: 317-232-9597. Business E-Mail: vesmith@iun.edu, h14@in.gov.

SMITH, VERNON LOMAX, economist, educator; b. Wichita, Kans., Jan. 1, 1927; s. Vernon Chessman and Lula Belle (Lomax) S.; m. Candace C. Smith, Mar. 13, 2002. BSEE, Calif. Inst. Tech., 1949; MA in Econs., U. Kans., 1952; PhD in Econs., Harvard U., 1955; D of Mgmt. (hon.), Purdue U., 1990. Asst. prof. econs. Purdue U., West Lafayette, Ind., 1955-58, assoc. prof., 1958-61, prof., 1961-65, Krannert prof., 1965-67; prof. Brown U., Providence, 1967-68, U. Mass., Amherst, 1968-75, U. Ariz., Tucson, 1975—2001, Regents' prof., 1988—2001; prof. econs. & law George Mason U., 2001—07; prof. econs. & law, George L. Argyros Endowed chair fin. and econs. Chapman U., Orange, Calif., 2008—. Contbr. articles to profl. jours. Fellow Ctr. for Advanced Study in Behavioral Scis., Stanford, Calif., 1972-73; Sherman Fairchild Disting. Scholar Calif. Inst. Tech., Pasadena, 1973-74; adj. scholar CATO Inst., Washington, 1983—; recipient Nobel prize in econs., 2002. Fellow AAAS, Am. Acad. Arts and Scis., Econometric Soc., Am. Econ. Assn. (Disting. fellow); mem. NAS, Pvt. Enterprise Edn. Assn. (Adam Smith award). Office: Chapman U Econ Sci Inst One University Dr Orange CA 92866 Office Phone: 714-628-2830. Office Fax: 714-628-2881. E-mail: vsmith@chapman.edu.*

SMITH, VERONICA LATTA, real estate company officer; b. Wyandotte, Mich., Jan. 13, 1925; d. Jan August and Helena (Hulak) Latta; m. Stewart Gene Smith, Apr. 12, 1952; children: Stewart Gregory, Patrick Allen, Paul Donald, Alison Veronica Hurley, Alisa Margaret Lyons, Glenn Laurence. BA in Sociology, U. Mich., 1948. Tchr. Coral Gables (Fla.) Pub. Sch. Sys., 1949—50; COO Latta Ins. Agy, Wyandotte, 1950—62; treas. L & S Devel. Co., Grosse Ile, Mich., 1963—84; v.p. Regency Devel., Riverview, Mich., 1984—. Active U. Mich. Bd. Regents, 1985-92, regent emeritus, 1993—; mem. Martha Cook Bd. Govs., U. Mich., pres., 1976-78; del. Rep. County Conv., Grand Rapids, Mich., 1985, 87, 89, 91, 92, 94, 96, Lansing, Mich., 1996, Detroit, 1986, 88, 90, 92, 97; mem. pres. adv. com. Campaign for Mich., 1992-97, mem. campaign steering com., 1992-97. Mem. Mich. Lawyers Aux. (treas. 1975, chmn. 1976, 77, 78, 79), Nat. Assn. Ins. Women (cert.), Faculty Women's Club U. Mich. (hon.), Radrick Farms Golf Club (Ann Arbor), Pres.'s Club U. Mich., Investment Club (pres. 1976, sec. 1974-75, treas. 1975-76), Alpha Kappa Delta. Home: 22225 Balmoral Dr Grosse Ile MI 48138-1403

SMITH, VIN, editor, small business owner, writer; b. Whittier, Calif., May 19, 1944; s. M. Clifford and Anna Eugenia (Hill) S.; m. Marthea Karen Callaham, May 15, 1969 (div. 1979); children: Jayare Smith, Eric Smith; m. Ginger Hammon, Oct. 20, 1984; children: Amy Michelle, Stacey Erin, Kellie Rae. Student, Columbia Sch. Broadcasting, San Francisco, 1967; AA, Cuesta Coll., 1974; grad., Am. Sch. of Piano Tuning, 1978; DD, Ancient Order of the WA, 2004. Sales mgr. Sta. KTAT, Frederick, Okla., 1967-69; announcer KOCY, Oklahoma City, 1969; owner Melmart Markets, San Luis Obispo, Calif., 1971-73, Am. Direct Sales, Grover City, Calif., 1973-79; instr. piano Valley View Acad., Arroyo Grande, Calif., 1977-78, Long Piano Co., San Luis Obispo, 1977-79, piano technician, 1978-79; owner Chocolate Piano, Yreka, Calif., 1979—; instr. piano Makah Indian Tribe, Neah Bay, Wash., 1981-82; sports editor New Words Digest, Bakersfield, Calif., 1988—. Cons., stress evaluator seminar Yreka Stress Therapy Clinic, 1986-87; founder Vinco Distbrs. (formerly Vinco Enhancement Sys.), 1998; chair piano dept. Bogus Sch., 1999-2004, internat. relationship counselor Ask Me com., 2000-03, askdrpiano.com., 2000. Author: (novel) Neon Streets, 2002, Lincoln Park, 2003, Ride the High Waves, 2004, Lucky Pierre's, 2004, The Outrageous Views of Professor Fogelman, 2004, a.k.a. Mandi Wire, 2004, A Bullet for Slade, 2005, Get Mandi Wire, 2005, Jimamon and the Air Kids, 2005; sports columnist New Words Digest, 1987-91; guest columnist Siskiyou Daily News, 1991-94; nat publicist chamber music concerts So. Oreg. State Coll., 1993—; host (TV Show) Vin and Friends, 2003; host, prodr. (nat. broadcast CRN Digital Talk, syndicated on Nat. Radio Network) Vin Smith's Midnight Bookworm, 2005—; contbr. articles to profl. jours. Chmn. heart fund Tillman County Okla., 1968; pub. co-chmn. Siskiyou County No-Prop 174, 1994; campaign worker Ken Jourdan for sheriff, Yreka, 1986; publicity dir. Gene Breceda for supr., 1993-94. Recipient Cert. of Appreciation, Siskiyou County, 1988, Achievement award, 1988, Golden Poet award World of Poetry, 1989, Living Treasure award Siskiyou County, 2003. Mem. Nat. Writers Club (chmn. student com. Yreka chpt. 1988), Author's Guild, Inc., Author's League of Am., Mystery Writers Am., Soc. Children's Book Writers, Jr. C. of C. (sgt.-at-arms Frederick chpt. 1967-69), Kiwanis, Moose. Democrat. Avocations: horse shoe pitching, photography, reading. Home: 710 Knapp St Yreka CA 96097-2343 Office: Chocolate Piano Prodns PO Box 447 Yreka CA 96097-0447 Personal E-mail: midnightbookworm@sbcglobal.net. Business E-Mail: drpiano@earthlink.net.

SMITH, VIRGINIA ELEANORE, psychologist, educator; b. Bklyn., Aug. 12, 1940; d. Valentine A. and Katherine V. (Angold) Pajer; m. Albert G. Smith, Aug. 12, 1961; children: Daniel, Douglas, Andrew, Katherine, James. BA, Neumann Coll., 1978; MS, Drexel U., 1984; PhD, Union Inst., Cin., 1994; postgrad. clin. tng., Gestalt Therapy Inst. Phila., 1991—. Lic. mental health counselor, Del., Pa. Med. social worker Delaware County Commn. Nursing Svc., Chester, Pa., 1983-84; counselor Manatee County Mental Health Agy., Bradenton, Fla., 1984-85; pvt. practice Wilmington, Del., 1990—; mental health counselor Correctional Med. Systems, Wilmington, Del., 1990—, AIDS Delaware, Wilmington, 2004—. Adj. prof. Delaware County CC, Media, Pa., 1985—, Widener U., Goldey Beacon Coll., Wilmington, 1987—, Neumann Coll., 2001-; assoc. dir. assessments CATCH, Phila., 1995-2003. Mem. AACD, Am. Sociol. Assn., Mental Health Counselors Assn., Assn. Humanistic Psychologists. Roman Catholic. Avocations: travel, hiking, photography, writing. Home: 830 S Walnut St Kennett Square PA 19348 Personal E-mail: virginiasmith173@comcast.net.

SMITH, VME EDOM (VERNA MAE SMITH), social sciences educator, freelance photographer, writer; b. Marshfield, Wis., June 19, 1929; d. Clifton Cedric and Vilia Clarissa (Patefield) Edom; children: Teri Smith Freas, Anthony Thomas. AB in Sociology, U. Mo., 1951; MA in Sociology, George Washington, 1965; PhD in Human Devel., U. Md., 1981. Tchr. Alcohol Safety Action Program Fairfax County, Va., 1973-75; instr. sociology No. Va. C.C., Manassas, 1975-77, asst. prof., 1977-81, assoc. prof., 1981-84, prof., 1984-94, prof. emerita, 1995, coord. coop. edn., 1983-89, Chancellor's Commonwealth prof., 1991-93; adj. faculty Tidewater C.C., 1996—2002; freelance writer, editor and photographer, 1965—; dir. Clifton and Vi Edom Truth With a Camera (photography workshops), 1994—2007; hon. dir., 2008—. Asst. prodr. history of photography program Sta. WETA-TV, Washington, 1965; rsch. and prodn. asst., photographer, publs. editor No. Va. Ednl. TV, Sta. WNVT, 1970—71; cons. migrant divsn. Md. Dept. Edn., Balt., 1977; rschr. photographer Roundabout presch. high sch. series Am. Values Sta. WNVT, 1970—71; documentary photographer Portsmouth (Va.) Redevel. and Housing Authority, 1998—2000; dir. Edom Found. Photojournalism Edn., 1994—; dir., sec. Edom Found. Author, photographer Middleburg and Nearby, 1988; co-author: Small Town America, 1993; contbr. photographs and articles to various publs.; author: Photojournalism, Child Growth and Development; exhibitions include Nat. Photographers Assn., Gordon Pks. Internat. Competition, others. Mem. ednl. adv. com. Head Start, Warrenton, Va. Recipient Emmy, Ohio State Children's Programming award; Fulbright-Hays Rsch. grantee, 1993, Va. Found. Humanities and Pub. Policy grantee, 1997—99. Mem.: Va. Assn. Coop. Edn. (com. mem.). Democrat.

SMITH, WADADA LEO See SMITH, ISHMAEL

SMITH, WALTER LLOYD, Middle School Educator; b. Scottsbluff, Nebr., Nov. 22, 1960; s. Henry Byrd and Sylvia Mae Smith; m. Kathryn Louise Hamer, June 26, 1990. BS, U. of Wyo., Laramie, Wyoming, 1980—84; MA, U. No. Colo., Greeley, 1990—94. Cert. tchr. Wyo., 1984, tech. edn. tchr., health edn. tchr. Wyo., 2009, CPR/AED/First Aid instr. ARC, 1999. Spl. edn. instr. Torrington Mid. Sch., Wyo., 1989—99, health edn. instr., 1999—. Volleyball coach Torrington Mid. Sch., 1989—2009, boys basketball coach, 1990—98, girls basketball coach, 1990—, track coach, 1990—, team leader, 1993—94, football coach, 2004; dist. collegial leader Goshen County Schs., Torrington, 1997—, dist. safe & drug free com. mem., 2000—, dist. arc cpr/first aid instr., 2000—, curriculum coordinating coun. mem., 2002—, dist. coop. learning instr., 2003—; wyo. health content & performance standards regional com. mem. Wyo. Dept. Edn., Douglas, 1999—2000, Laramie, 1999—2000, state writing com. for revision health standards, Cheyenne, 2002—03; torrington cmty. coalition com. City Torrington, 2000—01. Recipient Wyo. Jr High Coach of Yr. award, Wyo. Coaches Assn., 1999, Wyo. Health Tchr. of Yr. award, Wyo. Alliance for Health, Phys. Edn. & Dance, 2003, Wyo. Educator of Yr. award, Wyo. DARE Officers Assn., 2003; Curriculum grant, Goshen County Schs., 2004—05, 21st century grant award winner, 2009. Mem.: NEA, Wyo. Coaches Assn. (mid. sch. bd. dirs. 2004—), Am. Assn. Health Edn., Nat. Assn. Sport & Phys. Edn., Wyo. AAHPERD (v.p.-elect health 2003—04, vp. health 2004—05, pres.-elect 2005—06, pres. 2006—07, 2007—08), Am. AAHPERD, Goshen County Edn. Assn., Wyo. Edn. Assn. Office: Torrington Mid Sch 2742 W E St Torrington WY 82240 Office Fax: 307-532-8402. Business E-Mail: wsmith@goshen.k12.wy.us.

SMITH, WARREN ALLEN, writer, director, columnist; b. Minburn, Iowa, Oct. 27, 1921; s. Harry Clark and Ruth Marion (Miles) S. BA, U. No. Iowa, Cedar Falls, 1948; MA, Columbia U., NYC, 1949. Chmn. dept. Eng. Bentley Sch., NYC, 1949-54, New Canaan H.S., Conn., 1954-86; founder, pres., chmn. bd. Variety Sound Corp., NYC, 1961-90; pres. Afro-Carib Records, 1971-90, Talent Mgmt., 1982-90, AAA Rec. Studio, 1985-90; founder, pres. Variety Rec. Studio, 1961-96; founder Philosopedia.org, 2000—. Instr. Columbia U., 1961-62. Author: Who's Who in Hell, 2000, Celebrities in Hell, 2002, Cruising the Deuce, 2005, Gossip From Across the Pond, 2005; book rev. editor: The Humanist, 1953—58; editor: (jour.) Taking Stock, 1967—93, Pique, 1990—93, Van Rijn's Pad, 1991, Janestreeter, 1997—98; contbr. book revs. Libr. Jour.; editl. assoc.: Free Inquiry, 1992—2000, columnist: Gay and Lesbian Humanist, 1996—, GHQ Humanist, 2005—08, syndicated columnist: Manhattan Scene in W.I. newspapers; syndicated columnist Humanist Potpourri in Free Inquiry, 1994—98; drama critic: Brontë Newsletter, 1995—2000, book reviewer: New Humanist, 1997—2000, CD prodr.: Manuel Salazar: Costa Rica's Forgotten Tenor, writer: The Villager, 2002—05. Pres. Taursa Fund, 1971-73, bd. dirs. 31 Jane Street Corp. Treas. Secular Humanist Soc. NY, 1988-93; sec. Jane St. Corp., 1995-97, 98-99; with Jane Street Authors, 2000—; with ACT UP, Hume Soc.; founding mem. Voltaire Soc. Am. With AUS, 1942-46; signer Humanist Manifesto II, 1973, Humanist Manifesto, 2000, Humanist Manifesto III, 2003; mem. 1st Unitarian Ch. Des Moines. Recipient Leavey award Freedoms Found. at Valley Forge, 1985. Mem.: ASCAP, FANNY (co-pres. 1998—), chelCpress (pres. 2004—), NY Soc. Ethical Culture, Bertrand Russell Soc. (bd. dirs. 1973—, v.p. 1977—80), Brit. Humanist Assn., Conn. Edn. Assn., Rationalist Press Assn., Am. Unitarian Assn., Internat. Press Inst., NY Skeptics Soc. (bd. dirs. 1990—94), Asociación Iberoamericana Ético Humanista (hon.), Stonewall Vets. Orgn. (treas. 1998—99), Mensa, Omaha Beach Vets. Assn., Mensa Investment Club (chmn. 1967—2001), Hvmanist Book Clvb (pres. 1957—62). Unitarian Universalist. Avocation: teratology. Home and Office: 31 Jane St Apt 10 D New York NY 10014-1980

SMITH, WAYNE RICHARD, lawyer; b. Petoskey, Mich., Apr. 30, 1934; s. Wayne Anson and Frances Lynetta (Cooper) S.; m. Carrie J. Swanson, June 13, 1959; children: Stephen, Douglas (dec.), Rebecca. AB, U. Mich., 1956, JD, 1959. Bar: Mich. 1959. Asst. atty. gen. State of Mich., 1960-62; pros. atty. Emmet County (Mich.), 1963-68; dist. judge 90th Jud. Dist., Mich., 1969-72; city atty. City of Petoskey, 1976-98. Trustee North Central Mich. Coll., 1981-98, chmn., 1992-97; trustee/chmn. N. Ctrl. Mich. Coll. Found., 1999—; mem. No. Mich. Community Mental Health Bd., 1972-92, chmn., 1979-81. Mem. Emmet-Charlevoix Bar Assn. (pres. 1967), State Bar Mich., Mich. State Bar Found. Presbyterian. Home and Office: PO Box 4677 Harbor Springs MI 49740-4677 Personal E-mail: cardi@me.com.

SMITH, WAYNE THOMAS, healthcare company executive; b. Jan. 29, 1946; BS, Auburn Univ, 1968, MS, 1969; M in Hosp. Adminstrn., Trinity U.; postgrad., King's Fund Coll. Hosp. Adminstrn. With Trinity Univ, 1971-73, Humana Inc, Louisville, 1973-96, v.p. ctrl. hosp. region, 1978-80, sr. v.p., 1980-85, exec. v.p., 1985-86, pres., COO group health divsn., 1986-96, also bd. dirs.; exec. v.p. Humana Health Care Ops., Louisville, 1991-96; ret. Humana Inc., 1996; pres., CEO, Cmty. Health Sys., Brentwood, Tenn., 1996—, chmn. bd., 2001—. Exec. v.p. health plan ops., bd. dirs. Humana Health Plan, Inc., Louisville; pres. Humana Health Ins. Nev., Inc., Humana Health Plan Fla., Inc., Humana Health Plan Ohio, Inc., Humana Health Chgo. Ins. Co., Humana Kansas City, Inc.; pres., COO Humana Health Plan Tex., Prime Health Mgmt. Svcs.; pres., bd. dirs. HMPK, Inc.; bd. dirs. Praxair, Inc.; chmn. bd. Fedn. Am.'s Hosps. Bd. dirs. Gov.'s Scholars Program, Ky., Actors Theatre of Louisville, Ky. Ctr. for the Arts, The Louisville Orchestra; bd. overseers U. Louisville; mem. exec. com. Greater Louisville Fund for the Arts; past chair bd. dirs. Louisville Collegiate Sch. With U.S. Army, 1969-73, capt., 1973. Mem. Group Health Assn. Am. (bd. dirs.), Health Ins. Assn. Am. (bd. dirs.). Office: Community Health Sys 4000 Meridian Blvd Franklin TN 37067*

SMITH, WENDY HOPE, lawyer; b. NYC, Jan. 19, 1957; d. Morton and Doris Smith. AB, Smith Coll., 1978; JD, Boston U., 1981. Bar: N.J. 1981, U.S. Dist. Ct. 1981, U.S. Ct. Appeals (3d cir.), Supreme Ct. U.S. Law sec. to judge Superior Ct. N.J., Bergen County, 1981-82; assoc. firm Sellar, Richardson, Stuart & Chisholm, Roseland, N.J., 1982-89, ptnr., 1989-97, Sellar Richardson, P.C., 1997-2000, Marshall, Dennehey, Warner, Coleman & Goggin, Roseland, N.J., 2000—. Mem. adv. com. Inst. CLE, 1983—91. Mem. ABA, N.J. Bar Assn., Bergen County Bar Assn., Essex County Bar Assn., Mensa, Smith Coll. Alumnae Assn.

(fund rep. 1978-83). Home: 401 Hancock Ct Edgewater NJ 07020-1627 Office: Marshall Dennehey Warner Coleman & Goggin 425 Eagle Rock Ave Ste 302 Roseland NJ 07068 Office Phone: 973-618-4100.

SMITH, WENDY L., foundation executive; b. Chgo., Sept. 12, 1950; d. John Arthur and Dolores Mae (Webb) Rothenberger; m. Alan Richard Smith; children: Angela Fuhs, Erica Smith. Student, Oakton CC, Des Plaines, Ill., 1986, Mundelein Coll., 1990. Purchasing clk. AIT Industries, Skokie, Ill., 1975-76; purchasing agt. MCC Powers, Skokie, 1976-78; office mgr. Spartan Engring., Skokie, 1978-80, Brunswick Corp., Skokie, 1980—; successively sr. sec., coord. indsl. rels., dir. Brunswick Found., Lake Forest, Ill., 1982-89, pres., 1989—. Asst. sec. Brunswick Pub. Charitable Found., Lake Forest, 1989—; mem. adv. com. Found. for Ind. Higher Edn., Stamford, Conn., 1989—, Coun. Better Bus. Burs., Arlington, Va., 1988-90; bd. dirs. Associated Colls. of Ill., 1991—; bd. dirs., mem. trustees com., mem. compensation and benefits com. Donors Forum of Chgo., 1988-93. Bd. dirs. INROADS/Chgo., Inc., 1994—; mem. steering com. Dist. 57 Edn. Found., Mt. Prospect, Ill., 1996—. Recipient Pvt. Sector Initiative Commendation, U.S. Pres., 1987-89. Mem. Donors Forum Chgo. (treas. 1988-91, bd. dirs., mem. exec. com., chairperson audit and fin. com., mem. trustees com. 1992—), Coun. on Founds., Ind. Sector Suburban Contbns. Network (chairperson 1987-89), Women in Philanthropy Corp. Founds. (mem. cmty. rels. com. 1985-87), Chgo. Women in Philanthropy. Avocations: antique restoration, pleasure reading, bowling, golf.

SMITH, WILBUR LAZEAR, radiologist, educator; b. Warwick, NY, Oct. 11, 1943; s. Wilbur and Betty (Norris) S.; m. Rebecca Rowlands, June 19, 1965; children: Jason, Daniel, Joanna, Noah, Ethan, Jacob. BA, SUNY, Buffalo, 1965, MD, 1969. Diplomate Am. Bd. Radiology, Am. Bd. Pediat., Am. Bd. Pediatric Radiology. Intern, then resident Buffalo Children's Hosp., 1969-71; resident in pediatric radiology Cin. Gen. and Children's Hosp., 1971-74; asst. prof. pediatrics and radiology Ind. U., Indpls., 1975-78, assoc. prof., 1978-80, acting dir. pediatric radiology, 1979-80; assoc. prof. U. Iowa, Iowa City, 1980-82, prof., 1982—, dir. med. edn. in radiology, 1980-86, vice chmn. dept. radiology, 1986-94, interim head, 1994-96, dir. pediatric radiology, 1980-92; chmn. dept. radiology Henry Ford Health Sys., Detroit, 1998-99; prof. radiology Wayne State U., Detroit, 2000—, chmn. dept. radiology, 2002—; staff radiologist Mich. Children's Hosp., Detroit, 2000—. Vice chmn. radiology for academics Wayne State U., 2001, radiology residency dir., 01, prof., chmn. dept. radiology, 2002—. Assoc. editor Gastrointestinal Imaging in Pediatrics, Acad. Radiology, 1992—, Quar. Rev. Child Abuse, 1998, Radiology 101, co-author, 2d edit. 2004; exec. assoc. editor Acad. Radiology, 1997-2000, assoc. editor, 2000—02; contbr. articles to profl. jours. Vol. soccer coach, 1980-99; physician cons. in child abuse, 1980-; mem. equity adv. com. Iowa City Sch. Bd., 1983-87. With USAR, 1969—77, hon. discharge USAR. Fellow Am. Acad. Pediatrics, Am. Coll. Radiology; mem. AMA, Radiol. Soc. N.Am.(second v.p. 2004-05), Iowa Radiol. Soc. (pres. 1987-88), Assn. Univ. Radiologists (pres. 1995-96, sr. adv. 2001-08, Gold medal 2006), Soc. Pediat. Radiology (treas. 1995-98, rep. coun. Acad. Socs. of AAMC 1996-02), Mich. Radiol. Soc. (bd. dirs. 2004—). Mem. Soc. Of Friends. Avocation: photography. Home: 10124 Lasalle Blvd Huntington Woods MI 48070-1162 Office: Detroit Receiving Hosp Dept Radiology (3L8) 4201 St Antoine Detroit MI 48201 Home Phone: 248-582-1521; Office Phone: 313-745-4443, 313-745-3433. Business E-Mail: wlsmith@med.wayne.edu.

SMITH, WILBURN JACKSON, JR., retired bank executive; b. Charlotte, NC, June 13, 1921; s. Wilburn Jackson and Banna (Oswalt) S.; m. Terry Mosteller, Jan. 4, 1944; children: Kenneth M., M. Scott (dec.), Wilburn Jackson III, Curtis Todd. BS in Acctg., U. NC, 1943; postgrad. in comml. banking, Rutgers U., 1953, postgrad. in investment banking, 1956. With First Union Nat. Bank, Charlotte, 1946-74, exec. v.p., 1960-67, 1st exec. v.p., 1967-74; pres., mng. trustee Cameron-Brown Investment Group, Raleigh, N.C., 1974-78; chmn. loan policy com. N.C. Nat. Bank, Charlotte, 1979-88. Cons. in field. Served with USN, 1943-46. Recipient Citizenship award Charlotte Civitan, 1972. Mem. Robert Morris Assocs., Myers Park Country Club (Charlotte). Baptist. Home: 2222 Selwyn Ave 404 Charlotte NC 28207-2779

SMITH, WILL (WILLARD CHRISTOPHER SMITH JR.), actor, film producer; b. Phila., Sept. 25, 1968; s. Willard and Caroline Smith; m. Sheree Smith, May 9, 1992 (div. 1995); 1 child, Willard III; m. Jada Pinkett Smith, Dec. 31, 1997; children: Jaden Christopher Syre, Willow Camille Reign. Ptnr. Overbrook Entertainment. Albums (as The Fresh Prince with DJ Jazzy Jeff): And in this Corner..., 1989, Homebase, 1991, Rock the House, 1987, He's the DJ, I'm the Rapper, 1988, Code Red, 1993, Big Willie Style, 1997, Willennium, 1999, Maximum Will Smith, 2000, Born to Reign, 2002, Greatest Hits, 2002, Lost and Found, 2005; (singles) Just One of Those Days, 1987, Girls Ain't Nothing But Trouble, 1988, Brank New Funk, 1988, A Nightmare on My Street, 1988, Jazzy's Groove, 1989, I Think I Can Beat Mike Tyson, 1989, Parents Just Don't Understand, (Grammy award for Best Rap Performance, 1989), The Things That U Do, 1991, Summertime, 1991 (Grammy award), Ring My Bell, 1991, I'm Looking for the One (To Be With Me), 1993, Boom! Shake the Room, 1993; Actor: (TV series) The Fresh Prince of Bel-Air, 1990-96, (also exec. prodr. 1994-96), Happily Ever After: Fairy Tales for Every Child (voice), 1995, All of Us, 2003 (also writer, exec. prodr.); (TV appearances) Blossom, 1991, All of Us, 2003; (films) Where the Day Takes You, 1992, Made in America, 1993, Six Degrees of Separation, 1993, Bad Boys, 1995, Independence Day, 1996 (Blockbuster Entertainment award Favorite Actor Sci-Fi), Men In Black, 1997 (MTV Movie awards Best Fight, Best Movie Song, ASCAP award Most Performed Songs for Motion Picture, Blockbuster Entertainment award Favorite Actor Sci-Fi), Welcome to Hollywood, 1998, Enemy of the State, 1998, Wild Wild West, 1999, The Legend of Bagger Vance, 2000, Ali, 2001, Men in Black II, 2002, Bad Boys II, 2003, I, Robot, 2004 (also exec. prodr.), Shark Tale (voice), 2004, Hitch, 2005 (also prodr.), The Pursuit of Happyness, 2006 (also prodr.)(Choice Movie Actor: Drama, Teen Choice Awards, 2007), I Am Legend, 2007 (Best Male Performance, MTV Movie Awards, 2008, Choice Movie Actor: Horror/Thriller, Teen Choice Awards, 2008), Hancock, 2008, Seven Pounds, 2008 (Outstanding Actor in a Motion Picture, NAACP Image award, 2009); exec. prodr., Showtime, 2002, The Seat Filler, 2004; prodr. Saving Face, 2004, ATL, 2006. Recipient ShoWest Conv. awards Actor of Yr., 1999, Spl. Internat. Box Office Achievement award 1997, BET award for Best Actor, 2002, Am. Music Award, Favorite Male Artist, 2005; named one of 50 Most Powerful People in Hollywood, 2004-06, The 100 Most Influential People, Time Mag., 2006, The 100 Most Powerful Celebrities, Forbes.com, 2007, 2008, The Top 25 Entertainers of Yr., Entertainment Weekly, 2007, The 50 Smartest People in Hollywood, 2007, The Ten Most Fascinating People of 2008, Barbara Walters, Favorite Male Movie Star People's Choice Awards, 2009, Favorite Male Action Star, 2009; named to Power 150, Ebony mag., 2008. Office: Overbook Entertainment 450 N Roxbury Dr Fl 4 Beverly Hills CA 90210-4232

SMITH, WILLARD GRANT, psychologist; b. Sidney, NY, June 29, 1934; s. Frank Charles and Myrtle Belle (Empet) S.; m. Ruth Ann Dissly, Sept. 14, 1957; children: Deborah Sue Henri, Cynthia Lynn Koster, Andrea Kay Richards, John Charles. BS, U. Md., 1976; MS, U. Utah, 1978, PhD, 1981. Diplomate Am. Bd. Forensic Examiners, Am. Bd. Psychol. Specialities, Am. Bd. Disability Analysts, cert. forensic cons.; lic. psychologist Utah, cert. sch. psychologist nat. Tchg. asst. dept. ednl. psychology U. Utah; rsch. asst. U. Utah Med. Ctr., 1976-78; rsch. cons. Utah Dept. Edn., 1977; program evaluator Salt Lake City Sch. Dist.; program evaluator, auditor Utah State Bd. Edn., 1978; sch. psychologist Jordan Sch. Dist., Sandy, Utah, 1978-82, tchr., 1979-80; exec. dir. Utah Ind. Living Ctr., Salt Lake City, 1982-83; spl. edn. cons. Southeastern Edn. Svc. Ctr., Price, Utah, 1983-85; sch. psychologist Jordan Sch. Dist., Sandy, Utah, 1985-96; assoc. psychologist Don W. McBride & Assocs., Bountiful, Utah, 1989-91; pvt. practice Sandy, Utah, 1991—. Master sgt. USAF, 1953-76. Decorated Air Force Commendation medal with 2 clusters. Fellow Am. Coll. Forensic Examiners (life); mem. APA, Nat. Assn. Sch. Psychologists, Air Force Assn., Air Force Sgts. Assn., Ret. Enlisted Assn., Am. Legion, VFW, Phi Kappa Phi, Alpha Sigma Lambda. Home: 8955 Quail Hollow Dr Sandy UT 84093-1903 Office Phone: 801-942-5356. E-mail: dr_bill5@msn.com.

SMITH, WILLIAM, legislative staff member; married. Legis. dir., Rep. Harold Rogers US House of Reps., Washington, asst., appropriations com., chief of staff to Rep. Harold Rogers. Republican. Office: 2406 Rayburn House Office Bldg Washington DC 20515 Office Phone: 202-225-4601. Office Fax: 202-225-0940.*

SMITH, WILLIAM A., legislative staff member; b. Elwood, Ind., Jan. 2, 1962; m. Karen J. Knapp, Apr. 19, 1983; 5 children. Degree, Ball State U., Muncie, Ind., 1982, George Mason U., Fairfax. Va., 1984. Bd. dirs. Ind. Family Inst., 1989—, exec. dir., 1990—2000; chief of staff for Rep. Dan Burton US House of Reps., Washington, 1983—89, chief of staff for Rep. Mike Pence, 2001—. Mem.: Am. Family Assn. (bd. dirs. 2001—). Avocations: reading, football. Office: Office of Congressman Mike Pence 1431 Longworth House Office Bldg Washington DC 20515 Office Phone: 202-225-3021. Business E-Mail: william.smith@mail.house.gov.*

SMITH, WILLIAM HENRY PRESTON, freelance/self-employed writer, editor, former telecommunications industry executive; b. Pleasanton, Tex., Sept. 8, 1924; s. Sidney Newton and Willie Gertrude (Cloyd) S.; m. Frances Dixon, July 1, 1950; children: Juliet, Dixon, David. B.J., U. Tex., 1949. Reporter Dallas Morning News, 1949-52; advt. asst. Dallas Power & Light Co., 1952-55; dir. pub. relations Greater Boston C. of C., 1955-58; with New Eng. Telephone and Telegraph Co., Boston, 1958-86, asst. v.p., 1966-75, corp. sec., 1975-83, dir. pub. relations, 1983-86; free-lance writer Dover, Mass., 1986—. Editor: Bus. Ethics Resource Newsletter. Bd. dirs., v.p. Mass. Soc. for Prevention Cruelty to Children; bd. dirs. Bus. Ethics Found., Urban Dynamics Adv. Coun.; mem. support policies com. United Way Mass; bd. advisors to pres. Andover Newton Theol. Sch. With paratroopers U.S. Army, 1943-46. Decorated Purple Heart, U.S. Army, Bronze Star, U.S. Army. Mem. Am. Soc. Corp. Secs., Friars, Dedham Country and Polo Club, Down Town Club, Wellesley Coll. Club, Sigma Delta Chi, Delta Kappa Epsilon. Republican. Home and Office: 3236 Wingfield Lake Rd Williamsburg VA 23185-7519 Office Phone: 757-220-0970.

SMITH, WILLIAM REECE, JR., lawyer; b. Athens, Tenn., Sept. 19, 1925; s. William Reece and Gladys (Moody) S. BS, U. SC, 1946, LLD, 1981; JD, U. Fla., 1949; Rhodes scholar, Oxford U., 1949-52; LLD, U. So. Fla., 1973, Rollins Coll., 1980, U. Fla., 1980, Stetson U., 1985, Nova Southeastern U., 2005; DCL, Central Meth. Coll., 1980, New Eng. Coll., 1980; DHL, Calif. West Sch. Law, 1981; DBA, Tampa Coll., Fla., 1991; LHD, U. So. Fla., 1990. Bar: Fla. 1949. Mem. firm Carlton, Fields, Ward, Emmanuel, Smith and Cutler, Tampa, 1953—, now chmn. emeritus; interim pres. U. So. Fla., 1976-77; city atty. Tampa, 1963-72. Asst. prof. law U. Fla., 1952-53; adj. prof. law Stetson U., 1954-59, 91—; past pres. Fla. Legal Svcs., Inc., Tampa Philharmonic Assn., Fla. Gulf Coast Symphony, Inc. Sec. Fla. Rhodes Scholar Selection Com., 1969-94. Midshipman and ensign USNR, 1943—46. Named Outstanding Young Man of Tampa, 1961; named to Hall of Fame Stetson U. Coll. (inaugural mem.), Tampa Bay Bus. Hall of Fame, 2007; recipient Good Govt. award Fla. Jr. C. of C., 1965, Disting. Am. award Tampa Chpt. Nat. Football Found., 1977, Humanitarian award B'nai B'rith Found., 1977, Pres.'s award Fla. Assn. Retarded Citizens, 1978, Von Briesen award Nat. Legal Aid and Defender Assn., 1980, Brotherhood award NCCJ, 1980, Herbert Harley award Am. Judicature Soc., 1983, Citizen of Yr. award Civitan Club, 1986, Algernon Sydney Sullivan award, U. SC, 1987, Pub. Svc. award Stetson U. Coll. Law, 1990, C.H.I.E.F. award Fla. Ind. Colls. and Univs., 1990, Professionalism award Am. Inns of Ct., 2002, Tampa Bay Bus. Hall Fame, 2007. Fellow Am. Coll. Trial Lawyers, Internat. Acad. Trial Lawyers, Fla. Bar Found. (past pres.); mem. ABA (chmn. jr. bar conf. 1960-61, life, ho. dels., sec. 1967-71, pres. 1980-81, Gold medal 1989, Pro Bono Publico award 1994, award in recognition outstanding svc. profession pub. 2007), Am. Bar Found., Am. Bar Endowment, Internat. Soc. Barristers, Am. Law Inst. (mem. coun.), Internat. Bar Assn. (past pres.), Inter-Am. Bar Assn. (mem. exec. coun. 1972-77), Fla. Bar Assn. (pres. 1972-73), Hillsborough County Bar Assn. (pres. 1963, Outstanding Lawyer 2006), Nat. Conf. Bar Pres. (pres. 1978-79), Greater Tampa C. of C. (pres. 1986-87). Methodist. Home: PO Box 3239 Tampa FL 33601-3239 Office: Carlton Fields Ward Emmanuel Smith & Cutler Crp Ctr 3 10th Flr 4221 W Boy Scout Blvd Tampa FL 33607 Office Phone: 813-223-7000.

SMITH, WILLIAM S., JR., education association administrator; BS in Chemistry, Tex. A&M U., 1970, PhD in Chemistry, 1974. Postdoctoral rschr. U. Calif., Irvine, 1974—77; program mgr. FAA; graduate rsch. Tex. A&M U., 1971—74; phys. scientist FAA, U.S. Dept. Transp., 1977—85; sci. advisor subcom. on space, com. on sci., space and tech. U.S. Ho. of Reps., 1985—88, staff dir. subcom., 1988—94, dep. Dem. chief of staff, 1994—98; v.p. for programs Assn. Univs. for Rsch. in Astronomy, Inc., Washington, 1998—2000, interim pres., 1999—2000, pres., 2000—. Recipient Exceptional Svc. award, NASA, Sci. and Tech. Fellowship award, Dept. Commerce, 1984. Office: AURA Inc Ste 350 1200 New York Ave NW Washington DC 20005 E-mail: wsmith@aura-astronomy.org.

SMITH, YEARDLEY, actress; b. Paris, July 3, 1964; Voice of Lisa Simpson, Maggie Simpson and others The Simpsons, 1989—. Actor: (films) Heaven Help Us, 1985, The Legend of Billie Jean, 1985, Maximum Overdrive, 1986, Three O'Clock High, 1987, Listen to Me, 1989, Zwei Frauen, 1989, City Slickers, 1989, Toys, 1992, Jingle All the Way, 1996, Just Write, 1997, As Good As It Gets, 1997, (voice) We're Back! A Dinosaur's Story, 1993, The Simpsons Movie, 2007,: (TV films) Mom's On Strike, 1984, Tickets, Please, 1988; (TV series) Brothers, 1984, The Tracey Ullman Show, 1987—89, (voice) The Simpsons, 1989—, Herman's Head, 1991, Dharma & Greg, 1997—99, 2001—02, (TV guest appearance) Tales from the Darkside, 1986, Mama's Family, 1986, Mathnet, 1987, Sydney, 1990, Likely Suspects, 1992, Hey Hey, It's Sunday, 1994, Empty Nest, 1994, Smart Guy, 1997, Teen Angel, 1997, Sports Night, 1998, Nash Bridges, 1999, Becker, 2003; (plays) More, 2004, Balancing Act, 2007. Office: The Simpsons c/o Twentieth Television PO Box 900 Beverly Hills CA 90213

SMITH, YOSHIMI O., lawyer; d. Minol and Trinidad Ohye. JD, Hofstra U., Hempstead, NY, 1998. Bar: NY 1999, US Fed. Ct. NY, (ea. dist.) 1999, US Fed. Ct, NY (so. dist.) 1999, Fla. 2004. Atty. Rivkin Radler, LLP, Uniondale, NY, 1997—2005, Miller & O'Neill, Boca Raton, Fla., 2005—07, Duane Morris LLP, Boca Raton, 2007—. Sec., bd. mem. Kids New Directions, Boca Raton, 2007, com. mem., 2006—08, Kids In Distress, Delray Beach, Fla., 2006. Scholar, Adelante Assn., 1995. Mem.: Nassau County Bar Assn., South Palm Beach County Bar Assn. (chair probate com. 2007—), NY State Bar Assn., Palm Beach County Bar Assn. (Marikani planned giving com. mem. 2008—). Office: Duane Morris LLP Ste 300 2700 N Military Trail Boca Raton FL 33431-1808 Office Phone: 561-962-2110. Business E-Mail: yosmith@duanemorris.com.

SMITH, ZADIE (SADIE SMITH), writer; b. London, Eng., Oct. 27, 1975; m. Nick Laird, 2004. Grad. in English, Cambridge U., 1997; postgrad., Harvard U. Writer-in-residency Inst. Contemporary Arts; Radcliffe Inst. fellow Harvard U., 2002—03. Author: (novels) White Teeth, 2000 (First Book award, Guardian newspaper, Whitbread First Novel award, Commonwealth Writers prize, Ethnic and Multicultural Media Award, best book/novel, Ethnic and Multicultural Media Award, best female newcomer, James Tait Black Meml. prize for fiction, 2000, WH Smith award, best new talent, 2001, (UK miniseries, 2002; aired on PBS in US), The Autograph Man, 2002 (Wingate Literary prize for fiction, Jewish Quarterly, 2003), On Beauty, 2005 (Orange prize for fiction, 2006, Somerset Maugham award, 2006), (nonfiction) Fail Better, 2006; editor: (anthology) Pieces of Flesh, 2001; author of (introduction): The Burned Children of America, 2003. Named one of 100 Most Influential People, Time Mag., 2006. Mailing: c/o Georgia Garrett AP Watt Ltd 20 John St London WC1N 2DR England also: Hamish Hamilton Ltd c/o Penguin Ltd 80 Strand London WC2R ORL England Office Phone: 20 7405 6774. Office Fax: 20 7831 2154. E-mail: zsmith@literati.net.

SMITHART-OGLESBY, DEBRA LYNN, restaurant chain executive; b. Apr. 24, 1959; BA in Acctg., U. Tex.; MBA, So. Methodist U. Asst. contr. Brinker Internat., Inc., Dallas, 1985—86, contr., 1986—88, v.p., contr., 1988—91, v.p. fin., 1991, exec. v.p., CFO, 1991—97; pres. corp. services, CFO First Am. Autootive Inc., 1997—99; pres. Dekor, Inc., 1999—2000, O/S Partners, 2000—06; chmn. Denny's Corp., Spartanburg, SC, 2006—. Bd. dirs. Brinker Internat., Inc., 1991—97, Denny's Corp., 2003—, Noodles & Co. Office: Dennys Corp 203 E Main St Spartanburg SC 29319*

SMITH-BECKER, NANCY WOOLVERTON, public relations executive, art appraiser; b. San Antonio, July 31, 1947; d. Tillman Louis and Enid Maxine (Woolverton) Brown; m. William F. Pry II, Mar. 7, 1998 (div. July 31, 2003); m. Lawrence Becker, June 2, 2007; 1 child from previous marriage, Christina Elizabeth Woolverton Jones. Student, Ecole Nouvelle de la Suisse, Romande, Lausanne, Switzerland, 1962, Vanderbilt U., 1964; BA, So. Meth. U., 1968, postgrad., 1969-70. Cert. S.E. Paralegal Inst., Ancien Regime Christie's (London), antiques and residential contents. Tchr. spl. edn. Hot Springs Sch. Dist. (Ark.), 1970-72; reporter, soc. editor Dallas Morning News, 1974-82; soc./celebrity columnist Dallas Times Herald, 1982-91; owner, pub. High Society, Society Fax; bus. editor DFW Cmty. Newspapers divsn. Lionheart Newspapers Inc., Plano, Tex., 1999—2003; co-founder Decorative Arts Soc. Dallas, For Worth; pub. Decorative Arts Mag.; owner Personal Property Appraisal Svc., 2005—; realtor Keller Williams. Realtor, Ebby Halliday Realtors; stringer Washington Post, 1978; owner Nancy Smith Pub. Rels. Contbg. editor Ultra mag., Houston, 1981-82, Tex. Woman mag., Dallas, 1979-80, Profl. Woman mag., Dallas, 1979-80; mem. bd. advisors Ultra Mag., 1985—; columnist North Dallas People; appeared on TV series Jocelyn's Weekend, Sta. KDFI-TV, 1985. Bd. dirs. TACA arts support orgn., Dallas, 1980—, asst. chmn. custom auction, 1978-83; judge Miss Tex. USA Contest, 1984; bd. dirs. Am. Parkinson Disease Assn. (Dallas chpt.), mem. adv. bd. Cattle Baron's Ball Com., Dallas Symphony Debutante presentations; mem. bd. dirs. Dallas Opera Women's Bd., Northwood Inst. Women's Bd., Dallas Symphony Leauge; mem. Friends of Winston Churchill Meml. and libr., Dallas Theatre Ctr. Women's Guild, Childrens' Med. Ctr. Aux.; mem. women's com. Dallas Theatre Ctr.; hon. mem. Crystal Charity Ball Com.; mem. Cmty. Coun. Greater Dallas Cmty. Awareness Goals Com. Impact '88, 1985—; com. mem. Dallas Arboretum, Preservation Dallas; co-chmn. Multiple Sclerosis San Simeon Gala, 1988; celebrity co-chmn. Greer Garson Gala of Hope 1990-91; gala chmn. Greer Garson Gala of Hope for Am. Parkinson's Disease Assn., 1991-93; chmn. gala benefit Northwood U., 1994; co-chmn. star-studded stomp Mar. Dimes, 1994; mem. Femmes du Monde spl. activities com., 1999 luncheon com., com. Dallas Coun. World Affairs; bd. dirs. Dallas Ballet's Lone Star Adagio; pub. rels. vol. Habitat for Humanity, 2005. Mem.: DAR, Internat. Soc. Appraisers (accredited; antiques and residential contents cert.), Nat. Press Club, Soc. Profl. Journalists (v.p. coms. 1978—79), Winterthur, Mes Amis (1st v.p. 2007), Preservation Soc. Newport County, Flagler Mus., City of Plano Sister Cities Com., Daus. of Republic of Tex. (registrar 1972), Dallas So. Meml. Assn., Dallas County Heritage Soc. (bd. dirs.), Dallas Mus. Art League, Dallas Opera Guild, Lancaster Hist. Soc., French Heritage Soc., Decorative Arts Soc. Dallas/Ft. Worth (CEO, appraiser, co-founder), Dallas Glass Club, Bent Tree Country Club, Dallas Knife and Fork Club, S'Amuser, Kermis Club, Coterie Club, Thalia Club, Rondo/Carrousel Club, The 500 Club (Dallas), Argyle Club (sec. 1983—84, 1st v.p. 2005—, pres. 2008), Pub. Affairs Luncheon Club, Trippers Club (pres. elect, v.p.), Tower Club, Rotary (gala chmn. 2007). Home: 5727 Covehaven Dr Dallas TX 75252-4934 Home Phone: 972-381-0418; Office Phone: 214-625-1162. Personal E-mail: nancywoolvertonsmith@tx.rr.com, decorativeartssociety@gmail.com.

SMITH CANTER, LORA LEE, special education educator; b. Dayton, Ohio, May 24, 1963; d. Leslie and Margaret Smith; children: Cathleen Lorraine Canter, Patrick Joseph Canter. PhD, U. SC., Columbia, 2006. Cert. tchr. special edn. NC Dept. Pub. Instrn., 1985. Asst. prof. East Carolina U., Greenville, NC, 2004—. Contbr. chapters to books, articles to profl. jours. Mem.: Coun. Exceptional Children (regional coord. 2001—07). Office: East Carolina Univ 5th St Greenville NC 27858

SMITH-DIJULIO, KATHLEEN, psychosocial clinical nurse specialist; b. Milw., July 5, 1949; d. Richard L. and Jean M. (Carey) Smith; m. Donald A. DiJulio, Aug. 31, 1975; children: Carey Jean, Bianca Smith. BSN, U. Ariz., 1971; MA, U. Wash., 1975. Cert. clin. specialist adult psychiat.-mental health nursing. Asst. prof. U. Wash. Sch. Nursing, Seattle; coord. R & D, Alcoholism and Drug Abuse Inst., Seattle; crisis counselor Valley Med. Ctr., Renton, Wash.; psychiat. clin. nurse specialist Group Health Coop., Seattle, also dir. quality improvement, acting dir. nursing ops. Contbr. articles to profl. jours. Mem. AAACN, ACHE, Sigma Theta Tau (past pres. Psi chpt.), Phi Kappa Phi. Home: 1625 E McGraw St Seattle WA 98112-2135

SMITH-DOERR, LAUREL A., sociologist, educator; PhD, U. Ariz., Tucson. Asst. prof. sociology Boston U., 1999—2007, assoc. prof. sociology, 2007—; program dir. sci., tech. & soc. NSF, Arlington, Va., 2007—09; jean monnet fellow Robert Schuman Ctr. Advanced Study-European U. Inst., Florence, Italy, 2004—05. Author: (book) Women's Work: Gender Equity v. Hierarchy in the Life Sciences; contbr. articles to jours. (ASQ award, 2002). Mem.: Am. Sociol. Assn. (coun. mem. sci., knowledge and tech. sect. 2007—09). Mem. Congregational United Ch. Christ. Office: Boston Univ Sociology Dept 96 Cummington St Boston MA 02215 Business E-Mail: ldoerr@bu.edu.

SMITHER, HOWARD ELBERT, musicologist, educator; b. Pittsburg, Kans., Nov. 15, 1925; s. Elbert S. and Ethel (Schwab) S.; m. Doris J. Arvin (div. 1976); children: Thomas A., Jesse N. Woodsmith; m. Ann M. Woodward. AB magna cum laude, spl. honors in music, Hamline U., 1950; MA in musicology, Cornell U., 1952; postgrad., U. Munich, 1953-54; PhD in musicology, Cornell U., 1960. Instr. Oberlin Coll. and Conservatory of Music, Oberlin, Ohio, 1955-57, asst. prof., 1957-60, U. Kans., Lawrence, 1960-63; assoc. prof. Tulane U., New Orleans, 1963-68, U. N.C., Chapel Hill, 1968-71, prof., 1971-79, dir. grad. studies in music, 1977-79, 83-84, 86-88, James Gordon Hanes prof. humanities in music, 1979-92, James Gordon Hanes prof. emeritus humanities in music, 1992—; John Bird prof. of music U. Wales, Cardiff, 1993-95. Lectr., chmn. panels regional, nat. and internat. meetings, confs., symposiums, 1964-90. Author: A History of the Oratorio, Vol. 1, The Oratorio in the Baroque Era: Italy, Vienna, Paris, 1977 (transl. Italian), Vol. 2, The Oratorio in the Baroque Era: Protestant Germany and England, 1977 (Deems Taylor award ASCAP 1978), Vol. 3 The Oratorio in the Classical Era, 1987, Vol. 4, Oratorio in the 19th and 20th Centuries, 2000; editor Oratorios of the Italian Baroque, 1983—, The Italian Oratorio 1650-1800, Vols. 1-3, 6, 8, 11-13, 16, 18-20, 24-25, 27, 1986-87; Oratorios of the Italian Baroque, 1983—; editor, translator poems in Alfred Einstein's The Italian Madrigal, 1971; music rev. editor Notes, 1967-69; mem. editorial bd. Detroit Monographs in Musicology, 1971-87; chmn. editorial bd. Early Musical Masterworks: Editions and Commentaries, 1978-83; mem. editorial bd. Videodisc Music Series, NEH, 1982-86; contbr. articles to profl. jours. Fellow Cornell U., 1953-54, NEH, Italy, 1972-73, England, 1979-80, Guggenheim, 1984-85; Fulbright sr. rsch. grant in Italy, 1965-66, sr. Fulbright lectr. Moscow State Conservatory, 1990. Mem. Am. Mus. Soc. (hon; chmn. S.E. chpt. 1969-71, mem. coun. 1969-71, 75-77, bd. dirs. 1977-79, pres. 1980-82, del. to Am. Coun. Learned Socs. 1984-88, to Internat. Congress Strasbourg 1982), Music Libr. Assn. (bd. dirs. 1968-70), Soc. for Am. Music, Internat. Assn. Jazz Educators, Internat. Trumpet Guild. Avocations: hiking, jazz trumpet performance.

SMITHERAM, MARGARET ETHERIDGE, health facility administrator, director; d. Philip Fitzgerald and Mary Catharine (Dwyer) E.; m. Roy Charles McCracken, May 5, 1975; m. William Bertram Smitheram, Aug. 17, 1985. BA, Emory U., 1960; M in Health Adminstrn., Washington U., St. Louis, 1973. Registered record administr., 1960-71; spl. asst. to dir. VA Med. Ctr., Roseburg, Oreg., 1973-74; hosp. adminstrn. specialist VA Central Office, Washington, 1974-75; asst. dir. trainee VA Med. Ctr., Phila., 1976, assoc. dir. Hampton, Va., 1976--80, Buffalo, 1980-81; presdl. exchange exec. Kimberly Clark Corp., Neenah, Wis., 1981-82, Roswell, Ga., 1981-82; dir. VA Med. Ctr., Grand Island, Nebr., 1982-94; interim dir. Grand Island-Hall County Health Dept., 1996-97; instr. Cerritos Coll., 1969-70. Bd. dirs. Project 2M Coordinating Coun., Inc., Grand Island, 1985-87, Hall County Leadership Unlimited, Inc., 1990. Bd. dirs. Grand Island Area United Way, 1987-90 (pres. 1989), Grand Island Concert Assn. 1987-92, Ctrl. Nebr. Goodwill Industries, Inc., 1987-93 (pres. 1991-92). Fellow Am. Coll. Healthcare Execs. (life); mem. rev. bd. State of Nebr. Foster Care, Am. Hosp. Assn., Fed. Exec. Assn. (pres. Grand Island chpt. 1987), Nebr. Hosp. Assn., Grand Island C. of C. (bd. dirs. 1988-92, legis. affairs com 1984-85, priorities com. 1984-85, govtl. affairs com. 1984-88, nominating com. 1991-92, 94-95, audit com. 1992-93, pres. club 1993-94), Rotary Internat. Club #1485 (v.p. 1998-2000, pres. 2000-2001, District 5630 Group Study Exchange Team Leader to South Korea District 3710, 1999, Paul Harris fellow). Home: 221 Trail of the Flowers Georgetown TX 78633

SMITHERS, PAUL T (SMITHERS T), civil engineer, educator; b. June 16, 1950; s. Joan (Latue) and Marcus Smithers; m. Bernadette Vitale; 1 adopted child, Apple children: Alexis, Angelo. BS in Civil Engineering, U. Pa., 1972, MS in Civil Engineering, 1973. EIT Pa., 1973, cert. PE, Pa., 1980, concrete compression, Alaska, 1995. Asst. engr. Turner Constrn., Phila., 1974—76, jr. engr., 1976—80, design engr., 1981—90; assoc. prof. U. Alaska, Anchorage, 1991—95; co-owner/founder Smithers and Meriks Engring. Firm, Anchorage, 1996—. Design intern IMC Constrn., Pa., 1970—71; constrn. intern Turner, Pa., 1971—73; TA U. Pa. Engring. dept., Pa., 1973—74; adj. prof. U. Alaska, Anchorage, 1996—. Conservative. Catholic. Avocations: aquariums, board games, calligraphy. Office: Smithers and Meriks Engineering Firm 9101 Little Creek Dr Anchorage AK 99507-3920

SMITHIES, OLIVER, geneticist, educator; b. Halifax, Eng., June 23, 1925; naturalized; m. Nobuyo Maeda. PhD in Biochemistry, U. Oxford, Eng., 1951; DSc (hon.), U. Chgo., 1991, Duke U., Durham, NC, U. São Paulo, 2008. Postdoc. fellow phys. chemistry U. Wis., Madison, 1951—53, asst. prof. to prof. genetics/med. genetics, 1960—63, Leon J. Cole prof., 1971—80, Hilldale prof., 1980—88; Excellence prof. dept. pathology/lab. medicine U. NC Sch. Medicine, Chapel Hill, 1988—. Rsch. asst., assoc. Connaught Med. Rsch. Lab., Toronto, Canada, 1953—60; mem. nat. adv. med. sci. coun. NIH, 1985. Contbr. articles to profl. jours. Recipient William Allen Meml. award, Am. Soc. Human Genetics, 1964, Karl Landsteiner Meml. award, Am. Assn. Blood Banks, 1984, Gairdner Found. Internat. award, 1990, 1993, NC award for sci., 1993, Alfred P. Sloan award, GM Found., 1994, CIBA award, Am. Heart Assn., 1996, Cardiovasc./Metabolic Disease Rsch. award, Bristol-Meyers Squibb, 1997, Rsch. Achievement award, AHA, 1998, Internat. Okamoto award, Japan Vascular Disease Rsch. Found., 2000, Albert Lasker award for basic med. rsch., 2001, O. Max Gardner award, U. NC, 2002; co-recipient Wolf Found. prize in medicine, 2003, Nobel prize in physiology or medicine, 2007. Fellow: AAAS; mem.: NAS, Inst. Medicine, Genetics Soc. of America (v.p. 1974, pres. 1975), Am. Acad. Arts & Scis. Office: Univ N C Dept Pathology & Lab Med Chapel Hill NC 27599-0001 Office Phone: 919-966-6913. E-mail: oliver.smithies@pathology.unc.edu.*

SMITH II, LEON M., chemist; MS, Tenn. State U., Nashville, 1996. Assoc. scientist Amgen, Thousand Oaks, Calif., 1996—2001; scientist Imclone Sys., NYC, 2001—05; sr. rsch. scientist Bristol-Myers Squibb, Princeton, NJ, 2005—. Mem.: Am. Chem. Soc., Omega Psi Phi Frat., Inc.

SMITH-SANDERS, CAROL ANN, physical therapist, music therapist, psychologist; b. Montgomery County, Tenn., Apr. 19, 1951; d. Carl and Ruth (Gettinger) S. BME in Music Therapy, U. Kans., 1974; MA in Clin. Psychology, Mid. Tenn. State U., 1977; EdS in Human Svc. Mgmt., Vanderbilt U., 1979; EdD in Ednl. Adminstrn., Auburn U., 1997. Gen. therapeutic recreation specialist VA Med. Ctr., Murfreesboro, Tenn., 1973-79, music therapist Marion, Ind., 1979, chief recreation therapy service Tucson, 1979-84, chief recreation therapy Northport, N.Y., 1984-87, health systems specialist Dir.'s Office Cleve., 1987-88, adminstrv. asst. to assoc. dir., 1988-91, adminstrv. asst. to chief of staff Tuskegee, Ala., 1991-97; sr. health sys. specialist, med. dir. clin. programs Ctrl. Ala. Vets. Health Care sys., 1997—2008, dep. assoc., chief staff edn., dir. staff devel. Adj. instr. Mid. Tenn. State U., part-time 1978—; guest speaker, 1975—; facilitator AchieveGlobal. Contbr. articles to profl. jours. Mem. Am. Psychol. Assn. (assoc.), Nat. Assn. Music Therapy (cert.), NAFE, Phi Kappa Phi. Home: 1003 Wallace Ave Opelika AL 36801-6958 Office Phone: 334-725-3080. Business E-Mail: carol.sanders@va.gov.

SMITH-STERLING, CAROLYN LEOLA, technology educator; b. Beaumont, Tex., Mar. 21, 1954; d. Adam and Ruby Lee Smith; m. Paul Aaron Sterling, July 14, 1972; children: Paul Aaron Sterling Jr., Gregory Alan Sterling, Cicely Nicole Sterling-Bodwin. AAS in Gen. Office Tech., Houston CC, 1989; BS in Tech., U. Houston, 1994, MS in Tech., 1996; EdD, Tex. Southern U., Houston, 2006—. Lic. evangelist COGIC Tex. SE III, 1997. Prof. Lamar Inst. Tech., Beaumont, 1997—; acad. advisor, rsch. asst. U. Houston, Beaumont, 1988—94; tchr. Houston Ind. Sch. Dist., 1996—97. Adv. bd. mem. Lamar Inst. Tech. Office and Adm., Beaumont. Co-dir.: (plays) To Cast Her Own Shadow Women's Suffrage Movement in Tex. (1st Pl. Phi Theta Kappa State Conv., Tyler Tex., 1988). Pres. Minister's Wives Cir., Tex. SE III, Beaumont, Tex., 1993—97, Bus. and Profl. Women Orgn., Tex. SE III, Houston, 1994—97; pastor Non-denominational Ministry, 2001—08; precinct chair Jefferson County Election, Beaumont, 2008, del., county conv., 2008. Mem.: U. Houston Alumni Assn., Tex. CC Tchrs. Assn., Beta Gamma Phi, Phi Theta Kappa (advisor 1999—2003). Avocations: travel, reading. Office: Lamar Inst Tech 855 E Lavaca St Beaumont TX 77710 Office Fax: 409-839-2919. Business E-Mail: carolyn.sterling@lit.edu.

SMITH-THOMPSON, PATRICIA ANN, public relations consultant, educator; b. Chgo., June 7, 1933; d. Clarence Richard and Ruth Margaret (Jacobson) Nowack; m. Tyler Thompson, Aug. 2, 1992; children from previous marriage: Deborah, Kurt, Nancy, Janna, Gail, Lori. Student, Cornell U., 1951—52; BA, Centenary Coll., Hackettstown, NJ, 1983. Prodn. asst. Your Hit Parade Batten, Barton, Durstine & Osborne, 1953-54; pvt. practice polit. cons., 1954-66; legal sec., asst. Atty. John C. Cushman, 1966-68; field dep. L.A. County Assessor Office, 1968-69; pub. info. officer L.A. County Probation Dept., 1969-73; dir. consumer rels. Fireman's Fund, San Francisco, 1973-76; spl. projects officer L.A. County Transp. Commn., 1977-78; tchr. Calif. State U., Dominguez Hills, 1979-86. Editor, writer Jet Propulsion Lab., 1979—80; pub. info. dir. L.A. Bd. Pub. Works, 1980—82; pub. info. cons. City of Pasadena, Calif., 1982—84, pub. rels. cons., 1983—90; cmty. affairs cons. Worldport L.A., 1990—92; tchr. Kern County Schs., 2002—. Contbr. articles to profl. jours. Active First United Meth. Ch. Commn. Missions and Social Concerns, 1983—89; bd. dirs. Depot, 1983—87; mem. devel. com. Pasadena Guidance Clinics, 1984—85; pres. Cultural Arts Assn., Bear Valley Springs, 1999—2000, Calif. Press Women, Bay Area, 1975. Recipient Pro award, L.A. Publicity Club, 1978, Outstanding Achievement award, Soc. Consumer Affairs Profls. Bus., 1976, Disting. Alumni award, Centenary Coll., 1992. Mem.: Nat. Assn. Mental Health Info. Officers (3 regional awards 1986), Calif. Press Women (pres. Bay area 1975—76, award 1974, 1978, 1983, 1984, 1985, Cmty. Rels. 1st pl. winner 1986, 1987, 1988, 1989), Nat. Press Women (Calif. chpt. pres. 1975—76, Pub. Rels. award 1986), Pub. Rels. Soc. Am. (accredited mem., consumer program award 1977, 2 awards 1984, Joseph Roos Cmty. Svc. award 1985). Republican. Home and Office: 24145 Jacaranda Dr Tehachapi CA 93561-8309 Office Phone: 661-821-3804.

SMITS, EDWARD JOHN, historian, consultant; b. Freeport, NY, Dec. 11, 1933; s. Karl M. and Jennie (Spring) S.; m. Ruth K. Hall; children: E. John, Robert K., Theodore R. BA, Hofstra U., 1955; MA, NYU, NY, 1959. Curator Nassau County Hist. Mus., East Meadow, NY, 1956-70; dir. Div.sn Mus. Svc. Nassau County, Syosset, NY, 1971-92. Nassau County historian, 1985—; planning coord. Mus. at Mitchel Ctr., 1994-2001; chmn. Nassau County Centennial Com.; CEO, Museums at Mitchel Cradle of Aviation, 2002-04. Author: Long Island Landmarks, 1970, Creation of Nassau County, 1959, Nassau, Suburbia USA, 1974. Trustee Friends for L.I.'s Heritage, Nassau County Hist. Soc.; trustee, past pres. Levittown Libr. Bd. 1st lt. U.S. Army, 1955-56. Fulbright grantee, 1965; recipient Nassau County disting. svc. award, 1970, alumni disting. svc. award Hofstra U., 1970, Achievement award N.Y. State Historians, 2004 Mem. Am. Assn. Mus., Am. Assn. State & Local History. Avocations: book collecting, antique toys, golf. Home: 14 Wavy Ln Wantagh NY 11793-1202 Office Phone: 516-383-1557.

SMITS, JASPER, humanities educator; b. Nijmegen, Netherlands, Apr. 28, 1974; m. Jill Coody Smits, June 17, 2000. PhD, U. Tex. Austin, 2004. Asst. prof. So. Meth. U., Dallas, 2004—. Office: So Methodist Univ 64214 Hilltop Lane Dallas TX 75205

SMITS, KATHLEEN CURRAN, artist, educator; b. Urbana, Ill., Oct. 14, 1958; d. David James and Nancy (Judson) Curran; 1 child, Samuel. BS in Plant and Soil Scis., U. Mass., 1981; MA in Spirituality, Women's Leadership Inst., Hartford Sem., 2004. Cert. in digital arts Asnuntuck CC, 2008. Greenhouse mgr. Conn. Valley Biol. Supply Co., Southampton, Mass., 1982-85; bus. owner Mass., Tex., Conn., 1986-97; artist, tchr. Cheshire, Conn., 1996—; exhibit dir. Cheshire Acad., 2001—03. Tchr., cons. Housatonic Children's Ctr., Ansonia, Conn., 1997-98; art edn. dir. Wallingford (Conn.) Parks and Recreation, 1997-2000, dir. A Summer Arts Program, 2002—; tchr. Stratford (Conn.) Childs Ctr., 1999-2000; dir. art exhibit Cheshire (Conn.) Pub. Libr., 1999—2008; faculty fine arts dept. Cheshire Acad., 2000-03; adj. faculty, Manchester CC Digital Arts, Conn., 2008-. Exhibited at Salmagundi Club, NYC, Copley Square, Boston, Office of Sen. Joe Lieberman, Washington, West Hartford Art League (award), Housatonic Art League (award), Arts & Crafts Assn. (award), Meriden, Pioneer Valley Inst. (award), City Wide Open Studios, New Haven, others. Chair environ. com. Mansfield (Tex.) C. of C., 1990—93; chair Mansfield Area Fund, 1990—95; v.p. Mansfield C. of C., 1990—91; bd. dirs., ann. show chair Cheshire (Conn.) Art League, 1998, 2000, 2001, v.p. in charge of programs, 1998—2000. Recipient Citizen of Yr. award Mansfield C. of C., 1991, Unsung Hero award Trust for Pub. Land, 1992, Citizen's Excellence award City of Mansfield, 1996 Mem.: New Haven Arts Coun., New Britain Mus. Am. Art, Assn. Ctrl. Conn. Artists (founding pres. 1998), Arts and Crafts Assn. Meriden (bd. dirs. 1997), Am. Artists Profl. League. Avocations: gardening, environmental activist, cross country skiing, hiking, bird watching. Personal E-mail: kcsmits@kcsmitsgallery.com. Business E-Mail: Kcs1014@sbcglobal.net.

SMITS, RONALD FRANCIS, retired language educator, poet; b. Bayonne, NJ, Dec. 22, 1943; s. Edwin Joseph and Florence Ann Smits; m. Bonnie Lee Brown, June 10, 1970 (div. Mar. 1976); 1 child, Ronald Thomas. AB, Rutgers U., 1966; MS, Ind. State U., 1969; PhD, Ball State U., 1978. Instr. English, Kaskaskia Coll., Centralia, Ill., 1969-74; instr. Ball State U., Muncie, Ind., 1976-78; asst. prof. English, Indiana U. Pa., 1979-92, assoc. prof., 1992-96, prof., 1996—2009; ret. Contbr. poems to jours.; author: (poems book) Push. 1st lt. U.S. Army, 1966-68, Vietnam. Doctoral fellow Ball State U., 1974-78; Disting. Faculty Award, Creativ Arts, Indiana U. Pa, 1993; recipient Outstanding Faculty award English Assn. of Pa. State U., 2002. Avocations: walking, nature hikes, nature study, reading. Home: PO Box 466 Ford City PA 16226-0466 Home Phone: 724-763-7024. Personal E-mail: rfs2@windstream.net.

SMITTLE, NELSON DEAN, military analyst, artist; b. Peebles, Ohio, Sept. 19, 1934; s. Nelson John and Alma Katherine (Green) S.; m. Claire Wiggins, May 5, 1973. BS, BFA, U. Cin., 1962, MA, 1971. Commd. 2d lt. US Army, 1962; staff officer US Army Photo Agy. Pentagon, Washington, 1966; detachment comdr. tactical comms. Vietnam, 1967-68; commn. transferred to USAF, 1970; instr. art U. Cin., 1972; comdr. 907th communications squadron Rickenbacker AFB, Ohio, 1972; dir. ops. fixed communications Air Combat Command Langley AFB, Va., 1982; dir. info. systems AWACS Saudi Arabia, 1984-85; dep. chief of staff standard systems Air Material Command Wright-Patterson AFB, Ohio, 1985; comdr. engring. installation divsn. Tinker AFB, Okla., 1988; commd. col., ret. USAF, Cin., 1988, 91, ret., 1991; pres. Falcon Techs., Cin., 1991-98; tchr. Princeton City Sch. Dist., Cin., 1992-94; pres. Thumbs Up Aerospace Art, Cin., 1998—; instr. art history Cin. State Tech. & Cmty. Coll., 2000—; mil. analyst 700 WLW AM Radio, Cin., 2001—, WCPO TV, 2003—, WXIX TV, 2001—, WWNC AM Radio, 2006—, WNKU FM Radio, 2006—; lectr. Thumbs Up Am., Ams. at War, 2001—; asst. prof. fine arts Clermont Coll., Batavia, Ohio, 2007—. Lectr. USAF Mus., Ams. at War, 2002—; cons. Air War Coll., Air U., Maxwell AFB, Ala., 1987—, Def. Systems Mgmt. Coll., Ft. Belvoir, Va., 1988—; faculty Cin. Acad. Leadership U. Cin. Coll. Law, 2003—. Author: Army Visual Presentation, 1966 (medal 1966), Famous Moments in Aerospace History, 1997; exhibited in group shows Mus. of Flight, Seattle, 1997, Midland Arts Ctr., Mich., 1997, Wichita Ctr Arts, 1998, Ralice Studio, Cin., 1998, Master Works Exhibit, Cin., 1999, Cin. Mus. Ctr., 1998, Mus. Aviation, Warner Robbins, Ga., 1999, Pub. Libr. Cin., Hamilton County, Ohio, 1999, Cin. Art Club, 2001, Kathy McCoy Design Studio, Batavia, Ohio, 2004, The Miterbox Studio, Cin., 2005; mil. cons. costume dept. Across the Universe, film prodn., 2006; author cover art Jour. of League of World War I Aviation Historians, Jour. WWI Aviation Historians, 1999. Mem. Batavia City Coun., Ohio, 1972; pres. Ohio Buckeye Wing Assn., Columbus, 1973; mem. Air Force Policy Coun., Washington, 1978; congl. campaign mgr., 1993; bd. dirs. Cin. Art Club, 1995-96. Decorated Commendation medal; recipient Meritorious Svc. medal Dept. Def., 1986, 91. Mem.: VFW, DAV, Mil. Officers Assn. Am., Am. Soc. Aviation Artists, Res. Officers Assn., Air Force Assn., Cin. Warbirds, Spl. Ops. Warrior Found., 82d Airborne Assn., Aircraft Owners and Pilots Assn., Mil. Order Purple Heart (hon.). Avocations: writing, walking, science fiction. Home and Office: Thumbs Up America 198 Palisades Pointe Cincinnati OH 45238-5653 Office Phone: 513-922-6018.

SMOAK, EVAN L., lawyer; b. Columbia, SC, Jan. 30, 1967; s. Lewis E. and Phyllis Anderson. BAS cum laude, U. S.C., 1989; JD, U. Va., 1992. Bar: Conn. 1992, NY 1993, US Dist. Ct. (so. and ea. dists.) NY 1993, US Ct. Appeals (2d cir.) 2000, US Ct. Appeals (7th cir.) 2004. Actor S.C. Ednl. Television, Columbia, 1977-86; atty. Werner & Kennedy, NYC, 1992-97; assoc., ptnr. Barger & Wolen, NYC, 1997—. Art auction co-chair Empire State Pride Agenda, NYC, 1996-98, devel. com., 1999-2005, bd. dirs., 2000-2005, N100 fundraiser co-chair, 2001-02, exec. com. 2002-05, bd. counsel, 2002-04; vice-chair fall dinner fundraiser, 2002, co-chair, 2003; bd. dirs. Empire State Pride Agenda Found., 2005—06; arbitrator cert. com., AIDA Reinsurance and Insurance Arbitration Soc., 2005—07. Recipient Thomas Moore Craig award U. S.C., 1988; Carolina scholar, 1985-89, Nat. Merit scholar, 1985-89. Mem. ABA, Assn. Bar of City of N.Y., Phi Beta Kappa, Omicron Delta Kappa. Democrat. Office: Barger & Wolen LLP 10 E 40th St 40th Fl New York NY 10016 Home: 225 Fifth Ave New York NY 10010 Home Phone: 212-206-8734; Office Phone: 212-557-2800.

SMOAK, RANDOLPH DUNCAN, JR., surgeon; b. Bamberg, SC, May 5, 1933; MD, Med. Coll. S.C., 1959. Diplomate Am. Bd. Surgery. Intern Grady Meml. Hosp., Atlanta, 1959-60; resident surgery Med. U. S.C.-Teaching Hosps., 1962-65, resident, tchg. fellow, 1965-66; fellow surgery MD Anderson Cancer Ctr., Houston, 1966-67; surg. staff Orangeburg (S.C.) Calhoun Regional Hosp., 1967-87, emeritus staff, 1987; clin. prof. surgery Med. U. S.C., Charleston, 1987—, U.S.C. Sch. Medicine, Columbia, 86—. Fellow ACS; mem. AMA (pres. 2000-01), So. Med. Assn., Soc. Head and Neck Surgeons, So. Soc. Clin. Surgeons, Soc. Clin. Oncology. Office: 112 Cloister Cove Orangeburg SC 29115 Personal E-mail: randysmoak@earthlink.net. Business E-Mail: smoak@ama-assn.org.

SMOCK, RAYMOND WILLIAM, historian; b. Jeffersonville, Ind., Feb. 8, 1941; s. Richard and Lottie (Paciorek) S.; m. Phyllis Lee Chadwick, Feb. 12, 1961 BA, Roosevelt U., Chgo., 1966; PhD, U. Md., College Park, 1974. Rsch. asst. Md. Constl. Conv., Annapolis, 1967-68; lectr. in history U. Md., College Park, 1968-72; co-editor The Booker T. Washington Papers, 14 vols., 1972-83; pres. Instructional Resources Corp., Lanham, Md., 1976-83, Rsch. Materials Corp., College Park, 1982-83, dir., 1982-85; historian, dir. Office for Bicentennial, U.S. Ho. of Reps., Washington, 1983-89, Office of Historian, U.S. Ho. of Reps., Washington, 1989-95. Mem. editl. advisors Md. Historian, College Park, 1971—95; exec. dir. Robert C. Byrd Ctr. for Legis. Studies, Shepherd U., Shepherdstown, W.Va., 2002—. Author: A Talent for Detail: The Photographs of Miss Frances Benjamin Johnston 1889-1910, 1974, Booker T. Washington: Black Leadership in the Age of Jim Crow, 2009; co-editor: A Guide to Manuscripts in the Presidential Libraries, 1985, Masters of the House, 1998; editor: Booker T. Washington in Perspective: The Essays of Louis R. Harlan, 1988; author, editor: Landmark Documents on the U.S. Congress, 1998. Ford Found. fellow, 1970; recipient Philip M. Hamer award Soc. Am. Archivists, 1979 Mem. Nat. Coun. Pub. History, Assn. for Documentary Editing (pres. 1983-84), Orgn. Am. Historians, So. Hist. Assn., Soc. History in Fed. Govt. (v.p./pres.-elect 2000—), Assn. Ctrs. for Study of Congress (pres. 2005-08), W.Va. Humanities Coun. (bd. mem. 2006—), Nat. Hist. Publs. and Records Commn. Avocations: photography, astronomy. Office Phone: 304-876-5670. Personal E-mail: raysmock@aol.com. Business E-Mail: rsmock@shepherd.edu.

SMOKER, WENDY RUE KARTINOS, neuroradiologist, consultant, educator; b. Evanston, Ill., Feb. 28, 1948; d. Nicholas John and Marjorie (Smith) Kartinos; 1 child, Andrew Jason Smoker. BS, U. Iowa, 1971, MS, 1972, MD, 1977. Diplomate Am. Bd. Radiology, cert. added qualification in neuroradiology Am. Bd. Radiology. Asst. prof. radiology U. Iowa Hosps., Iowa City, 1982—86; assoc. prof. radiology U. Utah, Salt Lake City, 1986—90, acting dir. neuroradiology, 1989—90; prof. radiology Med. Coll. Va., Richmond, 1990—2001, dir. neuroradiology, neurology & neurosurgery, 1990—2000, prof. neurosurgery, 1997—2001, prof. otolaryngology, 1998—2001; prof. radiology U. Iowa Hosps., Iowa City, 2002—, dir. neuroradiology, 2002—. Contbr. chpts. to books; dep. editor Radiology, 1997-01; mem. editl. adv. bd. Am. Jour. Neuroradiology, 1989-97, The Radiologist, 1993-96, Stroke,

1996-97. Fellow: Am. Coll. Radiology; mem.: Radiol. Soc. N.Am. (program com. 1992—97), Am. Soc. Neuroradiology (sec. 1996—98), Am. Assn. Women Radiologists (treas. 1993—99, v.p. 2002—03), Am. Soc. Head and Neck Radiology (pres. 1998—99, 1st past pres. 1999—2000, councilor 1999—2005). Avocations: scuba diving, river rafting, jazz singing. Office: U Iowa Hosps Dept Radiology 200 Hawkins Dr 0453 G JCP Iowa City IA 52242 Business E-Mail: wendy-smoker@uiowa.edu.

SMOLANSKY, BETTIE MORETZ, sociology educator; b. Columbia, SC, June 1940; d. Walter Jennings Sr. and Opal (Ledford) Moretz; m. Oles M. Smolansky, Dec. 29, 1966; children: Alexandra Smolansky Zentmeyer, Nicholas Jennings. AB in Sociology, Lenoir-Rhyne Coll., 1962; MA in Sociology, Duke U., 1964; PhD in Sociology, Pa. State U., 1984. From instr. sociology to prof. Moravian Coll., Bethlehem, Pa., 1964—88, prof., 1988—2009, chmn. Dept. Sociology, 1991—97, 2005—09, interim dean faculty, 1998—99, dean acad. affairs, 2000—01. Trustee Moravian Coll., 1977-81, 91-95, sec. presdl. search com., 1996-97; NEH visitor core curriculum workshop Bklyn. Coll., 1985, mem. curriculum evaluation conf. 1988. Co-author: The USSR and Iraq, 1991 (Am. Assn. Advancement of Slavic Studies Marshall Schulman prize 1992), The Lost Equilibrium, 2001. Bd. dirs. Northampton County Area on Aging, Bethlehem, 1984-90, 2003—08; vice chair United Way Allocations Panel, Bethlehem, 1984-90; chair YWCA Commn. on Status of Women, Bethlehem, 1992-94; bd. dirs. YWCA of Bethlehem, 1993-97, 98-2002, 1st v.p., 1998-2000, pres., 2001-02. Recipient NDEA fellow, 1962-64, Disting. Alumnus award Lenoir-Rhyne Coll., 1995, Named YWCA Bethlehem Woman of Yr., 2008. Mem. Am. Sociol. Assn., Ea. Sociol. Assn., Lehigh Valley Assn. Acad. Women (pres. 1988-89, Woman of Yr. 1995-96), ODK (advisor 1987-90), AKD (advisor 1991—2009). Home: 3665 Walt Whitman Ln Bethlehem PA 18017-1553 Office: Moravian Coll Dept Sociology 1200 Main St Bethlehem PA 18018-6650 Office Phone: 610-861-1317. Business E-Mail: mebms01@moravian.edu.

SMOLEN, LEE M., lawyer; b. 1960; BS with highest honors, U. Ill., 1982; JD, U. Chgo., 1985. CPA; bar: Ill. 1985. Assoc. real estate group Sidley Austin LLP, 1985—93, ptnr. real estate group, 1993—. Chair Chgo. real estate group Sidley Austin LLP, 2004—, co-chair practice devel. com. Mem.: ABA. Office: One S Dearborn St Chicago IL 60603 Office Phone: 312-853-7823. Office Fax: 312-853-7036. Business E-Mail: lsmolen@sidley.com.

SMOLEN, ROBERT L. (BOB SMOLEN), federal agency administrator, retired military officer; married; 3 children. BA in Comm., Allegheny Coll., Meadville, Pa., 1974; student in Operational Readiness Tng., Vandenberg AFB, Calif., 1974; student, Air Command and Staff Coll., Maxwell AFB, Ala., 1984—85, Air War Coll., 1991—92; M in Pub. Adminstrn., U. Okla., 1976; M in Internat. Rels., Auburn U., 1985. Advanced through grades to maj. gen. USAF, 2003; Minuteman missile sys. crew mem., instr. and evaluator 91st Stategic Missile Wing, Minot AFB, ND, 1974—77; airborne missile ops. officer 4th Airborne Command Control Squadron, Ellsworth AFB, SD, 1977—79; aide to comdr. North Am. Aerospace Def. Command, Colorado Springs, 1979—80; congl. liaison officer to spl. asst. to dir. of legislative liaison Dept. Air Force, Washington, 1980—83; chief inter-agy. ops. plans branch, def. sys. mobilization planning activity US Dept. Def., 1983—84; internat. polit.-mil, affairs officer spl. actions branch Air Force Internat. Affairs, 1985—88; asst. chief of staff Air Tng. Command, Randolph AFB, Tex., 1988, exec. officer to comdr., 1988—89; dep. comdr. 12th Air Base Group, Randolph AFB, 1989—91; comdr. 750th Support Squadron, Onizuka AFB, Calif., 1992—93, 51st Support Group, Osan Air Base, Republic of Korea, 1993—95; chief inquiry divsn. Sec. of Air Force Office of Legis. Liaison, Washington, 1995, chief Senate Liaison Office, 1995—96; comdr. 72nd Air Base Wing, Tinker AFB, Okla., 1996—98; dep. dir. nuc. and counterproliferation Office of Dep. Chief of Staff of Air and Space Ops. Hdqs. USAF, Washington, 1998—99, dir. nuc. and counterproliferation, 2002—04; dir. manpower & personnel The Joint Staff, US Dept. Def., 2000—02; dir. strategic policy & arms control Nat. Security Coun., 2004—06; comdr. Air Force Dist. Washington, Bolling AFB, 2006—07; dep. adminstr. for def. programs Nat. Nuc. Security Adminstrn. US Dept. Energy, 2007—. Decorated Disting. Svc. medal USAF, Def. Superior Svc. medal with oak leaf cluster, Legion of Merit, Def. Meritorious Svc. medal, Meritorious Svc. medal with three oak leaf clusters, Joint Svc. Commendation medal, Air Fore Commendation medal with oak leaf cluster, Joint Svc. Achievement medal, Air Force Achievement medal, Combat Readiness medal, Nat. Def. Svc. medal with two bronze stars, Global War on Terrorism Svc. medal, Korea Def. Svc. medal; Nat. and Internat. Security Program fellow, John F. Kennedy Sch. Govt., Harvard U., 2000. Office: Nat Nuc Security Adminstrn US Dept Energy 1000 Independence Ave SW Washington DC 20585*

SMOLENSKI, LISABETH ANN, physician; b. Pitts., Oct. 1, 1950; d. Anthony Edward and Betty Jean (Gross) S.; m. William Ward Daniels, May 24, 1980; 1 child, Kathryn Elizabeth. BA, Carlow Coll., Pitts., 1972; MD, Hahnemann U., Phila., 1982. Diplomate Am. Bd. Family Practice. Resident in family practice West Jersey Health Sys., Voorhees, N.J., 1982-85; pvt. practice, Somerville, Tenn., 1985-90, Memphis, 1990—2003; with Spectrum Pain Clinics, Franklin-Nashville, Tenn., 2003—04, Cumberland Back Pain Clinic PC, Cookeville, Tenn., 2005—, Clarksville, Tenn., 2005—. Sec. exec. com. med. staff Meth. Hosp. Somerville, 1988-90. Fellow: Am. Acad. Family Physicians. Republican. Avocation: reading. Office: Cumberland Back Pain Clinic PC 480 Neal St Cookeville TN 38501 also: Cumberland Back Pain Clinic PC 271 Med Park Dr Clarksville TN 37043-6310 Office Phone: 931-520-8104, 931-647-5747. Business E-Mail: lsmolenski@painmgmtcenters.com.

SMOLENSKY, EUGENE, economics professor; b. Bklyn., Mar. 4, 1932; s. Abraham and Jennie (Miller) S.; m. Natalie Joan Rabinowitz, Aug. 16, 1952; children: Paul, Beth. BA, Bklyn. Coll., 1952; MA, Am. U., 1956; PhD, U. Pa., 1961. Prof. econs. U. Wis., Madison, 1968-88, chmn. dept., 1978-80, 86-88; dir. Inst. for Research on Poverty, U. Wis., 1980-83; dean Grad. Sch. Pub. Policy, U. Calif., Berkeley, 1988-97, prof. pub. policy, 1997—. Author: Public Expenditures, Taxation and the Distribution of Income: The U.S., 1950, 61, 70, 77. Mem. Nat. Acad. Pub. Adminstrn., 1994; mem. com. on child devel. rsch. and pub. policy NAS, Washington, 1982-87, mem. com. on status of women in labor market, 1985-87. With USN, 1952-56. Mem. Am. Econs. Assn. Democrat. Jewish. Avocation: master etching and lithograph collecting. Home: 669 Woodmont Ave Berkeley CA 94708-1233 Office: U Calif Dept Pub Policy 2607 Hearst Ave Berkeley CA 94720-7305 Office Phone: 510-643-3979. Business E-Mail: geno@berkeley.edu.

SMOLINSKI, BRYAN, professional hockey player; b. Toledo, Ohio, Dec. 27, 1971; m. Julie Smolinski, July 12. B. Broadcasting, Mich. State U. Center Boston Bruins, 1992-96, Pitts. Penguins, 1996, NY Islanders, 1996—99, LA Kings, 1999—2003, Ottawa Senators, 2003—06, Chgo. Blackhawks, 2006—07, Vancouver Canucks, 2007—. Mem. Team USA, World Cup of Hockey, 1996, 2004. Achievements include being a member of World Cup Champion Team USA, 1996.

SMOLLA, RODNEY ALAN, dean, law educator; b. Pueblo, Colo., Mar. 13, 1953; s. Richard Paul and Harriet (Waskowiak) S. BA, Yale U., 1975; JD, Duke U., 1978. Bar: Ill. 1979, US Supreme Ct. 1987. Law clk. to presiding judge U.S. Ct. Appeals, Jackson, Miss., 1978-79; assoc. Mayer, Brown & Pratt, Chgo., 1979-80; asst. prof. De Paul U. Sch. Law, Chgo., 1980-81, U. Ill. Coll. Law, 1981-83; prof. U. Ark. Sch. Law, 1983-87; vis. prof. U. Denver Coll. Law, 1987-88; Arthur B. Hanson prof. constl. law Coll. of William and Mary, Williamsburg, Va., 1988-98, dir. Inst. Bill of Rights Law, 1988-96; George E. Allen prof. U. Richmond Sch. Law, Va., 1998—2007, dean, 2003—07; dean, Roy. L. Steinheimer prof. law Wash. and Lee U. Sch. Law, Lexington, Va., 2007—. Author: Suing the Press: Libel, The Media & Power, 1986 (cert. of merit ABA 1987), Law of Defamation, 1986, Jerry Falwell V. Larry Flynt: The First Amendment on Trial, 1988; (with Banks and Braveman) Constitutional Law: Structure and Rights in Our Federal System, 1991, 3rd edit., 1996, Free Speech in an Open Society, 1992 (William O. Douglas Prize 1993), Smolla and Nimmer on Freedom of Speech, 1994, 3rd edit., 1996, Federal Civil Rights Acts, 1994; editor: A Year in the Life of the Supreme Court, 1995 (ABA Silver Gavel award), Deliberate Intent: A Lawyer Tells the True Story of Murder by the Book, 1999. Fellow, cons. Annenberg Washington Program in Comm., 1987-96; project dir. Annenberg Libel Reform Task Force, 1988-89; reporter Bill of Rights Adv. Com. to the Commn. on the Bicentennial of US Constitution, 1989. Recipient Recipient Disting. Prof. of Yr. award, U. Ark., 1986, Outstanding Faculty award, Va. State Coun. Higher Edn., 2002. Mem. ABA, AAUP (mem. litigation com.), Ill. Bar Assn. Office: Wash and Lee Univ Sch Law 506 Sydney Lewis Hall Lexington VA 24450-2116 Office Phone: 540-458-8501. Office Fax: 540-458-8488. Business E-Mail: smollar@wlu.edu.*

SMOLLER, BRUCE MELVYN, psychiatrist; b. Chgo., Sept. 19, 1944; s. Norman and Beatrice Betty (Janows) Smoller; m. Cosette Nieporent, Aug. 20, 1967; children: Jamie, Lauren. AB, Cornell U., 1965; MD, Tulane U., 1969. Diplomate Am. Bd. Psychiatry and Neurology. Intern Maimonides Med. Ctr., NYC, 1969-70; resident in orthopedic surgery Einstein Med. Ctr., NYC, 1970-73; resident in psychiatry Cornell Med. Ctr., NYC, 1973-76; pvt. practice in psychiatry with emphasis on clin. and rsch. aspects of pain Bethesda, Md., 1976—; chmn. dept. psychiatry Holy Cross Hosp., Silver Spring, Md., 1980-83; assoc. clin. prof. psychiatry George Washington U., 1977-91, clin. prof. psychiatry, 1991—. Cons. NIH, 1979—2001. Co-author: Pain Control: The Bethesda Program; editor: Md. Medicine, The State Med. Soc.'s Jour. With Med. Corps USAR, 1970—78. Mem.: Md. State Med. Soc. (pres. 2007—08), Montgomery County Med. Soc. (pres. 2004—05). Office: 5530 Wisconsin Ave Bethesda MD 20815-4404 Office Phone: 301-951-4466. E-mail: bsmoller@radix.net.

SMOLLETT, JURNEE DIANA, actress; b. NYC, Oct. 1, 1986; Actress (TV films) Sunday in Paris, 1991, Selma, Lord, Selma, 1999, Ruby's Bucket of Blood, 2001, (TV series) Hangin' with Mr. Cooper, 1992, Full House, 1992—94, On Our Town, 1995, Cosby, 1998—2000 (Outstanding Youth Actor/Actress, NAACP Image award, 1999, 2000), Wanda at Large, 2003, (films) Jack, 1996, Eve's Bayou, 1997 (Best Child Performance, Broadcast Film Critics Assn., 1998), Beautiful Joe, 2000, Roll Bounce, 2005, The Great Debaters, 2007 (Outstanding Actress in a Motion Picture, NAACP Image award, 2008), guest appearances on (TV series) Martin, 1992, NYPD Blue, 1996, Happily Ever After: Fairy Tales for Every Child, 1999, Strong Medicine, 2002, ER, 2002, House M.D., 2006. Mem. bd. dirs. Artists for a New South Africa.

SMOLTZ, JOHN ANDREW, professional baseball player; b. Warren, Mich., May 15, 1967; m. Dyan Smoltz, 1991 (div. 2007); children: John Andrew Jr., Rachel Elizabeth, Carly Maria, Kelly Christina; m. Kathryn Darden, 2009. Pitcher Atlanta Braves, 1988—2008, Boston Red Sox, 2009, St. Louis Cardinals, 2009—. Host John Smoltz Celebrity Pro-AM Golf Tournament; active Atlanta Cmty. Food Bank, Children's Healthcare of Atlanta; bd. chmn. Kings Ridge Christian Sch.; co-founder John and Dyan Smoltz Found., 1997—. Recipient Cy Young award, 1996, Silver Slugger award, 1997, Rolaids Relief award, 2002, Roberto Clemente award, 2005, Lou Gehrig Meml. award, 2005, Branch Rickey award, 2007; named Nat. League Championship Series MVP, 1992, Nat. League Pitcher of Yr., The Sporting News, 1996; named to Nat. League All-Star Team, 1989, 1992—93, 1996, 2002—03, 2005, 2007. Achievements include leading the National League in: starts, 1992, 1997, 2006; strikeouts, 1992, 1996; wins, 1996, 2006; innings, 1996, 1997; saves, 2002; member of the World Series Championship winning Atlanta Braves, 1995; being the only pitcher to accumulate 200 wins and 150 saves; recorded his 3,0000th strikeout, April 22, 2008; Major League Baseball's all-time leader in post-season wins (15). Avocations: golf, basketball. Office: St Louis Cardinals 700 Clark St Saint Louis MO 63102*

SMOOT, BURGESS HOWARD, federal official; b. Washington, Mar. 28, 1947; s. James Elias and Frances Galdinia (Hawkins) S.; m. Ann Louise Gordon, Aug. 9, 1982; children: Frederick Hawkins, Chanel Gordon, Ervine Gholston, Shemerrian. Cook Freedmans Hosp., Washington, 1968-70; mail & file clk. Asst. Chief of Staff Intelligence, Washington, 1970-74; adminstrv. asst. logistics Office Joint Chiefs of Staff, Pentagon, Washington, 1974-77, adminstrv. asst. policy & plans, 1977-80. Author: (poetry) Lost in the Beginning. Capt. Neighborhood Watch Group, Fort Washington, Md., 1995-97; presdl. election official, 2000—, primary election judge for Md., 2002, primary and gen. presdl. election judge, 2004; judge for Md. gov., 2002; pres. Sunday Schs. 12rs. through adult Capital Ward, 2002—04, libr., 2004—; judge primary and gen. elections Md., 2006. With U.S. Army, 1965-68, Civil Air Patrol, 1964-65. Decorated Army Commendation medal, Combat Infantry badge, Good Conduct medal, Nat. Def. medal, Vietnam Svc. medal, Vietnam Campaign ribbon, Sharp Shooter's Medal. Mem. Disabled Am. Vets. (comdr., svc. officer, sgt. at arms, hon. guard). Democrat. Mem. Lds Ch. Avocations: baseball, football, wrestling, bowling, pool. Home: 10103 Kathleen Dr Fort Washington MD 20744-2530

SMOOT, GEORGE FITZGERALD, III, astrophysicist; b. Yukon, Fla., Feb. 20, 1945; BS in Math and Physics, MIT, 1966, PhD in Physics, 1970. Rsch. physicist MIT, 1970; rsch. physicist, space sciences lab. Univ. Calif., Berkeley, Calif., 1971—, prof. physics, 1994—; rsch. physicist Lawrence Berkeley Lab., 1974—. Team leader, differential microwave radiometer experiment, COBE (Cosmic Background Explorer) satellite; mem. steering group on cosmic background explorer satellite, prin. investigator on isotrophy experiment (NASA), 1975; 80 mem. Mgmt. and Ops. Working Group for Shuttle Astronomy, 1976-80; mem. adv. com. White Mountain Rsch. Station, 1982; mem. superconducting magnet facility for the space station study team, 1985; mem. Ctr. for Particle Astrophysics, U. Calif. Berkeley, 1988; mem. adv. com. Radio Astronomy Lab., 1990. Author: (with Keay Davidson) Wrinkles in Time, 1993; contbr. articles to profl. jours. Recipient Space/Missiles Laurels award Aviation Week & Space Technology, 1992, Popular Sci. award, 1992, Disting. Scientist, ARCS Found., Inc., 1993, Kirby award, 1993, Golden Plate award, 1994, Ernesto Orlando Lawrence award US Dept Energy, 1994, Einstein medal, 2003, Grober prize with John Mather, 2006, Daniel Chalonge medak, 2006; co-recipient Nobel Prize in Physics, Nobel Found., 2006. Mem. Internat. Astron. Union, Am. Phys. Soc. (mem. com. on the safety comml. nuclear reactors, 1974-75), Am. Astron. Soc., Sigma Xi., AAAS. Office: Lawrence Berkeley Nat Lab 1 Cyclotron Rd 5OR5008 Berkeley CA 94720*

SMOOT, JULIANNA, political fundraiser; b. NC, 1967; Grad., Smith Coll., 1989. Fin. dir. Senator Tom Daschle, Senator John Edward's Campaign, 1998, Dem. Senatorial Campaign Com., 2006; nat. fin. dir. Barack Obama's 2008 Presdl. Campaign. Mem. Presdl. Inaugural Com. (PIC). Democrat.*

SMOOT, SKIPI LUNDQUIST, psychologist; b. Aberdeen, Wash., Apr. 10, 1934; d. Warren Duncan and Miriam Stephen (Bishop) Dobbins; m. Harold Richard Lundquist, June 2, 1951 (div. Mar. 1973); children: Kurt Richard, Mark David, Ted Douglas, Blake Donald; m. Edward Lee Smoot, June 14, 1975. BA in Psychology, Coll. of William and Mary, 1978; MA, Pepperdine U., 1980; PhD, Calif. Sch. of Profl., Psychology, San Diego, 1985. Lic. clin. psychologist, Calif.; lic. marriage and family therapist, Calif. Owner, operator McDonald's Restaurants, San Pedro and Torrance, Calif., 1965-76, Williamsburg, Va., 1965-76; psychotherapist Coll. Hosp., Cerritos, Calif., 1979-81, Orange County Child Guidance, Laguna Hills, Calif., 1981-82, Calif. State Police, Costa Mesa, 1982-83, Anaheim, 1983-84; psychologist Orange County Mental Health, Santa Ana, Calif., 1984-85, Psychol. Ctr., Orange and El Toro, Calif., 1985-91; clin. dir. Career Ambitions, Lake Forest, Calif., 1991-98, Psychol. Decisions, Irvine-Laguna Hills, Calif., 1991-94. Psychol. cons. seminars and workshops for bus., Irvine and Laguna Hills, 1991-98. Mem. APA, Calif. Psychol. Assn. Democrat. Avocations: music, travel, rsch. Office: Psychol Decisions Career Ambitions Unltd 10 McLaren Ste D Irvine CA 92618 Office Phone: 949-770-2675. Personal E-mail: skipilsmootphd@cox.net.

SMOOT, STEPHEN ANNESE, columnist, educator; b. Charleston, W.Va., Nov. 8, 1973; s. Stephen Annese Smoot and Mary Beth Wilson; m. Crystal Jane Fultz, May 1993; children: Emily Shannon, Jared Stephen. MA, Marshall U., Huntington, W.Va., 2001. Instr. Potomac State Coll., Keyser, W.Va., 2005—; columnist Mineral Daily News Tribune, Keyser, 2008. Vice chmn. Potomac Highlands Reps., 2007—08. Methodist. Home: 335 D St Keyser WV 26726 Office: Potomac State Coll Fort Ave Keyser WV 26726 Personal E-mail: smoot.stephen@gmail.com. Business E-Mail: sasmoot@mail.wvu.edu.

SMOTHERMON, PEGGI STERLING, middle school educator; b. Dallas, Nov. 11, 1948; d. Kiel Sterling and Ann C. (Wolfe) Sterling; m. William C. Smothermon Jr., June 20, 1981; children: Kirsten, Melinda, William III. BA, So. Meth. U., Dallas, 1973; MLA, So. Meth. U., 1978. Tchr. Richardson (Tex.) Ind. Sch. Dist., 1973-90, Coppell (Tex.) Ind. Sch. Dist., 1990-96, 2002—. J.J. Pearce scholar. Mem. NEA (faculty rep., membership chmn., sec.), Nat. Coun. Tchrs. Math., Tex. Tchrs. Assn., Assn. Coppell Educators, Tex. Computer Edn. Assn., Tex. Coun. Tchrs. Math., Kappa Delta Pi. Home: 408 Greenridge Dr Coppell TX 75019-5714 Office: Coppell Mid Sch N 120 Natches Trace Dr Coppell TX 75019

SMOTHERMON, REBA MAXINE, elementary school educator; b. Liberal, Kans., July 8, 1933; d. Albert Isaac and Georga Maxine (Long) Shank; m. Wendell Scott Smothermon, Sept. 6, 1953; children: Jennifer Lynn Smothermon Kirby, Wendell Brent Smothermon. BA in Edn., Wichita State U., 1955; MA in Ednl. Psychology and Guidance, U. No. Colo., 1959. Cert. tchr. Kans., Calif., Colo., arthritis instr. Tchr. second grade Unified Sch. Dist. 480/Washington Sch., Liberal, Kans., 1955-57, Adams County Dist. Skyline Vista Sch., Westminster, Colo., 1957-61; elem. tchr. Ventura Unified Santa Ana Sch., Ojai, Calif., 1964-80, Unified Sch. Dist. #480, Southlawn McKinley Schs., Liberal, 1980-95; ret., 1995. Literary coun. mem. Southwest Reading Coun., Liberal, 1985-95. Participant devel. sch. curriculum, 1977-79. Sec. to pres. Evergreen Garden Club, Liberal, 1980-05; youth sponsor, pres. women's group 1st United Meth. Ch., Liberal, 1945—; mem. Liberal Panhellenic, 1980-96; bd. dir., pres. Community Concerts of Liberal, 1987-91; pres. Liberal Woman's Club, 1995—; mem. Kans. Coun. on Travel and Tourism, 2002-05; pres. Book Club I, sec.-treas., tchr. swimming, arthritis support groups. Recipient Lifetime Achievement award, Southwest Daily Times, 2006. Mem. AAUW (pres. local chpt. 1980-2007, Woman of Yr. 1985, state chmn. internat. rels. com. 1985-90), DAR (regent chaplain 1972-), PEO (various to pres. 1985—), Aurora Club, Ladies' Oriental Shrine N.Am. Republican. Avocations: music, reading. Home: 830 S Clay F3 PO Box 470 Liberal KS 67905-0470 Home Phone: 620-624-4682. Personal E-mail: rwsmut@sbcglobal.net.

SMOTHERS, TOM, actor, singer; b. NYC, Feb. 2, 1937; s. Thomas B. and Ruth Smothers; children: Tom, Bo, Riley Rose; m. Marcy Carriker, Sept. 9, 1990. Student, San Jose State Coll. Owner winery, Kenwood, Calif. Nightclub appearances in Reno, Lake Tahoe, Las Vegas, Nev., and various venues in the U.S.; co-star TV situation comedy Smothers Brothers Show, 1965-66, Smothers Brothers Comedy Hour, CBS-TV, 1967-69, 70, weekly variety show The Smothers Brothers Show, NBC-TV, 1975; starred in films The Silver Bears, Get To Know Your Rabbit, A Pleasure Doing Business, Serial, There Goes the Bride, Pandemonium, Speed Zone; starred on Broadway in I Love My Wife, 1978-79; appeared in TV movie Terror at Alcatraz, 1982; starred in Smothers Brothers Spl. and Series, 1988-89. Office: Knave Prodns Ste 107B 6442 Coldwater Canyon Ave North Hollywood CA 91606-1137 Office Phone: 818-754-0351. E-mail: smobro1@aol.com.

SMOTRICH, DAVID ISADORE, architect; b. Norwich, Conn., Oct. 6, 1933; s. Max Z. and Ida (Babinsky) S.; m. Bernice D. Strachman, Mar. 25, 1956; children: Ross Lawrence, Maura Faye, Hannah. AB, Harvard Coll., 1955, MArch, 1960. Master planning team, Town of Arad, State of Israel, 1961-62; assoc. Platt Assocs., NYC, 1963-65; gen. ptnr. Smotrich & Platt, NYC, 1965-74, Smotrich Platt & Buttrick, NYC, 1975-76, Smotrich & Platt, NYC, 1976-85, David Smotrich & Ptnrs., NYC, 1985—. Cons. to Jerusalem Master Plan Office, Israel Ministry of Housing, 1967. Planning bd. Town of New Castle, N.Y., 1974-81; exec. bd. Road Rev. League, Bedford, N.Y., 1966-70. With AUS, 1955-57. Recipient Bard award, 1969, 85, Archtl. Record award, 1971, 73-75, 78, Design award HUD, 1980. Mem. AIA (Nat. Honor award 1969, N.Y. State Honor awards 1984, 94, Cmty. Design awards 1991, 93, AIA Coll. of Fellows 1993), Assn. Engrs. and Archs. in Israel, Phi Beta Kappa, Harvard Club (N.Y.C.). Home: 7 Mayberry Close Chappaqua NY 10514-1113 Office: David Smotrich & Ptnrs 443 Park Ave S New York NY 10016-7322 Office Phone: 212-889-4045. Personal E-mail: ds@dsmotricharch.com.

SMUCKER, RICHARD K., food products executive; m. Emily Delp; 1 child. BS, Miami U., Ohio, 1970; MBA, Wharton Sch. Bus., U. Penn, 1972. Mgmt. positions including treas., CAO, CFO & exec. v.p. The J.M. Smucker Co., Orrville, Ohio, pres., 1987—, co-CEO, 2001—, exec.

chmn., 2008—. Bd. dir. The J.M. Smucker Co., Wm. Wrigley Jr., Co., The Sherwin-Williams Co. Chmn. bd. trustees Miami Univ.; trustee Mus. Arts Assn. Cleveland Orch. Office: 1 Strawberry Ln Orrville OH 44667-1241

SMUCKER, TIMOTHY P., food products executive; m. Jennifer Coddington; 3 children. BS Economics, Coll. of Wooster, 1967; MBA Mktg., Wharton Sch. Bus., U Penn, 1969. Chmn. The J.M. Smucker Co., 1984—, co-CEO, 2001—. Bd. dirs. The J.M. Smucker Co., Huntington BancShares, Inc., Dreyer's Grand Ice Cream, Inc., Grocery Mfr. Am., Inc.; bd. trustees Coll. of Wooster; mem. steering com. Heartland Edn. Community. Office: 1 Strawberry Ln Orrville OH 44667-1241

SMUKAL, MICHAEL WILLIAM, musician, educator, composer; s. Paul Herbert and Carol Hannen Smukal; children: Michael Adam, Stephen Andrew. BA, MusM, U. Nev., Las Vegas, 1985. Dir. of bands Silvestri Jr. H.S., Clark County Sch. Dist., Las Vegas, 1985—. Composer, arranger Warner Bros. Music Publs., Las Vegas. Music arranger: educational jazz publs. Now Rock, Ye Rested Gentlemen (Editor's Choice, 2004), Song Of The Volga Boatmen, trombonist: with Elvis Presley, 1975—77, Elvis in Concert, CBS TV spl., Spring Tours '77, Elvis Presley, Moody Blue, Elvis Presley, Elvis: A Canadian Tribute, Elvis Presley, Platinum: A Life in Music, Elvis Presley, Elvis in Concert, Elvis Presley, This is Elvis, Elvis Presley, Elvis Aaron Presley. State pres. Nat. Assn. Of Jazz Educators, Las Vegas, Nev., 1984—86. Tech. sgt. USAF, 1971—75, Washington, DC. Named SW Region Disting. Educator of the Yr., Clark County Sch. Dist., 2003—04. Mem.: Internat. Assn. Jazz Educators, Nev. Music Educators Assn., Music Educator's Nat. Conf. Personal E-mail: smukal@cox.net.

SMUKSTA, MICHAEL J., history professor; b. Chgo., Ill., Sept. 21, 1950; m. Kris Richardson, Sept. 2, 1972; children: Jessica Albert, Matthew. PhD, Northern Ill. U., DeKalb, 1991. Assoc. prof. history Viterbo U., La Crosse, Wis., 1991—. Office: Viterbo Univ 900 Viterbo Dr La Crosse WI 54601 Business E-Mail: mjsmuksta@viterbo.edu.

SMULIAN, JOHN C., obstetrician; MD, Tulane U. Sch. Medicine Sch., New Orleans, LA, 1985; MPH, Tulane U. Pub. Health and Tropical Medicine, New Orleans, LA, 1985. Diplomate Am. Bd. Obstetrics Gynecology, 1991, cert. maternal fetal medicine Am. Bd. Obstetrics Gynecology, 1997. Prof., dept. obstetrics, gynecology reproductive scis. UMDNJ-Robert Wood Johnson Med. Sch., New Brunswick, NJ, 1994—2007; vice chairman, dept ob/gyn, chief-divsn. maternal fetal medicine Lehigh Valley Hosp., Allentown, Pa., 2008—; prof. dept. ob-gyn. Pa. State U. Coll. Medicine, 2008—. Author more than 120 rsch. articles in maternal fetal medicine. Named one of NJ. Top Dr., NJ. Mag., 2006—07. Office: Lehigh Valley Hosp Cedar Crest & I-78 Allentown PA 18105

SMUTNY, JOAN FRANKLIN, academic director, educator; b. Chgo. d. Eugene and Mabel (Lind) Franklin; m. Herbert Paul Smutny; 1 child, Cheryl Anne. BS, MA, Northwestern U. Tchr. New Trier H.S., Winnetka, Ill.; mem. faculty, founder, dir. Nat. H.S. Inst. Northwestern U. Sch. Edn., Chgo.; faculty, founder, dir. h.s. workshop critical thinking/edn. Nat. Coll. Edn., Evanston, Ill., exec. dir. h.s. workshops, 1970-75; founder, dir. Woman Power Through Edn. Seminar, 1969-74; dir. Right to Read Seminar in critical reading, 1973-74; dir. seminar gifted h.s. students, 1973; dir. gifted programs for 6th, 7th, 8th graders Evanston pub. schs., 1978-79; dir. gifted programs 1st-8th grade Glenview (Ill.) pub. schs., 1979—. Dir. gifted programs Nat.-Louis U., Evanston, 1980-82, dir. Ctr. for Gifted, 1982—; dir. Bright and Talented Project, 1986—, North Shore Country Day Sch., Winnetka, 1982—; dir. Job Creation Project, 1980-82; dir. New Dimensions for Women, 1973; dir. Thinking for Action in Career Edn. Program 1976-79; dir. TACE, dir. Humanities Program for Verbally Precocious Youth, 1978-79; co-dir., instr. seminars in critical thinking Ill. Family Svc., 1972-75; writer ednl. filmstrips in lang. arts and lit. Soc. Visual Edn., 1970-74; spkrs. bur. Coun. Fgn. Rels., 1968-69; adv. com. edn. professions devel. act U.S. Office Edn., 1969—; state team for gifted, Ill. Office Edn., Office of Gifted, Springfield, Ill., 1977; writer, cons. Radiant Ednl. Corp., 1969-71; cons. ALA, 1969-71, workshop leader and spkr. gifted edn., 1971—; coord. career edn. Nat. Coll.Edn., 1976-78, dir. Project 1987—, dir. Summer Wonders, 1986—, Creative Children's Acad., bd. dirs., Worlds of Wisdom and Wonder, 1978—; dir. Future Tchrs. Am. Seminar in Coll. and Career, 1970-72; cons. rsch. & devel. Ill. Dept. Vocat. Edn., 1973—; evaluation cons. DAVTE, IOE, Springfield, Ill., 1977, mem. Leadership Tng. Inst. Gifted, U.S. Office Edn., 1973-74; dir. workshops for h.s. students; cons., spkr. in field; dir. Gifted Young Writers and Young Writers confs., 1978, 79; dir. Project '92 The White House Conf. on Children and Youth; mem. adv. bd. Educating Able Learners, 1991—; chmn. bd. dirs. Barbereux Sch., Evanston, 1992—; asst. editor, editl. bd. Understanding our Gifted, 1994—. Author: Job Creation: Creative Materials, Activities and Strategies for the Classroom, 1982, A Thoughful Overview of Gifted Education, 1990, Your Gifted Child—How to Recognize and Develop the Special Talents in Your Child from Birth to Age Seven, 1987, paperback, 1991, Education of the Gifted: Programs and Perspectives, 1990, Teaching Gifted Young Children in the Regular Classroom, 1997, Gifted Girls, 1998, Stand Up For Your Gifted Child, 2001, Gifted Education: Promising Practices, 2003, Differentiated Instruction, 2003, Differentiating For the Young Child, 2004, Differentiating for the Young Child: Teaching Strategies Across the Content Areas, 2004, Acceleration for Gifted Learners, K-5, 2007; editor: The Young Gifted Child: Potential and Promise: An Anthology, 1998, Creativity Series Ablex, 1998—, Underserved Gifted Populations, 2003; contbg. editor: Roper Rev., 1994—; asst. editor: Understanding Our Gifted, 1995—; editor, contbr.: Maturity in Teching; editor: Jour. Ill. Assn. for Gifted, 1995—; mem. adv. bd. Gifted Edn. Press Quar., 1995—; writer: (ednl. filmstrips) The Brothers Grimm, How the West Was Won, Mutiny on the Bounty, Dr. Zhivago, Space Odyssey 2001, Christmas Around the World; contbr. editor numerous books in field; contbr. articles to profl. jours. including Chgo. Parent Mag.; reviewer programs for Gifted and Talented, US Office Edn., 1976-78. Mem. AAUP, Nat. Assn. Gifted Child (nat. membership chmn. 1991—, co-chmn. schs. and programs, co-editor newsletter early childhood divsn., Disting. Svc. award 1996), Nat. Soc. Arts & Letters (nat. bd., 1st and 3d v.p. Evanston chpt. 1990-92), Mortar Bd., Outstanding Educators of Am. 1974, Pi Lambda Theta, Phi Delta Kappa (v.p. Evanston chpt. rsch. chmn. 1990-92). Home: 633 Forest Ave Wilmette IL 60091-1713 Office Phone: 847-901-0173. Personal E-mail: joanfsm@aol.com. *Gifted education is particularly vital in that it discerns the needs of bright, talented children who have an immense amount to contribute to our country and our world. Gifted children are our country's most neglected resource--and most needed. It is my privilege to work in this area, to work with gifted children, their parents and teachers.*

SMYNTEK, JOHN EUGENE, JR., editor; b. Buffalo, Aug. 24, 1950; BA, U. Detroit, 1972. Asst. instr. Mich. State U., East Lansing, 1981; features editor Free Press, Detroit, 1985-92; dir. online svcs. and dir. libr. Free Press Plus, Detroit, 1992-95, spl. features and syndicate editor, 1995—2008; asst. instr. U. Detroit Mercy, 2000—01; columnist governewsdetroit.com, 2009—. Vis. fellow in journalism Duke U., 1988; profl. student publs. advisor U. Detroit Mercy, 1992—94; bd. visitors Wayne State U. Coll. Fine, Performing and Comm. Arts, 2001—05. Recipient Fine Arts Reporting award, Detroit Press Club, 1985. Roman Catholic.

SMYRE, CALVIN, state legislator; b. Ga., May 17, 1948; div.; 1 child. BS in Bus. Adminstrn., Fort Valley State U. Exec. v.p. corp. affairs Synovus Fin. Corp.; mem. Dist. 92 Ga. House of Reps., Atlanta, 1974—92, asst. adminstrn. floor leader Dist. 92, 1983, mem. Dist. 132, 1993—; mem. Dem. Nat. Com., 1984, adminstrn. floor leader. Chmn. univ. sys. Ga. com.; mem. appropriations com., rules com.; chmn. rules com., Ga. Dem. Party, 2001—; mem. appropriations com., ethics com., higher edn. com., spl. rules com. Nat. sec. Nat. Black Caucus State Legislators; bd. trustees Med. Coll. Ga. Found., Morehouse Sch. Med., Jack D. Hughston Found.; chmn. bd. trustees Fort Valley State U. Found.; former nat. pres. Fort Valley State U. Nat. Alumni Assn.; bd. advisors Atlanta U. Sch. Social Work. With U.S. Army. Served in US Army, 1970. Named to Power 150, Ebony mag., 2008. Democrat. Methodist. Office: Dist 132 PO Box 120 Columbus GA 31902-0120 also: 409-G Coverdell Legislative Office Atlanta GA 30334 Office Phone: 706-563-1794. Business E-Mail: calvinsmyre@synovus.com.*

SMYTH, DONALD MORGAN, chemistry professor, researcher; b. Bangor, Maine, Mar. 20, 1930; s. John Robert and Selma (Eubanks) S.; m. Elisabeth Luce, Aug. 1, 1951; children: Carolyn, Joanne. BS in Chemistry, U. Maine, 1951; PhD in Inorganic Chemistry, MIT, 1954. Sr. chemist Sprague Electric Co., North Adams, Mass., 1954-58, sect. head, 1958-61, dept. head, 1961-71; assoc. prof. Lehigh U., Bethlehem, Pa., 1971-73, prof., 1973-95, dir. Materials Rsch. Ctr., 1971-92, Paul B. Reinhold prof. materials sci., engring. and chemistry, 1988-95; emeritus, 1995—. Mem. various coms. Lehigh U., 1973-95; mem. materials rsch. adv. com. NSF, 1984-88, chmn., 1985-86, co-chair ad-hoc com. to brief dir., 1986; mem. coun. materials sci. Dept. Energy, 1986-90; presenter in field. Contbr. articles to profl. jours. Recipient Libsch Rsch. award Lehigh U., 1990, Buessem award Dielectrics Rsch. Ctr., Pa. State U., 1991; grantee in field. Fellow Am. Inst. Chemists, Am. Ceramic Soc. (com. edn. electronics divsn. 1974-78, chmn. Lehigh Valley sect. 1978-79, counselor 1982-00, assoc. editor jour. 1988-92, best paper award 1987, 95, Kraner award Lehigh Valley sect. 1990, Sosman lectr. 1996); mem. Am. Chem. Soc., Nat. Acad. Engring., Materials Rsch. Soc., Electrochem. Soc. (various coms., sec. dielectrics and insulation divsn. 1967-69, vice chmn. 1969-70, chmn. 1970-71, rsch. award battery divsn. 1960). Achievements include patents (with others) for Solid-State Battery Cell with Complex Organic Electrolyte Material, Capacitor with Dielectric Film Having Phosphorous-Containing Component Therein, Solid Barrier Electrolyte Incorporating Additive, others; research in defect chemistry and electrical properties of complex oxides. Home: 3429 Mountainview Cir Bethlehem PA 18017-1807 Office: Lehigh Univ Ctr Advanced Material and Nanotech 5 E Packer Ave Bethlehem PA 18015-3102 Home Phone: 610-867-6544; Office Phone: 610-758-3852. Business E-Mail: dms4@lehigh.edu.

SMYTH, ELLEN GRAY MENEES, systems support specialist; b. Clarksville, Tenn., Mar. 3, 1973; d. James Lee and Laverne Gregory Menees; m. Thomas Henry Menees, Mar. 14, 1998; children: Anne Katherine, Emily Baer. BS in Civil and Environ. Engring., Tenn. Technol. U., Cookeville, 1996, MS in Math., 0200. Mathematician Naval Surface Warfare Ctr., Dahlgren, Va., 2000—05; math instr. Austin Peay State U., Clarksville, 2005—07, course mgmt. sys. specialist, 2007—.

SMYTH, GLEN MILLER, management consultant; b. Abingdon, Va., July 26, 1929; s. Glen Miller and Kathleen (Dunn) S.; m. Cynthia Olson, Aug. 25, 1954 (div. 1967); children: Catherine Ellen, Glen Miller, III, Cynthia Allison; m. Lilian Castel Edgar, Oct. 31, 1968; children: Stephanie Castel, Kimberley Forsyth, Lindsay Dunn. BA, Yale U., 1951; MS in Psychology, Rutgers U., 1958. Mktg. rep. Wheeling Stamping Co., NYC, 1953-56; personnel dir. Celanese Internat., NYC, 1958-71; mgr. orgn. and Manpower Internat. and Can. group Gen. Electric Co., NYC, 1971-73; sr. v.p. human resources Northwest Bancorp., Mpls., 1973-82; sr. v.p. Calif. Fed. Savs., LA, 1983-85; v.p. Career Transition Group, LA, 1985-87; pres. Fuchs, Cuthrell & Co., Inc., LA, 1987-93, Fuchs & Co., LA, 1993-94; pres., CEO Smyth, Fuchs & Co., Inc., LA, 1995-99; v.p. Spherion, 1998—. Leader seminars. Co-author: International Career Pathing, 1971; Contbr. articles to profl. jours. Served with AUS, 1951-53. Mem. Am. Psychol. Assn., Nat. Fgn. Trade Coun. (founder, past chmn. human resources, orgn. com. 1966—), Human Resources Planning Soc., Employment Mgmt. Assn., Jonathan Club, Yale Club of N.Y., North Ranch Country Club, Phi Gamma Delta. Home: 1115 Westcreek Ln Westlake Village CA 91362-5467

SMYTH, JOEL DOUGLAS, newspaper executive; b. Renovo, Pa., Nov. 8, 1941; s. Bernard John and Eva Mae (Stone) S.; m. Madonna Robertson, Nov. 29, 1959; children: Deborah Sue, Susan Kelly, Michael Robertson, Patricia Ann, Rebecca Lee, Jennifer Neilia. Student, Lycoming Coll., 1959. Reporter Del. State News, Dover, 1960-62, news editor, 1962-65, mng. editor, 1965-70, editor, pres., 1970-78; editor Del. Sunday News, 1964-65; pres. Ind. Newspapers, Inc., Dover, 1970-89, chmn., CEO, 1989—. Founding pres. Valley Citizen's League, 1987-90. Recipient writing awards. Mem. AP Mng. Editors Assn. (dir.), Am. Soc. Newspaper Editors, Young Pres.'s Orgn., Sigma Delta Chi. Office: Independent Newspaper Inc PO Box 70001 Dover DE 19903 Home: 8306 E Calle Del Palo Verde Scottsdale AZ 85255-4212

SMYTH, JOSEPH PATRICK, retired military officer, physician; b. Norwalk, Conn., Mar. 2, 1933; s. Patrick and Helen (Heffernan) Smyth; m. Ursula Marie Kirwin, Feb. 22, 1961; children: Donna, Jennifer, Joseph. BA, Fairfield U., 1960; MD, Creighton U., 1964. Diplomate Am. Bd. Med. Examiners. Commd. ensign USN, 1963, advanced through grades to rear adm., 1988; intern Phila. Naval Hosp., 1964-65, internal medicine resident, 1965-68, staff physician, 1968-69; internist, chief of medicine U.S. Naval Hosp., DaNang, Vietnam, 1969-70, Orlando, Fla., 1970-76, chief of medicine, exec. officer Yokosuka, Japan, 1976-80, exec. officer Oakland, Calif., 1980-82, comdg. officer, 1984-86, Okinawa, Japan, 1982—84, Naval Med. Command European Region, London, 1986-90; dep. dir. for med. readiness The Joint Staff, Pentagon, Washington, 1990-92; retired US Navy, 1992; med. dir. Volusia County (Fla.) Dept. of Corrections, 1994—2005. Instr. medicine Jefferson Med. Coll., 1966—69; preceptor USN Physician Asst. Program, Orlando, 1971—76; instr. mgmt. course Navy Med. Dept., Washington, 1986; med. coord. entire Gulf War buildup to Joint Chief Staff chmn. Gen. Colin Powell Operation Desert Shield/Storm, Saudi Arabia, 1990—91; med. dir. Volusia County Dept. Corrections, Fla., 1994—2005. Physician Orange County Fla. Alcohol Ctr., Orlando, 1974—76. Decorated Def. Superior Svc. medal, Legion of Merit, Meritorious Svc. medals with 2 oak leaf clusters, Navy Commendation medal with combat V. Mem.: AMA, Orange County Med. Soc., Am. Acad. Physician Execs., Fla. Med. Assn., Am. Acad. Med. Adminstrs. (Levandowski award 1991), Assn. Mil. Surgeons U.S. Republican. Roman Catholic. Home: 400 Sweetwater Blvd Longwood FL 32779-3422

SMYTH, JOSEPH VINCENT, manufacturing executive; b. Belfast, Ireland, July 18, 1919; s. Joseph Leo and Margaret M. (Murray) S.; m. Marie E. Cripe, Mar. 22, 1941; children: Kevin W., Brian J., Ellen M., Vincent P. BS cum laude, U. Notre Dame, 1941. With Arnolt Corp., Warsaw, Ind., 1946-63, exec. v.p., gen. mgr., until 1963; pres., gen. mgr. Hills-McCanna Co., Carpentersville, Ill., 1963-72; pres. Lunkenheimer Co., Cin., 1972-79; v.p. Condec Flow Control Group, Chgo., 1979-82; cons., 1982—. Mem.: K.C. Address: 7656 Spring Bay Cove Orlando FL 32819-7208 Business E-Mail: j.smyth1@cfl.rr.com.

SMYTH, MICHAEL P., archaeologist, educator; b. Libertyville, Ill., Aug. 31, 1957; s. Paul H. and Edna M. Smyth; m. Pilar Suarez Valbuena, Dec. 20, 1984; children: Sean-Michael S., Sebastian S. PhD, U. N.Mex, Albuquerque, 1988. Vis. prof. anthropology U. Ky., Lexington, 1993—96; prof. anthropology Rollins Coll., Winter Pk., Fla., 1998—. Pres. Found. Am. Rsch. Inc., Winter Springs, Fla., 2008—. Contbr. articles to profl. jours. Mem.: Soc. Am. Archeology. Office: Found Am Rsch Inc PO Box 195553 1065 E State Rd 434 Winter Springs FL 32719-5553 Business E-Mail: info@farinco.org.

SMYTH, PAUL BURTON, lawyer; b. Phila., Aug. 15, 1949; s. Benjamin Burton and Florence Elizabeth (Tomlinson) S.; m. Denise Elaine Freeland, May 31, 1975. BA, Trinity Coll., 1971; JD, Boston Coll., 1974. Bar: Conn. 1974, D.C. 1975, U.S. Dist. Ct. D.C., 1980, U.S. Supreme Ct., 1985. With Dept. Interior, 1974—. Dep. assoc. solicitor for energy and resources Office of Solicitor, Washington, 1987—95, assoc. solicitor, divsn. mineral resources, 2009—; dep. assoc. solicitor for land and water resources Office of Hearings and Appeals, Arlington, 1995—2007, counselor to solicitor, 2007—09; lectr. environ. law George Washington U. Law Sch., Washington, 1997—2001. Editor: Federal Reclamation and Related Laws Annotated, Reclamation Reform Act Compilation, 1982—88; contbr. articles to legal pubs. Bd. dirs. EcoVoce, 1998—; trustee Rocky Mtn. Mineral Law Found., 1999—2001. Mem. ABA (coun. 1991-94, budget officer 1994-98, sec. natural resources, energy and environ. law, exec. editor Nat. Resources and the Environ. 1989-91). Office: Office of Solicitor Dept Interior 1849 C St Washington DC 20240-0001 Home Phone: 703-683-0322; Office Phone: 202-208-4307. Personal E-mail: paulb.smyth@verizon.net.

SMYTH, PETER HAYES, radio executive; b. Apr. 25, 1952; s. Arthur and Irene (McNamara) Smyth; m. Catherine Comerford, Aug. 8, 1976; children: Nancy, Colin, Kathleen. BA, Holy Cross Coll., Worcester, Mass., 1975; postgrad., Fordham U., 1975-76. Retail sales man Sta. WROR Radio, Boston, 1975-76, gen. sales mgr., 1976-83, Sta. WOR Radio, NYC, 1983-86; v.p. greater media radio sales, v.p. gen. mgr. Greater Boston Radio Stas., 1986-96; regional v.p., gen. mgr. Greater Boston Radio Group, 1996-98; group v.p. radio Greater Media Inc., Boston, 1998—, COO, pres., COO, 2000—02, pres., CEO, 2002—. Cons. Greater Media Cable, North Oxford, Mass., 1988—89; v.p. Radio Advt. Bur.; trustee, past pres. New England Media Assn. Bd. dir. Holy Cross Coll., Worcester, U. Club, Boston, United Way of Mass., 1993—94; bd. trustees Emerson Coll.; bd. dir. Police Athletic League. Named America's Best Broadcaster, Radio Ink, 2005; named one of Most Powerful People in Radio, 2001, 2003, 2004, 2005. Mem.: Country Music Assn., Nat. Assn. Broadcasters (chmn., Spectrum Task Force, bd. dirs.), New England Broadcast Assn. (bd. dirs. 1987 1987, pres. 1992, v.p.). Republican. Roman Catholic. Avocations: golf, swimming, skiing. Office: Greater Media Inc 35 Braintree Hill Pk Ste 300 Braintree MA 02184

SMYTH, RICH, publishing executive; b. Bronx, NY; married; 2 children. BA in Comm., Boston Coll. With Carnation Co. (now Nestle Foods), Dallas, 1985—88; joined Southern Living mag. Time Inc., 1988, nat. sales mgr. NYC, 1996—98, advt. dir., 1998—2000, v.p., 2000—, pub., 2003—. Office: Southern Living 20th Floor 1271 Ave of Americas New York NY 10020-1391 also: Southern Living PO Box 523 2100 Lakeshore Dr Birmingham AL 35209 Office Phone: 888-254-9654, 212-522-1212. Office Fax: 212-522-4199. E-mail: rich_smyth@timeinc.com.*

SMYTH, RUSSELL P., diversified financial services company executive, former food products executive; b. 1956; BS in Acctg., No. Ill. U., MBA. Various positions in the fin. arena McDonald's Corp., 1984—97, v.p. Latin Am. Group, 1996—99, sr. v.p., internat. relationship ptnr. for Southeast and Ctrl. Asia, 1999—2001; pres. McDonald's Ptnr. Brands, 2001—03, McDonald's Europe, 2003—05; pres., CEO H&R Block Inc., Kans. City, 2008—. Bd. dirs. H&R Block Inc., 2008—. Mem.: Ill. CPA Soc., Fed. Inst. of Cert. Pub. Accountants. Office: H&R Block Inc 1 H&R Block Way Kansas City MO 64105

SMYTH, RYAN, professional hockey player; b. Banff, Alta., Can., Feb. 21, 1976; m. Stacey Smyth. Left wing Edmonton Oilers, 1994—2007, NY Islanders, 2007, Colo. Avalanche, 2007—. Mem. Team Can., Olympic Games, Salt Lake City, 2002, Team Can., World Cup of Hockey, 2004. Named to NHL All-Star Game, 2007. Achievements include being a member of gold medal Canadian Hockey team, World Junior Championships, 1995, Salt Lake City Olympic Games, 2002; being a member of World Cup Champion Team Canada, 2004. Office: Colo Avalanche Pepsi Ctr 1000 Chopper Cir Denver CO 80204

SMYTHE, CHEVES MCCORD, internist, geriatrician, educator, dean; b. May 25, 1924; Student, Yale Coll., 1942—43; MD cum laude, Harvard, 1947. Diplomate Am. Bd. Internal Medicine, Am. Bd. Geriatrics. Intern, asst. resident Harvard Med. Svc., Boston City Hosp., 1947—49, chief resident, 1954—55; resident chest svc. Bellevue, 1949—50; rsch. fellow Presbyn. Hosp., NYC, 1950—52; assoc. medicine Med. Coll. S.C. Sch. Medicine, 1956—58, asst. prof. medicine, 1958—60, assoc. prof. medicine, 1960—66, dean, 1963—65; attending physician Wesley Meml., Cook County North Side VA Hosps., Chgo., 1967—70; with Aga Khan U. Hosp., Karachi, Pakistan, 1990—91; dean faculty health scis., prof. medicine Aga Khan U., Karachi, Pakistan, 1982—85, prof., chmn. dept. medicine, 1990—91; chief Med. Svcs. at LBJ Hosp., Houston, 1991—95; prof. divsn. gen. medicine dept. internal medicine U. Tex. Med. Sch., Houston, 1970—, dean, 1970—75, dean pro tem, 1995—96. Assoc. med. dir. Hermann Hosp., 1996—. Bd. dirs. Assn. Am. Assoc. Med. Colls., Office: U Tex Med Sch 6431 Fannin St 1-108 Houston TX 77030-1501

SMYTHE, WILLIAM RODMAN, physicist, researcher; b. LA, Jan. 6, 1930; s. William Ralph and Helen (Keith) S.; m. Carol Richardson, Nov. 27, 1954 (dec. Dec. 1987); children: Stephanie, Deborah, William Richardson, Reed Terry; m. Judith Brean Travers, Jan. 1, 1989. BS, Calif. Inst. Tech., 1951, MS, 1952, PhD, 1957. Engr. Gen. Electric Microwave Lab., Palo Alto, Calif., 1956-57; asst. prof. U. Colo., 1958-63, assoc. prof., 1963-67, prof., 1967-95, chmn. nuclear physics lab., 1967-69, 81-83, 90-92, prof. emeritus, 1995—. Mem. Am. Phys. Soc. Clubs: Colorado Mountain (Boulder). Achievements include inventing negative ion cyclotron. Home: 2106 Knollwood Dr Boulder CO 80302-4706 E-mail: Rod.Smythe@colorado.edu.

SMYTHE, WILLIAM ROY, surgeon; b. Temple, Tex., July 7, 1960; s. Royce Roy and Peggy Lucille Smythe; m. Allison Leigh Freund, Nov. 8, 2008; children: Meghan Dallaire, Durham Richard, Sebastian Alexander. MD, Tex. A&M U., Coll. Sta., 1989. Cert. Tex. State Med. Bd., 1998, diplomate Am. Bd. Surgery, 1998, Am. Bd. Thoracic Surgery, 2000. Assoc. prof. surgery U. Tex. M.D. Anderson Cancer Ctr., Houston, 1998—2004; prof. dept. surgery Scott & White Health Sys., Temple, 2004, Roney endowed chair surgery, 2004, dir., 2005; prof. molecular and cellular medicine Tex. A&M U., 2004. Trustee Scott & White Hosp. and Clinic, Scott, Sherwood and Brindley Found., Temple, 2005, bd. mem., 05. Contbr. articles to profl. jours. Dir. Sherwood and Brindley Found., Temple, Tex., 2005; founder Magic Carpet Found., Austin, Tex., pres. Named one of Best Dr. in America, 2003—08; Physician Scientist grant, U. Tex. MD Anderson Cancer Ctr., 2002—04, grant, NIH, 2002—08, NCI, 2002—08. Mem.: Soc. U. Surgeons, Tex. Surg. Soc., Soc. Clin. Surgery, Southern Surg. Soc., Am Assoc Thoracic Surgery, Soc. Thoracic Surgeons (com. mem. 2005). Office: Scott and White Tex A&M Coll Med 2401 South 31st St Temple TX 76504

SNADER, JACK ROSS, retired publishing company executive; b. Athens, Ohio, Feb. 25, 1938; s. Daniel Webster and Mae Estella (Miller) S.; m. Sharon Perschnick, Apr. 4, 1959; children: Susan Mae, Brian Ross. BS, U. Ill., 1959. Cert. mgmt. cons. With mktg. Richardson-Merrell, Cin., 1959-65, Xerox Corp., NYC, 1965-67, Sieber & McIntyre, Chgo., 1967-69; pres. Systema Corp., Northbrook, Ill., 1969—2008; ret., 2008. Mem. exec. adv. bd. bus. program Trinity Internat, U. Author Systematic Selling, 1987, The Sales Relationship, 1988. Mem. ASTD, Inst. Mgmt. Cons.

SNAPP, ELIZABETH, librarian, educator; b. Lubbock, Tex., Mar. 31, 1937; d. William James and Louise (Lanham) Mitchell; m. Henry Franklin Snapp, June 1, 1956 (div. Dec. 2001). BA magna cum laude, North Tex. State U., Denton, 1968, MLS, 1969, MA, 1977. Asst. to archivist Archive of New Orleans Jazz Tulane U., 1960-63; catalog libr. Tex. Woman's U., Denton, 1969-71, head acquisitions dept., 1971-74, coord. readers svcs., 1974-77, asst. to dean Grad. Sch., 1977-79, instr. libr. sci., 1977-88, acting Univ. libr., 1979-82, dir. librs., 1982—2002, dir. librs. emeritus, 2002—, univ. historian, 1995—2002; adj. prof. dept. history and govt. Tex. Woman's U., Denton, 2002—; rsch. assoc. Tex. Woman's U. Libr., Denton, 2002—. Chair-elect Tex. Coun. State U. Librs., 1988—90, chmn., 1990—92; adv. com. on libr. formula Coord. Bd. Tex. Coll. and Univ. Sys., 1981—92; Libr. Sys. Act adv. bd. Tex. State Libr. and Archives Commn., 1999—2002; del. OCLC Nat. Users Coun., 1985—87, by-laws com., 1985—86, com. on less-than-full-svcs. networks, 1986—87; trustee AMIGOS Libr. Svcs., 1994—2000, sec. bd. trustees, 1996—97, vice-chmn. bd. trustees, 1997—99, chair bd. trustees, 1999—2000; project dir. NEH consultancy grant on devel. core curriculum for women's studies, 1981—82; chmn. Blue Ribbon com. 1986 Gov.'s Commn. for Women to select 150 outstanding women in Tex. History; project dir. math./sci. anthology project Tex. Found. Women's Resources; co-sponsor Irish Lecture Series, Denton, 1968, 70, 73, 78. Asst. editor Tex. Academe, 1973—76; co-editor: Read All About Her! Texas Women's History: A Working Bibliography, 1995; contbg. author Women in Special Collections, 1984, Special Collections, 1986, book reviewer Libr. Resources and Tech. Svcs., 1973—2002; contbr. articles to profl. jours. Trustee, treas. Adult Day Care of North Tex., 2002—04, v.p., 2004; sec. Denton County Dem. Caucus, 1970. Recipient Ann. Pioneer award, Tex. Woman's U., 1986, Women's Studies Vision award, 1998. Mem.: AAUW (legis. br. chmn. 1973—74, br. v.p. 1975—76, br. pres. 1979—80, state historian 1986—88, treas. 1998—99), ALA (stds. com. 1983—85), AAUP, Tex. Assn. Coll. Tchrs. (pres. Tex. Woman's U. chpt. 1976—77), So. Conf. Brit. Studies, Women's Collecting Group (chmn. ad hoc com. 1984—86), Tex. Hist. Commn. (judge for Farenbach History prize 1990—93), Tex. Libr. Assn. (program com. 1978, Dist. VII chmn. 1985—86, archives and oral history com. 1990—92, co-chair conf. program com. 1994, Tall Texan selection com. 1995—96, treas. exec. bd. 1996—99, Centennial com. 2000—02), AAUW Ednl. Found. (rsch. and awards panel 1990—94), Alliance Higher Edn. (chair coun. libr. dirs. 1993—95), Rotary Internat. (sec. local chpt. 1999—2002), Soroptimist Internat. (pres. Denton chpt. 1986—88), Women's Shakespeare Club (pres. 1967—69), Pi Delta Phi, Alpha Lambda Sigma (pres. 1970—71), Alpha Chi, Beta Phi Mu (pres. chpt. 1976 1978, sec. nat. adv. assembly 1978—79, pres. 1979—80, nat. dir. 1981—83). Methodist. Office: TWU Sta PO Box 424093 Denton TX 76204-4093 Personal E-mail: esnapp@verizon.net. *The idealistic dreams of youth can be translated into making a difference in the work place and in your personal life if you develop a big picture that includes the ideas of individuals of diversity and if you give life your full attention, enthusiasm and courage and give a few your steadfast friendship.*

SNAPP, HARRY FRANKLIN, historian, educator; b. Bryan, Tex., Oct. 15, 1930; s. H.F. and Ethel (Manning) Snapp; m. Elizabeth Mitchell, June 1, 1956 (div. Dec. 20, 2001). BA, Baylor U., 1952, MA, 1953; PhD, Tulane U., 1963. Instr. U. Coll. Tulane U., 1960—62; asst. prof. history Wofford Coll., 1963—64, U. North Tex. (formerly North Tex. State U.), Denton, 1964—69, assoc. prof., 1969—94; dir. Tex. Rsch. Ctr. Biog. Study of Women, Denton, 1995—; pres., dir. Read All About Her Tex. Women's Biographic Ctr., Inc., 1995—. Editor: Brit. Studies Mercury, 1970—84, Tex. Acad., 1973—76; co-editor: Read All About Her! Texas Women's History: A Working Bibliography, 1995, enlarged edit., 1997; author (with others): West Texas Historical Assn. Year Book, 1994, 1996; contbr. articles to profl. jours. Mem. Bridwell Assocs. of So. Meth. U., Friends of Southwestern Art, Am. Com. Irish Studies; mem. adv. com. on acad. freedom and tenure policy, coord. bd. Tex. Coll. and Univ. System. Recipient North Tex. State U. Faculty Rsch. award, 1966, 1967. Mem.: AAUP (pres. North Tex. chpt. 1968—69, pres. Southwestern regional conf. 1971—72, pres. Tex. conf. 1974—76, nat. coun. 1976—86), Butler Soc. (Ireland), Northamptonshire Record Soc., Libr. History Round Table, Libr. Rsch. Round Table, Hist. Assn. (London), Tex. State Hist. Assn., Panhandle-Plains Hist. Soc., West Tex. Hist. Assn. (bd. dirs. 1997—), Am. Hist. Assn., So. Conf. Brit. Studies (sec.-treas. 1969—84), Tulane U. Alumni Assn., Lambda Chi Alpha, Alpha Chi. Democrat. Methodist. Home: 1904 N Lake Trl Denton TX 76201-0602 Office: Read All About Her Tex Women's Biographic Ctr Inc PO Box 424053 Denton TX 76204-4053

SNAPP, MARY E., computer software company executive, lawyer; b. Manhattan, Kans., Sept. 7, 1953; BS, U. Kans., 1974; MBA, Wayne State U., 1981; JD, U. Mich., 1984. Bar: Wash. 1984. Assoc. Preston, Thorgrimson, Ellis & Hollman, Seattle, 1984—88; corp. atty. Microsoft Corp., Redmond, Wash., 1988, assoc. gen. counsel, dep. gen. counsel, corp. v.p., dep. gen. counsel corp. affairs dept., 2002—. Bd. dirs. Greater Seattle C. of C., King County-Snohomish County YWCA, Artist Trust, ArtsFund; active in Food Lifeline, Ryther Child Ctr., Cath. Cmty. Services. Mem.: ABA, ABA Forum on Comm. Law (mem. governing com.), Wash. State Bar Assn., Seattle-King County Bar Assn., Phi Beta Kappa. Office: Microsoft Corp Law & Corp Affairs Dept 1 Microsoft Way Redmond WA 98052-6399 Office Phone: 425-882-8080. Office Fax: 425-936-7329.

SNAPPER, ERNST, mathematics professor; b. The Netherlands, Dec. 2, 1913; came to U.S., 1938, naturalized, 1942; s. Isidore and Henrietta (Van Buuren) S.; m. Ethel Lillian Klein, June 1941; children: John William, James Robert. MA, Princeton U., 1939, PhD, 1941; MA (hon.), Dartmouth Coll., 1964. Instr. Princeton, 1941-45, vis. asso. prof., 1949-50, vis. prof., 1954-55; asst. prof. U. So. Calif., 1945-48, asso. prof., 1948-53, prof., 1953-55; NSF post-doctoral fellow Harvard, 1953-54; Andrew Jackson Buckingham prof. math. Miami U., Oxford, Ohio, 1955-58; prof. math. Ind. U., 1958-63, Dartmouth, 1963—, Benjamin Pierce Cheney prof. math., 1971—79. Mem. Am. Math. Soc., Math. Assn. Am. (pres. Ind. sect. 1962-63, Carl B. Allendoerfer award 1980), Assn. Princeton Grad. Alumni (governing bd.), Soc. for Preservation Bridges of Konigsburg, Phi Beta Kappa (hon.), Pi Mu Epsilon (hon.). Home: PO Box 67 Norwich VT 05055-0067

SNAREY, JOHN ROBERT, psychologist, educator; BS, Geneva Coll., Beaver Falls, Pa., 1969; MA, Wheaton Coll., Ill., 1973; EdD, Harvard U., Cambridge, Mass., 1982. Postdoctoral rsch. fellow dept. psychiatry Harvard U., Cambridge, Mass., 1982-84; assoc. rsch. psychologist Wellesley Coll., 1984-85; assoc. prof. human devel. and edn. Northwestern U., Evanston, Ill., 1985-87; prof. human devel. and ethics Sch. Theology and dept. psychology Emory U., Atlanta, 1987—. Mem. senate Emory U., 2001—05, pres., 2003—04, dir. moral cognition and devel. lab., 2005—. Author: How Fathers Care for the Next Generation, 1993; contbr. articles to profl. jours.; editor: Conflict and Continuity: A History of Ideas on Social Equality and Human Development, 1981, Remembrance of Lawrence Kohlberg, 1988, Race-ing Moral Formation: African Am. Perspectives on Care and Justice, 2004; mem. editl. bd. Harvard Ednl. Rev., 1979—81, Jour. Psychology and Theology, 1986—90, Jour. Moral Edn., 1998—, Am. Ednl. Rsch. Jour., 2001—04, mem. editl. adv. bd. Lawrence Erlbaum Assocs., 1988—90. Recipient Exemplary Dissertation award, Nat. Coun. Social Studies, 1982, Kuhmereker Dissertation award, Assn. Moral Edn., 1983, Outstanding Human Devel. Rsch. award, Am. Ednl. Rsch. Assn., 1988, James D. Moran Book award, Assn. Family and Consumer Sci., 1994, Marie C. Keel, Excellence in Mentoring award, 2003. Fellow: APA, Am. Ednl. Rsch. Assn. (divsn. E exec. bd. 1990—2000, moral devel. and edn. spl. interest group co-chair 1994—96, sec. divsn. E 1997—99, Moral Devel. and Edn. Book award 2006); mem.: Assn. Moral Edn. (exec. bd. 1986—2007, program chair 1997, treas. 2001—04, pres. 2004—07). Office: Emory U 1531 Dickey Dr Ste 354 Atlanta GA 30322-0001 Office Phone: 404-727-4185. Business E-Mail: jsnarey@emory.edu.

SNEAD, GEORGE MURRELL, JR., military officer, research scientist, consultant; b. San Diego, Nov. 6, 1922; s. George Murrell and Helen (Olsen) S.; m. Kathleen Hill Dawson, Apr. 26, 1947; children: George Murrell III, James M., William M., John P., Edward W. BS, Va. Mil. Inst., 1943; MS, U. Ill., 1948; PhD, U. Va., 1953. Commd. 2d lt. U.S. Army, 1943, advanced through grades to brig. gen., 1969; with Central Germany campaign 805th Signal Co., Europe, 1945-46; Aleutian sector comdr. Alaska Communication System, 1948-50; sta. at Electronic Warfare Center Ft. Monmouth, N.J. and Ft. Huachuca, Ariz., 1953-56; student U.S. Army Command and Gen. Staff Coll., 1956-57; signal adviser MAAG Vietnam, 1957-58; signal officer Dept. Army, 1958-60; acting dir. research ballistic missile def. Advanced Research Projects Agy., 1960; with U.S. Army Satellite Communications Agy. Ft. Monmouth, 1960-63; student Nat. War Coll., 1963-64; div. signal officer 24th Inf. Div., 1964-65; comdg. officer 7th Signal Group, 1965; dir. Communication /ADP Lab. Ft. Monmouth, 1966-68; exec. asst. chief of staff Communications Electronics, Dept. Army, 1968; dir. army research Dept. Army Washington, 1968-71; comdr. Army Rsch. Offices-Europe, Asia and Durham, 1968—71; mem. Def. Rsch. Coordinating Com., 1968—71; chmn. Army Ops. Rsch. Symposia, 1969—71, Nat. Jr. Sci. and Humanities Symposia, 1969—71; dep. comdr. Army Strategic Communications Command, 1971-73; prin. scientist Gen. Research Corp. McLean, Va., 1973-82; pres. Nat. Sci. Ctr. Found., Burke, Va., 1982-84. Chmn. bd. Am. Fed. Savs. & Loan Assn., Lynchburg, Va., 1985-86; sci./bus. cons., 1986—. Active Boy Scouts Am., 1958-68; bd. dirs. Ctrl. Youth Summer Activities, Ft. Monmouth, 1960-63, Arthritis Found., Washington, 1981-84, Lynchburg Symphony, 1990-95; pres. Acad. Music Theatre, Lynchburg, 1985-95; trustee, vice chmn. bd. dirs. Westminster-Canterbury, Lynchburg, 1991-99; trustee Sci. Mus. Va., 1995-2001; elder Presbyn. Ch., 1986—. Decorated D.S.M., Legion of Merit with two oak leaf clusters, Six Campaign medals, Army Commendation medal with 4 oak leaf clusters, Galandry Cross, Republic Vietnam Civil Actions medal. Mem. Assn. U.S. Army, Armed Forces Communications and Electronics Assn. (sec. Washington chpt. 1968-69), Sigma Xi, Kappa Alpha. Office: PO Box 3306 Lynchburg VA 24503-0306

SNEARLEY, ED, biology professor; b. Charleston, Ill., Aug. 19, 1950; s. Earl and Marilyn Snearley; m. Rhonda Sue Grimes, Dec. 23, 1988; children: Ian McPheron, Travis McPheron, Megan McPheron, Bradley, Kevin. BS in Environ. Biology, Ea. Ill. U., Charleston, 1973, MS in Zoology, 1975; MS in Edn. Counseling, U. Texas, Pan Am., Edinburg, 1994. Prof. biology South Tex. Coll., McAllen, 1994—. Home: 2808 Jay Ave Mcallen TX 78504 Office: South Tex Coll 3201 Pecan Blvd Mcallen TX 78501 Personal E-mail: itm3@aol.com. Business E-Mail: snearley@southtexascollege.edu.

SNEDEKER, JOHN HAGGNER, university president; b. Plainfield, NJ, May 30, 1925; s. Alfred H. and Anna Marie (Ward) S.; m. Noreen I. Davey, Dec. 30, 1950; children— John D., Philip A., Patrick W. BS cum laude, N.Y. U., 1951, MA, 1951; Ed.D., Ind. U., 1959. Dir. lab. human devel. U. Mont., 1952-56; cons. psychologist research Purdue U., 1955; assoc. prof., dir. bur. research Ball State U., 1956-61; prof. higher edn., research asso. Ind. U., 1958; prof., dean Western Wash. State U., Bellingham, 1961-62; pres. Western N.Mex. U., Silver City, 1962—. Mem. exec. bd. Internat. Coun. Spl. Edn., 1952-56; Rocky Mountain regional rep. APA, 1953-56; mem. Gov. Wash. Com. Licensing Tchr. Edn., 1961, Wash. State Legislature Rsch. Tech. Com., 1961. Author or co-author rating scales, attitude and opinion measurement devices; contbr. jours. Bd. dirs. Nat. Sci. Fair; trustee N.Mex. Health Found. Served with U.S. Army, 1943-48. Fellow AAAS; mem. Midwest Psychol. Assn., Inter-Am. Soc. Psychology, Am. Ednl. Research Assn., Holland Soc. N.Y. Address: 2200 Pinon St Silver City NM 88061-7735

SNEE, CHRISTOPHER, professional football player; b. Edison, NJ, Jan. 8, 1982; s. Ed and Diane Snee; m. Katie Coughlin, July 2, 2004; children: Dylan, Cooper Christopher. B, Boston Coll., 2004. Guard NY Giants, 2004—. Active United Way, Susquehanna County, Pa. Named 1st Team All-Pro, AP, 2008; named to Nat. Football Conf. Pro Bowl Team, NFL, 2008. Mem.: French Nat. Honor Soc., Nat. Honor Soc. Achievements include member of Super Bowl XLII Championship winning New York Giants, 2008. Office: NY Football Giants Giants Stadium East Rutherford NJ 07073*

SNEE, LAWRENCE WARREN, geologist; b. Grove City, Pa., Dec. 6, 1947; s. William Warren and Ruth Elizabeth (Goehring) S.; m. Karen Ivy Lund, May 27, 1985 (div. Dec. 1994); children: Jens Erik, Torsten Anders. BS in Geology, Chemistry and Biology, Fla. State U., 1974; MS in Geology, Ohio State U., 1977, PhD in Geology, 1982. Geologist U.S. Geol. Survey, Reston, Va., 1981-83; prof. geology Oreg. State U., Corvallis, 1983-86; rsch. geologist U.S. Geol. Survey, Denver, 1986—. Supr. Argon geochronology lab. U.S. Geol. Survey, Denver, 1986—, mem. adv. bd., 1990—, rsch. chief, 1994—; chief scientist Nat. Coop. Geol. Mapping Team, Ctrl. REgion, 1995—. Author/editor: Emeralds of Pakistan, 1989; contbr. articles to profl. jours. Sgt. USMC, 1966-69, Vietnam. Decorated Bronze Star; Rsch. grantee NSF, U.S. Geol. Survey. Mem. Geo. Soc. Am., Am. Geophys. Union, Soc. Econ. Geologists. Avocations: skiing, hiking, reading, sports, travel. Office: US Geol Survey PO Box 25046 Denver CO 80225-0046

SNEED, LARRY ALLAN, history professor; b. Vincannes, Ind., Aug. 7, 1948; s. Lawrence Harding and Juanita Mae Sneed; m. Rebecca Bruner Adcock (div.); children: Travis, Shane; m. Barbara Vitale Sneed, June 13, 1995. BS in Hist. Edn., Ind. State U., Terra Houte, 1970; MEd in Hist. Edn., U. Ga., Athens, 1975, EDs in Hist. Edn., 1978. Cert. tchr. 2009. Sci. tchr. New Porterdale Elem. Sch., Covington, Ga., 1972—73; social studies tchr. Newton County High Sch., Covington, 1973—78, North Gwinnett High Sch., Suwanee, Ga., 1978—79, Parkview High Sch., Lilburn, Ga., 1979—2004, Mill Creek High Sch., Hoschton, Ga., 2004—. Home bound tchr. Oakland Ctr., Lawrenceville, Ga., 1987—2000; stadium announcer Parkview High Sch., Lilburn, 1980—2003. Author: No More Silence: An Oral History of the Assassination of President Kennedy, 1998. Guest speaker Kiwanis Club, Lilburn, Calif., 1987, 2001, Rotary Club, Duluth, Ga., 1999, Covington, Ga., 2001. Recipient DAR Am. History Tchr. of Yr., Gwinnett County, Ga, 1990—91; named Tchr. of Yr., Park View High Sch., 1990. Fellow: Dealey Plaza. Republican. Meth. Home: 3010 Clegg Farm Rd Social Circle GA 30025 Office: Mill Creek HS 4400 Braselton Hwy Hoschton GA 30548 Business E-Mail: snee1128@bellsouth.net.

SNEED, RONALD ERNEST, retired project engineer, educator; b. Oxford, NC, Nov. 23, 1936; s. Henry Ernest and Jewel Leigh (Hughes) S.; m. Shelba Jean Walters, June 8, 1958; children: Kathy Geneva Grosvenor, Jennie Leigh Berrier. BS in Agrl. Engring., N.C. State U., 1959, PhD in Biol. and Agrl. Engring., 1971. Registered profl. engr., NC; cert. irrigation designer, contractor, landscape irrigation auditor, and irrigation specialist. Sales trainee John Deere Co., 1959-60; ext. specialist NC State U., 1960-62, ext. instr., 1962-69, 70, ext. asst. prof., 1971-75, ext. assoc. prof., 1971-80, prof., 1980-92, prof. emeritus, 1993—; project engr. Agri-Waste Tech., Inc., 1993-2000, Irrigation Consulting, Inc., 1995—; project engr. divsn. soil and water NC Dept. Environment and Natural Resources, 1997-99, project engr. divsn. water quality, 2003—05, Carolina Turkeys, 2004—06, NC Dept. Adminstrn., 2004—05. Maj. gen. U.S. Army, 1960-95, ret. Recipient Outstanding Paper award So. region Am. Soc. Hort. Sci., 1986, 91; Ronald E. Sneed Irrigation Soc., Inc. scholarship established in his honor, 1991, Heermann Sprinkler Irrigation award, Am. Soc. Agrl. & Biol. Engrs., 2009. Fellow Am. Soc. Agrl.& Bio Engrs. (ednl. aids competition Blue Ribbon 1963-64, 68, 78-79, 85, 89, 91-92, Gunlogson Countryside Engring. award 1992, Outstanding Paper award 1984), The Irrigation Assn. (life tech. mem., Man of Yr. 1981), NC Irrigation Soc., Inc. (Oustanding Contbn. to Irrigation award 1973, former tech. advisor), Soil and Water Conservation Soc., Carolinas Irrigation Assn. (hon.), NC Irrigation Contractors Licensing Bd. (chairperson 2008-), Res. Officers Assn. (life), Civitan (Civitan of Yr. 1998). Democrat. Baptist. Office: 3405 Malibu Dr Raleigh NC 27607-6505 Office Phone: 919-782-7867. Business E-Mail: rsneed2@bellsouth.net.

SNEED, THOMAS K., oil industry executive; b. Dayton, Ohio; B in Computer and Info. Sci., Ohio State U. Computer applications programmer Marathon Oil Corp., Findlay, Ohio, 1981—84, data base mgmt., 1984—92, supr., corp. sys. and programming, 1992—97, mgr. info. tech. svcs., 1997—98; mgr. computer svcs. Speedway SuperAmerica, LLC, Enon, 1998—2000, v.p. info. tech. svcs., 2000—02; mgr. info. tech. svcs. Marathon Ashland Petroleum, LLC, Findlay, 2002—03; chief info. officer Marathon Oil Corp., Houston, 2003—. Office: Marathon Oil Corp Corp Headquarters 5555 San Felipe Rd Houston TX 77056-2723*

SNEERINGER, STEPHEN GEDDES, lawyer; b. Lancaster, Ohio, Mar. 27, 1949; s, Stanley Carlylle and Mary Eleanor (Fry) S.; m. Kristine Karen Serfling, Oct. 6, 1974; children: Mary Rhonda, Robyn Kathleen. BA magna cum laude, Denison U., Granville, Ohio, 1971; JD, Washington U., St. Louis, 1974. Bar: Mo. 1974. Sr. v.p. A.G. Edwards & Sons Inc., St. Louis, 1974—2007, cons., 2007—. Arbitrator N.Y. Stock Exch., NASD Dispute Resolution, Nat. Futures Assn., Am. Arbitration Assn. Editor: Urban Law Ann., 1973-74; bd. editors Securities Arbitration Commentator. Am. Jurisprudence scholar, 1974. Mem. ABA (dispute resolution sect., arbitration com.), Mo. Bar Assn., Securities Industries Assn. (arbitration com.), Futures Industries Assn., Nat. Assn. Securities Dealers (mem. nat. arbitration and mediation com. 1992-94, 2001-03).

SNEIDERMAN, CHARLES ALAN, medical researcher; s. Louis Robert and Mildred Sylvia Sneiderman; m. Constance Ellen Lawn, May 14, 2000. BS with honors, U. Md., Coll. Pk., 1969; MD, Duke U. Sch. Medicine, Durham, NC, 1975; PhD, Duke U. Grad. Sch., Durham, NC, 1975. Diplomate Am. Bd. Family Medicine, 1979. Med. officer Nat. Libr. Medicine, NIH, Bethesda, Md., 1979—. Contbr. scientific papers to profl. jours. Fellow: Am. Acad. Family Physicians (DC chpt. rsch. chair 1990); mem.: Phi Beta Kappa. Achievements include research in artificial intelligence in medicine. Home: 3622 Stanford Cir Falls Church VA 22041 Office: Nat Libr Medicine 8600 Rockville Pike Bethesda MD 20894

SNELBECKER, GLENN EUGENE, psychologist, educator; b. Dover, Pa., Sept. 24, 1931; s. William S. and Anna M. Snelbecker; m. Janice C. Fixler, Sept. 23, 1962; children: David M., Karen A., Laura B. BS, Elizabethtown Coll., Pa., 1957; MS, Bucknell U., Lewisburg, Pa., 1958; PhD, Cornell U., 1961. Lic. psychologist, Pa. Clin. psychology post-doctoral intern Brockton (Mass.) VA Hosp. and Boston U., 1961—62; clin. psychologist U.S. VA Hosp., Brockton, 1961—67; prof. Temple U., Phila., 1967—. Cons. Mgmt. Assn. Tech. Comm. and Health, Wyndmoor, 1963—; dir. project RAINBOW U.S. Dept. Edn., Phila Sch. Dist., Phila., 1995—2001; co-dir. model program elem., HS tchr.-technologists NSF, Phila., 1985—92; keynote spkr. Fifth Internat. Conf. on Tech. and Christian Edn., Seoul, 2004, Second Internat. Conf. Asia-Pacific Econ. Cooperation Cyber Cmty., Busan, 2004; subject An Interview with Glenn E. Snelbecker. Author: Learning Theory, Instructional Theory, 1985, (online learning book) Functional Relevance, 2008; contbr. chapters to books (Book of Yr. award, 1985, 1988), articles to profl. jours. Sgt. US Army, 1952—55. Fellow APA, Phila. Soc. Clin. Psychologists, Am. Ednl. Rsch. Assn. Avocation: travel. Office: Temple U TU-004-00 1301 Cecil Moore Ave Philadelphia PA 19122-6091 Office Phone: 215-204-6109. Personal E-mail: glenn.snelbecker@temple.edu. Business E-Mail: snelbeck@temple.edu.

SNELL, BRUCE M., JR., judge; b. Ida Grove, Iowa, Aug. 18, 1929; s. Bruce M. and Donna (Potter) Snell; m. Anne Snell, Feb. 4, 1956; children: Rebecca, Brad. AB, Grinnell Coll., 1951; JD, U. Iowa, 1956.

Bar: Iowa 1956, N.Y. 1958. Law clk. to presiding judge U.S. Dist. Ct. (no. dist.) Iowa, 1956-57; asst. atty. gen., 1961-65; judge Iowa Ct. Appeals, 1976-87; justice Iowa Supreme Ct., Des Moines, 1987—2001, sr. justice, 2001—. Comments editor: Iowa Law Rev. Mem.: ABA, Am. Judicature Soc., Iowa State Bar Assn., Order Coif. Methodist. Home: PO Box 192 Ida Grove IA 51445-0192

SNELL, LINDA S., internist, educator; b. Salford, Eng., Apr. 24, 1951; BA, U. Alta., 1971, MD, 1975; MHPE, U. Ill., Chgo., 1997. Assoc. dean continuing med. edn. McGill U., Montreal, 1994-2000, dir. divsn. gen. internal medicine, 1994—2004, vice-chair edn. dept. medicine, 2005—; assoc. physician-in-chief McGill U. Health Ctr., Montreal, 2004—; gov. Quebec ACP, 2007—. Fellow ACP, Royal Coll. Physicians Can.; mem. Can. Soc. Internal Medicine (pres. 1994-96), Can. Assn. Med. Edn. (treas. 2004-06). Office: McGill U Health Ctr Dept Medicine 687 Pine Ave W Rm M3-07 Montreal PQ Canada H3A 1A1 E-mail: linda.snell@mcgill.ca.

SNELL, MARILYN NELSON, psychologist, researcher; b. American Fork, Utah, Feb. 11, 1951; d. Ray C. and Affra M. Nelson; m. Paul Decker Snell, Aug. 13, 1969; children: Ben, Matt, Scott, Nelson, Jeff, Robby. BS in Psychology, Brigham Young U., 1972; MS in Counseling Psychology, U. Utah, 1996, PhD in Counseling Psychology, 1999. Postdoc. fellow, resident U. Counseling Ctr. and Dept. Family Preventive Medicine, U. Utah, Salt Lake City, 1999—2000; vis. asst. prof. U. Utah, Salt Lake City, 2000—02; pvt. practice Sandy (Utah) Counseling Ctrs., 2001—05, dir. rsch., 2001—05; chief psychologist Journey at Willow Creek, Utah, 2003—; prin., owner Snell Psychol. Svcs., Sandy, 2003—; co-owner Counseling and Assessments, LLC, Sandy, 2005—. Presenter in field; rev. manuscripts Covenant Pub., American Fork, 2002—; bd. dirs. Nat. Coalition for Emotional Abuse Awareness, 2005—; adj. faculty mem. dept. counseling psychology U. Utah, 2004—. Co-author: Quality Assurance in Residential Care: Organizational Assessment, 2001. Acad. scholar, Brigham Young U., 1969—72. Mem.: Assn. Women Psychologists, Utah Psychol. Assn., Am. Psychol. Assn. Mem. Lds Ch. Avocations: gardening, sports, travel, reading. Office: Counseling and Assessments LLC 11075 S State Ste 28 Sandy UT 84070 Home Phone: 801-733-4855; Office Phone: 801-501-8444.

SNELL, MARK A., utilities executive; B in acctg., San Diego State Univ. CPA. Sr. mgr. KPMG Peat Marwick; exec. v.p., CFO World Oil Corp.; CFO, CAO Latham & Watkins; exec. v.p., CFO Dames & Moore, Earth Tech, Long Beach, Calif.; v.p. planning & develop. Sempra Energy, San Diego, 2001; CFO Sempra Global, San Diego, 2001—04, group pres., 2004—06; exec. v.p., CFO Sempra Energy, San Diego, 2006—. Bd. dir. Venoco Inc. Office: Sempra Energy 101 Ash St San Diego CA 92101

SNELL, PATRICIA POLDERVAART, retired librarian, consultant; b. Santa Fe, Apr. 11, 1943; d. Arie and Edna Beryl (Kerchmar) Poldervaart; m. Charles Eliot Snell, June 7, 1966. BA in Edn., U. N.M., 1965; MSLS, U. So. Calif., 1966. Asst. edn. libr. U. So. Calif., LA, 1966—68; med. libr. Bedford (Mass.) VA Hosp., 1968—69; asst. law libr. U. Miami, Coral Gables, Fla., 1970—71; acquistions libr. U. N.Mex. Law Sch. Libr., Albuquerque, 1971—72; order libr. Los Angeles County Law Libr., 1972—76, cataloguer, 1976—90; libr. Parks Coll., Albuquerque, 1990—92; records technician Technadyne Engrng. Cons. to Sandia Nat. Labs., 1992—93; libr. Tireman Learning Materials Ctr. U. N.Mex., Albuquerque, 1993—96, instr. libr. sci. program Coll. Edn., 1991—2003; legal rsch. technician City of Albuquerque, 1996—2006, Bernalillo County, 2006—09, ret., 2009. Ch. libr. Beverly Hills Presbyn. Ch., 1974-90, ch. choir libr., 1976-90. Southwestern Library Assn. scholar, 1965. Mem.: ALA, N.Mex. Libr. Assn., Pi Lambda Theta. Avocations: travel, reading.

SNELL, RICHARD SAXON, anatomist; b. Richmond, Surrey, Eng., May 3, 1925; came to U.S., 1963; s. Claude Saxon and Daisy Lilian S.; m. Maureen Cashin, June 4, 1949; children: Georgina Sara, Nicola Ann, Melanie Jane, Richard Robin, Charles Edward. MB, BS, Kings Coll., U. London, 1949, PhD, 1955, MD, 1961. House surgeon Sir Cecil P.G. Wakeley, Kings Coll. Hosp. and Belgrave Hosp. for Children, London, 1948-49; lectr. anatomy Kings Coll., U. London, 1949-59, U. Durham, Eng., 1959-63; asst. prof. anatomy and medicine Yale U., 1963-65, assoc. prof., 1965-67, vis. prof. anatomy, 1969; prof., chmn. dept. anatomy N.J. Coll. Medicine and Dentistry, Jersey City, 1967-69; vis. prof. anatomy Harvard U., 1970, 71, 80, 86; prof. anatomy Coll. Medicine, U. Ariz., Tucson, 1970; prof., chmn. dept. anatomy George Washington U. Med. Ctr., Washington, 1972-88, prof. emeritus, 1988—. Author: Clinical Embryology for Medical Students, 1972, 3d edit., 1983, Clinical Anatomy for Medical Students, 1973, 6th edit., 2000, Clinical Anatomy, 7th edit., 2003, Clinical Anatomy By Regions, 8th edit., 2007, Atlas of Normal Radiographic Anatomy, 1976, Atlas of Clinical Anatomy, 1978, Gross Anatomy Dissector, 1978, Clinical Neuroanatomy, 1980, 7th edit., 2009, Student's Aid to Gross Anatomy, 1986, Clinical Anatomy for Anesthesiologists, 1988, Clinical Anatomy of the Eye, 1989, 2d edit., 1997, Gross Anatomy: A Review with Questions and Explanations, 1990, Neuroanatomy: A Review with questions and Explanations, 1992, Clinical Anatomy for Emergency Medicine, 1993, Clinical Neuroanatomy: An Illustrated Review with Questions and Explanations, 3d edit., 2001, Clinical Anatomy: An Illustrated Review with Questions and Explanations, 4th edit., 2003 Clinical Anatomy by Systems, 2006; contbr. articles to med. jours. Med. Rsch. Coun. grantee, 1959; NIH grantee, 1963-65 Mem. Anat. Soc. Gt. Britain, Am. Soc. Anatomists, Alpha Omega Alpha. Home: 518 Boston Post Rd Madison CT 06443-2930

SNELL, STEVEN LAYNE, lawyer, consultant; b. San Fernando, Calif., Nov. 21, 1959; s. Warren Everett and Betty Mae Snell. BA, Johns Hopkins U., Balt., 1982; JD, Northwestern U., Chgo., 1991; LLM, NYU, 1996, JSD, 2004. Registered: NY (Atty.) 1993. Atty. Haight, Gardner, Poor & Havens, NYC, 1991—93, Sonnenschein, Nath & Rosenthal, NYC, 1995—97; legal cons. self employed, Balt., 2001—. Del. Tex. Dem. Conv., Houston, 1988. Mem.: Selden Soc., Maritime Law Assn. the US, ABA Sect. Internat. Law (co-chmn. internat. transp. com. 2004—07). Avocation: travel. Office: 116 W University Pkwy Ste 534 Baltimore MD 21210

SNELL, WILLIAM E., JR., psychology professor, researcher; BA, MA, U. Tex., Austin, PhD, 1984. Prof. psychology SE Mo. State U., Cape Girardeau, 1986—. Contbr. articles to profl. publs. Recipient Tchg. award, SE Mo. State U. Office: SE Mo State Univ MS5700 One University Plz Cape Girardeau MO 63701 Business E-Mail: wesnell@semo.edu.

SNELLING, BARBARA W., retired state legislator; b. Fall River, Mass., Mar. 22, 1928; d. Frank Taylor and Hazel (Mitchell) Weil; m. Richard Arkwright Snelling, June 14, 1947 (dec. Aug. 1991); children: Jacqueline, Mark, Diane, Andrew. AB magna cum laude, Radcliffe Coll., Harvard, 1950; D of Pub. Svc. (hon.), Norwich U., 1981; LLD (hon.), Middlebury Coll., 1997; LLD (hon.), St. Michaels Coll., 2002. Pres. Snelling and Kolb, Inc., 1982-95; lt. gov. State of Vt., 1993-97; mem. Vt. Senate, Montpelier, Vt., 1997—99, 2001—02, ret., 2002. Bd. dirs. US Inst. Peace, 2001—07; mem. adv. bd. Westaff Inc. Vt., 1997—. Mem. bd. sch. dirs. Champlain Valley Union HS, 1962—69, chmn., 1962—68, others; mem. Vt. Edn. Adv. Coun., 1968—71, New Eng. Tchr. Edn. Adv. Com., 1968—70, Shelburne Sch. Bd., 1958—73, Vt. Alcohol and Drug Rehab., 1970—73, Vt. State Bd. Edn., 1971—77, Vt. Ednl. Partnerships, 1992—2000, New. Eng. Bd. Dollars for Scholars, 1997—2002, Champlain Valley Area Health Edn. Coun., 1997—2002; bd. dirs. Vt. Cmty. Found., 1986—94, Shelburne Mus., 1988—98, Vt. Program Quality, 1997—2002; trustee Champlain Coll., 1971—74, Radcliffe Coll., 1990—95; v.p. devel. and external affairs U. Vt., 1974—82. Recipient Laymen's award, Vt. Edn. Assn., 1965, Fanny G. Shaw award for Disting. Cmty. Svc., Burlington Cmty. Coun., 1972, Hope award, MS Cmty. Champion, 1996, Philanthropy Day award, Nat. Soc. Fundraising Execs., 1997, Susan B. Anthony award, YWCA Vt., 2001, Robert Skiff Cmty. Svc. award, Lake Champlain C. of C., 2002, Vt. Children's Trust Found. award, 2002, Patricia S. Walton award, Vt. Soc. Pub. Adminstrn., 2002, AHEC Bi State Primary Care Assn. award, 2002, Vt. Alzheimer's Assn. award, 2002, Gold heart, Am. Heart Assn., 2002; named Vt. Citizen of the Yr., Vt. State C. of C., 2002. Personal E-mail: ulfkiel@aol.com.

SNELLING, JAMES ANTHONY, biology professor, technologist; b. Omaha, Mar. 30, 1949; s. Lawrence Jack and Tina Maria Snelling; m. Mary Antionette Monico, Feb. 15, 1969; children: Kymberly Dawn Snelling-Donlan, Michelle Marie Dougherty, JoAnn Marie Higgins, Anthony James. BA in Biol. Scis., U. Nebr., Omaha, 1975, MA in Biol. Scis., 1978. Cert. med. technologist Am. Soc. Clin. Pathology, 1989. Med. technologist VA Med. Ctr., Omaha, 1970—2003, Alegent Health MV Hosp., Mo. Valley, Iowa, 2003—. Hospitalman, edn. staff USNR, Omaha, 1968—92; instr. Omaha Coll. Health Careers, 1981—2001; adj. instr. Met. C.C., Omaha, 2003—, Iowa We. C.C., Coun. Bluffs, Iowa, 2003—, Coll. St. Mary, Omaha, 2003—. With med. corps. USNR, 1970—71, Vietnam. Mem.: VFW, Am. Legion. Home: 815 Edgewood Blvd Papillion NE 68046 Personal E-mail: jamesandmary2@cox.net.

SNELLING, TROY WAYNE, history educator; b. Excelsior Springs, Mo., 1965; s. Kenneth Wayne and Shirley Louise Snelling. BA in History, Park Coll., 1991, MA in Edn., 1999. History tchr. Park Hill Sch. Dist., Kans. City, Mo., 1992—, chmn. HS dept. social studies, 1998—2007, sr. honors project coord., 2009—. Bd. dir. Tchg. History Through Reality, Kans. City. Named Area Tchr. of Yr., Mo. VFW, Kans. City, 2008—09. Mem.: Masons, Phi Alpha Theta. Republican. Episcopalian. Avocations: coin collecting/numismatics, antiques, trapshooting, vintage cars, reading. Home: 30422 NE 158th Excelsior Springs MO 64024 Office: Park Hill High School 7701 NW Barry Rd Kansas City MO 64153 Home Phone: 816-459-9892; Office Phone: 816-359-4110. Personal E-mail: snellingt@hotmail.com.

SNIDER, DAREN, educator; s. Kinard and Phyllis Price Snider; m. N. Ann Chumbley, Aug. 31, 1990; children: Colin, Christopher, Laura, Cameron. PhD, U. Utah, Salt Lake City, 2000. Cert. collaborative instl. tng. initiative U. Miami, 2007, US NIH, 2004. Assoc. prof. german U. Nebr., Kearney, 2006—, dir. gen. studies, 2006—, faculty senate pres., 2008—. Counselor LDS Ch., Salt Lake City, 1998—2000. Dee Fellowship, U. Utah., 1994—95. Mem.: Alpha Mu Gamma Nat. Fgn. Lang. Honor Soc. (Alpha Mu Gamma 2001), Nat. German Honor Soc. (Delta Phi Alpha 1990), Midwest Modern Langs. Assn. (chair, linguistics divsn. 1999—2002), Am. Coun. on Tchg. Fgn. Langs., Phi Kappa Phi Nat. Honor Soc. Conservative. Lds Ch. Avocations: travel, gardening. Office: Univ NE Thomas Hall 215 Kearney NE 68849 Business E-Mail: sniderd@unk.edu.

SNIDER, DARRYL, lawyer; BA, U. Mich., 1971, JD magna cum laude, 1974, PhD in Econ. with highest distinction, 1975. Bar: Calif., U.S. Supreme Ct., Am. Bar Assoc. Adjunct prof. Law Golden Gate Univ., 1977—78, Univ. San Francisco, 1979; atty., shareholder Heller, Ehrman, White, & McAuliffe LLP, Los Angeles, Calif., 1998—. Panel mem. Inst. Con. on Securities Litigation, 1996—97. Mem.: Phi Beta Kappa. Office: Heller Ehrman LLP 333 S Hope St Los Angeles CA 90071-1406 Office Phone: 213-689-7577. Office Fax: 213-614-1868. E-mail: dsnider@hewm.com.

SNIDER, EDWARD MALCOLM, professional sports team executive; b. Washington, Jan. 6, 1933; s. Sol C. and Lillian (Bonas) Snider; m. Christine Snider; children: Craig Alan, Jay Thomas, Lindy Lou, Tina Suzanne, Sarena Lynn, Samuel Everett. BS, U. Md., 1955; LHD (hon.), MCP Hahnemann U., 1985, Thomas Jefferson Hosp., 1999. CPA Md. Maj. stockholder, exec. v.p. Edge Ltd., Washington, 1957—63; v.p. Phila. Eagles Football Club, 1964—67; founder, owner Phila. Flyers Hockey Club, 1967—; chmn. bd. Spectrum Arena (Wachovia Spectrum since 2003), Phila., 1967—; bd. govs. NHL, 1967—. Established Spectacor (now Comcast-Spectacor), 1974, chmn. bd., 1996—; adv. bd. Sol C. Snider Entrepreneurial Ctr., U Pa.; bd. overseers Wharton Sch. U. Pa.; bd. dirs. Inst. Cancer and Blood Diseases, Hahnemann U., Simon Weisenthal Ctr.; bd. trustees Inst. Objectivist Studies. Founder Ed Snider Youth Hockey Found. Recipient Americanism award, Anti-Defamation League, 1999, Sports Leadership award, Temple U., 2001, William Penn award, Greater Phila. C. of C., 2005, Ellis Island Medal of Honor; co-recipient Lester Patrick Trophy for outstanding svc. to hockey in US, 1980; named Phila.'s greatest sports mover and shaker, Phila. Daily News, 1999; named to Hockey Hall of Fame, 1988, Phila. Flyers Hall of Fame, 1989, Phila. Sports Hall of Fame, Pa. Sports Hall of Fame, Phila. Jewish Sports Hall of Fame. Office: Comcast Spectator 3601 S Broad St Philadelphia PA 19148-5250*

SNIDER, JAMES RHODES, radiologist; b. Pawnee, Okla., May 16, 1931; s. John Henry and Gladys Opal (Rhodes) S.; m. Lynadell Vivion, Dec. 27, 1954; children: Jon, Jan. BS, U. Okla., 1953, MD, 1956. Intern Edward Meyer Meml. Hosp., Buffalo, 1956—57; resident radiology U. Okla. Med. Ctr., 1959—62; radiologist Holt-Krock Clinic and Sparks Regional Med. Ctr., Ft. Smith, Ark., 1962—66; dir. Fairfield Comty. Land Co., Little Rock, 1968—87, Fairfield Comtys., Inc., 1968—87. Assoc. editor: Computerized Tomography, 1976—88. Mem. Ark. Bd. Pub. Welfare, 1969—71; bd. visitors U. Okla.; bd. dirs. U. Okla. Assn., 1967—70, U. Okla. Alumni Devel. Fund, 1970—74. Lt. comdr. USNR, 1957—62. Mem.: AMA, Am. Roentgen Ray Soc., Radiol. Soc. N.Am., Am. Coll. Radiology, Phi Beta Kappa, Alpha Epsilon Delta, Beta Theta Pi. Home: 5814 Cliff Dr Fort Smith AR 72903-3845 Office: 1500 Dodson Ave Fort Smith AR 72901-5128

SNIDER, L. BRITT, federal official; b. Rocky Mount, NC, Jan. 12, 1945; s. Arnold Holmes and Kate Mills (Suiter) S.; m. Virginia Lansford, Aug. 24, 1974; 1 child, Britt Arnold. BA, Davidson Coll., NC, 1966; JD, U. Va., 1969. Counsel judiciary subcom. on constl. rights U.S. Senate, Washington, 1971-75, counsel select com. on intelligence, 1975-76; ptnr. Ketner & Snider, Salisbury, NC, 1976-77; counsel govt. ops. subcom. on govt. info. U.S. Ho. Reps., Washington, 1977; asst. dep. undersec. counterintelligence and security Dept. Def., Washington, 1977-87; minority counsel U.S. Senate Intelligence Com., Washington, 1987-89, gen. counsel, 1989-95, staff dir. commn. on roles and capabilities of U.S. Intelligence Cmty., 1995-96; sr. fellow Ctr. for Study of Intelligence, 1996-97; spl. counsel to dir. CIA, 1997-98, inspector gen., 1998-2001. Staff dir. Commn. to Rev. Security Practices and Procedures Dept. Def., Washington, 1985; adj. prof. Sch. Foreign Svc. Georgetown U., 2005 Served to capt. U.S. Army, 1969-71, Vietnam. Mem.: DC Bar Assn., Va. Bar Assn. Democrat. Episcopalian. Avocations: golf, jogging, reading.

SNIDER, ROBERT LARRY, management consultant; b. Muskogee, Okla., Aug. 10, 1932; s. George Robert and Kathryn (Smiser) S.; m. Gerlene Rose Tipton, Nov. 26, 1953; children: Melody Kathryn Porter, Rebecca Lee. BS in Indsl. Engring., U. Houston, 1955, postgrad., 1956, Pomona Coll., 1960. Cert. mgmt. cons. Instr. U. Houston Coll. Engring., 1955-56; sr. indsl. engr. Sheffield Steel Corp., Houston, 1955-59, Kaiser Steel Co., Fontana, Calif., 1959-60; cons. Arthur Young & Co., LA, 1960-61; mgmt. analyst Iranian Oil Exploration & Producing Co., Masjidi-Suliman, Iran, 1961—65; v.p., Dallas office mgr. operating methods divsn. Booz, Allen & Hamilton, Inc., 1966—68, v.p. internat. prodn. and inventory control divsn., 1968—69; prin., gen. cons. practice Peat Marwick Mitchell, CPAs, Houston, 1969-71; exec. v.p. mfg. Sterling Electronics Corp., Houston, 1971-72, COO, pres., 1972-77; CEO, pres. Rapoca Energy Corp., Cin., 1977-79; mng. ptnr., cons. Coopers & Lybrand, Southwest, Houston, 1979-81; mng. dir. S.W. region Korn Ferry Internat., Houston, 1981—83; ptnr.-in-charge Houston Mgmt. Cons. Practice, 1983—91; ptnr. cons. Southwest Enterprise Coopers & Lybrand, Houston, 1991-92, ptnr. S.W. Mfg. Cons. Process Improvement Group, 1992-93, internat. cons. ptnr., 1993-95; mng. ptnr. RLS Profl. Svcs. LLC, 1995—. Chmn., dir L&G Snacks, 1997—2000. Trustee Gene Cragg Caring Forever Found., 1997—99; sr. trustee R. Larry and Gerri R. Snider Native Am. scholarship trust Cullen Coll. Engring., U. Houston, 2004—; sr. trustee Melody Snider, Womens Indsl. Engring. scholarship trust U. Houston, Cullen Coll. Engring., 2006—; past chmn. bd. mem. found. bd. and adminstrv. bd. Chapelwood Meth.Ch.; former mem. adminstrv. bd. Memorial Dr. Meth. Ch., Houston, 1997—99; sr. trustee United Meth. Found. Remainder Trust, 2002—; mem. stewardship com., USCHR 1st United Meth. Ch., Conroe, Tex., 2005—; deacon, steward 1st Christian Ch., Conroe, Tex., 2003—05; past bd. dirs., exec. com. Houston Jr. Achievement; ret. exec. com. Houston Grand Opera, bd. dirs.; sr. trustee Tipton-Snider Minister Edn. Fund., 1999—; mem. Cullen Coll. Leadership bd. U. Houston, 1995—, mem. Bridge Builder Soc. Cullen Coll. Engring., 2006—, mem. dean's advisory com. Cullen Coll Engring., 2005—. With C.E. AUS, 1956. Recipient Outstandng Mil. Engr. award Soc. Mil Engrs., 1955; named Disting. Alumni, Cullen Coll. Engring., U. Houston, 1991, named Disting. Indsl. Engring. Alumni, 2005. Mem.: U. Houston Alumni Assn. (life; exec. com. 1985—94, pres. and chmn. bd. 1990—93, mem. Cir. of Excellence 2003—, bd. dir.), Phi Kappa Phi, Pi Theta Kappa. Home and Office: 9387 Escondido Dr Willis TX 77318-6621 Personal E-mail: rlarry32@yahoo.com.

SNIDER, ROWE WINSTON, lawyer; b. St. Louis, Feb. 11, 1954; s. Ralph W. and Evelyn A. Snider; m. Susan Health Crane, May 7, 1983; children: Mark, Brian, Elizabeth. BA, Ctrl. Meth. U., Fayette, Mo., 1976; JD, U. Chgo., 1979. Bar: Ill. 1979, US Dist. Ct. No. Dist. Ill. 1979, US Supreme Ct. 1989. Assoc. lawyer Friedman & Koven, Chgo., 1979—86, Locke, Lord, Bissell & Liddell LLP, Chgo., 1986—88, ptnr., 1989—. Chair dept. litigation Lord, Bissell & Brook, LLP, Chgo., 2005—07. Bd. dirs. Chgo. Vol. Legal Svcs., 1994—96, mem. adv. bd., 1996—2002. Mem.: Union League Club Chgo. Avocations: reading, photography. Office: Locke Lord Bissell & Liddell LLP 111 S Wacker Dr Chicago IL 60606 Office Phone: 312-443-0667. Office Fax: 312-896-6667. Business E-Mail: rsnider@lockelord.com.

SNIDER, STACEY, film company executive; b. Phila., Apr. 29, 1961; m. Gary Jones; children: Katie, Natalie. BA, U. Penn., 1982; JD, U. Calif. LA, 1985. Dir. of devel. Guber-Peters Entertainment Co., 1986—90, exec. v.p., 1990—92; pres. prodn. TriStar Pictures, 1992-96; co-pres. prodn. Universal Pictures, Universal City, Calif., 1996—98, pres. prodn., 1998—99, chmn., CEO, 1999—2006; co-chmn., CEO DreamWorks SKG, Glendale, Calif., 2006—. Bd. dirs. Am. Film Inst. Bd. dirs. Spl. Olympics of So. Calif.; bd. trustees Art Ctr. Coll. of Design, Pasadena, Calif. Recipient Dorothy and Sherrill C. Corwin Human Rels. Award, Am. Jewish Com., 2003; named one of The 100 Most Powerful Women in Entertainment, Hollywood Reporter, 2005—07, 100 Most Powerful Women, Forbes mag., 2005, 2009, 50 Most Powerful People in Hollywood, Premiere mag., 2004—05, 100 Most Powerful Women in Bus., Fortune mag., 2005—07, 50 Smartest People in Hollywood, Entertainment Weekly, 2007, America 's Top Women in Bus.-Game Changers, Pink mag. & Forté Found., 2007. Office: DreamWorks SKG 1000 Flower St Glendale CA 91201*

SNIDER, STEPHEN A., oil industry company executive; Gen. mgr., Air Compressor Ops. Tidewater Compression, 1975, worked, Western US Ops., 1981—83, sr. v.p., Compression, 1991; pres. Exterran GP LLC, 2006; COO Exterran Partners LP, 2008; pres., CEO Exterran Holdings Inc., 1998, pres., 2007—08, COO, 2008; pres. Universal Compression Holdings GP LLC, 2006; chmn. Universal Compression Holdings Inc., 2006; COO Universal Compression Holdings GP LLC, 2008, chmn., CEO, 2006—; chmn. Exterran Inc. (formerly Universal Compression Inc.), 2006—; CEO Exterran Holdings Inc. (formerly Universal Compression Holdings Inc.), 2007—. Former bd. dirs. T-3 Energy Svcs. Inc., 2003; bd. dirs. Exterran Holdings Inc., 1998—, Energen Corp., 2000—; chmn. UCO GP LLC, 2006—. Bd. dirs. Meml. Hermann Hosp. Sys. Office: Exterran Holdings Inc 16666 Northchase Dr Houston TX 77060 Office Phone: 281-836-7000.*

SNIFFEN, MICHAEL JOSEPH, hospital administrator; b. Ossining, NY, June 16, 1949; s. John Francis and Mary Agnes (Madden) S.; m. Anne Marie Gillick; children: Kevin, Kristina. BS, Fordham U., 1971; MBA in Hosp. Adminstrn., Baruch Coll., 1977. Dir. of fin. planning Westchester div. N.Y. Hosp., White Plains, N.Y., 1971-74, assoc. dir. NYC, 1974-80, sr. assoc. dir., assoc. dean Cornell Med. Ctr., 1980-87; pres., CEO Overlook Hosp., Summit, NJ, 1987-96; exec. v.p., COO Atlantic Health Sys., Florham Park, NJ, 1996—2000; pres., CEO BSCPC, Hoboken, NJ, 2001—05; mng. ptnr. The Manchester Group, Hoboken, 2005—. Exec. dir. Cornell Health Policy Program, N.Y.C., 1984-87; adminstr. program Commonwealth Fund, N.Y.C., 1978-81; adv. bd. Robert Wood Johnson Found.-Teaching Nursing Home Program, Princeton, N.J., 1980-86. Vol. March of Dimes, Tarrytown, N.Y., 1984-88; bd. dirs. St. Columbans Sch., Peekskill, N.Y., 1981-84; mem. various svc. clubs, Westchester County, N.Y., 1976-91. Fellow Am. Coll. Healthcare Execs.; mem. Hosp. Fin. Mgmt. Assn. (advanced mem.), Echo Lake Country Club (Westfield, N.J.), Baltusrol Country Club (Springfield, N.J.). Roman Catholic. Avocations: golf, college basketball. Home: 47 Murray Hill Sq New Providence NJ 07974-1531 Home Phone: 201-798-7396; Office Phone: 732-887-4012. Personal E-mail: michael_sniffen@hotmail.com.

SNIPE, TRACY DAVID, political science professor; s. Lukie and Mary Virginia Snipe. PhD, Ind. U., Bloomington, 1994. Assoc. prof. Wright State U., Dayton, Ohio, 2002—. Author: (book) Arts and Politics in Senegal. Judge NAACP, ACT Southern Program, Dayton, 2007—08. Mem.: SCASSI. Office: Wright State Univ 3640 Col Glenn Blvd Dayton OH 45435

SNIPES, SHEDRA AMY, research scientist; PhD, U. Wash., Seattle. W.k. kellogg health disparities scholar UT MD Anderson Cancer Ctr., 2006—08. Office: Univ Tex MD Anderson 1515 Holcombe Blvd Unit 639 Houston TX 77030 Office Fax: 713-563-2765. Business E-Mail: asnipes@mdanderson.org.

SNITZER, ELIAS, physicist; b. Lynn, Mass., Feb. 27, 1925; s. Isaac and Jenny (Sussman) Snitzer; m. Shirley Ann Wood, Nov. 22, 1950; children: Sandra, Barbara, Peter, Helen, Louis. BSEE, Tufts U., 1946; MS in Physics, U. Chgo., 1950, PhD, 1953. Rsch. physicist Honeywell Corp., Phila., 1954-56; assoc. prof. Lowell Technol. Inst., Mass., 1956-58; dir. rsch. Am. Optical Co., Southbridge, Mass., 1959-76; mgr. applied physics United Technologies Rsch., East Hartford, Conn., 1977-84; mgr. fiber optics Polaroid, Cambridge, Mass., 1984-88; prof. Rutgers U., 1989-97, prof. emeritus, 1997—. Contbr. articles to profl. jours. With USN, 1943—46. Fellow: Am. Phys. Soc., Ceramic Soc. (Corning Stookey Discovery award 2006), Optical Soc. Am. (John Tyndall award 1994); mem.: IEEE (George Morey award 1971, Quantum Electronics award 1979, Charles Townes award 1991, Otto Schott award 1999, Opto-Electronic Rank prize 2000, LEOS Millenium award 2001), NAE. Democrat. Jewish. Achievements include invention of glass laser; fiber laser amplifier. Home and Office: 78 Ivy Rd Wellesley MA 02482 Office Phone: 781-431-2605. Personal E-mail: snitzer27@yahoo.com, snitzer007@gmail.com.

SNIVELY, CAROLYN S., ancient language educator, archaeologist; b. Massillon, Ohio, Sept. 7, 1947; d. George Donald and Beulah Elizabeth (Snyder) Snively. BA, Mich. State U., Lansing, 1969; MA, U. Tex., Austin, 1973, PhD, 1979. Prof. classics Gettysburg Coll., Pa., 2001—. Am. co-dir. Konjuh Archaeol. Excavation Project, Kratovo, Macedonia, 1998—. Contbr. articles to profl. jour. Grant, Loeb Classical Libr. Found., 2006—08. Mem.: Archaeol. Inst. America. Office: Gettysburg Coll Dept Classics 300 N Washington St Gettysburg PA 17325 Business E-Mail: cnsively@gettysburg.edu.

SNIVELY, DAVID FREDERICK, agricultural products company executive, lawyer; b. Logansport, Ind., Apr. 26, 1954; s. Howard Woodrow Snively and Rebecca S. (Merrell) Hoover; m. Diane Marie Hepper, Aug. 7, 1976; children: Matthew David, Christine Marie, Evan David. BS magna cum laude, Ball State U., 1976; JD magna cum laude, Ind. U., 1979. Bar: Ind. 1979, Mo. 1987, US Dist. Ct. (so. dist. Ind.) 1979, US Ct. Appeals (7th cir.) 1979, US Supreme Ct. 1984. Assoc. Barnes & Thornburg, Indpls., 1979-84; litig. atty. Monsanto Co., St. Louis, 1984-87, asst. litig. counsel, 1987-89, assoc. litig. counsel, 1989-97, asst. gen. counsel litig., dep. gen. counsel, sr. v.p., sec., gen. counsel, 2006—. Note and devel. editor, contbr. Ind. Law Rev., 1978-79. Mem. ABA (co-chair subcommittee on product liability and toxic torts, com. on corp. counsel 1995—), Ind. Bar Assn., Mo. Bar Assn., Lawyers for Civil Justice (bd. dirs. 1990—), Def. Rsch. Inst. (co-chmn. corp. counsel sect.), Phi Delta Phi. Democrat. Roman Catholic. Avocations: marathon running, backpacking, skiing, rollerblading, bicycling. Office: Monsanto Co 800 N Lindbergh Blvd Saint Louis MO 63167-0001

SNIVELY, STEPHEN WAYNE, lawyer; b. Danville, Ill., Apr. 27, 1949; s. Roberts Eyster and Margaret Louise Snively; m. Heather Lea Patten, Mar. 19, 1988; children: Toby, Ben, Madeline, Taylor. BA, U. Ill., 1971, JD, 1975. Bar: Ill. 1975, US Supreme Ct., Fla. 1980. Assoc. Kavanagh, Scully, Sudow, White & Frederick, Peoria, Ill., 1975-80, Maguire, Voorhis & Wells, P.A., Orlando, Fla., 1980—; merged with Holland & Knight LLP, Orlando, 1998—. Seminar speaker, 1987, hon. consul Namibia, Fla., 2007-, founder, pres. scholarships Namibia, Inc. Contbr. articles to profl. jours. Bd. dirs. Found. for Orange County Pub. Schs., Orlando, 1987-96, officer, 1987-96, pres., 1993-94, chmn., 1994-96; bd. dirs. Found. for Hospice of Ctrl. Fla., Inc., 1995-96; treas., bd. dirs. HCF Found., Inc., 1996—, pres., 1998—. Mem. ABA (retail leasing com.), Fla. Bar (liaison to land surveyor com. 1982—), Orange County Bar Assn., Internat. Coun. Shopping Ctrs., Fla. C. of C. (Leadership Fla. 1991-92), Fla. Zool. Soc. (sec., bd. dirs. 1991-96), Tiger Bay Club, Phi Beta Kappa, Northland-A Ch. Distributed. Republican. Avocations: running, writing, photography. Office: Holland & Knight LLP 200 S Orange Ave Ste 2600 Orlando FL 32801-3453 Office Phone: 407-244-1112. E-mail: stephen.snively@hklaw.com.

SNODDY, JAMES ERNEST, education educator; b. Perrysville, Ind., Oct. 6, 1932; s. James Elmer and Edna May (Hayworth) S.; m. Alice Joanne Crowder, Aug. 15, 1954; children: Ryan Anthony, Elise Suzanne. BS, Ind. State U., 1954; MEd, U. Ill., 1961, EdD, 1967. Tchr. Danville (Ill.) Pub. Schs., 1954-57, prin., 1961-64; instr. U. Ill., Champaign, 1965-67; prof. edn. Mich. State U., East Lansing, 1967-72, 78-96, chmn. dept. elem. and spl. edn., 1972-78, ret., 1996, prof. emeritus, 1997—; dir. Program CORK, 1978-82. With U.S. Army, 1955-57. Mem. Am. Assn. for Adult and Continuing Edn., Commn. of Profs. of Adult and Continuing Edn. Methodist. Home: 1926 Creek Lndg Haslett MI 48840-8704 Office: Mich State U 419 Erickson Hall East Lansing MI 48824-1034 Office Phone: 517-339-6548. Business E-Mail: jsnoddy@msu.edu.

SNOEYINK, VERNON L., civil engineer, educator; BS in Civil Engring., U. Mich., 1984, MS in Sanitary Engring., 1966, PhD in Water Resource Engring., 1968. Asst. prof. sanitary engring. U. Ill., Urbana, 1969-73, from assoc. prof. to prof. environ. engring., 1973—, Ivan Racheff prof. environ. engring., 1989—2004, prof. emeritus, 2005—. Mem.: NAE. Office: U Ill Dept Civil Engring Newmark Civil Engring Lab 205 N Mathews Ave Urbana IL 61801 Home Phone: 217-352-0698. Business E-Mail: snoeyink@uiuc.edu.

SNOOK, PAUL, real estate company executive; b. Swindon, Wilt, Eng., Dec. 31, 1949; arrived in U.S., 1979; s. Eric Arthur and Eira Glynis Snook; m. June Chambers, Apr. 17, 1971 (div. Sept. 1977); m. Elizabeth Keefe, June 25, 1979 (div. Jan. 2003); children: Sarah, Erica. Student, Northamton (Eng.) Coll. Exec. property mgr. Zaremba Mgmt. Svcs. Inc., Cleve., 1979-85, dir. mktg. ops., 1985-88; sr. v.p. Riverview Mgmt. Co., Akron, Ohio, 1988-96; pres. Strategic Property Mgmt., Cleve., 1999—, Paul Snook & Assocs., Cleve. Contbr.: Professional Apartment Rental Techniques, 1999. Recipient Cmty. Improvement award City of Mayfield Heights, 1986. Mem. No. Ohio Apt. Assn. (life trustee, Mgr. of Yr. 1994, Pres. award 1987-90), Inst. of Real Estate Mgmt. (Pres. award 1987-90, cert. property mgr.), Cleve. Area Bd. of Realtors. Avocation: sailing.

SNOOK, STOVER HOFFMAN, retired social sciences educator; b. Ventnor, NJ, July 28, 1932; s. Stover Garfield and Leah Jane (Hoffman) Snook; m. Marie Melanie Rohrer, June 26, 1954; children: John Stover, Suzanne Marie, Linda Jeanne. BA, Hartwick Coll., 1954; MA, Fordham U., 1960; PhD, Tufts U., 1969. Lic. psychologist Mass., 1973; bd. cert. profl. ergonomist 1993. Staff psychologist Dunlap & Assoc., Stamford, Conn., 1956—62; asst. v.p. Liberty Mut. Ins. Co., Hopkinton, Mass., 1962—97; lectr. Harvard Sch. Pub. Health, Boston, 1974—2006. Com. human factors Nat. Rsch. Coun., Washington, 1984—87; adv. panel rsch. Am. Phys. Therapy Assn., Alexandria, Va., 1996—99; cumulative trauma com. Am. Nat. Stds. Inst., Chgo., 1990—97. Contbr. articles to profl. jours., chapters to books. Recipient Festschrift, Ergonomics, 1999, Kraft Innovation award, Human Factors and Ergonomics Soc., 1997, Extension award, McKenzie Inst. Internat., 2001. Fellow: Internat. Ergonomics Assn., Am. Psychological Soc. (fellow), Ergonomics Soc. (fellow, Ann. Lectr. 1978), Human Factors and Ergonomics Soc. (fellow, Tech. Group award 1992). Democrat. Unitarian. Achievements include development of psychophysical guidelines for manual handling tasks; guidelines for reducing low back pain and disability; incidence and cost data for industrial low back disorders. Avocations: travel, astronomy, history, music. Home: 7420 Willow Wood Ln Vero Beach FL 32966

SNOOP DOGG, (CALVIN BROADUS), vocalist, actor; b. Long Beach, Calif., Oct. 20, 1972; s. Beverly Tate; m. Shante Taylor, June 1997; 1 child, Corde Calvin Broadus;children from previous marriage: Cordell Broadus, Cori Broadus. Founder, owner Doggy Style Records, Inc. (formerly DoggHouse Records), 1999—. Musician: (albums) Doggystyle, 1993, Tha Doggfather, 1996, Da Game Is To Be Sold Not To Be Told, 1998, No Limit Top Dogg, 1999, Tha Last Meal, 2000, Doggy Style Allstars: Welcome to Tha House, 2002, Paid Tha Cost to Be da Bo$$, 2002, Soundtrack Raw N Uncut, Vol. 1, 2002, Welcome to Church: Mix Tape, Vol. 1, 2003, R&G - Rhythm and Gangster: The Masterpiece, 2004, Dogg Pound Mix, 2005, Me & My Homies, 2005, Tha Blue Carpet Treatment, 2006, The Chronicalz, Vol. 1: The Mixed Up Album, 2006, Ego Trippin', 2008; actor: (films) Half Baked, 1998, I Got the Hook Up, 1998, Ride, 1998, Caught Up, 1998, Urban Menace, 1999, The Wrecking Crew, 1999, Hot Boyz, 1999, Tha Eastsidaz, 2000, Baby Boy, 2001, Training Day, 2001, Bones, 2001, The Wash, 2001, Crime Partners, 2001, Malibu's Most Wanted, 2003, Old School, 2003, Starsky & Hutch, 2004, Soul Plane, 2004, (voice only) Racing Stripes, 2005,: (TV appearances) Just Shoot Me, 2001; co-author (with David Seay): Tha Doggfather: The Times, Trials, and Hardcore Truths of Snoop Dogg, 1999. Founder Snoop Youth Football League, Calif., 2005. Office: Doggy Style Records 1142 S Diamond Bar Blvd #504 Diamond Bar CA 91765

SNOW, ANDREW P, communications educator, researcher; s. Richard M Snow; m. Katherine B Badran; children: Andrew B, Jennifer N Petersen, Jeffrey M. PhD, U. Pitts., Pa., 1997. Rsch. asst. Old Dominion U. Rsch. Found., Norfolk, Va., 1970—72; lt. US Army, Signal Corps, Fayetteville, NC, 1972—75; capt. US Army Res., 1972—80; electronics engr. US Navy, Norfolk, 1975—77, FBI, Washington, 1977—79; v.p. ConTel Info. Sys., Fairfax, Va., 1979—86, Network Mgmt. Inc, Fairfax, 1986—92; chmn. CTX Corp., Fairfax, 1994—2002; asst. prof. Ga. State U., Atlanta, 1997—2004; prof. Ohio U., Athens, Ohio, 2002—. Contbr. articles to profl. jours. Treas. Lions Club Internat., Dumfries Va. Chpt., Dumfries, Va. Decorated Parachutist award US Army, Nat. Def. Svc. Medal, Army Commendation medal; grantee Telecom. Critical Infrastructure Protection, Homeland Security, 2007; Tchg. Fellow, U. Pitts., 1995. Mem.: IEEE, Internat. Telecom. Edn. and Rsch. Assn. (pres. and v.p. 2004—07, exec. com. and bd. mem. 2004—08, Pres. Emeritus 2007). Conservative. Achievements include invention of co-inventor of the local area network bridge. Avocations: walking, travel. Office: Ohio Univ Sch ITS Lindley Hall Athens OH 45701 Business E-Mail: asnow@ohio.edu.

SNOW, BRITTANY, actress; b. Tampa, Fla., Mar. 9, 1986; d. John and Cynthia Snow. Appearances on (TV series) All That, Sea Quest DSV, 1994—95, Safe Harbor, 1999, actress (TV films) Walt Disney World Inside Out, 1995, Murphy's Dozen, 2001, (films) Whisper of the Heart, 1995, The Pacifier, 2005, John Tucker Must Die, 2008, Hairspray, 2007 (Ensemble of Yr. Hollywood Film Festival, 2007), On the Doll, 2007, Prom Night, 2008, Finding Amanda, 2008, (TV miniseries) From the Earth to the Moon, 1998, (TV series) The Guiding Light, 1998—2001 (Best Performance in Daytime TV Series - Young Actress Young Artist Awards, 2001), American Dreams, 2002—05, Nip/Tuck, 2005, voice (video game) Kingdom Hearts II, 2005. Office: c/o ICM LA 10250 Constellation Blvd Los Angeles CA 90067

SNOW, DAVID B., JR., pharmaceutical executive; b. Manchester, NH, Nov. 30, 1954; BS in Sci. & Econs., Bates Coll., 1976; MS in Healthcare Adminstrn., Duke U., 1978. Sr. v.p. Am. Internat. Healthcare, Rockville, Md., 1988—89; pres., CEO Managed Healthcare Systems, Reston, Va., 1989—93; exec. v.p. Oxford Health Plans, Norwalk, Conn., 1993—98, WellChoice, Inc. (formerly Empire BlueCross & BlueShield), NYC, 1999—2001, pres., CEO, 2001—03; pres. Medco Health Solutions, Franklin Lakes, NJ, 2003—06, chmn., CEO, 2003—. Office: Medco Health 100 Parsons Pond Franklin Lakes NJ 07417*

SNOW, G. MURRAY, federal judge; b. Boulder City, Nev., 1959; BA magna cum laude, Brigham Young U., Provo, Utah, 1984, JD magna cum laude, 1987. Bar: US Dist. Ct. (Ariz. dist.) 1988, US Ct. Appeals (10th cir.) 1987, US Ct. Appeals (9th cir.) 1989, Ariz. Supreme Ct. 1987. Jud. clerk to Hon. Stephen H. Anderson US Ct. Appeals (10th Cir.), 1987—88; with Meyer, Hendricks, Victor, Osborn & Maledon, Phoenix, 1988—95; ptnr. Osborn Maledon, Phoenix, 1995—2002; judge Ariz. Ct. Appeals, 2002—08, US Dist. Ct. Ariz., 2008—. Adj. prof. polit. sci. Ariz. State U., 1992—99; mem. Ariz. Assn. Health Care Lawyers, 1991—2002. Mem.: State Bar Ariz. (com. on profl. rules conduct 1998—, ethical rules review grp. 2000—), J. Reuben Clark Law Soc. Mailing: US Dist Ct Ariz c/o G Murray Snow 401 W Wash St Phoenix AZ 85003 Office Phone: 602-322-7200.

SNOW, GARTH, professional sports team executive, former professional hockey player; b. Wrentham, Mass., July 28, 1969; m. Erica Snow; 1 child, Glenn. Grad., U. Maine, 1993. Goalie U. Maine, 1988—93, Quebec Nordiques, 1993—95, Phila. Flyers, 1995—98, Vancouver Canucks, 1998—2000, Pitts. Penguins, 2000—01, NY Islanders, 2001—06, gen. mgr., 2006—. Named to Second All-Star Team, Hockey East, 1992, 1993, Championship All-Tournament Team, NCAA, 1993, U. Maine Sports Hall of Fame, 2007. Office: NY Islanders Nassau Veterans Meml Coliseum 1255 Hempstead Turnpike Uniondale NY 11553

SNOW, JAMES BYRON, JR., otolaryngologist, research administrator, educator; b. Oklahoma City, Mar. 12, 1932; s. James B. and Charlotte Louise (Andersen) S.; m. Sallie Lee Ricker, July 16, 1954; children: James B., John Andrew, Sallie Lee Louise. BS, U. Okla., Norman, 1953; MD cum laude, Harvard U., Cambridge, Mass., 1956; MA (hon.), U. Pa., Phila., 1973. Diplomate Am. Bd. Otolaryngology (dir. 1972-90). Intern Johns Hopkins Hosp., Balt., 1956-57; resident Mass. Eye and Ear Infirmary, Boston, 1957-60; prof., head dept. otorhinolaryngology Sch. Medicine U. Okla., Oklahoma City, 1962-72; prof., chmn. dept. otorhinolaryngology and human communication U. Pa., 1972-90; dir. Nat. Inst. on Deafness and Other Comm. Disorders, NIH, Bethesda, Md., 1990-97; convener, corr. Tinnitus Rsch. Consortium, 1998—. Mem. nat. adv. coun. neurol. and communicative disorders and stroke NIH, 1972-76, 82-86; chmn. Nat. Com. Rsch. Neurol. and Communicative Disorders, 1979-80. Editor: Am. Jour. Otolaryngology, 1979-83; Contbr. articles to sci. and profl. jours. Officer, M.C., U.S. Army, 1960-62. Recipient Regents award for superior tchg. U. Okla., 1970, Golden award Internat. Fedn. Otorhinolaryngological Socs., 1989, Disting. Achievement award Deafness Rsch. Found., 1993, Presdl. Meritorious Exec. Rank award, 1994; named to Soc. Scholars Johns Hopkins U., 1991. Fellow Japan Broncho-Esophagological Soc. (hon.), Am. Laryngological Assn. (hon.); mem. ACS (regent 1982-90), AMA (coun. on sci. affairs 1975-86), Soc. Univ. Otolaryngologists (pres. 1975), Am. Acad. Otolaryngology-Head and Neck Surgery, Assn. Acad. Depts. Otolaryngology (pres. 1981-82), Am. Laryngol., Rhinol. and Otol. Soc., Am. Otol. Soc. (merit award 2003), Am. Laryngol. Assn. (editor 1983-89, pres. 1990-91), Am. Broncho-Esophagol. Assn. (editor trans. 1973-77, pres. 1979), Collegium Otorhinolaryngologicum (pres. 2000-02), Phi Beta Kappa, Alpha Omega Alpha. Home: 327 Greenbriar Ln West Grove PA 19390-9490 Personal E-mail: jandssnow@comcast.net.

SNOW, JOHN WILLIAM (JACK SNOW), investment company executive, former United States Secretary of the Treasury; b. Toledo, Aug. 2, 1939; s. William Dean and Catherine (Howard) S.; m. Fredrica Wheeler, June 11, 1964 (div. 1973); children: Bradley, Ian; m. Carolyn Kalk, Aug. 31, 1973; 1 child, Christopher. BA, Kenyon Coll./U. Toledo, 1962; PhD in Economics, U. Va., 1965; LLB, George Washington U., 1967. Asst. prof. econs. U. Md., College Park, 1965-67; assoc. Wheeler & Wheeler, Washington, 1967-72; asst. gen. counsel US Dept. Transp., Washington, 1972-73, dep. asst. sec. for policy, plans and internat. affairs, 1973-74, asst. sec. for govtl. affairs, 1974-75, dep. under sec., 1975-76; adminstr. Nat. Hwy. Traffic Safety Adminstrn., Washington, 1976-77; v.p. govt. affairs Chessie System Inc., Washington, 1977-80; sr. v.p. corp. services CSX Corp., Richmond, Va., 1980-84, exec. v.p., 1984-85; pres., CEO Chessie System R.R.s, Balt., 1985-86, CSX Rail Transport, Jacksonville, Fla., 1986-87, CSX Transp., Jacksonville, Va., 1987-88; pres., COO CSX Corp., Richmond, Va., 1988-89, pres., CEO, 1989-91, chmn., pres., CEO, 1991—2003; sec. US Dept. Treasury, Washington, 2003—06; chmn. Cerberus Capital Mgmt., L.P., NYC, 2006—. Adj. prof. law George Washington U., 1972-75; vis. prof. econs. U. Va., Charlottesville, spring 1977; vis. fellow Am. Enterprises Inst., Washington, spring 1977; bd. dirs. Marathon Oil Corp., 2006-, Verizon Comm. Inc., 2006- Ex officio trustee Nat. Gallery Art. Mem. Va. State Bar. Clubs: Chevy Chase, Metropolitan (Washington); Country of Va. (Richmond). Republican. Episcopalian. Office: Cerberes Capital Mgmt LP 299 Park Ave New York NY 10171*

SNOW, LINDA E., librarian; b. Mesa, Ariz., Oct. 16, 1945; d. Jon S. and Mary J. Snow. MA, U. Va., Charlottesville, 1972; MLS, ALA, 1978. Info. specialist US Dept. Energy, Washington, 1980—84; head, reference svcs. McDermott Libr., Richardson, Tex., 1984—. Dir. Bois D'Arc Rsch. Group, Dallas, 1990—. Advisor Tex. Early Music Soc., Austin, 2007—08. Recipient Ethel Ward-McLemore award, U. Tex. Dallas, 1991. Avocations: music, travel. Office: Univ Tex Dallas 800 W Campbell Rd Richardson TX 75080 Office Fax: 972-883-2473. Business E-Mail: snow@utdallas.edu.

SNOW, MARLON O., trucking executive, state agency administrator; m. Ann; children. Gen. mgr. spl. commodities Milne Truck Lines, Phoenix, LA, 1970-81; gen. mgr. spl. commodities, sales Motor Cargo, Salt Lake City, 1981-82; owner MST Trucking, Inc., Salt Lake City, 1982—. V.p. Utah Motor Carriers for State of Utah, 1997-98; mem. adv. bd. Zions Bank. Mem. State Bd. Edn., 1994-97, chair, 1995-97; trustee Utah Valley State Coll., 1998; mem. Ho. of Reps., Utah, 1999-2001; bd. regents Bd. Higher Edn. State of Utah, 2001—; bd. dirs. Children's Justice Ctr., State of Utah, 2002-, Riverside Country Club; mem. bd. I.H.C. Hosp. Utah County. Mem. Utah Valley State Coll. Found. (bd. dirs. 1991—), Alpine Sch. Dist. Found. (bd. dirs. 1990-94). Office: 1247 E 430 N Orem UT 84097-5400

SNOW, THEODORE PECK, astrophysics educator; b. Seattle, Jan. 30, 1947; s. Theodore P. and Louise (Wertz) S.; s. Constance M. Snow, Aug. 23, 1969; children: McGregor A., Tyler M., Reilly A. BA, Yale U., 1969; MS, U. Wash., 1970, PhD, 1973. Mem. rsch. staff Princeton (N.J.) U., 1973-77; prof. U. Colo., Boulder, 1977—, dir. Ctr. for Astrophysics and Space Astronomy, 1986-96, dir. Fiske Planetarium, 2000—. Mem. instrument devel. teams for far Ultraviolet Spectroscopic Explorer, 1999—, Cosmic Origins Spectrograph to be installed in Hubble Space Telescope. Author: (textbook) The Dynamic Universe, 1983, 4th edit., 1991, Essentials of the Dynamic Universe 4th edit., 1993 (textbook excellence award Text and Academic Authors Assn. 1994), Physics, 1986, Universe: Origins and Evolution, 1997; contbr. over 200 articles to profl. jours. Fellow Royal Astron. Soc.; mem. Am. Astron. Soc., Astron. Soc. Pacific, Sigma Xi. Achievements include discovery, through observations in ultraviolet visible, and infrared wavelengths, and through laboratory measurement of chemical reactions, of several important processes involving interstellar gas and dust, and their roles in star formation and late stages of stellar evolution. Office: U Colo Ctr Astrophysics Space Astronomy 389 UCB Boulder CO 80309-0389 Business E-Mail: tsnow@casa.colorado.edu.

SNOW, TOWER CHARLES, JR., lawyer; b. Boston, Oct. 28, 1947; s. Tower Charles and Margaret (Harper) S. BA in English, Dartmouth Coll., 1969; JD, U. Calif., Berkeley, 1973. Bar: Calif. 1973, US Dist. Ct. (no. dist.) Calif. 1973, US Ct. Appeals (9th cir.) 1973, US Supreme Ct. 1976, US Dist. Ct. (ea. dist.) Calif. 1979, US Ct. Appeals (fed. cir.) 1980, US Ct. Claims 1980, US Ct. Appeals (2d cir.) 1987, NY 1988, US Dist. Ct. (ea. and so. dists.) NY 1988, US Dist. Ct. (ctrl. dist.) Calif. 1989, US Dist. Ct. (no. dist.) Tex. 1995, US Dist. Ct. (so. dist.) Calif. 1996, US Dist. Ct. Ariz. 1996. Ptnr., chmn. litigation dept. Orrick, Herrington & Sutcliffe, San Francisco, 1973-89; ptnr. Shearman & Sterling, San Francisco, 1989-94; ptnr., chmn. securities litigation group, mem. policy com. Brobeck, Phleger & Harrison, LLP, San Francisco, 1995-97; chmn., CEO Brobeck, Phleger & Harrison, San Francisco, 1998—2001; ptnr., mem. Americas Mgmt. Group, Clifford Chance, LLP, 2002—04, cons., 2005—06; ind. cons., 2007—09; ptnr., dir. Howard Rice Nemerovski Canady Falk & Rabkin, San Francisco, 2009—. Arbitrator Nat. Assn. Securities Dealers, Am. Stock Exch., N.Y. Stock Exch., Pacific Coast Stock Exch., Superior Ct. City and County San Francisco, Am. Arbitration Assn.; lectr. in field. Author numerous law handbooks and articles to prof. jours. Mem. San Francisco Mus. Soc., San Francisco Symphony, San Francisco Ballet, San Francisco Opera, Am. Conservatory Theatre. Named Best Lawyer in the U.S. in his Field, Corp. Bd. Member Mag., 2001; named one of The 100 Most Influential Lawyers in America, Nat. Law Jour., 2000, The 100 Most Influential Lawyers in Calif., Calif. Law and Bus., 2000, 2002, Lawyer Mag. (U.K.), 2002, America's Leading Lawyers for Bus., Chambers USA, 2003, 2004, 2005; Rufus Choate scholar, Dartmouth Coll., 1969. Mem. ABA (chmn. subcom. pub. offering litig. 1984-88, co-chair task force on securities arbitration 1988-89, vice chair securities litig. com. 1986-88), Continuing Edn. Bar (bus. law inst. planning com. 1986), Securities Industry Assn., Nat. Inst. Trial Advocacy, San Francisco Bar Assn. (pres. securities litig. sect. 1995). Democrat. Avocations: travel, skiing, running, scuba diving, films. Office: Howard Rice Nemerovski Canady Falk & Rabkin Three Embarcadero Ctr Seventh Fl San Francisco CA 94111 Office Phone: 415-987-5877, 415-677-3475. Personal E-mail: tower.snow@gmail.com. E-mail: tsnow@howardrice.com.

SNOWBARGER, VINCE, former congressman; b. Kankakee, Ill., Sept. 16, 1949; s. Willis Edward and Wahnona Ruth (Horger) S.; m. Carolyn Ruth McMahon, Mar. 25, 1972; children: Jeffrey Edward, Matthew David. BA in History, So. Nazarene U., 1971; MA in Polit. Sci., U. Ill., 1974; JD, U. Kans., 1977. Bar: Kans. 1977, U.S. Dist. Ct. Kans. 1977, Mo. 1987. Instr. Mid-Am. Nazarene Coll., Olathe, Kans., 1973—76; ptnr. Haskin, Hinkle, Slater & Snowbarger, 1977—84, Dietrich, Davis, Dicus et al, 1984—88, Armstrong, Teasdale, Schafly & Davis, Overland Park, 1989—92, Holbrook, Heaven & Fay, P.C., Merriam, 1992—94, Snowbarger & Veatch LLP, Olathe, 1994—96; mem. 105th Congress from 3rd Kans. dist., 1997—99; exec. dir. Kans. Assn. Am. Educators, 2000—01; dep. dir. ops. Pension Benefit Guaranty Corp., Washington, 2002—. Mem. Kans. Legislature, Topeka, 1985-96; majority leader Ho. of Reps., 1993-96; mem. Olathe Planning Commn., 1982-84, Leadership Olalthe; divsn. chmn. United Way, Olathe, 1985-88, chmn. citizen rev. com., 1991-95. Mem. Olathe Area C. of C. (bd. dirs. 1984). Republican. Nazarene. Avocation: politics. Office: 1200 K St NW Washington DC 20005-4026 Home: 12676 Lace Falls Loop Bristow VA 20136-1295 Office Phone: 202-326-4010. Business E-Mail: snowbarger.vince@pbgc.gov.

SNOWDEN, FRANK MARTIN, III, history professor; b. Washington, June 22, 1946; s. Frank Martin Snowden, Jr. and Elaine Snowden; m. Margaret McClave, Sept. 4, 1999; children: Claire Brocklehurst, Jessica Lindsay. BA in Govt., Harvard U., Cambridge, Mass., 1968; BPhil in Politics, Oxford U., England, 1971, DPhil in Politics, 1975. Asst. prof. history Yale U., New Haven, 1975—78, prof. history, 1991—; lectr. history royal holloway coll. U. London, Egham, England, 1978—90, reader history, 1990—91. Author: (book) Violence and Great Estates in the South of Italy: Apulia 1900 - 1922, The Fascist Revolution in Tuscany, 1919-1922, Naples in the Time of Cholera, 1884 - 1911, The Conquest of Malaria: Italy, 1900 - 1962 (Helen and Howard Marraro prize Am. Hist. Assn., 2006); editor: Disastro! Disasters in Italy since 1860. Bd. dirs. Episc. Div. Sch., Cambridge, Mass., 2004—. Fellow, Am. Acad. Rome, 2003; scholar, Nat. Merit Scholarship Commn., 1964—68; Presdl. scholar, US, 1964, Marshall scholarship, Govt. UK, 1968—71. Mem.: Am. Hist. Assn., Phi Beta Kappa. Office: Dept History Yale Univ PO Box 208324 New Haven CT 06520-8324 Business E-Mail: frank.snowden@yale.edu.

SNOWDEN, LAWRENCE FONTAINE, retired air transportation executive, retired military officer; b. Charlottesville, Va., Apr. 14, 1921; s. Lawrence Fontaine Snoddy and Beatrice M. (Huffman) S.; m. Martha Roselyn Ham, Nov. 17, 1942; children: John Stephen, Brian Fontaine. Student, Stetson U., 1938-39; BS, U. Va., 1942; MA, Northwestern U., 1950; postgrad., Harvard U., 1968; grad., Indsl. Coll. Armed Forces, 1967. Commd. 2d lt. USMC, 1942, advanced through grades to lt. gen., 1975; comdr. 7th Marine Regt., Vietnam, 1966; ops. officer III Marine Amphibious Force, Vietnam, 1967; asst. dir. personnel Hdqrs. Marine Corps, Washington, 1968-69, dir. systems support group, 1969-70; dir. Marine Corps Devel. Ctr., Quantico, Va., 1970-72; chief of staff U.S. Forces, Japan, 1972-75; U.S. chmn. UN Bd., Japan, 1973-75; chief of staff Hdqrs. U.S. Marine Corps, 1977-79; ret., 1979; v.p. Far East Internat. Service Co. Hughes Aircraft Co., 1979-86, group v.p. Internat. Ground Systems Group Fullerton, Calif., 1986-88; pres. Snowden Internat. Assocs., Tallahassee, Fla., 1988—. Recipient Silver Beaver award Boy Scouts Am., Disting. Eagle Scout award; decorated Disting. Svc. medals (2), Legion of Merit (5), Army Commendation medal, Navy Commendation medal, Purple Heart (2), Cross of Gallantry (3) Vietnam, Second Order of Sacred Treasure Japan) Mem. Marine Corps League, U.S. Navy League, Am. C. of C. in Japan, Am.-Japan Soc., Marine Corps Assn., Econ. Club Fla., Sigma Nu. Clubs: Tokyo. Home Phone: 850-668-1433.

SNOWDEN, RUTH O'DELL GILLESPIE, artist; b. Gary, W.Va., Apr. 16, 1926; d. Haynes Thornton and Blanche Beaula (Boling) Gillespie; m. Eugene Louis Snowden, Dec. 21, 1946; children: Wanda Snowden Ballard, Eugene III, Ronald, Marian Snowden Warren, Jeffry. RN, Natharith Coll., 1946; student Sch. Art, Transylvania U., 1983-84, U. Ky., 1985-89. RN. Painter, publicity chmn. Artists's Attic Inc., Lexington, Ky., 1988-89. Exhibited in group shows at U. Ky. Art Mus., Lexington, 1988, 5th Internat. Juried Exhibition Pastels, Nyack, N.Y., 1988, Small Paintings Nat., Ky. Highlands Mus., Ashland, 1988, The Appalachian Cen., U. Ky., 1988, Ft. Wayne (Ind.) Mus. Art, 1986, John Howard Sanden Nat. Artists Seminar, Washington, Nat. Artists' Seminar, Chgo., Huntington (W.Va.) Galleries, Ashland Area Art Gallery, Guild Gallery, Lexington, Ky, Nat. Nursing Art Exhibit, Meth. Med. Cen., Peoria, Ill., Chautauqua Art Assn. Galleries, N.Y., 1990, Central Bank gallery, Chatauqua, 1990, Pastel & Chisel Acad. Fine Arts, 1990, Opera House Gallery, 1990, Sacramento Fine Arts Ctr., 1990, Ariel Gallery, Soho, N.Y., 1990, 91, Sumi-e Soc. Am., Inc., 1993, Watercolor Soc. Ala., 1994; represented in the Director of American Portrait Artists, Am. Portrait Soc., Huntington Harbour, Calif., Audubon Artists Exhibit, N.Y.C., 2003, 2004; numerous local and nat. shows; in pvt. collections. Recipient Assn. Alliance award Am. Frame Co., 1993, Elizabeth Morris Genious award, 2002, Winsor Newton Merchandising award Summie Soc. Am., 2002, Internat. Biographical Order of Merit, 2007, various others. Mem. Oil Pastel Assn., Winchester Art Guild, Lexington Art League, Ky. Watercolor Assn. (Bluegrass regional dir. 1988, 89, 90, 91, 92), Ky. Guild Artists and Craftsmen, Inc., Northwest Pastel Soc., Degas Pastel Soc., Pen & Brush Soc. (juried profl. mem. 2008, Perfect Proportion award), Audubon Artists (juried mem.) Avocations: golf, bowling. Home and Studio: 2800 Old Boonesboro Rd Winchester KY 40391-8805 Office Phone: 859-744-6693.

SNOWE, OLYMPIA J., United States Senator from Maine; b. Augusta, Maine, Feb. 21, 1947; d. George John and Georgia G. Bouchles; m. John McKernan. BA, U. Maine, 1969; LLD (hon.), U. Maine, Orono, 1981, Nasson Coll., 1981, U. Maine, Machias, 1982, Bowdoin Coll., 1982, Colby Coll., 1985; LHD (hon.), Thomas Coll., 1987; LLD (hon.), Suffolk U., 1994; DSc (hon.), Maine Maritime Acad., 1995; LLD (hon.), Colby Coll., 1996, U. New England, 1996; degree (hon.), Harvard U., 1997; LLD (hon.), Bates Coll., 1998. Businesswoman; mem. Maine Ho. of Reps., 1973-76, Maine Senate, 1976-78, 96th-103d Congresses from 2d Maine Dist., 1979-94, mem. budget com., foreign affairs com., com. on aging, 1979-94; co-chair Congl. Caucus for Women's Issues, 1983-94; U.S. senator from Maine, 1995—. Mem. Senate com. armed svcs., 1997-2001, chair, seapower subcom., Senate com. on commerce, sci. and transp., 1995—, chair, oceans and fisheries subcom., Senate Budget com., 1995—, Senate com. small business, 1995—, Senate com. Fgn. Rels., 1995-97; counsel to asst. majority leader, 1997—, House Budget com., 1991-95, House Fgn. Affairs com., 1979-95, House Aging com. 1979-95, Congl. Caucus on Women's Issues 1979-84, co-chair 1983-95; dep. Repub. Whip, 1984-95; dep. Whip, 1996-97; corporator Mechanics Savs. Bank. Recipient Homeric award for adv. of human rights Chian Fedn., 1999, award for "Excelling in Standing up for Choice" Women's Campaign Fund, 1999, Spirit of Enterprise award U.S. Chamber of Commerce, 1997, 99, Woman of Yr. award Glamour Mag., 1998, David and Sherry Huber award for leadership on family planning, women's health issues, Family Planning Assn. of ME, 1998, Golden Bulldog award Watchdogs of the Treasury, Inc., Wash., 1994, 96, 98, Guardian of Small Business award Nat. Fedn. Indep. Bus., Wash., 1994, 96, 98, Responsible Choices award Planned Parenthood of Am., 1998, Spl. honor Nat. Assn. Devel. Orgns., 1998, Disting. Pub. Svc. award Am. Legion, Wash., 1998, Neil W. Allen award Greater Portland Chamber of Commerce, 1997, Legis. award for outstanding svc. to schs. and pub. librs., White Ho. Conf. on Libr. and Info. Svcs. Task Force, Wash., 1997, Pub. Leadership award, Nat. Breast Cancer Coalition, 1997, Magnificent Seven award Bus. & Profl. Women/USA, Wash., 1997, Deborah Morton award Westbrook Coll., Portland, ME, 1997, Golden Gavel award U.S. Senate Leadership, Wash., 1996, Nat. Osteoporosis Assn. award for leadership, Wash., 1996, award for leadership U.S. Distance Learning Assn., Crystal City, Va., 1996, award for leadership United Hellenic Am. Cong., 1995, William H. Natcher Disting. Svc. award Com. for Edn. Funding, 1995, Pub. Svc. award Am. Coll. Obstetricians and Gynecologists, 1995, Nat. Security Leadership award Am. Security Coun., Wash., 1994, Thomas Jefferson award Nat. Am. Wholesale Grocers Assn./Internat. Foodsvc. Distbrs. Assn., 1994, Grace Caucus award Citizens Against Govt. Waste, 1994, Sound Dollar award Free Cong. Found., 1994, Appreciation award Agrl. Stblzn. and Conservation Com. Somerset County chpt., Lifetime Achievement award Am. Hellenic Inst., 1994, Golden Heart award Assn. for Children for Enforcement of Support, ME chpt., 1993, Am. Social Health Assn. award on behalf of women's health issues, 1993, Medal of St. Andrew presented by His All Holiness Dimitrios Ecumenical Patriarch of Constantinople, Wash., 1990, Congrl. Waste Watchers award Coalition to Reform the Davis-Bacon Act, 1990; named to "CQ 50" Congrl. Quarterly Mag., Wash., 1999, Maine Women's Hall of Fame, 1999, Washingtonian Mag. 100 Most Powerful Women, 1997, All Maine Women Honor Soc. U. Maine, 1996, Deficit Reduction Honor Roll Concord Coalition, 1994, Honor Roll for dairy farmer support Associated Milk Prodrs., 1993; named Taxpayer's Hero for preventing govt. waste Citizens Against Govt. Waste, 1997, No Nonsense Am. Women, No Nonsense Coun. on Women's Issues, 1995, Congresswoman of Yr. Nat. Assn. for Transp. Alternatives, 1986; honored by Nat. Coalition for Osteoporosis and Related Bone Diseases, 1999, Edn. and Libr. Networks Coalition, 1997, Am. Assn. Univ. Pres., 1996, Pub. Policy Com. for Hellenic-Am. Women, 1995, Nat. Vietnam Vet. Coalition, 1994; named one of most powerful women, Forbes mag., 2005. Mem.: Philoptochos Soc. Republican. Greek Orthodox. Office: US Senate 154 Russell Senate Bldg Washington DC 20510-1903 Office Phone: 202-224-5344. E-mail: olympia@snowe.senate.gov.*

SNOWHOOK, ANN LAFERTY, social services administrator; b. NYC, May 25, 1929; d. Paul Gause and Anna Gladys (Braun) Laferty; m. John David Snowhook, Sept. 13, 1952; children: Eileen M., Elizabeth J., David P., J. Jordan, Nancy P. BA in Math., UCLA, 1953, postgrad., 1965-70. Mathematician missiles divsn. The Rand Corp., LA, 1951-52; substitute tchr. math. Spastic Children's Found., LA, 1958-60; sec. women's aux. Exceptional Children's Found., LA, 1960-63; chmn. and treas. parents group, chmn. fundraising, substitute tchr. Exceptional Children's Class Pacific Palisades, LA, 1963-73; chmn. area guild, mgr. sch. lunch program Corpus Christi Ch., LA, 1972-74; statistician, rsch. asst. in mental retardation, family therapy and anorexia nervosa Neuropsychiatric Inst. UCLA, 1974-90; mem. program/policy bd. Kennedy Regional Ctr. for Developmentally Disabled, LA, 1974-78; del. program devel. fund grants review Los Angeles County Area Bd. X, 1978-82; del. We. Regional Ctr. Assn. Regional Ctr. Contracting Agys., LA, 1981-82; bd. dirs., pres., corp. sec. We. Regional Ctr. for Developmentally Disabled, LA, 1978-82; founding dir., corp. sec., treas. Home Ownership Made Easy, LA, 1988-91; bd. dirs., corp. sec., treas. Found. for Developmentally Disabled, LA, 1982—; bd. dirs., corp. treas. Marian Homes for Physically Handicapped and Devel. Disabled, LA, 1992—95. Rsch. assoc. Family Therapy: An Overview, 1980, Anorexia Nervosa: A Body Image Disturbance, 1978, Autism: A Study for Chromosomal Abnormalities, 1979, Family Therapy Today, Estrogen Therapy in Menopausal Women, 1991; rsch. cons. Estrogen Therapy in Menopausal Women, Family Therapy Today; bd. mem. Programs for the Developmentally Handicapped, 1995—, v.p. 1997-98, 2003-; bd. mem. Jay Nolan Cmty. Svcs., 1995-, v.p. 1997-98, chmn. human resources, 2001—, Jay Nolan v.p. 2005—, sec. 2003-05; program chair and bd. dirs. Easter Seals So. Calif., 1996—, treas., 2002—; mem. Calif. Legis. Blue Ribbon Commn. on Autism Sub-adult, 2006-07. Contbr. chapters to books. Mem. Autism Soc. L.A. (v.p., program chair 1993-95, pres. 1995-99, 2001-02). Roman Catholic. Avocations: reading, swimming, antiques. Home: 901 Iliff St Pacific Palisades CA 90272-3826

SNUSTAD, DONALD PETER, geneticist, educator; b. Bemidji, Minn., Apr. 6, 1940; s. Ole Snustad and Vera Grife; m. Judy Adams; 1 child, Eric. PhD, U. Calif., Davis, 1965. Prof. genetics U. Minn., St. Paul, 1965—2008. Author: (textbook) Principles of Genetics. Recipient Horse T. Morse-Amoco award, U. Minn., 1984, Stanley Dagley Meml. Tchg. award, 1990; NSF Coop. Grad. fellowship, 1963, NIH Predoc. Trainee fellowship, 1964—65, NSF & NIH Rsch. grants, 1967—2001. Fellow: AAAS (Elected Fellow Soc. 2005). Achievements include research in bacteriophage and plant genetics. Office: Univ Minnesota 1445 Gortner Ave Saint Paul MN 55108

SNYDER, ALLEGRA FULLER, dancer, film director, educator; b. Chgo., Aug. 28, 1927; d. R. Buckminster and Anne (Hewlett) Fuller; m. Robert Snyder, June 30, 1951 (div. Apr. 1975, remarried Sept. 1980); children: Alexandra, Jaime. BA in Dance, Bennington Coll., 1951; MA in Dance, UCLA, 1967. Asst. to curator, dance archives Mus. Modern Art, NYC, 1945-47; dancer Ballet Soc. of N.Y.C. Ballet Co., 1945-47; mem. office and prodn. staff Internat. Film Found., NYC, 1950-52; editor, dance films Film News mag., NYC, 1966-72; lectr. dance and film adv., dept. dance UCLA, 1967-73, chmn. dept. dance, 1974-80, 90-91, acting chair, spring 1985, chair of faculty Sch. of the Arts, 1989-91, prof. dance and dance ethnology, 1973-91, prof. emeritus, 1991—; pres. Buckminster Fuller Inst., Santa Barbara, Calif., chairwoman bd. dirs., 1984—. Vis. lectr. Calif. Inst. Arts, Valencia, 1972; co-dir. dance and TV workshop Am. Dance Festival, Conn. Coll., New London, 1973; dir. NEH summer seminar for coll. tchrs. Asian Performing Arts, 1978, 81; coord. Ethnic Arts Intercoll. Interdisciplinary Program, 1974-73, acting chmn., 1986; vis. prof. performance studies NYU, 1982-83; hon. vis. prof. U. Surrey, Guildford, Eng., 1983-84; cons. Thyodia Found., Salt Lake City, 1973-74; mem. dance adv. panel Nat. Endowment Arts, 1968-72, Calif. Arts Commn., 1974-91; mem. adv. screening com. Coun. Internat. Exch. of Scholars, 1979-82; mem. various panels NEH, 1979-85; core cons. for Dancing, Sta. WNET-TV, 1988—. Dir. film Baroque Dance 1625-1725, in 1977; co-dir. film Gods of Bali, 1952; dir. and wrote film Bayanihan, 1962 (named Best Folkloric Documentary at Bilboa Film Festival, winner Golden Eagle award); asst. dir. and asst. editor film The Bennington Story, 1952; created films Gestures of Sand, 1968, Reflections on Choreography, 1973, When the Fire Dances Between Two Poles, 1982; created film, video loop and text Celebration: A World of Art and Ritual, 1982-83; supr. post-prodn. film Erick Hawkins, 1964, in 1973. Also contbr. articles to profl. jours. and mags. Adv. com. Pacific Asia Mus., 1980-84, Festival of the Mask, Craft and Folk Art Mus., 1979-84; adv. panel Los Angeles Dance Currents II, Mus. Ctr. Dance Assn., 1974-75; bd. dirs. Council Grove Sch. III, Compton, Calif., 1976-81; apptd. mem. Adv. Dance Com., Pasadena (Calif.) Art Mus., 1970-71, Los Angeles Festival of Performing Arts com., Studio Watts, 1970; mem. Technology and Cultural Transformation com., UNESCO, 1977. Fulbright research fellow, 1983-84; grantee Nat. Endowment Arts, 1981, Nat. Endowment Humanities, 1977, 79, 81, UCLA, 1968, 77, 80, 82, 85; recipient Amer. Dance Guild Award for Outstanding Achievement in Dance, 1992. Mem. Am. Dance Therapy Assn., Congress on Rsch. in Dance (bd. dirs. 1970-76, chmn. 1975-77, nat. conf. chmn. 1972), Coun. Dance Administrs., Am. Dance Guild (chmn. com. awards 1972), Soc. for Ethnomusicology, Am. Anthrop. Assn., Am. Folklore Soc., Soc. Anthropology of Visual Comm., Soc. Humanistic Anthropology, Calif. Dance Educators Assn. (conf. chmn. 1972), L.A. Area Dance Alliance (adv. bd. 1978-84, selection com. Dance Kaleidoscope project 1979-81), Fulbright Alumni Assn. Home: 15313 Whitfield Ave Pacific Palisades CA 90272-2548 Office: Buckminster Fuller Institute 181 N 11th St Apt 402 Brooklyn NY 11211-1175

SNYDER, ARLEN DEAN, actor; b. Rice, Kans., Mar. 5, 1933; s. Glenn Arlen and Sylvia Thelma (Guiot) S.; m. Joanne Elizabeth Burke, May 8, 1983; 1 child, Kimble Burke. BA in Theater, U. Tulsa, 1957; MA in Theater, U. Iowa, 1959. Facilities designer Diamond Cir. Theatre, Durango, Colo., 1961, ptnr., mgr., actor, 1961—63. Instr. dept. cinema Hunter Coll., NYC, 1975-76. Dir.: (plays) Under Milkwood, 1974, Miss Pete, 1975; appeared in motion pictures including Yanks, 1978, Heartbreak Ridge, 1986, Bird, 1987, Internal Affairs, 1989, Marked For Death, 1990, Mommy's Day, 1996, The Overlookers, 2003, Lobster Farm, 2004; recurring roles (TV series) Dallas, TV 101, Eisenhower & Lutz, Designing Women; guest appearances (TV series) Hart to Hart, M*A*S*H, Murder She Wrote, Benson, Dynasty, Private Benjamin, St. Elsewhere, Quantum Leap, Trial By Jury, others; appeared in theatrical plays including The Candy Apple, 1970, Trial of the Catonsville Nine, 1972, Big Broadcast on E. 53rd, 1973, One World at a Time, 1973, The Poison Tree, 1974, 75, Streamers, 1976, The Trip Back Down, 1977, Curse of the Starving Class, 1978, Better Living, 1989, Mr Rickey Calls A Meeting, 1992, Madalyn Murray O'Hair in Exile, 2003; starred in TV series including Secret Storm, 1966-68, As The World Turns, 1968-69, Dear Detective, 1979, The Texas Rangers/Pilot, 1981, Trauma Center, 1983, One Life to Live, 1984, Macgruder and Loud/Pilot, 1984; actor (TV films) Young Love, First Love, 1979, Attica, 1979, Red Flag, 1980, RFK, 1981, Bus Stop, 1982, Night Partners, 1983, North & South Book II, 1986, The Oliver North Story, 1989, Frog Girl, 1989, Terror in Copper Valley, 1989, The Beach Boys' Story, 1990, Willing To Kill: The Texas Cheerleader Story, 1992, Cora Unashamed, PBS, 1999; recs. for Iowa's Books for the Blind and Handicapped. Bd. dirs. San Fernando Valley (Calif.) Arts Coun., 1987-88, mem. bd. advisors, 1989-90, pres., 1991. With US Army, 1953-55. Named Leading Male Performer, LA Weekly, Matrix Theatre, 1989. Mem. AFTRA, SAG (bd. dirs. 1991), Actors' Equity Assn., Players' Club (bd. dirs. 1974-76), Theta Alpha Phi. Independent. Avocations: anti-establishment commentary, set design, political history, farming, cabinet making. Office: 4580 Broadway Ste 4F New York NY 10040-2114 Office Phone: 212-304-3934. Business E-Mail: arlen@snarlin.com.

SNYDER, ARNOLD LEE, JR., retired military officer, research director; b. Washington, Oct. 12, 1937; s. Arnold Lee and Frances May (Humbert) S; m. Patricia Dorine Ward, July 6, 1963; children: Heinrick Jason, Sonya Doreen, Ross Nansen. BCE, George Washington U., 1960; MS, U. Colo., 1966; PhD, U. Alaska, 1972. Commd. 2d lt. USAF, 1960; advanced through grades to col., 1981; chief space environ. support sys. devel. sect. Air Force Global Weather Central, Offutt AFB, Nebr., 1972-76; chief ionospheric dynamics br. Geophysics Lab., Hanscom AFB, Mass., 1976-80; test dir. CONUS OTH-B radar system, Columbia Falls AFS, Maine, 1980-81, program dir. Hanscom AFB, 1981-85; dir. Office of Tech. Support, 1985-87; tech. dir. U. Lowell Ctr. Atmospheric Rsch., 1987-89; with The Mitre Corp., 1989-96; pvt. practice, 1996—. Adj. prof. U. Lowell, 1987-89. Contbr. articles to sci. jours. Recipient Legion of Merit, Meritorious Svc. medal with one oak leaf cluster, Commendation medal USAF, R&D award, 1981; Def. Value Engring. award, 1984; Henry Harding scholar, 1955-56. Mem. Am. Geophys. Union, Am. Meteorol. Soc., Air Force Assn., Sigma Xi. Home and Office: PO Box 530 Stockton Springs ME 04981 Home Phone: 207-567-3137. Personal E-mail: palsnyder@aol.com.

SNYDER, ARTHUR, publishing executive; b. Valley Stream, NY, Feb. 6, 1925; s. Arthur and Kathryn (Staubitzer) Snyder; m. Betty Lain Harper, July 8, 1950; children: Susan, Arthur, Betsy, Jack, Heidi, Bonnie. B in Metall. Engring., Cornell U., 1950, MBA, 1952. Mfg. engr. Norton Co., Worcester, Mass., 1952-56, chief acct., 1956-58, asst. contr., 1958-59, mgr. data processing, 1959-61, contr., 1961-65; exec. v.p. A.M. Best Co., Oldwick, NJ, 1965-67, pres., 1968—, chmn., 1971—. Author: (book) Principles of Inventory Control and Managing Capital Expenditures. 1st lt. AUS, 1942—45. Decorated Battlefield Commn., Bronze Star with oak leaf cluster, Purple Heart. Mem.: U.S. Srs. Golf Assn., Cornell Soc. Engrs., Fin. Execs. Inst., Lyford Cay Club (Nassau, Bahamas), Baltusrol Golf Club (Springfield, NJ). Presbyterian. Home: 111 Lloyd Rd Bernardsville NJ 07924-1710 Office: A M Best Company Inc Ambest Rd Oldwick NJ 08858 Office Phone: 908-439-3316. Business E-Mail: snydera2@ambest.com.

SNYDER, BARBARA ROOK, academic administrator; b. July 23, 1955; BA, Ohio State U., 1976; JD, U. Chgo., 1980. Bar: Ill. 1980. Law clk. for Judge Luther M. Swygert U.S. Ct. Appeals for the Seventh Cir.; with Sidley & Austin, Chgo.; joined law faculty Case Western Res. U., 1983, Ohio State U., Columbus, 1988, assoc. dean for acad. affairs, 2000—01, vice provost for acad. policy and human resources, 2001—03, interim provost, 2003—04, exec. v.p., provost, 2004—07, Joanne W. Murphy/Class of 1965 professorship Moritz Coll. Law; pres. Case Western Reserve U., Cleve., 2007—. Office: Case Western Reserve U Office of Pres 10900 Euclid Ave Cleveland OH 44106-7001 E-mail: barbara.snyder@case.edu.*

SNYDER, BURTON HAROLD, lawyer; b. York, Pa., Nov. 7, 1947; m. Carol A. Oyler. BA in math., Lehigh U., 1969; JD, Harvard U., 1975. Bar: Pa. 1975. Staff counsel Hershey Foods Corp., Hershey, Pa., 1979—82, sr. counsel, 1982—85, ops. dir., gen mgr. for Far East and Middle East Hershey Internat. Ltd., 1985—89; ptnr. McNees, Wallace & Nurick, Harrisburg, Pa., 1989—93; asst. gen. counsel Hershey Foods Corp., Hershey, Pa., 1993—2000, v.p., asst. gen. counsel, 2000—02, sr. v.p. pub affairs, gen. counsel, sec., 2002, sr. v.p. internat., gen. counsel, sec., 2002—03, sr. v.p., gen. counsel, sec., 2003—. Mem.: Assn. of Corp. Counsel, ABA. Office: The Hershey Co 100 Crystal A Dr Hershey PA 17033-0810

SNYDER, CHARLES AUBREY, lawyer; b. Bastrop, La., June 19, 1941; s. David and Shirley Blossom (Haas) S.; m. Sharon Rae Veta, Aug. 29, 1963; children: David Veta, Shelby Haas, Claire Frances. BBA, Tulane U., 1963; JD, La. State U., 1966. Bar: La. 1966. Assoc. firm. Milling Benson Woodward, LLP and predecessors, New Orleans, 1966-69, ptnr., 1969—. Bd. dirs. Terre aux Boeufs Land Corp., Kemper and Leila Williams Found., v.p., 2004-07, pres., 2007—. Bd. dirs. New Orleans Speech and Hearing Ctr., pres., 1978-80; bd. dirs. City Pk. Commn., 1991-98, pres., 1995, dir. emeritus, 1999—; bd. dirs. New Orleans Mus. Art, 1996-2002, 04—, v.p., 1998-99, 2007—m sec., 1999-2000. Fellow Am. Bar Found., La. Bar Found.; mem. ABA, La. Bar Assn. (chmn. sect. on corp. and bus. law 1982-83), New Orleans Bar Assn., Am. Law Inst., La. Law Inst. (coun. 2000—), Plimsoll Club, Bienville Club, Beta Gamma Sigma. Home: 74724 River Rd Covington LA 70435-2222 Office Phone: 504-569-7230. E-mail: csnyder@millinglaw.com.

SNYDER, CHARLES ROBERT, United States Senior Representative on Sudan; b. NYC, Sept. 19, 1947; s. Charles Theodore and Irene Virginia (Birnbaum) S.; m. Suzanne Elizabeth Carver, May 3, 1969; children: Jennifer, Amy, Jonathan. BA in Econs., Fordham U., 1969; MBA, Am. U., 1975; postgrad. in internat. rels., Cath. U. Am., 1981. Enlisted US Army, 1969, advanced through grades to lt. col., ret., 1991; Africa intelligence officer Chief of Staff Intelligence U. Army, Washington, 1978-80; security assistance officer, African affairs Dep. Chief Staff Ops., Washington, 1982-85; polit. and mil. advisor, bur. African affairs US Dept. State, Washington, 1985—91, nat. intelligence officer, Africa, 1992—95, dir. office regional affairs, 1995—2001, prin. dep., dep. asst. sec., 2001—03, acting asst. sec. of state African affairs, 2003—04, sr. rep. on Sudan, 2004—. Fellow Inter-Univ. Seminar on Armed Forces and Soc., Washington; disting. vis. lectr. Fgn Svc. Inst. Contbr. articles to profl. jours. Mem. African Studies Assn., Nat. Mil. Intelligence Assn., Fgn. Area Officers Assn. Republican. Roman Catholic. Office: US Dept State Bur African Affairs 2201 C St NW Washington DC 20520-0001*

SNYDER, CHARLES ROYCE, sociologist, educator; b. Haverford, Pa., Dec. 28, 1924; BA, Yale U., 1945, MA, 1949, PhD, 1954. Mem. staff Ctr. Alcohol Studies Yale U., 1950-60, asst. prof. sociology, 1956-60; prof. sociology So. Ill. U., Carbondale, 1960-85, chmn. dept., 1964-75, 81-85, prof. emeritus, 1985—. Vis. prof. human genetics Sackler Sch. Medicine, Tel Aviv U., 1980; cons. behavioral scis. tng. com. Nat. Inst. Gen. Med. Scis., NIH, 1962-64; mem. planning com., chmn. program 28th Internat. Congress Alcohol and Alcoholism, 1964. Author: Alcohol and the Jews, 1958; editor: (with D.J. Pittman) Society, Culture and Drinking Patterns, 1962; mem. editl. bd. Quar. Jour. Studies on Alcohol, 1957-83; assoc. editor Sociol. Quar., 1960-63. Mem. theol. commn. United Ch. of Christ, 1964-71; bd. dirs. Ill. Stewardship Alliance, 1990-95. With USNR, WWII. Fellow Am. Sociol. Assn.; mem. Soc. Study Social Problems (v.p. 1963-64, rep. to council Am. Sociol. Assn. 1964-66), Midwest Sociol. Soc. (bd. dirs. 1970-71), Pyrenees Homeowners Assn. (pres. 2009), AAUP. Home: 230 S Monaco & Pky 511 Denver CO 80224

SNYDER, CLAIR ALLISON, banker; b. Reading, Pa., June 12, 1921; s. Augustus M. and Estella G. (Bright) S.; m. Jean Doris George, June 27, 1948 (dec. Feb. 1997); children: Joan Marie Snyder Ferguson, Jerry George. Student, W.Va. U., 1943-44, U. Mich., 1944-45. With Meridian Bancorp, Inc. and Meridian Bank, Reading, 1938-43, 46-88, exec. v.p., gen. banking, 1973-78, exec. v.p., chmn. credit policy com., 1978-86; pvt. practice fin. cons. Snyder Svcs. Co., Reading, 1987—98. Asst. sec. Bi-Products, Inc., Fairfax, Va. Bd. dirs. Pa. divsn. Am. Cancer Soc., 1965-87, chmn. bd. dirs., 1975-77; chmn. Hope Lodge Com.; chmn. Property Mgmt. Com. With U.S. Army, 1943-46. Recipient Luther Halsey Gulick award Camp Fire Girls, 1966; div. Bronze medal Am. Cancer Soc., also Sword of Hope award Mem. Internat. Soc. for Philosophic Inquiry, Am. Bankers Assn. (cert.), Pa. Bankers Assn. (group chmn. 1972-73), Robert Morris Assocs. (pres. 1972-73), Am. Legion (post comdr. 1948-49). Republican. United Church Of Christ. also: 616 Sawgrass Rd Olde Point Hampstead NC 28443 Home: 2201 Ridgewood Rd Ste 180 Reading PA 19610-1190 Personal E-mail: rbdynsca@aol.com. *My life has been dedicated to personal achievement, but always with the knowledge that mankind's progress can only occur if each of us is willing to commit some of our efforts and resources to the future.*

SNYDER, DANIEL, professional sports team executive; b. Nov. 23, 1964; m. Tanya Snyder. Founder, chmn., CEO Snyder Communications, Inc. (sold to Havas), 1985—2000; chmn. bd., owner Washington Redskins, 1999—; non-exec. chmn. Six Flags Inc., 2005—; founder, investor Red Zone LLC, 2005—. Bd. dirs. McLeod USA, Ventiv Health; mem., broadcast com. and ventures com. NFL. Bd. dirs. Ctr. for Missing and Exploited Children, Parents in Charge; exec. leadership cabinet Martin Luther King, Jr. Nat. Meml. Found. Project; bd. dirs. Wash. Children's Nat. Med. Ctr.; founder Wash. Redskins Leadership Coun. Named one of The Most Influential People in the World of Sports, Bus. Week, 2007, The Most Powerful People in D.C., GQ mag., 2007. Mem.: Wash. Bd. Trade, Bus. Executives for Nat. Security. Office: c/o Washington Redskins 21300 Redskin Park Rd Ashburn VA 20147

SNYDER, DARIN W., lawyer; b. Kansas City, Mo., 1963; BA cum laude, Georgetown U., 1985; JD cum laude, U. Chgo., 1988. Bar: Calif. 1988, US Dist. Ct., (Ctrl, No., Ea., and So. Dists. of Calif.), US Ct. of Appeals (Ninth and Fed. Circuits), US Ct. Veterans Appeals. Co-chair patent and tech. litig. practice group O'Melveny & Myers LLP; mem. Policy Com. Dir. Bar Assn. San Francisco, Legal Aid Soc. Employment Law Ctr. Bradley Law & Government Fellow, 1987—88. Mem.: Am. Intellectual Property Law Assn., Santa Clara County Bar Assn., ABA (former co-chair intellectual property com., co-chair trade secrets subcommittee litig. sect. 1997—98). Office: O'Melveny & Myers LLP Embarcadero Ctr West 2 Embarcadero Ctr Ste 2800 San Francisco CA 94111-3903 Office Phone: 415-984-8846. Office Fax: 415-984-8701. Business E-Mail: dsnyder@omm.com.

SNYDER, DENISE, nutritionist, researcher; MS in Nutrition, U. Pa., 1997. Clinical trials mgr. Duke U. Sch. Nursing, 2000—. Office: Duke University School of Nursing Clipp Bldg Rm 1057 Durham NC 27710 Office Phone: 919-660-7580. E-mail: snyde023@mc.duke.edu.*

SNYDER, DONALD EDWARD, finance company executive; b. Rochester, NY, Nov. 10, 1928; s. Benjamin Orman and Arlien Henrietta (Wing) S.; m. Dorothy Edna Stanke, Oct. 16, 1954; children— Donald Edward, Anne Arlien Snyder Marone, Barbara Lynn Snyder Mitchell, Richard John Snyder. AB, Cornell U., 1950, JD, 1952; postgrad., Ind. U., 1962. Bar: N.Y. 1953. Pvt. practice law, 1953-56; with Eastman Savs. and Loan Assn., 1956-68, pres., 1970-75, chmn. bd., 1979-88; asst. to treas. Eastman Kodak Co., Rochester, 1968-70, gen. credit mgr., 1975-77, with Comptroller's div., 1977-78, asst. treas., 1978-79, treas., 1979-88; chmn. Eastman Kodak Credit Corp., 1985-88; chief exec. officer, chmn. bd., pres. Corp. Officers and Dirs. Assurance Ltd., Hamilton, Bermuda, 1990-93. Founding dir. & 1st. chmn. Nat. Assn. Corp. Treas. Bd. dirs. Greater Rochester chpt. Epilepsy Found. Am., 1979-85, Allendale Mut. Ins. Co., 1983-92; bd. dirs. Luth. Ch.-Mo. Synod, 1983-95; vice chmn. bd., chmn. fin. com., mem., chmn. audit com., 1989-95; bd. dirs., mem. exec. com. ACE Ltd., 1985-90, EXEL Ltd., 1985-90, CODA Ltd., 1986-93; mem. investment rev. com. United Way of Greater Rochester, 1979-2000; trustee Seneca Zool. Soc., 1983-90. With USNR, 1946-48. Mem. N.Y. State Bar Assn., Monroe County Bar Assn., Rochester C. of C. (trustee 1980-86), Cornell Club (Rochester), Phi Kappa Tau (nat. fin. advisor, mem. nat. coun. 1988-95, treas., mem. exec. com. Phi Kappa Tau Found. 1991-2001), Nat. Assn. Corporate Treas.(founding dir., first chmn. 1982). Home and Office: 14 Hidden Springs Dr Pittsford NY 14534-2897 also: 2700 N AIA Ste 705 Fort Pierce FL 34949 Home Phone: 585-218-0289.

SNYDER, DONALD IVANDALE, musician, educator; b. Fort Wayne, Ind., Jan. 5, 1956; s. Ivandale Everett and Helen Rachael Pauling Snyder. BS, U. Indpls., 1978; MusM, U. Houston, 1985. Certified Teacher Ind. Dept. of Pub. Instrn., 1978, Tex. Edn. Dept., 1981, SUNY-Dept. of Edn., 1987, NJ. Dept. of Edn., 1992. Music specialist Humble Ind. Sch. Dist., Tex., 1981—87, Greenburgh Ctrl. Sch. Dist. 7, Hartsdale, NY; vocal/gen. music specialist NYC Bd. of Edn., Brooklyn, 1990—97; music specialist Orange Twp. Bd. of Edn., NY, 1997—98; music specialist/guest lectr. Garfield Bd. of Edn., NJ, 1998—2003; music specialist/cons. East Brunswick Pub. Schs., 2004—. Music edn. cons. Beech Grove City Schs., Ind., 1986—; alumni guest lectr. U. of Indpls., 2000; guest lectr. Concordia Coll. of NY, Bronxville, 2000; conf. presenter NY State Sch. Music Assn., 2001, NJ Music Educators Assn., 2001, Ind. Music Educators Assn., Muncie, 2001; profl. choral musician Episcopal Ch. of Epiphany, New York, NY, 2003—; conf. presenter Music Educators Nat. Conf., Reston, Va., 2003—. Dir. of tour guide services St. Michael's Ch., New York, NY, 1996, dir. of aids outreach, 2001, parish coun. mem., 2002; mem. com. for certification and admission of new parishes Episcopal Diocese of NY, 2003; sales chair Kodaly Music Educators Orgn. of NY, 2000—04; sec. designate Diocesan Episcopal AIDS Com., New York, NY, 2000. Mem.: Am. Orff-Schulwerk Assn., Am. Orgn. of Kodaly Educators, Am. Choral Directors Assn., Music Educators Nat. Conf. (assoc.). Liberal. Episcopalian. Avocations: cooking, theater, art, bycling. Home: 1110 Fidler Lane #1622 Silver Spring MD 20910 Personal E-mail: dsnydermus@aol.com.

SNYDER, EDWARD ADAMS, dean, economics professor; b. Danville, Pa., July 3, 1953; s. Harry Coolidge and Fay (Adams) S.; m. Kimberly Marie Snyder; children: Alison Marie, Jeffrey Adams, Kevin James. Ba in Econs. and Govt., Colby Coll., 1975; M of Pub. Policy, U. Chgo., 1978, PhD in Econs., 1984. Staff economist antitrust div. US Dept. Justice, Washington, 1978—82; asst. prof. bus. econs. and pub. policy Sch. Bus. Adminstrn. U. Mich., Ann Arbor, 1982—90, assoc. prof. Sch. Bus. Adminstrn., 1990-94, prof. Sch. Bus. Adminstrn., 1994-98, chair bus. econ. and pub. policy, Sch. Bus. Adminstrn., 1992—95; dean Darden Bus. Sch. U. Va., Charlottesville, 1998—2001; dean U. Chgo. Booth Sch. Bus. (formerly U. Chgo. Grad. Sch. Bus.), 2001—, prof., 2001—02, George Pratt Shultz prof. economics, 2002—. Rsch. fellow Office for Study of Pub. and Pvt. Instns., U. Mich.; cons. Antitrust div. U.S. Dept. Justice, Chgo., 1982-85, Fed. Home Loan Bank Bd., Washington, 1989; antitrust expert, 1985—; John M. Olin vis. assoc. prof. U. Chgo., 1991-92; dir. William Davidson Inst. Mich. Bus. Sch., 1992-95. Author: Crisis Resolution in the Thrift Industry, 1989; contbr. articles to econ. jours. and law revs., 1985-98. Avocations: foreign policy, sports, sailing. Office: U Chgo Booth Sch Bus 5807 S Woodlawn Ave Chicago IL 60637 Office Phone: 773-702-1680. E-mail: tsnyder@chicagogsb.edu.*

SNYDER, GEORGE EDWARD, lawyer; b. Battle Creek, Mich., Feb. 7, 1934; s. Leon R. and Edith (Dullabahn) S.; m. Mary Jane Belt, July 27, 1957 (div. Sept. 23, 1982); children: Sara Lynn, Elizabeth Jane; m. Claudia Gage Brooks, Feb. 25, 1984 BS, Mich. State U., 1957; JD, U. Mich., 1960. Bar: Mich. 1961, U.S. Dist. Ct. (we. and ea. dists.) Mich. 1961. With Gen. Electric Co., 1957-58; assoc. firm Miller, Johnson, Snell & Commisky, Grand Rapids, 1960-62, Goodenough & Buesser, Detroit, 1962-66; partner firm Buesser, Buesser, Snyder & Blank, Detroit and Bloomfield Hills, 1966-85, Meyer, Kirk, Snyder & Lynch PLLC, Bloomfield Hills, 1985—2007; of counsel Meyer & Kirk, PLLC, 2007. Chmn. bd. dirs. Bill Knapps Mich., Inc., 1998-2000. Chmn. E. Mich. Environ. Action Council, 1974-78; pub. mem. inland lakes and streams rev. com. Mich. Dept. Natural Resources, 1975-76. Served as 2d lt. AUS, 1957. Named one of Best Lawyers in Am., Woodward White, 1992—2007, Mich. Super Lawyers, Law and Politics, 2006—07. Fellow Am. Acad. Matrimonial Lawyers (pres. Mich. chpt. 1991-92), Am. Coll. Family Trial Lawyers, Am. Bar Found., Internat. Acad. Matrimonial Lawyers, Mich. Bar Found; mem. ABA, Am. Judicature Soc., Am. Arbitration Assn. (panel arbitrators), State Bar Mich. (chmn. family law com. 1968-72, mem. rep. assembly 1972-78, chmn. rules and calendar com. 1977-78, mem. family law sect. coun. 1973-76, environ. law sect. coun. 1980-85, prepaid legal svcs. com. 1973-82, com. on judicial selection 1974, com. on specialization 1976-82), Detroit Bar Assn. (chmn. family law com. 1966-68), Oakland County Bar Assn., Delta Upsilon (chmn. trustees, alumni chpt. dep. 1965-70), Tau Beta Pi, Pi Tau Sigma, Phi Eta Sigma. Detroit Athletic Club, Birmingham (Mich.) Athletic Club, Bloomfield Hills Country Club. Episcopalian. Home: 32965 Outland Trl Bingham Farms MI 48025-2555 Office: Meyer & Kirk PLLC Ste 100 100 W Long Lake Rd Bloomfield Hills MI 48304-2773 Home Phone: 248-540-1698; Office Phone: 248-647-5111. Business E-Mail: gsnyder@meyerkirk.com.

SNYDER, HENRY LEONARD, historian, educator, writer; b. Hayward, Calif., Nov. 3, 1929; s. Henry Runyon and Mary (Rosenberg) Snyder; m. Janette Marie Hannus, July 21, 1961; children: Michael Jesse, Christopher Henry, David Lyle. BA, U. Calif., Berkeley, 1951, MA, 1960, PhD, 1963. Sr. buyer Dohrmann Comml. Co., San Francisco, 1951—59; instr. to prof. U. Kans., Lawrence, 1963—78, assoc. dean to dean rsch. adminstrn., 1967—78; dir. English Short Title Catalogue for N.Am., 1978—; prof. history, dean arts and scis. La. State U., Baton Rouge, 1979—86; prof. history U. Calif., Riverside, 1986—; dir. Ctr. for Bibliog. Studies, 1989—. Sigmund, Martin, Heller traveling fellow U. Calif., Berkeley, 1962—63; vis. lectr. Bedford Coll., U. London, 1965—66; sr. fellow Am. Council Learned Soc., 1969—70; Fulbright lectr., rsch. scholar U. Hamburg, Germany, 1974; dean humanities and social scis. U. Calif., Riverside, 1986. Co-editor: (book) The Marlborough Godolphin Correspondence, 1975, The Scottish World: History and Culture of Scotland, 1981; co-author: The English Heritage, 1988. United Way, 1977; pres. Baton Rouge Opera, 1981—83, Riverside Opera, 1987—90; bd. dirs. Arts and Humanities Com., Baton Rouge, 1981—85. Served with Nat. US Army. Recipient Nat. Humanities medal for digitizing the past, NEH, 2007. Fellow: Gt. Brit. Bibliog. Soc., Royal Hist. Soc.; mem.: Internat. Fed. Librs. (chair rarebooks sect. 1995—99), Am. Hist. Assn., Conf. Brit. Studies (exec. com. 1978—83), Am. Soc. 18th Century Studies (pres. 1980—81). Republican. Congregationalist. Home: 220 Trinity Ave Kensington CA 94708-1139 Office: U Calif Ctr For Bibliog Studies Riverside CA 92521-0154 Office Phone: 951-827-5841. Personal E-mail: hlsnyder@earthlink.net.

SNYDER, HOWARD ARTHUR, aerospace engineering educator, consultant; b. Palmerton, Pa., Mar. 7, 1930; s. Howard Franklin and Mary Rachel (Landis) S.; m. Nancy Jane Simon, Sept. 14, 1961 (div. Feb. 1975); m. Kaye Elizabeth Bache, Mar. 21, 1975. BS in Physics, Rensselaer Poly. Inst., 1952; MS in Physics, U. Chgo., 1957, PhD in Physics, 1961. From asst. prof. to assoc. prof. Brown U., Providence, 1961-68; from assoc. prof. to prof. aerospace engring. U. Colo., Boulder, 1968—. Cons. Storage Tech. Corp., Louisville, Colo., 1980-84, 89-91, Ball Aerospace Systems, Boulder, 1984-2002, Superconducting Super Collider, 1992-93. Contbr. articles to profl. jours. Served to lt. (j.g.) USN, 1948-55. Mem. Am. Phys. Soc., Colo. Mountain Club (Denver). Home: 251 Gay St Longmont CO 80501-5336 Office: U Colo PO Box 429 Boulder CO 80309-0429 Office Phone: 303-492-7635. Business E-Mail: howard.sndyder@colorado.edu.

SNYDER, JAMES C., JR., lawyer, consumer products company executive; BA, Wake Forest Univ.; JD, George Washington Univ. Bar: Ga., DC, Pa. Ptnr. litigation practice King & Spalding, Atlanta, 1989—2001; corp. counsel Home Depot, Atlanta, 2001—04, v.p. litigation, 2004—06, v.p., assoc. gen. counsel legal & risk mgmt., 2006—09, acting gen. counsel, 2007; sr. v.p., gen. counsel, sec. Family Dollar Stores, Inc., Matthews, NC, 2009—. Bd. dir. Spl. Olympics, Atlanta. Mem.: ABA, State Bar Ga. Mailing: Family Dollar Stores Inc PO Box 1017 Charlotte NC 28201-1017*

SNYDER, JAMES EUGENE, JR., lawyer; b. Lexington, NC, June 30, 1945; s. James Eugene and Sarah Frances (Olive) S.; m. Sandra Joyce Craver, June 25, 1966; children: Susan Courtney Snyder Brown, Sandra Elizabeth Snyder Lancaster. Bar: N.C. 1970, U.S. Dist. Ct. (mid. dist.) N.C. 1971, U.S. Ct. Appeals 1978, U.S. Supreme Ct. 1978, U.S. Tax Ct. 1971, U.S. Dist. Ct. (ea. dist.) N.C. 2007. Ptnr. Leonard and Snyder, Lexington, 1970-80; pvt. practice Lexington, 1980—. Mem. N.C. Ho. of Reps., Raleigh, N.C., 1971. Author: (books) Snyder N.C. Corporation Law, 1991, 4th edit., 2003, Snyder N.C. Corporation Law Forms, 1990, 4th edit., 2003, N.C. Automobile Law, 1988, 3d edit., 1999, Take Counsel, 2000, A Lawyer Prayes God's Will for His Clients, 2000, The Saga of Joe Monk, 2000, The Conservative Mind, 2004, Lexical Semantics, 2007. Chmn. Davidson County Rep. Exec. Com., Lexington, 1974; trustee Davidson County C.C., Lexington, 1973-81; candidate U.S. Senate, N.C., 2002; candidate for lt. gov., N.C., 2004. Mem. N.C. Bar Assn. Baptist. Avocations: painting, writing, athletics. Office: 16 W 1st Ave Lexington NC 27292-3304

SNYDER, JAMES M., JR., political science professor, economics professor; BA in Econs., Duke Univ., 1981; PhD, Calif. Inst. Tech., 1985. Asst. prof., dept. econs. Univ. Chgo., 1985—92; assoc. prof., polit. sci. MIT, 1992—97, prof., 1997—98, prof., polit. sci., econs., 1998—2001, Arthur and Ruth Sloan prof. polit. sci., prof. econs., 2001—. STICERD disting. vis. London Sch. Econs., 2003, 04, 06. Recipient Jack Walker award, Am. Polit. Sci. Assn., 2002, Heinz Eulau award, Am. Polit. Sci. Rev., 2003; grantee John Randolph Haynes and Dora Haynes Fellowship, 1984, Alfred P. Sloan Doctoral Dissertation Fellowship, 1984—85, Carnegie Mellon GSIA Postdoctoral Fellowship, 1990—91. Fellow: Am. Acad. Arts & Scis.; mem.: Nat. Bur. Econ. Rsch., Phi Beta Kappa. Office: Dept Polit Sci E53-457 MIT Cambridge MA 02142 Office Phone: 617-253-2669. Business E-Mail: millett@mit.edu.

SNYDER, JED C., foreign affairs specialist; b. Phila., Mar. 24, 1955; s. David and Lynn S. BA, Colby Coll., 1976; MA, U. Chgo., 1978, postgrad., 1978—79. Rsch. asst. U. Chgo., 1979; asst. rschr. Pan Heuristics divsn. R & D Assocs., Marina del Rey, Calif., 1979-80, assoc. rschr., asst. divsn. mgr., 1980-81, cons., 1982-83, Sci. Applications, Inc., 1979-81, Rand Corp., Santa Monica, Calif., 1979-81, Los Alamos (N.Mex.) Nat. Lab., 1984; sr. spl. asst. to dir. Bur. of Politico-Mil. Affairs, Dept. State, Washington, 1981-82; rsch. assoc. Internat. Security Studies Program, Woodrow Wilson Internat. Ctr. for Scholars, Smithsonian Instn., Washington, 1982-84; dep. dir. nat. security studies Hudson Inst., 1984-87; sr. rsch. fellow Nat. Strategy Info. Ctr., 1988-90; mgr. internat. strategic planing MPRI, Inc., 1997-2000; sr. nat. security advisor Dyncorp, 2001—02; sr. analyst CNA Corp., 2002—07; dir. operational net assessment HQ US Naval Forces Europe, 2007—08; sr. advisor to comdr. Pacific Command, 2008—. Cons. Rand Corp., 1983—88; founder, chmn. Washington Strategy Seminar, 1984—90, pres., corp. dir., 1984—93; appointee v.p. Bush's Adv. Task Force on Mid-East, 1987—88; cons. Office of Sec. of Def., 1988—92; apptd. supervisory rsch. prof., sr. fellow and team leader Inst. for Nat. Strategic Studies Nat. Def. U., 1992—97. Contbr. articles to profl. jours. Trustee Kents Hill (Maine) Sch., 1987-92. Comdr. USN, Europe, Italy. Recipient U.S. Navy award for Superior Civilian Svc., 2005, 2008; guest scholar Sch. Advanced Internat. Studies, Johns Hopkins U., 1982-83; fellow U. Chgo., 1979, Inter-Univ. Seminar on Armed Forces and Soc., 1980, MacArthur 1985-86, Herman Kahn fellowship, 1985-86, Smith Richardson fellowship, 1987-88, John M. Olin fellowship, 1987-88; selected as a Young Am. Leader, Am. Coun. on Fed. Republic of Germany, 1984. Mem. Internat. Inst. for Strategic Studies, Royal United Svcs. Inst., U.S. Naval Inst., Fgn. Policy Rsch. Inst., Coun. on Fgn. Rels. Office: 1718 M St NW #197 Washington DC 20036-4504 Office Phone: 703-824-2225. Personal E-mail: snyder7@attglobal.net.

SNYDER, JEFFREY SCOTT, chiropractor; b. Phila., Aug. 9, 1969; s. Ed and Elaine Snyder; m. Suzy Gail Weinberg, Apr. 9, 2000; children: Cameron, Emily. BS in Exercise and Sports Sci., Pa. State U., 1992; Dr. Chiropractic, Life U., 1998. Chiropractor Global Family Chiropractic, Roswell, Ga., 2000—01, Prog. Rehab., Oaks, Pa., 2001—07. Planner, mem. world congress chiropractic students Life U., Sch. Chiropractic, Marietta, Ga., 1996—97. Mem.: Internat. Chiropractor Assn. Libertarian. Avocations: fitness/exercise, photography, music, culinary. Office: Snyder Family Chiropractic 1003A Egypt Rd Oaks PA 19456

SNYDER, JOAN, painter; b. Highland Park, NJ, Apr. 16, 1940; d. Leon D. and Edythe A. (Cohen) S.; 1 child, Molly Fink. AB in Sociology, Douglass Coll., 1962; MFA, Rutgers U., 1966. Mem. faculty SUNY, Stony Brook, 1967-69, Yale U., 1974, U. Calif., Irvine, 1975, San Francisco Art Inst., 1976, Princeton U., 1975-77, Parsons, 1992, 93. One-woman exhbns. include, Paley and Lowe, New Brunswick, N.J., 1971, 73, Michael Walls Gallery, San Francisco, 1971, Parker 470, Boston, 1972, Los Angeles Inst. Contempory Art, 1976, Portland (Oreg.) Center Visual Arts, 1976, Carl Solway Gallery, NYC, 1976, Neuberger Mus., Purchase, N.Y., 1978, Hamilton Gallery Contemporary Art, 1978, 79, 82, 83, Nielson Gallery, Boston, 1983, 86, 91, Hirshl & Adler Modern Art Mus., NYC, 1985-87, 88, 90, 92, Compass Rose Gallery, Chgo., 1988, 89, Victoria Munroe, N.Y., 1990, Gibbs Mus. Art, Charleston, N.C., 1992, Artists Space, N.Y., 1992, Michael Walls Gallery, N.Y., 1992, Victoria Monroe Gallery, N.Y., 1993, Richard Anderson Gallery, N.Y., 1993, Nielson Gallery, 1993, 2002, Fine Arts Work Ctr., Mass., 1993, Allentown Art Mus., Pa., 1993, Nina Bransten Gallery, Calif., 1993, Jay Gorney Modern Art, NYC, 1993, Hirschl/Adler Modern, NYC, 1994, Nielsen Gallery, Mass., 1994, Rose Art Mus. Brandeis U., Waltham, Mass., 1994, Brooklyn Mus. Art, 1998, Robert Miller Gallery, NY, 2001, Elena Zang Gallery, NY, 2003, Betty

Cuningham Gallery, 2004, Alexandre Gallery, NY, 2004, Sawhill Gallery, James Madison Univ., Harrisburg, Va., 2005; travelling one-woman show, San Francisco Art Inst., Grand Rapids Art Mus., Renaissance Soc., U. Chgo., Anderson Gallery, Va. Commonwealth U., Richmond, 1979-80, The Jewish Mus., NYC, Danforth Mus., Framington, Mass., 2005—, group exhbns. include Whitney Ann., 1972, Whitney Bienniel, 1974, 80, Corcoran Bienniel, 1975, 87, Mus. Modern Art, NYC, Ann Jaffe Gallery, Bay Harbor Island, Fla., 1991, Cynthia Mcallister Gallery, NYC, Bixler Gallery, NYC, Parrish Art Mus., Southampton, N.Y., Acad. Arts and Letters, NYC, Tribeca 148 Gallery, NYC. Grantee Nat. Endowment Art, 1974; Guggenheim fellow, 1983; named a MacArthur fellow John D. and Catherine T. MacArthur Found., 2007.

SNYDER, JOEL BENNETT, engineering executive; b. NYC, Feb. 4, 1936; s. Sol and Anne (Bernstein) S.; m. Harriet Brenda Polinsky, Aug. 11, 1957; children: Eileen Schneyman, Jeffrey, Sharon Jones. BEE, Poly. Inst. Bklyn., 1956, MSEE, 1964. Registered profl. engr., N.Y.; chartered engr., U.K. Mathematician and programmer IBM, NYC, 1956—58; engr. Airborne Instruments Lab., Melville, NY, 1958—60; sr. project engr. Harman Kardon, Plainview, NY, 1960—63; ptnr. Snyder Assocs., Plainview, 1963—. Sr. industry prof. Poly. U., Bklyn., 1984-99; spkr. in field; bd. dirs. Motiontronics for Sci., NYC, 1990—, Multimedia for Sports, NYC, 1995—, Internet Golf Multimedia, NYC, United Engring. Found., NYC, 2002-06, Homeland Security Industries Assn., 2003-, Radio Frequency Identification Device Edn. Found., 2007—, Vehicular Tech. Soc., 2008-, Tech, Mgmt. Coun., 2009-. Editor: Data Systems Engineering Magazine, 1970; patentee video play counting techniques, 1986; contbr. numerous articles to profl. jours. Recipient George Gronner award Mid-Island Y, Plainview, N.Y., 1987, Achievement award Engrs. Joint Coun., 1998. Fellow Inst. Elec. Engrs.; mem. IEEE (sr. mem., citation of honor, 1979, Centennial medal, 1984, Gruenwal award, 1994, Millennium medal 2000, Larry K. Wilson Transnat. award 1999, pres. elect 2000, pres. 2001, v.p. prof. activities 1995-96, region 1 dir. 1992-93), Alumni Assn. Poly. U., Bklyn. (dedicated alumnus award 1989, disting. alumnus award, 2002, life. dir.). Office: Snyder Assocs 58 Diamond Dr Plainview NY 11803-2120 Office Phone: 516-349-1555. E-mail: jbsnyder@snyderassoc.com, j.snyder@ieee.org.

SNYDER, JOHN GORVERS, lawyer; b. Boston, June 20, 1960; s. Philip Francis and Sylvia (Gorvers) S.; m. Hinda Mala Simon, July 8, 1984; children: Monica Paige, Kimberly Blaine. BA, Johns Hopkins U., 1982; JD, Cornell U., 1987. Bar: Mass. 1988, U.S. Dist. Ct. Mass. 1989. Assoc. banking law, bus. law and corp. law dept. Craig and Macauley P.C., Boston, 1987—94, ptnr. banking law, bus. law and corp. law dept., 1995—2000; sr. v.p. and gen. coun. Simon Cos., LP, Braintree, Mass., 2000—. Lectr. New England Coll. Fin., 1994-2000. Active Combined Jewish Philanthropies, Boston, 1991—, Anti-Defamation League, Boston, 1993-94, Amherst Coll. Parents Fund, 2004—, Buckingham, Browne and Nichols Sch. Ann. Fund, 1999—. Mem. Mass. Bar Assn., Boston Bar Assn., Phillips Exeter Acad. Alumni Assn., B'nai Brith Realty Lodge, Phi Alpha Delta Internat., Omicron Delta Kappa (Johns Hopkins U. chpt., pres. 1981-82), Delta Upsilon (Johns Hopkins U. chpt.). Avocations: golf, tennis. Home: 7 Laurus Ln Newton Center MA 02459-3138 Address: The Simon Cos LP Attn: John G Snyder SVP 639 Granite St Braintree MA 02184-5366 E-mail: jsnyder@simoncompanies.com.

SNYDER, JOHN HENRY, computer science educator, consultant; b. Wichita, Kans., Mar. 16, 1947; s. Melvin Henry and Cathleen Ann (Collins) S.; m. Patricia Reilly, Mar. 11, 1984; children: Matthew Melvin George, Mark John Joseph. BA in English, Speech and Human Relations, U. Kans., Lawrence, 1970; MS in Computer Edn., Nova Southeastern U., Ft. Lauderdale, Fla., 1984. Cert. tchr. Nev., N.D. Computer sci. tchr. Hyde Park Jr. HS, Las Vegas, Nev., 1981-86, Chapparal HS, 1986-91, Cimarron Meml. HS, 1991-94, Meadows Sch., 1992—95, Advanced Tech. Acad., 1994—, Virtual HS, 2004—06. Copywriter pub. info. office CCSD, Las Vegas, 1982—84; chmn. gifted children spl. interest group Am. Mensa, 1984; mem. tech. com. Nev. State Network Internet Com., 1994—95; vice chair NW Accreditation Team, 2002—04; cons. Office Supt. Clark County Sch. dist., Las Vegas, 1984, Las Vegas, 85; systems analyst Homes & Narver, 1988; adminstrv. aide EG&G Energy Measurements, Las Vegas, 1989; adj. instr. computer sci., site co-adminstr. Nova U., 1984—93; adj. instr. computer sci. U. Nev., Las Vegas, 1990—, The Meadows Sch., 1991—96; with Nat. State Tchrs. of the Yr., 1993—, 2d v.p., 2001—02, nat. conv. chmn., 2002; nat. coord. Milken Educator States Network, 2000—, Milken Educator Listserve, 2001—. Newsletter editor Nat. State Tchrs. of Yr., 1991-93, nat. newsletter editor, webmaster, 1999—; contbr. articles to profl. jours. Co-chmn. Ednl. Exposition, Las Vegas, 1984; tech. cons. Harry Reid for U.S. Senate, 1986, 92; mem. Nevada 2000 Tech. Subcom., 1993, Nev. State Network Internet Com., 1993-96. With USAF, hon. discharge USAF, 1969. Recipient Innovative Teaching award Bus. Week Mag., 1990, Dolly Parton Chasing Rainbows award, 2003; named Tchr. of Yr., State of Nev., 1989-90, Burger King, 1989-90, U. Nev., Las Vegas, Southland Tchr. of Yr., 1990, Tandy Tech. Scholar, 1991, Nev. Educator of Yr., Milken Family Found., 1992, Nev. Tchr. of Yr. Microsoft Corp./Technology & Learning Mag., 1995; named to Nat. Tchr. Hall of Fame, 2007; Ward 5 grantee, Jr. League grantee, Impact Innovator grantee, 1996; McAuliffe fellow, 1994, 97. Mem.: KC (sec., v.p., pres., local lodge newsletter editor), Am. Legion, Phi Delta Kappa (newsletter editor Overall Excellence award 1990), Pi Lambda Theta, Kappa Delta Pi. Democrat. Roman Catholic. Avocations: programming, didjeridu, website construction, virtual reality. Office: Advanced Tech Acad 2501 Vegas Dr Las Vegas NV 89106-1643 Business E-Mail: jhsnyder@interact.ccsd.net.

SNYDER, JOHN JACOB, researcher; b. Harrisburg, Pa., Sept. 21, 1946; s. John Jacob and Evelyn R. (Gutshall) Snyder. BA., Dickinson Coll., 1968; MA., U. of Deleware, 1976. Hist. rsch. Loise Steinman Von Hess Found., Columbia, Pa., 1975—78; cons. arch. hist. Hist. Preservation Trust of Lancaster County, 1978—83, rsch. cons., 1983—. Bd. mem. James Buchanan Found., Lancaster, Pa., 1976—92, Heritage Ctr. Museum, Lancaster, Pa., 1988—97; cons. Montgomery House Restoration, Lancaster, 2004—. Co-author: Clocks of Lancaster County, 1977, Clocks of Berks County, 1995; contbr. articles to jour. Pres. Rock Ford Found., Lancaster, Pa., 1992—94, chmn. Acquisitions com., 1994—. Mem.: Hist. Soc. York County, Hist. Soc. Perry County, Hist. Soc. Lancaster County, Hist. Soc. Chester County, Hist. Soc. Berks County. Republican. Lutheran. Home and Office: PO Box 40 1938 Water St Washington Boro PA 17582 Office Phone: 717-684-6232.

SNYDER, JOHN JOSEPH, bishop emeritus; b. NYC, Oct. 25, 1925; s. John Joseph and Katherine Marie (Walsh) Snyder. Ordained priest Diocese of Bklyn., NY, 1951, sec. to bishops, 1957-72; assoc. pastor St. Mel's Parish, Flushing, NY, 1951-57; ordained bishop, 1973; aux. bishop Diocese of Bklyn., 1973—79; bishop Diocese of St. Augustine, Fla., 1979—2000, bishop emeritus, 2000—. Roman Catholic. Office: 5 Casa San Pedro 1714 State Rd 13 Ste 6 Jacksonville FL 32259 Office Phone: 904-262-3200. Office Fax: 904-262-0698.

SNYDER, JOHN LEIGHTON, lawyer; b. Atlanta, Ga., Jan. 28, 1969; s. Richard Albert and Mary Blair Snyder; m. Diane Paula Snyder; children: Elizabeth, Hannah, Gretchen. BA in Econ. and Polit. Sci., Ill. Wesleyan U., Bloomington, Ill., 1994; JD, U. Kans., Lawrence, 1994. Bar: Kans., Mo. Assoc. Levy & Craig, Kansas City, Mo., 1994—96, Bryan Cave LLP, Kansas City, 1996—2001; ptnr. Sonnenschein Nath & Rosenthal LLP, Kansas City, 2002—, chair real estate dept., 2002—, nat. chair bus. develop. and mktg., 2002—. Contbr. articles to profl. jours. Bd. dirs., v.p. Johnson County Housing Coalition, Olathe, Kans., 2001—06; bd. dirs. Ronald McDonald House Charities, Kansas City, 2006—; chair-elect Olathe EDC, Olathe, Kans., 2006. Named one of Best of the Bar, Kansas City Bus. Jour., 2002, Tope 40 Under Forty, Ingram's Mag., 2005. Mem.: Nat. Assn. Indsl. and Office Properties (bd. dits. 2006—), Urban Land Inst. (mem. exec. com. Kansas City chpt. 2005—), Kansas City Metro. Bar Assn. (vice chair real estate law sect. 2006—). Republican. Roman Catholic. Avocations: golf, running. Office Phone: 816-460-2668. Office Fax: 816-531-7545. Business E-Mail: jlsnyder@sonnenschein.com.

SNYDER, JON DAVID, dean; b. Portland, Mar. 14, 1953; s. Max M. and Nancy F. Snyder; 1 child, J. B. BA, Wash. State U., 1977, MA, 1980; EdD, Tchrs. Coll., 1992. Assoc. dir. honors program Wash. State U., Pullman, 1979—80; tchr. elem. sch. Vancouver Pub. Schs., Wash., 1977—84; mgr. product Hosts Corp., Vancouver, 1984—87; assoc. dir. rsch. Nat. Ctr. Restructuring Edn., NYC, 1990—92; sr. rschr. Nat. Commn. Tchg., NYC, 1997—2002; dir. tchr. edn. U. Calif., Santa Barbara, 1992—2001; dean Bank St. Coll., NYC, 2001—. Cons. Albertson's Found., Boise, 1997—2000. Author: Makers of Meaning in a Learning Centered School, Dare to Dream, 1996, A Teaching Quality System for Excellence in Equity, 1999. Commr. Calif. Coalition Tchr. Crediting, Sacramento, 1996—2000; cons. Ark. Tchr. Lic. Task Force, Little Rock, 1996, Nat. Assn. State Bds. Edn., Washington, 1992—93. Recipient EPIC award, Internat. Assn. Bus. Comm., 1996; scholar, Wash. State U., Pullman, 1977. Mem.: Nat. Soc. Study Edn., Am. Edn. Rsch. Assn., Phi Delta Kappa. Office: Bank St Coll 610 W 112th St New York NY 10025 Business E-Mail: jsnyder@bankstreet.edu.

SNYDER, JOSEPH JOHN, editor, lecturer, consultant, historian, writer; b. Aug. 27, 1946; s. Joseph John and Amy Josephine (Hamilton) S.; m. Sally Hale Walker, July 4, 1973; children: Lauren Elizabeth, Brian Joseph Seth. BA in Anthropology, George Washington U., 1968; MA in Anthropology, U. N.Mex., 1973. With U.S. CSC, Washington, 1974-77; editor, writer U.S. Nat. Pk. Svc., Harpers Ferry, W.Va., 1977-81; cons. editor Early Man mag., Evanston, Ill., 1978-83; spl. project editor Sea Power Mag., 1986-87, cons. editor, 1987—, Jour. Archaeoastronomy, 1987—. Freelance writer, 1978—; pres. Sta. at Shepherdstown Inc., 1992-2000; pres., chmn. bd. dirs., Atlantic & Pacific High Speed Railway, Inc., 1993—; pres. Duffields-Station Inc., 2003-; lectr. Maya archaeology Norwegian-Caribbean Lines, Miami, Fla., 1982; cons. in field. Author: Kenneth Westcott Jones Transport Menu Collection, 1998, A.D. 2025: Transportation in America, 1998, Musings from a New Manse, 1999, The Phaistos Disc, A Commentary, 1999, Fragments of My Fleece, 2000, 1859: Turning Point of the Modern Era, 2001, Miniatures of American History, 2005; editor: The Only Fight the Cops Could Not Stop, 1998; book rev. assoc. editor: Athena Rev., 1999—; contbr. articles to popular mags. Pres. Tourism Found., Inc., 1996—99; chmn. pks, com. Neighborhood Planning Adv. Group Croydon Pk., Rockville, Md., 1980—81; bd. dir. Agrl. R&D Orgn., 1985—; v.p. bd. dir. Hagerstown (Md.) Roundhouse Mus., 1989—91, Hagerstown-Washington County Conv. and Visitors Bur., 1993—96, sec., 1993—96. With US Army, 1969—71, Vietnam. Decorated Bronze Star. Mem.: Nat. Ry. History Soc., Nat. Geog. Soc. (cons. 1987—), Am. Com. to Advance Study of Petroglyphs and Pictographs (editor), Hakluyt Soc., Coun. Md. Archaeology, Internat. Assn. Torch Clubs, James Rumsey Torch Club (pres. 1997—99, 2003—05), Navy League of U.S. (pres. Frederick-Hagerstown coun. 1993—2006). Democrat. Home: 106 Ashley Dr Shepherdstown WV 25443-9767

SNYDER, LEE DANIEL, historian, educator; b. Waterbury, Conn., June 4, 1933; s. Clermont Jennings and Ethel Bentley Snyder; m. Anna Hopkins Givens, June 3, 1961; children: Rebecca Claire, Timothy Clermont. BA, Williams Coll., 1951—55; MDiv, Union Theol. Sem., NYC, 1959—61; PhD, Harvard U., 1955—66. Ordained elder United Meth. Ch., 1961. Asst. prof. Ithaca Coll., NY, 1963—64, Ohio Wesleyan U., Delaware, Ohio, 1964—69; prof. history New Coll. Fla., Sarasota, 1969—2003, prof. emeritus, 2004—09. Elder N.Y. Conf. United Meth. Ch., NYC, 1961—98; dir., medieval/renaissance studies New Coll. of Fla., Sarasota, 1982—2004. Author: (scholarly monograph) Macro-History, A Theoretical Approach to Comparative World History; contbr. articles to scholarly jours. Danforth Grad. fellow, 1955-63, Fulbright grantee, Mainz, Germany, 1956-57, NEH Summer Seminars and Insts. scholar, Nat. Humanities Found., 1978, 1981, 1985, 1989, 1991, 1994. Fellow: Internat. Soc. Comparative Study of Civilizations (pres. 2005—07); mem.: Am. Soc. Ch. History, Medieval Acad. Am. Home: 941 46th St Sarasota FL 34234 E-mail: lsnyder@ncf.edu, lldsnyder@aol.com.

SNYDER, LESLIE CROCKER, lawyer; b. NYC, Mar. 8, 1942; m. Fred Snyder; 2 children. AB, Radcliffe Coll., 1962; cert., Harvard-Radcliffe Program in Bus. Adminstrn., 1963; JD with honors, Case-Western Reserve Law Sch., 1966. Bar: Ohio 1966, NY 1967, US Ct. Appeals, Second Circuit 1967, US Dist. Ct. 1974, Ea. and So. Dist. NY 1974, US Supreme Ct. 1974. Asst. dist. atty. NYC; spl. asst. atty. gen. State of NY; justice NY Supreme State Ct., Criminal Term, 1986—2000; judge NY Ct. Claims, 2000—04; ptnr. Kasowitz, Benson, Torres & Friedman LLP, 2004—. Order of the Coif assoc. editor Case-Western Law Review; immediate past chair Criminal Procedure Law Adv. Com. to Chief Judge NY State, 1992—98. Author: 25 To Life: The Truth, the Whole Truth, and Nothing But the Truth, 2002; co-author: New York's Rape Shield Law. Trustee Kips Bay Boys and Girls Club, Bronx; bd. mem. NY Police Fire Widows' and Children's Orgn., DARE, NYC; mem. Citizen's Crime Commn., Moot Ct. Team. Recipient Hogan-Morganthau award, Florence Allen award, Disting. Alumnae award, Radcliffe Coll., Abraham House Justice & Compassion award, Frank S. Hogan Associates award, Ellis I. Medal of Honor. Mem.: Women's Bar Assn. (pres. 1982—83, past first v.p and third v.p.), Assn. Bar City NY (past mem. criminal justice counsel, past mem. com. on criminal advocacy, criminal cts., sex and law). Jewish. Office: Kasowitz Benson Torres & Friedman LLP 1633 Broadway New York NY 10019 Office Phone: 212-506-1754. Office Fax: 212-506-1800. Business E-Mail: lsnyder@kasowitz.com.*

SNYDER, LEWIS EMIL, astrophysicist, educator; b. Ft. Wayne, Ind., Nov. 26, 1939; s. Herman Lewis and Bernice (McKee) S.; m. Doris Jean Selma Lautner, June 16, 1962; children: Herman Emil, Catherine Jean. BS, Ind. State U., 1961; MA, So. Ill. U., 1964; PhD, Mich. State U., 1967. Research assoc. Nat. Radio Astronomy Obs., Charlottesville., Va., 1967-69; prof. astronomy dept. U. Va., Charlottesville, 1969-73, 74-75; vis. fellow Joint Inst. for Lab. Astrophysics, U. Colo., Boulder, 1973-74; prof. astronomy dept. U. Ill., Urbana, 1975—2005, prof. emeritus, 2005—, chair astronomy dept., 2002—05. Co-editor: Molecules in the Galactic Environment, 1973; contbr. articles to sci. jours. NASA-Am. Soc. Engring. Edn. summer fellow, 1972, 73; Alexander von Humboldt Found. sr. U.S. scientist award, 1983-84. Mem. AAAS, Am. Phys. Soc., Am. Astron. Soc., Internat. Astron. Union, Union Radio Scientifique Internationale, Alexander von Humboldt Assn. Am. Lutheran. Office: U Ill 1002 W Green St Urbana IL 61801-3074

SNYDER, LISA, social worker, consultant; d. John Lyman and Jennifer Warner Snyder; m. Jeffery Lee Irwin, May 30, 1987. BA, Humboldt State U., Arcata, Calif., 1983; MSW, San Diego State U., 1987. LCSW Calif., 1990; cert. in adlerian studies Alfred Adler Inst., 1990. Clin. social worker U. Calif. San Diego, Shiley-Marcos Alzheimer's Disease Rsch. Ctr., La Jolla, 1987—. Editor Perspectives Newsletter, La Jolla, 1995—. Author: (book) Speaking Our Minds. Mem. profl. adv. group Nat. Alzheimer's Assn., Chgo., 2006—07. Named Social Worker of Yr., NASW, Region, 2000, Profl. of Yr., Alzheimer's Assn., San Diego, Imperial County chpt., 2006. Mem.: Assn. Gerontology Educators Social Work, Gerontology Soc. America. Achievements include among the first to develop support groups for persons with early-stage Alzheimer's or a related disorder. Office: Univ Calif San Diego Shiley-Marcos Alzheimer's Rsch Ctr 8950 Villa La Jolla Dr Ste C-129 La Jolla CA 92037 Office Fax: 858-622-1012. Business E-Mail: lsnyder@ucsd.edu.

SNYDER, MARK A., marketing executive; Grad., U. Cin. Food/beverage mgr. Helmsley Hotels, 1980; v.p. brand mgmt. Harrah's Entertainment Inc.; gen mgr. Embassy Suites Hotel & Conf. Ctr., Portland, Oreg.; from regional dir. field mktg. to sr. dir. hotel mktg. support Embassy Suites Hilton Hotels Corp., 1999—2003; sr. v.p. worldwide brand mgmt. Holiday Inn Hotels & Resorts InterContinental Hotels Grp. PLC, 2003—08; chief mktg. officer Kmart Sears Holdings Corp., 2008—. Office: Sears Holdings Corp Hdqs 3333 Beverly Rd Hoffman Estates IL 60179 Office Phone: 847-286-2500.*

SNYDER, MARVIN, neuropsychologist; married; 1 child. BA (N.Y. State Regents scholar 1958-62, Meml. award psychology 1962), Bklyn. Coll., 1962; PhD (NDEA fellow 1962-65, USPHS fellow 1965-66, trainee 1966-67), Duke U., 1967. Rsch. psychologist NIMH, 1967—71, Nat. Eye Inst., 1971—72; program dir. neuroscis. Nat. Inst. Drug Abuse, 1974—79, dir. divsn. rsch., 1979—90, dir. Office of Sci. Policy, Edn. and Legislation, 1990—94, acting dep. dir., 1992—93; dir. life scis. rsch. office Fedn. Am. Socs. for Exptl. Biology, 1995—97; pres. Snyder Assocs., 1997—. Mem. NIH sr. exec. svc. USPHS exec. com. AIDS, 1983-85; mem. Dept. Health and Human Svcs. Orphan Products Bd., 1982-88; mem. The White House Task Force on Drug Abuse Health Issues; co-chmn. Interagy. Com. on Smoking and Health, Interagy. Com. on New Therapies for Pain and Discomfort; exec. sec. Interagy. Com. on Pain and Analgesia, chmn. subcom. on edn. and tng., 1985—; cons. to WHO on drug abuse policy issues, 1985-87, Ctr. Substance Abuse Treatment, 1999-2000, biosensor devel., 2000-02; testifier on drug abuse sci. and policy issues to U.S. Congress; mem. Fed. Coordinating Com. for Sci., Engring. and Technology, Com. on Brain and Behavior, 1990-91, Devel. Guidelines for Protecting Human Subjects in Drug Abuse Studies, 1991; sci. adv. Dynamac Corp., 1999—; adv. bd. Bus.-Higher Edn. Forum, Rsch. Collaboration Initiative, 1999—2001; cons. Los Alamos Nat. Lab. Found., 2007. Author papers and reports on comparative neurology, drug abuse, nutrition, and health and sci. policy. Recipient Devel. of Naltrexone award ADAMHA, 1985, Pub. Svc. award, 1986, Michael Morrison award for excellence in sci. adminstrn. Com. on Problems of Drug Dependence, 1988, Presdl. Meritorious Rank award 1990. E-mail: sibbaldus@comcast.net.

SNYDER, NATHAN, entrepreneur, investor; b. Hartford, Conn., Oct. 7, 1934; s. Saul and Betsy (Wand) S.; m. Geraldine Wolff, Dec. 27, 1964; children: Hannah Abigail, Alexander Lowell Wolff. AB, Harvard U., 1956; JD, Columbia U., 1963; postgrad. in bus., NYU, 1967-68. Bar: N.Y. 1963. Assoc. Paul, Weiss, Rifkind, Wharton & Garrison, NYC, 1963-66; v.p., sec. Randolph Computer Corp., Greenwich, Conn., 1966-69, exec. v.p., gen. counsel, bd. dirs., 1969-73; exec. v.p., chief operating officer BanCal Tri-State Corp. (holding co. Bank of Calif.), San Francisco, 1974-76; v.p. acquisitions CBS Inc., NYC, 1976-87; pres. VS & A Communications Ptnrs., NYC, 1987-89, The Snyder Co., New Canaan, Conn., 1989—. Lectr. mgmt. Golden Gate U., San Francisco, 1974-76, Annenberg Sch. Comms., Phila., 1982-87. Editor: Columbia Law Rev., 1962-63. Vol. legal services Office Econ. Opportunity, 1963; bd. dir. S.W. Regional Planning Agy. Served to lt. USNR, 1956-60. Harlan Fiske Stone scholar, 1964-65 Mem. Harvard Club (N.Y.C.), Harvard Club (bd. dirs. Fairfield County). Personal E-mail: naterun7@hotmail.com.

SNYDER, PATRICIA ANN, chemistry professor; b. NY, Sept. 24, 1940; d. Milton U. Snyder and Monica Edith McKernan; 1 child, Paul Milton. BS in Chemistry, Syracuse U., NY, 1962; PhD, U. Calif., La Jolla, 1970. Chemist DuPont, Town of Tonawanda, NY, 1962—64; rsch. asst. U. Calif. San Diego, 1964—70; rsch. assoc. Oreg. State U., Corvallis, 1970—73, instr., 1973—74; asst. prof. Baylor U., Waco, Tex., 1974—75; prof. Fla. Atlantic U., Boca Raton, 1976—. Cons. Brookhaven Nat. Lab., NY. Contbr. articles to profl. jours. Grant, NSF, Am. Chem. Soc. Mem.: Am. Chem. Soc., Sigma Xi. Achievements include first to measurements of circular and magnetic circular dichroism with synchrotron ratiation. Avocations: hiking, camping, swimming, travel, diving. Office: Fla Atlantic Univ Dept Chemistry and Biochemistry Boca Raton FL 33431 Business E-Mail: snyder@fau.edu.

SNYDER, PATRICIA DI BENEDETTO, theater director, producer; BA in English and Speech Edn., SUNY, Albany, 1967; MA in Theater Arts, Syracuse U., 1967; PhD in Arts and Humanities, NYU, 1991; DPub. Svc. (hon.), Sage Colls. Tchr. English, speech and drama West Genesee Sr. High Sch., Camillus, N.Y., 1962-64; tchr. English and drama, chair humanities teaching team Chestnut Hill Mid. Sch., Liverpool, (N.Y.), 1964-66; grad. asst. Syracuse (N.Y.) U., 1966-67; assoc. prof., theatre SUNY, Albany, 1967-74; spl. asst. to chancellor; founder, producing dir. Empire State Youth Theatre Inst. SUNY, Albany, 1975-92; exec. dir. Gov. Nelson A. Rockefeller Empire State Plz. Performing Arts Ctr. Corp., 1982-89; producing dir., CEO N.Y. State Theatre Inst. Corp., 1992—. Cons. Spanish and Portuguese Mins., Madrid and Lisbon, 1968, U.S. Office Edn. 1979, Spanish Min. Culture, 1982, Time Warner, Inc., 1991; mem. edn. bd. Saratoga Performing Arts Ctr., 1973; apptd. arts and humanities planning com. N.Y. State Edn. Dept., 1975; mem. arts task force on arts in edn. NEH, 1977; apptd. N.Y. State Edn. Commr.'s Adv. Coun., 1978; panelist U.S. Children's Lit. Assn., 1978; del. UNESCO Conf., Sibenek, Yugoslavia, 1979; lectr. Syracuse U., 1988; mem. acad. coun. Richard Porter Leach Fund for Arts, 1989; adj. prof. theatre Russell Sage Coll., 1992.; lectr. and presenter in field. Prodr. (stage prodns.) The Wizard of Oz, 1977, Lancashire Lad, 1980, Sleeping Beauty, 1981, 83, 90, Handy Dandy, 1985, Rag Dolly, 1986, Aladdin, 1987, Hizzoner!, 1988, 89, Beauty and the Beast, 1991, Slow Dance on the Killing Ground, 1993 (Best dir. theatre N.E. Metroland for '94); exec. prodr. (CD) Atlantic Theatre, A Tale of Cinderella, 1995 (Silver award, Worldfest, 1996, Chgo. Film Festival award, 1996); stage and video dir. A Tale of Cinderella, 1995; contbr. articles to profl. jours. Guest fellow Hungairan Theatre Inst., 1970, USSR Min. Culture, 1970,

84; recipient Mayor's medal City of Milan, Italy, 1977, Spl. Recognition award John F. Kennedy Ctr. for Performing Arts, 1978, 81, Recognition award NATAS, 1986, Albany League Arts award, 1986, Spl. Recognition award N.Y. State Theatre Edn Assn., 1993., Excellence award HRM Queen Noor of Jordan. Mem. Am. Theatre Assn. (commn. on theatre devel. 1976, Spl. Recognition citation 1973, 74, Jennie Heiden award 1985), Children's Theatre Assn. Am. (Zeta Phi Eta award 1972), League Am. Theatres and Prodrs., Soc. State Dirs. and Choreographers, Assn. Internat. du Theatre pour l'Enfants et al Jeunesse (del. 1968, 70, 74, 78, 79 congresses, exec. com. 1969, fundraiser 1972 conf., editor ofcl. report 1973, chair U.S. ctr. 1977), N.Y. Women in Film and TV, N.Y. League Profl. Theatre Women, U. Albany Alumni Assn. (Disting. Alumni award 1987), Cosmopolitan Club, Phi Delta Kappa, AATE (Sara Spencer award), US Ctr. ASSITEJ. Home: 722 N Broadway Saratoga Springs NY 12866-1621 Office: NY State Theatre Inst PO Box 28 Troy NY 12181-0028

SNYDER, PETER M., medical educator, medical researcher; BA in Biology summa cum laude, Luther Coll., 1984; MD, U. Iowa, 1989. Diplomate Am. Bd. Internal Medicine, Am. Bd. Cardiovasc. Disease. Resident in internal medicine U. Tex., Dallas, 1989—92; fellow in cardiovasc. diseases Dept. Internal Medicine U. Iowa Hosp. & Clinics, Iowa City, 1992—96, asst. prof. Dept. Internal Medicine, 1996—2000, assoc. prof. internal medicine and physiology and biophysics, 2000—. Contbr. articles to profl. jours. Recipient Clinician Scientist award, 1996, Katz Basic Sci. award, 1998; fellow, U. Iowa, 1985, Am. Heart Assn., 1987—88. Mem.: ACP, Alpha Omega Alpha. Achievements include research in sodium channel structure and function. Office: U Iowa Coll of Medicine Dept Internal Medicine 200 Hawkins Dr Iowa City IA 52242-1009

SNYDER, RICHARD GERALD, research scientist, administrator, educator, consultant; b. Northampton, Mass., Feb. 14, 1928; s. Grant B. and Ruth (Putnam) Snyder; m. Phoebe Jones, Mar. 2, 1949; children: Dorinda, Sherrill, Paul, Jeff, Jon, David. Student, Amherst Coll., 1946-48; BA, U. Ariz., 1956, MA, 1957, PhD, 1959. Diplomate Am. Bd. Forensic Anthropology (dir. 1978-84, 85-91, ret. 2008). Tchg. asst. dept. anthropology U. Ariz., Tucson, 1957-58, assoc. rsch. engr. Applied Rsch. Lab., Coll. Engring., 1958-60, mem. staff Ariz. Transp. and Traffic Inst., 1959-60, assoc. prof. sys. engring., 1960; chief phys. anthropology Civil Aeromed. Rsch. Inst. FAA, Oklahoma City, 1960-66, rsch. pilot, 1962-66, intermittent acting chief Protection and Survival Labs., 1963-66; mgr. biomechanics dept. Office Automotive Safety Rsch. Ford Motor Co., Dearborn, Mich., 1966-68, prin. rsch. scientist, 1968; rsch. scientist Hwy. Safety Rsch. Inst. U. Mich., Ann Arbor, 1968—82, rsch. scientist transp. rsch. inst., 1982—85, assoc. prof. anthropology Ann Arbor, 1968-73, head biomed. dept., 1969-84, prof., 1973-85, dir. NASA Ctr. Excellence in Man-Vehicle Sys., 1984-85, named chair, R.G. Snyder disting. univ. prof. indsl. and ops. engring, 2004—. Pres. Bio Dynamics Internat., Tucson, 1986—2007; pres., bd. dirs. George Snively Rsch. Found., 1992—98; assoc. prof. sys. engring. U. Ariz., 1960; adj. assoc. prof. U. Okla., 1963; rsch. assoc. Zoller Lab., U. Chgo., 1964—65, rsch. assoc. dept. anthropology, 1965—67; assoc. prof. Mich. State U., East Lansing, 1967—68; cons. USAF Aerospace Med. Rsch. Labs., NAS, US Dept. Transp., adv. com. Office Naval Rsch. Dept. Navy, numerous others. Assoc. editor Jour. of Comm., 1961—63, cons. editor Jour. Biomechanics, 1967—81, mem. editl. bd. Product Safety News, 1973, adv. bd. Aviation Space and Environ. Medicine, 1980—91, 1994, mem. editl. rev. bd. Stapp Car Crash Jour., 2001—03; contbr. chapters to books, numerous articles to profl. jours. Judge Internat. Sci. Fair, Detroit, 1968; mem. coun. Explorer Scouts, Ann Arbor, 1968—70; bd. dirs. Snell Meml. Found., 1990—, N.Mex. Rsch. Inst., 1996—2000. 1st lt. USAF, 1949—54, Korea. Decorated Disting. Flying Cross, 3 Air Medals; recipient Met. Life award, Nat. Safety Coun., 1970, Adm. Luis de Flores Flight Safety award, Flight Safety Found., 1981; named to Safety and Health Hall of Fame Internat., 1993, Ariz. Aviation Hall of Fame, 1998. Fellow: AAAS, AIAA (assoc.), Soc. Automotive Engrs. (Arch T. Colwell Merit award 1973, Aerospace Congress award 1982, Tech. Contbns. to Air Transport Safety), Am. Acad. Forensic Scis. (T. Dale Stewart award 1992), Royal Anthrop. Inst., Am. Anthrop. Assn., Aerospace Med. Assn. (Harry G. Moseley award 1975, Profl. Excellence award 1978, John Paul Stapp award in Aerospace Biomechanics 1994), Explorers Club; mem.: Aerospace Physiologists Soc., Internat. Soc. Aircraft Safety Investigators, Ariz.-Nev. Acad. Sci., Mach 3 Soc., Order of Daedalians, Sigma Xi, Phi Gamma Delta, Beta Beta Beta. Republican. Congregationalist. Avocations: aviation, aerospace medicine, forensic anthropology. Home: 3720 N Silver Dr Tucson AZ 85749-9709

SNYDER, RICHARD JOSEPH, lawyer; b. Boston, June 18, 1939; s. Harris H. and Ruth (Galner) Snyder; m. Joyce Marshall, Aug. 19, 1962 (div.); children: Robert M., Lauren E., John K.; m. Susana Gohiman, Apr. 11, 1982 (div.); stepchildren: Joanna Maixner-Goldstein, Adriana Maixner; m. Marilyn Bachelder, Sept. 28, 1997; stepchildren: Dexter Bachelder, Dayna Bachelder. BA with honors, Babson Coll., Wellesley, Mass., 1960, LLD (hon.), 1994; JD cum laude, Boston U. Sch. Law, 1963; LLM, Georgetown U. Law Ctr., Washington, 1966. Bar: Mass. 1963, US Ct. Claims 1964, US Tax Ct. 1966, US Dist. Ct. (Mass.) 1967, US Ct. Appeals (1st cir.) 1968, US Supreme Ct. 1968, Vt. 1988, Supreme Ct. Vt., Supreme Ct. Mass. Trial atty. US Dept. Justice, Washington, 1963-66; assoc. Epstein & Salloway, Boston, 1966-67, Cohn, Reimer & Pollack, Boston, 1967-69; assoc., then ptnr. Widett, Slater & Goldman, Boston, 1969-76; adminstrv. ptnr. Goldstein & Manello, Boston, 1976-88; pvt. practice, 1988—2003; ptnr. Duane Morris LLP, Boston, 2003—05, of counsel, 2006—. Law lectr. Babson Coll., 1967—76, guest lectr., 1991—; bd. advs. WBUR Pub. Radio, 1996—, mem. exec. com., 1996—2005, chmn. 'Newsmakers' orgn., 2001—05; mem. Town of Nahant, Mass. Planning Bd., 2001—, vice chmn., 2004—06, chmn., 2006—. Co-editor: Direct Sales Mag., 1976—78. Active Boston City to City Leadership Exchange, 1998—; mem. corp. com. Mass. Soc. Prevention Cruelty to Children, 1998—2001; bd. dirs. The Sunday Sch., Inc., 1974—84, pres., 1979—84; bd. dirs. Babson Coll. Recreation Ctr., Inc., 1982—96, Mass. Corp. Ednl. Telecomm., 1985—99, vice chmn., 1986—89, chmn., 1989—99; bd. dirs. Save the Harbor/Save the Bay, Boston, 2001—; mem. bd. trustees Babson Coll., 1977—89; mem. audit com. New Eng. Deaconess Hosp., 1993—96, Beth Israel Deaconess Med. Ctr., Boston, 1996—, mem. exec. com., 1999—2007. Named a Mass. SuperLawyer, Boston Mag. Fellow: Mass. Bar Found.; mem.: ABA, Babson Coll. Alumni Assn. (pres. 1977—79), North Atlantic Regional Bus. Law Assn. (pres. 1966—69), Am. Bus. Law Assn. (chmn. real property com. 1967—77), Nat. Assn. Coll. & Univ. Attorneys, Boston Bar Assn., Vt. Bar Assn., Mass. Bar Assn., US Supreme Ct. Hist. Soc., Greater Boston C. of C. (bd. dirs. 1999—). Avocation: boating. Office: Duane Morris LLP 470 Atlantic Ave Ste 500 Boston MA 02210 Office Phone: 857-488-4292. Office Fax: 857-401-3027. Business E-Mail: RJSnyder@duanemorris.com.*

SNYDER, RICK (RICHARD D. SNYDER), computer company executive; BGS with high distinction, Univ. Mich., 1977, MBA with high distinction, 1979, JD, 1982. CPA; bar: Mich. Acct. Coopers & Lybrand, 1982—88, ptnr., 1988—91; exec. v.p. Gateway, Inc., Irvine, Calif., 1991—97, pres. & COO, 1996—97, dir., 1991—97, chmn., 2005—, interim CEO, 2006; pres. Avalon Investments, 1997—2000; founder, CEO, chmn. Ardesta LLC, Ann Arbor, Mich., 2000—. Adj. prof. acctg. U. Mich., 1982—84; dir. Launch Media Inc. Trustee The Henry Ford; bd. mem. U. Mich. Coll. Engring. Nat. Adv. Com.; mem. tech. transfer nat. adv. com. U. Mich.; mem. Gov. e-Mich. Adv. Council; mem. adv. bd. Samuel Zell & Robert H. Lurie Inst. for Entrepreneurial Studies, NanoBus. Alliance; mem. vis. com. Purdue Univ. Sch. Engring.; chmn. Ann Arbor SPARK; mem. The Nature Conservancy, Mich. Chpt. Mem.: Mich. Bar Assn. Office: Gateway Inc 7565 Irvine Center Dr Irvine CA 92618

SNYDER, ROBERT LYMAN, materials scientist, educator; b. Plattsburgh, NY, June 5, 1941; s. George Michael and Dorothy (Lyman) M.; m. Sheila Nolan, Sept. 1, 1963; children: Robert N., Kristina Gardner. BA, Marist Coll., 1963; PhD, Fordham U., 1968. Postdoctoral fellow NIH U. Pitts., 1968; NRC fellow NASA Elec. Rsch. Ctr., Cambridge, Mass., 1969; asst. prof. ceramic sci. Alfred (N.Y.) U., 1970-77, assoc. prof., 1977-83, prof., 1983-96, dir. Inst. Ceramic Superconductivity, 1987-96; prof., chmn. dept. materials sci. and engring. Ohio State U., Columbus, 1996—2002; prof., chmn. Sch. Materials Scis. and Engring. Ga. Inst. Tech., Atlanta, 2003—. Vis. prof. Lawrence Livermore (Calif.) Lab., 1977, 78, U.S. Nat. Bur. Stds., Gaithersburg, Md., 1980, 81, Siemens AG Ctrl. Rsch. Labs., Munich, 1983, 91; invited prof. U. Rennes, France, 1995. Author: Introduction to X-Ray Powder Diffractometry, 1996; author, editor 8 books; contbr. chpts. to books and over 280 articles to profl. jours. Deputy mayor Village of Alfred, 1973-77; pres. Alfred Vol. Fire Co., 1979-88. Recipient Chancellor's award SUNY, 1980, numerous research grants; named Faculty Exch. scholar SUNY, 1978-96. Fellow Am. Ceramic Soc. (Outstanding Educator award 1999), Am. Soc. Metals (disting.), Internat. Ctr. Diffraction Data (Hanawalt award, 2004); mem. TMS (Leadership award 2002, Educator award 2008), NAS (U.S. nat. com. on crystallography 1991-95, Codata 2001—), Nat. Inst. Ceramic Engrs., Am. Crystallography Assn. (chmn. applied crystallography div. 1988-92), Materials Rsch. Soc., Ceramic Ednl. Coun., Internat. Ctr. Diffraction Data (bd. dirs. 1986-92, elected chmn. bd. dirs. 1996-2000), Internat. X-ray Analysis Soc. (pres. 2000-2001), Edward Orton Jr. Ceramic Found. (bd. dirs. 1996—), Alfred and Allegany County Fire Assn., Sigma Xi, Phi Kappa Phi. Democrat. Achievements include numerous patents for practical superconductors. Office: Ga Inst Tech Sch Materials Sci and Engring 771 Ferst Dr Atlanta GA 30332-0245 Home: 195 14th St NE Ste 1 Atlanta GA 30309-2682 Office Phone: 404-894-2888. Business E-Mail: robert.snyder@mse.gatech.edu.

SNYDER, RONALD R., lawyer; b. Louisville; s. Marion G. and Lois Esther (Berg) Snyder; m. Sarah Margaret Snyder; 1 child, Rebecca Anne Farris. BS in Law, U. Louisville, 1964, LLB, 1966, JD, 1969. Bar: Ky., U.S. Dist. Ct. Ky.; cert. real estate broker Ky. City atty. City of Jeffersontown, Ky., City of Houston Acres, Louisville; adminstrv. law judge Commonwealth of Ky., 1979—83. Hearing officer Workman's Compensation Bd., Louisville, 1979—83. State atty. gen. candidate Rep. Party, Ky., 1979. Mem.: Ky. Bar Assn. Republican. Home: 18700 Shelbyville Rd Fisherville KY 40023 Office: Long Run Bank Bldg Box 13 Eastwood KY 40018 Office Phone: 502-244-3837. Personal E-mail: lawyersnyder@compuserve.com. Business E-Mail: ron@sun-sand.cc.

SNYDER, SHARON VETA, management consultant, educator; d. G. John and Margaret Veta; m. Charles A. Snyder, Aug. 29, 1963; children: David Veta, Shelby Snyder Hammer, Claire Frances. BA, La. State U., Baton Rouge, 1965; MBA, U. New Orleans, 1981. Adj. faculty, coll. bus. adminstrn. U. New Orleans, 1985—; dir. to v.p. Veta Land and Investment, Inc., Wyo.; asst. vice chancellor, tech. transfer La. State U. Med. Ctr. (now La. State Health Scis. Ctr.), 1989—92; pres., founder SVS Inc. Mgmt. Consultants, Covington, La., 1992—2003. Contbr. articles to profl. jours. Com. mem. La. Philharm. Symphony, New Orleans, 2007. Mem.: New Orleans Mus. Art, Statewide Adv. Coun., Northshore Out-Reach (co chair 2008—), Rotary Club New Orleans (program chmn. 2004—05), Beta Gamma Sigma, Phi Kappa Phi. Office: U New Orleans COBA 2000 Lakaeshore Dr New Orleans LA 70148

SNYDER, SOLOMON HALBERT, neuroscientist, educator; b. Washington, Dec. 26, 1938; s. Samuel Simon and Patricia (Yakerson) Snyder; m. Elaine Borko, June 10, 1962; children: Judith Rhea, Deborah Lynn. B, Georgetown U., Washington, 1958, DSc (hon.), 1986; MD cum laude, Georgetown U. Med. Sch., 1962; PhD (hon.), Ben Gurion U., Israel, 1990; DSc (hon.), Northwestern U., 1981, Technion Inst., Israel, 2002, Mt. Sinai Med. Sch., 2004, U. Md., 2006, Charles U., Prague, 2008; DPhil (hon.), Albany Med. Coll., 1998. Intern Kaiser Found. Hosp., San Francisco, 1962-63; rsch. assoc. Nat. Inst. Mental Health, NIH, Bethesda, Md., 1963-65; asst. resident dept. psychiatry Johns Hopkins Hosp., Balt., 1965-68; assoc. prof. pharmacology/experimental therapeutics, assoc. prof. psychiatry Johns Hopkins Sch. Medicine, 1968-70, prof., 1970-77, disting. svc. prof. psychiatry/pharmacology, 1977-80, disting. svc. prof. psychiatry, pharmacology & neurosci., dir. dept. neurosci., 1980—; dir. dept. neurosci. Johns Hopkins Med. Sch., 1980—. Wellcome disting. prof. U. Wash., 1999. Author: (books) Uses of Marijuana, 1971, Madness and the Brain, 1973, The Troubled Mind, 1976, Biologic Aspects of Mental Disorder, 1980, Drugs and the Brain, 1986, Brainstorming, 1989; mem. editl bd. Molecular Medicine, FASEB Jour., Neurosci., Jour. Molecular Neurosci., Molecular Psychiatry, Jour. Nervous & Mental Diseases, Nitric Oxide Biology & Chemistry; contbr. articles to profl. jours. Recipient Outstanding Scientist award, Md. Acad. Scis., 1969, A.E. Bennett award, Soc. Biol. Psychiatry, 1970, Gaddum award, Brit. Pharm. Soc., 1974, F.O. Schmitt award in neurosci., MIT, 1974, Rennebohm award, U. Wis., 1976, Stanley Dean award, Am. Coll. Psychiatrists, 1978, Lasker award for clin. med. rsch., 1978, Wolf Found. prize in medicine, Israel, 1983, Dickson prize, U. Pitts., 1983, Sci. Achievement award, AMA, 1985, Ciba-Giegy-Drew award in biomed. rsch., 1985, Edward J. Sachar Meml. award, Columbia U., 1986, Sense of Smell award, Fragrance Rsch. Found., 1987, J. Allyn Taylor prize, 1990, Pasarow Found. award for biomed. rsch., 1991, Bower award, Franklin Inst., 1991, Joseph Priestley prize, Dickinson Coll., 1992, Baxter award, Am. Assn. Med. Colleges, 1995, Bristol-Myers-Squibb award for disting. achievement in neurosci., 1996, Gerard prize, Soc. Neurosci., 2000, Salmon prize, NY Acad. Medicine, 2001, Lieber prize, Nat. Alliance Rsch. Schizophrenia & Depression, 2001, Goldman-Rakic prize, 2003, Nat. Medal of Sci., 2003, Edward Perl award, U. NC, 2007, Albany Med. Ctr. prize in medicine & biomed. rsch., 2007. Fellow: Am. Philos. Soc., Am. Acad. Arts & Scis., Am. Coll. Neuropsychopharmacology (Daniel Efron award 1974), Am. Psychiat. Assn. (Hofheimer award 1972, Disting. Svc. award 1989, Judd Marmor award 2000); mem.: NAS (Sarnat prize in mental health 2001), Inst. Medicine, Am. Pharmacology Soc. (John Jacob Abel award 1970), Am. Soc. Biol. Chemists, Soc. Neurosci. (pres. 1979—80, Presdl. lectr. 2000). Office: Johns Hopkins U Sch Medicine Dept Neuroscis 725 N Wolfe St Rm 813 WBSB Baltimore MD 21205-2105 Office Phone: 410-955-3024. Office Fax: 410-955-3623. Business E-Mail: ssnyder@jhmi.edu.*

SNYDER, VIC, United States Representative from Arkansas, physician; b. Medford, Oreg., Sept. 27, 1947; m. Betsy Singleton; 1 child, Charles Pennington. BA in Chemistry, Willamette U., Salem, Oreg., 1975; MD, U. Oreg. Health Scis. Ctr., 1979; JD, U. Ark., Little Rock, 1988. Resident family practice U. Ark. Med. Scis., 1979-82; physician family practice Ark., 1982—; mem. Ark. State Senate, 1991-96, US Congress from 2d Ark. dist., 1997—; mem. armed srvc. com., veterans affairs com. Med. missions to Cambodian refugee camps, Thailand, El Salvadoran refugee camps, Honduras, Ethiopian refugee camps, Sudan; hosp. mission Sierra Leone, Africa. Served with USMC, 1967—69. Democrat. Methodist. Office: US Ho Reps 1330 Longworth Ho Office Bldg Washington DC 20515-0402 also: Dist Office Ste 150 1501 N Univ Little Rock AR 72207 E-mail: snyder.congress@mail.house.gov.*

SNYDER, WILLARD BREIDENTHAL, lawyer; b. Kans. City, Dec. 18, 1940; s. N.E. and Ruth (Breidenthal) S.; m. Lieselotte Dieringer, Nov. 10, 1970 (dec. Nov. 1975); 1 child, Rolf; m. T.J. Sewall, May 17, 1996. BA, U. Kans., 1962, JD, 1965; postgrad., Hague Acad. Internat. Law, The Netherlands, 1965-66, U. Dijon, France, 1966; grad., Command and Gen. Staff Coll., Ft. Leavenworth, Kans., 1977. Bar: Kans. 1965, Mo. 1986, U.S. Tax Ct. 1977, U.S. Ct. Mil. Appeals 1981, U.S. Dist. Ct. Kans. 1965, U.S. Supreme Ct. 1977. Atty., Kansas City, 1970-80, 85—; trust officer, corp. trust officer Security Nat. Bank., Kansas City, 1980-83, corp. sec., 1983—; pres. Real Estate Corp. Inc., Leawood, Kans., 1984—2006; adv. dir. United Mo. Bank, 1985-90. Bd. dirs. Blue Ridge Bank, mem. trust com. Bank Holding Co., 1991—; German Consul (Hon.) for Kans., Western Mo., 1972—. Mem. Platte Woods City Coun., Mo., 1983—84; bd. govs., past pres. Liberty Meml. Assn.; past pres. & trustee emeritus MacJannett Found., Talloires, France; chmn. Breidenthal-Snyder Found.; nominating and exec. com. Hoover Pres. Libr.; bd. dirs., v.p. Unicorn Theatre, 1998—2004; vice dean Kansas City Consular Corp.; bd. dirs., v.p. FBI Citizens Acad.; bd. dirs. Actors Theater of Kansas City; dir. Kansas City Metro Crime Commn., Truman Found., Kansas City; trustee St. Mary Coll., 1998—2001; bd. regents Rockhurst U., 2003—, trustee; bd. dirs., pres. The Nat. Navy UDT & SEAL Mus.; dir. and gen. counsel Army Command and GS Found.; bd. dirs. Air U. Found.; pres. Wy. Co. Cmty. Found., 2004—07. Col. inf. US Army, ret. USAR, ret. Kans. Army N.G. Decorated Bundesverdienst Kreuz I & II KL, Bundeswehr Kreuz (silver), Bundeswehr Kreuz (gold) Germany, Legion of Merit, KARNG medal of excellence, Mil. Order of WW award; recipient Golden Honour badge, German Vet. Orgn., Bavaria, 1988; named to Hon. Order Ky. Cols., OCS Hall of Fame. Mem. Mo. Bar Assn., Kansas City Bar Assn., Kansas City Hosp. Attys., Mil. Order of World Wars (chpt. comdr. 1983-84, regional comdr. 1987-91, Patrick Henry award), Nat. Eagle Scout Assn. Avocations: scuba diving, hunting, notgeld collections, cartridge collection. Office: 8014 State Line Rd Ste 203 Shawnee Mission KS 66208-3712 Business E-Mail: wbs11@kc.rr.com.

SNYDER, WILLIAM, library director; b. Balt., July 31, 1949; s. William and Miriam Tendvahl Snyder; m. Rebecca Snyder; 1 child, Catherine Cheek. MLS, East Carolina U., Greenville, NC, 1975. Libr. dir. Sampson County, Clinton, NC, 1979—89, Henderson County, NC, 1989—. Contbr. articles to profl. jours. Lt. gov. Kiwanis Carolina Dist., NC, 2000—01; pres. Hendersonville Kiwanis Club, 1997—98, NC Pub. Libr. Dir. Assn., 2003—04. Recipient Distinguished Lt. Gov. award, Kiwanis, Carolina Dist., 2001. Home: 121 Wells St Hendersonville NC 28739 Office: Henderson County Libr 301 N Washington St Hendersonville NC 28739 Business E-Mail: wsnyder@henderson.lib.nc.us.

SNYDER, WILLIAM BURTON, insurance company executive; b. Clarksburg, W.Va., July 9, 1929; s. William Burton and Mary Catherine (Cornwell) Snyder; m. Georgie Gaye, Oct. 27, 1951 (dec.); children: William Burton, Melissa Ann; m. Sally Marie Snyder, May 17, 2003. BBA in Acctg. cum laude, Tex. Tech U., 1955. With Travelers Ins. Co., 1955-77, v.p., 1970-77; with Govt. Employees Ins. Co., Washington, 1977-93; chmn., pres., CEO GEICO Corp., 1985-93. Dir. Nat. Capital Area coun. Boy Scouts Am. Capt. USAF, 1950—53. Decorated Air medal. Republican. Baptist.

SNYDER, WILLIAM W., corporate financial executive; m. Valerie Snyder; 2 children. BSBA, U. Mo., M in Accountancy. CPA. With pub. acctg. Deloitte & Touche; corp. contr. Enterprise Rent-A-Car, 1984—89, asst. v.p. to v.p. corp. acctg., 1989—94, v.p. fleet adminstrn., 1994—95, v.p. info. sys., 1995—98, sr. v.p., chief info. officer, 1998—2002, sr. v.p., CFO, 2002—03, exec. v.p., CFO, 2003—. Office: Enterprise Rent-A-Car 600 Corporate Park Dr Saint Louis MO 63105

SNYDER, ZACK, film director; b. Green Bay, Mar. 1, 1966; m. Denise Snyder (div.); m. Deborah Snyder, Sept. 25, 2004; 6 children. Grad., Art Ctr. Coll. Design, Pasadena, Calif.; student, Heatherlies Sch. Fine Art, London. Dir.: various sports and car commercials; (films) Dawn of the Dead, 2004, The Lost Tape: Andy's Terrifying Last Days Revealed, 2004, Watchmen, 2009; dir., writer (films) 300, 2006 (Hollywood Movie of Yr., Hollywood Film Festival, 2007, Saturn award for best direction, 2008). Recipient 2 Clio awards, Gold Lion award, Cannes Festival; named a Maverick, Details mag., 2008; named one of 50 Smartest People in Hollywood, Entertainment Weekly, 2007. Office: c/o Creative Artists Agy 2000 Ave of the Stars Los Angeles CA 90067*

SNYDERMAN, NANCY, surgeon, journalist; m. Doug Snyderman; 3 children. PhD in medicine, U. Nebr. Med. Sch. Cert. otolaryngology U. Pitts., UMDA. Resident in pediatrics and ear, nose, and throat surgery U. Pitts.; dir. head and neck surgery U. Ark. Med. Scis., 1983—87; surgical practice Calif. Pacific Med. Ctr., San Francisco, 1988—; med. corr. Good Morning Am., 1987—2003, 20/20, 1987—2003, ABC News, 1987—2003; v.p. med. affairs corp. staff Johnson & Johnson, 2003—06; chief med. editor NBC News, 2006—. Author: Dr. Nancy Snyderman's Guide to Good Health for Women Over Forty, 1996, Necessary Journeys: Letting Ourselves Learn from Life, 2001, Medical Myths That Can Kill You And the 101 Truths That Will Save, Extend and Improve Your Life, 2008; co-author: Girl in the Mirror: Mothers and Daughters in the Years of Adolescence, 2003; contbr. to med. jour. Mem.: Am. Acad. of Otolaryngology Head and Neck Surgery (bd. dirs.). Achievements include reporting on med. topics affecting both men and women; traveled and reported extensively from Eastern and Western Europe, Saudi Arabia during Persian Gulf War, Russia, Somalia, Kosovo, Pakistan, and Afghanistan. Office: NBC 30 Rockefeller Plz New York NY 10112

SNYDERS, DIRK JOHAN, electrophysiologist and biophysicist educator; b. Wilrijk, Antwerpen, Belgium, July 18, 1955; arrived in U.S., 1984; s. Godlief Stefaan and Mariette L. Snyders. BS in Med. Sci., U. Antwerp, Belgium, 1976, MD with great honor, 1980. Lic. physician, cert. cardiologist Belgium. Resident then fellow in internal medicine and cardiology Univ. Hosp. Antwerp, 1980—84; postdoctoral fellow U. Calif., San Francisco, 1984—85; instr. medicine Vanderbilt U., Nashville, 1986—87, asst. prof., 1987—95, assoc. prof. medicine and pharmacology, 1995—. With V.I.B. dept. biophysics and pharmacology Antwerp U., 1998—2003; prof. biochemistry U. Antwerp, 1998—, vice-chair dept. biochemistry, 1999—2001, chair dept. biomed. scis.,

2001—, prof. biomed. scis., 2001—, vice chair rsch. coun., 2004—. Co-author: The Heart and the Cardiovascular System, 1991; mem. editorial bd. Circulation Rsch.; reviewer Jour. Gen. Physiology, Cardiovascular Rsch., Jour. Molecular and Cellular Cardiology, Molecular Pharmacology, European Jour. Pharmacology, Biophys. Jour., Jour. Biol. Chemistry; contbr. articles to profl. jours. Lt. Med. Svc. Belgian Army, 1987—88. Recipient Specia award Specia NV., Belgium, 1980; hon. fellow Belgian Am. Ednl. Found., NATO rsch. fellow, 1984, med. rsch. fellow Alta. Heritage Found., 1984; rsch. grantee NIH, Am. Heart Assn. Fellow Am. Heart Assn. (basic sci. coun.); mem. AAAS, Biophys. Soc., Soc. Gen. Physiologists, European Working Group (cardiac cellular electrpmysiology bd. mem.) Achievements include research on mechanism of action of "specific bradycardiac agents", use-dependent unblocking and voltage clamp validation of modulated receptor theory (cardiac sodium channels and antiarrhythmic agents), electrophysiology and pharmacology of cloned channels molecular localisation of antiarrhythmic drug binding sites, cardiac potassium channels (including human), molecular ion channel structure-function relationships, molecular basis of congenital excitability disorders. Office: Antwerp U Dept Biomed Scis Universiteitsplein 1 T4 2160 Antwerp Belgium Address: Fazantenlaan 6 Antwerp B2610 Belgium Home Phone: 011-32-3-449-4374; Office Phone: 011-32-3-820-2335. E-mail: dirk.snyders@ua.ac.be.

SNYDER-SOWERS, MARY ANNE SARAH, performing company executive, choreographer, educator; b. Bristol, Tenn., Jan. 26, 1956; d. John Calvin and Pauline June Snyder; m. Lee E. Sowers, June 29, 1991; children: Mark Jason Sowers, Jeffrey Lee Sowers. BA, Va. Intermont Coll., Bristol, 1978; MEd, Milligan Coll., Tenn., 1997. Artistic dir. Bristol Ballet Co., Va., 1978—95; cert. tchr., first dance specialist Johnson City Schs., Tenn., 1995—. Dance grant rev. panelist Tenn. Arts Commn., Nashville, 2005—; prin. dancer Bristol Ballet Co., Va., 1968—82; regional evaluator Southeastern Regional Ballet Assn./Regional Dance Am., Atlanta, 1992—95; facutly mem. ballet dept. Va. Intermont Coll., Bristol, 1978—90; faculty summer arts camp Milligan Coll., 2000—; dir. Hardinge Ballet Ctr./Bristol Sch. Ballet, 1978—95; creative movement and dance specialist, artistic dir. ballet ensemble Mt. View Elem. Sch., Johnson City, 1995—. Dir.: (artisitc director) several ballet cos. Founding bd. mem. A! Mag. For The Arts, Bristol, Va., 1984—86; instr. liturgical dance St. Anne's Cath. Ch., Bristol; assoc. mem., dir. Southeastern Regional Ballet Assn./Regional Dance Am., Atlanta, 1991—95. Grantee, Johnson City Sports Found., 2005—06, Johnson City Area Arts Coun., 2005—06. Mem.: NEA, Tenn. Edn. Assn., Nat. Dance Edn. Orgn., Nat. Dance Edn. Assn. (assoc.), Tenn. Arts Commn. (assoc.; dance grant rev. panelist 2005), Johnson City Edn. Assn. (assoc.; com. chair 1992—2006, negotiating panel 2006). Home: 2859 Carroll Creek Road Johnson City TN 37615 Office: Johnson City Schools/Mountain View Elem 907 King Springs Road Johnson City TN 37601 Office Fax: 423-434-5596; Home Fax: 423-913-8183. Personal E-mail: maryanne@maryannesowers.com. E-mail: sowersm@jcschools.org.

SO, FRANKY, engineering educator; PhD, U. So. Calif., LA, 1991. Sr. scientist Hoeschst Celanese Rsch., Summit, NJ, 1991—93; mgr. Motorola Labs., Phoenix, 1993—2001; head rsch. OSRAM Opto Semiconductors, San Jose, Calif., 2001—05; assoc. prof. engring. U. Fla., Gainesville, 2005—. Bd. dirs. CBrite Corp., Santa Barbara, Calif., 2007. Contbr. research, reseach; mem. editl. bd. Materials Sci. and Engring. Reports, 2006—07. Recipient Disting. Inventor award, 1996, Master Innovator award, Motorola, 2000. Mem.: IEEE (sr.; assoc. editor Display Tech. 2006—07). Achievements include patents in field. Office: Univ Fla MSE Dept Gale Lamerand Dr Gainesville FL 32611-6400 Office Fax: 352-846-3355. Business E-Mail: fso@mse.ufl.edu.

SO, SAMUEL CHO YEE, therapeutic radiological physicist, physician; BA, St. Louis U., 1975; M Med. Sci., Emory U. Sch. Med., 1980; MD, Ross U. Sch. Med., 1986. Diplomate Am. Bd. Radiology, Am. Bd. Therapeutic Radiol. Physics, Am. Bd. Sci. in Nuclear Medicine, State Calif. cons. Radiological Physics. Nuclear medicine trainee nuclear medicine dept. Mallinkrodt Inst. Radiology, St. Louis, 1977-78; resident med. physicist dept. radiation oncology Emory U. Sch. Medicine, Atlanta, 1980-81; chief med. physicist dept. radiation oncology Grady Meml. Hosp., Atlanta, 1981; sr. radiol. physicist West Coast Cancer Found., San Francisco, 1987-97, assoc. dir., 1997—2001; dir. radiol. physics and dosimetry Seton Med. Ctr., Daly City, Calif., 2001—; dir. radiol. physics tng. Calif. Pacific Med. Ctr. Integrated Radiation Oncology Residency Program, 2002—. Cons. dept. radiation oncology St. Francis Med. Hosp., San Francisco, 1987—2002, St. Mary's Hosp., San Francisco, Seton Med. Ctr., Daly City, Calif., 1987—2001. Trustee Foshan U., China, 2002—. Mem. AAAS, Am. Coll. Radiology, Am. Assn. Physicists in Medicine, Am. Soc. Clin. Pathologists, Am. Bd. Med. Specialties, N.Y. Acad. Sci. Roman Catholic. Avocations: medicine, computers and technology. Office: Seton Med Ctr Dept Radiation Oncology 1900 Sullivan Ave Daly City CA 94015 E-mail: samuelso@dochs.org.

SO, SAMUEL KAI SUM, surgeon, researcher; s. Ching Chow and Helen So; m. Margaret Tao, Jan. 31, 1985; children: George, Richard, Phillip. BA summa cum laude, U. Minn., Mpls., 1973; MBBS, U. Hong Kong, 1978. Diplomate Am. Bd. Surgery. Intern, resident U. Hong Kong, 1978—80; intern and resident surgery U. Minn., Mpls., 1980—88, fellow multi-organ transplantation, 1988—89; asst. prof. surgery Washington U., St. Louis, 1989—92; assoc. dir. liver and pediat. kidney transplant programs Calif. Pacific Med. Ctr., San Francisco, 1992—95; assoc. prof. surgery Stanford U., Calif., 1995—2002, prof. surgery, 2003—; Lui Hac Minh endowed prof. Stanford Sch. Medicine. Co-founder, co-chair Studies in Pediat. Liver Transplantation, 1995—2001; founder, dir. Asian Liver Ctr. Stanford U., 1996—; dir. Liver Cancer Program Stanford U. Med. Ctr., 1998—; dir. Transplantation Program St Louis Children's Hosp., 1989—92; rsch. fellow Transplant Immunology U. Minn., 1983—86. Contbr. articles to profl. jours. and conf. procs. Cons. FDA Ctr. for Drug Evaluation, Bethesda, Md., 1998—; dir. (launcher) Jade Ribbon Campaign to prevent hepatitis B and liver cancer; mem. Com. Prevention And Control Viral Hepatitis In US, Inst. Medicine, 2008—; vol. Calif. divsn. Am. Cancer Soc., Oakland, 2002—, vol. No. Calif. Chinese unit Fremont, 2000—02; bd. mem. Population Health and Pub. Health Practice, Inst. Medicine, Washington; chair Nat. Hepatitis B Task Force, 2004—; co-founder Asia and Pacific Alliance to Eliminate Viral Hepatitis, 2008—. Recipient Disting. Physician award, Chinese Am. Physicians' Soc., 2000, Disting. Asian Leadership award, San Francisco Asian Bus. League, 2001, commendation, City and County of San Francisco, 2002, Santiago Ramon y Cajal award for outstanding rsch. in minority health, Nat. Minority Health Month, Washington, 2003, Ally award, San Francisco, Profile of Excellence award, ABC 7 TV, San Francisco, 2004, Cmty. Hero award, World Jour. Newspaper, 2004, Nat. Leadership award, NYU Ctr. Asian Am. Health, 2005, Cmty. Svc. Star award, 2007, Ann. award, Chinese Hosp., San Francisco, 2007, Fervent Global Love of Lives award, Chou-Ta Kuan Cultural and Edn. Found., 2008, Salute to Excellence award, Am. Liver Found., 2008, Ann. Asian Pacific Islander Heritage award, Calif. Legislature, 2009; named Local Hero of Yr., KQED Pub. Radio and TV, San Francisco, 2004; named one of Best Doctors in Silicon Valley, San Jose Mag., 1998—, Best Doctors in Am., Woodard/White Compendium, 1998—; grantee, Ctrs. Disease Prevention and Control, 2007, Office of Minority Health, Dept. Health & Human Svcs., 2007, Nat. Inst. Health, 2007. Fellow: ACS; mem.: Internat. Pediat. Transplant Soc., Internat. Liver Transplantation Soc., Transplantation Soc., Am. Assn. for Study of Liver Disease, Am. Soc. Transplantation, Am. Soc. Transplant Surgeons, San Francisco Surg. Soc. Achievements include research in genomics of liver and stomach cancers, developing novel approaches in the diagnosis and management of liver cancer, posttransplant lymphoproliferative disease; first to show growth improves after kidney transplantation in infants; successful treatment of infants with primary hyperoxaluria by combined liver and kidney transplantation. Office: Dept Surgery Stanford U 300 Pasteur Dr H3680 Stanford CA 94305 Business E-Mail: samso@stanford.edu.

SOARES, CARL LIONEL, quality assurance professional, metrologist; b. New Bedford, Mass., Sept. 14, 1944; s. Lionel Francis and Sarah Vincent (Flor) Soares; m. Jean Rosalee Bettencourt, Nov. 11, 1965 (div. Oct. 1974); children: Kevin Carl, Keith Christopher, Kenneth Craig; m. Maria T. Ortiz, July 9, 2005. Student in Indsl. Tech., Fitchburg State Coll., 1980—. Quality assurance specialist Cornell-Dubilier Electronics, Inc., New Bedford, Mass., 1965-66; computer controlled test equipment technician Raytheon Co., Waltham, Quincy, North Dighton, Mass., 1966-79, quality control supt. Waltham, 1982-85, metrologist, dept. quality dir., 1979-96; pres., treas., mgr. S&O Cleaning Corp. d/b/a The MAIDS, New Bedford, 1995—2006; dir. facilities svcs. SE Regional Network, 2006—. Former chmn. bd. dirs. New Bedford Coun. Substance Abuse; former clk. Southeastern Network; bd. dirs., treas., events chmn. Buttonwood Park Zool. Soc.; mem. Friends of Dartmouth Librs.; choir mem. St. James Ch. With USN, 1963—65. Mem.: Rotary Internat., Am. Legion. Roman Catholic. Avocations: gardening, bicycling, records and cds, computers, music. Home: 205 Maple St New Bedford MA 02740-3513 Office Phone: 508-997-0475 ext. 3161, 774-628-1061. Business E-Mail: carl.soares@hptc.org.

SOARES, LUCIANA, music educator; b. Goiânia, Goiás, Brazil, Dec. 10, 1971; d. Pedro Gonçalves and Elands Alarcão Soares. MusB in Piano Performance, U. Fed. Goiás, Goiânia, 1992; MusM, Ariz. State U., Tempe, 1998; MusD in Piano Performance and Pedagogy, U. Southern Miss., Hattiesburg, 2002. Asst. prof., piano Nicholls State U., Thibodaux, La., 2002—. Dir. Latin American Festival Nicholls, Thibodaux, 2007—. Recording artist (CD) Brasileira: Piano Music by Brazilian Women. Office: Nicholls State Univ 900 1st St Thibodaux LA 70310 Office Fax: 985-448-4674. Business E-Mail: luciana.soares@nicholls.edu.

SOBBOTT, SUSAN, diversified financial services company executive; b. NJ; 2 children. BA, Georgetown Univ.; MBA, Univ. Va. Joined strategic planning group Am. Express, 1990, sr. v.p., gen. mgr. OPEN Lending and Network Devel. group, pres. OPEN small bus. network NYC, 2004—, and global mgmt. team mem. Mentor Women Unlimited; bd. adv. Women's Leadership Exchange. Recipient NY Compass award, 2005; named one of America's Top Women in Bus.-Game Changers, Pink mag. & Forté Found., 2007. Avocations: bicycling, yoga. Office: OPEN Small Bus Network Am Express 200 Vesey New York NY 10281 Office Phone: 212-227-4262.

SOBECK, JOANNE L., social studies educator; PhD, Wayne State U., Detroit, 1999. Assoc. prof. Wayne State U., 1999—. Bd. mem. Am. Indian Health and Family Svcs. Southeastern Mich., Detroit, 1995. Office: Sch Social Work 4756 Cass Ave Detroit MI 48202

SOBEL, ALAN, electrical engineer, physicist; b. NYC, Feb. 23, 1928; s. Edward P. and Rose (Naftalison) S.; m. Marjorie Loebel, June 15, 1952; children: Leslie Ann, Edward Robert. BSEE, Columbia U., 1947, MSEE, 1949; PhD in Physics, Poly. Inst. Bklyn., 1964. Lic. Profl. Engr., N.Y. and Ill. Asst. chief engr. The Electronic Workshop, NYC, 1950-51; head, functional engr. Fairchild Controls Corp., 1951-56; project engr. Skiatron Electronics and TV Corp., 1956-57; sr. rsch. engr. Zenith Radio Corp., Glenview, Ill., 1964-78; v.p. Lucitron inc., Northbrook, Ill., 1978-87, pres., 1987; pvt. practice cons. Evanston, Ill., 1988—; v.p. Machine Vision and Control Internat. Inc., 1994—2003, LightWave Technologies Corp., 2000—. Asst., instr. Poly. Inst. Bklyn.,1957-64; mem. program coms. SID Internat. Symposium, Internat. Display Rsch. Conf., 1970—. Inventor: 14 patents on various display and electron devices; editor Jour. Soc. Info. Display, 1991-99, assoc. editor, 2000—; adv. editor Info. Display Mag., 1991-2003; assoc. editor: IEEE Trans. on Electron Devices, 1970-77; contbr. articles to profl. jours. NSF fellow, 1959, 60. Fellow Soc. Info. Display (Lewis and Beatrice Winner award 2002); mem. IEEE (sr., life), SPIE, Am. Phys. Soc., Sigma Xi. Democrat. Home and Office: 1307 Beechwood Dr Ann Arbor MI 48103 Office Phone: 734-995-8414. Personal E-mail: as1285@columbia.edu.

SOBEL, BURTON ELIAS, cardiologist, educator; b. NYC, Oct. 21, 1937; s. Lawrence J. and Ruth (Schoen) Sobel; m. Susan Konheim, June 19, 1958; children: Jonathan, Elizabeth. AB, Cornell U., 1958; MD magna cum laude, Harvard U., 1962. Intern Peter Bent Brigham Hosp., Boston, 1962-63, resident, 1963-64, 66-67; clin. asso., cardiology br. NIH, Bethesda, Md., 1964-66, 67-68; asst. prof. medicine U. Calif. at San Diego, La Jolla, 1968-71, asso. prof. medicine, dir. myocardial infarction research unit, dir. coronary care, 1971-73; asso. prof. medicine Barnes Hosp.-Washington U., St. Louis, 1973-75; adj. prof. chemistry Washington U., St. Louis, 1979-94; prof. medicine Barnes Hosp.-Washington U., 1975—, dir. cardiovascular div., 1973—, program dir. specialized ctr. rsch. ischemic heart disease, 1975-89, program dir. specialized ctr. rsch. in coronary and vascular diseases, 1990-94, program dir. principles in cardiovascular rsch., 1975-94; chmn. and E.L. Amidon prof. medicine, prof. biochemistry U. Vt., Burlington, 1994—2005, faculty mem. grad. coll., 2008—; physician-in-chief Med. Ctr. Hosp. Vt., Burlington, 1994—2005, Fletcher Allen Health Care, Burlington, 1995—2005; prof. medicine, dir. Cardiovasc. Rsch. Inst. U. Vt., Burlington, 2005—; faculty mem. cell and molecular biology program U. Vt., Burlington, 2008—, disting. prof. medicine, 2009—. Program dir. Collaborative Clin. Trial Therapy to Protect Ischemic Myocardium Washington U., 1977, prin. investigator Specialized Ctr. of Rsch. in Ischemic Heart Disease, 1975—95, program dir. Principles in Cardiovasc. Rsch., 1975—95, program dir. Nat. Rsch. and Demonstration Ctr. in Ischemic Heart Disease, 1985—95; chmn. cardio renal drugs US Pharmacopeial Conv., 1990—; prin. investigator BARI, II, NIH Fibrinalysis and Coagulation Core U. Vt., 2000; program dir. Cardiovascular Rsch. Inst./ Medtronic Corp./ U. Vt., 2006—, Disting. Rsch. Alliance / Medtronic Corp./ U. Vt., 2006—, Disting Rsch. Alliance/ Takeda Pharm./ U. Vt., 2008—; bd. dir. Scios Corp., Corvas Corp., Ariad Corp., Bristol Myers Squibb Corp., Fletcher Allen Health Care, New River Pharm., Inc, Nuvelo Corp., Clin. Data, Inc., Intrexon Corp., Area Biopharma, Inc.; scientific adv. bd. CV Therapeutics, Inc.; sci. adv. bd. Epix Med., Inc., New River Pharm., Inc.; chmn. HaptoGuird, Inc; co-prin. investigator NIH Regional Heart Failure Network Ctr., U. Vt., 2007—. Assoc. med. editor: Heart Bull, 1971—72; editor: Clin. Cardiology, 1971—74; mem. circulation bd. Clin. Guides to Med. Mgmt., 1971—; editor: Coronary Artery Disease, 1989—, Clin. Guides to Med. Mgmt., 1996—, Circulation, 1983—88; cons. editor Circulation; mem. editl. bd.: Circulation Rsch., 1974—, Annals Internal Medicine, 1976—, Am. Jour. Cardiology, 1976—, Cardiology Digest, 1976—77, Jour. Clin. Investigation, 1977—, Jour. Continuing Edn. Cardiology, 1978—, Am. Jour. Physiology: Heart and Circulatory Physiology, 1978—, Cardiology in Elderly, 1991—, Current Med. Lit., —, Churchill Livingstone edtl. adv. bd.: Internat. Seminars Cardiovascular Medicine, 1978—, Cardiology in Rev., 1992—; mem. editl. bd. Internat. Jour. Cardiology, Fibrinolysis, 1986; assoc. editor: Internat. Jour. Cardiology, Fibrinolysis, 1990—, mem. editl. bd.: Current Opinion in Cardiology, —; editor, 1989—; mem. editl. bd. Can. Jour. Cardiology, 1995—, Arteriosclerosis, Thrombosis, and Vascular Biology, 1996—, Clin. Therapeutics, 1996, Clin. Insights in Diabetes, 1999, Heart Disease, 2000, Diabetes Treatment Today, 2000, Am. Jour. Geriatric Cardiology, 2000, Diabetes Care, 2002—, Current Diabetes Revs., 2004—. Served to lt. comdr. USPHS, 1964—68. Recipient Career Rsch. Devel. award, USPHS, 1972, Internat. Recognition award, Heart Rsch. Found., 1981, Disting. Achievement award, Am. Heart Assn. Sci. Couns., 1984, award, Robert J. and Claire Posatow Found., 1988, Va. Heart Ctr., 1991, Drake award, Maine Heart Assn., 1992, E.L. Amidon Excellence in Tchg. award, U. Vt., 2007. Master: ACP, ASIM; fellow: AAAS (councilor 1997—), Am. Coll Angiology, Am. Coll. Cardiology (Disting. Scientist award 1987), Am. Heart Assn. (coun. on basic cardiovasc. scis., clin. coun., circulation and arteriosclerosis, thrombosis and vascular biology, James B. Herrick award 1992, Spl. Recognition award coun. on arteriosclerosis, thrombosis and vascular biology 1999), Molecular Medicine Soc., Royal Soc. Medicine; mem.: Inst. Biomed. Scis. and Tech., Internat. Acad. Cardiovascular Scis., Internat. Soc. Applied Cardiovasc. Biology, Soc. Exptl. Biology and Medicine (councilor 1998—, pres. bd. govs. 2002—, pres.-elect 2005—, pres. 2007—), Assn. Profs. Cardiology (pres.-elect 1992), Internat. Soc. Fibrinolysis and Thrombolysic (councilor), Western Soc. Clin. Rsch., Cardiac Muscle Soc., Am. Physiol. Soc., Assn. Am. Physicians, Am. Soc. Clin. Investigation (councilor, instnl. rep. 1997—), Assn. Univ. Cardiologists, Am. Fedn. Clin. Rsch. (councilor), Alpha Omega Alpha. Avocations: skiing, sailing. Home: 171 Lost Cove Rd Colchester VT 05446-7473 Office: U Vermont Colchester Rsch Facility 208 S Park Dr Colchester VT 05446

SOBEL, CLIFFORD M., United States Ambassador to Brazil; b. 1949; m. Barbara Sobel; 2 children. Student, U. Vt.; BS in Govt., NYU; LLD (hon.), Kean U., 1999. Founder, chmn. several cos. that designed, manufactured and imported fixtures in retail environments; founder, bd. mem. Norcrown Bank, NJ, 1985—91; chmn., pres. CMS Realty Co., SJJ Investment Corp.; chmn. Net2Phone, Inc.; co-chair ADIR; US amb. to the Netherlands US Dept. State, The Hague, Netherlands, 2001—05, US amb. to Brazil Rio de Janeiro, 2006—. Chmn. bd. overseer Alexis de Tocqueville Instn.; bd. dirs. Lexington Inst., Arlington, Va.; bd. dirs., mem. policy com. Bus. Execs. for Nat. Security. Bd. dirs. NJ Performing Arts Ctr.; bd. visitors Naval Post Grad. Sch., Monterey, Calif., 1993—97; mem. Holocaust Meml. Coun., 1994—95; adv. bds. Empower Am. and Rep. Leadership Coun.; del. Rep. Nat. Conv., 1996, 2000; NJ fin. chmn. George W. Bush Primary and Presdl. Campaigns, 2000; apptd. mem. US Govt. Industry Sector Internat. Trade Bd., 1987—89; exec. com. Prosperity NJ, United Jewish Fedn. Metrowest NJ. Office: DOS Amb 7500 Brasilia Pl Washington DC 20521-7500*

SOBEL, HOWARD D., dermatologist; b. 1950; MD, Albert Einstein Coll. of Medicine, Bronx, NY, 1973. Cert. in Dermatologic and Cosmetic Surgery. Residency in dermatology and dermatologic surgery Emory U. Sch. Medicine, Atlanta; clin. attending physician in dermatology and dermatologic surgery Lenox Hill Hosp., Beth Israel Hosp., and Cabrini Med. Ctr.; dir. Skin and Spa Cosmetic Surgery Ctr., NY. Editor-in-chief Internat. Jour. of Cosmetic Surgery and Aesthetic Dermatology, appeared on numerous television and radio programs (including: Sally Jesse Raphael Show, Home Show, Good Day NY, CNBC, MSNBC, New York 1, and Channels 2, 4, 5, and 7 News programs). Fellow: Am. Acad. Cosmetic Surgery; mem.: Am. Soc. Laser Surgery, Am. Soc. Hair Restoration Surgery, Am. Soc. Liposuction Surgery, Am. Acad. Dermatological Surgery, Am. Acad. Dermatology. Achievements include helping to pioneer the union of dermaology with cosmetic surgery; the first surgeon in 1986 to perform liposuction using the tumescent solution purely under local anesthesia; founder and chmn. of HDS Labs, the manufacturer if DDF (Doctor's Dermatologic Formula). Avocations: skiing, tennis. Office: Skin and Spa Cosmetic Surgery Ctr 960A Park Ave New York NY 10028 Office Phone: 212-288-0060. E-mail: hdsobel-md@nyc.rr.com.

SOBEL, MARK ESAR, pathologist, researcher; b. NYC, Apr. 14, 1949; s. Abraham David and Selma Etta (Spitzer) S. BA, Brandeis U., 1970; MD, Mt. Sinai Sch. Medicine, NYC, 1975; PhD in Biomed. Scis., CUNY, 1975. Diplomate Nat. Bd. Med. Examiners. Med. intern, clin. fellow in pediatrics Children's Hosp. Med. Ctr./Harvard U. Med. Sch., Boston, 1975-76; rsch. assoc. NIH, Bethesda, Md., 1976-79, 80-83; sr. investigator Nat. Cancer Inst., Bethesda, 1983-92, chief molecular pathology sect., 1992-2001; sr. exec. dir. Am. Soc. Investigative Pathology, Bethesda, 2001—. Vis. scientist Max Planck Inst. for Biochemistry, Martinsried bei Munchen, Germany, 1979-80; dir. Concepts in Molecular Biology course Am. Soc. Investigative Pathology, Rockville, Md., 1987-99. Contbr. more than 100 articles to profl. jours.; patentee in field. Capt. USPHS, 1975-2001. Recipient Commendation medal USPHS, 1989, other awards. Mem. Am. Soc. for Biochemistry and Molecular Biology, Am. Soc. Investigative Pathology (councilor 1995-97, vice pres.-elect 1997-98, v.p. 1998-99, pres. 1999-2000), Assn. for Molecular Pathology (sec.-treas. 1995-97, pres.-elect 1998, pres. 1999), Assn. Accreditation Human Rsch. Protections Programs (bd. dirs. 2001-08), Fedn. of Am. Soc. Exptl. Biology Minority Access Rsch. Careers (adv. bd. 2006-), PubMed Ctrl. (Nat. Adv. Com. 2007-), Phi Beta Kappa, Alpha Omega Alpha, Sigma Xi. Jewish. Avocations: classical music, history. Office: Am Soc Investigative Pathology 9650 Rockville Pike Bethesda MD 20814-3993 Business E-Mail: mesobel@asip.org.

SOBEL, MICHAEL, vascular surgeon, researcher; b. White Plains, NY, June 18, 1949; s. Raymond and Alma Sobel; m. Catherine G. Sobel; children: Alexander, Susan. BA cum laude, Harvard U., 1971; MD, Albert Einstein Coll. Medicine, Bronx, NY, 1975. Diplomate in gen. surgery and gen. vascular surgery Am. Bd. Surgery. Intern Beth Israel Hosp., Boston, 1975-76, resident in surgery, 1976-78, sr. and chief resident, 1980-82; resident in surgery Guys Hosp., London, 1979; fellow in peripheral vascular surgery NYU Med. Ctr., NYC, 1982-83; rsch. fellow in surgery Harvard Med. Sch., Boston, 1978-79; chief vascular surg. svc., dir. noninvasive vascular lab. McGuire VA Med. Ctr., 1984-97; attending surgeon Med. Coll. Va., 1984-97, Univ. Hosp. Health Scis. Ctr., SUNY, Syracuse, 1997—; chief of surgery Syracuse VA Med. Ctr., 1997—. Prof. surgery SUNY, Syracuse, 1997—. Mem. editl. bd. Vascular Surgery; reviewer for jours.; contbr. numerous articles to profl. jours. Fellow ACS; mem. Soc. for Vascular Surgery, Am. Assn. Vacsular Surgery, So. Assn. for Vascular Surgery, Am. Venous Forum, Assn. for Acad. Surgery, Assn. VA Surgeons. Office: U Wash Schl of Med 1660 S Columbian Way Seattle WA 98108 E-mail: Michael.sobel@med.va.gov.

SOBEL, SABRINA G., chemistry professor; d. John C. and Nancy Jane Godfrey; m. Ken Sobel, Aug. 15, 2000. PhD, U. Calif., Berkeley, 1993. Instr. Hofstra U., Hempstead, NY, 1992—, asst. prof., 1993—97, assoc. prof., 1997—2004, prof., 2004—, chair, chemistry dept., 2007—. Cons. Godfrey Sci. and Design, Huntingdon Valley, Pa., 1999—2006. Contbr. articles to profl. jours. Mem.: Am. Chem. Soc. Office: Dept Chemistry 151 Hofstra Univ Hempstead NY 11549-1510 Business E-Mail: sabrina.sobel@hofstra.edu.

SOBELLE, RICHARD E., lawyer; b. Cleve., Mar. 18, 1935; BA, Stanford U., 1956, JD, 1960; LLM, U. So. Calif., 1967. Bar: Calif. 1961, U.S. Supreme Ct. 1969. Exec. Tracinda Corp. Mem. ABA (corp., banking and bus. law sect. 1969-95), State Bar Calif. (del. to conf. state bar dels. 1965-77, exec. com. bus. law sect. 1977-78), L.A. County Bar Assn. (exec. coun., jr. barristers 1965-68, exec. com. bus. and corps. sect. 1973-75). Office: Tracinda Corp 150 S Rodeo Dr Ste 250 Beverly Hills CA 90212-2417 Office Phone: 310-271-0638.

SOBERON, PRESENTACION ZABLAN, state bar administrator; b. Cabambangan, Bacolor, Philippines, Feb. 23, 1935; came to U.S., 1977; naturalized, 1984; d. Pioquinto Yalung and Lourdes (David) Zablan; m. Damaso Reyes Soberon, Apr. 2, 1961; children: Shirley, Sherman, Sidney, Sedwin. Office mgmt., stenography, typing cert., East Cen. Colls., Philippines, 1953; profl. sec. diploma, Internat. Corr. Schs., 1971; A in Mgmt. Supervision, Skyline and Diablo Coll., 1979, LaSalle Ext. U., 1980-82; AA, cert. in Mgmt. and Supervision, Diablo Valley Coll. With U.S. Fed. Svc. Naval Base, Subic Bay, Philippines, 22 yrs, clerical, stenography and secretarial positions, 1955-73, adminstrv. asst., 1973-77; secretarial positions Mt. Zion Hosp. and Med. Ctr., San Francisco, 1977, City Hall, Oakland, Calif., 1978; with State Bar Calif., San Francisco, 1978-79; secretarial positions gen. counsel divsn. and state bar ct. divsn., adminstrv. asst. fin. and ops. divsn., 1979-81; office mgr. sects. and coms. dept., profl. and pub. svcs., 1981-83; appointment adminstr. office of bar rels., 1983-86; adminstr. state bar sects. bus. law sect., estate planning, trust and probate law sect., labor and employment law sect., office of bar rels., 1986-89; adminstr. antitrust and trade regulation law sect., labor and employment law sect., workers' compensation sect., edn. and meeting svcs., 1989-96; adminstr. criminal law sect., 1996—; labor and law employment law sect., 1996—; internat. law sect., 1996—; workers' compensation sect., 1996—; edn. and meeting svcs., 1996-98; ret., 1998. Lectr., min. Our Lady of the Queen of the World Ch.; disc jockey, announcer Radio Sta. DZYZ, DZOR and DWHL, Philippines, 1966-77. Organizer Neighborhood Alert Program, South Catamaran Circle, Pittsburg, Calif., 1979-80, vol. work, Kaiser and Cath. Parish Ch. Recipient 13 commendation certs., outstanding pers. awards, monetary awards, 20 Yr. U.S. Fed. Svc. cert., 1975, Nat. 1st prize award Nat. Inner Wheel Clubs Philippines, 1975, Kaiser Vol. Svc. award. Mem.: NAFE, Am. Soc. Assn. Execs., Our Lady Queen Ch. Filipino Assn., SRF Tigers No. Calif., Castillejos Assn. No. Calif., Olongapo-Subic Bay Assn. Am. (Pitts. rep. 1982—87, bus. mgr. 1988—89, pub. rels. officer 1993—94, bus. mgr. 1997—, bus. mgr. Ulo Ng Apo chpt. 2003—). Roman Catholic. Avocations: reading, travel, dance, singing, music, exercise. Home: 207 South Catamaran Circle Pittsburg CA 94565-3613 Office: State Bar of Calif 180 Howard St San Francisco CA 94105-1639 Personal E-mail: pzsoberon@comcast.net.

SOBERÓN MAINERO, JORGE, former commission administrator, ecology researcher, educator; b. Mexico City, Apr. 30, 1953; s. Jorge Soberon and Leticia (Mainero) S.; m. Aida Fernandez Hernandez, Mar. 25, 1979; children: Jorge, Pablo. BS, Nat. U., Mexico City, 1976, MS, 1979; PhD, London U., 1982. Diplomate Imperial Coll. Researcher, Inst. Ecology Nat. U. Mex., Mexico City, 1982—2005, coord. PhD ecology program, 1985-90, head grad. studies Sch. Scis., 1990-92; founding dir., exec. sec. Nat. Commn. on Biodiversity of Mexico (CONABIO) (now called Nat. Commn. for the Knowledge and Use of Biodiversity), 1992—2005; prof., divsn. ornithology U. Kans., Lawrence, Kans., 2005, sr. scientist, Biodiversity Rsch. Ctr., 2005—. Sci. v.p. Pronatura, A.C., Mex., 1994—; mem. sci. and tech. adv. panel Global Environment Fund., Nairobi, Kenya, 1995-98; vice-chair scientific com., Global Biodiversity Info. Facility; mem. scientific adv. coun. World Conservation Monitoring Centre, Internat. Centre for Insect Physiology and Ecology; mem. adv. bd. Network Nat. Ecol. Observatory Network; bd. dir. All Species Found., NatureServe, Pronatura. Author: Ecological and Epidemiological Games, 1979, Populations Ecology, 1990; contbr. several articles to profl. jours. Mem. Soc. Mex. Lepidopterologia, Soc. Bot. Mexicana, Soc. Conservation Biology, Academia Mexicana de Ciencias. Roman Catholic. Office: U Kans Divsn Ornithology 1345 Jayhawk Blvd Dyche Hall Lawrence KS 66045-7562 Office Phone: 785-864-3897. Office Fax: 785-864-5335. Business E-Mail: jsoberon@ku.edu.

SOBEY, DAVID FRANK, food company executive; b. Stellarton, NS, Can., 1931; s. Frank Hoyse and Irene S.; m. Faye B. Naugle, June 2, 1953; children: Paul David, Janis Irene Hames. D of Commerce (hon.), St. Mary's U., 1991. With Sobeys Inc., Stellarton, 1949—, store mgr., dir. merchandising and advt., v.p., exec. v.p., pres., dep. chmn., chief exec. officer, dir., 1981-85, chmn., 1985—2001, chmn. emeritus, 2001—. Mem. Order of Can., 1996; chancellor, St. Mary's U., 2008; bd. dirs. Empire Co. Ltd., Sobeys Inc.; chmn. The Sobey Found., Frank H. Sobey Fund for Excellence in Bus. Studies. Bd. dirs. The Sobey Art Found., Atlantic Salmon Fedn. Named to Canadian Bus. Hall Fame, 2007. Mem.: Abercrombie Golf Club, City Club (New Glasgow), Halifax Club. Office: Sobeys Inc 115 King St Stellarton NS Canada B0K 1S0

SOBEY, EDWIN J. C., museum director, oceanographer, consultant; b. Phila., Apr. 7, 1948; s. Edwin J. and Helen (Chapin) S.; m. Barbara Lee, May 9, 1970; children: Ted Wooddall, Andrew Chapin. BS, U. Richmond, 1969; MS, Oreg. State U., 1974, PhD, 1977. Rsch. scientist Sci. Applications, Inc., Boulder, Colo., 1977-79, divsn. mgr., 1979-81; exec. dir. Sci. Mus., West Palm Beach, Fla., 1981-88, Mus. Sci. and History, Jacksonville, Fla., 1988, Nat. Invention Ctr., Akron, Ohio, 1989-92, Fresno Met. Mus., Calif., 1993-95; ednl. cons., 1995—. Exec. dir. A.C. Gilbert's Discovery Village, Salem, Oreg., 1997-99; pres. Northwest Invention Ctr., 1999—; founder Nat. Toy Hall of Fame, 1998; instr. mus. mgmt. U. Wash., 1998-2001. Author: Complete Circuit Training Guide, 1980, Strength Training Book, 1981, The Whole Backpacker's Catalog, 1988, Increasing Your Audience, 1989, Inventing Stuff, 1995, Wrapper Rockets and Trombone Straws-Science at Every Meal, 1996, Car Smarts, 1997, Just Plane Smart, 1998, Young Inventors at Work, 1999, How to Enter and Win an Invention Contest, 1999, Fantastic Flying Fun with Science, 2000, Wacky Water Fun with Science, 2000, Inventing Toys: Kids Having Fun Learning Science, 2001, How to Build Your Own Prize-Winning Robot, 2002, Loco-Motion, 2005, Rocket-Powered Science, 2005, A Field Guild to Roadside Technology, 2006, A Field Guide to Office Technology, 2007, Wax Toys Work, 2008; co-author: Aerobic Weight Training Book, 1982; mem. editl. adv. bd. Invent Mag., 1989—92; exec. prodr.: (TV show) Idea Factory, Sta. KFSN-30, 1995—97; co-host (ednl. TV show) Blow the Roof Off, 1992. Alumni v.p. Leadership Palm Beach County; expdn. leader Expdn. Tng. Inst., S.E. Alaska, 1980; mem. U.S. Antarctic Rsch. Program, 1974; founder, bd. dirs. Visually Impaired Sports Program, Boulder, 1978-81; fitness instr. YMCA Boulder, 1977-81; convener 1st Nat. Conf. Sports for the Blind, 1979; bd. dirs. Leadership Palm Beach; vice chmn. County Com. on Artificial Reefs; treas. Leadership Akron Alumni Assn., 1990-91, class pres. Leadership Akron; v.p. Ohio Mus. Assn., 1991-92, pres., 1992-93; bd. dirs. Fla. Mus. Assn., 1988-89; mem. adv. bd. Marine Sci. Inst., 1990—. Lt. USN, 1970-73. Recipient Disting. award, Akron Coun. Engring. and Scientific Socs., 1992, award, Ohio Ednl. Broadcasting Network Commn., 1994, Congl. award for inventing equitable futures, 2005; named to Nonfiction Honor List, Voice of Youth Activities, 2003. Fellow Explorers Club (chair Pacific Midwest chpt. 2002-07); mem. Marine Tech. Soc. (sect. chmn. 1982-84), Coral Reef Soc. (chpt. pres. 1982-87), Nat. Inventive Thinking Assn. (bd. dirs. 1989—). Home: 2420 178th Ave NE Redmond WA 98052-5820 Office Phone: 425-861-8685. Personal E-mail: sobey@gte.net.

SOBIESKI, JAROSLAW, aerospace engineer; b. Wilno, Poland, Mar. 11, 1934; came to U.S., 1966; naturalized, 1971. s. Stanislaw and Sabina Sobieszczanski; m. Wanda Dlugosz, Dec. 31, 1958; children: Margaret Ann, Ian Patrick. BS aeros., Tech. U. Warsaw, 1955, MS aeros., 1957, DEng, 1964. Cons. Polish Aircraft Industries, Warsaw, 1957-64; asst. and adj. prof. Tech. U. Warsaw, Warsaw, 1955-64; rsch. assoc. Tech. U. Norway, Trondheim, 1964-66; assoc. prof. St. Louis U., 1966-71; aerospace engr. NASA Langley Rsch. Ctr., Hampton, Va., 1971-89, head rsch. office, 1979-93, chief scientist, 1993—96, multidisciplinary rsch. coord., 1994—2001, mgr. Computational AeroScis. team, 1996—2001, sr. rsch. scientist, 2001—06, disting. rsch. assoc., 2006—. Mem. faculty George Washington U., 1971-2003, U. Va., 1992-99, Va. Poly. Inst., 2004—; pres. and cons. engr. Tech. Analysis Optimization, Inc. Hampton, Va., 1982-02, lectr. presentations USA UK Australia, China, Japan, Brasil. Germany, Norway, Denmark, Holy, France, Portugal, Belgium, & Holland. Co-editor: Structural Optimization jour., 1989-2005; contbr. articles to profl. jours. Recipient Wright Bros. medal, SAE, 2000. Fellow AIAA (mem. tech. com., Nat. Multidisciplinary Design Optimization award 1996); mem. International Soc. for Structural and Multidisciplinary Optimization (founding mem. exec. bd. 1992—2003). Achievements include research in and problem solving for aeronautics, space flight, and high performance computing; multidisciplinary design optimization. Home: 518 Elizabeth Lake Dr Hampton VA 23669-1724 Office: NASA Langley Rsch Ctr MS 188E Hampton VA 23681-0001 Home Phone: 757-851-8690. Personal E-mail: xsobieskix@aol.com. E-mail: jaroslaw.sobieski-1@nasa.gov.

SOBIESKI, LEELEE (LILIANE RUDABET GLORIA ESLVETA SOBIESKI), actress; b. NYC, June 10, 1983; d. Jean Sobieski and Elizabeth Soloman. Attended, Brown U. Actress (TV films) Reunion, 1994, A Horse for Danny, 1995, Joan of Arc, 1999 (Best Performance by a Young Actress in a Mini-Series/Made for TV Film, YoungStar award, 1999), Uprising, 2001, Hercules, 2005, (TV series) Charlie Grace, 1995, (films) Jungle 2 Jungle, 1997, Deep Impact, 1998, A Soldier's Daughter Never Cries, 1998, Never Been Kissed, 1999, Eyes Wide Shut, 1999, Here on Earth, 2000, My First Mister, 2001, Joy Ride, 2001, Glass House, 2001, The Idol, 2002, Max, 2002, Lying, 2006, Heavens Fall, 2006, In a Dark Place, 2006, The Wicker Man, 2006, The Elder Son, 2006, In the Name of the King: A Dungeon Siege Tale, 2007, 88 Minutes, 2007, Walk All Over Me, 2007, Acts of Violence, 2008, (TV miniseries) Dangerous Liaisons, 2003, voice (films) Coven, 2006. Named Superstar of Tomorrow - Female, Young Hollywood Awards, 2000. Avocations: painting, ceramics, poetry, martial arts, horseback riding. Office: c/o Pinnacle PR 8265 Sunset Blvd Ste 201 Los Angeles CA 90046

SOBIN, LESLIE HOWARD, pathologist, educator; b. NYC, Feb. 10, 1934; s. Martin L. and Kitty N. Sobin; m. Margareta E.D. Ahlstrom, Dec. 21, 1962; 1 child, Annika D. BS, Union Coll., 1955; MD, SUNY, NYC, 1959. Diplomate Am. Bd. Pathology. Instr. pathology Cornell U. Med. Coll., NYC, 1962-65, asst. prof. pathology, 1965; WHO visiting prof. pathology Univ. Kabul, Afghanistan, 1965-68; assoc. prof. pathology Cornell U. Med. Coll., 1968-70; pathologist WHO, Geneva, 1970-81; prof. pathology Uniformed Svcs. Univ. Health Scis., Bethesda, Md., 1984—; head WHO collaborating ctr. tumor classification Armed Forces Inst. Pathology, Washington, 1983—99, dir. sci. publs., 1987—, chief gastrointestinal pathology, 1991—, co-chmn. dept. hepatic/gastrointestinal pathology, 2004—. Adj. prof. pathology Cornell U. Med. Coll., 1980-2001, Georgetown U. Med. Coll., 1992—; expert, panel on cancer WHO, Geneva, 1981—. Author: Pathology Primer in Verse, 1978, 91, Tales of the Ampulla of Vater, 1994, The Last Examination: The Prosecutor's Guide to the Autopsy-In Verse, 1996; editor: International Histological Classification of Tumors, 1970-2002; co-editor: WHO Classification of Tumors, 2000-06, TNM Classification of Tumors, 1987, 97, 2002, Prognostic Factors in Cancer, 1995, 2001, 06; adv. editor (oncology) International Dictionary of Medicine and Biology, Churchill's Medical Dictionary. Recipient Sr. Exec. Svc. award Dept. of Army, 1990, Meritorious Presdl. Rank award, 1991. Fellow Royal Coll. Pathologists; mem. Internat. Acad. Pathology (sec. 1982-88).

SOBKOWICZ, HANNA MARIA, retired neurologist; b. Warsaw, Jan. 1, 1931; arrived in U.S., 1963; d. Stanislaw and Jadwiga (Ignaczak) S.; m. Jerzy E. Rose, Mar. 12, 1972. BA, Girls State Lyceum, Gilwice, Poland, 1949; M.D, Med. Acad., Warsaw, 1954, PhD, 1962. Intern. 1st Internal Med. Clinic Med. Acad., Warsaw, 1954-55; resident 1st Internal Med. Clinic, Med. Acad., Warsaw, 1955-59, Neurol. Clinic, Med. Acad., 1959, jr. asst., 1959-61, sr. asst., 1961-63; research fellow neurology Mt. Sinai Hosp., NYC, 1963-65; Nat. Multiple Sclerosis Soc. fellow Columbia U., NYC, 1965-66; asst. prof. neurology U. Wis., Madison, 1966-72, assoc. prof., 1972-79, prof., 1979—2006, prof. emerita, 2006—. Contbr. articles to profl. jours. NIH rsch. grantee, 1968—2002. Mem. Internat. Brain Rsch. Orgn., Soc. Neurosci., Internat. Soc. Devel. Neurosci. (editl. bd. 1984—). Business E-Mail: hmsobkow@wisc.edu.

SOBOL, ELISE SCHWARCZ, music educator; b. Chgo., June 12, 1951; d. Morton and Harriet Jacobsohn Schwarcz; m. Lawrence Paul Sobol, Aug. 21, 1977 (div. Sept. 1989); children: Marlon I., Aaron L. AA, Simon's Rock Bard Coll., 1971; student, Mannes Coll. Music, 1971—73, Juillard Sch. Music, 1973—74; BA, New Sch. Social Rsch., 1985; MA, Columbia U., 1987. Staff auditorium events, concerts, lectures Met. Mus. Art, 1972-73; sec. to pres. Harry Beall Mgmt. Inc., NYC, 1973-76; sales rep. M.L. Falcone Pub. Rels., NYC, 1976-77; asst. to pres. Jacques Leiser Artist Mgmt., NYC, 1977-78; artist rep. Elise Sobol Mgmt. Inc., South Huntington, NY, 1978-82; dir. early musical devel. program children Calling All Kids, South Huntington, 1981—86; tchr. music Roslyn Mid. Sch., 1987—88, Nassau Boces Divsn. Spl. Edn., 1988—; dir. LI Music Workshop, 1992—. Tchr. young and adult piano students, 1968—; instr. SUNY, Farmingdale, 1993—98; piano adjudicator, NY, 1993—; guest lectr. NYU, NYC, 1999; adj. prof. NYU, Steinhardt Sch. Edn., NYC, 2000—; advisor arts and humanities Internat. Biog. Ctr., Cambridge, England; exec. dir. United Cultural Convention, Am. Biog. Inst., Raleigh, NC, 2004—; guest lectr. Hofstra, 2000; adj. music edn. faculty C.W. Post Coll. LI U., 2000. Musician: (piano concerts) Chamber Music series at U.S. Mil. Acad., NY/NJ met. area concerts, Disting. Artists series, 2002—03, Met. Area Concerts, 2003, Am. Assn. Univ. Women Commentary and Concerts, 2003; musician: (commentary and concert) A Gentlewoman's Pursuit, AAUW, 2003, concerts in New Zealand, Australia, Eng., Ireland, Can. and US; contbg. author: Spotlight in Making Music with Special Learners, 2004; author, author: An Attitude and Approach for Teaching Music to Special Learners, 2001, author, 2008. Active Nassau Boces Elem. Program PTA, cultural arts coord., 1988—2005. Recipient Honor award, LI Very Spl. Arts Festival, 1993, Spl. citation, NY State Assembly Ames Elem. Program, 1998, Spl. recognition, Nassau Music Educators Assn., 1999, 1st prize, Dr. Martin Luther King Jr. Performing Arts Competition, 1999—2001, Internat. Peace prize, United Cultural Conv., 2002, citation, Town of Oyster Bay, 2002, award, Ernest Kay Internat. Found., Dublin, 2004; named an Outstanding Am. Tchr., Nat. Honor Roll, 2005—06; named one of Am.'s Outstanding Tchrs., 2005—06; nominee, NY Senate Women of Distinction Program, 2003. Mem.: AAUP, ASCD, NAFE, Music Educators Nat. Conf., NY State Sch. Music Assn. (chair music spl. learners 1993—). Home: 21 Saxon St Melville NY 11747 Office Phone: 516-662-1250. Business E-Mail: es86@nyu.edu.

SOBOLEWSKI, JOHN STEPHEN, computer scientist, director, consultant; b. Krakow, Poland, July 14, 1939; came to U.S., 1966; s. Jan Zygmund and Stefania (Zwolinska) S.; m. Helen Skipper, Dec. 17, 1965 (div. July 1969); m. Carole Straith, Apr. 6, 1974; children: Anne-Marie, Elisa, Martin. BE, U. Adelaide, Adelaide, South Australia, 1962, ME, 1966; PhD in Computer Sci., Wash. State U., 1971. Sci. officer Weapons Research Establishment, Salisbury, South Australia, 1964-66; asst. prof. computer sci. Wash. State U., Pullman, 1966-73; dir. research, assoc. prof. U. Wash., Seattle, 1973-80, dir. computer svcs., 1980-88; assoc. v.p. computing U. N.Mex., Albuquerque, 1988—. Cons. govt. and industry, Seattle, 1973—; mem. bd. trustees Fisher Found., Seattle, 1984—. Author: Computers for the Dental Office, 1986; contbr. articles to profl. jours. Served as engr. with Royal Australian Army, 1957-60. Australian govt. scholar, 1954-60, Elec. Res. Bd. scholar CSIRO, Melbourne, Australia, 1961-64. Mem. IEEE, Computer Soc. Roman Catholic. Avocation: mineral collecting. Home: 18422 57th Ave NE Kenmore WA 98028 Personal E-mail: nwminerals@hotmail.com.

SOBOLEWSKI, MICHAEL VLADYSLAV, computer scientist; b. Morag, Poland, Apr. 16, 1947; m. Irena Wanda Jarocka, Aug. 18, 1946; 1 child, Monika Beata Sobolewska. Diploma with distinction, St. Petersburg Electro-technical U., Russia; MS in Computer Engring., Gdansk U. Tech., Poland; PhD, Polish Acad. Sciences. Rsch. prof. Polish Acad. Sciences, Warsaw, 1971—89; rsch. assoc. Concurrent Engring. Rsch. Ctr., W. Va. U., Morgantown, 1989—94; sr. computer scientist GE Global Rsch. Ctr., Schenectady, NY, 1994—2002; prof. computer sci. Tex. Tech U., Lubbock, 2002—. Recipient GE Managerial awards, GE Global Rsch. Ctr., 1998—2000, Oustanding Svc. award, W. Va. U., 1994; named Hon. Prof. Computer Sci., Academic Coun. Ulyanovsk State U., 2007; Air Force Summer Faculty fellowship, 2006, 2007. Fellow: Internat. Soc. Productivity Enhancement (life Oustanding Svc. award 1995—96, Leadership award 1996, Outstanding Svc. award 2004—05); mem.: IEEE (assoc.), ACM (assoc.). Achievements include first to metacomputing globally distributed systems, exertion-oriented programming, percept calculus for knowledge representation. Office: Texas Tech Univ 4th St and Boston Lubbock TX 79409 Home: PO Box 64514 Lubbock TX 79464-4514 Personal E-mail: mwsobol@gmail.com. Business E-Mail: sobol@cs.ttu.edu.

SOBOYEJO, WINSTON OLUWOLE, materials engineering educator, researcher; b. Palo Alto, Calif., Oct. 13, 1964; s. Alfred Babatunde Olalya and Anthonia Adesiyan (Aileru) S. BSc in Mech. Engring., London U., 1985; PhD in Materials Sci and Metallurgy, Cambridge U., Eng., 1988. Rsch. scientist McDonnell Douglas, St. Louis, 1988-92; prin. rsch. engr. Edison Welding Inst., Columbus, Ohio, 1992; prof. Ohio State U., Columbus, 1992-99, Princeton U., NJ, 1999—; pres. to chair African Renaissance Inst. Sci. and Tech.; pres. Mateng Inc.; dir. undergrad. program in materials Princeton U., NJ. Cons. McDonnel Douglas, St. Louis, 1992—, Allison Gas Turbines, Indpls., 1993, Ohio Dept. Transp., 1996; bd. dirs. Mateng, Inc., Skillman, NJ, Abuja Tech. Village; vis. Martin Luther King assoc. prof. MIT, 1997-98; chair African sci. com., dir. US/Africa Materials Inst. Editor Conf. Procs., 1994, 95, 96. Recipient Rsch. Initiation award NSF, 1993, Nat. Young Investigator award, NSF, 1994, Young Investigator award Office of Naval Rsch., 1994. Fellow ASME, Nigerian Acad. Sci.; mem. ASM Internat. (local chpt. chair 1995-96, Bradley Stoughton award 1998), Materials Rsch. Soc., Minerals, Metals and Materials Soc. (local chpt. chair 1995-96). Achievements include contributions to the use of nanotechnology and BioMEMS in cancer detection and treatment, the design of cold welded organic electronics structures, and the design of bio-inspired dental/orthopedic multilayers. Avocations: piano, current affairs, keeping fit. Office: Princeton U Olden St Princeton NJ 08544-0001

SOCHET, MARY ALLEN, psychotherapist, educator, writer; b. Plattsburgh, NY, Feb. 10, 1938; d. Edwin Elisha and Mary Elizabeth (Thomson) Allen; m. Marvin J. Sochet, 1963; children: Melorra, David. BS in Childhood Edn., SUNY, Plattsburgh, 1958; MA in Human Rels., NYU, 1961, PhD in Human Devel., 1963. Tchr. kindergarten L.I. Pub. Schs., 1958-62; tchr. N.Y.C. Pub. Schs., 1962-64; prof. early childhood edn., child devel. and psychology Bklyn. Coll., 1964-71; program dir., acting exec. dir. Newark Pre-Sch. Coun., 1965-66; psychotherapist N.Y.C. Community Guidance Svc., 1966-78; staff cons. Human Resources Inst., 1966—; pvt. practice psychotherapy NYC, 1966—. Writer, lectr., ednl. cons. and editorial cons. in field. Author: (with Robert Allen) Toward a Caring Community, 1980; contbr. articles on edn., community orgns., peace and mental health to various jours. Founding mem. Community Loft, 1971-74, Neighbor's Network, 1979—; organizing mem. Children's Free Sch., 1969-81; co-chair Perhaps Kids Meeting Kids Can Make a Difference, 1982—. NCCJ fellow, 1961-61; recipient Founder's Day award NYU, 1963. Mem. Am. Psychol. Assn., Soc. Psychol. Study Social Issues, Psychologists for Social Responsibility. Home and Office: 380 Riverside Dr New York NY 10025-1858 Business E-Mail: kidsmtgkids@igc.org.

SOCKOLOW, ROBBYN ELLEN, pediatrician; d. Harry Sockolow; m. Brian Keith Maier, Nov. 18, 1989. BA, Emory U., Atlanta, 1978, BA, 1982; MD, NY Med. Coll., Valhalla, 1986. Cert. in pediat. 2005, in pediatric gastroenterology and nutrition 2003, physician nutrition specialist. Internship in pediat. Montefiore Med. Ctr., Bronx, NY, 1986—87, residency in pediat., 1987—89, fellowship in gastroenterology, asst. attending pediatrician, 1990—92; fellowship in gastroenterology Mt. Sinai Hosp., NYC, 1989—90; attending pediatrician North Ctrl. Bronx Med. Ctr., Bronx Mcpl. Med. Ctr.; cons. attending pediat. South Nassau Cmtys. Hosp., Oceanside, NY; asst. prof. pediat. Albert Einstein Coll. Medicine, Bronx, Stony Brook U. Coll. Medicine, NY, Weill Cornell Med. Coll., NYC, 2004—, sect. chief, divsn. pediatric gastroenterology and nutrition, 2004—, assoc. prof. clin. pediat., assoc. attending pediatrician. Contbr. articles to profl. jours., chapters to books. Profl. adv. bd. David Ctr.; bd. trustees LI Chpt., Crohn's and Colitis Found. America. Recipient Chmn.'s Recognition award, 1989; named to America's Top

Doctors, Castle Connolly Med., Ltd., 1999—. Mem.: Am. Acad. Pediat., Am. Coll. Gastroenterology, Bockus Soc., Am. Gastroenterol. Assn., N.Am. Soc. Pediatric Gastroenterology, Hepatology, and Nutrition. Office: NY Presbyn Hosp Weill Cornell Med Ctr Divsn Pediat Gastroenterology Nutrition 428 E 72nd St Oxford Bldg Ste 100 New York NY 10012 Office Phone: 212-746-3520. Office Fax: 212-746-8577.

SOCOL, MICHAEL LEE, obstetrician, gynecologist, educator; b. Chgo., Oct. 3, 1949; s. Joseph and Bernice (Bofman) S.; m. Donna Kaner, Dec. 17, 1972. BS, U. Ill., 1970; MD, U. Ill., Chgo., 1974. Diplomate Am. Bd. Ob-Gyn., Am. Bd. Maternal-Fetal Medicine. Resident obstetrics and gynecology U. Ill. Hosp., Chgo., 1974-77; clin. rsch. fellow dept. obstetrics and gynecology L.A. County-U. So. Calif. Med. Ctr., 1977-79; assoc. attending physician Northwestern Meml. Hosp., Chgo., 1980-86, attending physician dept. ob-gyn., 1986—; co-dir. Northwestern Perinatal Ctr., Chgo., 1987—; chief obstetrics Northwestern Meml. Hosp., Chgo., 1987—, dir. maternal-fetal medicine fellowship program, 1987-99, asst. prof. obstetrics and gynecology, 1979-84, assoc. prof., 1984-92, prof., 1992—. Vice chmn. dept. ob-gyn Northwestern Meml. Hosp., Chgo., 1992—. Author: (with others) Clinical Obstetrics and Gynecology, 1982, 1984, Diagnostic Ultrasound Applied to Obstetrics and Gynecology, 1987, Principles and Practice of Medical Therapy in Pregnancy, 1992; peer reviewer Am. Jour. Obstetrics and Gynecology, 1980—, Obstetrics and Gynecology, 1984—; contbr. numerous articles to profl. jours. Fellow Am. Coll. Ob-Gyn., Soc. Maternal-Fetal Medicine, Soc. for Gynecol. Investigation, Am. Gynecol. and Obstet. Soc.; mem. Assn. Profs. Gynecology and Obstetrics. Avocation: marathon running. Home: 30 W Oak St Apt 20 B Chicago IL 60610 Office: 250 E Superior St Ste 3-2307 Chicago IL 60611-3015

SOCOL, SHELDON ELEAZER, university official; b. NYC, July 10, 1936; s. Irving and Helen (Tuchman) S.; m. Genia Ruth Prager, Dec. 26, 1959; children: Jeffrey, Steven, Sharon, Robyn, Leslie, Steven Warren. BA, Yeshiva U., 1958; JD, NYU, 1963. From asst. bursar to dir. student fins. Yeshiva U., NYC, 1958-70, sec., 1970—, chief fiscal officer, 1971-72, v.p. bus. affairs, 1972—2003, v.p. and counselor to the pres., 2003—05; exec. asst. to chmn. Bd. of Overseers, 2006—07; advisor to dean Med. Sch., 2007—08; advisor Office of Pres., 2008—09. Mem. N.Y. State Adv. Coun. on Fin. Assistance to Coll. Students, 1969-76; asst. dir. Tng. Inst. for Fin. Aid Officers, Hunter, Coll., CUNY, 1970-71; mem. presdl. adv. com. Temple U., 1986; mem. regents adv. task force N.Y.C. Regional Plan for Higher Edn., 1971-73; bd. dirs. N.Y. Structural Biology Ctr., 2000-08; spkr. in field. Pres. Minyon Park Estates, Inc., 1966—2006. Mem. NEA, Nat. Assn. Coll. and Univ. Attys., Met. N.Y.C. Fin. Aid Adminstrs. Assn., Ea. Assn. Student Fin. Aid Officers, Am. Mgmt. Assn., Am. Assn. for Higher Edn., Nat. Assn. Coll. and Univ. Bus. Officers, Soc. Coll. and Univ. Planning, Mid. States Assn. Colls. (evaluation team Commn. on Higher Edn., U. Medicine and Dentistry N.J., 1985, Upstate Health Sci. Ctr. 1986, Carnegie-Mellon U. 1988, Albany Med. Ctr. 1989). Office Phone: 718-263-6519. Business E-Mail: dses@yu.edu.

SOCOLAR, JOSHUA E. S., physics professor; b. Paris, Sept. 16, 1958; s. Milton J. and Marlyn Socolar; m. Rebecca R. S. Sheline, Sept. 3, 1983 (dec. Jan. 13, 2009); children: S. Jacob, Yvonne M. BA, Haverford Coll., Pa., 1980; PhD, U. Pa., Phila., 1987. Tchr. George Sch., Newtown, Pa., 1981—82; jr. fellow Harvard U. Soc. Fellows, Cambridge, Mass., 1987—90; vis. scientist IBM Watson Rsch. Lab., Yorktown Heights, NY, 1990—92; asst. prof. Duke U., Durham, NC, 1992—99, assoc. prof., 1999—. Mem.: Am. Phys. Soc. Avocations: piano, puzzles, singing, hiking, tennis. Office: Duke Univ Physics Dept Durham NC 27708

SOCOLOW, ARTHUR ABRAHAM, geologist; b. Bronx, NY, Mar. 23, 1921; s. Samuel and Yetta (Solomon) S.; m. Edith S. Blumenthal, Apr. 10, 1949; children: Carl, Roy. Jeff. BS, Rutgers U., 1942; MA, Columbia U., 1947, PhD, 1955. Reg. profl. geologist, Commonwealth Pa. Photogrammetrist, U.S. Army Air Corps, 1942-46; with Eagle Picher de Mexico, 1947; instr. geology So. Methodist U., 1948-50; dir. geology field camp Colo., 1948-50; asst. prof. Boston U., 1950-55; geologist Def. Minerals Exploration Authority, Alaska, 1952; assoc. prof. U. Mass., 1955-57; econ. geologist Pa. Geol. Survey, 1957-61, dir., state geologist, 1961-86; cons. geologist Gloucester, Mass., 1986—; prof. environ. geology Salem (Mass.) State Coll., 1993-98; dir. New Eng. Govs. Conf. Project on Aggregate Resources New Eng., 1990-97. Mem. Outer Continental Shelf Policy Com., 1974-88, Pa. rep., 1978-88; lectr. mineral conservation Pa. State U., 1959-75; mem. conf. earth sci. source materials NSF, 1959; chmn. ann. field conf. Pa. Geologists, 1961-86; past mem. U.S. Nat. Com. on Tunnelling Tech.; mem. com. on N.Y. State low level waste program Nat. Acad. Sci.; past mem. gov.'s adv. com. Nat. Coun. on Environ. Quality; past chmn. Pa. Water Resources Coordinating Com.; geol. advisor Boston Mus. Sci., 1955-57. Former editor Pa. Geol. Bull.; mem. editorial bd. Northeastern Geol. Jour.; contbr. over 100 publs. and papers on environ. and econ. geology to profl. jours. Served with USAAF, 1942-46. Fellow AAAS (past pres. geography-geology sect.), Geol. Soc. Am. (sec.-treas. N.E. sect., past nat. councilor), Mineral Soc. Am., Soc. Econ. Geologists; mem. AAUP, Am. Geol. Inst. (Geology Svc. Profl. Campbell medal 2008), Nat. Assn. Geology Tchrs. (past regional pres., Ralph Digman award for contbns. to geologic edn. 1980), Am. Meteoritical Soc., Assn. Am. State Geologists (past pres., editor, compiler State Geol. Surveys-A History 1988, Disting. Svc. award 2004), Am. Geophys. Union, Am. Commn. Stratigraphic Nomenclature (past chmn.), Gloucester Conservation Commn. (chmn.), Fgn. Policy Assn. (past chpt. pres.), Sigma Xi. Clubs: Internat. Torch (past pres. chpt.). Home and Office: 26 Salt Island Rd Gloucester MA 01930-1945 Home Phone: 978-283-7490. Personal E-mail: artsoc@verizon.net. *I have great respect for the individualism of man in the midst of a society and a world where there is an unavoidable interrelationship and interdependence of man upon man, and of man upon his environment. While we strive to maintain our individualism, we must share our common resources and our common aspirations. This is the challenge that makes our lives worth living.*

SOCOLOW, ROBERT HARRY, engineering educator, physicist; b. NYC, Dec. 27, 1937; s. A. Walter and Edith (Gutman) S.; m. Elizabeth Anne Sussman, June 10, 1962 (div. Apr. 27, 1982); children: David, Seth; m. Jane Ries Pitt, May 25, 1986 (dec. Apr. 16, 2003); stepchildren: Jennifer, Eric; m. Emily Elizabeth Mathuws, Oct. 26, 2003. BA summa cum laude in Physics, Harvard Coll., 1959; MA in Physics, Harvard U., 1961, PhD in Physics, 1964. NSF predoctoral fellow, 1960—64; NSF postdoctoral fellow physics U. Calif. Berkeley and European Ctr. Nuc. Rsch. (CERN), 1964—66; asst. prof. dept. physics Yale U., New Haven, 1966-71; assoc. prof. dept. aerospace and mech. scis., mem. Ctr. Environ. Studies Princeton U., NJ, 1971-77, prof., 1977—79, assoc. dir. Ctr. for Environmental Studies, 1977—78, acting dir. Ctr. for Environmental Studies, 1978—79, prof. dept. mech. and aerospace engring., 1979—, co-dir. Carbon Mitigation Initiative, 2000—. Rsch. assoc. dept. geology and geophysics Yale U., 1971; mem. Inst. Advanced Study Princeton U., 1971; dir. Princeton U. Ctr. Environ. Studies, 1977—78, acting dir., 1978—79; dir. Princeton U. Ctr. Energy and Environ. Studies, 1979—98; chmn. bd. Am. Coun. Energy Efficient Econ., 1989—93; bd. dirs. Nat. Audubon Soc., 1992—99; mem. environ. sci. adv. com. Environ. Def. Fund, 1999—2001; mem. various com. U.S. Dept. of Energy, 1995—2000; mem. various com. including energy and environmental sys. com., panel on carbon sequestration & com. on alt. and strategies for future hydrogen prod. Nat. Rsch. Council, 1993—2006. Contbr. articles to profl. jours., chapters to books; co-editor: Patient Earth, 1971, Efficient Use of Energy, 1975, Boundaries of Analysis: An Inquiry into the Tocks Island Dam Controversy, 1976, Indsl. Ecology and Global Change, 1994, Environmentally Significant Consumption, 1997; editor: Saving Energy in the Home: Princeton's Expts. at Twin Rivers, 1978; assoc. editor: Ann. Rev. Energy and Environment, 1988—92; editor, 1992—2002; contbg. editor: Environment, 1999—, mem. mng. bd.: Jour. Indsl. Ecology, mem. editl. bd.: Perspectives in Energy, Energy and Bldgs. Recipient Axelson Johnson Commemorative Lecture award, 2005; named Lifetime Nat. Assoc. of Nat. Acad., 2004; grantee John Simon Guggenheim fellowship, 1976—77, German Marshall Fund fellowship, 1976—77. Fellow: Am. Phys. Soc. (Leo Szilard Lectureship award 2003), AAAS. Jewish. E-mail: socolow@princeton.edu.

SODAL, INGVAR EDMUND, retired electrical engineer, science administrator; b. Hemne, Norway, Feb. 12, 1934; came to U.S., 1962; s. Ingebrigt L. and Johanna Sodal; m. Sally Rollins; 1 child, Silje M. Degree in elec. engring., Trondheim Tech. Coll., Norway, 1959; BSEE, U. Colo., 1964. Engr. Fjeldseth Engring., Trondheim, 1959-61; rsch. engr. U. Norway, Trondheim, 1961-62, U. Colo. Med. Ctr., Denver, 1964-66, rsch. assoc., 1966-75, instr., lectr., 1975-79; vis. rsch. assoc. dept. engring. U. Colo., Boulder, 1974-75, lectr., 1975-76; asst. prof., div. head. Ohio State U., Columbus, 1979-82, mem. grad. faculty, 1982; pres., chief exec. officer Masstron, Inc., Boulder, Colo., 1983-87; chief scientist Paradygm, Boulder, 1987-89; pres. Pacemark, Inc., Boulder, 1989-90, Med. Physics Colo., Inc., 1991—; ret. Contbr. articles to profl. jours., chpts. to books; holder 6 patents in field. Instr. and/or program coord. in Scandinavian folklore and folk dancing for numerous groups and instns. throughout U.S., Can., and Norway, 1959—. Grantee, NIH, others. Mem. Village Arts Coalition, Sons of Norway. Office: 1550 Moss Rock Pl Boulder CO 80304-1543 E-mail: sodaling@norsk.us, ingvarsodal@netscape.net.

SODD, MARY JO, theatre educator; b. Mpls., May 19, 1952; d. Joe and Nancy Joan Sodd; 1 child, Vanessa Joan. BA, St. Catherine U., St. Paul, Minn., 1975; MA, U. Minn., Mpls., 1989; PhD, U. Colo., Boulder, 1993. Asst. prof. theatre Susquehanna U., Selinsgrove, Pa., 1992—96; prof. theatre Ctrl. Coll., Pella, Iowa, 1996—. Bd. mem. Pella Shakespeare Co., 2004—. Dir.: (classical and contemporary stage performances). Recipient David Crichton Tchg. award, Ctrl. Coll., 1999. Office: Ctrl Coll 812 University Ave Pella IA 50219 Business E-Mail: soddmj@central.edu.

SODEN, RICHARD ALLAN, lawyer; b. Feb. 16, 1945; s. Hamilton David and Clara Elaine (Seale) S.; m. Marcia LaMonte Mitchell, June 7, 1969; children: Matthew Hamilton, Mark Mitchell. AB, Hamilton Coll., 1967; JD, Boston U., 1970. Bar: Mass. 1970. Law clk., Hon. George C. Edwards Jr. U.S. Ct. Appeals (6th cir.), 1970-71; assoc. firm Goodwin, Procter & Hoar LLP, Boston, 1971-79; ptnr., bus. law dept. Goodwin Procter LLP (formerly Goodwin, Procter & Hoar LLP), Boston, 1979—; mem., diversity com. Goodwin Procter LLP, Boston. Instr. Law Sch. Boston Coll., Chestnut Hill, Mass., 1973-74. Mem. South End Project Area Com.; hon. dir. United South End Settlements, pres., 1977-79; chmn. Boston Mcpl. Rsch. Bur., 1996-97, pres., 1997-99; pres. Boston Minuteman coun. Boy Scouts Am.; trustee Judge Baker Children's Ctr., chmn., 1994-96, pres., 1992-94; trustee New Eng. Aquarium, Boston U., 1995-2001; bd. visitors Boston U. Goldman Sch. Grad. Dentistry; mem. bd. overseers WGBH; mem. Mass. Minority Bus. Devel. Commn.; mem. Adv. Task Force on Securities Regulation; mem. Adv. Com. on Legal Edn.; steering com. Lawyers Com. for Civil Rights under Law, chmn., 1992-94. Mem. ABA (chmn. standing com. on bar svcs. and activities, Commn. on Lawyer Assistance Programs Adv. Coun. on Diversity 1998-2000, bd. govs. 2008-), Nat. Bar Assn., Mass. Bar Assn. (past vice chmn. bus. law coun. 1990-91), Boston Bar Assn. (pres. 1994-95), Mass. Black Lawyers Assn. (pres. 1980-81), fellow Am. Bar Found., Boston Bar Found. Office: Goodwin Procter LLP Exchange Pl 53 State St Boston MA 02109-2803 Office Phone: 617-570-1533. Office Fax: 617-523-1231. Business E-Mail: rsoden@goodwinprocter.com.

SODERBERG, HERMAN ALBERT, minister, educator; b. Bklyn., Dec. 31, 1931; m. Audrey Carol Soderberg. BS in Math. and Physics, Wagner Coll., SI, 1961; MDiv, Drew U., Madison, NJ, 1965; postgrad., Duke U., Durham, NC, 1982. Min. United Meth. Ch., NJ, 1962—, NC; instr. Meth. Coll., Fayetteville, NC. Sr. adj. instr. Burlington County Coll., NJ, 1993—2006; adj. instr. Camden County Coll., NJ, 1994—2006, Fayetteville Tech. CC, NC, 2008—. With USN, 1951—55. Mem.: ASME, IEEE (life), Am. Chem. Soc., Inst. Radio Engrs., Am. Soc. Testing Materials. Avocations: photography, coin collecting/numismatics, camping, chess, travel. Home: 240-20 Sawtooth Dr Fayetteville NC 28314 Home Phone: 910-860-8382.

SODERBERG, NANCY, former ambassador; b. San Turce, PR, Mar. 13, 1958; d. Lars Olof and Nancy (MacGilvrey) S. BA in French and Econs., Vanderbilt U., 1980; MS in Fgn. Svc., Georgetown U., 1984. Del. selection asst. Mondale-Ferraro Com., Washington; dep. issues dir. fgn. policy Dukakis for Pres. Com., Boston, 1988; fgn. policy advisor to Senator Edward M. Kennedy US Senate, Washington, 1985-88, 89-92; fgn. policy dir. Clinton/ Gore Campaign, Little Rock, 1992; dep. asst. dir. transition nat. security Bill Clinton Presdl. Transition Team, Little Rock, 1992-93; dep. asst. to Pres. for nat. security affairs NSC, Washington, 1993—97; amb. (alt. rep.) to UN US Dept. State, NYC, 1997—2001; v.p., dir. Internat Crisis Group, NYC, 2001—05; dist. vis. scholar U. North Fla., Jacksonville, 2006—; pres., CEO Soderberg Global Solutions, Jacksonville, Fla., 2007—; pres. Connect US Fund, Washington, 2009—. TV and radio commentator MSNBC; mem. advisory bd., Nat. Com. on Am. Fgn. Policy, Tannenbaum Ctr.; adj. prof., Columbia U. Sch. Internat. & Pub. Affairs Author: The Superpower Myth: The Use and Misuse of American Might, 2005; co-author (with Brian Katulis): The Prosperity Agenda: what world wants from America and what we need in Return. Bd. mem. Concern Worldwide; pres. Sister City Program, NYC, 2002—06. Mem.: Coun. Fgn. Rels. Office Phone: 904-233-5023, 904-233-5021. Personal E-mail: ptarleton@bellsouth.net, nsoderberg@comcast.net.

SODERBERG, PETER H., health products executive; B in Engring., Yale Univ., New Haven. Mgmt. positions Johnson & Johnson, 1968—89; pres. Johnson & Johnson Health Mgmt., 1989—93; group v.p., COO Welch Allyn Inc., Skaneateles Falls, NY, pres., CEO, 2000—06, Hillenbrand Industries Inc., Batesville, Ind., 2006—, Hill-Rom, 2006—. Bd. dir. Greatbatch Inc., AdvaMed; bd. dirs. Hill-Rom Holdings, Inc., Constellation Brands, Inc., 2007—. Vice-chmn. Syracuse Symphony Orch., Met. Develop. Authority Ctrl. NY; chmn. CNY Medtech. Office: Hill-Rom Holdings Inc 1069 State Route 46 E Batesville IN 47006 Office Phone: 812-934-7777. Office Fax: 812-934-8189.*

SODERLIND, STERLING EUGENE, publishing executive, consultant; b. Rapelje, Mont., Sept. 6, 1926; s. William John and Florence (Longbotham) S.; m. Helen Boyce, Apr. 9, 1955; children: Steven (dec.), Sarah, Lori. BA, U. Mont., 1950; Rhodes Scholar, Oxford U., Eng., 1950-52. Reporter Mpls. Tribune, 1952-55; reporter Wall St. Jour., Chgo., 1955-56, Southeastern bur. chief Jacksonville, Fla., 1956-57, mem. page one editing staff NYC, 1957-65, asst. mng. editor, 1966-70, mng. editor, 1970; econs. editor Dow Jones & Co., Inc., NYC, 1970-77, asst. to pres., 1975-77, v.p., 1977-91; newspaper industry cons., 1992—2007. Served with USNR, 1944-46. Congregationalist. Home: Crane's Mill 459 Passaic Ave Cottage 308 West Caldwell NJ 07006

SODERSTRAND, MICHAEL ALAN, mathematics professor, electrical engineer; b. Berkeley, Calif., July 31, 1946; s. Joseph Norman Soderstrand and Helen Irene DeWees; m. Eunyoung Kim, June 27, 1992; children: Grace Yoona Cho, Matthew Alan West. AA in Engring., Sacramento City Coll., 1966; BSEE, U. Calif., Davis, 1968; MSEE, U. Calif., 1969, PhD, 1972; cert. in Edn. for Ministry, U. South, Swanee, Tenn., 2004. Registered profl. engr., Calif., 1968. Continuity dir. KROY Radio, Sacramento, 1962—63; radio engr. KJAY, Sacramento, 1963—67; audio engr. KXTV TV, Sacramento, 1964—68; mem. tech. staff Sandia Nat. Labs., Livermore, Calif., 1968—79; prof. elec. & computer engring. U. Calif., 1972—98; vis. prof. elec. & computer engring. Seoul Nat. U., Republic of Korea, 1997—98; prof. & head elec. & computer engring. dept. Okla. State U., Stillwater, 1998—2004; inmate tutor Fed. Med. Ctr., Ft. Worth, 2004—06; dir. product devel. Synapse Internat., LLC, Okla. City, 2004—; adj. prof. math. & stats. DeVry Keller Sch. Mgmt., Okla. City, 2006—. Cons. Lawrence Livermore Nat. Lab., Livermore, 1979—92. Co-author (with M.A. Soderstrand and G.F. Ford): (textbook) Analog Electronics Circuits and Systems, 2007; contbr. scientific papers in field. Staff mem. Hand-Up Ministries, Okla. City, 2006; bd. mem. Korean Lang. & Culture Sch., Sacramento, 1992—97. Recipient Outstanding Engring. Tchr. at Large award, U. Calif., 1980, Outstanding Elec. & Computer Engring. Tchr. of Yr. award, 1994, Myril B. Reed Best Paper award, IEEE Midwest Symposium Circuits Sys., 2001. Fellow: IEEE (v.p. Circuits & Sys. Soc. 1995—96). D-Liberal. Episcopal. Achievements include patents for active-R filters; adaptive removal of resonance induced noise; removal of resonance induced noise; early pioneer of active R filter design and residue number arithmetic. Home and Office: Synapse Internat LLC 2500 SW 141st St Oklahoma City OK 73170-5787 Office Fax: 405-200-1989; Home Fax: 405-200-1989. Personal E-mail: soderstrand@ieee.org. Business E-Mail: soderstrand@synapse-int.com.

SODEY, ANGELA ANN, gifted and talented educator; b. Freeport, Ill., Sept. 26, 1949; d. John Francis and Carolyn Lola McKenna; m. James Carleton Sodey, Sept. 5, 1970; children: Jay Carleton, Christopher John. BA, U. Iowa, Iowa City, 1971; MSE Reading Specialist, Drake U., Des Moines, Iowa, 1978. Tchr. grade 4 Ottumwa (Iowa) Schs., 1971; tchr. grades 5,6 Des Moines Pub. Schs., 1972—75, reading specialist, 1975—77, tchr. grade 3, 1977—79, tchr. grades 4, 5, 6 lang. arts, 1980; kindergarten tchr. Boone (Iowa) Pub. Schs., 1980; tchr. h.s. reading Jefferson County Schs., Denver, 1981—83; elem. talented and gifted tchr. Spencer (Iowa) Pub. Schs., 1984—85, Ft. Madison (Iowa) Pub. Schs., 1985—88, TAG coord., 1988—92, tchr. mid. sch. reading, 1992—98, tchr. grade 6, 1998—2004, elem. talented and gifted tchr., 2004—. Bd. dirs. Shining Trail coun. Girl Scouts Am., Burlington, Iowa, 2003—07. Grantee, Wal-Mart, 2004—05. Mem.: Lee County Reading Assn., Iowa Reading Assn. (pres.-elect, pres. 2003—05), Ft. Madison Country Club (bd. dirs. 1994—96), Delta Kappa Gamma (sec. 1992). Independent. Methodist. Avocations: boating, reading, knitting, bicycling, hiking, exercise, travel. Home: 612 Ave G Fort Madison IA 52627

SODHANI, ARVIND, computer company executive; Bachelor's, Master's, U. London; MBA, U. Mich., 1978. Asst. treas. Intel Europe Intel Corp., 1981—84, asst. treas., 1984—88, treas., 1988—90, v.p. and treas., 1990—2005, sr. v.p., pres. Intel Capital, 2005—07, exec. v.p., pres. Intel Capital, 2007—. Office: 2200 Mission College Blvd Santa Clara CA 95052*

SODINI, PETER J., food service executive; b. Jan. 26, 1941; With Fazio's div. of Fisher Foods Inc., 1976-78, Boys Markets Inc., LA, 1978-1990, Buttrey Food & Drug Co., Great Falls, Mo., 1990-91; pres., CEO Purity Supreme, North Billerica, Mass., 1991-98, The Pantry Inc., Sanford, NC, 1998—. Office: Pantry PO Box 1410 Sanford NC 27331-1410*

SODOLSKI, JOHN, retired professional society administrator; b. Menasha, Wis., Apr. 11, 1931; s. L.V. and L.W. (Pinkowski) S.; m. C.J. Eppard BS, U. Wis., 1953. Vice pres. Electronic Industries Assn., Washington, 1961-83; pres. U.S. Telephone Assn., Washington, 1983-93; ret., 1993. Served to 1st lt. USMC, 1955 Home: PO Box 1014 Middleburg VA 20118-1014

SODREL, MICHAEL EUGENE, former congressman, small business owner; b. Louisville, Dec. 17, 1945; s. Robert Eugene Sodrel and Nora Baily (Vermillion) Keller, m. Marquita Dean, Nov. 24, 1967; children: Michael Noah, Keesha. Student, Ind. U., Jeffersonville, 1963. Dir. maintenance Sodrel Truck Lines, Inc., Jeffersonville, 1969-72, dir. ops., 1972-74, v.p., 1974-76, exec. v.p., 1976-81, pres., CEO, 1981—2004; mem. US Congress from 9th Ind. dist., 2005—07; mem. sci. com., small bus. com., transp. and infrastructure com. Pres., chief exec. officer, Salem Stage, Inc., Jeffersonville, 1974-2004, The Free Enterprise System, Inc., 1976-2004. Bd. dirs. George Rogers Clark council Boy Scouts Am., New Albany, Ind., 1988—. Served to staff sgt. Nat. Guard US Army, 1966—73. Recipient Spl. Tourism award State of Ind., 1987; named to Hon. Order Ky. Col, 1983. Mem. Nat. Star Route Mail Contractor's Assn. (pres., chmn. bd. 1978-88), Am. Bus. Assn. (bd. dirs. 1987—), So. Ind. C. of C. Clubs: Skal (pres. 1986-87). Lodges: Rotary (pres. 1988—, Paul Harris fellow 1976). Republican. Presbyterian. Mailing: PO Box 1505 Jeffersonville IN 47131*

SODROSKI, JOSEPH G., medical educator; b. Coaldale, Pa. BS, Allentown Coll., 1976; MD, Jefferson Med. Coll., 1980. Intern in medicine New Eng. Deaconess Hosp., Boston, 1980—81; rsch. fellow in microbiology Dana-Farber Cancer Inst., Sch. Pub. Health Harvard U., Boston, 1981—84, from instr. to assoc. prof. div. human retrovirology Dana-Farber Cancer Inst., 1984—96, prof. div. human retrovirology Dana-Farber Cancer Inst., 1996—97, from instr. assoc. prof. dept. pathology Med. Sch., 1984—96, prof. dept. pathology Med. Sch., 1996—, assoc. prof. dept. cancer biology Sch. Pub. Health, 1992—96, prof. dept. cancer biology Sch. Pub. Health, 1996—97, prof. dept. cancer immunology and AIDS Dana-Farber Cancer Inst., 1997—, prof. dept. immunology and infectious diseases Sch. Pub. Health, 1997—. Chief div. human retrovirology Dana-Farber Cancer Inst. Harvard U., Boston, 1993—97; dir. Ctr. AIDS rsch. Dana-Farbert Inst. Beth Israel Deaconess Med. Ctr./Children's Hosp., Boston, 1994—; mem. sci. adv. bd. Ariel Project for prevention on HIV transmission from mother to infant, 1992—; mem. various coms. confs. in field; mem. external sci. adv. com. div. infectious diseases Mass. Gen. Hosp., 2000; mem. various coms.

NIH; mem. sci. adv. bd. Aaron Diamond AIDS Rsch. Ctr. City N.Y., 1989—; mem. sci. adv. bd. Ctr. Human Retrovirology Thomas Jefferson U., 1995. Editor: Jour. Virology, 1993—98; editor: (assoc. editor) AIDS Scis., 1995—; reviewing editor AIDS, 1987—90, Jour. AIDS, 1988— (Howard Temin award for basic sci., 1993), AIDS Rsch. and Human Retroviruses, 1990—, Virology, 1991—, Jour. Virology, 1998—. Recipient David Gottlieb Meml. Lectureship, U. Ill., 1993, Best of What's New award, Popular Sci. mag., 1998, Harvey Lectr., 2005, Retrovirology prize, 2006; grantee, NIH, 1986—2005, Dept. Army, 1987—90, Am. Found. AIDS Rsch., 1987—88; fellow, Damon Runyon-Walter Winchell Found., 1982, Am. Found. AIDS Rsch., 1986; scholar, Leukemia Soc. Am., 1986; postdoctoral fellow, NIH, 1981, Spl. fellow, Leukemia Soc. Am., 1985, Stohlman Meml. scholar, 1991. Mem.: AAAS, Clin. Immunology Soc., Am. Soc. Virology, Am. Soc. Microbiology, Delta Epsilon Sigma, Alpha Omega Alpha, Sigma Xi. Office: Dana-Farber Cancer Inst Dept Cancer Immunology and AIDS 44 Binney St Ctr Life Scis Bldg Rm 1009 Boston MA 02115 Office Phone: 617-632-3371. Business E-Mail: joseph_sodroski@dfci.harvard.edu.

SOE, KYAW K., medical educator; s. Kyi Soe; m. Kyawt Win Shwin. MBBS, Inst. Medicine, Yangon, Burma, MD, 2001. Diplomate Am. Bd. Internal Medicine, 2007. Asst. clin. prof. medicine SUNY Downstate Coll. Medicine, 2007—. Pres. MedAid Internal Found. Inc, NYC, 2007—; co-chair fin. com. Myanmar Am. Med. Edn. Soc., NYC, 2007—. Recipient award, Myanmar Am. Med. Edn. Soc., Inc, 2007; Govt. State scholar, Ministry Edn. Burma, 1990. Achievements include research in hepatitis C and cardiovascular risk. Business E-Mail: kyaw.soe@downsate.edu.

SOENS, LAWRENCE DONALD, bishop emeritus; b. Iowa City, Aug. 26, 1926; Student, Loras Coll., Dubuque, Iowa, St. Ambrose Coll., Davenport, Iowa, Kenrick Sem., St. Louis, U. Iowa. Ordained priest Diocese of Davenport, Iowa, 1950; ordained bishop, 1983; bishop Diocese of Sioux City, 1983—98, bishop emeritus, 1998—. Roman Catholic. Office: Chancery Office PO Box 3379 1821 Jackson St Sioux City IA 51102-3379 Office Phone: 712-233-7512. Office Fax: 712-233-7598.

SOERGEL, KONRAD HERMANN, physician; b. Coburg, Germany, July 27, 1929; came to U.S., 1954, naturalized, 1962; s. Konrad Daniel and Erna Henrietta (Schilling) S.; m. Rosina Klara Rudin, June 24, 1955; children: Elizabeth Ann, Karen Theresa, Marilyn Virginia, Kenneth Thomas. MD, U. Erlangen, Germany, 1954, Dr. med., 1958. Intern Bergen Pines County Hosp., Paramus, NJ, 1954-55; resident in pathology West Pa. Hosp., Pitts., 1955-56; rsch. asst. U. Erlangen, Germany, 1956-57; resident in medicine Mass. Meml. Hosp., Boston, 1957-58; fellow in gastroenterology Boston U. Med. Sch., 1958-60, instr., 1960-61; mem. faculty Med. Coll. Wis., Milw., 1961—, prof. medicine, 1969—2002, prof. medicine emeritus, 2003—, prof. physiology, 1993—2002, chief sect. gastroenterology, 1961-93. Chmn. gastroenterology and clin. nutrition study sect. NIH, 1979-80 Contbr. articles to profl. jours., chpts. to books. Recipient Rsch. Career Devel. award USPHS, 1963-72; Alexander von Humboldt Found. sr. fellow, 1973-74 Mem. Am. Gastroenterol. Assn., Am. Soc. Clin. Investigation, Am. Assn. Physicians, German Soc. for Digestive and Metabolic Disorders (hon.), Ger. Soc. Internal Medicine (hon.). Home: 14245 Hillside Rd Elm Grove WI 53122-1677 Office: Med Coll Wis 9200 W Wisconsin Ave Milwaukee WI 53226-3522

SOERGEL, PHILIP MARK, history professor; b. Pitts., May 23, 1959; s. Ray Clair and Donna Lee Soergel; m. Marcia Irene Willis, May 28, 1983; children: Elizabeth Lee, William James. BA, Muskingum Coll., New Concord, Ohio, 1980; AM, U. Mich., Ann Arbor, 1982, PhD, 1988. Asst. prof. history Ariz. State U., Tempe, 1989—94, assoc. prof. history, 1994—2005, U. Md., Coll. Pk., 2005—. Author: (books) Arts and Humanities Through the Eras, 2004, Wondrous in His Saints, 1993; editor: Sexuality and Culture in Medieval and Renaissance Europe, 2006; contbr. articles. Mem., editl. bd. Studies Medieval and Renaissance History, Tempe, 2005—08. Mem.: Soc. Reformation Rsch. (chair and mem., nominating com. 1995—98), Sixteenth Century Studies Soc., Am. Hist. Assn. (chair 2007—07, Leo Gershoy Prize Com.). Avocations: reading, travel, gardening. Home: 11002 Willow Bottom Dr Columbia MD 21044 Office: Univ Md Dept History College Park MD 20742 Office Fax: 301-314-9399. Business E-Mail: psoergel@umd.edu.

SOETEBER, ELLEN, journalist, editor; b. East St. Louis, Ill., June 14, 1950; d. Lyle Potter and Norma Elizabeth (Osborn) S.; m. Richard M. Martins, Mar. 16, 1974. BJ, Northwestern U., 1972. Edn. writer, copy editor Chgo. Today, 1972-74; reporter Chgo. Tribune, 1974-76, asst. met. editor, 1976-84, assoc. met. editor, 1984-86, TV and media editor, 1986, met. editor, 1987-89, assoc. mng. editor for met. news, 1989-91, dep. editor editorial page, 1991-94; mng. editor South Fla. Sun-Sentinel, Ft. Lauderdale, 1994-2001; editor St. Louis Post-Dispatch, 2001—05. Vis. faculty Poynter Inst. Journalism Studies, 2006-; presenter in field; Gaylord vis. prof. journalism and ethics, Ariz. State U., 2008. Named to Hall of Achievement, Medill Sch. Journalism, 2003; Journalism fellow, U. Mich., Ann Arbor, 1986—87. Office Phone: 954-533-2948. Personal E-mail: ellsoeteber@aol.com.

SOFAER, ABRAHAM DAVID, lawyer, former federal judge, educator, consultant; b. Bombay, May 6, 1938; arrived in U.S., 1948, naturalized, 1959; m. Marian Bea Scheuer, Oct. 23, 1977; children: Daniel E., Michael J., Helen R., Joseph S., Aaron R., Raphael J. BA in History magna cum laude, Yeshiva Coll., 1962; LLB cum laude, NYU, 1965. Bar: N.Y. 1965, D.C. 1988. Law clk. to Hon. J. Skelly Wright U.S. Ct. Appeals (DC cir.), Washington, 1965-66; law clk. to Hon. William J. Brennan Jr. US Supreme Ct., Washington, 1966-67; asst. U.S. atty. (so. dist.) NY US Dept. Justice, NYC, 1967-69; prof. law Columbia U., NYC, 1969-79; judge US Dist. Ct. (so. dist.) NY, 1979-85; legal adv. US Dept. State, Washington, 1985-90; ptnr. Hughes Hubbard & Reed, Washington, 1991-94; George P. Shultz disting. scholar, sr. fellow Hoover Instn., Stanford U., 1994—. Hearing officer N.Y. Dept. Environ. Conservation, 1975-76. Author: War, Foreign Affairs and Constitutional Power: The Origins, 1976; contbr. articles to legal, polit., fgn. jours.; editor-in-chief: NYU Law Rev, 1964-65. Served with USAF, 1956-59. Root-Tilden scholar NYU, 1965. Mem. ABA, Fed. Bar Assn., N.Y.C. Bar Assn., N.Y. Bar Assn., Am. Law Inst. Jewish. Office: Stanford Univ The Hoover Instn Stanford CA 94305-6010 Office Phone: 650-725-3763. Office Fax: 650-723-2103. Business E-Mail: sofaer@hoover.stanford.edu.

SOFGE, STEVE WAYNE, biology professor; MS, U. Tex., Permian Basin, Odessa, 1981. Instr. Odessa Coll., Tex., 1993—. Recipient Outstanding Tchg. award, Odessa Coll. Office: Odessa Coll 201 W University Odessa TX 79764

SOFMAN, MICHAEL S., dermatologist; b. Newark, Mar. 3, 1959; s. Howard and Harriet Sofman; m. Susan Abano, Sept. 20, 1987; children: Sarah, Andrew. BS in Biology, Georgetown U., Washington, 1981; MD, U. Med. and Dentistry NJ, 1985. Diplomate Am. Bd. Dermatology. Intern U. Pitts., 1985—86; resident SUNY Downtown Med. Ctr., 1986—88, chief resident NY, 1988—89; physician Sobel and Sofman, MD, PA, Hollywood, Fla., 1989—. Fellow: Am. Acad. Dermatology. Office: Sobel and Sofman MD PA 4340 Sheridan St Hollywood FL 33021 Business E-Mail: msofman@sobelandsofmanderm.com.

SOFRONIEW, MICHAEL VICTOR, medical educator; b. Detroit, July 30, 1952; s. Bojan Minko and Irmina Theresea Sofroniew; m. Patricia Eva Campbell, July 3, 1979; children: Alexandra Katherina, Nicholas James. BSc, Loyola U., LA, 1974; MD, Ludwig-Maximillians U., Munich, 1981; DPhil, U. Oxford, Eng., 1984. Demonstrator anatomy U. Oxford, 1984—85; surg. resident Johns Hopkins U., Balt., 1985—86; lectr. U. Cambridge, England, 1986—87, reader, 1997—99; prof. UCLA Sch. Medicine, 1999—. Recipient Demuth Young Investigator award, Internat. Brain Rsch. Orgn., 1984. Office: UCLA Sch Medicine 10833 Le Conte Ave Los Angeles CA 90095-1763 Business E-Mail: sofroniew@mednet.ucla.edu.

SOFTLI, TONY, professional sports team executive; b. Bellevue, Wash. s. Tony Softli. Attended, Walla Walla Jr. Coll., Wash., U. Wash., Seattle. Semi-pro football player Seattle Cavaliers, 1980—82, head football coach, dir. player pers.; semi-pro football player Eastside Express, 1983—85; assoc. Nordstrom's; purchasing dept. U. Wash., grad. asst., running backs coach, jr. coll. recruiting coord., 1991—93; computer systems analyst Boeing; head football coach Blackpool Falcons, England; regional scout Carolina Panthers, 1995—2000, dir. coll. scouting, 2000—05; v.p. player pers. St. Louis Rams, 2006—. Office: St Louis Rams One Rams Way Saint Louis MO 63045*

SOFTNESS, BARNEY, pediatrician, educator; b. Coral Gables, Fla., 1954; BA, Amherst Coll., Mass.; MD, Columbia U., NYC. Cert. in pediat. Am. Bd. Med. Specialties, 1986, in pediatric endocrinology Am. Bd. Med. Specialties, 1986. Intern in pediat. Babies Hosp., NYC, 1980—81, resident in pediatric endocrinology & metabolism, 1981—83; fellow NY Hosp.-Cornell, NYC, 1983—85; asst. clinical prof. pediatric endocrinology Columbia U. Coll. Physicians and Surgeons; pediatric endocrinologist Naomi Berrie Diabetes Ctr. NY Presbyn. Hosp., Columbia U. Med. Ctr. Named to America's Top Doctors, 2006, NY Mag. Best Doctors, 2006. Office: Naomi Berrie Diabetes Ctr Columbia U 1150 St Nicholas Ave New York NY 10032 also: NY Presbyn Hosp 450 W End Ave New York NY 10024 Office Phone: 212-851-5494. Office Fax: 212-851-5493.

SOFTNESS, DONALD GABRIEL, marketing professional, manufacturing executive; b. Bklyn. s. Burt H. and Ida (Kaiser) S.; m. Sydell Meyerson; children: Michael, Anita May, Beth. AB, NYU, 1949, MBA, 1959; L.H.D., St. John's U., 1979. Chmn. Softness Group, Inc., NYC, 1960-79; pres. Softness Groupe, NYC, 1979—, SecureVue, Inc., NYC, 1984—. V.p., maj. prin. Radio Stas. WVJ-AM-FM, Newark and NYC; mem. faculty Advt. Week seminars Advt. Age; prodr., promoter Bklyn. Rollathon (skating marathon). Co-author: Cardiologists' Guide to Health and Fitness Through Exercise, 1979; contbr. articles to bus. and trade jours. Patentee in mech. field. Served with USN. Mem. Public Relations Soc. Am., Internat. Radio TV Soc., Am. Coll. Sports Medicine Clubs: N.Y. Yacht. Home and Office: 28 Trues Dr West Islip NY 11795-5139 Office: SecureVue Inc 251 E 51st St New York NY 10022-6534 Office Phone: 212-752-5960. Business E-Mail: don@securevue.net, don@securevue.com. E-mail: softdon@aol.com.

SOFTNESS, JOHN, public relations executive; b. Bklyn., Nov. 7, 1930; s. Burt H. and Ida (Kaiser) S.; m. Leona R. Softness (dec.); m. Carol Brady Blades; children: Barney, David, Daniel. BA, U. Miami, 1955. Reporter Miami Herald, 1953; reporter Sta. WTVJ, Miami, Fla., 1954; pub. relations dir. aviation dept. Shell Oil Co., NYC, 1958-60; pres., chief exec. officer The Softness Group, Inc., NYC, 1960-91, chmn., 1992-98; spl. asst. to dean Sch. Bus. U. Miami, 1998-2000; speechwriter Mayor Alex Penelas, Miami-Dale, Fla. Spl. counselor to Bklyn. Borough pres., 1966-76; adj. prof. comm. arts St. John's U., 1981-98; adj. prof. speechwriting U. Miami, 2006; counselor comms. com. N.Y. Heart Assn.; mem. comm. coun. U. Miami. Author: (autobiography) Boy Outta Brooklyn. Dir. Alliance for Ethical Govt., Miami. Served to capt. USAF, 1955-59. Mem. Pub. Rels. Soc. Am., Pride and Alarm (chmn.), Counselors' Acad. Home and Office: 2 Grove Isle Dr Apt 210 Coconut Grove FL 33133-4102 Personal E-mail: softysr@aol.com.

SOGG, WILTON SHERMAN, lawyer; b. Cleve., May 28, 1935; s. Paul P. and Julia (Cahn) S.; m. Saralee Frances Krow, Aug. 12, 1962 (div. July 1975); 1 child, Stephanie; m. Linda Rocker Lehman, Dec. 22, 1979 (div. Dec. 1990); m. Nancy Rosenfield Walsh, June 2, 1991. AB, Dartmouth Coll., 1956; JD, Harvard U., 1959; postgrad., London Grad. Sch. Bus. Studies, 1974-76. Bar: (Ohio) 1960, (Fla) 1970, (U.S. Tax Ct.) 1961, (U.S. Supreme Ct.) 1969. Assoc. Gottfried, Ginsberg, Guren & Merritt, 1960-63, ptnr., 1963-70, Guren, Merritt, Feibel, Sogg & Cohen, Cleve., 1970-84; of counsel Hahn, Loeser, Freedheim, Dean and Wellman, Cleve., 1984-85; ptnr. Hahn Loeser & Parks LLP, Cleve., 1986-2000; of counsel McCarthy, Lebit, Crystal & Liffman Co., Cleve., 2001—. Trustee, pres. Cleve. Jewish News; adj. prof. Cleve. State U. Law Sch., 1960—; lectr. Harvard U. Law Sch., 1978-80. Author: (with Howard M. Rossen) new and rev. vols. of Smith's Review Legal Gems series, 1969—; editor: Harvard Law Rev.; contbr. articles to profl. jours. Trustee Jewish Cmty. Fedn. of Cleve., 1966-72, Black Swamp Bird Obs., 2007-; bd. overseers Cleveland Marshall Coll. Law, Cleve. State U., 1969—, vis. com. Coll. Bus. Adminstrn., 1996-2001, 2003-; mem. U.S. and State of Ohio Holocaust commns.; pres. bd. trustees Ohio Audubon Adv. Bd., 2005-07. Fulbright fellow U. London, 1959-60. Mem. Ohio Bar Assn., Fla. Bar Assn., Germany Philatelic Soc., Chagrin Valley Hunt, Rowfant Club, Phi Beta Kappa. Home: PO Box 278 Gates Mills OH 44040-0278 Office: McCarthy Lebit Crystal & Liffman 101 W Prospect Ave Ste 1800 Cleveland OH 44115-1088 Home Phone: 440-423-1809; Office Phone: 216-696-1422. Business E-Mail: wss@mccarthylebit.com.

SOH, CHUNGHEE SARAH, anthropology educator; b. Taegu, Korea, May 1, 1947; came to U.S., 1970; d. Sang Yung and Ock Yun (Choi) S.; m. Jerry Dee Boucher. BA in English summa cum laude, Sogang U., 1971; postgrad., U. Calif., Berkeley, 1971; MA in Anthropology, U. Hawaii, 1983, PhD in Anthropology, 1987. Staff instr. English Korean Air Lines, Edn. & Tng. Ctr., Seoul, 1978-79; instr. anthropology Ewha Womans U., Seoul, 1985; post-doctoral assoc. Inst. of Culture and Comm., East-West Ctr., Honolulu, 1987; asst. prof. U. Hawaii, 1990; asst. prof. anthropology Southwest Tex. State U., San Marcos, 1991-94, San Francisco State U., 1994-96, assoc. prof. anthropology, 1996—2006, prof., 2006—. Guest lectr. Chaminade U. Honolulu, 1988; vis. asst. prof. anthropology U. Ariz., 1990-91; adj. prof. Intercultural Inst. Calif., 1996-98, The Comfort Women Sexual Violence and Postcolonial Memory in Korea & Japan, 2008; cons. in field. Author: The Chosen Women in Korean Politics: An Anthropological Study, 1991, Women in Korean Politics, 1993, The Comfort Women: Sexual Violence and Postcolonial Memory in Korea and Japan, 2008; contbr. articles to profl. jour. Bd. dirs. Women Devel. Inst. Internat., 2000—. Grantee East-West Ctr., 1981-87, NSF, 1985-86; fellow Korea Found., 1993, Japan Found., 1997-98, Inst. Social Sci., U. Tokyo, 1997-98, Leiden U. Internat. Inst. for Asian Studies, The Netherlands, 1998, Inst. for Corean-Am. Studies, 1998—; Hoover Inst. scholar, 1996-97, Stanford U. Inst. for Rsch. on Women and Gender scholar, 2000-01; Rsch. and Writing grantee John D. and Catherine T. MacArthur Found., 2000-01, Fulbright Scholor grant, 2008. Fellow Am. Anthrop. Assn. (treas. East Asia sect. 2001-03), Inst. for Corean-Am. Studies; mem. Am. Ethnological Soc., Soc. Psychol. Anthropology, Assn. Asian Studies (exec. bd. Com. Women Asian Studies 1995-97), Korean Assn. Womens Studies, Royal Asiatic Soc. Korean Br. Office: San Francisco State U Dept Anthropology 1600 Holloway Ave San Francisco CA 94132-1722 Business E-Mail: soh@sfsu.edu.

SOH-HARBIN, JULIE, music educator; b. Medan, Sumatra, Indonesia, July 3, 1957; arrived in U.S., 1976; d. Hock Eng and Giok Eng Soh; m. James William Harbin, Jr., July 22, 2000; children: Vernon Mui, Vincent Mui. AA, DeKalb Coll., 1981; MusB, Mercer U., 1984; MusM, Ga. State U., 1996. Nat. cert. tchr. music. Pvt. piano tchr. Julie Piano Studio, Woodstock, Ga., 1984—. Judge for auditions Fedn. Music Clubs, Ga., 2003—. Mem.: North Fulton Music Tchrs. (audition chmn. 1998—2000, v.p. 2006—), North DeKalb Music Tchrs. (pres. 2003—05, v.p. 2006—08), Ga. Music Tchrs. Assn. (ind. music tchr. 2003—04, chair 2009—). Avocations: piano, travel, harp, yoga. Home: 812 Arnold Mill Rd Woodstock GA 30188 Business E-Mail: julieharbin@gmail.com.

SOHLMAN, MICHAEL, foundation administrator; b. Stockholm, 1944; s. Rolf R. and Zinaida (Yarotskaya) S. BA, U. Uppsala, Sweden, 1964, postgrad. in econs. and polit. sci., 1968, U. Stockholm, 1968. Asst. sec. to Commn. Environ. Problems, 1969; with Ministry of Industry, 1972-74; with internat. divsn. Ministry of Fin., 1974-76, with budget dept., 1976, head of planning econ. dept., 1982-84, dir. of budget, 1985-87; fin. counsellor, permanent Swedish del. OECD, 1977-80; with rsch. dept. Social-Dem. Parliamentary Group, 1981-82; under-sec. of state Ministry of Agriculture, 1987-89; under-sec. of state for fgn. affairs Ministry for Fgn. Affairs, 1989-91; exec. dir. Nobel Found., Stockholm, 1992—. Chmn. bd. dirs. Royal Dramatic Theatre, Stockholm, 1993-96; chmn. bd. dirs. Post Pension Fund; bd. dirs. Axel Johnson Internat. Mem. Royal Swedish Acad. Scis., Acad. of Engring. Scis. Office: Nobel Foundation PO Box 5232 102 45 Stockholm Sweden

SOHM, ALDO, Sommelier; With Alberg Hopiz, Austria, Bio Hotel Stanglwirt; wine dir., sommelier Le Bernardin, NYC, 2007—. Recipient Outstanding Wine Svc. award, James Beard Found., 2009; named Best Sommelier in Austria, 2002, 2003, 2004, 2006, Best Sommelier in the World, Worldwide Sommelier Assn., 2008. Office: Le Bernardin 155 W 51st St New York NY 10019*

SOHMER, BERNARD, mathematics professor, administrator; b. NYC, July 16, 1929; s. Sol and Florence (Schonfeld) S.; m. Margot Rosette, July 27, 1952; children: Emily Sohmer Tai, Olivia Sohmer Rosenbaum. BA, NYU, 1949, MS, 1951, PhD, 1958. Lectr. CCNY, NYC, 1952—57; asst. prof. NYU, NYC, 1957—58; faculty CCNY, NYC, 1958—2005, prof. math., 1969—2005, prof. emeritus, 2005—. Founding mem. SEEK program CCNY, NYC, 1964, dean students, 1969—72, v.p. student affairs, 1972—75, chmn. faculty senate, 1977—79, NYC, 1985—91, NYC, 2002—03, chmn. liberal arts and sci. faculty coun., 1979—85, ombudsman, 1991—98, NYC, 2002—03; trustee PSC-CUNY Welfare Fund, 1982—97; pres. Hillel, 1988—2001; sec. U. Faculty Senate CUNY, NYC, 1992—94, vice chair, 1994—98, chair, 1998—2002, ex officio bd. trustees, 1998—2002. Mem. AAAS, AAUP (pres. CCNY chpt. 1966-67, sec. 1977-78), Am. Math. Soc., Math. Assn. Am. (pres. elect NY Met. sect. 1989-90, pres. 1992-93, past pres. 1993-94, gov. 1996-98), Profl. Staff Congress (chair CCNY chpt. 1993-96, exec. coun. 1997-2000). Home: 176 E 77th St New York NY 10021 E-mail: bsohmer@earthlink.net.

SOHN, HANSUK, research scientist, educator; b. Seoul, Republic Of Korea; s. Jik-Soo Sohn and Sang-Hee Kim; m. Jeehye Seo; 1 child, Christine Joohee. BS, Sung Kyun Kwan U., Seoul, 1992; MS, U. Iowa, Iowa City, 1995, PhD, 2004. Rsch. assoc. U. Iowa, 2004—05; asst. prof. N.Mex State U., Las Cruces, 2006—. Mem.: Inst. Supply Mgmt., OR Soc., Am. Soc. Engring. Edn., Inst. Indsl. Engrs., Inst. Ops. Rsch. and Mgmt. Scis., Alpha Pi Mu. Office: NMex State U Indsl Engring MSC 4230 Las Cruces NM 88003 Office Fax: 575-646-2976. E-mail: hsohn@nmsu.edu.

SOHN, HONG YONG, chemical and metallurgical engineer, educator; b. Kaesung, Kyunggi-Do, Republic of Korea, Aug. 21, 1941; arrived in U.S., 1966; s. Chong Ku and Soon Deuk (Woo) Sohn; m. Victoria Bee Tuan Ngo, Jan. 8, 1971; children: Berkeley Jihoon, Edward Jihyun. BSChemE, Seoul Nat. U., Republic of Korea), 1962; MSChemE, U. NB, Can., 1966; PhD, U. Calif., Berkeley, 1970. Engr. Cheil Sugar Co., Busan, Republic of Korea, 1962-64; rsch. assoc. SUNY, Buffalo, 1971-73; rsch. engr. DuPont Co., Wilmington, Del., 1973-74; prof. metall. engring., adj. prof. chem. engring. U. Utah, Salt Lake City, 1974—. Cons. Lawrence Livermore Nat. Lab., 1976—, Cabot Corp., 1984—, DuPont Co., 1987—, Utah Power and Light Co., 1987—, H. C. Starck, 1997—. Co-author: (book) Gas-Solid Reactions, 1976; co-editor: Rate Processes of Extractive Metallurgy, 1979, Extractive Metallurgy of Refractory Metals, 1980, Advances in Sulfide Smelting, 2 vols., 1983, Recycle and Secondary Recovery of Metals, 1985, Gas-Solid Reactions in Pyrometallurgy, 1986, Flash Reaction Processes, 1988, Metallurgical Processes for the Year 2000 and Beyond, 1988, Metallurgical Processes for the Early Twenty-First Century, 2 vols., 1994, Proceeding of the Julian Szekely Memorial Symposium on Materials Processing, 1997, Value-Addition Metallurgy, 1998, Sulfide Smelting, 2002, Metallurgical and Materials Processing: Principles and Technologies, 3 vols., 2003; contbr. articles to profl. jours. Recipient Fulbright Disting. lectureship, 1983; Camille and Henry Dreyfus Found. Tchr. scholar, 1977, Japan Soc. Promotion Sci. fellow, 1990. Fellow: Minerals, Metals and Materials Soc. (past dir., Extractive Metallurgy Lectr. award 1990, Extraction and Processing Sci. award 1990, champion H. Mathewson Gold medal award 1993, Extraction and Processing Sci. award 1994, 1999, 2007, symposium named in his honor); mem.: AIChE, AIME (James Douglas Gold medal 2001), Korean Inst. Chem. Engrs., Korean Acad. Sci. and Tech. (Fellow award 1998). Achievements include patents for process for treating sulfide-bearing ores, continuous solvent extraction with bottom gas injection; hydrogen-storage materials. Office: U Utah 135 S 1460 E Rm 412 Salt Lake City UT 84112-0114 Office Phone: 801-581-5491. Business E-Mail: h.y.sohn@utah.edu. *Fortunate are those who earn a living by doing what they would rather be doing even if they do not have to do it to earn a living. Material wealth accumulated by doing what one does not enjoy doing is not worth the effort.*

SOHN, JUNGYUL, geographer; b. Seoul, Korea (South), Oct. 11, 1968; s. Dongin Sohn and Youngsoo Kim; m. Soo Kyoung Oh, Jan. 7, 2006; 1 child, Yeran. BA with honors, Seoul Nat. U., 1987—91, MA, 1991—93; PhD, U. of Ill., 1996—2002. Rsch. asst. U. Md., College Park, 2002—04; asst. prof. U. Memphis, 2004—06, Seoul Nat. U.,

2006—, assoc. prof., 2008—. Affiliate prof. U. Md., 2004—06; dep. to sec. gen. Internat. Geog. Union, 2007—; mem. adv. bd. BK Global and Regional Econ. Analysts Program, 2007—; urban landscape com. mem. Inchehon Free Editl. Zone Authority, 2008—; assoc. dir. pub. rels. Korean Geographers Soc., 2009—; auditor Korean Regional Sci. Assn., 2009—; dir. rsch. Korean Urban Geographical Soc., 2008—. Mem. editl. bd. Geog. Jour. of Korea, 2003—08, Korean Jour. Regional Sci., 2007—; contbr. articles to profl. jours., chapters to books. With Korean Army, 1993—95. Finalist 16 Competiton Trbout prize in regional sci., 2002; scholar, Woosan Found., 1991—93; workshop scholar, CSISS, 2004—06. Mem.: Korean Academic Soc. of Indsl. Cluster (mem. editl. bd. jour. 2007—), Regional Sci. Assn. Internat. Avocations: travel, movies, sports. Office: Seoul Nat Univ Dept Geography San 599 Gwanangno Seoul Republic of Korea Office Fax: 82-2-876-9498. Business E-Mail: jsohn@snu.ac.kr.

SOHN, LIVIA, music educator; d. Woochung Sohn; m. Geoff Nuttall, June 11, 2000; 1 child, Jack Nuttall. MusB, Juilliard Sch., NYC, 1998. Lectr. Stanford U., Calif., 2005—. Musician: (CD) Opera Fantasies. Liberal. Avocations: cooking, reading. Business E-Mail: livia@liviasohn.com.

SOHN, SUNG WON, former bank executive; b. 1945; Grad., U. Pitts., Harvard U. Sr. economist Coun. Econ. Advisors, Exec. Office of the Pres.; exec. v.p., chief econ. officer Wells Fargo Banks; pres., CEO Hanmi Fin. Corp., 2005—08. Prof. Pa. State U. Sys. Bd. dirs. LA World Affairs Coun., Children's Bur., Claremont Grad Sch. Named most accurate forcaster for We. U.S., Blue Chip Publications, 2002, most accurate economist in U.S., Wall Street Jour., 2006; named one of five most accurate forcasters in U.S., 2001, 100 most influential Minnesotans of 20th century, The Star Tribune; named to Board of Economists, Time mag., 2001.

SOHN, YOUNGKU, chemistry professor; PhD, U. BC, Vancouver, Can., 2004. Postdoc. rschr. U. Tex., Austin, 2005—, U. Waterloo, Ontario, Canada, 2007—08. Achievements include research in physical chemistry. Office: Yeungnam Univ Dept Chemistry Daedong 214-1 Gyeongsan Gyeongbuk 712-749 Republic of Korea Business E-Mail: youngkusohn@ynu.ac.kr.

SOHRABJI, FARIDA, neuroscientist, educator; PhD, U. Rochester, NY, 1990. Assoc. prof., dept. head Tex. A&M Health Sci. Ctr. Coll. Medicine, Coll. Sta., 2004—. Dir. Women's Health Neurosci. Program. Mem.: Tex. Brain and Spine Inst. (Coll. Sta.), Endocrine Soc., Soc. Neurosci. Office: Tex A&M Health Sci Ctr 228 Reynolds Medical Bldg College Station TX 77843 Business E-Mail: sohrabji@medicine.tamhsc.edu.

SOIFER, AVIAM, dean, law educator; b. Worcester, Mass., Mar. 18, 1948; married; 2 children. BA cum laude, Yale U., 1969, MA in Urban Studies, 1972, JD, 1972. Bar: Conn. 1974, U.S. Dist. Ct. Conn. 1974, U.S. Supreme Ct. 1994. Law clk. to Judge Jon O. Newman US Dist. Ct. Conn., 1972-73; asst. prof. U. Conn. Sch. Law, 1976-77, assoc. prof., 1977-78, prof., 1978-80, Boston U. Sch. Law, 1980—93; dean Boston Coll. Law Sch., 1993-98; prof. U. Hawaii Sch. Law, Honolulu, 1998—2003, dean, prof. law, 2003—. Vis. prof. Boston U. Sch. Law, 1979-80; vis. colleague William S. Richardson Sch. Law, 1999-2000. Author: Law the the Company We Keep, 1995 (Alpha Sigma Nu Nat. Jesuit Book Prize, 1998); contbr. articles to profl. jours. Vice chair Supreme Jud. Ct. Mass. Task Force on Jud. Edn., 1996-2001; mem. steering com. 1st Cir. Task Force on Gender, Race and Ethnicity, 1995-99; trustee New Eng. Med. Ctr., 1997-2002, Cambridge Health Alliance, 2002-03. Recipient Disting. Sr. Rsch. award Boston Coll., 2001-02; named Disting. Scholar Legal Studies Inst., U. Wis., 2001-; Harvard Program in Law and Humanities fellow, 1976-77; Kellog Nat. fellow, 1981-84. Mem. ABA (commn. on coll. and univ. legal studies 1996-2000. Office: William S Richardson Sch Law U Hawaii 2515 Dole St Honolulu HI 96822 Office Phone: 808-956-6343. E-mail: soifer@hawaii.edu.*

SOIFER, SCOTT JAY, pediatrician; b. 1952; MD, SUNY Upstate Med. Ctr., Syracuse, 1977. Cert. in pediat. 1981, in pediatric cardiology 1981, in pediatric critical care medicine 2002. Residency in pediat. Yale U., New Haven; fellowship in pediatric cardiology U. Calif. Med. Ctr., San Francisco, program and clin. med. dir., pediatric intensive care unit, vice chair clin. affairs, dept. pediat. Contbr. articles to profl. jours. Office: Univ Calif Med Ctr Pediatric Critical Care Medicine 505 Parnassus Ave Box 0106 San Francisco CA 94143 Office Phone: 415-476-5153. Office Fax: 415-476-6083. Business E-Mail: SoiferS@peds.ucsf.edu.

SOILEAU, MONICA MARIE, economist; d. Freddie George Singleton and Molly Anne Guillory; m. Rolland Soileau, May 13, 1995; children: Hailey Paige, Heather Elaine. Student, U. Phoenix Online, 2000—07. Cert. therapon belief therapist The Therapon Inst., 2007; Christian marriage and family therapist Am. Soc. Christian Therapists, 2007. Operator process unit ConocoPhillips, Westlake, La., 1993—98; optimization economics analyst ConocoPhillips Oil Refinery, Westlake, 1998—. Planning staff ConocoPhillips, Westlake, 1998—. Author: The Forgotten Victims. Vol. The Women's Shelter, Lake Charles, La., 2000—07, ARC, Lake Charles, 2000—07; fund raiser com. & vol. Am. Heart Assn., Lake Charles, 2003—07; vol. and fund raiser Am. Cancer Soc., Lake Charles, 2003—07; loaned exec. United Way, Lake Charles, 2006—07; vol. Partners In Edn., Westlake, 2005—07. Named Outstanding Vol., ConocoPhillips, 2004, 2005, 2006. Personal E-mail: monica_conoco@yahoo.com.

SOILEAU, VERONICA DEMORUELLE, counselor, educator; d. Joseph Edison Demoruelle and Vernice Marie La Haye-Demoruelle; m. Robert B. Soileau (div.); children: Blaine Philip, Alyson Camille, Shanon Gerard. BA, U. Southwestern La., Lafayette, 1963; MEd, McNeese State U., La., 1992. Lic. profl. counselor LA Bd. Examiners, 1994, nat. cert. counselor Nat. Bd. Cert. Counselors, N.C., 1995, lic. profl. counselor Tex. Bd. Examiners of LPC Prin. PR-12 cir., 2005. Dir. counseling ctr. Charter Lake Charles, Lake Charles, La.; clin. mgr. Vol. of Am., Lake Charles, La.; sch. counselor Goose Creek Ind. Sch. Dist., Baytown, Tex., 2002—. Avocations: travel, reading. Office: Robert E Lee HS 1809 Market St Baytown TX 77520 Home Phone: 281-426-8589. Personal E-mail: vsoileau@comcast.net. Business E-Mail: vdsoileau@gccisd.net.

SOJKA, GARY ALLAN, biologist, educator, academic administrator; b. Cedar Rapids, Iowa, July 15, 1940; s. Marvin F. and Ruth Ann (Waddington) Sojka Green; m. Sandra Kay Smith, Aug 5, 1962; children: Lisa Kay, Dirk Allan. BS, Coe Coll., 1962; MS, Purdue U., 1965; PhD, Purdue U., Lycoming Coll., 1967; DL (hon.), Purdue U., 2002; DSc (hon.), Lycoming Coll. Bucknell U., 1995; DHL (hon.), 2009. Rsch. assoc. Ind. U., Bloomington, 1967-69, asst. prof., 1969-73, assoc. prof., 1973-79, prof., 1979-84, assoc. chmn. biology, 1977-79, chmn. biology, 1979-81, dean arts and scis., 1981-84; pres. Bucknell U., Lewisburg, Pa., 1984-95, prof. biology, 1984—2006, prof., pres. emeritus, 2006; interim pres. Assn. Coll. & Univs., Pa., 1995—97; commr. Pa. Gaming Control Bd., 2007—. Mem. higher edn. commn. Mid. States Assn. Colls. and Schs., 1992-96, chmn. task force on instnl. effectiveness, 1999-2000; chmn. tax policy subcom. Nat. Assn. Ind. Colls. and Univs., 1991-93; mem. study group on internat. edn. Am. Coun. Edn., 1992-94. Mem. So. Ind. Health Sys. Agy., Bedford; emeritus bd. dir. Geisinger Health Sys.; vice-chair Am. Livestock Conservancy, 2003—05, chmn. bd., 2005—07; bd. trustee Coe Coll., 2009—; chmn. bd. dirs. Stone Belt Coun. Ret. Citizens, Bloomington, 1977—78; mem. nominating com. Ind. Assn. Ret. Citizens, Indpls., 1979; bd. dirs. Geisinger Med. Found., Danville, Pa., 1985—97, 2003—06, mem. regional bd., 1997—2003; chmn. Pa. Assn. Ind. Colls. and Univs., 1989—90; mem. pres.'s commn. NCAA, 1993—95; mem. planning adv. com. Snyder County, Pa., 1996—98, mem. planning commn., 2001—; bd. dirs. Bethesda Found., Lewisburg, 1996—98; trustee, bd. dirs. Am. Livestock Conservancy, 2001—08, vice chair, 2003—05, chair bd., 2006—08; dir. WITF Public Broadcasting, Harrisburg, bd. trustees, 2003—06; commr. Pa. Gaming Control Bd., 2007; gov. Inst. European Studies, 0989—1994, Citizen for the Future of Pa., 1999—. Recipient Ind. U. Sr. Class Tchg. award, 1975, Frederick B. Lieber award, 1977, Coe Coll. Alumni award of merit, 1982, Gary A. Sojka award Bucknell U., 1992, Cmty. Leadership award Susquahanna Valley Boy Scouts, 1994, Sheepskin award for Disting. Svc. to Higher Edn. Pa. Assn. Colls. and Univs., 2000, ECAC Appreciation award, Bucknell U., 2003, Adam Smith award Econ. Pa., 2003, Disting. Svc. medal Reading (Pa.) Ind. Day Coms., 2004; named to Coe Coll. Athletic Hall of Fame, 1988, Bucknell U. Athletic Hall of Fame, 2006; Gary A. Sojka Pavillion named in his honor, 2003. Mem.: AAAS, Pa. Assn. Coll. and Univs. (interim pres. 1997—98, exec. com., pres., Sheepskin award 1999), Phila. Soc. Promotion of Agriculture (pres. 2006—07), Am. Coun. Edn. (study group on internat. edn. 1992—94), Nat. Assn. Independent Colls. and Univs. (subcom. chmn. 1991—93), Am. Soc. Biol. Chemists, Am. Acad. Microbiology, Am. Soc. Microbiology, Phi Beta Kappa (hon.; pres. 2007—), Omicron Delta Kappa, Sigma Nu, Sigma Xi. Baptist. Business E-Mail: gsojka@bucknell.edu.

SOJKA, NICKOLAS JOSEPH, JR., lawyer; b. Durham, NC, Aug. 30, 1962; s. Nickolas Joseph and Eleanor Cox Sojka; m. Lucy Purcell, Apr. 13, 1991; children: Eleanor Purcell, Joseph Augustus. BA, Coll. William and Mary, Williamsburg, Va., 1984; JD, U. Va., Charlottesville, Va., 1987. Bar: N.C. 1987, S.C. 1993, U. S. Dist. Ct. (we. dist.) N.C. 1987, U. S. Dist. Ct. (mid. dist.) N.C. 1988, U. S. Dist. Ct. (ea. dist.) N.C. 1989, U. S. Ct. Appeals (4th cir.) 1995. Assoc. Parker Poe Adams & Bernstein, LLP, Charlotte, NC, 1987—93; ptnr. Williamson, Dean, Williamson & Sojka, LLP, Laurinburg, NC, 1993—. Contbr. chapters to books. Co-chmn. local area campaign St. Andrews Presbyn. Coll., Laurinburg, 2001—02; leader webelos den Cub Scout Pack 420, Laurinburg, 2003—05; chmn. bd. deacons Laurinburg Presbyn. Ch., 2002—03, elder, 2005—08; chmn. Laurinburg Downtown Revitalization Corp., NC, 2003—04; chmn. Scotland County chpt. ARC, Laurinburg, 2004—05; chmn. Scotland County Tourism Devel. Authority, Laurinburg, 2006—. Mem.: ABA, N.C. Coun. Sch. Attys., N.C. Bar Assn., Laurinburg Jaycees (pres. 1995—96). Presbyn. Avocation: history. Home: 701 Morrison Ln Laurinburg NC 28352 Office: Williamson Dean Williamson & Sojka 213C East Cronly St Laurinburg NC 28352 Office Fax: 910-276-1011. Personal E-mail: lpsojka@live.com. Business E-Mail: nsojka@williamsondean.com.

SOJKA, PAUL E., engineering educator; b. Detroit, Apr. 10, 1954; s. John Frank and Barabara Ann Sojka; m. Karole Anne Timmons, Apr. 13, 2002; children: Jason Matthew Shamp, Joseph Michael Shamp, Ellen Eileen, Kayla Denise Shamp, Ann Elizabeth, Phillip Christopher. PhD in Mech. Engring., Mich. State U., 1983. Adj. assoc. prof. mech. and indsl. engring. U. Ill. Urbana-Champaign; asst. prof. Purdue U., West Lafayette, Ind., 1983—89, assoc. prof., 1989—99, prof. mech. engring., 1999—, co-dir. bio-sprays ctr., 2000—; SEW vis. prof. Tech. U., Karlsruhe, Baden-Wurtemburg, Germany, 2008. Faculty fellowship, Am. Western Univs., 1991. Mem.: ASME. Achievements include patents for consumer product package incorporating a spray device utilizing large diameter bubbles. Office: Purdue Univ Sch Mech Engring West Lafayette IN 47907 Office Fax: 765-494-1536. Business E-Mail: sojka@ecn.purdue.edu.

SOKAL, ROBERT REUVEN, biology professor, writer; b. Vienna, Jan. 13, 1926; came to U.S., 1947, naturalized 1958; s. Siegfried and Klara (Rattner) S.; m. Julie Chen-Chu Yang, Aug. 12, 1948; children: David Jonathan, Hannah Judith. BS in Biology, St. John's U., Shanghai, China, 1947; PhD in Zoology, U. Chgo., 1952; DSc (hon.), U. Crete, Greece, 1990. From instr. to prof. U. Kans., Lawrence, 1951-69; prof., then leading prof., Disting. prof. SUNY, Stony Brook, 1969-95, dept. chmn., 1980-83, vice provost for rsch. and grad. studies, 1981-82, disting. prof. emeritus, 1995. Fulbright vis. prof. Hebrew/Tel Aviv U., Israel, 1963-64, U. Vienna, Austria, 1977, 78, 84; vis. prof. Inst. Adv. Studies, Oeiras, Portugal, 1971-80; vis. disting. prof. U. Mich., 1975-76; vis. prof. Coll. de France, Paris, 1989. Author: Principles of Numerical Taxonomy, 1963, Biometry, 1969, 3d rev. edit., 1995, Statistical Tables, 1969, 3rd rev. edit. 1995, Introduction to Biostatistics, 1973, 2d rev. edit., 1987-2004, Numerical Taxonomy, 1973; editor Am. Naturalist, 1969-74. Recipient Charles Darwin Lifetime Achievement award in phys. anthropology, 2004; Career investigator NIH, 1964-69; sr. fellow NSF, 1959-60, NATO fellow, 1974, Guggenheim fellow, 1975-76, 84; Ctr. Advanced Study in Behavioral Sci. fellow, 1992-93. Fellow AAAS, Am. Acad. Arts and Scis.; mem. Soc. Study Evolution (pres. 1977), Am. Soc. Naturalists (hon. mem., pres. 1984), The Classification Soc. (pres. 1969-71), Internat. Fedn. Classification Socs. (pres. 1988-89), Nat. Acad. Scis., Linnean Soc. London (fgn.), Soc. Systematic Zoology (hon.), Natural History Mus. (Paris, corr. mem.), B'nai Brith Lodge (pres. 1966). Democrat. Jewish. Office: Stony Brook Univ Dept Ecology and Evolution Stony Brook NY 11794-5245

SOKOL, DAVID LEE, utilities company executive; b. Omaha, Nebr., 1956; m. Peggy Sokol; children: D.J.(dec.), Kelly. BSCE, U. Nebr., Omaha, 1978; Ph.D (hon.), Bellevue U., Nebr., 1997. With Henningson, Durham and Richardson, Inc. (HDR, Inc.), 1978—82, Citicorp, 1982—83; pres., CEO Ogden Projects, Inc., 1983—91, Peter Kiewit Energy Company, 1991; chmn., pres., CEO MidAmerican Energy Holdings Co. (formerly CalEnergy Co., Inc.), Des Moines, 1991—2008, chmn., 2008—; interim chmn., CEO NetJets Inc. (formerly Exec. Jet, Inc.), Woodbridge, NJ, 2009—. Co-chmn. for Campaign Nebr., U. Nebr. Found., chmn. Omaha Met. Entertainment & Convention Authority; bd. dirs. Creighton U., Coll. World Series Omaha, Inc., Omaha Airport Authority, Strategic Command Consultation Co., Joslyn Art Mus., River City Roundup and Rodeo, Nebr. Easter Seal Soc., Mt. Michael Abbey H.S., Archdiocese of Omaha, Girls, Inc., Mid-Am. Coun. Boy Scouts Am., Muscular Sclerosis Soc.-Midlands Chpt., United Way Midlands, Edison Electric Inst.; mem. bd. dirs. NCAA Leadership Advisory Recipient Alumnus Achievement award, U. Nebr. Alumni Assn., 1992, Whitney M. Young, Jr. award, Boy Scouts America-Mid. America Coun., 1993, Heritage Patron award, 1993, Silver Beaver award, 1996, Viking of Distinction award, Omaha North H.S., 1996, Industrial Entrepreneur of Yr., Iowa/Nebr. Region, 1997, Disting. Grad. award, Nat. Catholic Edn. Assn., 1998, Order of the Tower award, U. Nebr., 1998, Community Svc. award, Chancellor's Commn. on Status of Women, U. Nebr., 1999, Mancuso award, Omaha Sportscasters Assn., 2000, Individual Achievement award, The Energy Daily, 2001, Omaha Bus. Hall of Fame award, Greater Omaha Found., 2004, Waite Medal for Leadership award, Creighton U., 2004; named Exec. of Yr., Alternative Sources Energy mag., 1988, Maverick Man of Yr., U. Nebr., 1996, CEO of Yr., Financial Times Energy, 2000, Volunteer of Yr., Greater Omaha C. of C., 2001; named one of 40 Under 40, Crain's NY Bus., 1990. Mem. Del. Assn. Profl. Engrs., Neb. Soc. Profl. Engrs.; life mem., Omicron Delta Kappa U. Nebr., 1994-, Horatio Alger Assn., 2004-; bd. govs. Knights of Ak-Sar-Ben Avocations: hockey, hunting, fishing, running, horseback riding. Office: MidAm Energy Holdings Co 666 Grand Ave PO Box 657 Des Moines IA 50303-0657*

SOKOL, ERIC RUSSELL, urogynecologist, reconstructive surgeon, educator; b. Rapid City, SD, Jan. 18, 1972; s. Robert James and Roberta Sue Sokol; m. Karin Nicole Stitt, Aug. 25, 2001; children: Aria Helene, Zachary Eli. MD, Wayne State U., Detroit, 1998. Diplomate Am. Bd. Ob-Gyn. Ob-gyn resident Northwestern U., Chgo., 2002, resident physician, 1998—2002; tchg. fellow, urogynecology & reconstructive pelvic surgery Brown U. Sch. Medicine, Providence, 2002—05; asst. prof. ob-gyn, co-dir. urogynecology & pelvic reconstructive surgery Stanford (Calif.) U. Sch. Medicine, 2005—. Mem. grad. med. edn. com. Med. Sch. Brown U., Providence, 2003—05, instr. surg. skills course, 2003; dir. gyn. clinics Stanford Hosps. and Clinics, 2006—. Editor: The Requisites - Gynecology. Vol. physician Hosp. Maternidad, Dominican Republic, 2003. Recipient Alpha Omega Alpha, Wayne State U. Sch. of Medicine, 1998, Undergraduate Med. Edn. Rsch. Award, APGO/Ortho-McNeil, 2004. Mem.: ACOG (assoc.), Am. Assn. Gynecologic Laparoscopists (assoc.), Assn. Profs. Gynecology and Obstetrics (assoc.), Am. Urogynecologic Soc. (assoc.; lectr. 2004—), Phi Beta Kappa. Achievements include research exploring novel minimally invasive surgical treatment options for incontinence and prolapse. Avocations: travel, gourmet cooking, art, hockey. Office: Stanford U Sch Medicine 300 Pasteur Dr Rm HH333 MC: 5317 Stanford CA 94305 Office Fax: 650-723-7737. Business E-Mail: esokol@stanford.edu.

SOKOL, JASON, historian; s. Frederic and Betsy Pirtle Sokol; life ptnr. Nina Louise Morrison. BA, Oberlin Coll., Ohio, 1999; PhD, U. Calif., Berkeley, 2006. Mellon postdoc fellow U. Pa., Phila., 2008—; vis. asst. prof. Cornell U., Ithaca, NY, 2006—08. Author: (book) There Goes My Everything: White Southerners in the Age of Civil Rights (Top 10 books of Yr., Jonathan Yardley, Wash. Post, 2006). Recipient James Kettner Grad. prize, U. Calif., Berkeley, 2006; Jacob K. Javits fellowship, US Dept. Edn., 2001—05. Mem.: Am. Hist. Assn., Phi Beta Kappa. Avocation: basketball. Office: Univ Pa 3619 Locust Walk Philadelphia PA 19104-6213 Personal E-mail: jasonsokol@hotmail.com.

SOKOL, JENNIFER MARIE, musician, writer; b. Seattle, Mar. 26, 1958; d. Vilem and Agatha Sokol. BA in violin performance, Ind. U. Founder, first violinist, mgr. Cameo String Quartet. Author: Six Years of Grace: Caregiging Episodes With My Mother, 2007; freelance writer: Cath. Northwest Progress; contbr. articles various profl. jours. Recipient Pres. award for Literary Excellence, Nat. Authors Registry, 2004. Roman Cath. Avocations: reading, ballet, outdoor recreation. Home: 6303 NE 185th St Kenmore WA 98028 Office Phone: 425-485-8380. E-mail: jennifermsokol@aol.com.

SOKOL, MARIAN, medical association administrator; PhD in Early Childhood Spl. Edn., Univ. Tex., Austin; postdoctoral M in Pub. Health, Univ. Tex. Health Sci. Ctr., Houston. Founding dir. Any Baby Can Inc., 1982—2003; pres. First Candle/SIDS Alliance, 2003—. Vice chair Gov. Commn. for Women, Tex., 1991—93; commr. Nat. Adv. Comn. on Childhood Vaccines, 1995, chair, 97, 98; bd. chair Nat. SIDS Alliance. Founding chair Tex. Network for Medically Fragile and Chronically Ill Children. Recipient Imagineeer award, Mind Sci. Found., 1987, Excellence 90 Health Care Profl. award, Women's Coalition, Prudential HealthCare's Salute to San Antonio's Good Health award, 1996, San Antonio Cmty. of Churches award, 2001; named to San Antonio Women's Hall of Fame. Office: First Candle/SIDS Alliance Ste 210 1314 Bedford Ave Pikesville MD 21208 Office Phone: 800-221-7437. Business E-Mail: marian.sokol@firstcandle.org.*

SOKOL, ROBERT JAMES, obstetrician, gynecologist, educator; b. Rochester, NY, Nov. 18, 1941; s. Eli and Mildred (Levine) S.; m. Roberta Sue Kahn, July 26, 1964; children: Melissa Anne, Eric Russell, Andrew Ian. BA in Philosophy with highest distinction, U. Rochester, 1963, MD with honors, 1966. Diplomate Am. Bd. Ob-gyn. (assoc. examiner 1984-86), Sub-Bd. Maternal-Fetal Medicine. Intern Barnes Hosp., Washington U., St. Louis, 1966—67, resident in ob-gyn., 1967—70, asst. in ob-gyn., 1966—70, rsch. asst., 1967—68, instr. clin. ob-gyn., 1970; Buswell fellow in maternal fetal medicine Strong Meml. Hosp.-U. Rochester, 1972—73; fellow in maternal-fetal medicine Cleve. Met. Gen. Hosp.-Case Western Res. U., 1974—75, assoc. obstetrician and gynecologist, 1973—83, asst. prof. ob-gyn., 1973—77; asst. program dir. Perinatal Clin. Rsch. Ctr., 1973—78, co-program dir., 1978—82, program dir., 1982—83, acting dir. obstetrics, 1974—75, co-dir., 1977—83, assoc. prof., 1977—81, prof., 1981—83, assoc. dir. dept. ob-gyn., 1981—83; prof. ob-gyn. Wayne State U., Detroit, 1983—2000, dist. prof. ob-gyn., 2000—, chmn. dept. ob-gyn., 1983—89, mem. grad. faculty dept. physiology, 1984—, interim dean Med. Sch., 1988—89, dean, 1989—99, pres. Fund for Med. Rsch. and Edn., 1988—99, interim dir. Applied Genomics Ctr., 2004—; chief ob-gyn. Hutzel Hosp., Detroit, 1983—89; interim chmn. med. bd. Detroit Med. Ctr., 1988—89, chmn. med. bd., 1989—99, sr. v.p. med. affairs, 1992—99, trustee, 1990—99; past pres. med. staff Cuyahoga County Hosps.; mem. profl. adv. bd. Educated Childbirth Inc., 1976—80; dir. C.S. Mott Ctr. for Human Growth and Devel., 1983—89, 1999—, John M. Malone Jr. MD endowed chair & dir, 2009—. Sr. obstet. cons. Symposia Medicus; cons. Grant Planning Task Force Robert Wood Johnson Found., Nat. Inst. Child Health and Human Devel., Nat. Inst. Alcohol Abuse and Alcoholism, Ctr. for Disease Control, NIH, Health Resources and Svcs. Adminstrn., Nat. Clearinghouse for Alcohol Info., APA; mem. alcohol psychosocial rsch. rev. com. Nat. Inst. Alcohol Abuse and Alcoholism, 1982-86; mem. ob-gyn. adv. panel U.S. Pharmacopial Conv., 1985-90, adv. com. on policy Am. Jour. Ob-gyn., 1999-2001, internat. adv. bd. Karmanos Cancer Inst., Detroit, Mich., 2002-04; mem. clin. rsch. task force Assn. Am. Med. Colls., 1998-2000; mem. WSU Faculty Devel. Coun., 2003—. Mem. internat. editl. bd. Israel Jour. Obstetrics and Gynecology; reviewer med. jours.; mem. editl. bd. Jour. Perinatal Medicine; editor-in-chief Interactions: Programs in Clinical Decision-Making, 1987-90; rschr. computer applications in perinatal medicine, alcohol-related birth defects, perinatal risk and neurobehavioral devel.; contbr. chpts. to books and articles to profl. jours. Mem. Pres.'s leadership coun. U. Rochester, 1976—80, permanent trustee, 1986—; mem. exec. com. bd. trustees Southeast Mich. Ctr. Med. Edn., 1987—2000; chmn. Friends of the Grand Theatre, 2005—; mem. rsch. adv. com. Wayne State U., 2005—; mem. fetal alcohol spectrum disorders prevention adv. com. CDC and Prevention, 2005—07, mem. sci. review group, 2007; bd. dirs. Am. U. Caribbean,

2001—, vice chair, 2007—, 2004; trustee Stratford Am., 2004—, pres., 2007—, Grand Theatre, London, Ont., Canada, 2007, bd. dirs., 2002—. Maj. M.C. USAF, 1970—72. Recipient 15 sci. rsch. awards, 1986—, Disting. Svc. award, Wayne State U., Sch. Medicine, 2004. Mem.: APHA, ACOG (chmn. steering com. drug and alcohol abuse contract 1986—87, rep. ctr. for disease control & prevention task force 2000—07, editor-in-chief ACOG Update 2001—, Outstanding Dist. Svc. Excellence award 2006), NAS (Inst. of Medicine, com. to study fetal alcohol syndrome 1994—96), AMA, Am. Bd. Addiction Medicine, Soc. Maternal-Fetal Medicine Found. (found. bd. chmn. 2003—06, award for dedication and leadership 2007), Soc. Physicians Reproductive Choice and Health, World Assn. Perinatal Medicine, Internat. Soc. Computers in Obstetrics, Neonatology, Gynecology (v.p. 1987—89, pres. 1989—92), Soc. for Neuroscis. (Mich. chpt.), Am. Med. Soc. on Alcoholism and Other Drug Dependencies, Am. Gynecol. and Obstet. Soc., Neurobehavioral Teratology Soc., Soc. Perinatal Obstetricians (pres.-elect 1987—88, pres. 1988—89, v.p., Achievement award 1995), Rsch. Soc. Alcoholism, Ctrl. Assn. Obstetricians-Gynecologists (pres.-elect 1997—99, pres. 1999—2000), Detroit Acad. Medicine (pres.-elect 1999—2001, pres. 2001—02), Wayne County Med. Soc., Mich. Med. Soc., Royal Soc. Medicine, Assn. Profs. Ob-gyn., Perinatal Rsch. Soc., Soc. Gynecologic Investigation, Am. Med. Informatics Assn., Chgo. Gynecol. Soc. (hon.), Detroit Physiol. Soc. (hon.), Wayne State U. Acad. Scholars (pres. 2006—07), Alpha Omega Alpha, Sigma Xi, Phi Beta Kappa. Republican. Jewish. Achievements include named chair of molecular and obstetrics and gynecology, WSV. Home: 7921 Danbury Dr West Bloomfield MI 48322-3581 Office: Wayne State U CS Mott Ctr for Human Growth and Devel Detroit MI 48201 Office Phone: 313-577-1337. Business E-Mail: rsokol@moose.med.wayne.edu. *The drive for academic accomplishment was instilled early in childhood in a home environment which placed value on a multiplicity of interests in science and the arts. My parents taught me what to do. In retrospect, exposure to strong role models-professors of philosophy, pathology, psychiatry and obstetrics-gynecology-takes on increased importance-these individuals showed me how to do it. My family continues to support me in seeking and meeting new challenges. The opportunity to develop and transmit new knowledge sustains a high level of activity. I enjoy what I do.*

SOKOL, RONALD JAY, pediatric gastroenterologist, researcher; b. Chgo., July 18, 1950; s. Max Charles and Edith Sokol; m. Lori Lubman, Aug. 20, 1989; children: Skylar Paul, Jared Todd. BS, U. Ill., 1972; MD, U. Chgo., 1976. Diplomate Am. Bd. Pediat., Am. Bd. Pediatric Gastroenterology. Asst. prof. pediat. U. Colo., Denver, 1983—88; assoc. prof. pediat. U. Colo. Sch. Medicine, Denver, 1989—95, prof. pediat., 1995—, vice chair pediat., 1999—. Program dir. Pediatric Gen. Clin. Rsch. Ctr., Denver, 1998—2008, head sect. pediat. gastroenterology, hepatology and nutrition, 2006—; dir. and prin. investigator Colo. Clin. and Translational Scis. Inst., 2008—. Editor: (med. textbook) Liver Disease in Children. Chair children's liver coun. Am. Liver Found., NYC, 1997—2003. Rsch. grantee, NIH, 1985—. Fellow: Am. Acad. Pediat. (nutrition rsch. award 2003); mem.: Am. Pediat. Soc., N. Am. Soc. for Pediat. Gastroenterology, Hepatology and Nutrition (pres. 1996—98), Am. Assn. for Study of Liver Disease, Soc. Pediat. Rsch., Am. Gastroent. Assn. Achievements include patents for antioxidant solution for treatment of cholestatic liver disease and for treatment of non-alcoholic steatohepatitis. Business E-Mail: sokol.ronald@tchden.org.

SOKOLOFF, LOUIS, retired physiologist, neuroscientist; b. Phila., Oct. 14, 1921; married; 2 children. BA, U. Pa., 1943, MD, 1946; MD (hon.), U. Lund, Sweden, 1980; ScD (hon.), Yeshiva U, NY, 1982, U. Glasgow, UK, 1989, Philipps U. Marburg, Germany, 1990; MD (hon.), U. Rome, 1992; ScD (hon.), Georgetown U., Washington, 1992, Mich. State U., Lansing, 1993, U. Pa., Phila., 1997. Intern Phila. Gen. Hosp., 1946-47; rsch. fellow in physiology U. Pa. Grad. Sch. Medicine, 1949-51, instr., then assoc., 1951-56; assoc. chief, then chief sect. cerebral metabolism NIMH, Bethesda, Md., 1953-68, chief lab. cerebral metabolism, 1968—2004, emeritus scientist, 2004—. Chief editor Jour. Neurochemistry, 1974-78. Pvt. 1st class US Army, 1943—46, capt. MC US Army, 1947—49. Recipient F.O. Schmitt medal in neurosci., 1980, Albert Lasker clin. med. research award, 1981, Karl Spencer Lashley award Am. Philos. Soc., 1987, Disting. Grad. award U. Pa., 1987, Nat. Acad. Scis. award in Neurosci., 1988, Georg Charles de Hevesy Nuclear Medicine Pioneer award Soc. Nuclear Medicine, 1988, Mihara Cerebrovascular Disorder Rsch. Promotion award, 1988, Ralph Gerard award Soc. Neuroscience, 1996, Lifetime Achievement award Internat. Soc. Cereb and Mental Health, 1999. Mem. NAS, Inst. Medicine (sr.), Am. Physiol. Soc., Assn. Rsch. Nervous and Mental Diseases, Am. Biophys. Soc., Am. Neurol. Assn., Am. Philos. Soc., Am. Acad. Arts & Sci., Am. Soc. Biol. Chemists, Am. Soc. Neurochemistry, Internat. Soc. Neurochemistry, Internat. Soc. Cereb Blood Flow & Metab. Independent. Jewish. Achievements include development of methods for measurement of cerebral blood flow, metabolism and imaging of local functional activity in the brains of animals and man, and application of this for functional imaging in the brains of animals and man. Office: NIMH/NIH Bldg 49 Rm 1B80 9000 Rockville Pike Bethesda MD 20892-4030 Office Phone: 301-496-1371. Business E-Mail: louissokoloff@mail.nih.gov.

SOKOLOV, RICHARD SAUL, real estate company executive; b. Phila., Dec. 7, 1949; s. Morris and Estelle Rita S.; m. Susan Barbara Saltzman, Aug. 13, 1972; children: Lisa, Anne, Kate. BA, Pa. State U., 1971; JD, Georgetown U., 1974. Assoc. Weinberg & Green, Balt., 1974-80, ptnr., 1980-82; v.p., gen. counsel The Edward J. DeBartolo Corp., Youngstown, Ohio, 1982-86, sr. v.p. devel., gen. coun., 1986-94; pres., CEO DeBartolo Realty Corp., Youngstown, Ohio, 1994-96; pres., COO Simon DeBartolo Group, Indpls., 1996-98; pres, COO Simon Property Group, Indpls., 1998—. Mem. investment com. Jewish Fedn., Youngstown, 1992—; trustee U. Wis.-Madison Ctr. for Urban Land Econs. Rsch., Youngstown/Mahoning Valley United Way. Alumni fellow Pa. State U., 2000. Mem. Internat. Coun. Shopping Ctrs. (trustee 1994—, chmn. 1998-99), Am. Jewish Com. (bd. govs.). Office: Simon Property Group 225 W Washington St Indianapolis IN 46204-3464

SOKOLOV, YURI, engineer; b. Kaliningrad, Russia, Mar. 20, 1947; s. Vladimir Ivanovich Sokolov and Zoya Michailovna Sokolova; m. Rita Perelzvaig; children: Dmitry, Vladimir. PhD in Physics, Poly. U., Kharkov, Ukraine, 1974. Physics analytical lab. leader Poly. U., 1976—97, assoc. prof., physics, 1979—97; staff process engr. Fairchild Semiconductor, West Jordan, Utah, 2002—. Contbr. scientific papers. Recipient J. Soros award, 1997, Build-In Quality award, 2003—08. Mem.: Electrochem. Soc. Achievements include 5 patents. Home: 8055 Angel St Sandy UT 84070 Personal E-mail: yusokol@hotmail.com

SOKOLOWSKI, THOMAS WILLIAM, museum director; b. Chgo. BA in Art History, U. Chgo., 1972; MA, Inst. Fine Arts, NYU, 1974, PhD, 1976. Curator, European painting and sculpture Chrysler Mus., 1981—82, chief curator, 1982—84; dir. Grey Art Gallery & Study Ctr., NYU, 1984—96, Andy Warhol Mus., Pitts., 1996—. Bd. dirs. MacDowell Colony, 1991—95. TV arts corr.: F/X Cable TV Network, 1994—; mem. editl. bd.: Art + Text, 1993—. Bd. dirs. Penny McCall Found., 1989—, Artist & Homeless Collaborative, 1991—93, Visual AIDS, 1990—94, bd. pres., 1992—94; bd. dirs. Dance Alloy, Pitts., 1996—, Pitts. AIDS Task Force, 1998—. Mem.: Greater Pitts. Art Alliance. Office: Andy Warhol Mus 117 Sandusky St Pittsburgh PA 15212 Office Phone: 412-237-8354. Office Fax: 412-237-8340. Business E-Mail: sokolowskit@warhol.org.

SOKOLSKY, ROBERT LAWRENCE, journalist; b. Boston, May 18, 1928; s. Henry and Lillian (Gorodetzky) S.; m. Sally-Ann Moss, Aug. 11, 1955; 1 son, Andrew E. AB, Syracuse U., NY, 1950. Reporter Springfield (Mass.) Union, 1950; asst. dir. pub. info. ARC, Syracuse, 1952-54; entertainment editor Syracuse Herald-Jour., 1954-61, Buffalo Courier Express, 1961-72, Phila. Bull., 1972-82; entertainment writer Riverside (Calif.) Press-Enterprise, 1983-2000; syndicated TV columnist Ottaway News Svc., 1988-96, Scripps Howard, 1996-2000; freelance writer, radio commentator pub. radio, 2000—; columnist San Bernardino Sun, 2001—08; entertainment editor Inland Empire News Radio, 2001—; feature writer instantriverside.com, 2005—. Radio show host; freelance writer; guest lectr. Contbr. columns in newspapers, 2001, articles to profl. jours. Bd. dirs. Brush Hollow Civic Assn., Evesham Twp., N.J. Served with U.S. Army, 1950-52. Recipient Sigma Delta Chi award for feature writing, 1950, award for entertainment coverage Twin Counties Press Club, 1984, 87, Lifetime Achievement award Inland Theatre League, 2001. Mem. Am. Newspaper Guild (Page One award for opinion writing), Syracuse Press Club, Greater Buffalo Press Assn., TV Critics Assn., Soc. Profl. Journalists (Excellence in Journalism award 1989, 93), Pen and Pencil Club of Phila., Variety Club. Republican. Jewish. Home and Office: 3080 Saratoga St Riverside CA 92503-5435 Home Phone: 951-785-0798. Personal E-mail: bsokolsky@gmail.com. E-mail: rsokolsky@charter.net.

SOKULSKI, GARY A., lawyer; BSBA, Robert Morris Coll., 1979. CPA Price Waterhouse, 1981—92; joined Reed Smith LLP, Pitts., 1992, now COO, mem. mgmt. com. & exec. com. Mem.: Pitts. Legal Administrators Assn., Pa. Inst. CPAs, Assn. Legal Administrators, Am. Inst. CPAs. Office: Reed Smith LLP 435 Sixth Ave Pittsburgh PA 15219 Office Phone: 412-288-4232. Office Fax: 412-288-3063. Business E-Mail: gsokulski@reedsmith.com.

SOLA, JURE, electronics executive; BSEE, San Jose State U., 1972. Various mgmt. positions Lika Corp., Stockton, Calif., 1972-80; co-founder, held various mgmt. positions Sanmina Corp. and predecessor, 1980—, pres. & chmn., 1991—2001; co-chmn. Sanmina-SCI, 1999—2002, CEO, 2001—, chmn., 2002—. Recipient Ernst & Young Master Entrepreneur of Yr. award, 2004. Office: Sanmina SCI Corp 2700 N 1st St San Jose CA 95134-2015

SOLÁ, VICTORIA M., announcer, writer; b. Englewood, NJ, Nov. 11, 1952; d. Salvador Felix and Hedda Blanc (Westhead) Solá; 1 child, Frank Salvador Solá Grillo. Student, Fairleigh Dickinson U., NJ, 1970—72. Radio host and prodr. jazz WFDU-FM Radio, Teaneck, NJ, 1981—83, jazz dir., 1982—86, radio host and prodr. Latin, 1983—, Latin music dir., 1983—. Contbg. editor Descarga Catalog, NYC, 1996—2002; columnist Latin Beat Mag., Gardena, Calif., 1998, Latin London Mag., 1999; Latin jazz planning com. adv. Smithsonian Inst. Traveling Exhbn. Svc., Washington, 1999—2002, narrator, 2002. Coord. ann. on-air fundraiser for Latin music programming WFDU-FM, Teaneck, NJ, 1983—; participant on-air blood donor drive Bergen Cmty. Regional Blood Ctrs., Paramus, NJ, 1986; vol. fund raiser Operation Rescue North Shore Animal League Am., 2006. Mem.: Internat. Latin Music Hall of Fame (adv. com. 1999—, Spl. Recognition award 2001). Democrat. Avocations: reading, photography, drawing, writing. E-mail: vickisola1@aol.com.

SOLANO, CARL ANTHONY, lawyer; b. Mar. 26, 1951; s. Nick and Catherine A. (Occhiato) Solano; m. Nancy M. Randazzo, 1989; children: Melanie A., Carla Nicole. BS magna cum laude, U. Scranton, 1973; JD cum laude, Villanova U., 1976. Bar: Pa. 1976, U.S. Dist. Ct. (ea. dist.) Pa. 1978, U.S. Ct. Appeals (3d cir.) 1980, U.S. Ct. Appeals (5th cir.) 1981, U.S. Supreme Ct. 1982, U.S. Ct. Appeals (9th cir.) 1986, U.S. Dist. Ct. (mid. dist.) Pa. 1988, U.S. Ct. Appeals (6th cir.) 1988, U.S. Ct. Appeals (fed. cir.) 1989, U.S. Ct. Appeals (7th cir.) 1996. Law clk. Hon. Alfred L. Luongo U.S. Dist. Ct. (ea. dist.) Pa., Phila., 1976—78; assoc. Schnader, Harrison, Segal & Lewis, Phila., 1978—84, ptnr., 1985—. Adj. prof. Villanova U. Sch. Law, 1999—2001. Contbg. author: Federal Appellate Procedure Third Circuit, 1996, MLRC State Survey: Media Libel Law, 1984—, Third Circuit Appellate Practice Manual, 2007, 2009. Recipient Legal Achievement award, Burton, 2007, Pro Bono award, Pa. Bar Assn., 2008; named Pa. Super Lawyer, 2004—09; named one of Best Lawyers in Am. for Appellate Law, First Amendment Law, 2006—08, Best Lawyers in Phila. for Appellate Law, First Amendment Law, 2009. Mem.: ABA (TIPS 3rd ctr. reporter 2007—), Justinian Soc. (bd. govs. 2008—), St. Thomas More Soc., Phila. Bar Assn. (chair bar news media com. 2003), Pa. Bar Assn. (statutory law com. 1980—95, Appellate Adv. Com. chair 2008—09), Am. Law Inst., Order of Coif, Pi Gamma Mu. Roman Catholic. Home: 5 Barrister Ct Haverford PA 19041-1137 Office: Schnader Harrison Segal & Lewis LLP 1600 Market St Ste 3600 Philadelphia PA 19103-7286 Office Phone: 215-751-2202. Business E-Mail: CSolano@Schnader.com.

SOLANO, HENRY L., lawyer; m. Janine Solano; children: Mateo, Amalia, Guadalupe. BS in Mech. Engring., U. Denver; JD, U. Colo.; LLD (hon.), U. Denver. Asst. atty. gen. Human Resources divsn. Colo. Dept. Law, 1977-82; asst. U.S. atty. Dist. Colo., 1982-87; U.S. atty. for Colo. U.S. Dept. Justice, Denver, 1994-98; solicitor U.S. Dept. Labor, Washington, 1998-2001; ptnr. LeBoeuf, Lamb, Greene & MacRae L.L.P., Denver, 2001—. Exec. dir. Colo. Dept. Instns., 1987-91, Colo. Dept. Regulatory Agys., 1987; acting exec. dir. Colo. Dept. Corrections, 1989-90; chair Cabinet Coun. on Families and Children, 1990-91; mem. adv. com. U.S. Atty. Gen., 1994-95; lectr. Kennedy Sch. Govt. Bd. dirs. Nat. Latino Children's Inst., Nat. Hispana Leadership Inst., Mex.Am. Legal Def. Edn. Fund, Denver Housing Authority, Denver Women's Commn., Colo. Dept. Social Svcs., Colo. Transit Constrn. Authority, Regional Transit Dist. Office: LeBoeuf Lamb Greene & MacRae 125 West 55th St New York NY 10019-5389 Office Phone: 202-986-8056. Business E-Mail: hsolano@llgm.com.

SOLANO, JULIO RAFAEL, priest, educator; b. Barranquilla, Atlantico, Colombia, Sept. 12, 1946; came to US, 1971; s. Domingo Rafael Solano and Christine Balderrama. Degree in acctg., Centro Intensificacion Comml., Bogota, Colombia, 1970; BA, St. John Vianney Coll. Sem., Miami, Fla., 1989; MDiv, St. Vincent de Paul Regl. Sem., Boynton Beach, Fla., 1993. Transitional deacon St. Louis Cath. Ch., Miami, 1992—93; asst. pastor St. Elizabeth Cath. Ch., Pompano Beach, Fla., St. Patrick Cath. Ch., Miami Beach, Fla., 1996—98; parochial vicar St. Coleman Cath. Ch., Pompano Beach, 1998—99, St. Elizabeth of Hungary Cath. Ch., Pompano Beach, 1999—2001, St. Vincent Cath. Ch., Margate, Fla., 2001—02; pastor Our Lady Queen of Heaven Cath. Ch., North Lauderdale, Fla., 2002—06, Little Flower Cath. Ch., Hollywood, Fla., 2006—. Tchr. La Salle HS, Miami, 1996—98; asst. chaplain Serra Club Internat. Pompano Beach, 1994-95; co-host radio program Abuelito Pepito, Radio Maria, Peru, Colombia, 2008-. Mem. KC, Assn. Sacerdotes Hispanos. Democrat. Roman Catholic. Avocations: travel, reading, writing, stamps, coins. Office Phone: 954-922-3517. Personal E-mail: frsolano@bellsouth.net. E-mail: jrsb@att.net.

SOLARZ, STEPHEN JOSHUA, former congressman; b. NYC, Sept. 12, 1940; s. Sanford and Ruth (Fertig) S.; m. Nina Koldin, Feb. 5, 1967; children: Randy, Lisa. BA, Brandeis U., 1962; MA, Columbia U., 1967. Mem. NY State Assembly from 45th Dist., 1968-74, US Congress from 13th NY Dist., 1975—93, mem. fgn. affairs com., chmn. fgn. affairs subcom. on Asian and Pacific affairs and chmn. subcom. on Africa, mem. merchant marine and fisheries com., mem. joint econ. com.; mem. Permanent Select Com. on Intelligence; Congl. del. UN Gen. Assembly, 1983; chmn. Ctrl. Asian-American Enterprise Fund, 1993—98; founder (with George Mitchell and Morton Abramowitz) Internat. Crisis Group, 1995—, vice chmn.; pres. Solarz Associates; sr. counselor APCO Worldwide; co-chmn. Am. Com. for Peace in Chechnya. Instr. Bklyn. Coll., 1966—69, CUNY; vis. prof. George Washington U., Washington, 1994—95; disting. cons. Carnegie Endowment for Internat. Peace. Editor, Newsfront; assoc. editor, Greater Philadelphia. Mem. governing coun. Am. Jewish Congress; trustee Brandeis U. Democrat. Office: APCO Worldwide Ste 800 700 12th St NW Washington DC 20005 also: Solarz Associates 1120 Bellview Rd Mc Lean VA 22102-1104

SOLBERG, AMY KATHLEEN, director; b. Chester, Mont., Mar. 11, 1977; d. Timothy and Kathleen Solberg. MusB, Concordia Coll., Moorhead, Minn., 1999; MusM, U. Houston, 2005. Cert. tchr. Tex., N.Mex. Choir dir. Valley HS, Albuquerque, 1999—2003; music dir. Minot State U. Theatre, ND, 1999—2003; tchg. asst. U. Houston, 2003—05; choir dir. Bellaire HS, 2005—. Staff singer St. John's Episcopal Cathedral, Albuquerque, 2001—03, Bellaire Presbyn. Ch., 2003—07, Christ Ch. Episcopal Cathedral, Houston, 2007—. Singer: Cantare Houston, Mercury Baroque, Santa Fe Desert Chorale; mus. dir.: Guys and Dolls, Oklahoma, Anything Goes!, Into the Woods; mus. dir.: Children of Eden; mus. dir.: Forever Plaid, Nunsense, Music Man, Oliver, A Funny Thing Happened on the Way to the Forum, The Fantasticks, Smoking Joe's Cafe The Frogs. Sect. leader Bellaire (Tex.) Presbyn. Ch., 2003—06. Recipient Excellence in Tchg. award, Valley HS, 2002; named Most Inspirational Tchr., Valley HS Acad., 2002, Nat. Honor Roll, Outstanding Tchrs. America, 2005; fellow, U. Houston, 2003—05; Music Performance scholar, Concordia Coll., 1995—99, Faculty scholar, 1995—99, Music scholar, U. Houston, 2003—05. Mem.: Chorus America, Tex. Music Educators' Assn., Music Educators' Nat. Conf., Tex. Choral Directors' Assn., Am. Choral Directors' Assn. Avocations: reading, travel, dance.

SOLBERG, RONALD LOUIS, investment adviser, portfolio manager; b. Madison, Wis., May 15, 1953; s. Carl Louis and Gladys Irene Evelyn (Oen) S.; m. Anna Maria Teresa Gorgol, May 16, 1983 (div. Aug. 1992); m. Elizabeth Catherine Gillett, Dec. 24, 1996 (div. Oct. 2001). BA in Econs. with honors, U. Wis., 1975; MA, U. Calif., Berkeley, 1977, PhD, 1984. Country risk analyst Wells Fargo Bank, San Francisco, 1978-79; asst. v.p., economist Wells Fargo Ltd., London, 1979-81; cons. RAND Corp., Santa Monica, Calif., 1982-84; acting instr. econs. U. Calif., Berkeley, 1983; 1st v.p., portfolio risk policy mgr. Security Pacific Corp., LA, 1984-92; internat. fin. cons., 1992-94; v.p., fixed-income credit rschr. Pacific Investment Mgmt. Co., 1994-95; mng. dir. head Asian econ. rsch. Chase Manhattan Bank, Hong Kong, 1995-98; acting head of emerging markets securities Asia, Chase Manhattan Asia Ltd., 1996-98; mng. dir., head mkt. and credit rsch. group Tokyo-Mitsubishi Internat. plc, London, 1998—2000; prin. Viking Asset Mgmt., Laguna Beach, Calif., 2001—08; co-founder Armored Wolf LLC, Aliso Viejo, Calif., 2008—. Adj. asst. prof. U. So. Calif., L.A., 1985-92. Author: (monograph with G. Grossman) The Soviet Union's Hard-Currency Balance of Payments and Creditworthiness in 1985, 1983; (book) Sovereign Rescheduling: Risk and Portfolio Management, 1988, Country Risk Analysis, 1992; contbr. articles to profl. jours. Research fellow Inst. Internat. Studies, Berkeley, 1982-84. Mem. Am. Econ. Assn., Asia Soc., Nat. Assn. for Bus. Economists, Soc. for Internat. Devel. Avocations: fly fishing, cross country skiing, squash, billiards. Office Phone: 949-291-4643. E-mail: rsolberg@cox.net.

SOLBERG, WINTON UDELL, historian, educator; b. Aberdeen, SD, Jan. 11, 1922; s. Ole Alexander and Bertha Georgia (Tschappat) S.; m. Ruth Constance Walton, Nov. 8, 1952; children: Gail Elizabeth, Andrew Walton, Kristin Ruth. AB magna cum laude, U. S.D., 1943, LHD (hon.), 1987; student, Biarritz Am. U., France, 1946; A.M., Harvard, 1947, PhD, 1954. Instr., then asst. prof. social scis. U.S. Mil. Acad., 1951-54; instr., then asst. prof. history Yale U., 1954-58; fellow Pierson Coll., 1955-58, Morse fellow, 1958; James Wallace prof. history Macalester Coll., 1958-62; vis. prof. U. Ill., 1961-62, assoc. prof. history, 1962, prof., 1967—, chmn. dept. history, 1970-72. Rsch. fellow Ctr. Study History of Liberty in Am., Harvard U., 1962-63; rsch. scholar Henry E. Huntington Library, San Marino, Calif., 1959; dir. Coe Found. Am. Studies Inst., summers 1960-62; lectr., cons. Army War Coll., 1959-62; lectr. U.S. Command and Gen. Staff Sch., 1963-64; Fulbright prof. Johns Hopkins U. Bologna, 1967-68, Moscow (USSR) State U., 1978, U. Calcutta India, 1993; vis. prof. Konan U., Kobe, Japan, 1981; USIA Lectr., Korea and Malaysia, 1985, Korea, 1992. Author: The Federal Convention and the Formation of the Union of the American States, 1958, The Constitutional Convention and the Formation of the Union, 1990, The University of Illinois, 1867-1894, An Intellectual and Cultural History, 1968, Redeem the Time: The Puritan Sabbath in Early America, 1977, History of American Thought and Culture, 1983, Cotton Mather, The Christian Philosopher, 1994, The University of Illinois, 1894-1904: The Shaping of the University, 2000, Reforming Medical Education:The University of Illinois, Coll. Medicine 1880-1920, 2009; also articles. Mem. Ill. Humanities Council, 1973-75; sec. Council on Study of Religion, 1981-85. Maj. inf. AUS, 1943-46, 51-54; lt. col. U.S. Army Res. Recipient Faculty Achievement award Burlington No. Found., 1986, Disting. Teaching award U. Ill. Coll. Liberal Arts and Scis., 1988; NEH sr. fellow, 1974-75; Rsch. grantee NSF, 1981-82 Mem. Am. Hist. Assn., So. Hist. Assn., Orgn. Am. Historians, Am. Studies Assn. (pres. Mid-Am. 1985-86), Am. Soc. Ch. History (pres. 1985-86), AAUP (chpt. pres. 1965-66, mem. council 1969-72, 1st v.p. 1974-76), Phi Beta Kappa. Episcopalian. Home: 8 Lake Park Rd Champaign IL 61822-7101 Office: U Ill History Dept Urbana IL 61801 Home Phone: 217-244-2075; Office Phone: 217-333-4193. Business E-Mail: wsolberg@illinois.edu.

SOLBRIG, INGEBORG HILDEGARD, retired literature educator, writer; b. Weissenfels, Germany, July 31, 1923; arrived in U.S., 1961, naturalized, 1966; d. Reinhold J. and Hildegard M. A. (Ferchland) Solbrig. Grad. in chemistry, U. Halle, Germany, 1948; student, Delmar Coll., 1961; BA summa cum laude, San Francisco State U., 1964; postgrad., U. Calif., Berkeley, 1964-65; MA, Stanford U., 1966, PhD in Humanities and German, 1969. Asst. prof. U. R.I., 1969-70, U. Tenn., Chattanooga, 1970-72, U. Ky., Lexington, 1972-75; assoc. prof. German U. Iowa, 1975-81, prof., 1981-93, prof. emerita, 1993—2009. Domestic and abroad lectr.; former presenter The Light from the East, Coptic Christians/Egypt, 2004. Author: Hammer-Purgstall und Goethe, 1973,

Orient-Rezeption, 1996, Orient-Rezeption, Fischer Lexikon Literatur, 1996, 2d edit., 2000, Modulationen von Gold und Licht in Goethes Kunstmärchen, 1997, Momentaufnahmen, 2000, J.G. Herder: Echo of the Cultural Philospher's Ideas in Early African-American Intellectual Writing, 2000, Maria Sibylla Merian..., 2001; main editor: Rilke Heute, Beziehungen und Wirkungen, 1975; editor (and translator): Reinhard Goering: Seeschlacht/Seabattle, 1977; mem. editl. bd.: Kairoer Germanistische Studien, vol. 9 & 10, 1998; contbr. articles to profl. jours., chpts. to books. Mem. Iowa Gov.'s Com. 300th Anniversary German-Am. Rels. 1683-1983, 1983. Recipient Hammer-Purgstall Gold medal, Austria, 1974; named Ky. Col., 1975; fellow, Stanford U., 1965—66, 1968—69, Austrian Ministry Edn., 1968—69; Delta Phi Alpha Deutsche Ehrenverbindung, U. Ky., 1973, Old Gold fellow, Iowa, 1977, Am. Coun. Learned Socs. grantee, German Acad. Exch. Svc. grantee, 1980, Sr. Faculty Rsch. fellow in humanities, 1983, NEH grantee, 1985, May Brodbeck fellow in humanities, 1989, numerous summer faculty rsch. grants. Mem.: MLA (life), Soc. for History Alchemy and Chemistry, Internat. Herder Soc. (founding mem.), Goethe Soc. N.Am., Inc., Can. Soc. 18th Century Studies, Am. Soc. 18th Century Studies, Deutsche Schiller Gesellschaft, Goethe Gesellschaft, Internat. Vereinigung fur Germanische Sprach und Lit. Wiss., Egyptian Soc. Lit. Criticism (hon.), World Peace and Diplomacy Forum (life). Avocations: horseback riding, photography, writing, travel, theology. Home: 1126 Pine St Iowa City IA 52240-5711 Home Phone: 319-339-1427. *The circumstances of my life took me to many places and cultures. Despite the discord and problems plaguing many parts of this planet, let us not forget that it's the home of the human family, our home. Always remember: Life is, by definition, change.*

SOLDNER, PAUL EDMUND, artist, ceramist, educator; b. Summerfield, Ill., 1921; s. Grover and Beulah (Geiger) S.; m. Virginia I. Geiger, June 15, 1947; 1 child, Stephanie. BA, Bluffton Coll., 1946; MA, U. Colo., 1954; MFA, L.A. County Art Inst., 1956; DFA (hon.), Westminster Coll., 1992. Tchr. art Medina (Ohio) County Schs., 1946-47; supr. art, asst. county supr. Wayne County Schs., Wooster, Ohio, 1951-54; tchr. adult edn. Wooster Coll., 1952-54; vis. asst. prof. ceramics Scripps Coll., 1957-66, prof., 1970-91, prof. emeritus, 1991. Prof. Claremont (Calif.) Grad. Sch., 1957-66, prof., 1970-92; prof. U. Colo., Boulder, 1966-67, U. Iowa, Iowa City, 1967-68; pres. Soldner Pottery Equipment, Inc., Aspen, Colo., 1956-2008; mem. steering com. Internat. Sch. Ceramics, Rome, 1965-77; advisor Vols. for Internat. Assistance, Balt., 1966-75; craftsman, trustee Am. Craft Coun., N.Y.C., 1970-74, trustee emeritus, 1976-2008; dir. U.S. sect. World Craft Coun., 1970-74; dir. Anderson Ranch Ctr. for Hand Art Sch., 1974-76; speaker 6th Internat. Ceramics Symposium Syracuse, 1989; participant Internat. Russian Artists Exchange Program, Riga, Latvia, 1989; cons. in field. Author: Kilns and Their Construction, 1965, Raku, 1964, Paul Soldner, A Retrospective View, 1991; contbr. articles to profl. jours.; subject of 5 films; 160 one-man shows including Cantini Mus. Modern Art, Marseille, France, 1981, Thomas Segal Gallery, Boston, 1982, Elements Gallery, N.Y., 1983, Louis Newman Gallery, L.A., 1985, Susan Cummins Gallery, Mill Valley, Calif., 1989, Great Am. Gallery, Atlanta, 1986, Patricia Moore Gallery, Aspen Colo., 1987, Coleg Prifysgol Cymru, Aberystwyth, Wales, 1987, Joan Hodgell Gallery, Sarasota, Fla., 1988, Esther Saks Gallery, Chgo., 1986, 88, El Camino Gallery Art, Toraance, Calif., 1987, San Antonio Art Ctr., San Angelo, Tex., 1988, traveling exhibit, 12 U.S. mus., 1992—, Besson Gallerie, London, 1996, Bernard Palissy Mus., France, 1996; 400 group shows including Nelson-Atkins Mus., Kansas City, Mo., 1983, Los Angeles Mcpl. Art Gallery, 1984, 27th Ceramic Nat. Exhibition, Everson Mus. Art, Syracuse, N.Y., 1986, Victoria & Albert Mus., London, 1986, Chicago Internat. New Art Forms Exposition, 1986, Hanover Gallery, Syracuse, N.Y., 1987, L.A. County Mus. of Art, 1987, Crain/Wolov Gallery, Tulsa, 1987, Contem Crafts Gallery, Portland, Oreg., 1988, Oakland (Calif.) Art Mus., 1988, Munson Gallery, Santa Fe, 1988, Japanese Influence on Am. Ceramics, Everson Mus., Syracuse, N.Y., 1989, traveling retrospective, 1991-93; hon. vis. artist Shigaraki Ceramic Cultural Park, Japan, 1994; works in permanent collections, Nat. Mus. Modern Art, Kyoto, Japan, Victoria and Albert Mus., London, Smithsonian Instn., Washington, Los Angeles County Mus. Art, Oakland Art Mus., Everson Mus. Art, Syracuse Australian Nat. Gallery, Taipei Fine Arts Mus.; curator Mirror Images Exhibit, Craft Alliance Gallery, St. Louis, 1989, Am. Mus. Ceramic Arts Pomma, Calif., Amaroussion Olympic Collection Ceramic Sculptures, Athens, Greece; (book) Nothing to Hide Exposures Disclosers, Relections; (videos and CD) Playing with Fire, The Courage to Explore, Thrown and Altered Clay. Served with U.S. Army, 1941-46, Decorated Purple Heart; grantee NEA, 1991, Louis Comfort Tiffany Found., 1966, 72, Nat. Endowment for Arts, 1976, Colo. Gov.'s award for the Arts & Humanities, 1975; voted one of Top Twelve Potters World-Wide, Ceramics Monthly mag., 1981; Scripps Coll. Faculty Recognition award, 1985; named Hon. Mem. Coun., Nat. Coun. on Edn. for Ceramic Arts, 1989, Aileen Osborn Webb Gold Medal award, Am. Crafts Coun. NY, 2008, grant NEA. Fellow Collequim of Craftsmen of the U.S.; mem. Internat. Acad. Ceramics, Nat. Coun. on Edn. for Ceramic Arts. Achievements include being the originator of Am. Raku philosophy and techniques in ceramics. Home: PO Box 90 Aspen CO 81612-0090 Home Phone: 970-925-7436. Personal E-mail: dreamindigo@gmail.com.

SOLE, MICHAEL JOSEPH, cardiologist; b. Timmins, Ont., Can., Mar. 5, 1940; s. Fred and Lillian Sole; m. Susan Karen Samuels, May 26, 1964; children: David Frederick, Leslie Meredith. BSc, U. Toronto, Ont., Can., 1962, MD, 1966. Cert. Coll. Physicians and Surgeons Ont.; diplomate Am. Bd. Internal Medicine. Rotating intern, jr. asst. resident, sr. asst. resident in internal medicine Toronto Gen. Hosp., 1966-69; cardiology fellow Cardiovasc. Rsch. Inst., U. Calif., San Francisco, 1969-71; cardiology fellow Peter Bent Brigham Hosp., Boston, 1971-73, jr. assoc. medicine, 1973-74; rsch. assoc. MIT, Cambridge, 1973-74; instr. medicine Harvard Med. Sch., 1973-74; from asst. to assoc. prof. medicine U. Toronto, 1974-83, prof. medicine and physiology, 1983—, mem. staff inst. med. sci., 1978—, dir. cardiology rsch., 1987-89, dir. centre cardiovasc. rsch., 1989-99, Searle chair cardiovasc. rsch., 1998—; staff cardiologist Toronto Hosp., 1974-89, dir. non-invasive cardiology, 1974-79, dir. cardiology rsch., 1979-89, dir. divsn. cardiology, 1989-98, dir. cardiovasc. program, 1992—97, dir. Peter Munk Cardiac Ctr., 1992-97. Vis. prof. Harvard U., 1975, NIH, Bethesda, Md., 1981, U. B.C., 1982, 91, 92, Capital Med. Sch. and Beijing Hosp., 1985, U. Tokyo, 1992, others; mem. Can. Govt. Task Force Diagnostic Ultrasound, 1976-78; vice-chmn. econs. com. dept. medicine Toronto Gen. Hosp., 1977, chmn., 1978, 79, chmn. emeritus, 1980, mem. various coms., 1981-98, chmn. cardiology rsch. com., 1988-89, mem. cardiovasc. collaborative practice group, 1989-92; rsch. assoc. Ont. Heart Found., 1979-89; assoc. rsch. inst. pediat. Hosp. Sick Children, Toronto, 1979—; mem. med. staff Mt. Sinai Hosp., Toronto, 1979—; mem. adv. bd. Merck Pharms., 1983—, Boots Pharms., 1992-93; mem. Health Rsch. and Devel. Coun., Province of Ont., 1983-86, mem. exec. com., 1984-86; Levesque lectr. Montreal Heart Inst., 1984; mem. cardiovasc. panel Med. Rsch. Coun. Can., 1985-87; mem. heart and blood vessel rsch. adv. com. Toronto Hosp., 1986-89; chmn. cardiovasc. rsch. adv. com. faculty medicine U. Toronto, 1986-87, mem. various coms., 1987—, chmn. rsch. com. dept. medicine, 1987-88, mem. rsch. adv. bd., 1989-97, chair life scis. com., 1990-92, chair decanal promotions com. faculty medicine, 1992-94; mem. exec. com. Centre Cardiovasc. Rsch., 1998-99, chmn. sci. com., 1989-99, mem. exec. com. cardiovasc. clin. rsch. lab., 1992-99, chmn. rsch. com., 1992-99; Pfizer vis. fellow Clin. Rsch. Inst., Montreal, 1988; mem. sr. adv. com. Toronto Western Hosp., 1989-90; Katz vis. prof. U. Chgo., 1989; mem. provincial working group cardiovasc. svcs. Ministry of Health, 1990-91, mem. ctrl. east region cardiovasc. patient care mgmt. group, 1990-91; mem. trial devel. com. diabetes atherosclerosis intervention study WHO and Fournier Pharms., 1991-93, mem. trial exec. com., 1993-2000; mem. Joint Med. Rsch. Coun. Can./Pharm. Mfrs. Assn. Can. Adv. Com. Sci., 1993; mem. organizing coms. various sci. meetings; presenter in field. Mem. editl. bd. Can. Jour. Cardiology, 1988—, Index and Revs. Congestive Heart Failure, 1988-90, Hypertension Can., 1988-90, European Jour. Pharmacology, 1992-96, Cardiosci., 1993, Jour. Heart Failure, 1994—, Circulation, 1996—, Jour. Molecular Medicine, 1996—, Jour. Molecular Cell Cardiology, 1999-2001; mem. internat. editl. bd. Cardiology Digest, 1992—; contbr. chpts. to books and articles to profl. jours.; patentee in field. Recipient Robert Beamish Leadership award, Inst. CV Sci., U. Man., 2001; grantee Grantee, Heart & Stroke Found. Ont., 1969—, Med. Rsch. Coun. Can., 1982—92, 1994—97; fellow Ivan Smith Rsch. fellow, U. Toronto, 1964, Hunter fellow, Ont. Heart Found., 1973; scholar Walter Watkins scholar, U. Toronto, 1962. Fellow Am. Coll. Cardiology (abstract reviewer 1989, 91), Royal Coll. Physicians and Surgeons, Can. Acad. Health Sci.; mem. Am. Soc. Clin. Investigation, Assn. Am. Physicians, Am. Heart Assn. (fellow couns. clin. cardiology, hypertension, circulation and basic sci., mem. exec., basic sci. coun. 1986-89, mem. Katz prize selection com. 1988-90), Can. Inst. Acad. Medicine, Can. Soc. Clin. Investigation, Can. Cardiovasc. Soc. (mem. young investigators award panel 1982-84, mem. student presentation award com. 1988-90, mem. nat. task force cardiovasc. sci. 1992-93, Ann. Rsch. award 1975, Rsch. Achievement award 1989), Heart and Stroke Found. Can. (mem. sci. rev. bd. 1976-79, vice-chmn. 1980-83, chmn. hypertension and cardiovasc. pharmacology panel 1982-83, chmn. molecular biology, biochemistry, pathology panel 1989-90), Can. Med. Assn. (mem. coun. 1982-87), Am. Fedn. Clin. Rsch., Ont. Med. Assn. (alt. del. Toronto Gen. Hosp. bd. 1988-90), Heart and Stroke Found. Ont. (mem. med. rsch. com. 1978-81, bd. dirs. 1986-92, 96—, mem. fin. com. 1986-90, 96-97, mem. corp. rels. com. 1990-92, mem. rsch. policy com. 1991-93, 96-97, chmn. 1997-99, mem. exec. com. 1997-99, nomination com. 1997-99, chmn. 50th anniversary com., mem. audit com., Disting. Rsch. prof. 1989-96, Murray Robertson Meml. lectr. 1989), Internat. Soc. Heart Rsch. (exec. Am. sect. 1979-88, lectr. Latin Am. sect. 1995), Banting Rsch. Found. (hon. sec.-treas. 1979-81), Gairdner Found. (mem. rev. panel 1979-94), Heart Failure Soc. Am. (publs. com. 2000-03, nominating com. 2001-04), Maple Downs Golf and Country Club (Toronto; bd. dirs. 2001-06, exec. bd. 2003-06), Alpha Omega Alpha. Office: Toronto Gen Hosp 585 University Ave Rm 4N488 Toronto ON Canada M5G 2N2 Office Phone: 416-340-3471. Business E-Mail: michael.sole@uhn.on.ca.

SOLECKI, R. STEFAN, anthropologist, educator; b. Bklyn., Oct. 15, 1917; s. Kazimierz John and Mary (Tarnawski) S.; m. Rose Muriel Lilien, June 24, 1955; children: John Irwin, William Duncan. BSc, CCNY, 1941; MA, Columbia U., NYC, 1950, PhD in Anthropology, 1958. Archaeologist Smithsonian Instn., 1948-54; archaeol. asst. anthropology Columbia U., NYC, 1954-55, mem. faculty, 1959-88, prof. anthropology, 1965-88, prof. emeritus, 1989—, chmn. dept., 1975-78; adj. prof. dept. anthropology Tex. A&M Univ., College Station, 1989—; assoc. curator old world U.S. Nat. Mus., 1957-59. Archael. expdns. to Alaska, 1949, 61, Iraq, 1950-51, 53, 56-57 (field dir.), 60, 78, Sudanese Nubia, 1961, Turkey, 1963, Syria, 1963, 64, 65, 88, 89, Iran, 1968, Lebanon, 1969-73, France, 1975, Ea., Midwestern and Western US; collaborator in archaeology Smithsonian Instn., 1953; cons. UNESCO, 1959. Served with AUS, 1943-45. Fulbright scholar, Iraq, 1952-53; William Bayard Cutting travelling fellow Columbia, 1956-57; Fulbright-Hays faculty research awardee Syria, 1980-81; Fulbright fellow, Iraq, 1988-89. Fellow Am. Anthrop. Assn., Arctic Inst. Am., NY Acad. Scis. (chmn. anthropology sect. 1977-79); mem. NY Archaeol. Assn. (pres. 1960-62), NY Oriental Club (pres. 1965), Profl. Archeologists of NYC (pres. 1980-81), Soc. Archaeology, Am. Schs. Oriental Research (assoc. trustee 1969-71), Prehistoric Soc., Deutsches Archaeologisches Inst., Soc. Préhistorique Français, Archaeol. Inst. Am. (exec. com. 1968-70), Assn. Field Archaeology (pres. 1972-74). Home: 86 Park Pl South Orange NJ 07079-2303 Office: Columbia U Dept Anthropology New York NY 10027

SOLES, WILLIAM ROGER, insurance company executive, director; b. Whiteville, NC, Sept. 16, 1920; s. John William and Margaret (Watts) S.; m. Majelle Marrene Morris, Sept. 22, 1956 (dec. 1993); children: William Roger, Majelle Janette. BS in Commerce, U. N.C., 1947, postgrad., 1956; LLD, Campbell U., 1981; DHL, High Point U., 1996. With Jefferson Standard Life Ins. Co., Greensboro, N.C., 1947—, v.p., mgr. securities dept., 1962-64, asst. to pres., 1964-66, exec. v.p., mgr. securities dept., 1966, pres., also dir., 1967-86; chmn., pres., chief exec. officer Jefferson-Pilot Life Ins. Co.; retired, 1993; chmn., pres. Jefferson-Pilot Corp., retired, 1993. Trustee, past chmn. High Point U.; past chmn. Wesley Long Community Hosp.; trustee, past chmn. Ind. Coll. Fund N.C.; past pres. Bus. Found. of N.C.; bd. dirs., past chmn. N.C. Ins. Edn. Found. Served with USAAF, 1941-45. Mem. N.C. Citizens for Bus. and Industry (past chmn.), Am. Council Life Ins. (past chmn., dir.), Beta Gamma Sigma. Clubs: Greensboro Country. Office: Jefferson-Pilot Corp PO Box 21008 Greensboro NC 27420-1008 Home: 621 Woodland Dr Greensboro NC 27408-7416

SOLET, MAXWELL DAVID, lawyer; b. Washington, May 15, 1948; s. Leo and Pearl (Rose) S.; m. Joanne Marie Tolksdorf, Sept. 27, 1970; children: David Marc, Paul Jacob. AB, Harvard U., 1970, JD, 1974. Bar: Mass. 1974, U.S. Tax Ct. 1976, U.S. Ct. Claims 1976, U.S. Supreme Ct. 1976. Assoc. Gaston Snow & Ely Bartlett, Boston, 1974-79, Mintz, Levin, Cohn, Ferris, Glovsky & Popeo, P.C., Boston, 1979-82, ptnr., 1982—. Mem. adv. com. tax exempt and gov. entities IRS, 2005—08, chmn. adv. com. tax exempt and gov. entities, 2007—08. Mem.: ABA, Cambridge Health Alliance (bd. mem. 2005—), Nat. Assn. Bond Lawyers (mem. steering com. bond atty.'s workshop 1992—95, 2007—), Boston Bar Assn. (chmn. tax sect. 1987—89, mem. multidisciplinary practice task force 2000—01, mem. audit com. 2003—), Mass. Bar Assn., Cambridge Hist. Soc. (bd. mem. 1999—2000, sec. 2001—05, v.p. 2005—08, advisor 2008—). Home: 15 Berkeley St Cambridge MA 02138-3409 Office: Mintz Levin Cohn Ferris Glovsky & Popeo PC One Financial Ctr Boston MA 02111 Home Phone: 617-547-3250; Office Phone: 617-348-1739. Business E-Mail: msolet@mintz.com.

SOLEY, ROBERT LAWRENCE, plastic surgeon; b. NYC, Feb. 26, 1935; s. Max and Saide (Leader) S.; m. Judy Wasserman, June 16, 1963; children: John, Jill. BS, Yale U., 1956; MD, NYU, 1959. Diplomate Am. Bd. Surgery, Am. Bd. PLastic Surgery. Intern Bellevue Hosp., NYC, 1955—60; resident in gen. surgery Mt. Sinai Hosp., NYC, 1960—65; resident in plastic surgery Hosp. U. Pa., Phila., 1967—69; practice medicine specializing in plastic surgery White Plains, NY, 1969—. Mem. staff, mem. med. bd. White Plains Hosp., 1985—88, chief sect. plastic surgery, 1988—94. Contbr. articles to profl. jours. Capt. M.C., USAF, 1965-67. Grantee USPHS, 1968-69. Fellow ACS; mem. Am. Soc. Plastic Reconstructive Surgery, Am. Soc. Aesthetic Surgery, N.Y. State Med. Soc. (ho. of dels.), Westchester County Med. Soc. (pres. 1996-97, bd. dirs.), Rotary (bd. dirs. White Plains chpt. 1982-85). Home: 30 Griffin Ave Scarsdale NY 10583-7661 Office: Associated Plastic Surgeons Westchester PC 30 Griffen Ave Scarsdale NY 10583-7661

SOLGANIK, MARVIN, real estate executive; b. Chgo., Nov. 7, 1930; s. Harry and Dora (Fastoff) S.; m. Judith Rosenberg, Sept. 11, 1960; children: Randall, Janet, Robert. BBA, Case Western Res. U., 1952. Real estate broker, Cleve., 1950-65, Herbert Laronge Inc., Cleve., 1965-68; sr. v.p. real estate Revco D.S., Inc., Twinsburgh, Ohio, 1968—, corp. dir., 1974—. Adj. prof. Ohio No. U.; guest lectr. Cleve. State U., Case Western Res. U. Sch. Law, Cuyahoga C.C., Ohio No. U., Cleve. Real Estate Bd., CASE Sch. Law. Vol. jewish Welfare Fund, Shaker heights, Ohio; chmn. capital and budget coms. Jewish Fedn.; chmn. Agnon Sch. Bdlg. Com.; bd. dirs. Bellfair-J.C.B.-Home for Emotionally Disturbed Children, Visconsi Cos, Cleve. Inst. Music. Recipient Appreciation award Am. Soc. Real Estate Appraisers, Akron-Cleve. chpt., 1971 Mem. Nat. Assn. Corp. Real Estate Officers, Internat. Council Shopping Ctrs. Office: D S Revco 22925 Holmwood Rd Shaker Heights OH 44122-3005

SOLIDUM, JAMES, finance and insurance executive; b. Honolulu, Mar. 12, 1925; s. Narciso and Sergia (Yabo) S.; m Vickie Mayo, Aug. 14, 1954; children: Arlin James, Nathan Francis, Tobi John, Kamomi Teresa. Student, U. Hawaii, 1949-50; BA, U. Oreg., 1953. CLU, Am. Coll. Life Underwriters, 1975. Promotional salesman Tongg Pub. Co., 1953—54; editor Fil-Am. Tribune, 1954—55; master planning technician Fed. Civil Svc., 1955—57; publs. editor Hawaii Sugar Planters Assn., 1957; field agt. Grand Pacific Life Ins. Co., 1957—59, home office asst., 1959—60, supr., 1960—62, asst. v.p., 1962—64; propr. J. Solidum & Assoc., Honolulu, 1964—; pres. Fin. Devel. Inst., 1967—. Contbg. writer Paradise of Pacific Mag., 1957-58, Hawaii Agrl. Mag., 1957-58; gen. ptrn. R.Z. Limited Partnership, 1981—; v.p. Grand Pacific Life Ins. Co., 1983-90; bd. dirs. Hawaii Econ. Devel. Corp., 1982-89; mem. adv. com. Honolulu dist. SBA, 1971-77; bd. advisors Philippine Consulate of Hawaii, 1959. Pres. Keolu Elem. PTA, 1960-62; mem. satisfaction com. Hawaii Visitors Bur., 1963-66; chmn. budget and rev. panel IV, Aloha United Way, 1966-72, bd. dir., 1971-77, 82-88, chmn. bd., 1984; mem. mgmt. svcs. com., 1977, mem. cen. com., 1977-82, chmn. budget and allocations com., 1982-84; chmn. Kamehameha Dist. fin. com. Aloha coun. Boy Scouts Am., 1966; vice chmn. Businessmen's Cancer Crusade, 1965; chmn. Operation Bayanihan, Hawaii Immigration Task Force, 1970; participant Oahu Housing Workshop, State of Hawaii, Hawaii chpt. HUD, 1970; mem. task force on housing and transp. Alternative Econ. Futures for Hawaii, 1973; chmn. Bicentennial Filipiniana, 1976; campaign chmn. State Rep. Rudolph Pacarro, 1964-68; mem. exec. com. Campaign for Reelection U.S. Senator Hiram L. Fong, 1970, Gov. William Quinn for U.S. Senate, 1976; Rep. candidate for Hawaii Ho. of Reps., 1972; mem. Rep. Citizens Task Force on Housing, 1973; trustee St. Louis Alumni Found., 1970—, Kuakini Med. Ctr., 1984-86, Palama Settlement, 1975-82, v.p., 1976, treas., 1980-82; bd. mgrs. Windward YMCA, 1964-67; bd. advisers St. Louis H.S., 1963-64; bd. gov. Goodwill Industries, 1964; bd. dir. Children's Ctr., Inc., 1975-77, Hawaii Multi-Cultural Arts Ctr., 1977-81, treas., 1979; fin. chmn. St. Stephen's Parish Coun., 1974—; bd. dir. St. Louis Fine Arts Ctr., 1985-88; mem. steering com. Conf. Filipino Voter Registrars, 1962. With U.S. Army, 1945-47. Recipient Man of Yr. award Filipino C. of C., 1965, cert. of merit Aloha United Way, 1971, Honor award Wisdom mag., 1974, Outstanding Alumnus honor medal St. Louis HS, 1976, Island Treasure award Cath. Ch. Hawaii, 2003. Mem. Hawaii State C. of C. (bd. dir. 1964-67, chmn. legis. com. 1966-67, v.p. 1970, chmn. election judges 1971, mem. ad hoc com. bus.-youth rels. 1970—), Filipino C. of C. (past pres. 1965, com. chmn.), Am. Soc. CLU, Soc. Fin. Svcs. Profls., Honolulu Assn. Life Underwriters (bd. dir. 1963-66, del. nat. conv. 1967, chmn. life underwriters tng. coun. 1962-67), Hawaii Estate Planning Coun., Hawaii Plantation Indsl. Editors Assn. (sec.-treas. 1957), St. Louis Alumni Assn. (bd. dir., chmn. fin. 1969-75, pres. 1976, treas. 1977—), Phi Kappa Sigma. Republican. Roman Catholic. Home: 2622 Waolani Ave Honolulu HI 96817-1362 Office: 225 Queen St Apt 12-A Honolulu HI 96813-4603

SOLIMAN, ELSAYED Z., cardiologist, educator; s. Zohair Elsayed and Ratieba Mohy Koura; m. Omaima A. Shalash; children: Karim, Islam, Mai. Cert. cardiologist Egyptian Med. Syndicate, 1997. Med. advisor Africa Egyptian Ministry Fgn. Affairs; asst. prof. Wake Forest U. Sch. Medicine, Winston Salem, NC, 2008—. Head of dept., medicine Mzuzu Ctrl. Hosp., Malawi. Recipient Young Investigator award, Egyptian Soc. Cardiology, 1997—98. Mem.: Am. Heart Assn. Achievements include patents pending for electrocardiograph cable modification. Home: 608 Alpine Rd Winston Salem NC 27104 Office: Wake Forest Univ 2000 W First St Ste 505 Winston Salem NC 27104 Office Fax: 336-716-0834. Business E-Mail: esoliman@wfubmc.edu.

SOLIMON, RONALD JAMES (RON SOLIMAN), museum administrator; m. Elaine Solimon; children: Kristin, Justin. BBA, N.Mex State U., 1973; JD, U. N.Mex Law Sch., 1976. Pres., CEO Indian Pueblo Cultural Ctr., Albuquerque, Indian Pueblos Mktg., Inc., Albuquerque. Bd. mem. Nat. Ctr. Am. Indian Enterprise Devel., Walking Shield, N.Mex Workforce Devel. Bd., N.Mex Comm. on Community Volunteerism, Laguna Devel. Corp., Pueblo Tesuque Devel. Corp. Bd. mem. Albuquerque Conv. & Visitors Bur. Mem.: Tourism Assn. N.Mex (bd. mem.). Office: Indian Pueblo Cultural Ctr Inc 2401 12th St NW Albuquerque NM 87104

SOLIS, CARLOS, lawyer; b. Managua, Nicaragua, May 15, 1945; came to US, 1952; s. Carlos and Luisa (Serrano) S. BA, U. San Francisco, 1967, JD, 1969. Bar: Calif. 1970, US Dist. Ct. (cen. and no. dists.) Calif. 1970, US Ct. Appeals (9th cir.) 1970, US Dist. Ct. (ea. dist.) Calif. 1972, US Dist. Ct. (so. dist.) Calif. 1973, US Supreme Ct. 1973. Assoc. Kindel & Anderson, LA, 1969—76, ptnr., 1976—96, Heller Ehrman LLP, 1996—2005; pvt. practice, 2005—. Exec. legal counsel, bd. dirs. internat. student ctr. UCLA, 1976-86, exec. v.p., 1981-86; instr. atty. asst. program UCLA, 1977-79; bd. advisors LA Internat. Trade Devel. Corp., 1981-87; bd. dirs. Pub. Counsel of LA, 2003-05. Assoc. editor U. San Francisco Law Rev., 1968-69; contbr. articles to profl. jours. Bd. dirs. ARC, LA, 1978-93, 95-05, chmn. audit com., 1985-88, bd. advisors, 1993-05; bd. dirs. March of Dimes, LA, 1982-87, LA Pub. Theater Found., 1978-81, Young Musicians Found., 1979-80, Boys and Girls Club East LA, 1986-89; bd. dirs. Am. Diabetes Assn., LA, 1986-93, chmn., 1989-91, bd. dirs. Calif., 1988-93, chmn., 1992-93, mem. nat. minority initiative task force, 1986-92, bd. dirs. Nat., 1993-95; vice chmn. bd. LA United Way, 1982-83, bd. dirs., 1980-03, corp. bd. dirs., 1982-86, treas., 1989-93; pres. LA Open Golf Found., 1979-80. Recipient Alumni Award U. San Francisco, 1969, Province award Phi Delta Phi, 1969. Mem. LA Jr. Chamber (pres., chmn. bd. dirs. 1980-81, Most Improved com. award 1975, Dir. of Yr. award 1977, Outstanding Bus. Leader award 1980), Assocs. LA C. of C., LA Area C. of C. (bd. dirs. 1979-80), U. San Francisco Alumni Assn. (pres. San Gabriel Valley chpt. 1976-80), Latin Am. Ctr. Assocs. (pres. 1980-82, bd. advisors 1980-88), Alpha Sigmu Nu, Phi Delta Phi. Avocation: travel. Home: 201 La Vereda Rd Pasadena CA 91105-1227 Personal E-mail: carlossolis1000@yahoo.com.

SOLIS, DANIEL S., alderman; Tchr., Chgo.; founder, exec. dir. Latino Youth Alternative HS, Chgo.; exec. dir. Pilsen Neighbors Cmty. Coun., Chgo.; co-founder, exec. dir. United Neighborhood Org., Chgo.; alderman, 25th ward Chgo. City Coun., 1996—, pres. pro tempore, 2001—. Committeman 25th Ward, Chgo.; chmn. Citizenship Assistance Coun., Chgo., 1995; bd. dirs. Eighteen St. Devel. Corp., Chgo., Gads Hill Ctr., Chgo.; bd. trustees Regional Transit Authority, Chgo. Housing Authority; mem. Fannie Mae Nat. Adv. Bd. Democrat. Office: 2439 S Oakley Ave Chicago IL 60608 also: City Hall 121 N LaSalle St Rm 203 Office 14 Chicago IL 60602 Office Phone: 773-523-4100, 312-744-6845. Office Fax: 773-523-9900. Business E-Mail: dsolis@cityofchicago.org.*

SOLIS, HILDA LUCIA, Secretary of Labor, former United States Representative from California; b. LA, Oct. 20, 1957; d. Raul and Juana (Sequiera) Solis; m. Sam H. Sayyad, June 26, 1982. BA in Polit. Sci., Calif. State Polytechnic U., 1979; MA in Pub. Adminstrn., U. So. Calif., 1981. Interpreter Immigration Naturalization Svc., LA, 1977-79; editor in chief Office Hispanic Affairs White House, Washington, 1980-81, mgmt. analyst civil rights. divsn. Office Mgmt. and Budget, 1981-82; field rep. Office Assemblyman Art Torres, LA, 1982; dir. Calif. Student Opportunity & Access Prog., Whittier, 1982—; rep. 57th assembly dist. Calif. State Assembly, Sacramento, 1992-94; mem. Calif. Senate from 24th dist., 1994-2000, US Congress from 32nd Calif. dist., Washington, 2001—09, sr. whip, So. Calif. regional whip, mem. resources com., energy & commerce com., former mem. edn. & workforce com.; sec. US Dept. Labor, Washington, 2009—. Mem. Progressive Caucus, Nat. Women's Polit. Caucus, Mex.-US Interparliamentary Grp., LA County Commn. on Ins., Dem. Women's Working Grp., Congl. Asian Pacific Islander Caucus, Commn. Security & Co-operation in Europe, Congl. Hispanic Caucus; co-vice chair Dem. Steering & Policy Com.; Dem. chair Congl. Caucus Women's Issues, 2005—06; cons. South Coast Consortium, LA, 1986—; bd. dirs. Calif. Commn. Status of Women, 1993—. Bd. trustees Rio Hondo CC, 1985—92; corr. pres. Friendly El Monte Dem. Club, Calif., 1986—. Recipient Meritorious Svc. award, Dept. Def., 1981, Profile in Courage award, John F. Kennedy Libr. Found., 2000. Mem.: El Monte C. of C., El Monte Bus. & Profl. Women's Orgn. (Young Careerist award 1987), Comision Feminil LA (bd. dirs. 1983—84, edn. chmn.), Western Assn. Ednl. Opportunity Pers. (sec. bd. dirs. 1986—), Women of Moose. Democrat. Roman Catholic. Office: US Dept Labor Frances Perkins Bldg 200 Constitution Ave NW Washington DC 20210 Office Phone: 202-693-6001.*

SOLIS, JORGE A., state banking agency administrator; married. BS in Acctg., U. Detroit, MBA in Fin., 1975. With Nat. Bank Detroit (later Chgo. NBD and Bank One), 1975—2002; sr. v.p., divsn. head middle mktg. comml. banking LaSalle Bank, Chgo., 2002; dir. divsn. banking Ill. Dept. Fin. Profl. Regulation, Springfield, Ill., 2007—. Mem. bd. dirs. US/Mex. C. of C. Mem. bd. trustees U. Chgo. Hosps. and Health System, 2005; mem. bd. dirs. Peggy Notebaert Nature Mus., The Joffrey Ballet, Chgo. Pub. Libr. Found., Lawson House YMCA; pres. bd. dirs. Luna Negra Dance Theater. Office: Ill Dept Fin Profl Regulation Divsn Banking 320 W Washington St Springfield IL 62786 Office Phone: 217-785-2900. Office Fax: 217-557-0330. E-mail: jorge.solis@illinois.gov.

SOLÍS, MARCO ANTONIO, singer, composer; b. Ario de Rosales, Michoacan, Mexico, Dec. 29, 1959; Co-founder Los Hermanitos Solis, 1962; co-founder, singer & songwriter Los Bukis, 1975—95; solo career, 1995—. Singer: (albums) (with Los Bukis) Falso Amor, 1975, Yo Te Necesito, 1984, Adonde Vas, 1985, Juntos Otra Ves, 1989, Y Para Siempre, 1989, Travez de Tus Ojos, 1991, Me Volvi a Acordarme de Ti, 1991, Si Me Recuerdas, 1991, Quiereme, 1992, Inalcanzable, 1993, Casas de Carton, 1994, Frente a Frente, 1994, Nortenas Y Chicanas, A Donde Vas, 1995, Triste Imaginar, 1995, A Bailar Con, 1996, Romanticos, 1996, (solo albums) Por Amor a Mi Pueblo, 1995, Romanticos de Corazon, 1996, En Pleno Vuelo, 1996, Marco, 1997, Recuerdos, Tristeza y Soledad, 1998, Trovos de Mi Alma, 1999, En Vivo, 2000, Mas de Mi Alma, 2001, En Concierto, 2001, Ty Amor o Tu Desprecio, 2003, Razon de Sobra, 2004, Dos Idolos, 2005, No Molestar, 2008; actor: (films) La Coyota, 1987, Como Fui a Enamorarme de Ti, 1991. Recipient Latin Grammy award for Best Regional Mex. Song, 2004, Lifetime Achievement award, Billboard Music Awards, 2005, Super Artist Sales award, Chile, 2006, Male Artist of Yr. award, Premio Lo Nuestra Música Latina, 2006, Spl. Recognition award, 2006, Greatest Hits Album of Yr. award, Billboard Latin Music Awards, 2006, Songwriter of Yr., 2008, Latin Songwriter of Yr. award, ASCAP, 2007. Office: c/o Elizabeth Sobol Gomez IMG Artists 152 W 57th St 5th Fl New York NY 10019

SOLIS, OSCAR AZARCON, bishop; b. San Jose City, Philippines, Oct. 13, 1953; arrived in US, 1984; s. Anselmo dela Fuente Solis and Antonio Ortega Azarcon. BST cum laude, U. Santo Tomas, Manila, 1978. Ordained priest Diocese of Cabanatuan, Philippines, 1979; assoc. pastor St. Rocco Ch., Union City, NJ, 1984—98, St. Joseph Co-Cathedral, Thibodaux, La., 1988—92, pastor, 1999—2003, Our Lady of Prompt Succor Ch., Golden Meadow, La., 1993—99, St. Luke Ch., Thibodaux, La., 1999—2003; ordained bishop, 2004; aux. bishop Archdiocese of LA, 2004—, coord. ethnic ministries. Roman Catholic. Achievements include becoming first Filipino-American bishop ordained in the US. Office: Archdiocese of LA 3424 Wilshire Blvd Los Angeles CA 90010-2202 Office Phone: 213-637-7000. E-mail: info@la-archdiocese.org.

SOLIS DOYLE, PATTI, political campaign worker; b. Chgo., Aug. 23, 1965; d. Santiago and Alejandrina (Ortega) S. BA in Comm., Northwestern U., 1990. Asst. to treas. City of Chgo., 1989-91; dir. of scheduling for Hilary Rodham Clinton Clinton-Gore Campaign, Little Rock, 1991-92, Clinton Transition Team, Little Rock, 1992-93; spl. asst. to Pres., dir. of scheduling for First Lady The White House, Washington, 1993—2001; campaign asst. Hillary Clinton 2000 Election Campaign, 2000—01; exec. dir. HILLPAC; campaign mgr., sr. advisor Hillary Clinton 2008 Presdl. Campaign, 2006—08; chief of staff to the v.p. candidate Barack Obama 2008 Presdl. Campaign, 2008. Recipient Latinas of Excellence award, Hispanic Mag., 2007; named one of The 50 Most Powerful Women in NYC, NY Post, 2007. Democrat. Roman Catholic. First Hispanic woman to lead U.S. presidential campaign. Office: 4420 N Fairfax Dr Arlington VA 22203*

SOLIZ, EUSEBIO, military officer; b. San Juan, Tex., Apr. 25, 1979; s. Eusebio and Joangela (Sanchez) Soliz; m. Joangela Sanchez; children: Richard Sanchez, Eusebio, Emma Felicity, Nicholas Sanchez, Michelle Pilar. Enlisted USN, 1997, supr. Ingleside, Tex., 1997—. Decorated Navy Achievement medal. Home: 1011 Espana Dr Portland TX 78374 Personal E-mail: soliz53@yahoo.com.

SOLJACIC, MARIN, physicist, educator; b. Zagreb, Croatia, Feb. 7, 1974; arrived in U.S., 1992; s. Ivo and Marija Soljacic; m. Mihaela Papa, Apr. 2, 1976; 1 child, Fran Daniel. BA in Physics, MIT, 1996, BA in Elec. Engring., 1996; PhD, Princeton U., 2000. Pappalardo fellow MIT, Cambridge, Mass., 2000—03, prin. rsch. scientist, 2003—05, asst. prof., 2005—. Founder Witricity Corp., 2007—; spkr. in field. Contbr. chapters to books, articles to sci. jours. Recipient Adolph Lomb medal, Optical Soc. Am., 2005, TR35 award, Tech. Rev., 2006; named a MacArthur Fellow, The John D. and Catherine T. MacArthur Found., 2008. Mem.: Phi Beta Kappa. Achievements include 15 patents. Office: MIT Room 6C-419 77 Mass Ave Cambridge MA 02139

SOLKOFF, JEROME IRA, lawyer, educator; b. Rochester, NY, Feb. 15, 1939; s. Samuel and Dorothy (Krovetz) S.; m. Doreen Hurwitz, Aug. 11, 1963; children: Scott Michael, Anne Lynn. BS Sch. Indsl. Rels. and Labor Rels., Cornell U., 1961; JD, U. Buffalo, 1964. Bar: N.Y. 1965, Fla. 1974, U.S. Dist. Ct. (we. dist.) N.Y. 1965; cert. elder law atty., Fla. Bar, Nat. Elder Law, Found. of Nat. Acad. of Elder Law Attys., ABA. Assoc. Nusbaum, Tarricone, Weltman, Bilgore & Silver, Rochester, N.Y., 1964-66, Mousaw, Vigdor, Reeves, Heilbronner & Kroll, Rochester, 1966-70; sr. mcpl. atty. Urban Renewal Agy., Rochester, 1970-73; sole practice Rochester, 1970-73; chief legal counsel Arlen Realty Mgmt., Inc., Miami, Fla., 1973-75; assoc. Britton, Cohen, Kaufman, Benson & Schantz, Miami, 1975-76; chief legal counsel First Mortgage Investors, Miami Beach, Fla., 1976-79; ptnr. Cassel & Cassel, P.A., Miami, 1979-82; sole practice Deerfield Beach, Fla., 1982—. Lectr. on fgn. investment practices in U.S., Eng., 1981, estate planning, 1982—, medicaid law and elder law, 1988—. Author: Fundamentals of Foreign Investing in American Real Estate and Businesses, 1981, Checklist of N.Y. Mortgage Foreclosure Procedures, 1970, History of Municipal Employee Unions, 1964, Practice Guide for Florida Elder Law, 1996, National Elder Law Forms Manual, 2005, and yearly supplements Thomson West Bd. dirs. Broward Homebound Program, 1990-2001, pres. 1998-99; bd. dirs. Jewish Cmty. Ctrs. of South Broward, Fla., 1979-90, NE Alzheimers Daycare Ctr., Inc., 1990-92; mem. exec. bd. dirs. Broward Alzheimers Assn., 1995—; co-chair Fla. Alzheimers Pub. Policy steering com., 1999-2001. Named Advocate of Yr., Broward County Legal Aid Assn., 2003. Mem. ABA (mem. sects. real property, trust and probate law), Fla. Bar Assn. (sects. real property, trust and probate law, vice-chmn. com. on the elderly 1987-91, lectr. estate planning for the aging and disabled 1989—, founder, chmn. elder law sect. 1994-95, elder law sect., chmn. ethics com. 1998-2000), Nat. Acad. Elder Law Attys., Elder Law Attys., Fla. Acad. Elder Law Attys.

SOLL, JACOB, history professor; b. Madison, Wis., Dec. 22, 1968; s. David R. and Beth Bronfenbrenner Soll; m. Ellen Wayland-Smith, Aug. 26, 1999; children: Sophia Cornelia, Lydia Augusta. BA, U. Iowa, Iowa City, 1991; DEA, EHESS, Paris, 1995; PhD, Cambridge U., Eng., 1998. Lectr. Princeton U., NJ, 1997—99; assoc. prof. Rutgers U., Camden, NJ, 1999—; Fernand Braudel prof. EUI, Fielsole, Florence, Toscana, Italy, 2007—08. Author: (book) Publishing The Prince: History, Reading, and the Birth of Political Criticism (Jacques Barzun prize, Am. Philos. Soc., 2005), The Information Master: Jean-Baptiste Colbert's Secret State Intelligence System. Recipient Forkosch prize, Jour. History Ideas, 2000; Franklin grant, Am. Philos. Soc., 2004, fellowship, Nat. Endowment for the Humanities, 2005—06, Guggenheim fellowship, 2009. Mem.: Renaissance Soc. America, French Hist. Soc., Am. Hist. Soc. Avocations: cooking, winecollecting, snorkeling. Office: Rutgers Univ Dept History Camden NJ 08102 Business E-Mail: soll@crab.rutgers.edu.

SOLLECITO, LARRY A., energy executive; b. Feb. 1952; BS in Computer Sci. and Systems Engring., Union Coll. Joined GE Co., 1975, gen. mgr. e-Business and global sourcing gen. mgr. in businesses within GE Consumer and Industrial and GE Enterprise Solutions, pres., gen. mgr. Multilin a business within GE Consumer & Industrial, pres., CEO Enterprise Solutions, a business within GE Tech. Infrastructure, 2009—. Office: GE Digital Energy 170 Science Pkwy Rochester NY 14620

SOLLENDER, JOEL DAVID, accountant, consultant, financial executive; b. NYC, Nov. 11, 1924; s. Samuel and Flora (Blumenthal) S.; m. Dorothy Leaf, Aug. 6, 1958; children: Jeffrey D., Jonathan L. BS, N.Y. U., 1946. CPA N.Y., 1947. Staff auditor Ernst & Young, NYC, 1946-50; with United Mchts. & Mfrs., Inc., NYC, 1950-86, chief acctg. officer, 1976—, corp. contr., 1977—, sr. v.p., 1980—, mem. exec. mgmt. com. also bd. dirs. subsidiary cos.; assoc. dir. N.Y. Hist. Soc., NYC, 1986—89; mem. adv. coun. to Office of Charities Registration Dept. State, N.Y. State, 1988-89; v.p. fin. Piedmont Industries, NYC, 1989-90; exec. v.p., CFO Earthworm Inc., 1990—92; fin. mgmt. cons.; sr. cons. Internat. Exec. Svc. Corps Agy. for Aid for Internat. Devel., Kazakstan, 1996—. Adv. coun. San Diego State U., 1997—; audit com. San Diego Mus. Art, 1997-2002; fin. com. Globe Theater, 2003-04, audit com., 2004—; fin. com. mem. SD Youth Symphony, 2009. With US Army, 1943—45, WW II. Decorated Combat Infantry Badge, Purple Heart with oak leaf cluster, Prisoner of War medal, Bronze Star medal. Mem. AICPA, N.Y. State Soc. CPAs (chief fin. officer com.), Am. Inst. Corp. Contrs., Rancho Bernardo (Calif.) Men's Club, Bailiwick Club (Greenwich, Conn.), Greenhaven Yacht Club (Rye).

SOLLERS, JOSEPH SEDWICK, III, lawyer; b. Balt. AB, Princeton Univ., 1977; JD with honors, Univ. Md., 1982. Bar: D.C. 1983. Law clk. Judge Norman P. Ramsey, US Dist Ct. Md.; mng. ptnr., Spec. Matters & Govt. Investigations Practice Group King & Spalding LLP, Washington. Fellow: Am. Col. Trial Lawyers (co-chmn. D.C. subcom., Criminal Litigation com.); mem.: ABA. Office: King & Spalding LLP 1700 Pennsylvania Ave NW Washington DC 20006 Office Phone: 202-626-5612. Office Fax: 202-626-3737. Business E-Mail: wsollers@kslaw.com.

SOLLINS, SUSAN, curator, television producer; m. Earle Brown (dec., 2002). BA, Sarah Lawrence Coll.; postgrad., Columbia U. Dir. studio art program Barnard Coll., U. Columbia, NYC, 1964-66; editor Harry N. Abrams, Inc., NYC, 1967; curator of Edn. Nat. Mus. Am. Art, Smithsonian Inst., Washington, 1968-71; producer arts interviews Nat. Pub. Radio, 1972-74; exec. dir., co-founder, curator Independent Curators Inc., NYC, 1974—94; exec. prodr., curator Art:21, PBS, 2001—. Dir. Inner City Art Program, Collegiate Sch., NYC, 1965; instr. Art History, NYU, 1965-66; guest curator Balt. Mus. of Art, 1972-73; cons. Balt. Pub. Schs., 1972, San Francisco Mus. of Art, 1975, Am. Assn. of Mus., 1975, London (Ontario) Art Gallery, 1976, Neuberger Mus., SUNY Purchase, 1976, Denver Art Mus. 1976, Portland (Oreg.) Art Mus., 1977, Georgetown U., 1988 and numerous other museums, ednl insts. and art galleries; curator contemporary art Art in Landscape, 1975, New Work, NY, 1977, Supershow!, 1979, New Sculpture: Icon and Environment, 1983, Points of View: Four Painters, 1985, Eternal Metaphors: New Art from Italy, 1988, Team Spirit, 1990. Author (tchr. instructional materials on art and art history) Great Ideas, 1976, The City-Project Ideas, 1977, The Decordova Lessons, 1979; (films) You're It, 1971, Learning to Look, 1977; contbr. articles to profl. jours., mags. and newspapers; exec. prodr. and curator: (TV series) Art:21: Art in the Twenty-First Century, 2001, 2003, 2005, 2007. Nat. Jury Awards in the Visual Arts, Southeastern Ctr. for Contemporary Art, 1988; pres. Earl Brown Music Found., Rye, NY, 1996-. Recipient Gov.'s award for Outstanding Service to Artists, Skowhegan, 2008. Mem. Mass. Arts Coun., NY State Arts Coun., Art Table, Inc. (bd. dirs. 1984-87), Ivy Labs. (bd. dirs., chmn. 1991). Office: Earl Brown Music Found 52 Brevoort Ln Rye NY 10580

SOLLORS, WERNER, literature and language educator; PhD, Freie U., Berlin, 1975. Wissenschaftlicher asst., asst. prof. John F. Kennedy Inst. Freie U., Berlin; from asst. to assoc. prof. English and Comparative Lit. Columbia U.; Henry B. and Anne M. Cabot Prof. English Lit., prof. Afro-Am. studies Harvard U., Cambridge, Mass. Author: Amiri Baraka/LeRoi Joines: The Quest for a Populist Modernism, 1978, Beyond Ethnicity: Consent and Descent in American Culture, 1986, Neither Black Nor White Yet Both: Thematic Explorations of Interracial Literature, 1997, Schiesswerder 29, 2006, Ethnic Moderism, 2008; contbr. chapters to books Das amerikanische Drama der Gegenwart, 1976, The Harvard Encyclopedia of American Ethnic Groups, 1980, Reconstructing American Literary History, 1986, 1986, Columbia Literary History of the United States, 1988, 1988, Critical Terms for Literary Study, 1990, 1990, Looking Inward, Looking Outward: From the 1920s through the 1940s, 1990, 1990, Nationale und kulturelle Identitat: Studien zur Entwicklung des kollektiven Bewusstseins in der Neuzeit, 1991, Immigrants in Two Democracies: French and American Experience, 1992, Intersecting Boundaries: The Theatre of Adrienne Kennedy, 1992, Il razzismo e le sue storie, 1992, Swedes in America: Intercultural and Interethnic Perspectives on Contemporary Research, 1993, Multiculturalism and the Canon of American Culture, 1993, Configurations de l'ethnicite aux Etats-Unis, 1993, History & Memory in African-American Culture, 1994, Thematics: New Approaches, 1995, Thematics Reconsidered: Essays in Honor of Horst Jr. Daemmrich, 1995, Performances in American Literature and Culture, 1995, New Essays on Henry Roth's Call It Sleep, 1996, Families, 1996, Cultural Difference and the Literary Text, 1996, Beyond Pluralism, 1998, The Sally Hemings-Thomas Jefferson Relationship, 1999, Columbia Companion to 20th Century American Short Fiction, 2001, Dream-Fluted Cane: Essays on Jean Toomes and the Harlem Renaissance, 2001, Not English Only: Redefining "American" in American Studies, 2001, American Studies and Peace, 2001, Mixed-Race Literature, 2001; editor: A Bibliographic Guide to Afro-American Studies, 1972, A Bibliographic Guide to Afro-American Studies Supplement I, 1974; co-editor: Bibliographie amerikanistischer Veröffentlichungen in der DDR bis, 1968, 1976, Varieties of Black Experience at Harvard, 1986, The Invention of Ethnicity, 1989, The Life Stories of Undistinguished Americans as Told by Themselves, 1990, 1999, The Return of Thematic Criticism, 1993, Cane, 1993, Blacks at Harvard: A Documentary History of African-American Experience at Harvard and Radcliffe, 1993, The Black Columbiad: Defining Moments in African-American Literature and Culture, 1994, Theories of Ethnicity: A Classical Reader, 1996, The Promised Land, 1997, Multilingual America: Transnationalism, Ethnicity and the Languages of American Literature, 1998, The Multilingual Anthology of American Literature, 2000, The Norton Critical Edition of Olaudah Equiano, 2000, Interracialism: Black-White Intermarriage in American History, Literature and Law, 2000, The Adrienne Kennedy Reader, 2001, German? American? Literature?: New Directions in German-American Studies, 2002, Interracial Literature: An Anthology of Black-White Contacts in the Old World and the New, 2004, Frank J. Webb: Fiction, Essays and Poetry, 2005, Georges, 2007, The Autobiography of W.E.B. Du Bois, 2007, A New Literary History of America, 2009. Recipient Constance Rourke prize Am. Studies Assn., 1990; John Simon Guggenheim Meml. fellow, Andrew W. Mellon faculty fellow Harvard U., Walter Channing Cabot fellow Harvard U., 1997-98; NEH fellow, 1999-00. Fellow: Am. Acad. of Arts and Scis. Office: Harvard U Barker Center 12 Quincy St Cambridge MA 02138-3804 Office Phone: 617-495-4116.

SOLLS, MARK A., lawyer; b. 1956; married; 3 children. BA in Fin., U. Ill., 1977; JD, So. Ill. U., 1980. Bar: Ill. 1980, Tex. 1982, cert.: mediator. Pvt. practice; v.p., gen. counsel, sec. Pronet, Inc., 1993—97, Dal-Tile Internat., Inc., 1998—2002; exec. v.p., general counsel, sec. Wyndham Internat., Inc., Dallas, 2002—.

SOLLY, RICHARD PETER, music educator; s. Richard Gibson and Jane Ruth Solly. BA, Coll. NJ, 1975, MA, 1976. Cert. tchr. Pa., NJ. Asst. organist Trinity Episcopal Cath., Trenton, NJ, 1975—77; organist, choirmaster, dir. St. Paul's Luth. Ch., Doylestown, Pa., 1972—; tchr. music North Penn Sch. Dist., Lansdale, 1978—. Adj. faculty Bucks County CC, Newtown, Pa., 1977—78; program annotator Bucks County Symphony Orch., Doylestown, 1988—. Composer: The Hymnal, 1982, Hymnal for the Hours, 1989. Recipient Srs. Choice award, North Penn Sch. Dist., 1996, 1997, 1998. Mem.: Organ Hist. Soc., Am. Guild Organists, Kappa Delta Pi. Avocations: travel, baseball, railroading. Home: PO Box 264 Doylestown PA 18901-0264

SOLMSSEN, PETER, retired academic administrator; b. Berlin, Nov. 1, 1931; m. Kathleen Mailliard, Dec. 2001. AB, Harvard U., 1952; JD, U. Pa., 1959. Atty. Ballard, Spahr, Andrews & Ingersoll, Phila., 1959-60; with U.S. Fgn. Service, 1961; vice consul Singapore, 1962-63; asst. to under sec. of state, 1963-65; 2d sec. Rio de Janeiro, 1965-67; Cultural attache U.S. Dept. State, Sao Paulo, Brazil, 1967-70; adviser on arts Washington, 1974-80; dep. ambassador at large for cultural affairs, 1981-83; pres. Phila. Coll. Art, 1983-87, U. of the Arts, Phila., 1987-2000. One-man photography exhbns. include: Mus. Art, Sao Paulo. Author and illustrator. Mem.: Philadelphia; Century Assn.

SOLO, ASHU M. G., engineer, researcher; b. Saskatoon, Sask., Can., Sept. 19, 1971; USA; s. Madan M. and Suman Gupta. BSc in Elec. and Computer Engring., U. Waterloo, Ont. Can. Intern engr. Bell-Northern Rsch Ltd., Ottawa, Ont., 1989; undergrad. rsch. asst., VLSI group U. Waterloo, 1990, undergrad. rsch. asst., computer architecture lab., 1990, intern engr. hardware design lab., math faculty computing facility, 1992; intern engr. Allied Signal Aerospace Can., Etobicoke, Ont., 1992, Automation Engring. Assocs. Ltd., Toronto, Ont., 1993; prin. Maverick Techs. America Inc., 1994—, r & d engr., 1994—; IT ptnr. Foreign Workers Alliance, 2007—. Undergrad. rsch. asst. VLSI Group, U. Waterloo, 1990. Contbr. articles to profl. jours., chapters to books. Officer cadet Res. Infantry Can. Army, 1995—96, Brampton, Ont. Recipient Achievement award, Worldcomp, 2006—07, Disting. Svc. award, World Congress Computer Sci., 2008. Achievements include research in methods for maintaining power flow to customers during reconfiguration of radial power distribution systems; methods for multiobjective optimization of power distribution system operations. Avocations: kickboxing, martial arts, motorcycling, sports, exercise. Office: Maverick Techs America Inc Ste 201 100 Alta St San Francisco CA 94133 Business E-Mail: amgsolo@mavericktechnologies.us.

SOLO, JOYCE RUBENSTEIN, volunteer; b. Buffalo, Feb. 14, 1924; d. Jay Harry and Rose (Maisel) Rubenstein; m. Richard D. Solo, Jan. 6, 1946; children: Harry Jay Solo, Eleanor Solo, Sally Solo. BA, Wellesley Coll., 1945. Mem. S.E. Pa. Health Coord. Coun., 1978—84; chair reach to recovery Phila. divsn. Am. Cancer Soc., 1985—87; sec. Sarasota County Health Care Coord. Adv. Coun., Fla., 1993—95; chair sr. adv.

com. Sarasota Meml. Hosp., 1996—98; vol. Reach to Recovery Breast Cancer Task Force, Manatee County Am. Cancer Soc.; mem. numerous other health and civic orgn. activities; pres. women's bd. Temple Beth Israel, 1996—98, bd. dirs., 1998—2000; mem. governing bd. Health Systems Agy. S.E. Pa., 1977—86. Mem.: LWV (v.p. Pa. chpt. 1969—73, pres. Phila. 1975—77, pres. Sarasota County 1990—92, healthcare com. chair 1988—90, 1992—), Phi Beta Kappa. Home: 1570 Tower Blvd Apt 119 North Mankato MN 56003 Personal E-mail: rjoysolo#1@hotmail.com.

SOLO, ROBERT ALEXANDER, economist, educator; b. Phila., Aug. 2, 1916; s. Louis C. and Rebecca (Muchnick) S.; m. Roselyn Starr; 1 dau., Tova Maria. BS, Harvard U., 1938; MA, Am. U., 1941; PhD, Cornell U., 1953. Economist fed. and war agys., 1939-41; author, script chief Sta. WCAU-TV, Phila., 1949-50; mem. faculty Rutgers U., New Brunswick, N.J., 1953-55, McGill U., Montreal, Que., Can., 1955-56, CCNY, 1956-58; sr. research economist Princeton U., 1965-66; prof. dept. econs. Mich. State U., East Lansing, 1966-87, prof. emeritus, 1987—; dir. Inst. Internat. Bus. and Devel. Studies, 1966-68. Mem. faculty Johns Hopkins U., Balt., summer 1953, U. Mich., Ann Arbor, summer 1958; lectr. L'Ecole Practique des Hautes Etudes, Sorbonne, Paris, 1964-65; research Institut Recherch Economique et Planification, lectr. U. Grenoble, France, 1972-73; prof. associe U. Paris IV, Dauphine, 1971, 73; cons. NASA, 1965-67, OECD, 1963-65, Commonwealth of P.R., 1959-61, U.S. Dept. Justice, 1994-96; project chmn. Study on Info. Tech., Nat. Conf. Bd., 1969-72; project dir. Nat. Planning Assn., Washington, 1961-63; U.S. del. Yugoslavian Conf. on Transfer of Tech., Belgrade, 1974; mem. Alan T. Waterman award Com., 1976-77; expert witness Dept. Justice, Washington, L.A., 1995-97. Author: Economics and the Public Interest, 1955, Synthetic Rubber: A Case Study in Technological Development under Public Direction, 1959 (reprinted as Across the High Technology Threshold 1980), Economic Organizations and Social Systems, 1967 (reissued 2001), (with Everett Rogers) Inducing Technological Change for Economic Growth and Development, 1973, The Political Authority and the Market System, 1974, Organizing Science for Technology Transfer in Economic Development, 1975, The Positive State, 1981, (with Charles Anderson) Value Judgement and Income Distribution, 1981, Opportunity Knocks: American Economic Policy after Gorbachev, 1991, The Philosophy of Science and Economics, 1991, The Super Power and the Serb, 1998, The Song of Songs: The Harvard Version, 1998, also other books in field; contbr. chpts. to books, articles to profl. jours. Fulbright fellow, 1972-73 Mem. Council European Studies (steering com., exec. com., chmn. research com. 1974-77). Home: 4609 Chippewa Dr Okemos MI 48864-2009 Personal E-mail: solo@msu.edu.

SOLOMON, ABRAHAM LEV, mathematics professor; b. Columbus, Ohio, Mar. 14, 1980; s. Ronald Mark and Myriam Huberman Solomon. BS in Engring. Physics, U. Calif. Berkeley, 2001; MS in Math., Ohio State U., Columbus, 2003; attending in Atmospheric Sci., U. Chgo., 2005—. Lab mgr. Superconductive Somponents Inc., Columbus, 1997—99; math lectr. Fla. Internat. U., Miami, 2003—05. McCormick fellowship, U. Chgo., 2005—06. Avocations: skiing, bicycling, reading, soccer, basketball. Business E-Mail: solomona@uchicago.edu.

SOLOMON, ANDREW P., lawyer; b. Newark, 1953; BA, Brown U., 1975; JD, Harvard U., 1984. Bar: NY 1985. Ptnr. Sullivan & Cromwell, NYC, 1992—, now mng. ptnr. tax group. Mem.: NY State Bar Assn. (tax section exec. com., co-chair, com. of fin. intermediaries). Office: Sullivan & Cromwell LLP 125 Broad St New York NY 10004-2489 also: Sullivan & Cromwell LLP 1 New Fetter Ln London EC4A 1AN England Office Phone: 212-558-4000, 44 20 7959 8900. Office Fax: 212-558-3588. Business E-Mail: solomona@sullcrom.com.

SOLOMON, ARTHUR CHARLES, pharmacist; b. Gary, Ind., May 30, 1947; s. Laurence A. and Dorothy B. (Klippel) S.; m. Janet Evelyn Irak, Aug. 23, 1969; children: Thomas, Michael, Mark, Jill. BS in Pharmacy, Purdue U., 1970, MS in Clin. Pharmacy, 1972; PharmD. Registered pharmacist; cert. nuclear pharmacist. Clin. prof. pharmacy U. Tex., Austin, 1972-75; v.p. Nuclear Pharmacy, Inc., Atlanta, 1975-83; exec. v.p., COO Diagnostek, Inc., Albuquerque, 1983-95; pres. Health Care Svcs., Inc., 1990-95; exec. v.p., COO Value Rx, Albuquerque, 1995-96; pres. Solomon and Assocs., Albuquerque, 1996-97; pres., CEO, dir. SP Pharms. LLC, Albuquerque, 1997—2001; sr. v.p. Cardinal Health, Albuquerque, 2001—04; COO PharmaFab, Grand Prairie, Tex., 2004—. Adj. prof. U. N.Mex., 1992—. Contbr. articles to profl. jours. Named Disting. Alumnus Purdue U., 1998. Fellow Am. Soc. Cons. Pharmacists, Parental Drug Assn.; mem. Am. Pharm. Assn., Am. Assn. Pharm. Scis., Am. Soc. Hosp. Pharmacy, Nat. Assn. Retail Druggists, Nat. Coun. Prescription Drug Programs, Am. Managed Care Pharmacy Assn. (pres., dir.), Rho Chi, Pi Kappa Phi. Republican. Roman Catholic. Avocations: golf, woodworking, gardening. Home: 6709 Alpine Ln Colleyville TX 76034-7290 Office: ThermaFab 2940 N Hwy 360 Grand Prairie TX 75050 E-mail: asolomon@pharmafab.com.

SOLOMON, BARRY J., human services administrator, consultant; b. Boston, May 16, 1934; s. Samuel and Ethel (Fleishman) Solomon; m. C. Priscilla Fugate, June 29, 1958; children: R. Stephen, Jon, Julie Ellen. BS in Biology and Chemistry, Tufts U., Medford, Mass., 1955; MBA in Health Care Adminstrn., Xavier U., Cin., 1960; MPH in Health Care Adminstrn., U. NC, 1989. Chief med. record adminstr. USPHS Hosp., Lexington, Ky., 1956-59; asst. dir. Union Meml. Hosp., Balt., 1960-61; asst. adminstr. James Lawrence Kernan Hosp., Balt., 1961-67; asst. to dean, lectr. health edn. and med. care sects. Yale U. Sch. Medicine, New Haven, 1967-70; dir. health svcs., clin. asst. prof. pharmacy adminstrn. U. RI, Kingston, 1970-76; assoc. dir. for adminstrn. USPHS Hosp., Norfolk, Va., 1976-81; dir., COO, sr. fellow in social medicine Montefiore Hosp., Bronx, NY, 1981-84; assoc. v.p. for med. affairs, mem. exec. coun. of Med. Sch. U. South Fla., Tampa, 1984-89; assoc. prof., acting chmn. dept. comprehensive medicine U. So. Fla., Tampa, 1984-89, assoc. prof. Coll. Pub. Health, 1984-89; cons. in health adminstrn., Columbia, Md., 1989-93; v.p. for acad. affairs North Broward Hosp. Dist., Ft. Lauderdale, Fla., 1993-96; chmn. bd. dirs. Sr. Benefit Ctrs. Am., Inc., 1998-2000. 1st v.p. bd. trustees, CEO Count and Countess de Hoernle Alzheimer's Pavillion, 2000—06, cons. to bd. dirs., 2006—; pres. Villa D'Este Condominium, Inc., 1999—2001; exec. com., nominating com. Vis. Nurse Assn. Tampa Bay, 1987—90; planning com. bd. trustees Hillsborough County Hosp. Authority, 1986—88; profl. affairs com. bd. trustees H. Lee Moffitt Cancer Ctr. and Rsch. Inst., 1986—88; affiliation com. S.W. Fla. Blood Bank, 1988—89; instr. hosp. adminstrn. Xavier U., 1960; course asst., instr. Am. Med. Record Assn., 1962—72; instr. Howard U. Coll. Continuing Edn., Washington, 1993; cons. St. Elizabeth Hosp., Covington, Ky., 1959, City Hosp. Ctr. Elmhurst, 1965, Hall-Brooke Hosp., Westport, Conn., 1968—69, Conn. Mental Health Ctr., New Haven, 1969—70, South County Hosp., Wakefield, RI, 1970—76, Centurion Hosp., Tampa, 1989, Primary Care Svcs., Tampa, 1991, Holland & Knight, Tampa, 1991, NCC Internat., Colchester, England, 1991, F. W. Assocs., Tampa, 1989—92, Decking Design, Norfolk, 1986—93, SMinc., Columbia, 1993, Internat. Flooring & Protective Coatings, Inc., Norfolk, 1993—; sr. cons. Meisel Assocs., Inc., NYC, 1983—; bd. dirs. Care Source, Inc., 2007—; patient safety strategic team North Broward Med. Ctr., 2007—. Contbr. articles to profl. jours. Mem. Nat. Com. Religion and Health, 1982—84; mem., vice chmn. Chariho Sch. Bd., Richmond, RI, 1974—76; mem. Broward Econ. Devel. Coun., Inc.; trustee Montefiore-Mosholu Cmty. Ctr., 1981—84. Lt. USPHS, 1956—59, capt. USPHS, 1976—81. Recipient citation, Suncoast chp. Am. Heart Assn., 1988. Fellow: Am. Coll. Healthcare Execs.; mem.: APHA. Avocation: tennis. Home: 2863 Via Venezia Deerfield Beach FL 33442-8633

SOLOMON, CALEB P., editor; b. Mar. 3, 1959; BA, Columbia Coll., 1980; MA, Columbia U. Grad. Sch. Journalism, 1981. Reporter The Wall St. Jour., Houston, head of Tex. region; editor The Wall St. Jour. New Eng., Boston, 1997—2000; tech., media, mktg. and mgmt. editor The Wall St. Jour. Europe, Brussels, 2000—01, asst. mng. editor, 2001—02, The Boston Globe, 2003—08, Page One editor, 2007—, mng. editor news, 2008—. Fellow Sulzberger Exec. Leadership Program, 2007. Office: Boston Globe PO Box 55819 Boston MA 02205-5819 Office Phone: 617-929-3058. E-mail: solomon@globe.com.

SOLOMON, DARLENE J.S., electronics executive; BS, Stanford Univ.; PhD, MIT; grad. exec. develop. program, Stanford Univ. Rsch. & mgmt. positions Hewlett-Packard Laboratories, 1984—99; dir. Life Sciences Technologies Lab. & sr. dir. rsch. & develop. tech. life sciences & chem. analysis Agilent Technologies, Palo Alto, Calif., 1999—2003, v.p. Agilent Labs & chief tech. officer, 2003—. Chair. R&D Calif. Blue Ribbon Task Force on Nanotechnology; mem. adv. bd. NSF Nanobiotechnology Ctr., A-STAR Singapore Econ. Develop., Univ. Calif. Davis, Viterbi Sch. Engring. Univ. So. Calif., Joint Venture Tech. Convergence Consortium, Bay Area Sci. & Innovation Consortium. Recipient Tribute to Women and Industry award, YWCA, 2004; named one of Women Worth Watching, Diversity Jour., 2007; named to Women in Tech. Internat. Hall of Fame, 2001. Achievements include patents in field. Office: Agilent Technologies Inc 5301 Stevens Creek Blvd Santa Clara CA 95051-7201

SOLOMON, DAVID HARRIS, geriatrician, educator; b. Cambridge, Mass., Mar. 7, 1923; s. Frank and Rose (Roud) Solomon; m. Ronda L. Markson, June 23, 1946; children: Patti Jean Sinaiko, Nancy Ellen. AB, Brown U., 1944; MD, Harvard U., 1946. Intern Peter Bent Brigham Hosp., Boston, 1946—47, resident, 1947—48, 1950—51; fellow endocrinology New Eng. Center Hosp., Boston, 1951—52; faculty UCLA Sch. Medicine, 1952—, prof. medicine, 1966—93, vice chmn. dept. medicine, 1968—71, chmn. dept., 1971—81, assoc. dir. geriatrics, 1982—89; dir. UCLA Ctr. on Aging, 1991—96; prof. emeritus UCLA, 1993—. Chief med. svc. Harbor Gen. Hosp., Torrance, Calif., 1966—71; cons. Wadsworth VA Hosp., LA, 1952—93, Sepulveda VA Hosp., 1971—93; cons. metabolism tng. com. USPHS, 1960—64, endocrinology study sect., 1970—73; cons. RAND Corp., 1997—. Editor: Jour. Am. Geriatric Soc., 1988—93; contbr. numerous articles to profl. jours. Recipient Ollie Randall award, Nat. Coun. on the Aging, 2004. Master: ACP (John Phillips Meml. award 2002); mem.: AAAS, Gerontol. Soc. Am. (Freeman award 1997), Am. Geriatrics Soc. (bd. dir. 1985—93, Milo Leavitt award 1992, Disting. Svc. award 1993, Edward Henderson award 1999, David H. Solomon Disting. Svc. award named in his honor), Am. Fedn. Aging Rsch. (Irving S. Wright award 1990), Western Assn. Physicians (councillor 1972—75, pres. 1983—84), Inst. Medicine Nat. Acad. Sci., Am. Thyroid Assn. (pres. 1973—74, Disting. Svc. award 1986), Endocrine Soc. (Robert H. Williams award 1989), We. Soc. Clin. Rsch. (councillor 1963—65, Mayo Soley award 1986), Am. Soc. Clin. Investigation, Assn. Am. Physicians, UCLA Med. Alumni Assn. (Extraordinary Merit award 2002), Assn. Profs. of Medicine (pres. 1980—81), Alpha Omega Alpha, Sigma Xi, Phi Beta Kappa. Achievements include The Parlow-Solomon Chair on Aging named in his honor at UCLA School of Medicine. Home: 3640 Dragonfly Dr Apt 202 Thousand Oaks CA 91360-8445 Home Phone: 805-241-4789. Personal E-mail: dsolomon1@earthlink.net.

SOLOMON, EDWARD IRA, chemistry professor, researcher; b. NYC, Oct. 20, 1946; s. Mordecai L. and Sally S. Solomon; m. Darlene Joy Spira, Sept. 15, 1984; children: Mitchell Landau, Paige Elana. BS, Rensselaer Poly. Inst., 1968; PhD, Princeton U., 1972. Rsch. assoc. Princeton U., NJ, 1972-73; postdoctoral fellow H.C. Ørsted Inst., Copenhagen, 1973-74, Calif. Inst. Tech., Pasadena, 1974-75; asst. prof. MIT, Cambridge, Mass., 1975-79, assoc. prof., 1979-81, prof., 1981-82, Stanford U., Calif., 1982-91, Monroe E. Spaght prof. humanities and sci., 1991—, SSRL prof., 2005—. Cons. prof., World Bank lectr. Xiamen U., People's Republic of China, 1984: O.K. Rice lectr. U. NC, 1984, Reilly lectr. U. Notre Dame, 1985; invited prof. U. Paris, 1987; 1st Glen Seaborg lectr. U. Calif., 1990; Frontiers in Chem. Rsch. lectr. Tex. A&M U., 1990; ACS lectr., Argentina, 1992; invited prof. Tokyo Inst. Tech., 1992; Xerox lectr. U. Alta., 1993; lectr. NSC Republic of China, 1993; Leermakers lectr. Wesleyan U., 1994; Amoco lectr. Ind. U., 1995; Kahn lectr. U. N.Mex., 1996, Golden Jubilee invited prof. Tata Inst., India, 1996; Karcher lectr. U. Okla., 1997; Colloquium 3eme Cucle, Switzerland, 1998; FMC lectr. Princeton U., 1998; A.D. Little lectr. MIT, 1998, Nobel Found. lectr. Stockholm U., 2000; invited prof. Tata Inst. Bombay, India, 2000; Crawford lectr. in spectroscopy U. Minn., 2004; McElvain lectr. U. Wis.; Walton lectr. Purdue U., Hill Meml. lectr., Cady lectr., U. Wash.; Kieler Woche lectr., Kiel U., Dawson lectr., U. Ky.; Andreas Albrecht Lectureship, Cornell U., 2009; Proctor & Gamble Lectr., U. Ariz., 2008; Thomas Chemistry Scholar, U. Mo.- Columbia, 2007; Frontiers Lecturer, Tex. A & M U., 2007, Mans B. Jonasson Lectr., 2009, Andreas Albrecht Lectr., 2009, Harteck Lectr., 2009, Sunney Chan Lectr., 2009, Highly Cited rschr.; Inst. Sci. Info., 2005. Assoc. editor Inorganic Chemistry, 1985—; bd. editors Jour. Inorganic Biochemistry, 1991-; mem. editl. bd. Chem. Revs., 1990—, Chemtracts Inorganic Chemistry, 1992-, Chemistry Biology, 1993-94, Jour. Biol. Inorganic Chemistry, 1995-03, Coord. Chem. Revs., 1996-, Indian Jour. Chemistry, 2001-, Ctrl. European Jour. Chemistry, 2003-, Inorganica Chemica Acta, 2005-, Metal Based Drugs, 2006-, Chemistry Ctrl. Jour., 2007-; contbr. articles to profl. 4 jours. including Jour.; numerous other lectureships; Am. Chem. Soc., Inorganic Chemistry, Procs. of NAS, Phys. Rev. Sci. Mem. panels NIH, NSF, Washington; mem. vis. coms. Exxon, U. Calif., Santa Cruz. Recipient Dean award for disting. tchg., 1990, Remsen award Md. ACS and Johns Hopkins U., 1994, NIH Merit award, 1995, G.W. Wheland medal, U. Chgo., 2001, Aldrich Sponsored lectureship, Northwestern, 2001, Frontiers Biol. Chem. award, Max Planck Inst., NIH Merit award, 2002, Centenary medal and lectureship Royal Soc. UK, 2003, Chakravorty award & lectr., Chemical Rsch. Soc. India, 2008, Bailar medal, U. Ill., 2007, Solomon award, Symposium Nat. ACS Meeting, San Diego, 2001, Atlanta, 2006, ACS award, Disting. Svc. Advancement Inorganic Chemistry, 2006, Endicott/Rorabacker Frontiers lecturership, Wayne State U., 2006. Fellow AAAS, NAS, Japan Soc. for Promotion of Sci., Am. Acad. Arts and Scis.; mem. Am. Chem. Soc. (chmn. bioinorganic divsn.), Am. Phys. Soc., Internat. EPR Soc., Soc. Biol. Inorganic Chemistry, Sigma Xi. Achievements include research in physical-inorganic and bioinorganic chemistry emphasizing application of a wide variety of spectroscopic and computational methods to determine the electronic structure of transition; metal complexes to define in detail electronic structure high symmetry small molecule complexes to define in detail electronic structure contributions to chemical and physical properties, and metal ion; active sites in catalysis to understand their unusual spectral features in terms of electronic and geometric structure and to evaluate these structural contributions to reactivity; fundamental problems in bioinorganic chemistry. Office: Stanford U Dept Chemistry 333 Campus Dr Stanford CA 94305 Office Phone: 650-723-9104. Business E-Mail: edward.solomon@stanford.edu.

SOLOMON, ELINOR HARRIS, economics professor; b. Boston, Feb. 26, 1923; d. Ralph and Linna Harris; m. Richard A. Solomon, Mar. 30, 1957; children: Joan S. Griffin, Robert H., Thomas H. AB, Mt. Holyoke Coll., 1944; MA, Radcliffe U., 1945; PhD, Harvard U., 1948. Jr. economist Fed. Res. Bank Boston, 1945-48; economist Fed. Res. Bd. Govs., Washington, 1949-56; internat. economist U.S. State Dept., Washington, 1957-58; professorial lectr. Am. U., Washington, 1964-66; sr. economist antitrust div. U.S. Dept. Justice, Washington, 1966-82; prof. econs. George Washington U., Washington, 1982—. Econ. cons., Washington, 1982—; expert witness antitrust, fin. networks, electronic funds transfer cases, Washington, 1988—. Author: Virtual Money, 1997; author, editor: Electronic Funds Transfers and Payments, 1987, Electronic Money Flows, 1991; contbr. articles on econs., banking and law to profl. jours. Mem. Am. Econs. Assn., Nat. Economists Club (bd. govs. 1997-98), The Cosmos Club (chmn. program com. 2004-06, bd. mgmt. 2006—, Frontiers of Sci. 2001-04). Home: 6805 Delaware St Chevy Chase MD 20815-4164 Office: George Washington U Dept Econ Washington DC 20052-0001 Personal E-mail: rsolomonhome@earthlink.net.

SOLOMON, ELLEN JOAN, business owner, consultant; b. Orange, NJ, Aug. 26, 1943; d. Abram Shrier and Mildred Elizabeth (Berger) Solomon. BA in Psychology, U. NC, 1965; MS in Human Resource Devel., Am. U., 1985. Cert. Women owned bus. enterprise 2004. Contract writer Conn. Gen. Life Ins. Co., Bloomfield, 1965—66; mgmt. trainee, asst. buyer G. Fox & Co., Hartford, Conn., 1966—68; account exec. WLAE-FM, Hartford, 1968; sr. analyst Travelers Ins. Co., Hartford, 1968—70; job analyst Conn. Blue Cross, New Haven, 1970—71; sr. ops. auditor Govt. Employees Ins. Co., Washington, 1972—75; employee devel. specialist Employment Stds. Adminstrn., U.S. Dept. Labor, Washington, 1975—81, mgmt. analyst, 1981—82, supervisory mgmt. analyst, 1982—87; program designer, cons. Eastman Kodak Co., Rochester, NY, 1987—89, mgr., 1989, sr. orgnl. cons., 1990—93; pres., CEO Strategic Change, Inc., Fairfax, 1993—. Adj. faculty Rochester Inst. Tech., 1993—2001; conf. spkr.; workshop leader; cons. Recipient spl. achievement award, U.S. Dept. Labor, 1977, 1978, 1983, 1985; named Women in Bus. Advocate of Yr., SBA NC, 2003; named one of Bus. Leaders Impact 100, Bus. Leader Mag., 2003. Mem.: NOW, Rochester Women's Network (bd. dirs. 1990—92, v.p. 1991—92, Pres.'s award 1992), NAWBO (chpt. pres. 2002—03), NTL Inst. Applied Behavioral Sci., Leadership Am. NC, Leadership Am., Leadership Triangle, U. N.C. Alumni, Alpha Gamma Delta. Democrat. Jewish. Office: Strategic Change Inc 4094 Majestic Ln Fairfax VA 22033 Home: 1105 Sch St Cambridge MD 21613 Office Phone: 703-263-2702, 703-887-7498.

SOLOMON, ERIC, federal agency administrator; AB, Princeton U.; JD, U. Va.; LLM, NYU. Ptnr. Drinker Biddle & Reath LLP; tax atty. Cadwalader Wickersham & Taft LLP; ptnr. Ernst & Young LLP; asst. chief counsel (corp.) IRS US Dept. Treasury, dep. asst. sec. regulatory affairs, asst. sec. for tax policy, 2006—. Adj. prof. Georgetown U. Office: US Dept Treasury 1500 Pennsylvania Ave NW Rm 3120 Washington DC 20220 Office Phone: 202-622-0050. Office Fax: 202-622-0605.*

SOLOMON, GLORIA LEE, educational consultant; b. NYC, Nov. 22, 1937; d. George and Nellie Rosen Shapiro; m. Allen Bennett Solomon, Dec. 23, 1955; children: Mark David, Robert Joel. BS, Samford U., 1972; MS, U. Ala., 1975, supt. and prin.'s cert., 1979, EdD, 1981; student summer inst., Columbia U., 1984, Harvard U., 1985; student summer session, Vanderbilt U., 1986. Tchr. Hillview Elem., Birmingham, 1972—79, prin., 1979—86, Hewitt Elem., Birmingham, 1986—89, Pinson Elem. Sch., Birmingham, 1989—92, Hoover Sch. Sys., Ala., 1992—93, asst. supt., 1993—2000, cons., 2000—04; early coll. enrollment cons. Jefferson State CC, Birmingham, 2004—. Contbr. numerous to profl. publs. Bd. dirs. Birmingham Children's Theatre, 1998—2003, Ctr. for Law and Civic Edn., Birmingham, 1998—2004, Ala. Ctr. for Law and Civic Edn., Law Acad., Hoover H.S., Hoover, 2003—04, Ala. Grief Support Found., Birmingham, 2002—05. Recipient Alumni Golden Apple award for Outstanding Adminstr. of Yr., Samford U., 1989, Outstanding Adminstr. of Yr. award, Jefferson County Coun. PTAs, 1990, Outstanding PTA unit award, State of Ala., 1990, Blue Ribbon Sch. award, U.S. Dept. Edn., 1992; nominee award for Creative Leadership in Promoting Women's Rights, Nat. Edn. Assn., 1987. Mem.: Assn. for Supervision and Curriculum Devel., New Horizons at U. Ala. Birmingham (co-chair curriculum com. 2003—05), Phi Delta Kappa. Office: Jefferson State Cmty Coll 4600 Valleydale Rd Birmingham AL 35242 Business E-Mail: gsolomon@jeffstateonline.com.

SOLOMON, HENRY, university dean; b. Bronx, NY, Nov. 28, 1926; s. Max and Tillie (Gilerowitz) S.; m. Jacqueline Mona Cohen, May 31, 1953; 1 son, Michael Robert. BA, Bklyn. Coll., 1949; MA, NYU, 1950, PhD, 1960. Rsch. assoc., then sr. staff investigator and dep. prin. investigator Logistics Rsch. Project George Washington U., 1950—66, prof. econs., chmn. dept., 1962—74, 1991—96, dean Grad. Sch. Arts and Scis., 1974—90, prof. and dean emeritus, 1996—. Dep. asst. adminstr. econs., acting asst. adminstr. planning, research and analysis SBA, 1966-67; cons. in field. Assoc. editor: Naval Research Logistics Quar., 1957-90. Served with U.S. Army, 1945-46. Recipient Founder's Day award N.Y. U., 1960 Mem.: Am. Econ. Assn. Home: # 603 5450 Whitley Park Terr Bethesda MD 20814 E-mail: henry20814@aol.com.

SOLOMON, HOWARD, pharmaceutical executive; b. Aug. 12, 1927; s. David and Faye (Gussow) Solomon; m. Carolyn Ruth Bower, Dec. 17, 1961 (dec. 1991); children: Andrew Wallace, David Frederick; m. Sarah Durie Billinghurst, Aug. 27, 2003. BA, CCNY, 1949; LLB, Yale U., New Haven, Conn., 1952. Bar: NY 1952. Atty. Moses & Singer, NYC, 1952-55, Kay Scholer, Fierman Hays & Handler, NYC, 1956-60; pres. Hildred Mgmt. Corp., NYC, 1967-83; dir. Forest Laboratories Inc., NYC, 1964—, CEO, 1977—98, chmn., CEO, 1998—. Bd. trustees NY-Presbyn. Hosp. Bd. dirs. Met. Opera, Lincoln Ctr. for Performing Arts; exec. com. mem., chmn. emeritus NYC Ballet; mem. Sch. AM. Ballet. Mem. NY State Bar Assn., Yale Club, Harmonie Club of NY. Office: Forest Labs Inc 909 3rd Ave New York NY 10022-4731

SOLOMON, JACK AVRUM, JR., lawyer, automotive executive, art dealer; b. Omaha, Oct. 25, 1928; s. John A. and Matilda (Bienstok) S.; m. Josephine J. Kleiman, June 1948 (div. Mar. 1971); children: Debra, Alisa, Michael, Rena; m. Carolyn Summers, Dec. 1973. BS, U. Nebr., 1950, LLB cum laude, 1952; LLM (Cook fellow), U. Mich., 1953. Bar: Nebr. 1950, Ill. 1951. Practice law, Chgo., 1950—; with firm Stiefel, Greenberg, Burns, Baldridge & Solomon, 1953-66, ptnr., 1958-66, Solomon, Rosenfeld, Elliot & Stiefel, and predecessor, 1966—, sr. ptnr.,

1966—. Bd. dirs. Amco Industries, Inc., Chgo., chmn. bd., 1968-69, sec., gen. counsel, 1969-72; sec. Mogen David Wine Corp., Chgo., 1964-71; chmn. bd. Arts and Leisure Corp., 1969-76; pres., chmn. bd. Circle Fine Art Corp., 1968-94; chmn. bd. dirs. S2 Art Group, Ltd., 1996—, Re Soc., 1997—, Art of the Movies.com, 1999—; pres. Las Vegas Art Dist., 2002-05; mng. dir. C&J Properties LLC, 2005-, Carjack Properties LLC, 2005—; chmn., CEO Jack Gallary, Inc., 2005— Commr. City of Las Vegas Arts Commn., 2005—; pres. temple, 1959—61; bd. dirs. Boulder Plz. Sculpture Park Found. Mem. Ill., Nebr. Bar Assns., Fine Art Pubs. Assn. (pres. 1982—, Lifetime Achievement award, Art Expo and Art Bus. News)), Order of Coif.; Club: Nat. Arts (NYC). Jewish. Home: 2870 Augusta Las Vegas NV 89109 Office: 1 E Charleston Las Vegas NV 89104 Office Phone: 702-868-7880. Personal E-mail: jsolomon@s2art.com.

SOLOMON, KERRY D., ophthalmologist, surgeon, consultant; s. Alan M. and Sheila M. Solomon; m. Cynthia Loiacano Solomon, June 12, 1992; children: Brandon, Coleman. BA in Psychology, U. Vt., 1983, MD, 1987. Diplomate Am. Bd. Ophthalmology, 1993, lic. ophthalmologist SC, 1993. Felow in ophthalmic pathology U. Utah, Salt Lake City, 1987—88; intern Yale U. Hosp. St. Raphael, New Haven, 1988—89; resident in ophthalmology U. Ky., Lexington, 1989—92; fellow in cornea, external disease, anterior segment surgery Wilmer Inst. Johns Hopkins Hosp., Balt., 1992—93; staff Med. U. SC, 1993—, from asst. prof. to assoc. prof. ophthalmology, 1993—2002, prof. ophthalmology, 2002—. Dir. Magill Laser Ctr., SC, 1994—, ophthalmology ambulatory care com. liaison, 1994—99; chmn. hosp. laser com. Med. U. SC, 1999—, dir. cornea/refractive surgery svc., SC, 2000—; co-med. dir. SC Lions Eye Bank, 1996—2001, Magill Rsch. Ctr., SC, 2000—; lectr., presenter in field. Editor: Refractive Surgery Quar.; mem. editl. bd.: Ocular Surgery News, Phaco and Foldables, Ocular Therapeutics, Ophthalmic Practice, Cataract and Refractive Surgery Today; contbr. articles to profl. jours. Ednl. com. Internat. Soc. Refractive Surgery. Recipient Pierre Guatier Jenkins award, Med. U. SC, 2006—07; grantee, Allergan, 1994—95, 1998—2001, Chiron Vision, 1994—97, Akorn, Inc., 1997—99, Alcon Labs., 1997—, Pharmacia and Upjohn, 1997—98, Pharmacia, 1999—2000, JAEB Ctr. for Health Rsch., 1999—2004, Otsuka Md. Rsch. Inst., 2004—05, Advanced Med. Optics, 2004—; fellow, Heed Ophthalmic Found., Wilmer Eye Inst., Johns Hopkins Hosp., 1992; Rsch. grant, Nat. Soc. to Prevent Blindness, Wilmer Eye Inst., Johns Hopkins Hosp., 1992. Fellow: Am. Acad. Ophthalmology (Honor award 1998, Sr. Achievement award 2005); mem.: Charleston County Med. Soc., Charleston Ophthalmol. Soc., SC Soc. Ophthalmology, SC Med. Assn., Wilmer Resident Assn., Refractive Surgery Interest Group, Johns Hopkins Univ. Sch. Medicine Alumnae, Internat. Soc. Refractive Keratoplasty, Heed Ophthalmic Found., Eye Bank Assn. Am., Assn. for Rsch. in Vision and Ophthalmology, Am. Soc. Cataract and Refractive Surgery (program com., practice mgmt. com., FDA com., Best Paper award 1995, Grand prize 1997, Video award 1998, Best Paper award 2000, Lee T. Nordan Achievement award 2006). Avocations: golf, travel. Office: Storm Eye Inst 167 Ashley Ave Charleston SC 29403-5836*

SOLOMON, MARK RAYMOND, lawyer, educator; b. Pitts., Aug. 23, 1945; s. Louis Isadore and Fern Rhea (Josselson) S. BA, Ohio State U., 1967; MEd, Cleve. State U., 1971; JD with hons., George Washington U., 1973; LLM in Taxation, Georgetown U., 1976. Bar: Ohio, Mich., U.S. Dist. Ct. (ea. dist.) Mich., U.S. Ct. Appeals (6th cir.), U.S. Tax Ct., U.S. Ct. Fed. Claims. Tax law specialist corp. tax br. Nat. Office of IRS, 1973—75; assoc. Butzel, Long, Gust, Klein & Van Zile, Detroit, 1976—78; dir., v.p. Shatzman & Solomon, P.C., Southfield, Mich., 1978—81; prof., chmn. tax/bus. law dept., dir. MS in Taxation Program Walsh Coll., Troy, Mich., 1981—; of counsel in tax matters Meyer & Kirk, PLLC, Bloomfield Hills, Mich., 1981—. Adj. prof. law U. Detroit, 1977-81. Editor: Cases and Materials on Consolidated Tax Returns, 1978, Cases and Materials on the Application of Legal Principles and Authorities to Federal Tax Law, 1990. Mem.: Mich. Bar Assn., Phi Eta Sigma. Avocation: bridge (life master). Home: 2109 Golfview Dr Apt 102 Troy MI 48084-3926 Office: Meyer & Kirk PLLC 100 W Long Lake Rd Ste 100 Bloomfield Hills MI 48304-2773 also: Walsh Coll 3838 Livernois Rd Troy MI 48083-5066 Office Phone: 248-647-5111, 248-823-1277. Business E-Mail: msolomon@walshcollege.edu.

SOLOMON, MARSHA HARRIS, draftsman, artist; b. Tulsa, Oct. 21, 1940; d. Ruel Sutton and Anna May (Fellows) Harris; m. Robert E. Collier, Aug. 13, 1960 (div. Dec. 1968); 1 child, Craig Robert Collier; m. Louis G. Solomon, Sept. 5, 1984. Student, U. Tex., 1958-61; BFA, U. Houston, 1966. Chief draftsman Internat. Paper, Petroleum and Minerals Divsn., Houston, 1985—2003; artist, ptnr. Archway Gallery, Houston, 1994. Mem. Nat. Mus. Women in Art (charter). Mem. Watercolor Art Soc. Houston (bd. dirs. 1984-91, treas. 1987-89, pres. 1990-91, signature mem. 2008), Tex. Watercolor Soc. (signature mem., Purple Sagebrush), N.Mex. Watercolor Soc. (signature mem.), Okla. Watercolor Soc. (signature mem.), Ariz. Watercolor Soc. (signature mem., Royal Scorpion mem.). Home: 5832 Valley Forge Dr Houston TX 77057-2248

SOLOMON, MICHAEL BRUCE, lawyer; b. Chgo., Nov. 8, 1945; s. Arthur J. and Ruth H. (Halpert) S.; m. Tunny Jamri, Dec. 17, 1983. BA, U. Miami, Coral Gables, Fla., 1967, JD, 1970. Bar: Fla. 1970; U.S. Dist. Ct. (so. dist.) Fla. 1972; U.S. Ct. Appeals (5th cir.) 1989, U.S. Ct. Appeals (11th cir.) 1990. Assoc. Theodore M. Trushin P.A., Miami Beach, Fla., 1970-77; ptnr. Klein, Oshinsky & Solomon, Hallandale, Fla., 1978-87; pvt. practice North Miami, Fla., 1988—, 1998—, Hallandale, 1988-98. Spl. asst., pub. defender, Dade County, Fla., 1972-78; ombudsman Dade County pub. defender's office, Miami, 1972. Contbr. article to profl. jour. Mem. So. Dist. Fla. Trial Bar (sec.). Home: 1090 Kane Concourse Ste 202 Bay Harbor Islands FL 33154-2129 E-mail: mbslaw@netrox.net.

SOLOMON, NAMALA, economics professor; Assoc. prof. Cerritos Coll., Norwalk, Calif., 1999—. Office: Cerritos Coll 11110 Alondra Blvd Norwalk CA 90650

SOLOMON, PHYLLIS LINDA, social work educator, researcher; b. Hartford, Conn., Dec. 6, 1945; d. Louis Calvin and Annabell Lee (Nitzberg) S. BA in Sociology, Russell Sage Coll., 1968; MA in Sociology, Case Western Res. U., 1970, PhD in Social Welfare, 1978. Lic. social worker Pa. Rsch. assoc. Inst. Urban Studies Cleve. State U., 1970-71; program evaluator Cleve. State Hosp., 1971-74; project dir. Ohio Mental Health and Mental Retardation Rsch. Ctr., Cleve., 1974-75; rsch. assoc. Psychiat. Rsch. Found. of Cleve., 1975; project dir. Ohio Mental Health and Mental Retardation Rsch. Ctr., 1977-78; rsch. assoc. dirs. rsch. and mental health planning Fedn. for Cmty. Planning, 1978-88; prof. dept. mental health scis., dir. sect. mental health svcs. and systems rsch. Hahnemann U., Phila., 1988-94; prof. Sch. Social Work U. Pa., Phila., 1994—. Secondary appointment Prof. Social Work in Psychiatry U. Pa. Sch. Medicine, 1994—; adj. prof. dept. psychiatry Allegheny U., 1994—97. Author (with others): Community Services to Discharged Psychiatric Patients, 1984, Principles and Practice of Psychiatric Rehabilitation: An Empirical Approach, 2008, Randomized Controlled Trials: Design and Implementation for Community Based Psychosocial Interventions, 2009; co-editor: New Developments in Psychiatric Rehabilitation, 1990, Psychiatric Rehabilitation in Practice, 1993, Research Process in the Human Services, 2005; mem. editl. adv. bd. Community Mental Health Jour., 1988—, mem. editl. bd. Jour. Rsch. in Social Work Practice, 1997—2000, Social Work Forum, 1997—, Health and Social Work, 1998—2000, Psychiat. Rehab. Jour., 1999—2008, Mental Health Svcs. Rsch. Jour., 2001—08, Brief Treatment and Crisis Intervention, 2001—08, Social Work, 2003—, Am. Psychiat. Rehab. Jour., 2006—; contbr. articles to profl. jours. Trustee Cleve. Rape Crisis Ctr., 1981-84, CIT Mental Health Svcs., Cleve., 1985-88; mem. citizen's adv. bd. Sagamore Hills (Ohio) Children's Psychiat. Hosp., 1984-88; bd. dirs. Plan of Pa., 2004—. Named Evaluator of the Yr., Ohio Program Evaluators Group, 1987; recipient Ann. award Cuyahoga County Cmty. Mental Health Bd., 1988, Armin Loeb award Internat. Assn. Psychosocial Rehab. Svcs., 1999, Outstanding Non-Psychiatrist award Am. Assn. Cmty. Psychiatrists, 2002, Knee/Wittman Outstanding Lifetime Achievement award Nat. Assn. Social Workers Found., 2005, Tchg. & Mentoring award, U. Provost, 2009. Mem. NASW, U.S. Psychiat. Rehab. Assn., Soc. for Social Work and Rsch. (1st place award for pub. article 1997). Jewish. Home: 205 Governor's Ct Philadelphia PA 19146 Office: U Pa Sch Social Policy & Practice 3701 Locust Walk Philadelphia PA 19104-6214

SOLOMON, RANDALL LEE, lawyer; b. Dayton, Ohio, June 8, 1948; BA summa cum laude, Wright State U., 1970; JD, Case Western Res. U., 1973. Bar: Ohio 1973, U.S. Dist. Ct. (no. dist.) Ohio 1973, U.S. Ct. Appeals (6th cir.) 1973, U.S. Ct. Appeals (fed. cir.) 1988, U.S. Supreme Ct. 2002. Ptnr. Baker & Hostetler, Cleve. Life mem. Sixth Circuit Jud. Conf., Eighth Dist. Jud. Conf., Ohio; speaker in field. Fellow Am. Coll. Trial Lawyers; mem. ABA (mem. litigation, tort and ins. practice sects.), Ohio State Bar Assn., Cleve. Bar Assn. (chair litig. sect. 1991-92), Nat. Inst. Trial Advocacy (mem. nat. session 1978), Def. Rsch. Inst., John M. Manos Inn. of Ct. (master). Office: Baker & Hostetler LLP 3200 Nat City Ctr 1900 E 9th St Ste 3200 Cleveland OH 44114-3475 Office Phone: 216-861-7327. Business E-Mail: rsolomon@bakerlaw.com.

SOLOMON, RAYMAN LOUIS, dean, law educator; b. Helena, Ark., June 5, 1947; s. David and Miriam (Rayman) S.; m. Carol Avins, Aug. 10, 1975. BA, Wesleyan U., 1968; MA in History, U. Chgo., 1972, JD, 1976, PhD in History, 1986. Bar: Ill. 1976, U.S. Ct. Appeals (7th cir.) 1978, U.S. Ct. Appeals (6th cir.) 1979. Dir. court history project U.S. Ct. Appeals (7th cir.), Chgo., 1976-78; law clk. to presiding judge U.S. Ct. Appeals (6th cir.), Cin., 1978-79; Bigelow fellow instr. U. Chgo. Law Sch., 1979-80; research fellow Am. Bar Found., Chgo., 1980-89, assoc. dir., 1986-89; assoc. dean Northwestern U. Sch. Law, Chgo., 1989—98; prof. law Rutgers U. Sch. Law, Camden, NJ, 1998—, dean, 1998—. Instr. Kent-Ill. Inst. Tech. Coll. Law, Chgo. 1982, Northwestern U., Evanston, Ill. 1986. Author: History of the Seventh Circuit, 1981; editor Am. Bar Found. Rsch. Jour., 1985-87. Bd. dirs. Family Counseling Svc. of Evanston, 1985—, BPI, 1990—. Served with USN, 1969-70. Mem. ABA, Law and Soc. Assn., Selden Soc., Am. Soc. Legal Hist. (bd. dirs. 1985-88). Democrat. Jewish. Office: Rutgers State U Sch Law 217 North Fifth St Camden NJ 08102 Office Phone: 856-225-6191. Office Fax: 856-225-6487. E-mail: raysol@camlaw.rutgers.edu.*

SOLOMON, RICHARD, pediatrician; b. Cleve., Sept. 3, 1949; s. Edward None Solomon and Rita Elaine Goldstein; m. Linda Joy Lerner, Feb. 9, 1949; children: Gabriel None, Onna Lynn. BS, U. Mich., Ann Arbor, 1971, MD, 1981. Cert. in pediat. Mich. State U., 1984, in devel. behavioral pediat. Mich. State U., 1986. Med. dir. Ann Arbor Ctr. Dev. Beh. Pediat., Mich., 2001—; sect. head devel. behavioral. pediat. U. Mich. Med. dir. The PLAY Project, Ann Arbor, 1998—2008. Author: (non fiction book) Residential Home Management. Named Profl. of Yr., Assoc. Retarded Citizens, Pa., 1988; grantee Pediatric Pain Mgmt. grant, NIH, 1992—95; Family Growth Ctr. Child Abuse Prevention grant, Maternal Child Health Bur., 1990—95. Mem.: Am. Acad. Pediat. Office: Ann Arbor Ctr Dev Beh Pediatrics 1601 Briarwood Cir #500 Ann Arbor MI 48108 Office Fax: 734-997-9211. Business E-Mail: drrick@aacenter.org.

SOLOMON, RICHARD HARVEY, think-tank executive; b. Phila., June 19, 1937; s. Bertram Harvey and Ellen (Harris) S.; m. Anne G. Keatley, Dec. 16, 1991. Student, Harvard U., 1959-63, Yale U., 1961, 63-64; SB, MIT, 1960, PhD, 1966. Tech. photographer, lab. worker Photon, Inc., Cambridge, Mass., 1957; rschr. Polaroid Corp., 1959-61; rsch. assoc. Ctr. for Chinese Studies U. Mich., Ann Arbor, Mich., 1966-71, from asst prof. to prof. polit. sci., 1966-71; staff mem. NSC, Washington, 1971-76; head. polit. sci dept. The Rand Corp., Santa Monica, Calif., 1976-86, program dir. Internat. Security Policy Research, 1977-83; mem. Pres.' Commn. on Fgn. Lang. and Internat. Studies Washington, 1978-80; mem. Chief of Naval Ops. exec. panel, 1983—; dir. policy planning staff Dept. of State, Washington, 1986-89, asst. sec. of state for East Asian and Pacific affairs, 1989-92; U.S. ambassador to Philippines, 1992-93; pres. U.S. Inst. of Peace, Washington, 1993—. Author: Mao's Revolution and the Chinese Political Culture, 1999, Chinese Political Negotiating Behavior, 1999, Exiting Indochina, 2000; contbr. articles to profl. jours. Office: US Inst of Peace 1200 17th St NW Ste 200 Washington DC 20036-3011 Office Phone: 202-457-1700. Business E-Mail: usip_requests@usip.org, info@usip.org.

SOLOMON, ROBERT, economist; b. NYC, May 2, 1921; s. Sol and Betty (Brownstone) S.; m. Fern Rice, Sept. 11, 1946 (dec. 2001); children: Carol Ann, Barbara Betty, Anne Eleanor. BA, U. Mich., 1942; MA, Harvard U., 1947, PhD, 1952. With Fed. Res. Bd., 1947-76, assoc. adviser research div., 1963-65, adviser research div., 1965, adviser to bd. govs., 1965-76, dir. div. internat. fin., 1966-72; sr. fellow Brookings Instn., Washington, 1976-80, guest scholar, 1980—. Pres. RS Assos., 1981—2005; vice chmn. deps. of com. of 20 IMF, 1972-74; adj. prof. Am. U., 1962-67; sr. staff economist Coun. Econ. Advisers, 1963-64 Author: The International Monetary System, 1945-81, 1982, Partners in Prosperity, 1991, Money on the Move, 1999, The Transformation of the World Economy, 1999; contbr. articles to profl. jours. 1st lt. USAAF, 1942—45. Decorated D.F.C., Air medal; named Officier Legion of Honor France; recipient Rockefeller Pub. Service award, 1971. Mem. Am. Econ. Assn., Coun. on Fgn. Relations. Clubs: Cosmos (Washington). Home and Office: 8502 W Howell Rd Bethesda MD 20817-6827 Personal E-mail: rsolo52178@aol.com.

SOLOMON, SEAN CARL, geophysicist, lab administrator; b. LA, Oct. 24, 1945; BS geophysics, Calif. Inst. Tech., 1966; PhD geophysics, MIT, 1971. From asst. prof. to prof. geophysics MIT, Cambridge, 1972-92; dir. Dept. Terrestrial Magnetism Carnegie Instn. Washington, 1992—. Vis. scientist Lunar Sci. Inst., 1975, Lawrence Livermore Nat. Lab., 1978, Jet Propulsion Lab., 1990—91; guest investigator Woods Hole Oceanographic Inst., 1979—92; vis. faculty Inst. Geophysics and Planetary Physics, dept. earth and space scis. UCLA, 1982—83; Roland and Jane Blumberg vis. prof. planetary scis. U. Tex., Austin, 1988; vis. assoc. divsn. geol. and planetary scis. Calif. Inst. Tech., 1990—91; mem. various groups, teams, coms. NASA, 1974—; earthquake hazards reduction program peer rev. panel U.S. Geol. Survey, 1975, 85; lunar and planetary sci. coun. Univs. Space Rsch. Assn., 1978—80, 1991—93; tech. rev. panel, geophysics rev. panel Dept. Def., 1981—86; chmn. steering com. space sci. working group Assn. Am. Univs., 1987—89; rev. panelist NSF, 1986, 88, 95, 96, 2001, 03, 2006—; chmn. standing com. global seismic network Inc. Rsch. Instns. Seismology, 1988—90; participant numerous oceanographic expeditions, 1967—88. Editor (assoc. editor): Proceedings of the Lunar and Planetary Sci. Conf., 1976, 1978, Jour. Geophys. Rsch., 1976—78, Physics of the Earth and Planetary Interiors, 1977, Eos Transactions of Am. Geophys. Union, 1979—81, Geophys. Rsch. Letters, 1986—88; editor: Tectonophysics, 1981; mem. editl. bd.: Physics and Chemistry of Earth, 1981—85, Astrobiology, 2001—, Earth and Planetary Sci. Letters, 2001—07, mem. editl. com.: Ann. Rev. Earth and Planetary Scis., 1993—97; contbr. articles to profl. jours. Recipient Arthur L. Day prize, NAS, 1999, Public Svc. medal, NASA, 2004, Disting. Alumni award, Calif. Inst. Tech., 2006; fellow Grad., NSF, 1966—68, Postdoctoral, 1971—72, Fannie and John Hertz Found., 1968—71, Alfred P. Sloan Rsch., 1977—81, John Simon Guggenheim Meml., 1982—83. Fellow: AAAS, Geol. Soc. Am. (G.K. Gilbert award 1999), Am. Geophys. Union (pres. elect and pres. 1994—98, pres. planetology sect. 1984—88, chmn. geophys. monograph bd. 1983—84, numerous coms., H.H. Hess medal 2005), Am. Acad. Arts and Scis.; mem.: NAS, Seismol. Soc. Am., Am. Astron. Soc. (divsn. planetary scis.), Tau Beta Pi. Office: Carnegie Instn Dept Terrestrial Magnetism 5241 Broad Branch Rd NW Washington DC 20015-1305 Office Phone: 202-478-8850. E-mail: scs@dtm.ciw.edu.

SOLOMON, STEPHEN L., lawyer; b. NYC, Aug. 15, 1942; s. Sam and Ruth (Goldblum) S.; m. Regina Fisher, Aug. 16, 1969; children: Todd, Lisa. AB, Columbia Coll., 1964; LLB, NYU, 1967. Bar: N.Y. 1967, U.S. Dist. Ct. (so. and ea. dists.) 1969, U.S. Ct. Customs 1970, U.S. Supreme Ct. 1975. Assoc. Burns, Jackson, Summit, NYC, 1969-74; ptnr. Miller, Singer, Michaelson & Raives, NYC, 1974-79; pres. Jarblum, Solomon & Fornari, PC, NYC, 1979-97; ptnr. Rubin Baum LLP, NYC, 1997—2002, Sonnenschein Nath & Rosenthal, NYC, 2002—08. Contbr. articles to profl. jours. Active Com. on Philanthropic Orgns., N.Y.C., 1980-83; bd. dirs. Emanu-El Midtown YM/YWHA, N.Y.C., 1979-85, Columbia Coll. Alumni Assn. Mem. Assn. Bar City of N.Y. Democrat. Home: 302 Region Dr Jupiter FL 33477 Personal E-mail: stephensolomonnyc@yahoo.com.

SOLOMON, SUSAN, atmospheric chemist; d. Leonard Marvin and Alice Solomon. BS in Chemistry, Ill. Inst. Tech., 1977; MS in Chemistry, U. Calif., Berkeley, 1979, PhD in Chemistry, 1981; D (hon.), Tulane U., Williams Coll., SUNY at Stony Brook, Ill. Inst. Tech., U. Colo. Sr. scientist aeronomy lab. NOAA, Boulder, Colo., 1981—, program leader middle atmosphere group aeronomy lab., 1988—. Adj. faculty U. Colo., 1982—; head project sci. Nat. Ozone Expdn., McMurdo Station, Antarctica, 1986, McMurdo Station, Antarctica, 87; co-chair Intergovernmental Panel on Climate Change. Co-author: Aeronomy of the Middle Atmosphere, 1984; contbr. articles to sci. jours. Recipient Gold medal, US Dept. Commerce, 1989, Nat. Medal of Sci., 2000, Victor Moritz Goldschmidt Medal, Geochemical Soc., 2006, Arthur S. Flemming award, Common Wealth Trust award, Ozone award, UN Environ. Programme; named Scientist of Yr., 1992, Solomon Glacier and Solomon Saddle in honor of leadership in Antarctic rsch., 1994, CIRES Fellow; named one of The 100 Most Influential People in the World, TIME mag., 2008; named to Women in Tech. Inst. Hall of Fame, 2004, Colo. Women's Hall of Fame, 2006. Fellow: Am. Geophys. Union (J.B. McElwane award 1985), Am. Meteorol. Soc. (Henry G. Houghton award, Carl-Gustaf Rossby award 2000), Royal Meteorol. Soc.; mem.: NAS, European Acad. Scis. (foreign assoc.), French Acad. Scis. (foreign assoc.), US Nat. Acad. Scis., Am. Acad. Arts and Scis. Avocations: creative writing, crafts, scuba diving. Office Phone: 303-497-3483. Business E-Mail: ssolomon@al.noaa.gov.

SOLOMON, TERRI MARCIA, lawyer; b. Passaic, NJ, July 22, 1955; d. Sol and Arlene (Stiskin) S.; m. Howard Michael Topaz, July 4, 1982; children: Richard Harris Topaz, Jonathan Shaun Topaz. BA summa cum laude, U. Mass., 1976; JD, U. Pa., 1979. Bar: NJ 1979, US Dist. Ct. NJ 1979, NY 1980, US Dist. Ct. (so. dist.) NY 1980, US Dist. Ct. (ea. dist.) NY 1980, US Dist. Ct. (no. dist.) NY, 1997, U.S. Ct. Appeals (2d cir.) 1981, US Ct. Appeals (3d cir.) 1981. Assoc. Simpson, Thacher & Bartlett, NYC, 1979-87, counsel, 1988-93; ptnr. Grotta, Glassman & Hoffman, PA, NYC, 1993-96, Littler Mendelson, PC, NYC, 1996—. Fellow Coll. Labor and Employment Attys.; mem. ABA, NY State Bar Assn. (labor employment sect., ADR com.), Assn. Bar of City NY (labor employment sect.). Democrat. Jewish. Office: Littler Mendelson PC 900 3rd Ave Fl 20 New York NY 10022-4883 Home Phone: 212-879-8527; Office Phone: 212-583-9600. Business E-Mail: tsolomon@littler.com.

SOLOMON, WILLIAM B., JR., lawyer, finance company executive; b. Detroit, Jan. 1, 1953; BA in Polit. Sci. with honors, U. Detroit, 1973; MA in Polit. Sci. with honors, McMaster U., Hamilton, Ont., Can., 1974; JD, U. Notre Dame, Ind., 1978. Law clerk Mich. Ct. of Appeals, 1978—80; regional staff atty. Ford Motor Credit Co., 1980—85; gen. counsel Vixen Motor Co., Pontiac, Minn., 1985—88; atty., practice area mgr. Gen. Motors Corp., 1988—99; gen. counsel GMAC Fin. Services, Detroit, 1999—, group v.p., 2004—. Lectr. in comml. lending, bankruptcy and workouts Bratislava, Weisbaden and Madrid. Contbr. articles to profl. jours. Mem.: ABA, Mich. Bar Assn. Office: GMAC Fin Services 200 Renaissance Ctr Detroit MI 48265-2000 Office Phone: 313-556-5000. Office Fax: 815-282-6156.*

SOLOMONOFF, GALIA, architect; BS in Architecture magna cum laude, CUNY City Coll.; MArch, Columbia U., NYC, 1994. With Office Met. Architecture/Rem Koolhaas, Rotterdam, Germany; project designer Bernard Tschumi Archs., Rafael Vinoly Archs.; prin. OpenOffice, Galia Solomonoff Architecture, NYC. Louis Kahn chair Yale U., New Haven, 2004; adj. asst. prof. architecture Columbia U. Grad. Sch. Architecture; ptnr.-in-charge Dia:Beacon. Office: Solomonoff Architecture Studio 530 W 25th St Rm 409 New York NY 10001 Office Phone: 212-337-3700. Office Fax: 212-337-3730. E-mail: Galia@solomonoff.com.

SOLOMONS, GUS, JR., (GUSTAVE MARTINEZ), choreographer, dancer, writer; b. Boston; s. Gustave Martinez and Olivia Mae. Student, Boston Conservatory of Music, 1956-59; BArch, MIT, 1961; postgrad., Martha Graham Sch., NYC, 1961-66. Dance soloist Martha Graham Co., NYC, 1964-65, Donald McKayle Co., 1961-64, Merce Cunningham Co., NYC, 1965-68; artistic dir. The Solomons Dance Co., NYC, 1972—; dean, artistic dir. Calif. Inst. of the Arts, Valencia, 1976-78; founder art dir. PARADIGM, 1996—; arts prof. NYU, NYC, 2005. Vis. artist-in-residence U. Calif., Santa Cruz, Calif. State U., Long Beach, others; dance panelist Nat. Endowment Arts; various other other state art couns., 1983—; assoc. prof. dance numerous colls., univs., including UCLA, Un. Nev.-Las Vegas, Tex. Christian U., York, Simon Fraser, Tisch Sch. Arts, 1994-, prof., 2005-; USIA cons. to Nat. Dance Co., Tanzania, East Africa, 1988, Argentina, 1994. Appearances on TV networks, WGBH-TV, Boston; choreographr for various univs. and dance cos.; writer dance criticism for Metro Daily, Dance Mag., others. Grantee Nat. Endowment for Arts, 1983—, N.Y. State Coun. on the Arts, 1972—; fellow Nat. Endowment for Arts, 1978-80; recipient Master

Tchr. award NYU/Tisch, 1996, Bessie award, 2000, Robert A. Muh award for disting. MIT artist/alumnus, 2001, Balasaraswat/Beineke Disting. Tchg. award, 2004; named Vis. Scholar, Phi Beta Kappa, 2006. Studio: 889 Broadway New York NY 10003-1212 E-mail: gus.solomonsjr@nyu.edu. *The content of a good dance is the truth about its maker. Performing it is a confession to the audience. The dancer places himself in the position of ultimate vulnerability each time he performs; it is at once cleansing, fulfilling, and courageous.*

SOLOMONS, MARK ELLIOTT, lawyer, art dealer, entrepreneur; b. Buffalo, Mar. 4, 1946; s. Alvin and Trude (Salant) Solomons; m. Jill E Kent, Aug. 20, 1978. BA, U. Rochester, 1967; JD, U. Pa., 1970; LLM, George Washington U., 1973. Staff atty. U.S. Dept. Labor, Washington, 1970-73, counsel coal miners benefits, 1973-77, legis. counsel, 1977-80; prin. Kilcullen Wilson & Kilcullen, Washington, 1980-86; ptnr. Arter and Hadden, Washington, 1986-2001, mem. exec. com., 1989-98; prin. shareholder Greenberg Traurig, Washington, 2001—, nat. co-chair appellate practice group. Guest lectr law and hist SUNY, Stony Brook, 1970—76, Univ Mich, 1977—78, Hobart Col, 1972—76; prin Coun for Excellence in Govt, 1991—; co-owner Frogeye Co; chmn Atlantic Threadworks, 1998—2001; del Atlantic Treaty Asn Gen Assembly, 2000—. Contbr. articles to profl jours. Trustee China Found, 1997—, chair, nominating com., 1997—, v.p., 2003—; mem. US Delegation to Gen. Assembly Atlantic Treaty Assn., 2001—08. Master: Am Inn of Ct (counselor 1996—97); mem.: ABA (chair workers compensation and employers liability comt 1987—88, sr. vice chair 1988—2004, vice chair appellate advocacy comt), NY Bar Asn, DC Bar Asn, Fed Bar Asn (chair regulatory reform comt 1988—89). Republican. Office: Greenberg Traurig LLP 2101 L St NW Washington DC 20038 Home Phone: 202-483-7209; Office Phone: 202-533-2361. Business E-Mail: solomonsm@gtlaw.com.

SOLOMONSON, MICHAEL, performing arts, department chairman; s. Don Solomonson and Ruth (Sveen) Bachman; married. BA, Northwestern Coll., Orange City, Iowa, 1987; MA, Kans. State U., Manhattan, 1991; PhD, U. Nebr., Lincoln, 1996. Faculty-speech, theatre, film Northland Pioneer Coll., Snowflake, Ariz., 2000—; entertainment dir. Old Tucson Studios, Tucson, 1998—2000. Co-author: (plays) Intimations From The Brook. Mem.: Susan Glaspell Soc., Assn. Theatre in Higher Edn. Office: Northland Pioneer Coll PO Box 610 Holbrook AZ 86025

SOLÓRZANO, ROSALÍA, sociologist, educator; b. El Paso, Tex., Mar. 18, 1953; d. Isidro and Isaura (Torres) S. BA in Psychology, U. Tex., El Paso, 1977; MA in Sociology, U. Tex., 1979; postgrad., Colegio de Mex., Mexico City, 1983; PhD in Sociology, Mich. State U., 1991; MA in Counseling, Webster U., 1992. Rsch. assoc. Ctr. for U.S. Mex. Studies, La Jolla, Calif., 1981-83; assoc. dir. Ctr. for Inter-Am. and Border Studies, U. Tex., El Paso, 1983-85; vis. lectr. U. Colo., Boulder, 1985-87; instr. sociology, counselor El Paso Community Coll., 1988—. Cons. in field. Author poems and contbg. author chpts. to books. Mem. bd. Chicano Humanities and Arts Coun., Denver, 1986-87. Nat. Minority Doctoral Competitive fellow, 1979-83, Tinker fellow, 1981-83, U. Mich. fellow, 1987, Stanford U. fellow, 1987, S.W. Inst. Rsch. for Women, U. Ariz., 1989., Pew fellow Tomas Rivera Ctr., 1991. Mem. Assn. for Borderlands Scholars Conf., Western Social Svc. Assn. (site com.), Nat. Assn. Chicano Studies, Mujeres Activas en Letras (steering com. 1989-90, nat. com. coord. 1989-90), Phi Kappa Phi, Sigma Delta Pi (pres. 1975-76). Democrat. Roman Catholic. Office: El Paso Community Coll Women's Ctr El Paso TX 79998

SOLOSKI, JOHN, journalism and communications educator; AB cum laude, Boston Coll., 1974; MA in Journalism, U. Iowa, 1976, PhD, 1978. Copy editor, reporter Iowa City Press Citizen, 1977-78; instr. Univ. Iowa, 1977-78, asst. prof. sch. journalism and mass communication, 1978-84, assoc. prof. sch. journalism and mass communication, 1984-85, assoc. prof., head of grad. studies, 1985-92, prof., head of grad. studies, 1992-94, prof., acting dir., 1994-95, prof. sch. of journalism and mass communication, 1995-96, prof., dir. sch. of journalism and mass communication, 1996—, prof. law, 1996—2001; dean Grady Coll. Journalism and Mass Comm. U. Ga., 2001—04, prof. Grady Coll. Journalism and Mass Comm., 2004—. Con. Ottumwa Courier, 1976-77, Iowa City Press-Citizen, 1976-77; speaker in field; vis. prof. Univ. Tech., Sydney, Australia, 1995. Co-author: Reforming Libel Law, 1992, Libel and the Press: Myth and Reality, 1987, Taking Stock: Journalism nad the Publicly Traded Newspaper Company, 2001; contbr. numerous articles to profl. jours.; editor: Journalism and Communication Monographs, 1994—. Recipient Soc. of Profl. Journalists Disting. Svc. award, 1988; numerous rsch. grants. Mem.: Assn. Schs. Journalism and Mass Comm. (pres. 2003—04). Office: Henry W Grady College of Journalism and Mass Communication The University of Georgia Athens GA 30602-3018 Office Phone: 706-542-1704. Business E-Mail: jsoloski@uga.edu.

SOLOVY, JEROLD SHERWIN, lawyer; b. Chgo., Apr. 10, 1930; s. David and Ida (Wilensky) S.; m. Kathleen Hart; children: Stephen, Jonathan. BA with honors, U. Mich., 1952; LLB cum laude, Harvard U., 1955. Bar: Ill. 1955, DC 1955. Mem. bd. of editors Harvard Law Review, 1953—55; mem. visiting com. Harvard Law Sch., 1986—92; mem. Harvard Com. U. Resources, 1993—98; assoc. Jenner & Block LLP, Chgo., 1955-63, ptnr., 1963—, chmn., 1991—2007, chmn. emeritus, 2007—. Chmn. Spl. Commn. on Adminstrn. Justice in Cook County, 1984-91, Ill. Supreme Ct. Spl. Commn. on Adminstrn. of Justice, 1992-93, Criminal Justice Project of Cook County, 1987-91. Mem. Cook County Jud. Adv. Council, Chgo., 1975-77, 82-89, chmn., 1989-91; trustee U.S. Supreme Ct. Hist. Soc., 1993—. Recipient Pro Bono Award, Seventh Cir. Bar Assn., 1993, Professionalism Award, Am. Inns of Ct., 2004, Lifetime Achievement Award, Decalogue Soc. of Lawyers, 2004, John Minor Wisdom Pub. Svc. and Professionalism Award, Am. Bar Assn., 2005, Lifetime Achievement award, The Am. Lawyer mag., 2007; named one of 100 Most Influential Lawyers, Nat. Law Jour., 1991, 1994, 1997, 2000, 2006, 500 Leading Leading Lawyers in Am., Lawdragon Mag., 2005, 2006, 500 Leading Litigators in Am., 2006. Fellow Am. Coll. Trial Lawyers; mem. ABA, Chgo. Bar Assn., Ill. State Bar. Assn., Am. Law Inst. Clubs: Standard; Lake Shore Country (Chgo.), Phi Eta Sigma, Phi Kappa Phi, Phi Beta Kappa, Pi Sigma Alpha. Office: Jenner & Block 330 N Wabash Avenue Chicago IL 60611-7603 E-mail: jsolovy@jenner.com.

SOLOW, MICHAEL BARRY, lawyer; b. Chgo., Jan. 6, 1959; s. Gilbert and Eunice (Eres) S.; m. Dale Susan Weinbaum, Aug. 21, 1983; children: Corey Francis, Andrew Wenbaum. AB summa cum laude, U. Ill., 1981; JD, Harvard U., 1984. Bar: Ill. 1984, NY 2003, U.S. Dist. Ct. (no. dist.) Ill. 1984, U.S. Dist. Ct. (no. dist.) Tex. 1987, U.S. Dist. Ct. Ariz. 1991, U.S. Dist. Ct. (we. dist.) Mich. 2003, U.S. Dist. Ct. (so. dist.) NY 2004, U.S. Ct. Appeals (7th cir.) 1984, U.S. Ct. Appeals (8th cir.) 1992, U.S. Ct. Appeals (4th cir.) 1993, U.S. Ct. Appeals (6th cir.) 1997, U.S. Supreme Ct. 1993. Law clk. to presiding justice Ill. Supreme Ct., 1984-85; assoc. Hopkins and Sutter, Chgo., 1985-90, ptnr., 1990—2001; ptnr., co-chair Bus. Reorganization and Creditors' Rights Dept., mem. Exec. Com. Kaye Scholer LLP, Chgo., NYC, 2001—. Mem. ABA, Chgo. Bar Assn., Phi Betta Kappa. Office: Kaye Scholer LLP 3 First Nat Plaza, Ste 4100 70 West Madison St Chicago IL 60602 also: 425 Park Ave New York NY 10022 Home Phone: 847-940-7691; Office Phone: 312-583-2310, 212-836-7240. Business E-Mail: msolow@kayescholer.com.

SOLOW, ROBERT MERTON, economist, educator; b. Bklyn., Aug. 23, 1924; s. Milton Henry and Hannah Gertrude (Sarney) Solow; m. Barbara Lewis, Aug. 19, 1945; children: John Lewis, Andrew Robert, Katherine. BA, Harvard U., 1947, MA, 1949, PhD, 1951, DLitt (hon.), 1992; LLD (hon.), U. Chgo., 1967, Brown U., 1972, U. Warwick, 1976, Tulane U., 1983, Dartmouth Coll., 1990, Rensselaer Poly. Inst., 2003, U. Rochester, NY, 2007; DLitt (hon.), Williams Coll., 1974, Lehigh U., 1977, Wesleyan U., 1982, Boston Coll., 1986, Harvard U., 1992, Colgate U., 1990; DSc (hon.), U. Paris, 1975, U. Geneva, 1982, Bryant Coll., 1988; D of Social Sci. (hon.), Yale U., 1976, U. Mass., Boston, 1989; D Social Sci. (hon.), U. Helsinki, 1990, SUNY, Albany, 1991, U. Glasgow, 1992, Rutgers U., 1994; D (hon.), U. Chile, 1992; Conservatoire, Nat. des Arts et Mètiers, Paris, 1994; D in Engring., Colo. Sch. Mines, 1996; postgrad, U. Buenos Aires, 1999; D in Lit. Humanities, NYU, 2000, New School U., 2006. Mem. faculty MIT, 1949—95, prof. econs., 1958—95, inst. prof., 1973—95, prof. emeritus, 1995—; W. Edwards Deming prof. NYU, 1996—97. Sr. economist Coun. Econ. Advisers, 1961—62, cons., 1962—68, RAND Corp., 1952—64; Marshall lectr., fellow commoner Peterhouse Cambridge (Eng.) U., 1963—64; Eastman vis. prof. Oxford U., 1968—69; overseas fellow Churchill Coll., Cambridge; sr. fellow Soc. Fellows, Harvard U., 1975—89; bd. dirs. Boston Fed. Res. Bank, 1975—80, chmn., 1979—80; active President's Commn. on Income Maintenance, 1968—70, President's Com. on Tech., Automation and Econ. Progress, 1964—65, Carnegie Commn. Sci., Tech. and Govts., 1988—93, Nat. Sci. Bd., 1994—2000; found. fellow Russell Sage Found., 2001—. Author (with R. Dorfman, P. Samuelson): Linear Programming and Economic Analysis, 1958; author: Capital Theory and the Rate of Return, 1963, The Sources of Unemployment in the United States, 1964, Growth Theory, 1970, Price Expectations and the Behavior of the Price Level, 1970; author: (with M. Dertouzos, R. Lester) Made in America, 1989; author: The Labor Market as a Social Institution, 1990; author: (with F. Hahn) A Critical Essay on Modern Macroeconomic Theory, 1995; author: Learning from "Learning by Doing", 1997; author: (with J. Taylor) Inflation, Unemployment and Monetary Policy, 1998; author: Monopolistic Competition and Macroeconomic Theory, 1998, Work and Welfare, 1998; editor (with Alan Krueger): The Roaring Nineties, 2002. Bd. dirs., mem. exec. com. Nat. Bur. Econ. Rsch.; trustee Inst. for Advanced Study, Princeton U., 1972—78, Woods Hole Oceanographic Inst., 1988—, Alfred P. Sloan Found., 1992—, Resources for the Future, 1994—2003, Urban Inst., 1994—, German Marshall Fund of U.S., 1994—2002, Ctr. Advanced Study Behavioral Scis., 1982—95, chmn., 1987—95. With US Army, 1942—45. Decorated Bronze Star U.S. Army; recipient David A. Wells prize, Harvard U., 1951, Seidman award in polit. economy, 1983, Nobel prize in Econs., 1987, Nat. Medal of Sci., 2000; fellow, Ctr. Advanced Study Behavioral Scis., 1957—58, Russell Sage Found., 2000—. Fellow: Am. Acad. Arts and Scis., Brit. Acad. (corr.); mem.: NAS (coun. 1977—80, 1995), AAAS (v.p. 1970), Internat. Econ. Assn. (pres. 1999—2002), Econometric Soc. (pres. 1964, exec. com.), Am. Econ. Soc. (exec. com. 1964—66, v.p. 1968, pres. 1979, John Bates Clark medal 1961), Royal Irish Acad. (hon.), Order Pour le Merite (Germany), Acad. dei Lincei, Am. Philos. Soc. Home: 528 Lewis Wharf Boston MA 02110-3920 Office: MIT Dept Econs Cambridge MA 02139*

SOLOW, SHELDON H., real estate developer; b. July 20, 1928; m. Mia Solow; children: Stefan, Nikolai. Founder, pres. Solow Bldg. Co., NYC. Bd. trustees Inst. Fine Arts, NY, 1987—2003, chmn. bd. trustees, NY, 1993—2003, emeritus trustee, NY, 2003—; bd. trustees NYU; vice chmn. bd. dirs. Benjamin N. Cardozo Sch. Law; mem. chmn.'s coun. Met. Mus. Art. Founder Solow Art and Architecture Found., 1991. Jewish. Office: Solow Bldg Co 70 Washington Sq S New York NY 10012-1019 Office Phone: 212-998-1212. Office Fax: 212-995-4902.*

SOLOWAY, ALBERT HERMAN, medicinal chemist; b. Worcester, Mass., May 29, 1925; s. Bernard and Mollie (Raphaelson) S.; m. Barbara Berkowicz, Nov. 29, 1953; children: Madeleine Rae, Paul Daniel, Renee Ellen. Student, U.S. Naval Acad., 1945-46; BS, Worcester Poly. Inst., 1948; PhD, U. Rochester, 1951. Postdoctoral fellow Nat. Cancer Inst. at Sloan-Kettering Inst., NYC, 1951-53; research chemist Eastman Kodak Co., Rochester, NY, 1953-56; asst. chemist Mass. Gen. Hosp., Boston, 1956-61, asso. chemist, 1961-73; asso. prof. med. chemistry Northeastern U., Boston, 1966-68, prof. medicinal chemistry, chmn. dept., 1968-71, prof. medicinal chemistry and chemistry, chmn. dept. medicinal chemistry and pharmacology, 1971-74; dean Coll. Pharmacy and Allied Health Professions, 1975-77; dean Coll. Pharmacy Ohio State U., Columbus, 1977-88, prof. medicinal chemistry, 1977-98, Kimberly prof. pharmacy, 1997-2000, dean, prof. emeritus, 1998—. Author rsch. in medicinal chemistry, boron neutron capture therapy of cancer. Recipient Disting. Achievements in Boron Sci. award, Boron USA, 1994. Fellow AAAS, Acad. Pharm. Soc.; mem. AHS (50 Yr. mem.), Am. Chem. Soc., Am. Assn. Coll. Pharmacy, Am. Assn. Cancer Rsch., Torch Club Columbus (pres. 2004-05) Office: Ohio State U 500 W 12th Ave Columbus OH 43210-1214 Business E-Mail: soloway.1@osu.edu.

SOLOWAY, DANIEL MARK, lawyer; b. Buffalo, Jan. 21, 1959; s. Sol Murray and Shirley (Prashker) S.; m. Natalie Ann-Marie Chin, June 10, 1989; children: Rachael Ann, Rebecca Leigh. BA cum laude, SUNY, Buffalo, 1982; JD with honors, Fla. State U., 1985. Bar: Fla. 1985, U.S. Dist. Ct. (no. dist.) Fla. 1985, (mid. dist.) Fla. 1995, (so. dist.) Ala. 1986, U.S. Ct. Appeals (11th cir.) 1985, U.S. Supreme Ct. 1989; bd. cert. in civil trial law, Fla.; cert. Nat. Bd. Trial Advocacy, 1998, civil ct. mediator, 2000. Law clk. Circuit Judge, Tallahassee, 1983-84, Douglass, Davey, Cooper & Coppins, Tallahassee, 1984-85; ptnr. McKenzie & Soloway, Pensacola, Fla., 1985-98; owner Soloway Law Firm, Pensacola, 1998—; adj. prof. Fla. State U. Coll. Law, 2008—. Author: Criminal Justice: An Analysis Toward Reform, 1981; contbr. articles to profl. jours.; editor Escambia-Santa Rosa Bar Assn. newsletter, 1989-90, Dry Shoes, Fla. Bar Jour., 1992. Profl. adv. bd. N.W. Fla. Epilepsy Soc., Pensacola, 1989—; speaker on AIDS, State of Fla. Dept. HRS, 1988—; active Escambia County Human Rels. Commn., 1996-98. Recipient Pro Bono Svc. award Escambia-Santa Rosa Bar, 1989-90, Pro Bono Svc. Pres.'s award Fla. Bar, 1990. Mem. Million Dollar Advocates Forum (diplomat), ABA, Assn. Trial Lawyers Am., Escambia-Santa Rosa Bar Assn. (editor newsletter 1989-90), Acad. Fla. Trial Lawyers (speaker 1993—), Nat. Orgn. Social Security Claimants Reps. Democrat. Jewish. Avocation: writing. Office: 1013 Airport Blvd Pensacola FL 32504 Office Phone: 850-471-3300.

SOLSO, THEODORE M., manufacturing executive; m. Denny; 3 children. BA, DePauw U., 1969; MBA, Harvard U., 1971. Asst. to v.p. personnel Cummins Engine Co., Inc., Columbus, Ind., 1971—72; employment dir. Holset Engring. Co., Ltd. (Cummins' U.K. subs.), Columbus, 1972—74, dir. devel. & tng., 1974—77; exec. dir. personnel Cummins Engine Co., Inc., Columbus, 1977-80; v.p., mng. dir. Holset Engrng. Co., Ltd. (Cummins' U.K. subs.), 1980-84; v.p. spl. engine markets Cummins Engine Co., Inc., Columbus, 1984-86, v.p. mktg., 1986-88, v.p., gen. mgr. engine bus., 1988-92, exec. v.p. opers., 1992—94, exec. v.p. & COO, 1994—95, pres. & COO, 1995-00, chmn., CEO, 2000—. Bd. dirs. Ashland, Inc., Cyprus Amax Minerals, Inc. Bd. trustees DePauw U.; bd. advisors U. Mich. Sch. Bus.; past bd. dirs. Heritage Fund Bartholomew County, Ind.; chmn. campaign Bartholomew County United Way; bd. dirs. Otter Creek Golf Course, Columbus, Ind. Mem. Mfrs. Alliance (bd. trustees). Office: Cummins Inc 500 Jackson St Columbus IN 47201

SOLTAN, KAROL EDWARD, political science professor, director; b. Warsaw, Nov. 25, 1950; s. Jerzy Wladyslaw and Hanna Soltan; m. Margaret Rapp, Mar. 1, 1987; 1 child, Anna (Ania) Livia. AB, Harvard Coll., Cambridge, Mass., 1972; MA, U. Chgo., PhD, 1983. Instr. to asst. prof. U. Rochester, NY, 1980—83; asst. prof. to assoc. prof. U. Md., Coll. Pk., 1983—; vis. rsch. prof. George Mason U., Faifax, Va., 1989; vis. prof. U. Warsaw, 1992—93, Nat. Sch. Pub. Adminstrn., Warsaw, 1992—95; codir., lectr. Internat. Summer Sch. Polit. Sci. & Internat. Rels., Poland, 1994—98; vis. scholar Faculty Law, U.Toulouse, 2003; adj. prof. U. Md. Law Sch., 2008—; dir., com. politics, philosophy, pub. policy U. Md., Coll. Pk., Md., 2008—; codir. Summer Inst. Civic Studies, Tufts U., Medford, 2009—. Cons. Pres. Lech Walesa's Coun. Econ. Devel., Poland, 1993; dep. dir. & acting dir. Office Polit., Constl. & Electoral Affairs, UNTAET, Dili, East Timor, 2000; dir., recovered states task force IRIS Project Fragile States, USAID, 2003—05; advisor Kurdistan Govt., Erbil, Iraq, 2005—07. Author: (book) Causal Theory of Justice; editor: A New Constitutionalism, The Constitution of Good Societies, New Institutionalism: Institutions and Social Order, Citizen Competence and Democratic Institutions, Politics from Anarchy to Democracy, Global Democracy and Its Difficulties. Coun. man, Garrett Pk, Md., 2005—07. Home: PO Box 518 Garrett Park MD 20896 Office: Dept Govt & Politics Univ Md College Park MD 20742 Business E-Mail: ksoltan@umd.edu.

SOLTANI, AZITA, director of research; d. Ahmad Ali Soltani and Sorraya Tehrani; m. Nader Noorfeshan; 1 child, Sahm Noorfeshan. PhD in Med. Biophysics, Vienna U. Applied Tech., MS in Applied Physics. Cert. in clinical trials U. Wash. Rsch. assoc. Austrian U. Inst. Nuc. Rsch., Vienna, 1993—95; rsch. fellow U. Wash., Seattle; tissue optic engr. scientist Light Scis. Inc., Issaquah, Wash.; rsch. dir. EKOS Corp. Prin. investigator NIH Funded Grants. Contbr. articles to profl. jours. Hammer Purgstall scholarship, Austrian Orient Soc., 1986—96. Mem.: ACRP. Achievements include patents for catheter with multiple ultrasound radiating members; treatment of vascular occlusions using ultrasonic energy and microbubbles; power parameters for ultrasonic catheter; ultrasound catheter with cavitation promoting surface. Office: EKOS Corp 11911 N Creek Parkway S Bothell WA 98011 Business E-Mail: info@ekoscorp.com.

SOLTERO-HARRINGTON, LUIS RUBÉN, retired surgeon, educator; b. San Juan, Sept. 4, 1925; s. Augusto Rafael Soltero and Anna Lila Harrington; m. Alice Joyce Carpenter, Apr. 24, 1958; children: Luis Ruben, Kathleen Ann, Susan Joyce, Robert Richard, Sharon Theresa. BS in Agr., U. P.R., Rio Piedras, 1945; BM, MD, Northwestern U., Chgo., 1949. Diplomate Am. Bd. Surgery, Nat. Be. Med. Examiners, P.R. Rd. Med. Examiners. Intern Michael Reese Hosp., Chgo., 1949-50; resident in gen. surgery Aguadilla (P.R.) Dist. Hosp., 1950-51; resident in gen. surgery, instr. Baylor U. Coll. Medicine and Affiliated Hosps., Houston, 1954-59; resident in gen. surgery Jefferson Davis, VA and M.D. Anderson Hosps., Houston, 1954-57; resident in pediatric, thoracic and cardiovasc. surgery St. Luke's-Tex. Children's Hosp., Houston, 1957-59; asst. prof. surgery U. P.R. Sch. Medicine, 1960-64, assoc. clin. prof., 1972-73, assoc. clin prof., 1973—, in charge devel. heart surgery program, 1960-64, dir. surgery residency tng. program, 1961-64; pvt. practice San Juan, 1959—2003; ret., 2003; prof. San June Bautisa Sch. Medicine, 2006—. Prof. surgery U. del Caribe Sch. Medicine, Cayey, P.R., 1981—, San Juan Bautista Sch. Med., 2006-; cons. in cardiovasc. and thoracic surgery Med. Examing Bd. P.R., San Juan, 1989; chief thoracic and cardiovasc. surgery Tchrs. Hosp., San Juan, from 1959; dir. surgery residency tng. program Univ. Hosp., Rio Piedras, from 1961; cons. in thoracic and cardiovasc. surgery San Juan City Hosp., 1962—, cons. in surgery, 1964—; cons. in surgery Presbyn. Hosp., 1972—, Mimiya's Hosp., 1987—; cons. in thoracic and cardiovasc. surgery Indsl. Hosp., San Juan, 1975—, Hosp. Met., 1982—, Clinic Fernández García, 1983—; chief surgery Ruiz Arnau Hosp., Bayamon, P.R., 1978—; asst. dir. ICU, Hosp. del Maestro, 1987—; bd. dirs. Rsch. Found. Cardiovasc. Surgery Tex., 1984—, Am. Cancer Soc., 1974; mem. Nat. Adv. Cun. Mended Hearts, Inc., 1969. Author: (textbook) The Management of the Acutely Ill Patient, 2002; contbr. articles to med. jours.; patentee partial occlusion vascular clamp to be used in small blood vessels; inventor respirator for infants based on electronic equipment. Capt., M.C., USAF, 1953-54. Recipient award for outstanding work in cardiovasc. surgery Lions Club, Hato Rey, 1961. Fellow Am. Acad. Pediat., Am. Coll. Legal Medicine (assoc.); mem. AMA (physician recognition award 1986); mem. Denton A. Cooley Cardiovasc. Surg. Soc., Michael E. De Bakey Internat. Cardiovasc. Soc., Pan Am. Med. Assn. (coun. pediatric surgery), P.R. Soc. Cardiology, Am. Heart Assn., P.R. Hear Assn., Phi Chi. Avocations: travel, horticulture, bridge.

SOLTESZ, STEFAN, conductor; b. Nyiregyhaza, Hungary, Jan. 6, 1949; arrived in Austria, 1956. s. Stefan and Auguste S.; m. Diana Roselind, Feb. 1, 1974. Student, Hochschule fuer Musik und Darstellende Kunst, Vienna; studied with Prof. Hans Swarowsky. Condr. Theater an der Wien, Vienna, 1971-73; coach, condr. Vienna State Opera, Vienna, 1973-83; guest condr. Opera of Graz, Austria, 1979-81; musical asst. to Karl Böhm, Christoph von Dohnányi, and Herbert von Karajan Salzburg Music Festivals, Austria, 1978, 79, 83; permanent condr. Hamburg State Opera, Germany, 1983-85, Deutsche Oper Berlin, Berlin, 1985-97; music dir. State Theater of Brunswick, Germany, 1988-93, Flanders Opera of Antwerp, Ghent, Belgium, 1992-97, Essen Philharmonic Orchestra, 1997—; gen. and artistic dir. Aalto Music Theater, Essen, Germany, 1997—. Guest condr. Bavarian State Opera, Munich, Opera of Bonn, Opera of Frankfurt, Hamburg Opera, State Opera Stuttgart, Vienna State Opera, Teatro Bellini Catania, Washington Opera at the Kennedy Ctr., United States, Semper Opera, Dresden, Teatro Colón, Buenos Aires, Opera Bilbao, Spain, Royal Opera House, Covent Garden, London, San Francisco Opera, Zurich Opera, Japan, Festivals in Montpellier, Aix-en, Savonlinna, Finland, symphony concerts, Paris, Montpellier, Vienna, Bremen, Dresden, Leipzig, Catania, Rome, Milan, Genua, Basel, Graz, Hannover, Saarbrücken, Trieste, Verona, Bern, Berlin, Budapest, Zaino, Nederlandse Opera Amsterdam. Recordings: Puccini's La Boheme, Gazzaniga's Don Giovanni, The Chalk Circle; recordings of arias and lieder with Grace Bumbry, Lucia Popp and Dietrich Fischer-Dieskau; musical dir., pianist Doppleriade: Compositions for Flute by F. and K. Doppler. Recipient Cultural prize, Found. Savings Banks, The Rhineland, Germany, 2004, Orchestra of Yr., Essen Philharmonic Orchestra, 2003—08; named Opera House of Yr., Operawelt, 2008. Office: Aalto Musiktheater Opernplatz 10 D-45128 Essen Germany

SOLTIS, KATHERINE, editor; b. Pitts., Apr. 15, 1950; d. John Andrew and Katherine (Hnidec) Goidich; m. Patrick T. Soltis, July 27, 1973 (div. 1998). BA, Mich. State U., 1972; MA in English/Linguistics, Case Western Res. U., 1982. Part time clk. Case Western Res. U., Cleve., 1974-83; lexicographer Webster's New World Dictionaries, Wiley Pub., Cleve., 1983—. Freelance copy editor. Editor: Webster's New World Vest Pocket Dictionary, 2nd edit., 1994; style guide editor, Webster's New World Desk Dictionary and Style Guide, 2d edit. Trustee Cleve.-Volgograd Ptnr. Cities, 1990-2001; pres. Women Speak Out for Peace & Justice/Women's Internat. League for Peace & Freedom, 1993-95, chair program com., 1995-2001; orgn. rep. Cleve. Coalition Against the Death Penalty, 1981-, chair, 2002-; supporter Ariz. death row inmate, 1981-; mem. Cleve. Pro-Choice Action League, 1996-, Windsong Cleve. Feminist Chorus, 1998-, Ohioans to Stop Executions. Mellon fellow Case Western Res. U. Mem.: Phi Beta Kappa. Soc. Of Friends. Avocations: reading, music, gardening, composting/recycling, foreign travel. Home: 896 Englewood Rd Cleveland Heights OH 44121-2042 Office: Websters New World 1228 Euclid Ave Ste 1010 Cleveland OH 44115-1816 Personal E-mail: kssoltis@yahoo.com.

SOLUM, JOHN HENRY, flutist, educator, author, advocate for arts; b. New Richmond, Wis., May 11, 1935; s. Irwin M. and Helen L. (Anderson) S.; m. Millicent Kemp Hunt, July 30, 1960; children: Eric, Andrew. AB, Princeton U., 1957. Concert flutist, 1957—; tchr. Ind. U., Bloomington, 1973, Vassar Coll., Poughkeepsie, NY, 1969-71, 77—, Oberlin (Ohio) Conservatory, 1976. Dir. Bath (Eng.) Summer Sch. Baroque Music, 1979-89; artistic dir. Conn. Early Music Festival, New London, 1982-99; pres. N.Y. Flute Club, 1983-86; mem. music adv. panel NEA, 1990-93; arts adv. panel N.H. Arts Coun., 1995-98. Composer Cadenzas for Mozart's Flute Concertos, 1964; editor flute music; music critic for Notes, Pro Musica, The Consort; author: The Early Flute, 1992; contbg. author: New Grove Dictionary of Musical Instruments, New Grove Dictionary of Music and Musicians, Lexikon der Flöte; contbr. articles to Mus. Am., Flutist Quar., Flute Talk, Hist. Performance Mag., Woodwind World, Traversieres, Revue de la Société Liégeoise de Musicologie, Pan; flutist throughout N.Am., 1957—, Europe, 1962—, Asia, 1969—, S.Am., 1978—, Russia, 1983—; rec. artist Albany, Arabesque, Boston Skyline, Brunswick, Cambridge, Centaur, Chesky, Columbia, CRI, Decca Gold Label, EMI, Epiphany, Innova, MCA Westminster, MSR, Philips, RCA, Seraphim, Smithsonian, Vanguard, others. Chmn. Hanoverian Found., 2000—. Recipient Phila. Orch. Youth Contest award, 1957, Conn. Commn. Tourism Disting. Advocates award, 2008. Mem. Nat. Flute Assn. (treas. 1989-94, Disting. Svc. award 1998), Dolmetsch Found. (bd. dirs.), Am. Musical Instrument Soc., Century Assn. (N.Y.). Home: 10 Bobwhite Dr Westport CT 06880-1001 E-mail: jhsolum@optonline.net.

SOLYMOSY, EDMOND SIGMOND ALBERT, marketing professional, retired military officer; b. Budapest, Pest, Hungary, Sept. 3, 1937; came to U.S., 1949; s. Sigmond Ladislas and Gabrielle (Lindelof) S.; m. Mary Ellen Via, Sept. 9, 1961; children: Edmond S.A. Jr., Stephan G., Philip A. BSME, Tex. A&M U., 1960, BBA, 1961, MBA, 1970; postgrad., Mich. U., 1985, Harvard U., 1991. Commd. 2d lt. U.S. Army, 1961, advanced through grades to gen., 1985; student Nat. Def. U., Washington, 1980-81; comdr. 1st Air Def. Arty. Brigade, Ft. Bliss, Tex., 1981-83; chief of staff U.S. Army Air Def. Ctr., Ft. Bliss, 1983; dir. Human Resources Directorate, Hdqrs. Dept. Army, Washington, 1983-85; dep. comdr. U.S. Army Community and Family Support Ctr., Alexandria, Va., 1985-86; chief of staff U.S. Army I Corps, Ft. Lewis, Wash., 1986-88; chief exec. U.S. Office of Def. Coop., Athens, Greece, 1988-91; ret., 1991; pres. Global Project Mgmt., Houston, 1991—, Am. Southwest Properties Inc., 1993-95, Prime Daniel Asset Mgmt. Corp., 1997-2001; sr. ptnr. Solymosy Investment Assocs., 2000—; owner Bar-O-S Ranch. Advisor Sec. of Army Panel, Washington, 1983-86, Hellenic-Am. C. of C., Athens, 1988-91; bd. dirs. Am. Ikarus Inc., Maxoil Inc., So. Nat. Bank Tex., SNB Bankshares, Tex. A&M U. Rsch. Found., Fin. Literacy Found.; hon. consul Republic of Hungary; chmn. Houston Com. on Fgn. Rels. Author: Continental Economic Alliances, 1981. Sponsor Spl. Olympics, Ft. Lewis, 1986; advisor Mil. Mus., Ft. Lewis, 1986-88; regional v.p. Mediterranean coun. Boy Scouts Am., Athens, 1988-91; mem. devel. com. Tex. A&M U., College Station, 1991, advisor Ctr. for Internat. Bus.; mem. bd. advisors Mosher Inst. for Internat. Policy Studies; mem. Mil. Com., Houston. Decorated D.S.M., Def. D.S.M., Combat Infantryman's Badge, Airborne Parachutist's Badge, Army Ranger, Legion of Merit (3); recipient U.S. and Vietnamese awards for heroism, Greek Disting. Svc. award, 1991. Mem.: VFW, Assn. U.S. Army (Svc. to Soldiers award 1985), Am. Quarter Horse Assn., Armed Forces YMCA (chmn. com. 1982, nat. vol. of yr. award 1983), Am. Palomino Horse Breeders Assn., Internat. Propeller Club (Greece advisor 1989), Kiwanis Club Houston, Hungarian Knights Hospitaller of Order of St. John. Republican. Lutheran. Avocations: sports, jogging, sailing, fishing, hunting, western horsemanship. Home: 10150 Dogwood Tr College Station TX 77845-6740 Personal E-mail: essglobal@aol.com.

SOLYOM, ANTAL ENDRE, retired psychiatrist; arrived in US, 1966, naturalized, 1972; s. Antal Solyom and Ilona Molnar; m. Gwen Ellen Cattle, Oct. 30, 1971; 1 child, Alexander Istvan. MD summa cum laude, Med. U. Szeged, Hungary, 1960; PhD in Biochemistry, U. Okla., Norman, 1970; MA in Bioethics, U. Va., Charlottesville, 2003. Diplomate in psychiatry Am. Bd. Psychiatry and Neurology, 1976, in child psychiatry Am. Bd. Psychiatry and Neurology, 1978, cert. in addiction medicine Am. Soc. Addiction Medicine, 1988. Rsch. assoc. dept. pharmacology Rsch. Inst. Pharm. Industry, Budapest, Hungary, 1960—64; vis. scientist inst. pharmacology and therapy U. Milano, Italy, 1964—66; postdoctoral fellow Okla. Med. Rsch. Found., Okla. City, 1966—70; rsch. fellow, neurochemistry NIH, Bethesda, Md., 1970—72; dir., children's outpatient svc. Detroit Psychiat. Inst., 1975—77; asst. prof. psychiatry sch. medicine Wayne State U., 1975—77; dir. infant study and infant psychiatry program med. sch. U. Mich., Ann Arbor, 1977—85, asst. prof. psychiatry med. sch., 1977—85; co-dir. Eleonore Hutzel recovery ctr. sch. medicine Wayne State U., Detroit, 1985—87, assoc. prof. psychiatry sch. medicine, 1985—89; dir. child-adolescent psychiatry edn. Fairlawn Ctr. Child/Adolescent Psychiat. Svcs., Pontiac, Mich., 1987—89; clin. prof. family medicine sch. medicine U. Va., 1989—2002; med. dir. bridges child-adolescent treatment ctr. Centra Health, Inc., Lynchburg, Va., 1989—2002, ret., 2002. Adj. affiliate ctr. biomedical ethics and humanities U. Va. Health Sys., Charlottesville, Va., 2003—; locum tenens psychiatrist Staff Care, Inc., Irving, Tex., 2004—. Contbr. more than 40 articles to profl. jours. Fellow: Am. Acad. Child and Adolescent Psychiatry (life); mem.: AMA (life), Am. Soc. Bioethics and Humanities, World Fedn. Mental Health, Am. Psychiat. Assn. (life). Achievements include research in pharmacological and hormonal regulation of lipid metabolism, particularly the effect of androgens on serum lipoproteins; research on the development and regulation of affects in infants and toddlers; postulated the affect-balance principle to understand the attachment to pecific persons or objects, and conceptualized the disease of addiction as a maladaptive/pathological attachment; the ethical challenges to the integrity of physicians regarding financial conflicts of interest in clinical research and in the use of assisted reproductive technologies; proposed special bioethical sonsiderations regarding clinical research in children/adolescents with psychiatric disorders, and in people with decisional impairments needing surrogate decision makers. Avocations: chess, classical music, travel, reading, swimming. Home: Po Box 3620 Lynchburg VA 24503

SOM, PETER M., radiologist; s. Max L. and Ethel S. Som; m. Judith S. Som, July 23, 1978; 1 child, Jamie E. Lindenbaum. MD, NYU Sch. Medicine, 1967. Chief head, neck imaging, dept. radiology Mt. Sinai Hosp., NYC, 1970—; prof., radiology, otolaryngology and radiation oncology Mt. Sinai Sch. Medicine, NYU, NYC. Maj. US Army, 1971—73, Fort Dix, NJ. Recipient Gold Medal, Am. Soc. Head and Neck Radiology, 2004. Mem.: Royal Coll. Medicine. Office: Mount Sinai Sch Medicine One Gustave Levy Pl New York NY 10029 Personal E-mail: drpsom@aol.com. Business E-Mail: peter.som@mssm.edu.

SOMASEGAR, SIVARAMA KICHENANE, computer software company executive; b. 1965; m. Akila Somasegar; children: Sahana, Archana. BSEE, Anna U., India; MS in Computer Engring., La. State U.; PhD (hon.), Anna U., India, 2006. From software design engr. to v.p. Microsoft Corp., Redmond, Wash., 1989—2000, dir. India Devel. Ctr. Hyderabad, 1998—, dir. Can. Devel. Ctr. Vancouver, v.p. Windows engring. solutions & svc. group, 2000—04, corp. v.p. developer divsn., 2004—08, sr. v.p. developer divsn., 2008—. Recipient Asian Am. Engr. of Yr. award, Chinese Inst. Engrs., USA, 2008. Office: One Microsoft Way Redmond WA 98052-6399

SOMASUNDARAN, PONISSERIL, surface and colloid engineering educator; b. Pazhookara, Kerala, India, June 28, 1939; arrived in U.S., 1961; s. Kumara Moolayil and Lakshmikutty (Amma) Pillai; m. Usha N., May 25, 1966; 1 child, Tamara. BS, Kerala U., Trivandrum, India, 1958; BE, Indian Inst. Sci., Bangalore, 1961; MS, U. Calif., Berkeley, 1962, PhD, 1964. Rsch. engr. U. Calif., 1964, Internat. Minerals & Chem. Corp., Skokie, Ill., 1965-67; rsch. chemist R.J. Reynolds Industries, Inc., Winston-Salem, NC, 1967-70; assoc. prof. Columbia U., NYC, 1970-78, prof. mineral engring., 1978-83, La Von Duddleson Krumb prof., 1983-97; dir. NSF Industry U. Coop. Rsch. Ctr. in Novel Surfactants, 1998—; hon. prof. Wuhan Inst. Chem. Tech., 2001—. Chmn. Henry Krumb Sch. Chem. Engring., Materials Sci. and Mining Engring., Columbia U., 1988—97; dir. Langmuir Ctr. for Colloids and Interfaces Columbia U., 1987—; mem. panel NRC; chmn. numerous ianternat. symposia and NSF workshops; mem. adv. panel Bur. Mines Generic Ctr., 1983—91; keynote and plenary lectr. internat. meetings; hon. prof. Ctrl. South U. Tech., China; Brahm Prakash prof. metallurgy and material sci. Indian Inst. Sci., Bangalore, 1990; hon. rsch. advisor Beijing Gen. Rsch. Inst., 1991—; Henry Krumb lectr. AIME, 1988; cons. in field; hon. prof. Amrita U., 2008—; chmn. Internat. Colloid and Surface Sci. Symposium & 83rd Am. Chem. Soc. Colloid and Surface Sci. Symposium; fellow Am. Inst. Chem. Engrs., 2009—; chmn. 13th Internat. Conf. Colloid & Surface Scis. Editor: Fine Particles Processing, 1980; editor-in-chief: Encyclopedia of Surface and Colloid Sci.; hon. editor-in-chief Colloids and Surfaces, 1980—; contbr. articles to profl. jours. Pres. Keralasamajam of Greater NY, NYC, 1974-75; bd. dirs. Fedn. Indian Assocs., NYC, 1974-95, Vols. in Svc. to Edn. in India, Hartford, Conn., 1974—; mem. planning bd. Village of Piermont, NY, 1995-2000, mem. zoning bd. appeals, 2000—, mem. citizens adv. com., 2000—. Recipient Disting. Achievement in Engring. award, AINA, 1980, Antoine M. Gaudin award Soc. Mining Engrs.-AIME, 1983, Achievements in Applied Sci. award 2d World Malayalam Conf., 1985, Robert H. Richards award, AIME, 1986, Arthur F. Taggart award Soc. Mining Engrs.-AIME, 1987, honor award Assn. Indian in Am., 1988, VHP award of Excellence, Ellis Island medal of Honor, 1990, Commendations citation State of N.J. Senate, 1991; named Mill Man of Distinction, Soc. Mining Engrs.-AIME, 1983, Disting. Alumnus award Indian Inst. Sci., Bangalore, 1989, Outstanding Contbns. and Achievement award Cultural Festival India, 1991, Recognition award SIAA, 1992, Asian-Am. Heritage award Asian Am. Higher Edn. Coun., 1994, award for outstanding contbn. to sci. and tech. Hudson Valley Malayalee Assn., 2005, AIME Edn. award, 2006, Malayalee Engr. of Yr. award, 2007, Columbia Disting. Achievement award, 2007, Columbia Asian Alumni award, 2007, Disting. Contbr. award ACAA, 2007, Disting. Alumni award; named Engr. Yr. MEANA, 2007. Fellow Russian Acad. Nat. Scis. (fgn.), Chinese Acad. Engring. (fgn.) Indian Nat. Acad. Engring., Instn. Mining and Metallurgy (UK); mem. AICE, NAE, Soc. Mining Engrs. (bd. dirs. 1982-85, Disting. mem. award, also others), Engring. Found. (chmn. bd. 1993-95, chmn. conf. com. 1985-88, bd. exec. com. 1985-88, bd. dirs. 1991—, Frank Aplan award 1992), Am. Chem. Soc., NY Acad. Scis., Russian Acad. Natural Scis. (fgn.), Internat. Assn. Colloid and Surface Scientists (councillor 1989-92), Indian Material Rsch. Soc. (hon.), Sigma Xi, Backan Acad. Scis. Mineral Tech. Achievements include patents in field. Office Phone: 212-854-2926. E-mail: ps24@columbia.edu.

SOME-GUIEBRE, WEN-YAM ESTHER, language educator; b. Ouagadougou, Kadiogo, Burkina Faso, Sept. 10, 1975; d. Napougba Robert Guiebre and Elizabeth Lingani; m. Batamaka Some, May 6, 2000; children: Saanbe Alvyn Joslin Some, Baryen Betsy Some. PhD student in Curriculum and Instrn., U. Ill., Urbana Champaign, 2007—. HS tchr. Lycee Nelson Mandela, Ouagadougou, 2000—04; tchg. asst. U. Ill., 2006—. Organizing sec. Africa Student Orgn., Urbana Champaign, 2008. Parent rep. headstart Policy coun., Urbana Champaign, 2005—06. Office: Dept Linguistics 707 S Mathews Ave MC 168 Urbana IL 61801

SOMER, ROBERT A., physician, educator; b. Bronx, NY, Nov. 22, 1971; s. Richard B. Somer; m. Athena F. Zuppa, May 4, 1997; 1 child, Anna Rose. MD, SUNY, Stony Brook, 1997. Asst. prof. medicine Robert Wood Johnson Sch. Medicine, New Brunswick, NJ, 2003—; dir. Cooper Prostate Cancer Ctr. Cooper U. Hosp., Camden, NJ, 2003—; dir. med. oncology clin. trials ctr. CINJ at Cooper, Voorhees, NJ, 2004—. Mem.: ACP (assoc.), AMA (assoc.), Am. Soc. Hematology (assoc.), Am. Soc. Clin. Oncology (assoc.). Office: CINJ at Cooper Ste M2 900 Centennial Blvd Voorhees NJ 08043 Home: 26 High Point Dr Medford NJ 08055-3816 Office Fax: 856-325-6777. Business E-Mail: somer-robert@cooperhealth.edu.

SOMER-GREIF, PENNY LYNN, lawyer; b. New Hyde Park, NY, Mar. 30, 1970; d. Stanley Jerome and Janice Somer; m. Brian Scott Greif; 1 child, David Joseph Somer Greif. BS, SUNY, Binghamton, 1992; JD, Am. U., 1995. Bar: NJ 1996, NY 1996, DC 2000, Md. 2006, Pa. 2008. Atty., advisor US SEC, Washington, 1995—2000; assoc. Arnold & Porter LLP, Washington, 2000—06, Ober, Kaler, Grimes & Shriver, Balt., 2006—. Avocations: reading, exercise. Office: Ober Kaler Grimes & Shriver 120 E Baltimore St Baltimore MD 21202-1643 Office Phone: 410-347-7341. Business E-Mail: psomergreif@ober.com.

SOMERHALDER, JOHN W., II, energy executive; m. Rebecca Somerhalder; 4 children. BSCE, Univ. Ariz. Sr. v.p. El Paso Corp., Houston, 1992—96, pres. El Paso Energy Resources Co., 1996, exec. v.p. pipeline group, pres. pipeline group, 2001—05, exec. v.p., 2001—05; pres., CEO AGL Resources Inc., Atlanta, 2006—07, chmn., pres., CEO, 2007—. Bd. dir., past chmn. Interstate Natural Gas Assn. Am.; bd. dir. Interstate Nat. Gas Assn. Am.; bd. mem. Am. Gas Assn. Bd. mem. Metro Atlanta C. of C., Ga. C. of C. Office: AGL Resources Inc 10 Peachtree Pl Atlanta GA 30309 Mailing: AGL Resources Inc PO Box 4569 Atlanta GA 30302-4569

SOMERO, GEORGE NICHOLLS, biology educator; b. Duluth, Minn., July 30, 1940; s. George Theodore and Mary Elizabeth (Nicholls) S.; m. Amyelin Anderson, July 2, 1988. BS, Carleton Coll., Northfield, Minn., 1962; PhD, Stanford U., 1967. Postdoctoral fellow U. B.C., Vancouver, 1967-70; asst. prof. Scripps Inst. Oceanography, La Jolla, Calif., 1970-76, assoc. prof., 1976-80, prof., 1980-91; prof. dept. zoology Oreg. State U., 1991-95; David and Lucile Packard chair of Marine Sci. Hopkins Marine Sta., Stanford U., Pacific Grove, Calif., 1995—. Co-author: Biochemical Adaptation, 1974, 84. Endowed chair named in his honor U. Calif., San Diego, 1984, Wayne and Gladys Valley chair of Marine Biology, Oreg. State U. Fellow AAAS; mem. NAS. Home: 25010 Outlook Dr Carmel CA 93923-8960 Office: Hopkins Marine Sta Pacific Grove CA 93950

SOMERS, LOUIS ROBERT, retired food company executive; b. Pontiac, Mich., Aug. 8, 1926; s. Jay G. and Maggie (Gee) S.; m. Rynda Horinga, July 28, 1950; children: Linda, Laurie. BS, Mich. State U., 1950. With Kellogg Co., Battle Creek, Mich., 1955-88; controller Kellogg Internat., 1967-70, 72-75; fin. dir. Kellogg Gt. Brit. Ltd., 1970-72; v.p. fin., treas. Kellogg Co., 1975-85, sr. v.p. fin., 1985-88. Trustee Alma Coll., 1982—2001; bd. govs. ARC, 1985—92, chmn. audit com.; bd. dirs. Mich. State U. Devel. Fund, 1983—88.

SOMERVILLE, CHRISTOPHER ROLAND, biochemist, educator; b. Oct. 11, 1947; naturalized, US, 1995; BSc in Math., U. Alta., Can., 1974, MSc in Genetics, 1976, PhD in Genetics, 1978; DSc (hon.), Queen's U., 1993, U. Alta., 1997, Wageningen U., 1998. Rsch. assoc. dept. agronomy U. Ill., 1978—81; asst. prof. dept. genetics U. Alta., 1981; assoc. prof. dept. botany and plant pathology Mich. State U., 1982-86, prof., 1986—93; prof. dept. biol. scis. Stanford U., Calif., 1994—2008; dir. dept. plant biology Carnegie Instn. Washington, Stanford, Calif., 1994—2008; dir. Energy Bioscis. Inst., Uc Berkeley, Calif., 2007—, prof., 2007—. Panel mem. fed. support for soybean rsch. USDA-ARS, 1981; mem. adv. bd. molecular genetics Mass. Gen. Hosp., 1989—92; mem. plant adv. group Cold Spring Harbor Lab., 1990; mem. adv. bd. The Inst. Genomic Rsch., 1992—, Noble Found., 1993—97, Danforth Ctr., 1999—2001; mem. bd. agr. NRC, 1994—96; mem. vis. com. Swedish Found. for Strategic Rsch., 1995, Cornell U. Plant Biology, 1998; mem. President's Adv. Panel on Plant Biodiversity, 1997—98, Alta. Heritage Found., 2000—04; vis. prof. U. Glasgow, 1998—2006; mem. sci. adv. bd. Wellcome Trust, 1999—2001; mem. adv. com. life scis. Cornell U., 2001—04; mem. adv. com. U. Wis. Structural Biology Ctr., 2001—04; CEO Mendel Biotech., 2002—07. Contbr. articles to sci. jours.; mem. editl. com.: Photosynthesis Rsch., 1984—87, Plant Physiology, 1985—91, Development, 1986—93, Archives Biochemistry and Biophysics, 1986—2003, Devel. Genetics, 1989—91; editor: The Plant Jour., 1990—94; co-editor: Biochemistry and Molecular Biology of Membrane and Storage Lipids of Plants, 1993, Arabidopsis, 1994, The Arabidopsis Book, 2002; assoc. editor: Ann. Rev. Plant Physiology and Plant Molecular Biology, 1993—97, The Plant Cell, 1995—2000, mem. editl. bd.: Current Biology, 1996—97, Procs. NAS, 1997—2000, mem. bd. reviewing editors: Science, 1996—2007, mem. sr. editl. com.:, 2001—; editor: Current Opinion in Plant Sci., 1997—2000. Recipient Young Presdl. Investigator award, NSF, 1984, Humboldt Sr. Rsch. award, 1992, Kuhmo award, 2001, Mendel medal, Genetics Soc., 2004, Balzan award, 2006. Fellow: AAAS, Royal Soc. London, Royal Soc. Can.; mem.: Internat. Soc. Plant Molecular Biology, Academia Europaea, NAS (bd. mem. 1993—97), Am. Soc. Plant Physiologists (mem. publ. com. 1989—91, Gibbs medal 1993, Schull award 1987). Business E-Mail: crs@berkeley.edu.

SOMERVILLE, DAPHINE HOLMES, retired elementary school educator; b. Clinton, NC, Jan. 19, 1940; d. George Henry and Mamie Estelle (Streeter) Holmes; m. Kalford Burton Somerville, Dec. 26, 1970 (div. Sept. 1992); 1 child, Daria Lynn. AA, Blackburn Coll., Carlinville, Ill., 1959, BA, 1961; MS in Edn., Hofstra U., Hempstead, NY, 1967; postgrad., Columbia U., NYC, 1971, SUNY, Farmingdale, 1999-2000. Cert. elem. tchr. Tchr. East Islip Sch. Dist., NY, 1961-99, ret. NY, 1999; tchr. computer/writing Opportunities Industrialization Ctr., 1998—2003, webmaster, 2000—04; field supr. dept. edn. Dowling Coll., 2006—. Mem., instr. Outcome Based/Mastery Learning/Excellence in Learning Com., East Islip, 1984—89; mentor East Islip Sch. Dist., 1987—88, mem. sch. improvement team, 1989—91, staff devel. com., 1992—96; chair Ptnrs. in Edn., 1991—2001; instr. AARP's Driver Safety, 2001—03; election insp., 2001—. Author: Beaman Family Reunion Journal, 2001, Baptist Training Union Study Guide; founder, co-author: tutoring program Adopt-A-School Child/Family, 1990. A founding mem. Nat. Dr. Martin L. King Jr. Meml., Washington, 2005; Mem. Bay Shore Civic Assn. and Bay Shore Pub. Schs. Task Force for Advancement Equality Ednl. Opportunity, NY, 1967—69; sec. Islip Town NAACP, Bay Shore, 1965—90; dir. Bapt. Tng. Union, 1974—81; trustee First Bapt. Ch., Bay Shore, 1972—90, vice chair revitalization com., 2000—04. Recipient Cmty. Svc. award, Town Bd.-Town of Islip, Suffolk County, 1982, Recognition award, Islip Town NAACP, 1987, Disting. Svc. award, LI Region NAACP, 1993, Dedicated Svc. award, Ptnrs. in Edn. First Bapt. Ch. Bay Shore, 1995, 1996, recognition, Congressman Rick Lazio, 1997, African-Am. Educators award, Martin L. King Commn. Suffolk County, 1997, Editors Choice award, Nat. Libr. Poetry, 1999, citation, Town of Islip, 1999; LI Sch. to Career Partnership for Proposed Sch./Bus. Govt. Project grantee, 1996. Mem.: NAACP (Islip) (silver life mem. 2006, founding mem. 2008, Islip Town award 2008), NY State United Tchrs., East Islip Tchrs. Assn. (past bldg. rep.), Nat. Coun. Negro Women (life Ednl. Involvement award 1993), Huntington Christian Women's Club (fin. coord. 2003—). Democrat. Avocations: theater, writing, tennis, reading, travel. Home: 130 Carman Rd Dix Hills NY 11746-5648 Personal E-mail: dsomer4@verizon.net.

SOMERVILLE, RICHARD CHAPIN JAMES, atmospheric scientist, educator; b. Washington, May 30, 1941; s. James William and Mollie (Dorf) S.; m. Sylvia Francisca Bal, Sept. 17, 1965; children: Anatol Leon, Alexander Chapin. BS in Meteorology, Pa. State U., 1961; PhD in Meteorology, NYU, 1966. Postdoctoral fellow Nat. Ctr. Atmospheric Rsch., Boulder, Colo., 1966-67; rsch. assoc. geophysical fluid dynamics lab. NOAA, Princeton, NJ, 1967-69; rsch. scientist Courant Inst. Math. Scis., NYC, 1969-71; meteorologist Goddard inst. space studies NASA, NYC, 1971-74; adj. prof. Columbia U., NYU, 1971-74; head numerical weather prediction sect. Nat. Ctr. Atmospheric Rsch., Boulder, 1974-79; prof. meteorology Scripps Inst. Oceanography, U. Calif.-San Diego, La Jolla, 1979—. Author: The Forgiving Air: Understanding Environmental Change, 1996. Fellow: AAAS, Am. Meteorol. Soc.; mem.: Am. Geophys. Union. Office: U Calif San Diego Scripps Inst Oceanography 9500 Gilman Dr Dept 0224 La Jolla CA 92093-0224

SOMES, JOAN MARIE, emergency nurse practitioner; b. St. Paul, Aug. 17, 1952; d. Richard and Jane (Blaiser) Friesen; m. Michael Somes, Nov. 15, 1975. BA in Nursing, Coll. of St. Catherine, St. Paul,

1974; paramedic cert., Inver Hills C.C., Inver Grove Heights, Minn., 1976; MSN, U. Minn., 1989; PhD in Health Adminstrn., Columbia So. U., Orange Beach, Ala., 2002. RN, Minn.; cert. emergency nurse, getiatrics nurse; nat. registered EMT-paramedic; cert. ACLS instr., PALS instr.; cert. TNCC instr.; cert. CATN instr., ENPC instr.; cert. ACLS-EP instr.; cert. pediat. emergency nurse. Paramedic A.L.F. Ambulance, Apple Valley, Minn., 1987-97; charge nurse emergency dept. Divine Redeemer Hosp., South St. Paul, Minn., 1974-94; staff nurse emergency dept. St. Joseph's Hosp., St. Paul, 1994—, emergency dept. educator/staff nurse, 1999—. Instr. numerous local cmty. colls., hosps. and ambulance svcs.; item writer CEN exam., 1994-96, 96-98; edn. specialist Regions Emergency Med. Svcs., 1994—; spkr. in field; co-chair Cornerstones Emergency Nursing Conf., 2000; mem. regional faculty PALS Am. Heart Assn., 2004—; regional faculty PALS & ACLS, 2009-; mem. magnet steering com. Health East Hosp. Sys., 2005—; v.p. Emergency Care Instructing LLP, 2006-. Author nursing home study courses; consulting editor Man. of Emergency Dept. and Urgent Care Instrns., 2001--; contbr. articles to profl. jour. Mem. steering com. Minn. Lit. Partnership, 2006—07. Grantee Glaxo Pharm. Co., 1989, Health East Found. 1991, 94, 97, 98, 2006; recipient Mary Piner award Minn. Emergency Nurses Assn. State Coun. 1994-2006 Fellow: Acad. Emergency Nurses; mem.: Vision Coun. for Profl. Devel., Nat. Emergency Nurses Assn. (chair geriatric com. 2003—04, exam item writer com. 2003—05, geriat. com. 2005—, scholarship selection com. mem. 2009, State Achievement award 2008), Emergency Nurses Assn. (chair state trauma com. 1994—95, sec. treas. Minn. state coun. 1994—95, sec. 1996—98, sec.-treas. Minn. state coun. 1997—2000, pres. Greater Twin Cities chpt. 2001—02, state coun. rep. 2001—03, sec.-treas. Minn. state coun. 2004—07, pres. Minn. emergency nurses assn. state coun. 2008—, dir./state coun. liaison Greater Twin Cities chpt., geriat. com. mem. 2009, Nurse Competency in Aging award 2005, Deanna Earle award Greater Twin Cities chpt.).

SOMMA, LOUIS A., biologist; b. Eglin Air Force Base, Fla., July 31, 1960; s. Salvatore F. and Nancy M. Somma. BS in Biology, U. Nebr., Omaha, 1982, MA in Biology, 1985. Cert. in appreciation, dedicated svc. & contbn. Fla. Dept. Agr. & Consumer Svcs., 2006. Tchg. asst. Dept. Biology, U. Nebr., 1982—84, Dept. Zoology, U. Fla., Gainesville, 1985—2001; OPS biologist Nat. Fisheries Rsch. Ctr., US Fish & Wildlife Svc., Gainesville, 1991—92; adj. faculty to instr. Santa Fe CC, Gainesville, 1994—96; rsch. assoc., lab technician Fla. State Collection Arthropods, Fla. Dept. Agr. & Consumer Svcs., Gainesville, 2003—. Author: (book) Parental Behavior in Lepidosaurian and Testudinian Reptiles. A Literature Survey; contbr. chapters to books, articles to profl. jours. Presdl. Grad. fellowship, Grad. Sch., U. Nebr., 1984—85, fellowship, Linnean Soc. London, 1991—. Mem.: AAAS, Internat. Soc. History & Bibliography Herpetology, Soc. Study Amphibians & Reptiles, Herpetologists League, Am. Soc. Ichthyologists & Herpetologists. Office: Fla State Collection Arthropods 1911 SW 34th St PO Box 147100 Gainesville FL 32614-7100

SOMMARUGA, CORNELIO, foundation administrator, diplomat; b. Rome, Dec. 29, 1932; s. Carlo and Anna Maria (Valagussa) S.; m. Ornella Marzorati; 6 children. LLD, U. Zurich, Switzerland, 1957; D of Polit. Affairs (hon.), U. Fribourg, Switzerland, 1985; D in Internat. Rels. (hon.), U. Minho, Portugal, 1989; D of Medicine (hon.), U. Bologna, Italy, 1991; D in Law (hon.), U. Nice, Sophia-Antipolis, France, 1992, Seoul Nat. U., 1992; PhD in Law (hon.), Geneva U., 1997; LHD (hon.), Webster U., St. Louis, 1998; LLD (hon.), U. Insubria, Como, Italy, 2008. Various diplomatic positions Swiss Confedn.'s Svc., 1960-73; dep. sec. gen. European Free Trade Assn., Geneva, 1973-75; minister plenipotentiary Dept. Pub. Economy, Berne, Switzerland, 1976-77, amb. plenipotentiary, 1977-80, del. Swiss Govt. for Trade Agreements, 1980-83, state sec. external econ. affairs, 1984-86; pres. Internat. Com. Red Cross, Geneva, 1987-99; hon. chair. Assn. Initiatives of Change Internat., Caux, Switzerland, 2007. Hon. pres. Geneva Internat. Ctr. for Humanitarian Demining, 2003—. Vice chair Found. for Future, 2006—; pres. bd. Found. Internat. Union Against Cancer, Geneva, 2006—. Recipient Presdl. award Tel-Aviv U., 1995, North-South prize Coun. of Europe, 2001, Dr. Jean Mayer Global Citizenship award Tufts U., 2003. Home: 16 chemin Crets-de-Champel CF-1206 Geneva Switzerland Business E-Mail: cornelio.sommaruga@bluewin.ch.

SOMMER, ALFRED, ophthalmologist, medical educator, researcher; b. NYC, Oct. 2, 1942; s. Joseph and Natalie Sommer; m. Jill Abramson Sommer, Sept. 1, 1963; children: Charles Andrew, Marni Jane. BS summa cum laude, Union Coll., 1963; MD, Harvard U., 1967; MHS in Epidemiology, Johns Hopkins U., 1973. Diplomate Am. Bd. Ophthalmology, Nat. Bd. Med. Examiners. Tchg. fellow in medicine Harvard U. Med. Sch., Boston, 1968—69; dir. Nutritional Blindness Prevention Rsch. Program, Bandung, Indonesia, 1976—79; vis. fellow Inst. Ophthalmology U. London, 1979—80; founding dir., Dana Ctr. for Preventive Ophthalmology Johns Hopkins Med. Insts., Balt., 1980—90; assoc. prof. Johns Hopkins U., Balt., 1981—85, prof. ophthalmology, epidemiology and internat. health, 1985—, dean Johns Hopkins Sch. Hygiene and Pub. Health, 1990—2005, dean emeritus, 2005—. Vis. prof. ophthalmology U. Padjadjaran, Indonesia, 1976—79; cons., advisor Helen Keller Internat., NYC, 1973—; cons., chmn. com. NIH, Bethesda, Md., 1981—; bd. dirs. Internat. Agy. for the Prevention of Blindness, Geneva; cons., com. mem. NAS, Washington, 1989; chmn. program adv. group on blindness prevention WHO, Geneva, 1989—90, com. mem., 1978—90, expert com., 1990—; chmn. steering com. Internat. Vitamin A Cons. Group Micronutrient Forum, Washington, 1975—; pres. Internat. Fedn. of Tissue Banks; chmn. sci. adv. bd. Edna McConnell Clark Found.; mem. Internat. Coun. Ophthalmology; dir. Becton Dickenson Corp., 1998—, T. Rowe Price Group, 2003—, Internat. Trachoma Initiative Found. of NIH, 2004—, chmn.; dir. Lasker Found., 2004—, chmn., 2008—; chair expect cmty. health global governance initiative World Econ. Forum; lectr. in field. Author: Epidemiology and Statistics for the Ophthalmologist, 1980, Nutritional Blindness: Xerophthalmia and Keratomalacia, 1982, Vitamin A Deficiency: Health, Survival and Vision, 1995, Detection and Control of Vitamin A Deficiency and Xerophthalmia, 1978, 1982, 1995; chmn. bd. overseers Am. Jours. Epidemiology and Epidemiologic Revs., 1990—2005, also bd. dirs., —; contbr. articles to profl. jours. Recipient Charles A. Dana Found. award for Pioneering Achievement in Health, 1988, Disting. Svc. award for Contbn. to Vision Care, APHA, 1988, E.V. McCollum Internat. Lectureship in Nutrition, Am. Inst. Nutrition, 1988, Second Ann. Am. Coll. Advancement in Medicine Achievement award in Preventative Medicine, 1990, Disting. Contbn. to World Ophthalmology award, Internat. Fedn. Ophthal. Socs., 1990, Smadel award, Infectious Diseases Soc. Am., 1990, Doyne Meml. medal, Oxford, 1995, Albert Lasker award Clin. Rsch., 1997, Helmut Horten Rsch. award, 1997, Gold medal, Singapore Ophthalmology Soc., 1997, Duke Elder Gold medal, Internat. Coun. Ophthalmology, 1998, Prince Mahidol award for contbns. to pub. health, 1998, Bristol-Meyers Nutrition Rsch. award, 2001, Danone Internat. award in nutrition rsch., 2001, Warren Alpert Found. prize, Harvard Med. Sch., 2003, Howe medal, Am. Opthal. Soc., 2003, Pollin prize, Columbia U., 2004, Helen Keller Rsch. Found prize, 2006, Gonin medal, Internat. Coun. Oph., 2007, First prize, Contbn. to Health, 2009. Mem.: IOM, NAS, Inst. Medicine, Internat. Coun. Ophthalmology, Chgo. Ophthal. Soc., Assn. Schs. of Pub. Health (pres.), Internat. Assn. to Prevent Blindness (bd. dirs. 1978—2005), Nat. Soc. to Prevent Blindness (bd. dirs. 1984—94), Am. Acad. Ophthalmology (chmn. pub. health com. 1982—88, chmn. Quality of Care/Clin. Guidelines 1986—90). Achievements include first to detail and publish epidemiologic approach disaster assessment; nutritional indices predict subsequent mortality in children, surveillance and containment is effective intervention strategy for controlling smallpox vaccenation effective 5 days after exposure; vitamin A deficiency increases childhood mortality and vitamin A supplementation decreases childhood mortality; nerve fiber layer is valuable diagnostic and prognostic sign of early glaucoma; routine preventive services cost-effective in eye disease; clinical guideline development and importance of outcome assessment; research in epidemiologic and public health approaches to ophthalmology, blindness prevention, and improved health and survival. Office: Johns Hopkins U Bloomburg Sch Pub Health 615 N Wolfe St Rm 1041 Baltimore MD 21205-2103 Office Phone: 410-502-4169. Office Fax: 410-502-4167. Business E-Mail: asommer@jhsph.edu.

SOMMER, BOB (ROBERT G. SOMMER), public relations executive, lobbyist; Presdl. mgmt. asst. EPA, 1983; cons. House Commerce Com. US Ho. of Reps., 1984—87; exec. v.p., dir. pub. affairs MWW Group Inc., 1988—2006; pres. Observer Media Group, 2007—09, Devils Arena Entertainment, LLC, Newark, 2009—. Lectr. Bloustein Sch. Planning and Pub. Policy, Rutgers U. Office: Devils Arena Entertainment LLC Prudential Ctr 165 Mulberry St Newark NJ 07102*

SOMMER, CAROL R., elementary school educator; b. Miller, SD, June 7, 1950; d. Earl C. and Alice E. Horn; m. Terry J. Sommer, Aug. 22, 1970; children: Riley R., Tara J., Megan B. BS, No. State U., Aberdeen, SD, 1973—77. Tchr. Christ King Sch., Sioux Falls, SD, 1994—2004, Holy Spirit Sch., Sioux Falls, 2004—. Grantee Japan Fulbright Meml. Fund Tchr. Program fellowship, Govt. Japan, 2005. Mem.: Alpha Delta Kappa (chaplain 2006—08, treas. 2008—). Roman Catholic. Avocations: reading, walking, travel, exercise. Office: Holy Spirit Sch 4309 S Bahnson Ave Sioux Falls SD 57103 Business E-Mail: csommer@sfcss.org.

SOMMER, JAMES STEVEN, psychologist; b. Denver, Mar. 19, 1965; s. Jay Monroe and Vivian Chantel Sommer; m. Teri Diane Atkison, Aug. 7, 1993; children: Jamon Lee, Lenzie Brianne. MS in Clin. Psychology, Ft. Hays State U., Hays, Kans., 1991. Lic. clin. psychotherapist Kans., 2000. Lic. master level psychologist Wichita Child Guidance Ctr., Kans., 1991—99; lic. clin. psychotherapist Family Consultation Svc., Wichita, 1999—2001; clin. psychology svcs. coord. USD 259, Wichita Pub. Schs., 2001—. Cons. Rescue Zone, Wichita, 2008—. Dir.: (gang prevention therapy group) Cmty. Youth Acad. Recipient Outstanding Achievement award, NASA, 1983, Good Apple award, USD 259, Wichita Pub. Schs., 2006. Mem.: Nat. Assn. Master Psychologists, Tripoli Rocketry Assn., Masons (sr. deacon 2009—), Psi Chi Honor Soc., Midian Shrine, York Rite, Wichita Scottish Rite. Democrat. Home: 1424 N Burns Wichita KS 67203 Office: USD 259 Wichita Pub Schs 2400 Wassall Wichita KS 67216 Office Fax: 316-973-1610. Personal E-mail: fasolstice@cox.net. Business E-Mail: jsommer@usd259.net.

SOMMER, JAY, writer, literature and language educator; b. Germany, 1927; arrived in US, 1948; m. Shirley Sommer; 1 child. BA, Bklyn. Coll.; MA in Spanish Lang., Lit., Hunter Coll.; MA in Russian, Fordham Univ.; PhD in Comparative Lit., NYU; LHD (hon.), Fontbonne Coll., St. Louis, 2001. Fgn. lang. tchr. New Rochell H.S., NY; ret. Adj. prof., modern lang. Fairfield Univ.; comn. mem. Nat. Comn. on Excellence in Edn., 1983. Author: Journey to the Golden Door. Named Nat. Tchr. of Yr., 1981. Fluent in 10 languages; Holocaust survivor. Mailing: 11 Lakeside Dr New Rochelle NY 10801

SOMMER, KENNETH, finance company executive; BA in acctg., Mich. State Univ., 1980. V.p., CFO global ops. & tech. div. Citigroup Inc., CFO, corp. & investment bank, Latin Am.; exec. v.p., chief adminstrv. officer Visa Internat., Foster City, Calif., 2000—06, CEO, 2006—. Mailing: Visa Internat PO Box 8999 San Francisco CA 94128-8999 Office: Visa Internat 900 Metro Ctr Blvd Foster City CA 94404

SOMMER, MIRIAM GOLDSTEIN (MIMI G. SOMMER), writer, photographer; b. Springfield, Mass., May 2, 1929; d. Nathan E. and Anna (Ginsberg) Goldstein; children: Babette, Anne. BA, Wells Coll., 1950; rsch. cert., London Sch. Econs., 1953; MS in Art History, So. Conn. State U., 1977. Music dept. adminstr. Yale U., 1963-83; free-lance travel writer, photographer New Haven, 1984—. Mem. Creative Arts Workshop, New Haven, 1960—; mem. New Haven Arts Coun., 1970—, Met. Mus. Art/Yale U. Art Galleries, Rockport Art Assn.; guest lectr. Journalism dept., So. Conn. State U., 1989-05; mem. Alumna Experiment Internat. Living-World Learning, France, 1950, Brattleboro, Vt. Contbr. articles and photography to profl. mags. including Colonial Homes mag., Family Fun mag., Touring Am. mag., Coastal Living mag., Conn. mag., Early American Life, Travel Agent mag., Jax Fax Travel Mktg. mag.; also newspapers including NY Times, LA Times, New Haven Register, Hartford Courant, Vineyard Gazette, Norwalk Hour, Connecticut Traveler; guest columnist Northhampton Daily Hampshire Gazette, 1998. V.p. Decade Alumni Coun., Williston Northampton Sch., Easthampton, Mass., 1989, co-founder, panelist career day; bd. mem., co-dir. Assn. Handicapped Artists, New Haven, 1989; co-founder Creative Arts Workshop course handicapped artists; vice-chmn. Cultural Affairs Commn., 2006-08, City of New Haven, 2001-09, commr.; substitute tchr. Worthington Hooker Elem. Sch., New Haven, Conn. Recipient Commendation Thesis with Distinction, Image Of Woman in Am. Film. Mem. Soc. Profl. Journalists (Excellence in Journalism First Prize Winner 1991 for best mag. spl. supplement feature "Designing Woman, Conn. Mag.), Am. Soc. Journalists and Authors, Soc. Profl. Journalists (Excellence in Journalism, 2002, 1st Pl. and 2nd Pl. Mag. Featured Photo awards competition), Rockport Art Assn. Avocations: pottery, movies, theater, antiques, citizenship. Home: 603 Prospect St New Haven CT 06511-2146 E-mail: miriam.sommer@yale.edu.

SOMMER, SCOTT WILLIAM, control systems integrator manager; b. Peoria, Ill., Mar. 26, 1959; s. William Alvin and Claudia (Almand) S.; m. Julia Ann Kyburz, May 19, 1984; children: Meghann Claire, Logan Scott. BSChemE, U. Ill., 1981; M in Engring. Chem. Engring., McNeese State U., 1983; postgrad., U. Phoenix, 1994—. Registered profl. engr., Ohio, Ill. Process engr. Conoco Chems. Co., Westlake, La., 1981-84; sys. engr. Celanese, Bishop, Tex., 1984-85; sr. automation engr. Fluor-Daniel, Cin., 1985-88; project mgr. Asea-Brown-Boveri, Columbus, Ohio, 1988-90; v.p. The Delta Group, Cin., 1990-93, 95—; dir. ops. PID, Inc., Cin., 1993-95, bus. process improvement leader, sr. tech. cons., 1995. Mem. NSPE, AICE, Instrument Soc. Am., Tau Beta Pi. Republican. Evangelical. Office: The Delta Group 9933 Alliance Rd Ste 200 Cincinnati OH 45242-5642

SOMMERFELD, JUDE THOMAS, chemical engineer, educator; b. Cin., Ohio, Feb. 4, 1936; s. Henry Anthony and Hilda Catherine (Diffley) S.; m. Rosemary Sniatkowski, May 17, 1958 (div. 1983); children: Loretta, Margaret, Maria, Joanna; m. Elizabeth Ryder, Apr. 18, 1992. B in Chem. Engring., U. Detroit, 1958; MS in Engring., U. Mich., 1960, PhD, 1963. Registered profl. engr., Ga. Sys. engr. Monsanto Co., St. Louis, 1963-66; dir. process engring. BASF-Wyandotte Corp., Mich., 1966-70; assoc. prof. Ga. Inst. Tech., Atlanta, 1970-75, prof., 1975—2002, cons., 2002—. Contbr. numerous articles to profl. jours. Fellow AIChE. Roman Catholic. Avocations: tennis, guitar, classical music, whitewater rafting. Business E-Mail: jude.sommerfeld@che.gatech.edu.

SOMMERFELDT, JOHN ROBERT, historian, educator; b. Detroit, Feb. 4, 1933; s. Melvin John and Virginia Zita (Gruenheck) S.; m. Patricia Natalie Levinske, Aug. 25, 1956; children: Ann, James, John, Elizabeth. AB, U. Mich., 1954, AM, 1956, PhD, 1960. Instr. history Stanford U., 1958-59; from instr. to prof. Western Mich. U., 1959-78; prof. history U. Dallas, 1978—, chmn. dept. history, 1984-87, univ. pres., 1978-80. Dir. Medieval Inst., Western Mich. U., 1961-76; exec. dir. Inst. Cistercian Studies, 1973-78; dir. Center Contemplative Studies, 1976-78; pres. Cistercian Publs., 1973-79, chmn. bd., 1976-79. Author: The Spiritual Teachings of Bernard of Clairvaux, 1991, Bernard of Clairvaux On the Life of the Mind, 2004, Bernard of Clairvaux On the Spiritualty of Relationship, 2004, Aelred of Rievaulx: Pursuing Perfect Happiness, 2005, Aelred of Rievaulx On Love and Order in the World and in the Chuch, 2006, Christianity in Culture, 2009; editor: Studies in Medieval Culture, 12 vols., 1964-78, Studies in Medieval Cistercian History, II, 1977, Cistercian Ideals and Reality, 1978, Simplicity and Ordinariness, 1980, The Chimaera of His Age: Studies in Bernard of Clairvaux, 1980, Abba: Guides to Wholeness and Holiness, East and West, 1981, Erudition at God's Service, 1987, Bernardus Magister, 1992, Studiosorum Speculum, 1993, Studies in the Theology of St. Thomas Aquinas, 1995. Fulbright scholar, 1954-55; Univ. fellow U. Mich., 1956-57. Mem. Medieval Acad. Am., Am. Catholic Hist. Assn., Am. Soc. Ch. History, Phi Beta Kappa, Phi Eta Sigma, Phi Kappa Phi. Republican. Roman Catholic. Home: 2809 Warren Cir Irving TX 75062-8938 Office: U Dallas Dept History 1845 E Northgate Dr Irving TX 75062-4736 Home Phone: 972-255-0608; Office Phone: 972-721-5370. Business E-Mail: jrsommer@udallas.edu.

SOMMERLAD, ROBERT EDWARD, environmental research engineer; b. Jersey City, Aug. 27, 1937; s. Herman Francis and Helen Rita (Joyce) S.; m. Margaret Doreen Breen, Sept. 9, 1961; children: Sharon K., Michael E., Ellen J. BSME, N.J. Inst. Tech., 1960, MSME, 1963, postgrad., 1965. Cert. profl. engr., State of NJ, 1964. V.p. contract ops. Foster Wheeler Devel. Corp., Livingston, 1974-84; pres. Enviresponse Inc., Livingston, 1985-86; dir. bus. devel. Energy and Environ. Rsch. Corp., Edison, NJ, 1987-88; cons., 1988-89; dir. environ. bus. devel. Midwest Rsch. Inst., Falls Church, Va., 1989-90; mgr. combustion tech. Rsch.-Cottrell Cos., 1990-92, cons., 1992-93; mktg. dir. PSI Powerserve, Andover, Mass., 1993-94, cons., program mgr., 1994-95; cons. Gas Rsch. Inst., Chgo., 1995-98, GE Energy and Environ. Rsch. Corp., Gurnee, Ill., 1998—2003; pvt. cons., 2003—; cons. Coll. Lake County, GraysLake, Ill., 2004—; head air pollution control sect. Foster Wheeler Energy Corp., Livingston, 1971-74, devel. engr., rsch. assoc., 1960-71; strategic acct. mgr. Loesche Energy Systems Ltd., 2005—08. Mem. coal combustion and applications working group U.S. Dept. Energy U. San Diego, 1981-84. Patentee in field. V.p. Cranford (N.J.) Cmty. Pools Parents Assn., 1975-77, 86-87, pres., 1977-79, 84-89; chmn. N.J. Swimming and Diving Conf., Cranford, 1986-89; v.p. Stonebrook Crossings Homeowners Assn., Gurnee, 1998-2000, pres., 2000—; com. for family aquatic ctr. Gurnee Park Dist., 1996-2002; mem. dept. pub. works com. Village of Gurnee, 2002—; mem. St. Paul the Apostle Choir, 2000-, Parish Pastoral Coun., 2003-. Recipient Outstanding Achievement award Westfield YMCA, 1975. Fellow ASME (mem. rsch. com. energy environ & waste 1971—, vice chmn. 1972-74, sec. 1987-91, mem. environ. affairs com. 1982-92, mem. dioxin com. 1985-92, mem. bd. performance test codes 1986-97, mem. emeritus 1998-, chmn. boiler-calorimeter com. 1986-89, numerous com. and conf. chairmanships, Cert. Achievement, Bd. on Codes and Standards, 1997); mem-.(life) Air and Waste Mgmt. Assn. (mem. AE-1 com. on particulate and associated acid gases, sec. 1991-94, vice chair 1996), Watchung Amateur Ski Club (mem. exec. bd. 1986-87); Bd. Cert. environ. engr. Am. Acad. Environ. Engr. (bd. trustees 2003-2008). Roman Catholic. Home: 1368 Knottingham Dr Gurnee IL 60031-5632 Office Phone: 847-856-1390.

SOMMERS, GEORGE R., lawyer; b. NYC, Jan. 27, 1955; BA, U. So. Fla., 1975; JD, NYU, 1987. Bar: NJ 1987, US Dist. Ct. NJ 1987, NY 1988, US Dist. Ct. (all dists.) NY 1988, US Ct. Appeals (3d cir.) 1988, US Ct. Appeals (2d cir.) 1989, US Supreme Ct. 1992. Assoc. Sullivan & Cromwell, NYC, 1987-90; pvt. practice lawyer NYC, 1990—. Pres. Bill of Rights Found., NYC, 1994—. Seidler scholar NYU Sch. Law, NYC, 1985. Mem. Hoboken Bar Assn. (pres. 1994). Jewish. Avocations: boxing, chess. Office: 51 Newark St Hoboken NJ 07030-4548 Home Phone: 201-344-3338; Office Phone: 212-709-8389, 201-656-6575.

SOMMERS, JILL ELAINE, commissioner; b. Ft. Scott, Kans., 1968; m. Michael J. Sommers; 3 children. BA, U. Kans. Intern to Senator Robert J. Dole US Senate, Washington DC, 1991—95; legis. aide Clark & Muldoon, P.C., Taggard & Associates; assoc. dir. govt. affairs Chgo. Mercantile Exch.; policy dir., head of govt. affairs Internat. Swaps and Derivatives Assn., 2005—07; commr. Commodity Futures Trading Commn. (CFTC), 2007—, chmn., designated fed. ofcl. global markets adv. com., 2008—. Commn. mem. Fin. Literacy and Edn. Commn. Office: Commodity Futures Trading Commn Three Lafayette Ctr Washington DC 20581 Office Phone: 202-418-5000. Office Fax: 202-418-5514.*

SOMMERS, MARK, lawyer; b. Chgo., Mar. 29, 1956; BA, Ohio Wesleyan U., 1978; JD, U. Northern Ill., 1982; LLM, U. London, Eng., 1983. Bar: Ill. 1982, NY 1985, Mass. 1985, DC 1989. Ptnr. Finnegan, Henderson, Farabow, Garrett & Dunner LLP, Washington, leader, Trademark & Copyright Sect. Named top 5 trademark attys. in US, Mng. Intellectual Property, top 10 trademark attys. in world. Office: Finnegan Henderson Farabow Garrett & Dunner LLP 901 New York Ave NW Washington DC 20001-3315 Office Phone: 202-408-4000. Office Fax: 202-408-4400. Business E-Mail: mark.sommers@finnegan.com.

SOMMERS, STEPHEN, film director, producer, scriptwriter; b. Indpls. Motion picture dir., writer, prodr. Writer, dir. Catch Me If You Can, 1989, The Adventures of Huck and Finn, 1993, The Jungle Book, 1994, Deep Rising, 1998, The Mummy, 1999; The Mummy Returns, 2001; writer, prodr. Tom and Huck, 1995, The Scorpion King, 2002; writer, prodr., dir., Van Helsing, 2004; prodr. T.V. movie Oliver Twist, 1997; dir. Terror Eyes, 1989, G.I. Joe: The Rise of Cobra, 2009; writer Gunmen, 1994. Office: c/o Jim Wiatt William Morris Agy 151 El Camino Dr Beverly Hills CA 90212*

SOMMESE, ANDREW JOHN, mathematics professor; b. NYC, May 1948; s. Joseph and Frances S.; m. Rebecca Rooze DeBoer, June 7, 1971; children: Rachel, Ruth. BA in Math., Fordham U., 1969; PhD in Math., Princeton U., 1973. Gibbs instr. Yale U., New Haven, 1973-75; asst. prof. Cornell U., Ithaca, NY, 1975-79; assoc. prof. U. Notre Dame, Ind., 1979-83, prof. of math. Ind., 1983—, chair dept. math. Ind., 1988-92, Vincent J. Duncan and Annamarie Micus Duncan chair math. Ind., 1994—, dir. Ctr. Applied Math. Ind., 2005—. Mem. Inst. for Advanced Study, Princeton, N.J., 1975-76; guest prof. U. Bonn, Germany, 1978-79; guest rschr. Max Planck Inst. for Math., Bonn, 1992-93; cons. GM Rsch., Warren, Mich., 1986-97. Editor: Manuscripta Mathematica jour., 1986-93, Advances in Geometry, 2000;mem. editl. bd. Milan Jour. Math., 2002; contbr. articles to profl. publs. Recipient Rsch. award for Sr. U.S. Scientists, Alexander Von Humboldt Found., 1993; A.P. Sloan Found. rsch. fellow, 1979. Mem. Am. Math. Soc., Soc. for Indsl. and Applied Math., Phi Beta Kappa. Office: U Notre Dame Dept Math Notre Dame IN 46556

SOMORJAI, GABOR ARPAD, chemist, educator; b. Budapest, Hungary, May 4, 1935; came to US, 1957, naturalized, 1962. s. Charles and Livia (Ormos) S.; m. Judith Kaldor, Sept. 2, 1957; children: Nicole, John. BS, U. Tech. Scis., Budapest, 1956; PhD, U. Calif., Berkeley, 1960; Dr. Honoris Causa (hon.), Tech. U., Budapest, 1989, U. Pierre et Marie Curie, Paris, 1990, U. Libre Brussels, 1992, U. degli de Ferrara, Italy, 1998, Jozsef Attila U., Szeged, Hungary, 1999, Royal Inst. Tech., Stockholm, 2000; D (hon.), U. Manchester, Eng., 2001. Mem. rsch. staff IBM, Yorktown Heights, NY, 1960-64; dir. Surface Sci. and Catalysis Prog. Lawrence Berkeley Lab., Calif., 1964—; mem. faculty dept. chemistry U. Calif., Berkeley, 1964—, assoc. prof., 1967-72, prof., 1972—, Miller prof., 1978, univ. prof., 2002. Unilever prof. dept. chemistry U. Bristol, Eng., 1972; vis. fellow Emmanuel Coll., Cambridge, Eng., 1989; Baker lectr. Cornell U., Ithaca, NY, 1977; edit. bd. mem. Catalysis Reviews J. Am. Chem. Soc., 2004—; hon. fellow Cardiff U., 2006. Author: Principles of Surface Chemistry, 1972, Chemistry in Two Dimensions, 1981, Introduction to Surface Chemistry and Catalysis, 1994; editor-in-chief Catalysis Letters, 1988—; contbr. articles to profl. jours. Recipient Emmett award Am. Catalysis Soc., 1977, Kokes award Johns Hopkins U., 1976, Albert award Precious Metal Inst., 1986, Sr. Disting. Scientist award Alexander von Humboldt Found., 1989, E.W. Mueller award U. Wis., Chem. Pioneer award Am. Inst. Chemists, 1995, Von Hippel award Materials Rsch. Soc., 1997, Wolf prize in chemistry, Wolf Found., Israel, 1998; Guggenheim fellow, 1969; hon. fellow Cardiff U., 2006, Priestley medal, 2008. Fellow: AAAS, Am. Phys. Soc. (Langmuir award 2007); mem.: NAS (Irving Langmuir prize in Chem. Physics 2007), Catalysis Soc. N.Am., Am. Chem. Soc. (chmn. colloid and surface chemistry 1981, Surface and Colloid Chemistry award 1981, Peter Debye award 1989, Arthur W. Adamson award 1994, Award for creative rsch. in homogeneous and heterogeneous catalysis 2000, Cotton medal 2002, Remsen award 2006, Priestley medal 2008), Hungarian Acad. Scis. (hon. Pauling medal 2000, Nat. Medal of Sci. 2001), Am. Acad. Arts and Scis. Home: 665 San Luis Rd Berkeley CA 94707-1725 Office: U Calif Dept Chemistry D 58 Hildebrand Hl Berkeley CA 94720-0001 E-mail: somorjai@socrates.berkeley.edu.

SOMSOUK, MA, gastroenterologist; m. Jennifer Tan. BA, Pomona Coll., Claremont, 1997; MD, Harvard U., Boston, 2002; MAS, U. Calif., San Francisco, 2008. Asst. prof. U. Calif., 2008. Office: Univ Calif San Francisco 1001 Potrero Ave 3D-2 San Francisco CA 94110

SON, TAE W., physics professor; b. Seoul, Republic of Korea, May 13, 1975; s. Yoon Ho Son and Chong Hui Yun. MS, U. Tex. Dallas, Richardson, 2002. Adj. prof. physics Richland Coll., Dallas, 2004—; assoc. prof. physics Collin County CC, Plano, Tex., 2007—. Mem.: Soc. Physics Students (v.p. 1996—97). Office: Richland Coll 12800 Abrams Rd Dallas TX 75243-2199

SON, YOUNG K., engineering educator; PhD, Auburn U. Assoc. prof. Baruch Coll., NYC, 1987—; doctoral faculty Grad. Ctr., CUNY, NYC, 1992—. Dir. Samsung-Baruch Program, NYC, 1994—97. CCD program dir. Notre Dame Ch. Korean Cmty., New Hyde Pk., NY, 1998; fundraising com. chmn. St. Brigid's Ch. Korean Cmty., Westbury, NY, 1989. Recipient Alfred V. Bodine award, Soc. Mfg. Engrs., 1987, Eugene L. Grant award, Am. Soc. Engring. Edn., 1990, Romey Everdell award, Am. Prodn. and Inventory Control Soc., 1991, Outstanding Publ. award, Inst. Indsl. Engrs., 1991, Award of Merit, Soc. Tech. Communication, 1998. Office: Zicklin Sch Bus Baruch Coll One Bernard Baruch Way New York NY 10010-5585

SON, YOUNGJIN, mechanical engineer; s. Yonghun Son and Sukja Ko; m. Jiyoung Lee; 1 child, Hans Hyungseok. BS, Seoul Nat. U., Republic of Korea, 1992, MS, 1994; PhD, U. Southern Calif., LA, 2004. Jr. rsch. engr. Mando Machinery Corp., Gunpo, Kyunggi, Republic of Korea, 1994—99; rsch. assoc. U. Southern Calif., 2004—06; sr. engr. Hyundai Motor Co., Yongin, Kyunggi, 2006—08, Caterpiller Inc., Mossville, Ill., 2008—. External tech. cons. Firefighter LLC., Ont., Calif., 2004—05. Contbr. scientific papers. With Korean Army, 1997. Recipient Best Rsch. Team award, Mando Machinery Corp., 1998, Excellence award, Seoul Nat. U., 1992, Excellent Tchg. award, U. Southern Calif., 2000, Best Paper award, Star-CD Korea, 2007; fellowship, Mando Machinery Corp., 1991. Mem.: AIAA, SAE Internat., Combustion Inst. Achievements include research in microgravity combustion; design of fuel cell system design improvement for automotive application; development of diesel particulate trap system for small gabage truck. Office: Caterpillar Inc 14009 Old Galena Rd Mossville IL 61615 Business E-Mail: son_youngjin@cat.com.

SONBERG, STEVEN, lawyer; b. NYC, May 10, 1947; BS in Acctg., NYU Leonard N. Stern Sch. Bus., 1969; JD, U. Miami Sch. Law, 1972; LLM in Taxation, NYU Sch. Law, 1973. Bar: Fla. 1972, US Tax Ct. 1979. Ptnr. Holland & Knight LLP, Miami, Fla., 1992—, chair, bus. law sect., 2003—, co-chair, corp. governance nat. practice group, mng. ptnr., 2008—. Spkr. in field. Contbr. articles to profl. jours. Bd. trustee U. Miami; bd. dir. Diabetes Rsch. Inst. Found., Inc., 1980—, pres., 1984—86, chmn. bd. dirs., 1990—96. Mem.: Am. Bar Found., Fla. Bar (mem. bus. law sect., internat. law sect., tax sect.), ABA (mem. bus. law, internat. and tax sects.), Dade County Bar Assn., Broward County Bar Assn. Office: Holland & Knight LLP 701 Brickell Ave Ste 3000 Miami FL 33131 Address: Holland & Knight LLP One East Broward Blvd Ste 1300 Fort Lauderdale FL 33301 Office Phone: 305-789-7794, 954-468-7816. Business E-Mail: ssonberg@hklaw.com.

SONDAY, ARLENE W., educational consultant; d. Rudolph Anselm and Ebba Isabelle Linnea Waxlax; m. Ralph E. Sonday, July 30, 1955; children: Barbara Ann Sonday Neafus, Bradley Allen, Karen Lee, David Ralph. BA, Gustavus Adolphus Coll., 1954; MA, U. St. Thomas, 1976. Cert. learning disabilities State of Minn., 1973. Founder, academic dir. summer sch. St. Paul Acad., 1975—93, faculty, 1975—85; tchr. educator Scottish Rite Children's Learning Ctr., various cities in Pa and Ohio, 1997—2003; tchr. tng. Winsor Learning, Inc., St. Paul, 1999—. Lectr., workshop leader, 1972—; adj. faculty Fairleigh Dickinson U., Teaneck, 1988—2005, adv. com. dyslexia specialist cert. program, 1988—; adj. faculty Hamline U., St. Paul, 1988—; adv. bd. curriculum stds. Scottish Rite Children's Learning Ctr., Lexington, Mass., 1997—2003; conf. workshop leader Egyptian Learning Disabilities Assn., Cairo, 2005—, Coun. Exceptional Children, Beijing, 2004, Children 2002, Chennai, India, 2002; workshop leader, Mumbai, Puna, Nasik, New Delhi, Chennai, India, 2004—05. Author: (curriculum writer) Sonday System-Let's Play Learn; Sonday System Learning to Read; Sonday System II. V.p., bd. dirs. Internat. Dyslexia Assn., Balt., 1982—93, pres., bd. dirs., bd. advisors upper midwest br. Mpls., 1969—2005. Recipient Betty Jones Dedicated Svc. award, Minn. Assn. Children with Learning Disabilities, 1989. Fellow: Acad. Orton-Gillingham Practitioners and Educators (bd. dirs., chair organizing com. 1993—2000, pres. 1996—97); mem.: European Dyslexia Assn., Thailand TESOL, Jamaican Dyslexia Assn., Brit. Dyslexia Assn., Coun. for Exceptional Children, Learning Disabilities Am., Internat. Reading Assn., Internat. Dyslexia Assn. (v.p. 1987—93, Outstanding Svc. award 1993), Children 2002. Avocations: travel, reading, needlecrafts, exercise. Home: 1585 Dodd Rd #303 Saint Paul MN 55118 Office: Winsor Learning 1620 W 7th St Saint Paul MN 55102 Office Phone: 800-321-7585. Office Fax: 651-222-3969. Personal E-mail: asonday@comcast.net.

SONDEL, PAUL MARK, pediatric oncologist, educator; b. Milw., Aug. 14, 1950; s. Robert F. and Audrey J. (Dworkus) S.; m. Sherie Ann Katz, Jan. 1, 1973; children: Jesse Adam, Beth Leah, Elana Rose, Jodi Zipporah. BS with honors, U. Wis., Madison, 1971, PhD in Genetics, 1975; MD magna cum laude, Harvard Med. Sch., Boston, 1977. Diplomate Nat. Bd. Med. Examiners, Am. Bd. Pediatrics; lic. physician, Wis. Postdoctoral rsch. fellow Harvard Med. Sch., Boston, 1975-77; intern in pediatrics U. Minn. Hosp., Mpls., 1977-78; resident in pediatrics U. Wis. Hosp. and Clinics, Madison, 1978-80; asst. prof. pediatrics, human oncology and genetics U. Wis., Madison, 1980-84, assoc. prof., 1984-86, prof. pediatrics, human oncology and genetics, 1987—, head divsn. pediatric hematology/oncology, program leader, 1990—; assoc. dir. U Wisc. Cancer Ctr., 1996-99, U. Wis. Cancer Ctr., 2006—; vice chair rsch. dept. pediatrics U. Wis., Madison, 2006—. Sub-fellow pediat. oncology; Midwest Children's Cancer Ctr., Milw., 1980; vis. scientist dept. cell biology Weizmann Inst. Sci., Rehovot, Israel, 1987, 2000; chmn. immunology com. Children's Cancer Group 1990-2001; cancer ctr. rev. com. Nat. Cancer Inst., 1997-2000, bd. sci. counselors, 2005—. Sr. editor Clin. Cancer Rsch., 1996-99; mem. editl. bd. Jour. Immunology, 1985-87, Jour. Nat. Cancer Inst., 1987—, Jour. Biol. Response Modifiers, 1990—, BLOOD, 1992—, Natural Immunity, 1992—; contbr. articles to Jour. Exptl. Medicine, Jour. Immunology, Cellular Immunology, Immunol. Revs., Med. Pediatric Oncology, Wis. State Med. Jour., Jour. Biol. Response Modifiers, Jour. Pediatrics, Jour. Clin. Oncology, Jour. Clin. Investigation, others State of Wis. Regents scholar, 1968; J.A. and G.L. Hartford Found. fellow, 1981-84. Mem. Am. Assn. Immunologists, Am. Assn. Clin. Histocompatibility Typing, Am. Fedn. Clin. Rsch., Am. Soc. Pediatric Hematology/Oncology, Am. Assn. Cancer Rsch., Am. Soc. Transplant Physicians, Am. Soc. Clin. Oncology, Am. Acad. Pediatrics, Leukemia Soc. Am. (bd. dirs. Wis. chpt. 1987-90 Achievements include patent for Typing Leukocyte Antigens; research on clinical and immunological effects of human recombinant Interleukin-2 and monoclonal antibodies. Home: 1114 Winston Dr Madison WI 53711-3161 Office: U Wis K4/448 Clin Sci Ctr 600 Highland Ave Madison WI 53792-3284 Business E-Mail: pmsondel@humonc.wisc.edu.

SONDERBY, SUSAN PIERSON, federal judge; b. Chgo., May 15, 1947; d. George W. and Shirley L. (Eckstrom) Pierson; m. James A. De Witt, June 14, 1975 (dec. 1978); m. Peter R. Sonderby, Apr. 7, 1990. AA, Joliet Jr. Coll., Joliet, Ill., 1967; BA, U. Ill., 1969; JD, John Marshall Law Sch., 1973. Bar: Ill., 1973; U.S. Dist. Ct. (cen. and so. dists.) Ill., 1978,; U.S. Dist. Ct. (no. dist.) Ill., 1984; U.S. Ct. Appeals (7th Cir.), 1984. Assoc. O'Brien, Garrison, Berard, Kusta, and De Witt, Joliet, Ill., 1973-75, ptnr., 1975-77; asst. atty. gen. consumer protection div., litig. sect. Office of the Atty. Gen., Chgo., 1977-78, asst. atty. gen., chief consumer protection divsn. Springfield, Ill., 1978-83; U.S. trustee (no. dist.) Ill. Chgo., 1983-86; judge U.S. Bankruptcy Ct. (no. dist.) Ill., Chgo., 1986—, chief fed. bankruptcy judge, 1998—2002. Mem. law faculty Fed. Jud. Tng. Ctr., Ill., Practicing Law Inst., Ill., U.S. Dept. Justice, Ill., Nat. Bankruptcy Inst., Ill., Ill. Continuing Edn.; spl. asst. atty. gen., Ill., 1972—78; adj. faculty De Paul U. Coll. Law, Chgo., 1986; past mem. U.S. Trustee adv. com., Ill.; consumer adv. coun. Fed. Res. Bd., Ill.; past sec. of State Fraudulent I.D. com. Dept. of Ins. Task Force on Improper Claims Practices, Ill.; former chair pers. rev. bd., mem. task force race and gender bias, U.S. Dist. Ct.; jud. conf. planning com. 7th Cir. Jud. Conf.; former mem. Civil Justice Reform Act Adv. Com., Adminstrv. Office of the U.S. Cts. Bankruptcy Judges Adv. Group, Ct. Security com., Adminstrv. Office of the U.S. Cts. Budget and Fin. Coun.; mem. US Bankruptcy Judges, 2008. Contbr. articles to profl. jour. Mem. Fourth Presbyn. Ch., Art Inst. Chgo.; past mem. Westminster Presbyn. Ch., Chgo. Coun. of Fgn. Rels.; past bd. dirs. Land of Lincoln Coun. Girl Scouts U.S.; past mem. individual guarantors com. Goodman Theatre, Chgo.; past chair clubs and orgns. Sangamon County United Way Capital campaign; past bd. dirs., chair house rules com. and legal subcom. Lake Point Tower; past mem. Family Svc. Ctr., Aid to Retarded Citizens, Henson Robinson Zoo. Recipient Spl. Achievement Award, Dept. Justice, 1984, Disting. Svc. Alumni Award, Joliet Jr. Coll., 1987, Disting. Alumni Award, John Marshall Law Sch., 1988, Dir. Award, Exec. Office U.S. Trustee, Leadership Award, Internat. Orgn. Women Exec., Outstanding Svc. to Bench, Am. Bankruptcy Inst., 1990; named Young Career Woman, Bus. and Profl. Women, One of Ten Outstanding Bankruptcy Judges, Turnarounds and Workouts, 2002; named one of 500 Leading Judges in Am., Law Dragon mag., 2006. Master: Abraham Lincoln Marovitz Inn of Ct. (former pres., membership com.); fellow: Am. Coll. Bankruptcy (circuit admissions com.); mem.: ATLA, Comml. Law League Am. (former exec. coun. mem., bankruptcy and insolvency sect., coord. with nat. conf. bankruptcy judges com.), Nat. Conf. Bankruptcy Judges (co-chair edn1. program com. conf. 2001, judge advisor Mgmt. Manual US Bankrupty Cts. 2009, liaison with bankruptcy rev. commn. com.), Bar Assn. (7th cir.) (former treas., judicial conf. planning com.), Am. Bankruptcy Inst., Fed. Bar Assn. (bd. dirs. chgo. chpt.), Chgo. Archtl. Found., John Marshall Law Sch. Alumni Assn. (bd. dirs.), Nordic Law Club (past legis. com.), Lawyers Club Chgo. (hon.). Avocations: travel, flying, interior decorating. Office: US Bankruptcy Ct 219 S Dearborn St Ste 638 Chicago IL 60604-1702

SONDHEIM, STEPHEN JOSHUA, composer, librettist, lyricist; b. NYC, Mar. 22, 1930; s. Herbert and Janet (Fox) Sondheim. BA, Williams Coll., 1950. Composer, lyricist. Vis. prof. comtemporary theatre Oxford U., England. Lyricist West Side Story, 1957 (Tony award), Gypsy, 1959, Do I Hear a Waltz?, 1965, Evening Primrose, 1966, Bounce, 2003, music and lyrics A Funny Thing Happened on the Way to the Forum, 1962, Anyone Can Whistle, 1964, Company, 1970 (Tony award, 1971), Follies, 1971 (Tony award, 1972), A Little Night Music, 1973 (Tony award, 1973), The Frogs, 1974, Pacific Overtures, 1976, Sweeney Todd, 1979 (Tony award, 1979), Merrily We Roll Along, 1981, Sunday in the Park with George, 1984 (Pulitzer prize, 1985), Into the Woods, 1987 (Tony award, 1988), Assassins, 1991, Putting It Together, 1992, Passion, 1994 (Tony award, 1994), Chita Rivera: The Dancer's Life, 2005; music and lyrics: Road Show, 2008 (Drama Desk award for Outstanding Lyrics, 2009, Obie award for Music and Lyrics, 2009); (incidental music) Girls of Summer, 1956, incidental music Invitation to a March, 1961, Twigs, 1971, additional lyrics Candide, 1973, (anthologies) Side by Side by Sondheim, 1976, Marry Me a Little, 1981, You're Gonna Love Tomorrow, 1983, (film scores) Stavisky, 1974, Reds, 1981; composer: songs for film Dick Tracy, 1990 (Acad. award); co-author: (films) The Last of Sheila, 1973, Birdcage, 1996, Getting Away with Murder, 1996. Founder Young Playwrights Inc., 1981—. Recipient Creative Arts medal, Brandeis U., 1982, Grammy awards, 1970, 1973, 1975, 1979, 1984, 1988, Kennedy Ctr. Honor for Lifetime Achievement, 1993, Nat. Medal of Arts, NEA, 1997, Praemium Imperiale, 2000, The Jason Robards award for excellence in theatre, Roundabout Theatre Co., 2005, Golden Plate award, Acad. Achievement, 2005, Spl. Tony award for Lifetime Achievement in Theatre, 2008. Mem.: Am. Acad. and Inst. Arts and Letters.*

SONDOCK, RUBY KLESS, retired judge; b. Apr. 26, 1926; d. Herman Lewis and Celia (Juran) Kless; m. Melvin Adolph Sondock, Apr. 22, 1944; children: Marcia Cohen, Sandra Marcus. AA, Cottey Coll., Nevada, Mo., 1944; BS, U. Houston, 1959, LLB, 1961. Bar: Tex. 1961, U.S. Supreme Ct. 1977. Pvt. practice, Houston, 1961-73, 89—; judge Harris County Ct. Domestic Rels. (312th Dist.), 1973-77, 234th Jud. Dist. Ct., Houston, 1977-82, 83-89; justice Tex. Supreme Ct., Austin, 1982; of counsel Weil Gotshal and Manges, 1989-93, Houston Ctr., 1993—. Mem. ABA, Tex. Bar Assn., Houston Bar Assn., Houston Assn. Women Lawyers, Order of Barons, Phi Theta Phi, Kappa Beta Pi, Phi Kappa Phi, Alpha Epsilon Pi. Address: 1111 Caroline St #2608 Houston TX 77010 Office Phone: 713-655-1111.

SONE, HIRO, chef, restaurant owner, writer; b. Ichihasama, Japan; m. Lissa Doumani. Grad., Ecole Technique Hoteliere Tsuji, Osaka, Japan. From dishwasher to sous chef Italian restaurant, Tokyo; from mem. staff to head chef Spago, LA, former sous chef Tokyo; co-owner, chef Terra, St. Helena, Calif., 1988—. Author (with Lissa Doumani): Terra, Cooking from the Heart of the Napa Valley, 2001. Recipient Best Chef Calif. award, James Beard Found., 2003, Outstanding Svc. award (with Lissa Doumani), 2008; nominee Am. Express Best Chef, Calif., 2001. Office: Terra 1345 Railroad Ave Saint Helena CA 94574

SONEGO, IAN G., retired assistant attorney general; b. Louisville, May 27, 1954; s. Angelo and Zella Mae (Causey) S. BA in Polit. Sci. with high honors, U. Louisville, 1976, JD, 1979. Bar: Ky. 1979, U.S. Dist Ct. (ea. dist.) Ky. 1980, U.S. Dist. Ct. (we. dist.) Ky. 1989, U.S. Ct. Appeals (6th cir.) 1989, U.S. Supreme Ct. 1990. Asst. atty. Office Commonwealth's Atty. Pike County, Pikeville, Ky., 1980, sr. asst. atty., 1988-89; assoc. John Paul Runyon Law Firm, Pikeville, 1981-87; asst. atty. gen. Office Atty. Gen., Frankfort, Ky., 1989—2008. Lectr. criminal law Ky. Bar Assn., Jenny Wiley Park, 1981, Ky. Prosecutors Confs., 1989, 93; mem. Atty. Gen.'s task force child sexual abuse, 1992-94, Nat. Conf. on Domestic Violence, 1996. Contbg. editor Ky. Prosecuter Newsletter, 1991—. Recipient Kesslman award, U. Louisville, 1975, Bd. trustee award, 1979, Outstanding Prosecutor award, Ky. Atty., Award Outstanding Advocacy, Assn. Govt. Attys. in Capital Litigation, 2001, Disting. Svc. award, Ky. Prosecutors Coun., 2008. Mem.: Assn. Govt. Attys. in Capital Litig., Ky. Commonwealth's Attys. Assn. (hon.; lectr. 1987, 90, chmn. com. ethics 1984—86, bd. dirs. 1983—85, Spl. award 1987). Personal E-mail: sonegoian@bellsouth.net.

SONFIELD, ROBERT LEON, JR., lawyer; b. Houston, Oct. 28, 1931; s. Robert Leon and Dorothy Harriett (Huber) S.; 1 dau., Sheree. BA, U. Houston, 1956, LLB, JD, 1959; PhD (hon.), U. Eastern Fla., 1962; LLD (hon.), London Inst. Applied Rsch., 1973; cert. fed. taxation, NYU, 1973; cert. securities regulation, Harvard U., 1983. Bar: Tex. 1959, U.S. Supreme Ct. 1959, U.S. Dist. Ct. Tex. 1960, U.S. Tax Ct. 1960, U.S. Ct. Appeals 1960, U.S. Ct. Claims 1974. Mng. dir. Sonfield & Sonfield, Houston, 1959—. Mem. nat. adv. coun. Nat. Fedn. Ind. Bus. Author: Corporate Financing by Sale of Securities to the Public, 1969, Mergers and Acquisitions, 1970, Student Rights, 1971, The Limited Partnership as a Vehicle for Real Estate Investment, 1971, Integration of Partnership Offerings, 1974, The Grantor Trust Rules After The Tax Reform Act of 1986, Incentive Equity Program, Corporate Name Protection Along With Name Registration, A Guide to SEC Corporate Filing, Organizational Professionals' Residual Litigation and Investment Strategy, Comparing California, Delaware and Nevada: Corporate Laws in Light of California Corporations Code Section 2115 and Offering of Unregistered Securities Only to Accredited Investors, Disclosure Policies, Practices and Procedures For Public Companies, Regulation of Franchises, How to Become a Publicly Held Company Via the Registered Distribution of a Percentage of Your Company's Stock to Shareholders, numerous others. Recipient St. John Garwood award, 1957, Frio-Finnegan Outstanding Alumnus award, 1970-71, citation for outstanding contbn. to legal profession, 1971. Mem. Am. Tax Lawyers Assn. (pres.), Lawyers Soc. Houson, Am. Judicature Soc., ABA, Tex. Bar Assn. (dist. com. on admission to state bar, chmn. clients security fund com.), Houston Bar Assn. (com. chmn. coun., tax sect.), Tex. Equal Access to Justice Found., Houston Bar Found., Real Estate Securities and Syndication Inst., Huguenot Soc. of London, Order Stars and Bars, SAR, Sons Confederate Vets., Mil. Order World Wars, Mil. and Hospitaller Order St. Lazarus of Jerusalem, Knightly Assn. St. George the Martyr, Smithsonian Assocs., Houston Heritage Soc., Houston Mus. Fine Arts, Newcomen Soc. N.Am., Phi Delta Phi, Delta Sigma Phi, Met. Club (N.Y.C.), Argyle Club (San Antonio), Houston Club, Houstonian Club. Office: Sonfield & Sonfield 770 S Post Oak Ln Houston TX 77056-6665 Home Phone: 713-850-0918; Office Phone: 713-877-8333. Personal E-mail: robert@sonfield.com.

SONG, BYOUNG-JOON, pharmacologist, biochemist; b. Inchon, Republic of Korea, Mar. 4, 1950; PhD, U. Minn. Med. Sch., Mpls., 1982. Sr. staff fellow NIH, Bethesda, Md., 1986—92, sr. investigator, 1993—. Master: Am. Assn. Biochemistry and Molecular Biology. Office: NIH 9000 Rockville Pike Bethesda MD 20892-9410

SONG, BYUNG YOUN, electronics executive, consultant; b. Pusan, Republic of Korea, Dec. 30, 1973; s. Myung June Song and Tae Sook Kwak; m. Youngmi Kim; children: Jisu, Yeonsu. PhD, Seoul Nat. U., Republic Of Korea, 2009. Rsch. staff Doosan Infracore Co. Ltd., Changwon, Republic of Korea, 1998—2000; sr. rsch. staff Samsung Electronics Co. Ltd., Suwon, Republic of Korea, 2000—04; chief rsch. staff Toshiba Samsung Storage Tech., Suwon, 2004—; vis. scholar UCLA, 2007—. Cons. MuTAS Inc., Suwon, 2005—, PowerMEMS Inc., Cupertino, Calif., 2007—. Recipient Good Co. award, Samsung Electronics Co. Ltd., 2003. Mem.: Korea Soc. Noise and Vibration. Achievements include design of infantry fighting vehicle; patents for optical pickup actuator damper design; development of ultra slim optical and blue-ray disc optical actuator; patents pending for silicon photonic volatile memory device. Personal E-mail: lucsong@gmail.com. Business E-Mail: bsong@seas.ucla.edu, lucsong9@snu.ac.kr.

SONG, DAVID, plastic surgeon, medical educator; b. 1970; MD, UCLA. Cert. Plastic Surgery. Surg. resident Univ. Chgo. Hospitals, plastic surgeon, chief plastic surgeon, 2004—. Spkr. in field; bd. mem. Med. Aid for Children of Latin Am. Contbr. articles to numerous profl. jours. Med. Aid for Children Latin Am. Named one of 40 Under Forty, Crain's Bus. Chgo., 2005. Mem.: Am. Coll. Plastic Surgeons, Am. Coll. Surgeons. Office: Univ Chgo Hosps MC 6035 5841 S Maryland Ave Chicago IL 60637 Office Phone: 773-702-6302. Office Fax: 773-702-1634. E-mail: dsong@surgery.bsd.uchicago.edu.

SONG, JANE INYOUNG, lawyer; b. Seoul, Jan. 3, 1970; arrived in US, 1981; d. Key Oh and Inja Song; m. Paul Edward James Whitworth, Oct. 7, 1995. BS, MIT, Cambridge, 1991, MS, 1993; JD, Columbia U., NYC, 1996. Bar: Mass. 1996, Calif. 2000, US Dist. Ct. (ea. dist.) Mass. 1999. Assoc. Testa, Hurwitz & Thibeault LLP, Boston, 1996—2000, Cooley & Godward LLP, Palo Alto, San Diego, 2000—04, Paul Hastings LLP, San Diego, 2004—. Spkr. in field. Contbr. articles to profl. jours. Mem.: Licensing Exec. Soc., Am. Intellectual Property Law Assn., Calif. Bar Assn. (licensing com. 2005—, intellectual property sect.). Office: Paul Hastings LLP 4747 Executive Dr 12th Fl San Diego CA 92121 Office Fax: 858-450-3143.

SONG, JOSEPH, pathologist, educator; b. Pyong Yang, Korea, May 11, 1927; s. Ha Ju and Hwa Soon (Koh) S.; m. Kumsan Ryu, Apr. 12, 1958; children: Patricia, Michael, Jeff. MD, Seoul U. Sch. Medicine, 1950; MS in Pathology, U. Tenn., Memphis, 1956; MD, U. Ark. Med. Sch., 1965. Diplomate Am. Bd. Pathology. Pathologist in charge State Cancer Detection Survey, Providence, 1956—59; assoc. pathologist Providence Lying-In Hosp., 1958—61; assoc. prof. pathology U. Ark. Med. Ctr., Little Rock, 1961—64; dir. lab. Mercy Hosp., Des Moines, 1965—92, rschr. cancer, 1993—95; clin. prof. pathology Creighton U. Sch. Medicine, Omaha, 1968—95; med. dir. Corning Clin. Labs., Des Moines, 1995—97; ret., 1997. Cons. EPA, Washington, 1975-85; pres. med. staff Mercy Hosp., Des Moines, 1981 Author: (book) The Human Uterus, 1964, Pathology of Sickle Cell Anemia, 1971 (award 1975), Beyond the Horizon, 1995. Elder Winsdor Presbyn. Ch., Des Moines, 1964; com. mem. Aldersgate Meth. Ch., Des Moines, 1995. Major Med. Corps, 1950-52, Korea. Recipient Martin Luther King Med. Achievement award, So. Christian Leadership Conf., Statesmanship award Am. Assn. Med. Adminstrs., Las Vegas, Nev., 1987. Fellow ACP, Coll. Am. Pathologists, Am. Soc. Clin. Pathology, Am. Assn. Cancer Rsch. Methodist. Avocation: classical music. Home: 2345 Park Ave Des Moines IA 50321-1505 Home Phone: 515-243-7748.

SONG, JUNFENG JOHN, engineer, researcher; b. Chongqing, Sichuan, China, May 20, 1942; s. Hengtai Jilong Song and Fengying Cheng; m. Fang Helen Hou, Jan. 6, 2004; children: Jane Ysabelle, Jiajie Jack. MS, Harbin Inst. Tech., China, 1981. Sr. engr. Changcheng Inst. Metrology and Measurement, Beijing, 1985—87; sr. rsch. engr. Nat. Inst. Stds. and Tech., Gaithersburg, Md., 1987—. Postdoc. rsch. advisor NRC US Nat. Acad. Sci., Washington, 1997—. Inventor (engring. stds.) A Metrological Approach to Unifying International Rockwell Hardness Scales published in Metrologia, Vol. 34, 1997; contbr. articles to profl. jours. Recipient Bronze Medal award, Nat. Inst. Stds. Tech., 1994, E. B. Rosa award, 1996, Judson C. French award, 2002. Mem.: Am. Soc. Precision Engring., Internat. Com. Measurements and Instrumentation, CIPM (BIPM) Consultative Com. Mass and Related Quantities - Working Group Hardness, Vivian Kwok Seasharp Music Club. Achievements include patents for random profile precision roughness calibration specimens; invention of standard reference material 2460-2461 standard bullets and casings; design of 2D and 3D topography measurement system and US national ballistics measurement traceability and quality system. Avocations: piano, rollerskating, skiing, swimming. Home: 13105 Lake Geneva Way Germantown MD 20874 Office: Nat Inst Stds Tech 100 Bureau Dr Stop 8212 Gaithersburg MD 20899-8212 Home Phone: 301-972-2764; Office Phone: 301-975-3799. Office Fax: 301-869-0822. Business E-Mail: junfeng.song@nist.gov, song@nist.gov.

SONG, KIT M., orthopedist, educator; b. Mpls., May 30, 1958; m. Kwi-Yong Lee, Aug. 6, 2005; children: Michael, Rebecca. BA in Chemistry with highest distinction, U. Iowa, 1980, MD, 1985. Diplomate Am. Bd. Orthop. Surgery. Pathology externship U. Iowa, Iowa City, 1983; gen. surg. intern UCLA, 1985—86; resident dept. orthop. surgery U. Wash., 1986—91; pediat. orthop. fellow Tex. Scottish Rite Hosp. for Children, Dallas, 1991—92, staff orthop. surgeon, 1992—95, med. dir. Gait Analysis Lab., 1992—95; staff pediat. orthop. surgeon Parkland Hosp. and U. Tex. Southwestern Med. Ctr., Dallas, 1992—95; asst. dir. pediat. orthop. Children's Hosp. and Regional Med. Ctr. Seattle, Seattle, 1995—; asst. prof. dept. orthop. surgery U. Tex. Southwestern Med. Ctr., Dallas, 1992—95; asst. prof. dept. orthop. surgery Sch. Medicine U. Wash., Seattle, 1995—2000, assoc. prof. dept. orthop. surgery Sch. Medicine, 2000—. Cons. pediat. orthop. surgeon Children's Med. Ctr., Dallas, 1992—95; mem. program com. numerous symposiums and confs. in field; invited spkr. in field; mem. contracting com. Children's Univ. Med. Group, 2002—, mem. physician edn. and compliance com., 2001—, bd. dirs. Cons. reviewer: Jour. Pediat. Orthop., 1998—, reviewer pediat. sect.: Jour. Am. Acad. Orthop. Surgery, 1998—, guest reviewer: Jour. Bone and Joint Surgery, 2000—; contbr. articles to profl. jours. Recipient Honors Cert. of Achievement, U. Iowa, 1980, Faculty award, Dept. Chemistry, U. Iowa, 1980, Dept. Pathology award, U. Iowa, 1985, Caring for Children award, Children's Hosp. Seattle, 2001, Children's Orthop. Day Resident award for outstanding rsch., U. Wash., 1989; named one of Best Physicians in Seattle, Seattle Mag., 2000; grantee, Tex. Scottish Rite Hosp. for Children, 1991, NIH, 1995—96, Bionix Corp., 1997, Children's Hosp. and Med. Ctr. Rsch. Endowment, 1997, Pediat. Orthop. Soc. N.Am. Rsch., 1999, Nat. Ctr. Injury Prevention and Control, 1999, Scoliosis Rsch. Soc., 1999, Synthes Corp.; Rsch. fellow, U. Iowa, 1980, 1981. Mem.: Am. Acad. Pediat. (mem. Wash. State chpt.), N.Am. Soc. Gait and Clin. Movement Analysis, Am. Acad. Cerebral Palsy and Devel. Medicine, Scoliosis Rsch. Soc., Pediat. Orthop. Soc. N.Am. (bd. dirs. 1998—99, mem. awards com. 1998—99, mem. long range planning com. 1999—2000, mem. program com. 2001—), Am. Acad. Orthop. Surgery, Alpha Omega Alpha, Phi Beta Kappa. Office: Children's Hospital Regional Medical Center 4800 Sand Point Way NE Seattle WA 98105 Office Fax: 206-987-3852. Business E-Mail: kit.song@seattlechildrens.org.

SONG, LIANFA, educator; s. Jiyao Song and Guizheng Yuan; m. Fuxia Li, Jan. 11, 1957; children: Lisa Qian, Julie Jia. B, Peking U., Beijing, China, 1982, M, 1984; PhD, UCLA, 1993. Asst. prof. Hong Kong U. Sci. and Tech., 1996—2000; assoc. prof. Nat. U. Singapore, 2000—. Achievements include research in theory on concentration polarization, fouling dynamics, and process optimization in membrane technology. Office: Texas Tech Univ 10th and Akron Lubbock TX 79409 Home: 6008 90th St Lubbock TX 79424 Business E-Mail: eseslf@nus.edu.sg.

SONG, MI-YEON, education educator, physician; b. Seoul, Republic of Korea, Dec. 21, 1971; d. Young-Ho Song and Jung-Hee Park; m. Sang-Hyun Moon; children: Chai-ho Moon children: Chai-jung Lim, Chai-hyun Lim. MD (Korean Medicine), KyungHee U., Seoul, 1996, PhD, 2001. Diplomate Nat. Cert. Commn. for Accupuncture and Oriental Medicine. Intern KyungHee Med. Ctr., Seoul, 1996—97, resident, 1998—2000; postdoc. fellow Columbia U., NY, 2001—03; instr. KyungHee U., Seoul, 2003—05, asst. prof., 2005—; postdoc. fellow John's Hopkins U., Balt. Contbr. chapters to books. KyungHee Rsch. Fund grantee, KyungHee U. Mem.: Soc. for Korean Med. Study of Obesity (life), Acad. Oriental Rehab. Medicine (life). Achievements include research in obesity and body composition, complementary and alternative medicine. Home: 7266 Calm Sunset Columbia MD 21046 Office: Kyung Hee U Dept Oriental Rehab Med 1 Hoegi-dong Dongdoemun-gu 13070 Seoul Republic of Korea Personal E-mail: mysong@khmc.or.kr.

SONG, QI, electrical engineer; s. Wen-pu Song and Sa Li. Attending, UC Irvine, 2007—. Rschr. CIOMP, Changchun, Jilin, China, 2005—07. Mem.: OSA.

SONG, SANG-HYUN, judge, law educator, consultant; b. Seoul, Korea, Dec. 21, 1941; s. Youngsoo and Hyunsoo (Kim) S.; m. Myungshin Kim Song, Nov. 4, 1971; children: Jay, Yoo-Jean. JD, Seoul Nat. U., 1963, LLM, 1965, Tulane Law Sch., New Orleans, 1968; diploma, U. Cambridge, Eng., 1969; JSD, Cornell Law Sch., Ithaca, NY, 1970. Fgn. atty. Haight, Gardner, Poor & Havens, NYC, 1970—72; vis. prof. law U. Melbourne, Australia, 1990, 92, 94, Harvard Law Sch., Cambridge, Mass., 1991, 95, 99, 2003; disting. prof. law NYU Law Sch., 1994—; dean of law sch. Seoul Nat. U., 1996-98, prof. law, 1972—; judge Internat. Criminal Ct., The Hague, Netherlands, 2003—. Pres. Koreal Intellectual Property Rsch. Soc., Inc., Seoul, Korea, 1986-96, Korean Internat. Trade Law Assn., Seoul, Korea, 1991-94; mem arbitrator Internat. Ctr. for Settlement of Investment Disputes, World Bank, Washington, 1986—; mem. arbitration consultative com., World Intellectual Property Orgn., Geneva, Switzerland, 1994—. Author: A Comparative Study on Maritime Cargo Carrier's Liability Under Anglo-American and French laws, 1970, Introduction to the Law and Legal System of Korea, 1983, An Introduction to Law and Economics, 1983, Korean Law in the Global Economy, 1996, The Korean Civil Procedure, 2003. Auditor Korea-US Ednl. and Cultural Found., 1991—; pres; Children's Leukemia Found., Korea, 1999-; mem., v.p., bd. dirs. UNICEF, Korea, 1998-; pres. Korean Law Profs. Assn., Seoul, Korea, 1999. Recipient Disting. Alumni award Cornell U., Ithaca, NY, 1994, Decoration of Moran, Korean Govt., Seoul, Korea, 1997, The Legal Culture award Korean Fed. Bar Assn., 1998. Mem. Korean Fed. Bar Assn., Seoul-Hangang Rotary Club. Avocations: golf, gardening, hiking. Office: Seoul Nat Univ Law Sch Seoul 151-743 Republic of Korea also: Internat Criminal Ct PO Box 19519 2500 CM The Hague Netherlands E-mail: koreansong@hotmail.com.

SONG, SEOK GOO, geophysicist; PhD in Geophysics, Stanford U., Calif., 2007. Seismologist URS Corp., Pasadena, Calif., 2007—. Overseas scholarship, Korean Govt., 2001. Mem.: Am. Geophys. Union. Achievements include development of unified source model for the 1906 San Francisco earthquake. Office: URS Corp 566 El Dorado St Pasadena CA 91101-2560

SONG, WON JAY, electrical engineer, educator; b. Seoul, Republic of Korea, Nov. 4, 1972; s. Kang Il Song and Young Ja Kim; m. Seung Heui Chung, Nov. 22, 1997; 1 child, Sung Jean. MS, Kwangju Inst. Sci. and Tech., 1997, PhD, 2003. Sr. rschr. Kwangju (Republic of Korea) Inst. Sci. and Tech., 1997—2000; sr. cons. Simulation Tech. Lab., Seoul, Republic of Korea, 2000—01, Electronic Design Automation Lab., Daejeon, Republic of Korea, 2001—02; sr. rschr. Chungnam Nat. U., Daejeon, 2002—03, Info. and Comms. U., Daejeon, 2003—. Contbr. articles to profl. jours. Scholar, Ministry Sci. and Tech., 1995—2003. Office: Univ of Colorado at Boulder Interdisciplinary Telecommunications Boulder CO 80309

SONG, XIANGZHI, research scientist; s. Shuangjv Song and Yufeng Zhang; m. Yantao Song; children: Sophia, Jeffrey. PhD, Peking U., Beijing, 2002. Postdoc. assoc. Rowland Inst., Harvard U., Cambridge, Mass., 2003—05, rsch. assoc., 2005—. Rsch. asst. Peking U., 1999—2002. Contbr. scientific papers. Mem.: Sigma Xi. Office: Rowland Inst Harvard Univ 100 Edwin H Land Blvd Cambridge MA 02142 Office Fax: 617-497-4627. Personal E-mail: xiangzhisong@gmail.com. Business E-Mail: song@rowland.harvard.edu.

SONG, XIAODONG, geophysicist, seismologist; m. Shoumin Liang; children: Thomas W., Angela F. PhD, Calif. Inst. Tech., 1994. Storke-Doherty lectr. Lamont-Doherty Earth Obs. of Columbia U., Palisades, NY, 1996—99; prof. U. Ill., Urbana, 1999—. Recipient Doornbos prize, Internat. Union Geophysics and Geodesy, 1996, Breakthrough of Yr. award, Sci. Mag., 1996, Sci. and Tech. award, Popular Sci. Mag., 1996, Outstanding Young Scientist award, Nat. Natural Sci. Found. China, 1998; named one of Most Important Discoveries in 20th Century, Discover Mag., 2000, Top 100 Sci. Stories of Yr., 2005; Sci. and Tech. Agy. fellow, Rsch. Devel. Corp. Japan, 1997. Mem.: Am. Assn. Advancement Scis., Seismol. Soc. Am., Am. Geophys. Union. Achievements include discovery of the rotation of the Earth's inner core using seismic waves; the Earth's inner core itself is layered with isotropic upper inner core and anisotropic lower inner core; differential inner core rotation using repeated earthquakes. Avocations: travel, reading, swimming. Office: Univ Ill 1301 W Green St 245 NHB Urbana IL 61801 Office Fax: 217-244-4996. Business E-Mail: xsong@uiuc.edu.

SONG, XUBIN, mechanical engineer, researcher; b. Yi Wu, China; arrived in US, 1994; s. Sengui Song and Yueqing Hu; m. Rongrong Zhou; 1 child, Justin Jia-Wen. BS in Engring., Nanjing U. Aeronautics and Astronautics, Nanjing, China, 1986; MS in Engring., China Acad. Launch Vehicle Tech., Beijing, China, 1988; MS in Mech. Engring., NC A&T State U., Greensboro, 1996; PhD, Va. Tech. U., 1999. Engr. China Acad. Launch Vehicle Tech., Beijing, 1988—94, MSX Internat., Auburn Hills, Mich., 1999—2000; tech. profl. Visteon Corp, Dearborn, Mich., 2000—04; prin. engr. Eaton Corp, Southfiled, Mich., 2004—. Gen. mgr. XYZ Tech. Corp., Canton, Mich., 2003—. Contbr. more than 40 articles to profl. jours. and confs. Mem.: ASME (mem. vehicle design com. 2003—), IEEE, Detroit Chinese Bus. Assn. (sr. bus. mgr. 2001—08), Soc. Automotive Engrs. (mem. SAE drivetrain/powertrain transmission com. 2004—, SAE driveline stds. com. 2007—, vice chair 2008—, chair 2009—), Phi Kappa Phi. Achievements include seven patents in field; development of torsional vibration control for commercial vehicles; adaptive control for magneto-rheological damper based suspension systems; research in automated optimization design and control of large nonlinear flexible structures; four patents pending; more than twenty inventions related to powertrain control under patent application. Office: Eaton Corp 26201 Northwestern Highway Southfield MI 48076 Personal E-mail: xusong@vt.edu. Business E-Mail: xubinsong@eaton.com.

SONG, YONGYI, librarian; b. Shanghai, Dec. 15, 1949; arrived in U.S., 1989; s. Changrui Song and Meiqing Jia; m. Xiaohua Helen Yao, Jan. 1, 1980; 1 child, Xiao. BA, Inst. Shanghai Edn., 1985; MA, U. Colo., 1992; MLS, Ind. U., 1995. Instr. comparative lit. Pa. State U., State College, 1992—93; Chinese bibliographer U. Pitts., 1995—97; sr. libr. East Asian studies/langs. and area studies Dickinson Coll., Carlisle, Pa., 1997—2004; libr. tch. svcs. and collection devel. Calif. State U., LA, 2004—. Author: The Cultural Revolution: A Bibliography, 1966-1996, 1998, The Cultural Revolution and Heterodox Thoughts, 2001, Historical Dictionary of the Chinese Cultural Revolution, 2006; chief editor The Chinese Cultural Revolution Database Online, 2002—09. Recipient 21st Century Nat. Libr. award, Syracuse U. Sch. Info. Studies, NY, 2004; grantee, Chan's Journalism and Culture Found., NYC, 2000; scholar, Pa. Libr. Assn., 2001. Mem.: ALA (Paul Howard award 2005). Office: Calif State U 5151 State Univ Dr Los Angeles CA 90033 Business E-Mail: ysong2@calstatela.edu.

SONG, YULIN, physicist; s. Jinbo Song and Lianying Wang; m. Fan Jiang; children: Yuanyuan, Rudy. BS, Beijing U., 1982; MS, Sam Houston State U., Huntsville, Tex., 1993, U. Tex., Dallas, 1997, PhD, 2001. Cert. therapeutic med. physicist NY State, 2006. Lectr. Tianjian Radio Tech. Sch., China, 1982—90; asst. tchr. Sam Houston State U., Huntsville, 1991—93; physicist Super Conducting Super Collider Lab., Dallas, 1993—94; rsch. fellow U. Tex. Southwestern Med. Ctr., 1997—2001; postdoc. fellow, dept. radiation oncology Stanford Univ Sch. Medicine, Palo Alto, Calif., 2001—03; asst. attending clin. mem. Meml. Sloan-Kettering Cancer Ctr., NYC, 2003—. Guest editor Internat. Jour. Biomed. Engring. and Tech., 2007—08. Contbr. chapters to books, scientific papers. Student fellowship, Nat. Osteoporosis Found., 1996, Rsch. fellowship, Dept. Def. Breast Cancer, 1997—2001, 2001—03. Mem.: IEEE, Engring Medicine and Biology Soc., Am. Assn. Physicists Medicine (NJ Chpt.) (treas. 2006—08), Am. Assn. Physicists Medicine. Home: 114 Janelle Blvd Parsippany NJ 07054 Office: Meml Sloan-Kettering Cancer Ctr 777 North Broadway Ste 100 Sleepy Hollow NY 10591 Personal E-mail: yulinsongmskcc@yahoo.com. Business E-Mail: songy@mskcc.org.

SONG, ZHEN, electrical engineer, researcher; b. Beijing, Mar. 10, 1975; s. Kongzhi Song and Xiaoxia Yan; m. Hong Yan; 1 child, Calla Xueyan. MS, Utah State U., Logan, 2003, PhD, 2007. Cert. IRB tng., Utah State U., 2004, Responsible conduct of rsch., Utah State U., 2004. With Siemens Corp. Rsch., Princeton, NJ, 2006—. Contbr. scientific papers to profl. jour. Recipient 2nd Pl. of Smart Dust Challenge, Crossbow Inc., 2005. Mem.: IEEE (3d pl. Student Paper/Poster award 2007, 3d pl. Best Paper award 2006), Assn. Computing Machinery. Achievements include research in wireless sensor network; development of robots. Office: Siemens Corp Rsch 755 Coll Rd E Princeton NJ Home: 1807 Fox Run Dr Plainsboro NJ 08536 Office Phone: 609-734-3589. Personal E-mail: zhensong@ieee.org.

SONI, JAYSHRI, science educator, director; arrived in U.S., 1989; d. Mangilal and Krishnabai Soni; m. Komal Soni, May 28, 1988; children: Kishen K., Reema K. MSc in Botany, Sagar U., Khandwa, India, 1989, BSc in Biology, 1987; BSc in Edn., Lander U., Greenwood, SC, 1995. Cert. tchr. biology S.C., 1995. Tutor McCormick County Literacy Assn., SC, 1989—95; tchr. sci. Long Cane Acad., McCormick, SC, 1996—98; tchr. math. John de la Howe Sch., McCormick, SC, 2002—04, tchr. sci., 2004—; program dir. Gurukul L.L.C., McCormick, 2005—. Mentor to mid. sch. sci. tchrs. John de la Howe Sch., 2004—. Recipient Nominated Presdl. award, Excellence in Tchg. Sci, 2006—07; grantee, Am. Aeronautics Assn., 2004-05, Donorschoose.org, 2005-06, 2006—07. Mem.: S.C. State Employees Assn. Home: 4098 Hwy 378 W Mc Cormick SC 29835 Office: 119 N Pine St Mc Cormick SC 29835 Home Fax: 864-852-2865. Personal E-mail: ksoni@wctel.net. Business E-Mail: gurukul@wctel.net.

SONKUSALE, SAHCIN RAMRAO, electrical engineer; b. Bhavnagar, Gujarat, India, May 30, 1978; s. Ramrao Ganpatrao and Anita Ramrao Sonkusale. PhD, NC State U., Raleigh, 2006. Rsch. asst. NC State U., 2000—01, 2003—06, tchg. asst., 2001—03; device engr. DSM Solutions Inc., Los Gatos, Calif., 2006—. Mem. & participant Art Living Soc., Raleigh, 2001—06. Mem.: IEEE Electron Device Soc. (asst. sec. 2007—, Santa Clara Valley chpt.). Achievements include invention of planar edge defined alternate layer process, an unconventional way to fabricate waferscale aligned sub 25nm metal nanowires and nanowire imprint templates; patents for JFET using germanium buil on silicon; patents pending for junction field effect transistors having isolated well region and method of fabrication; junction field effect transistor with low temperature sensitivity; junction field effect transistors in germanium and silicon-germanium alloys and method of making and using. Home: 105 Massol Ave Apt 203 Los Gatos CA 95030 Office: DSM Solutions Inc 130D Knowles Dr Los Gatos CA 95032 Business E-Mail: sachin.sonkusale@gmail.com.

SONNEBORN, WILLIAM CHARLES, diversified financial services company executive; b. 1970; BA with honors, Georgetown U., Washington. Cons. KPMG Peat Marwick, Washington; various corp. fin. positions Goldman, Sachs & Co., NY, Hong Kong, 1992—98; mng. dir., CFO TCW Group Inc., 1998—2001, COO, 2001—08, pres., 2005—08; CEO The TCW Funds, Inc., 2005—08; CEO, bd. dirs., head asset mgmt. divsn. KKR Fin. Holdings LLC (Kohlberg Kravis Roberts & Co.), San Francisco, 2008—. Bd. dirs. Sompo Japan Asset Mgmt., Tokyo; mem. internat. exec. com. Société Générale Asset Mgmt., S.A., Paris. Trustee St. John's Health Ctr. Found., Santa Monica, Calif.; bd. dirs., mem. exec. com. LA Coun. Boy Scouts of America. Served in Naval ROTC, Washington. Office: KKR Asset Mgmt 555 California St 50th Fl San Francisco CA 94104 Office Phone: 415-315-3620.*

SONNEDECKER, GLENN ALLEN, pharmaceutical historian, educator; b. Creston, Ohio, Dec. 11, 1917; s. Ira Elmer and Leta (Linter) S.; m. Cleo Bell, Apr. 3, 1943; 1 child, Stuart Bruce. BS, Ohio State U., 1942, DSc honoris causa, 1964; MS, U Wis., 1950, PhD, 1952; DSc honoris causa, Phila. Coll. Pharmacy and Sci., 1989; PharmD honoris causa, Mass. Coll. Pharmacy, 1974. Lic. pharmacist. Mem. editorial staff Sci. Service, Washington, 1942-43; editor Jour. Am. Pharm. Assn. (practical pharmacy edit.), Washington, 1943-48; asst. prof. U. Wis., 1952-56, asso. prof., 1956-60, prof., 1960-81, Edward Kremers prof., 1981-86; sec. Am. Inst. History of Pharmacy, 1949-57, dir., 1957-73, 81-85, hon. dir. life, chmn. bd., 1988-89; editor-in-chief RPh, 1978-80. Sec., bd. dirs. Friends of Hist. Pharmacy, 1945-49; chmn. Joint Com. on Pharmacy Coll. Librs., 1960-61; US del. Internat. Pharm. Fedn., 1953, 55, 62; US rep. to Mid. East Pharm. Congress, Beirut, 1956; sec. sect. history of pharmacy and biochemistry Pan-Am. Congress Pharmacy and Biochemistry, 1957. Co-author books; contbr. to pharm. and hist. publs. Recipient Edward Kremers award (for writings), 1964, Nat. award Rho Chi, 1967, Schelenz plaquette Internat. Soc. for History of Pharmacy, 1971, Remington honor medal Am. Pharm. Assn., 1972, Urdang medal, 1976, Folch Andreu prize, Spain, 1985, Profile award Am. Found. Pharm. Edn., 1994; Am. Found. fellow, 1948-52, Guggenheim fellow, 1955, Fulbright Rsch. scholar, Germany, 1955-56. Mem. Am. Pharm. Assn. (life; sec. sect. history of pharmacy 1949-50, vice chmn. 1950-51, chmn. 1951-52, rsch. assoc. 1964-65, chmn. joint task force with Acad. Pharm Scis. 1985, hon. chmn. bd. trustees 1985), Internat. Acad. History Pharmacy (1st v.p. 1970-81, pres. 1983-91, hon. pres. 1991—), Am. Assn. History of Medicine (exec. coun. 1966-69), Internat. Gesellschaft fur Geschichte der Pharmazie (exec. bd. 1965-89), hon. mem. socs. for history of pharmacy of Italy, Benelux, Spain; mem. Sigma Xi, Rho Chi (mem. nat. exec. coun. 1957-59), Phi Delta Chi. Unitarian. Home: 2030 Chadbourne Ave Madison WI 53726-4047

SONNEMAN, EVE, artist; b. Chgo., 1946; d. Eric O. and Edith S. BFA, U. Ill., 1967; MFA, U. N.Mex., 1969. One-woman shows include Castelli Gallery, N.Y.C., 1976, 78, 80, 82, 84-86, Tex. Gallery, Houston, 1976, 78, 80, 82, 85, Galerie Farideh Cadot, Paris, 1978, 80, 83, François Lambert Gallery, Milan, Italy, 1980, 87, Mpls. Inst. Arts, 1980, La Noveau Musèe, Lyon, France, 1980, Musèe de Toulon, France, 1983, Centre Georges Pompidou, Paris, 1984, Circus Gallery, L.A., 1989, 97, Jones Troyer Fitzpatrick, Washington, 1989, Zabriskie Gallery, N.Y., 1990, Gloria Luria Gallery, Miami, 1990, Grand Central Terminal, N.Y.C., 1991, Charles Cowles Gallery, 1992, Sidney Janis Gallery, N.Y.C., 1996, La Geode Mus., Paris, 1996, Cirrus Gallery, 1997, Bruce Silverstein Gallery, N.Y., 2002, Jadite Gallery, N.Y., 2002, 03, 04, 05, 06,07, Galeria Turchi, Siena, Italy, 2002, I Space, Chgo., 2005, Mingle Salon, Tokyo, 2005-2007; author: America's Cottage Gardens, 1990, Where Birds Live, 1992; co-author: How To Touch What, 2000; photographs subject of book Real Time, 1976. Grantee Nat. Endowment Arts, 1971, 78, Polaroid Corp., 1978; Cartier fellowship, France, 1989. Address: 446 W 47th St Apt 5C New York NY 10036-2381 Office Phone: 212-582-9375. Personal E-mail: evesonneman@earthlink.net.

SONNEMANN, HARRY, electrical engineer, consultant; b. Munich, Sept. 3, 1924; came to U.S., 1938, naturalized, 1944; s. Leopold and Emmy (Markus) S.; m. Shirley E. Battles, Nov. 25, 1949; children: Carol Jean, Joyce Elaine, Patricia Ann. BS, Poly. Inst. Bklyn., 1954. Research electroence-phalography, 1944-47; asst. to dir. electronics dept. AEC contract, Columbia U., 1947-50; supr. electronics shop Columbia Hudson Labs., 1951-53, head electronics dept., 1954-59; asst. dir. Project Artemis, 1959-64, Project Artemis (Hudson labs.), 1961-64; asst. dir. field engring. Advanced Research Projects Agy., Nuclear Test Detection Office, 1964-67; acting dep. dir. Nuclear Test Detection Office, 1967-68; spl. asst. in electronics to asst. sec. navy for research and devel. Navy Dept., 1968-76, spl. asst. to asst. sec. navy for research and devel., 1976-77; asst. to chief engr. NASA, 1977-78, dep. chief engr., 1978-84, asst. chief engr., 1984-86, cons., 1986—2000; pres. SBC Assocs., McLean, Va., 1988-95. Chmn. Dept. Def. Tactical Satellite Exec. Steering Group, 1968-69, chmn. Dept. Def. nav. satellite exec. steering group, 1969-70, 72-73 Treas. Art League. No. Va., 1967-68; pres. Rotonda Condominium Unit Owners Assn., 1982-84, 97-98, 99-2000. Mem.: Washington Figure Skating (dir. 1968-73, treas. 1969-72), Ice Club of Washington (pres. 1974-76). Home and Office: 7452 Spring Village Dr # 434 Springfield VA 22150-4951 E-mail: hssbc@aol.com.

SONNENBERG, HARDY, data processing executive, researcher, electrical engineer; b. Schoensee, Fed. Republic Germany, Apr. 12, 1939; s. Gustav and Wanda (Neumann) S.; m. Doris Linda Adam, June 20, 1964; children: Kevin, Denise. BS, U. Alta., 1962; MS, Stanford U., 1964, PhD, 1967. Registered profl. engr., Ont. Advanced devel. engr. GTE Sylvania, Mountain View, Calif., 1966-68, engring. specialist, 1968-70, sect. mgr., 1970-73; dir. rsch. Optical Diodes Inc., Palo Alto, Calif., 1973-74; mem. rsch. staff Xerox Rsch. Centre Can., Mississauga, Ont., 1975-78, area mgr., 1978-80, lab. mgr., 1980-86, mgr. rsch. ops., 1986-87, mgr. tech. and engring. systems, 1987-94, v.p. rsch. and tech., 1994-96; pres. Calixo Cons., Freelton, Ont., 1997—. Chmn. indsl. adv. coun. McMaster U., Hamilton, Ont., 1990-93, active, 1987-94. Contbr. articles to profl. jours.; patentee in field. Chmn. bd. dirs. local ch., Hamilton, Ont., 1983-85, 89-93, 98-2002; pres. Sheridan Park Assn., Mississauga, 1988-89; chmn. Conf. Bd. Can. Rsch. Mgrs. Forum, 1991-93. Recipient cert. of recognition for invention NASA, 1973, 74, Achievement award Xerox Corp., 1981, Charles E. Ives Engring. award, 1983. Mem.: IEEE (sr.), Assn. Profl. Engrs. Ont., Am. Phys. Soc., sigma Xi. Avocations: outdoor activities, singing, church participation. Home and Office: 900 Hwy 97 Freelton ON Canada L0R 1K0 E-mail: hsonnenb@ieee.org.

SONNENFELD, ALBERT, retired French literature and comparative literature educator, food historian; b. Berlin, July 22, 1934; came to U.S. 1938; s. Arthur and Anni (Lichtenstein) S.; m. Portia B. Leys, June 15, 1955 (div. 1986); children: Mark David, Carole Marie Geithner; m. Noel Riley Fitch, Aug. 23, 1987. AB, Oberlin Coll., Ohio, 1955; AM, Princeton U., 1957, PhD, 1958. Prof. French and comparative lit. Princeton U., 1958-86; M.F. Chevalier prof. French and dept. chmn. U. So. Calif., LA, 1986—2004; prof. emeritus, 2004—. Vis. prof. Dartmouth Coll., UCLA, U. Wis., NYU, CUNY, also others; cons. Linguaphone Inst., London, 1974—; food critic; restaurant cons.; chmn. exec. bd. City Smarts, Inc., 1996—. Author: L'Oeuvre poetique de Tristan Corbiere, 1961, Crossroads, 1982, Thirty-Six French Poems, 1961; co-author: Temoins de l'Homme, 1965; editor (series) Arts of the Table, Columbia U. Fulbright fellow, 1966-67; NEH fellow, 1978-79, 80, 83; recipient Raubenheimer Outstanding Faculty award, U. So. Calif., 1990. Mem. Am. Inst. Wine and Food (bd. dirs. 1989-2004), The Athenaeum (London), Phi Beta Kappa. Avocations: classical music, folksinging. Home: 11829 Mayfield Ave Apt 303 Los Angeles CA 90049-5790 Office: U So Calif 126 University Park Los Angeles CA 90089-0359 Personal E-mail: albertsonn@aol.com.

SONNENFELD, BARRY, director, cinematographer; b. NYC, Apr. 1, 1953; m. Susan Ringo, 1989; 1 child. Grad., NY U., 1978. Cinematographer (films) In Our Water, 1982, Blood Simple, 1984, Compromising Positions, 1985, Three O'Clock High, 1987, Raising Arizona, 1987, Throw Momma from the Train, 1987, Big, 1988, When Harry Met Sally..., 1989, Miller's Crossing, 1990, Misery, 1990, (TV movies) How to Be a Perfect Person In Just Three Days, 1983, Out of Step, 1984 (Emmy award best cinematography 1984), Double Take, 1985, Welcome Home, Bobby, 1986, Classified Love, 1986; dir. (films) The Addams Family (uncredited cameo appearance), 1991, Addams Family Values (also actor), 1993, Get Shorty, 1995 (also exec. prodr., actor), Men In Black, 1997, Maximum Bob (TV series, also exec. prodr.), 1998, Wild Wild West, 1999 (also prodr.), Chippendales, 2000, Men In Black II, 2002 (also actor), R.V., 2006; dir., co-prodr.: For Love or Money, 1993; exec. prodr.: (films) Out of Sight, 1998, Lemony Snicket's A Series of Unfortunate Events, 2004, (TV Series) Fantasy Island, 1998, Pushing Daisies (also dir.)(Outstanding Directorial Achievement in Comedy Series for 2007, Directors Guild Am., 2008, Primetime Emmy for Outstanding Directing for a Comedy Series, Acad. TV Arts and Scis., 2008), (TV) Partners, 1999; prodr. (TV Series) Secret Agent Man, 2000 (also creator), The Tick, 2001 (also dir.), Karen Sisco, 2003, (film) The Crew, 2000, Big Trouble, 2002 (also dir.), Ladykillers, 2004. also: United Talent Agency 9560 Wilshire Blvd Fl 5 Beverly Hills CA 90212-2401

SONNENFELD, GERALD, microbiology and immunology educator; b. NYC, Oct. 14, 1949; s. Otto Arthur and Ann (Perelman) S.; m. Elizabeth; 3 children, Jennifer, Jessica, Susan. BS, CCNY, 1970; PhD, U. Pitts., 1975. Postdoctoral fellow Stanford (Calif.) U. Sch. Medicine, 1976-78; assoc. guest worker Ames Rsch. Ctr. NASA, Moffett Field, Calif., 1976-78; asst. prof. microbiology and immunology U. Louisville, 1978-83, from assoc. prof. to prof. microbiology and immunology, 1983-93; dir. rsch. immunology Carolinas Med. Ctr., Charlotte, NC, 1994—98. Prof. & chair dept. microbiology and immunology Morehouse Sch. Med., Atlanta, 1999-2004, assoc. dean basic scis. & grad. studies, v.p. rsch. Binghamton U., SUNY, 2004-. Assoc. editor Jour. Interferon Cytokine Rsch., 1981—; contbr. over 150 articles to profl. jours. Grantee NASA, 1978—, Environ. Protection Agy., 1980-82, U.S. Army, 1983-87, NIH, 1984-87. Mem. Internat. Soc. for Interferon Rsch. (pubs. com. 1988—), Am. Assn. Immunologists, Am. Soc. Microbiology, Am. Soc. Gravitational and Space Biology (governing bd. 1992-95, pres.-elect 1996-97, pres. 1997-1998), Sigma Xi. Avocation: railroading. Office: VP Rsch Binghamton Univ SUNY PO Box 6000 Binghamton NY 13902 Office Phone: 607-777-4818.

SONNENFELD, STEFAN, film editor; b. LA; Grad., Boston U. Asst. colorist Image Transform, LA; colorist The Post Group, Pacific Ocean Post; co-founder, pres., mng. dir. Company 3, Santa Monica, 1997—. Named one of 50 Smartest People in Hollywood, Entertainment Weekly, 2007. Office: Company 3 1661 Lincoln Blvd Ste 400 Santa Monica CA 90404 Office Phone: 310-255-6644. Business E-Mail: ssonnenfeld@company3.com.

SONNENFELDT, HELMUT, former government official, educator, consultant, writer; b. Berlin, Sept. 13, 1926; came to U.S., 1944, naturalized, 1945; s. Walther H. and Gertrud (Liebenthal) S.; m. Marjorie Hecht, Oct. 4, 1953; children: Babette Sonnenfeldt Lubben, Walter H., Stewart H. AB, Johns Hopkins, 1950, MA, 1951. With Dept. State, Washington, 1952-77; formerly dir. Office Rsch. and Analysis for USSR and Eastern Europe, 1965-69; lectr. Sch. Advanced Internat. Studies, Johns Hopkins U., 1958-69, vis. scholar, 1977-78; guest scholar Brookings Instn., Washington, 1978—. Sr. mem. Nat. Security Coun., 1969-74; counselor Dept. State, 1974-77; mem. exec. panel chief naval ops. USN, 1971—. Former gov. UN Assn. of U.S.; dir. Atlantic Coun. of U.S., World Affairs Coun. Washington; trustee Johns Hopkins U. With AUS, 1945-46. Mem. Coun. on Fgn. Rels. N.Y. Home: 5600 Wisconsin Ave Apt 1505 Chevy Chase MD 20815-4412 Office: Brookings Instn 1775 Massachusetts Ave NW Washington DC 20036-2103 Office Phone: 202-797-6028. Business E-Mail: hsonnenfeldt@brookings.edu.

SONNENSCHEIN, HUGO FREUND, academic administrator, writer, economist, educator; b. NYC, Nov. 14, 1940; s. Leo William and Lillian Silver Sonnenschein; m. Elizabeth Gunn, Aug. 26, 1962; children: Leah, Amy, Rachel. AB, U. Rochester, 1961; MS, Purdue U., 1963, PhD, 1964, PhD (hon.), 1996; PhD (hon.), Tel Aviv U., 1993; D (hon.), U. Autonoma Barcelona, Spain, 1994; PhD (hon.), Lake Forest Coll., 1995, North Ctrl. Coll., 2001, U. Chgo., 2002. Faculty dept. econs. U. Minn., 1964—70, prof., 1968—70; prof. econs. U. Mass., Amherst, 1970—73, Northwestern U., 1973—76, Princeton (N.J.) U., 1976—87, Class of 1926 prof., 1987—88, provost, 1991—93; dean, Thomas S. Gates prof. U. Pa. Sch. Arts & Scis., Phila., 1988—91; pres. U. Chgo., 1993—2000, Hutchinson disting. prof., pres. emeritus, 2000—. Vis. prof. U. Andes, Columbia, 1965, Tel Aviv U., 1972, Hebrew U., 1973, U. Paris, 1978, U. Aix-en-Provence, France, 1978, Stanford U., 1984—85; bd. dirs. Van Kampen Mutual Funds. Editor: Econometrica, 1977—84; mem. editl. bd.: Jour. Econ. Theory, 1972—75, Jour. Math. Econs., 1974—, SIAM Jour., 1976—80; contbr. articles to profl. jours. Trustee U. Rochester, 1992—, U. Chgo., 1993—. Fellow, Social Sci. Rsch. Coun., 1967—68, NSF, 1970—, Ford Found., 1970—71, Guggenheim Found., 1976—77. Fellow: Econometric Soc. (pres. 1988—89), Am. Acad. Arts and Scis.; mem.: NAS, Am. Philos. Soc. Business E-Mail: h-sonnenschein@uchicago.edu.

SONNETT, NEAL RUSSELL, lawyer; b. Bklyn., Nov. 29, 1942; s. Douglas Murray Sonnett and Carol (Brown) Sonnett Rosen; m. Pat D. Sallee, June 10, 1979; 1 child, Gary. BA, U. Miami, 1964, JD, 1967. Bar: Fla. 1967, US Dist. Ct. (so. dist.) Fla. 1967, US Ct. Appeals (5th cir.) 1971, US Ct. Appeals (11th cir.) 1981, US Ct. Appeals (9th cir.) 1982, US Supreme Ct. 1971, US Dist. Ct. (ea. dist.) Mich. 1984. Asst. US atty. So. Dist. Fla., 1967—72, chief criminal divsn., 1971—72; ptnr. Sonnett, Sale & Kuehne PA, Miami, Fla., 1972—93; founder Neal R. Sonnett PA, 1993—. Legal counsel Fla. Jaycees, 1971—72; Fla. Regional bd. dirs. Anti-Defamation League B'nai B'rith, 1972, 82; pres. Fraternal Order Police Assocs., 1972, Transition Inc., 1976; chmn. Met. Dade County Ind. Rev. Panel, 1981—84; lectr. immigration law and advanced fed. criminal practice U. Miami Sch. Law; lectr. cross-exam. techniques Fed. Law Enforcement Tng. Ctr., 1983; chmn. Cmty. Task Force on Jury Selection, 1984. Host (TV series) To the Point, Sta. WCIX-TV, 1980—82. Recipient Outstanding Svc. Award, Jewish War Vets of US, Disting. Svc. Award, Dade County Pub. Interest Law Bank, 1983; named Outstanding Young Man of Miami, Greater Miami Jaycees, 1970, Outstanding Fed. Employee South Fla., 1971—72, Outstanding Young Law Enforcement Officer, South Miami Jaycees, 1971—72; named one of Five Outstanding Young Men of Fla., Fla. Jaycees, 1971—72. Mem.: ABA (mem.-at-large bd. govs. criminal justice sect. 2009—), Acad. Fla. Trial Lawyers, Am. Trial Lawyers Am., Nat. Assn. Criminal Def. Lawyers, Am. Immigration Lawyers Assn., Fed. Bar Assn., Dade County Bar Assn. (pres. 1983—84), Fla. Criminal Def. Attys. Assn. (treas. 1983—84, pres. 1984—85), Calif. Attys. for Criminal Justice, Met. Bar Leaders Caucus, Inter-Am. Bar Assn., Elks, Optimist, Footlighter. Democrat. Jewish. Office: Neal R Sonnett PA 1 Biscayne Tower 26th Fl 2 S Biscayne Blvd Miami FL 33131-1804 Office Phone: 305-358-2000. Office Fax: 305-358-1233.*

SONNHALTER, CAROLYN THERESE, physical therapist, consultant; b. Bedford, Ohio, Apr. 26, 1942; d. Gabriel Edward Jr. and Josephine Irene (Kubera) Farkas; m. Donald Joseph Lippert, June 11, 1966 (div. June 1981); 1 child, Kevin Michael; m. Robert Louis Sonnhalter, Aug. 31, 1985. BS, Ohio State U., 1964. Lic. phys. therapist, Ohio. Staff and sr. phys. therapist Akron (Ohio) City Hosp., 1964-69; asst. dir. phys. therapy Akron Gen. Med. Ctr., 1975-82; dir. phys. therapy Litchfield Rehab. Ctr., Akron, 1983-87; phys. therapist HMO Health Ohio, Akron, 1987-97, Phoenix-Hudson Corp., Middleburg Heights, Ohio, 1993-98; dir. phys. therapy Tri-County Home Nursing, Mogadore, Ohio, 1997-99; phys. therapist VNS, Kent, Ohio, 1999—. Revel. phys. therapy first outpatient Chronic Pain Mgmt. Program, Ohio, 1983; cons. video animation on mechanism of whiplash for use by med. and legal profls., Ohio, 1996. Mem. Am. Phys. Therapy Assn., Alpha Gamma Delta. Avocations: traveling ohio and nearby states in search of antiques, gardening. Home: 3631 Oak Rd Stow OH 44224-3934 Office: VNS 234 S Water St Kent OH 44240-3526

SONSINI, LARRY W., lawyer; b. Rome, NY, Feb. 5, 1941; AB, U. Calif., Berkeley, 1963, LLB, 1966; PhD (hon.), Pacific Grad. Sch.of Psychology. Bar: Calif. 1966. Assoc. McCloskey Wilson & Mosher, Palo Alto, 1966—73, ptnr., 1973—78; mng. ptnr., chmn. CEO Wilson, Sonsini, Goodrich & Rosati, Palo Alto, 1978—; prof. securities regulation Boalt Hall Sch. law U. Calif., Berkeley, 1985—. Bd. dirs. NY Stock Exchange (NYSE), 2001—03, Silicon Valley Bancshares, 2003—, Brocade Communications Systems, Inc., Echelon Corp., LSI Logic Corp., Lattice Semiconductor Corp., Pixar, Inc., Tesla Motors, Inc., 2008—; chmn. Regulation, Enforcement and Listing Standards Com., Legal Adv. Com., 2003—. Trustee Santa Clara U. Recipient Spl. Achievement Award in Commerce and Law, Nat. Italian Am. Found. (NIAF), 2003, Cmty. Svc. Award exemplary leadership, Nat. Conf. Cmty. & Justice, 1993, Visionary Award, Software Devel. Forum, 2000, Dir.'s Award, San Francisco Exploratorium, Boalt Hall Sch. of Law Citation Award, U. Calif., Berkeley, Bus. Hall of Fame Award, Bay Area Coun.; named Bus. Leader of the Yr., Harvard Bus. Sch. Assn. of No. Calif., 2005; named one of Top Ten Lawyers in Bay Area, San Francisco Chronicle, 2003, 100 Most Influential Lawyers, Nat. Law Jour., 2006. Mem.: ABA (com. on fed. regulation securities, subcom. on registration statements), Am. Acad. Arts and Scis., Am. Law Inst. Office: Wilson Sonsini Goodrich & Rosati 650 Page Mill Rd Palo Alto CA 94304-1050 Office Phone: 650-493-9300. Office Fax: 650-493-6811. E-mail: lsonsini@wsgr.com.

SONSTENG, KATHLEEN A., education educator; b. St. Paul, Feb. 16, 1954; d. Allan G. and Dolores H. Sonsteng; m. Jeffrey J. Peura; children: Aaron P. Furuseth, Joseph A. Furuseth. MS in Edn, Bemidji State U., Minn., 1998; EdD, U. ND, Grand Forks, 2006. Tchr. Red Lake Schs., Red Lake, Minn., 1976—79, Northome Sch., Minn., 1979—97; in-str.,dept. chair Leech Lake Tribal Coll., Cass Lake, Minn., 1998—2000; asst. & assoc. prof. Bemidji State U., Minn., 2000—. Presenter Campus Childcare Ctr., Bemidji, Minn., 2002—03, 2008, Stephen-Argyle Schs., Minn., 2006, Early Childhood Adminstr. Conf., St. Cloud, Minn., 2007, Region V Head Start Tng. Inst., St.Paul, 2007, Cmtys. Collaborative Conf., Mahnomen, Minn., 2007, Bemidji State U. Summer Workshop, Minn., 2008, Head Start Parenting Workshop, Bemidji, Minn., 2008, Early Childhood MEGA Conf., Bemidji, 2008, United Children Conf., Park Rapids, Minn., 2008. Evaluation team mem. Growing Up Healthy: Kids & Cmty. Project, Bemidji, 2007—09. Mem.: ASCD, Minn. & Nat. Assn. Early Childhood Tchr. Educators, Assn. Childhood Edn. Internat., Nat. Assn. Edn. Young Children. Office: Bemidji State Univ 1500 Birchmont Dr NE #35 Bemidji MN 56601

SONTAG, JAMES MITCHELL, oncologist, researcher; b. Denver, Dec. 8, 1939; s. Samuel Henry and Rose Hazel (Silverman) S.; m. Elizabeth Crockett Tunis; children: Ariella, Eythan. BS, Lamar State Coll. Tech., Beaumont, Tex.; MS, U. Ill., 1967; PhD, Weizmann Inst. Sci., Rehovot, Israel, 1971; MPH, Harvard U., 1982. Postdoctoral fellow Damon Runyon Meml. Fund Cancer Rsch., 1971-72; guest worker Nat. Cancer Inst., NIH, Bethesda, Md., 1972-73, staff fellow, 1973-74, exptl. oncologist, 1973-76, mgr. carcinogen bioassay program, 1973-76, asst. to divsn. dir. cancer cause and prevention, 1976-80; exec. sec. Clearinghouse on Environ. Carcinogens, 1976-80, asst. dir. for interagy. affairs Office of Dir., 1980-82, spl. asst. epidemiology and biostatistics program, 1982-96; chief office divsn. ops. & analysis divsn. cancer epidemiology and genetics Nat. Cancer Inst., 1996-99; vol. Grassroots Artisans, Med. Mission, L.Am., 1999—. Author, editor in field. ESL tchr. 2004-; Served with AUS, 1956-59. Beaumont LWV scholar, 1963-65 Mem. Beta Beta Beta. Personal E-mail: jim18y@msn.com.

SOOCHER, STAN, editor, lawyer; b. Bangor, Maine, Jan. 10, 1951; BA in English, U. Fla., 1973, MA in English, 1974; JD, N.Y. Law Sch., 1983. Bar. N.Y. 1984. Entertainment journalist Musician Mag., Rolling Stone, Miami Herald, etc., NYC, 1976—; assoc. editor Circus Mag., NYC, 1978-79; staff writer Nat. Law Jour., NYC, 1981—; founding editor Entertainment Law & Finance, NYC, 1985—. Recipient Deems Taylor Journalism awards ASCAP, 1986, 91. Avocations: song writing, playing drums. Office: Entertainment Law & Finance 345 Park Ave S Fl 8 New York NY 10010-1707

SOOD, ANIL K., oncologist, researcher; MD, U. N.C., 1991. Diplomate Am. Bd. Obstetrics and Gynecology 1999. Intern in ob-gyn. U. Fla., Gainesville, Fla., 1991—93, resident in ob-gyn., 1993—95; fellow in gynecol. oncology U. Iowa, Iowa City, 1995—98; asst. prof. U. of Iowa, 1998—2002; assoc. prof. gynecologic oncology and cancer biology M.D. Anderson Cancer Ctr., U. Tex., Houston, 2002—06, dir. ovarian cancer rsch., 2005—, prof. gynelogic oncology and cancer biology, 2006—. Editl. adv. bd. Cancer, 2003—; editl. bd. Current Cancer Therapy Reviews, 2003—, Cancer Biology and Therapy, 2005—, Obstetrics and Gynecology, 2006—. Recipient Reproductive Scientist Devel. award, NIH, 1999—2001, Rsch. award, Gynecologic Cancer Found., 2001, Am. Cancer Soc./U. Iowa, 1998, phase 2 RSDP award, Gynecologic Cancer Found., 2001, James F. Nolan award, Western Assn. Gynecologic Oncologists, 2002, 2004, Charles A. Hunter Jr. prize, Am. Gynecological and Obstetrical Soc., 2003, Faculty Scholar award, M.D. Anderson Cancer Ctr., 2006—09. Mem.: ACOG, Am. Soc. Clin. Investigation, Am. Soc. Clin. Oncology, Soc. of Gynecologic Oncologists, Am. Assn. for Cancer Rsch. Office: UTMD Anderson Cancer Ctr Dept Gyn Oncology 1515 Holcombe Blvd 440 Houston TX 77030

SOOD, NAMITA, medical educator; b. Chandigarh, India, Mar. 29, 1964; MD, Alfateh U., Tripoli, 1987. Assoc. prof. Ohio State U., Columbus, Ohio, 2008. Named one of Best Doctors in Am., 2005, 2007. Office: Ohio State Univ 201 Heart &Lung Rsch Ctr 12th W Columbus OH 43215

SOODIK, LYNN, lawyer; b. Pitts., Aug. 6, 1956; BS with distinction, Pa. State U., 1978; student, Durham U., Eng.; JD, U. Calif. Hastings Coll. Law, San Francisco, 1982. Bar: Calif. 1982, cert.: State Bar Calif. Bd. Legal Specialization (family law) 1988. Prin. Law Offices of Lynn Soodik, P.C., Santa Monica, Calif. Instr., mentor Harriet Buhai Ctr. Family Law, 1990—93. Assoc. articles editor: COMM/ENT, A Jour. of Comm. and Entertainment Law, 1980—82; contbr. articles to profl. jours. Mem.: Beverly Hills Bar Assn., LA County Bar Assn. (sec. 1995—96, vice chair 1996—97, chair-elect 1997—98, chair family law sect. 1998—99, mem. exec. com. 1986—99). Office: Law Offices of Lynn Soodik 233 Wilshire Blvd Ste 525 Santa Monica CA 90401-1205 Office Phone: 310-393-8000. Office Fax: 310-394-8182. Business E-Mail: info@lynnsoodik.com.

SOO HOO, TSUNG (BILL) YAO, security studies educator, consultant; s. Yin and Chui Woo Soo Hoo; m. Rachel Ann Cammorato, Nov. 3, 1984; 1 child, Carolyn Yu-yi. PhD, Seton Hall U., 2007. Cert. firearms instr. N.J., 1986. Spl. agt. FBI, West Paterson, NJ, 1970—2001; chair profl. security studies dept. NJ City U., 2002—. Exec. com. Am. Soc. Indsl. Security, Ltd., Internat., NJ, 2002—. Author: An Alternative Problem-based Collaborative Learning Model and Student Experiences. Recipient US Nat. Intelligence medal of achievement. Mem.: AAUP, US Dept. Homeland Security-Def. Edn. Consortium, Soc. Former Spl. Agents the FBI, Fed. Law Enforcement Officers Assn., Assn. Intelligence Officers, Am. Soc. Indsl. Security (exec. bd. mem. 2005), US Bowling Congress. Office: NJ City U 2039 Kennedy Blvd Rm P449 Jersey City NJ 07305-1597 Office Fax: 201-200-2279. Business E-Mail: bsoohoo@njcu.edu.

SOON-SHIONG, PATRICK, pharmaceutical executive; m. Michele Chan; 2 children. MSc, U. Brit. Columbia; MD, U. Witwatersrand. CEO, chmn. bd. VivoRx, Inc., 1994—98; pres., CFO, dir. Am. BioScience,

Inc., 1994—; CEO, chmn. bd. Am. Pharm. Partners, Inc. (renamed Abraxis BioScience in 2006), Schaumburg, Ill., 1996—, pres., 2001—. Named one of Forbes' Richest Americans, 2006. Fellow: ACS, Royal Coll. Physicians and Surgeons Can. Achievements include patents in field; invention of cancer treatment Abraxane. Office: Am Pharmaceutical Partners Ste 300 E 1501 E Woodfield Rd Schaumburg IL 60173-5837

SOORIYAARACHCHI, GAMINI SARATHCHANDRA, oncologist, hematologist, educator; b. Kosgama, Sri Lanka; m. Chandrika Senerath; children: Jasmine, Marcus. MBBS with honors, U. Ceylon, Colombo, Sri Lanka, 1970; diploma in child health, Conjoint Bd. Examiners, London, 1975; diploma in obstetrics, Royal Coll. Ob-Gyn Gt. Britain, 1975; MBA, U. Tenn., Knoxville, 2004. Diplomate Am. Bd. Internal Medicine, Am. Bd. Geriatric Medicine, Am. Bd. Med. Oncology, Am. Bd. Hematology, cert. physician exec. Cert. Commn. Med. Mgmt., 2005. Intern U. Ceylon Tchg. Hosps., 1970-71; sr. house officer Guildford Hosps., England, 1971-73; registrar St. Helens Hosp., England, 1974-75; sr. house officer Royal Marsden Hosp. and Inst. Cancer Rsch., Sutton, England, 1973-74; fellow in med. oncology and hematology U. Wis. Comprehensive Cancer Ctr., Madison, 1975-77; cons. med. oncologist and hematologist Rockford Clinic and Rockford Meml. Hosp., Ill., 1977-83, Oncology Hematology West and Alegent Bergan Mercy Cancer Ctr., Omaha, 1983—; med. dir. Alegent Bergan Mercy Cancer Ctr., Omaha, 1984—; co-dir. bone marrow transplantation program Oncology Hematology West and Alegent Bergan Mercy Med. Ctr., Omaha, 1993—. Asst. clin. prof. medicine U. Ill. Sch. Medicine, Rockford, 1977—83; bd. dirs. Cancer Biotherapy Rsch. Group, Franklin, Tenn.; mem. at-large med. exec. com. Alegent Bergan Mercy Med. Ctr., 2002—03, pres.-elect, vice chmn., 2003—04; pres., chief med. staff Alegent Bergan Mercy Med. Ctr, 2005—07; bd. dirs. Missouri Valley Cancer Consortium, Omaha, pres., 1999—2001, prin. investigator, 2006—; assoc. clin. prof. medicine Creighton U. Sch. Medicine, Omaha, 1984—96, clin. prof., 1996—; chmn. prof. edn. Am. Cancer Soc., 1986, Nebr. divsn., 87, bd. dirs. Douglas and Sarpy Counties, Neb., 86, Nebr. divsn., 87; med. dir., founding mem. No. Ill. Hospice Assn., Rockford, 1980—83; mem. exec. com., novel therapeutics com., audit com., ethnic diversity com., by-law com. North Ctrl. Cancer Treatment Group, Mayo Clin., Rochester, Minn.; mem. head and neck cancer steering com., alt. mem. breast cancer steering com. Nat. Cancer Inst., Bethesda, Md.; chmn. Am. Med. Assn. Sec. of Internat. Med. Graduates, 2007—; alt. rep. AMA Commn. to End Healthcare Disparities; mem. Coun. Long Range Planning & Devel, AMA. Contbg. author: Cancer Genetics in Women, 1987; contbr. over 60 articles and astracts to med. jours., including Jour. Clin. Oncology, Blood, Archives Surgery, Jour. Immunotherapy, Cancer Investigation, Annals Pharmacotherapy, Jour. Am. Acad. Dermatology, Jour. Clin. Pathology. Recipient Spirit Mission award, Alegent Health System, 2005, Leadership award (Internat. Med. Grad. Physician), AMA Found., 2006, Candle Light award, Alegent Bergan Mercy Med. Ctr., 2007. Fellow ACP, Royal Coll. Physicians (London), Soc. for Biol. Therapy; mem. AMA (alt. del. to House of Dels. 2006-, alt. rep. Commn. to End Healthcare Disparities 2006-), Royal Coll. Surgeons (Eng.), Am. Soc. Clin. Oncology, Am. Soc. Hematology (com. on practice), Am. Soc. for Blood and Marrow Transplantation, Nebr. Med. Assn., Am. Soc. Hematology(practise com.), Am. Soc. Clin. Oncology(by-law com. mem.), Am. Hosp. Pharmacists Assn.(oncology expert panel mem.) Office: Alegent Health Bergan Mercy Cancer Ctr 7710 Mercy Rd Ste 122 Omaha NE 68124-2346

SOOUDI, MATTHEW M., retired surgeon; b. Iran, Oct. 24, 1934; came to U.S., 1962; s. Yahya and Iran (Nicknejad) S.; m. Joyce J. Sooudi, Oct. 2, 1965; 2 children. MD, U. Iran, 1962. Diplomate Am. Bd. Surgery, Am. Bd. Colon and Rectal Surgery, Internat. Bd. Proctology. Intern. Bon Secours Hosp., Grosse Pointe, Mich., 1962-63; resident Grace Hosp., Detroit, 1963-67, Ferguson Clinic, Grand Rapids, Mich., 1967-68; pvt. practice St. Elizabeth Hosp., Tex., Beaumont (Tex.) Med. Hosp., Bapt. Hosp., Tex.; ret., 1996. Fellow ACS, Am. Soc. Colon and Rectal Surgeons, Internat. Assn. Proctologists; mem. AMA, Am. Assn. Phys. Surgeons, So. Med. Assn., Tex. Med. Assn., Tex. Soc. Colon and Rectal Surgeons. Address: 980 Thomas Rd Beaumont TX 77706-4621

SOPER, JEANNINE, real estate agent; b. NYC, Nov. 24, 1929; d. Antonio Bruno and Marie Kapuscinski; widowed; children: Erik, Wayne. Grad., Scudder Secretarial Coll., 1948, Realtors Inst., 1970. Sec. Std. Brands Inc., NYC, 1948—52, Armstrong Rubber Co., Norwalk, Conn., 1952—53; real estate sales assoc. V, Ducale Real Estate, Norwalk, 1960—63; owner Sopers Real Estate, Norwalk, 1963—66; owner, ptnr. Siegel and Soper, Realtors, Norwalk, 1966—86; realtor, sales mgr. Prudential Real Estate, Norwalk, 1986—91; realtor Wm. Pitt Real Estate, Norwalk, 1991—. Pres. Women's Coun. Realtors, Conn., 1970, Norwalk Bd. Realtors, 1979. Exhibited in group shows at Rowayton Art Ctr., Darien Art Ctr., others. Chmn. Bd. Assessment Appeals, Norwalk, 1989—; pres., treas. Rowayton (Conn.) Art Ctr., 2000—. Mem.: Wilson Cove Yacht Club (life 1st Woman Commodore 1991). Office: Wm Pitt Sothebys Internat Real Estate 162 East Ave Norwalk CT 06851 Office Phone: 203-838-0018. Personal E-mail: jlsoper@optonline.net.

SOPHER, VICKI ELAINE, appraiser; b. Streator, Ill., May 22, 1943; d. Donald Bird and Thelma Elsie (Saxton) Watson; m. Terry Ray Sr., Jan. 20, 1962 (div. July 1982); 1 child, Terry Ray Jr. AA, No. Va. Community Coll., 1973; BA, Am. U., 1976; MS, Bank State Coll. Edn., 1986; Cert., Getty Mus. Mgmt. Inst., 1998. Cert. in appraisal courses George Washington U., 2004. Adminstrv. asst. Decatur & Wilson House, Washington, 1977-81; asst. dir. Decatur House/Nat. Trust for Hist. Preservation, Washington, 1981-84, dir., 1984-95; exec. dir. Hammond-Harwood House Assn., Annapolis, Md., 1996-98; curator Nat. Am. Red Cross, Washington, 1999—2004; pres. Vintage Appraisals, Inc., Tampa, Fla., 2005—. Cons.; founder, pres. Historic House Mus. Met. Washington. Mem. Am. Assn. Mus., Mid-Atlantic Assn. Mus., Am. Assn. State and Local History, Victorian Soc. Am. (bd. dirs.), Am. Soc. Appraisers. Home and Office: Vintage Appraisals 3118 W Wallcraft Ave Tampa FL 33611-1943 Office Phone: 815-300-9200. Personal E-mail: vsopher@verizon.net.

SOPP, MARK W., corporate financial executive; B in acctg., New Mex. State Univ., 1987. CPA. CPA Arthur Andersen & Co., 1987—90; sr. acct. through dir. & internat. controller Taylor Made Gold Co., 1990—98; dir. fin. & bus. ops. Titan Systems Corp., 1998—99, v.p. fin. & bus. ops., 1999—2001; sr. v.p., CFO, treas. Titan Corp., 2001—05; exec. v.p., CFO Sci. Applications Internat. Corp., San Diego, 2005—. Office: SAIC 10260 Campus Point Dr San Diego CA 92121

SOPRANZETTI, BEN J., finance educator, investment banker; PhD, U. Ill. Urbana-Champaign, Ill., 1995. Prof. Rutgers Bus. Sch., Piscataway, NJ, 1997—. Prin. Innovative Fin. Solutions, Beijing, 2001—. Office: Rutgers Bus Sch 94 Rockafeller Rd Piscataway NJ 08854 Personal E-mail: sopranzetti@gmail.com.

SORAN, Z. OZLEM, medical educator; m. Atilla Soran. MD, Ankara U., Turkey, 1989; MPH, U. Pitts., 2004. Cert. cardiology Turkish Ministry Health, 1996. Chief resident cardiology Dr. MU Tchg. and Rsch. Hosp., Ankara, 1994—95, chief instr., attending cardiologist, 1996—97, attending cardiologist, nterim co-dir. cardiology dept., 1999—2001; instr., post doctoral fellow U. Pitts., Cardiovasc. Inst., 1997—99; asst. prof. medicine U. Pitts., 2001—03, assoc. prof. medicine, assoc. prof. epidemiology/rsch., 2003—. Dir. EECP rsch. lab. U. Pitts., 2001—. Contbr. articles to profl. jours. Recipient Turkey's Best Physician/Scientist award, Anatolian Press Assn., 1999, Mediterranean Press Assn., 2002, Women of Distinction award, Daughters of Ataturk, 2004; named one of Top Forty Rsch., The Astra Zeneca Cardiovasc. Young Investigators' Forum, 2002; grantee HFHC Project, Ctr. for Medicare and Medicaid Svcs., 2001—07; scholar, Turkish Med. Assoc., Internat. Fedn. Med. Students Assn., 1987, Japanese Govt., 1991. Fellow: European Soc. Cardiology, Am. Coll. Cardiology; mem.: AMA (Women Physician Congress), Am. Heart Assn. (clin. cardiology coun.), Turkish Med. Assn., Chamber of Medicine of Ankara, Turkish Cardiology Assn., So. Med. Assn. Home Phone: 724-443-6388; Office Phone: 412-647-4411. Office Fax: 412-647-7005. Business E-Mail: osoran@lycos.com, soranzo@upmc.edu.

SORBY, DONALD LLOYD, retired dean; b. Fremont, Nebr., Aug. 12, 1933; s. Lloyd A. and Orpha M. (Simmons) S.; m. Jacquelyn J. Burchard, Nov. 7, 1959; children: Thomas, Sharon. BS in Pharmacy, U. Nebr., 1955; MS, U. Wash., 1958, PhD, 1960. Dir. pharm. services U. Calif., San Francisco, 1970-72; chmn. dept. pharmacy practice Sch. Pharmacy, U. Wash., Seattle, 1972-74; dean Sch. of Pharmacy, U. Mo., Kansas City, 1974-84, Sch. of Pharmacy, U. Pacific, Stockton, Calif., 1984-95, dean emeritus, 1995—. Contbr. articles to profl. jours. Named Disting. Alumnus, U. Nebr. Coll. Pharmacy, 2000. Am. Assn. Colls. of Pharmacy (pres. 1980-81), Calif. Pharm. Assn., Calif. Soc. Health-Sys. Pharmacists, Sigma Xi, Phi Kappa Phi, Rho Chi. Home: 4362 Yacht Harbor Dr Stockton CA 95204-1126 Business E-Mail: donsorby@sbcglobal.net.

SOREL, EDWARD, artist; b. NYC, Mar. 26, 1929; s. Morris and Rebecca (Kleinberg) Schwartz; m. Nancy Caldwell, May 29, 1965; children: Jenny, Katherine; children by previous marriage: Madeline, Leo. Diploma, Cooper Union, 1951; DFA (hon.), Art Inst. Boston, 1998. Co-founder Pushpin Studio, 1953; free-lance artist, 1956—; syndicated Sorel's News Service, 1969-70, King Features. Author, illustrator: Making the World Safe for Hypocrisy, 1972; exhibited in Pushpin Studio retrospective at the Louvre, 1970, other European galleries, 1970-71; exhibited one-man show, Graham Galleries, NYC, 1973, 78, Galerie Bartsch & Chariau, Munich, 1986, Retrospective Exhibition Cooper Union, 1987, Susan Conway Galleries, Washington, 1992, Soc. Illustrators Am. Mus. Illustration, NYC, 1993, Davis and Langdale Galleries, NYC, 1994, 97, 2006, Nat. Portrait Gallery, Washington, 1999; illustrator: Pablo Paints a Picture, 1961, Gwendolyn the Miracle Hen, 1963 (NY Herald Tribune Book award for illustration 1962), What's Good for a Five-Year-Old, 1969, The Duck in the Gun, 1969, Word People, 1970, Magical Storybook, 1972, Superpen, 1978, The Zillionaire's Daughter, 1990, First Encounters, 1994, Unauthorized Portraits, 1997, Johnny on the Spot, 1998, The Saturday Kid, 2000, Literary Lives, 2006; The Mural at the Waverly, 2008, Certitude, 2009; muralist: Waverly Inn, Greenwich Village, NY, 2007, The Monkey Bar, NY, 2009; contbr. to Nation, New Yorker, Vanity Fair, American Heritage and Atlantic monthly mags. Recipient awards Soc. Illustrators, Art Dirs. Club N.Y.; Augustus St. Gauden's medal Cooper Union; George Polk award for satiric drawing, 1981; Page One award Newspaper Guild of N.Y. for best editorial cartoon (magazines), 1988, Hamilton King award Soc. Illustrators, 1990, John Singleton Copley medal Smithsonian Instn., 1999, Art Dirs. Hall of Fame, 2001, Karikaturpreis Deutschen Anwaltschaft 2002. Office Phone: 212-665-0698. Office Fax: 212-665-0699. Personal E-mail: edwardsorel@gmail.com.

SORELLE, JAMES, history professor; b. Waco, Tex., Feb. 1, 1950; s. Jack Martin and Patricia Murphy SoRelle; m. Cynthia Marie Sigerman, July 23, 1973; children: Mallory Elizabeth, Elliott Daniel. PhD, Kent State U., Ohio, 1980. Prof. history Baylor U., Waco, 1980—. Mem.: Southern Hist. Assn., Orgn. Am. Historians. Home: 2926 Maple Ave Waco TX 76707 Office: Baylor Univ One Bear Pl 97306 Waco TX 76798 Business E-Mail: james_sorelle@baylor.edu.

SOREN, DAVID, archaeologist, educator, writer, filmmaker; b. Phila., Oct. 7, 1946; s. Harry Friedman and Erma Elizabeth (Salamon) Soren; m. Noelle Louise Schattyn, Dec. 22, 1967. BA, Dartmouth Coll., 1968; MA, Harvard U., 1972, PhD, 1973. Cert. Rome Classics Ctr. Curator of coins Fogg Art Mus., Cambridge, Mass., 1972; asst. prof. U. Mo., Columbia, 1972-76, assoc. prof., dept. head, 1976-81; prof. U. Ariz., Tucson, 1982-97, Regents prof., 1997—, dept. head, 1984-89. Guest curator Am. Mus. Natural History, NYC, 1983—90, lectr, 1993—; creator, dir. Kourion Excavations, Cyprus, 1982—89, Portugal, 1983—84, Am. Excavations, Lugnano, Italy, 1988—93; pot cons., field dir. Tunisa Excavations, Chgo. Oriental Inst./Smithsonian Instn., 1973—78; dir. excavations Chianciano, Terme, Italy, 1995—; dir. Orvieto (Italy) Inst. Classical Studies, 2002—; resident in classical archaeology Am. Acad., Rome, 2002. Author: (book) Unreal Reality, 1978, Rise and Fall of Fantasy Film, 1980, Carthage, 1990, Carthage, French edit., 1994, Vera-Ellen: The Magic and the Mystery, 1999, 2d edit., 2003, Lugnano! Excavation of a Roman Villa, 1999, Kourion: Search for a Lost Roman City, 1988, Corpus des Mosaiques de Tunisie, 1972, Corpus des Mosaiques de Tunisie, 3d rev. edit., 1986, Carthage: A Mosaic of Ancient Tunisia, 1987; editor: Excavations at Kourion I, 1987; contbg. editor: Archaeology Mag.; prodr.: (films) Carthage: A Mirage of Antiquity, 1987; creator, guest curator (internt traveling exhbn.) Carthage: A Mosaic of Ancient Tunisia, 1987—92; editor, founder: Roscius, 1993—95; creative cons. (TV miniseries) Lost Civilizations, 1994; contbr. articles to profl. jours.; prodr.: (documentaries) BBC-TV documentary Malaria and the Fall of Rome, 2002; author: Vera-Ellen: The Magic and the Mystery; 2d edit., 2003; cons.: The History Channel, 2004; cons., on-screen contbr. The Colosseum, History Channel, 2005, Where Did it Come From? 3rd Episodes for History Channel As On Screen Personality and Creative Consultaut, 2006; editor: (reports) Archaeological Excavations, 2007; prodr.: (TV reality show) Forgotten Lives, 2008. Recipient Cine Golden Eagle, 1980, Angenieux Film award, Indsl. Photography Mag., 1980, Oustanding Am. Under 40 award, C. Johns Hopkins-Britain's Royal Inst. Internat. Affairs, 1985; named Outstanding Am. Under 40, Esquire Mag., 1985, hon. Italian citizen, Lugnano, Italy, 1989; grantee, NEH, 1979, 1987, Fulbright, Lisbon, 1983. Fellow: Brit. Royal Inst. Internat. Affairs; mem.: Am. Acad. Rome (mem. internat. com. 2003—, bd. dirs. 2003—), Luso-Am. Commn. (citation 1983—84), Archaeol. Inst. Tucson (pres. 1983—86), Am. Sch. Oriental Rsch. (dept. rep. 1981—85), Nat. Geog. Soc. (project dir. 1983—84). Office: Univ Ariz Dept Classics PO Box 210105 206 Learning Svcs Bldg Tucson AZ 85721-0001 Office Phone: 520-621-1689. Business E-Mail: soren@u.arizona.edu.

SORENSEN, ANDREW AARON, retired academic administrator; b. Pitts., July 20, 1938; s. Albert Aaron and Margaret (Lindquist) S.; m. Donna Ingemie, Aug. 4, 1968; children: Aaron Ashley, Benjamin Samuel. BA, U. Ill., 1959; BDiv, Yale U., 1962, MPh, 1970, PhD, 1971; MPH, U. Mich., 1966. Asst. prof. Cornell U., Ithaca, NY, 1971-73, U. Rochester, NY, 1973-76, assoc. prof. NY, 1976-83; prof., dean U. Mass., Amherst, 1983-86, Johns Hopkins U., Balt., 1986-90, exec. dir. AIDS Inst.; provost, v.p. acad. affairs U. Fla., Gainesville, 1990-96; pres. U. Ala., Tuscaloosa, 1996—2002, U. SC, Columbia, 2002—08, prof. Sch. Medicine, 2008—. Vis. fellow U. Cambridge, 1979—80, 2008—09; pres. bd. Preservation Inst. Nantucket, 1990—96. Author 8 books; chmn. editl. bd. U. Press., Fla., 1990-96; contbr. over 100 articles to profl. jours. Vice-chmn., bd. dirs. Chautauqua Instn., 1996-98; bd. mem. Nat. Sci. Advisory Bd. for Biosecurity, 2005—; chmn. bd. dirs. SC Gov. Sch. Sci. & Math. 2009-. U.S. Dept. Edn. fellow Lincoln U., 1966-67, NSF fellow Harvard U., 1975-76; named Amb. of Yr., Greater Columbia C of C. Mem.: So. Univ. Conf. (past pres.), Univ. Rsch. Assn. (trustee), Southeastern Univs. Rsch. Assn. (past chmn. coun. presidents, pres. conf.). Presbyterian. Office: USC Sch Medicine 6311 Garners Ferry Rd Columbia SC 29209 Home Phone: 803-777-3104. Business E-Mail: sorensen@sc.edu.

SORENSEN, CARL EDWARD, manufacturing executive; b. San Diego, Sept. 21, 1964; s. Carl Edward and Bonnie Jean Sorensen; m. Cynthia Ann Sorensen, June 5, 1987; 1 child, Carl Edward. B Bus. Mgmt., St. Leo Coll., Norfolk, Va., 1995; M Bus. Fin. and Acctg., Mont. State U., Bozeman, 1998. Commd. USN, 1983, advanced through grades to comdr., 1998; owner, pres., CEO Sorensen Enterprises Inc., Virginia Beach, Va., 1998—. Adv. bd. chmn. Rural Bus. Enhancement, Virginia Beach; chmn. Pennys From Heaven, Sunbury, S.C. Mem. DAV, WW II Meml. Fund, Elks. Republican. Methodist. Avocations: buying small companies, improving and selling them, antique collecting. Office Phone: 828-494-2049.

SORENSEN, CHRISTOPHER MICHAEL, physics professor, researcher; b. Omaha, Oct. 1, 1947; s. Nels Anton and Lyla Fern (Johnson) S.; m. Georgia Gold, Nov. 15, 1975; 1 chld, Hali Paige. BS, U. Nebr., 1969; MS, U. Colo., 1973, PhD, 1977. Asst. prof. physics Kans. State U., Manhattan, 1977-82, assoc. prof., 1982-86, prof. physics, 1986—2000, adj. prof. chemistry, 1987—, Univ. disting. prof., 2000—. Contbr. articles to profl. jours. With U.S. Army, 1969-71, Vietnam. Recipient Presdl. Tchg. Award, US Professor of Yr. award for Doctoral and Rsch. Universities, Carnegie Found. for Advancement of Tchg. and Coun. for Advancement and Support of Edn., 2007, Norlin Disting. Achievement award, U. Colo., 2008; Woodrow Wilson fellow, 1969. Mem. Am. Phys. Soc., Am. Chem. Soc., Am. Assn. Aerosol Rsch. (pres. 2007, 2008, David Sinclair award), Gesellschaft fur Aerosolforschung, Phi Beta Kappa. Avocations: amateur astronomy, running, rugby. Home: 3925 Snowyreach Manhattan KS 66503-7559 Office: Kans State U 325A Cardwell Hall Manhattan KS 66506 Office Phone: 785-532-1626. Office Fax: 785-532-6806. E-mail: sor@phys.ksu.edu.

SORENSEN, GILLIAN MARTIN, United Nations official; b. Columbus, Ohio, Mar. 4, 1941; d. John Butlin and Helen (Hickam) Martin; m. Theodore C. Sorensen, June 28, 1969; 1 child, Juliet. BA, Smith Coll., 1963. Commr. NYC Commn. UN and Consular Corps, 1978-90; pres. Nat. Conf., 1990-93; undersec gen., spl. advisor for pub. policy UN, NYC, 1993-97, asst. sec. gen. external rels., 1997—2003; sr. advisor UN Found., NYC, 2003—. Fellow Harvard U. Kennedy Sch. Govt. Inst. Politics. Del. Dem. Nat. Conv., 1976, 84, 88. Mem.: Women's Forum, Coun. on Fgn. Rels. Democrat. Office: UN Found 801 Second Ave 13th Fl New York NY 10023 Office Phone: 212-697-3315. Business E-Mail: gsorensen@unfoundation.org.

SORENSEN, JACK, computer game company executive; BA, Brandeis U., Waltham, Mass.; MBA, U. Calif., Berkeley. Mgr. product devel. and internat. and bus. ops. LucasArts Entertainment Co., pres.; exec. v.p. worldwide studios THQ Inc., Calabasas, Calif., 2001—.

SORENSEN, JOHN B., surgeon; s. Bruce F. and Suzanne B. Sorensen. MD, Temple U., 1986. Cert. surgery Am. Bd. Surgery, 1992, critical care Am. Bd. Surgery, 1995, transplantation surgery U. Pitts., 1993. Dir. transplantation LDS Hosp., Salt Lake City, 1993—2005; chief sect. transplantation dept. surgery U. Utah, Salt Lake City, 2005—. Med. dir. Intermountain Donor Services, Salt Lake City, 2004—. Col. US Army, 2002. Decorated Combat Med. Badge, Bronze Star U.S. Army. Fellow: ACS; mem.: Am. Soc. Transplant Surgeons, Sigma Chi. Mem. Lds Ch. Office: Univ Utah Dept Surgery 30 North 1900 East Salt Lake City UT 84132

SORENSEN, LINDA, lawyer; b. Eureka, Calif., Mar. 3, 1945; BS, U. Wis., 1967; JD, U. Calif., 1976. Bar: Calif. 1976, U.S. Dist. Ct. (no. dist.) Calif. 1976, U.S. Ct. Appeals (9th cir.) 1976, U.S. Dist. Ct. (ea. dist.) Calif. 1977. Assoc., ptnr. Rothschild, Phelan & Mortali, San Francisco, 1976-88; dir. Howard, Rice, Nemerovski, Canady, Falk & Rabkin, San Francisco, 1988-95; shareholder Feldman, Waldman & Kline, P.C., San Francisco, 1997-99; pvt. practice Berkeley, Calif., 1999—; of counsel Stromsheim & Assoc., 2001—. Mem. ABA (mem. subcom. on avoiding powers, bus. bankruptcy com. 1983-95), Bar Assn. of San Francisco (chmn. comml. law and bankruptcy sect. 1984, editor fed. cts. com., no. dist. Calif. digest 1979-82). Office: PO Box 325 Bodega Bay CA 94923 Office Fax: 707-875-9287. Personal E-mail: lindasorensen@earthlink.net.

SORENSEN, TED (THEODORE CHAIKIN SORENSEN), lawyer, former federal official; b. Lincoln, Nebr., May 8, 1928; s. Christian Abraham and Annis (Chaikin) Sorensen; m. Gillian Martin, June 28, 1969; 1 child, Juliet Suzanne; children from previous marriage: Eric Kristen, Stephen Edgar, Philip Jon. BS in Law, U. Nebr., 1949, LLB, 1951, LLD, 1969, U. Canterbury, 1966, Alfred U., 1969, Temple U., 1969, Fairfield U., 1969, U. Wis., Stout, 1998. Bar: Nebr. 1951, NY 1966, US Supreme Ct. 1966, DC 1971. Atty. Fed. Security Agy., 1951-52; mem. staff joint com. r.r. retirement US Senate, 1952, asst. to Senator John F. Kennedy, 1953-61; sec. New Eng. Senators' Conf., 1953-59; spl. counsel to Pres. John F. Kennedy The White House, 1961-64; sr. counsel Paul, Weiss, Rifkind, Wharton & Garrison, NYC, 1966—2002, chmn. internat. practice com., of counsel, 2002—. Mem. Pres.'s Adv. Com. Trade Negotiations, 1978; chmn. Gov.'s panel on NY State Export Credit Agy., 1982. Author: Decision Making in the White House, 1963, Kennedy, 1965, The Kennedy Legacy, 1969, Watchmen in the Night: Presidential Accountability After Watergate, 1975, A Different Kind of Presidency, 1984, Counselor: A Life at the Edge of History, 2008; co-author (with Ralf Dahrendorf): A Widening Atlantic? Domestic Change and Foreign Policy, 1986; editor: Let the Word Go Forth: The Speeches, Statements and Writings of John F. Kennedy, 1988, Why I Am A Democrat, 1996. Dem. candidate for US Senate, 1970; chmn. Dem. Nat. Com. task force on polit. action, 1981-82, mem. task force on fgn. policy, 1986; nat. co-chair Gary Hart's Presdl. Campaign, 1984; mem. Internat. Trade Roundtable, 1985; chmn., 1994-99, dir. Twentieth Century Found., 1984—, Coun. on Fgn. Rels., 1993-2004, Ctrl. Asian-Am. Enterprise Fund, 1995-99, Nat. Dem. Inst. for Internat. Affairs,

1993-99; trustee NY Acad. Medicine, 1991-97; advisor Russian-Am. Press and Info. Ctr., pres's Commn. on White House Fellows; chmn. adv. bd. Brandeis Internat. Ctr. Ethics, Justice and Pub. Life; mem. adv. bd. Partnership a Secure America; hon. co-chair ABA Commn. on the Renaissance of Idealism in the Legal Profession. Named one of Ten Outstanding Young Men of Yr., Jr. C. of C., 1961; fellow Inst. Politics, Harvard U. Kennedy Sch. Govt., 2002. Mem. Order of Coif, Phi Beta Kappa. Office: Paul Weiss Rifkind Wharton & Garrison Rm 200 1285 Avenue Of The Americas New York NY 10019-6065*

SORENSON, ARNE M., hotel executive; b. Tokyo, 1958; m. Ruth Sorenson; 4 children. BA, Luther Coll., 1980; JD, U. Minn., 1983. Law clk. to Hon. Ellsworth Van Graafeiland US Ct. Appeals (2nd Cir.), 1983—84; assoc. Latham & Watkins, Washington, 1984—90; ptnr. Latham & Watkins, Washington, 1990—96; sr. v.p. bus. devel. Marriott Internat., Inc., Washington, 1996-98, exec. v.p., CFO, 1998—2009, pres., continental European lodging, 2003—09, pres., COO Bethesda, Md., 2009—. Office: Marriott International Inc 10400 Fernwood Rd Bethesda MD 20817*

SORENSON, JAMES ROGER, public health educator; b. Yakima, Wash., Feb. 9, 1943; s. Paul Olaf and Helen Leona (Anderson) S.; m. Nancy Ellen O'Neal, May 24, 1968;1 child, Peter Matthew. BA in Sociology, U. Wash., 1965, MA in Sociology, 1966; PhD in Sociology, Cornell U., 1970. Asst. prof. Princeton (N.J.) U., 1969-74; assoc. prof. Boston U. Sch. of Medicine, 1974-84, Boston U. Sch. of Pub. Health, 1979-84; prof. Boston Univ. Schs. of Medicine and Pub. Health, 1984-85; prof. Sch. Pub. Health U. N.C., Chapel Hill, 1985—. Cons. NIMH (Changing Role of Women Com.), 1971, Rutgers U. Ednl. Decision Making Project, 1970-74, Nat. Inst. Child Health and Human Devel., 1977-79, Nat. Heart, Lung and Blood Inst., Sickle Cell Br., 1977-80, 1991-92, Boston Comprehensive Sickle Cell Ctr., 1979-85, Nat. Ctr. for Human Genome Rsch., 1990-91; com. mem. Ea. Sociol. Soc. Papers Com., 1970-73, Genetics Core Group, Inst. for Soc., Ethics and the Life Scis., 1971-76, NYU com. on Med. and Ethical Issues in Treating Spina Bifida, 1973-74, Nat. Found. March of Dimes Clin. Rsch. (Human) adv. com. 1974-75; sci. assoc. Boston City Hosp., 1975-85, N.E. Group on Med. Edn., 1976-77; also many coms. at U. N.C. including Dean's Cabinet Sch. of Pub. Health, 1985—; dir. and chair steering com. Sch. of Pub. Health Promotion/Disease Prevention Program, 1986-89; adv. bd. Injury Prevention Rsch. Ctr., many others. Author: (with others) In Sickness and in Health: Social Dimensions of Medical Care, 1981, Reproductive Pasts, Reproductive Futures: Genetic Counseling and Its Effectiveness, 1981; also numerous articles to profl. jours. and chpts. to books; reviewer Am. Jour. Med. Genetics, Am. Jour. Preventive Medicine, Am. Jour. Pub. Health, Archives of Pathology and Laboratory Medicine, Human Relations, Jour. of Health and Social Behavior, Jour. Am. Geriatrics Soc., Milbank Meml. Fund Quarterly, New Eng. Jour. of Medicine, Patient Edn. and Counseling, Prenatal Diagnosis, Sci., Tech. and Human Values, Social Sci. and Medicine; exec. editor: Health Edn. Rsch., 1996—. Mem. adv. coun. Com. to Combat Huntington's Disease, Mass. chpt., 1979-85, edn. and comty. adv. bd. Am. Heart Assn., N.C. affiliate, 1986-89. Named fellow NIMH, Cornell U., 1967-69, Inst. of Soc., Ethics and Life Scis; named Falk lectr. Ea. Sociol. Soc., 1975-76; recipient Disting. Alumnus award Yakima Valley Coll., 1985; grantee; Mass. Dept. Pub. Health, Nat. Found., March of Dimes, NIDA, Nat. Cancer Inst. and others (19 grants in all). Mem. Am. Pub. Health Assn., Soc. Profl. Health Educators, N.C. Soc. Profl. Health Educators, Coun. on Health Edn. in Higher Edn., N.C. Pub. Health Assn., Phi Beta Kappa, Delta Omega. Avocations: music, theater. Office: U NC Sch Pub Health 326 Rosenau Hall 7400 Chapel Hill NC 27599-0001 Home: 214 Sandfiddler E Emerald Isle NC 28594-2285

SORENSON, STEPHEN JAY, lawyer; b. Salt Lake City, Aug. 9, 1949; s. Peter Jay and Jeannette (Hanks) S.; m. Corinne Clyde, Jan. 24, 1974; children: Jeannette, Peter, Richard, Michael, Rebecca. Student, Yale U., 1967-69; BA, U. Utah, 1973, JD, 1977. Bar: Utah 1977, U.S. Dist. Ct. Utah 1977, U.S. Ct. Appeals (10th cir.) 1982. Asst. atty. gen. State of Utah, Salt Lake City, 1977-90, chief litig. divsn., 1986-90; asst. US atty. Dist. Utah US Dept. Justice, Salt Lake City, 1990—, chief civil divsn., 1995-98, 2006—09, first asst. US atty., 1998—2006, acting US atty., 2006. Mem. Utah Bar Assn. Office: US Atty's Office 185 S State St Ste 300 Salt Lake City UT 84111-1552 Office Phone: 801-325-3218.

SORENSON, STEVEN P., insurance company executive; AB, Harvard Univ.; MBA, Univ. Chgo. Engagement mgr. McKinsey & Co., Chgo., Houston, London; gen. mgr. Progressive Ins. Co.; prod. v.p. Allstate Ins. Co., Northbrook, Ill., 2000—02, v.p., co-leader field ops., 2002—07, sr. v.p. protection distbn., 2007—08, sr. v.p. product ops., 2008—. Office: Allstate Corp 2775 Sanders Rd Northbrook IL 60062*

SORENSTAM, ANNIKA, retired professional golfer; b. Stockholm, Oct. 9, 1970; d. Tom and Gunilla Sorenstam; m. David Esch, Jan. 4, 1997 (div. 2005); m. Michael McGee, Jan. 10, 2009; 1 child, Ava Madelyn. Student, U. Ariz. Profl. golfer Ladies European Tour, 1992—2008, LPGA, 1993—2008; mem. Swedish Nat. Team, 1987-92, Solheim Cup Team, 1994, 96, 98; playing editor Golf Digest, 2006—, Golf for Women, 2006—. Recipient Vare Trophy award, 1998, ESPY award, Best Female Golfer, ESPN, 1996, 1998, 1999, 2002-04, ESPY award, Best Female Athlete, 2006; named Rolex Player of Yr., 1995, 97, 98, 2000-03, Female Athlete of Yr., AP, 2003. Achievements include 72 LPGA Tour victories, 14 Ladies European Tour victories; Major tournament wins: US Women's Open, 1995, 96, 2006, Kraft Nabisco Championship, 2001, 02, 05, Women's British Open, 2003, LPGA Championship, 2003-05; becoming the first woman since 1945 to appear in a PGA Tour event, 2003; induction into the World Golf Hall of Fame, 2003.*

SORGE, KAREN LEE, printing company executive, consultant; b. Warwick, NY, May 27, 1958; d. Wesley Thomas and Margaret Anne (Storms) Kervatt; m. David W. Farquhar, July 16, 1982 (div. Feb. 1990); 1 child: Lauren Nicole; m. Thomas E. Sorge, May 16, 1997; children: Natalie MaKalen Sorge, Ryan Thomas. AS, Roger Williams Coll., 1978, BS cum laude, 1980. Office mgr. Price-Rite Printing Co., Dover, NJ, 1975—76; cons. SBA, Bristol, RI, 1978—80; account exec. P.M. Press Inc., Dallas, 1980—90, sales trainer, 1984—85; v.p. KDF Bus. Forms Inc., Dallas, 1984—90; account exec. Jarvis Press, Dallas, 1990—2008, Ussery Printing, Dallas; pres. Print Trends, Dallas, 1990—. Printer Tex. Aux. Charity Auction Orgn., Dallas, 1985, Cystic Fibrosis, Dallas, 1989—93, Life Enhancement Assn. Programs Found., 1992—, Dallas Soc. Visual Comm., 1992, AIDS Resources Com., Dallas chpt. Cerebral Palsy, 1994, Lloyd-Paxton AIDS Benefit, 1994, Feast for the Eyes Gala-Benefit to Prevent Blindness, 2001, Genesis Women's Shelter, 2002, others. Recipient award, Clampitt Paper Co., Dallas, 1982, P.M. Press Inc., 1983—89, Mead Paper Co., 1985—96, Feast for the Eyes Gala, 2001, Gold award, Adrian Advt., 2004, Silver award, 2005, 2006. Mem. Printing Industry in Am. (recipient Judges Favorite award 1992, Best of Show Hon. Mention award 1994, gold award Best of Tex. 1996), Internat. Assn. Bus. Communicators, Nat. Bus. Forms Assn. Republican. Baptist. Avocation: piano. Home: 2600 Raintree Dr Southlake TX 76092-5536 Office Phone: 817-424-5252. Business E-Mail: printtrends@mac.com.

SORHANNUS, ULF MIKAEL, biology professor; s. Tage and Gotel Sorhannus; m. Lucia Mancini; 1 child, John Joseph. PhD, CUNY: Borough of Manhattan CC, NYC, 1989. Assoc. prof. Edinboro U. Pa., 1995—. Contbr. articles to profl. sci. jours. Achievements include research in evolutionary and systematic work. Office: Edinboro Univ Pennsylvania Scotland Rd Fairview PA 16415

SORIANO, ALFONSO GUILLEARD, professional baseball player; b. San Pedro De Macoris, Dominican Republic, Jan. 7, 1976; Player NY Yankees, 1999—2004, Tex. Rangers, 2004—05, Wash. Nationals, 2005—06, Chgo. Cubs, 2007—. Recipient Silver Slugger award, 2002, 2004—06; named All-Star Game MVP, 2004; named to Am. League All-Star Team, 2002—05, Nat. League All-Star Team, 2006—08. Achievements include leading the Am. League in hits (209), runs scored (128), and stolen bases (41), 2002. Mailing: c/o Chgo Cubs Wrigley Field 1060 W Addison St Chicago IL 60613-4397

SORIOT, PASCAL, pharmaceutical executive; MBA, HEC, Paris, 1986. Fin. contr. Asia Pacific region Roussel Uclaf, 1986; dist. sales mgr. Roussel New Zealand, 1987; sales and mktg. mgr. Roussel Australia, 1989, gen. mgr.; divsn. global mktg. dir. Roussel Uclaf Pharmaceuticals, 1994; gen. mgr. Hoechst Marion Roussel Australia, 1996—97; regional v.p. Asia Pacific Hoechst Marion Roussel Tokyo, 1997—2000; sr. v.p., head global mktg. and med. affairs Aventis Bridgewater, 2000—02; COO Aventis US, 2002—06; head strategic mktg. Roche, 2006; head. comml. ops., mem. Enlarged Corp. Exec. Com., 2007; CEO Genetech, Inc., 2009. Mem. Roche Corp. Exec. Com. Office: Genetech Inc 1 DNA Way South San Francisco CA 94080*

SORKIN, AARON, scriptwriter, television producer, playwright; b. NYC, June 9, 1961; m. Julia Bingham, Apr. 13, 1996 (div. 2006); 1 child, Roxy. Student, SUNY, Purchase; BFA in Musical Theatre, Syracuse U. Creator, prodr. (TV series) Sports Nights, 1998—2000 (Humanitas prize, 1999); creator, writer, exec. prodr.: TV series The West Wing, 1999—2003 (Emmy award for Best for Outstanding Writing in a Drama Series, 2000, 2001, 2002, 2003, Humanitas prize, 2000, 2002, Writer Guild Am. award, 2001, Television Prodr. of the Yr. Producers Guild Am. Golden Laurel award, 2002); creator, writer, exec. prodr. (TV series) Studio 60 on the Sunset Strip, 2006—07; writer: screenplays A Few Good Men, 1992, Malice, 1993, Charlie Wilson's War, 2007; writer: (films) The American President, 1995; writer: Broadway plays A Few Good Men, 1989 (Outer Critics Circle award as Outstanding American Playwright, 1989), Hidden in this Picture, 1990, Making Movies, 1992.

SORKIN, ALAN LOWELL, economist, educator; b. Decatur, Ill., Nov. 2, 1941; s. Martin and Sally Eileen (Steinberg) S.; m. Sylvia Jean Smardo, Sept. 9, 1967; children: David, Suzanne. BA, Johns Hopkins U., 1963, MA, 1964, PhD, 1966. Rsch. assoc. Brookings Instn., Washington, 1967-69; asst. prof. internat. health and econs. Johns Hopkins U., Balt., 1969-72, assoc. prof. internat. health and econs., 1972-74, adj. prof. dept. internat. health sch. Hygiene and Pub. Health, 1986—; prof., chmn. dept. econs., 1974—; also adj. prof. preventive and social medicine Med. Sch., U. Md., 1974—. Author: Education, Unemployment and Economic Growth, 1974, Health Economics: An Introduction, 1975, 2d edit., 1983, 3d edit., 1992. The Urban American Indian, 1978, Economic Aspects of Natural Hazards, 1982, Health Care and the Changing Economic Environment, 1986, Monetary and Fiscal Policy and Business Cycles in The Modern Era, 1988, Public Health and Development, 1988, (with others) Female Labor Force and Development, 1990, Nutrition, Food Policy and Development, 1995, (with Irina Farquhar) Economic and Social Aspects of Occupational and environmental Health, 1998, others; contbr. articles to profl. jours. Mem. Am. Econs. Assn., Phi Beta Kappa, Delta Omega. Republican. Lutheran. Home: 1694 Campbell Rd Forest Hill MD 21050-2342 Office: Univ Md Dept Econ 1000 Hilltop Cir Baltimore MD 21250 Home Phone: 410-893-1728; Office Phone: 410-455-2173, 410-502-0413. Business E-Mail: sorkin@umbc.edu, asorkin@jhsph.edu. *Personal relationships are more important than material possessions. Persons with many friends have a sense of well-being that can never be embodied in materialism.*

SORKIN, DAVID JAMES, lawyer; b. NYC, June 26, 1959; s. Sol Sorkin; m. Susan Anne Meisel, May 1, 1993. BA, Williams Coll., 1981; JD, Harvard U., 1984. Bar: NY 1985. Law clk. to Hon. Charles M. Merrill US Ct. Appeals (9th Cir.), San Francisco, 1984-85; assoc. Simpson Thacher & Bartlett, NYC, 1985-92, ptnr., 1993—2007; gen. counsel Kohlberg Kravis Roberts & Co., NYC, 2007—. Office: Kohlberg Kravis Roberts & Co 9 W 57th St Ste 4200 New York NY 10019

SORKIN, IRA LEE (IKE SORKIN), lawyer; b. NYC, May 30, 1943; s. Nathan and Rosalie (Cohen) S.; m. Ellen M. Sorkin, Aug. 24, 1969; children: Roger David, Peter Neil. BA, Tulane U., 1965; JD, George Washington U., 1968. Trial atty. SEC, NYC, 1968-71, dir., 1984—86; asst. U.S. atty. (so. dist.) N.Y. US Dept. Justice, 1971-76, dep. chief, criminal divsn., 1976; ptnr. Squadron Ellenoff Plesent & Lehrer, NYC, 1977-84, Squadron Ellenoff Plesent & Sheinfeld, NYC, 1986—95, Squadron, Ellenoff, Plesent & Sheinfeld LLP, NYC, 1997—2002; chief legal officer Nomura Securities Internat. Inc., NYC, 1995-97; ptnr. Carter, Ledyard & Milburn LLP, NYC, 2002—05, Dickstein Shapiro LLP (formerly Dickstein Shapiro Morin & Oshinsky LLP), NYC, 2005—. Lectr. Nat. Inst. Trial Advocacy, N.Y.C., 1981-91, Securities Industry Assn. Contbr. articles to profl. jours. Tutor inner city students N.Y.C. Sch. Sys., 1996-97; pres. Am. Friends of the Hebrew U. of Jerusalem Mem. ABA, N.Y. Coun. Def. Lawyers, Assn. of the Bar for the City of N.Y., Leardning Leaders Avocations: golf, reading. Office: Dickstein Shapiro LLP 1633 Broadway New York NY 10019-6708 Office Phone: 212-277-6576. Business E-Mail: sorkini@dicksteinshapiro.com.*

SORKIN, LAURENCE TRUMAN, lawyer; b. Bklyn., Oct. 20, 1942; s. Sidney and Lilly (Kowensky) S.; m. Joan Carol Ross, June 25, 1972; children: Andrew Ross, Suzanne Ross. AB summa cum laude, Brown U., 1964; LLB, Yale U., 1967; LLM, London Sch. Econs./Polit. Sci., 1968. Law clk. to Judge J. Joseph Smith U.S. Ct. Appeals (2d cir.), 1968-69; assoc. Cahill Gordon & Reindel, NYC, 1969-75, ptnr., 1975—. Vis. lectr. Yale U., 1972, 73; lectr. various profl. orgns.; rsch. asst. to Lester and Bindman for book Race and Law in Great Britain, 1972; adj. prof. law Fordham Law Sch., 2007-; adv. bd., Inst. Consumer Antitrust Studies, Loyola U. Sch. Law, 2008-. Contbr. to State Antitrust Law (Lifland), 1984; author: (with Lifland, Sorkin and Van Cise) Understanding the Antitrust Laws, 1986; mem. bd. editors Lexis/Nexis Antitrust Report, 2004—. Bd. dirs. Legal Aid Soc., N.Y.C., 1988-94, N.Y. Lawyers for Pub. Interest, 1990-93, adv. bd. mem., BNA Antitrust & Trade Reputation Reports, 2008-. Fulbright scholar, 1967-68. Mem. ABA (antitrust law sect. 1978—), N.Y. State Bar Assn. (antitrust sect., chmn. com. on legislation 1978-79, sect. sec. 1979-80, chmn. com. on mergers 1987-89, chmn. Clayton Act com. 1989-94, exec. com. 1989-94, comml. and fed. litigation sect. chmn. com. antitrust 1996-98), Assn. Bar City N.Y. (com. trade regulation 1974-77, 95-98, com. on electronic funds transfer 1979-80), Yale Law Sch. Assn. (pres. 2007-09, exec. com. 2000—, chmn. 2009-), Phi Beta Kappa. Office: Cahill Gordon & Reindel 80 Pine St Fl 17 New York NY 10005-1702 Office Phone: 212-701-3209. Business E-Mail: lsorkin@cahill.com.

SORKIN, ROBERT DANIEL, psychologist, industrial engineer, educator; b. NYC, May 24, 1937; s. Harry and Cynthia (Erdreich) S.; m. Nancy Jayne Sloan, July 3, 1960; children: David, Susan. BEE, Carnegie Inst. Tech., 1958; PhD, U. Mich., 1965. Engr. human factors Martin Co., Balt., 1958—60; assoc. rsch. engr. Cooley Labs. U. Mich., Ann Arbor, 1960—65; asst. prof. psychology Purdue U., West Lafayette, Ind., 1965—68, assoc. prof., 1968—73, prof. dept. psychol. scis., 1973—88; prof., chair dept. psychology U. Fla., Gainesville, 1988—95, prof. dept. psychology, indsl. and sys. engrng. dept., 1995—2008, emeritus prof., dept. psychology, indsl. and system engrng., 2008—. Asst. dean sch. humanities, social scis. and edn. Purdue U., 1973-75; dir. psychobiology program NSF, Washington, 1975-76; chair Coun. Grad. Depts. Psychology, Blacksburg, Va., 1994-95; mem. com. on hearing and bioacoustics NRC, Washington, 1987-90; mgr. cognition program Air Force Office Scientific Rsch., Va., 2002-2005; sr. scientist Human Effectiveness Directorate, Air Force Rsch. Lab., Wright-Patterson AFB, Ohio, 2005-07. Author: (software) Laboratory Projects in Experimental Psychology, 1998; co-author: Human Factors: Understanding People-System Relationships, 1983; contbr. articles to profl. jours.Jour. Acoustical Soc. Am., Perception and Psychophysics, Jour. Exptl. Psychology, Human Factors, Psychol. Rev., Psych. Sci. With US Army, 1960. Fellow Acoustical Soc. Am., APA, Am. Psychol. Soc.; mem. Human Factors Soc., European Assn. Decision Making, Soc. for Judgment and Decision Making Home: 159 Marine St Apt 205 Saint Augustine FL 32084

SOROKA, STEFAN, archbishop; b. Winnipeg, Man., Can., Nov. 13, 1951; s. Ivan and Anna Soroka. B in Social Work, U. Man., Winnipeg, Can., 1973, M in Social Work, 1978; STB, Catholic U. of Am., Washington, DC, 1982, D in Social Work, 1985. Corrections officer Headingley Correctional Inst., Winnipeg, Manitoba, Canada, 1971—72; social worker Probation Svcs., Manitoba, 1973—79; ordained priest Archeparchy of Winnipeg (Ukrainian), Canada, 1982; asst. priest Holy Family Ukrainian Catholic Nat. Shrine, Washington, Blessed Virgin Mary, Winnipeg, 1984—86; vice-chancellor Archeparchy of Winnipeg (Ukrainian), 1985—94, vocations dir., 1985—2000, chancellor, 1994—96, econome, 1994—98, auxiliary bishop, 1996, auxiliary bishop, vicar gen., 1996—2000; parish priest Ukrainian Catholic Ch. of the Assumption, Portage La Prairie, 1986—87, St. Anne Ukrainian Catholic Ch., Winnipeg, 1987—95; ordained bishop, 1996; archbishop Archeparchy of Phila. (Ukrainian), 2001—. Judge Archieparchial Marriage Tribunal, 1984—93; chaplain, nat. exec. Ukrainian Catholic Youth of Can., 1989—92; chmn, bd. dirs. Asset Protection Group Insurance Corn. for Western and Northern Can. Dioceses/Eparchies, 1998—2000; chaplain Ukrainian Catholic Women's League Can. (Winnipeg Archeparchy), 1998—2000; mem. Ad Hoc com. on Aid to Ch. in Ctrl. and Eastern Europe, 2001—, Permanent Synod of Bishops of Ukrainian Catholic Ch., 2002—07; mem. Ad Hoc com. on Sexual Abuse US Conf. Catholic Bishops, 2002—08, mem. Task Force on Content and Flow of Gen. Meeting, 2003—04, mem. Task Force to Establish Guidelines, 2003—04, mem. Com. on Rels. between Eastern and Latin Catholic Churches, 2003—. Editor: Progress Ukrainian Catholic Newspaper, 1996—2000. Recipient St. Dominic medal, Dominican House of Studies, Washington, DC, 2001. Mem.: Consecrated Life and Lay Assn. (mem. com. rels. with clergy 1997—2000), Catholic Health Assn. Man. (bishops' rep. 1988—90), Knights of Columbus (chaplain St. Josaphat Coun. 1986—89, chaplain St. Anne Coun. 1987—95, chaplain St. Josaphat Coun. 1995—97). Roman Catholic. Office: Archeparchy of Phila 827 N Franklin St Philadelphia PA 19123-2097

SOROKIN, ETHEL SILVER, lawyer; b. Hartford, Conn., 1928; d. Jacob M. and Jennie (Klein) Silver; m. Milton Sorokin, June 25, 1950; children: Rachel B., Sharon L., Leo T. BA, Vassar Coll., 1950; LLB with honors, U. Conn., 1953. Bar: Conn. 1953, US Dist. Ct. Conn. 1955, US Ct. Appeals (2d cir.), US Supreme Ct. 1960. Assoc. Levine & Katz, Hartford, Conn., 1953-56; ptnr. Sorokin & Sorokin, Hartford, Conn., 1956-89, Sorokin, Gross & Hyde PC, Hartford, Conn., 1989-93, of counsel, 1994—2001. Lectr. law, advisor law rev. U. Conn., 1955-58, 61-66; sec. Conn. Jud. Rev. Coun., 1978-92; spkr. in field. Editor-in-chief U. Conn. Law Rev., 1953; mem. editl. bd. Conn. Bar Jour., 1951-56; contbr. articles to profl. jours. Trustee U. Conn. Law Found., Hartford, 1976-92, pres., 1978-79; dir. treas. Ctr. for First Amendment Rights, Inc., 1993-96, pres., 1996-2004, pres. emerita, 2005-08. Recipient U. Conn. Law Review award for scholarship svc., 1996, Dean C. Avery award, The Day of New London, 1997, Disting. Svc. award, U. Conn. Sch. Law, 1989, Pub.'s award for enhancement of first amendment and media, Ct. Law Tribune, 2004, Disting. Grad. award, West Hartford Found. Pub. Edn., 2008. Mem. ABA (media law com., 1st amendment com.), Conn. Bar Assn. (family law sect., chmn. legis. com. 1984-87, chmn. UMPA study com. 1986, media-law com. 1992—, Media Law award 1996). Office: 13rd Fl 90 Statehouse Sq Hartford CT 06103-3708 Office Phone: 860-541-3339. Business E-Mail: ethel@freedomprojects.com. E-mail: esorokin@pullcom.com.

SOROKINE, ALEXANDRE, geographer, researcher; married. PhD in Geography, SUNY, Buffalo, 2004. Rschr. Regional Sci. Inst., Sapporo, Japan, 1996—2000; r&d staff mem. Oak Ridge Nat. Lab., Tenn., 2004—. Mem.: Assn. Am. Geographers. Avocation: hiking. Office: Oak Ridge Nat Lab 1 Bethel Valley Rd Oak Ridge TN 37831-6017

SOROKO, JOHN J., lawyer; b. NYC, May 13, 1951; AB, Haverford Coll., 1973; JD, NYU, 1977; Grad., Harvard Bus. Sch. Leading Profl. Svc. Firms Program, 2007. Bar: Pa. 1977, US Ct. Appeals 3rd Cir., US Ct. Appeals 4th Cir., US Dist. Ct. Ea. Dist. Pa. Assoc. Duane Morris LLP, Phila., 1977—84, ptnr., 1985—, mem. firm partners bd., 1996—, chair Trial Practice Group, 2002—08, vice chair, 2005—08, chmn., CEO, 2008—. Arbitrator Phila. Stock Exchange; mem. editl. bd. The Legal Intelligencer. Contbr. articles to law jours. Mem. Phila. Vol. Lawyers for the Arts. Mem.: ABA, The Federalist Soc. for Law & Pub. Policy Studies (co-founder & chmn. Phila. Lawyers' Chpt.), Phila. Bar Assn., Pa. Bar Assn. Office: Duane Morris LLP 30 S 17th St Philadelphia PA 19103-4196 Office Phone: 215-979-1124. Office Fax: 215-689-3449. Business E-Mail: soroko@duanemorris.com.*

SOROKOWSKI, ANDREW DENNIS, lawyer, historian; b. Hartford, Conn., Aug. 29, 1950; s. George Wsewolod and Nadia Sorokowski; m. Oksana Bachynska, Mar. 5, 1993. BA, U. Calif., Berkeley, 1972; MA, Harvard U., 1975; JD, Hastings Coll., 1979; PhD, U. London, 1991. Bar: Calif. 1980. Mem. rsch. staff Keston Coll., Kent, U.K., 1984—87; dir. rsch. and documentation Archdiocese of L'viv, Rome, 1989—90; atty. Jaffe, Trutanich, Scatena & Blum, San Francisco, 1990—93; mng. editor, rsch. assoc. Harvard Ukrainian Rsch. Inst., Cambridge, Mass.,

1993—97; instr. St. Basil Coll., Stamford, Conn., 1998—99; adj. lectr. U. Mass., Boston, 1999—2000; hist. rsch. specialist U.S. Dept. Justice, Washington, 2000—. Editor: A Millennium of Christian Culture in Ukraine, 1988; co-editor: A Thousand Years of Christianity in Ukraine, 1988. Sec. Shevchenko Sci. Soc., Washington, 2001; bd. dirs. The Washington Group, 2001. Grantee, Internat. Rsch. Exchg. Bd., Poland, 1988. Mem.: Am. Cath. Hist. Assn., Am. Assn. Ukrainian Studies. Office: US Dept Justice ENRD-EDS PO Box 23986 Washington DC 20026-3986

SOROKULOVA, IRYNA, microbiologist, educator; b. Kiev, Ukraine, June 3, 1949; d. Boris Kalmanovsky and Varvara Khomenko; m. Valeriy Sorokulov, Aug. 10, 1973; 1 child, Volodymyr Sorokulov. Degree summa cum laude, Kiev U., 1971; PhD, Inst. Microbiology and Virology, Kiev, 1983, DSc, 1999. Cert. WHO, 1998. Asst. prof. Inst. Microbiology and Virology, 1974—91, assoc. prof., 1991—2000, prof., 2000—02; vis. prof. Auburn U., Ala., 2002—07, rsch. prof., 2007—. Head dept. Com. Biol. Products, Kiev, 1996—2002. Author: (book) Guide for Isolation and Identification of Bacteria of the Bacillus Genus from Human and Animals, Probiotic Subalin — New Approach to Treatment of Bacterial and Viral Infections; contbr. articles to numerous profl. jours. Recipient State prize, Ukraine Sci. and Tech., Govt. of Ukraine, 1995, Cert. of Recognition, Ministry of Health Ukraine, 2001, Mechnikov's prize, NAS Ukraine, 2002; grantee, Ukrainian Ministry of Sci. and Tech., 1997—98, NIH, 2003—05. Russian Orthodox. Achievements include patents for biosporin for prophylaxis and treatment of human enteric diseases; method of correction of vaginal microflora; method of cubiotic Biosporin production; probiotic preparation with complex activity; bacillus licheniformis strain with antiviral and antibacterial activity; souche bacillus subtilis CU1, son utilization comme agent immunomodulateur du systeme immunitaire et vaccin vivant recombinant contre Helicobacter pylori la contenant; method for enhancing the efficacy of antitumor vaccine; phage ligand sensor devices and uses theirof; strain of bacillus subtilis exhibiting the antiviral and antibacterial activity. Avocation: travel. Office: Auburn Univ 109 Greene Hall Auburn AL 36849 Business E-Mail: sorokib@auburn.edu.

SOROS, GEORGE, hedge fund manager, entrepreneur, philanthropist; b. Budapest, Hungary, Aug. 12, 1930; arrived in US, 1956; s. Tivadar and Elisabeth (Szucs) Soros; m. Annaliese Witschak, Sept. 17, 1960 (div. June 1983); children: Robert, Andrea, Jonathan; m. Susan Weber, June 19, 1983 (div.); children: Alexander, Gregory. BS, London Sch. Econs., 1952; D. Civil Law (hon.), U. Oxford, Eng., 1980; LLD (hon.), New Sch. for Social Rsch., NYC, 1990; LHD (hon.), Yale U., New Haven, 1991; degree (hon.), U. Bologna, Italy, 1995, Corvinus U. Budapest. Arbitrage trader F.M. Mayer, NYC, 1956-59; analyst Wertheim & Co., NYC, 1959-63; v.p. Arnhold & S. Bleichroeder, NYC, 1963-73; founder Soros Fund Mgmt., LLC, NYC, 1969—, chmn., 1996—, co-founder, prin. adv. Quantum Fund, 1970—. Author: The Alchemy of Finance, 1987, 2nd edit, 1994, Opening the Soviet System, 1990, Underwriting Democracy, 1991, Soros on Soros: Staying Ahead of the Curve, 1995, The Crisis of Global Capitalism: Open Society Endangered, 1998, Open Society: Reforming Global Capitalism, 2000, George Soros on Globalization, 2002, The Bubble of America Supremacy: Correcting the Misuse of American Power, 2004, The Age of Fallibility: Consequences of the War on Terror, 2006, The New Paradigm for Financial Markets: The Credit Crisis of 2008 and What It Means, 2008; contbr. articles to mags. and newspapers. Chmn. Open Soc. Fund, 1981; founder, chmn. Open Soc. Inst., 1993—; chmn., founding pres. Ctrl. European U., Budapest, 1991; bd. dirs. Ctr. Am. Progress, Washington, 2003. Recipient Internat. Ctr. Fin. award, Yale Sch. Mgmt., 2000; named one of World's Richest People, Forbes Mag., 1999—, Forbes Richest Americans, 1999—, NY's Influentials, NY Mag., 2006. Mem.: Royal Inst. Internat. Affairs London, Coun. Fgn. Rels. Avocations: tennis, skiing, chess, backgammon. Office: Open Soc Inst 400 W 59th St New York NY 10019 also: Soros Fund Mgmt 888 7th Ave Ste 3300 New York NY 10106-0001 Business E-Mail: gsoros@soros.org.*

SOROSKY, JERI P., academic administrator; b. Chgo. d. Hans S. and Florence J. (Hurwitz) Pakula; m. Gene E. Sorosky; children: Cindi, Dana, Lesli. BA, Roosevelt U., Chgo., 1952; MEd, Fla. Atlantic U., Boca Raton, 1967; EdS, Nova Southeastern U., Ft. Lauderdale, Fla., 1972; EdD, MS, Nova Southeastern U., 1981. Cert. adminstr., supr., media specialist, gifted and elem. educator, Fla. Chairperson Elem. Highland Oaks, North Miami Beach, Fla., 1967-75; mem. faculty gifted program Highland Oaks Gifted Ctr., North Miami Beach, 1975-85; chairperson gifted program Miami (Fla.) Dade C.C., 1985-2000; site adminstr. grad. tchr. edn. program Nova. Southeastern U., Ft. Lauderdale, 1992—2004. Adj. prof. Nova Southeastern U., Ft. Lauderdale, 1979-87, adv. doctoral practicums, 1985-00, cluster coord., 1987-03, admissions com. doctoral programs Tech. and Distance Edn. and Child and Youth Studies, 1996-03, adj. prof. innovative math, 2004-, adj. prof. early childhood, 2004-; chairperson gifted edn. Dade County Schs., Miami, 1990-93; mem. com. State Gifted Task Force, Tallahassee, 1992; presenter in field. Author: GEM Major Module in Gifted Education, 1981, Ideas Unlimited, 1985, Guide for Elementary Educators, 1995, Technology in the Curriculum, 1998; editor: Readings: Gifted Education, 1991, Early Childhood Education, 1982. Project chairperson Kids in Distress, Ft. Lauderdale, 1989. Named Woman of Yr. Bus. Profl. Women, 1985. Mem. Fla. Assn. Gifted (charter, v.p. 1975-97), Nova Southeastern U. Alumni (bd. dirs. 1981-97), AAUW, Phi Delta Kappa (chairperson newsletter 1985-97). Avocations: dance, technology. Office: Nova Southeastern U 1750 NE 167th St North Miami Beach FL 33162-3017 Business E-Mail: jeris@nova.edu.

SOROSKY, SHELDON M., lawyer; b. Chgo., Oct. 28, 1941; s. Saul and Nettie (Gordon) S.; m. Nancy Bowen, Dec. 7, 1984; 1 child, Nicholas. BS, Loyola U., 1964; JD, De Paul U., 1967. Asst. states atty. Cook County States Atty. Office, Chgo., 1967-72; ptnr. Kaplan, Sorosky & Hoffman, Chgo., 1973-84, Kaplan & Sorosky Ltd., Chgo., 1984—. Office: Kaplan & Sorosky 158 W Erie St Chicago IL 60610-3703*

SORRELL, MARTIN STUART, advertising and marketing executive; b. London, Feb. 14, 1945; s. Jack and Sally (Goldberg) Sorrell; m. Sandra Carol Ann Finestone, Apr. 25, 1971; children: Mark, Robert, Jonathan. BA, Cambridge U., Eng., 1966, MA, 1970; MBA, Harvard U., 1968. Cons. Glendinning Assoc., Conn., 1968-70; v.p. Mark McCormack Orgn., London, 1970-74; dir. James Gulliver Assoc., London, 1975-77; group fin. dir. Saatchi & Saatchi, London, 1977-86; group chief exec. WPP Group PLC, London, 1986—. Non-exec. dir. Colefax & Fowler, 1997—; mem. adv. bd. IBM, 1997—; mem. dean's adv. coun. Boston U. Sch. Mgmt., 1998—; bd. dirs. assoc. Harvard Bus. Sch., 1998; judge, panel mem. Inst. Mgmt. Studies; mem. governing body London Bus Sch.; dep. chmn. and mem. adv. bd. Ins. Estudios Superiores Empresa. Trustee U. Cambridge Found. Recipient Alumni Achievement award, Harvard Bus. Sch., 2007; named one of World's 100 Most Influential People, Time Mag., 2005. Avocations: cricket, skiing. Office: WPP Group PLC 27 Farm St London W1X 6RD England E-mail: msorrell@wpp.com.

SORRELL, MICHAEL E., consulting company and hospitality management executive; b. Pasadena, Calif., Mar. 31, 1945; s. James Hendrick Sorrell and Marie Vivian Bristow. AA, Normandale Coll., Bloomingdale, Minn., 1992; BA, Concordia Coll., St. Paul, Minn., 1994. Pres., CEO, owner Daggers/La. Inc., Metairie, La., 1987-89, Mesa Cons. Svcs./MN/Inc., Mpls., 1989-94, Mesa Cons. Svcs., Inc., Las Vegas, Nev., 1994—; pres., CEO, majority ptnr. S&W Hospitality Group, Inc., Las Vegas, 1999—; ptnr., dir. S.R. Owl Inc., 1999—; chmn., CEO Bristow-Norwich Group Internat., Las Vegas, 2000—08; mgr. Bristow-Sorrell Family Trust, 2008; chmn. Bristow-Sorrell Philanthropies, Inc, 2008. With USAF, 1963-69, USN, 1972-89. Mem. VFW, Nat. Assn. Small Bus., Nat. Lic. Beverage Assn., Inst. Mgmt. Cons., Soc. Human Resources Mgmt., Soc. Hospitality Cons., Am. Legion, Fleet Res. Assn., Navy League US, U.S. Naval Inst., Amateur Athletic Union of U.S., Marines' Meml. Club, Victory Svcs. Club. Roman Catholic. Avocations: golf, hiking, tennis. Office: Bristow-Norwich Group Internat 3888 W Sahara Ave Ste 33 Las Vegas NV 89102-0505 Office Phone: 702-364-0989. Business E-Mail: mesaconsultant@aol.com, bristownorwich1@aol.com.

SORRELL, ROZLYN, singer, actress, theater director, educator; b. Bklyn. d. Nathaniel Otis and Cupid Viola (Logan) S. BA in Theatre, CUNY, 1976, MS in Edn., 1985. Cert. tchr. Calif., NY. Tchr. LA Unified Sch. Dist., 1997, Sylvan Learning Ctr., LA, 1998, Westmark Sch., Encino, Calif., 2000, Achievement Sch., Raleigh, NC, 2002, Easter Seals UCP, NC, 2006. Bus. cons., LA, 1989—; voice tchr., LA, 1992—; mem. Albert McNeil Jubilee Singers, LA, 1994—2000. Actress various TV programs, commls., stage prodn. and films, 1986—; soloist Temple of Music and Art, Tucson, 1990, El San Juan (PR) Hotel, 1985, Hour of Power, Glory of Christmas, Glory of Easter, Garden Grove, Calif., 1994—, Miyazaki Civic Culture Hall, Japan, 1996, Anaheim Pond, Calif., 1997, Honolulu Symphony, 1998, Hollywood Bowl, Calif., 1998, Gospel Recording Artist, 2000, Harris Teeter Harvest Festival, Raleigh Conv. Ctr., 2004, Carolina Theatre, Durham, NC, 2005, Spiritual Awakening, WRAL-TV, NC, 2004, Pops in the Park, Regency Theatre, Cary, NC, 2004, 05, 06, Summerfest, Koka Booth Amphitheater, Cary, NY,2008, African Am. Cultural Ctr., Raleigh, NC, 2004, Greensboro Coliseum, 2005, Progress Energy Ctr. Performing Arts, Meymandi Concert Hall, Raleigh, NC, 2006, 07, 08, Mint Raleigh NC 2008, NC Fairgrounds, 2006, Hayes Barton Baptist, Raleigh, NC, 2007, 09, Garner Hist. Auditorium, NC, 2007, 2008; guest artist, soloist NC Symphony, 2006, 08, 1st Annual Gospel Christians Spectacular NC Symphony, 2007, Blues in the Night Summerfest Koka Booth Amphitheatre, 2008; soloist NC Theatre Cabaret Night, 2008, CMP Gospel Showcase, Dallas Conv. Ctr., 2007; featured soloist Artsplosure Moore Square Park, Raleigh, 2007; solo concert Where The Spirit Leads, Sampson Ctr. Stage, Clinton, NC, 2008; dir. Storms of Life, 2005, Country Club NC (Pinehurst), Clover Sch. Dist. Audition Clover (SC), Hampton St. Audition Waterboro (SC), 2009 Mem. AFTRA, SAG, Actors Equity Assn, Country Club NC (Pinehurst), Clover Sch. Dist. Audition Clover (SC), Hampton St. Audition Waterboro (SC), Theater Pk. Raleigh, NC, Performing Arts Exchange Juried Showed Roper Performing Art Ctr. Norfolk, Va. Avocations: dance, walking, theater, exercise. Office: 3745 Junction Blvd Raleigh NC 27603 Office Phone: 866-686-0713, 919-665-4200. Personal E-mail: rozlyn@rozlynsorrell.com. Business E-Mail: info@vocalprecision.com.

SORRELL, WILLIAM H., state attorney general; b. Burlington, Vt., Mar. 9, 1947; s. Marshal Thomas and Esther Sorrell; children: McKenzie, Thomas. AB, U. Notre Dame, 1970; JD, Cornell U., 1974. Dep. state's atty. Chittenden County State of Vt., 1975—77, state's atty. Chittenden County, 1977—78, 1989—92; ptnr. McNeil, Murray & Sorrell, 1978—89, sec. adminstrn., 1992—97; atty. gen. State of Vt., 1997—. Pres. United Cerebral Palsy Vt.; sec. Vt. Coalition Handicapped; bd. dirs. Winooski Valley Pk. Dist., Am. Legacy Found. Mem.: Nat. Assn. Attys. Gen. (past chmn., past pres.). Democrat. Office: Office Atty Gen 109 State St Montpelier VT 05609-1001 Office Phone: 802-828-3173. Business E-Mail: mkswanson@atg.state.vt.us.*

SORRELLS, FRANK DOUGLAS, retired mechanical engineer; b. Toccoa, Ga., May 14, 1931; s. Ralph Price and Ila B. (Freeman) S.; m. Alma M. West, June 19, 1954; 1 child, Desiree G. BSME, U. Tenn., 1957, MS, 1968. Registered profl. engr., Tenn. Chief engr. Formex Co., Greeneville, Tenn., 1960-67; exec. v.p. Charles Lee Assoc., Knoxville, Tenn., 1967-76; pvt. practice consulting engr. Knoxville, Tenn., 1976-78, 83-88; dir. engring. Cole Nat. Corp., Knoxville, Tenn., 1978-83; mgr. tech. transfer Valmet Paper Machinery div. Valmet-Enerdry, Knoxville, Tenn., 1988-93; pres. PEPE Software LLC, Knoxville, Tenn., 1996-98. Cons., Knoxville, 1976—; mem. Advanced Toroidal Facility Design Team, cons. Oak Ridge (Tenn.) Nat. Lab., 1984-85. Inventor, patentee of 8 patents and co-inventor, patentee of 14 patents in fields of filtration, web processing, plastic forming and lens processing; developer and author copyrighted technical software. Staff sgt. USAF, 1950—54. Mem.: ASME (Energy Resources Rsch. award 1987), Tenn. Soc. Profl. Engrs. Achievements include patents for on fields of filtration; on web processing; on plastic forming; on lens processing; developer and author copyrighted technical software version 5.0. Avocations: fishing, boating. Home: 8881 Lennox View Way Knoxville TN 37923-6042 Office Phone: 865-693-4991. E-mail: fdsorrells@hotmail.com.

SORRELS, CAROLYN JEAN, assistant to CIO; b. Waco, Tex., Aug. 20, 1953; d. Carroll Eugene and Wincie Iona Cannon; children: Christopher Jason, Robyn Lynn. BBA magna cum laude, Davenport U., 2000; MS, Ctrl. Mich. U., 2002; degree in Edn., U. Cambridge, 2003; student in Ednl. Adminstrn., Tex. A&M U., 2006—. Adj. instr. North Harris Montgomery C.C. Dist., Tomball, Tex., 1991—99; office mgr. Profl. Counseling Ctr., Lapeer, Mich., 2001—03; asst. to chief investment officer Baylor U., Waco, Tex., 2003—. Vol. Baylor U., Waco, Tex., 2003—06. Mem.: Am. Assn. C.C.s, Kappa Delta Pi (assoc.). Republican. Methodist. Avocations: reading, walking, gardening. Home: PO Box 463 Waco TX 76703 Office: Baylor University One Bear Place 97030 Waco TX 76798 Office Fax: 254-710-8798. Business E-Mail: carolyn_sorrels@baylor.edu.

SORRENTI, MARIO, photographer; b. Naples, Italy, 1971; arrived in US, 1981; B in Social Anthropology, Edinburgh Univ. Fashion photographer French, Italian Vogue, W, V, Vanity Fair, Harper's Bazaar, Arena Homme, mags.; photographer, advt. campaigns Dolce & Gabbana, Giorgio Armani, Hermes, Jil Sander, Yves Saint Laurent, Prada, Lancome, Calvin Klein, others. Dir.: (music video) Daughters by John Mayer, (commercials) Calvin Klein, Davidoff, Lancome, Benetton; Exhibited in group shows at Fashioning Fiction, Mus. Modern Art, NYC, 2004, Face of Fashion, Wolfson Gallery, Nat. Portrait Gallery, 2007. Studio: Art Partner FI 15 155 Sixth Ave New York NY 10013

SORSBY, JAMES LARRY, home building company executive; b. Houston, May 31, 1955; s. J.B. Jr. and Viola (Lueckemeyer) S.; m. Terry Prince, July 28, 1984; children: Carson Drew, Cameron Brent. BBA, Stephen F. Austin State U., 1977. Loan officer 1st Mortgage Co. Tex., Houston, 1977-82; pres. The MortgageBanque, Inc., Houston, 1982-88; sr. v.p., treas. Hovnanian Enterprises, Inc., Red Bank, NJ, 1991—96, sr. v.p., CFO, treas., 1996—2000, exec. v.p., CFO, 2000—. Bd. dirs. Am. S.W. Fin. Corp., Phoenix. Office: Hovnanian Enterprises Inc 110 W Front St Red Bank NJ 07701

SORSTOKKE, ELLEN KATHLEEN, marketing executive, educator; b. Seattle, Mar. 31, 1954; d. Harold William and Carrol Jean (Russ) Sorstokke. MusB with distinction, U. Ariz., 1976; postgrad., UCLA Extension, 1979-83, L.A. Valley Coll., 1984-85, Juilliard Extension, fall 1987, U. Calif. Berkeley Extension, 1992-93. Pvt. practice music tchr., Tucson, 1975—77, Whiteriver, Ariz., 1977—78, LA, 1980—85, SI, NYC, 1986—89; music tchr. Eloy Elem. Schs., Ariz., 1976-77, Whiteriver Pub. Schs., Ariz., 1977-78; svc. writer, asst. svc. mgr. Alfa of Santa Monica, Calif., 1978-79; purchasing agt. Advance Machine Corp., LA, 1979-80; asst. mgr. Atlantic Nuc. Svcs., Gardena, Calif., 1980-81; mgr. Blue Lady's World Music Ctr., LA, 1981-83; instrument specialist Baxter-Northup Music Co., Sherman Oaks, Calif., 1983-85; dir. mktg. Mandolin Bros., Ltd., SI, N.Y., 1985-89; product mgr. Gibson Guitar Corp., Nashville, 1989; sales mgr. Saga Musical Instruments, South San Francisco, Calif., 1990-91, mktg. dir., 1991-95, mktg. strategist, 2002—. Freelance mktg. cons., S.I., Foster City, Atlanta, 1986—; freelance cons. www.fussycuts.com, 2002; music cons. 20th Century Fox, L.A., 1984; freelance music copyist and orchestrator, Tucson, L.A., N.Y.C., 1972-89; freelance graphic designer and advt., N.Y.C., S.I., Foster City, Atlanta, 1986—. Contbr. articles to profl. jours. Campaign worker Richard Jones for Supr., Tucson, 1972; mem., program book designer Marina Del Rey-Westchester Symphony Orch., L.A., 1981-83. Scholar U. Ariz., 1973-76, ASCAP scholar UCLA, 1980-81. Mem. Tucson Flute Club (publicity chmn. 1974-75, v.p. 1975-76). Republican. Home Phone: 770-932-5281. Personal E-mail: esorstok@bellsouth.net.

SORTE, JOHN FOLLETT, investment firm executive; b. Boston, June 30, 1947; s. Martin Eugene and Elizabeth Foster (Bradley) S.; m. Colleen Sarah Costello, July 28, 1979; children: Bradley Follett, Laura Elizabeth, Kathryn Clare. BAChemE, Rice U., 1969, M in Chem. Engring., 1970; MBA, Harvard U., 1972. Assoc. Shearson Hammill & Co., Inc., NYC, 1972-74; v.p. Shearson Hayden Stone, Inc., NYC, 1974-79; 1st v.p. Shearson Loeb Rhoades, Inc., NYC, 1979-80, Drexel Burnham Lambert, Inc., NYC, 1980-82, mng. dir., 1982-88, exec. v.p., 1989-90, pres., CEO, dir., 1990-92; pres., CEO New Street Capital Corp., NYC, 1992-94; pres. New Street Advisors L.P., NYC, 1994—2001; pres., CEO, dir Morgan Joseph & Co. Inc., NYC, 2001—. Chmn. NY Media Group, Inc., 1995-2001; bd. dirs. Vail Resorts, Inc., Shorts Internat. Ltd. Office: Morgan Joseph & Co Inc 600 Fifth Ave 19th Fl New York NY 10020-2302 E-mail: jsorte@morganjoseph.com.

SORTER, GEORGE HANS, accounting and law educator, consultant; b. Vienna, Dec. 2, 1927; came to U.S., 1938; s. Alfred and Hertha (Kohn) S.; m. Dorienne Lachman, Aug. 18, 1966; children: David, Ivan, Adrienne. Ph.B., U. Chgo., 1953, MBA, 1955, PhD, 1963. C.P.A., N.Y. Instr. U. Chgo., 1955-58, asst. prof., 1959-63, assoc. prof., 1963-65, prof., 1966-74; Vincent C. Ross prof. acctg., prof. of law NYU, 1974—2003, prof. emeritus, 2003—. Arthur Young prof. U. Kans., 1969; Coopers & Lybrand prof. Tuck Sch. Dartmouth Coll., 1982; bd. dirs. NYU Credit Union, 1982-85; dir. Greater N.Y. Savs. Bank, N.Y.C., 1983-97; audit com. City of N.Y., 1985-94. Author: Accounting Theory, 1963, Accounting Thoughts of W.W. Werntz, Boundaries of Accounting Universe, 1978, Relevant Financial Statements, 1978, Financial Accounting: An Events and Cash Flow Approach, 1990, The Mix-Max Co., 1990. Mem. Ill. Sch. Bd. Dist. 233, Flossmoor, 1970-74; bd. dirs. Sch. Emotionally Disturbed Children, Chgo., 1960-74, Renaissance Soc., 1956-74, Found. Acctg. Edn., N.Y.C., 1975-79. Erskine fellow U. Canterbury, 1979 Mem. Am. Acctg. Assn. (v.p 1980-81 Outstanding Acctg. Educator), N.Y. State Soc. C.P.A.s (dir. 1980-82), Am. Inst. C.P.A.s, Fin. Acctg. Standard Adv. Com. Home: 375 S End Ave Apt 15E New York NY 10280 Office: 415 Vanderbilt NYU 40 Washington Sq S New York NY 10012 Business E-Mail: g.sorter@stern.nyu.edu.

SORTLAND, PAUL ALLAN, lawyer; b. Powers Lake, ND, July 30, 1953; s. Allan Berdette and Eunice Elizabeth (Nystuen) S.; m. Carolyn Faye Anderson, June 23, 1979; children: Joseph Paul, Martha Marie, Nicholas John, Benjamin David. BA, St. Olaf Coll., 1975; JD, U. Minn., 1978. Bar: Minn. 1978, N.D. 1981, U.S. Dist. Ct. Minn. 1979, U.S. Dist. Ct. N.D. 1980, U.S. Ct. Appeals (8th cir.) 1987, U.S. Supreme Ct. 1991. Assoc. Alderson, Ondov, Leonard & Sween, PA, Austin, Minn., 1978-80, Qualley, Larson & Jones, Fargo, N.D., 1980-83; ptnr. Holand, Lochow & Sortland, Fargo, 1983-85; pres. Sortland Law Office, Fargo, 1985-88; ptnr. Messerli & Kramer, Mpls., 1988-92; Sortland Law Office, Mpls., 1993—. Adj. prof. bus. law Moorhead State U., 1987. Mem. ATLA, ND Bar Assn., Minn. Bar Assn. (cert. civil trial specialist), Kiwanis, Million Dollar Advocates Forum, Upper Lake Minnetonka Yacht Club, Gamma Eta Gamma. Lutheran. Home: 120 Quebec Ave S Minneapolis MN 55426-1509 Home Phone: 763-542-1907; Office Phone: 612-375-0400. Business E-Mail: sortland@sortland.com.

SORVINO, MIRA, actress; b. Tenafly, NJ, Sept. 28, 1967; d. Paul Sorvino and Lorraine Davis; m. Christopher Backus, June 11, 2004; children: Mattea Angel, Johnny Christopher King, Holden Paul Terry. BA in Asian Studies, Harvard U., 1990. Actress (films) The Obit Writer, 1993, Amongst Friends, 1993, Quiz Show, 1994, Barcelona, 1994, The Dutch Master, 1994, Mighty Aphrodite, 1995 (Acad. award for Best Supporting Actress, Golden Globe award for Best Supporting Actress), Blue in the Face, 1995, Beautiful Girls, 1996, Tales of Erotica, 1996, Sweet Nothing, 1996, Tarantella, 1996, Romy and Michele's High School Reunion, 1997, Mimic, 1997, The Replacement Killers, 1998, Lulu on the Bridge, 1998, Too Tired to Die, 1998, Free Money, 1998, At First Sight, 1999, Summer of Sam, 1999, The Grey Zone, 2001, The Triumph of Love, 2001, WiseGirls, 2002, Semana Santa, 2002, Gods and Generals, 2003, The Final Cut, 2004, Reservation Road, 2007, Leningrad, 2007, (TV films) Parallel Lives, 1994, The Second Greatest Story Ever Told, 1994, Jake's Women, 1996, Norma Jean & Marilyn, 1996 (Golden Globe award nominee), The Great Gatsby, 2000, (TV series) House, 2008, (TV miniseries) The Buccaneers, 1995, Human Trafficking, 2005 (Golden Globe award nominee), The Last Templar, 2009, TV appearances include Guiding Light, 1991, Swans Crossing, 1992, 1995, Will & Grace, 2003. Office: c/o Untitled Entertainment 1801 Century Park E Ste 700 Los Angeles CA 90067*

SORVINO, PAUL, actor; b. NYC, 1939; Attended, Am. Musical and Dramatic Acad. Artistic dir. Am. Stage Co., Teaneck, NJ 1986-90. N.Y.C. stage debut in Bajour, 1964; actor in (plays) including The Baker's Wife, Mating Dance, Skyscraper, That Championship Season, King Lear, An American Millionaire, For My Last Number, We'll Get By, Philemon, (films) The Gambler, 1970, Where's Poppa, 1970, Panic in Needle Park, 1971, Cry Uncle, Made for Each Other, 1971, The Day of the Dolphin, 1973, A Touch of Class, 1973, I Will, I Will... For Now, 1976, Oh God!, 1977, The Brink's Job, 1978, Shoot It, Black, Shoot It, Blue, Slow Dancing in the Big City, 1978, The Bloodbrothers, 1979, Lost and Found, 1979, Cruising, 1980, Reds, 1981, That Championship Season, 1982, I, The Jury, 1982, Off the Wall, Turk 1982, A Fine Mess, 1985, The Stuff, 1986, Vasectomy, 1986, Dick Tracy, 1990, Goodfellas,

1990, The Rocketeer, 1991, The Firm, 1993, Nixon, 1995, Romeo and Juliet, 1996, Love Is All There Is, 1996, Escape Clause, 1996, Dog Watch, 1996, Love is All There Is, 1996, Romeo and Juliet, 1996, Men with Guns, 1997, Money Talks, 1997, American Perfekt, 1997, Most Wanted, 1997, Bulworth, 1998, Knock Off, 1998, Ringside, 1999, That Championship Season, 1999, Prince of Central Park, 1999, Harlem Aria, 1999, Goodnight Joseph Parker, 1999, Dead Broke, 1999, Amati Girls, 2000, Family Man, 2000, Longshot, 2000, Perfume, 2001, See Spot Run, 2001, Plan B, 2001, Witches to the North, 2001, Rhode Island Blue, 2001, Irishman: The Legend of Danny Greene, 2001, Ciao America, 2002, Hey Arnold! (voice), 2002, The Cooler, 2003, Mambo Italiano, 2002, Goodnight, Joseph Parker, 2004, Mr. 3000, 2004, The Wild Stallion, 2006, Mr. Fix It, 2006, Greetings from the Shore, 2007, Last Hour, 2008, Carnera: The Walking Mountain, 2008, Repo! The Genetic Opera, 2008; (TV miniseries) Seventh Avenue, 1977, (TV movies) Tell Me Where it Hurts, 1974, It Couldn't Happen to a Nicer Guy, 1974, Dummy, 1979, A Question of Honor, 1982, Chiefs, 1983, My Mother's Secret Life, 1984, With Intent to Kill, 1984, Surviving, 1985, Betrayed by Innocence, 1986, Don't Touch My Daughter, 1991, Perry Mason: The Case of the Wicked Wives, 1993, Parallel Lives, 1994, The Art of the Cigar (host), 1996, Joe Torre: Curveballs Along the Way, 1997, That Championship Season, 1999, The Thin Blue Lie, 2000, Mafia Doctor, 2003; (TV series) We'll Get By, 1975, Bert D'Angelo/Superstar, 1976, The Oldest Rookie, 1987, Law and Order, 1991-92, Star Trek: The Next Generation (guest appearance), 1994, That's Life, 2000-02. Office: Gersh Agy c/o Larry Taube 232 N Canon Dr Beverly Hills CA 90210-5302*

SOSA, ERNEST, philosopher, educator; b. Cardenas, Cuba, June 17, 1940; s. Ernesto and Maria (Garriga) S.; m. Sara Mercedes, Dec. 21, 1961; children: E. David, Adrian J. BA, U. Miami, 1961; MA, U. Pitts., 1962, PhD, 1964. Instr. U. Western Ont., London, Canada, 1963-64, asst. prof., 1966-67; instr. U. Pitts., 1964; postdoctoral fellow Brown U., Providence, 1964-66, asst. prof. to full prof., 1967-74, chmn. of philosophy, 1970-76, full prof., 1974—, Romeo Elton prof., 1981—2007; prof. Rutgers U., 2007—08, bd. Govs. prof., 2008. Vis. prof. U. Miami, 1970, Nat. U. Mexico, 1979, 80, 81, Harvard U., Cambridge, Mass., 1982, U. Salamanca, 1995, 98, Oxford U., 1997; disting. vis. prof. Rutgers U., 1998-2007; John Locke lectr. Oxford U, 2005; co-chair program com. 20th World Congress of Philosophy, 1998. Author: Knowledge in Perspective, 1991, A Virtue Epistemology, 2007, reflective Knowledge, 2009; gen. editor book series, Cambridge Univ. Press, 1990—2002, Blackwell Publishers, 1991—; editor Philosophy and Phenomenol. Rsch.; editor: Nous; contbr. numerous articles to profl. jours. Grantee NSF, 1970-72, Exxon Ednl. Found., 1980-82; recipient Sr. fellowship NEH, 1988-89. Mem. Am. Acad. Arts and Scis., Am. Philos. Assn. (sec.-treas. 1974-82, chair internat. coop. com. 1984-89, ea. divsn. rep. 1995-98, pres. ea. divsn. 2004-05, v.p. ea. divsn. 2003-04 bd. chair 2005—), Am. Coun. Learned Socs./Soviet Acad. Commn., Internat. Fedn. Philos. Soc. (steering com. 1988-98, v.p. 1988-93), Institut Internat. de Philosophie (exec. com. 1993-96). Business E-Mail: sosa@brown.edu.

SOSA, JORGE LUIS, surgeon; s. Eduardo and Elsa Sosa; children: Sarah Elizabeth, Gladys Michelle. MD, U. South Fla., Tampa, 1987. Board Certified in Surgical Critical Care Am. Bd. of Surgery, 1994. Asst. prof. of surgery U. Miami Jackson Meml. Hosp., Fla., 1993—95; trauma attending Delray Hosp., Delray Beach, Fla., 1995—2002; surgeon, pres. Laparoscopic Inst. of South Fla., Hialeah, 1995—. Dir. bariatric surgery Hialeah Hosp., Fla., 2002—05, Palmetto Gen. Hosp., Hialeah, Fla., 2005—. Fellow: Am. Coll. Surgeons; mem.: Am. Soc. for Bariatric Surgery. Conservative. Office: Laparoscopic Inst S Fla 3499 W 4th Ave Ste 201 Hialeah FL 33012 Office Fax: 305-863-3802.

SOSA, JULIE A., medical educator; AB, Princeton U., NJ, 1988; MA, U. Oxford, Eng., 1990; MD, Johns Hopkins U. Sch. Medicine, Balt., 1994. Diplomate in surgery Am. Bd. Surgery, 2004. Asst. prof. surgery and clin. epidemiology Yale U. Sch. Medicine, New Haven, 2002—08, assoc. prof. surgery, 2008—. Mem., editl. bd. Jour. Clin. Endocrinology and Metabolism, 2009—. Recipient Dennis Jahnigen Career Devel. award, Am. Geriat. Soc., 2006—09, Clin. and Cmty. Health Issues Program award, Patrick and Catherine Weldon Donaghue Med. Rsch. Found., 2005—09, Rsch. Career Devel. award, Pepper Ctr., Yale U. Sch. Medicine, 2005—07, John G. Haddad, Jr. award, Paget Found., 2004—05. Fellow: ACS; mem.: Soc. Surg. Oncology, Assn. Acad. Surgery (J. J. Roslyn Faculty Rsch. award 2005—09), New Eng. Surg. Soc., Soc. U. Surgeons, Am. Assn. Endocrine Surgeons (exec. coun. 2008).

SOSEMAN, ELEANOR DOUGLASS, volunteer; b. Creston, Iowa, May 7, 1930; d. John Wayne and Ruby Neill Douglass; m. Floyd William Soseman, Jr., Aug. 17, 1952 (dec. Aug. 2003); children: Douglass John, Amy Lynn Stover, Elizabeth Kistenmacher, Thomas William. BA, Grinnell Coll., Iowa, 1952. Past mem. We. Iowa Tech. Adv. Bd., Sioux City. Co-editor: Holstein Centennial Book, 1982. Active Girl Scouts USA, 1938—; trustee Stubbs Meml. Libr., Holstein, 1959—94; vol. Holstein Cmty. Betterment, 1984—87. Recipient Gov.'s Leadership award, Planning Coun., Holstein, 1982, Gov.'s Vol. award, Gov.'s Office, Des Moines, 2002. Mem.: AAUW, United Meth. Women, Gen. Fedn. Women Clubs, Philanthropic Ednl. Orgn. Sisterhood. Democrat. United Methodist. Avocations: reading, doll collecting, travel. Home: 510 E 2nd Box 470 Holstein IA 51025 Office: Agnew-Soseman Ins Holstein IA 51025

SOSLAU, GERALD, biochemistry professor; b. NYC, Jan. 22, 1944; married. PhD, U. Rochester, NY, 1970. Prof., sr assoc dean Drexel U. Coll Medicine, Phila., 1975—. Contbr. chapters to books. HCOP grant, US Dept. Health and Human Svc., 2005—07. Mem.: Am. Assoc. U. Prof. (pres. state divsn. 2004—06). Achievements include patents for several dealing with human platelets. Office: Drexel Univ Coll Medicine 245 N 15th St MS 344 Philadelphia PA 19102

SOSNE, GABRIEL, ophthalmologist, educator; b. Phila., June 10, 1967; s. Zelman and Eleanor Sosne; m. Aliza Sosne, Dec. 27, 1989; children: Elchanan, Betzalel, Ariel, Eitan, Adina, Hadassah, Batsheva. MD, Albert Einstein Coll. Medicine, Bronx, NY, 1994. Diplomate Am. Bd. Ophthalmology, 2001. Sr. staff ophthalmologist Henry Ford Hosp., Detroit, 1999—2002; assoc. prof. Wayne State U. Sch. Medicine, Detroit, 2002—. Bd. mem. Yeshiva Beth Yehudah, Southfield, Mich., 2002—. Rsch. grant, NIH, 2000—06. Fellow: Am. Acad. Ophthalmology. Achievements include research in corneal wound healing. Avocation: exercise. Office: Kresge Eye Inst 4717 St Antoine Detroit MI 48201 Office Fax: 313-577-3125. Business E-Mail: gsosne@med.wayne.edu.

SOSNOW, LAWRENCE IRA, health care company executive; b. Newark, Mar. 7, 1935; s. Emanuel and Edith (Grunt) S.; m. Ellen N. Rosenthal, May 30, 1965; children: Peter, Meg. BBA, Upsala Coll., East Orange, NJ, 1957; postgrad., NYU Grad. Sch. Bus., 1958. Pres. Sosnow & Co., Inc., Newark, 1960-66; chmn., pres. Spade & Archer, NYC, 1966-69; chmn. Gilbert Youth Research, NYC, 1968-69; pres. MIND, Inc., NYC, 1969-74, vice chmn., 1974-75; chmn. Patient Care Inc., West Orange, NJ, 1975-95, vice-chmn., 1995; dir. Home Health Agy. Assembly of N.J., 1985-88; chmn. I.V. Therapy Products, Inc., 1989-92; founder, chmn. SeniorBridge, NYC, 2000—, pres., CEO, 2000—07. Mem. N.Y. State Dept. Health Adv. Com. on Licensure, 1985-86, Home Care Assn. N.Y. Legis. Commn., 1992—. Bd. govs. Boy's Athletic League, N.Y.C., 1969-85, United Cerebral Palsy No. N.J., 1983-86, McBurney Sch., 1985-86. Served with AUS, 1957, 61-62. Mem. Nat. Assn. Home Care (dir. 1979-82) Office: 845 Third Ave New York NY 10022 Office Phone: 212-994-6100.*

SOSOWER, MARK LAWRENCE, educator; b. Teaneck, NJ, Apr. 26, 1949; s. Leon Sosower and Evelyn Malek; m. Mary Julia Linehan, June 15, 1980; children: Deborah Linehan, Robert Linehan. PhD, NYU, 1981. Vis. lectr. NC State U., Raleigh, 1982—85, disting. prof. Author: (monograph) Palatinus Graecus 88 and the Manuscript Tradition of Lysias. Home: 3437 Dixon Rd Durham NC 27707 Office: NC State Univ FLL 101 Lampe Dr Raleigh NC 27695 Business E-Mail: mlsfll@unity.ncsu.edu.

SOSTARICH, MARK EDWARD, lawyer; b. Milw., Apr. 10, 1953; s. Edward Michael and Sophia (Hibler) S.; m. Karen Sue Baranek, June 12, 1976; children: Samantha Nicole, Alex Edward. BA with distinction, U. Wis., Madison, 1975, JD cum laude, 1978. Bar: Wis. 1978, U.S. Dist. Ct. (ea. and we. dists.) Wis. 1978, U.S. Trademark Trial and Appeal Bd. 1995. Assoc. Godfrey & Kahn, Milw., 1978-84, ptnr., 1984-96, Petrie & Stocking SC, Milw., 1997—2004; pvt. practice Elkhorn, 2004—. Editor-in-chief U. Wis. Law Rev., 1978, mem., 1977. Mem. bd. visitors U. Wis., Madison, 1983-88; commr. South Milw. Housing Authority, 1985-86; mem. South Milw. Fire and Police Commn., 1986-92, sec., 1987-91, pres., 1991-92; mem. Wis. Elections Bd., 1987-95, vice chmn., 1990, chmn., 1991; mem. Dem. Nat. Com., 1993, 1995-97; mem. platform and resolutions com. Wis. Dem. Party, 1984-97, 1st vice chmn., 1984, chmn., 1985-97; chmn. Wis. Dem. Party, 1995-97; mem. Assn. State Dem. Chairs, 1993, 95-97; chmn. Milw. County Dem. Party, 1986-97, v.p., 2001, pres., 2001-04; mem., usher, HS Sunday sch. tchr., chmn. organ fundraising com. Trinity Luth. Ch., South Milw.; bd. dirs. Arthritis Found. Wis., 2000-03. Mem.: ABA, Walworth County Bar Assn., 7th Cir. Ct. Appeals Bar Assn., Milw. Bar Assn., Wis. Bar Assn. Avocations: politics, photography, art. Home: 1785 Tamarack St South Milwaukee WI 53172-1048 Office: 6 South Church St Elkhorn WI 53121 Office Phone: 262-723-5041. Personal E-mail: msostarich@charterinternet.com.

SOSTEK, BRUCE STEVEN, lawyer; b. Boston, Dec. 16, 1953; s. Alan Bernard Sostek and Cecily Sostek Sallen; m. Joan C. Sprince, 1990; children: Alan Brewer, Rebecca Hali. BA, Union Coll., Schenectady, NY, 1975; MA, SUNY, Albany, 1977; JD, Emory U., Atlanta, 1981. Bar: U.S. Supreme Ct. 2003, Tex. 1981, Mass. 1989, D.C. 2004, N.Y. 2006, U.S. Dist. Ct. (no. dist.) Tex. 1981, U.S. Dist. Ct. (ea. dist.) Tex. 1993, U.S. Dist. Ct. (so. dist.) Tex. 1993, U.S. Dist. Ct. (we. dist.) Tex. 1993, lic.: U.S. Internat. Trade Commn., Washington (United States International Trade Commission) 1990, bar: U.S. Ct. Appeals (5th cir.) La. 1989, U.S. Ct. Appeals (fed. cir.) D.C. 1991, U.S. Ct. Appeals (6th cir.) Ohio 2001. Sr. ptnr. Thompson & Knight LLP, Dallas, 1981—. Mem. exec. com. Inst. Law and Tech., Ctr. Am. and Internat. Law, Dallas. Author: Doing Business in Texas (Intellectual Property Section), 2003. Named one of Best Lawyers in Dallas, D Mag., 2003, 2004, 2005, 2006, Tex. Super Lawyers, Tex. Monthly Mag., 2003, 2004, 2005, 2006, Am.'s Leading Lawyers for Bus., Chambers & Partners, Chambers USA, 2004, 2005, Best Lawyers in Am., Woodard White Best Lawyers in Am., 2005, 2006, The 500 Leading Lawyers in Am., The Lawdragon 500, 2006. Fellow: Tex. Bar Found., Dallas Bar Found.; mem.: ABA, State Bar Tex., Fed. Cir. Bar Assn., Am. Intellectual Property Lawyers Assn. Avocations: fishing, sailing, hockey, home repairs. Office: Thompson & Knight LLP One Arts Plz 1722 Routh St Ste 1500 Dallas TX 75201 Office Fax: 214-880-3252; Home Fax: 214-880-3252. Business E-Mail: bruce.sostek@tklaw.com.

SOSTILIO, ROBERT FRANCIS, office equipment marketing consultant; b. Boston, Nov. 17, 1942; s. Natale J. and Louise Sostilio; m. Gail Marie McGuinness, Apr. 17, 1966. Student, U. Maine, 1960—61, Broward Jr. Coll., Ft. Lauderdale, 1967—70, Miami-Dade Jr. Coll., 1979. Product assurance engr. Saxon Copystatics, Miami, Fla., 1970-77; internat. svc. mgr. Saxon Export Corp., Miami, 1977-80; nat. svc. mgr. Cybernet Internat., Warren, N.J., 1980-81; mgr. nat. copier svc. Monroe Systems for Bus., Morris Plains, N.J., 1981-82; nat. OEM mgr. Panasonic Indsl. Co., Secaucus, N.J., 1982-86; assoc. dir. copier rsch. Dataquest, San Jose, Calif., 1987-90; mgr. product program Ricoh Corp., West Caldwell, N.J., 1986-87, dir. copier mktg., 1990-94, dir. strategic planning, 1994-96; group svc. dir. converging digital peripherals Cap Ventures, 1996—2000; pres., CEO Sostilio and Assocs. Internat. Inc., Ocala, Fla., 2002—. Editor: (newsletter) Multifunctionality, 1987, Color Copiers, 1989. Block capt. Meadow Ridge Civic Assn., Basking Ridge, NJ, 1985—87; sgt.-at-arms UNICO Nat., San Jose, 1990. With USN, 1964—67. Roman Catholic. Avocations: woodworking, home remodeling, dog breeding, travel, cooking. Office: Sostilio & Assocs Internat PO Box 830190 Ocala FL 34483 Office Phone: 352-624-2625. E-mail: sostilio@flash.net.

SOSTMAN, DIRK, physician, clinical researcher, medical educator; b. NYC, Nov. 20, 1948; s. Henry and Theodora (Slokker) S.; m. Maria Preka, Sept. 1, 2003; 1 child Erik Alexandros. MD, Yale University, New Haven, 1977. Diplomate Am. Bd. Radiology, Nat. Bd. Med. Examiners. Intern and resident Yale-New Haven Hosp., 1977—82; prof., chair Weill Med. Coll. Cornell U., NYC, 1995—2005, exec. vice dean, 2003—; exec. v.p. The Meth. Hosp., Houston, 2005—; CEO Meth. Physician Orgn., 2006—. Mem. lung scan interpretation panel and nuclear medicine working group Prospective Investigation of Pulmonary Embolism Diagnosis Study, Nat. Heart, Lung and Blood Inst., 1984-88; cons. Fluoromed Pharms, 1988, Am. Cancer Soc., 1992; mem. Duke Comprehensive Cancer Ctr., 1993—; program dir. Duke Winter Imaging Course, 1993-94; vis. prof. U. Pisa, 1993, U. Milan, 1993; dir. Imaging Rsch. Lab. Yale U. Sch. Medicine, 1981-84, dir. MR Imaging, 1983-87; mem. numerous adv. panels. Assoc. editor: Yearbook of Nuclear Medicine, 1984-92; mem. editorial bd.: Investigative Radiology, 1984—, Magnetic Resonance Imaging, 1985—, Jour. Thoracic Imaging, 1985—; manuscript referee; contbr. chpts. to books and numerous articles to profl. jours. Recipient Fales prize Rutgers U., 1972, Dolgan Meml. award Yale U., 1972; Yale U. summer fellowship, 1975, Lamport Biomed. Rsch. award, 1976; Winchester Chest fellow in radiology; grantee in field. Fellow Am. Coll. Chest Physicians, Am. Coll. Radiology; mMem. Fleischner Soc. (George Simon Meml. award 1982, exec. com. 1987-90, mem. Simon award com. 1991—), Soc. MRI (edn. com. 1984-86), Assn. Univ. Radiologists (Pres. 2001, Stauffer award 1988, Stauffer award com. 1983), Radiol. Soc. N.Am., Soc. Thoracic Radiology (founding mem.), Sigma Xi, Phi Beta Kappa, others. leadership in major clinical trials of venous thromboembolism diagnosis. Office: Dunn 200 6565 Fannin St Houston TX 77030 Office Phone: 713-441-2192. Business E-Mail: dsostman@tmhs.org.

SOTELO, EDUARDO (EL PIOLÍN), radio personality; b. Ocotlán, Jalisco, Mexico, 1971; arrived in US, 1986, permanent resident, 1996; Broadcaster local radio stations, Calif., 1991—2003, KSCA FM101.9, LA, 2003—; with Univision Radio, LA, 2003—. Host (radio shows) Piolín por la Mañana, 2003—. Recipient Marconi Radio award for Spanish Format Personality of Yr., Nat. Assn. Broadcasters, 2006, 2008. Achievements include support and organization of demonstrations for immigrants' rights through radio broadcasts. Office: La Nueva #2500 655 N Central Ave Glendale CA 91203 Office Phone: 818-500-4500. Office Fax: 818-500-4550. E-mail: elshowdepiolin@univision.com.

SOTELO-DYNEGA, MARLENE, psychologist, professor; b. Flushing, NY, Sept. 16, 1976; d. Mary and Manuel Sotelo; m. David Dynega, May 26, 2002. BS, Iona Coll., NY, 1998, MA, 2001; D of Psychology, St. John's U., NY, 2007. Cert. sch. psychologist NY, 2003, Bilingual Ext. (Spanish) Sch. Psychologist NY. Sch. psychologist LMT Sch. for Child Devel., Riverdale, NY, 2001—02; bilingual sch. psychologist Port Chester-Rye Union Free Sch. Dist., Port Chester, NY, 2002—07; asst. prof. sch. psychology St. John's U., 2007—. Mem.: APA, NASP, NYASP. Office: St Johns Univ 500 Montauk Hwy Oakdale NY 11769 Business E-Mail: sotelodm@stjohns.edu.

SOTIROPOULOS, CAROL STRAUSS, language educator; b. Newark, July 24, 1950; d. Frederick and Helen May Strauss; m. Theodore Demetrios Sotiropoulos, Apr. 19, 1975; children: Demetrios Frederick, Michael Theodore, Peter Aaron. BA, Clark U., Worcester, Mass., 1972, MA, 1975; PhD, U. Conn., Storrs, 2001. Assoc. prof. Northern Mich. U., Marquette, 2001—. Contbr. chapters to books, articles to profl. jour., monograph. Mem. Marquette Citizens Peace and Justice, 2001, Amnesty Internat. Recipient Outstanding Tchg. award, U. Conn., 1999; grant, Northern Mich. U., 2002, 2005, 2007—08. Mem.: MLA, Women in German, Am. Soc. Eighteenth-Century Studies, Am. Assn. Tchrs. German, Phi Beta Kappa. Office: Northern Mich Univ 1401 Presque Isle Ave Marquette MI 49855 Office Fax: 906-227-2533. Business E-Mail: csotirop@nmu.edu.

SOTO, CLAUDIO, medical educator; b. Santiago, Chile, July 5, 1965; came to U.S., 1994; s. Guillermo O. and Sylvia G. (Jara) S.; m. Soledad de la Cerda, May 12, 1988; children: Claudia, Andres. BS, U. Chile, Santiago, 1986, PhD, 1992. Asst. investigator Cath. U. Chile, Santiago, 1992-94; assoc. investigator Internat. Ctr. for Cancer and Devel. Biology, Santiago, 1993-94; asst. prof. NYU Med. Ctr., NYC, 1995—. Mem. sci. adv. bd. Axonyx Inc., Stevenson, Wash., 1993—; adv. hoc. reviewer Jour. Biol. Chemistry, Proc. NAS, Exptl. Cell Rsch., Amyloid, Am. Jour. Pathology, Neurobiology of Aging; editor-in-chief Alzheimer's News, 1993-94. Contbr. chpts. to books in field, over 20 articles to profl. publs. Recipient award Andes Found., 1988-92, Internat. Union Biochemistry and Molecular Biology, 1991, Otsuka Pharm. Co., 1996; grantee Alzheimer's Disease Found., Am. Fedn. for Aging Rsch., Wellcome Trust Found., NIH, 1994-95, Sandoz Found. for Gerontol. Rsch., 1993-95, Nat. Fund. for Sci. and Tech. Rsch. Chile, 1987, 90, 89-91, 90-92, 93-95, U. Chile, 1991. Mem. Am. Soc. Neurosci., N.Y. Acad. Scis., Chilean Soc. Biochemistry. Achievements include development of novel therapeutic approach for Alzheimer's and Prion-related diseases; 3 patents in field. Home: 595 Main St Apt 1012 New York NY 10044-0046 Office: NYU Med Ctr 550 1st Ave Rm Th427 New York NY 10016-6402

SOTO, GEOVANY, professional baseball player; b. San Juan, Jan. 20, 1983; Catcher Chgo. Cubs, 2005—. Mem. Puerto Rican nat. team World Baseball Classic, 2009. Named Rookie of Yr., The Sporting News, 2008, Nat. League Rookie of Yr., MLB, 2008; named to Nat. League All-Star Team, 2008. Achievements include being the first rookie catcher in Major League Baseball history to start in the All-Star Game, 2008; catching Carlos Zambrano's no-hitter against the Houston Astros, September 14, 2008. Office: Chgo Cubs Wrigley Field 1060 W Addison Chicago IL 60613*

SOTO, GILBERTO D., music educator; b. Torreon, Mex., May 9, 1961; arrived in U.S., 1983; s. Enrique Soto-Ruiz and Maria Martinez; m. Blanc C. Ramirez, Aug. 23, 1986; children: Daney, Erika. BA in Edn., U. del Noreste, Torreon, 1983; BA in Music, Abilene Christian U., 1986; MusM, U. So. Miss., 1988, PhD in Music Edn., 1995. Music instr. Miss. Coast Coll., 1986—90; prof., chair Laredo C.C., Tex., 1990—2001; assoc. prof., chair Tex. A&M U., Laredo, 2001—05. Tchr. asst. U. So. Miss., Hattiesburg, 1981—90. Co-author: Spotlight on Music, 2005; author: Fiesta De Canciones, 2005. Mem.: Music Educators Nat. Conf., Tex. Music Edn. Assn. Roman Catholic. Home: 8627 Northridge Loop Laredo TX 78045 Office: Tex A&M Univ 5201 University Blvd Laredo TX 78041 Office Phone: 956-726-4006.

SOTO, JAIME, bishop; b. Inglewood, Calif., Dec. 31, 1955; BA in Philosophy, St. John's Sem. Coll., Camarillo, Calif., 1978, MDiv, 1982; MSW, Columbia U. Sch. Social Work, 1986. Ordained priest Diocese of Orange, Calif., 1982; assoc. pastor St. Joseph Ch., Santa Ana, 1982—84; assoc. dir. Cath. Charities of Orange, 1986, dir. immigration & citizenship services, 1986—89; episcopal vicar for Hispanic cmty. Diocese of Orange, 1989—2000, vicar for charities, 1999—2000; ordained bishop, 2000; aux. bishop Diocese of Orange, 2000—07; coadjutor bishop Diocese of Sacramento, 2007—08, bishop Calif., 2008—. Roman Catholic. Office: Pastoral Ctr 2110 Broadway Sacramento CA 95818 Office Phone: 916-733-0100.*

SOTO, JOSE ANTONIO, family medicine physician; b. Cienfuegos, Cuba, Sept. 20, 1963; s. Antonia Sara Padron and Jose Antonio Soto; m. Alicia Soto, Jan. 30, 1987; children: Jose Antonio, Jorge Luis. MD, Inst. Superior Ciencias Medicas Habana, Havana, 1987. Diplomate U. La Habana, 1987. Cardiology resident Inst. Cardiology and Cardiovasc. Surgery. Havana. Cuba, 1989—92; resident physician U. Miami, Jackson Meml. Hosp., Fla., 1996—99; md. family medicine Soto Med. Assoc., Inc, Sunny Isles Beach, Fla., 2000—, md, 2000—. Author: (science and nature book) Marine Therapy Health Benefits of Seawater Minerals, Seawater Treatment Respiratory Diseases, Pharmaceutical Speaker. Mem. Inst. Cuban and Cuban Am. Studies, Miami, 2008—. Fellowship, Harvard Pilgrim Health Care. Conservative. Roman Catholic. Avocations: boating, travel. Office: Soto Med Assoc Inc 179 Sunny Isles Boulevard North Miami Beach FL 33160

SOTOMAYOR, SONIA, United States supreme court justice; b. South Bronx, NY, June 25, 1954; d. Juan and Celina (Baez) Sotomayor; m. Kevin Edward Noonan, Aug. 14, 1976 (div. 1983). BA summa cum laude, Princeton U., 1976; JD, Yale U., 1979; LLD (hon.), Herbert H. Lehman Coll., 1999; JD honoris causa (hon.), Princeton U., 2001, Bklyn. Law Sch., 2001. Bar: NY 1980, US Dist. Ct. (ea. and so. dists.) NY 1984. Asst. dist. atty. Office of Dist. Atty. County of NY, NYC, 1979—84; assoc. Pavia & Harcourt, NYC, 1984—87, ptnr., 1988—92; judge US Dist. Ct. (so. dist.) NY, NYC, 1992—98, US Ct. Appeals (2nd Cir.), NYC, 1998—2009; assoc. justice US Supreme Ct., Washington, 2009—. Adj. prof. NYU Sch. Law, 1998—2007; lectr. law Columbia Law Sch., 1999—. Editor: Yale U. Law Rev., 1979. Mem. State Adv.

Panel on Inter-Group Rels., NYC, 1990—92, 1990—91; bd. dirs. P.R. Legal Def. and Edn. Fund, NYC, 1980—92, State of NY Mortgage Agy., NYC, 1987—92, NYC Campaign Fin. Bd., 1988—92. Co-recipient M. Taylor Pyne prize, Princeton U.; named one of 100 Most Powerful Women, Forbes mag., 2009. Mem.: ABA, Assn. Hispanic Judges, Am. Philos. Soc., NY Women's Bar Assn., P.R. Bar Assn., Hispanic Bar Assn., Phi Beta Kappa. Roman Catholic. Office: US Supreme Ct One First St NE Washington DC 20543*

SOTOMORA-VON AHN, RICARDO FEDERICO, pediatrician, educator; b. Guatemala City, Guatemala, Oct. 22, 1947; s. Ricardo and Evelyn (von Ahn) S.; m. Eileen Marie Holcomb, May 9, 1990; m. Victoria Monzon, Nov. 26, 1971; children: Marisol, Clarisa, Ricardo III, Charlotte Marie. MD, San Carlos U., 1972; MS in Physiology, U. Minn., 1978. Diplomate Am. Bd. Pediats., Am. Bd. Pediat. Cardiology, Am. Bd. Neonatology-Perinatal Medicine. Rotating intern Gen. Hosp., Guatemala, 1971-72; pediat. intern U. Ark., 1972-73, resident, 1973-75; fellow in pediat. cardiology U. Minn., 1975-78; rsch. assoc. in cardiovasc. pathology United Hosps., St. Paul, 1976; fellow in neonatal-perinatal medicine St. Paul's Children's Hosp., 1977-78, U. Ark., 1981-82; instr. pediats. U. Minn., 1978-79; pediat. cardiologist, unit cardiovasc. surg. Roosevelt Hosp., Guatemala City, 1979-81; asst. prof. pediats. cardiology and neonatology U. Ark., Little Rock, 1981-83; pvt. practice Little Rock, 1983—. Fellow: Am. Coll. Angiology, Am. Coll. Chest Physicians, Am. Coll. Cardiology, Am. Acad. Pediat.; mem.: AAAS, ABA, Soc. Critical Care Medicine, So. Soc. Pediat. Rsch., Ctrl. Ark. Pediat. Soc., Guatemala Coll. Physicians and Surgeons, Soc. Pediat. Echocardiology, Am. Heart Assn., NY Acad. Scis., Ark. Med. Soc., Soc. Genealogists London, Guatemala Acad. Genealogy, Heraldry and Hist. Studies (corr.), The Country Club of Little Rock. Home: 3 River Ridge Ct Little Rock AR 72227-1523 Office: Evergreen Pl 1100 N Univ Ste 142 Little Rock AR 72207 E-mail: rfsotomora@aol.com.

SOTOS, JOHN GEORGE, cardiologist, writer; b. Homer, Alaska, Feb. 11, 1955; s. Luigi Vito and Bettina (Squalidozzi) S. B in Chemistry and Math., Dartmouth Coll.; M in Computer Sci. (artificial intelligence), Stanford U.; MD, John Hopkins U., 1980. Intern cardiology John Hopkins Hosp., Balt., 1983—84, resident, 1984—86, fellow transplantation cardiology and gen. cardiology, 1988—92; co-founding mem. to chief med. engr. Healtheon (now called WebMD); prin. scientist DNA Sciences; CEO Apneos Corp. Author: Zebra Cards: An Aid to Obscure Diagnoses, 1989, (web encyclopedia) The Medical History of American Presidents, The Physical Lincoln, 2008; technical advisor (TV series) House, MD. Lt. col. U.S. Air N.G., 1984—. Fellow RACC, Am. Coll. Cardiology; mem. Am. Acad. Sleep Medicine, American Sleep Apnea Assn. (bd. dirs.) In 2003 established that President William Howard Taft had severe obstructive sleep apnea during his Presidency. In 2008 requested President Abraham Lincoln's DNA to prove that Lincoln had a rare genetic cancer syndrome called MEN2B.*

SOTO-WRIGHT, VALENA, gynecologist, director; m. Ivan Soto-Arape, Dec. 28, 1989. MD, Dalhousie U., Nova Scotia. Diplomate Am. Bd. Ob-Gyn., 1998. Dir. minimally invasive gynecologic surgery Lahey Clinic, Burlington, Mass., 2008—, gynecologic resident, 2005—, fellowship program dir., 2005—. Office: 41 Mall Rd Burlington MA 01805 Office Fax: 781-744-5398. Business E-Mail: valena_soto_wright@lahey.org.

SOTTILE, JAMES, lawyer; b. Gainesville, Fla., Sept. 20, 1960; s. James and Judith Sottile; m. Noell Harris; children: James Eliot, David William. BS, U. Fla., Gainesville, 1982; JD, Georgetown U., Washington, 1985. Assoc. Wilmer, Cutler & Pickering, Washington, 1985—87, Nussbaum Owen & Webster, Washington, 1987—89; from assoc. to ptnr. Caplin & Drysdale, Washington, 1989—99; ptnr. Baach Robinson & Lewis, Washington, 1999—2004, Zuckerman Spaeder LLP, Washington, 2004—. Jr. warden St. Alban's Episcopal Ch., Washington, 2007—. Episcopalian. Home: 3508 Cummings Ln Chevy Chase MD 20815 Office: Zuckerman Spaeder LLP 1800 M St NW Washington DC 20036

SOTTILE, JOSEPH JAMES, elementary school educator, poet; b. Queens, NY; s. Anthony and Mary Sottile; m. Marilyn Dufford, June 24, 1967; children: Mary Lou, April. AA, Suffolk County CC, Selden, NY, 1964; BS, SUNY, Plattsburgh, 1967; postgrad., SUNY, Brockport, 1971. Tchr. Gates Chili Sch. Dist., Rochester, NY, 1967—2000, tutor out of sch. suspension program, 2001—. Adj. faculty Rochester Inst. Tech., 1980—90; presenter in field. Author: Bathroom Vacation, 1998, Picture Poetry on Parade!, 2004, Waiting to See the Principal and Other Poems, 2007, numerous poems; contbr. articles to popular mags., local newspapers. Mem.: Ret. Tchrs. Orgn. Rochester and Vicinity, Rochester Writers and Books, Rochester Area Children's Writers and Illustrators, Soc. Children's Book Writers and Illustrators. Avocations: bicycling, golf, tennis, racquetball, reading. Personal E-mail: jsottile@frontiernet.net.

SOTTILE, KATHLEEN M., principal, music educator; b. Washington, Aug. 23, 1960; d. Edward R. Scartelli and Marilyn Coyne; m. Lou Sottile, July 1, 1983; children: Luigi, Mia. BA in Music Edn., Marywood U., Scranton, Pa., 1989, MA in Music Edn., 2001; prins. cert., Temple U., Phila., 2002; postgrad., Indiana U., Strousburg, Pa. Customer svc. rep. Third Nat. Bank, Chinchilla, Pa., 1986—90; owner Hyde Park Nursery Sch., Scranton, Pa., 1990—94; tchr. gen. music and choral grades 1-8 St. Patrick's Elem. Sch., Scranton, 1993—97; instrumental music tchr. South Scranton Intermediate Sch., 1997—98, music tchr., 1998—2002; asst. prin. grades 11-12 Delaware Valley H.S., Milford, Pa., 2002—03; asst. prin. grades 9-12 Scranton H.S., 2003—05; prin. grades 7-12 Floral Park Meml. H.S., NY, 2005—. Pvt. piano tchr., Scranton, 1980—; presenter in field. Bd. dirs. Pa. Alliance for Arts in Edn. Mem.: Sch. Adminstrn. Assn. NY, Nat. Assn. Secondary Sch. Principals, Nat. Guild Piano Tchrs. and Judges. Office: Sewanhaka Ctrl HS Dist 210 Locust St Floral Park NY 11001

SOUBA, WILEY WILLIAM, JR., medical educator, researcher, dean; b. Caracas, Venezuela, May 17, 1953; came to the U.S., 1968; s. Wiley William and Phyllis (Rowe) S.; m. Lynne Hayes, Mar. 26, 1983; children: Matthew, Julia. BS in Chemistry, Muskingum Coll., New Concord, Ohio, 1975; MD, U. Tex., 1978; ScD in Nutritional Biochemistry, Harvard U., 1984, MS, 1994; MBA, Boston U., 1998. Assoc. prof. physiology U. Fla. Coll. Medicine, Gainesville, 1991-92, assoc. prof. biochemistry/molecular biology, 1991-92, prof. surgery, 1993, prof. biochemistry/molecular biology/physiology, 1993; prof. surgery Harvard U., Boston, 1993—99, prof. nutrition, 1996—99; assoc. dir. cancer ctr. Mass. Gen. Hosp., Boston, 1993—, dir. nutrition support svcs., 1993—99, dir. surg. oncology rsch. labs., 1993—99, chief Divsn. Surg. Oncology, 1993—99, chair Dept. Surgery Practice Coun., 1999; adj. prof. mgmt. policy Boston U., 1999; Waldhausen prof. chmn. Dept. Surgery Pa. State U. Coll. Medicine, University Park, 1999—2006, interim chair Dept. Ophthalmology, 2001—02, interim dir. Pa. State Cancer Inst., 2001—03, dir. Hershey Ctr. for Leadership Devel., 2002—06, prof. cellular and molecular physiology, 2002—06; dean, chief academic officer Ohio State U. Coll. Medicine, Columbus, 2006—, prof. surgery, 2006—. Bd. dirs. Mass. Gen. Hosp. Cancer Ctr. Contbr. 160 articles to profl. jours.; author: 40 book chpts. Eagle Scout, Boy Scouts Am., 1967; named one of Top Drs. Am., 1992—; recipient NIH rsch. grants, 1990-95, 94-99, Shriners Burn Inst. (Boston Unit) rsch. grant, 1995-97. Fellow ACS; mem. AMA, Assn. Acad. Surgery (pres. 1994), Am. Soc. Parenteral and Enteral Nutrition, Surg. Infection Soc., Soc. Univ. Surgeons, Am. Soc. Clin. Oncology, Soc. Surg. Oncology, Collegium Internationale Chirurgiae Digestivae, Am. Coll. Nutrition, Am. Physiol. Soc., Am. Soc. for Clin. Nutrition, Am. Fedn. for Clin. Rsch., Soc. for Surgery of the Alimentary Tract, Am. Assn. for the Surgery of Trauma, Soc. Clin. Surgery, So. Surg. Assn., Ea. Assn. for Surgery of Trauma, Am. Surg. Assn., Alpha Omega Alpha. Achievements include rsch. in molecular regulation of the altered glutamine transport and metabolism that occurs during critical illness. Office: Ohio State U Coll Medicine 250 Meiling Hall 370 W 9th Ave Columbus OH 43210 Office Phone: 614-292-2600. E-mail: souba.1@osu.edu.*

SOUDER, MARK EDWARD, United States Representative from Indiana; b. Ft. Wayne, Ind., July 18, 1950; s. Edward Getz and Irma (Fahling) Souder; m. Diane Kay Zimmer, July 28; children: Brooke Diane, Nathan Elias, Zachary. BS, Ind. U., Ft. Wayne, 1972; MBA, U. Notre Dame, 1974. Mgmt. trainee Crossroads Furniture Co., Houston, 1974; mktg. mgr. Gabberts Furniture & Studio, Mpls., 1974-76; mktg. mgr., exec. v.p. Souder's Furniture & Studio, Grabill, Ind., 1976-80, pres., 1981-84; econ. devel. liaison for U.S. Rep. Dan Coats, from 1983; mem. U.S. Congress from Ind. 3rd Dist. (formerly 4th), 1995—, Ho. Select Com. on Homeland Security, edn./workforce com., govt. reform/oversight com., small bus. com., natural resources com. Mem. bus. alumni adv. com. Ind. U.; mem. Ind. Area Devel. Coun.; publicity chmn. Grabill County Fair; adv. Dan Coats for Congress Com., 1980—81; mem. Apostolic Christian Ch. Mem.: U. Notre Dame Alumni Assn., Ind. U. Alumni Assn. (dir., past pres.), Allen County Hist. Soc., Grabill C. of C., Ft. Wayne C. of C., Midwest Home Furnishings Assn. (dir. 1976—84, past treas., exec. v.p.). Republican. Home: 13733 Ridgeview Ct Grabill IN 46741 Office: US Ho Reps 2231 Rayburn Ho Office Bldg Washington DC 20515-1403 Office Phone: 202-225-4436. Office Fax: 202-225-3479. E-mail: souder@mail.house.gov.*

SOUDERS, PATRICK J., legislative staff member; b. Quincy, Ill., Jan. 20, 1969; BA in Broadcast Comm., Marquette U., Milw., 1991; MA in Liberal Studies, Georgetown U., Washington, 1998. Legis. asst., Senator Richard Durbin US Senate, Washington, 1990—96, projects dir., Senator Richard Durbin, 1997—2004, chief of staff, asst. Dem. leader's office, 2005—07, chief of staff to Senator Richard Durbin, 2007—. Mem.: Marquette Univ. Alumni Assn. Democrat. Roman Catholic. Avocations: running, tennis. Office: 309 Hart Senate Office Bldg Washington DC 20510-1304 Office Phone: 202-224-2152.*

SOUDERS, ROBERTA BELSHAW, literature and language educator; b. Bethlehem, Pa., Sept. 25, 1954; d. Samuel James and Josephine Porazzi Belshaw; m. Peter Malcolm Souders, Feb. 27, 1986; children: Zac Peter, Samantha Jo. M in Secondary Edn./Reading, West Chester U., Pa., 1978. Project Discovery ptnr. Peoples' Light and Theatre, Malvern, Pa., 1996—; comm. arts dept. chair Octorara HS, Atglen, Pa., 1999—2008; vol. Epilepsy Found., 2008—. Vol. March of Dimes, Parkesburg, Pa., 2000—; Sunday sch. tchr. Episc. Ch., Parkesburg, 1992—2001. Mem.: Nat. Orgn. Tchrs. (life). Episcopalian. Avocations: reading, writing, swimming, gardening. Office: Octorara HS 226 Highland Rd Atglen PA 19310 Business E-Mail: rsouders@octorara.org.

SOUGANIDIS, PANAGIOTIS EMMANUEL, mathematician, educator; s. Emmanuel Souganidis and Stella Michailatsou; m. Thaleia Zariphopoulou-Souganidis, July 14, 1987; children: Ellie Stella, Emmanuel Panagiotis. PhD, U. Wis., Madison, 1983. Asst. prof. Brown U., Providence, 1983—91; prof. U. Wis., Madison, 1991—2000, U. Tex., Austin, 2000—. Recipient Presdl. Young Investigation award, NSF, 1987, Academic prize, Bodossaki Found., 1995; fellow, Sloan Found., 1989. Mem.: Am. Math. Soc.

SOUHAM, GÉRARD, communications executive; b. Paris, May 30, 1928; s. Lucien and Mary-Françoise (Husson) S.; m. Eliane Meyrat, June 23, 1951; children: Glenn (dec.), Yan, Philip. Diploma, Am. Community Sch., Paris, 1948. Cert. Ecole Commerciale de Paris. Chargé de mission State Dept., Europe, 1950-52; pub. info. officer Allied Air Forces NATO, Fontainebleau, 1953-55; chmn. bd., chief exec. officer J. Walter Thompson, Paris, 1955-75, v.p. NYC, 1970-75; prin. S3C Gerard Souham Group Communication Cos., Paris and Lausanne, Switzerland, 1975—, NYC, 1979—. Bd. dirs. Am. Overseas Meml., I.T. Fin., AVON, France, Mattel-France; chmn. bd. Turner Prodn. Europe, 1994—98; vice chmn. bd. Avon. Author: Général Souham Comte de l'Empire, 1964, Impressions sur..., 1970, Souham, 1989, Sur les Champs de Bataille de la Révolution et de l'Empire, 1990. Mem. pvt. sector internat. and pub. rels. coms. USIA, 1985; mem. world bd. govs. USO, Washington, 1984, chmn. fundraising com., 1989—, pres., Paris, 1995, bd. dirs. 2000—. Decorated officer Legion of Honor (France); officer Order of Leopold, knight Belgian Crown (Belgium). Mem. Am. Air Mus. Eng. (founding mem.), Internat. Inst. Strategic Studies London, France, USA (bd. dirs.), Am. Overseas Meml. Assn. (bd. dirs. 1988—), USAF Assn. (life), HM Guards Polo (Windsor, Eng.) (life), Polo de Bagatelle (Paris), NY Athletic, Yacht of Monaco. Roman Catholic. Avocation: collecting fine bindings. Office: Souham Group Comm 500 5th Ave New York NY 10110-0002

SOULE, GEORGE ALAN, literature educator; b. Fargo, ND, Mar. 3, 1930; s. George Alan and Ruth Georgia (Knudsen) S.; m. Carolyn Richards, Nov. 24, 1961; 1 child, Katherine. BA, Carleton Coll., 1951; postgrad., Corpus Christi Coll., Cambridge U., Eng., 1952-53; MA, Yale U., 1956, PhD, 1960. Instr. English lit. Oberlin (Ohio) Coll., 1958-60; asst. prof. U. Wis., Madison, 1960-62; from asst. prof. to prof. Carleton Coll., Northfield, Minn., 1962-95, prof. emeritus, 1995—, chair English dept., 1980—83; tchr. Cannon Valley Elder Collegium, 1998—, vice chair, 2003—05, chair, 2005—07, also bd. dirs. Cons. Ednl. Testing Svc., Princeton, NJ, 1967-84, 94-97; lectr. Wordsworth Winter Sch., Grasmere, UK, 2003-07. Author: Four British Women Novelists: An Annotated and Critical Secondary Bibliography, 1998; editor: Theatre of the Mind, 1974; contbr. articles to profl. jours. Libr. bd. City Northfield, 1997-00; bd. dirs. Northfield Area Found., 2001-02. With US Army, 1954-55. Internat. fellow Rotary, 1952-53, Sterling pre-doctoral fellow Yale U., 1957-58. Mem.: Friends Wordsworth Conf. Found., Anthony Powell Soc., The Iris Murdoch Soc., Friends of Dove Cottge, Boswell Soc. of Auchinleck, Johnson Soc. of Lichfield, Mayflower Soc., Oxford and Cambridge Club, Rotary, Phi Beta Kappa. Episcopalian. Avocations: cooking, travel, Jeopardy (Champion Sr. Tournament 1990). Home: 313 Nevada St Northfield MN 55057-2346 Home Phone: 507-645-8285. Fax: 507-645-5099. Personal E-mail: gsoule@charter.net.

SOULE, HOWARD R., medical association administrator; PhD in Virology & Epidemiology, Baylor Coll. Medicine. Fellow in immunology & vascular biology Scripps Rsch. Inst.; sr. rsch. & devel. exec. Corvas Internat.; mng. dir. Knowledge Universe Health & Wellness Group; exec. vice pres. & chief science officer Prostate Cancer Found., 1997—2004, exec. vice pres. discovery & translation, 2007—. Office: 1250 Fourth St Santa Monica CA 90401 Office Phone: 310-570-4700. Office Fax: 310-570-4701. E-mail: info@pcf.org.*

SOULER, BENJAMIN KERWIN, retired research chemist, pharmacist, consultant; b. Woonsocket, RI, Aug. 8, 1917; s. Harry Nelson and Elizabeth (Kerwin) Souler; m. Cornelia Carruthers, Mar. 26, 2005; m. Priscilla Jepson, Feb. 7, 1942 (dec. Sept. 20, 1999); children: Mary Elizabeth Hardwich, Priscilla Ann Henry. BS, U. RI, Kingston, 1939; MS, U. So. Calif., LA, 1941. Rsch. chemist United Rexall Drug Co., Boston, 1941—46; lab. dir. Am. Home Foods Co., Boston, 1946—47, Elkhart, Ind., 1946—47; sr. rsch. scientist Bristol-Myers Squibb Co., Syracuse, NY, 1947—72; pharmacist cons. various pharmacies Cape Cod, Mass., 1972—86, Orleans Convalescent and Retirement Ctr., Mass., 1986—86; ret. Spkr. in fielf. Candidate US congress NY State Conservative Party, Onadaga County, NY. Pvt. 243rd regiment coastal arty. RI N.G., 1935—38, Woonsocket, pvt. coastal gun crew RI N.G., 1935—38, Ft. Henry G. Wright, Fishers Island, NY, pharmacist's mate USN, 1943—44, lt. comm. cryptographic officer USN, 1944—46, lt. officer courier USN, 1944—46, lt. tng. officer USN, 1952—53. Mem.: DAV, Sampson WWII Sailors, Am. Legion, Bristol Employee's Assn. (pres. 1962), Syracuse Lions Club (pres. 1954). Achievements include patents for war gas (lewisite) decontaminant; highly stable ointment base. Avocations: history, botany, stamp collecting/philately.

SOULES, ALINE, librarian, writer; arrived in U.S., 1971; d. Stanley and Harriet Flora (Craig) Stannard; m. Donald Keith Soules (dec.); 1 child, Craig. BA with honors, U. Windsor, Can., 1969, MA, 1970; MLS, Wayne State U., 1973; MFA, Antioch U., 2003. Libr. Lawrence Tech. U., Southfield, Mich., 1974—76; dept. head U. Windsor, Ont., Canada, 1976—88; mgr. tech. svc. and automation U. Mich. Bus. Sch., Ann Arbor, 1988—93, dir. libr., 1993—2000, mgr. rsch. support, 2000—02; assoc. univ. libr. Calif. State U., Hayward, 2002—06, prof. East Bay, 2006—. Presenter in field; guest lectr. Sch. Info., U. Mich., 1995; mem. adv. bd. NSF, Washington, 2001; cons. Cleary Coll. Libr, 1995, 99. Author numerous poems; co-author: Variations on the Ordinary, 1995; co-author: (with Nancy Ryan) The Size of the World/The Shape of the Heart, 2000; contbr. articles to profl. jours. Recipient Dist. Svc. award, U. Mich., 2003, 3rd pl. Poetry award, Inland Empire Br. Calif. Writers Club, 2004, 2d pl. open short story award, N.Am. Internat. Auto Show, 3d pl., Poet Hunt, 1993. Mem.: Am. Assn. U. Prof., ALA (libr. higher edn. and campus adminstrn. com. 1994—96, mem. current topics planning com. 1997—99, subcom. intellectual property 2001—), ACRL (govt. rel. com. 1997—2001, legis. network rep. to Mich. 1998—2002, chair current topics planning com. 1999—2001, conf. planning com. 1999—2002, copyright com. 2001—05, legis. network rep. to Calif. 2002—08, chpts. coun. leg liaison 2008—), Calif. Acad. Rsch. Libr. (legis. liaison, ex-officio mem. bd. 2002—08, Com. Rsch. award 2008—), Mich. Libr. Assn. (chair-elect acad. and rsch. libr. divsn. 1992—93, chair acad. endowment fund com. 1992—94, chair acad. and rsch. libr. divsn. 1993—94, past chair acad. and rsch. libr. divsn. 1994—95, leadership acad. oversight com. 1994—95, long range planning com. 1994—95, conf. planning com. 2000—01, pub. chair 2000—01, pub. policy com. 2000—02), Beta Phi Mu. Avocation: singing. E-mail: aline.soules@csueastbay.edu.

SOUNEY, PAUL FREDERICK, pharmacist; b. Bristol, Conn., Mar. 29, 1947; s. Frederick Raymond and Julia Yvonne (Weeks) S.; m. Billie Lorraine Petersen, Apr. 7, 1972; children: Jared Paul, Jeremy Christian. BS, Northeastern U., 1971, MS, 1984. Drug info. pharmacist Hartford (Conn.) Hosp., 1971-77; pharmacy supervisor Boston Hosp. for Women, 1977-81; clin. rsch. pharmacist Channing Labs./Harvard Med. Sch., Boston, 1981-92; dir. drug info. Brigham and Women's Hosp., Boston, 1981—90, dir. clin. pharmacy, 1985—92; med. info. scientist Astra Merck Inc., Providence, 1992-97; field sci. ptnr. N.E. Customer Ctr. Astra Pharms., L.P., Providence, 1997-99; med. mktg. scientific leader AstraZeneca Pharms., Wayne, Pa., 1999-2000, group dir. med. mktg., 2000, nat. sci. dir. GI, 2000—03, sr. dir. med. affairs, 2003—04; prin. Sci. Commercialization LLC, Kennett Square, Pa., 2004—06; nat. dir. med. affairs Berlex Labs., Kennett Square, 2006—07; nat. dir. med. affairs, Neurosci. Bayer Healthcare Pharmaceuticals, 2007; exec. dir. med. affairs Prism Pharmaceuticals, 2007—. Cons. in field. Editor: Comprehensive Pharmacy Review, 7th edit., 2009; contbr. articles to profl. jours.; editl. adv. panelist Internat. Pharm. Abstracts, Pharmacy Practice News, Am. Jour. Gastroenterology. Treas. men's club First Congl. Ch., 1993-2000; vol. Mansfield (Mass.) Animal Shelter, 1990-94. Mem. Am. Coll. Clin. Pharmacy, Am. Soc. Health Sys. Pharmacists, Am. Pharmaceutical Assn., Acad. Managed Case Pharmacy, New Eng. Coun. Hosp. Pharmacists, Northeastern Univ. Alumnae Assn. Office: Prism Pharmaceuticals 1150 First Ave King Of Prussia PA 19406 Office Phone: 610-994-0096. Business E-Mail: psourey@prismpharma.com.

SOURAY, SHELDON, professional hockey player; b. Elk Point, Alta., Can., July 13, 1976; m. Angelica Bridges (div.); children: Valentina Raine, Scarlett Skye. Defenseman NJ Devils, 1997—2000, Montreal Canadiens, 2000—07, Edmonton Oilers, 2007—. Co-owner La Pizzeria etc., Montreal. Named to NHL All-Star Game, 2004, 2007, 2009. Achievements include setting NHL record for most powerplay goals scored by a defenseman in a single season, 2007. Office: Edmonton Oilers Hockey Club 11230 - 110 St Edmonton AB Canada*

SOURIAL, ALFY SAIF, surgeon; b. Tanta, Egypt, Jan. 10, 1928; s. Saif and Erada Atiah (El-Sanady) S.; m. Elizabeth Ann Siebert, 1960; children: Edward S., Wynn Heather; m. Shirley Ann Maniscalco, Oct. 7, 1971; children: Dean Michael, Jill Soraya. MD, Cairo U., 1950. Diplomate Am. Bd. Surgery. Intern Doctors Hosp., Cleve., 1955-56, resident in surgery, 1956-57, Huron Rd. Hosp., Cleve., 1957-60; fellow in surgery Case Western Res. U., Cleve., 1960-61; surgeon Valley Hosp., Pomona, Calif., 1962-72; pvt practice Thousand Oaks, Calif., 1970-93; active staff Los Robles Hosp., Thousand Oaks, 1968-92, hon. staff, 1992—. Author: Beyond Mathematics, A Standard Physical Particle and the Unified Field of Energy; patentee in field. Lt. col. USAF, 1982-87. Fellow ACS; mem. AMA. Office Phone: 909-336-7240. Personal E-mail: asourial@aol.com.

SOURIAN, PETER, writer, educator; b. Boston, Apr. 7, 1933; s. Zareh Missak and Zabelle (Bayentz) S.; m. Eve Jeanne Pocquet, Sept. 25, 1971; children: Mark, Delphine. BA, Harvard U., 1955. Lectr. ext. divsn. NYU, NYC, 1963-65; from instr. English to prof. Bard Coll., Annandale-on-Hudson, NY, 1965—75, prof., 1975—, co-dir. Writing Program, 1980—. Faculty New Sch. Social Rsch., NYC, 1975-2000; TV critic Nation mag., NYC, 1975-81; mem. Anahit Prize Com., 1988—; nat. adv. panel George Polk Awards Com., 1979-92, nat screening com. mem. US Student Fulbright Program, 2008-09. Author:(novels) Miri, 1957, The Best and Worst of Times, 1961, The Gate, 1965, (essays and criticism) At The French Embassy in Sofia, 1992; mem. editl. bd. Ararat Quar., 1975—; contbr. articles and fiction to popular mags, profl. jours. and collections. Bd. dirs. Armenian Ctr. Columbia U., N.Y.C., 1988-97; mem. Clemente Course Humanities Adv. Bd., 1999—. With U.S. Army, 1957-59. Recipient Bardian award Bard Coll. Alumni, 2000; Lilly Endowment grant, 1976, Kellogg Found. grant, 1977. Mem. MLA, PEN,

Nat. Book Critics Circle, Century Assn. Home: 30 E 70th St New York NY 10021-4942 Office: Bard Coll Annandale on Hudson Annandale On Hudson NY 12504 Office Phone: 845-758-6822.

SOURIRAJAN, KARTHIK, research scientist; s. Sourirajan Srinivasa-rangan and Padmini Sourirajan; m. Anuradha Jayaraman, Dec. 8, 2004. BS in Mech. Engring. with honors, Birla Inst. Tech. and Sci., Pilani, India, 2000; MS in Indsl. Engring., Purdue U., West Lafayette, Ind., 2002, PhD, 2006. Rschr. IBM TJ Watson Rsch. Ctr., Yorktown Heights, NY, 2006—. Recipient Outstanding Tech. Achievement award, IBM, 2008. Mem.: Inst. Ops. Rsch. and Mgmt. Scis. Achievements include patents pending in field.

SOURKES, THEODORE LIONEL, biochemistry professor; b. Montreal, Que., Can., Feb. 21, 1919; s. Irving and Fannie (Golt) S.; m. Shena Rosenblatt, Jan. 17, 1943; children: Barbara, Myra. B.Sc., McGill U., 1939, M.Sc. magna cum laude, 1946; PhD, Cornell U., 1948; D.U. honoris causa, U. Ottawa, Can., 1990. Asst. prof. pharmacology Georgetown U. Med. Sch., 1948-50; research asso. dept. enzyme chemistry Merck Inst. Therapeutic Research, Rahway, NJ, 1950-53; sr. research biochemist Allan Meml. Inst., Montreal, 1953-65; dir. lab. neurochemistry Allan Meml. Inst. Psychiatry, 1965—91; mem. faculty McGill U., Montreal, 1954—, prof. biochemistry, 1965—, prof. psychiatry, assoc. dean of medicine for research Faculty Medicine, 1972-75; prof. pharmacology, 1990—; emeritus, 1991. Mem. Que. Med. Rsch. Coun., 1971-77; sr. fellow Parkinson's Disease Found., N.Y.C., 1963-66. Author: Biochemistry of Mental Disease, 1962, Nobel Prize Winners in Medicine and Physiology, 1901-1965, 1967, Life and Work of J.L.W. Thudichum, 1829-1901, 2003; sect. editor Internat. Jour. of the History of Neuroscis., 1996—. Decorated officer Order of Canada, Venezuelan Order Andrés Bello; laureate of the Wilder Penfield Prix du Que. for Biomed. Sci., 1998. Fellow Royal Soc. Can.; mem. Canadian Biochem. Soc., Pharmacol. Soc. Can., Canadian Coll. Neuropsychopharmacology (Heinz Lehmann award 1982, medal 1990), Am. Soc. Biol. Chemists, Am. Soc. Pharmacology and Exptl. Therapeutics, Am. Soc. Neurochemistry, Internat. Soc. History of Neuroscis. (medal 2001, Lifetime Contbn. award 2009), Internat. Soc. Neurochemistry, Internat. Brain Research Orgn., Sigma Xi. Achievements include research and publs. on drugs for treatment high blood pressure; 1st basic research on methyldopa; elucidation of role of dopamine and other monamines in nervous system; first trials of L-dopa in Parkinson's disease, biochemistry of mental depression, pathways of stress in the nervous system, imaging serotonin in brain, history of biochemistry. Home: 3033 Sherbrooke St W # 303 Montreal PQ Canada H3Z 1A3 Office: McGill U 1033 Pine Ave W Montreal PQ Canada H3A 1A1 Office Phone: 514-398-7316. E-mail: theodore.sourkes@mcgill.ca.

SOURS, DAVID A., legislative staff member; BBA in Bus. IT, Coll. William and Mary, Williamsburg, Va., 2001. Risk tech. Deutsche Bank, 2001; mortgage banker GRL, 2003—05; staff asst., Rep. Phil Gingrey US House of Reps., Washington, 2005, legis. correspondent, Rep. Phil Gingrey, 2005—06, legis. asst., Rep. Phil Gingrey, 2006—07, legis. dir., Rep. Phil Gingrey, 2007—09, chief of staff to Rep. Phil Gingrey, 2009—. Mem.: Pi Kappa Alpha. Republican. Office: 119 Cannon House Office Bldg Washington DC 20515 Office Phone: 202-225-2931. Office Fax: 202-225-2944.*

SOUSSLOFF, ANDREW D., lawyer; b. Providence, Sept. 21, 1953; s. Dimitri Gregory and Barbara Lucy (Farr) S.; m. Patricia James, June 7, 1986. BA, MA, U. Pa., 1975, JD cum laude, 1979. Bar: NY 1980, Calif. 1987. Assoc. Cadwalader Wickersham & Taft, NYC, 1979-80, Sullivan & Cromwell LLP, NYC, 1981-86, ptnr., 1986—, former co-mng. ptnr. gen. practice group. Mem.: Brearley Sch., NYC (trustee), Internat. Bar Assn. (co-chmn., securities law com. 2000—03, chmn., capital mkts. forum 2005—06). Office: Sullivan & Cromwell LLP 125 Broad St New York NY 10004-2489 Office Phone: 212-558-4000. Office Fax: 212-558-3588. Business E-Mail: soussloffa@sullcrom.com.

SOUTAS-LITTLE, ROBERT WILLIAM, mechanical engineer, educator; b. Oklahoma City, Feb. 25, 1933; s. Harry Glenn and Mary Evelyn (Miller) Little; m. Patricia Soutas, Sept. 3, 1982; children: Deborah, Catherine, Colleen, Jennifer, Karen. BS in Mech. Engring, Duke U., 1955; MS, U. Wis., 1959, PhD, 1962. Design engr. Allis Chalmers Mfg. Co., Milw., 1955-57; instr. mech. engring. Marquette U., 1957-59; instr. U. Wis., Madison, 1959-62, asst. prof., 1962-63, Okla. State U., 1963-65; prof. Mich. State U., 1965—2001, chmn. dept. mech. engring., 1972-77, chmn. dept. biomechanics, 1977-90; dir. biomechanics evaluation lab., 1989—; prof. emeritus Mich. State U., Lansing, 2001—. Cons. A. C. Electronics Co., Ford Motor Co., CBS Research Lab., B. F. Goodrich Co.; lectr. AID, India, 1965 Author: Elasticity, 1973, Engineering Mechanics: Statics, 1999, Computational Edit., 2007, Engineering Mechanics: Dynamics, 1999, Computational Edit., 2008; contbr. articles to profl. jours. Vice pres. Okemos (Mich.) Sch. Bd., 1967-72; mem. Meridian Twp. (Mich.) Charter Commn., 1969-70, Meridian Twp. Zoning Bd. Appeals, 1969-71. Recipient award for excellence in instrn. engring. students Western Electric Co., 1970-71, Disting. Faculty award, 1996; NSF grantee, 1964-69, 79, NIH grantee, 1973-75, 79—. Fellow ASME; mem. Soc. Engring. Sci., Am. Soc. Biomechanics, Internat. Soc. Biomechanics, N.Am. Soc. Clin. Gait and Movement Analysis, Sigma Xi, Pi Tau Sigma, Ta Beta Pi. Home: 187 S Highland Dr Leland MI 49654-1143 Office: PO Box 1143 Leland MI 49654-1143 Home Phone: 231-256-7646; Office Phone: 231-256-7646. Business E-Mail: soutas@egr.msu.edu.

SOUTER, DAVID HACKETT, retired United States supreme court justice; b. Melrose, Mass., Sept. 17, 1939; s. Joseph Alexander and Helen Adams (Hackett) Souter. BA, Harvard U., 1961, LLB, 1966; BA, MA in Jurisprudence, Oxford U., 1989. Bar: NH 1967. Assoc. Orr & Reno, Concord, NH, 1966—68, Lowell House, Harvard Coll.; asst. atty. gen. State of NH, 1968—71, dep. atty. gen., 1971—76, atty. gen., 1976—78; assoc. justice NH Superior Ct., 1978—83, NH Supreme Ct., 1983—90; judge US Ct. Appeals (1st Cir.), NH, 1990; assoc. justice US Supreme Ct., Washington, 1990—2009. Mem. Maine-NH Interstate Boundary Commn., 1971, NH Police Stds. and Training Coun., 1976—78, NH Jud. Coun., 1976—78, NH Governor's Commn. Crime and Delinquency, 1976—78, 1979—83. Trustee Concord Hosp., 1972—85, pres., 1978—84; trustee NH Hist. Soc., 1976—85; v.p., 1980—85; overseer Dartmouth Med. Sch., 1981—87. Rhodes scholar, Magdalen Coll., Oxford U., 1963, Honorary fellow. Master: Gray's Inn (London) (hon.); fellow: American Acad. Arts and Sciences, Mass. Historical Soc., American Coll. Trial Lawyers (hon.), American Bar Found. (hon.); mem.: American Antiquarian Soc., American Philos. Soc., New Eng. Historical Geneal. Soc. (hon.), Pilgrim Soc. (hon.), Merrimack County Bar Assn., NH Bar Assn., NH Hist. Soc. (v.p. 1980—85, trustee 1976—85), Phi Beta Kappa. Republican. Episcopalian.*

SOUTH, FRANK EDWIN, physiologist, educator; b. Norfolk, Nebr., Sept. 20, 1924; s. Frank Edwin and Gladys (Brinkman) S.; m. Berna Deane Phyllis Casebolt, June 23, 1946; children: Frank Edwin, Robert Christopher. AB, U. Calif., Berkeley, 1949, PhD, 1952. Asst. prof. physiology U. P.R. Sch. Medicine, 1953-54, U. Ill. Coll. Medicine, 1954-61; assoc. prof. Colo. State U., 1961-62, prof., 1962-65, U. Mo., 1965-76; prof., dir. Sch. Life and Health Scis., U. Del., Newark, 1976-82; prof. emeritus U. Del., Newark, 1989, Sch. Life and Health Scis., U. Del., Newark, 1989—. Mem. governing bd., dir. Hibernation Info. Exchange, 1959— Mem. editorial bd. Cryobiology, 1989; contbr. numerous articles on physiology of hibernation, temperature regulation, renal function, marine mammals, artificial atmospheres, and sleep to profl. jours. Bd. dirs. Del. Lung Assn., 1976-82, Del. Cancer Network, 1977-82; mem. research com. Del. Heart Assn., 1977-82; mem. N.E. regional research com. Am. Heart Assn.; mem. med. adv. bd. A.I. DuPont Inst., Wilmington, Del., 1978-83. Served with AUS, 1943-45. Decorated Purple Heart with oak leaf cluster, Bronze Star with oak leaf cluster, Pres. unit citation, Croix de Guerre (unit); NIH career devel. awardee, 1961-65; recipient European African Mid East campaign medal with bronze spear head and silver star, World War II victory medal, Army of Occupation medal with Germany clasp, combat med. badge. Fellow AAAS, Sigma Xi; mem. Am. Physiol. Soc.; Clubs: Ranger Bns. Assn. World War II (pres. 2005-06, 2008-09), Haven Yacht Club. Episcopalian. Business E-Mail: fsouth@udel.edu.

SOUTH, GAIL, business and mathematics professor; b. Paterson, NJ, Mar. 14, 1963; d. Harmon Carlisle and Deanna Merle Zacune; m. Steve South, Sept. 8, 1985; children: Raienne Alyse, Danielle Vincent. BSIM, MSIA, Purdue U., W. Lafayette, IN, 1984. Cert. Montgomery Coll. Germantown, Md., 2002. Mgr. Procter & Gamble, Staten Island, NY, 1984—87; cons. Rockville, Md., 1988—2000; tutor, 2003—; prof. Montgomery Coll., Germantown, Md., 1988—. Parent vol. Upper County Swim Team, Gaithersburg, Md., 1991—2004, MCPS, Rockville, Md., 1991—2005; vol. All-Breed Rescue, Rockville, 2005. Recipient Outstanding Faculty Svc., Montgomery Coll., 2006, Outstanding Faculty award, Nat. Inst. Staff and Orgnl. Devel., 2000, 2006. Office: Montgomery Coll 20200 Observation Dr Germantown MD 20876 Office Fax: 240-567-7723. Personal E-mail: south_family@verizon.net. Business E-Mail: gail.south@montgomerycollege.edu.

SOUTH, LISA, nursing educator; d. Pm and Ida South; children: Nathaniel, Emily. DSN, U. Ala., Birmingham, 1995. Cert. ELNEC, 2004. Asst. prof. U. Ala., Huntsville, 1996—2004, 2004—. Health ministry 1st Baptist Ch. Arlington, Alabaster, Ala., 2006—08. Mem.: Ala. Asthma Coalition. Baptist. Office: Univ AL Birmingham Sch Nursing Birmingham AL 35201

SOUTH, MICHAEL SHANE, oncologist; b. Pensacola, Fla., Sept. 14, 1965; s. James Coleman South and Alice Fawnell Powell; m. Raquel Herrera South, May 26, 1996; children: Joshua Michael, Keilah Isabel. Degree in Biology, San Jacinto Coll., Houston, 1996; BS, Thomas Edison State Coll., Trenton, NJ, 2000. Cert. Med. Dosimetry Credentialing Bd., 2000. Radiation safety specialist U. Tex. M. D. Anderson Cancer Ctr., Houston, 1988—97; med. dosimetrist Meth. Hosp., Houston, 2000—08, radiation oncology mgr. clin. ops., 2008—. Contbr. articles to profl. jours. With US Navy, 1983—88, Groton. Named to Nat. Dean's List, Edn. Comm. Inc., 1995—96. Mem.: Am. Assn. Med. Dosimetrists, ASTRO. Avocations: reading, travel.

SOUTHARD, WILLIAM G., lawyer; b. Toledo, May 6, 1953; s. James Theodore and Dorothy (Fergusson) S.; m. Martha Donelan, Aug. 14, 1976. BA, Williams Coll., 1975; JD, Columbia U., 1978. Bar: U.S. Dist. Ct. Ill. 1979, Mass. 1981, U.S. Dist. Ct. Mass. 1981, U.S. Ct. Appeals (1st cir.) 1985. Assoc. Schiff Hardin & Waite, Chgo., 1978-81, Bingham, Dana & Gould LLP, Boston, 1981-85, ptnr., 1985—2002, dep. chmn. litig., 1994-2000, chmn. litig., 2000—02; ptnr. Bingham McCutchen LLP, 2002—, dep. chair litig., 2002—. Assoc. editor Columbia Jour. Transnat. Law, 1978; contbr. articles to profl. jours. Mem. ABA, ASTM, Boston Bar Assn. Office: Bingham McCutchen LLP 150 Federal St Fl 15 Boston MA 02110-1745 Office Phone: 617-951-8232. Business E-Mail: william.southard@bingham.com.

SOUTHERLAND, S. DUANE, manufacturing executive; b. Durham, NC, Apr. 24, 1949; s. Sydney Duane and Beatrice Marie (Carver) S.; m. Linda F. Lewis, Jan. 5, 1974, 1 child, S. Duane III. BSE, Duke U., 1971, MS in Engring., 1973, MBA, 1974. Ops. analyst Cooper Group Div. Cooper Industries, Apex, NC, 1974-78, planning analyst Houston, 1978-81, dir. fin. Cooper Electronics Div. Nashua, NH, 1981-83, gen. mgr. Conn. ops. Kirsch Div. Beacon Falls, Conn., 1983-87, pres. Kirsch Div. Sturgis, Mich., 1987-94; pres., CEO Conso Products Co., Union, SC, 1995-98; pres., CEO, dir. Equality Specialties, Inc., NYC, 1999—2001; pres., CEO Conso Products, Union, SC, 2002—, Taos, LLC, Spartanburg, 2005—. Republican. Baptist.

SOUTHERN, DAVID W., history professor; b. Great Bend, Kans., Feb. 19, 1938; s. Arnett D. Southern and Maxine Loretto Windon; m. Judith Marie Jarvis (div.); 1 child, Sheri Lee. BA, Alderson-Boraddus Coll., W.Va., 1964; MA, Wake Forest U., NC, 1965; PhD, Emory U., Atlanta, 1971. Instr. N.C. Wesleyan Coll., Rocky Mount, NC, 1965—66; prof. Westminster Coll., Fulton, Mo., 1970—2005. Author: The Malignant Heritage: Yankee Progressives and the Negro Question, 1901-1914, 1968, Gunnar Myrdal and Black-White Relations, 1987, John LaFarge and the Limits of Catholic Interracialism, 1911-1963, 1996, The Progressive Era and Race: Reaction and Reform, 1900-1917, 2005; contbr. book revs. to jours., articles to profl. jours. With USAF, 1956—60. Recipient Gustavus Myers award, U. Ark., 1987, 1996; fellow, NEH, 1982—83; Grant, ACLS, APS, CUSHWA. Mem.: So. Hist. Assn., Orgn. Am. Historians. Democrat. Avocations: tennis, basketball, running, gardening, jazz. Home: 116 Merino Canonsburg PA 15317 Personal E-mail: dwsouthern@comcast.net.

SOUTHERN, NANCY C., utilities executive; m. Jonathan Asselin; children: Kelly Asselin, Kyle Asselin, Benjamin Asselin. Dir. corp. ATCO Ltd. and Can. Utilities Ltd., Calgary, Alba., dep. chair, 1989—96, dep. CEO, 1996—98, co-chair, CEO, 1998—2000, dep. chair, 2000—03, 2008—, pres., CEO, 2003—. Exec. v.p. Spruce Meadows; bd. dirs. Akita Drilling Ltd., Sentgraf Enterprises Ltd.; dir., risk rev. com. Bank of Montreal. Mem. Calgary Econ. Devel. Authority. Named Bus. Woman of Yr., Consumer's Choice Awards, 2005. Mem.: U. Calgary & C.D. Howe Inst., N.Am. Competitiveness Coun., Bus. Coun., Can. Coun. Chief Execs., Chancellor's Club. Office: ATCO Ltd 1600 909 11th Ave SW Calgary AB Canada T2R 1N6

SOUTHERN, ROBERT ALLEN, lawyer; b. Independence, Mo., July 17, 1930; s. James Allen and Josephine (Ragland) S.; m. Cynthia Agnes Drews, May 17, 1952; children: David D., William A., James M., Kathryn S. O'Brien. BS in Polit. Sci., Northwestern U., 1952, LL.B., 1954. Bar: Ill. 1955. Assoc. Mayer, Brown & Platt (now Mayer, Brown, Rowe & Maw), Chgo., 1954-64, ptnr., 1965-96, mng. ptnr., 1978-91, LA, 1991-96; CEO So. Assocs., Grayslake, Ill., 1997—, Chapel Hill, NC, 2004—. Editor in chief Northwestern U. Law Rev., 1953-54. Trustee, v.p., gen. counsel LaRabida Children's Hosp. and Rsch. Ctr., Chgo., 1974-89; trustee Kenilworth (Ill.) Union Ch., 1980-88; pres. Joseph Sears Sch. Bd., 1977-79; trustee Rush U. Med. Ctr., 1983-91, life trustee, 1991—; bd. dirs. Boys and Girls Clubs Chgo., 1986-91; governing mem. Orchestral Assn. Chgo., 1988-93. With U.S. Army, 1955-57. Mem. Chgo. Bar Assn., Lawyers Club Chgo., Order of Coif, Govs. Club (Chapel Hill, N.C.), Chgo. Club. Home: 60116 Davie Chapel Hill NC 27517-8466 Office Phone: 919-969-8292. Personal E-mail: rsouthern@nc.rr.com.

SOUTHERN, TERRY KEITH, engineering executive; b. Shelbyville, Tenn., USA, Aug. 29, 1954; s. Harry Jerome Southern and Mary Millinea Jones; m. Tinya Leigh Rose Butler, Dec. 1981 (div. Sept. 12, 1988); children: Jeremy Ryan, James Aaron, Amanda Renee. BS in Aviation Mgmt., Southern Ill., 1989; BS in Fire Sci., Norcross, Ga., 2007; degree in Fire Sci., Ala. Fire Coll., Tuscaloosa. Cert. fire ins., fire fighter II, fire instr. I/II, fire officer I. Master sgt. US Marine Corps., Wash., DC, 1971—92; fire commander Fire Dept. Lexington, Ala., 1995—2000; fire engr. insp. Killen Fire Dept., Killen, Ala., 2000—07; fire officer Boeing Aircraft, Ala., 2002—05; fire engr. insp. Wackenttut IRAQ, 2005—. Pres. Enferno Marina Del Rey, Calif., 2007—. Decorated Navy Cotmnendation medal, Marine Corps Expeditionary medal, Presidential Svc. Badge, Nat. Defense medal, Overseas Deployment Ribbon; recipient award, Am. Assn. Airport Executives, 1980, Fire Dept. Safety Assn., 2007, Congressional Fire Svcs. Inst., 2008, Marine Corps Good Conduct medal. Mem.: Congressional Fire Svc. Inst., Fire Dept. Safety Officers Assn., Am. Assn. Airport Executives, Pine Ridge Hunt Club. Avocations: hunting, fishing, woodworking. Office: Wackenhut Svcs WSI Fire Emergency Svcs Mosul Fire Dept St 2 Mosul AL 09334 Home Phone: 818-451-8414. Personal E-mail: tksouth4@yahoo.com.

SOUTHWELL, DONALD G., insurance company executive; Grad., We. Mich. U. Mgmt. positions through pres. ins. & fin. svcs. Prudential Ins. Co. Am., 1974—96; pres. life & health ins. group Unitrin, Inc., Chgo., 1996—99, v.p., 1998—99, sr. v.p., pres. ins. ops., 1999—2002, pres., COO, 2002—06, pres., CEO, 2006—. Bd. dirs. Unitrin, Inc., 2002—. Office: Unitrin Inc One E Wacker Dr Chicago IL 60601

SOUTHWICK, CHARLES HENRY, zoologist, educator; b. Wooster, Ohio, Aug. 28, 1928; s. Arthur F. and Faye (Motz) S.; m. Heather Milne Beck, July 12, 1952; children: Steven, Karen. BA, Coll. Wooster, 1949; MS, U. Wis., 1951, PhD, 1953. NIH fellow, 1951-53; asst. prof. biology Hamilton Coll., 1953-54; NSF fellow Oxford U., England, 1954-55; faculty Ohio U., 1955-61; assoc. prof. pathobiology Johns Hopkins Sch. Hygiene and Pub. Health, Balt., 1961-68, prof., 1968-79; assoc. dir. Johns Hopkins Internat. Ctr. for Med. Rsch. and Tng., Calcutta, India, 1964-65; chmn. dept. environ., population and organismic biology U. Colo., Boulder, 1979-82, prof. biology, 1979—, prof. emeritus, 1993—. Rschr. and author publs. on animal social behavior and population dynamics, influences animal social behavior on demographic characteristic mammal populations, primate ecology and behavior, estuarine ecology and environ. quality, Global Ecology in Human Perspective; mem. primate adv. com. Nat. Acad. Sci.-NRC, 1963-75, com. primate conservation, 1974-75; mem. Gov.'s Sci. Adv. Com. State of Md., 1975-78; mem. com. on rsch. and exploration Nat. Geog. Soc., 1979-2000; mem. adv. bd. Caribbean Primate Rsch. Ctr., 1987-99, Wis. Primate Rsch. Ctr., 1990-98; mem. Integrated Conservation Rsch., 1989-2002; mem. or leader of more than 85 rsch. expdns. on five continents. Editor, author: Primate Social Behavior, 1963, Animal Aggression, 1970, Nonhuman Primates in Biomedical Research, 1975, Ecology and the Quality of Our Environment, 1976, Global Ecology, 1985; Ecology and Behavior of Food-Enhanced Primate Groups, 1988; author: Global Ecology in Human Perspective, 1996. Recipient Fulbright Rsch. award, India, 1959—60, Tchg. Excellence award, U. Colo., 1993. Fellow AAAS, Acad. Zoology, Animal Behavior Soc.; mem. Am. Soc. Zoologists, Ecol. Soc. Am., Am. Soc. Mammalogists, Am. Soc. Primatology (Disting. Primatologist award 1994), Internat. Primatology Soc., Am. Inst. Biol. Scis. Home: 6507 Baseline Rd Boulder CO 80303-3065

SOUTHWICK, LESLIE HARBURD, federal judge, lawyer; b. Edinburg, Tex., Feb. 10, 1950; s. Lloyd M. and Ruth (Tarpley) S.; m. Sharon E. Polasek, Aug. 18, 1973; children: Philip, Catherine. BA cum laude, Rice U., 1972; JD, U. Tex., 1975. Bar: Tex. 1975, Miss. 1977. Law clk. to Hon. John F. Onion Jr. Tex. Ct. Criminal Appeals, Austin, 1975-76; law clk. to Hon. Charles Clark US Ct. Appeals (5th cir.), Jackson, Miss., 1976-77, judge, 2007—; assoc. Brunini, Grantham, Grower & Hewes, Jackson, 1977-83, ptnr., 1983-89; dep. asst. atty. gen. civil divsn. US Dept. Justice, Washington, 1989—93; judge Miss. Ct. Appeals (Dist. 4), 1995—2006. Adj. prof. Miss. Coll. Sch. Law, Jackson, 1985-89, 98-; mem. Miss. Constn. Study Commn., 1985-86. Author: Presidential Also-Rans and Running Mates, 1984, 2nd edit, 1998 (ALA Best Reference Book award 1985). Pres. Hinds County Mental Health Assn., Jackson, 1981-82, Jackson Servant Leadership Corp.; Miss. campaign mgr. George Bush for Pres., 1980, 88; alternate del. Rep. Nat. Conv., 1984, del., 1988; mem. State Rep. Exec. Com., 1988. Served in USAR, 1992—97 Miss. Army Nat. Guard, 1997—, dep. staff judge advocate US Army, 2004—05, staff judge advocate, 2006. Named Vol. of Yr., Hinds County Mental Health Assn., 1981, 85; recipient Miss. Bar Jud. Excellence award, 2004. Mem. ABA, Miss. Bar Assn. Lodges. Roman Catholic. Office: US Ct Appeals 245 E Capital St Jackson MS 39201*

SOUTHWICK, PAUL, retired public relations executive; b. West Newton, Mass., Mar. 27, 1920; s. Alfred and Pauline (Winkler) S.; m. Susan Barbara Heider, Feb. 24, 1947; children: Thomas Paul, Peter Alfred, Linda Susan. AB in Econs. cum laude, Harvard Coll., 1943. Coor. AP, Concord, NH, 1947-49; UP UPI, Washington, 1949-57; mem. profl. staff govt. info. subcom. U.S. Ho. Reps., 1957-59; legis. asst., adminstrv. asst. U.S. Senator Long of Hawaii, 1959-62; dep. adminstr. charge accelerated pub. works program Area Redevel. Adminstrn., 1962-63; spl. asst. The White House, 1963-65; spl. asst. for congl. rels. Office of U.S. Sec. Commerce, 1965-67; v.p. Newmyer Assocs., Inc., Washington, 1967-87; ind. cons., 1987-93; ret., 1993. With USNR, 1941-45, PTO. Democrat. Home: 102 Brooksby Village Dr Unit 513 Peabody MA 01960

SOUTHWORTH, ROBERT ALEXANDER, JR., education researcher, educator; b. NYC, Jan. 6, 1959; s. Robert Alexander Southworth, Sr. and Katherine Hobson Southworth; m. Linda Estelle Fischl, Sept. 11, 1994; children: Ekaterina Sophia, Anna Natalya, Robert Alexander III. AB, Dartmouth Coll., 1981; EdM, Tufts U., 1983; EdD, Columbia U. Tchrs. Coll., 1999. Secondary sch. tchg. cert. Mass., 1983, cert. advanced study. Apprentice tchr. Shady Hill Sch., Cambridge, Mass., 1982—83; theater tech dir. Colo. Acad., Denver, 1983—86; asst. dir. Denver Ctr. Performing Arts, 1986—87, Am. Conservatory Theater, San Francisco, 1988—89; asst. rschr. Nat. Ctr. for Restructuring Edn., Schools and Tchg., Teachers Coll., NYC, 1993—96; pres. The School-Works Lab, Inc., NYC, 2002—. Cons. Fenway Mid. Coll. H.S., Boston, 1990—92; adj. prof. Adelphi U. Grad. Sch. Edn., NYC, 1996—99, Bank St. Coll. Edn., NYC, 1998—2002; adj. asst. prof. Teachers Coll. Columbia U., NYC, 1998—2005. Named Bus. Man of Yr., US Congress, 2003. Mem.: Nat. Soc. Study of Edn., Am. Evaluation Assn., Am. Edn. Rsch. Assn., Phi Delta Kappa (v.p. 1997—2000), Kappa Delta Pi. Achievements include research in the positive effect on student scores in

Music, ELA and Math due to music; development of a new website to help the public understand school reform; a process to improve teacher learning called Assessment Data Gathering; statewide system of accountability for 84 funded arts partnerships in New York. Home: 19 Atlantic Ave North Hampton NH 03862-2305 Office Fax: 212-768-8700. Business E-Mail: rasouth@edspeak.org.

SOUTHWORTH, WILLIAM DIXON, retired education educator; b. Union City, Tenn., Dec. 28, 1918; s. Thomas and Gertrude (Dyer) S.; m. Violet Kuehn, July 22, 1944 (dec. 2006); 1 child: Linda Jean. PhB, Marquette U., Milw., 1948, MEd, 1950; PhD, NYU, 1961. Tchr., coach La Follette Sch., Milwaukee County, Wis., 1948-51; teaching dist. prin. Grand View Sch., Milwaukee County, 1951-56; supervising dist. prin. Maple Dale Sch., Milwaukee County, 1956-58; bldg. prin. Main St. Sch., Port Washington, NY, 1958-65; asst. supt. for elem. edn. Huntington pub. schs., NY, 1965-67; assoc. prof., acting head dept. adminstrn. and supervision St. John's U., Jamaica, NY, 1967, chmn. dept., 1968-73, prof., 1968-84. Parliamentarian for 35 internat., nat. regional orgns., expert witness, pub. moderator, and workshop leader. Author: Care and Nurture of the Doctoral Candidate, 1968, 74, Q The Story of Captain Quimby Scott, U.S. Navy WWII, 1997, The Art of Successful Meetings, 1997, Murder on the Flagship, 1998, Corpsman!, 1998, Murder Impossible, 2002, The Wonderful World of Words: How to Build and Retain a Superior Vocabulary, 2002, The Sensual Sailor, 2003, Murders in Old Main, 2004; contbr. over 270 articles to ednl. jours., condominium and parliamentary publs. With USN, 1938—44. Lutheran. Home: 2650 1st Ave S St Saint Petersburg FL 33712 Home Phone: 727-898-5697. Personal E-mail: drwilliamsouthworth@gmail.com. *In the conflicting demands of self and society, one must strike a balance by retaining the uniqueness of one's individuality while serving the society that nurtured that uniqueness. It is in the balance thus struck that the complete person evolves self-esteeming, and socially involved.*

SOUTO, FRANCISCO JAVIER, nuclear engineer, researcher; b. Mex. City, May 21, 1958; s. Arturo Souto and Matilde de Souto; life ptnr. Claudia Reyes; children: Rodrigo, Marina. PhD, U. N.Mex., Albuquerque, 2002. Grad. rsch. asst. Los Alamos Nat. Lab., N.Mex., 2000—02, tech. staff mem., 2002—. Mem.: Am. Nuc. Soc. Achievements include research in radiolytic gas bubbles in solution reactors. Home: 3000 Trinity Dr Apt 93 Los Alamos NM 87544 Office: Los Alamos Nat Lab PO Box 1663 MS T086 Los Alamos NM 87545 Personal E-mail: fjsouto@yahoo.com.

SOUTTER, THOMAS DOUGLAS, retired lawyer; b. NYC, Nov. 1, 1934; s. Thomas G. and Hildreth H. (Callanan) S.; m. Virginia Hovenden; children: Alexander D., Christopher A., Hadley H. BA, U. Va., 1955, LL.B., 1962; postgrad., Advanced Mgmt. Program, Harvard U., 1980. Bar: N.Y. 1962, R.I. 1969. Atty. Breed, Abbott & Morgan, NYC, 1962-68; with Textron Inc., Providence, 1968-95, gen. counsel, 1970-95, v.p., 1971-80, sr. v.p., 1980-85, exec. v.p., gen. counsel, 1985-95; cons., 1995-97. Mem. adv. bd. Internat. and Comparative Law Ctr., 1975-95; mem. Assn. Gen. Counsel; bd. dirs. Avco Fin. Svcs., Inc., 1985-95, Paul Revere Corp. 1993-95; trustee New England Legal Found. Nat. chmn. ann. giving campaign U. Va. Law Sch., 1992-94, mem. exec. com. campaign, 1995-2000; former trustee Providence Preservation Soc., Providence Performing Arts Ctr.; mem. U. Va. Arts and Scis. Alumni Coun.; mem. Narragansett coun. Boy Scouts Am. Lt. USNR, 1955-59. Mem. ABA, N.Y. State Bar Assn., R.I. Bar Assn., Internat. Bar Assn. Office: 2 White Birch Ln Barrington RI 02806-4932 E-mail: tdsout@aol.com.

SOUW, BERNARD ENG-KIE, physicist, researcher, engineer, consultant; b. Pekalongan, Java, Indonesia, Jan. 7, 1942; came to US, 1984, naturalized citizen, 1990; s. Tjwan-Ling and Pek-Liang (Kwee) S.; m. Martha Tjoei-Lioe Lim, July 17, 1967; children: Victor, Verena. Diploma in Physics, Tech. U. Clausthal, Germany, 1972; PhD, U. Duesseldorf, Germany, 1981. Rsch. assoc. U. Duesseldorf, 1973-83; rsch. scientist Isotope Rsch. Inst., Haan, Germany, 1983; univ. asst. Free U., Berlin, 1984; vis. scientist Air Force Wright Aero. Labs., Wright-Patterson AFB, Ohio, 1984-85; rsch. scientist Brookhaven Nat. Lab., Upton, NY, 1985-97, rsch. scientist star wars project neutral particle beam, prin. investigator, DOE in nuclear detector devel.; rsch. scientist Phys. Scis. Inc., Alexandria, Va., 1997-98; patent examiner US Patent and Trademark Office, Arlington, Va., 1998-2000, primary examiner, 2002—; sr. engring. scientist, optical free-space comm. specialist ITT Industries, Advanced Engring. & Scis., Reston, Va., 2000—02; prin. rsch. scientist, optical comm. & biophotonics BMS Enterprises, Sterling, Va., 2003—. Consulting team leader Vactronic Lab Equipment Bohemia, NY, 1992-97; adj. full prof. applied physics NJ Inst. Tech., Newark, 1993-97, team leader in collaboration with Northrop-Grumman Corp. 1993-96. Contbr. articles to profl. jours. including SPIE Jour. Optical Engring., Jour. Applied Physics, Jour. Quantitative Spectroscopy and Radiation Transfer, Jour. Plasma Physics, Plasma Physics and Controlled Fusion, Physica, Jour. Vac. Sci. Tech. Mem. Soc. Photo-Optical Instrumentation Engrs., Am. Phys. Soc. Office: BMS Enterprise Inc PO Box 650016 Sterling VA 20165-0016 Office Phone: 703-406-9831. Business E-Mail: bms@usa.com.

SOUZA, FREDERICO FERREIRA, radiologist; b. Sao Paulo, Brazil, July 22, 1976; s. Antonio Carlos Ferreira and Ana Luiza Castro Souza; m. Ana Ferreira Loviat. MD, Faculdade Ciencias Medicas Santos, 2001. Radiologist Brigham and Womens Hosp., Boston, 2006—. Recipient Douglass Adams award, Abdominal Imaging and Intervention Sect.-Brigham and Women's Hosp., 2007. Mem.: ARRS, RSNA. Home: 400 Brookline Ave Apt 14E Boston MA 02215 Office: Brigham and Women's Hosp 75 Francis St Boston MA 02115 Personal E-mail: ffsouza@partners.org.

SOUZA, KATHLEEN ANNE, middle school educator; b. New Bedford, Mass., Nov. 15, 1960; d. Ronald Joseph and Marjorie N. Souza; m. Randell Arthur Pontes, Aug. 7, 2004; children: Sean Randell Pontes, Katherine Elizabeth, Daniel Robert Trifone. Degree, So. Conn. State Coll., New Haven, 1982, Sacred Heart U., Fairfield, Conn., 1997. Cert. in mid. sch. curriculum Conn. & Mass. State Dept. Edn., 1997, in mid. sch. English Conn. & Mass. State Dept. Edn., 2005, in early childhood edn. Conn. State Dept. Edn., 1982. Edn. coord. Child Care Ctr., Inc., Stamford, Conn., 1982—86; elem. sch. tchr. Stamford Pub. Schs., 1986—90; day care provider Dept. Human Resources, Norwalk, Conn., 1990—93; sch. vol. coord., pub. rels. Supt. Schs., Norwalk, 1994—96; 8th grade English tchr. Dartmouth Pub. Sch, Mass., 1997—. English tutor Dartmouth Mid. Sch., 1997, talent show coord., 1999—2004, performance improvement team mem., 2005, young readers club advisor, 2005—07, drama club advisor, 2006—. Lector St. Matthew's Ch., Norwalk, 1992—96, children's liturgy coord., 1993—95. Recipient Excellence in Edn. award, New Bedford Regional Vocat. HS, 2006. Mem.: NEA, Dartmouth Educators Assn., Bristol County Educators Assn., Mass. tchr.assn., Nat. Coun. Tchr. English. Office: Dartmouth Mid Sch 366 Slocum Rd Dartmouth MA 02747 Business E-Mail: ksouza@dartmouthps.org.

SOVERN, MICHAEL IRA, law educator; b. NYC, Dec. 1, 1931; s. Julius and Lillian (Arnstein) S.; m. Lenore Goodman, Feb. 21, 1952 (div. Apr. 1963); children: Jeffrey Austin, Elizabeth Ann, Douglas Todd; m. Eleanor Leen, Aug. 25, 1963 (div. Feb. 1974); 1 child, Julie Danielle; m. Joan Wit, Mar. 9, 1974 (dec. Sept. 1993); m. Patricia Walsh, Nov. 12, 1995. AB summa cum laude, Columbia U., 1953, LLB (John Ordronaux prize), 1955, LLD (hon.), 1980; PhD (hon.), Tel Aviv U., 1982; LLD (hon.), U. So. Calif., 1989. Bar: N.Y. 1956, U.S. Supreme Ct. 1976. Asst. prof., then assoc. prof. law U. Minn. Law Sch., 1955-58; mem. faculty Columbia Law Sch., 1957—, prof. law, 1960—, Chancellor Kent prof., 1977—, dean Law Sch., 1970-79; chmn. exec. com. faculty Columbia U., 1968-69, provost, exec. v.p., 1979-80, univ. pres., 1980-93, pres. emeritus, 1993. Rsch. dir. Legal Restraints on Racial Discrimination in Employment, Twentieth Century Fund, 1962-66; spl. counsel to gov. N.J., 1974-77; cons. Time Mag., 1965-80; mem. panel of arbitrators N.J. Bd. Mediation, Fed. Mediation and Conciliation Svc.; bd. dirs. Asian Cultural Coun., Shubert Orgn., Comcast Corp., Sta. WNET-TV, NAACP Legal Def. Fund, 1976-97, Freedom Forum Newseum; chmn. N.Y.C. Charter Revision Commn., 1982-83; co-chmn. 2d Cir. Commn. on Reduction of Burdens and Costs in Civil Litigation, 1977-80; chmn. Commn. on Integrity in Govt., 1986; pres. Italian Acad. Advanced Studies in Am., 1991-93, Shubert Found., 1996—; chmn. Japan Soc., 1993-2004, hon. chmn., 2004—; chmn. Am. Acad. Rome, 1993-2005, chmn. emeritus, 2005—; chmn. Sotheby's, 2000—; chmn. nat. adv. coun. Freedom Forum Media Studies Ctr., 1993-2001. Author: Legal Restraints on Racial Discrimination in Employment, 1966, Law and Poverty, 1969, Of Boundless Domains, 1994; host Sta. WNET-TV series Leading Questions. Mem. Pulitzer Prize Bd., 1980-93, chmn. pro tem, 1986-87; trustee Kaiser Family Found., 1994-2002, Presdl. Legal Expense Trust, 1994-98; chmn. Sotheby's, 2000. Decorated commendatore Order of Merit (Italy), Order of the Rising Sun, Gold and Silver Star (Japan); recipient Alexander Hamilton medal Columbia Coll., 1993, Citizens Union Civic Leadership award, 1993, Town Hall Friend of the Arts award, 2001, Centennial medal Am. Acad. Rome, 2006. Fellow Am. Acad. Arts and Scis.; mem. ABA, Coun. Fgn. Rels., Assn. Bar City N.Y., Am. Philos. Soc., Am. Arbitration Assn. (panel arbitrators), Am. Law Inst., Econ. Club, Nat. Acad. Arbitrators. Office: Columbia U Sch Law 435 W 116th St New York NY 10027-7297 Office Phone: 212-854-7848. Business E-Mail: mem11@columbia.edu. E-mail: msovern@law.columbia.edu.

SOVIK, EDWARD ANDERS, architect, consultant; b. Honan, China, June 9, 1918; s. Edward Anderson and Anna (Tenwick) S.; m. Genevieve Elaine Hendrickson, June 29, 1946 (dec.); m. Anne Running, Mar. 25, 2001; children: Rolf, Martin, Peter. BA, St. Olaf Coll., Northfield, Minn., 1939; student, Art Students League N.Y., 1939-40, Luther Theol. Sem., 1940—41; MArch, Yale U., New Haven, Conn., 1949; DFA (hon.), Concordia Coll., 1981. Ret. chmn. SMSQ, Architects and predecessors, Northfield, Minn.; prof. art emeritus St. Olaf Coll., Northfield. Lectr. on ch. design at various confs., schs., univs.; participant, planner, del. numerous domestic and fgn. confs. on religion and architecture; mem., officer various profl., religious and pub. bds. and commns. Author: Architecture for Worship; Contbr. numerous articles to mags., anthologies.; works include chs., coll. and univ. bldgs., instns. With USMC, 1942-45; maj. Res. Decorated D.F.C., Purple Heart, Air medals; recipient Diekmann award, N.Am. Acad. Liturgy, 2003. Fellow AIA; mem. AIA Minn. (pres. 1977, Gold medal 1981), Phi Beta Kappa. Democrat. Lutheran. Home: 711 Summit Ave Northfield MN 55057-1568 Personal E-mail: sovik@charter.net.

SOVYANHADI, YOEDONO, biology professor; s. Soeyanto and Suzana Magdalena; m. Marta Lukas Sovyanhadi, June 29, 1980; children: Alpha Benevolence, Zeta Benevolence. PhD, Loma Linda U., Calif., 1995. Operation mgr. HHS, Long Beach, Calif., 1996—99; faculty Oakwood U., Huntsville, Ala., 1999—. Contbr. articles to profl. jours. (Rsch. grant, 2000, UNCF grant, 2004, 2005). Recipient Travel award, FASEB, 2002, Tng. award, UNCF, 2002, Travel award, AACR, 2008. Mem.: Am. Assn. Cancer rsch. Avocations: swimming, gardening. Home: 3809 McEwen Dr NW Huntsville AL 35810 Office: Oakwood Univ 7000 Adventist Blvd NW Huntsville AL 35896

SOWA, GRZEGORZ, pharmacologist, educator; s. Kazimierz Krzysciak and Jozefa Sowa; m. Beata Paw, Feb. 8, 1997. MS in Biology, Jagiellonian U., Krakow, Poland, 1989; PhD in Pharmacology, Inst. Pharmacology Polish Acad. Scis., Krakow, 1994. Assoc. rsch. scientist Dept. Pharmacology Yale U., New Haven, 2001—05; asst. prof. Dept. Med. Pharmacology and Physiology, U. Mo., Columbia, 2008—. Contbr. scientific papers to profl. jours. Grantee Scientist Devel. Grant, Am. Heart Assn., 2003—07, 2008—. Mem.: Am. Soc. Biochemistry and Molecular Biology. Office: Univ Mo 1 Hosp Dr Columbia MO 65212

SOWADA, ALPHONSE AUGUSTUS, bishop emeritus; b. Avon, Minn., June 23, 1933; s. Alphonse B. and Monica (Pierskalla) Sowada. Student, Onamia Sem., Minn., 1947-53; grad., Crosier House of Studies, Ft. Wayne, Ind., 1959; MA, Cath. U. Am., 1961. Ordained priest Canons Regular of the Holy Cross, 1958; arrived in Irian Jaya to work among Asmat, 1961; selected as mission superior, 1966; ordained bishop, 1969; bishop Diocese of Agats-Asmat, Indonesia, 1969—2001, bishop emeritus, 2001—. Mem. exec. com. Indonesian Conf. of Bishops, 1991—. Contbr. to: Nat. Geog. Yearbook, 1968, other publs. Mem. Order of Alhambra, Crosier Order, Kappa Delta Gamma. Roman Catholic. Mailing: c/o Diocese of St Cloud 214 3d Ave S Saint Cloud MN 56301

SOWALD, HEATHER GAY, lawyer; b. Columbus, Ohio, Dec. 26, 1954; d. Martin M. and Beatrice (Kronick) S.; m. Robert Marc Kaplan, June 12, 1977; children: Andrew Scott, Alexis Beth. BA, Case Western Res. U., 1976; JD, Capital U., 1979. Bar: Ohio 1979, U.S. Dist. Ct. (so. dist.) Ohio 1980, U.S. Ct. Appeals (6th cir.) 1981, U.S. Supreme Ct., 1987. Ptnr. Sowald & Sowald, Columbus, 1979-85, Sowald & Daneman, Columbus, 1985-1987, Sowald, Sowald & Mas, Columbus, 1988, Sowald, Sowald & Clouse, Columbus, 1991—2007, Sowald, Sowald, Anderson & Hawley, 2008—. Hearing officer Cert. Need Rev. Bd. State of Ohio, 1982—, Dept. Adminstrv. Services, 1982—, Dept. Mental Health, 1986—, Dept. Mental Retardation, 1986-88, Dept. Health, 1986-89, Ohio Dept. Liquor Control, 1989—. Bd. dirs. Wilderness Bond, Inc., Franklin County, Ohio, 1982-86, Youth Svcs. Adv. Bd., Franklin County, 1984—, chmn. 1987—, Ohio Bd. of Nursing, 1988—; legal advisor United Way League Against Child Abuse, Franklin County, 1986-87. Mem. Ohio State Bar Assn. (council of dels. 1986, pres. 2004, mem. family law com.), Columbus Bar Assn. (chmn. juvenile law com. 1982-84, chmn. admissions to bar 1984-86, 2005-07, chmn. publications com., 1987-88, chmn. family law com. 1988—, ethics com. 1988—, pres. 1998-99), Franklin County Trial Lawyers Assn. (trustee 1985-88, treas. 1988-89. pres.-elect 1989—, pres. 1989-90), Women Lawyers of Franklin County (pres. 1984-85), Capital U. Law Sch. Alumni Assn. (pres. 1984-86), Ohio State Bar Found. (trustee 2003—), Columbus Bar Found. (trustee 1999—, mem. grants com. 2007—), Legal Aid Soc. Columbus Ohio (trustee 2006—). Democrat. Jewish. Office: Sowald Sowald Anderson & Hawley One Americana 400 S 5th St Ste 101 Columbus OH 43215

SOWANDE, BEVERLY FOLASADE, lawyer, educator; d. Olufela Charles and Mildred Bernice (Marshall) Sowande. BA, CUNY, 1963, MS, 1966; PhD, NYU, 1974; JD, Yeshiva U., 1980. Bar: N.Y., U.S. Dist. Ct. (so. dist., ea. dist.), U.S. Ct. Appeals (2d cir.), U.S. Supreme Ct. Lectr., assoc. prof. Hunter Coll. CUNY, 1970—88; pvt. law practice NYC, 1986—88, 1992—; assoc. counsel Office Gen. Counsel CUNY, 1988—90; 1st dep. gen. counsel Human Resources Adminstrn., NYC, 1990—92. From. lectr. to assoc. prof., dept. academic skills Hunter Coll. CUNY, 1970—92, adj. assoc. prof., women's studies program and dept. polit. sci., 1982—86, NYC, 1995—96, adj. lectr., 1971—73, adj. asst. prof. dept. comm., 1973—74; adj. assoc. prof., consortium for worker edn. City Coll., CUNY, 1987—88; panel mem. departmental disciplinary com. 1st Jud. Dept., 1993—98; presenter in field. Pro bono atty. for indigent and abused women and men Coun. NY Law Assocs. and NYU Law Project for Battered Women, 1986—88; vol. atty. NY Civil Liberties Union, NYC, 1986—88; adv. bd. Sanctuary for Families Legal Advocacy Ctr., NYC, 1988—90; v.p. Wistarians Alumni, Hunter Coll. CUNY, 1986—88, pres., 1988—90; bd. dirs. Coun. NY Law Assocs., 1986—92; chair Bd. Com. on Not-for-Profit Law Project, 1988—92; coord. Pro Bono Domestic Violence Panel Family Ct. Project, with Victim Svcs. Agy., 1989—93; mem. NYC Conditional Release Commn., 1989—96; bd. dirs. Scholarship and Welfare Fund Hunter Coll., CUNY, 1980—97; bd. dirs. Alumni Assn. Hunter Coll., CUNY, 1977—78, sec., 1978—81, 2nd v.p., 1981—84, 4th v.p., 1984—87, 2nd v.p., 1987—90; chair Bylaws Revision Com., 1987—93; 1st v.p., 1990—93; pres., 1993—96; chair, Com. on Battered Women NY Women's Bar Assn., 1987—91; coord. Pro Bono Domestic Violence Project, 1987—89, bd. dirs., 1988—92; chair Continuing Legal Edn. Com., 1991—94, corr. sec., 1992—93, recording sec., 1993—94; mem. Com. on Minorities NY County Lawyers Assn., 1992; mem. Crime Victim's Com. Assn. Bar. City of NY, 1992, mem. Matrimonial Law Com., 1992—93; dir. Lawyers Com. on Violence, Inc., 1994—96, mem. Com. Profl. Responsibility, 1997—98; bd. dirs. Roosevelt House, Hunter Coll., 1993—97, Lenox Hill Neighborhood Assn., Inc., NYC, 1993—96; trustee Urban Resource Inst., Bklyn., 1994—97, sec. bd. trustees, 1997—98; adv. bd. Rosen Scholars Program, NYC, 1996—97; cert. rape crisis counselor, Sexual Assault and Violence Intervention Program Mt. Sinai Med. Ctr., NYC, 2004—. Recipient Cert. Appreciation for Pro Bono Activities, Coun. NY Law Assocs., 1988, Cert. Appreciation, Urban Women's Retreat, 1991, Pres.'s Pro Bono Svc. award, NY State Bar Assn., 1989; named to Hunter Coll. Hall of Fame, CUNY, 1987; Univ. Founder's scholar, NYU, 1974, Danforth Found. fellow, 1974. Achievements include being the coordinator of the Pro Bono Domestic Violence Panel Family Court Project with Victim Services Agency which received an Award of Merit from the New York State Bar Association. Avocation: baking. Personal E-mail: bsowande@aol.com.

SOWDER, ROBERT ROBERTSON, architect; b. Kans. City, Dec. 29, 1928; s. James Robert and Agnes (Robertson) S.; m. Joan Goddard, July 26, 1954; 1 dau., Lisa Robertson Lee. BA, U. Wash., 1953; B.Arch., U. Va., 1958; grad. diploma in Architecture, Ecole Des Beaux Arts, Fontainebleau, France, 1952. Designer Architects Collaborative, Boston, 1958-59, Peirce & Pierce (architects), Boston, 1959-63; asso. Fred. Bassetti & Co. (architects), Seattle, 1963-67; partner Naramore, Bain, Brady & Johanson (architects), Seattle, 1967-81; pres. NBBJ Internat., 1976-81; architect TRA, Seattle, 1981-83; v.p. Daniel, Mann, Johnson & Mendenhall, San Francisco, 1983-93; prin. RRS Consulting, 1993—. Archtl. design critic Boston Archtl. Ctr., 1961-62. Important works include Ridgeway III Dormitories, Bellingham, Wash. (Dept. Housing and Urban Devel. Honor award), Seattle Rapid Transit (HUD Excellence award), Safeco Ins. Co. Home Office Complex, Seattle, King County Stadium, Balt. Conv. Ctr., Oreg. Conv. Ctr., San Francisco (Moscone) Conv. Ctr. Expansion, Honolulu Conv. Ctr., Wilmington (Del.) Conv. Ctr. Mem. Redmond (Wash.) Design Rev. Bd., 1996-2000. Served with CIC U.S. Army, 1954-56, Thomas Jefferson Soc., U. Va. Recipient Premier Prix D'Architecture Ecole Des Beaux Arts, Fontainebleau, 1951, 52, Prix D'Remondet Fontainebleau, 1952 Mem. AIA (emeritus), Internat. Assn. Assembly Mgrs., Seattle Tennis Club, Seattle Rainier Club, Scarab, Sigma Chi. Episcopalian. Home and Office: 17032 NE 135th Ct Redmond WA 98052-1715

SOWELL, LAVEN, retired music educator; b. Wewoka, Okla., Jan. 9, 1933; s. Vestal Laven and Viola Jane Sowell. MusB, U. Okla., 1955; MA, Columbia U., 1964; postgrad., Manhattan Sch. Music, 1956—57, Conservatoire de Musique de Fontainebleu, France, 1966; studied with Clark Snell, Martial Singher, Joseph Benton, John Brownlee, Samuel Margolis, Nadia Boulanger, studied choral conducting with Harry Robert Wilson. Choral condr. Edison H.S., Tulsa, 1961—70; chorus master Tulsa Opera, 1962—94, chorus master emeritus, 1994—; dir. music 1st Presbyn. Ch., Tulsa, 1969—85; prof. music U. Tulsa, 1970—91. Vocal adjudicator various mus. orgns.; tchr. pvt. voice lessons. Co-author: Tulsa Opera Chronicles, 1992; author: My Music Notebook, 2000, With Affection, 2006. Bd. dirs. Tulsa Opera. Recipient Gov.'s Arts award, State of Okla., 1991. Mem.: Tulsa Accredited Music Teacher's Assn., Okla. Music Teacher's Assn. Democrat. Presbyterian. Avocations: travel, reading, opera. Home: 3800 W 71st Apt 2312 Tulsa OK 74132-2153 Office Phone: 918-388-4461.

SOWERS, MARYFRAN, epidemiologist, gynecologist, educator; BA in Nutrition, Emporia State U., 1968; MS in Nutrition, Okla. State U., 1973; PhD in Epidemiology, U. Iowa, 1984. Fellow U. Iowa, 1985, rsch. coord. in pediatric cardiology, 1978—80; asst. prof. divsn. nutritional sciences Cornell U., 1986—87; asst. prof. dept. epidemiology U. Mich. Sch. Pub. Health, 1987—92, assoc. prof. dept. epidemiology, 1992—96, prof. dept. epidemiology, 1996—; adj. prof. obstetrics & gynecology UMDNJ, 1995—; adj. assoc. prof. obstetrics & gynecology U. Mich., 1995—99, adj. prof. obstetrics & gynecology, 1999—, adj. prof. internal medicine, 1999—. Mem.: Soc. Epidemiologic Rsch., Osteoarthritis Rsch. Soc., Endocrine Soc., Am. Soc. for Clinical Nutrition, Am. Soc. Bone & Mineral Rsch., Am. Pub. Health Assn., Am. Inst. Nutrition. Office: 1846 SPH I 109 Observatory St Ann Arbor MI 48109-2029 Office Phone: 734-936-3892. Office Fax: 734-763-4552. E-mail: mfsowers@umich.edu.*

SOWMAN, HAROLD GENE, ceramics engineer, researcher; b. Murphysboro, Ill., July 21, 1923; s. Harold Thomas and Thelma (Crombar) S.; m. Gladys May Wright, Dec. 8, 1945; children: Letitia Ann, Daniel Patrick BS in Ceramic Engring., U. Ill., 1948, MS in Ceramic Engring., 1949, PhD in Ceramic Engring., 1951. Assoc. ceramist Titanium Alloy, Niagara Falls, NY, 1951-52; research assoc. Knolls Atomic Power Lab., Gen. Electric Co., Schenectady, 1952-57; various supervisory and mgmt. positions in nuclear materials research and devel. 3M Co., St. Paul, 1957-65, research specialist, 1965-67, sr. research specialist, 1967-70, corp. scientist, 1970-87. Friedberg Meml. lectr. Nat. Inst. Ceramic Engrs., 1988. Contbr. articles to profl. jours. Served to 2d lt. AUS, 1943-46 Recipient Hon. Alumni award for disting. service in engring. U. Ill. Coll. Engring., 1983 Fellow Am. Ceramic Soc. (John Jeppson medal 1985, Samuel Geijsbeek award 1989); mem. Nat. Acad. Engring., Acad. of Ceramics, 3M Carlton Soc., Tau Beta Pi (chpt. Eminent Engr. award 1983). Achievements include patents in field; development of ceramic and nuclear materials. Home: 2275 Harmony Ln #102 Naples FL 34109

SOX, HAROLD CARLETON, JR., physician, educator, editor; b. Palo Alto, Calif., Aug. 18, 1939; s. Harold Carleton and Mary (Griffiths) Sox; m. Carol Helen Hill, Aug. 26, 1962; children: Colin Montgomery, Lara Katherine. BS, Stanford U., 1961; MD cum laude, Harvard U., 1966. Diplomate Am. Bd. Internal Medicine. Intern and resident Mass. Gen. Hosp., Boston, 1966—68; clin. assoc. Nat. Cancer Inst., Bethesda, Md., 1968—70; instr. Dartmouth Med. Sch., Hanover, NH, 1970—73; asst. prof. medicine to prof. clin. medicine Stanford U. Sch. Medicine, Calif., 1973—88; Joseph Huber prof., chmn. dept. medicine Dartmouth Med. Sch., 1988—2001; editor, Annals Internal Medicine ACP, Phila., 2001—09. Pretest writing com. Am. Bd. Internal Medicine, 1992—94; panel mem. Nat. Bd. Med. Examiners, Physician Assts. Nat. Certifying Exam., 1973—76; chair com. on priority-setting for health tech. assessment Inst. Medicine, 1990—91, US preventive svcs. task force chair, 1990—95, chair com. on HIV and U.S. blood supply, 1994—95, chair IOM com. health effects Persian Gulf War svc., 1998—2000, mem. complementary and alternative medicine IOM com., 2003—04, mem. IOM com. evidence framework obesity prevention & vice chmn. IOM com. high value health svcs., 2006—07, co-chair com. priority-setting for comparative effectiveness rsch., 2009, IOM com. stds. systematic revs., 2009—; chair task force to revise internal medicine residency curriculum Federated Coun. Internal Medicine, 1993—97; nat. adv. com. generalist physician Scholars Program Robert Wood Johnson Found., 1992—2008, chmn., nat. adv. com. physician Faculty Scholar Program, 2005—; physician Leaders Nat. Drug Policy, 1997—; founding chair exec. com. Medicare Coverage Adv. Com., 1999—2003; report rev. com. NRC, 2000—05. Author: Medical Decision Making, 1988; editor: Common Diagnostic Tests, 1987, 2d edit., 1990; mem. editl. bd.: Med. Decision Making, 1980—87, Jour. Gen. Internal Medicine, 1985—87, New Eng. Jour. Medicine, 1990—97, cons. assoc. editor: Am. Jour. Medicine, 1988—95, assoc. editor: Sci. Am. Medicine, 1995—2001; contbr. chapters to books, articles to profl. jours. Bd. dirs. Found. Informed Med. Decision Making, 2002—; internat. adv. bd. Clin. Trial Registration Platform program WHO, 2005—08. Master: ACP (clin. efficacy assessment subcom. 1985—92, bd. regents 1991—2000, chmn. ednl. policy com. 1994—97, pres. 1998—99); fellow: AAAS, Coll. Physicians Phila. (bd. trustees 2006—09), Royal Australasian Coll. Physicians (hon.); mem.: Internat. Com. Med. Jour. Editors, Inst. Medicine Nat. Acads., Assn. Am. Physicians, Soc. Med. Decision Making (trustee 1980—83, pres. 1983—84, Career Achievement award 1998, John Eisenberg award 2007), Soc. Gen. Internal Medicine (coun. 1980—83, Robert J. Glaser Career Achievement award 2000), Alpha Omega Alpha. Home: 31 Faraway Ln West Lebanon NH 03784

SOYER, DAVID, cellist, music educator; b. Phila., Feb. 24, 1923; s. Samson and Esther (Faggin) Soyer; m. Janet Putnam, June 23, 1957; children: Daniel, Jeffrey. Student pub. schs., NYC; DFA (hon.), U. South Fla., 1976, SUNY, 1983. Prof. cello Curtis Inst. Music, 1967; prof. music U. Md.; prof. Manhattan Sch. Music Boston U.; prof. Juilliard Sch. Music, NYC. Musician (cellist): Bach Aria Group, 1948—49, Guilet Quartet, 1949—51, New Music Quartet, 1954—55, Guarneri String Quartet, 1964— (5 Grammy awards for Guarneri Quartet recs.). With USNR, 1942—46. Mem.: Century Assn. Jewish. Home: 6 W 77th St New York NY 10024-5125 Office: Herbert Barrett Mgmt 266 W 37th St Fl 20 New York NY 10018-6648

SOYLU, ALI, finance educator; b. Elazig, Turkey, Feb. 2, 1967; s. Abdullah and Sultan Soylu; m. Sultan Soylu; children: Sena, Lanenur, Miray Sevde, Abdullah Baran. MBA, Drexel U., Phila., 2007; PhD, Temple U., Phila., 2007. Adj. faculty Temple U., 2004—07; asst. prof. mgmt. Cameron U., Lawton, Okla., 2007—. Home: 5308 SW Inwood Cir Lawton OK 73505 Office: Cameron Univ 2800 W Gore Blvd Lawton OK 73505

SOZAN, MICHAEL L., legislative staff member; B, Coll. William and Mary, Williamsburg, Va.; JD, George Wash. U. Law Sch., Washington, 1994. Law clk., Judge Larry Elder Va. Ct. Appeals, 1994—96; atty. Dept. Justice, 1996—99, FCC, 2000—01; assoc. Arnold and Porter, 2001—03; counsel, Senator Bill Nelson US Senate, Washington, 2004—06, legis. dir., Senator Jim Webb, 2007—08, chief of staff to Senator Mark Udall, 2009—. Democrat. Office: Dirksen Senate Office Bldg Ste SD-B40E Washington DC 20510 Office Phone: 202-224-5941. Business E-Mail: michael_sozan@udall.senate.gov.*

SOZER, SADRI OZAN, plastic surgeon; s. Yalcin and Deniz Sozer; m. Mariaelena Gonzalez; children: Selin, Lara, Kaan. MD, EGE U. Sch. Medicine, Turkey, 1991. Cert. in plastic surgery ASPS, 2003, diplomate Am. Bd. Plastic Surgery, 2003. Owner, pres. El Paso Cosmetic Surgery, Tex., 2001—. Tchr. Tex. Tech U. Health Scis. Ctr., El Paso, 2008. Contbr. articles to profl. jour. Recipient Sherrell J. Aston award, Am. Soc. Aesthetic Plastic Surgery, 2005, Best Cosmetic Surgeon, El Paso Mag.-Readers Poll, 2007—08, Future 15 award, El Paso Hispanic C. of C., 2008. Achievements include invention of buttock augmentation with autoprosthesis. Avocations: travel, running, reading. Office: El Paso Cosmetic Surgery 651 S Mesa Hills Dr El Paso TX 79912 Office Fax: 915-351-8790. Business E-Mail: doctor@elpasoplasticsurgery.com.

SPACE, ZACK (ZACHARY T. SPACE), United States Representative from Ohio; b. Dover, Ohio, Jan. 27, 1961; s. Socrates and Sandra (Gallion) Space; m. Mary Wade, 1988; children: Gina, Nicholas. BA in Polit. Sci., Kenyon Coll., Gambier, Ohio, 1983; JD, Ohio State U., Columbus, 1986. Atty. Space & Space Co., LPA, 1986—, Pub. Defender's Office; spl. counsel to Ohio Attys. Gen. Anthony Celebrezze and Lee Fisher State of Ohio; law dir. City of Dover, Ohio, 2000—06, city atty. Ohio, 2000—06; mem. US Congress from 18th Ohio dist., 2007—, mem. agr. com., transp. & infrastructure com., vets.' affairs com. Mem. St. George Greek Orthodox Ch., Massillon, Ohio. Democrat. Greek Orthodox. Office: 315 Cannon Ho Office Bldg Washington DC 20515 also: 137 E Iron Ave Dover OH 44622 Office Phone: 330-343-2430, 202-225-6265, 330-364-4300. Office Fax: 330-364-2599, 330-364-4330.*

SPACEK, SISSY (MARY ELIZABETH SPACEK), actress; b. Quitman, Tex., Dec. 25, 1949; d. Edwin S. and Virginia S.; m. Jack Fisk, 1974; children: Schuyler Elizabeth, Virginia Madison. Attended, Lee Strasberg Theatrical Inst. Motion picture appearances include Prime Cut, 1972, Badlands, 1974, Carrie, 1976 (Acad. award nomination for best actress 1976), Three Women, 1977 (Best Supporting Actress 1977), Welcome to L.A., 1977, Heartbeat, 1980, Coal Miner's Daughter, 1980 (Acad. award best actress 1980, Golden Globe best actress 1980, Brit. Acad. award nomination best actress 1980, L.A. Film Critics for best actress 1980, Nat. Soc. Film Critics best actress 1980), Raggedy Man (Golden Globe nomination best actress 1981), 1981, Missing, 1982 (Acad. award nomination best actress, Golden Globe nomination best actress 1982, Brit. Acad. award nomination best actress 1982), The River, 1984 (Acad. award nomination best actress), Marie, 1985, Night Mother, 1986, Crimes of the Heart, 1986 (Acad. award nomination best actress, Golden Globe best actress 1986), Violets Are Blue, 1986, JFK, 1991, The Long Walk Home, 1990, Hard Promises, 1992, Trading Mom, 1994, The Grass Harp, 1995, Affliction, 1997, Blast From the Past, 1998, Songs in Ordinary Time, 2000, In the Bedroom, 2001 (Best Actress in Drama Golden Globe 2001, Am. Film Inst. award, Ind. Spirit award, Broadcast Critics award, Chgo. Film Critics award, Fla. Film Critics award, Golden Satellite award, Sundance Film Festival award, Southeastern Film award, N.Y. Film Critics award, L.A. Film Critics award 2001), Last Call, 2002 (nominee Outstanding Supporting Actress in Miniseries or Movie Emmy award) Tuck Everlasting, 2002, A Home at the End of the World, 2004, Nine Lives, 2005, The Ring Two, 2005, Summer Racing: The Race to Cure Breast Cancer, 2005, North Country, 2005, An American Haunting, 2006, Gray Matters, 2006, Hot Rod, 2007, Lake City, 2008, Four Christmases, 2008; TV movie appearances include Straight Story, 1999, In the Bedroom, 2001 (Acad. award nomination best actress 2001, Brit. Acad. award nomination best actress 2001, Brit. Film Critics Choice award best actress 2001, Sundance Film Festival Spl. prize 2001, Golden Globe best actress 2001, Ind. Spirit award best felmale lead 2001, AFI, Actress of Yr. 2001, L.A. Film Critics best actress 2001, N.Y. Film Critics best actress 2001, SAG nomination best actress 2001, nominee Best Actress Acad. award 2001), The Migrants, 1973, Katherine, 1975, Verna: USO Girl, 1978, A Private Matter, 1992, A Place for Annie, 1994, The Good Old Boys, 1995, Streets of Laredo, 1995, If These Walls Could Talk, 1996, Beyond the Call, 1996, Songs in Ordinary Time, 2000, Midwives (SAG nomination best actress 2001), 2001; guest host TV show Saturday Night Live, 1977; appeared in episode TV show The Waltons. Home: 1505 10th St Santa Monica CA 90401 Office Phone: 310-656-0400.*

SPACEY, KEVIN, actor; b. South Orange, NJ, July 26, 1959; s. Thomas and Kathleen Fowler. Student, Juilliard Sch., 1979-81. Actor Old Vic Theatre, England, 2003—, artistic dir., 2004—; Cameron Mackintosh vis. prof. contemporary theatre St. Catherine Coll., Oxford U., 2008—. Stage appearances include Henry IV, part I, 1981, Barbarians, 1982, Hurlyburly, 1985, Long Days Journey into Night, 1986, National Anthems, 1988, Lost in Yonkers, 1991 (Tony award for Best Featured Actor, 1991, Drama Desk award, 1991), Playland, 1993, The Iceman Cometh, 1997 (Tony award Best Male Performance/Drama 1999), The Philadelphia Story, 2005, Richard II, 2005, A Moon for the Misbegotten, 2007; actor: (films) Heartburn, 1986, Working Girl, 1988, Rocket Gibraltar, 1988, Dad, 1989, See No Evil, Hear No Evil, 1989, A Show of Force, 1990, Henry and June, 1990, Glengarry Glen Ross, 1992, Consenting Adults, 1992, Iron Will, 1994, The Ref, 1994, Outbreak, 1995, The Usual Suspects, 1995 (Acad. award for best supporting actor, 1996), Seven, 1995, A Time to Kill, 1996, Looking for Richard, 1996, Midnight in the Garden of Good and Evil, 1997, L.A. Confidential, 1997, Hurlyburly, 1998, The Negotiator, 1998, (voice only) A Bug's Life, 1998, American Beauty, 1999 (Acad. award for best actor, 2000), (voice only) Its Tough to Be a Bug, 1999, Ordinary Decent Criminals, 2000, Pay It Forward, 2000, K-PAX, 2001, The Shipping News, 2001, (voice only)The Tower of Babble, 2001, The Life of David Gale, 2003, Edison, 2005, Superman Returns, 2006, Fred Claus, 2007, 21, 2008, (voice only) Moon, 2009; actor, dir., prodr., writer, Beyond the Sea, 2004; actor, prodr. (films) Swimming With Sharks, 1994, The Big Kahuna, 1999, The United States of Leland, 2003; dir. (films) Albino Alligator, 1994; prodr. (films) Triggerstreet.com, 2004, The Sasquatch Dumpling Gang, 2006, Mini's First Time, 2006; exec. prodr. (films) Interstate 88, 2000, Uncle Frank, 2002, Mr. Gibb, 2006; actor: (TV series) Wiseguy, 1987-88, Nat. Anthems, 2005; (TV films) The Murder of Mary Phagan, 1988, Fall From Grace, 1990, When You Remember Me, 1990, Darrow, 1991, Doomsday Gun, 1994, Recount, 2008 Address: William Morris Agy 151 S El Camino Dr Beverly Hills CA 90212-2704 Office: Old Vic The Cut London SE1 8NB England*

SPACH, JULE CHRISTIAN, church executive; b. Winston-Salem, NC, Dec. 21, 1923; s. Jule Christian and Margaret Stockton (Coyner) S.; m. Nancy Clendenin, Sept. 18, 1948; children: Nancy Lynn Lane, Margaret Cuningham, Ann Thomerson, Cecelia Welborn, Robert Spach. Student, Va. Mil. Inst., 1942-43; BSChemE, Ga. Inst. Tech., 1949; postgrad., Union Theol. Sem., Richmond, Va., 1951-52, Duke U., 1955-56; MA in Ednl. Adminstrn., U. N.C., Greensboro, 1976; LHD (hon.), Stillman Coll., Tuscaloosa, Ala., 1977; LittD (hon.), Belhaven Coll., Jackson, Miss., 1977; LLD, King Coll., Bristol, Tenn., 1977. Salesman Mengle Corp. subs. Internat. Container Corp., Winston-Salem, 1950-52; from prof. scis., athletic dir. to pres. Quinze de Novembro Coll., Garanhuns, Pernanbuco, Brazil, 1952-64; edn. dir. Cruzada ABC-Recife, Pernanbuco, 1965-70, pres., 1969-70; exec. sec. Parliamentary Christian Leadership, Brasilia, Fed. Dist., Brazil, 1970-73; exec. dir. Presbyn. Mission in Brazil, Campinas, Sao Paulo, 1973-75; moderator Gen. Assembly of Presbyn. Ch. in U.S., Atlanta, 1976-77; exec. dir. Triad United Meth. Home, Inc., Winston-Salem, 1977—. Bd. dirs. First Home Fed. Savs. and Loan. Author: (biography) Every Road Leads Home, 1997. Bd. dirs. Instituto Gammon, Presbyn. Ch. U.S., Forsyth County Coun. on Aging Forsyth County Sr. Svcs. Forsyth County, Covenent Fellowship of Presbyns., William Black Lodge, Synod of N.C., Presbyn. Ch. U.S.A.; bd. visitors Lee's McRae Coll., Montreat Anderson Coll.; mem. cabinet United Way, 1987; chmn. Winston-Salem Forsyth County Coun. on Svcs. to Homeless; chmn. bd. dirs. Sr. Svcs., Inc., Winston-Salem, Missionary Family Counseling Svc. With USAAF, 1943-45, prisoner of war, Poland. Decorated Purple Heart; recipient Jefferson award, 1991; named Hon. Citizen of Garanhuas, Brazil. Mem. Sertoma Club (3 Svc. awards), Lions, Rotary. Republican. Home: Arbor Acres 1244 Arbor Rd Apt 197 Winston Salem NC 27104-1199 Office: 1240 Arbor Rd Winston Salem NC 27104-1106 Business E-Mail: jspach1@triad.rr.com. *The Christian faith teaches us that the greatest of all gifts is love. This gift comes from God, and it is ours through the presence of His spirit dwelling in us. This love gives man peace within and with his fellow man.*

SPACK, RUTH KARTEN, literature educator; b. Providence, Feb. 12, 1947; m. Norman Paul Spack; children: Rebecca Spack Sneider, Jonathan Baidell. BA, U. Rochester, NY; MA, Simmons Coll., Boston; PhD, Lesley U., Cambridge, 1998. Prof., english Bentley U., Waltham, Mass., assoc. prof., 1998—2005. ESL tchr. Watertown Pub. Schs., 1970—71; ESL tchr., adult edn. dept. Prince George's County, Marlboro, Md., 1973—74; ESL tchr. Brookline Adult & Cmty. Edn., Brookline, 1974—79; lectr., dept. english Boston U., 1978—88; lectr., dir. ESL composition, dept. english Tufts U., Medford, 1980—98. Author: (book) Guidelines: A Cross-Cultural Reading/Writing Text, 3rd ed., America's Second Tongue: American Indian Education and the Ownership of English, 1860-1900 (Mina P. Shaughnessy prize, 2003), Teaching Writiing for ESL Students, 4th ed., The International Story: An Anthology with Guidelines for Reading and Writing about Fiction; co-editor (book) Crossing the Curriculum: Multilingual Learners in College Classrooms, Enriching ESOL Pedagogy: Readings and Activities for Engagement, Reflection, and Inquiry, Negotiating Academic Literacies: Teaching and Learning Across Languages and Cultures, Language Lessons: Stories for Teaching and Learning English; contbr. articles to profl. jours, chapters to books. Mem., kehillah project, english lang. com. Jewish Cmty. Rels. Coun., Boston; pen pal, timilty mid. sch. Promising Pals; mem., fulbright nat. screening com. Inst. Internat. Edn., NYC, 2005—07; mem., editl. adv. bd. Jour. Basic Writing, Jour. Second Lang. Writing, 1990—2006, TESOL Quar., 1986—89; mem., dean's adv. coun. Simmons Coll.; mem., vis. com. Mt. Ida Coll., Newton. Recipient Freedom to Learn award, Mass. Assn. Tchrs., 2003, CHOICE Outstanding Acad. Title, Assn. Coll. & U. Rsch. Librs., 2003, Tchg. award, Bentley U., 2001, Mina P. Shaughnessy prize, MLA, 2003; grantee Rsch. grant, Bentley U., 2008; Faculty Affairs Com. grant, 2005—06, Rsch. grant, 2003, Women's Leadership Inst. grant, Bentley U. & Patrina Found., 2005. Mem.: TESOL (exec. bd. mem. 1989—92), MLA, Soc. Study Am. Women Writers, Nat. Coun. Tchrs. English, Assn. Study Am. Indian Lits. Avocations: creative writing, reading, travel. Office: English Dept Bentley Univ 175 Forest St Waltham MA 02452 Office Fax: 781-891-2896. Business E-Mail: rspack@bentley.edu.

SPACKMAN, THOMAS JAMES, radiologist; b. Oak Park, Ill., Apr. 24, 1937; s. Thomas Frederick and Louise Mary (Kaiser) Spackman; m. Donna S. Stewart, June 25, 1960; children: Kirsten, Thomas James, Victoria. BA, DePauw U., 1959; MD, Western Res. U., 1964; diploma in bus. studies, London Sch. Econs., 1987. Intern, then resident in internal medicine Yale-New Haven Med. Ctr., 1964-66, resident in diagnostic radiology, 1966-68, fellow clin. rsch. tng. unit, 1968-69; instr., then asst. prof. radiology Yale U. Med. Sch., New Haven, 1969-74; assoc. prof. U. Pa. Med. Sch., 1974-78; prof. radiology U. Conn. Med. Sch., Farmington, 1978—, head dept., 1978-90; dir. radiology St. Francis Hosp. and Med. Ctr., Hartford, Conn., 1992-93; pres. Elscint, Inc., Hackensack, NJ, 1993-97; sr. v.p. Elscint, Ltd., Haifa, Israel, 1993-97; pres. Spackman Assocs., Vero Beach, Fla., 1997—; chmn. Xicon Technologies LLC, Vero Beach, 1997-98; v.p. physician affairs Quorum Health Resources, 2000—02, Cambio Health Solutions LLC, 2002—05; chmn. Navix Diagnostix, Inc., 2002—; mng. dir. FTI Cabmrio Health Solutions, 2005—07. Mem. Conn. Med. Exam. Bd., 1980—86; bd. dirs. Elscint, Inc. Mem. editl. adv. bd. Diagnostic Imaging, 1989—92; contbr. articles to profl. jours., chapters to books. Fellow: Am. Coll. Radiology; mem.: Indian River County Hosp. Dist. (Fla.) (trustee 2009—), Environ. Learning Ctr. (trustee 2007—), Soc. Pediatric Radiology, Assn. U. Radiolgoists. Office Phone: 772-388-4631. Business E-Mail: tspackman@bellsouth.net.

SPADA, JAMES, writer, photographer, publishing executive; b. S.I., NY, Jan. 23, 1950; s. Joseph Vincent and Mary Ruberto Spada. Student, Wagner Coll., SI, 1968—71, Calif. State U., LA, 1979—80. Pres. Spada Publs., LA; pub. Barbra Quar., LA, 1980-83. Author: Barbra: The First Decade - The Films and Career of Barbra Streisand, 1974, The Films of Robert Redford, 1977, The Spada Report, 1979, Streisand - The Woman and the Legend, 1981, Monroe - Her Life in Pictures, 1982, Judy and Liza, 1983, Hepburn: Her Life in Pictures, 1984, The Divine Bette Midler, 1984, Fonda: Her Life in Pictures, 1985, Shirley and Warren, 1985, Grace: The Secret Lives of a Princess, 1987, Peter Lawford: The Man Who Kept the Secrets, 1991, More than a Woman: An Intimate Biography of Bette Davis, 1993, Streisand: Her Life, 1995, Jackie: Her Life in Pictures, 2000; photographer, pub.: Black & White Men, 2000, Ronald Reagan: His Life in Pictures, 2001, John and Caroline: Their Lives in Pictures, 2001, Edwardian Men, 2004, Julia: Her Life, 2004, The Bush Family, 2004, The Romantic Male Nude, 2007; book packager The 1984 Marilyn Monroe Pin-Up Calendar, 1983, The Telephone Book, 1984, Elizabeth Taylor: A Biography in Photographs, 1984, Bette Davis: A Biography in Photographs, 1985, Natalie Wood: A Biography in Photographs, 1986; one-man shows include Against the Grain Gallery, Cape Cod, 1998, Gallery One, Boston, 2000, Radiant Light Gallery, Portland, Maine, 2001. Democrat. Home: 622 South St Roslindale MA 02131 Personal E-mail: jamesspada2@verizon.net.

SPADAFOR, CHRISTINE J., management consultant; b. 1955; JD, Harvard Law Sch.; MSc, Harvard Sch. Pub. Health. Lic. atty., registered nurse. Prin., ptnr. with global mgmt. consulting; pres., CEO SpadaforClay Group Inc., 2004—. Bd. dirs. Boyd Gaming Corp., 2009—. CEO St. Jude's Ranch for Children, Boulder City, Nev., 2006—. Office: St Jude's Ranch for Children 100 St Jude's St Boulder City NV 89005 Office Phone: 702-294-7100. Office Fax: 702-294-7171. E-mail: cspadafor@stjudesranch.org.*

SPADAFORA, DAVID CHARLES, historian, educator; b. Hamilton, Ohio, June 4, 1951; s. Samuel Charles and Dorothy (Hardy) S.; m. Carolyn Elizabeth Gaugler, Mar. 24, 1973; children: Andrew, Claire. BA, Williams Coll., 1972; PhD, Yale U., 1981; D of Letters (hon.), Lake Forest Coll., 2001. Instr. Simon's Rock Coll., Great Barrington, Mass., 1977-78; lectr. Univ. Conn., West Hartford, 1978-80; research analyst Conn. Gen. Assembly, Hartford, 1980-81; dean of Morse Coll. Yale U., 1982, lectr. in history, 1982—90, dean of Calhoun Coll., 1982-85, assoc. dean of grad. sch., 1985—90; prof. history Lake Forest Coll., Lake Forest, Ill., 1990—2007, dean of faculty, 1990—93, pres., 1993—2007, adj. prof., 2007—; pres., libr. Newberry Libr., Chgo., 2005—. Author: The Idea of Progress in Eighteenth-Century Britain, 1990; contbr. articles to profl. jours. Bd. dirs. Yale Coop, New Haven, 1987-90, Recordings for the Blind and Dyslexic Ill. Unit, 1998-2001, Assoc. Colls. of the Midwest, 1993-2001, chmn. 2000-01; bd. dirs. CROYA, Lake Forest, Ill., 1993-2001. Recipient award for Meritorious Svc., Conn. Gen. Assembly, 1981; named Alumnus of Yr., Cin. Country Day Sch., 1994. Fellow: British-Am. Project; mem.: Am. Antiquarian Soc., Grolier Club, Mid-Am. Club, Caxton Club, Phi Beta Kappa. Avocations: golf, tennis.

SPADE, DAVID (DAVID WAYNE SPADE), actor; b. Birmingham, Mich., July 22, 1964; s. Wayne Spade and Judy Todd; 1 child. BBA, Ariz. State U., 1986. Comml. spokesperson Sierra Mist soda, Capital One credit cards. Cast mem. & writer, Saturday Night Live, 1990; actor (TV series) (voice) Beavis and Butt-Head, 1994-97, Just Shoot Me, 1997-2003, 8 Simple Rules...For Dating My Teenage Daugher, 2004-05, Rules of Engagement, 2007-; (TV host) The Showbiz Show With David Spade, 2005-; appeared in films: Police Academy 4: Citizen on Patrol, 1987, Coneheads, 1993, PCU, 1994, Tommy Boy, 1995, Black Sheep, 1996, A Very Brady Sequel, 1996, Eight Heads in a Duffel Bag, 1997, Senseless, 1998, The Rugrats Movie (voice), 1998, Lost & Found (also writer, exec. prodr.), 1999, Little Nicky, 2000, The Emperor's New Groove (voice), 2000, Joe Dirt, 2001, Dickie Roberts: Former Child Star, 2003, (voice) Racing Stripes, 2005, Grandma's Boy, 2006, The Benchwarmers, 2006; actor, writer, exec. prodr. David Spade: Take the Hit (TV), 1998; exec. prodr. Jerome, 1999; appeared on TV shows The Facts of Life, ALF, The Larry Sanders Show, The Dennis Miller Show, Beavis and Butt-head (voice), The Daily Show, BioRhythm, Comedy Central Roast of Pamela Anderson, 2005. Named to Hollywood Walk of Fame, 2003. Office: c/o Brillstein-Grey Entertainment 9150 Wilshire Blvd Ste 350 Beverly Hills CA 90212

SPADE, KATE (KATHERINE NOEL SPADE), apparel designer; b. Kansas City, Mo., 1962; m. Andy Spade, 1994. BA in Journalism & Broadcasting, Ariz. State U., 1985. From asst. to accessories editor Mademoiselle mag., 1985—92; co-founder, designer Kate Spade Inc., NYC, 1993—; designer Kate Spade paper and social stationary, 1998—, Kate Spade shoe collection, 1999—, Kate Spade glasses, 2001, Kate Spade beauty, 2002—; co-founder Jack Spade, 1999—, Kate Spade Home, 2002—. Designer (uniforms) Song Airlines (subs. Delta Airlines), 2004. Recipient Perry Ellis award, New Fashion Talent, Coun. Fashion Designers of Am., 1996, Accessory Designer of the Year, 1998, FiFi award for Bath & Body Star of the Year, US Fragrance Found.,

2003, FiFi award for Best Fragrance in Ltd. Distribution, U.K. Fragrance Found., 2003, Giants of Design award for Tastemaker, House Beautiful, 2004, Am. Food & Entertaining award for Designer of Yr., Bon Appetit, 2004, Elle Decor Internat. Design award for bedding, 2004. Achievements include stores opening in NYC in 1996, Boston and LA in 1998, and Chgo. and San Francisco in 2000. Office: Kate Spade Inc 48 W 25th St New York NY 10010

SPADE-SHENKER, GEORGE LAWRENCE (GEORGE SHENKER), research scientist; b. Sioux City, Iowa, Dec. 14, 1945; s. Walter Charles and LaVancha May (Green) S.; m. Carol Margaret Deaton, Mar. 14, 1966 (div. June 1985); children: Aaron Michael, Margaret. Mem. earthquake study group for China, U.S. Citizen Amb. Programs, 1989. Contbr. articles to profl. jours. Mem. AAAS, Internat. Soc. Philos. Enquiry, Am. Math. Soc., Math. Assn. Am., N.Y. Acad. Scis., Mensa. Avocations: poetry, painting, music. Home and Office: PO Box 2260 Columbia Falls MT 59912-2260

SPADY, JOANNE SMITH, secondary school educator; b. Phila., Jan. 17, 1935; d. Houston Thomas and Odeas Frances (Ewell) Savage; m. Sydney thomas Smith, June 1, 1963 (dec. July 1989); children: Deborah, Gregory; m. Lester Herbert Spady Sr., Apr. 3, 1994. AS, Norfolk State U., 1954; BA, U. Md., 1956. Choral, band tchr. Worcester County H.S., Snow Hill, Md., 1956-57; tchr. choral, history Acomac County, Mary N. Smith H.S., Accomac, Va., 1957-73; part-time tchr. Montgomerycounty Dept. Edn., Rockville, Md., 1973-76; asst. mgr. csh office Bradlees Inc., Rockville, 1976-86; tchr. fine arts Northampton County Dept. Edn., Eastville, Va., 1987-97. Vice chmn. planning commn. City of Cape Charles; sec. Arts Coun.; me. AFS BlackCoalition; bd. dirs. Eastern Shore C.C., Melfa, Va., 1989—. Named 1st Female High Sheriff, J. William Cultural Club. Mem. NEA, NAACP, Northampton County Edn. Ass., Edn.Assn. Va., Assn. Am. Choral Dirs., Va. Music Educators Assn., Nat. Music Educators Assn., Nat. Assn. Female Execs., Nat. Assn. Colored Women, Progressive Women eastern Shore (pres.), CWC Inc. Democrat. Methodist-Episcopalian. Avocations: music teaching, creative needle work. Home: PO Box 170 Capeville VA 23313-0170

SPAEDER, ROGER CAMPBELL, lawyer; b. Cleve., Dec. 20, 1943; s. Ferdinand N. and Luceil (Campbell) S.; m. Frances DeSales Sutherland, Sept. 7, 1968; children: Michael, Matthew. BS, Bowling Green U., 1965; JD with honors, George Washington U., 1970. Bar: DC 1971, US Dist. Ct. DC 1971, US Ct. Appeals (DC cir.) 1971, US Ct. Claims 1979, US Dist. Ct. Md. 1984, US Ct. Appeals (2d and 4th cirs.) 1985, US Supreme Ct. 1976. Asst. U.S. atty. D.C., Washington, 1971-76; ret.; ptnr. Zuckerman Spaeder LLP, Washington, 1976—2009. Faculty Atty. Gen. Advocacy Inst., 1974-76, Nat. Inst. Trial Adv., 1978-79; adj. faculty Georgetown U. Law Ctr., 1979-80, Am. U. Ctr. Adminstrn. Justice, 1976-79; lectr. DC Bar Continuing Legal Edn. Programs, 1980-90; Cardozo Prize judge Yale Law Sch., 1992; master Edward Bennett Williams Inn of Ct., 1996—; mem. DC Cir. Jud. Conf., 1991. Contbr. articles to profl. jours. and chpts. to books. Recipient Spl. Achievement award Dept. Justice, 1971. Fellow Am. Coll. Trial Lawyers; Mem. ATLA, ABA (co-chair com. on complex crimes litigation 1989-92, divsn. co-dir. sect. litigation 1992-94), Bar Assn. DC (lectr. Criminal Practice Inst. 1977-80), DC Bar (com. criminal jury instrns. 1972, divsn. cts. lawyers, adminstrn. of justice 1976-78; adv. com. continuing legal edn. 1986), Def. Rsch. Inst., Assn. Plaintiffs' Trial Attys., Nat. Assn. Criminal Def. Lawyers, Omicron Delta Kappa. Home: 7624 Georgetown Pike Mc Lean VA 22102-1412 Office: Zuckerman Spaeder LLP 1800 M St NW Ste 1000 Washington DC 20036-5802 Office Phone: 202-778-1806.

SPAEPEN, FRANS AUGUST, physicist, educator; b. Mechelen, Belgium, Oct. 29, 1948; arrived in U.S., 1971; s. Jozef F. M. and Ursula (Roppe) Spaepen; m. Moniek Steemans, Aug. 21, 1973; children: Geertrui M., Elizabet U., Hendrik J. L. Burgerlijk Metaalkundig Ingenieur, U. Leuven, Belgium, 1971; PhD, Harvard U., 1975. IBM postdoctoral fellow Harvard U., Cambridge, Mass., 1975-77, asst. prof. applied physics, 1977-81, assoc. prof., 1981-83, Gordon McKay prof. applied physics, 1983—2002, Franklin prof. applied physics, 2002—, dir. Materials Rsch. Lab., 1990—98, dir. Rowland Inst., 2002—; interim dean Harvard Sch. Enqring. & Applied Scis., 2008—09, Ctr. Nanoscale Sys., Harvard, 2009—. Vis. prof. U. Leuven, 1984, 2007, Deutsches Zentrum für Luft-und Raumfahrt-Köln, 2000, Forschungszentrum Jülich, 2001; chmn. Gordon Conf. on Phys. Metallurgy, 1988; NRC com. on solid state scis., 1990—93; NRC com. on condensed matter and materials physics, 1996—98; Krengel lectr. Technion, Israel, 1994; mem. summer rsch. group Los Alamos Nat. Lab., 1986—99; mem. sci. and tech. steering com. Brookhaven Nat. Lab.; chmn. scientific adv. bd. Netherlands Inst. for Metals Rsch.; J.B. Cohen lectr. Northwestern U., 2004. Co-editor: (series) Solid State Physics; mem. editl. bd. Jour. Applied Physics, Applied Physics Letters, 1990—93, 1999—2001, Applied Physics Revs., 1991—97, Phys. Rev., 1994—99, Jour. Non-Crystalline Solids, 1990—94; editor (prin. editor): Jour. Materials Rsch., 2001—; contbr. articles to profl. jours., chpts. to books. Recipient Best Paper award, Acta Metallurgica, 1994, Humboldt award, 1999, R.F. Mehl award, TMS Inst. Metals, 2002, Heyn medal, German Soc. Materials Sci., 2005. Fellow: AIME-The Metall. Soc., Materials Rsch. Soc. (councillor 1986—88, co-chmn. fall meeting Boston 1990, councillor 1990—92, chmn. program com. 1993—2000, Woody award 1998), Am. Phys. Soc. (chmn. divsn. materials physics 1992); mem.: Nat. Acad. Engring., Max Planck Soc. (external mem.), Vlaamse Academie voor Wetenschappen en Kunsten, Orde van den Prince, Vlaamse Ingenieurs Vereniging, Am. Soc. Metals. Office: Harvard Univ Divsn Engring and Applied Scis 29 Oxford St Cambridge MA 02138-2901 Business E-Mail: spaepen@seas.harvard.edu.

SPAETH, EDMUND BENJAMIN, JR., retired lawyer, retired law educator, former judge; b. Washington, June 10, 1920; s. Edmund B. and Lena (Link) S. AB magna cum laude, Harvard U., Cambridge, Mass., 1942; LLB, Harvard U., 1948. Bar: Pa. 1949. Judge Ct. of Common Pleas, Phila., 1964-73, Superior Ct of Pa., 1973-86, pres. judge, 1983-86; of counsel Pepper Hamilton LLP, Phila., 1986—2002. Adj. prof. U. Pa. Law Sch., 1976-97; chair Pennsylvanians for Modern Cts., 1987-2000. Fellow Am. Bar Found. (life); mem. Am. Law Inst. (life), Am. Judicature soc., Order of Coif, Phi Beta Kappa. Home: Cathedral Village Apt L-206 600 E Cathedral Rd Philadelphia PA 19128-1933

SPAETH, GEORGE LINK, ophthalmologist, educator, writer; b. Phila., Mar. 3, 1932; s. Edmund Benjamin and Lena Marie (Link) S.; m. Ann Ward, May 17, 1958; children: Kristin Lea Crowley, George Link Jr., Eric Edmund. BA magna cum laude, Yale U., 1954; MD cum laude, Harvard U., 1959; postgrad., U. Mich., 1960, U. Pa., 1961. Resident surgeon Wills Eye Hosp., Phila., 1961-63, attending surgeon, 1970—, dir. glaucoma svc., 1968—2007, dir. emeritus, 2007—; clin. fellow NIH, Bethesda, Md., 1963-65; instr. U. Pa., Phila., 1965-68; pvt. practice Phila., 1965-68; prof. ophthalmology Temple U. Med. Sch., Phila., 1968-75, Jefferson Med. Coll., Phila., 1975—, Louis Esposito glaucoma rsch. prof., 2000—. Ophthalmologist Chestnut Hill Hosp., Phila., 1975—; attending surgeon, Graduate Hosp.; cons., Bryn Mawr Hosp., Wills Eye Hosp., Hosp. Jefferson Med. Coll. Author: 19 books in ophthalmology, surgery, and med. ethics, 1970—, Poetry and Essays; contbr. over 600 articles to profl. jours.; editor Ophthalmic Surgery jour., 1985-96; editl. editor Ophthalmic Surgery and Lasers; mem. editl. bd. Jour., Ocular Surgery News, Jour. Glaucoma, Jour. Evidence-Based Ophthalmology, Glaucoma Abstracts; manuscript reviewer, New Eng. Jour. Medicine, Med. Letter Drugs and Therapy, others; patentee differometer, tonometer tip cover. Pres. Chestnut Hill Cmty. Assn., Phila., 1970-72; founder, CEO Internat. Soc. Spaeth Fellows, 1975—; trustee, founder, pres. E.B. Spaeth and Glaucoma Svcs. Found., 1978—, Profls. for Nuclear Army Control, 1985-88; trustee, treas. Thomas Skelton Harrison Found., Inc., 1984—; interviewer Yale Alumni Schs. Com., Phila., 1965—; Yale Class coun., 1968—, Yale Assn. Alumni Reps., 1996-2002; trustee Recording for the Blind and Dyslexia, 1996-2002, Internat. Arts-Medicine Assn., Pa. Ballet, 2002—, Bach Festival of Phila., 2002-2005, Squirrel Island Chapel, Maine; curriculum com. Jefferson Med. Coll., 1987-90; institutional review bd. Jefferson Med. Coll., 1990-95; pres. Phila. Glaucoma Inst., 1997—. Lt. comdr. USPHS, 1963-68. NIH grantee, 1968—; recipient Pub. Svc. medal Chestnut Hill Coll., 1972, Sir Stuart Duke Elder Glaucoma award Internat. Glaucoma Soc., 1986, Newberg award Lawyers Alliance for World Security, 1995, Derrick Vail award Internat. Soc. Prevention Blindness, 1996, Trantas award Greek Ophthalmol. Soc., 2000, Frominopolous prize Greek Glaucoma Soc., 2003, Large Flower and Vegetable Garden 1st Pl. award Pa. Horticultural Soc., 2004, Nizankowska award Polish Glaucoma Soc., 2006, Mildred Weisenfeld award, Assn. Rsch. Vision Ophthalmology, 2009; named Ophthalmic Visionary, Ocular Surgery News, 2003, Bausch & Lomb, 2005, Goldmann medal, Internat. Glaucoma Rsch. Soc., 2007, Silver fellowship, Assn. Rsch. Vision Ophthamology, 2009. Fellow Am. Acad. Ophthalmology (chmn. ethics com. San Francisco 1987-95, coun. 1980-93, vice chmn. residency rev. com. Chgo. 1982-88, Sr. honor award 1988, life time achievement award 1999), Am. Assn. Rsch. in Vision and Ophthalmology, Royal Coll. Ophthalmologists U.K., Danish Ophthalmol. Soc., Ind. Soc. of Ophthalmology; mem. Am. Glaucoma Soc. (pres. 1983-85), Coll. Physicians Phila. (sec. 1976-84), Phila. County Med. Soc., Pa. Acad. Ophthalmology (pres. coun.), German Ophthalmol. Congress, Physicians for Social Responsibility (pres. emeritus Phila. chpt.), ACS (bd. govs. emeritus, chmn. emeritus adv. coun. for ophthalmology), Phila. Club, Phila. Cricket Club, Phi Beta Kappa, Alpha Omega Alpha. Democrat. Avocations: composing music, piano, sports, photography, gardening. Office: Wills Eye Hosp 11th Fl 840 Walnut St Philadelphia PA 19107-5109 Home Phone: 215-242-3285; Office Phone: 215-928-3960. Business E-Mail: gspaeth@willseye.org.

SPAETH, JAN MILLS, jury consultant; b. Grinnell, Iowa, July 17, 1951; d. Paul Herbert and Joyce Carol Broadwell; m. Paul Vincent Spaeth, May 26, 1988. BA with honors, U. Wis., Madison, 1973; MA, U. Ariz., 1996; PhD, Calif. Coast U., 1999. Social worker Cass County Dept. Social Svcs., Walker, Minn., 1973—75; dir. rsch. Lakehead Social Planning Coun., Thunder Bay, Ont., Canada, 1975—76; social worker Thunder Bay Social Svcs. Dept., 1976—78; free-lance workshop coord. Duluth, Minn., 1979; freelance litig. cons. Tucson, 1980—. Educator Tucson Free U., 1980, Pima County Jail, Tucson, 1981, Pima County Juvenile Ct. Ctr., Tuscon, 1981; instr. U. Ariz., Tuscon, 1980—94, Pima C.C., Tucson, 1990—94, Cochise C.C., Sierra Vista, Ariz., 1991; supplemental juror questionnaire subcom. Supreme Ct. Ariz., Phoenix, 1995; spkr. in field. Contbr. articles to profl. jours. Recipient Appreciation award, Pima County Juvenile Ct. Ctr., 1982. Mem.: APA, Ariz. Attys. for Criminial Justice, Am. Coll. Forensic Examiners, Am. Soc. Trial Cons. Avocations: hiking, travel, golf, research, writing. Office: Ariz Jury Rsch PO Box 91410 Tucson AZ 85752 Office Phone: 520-297-4131.

SPAETH, KARL HENRY, retired chemicals executive, lawyer; b. Phila., Mar. 12, 1929; s. Edmund Benjamin and Lena Marie (Link) S.; m. Ann Dashiell Wieland, Sept. 14, 1963; children: Karl Henry, Edmund Alexander, Christopher Philip. AB, Haverford Coll., 1951; postgrad., Oxford U., 1955; JD, Harvard U., 1958. Bar: Pa. 1959, U.S. Ct. (ea. dist.) Pa. 1959, U.S. Ct. Appeals (3d cir.) 1959. Assoc. MacCoy, Evans & Lewis, Phila., 1959-62; counsel for fgn. ops. Scott Paper Co., Phila., 1962-69; v.p., corp. sec. Quaker Chem. Corp., Conshohocken, Pa., 1969-95, ret. v.p., 1995, ret. corp. sec., 1998. Bd. dirs. Greater Phila. Devel. Corp., 1991-98; bd. dirs., sec.-treas. Edmund B. Spaeth Clin. Rsch. Found., 1982—; chmn. bd. dirs. Pa. Chem. Industry Coun., 1984-86. Chmn. bd. trustees Quaker Chem. Found., 1982-2003; bd. overseers Univ. Mus., U. Pa., Phila., 1983-89, 90-96; bd. dirs. Opera Co. Phila., 1988-2003; bd. dirs. Chestnut Hill Acad., Phila., 1976-83, pres. 1979-83; mem. Whitemarsh Twp. Bd. Suprs. Pa., 1969-75, chmn., 1972-74; mem. Com. of Seventy, Phila., 1984-96. Comdr. USNR, 1952-55, ret. Mem. Pa. Bar Assn. (chmn. sect. on internat. and comparative law 1980-92), Phila. Com. on Fgn. Rels. (exec. com., sec. 1984-94, chmn. 2001-04), Phila. Club, Phila. Athenaeum, Libr. Co. of Phila., Phila. Cricket Club, Oxford Union Club, Univ. Barge (sec. 1988-94), Mil. Order Fgn. Wars (registrar 1989-91, vice commdr. 1991-93), German Soc. Pa. (bd. dirs. 2001-, sec. 2007-). Republican. Anglican. Home: 2129 Harts Ln Conshohocken PA 19428-2416 E-mail: khspaeth@comcast.net.

SPAETH, MARY SHEPARD, marketing communications executive; b. Evanston, Ill., Apr. 25, 1957; d. Kenneth Sihler and Helen (Reis) Shepard; m. Alan Colin Spaeth, May 27, 1978; children: Erika Leigh, Daniel Barrett. BA in English, So. Meth. U., 1978, MA, 1982. Cert. secondary edn. tchr., Tex., Ill. Pub. info. officer Hockaday Sch. for Girls, Dallas, 1978-79; French tchr. Episcopal Sch. Dallas, 1979-80; tchg. fellow So. Meth. U., Dallas, 1980-82, English instr., 1982-83; English lectr. Loyola U., Chgo., 1984-92; pres. Comm. Resource Group, Evanston, 1989—; dir. pub. rels. Northwestern U./Evanston Rsch. Park, 1994—; econ. devel. tech. transfer cons. and advisor, 1995—. Ind. cons. mktg. and econ. devel.; English dept. writing com. Loyola U., Chgo., 1987-89; pres. Savoy-aires Light Opera Co., 1990-94; adj. prof. Nat. Louis U., Evanston, 1989—. Author: The Fiery Collaboration of Gilbert and Sullivan, 1991; author numerous articles and poems; editor: Hockaday, 1978-79; assoc. editor: Brides Today, 1993-94. Active Chgo. Coun. on Fgn. Rels., 1993—; chair Lincoln Sch. PTA Lang. Bd., 1990-97. 1st lt. CAP. Loyola U. fellow, 1990-91; named one of Outstanding Young Women of Am., 1991. Mem. MLA, DAR, Internat. Assn. Bus. Communicators, Nat. Coun. Tchrs. English, Westminster Club, Technology Execs. Roundtable (bd. dirs.), Young Execs. Club Chgo. (v.p. comms. 1992-94, exec. v.p. 1994-95, dir. 1995-96, v.p. pub. rels. 1996—), Chgo. Playwrights Ctr. (bd. dirs.), Sigma Tau Delta, Pi Delta Pi. Avocations: singing, acting, directing, writing, reading. Home: Döbelnsgatan 33 113 58 Stockholm Sweden Office: Transmera AB Teknikringen 7 583 30 Linköping Sweden also: Royal Inst Tech Kungliga Tekniska högskolan Inst Ind Mgmt (INDEK) Lindstedtsvägen 30 SE-100 44 Stockholm Sweden

SPAETH, VIRGINIA ANN, biology professor; b. Chgo., Ill., Mar. 28, 1935; d. Ralph and Erma Spaeth. BS in Biology, U. Chgo., 1957, MS in Biology, 1962; PhD in Zoology, U. Wis. Madison, 1982. Tchr. gen. sci. & biology Thornton Twp. HS, Harvey, Ill., 1957—58; rsch. asst., dept. zoology Univ Chgo., 1961—62; lectr. gen. biology Chgo. City Jr. Coll., 1962—63; asst. & instr. U. Ill. Navy Pier & Chgo. Cir., Chgo., 1962—67; tchr. Faulkner Sch., Chgo., 1972—73; instr. biology U. Tenn. Nashville, 1975—77; tchr., gen. biology, human anatomy & physiology Madison Area Tech. Coll., Wis., 1977—80; tchg. asst. Dept. Genetics, U. Wis., Madison, 1980; tchr., biology, anatomy, physiology Gateway Tech. Inst., Racine, Wis., 1983—84; biology instr. U. Wis., Plateville, 1984; instrnl. specialist, sci. tutor U. Wis. Sch. Nursing, Madison, 1985—92; biology, anatomy & physiology instr. Coll. DuPage, Glen Ellyn, Ill., 1989—92; asst. prof. biology Oakton CC, DesPlaines, Ill., 1992—95; adj. instr. biology Roosevelt U., Chgo., 1995—; instr. biology Northeastern Ill. U., Chgo., 1996—. With Entomol. Soc. Am., Portland, Oreg., 1966, Tenn. Acad. Scis., Chattanooga, 1976, Internat. Congress Zoology, 1976. Contbr. articles to profl. jours. Vol. Radio Sta. WFMT, Chgo., 2005—08. Grant, U. Ill. Rsch. Bd., 1965. Jewish. Avocations: music, swimming, movies. Office: Roosevelt Univ Biology Dept 430 S Michigan Ave Chicago IL 60605 Office Fax: 847-619-8555. Business E-Mail: vspaeth@roosevelt.edu.

SPAFFORD, MICHAEL CHARLES, artist; b. Palm Springs, Calif., Nov. 6, 1935; BA, Pomona Coll., 1959; MA, Harvard U., 1960. Artist-in-residence Dartmouth Coll., 2005. One man shows include Seattle Art Mus., 1982, 86, Reed Coll., 1984, Whtcom county Mus., 1987, U. Puget Sound, Tacoma, Wash., 1973, Tacoma Art Mus., 1975, 86, Utah Mus. Fine Arts, Salt Lake City, 1975, Francine Seders Gallery, Seattle, 1965—, Bellevue Art Mus., 1991, Cheney-Cowles Mus., Spokane, Wash., 1994, Hallie Ford Mus. Art, Willamette U., Salem, Oreg., 1999; exhibited in group shows at Wilcox Gallery, Swarthmore Coll., Pa., 1977, Seattle Art Mus., 1977, 80, 84, Am. Acad. and Inst. Arts and Letters, N.Y.C., 1980, 83, 89, 95, Kobe, Japan, 1981, Eastern Wash. U., 1982, Henry Art Gallery, 1982, 86, Bellevue Art Mus., 1987, 95, Cheney Cowles Mus., 1988, Holter Mus. of Art, Helena, Mont. Recipient Rome Prize Am. Acad. in Rome, 1967-69, award Am. Acad. and Inst. Arts and Letters, 1983, Lifetime Achievement in Arts award Corp. Coun. Arts, Seattle, 1999. Flintridge Found. award for visual artists, 2006; Louis Comfort Tiffany Found. grantee, 1965-66; Neddy fellow, 1996. Address: c/o Francine Seders Gallery 6701 Greenwood Ave N Seattle WA 98103-5225

SPAGNOLETTI, ROBERT JAMES, lawyer, former attorney general; b. 1962; 1 adopted child, Hunter. BS in Mathematics & History, Lafayette Coll., 1984; JD, Georgetown U., 1987. Bar: NJ, NY, Washington, DC. Litig. assoc. Mayor Day Caldwell & Keaton, Houston, Skadden, Arps, Salte, Meagher & Flom, NY & DC; asst. US atty. DC US Dept. Justice, Washington, 1990—2003, chief domestic violence unit, 1995—98, chief sex offence & domestic violence section, 1998—2003; atty. gen. Washington, DC, 2003—06; ptnr. Schertler & Onorato LLP, Washington, 2006—. Prof. law Georgetown U. Law Ctr. Recipient Young Lawyer of Year award, Bar Assn. of DC, 1997, Sullivan Award, Asst. US Atty. Assn., 2002. Democrat. Office: Schertler & Onorato LLP 601 Pennsylvania Ave NW Washington DC 20004

SPAGNOLO, SAMUEL VINCENT, internist, pulmonary specialist, educator; b. Pitts., Sept. 3, 1939; s. Vincent Anthony and Mary Grace (Culotta) S.; children: Samuel, Brad, Gregg; m. Dorcas R. Hardy, Sept. 29, 1996. BA, Washington & Jefferson Coll., 1961; MD, Temple U., 1965. Diplomate Am. Bd. Internal Medicine, Bd. Pulmonary Disease, lic. physician Fla., Calif., Md., D.C., Va., Ariz., Pa., Mass. Sr. resident in medicine VA Med. Ctr., Boston, 1969-70, chief resident in medicine, 1970-71; Harvard Clin. and Rsch. fellow in pulmonary diseases Mass. Gen. Hosp., Boston, 1971-72; asst. chief med. svc. VA Med. Ctr., Washington, 1972-75, acting chief med. svc., 1975-76, chief pulmonary disease sect., 1976-94, chief of staff, 1998-99, dir. respiratory care and sr. attending in pulmonary diseases, 1999—; instr. in medicine Boston U. Sch. of Medicine, Tufts U. Sch. Medicine, Boston, 1970-71; clin. and rsch. fellow in pulmonary diseases Harvard U. Sch. of Medicine, Mass. Gen. Hosp., Boston, 1971-72; attending physician George Washington U. Med. Ctr., 1972—; clin. asst. prof. medicine Georgetown U., Washington, 1975-77; asst. prof. medicine George Washington U. Sch. of Medicine and Health Scis., Washington, 1972-75, assoc. prof., 1975-81, prof. medicine, 1981—, dir. divsn. pulmonary diseases and allergy, 1978-93; assoc. chmn. dept. medicine George Washington U. Med. Ctr., Washington, 1986-89. Cons. in pulmonary diseases The Washington Hosp. Ctr., Washington, DC, 1977—, Will Rogers Inst., White Plains, NY, 1980—, US Dept. Labor, Washington, 1980—, Walter Reed Army Med. Ctr., Washington, 1987-90; rep. Am. Coll. Chest Physicians to Am. Registry Pathology, Washington, 1981-92; radio tv appearances on Health Oriented Programs; invited lectr. in U.S., Russia, Jordan; med. chest cons. in attempted assasination of former Pres. Reagan; presenter in field. Author: Clinical Assessment of Patients with Pulmonary Disease, 1986; co-author: (with A.E. Medinger) Handbook of Pulmonary Emergencies, 1986, Handbook of Pulmonary Drug Therapy, 1993, (with Witorsch, P.) Air Pollution and Lung Disease in Adults, 1994; mem. editl. bd. CHEST Jour., 2002-06; mem. editl. bd. Chest, 2006—; contbr. numerous articles to profl jours. including Med. Clin. N.Am., Chest, So. Med. Jour., Am. Jour. Cardiology, Jour. Am. Med. Assn., Clin. Rsch., Am. Rev. Respiratory Disease, Am. Lung Assn. Bull., Clin. Notes on Respiratory Diseases, Jour. Nuc. Medicine, Drug Therapy. Pres., chmn. Found. Vets. Health Care, 1998—. Lt. comdr. USPHS, 1966-68. Decorated cavaliere Order of Merit, Republic of Italy; nominated for Golden Apple award by med. students George Washington Sch. Medicine, Phila., 1977; recipient cert. appreciation D.C. Lung Assn., 1983. Fellow ACP (coun. critical care 1983-85), Am. Coll. Chest Physicians (gov. DC, coun. of govs. 1989-96); mem. Am. Thoracic Soc. (exec. com. DC chpt. 1978, 85, 89, mem. adv. com. Tb control, 1978-84, pres. DC chpt. 1981-83), Nat. Assn. VA Physicians (sec. 1987-89, v.p. 1989-91, pres. 1992-98), Internat. Lung Found. (pres. 1991—). Achievements include first major review of patient outcome during early history of intensive care units; an analysis of mechanisms of hypoxemia in patients with chronic liver disease; first report of Pneumocystis Carinii Pneumonitis in patients with lung cancer; first prospective evaluation of short course therapy reported in U.S. using Isoniazid and Rifampin; first American report using laser through fiberoptic bronchoscope to treat lung cancer; first report to evaluate continuous intravenous morphine to control pain in cancer patients; description of a simple technique to measure the total lung volume non-invasively using the routing chest x-ray. Office: George Washington U 5-425 2150 Pennsylvania Ave NW Washington DC 20037-3201 Office Phone: 202-741-2237.

SPAGNUOLO, LOUIS D., banker; b. Boston, June 22, 1971; s. Louis D. and Beverly A. Spagnuolo. Degree in fin., U. Miami, Coral Gables, Fla., 1992. Cert. in life health & v ariable annuity Fla., 2006. Mortgage banker Royal Bank Can., Boca Raton, Fla., 2003—05; sr. mortgage banker Home 123 Financial, Boca Raton, 2005—07; v.p. mortgage banking WCS Lending, Boca Raton, 2007. Pres. JRS Holdings LLC, Ft. Lauderdale, Fla., 2006. Contbr. articles to profl. jours. Contbr. I Have A Dream Orgn., N.Miami Beach, 2004. Recipient Pres. award, Royal Bank Can., 2004—05, Home 123 Mortgage, 2006. R-Conservative. Avocation: travel. Office: Wealth Capital Solutions Lending 6501 Congress Ave 3d Fl Boca Raton FL 33487 Home: 411 N New River Dr E Fort Lauderdale FL 33301 Office Fax: 561-864-2818. Personal E-mail: sld7@aol.com. Business E-Mail: lspagnuolo@wcslending.com.

SPAGNUOLO, MARK MARIO, retired dentist; b. Midland, Mich., July 24, 1928; s. Anthony and Rose Spagnuolo; m. Sarah Frances Novello, Aug. 7, 1954; children: Christina Marie, Anthony Mark, Natalie Louise. BS, Ctrl. Mich. U., Mt. Pleasant, 1951; MS, U. Detroit, 1952, DDS, 1956. Lab. asst. Ctr. Mich. U., 1949—51; instr. U. Detroit, 1951—53; dentist pvt. practice, Ferndale, 1956—57, Lansing, 1959—92; ret., 1992. Pres. Ceatnal Supply Co., Spagnulo Builders, 1982—. Contbr. articles to profl. jours. Co-chair Mich. Com. for Re-election of Nixon, 1972; chmn. Mich. Dentists for Reagan, 1980, 1984; pres. Anthony Apts., 1959—, Park Laynes Gardens Apt., 1993—. Capt. US Dental Corps., 1957—59, cmdr. Army Mobile Dental Svc. Recipient Eagle Scout, 56 merit badges, 3 palms. Fellow: Am. Acad. Gen. Dentistry, Royal Soc. Health, London (pres.); mem.: Nat. Italian-Am. Found., Internat. Platform Assn., Nat. Acupuncture Rsch. Soc., Acad. Gen. Dentistry, Internat. Acad. Orthodontice, Fedn. Dentare Internationale, Assn. Mil. Surgeons US, Mich. Soc. Dentistry Children, Am. Dental Assn. (produced, directed, wrote ednl. film), Mich. Dental Assn., Ctrl. Dist. Dental Soc., Chgo. Dental Soc., Detroit Dist. Dental Soc., Mich. Fedn. Physicians and Dentists (chmn. peer rev. com. 1974—92, bd. dirs. 1975—92, chmn. legis. com. 1975—92, chmn. travel sem. 1976—92), Century Club (founder), Rotary. Republican. Roman Catholic. Home: 1724 Old Mill Rd East Lansing MI 48823

SPAGNUOLO, STEVE, professional football coach; b. Whitinsville, Mass., Dec. 21, 1959; m. Maria Spagnuolo. B in Phys. Edn., Springfield Coll., Mass.; M in Sports Mgmt., U. Mass. Grad. asst. U. Mass. Minutemen, 1982—83; player pers. intern Washington Redskins, 1983; defensive line, spl. teams coach Lafayette Coll. Leopards, Pa., 1984—86; defensive coord., defensive backs coach U. Conn. Huskies, 1987—91; defensive line, spl. teams coach Barcelona Dragons, Spain; scout San Diego Chargers, 1993; defensive coord., defensive backs/linebackers coach U. Maine Black Bears, 1993—94; defensive backs coach Rutgers U. Scarlet Knights, NJ, 1994—95, Bowling Green State U. Falcons, Ohio, 1996—97; defensive coord., linebackers coach Frankfurt Galaxy, Germany, 1998; defensive asst. Phila. Eagles, 1999—2000, defensive backs coach, 2001—03, linebackers coach, 2004—06; defensive coord. NY Giants, 2007—09; head football coach St. Louis Rams, 2009—. Recipient Male Scholar Athlete award, AAUP, 1982. Achievements include member of Super Bowl XLII Championship winning New York Giants, 2008. Office: St Louis Rams 1 Rams Way Saint Louis MO 63045*

SPAHN, GARY JOSEPH, lawyer; b. NYC, July 23, 1949; s. Harry G. and Mary (Hopkins) S.; m. Lois Luttinger, Aug. 9, 1975; children: Gary J. Jr., Lori J. BA, L.I. U., 1971, MA, 1976; JD, U. Richmond, 1975. Bar: Va. 1975, U.S. Ct. Appeals (4th cir.) 1975, U.S. Supreme Ct. 1980. Law clk. to Hon. Judge Dortch U.S. Dist. Ct. (ea. dist.) Va., Richmond, 1975—77; from assoc. to ptnr. Troutman Sanders LLP (formerly Mays & Valentine), Richmond, 1977—; now ptnr. Troutman Sanders LLP, Richmond, past chmn. products liability and ins. sect. Lectr. in field, 1980—; mem. jud. conf. U.S. Ct. Appeals (4th cir.). Co-author: Virginia Law of Products Liability, 2000 Pres. Southhampton Citizens Assn., Richmond, 1982-85; bd. dirs. Southhampton Recreation Assn., Richmond. 1983, Chesterfield County Crime Solvers. With USAF, 1967-73. Named to Best Lawyers Am. Products Liability, 2007. Mem. ABA (litig. and tort and ins. sects.), Internat. Assn. Def. Counsel (co-chair litig. sect. Products Liability com.), Def. Rsch. Inst., Va. Assn. Def. Attys., Va. Mfrs. Assn., Products Liability Adv. Counsel, Va. Power Boat Assn. (commodore). Avocations: boating, basketball, racquetball, guitar. Office: Troutman Sanders LLP PO Box 1122 1001 Haxall Point Richmond VA 23218-1132 Office Phone: 804-697-1400. Business E-Mail: gary.spahn@troutmansanders.com.

SPAHN, JAMES FRANCIS, marketing professional; b. Dubuque, Iowa, Oct. 4, 1957; s. Ervin Henry and Denise Marie (Shuhert) S.; m. Beverly Joan Burns, Oct. 22, 1983. Grad., Brown Inst. Tech., 1977. Lic. real estate commn.; cert. mktg. dir. Mktg. dir., cert. shopping ctr. mgr. The Cafaro Co., Dubuque, 1979-80; mktg. dir. The Herring Marathon Group, Dallas, 1980-83, Dusco Property Mgmt., Inc., Lancaster, Pa., 1983-87, Jim Wilson and Assocs., Montgomery, Ala., 1987—2004; dir. mktg. Bayer Properties Inc., Birmingham, Ala., 2004—07; v.p. mktg. Colonial Properties Trust, Birmingham, 2007—. Co-author: Operating Shopping Centers, 1984. Mem. Cen. Bus. Dist. Revitalization Task Force, Savannah, Ga., 1984-86, Transit Task Force, Savannah, 1985-86; bd. dirs. Conv. and Vis. Bur., Savannah, 1986-87. Recipient Addy awards Dubuque Advt. Club, 1980. Mem. Internat. Coun. Shopping Ctrs. (Maxi award 1982, Maxi finalist 1987, 89, 90, 94, 2002, 03), Savannah Advt. Club (bd. dirs. 1984-87), Birmingham Advt. Club (Addy awards 1983-87, 89). Roman Catholic. Avocations: camping, bicycling. Home: 7375 Thomas Hall Dr Trussville AL 35173-1851

SPAHR, RONALD W., finance educator, department chairman; s. Wesley C. and Pearl M. Spahr; m. Helen R. Murphy, Oct. 16, 2004; children: R. Scott, Laton A., Matthew R. PhD in Fin., U. Wis., Madison, 1976. Prof. U. Wyo., 1976—88; Belk disting. prof. fin. U. NC, 1998—2001; nat. city disting. prof. banking and fin. U. Ill., Springfield, 2001—05; prof. and chair dept fin., ins. and real estate U. Memphis, 2005—. Pres. Montis West Corp., Cordova, Tenn., 1985—. Contbr. articles to profl. jours. Treas. U.Wyo., Laramie, 1980—98. Capt. USAF, 1966—70, Malmstrom AFB, Mont. Grants, 1980—98. Mem.: Beta Gamma Sigma (life), Omicron Delta Kappa (life), Lambda Alpha (life). Home: 7808 Woodchase Dr Cordova TN 38016 Office: Univ Memphis Dept Fin Ins and Real Estate Memphis TN 38152 Office Phone: 901-678-5930. Business E-Mail: rspahr@memphis.edu.

SPAHT, CARLOS G., II, mathematics educator; b. New Orleans, June 22, 1943; s. Carlos Gustave and Loretta Andrus Spaht; children: Elizabeth, Carolyn. BS in Math. with honors, La. State U., 1964, MS in Math., 1966, PhD in Math., 1970. Asst. prof. math. La. State U., Shreveport, 1972—80, prof., 1980—, chmn. Dept. Math., 1981—86, 1996—2001, dir. La. Preparatory Program (LaPREP), 1992—. Founder, dir. Math Helpers, Inc., 1996—; spkr. in field. Capt. US Army, 1970—72. Recipient La./Miss. Disting. Tchg. award, Math. Assn. Am., 1997, Jefferson award, Jacqueline Kennedy Onassis Found., 1998, Jacqueline Kennedy Onassis award, 1998, Presdl. award, NSF, 2000, US Professors of Yr. Award for Outstanding Master's Universities and Colleges Prof., Carnegie Found. for Advancement of Tchg. and Coun. for Advancement and Support of Edn., 2007; named La. Prof. of Yr., Carnegie Found., 1997. Office: La State U Math Dept One University Pl Shreveport LA 71115 Office Phone: 318-797-5377. E-mail: cspaht@lsus.edu.

SPAIN, JAMES DORRIS, JR., biochemist, educator; b. Washington, Feb. 3, 1929; s. James Dorris and Frances (Pitkin) S.; m. Patricia Mann, Oct. 3, 1952; children: James Williamson, Caryn Ann, Mary Alisa. Student, Tulane U., 1947-48; BS, Mich. Technol. U., 1951; MS, Med. Coll. Va., 1953; PhD, Stanford, 1956. Research fellow biochemistry U. Tex.-M.D. Anderson Hosp. and Tumor Inst., 1955-56; assoc. prof. dept. chemistry Mich. Technol. U., Houghton, 1956-62, head dept. biol. scis., 1962-68, prof. biochemistry, 1962-84, prof. emeritus, 1985—. Dir. Ctr. for Instrnl. Computing, Ea. Mich. U., Ypsilanti, 1984-85; vis. prof. Clemson U., S.C., 1985-94; pres. Electronic Homework Sys., Inc., 1994—; cons. Computer Applications in Biology and Chemistry; dir. SUMIT Courseware Devel. Project, 1979-82. Author: Some Computer Programs for Biology, 1970, Biological Simulation Techniques, 1972, Lake Superior Basin Bibliography, 1976, BASIC Computer Models in Biology, 1978, Basic Microcomputer Models in Biology, 1982, Developing Chemical Skills with Computerized Instruction, 1990, Computer Simulation in Biology: A Basic Introduction, 1992, Chemi-Skill-Bildr Electronic Homework System, 1994, ChemSkill Builder for Windows, 1997, ChemSkill Foundations, 1998, Chem Skill Builder/2000, 1999, GOB-ChemSkills, 2002, ChemSkill Builder/3000, 2005; contbr. articles to profl. jours. Chmn. adv. council St. Josephs Hosp. Sch. Nursing, 1967; Trustee, pres. Portage Twp. Sch. Bd., 1968-76; trustee Copper Country Intermediate Sch. Dist., 1975-78. Recipient Faculty Rsch. award, Mich. Technol. U., 1965. Mem. Am. Chem. Soc. (past sect. v.p., chmn.), Rotary, Sigma Xi, Phi Lambda Upsilon. Clubs: Miscowaubik (gov. 1971-74, 79-82), Boscobel Country. Episcopalian. Home: 42498 Lakeshore Dr Chassell MI 49916-9006 also: 129 Leslie Ln Pendleton SC 29670 Home Phone: 800-836-3949. Personal E-mail: jspain.chemskil@prodigy.net.

SPAIN, JIM C., environmental engineer, educator; b. Dallas, Sept. 15, 1948; life ptnr. Catherine M. Vogel. BS, U. Tex., Arlington, 1973; PhD, U. Tex., Austin, 1979. Postdoc. rsch. assoc. EPA Rsch. Lab., Gulf Breeze, Fla., 1979—82; sr. rsch. microbiologist Air Force Rsch. Lab., Panama, Fla., 1984—87, chief, environ. bio-tech. rsch., 1988—2004; sabbatical ETH Inst. Bio-tech., Zurich, Switzerland, 2000; prof., environ. engring. Ga. Inst. Tech., Atlanta, 2005—. Sci. adv. com. mem. EPA Hazardous Substance Rsch. Ctr., 1992—2000, 2002—05; sci. adv. bd. mem. U. Iowa Ctr. Biocatalysis and Bioprocessing, 2002—05, Rice U. NSF Ctr. Biol. and Environ. Nano-tech., 2004—07, DuPont Chambers Works Sci. Adv. Bd., 2005—. Contbr. articles to profl. jours. Recipient Applied and Environ. Microbiology award, Proctor and Gamble, 2008. Fellow: Am. Acad. Microbiology; mem.: AAAS, Am. Chem. Soc., Am. Soc. Microbiology. Achievements include 6 Patents. Office: Ga Inst Tech Civil & Environ Engring 311 Ferst Dr Atlanta GA 30332-0512 Office Fax: 404-894-8266. Business E-Mail: jspain@ce.gatech.edu.

SPAIN, THOMAS B., retired state supreme court justice; Judge 4th Judicial Cir., Hopkins and Caldwell Counties, 1973—91; justice Ky. Supreme Ct, Frankfort, 1991-95; ret., 1995; of counsel Whitfield & Cox P.S.C. Office: Whitfield & Cox PSC 29 E Center St Madisonville KY 42431-2037 Home Phone: 270-821-4821; Office Phone: 270-821-0656.

SPAINHOUR, J. PATRICK (JAMES PATRICK SPAINHOUR), outsourcing company executive, former apparel executive; b. 1950; married. B, Miss. State Univ., 1972. Positions through v.p. fin. & adminstrn. Kellwood Co., 1972—83; exec. v.p. fin. & ops. Seminole Mfg. Co., 1983; sr. v.p. sourcing Gap Inc., 1988—93; exec. v.p. fin. & ops. Stride Rite Corp., 1993—94; exec. v.p., CFO Donna Karen Co., 1994—96; pres., COO Ann Taylor Stores Corp., 1996, chmn., CEO, 1996—2005; interim chmn., CEO Servicemaster Co., Downers Grove, Ill., 2006, chmn., CEO, 2006—07; CEO Servicemaster Co., Servicemaster lLobal Holdings, Downers Grove, Ill., 2007—. Bd. dir. Tupperware Corp., Circuit City Stores Inc., 2004—, Servicemaster Co., 2005—.

SPAINHOWER, JAMES IVAN, retired college president; b. Stanberry, Mo., Aug. 3, 1928; s. Elmer Enoch and Stella Irene (Cox) S.; m. Joanne Steanson, June 10, 1950; children: Janet Dovell, James Jeffrey. BA, Phillips U., Enid, Okla., 1950, LLD (hon.), 1967; BD, Lexington Theol. Sem., Ky., 1953; MA in Polit. Sci., U. Mo., Columbia, 1967, PhD, 1971, U. Ark., 1954; diploma, U. Pacific Sch. Religion, Berkeley, Calif., 1958; DPA (hon.), Culver-Stockton Coll., 1973; LL.D. (hon.), Maryville Coll., St. Louis, 1976; Litt.D. (hon.), Kirksville Coll. Osteo. Medicine, Mo., 1977; D.H.L. (hon.), Mo. Valley Coll., 1984; LLD (hon.), Eureka Coll., 1989, Lynchburg Coll., 1993. Ordained to ministry Christian Ch. (Disciples of Christ), 1950; pastor chs. in Ark. and Mo., 1953-70; mem. Mo. Ho. of Reps. from, Saline County, 1963-70; pres. Asso. Med. Schs. Mo., Jefferson City, 1970-72; part-time prof. polit. sci. Lincoln U., Jefferson City, 1970-72; treas. State of Mo., 1973-80; pres. Sch. of Ozarks, Point Lookout, Mo., 1981-82, Lindenwood Coll., St. Charles, Mo., 1983-89; pres. divsn. higher edn. Christian Ch. (Disciples of Christ), 1989-93. Author: Pulpit, Pew and Politics, 1979. Chmn. Mo. del. Dem. Nat. Conv., 1976; elected mem. Acad. Squires, 1981; 1st chmn. Mo. Children's Trust Fund, 1984-86. Recipient Mental Health award Mo. Mental Health Assn., 1967, Meritorious Service award St. Louis Globe Dem., 1968, Harry S. Truman award Saline County Young Democrats, 1970, citation of merit Alumni Assn. U. Mo., 1975; named Mo. Lay Educator of Year Mo. chpt. Phi Delta Kappa, 1968 Home and Office: 1616 W Long Blvd Raymore MO 64083

SPAKE, MARY BARBARA, music educator; b. Mpls., Apr. 7, 1919; d. Donald Nivison Ferguson and Arline Calista (Folsom); m. Virgil F. Spake, July 2, 1978. BS, U. Minn., 1942, M. Music Edn., 1949. Tchr. Grand Marais (Minn.) Pub. Schs., 1942-43, Litchfield (Minn.) Pub. Schs., 1943-45, Mpls. Pub. Schs., 1945-79, Mpls. Coll. Music, 1949-55, Macalestar Coll., St. Paul, 1950-56; pvt. music tchr. Golden Valley, Minn., 1949—, Asst. choir dir. Cen. Luth. Ch., Mpls., 1946-56; choir dir. Grace U. Luth. Ch., Mpls., 1950-55. Mem. Retired Tchrs. Mpls., Music Educators Nat. Conf., Nat. Assn. Tchrs. of Singing, Sigma Alpha Iota. Avocation: dress making. Home and Office: 5825 Saint Croix Ave N 174 Golden Valley MN 55422-4763

SPAKE, REUBEN MICHAEL, mathematics professor, researcher; b. Spokane, Wash., Mar. 20, 1957; s. William Jack and Georgia Geraldine (Christensen) S.; m. Cynthia Spake. BS, U. Calif., Davis, 1978, MA, 1984, PhD, 1986. Mathematician, Edwards AFB, Calif., 1976-79; computer programmer analyst Mgmt. Info. Svcs., Fairfield, Calif., 1979—83; math. teaching asst. U. Calif., Davis, 1983-86; prof. Coll. Charleston, SC, 1987—93; prof. math. Solano CC, Fairfield, Calif., 1993—, Consumnes River Coll., Sacramento, 1994—, San Jacquin Delta Coll., Stockton, Calif., 1994—, Los Medanos Coll., Pitts., 1994—. Pub. power semigroup rsch., 1985—. Recipient Math. Achievement award Bank Am., 1974; Kraft scholar U. Calif., Davis, 1975. Mem. AAAS, SAR, Am. Math. Soc., Math. Assn. Am., NY Acad. Scis., Hereditary Order of First Families Mass., Sons and Daus. of Pilgrims, Sons of the Am. Revolution, Magna Charta Barons, Pi Mu Epsilon, Mu Alpha Theta. Avocations: guitar, music, travel. Office: Solano CC 4000 Suisun Valley Rd Fairfield CA 94534 Personal E-mail: rmspake@yahoo.com.

SPALDING, ANDREW FREEMAN, lawyer; b. Toledo, June 24, 1951; s. Dean and Shirley Louise (Maitland) S.; m. Adele Taylor, May 17, 1980; children: Amy Louise, Adam Freeman, Audrey Wade, Abigail Maitland. BA, U. Calif., Berkeley, 1973; JD, So. Meth. U., 1977. Bar: Tex. 1977, NY 2006, US Dist. Ct. (so., ea. and we. dists.) Tex. 1978, US Ct. Appeals (5th cir.) 1978; bd. cert. civil trial law, personal injury trial law. Assoc. Bracewell & Giuliani, LLP, Houston, 1977-84, ptnr., 1985—. Notes and comments editor So. Meth. U. Law Jour., Dallas, 1976-77. Fellow Tex Bar Found., Houston Bar Found.; mem. State Bar Tex., Houston Bar Assn., Tex. Assn. Def. Counsel, Def. Rsch. Inst., Am. Bd. Trial Advocates (assoc.), Knights Momus, Krewe Maximilian, Pan Tex. Assembly, Allegro, Houston Country Club. Office: Bracewell & Giuliani LLP 2300 S Tower Pennzoil Pla 711 Louisiana St Ste 2300 Houston TX 77002-2770 Office Phone: 713-221-1220. Business E-Mail: Andrew.Spalding@bgllp.com.

SPALDING, JAMES STUART, retired telecommunications industry executive; b. Edinburgh, Nov. 23, 1934; arrived in Can., 1957, permanent resident, 1962; Student, Edinburgh U., 1951-52, Glasgow U., 1953. Gen. mgr., dir. United Corps. Ltd., Montreal, Que., Canada, 1970-72; from pension fund mgr. to exec. v.p. fin. BCE, Inc., Montreal, 1972-90. Mem. Inst. Chartered Accts. Scotland, Inst. Chartered Accts. Ont., Fin. Execs. Inst. Can. (past chmn.), Montreal Soc. Fin. Analysts (past pres.). Home: 126 King St E Brockville ON Canada K6V 1B9 Personal E-mail: stuart231134@aol.com.

SPALDING, ROBERT STEELE, II, systems administrator; b. Denver, May 9, 1968; s. Robert Harry and Barbara Spalding; m. Diane Marie Krenowicz, Sept. 15, 2001; 1 child, Julie Marie. MCSE 1999, CSSP Soinc Wall, 2008. Sys. adminstr. Vangard Tech., Englewood, Colo., 1996—97, Commnet Cellular, Englewood, Colo., 1997—99, MoneyGram Internat., Lakewood, Colo., 1999—2004; pres., CTO Avail Computer LLC, Littleton, Colo., 2004—. Fellow: Rotary Internat. (bd. mem. 2005—07, coord. 2005—07, Paul Harris fellowship 2008). Conservative. Avocation: hiking. Office: Avail Computer LLC 11757 W Ken Caryl Ave #F357 Littleton CO 80127

SPALDING, TIM, Internet company executive; m. Lisa Carey; 1 child, Liam Patrick. Grad., U. Mich. Freelance web developer, web pub. Houghton Mifflin, Boston; founder www.isidore-of-seville.com, www.ancientlibrary.com, www.bramblestory.com, LibraryThing, 2005—. Home: 28 Atlantic St Portland ME 04101 Business E-Mail: tim@librarything.com.

SPALTY, EDWARD ROBERT, lawyer; b. New Haven, Oct. 1, 1946; s. Kermit and Elinor Turgeon; m. Suzy Clune; children: Thomas John, Kathleen Tess. BA, Emory U., 1968; JD, Columbia U., 1973. Bar: Mo. 1975, Nebr. 1997, Kans. 1998, Colo. 2003, U.S. Dist. Ct. (we. dist.) Mo. 1975, U.S. Ct. Claims 1977, U.S. Ct. Appeals (8th cir.) 1984, U.S. Ct. Appeals (10th cir.) 1999, U.S. Supreme Ct. 1994, U.S. Dist. Ct. (ea. dist.) Wis. 2004, US Ct. Appeals (9th cir.) 2009. Assoc. Webster & Sheffield, NYC, 1973-74; mng. ptnr. Armstrong Teasdale LLP, Kansas City, Mo., 1991-2001, ptnr., 1980—. Contbr. articles to profl jours. Chmn. bd. dirs. Mo. Easter Seals, 1990—92; founding mem. Heartland Franchise Assn.; bd. dirs., mem. exec. com. Easter Seal, 1992—98, 2002—08; bd. dirs. Mo. Easter Seals, 1984—2008. With US Army, 1968—70. Recipient Client Svc. award, Chambers USA, 2008, 2009; named Best of the Bar, Kans. City Bus. Jour., 2006; named a Superlawyer, Mo., 2006, Kans., 2006—; named one of Best Lawyers in Am., Chambers USA, 2007—, Woodward White, 1995—. Mem.: ABA (litigation sect, franchising forum comt), Easter Seals Inc. (gen. counsel), Intern. Rels. Coun. Kansas City, Def. Rsch. Inst., Mo. Orgn. Def. Attys., Lawyers Assn. Kansas City, Kansas City Met. Bar Assn. (chmn antitrust and franchise law comt, co-chair 14th and 16h ann Nat Franchise Law Inst), Mo. Bar Assn. (civil rules and procedures comt), Lex Mundi (regional vice chair N.Am. dispute resolution, antitrust practice group), German-Am C. of C. (v.p. Kansas City chpt), Nat. Golf Club Kansas City (founder), Phi Delta, Pi Sigma Alpha, Sigma Nu. Home: 13703 NW 73rd St Parkville MO 64152-1120 Office: Armstrong Teasdale LLP 2345 Grand Blvd Ste 2000 Kansas City MO 64108-2617 Office Phone: 816-221-3420. Business E-Mail: espalty@armstrongteasdale.com.

SPALVINS, JANIS GUNARS, steamship company executive; b. Riga, Latvia, May 26, 1936; arrived in Australia, 1949; s. Peter Spalvins and Hilda (Dritmanis) Blumentals; m. Cecily Westall Rymill, Dec. 16, 1961; children: John Rymill and Richard Rymill. B in Econ. Group sec., dir. Camelec Group of Cos., South Australia, 1955-73; asst. gen. mgr. The Adelaide Steamship Co. Ltd., South Australia, 1973-77, chief gen. mgr., dir., 1977-81, mng. dir., 1981-90; dir., chief exec. David Jones Ltd., Australia, 1980, 1988—91; dir. Macmahon Holdings, Ltd., 1987—92; chmn., dir. Galufo Pty, Ltd., 1991—. Fellow Australian Inst. Mgmt., Australian Soc. CPAs, Inst. Chartered Accts., Inst. Dirs., Chartered Inst. Secs., Cruising Yacht of SA. Avocations: sailing, tennis, snow and water skiing. Home: 2 Brookside Rd Springfield SA 5061 Australia Office Phone: 618 418821900. Personal E-mail: jgspalvins@bigpond.com.

SPANAKI, MARIANNA V., neurologist, educator; d. Vlassios E. Spanakis and Ekaterini I. Trantalidi; m. Panayiotis N. Varelas, Oct. 7, 1995; 1 child, Eleni Nefeli Varelas. MD, Patras Med. Sch., Greece, 1988; PhD, Athens Med. Sch., Greece, 1998; MBA, U. Tenn., Knoxville, 2008. Asst. prof., neurology Med. Coll. Wis., Milw., 2001—05; sr. staff, neurologist Henry Ford Health Sys., Detroit, 2005—, dir., epilepsy monitoring unit, neurology dept., 2008—; assoc. prof., neurology Wayne State U. Med. Sch., Detroit, 2006—. Bd. mem., examiners baldrige Nat. Inst. Stds. & Tech., Washington, 2009; adv. bd. mem. to sec. Lansing, Mich., 2009. Recipient award, Milw. Bus. Jour., 2004. Mem.: AMA (Early Career Leadership award 2008), Mich. State Med. Soc., Am. Epilepsy Soc., Am. Acad. Neurology (active mem.), Phi Kappa Phi. Office: Henry Ford Health Sys Neurology 2799 W Grand Blvd Detroit MI 48202

SPANDORFER, MERLE SUE, artist, educator, writer; b. Balt., Sept. 4, 1934; d. Simon Louis and Bernice P. (Jacobson) S.; m. Lester M. Spandorfer, June 17, 1956; children: Cathy, John. Student, Syracuse U., 1952-54; BS, U. Md., 1956. Mem. faculty Cheltenham (Pa.) Sch. Fine Arts, 1969—; instr. printmaking Tyler Sch. Art Temple U., Phila., 1980-84; faculty Pratt Graphics Ctr., NYC, 1985-86. One woman shows include Richard Feigen Gallery, N.Y.C., 1970, U. Pa., 1974, Phila. Coll. Textiles and Sci., 1977, Ericson Gallery, N.Y.C., 1978, 79, R.I. Sch. Design, 1980, Syracuse U., 1981, Marian Locks Gallery, Phila., 1973, 78, 82, Temple U., 1984, Tyler Sch. Art, 1985, University City Sci. Ctr., 1987, Gov.'s Residence, 1988, Wenninger Graphics Gallery, Provinceton, Mass., 1989, Widener U. Art Mus., 1995, Gloucester County Coll., 1996, Mangel Gallery, 1992, 97, 2000, 03, 06, Cabrini Coll., 1999, Mangel Gallery, 2006, Fireside Gallery, Devon, Pa., 2007; group shows Bklyn. Mus. Art, 1973, San Francisco Mus. Art, 1973, Balt. Mus. Art, 1970, 71, 74, Phila. Mus. Art, 1972, 77, Fundacio Joan Miro. Barcelona, Spain, 1977, Del. Mus. Art, Wilmington, 1978, Carlsberg Glyptotek Mus., Copenhagen, 1980, Moore Coll. Art, Phila., 1982, Tyler Sch. Art, 1983, William Penn Meml. Mus., Harrisburg, Pa., 1984, Ariz. State U., 1985, Tiajin Fine Arts Coll., China, 1986, Beaver Coll., Phila., 1988, The Port of History Mus., Phils., 1987, Sichuan Fine Arts Inst., Chong Qing, China, 1988, Glynn Vivian Mus., Swansea, Wales, 1989, Phila. Mus. Art, 1990, Fgn. Mus., Riga, Latvia, 1995, Woodmere Art Mus., Phila., 1996, Am. Coll., 1997, Cheltenham Ctr. for the Arts, Phila., 1997, Rowan Coll., 1997, Villanova U., 1998, U. Pa., 1999, U. of the Arts, 2001, Rosemont Coll., 2008, State Mus. PA, 2008, Ambre Gallery, Bethlehem, 2009. others; represented in permanent collections Met. Mus. Art, N.Y.C., Whitney Mus. Am. Art, N.Y.C., Paper Mus., Kyoto,

Japan, Mus. Modern Art, N.Y.C., The Israel Mus., Balt. Mus. (gov.'s prize and purchase award 1970), Phila. Mus. Art (purchase award 1977), Toyoh Bijutsu Gakko, Tokyo, Library of Congress, Temple U., Colgate U., Reading Mus.; commd. works represented in U. Pa. Inst. Comtemporary Art, 1991; co-author: Making Art Safely, 1993, State Mus. Penn., 2009 Recipient award Balt. Mus. Art/Md. Inst. Art, 1971, Govs. prize and Purchase award Balt. Mus. Art, 1970, Outstanding Art Educators award Pa. Art Edn. Assn., 1982, Purchase award Berman Mus., 1995, Artist Equity award, 1996; grantee Pa. Coun. Arts, 1989. Mem. Am. Color Print Soc., Pa. Art Edn. Assn. Jewish. Office: 307 E Gowen Ave Philadelphia PA 19119-1023 Home Phone: 215-379-2813. Personal E-mail: merlespandorfer@comcast.net.

SPANFELLER, JAMES JOHN, JR., former publishing executive; b. Phila., Aug. 25, 1956; s. James John and Patricia Ann (Durkin) Spanfeller. BA, Union Coll., Schenectedy, NY, 1979. Assoc. pub. Soho News, NYC, 1979-81; dir. Alan Western Comm., NYC, 1981-83; pub. Newsweek on Campus, NYC, 1983-86; nat. sales mgr. Newsweek, NYC, 1986, sales dir., 1987-89; assoc. pub. Playboy, sr. v.p. Playboy Enterprises Pub. Group, 1989-93; pub. Inc. mag., 1993—96; pub. Yahoo! Internet Life mag. Ziff-Davis Inc., 1996—98, v.p. Yahoo! Internet Life, 1998—2000; pres., CEO Forbes.com, 2000—09. Bd. dirs. Mag. Pub. Assoc., 1999—2000; bd. dirs. Am. Bus. Media, Freedom Comm., Inc. Named a Top Innovator in Bus. Pub., BtoB Media Bus., 2006; named one of 21 Most Intriguing People, MinOnline mag., 2003, Top 25 Newsmakers, BtoB Media Bus., 2005; named to Digital Hall of Fame, MinOnline mag., 2006. Mem.: Interactive Advt. Bur., Online Pub. Assn. Office Phone: 212-366-8999. Office Fax: 212-366-8801.*

SPANFELNER, DEBORAH CALABRO, college librarian; BA in Modern Fgn. Langs., Nazareth Coll., Rochester, NY, 1977; MA in Comparative Lit., Binghamton U., NY, 1979, PhD in Comparative Lit., 2007; MLS, Syracuse U., NY, 1986. Spanish, French tchr. Seton Cath. Ctrl. HS, Binghamton, 1980—84; ref. and instrn. libr. Broome CC, Binghamton, 1987—. Author (Dissertion): VDM Verlag Dr. Muller, Helene Cixious: A Space For The Other, 2008. Bd. mem. Binghamton La-Teste France Sister Cities Program, 1997—. Recipient Chancellor's Librarianship award, SUNY, 2000. Mem.: SUNY Libr. Assn. Office: Broome CC Libr PO Box 1017 Binghamton NY 13902 Business E-Mail: spanfelner_d@sunybroome.edu.

SPANGENBERG, NORMAN EARL, retired hydrologist educator; b. Porterville, Calif., Sept. 10, 1939; m. Lillian Spangenberg. PhD, Colo. State U., Fort Collins, 1972. Lic. in profl. hydrologist State Wis. Prof. U. Wis. Stevens Point Coll. Natural Resources, 1971—2006, prof. emeritus, 2006—. Editor-in-chief Water Resources Impact, Am. Water Resources Assn., Middleburg, Va., 1999—; exec. sec. Wis. Conservation Hall of Fame Found., Inc., Stevens Point, 2007—. 1st lt. USAF, 1962—66. Fellow: Am. Water Resources Assn. (past pres., bd. mem., editor); mem.: Wis. Sect. Am. Water Resources Assn., Soil and Water Conservation Soc. Liberal. Episcopalian. Avocations: travel, gardening, walking.

SPANG-HANSSEN, HENRIK STAKEMANN, lawyer, researcher; b. Copenhagen, Oct. 31, 1953; arrived in US, 1998; s. Henning and Bente Lise (Stakemann) Spang-Hanssen. Attended, Tech. U. Denmark, 1973—75; LLM, Copenhagen U., Denmark, 1980, Santa Clara U., Calif., 2005, cert. in US Law, 2002; Merconom in Acctg., Danish Comml. Schs., Copenhagen, 1988. Bar: Denmark 1983, Ct. Appeals 1988, Danish Supreme Ct. 1994. Reporter Dist. Atty. Zealand office, 1978—80; lawfirm John Richter & A Klastrup Hansen, Nykøbing Sjaelland, Denmark, 1980—83; with Danish Law Soc., 1983—85; barrister, solicitor, own lawfirm Copenhagen, 1985—99; sr. rschr. Santa Clara U., Silicon Valley, Calif., 1998—, vis. scholar, 1998—99, 2005—06, Stanford U., Calif., 1999, Oxford U., England, 2000, U. Oslo, 2000—04; project leader Vienna U., Austria, 2008. Clerk for Chief Justice of Supreme Ct., Denmark, 1984—85; owner, mng. dir. real estate mgmt. co., Copenhagen, 1987—99; co-owner, mgr. legal affairs in a franchise co., Copenhagen City, 1990—95; CEO Apple Co., Copenhagen, 1994—95; v.p. Danish Merc. Assn., 1989—90, exec. mem., 1990—91; foreclosure actions, debt-collecting bus. bankruptcy, moratorium com. mem. Danish Law Soc., 1989—92, mem. disciplinary com. dist. Copenhagen, 1989—94; chmn. spl. debt-collecting bus. com., 1991—92; judge Jessup Internat. Law Moot Ct. Competition, 2002—04, lectr., presenter, 1986—. Author: (books) Reduction, exchange, and addition concerning mortgage and pledge, 1980, Lawyers' fee - presentation, practice and policy, 1985, Legal Ethics/Precepts for Lawyers - presentation and discussion, 1996, Cyberspace Jurisdiction in the US - The International Dimension of Due Process, 2001, Cyberspace & International Law on Jurisdiction - Possibilities of Dividing Cyberspace into Jurisdictions with help of Filters and Firewall Software, 2004, Public International Computer Network Law Issues, 2006, Legal Research Methods in the US & Europe, 2007, 2009, The Study of the Intersection of Public International Law & Public International Computer Networks; contbr. articles and papers to profl. pubs., chapters to books. Bd. mem., elected internal acct. Danish Leprosy Mission, 1997—2009. Mem.: ABA (assoc.; cyberspace law com. 2002), Am. Soc. Internat. Law, Internat. Law Assn., Norwegian Assn. Law and Edn., Computer Law Assn., Lions Club of Copenhagen (pres. 1996—99). Home and Office: 521 Del Medio Ave APT 218 Mountain View CA 94040

SPANGLER, ARTHUR STEPHENSON, JR., psychologist; b. Boston, June 20, 1949; s. Arthur Stephenson and Barbara Louise (Fellows) Spangler; m. Deborah A. Kauders, Nov. 27, 1971; children: Heather Anita, Rebecca Haley. BS, Hobart Coll., 1971; MEd, Boston Coll., 1974; ScD, Boston U., 1985. Diplomate Am. Acad. Pain Mgmt.; lic. psychologist, Mass., clin. social worker, Mass.; bd. cert. rehab. counselor, Mass. Mass. counselor Met. State Hosp., Waltham, 1971-73; rehab. counselor J.T. Berry Rehab. Ctr., North Reading, Mass., 1974-75; program coord. Shore Collaborative, Medford, Mass., 1975-76; dir. instl. sch. programs South Shore Collaborative, North Weymouth, Mass., 1976-79; dir. mental retardation program South Shore Mental Health Ctr., Quincy, Mass., 1979-85; coord. outpatient clinic Boston Pain Ctr., Spaulding Rehab. Hosp., 1985-86; v.p., dir. behavioral medicine svcs. Mass. Bay Counseling, Quincy, 1985—; dir. indsl. disability mgmt. svcs., psychologist chronic pain program Miriam Hosp., Providence, 1987-88; psychologist John Graham Headache Ctr. Faulkner Hosp., Boston, 1992-94. Adj. prof. Sargent Coll., Boston U., 1990—99; med. cons. Social Security Adminstrn., Disability Determination Services, Boston, 2006—. Vol. counselor Multi-Svc. Ctr., Newton, Mass., 1973-75; bd. dirs. Newton-Wellesley-Weston-Needham Cmty. Mental Health and Mental Retardation Ctr., Newton, 1976-80, pres. 1979-80; mem. Boston Symphony Assn. Vols. Recipient award Nat. Assn. Retarded Citizens, 1974. Mem.: ACA, APA (assoc.), New Eng. Pain Assn., Soc. Behavioral Medicine, Internat. Assn. for Study of Pain, Assn. for Study of Pain. Episcopalian. Home: 151 Tremont St # 11P Boston MA 02111-1110 Office: 234 Copeland St 3rd Fl Quincy MA 02169 Office Phone: 617-786-0137. Business E-Mail: sspangler.mbc@comcast.net.

SPANGLER, BEULAH STARK (BES SPANGLER), retired literature and language professor; b. Wilson, NC, Dec. 11, 1937; d. James Luther Stark and Annabelle Stark Martin; m. John Barringer Spangler, Aug. 12, 1967; 1 child, Haywood Barringer. PhD, U. NC, Chapel Hill, 1983. English prof. Peace Coll., Raleigh, NC, 1982—2008. Lectr. NC Humanities Coun., Greenboro, 1988—2008. Contbr. chapters to books. Edn. com. mem. Christ Episcopal Ch., Raleigh, 1998—2005. Recipient Alumnae Disting. Prof. award, Peace Coll., 1998—2000, Janice Edwards Svc. award, 2005; Summer Inst. scholar, Nat. Humanities Coun., 1985. Mem.: Soc. Study Southern Lit. (pres. coll. English assn. 1986—87), Thomas Wolfe Soc., Southeastern MLA. Democrat. Avocations: travel, reading.

SPANGLER, CLEMMIE DIXON, JR., construction company executive; b. Charlotte, NC, Apr. 5, 1932; s. Clemmie Dixon and Veva C. (Yelton) S.; m. Meredith Jane Riggs, June 25, 1960; children: Anna Wildy, Abigail Riggs. BS, U. N.C., 1954; MBA, Harvard U., 1956; LHD (hon.), Queens Coll., 1985; LLD (hon.), Davidson Coll., 1986, Furman U., 1993; LLD U. N. Carolina (hon.), 2003. Pres. C.D. Spangler Constrn. Co., Charlotte, 1958-86, Golden Eagle Industries, Inc., 1968-86; chmn. bd. Bank of N.C., Raleigh, 1973-82; dir. NCNB Corp., 1983-86; chmn. N.C. Bd. Edn., 1982-86; pres. U. N.C., Chapel Hill, 1986-97; CEO, chmn. C.D. Spangler Constrn. Co., Charlotte, 1997—. Bd. dirs. BellSouth Corp., Atlanta; chmn. bd. dirs. Nat. Gypsum Co., Charlotte. Past deacon Myers Park Bapt. Ch., vice-chmn. Charlotte-Mecklenburg Bd. Edn., Charlotte, 1972-76; past trustee Charlotte Symphony Orch., Crozer Theol. Sem.; past chmn. Charlotte adv. bd. Salvation Army; past bd. dirs. YMCA, Equitable Life Assurance Soc., Jefferson-Pilot Corp.; pres. bd. trustees Mint Mus. Art; bd. dirs. Union Theol. Sem., 1985-90, Assocs. Harvard Bus. Sch.; pres. bd. overseers Harvard Coll., 2003. With U.S. Army, 1956-58. Recipient Liberty Bell award Mecklenburg County Bar Assn., 1985, Alumni Achievement award Harvard Bus. Sch., 1988; named one of Forbes' Richest Americans, 2006. Mem. Assn. Am. Univs., Bus. Higher Edn. Forum, Harvard Club (N.Y.C.), Univ. Club (N.Y.C.), Quail Hollow Country Club (Charlotte). Office: CD Spangler Constrn Co Office of Chmn Box 36007 Charlotte NC 28236-6007

SPANGLER, COLLEEN ANN, marketing professional; b. Toledo, Aug. 14, 1938; d. Irvin Frederick Callahan and Eileen Rose Carey-Callahan; m. Richard Leon Blass, Jan. 14, 1956 (dec.); children: Edie Davenport, Vicki Schramm, Rick Blass, Tracy; m. Joseph Carl Spangler, Dec. 12, 1977 (dec.); 1 child, Scott Splanger. Vol. coord. Lucas County Dem., Toledo, 1986—89; exec. dir. Arcadia Main St. Program, Fla., 1991—93, Arcadia C. of C., 1993—95; promotion dir. Up River Adventure, Nocatee, Fla., 1995—98; mktg. specialist Suncoast Cmty. Blood Bank, Arcadia, 1995—98; mktg. dir. Arcadia Oaks Assisted Living, 1997—2000; mktg. specialist Suncoast Cmty. Blood Bank, Arcadia, 2000—; democrate exec. comm. State Cmty. Woman DeSoto County. Pub. rels. officer Arcania DeSoto Habitat Humanity; bd. mem. DeSoto County Econ. Devel. Coun. Mem. DeSoto Home Health Profl. Adv. Com.; adv. coun. mem. DeSoto County Sr. Friendship Ctr.; bd. mem. Voluntary Orgns. Active in Disaster; adv. coun. Tidewell Hospice Shepherds Watch; mem. Notary Pub.; past chair Desoto Dec; chair DeSoto County Dem. Exec. Com.; mem. Dem. Nat. Com.; Eucharistic min., parish coun. mem. St. Paul Cath. Ch.; bd. dirs. DeSoto County Econ. Devel. Coun. Named Democrat of Yr, DeSoto County Democrat. Mem.: Fawcett Hosp. Family Advisory Coun., Coun. of Catholic Women Assn., Amvet Aux., Ladies of Moose. Democrat. Roman Catholic. Avocations: reading, needlecrafts, cooking, travel. Home: 1269 SE Tangelo Dr Arcadia FL 34266 Home Phone: 863-993-1720. Personal E-mail: capangler1938@embargmail.com.

SPANGLER, DAVID SHERIDAN, composer, director, creative arts educator, writer; b. Belleville, Kans., June 3, 1948; s. Robert Richard Spangler and Marjorie Claire (Forman) Barrett; m. Cynthia Adler (div. 1981); m. Martha Helen Obrecht; children: Marjorie Anne, Catherine Helen, Isadora Maxine, Sheridan Rose. BFA, Carnegie-Mellon U., 1970. Instr. jazz U. Pitts., 1971-72; pres. Spangler Prodns., Inc., Ft. Lauderdale, Fla., 1974—; music dir., producer AC & R Advt., Inc., NYC, 1975-77; assoc. music dir. Grey Advt., Inc., NYC, 1977-79; producer, writer MZH & F Music Prodns., Inc., NYC, 1980-85; founder, dir. Lovewell Inst. for the Creative Arts, Ft. Lauderdale, Kans., 1987—; artistic dir. The Drama Ctr., Deerfield Beach, Fla., 1992. Conducted seminars in creative edn., 1990-00. Composer, lyricist: (film) So Fine, 1981, (TV series, records, videos) Romper Room, 1982—; composer (Broadway show) Elizabeth 1, 1974, Nefertiti, 1977, Chgo. 2004; soloist (original live tour) Bernstein's Mass, 1974; co-writer, dir. Dancing Animals, 1988, Children of the Sun, 1989; dir. The Cover of Life, 1992. On-site evaluator, panelist Fla. Dept. State divsn. Cultural Affairs - Theatre & Arts Instns., 1998-00; bd. dirs. Miami City Ballet, 2000; v.p. Theatre League S. Fla.; program adminstr./artistic dir. of interdisciplinary arts master's program Nova-Southeastern Univ., 2004—. Recipient Merit award Awards for Creative Excellence in Communications, 1971, Big Apple Radio award N.Y. Market Radio Broadcasters Assn., 1983. Mem. Nat. Acad. Rec. Arts and Scis., Dramatist Guild. Clubs: N.Y. Athletic (N.Y.C.). Libertarian. Home and Office: 1600 NE 18th Ave Fort Lauderdale FL 33305-3446 Home Phone: 954-537-7508; Office Phone: 954-262-8363.

SPANGLER, NITA REIFSCHNEIDER, volunteer; b. Ukiah, Calif., Apr. 17, 1923; d. John Charles and Olga Augusta (Wuertz) Reifschneider; m. Raymond Luper Spangler, Sept. 22, 1946 (dec.); children: Jon Martin, Mary Raymond, Thor Raymond. BA, Univ. Nev., 1944. News reporter Redwood (Calif.) City Tribune, 1944-46, Country Almanac, Woodside, Calif., 1969-77. Mem. bd. dirs. San Mateo (Calif.) County Hist. Assn., 1961-68, pres., 1964-66; founder, 1st pres. Portolá Expedition Bicentennial Found., 1966-70; chmn. San Mateo County Scenic Rds. Com., 1967-76; mem. San Mateo County Hist. Resource Adv.; mem. commn. San Mateo County Parks and Recreation, 1983-97, past chmn.; cons. hwy. aesthetics Cal Trans., 1981-83; mem. sch. coms. Recipient Commendation, County Bd. Suprs., 1968, 1977, 92. Mem. Sierra Club, Western History Assn., Mormon History Assn., Nev. State Hist. Soc. (life), San Mateo County Hist. Assn. (life), Resolution of Thanks 1968, 76, 94), Friends Redwood City, Kappa Alpha Theta. Democrat. Episcopalian. Avocation: historic preservation. Home: 970 Edgewood Rd Redwood City CA 94062-1818

SPANGLER, RONALD LEROY, retired television and aircraft executive, automobile consultant; b. York, Pa., Mar. 5, 1937; s. Ivan L. and Sevilla (Senft) S.; m. Svetlana Gavrilova; children: Kathleen, Ronald Jr., Beth Anne, Pavel. Student, U. Miami, Coral Gables, 1955-59. Radio announcer Sta. WSBA, York, 1955-59; TV prodr. Sta. WBAL-TV, Balt. and NBC TV, 1958-65; pres., chmn. bd. LewRon Television, NYC, Hollywood, Calif., 1965-78, Spanair Inc.; distbr. Rockwell bus. aircraft, 1975-85. Owner Prancing Horse Farm; dealer vintage and modern Ferrari automobiles; racer numerous courses including LeMans, Daytona, Sebring; racer vintage and modern Ferrari automobiles; Ferrari cons. (PBS show) Motorweek; cons. Bentley Motor Cars, Pininfarina S.P.A.; North Am. rep. Pinin Farina Automotive Design, 2005—. Mem. Video Tape Producers Assn. NYC, Rolls Royce Owners Club, Ferrari Clubs Am. and Italia, Mercedes Benz Club Am., Porsche Club Am. Avocation: antique automobile collector. Home: Prancing Horse Farm 3710 Ady Rd Street MD 21154-1432 Office Phone: 410-452-5500. Personal E-mail: phfarmferrari@aol.com.

SPANGRUDE, GERALD JOHN, hematologist, researcher; b. Helena, Mont., July 5, 1953; s. George Randolf and Lila Viola (Machulda) S.; m. Paula Elizabeth Braun, Sept. 15, 1984; children: Tegan Elizabeth, Carl Erik. BS in Microbiology, U. Mont., 1979; PhD, U. Utah, 1984. Post doctoral fellow Stanford U., Stanford, Calif., 1984-88; post doctoral fellow Hall Inst., Melbourne, Australia, 1988-89; NIAID investigator NIH, Hamilton, Mont., 1989-94; assoc. prof. U. Utah, Salt Lake City, 1994—. Cons. Systemix Inc., Palo Alto, Calif., 1989—; ad hoc advisor NIH, Bethesda, Md., 1994—. Inventor stem cell enrichment, 1988. Post doctoral fellowship Am. Cancer Soc., 1984-86; spl. fellow Leukemia Soc. Am., 1987-90. Mem. AAAS, Am. Soc. Hematology, Internat. Soc. of Exptl. Hematology. Office: Dept Pathology U Utah 50 N Medical Dr Salt Lake City UT 84132-0001

SPANIER, GRAHAM BASIL, academic administrator; b. Capetown, South Africa, July 18, 1948; s. Fred and Rosadele (Lurie) Spanier; m. Sandra Kay Whipple, Sept. 11, 1971; children: Brian Lockwood, Hadley Alison. BS, Iowa State U., 1969, MS, 1971, Doctorate (hon.), 2006; PhD, Northwestern U., 1973. Assoc. dean, prof. in charge Pa. State U., University Park, 1973—82, pres., 1995—; vice-provost, prof. SUNY, Stony Brook, 1982—86; provost, v.p. for acad. affairs Oreg. State U., 1986—91; chancellor U. Nebr., Lincoln, 1991—95. Chmn. Presdl. Adv. Group on Info. Tech., 1997—99, Kellogg Commn. on Future of State and Land-Grant Univs., 1997—2000; bd. dirs. Univ. Corp. for Advanced Internet Devel., U.S. Dept. Edn. Commn. on Opportunity in Athletics, 2002—03; host TV and radio programs, 1973—; bd. dirs. Citizens Fin. Group, Jr. Achievement Worldwide; trustee Univs. Rsch. Assn., 2001—05; vice-chmn. Worldwide Univ. Network, 2003—07; chair Nat. Security Higher Edn. Adv. Bd., 2005—. Founding editor: Jour. Family Issues. Del. White House Conf. on Families, Washington, 1980; chmn. bd. dirs. Christian Children's Fund, Richmond, Va., 1985—94; bd. dirs. Nat. 4H Coun., 1997—2000. Named Outstanding Young Alumnus, Iowa State U., 1982, Disting. Alumnus, 2005; Woodrow Wilson fellow, 1972. Mem.: Assn. Am. Univs. (com. intellectual property 1997—), Acad. Health Ctrs. (commn. on future of acad. health ctrs. 1996—98), Am. Assn. State Colls. and Univs. (joint commn. on accountability report 1993—95), Nat. Collegiate Athletic Assn. (pres. commn. 1995—97, bd. dirs., exec. com. 1997—2001, divsn. I bd. dirs., chmn. 1998—2001), Am. Coun. on Edn. (commn. on women 1992—95), Nat. Assn. State Univs. and Land Grant Colls. (exec. com. coun. on acad. affairs 1990—91, bd. pres. commn. on info. technologies 1993—99, chmn. 1996—99, bd. dirs. 1997—, chmn. coun. of pres. 1999—2000, bd. chair 2002), Am. Assn. Family and Consumer Scis. (Moran award 1972), Am. Sociol. Assn. (family sect. chmn. 1983—84), Population Assn. Am., Nat. Coun. Family Rels. (pres. 1987—88, Outstanding Grad. Student award 1972), Am. Assn. for Marriage and Family Therapy. Democrat. Avocations: aviation, magic, athletics, public broadcasting. Office: Pa State Univ Office of Pres 201 Old Main University Park PA 16802-1503 Office Phone: 814-865-7611. E-mail: president@psu.edu.

SPANIER, JOSHUA, advertising agency executive, director; b. London; Grad., U. Sussex, Eng. Media planner ZenithOptimedia UK; from assoc. media dir. to grp. comm. strategist, now dir. media/comm. strategy Goodby, Silverstein & Ptnrs., San Francisco, 2003—. Office: Goodby Silverstein & Ptnrs 720 Calif St San Francisco CA 94108 Office Phone: 415-392-0669. Office Fax: 415-788-4303.*

SPANIOL, LEROY, retired psychologist; b. Milw., Oct. 22, 1938; married. PhD, U. Wis., Madison, 1974. Adj. prof. Boston U., 1974—2005; pres. NAMI Cape Cod, Hyannis, Mass., 2006—. Contbr. articles to profl. jours., chapters to books. Mem.: APA. Avocations: chess, writing, gymnastics. Home: 405 Old Kings Hwy Wellfleet MA 02667 Personal E-mail: lspaniol405@comcast.net.

SPANN, GEORGE WILLIAM, management consultant; b. Cuthbert, Ga., July 21, 1946; s. Glinn Linwood and Mary Grace (Hiller) S.; m. Laura Jeanne Nason, June 10, 1967; children: Tanya Lynne, Stephen William. BS in Physics with honors, Ga. Inst. Tech., 1968, MS, 1970, MS in Indsl. Mgmt., 1973. Engr. Martin Marietta Corp., Orlando, Fla., 1968-70; rsch. scientist Engring. Exptl. Sta., Ga. Inst. Tech., 1970-75; v.p., dir. Metrics, Inc., mgmt. and engring. cons., Atlanta, 1973-78, pres., dir., 1978—; v.p., dir. Exec. Data Sys., Inc., 1981—. Mem. Ga. Energy Policy Coun., Ga. Metrication Coun., NASA applications survey group for Landsat follow-on; mem. com. on practical applications of remote sensing from space Space Applications Bd. NRC; market rsch. cons. NOAA, NASA, pvt. cos. Contbr. articles to profl. jours. Regents scholar, 1964. Mem. Am. Soc. Photogrammetry, Urban and Regional Info. Sys. Assn., Atlanta Jaycees, Tau Beta Pi, Phi Kappa Phi, Sigma Pi Sigma. Home: 3475 Clubland Dr Marietta GA 30068-2509 Office: Bldg 27 #100 1640 Powers Ferry Rd SE Marietta GA 30067-5491

SPANO, ROBERT, conductor, music director; b. Conneaut, Ohio, May 7, 1961; Grad., Oberlin Conservatory Music, Ohio; student, Curtis Inst. Music, Phila.; D (hon.), Bowling Green State U., 2004. Dir. orchestral activities Bowling Green State U., Ohio, 1985—89; faculty Oberlin Conservatory Music, 1989—; asst. condr. Boston Symphony Orch., 1990—93; music dir. Bklyn. Philharm. Orch., 1996—2004, artistic adv., prin. guest condr., 2004—07; music dir. Atlanta Symphony Orch., 2001—. Head conducting fellowship program Tanglewood Music Ctr., Mass., 1998—2002, dir. Festival Contemporary Music, 2003—04; guest condr. Chgo. Symphony Orch., Boston Symphony Orch., Houston Symphony Orch., San Francisco Symphony Orch., Cleve. Orch., LA Philharm., Nat. Symphony Orch., Phila. Orch., Royal Opera Covent Gardens, Welsh Nat. Opera, Orch. Filharmonica della Scala, City of Birmingham Symphony. Musician (piano): (chamber concerts) Atlanta Symphony, Brooklyn Philharm, Boston Symphony, Oberlin Conservatory; recordings include Rimsky-Korsakov: Scheherazade and Vaughan Williams: A Sea Symphony, Del Tredici: Paul Revere's Ride and Theofanidis: The Here and Now, Berlioz Requiem, Atlanta Symphony Orch. (Grammy award for Best Choral Performance, 2005), Golijov's Ainadamar: Fountain of Tears (Grammy award for Best Opera Performance, 2007), featured on (TV series) City Arts, PBS, Breakfast with the Arts, A&E, Late Show with David Letterman, CBS, Sunday Morning, (TV special) Sound Choices - Inside the ASO with Monica Kaufman, WSB-TV. Recipient Conductors award, Seaver Inst./NEA, 1994, Ditson Conductor's award, Columbia U., 2008. Office: Atlanta Symphony Hall 1280 Peachtree St NE Atlanta GA 30309-3552 Mailing: c/o Jason Bagdade Opus 3 Artists 470 Park Ave 9th Fl N New York NY 10016*

SPANOGLE, ROBERT WILLIAM, marketing and advertising company executive, association administrator; b. Lansing, Mich., Nov. 13, 1942; s. William P. and Mary A. (Lenneman) S.; m. Ruth Ann Long, Jan. 14, 1967; children: John Paul Stephen Donald, Amy Lynn. AA, Lansing C.C., 1969; BA, Mich. State U., 1971; postgrad., U. Pa., 1985. Cons. Nat. League Cities, Washington, 1971-72, Am. Legion, Indpls., 1972-75, dir. membership, 1975-79, exec. dir. Washington, 1975-81, nat. adjutant,

1981—; chmn. HP Direct, Inc., Indpls., 1985—, chmn. exec. com. Washington, 1989—. Mem. individual investors adv. com. N.Y. Stock Exch., N.Y.C., 1989-92. Bd. govs. USO, Washington, 1986-92, Childrens Miracle Network, 2001—; trustee St. Mary of the Woods Coll., Terre Haute, Ind., 1991-2001; treas. Civil War Battle Flags Commn. State of Ind., Indpls., 1994—; sec. 500 Festival Assocs., Indpls., 1985-91; mem. Vet.'s Day Coun., Indpls., 1989; bd. dirs. Indpls. Athletic Club, 1989-93, Crossroads Coun. Boy Scouts Am., 1985-92; civilian aide Sec. Army India, 2003-. With U.S. Army, 1962-65. Recipient Silver Buffalo award, Nat. Council Boy Scouts Am., 2004. Mem. Am. Legion of Mich. (Hon. Comdr. 1985), Kiwanis (exec. com. 1989-92). Roman Catholic. Avocations: golf, hunting, reading. Home: 7420 Killarney Dr Indianapolis IN 46217-5472 Office: Am Legion 700 N Pennsylvania St Indianapolis IN 46204-1129 Office Phone: 317-630-1236.

SPANOS, ALEXANDER GUS, construction and professional sports team executive; b. Stockton, Calif., Sept. 28, 1923; m. Faye Spanos; children: Dean, Dea Spanos Berberian, Alexis Spanos Ruhl, Michael. LLD (hon.), U. Pacific, 1984, Eureka Coll., 1984; DHL (hon.), Wayne State Coll., 2003, Calif. Polytechnic State U., 2004, Anatolia Coll., Thessaloniki, Greece, 2004; HHD (hon.), Hellenic Coll., 2004, Holy Cross Greek Orthodox Sch. Theology, 2004. Chmn. bd. dirs. A.G. Spanos Constrn. Inc., Stockton, Calif., 1960—; chmn. bd. dirs. A.G. Spanos Mgmt. Inc., Stockton, Calif., 1967—, A.G. Spanos Enterprises Inc., Stockton, Calif., 1971—, A.G. Spanos Devel. Inc., Stockton, Calif., 1973—, A.G. Spanos Realty Inc., Stockton, Calif., 1978—, A.G.S. Fin. Corp., Stockton, Calif., 1980—, A.G. Spanos Securities Corp., Stockton, Calif., 1981—, San Diego Chargers, 1984—. Chmn. bd. dirs. AGS Internat. Corp., Stockton, Calif., The Spanos Corp., Stockton, A.G. Spanos Ventures, Stockton, AGS Comms., LLC, Stockton. Former trustee Children's Hosp., San Francisco, San Francisco Fine Arts Mus.; trustee Eisenhower Med. Ctr., Rancho Mirage, Calif., John F. Kennedy Ctr. Performing Arts; hon. regent U. Pacific, Stockton, 1972-82; gov. USO, Washington, 1982—; former gov. Ronald Reagan Presdl. Found.; chmn. U.S. chpt. U.S. Greece bus. coun. Served with USAF, 1942-46. Recipient Albert Gallatin award Zurich-Am. Ins. Co., 1973, Horatio Alger award Horatio Alger Found., 1982, medal of Honor Statue of Liberty-Ellis Islan Found., 1982; named one of Forbes' Richest Americans, 2006. Mem. Am. Hellenic Ednl. Progressive Assn., Calif. C. of C. (bd. dirs. 1980-85). Republican. Greek Orthodox. Avocation: golf. Office: San Diego Chargers Qualcomm Stadium PO Box 609609 San Diego CA 92160-9609 also: A G Spanos Cos 10100 Trinity Pkwy 5th Fl Stockton CA 95219 Business E-Mail: agspr@agspanos.com.

SPAR, DEBORA LYNN, academic administrator; b. June 16, 1963; BSFS, Georgetown U., 1984; AM, Harvard U., 1986, PhD in Govt., 1990, PMD, 1991. Spangler Family prof. Harvard Bus. Sch., Boston; former sr. assoc. dean, dir. rsch. Harvard U., Boston, chair Univ. Com. on Human Rights Studies; pres. Barnard Coll., NYC, 2008—. Chair Making Markets Work. Co-author (with Raymond Vernon): Beyond Globalism: Remaking American Foreign Economic Policy, 1988; author: The Cooperative Edge: The Internal Politics of International Cartels, 1994, Ruling the Waves: Cycles of Discovery, Chaos, and Wealth from the Compass to the Internet, 2001, The Baby Business: How Money, Science, and Politics Drive the Commerce of Conception, 2006; contbr. articles to profl. jours. Avocations: reading, gardening. Office: Barnard Coll Office of Pres 109 Milbank Hall New York NY 10027 Office Phone: 617-495-6035, 212-854-2021. E-mail: dspar@hbs.edu, dspar@Barnard.edu.*

SPARANO, TONY, professional football coach; b. West Haven, Conn., Oct. 7, 1961; m. Jeanette Sparano; children: Tony, Andrew, Ryan Leigh. BA in Criminal Law, U. New Haven, West Haven, Conn., 1982. Offensive line coach, recruiting coord. U. New Haven, 1984—87, head coach, 1994—98; offensive line coach, recruiting coord., acad. liasion Boston U., 1988—89, offensive coord., 1989—93; offensive quality coach Cleve. Browns, 1999, offensive line coach, 2000; tight ends coach Washington Redskins, 2001, Jacksonville Jaguars, 2002, Dallas Cowboys, 2003—04, running game coord., 2005—06, offensive line coord., 2005—07, asst. head coach, 2006—07; head coach Miami Dolphins, 2008—. Named Divsn. II/III Coach the Yr., New Eng. Football Writers, 1995, 1997, Divsn. II Coach the Yr., NY Metro. Football Writers, 1997. Office: Miami Dolphins 7500 SW 30th St Davie FL 33314

SPARBERG, MARSHALL STUART, gastroenterologist, educator; b. Chgo., May 20, 1936; s. Max Shane and Mildred Rose (Haffron) S.; m. Eve Gaymont Enda, Mar. 15, 1987. BA, Northwestern U., 1957, MD, 1960. Intern Evanston Hosp., Ill., 1960-61; resident in internal medicine Barnes Hosp., St. Louis, 1961-63; fellow U. Chgo., 1963-65; practice medicine specializing in gastroenterolgy Chgo., 1967—; asst. prof. medicine Northwestern U., 1967-72, assoc. prof., 1972-80, prof. medicine, 1980—; instr. Wash. U., St. Louis, 1961-63, U. Chgo., 1963-65. Author: Ileostomy Care, 1969, Primer of Clinical Diagnosis, 1972, Ulcerative Colitis, 1978, Inflammatory Bowel Disease, 1982; contbr. numerous articles to profl. jours. Pres. Fine Arts Music Found., 1974-76, Crohn's Disease and Colitis Found. of Am., pres. Ill. chpt., 1994-97; bd. dirs. Lyric Opera Guild, 1974-94, Chamber Music Soc. North Shore Chgo., 1984—; physician to Chgo. Symphony Orch., 1981-97. With USAF, 1965-67. Named Outstanding Tchr. Northwestern U. Med. Sch., 1972 Mem. AMA, ACP, Am. Gastroent. Assn., Am. Coll. Gastroent. (bd. govs.), Chgo. Med. Soc., Chgo. Soc. Internal Medicine, Chgo. Soc. Gastroenterology (pres.), Chgo. Soc. Gastrointestinal Endoscopy (pres.) Office: 676 N Saint Clair St Ste 1525 Chicago IL 60611-2862 Office Phone: 312-944-7080.

SPARBY, DAVID M., energy executive; BA, Coll. St. Scholastica; JD, William Mitchell Coll.; MBA, Univ. St. Thomas. Joined as staff atty. Northern States Power Co. Minn. (Xcel Energy subs.), 1982; legal & mgmt. positions Xcel Energy, Mpls., 1982—2000; v.p. govt. & regulatory affairs Xcel Energy Services, 2000—07; exec. v.p., acting pres. & CEO Northern States Power Co. Minn., 2007—08, pres., CEO, 2008—09; CFO Xcel Energy, 2009—. Mem. Midwestern Greenhouse Gas Accord adv. group, 2008—; Minn. Climate Change adv. group; bd. trustee Metro. State Univ.; mem. external adv. coun. Univ. Minn. Initiative for Renewable Energy & Environ. Office: Xcel Energy 414 Nicollet Mall Minneapolis MN 55401*

SPARGO, BENJAMIN H., renal pathologist, educator; b. Six Mile Run, Pa., Aug. 11, 1919; s. Benjamin H. and Lillian (Rankin) S.; m. Barbara Scollard, Mar. 12, 1942; children— Janet, Patricia. BS in Biol. Scis, U. Chgo., 1948, MS in Pathology, 1952, MD with honors, 1952. Intern Univ. Hosp., Ann Arbor, Mich., 1953-54; resident pathology U. Chgo. Med. Sch., 1954-55, mem. faculty, 1954—, prof. renal pathology, 1964-95; prof. pathology emeritus, 1995—; assoc. chmn. dept., 1974-80. Cons. Armed Forces Inst. Pathology, 1975-79, Midwest Regional Organ Bank of Ill., 1989-94. Served with USAAF, 1941-46. Recipient Rsch. Career award Nat. Heart Inst., 1964-99, Disting. Svc. award Kidney Found. Ill., 1991, Disting. Lifetime Achievement award Renal Pathology Soc., 1996. Mem.: US-Can. Acad. Pathology (chmn. edn. com. 1975—77). Home: 5550 S South Shore Dr Chicago IL 60637-5051

SPARGO, R. CLIFTON, literature and language professor; s. Robert Clifton and Joan Elaine (Fitzgibbon) Spargo. BA, U. Ill., Urbana-Champaign, 1987; MSc, Edinburgh U., 1989; MA, Yale U., New Haven, 1990, PhD, 1995. Assoc. prof. English Marquette U., 1995—; vis. lectr. creative writing Yale U., 2003, vis. assoc. prof. English, 2009. Author: (short story) Anne, Afterward, SOMA, The Duck Pond, Green Mountains Review, The Death of Animals, Glimmer Train (Fiction Open award, 2004), A History of Minor Trespasses, Glimmer Train (Short Story award, 2001), American Women, Fiction, The Empty Center, The Antioch Review, Second Sorrow, The Connecticut Review, Bluefish, South of Plymouth, Glimmer Train, Sincerity, Fiction; co-author (with John Hopkins): (book) The Ethics of Mourning, 2004, Vigilant Memory, 2006; co-editor: After Representation?, 2009. Ethics lit. advisor Voices & Faces Project, Chgo. Finalist Hiett prize in the Humanities, Dallas Inst. Humanities, 2005; Pearl Resnick fellowship, US Holocaust Meml. Mus., 2000—01. Mem.: Modernist Studies Assn., MLA (exec. com. mem. 2008—). Roman Catholic. Avocations: contemporary rock music, guitar. Home: PO Box 5337 Chicago IL 60680 Personal E-mail: rcspargo@aol.com. Business E-Mail: clifton.spargo@mu.edu.

SPARKMAN, BRANDON BUSTER, educator, consultant, writer; b. Hartselle, Ala., Aug. 2, 1929; s. George Olan and Mary Louise (Jones) S.; m. Wanda Phillips, Sept. 13, 1952; children— Ricky Brandon, Rita Sharon, Robert Lee. BS, U. North Ala., 1952; MA, U. Ala., 1958, EdS, 1961; EdD, Auburn U., Ala., 1970. Tchr., asst. prin. Phllips High Sch., Bear Creek, Ala., 1954-57; prin. Tuscumbia, Ala., 1957-65; asst. supt., 1965-69; ednl. cons. Auburn Center, 1969-70; mem. faculty dept. sch. adminstrn. Auburn U., 1970; asst. supt. for staff personnel devel. Jackson (Miss.) Pub. Schs., 1970-71, supt., 1971-73; sch. supt. Richland County Sch. Dist. 1, Columbia, SC, 1973-75; asst. supt. instruction Hartselle (Ala.) City Schs., 1975-80; supt. Guntersville (Ala.) City Schs., 1980-88; CEO The Right Combination Pub. & Ednl. Svcs. Corp., Guntersville, Ala., 1984-93. Adj. prof. U. Ala., Birmingham, 1998-2000; writer, cons. in field. Sr. author: Blueprint for a Brighter Child, 1973, STEPS (System for Teacher Evaluation of Pre-reading Skills), 1974; co-author: Preparing Your Preschooler for Reading, 1977, Competency Tests for Basic Reading Skills, 1978, Soaring High with Science, 1985, Soaring High with Social Studies, 1985; author: How Well Does Your Child Read, 1979, Writing Composition Made Easy, 1991, Blueprint for Expository Writing, 1993, Reading Skills Competency Tests, 1999; editor: The In-Between Years, 1979; creator: CORE (Program Management Through Computer Systems), 1975; editor, contbg. author: The Advantaged, A Preschool Program for the Disadvantaged, 1969; contbr. articles to profl. jours. Bd. dirs. Morgan County chpt. ARC, United Givers Fund, Colbert-Lauderdale Child Study Center, Sheffield-Tuscumbia Credit Union; bd. govs. Jackson Symphony Orch.; adv. bd. Jackson Mental Health Center. Served with AUS, 1952-54. Recipient Human Relations award Jackson. Mem. Am., Ala assns. sch. adminstrs. (past pres.), Ala. Council Sch. Adminstrn. and Supervision (past pres.), Assn. Supervision and Curriculum Devel., Ala. Assn. Supervision and Curriculum Devel. (past pres.), Florence State U. Alumni Assn. (past pres.) Methodist (ch. sch. tchr., supt., chmn. ofcl. bd., chmn. commn. edn.). Home and Office: 2401 Northfield Dr Jasper AL 35504 Office Phone: 205-387-9222.

SPARKMAN, LYLE BRUCE, academic administrator, education educator; b. Springfield, Mo., Sept. 2, 1947; s. Etsyl J. and Rayma LaVern Sparkman; m. Martha Rothrock, Mar. 17, 1984; 1 child, Sarah Anne. BA in English Philosophy, Drury Univ., Springfield, Mo., 1972; MEd Instructional Adminstrn., Univ. Ark., Fayetteville, Ark., 1985, EdS Ednl. Specialist, 1999. Cert. tchg., adminstrn. Mo., Ark. News dir. KMTC TV (channel 27), Springfield, Mo., 1973—74; tchr. 3rd grade Kana. City Mo. Schs., Kans. City, South West R-5, Washburn, 1978—83; prin. Rose Bud Elem., Ark., 1984—88, Green Forest Sch., 1988—2002; asst. supt. East newton R.V.I, Granby, Mo., 2002—. Adj. prof. Lindenwood Univ., Granby, 2002—; grant reader USDE Office Migrant Edn, Washington, 2000—02, Washington, 2004; v.p. Crowder Coll. Admin. Adv. Coun., Mo., 2004—06; nat. pilot leader AIM Project Migrant Families, 1997—2002; adv. bd. mem. project SPEAK Mo. Southern State U., 2007—. Co-author: The Heritage of the Ozarks, 1984; prodr.: (plays) The Toby Show, 1972;, performer folk music. Patron Wilson's Creek Nat. Found., Springfield, 1991—2008, Nat. Mil. Pk. Found., Pea Ridge, Ark., 2005—08; pub. info. officer Am. Legion post 163, Neosho, 2005—06. Specialist 5th class US Army, 1969—71, with USAR, 1971—75. Documenting Past grant, US Dept. Edn., 2005—09. Mem.: ASCD, Mo. Archl. Soc. (pres.), Phi Delta Kappa. Avocations: archaeology, music, comparative folklore. Office: E Newton R VI 22808 F Hwy 86 Granby MO 64844 Business E-Mail: sparkmanl@mail.enr6.k12.mo.us.

SPARKMAN, ROBIN HAMILTON, editor; b. Apr. 29, 1969; d. Nicholas P. and Beatrice S. (Page) Sparkman; m. Howard Zachary Robbins, June 21, 1997. Grad. magna cum laude, Wellesley Coll.; MA in Journalism, Columbia U., 1996. Reporter Newsweek mag.; bus. editor MSNBC Online, 1996—2001; editor-in-chief Corp. Counsel mag., 2001—08; dep. editl. dir. ALM, 2007—08; exec. editor The Am. Lawyer mag., 2008—. Co-recipient Nat. Editorial Award. Office: The American Lawyer 105 Madison Ave 7th Fl New York NY 10016

SPARKMAN, STEVEN LEONARD, lawyer; b. Sarasota, Fla., May 30, 1947; s. Simeon Clarence and Ursula (Wahlstrom) S.; m. Terry Jeanne Gibbs, Aug. 23, 1969; children: Joanna Jeanne, Kevin Leonard. BA, Fla. State U., 1969, JD, 1972. Bar: Fla. 1972. Legal rsch. asst. Office Gen. Counsel, Fla. Dept. Revenue, Tallahassee, 1971; legis. intern com. on cmty. affairs Fla. Ho. of Reps., Tallahassee, 1971-72; jud. rsch. aide Fla. 2d Dist. Ct. Appeals, Lakeland, 1972-73; asst. county atty. Hillsborough County, Tampa, Fla., 1973-75; assoc. Carlton, Fields, Ward, Emmanuel, Smith & Cutler, P.A., Tampa, 1975-80, sr. atty., 1980-2001; pvt. practice Plant City, Fla., 2001—. Mem. bd. visitors Fla. State U. Coll. Law, 1994—2000. Trustee Fla. Bapt. Children's Homes, Inc., 2004—09; deacon 1st Bapt. Ch., Plant City, 1980—; sec., bd. dirs. Bapt. Towers Plant City, Inc., 1981—84; bd. dirs. Tampa Kiwanis Found., 1997—2000. 1st lt. USAFR, 1973. Mem.: ABA, Plant City Bar Assn. (sec. treas 2003—05, treas. 2005—08, v.p. 2008—), Fla. Bar Assn. (exec. coun. local govt. law sect. 1978—79), Kiwanis (bd. dirs. 2003—06). Democrat. Office: 102 W Reynolds St Ste 201 Plant City FL 33563 Office Phone: 813-759-1444. Business E-Mail: sls@sparklaw.com.

SPARKS, CHARLES EDWARD, pathologist, educator; b. Peoria, Ill., July 29, 1940; s. William Joseph and Meredith (Pleasants) S.; m. Janet Lindsay Dehoff, Aug. 18, 1977; children: William, Debra, Robert. BS in Biology, MIT, 1963; MD, Thomas Jefferson U., 1968. Diplomate Am. Bd. Pathology, Am. Bd. Clin. Chemistry. Rsch. asst. Mass. Gen. Hosp., Boston, 1963; intern NY Hosp., Cornell Naval Hosp., St. Albans, 1968-69; resident in clin. pathology Hosp. of U. Pa., 1972-75; fellow in cardiopulmonary medicine U. Pa., Phila., 1975-76, asst. instr., 1972-75; fellow in biochemistry Med. Coll. Pa., Phila., 1976-77, instr., 1976-77, asst. to assoc. prof. biochemistry and physiology, 1977-82; assoc. prof. pathology U. Rochester (NY), 1982-88, prof. pathology, 1988—. Advisor med. scientist tng. program U. Rochester, 1984-92; attending pathologist, dir. clin. chemistry unit Strong Meml. Hosp., 1982—, chair rsc. adv. com., assoc. chair pathology, 1994—, dir. grad. studies in Integrative Biomed. Scis., 1998—. Contbr. articles to profl. jours.; patentee in field. Chairperson Endocrinology VA Merit Rev. Study Sect., 2000—. Lt. comdr. USN, 1969—72. Postdoctoral fellow NIH, 1975-77. Mem. AAAS, Am. Diabetes Assn. (co-chmn. nat. symposium meeting 1988), Acad. Clin. Lab. Physicians and Scientists, Am. Heart Assn. (fellow coun. on arteriosclerosis, mem. nominating com.). Office: Dept Pathology U Rochester 601 Elmwood Ave Rochester NY 14642-0001 Home Phone: 585-381-9549; Office Phone: 585-275-8236.

SPARKS, DALE BOYD, allergist, health facility administrator; b. Springfield, Mo., July 14, 1929; s. Roscoe R. and Ruby V. (Boyd) S.; children: Susan L., Laura A., Lisa M., Jennifer G.; m. Leeanna M. Molccyk Priboy, Apr. 21, 2001. AB, BS, Southwest Mo. State U., 1951; BS in Medicine, U. Mo., 1953; MD, St. Louis U., 1955. Diplomate Am. Bd. Allergy and Immunology. Intern Kansas City (Mo.) Gen. Hosp. U. Med. Ctr., 1955-56; resident U. Mo. Hosp., 1958-60; fellow in allergy and immunology Northwestern U., 1960-61; mem. cons. staff Parkview Cmty. Hosp., 1961—; mem. med. staff Riverside County Regional Med. Ctr., 1961-2000, dir. respiratory therapy, 1968-85, dir. respiratory therapy and diagnostic svcs., 1965—, chmn. dept. medicine, 1978-98, chief med. staff, 1990-98; acting dir., health officer Riverside Pub. Health Dept., 1991-93; ret., 1993. Clin. prof. medicine Loma Linda U. Mem. editl. bd. Immunology and Allergy in Practice, 1980—. Lt. USNR. Fellow ACP (coun. subsplty. socs. 1988—), Am. Coll. Allergy and Immunology (disting., bd. regents 1989-93, pres. 1990-91, chmn. fin. com., treas. 1990-93, recert. com.), Coll. Allergy, Asthma and Immunology; mem. AMA, Am. Lung Assn. (bd. dirs. 1990-95), Am. Heart Assn. (bd. dirs. 1964-70, pres. 1966), Joint Coun. Am. Allergy and Immunology (bd. dirs. 1985-90), Calif. Med. Assn., Calif. Soc. Allergy, Inland Soc. Internal Medicine, Riverside County Med. Assn. (bd. councilors 1980-99, del. CMA 1988-99), Riverside County Found. Med. Care (sec., past pres.). Home and Office: 29368 Big Range Rd Canyon Lake CA 92587 Personal E-mail: dsparksmd@aol.com.

SPARKS, DONALD LEWIS, soil chemistry educator; b. Paris, Ky., June 26, 1953; s. Elmer Johnston and Christine (McKenzie) Sparks; m. Joy Lynn Gooden, Sept. 14, 1984. BS, U. Ky., Lexington, 1975, MS, 1976; PhD, Va. Poly. Inst. and State U., Blacksburg, 1979. Asst. prof. soil chemistry U. Del., Newark, 1979-83, assoc. prof., 1983-87, prof., 1987—, chmn. dept. plant and soil scis., 1989—, disting. prof., 1994—, Francis Alison prof., 1996—, T.A. Baker prof., 2001—02, S. Hallock duPont chair, 2002—. Cons. DuPont Corp., Wilmington, Del., 1981—. Author: Kinetics of Soil Chemical Processes, 1989, Environmental Soil Chemistry, 1995, 2d edit., 2002; editor: Soil Physical Chemistry, 1986, rev. 2d edit. 1998, Rates of Soil Chemical Processes, 1991, Method of Soil Analysis: Chemical Methods, 1996; mem. editl. bd. Am. Jour. Soil Sci. Soc., 1984-93, Geoderma, 1986—, Soil Sci., 1987—, Pedosphere, 1999—, Geochimica Cosmochimica Acta, 1999—, Vadose Zone Jour., 2002—Chemical Geology, 2009-; editor: Advances in Agronomy, 1990—; contbr. over 171 articles and 40 book chpts. to profl. publs. Pres. Torch Club of Del., Newark, 1989—. Recipient U. Dl. Doctoral Advising and Mentoring award. Fellow AAAS, Am. Soc. Agronomy (Environ. Quality Rsch. award, N.E. br. Rsch. award 1986, Francis Alison award 1996), Soil Sci. Soc. of Am. (pres.-elect 1998-99, pres. 1999-00, Soil Sci. Rsch. award 1994, M.L. and Chrystie M. Jackson Soil Sci. award), Geochem. Soc. European Assn. Geochemists; mem. Internat. Union Soil Sci. (pres.-elect 2000-02, pres. 2002-06), Am. Chem. Soc., Clay Minerals Soc., Geochem. Soc. Mem. Christian Ch. (Disciples Of Christ). Achievements include pioneering application of chemical kinetics to soil systems. Office: U Del Dept Plant and Soil Scis Newark DE 19717-1303 Business E-Mail: dlsparks@udel.edu.

SPARKS, DONALS L., economics professor; life ptnr. Katherine Saenger; children: Sally, Laker. PhD, U. London, 1985. Regional economist Africa US Dept. State, Washington, 1977—84; prof. internat. economics Citadel, Charleston, SC, 1986—. V.p. League Am. Bicyclists, Washington, 2002—08. Fulbright fellowship, 1986, 1993, 2005. Liberal. Office: Citadel 171 Moultrie St Charleston SC 29409 Office Phone: 843-953-5159. Business E-Mail: sparksd@citadel.edu.

SPARKS, GEORGE, museum administrator; BS, USAF Acad.; MS in Aeronautics and Astronautics, MIT. Asst. prof. aeronautics USAF Acad.; with Hewlett-Packard, 1979—99, divsn. gen. mgr.; v.p. Agilent Technologies, 1999—2003; ptnr. NorthStone Group, Louisville, Colo.; pres., CEO Denver Mus of Nature and Sci., 2004—. Bd. mem. U. Colo. at Boulder's Pres. Leadership Class, Colo. MESA, Colo. Forum, Pub. Edn. and Bus. Coalition, Colo. Bright Beginnings, Colo. Adv. Coun. of the Trust for Public Lands; mem. Early Childhood Edn. Leadership Team. Office: Denver Mus of Nature and Sci 2001 Colorado Blvd Denver CO 80205

SPARKS, HARVEY VISE, JR., physiologist; b. Flint, Mich., June 22, 1938; s. Harvey Vise and Ellen Louise (Paschall) S.; m. Barbara M. Taylor, Jan. 17, 1959; children— Matthew Taylor, Catherine Elliott, Wendy Sue, Harvey Vise. Student, U. Mich., 1956-59, MD, 1963. Postdoctoral fellow dept. physiology Harvard Med. Sch., Boston and; U. Goteborg, Sweden; instr. U. Mich., 1966-67, asst. prof. physiology, 1967-70, assoc. prof., 1970-74, prof., 1974-78; asst. to dean U. Mich. (Med. Sch.), 1970-71, asst. dean, 1971-72; prof. physiology Mich. State U., East Lansing, 1978—, chmn. dept., 1978-89, vice provost human health programs, 1989-93, univ. disting. prof., 1997—. Fulbright lectr. U. Zimbabwe, 1986-87; vis. prof. U. Zimbabwe, 1995; mem. survey team, liaison com. on med. edn. AMA Am. Assn. Med. Colls.; mem. rev. teams NIH. Author: Casebook of Physiology, 1973, Essentials of Cardiovascular Physiology, 1987; contbr. numerous articles to profl. jours.; editor: (with others) Handbook of Physiology, 1979. Recipient Meritorious Service award Mich. Heart Assn., 1962, Borden award for med. student research, 1963, Merit award NIH, 1988; Mich. Heart Assn. student fellow, 1962-63; John and Mary Markle scholar, 1967-72; USPHS postdoctoral fellow, 1963-66; U. Mich. student research fellow, 1960-61; USPHS grantee, 1963— Fellow Royal Soc. Medicine; mem. AAAS, Am. Physiol. Soc. (pres. 1987-88, editl. bd. Am. Jour. Physiology 1974-88), Microcirculatory Soc., Am. Heart Assn. (coun. on circulation, editl. bd. Circulation Rsch.), Mich. Pub. Health Inst. (bd. dirs. 1989-94), Internat. Union Physiol. Scis. (treas. 1990-97), Coun. Internat. Exch. Scholars (Africa area com. 1988-91), Russian Acad. Sci. (fgn.), Victor Vaughn Soc., Alpha Omega Alpha, Phi Kappa Phi, Phi Zeta. Home: 8122 W Lovejoy Rd Perry MI 48872-8902 Office: Mich State U Dept Physiology East Lansing MI 48824

SPARKS, JACK NORMAN, dean; b. Lebanon, Ind., Dec. 3, 1928; s. Oakley and Geraldine Ruth (Edrington) S.; m. Esther Lois Bowen, Apr. 11, 1953; children: Stephen Michael, Robert Norman, Ruth Ann, Jonathan Russell. BS, Purdue U., 1950; MA, U. Iowa, 1951, PhD, 1960. Tchr. math. Leyden Cmty. H.S., Franklin Park, Ill., 1954—58; rsch. asst. U. Iowa, Iowa City, 1958—60; assoc. prof. applied stats., dir. bur. of rsch. U. No. Colo., Greeley, 1960—65; assoc. prof. ednl. psychology Pa. State U., State College, 1965—68; dir. corr. Campus Crusade for Christ, San Bernardino, Calif., 1968—69; dir. Christian World Liberation Front,

Berkeley, Calif., 1969—75; pastor, ch. overseer New Covenant Apostolic Order, Berkeley, 1975—77; dean St. Athanasius Acad. Orthodox Theology, Santa Barbara, Calif., 1977—87, St. Athanasius Coll., Santa Barbara, 1987—93, St. Athanasius Acad. Orthodox Theology, Elk Grove, Calif., 1996—2005, St. John's Orthodox Cathedral, Eagle River, Alaska, 2005—. Cons. Measurement Rsch. Ctr., Iowa City, 1959-60, We. States Small Schs. Project, Greeley, 1962-65, Colo. Coun. Ednl. Rsch., Denver, 1963-65; project dir. Orthodox Study Bible Old Testament, 1998—2008. Author: Letters to Street Christians, 1971, The Mind Benders, 1977, 79, The Resurrection Letters, 1978, The Preaching of the Apostles, 1987, Victory in the Unseen Warfare, 1993; editor: Apostolic Fathers, 1978, 88; gen. editor: The Orthodox Study Bible, 1993, Virtue in the Unseen Warfare, 1995, Prayer in the Unseen Warfare, 1996, Christ Is Our Holiness, 1996, The Coming of the Prince, 1997, Tradition in the Early Church, 1997, The Letters of St. Ignatius, 1998, Faith and Godliness, 1999, Pentecost: A Homily of St. John Chrysostom, 2000, No Graven Image, 2000, The Valley of the Shadow of Death, 2000, Death, Fear of Death, Hope of Resurrection, 2000, Kindling the Fire Within, 2000, How Can Jesus Be Both God and Man, 2001, The Annunciation, 2001, The Bride of Christ, 2001, The Boundless Beauty, 2001, Walking Through the Night, 2001, Out of the Depths, 2002, Redemption and Reconciliation, 2002, A Family Baptized, 2003, Zeal and Patience, 2003, The Biblical Story of Esther, 2006; project dir., gen. editor: Orthodox Study Bible, Old and New Testaments, Thomas Nelson Pubs., 2008. Trustee Rock Mont Coll., Denver, 1962-77, Thomas Nelson Co., Nashville, 1977-78. 1st lt. U.S. Army, 1952-54 Mem. Am. Sci. Affiliation, Assn. Orthodox Theologians, Conf. on Faith and History, Phi Delta Kappa (pres. Epsilon chpt. 1959-60) Republican. Orthodox Christian. Home: 19042 Monastery Dr Eagle River AK 99577 Office Phone: 907-696-2002. Business E-Mail: frjack@saaot.edu.

SPARKS, JANET LINDSAY DEHOFF, pathologist, educator; b. Lawrence, Mass., Sept. 13, 1950; d. Ronald Lee and Barbara Isabelle (Platt) DeHoff; m. Charles Edward Sparks, Aug. 18, 1977; 1 child, Robert. BA in Biology, BS in Med. Tech., U. Pa., 1972, PhD in Pathology, 1980. Cert. med. technologist Am. Soc. Clin. Pathologists. Instr. clin. chemistry U. Pa., Phila., 1974-76; fellow Wistar Inst. Anatomy and Biology, Phila., 1975-80; postdoctoral fellow U. Rochester (N.Y.), 1983-85, scientist, 1985-94, asst. prof. pathology and lab. medicine, 1994-96, assoc. prof. pathology and lab. medicine, 1996—2008, prof. pathology and lab. medicine, 2008—. Cons. NIH, Indpls., 1994-96. Contbr. numerous articles to profl. jours.; patentee in field. Nat. NIDDK RO1 grantee, 1995—. Fellow Coun. on Arteriosclerosis Thrombosis and Vascular Biology; mem. AAAS, Am. Soc. Clin. Pathologists, Am. Diabetes Assn., Am. Heart Assn. (coun. on arteriosclerosis, coun. on clin. cardiology), N.Y. Lipid Club, N.Y. Acad. Scis., Am. Physiol. Soc. Office: U Rochester Dept Pathology 601 Elmwood Ave # 626 Rochester NY 14642-0001 Business E-Mail: janet_sparks@urmc.rochester.edu.

SPARKS, JOHN EDWARD, lawyer; b. Rochester, Ind., July 3, 1930; s. Russell Leo and Pauline Anna (Whittenberger) S.; m. Margaret Joan Snyder, Sept. 4, 1954; children: Thomas Edward, William Russell, Kathryn Chapman McCarthy. AB, Ind. U., 1952; LL.B., U. Calif., Berkeley, 1957; postgrad., London Sch. Econs., 1957-58. Bar: Calif. 1958, U.S. Supreme Ct., 1968. Assoc. Brobeck, Phleger & Harrison, San Francisco, 1958-66, ptnr., 1967-95, of counsel, 1996—2003; pvt. practice, 2003—. Adj. prof. law U. San Francisco, 1967-69; pres. Legal Aid Soc. San Francisco, 1978-79, dir., 1971-81. Editor U. Calif. Law Rev., 1956-57. Served to 1st lt. Q.M.C. U.S. Army, 1952-54, Korea. Recipient Wheeler Oak Meritorious award U. Calif., Berkeley, 1986. Fellow Am. Bar Found., Am. Coll. Trial Lawyers; mem. ABA, State Bar Calif., Bar Assn. San Francisco (bd. dirs. 1974-75), Boalt Hall Alumni Assn. (pres. 1983-84). Democrat. Home Phone: 510-524-6106; Office Phone: 510-524-5404. E-mail: jsparks458@aol.com.

SPARKS, JOHN WESLEY, physician; b. Elizabeth, NJ, Sept. 14, 1946; s. William Joseph and Meredith (Pleasant) S.; m. Patricia Bauman, Aug. 19, 1967; children: Rebecca, Michael, Sarah. BS in Life Scis., MIT, 1968; MD, Harvard Med. Sch., 1972. Diplomate Nat. Bd. Med. Examiners, Am. Bd. Pediatrics, Sub-specialty bd. Neonatal-Perinatal Medicine. Research assoc. NIH, Bethesda, Md., 1974-76; resident in pediatrics U. Colo., Denver, 1972-74, 76-77, fellow in perinatal medicine, 1977-79, asst. prof. pediatrics, 1979-84, assoc. prof. pediatrics, 1984—; dir. newborn services U. Colo. Hosp., Denver, 1980—. Contbr. articles and revs. to profl. jours. Served with USPHS, 1974-76. Grantee NIH, 1979—. Mem. Soc. Pediatric Research, Perinatal Research Soc., Western Soc. Pediatric Research. Home: 4001 Oberlin St Houston TX 77005-3637 Office: Newborn Svc B-195 4200 E 9th Ave Denver CO 80220-3706

SPARKS, JORDIN BRIANNA, singer; b. SI, NY, Dec. 22, 1989; d. Phillippi and Jodi (Weidmann) Sparks. Model for Torrid; toured with Michael W. Smith, 2005, 2006; winner Ariz. Idol competition Fox 10, Phoenix, 2006; contestant & first-place winner American Idol Season 6, 2007; signed to Arista Records/19 Entertainment, 2007—. Actor: (plays) The Wiz, Cinderella, Valley Youth Theatre, Phoenix, 2002; appeared in (TV series) America's Most Talented Kids, 2005, American Idol: The Search for a Superstar, 2007; singer: (albums) For Now, 2006, Jordin Sparks, 2007, (singles) This is My Now, 2007. Recipient Image award for Outstanding New Artist, NAACP, 2008, Favorite Adult Contemporary Artist award, Am. Music Awards, 2008, Favorite Combined Forces (with Chris Brown), People's Choice Awards, 2009; named Spotlight Overall winner, Gospel Music Assn. Acad., 2004. Achievements include becoming the youngest winner of American Idol.

SPARKS, MARVIN ROOSEVELT, JR., music educator; b. Chgo., Mar. 5, 1954; s. Marvin Sparks, Sr. and Bernice Sparks; m. Melba Denise Warren, Apr. 26, 1990; 1 child, Deron Warren. MusB, U. Ill., Champaign-Urbana, 1976; MA, Ea. Ill. U., Charleston, 1988. Instr. percussion Am. Conservatory Music, Chgo., 1976—77; staff rec. musician Hershal Comml. Prodns., Chgo., 1977—86; freelance studio and live musician Chgo., 1977—86; mgr. pro sound and drum Guitar Ctr., Chgo., 1986—86; lectr. black am. music, asst. percussion, jazz Ea. Ill. U., Charleston, Ill., 1986—89; asst. dir. band Kastner intermediate sch. Clovis Ind. Sch. Dist., Calif., 1989—90; dir. percussion studies U. Houston, 1990—96; dir. jazz and percussion studies U. Mo., St. Louis, 1996—98; itinerant music specialist North Forest Ind. Sch. Dist., Houston, 1998—2008; adj. prof. Lone Star Coll. Kingwood, Contemporary Sch. Fine Arts, 2007—. Endorsee VicFirth Mallets and Sticks, Boston, 1990—, Aquarian Drumheads, Anaheim, Calif., 1992—2006, Sabian Cymbals, Marshfield, Mass., 1992—, LP/Kaman Percussion, Garfield, NJ, 1992—, Evans Drumheads, Farmingdale, NY, 2007—; dir. Afro Cuban ensemble internat. festival Latin stage U. Houston, 1995; pit instr. Clovis HS-Clovis Unified Sch. Dist., Fresno, Calif., 1989—90; adjudicator jazz festival Purdue U., West Lafeyette, Ind., 1995; instr. percussion summer camps Ea. Ill. U., 1987—99; adj. prof. Tex. So. U., Houston, 2001—; clinician, ednl. advisor in field; presenter in field; cons. in field. Musician (musical dir., prodr.): (albums) The Calvin Owens Show: Aint Gonna Be Yo Dog No More, 2005, The Calvin Owens Hip Hop Orchestra: Say Boy How You Do That Thang, 2005, Trudy Lynn: I'm Still Here, 2005; musician: Your Love Looks Good on Me, 1985, Here's To Love, 1981, Christ Universal Temple, 1981, Kitty Haywood and Haywood Singers, 1981, Vibrations, 1976, Texas Master Chorale Live, 2005, Calvin Owens Blues Orchestra: The Calvin Owens Show, Vol 1, 2004, Lakewood Church Live: We Speak To Nations, 2001, Make Up Your Mind-Gavin Christopher, 1985, Phenix Horns-Phenix Horns, 2004, Calvin Owens Blues Band: Live at Kemah Jazz Festival, 1984, Journey Thru Forever, 1984, Virginity-Yvonne Gage, 1984, Willie Clayton-Willie Clayton, 1983, Albertina Walker with the Christ Universal Temple Choir Live, 1983, Ice N Hot, 1982, Maxx Traxx-Maxx Traxx; Pulse Records, 2005; musician: (prodr.) Calvin Owens Show Vol. 3: Calvin Owens Blues Orchestra; musician: (live performances) U Ill., 1971—73, Ward Ames Production: Ray Charles, 2000, (live performance) Bace Productions: Music of Motown and Beyond, 1993—, Barrie Lee Hall Ensemble: Kemah Jazz Festival, 2005, Seabreeze, (plays) Christmas Goes Uptown, 1998—, Ragtime: The Musical, 2006, Will Rodgers Follies, 1992, Pippin: Houston Community College, 1999—2000, Titanic: The Musical, 2003, Get Ready, 2006. Mem. judging panel grant allocation Cultural Arts Coun. Houston, Houston, 1993—94; music ministry Met. CME Ch., Houston, 1994—2006, Lakewood Ch., Houston, 2000—03. Named one of Outstanding Young Men Am., U.S Jr. C. of C., 1979; grantee, U. Houston, 1993, 1994, Cultural Arts Coun. Houston, Tex. Commn. Arts, 1994; fellow, Ill. Consortium Ednl. Opportunity Program, 1986—88; scholar, Urban League, 1970—71, U. Ill., 1972; Pullman scholarship, 1972. Mem.: Internat. Assn. Jazz Edn. (chmn. jazz selection panel drums 2006, 2000, chmn. selection com. all state jazz band percussion 2006), Nat. Assn. Study and Performance African Am. Music (assoc.), Tex. Music Educators Assn. (assoc.), Houston Profl. Musicians Assn. Local (assoc.), Percussive Arts Soc. (assoc.), U. Ill. Alumni Assn. (life), Phi Kappa Delta, Omega Psi Phi (licentiate; basilus/chpt. pres. 1973—74). Home: 2814 Creek Manor Dr Kingwood TX 77339 Office: Texas So Univ Dept Music 3100 Cleburne Ave Houston TX 77339 Personal E-mail: msparkdrm@aol.com.

SPARKS, NICHOLAS, writer; b. Omaha, Dec. 31, 1965; s. Patrick Michael and Jill Emma Marie (Thoene) Sparks; m. Catherine Sparks, 1989; children: Miles, Ryan, Landon, Lexie, Savannah. BBA with high honors, U. Notre Dame, 1988. Author: (novels) The Notebook, 1996 (Publishers Weekly bestseller), Message In a Bottle, 1998, A Walk To Remember, 1999, The Rescue, 2000, A Bend in the Road, 2001, Nights in Rodanthe, 2002 (Publishers Weekly bestseller), The Guardian, 2003, The Wedding, 2003 (Publishers Weekly bestseller), True Believer, 2005 (Publishers Weekly bestseller), At First Sight, 2005 (Publishers Weekly bestseller), Dear John, 2006, The Choice, 2007 (Publishers Weekly bestseller), The Lucky One, 2008 (No. 1 Publishers Weekly bestseller); co-author (with Micah Sparks) Three Weeks With My Brother, 2004. Office: c/o Author Mail Warner Books 1271 Ave of Americas New York NY 10020

SPARKS, NICHOLAS B., lawyer; b. Jasper, Ala., Feb. 2, 1980; s. Gary and Evelyn Sparks. AS in Bus. Adminstrn., Bevill State CC, 2001; BS in Fin., U. Ala., Birmingham, 2003; JD, Birmingham Sch. Law, 2007. Bar: Ala. Ptnr. Sparks & Diamond, LLP, 2008; pvt. practice Jasper, Ala., 2008—. Mem.: Ala. State Bar. Democrat. Office: PO Box 1467 Jasper AL 35502 Office Phone: 205-387-8282. Office Fax: 205-221-1067.*

SPARKS, ROBERT DEAN, medical administrator, gastroenterologist; b. Newton, Iowa, May 6, 1932; s. Albert John and Josephine Emma (Kleinendorst) S.; children: Steven Robert, Ann Louise, John James. BA, U. Iowa, 1955, MD, 1957; D of Humanitarian Svc. (hon.), Creighton U., 1978. Diplomate Am. Bd. Internal Medicine. Intern Charity Hosp. of La., New Orleans, 1957-58, resident in internal medicine, 1958-59, asst. in medicine, 1958-59; fellow in gen. medicine and gastroenterology Tulane U. Sch. Medicine, 1959-62, instr. medicine, 1959-63, asst. prof., 1963-64, assoc. prof., 1964-68, prof., 1968-72, asst. dean, 1964-67, assoc. dean, acting dean, 1967-68, vice dean, 1968-69, dean, 1969-72, chief sect. gastroenterology, 1968-72; chancellor Med. Ctr. U. Nebr., 1972-76, prof. medicine, 1972-76; v.p. U. Nebr. System, 1972-76; health program dir. W.K. Kellogg Found., Battle Creek, Mich., 1976-81, v.p. programming, 1981-82, sr. v.p., 1982, pres., chief programming officer, 1982—88, trustee, 1988, pres. emeritus, cons., 1988-92; pres., CEO, Calif. Med. Assn. Found., Sacramento, 1995-98, sr. assoc., 1998—; dir. OMNI Med., Waban, Md., 2000—; with Great Plains Pub. Health Leadership Inst. Adv. Coun., 2002; dean coun. Tulane U. Sch. Medicine; hon. mem. Centro de Estudios en Medicina Familiar " Ian Mc Whinney", Buenos Aires, 2007. Cons. U. Tenn. Health Sci. Ctr., 1988-90, Boston U. Health Policy Inst., 1989-90; mem. sci., compensation and trust rev. coms. Syntex Corp., Palo Alto, Calif., 1987-91, v.p. product safety and compliance, 1991-93; mem. overseers com. to visit Harvard U. Med. and Dental Schs., 1984-90; mem. vis. com. U. Miami Sch. Medicine, 1982-86; assoc. med. dir. for addiction treatment svcs., dir. for edn. and rsch., Battle Creek Adventist Hosp., 1990-91; v.p. Howe-Lewis Internat Inc., Menlo Park, N.Y., 1993-94, cons., 1994-95; mem. adv. coun. to dean Tulane U. Sch. Medicine, 2004—. Mem. editl. bd. Alcoholism Treatment Quar., 1985--; contbr. articles to profl. jours. Bd. dirs. Nat. Coun. on Alcoholism and Drug Dependence, NYC, 1982-93, treas., 1986-88, chmn., 1989-90, past chmn., 1991-92; bd. dirs. Battle Creek Symphony Orch., 1981-88, Lakeview Sch. Dist., Battle Creek, 1979-83, 88-91, Omni Med, 2001-; trustee Monsour Med. Found., Jeannette, Pa., 1976-90, interim pres. 1989, chmn. bd., pres., 1989-90; mem. President's Adv. Bd. on Pvt. Sector Initiatives, Washington, 1986-89; chmn. bd. dirs. Bard Coll. Health Policy and Practice Inst., 1988-96, Consumer Health Info. Rsch. Inst., 1990-95, Chelsea-Arbor Treatment Ctr., 1990-91; bd. dirs. Calhoun County Bd. Health, 1988-91, chmn., 1989-91; mem., bd. dirs. Mental Health and Addictions Found. Mich., Battle Creek, 1991-93; mem. adv. coun. CMA Found., 2004-07; mem. cmty. adv. com., Taser Found., Scottsdale, Ariz., 2005—, bd. dirs. 2006—, chair, 2006—. Recipient Harvard Dental award Harvard U. Sch. Dental Medicine, 1992, Disting. Alumni award for achievement U. Iowa Coll. Medicine, 1998, U. Iowa Alumni Assn, 2009, Disting. Alumni Achievement award, annual Robert D. Sparks Cmty. Health Leadership Achievement award CMA Found., 1997— Fellow ACP; mem. AMA, Nat. Acad. Scis. Inst. Medicine (com. study of treatment and rehab. svcs. for alcoholism and alcohol abuse, bd. mental health and behavioral medicine), Coun. Mich. Founds. (trustee 1986-88), Assn. Am. Med. Colls. (disting. svc. mem. 1975—), Phi Eta Sigma, Alpha Omega Alpha, Ph Kappa Psi. Republican. Methodist. Avocations: tennis, bridge, reading, travel. Home and Office: 5004 Gresham Dr El Dorado Hills CA 95762-7703 Office Phone: 916-230-0719. Personal E-mail: rdsparksmd1@earthlink.net.

SPARKS, ROBERT RONOLD, JR., lawyer; b. Bklyn., Dec. 4, 1946; s. Robert Ronold Sr. and Marjorie Anne (Boehm) S. BA, Va. Mil. Inst., 1969; JD, U. Va., 1972. Bar: U.S. Dist. Ct. (D.C. cir.) 1979, U.S. Dist. Ct. (ea. dist.) Va. 1979, U.S. Ct. Appeals (2d cir.) 1986, U.S. Ct. Appeals (D.C. cir.) 1975, Va. 1972, U.S. Ct. Appeals (4th cir.) 1982, U.S. Ct. Mil. Appeals 1976, U.S. Tax Ct. 1978, U.S. Supreme Ct. 1981. From assoc. to ptnr. Sedam & Herge, McLean, Va., 1977-85; ptnr. Herge, Sparks & Christopher, McLean, 1985—2004, Sparks & Craig, McLean, 2005—. Mem. Bd. Regents James Monroe Law Office Mus. and Meml. Library, Fredericksburg, Va., 1983-86; chmn. Fairfax County Electoral Bd., 2006-09. Mem. Fairfax County Redevel. and Housing Authority, Fairfax, Va., 1981—82; commr. Fairfax County Indsl. Devel. Authority, 1980—81, Fairfax County Planning Commn., 1983—89. Lt. USNR, 1972—77, Philippines. Mem. Va. Bar Assn., D.C. Bar Assn., Rotary (treas., bd. dirs. 1978-80). Roman Catholic.

SPARKS, ROBERT WILLIAM, retired publishing executive; b. Seattle, Dec. 30, 1925; s. James Donald and Gladys (Simmons) S. Student, U. Wash., 1947-50; BA, U. Hawaii, 1954, MA, 1965. Editor, various publs., 1947-64; mng. editor U. Hawaii Press, 1964-66, dir., 1967-87. Cons. East-West Ctr., Jour. Hawaiian History, Japanese and Chinese book pubs., 1987-92; advisor New World Press, Beijing, 1986; mem. adv. bd. to pres. Kamehameha Schs. Author: Seattle, Sitka, San Francisco, 1955, Letters From an Island, 1962, New Endings, 1989, Riding Backwards, 2009; contbr. articles to internat. pub. jours. Served with AUS, 1944-46, PTO. Recipient McInerny editorship, 1953; Pacific House citation Pacific and Asian Affairs Council, 1974 Mem. Assn. Am. Univ. Presses, Assn. Am. Publishers, Internat. Assn. Scholarly Publishers, Soc. for Scholarly Pub., Hawaiian Hist. Soc., Hawaii Found. History and Humanities, Honolulu Acad. Arts, Bishop Mus. Assn. Home: 66 Queen St PH4102 Honolulu HI 96813-4449 Personal E-mail: nihipali@hawaii.rr.com.

SPARKS, THOMAS E., JR., lawyer; b. Little Rock, Jan. 11, 1942; children: Thomas Gunnar, Erik Richard, Andrew Pal. BS, Washington and Lee U., 1963; JD, U. Ark., 1968; LLM, Harvard U., 1970. Bar: Ark. 1968, Calif. 1970. Assoc. Pillsbury Madison & Sutro, San Francisco, 1970-76; ptnr. Pillsbury, Madison & Sutro, San Francisco, 1977-84, Baker & McKenzie, San Francisco, 1984-87, Pillsbury Madison & Sutro, San Francisco, 1987-2000, Pillsbury Winthrop, San Francisco, 2001—. Trustee Grace Cathedral, San Francisco. 1st lt. U.S. Army, 1965. Mem. ABA, Calif. Bar Assn., Calif. Tennis Club (pres. 2000). Office: Pillsbury Winthrop LLP 50 Fremont St San Francisco CA 94105-2230

SPARLING, PHILIP FREDERICK, medical educator; b. Evanston, Ill., Sept. 7, 1936; s. Philip Sparling and Catherine Carnahan; m. Joyce W. Whitaker; children: Whitaker Rand, Frederick Bradford, Rebecca Wynne, Mark Aldrich. AB, Princeton U., NJ, 1958; MD, Harvard, Boston, 1962. Diplomate Internal Medicine, 1973, Infectious Diseases, 1976. Asst. prof. U. NC, Chapel Hill, 1969—73, assoc. prof., 1973—76, prof., 1976—. Chmn. Chair, Dept Microbiology & Immunology, Chapel Hill, 1981—89, Dept. Medicine, Chapel Hill, 1989—99; dir. SE Sexually Transmitted Infections Coop. Rsch. Ctr., Chapel Hill, 1992—, SE Regional Ctr. Biofense & Emerging Infections, Chapel Hill, 2005—. Contbr. scientific papers to publ. Recipient Maxwell Finland award, Infectious Diseases Soc. Am., 2002. Fellow: ACP; mem.: Assn. Am. Physicians. Achievements include research in patents related to vaccines for Gonorrhea. Avocations: canoeing, art, fly fishing. Office: Univ NC 130 Mason Farm Rd Chapel Hill NC 27599-7537

SPARROW, ALISON KIDDER, painter, sculptor; b. Grosse Pointe, Mich., Feb. 13, 1974; d. Herbert George and Nancy Woodruff Sparrow. BFA, RISD, 1997. Fellow Va. Ctr. for the Creative Arts, Lynchburg, 2002, 2004; artist in residence Mary Anderson Ctr. for the Arts, Mt. St Francis, Ind., 2002—05; Hambidge fellow, 2003; artist in residence Contemporary Artist Ctr., North Adams, Mass., 2006. Exhibitions include Inst. for Unpopular Culture of San Francisco, Detroit Artists Market, Scarab Club of Detroit, Moore Art Gallery of St. Clair, Nat. Scholastic Hallmark award (Best of Show (Mich. region), Internat. Salon Exhbn. of Small Works, 2002—06, Mike Kelley Selects, 2004, Member Show, 2006, Great Frame UP Gallery St. Clair Shores, Mich., 2008, Represented in permanent collections Mary Anderson Ctr., Mt. St. Francis, Ind., Vt. Studio Ctr., Johnson. Tchr. Literacy Volunteers of Am., Detroit, 2000—03; vol. Inst. for Unpopular Culture, San Francisco, 1999—2002, Providence Pub. Schools, 2001, Detroit Inst. of Arts. Recipient Advanced Standing, RISD, 1996; grantee, Vt. Studio Ctr., 2002, 2004, 2006, 2008; fellow, Woodstock Guild, 2002, 2003, 2006. Fellow: Scarab Club (assoc.); mem.: Nat. Mus. of Women in the Arts (records stored in archives). Green Party. Protestant. Avocation: writing. Personal E-mail: sparrow_alison@yahoo.com.

SPARROW, BARTHOLOMEW HUNTINGTON, political scientist, educator; b. Brunswick, Maine, Aug. 2, 1959; s. Edward Grant and Lydia Huntington Sparrow. AB, Dartmouth Coll., 1981; AM, U. Tex., 1984; PhD, U. Chgo., 1991. Instr. U. Chgo., 1990-91; asst. prof. U. Tex., Austin, 1991-99, assoc. prof., 1999—, prof., 2008. Author: (books) From the Outside In, 1996, Uncertain Guardians, 1999, The Insular Cases and the Emergence of American Empire, 2006; contbr. articles to profl. jours. Bd. mem. Hostelling Internat. S.W. Tex. Coun., Austin, 1996—. Recipient Scholar's award Harry Truman Libr., 1992; jr. fellow Brit. Studies, 1998, fellow Joan Shorenstein Ctr. on Press, Politics and Pub. Policy, Harvard U., Cambridge, Mass., 1996, Woodrow Wilson Internat. Ctr. Scholars, 2008-09 Mem. Am. Polit. Sci. Assn. (Leonard D. White award 1992, Franklin L. Burdette award 1991), Acad. Polit. Sci. Office: U Tex Burdine 536 Austin TX 78712 E-mail: bhs@email.la.utexas.edu.

SPARROW, CAROL SWEENEY, music educator; d. LeRoy Edward and Louise Woodlieff Sweeney; m. Randolph Howard Locke, Aug. 24, 2005. MusB, U. NC, Greensboro, 1977; MusM, U. NC, Cin., 1979. Opera singer in various cos., 1979—; mem. music faculty Manatee CC, Bradenton, Fla., 2007—. Singer: (Operas) Works of Puccini, Verdi, Bizet, Mascagni, Wagner, Strauss (Stanley Tausend award, 1986). Co-founder, pres. Opera Animals, Singing Is Saving, Sarasota, Fla., 2001—. Avocations: golf, travel. Office: Opera Animals Singing Is Saving 8437 Tuttle Ave #333 Sarasota FL 34243 Personal E-mail: cssparrow@aol.com. Business E-Mail: operaforanimals@aol.com.

SPARROW, EPHRAIM MAURICE, engineer, educator; b. Hartford, Conn., May 27, 1928; s. Charles and Frieda (Gottlieb) S.; m. Ruth May Saltman, Nov. 2, 1952; 1 child, Rachel Bernarr. BS, MIT, 1948, MS, 1949; MA, Harvard U., 1950, PhD, 1956; PhD (hon.), U. Brazil, 1967. Heat transfer specialist Raytheon Mfg. Co., 1952-53; rsch. specialist Lewis Rsch. Ctr., NASA, Cleve., 1953-59; prof. mech. engring. U. Minn., 1959—, Inst. prof., 1994—, chmn. fluid dynamics program, 1968-80, Morse alumni disting. tchg. prof., 1980—. Program dir. NSF, 1986-87, dir. chem., biochem. and thermal engring. divsn., 1986-88; vis. prof., chief AID mission U. Brazil, 1966-67; adv. prof. Xi'an Jiaotong U., 1984—; cons. in field, 1960—; pres. 1st Brazilian Symposium on Heat Transfer and Fluid Mechanics, 1966; mem. solar energy panel Fed. Coun. on Sci. and Tech., 1972; U.S. sci. committeeman 5th Internat. Heat Transfer Conf., 1973-74. Author: (with R.D. Cess) Radiation Heat Transfer, 1966, 2nd edit., 1978; editor: Handbook of Numerical Heat Transfer, 1988, Advances in Numerical Heat Transfer, vol. 1, 1997, vol. 2, 2000, vol. 3, 2009; hon. mem. editl. bd. Internat. Jour. Heat Mass Transfer, 1964—, Internat. Comm. in Heat Mass Transfer, 1975—; sr. editor Jour. Heat Transfer, 1972-80; editor Series in Computational and Phys. Processes in Mechanics and Thermal Scis., 1980—; chmn. editl. adv. bd. Numerical Heat Transfer, 1978—; contbr. over 650 tech. articles to profl. jours. Recipient Ralph Coates Roe award Am. Soc. Engring. Edn., 1978, Outstanding Teaching award U. Minn., 1985, Fed. Engr. of Yr. award NSF, 1988, Sr. Rsch. award Am. Soc. Engring. Edn., 1989, Horace T. Morse award for outstanding contbns. to undergraduate teaching, 1993, Disting. Tchg. award Acad. Disting. Tchrs., U. Minn., 1997, 99, Donald Q. Kern award, Am. Inst. Chemical Engrs., 1999; named George Hawkins Disting. lectr. Purdue U., 1985. Fellow ASME (Meml. award for outstanding contbn. to sci. heat transfer 1962, Max Jakob award for eminent contbn. 1976, Centennial medal 1980, Disting. Svc. award heat transfer divsn. 1982, Charles Russ Richards Meml. award 1985, Worcester Reed Warner medal 1986, 50th Anniversary award heat transfer divsn. 1988, Disting. lectr. 1986-91, 93-94); mem. NAE, Biomed. Engring. Soc. (faculty advisor 1994—), Sigma Xi (Monie A. Ferst medal for contbn. to rsch. through edn. 1993), Pi Tau Sigma. Home: 2105 West Hoyt Ave Saint Paul MN 55108-1314 Office: U Minn Dept Mech Engring Minneapolis MN 55455-0111 Home Phone: 651-647-0787; Office Phone: 612-625-5502. Business E-Mail: esparrow@umn.edu.

SPARROW, HERBERT GEORGE, III, lawyer, educator; b. Ft. Bragg, NC, May 26, 1936; s. Herbert George and Virginia (Monroe) S.; m. Nancy Woodruff, Mar. 4, 1962; children: Amy Winslow, Edward Harrison, Herbert G. IV, Alison Kidder. AB cum laude, Princeton U., 1958; JD, U. Mich., 1961. Bar: Mich. 1961, Calif. 1964, D.C. 1979, U.S. Ct. Claims 1982, U.S. Tax Ct. 1983, U.S. Ct. Mil. Appeals 1962, U.S. Supreme Ct. 1976. Assoc. Dickinson Wright PLLC, Detroit, 1965-70, ptnr., 1970—. Adj. prof. Detroit Coll. Law, Mich. State U., 1977-99. Author numerous articles environ. law.; speaker in field. Bd. dirs. Family Life Edn. Coun., Grosse Pointe, Mich., 1982-88, Adult Well-Being Svcs., Inc., Detroit, 1995-2001; cons. Adult Well-Being Svcs. Inc., 2001—. Capt. JAGC, U.S. Army, 1962-65. Mem. Mich. Bar Assn. (rep. assembly 1979-85, environ. law sect. coun. 1985-91), Calif. Bar Assn., Detroit Bar Assn., Am. Arbitration Assn. (panel arbitrators 1975—), Mich. State Bar Found. (fellow 1989-93), Environment Law Inst. (former assoc.), Phi Delta Phi (pres. Kent Inn Assn., Ann Arbor 1985-97). Office: Dickinson Wright PLLC 500 Woodward Ave Ste 4000 Detroit MI 48226-3416

SPARROW, JOSHUA D., child psychiatrist; married; 2 children. BA, Wesleyan U.; MD, Yale Med. Sch. Assoc. prof. psychiatry Univ. Marseille Sch. Med., France; asst. prof. psychiatry Harvard Med. Sch., Boston, clin. prof. pediat. emeritus; supr. inpatient psychiatry unit Children's Hospital, Boston, founder Child Devel. Unit; assoc. dir. Brazelton Touchpoints Ctr., dir. spl. initiatives. Cons. Harlem Children's Zone, NYC, Am. Indian Early Head Start Programs, Careplus HMO, NYC; mem. adv. bd. Ready, Set, Learn, 2005—. Co-author (with Dr. T. Berry Brazelton): (NY Times syndicated column) Families Today, 1999—, (books) Touchpoints: Three to Six, 2001, Brazelton Way book series, 2004—; cons. (TV series) Brazelton on Parenting, 2000, Ready, Set, Learn, 2005—, contbr. Family Circle mag., Family & Child mag. Coach girls' soccer team, Brookline, Mass. Office: Children's Hospital Ste 320 1295 Boylston St Boston MA 02215 also: Children's Hospital 300 Longwood Ave Boston MA 02215 also: NY Times Syndication Sales Corp 14th Fl 122 E 42nd St New York NY 10168 Office Phone: 617-355-7639. Office Fax: 617-859-7215, 212-499-3382. E-mail: joshua.sparrow@tch.harvard.edu, nytsyn-families@nytimes.com.

SPARROW, KATHLEEN GAIL, retired secondary school educator; b. Akron, Ohio, Apr. 20, 1948; d. Richard Donald and Eldean Kathryn Kraft Sparrow; m. Philip Heiner Gross, May 5, 1988. BA, Miami U., Oxford, Ohio, 1970; MA, U. Akron, 1974, PhD, 1987. Sci. tchr. Akron Pub. Schs., 1970—92, sci. learning specialist k-12, 1992—2006. Praxis III evaluator Ohio Dept. Edn., Columbus, 2003—; nat. selection com. presdl. awards math. and sci. NSF, Washington, 1998—98; mem. global polymer acad. steering com. U. Akron, 2001—; co-prin. investigator NSF gk-12 grant U. Akron and Akron Pub. Schs., 2001—04; co-prin. investigator NSF comprehensive partnership math. and sci. achievement Akron Pub. Schs., 1996—2001; mem. content rev. com. Ohio graduation test Ohio Dept. Edn., Columbus, 2003—, mem. sci. content rev. com.ohio graduation test, 1999—2000, mem. sci. content standards adv. bd., 2001—02, mem. sci. program model writing com., 2005—; adj. prof. U. Akron, 1994—2005, Ashland U., 1996—. Mem. humane commn. County of Summit, Akron; leadership cir., mem. Humane Soc. Greater Akron, Peninsula. Recipient Nat. Sci. Supr. award, Nat. Sci. Ednl. Leadership Assn., 1999, Disting. award Coun., Akron Coun. Engring. and Sci. Socs., 2001, Friend Sci. award, Sci. Edn. Coun. Ohio, 2001; scholar, Martha Holden Jennings Found., 2002. Mem.: ASCD (assoc.), Nat. Sci. Ednl. Leadership Assn. (assoc.; pres. 2000—01, dir. region E 1996—99, coun. mem. 1999—2001), Nat. Sci. Tchrs. Assn. (assoc.), Phi Delta Kappa (pres. 1987—88, 1996—99, Svc. Key 1989). Independent. Home: 7047 Imperial Beach Cir Delray Beach FL 33446-5632 Personal E-mail: ksparrow@adelphia.net.

SPATAFORA, MARCELLO, ambassador; b. Innsbruck, Austria, 1941; married; 1 child. Grad. in Internat. Law, U. Pisa, Italy, 1962. With diplomatic corps Italian Ministry Fgn. Affairs, 1964, vice consul Paris, 1968—70, counselor Belgrade, Serbia, 1970—73, counselor, Chargé d'Affaires Beirut, 1975—77, with Office of Sec.-Gen. Rome, 1977—80, amb. to Malaysia, 1980—86, amb. to Malta, 1986—89, chief. Italian del. responsible for organizing Italy's presidency to the European Econ. Cmty., 1989—90, head arms export licensing unit Rome, 1991—93, amb. to Australia, 1993—97, amb. to Albania, 1997—99, gen. dir. multilateral econ. and fin. cooperation Rome, 2000—03, amb., permanent rep. to UN NYC, 2003—08. Office: Permanent Mission of Italy to UN 1 United Nations Plz 24th Fl New York NY 10017 Office Phone: 212-486-9191. Office Fax: 212-486-1036.

SPATT, CHESTER S., finance educator; b. Bklyn., Jan. 12, 1954; s. Owen and Shirley Spatt; m. Ellen Gordon Spatt (dec.); 1 child, Samuel. AB in Economics, Princeton U., NJ, 1975; AM, U. Pa., Phila., 1976, PhD, 1979. Asst. prof., economics Carnegie Mellon U., Pitts., 1979—84, assoc. prof., economics & fin., 1984—86, prof., economics & fin., 1987—96, mellon bank prof., fin., 1996—2008, Dunn prof. fin., 2008—; vis. asst. prof. Princeton U., 1984; Leslie Wong disting. vis. prof., fin. U. BC, Vancouver, 1986; vis. prof. Toulouse U., France, 1996. Exec. editor Review Fin. Studies, 1990—93; chief economist & dir., Office Economic Analysis Securities Exch. Comm., Washington, 2004—07; rsch. assoc. Nat. Bur. Economic Rsch., 2008—. Contbr. articles to profl. jours. Mem. Fin. Economists Roundtable, 2006—, Shadow Fin. Regulatory Com., 2007—. Co-recipient Michael Brennan award, Barclays Global Investors, 2001; grants, Nat. Sci. Found., Inst. Quantitative Rsch. in Fin. Fellow: TIAA-CREF Inst. (Paul Samuelson award 2004); mem.: Western Fin. Assn. (pres. 1995—96), Soc. Fin. Studies (pres. 1993—96, co-founder). Office: Carnegie Mellon Univ Tepper Sch Bus Posner Hall Rm 253A Pittsburgh PA 15213 Office Phone: 412-268-8834. Office Fax: 412-268-8896. Business E-Mail: cspatt@andrew.cmu.edu.

SPATT, HARTLEY STEVEN, humanities educator; b. Bklyn., Nov. 21, 1947; s. Milton E. and Blanche S. (Bakstansky) S.; m. Wendy Doroshkin, June 13, 1971; children: Martin, Samantha. BA summa cum laude, Colgate U., 1970; MA, NYU, 1971, Johns Hopkins U., 1973, PhD, 1975. Asst. prof. Towson State U., Balt., 1974-76, SUNY Maritime Coll., Bronx, 1976-81, assoc. prof., 1981-87, prof., 1987—, Disting. Tchg. prof., 2004—, assoc. v.p. for acad. affairs, 1999—2002. Writer, editor A.L. Fierst, Greatneck, N.Y., 1977-80, Reference Works, 1993-2001; bus. mgr. Victorian Studies Bull., N.Y.C., 1983—2007; writer Chernow Editl. Svcs., N.Y.C., 1985-90. Contbr. articles to Victorian Poetry, Walt Whitman Rev., other profl. jours. NEH fellow, 1979, 82, 86, 2004. Mem. MLA, N.E. Victorian Studies Assn. (chair nominations 1985—), William Morris Soc. U.S. (sec.-treas. 1984-2006, v.p. 2007-), Phi Beta Kappa. Republican. Jewish. Office: Maritime Coll Suny Bronx NY 10465 Office Phone: 718-409-7250. E-mail: hspatt@sunymaritime.edu.

SPATT, ROBERT EDWARD, lawyer; b. Bklyn., Mar. 26, 1956; s. Milton E. and Blanche S. Spatt; m. Lisa B. Malkin, Aug. 11, 1979; 1 child, Mark Eric. AB, Brown U., 1977; JD magna cum laude, U. Mich., 1980. Bar: N.Y. 1981. Assoc. Simpson Thacher & Bartlett, NYC, 1980-87, ptnr., 1987—. Mem. ABA, N.Y. State Bar Assn., City of N.Y. Bar Assn., Order of Coif. Avocations: photography, boating, reading. Office: Simpson Thacher & Bartlett 425 Lexington Ave New York NY 10017-3954 Office Phone: 212-455-2685. E-mail: RSpatt@stblaw.com.

SPATZ, KENNETH CHRIS(TOPHER), JR., statistics educator; b. Tyler, Tex., Mar. 25, 1940; s. Kenneth Christopher and Mary E. (Harton) S.; m. Thea Siria, May 31, 1961; children: Mark C., Kenneth S., Arr Spatz Nichols BA, Hendrix Coll., 1962; PhD, Tulane U., 1966. Asst. prof. U. of South, Sewanee, Tenn., 1966-69; assoc. prof. U. Ark., Monticello, 1971-73, Hendrix Coll., Conway, Ark., 1973—85, prof., 1985—2003. Author: Basic Statistics: Tales of Distributions, 1976, 9th edit., 2008; co-author: Research Methods in Psychology: Ideas, Techniques and Reports, 2008. Fellow U. Calif., Berkeley, 1969-71. Office: Hendrix Coll Dept Psychology Conway AR 72032 Home: 615 Davis St Conway AR 72034 Business E-Mail: Spatz@hendrix.edu.

SPAULDING, ANNE C., epidemiologist, educator; d. Wallace and Dorothy Spaulding; married. BSc, Brown U., Providence RI; MPH, Johns Hopkins, Balt.; MD, Med. Coll. Va., Richmond. Asst. prof. epidemiology Emory U. Rollins Sch. Pub. Health, Atlanta, 2005—. Recipient Armand Start award,Correctional Medicine, Soc. Correctional Physicians, 2008. Personal E-mail: docspauldingwild@aol.com.

SPAULDING, DAN, public relations executive; BA, MA, U. Mich. Lt. USN; aide, pub. affairs officer to comdr. Tng. Command U.S. Pacific Fleet, San Diego, 1969-72; news anchor/prodr./reporter Staf. WFRV-TV, Green Bay, Wis., Sta. WEYI-TV, Flint-Saginaw, Mich.; mem. faculty U. Wis., Green Bay; news dir. Sta. KOMU-TV, Columbia, Mo., Sta. WOTV-TV 8; with Seyferth & Assocs., Inc., Grand Rapids, Mich., 1989-94, exec. v.p., 1994—. Active West Mich. Environ. Action Coun. Mem. Pub. Rels. Soc. Am. (accredited). Office: Seyferth Assocs Inc 40 Monroe Center NW Ste 202 Grand Rapids MI 49503-3003 Business E-Mail: info@seyferthpr.com.

SPAULDING, JEB (GEORGE B. SPAULDING), state treasurer; b. Washington, Dec. 28, 1952; m. Susan Spaulding; 2 children. BA, Antioch Coll., 1975; MEd, U. Vt., 1993. Owner & mgr. radio sta.; operator Black Angus breeding farm; dir. Vt. Acad. Sci. & Tech. Vt. Tech. Coll.; gen. ptnr. Precision Media Inc.; dir., career and workforce develop. Vt. Dept. Edn.; mem. Edn. Commn. States; del. Dem. Nat. Conv., 1988; mem. Vt. Senate, 1985—2000; state treas. State of Vt., 2002—. Adj. instr. Norwich Univ. Mem., past bd. dirs. Cen. Vt. chpt. ARC, United Way; mem. Gov.'s Snowmobile Adv. Coun.; bd. dir. Red Cross, United Way Washington County 4-H Found., Woodbury Coll.; mem. Ctrl. Vt. Adult Basic Edn., Child Care Fund Vt. and Woodbury Coll. Mem. Nat. Assn. Broadcasters, Vt. Assn. Broadcasters, Vt. Angus Assn., Vt. Red Cross, Green Mt. United Way, New Eng. Bd. Higher Ed. Address: 109 State St Montpelier VT 05609 Office Phone: 802-828-2301. Office Fax: 802-828-2772.*

SPAULDING, KARLA RAE, lawyer; b. Breckenridge, Mich., Feb. 22, 1954; d. Donald Hugh and Shirley Ann (Federspiel) S. BA magna cum laude, Western Mich. U., 1975; JD, Northwestern U., 1980. Bar: Ohio 1980, Fla. 1987. Vis. prof. Grand Valley State Colls., Allendale, Mich., 1975-76; assoc. Baker & Hostetler, Cleve., 1980-83; asst. U.S. atty. U.S. Atty. Office, Tampa, Fla., 1983-88, Grand Rapids, Mich., 1988-89, chief maj. drug trafficking sect. Mid. Dist. Fla. Tampa, 1989-90, chief appellate div. Mid. Dist. Fla., 1990-92; chief fraud and econ. crime sect. So. Dist. Tex. U.S. Atty. Office, Houston, 1992-93; ptnr. Holland & Knight, Tampa, Fla., 1994; pvt. practice Tampa, 1994-97; U.S. magistrate judge U.S. Dist. Ct. (mid. dist.) Fla., Orlando, 1997—. Bd. editors, dep. editor-in-chief Fed. Bar Jour., 1992-95; exec. editor Jour. Criminal Law and Criminology; contbr. articles to profl. publs. Recipient Dir.'s award IRS, 1988. Mem. FBA, Orange County Bar Assn., Hillsborough County Bar Assn. Office: US Courthouse 401 W Ctrl Blvd Ste 5-500 Orlando FL 32801-0550

SPAULDING, WILLIAM D., psychologist, educator; m. Mary E. Sullivan, Aug. 8, 1985. PhD, Univ. Ariz., Tucson, 1976. Lic. Psychologist NE, 1980. Prof. psychology, clin. tng. program U. Nebr. - Lincoln, 1993—. Cons. mental health and psychiat. rehab. in fields. Author: (book) Treatment and rehabilitation of severe mental illness. Mem.: APA. Office: Dept of Psychology Univ Nebraska - Lincoln Lincoln NE 68588-0308 Business E-Mail: wspaulding@unl.edu.

SPAULDING, WILLIAM ELLIS, finance educator, consultant; m. Lois Marie Metzger; 1 child, Joanne Marie. MBA, Ctrl. Mich. U., Mt. Pleasant, 1986. Cert. CHE Ednl. Inst., 1988. Dist. food, beverage dir. Holiday Inn, Memphis, 1972—76; dept. chair Grand Valley State U., Grandville, Mich., 1990—95. Ptnr. Hospitality Consulting Svc., Midland, Mich., 1980—90. Mem. Mich. Hotel Tourism Assn., Lansing, 1977—2008. Mem.: Michrie (pres. 1984—85), Delta Zeta (Outstanding Faculty award 1988). Home: 8670 Wilderness Freeland MI 48623 Office: Northwood Univ 4000 Whiting Dr Midland MI 48640

SPAYD, ELIZABETH TERRY (LIZ SPAYD), editor; b. 1958; BA in Technical Journalism, Colo. State U., 1981. Asst. editor nat. bus. coverage The Washington Post, 1988—91, metro reporter, 1991, reporter Outlook, social policy editor, nat. editor, asst. mng. editor nat. news, 2000—07, editor washingtonpost.com, 2007—09, mng. editor, 2009—. Office: The Washington Post 1150 15th St NW Washington DC 20071*

SPAZIANI, FRANK, college football coach; m. Laura Heikel; children: Joseph, Avery, Andrew. B, Pa. State U., 1969. Grad. asst. Pa. State U. Nittany Lions, 1969; asst. HS coach; head football coach Hempstead HS Tigers, NY, 1973, Raritan HS Rockets, NJ, 1974; offensive asst. US Naval Acad. Midshipman, 1975—82; defensive backs coach U. Va. Cavaliers, 1982—86, defensive coord., 1986—91, Winnipeg Blue Bombers, Can. Football League, 1991—93, Calgary Stampeders, Can. Football League, 1993—96; running backs coach Boston Coll. Eagles, 1996—98, defensive coord., 1998—2008, head football coach, 2009—. Office: Boston Coll Athletic Assn Conte Forum 140 Commonwealth Ave Chestnut Hill MA 02467 Office Phone: 617-552-3010. Business E-Mail: spaziani@bc.edu.*

SPEAR, HARVEY M., lawyer; b. Providence, May 24, 1922; s. Alfred and Esther S.; m. Ruth Abramson, June 27, 1965; children: Jessica, Elizabeth Rogers. AB, Brown U., 1942; LL.B., Harvard, 1948; MA, George Washington U., 1949, LL.M., 1952, SJD, 1955. Bar: Mass. 1948, D.C. 1948, N.Y. 1954, U.S. Supreme Ct. 1954; CPA, Md. Asst. U.S. atty. D.C., 1945; legal asst. to chmn., asst. to vice chmn. SEC, 1948—50; spl. asst. to atty. gen. Dept. Justice, 1951—54; pvt. practice law NYC and Washington, 1956—; counsel Cadwalader Wickersham & Taft, NYC, 1996—. Contbr. articles to profl. jours. Mem.: ABA, Assn. of Bar of City of NY. Home: 765 Park Ave New York NY 10021-4254 also: 78 Hither Ln East Hampton NY 11937 Office: One World Fin Ctr New York NY 10281 Business E-Mail: harvey.spear@cwt.com.

SPEAR, RICHARD EDMUND, art history educator; b. Michigan City, Ind., Feb. 3, 1940; s. Irving S. and Esther Marion (Lieber) S.; m. Athena Tacha, June 11, 1965. BA, U. Chgo., 1961; MFA, Princeton U., 1963, PhD, 1965. Mem. faculty Oberlin (Ohio) Coll., 1964-2000, prof. art history, 1975-83, Mildred Jay prof. art history, 1983-2000; dir. Allen Meml. Art Mus., 1972-83; vis. disting. prof. U. Md., College Park, 1998—. Harn Eminent Scholar prof. U. Fla., 1997-98; disting. vis. prof. George Washington U., Washington, 1983-84; trustee Intermuseum Conservation Assn., 1972-83, pres., 1975-77. Author: Caravaggio and His Followers, 1971, 75, Renaissance and Baroque Paintings from the Sciarra and Fiano Collections, 1972, Domenichino, 1982, Domenichino, 1581-1641, 1996, The Divine Guido, 1997, From Caravaggio to Artemisia, 2002; editor-in-chief Art Bull., 1985-88; contbr. articles to profl. jours. Regional exec. bd. ACLU, 1974-76. Recipient Premio Daria Borghese Gold medal, 1972; Fulbright scholar Italy, 1966-67; Am. Coun. Learned Socs. fellow, 1971-72; NEH fellow, 1980-81, sr. fellow Ctr. Advanced Study in Visual Arts Nat. Gallery Art, 1983-84, Guggenheim fellow, 1987-88; Nat. Humanities Ctr. fellow, 1992-93, Rockefeller Found./Bellagio Ctr. fellow, 1996, Bogliasco Found./Liguria Study Ctr. fellow, 2003; Rockefeller Found./Bellagio Ctr. fellow, 2007. Mem. Coll. Art Assn. Am. Democrat. Home: 3721 Huntington St NW Washington DC 20015-1817 Office: U Md Dept Art History & Archeol College Park MD 20742-0001 Office Phone: 202-362-2347. Business E-Mail: rspear@umd.edu.

SPEAR, SCOTT LAWRENCE, plastic surgeon; b. Chgo., Aug. 25, 1948; s. Louis and Esther S.; m. Cynthia Staley Spear; children: Alexandra, Geri, Louis. BA (hon.), U. Mich., Ann Arbor, 1968; MD, U. Chgo., 1972. Cert. Mass., 1986, Calif., 1992, Fla., 1990, Washington, 1981—, Md., 1982—, Va., 1982—, Am. Bd. Surgery, Am. Bd. Plastic Surgery, Am. Bd. Med. Examiners. Intern Beth Israel Hosp., Boston, 1972-73; jr. residency San Francisco Gen. Hosp., 1973-74, Beth Israel Hosp., Boston, 1974-75, sr. residency, 1976-78; plastic surgery residency U. Miami, 1978-80; asst. prof. plastic surgery U. Fla., Gainesville, 1980-81, Georgetown U. Sch. Medicine, Washington, 1981-86, assoc. prof. plastic surgery, 1988-90; dir. Georgetown Univ. Hosp. Plastic Surgery training program, 1992—; prof. plastic surgery Georgetown U. Sch. Medicine, Washington, 1990—, and chief, dept. plastic surgery. Dir. Nat. Capitol Tng. program, Washington, 1992—, Divsn. of Plastic and Reconstructive Surgery, Georgetown U. Sch. Medicine, Washington, 1992—; vis. prof. U., Tex., 1982, U. Fla., 1982, 84, 85, 86, 87, Nat. Naval Med. Ctr., 1983, 85. Author, Surgery of the Breast; sect. editor, Jour. Plastic and Reconstructive Surgery; featured in NY Times, Washington Post, NPR, ABC, NBC, CBS; contbr. more than 225 articles to profl. jours. Named a Top Doctor, Washingtonian mag., 1986-. Mem. ACS, Med. Soc. of D.C., Plastic Surgery Ednl. Found. (past bd. dir.), Am. Cleft Palata Assn., Nat. Capital Soc. of Plastic Surgeons, Am. Soc. of Maxillofacial Surgeons, Am. Soc. of Plastic and Reconstructive Surgeons, Northeastern Soc. of Plastic and Reconstructive Surgeons (past pres.), Am. Assn. Plastic Surgeons (past pres., bd. dir.), Am. Soc. for Aesthetic Plastic Surgery (past. bd. dir.), Royal and Ancient Soc. Am. Plastic Surgeons (founder, pres.). Has testified before FDA, Congress as expert regarding breast implants. Office: Georgetown Univ Med Ctr Dept Plastic Surgery 1st Fl PHC Bldg 3800 Reservoir Rd NW Washington DC 20007-2113 Office Phone: 202-444-8612. Office Fax: 202-444-7204. Business E-Mail: spears@gunet.georgetown.edu.

SPEAR, SUSAN, legislative staff member; b. NYC; Mem., dep. minority leader, minority whip NH House of Reps., 1985—92; dir. consumer affairs Verizon Comm. Inc.; dist. dir. to congressman John Hall US House of Reps., 2007—, chief of staff, 2009—. Mem. exec. com. NY State Dem. Com.; past chair Putnam County Dem. Com. Democrat. Mailing: US House Reps 1217 Longworth House Office Bldg Washington DC 20515 Office Phone: 202-225-5441. Office Fax: 202-225-3289.*

SPEARING, ANTHONY COLIN, English literature educator; b. London, Jan. 31, 1936; came to U.S., 1987; s. Frederick and Gertrude (Calnin) S. MA, Cambridge U., Eng., 1960. W.M. Tapp rsch. fellow Gonville-Caius Coll. Cambridge U., 1959-60, asst. lectr. in English, 1960-64, official fellow Queens' Coll., 1960-87, life fellow, 1987—, dir. studies in English, 1967-85, lectr. in English, 1964-85, reader in medieval English lit., 1985-87; vis. prof. English U. Va., Charlottesville, 1979-80, 84, prof. English, 1987-89, Kenan prof. English, 1989—. William Matthews lectr. Birkbeck Coll., London, 1983—84; invited lectr. numerous colls. and univs. Eng., Europe, Can., U.S.; Lansdowne vis. fellow U. Victoria, 1993; Benjamin Meaker vis. prof. U. Bristol, 2003; Conway lectr. U. Notre Dame, 2007. Author: Criticism and Medieval Poetry, 1964, rev. edit., 1972; (with Maurice Hussey and James Winny) An Introduction to Chaucer, 1965; The Gawain-Poet: A Critical Study, 1970, Chaucer: Troilus and Criseyde, 1976, Medieval Dream-Poetry, 1976, Medieval to Renaissance in English Poetry, 1985, Readings in Medieval Poetry, 1987, The Medieval Poet as Voyeur, 1993, Textual Subjectivity, 2005; editor: The Pardoner's Prologue and Tale (Chaucer), 1965, rev. edit., 1994, The Knight's Tale (Chaucer), 1966, rev. edit., 1995, The Franklin's Prologue and Tale (Chaucer), 1966, rev. edit., 1994; co-editor: (with Elizabeth Spearing) Shakespeare: The Tempest, 1971, Poetry of the Age of Chaucer, 1974, The Reeve's Prologue and Tale (Chaucer), 1979, Julian of Norwich: Revelations of Divine Love, 1998; translator: The Cloud of Unknowing and Other Works, 2001; contbr. numerous articles to profl. jours. Mem. Medieval Acad. Am., Internat. Assn. U. Profs. English, New Chaucer Soc. (trustee 1986-90). Office: Univ Va Dept English 219 Bryan Hall PO Box 400121 Charlottesville VA 22904-4121 Business E-Mail: acs4j@virginia.edu.

SPEARMAN, DAVID HAGOOD, retired veterinarian; b. Greenville, SC, Nov. 16, 1932; s. David Ralph and Elizabeth (Hagood) S.; m. Patsy Lee cordle, Dec. 18, 1954; children: Kathleen Elizabeth, David Hagood. Student, Clemson Coll., 1950-52, BS, 1975; DVM, U. Ga., 1956. With Cleveland Park Animal Hosp., Greenville, 1956-57; individual practice vet. medicine Easley, SC, 1957—2004, Powdersville, SC, 1987—96. Advisor Pickins County Planning and Devel. Bd., 1972; pres. Northside Parent-Tchr. Orgn., 1965-67; mem. adv. bd. vet. technicians program

Tri-County Tech., 1975-06; mem. admissions com. Vet. Coll., U. Ga., 1975; chmn. Easley Zoning Bd., 1980-83; mem. S.C. Bd. Vet. Examiners, 1982-89, chmn., 1987. Mem. AVMA (alt. del. 1992-95, S.C. del. 1996-99), Blue Ridge Vet. Med. Assn. (founder, pres., sec.), S.C. Assn. Veterinarians (pres. 1974-75, publicity chmn. 1975—, chmn. animal health technician com., Veterinarianof Yr. 1985), Am. Animal Hosp. Assn. (assoc.), S.C. Wildlife, Pickens County Horse, Cattle and Fair Assn. (pres.), Jr. C. of C. (past officer, Key Man award 1959), Trout Unltd. (state dir.), Pickens County Foxhunters Assn., Clemson U. Tiger Letterwinners Assn., Easley Boosters Club, Easley C. of C., World Wildlife Fund, Nat. Wildlife Fedn., Audubon Soc., Nature Conservancy, Internat. Platform Assn., Pickens County Hist. Soc., Lions (pres., internat. del. 1971, 73), Pendleton Farmers Soc., Eastatoee Valley Cmty. Club, Commerce Club, Cliffs at Glassy, Alpha Psi, Alpha Zeta. Presbyterian (deacon, elder, youth leader 1972-74, chmn. orgn. com. 1973-75, 83-85, pulpit com., chmn. nursery bldg. com., stewardship com.). Avocations: photography, fly fishing, bridge. Home: Burdine Springs PO Box 1711 Easley SC 29641-1711

SPEARMAN, DIANE NEGROTTO, art/special education educator; b. New Orleans, Nov. 22, 1949; d. Allen Jules and Constance Lenora (Hinkel) Negrotto; m. Joe Dalton Spearman, June 26, 1971; children Brett Dalton, Eric Clayton, Scott Brandon. BS in Art Edn., La. State U., 1971, MA in Art Edn., 1991, Ed. Spl. Education, 1994. Cert. tchr. La. art, English, spl. edn., 1-12, supr. student tchrs. Art tchr. E. Baton Rouge Schs., 1971-72, 1973-78, 1981-83, 1990—. Presenter state confs. gifted and spl. edn., Baton Rouge, 1985, 94; mem. art edn. curriculum revision com., La. State U., 1994; mem. com. to write art edn. and to revise art edn. curriculum Holmes Program La. State U., Baton Rouge, 1995, supr. student tchrs., 1992-96, cons. art and spl. edn., 1991-96. Products of students sold to fund art program have been featured in newspaper and mag. articles. Leadership positions Cub Scouts Pack 37, Boy Scouts Troop 478, Boy Scouts Am., 1982-95; scoutmaster Troop 93 (handicapped boys), Baton Rouge, 1992-2008. Named Arlington Tchr. of Yr. East Baton Rouge Parish Schs., 1993-94; grantee Arts Coun. of Greater Baton Rouge, Jr. League, 1991, 92, 93. Mem. Nat. Art Edn. Assn., Am. Legion Auxiliary. Republican. Roman Catholic. Avocations: travel, pokeno, motorcycling. Home: 14628 Bailey Dr Baton Rouge LA 70816-1201 Office: Arlington Prep Acad 931 Dean Lee Dr Baton Rouge LA 70820-5102

SPEARMAN, ROBERT WORTHINGTON, lawyer; b. Durham, NC, Jan. 24, 1943; s. Walter and Mary Elizabeth (Dale) S.; m. Patricia Hinds, June 2, 1973; children: Madolyn Marschall, Dorothy Marschall. BA in Polit. Sci., U. N.C., 1965; MA in Philosophy/Econs., Oxford U., 1967; LLB, Yale U., 1970. Bar: NC 1971, DC 1979, U.S. Dist. Ct. (ea., mid. and we. dists. NC), U.S. Ct. Appeals (4th and 5th cirs.), U.S. Supreme Ct. Law clk. to Justice Hugo L. Black U.S. Supreme Ct., Washington, 1971; assoc. Adams, McCullough & Beard, Raleigh, 1971-75, ptnr., 1975—90; ptnr. litig., antitrust & bus. torts practice group leader Parker Poe Adams & Bernstein LLP, Raleigh, 1990—. Adj. prof. Law Sch., U. N.C., Chapel Hill, 1982-83. Vice chmn. corrections planning com. N.C. Crime Control Commn., 1979-81; chmn. Wake County Democratic Com., 1979-81, N.C. Elections Bd., 1981-85. Vice chmn. corrections planning com. N.C. Crime Control Commn., 1979-81; chmn. Wake County Dem. Com., 1979-81, N.C. Elections Bd., 1981-85. Morehead Found. scholar, 1961, Rhodes scholar, 1965; Razor Walker award, 2002, Defender Justice award NC Justice Ctr., 2004; named one of Woodward White's Best Lawyers in Am., 2000-08, Legal Elite, NC, 2003-08. Fellow Am. Coll. Trial Lawyers (mem. NC State Com. 2003-05); mem. ABA, N.C. Bar Assn. (chmn. comml. litigation com. 1982-83), Phi Beta Kappa. Presbyterian. Office: Parker Poe Adams & Bernstein LLP Ste 1400 150 Fayetteville St PO Box 389 Raleigh NC 27602-0389 Office Phone: 919-828-0564. Office Fax: 919-835-4560. Business E-Mail: bobspearman@parkerpoe.com.

SPEARS, BRITNEY, singer; b. McComb, Miss., Dec. 2, 1981; d. Jamie and Lynne Spears; m. Jason Alexander, Jan. 2, 2004 (annulled Jan. 5, 2004); m. Kevin Federline, Sept. 18, 2004 (div. July 30, 2007); children: Sean Preston, Jayden James stepchildren: Kori, Kaleb. Released signature fragrance Curious Britney Spears, 2004, Britney Spears: Fantasy, 2005, In Control, 2006. Singer: (albums) Baby One More Time, 1999, Oops! I Did It Again, 2000 (Billboard Album artist of the Year, 2000), Britney, 2001, In the Zone, 2003, Britney Spears Greatest Hits: My Prerogative, 2004, B In The Mix, The Remixes, 2005, Blackout, 2007, Circus, 2008, (songs) Baby, One More Time (Choice Music Single, Teen Choice Awards, 1999), Toxic (Choice Music Single, Teen Choice Awards, 2004, Grammy award for Best Dance Recording, 2005), Me Against the Music, feat. Madonna (Hot Dance Sales Single of Yr., Billboard, 2004), Piece of Me (Best Female Video, Best Pop Video, Video of Yr., MTV Video Music Awards, 2008); composer (for film Drive Me Crazy) You Drive Me Crazy, 1999, (for film Pokémon the First Movie: Mewtwo Strikes Back) Soda Pop, 1999, (for film On The Line) Let Me Be, 2001, (for film Jimmy Neutron: Boy Genius) Intimidated, 2001, (for film Austin Powers in Goldmember) Boys, 2002; actor: (films) Longshot, 2000, Crossroads, 2002, (TV appearances) How I Met Your Mother, 2008, (voice only): (TV films) Hooves of Fire, 1999, Legends of the Lost Tribe, 2002; appeared in (TV series) Britney And Kevin: Chaotic, 2005, (TV spl.) Britney: For The Record, 2008. Founder, supporter Britney Spears Found., 1999—. Recipient Female Artist of the Year, Billboard, 1999, New Artist of the Year, 1999, Choice Hottie Female & Choice Female Artist, Teen Choice award, 2000, 2002, Choice Female Artist, 2001, Best New Artist, Am. Music Awards, 2000. Office: Jive Records 550 Madison Ave New York NY 10022-3211

SPEARS, GLENNA ELLEN, psychologist; d. Herbert Glenn and Willa Gertrude Spears. MS in Edn., U. Wis., Superior, 1980. Cert. Ncsp NASP, 1989. Sch. psychologist Osceola Dist. Schs., Kissimmee, Fla., 1989—, mentor sch. psychology, 2005—09. Independent. Avocations: travel, camping. Office: 817 Bill Beck Blvd Kissimmee FL 34744 Personal E-mail: glennaespears@hotmail.com. Business E-Mail: spearsg@osceola.k12.fl.us.

SPEARS, JAE, state legislator; b. Latonia, Ky. d. James and Sylvia (Fox) Marshall; m. Lawrence E. Spears; children: Katherine Spears Cooper, Marsha Spears-Duncan, Lawrence M., James W. Student, U. Ky. Reporter Cin. Post, Cin. Enquirer newspapers; rschr. Stas. WLW-WSAI, Cin.; tchr. Jiya Gakuen Sch., Japan; lectr. U.S. Mil. installations East Anglia, England; del. State of W.Va., Charleston, 1974-80; mem. W.Va. Senate, Charleston, 1980-1993. Mem. vis. com. W.Va. Extension and Continuing Edn., Morgantown, 1993-2000; advising bd. mem., W.Va. U. Sch. Medicine, 1992—; with state sen., 1980-93; apptd. to Jud. Hearing Bd., 1993-2000. Chmn. adv bd. Sta. WNPB, 1992-94; congl. liaison Am. Pub. TV Stas. and Sta. WNPB-TV, 1992-97; mem. coun. W.Va. Autism Task Force, Huntington, 1981-90; mem. W.Va. exec. bd. Literacy Vols. Am., 1986-90, 94—, pres., 1990-92; mem. Gov.'s State Literacy Coun., 1991-97; bd. dirs. Found. Ind. Colls. W.Va., 1986—; mem. regional adv. com. W.Va. Gov.'s Task Force for Children, Youth and Family, 1989; mem. USS W.Va. Commn., 1989; mem. exec. com. W.Va. Employer Support Group for Guard and Res., 1989, mem. steering com., 1990-92. Decorated Purple Heart (hon.); recipient Susan B. Anthony award NOW, 1982, edn. award Profl. Educators Assn. W.Va., 1986, ann. award W.Va. Assn. Ret. Sch. Employees, 1985, Meritorious Svc. award W.Va. State Vets. Commn., 1984, Vets. Employment and Tng. Svc. award U.S. Dept. Labor, 1984, award W.Va. Vets. Coun., 1984; named Admiral in N.C. Navy, Gov. of N.C., 1982, hon. Brigadier Gen. W.Va. N.G., 1984, One of 11 Women Pioneers of W.Va. Legislature, W.Va. U. Inst. for Pub. Affairs, 1997, Disting. West Virginian, Gov. W.Va., 2005, Comm. award W.Va. Womens Comm., 2006. Mem. DAR, VFW (aux.), Bus. and Profl. Women (Woman of Yr. award 1978), Nat. League Am. Pen Women (Pen Woman of Yr. 1984), Nat. Order Women Legislators, Am. Legion (aux.), Delta Kappa Gamma, Alpha Xi Delta. Democrat. Home and Office: PO Box 98 Shinnston WV 26431 Office Phone: 304-558-0070.

SPEARS, JAMES RICHARD, cardiologist; b. Fargo, ND, Jan. 23, 1945; s. John Hugh and Jacqueline Patricia Spears; m. Zhanna Tsiukhai, Oct. 15, 2002; children: Kimberly Lynn, Eric Richard, Katrina Arielle. BA, Queens Coll., NYC, 1966; MD, SUNY Downstate Med. Ctr., Bklyn., 1970. Diplomate Am. Bd. Internal Medicine, 1985, in cardiovasular disease 1987, in interventional cardiology 1999. Asst. prof., medicine Harvard Med. Sch., Boston, 1980—87; assoc. prof., medicine Wayne State U., Detroit, 1987—92, dir., cardiovasc. laser lab., 1987—2007, prof., medicine, 1992—2007; dir., cardiac catheterization lab. Harper U. Hosp. WSU, Detroit, 1997—2005, interim chief, divsn. cardiology, 2005—06. Editl. bd. Jour. Coronary Artery Disease, 1987—97, Jour. Lasers Surgery & Medicine, 1987—99, Jour. Amer Soc. Art Inst. Organs, 2006. Contbr. scientific papers to profl. publs. Rsch. grant, NIH, 1982—92, USCI Therox, 1995—2000. Fellow: Am. Coll. Cardiology. Achievements include discovery of intravascular delivery of oxygen and application of aqueous oxygen infusion into coronary arteries; patents in field; first to perform coronary angioscopy experimentally and clinically; discovery of affinity of hematorporphyrin for atheromatous plaques; development of local application of heparin to arteries and first to perform procedure experimentally and clinically; discovery of collagen cross-linking as important cause of restenosis after angioplasty. Avocations: golf, piano. Home: 615 Bridle Path Ct Bloomfield Hills MI 48304 Office: Rochester Med Ctr 610 Main St PO Box 82177 Rochester MI 48307 Office Fax: 248-651-0355. Personal E-mail: jrspears2008@gmail.com.

SPEARS, RONALD E., telecommunications industry executive; Grad., US Mil. Acad., West Point, NY; M in Pub. Svc., We. Ky. U. Mgr. AT&T Long Lines, 1978; pres. Midwest divsn. MCI WorldCom, Inc., 1984—90; corp. v.p. Citizens Utilities Co., 1995—98; pres., COO e.spire Comm. Inc., 1998—99; pres., CEO CMGI Solutions, 1999—2000, Vaultus, Inc., 2000—02; v.p. signature client grp. AT&T Inc., 2002—06, exec. v.p. bus. sales, 2006—07, grp. v.p. global bus. svcs., 2007—08, pres., CEO bus. solutions, 2008—. Bd. dirs. MCF Corp., San Francisco, 2000—08, RateXchange, Inc., 2000—, USA Broadband, Inc., 2002—. Officer US Army, 1970—78. Office: AT&T Hdqs 208 S Akard St Dallas TX 75202 Office Phone: 210-821-4105. Business E-Mail: respears@att.com.*

SPEARS, SALLY, lawyer; b. San Antonio, Aug. 29, 1938; d. Adrian Anthony and Elizabeth (Wylie) S.; m. Tor Hultgreen, July 15, 1961 (div. Jan. 1983); children: Dagny Elizabeth, Sara Kirsten, Kara Spears. BA, U. Tex., 1960, LLB, 1965. Bar: Tex. 1961, Ill. 1971. Practice law, Stamford, Conn., 1966-67, Chgo., 1970-71, Northbrook, Ill., 1972-73, Toronto, Ont., Canada, 1973-81; assoc. firm Cummings & Lockwood, Stamford, 1966-67, Kirkland & Ellis, Chgo., 1970-71; sr. atty. Allstate Ins. Co., Northbrook, Ill., 1971-73; gen. counsel, sec. Reed Paper Ltd., Reed Ltd., Toronto, 1973-78, Denison Mines Ltd., Toronto, 1978-81; pvt. practice law San Antonio, 1981—. Apptd. by Sec. of Def. to serve on Def. Adv. Com., Women in the Svcs., 1997—99. Author: Call Sign Revlon: The Life and Death of Navy Fighter Pilot Kara Hultgreen, 1998. Mem. Tex. Bar Assn., San Antonio Bar Assn., Bankruptcy Bar Assn., San Antonio Country Club, The Club at Sonterra. Home: 433 Evans Ave San Antonio TX 78209-3725 Office: Ste 106 8151 Broadway San Antonio TX 78209-1938 Home Phone: 210-822-4682; Office Phone: 210-826-7020. Personal E-mail: sespears@swbell.net.

SPECHALSKE, FRANK HERMAN, retired educational administrator; b. Berea, Ohio, Sept. 16, 1923; m. Phyllis June Valand, June 18, 1954 (dec.); children: Richard, Janine, Jon, Robert. BS in Edn., Kent State U., Ohio, 1948, MEd, 1950; EdD, Temple U., 1969. Basketball coach, athletic dir. John Marshall High Sch., Cleve., 1951-58; asst. prof. phys. edn., basketball coach Western Res. U., Cleve., 1958-65; prof. phys. edn., dir. athletics Ea. Mont. Coll., Billings, 1968-77; doctoral fellow Temple U., Phila., 1965-68; exec. dir., alumni assoc. U.S. Sports Acad., Daphne, Ala., 1989-92, dean acad. adminstrn., 1985-89, prof. sport mgmt., 1977-92; prof. emeritus, 1992; v.p. spl. projects Am. Acad. for Distance Learning, Scranton, Pa., 1992-95; v.p., CEO All Am. Boy/Girl Inc., 1995; mgmt. cons., U.S. coord. C&G Hotel and Catering Sch., Kuala Lumpur, Malaysia, 1995. Cons., presenter in field. Contbr. articles to profl. jours. Exec. com., chmn. basketball com. U.S. Olympic Com.; exec. com., chmn. basketball com. Amateur Athletic Union; mem. Mont. Gov.'s Coun. on Phys. Fitness and Sport; Southeastern AAU basketball chmn., 1977-83, nat. conv. del., 1977-81; active bd. dirs. Boy Scouts Am. Grantee, Internat. Communication Agy. of U.S. Dept. State 1981, 82, Mobile County (Ala.) Bd. Edn., 1979, Okaloosa County (Fla.) Bd. Edn., 1979, Santa Rosa County (Fla.) Bd. Edn., 1979. Mem. Nat. Assn. Collegiate Dirs. Athletics (bd. dirs.), Nat. Assn. for Intercollegiate Athletics, Amateur Basketball Assn. of U.S. (sec., bd. dirs.), AAHPERD (chmn. task force on Club sports, conv. panelist), Internat. Amateur Basketball Fedn. (assoc. sec. gen., mem. cen. bd.), Phi Delta Kappa. Home: 3771 Swansea Dr Mobile AL 36608-1779 Home Phone: 251-343-7248. E-mail: frankmobil@bellsouth.net.

SPECHT, ALICE WILSON, university libraries dean; b. Caracas, Venezuela, Apr. 3, 1948; (parents Am. citizens); d. Ned and Helen (Lockwood) Wilson; m. Joe W. Specht, Dec. 30, 1972; 1 child, Mary Helen. BA, U. Pacific, 1969; MLS, Emory U., 1970; MBA, Hardin-Simmons U., 1983. Libr. social scis. North Tex. State U., Denton, 1971-73; reference libr. Lubbock (Tex.) City and County Libr., 1974-75; system coord. Big Country Libr. System, Abilene, 1975-79; assoc. dir. Hardin-Simmons U., 1981-88, dir. univ. librs., 1988—, dean univ. librs., 2002—. Apptd. Mayor's Task Force Libr. Svcs., 1995-96; mem. adv. bd. Libr. Sys. Act, 2001-07; mem. vision task force TLA, 2007-. Author bibliog. instrn. aids, 1981-90; editor; The College Man, For Pilots Eyes Only. Mem. mayor's task force Abilene Pub. Libr., 1995—96; mem. Libr. Sys. Act. Bd., Tex., 2000—07. Recipient Boss of Yr., Am. Bus. Women's Assn., 1994. Mem.: ALA, Abilene Libr. Consortium (chair adminstrv. com. 1990, coord. nat. conf. 1991, 1993, librart sys. act adv. bd. 2001—, coord. nat. conf. 2002, chair adminstrv. com. 2006), Tex. Libr. Assn. (chair com. 1978—84, sec.-treas. coll. and univ. librs. divsn. 1993—94, legis. com. 1994—, exec. bd. 2009—), Texshare Ednl. Working Group (chair 1999). Home: 918 Grand Ave Abilene TX 79605-3233 Office: Hardin-Simmons U PO Box 16195 2341 Hickory St Abilene TX 79698-6195 Business E-Mail: aspecht@hsutx.edu.

SPECHT-JARVIS, ROLAND HUBERT, fine arts and humanities educator, dean; b. Dortmund, Germany, Oct. 31, 1954; came to U.S., 1982; s. Otto and Waltraud Specht; m. Shawn Cecilia Jarvis, June 15, 1982; children: Alex Jarvis, Elly Jarvis. Staatsexamen in German and pedagogy, Ruhr U. Bochum, Germany, 1982, Staatsexamen in Law and German, 1982, PhD, 1988. Instr. German St. Cloud (Minn.) State U., 1982-87, asst. prof. German, 1987-89, assoc. prof. German, 1989-92, prof. German, 1992—, dir. Ingolstadt program dept. fgn. langs. and lit., 1984-97, chmn. and dir. dept. fgn. langs., 1988-94, dir. quality enhancement programs State Minn., 1994-97, dean Coll. Fine Arts & Humanities, 1997—. Author: (with H. Walbruck) Deutsch Gestern und Heute, 1986, tchrs. annotated edit., 1986, audio tape program and manual, 1987, workbook, 1987, test series, 1988, Deutsch Aktuell 3 tchrs. edit., 1993, 4th edit. workbook, 1999, Compendium College of Fine Arts and Humanities, 1998, 2000, student edit., 1993, workbook, 1993, tape program manual, 1993, Microsoft Word. Textverarbeitung mit dem Macintosh, 1990, Die Ausbildung des Literarischen Diskurses Friedrich Schlegels zur Zeit der Herausgabe des Athenaeums, 1994, (with Shawn C. Jarvis and Isolde Mueller) Deutsch Aktuell 3, 1998, 5th edit., 2003. V.p., founder Förderverein Ingolstadt-St. Cloud, 1985; bd. dirs. Alexandria-St. Cloud Performing Arts Found., 1997—, St. Cloud State U. Alumni Assn., 1995, Theatre L'Homme Dieu, 1997—, St. Cloud Symphony Orch., 1998-2002, Herberger Coll. Bus., 2000—; mem. coun. Coll. of Arts and Scis., 1995. Mem. St. Cloud Rotary (sec. 1998-99, v.p. 2001-02, pres. 2002-03), Amnesty Internat. Avocations: outdoors, chess, racquetball, motorcycles. Home: 1922 9th Ave SE Saint Cloud MN 56304-2118 Office: St Cloud State Univ 720 4th Ave S Saint Cloud MN 56301-4498 Office Phone: 320-308-3093. E-mail: roland@stcloudstate.edu.

SPECK, EUGENE LEWIS, internist; b. Boston, Dec. 17, 1936; s. Robert A. and Anne (Rosenberg) S.; m. Rachel Shoshana; children: Michael Robert, Keren Sara. AB, Brandeis U., Waltham, Mass., 1958; MS, U. Mass., 1961; PhD, George Washington U., 1966, MD, 1969. Diplomate Am. Bd. Internal Medicine with subspecialty in infectious diseases. Intern N.Y. Hosp.-Cornell, 1969-70; rsch. assoc. NIH, Bethesda, Md., 1970-72; resident Barnes Hosp.-Washington U., 1972-73; instr. medicine Washington U., St. Louis, 1972-73; fellow Strong Meml. Hosp.-U. Rochester, 1973-75; instr. medicine U. Rochester, N.Y., 1973-75, asst. prof. medicine N.Y., 1975-80, U. Nev., Las Vegas, 1980-85, assoc. prof., 1985-95, prof. medicine, 1995—; dir./co-dir. infectious disease unit U. Med. Ctr. of So. Nev., Las Vegas, 1980—; ptnr. Infectious Diseases Consultants, 1983—. Cons. Clark County Health Dept., Las Vegas, 1980—, U. Med. Ctr. So. Nev., Las Vegas, 1980—, Sunrise Hosp., Las Vegas, 1980—, Valley Hosp., Las Vegas, 1980—; Am. coll. physicians gov., State Nev. Contbr. articles to profl. jours., chpts. to books. Recipient Disting. Physician award, State of Nev., 2002. Fellow ACP (elected gov. Nev.), Infectious Disease Soc. Am.; mem. Am. Soc. Microbiology, Alpha Omega Alpha. Avocations: tennis, skiing, racquetball. Home: 2228 Chatsworth Ct Henderson NV 89074-5309 Office: Infectious Diseases Cons 3006 S Maryland Pkwy Ste 780 Las Vegas NV 89109-2292 Office Phone: 702-737-0740.

SPECK, SAMUEL WALLACE, JR., federal official; b. Canton, Ohio, Jan. 31, 1937; s. Samuel Wallace Sr. and Lois Ione (Schneider) S.; m. Sharon Jane Anderson, Jan. 20, 1962; children: Samuel Wallace III, Derek Charles. BA, Muskingum Coll., 1959; postgrad., U. Zimbabwe, 1961; MA, Harvard U., 1963, PhD, 1968. Prof. polit. sci. Muskingum Coll., New Concord, Ohio, 1964-83, asst. to pres., 1986-87, exec. v.p., 1987, acting pres., 1987-88, pres., 1988-99; assoc. dir. Fed. Emergency Mgmt. Agy., 1983-86; mem. Ohio Ho. of Reps., 1971-76, Ohio State Senate from 20th Ohio Dist., 1977-83; dir. Dept. Natural Resources, mem. Gov.'s cabinet State of Ohio, 1999—2007. Bd. dirs. Camco Fin. Corp., Cambridge, Ohio, 1990-2007; pres. Eastern Ohio Devel. Alliance, 1990-92; Fund for Improvement of Postsecondary Edn., 1990-92, chmn. 1991. Contbr. numerous articles on African and Am. govt. and pub. policy. Bd. dirs. Ohio Tuition Trust Authority, 1991-93, Internat. Ctr. for Preservation Wild Animals, 1988-99, Lake Erie Commn., 1999-2007; bd. dirs., chmn. Ohio Water Resources Coun. 1999-2005; mem. Great Lakes Commn., 1999-2007, chmn., 2002-04; mem. Ohio Power Siting Bd., 1999-2007; mem. Ohio Pub. Works Commn., 2003-07; chmn. coun. Great Lakes water mgmt. working group, 2002-05; mem. Ohio Higher Edn. Facility Commn., 2007—, Battelle for Kids Bd., 2006-, commr. Internat. Jt. Commn., 2008-. Recipient Outstanding Legislator award VFW/DAV/Am. Legion, Conservation Achievement award State of Ohio, Disting. Svc. award, Nat. Gov. Conf., 2004, Conservation Leadership award, Ohio Nature Conservancy. Home: 240 Greenbriar Ct Worthington OH 43085-3055

SPECK, WILLIAM T., former physician, health facility administrator; BS, Rutgers U.; MD, Wake Forest U. Sch. Medicine, 1968. Resident Columbia U., NYC, fellow, with dept. pediat. and microbiology; with dept. pediat. Case Western Reserve U., Cleve., prof., dept. pediat., chmn., dir., dept. pediat.; CEO Rainbow Babies and Children's Hosp., Cleve., 1982—92; pres., CEO Presbyn. Hosp. in NYC/Columbia-Presbyn. Med. Ctr., 1992—99; interim dir., CEO Marine Biol. Lab., Woods Hole, Mass., 2000—01, chmn., CEO, 2001—06. Bd. trustees Marine Biol. Lab., 1994—; mem. MBL Corp. Office: Marine Biol Lab 7 MBL St Woods Hole MA 02543

SPECKHARD, DANIEL V., United States Ambassador to Greece; m. Anne Speckhard; 3 children. BA with distinction, U. Wis., Madison, MA in Pub. Policy and Adminstrn., MS in Econs. Staff mem. Small Bus. Adminstrn., US Agency Internat. Devel., US Senate Small Bus. Com., 1982—84; with internat. affairs divsn. Office Mgmt. and Budget, Washington, 1984—90; advisor to dep. sec. of state US Dept. State, Washington, 1990—92, dir. policy & resources, 1992—93, dep. to the amb.-at-large for the new ind. states, 1993—97, US amb. to Belarus, 1997—2000, dir. Iraq reconstruction mgmt. office Baghdad, Iraq, 2005—06, dep. chief of mission, 2006—07, US amb. to Greece Athens, 2007—; dep. asst. sec. gen. polit. affairs NATO, 2000—03, dir. policy planning, 2003—05. Recipient Svc. medal, NATO. Office: DOS Amb 7100 Athens Pl Washington DC 20521-7100*

SPECTER, ARLEN, United States Senator from Pennsylvania; b. Wichita, Kans., Feb. 12, 1930; s. Harry and Lillie (Shanin) S.; m. Joan Lois Levy, June 14, 1953; children: Shanin, Stephen. Student, U. Okla., 1947-48; BA Internat. Rels., U. Pa., 1951; LLB, Yale U., 1956. Asst. counsel Warren Commn., Washington, 1964; magisterial investigator Commn. of Pa., 1965; asst. dist. atty. City of Phila., 1959-63, dist. atty., 1966-74; ptnr. Dechert Price & Rhoads, Phila., 1956-66, 74-80; US Senator from Pa., 1981—; mem. US Senate Appropriations Com., US Senate Environment & Pub. Works Com., US Senate Judiciary Com., chmn., 2005—07, US Senate Select Com. on Intelligence, 1995—97; mem. US Senate Veterans Affairs Com., chmn., 1997—2001, 2001, 2001—03; mem. US Senate Spl. Com. on Aging. Asst. counsel, Commn. on the Assassination of President Kennedy (Warren Commn.), 1964; lectr. Temple U. Law Sch., 1972-75, U. Pa. Law Sch., 1968-72 Author: Police Guide to Search and Seizure, Interrogation, and Confession, 1967; co-author: (with Charles Robins) Passion for Truth: From Finding JFK's Single Bullet to Questioning Anita Hill to Impeaching Bill

Clinton, 2000, (with Frank J Scaturro) Never Give In: Battling Cancer in the Senate, 2008; contbr. articles to profl. jours. 1st lt. USAF, 1951—53. Recipient Youth Svcs. award B'nai B'rith, 1966; recipient Sons of Italy award, 1968, Community Humanitarian award Bapt. Ch., 1969, man of Yr. award, Temple Beth Ami, 1971, N.E. Cath. High Sch. Outstanding Achievement award, 1973, Congl. award, Am. Soc. of Nephrology, 1998, Legis. of the Year award Nat. Assn. of Alcoholism & Drug Abuse Counselors, 1999, Pub. Policy Leadership award, Am. Cancer Soc., 2000, Spl. Recognition award, Am. Heart Assn., 2003, Lead On! award, Nat. Org. on Disability, 2004. Mem. ABA, Pa. Bar Assn., Phila. Bar Assn., Phi Beta Kappa. Democrat. Jewish. Office: US Senate 711 Hart Senate Office Bldg Washington DC 20510-0001 also: District Office Ste 9400 600 Arch St Philadelphia PA 19106 Office Phone: 202-224-4254, 215-597-7200. Office Fax: 202-228-1229, 215-597-0406. E-mail: senator_specter@specter.senate.gov.*

SPECTER, RICHARD BRUCE, lawyer; b. Phila., Sept. 6, 1952; s. Jacob E. and Marilyn B. (Kron) S.; m. Jill Ossenfort, May 30, 1981; children: Lauren Elizabeth, Lindsey Anne, Allison Lee. BA cum laude, Washington U., St. Louis, 1974; JD, George Washington U., 1977. Bar: Mo. 1977, U.S. Dist. Ct. (ea. and we. dists.) Mo. 1977, U.S. Ct. Appeals (8th cir.) 1977, Ill. 1978, Pa. 1978, U.S. Dist. Ct. (ea. dist.) Ill. 1979, U.S. Ct. Appeals (7th cir.) 1979, Calif. 1984, U.S. Dist. Ct. (cen. dist.) Calif. 1985, U.S. Ct. Appeals (9th cir.) 1986, U.S. Dist. Ct. (so. dist.) Calif. 1987, U.S. Dist. Ct. (no. dist.) Calif. 1988, U.S. Supreme Ct. 1999. Assoc. Coburn, Croft, Shepherd, Herzog & Putzell, St. Louis, 1977-79; ptnr. Herzog, Kral, Burroughs & Specter, St. Louis, 1979-82; exec. v.p. Uniqey Internat., Santa Ana, Calif., 1982-84; pvt. practice LA and Irvine, Calif., 1984-87; ptnr. Corbett, Steelman, & Specter, Irvine, 1987—. Instr. Nat. Law Ctr. George Washington U. 1975; dir. Javo Beverage Co., 2001-. Mem. ABA, Ill. Bar Assn., Mo. Bar Assn., Pa. Bar Assn., Calif. Bar Assn. Jewish. Office: 18200 Von Karman Ave Ste 900 Irvine CA 92612-1086 Home: 2 Serenity Newport Coast CA 92657 Office Phone: 949-553-9266. Business E-Mail: rspecter@corbsteel.com.

SPECTOR, DANIEL EARL, historian, educator; b. Pensacola, Fla., Dec. 19, 1942; s. Joseph and Dorothy Margaret (Givens) S.; m. Esta Gelda Rappaport, Aug. 9, 1964; children: Warren Leigh, Susan Artemis (dec.). BA, George Washington U., 1963; postgrad., U. Fla., 1963-64; MA, U. Tex., 1972, PhD, 1975. Adj. instr. Jacksonville (Ala.) State U., 1975-77; chief skill qualification test br. U.S. Army Mil. Police Sch., Ft. McClellan, Ala., 1975-80; supr. edn. specialist U.S. Army Chem. Sch., Ft. McClellan, 1980-82; chief U.S. Army Chem. Sch. Standardization & Analysis Div., Ft. McClellan, 1982-84; dep. dir. U.S. Army Chem. Sch. Directorate of Tng. & Doctrine, Ft. McClellan, 1984-88; adj. prof. U. Ala., Birmingham, 1986—2001; chem. corps historian U.S. Army Chem. Sch., Ft. McClellan, 1988-94; adj. prof. Troy State U., Ft. Benning, Ga., 2003—05. Accreditation coord. U.S. Army Chem. Sch., Ft. McClellan, 1984-90; accreditation team chief So. Assn. Colls. and Schs., Atlanta, 1985-90; U.S. Army rep. EURO-NATO nuc., biol. and chem. workgroups, 1984-90. Author: Chemical School Annual Historial Reviews, 1988—92; contbr. numerous revs., articles and ency. entries to several profl. jours. and encyclopedias pubs. Mem. Jacksonville Kiwanis, 1981-92. Alumni scholar George Washington U., 1959-63, Road scholar Ala. Humanities Found., 2002-; NDEA fellow U. Fla., 1963-64, NDFL fellow U. Tex. 1972-73. Mem. Middle Eastern Studies Assn., Middle East Inst., Am. Hist. Assn., Soc. Mil. History, Ala. Assn. Historians, MENSA, Temple Beth-El, Scottish Rite, Hiram Lodge, Ala. Master Gardener, Calhoun County Sheriff's Garden (advisor), Legion of Honor, Chapel of Four Chaplains, Phi Alpha Theta. Democrat. Jewish. Avocations: gardening, fishing. Home: 1317 7th Ave NE Jacksonville AL 36265-1174 Personal E-mail: drspector@cableone.net.

SPECTOR, DAVID M., lawyer; b. Rock Island, Ill., Dec. 20, 1946; s. Louis and Ruth (Vinikour) S.; m. Laraine Fingold, Jan. 15, 1972; children: Rachel, Laurence. BA, Northwestern U., 1968; JD magna cum laude, U. Mich., 1971. Bar: Ill. 1971, U.S. Dist. Ct. (no. dist.) Ill. 1971, U.S. Ct. Appeals (7th cir.) 1977, U.S. Ct. Appeals (4th cir.) 1984, U.S. Dist. Ct. (cen. dist.) Ill. 1984, U.S. Supreme Ct. 1999, N.Y. 2002, U.S. Ct. Appeals (2d cir.) 2002. Clk. Ill. Supreme Ct., Chgo., 1971-72; ptnr., assoc. Isham, Lincoln & Beale, Chgo., 1972-87; ptnr. Mayer, Brown & Platt, Chgo., 1987-97, Hopkins & Sutter, Chgo., 1997-2001, Schiff, Hardin LLP, Chgo., 2001—. Chmn. ABA Nat. Inst. on Ins. Co. Insolvency, Boston, 1986; co-chmn. ABA Nat. Inst. on Internat. Reins.: Collections and Insolvency, NY, 1988; chmn. ABA Nat. Inst. on Life Ins. Co. Insolvency, Chgo., 1993; spkr. in field. Editor: Law and Practice of Insurance Company Insolvency, 1986, Law and Practice of Life Insurer Insolvency, 1993; co-editor: Law and Practice of International Reinsurance Collections and Insolvency, 1988; contbr. articles to profl. jour. Mem. ABA (chair Nat. Inst. on Life Insurer Insolvency 1993), Chgo. Bar Assn., Lawyer's Club of Chgo. Office: Schiff Hardin LLP 6600 Sears Tower Chicago IL 60606 Home: 1418 N Lake Shore Dr Chicago IL 60610-1642 Office Phone: 312-258-5552. Business E-Mail: dspector@schiffhardin.com.

SPECTOR, ELEANOR RUTH, manufacturing executive; b. NYC, Dec. 2, 1943; d. Sidney and Helen Lebost; m. Mel Alan Spector, Dec. 10, 1966; children: Nancy, Kenneth. BA, Barnard Coll., 1964; postgrad. sch. pub. adminstrn., George Washington U., 1965-67; postgrad sch. edn., Nazareth Coll., 1974. Indsl. investigator N.Y. State Dept. Labor, White Plains, 1964-65; mgmt. intern Navy Dept., Washington, 1965, contract negotiator, 1965-68, contract specialist, 1975-78, contracting officer/br. head, 1978-82, dir. div. cost estimating, 1982-84; dep. asst. sec. def. for procurement Washington, 1984-91; dir. Def. Procurement, Washington, 1991-2000; v.p. contracts Lockheed Martin Corp., Bethesda, Md., 2000—. Advisor Nat. Contract Mgmt. Assn., 1984—, Fed. Contracts Report, 2000—. Recipient Def. Meritoroius Civilian Svc. medal, 1986, 93, 96, Meritorious Svc. Presdl. award, 1989, 94, Disting. Civilian Svc. Presdl. award, 1990, 97, Def. Disting. Civilian Svc. medal, 1991, 94, 2000, Nat. Pub. Svc. award, 1998, Sec. Def. award for Excellence, 1997. Office: Lockheed Martin Corp MP 110 6801 Rockledge Dr Bethesda MD 20817-1877

SPECTOR, GERSHON JERRY, otolaryngologist, educator, researcher; b. Rovno, Poland, Oct. 20, 1937; came to U.S., 1949; naturalized, 1956; m. Patsy Carol Tanenbaum, Aug. 28, 1965. BA, Johns Hopkins U., 1960; MD cum laude, U. Md., 1964. Intern Beth Israel Hosp., Boston, 1964-65; resident in surgery Sinai Hosp., Balt., 1965-66; resident in otolaryngology Mass. Eye and Ear Infirmary, Boston, 1966-69, Peter Bent Brigham Hosp., Boston, 1968-69; teaching fellow in otolaryngology Harvard U. Med. Sch., Boston, 1968-69; assoc. physician Ill. Crippled Children's Svc., Carbondale, 1971; mem. faculty Washington U. Med. Sch., St. Louis, 1971—, assoc. prof. otolaryngology, 1974-76, prof., 1976—; chief dept. otolaryngology St. Louis County Hosp., 1971-77. Mem. staff Washington U. Med. Ctr., Barnes Hosp.; dir. temporal bone bank, 1971-81; guest examiner Am. Bd. Otolaryngology, 1975-77; rsch. cons. neurosci. group, G.D. Searle Pharm. Corp. Mem. editl. bd. Laryngoscope, 1978, editor-in-chief, 1984-94; contbr. articles to med. jours. With U.S. Army, 1969-71. Hancock scholar, 1962. Fellow ACS; mem. AAAS, AMA, Am. Acad. Ophthalmology and Otolaryngology (Honor award 1979), St. Louis Med. Soc., St. Louis County Med. Soc., Am. Coun. Otolaryngology, St. Louis Ear, Nose and Throat Club (pres. 1986), So. Med. Assn., Deafness Rsch. Found., Pan. Am. Assn. Otorhinolaryngology and Broncho Esophagology, Am. Soc. Head and Neck Surgery, Soc. Univ. Otolaryngologists, Am. Laryngol., Rhinol. and Otol. Soc. (Edmund Prince Fowler award 1974), Am. Soc. Cell Biology, Electron Microscopy Soc., N.Y. Acad. Scis., Am. Assn. Anatomists, Am. Acad. Facial Plastic and Reconstructive Surgery, Am. Neuro-Otology Soc., Gesellschaft fur Neurootologie und Aequilibrimoetrie A.V., Barany Soc., Am. Radium Soc., Assn. Acad. Surgery, Am. Fedn. Clin. Oncologic Socs., Am Otol. Soc., Acoustical Soc. Am., Soc. for Neurosci., Internat. Skull Base Soc. (founding), Brazilian Skull Base Soc. (hon.), Centurion Club, Alpha Omega Alpha, Psi Chi. Home: 7365 Westmoreland Dr Saint Louis MO 63130-4241 Office: Washington U Med Sch Saint Louis MO 63110 Office Phone: 314-362-7252. Business E-Mail: spectorg@wustl.edu.

SPECTOR, JASON A., plastic surgeon, educator; b. NYC, Jan. 24, 1970; s. Bernard Robert Spector and Evelyn Rose Jefferies, Bryan Reginald Jefferies (Stepfather); m. Beth Chartoff, Nov. 21, 1998; children: Joshua Andrew, Samuel Benjamin. Grad., Cornell U., 1991; MD, NY U. Sch. Medicine, 1996. Diplomate Am. Bd. Plastic Surgery, 2007. Intern, resident & fellow NYU Med. Ctr., rsch. fellow Lab. Devel. Biology & Repair; asst. prof. Weill Cornell Med. Coll., NYC, 2006—; asst. attending surgeon NY Presbyterian Hosp. Mem.: Plastic Surgery Rsch. Coun., NY Regional Soc. Plastic Surgeons (Best Rsch. Presentation award 2003), Northeastern Soc. Plastic Surgeons (Best Resident Rsch. Presentation award 1999), Alpha Omega Alpha. Office: Weill Cornell Medical Coll 525 East 68th St Payson 709-A New York NY 10065 Office Fax: 212-746-8952. Business E-Mail: jas2037@med.cornell.edu.*

SPECTOR, JUDITH ANN, retired english educator; b. Klamath Falls, Oreg., Apr. 6, 1945; d. Samuel and Lillian (Hutchinson) S.; m. Sandor P. Vaci, May 14, 1966 (div. 1971); m. Thomas E. Ward, May 30, 1978 (div. 1985); m. John Michael Partridge, Sept. 15, 1989. BA in English magna cum laude, U. Mich., 1967; MA in English, Ind. U., 1975, PhD in English, 1977. Cert. tchr. ESL, Internat. House, London. Tchr. ESL The London Sch. English, 1967-70; assoc. instr. Ind. U., Bloomington, 1974-76; vis. asst. prof. Ind. U./Purdue U., 1977-78, asst. prof., 1978-83, assoc. prof., 1983-97, prof. Columbus, 1997—, emeritus prof., 2009. Editor, contbr.: Gender Studies: New Directions in Feminist Criticism, 1986; contbr. articles to profl. jours. Mem. MLA, Nat. Coun. Tchrs. English, Assn. for Humanistic Psychology, Phi Beta Kappa. Avocation: ballroom dance. Office: Ind U/Purdue U 4601 Central Ave Columbus IN 47203-1769 Home: 3614 E Tamarror Dr Bloomington IN 47408 Office Phone: 812-348-7213. E-mail: jspector@iupui.edu.

SPECTOR, MELBOURNE LOUIS, retired foreign service officer; b. Pueblo, Colo., May 7, 1918; s. Joseph E. and Dora (Bernstein) S.; m. Louise Vincent, Nov. 23, 1948; 1 son, Stephen David. BA with honors, U. N.Mex., 1941. Intern U.S. Bur. Indian Affairs, 1941, Nat. Inst. Pub. Affairs, 1941; personnel asst. Office Emergency Mgmt., 1941-42; chief classification div. War Relocation Authority, 1942-43, Hdqrs. USAAF, 1943-45; employment officer UNRRA, 1945-46; pvt. employment, 1946-47; personnel officer Dept. State, 1947-49; detail Econ. Coop. Adminstrn., 1948; dep. dir. personnel Econ. Coop. Adminstrn., Marshall Plan, Paris, 1949-51; dep. dir., acting dir. personnel Econ. Coop. Adminstrn., Mut. Security Adminstrn., FOA, 1951-54; asst., dep. dir. Mission to Mexico, ICA, 1954-57, acting dir., 1957-59; chief C. Am., Mex. and Caribbean div. ICA, 1959-61; dir. Office Personnel Mgmt., AID, 1961-62; exec. dir. Bur. Inter-Am. Affairs, Dept. State, 1962-64; commd. consul gen., sec., 1964; counselor for adminstrv. affairs Am. embassy, New Delhi, India, 1964-66; seminarian Sr. Seminar Fgn. Policy, Dept. State, 1966-67; exec. dir. U.S.-Mex. Commn. for Border Devel. and Friendship, 1967-69, Am. Revolution Bicentennial Commn., 1969-71; mem. mgmt., policy and coordination staffs Dept. State, 1971-73; ret., 1973; cons., 1973—. Mem. Fgn. Svc. Grievance Bd., 1976-77; advisor Peace Corps Dir., 1979-80; exec. dir. Am. Consortium for Internat. Pub. Adminstrn., 1980-84, 93-94, dir. Marshall Plan Oral History Project, 1987-97. Mem. Cosmos Club, Am. Soc. Pub. Adminstrn., Pi Kappa Alpha, Phi Kappa Phi. Home: 5111 Connecticut Ave NW # 407 Washington DC 20008-2004

SPECTOR, MICHAEL JOSEPH, agribusiness executive; b. NYC, Feb. 13, 1947; s. Martin Wilson and Dorothy (Miller) S.; m. Margaret Dickson, Sept. 14, 1977. BS in Chemistry, Washington and Lee U., 1968. Rsch. chemist Am. Viscose, Phila., 1968-69; pres. MJS Entertainment Corp., Miami, Fla., 1970-84; also MJS Internat., Inc.; ptnr. Old Town Key West Devel. Ltd., Fla., 1977—2002. Pres. MJS Entertainment of Can., Inc., Toronto, Margo Farms, MJS Prodns., Inc., NYC; chmn., CEO Margo Caribe, Inc., Dorado, PR, 1981—, bd. dir.; pres. Costa Del Norte Devel., Inc., Dorado, 1998—; bd. dir. Goodwill Industries So. Fla., v.p. fin., 1980; bd. dir. Plz. Bank of Miami; hon. Consul Belgium in P.R., U.S. V.I., Turks & Caicos Islands, West Indies, 2000—; dir. Consular Corp. of P.R., 2002, vice-dean, 2003—04, dean, PR, 2004. Internat. judge The Floralies Exhbn., Gent, Belgium, 1995, 2000, 05; knight Sociedad Heraldica Espanola, 2003—. With AUS, 1969-70. Robert E. Lee rsch. grantee Washington and Lee U., 1967-68; named Agri-bus. Exec. of Yr., Govt. of P.R., 1999; knighted Order of King Leopold II, King of Belgium, 2005. Mem. Nat. Assn. Record Merchandisers (dir. Nova divsn., chmn. one-stop distbn. com. 1982-83), Country Music Assn., Dorado Beach Golf and Tennis Club, Bankers Club P.R., Ocean Reef Club. Achievements include patent for synthetic stretching process. Home: Call Box 1370 Dorado PR 00646-1370 Business E-Mail: mspector@margocaribe.com.

SPECTOR, NANCY, curator; With Solomon R. Guggenheim Mus., NYC, 1989—, chief curator; asst. curator edn. Albright-Knox Art Gallery, Buffalo, 2001—. Adj. curator Venice Biennale, 1997, Am. commr., 2007; co-organizer Berlin Biennial, 1998. Curator (exhibitions) Gary Hill, Solomon R. Guggenheim Mus., NYC, 1995, Felix Gonzalez-Torres Retrospective, 1995, Robert Rauschenberg: Performance, 1997, Andreas Slominski, 1999, Matthew Barney: The Cremaster Cycle, 2003, Moving Pictures, 2003, Singular Forms (Sometimes Repeated), 2004, Marina Abramovic: Seven Easy Pieces, 2006, Richard Prince Retrospective, 2007, the anyspacewhatsoever, 2008, Louise Bourgeois Retrospective, 2008, Monument to Now, Dakis Joannou Collection, Athens, Everything in the Present Must Be Transformed, Deutsche Guggenheim, Berlin, 2005, Felix Gonzales-Torres: America, Venice Biennale, 2007. Recipient Peter Norton Family Found. Curators award. Office: Solomon R Guggenheim Mus 1071 5th Ave New York NY 10128-0173 Office Phone: 212-423-3500.*

SPECTOR, PHILLIP LOUIS, lawyer; s. Everett L. Spector and Rebecca Newman; m. Carole Sue Lebbin, May 11, 1980; children: Adam, David. Student, U. Birmingham, Eng., 1970—71; BA with highest honors, U. Calif., Santa Barbara, 1972; M in Pub. Policy, Harvard U., 1976, JD magna cum laude, 1976. Bar: Calif. 1976, DC 1978, US Ct. Appeals (DC cir.) 1983, US Supreme Ct. 1983, US Dist. Ct. DC 1985. Law clk. U.S. Ct. Appeals (2d cir.), Brattleboro, Vt., 1976-77; law clk. to U.S. Supreme Ct., 1977-78; assoc. asst. to Pres. U.S., 1978-80; assoc. Verner, Liipfert, Bernhard & McPherson, 1980-83; ptnr. Goldberg & Spector, 1983-92, Paul, Weiss, Rifkind, Wharton & Garrison, Washington, 1992—2005, mng. ptnr. Washington office, 2001—05; exec. v.p. bus. develop., gen. counsel Intelsat Global, Ltd., 2005—. Bd. dirs. Global Relief Techs., Inc., WildBlue Comm. Inc., Appleseed Found. Co-author: Communications Law and Practice, 1995, Communications and Techology Alliances: Business and Legal Issues, 1996; contbr. articles to profl. jours. Mem. Coun. on Fgn. Rels., NYC, 1980-85; moot ct. judge Nat. Assn. Attys. Gen., Washington, 1987—; adviser Dem. caucus US House Reps., Washington, 1981-83; speechwriter, podium prodr. Dem. Nat. Convs., NYC, 1980, Phila., 1982, San Francisco, 1984, Atlanta, 1988, NYC, 1992, Chgo., 1996, LA, 2000, Boston, 2004. Recipient Disting. Achievement in Pub. Svc. Medal U. Calif., Santa Barbara, 1981, Close-Up Found. awards Via Satellite Mag., Vol. Recognition award Nat. Assn. Attys. Gen., 1993, Unsung Hero award, Appleseed Found., 2008; named Leading Satellite Specialist in Washington, European Counsel, 2000. Mem. ABA (former chair internat. comm. law com.), Fed. Comms. Bar Assn., Bethesda Country Club, Addison Res. Country Club, Mid Ocean Club (Bermuda), Seagate Beach Club, Phi Beta Kappa. Jewish. Office: 3400 International Dr Washington DC 20008-3006 Office Phone: 202-944-7340. Business E-Mail: phil.spector@intelsat.com.

SPECTOR, ROSE, former state supreme court justice; BA, Columbia U.; JD, St. Mary's Sch. Law, 1965. Judge County Ct. at Law 5, 1975-80, 131st Dist. Ct., 1981-92; justice Tex. Supreme Ct., 1993-98; atty. Bickerstaff, Heath, Delgado, Acosta, LLP, Austin, Tex., 1998—. Office Phone: 512-404-7867.

SPEECE, RICHARD EUGENE, civil engineer, educator; b. Marion, Ohio, Aug. 23, 1933; s. Irvin Ward S. and Desta May (Speece); m. Jean Margaret Edscorn, Nov. 15, 1969; children: Eric Jordan, Lincoln Dana. BCE, Fenn. Coll., 1956; M of Engring., Yale U., 1958; PhD, MIT, 1961. Assoc. prof. civil engring. U. Ill., Urbana, 1961-65; prof. N.Mex. State U., 1965-70, U. Tex., Austin, 1970-74; Betz chair prof. environ. engring. Drexel U., Phila., 1974-88; Centennial prof. Vanderbilt U., Nashville, 1988—. Vis. scholar Cambridge (Eng.) U., 1994; cons. to govt., industry. Contbr. articles to profl. jours.; patentee in field. Recipient hon. mention for best paper Trans. Am. Fisheries Soc., 1973, Founders award Assn. Environ. Engrs. Profs., 2005., Assoc. Environ. Engr. Profs. Founders award 2005. Mem. ASCE (J. James Cross medal 1983), Assn. Environ. Engring. and Sci. Profs. (disting. lectr. 1978, trustee 1981-83, Disting. Faculty award 1970, Engring. Sci. award 1982, Founders award 2005, 06), Am. Soc. Microbiologists, Water Environ. Fedn. (Harrison Prescott Eddy medal 1966), U.S. ANC (Founders award 1991), Internat. Assn. on Water Pollution Rsch. and Control. Office: Vanderbilt Univ Dept Civil Engring Nashville TN 37235 Office Phone: 615-343-6328. Business E-Mail: dick.speece@vanderbilt.edu.

SPEED, BONNIE ANNE, museum director; b. Skowhegan, Maine, 1955; d. Andrew Walker Speed and Roberta Irene Allen. BS, U. So. Maine, 1979; MA, U. Kans., 1990. Dir. visual arts Mitchell Mus. at Cedarhurst, Mt. Vernon, Ill., 1991—2000; dir. Trammell & Margaret Crow Collection Asian Art, Dallas, 2000—02; dir. Michael C. Carlos Mus. Emory U., Atlanta, 2002—. Mem. adv. bd. Sch. Art U. North Tex., Denton, 2000—02; cons. Ramesses I mummy Emory U., 2003. Editor: Patronage in Chinese Art, 1989. Mem.: U.S. Dressage Assn., Art Table, Am. Assn. Mus. Avocation: dressage. Office: Michael C Carlos Mus at Emory U 571 South Kilgo Cir Atlanta GA 30322 Office Phone: 404-727-0573. Office Fax: 404-727-4292. Business E-Mail: baspeed@emory.edu.

SPEED, CYNTHIA AGNES, retired mathematics professor; d. Carter Coleman and Lillian Jeannette Speed. BA, Calif. State U., Sacramento, 1962; MA, Stanford U., 1967. C.C. Supr. credential Calif., 1980, C.C. Instr. credential Calif., 1973, gen. secondary tchg. credential Calif., 1963. Tchg. asst. in ednl. stats. U. of Calif., Berkeley, Calif., 1963; math. instr. Hiram W. Johnson Sr. H.S., Sacramento, 1963—67, John F. Kennedy Sr. H.S., Sacramento, 1967—69; math. lectr. Calif. State U., Sacramento, 1969—69, Calif. Poly. State U., San Luis Obispo, Calif., 1969—71; math. instr. Santa Rosa Jr. Coll., Calif., 1973—73; math. instr. and dept. chair Mendocino Coll., Ukiah, Calif., 1973—2003; ret., 2003. Exec. com. mem. Tech. in the Redwoods Conf., Ukiah, Calif., 1988—89; course descriptors com. mem. Calif. Articulation Number Sys., Sacramento, 1986—88; chairperson, creator, and organizer Math. Contest for Jr. and Sr. H.S. Students in Mendocino and Lake Counties, Ukiah, Calif., 1975—79. Author: (computer program) Technology in the Redwoods Computer Contest Prize Winners, Lake View Water Co. Billing Program, Black Bart Trail Rd. Assn. Dues Assessment Program. Vol. Legal Svcs. Northern Calif., 2007; mem. East Sacramento Preservation Task Force, 2007—; chairperson Sacred Heart Ch. Ministry to the Homebound, 2006—; v.p. and mem. Lake View Mut. Water Co., Redwood Valley, Calif., 1977—; treas. and mem. Black Bart Trail Rd. Assn., Redwood Valley, Calif., 1977—. Mem.: AAUW, NEA, Cath. Alumni Club Sacramento (treas. 2005—), Calif. Ret. Tchrs. Assn. (treas. 2007—), Calif. Teachers Assn., Nat. Coun. of Teachers of Math., Calif. Math. Coun., Math. Assn. of Am., Calif. Math. Coun., Cmty. Colls. Found. (pres. 2005—), Calif. State U. Sacramento Alumni Assn., Stanford Alumni Assn., Delta Kappa Gamma. Democrat. Roman Catholic. Avocations: piano, swimming, golf, dance, bicycling. Home: 1232 43rd St Sacramento CA 95819 Office: 4949 Black Bart Trail Redwood Valley CA 95470 Personal E-mail: sac67449@saclink.csus.edu. Business E-Mail: cspeed@mendocino.edu.

SPEEDIE, MARILYN KAY, microbiologist, dean, educator; b. Salem, Oreg., Nov. 13, 1947; d. Arthur Alexander and Eleanor Ruth (Todd) Wilson; m. Stuart Mitchell Speedie, July 18, 1968; children: Andrea Elizabeth, Christopher Todd. BS in Pharmacy, Purdue U., West Lafayette, Ind., 1970, PhD, 1973. Asst. prof. Oreg. State U., Corvallis, 1973-75; asst. prof. then prof., dept. chmn. U. Md., Balt., 1975-91, prof. Sch. Pharmacy, 1991—96; prof. dept. medicinal chemistry, dean U. Minn. Coll. Pharmacy, Mpls., 1996—. Contbr. articles to profl. jours. Mem.: US Pharmacopoeia, Am. Pharm. Assn., Am. Soc. Health Sys. Pharmacists, Am. Chem. Soc., Am. Assn. Colleges of Pharmacy (bd. dirs., pres. 2006—07), Am. Soc. Pharmacognosy (exec. com. 1987—89, 1999—2000), Soc. Indsl. Microbiology, Am. Soc. Microbiology, Rho Chi. Office: U Minn Coll Pharmacy 5 130 Weaver Densford Hall 308 Harvard St SE Minneapolis MN 55455-1142 Office Phone: 612-624-1900. Business E-Mail: speed001@umn.edu.

SPEEDY, MIKE, councilman, real estate consultant; b. Indpls. m. Amanda Speedy; 3 children. BS in Real Estate Fin., Ind. U. Sch. Bus., Bloomington; JD, Ind. U. Sch. Law, Indpls. Bar: Ind. Owner real estate cons. and devel. firm; councillor, dist. 24 Indpls.-Marion County City-County Coun., 2003—. Chmn. cmty. affairs com. Indpls.-Marion County City-County Coun. Active Perry Twp. Fire Dept. Found., Big Brothers Big Sisters, Greater Indpls., Living Logos Ch. Republican. Avocations: exercise, golf, skiing, sailing. Office: 4733 Moss Creek Ter

Indianapolis IN 46237 also: Indpls Marion County City County Coun 241 City County Bldg 200 E Washington St Indianapolis IN 46204 Office Phone: 317-786-6689, 317-327-4242. Business E-Mail: m.speedy@sbcglobal.net.*

SPEELMAN, PATRICK J., history professor; b. Van Wert, Ohio, Nov. 14, 1970; s. David L. and Nancy M. Speelman; m. Jennifer Coleman. PhD, Temple U., Phila., 2000. Vis. prof. history Coll. Charleston, SC, 2002—06, Citadel, Charleston, 2006—. Contbr. articles to profl. jours. Mem.: Soc. Mil. History. Business E-Mail: patrick.speelman@citadel.edu.

SPEER, BROWNLOW MAIN, lawyer; b. Delhi, NY, Aug. 24, 1938; s. James Robert and Elizabeth Main Speer; m. Doris Pulver Speer, Jan. 22, 1965; children: James, Andrew(dec.). BA, Haverford Coll., Pa., 1960, Oxford U., Eng., 1962, MA, 1969; JD, Harvard Law Sch., Cambridge, 1970. Bar: Mass. 1970, US Dist. Ct., Dist. Mass. 1971, US Ct. Appeals, 1st Circuit 1974, US Supreme Ct. 1995. Assoc. Palmer & Dodge, Boston, 1970—72; staff atty. Lawyers' Com. for Civil Rights, Boston, 1972—74; dir. of tng. Mass. Defenders Com., Boston, 1974—79, chief appellate atty., 1979—, Com. for Pub. Counsel Svcs., 1984—. Co-author (with Blumenson and Kanstroom): Massachusetts Criminal Practice, 2001; co-author: (with Herrmann) (jour. publ.) Facing the Accuser: Ancient and Medieval Precursors of the Confrontation Clause, 1994, Standing Mute at Amest as Evidence of Guilt: The Right to Silence Under Attack, 2007; assoc. editor Mass. Law Rev., 2003—. Pres., bd. mgrs. First Parish in Waltham (Mass.) U-U, 1995—97; bd. dirs. Waltham Alliance to Create Housing, Mass., 2003—09; publicity com. Cmty. Works, Boston, 2003—; mem. Otto M. Stanfield Law Scholarship Com., 2005—. With US Army, 1962—66. Recipient Kutak-Dodds Defender prize, Nat. Legal Aid and Defender Assn., 2005, Mass. Super Lawyer, 2005, 2008—09. Mem.: Am. Acad. Appellate Lawyers, Boston Bar Assn. (mem. coun. 1986—89, John G. Brooks award 1996), ABA, Mass. Bar Assn., Mass. Assn. Criminal Def. Lawyers. Democrat. Unitarian Universalist. Avocations: legal history, language study. Home: 141 Barbara Rd Waltham MA 02453 Office: Com for Pub Coun Svcs 44 Bromfield St Boston MA 02108 Office Fax: 617-988-8485. Business E-Mail: bspeer@publiccounsel.net.

SPEER, DAVID BLAKENEY, chemicals executive; b. Sault Ste. Marie, Ont., Apr. 6, 1951; s. Richard Norwood and Mary (Davis) S.; m. Barbara Ann Brugenhemre, June 22, 1974; children: Blake, Sarah. BS in Indsl. Engring., Iowa State U., 1973; MBA, Northwestern U., 1977. Sales engr. Precision Paper, Wheeling, Ind., 1976-78, sales mgr., 1976-78; regional sales mgr. ITW Buildex, Itasca, Ill., 1978-81, nat. sales mktg. mgr., 1981-84, v.p., gen. mgr., 1984-92, ITW Paslode, Lincolnshire, Ill., 1992; group v.p., constrn. products Ill. Tool Works Inc. (ITW), 1994—95, exec. v.p. global constrn. products bus. Glenview, Ill., 1995—2004, exec. v.p. finishing systems bus., 1997—2004, exec. v.p. global Wilsonart laminate bus. unit, 2003—04, pres., 2004—06, CEO, 2005—, chmn., 2006—. Bd. dirs. Rockwell Automation, Inc. Mem. adv. bd. Northwestern U. Master of Mgmt. and Mfg. program. Mem. Am. Mgmt. Assn., Am. Mktg. Assn., Am. Soc. Indsl. Engrs., Midwest Indsl. Mfg. Assn. Achievements include brokering historic number of acquisitions within company, 2006. Office: Ill Tool Works Inc 3600 W Lake Ave Glenview IL 60026-1215 Office Phone: 847-724-7500. Office Fax: 847-657-4572.*

SPEER, JACK ATKESON, publisher; b. Wichita, Kans., July 3, 1941; s. Jack Shelley and Shannon C. Speer; m. Judith Ann Fuller, Aug. 5,1967; children: Martin Fuller, Elizabeth Speer Goodwin. BS in Bus. Adminstrn., Kansas State U., 1966, ML, 1967; postgrad., U. Mo., 1967, U. So. Calif., 1969; IBM Pres.'s Class, Harvard U., 1980. Mem. advt., editorial, mech. staffs Wichita Eagle-Beacon, 1954-64; editorial asst. Emporia (Kans.) Gazette, 1964-65; supr. libr. data processing Kans. State U., Emporia, 1965-67, mgr. data processing ctr. Manhattan, 1967-69; mgr. systems and programming John Wiley Inc.-Becker & Hayes Inc., Bethesda, Md., 1969-72; dir. libr. info. systems Informatics Inc. Info. Systems Group, Rockville, Md., 1972-77; v.p. ops. Arcata Real Estate Data Inc., Miami, Fla., 1977-79; mgr. electronic info. systems Arcata Publs. Group, Norwalk, Conn., 1979-83; v.p. mktg./sales, data imaging group The William Byrd Press, Richmond, Va., 1983-84; sr. v.p. ops. NewsBank Inc., New Canaan, Conn., 1984-85; pres., pub. Buckmaster Pub., Mineral, Va., 1986—. Mem. faculty Cath. U. Am. Libr. Sch., Kans. State U. Libr. Sch.; customer adv. coun. U.S. Postal Svc., 1996—. Author: Amateur Radio Call Directory Ham Call, 1982—, Buckmaster's Ann. Stockholder Reports, 1986—, Front-Page-News (CD-ROM and Internet), 1989, HamCall (CD-ROM and Internet), 1988—; compiler Libraries and Automation: A Bibliography, 1967, The Living Bible Concordance, 1972. Trustee Jefferson-Madison Regional Libr., 1990-91; commr. Louisa County Planning Commn. 1992-; pres. Louisa County Libr. Found. 2003-; with J. Sargeant Reynolds CC, 2009-. Mem. ALA, NRA, Am. Radio Relay League, Nat. Info. Standards Orgn. (CD-ROM com), D.C. Libr. Assn. (pres.), Rotary, Sigma Tau Gamma. Office: Buckmaster Pub 6196 Jefferson Hwy Mineral VA 23117-3425 E-mail: speerj@buck.com.

SPEER, KEVIN PAUL, surgeon; b. Evansville, Ind., June 8, 1959; m. Marcy Carlson Speer, Mar. 24, 1984; children: Casey, Kira. MD, Johns Hopkins U., 1985. Lic. physician N.C., 1992. Assoc. prof. orthopedics Duke U. Med. Ctr., Durham, NC, 1992—2000; pvt. practice Southeastern Orthopedics, Raleigh, NC, 2000—. Fellow, Am. Orthop. Assn., 1992. Fellow: AAOS. Office: Southeastern Orthopedics 3404 Wake Forest Rd Ste 201 Raleigh NC 27609 Business E-Mail: kspeer@nc.rr.com.

SPEER, MICHAEL EMERY, neonatologist, educator; b. San Diego, Oct. 2, 1942; s. Emery and Meryl Elizabeth (Winn) S.; m. Mary Elizabeth Swiler, Apr. 26, 1969; children: James A., Mark S. BS in Biology, Occidental Coll., LA, 1964; MD, Baylor Coll. Medicine, 1968. Diplomaed Am. Bd. Pediatrics, Sub-Bd. Neonatal-Perinatal Medicine; lic. neonatologist, Calif., Tex. Intern Ben Taub Gen. Hosp. and Jefferson Davis Hosp., Houston, 1968-69; resident in pediatrics Baylor Affiliated Hosps., Houston, 1969-70, 72-73; fellow in infectiour disease Baylor Coll. Medicine, Houston, 1973-74, fellow in neonatology, 1974-76, instr. pediatrics, 1976, asst. prof. pediatrics, 1976-89, assoc. prof. pediatrics, 1990—. Mem. staff Woman's Hosp. Tex., 1976—, dep. dir. neonatology, 1976-81; attending neonatologist Harris County Hosp., 1977—, Tex. Children's Hosp., 1977—; med. dir. quality and outcomes mgmt. dept. Tex. Children's Hosp., 1993—; attending neonatologist St. Luke's Episc. Hosp., 1977—, assoc. chief newborn and premature svc., 1994—; dir. neonatology svcs. Meth. Hosp., 1981—, dep. chief pediat. svcs., 1993—; clin. coord. health care practice and quality of care Tex. Children's Hosp. and Baylor Coll. Medicine, 1993—; chair quality mgmt. com. Baylor MedCare, Baylor Coll. Medicine, 1995—. Reviewer Jour. of Infectiour Disease, 1984—, Pediatric Rsch., 1987—, Pediatrics, 1990—, Hosp. Formulary, 1990—, Acta Paediatrica Scandinavica, 1991—; contbr. numerous articles and abstracts to publs. Mem.-at-large, dist. com. Golden Arrow dist. Sam Houston Area coun. Boy Scouts Am.; bd. dirs. Friends of Jesse H. Jones Libr., 1992—. Lt. comdr. USN, 1970-72, USNR, 1972-79. Mem. AMA, Am. Acad. Pediats. (mem. fetus, newborn com.), Tex. Med. Assn. (mem. coms., mem. coun. sci. affairs), Tex. Perinatal Assn. (exec. bd. 1991—, pres. 1994-95), Tex. Pediatric Soc. (mem. fetus, newborn com., chmn. dist. 1995—), Harris County Med. Soc. (exec. bd. 1988-94), Houston Pediatric Soc. (pres. 1990-91, exec. bd. 1984-95), Houston Acad. Medicine (trustee 1988-94, pres. 1994), Houston Acad. Medicine Meml. Edn. and Rsch. Found. (bd. dirs. 1990-94, pres. 1994), So. Soc. Pediatric Rsch., Medserv (bd. dirs. 1991—), Houston Acad. Medicine/Tex. Med. Ctr. Libr. (bd. dirs. 1993—, chmn. 1994, 95). Avocations: skiing, scuba, camping, reading. Home: 6031 Fordham St Houston TX 77005-3125 Office: Baylor College Of Medicine 1 Baylor Plz Houston TX 77030-3411 Office Phone: 832-826-1380.

SPEER, RICHARD ALLAN, library director; s. George Allan and Elizabeth Jean Speer; m. Judith G. Frost, Sept. 10, 1983; 1 child, Kathryn L. BS, Millersville U. Pa., 1974; MLS, U. Pitts., 1977. Head libr. Cmty. Libr. Alleghany Valley, Tarentum, Pa., 1975—77; dist. cons. libr. Warren County Libr., Pa., 1977—80; dir. Oil City Libr., Pa., 1980—84, Lewiston Pub. Libr., Maine, 1984—. Recipient New Libr. award, Pa. Libr. Assn., 1982, NY Times Libr. award, NY Times, 2004, ProQuest SIRS Intellectual Freedom award, Maine Libr. Assn., 2008. Mem.: ALA, Maine Libr. Assn., Josselyn Bot. Soc. (corr. sec. 2001—). Office: Lewiston Public Library 200 Lisbon Street Lewiston ME 04240 Business E-Mail: rspeer@ci.lewiston.me.us.

SPEER, RICHARD JOHN, security consultant; b. Oxnard, Calif., Aug. 21, 1958; s. Richard McCord Speer and Betty Jean Wilson. Grad. H.S., Las Vegas, Nev. Enlisted U.S. Army, 1976, advanced through grades to sgt. first class, 1990, infantryman 82nd Airborne Divsn. Ft. Bragg, NC, 1976—81, infantry squad leader, 1981—87, infantry squad leader 4th Infantry Divsn. Ft. Carson, Colo., 1987—88, heavy weapons specialist Spl. Forces Ft. Bragg, 1988—94, project mgr. spl. projects, 1995—98, ret., 1998; ops. support mgr., nuclear security cons. Securitas Security Svcs., NJ, 1998—2008; lead security specialist corp. ops. nuc. dept. Progress Energy Svcs. Co., LLC, 2008—. Life mem. Rep. Nat. Com., Washington, 1994-, Nat. Rep. Congl. Com., 2003-, Nat. Rep. Senatorial Com., 2003-, Rep. Presdl. Task Force, 2005—. Decorated Army Commendation medal 3rd award U.S. Army, 1984, Meritorious Svcs. medals U.S. Army, 1991, 96, 98. Mem. Heritage Found., N.Am. Hunting Club (life), Am. Legion. Avocation: amateur philatelist.

SPEER, WILLIAM DALE, lab administrator, biology professor; b. Conrad, Mont., Aug. 24, 1957; s. Wayne Arthur Speer and Janet Lou Jordan; m. Victoria Joan Wiser; children: Savannah Victoria, William Gerald. Degree in Arts, Scis. summa cum laude, Patrick Henry CC, Martinsville, Va., 1991; BS cum laude, Va. Poly. Inst. & State U., Blacksburg, 1994, MS, 1997. Biology lab coord. Salt Lake CC, 2002—, biology adj. instr., 2003—. Contbr. articles to sci. profl. jours. Mem.: Am. Fern Soc. Office: Salt Lake CC 4600 S Redwood Rd Salt Lake City UT 84130 Business E-Mail: william.speer@slcc.edu.

SPEERS, ROLAND ROOT, II, lawyer; b. Jacksonville, Fla., Oct. 8, 1933; s. Roland Root and Alice (Calkins) S.; m. Florence Briscoe, Dec. 18, 1954; children: Kirsten, Guy, Gina Marie. BA cum laude, UCLA, 1955, JD, 1958. Bar: Calif. 1958, D.C. 1978. Dep. commr. corps. Calif. Dept. Corps., Los Angeles, 1958-59; sec., gen. counsel Suburban Cos., Pomona, Calif., 1959-64; sec. Amcord, Inc., Los Angeles, 1964-66, asst. to pres., 1968, v.p. corp. devel., 1969, v.p., gen. counsel Newport Beach, Calif., 1970, sr. v.p., 1971, exec. v.p., 1972-75, pres., 1975-94; ptnr. Speers, Dana, Teal Balfour & MacDonald, Costa Mesa, Calif., 1977-97. Dir. Logicon, Inc., Torrance, Calif., Twelve Eleven Press, Newport Beach, Calif. Co-author: The Malloy Chronicles: The Hidden Empire, 2003, The Malloy Chronicles: The Rheingold Legacy, 2006, The Malloy Chronicles: The Catalyst, 2007. Trustee Pitzer Coll., Pomona, 1975-80; bd. councillors Center Pub. Affairs U. So. Calif., 1976-81; bd. dirs. Newport Harbor Art Mus., 1977-82; sr. warden St. James Episcopal Ch., 1993; mem rectors counsel St. James Anglican Ch., 2004—; chmn. Assn. Western Anglican Congregations, 2007-; bd. visitors Pepperdine U. Sch. Pub. Policy, 2008; governance com. mem. Anglican Ch. N.Am., 2008-, pres. dir., Western Anglicans Anglican Ch. N. America. Mem. D.C. Bar Assn., State Bar Assn. Calif., UCLA Alumni Assn., UCLA Law Sch. Alumni Assn., Phi Alpha Delta. Clubs: Big Canyon Country (Newport Beach).

SPEERT, ARNOLD, academic administrator, chemistry educator; b. Bronx, NY, June 19, 1945; s. David Jack and Dorothy Bernice (Feldman) S.; m. Myrna Goldstein, June 11, 1967; children: Alan Michael, Debra Beth. BS, CCNY, 1966; PhD, Princeton U., 1971. Asst. to dean grad. and rsch. program William Paterson Coll., Wayne, NJ, 1970-71, from asst. to assoc. prof. chemistry, 1970-80, prof., 1980-85, asst. to v.p. acad. affairs, 1971-78, assoc. dean acad. affairs, 1978-79, v.p. acad. affairs, 1979-85; pres. William Paterson U., Wayne, NJ, 1985—. Bd. dirs. State Farm Indemnity Co. Trustee Barnert Hosp., Paterson, 1986—, chmn. bd. trustees, 1998—; trustee Jewish Fedn. North Jersey, Wayne, 1986-96, YM & YWHA No. N.J., Wayne, 1988—, Respiratory Health Assn., 1990-93; bd. dirs. William Paterson Univ. Found., 1985—. Mem. Am. Assn. State Colls. and Univs. (bd. dirs. 1993-95), Tri-County C. of C. (bd. dirs. 1986-94), N.J. State Bd. Examiners, N.J. Pres.'s Coun. (chair 1996—). Home: 48 Brandon Ave Wayne NJ 07470-6032 Office: William Paterson Univ 300 Pompton Rd Wayne NJ 07470-2152*

SPEESE, MARK E., rental company executive; Student, Western Mich. U. Regional mgr. Thorn Americas, 1979—86; from v.p. N.J. Ops. to chmn., CEO Rent A Center, Plano, Tex., 1986—2001, chmn., CEO, 2001—. Bd. dirs. Rent A Ctr. Office: Rent A Center 5501 Headquarters Dr Plano TX 75024-5837

SPEICHER, CARL EUGENE, pathologist; b. Carbondale, Pa., Mar. 21, 1933; s. William Joseph and Elizabeth Marcella (Connolly) S.; m. Mary Louise Walsh, June 21, 1958; children: Carl E. Jr., Gregory, Erik. BS in Biology, King's Coll., 1954; MD, U. Pa., 1958; student, Sch. of Aerospace Medicine, Brooks AFB, Tex., 1969. Diplomate Am. Bd. Pathology. Intern U. Pa. Hosp., Phila., 1958-59, resident, 1959-63; chief lab. svcs. USAF Hosp., London, Eng., 1963-66, USAF Med. Ctr. Wright Patterson, Dayton, Ohio, 1966-70; dir. clin. labs. and chmn. dept. pathology Wilford Hall USAF Med. Ctr., San Antonio, 1971-77; prof. dept. pathology Ohio State U., Columbus, 1977—2000, vice chair dept. pathology, 1992—2000, prof. emeritus dept. pathology, 2000—; dir. clin. svcs. Ohio State U. Med. Ctr., Columbus, 1977—2000; dir. clin. lab. Stoneridge Med. Ctr., Ohio State U., 2000—. Co-author: Choosing Effective Laboratory Tests, 1983; author: The Right Test, 1990, 3d edit., 1998. Col. USAF, 1956-77. Decorated Legion of Merit; fellow in med. chemistry SUNY, Syracuse, 1970-71. Mem. AMA, Ohio Soc. Pathologists, Ctrl. Ohio Soc. Pathologists, Am. Assn. for Clin. Chemistry, Assn. Clin. Scientists, Coll. Am. Pathologists, Am. Soc. Clin. Pathologists, Alpha Omega Alpha.

SPEIDEL, JOHN JOSEPH, public health professional, educator; b. Iowa City, Iowa, Sept. 17, 1937; s. Thomas Dennis and Edna (Warweg) Speidel; m. Melissa Jane Webster, Oct. 7, 2001; 1 child from previous marriage, Sabrina Brett. AB cum laude, Harvard U., 1959, MD, 1963, MPH, 1965. Diplomate Nat. Bd. Med. Examiners, Am. Bd. Preventive Medicine. Intern St. Luke's Hosp., NYC, 1963-64; resident N.Y.C. Dept. Health, 1965-67, dep. dir. maternal and infant care project, 1966-67; chief rsch. divsn. Office Population, AID, Dept. of State, Washington, 1969-76, assoc. dir., 1977, dep. dir., acting dir. office, 1978-83; v.p. Population Action Internat. (formerly Population Crisis Com.), 1983-87, pres., 1987-95; program dir. population Hewlett Found., 1995—2003; prof. Bixby Ctr. Global Reproductive Health U. Calif., San Francisco, 2003—. Lectr. population and family planning Georgetown U., 1973—75. Editor (with others): (book) Female Sterilization, 1971, Hysteroscopic Sterilization, 1974, Intrauterine Devices, 1974, Control of Male Fertility, 1975, Advances in Female Sterilization Technology, 1976, Risks, Benefits and Controversies in Fertility Control, 1978, Reversal of Sterilization, 1978, Pregnancy Termination, 1979, Vaginal Contraception, 1979; contbr. articles to profl. jours. Served to maj. US Army, 1967—69. Recipient Meritorious Unit citiation, Office of Population, 1969—71, Arthur S. Flemming award, Washington Downtown Jaycees, 1972, Family Planning Visionary award, Nat. Family Planning & Reproductive Health Assn., 2008, Allan Rosen Guild award, Internat. Family Planning Soc. Family Planning, 2009. Mem.: Population Assn. Am., Am. Pub. Health Assn. (Carl S. Shultz award 1982). Office: U Calif San Francisco BCGRH Dept Ob Gyn 3333 California St Ste 335 Box 0744 San Francisco CA 94118 Office Phone: 415-502-3928. Business E-Mail: speidelj@obgyn.ucsf.edu.

SPEIER, JACKIE (KAREN LORRAINE JACQUELINE SPEIER), United States Representative from California, former state senator; b. San Francisco, May 14, 1950; m. Steven K. Sierra, 1987 (dec. 1994); children: Jackson Kent, Stephanie Katelin; m. Barry Dennis, 2001. BA, U. Calif., Davis, 1972; JD, U. Calif. Hastings Coll. Law, 1976. Legal coun., legis. asst. to Rep. Leo J. Ryan US Congress, 1973-78; mem. San Mateo County Bd. Suprs., Calif., 1980—84, chair Calif., 1985—86; mem. Calif. State Assembly from Dist. 19, 1987—96, majority whip, 1988—92, chair consumer protection com., 1991-95; v.p. govtl. & cmty. affairs Electronic Arts Inc., 1996—98; dir. govtl. & corp. affairs Poplar ReCare, 1996—98; mem. Calif. State Senate from Dist. 8, 1999—2006; of counsel Hanson, Bridgett, Marcus, Viahos, & Rudy LLP, San Francisco, 2007—08; mem. US Congress from 12th Calif. Dist., 2008—, US House Financial Services Com., 2009—, US House Oversight & Govt. Reform Com., 2009—, US House Spl. Com. on Energy Independence & Global Warming, 2009—. Author: This Is Not the Life I Ordered: 50 Ways to Keep Your Head Above Water When Life Keeps Dragging You Down, 2007. Named Legis. of Yr., Met. Transp. Commn., 2004. Democrat. Roman Catholic. Office: US Congress 2413 Rayburn Ho Office Bldg Washington DC 20515 also: 400 S El Camino Real Ste 410 San Mateo CA 94402*

SPEIGHT, JOHN BLAIN (JACK SPEIGHT), lawyer; b. Cheyenne, May 29, 1949; s. Jack B. and Kathryn Elizabeth (Schmidt) S.; m. Sally Karolee Sullivan, Aug. 20, 1960; children— Sheryl, Tricia, Jackie; m. Carol Ann McBee, Sept. 16, 1979. BA, U. Wyo., 1962, JD, 1965. Bar: Wyo. 1966, U.S. Dist. Ct. Wyo. 1967, U.S. Dist. Ct. Colo. 1967, U.S. Ct. Appeals (10th cir.) 1967, U.S. Supreme Ct. 1970; diplomate Am. Bd. Trial Attys. Atty., Standard Oil Co. of Calif., 1965-67; asst. atty. gen. State of Wyo., 1967-69; adminstrv., legal asst. to Gov. Wyo., 1969-71; atty. for Reorgn. Commn., State of Wyo., 1969-71; asst. U.S. atty. Litigation divsn., 1971-72; cons. sec. interior, 1975; ptnr. Speight McCue & Crank, Cheyenne, 1972—; bd. dirs. First Wyo. Bank, East Cheyenne, Laramie County Legal Svc. Inc. Bd. dirs. Laramie County United Fund.; Best Lawyers in America U. Wyo.; Mem. Wyo. Bar Assn., ABA, Wyo. Trial Lawyers Assn., Am. Trial Lawyers Assn., Laramie County United Fund. Mem. Wyo. Bar Assn., ABA, Wyo. Trial Lawyers Assn. (bd. dirs. 1982—), Am. Trial Lawyers Assn., Laramie County Bar Assn. (pres. 1982-83), Commrs. for Uniform State Laws from the State of Wyo., Jud. Supervisory Commn. (chmn.), Cheyenne Kiwanis Club (bd. dirs.) Young Men's Lit. Club (Outstanding Alumni Law Cmty Svc. award, 2008). Republican. Roman Catholic. Home: 4021 Snyder Ave Cheyenne WY 82001-1170 Office: PO Box 1709 Cheyenne WY 82003-1709 Office Phone: 307-634-2994. Business E-Mail: jspeight@speightmccue.com.

SPEIGHT, JOYCELYN, oncologist; b. Calif. MD, PhD. Asst. prof. dept. radiation oncology U. Calif., San Francisco, 2000—, asst. prof. dept. urology, program dir. radiation oncology resident and fellows program, 2007—. Office: Univ Calif San Francisco Box 1708 1600 Divisadero St H1031 San Francisco CA 94143-1708

SPEIR, MARCIA ANN, retired accountant; b. Tulsa, Oct. 20, 1935; d. Charles Henry and Pearl Jewell (Palmer) Hall; m. Jack Wesley Speir, June 17, 1955; 1 child, Andrea Renee. Student, Northeastern State Coll., Tahlequah, Okla., 1953-56, Am. River Coll., Sacramento, Calif., 1974-76. Acct. Commonwealth Life Ins. Co., Tulsa, 1953-56, Okla. Natural Gas Co., Tulsa, 1957-62; acct., systems analyst Shell Oil Co., Tulsa, 1962-69; staff acct. Trane Heating and Air Conditioning, Sacramento, 1975-79; owner Arapahoe County Steamway Carpet & Upholstery Cleaning Co., Denver, 1969-74; acct., office mgr. Sureway Corp., Sacramento, 1980-89; on med. leave, 1989—. Career counselor Am. River Coll., 1974-76; active in cancer support groups. Mem. NAFE, Sacramento Employer Adv. Group. Republican. Mem. Christian Ch. Avocations: tennis, walking, sewing, piano. Home: 4930 Andrew Cir Carmichael CA 95608 Office Phone: 916-485-2459. Personal E-mail: mspeir@att.net.

SPEIRN, STERLING K., foundation administrator; BA in Polit. Sci., Stanford U., Calif., 1970; LLB, U. Mich., Flint, 1973. Tchr., counselor Univ. Sch., Shaker Heights, Ohio, 1974-76; law clk. Office Hearings & Appeals US Dept. Interior, Washington, 1977-78; staff atty. North Ctrl. Legal Assistance Program, Durham, NC, 1979-81; dep. dir. Humboldt Open Door Clinic Cmty. Health Ctr., Arcata, Calif., 1982-85; intern Peninsula Cmty. Found., Burlingame, Calif., 1986; program officer cmty. leagal affairs dept. Apple Computer, Inc., Cupertino, Calif., 1986-90; program officer Peninsula Cmty. Found., San Mateo, Calif., 1990, acting exec. dir., 1991, sr. v.p., 1991-92, pres., CEO, 1992—2005, co-founder Peninsula Partnership for Children, Youth & Families, 1994, co-founder, dir. Ctr. Venture Philanthropy, 1999—2005; pres., CEO W.K. Kellogg Found., Battle Creek, Mich., 2006—. Bd. dirs. Kellogg Co., 2007—, W.K. Kellogg Found. Trust, 2007—, No. Calif. Grantmakers, San Jose, chmn. bd. dirs., 1987—90; guest lectr. U. Calif. Berkeley Haas Sch. Bus., Harvard Bus. Sch., U. Santa Clara, U. San Francisco, Northwestern U. Kellogg Sch. Mgmt. Mem. adv. coun. Global Philanthropy Forum; past bd. dirs. Am. Leadership Forum Silicon Valley. Avocations: hiking, gardening, running, swimming, camping. Office: WK Kellogg Found One Michigan Ave E Battle Creek MI 49017-4012 Office Phone: 269-968-1611. Office Fax: 269-968-0413.*

SPEIRS, DEREK JAMES, diversified financial services company executive; b. Montreal, Que., Can., Dec. 21, 1933; s. James B. and Marie C. (Hunt) S.; m. Carol Alice Cumming, Dec. 8, 1967 (div. Feb. 1989); children: Lara Marie, Gregory Ross, Scott Lawrence Gordon. B. Commerce with honors in Econs., McGill U., 1954, MBA, 1959. Chartered acct., Can., chartered corp. sec. Devel. dir. fine papers, corp. acctg. dir. Domtar, Inc., Montreal, 1970-72, dir. corp. devel., 1976-78, v.p. fin., corp. devel., 1978-89, sr. v.p. fin. and corp. devel., 1989-91; v.p., sec. fin. Consoltex, Montreal, 1972-76, bus. cons., 1991—; pres. Speirs Fin. Inc., Speirs Cons. Inc., Speirs Capital Inc. Mem. Can. Inst. Chartered Accts., Fin. Execs. Inst., C.D. Howe Inst., Lac Marois Country Club, St. James Club, Montreal Amateur Athletic Assn. Avocations: travel, skiing. Home: 365 Stanstead Ave Mont-Royal Montreal PQ Canada H3R 1X5 Office: Ste 1100 2 Pl Alexis Nihon Montreal PQ Canada H3Z 3C1 Office Phone: 514-342-3857. E-mail: speirsco@videotron.ca.

SPEIRS, GREG, sports artist; Art dir. Grooves Mag., NYC, 1977—79, Changes, Inc., 1980—85. Artwork, Panther Dream Ski for K-2 Corp., 1992, Original Lithuanian Olympic Basketball Jerseys, Am. Eagle Artwork U.S. Olympic Team Bobsleds, 2002, prin. works include for Prince Albert of Monaco Monaco Olympic Bobsled Team. Named to Soc. Illustrators, N.Y., N.Y., 1975, 1976. Achievements include design of first 'Extreme Sports' licensed property character, Scully A.K.A. Skullman. Office: No Rules Graphics and Slammin Sports Box #125 Yonkers NY 10710 Personal E-mail: skully@skullman.com. E-mail: greg@skullman.com.

SPELFOGEL, EVAN J., lawyer, educator; b. Boston, Jan. 28, 1936; s. Morris R. and Helen S. (Steinberg) S.; m. Beverly Kolenberg; children: Scott, Douglas, Karen. AB, Harvard U., 1956; JD, Columbia U., 1959. Bar: Mass. 1959, N.Y. 1964, U.S. Supreme Ct. 1969. Atty. Office of Solicitor, U.S. Dept. Labor, Washington, Boston, 1959-60, NLRB, Boston, NYC, 1960-64; assoc. Simpson, Thacher & Bartlett, NYC, 1964-69, Dewey, Ballantine, NYC, 1969-77; ptnr. Fellner, Rovins & Gallay, NYC, 1977-80, Summit, Rovins & Feldesman, NYC, 1981-91, Epstein Becker and Green, P.C., NYC, 1991—. Adj. prof. law Baruch Coll., CCNY. Bd. editors Developing Labor Law: The Board, The Courts and the National Labor Relations Act, also co-editor-in-chief Supplements; bd. sr. editors Employee Benefits Law; contbr. articles to profl. jours. Fellow Coll. Labor and Employment Lawyers; mem. ABA (sect. on labor and employment law, exec. coun. 1978-86, co-editor sect. newsletter 1976-92, editl. bd. The Labor Lawyer 1986—2009, mem. ho. dels. 1987-90, sect. dispute resolution 1992—), FBA (coun. on labor law), N.Y. State Bar Assn. (chmn. labor and employment law sect. 1977-78, exec. coun. 1975—, dispute resolution sect. charter mem. exec. com., 2009-, ho. dels. 1978-79, 2008-09, com. on profl. discipline 1987-90), Special Comm. on the Bar Exam., 2006-, NYC Bar Assn. (labor com. 1968-71, 87-90, employee benefits com. 1992-96, Enhance Diversity in Profession Com., 2007-), Labor and Employment Rels. Assn. (sec. N.Y. chpt. 1999-2000, pres. 2000-01), Am. Arbitration Assn. (nat. panel labor arbitrators), Harvard Varsity Club, Phi Alpha Delta. Home: 17 Parkside Dr Great Neck NY 11021-1042 Office: Epstein Becker & Green, PC 250 Park Ave New York NY 10177-0001 Office Phone: 212-351-4539. Business E-Mail: espelfogel@ebglaw.com.

SPELKE, ELIZABETH SHILIN, psychology professor; b. NYC, May 28, 1949; d. Alan Shilin and Ruth (Simon) Spelke; m. Elliott M. Blass, Oct. 23, 1988; children: Mae Bridget, Joseph Alan. BA in Soc. Rels., Radcliffe Coll., 1971; PhD in Psychology, Cornell U., 1978; PhD honoris causa, Umeå U., Sweden, 1993, Ecole Pratique des Hautes Etudes, Paris, France, 1999. Asst. prof., dept. psychology U. Pa., 1977—81, assoc. prof., dept. psychology, 1981—86; prof., dept. psychology Cornell U., Ithaca, NY, 1986-96; prof., dept. brain and cognitive sciences MIT, Cambridge, Mass., 1996—2001; prof., dept. psychology Harvard U., Cambridge, 2001—05, co-dir., Mind, Brain and Behavior Inter-faculty Initiative, 2003—, Marshall L. Berkman Prof. Psychology, 2005—. Contbr. articles to profl. sci. jours. Recipient Boyd McCandless Young Scientist Rsch. award, Am. Psychological Assn., 1984, NIH MERIT award, 1993, James McKeen Cattell Fellowship, 1992, Ipsen Prize in Neuronal Plasticity, 2001; Fulbright-Hays Sr. Rsch. Fellowship, 1983, Guggenheim Meml. fellow, 1988-89, James McKeen Cattell fellow, 1992-93; named one of America's Best in Sci. and Medicine, Time mag., 2001. Fellow AAAS, Am. Psychol. Soc. (William James award, 2000, Disting. Scientific Contribution award, 2000), Soc. Exptl. Psychologists; mem. NAS, Cognitive Neurosci. Soc., Psychonomic Soc., Am. Acad. Arts and Scis., Phi Beta Kappa, Sigma Xi Achievements include research on early development of perception by human infants; rsch. on devel. of reasoning about objects, space, and number by children. Office: Dept Psychology Harvard U 1130 William James Hall 33 Kirkland St Cambridge MA 02138 Office Phone: 617-495-3876. Office Fax: 617-384-7944. E-mail: spelke@wjh.harvard.edu.

SPELLACY, WILLIAM NELSON, obstetrician, gynecologist, educator; b. St. Paul, May 10, 1934; s. Jack F. and Elmyra L. (Nelson) Spellacy; m. Lynn Larsen; children: Kathleen Ann, Kimberly Joan, William Nelson. BA, U. Minn., 1955, BS, 1956, MD, 1959. Diplomate subsplty. cert. in maternal and fetal medicine Am. Bd. Ob-Gyn. Intern Hennepin County Gen. Hosp., Mpls., 1959—60; resident U. Minn., Mpls., 1960—63; practice medicine specializing in ob-gyn. Mpls., 1963—67, Miami, Fla., 1967—73, Gainesville, Fla., 1973—79, Chgo., 1979—88; prof., dept. head U. Ill. Coll. Medicine, Chgo., 1979—88; dept. chmn. U. So. Fla. Coll. Medicine, Tampa, 1988—2002, prof., 1988—. Prof. dept. ob-gyn. U. Miami, 1967—73; prof., chmn. dept. U. Fla., 1973—79. Contbr. articles to med. jours. Mem.: ACOG, AMA, Inst. Medicine, Ill. Med. Soc., Soc. Perinatal Obstetricians, Ctrl. Assn. Obstetrics and Gynecology, South Atlantic Soc. Obstetrics and Gynecology, Perinatal Rsch. Soc., Am. Diabetes Assn., Assn. Profs. Gynecology and Obstetrics, Am. Fertility Soc., Endocrine Soc., Am. Assn. Obstetricians and Gynecologists, Soc. Gynecol. Investigation, Am. Gynecol. and Obstet. Soc., Am. Gynecol. Soc., Rotary. Episcopalian. Home: 845 Seddon Cove Way Tampa FL 33602-5704 Office: Univ South Fla Coll Medicine Dept OBGYN 2A Tampa General Cir Tampa FL 33606-3589

SPELLING, TORI (VICTORIA DAVEY SPELLING), actress; b. LA, May 16, 1973; d. Aaron and Carol Jean Spelling; m. Charlie Shanian, July 3, 2004 (div. Apr. 20, 2006); m. Dean McDermott, May 7, 2006; children: Liam Aaron, Stella Doreen stepchildren: Jack Montgomery, Lola. Actor: (TV films) Shooting Stars, 1983, The Three Kings, 1987, A Friend to Die For, 1994, Awake to Danger, 1995, Deadly Pursuits, 1996, Co-ed Call Girl, 1996, Mother, May I Sleep with Danger?, 1996, The Alibi, 1997, Way Downtown, 2002, A Carol Christmas, 2003, Hush, 2005, The Family Plan, 2005, Mind Over Murder, 2006; (TV series) Beverly Hills, 90210, 1990—2000, So noTORIous, 2006, Tori & Dean: Inn Love, 2007, Tori & Dean: Home Sweet Hollywood (a.k.a. Tori & Dean: Still In Love), 2008—, (TV appearances) So Downtown, 2003, Less than Perfect, 2004, The Help, 2004, Smallville, 2007, 90210, 2009; (films) Troop Beverly Hills, 1989, The House of Yes, 1997, Scream 2, 1997, Perpetrators of the Crime, 1998, Trick, 1999, Sol Goode, 2001, Scary Movie 2, 2001, Evil Alien Conquerors, 2002, 50 Ways to Leave Your Lover, 2004, Cthulhu, 2006, Kiss the Bride, 2007; co-author (with Hillary Liftin): sTORI Telling, 2008 (Publishers Weekly bestseller), Mommywood, 2009 (Publishers Weekly bestseller). Office: c/o United Talent Agy Ste 500 9560 Wilshire Blvd Beverly Hills CA 90212-2401

SPELLINGS, MARGARET LAMONTAGNE, former United States Secretary of Education; b. Ann Arbor, Mich., Nov. 30, 1957; d. John and Peg Dudar; m. Robert Spellings, 2001; children: Mary, Grace. BA in Polit. Sci. & Journalism, U. Houston, 1979. Worked for Tex. Gov. William P. Clements; assoc. exec. dir. Tex. Assn. Sch. Bds.; polit. dir. Gov. George W. Bush gubernatorial campaign, Tex., 1994; sr. advisor to Gov. George W. Bush State of Tex., 1994—2000; asst. to Pres. for domestic policy The White House, Washington, 2001—05; sec. US Dept. Edn., Washington, 2005—09; sr. adv. to pres. US C. of C., 2009—. Host online interactive forum Ask the White House. Recipient Golden Plate award, Acad. Achievement, 2006; named one of The 100 Most Powerful Women in Washington, Washingtonian mag., 2001. Republican. Achievements include one of the principal authors of the No Child Left Behind Act, 2001. Office: US Chamber of Commerce 1615 H St NW Washington DC 20062*

SPELLMAN, MITCHELL WRIGHT, surgeon, academic administrator, educator; b. Alexandria, La., Dec. 1, 1919; s. Frank Jackson and Altonette Beulah (Mitchell) S.; m. Billie Rita Rhodes, June 27, 1947 (dec.); children: Frank A., Michael A. (dec.), Mitchell A., Maria S. Weaver, Melva A., Mark A., Manly A. (dec.), Rita S. Parks; m. Adrienne Foster Williams, Feb. 14, 2001 (dec. Dec. 2001). AB magna cum laude, Dillard U., 1940, LLD (hon.), 1983; MD, Howard U., 1944; PhD in Surgery, U. Minn., Mpls., 1955; DSc (hon.), Georgetown U., 1974, U. Fla., 1977. Intern Cleve. Met. Gen. Hosp., 1944-45, asst. resident in surgery, 1945-46, Howard U. and Freedmen's Hosp., Washington, 1946-47, chief resident in thoracic surgery, 1947-48, tchg. asst. in physiology, 1948-49, chief resident in surgery, 1949-50, tchg. asst. in surgery, 1950-51; asst. prof. surgery Howard U., 1954-56, assoc. prof., 1956-60, prof., 1960-68; dir. Howard surgery svc. at DC Gen. Hosp., 1961-68; fellow in surgery U. Minn., 1951-54; sr. resident in surgery U. Minn. Med. Sch. and Hosp., 1951—54; dean Charles R. Drew Postgrad. Med. Sch., LA, 1969-77, prof. surgery, 1969-78; asst. dean, prof. surgery Sch. Medicine, UCLA, 1969-78; clin. prof. surgery Sch. Med., U. So. Calif., 1969-78; dean for med. svcs., prof. surgery Harvard Med. Sch., Boston, 1978-90, dean emeritus for med. svcs., 1990—, dean emeritus for internat. projects, 1990—, prof. surgery emeritus, 1990—; dir. internat. exch. programs Harvard Med. Internat., 1995—; exec. v.p. Harvard Med. Ctr., 1978-90. Fellow Ctr. for Advanced Study in Behavioral Scis.; vis. prof. Stanford U., 1975-76; bd. dirs. Kaiser Found. Hosps., Kaiser Found. Health Plan, 1971-89; mem. DC Bd. Examiners in Medicine and Osteopathy, 1955-68; mem. Nat. Rev. Com. for Regional Med. Programs, 1968-70; spl. med. adv. group, nat. surg. cons. VA, 1969-73; mem. Commn. for Study Accreditation of Selected Health Ednl. Programs, 1970-72; chmn. adv. com. br. med. devices Nat. Heart and Lung Inst., 1972; Am. health del. to visit People's Republic of China, 1973; hon. dir. State Mut. Cos., 1990—; mem. com. mandatory retirement in higher edn. NAS/NRC, 1989-91; panel on internat. programs Nat. Libr. Medicine, 1996-97; adv. bd. faculty medicine and health scis. United Arab Emirates U., 2004—. Mem. editl. bd.: Jour. Medicine and Philosophy, 1977-90; contbr. articles on cardiovasc. physiology and surgery, measurement of blood volume, and radiation biology to profl. jours. Past bd. dirs. Sun Valley Forum on Nat. Health; mem. ethics adv. bd. HEW, 1977-81; bd. dirs. Harvard Cmty. Health Plan, 1979-84; former trustee Occidental Coll.; former bd. overseers com. to visit univ. health svc. Harvard, bd. overseers Harvard Cmty. Health Plan, 1984-95; former regent Georgetown U., bd. dirs., 1986-92; former vis. com. U. Mass. Med. Ctr.; mem. bd. visitors UCLA Sch. Medicine; mem. corp. MIT; adv. bd. PEW Scholars Program in Biomed. Scis., 1984-86; bd. dirs. Med. Edn. for South African Blacks, 1985—; adv. bd. United Arab Emirates U. Faculty of Medicine and Health Scis., 2004-. Recipient Disting. Alumnus award Dillard U., 1963, Disting. Postgrad. Achievement award Howard U., 1974, Outstanding Achievement award U. Minn., 1979, Surg. Alumnus of Yr. award U. Minn., 1991, Disting. Support citation Charles R. Drew U. of Medicine, 2002; named U. Minn. Dept. Surgery Alumnus of Yr., 1991; Markle scholar in med. scis., 1954-59; Commonwealth Fund fellow, U. Minn., Mpls., 1955. Mem. AMA, AAAS, AAUP, ACS, Nat. Med. Assn. (William A. Sinkler Surgery award 1968), Soc. Univ. Surgeons, Am. Coll. Cardiology, Am. Surg. Assn., Inst. Medicine of NAS (chmn. program com. 1977-79, governing coun. 1978-80), Nat. Acad. Practice in Medicine, Am. Assn. Sovereign Mil. Order of Malta (Knights and Dames of Malta), Soc. Black Acad. Surgeons, MIT Corp. (life mem. emeritus), Cosmos Club. Roman Catholic.

SPELLMAN, THOMAS JOSEPH, JR., lawyer; b. Glen Cove, NY, Nov. 11, 1938; s. Thomas J. and Martha H. (Erwin) S.; m. Margaret Mary Barth, June 23, 1962; children: Thomas Joseph, Kevin M., Maura N. BS, Fordham U., Bronx, NY, 1960, JD, 1965. Bar: NY 1966, US Dist. Ct. (so. and ea. dist.) NY 1968, US Ct. Appeals (2nd cir.) 1980, US Supreme Ct. 1981. Staff atty. Allstate Ins. Co., NYC, 1966-69; trial atty. Hartford Ins. Co., Hauppauge, NY, 1969-71; ptnr. Wheller & Spellman, Farmingville, NY, 1971-76, Devitt Spellman Barrett, LLP, Smithtown, NY, 1976—. Mem. grievance com. 10th Jud. Dist., Westbury, NY, 1984-92. Trustee Acad. St. Joseph, Brentwood, NY, 2000-04; bd. trustees, exec. com. St. Catherine of Sienna Med. Ctr., Smithtown, NY, 2002-07. Capt. USAR, 1960-68. Fellow: NY Bar Found., Am. Bar Found.; mem.: NY Bar State Bar Assn. (ho. of dels. 1989—2005, nominating com. 1992—93, v.p. 1996—98), Suffolk County Bar Assn. (bd. dirs., sec.-treas. v.p. 1982—, pres. 1992—93), Swordfish Club. Westhampton Beach, NY (bd. dirs., sec. 2000—01). Home: 8 Highwoods Ct Saint James NY 11780-9610 Office: Devitt Spellman Barrett LLP 50 Route 111 Ste 314 Smithtown NY 11787-3700 Office Phone: 631-724-8833. Business E-Mail: info@devittspellmanlaw.com.

SPELLMAN SWEET, JULIE T., lawyer; b. Orange, Calif., Oct. 11, 1967; BA, Claremont McKenna Coll., 1989; JD, Columbia Univ., 1992. Bar: NY 1993. Assoc. Cravath Swaine & Moore LLP, NYC, 1992—2000, ptnr., corp., 2000—. Bd. trustees Claremont McKenna Coll.; bd. dir. Drew Found. Recipient Harlan Fiske Stone Scholar, 1992; named a Dealmaker of Yr., The Am. Lawyer mag., 2007. Mem.: NY Lawyers for the Pub. Interest, Disability Rights Task Force, Phi Beta Kappa. Fluent in Mandarin Chinese. Office: Cravath Swaine & Moore LLP Worldwide Plz 825 Eighth Ave New York NY 10019-7475 Office Phone: 212-474-1572. Office Fax: 212-474-3700. Business E-Mail: jspellmansweet@cravath.com.

SPELLMIRE, GEORGE W., lawyer; b. Oak Park, Ill., June 10, 1948; Student, Brown U.; BA, Ohio State U., 1970; JD, De Paul U., 1974. Bar: Ill. 1974, US Dist. Ct. (no. dist.) Ill. 1974, US Tax Ct. 1984, US Ct. Appeals (7th cir.) 1984, US Supreme Ct. 1994. Ptnr. Hinshaw & Culbertson, Chgo., 1982-98, D'Ancona & Pflaum, Chgo., 1998—2003, Spellmire & Sommer, Chgo., 2003—. Author: Attorney Malpractice: Prevention and Defense, 1988, supplemental edit., 1990; co-author: Accounting, Auditing and Financial Malpractice, 1998, supplemental edit., 2000, Accountants' Legal Liability Guide, 1990, Illinois Handbook on Legal Malpractice, 1982, Associates Primer for the Prevention of Malpractice, 1987. Mem. ABA, Am. Coll. Trial Lawyers, Soc. Trial Lawyers, Fed. Trial Bar, Internat. Assn. Def. Counsel (legal malpractice com., def. counsel practice mgmt. com.), Ill. State Bar Assn. Office: 77 W Wacker Dr Ste 4800 Chicago IL 60601-1664 Office Phone: 312-606-8722. Business E-Mail: gws@spellmireSommer.com.

SPELMAN, NANCY LATTING, developmental psychologist; b. Oklahoma City, Sept. 13, 1945; d. Trimble Baggett and Patience Francelia (Sewell) Latting; m. Douglas Gordon Spelman, Jan 21, 1970; children: Brooke Patience, Erin Latting. BA in Polit. Sci., Boston U., 1967; MA in Psychology, Bucknell U., 1972; PhD in Psychology, U. Hong Kong, 1987. Tour guide UN, NYC, summer 1966; tchr. emotionally disturbed and retarded pre-sch. children Mass. Dept. Mental Health, Boston, 1968-70; coord. vols. campaign for mayor Patience Latting, Oklahoma City, 1971; lectr. psychology Petaling Jaya Community Coll., Kuala Lumpur, Malaysia, 1987-88, George Mason U., Fairfax, Va., 1989; interactive skills observer, facilitator mgmt. programs Xerox Corp. Edn. and Tng., Leesburg, Va., 1989-91; pers. officer Am. Inst. in Taiwan, Taipei, 1993-95; tchr. psychology U. Hong Kong, 1996-99; adj. fellow psychology Nat. U. Singapore, 2000—01. Bd. dirs. Internat. Sch. Kuala Lumpur, 1986-87, sec., 1987-88, Golf Course Square Cluster, Reston, Va., 1991, Shanghai Am. Schs., 2003-2004; com. mem. Hong Kong Soc. for Disabled, 1976-77; Half the Sky Found., 2004—, sec., 2007-. Avocations: hiking, tennis. E-mail: dougnancyspelman@yahoo.com.

SPELMAN, WILLIAM, social studies educator; b. Burbank, Calif., June 9, 1957; s. Dennis Glenn and Julia Power Spelman; m. Niyanta Patel, Apr. 19, 1997; children: Jasiel Ramesh, Ronan Ramesh. AB, UCLA, 1977; MPP, Harvard Kennedy Sch., Cambridge, Mss., 1984; PhD, Harvard Kennedy Sch., 1988. Market analyst and graphic artist Calif. Rsch. Corp., Santa Monica, 1977; rsch. assoc. Police Exec. Rsch. Forum, Washington, 1978—81; jr. fellow Harvard Law Sch., 1981—84; sr. rsch. assoc. Police Exec. Rsch. Forum, Washington, 1984—88; asst. prof., LBJ sch. pub. affairs U. Tex., Austin, 1988—93, assoc. prof., LBJ sch. pub. affairs, 1993—2004, prof., LBJ sch. pub. affairs, 2004—, exec. dir., tex. inst. pub. problem solving, 1997—2005; council mem. City Austin, 1977—2000. Profl. trainer Various Pub. Agencies Worldwide, 1988—. Author: (nonfiction book) Calling the Police, Dangerous Offenders, Problem Solving, Repeat Offender Programs, Criminal Incapacitation; contbr. articles to profl. jours. Commr. Water and Wastewater Commn., Austin, 1995—97; chair Task Force Citizen Participation, Austin, 2001—04, Waller Creek Adv. Bd., Austin, 2007—; mem. Travis County Dispute Resolution Ctr., Austin, 1996—98; founder and chair Liveable City, Austin, 2002—03. Recipient Excellence Tchg. award, U. Tex., 1992, Raymond Vernon Meml. prize, 2005. D-Conservative. Unitarian Universalist. Achievements include research in effects of incarceration on crime; effectiveness of community crime prevention; effects of stability on urban economies. Avocations: camping and hiking, whitewater canoeing, playing piano. Home: 3802 Ave F Austin TX 78751 Office: Univ Texas PO Box Y Austin TX 78713-8925 Office Fax: 512-471-1835. Business E-Mail: spelman@mail.utexas.edu.

SPELTS, RICHARD JOHN, lawyer; b. Yuma, Colo., July 29, 1939; s. Richard Clark and Barbara Eve (Pletcher) S.; children: Melinda, Meghan, Richard John Jr.; m. Gayle Merves, Nov. 14, 1992. BS cum laude, U. Colo., 1961, JD, 1964. Bar: Colo. 1964, U.S. Dist. Ct. Colo. 1964, U.S. Supreme Ct. 1968, U.S. Ct. Appeals (10th cir.) 1970, U.S. Dist. Ct. (ea. dist.) Mich. 1986. With Ford Motor Internat., Cologne, Germany, 1964-65; legis. counsel to U.S. Senator, 89th and 90th Congresses, 1967-68; minority counsel U.S. Senate Subcom., 90th and 91st Congresses, 1968-70; asst. U.S. atty., 1st asst. U.S. atty. Fed. Dist. of Colo., 1970-77; pvt. practice Denver, 1977-89; risk mgr. sheriff's dept. Jefferson County, Golden, Colo., 1990-91. Selected for Leadership Denver, 1977; recipient cert. for outstanding contbns. in drug law enforcement U.S. Drug Enforcement Adminstrn., 1977, spl. commendation for criminal prosecution U.S. Dept. Justice, 1973, spl. commendation for civil prosecution U.S. Dept. Justice, 1976. Mem. Fed. Bar Assn. (chmn. govt. torts seminar 1980), Colo. Bar Assn. (bd. govs. 1976-78), Denver Bar Assn., Colo. Trial Lawyers Assn., Denver Law Club, Order of Coif. Republican. Methodist. Home and Office: 9715 Sunset Hill Cir Lone Tree CO 80124-6716

SPENCE, ANDREW, artist, painter; b. Bryn Mawr, Pa., Oct. 4, 1947; s. Thomas and Elizabeth Spence; m. Mary Stewart Stoll, June 24, 1977. BFA, Temple U., 1969; MFA, U. Calif., Santa Barbara, 1971. Prof. art Bennington Coll., Vt., 1994—. One-man shows include TransAvant Garde Gallery, Austin, Tex., 1989, Barbara Krakow Gallery, Boston, 1989, Barbara Toll Fine Arts, NYC, 1982-83, 85, 87-88, 90, Compass Rose Gallery, Chgo., 1990, James Corcoran Gallery, LA, 1990, Max. Protetch Gallery, NYC, 1992-93, Barbara Scott Gallery, Miami, 1993, 96, Worcester Art Mus., Mass., 1991, Morris Healy Gallery, NYC, 1996, Art Resources Transfer, NYC, 2000, Edward Thorp Gallery, NYC, 2001, 02, Ulrich Mus. Art, Wichita, Kans., 2005, Edward Thorp Gallery, NYC, 2006; exhibited in group shows including Corcoran Gallery of Art, Washington, 1987, Hirshhorn Mus. and Sculpture Garden, Smithsonian Instn., Washington, 1989, 04, Whitney Mus. Am. Art, NY, 1989, 91-92, Met. Mus. Art, NYC, 1993, Am. Acad. Arts and Letters, NYC, 1994, 2008, Wall Street Rising, NYC, 2002, Wayne State U., Detroit, 2004, Andrew Kreps Gallery, NYC, 2006, Lennon Weinberg, NYC, 2007, Am. Acad. Arts and Letters, NYC, 2008; represented in permanent collections including Addison Gallery Am. Art, Albright Knox Art Gallery, Balt. Mus. Art, Carnegie Mus. Art, Pitts., Cleve. Mus. Art, Cin. Art Mus., Hirshhorn Mus. and Sculpture Garden, Austin Mus. Art, Mus. Modern Art, NY, Met. Mus. Art, NYC, San Diego Mus. Contemporary Art, Walker Art Ctr., Whitney Mus. Am. Art, NYC. Painting grantee Nat. Endowment for Arts, 1987, Purchase award, AAAL, 2008; Guggenheim fellow, 1994.

SPENCE, ANDREW MICHAEL, former dean, finance educator; b. Montclair, NJ, 1943; m. Ann Bennett (div.); children: Graham, Catherine, Marya; m. Monica Spence. BA in Philosophy summa cum laude, Princeton U., 1966; BA, MA in Maths., Oxford U., 1968; PhD in Econs. with honors, Harvard U., 1972. Asst. prof. polit. econ. Kennedy Sch. Govt. Harvard U., Cambridge, Mass., 1971-75, hon. rsch. fellow, 1975—76, vis. prof. econs. dept., 1976-77, prof. econs., 1977-83, prof. bus. adminstrn., 1979-83, George Gund prof. econs. and bus. adminstrn., 1983-86, chmn. bus. econs. PhD program, 1981-83, chmn. econs. dept., 1983-84, dean Faculty Arts and Scis., 1984-90; assoc. prof. dept. econs. Stanford U., Calif., 1973-75, Philip H. Knight Prof., dean Grad. Sch. Bus. Calif., 1990-99, Philip H. Knight Prof. Emeritus, prof. mgmt. Calif., 1999—; ptnr. Oak Hill Venture Ptnrs. and Oak Hill Capital Ptnrs., Menlo Park, Calif., 1999—. Bd. dirs. Gen. Mills, Inc., Nike, Inc., Exult Inc., Siebel Sys. Inc., Blue Martini Software, Torstar Corp., ITI Edn.; mem. econs. adv. panel NSF, 1977-79; chmn. Nat. Rsch. Coun. Bd. on Sci., Tech. and Econ., Policy, 1990-97. Author: Market Signaling: Informational Transfer in Hiring and Related Processes, 1974; Co-author: Industrial Organization in an Open Economy, 1980, Competitive Structure in Investment Banking, 1983; past mem. editl. bd. Am. Econs.

Rev., Bell. Jour. Econs., Jour. Econ. Theory and Pub. Policy; contbr. over 50 articles to profl. jours. Mem. econs. adv. com. Sloan Found., 1979—. Recipient J.K. Galbraith prize for excellence in tchg., 1978, Nobel prize in econ. scis., 2001, Golden Plate award, Acad. Achievement, 2006; Danforth fellow, 1966, Rhodes scholar, 1966. Fellow Am. Acad. Arts & Scis., 1983-, Econometric Soc.; mem. Am. Econ. Assn. (John Bates Clark medal 1981). Office: Stanford U Grad Sch Bus Bldg 350 Memorial Way Stanford CA 94305-5015 also: Oak Hill Venture Partnership 2775 Sand Hill Rd Ste 220 Menlo Park CA 94025-7085*

SPENCE, GERRY (GERALD LEONARD SPENCE), lawyer, writer; b. Laramie, Wyo., Jan. 8, 1929; s. Gerald M. and Esther Sophie (Pfleeger) S.; m. Anna Wilson, June 20, 1947; children: Kip, Kerry, Kent, Katy; m. LaNelle Hampton Peterson, Nov. 18, 1969. BSL, U. Wyo., 1949, LLB, 1952, LLD (hon.), 1990. Bar: Wyo. 1952, U.S. Ct. Claims 1952, U.S. Supreme Ct. 1982. Sole practice, Riverton, Wyo., 1952-54; county and pros. atty. Fremont County, Wyo., 1954-62; ptnr. various law firms, Riverton and Casper, Wyo., 1962-78; sr. ptnr. Spence, Moriarity & Schuster, Jackson, Wyo., 1978—2002, Spence, Moriarity & Shockey, 2002—03, Spence Law Firm, 2004—. Founder Trial Lawyers Coll.; lectr. legal orgns. and law schs. Author: (with others) Gunning for Justice, 1982, Of Murder and Madness, 1983, Trial by Fire, 1986, With Justice for None, 1989, From Freedom to Slavery, 1993, How To Argue and Win Every Time, 1995, The Making of a Country Lawyer, 1996, O.J.: The Last Word, 1997, Give Me Liberty, 1998, A Boy's Summer, 2000, Gerry Spence's Wyoming: The Landscapes, 2000, Half Moon and Empty Stars, 2001, Seven Simple Steps to Personal Freedom, 2001, The Smoking Gun, 2003, Win Your Case, 2005, Bloodthirsty Bitches and Pious Pimps of Power: The Rise and Risk of the New Conservative Hate Culture, 2006. Recipient Lifetime Achievement award, Consumer Attys. Calif. (formerly Calif. Trial Lawyers Assn.), 2008; inducted to, Am. Trial Lawyers Hall of Fame, 2009. Mem. ABA, Wyo. Bar Assn., Wyo. Trial Lawyers Assn., Assn. Trial Lawyers Am., Nat. Assn. Criminal Def. Lawyers Office: The Spence Law Firm LLC PO Box 548 Jackson WY 83001-0548 Office Phone: 307-733-7290. Office Fax: 307-733-5248. Business E-Mail: infointake@spencelawyers.com.*

SPENCE, JAMES ROBERT, JR., broadcast executive, educator, mediator; b. Bronxville, NY, Dec. 20, 1936; s. James Robert and Mary Jeffrey (Grant) Spence; m. Betsy Jo Viener, June 16, 1992. BA, Dartmouth Coll., 1958. Prodn. asst. ABC Sports, Inc. (known as Sports Programs, Inc. through 1966), NYC, 1960-63; asst. to exec. prodr. ABC's Wide World of Sports, 1963-66, coordinating prodr., 1966-70; v.p. program planning ABC Sports, Inc., 1970-78, sr. v.p., 1978-86; pres. Sports TV Internat. Inc., NYC, 1986—2006, exec. prodr., 1986—2006. Adj. assoc. prof. broadcasting NYU Sch. Continuing and Profl. Studies, NYC, 1999—2003; vis. scholar Coll. William and Mary, Williamsburg, Va., 2004—; cert. mediator Gen. Dist. Ct., Va., 2008—. Author: Up Close and Personal - The Inside Story of Network Television Sports, 1988. With US Army, 1958—60. Mem.: Two Rivers Country Club (Williamsburg, Va.), Westchester Country Club (Rye, NY).

SPENCE, JEAN LOUISE, biology professor, researcher; b. Jacksonville, Fla., Apr. 11, 1952; d. John Roger and Irene Spence; life ptnr. John Robert Leek. PhD, U. Utah, Salt Lake City, 1983—88. Founder Omnitron Bioscis., San Diego, 2005—08. Contbr. articles to profl. jours. Achievements include discovery of K-63 linked multi ubiquitin chains; role of ubiquitination in facilitating translation or protein synthesis; identified messenger RNAss that are differentially translated in oncogenically transformed cells; bioinformatic platform for analyzing mRNA non coding regions. Home: 3090 Admiral Ave San Diego CA 92123 Personal E-mail: jlspence@san.rr.com. Business E-Mail: jspence@swccd.edu.

SPENCE, JOSEPH THOMAS, biochemist; b. Bklyn., May 7, 1951; s. Joseph B. and Mary Spence; m. Marlene Spence; children: Joseph, Laura. BS, St. Francis Coll., Bklyn., 1973; MNS., Cornell U., Ithaca, NY, 1975, PhD, 1977. Postdoc. fellow McArdle Lab Cancer Rsch., Madison, Wis., 1977—80; asst. prof. SUNY, Buffalo, 1980—85, assoc. dean rsch. & grad. studies, Sch. Med & Biomed. Scis., 1988—93. Health scientist adminstr. Natl Heart, Lung and Blood Inst., NIH, Bethesda, Md., 1985—88; dir. Beltsville Human Nutrition Rsch. Ctr., 1993—2004; dep. adminstr. Agrl. Rsch. Svc., USDA, Beltsville, 2004—08; dir. Beltsville Agrl. Rsch. Ctr., 2008—. Recipient Presdl. Rank award, US Govt., 1997, 2003. Mem.: Soc. Exptl. Biology & Medicine, Am. Soc. Nutrition. Achievements include research in regulation of gene expression of enzymes in response to diet and hormones. E-mail: joseph.spence@ars.usda.gov.

SPENCE, KENNETH F., III, lawyer, insurance company executive; b. Balt., Apr. 18, 1955; BA summa cum laude, Dickinson Coll., 1977; JD with honors, U. Md., 1982. Bar: Md. 1982, US Fed. Ct. 1982. Mem. litig. dept. Miles & Stockbridge, Balt., 1983—96, ptnr., 1990—96; with USF&G (merged with St. Paul Cos. Inc.), 1996—98; v.p. corp. litig. St. Paul Cos. Inc. (merged with Travelers Property Casualty Corp.), 1998—2004; v.p. legal services divsn., dep. gen. counsel St. Paul Travelers Cos. Inc., 2004, exec. v.p., gen. counsel, 2004—. Mem.: Md. State Bar, Minn. State Bar. Office: St Paul Travelers Companies Inc 385 Washington St Saint Paul MN 55102*

SPENCE, NANCY ELIZABETH, workshop developer, psychology educator, literature educator, writer; d. Frederick Richard and Elizabeth M. R. (Harter) Spence; m. Earl Arthur Crossland, Mar. 14, 1970 (div. 1985); children: Catherine Elise Spence Crossland Davison, Susannah Elizabeth Spence Crossland-Dwyer; m. Benjamin Lee Hemingway, Aug. 5, 1991. BA in English Lang. and Lit., Pa. State U., 1970; MA in Libr. Sci., U. Mich., 1973, MA in Am. Culture, 1974; PhD in East/West Psychology, Union Inst., Cin., 1994. Adj. instr. English Schoolcraft C.C., Livonia, Mich., 1974—77; ethnic studies bibliographer U. Cin., 1977—78, dir., office women's programs and svcs., 1985—98, adj. instr. counseling, 1987—97; adj. asst. prof. English Xavier U., Cin., 1978—82; freelance spkr., writer, editor, workshop developer Cin., 1998—. Chief writer, editor, cons. Pro-Ohio, Cin., 1998—; adj. prof. Union Inst. U., Cin., 1999—2007; co-founder Ikigai, 2005—. Editor: Life Medicine: Wisdom for Extraordinary Living, 1997, 4th edit., 2006. Recipient Margaret Mann award, U. Mich., 1973, Golden Rule award, Greater Cin. United Way, 1993, U.S. Presdl. citation, Point of Light Found., 1994. Mem.: ACA, Internat. Positive Psychology Assn., Internat. Assn. Applied Psychology, Am. Coll. Pers. Assn., Beta Phi Mu, Phi Beta Kappa (life). Avocations: reading, bicycling, yoga, writing, travel.

SPENCE, ROBERT JAMES, plastic surgeon; b. Troy, NY, Mar. 9, 1947; s. James Robert and Ruth Elizabeth (Swanker) S.; m. Cressy Ann Starkweather, Aug. 14, 1971; children: Courtney Ann, Erin Elizabeth, Kevin Robert. BA, Johns Hopkins U., 1969, MD, 1972. Diplomate Am. Bd. Plastic Surgery, Am. Bd. Surgery. Asst. prof. plastic surgery U. Md., Balt., 1980-85, Johns Hopkins Med. Sch., Balt., 1985—; assoc. prof. plastic surgery; chief of plastic surgery Johns Hopkins Bayview Medical Ctr., Balt., 1985—. Dir. Ctr. for Burn Reconstrn., Balt., 1990—; med. dir. Md. Tissue Bank, Balt., 1984—; co-dir. Balt. Regional Burn Ctr., 1985—. Patentee in field; contbg. author four books; contbr. articles to profl. jours. Bd. dirs., v.p. Transplant Resource Ctr. of Md., Balt., 1991-92; bd. dirs. Balt. Regional Burn Ctr. Fund, 1986—, exec. v.p., 1993. Recipient Henry Strong Denison scholarship for med. rsch., 1970. Fellow ACS; mem. Am. Soc. Plastic and Reconstructive Surgeons, Northeastern Soc. Plastic Surgeons (bd. dirs. 1990-92), John Staige Davis Soc. Plastic Surgeons (sec. 1984-86, pres. 1991-92), Am. Assn. Tissue Banks, Am. Burn Assn. (chmn. edn. com. 1996-99), Balt. Acad. Surgery (sec. 1993-95, v.p. 1995-96, pres. 1996-97). Avocations: photography, tennis. Office: Johns Hopkins Bayview Med Ctr 4940 Eastern Ave Baltimore MD 21224-2735

SPENCE, ROBERT LEROY, publishing executive; b. Carlisle, Pa., Sept. 13, 1931; s. Leroy Oliver and Esther Helen (Lau) S.; m. Barbara Amelia Hunter, Sept. 1, 1954 (div. Sept. 1978); children— Robert Roy, Bonnie Leigh; m. 2d, Maryanne Elizabeth Yacono, Jan. 10, 1979 BA, Dickinson Coll., 1953; postgrad, Temple U., 1955-57, Rutgers U., 1956, 59-60, U. Pa., 1960. Cert. tchr., N.J. Chmn. dept. math. Haddon Heights High Sch., NJ, 1954-62; sr. editor Silver Burdett Co., Morristown, NJ, 1962-64; editor-in-chief Harcourt Brace Jovanovich, Inc., NYC, 1964-81; v.p., pub. Harper & Row Publishers, Inc., NYC, 1981-85, Scribner Ednl. Pubs. div. Macmillan, Inc., NYC, 1985; pres. R&M Spence, Inc., Sparta, NJ, 1985—. Author textbook series: Growth in Mathematics, 1978, Excel in Mathematics, 1989-90, Mathematics Plus: Multicultural Projects, 1993; editor: Financial Planning for The Baby Boomer Client, 2000, 2d edit., 2004, Money Forever, 2002. Mem. Assn. Am. Pubs. (mem. exec. com. 1981-84), Nat. Council Tchrs. Math., Internat. Reading Assn., Am. Numismatic Assn. Avocations: rare coin collecting, coin newsletter author and publisher, artist, writer. Home and Office: 37 Heather Ln Sparta NJ 07871-3538

SPENCE, ROY MILAM, JR., advertising executive; b. Brownwood, Tex., Oct. 10, 1948; m. Mary Spence; children: Courtney, Ashley, Shay. BA in Govt., U. Tex., 1971. Co-founder GSD&M's Idea City (formerly GSD&M Advt.), Austin, Tex., 1971, pres., 1971—2007, chmn., CEO, 2007—. Mem. devel. bd. U. Tex., Austin, mem. adv. coun. McComb Sch. Bus. Featured in Fortune, The Wall St. Jour., The New York Times, USA Today. Mem. Wal-Mart Lit. Coun. Recipient Disting. Alumnus award, U. Tex., 2004. Office: GSD&M's Idea City 828 W 6th St Austin TX 78703-5420

SPENCE, SANDRA, retired trade association administrator; b. McKeesport, Pa., Mar. 25, 1941; d. Cedric Leroy and Suzanne (Haudenshield) S. BA, Allegheny Coll., 1963; MA, Rutgers U., 1964. With Pa. State Govt., Harrisburg, 1964-68, Appalachian Regional Commn., Washington, 1968-75; legis. rep. Nat. Assn. Counties, Washington, 1975-77; fed. rep. Calif. Dept. Transp., Washington, 1977-78; dir. congl. affairs Amtrak, Washington, 1978-81, corp. sec., 1981-83, dir. computer svcs., 1983-84; co-owner Parkhurst-Spence Inc., 1985; owner The Spence Group, 1986-90; v.p. Bostrom Corp., Washington, 1990-92; exec. dir. Soc. Glass and Ceramic Decorators, 1992-2000. Chmn. legis. com. Womens Transp. Seminar, 1977-79, dir., 1982-83, v.p., 1983-84, chmn. edn. com., 1982-83; com. on edn. and tng. Transp. Rsch. Bd., 1982-85; mng. ptnr. Cambio Capital Club, 1996. Contbr. articles to profl. jours. Commnr. DC Commn. for Women, 1983—88, sec., 1983—88; pres. Found. for Work of Laity, 2001—06; coun. mem. Agenda for Del. Women, 2006—08; del. Ward III Dem. Com., 1982—90, 1st vice chmn., 1987—88; bd. dir. DC Habitat for Humanity, 1998—2002, chmn. devel. com., 1998—2000, sec., 2000—01, Sussex County Habitat for Humanity, Del., 2003—05, bd. dirs., 2003—06, treas., 2005—06, housing adv., 2007—08; bd. dirs. Del. Housing Coalition, 2007—; treas. League Women Voters DE, 2007—09, pres., 2009—. Fellow Eagleton Inst. Politics, 1963-64; recipient Achievement award Transp. Seminar, 1982, 83 Mem. LWV (treas. Del. chpt. 2007-), Greater Washington Soc. Assn. Execs. (vice-chair law and legis. com. 1989-90, chmn. 1990-91, chmn. scholarship com. 1992-93, bd. dirs. 1993-96, Rising Star award 1989, Chmn.'s award for Govt. Rels. 1991), Am. Soc. Assn. Execs. (mgmt. cert. 1987), Phi Beta Kappa. Home: 18471 Seashell Blvd Lewes DE 19958 Personal E-mail: sandyspence325@gmail.com.

SPENCE, SIQUE (MARY STEWART SPENCE), art dealer; b. Balt., Aug. 16, 1946; d. Joseph Adolphus and Nell Orum (Jones) Stoll; m. Ronald A. Kuchta, Nov. 2, 1969 (div. 1975); m. Andrew R. Spence, June 24, 1977. Dir. Galeria del Sol/Fairtree Fine Crafts Inst., Santa Barbara, Calif., 1970-75; asst. to dir. Arco Ctr. for the Visual Arts, LA, 1975-77; registrar Droll/Kolbert Gallery, NYC, 1977-78; gallery asst. Nancy Hoffman Gallery, NYC, 1978-81, dir., 1981—. Office: Nancy Hoffman Gallery 429 W Broadway New York NY 10012-3799 Fax: 212-334-5078. Business E-Mail: sique@nancyhoffmangallery.com.

SPENCE, WILLIAM H., electric power industry executive; BS, Pa. State Univ.; MBA, Bentley Coll. Mgmt. positions through v.p. trading Delmarva Power, 1987—2000; sr. v.p. Conectiv Holdings, 2000—06, Pepco Holdings Inc., 2002—06; exec. v.p., COO PPL Corp., Allentown, Pa., 2006—. Office: PPL Corp 2 N 9th St Allentown PA 18101

SPENCER, ALAN C., legislative staff member; b. Dec. 15, 1953; m. Leanne Spencer, May 15, 1976. BS in Bus. Adminstrn., U. Ala., 1975; MA in Pub. Adminstrn., Webster U., 1978; attended, Mil. War Coll., 1992. Sr. cons., program mgr. Digital Sys. Internat. Corp., Arlington, Va., 1997—2001; dep. chief staff for Rep. Sonny Callahan, US House of Reps., 2001—02, chief of staff, 2002, Rep. Jo Bonner, 2003—. Served in USAF, 1976—97. Mem.: Retired Officers Assn., Nat. Contract Mgmt. Assn., Ala. State Soc., Nat. Rep. Party, Nat. Eagle Scout Assn. Office: Office of Congressman Jo Bonner 2236 Rayburn House Office Bldg Washington DC 20515 Office Phone: 202-225-4931. Office Fax: 202-225-0562. E-mail: alan.spencer@mail.house.gov.*

SPENCER, ALBERT FRANKLIN, physical education educator; b. Pitts., Pa., Dec. 31, 1943; s. Albert Clair and Ann Mary (Kielbas) Spencer; m. Sue Spencer; stepchildren: Flannery Heath, Russell Yopp. BS in Edn., Slippery Rock State Coll., Pa., 1966; MS in LS, Clarion State U., Pa., 1981; PhD in LS, Fla. State U., Tallahassee, 1985, PhD in Phys. Edn., 1991. Mgr. Kmart, New Kensington, Pa., 1972, departmental dir., 1973—74; phys. edn. tchr., libr., coach St. John's Indian Sch., Komatke, Ariz., 1976-77, Duncan HS, Ariz., 1977-79; tchr. math. and sci. Army and Navy Acad., Carlsbad, Calif., 1979-80; phys. edn. tchr., libr., coach Baboquivari HS, Sells, Ariz., 1980-81; asst. men's intercoll. basketball coach Fla. State U., Tallahassee, 1981-83; asst. prof. phys. edn., dir. audiovisual svcs. St. Leo Coll., Fla., 1983-86; asst. prof. Atlanta U. and Emory U., Atlanta, 1986-87; assoc. prof. phys. edn./athletics, libr. dir., coach Ga. Mil. Coll., Milledgeville, 1987-90; asst. prof. edn. U. Nev., Las Vegas, 1991-94, 2000; asst. prof. phys. edn., dept. human performance/health scis. Rice U., Houston, 1994—98; prof. phys. edn. & sport mgmt. Limestone Coll., 2000—. Dir. athletics YMCA, Kittanning, Pa., 1969; cons. ednl. tech. Atlanta Pub. Schs., 1986-87; profl. basketball scout Bertka Agy. and LA Lakers, 1985-91; chair ethics com. Am. Alliance for Health, Phys. Edn., Recreation and Dance, 2005-08. Contbg. author: Twentieth-Century Young Adult Writers, 1994; contbr. articles and revs. to profl. jours. Fundraiser KC, Las Vegas, patriotic degree and recruitment dir., 1991-; vol. coach for youth league St. Anthony Elem. Sch., San Antonio, Fla.; asst. scoutmaster Boy Scouts America, New Kensington, 1968-70; fundraiser St. Jude's Children's Hosp., 1968-70; mem. Southeastern Cherokee Fedn.; vol. elem. sch. reader Reading is Fundamental, 1991-; event. coord. Spl. Olympics, Limestone Coll., Cherokee County, SC, 2000-08; with US House Reps. SC, 2004-08. Mem. AAHPERD, ALA, Am. Libr. and Info. Sci. Educators, Fla. Assn. for Health, Phys. Edn., Recreation and Dance, Tex. Assn. for Health, Phys. Edn., Recreation and Dance, U.S. Phys. Edn. Assn., Tex. Faculty Assn., Beta Phi Mu, Omicron Delta Kappa. Republican. Roman Catholic. Avocations: writing, golf, basketball, hiking. Office: 109 Ridgeway Rd Gaffney SC 29340-3615 Home Phone: 864-489-4300; Office Phone: 864-488-4563. Business E-Mail: spencer@spencer4congress.com, uspencer@limestone.edu.

SPENCER, BENNION L., college instructor; b. Ogden, Utah, Oct. 26, 1952; m. Malinda Spencer; children: Jonathan, Jason, Jesse, Jodi. BA in Broadcast Comm., Weber State U., 1985; MA in Internat. Rels., Utah State U., 1993. TV news reporter KTVX 4 Utah, 1980—85; TV news prodr. KSL TV, 1985—96; TV news dir. KBMT TV, 1996—98; instr. Utah Valley U., 2000—07; student media ctr. advisor Salt Lake Cmty. Coll., 2002—05; gen. mgr. KCSG, 2005—07; instr. Neumont U. Adv. Riverton Youth Coun. Democrat. Avocations: reading, swimming, weightlifting.

SPENCER, C. STANLEY, insurance company executive; b. Canton, Pa., Sept. 24, 1940; s. Clarence N. and Maude E. (Phipps) S.; m. Carol M. Vest, Aug. 23, 1962; children: Greg, Mike. BS in Agrl. Engring., Pa. State U., 1961. Regional sales mgr. W.T. Grant Co., NYC, 1966-76; engr. Hoover Well Service, Zion, Ill., 1976-80, Nielson Iron Works, Racine, Wis., 1980-82; spl. agent Prudential Ins. Co., Racine, 1982-84, div. mgr., from 1984; v.p. legal dept. Am. Family Mut. Ins. Co., Madison, Wis. Recipient 1st Place Barbershop Chorus award, Racine, 1984, Kenosha, 1985, Manitowoc, 1986, 1st Place Barbershop Quartet award, Kenosha, Wis., 1986. Mem. Life Underwriters Assn. (v.p. 1985-86), Soc. for the Preservation and Encouragement of Barber Shop Quartet Singing in Am. (pres. Racine 1984-85). Clubs: Toastmasters (1st Place 1985). Republican. Office: American Family Mutual Insurance Company 6000 American Pkwy Madison WI 53783-0001 Home: 578 County Route 93 Slate Hill NY 10973-4106

SPENCER, CATHERINE ELLEN, academic administrator; b. Englewood, NJ, Apr. 17, 1959; d. Donald Mansfield and Lois Anne Spencer. BS in Edn., U. Steubenville, Ohio, 1981; MS in Edn. Adminstrn., Franciscan U. of Steubenville, Ohio, 1996. Tchr. St. Francis Cath. Sch., Toronto, Ohio, 1981—82, St. Peter Sch., Steubenville, Ohio, 1982—92; tchr., asst. prin. Lincoln Internat. Acad., Managua, Nicaragua, 1992—93; residence dir. Franciscan U. of Steubenville (Ohio), 1993—96; prin. All Saints Sch., Steubenville, Ohio, 1996—2004; asst. supt. Diocese of Wheeling-Charleston, Wheeling, W.Va., 2004—08; dir. Curriculum Archdiocese, Washington, 2008—. Mem. bd. trustees North Ctrl. Assn. Commn. on Accreditation and Sch. Improvement, Tempe, Ariz., 2004—08; bd. of dirs. Holy Family Child Care and Devel. Ctr., Wheeling, W.Va. Missionary Dene Indian Reservation, Assumption, Canada, 1990—90. Recipient John Vaughn award, North Ctrl. Assn. Commn. on Accreditation and Sch. Improvement, 2006. Mem.: Chief Administrs. of Cath. Edn., Ohio Geneal. Soc., Kappa Delta Pi (life), Alpha Chi (life), Delta Zeta Sorority (life; pres. 1980—81). Office: Archdiocese of Wash 5001 Eastern Ave PO Box 29260 Hyattsville MD 20782-3447 Home: 14252 Long Green Dr Silver Spring MD 20906 Office Phone: 301-853-4590. Business E-Mail: spencer@adw.org.

SPENCER, CHARLES S., anthropologist; BA in Anthropology, Rice U., 1972; MA in Anthropology, U. Mich., 1976, PhD in Anthropology, 1981. Assoc. prof. anthropology U. Conn.; assoc. curator divsn. anthropology Am. Mus. Natural Hist., NYC, 1991—94, chair, curator, 1994—. Adj. prof. anthropology dept. Columbia U., adj. sr. rsch. scientist Ctr. Environ. Rsch. and Conservation. Contbr. articles to profl. jours., chapters to books. Fellow: Am. Acad. Arts & Scis.; mem.: NAS, AAAS, Soc. Am. Archaeology, Sigma Xi. Office: Divsn Anthropology Am Mus Natural Hist Ctrl Pk West at 79th St New York NY 10024-5192 E-mail: cspencer@amnh.org.

SPENCER, CHERYL L., literature and language educator; BA, Edgewood Coll., 1969; MA in Theater and Drama, U. Wis., Madison, 1993. Cert. tchr. secondary education, English Wis., 1974. Affirmative action asst. officer City of Madison, Wis., 1985—86; English tchr. Madison Met. Sch. Dist., 1969—, English tchr. diploma completion program, 1977—84, English tchr. summer sch., 1975. Sys. strategic planning in tchr. edn. com. U. of Wis., 1989—92; minority student achievement com. Madison Met. Sch. Dist., 1977—79, graduation stds. com., 1999—2000; pres. faculty senate Madison Meml. H.S., 1980—84, scholarship com., 2003—; tchr. edn. rev. panel U. Wis.-Plattville Dept. of Pub. Instrn., State of Wis., Madison, 2003. Producer- organizer, media person (traveling theatre group performances); dir.: (high school play) Plautus' The Captives. Bd. dirs. Urban League of Greater Madison, 1992—94. Recipient Outstanding H.S. Tchr. award, U. of Chgo., 1998. Mem.: Nat. Coun. of Tchrs. of English, Wis. Edn. Assn. Coun. (rep. to state rep. assembly 1977—80), Madison Tchrs. Inc. (bd. dirs., com. chair 1980—94). Office: Madison Memorial High School 201 S Gammon Rd Madison WI 53717 E-mail: cspencer@madison.k12.wi.us.

SPENCER, CHRISTOPHER S., lawyer, insurance company executive; b. Boston, Mass., Apr. 29, 1946; BA, Beloit Coll., 1969; JD, Univ. Wis., Madison, 1972. Bar: Wis. 1972. V.p., legal Am. Family Ins. Group, Madison, Wis. Office: American Family Insurance Group Legal Dept 6000 American Pkwy Madison WI 53783-0001 Office Phone: 608-249-2111. Office Fax: 608-243-4917.

SPENCER, EDGAR WINSTON, geology educator; b. Monticello, Ark., May 27, 1931; s. Terrel Ford and Allie Belle (Shelton) S.; m. Elizabeth Penn Humphries, Nov. 26, 1958; children: Elizabeth Shawn, Kristen Shannon. Student, Vanderbilt U., Nashville, 1949—50; BS, Wash. and Lee U., Lexington, Va., 1953; PhD, Columbia U., NYC, 1957. Lectr. Hunter Coll., 1954-57; mem. faculty Washington and Lee U., 1957—, prof. geology, head dept., 1962-95, Ruth Parmly prof. Pres. emeritus Rockbridge Area Conservation Coun., 1978-79, co-pres. 1992-98; NSF sci. faculty fellow, New Zealand and Australia; dir. grant for humanities and pub. policy on land use planning Va. Found., 1975; dir. grant Petroleum Rsch. Fund, 1981-82; leader field trip Ctrl. Appalachian Mts. Internat. Geol. Congress, 1989. Author: Basic Concepts of Physical Geology, 1962, Basic Concepts of Historical Geology, 1962, Geology: A Survey of Earth Science, 1965, Introduction to the Structure of the Earth, 1969, 3d edit., 1988, The Dynamics of the Earth, 1972, Physical Geology, 1983, Geologic Maps, 1993, 2nd edit., 2000, Geologic Maps of the Buena Vista and Glasgow Quadrangle, Virginia, 2000; co-author: Geologic Map and Report on the Geology of Rockbridge County, Virginia, 2007; author: Earth Science-Understanding Environmental Systems, 2003. Recipient Va. Outstanding Faculty award Va. Coun. of Higher Edn., 1990. Fellow Geol. Soc. Am., AAAS; mem. Am. Assn. Petroleum Geologists (dir. field seminar on fold and thrust belts 1987, 88-91), Am. Inst. Profl. Geologists, Am. Geophys. Union, Yellowstone-

Bighorn Rsch. Assn., Phi Beta Kappa (hon.), Omicron Delta Kappa (hon.), Sigma Xi. Home: PO Box 1055 Lexington VA 24450-1055 Office Phone: 540-458-8866. E-mail: spencere@wlu.edu.

SPENCER, ELIZABETH, writer; b. Carrollton, Miss., 1921; d. James Luther and Mary James (McCain) S.; m. John Arthur Blackwood Rusher, Sept. 29, 1956. BA, Belhaven Coll., 1942; MA, Vanderbilt U., 1943; LittD (hon.), Southwestern U. at Memphis, 1968; LLD (hon.), Concordia U. at Montreal, 1988; LittD (hon.), U. of the South, 1992; DLitt (hon.), U. NC, Chapel Hill, 1998, Belhaven Coll., 1999. Instr. N.W. Miss. Jr. Coll., 1943-44, Ward-Belmont, Nashville, 1944-45; reporter The Nashville Tennessean, 1945-46; instr. U. Miss., Oxford, 1948-51, 52-53. Vis. prof. Concordia U., Montreal, Que., Can., 1976-81, adj. prof., 1981-86; vis. prof. U. NC, Chapel Hill, 1986-92. Author: Fire in the Morning, 1948, This Crooked Way, 1952, The Voice at the Back Door, 1956, The Light in the Piazza, 1960, Knights and Dragons, 1965, No Place for an Angel, 1967, Ship Island and Other Stories, 1968, The Snare, 1972, The Stories of Elizabeth Spencer, 1981, Marilee, 1981, The Salt Line, 1984, Jack of Diamonds and Other Stories, 1988, (play) For Lease or Sale, 1989, On the Gulf, 1991, The Night Travellers, 1991, (memoir) Landscapes of the Heart, 1998, The Southern Woman, 2001; contbr. short stories to mags. and anthologies. Recipient Women's Dem. Com. award, 1949, recognition award, Nat. Inst. Arts and Letters, 1952, Richard and Hinda Rosenthal Found. award, Am. Acad. Arts and Letters, 1957, Fortner award for lit., 1998, Award of Merit medal for the short story, 1983, 1st McGraw-Hill Fiction award, 1960, Henry Bellamann award for creative writing, 1968, Salem award for lit., 1992, Dos Passos award for fiction, 1992, NC Gov.'s award for lit., 1994, Corrington award for lit., 1997, Richard Wright award for lit., 1997, award for non-fiction, Miss. Libr. Assn., 1999, Brooks medal, Fellowship of So. Writers, 2001, Thomas Wolfe award for lit., 2002, William Faulkner award for lit. excellence, 2002, Miss. Gov.'s award for excellence in the arts, 2006, Pen/Malamud award for short fiction, 2007, Lifetime Achievement award, Miss. Inst. Arts & Letters, 2009; named to NC Hall of Fame, 2002; fellow, Guggenheim Found., 1953; Kenyon Rev. fellow in fiction, 1957, Bryn Mawr Coll. Donnelly fellow, 1962, Nat. Endowment for Arts grantee in lit., 1983, Sr. Arts Award grantee, Nat. Endowment for the Arts, 1988. Mem. Am. Acad. Arts and Letters, Fellowship of So. Writers (charter; vice chancellor 1993-97). Home: 402 Longleaf Dr Chapel Hill NC 27517-3042 Office Phone: 919-929-2115. E-mail: elizabeth0222@earthlink.net.

SPENCER, ESTELLE HEIDI, library director; b. Camden, Maine, Feb. 2, 1969; m. James Spencer, Sept. 18, 2004. BA in English, Fairleigh Dickinson U., Teaneck, NJ, 1992; MLIS, Simmons Coll., Boston, 2004. Data collection supr. Market St. Rsch., Northampton, Mass., 1995—2001; serials supr. Am. Internat. Coll., Springfield, Mass., 2001—03, reference libr., 2003—06, asst. dir. libr. svcs., 2006—07, dir. libr. svcs., 2007—. Pres. Cooperating Librs. Greater Springfield, 2008—. Independent. Avocations: running, reading, cooking, knitting, travel. Office: Am Internat Coll 1000 State St Springfield MA 01109 Business E-Mail: estelle.spencer@aic.edu.

SPENCER, FITZGERALD, medical educator; s. Fitzclarence and Mayotte Spencer; children: Simbonika N., Geraldo. BS, Southern U., Baton Rouge, La., 1961; MEd, Utah State U., Logan, 1965; MS, U. Northern Colo., Greeley, 1970; PhD, U. Kans., Lawrence, 1974. Cert. biomed. kndocrinology U. Kans., 1974, biomed. endocrinology. Fulbright scholar US Congress, Washington, 1991—; prof. chancellor rsch. fellow Southern U., 1995—. Contbr. articles to profl. jours. Achievements include research in uterine implantation decidualization & placentation, Pineal circadian regulation of uterine function, effects of environmental toxins, xenoestrogens & synthesys hormones on decidualization. Office: Southern Univ Harding Blvd Baton Rouge LA 70813-5001 Office Phone: 2257713611 5210.

SPENCER, GEORGE HENRY, lawyer; b. Vienna; s. Frank Henry and Lillian (Godin) S.; m. Joan Betty Spencer, Sept. 16, 1956 (dec.); children: Lucy, Margaret, Robert, Nancy; m. Mollie Cole Sabol, Oct. 31, 1987; stepchildren: Jeanne, Marta. BE, Yale U., 1948; JD, Cornell U., 1952. Bar: D.C., N.Y. Examiner U.S. Patent Office, 1952-54; sole practice NYC, Washington, 1954-62; ptnr. Spencer & Frank, Washington, 1962-98, Venable, LLP, Attys. at Law, Washington, 1998—2003; counsel Fitch, Even, Tabin & Flannery, Washington, 2003—06, Dennison, Schultz & MacDonald, Washington, 2007—. Master of bench Prettyman-Leventhal Am. Inn of Ct.; lectr. World Trade Inst. Served to capt. JAGC, U.S. Army, 1956-62. Mem. ABA, Am. Patent Law Assn., Lawyer-Pilots Bar Assn., World Intellectual Property Orgn. (panel of arbitrators and mediators), Cosmos Club (Washington). Avocations: aviation, music, German and French language studies, poetry. Home: 1102 Flor Ln Mc Lean VA 22102-1737 Office: Dennison, Schultz & MacDonald Ste 105 1727 King St Ste 105 Alexandria VA 22314 Office Phone: 703-837-9600 ext. 17. Personal E-mail: specole@aol.com. Business E-Mail: gspencer@dennisonlaw.com.

SPENCER, HERBERT HARRY, structural engineer, researcher, computer analyst; b. Vienna, Jan. 2, 1928; arrived in US, 1953; s. Ingenieur Oskar and Bronia (Steinberger) Schnabel; m. Margot Goldrei (div.); m. Sara Slomka, July 24, 1992. BSc, U. London, 1948; MS, Poly. Inst. Bklyn., 1955; PhD, U. London, 1976. Asst. jr. engr. Tarmac Ltd., Coventry, England, 1944—45, Wimpey & Co., Coventry, 1945—46, Kershaw & Kaufman, London, 1946—48; engr. Halcrow & Ptnrs., London, 1948—49, Hydraulic Dept., Nazareth, Israel, 1949—50, Quibuts Eyn HaShofet, Galilee, Israel, 1950—51, Rendel Palmer & Tritton, London, 1951—53; rsch. asst. Poly. Inst. Bklyn., 1953—55; instr. Yale U., New Haven, 1955—56; rsch. asst., lectr. Columbia U., NYC, 1956—59; asst. prof. San Diego State Coll., 1959—61; rsch. assoc. Caltech, Pasedena, Calif., 1961—62; asst. prof. U. So. Calif., LA, 1961—65; sr. scientist Ford Instrument Co., Sperry Gyro, L.I. City, NY, 1965—66, Tech. Rsch. Group, Melville, NY, 1966—67; engr. cons. Spencer Rsch., NYC and London, 1967—77; sr. lectr. Hatfield Poly., England, 1970—77; vis. assoc. prof. U. Pitts., 1976—77; assoc. prof. La. State U., Baton Rouge, 1977—79; vis. rsch. cons. Columbia U., NYC, 1979; asst. prof. Rutgers U., New Brunswick, NJ, 1979—82. Pres. Spencer Sci. Computing, New Brunswick, 1982—; vis. prof. Aero Lab., Technion, Haifa, Israel, 1988, Rutgers U., Piscataway, N.J., 1998-2003 Contbr. articles to profl. jours. Mem. ASCE, ASME, Israeli Soc. Engrs. and Architects, Gesellschaft für Angewandte Mathematik und Mechanik, Structural Rsch. Coun., Mensa, Intertel. Home: 10-8M Landing Ln New Brunswick NJ 08901 Office: Spencer Sci Comp PO Box 4191 Highland Park NJ 08904-4191 Office Phone: 732-246-0499. Business E-Mail: sscc@isp.com.

SPENCER, JAN B., health products executive; b. Rostrup, Germany, 1955; m. Miriam Spencer; 3 children. B in Textile Tech. and Mgmt. Scis., U. Manchester Inst. Sci. and Tech. Comml. sales rep. Kimberly-Clark Corp., Manchester, England, 1979, product mgr. to bus. analyst to bus. mgr., 1980—88, various positions including dir. washroom bus., VSE to UCTAD project mgr. and Scott merger integration mgr., 1988—96, v.p. rsch., devel. & engring. Away From Home, 1996—98, v.p. wiper bus., 1998—2000, v.p. European Ops., Engring., Supply Chain in Profl. sector, 2000—02, pres. Kimberly-Clark Profl. Europe, 2002—03, pres. Kimberly-Clark Profl. N.Am., 2003—04, pres. Kimberly-Clark Profl. North Atlantic, 2004—06, pres. Global Kimberly-Clark Profl., 2006—. Office: Kimberly Clark Corp 1400 Holcomb Bridge Rd Roswell GA 30076

SPENCER, JOHN DANIEL, former mayor; b. White Plains, NY, Nov. 17, 1946; s. Edward and Ann (McGlinchy) Spencer; m. Eileen Looney, May 8, 1971 (div.); children: John, Jr., Jennifer; m. Kathy Spring, 2003; children: Kaitlyn, Patrick, James Grad., Westchester C.C., 1966. Sr. property mgr. Cushman & Wakefield, Inc., 1977-84; v.p. for real estate mgmt. Bankers Trust Co., 1984-91; city councilman City of Yonkers, 1990—95, mayor, 1996—2004. Commr. Human Rights Commn., City of Yonkers, 1983-86; bd. dirs. Northwest Yonkers Civic Assn., 1987-91; pres. North Yonkers Boys and Girls Club, 1987-88, bd. dirs. 1982-84, 87-90; treas. Amackassin Club, 1988-90; counsel Am. Irish Assn. of Westchester; mem. Westchester Irish Com., others. Served in US Army, 1966—69, Vietnam. Decorated Bronze Star, Combat Infantryman's badge; recipient Sen. John E. Flynn Disting. Svc. award, 1987, Ellis Island medal of honors, 1997. Mem. Vietnam Vets. of Am., Am. Legion, VFW. Avocations: golf, reading. Home Phone: 914-963-9126; Office Phone: 914-263-8277. Personal E-mail: jspencergroup@aol.com.

SPENCER, JOHN HEDLEY, biochemistry educator; b. Stapleford, Eng., Apr. 10, 1933; emigrated to Can., 1956; s. Thomas and Eva (Johnson) S.; m. Magdeliene Vera Kulin, Sept. 16, 1958; children: Robin Anne, David Thomas, Mark Stewart. BSc, U. St. Andrews, Scotland, 1955, BSc with honors, 1956; student, Montreal Cancer Rsch. Soc., 1956-59; PhD, McGill U., 1960. Damon Runyon Meml. Fund postdoctoral fellow Columbia U., NYC, 1959-61; mem. faculty McGill U., Montreal, 1961-78, assoc. prof. biochemistry, 1966-71, prof., 1971-78; prof. biochemistry Queen's U., Kingston, Ont., 1978-98, head biochemistry, 1978-90, prof. emeritus, 1998—. Vis. scientist NICHHD/NIH, Bethesda, Md., 1987-88; vis. prof. U. Montreal, 1992-93. Author: The Physics and Chemistry of DNA and RNA, 1972; co-editor: Planet Earth: Problems and Prospects, 1995. Recipient Ayerst award Can. Biochem. Soc., 1972 Fellow Royal Soc. Can., 1985; mem. Can. Biochem. Soc. (treas. 1966-69, pres. 1979-80), Can. Fedn. Biol. Socs. (pres. 1981-82), Canadians for Health Rsch. (bd. dirs. 2001-06), Biochem. Soc., Am. Soc. Biochemistry and Molecular Biology, Royal Soc. Can., Sigma Xi. Home: 36 Kenwoods Cir Kingston ON Canada K7K 6Y1

SPENCER, MELISSA JOHANNA, psychotherapist, special education educator; b. Durham, NC, Sept. 13, 1951; d. Joseph Whitney and Regina Colleen (Barnett) Spencer; m. Charles Ray Barrow, Aug. 21, 1972; children: Matthew R. Barrow, Christine N. Gonzales, Charlotte D. Barrow. Attended, U. Hawaii-Manoa, 1986—88; BA in Psychology, Tex. Tech. U., Lubbock, 1990, MEd in Counseling, 1994, EdD in Counselor Edn., 1999. Lic. profl. counselor NC, 2000, cert. spl. edn. educator 2006. Dir. vols. Rappahannock Coun. Domestic Violence, Fredericksburg, Va., 1999—2000; asst. prof. U. NC-Pembroke, 2000—02; pvt. practice psychotherapy Southeastern Psychol. Svcs., Fairmont, NC, 2002—; tchr. exceptional children with autism Seventy-First HS, Fayetteville, NC, 2003—06, Robeson County Pub. Schs., Lumberton, NC, 2006—. Adv. bd. Substance Abuse & Traumatic Brain Injury Linking Svcs., Fairmont, NC, 2005—06. Recipient Tchg. Excellence award, Jiffy Lube, 2005. Mem.: NEA, Assn. Counselor Edn. and Supervision, Assn. Specialists Group Work, Internat. Assn. Marriage & Family Counselors, Am. Counseling Assn. Office: Southeastern Psychol Svcs 302 N Main Fairmont NC 28340 Personal E-mail: dr_melissajspencer@yahoo.com.

SPENCER, MELVIN JOE, retired health facility administrator, lawyer, consultant; b. Buffalo Center, Iowa, Jan. 2, 1923; s. Kenos W. and Jennie (Michaelson) S.; m. Dena Joyce Butterfield, Mar. 1, 1952; children: Dennis Norman, Gregory Melvin, Shelly Lynn Spencer Goodnight. AB, U. Mich., 1948, JD, 1950. Bar: Iowa 1950, Mo. 1950, Okla. 1961. Practiced in, Kansas City, Mo., 1950-61, Oklahoma City, 1961—; assoc., then ptnr. Watson, Ess, Marshall & Enggas, 1950-61; ptnr. Miller & Spencer (and predecessor firm), 1961-75, of counsel, 1975-80; adminstr. Deaconess Hosp., 1975-92, cons., 1992-93; ret., 1993. Dir. Union Bank & Trust Co., Oklahoma City, 1977-88, 89-96, adv. dir., 1996-99; dir., sec. Hosp. Casualty Co., 1977-92; dir., treas. VHA Okla., Inc., 1986-92 Assoc. editor Mich. Law Rev., 1949-50. Mcpl. judge City of Roeland Park, Kans., 1952, city coun., 1954; area Rep. precinct chmn., 1968-69; del. Rep. State Conv., 1968, 96; bd. dir. Deaconess Hosp., Oklahoma City, 1966-2005, Christian Counseling Ctr., 1973-75, Witteman Corp., 2005-07, Butterfield Meml. Found., 2005—; trustee Okla. Hosp. Assn., 1978-84, chmn. bd. trustees, 1983, trustee Okla. Co. Med. Soc. Found., 2002—; trustee, vice chmn. bd. dir. Ctrl. Coll., McPherson, Kans., 1972-86; trustee Okla. Ambulance Trust, 1984-87; adv. bd. Okla. State U. Tech. Inst., 1980-92; bd. dir. Emergency Med. Svcs. Ctrl. Okla., 1975-78, FMC Ministries, Inc.; const. coun. Free Meth. Ch. World Fellowship, 1975-95; chmn. Free Meth. Found., 1988-99; gen. counsel Free Meth. Ch. N.Am., 1969-95, bd. adminstrn., 1969-99, sec., 1985-95, investment com., 1976-88, chmn. investment com., 1986-88. Capt. USAAF, 1943-46 Named Layman of Yr., Free Meth. Ch. N.Am., 1984; recipient W. Cleveland Rodgers Disting. Svc. award Okla. Hosp. Assn., 1985; fellow Cen. Coll. Acad. of Achievers, 1990. Mem. Okla. Bar Assn., Oklahoma County Bar Assn., Order of Coif, Phi Beta Kappa, Phi Kappa Phi Home: 5910 N Shawnee Ave Oklahoma City OK 73112-1627

SPENCER, MICHAEL C., lawyer; b. Sept. 10, 1951; BA magna cum laude, Yale U., 1973; JD cum laude, Harvard Law Sch., 1976. Bar: N.Y. 1978, Calif. 1978. Law clk. to Hon. William Matthew Byrne, Jr. U.S. Dist. Ct. (cen. dist.) Calif., LA, 1976-77; assoc. atty. Cravath, Swaine & Moore, NYC, 1977-86; assoc. Milberg LLP, NYC, 1986—87, ptnr., 1987—. Office: Milberg LLP 1 Pennsylvania Plz 49th Fl New York NY 10119 Office Phone: 212-946-9450. Office Fax: 212-273-4395. Business E-Mail: mspencer@milberg.com.

SPENCER, ROGER FELIX, psychiatrist, educator; b. Apr. 19, 1934; came to U.S., 1941; s. Eugene S. Spitzer and Santa Spencer; m. Barbara Ann Houser, Aug. 18, 1958; children: Geoffrey, Jennifer, Rebecca. BS, Yale Coll., 1956; MD, Harvard Med. Sch., 1959. Diplomate Am. Bd. Psychiatry. Intern N.C. Meml. Hosp., Chapel Hill, 1959-60, resident in psychiatry, 1960-63; instr. U. N.C. Sch. Medicine, Chapel Hill, 1963-66, asst. prof., 1966-69, assoc. prof., 1969-76, prof., 1976—. Dir. of liaison and cons., U. N.C., 1967-77, dir. out patient psychiatry, 1977-95. Contbr. articles to profl. jours.;, author short stories. Recipient Career Tchr. award NIMH, 1965-67. Fellow Am. Psychiat. Assn. (life), Am. Psychoanalytic Assn.; mem. N.C. Psychoanalytic Soc. (past pres.), N.C. Psychiat. Assn. (past pres.). Office: UNC Hosps Dept Psychiatry CB 7160 Chapel Hill NC 27599-7160 Home Phone: 919-929-6192; Office Phone: 919-966-5772. Office Fax: 919-843-6102. Business E-Mail: roger_spencer@med.unc.edu.

SPENCER, ROGER WAYNE, economics professor; b. Lynchburg, Va., Feb. 4, 1939; s. Emmet Snead and Roxie Boyd Spencer; m. Susan Kay Spencer; children: Kara Lynn Payne, Jeffrey Lee, Tanya Kay, Matthew Jay. PhD, U. Va., Charlottesville, 1969. Sr. economist Fed. Res. Bank St. Louis, 1968—76; rsch. chief, economics Securities & Exch. Commn., Washington, 1978—79; dean, bus. and adminstrv. divsn. Trinity U., San Antonio, 1980—85, Vernon Taylor prof., economics, 2008—. Contbr. articles. Chmn. SEC Transition Team, Washington, 1980. Ret. capt. US Army, 1962—65, Germany. Home: 356 Long Meadow Spring Branch TX 78070 Office: Trinity Univ 1 Trinity Pl San Antonio TX 78212 Business E-Mail: rspencer@trinity.edu.

SPENCER, TRICIA JANE, writer; b. Springfield, Ill., Dec. 8, 1952; d. Frank Edward and LaWanda (Edwards) Bell; m. Mark Edward Spencer, Aug. 21, 1982. Student pub. schs. Instr. Falcons Drum & Bugle Corps, Springfield, 1969-72; concert, stage, TV performer, 1970-82; guest dir. Sing Out, Salem, Ohio, 1973; legal sec. to pvt. atty. Tustin, Calif., 1980-82; owner Am. Dream Balloons & Svcs., Orange, Calif., 1982-89; founder, corp. pres. Am. Dream Limousine Svc., Inc., Orange, 1983-90; founder, designer Am. Dream Creations Co., Inc., Irvine, Calif., 1988—96; founder Am. Dream Bride's Mus., 1992; established Lilac Bloom Press, Riverside, Calif., 2002. Designer greeting cards, t-shirts, wedding related gifts, one-of-a-kind automobile; mediator Limousine and Chauffeur Coun., Orange County, 1984-85. Author: TIPS - The Server's Guide to Bringing Home the Bacon, 1987 (Winner 1999 Best Non-Fiction Book S.W. Writers Workshop Ann. Competition 1999), There's a Bunny in the House, 1992, Real Rabbitts Don't Eat Lettuce, 1992, Elysium, 1996, Miracle Man, 1997, (winner Cloak and Dagger Mystery Short Story Contest, 2005), Deviled Eggs, 1998 (winner L. Ron Hubbard's Writer's of the Future Competition for Sci. Fiction award 2000, Winner Crossquarter Publish Competition 2002), Tourist Attraction, 2004, Shamrock, 2004, DMV, 2004, Brave Destiny, 2005, Noses, Toes and Elbows, 2005 (winner Scribes Valley Publ. Short Story Competition, 2005), Once Upon an eBay Moon, 2005, Rush Hour, 2007, Empty Shoes (Winner Scribes Valley Short Story Competition, 2008), Miss Galaxy, 2008, Beauty, 2008; performer Up With People, 1972-73; contbr. Saddle Tramps Wild West Revue, 1977-79, Spirit Prayers for Joyfulliving, 2007, Empty Shoes(Scribes Valleypubl Short Story award) Organizer Bicentennial Com. Springfield, 1976; vol. Orange County Performing Arts Soc. Recipient Appreciation, Achievement awards Muscular Dystrophy Assn., 1977-79, Transp. Partnership award, 1988, 7 songwriting and vocal performance awards Music City Song Festival, 1989, Outstanding Booth Display award Chgo. Gift Show, 1991; named one of top 10 Bridal Cos. Assn. Bridal Cons. Mem. Greenpeace, World Wildlife Fedn., Nature Conservancy. Avocations: music, writing. Business E-Mail: zenword@aol.com.

SPENCER, VICKI CAROL, elementary school educator; d. Harvey Leon and Linda Carol Spencer. BS in Edn., Lamar U., Beaumont, Tex., 1982. Tchr. Pt. Arthur Ind. Sch. Dist., 1982—87, Waco Ind. Sch. Dist., Tex., 1987—. Home: 2736 Lake Shore Dr Apt 2601 Waco TX 76708

SPENCER, VIVIAN L., gallery director; BA in Art Edn., U. West Fla., Pensacola; MFA, Md. Inst. Coll. Art, Balt. Profl. tchg. cert. Fla. Chair, instr., art dept. Washington HS, 1984—2001; edn. curator Pensacola Mus. Art, 2001—03; exec. dir. Belmont Arts and Cultural Ctr., 2003—05; gallery dir. Pensacola Jr. Coll., 2005—. Adj. prof. Pensacola Jr. Coll., 1997—, U. West Fla., 2003—05; vis. artist, Hagiwara, Japan, 1998, Hagiwara, 2000. Contbr. articles to profl. jours. Vol. Big Brothers and Big Sisters, Belmont Arts and Cultural Ctr., Arts Coun. Northwest Fla. Recipient Centerstage award, Arts Coun. Northwest Fla., 1999, Edna Rivers Humanitarian award, Washington HS, 2000. Mem.: Fla. Arts in Edn., Fla. Art Edn. Assn., Nat. Art Edn. Assn., Alpha Delta Kappa. Office: Anna Lamar Switzer Ctr for Visual Arts Pensacola Jr Coll 1000 College Blvd Pensacola FL 32504 Office Phone: 850-484-2048. Office Fax: 850-484-2564. Business E-Mail: vspencer@pjc.edu.

SPENCER, WILLIAM EDWIN, retired telecommunications industry executive, engineer; b. Mar. 22, 1926; s. Erwin Blanc and Edith Marie (Peterson) S.; m. Ferne Arlene Nieder, Nov. 14, 1952; children: Elizabeth Ann, Gary William, James Richard, Catherine Sue. Student, U. Kansas City, 1942; AS, Kansas City Jr. Coll., 1945; BSEE, U. Mo., 1948; postgrad., Iowa State U., 1969. Registered profl. engr., Kans. With Southwestern Bell Telephone Co., Kansas City, Mo., 1948-50, Topeka, 1952-61, sr. engr., 1966-69, equipment maintenance engr., 1967-76, engring. ops. mgr., 1976-79, dist. mgr., 1979—86, ret., 1986. Mem. tech. staff Bell Telephone Labs., N.Y.C., 1961-62, Holmdel, N.J., 1962-66; pres., owner W.E. Spencer Co.; mem. U.S. Senatorial Club, 1985—. Patentee in field. Mem. Rep. Presdl. Task Force, 1984—; supervising judge Shawnee County Election Commn.; trustee, bd. dirs. Brookwood Covenant Ch., also pres. Joy Sr. Group. With AUS, Pentagon, Washington, 1950-52. Recipient Best Kans. Idea award Southwestern Bell Telephone Co., 1972, cert. of appreciation Kans. Miss Teen Pageant, 1984, Rep. Presdl. League of Merit, 1992—. Mem. IEEE, NSPE, Kans. Engring. Soc., Topeka Engrs. Club (pres.), Telephone Pioneers Assn. (life mem., rep., Sunflower and Heartland chpt., Topeka life mem., coun. pres. and club pres.), Nat. Geog. Soc., Kans. Hist. Soc., Am. Assn. Ret. Persons, U. Mo.-Columbia Alumni Assn., Nat. Travel Club, Topeka Geog. Soc., Active Prime Timer (historian). Republican. Home: 3201 SW Macvicar Ct Topeka KS 66611-1800 Office: 220 SE 6th Ave Topeka KS 66603-3507 Home Phone: 785-266-4236.

SPENDER, PHILIP G., automotive executive; b. New Zealand; Cert. in engring., Ctrl. Inst. Tech., New Zealand; grad., Grad. Sch. Mgmt., Melbourne U., Australia; doctorate in bus. adminstrn. (hon.), Burkes U. With Ford New Zealand, 1975—85, Ford Australia, 1985—98; mng. dir., CEO Mahindra Ford, India, 1998—2001; pres., CEO Auto Alliance Internat., 2001—05, Chang'an Ford (now Chang'an Ford Mazda Automobile Co.), China, 2005; COO Ford Motor (China) Ltd.; exec. v.p. Mazda Motor Corp., 2008—; v.p. Ford Motor Co., 2008—. Office: Ford Motor Co PO Box 6248 Dearborn MI 48126*

SPENIK, JAMES L., research scientist; b. Mogantown, W.Va., Mar. 5, 1958; s. John L. and Frances Spenik; 1 child, Katheryn. BSAE, W.Va. U., Morgantown, 1980; MSME, W.Va. U., 1989, PhD, 1998. Cert. profl. engr., W.Va., 1989. Rsch. engr. REM Engring., Morgantown, 2000—, USDOE, Morgantown, 1998—2000. Contbr. articles to profl. jours. Mem.: ASME. Achievements include patents pending for probe for detection of anomalies in buried plastic natural gas pipelines. Home: 486 Brookhaven Rd Morgantown WV 26508 Office: Nat Energy Tech Lab PO Box 880 Morgantown WV 26507 Personal E-mail: jamspn9@aol.com. Business E-Mail: spenik@re.netl.doe.gov.

SPENNER, RICHARD LEE, media specialist; m. Jill C. Spenner; children: Allison, Emily. BA in Theatre, Ind. U., Bloomington, 1981, BS in Edn., 1982, MLS, 1983. Cert. in tchg. Ind., 1983. Elem. media specialist Huntington County Cmty. Sch. Corp., Ind., 1983—87, HS drama & english media specialist, 1987—. Office: Huntington N HS 450 Mc Gahn St Huntington IN 46750 Business E-Mail: rspenner@hccsc.k12.in.us.

SPENSER, IAN DANIEL, chemistry professor; b. Vienna, June 17, 1924; m. Anita Fuchs, Sept. 5, 1951; children: Helen Ruth, Paul Andrew. BSc with honors, U. Birmingham, Eng., 1948; PhD in Biochemistry, U. London, 1952, DSc in Organic and Biochemistry, 1969; DSc (hon.), McMaster U., 2004. Demonstrator in biochemistry King's Coll., U. London, 1948-52, asst. lectr. in biochemistry Med. Coll. St. Bartholomew's Hosp., 1952-54, lectr., 1954-57; postdoctoral fellow div. pure chemistry NRC Can., Ottawa, Ont., 1953-54; asst. prof. biochemistry McMaster U., Hamilton, Ont., Can., 1957-59, assoc.prof., 1959-64, prof., 1964-68, prof. chemistry, 1968-89, prof. emeritus, 1989—; Akademischer Gast Laboratorium für Organische Chemie/Eidgenössische Technische Hochschule, Zürich, Switzerland, 1971, 89; vis. prof. Inst. Organic Chemistry, Tech. U. Denmark, Lyngby, 1977, Inst. Organische Chemie/Univ. Karlsruhe, Fed. Republic Germany, 1981, Institut für Pharmazeutische Biologie, Universität Bonn, Federal Republic of Germany, 1989. Research in biosynthesis of alkaloids, biosynthesis of vitamin B1 and vitamin B6 Recipient Sr. Scientist award NATO, 1980; recipient Can.-Japan Exchange award, 1982-83, Univ. Club of Hamilton award, 1990. Fellow Royal Soc. Can., Chem. Inst. Can. (John Labatt Ltd. award 1982-83, R.U. Lemieux award 2005), Royal Soc. Chemistry (U.K.); mem. Biochem. Soc., Am. Soc. Biochemistry Molecular Biology, Am. Soc. Pharmacognosy, Phytochem. Soc. N. Am. Office: McMaster U Dept Chemistry Hamilton ON Canada L8S 4M1 Business E-Mail: spenser@mcmaster.ca.

SPERA, DOMINIC GREGORIO, music educator, writer; b. Kenosha, Wis., Apr. 18, 1932; s. Costanzo and Anita Spera; m. Patty Jean Graber, Jan. 22, 1956; children: Gregory Allen, Mark Christopher. MusB in Edn., Ind. U., 1967, MusB in Trumpet, 1967, MusM in Edn., 1968. Bandsman U.S. Army, Fort Sheridan, Ill., 1953—56; profl. musician NYC, 1957—67; dir. of instrumental music U. Jr. and Sr. HS, Bloomington, Ind., 1967—68; prof. of music U. of Wis., Eau Claire, Wis., 1968—77; prof. of music Sch. Music Ind. U., Bloomington, 1977—97, prof. emeritus Sch. Music, 1997—. Profl. trumpet player various TV shows, NYC, 1958—66, Radio City, NYC, 1958—66, City and Roxy Theaters, Bands of Lionel Hampton, Charlie Barnet, Benny Goodman, Tito Puente, Tommy Dorsey Bands, NYC, 1958—66; profl. trumpet player with Burt Bacharach, Johnny Mathis, Henry Mancini, Andy Williams, Frank Sinatra, International Locations, 1966—92. Composer: (songs) more than 100 pub. compositions; author: Blues and the Basics, Making the Changes, 1973, Take the Lead, 1981, Stretching Out, 1985; trumpet soloist and composer (albums) Yamaha Trumpet Series, trumpet soloist, composer, producer Make a Joyful Noise, Chops Don't Fail Me Now; trumpet soloist, composer, producer: albums Dominic Spera Big Band, soloist, condr., edn. dir.: Hawaii Internat. Jazz Festival, 1997—2000, guest soloist, clinician: Jazz Festival, 2003, soloist, guest lectr.: Escuela de Música, 2008; composer: Dominic Spera Writes for the Brass Quintet, 2005; arranger: CD Dominic Spera Presents the American Popular Songbook for Brass Quintet, 2006. Dir. Eau Claire (Wis.) Jazz Festival, 1968—77; founder, dir. U. Alta. Summer Jazz Camp-, Edmonton, Alberta, Canada, 1979—2002, Bloomington (Ind.) Jazz Festival, 1981—2002. Pvt. first class US Army, 1953—56. Recipient awards, 19 US States, Can., and Australia, 1968—2002, Outstanding Svc. award, Internat. Assn. of Jazz Educators, 1974, 1982; grantee, NEA, 1976. Mem.: Internat. Trumpet Guild (life), Internat. Assn. of Jazz Educators (life), Music Educators Nat. Conf. (life). Achievements include first to publish jazz composition utilizing the 12 tone system of composition introduction and allegro for jazz ensemble and percussion; publish theme and variations for jazz ensemble. Avocations: painting, travel. Home and Office: 3704 Grasstree Ct Bloomington IN 47401

SPERBER, ALAN B., urologist; s. Fred and Liselotte Sperber; m. Elizabeth Ann Pinck, June 6, 1982. BA, NYU, NYC, 1963, MD, 1967. Diplomate Am. Bd. Urology, 1977. Surg. intern Albert Einstein Coll. Medicine, Bronx, 1967—68, surg. resident, 1968—69; urology resident NYU Med. Ctr., 1971—75; attending physician Bellevue Hosp., 1975—78; asst. attending urologist NYU Med. Ctr., 1978—2008, vis. staff physician, dept. urology, 2008—; clin. assoc. prof. urology NYU Sch. Medicine, 1992—. Contbr. articles to profl. jours. Maj. US Army, 1969—71, Vietnam. Fellow: ACS; mem.: Am. Urol. Assn. Avocations: classical music, skiing, hiking, sports, reading. Home: 250 W 94th St Apt 7-B New York NY 10025

SPERBER, MARTIN, pharmaceutical company executive, pharmacist; b. NYC, Aug. 6, 1931; s. David and Gertrude (Besen) S.; m. Ellen Claire Marx, June 7, 1953; children— Steven Jay, Susan Barbara Parnes. BS, Columbia U., NYC, 1952. Registered pharmacist. Pharmacist, dir. sales and mktg. Henry Schein, Inc., NYC, 1953-65, v.p., 1965-80, pres., COO Melville, NY, 1980-89, vice chmn., 1989-93, also bd. dirs.; pres., COO Schein Pharm., Inc., Florham Park, NJ, 1985-89, chmn., chief exec. officer, 1989—, chmn., CEO, pres., also bd. dirs.; chmn., CEO Danbury Pharm. Inc. (owned by Schein Pharm., Inc.), Carmel, NY, 1989—, also bd. dirs.; chmn., CEO Schein Pharm. Inc., Phoenix, 1989—; also bd. dirs. Steris Labs., Inc. (owned by Schein Pharm., Inc.), Phoenix. Mem. coun. of overseers Arnold and Marie Schwartz Coll. Pharmacy, L.I. U.; bd. dirs. Am. Found. for Pharm. Edn. Mem. Am. Pharm. Assn. Office: Watson Pharma Inc PO Box 1953 Morristown NJ 07962-1953

SPERBER, WILLIAM HENRY, microbiologist, writer; b. Sturgeon Bay, Wis., Feb. 15, 1941; s. Archibald Valentine and Doris Estelle (Kath) Sperber; m. Renate Linda Wolf, Apr. 13, 1963; children: Linda Christine, Trent William. BS, U. Wis., Madison, 1964, MS, 1967, PhD, 1969. Mgr., microbiology & chemistry CPC Internat., Waltham, Mass., 1969—70; mgr. microbiology Best Foods, Union, NJ, 1970—72; dir. microbiology & food safety The Pillsbury Co., Mpls., 1972—95; sr. corp. microbiologist Cargill, Inc, Minnetonka, Minn., 1995—; secretariat Safe Supply of Affordable Food Everywhere, Inc., St. Paul, 2006—08. Cons. Solar Cookers Internat., Sacramento, 1984—95. Contbr. articles to profl. jours., chapters to books. Creator William H. and Renate L. Sperber Undergrad. Scholarship Endowment, U. Wis., Madison, 2007; donor numerous ednl., artistic and environ. orgns.; nat. adv. com. mem. Microbiological Criteria for Foods, 1990—96, 1998—2002; exec. com. mem. Noordwijk HACCP & Food Safety Forums, 1997—2002, Nat. Acad. Sci. Coms., 2008—. Hosp. corpsman USN Res., 1959—65, Madison. Recipient Harold Barnum Industry award, Internat. Assn. Food Protection, 2001, Scientific Achievement award, Am. Meat Inst., 2002, Disting. Svc. award, Food Safety Magazine, 2004; named W.C. Frazer Meml. Lectr., Food Rsch. Inst., U. Wis., 2004, John H. Silliker Lectr., Internat. Assn. Food Protections, 2006. Mem.: Food Microbiology Rsch. Conf. (chmn. 1987—91), Inst. Food Technologists (chmn. food microbiology divsn. 1986), Am. Soc. Microbiology, Internat. Assn. Food Protection, Phi Eta Sigma. Liberal. Achievements include patents for related to food processing. Avocations: music, writing, reading, fitness training, travel. Home: 5814 Oakview Cir Minnetonka MN 55345 Personal E-mail: brsperber@comcast.net.

SPERELAKIS, NICHOLAS, SR., retired physiology and biophysics educator, researcher; b. Joliet, Ill., Mar. 3, 1930; s. James and Aristea (Kayaidakis) S.; m. Dolores Martinis, Jan. 28, 1960; children: Nicholas Jr., Mark (dec.), Christine, Sophia, Thomas, Anthony. BS in Chemistry, U. Ill., 1951, MS in Physiology, 1955, PhD in Physiology, 1957. Cert. in electronics, radio and radar US Navy & Marine Corps Electronics Sch., 1952. Tchg. asst. U. Ill., Urbana, 1954-57; instr. Case Western Res. U., Cleve., 1957-59, asst. prof., 1959-66, assoc. prof., 1966; prof. U. Va., Charlottesville, 1966-83; Joseph Eichberg prof. physiology Coll. Medicine U. Cin., 1983-96, chmn. dept., 1983-93, Eichberg prof. emeritus, 1996—. Cons. NPS Pharm., Inc., Salt Lake City, 1988-95, Carter Wallace, Inc. Cranbury, N.J., 1988-91; vis. prof. U. St. Andrews, Scotland, 1972-73, U. San Luis Potosi, Mex., 1986, U. Athens, Greece, 1994; Rosenblueth prof. Centro de Investigacion y Avanzades, Mex., 1972; mem. sci. adv. com. several internat. meetings, editl. bds. numerous sci. jours. Co-editor: Handbook of Physiology: Heart, 1979; editor: Physiology and Pathophysiology of the Heart, 1984, 2d edit., 1988, 3rd edit., 1994, 4th edit., 2000, Calcium Antagonists: Mechanisms of Action on Cardiac Muscle and Vascular Smooth Muscle, 1984, Cell Interactions and Gap Junctions, vols. I and II, 1989, Frontiers in Smooth Muscle Research, 1990, Ion Channels in Vascular Smooth Muscle and Endothelial Cells, 1991, Essentials of Physiology, 1993, 2d edit., 1996, Cell Physiology Source Book, 1995 (Outstanding Acad. Book, Choice Am. Libr. Assn. 1996, 98), 3d edit., 2001, Electrogenesis of Biopotentials, 1995; assoc. editor Circulation Rsch., 1970-75, 75-80, Molecular Cellular Cardiology; regional editor Current Drug Targets, 2000-02; contbr. more than 500 articles to profl. jours. Lectr. Project Hope, Peru, 1962. Sgt. USMC, 1951—53, Korean War, with USMCR, 1953—59. Recipient Disting. Alumnus award Rockdale (Ill.) Pub. Schs., 1958, Rsch. Excellence award Am. Heart Assn. Ohio, 1995, Visionary award Am. Heart Assn., S.W. Ohio, 1996; U. Cin. Grad. fellow, 1989; NIH grantee, 1959-99. Mem. IEEE, Engring. in Medicine and Biology, Am. Physiol. Soc. (chair steering com. sect. 1981-82), Biophys. Soc. (coun. 1990-93), Am. Soc. Pharmacology and Exptl. Therapeutics, Internat. Soc. Heart Rsch. (coun. 1980-89, 92-98), Am. Hellenic Ednl. Progressive Assn. (pres. Charlottesville chpt. 1980-82), Ohio Physiol. Soc. (pres. 1990-91), Phi Kappa Phi. Independent. Greek Orthodox. Avocations: ancient Greek coins, stamp collecting/philately. Personal E-mail: nicksperel@aol.com.

SPERGEL, IRVING ABRAHAM, social worker, researcher; b. NYC, Jan. 17, 1924; s. Julius and Frieda Mann Spergel; m. Bertha Jampel Spergel, June 27, 1949 (dec. Nov. 1989); children: Barry Alexander, Mark Jonathan, Daniel Jeremy; m. Annot Mary McGiffin, Oct. 5, 1996. BSS, CCNY, 1946; MA, Columbia U., NYC, 1948, PhD in Social Work, 1960; MSW, U. Ill., 1952. Program asst. YM-YWHA, Wilmington, Del., 1948—49; gang worker, supr. NYC, 1950, 1952; ct. rep. Youth Bd., NYC, 1954, 1958, 1960; dir. Neighbors United St. Club project Lenox Hill Neighborhood House, NYC, 1954—57; from asst. to assoc. prof. U. Chgo., 1960—66, prof., 1967—92, George Herbert Jones prof., 1993—2002, George Herbert Jones prof. emeritus, 2002—. UN youth adv. Hong Kong Govt., 1970—71; external examiner social work Chung Chi Coll., 1978—97; cons. Hong Kong Coun. Social Svc., 1978—97; cons., rschr. in field. Author: Racketville, Slumtown, Haulberg, 1964, Street Gang Work, 1966, Community Problem Solving, 1969, The Youth Gang Problem: A Community Approach, 1995, Reducing Youth Gang Violence, 2007. Mem. Ill. Gov.'s Commn. on Gangs, 1995—96, Nat. Youth Gang Adv. Com., Boys and Girls Clubs Am., 1989—91; mem. acad. adv. com. Ill. Criminal Justice Info. Authority, 1989—. With US Army, 1943—46, ETO. Grantee, Ford Found., 1960, NIMH, 1960—61, US Dept. Justice, 1987—2003. Jewish. Office: U Chgo Sch Social Svc Adminstrn 969 E 60th St Chicago IL 60637 Office Phone: 773-702-1134. Business E-Mail: iasperge@uchicago.edu.

SPERLING, GENE B., economist, former federal official; b. Ann Arbor, Mich., 1958; m. Allison Abner Sperling. B summa cum laude, U. Minn.; student, Wharton Bus. Sch.; JD, Yale U. Econ. adv. to Gov. State of NY, Albany, 1990—92; dep. dir. econ. policy for presdl. transition & econ. policy dir. Clinton/Gore Campaign, 1992—93; dep. asst. to Pres. for econ. policy The White House, 1993—96, asst. to Pres. for econ. policy, 1997—2001; dep. dir. Nat. Econ. Coun., 1993—97, dir., 1997—2001; sr. fellow econ. studies, dir. Ctr. for Universal Edn. Coun. on Foreign Rels. Keynote spkr. UN World Edn. Forum, Dakar, Senegal, 2000; mem. edn. expert group Global Governance Initiative World Econ. Forum, 2003—04; sr. fellow econ. policy Ctr. for Am. Progress; US chair Global Campaign for Edn.; mem. FTI Task Team on Edn. in Fragile States; mem. adv. bd. Gates Found./Hewlett Partnership on Quality Edn.; gov. Phila. Stock Exchange Bd. Author: The Pro-Growth Progressive: An Economic Strategy for Shared Prosperity, 2005; contbg. editor, columnist: Bloomberg News, former cons., contbg. writer: TV series The West Wing. Adviser Senator Hillary Clinton's Presdl. Campaign. Office: Coun on Foreign Rels 58 E 68th St New York NY 10021 Office Phone: 212-434-9400. Office Fax: 212-434-9800. E-mail: gsperling@cfr.org.*

SPERLING, GEORGE, psychologist, educator; s. Otto and Melitta Sperling BS in Math., U. Mich., 1955; MA in Psychology, Columbia U., 1956; PhD in Psychology, Harvard U., 1959. Rsch. asst. in biophysics Brookhaven Nat. Labs., Upton, NY, summer 1955; rsch. asst. in psychology Harvard U., Cambridge, Mass., 1957-59; mem. tech. rsch. staff Acoustical and Behavioral Rsch. Ctr., AT&T Bell Labs., Murray Hill, NJ, 1958-86; prof. psychology and neural sci. NYU, NYC, 1970-92; disting. prof. cognitive scis., neurobiology and behavior U. Calif., Irvine, 1992—. Instr. psychology Washington Sq. Coll., NYU, 1962-63; vis. assoc. prof. psychology Duke U., spring 1964; adj. assoc. prof. psychology Columbia U., 1964-65; acting assoc. prof. psychology UCLA, 1967-68; hon. rsch. assoc. Univ. Coll., U. London, 1969-70; vis. prof. psychology U. Western Australia, Perth, 1972, U. Wash., Seattle, 1977; vis. scholar Stanford (Calif.) U., 1984; mem. sci. adv. bd. USAF, 1988-92. Recipient Meritorious Civilian Svc. medal USAF, 1993; Gomberg scholar U. Mich., 1953-54; Guggenheim fellow, 1969-70, APS fellow. Fellow: APA (Disting. Sci. Contbn. award 1988), AAAS, Am. Psychol. Soc. (William James fellow), Optical Soc. Am. (Tillyer award 2002), Am. Acad. Arts and Sci.; mem.: NAS, Internat. Neural Network Soc. (founding mem., mem. governing bd. 1987—91, Helmholtz award 2004), Soc. Math. Psychology (exec. bd. 1979—85, chmn. 1983—84), Soc. Exptl. Psychologists (Warren medal 1996), Psychonomic Soc., Soc. Computers in Psychology (steering com. 1974—78), Eastern Psychol. Assn. (bd. dirs. 1982—85), Ann. Interdisciplinary Conf. (organizer 1975—, founder), Assn. Rsch. in Vision and Ophthalmology, Sigma Xi, Phi Beta Kappa. Office: U Calif SS Plz A Dept Cognitive Scis Irvine CA 92697-5100 E-mail: sperling@uci.edu.

SPERLING, GODFREY, JR., retired journalist; b. Long Beach, Calif., Sept. 25, 1915; s. Godfrey and Ida (Bailey) Sperling; m. Betty Louise Feldmann, June 22, 1942; children: Mary McAuliffe, John Godfrey. BS, U. Ill., 1937; JD, U. Okla., 1940. Bar: Ill. 1940. Pvt. practice, Urbana, Ill.; reporter Champaign-Urbana News-Gazette, 1940-41; mem. staff Christian Sci. Monitor, 1946—2005, Midwest bur. chief, 1957-62, N.Y. bur. chief, 1962-65, news mgr., asst. chief Washington bur., 1965-73, nat. polit. corr., 1970-83, chief Washington Bur., 1973-83, sr. Washington columnist, 1971—2005; ret. Served to maj. USAF, 1941—46, col. USAF Res., 1960—. Recipient Alumni Achievement award, U. Ill., 1987, Spl. citation, Nat. Press Found. for unique contbn. Am. journalism, 1994; named Alumni Hall Of Fame, U. Ill., 2008; fellow, Woodrow Wilson Found., 1976—; Sperling Journalism fellow, U. Ill., 2003. Mem.: Fort Myer Officers Club, Overseas Writers Club (Washington), Nat. Press Club (Washington), White House Press Corr. Assn., Congl. Press Corr. Assn., Mass. Bar Assn., Ill. Bar Assn., Okla. Bar Assn., Sperling Breakfast Group (host 1966—2001), Cosmos Club (Washington), Gridiron Club Washington (pres. 1991), Sigma Delta Chi. Christian Scientist. Home: Knollwood 6200 Oregon Ave NW Apt 108 Washington DC 20015-1530

SPERLING, JOHN GLEN, educational services company executive; b. Willow Springs, Mo., Jan. 9, 1921; s. Leon Birchfield and Lena (McNama) S.; m. Virginia Vandergrift, June 1951 (div. 1965); 1 child, Peter Vandegrift. BA, Reed Coll., 1948; MA, U. Calif., 1952; PhD, U. Cambridge, Eng., 1955. Mem. faculty Northern Ill. U.; instr. U. Md., Europe, 1955-57; asst. professor Ohio State U., Columbus, 1957—61; prof. Humanities San Jose (Calif.) State U., 1961—73, dir., Right to Read Project, dir., NSF Cooperative Coll.-Sch. Sci. Prog in Econ.; pres. Inst. Profl. Devel., San Jose, 1972-76; founder, pres. U. Phoenix, 1976-80; founder, dir. Apollo Group Inc., Phoenix, 1973—, pres., 1973—98, CEO, 1973—2001, chmn., 1973—2004, acting exec. chmn., 2006—08, exec. chmn., 2008—. Author: The South Sea Company, 1964, Great Depressions: 1837, 1893, and 1929, 1966, Against All Odds, 1989, Rebel With a Cause: The Entreprenur Who Created the University of Phoenix and the For-Profit Revolution in Higher Education 2000, The Great Divide: Retro vs. Metro America, 2004; co-author: (with Peter Dixon) War Finance 1698-1714, (with Suzanne Helburn) Economic Concepts and Institutions, 1974, Industry Performance, 1974, National Economic Policies, 1974, Social and Economic Priorities, 1974, Communist Economics, 1974, Third World Economics, 1974, (with Robert Tucker) For Profit Higher Education: Developing a World Class Workforce, 1997; contbr. articles to profl. jours. including Hist. Jour., Econ. History Rev., Bull. NASSP, Rule Mag., among others. Cons. Combating Juvenile Delinquency, Sunnyvale, Calif., 1972-75. Recipient Ehrman Studentship, Kings Coll., Cambridge U., 1953-55, Acad. Freedom award Calif. Fedn. Tchrs., L.A., 1988; named of Forbes Richest Americans, 2006. Mem. Arizona Club. Democrat. Founder the U. Phoenix, which has established itself as a leading provider of higher education programs for working adults by focusing on servicing the needs of the working adult; Primary investor in Genetic Savings and Clone, Inc., "Missyplicity Project" (cloned dog) and "Operation CC" (cloned cat that was created was called CopyCat), made first sale: a cloned male kitten, for $50,000 in December, 2004; latest quest: to research, develop, and sell the new science of longevity; opponent of drug prohibition and is actively financing initiatives to legalize medical marijuana in the US. Office: Apollo Group Inc 4615 E Elwood St Phoenix AZ 85040-1958 Office Phone: 480-921-5394.*

SPERLING, REISA A., neurologist, researcher; MD, Harvard U., 1991. Cert. Neurology, 2007. Intern Brigham and Women's Hosp., Boston, 1992, now neurologist; chief resident Longwood Residency Program, Boston; fellowship Harvard Longwood Neurology Training Program, Boston, 1997; dir. clin. rsch., staff physician Memory Disorders Unit Brigham Behavioral Neurology Group, Boston. Recipient award, AAN, Memory Ride award, Alzheimer's Assn.; grantee Am. Acad. Neurology Clin. Rsch. Training Fellowship; fellow Harvard/MIT Clin. Investigator Training Program; scholarship, AFAR Beeson. Office: Brigham Behavioral Neurology Group 221 Longwood Ave Boston MA 02115 Office Phone: 617-732-8060. Office Fax: 617-738-9122. E-mail: rasperling@bics.bwh.harvard.edu.

SPERLING, SHELDON J., prosecutor; m. Marvetta Sperling; 2 children. BA, Northeastern State Coll., 1971; JD, U. Tulsa, 1979. Pvt. practice, Tulsa, 1979—82; asst. dist. atty. Okla. Dist. Atty.'s Office, 1983—85; asst. US atty. (ea. dist.) Okla. US Dept. Justice, 1985—89, 1st asst. US atty., criminal chief, 1989—2000, US atty. (ea. dist.) Okla., 2000—. Mem. Tulsa County Bar Assn., 1979—82, Am. Bar Assn., 1979—86, Okla. Dist. Atty.'s Assn., 1983—85, Nat. Dist. Atty.'s Assn., 1984, Nat. Assn. Asst. US Attorneys, 1994—2001, exec. dir., regional dir., del. Recipient Special Commendations, FBI Dir. William S. Sessions, 1993, FBI Dir. Louis J. Freech, 1998, FBI Dir. Robert S. Mueller III, 2002, Dept. Justice Dir. award, 1994. Mem.: Bar of Northern Dist. Okla., Bar of Eastern Dist. Okla., Phi Rho Pi, Rho Theta Sigma, Delta Theta Phi. Office: US Attys Office 1200 W Okmulgee St Muskogee OK 74401*

SPERO, JOAN EDELMAN, foundation administrator; b. Davenport, Iowa, Oct. 2, 1944; d. Samuel and Sylvia (Halpern) Edelman; m. C. Michael Spero, Nov. 9, 1969; children: Jason, Benjamin. Student, L'Inst. d'Etudes Politiques, Paris, 1964-65; BA in Internat. Rels. with honors, U. Wis., 1966; MA, Columbia U., 1968, PhD, 1973; LLD (hon.), Amherst Coll., 1997. Asst. prof. Columbia U., NYC, 1973-79; amb. of U.S. to UN Econ. and Social Coun., NYC, 1980-81; v.p. Am. Express Co., NYC, 1981-83, sr. v.p. internat. corp. affairs, 1983-89; treas., sr. v.p., 1989-91; exec. v.p. corp. affairs and communications Am. Express Co., 1991-93; under sec. for econ., bus. and agrl. affairs Dept. of State, Washington, 1993-97; pres. Doris Duke Charitable Found., NYC, 1997—. Vis. scholar Fed. Res. Bank NY, 1976—77; bd. dirs. IBM Corp., ING; internat. adv. bd. Toyota Motor Corp.; hon. trustee The Brookings Inst. Author: The Politics of International Economic Relations, 6th edit., 2003, The Failure of the Franklin National Bank, 1980; contbr. articles to profl. jours. Trustee Wis. Alumni Rsch. Found., 1997—, Columbia U., 1998; trustee emeritus Amherst Coll.; bd.dir. Coun. Fgn. Rels.; mem. Coun. Am. Ambs. Recipient Woodrow Wilson fellow. Mem. Am. Acad. Diplomacy, Found. Execs. Group, Coun. on Fgn. Rels. (bd. dirs.), Am. Philos. Soc., Phi Beta Kappa. Democrat. Jewish. Avocations: writing, swimming. Office: Doris Duke Charitable Found 650 5th Ave 19th Fl New York NY 10019-6108 Office Phone: 212-974-7000.

SPERO, NANCY, artist; b. Cleve., 1926; BFA, Sch. Art Inst. Chgo., 1949; student, Ecole des Beaux-Arts, Paris, 1950, Atelier Andre l'Hote, 1950. One-woman shows include Hewlett Gallery, Carnegie-Mellon U., Pitts., 1989, Rhona Hoffman Gallery, Chgo., 1986, 94, Inst. Contemporary Art, London, 1987, Everson Mus. Art, Syracuse, NY, 1987, Mus. Contemporary Art, LA, 1988, Smith Coll. Mus. Art, Northampton, Mass., 1990, Haus am Walsee, Berlin, Germany, 1990, Barbara Gross Galerie, Munich, 1991, 95, 97-98, Salzburger Kunstverein, Austria, 1991, Christine König Gallery, Vienna, Austria, 1992, Ulmer Mus., Ulm, Germany, 1992, Josh Baer Gallery, NYC, 1993, Nat. Gallery Can., Ottowa, 1993, Greenville (SC) County Mus. Art, 1993, Printworks, Chgo., 1994, Kunststichting Kanaal Art Found., Kortrijk, Belgium, 1994, Malmö (Sweden) Konsthall, 1994, Am. Ctr., Paris, MIT List Visual Arts Ctr., Cambridge, 1994, Arthur M. Sackler Mus., Harvard U., 1995, Fine Arts Gallery, U. Md. Baltimore County, 1995, NY Kunsthalle, 1996, Vancouver Art Gallery, 1996, Hiroshima City Mus. Contemporary Art, 1996, Jüdisches Mus. der Stadt Wien, 1996, Heeresspital, Innsbruck, Tyrol, 1996, Jack Tilton Gallery, NYC, 1996, PPOW Gallery, NYC, 1996, Galerie im Taxispalais, Innsbruck, 1996, Elaine C. Jacob Gallery, Wayne State U., Detroit, 1997, Documenta X, Kassel, Germany, 1997, Crown Gallery, Brussels, 1997-98, Ikon Gallery, Birmingham, Eng., 1997-98, Internat. Biennale of Cairo, 1998, Festpielhaus Hellerau, Dresden, 1998, Galerie Montenay-Giroux, Paris, 1998, Barbara Gross Galerie, Munich, 1998, Miami U., Oxford, Ohio, 2000, others; exhibited in group shows at The Biennial of Sydney, Australia, 1986, Mus. Modern Art, NYC, 1988, The Bertha and Karl Leubsdorf Art Gallery, Hunter Coll., NYC, 1988, Le Grande Halle de La Villette, Paris, 1989, Bullet Space, NYC, 1989, Ctr. Internat. d'Art Contemporain, Montreal, 1990, Dum Umeni Mesta Brna, Brünn, Czechoslowakia, 1991, Boston U. Art Gallery, 1991, Mus. der Stadtentwässerung, Zurich, 1994, Stichting Artimo, Beurs van Berlage, Amsterdam, 1994, Sch. Art Inst. Chgo., Betty Rymer Gallery, Chgo., 1994, MIT List Visual Arts Ctr., Cambridge, 1995, Southeastern Ctr. for Contemporary Art, Winston-Salem, NC, 1995, Ctr. Georges Pompidou, Paris, 1995, Uffizi Gallery, Florence, Italy, 1995, Mus. Modern Art, NYC, 1996, Whitney Museum Am. Art, NYC, 1999, Venice Biennale, 2007, numerous others; represented in permanent collections Art Inst. Chgo., Australian Nat. Gallery, Boston Museum of Fine Arts, Brooklyn Museum, NY, Centro Cultural, Mex. City, Frac Nord Pas de Calais, France, Harvard U. Art Museums, Hiroshima City Museum of Contemporary Art, MIT List Visual Arts Ctr., Madison Art Ctr., Musée des Beaux-Arts de Montreal, Nat. Gallery of Canada, Ottowa, Phila. Museum of Art, Museum of Modern Art, NYC, U. Art Museum, Berkeley, Calif., Vancouver Art Gallery, Whitney Museum Am. Art, NYC. Mem.: Am. Acad. Arts and Letters (acad. 2004).*

SPERRY, LEN THOMAS, psychiatrist and preventive medicine educator; b. Milw., Dec. 1, 1943; s. Leonard V. and Wanda R. (Sadowski) S.; m. Patricia L. Garcia, June 11, 1977; children: Tracey, Christen, L. Timothy, Steven, Jonathon. BA, St. Mary's U. Minn., Winona, Minn., 1966; PhD, Northwestern U., 1970; MD, CETEC U., 1981; MA, Loyola U., 1984; D in Ministry, Barry U., 2001. Diplomate Am. Bd. Profl. Psychology, Am. Bd. Psychiatry and Neurology, Am. Bd. Preventive Medicine. Asst. prof. Marquette U., Milw., 1971-74; assoc. prof. U. Wis., Milw., 1974-75, U.S. Internat. U., San Diego, 1976-78; resident in psychiatry and preventive medicine Med. Coll. Wis., Milw., 1982-85; fellow in behavioral medicine U. Wis. Med. Sch., Milw., 1984-85; assoc. prof. psychiatry, preventive medicine Med. Coll. Wis., Milw., 1986-92, prof., 1992-2000, prof. cmty. and family medicine, 1998-2000, vice chair dept. psychiatry, 1997-2000, clin. prof. psychiatry, 2000—; prof. health adminstrn., prof. psychology Barry U., Miami Shores, Fla., 2000—02, dir. doctoral program in counseling, 2003; prof. Fla. Atlantic U., 2003—. Author: Learning Performance and Individual Differences, 1972, Contract Counseling, 1974, You Can Make It Happen: Self-Actualization and Organization, 1977, Together Experience, 1978, Aderian Counseling and Psychotherapy, 1987, Psychiatric Case Formulations, 1992, Psychopathology and Psychotherapy, 1993, 2d edit., 1996, Psychiatric Consultation in the Workplace, 1993, Handbook of Diagnosis and Treatment of DSM-IV Personality Disorders, 1995, Psychopharmacology and Psychotherapy, 1995, Treatment Outcomes in Psychotherapy and Psychiatric Interventions, 1996, Aging in the 21st Century, 1996, Family Therapy: Ensuring Treatment Efficacy, 1997, The Disordered Couple, 1997, The Intimate Couple, 1998, Brief Therapy Strategies with Individuals and Couples, 2000, Ministry and Community, 2000, Integrative and Biopsychosocial Therapies, 2000, Spirituality in Clinical Practice, 2001, Transforming Self and Community, 2002, Effective Leader, 2002, Becoming an Effective Therapist, 2003, Becoming an Effective Health Care Manager, 2003, Sex, Priestly Ministry and the Church, 2003, Executive Coaching, 2004, Spiritually-Oriented Psychotherapy, 2005, Couple and Family Assessment, 2005, Health Promotion and Health Counseling, Couples Therapy (2d edit.), 2005, Family Therapy Techniques, 2005, Cognitive Behavior Therapy of DSM-TR Pesonality Disorders, 2006, Psychological Treatment of Chronic Illness, 2006, The Ethical and Professional Practice of Counseling and Psychotherapy, 2007, Dictionary of Ethical and Legal Terms and Issues, 2007, Treatment Chronic Med. Conditions, 2008, Highly Effective Therapy Developing Essential Clinical Conptency,2009; contbr. articles to profl. jours. Bd. dirs. Am. Coun. on Sci. and Health, Nat. Acad. for Certified Family Therapists, St. Camillus Health Ctr., 1996-2000, Cath. Health Svcs., 2001—; cons. dir. Staff Devel. Am. Appraisal Assn., Milw., 1972-76. Northwestern U. fellow, 1969, Med. Coll. Wis. grantee, 1981. Fellow APA (Harry Levinson award 1998), Am. Psychiat. Assn. (chair com. on psychiatry in workplace 1998—, fellow, 1987-2001, distinguished fellow, 2001-), Am. Coll. Preventive Medicine, Am. Coll. Psychiatrists, Am. Bd. Profl. Psychology, Am. Bd. Psychiatry and Neurology, Acad. Orgnl. and Occupational Psychiatry (v.p. 1993-96, Alan McLean lifetime achievement award 2000), Group for Advancement of Psychiatry, Coalition for Family Diagnosis. Avocations: reading, racquet sports, music. Office: Fla Atlantic U 777 Glades Rd Boca Raton FL 33431 Business E-Mail: lsperry@fau.edu.

SPETH, ANDREW D., legislative staff member; married; 5 children. Chief of staff to Rep. Paul Ryan US House of Reps., Washington. Sr. airman 440th Air Lift Wing USAFR, 2005—06, Operation Iraqi Freedom. Republican. Office: 1113 Longworth House Office Bldg Washington DC 20515 Office Phone: 202-225-3031. Office Fax: 202-225-3393.*

SPETH, JAMES GUSTAVE, dean, environmental studies educator, lawyer; b. Orangeburg, SC, Mar. 4, 1942; s. James Gustave and Amelia St. Clair (Albergotti) S.; m. Caroline Cameron Council, July 3, 1965; children: Catherine Council, James Gustave, Charles Council. BA summa cum laude, Yale U., 1964, LLB, 1969; MLitt, Oxford U., 1966; LLD (hon.), Clark U., 1995; MSE (hon.), Coll. of the Atlantic, 2001; LLD (hon.), Vt. Law Sch., 2005; Degree in Sci. (hon.), Middlebury, Verment. Law clk. to Justice Hugo L. Black U.S. Supreme Ct., 1969-70; sr. staff atty. Natural Resources Def. Council, Washington, 1970-77; mem. Council Environ. Quality, Washington, 1977-79, chmn., 1979-81; prof. law Georgetown U. Law Ctr., Washington, 1981-82; pres. World Resources Inst., Washington, 1982-93; adminstr. UN Devel. Program, NYC, 1993-99; dean, prof. Yale Sch. Forestry and Environ. Studies Yale U., 1999—. Founded World Resources Inst.; organized Western Hemisphere Dialogue environ. and devel., 1990; chaired U.S. Task Force internat. devel. and environ. security. Contbr. articles to profl. jours.; speaker in field. Bd. dirs. World Resources Inst., Nat. Resources Def. Coun Recipient Resources Def. award Nat. Wildlife Fedn., 1976, Barbara Swain award of honor Nat. Resources Coun. Am., 1992, Environ. Law Inst. Lifetime Achievement award, 1999, Blue Planet prize, 2002; named to Global 500 Honor Role UN Environ. Program, 1988; Rhodes scholar, 1964-66. Mem. Coun. on Fgn. Rels. (N.Y.C.), Rockefeller Brothers Fund and Population Action Internat.(bd. mem.) Episcopalian. Home: 986 Forrest Rd New Haven CT 06515-2501 E-mail: gus.speth@yale.edu.

SPEVACK, MARVIN, language educator; b. NYC, Dec. 17, 1927; s. Nathan and Miriam (Propper) S.; m. Helga Husmann, May 28, 1962; 1 child, Edmund Daniel (dec.). BA, CCNY, 1948; MA, Harvard U., 1950, PhD, 1953. Instr. English CCNY, 1955-61; asst. prof. City Coll. N.Y., 1961-63; prof. English, U. Muenster, Germany, 1963-89, dir. English seminar, 1964-89, dir. Inst. Erasmianum, 1974-89; Fulbright lectr. U. Münster, Germany, 1961-62; vis. rsch. fellow Inst. U. London. Vis. prof. U. Munich, 1962-63, NYU, summer 1966, Harvard U., summer 1973, U. N.Mex., 1985-86, Bowling Green State U., fall 1989; fellow Folger Shakespeare Libr., 1970, 98; hon. rsch. fellow Univ. Coll., London, 1980-81, 94—; vis. fellow Wolfson Coll., Cambridge (Eng.) U., 1984; scholar-in-residence Ctr. for Renaissance and Baroque Studies, U. Md., spring 1989; vis. rsch. fellow Inst. for Advanced Studies in Humanities, U. Edinburgh, Scotland, 1991., U. London, 2008, biographers, Shakespearean, comparatist, educator Sydney Lee, 2009. Author: Harvard Concordance to Shakespeare, 1973, A Complete and Systematic Concordance to the Works of Shakespeare, 9 vols., 1968-80, Robert Burton, Philosophaster, 1984, Shakespeare: The second, Third, and Fourth Folios, 1985, New Cambridge Julius Caesar, 1988, Shakespeare-Text, Language and Criticism: Essays in Honor of Marvin Spevack, 1988, New Variorum Antony and Cleopatra, 1990, A Shakespeare Thesaurus, 1993, James Orchard Halliwell- Phillipps: A Classified Bibliography, 1997, A Victorian Chronicle: The Diary of Henrietta Halliwell-Phillipps, 1999, James Orchard Halliwell-Phillipps: The Life and Works of the Shakespearean Scholar and Bookman, 2001, Isaac D'Israeli on Books: Pre-Victorian Essays on the History of Literature, 2004, Curiosities Revisited: The Works of Isaac D'Israeli, 2007; also articles and editions. Served with AUS, 1953-55. Guggenheim fellow, 1973-74, Andrew W. Mellon Found. fellow Huntington Libr., 1992, Ctr. for Book fellow Brit. Libr., London, 1994-95. Mem. MLA, Internat. Assn. Univ. Profs. English, Internat. Shakespeare Assn., The Bibliog. Soc., Deutsche Shakespeare Gesellschaft W., Shakespeare Assn., Harvard Club (N.Y.C.), Harvard of Rhein-Ruhr Club (Germany), Phi Beta Kappa. Home: 14 Potstiege 48161 Münster Germany Office: 12-20 Johannisstrasse 48143 Münster Germany

SPEVAK, ERIC SCOTT, lawyer; b. Syracuse, NY, Feb. 28, 1959; s. Mannie and Sylvia Spevak. BA cum laude, Hobart Coll., 1981; JD, Villanova U. Sch. Law, 1984. Bar: Pa. 1984, NJ 1984. Assoc. Archer & Greiner, P.C., Haddonfield, NJ, 1984-86; ptnr. Gerstein, Cohen Kurtzman & Spevak, P.A., Haddonfield, NJ, 1986-90, Adinolfi & Spevak, P.A., Haddonfield, NJ, 1990—. Instr. NJ Inst. for CLE, 1995—; mem. NJ Dist. IV Ethics Com., 2002-; co-host The Law and You, 1994-1999; cert. divorce mediator, South Jersey Mediation Ctr.; lectr. ATLA, Am. Acad. Matrimonial Lawyers; legal commentator NBC Today Show, CNN, MSNBC News, Fox News with Paula Zahn, ABC Sunday Morning with Wally Kennedy, CNN's The Point with Greta Van Susteran, MSNBC's Hardball with Chris Matthews, Court TV's Catherine Cryer Live, CNN Headline News. Contbr. articles to profl. jours. Head coach Cherry Hill Lightening Boys Soccer, 1997—2001; mgr. Syracuse Sky Chiefs World Series Little League Champions, CHALL, 1999; coach South Jersey Maccabi Girls Soccer, Richmond, 2000, Miami, 2001; chairperson Cherry Hill Twp. Com. Recreation and Veteran's Affairs, 2005; appointed NJ WWII commr., 2006; mayor's liaison vet. affairs Cherry Hill Twp. Recipient Commendation medal, NJ, 2006, Meritorious Svc. medal, 2006, Patrick Henry award, Nat. Guard Assn. US, 2006, Cert. of Appreciation for meritorious pub. svc., NJ Supreme Ct., 2006; named NJ Super Lawyer, NJ Monthly Mag., 2005, 2006—08, Citizen of Yr., Jewish War Vets. USA, Dept. NJ, Inc., 2005, Hon. Comdr., Fort Dix NJ, 2006—, Top Atty., South Jersey Mag., 2006—08, Awesine Atty., 2007—08; named one of Ten Leading Divorce Attys. in So. NJ, Digital Press Internat., 2005, Listed Atty. 10 Leaders, 2005—08. Fellow: Am. Acad. Matrimonial Lawyers; mem.: NJ State Family Law Assn. (exec. com. 1995), Haddonfield Bus. and Profl. Assn. (solicitor/bd. mem. 2000—01), Burlington County Bar Assn. (mem. family law com. bd. dirs. 1993—95, matrimonial early settlement panelist, lectr.), NJ Bar Assn. (mem. family law exec. com. 1994—95), South Jersey Family Law Assn. Inns of Ct. (vice chmn. 1995—2002, v.p. 1997—), Camden County Bar Assn. (trustee 1988—92, co-chairperson family law com. 1989—94, bd. trustees 1989—94, chmn. family law com. 1989—94, co-chair 1999, co-chairperson family law com. 1999—2002, co-chair 2000, bd. trustees 2001—04, sec. 2002—03, chairperson family law com. 2002—, treas. 2003—04, second v.p. 2004—05, first v.p. 2005—06, pres. 2007—, Blue Ribbon panelist, lectr., pres. 2007—08). Avocations: soccer coach, baseball coach, basketball official. Office: Adinolfi & Spevak PA 4 Kings Hwy E Haddonfield NJ 08033-2463 Office Phone: 856-428-8334. Business E-Mail: adinolspev@aol.com, espevak@aandglawyers.com.

SPEYER, JERRY I., real estate company executive; b. June 23, 1940; m. Lynne Tishman, 1987 (div.); children: Valerie, Holly; m. Katherine G. Farley, 1991; 1 child, Laura. BA, Columbia Coll., 1962; MBA, Columbia U., 1964. Co-founder, pres., CEO Tishman Speyer Properties, NYC, 1978—. Chmn. Fed. Res. Bank NY, 2007—; chmn. emeritus Columbia U., Real Estate Board of NY; bd. mem. Siemens AG, Yankees Global Enterprises, Real Estate Roundtable, Urban Land Inst.; mem. Council on Foreign Relations. Vice chmn. Museum of Modern Art, NYC, NY Presbyterian Hospital; co-chair NYC Partnership. Named one of Top 200 Collectors, ARTnews Mag., 2004—08. Mem.: Economic Club of NY. Avocation: Collector of Contemporary Art. Office: Tishmanspeyer Properties 45 Rockefeller Plz Fl 12 New York NY 10111-1299 Office Phone: 212-715-0300.*

SPEYRER, JUDE, bishop emeritus; b. Leonville, La., Apr. 14, 1929; Student, St. Joseph Sem., Covington, La., Notre Dame Sem., New Orleans, Gregorian U., Rome. Ordained priest Diocese of Lafayette, La., 1953; ordained bishop, 1980; bishop Diocese of Lake Charles, La., 1980—2001. Roman Catholic. Office: Diocese of Lake Charles PO Box 3223 Lake Charles LA 70602 Office Phone: 337-439-7400. Office Fax: 337-439-7413. E-mail: jude.speyrer@lcdiocese.org.

SPEZZA, JASON, professional hockey player; b. Mississauga, Ont., Can., June 13, 1983; Center Binghamton Senators (Am. Hockey League), 2002—03, 2004—05, Ottawa Senators, 2002—. Recipient John B. Sollenberger Trophy, Am. Hockey League, 2005, Les Cunningham Plaque, 2005, NHL All-Star Game, 2008; named to All-Rookie Team, Am. Hockey League, 2003, First All-Star Team, 2005. Office: Ottawa Senators Scotiabank Place 1000 Palladium Dr Kanata ON K2V 1A5 Canada

SPHIRE, RAYMOND DANIEL, anesthesiologist, educator; b. Detroit, Feb. 12, 1927; s. Samuel Raymond and Nora Mae (Allen) S.; m. Joan Lois Baker, Sept. 5, 1953; children: Suzanne M., Raymond Daniel, Catherine J. BS, U. Detroit, 1948; MD, Loyola U., Chgo., 1952. Diplomate Am. Bd. Anesthesiology. Intern Grace Hosp., Detroit, 1952-53; resident Harvard Anesthesia Lab.-Mass. Gen. Hosp., 1953-55; attending anesthesiologist Grace Hosp., Detroit, 1955-72, dir. dept. inhalation therapy, 1968-70; sr. attending anesthesiologist, dir. dept., dir. dept. respiratory therapy Detroit-Macomb Hosps. Assn., 1970—, trustee, 1978—, chief of staff, 1980—. Clin. asst. prof. Wayne State U. Sch. Medicine, 1967—; clin. prof. respiratory therapy Macomb Community Coll., Mount Clemens, Mich., 1971—; examiner Am. Registry Respiratory Therapists, 1972—; insp. Joint Rev. Com. Respiratory Therapy Edn., 1972— Co-author: Operative Neurosurgery, 1970, First Aid Guide for the Small Business or Industry, 1978 With AUS, 1944-45; 1st lt. M.C., USAF, 1952 Fellow Am. Coll. Anesthesiologists, Am. Coll. Chest Physicians; mem. AMA, Am. Soc. Anesthesiologists, Wayne County Soc. Anesthesiologists (pres. 1967-69), Am. Assn. Respiratory Therapists, Soc. Critical Care Medicine, Country Club of Detroit, Grosse Pointe Club, Cumberland Club (Portland, Maine), Severance Lodge. Roman Catholic. Home and Office: 36 Sunningdale Dr Grosse Pointe Shores MI 48236

SPICER, EMILY TAYLOR, retired educational administrator; b. Versailles Ky., July 25, 1926; d. Larry Duncan and Arega (Twyman) Harris; m. Mac Cecil Watkins; 1 son, Mac Duncan Watkins; m. 2d, Roy James Spicer, Dec. 18, 1976. B.S. in Edn., U. Cin., 1948, M.Ed., 1963. Tchr. Lincoln Heights High Sch., Cin., 1958-59, Heinold Jr. High Sch., Cin., 1959-62, Aiken High Sch., Cin., 1962-65, counselor, 1965-68; postgrad. work supr. adminstrn. Xavier U., 1964, adj. prof., 1984-85; bd. mem. Lincoln Heights Cmty. Sch., 1990, bd. dirs. project grad., 2007; guidance coordinator Woodward High Sch., Cin., 1968-71, asst. prin., 1976-78; prin. Merry Jr. High Sch., Cin., 1976-78, Taft High Sch., Cin. Pub. Sr. HS, Queen City Vocat. Ctr., 1978-81; dir. staff devel. Cin. Pub. Schs., 1981-82; dir. secondary edn., Cin., 1982—1983; co-chaired Girlz Hard Leadership Acad., 2007, The Scholarship BanquetProject Grad., 2008; co-chair 35th Ann. NCACP Freedom Fund Dinner, 2008. Bd. dirs. YMCA, YWCA, Black Career Women, Inc.; bd. youth services juvenile ct.; mem. planning com. Cin. Presbytery; founding mem. Cin. Reads, Hamilton County Math. and Sci. Acad.; mem. South Avondale Local Sch. Decision Making Com., Citizens Sch. Com.; chair Edn. Task Force Amos Project, 1999—. Recipient Outstanding Profl. Woman award Iota Phi Lambda, 1977, Outstanding Educator award Ohio Elks Assn., 1979, YMCA Black Achiever award Cin. Bd. Edn., 1979, Service in Edn. award NAACP, 1980, YWCA Career Woman Achiever award, 1980, Ethelrie Harper human relations award Cin. Human Relations Commn., 1980, Cin Enquirers One of Ten Women of Yr. award, 1980, Service to Edn. and Community award Shriners, 1981, Glorifying the Lion award Cin. Urban League, 1989, Faith in Action award Coun. Christian-Commons, 1997, Living the Vision award Amas Project, 2001, Charles P. Taft award Coun. Christian Commons, 2006, Cmty. Svc. award YMCA Black Achievers, 2006, Yrs. of Svc. award in Arts and Edn., Cin. Black Theatre Midwest Regional Festival, 2006, Parents Choice award Cin. Parents Pub. Schs., 2008; named Great Living Cincinnatian, Cin. C. of C., 2002; featured on TV show PM Mag., 1978, Hon. Co-chair YMCA Black Achievers Banquet, 2008. Mem. Ohio Assn. Supervision and Curriculum Devel., Ohio Edn. Assn., NEA, Cin. Assn. Adminstrs. and Suprs., Nat. Assn. Secondary Sch. Prins., NAACP, Delta Kappa Gamma, Delta Sigma Theta (sonority women world ministry), Phi Delta Kappa. Clubs: Top Ladies of Distinction, Woman's City, Winton Woods Bd. Edn. (elected pres. 1986-90), Leadership Cin. (hon. mem. 2004), Cin. Black Family Reunion (charted steering com. 1990) Home: 693 Bridle Path Cincinnati OH 45231-7005

SPICER, HAROLD OTIS, retired English language educator, communications educator; b. Gosport, Ind., Dec. 10, 1921; s. Otis R. and Hattie Grace (Wampler) S.; m. Hilda Jane Templeton, June 21, 1946 (dec. Nov. 1994); children: Sherry Lynne (dec. May 1987), Sylvia Jean, Stephen Michael, Zachary Ian. BA, DePauw U., 1947, MA, 1949; PhD, Ind. U., 1962. Instr. English DePauw U., Greencastle, Ind., 1947-49, asst. prof. English, 1957-63; from instr. to prof. English We. Ill. U., Macomb, 1949-57; adj. prof. English Ind. U., Indpls., 1960-63; founder ISU Chpt. SPJ Journalism Fraternity, 1964; assoc. prof. to prof. English Ind. State U., Terre Haute, 1963-85; ret., 1985. Sec. Main Street, Greencastle, 1993-95. Author: Covered Bridges of Putnam County, 1989, Organizational Handbook for Council on Aging, 1989 (Ameritech Tchr. Vol. award, 1989), James Whitcomb Riley: Hoosier Poet, 1993; co-author: DePauw: Pictorial History, 1987; editor: Ten O'Clock News, a museum newsletter, 2003—05; author, narrator, interviewer: 20th Century Golden Memories, 2001—02. Pres. Ret. Tchrs. Putnam County, Greencastle, 1988-90, 2005-06, Putnam County Coun. on Aging, 1990-96 (Man of Yr. award 1994); bd. dirs. Heritage Preservation Soc., Greencastle, 1993—, Putnam County Found., 1995-02, sec., 2000-03; pres. West Ctrl. Ind. Area Agy. on Aging, 2000, 06; coach DePauw U. team Gen. Electric Co. Coll. Bowl Program, 1962, coach Ind. State U. team, 1963. Recipient Danforth Tchr. grant, 1959, Man of Yr. award Area 7 Agy. on Aging West Ctrl. Ind. Econ. Devel. Dist., Terre Haute, 1994; named Older Hoosier of Yr. Ind. Gov.'s Conf., Indpls., 1994, RSVP Vol. of Yr., 1995, Ameritech Vol. Tchr. of Yr., 1989, Martin H. Miller Vol. of Yr. award Ind. Family and Social Svcs. Adminstrn., 1999, Outstanding Leadership award in area/agy. on aging Ind. Assn. Area Agys. on Aging, 2000, named Man of Yr., SPJ. Mem.: VFW (life), Am. Assn. Ret. Persons (pres. Putnam County chpt. 1995—96, 1999—2002, 2005—06), Kiwanis Club Greencastle, West Ctrl. Ind. Civil War Roundtable (v.p. 1998—2000), Greencastle C. of C. (bd. dirs. 1995—99, Putnam County Citizen of Yr. 1996), Am. Legion. Avocations: music, writing, travel. Home: PO Box 892 Greencastle IN 46135-0892 Personal E-mail: h.spicer@comcast.net.

SPICER, HOLT VANDERCOOK, retired theater educator; b. Pasadena, Calif., Feb. 1, 1928; s. John Lovely and Dorothy Eleanor (Clause) S.; m. Marion Arel Gibson, Aug. 16, 1952; children: Mary Ellen, Susan Leah, Laura Alice, John Millard. BA, U. Redlands, 1952, MA, 1957; PhD, U. Okla., 1964. From instr. speech and theatre to prof. S.W. Mo. State Coll., 1952-93, emeritus prof., 1993—, head dept. speech and theatre, 1967-71, dean Sch. Arts and Humanities, 1971-85. Chmn. Dist. 4 Nat. Debate Tournament Com., 1955, 58, 64, 68 Vestryman Episcopalian Ch., 1981—85, 1998—2001; bd. dirs. Springfield (Mo.) Cmty. Ctr., 1981—. Named Debate Coach of Decade U.S. Air Force Acad., 1965, Holt V. Spicer Debate Forum, 1988, Wall of Fame, Mo. State U., 2002; recipient Alumni Achievement award in Speech and Debate U. Redlands, 1991, Alumni award of appreciation S.W. Mo. State U., 1996; team won CEDA Nat. Debate championship, 1992. Mem.: AAUP, Am. Forensic Assn., Speech Communication Assn. Episcopalian. Home: 2232 E Langston St Springfield MO 65804-2646 E-mail: holtspicer9@mchsi.com.

SPIDLE, JAKE W., history professor; b. Memphis, Aug. 25, 1941; s. Jake Wilton and Irma Bright Spidle; m. Gail B. Gillock, Oct. 1, 2005; children: Christopher P., Susan S. Dicks, Joseph A. PhD, Stanford U., Calif., 1972. Assoc. prof. dept. history UNM, Albuquerque, 1970—. Author: (book) Doctors of Medicine in New Mexico: A History of Health and Medical Practice (Gilberto Espinosa award, 1988). Home: 1912 Shirlane Pl NE Albuquerque NM 87112 Office: UNM Dept History Albuquerque NM 87112 Office Fax: 505-277-6023. Business E-Mail: jspidle@unm.edu.

SPIDLIK, TOMAS CARDINAL, cardinal, priest, theologian; b. Boskovice, Czech Republic, Dec. 17, 1919; Attended, Univ. Brno; D, Pontifical Oriental Inst., Rome, 1955; D (hon.), Sacred Heart Univ., 2006. Professed Soc. of Jesus, 1939, ordained priest, 1949; prof. patristic & spiritual theol. various universities; collaborator Vatican Radio, Rome, 1951—; spiritual dir. Pontifical Nepomuceno Seminary, 1968—; elevated to cardinal, 2003; cardinal-priest S. Agata de' Goti, 2003—. Author: numerous works on patristic and spiritual theology. Recipient Order of Masaryk, Czech Republic, 1998. Roman Catholic.

SPIEGEL, ALLEN MICHAEL, dean, internist; b. Lundsberg, Germany, May 18, 1946; BA summa cum laude, Columbia U., NYC, 1967; MD cum laude, Harvard U., Boston, 1971. Intern/resident internal medicine Mass. Gen. Hosp., Boston, 1971—73; mem. endocrinology rsch. tng. prog., Nat. Inst. Diabetes & Digestive & Kidney Disease (NIDDK) NIH, 1973—76, sr. investigator metabolic diseases br., 1977—84, chief molecular pathophysiology sect., 1985—88, chief metabolic diseases br., 1988, sci. dir. NIDDK, 1990—99, dir., 1999—2006; dean Albert Einstein Coll. Medicine Yeshiva U., NYC, 2006—. Recipient Jacobaeus prize, Novo Nordisk Insulin Found., 1990, Komrower Meml. Lecture award, Soc. Study of Inborn Errors of Metabolism, 1996, Edwin B. Astwood Lecture award, Endocrine Soc., 1998. Mem.: Inst. Medicine, Assn. Am. Physicians, Am. Soc. Clin. Investigation. Office: Albert Einstein Coll Medicine Jack & Pearl Resnick Campus 1300 Morris Park Ave Bronx NY 10461*

SPIEGEL, COLLEEN, electric power industry executive; d. Chris and Shirley O'Brien; m. Brian Spiegel, June 25, 2005. PhD, U. South Fla., Tampa, 2008. Pres. Clean Fuel Cell Energy, LLC, Clearwater, Fla., 2006—. Author: (book) Designing and Building Fuel Cells. Office: Clean Fuel Cell Energy LLC 1737 Prince Philip St Clearwater FL 33755 Office Fax: 888-852-6501. Business E-Mail: colleen@cleanfuelcellenergy.com.

SPIEGEL, EVELYN SCLUFER, biology professor; b. Phila., Mar. 20, 1924; d. George and Helen (Laurantos) Sclufer; m. Melvin Spiegel, Apr. 16, 1955; children: Judith Ellen, Rebecca Ann. BA, Temple U., 1947; MA, Bryn Mawr Coll., 1951; PhD, U. Pa., 1954. Asst. program dir. for regulatory biology NSF, Washington, 1954-55; instr. in biology Colby Coll., Waterville, Maine, 1955-59; rsch. assoc. Dartmouth Coll., Hanover, N.H., 1961-74, rsch. assoc. prof. biology, 1974-78, rsch. prof. biology, 1978-91; rsch. prof. biology emerita, 1991—. Vis. scholar Calif. Inst. Tech., Pasadena, 1964-65, U. Calif.-San Diego, La Jolla, 1970, Nat. Inst. for Med. Rsch., Mill Hill, Eng., 1971, NIH, Washington, 1975-76, U. Basel (Switzerland) Biocenter, 1979, 80, 81, 82, 85. Contbr. numerous articles to profl. jours., chpts. to books and book reviews. Mem. Soc. for Devel. Biology, Marine Biol. Lab. Corp. (trustee 1981-86, 88-92). Office: Dartmouth Coll Dept Biol Scis Hanover NH 03755

SPIEGEL, H. JAY, lawyer; b. Cleve., July 7, 1952; s. Martin and Thea (Lange) S BS, Cornell U., 1974; JD, George Mason U., 1981. Bar: Va. 1981, U.S. Patent Office 1982, DC 1986, U.S. Ct. Appeals (fed. cir.) 1982, U.S. Dist. Ct.(ea. dist.) Va. 1982, U.S. Dist. Ct. DC 2001, U.S. Ct. Appeals (DC cir.) 2003, U.S. Ct. Appeals (2d cir.) 2003, U.S. Ct. Appeals (4th cir.) 2003, U.S. Supreme Ct. 1984. Primary and asst. examiner U.S. Patent and Trademark Office, Arlington, Va., 1974—82; assoc. Sherman & Shalloway, Alexandria, Va., 1982—88, of counsel, 1988; pvt. practice. Alexandria, 1988—96; pvt. practice Mt. Vernon, Va., 1996—. Owner, pres. Premium Products, Inc., Alexandria, 1984—, Jumpstart, 1990—. Named to Disting. Alumni Hall of Fame, Cleve. Heights H.S., 2004. Mem.: Licensing Exec. Soc., Am. Intellectual Property Law Assn. Achievements include patents for sporting goods and jewelry; being co-inventor of 26 US patents. Avocations: boating, travel. Office: H Jay Spiegel & Assocs PC PO Box 11 Mount Vernon VA 22121-0011 Office Phone: 703-619-0101. Personal E-mail: jayspiegel@aol.com.

SPIEGEL, JAYSON LESLIE, lawyer, educator, professional society administrator; b. NYC, Mar. 1, 1959; s. Jack and Frieda Rhoda (Michaelson) S.; m. Deborah Marie Scott, Nov. 1, 1986; children: Kyle Reid, Alicia Jean. AB, Georgetown U., 1980; JD, U. Va., 1983; postgrad., USMC Command and Staff Coll., 1991, Army Command and Gen. Staff Coll., 1996; MS in Strategic Studies, US Army War Coll., Carlisle, Pa., 2006. Bar: Md. 1984, D.C. 1985, U.S. Ct. Appeals (D.C. cir.) 1986, U.S. Ct. Mil. Appeals 1987, U.S. Ct. Appeals (4th cir.) 1987, U.S. Supreme Ct. 1988, U.S. Ct. Claims 1990. Law clk. to assoc. judge Md. Ct. Appeals, Balt., 1983—84; assoc. Jordan, Coyne, Savits & Lopata, Washington, 1985—91, ptnr., 1991—94; dep. asst. sec. U.S. Army, 1994—99, acting asst. sec., 1997—98; exec. dir. Res. Officers Assn., 1999—2003; sr. nat. def. counsel Ball Janik, LLP, 2003—05; prin. tech. dir. General Dynamics Info. Tech. (and predecessor corp.), 2005—. Lectr. law and transfusion medicine NIH, 1989, 91-94. Contbr. articles to profl. jours. Mem. recreation adv. bd. Montgomery County, Md., 1989-93. With USAR, 1981—, Desert Shield/Desert Storm, 1990-91. Mem.: ABA (young lawyers mem. com. on law and nat. security, vice chair internat. criminal law com. 1991—94), Conf. of Def. Assn. (Can.), Nat. Def. Indsl. Assn., Md. Bar Assn., D.C. Bar Assn. (founder, chmn. com. on law and nat. security 0197—1994, Com. Chmn. of Yr. 1988, 1991), U.S. C. of C. (com. of 100 assn. execs. 2000—03), Mil. Coalition (bd. dirs. 1999—2003), Res. Officers Assn. (life), Army and Navy club. Avocations: running, tennis. Office Phone: 202-292-1856, 703-253-3178. Personal E-mail: jayson.spiegel@gdit.com. Business E-Mail: jspiegel@anteon.com.

SPIEGEL, JEFFREY H., plastic surgeon; m. Onir Leshem. MD, U. Mich., Ann Arbor, 1994. Chief, facial plastic and reconstructive surgery Boston U. Sch. Medicine, 2000—. Recipient Sir Harold Delf Gillies award, Am. Acad. Facial Plastic and Reconstructive Surgery, 2000. Office: Boston Univ Sch Medicine 830 Harrison Ave Ste 1400 Moakley Boston MA 02118

SPIEGEL, JOHN FRANKLIN, theater educator; AB in Liberal Arts, Davidson Coll., NC, 1993; MFA in Theatre, U. NC, Greensboro, 2003. Dir. theatre Andrew Coll., Cuthbert, Ga., 2003—05, asst. prof., 2003—05; theater prof. Presbyn. Coll., Clinton, SC, 2005—. Divsn. vice chair Southeastern Theatre Conf.; divsn. chair SC Theatre Assn., Columbia, 2008. Office: Presbyn Coll 503 South Broad St Clinton SC 29325

SPIEGEL, JOHN WILLIAM, banker; b. Indpls., Mar. 14, 1941; s. William Sordon and Elizabeth (Hall) S.; children: W. Robert, John F., Bradley H. BA, Wabash Coll., 1963; MBA, Emory U., 1965; postgrad., Nova Southeastern U., 1993—99. Rsch. assoc. IMEDE (Mgmt. Inst.), Lausanne, Switzerland, 1965-66; mgmt. trainee Trust Co. Bank, Atlanta, 1966-67, bond portfolio mgr., 1967-72; data processing mgr. Trust Co. Ga., Atlanta, 1972-78, treas., 1978-85; vice chmn., CFO SunTrust Banks Inc., Atlanta, 1985—. Mem. exec. com. CFO divsn. ABA, 1987-90, chair, 1989-90; former instr. Morehouse Coll. and Banking Schs.; bd. dirs. Bentley Pharms., Colonial Properties. Mem. exec. com., bd. dirs. Alliance Theatre, Atlanta, 1985—92, pres., 1989—91; bd. dirs. High Mus. Art, Atlanta, 1985—, chmn., 1997—98; founding pres. Young Audiences Atlanta, Inc., 1982—84, mem. adv. bd., 1985—; pres. bd. vis. Grady Meml. Hosp., 1983—90; v.p. exec. bd. Atlanta Area coun. Boy Scouts Am., 1983—92, treas., 1989—91, mem. adv. bd., 1992; mem. adv. coun. Ga. State U. Sch. Accountacy, 1981—85, chmn. curriculum subcom., 1983—84; mem. exec. com., trustee Morehouse Sch. Medicine, 1984—93, chmn. fin. com., 1987—90, chmn., 1990—92; mem. Leadership Atlanta, 1976—, trustee, 1990—94; trustee, mem. exec. com. Robert W. Woodruff Arts Ctr., Inc., 1976—2001, treas., 1976—83, chmn. fin. com., 1984—89, 1993—97, chmn., 1998—2001; chmn. fin. com., bd. dirs. Schenck Sch., 1986—88; exec. vice chmn. bd. trustees Holy Innocents Episcopal Sch., 1976—79, bd. dirs., treas., 1987—90; bd. dirs. Atlanta Opera, 1986—98, United Way Met. Atlanta, 1994—98, Rock Tenn. Co., 1989—, Sallie Mae, 1993—97, Suburban Lodges Am., Inc., 1999—2002; mem. bd. visitors Emory U., 1991—95; trustee ESR Children's Health Care System, Inc., 1997—, bd. dirs., 1999—; trustee Wabash Coll., 1997—99; mem. dean's adv. coun. Goizueta Bus. Sch., Emory U., 1994—; bd. dirs., chmn. fin. com. Am. Cardiovasc. Rsch. Inst., 2002—03; bd. dirs. and mem. exec. com. Atlanta Coll. Art, 2003—. Mem. Bank Adminstrn. Inst. (bd. dirs. 1987-92, 99-, rsch. oversight com. 1992-98, treas. 1999, chmn. 2000-03). Home: 3745 Randall Mill Rd NW Atlanta GA 30327-2747 Office: SunTrust Banks Inc 303 Peachtree St NE Atlanta GA 30308-3201

SPIEGEL, JOSEPH, medical educator; b. Philadelphia, Pa., July 8, 1956; s. Henry and Anne Spiegel; m. Jill Steinslofer, Aug. 19, 1978; children: Lauren Amy, Samuel Ryan, Hannah Leah, Joseph. MD, Jefferson Med. Coll., Philadelphia, 1979. Diplomate Am. Bd. Otolaryngology Head & Neck Surgery, 1985. Resident physician U. Mich., Ann Arbor, 1981—85; assoc. prof. otolaryngology Thomas Jefferson U., Philadelphia, 1985—. Dir. jefferson ctr. voice & swallowing Thomas Jefferson U., Philadelphia, 2008—. Fellow: ACS, Am. Soc. Head & Neck Surgeons. Achievements include patents for portable video endoscopy system. Avocation: golf. Office: Thomas Jefferson Univ 925 Chestnut St 6th Fl Philadelphia PA 19107 Business E-Mail: joseph.spiegel@jefferson.edu.

SPIEGEL, LAWRENCE HOWARD, advertising executive; b. NYC, Oct. 9, 1942; s. Melvin Arthur and Rose (Black) S.; m. Christy Mansfield; children from previous marriage: Robert, David. BA, NYU, 1963. Print buyer William Esty Co., NYC, 1964-65, broadcast buyer, 1965-66; media planner Batten, Barton, Durstine & Osborn, Inc., NYC, 1966-67, media supr., 1967-68, assoc. media dir., 1969-72, v.p., 1972-74; media group head Jack Tinker & Ptnrs., NYC, 1968-69; v.p. Tracy-Locke, Dallas, 1974-80, sr. v.p., 1980-84, exec. v.p., 1984-89; prin. The Richards Group, Dallas, 1989—. Pres. Tex. Coun. Advt., 1991-97, Leading Agy. Network, 1997—; dir. Dream Fund, 1999—; charter mem. broadband video adv. bd. AOL. Guest editor Mktg. and Media Decision mag., June 1982. Mem. Dallas Cable Bd., 1983-86; chmn. mktg. com. U. Tex., Dallas, 1984-89; pres. Cable Access Dallas, Inc., 1985-86; trustee Dallas Symphony Assn., 1978—; bd. dirs. Equest Inc., 1991-92, DREAM Fund, 1999—. Staff sergeant US Army. Recipient Excellence award, Am. Women in Radio and TV, 2006. Mem. Assn. Broadcasting Execs. Tex. (pres. 1975-76), Am. Women in Radio and TV, Inc. (bd. dirs. 1992-93), Dallas Ad League. Republican. Avocations: skiing, sailing. Office: The Richards Group 8750 N Central Expy Ste 1200 Dallas TX 75231-6436 Office Phone: 214-891-5843. Personal E-mail: larry_spiegel@embarqmail.com.

SPIEGEL, MATTHEW, finance educator; PhD, Princeton U., NJ, 1987. Prof. U. Calif., Berkeley, 1992—99, Yale Sch. Mgmt., New Haven, 1999—. Co-editor, co-founder Jour. Fin. Markets, San Diego, 1997—2005; exec. editor Rev. Fin. Studies, New Haven, 2005—. Contbr. articles rsch. paper (Michael Brenan Best Paper prize, 2008). Mem., dept. corps. Calif. State Commr.'s Adv. Com., Sacramento, 1997—99; mem. NASDAQ Econ. Adv. Bd., NYC, 2003—06. Recipient Citation Excellence award, ANBAR Mgmt. Intelligence, 1998. Fellow: Columbia U. Program Law and Economics Capital Markets. Avocations: skiing, running. Office: Yale Sch Mgmt PO Box 208200 New Haven CT 06520 Office Fax: 203-432-8931. Business E-Mail: matthew.spiegel@yale.edu.

SPIEGEL, MELVIN, retired biology professor; s. Philip Edward and Sadie (Friedman) S.; m. Evelyn Sclufer, Apr. 16, 1955; children: Judith Ellen, Rebecca Ann. BS, U. Ill., 1948; PhD, U. Rochester, 1952; MA (hon.), Dartmouth Coll. Research fellow U. Rochester, 1952-53, Calif. Inst. Tech., 1953-55, 64-65; asst. prof. Colby Coll., 1955-59; mem. faculty Dartmouth Coll., Hanover, NH, 1959—, prof. biology, 1966-93; prof. emeritus Dartmouth Coll, Hanover, NH; chmn. dept. biol. scis. Dartmouth Coll., Hanover, NH, 1972-74. Summer investigator Marine Biol. Lab., Woods Hole, Mass., 1954—; sr. rsch. biologist U. Calif.-San Diego, 1970-71; vis. prof. biochemistry Nat. Inst. Med. Rsch., Mill Hill, London, 1971; vis. prof. Biocenter, U. Basel, 1979-82, 85; Wilson Meml. lectr. U. N.C., 1975; program dir. developmental biology NSF, 1975-76; mem. cell biology study sect. NIH, 1966-70 Editl. bd.: Biol. Bull., 1966-70, 71-75, Cell Differentiation, 1979-88; contbr. articles to profl. jours. Trustee Marine Biol. Lab. Corp.; mem. exec. com., trustee Marine Biol. Lab., 1976-80. Fellow AAAS; mem. Am. Soc. Cell Biology, Am. Soc. Devel. Biology, Internat. Soc. Devel. Biologists (sec.-treas. 1977-81, bd. dirs. 1981-85). Home Phone: 603-643-4353. E-mail: melvin.spiegel@dartmouth.edu.

SPIEGEL, PHYLLIS, public relations consultant, journalist; b. Bronx, NY; d. Bernard and Lillian (Horowitz) Finkelberg; m. Stanley Spiegel, Sept. 20, 1959 (div. 1981); children: Mark, Adam. BA, NYU. Feature writer various newspapers, pubs., 1960—70, 2000; dir. pub. rels. Mort Barish Assocs., Princeton, NJ, 1975-80; account exec. pub. rels. Keyes Martin, Springfield, NJ, 1980-84; pres. Phyllis Spiegel Assocs., Plainsboro, NJ, 1984—. Pub. rels. dir., founder Red Oak Coop. Nursery Sch., Middletown, N.J., 1960's, Matawan (N.J.) Student Enrichment Program, 1960s-70s; pub. rels. cons., event organizer New Philharm. of N.J., Morristown, 1991-93; mem. Child Placement Rev. Bd. of Family Ct., Mercer County, N.J., 1994-98. Recipient Commendation from Gov. N.J. for U. Med. and Dentistry of N.J. campaign, 1983, Commendation for N.J. Pharm. Assn. campaign Pub. Rels. News Assn., 1979. Mem.: Soc. Humanistic Judaism (bd. dir. 1983—85). Avocations: film and theatre, classical music, reading, travel, walks. Office: Phyllis Spiegel Assocs PO Box 243 Plainsboro NJ 08536-0243

SPIEGELBERG, EMMA JO, business education educator, academic administrator; b. Mt. View, Wyo., Nov. 22, 1936; d. Joseph Clyde and Dorcas (Reese) Hatch; m. James Walter Spiegelberg, June 22, 1957; children: William L., Emory Walter, Joseph John. BA with honors, U. Wyo., 1958, MEd, 1985; EdD, Boston U., 1990. Tchr. bus. edn. Laramie H.S., Wyo., 1960—61, 1965—93, adminstr., 1993—97; prin. McCormick Jr. H.S., Cheyenne, 1997—2002; exec. dir. Wyo. Assn. Secondary Sch. Prins., 2001—. Author: Branigan's Accounting Simulation, 1986, London & Co. II, 1993; co-author: Glencoe Computerized Accounting, 1993, 2d edit., 1995, Microcomputer Accounting: Daceasy, 1994, Microcomputer Accounting: Peachtree, 1994, 3d edit., 2000, Microcomputer Accounting: Accpac, 1994, Computerized Accounting with Peachtree, 1995, 2000, 02. Bd. dir. Cathedral Home for Children, Laramie, 1967-70, 72—, pres., 1985-88, Laramie Plains Mus., 1970-79. Named Wyo. Bus. Tchr. of Yr., 1982, Disting. Alumni, 2008, Wyo. Asst. Prin. of Yr., 1997. Mem.: NASSP, NEA, U. Wyo. (disting. alumni 2008), Wyo. Ret. Ednl. Pers. (pres. 2008—), Wyo. Territorial Prison Hist. Assn. (pres. 2009—), Wyo. Territorial Prison-State Hist. Site (sec. 2008, bd. dirs. 2008—, pres. 2009), Wyo. Assn. Secondary Sch. Prins. (sec., treas. 1997—2001), Albany County Edn. Assn. (sec. 1970—71), Wyo. Edn. Assn., Wyo. Bus. Edn. Assn. (pres. 1979—80, Hall of Fame 2004), Internat. Soc. Bus. Edn. (rep. Mt. Plains chpt. 2006—07), Mt. Plains Bus. Edn. Assn. (Wyo. rep. to bd. dirs. 1982—85, pres. 1987—88, Sec. Tchr. of Yr. 1991, Leadership award 1992), Nat. Bus. Edn. Assn. (bd. dir. 1987—88, 1991—96, Sec. Tchr. of Yr. 1991), Wyo. Vocat. Assn. (exec. bd. 1978—80, pres. 1981—82, exec. sec. 1986—89, Outstanding Contbns. to Vocat. Edn. award 1983, Tchr. of Yr. 1985), Am. Vocat. Assn. (policy com. region V 1984—87, region V Tchr. of Yr. 1986), U. Wyo. Alumni Assn. (bd. dir. 1985—90, pres. 1988—89, named Disting. Alumna 2008), Laramie C. of C. (bd. dir. 1985—88), Zonta (v.p. 2002—03, pres. 2003—04, dist. 12 parliamentarian 2004—06, bd. dirs. 2007—09), Delta Pi Epsilon, Pi Lambda Theta, Chi Omega, Alpha Delta Kappa (state pres. 1978—82), Phi Delta Kappa, Kappa Delta Pi. Episcopalian. Home: 3301 Grays Gable Rd Laramie WY 82072-5031 Personal E-mail: jwejspiegelberg@aol.com.

SPIEGELBERG, MARC STEVEN, secondary school educator; b. Seattle, July 5, 1954; s. Carl Harvey and JoAnn Stover Spiegelberg; m. Janet Erickson, June 14, 1975 (dec. Oct. 10, 1996); children: Jason Thomas Ruiz, Peter Carl, Arla Rose Ruiz, Avarie Phyllis Ruiz, Jarin Luis Ruiz, Jardan Jose Ruiz, Keith David, John Steven; m. Jeanette Ann Knutson, Dec. 27, 1997. EdB, Ctrl. Wash. State Coll., Ellensburg, 1976; MEd, Western Wash. U., Bellingham, 1990. Indsl. arts tchr. Shelton Sch. Dist., Wash., 1976—82; indsl. arts/tech. edn. tchr. Tenino Sch. Dist., Wash., 1982—91, Rochester Sch. Dist., Centralia, Wash. Sec. property/fin. com. Centralia Cmty. Ch. of God, 2000—06; cemetery dist. bd. Grand Mound Cemetery, Rochester, 1996—2006. Recipient 25 Yr. Svc. award, Wash. Tech. Edn. Assn., 2006. Mem.: Wash. Edn. Assn. (life). Republican. Church Of God. Home: 6639 Prather Rd SW Centralia WA 98531 Office: Maple Lane HS 20311 Old Hwy 9 SW Centralia WA 98531 Office Fax: 360-273-5012. Personal E-mail: spiegelbergm@reachone.com. Business E-Mail: mspiegelberg@rochester.wednet.edu.

SPIEGELMAN, ART, writer, cartoonist; b. Stockholm, Feb. 15, 1948; s. Wladek and Andzia (Zylberberg) S.; m. Francoise Mouly, July 12, 1977; children: Nadja, Dashiell. Student, Harpur Coll. (now SUNY), Binghamton, NY. Creative cons., artist, designer, editor, writer Topps Chewing Gum, Inc., Bklyn., 1966-88; editor Douglas Comix, 1972; contbg. editor Arcade, the Comics Revue, 1975-76; founding editor Raw, 1980—; artist, contbg. editor New Yorker, 1992—2003. Instr. San Francisco Acad. Art, 1974-75, NY Sch. Visual Arts, 1979-87. Author, illustrator: The Complete Mr. Infinity, 1970, The Viper Vicar of Vice, Villainy, and Vickedness, 1972, Ace Hole, Midge Detective, 1974, The Language of Comics, 1974, Breakdowns: From Maus to Now: An Anthology of Strips, 1977, Work and Turn, 1979, Every Day Has Its Dog, 1979, Two-Fisted Painters Action Adventure, 1980, Maus: A Survivor's Tale, 1986 (Joel M. Cavior award for Jewish Writing 1986, Nat. Book Critics Cir. nomination 1986, Pulitzer prize 1992), Maus, Part Two, 1992 (Nat. Book Critics Cir. nomination 1992, Pulitzer prize 1992, Eisner award, 1992, Harvey award, 1992), Open Me...I'm a Dog!, 1997; (with J.M. March) The Wild Party, 1994, Kisses from New York; (with F. Mouly) Read Yourself Raw, 1987, In the Shadow of No Towers, 2004 (named one of the 100 Notable Books of 2004, NY Times Book Review), Breakdowns: Portrait of the Artist as a Young %@&*!, 2008; contbr. The Apex Treasury of Underground Comics, 1974; compiling editor (with B. Schneider) Whole Grains: A Book of Quotations, 1972; creator (with composer Phillip Johnston) Drawn to Death: A Three Panel Opera, Am. Repertory Theatre Co., Cambridge, Mass.; editor (comic series) Little Lit, 2000-03; exhbns. include NY Cultural Ctr., Inst. Contemporary Art, London, Seibu Gallery, Tokyo, Mus. Modern Art, NYC, 1991, Galerie St. Etienne, NYC, 1992, Ft. Lauderdale Mus. Art, 1993, LA Mus. Contemporary Art, 2005; creator Wacky Packages, Garbage Pail Kids and other novelties; contbr. to numerous underground comics. Named one of Time Mag. 100 Most Influential People, 2005; named to Will Eisner Award Hall of Fame, 1999, Art Dir.'s Club Hall of Fame, 2006; recipient Playboy Editorial award for best comic strip, 1982, Yellow Kid award for best comic strip author, 1982, Regional Design award, Print mag., 1983, 1984, 1985, Inkpot award, San Diego Comics Conv., 1987, Stripschappening award for best fgn. comics album, 1987, Alpha Art award, Angoulerne, France, 1993, Chevalier de l'Ordre des Arts et des Lettres, France, 2005. Fellow: Am. Acad. Arts and Sciences. Office: c/o The Steven Barclay Agency 321 Pleasant St Petaluma CA 94952-2648 Office Phone: 888-965-7323.*

SPIELBERG, STEPHEN PAUL, pediatrician, medical educator, former dean; b. 1945; m. Laurel A. Spielbery. AB, Princeton U., 1966; PhD in pharmacology, U. Chgo., 1971; MD, U. Chgo. Pritzker Sch. Medicine, 1973. Pediat. resident Children's Hosp. Med. Ctr., Boston, 1974—75; instr. to asst. prof. pediat. & pharmacology Johns Hopkins U. Sch. Medicine, 1971—81; assoc. prof. to prof. pediat. & pharmacology U. Toronto, 1981—92, dir. Ctr. for Drug Safety Rsch., 1988—92; sr. scientist rsch. inst. Hosp. for Sick Children, Toronto, established & headed div. pediat. clin. pharmacology and toxicology, 1987—92; exec. dir. exploratory biochemical toxicology and clin. and regulatory develop. Merck Labs., 1992—97; v.p. pediat. drug develop. Johnson & Johnson Pharm. Rsch. & Develop., Titusville, NJ, 1997—2003, established dept. of pediat. drug develop.; v.p. health affairs Dartmouth Coll., 2003; dean & prof. pediat. and pharmacology and taxicology Dartmouth Med. Sch., 2003—08, prof. pediat., pharmacology and toxicology; prin. investigator Inst. Pediatric Innovation, Hanover, NH, 2007; dir. Ctr. Personalized Medicine and Therapeutic Innovation, Children's Mercy Hosp., Kansas City, Mo., 2009—; Marion Merrell Dow chair in Pediatric Pharmacogenomics U. Mo.-Kansas City Sch. Medicine. Adj. prof. pediat., medicine and pharmacology Thomas Jefferson U.; adj. prof. pediat. Robert Wood Johnson Med. Sch.; mem. adv. bd. PediaLink; mem. Fed. Adv. Com., Nat. Children's Study, Nat. Inst. of Child Health and Human Develop.; chair Pediat. Task Force, Pharm. Rsch. and Mfr. of Am.; bd. dirs. Found. for NIH; mem. panel on ethics and pediat. clin. trials Inst. Medicine; mem. pediat. adv. subcom. FDA; mem. sci. adv. bd. Elizabeth Glaser Pediat. Rsch. Network. Recipient Rawls-Palmer Award, Am. Soc. for Clin. Pharmacology and Therapeutics, 1992, Werner Kalow Award for Pharmacogenetics and Drug Safety, 1995, William B. Abrams Award and Lectureship, FDA & Am. Soc. for Clin. Pharmacology and Therapeutics, 2001, Exceptional Service Award, Pharm. Rsch. and Mfr. of Am., 2003. Fellow: Nat. Inst. of Child Health and Human Develop. (mem. of month 2008); mem.: Am. Soc. Clin. Pharmacology and Therapeutics. Office: Children's Mercy Hospitals & Clinics 2401 Gillham Rd Kansas City MO 64108 Office Phone: 816-234-3059.*

SPIELBERG, STEVEN ALLAN, film director, producer; b. Cin., Dec. 18, 1946; m. Amy Irving, Nov. 27, 1985 (div. Feb. 2, 1989); 1 child: Max Samuel; m. Kate Capshaw Oct. 12, 1991; children: Theo (adopted), Sasha, Sawyer, Mikaela (adopted), Destry, Jessica (stepchild). BA, Calif. State U., Long Beach; D of Creative Arts (hon.), Brandeis U., 1986; DHL (hon.), Yale U., 2002; LHD (hon.), Boston U., 2009. Founder Amblin Entertainment, 1984—; co-founder (with Jeffrey Katzenberg & David Geffen), ptnr. DreamWorks SKG, Universal City, 1994—. Co-founder DreamWorks SKG, 1995—2005; co-creator of concept, story and design of new game franchises EA Games, LA, 2005—; artistic adv. 2008 Olympic Games, Beijing, 2007—08. Dir.: (films) The Last Gun, 1959, Jaws, 1975, 1941, 1979, Raiders of the Lost Ark, 1981 (Acad. Award nomination for best dir., 1982), Indiana Jones and the Temple of Doom, 1984, Indiana Jones and the Last Crusade, 1989, Hook, 1991, Jurassic Park, 1993, The Lost World: Jurassic Park, 1997, Minority Report, 2002, War of the Worlds, 2005, Indiana Jones and the Kingdom of the Crystal Skull, 2008; dir., prodr. (films) E.T. the Extra-Terrestrial, 1982 (Acad. Award nomination for best dir., 1983, Acad. Award nomination for best picture, 1983), Twilight Zone: The Movie, 1983; dir.: (TV films) Columbo: Murder by the Book, 1971, Duel, 1971,

Something Evil, 1972, Savage, 1973, (episodes for TV series) The Name of the Game, 1968, Marcus Welby, M.D., 1969, Night Gallery, 1970, The Psychiatrist, 1971, Owen Marshall: Counselor at Law, 1971; exec. prodr.: (films) I Wanna Hold Your Hand, 1978, Used Cars, 1980, Continental Divide, 1981, Gremlins, 1984, Back to the Future, 1985, Young Sherlock Holmes, 1985, The Money Pit, 1986, An American Tail, 1986, Innerspace, 1987, *batteries not included, 1987, Who Framed Roger Rabbit, 1988, The Land Before Time, 1988, Tummy Trouble, 1989, Dad, 1989, Back to the Future Part II, 1989, Joe Versus the Volcano, 1990, Yume, 1990, Back to the Future Part III, 1990, Roller Coaster Rabbit, 1990, Gremlins 2: The New Batch, 1990, Arachnophobia, 1990, Trail Mix-Up, 1993, We're Back! A Dinosaur's Story, 1993, I'm Mad, 1994, The Flinstones, 1994, Casper, 1995, Balto, 1995, Twister, 1996, The Lost Children of Berlin, 1997, Men in Black, 1997, Deep Impact, 1998, The Mask of Zorro, 1998, The Last Days, 1998, The Haunting, 1999, Eyes of the Holocaust, 2000, Jurassic Park III, 2001, Price for Peace, 2002, Men in Black II, 2002, The Legend of Zorro, 2005, Monster House, 2006, Disturbia, 2007, Transformers, 2007; (TV films) Class of '61, 1993, Survivors of the Holocaust, 1996, Shooting War, 2000, Semper Fi, 2001, We Stand Alone Together, 2001, Burma Bridge Busters, 2003, Dan Finnerty & the Dan Band: I Am Women, 2005; (TV miniseries) Band of Brothers, 2001 (Emmy for outstanding miniseries, 2002), Broken Silence, 2002, Taken, 2002 (Emmy for outstanding miniseries, 2003), Into the West, 2005; (TV series) The Plucky Duck Show, 1992, Family Dog, 1992, SeaQuest DSV, 1993—96, ER, 1994, Pinky and the Brain, 1995—98, Freakazoid!, 1995—97, Toonsylvania, 1998—2000, Pinky, Elmyra & the Brain, 1998, On the Lot, 2007; prodr.: (films) An American Tail: Fievel Goes West, 1991; writer (films) Ace Eli and Rodger of the Skies, 1973, dir., prodr. The Color Purple, 1985 (Acad. Award nomination for best picture, 1986), Empire of the Sun, 1987, Always, 1989, Schindler's List, 1993 (Acad. Award for best dir., 1994, Acad. Award for best picture, 1994, Golden Globe for best dir., 1994), Amistad, 1997, Saving Private Ryan, 1998 (Acad. Award for best dir., 1999, Acad. Award nomination for best picture, 1999, Golden Globe for best dir., 1999, Disting. Pub. Svc. Award USN, 1999), Catch Me If You Can, 2002, The Terminal, 2004, Munich, 2005, dir., writer Fighter Squad, 1961, Escape to Nowhere, 1961, Firelight, 1964, Slipstream, 1967, Amblin', 1968, The Sugarland Express, 1974, Close Encounters of the Third Kind, 1977 (Acad. Award nomination for best dir., 1978); prodr.: (films) Memoirs of a Geisha, 2005, Flags of Our Fathers, 2006, Letters from Iwo Jima, 2006; prodr., writer (films) Poltergeist, 1982, exec. prodr., writer The Goonies, 1985, (TV series) Amazing Stories, 1985—87, Tiny Toon Adventures, 1990—92, Animaniacs, 1993—98, consulting prodr. The Unites States of Tara, 2009—, dir., prodr., writer (films) Artificial Intelligence: AI, 2001, asst. dir. action scenes Star Wars III: Revenge of the Sith, 2005. Mem. adv. bd. Sci. Fiction Mus. and Hall of Fame. Recipient Man of Yr. award Hasty Pudding Theater, Harvard U., 1983, Outstanding Directorial Achievement award for feature films Dirs. Guild Am., 1985, Film award Brit. Acad. Film and TV Arts, 1986, Irving Thalberg Mem. award Acad. Motion Picture Arts and Scis., 1987, Golden Lion award for career achievement Venice Film Festival, 1993, Life Achievement award Am. Film Inst., 1995, John Huston award Artists Rights Found., 1995, Lifetime Achievement award, Dir. Guild America, 2000, Liberty Kennedy Ctr. Honor, John F. Kennedy Center for Performing Arts, 2006, The French Legion of Honor, 2008, Cecil B. DeMille award, Hollywood Fgn. Press Assn., 2009, Liberty medal, Nat. Constitution Ctr., 2009; named Entertainment Weekly's Most Powerful Person in Entertainment, 1997; named one of The 50 Most Powerful People in Hollywood Premiere mag., 2004-06, Forbes' Richest Americans, 1999—, World's Richest People, Forbes mag. 2001—, 100 Top Celebrities, Forbes mag., 2001—, The 100 Most Powerful Celebrities, 2007, 2008, Forbes.com, 50 Smartest People in Hollywood, Entertainment Weekly, 2007, America's Best Leaders, US News & World Report, 2008; named a Comdr. of the Order of the British Empire (CBE), Her Majesty Queen Elizabeth II, 2001. Fellow Brit. Acad. Film and TV Arts. Achievements include winning film contest with 40-minute war movie, Escape to Nowhere, at age 13; made film Firelight at age 16, and made 5 films while in coll.; became TV dir. at Universal Pictures at age 20. Office: c/o Dreamworks SKG 100 Universal City Plz Bldg 477 Universal City CA 91608-1002

SPIELBERGER, CHARLES DONALD, psychologist, educator; b. Atlanta, Mar. 28, 1927; s. A.R. and Eleanor (Wachman) S.; m. Carol Lee, June 4, 1971. BS, Ga. Inst. Tech., 1949; BA, U. Iowa, 1951, MA, 1953, PhD, 1954. Asst. prof. med. psychology Duke U., Durham, N.C., 1955-58, from asst. prof. to assoc. prof. psychology, 1955-63; prof. psychology Vanderbilt U., Nashville, 1963-66; tng. specialist in psychology NIMH, Bethesda, Md., 1965-67; prof. psychology, dir. clin. training program Fla. State U., Tallahassee, 1967-72; prof. psychology U. South Fla., Tampa, 1972—85, dir. clin. tng., 1972—78, disting. univ. rsch. prof., 1985—. Fellow Netherlands Inst. for Advanced Study, Wassenaar, 1979-80, 85-86; cons. FAA, NIMH, VA, USAF, others. Author: Anxiety and Behavior, 1966, Understanding Stress and Anxiety, 1979, Anxiety in Sports, 1989, Test Anxiety: Theory, Assessment and Treatment, 1995; editor: Stress and Anxiety Series, 1975; editor: (gen.) Centennial Psychology Series, 1979—; editor: (in-chief) Encyclopedia of Applied Psychology, 2004—. Named Disting. scholar U. South Fla., 1973, Disting. Sci. Contbr., Fla. Psychol. Assn., 1977, 88, Outstanding Faculty Rschr., U. South Fla., 1985. Fellow APA (pres. 1991-92, nat. treas. 1987-90, nat. coun. v.p. 1994-99, 2001-, pres. divsn. clin. psychology 1989, pres. divsn. cmty. psychol. 1975-76, pres. divsn. internat. psychol., 2002, Disting. Sci. Contbr. to Cmty. Psychology 1982, Disting. Sci. and Prof. Contbr. Clin. Psychology 1989, Disting. Contbr. Edn. Psychology 1992, Disting. Contbr. Profl. Practice 1993, APA/APF Gold Medal Disting. Contbr., 2003, Disting. Contbr. Internat. Psychology, 2005 pres. divsn. media psychol., 2005); mem. Southeastern Psychol. Assn. (pres. 1975-76), Soc. for Personality Assessment (pres. 1986-89, Disting. Sci. Contbr. 1990), Nat. Coun. Sci. Soc. Presidents (chair 1996-2000), Internat. Stress Mgmt. Assn. (pres. 1992-2000), Internat. Coun. Psychologists (pres. 1986-87), Internat. Assn. Applied Psychology (pres. 1998-2002, Wundt James Disting. Contbr. award), Stars & Anxiety Rsch. Soc. (pres. 1980-84), Psi Chi (nat. pres. 1980-83). Home: 11313 Carrollwood Dr Tampa FL 33618-3703 Office: U South Fla Dept Psychology Tampa FL 33620 Business E-Mail: spielber@cas.usf.edu.

SPIELER, EMILY A., dean, law educator; AB, Radcliffe Coll., Harvard U., 1969; JD, Yale U., 1973. Ptnr. Women's Law Collective, Cambridge, Mass.; spl. asst. atty. gen. Mass. Dept. Pub. Health's Lead Poisoning Prevention Div.; commr. W.Va. Workers' Compensation Fund; first dep. atty. gen. for civil rights Govt. W.Va., mem. Human Rights Commn.; Hale J. and Roscoe P. Posten Prof. Law W.Va. U., 1990—2002; dean Northeastern U. Sch. Law, Boston, 2002—. Mem., pres. Obama's Transition Team, US Dept. Labor; com. chair US Dept. Energy, Nat. Inst. Occupl. Safety and Health. Contbr. articles to law jours. Recipient Fulbright award, 2001, Martin Luther King Jr. Advocacy of Justice award. Mem.: NAS, Nat. Acad. Soc. Insurance. Office: Northeastern U Sch Law 120 Knowles Ctr 400 Huntington Ave Boston MA 02115 Office Phone: 617-373-3307. Office Fax: 617-373-8793. Business E-Mail: e.spieler@neu.edu.*

SPIELER, JEFF, public health service officer; BS in zoology, U. Fla., 1967, PhD (hon.) in pub. svc., 2002; MS in zoological sciences and reproductive biology, Rutgers U., 1971. Scientist Lederle Labs. Pharm. Co., Pearl River, NY, WHO, Geneva; sr. biomedical rsch. advisor in pop. Office Pop. and Reproductive Health, US Agy. Internat. Devel., 1983—93, chief rsch., tech. and utilization divsn., 1993—2007, sr. sci. advisor, 2007—. Office: US Agy Internat Devel Off Pop and Reproductive Health 1300 Pennsylvania Ave NW Washington DC 20523*

SPIELER, RICHARD EARL, oceanographer, educator; b. Washington, Mar. 11, 1942; s. Ernst Henry Spieler and Gladys Gnegy; m. Janice Schacht (div.); children: Lara L., Lisel R. BA, U. Md., 1963; BS, Ark. State U., 1970, MS, 1971; PhD, La. State U., 1975. Curator fishies Milw. Pub. Mus., 1975—91; assoc. prof. Nova S.E. U., Ft. Lauderdale, Fla., 1991—96, prof., 1996—, dir. Guy Harvey Rsch. Inst., 1999—2002, dir. acad. programs, 2006—. Cons. fish ecology, physiology, 1991—. Contbr. articles to profl. jours. Lt. col. USAFR, 1963—92. Avocations: sailing, scuba diving, reading, hiking. Office: Nova Southeastern Univ Oceangraphic Ctr 8000 N Ocean Dr Dania Beach FL 33004 Office Phone: 954-262-3613.

SPIELMAN, RICK, professional sports team executive; m. Michele Spielman; children: Juan, Luis, Ronnie, J.D., Omie, Whitney. B, So. Ill. U.; M, Ohio State U. Coll. scout Detroit Lions, 1990—94, pro scout, 1995—96; dir. pro pers. Chgo. Bears, 1997—99; v.p. player pers. Miami Dolphins, 2000—02, sr. v.p. football ops., player pers., 2002—04, gen. mgr., 2004—05; football analyst ESPN, 2005—06; v.p. player pers. Minn. Vikings, 2006—. Office: Minn Vikings 9520 Viking Dr Eden Prairie MN 55344*

SPIELVOGEL, SIDNEY MEYER, retired investment banker; b. NYC, July 14, 1925; s. Hyman and Rae (Mandel) S.; m. Beverly Anne Gold, Dec. 18, 1960; 1 son, Peter James. BSS., CCNY, 1944; A.M., Harvard U., Cambridge, Mass., 1946, MBA, 1949. Economist Treasury Dept., Washington, 1946-47; assoc. dept. mgr. Alexander's Dept. Stores, 1949-53; asst. to mdse. mgr., dept. mgr. Bloomingdale's Dept. Store, 1953-56; with Prudential-Bache Securities Inc., 1956-88, 1st v.p., 1971-75, sr. v.p., 1975-85, mng. dir., 1986-88. Dir. MoneyMart Assets Inc., 1976-96, pres., 1981-87; lectr. Hunter Coll., N.Y.C., 1963-68, The New Sch., 1993-96. Bd. dirs. Emanu-el Midtown YM-YWHA, N.Y.C., 1975-91; mem. Harvard Grad. Sch. Coun., 1983-88, 89-92, 94—, chmn., 1985-87. Recipient Outstanding Svc. award, Harvard Alumni Assn., 2006. Mem. Harvard Club (N.Y.C.), Harvard Bus. Sch. Club (N.Y.C.), World Trade Center Club (N.Y.C.), Phi Beta Kappa. Home: 245 E 19th St New York NY 10003-2639

SPIER, GUY SELMAR, investment advisor; b. Pietermaritzburg, Natal, Republic of South Africa, Feb. 4, 1966; s. Simon Gustav and Marylin Eda (Pearse) S. BA with first class honors, Oxford U., Eng., 1988; MBA, Harvard U., 1993; MA, Oxford U., 1998. Rsch. assoc. Braxton Assocs., London, 1988-89, Paris, 1989-90; project mgr. Aquamarine B.V., London, 1990-91; advisor to pres. European Commn., Brussels, 1991; CEO Aquamarine Capital Mgmt. LLC, NYC. Baker Found. scholar Harvard U. Mem. Am. Econ. assn., Amnesty Internat., Greenpeace. Mem. Coonservative Party. Office: Aquamarine Capital Mgmt LLC 152 W 57th St 25th fl New York NY 10019

SPIER, KATHRYN ELIZABETH, economist, educator; b. Port Washington, NY, July 16, 1963; d. Peter Edward and Kathryn Madeleine Spier; m. James Dwight Dana Jr., June 8, 1991; 1 child, James Dwight Dana. BA summa cum laude, Yale U., 1985; PhD, MIT, 1989. Assoc. prof. Harvard U., Cambridge, Mass., 1989—94; vis. prof. U. Chgo., 1993—94; prof. Northwestern U., Evanston, Ill., 1994—. Bd. dirs., exec. com. Am. Law and Econs. Assn., New Haven, 1997—2000; rsch. assoc. Nat. Bur. Econ. Rsch. Contbr. articles to profl. jours.; mem. editl. bd. Jour. Law Econs. and Orgn., 1996—; editor (assoc.): Rand Jour. Econs., 1996—. Grantee, NSF, 1985—88, 1991—93; fellow, Olin Found., 1988—89, 1992—94. Office: Northwestern U Kellogg Sch 2001 Sheridan Rd Evanston IL 60208 Business E-Mail: k-spier@kellogg.northwestern.edu.

SPIERKEL, GREGORY M., information technology executive; b. 1957; BA, Carleton U., Ottawa, Can.; MBA, Georgetown U.; attended, Advanced Manufacturing Program at INSEAD, Fontainbleau, France. Mng. dir. Mitel Telecom, United Kingdom, 1986—89; gen. mgr. Mitel Far East Ltd., Hong Kong, 1989—90; pres., CEO, N. Am. Mitel Inc., Reston, Va., 1992—96, v.p., global sales and marketing Canada, 1996—97; sr. v.p., pres. Ingram Micro Inc., Santa Ana, Calif., 1997—99; pres. Ingram Micro Asia-Pacific, 1997—99; exec. v.p. Ingram Micro Inc., 1999—2004, officer, 1997—; pres. Ingram Micro Europe, 1999—2004, Ingram Micro Inc., 2004—05, CEO, 2005—. Bd. dir. PACCAR Corp., 2008—. Bd. mem. Sch. Bus., U. Calif., Irvine. Office: Ingram Micro Inc 1600 E St Andrew Pl Santa Ana CA 92705-4931 Office Phone: 714-566-1000. Office Fax: 714-566-7900.*

SPIERS, RONALD IAN, diplomat; b. Orange, NJ, July 9, 1925; s. Thomas Hoskins and Blanca (De Ponthier) S.; m. Patience Baker, June 11, 1949; children: Deborah Wood, Peter, Martha, Sarah. BA, Dartmouth Coll., 1948; M in Pub. Affairs, Princeton U., 1950. With AEC, 1950-54; officer-in-charge disarmament and arms control Dept. State, Washington, 1955-61, dir. NATO affairs, 1962-66; polit. counselor Am. Embassy, London, 1966-69; asst. sec. for Politico-Mil. Affairs U.S. Dept. State, 1969-73; amb. to Bahamas, Am. Embassy, Nassau, 1973-74, dep. chief of mission London, 1974-77; U.S. permanent rep. to CENTO Coun., 1977-79; amb. to Turkey, Am. Embassy, Ankara, 1977-80; asst. sec. for intelligence and rsch., mem. U.S. Intelligence Bd. U.S. Dept. State, Washington, 1980-81; amb. to Pakistan, Am. Embassy, Islamabad, 1981-83; under-sec. for mgmt. U.S. Dept. State, 1983-89; under-sec. gen. for polit. affairs UN, NYC, 1989-92; internat. affairs cons. Dept. State, 1992—. Career ambassador U.S. Fgn. Svc., 1984. Served to lt. (j.g.) USN, 1943-46, PTO. Woodrow Wilson fellow Princeton U., 1948. Fellow Nat. Acad. of Pub. Adminstrn.; mem. Am. Fgn. Svc. Assn., Internat. Inst. Strategic Studies, Coun. on Fgn. Rels., Am. Acad. of Diplomacy, Washington Inst. Fgn. Affairs. Home: 1320 Middletown Rd South Londonderry VT 05155-9145 E-mail: rispiers@comcast.net.

SPIERS-LOPEZ, PERNILLE (PERNILLE LOPEZ), consumer products company executive; b. Aarhus, Denmark; arrived in US, 1984; m. Jason Lopez, 1989; 2 children. With Door Store, Coral Gables, Fla., Stor (purchased by IKEA); sales mgr. West Coast stores IKEA, 1991—93, store mgr. Pitts., 1993—97, head, human resources, 1997—2003; pres. IKEA N. Am., Plymouth Meeting, Pa., 2001—. Bd. trustees Save the Children. Recipient Nat. Working Parent award, Terri Lynne Lokoff Child Care Found., 2005; named one of America's Top Women in Bus.-Game Changers, Pink mag. & Forté Found., 2007. Office: Ikea N America Services LLC 420 Alan Wood Rd Conshohocken PA 19428-1141 Office Phone: 800-434-4532.

SPIESS, ELIOT BRUCE, biologist, educator; b. Boston, Oct. 13, 1921; s. George Nicholas and Rena (Bunce) S.; m. Luretta Davis; children: Arthur Eliot, Bruce Davis. AB cum laude, Harvard Coll., 1943; AM, Harvard U., 1947, PhD, 1949. Instr. biology Harvard U., Cambridge, Mass., 1949-52; asst. prof. U. Pitts., 1952-56, assoc. prof., 1956-65, prof., 1965-66, U. Ill., Chgo., 1966-89, prof. emeritus, 1989—. Editor: Papers on Animal Polulation Genetics, 1962; author: (book) Genes in Populations, 1977, 2d edit., 1989; contbr. articles to profl. jours. 1st lt. U.S. Army Air Force, 1943-45. Grantee NSF, 1972-83, U.S. Atomic Energy Commn., 1966-72. Fellow AAAS; mem. Soc. for the Study of Evolution (assoc. editor 1956-58, 67-69, editor of Evolution 1975-78), Am. Soc. Naturalists (pres. 1981). Avocations: piano, photography, writing, reading, birding, hiking. Personal E-mail: elspiess@aol.com.

SPIGARELLI, JAMES L., science administrator; BA in Chemistry, MS in Chemistry, PhD in Chemistry, Kans. State Coll. Various positions Midwest Rsch. Inst., Kansas City, Mo., 1961—78, v.p., 1978—91, sr. v.p., 1991—97, exec. v.p., 1997—98, COO, 1998—99, pres., CEO, 1999—. Bd. dirs. Sci. City at Union Sta., Kansas City Mus., KCCatalyst, Brush Creek Cmty. Ptnrs., Sci. Pioneers; founding bd. mem. Kansas City Area Life Sci. Inst., Inc., 2000; trustee Univ. Mo.-KC, Avila Coll., Rockhurst Univ. R&D task force Kansas City Area Life Scis. Inst., 1999; trustee U. Mo., Kansas city, Avila Coll., Rockhurst U.; bd. dirs. Kansas City Area Life Scis. Inst., 2000. Lt. Chemical Corps US Army, Rocky Mt. Arsenal. Recipient Meritorious Achievement award, Pitts. State U., 1993; named Tech. Leader of Yr., Silicon Prairie Tech. Assn., 2000. Fellow: Coll. Arts and Scis. Alumni, Kans. State U. Office: Midwest Rsch Inst 425 Volker Blvd Kansas City MO 64110

SPIKES, PATRICIA WHITE, medical technologist; b. Houston, Nov. 30, 1951; d. Albert Carr and Willie Mae (Sneed) White; m. Herbert Charles Pete, May 24, 1980 (div.); 1 dau., Sheatri Denise; m. John Ray Spikes, Sept. 7, 1991; 1 child, John Ray II. BS Tex. Christian U., Ft. Worth, 1974. Med. technologist, edn. coordinator Riverside Gen. Hosp., Houston, 1974-76; chief lab. technologist Almeda Med. Lab., Houston, 1976-80; med. technologist Jefferson Davis Hosp., Harris County Hosp. Dist., Houston, 1980—, Lyndon B. Johnson Hosp., Harris City Hosp. Dist. Founder Coalition of Pre-Sch. Dirs., 1982—; dir. Parents Calling Parents, Houston, 1980—; and 3d v.p. Vols. in Pub. Sch. Adv. Bd., Houston, 1981, 2d v.p., 1983, pres. 1986-89, v.p. tng. chair, 1990-92, v.p. community coalitions, 1993; mem. Tex. State Bd. for Vols. in Pub. Sch., 1982—, sec., 1988—, 1st v.p., 1985, pres., 1986, sec. 1987—; chairperson Bucks for Belts Coalition for Sch. Bus Seat Belts, 1985; chair awards com. Salute to Sch. Vols.; mem. Mayor's Task Force on Edn., Houston, Mayor's Com. on Child Abuse Prevention; panelist Regional IV Svc. Ctr. State Seminar; mem. adv. bd. Blueridge Health Dept., Attucks Community Coll.; pres. Reynolds Elem. Parent Tchr. Orgn., 1982, treas., 1984; sec. Pershing Middle Sch., PTO, 1985, Class of 1969 Worthing High Sch. Reunion; candidate for Houston Ind. Sch. Dist. Bd. Edn., 1989; pres. Kings Row Child Care Parent Tchrs. Orgn., 1978; mem. Nat. Sch. Vol. Program 1982—, Mo. City Space; panelist Houston Area Black Sch. Educators, 1987; bd. dirs. Women in Action, 1984-85; mediator Dispute Resolution Ctr., 1984—, Women of Vision, Chs. Interested in Premature Parentage; city wide adv. com. Houston Ind. Sch. Dist., 1988; edn. adv. com. Family Life; pres. adv. com. Inner City 4-H, 1989—; chmn. adult leaders adv. bd. Harris County 4-H, 1989-91, treas. 1890 program, 1991-93; chmn. Northeast Adolescent Program, 1990-92; computer maintenance adv. com. Reagan High Sch., 1988—; chair Salute to Sch. Vols., 1984-86; speaker career day Houston Ind. Sch. Dist., 1989—; chmn. adv. bd. Sunnyside Multi-Svc. Ctr./Health Ctr., 1991—; mem. steering com. Tex. Cancer Coun., 1992—; spkr., active Teen Health Symposium Prairie View Adminstrn. 1980 4-H Program, 1992, 93; coord. baby buddy program Sunnyside Clinic City of Houston Health Dept., 1989—; mem. S.E. br. adv. bd. ARC, 2000-, chair, 2004-06, membership com. Greater Houston coun., 2004-; mem. membership com. Nat. Healthy Start Assn., 1974—; consortium chmn. Sunny Futures Healthy Start Program, Houston, 1998-2003; coord. Girls Rite of Passage, 2000-02; chmn. Prairie View A&M Coll. Coop. Extension Project H.O.P.E., 2001—; cons. Families Under Urban and Social Attack Non Profit Devel., 2002—; CEO, founder S&J Literary Works, 2003, Rewriting the Script Through Connections, 2005; mem. Syphilis Elimination Adv. Task Force, 2003—; chair Syphilis Elimination Bd., ARC, 2004-06; mem. program svcs. com.; mem. Sunnyside Pride, 2005; mem. Healthy Minority Marriage Initiative, 2006; mem. City of Houston HIV/AIDS Task Force, 2003—; workshop trainer Families Under Urban and Social Attack, 2004-; presenter, cons., spkr. in field, pres. SE Br. America Red Cross Bd., vol. Com. Houston Am. Red Cros Bd., founder S & J Literary Works. Recipient Vols. in Pub. Sch. Spl. Service cert., 1984; recipient numerous certs. of appreciation. Author Band Aids for Peace. Mem. NAACP, Delta Sigma Theta. Recipient Cert. of Appreciation, Vols. Am., 1980, Vols. in Pub. Schs., 1986, 87, Houston Ind. Sch. Dist., 1981, 82, 83, pres.' award Vols. in Pub. Schs., 1986-95; Outstanding Service award Reynolds Sch., 1982, cert. recognition Training Tchrs. and Adminstrs. Parent Involvment, 1986, Kay On-going Edn. Ctr., Pershing Mid. Schs., 1987, Neighborhood Ctrs. Crystal House Cmty. Svc. award, 2005, Vol. award Prairie View A&M U. project H.O.P.E. Democrat. Baptist. Mem. Top Ladies of Distinction. Home: 3134 Sunbeam St Houston TX 77051-3526 Personal E-mail: pspikes30@aol.com.

SPIKES, TAKEO, professional football player; b. Sandersville, Ga, Dec. 17, 1976; Student, Auburn U., 1995—97. Linebacker Cin. Bengals, 1998—2002, Buffalo Bills, 2003—07, Phila. Eagles, 2007—08, San Francisco 49ers, 2008—. Named First Team All-Pro, NFL, 2004; named to Nat. Football Conf. Pro-Bowl Team, 2003—04. Office: San Francisco 49ers 4949 Centennial Blvd Santa Clara CA 95054*

SPIKOL, EILEEN, artist; b. Sarasota, Fla. 1 child, Hannah. BA in Fine Arts, Fordham U., 1975; MFA in Sculpture, City Coll., NYC, 1977. Supr. reproduction studio Am. Mus. Natural History, NYC, 1971-78; tchr. painting and drawing grades 7-12 Fieldston Sch., Riverdale, N.Y., 1977-79; tchr. molding, casting, patina workshop Children's Mus. Manhattan, NYC, 1979-80; tchr. art spl. edn. Sch. Visual Arts, NYC, 1982; tchr. drawing, painting, sculpture, printmaking Studio in a Sch., NYC, 1987-90; instr. Bronx (N.Y.) Mus. Arts, 1990-91. Tchr. sculpture Md. Ctr. Arts Goucher Coll., Towson, 1986; adj. prof. art edn., spl. edn. Bkyln. (N.Y.) Coll., 1979-85, field supr.; adj. prof. fine arts St. Johns U., Queens, N.Y., 1991-93; artist in residence Found. Michel Karolyi, Vence, France, 1989, Domiciliary Care Program for Homeless Vets., St. Albans (N.Y.) VA Ctr., 1997—; adj. prof. in art edn., spl. edn. Nat. History N.Y.C., 1979-85; lectr. in field. One woman exhbns. include Soho 20 Gallery, N.Y.C., 1974, 75, 77, 78, Maples Gallery Fairleigh Dickinson U., Teaneck, N.J., 1980, 84, Islip Art Mus., E. Islip, N.Y., 1986, Bronx (N.Y.) Mus. Arts, 1988; group exhbns. include One Hundred Acres Gallery, N.Y.C., 1972, Aldrich Mus., Ridgefield, Conn., 1974, New Britain (Conn.) Mus., 1974, Hera Gallery, Wakefield, R.I., 1976, Bronx (N.Y.) Mus. Arts, 1979, 1980, Landmark Gallery, N.Y.C., 1979, Nobe' Gallery, N.Y.C., 1979, Walnut St. Galleries, Phila., 1979, Blaffer Gallery U. Houston, 1980, Mus. Natural History, N.Y.C., 1982, The Fine Arts Ctr. SUNY, Stony Brook, 1982, Fed. Plz., N.Y.C., 1982,

Freedman Gallery Albright Coll., Reading, Pa., 1982, The New Mus., N.Y.C., 1984, Henry Street Settlement, N.Y.C., 1986, Artspace Gallery, New Haven, Conn., 1992, Leopold-Hoesch-Mus., Duren, Ger., 1992, B4A Gallery, N.Y.C., 1993; featured in Arts Mag., Soho Weekly News, Womanart, The Nation, The Village Voice, Coll. Art Jour., N.Y. Times, Newsday, New Haven Register. Home: 175 W 72nd St New York NY 10023-3203

SPILKER, LINDA JOYCE, aerospace scientist; b. Mpls., Apr. 26, 1955; d. Arthur Elzear and Bonnie Joy (Jansen) Bies; m. John Leonard Horn, Jr., July 31, 1976 (div.); children: Jennifer, Jessica; m. Thomas Richard Spilker, 1997. BA in Physics, Calif. State U., Fullerton, 1977; MS in Physics, Calif. State U., LA, 1983; PhD in Geophysics and Space Physics, UCLA, 1992. Rep. Voyager Infrared Radiometer and Spectrometer expt. Jet Propulsion Lab., Pasadena, Calif., 1977-90, sci. assoc. Voyager Photopolarimeter, 1984-90, sc. assoc. Voyager Infrared Radiometer and Spectrometer, 1988-90, study scientist Cassini asst., 1988-90, co-investigator Cassini Composite Infrared Spectrometer, 1990—, dep. project scientist Cassini mission, 1990—, prin. investigator planetary geology and geophysics, 1993—. Mem. planetary sci. data steering group NASA, Washington, 1991-95, adv. coun. for planetary data sys. ring node, Moffett Field, Calif., 1990—. Contbr. chpt. Van Nostrand Encyclopedia of Planetary Science, 1994; contbr. jour. articles Icarus. Pres. North San Gabriel Valley Dem. Club, Monrovia, Calif., 1992-94. Recipient Exceptional Svc. medal, NASA, 1990, Sci. Achievement award, 1992, Disting. Alumna award, Calif. State U., L.A., 1996, Calif. State U., Fullerton, 2005; named one of Hottest 25 in Orange County, Orange County Metro mag., 2004; named to Hall of Fame, Placentia-Yorba Linda Unified Sch. Dist., 1998—99. Mem. AAAS, AAUW, Divsn. of Planetary Sci. Democrat. Presbyterian. Avocations: hiking, astronomical observing, piano, jogging. Home: 457 Granite Ave Monrovia CA 91016-2324 Office: Jet Propulsion Lab MS 230-205 4800 Oak Grove Dr Pasadena CA 91109-8001 Business E-Mail: Linda.J.Spilker@jpl.nasa.gov.

SPILLANE, DENNIS KEVIN, lawyer; b. NYC, Sept. 15, 1953; s. Denis Joseph and Mary Kate (Sullivan) S. BA magna cum laude, Manhattan Coll., 1974; JD, N.Y. Law Sch., 1978; MS in Taxation, Pace U., 1986, post-masters cert. in bus., 1992. Bar: N.Y. 1979, U.S. Dist. Ct. (ea. and so. dists.) N.Y. 1979, U.S. Tax Ct. 1986, D.C. 1988, U.S. Ct. Appeals (2d cir.) 1988, U.S. Supreme Ct. 1988, Conn. 1989. Asst. dist. atty. Borough of Bronx, NYC, 1978-85; prin. atty. N.Y. State Tax Dept., NYC, 1985-87; supervising atty. Office of Profl. Discipline, N.Y. State Edn. Dept., 1987—. Prof. law and taxation Pace U., 1987—. Contbr. articles to profl. jours. Mem. Conn. Bar Assn, N.Y. State Bar Assn., D.C. Bar Assn. Conservative. Roman Catholic. Office: NY State Edn Dept 475 Park Ave S Front 3 New York NY 10016-6901 Business E-Mail: dspillan@mail.nysed.gov.

SPILLANE, NANCY MARIE, primary school educator; b. Muskegon, Mich., July 23, 1952; d. Carl Fritz and Genevieve Helen Reinhold; m. James Mason Spillane, July 2, 1977; children: Johnny Mason, Katica Genevieve, Samuel Durward. BS, Mich. State U., 1974; MEd, Mich. State U., E. Lansing, 1976—78. Tchr. Steamboat Springs Sch. Dist., Colo., 1985—93; founder/head sch. Lowell Whiteman Primary Sch., Steamboat Springs, 1993—. Mem.: Assn. Colo. Ind. Schs. (v.p. 2004—), Colo. Coun. Internat. Reading Assn., Internat. Reading Assn., Hist. Routt County, Rotary Internat. Achievements include founding a K-8 independent school.

SPILLANE, ROBERT RICHARD, school system administrator; b. Lowell, Mass., Oct. 29, 1934; s. John Joseph and Catherine (Barrett) S.; children: Patricia, Robert Jr., Kathleen, Maura. BS, Ea. Conn. State Coll., 1956; MA, U. Conn., 1959, PhD, 1967. Elem. and secondary tchr., Storrs, Conn., 1956-60, Chaplin, Conn., 1960-62; elem. prin. Trumbull, Conn., 1962-63; secondary prin., 1963-65; asst. supt. Glassboro Pub. Schs., NJ, 1966-68, Roosevelt Schs., Long Island, NY, 1968-70, New Rochelle Pub. Schs., NY, 1970-78; dep. commr. NY State Dept Edn., Albany, NY, 1978-81; supt. Boston Pub. Schs., 1981-85, Fairfax County Pub. Schs., Va., 1985—97; regional officer Office Overseas Schs. US Dept. State, 1997—. Bd. dirs. Council Great City Schs.; mem. adv. bd. Met. Ctr. Ednl. Research, Devel. and Tng. NYU, Instr. Mag.; chmn. pres.' adv. bd. Tchrs. Coll. Columbia U.; co-chmn. adminstrs. com. study on edn. and edn. of tchrs. US Office Edn., Washington; mem. N.Y. State Sch. Officers Resolutions Com. on Legislation, Westchester County Chief Sch. Officers Legis. Com.; bd. dirs. Curriculum Devel. Council So. NJ, Impact II, NYC; adj. prof. sch. edn. Fordham U., NYC, Iona Coll., New Rochelle, Bank St. Coll. Edn., NYC, Glassboro State Coll.; instr. NYU; vis. lectr. U. Bridgeport, Conn. Author: You and Smoking, 1970, Management by Objectives in the Schools, 1978; contbr. articles to profl. jours. Trustee Mus. Fine Arts, Boston; bd. dirs. Jr. Achievement Ea. Mass., Inc.; mem. adv. com. Boston Pub. Library, The Statue of Liberty-Ellis Island Found., Inc., commn. on Bicentennial U.S. Constitution. Recipient Disting. Alumni award Ea. Conn. State Coll., 1969, Disting. Alumni award U. Conn., 1986; named one of Outstanding Young Men of Am. Mem. Am. Assn. Sch. Adminstrs. (named Nat. Supt. of Yr., 1995), Mass., Conn., NJ, NY Assns. Sch. Adminstrs., Sch. Mgmt. Study Group (pres. 1971-73, Hall of Fame award 1974), Assn. Supervision and Curriculum Devel., Nat. Sch. Pub. Relations Assn., Phi Delta Kappa. Avocations: swimming, sailing, skiing, theater and the arts, entertaining. Office: Office Overseas Sch US Dept State 2401 East St Rm H328 SA 1 Washington DC 20522 Office Phone: 202-261-8210. Office Fax: 202-261-8224. E-mail: spillanerr2@state.gov.

SPILLER, PABLO TOMAS, economics and public utilities educator; b. Montevideo, Uruguay, Apr. 30, 1951; came to U.S., 1976; s. Andres and Elizabeth (Kweksilber) S.; m. Silvia Treibich, June 8, 1972; children: Addy, Elisheba. BA in Econs., Hebrew U., Jerusalem, 1974, MA in Econs., 1976, U. Chgo., 1978, PhD in Econs., 1980. Asst. prof. econs. U. Pa., Phila., 1980-84; sr. rsch. fellow Hoover Instn., Stanford (Calif.) U., 1984-87; vis. assoc. prof. Stanford (Calif.) U., 1987; William B. McKinley prof. econs. and pub. utilities U. Ill., Champaign, 1987-94, prof. govt. and pub. affairs, 1992-94. Vis. assoc. prof. U. Calif., Berkeley, 1986, vis. prof. bus. and pub. policy, 1991-92, 93-95, Joe Shoong prof. internat. bus. and pub. policy, 1995—; vis. prof. Grad. Sch. Bus., U. Chgo., 1989; cons. World Bank, Washington, 1982—, UN, N.Y.C., 1982, 83, FTC, Washington, 1984-89; mem. internat. adv. bd. CERES, Montevideo, 1989—. Assoc. editor Jour. Indsl. Econs., 1992—, Jour. Policy Reform, 1994—; co-editor Jour. Law, Econ. and Orgn., 1992—, Jour. Econ. and Mgmt. Strategy, 1992—. Grantee Olin Found., 1977-80, NSF, 1990-95, Bradley Found.; fellow Tinker Found., 1983, Ctr. for Study of Economy and State, U. Chgo., 1989, Inst. for Policy Reform, 1992—. Mem. Am. Econ. Assn., Econometric Soc., European Assn. for Ind. Econ. Rsch. Office: U Calif Haas Sch Bus Berkeley CA 94720-0001 Home: 1076 Carol Ln Apt 43 Lafayette CA 94549-4739

SPILLERS, WILLIAM RUSSELL, civil engineering educator; b. Fresno, Calif., Aug. 4, 1934; s. William Horton and Marguerite Ester (Johnson) S.; m. Priscilla Watson, Sept. 10, 1960 (div. 1981); children: Sarah, William, Lars; m. Sandra Lynn Newsome, July 15, 1983 (div. 1995); m. Joy Bechard, Mar. 13, 2000. Student, Fresno State Coll., 1951-53; BS, U. Calif., Berkeley, 1955, MS, 1956; PhD, Columbia U., 1961. Registered profl. engr., N.Y., N.J. Structural engr. John Blume Assocs., San Francisco, 1956-57; teaching asst. Columbia U., NYC, 1957-61, prof. civil engring. and engring. mechanics, 1961-76; prof. civil engring. Rensellaer Poly. Inst., Troy, NY, 1976-90; prof., chmn. civil and environ. engring. N.J. Inst. Tech., Newark, 1990—, disting. prof. civil and environ. engring., 1995—. Cons. Weidlinger Assoc., N.Y.C., 1957-76, Geiger Berger Assoc., N.Y.C., 1957-76, DeLeuw Oh Eocha, Manchester, Eng., 1974, Parsons Hawaii, L.A., 1983, Horst Berger Ptnrs., N.Y.C., 1980; organizer NSF workshop on design theory, Troy, N.Y., 1988. Author: Automated Structural Analysis, 1972, Iterative Structural Design, 1975, Intro Structures, 1985; (with R. Levy) Analysis of Geometrically Nonlinear Structures, 1995, 2d edit., 2003, Introduction to Structures, 2002, Structural Optimization, 2009; editor 4 books including Design Theory, 1988; contbr. over 140 articles to profl. jours. Named Educator of Yr. award, Cons. Engrs. Coun. N.J., 1998; NSF fellow, 1976, Guggenheim fellow, 1968. Mem. ASCE (numerous coms., chmn. exec. com. TCCP, 1987), Internat. Assn. Bridge & Structural Engrs. Democrat. Achievements include contribution to the development of fabric structures; initiated the science of design theory; participated in development of applications of digital computers to large structural systems. Home: 7 Oak Ave West Orange NJ 07052-2409 Office: NJ Inst Tech Dept Civil & Environ Engring Newark NJ 07102 Office Phone: 973-596-2479. E-mail: spillers@njit.edu.

SPILLETT, ROXANNE, social services administrator; 1 son, Keith. BA in Edn., SUNY; postgrad., St. Lawrence U., Hunter Coll., NYC. Tchr., curriculum writer NY State Schs., 1971-73; program specialist Girl Scouts USA, 1973; dir. nat. health project Boys & Girls Clubs Am., Atlanta, 1978-79, dir. program svcs., 1979-91, asst. nat. dir. program svcs., 1991-1995, v.p. N.E. regional office, 1995, acting pres., 1995-96, pres., 1996—. Vice chair bd. dirs. Nat. Assembly of Health and Human Svc. Orgns. Office: Boys & Girls Clubs Am 1275 W Peachtree St NE Atlanta GA 30309-3404

SPILLIAS, KENNETH GEORGE, lawyer; b. Steubenville, Ohio, Nov. 8, 1949; s. George and Angeline (Bouyoucas) S.; m. Monica Mary Saumweber, May 10, 1975; children: Geoffrey David, Alicia Anne, Stephanie Marie BA, Pa. State U., 1971; JD magna cum laude, U. Pitts., 1974. Bar: Pa. 1974, Fla. 1978, U.S. Supreme Ct. 1978, U.S. Ct. Appeals (2d, 3d, 4th, 5th, 6th cirs.) 1975, (11th cir.) 1981, U.S. Dist. Ct. (mid. dist.) Fla. 1979, U.S. Dist. Ct. (so. dist.) Fla. 1978. Trial atty. U.S. Dept. Justice, Washington, 1974—76; asst. dist. atty. Dist. Atty. Allegheny County, Pitts., 1976—78; asst. atty. gen. Fla. Dept. Legal Affairs, West Palm Beach, 1978—79; ptnr. Spillias & Mitchell, West Palm Beach, 1979—82, Considine & Spillias, West Palm Beach, 1982—83, Schneider, Maxwell, Spillias et al, West Palm Beach, 1984—86, Wolf, Block, Schorr et al, West Palm Beach, 1986—88, Shapiro & Bregman, West Palm Beach, 1988—91; of counsel Greenberg, Traurig et al, West Palm Beach, 1991; pvt. practice West Palm Beach, 1991—97; ptnr. Lewis, Longman & Walker, P.A., West Palm Beach, 1997—. Instr. bus. law Coll. of Palm Beaches, West Palm Beach, 1980-81; lectr. in field County commr. Bd. County Commrs., Palm Beach County, 1982-86; co-founder, mem. Children's Svcs. Coun., Palm Beach County, 1986-91; steering com. Fla. Atlantic U. Inst. Govt., Boca Raton, 1983-94; bd. dirs. The Literacy Coalition Palm Beach County, West Palm Beach, 1990-, pres., 1992-93, health and human svcs. Fla. Dist. IX, 1995-98, Ctr. Family Svc., West Palm Beach, 1992-96, Palm Beach County Coun. Arts, 1987-88; mem. West Palm Beach Planning Bd., 1997—, chmn., 2001—; mem. policy coun. Fla. Inst. Govt., Tallahassee, 1985-86; fund raising chmn. United Cerebral Palsy Telethon, West Palm Beach, 1984-85; judge Palm Beach Post Pathfinders Awards, 1992-98; bd. dirs. South Fla. Fair, 2003-08, Palm Beach County Film and TV Commn., 2004-, chmn. 2005—, Bob Carter's Actors Workshop and Repertory Theater, 2005-08, Econ. Coun. Palm Beach County, 2006-08, Housing Leadership Coun. Palm Beach County, Fla., 2008-. Recipient Cmty. Svc. award Downtown Civitan Club, West Palm Beach, 1983, Man of Day award United Cerebral Palsy, 1986, Spl. Honoree award Palm Beach County Child Advocacy Bd., 1986, Children's Trust award Exch. Club/Dick Webber Ctr. for Prevention Child Abuse, 1991, Up and Comers award in Law, South Fla. Bus. Jour./Price Waterhouse, 1988, Achievement award Nat. Assn. Counties, 1986, Employment Law award Palm Beach County Legal Aid Soc., 2002; named Outstanding Young Men Am., U.S. Jaycees, 1975, 84, Fla. Super Lawyers, 2008. Mem. ABA, Palm Beach County Bar Assn. (appellate practice com. 1990—), Am. Hellenic Ednl. Progressive Assn. (pres. 2001-02), Fla. Bar Assn. (appellate advocacy and city, county and local govt. sects.), Order of Coif, Kiwanis. Avocations: sports, writing, theater, reading, music. Home: 147 Gregory Rd West Palm Beach FL 33405-5029 Office: Ste 1000 1700 Palm Beach Lakes Blvd West Palm Beach FL 33401-2006 Office Phone: 561-640-0820. Business E-Mail: kspillias@llw-law.com.

SPILLMAN, JANE SHADEL, curator, writer, researcher; b. Huntsville, Ala., Apr. 30, 1942; d. Marvin and Elizabeth (Russell) Shadel; m. Don Lewis Spillman, Feb. 18, 1973 (dec. Jan. 1999); children: K. Elizabeth, Samuel Shadel. AB, Vassar Coll., 1964; MA, Cooperstown Grad. Program, 1965. Rsch. asst. Corning (N.Y.) Mus. Glass, 1965-70, asst. curator, 1971-73, assoc. curator Am. glass, 1974-77, curator, 1978—, head of curatorial dept., 1994-99, dep. dir. collections, 1999—2004. Cons. The White House Curator's Office, Washington, 1987-90, other museums. Author: Complete Cut and Engraved Glass of Corning, 1979, rev. edit., 1997, Knopf Collectors Guide to Glass, Vol. 1, 1982, Vol. 2, 1983, White House Glassware, 1989, Masterpieces of American Glass, 1990, The American Cut Glass Industry: T.G. Hawkes and His Competitors, 1996, European Cut Glass Furnishings for Eastern Palaces, 2006, also 6 other books, numerous articles; editor The Glass Club Bull., 1999—. Mem. Am. Assn. Mus. (chair curators com. 1989-93), Nat. Early Am. Glass Club (bd. dirs. 1989-95), Glass Circle of London, Internat. Assn. for the History of Glass (gen. sec. 2003—), ICOM-GI (sec. 2007-). Office: Corning Mus Glass 1 Museum Way Corning NY 14830-2253

SPILLMAN, MARJORIE ROSE, theater producer, dancer; b. Norfork, Va., Jan. 5, 1958; d. William Bert and Rose Marjorie (Naperski) S.; m. David E. Marks, Apr. 4, 1985 (dec. July 1997); children: F. Oscar Marks, Miranda Rose. AS, Mt. Ida Jr. Coll., 1974; CT, Northeastern U., 1975; BS in Nursing, U. Mass., 1977; CPE, Baystate Med. Ctr., Springfield, Mass., 2007; Clin. Pastoral Edn., Chaplain Resident, 2009; MAAT, Elms Coll., 2008. RN, Mass. Charge nurse VA Med. Ctr., Northampton, Mass., 1977-82; dancer N.E. Am. Ballet, Northampton, 1982, Ballet Theater Sch., Springfield, Mass., 1982-84, Smith Coll., Northampton, 1984-96; sales rep. Winthrop Pharm., NYC, 1982-94, Nycomed, NYC, 1994-96; dir. mktg. and devel. The Northampton Ctr. for the Arts, 1997. Prin. dancer Project Opera, Northampton, 1984—86; dancer Polobulus East St. Dance, Hadley, Mass., 1985; dance and theatre reviewer Holyoke T. Telegram, 1991—92; theater critic Daily Hampshire Gazette, 1993—96; dance panelist Mass. Cultural Coun., 1998; curator The Refrigerator Door art exhibit Smith Coll., 1999—2001; prodr. Pioneer Valley Performing Arts H.S., 1998; founder Open Door Prodns., 1999; cons. Organic Trade Assn., 1999, New Eng. Artist Trust, 1999—; organizer Congl. Edn. Day in Washington, D.C.; tchr. Easthampton HS, 2000—. Dancer, creator part of Carmen in Carmen, 1985, Ruth St. Denis in the House of Ruth Ted and Martha, 1994; dancer, choreographer A Victorian Evening, 1986; dancer Nutcracker Ballet, Pioneer Valley Ballet, 1988; creator, prodr. The Halloween House at Sunnyside, 1990, producing dir., 1991-92; actor, author play Mary P. Wells Smith Narrates, 1987; founder, prodr., dir. Northampton Children's Theater, 1993—; prodr. Northampton's First Night Children's Parade, 1996, dir. First Night Northampton, 1997-98, Saturday As a Work of Art—Summer Series, 1997; contbg. writer Healthy & Natural Mag. Theater panelist Mass. Cultural Coun., 1997, 2000; devel. com. Cooley Dickerson Hosp., 1999; religious tchr. St. Mary of the Assumption, 2001-04, 2005—; dir. Nothing Scary Halloween House, East St. Studios, 2004, RCIA for Children, 2001-. Democrat. Roman Catholic.

SPILLMAN, ROBERT ARNOLD, architect; b. Bethlehem, Pa., May 21, 1931; s. Otto Henry and Ruth Meredith (Miller) S.; m. Cidney Jane Brandon, July 7, 1956; children: Catherine, Sarah, Peter. BArch, Cornell U., 1954. Registered arch., Pa., N.J. Archtl. designer Office Douglass Orr, New Haven, 1956-58; ptnr. Lovelace & Spillman, Archs., Bethlehem, 1959-70; sr. ptnr. Spillman Farmer Archs., Bethlehem, 1971-82; pres. Spillman Farmer Shoemaker Pell Whildin, P.C., Bethlehem, 1983—96, sr. prin., 1997—. Trustee Laros Found., Bethlehem, 1970-2007; pres. Bethlehem Libr. Bd., 1970-74, United Way Northampton and Warren Counties, 1979-81, Lehigh River Found. Lehigh Valley Indsl. Parks bd., 1985-96, pres., 1996-2001; chmn. Bethlehem Bd. Hist. Archtl. Rev., 1961-82; mem. pres.'s coun. Lehigh Valley Partnership, 2001—; bd. dirs. KidsPeace, 2003-2007; Olympic torchbearer, 1996. 1st lt. USAF, 1954-56. Fellow AIA (pres. Ea. Pa. chpt. 1969-70); mem. Pa. Soc. Archs. (disting. bldg. awards 1971, 76, 78, 94, 2001, 02, 04, 05, 06, 07), Soc. Coll. and Univ. Planners, Bay Head Yacht Club (N.J.) (rear commodore 1985-87, vice commodore 1999-2001, commodore 2001-03). Democrat. Episcopalian. Office: Spillman Farmer Shoemaker Pell Whildin 1720 Spillman Dr Bethlehem PA 18015 Business E-Mail: rspillman@spillmanfarmer.com.

SPILMAN, JANET LYNNE, special education educator; b. Marysville, Calif., Nov. 29, 1957; d. Mary Elizabeth and James Maurice Spilman. BA in Hist. and Polit. Sci., Jamestown Coll., ND, 1980; BS in Spl. Edn., Moorhead State U., Minn., 1983; MEd, U. La Verne, Calif., 2004. Specialist Instrn. Credential: Learning Handicapped Commn. on Tchr. Credentialing, Calif., 1989, Single Subject Tchg. Credential: Soc.Sci. Commn. on Tchr. Credentialing, Calif., 1989, Resource Specialist Cert. Commn. on Tchr. Credentialing, Calif., 2000, Nat. Cert. In Assistive Tech. Calif. State U. Northridge, 2000. Case mgr., behavior analyist Fraser Hall, Inc, Fargo, ND, 1983—85; spl. edn. tchr. Yuma Union H.S. Dist. - Kofa H.S., Yuma, Ariz., 1985—89; job coord. Job Tng. Partnership Act - Summer Youth Program, 1986—88; tchr. (govt.) Yuma Union H.S. Dist., Migrant Edn. Dept., Yuma, Ariz., 1987—89; resource specialist Live Oak Unified Sch. Dist., Calif., 1989—94; ind. living instr. Cmty. Resource Svcs., Marysville, Calif., 1994—96; spl. day class tchr., emotionally disturbed program Milhous Sch., Inc., Sacramento, 1996—97; resource specialist Wash. Unified Sch. Dist., West Sacramento, Calif., 1997—2002, Sacramento City Unified Sch. Dist., Sacramento, 2002—. Mem.: ASCD, Vocat. Evaluation and Work Adjustment Assn., Nat. Rehab. Assn., Assn. for Children and Adults with Learning Disabilities, Coun. for Children with Behavioral Disorders, Calif. Assn. for Resource Specialists, Phi Delta Kappa, Assn. Calif. Sch. Adminstrs., Am. Assn. Sch. Adminstrs., Prader Willi Assn., Coun. For Exceptional Children. Avocations: working cattle, packing (horse and burro), hiking, photography, gardening, horseback riding. Home: 9524 North Butte Rd Live Oak CA 95953 Personal E-mail: spilmanrsp@comcast.net.

SPILMAN, ROBERT HENKEL, furniture company executive; b. Knoxville, Tenn., Sept. 27, 1927; s. Robert Redd and Lila (Henkel) S.; m. Jane Bassett, Apr. 2, 1955; children: Robert Henkel Jr., Virginia Perrin, Vance Henkel. BS, N.C. State U., 1950. With Cannon Mills, 1950-57; with Bassett Table Co., Va., 1957-60; dir. Bassett Furniture Industries Inc., 1960—97, exec. v.p., 1966, pres., 1966-89, CEO, 1979—97, chmn., 1982—97; ret., 1997. Adv. bd. Liberty Mut. Ins. Co Trustee Va. Found. Ind. Colls.; bd. dir. Blue Ridge Airport Authority. Lt. U.S. Army, WWII and Korea. Recipient Best CEO Home Furnishing Industry award, Wall Street Transcript, 1981, 1982; named Humanitarian of Yr., City of Hope, 1982; named to Furniture Hall of Fame, 2005. Mem. Am. Furniture Mfrs. Assn. (James T. Ryan award 1984), Nat. Furniture Mfrs. Assn. (bd. dir., past pres.), Furniture Factories Mktg. Assn. (past chmn., bd. dirs.), Va. Mfrs. Assn. (past dir. exec. com.), Bassett Country Club, Commonwealth Club, Kinloch Golf Club, Linville Golf Club, Grandfather Golf and Country Club (Linville, N.C.), The Country Club Va., Olde Farm (Bristol, Va.). Episcopalian. Avocation: fishing. Office: Spilman Properties PO Box 880 Bassett VA 24055 Personal E-mail: bspilman@sitestar.net.

SPINA, ANTHONY FERDINAND, lawyer; b. Chgo., Aug. 15, 1937; s. John Dominic and Nancy Maria (Ponzio) S.; m. Anita Phyllis De Orio, Jan. 28, 1961; children: Nancy M. Spina Okal, John D., Catherine M. Spina Samatas, Maria J. Spina Samatas, Felicia M. Spina DiGiovanni. BS in Social Sci., Loyola U., Chgo., 1959; JD, DePaul U., Chgo., 1962. Bar: Ill. 1962; US Supreme Ct. 2005. Assoc. Epton, Scott, McCarthy & Bohling, Chgo., 1962-64; pvt. practice Elmwood Park, Ill., 1964-71; pres. Anthony & Spina, PC, 1971-84; arbitrator Circuit Ct. of Cook County, 1990—98; pres. Spina, McGuire & Okal, PC, Elmwood Park, 1985—. Codifier Rosemont Village Ordinances, 1971, Elmwood Park Bldg. Code, 1975, Leyden Twp. Codified Ordinances, 1987. Mem. Elmwood Pk. Bldg. Code Planning Commn. Bd. Appeals; bd. dirs. Sheridan Carrol Charitable Works Fund, 1994—; atty. Leyden Twp., Ill., 1969—89, Village of Rosemont, Ill., 1971; counsel for Pres. and dir. Cook County Twp. Ofcls. Ill., 1975—96; counsel for exec. dir. Ill. State Assn. Twp. Ofcls., 1975—96; counsel Elmwood Park Village Bd., 1967—89, Norwood Park St. Lighting Dist., 1988—, various Cook County Twps. including DuPage, 1980—82, Maine, 1981—97, Norwood Park, 1982—, Wayne, 1982—84, Berwyn Twp., 1997—99, Hanover Twp., 1997, Cook County Hwy. Commrs. Traffic Fine Litigation, 1974—96, 1999—2001, Hanover Twp. Mental Health Bd., 1991—2002, Glen Edens Assn., 1994—99, Berwyn Twp. Mental Health Bd., 1997—2002. Recipient Lacodaire medal Deans Key Loyola U., Loyola U. Housing awards, 1965, 71, 76; Appreciation award Cook County Twp. Ofcls., B. Scidmore award Ill. Twp. Attys. Assn., 2002. Mem. ABA, Ill. Bar Assn., Chgo. Bar Assn., West Suburban Bar Assn. Cook County (past chmn. unauthorized practice law sect.), Am. Judicature Soc., Justinian Soc. Lawyers, Ill. State Twp. Attys. Assn. (past v.p., pres. 1982-86, dir. 1996-99, dir. emeritus 1999—), Nat. Inst. Town and Twp. Attys. (past v.p., pres. 1993-95, Ill. del.), Montclare/Leyden C. of C., Edgebrook C. of C. (past bd. dirs.), Nat. Assn. Italian Am. Lawyers, Nat. Italian Am. Bar Assn., Joint Civic Com. Chgo. (exec. com.), World Bocce Assn. (dir. 1994-2002), St. Rocco Soc. Simbario, KC (scribe, trustee, past Grand Knight, bldg. corp. dir. 1967-91, dir., Charitable Words Fund 1991-), Calabresi in Am. Orgn. (bd. dirs. 1991—), Fra Noi

Ethnic Publ. (dir. 1995—), Blue Key, Delta Theta Phi, Tau Kappa Epsilon, Pi Gamma Mu. Roman Catholic. Office: 7610 W North Ave Elmwood Park IL 60707-4100 Office Phone: 708-453-2800. Business E-Mail: aspina@smolaw.com.

SPINA, FRANCIS X., state supreme court justice; b. Pittsfield, Mass., Nov. 13, 1946; m. Sally O'Donnell; 2 children. BA, Amherst Coll.; JD, Boston Coll. Law Sch. With Western Mass. Legal Services, 1972—74; asst. city solicitor Pittsfield Law Dept., 1975—77; second asst. dist. atty. Berkshire County Dist. Attorney's Office, Mass., 1979—83; atty. Reder, Whalen, and Spina, 1983—87, Katz, Lapointe, and Spina, 1987—93; judge Mass. Superior Ct., 1993-97, Appeals Ct., Pittsfield, 1997-99; assoc. justice Mass. Supreme Jud. Ct., Boston, 1999—. Mem. Mass. Standing Com. on Pro Bono Legal Services. Mem.: Boston Bar Assn., Mass. Bar Assn. Office: Supreme Judicial Court 1 Pemberton Sq Ste 2-500 Boston MA 02108-1717*

SPINDLER, GEORGE DEARBORN, anthropologist, educator, writer; b. Stevens Point, Wis., Feb. 28, 1920; s. Frank Nicholas and Winifred (Hatch) S.; m. Louise Schaubel, May 29, 1942 (dec. Feb. 1997); 1 dau., Sue Carol Spindler Coleman. BS, Central State Tchrs. Coll., Wis., 1940; MA, U. Wis., 1947; PhD, U. Calif. at Los Angeles, 1952. Tchr. sch. in, Wis., 1940-42; rsch. assoc. Stanford U., 1950-51, prof. anthropology and edn., 1954—2006, exec. head dept., 1963—67. Cons. editor Holt, Rinehart & Winston, 1965-91, Harcourt, 1991-99, Wadsworth-Thomson, 2002-; vis. prof. U. Wis., 1979-85, U. Calif., Santa Barbara, 1986-91, Harvard U., 1999. Author: Menomini Acculturation, 1955, (with A. Beals and L. Spindler) Culture in Process, 1967, rev. edit., 1973, Transmission of American Culture, 1959, (with L. Spindler) Dreamers Without Power, 1971, rev. edit., 1984, Burgbach: Urbanization and Identity in a German Village, 1973, (with Louise Spindler) The American Cultural Dialogue and its Transmission, 1990, (with Lorie Hammond) Innovations in Educational Ethnography, 2006; editor: Education and Anthropology, 1955, (with Louise Spindler) Case Studies in Cultural Anthropology, 1960—, Am. Anthropologist, 1962-66, Methods in Cultural Anthropology, 1965-71, Case Studies in Education and Culture, 1966-72, Basic Units in Anthropology, 1970, (with Janice Stockard) Globalization and Urbanization in Fifteen Cultures-Born in One World, Living in Another, 2006; editor, contbr.: Education and Culture, 1963, Being An Anthropologist, 1970, Education and Cultural Process, 1974, rev. edit., 1987, 97, The Making of Psychological Anthropology, 1978, 2nd edit., 1994, Doing the Ethnography of Schooling, 1982, Interpretive Ethnography of Schooling at Home and Abroad, 1987, Pathways to Cultural Awareness: Cultural Therapy with Students and Teachers, 1994, Fifty Years of Anthropology and Education: A Spindler Anthology, 2000. Pres. Peninsula Sch. Bd., Menlo Park, Calif., 1954-56. Served with AUS, 1942-45. Recipient Lloyd W. Dinkelspeil award Stanford U., 1978, Disting. Svc. award Soc. Internat. Diplomacy and Third World Anthropologists, 1984, Disting. Career Contbn. award Com. on Role and Status of Minorities, Am. Edn. Rsch. Assn., Nat. Acad. Edn., 1994, Father of Ednl. Ethnography award Nat. Ednl. Ethnography Conf., 2000, George and Louise Spindler Excellence award Stanford U., 2001; fellow Ctr. Advanced Study of Behavioral Scis., 1956-57; subject of Vol. 17 Psychoanalytic Study of Soc. essays, 1992. Fellow Am. Anthrop. Assn.; mem. Southwestern Anthrop. Assn. (pres. 1962-63), Coun. for Anthropology and Edn. (pres. 1982, George and Louise Spindler award for outstanding contbns. to ednl. anthropology 1987, disting. Scholar award 1998), Nat. Acad. Edn. Office: Ethnographics 1247 Alice St Davis CA 95616-2174 Personal E-mail: geospinner@aol.com. *My major aims as a professional observer and interpreter of human behavior are to acquire knowledge by research and disseminate understanding to others by teaching, writing, and editing. As a person I try to keep love, work, play in balanced relationship to each other, and strive for tolerance at least, and hopefully appreciation for others who are different than myself.*

SPINDLER, JAMES ANDREW, not-for-profit executive; b. Morgantown, W.Va., Oct. 20, 1950; s. Garold Ralph and Elizabeth (Carroll) Spindler; m. Ann Bailie Trautman; children: James Andrew Jr., Emma Carroll, Eliza Bailie. AB, Harvard Coll., Cambridge, Mass., 1972; MPA, Princeton U., 1975, PhD, 1983. Bus. fellow The Brookings Instn., Washington, 1980—82; v.p. Continental Ill. Nat. Bank., Chgo., 1984—85, Fed. Res. Bank of N.Y., NYC, 1985—89, sr. v.p., 1989—93; mng. dir. Fin. Svcs. Vol. Corps, NYC, 1993—95, exec. dir., 1995—2005, pres. & CEO, 2005—. Mem. Basle Com. on Banking Supervision, Switzerland, 1991—93, G10 Com. on Payment and Settlement Sys., Basle, 1991—93; prin. investigator Russia Initiative Project of the Carnegie Corp. of NY, NYC, 2000—01; mem. bd. dirs. Dubai Fin. Svc. Authority, United Arab Emirates, 2004—. Author: The Politics of International Credit: Private Finance and Foreign Policy in Germany and Japan, 1984, (Op-Ed Pieces) International Herald Tribune, San Francisco Chronicle, and The Jakarta Post, 2001. Recipient Medal of Svc. for assistance in developing Russian fin. mkts., Ctrl. Bank of Russia and the Russian Finance Ministry, 1996. Mem.: Bretton Woods Com., Am. Coun. on Germany, Coun. on Fgn. Rels. Presbyterian. Avocations: classical music, travel, running. Office: Financial Services Volunteer Corps 800 3d Ave 11th Fl New York NY 10022 Office Phone: 212-771-1412. Business E-Mail: jspindler@fsvc.org.

SPINELLI, CHRISTOPHER JOHN, military officer; b. Abilene, Tex., Feb. 15, 1974; s. Joseph John and Elizabeth Ann Spinelli; m. Amy Kay Baker, Jan. 24, 1998; children: Luke Joseph, Simon Paul, Leigh Faith. MS in Computer Sci., Air Force Inst. Tech., Wright-Patterson AFB, Ohio, 2006. Cert. pilot USAF, 1998, experimental test pilot USAF, 2006, in test and evaluation level 2 Def. Acquisition U., 2007. Maj. USAF, Multiple, 1992—2008; exptl. f-16 test pilot 416th Flight Test Squadron, 2006—08; exec. officer Air Force Flight Test Ctr., Edwards, Calif., 2008—. Contbr. scientific papers (AFIT Nav. Rsch. Excellence Award, 2006). Decorated Air medal Dept. Def., Aerial Achievement medal, Air Force Achievement medal, Joint Svc. Achievement medal. Mem.: Inst. Nav., Order of Daedalians, Soc. Experimental Test Pilots, Tau Beta Pi. Church Of Christ. Avocations: cycling, running. Office: Air Force Flight Test Ctr 1 S Rosamond Blvd Bldg 1 Edwards CA 93524

SPINELLI, HENRY MICHAEL, plastic surgeon; b. NYC, Mar. 21, 1956; B, Johns Hopkins Univ.; MD, NYU Sch. Med., 1981. Cert. Am. Bd. Ophthalmology, 1987, Am. Bd. Plastic Surgery, 1993. Intern in ophthalmology NYU Med. Ctr., 1981—82; resident in surgery Manhattan Eye Ear & Throat Hosp., 1982—85; resident in plastic reconstructive surgery Columbia Presbyterian Hosp., NYC, 1985—88; resident in craniofacial surgery NYU Med. Ctr., 1988—90, fellow in plastic surgery, 1990—91; asst. prof. surgery, dir. craniofacial surgery Yale Univ., 1991—96; attending surgeon Lenox Hill Hosp., 2000; clin. assoc. prof. surgery Cornell Univ. Med. Ctr.; staff mem. NY Eye & Ear Infirmary, Manhattan Eye Ear & Throat Hosp., NY Hosp. Cornell Med. Ctr.; private practice in plastic surgery NYC. Contbr. articles to profl. jours. Mem.: Am. Soc. Plastic Surgeons & other profl. societies. Office: 875 5th Ave New York NY 10021 Office Phone: 212-570-6235. Office Fax: 212-570-4168. Business E-Mail: hmspinelli@aol.com.

SPINETTA, JEAN-CYRIL, airline executive; b. Paris, Oct. 4, 1943; s. Adrien Spinetta and Antoinette Brignoli; m. Nicole Ricquebourg, Nov. 22, 1969; children: Eric, Isabelle, Cécile, Adrien. Postgrad degree, Public Law Paris, 1968; diploma, Inst. Internat. Politics, Paris; graduate, Ecole Nat. d'Administrn., 1972. Bur. chief dept. investments and planning Nat. Edn. Adminstrn., 1972—76; auditor State Coun. Govt., 1976—78; adv. French Govt., 1978—81; info. svc. chief Prime Min. of France, 1981—83; CoS minister Min. Labour, Employment and Profl. Devel., 1984—86; inspector gen. Nat. Edn. Adminstrn., 1986—88; CoS minister Min. Social Affairs and Employment, Min. Planning Devel., Housing & Transport, 1988—90; chair, CEO Air Inter, 1990—93; indsl. advisor Presidency of the Republic, 1994—95; govt. adminstr. Public Svc., 1995; chmn., CEO Air France, 1997—; chmn. & CEO Air France-KLM Group, 2004—. Decorated officer Legion of Honor, comdr. Nat. Order of Merit (France), Officier des Palmes Académiques, Nat. Edn. Ministry, Comdr. in the Dutch Order of Orange-Nassau, Netherlands. Mem.: IATA (chmn. 2004), Assn. European Airlines (pres. 2001). Avocations: tennis, skiing. Office: Air France 45 rue de Paris Roissy France Office Phone: 33141566164. Office Fax: 33141566159.

SPINKA, WILLIAM J., art educator; b. Bridgeport, Conn., Oct. 3, 1920; s. Jacob J. Spinka and Anna M. Syrotiak; m. Valerie A. Lauten, June 19, 1943; children: Kenneth W., Caryl V. BS in Edn., CCNY, 1942, MS in Edn., 1945. Tchr., phys. edn. dir. Birch Wathen Sch., NYC, 1942—44; instr. engring. USMcht. Marine Acad., Kings Point, 1944—45; instr. art CCNY, 1946—60, asst. prof. art, 1961—66, assoc. prof., 1967—81, prof., 1981—85, prof. emeritus, 1986, archtl. design rsch. projects, 1986—. Ednl. affiliate Am. Soc. Interior Design, NYC, 1976—88; profl. mem. Nat. Soc. Interior Designers, 1960—75; sculptor; painter. Exhibitions include Salmagundi Club, Nat. Arts Club, Nat. Acad., NY, 1976—99, Corcoran Gallery, 1946, Lever House Gallery, 1986—95, one-man shows include Canton Artists Guild, Conn., 1979, works pub. in mags. Ensign US Maritime Svc., 1944—46. Mem.: Audubon Artists Inc. (v.p. sculpture 1987—93, sr. v.p. 1994—98, Gold medal of honor 1988, Silver medal of honor 1992). Avocations: construction, landscape design, athletics. Home: 4658 Grosvenor Ave Bronx NY 10471

SPINNER, LEE LOUIS, accountant; b. Hillsboro, Ill., Nov. 9, 1948; s. John Louis and Clara Mae (Brown) Spinner; m. Rosemary T. Dean, Mar. 2, 2002. BS in Acctg., U. Ill., 1971, MAS in Acctg., 1972; MS in Taxation, DePaul U., 1983. CPA, Ill. Sr. tax acct. Ernst & Young, Chgo., 1972-78; dir. tax returns and audits Sunbeam Corp., Chgo., 1978-82; dir. tax compliance Sara Lee Corp., Chgo., 1982-83; mgr. tax compliance AM Internat., Inc., Chgo., 1983-85; mgr. taxes Household Mfg., Inc., Prospect Heights, Ill., 1985-89; mgr. internat. taxes Pittway Corp., Chgo., 1990-2000; dir. taxes Methode Electronics, Inc., Harwood Heights, Ill., 2000—. Instr. tax tng. program Ernst & Young, 1975-78; tax advisor Sta. WIND, Call Your Acct., Chgo., 1977-78. Sec. Grant Park Accts. Softball League, Chgo., 1976-77. Mem. AICPA, Ill. CPA Soc., U. Ill. Alumni Assn. (bd. assoc., audit com. 1997—), Top Social Athletic Club, Moose, KC. Democrat. Roman Catholic. Home: 435 W Wilshire Dr Palatine IL 60067-4788

SPINNER, MARINA A., lawyer; d. Ralph Salvatore and Phyllis Bussola; m. Dennis H. Spinner, July 2, 1988; children: Alexandra, Skylar. BA, Columbia U., NYC, 1988; JD, Pace U., White Plains, NY, 1994. Bar: NJ 1994, NY 1995, DC 2006, US Dist. Ct. (so. dist.), NY, U.S. Ct. Appeals. Assoc. Turner & Owen, NYC, 1994—95; ptnr. Nicoletti, Gonson, Spinner & Owen, LLP, NYC, 1995—. Mem.: ABA, NY State Trial Lawyers Assn., Assn. Profl. Insurance Women. Office: Nicoletti Gonson Spinner & Owne LLP 555 Fifth Ave New York NY 10017

SPINNER, NANCY BETTINA, medical educator, director; b. Bklyn., Feb. 19, 1954; d. Sidney and Mildred Spinner; m. Ian Daniel Krantz, Mar. 9, 2002; children: Alexander Charles Kadesch, Hanna Elisabeth Kadesch, Sarah Rose Krantz. PhD, U. Calif., Berkeley, 1984. Diplomate in med. genetics 1987. Postdoc. fellow Children's Hosp. Phila., 1984—86; dir., cytogenetics lab. Albert Einstein Med. Ctr., 1986—91; dir., cytogenomics lab. Children's Hosp. Phila., 1991—; prof. U. Pa., Sch. Medicine, 1991—. Recipient Dean's award, U. Pa. Sch. of Medicine, 1997; Molecular Analysis Alagille Syndrome, NIH, 1997—2008, Genetic Analysis Ring Chromosome 20, Ring Chromosome 20 Found., 2007—09, Genetic Mechanisms Pediatric Heart Disease, NIH, 1999—2008. Fellow: Am. Coll. Med. Genetics; mem.: Am. Soc. Human Genetics (program com. 2001—04). Achievements include discovery of identified Jagged1 role in causing Alagille syndrome. Office: Children's Hosp Phila 3615 Civic Ctr Blvd Philadelphia PA 19104 Office Fax: 215-590-3850. Business E-Mail: spinner@mail.med.upenn.edu.

SPINNER, STEVEN L., food products executive; With AFI Foodservice Distributors Performance Food Group, Richmond, Va., 1985—89; v.p. AFI Foodservice Distributors, 1989—97, pres., 1997—2000; regional pres. Broadline div. Performance Food Group, Richmond, Va., 2000—01, pres. Broadline div., 2001—02, sr. v.p., CEO Broadline div., 2002—05, pres., COO, 2005—06, pres., CEO, 2006—08, United Natural Foods Inc., Dayville, Conn., 2008—. Office: United Natural Foods 260 Lake Rd Dayville CT 06241*

SPINRAD, MICHAEL IRWIN, social studies educator; s. Hyron Zeleg and Bette Louise Spinrad; m. Caroline Beth Kreitzberg, Sept. 1, 1985 (div. 2009); children: Samuel Emanuel, William Kreitzberg, Rebecca Felice, Elaine Alexandra, Joseph Shalom. AB, U. Calif., Berkeley, 1982; MA, St. Mary's Coll., Moraga, Calif., 2002. Freelance musician, Kentfield, Calif., 1982—; asst. tchr. music Kent Mid. Sch., Kentfield, 1996—2001; tchr. social studies San Marin H.S., Novato, 2003—, chmn. dept. social studies, 2006—. Presenter in field. Composer: (percussion music) Paradiddle Madness, Expanding on a Three-Over-Four Beat Idea; composer: (musician) (musical recording) It's Morning, Light and Easy; musician: (music recording) Marshal Fields, (musical recording) Rio Lindo, Sweet Romance. Recipient Award of Excellence, Outstanding Tchr. Recognition Program, U. Calif. San Diego, 2006, Outstanding Tchr. award, Rotary Novarto, 2007. Mem.: Percussive Arts Soc., Calif. Coun. Social Studies, Nat. Coun. Social Studies. Jewish. Avocations: music, running, chess. Home: PO Box 61 Kentfield CA 94914 Office: San Marin High School 15 San Marin Dr Novato CA 94945 E-mail: mspinrad@nusd.org.

SPINRAD, RICHARD WILLIAM, federal agency administrator, oceanographer; b. NYC, Apr. 6, 1954; s. Leonard William and Thelma (Zipkin) S.; m. Alanna Wynn Thompson, June 1, 1980; 1 child, Gary Brian. BA, Johns Hopkins U., 1975; MS in Phys. Oceanography, Oreg. State U., 1978, PhD in Marine Geology, 1982. Rsch. asst. Oreg. State U., Corvallis, 1975-82; rsch. scientist Bigelow Lab. for Ocean Sci., West Boothbay Harbor, Maine, 1982-86, prin. investigator, 1986—94; pres. Sea Tech., Inc., Corvallis, 1986-87; program mgr. optical oceanography Office of Naval Research, Arlington, Va., 1987-89; div. dir. Office of Naval Rsch., Arlington, Va., 1989-94; dir. Consortium for Oceanographic Rsch. & Edn. (CORE), 1994—99; tech. dir. Oceanographer of the Navy, 1999—2003; asst. adminstr., Nat. Ocean Svc. Nat. Oceanic and Atmospheric Adminstrn., Washington, 2003—05, asst. adminstr., Office of Oceanic and Atmospheric Rsch., 2005—. Adj. faculty George Mason U., 1994-97, U.S. Naval Acad., 1997-99; trustee Bigelow Lab. for Ocean Scis., 1995-; led develop. Nat. Ocean Sciences Bowl for HS Students, CORE; US permanent rep., Intergovernmental Oceanographic Commn., UNESCO, 2004-; co-chair, White House Joint Subcommittee on Ocean Sci. and Tech. Editor-in-chief: Oceanography; co-author with Admiral James D. Watkins, Oceans 2000: Bridging the Millennia; contbr. sci. articles to profl. jours. Recipient Disting. Civilian Svc. award, Dept. Navy, 2003, Presdl. Rank award. Mem. NAS, AAAS, Am. Soc. Limnology and Oceanography, Am. Geophys. Union, Oceanography Soc., Optical Soc. Am. (Johns Hopkins U. Schs. com.), Oceanography Soc. (coun. 1994-97, pres.-elect), Am. Meteorological Soc., Navy League Democrat. Jewish. Avocations: banjo, outdoor activities, woodworking. Office: NOAA Office of Oceanic and Atmospheric Rsch 1315 East-West Hwy Silver Spring MD 20910 Office Phone: 301-713-2458. Office Fax: 301-713-0163.

SPINRAD, ROBERT JOSEPH, computer scientist; b. NYC, Mar. 20, 1932; s. Sidney and Isabel (Reiff) S.; m. Verna Winderman, June 27, 1954; children: Susan Irene, Paul Reiff. BS, Columbia U., 1953, MS (Bridgham fellow), 1954; PhD (Whitney fellow), MIT, 1963. Registered profl. engr., N.Y. Project engr. Bulova Research & Devel. Lab., NYC, 1953-55; sr. scientist Brookhaven Nat. Lab., Upton, NY, 1955-68; v.p. Sci. Data Systems, Santa Monica, Calif., 1968-69; v.p. programming Xerox Corp., El Segundo, Calif., 1969-71, dir. info. scis., 1971-76, v.p. systems devel., 1976-78, v.p. research Palo Alto Rsch. Ctr., 1978-83, dir. systems tech., 1983-87, dir. corp. tech., 1987-92, v.p. tech. analysis and devel., 1992-94, v.p. technology strategy, 1994-98; ret.; cons. in field, Palo Alto, Calif., 1998—. Contbr. articles to profl. jours. Fellow Am. Acad. Arts & Scis.; mem. Nat. Acad. Engring., Calif. Coun. on Sci. and Tech., Sigma Xi, Tau Beta Pi. Achievements include patents in field. E-mail: robert@spinrad.com.

SPIOTTO, JAMES ERNEST, lawyer; b. Chgo., Nov. 25, 1946; s. Michael Angelo and Vinnetta Catherine (Henninger) S.; m. Ann Elizabeth Humphreys, Dec. 23, 1972; children: Michael Thomas, Mary Catherine, Joan Elizabeth, Kathryn Ann. AB, St. Mary's of the Lake, 1968; JD, U. Chgo., 1972. Bar: Ill. 1972, U.S. Dist. Ct. (no. dist.) Ill. 1973, U.S. Ct. Appeals (7th cir.)1974, US Ct.Appeal(3d cir.), 1992, U.S. Supreme Ct. 1978, U.S. Ct. Appeals (9th cir.) 1984, U.S. Dist. Ct. (so. dist.) Calif. 1984. Exclusionary rule study-project dir. Law Enforcement Assistance Agy. Grant, Chgo., 1972; law clk. to presiding justice U.S. Dist. Ct., Chgo., 1972-74; assoc. Chapman and Cutler, Chgo., 1974-80, ptnr., 1980—. Chmn. program on defaulted bonds and bankruptcy Practising Law Inst., 1982—, chmn program on troubled debt financing, 1987— Author: Troubled Debt Financing: Litig. Bankruptcy, 1987, Defaulted Bonds and Bankruptcy, 1988, Defaults, Litig., Bankruptcy, and Workouts, 1988, Troubled Debt Securities, 1988, The Problems of Indenture Trustees and Bondholders, 1988, Bonds and Bankruptcy, 1989, Defaulted Securities, 1990; co-author with Joseph C. Daley Current Disclosure of Obligations for Mcpl. Securities, 1988, Mcpl. Bond Disclosure, 1987, The Law of State and Local Govt. Debt Financing, 2001; contbr. numerous articles to profl. jours. With USAR, 1969-75. Recipient Mcpl. Industry Contbn. award, Nat. Fedn. of Mcpl. Analysts, Carlson Prize, 1995. Mem. ABA, Chgo. Bar Assn., Econ. Club of Chgo, Nat. Assn. Bond Lawyers, Soc. Mcpl. Analysts, Law Club of City of Chgo., Union League, Econs. Club Chgo. Roman Catholic. Office: Chapman and Cutler 111 W Monroe St Ste 1700 Chicago IL 60603-4006 Office Phone: 312-845-3000. Office Fax: 312-701-2361.

SPIRA, MICHAEL, legislative staff member; Temp. employee to congressmen Steven Rothman and Sam Farr US House of Reps., Washington, 2001, staff asst. to congressman Bob Filner, 2001—02, legis. corr. to congresswoman Carolyn McCarthy, 2002—03, legis. asst., 2003—07, legis. dir., 2007—08, legis. dir./chief of staff, 2008, chief of staff, 2008—. Democrat. Mailing: US House Reps 2346 Rayburn House Office Bldg Washington DC 20515 Office Phone: 202-225-5516. Office Fax: 202-225-5758.*

SPIRA, PATRICIA GOODSITT, retired association executive; b. Milw. d. Lawrence Manfred and Ruth Pauline (Miller) Goodsitt; m. Marvin Alfred Spira, July 12, 1952; children: David, James, Ann, Ellen. BA in History, U. Wis., Milw., 1967. Dir. group sales Swan Theatre and Supper Club, Milw., 1962-63; mgr. box office Performing Arts Ctr., Milw., 1969-80; dir. devel. St. Louis Conservatory and Schs., 1980-81; pres. The Internat. Ticketing Assn., NYC, 1981—2002; ret., 2002. Tchr. Creative Dramatics, Milw., 1962-66; adv. coun. Town Hall, N.Y.C., 1989—; bd. dirs. Theatre and Dance Co., N.Y.C., 1986-89. Bd. dirs. Milw. Chamber Music Soc., 1974-80, Soc. Preservation Profl. Touring Entertainment History, 1998; bd. dirs. Sledgehammer Theatre, 2003-, mng. dir., 2004-; chair bd. dirs. Great Am. Children's Theatre, 1977-80. Mem. Am. Soc. Assn. Execs. (cert.). Avocations: reading, travel, theater. Home: 645 Front St unit 607 San Diego CA 92101 Office Phone: 619-544-1484. Personal E-mail: pspira@cox.net. Business E-Mail: pspira@sledgehammer.org.

SPIRES, DIANE HAYES, music educator; b. Portland, Maine, Nov. 19, 1949; d. Erwin Roland and Doris Louise Hayes; m. Terrance Tyrone Spires, July 29, 1972; children: James Michael, Jeffrey Hayes. MusB, Heidelberg Coll., Tiffin, Ohio, 1972; MS, Butler U., Indpls., 1976. Cert. commd. music min. United Ch. Christ, NH, 1999. Music tchr. Indpls. Pub. Schs., 1973—80, Kensington Elem. Sch., NH, 1985—86, East Kingston Elem. Sch., 1985—86, Stratham Elem. Sch., NH, 1985—88, Raymond Elem. Sch., NH, 1989—2001; ch. organist NE UCC, Indpls., 1975—81; min. music Lee Ch. UCC, NH, 1982—; music tchr. Horne Street Sch., Dover, NH, 2001—. Musician: (dir. music conf.) Women's Celebration- UCC. Mem.: Descs. of Mayflower. Democrat. Mem. Christian Ch. Avocations: travel, camping, reading. Home: 6 Decato Dr Lee NH 03824 Office: Horne Street Sch 78 Horne St Dover NH 03820 Business E-Mail: d.spires@dover.k12.nh.us.

SPIRO, HERBERT JOHN, political scientist, ambassador; b. Hamburg, Germany, Sept. 7, 1924; came to U.S., 1938, naturalized, 1944; s. Albert John and Marianne (Stiefel) S.; m. Elizabeth Anna Petersen, June 7, 1958 (div.); children: Peter John, Alexander Charles Stiefel; m. Marion Ballin, July 22, 1985. Student, San Antonio Jr. Coll., 1942-43; AB summa cum laude, Harvard U., 1949, MA, 1950, PhD, 1953; MA (hon.), U. Pa., 1971. Adminstrv. asst. U.S. War Dept., Vienna, 1945-46; mem. faculty Harvard U., Cambridge, Mass., 1950-61, asst. prof., 1957-61; assoc. prof. polit. sci. Amherst (Mass.) Coll., 1961-65; prof. polit. sci. U. Pa., Phila., 1965-73; mem. policy planning staff Dept. State, Washington, 1970-75; ambassador to Cameroon, 1975-77; amb. to Equatorial Guinea, 1975-76; fellow Woodrow Wilson Internat. Ctr. for Scholars, Smithsonian Instn., Washington, 1978; vis. prof. polit. sci. Def. Intelligence Sch., Washington, 1979-80; univ. prof. polit. sci. John F. Kennedy Inst. for N.Am. Studies, Free U. Berlin, 1980-89. Fulbright sr. rsch. prof. U. Coll. Rhodesia and Nyasaland, 1959-60; cons. Brit. Commn. to Rev. Constn., Fedn. Rhodesia and Nyasaland, 1960, Japanese Commn. on Revision Constn., 1962; vis. assoc. prof. U. Chgo.,

1961, Stanford (Calif.) U., 1963; chmn. Asian and African Studies program, Amherst-Smith-Mt. Holyoke Colls., U. Mass., 1964-65; vis. prof. internat. affairs Woodrow Wilson Sch., Princeton (NJ) U., 1966; adv. coun. polit. sci. Haverford Coll., 1966-71; affiliated with Nuffield Coll., Oxford (Eng.) U., 1967-68; resident scholar Rockefeller Found. Study Ctr., Bellagio, Italy, 1968, 78; vis. prof. govt., guest scholar Ctr. for Internat. Affairs, Harvard U., 1983; vis. scholar U. Tex., Austin, 1984-89; life mem. Brit. studies faculty seminar U. Tex., Austin, 1983—; rschr. Lyndon Baines Johnson Presdl. Libr., 1985-86; fellow Aspen (Colo.) Inst. Humanistic Studies, 1986; adj. prof. govt. U. Tex., Austin, 1989-91; participant internat scholarly and diplomatic confs.; founder Brackenridge H.S.-Wilhelm Gymnasium Exchange; lectr. in field. Author: Politics of German Codetermination, 1958, (with others) Patterns of Government, 1958, 2d edit., 1962, Government by Constitution, 1959, Politics in Africa, 1962, 2d edit., 1975, Five African States, 1963, World Politics: The Global System, 1966, (with others) Authority, Nomos I, 1958, Responsibility, Nomos III, 1960, Privacy Nomos XIII, 1971, Why Federations Fail, 1968, Responsibility in Government, 1969, The Dialectic of Representation 1619-1969, 1969, Politics as the Master Science: From Plato to Mao, 1970 (with others), Theory and Politics, 1971 (with others), Between Sovereignty and Integration, 1974, A New Foreign Policy Consensus?, 1979, (with others) The Legacy of the Constitution, 1987, (with others) Anti-Americanism, 1988; editor, contbr.: (with others) Africa: The Primacy of Politics, 1966, Patterns of African Development, 1967, 'Privatization' of U.S. Foreign Relations, 1995; contbr.: World Book Ency., Ency. Britannica, Intern. Ency. of the Social Scis.; host Spiro's Conversations, Austin Community TV, 1992-97, San Antonio TimeWarner Access TV channel 20, 1999-2006; contbr. articles to profl. jours. Del. Tex. State Rep. Conv., 1990-92; precinct chmn. Travis County; Rep. cand. for Tex. Ho. of Reps., 1991, U.S. House of Reps., 1992, 94, U.S. Senate, 1993. Decorated Bronze Star medal with oak leaf cluster, Purple Heart; grand officer Legion of Valor Cameroon, 1977; recipient Detur prize Harvard Coll., 1948, Bowdoin prize, 1952; John Harvard scholar, 1949-51, Holzer scholar, 1949-51; Guggenheim fellow, 1959-60, Social Sci. Research Council faculty fellow, 1962, 67-68, Rockefeller Found. fellow, 1958, Sheldon travelling fellow Harvard U., also Fulbright fellow, 1953-54; Moody grantee Lyndon Baines Johnson Found., 1985. Fellow Assn. for Diplomatic Studies; mem. African Studies Assn., Am. Polit. Sci. Assn. (coun. 1968-70, chmn. election com. 1969), Internat. Polit. Sci. Assn., Am. Soc. Polit. and Legal Philosophy, Coun. Fgn. Rels., Coun. Am. Ambs., Am. Fgn. Svc. Assn., Mil. Order Purple Heart, San Antonio World Affairs Coun., Harvard Alumni Assn. (apptd. regional dir. Tex. 1994-97), San Antonio Coll. Alumni Assn. (dir. 1999—, Disting. Former Student award 2000), Wissenschaftliche Gesellschaft Berlin, Signet Soc., Harvard U. Faculty Club, Harvard Club (N.Y.C., del. to Tex.), Harvard Club Berlin (pres. 1985-89), Harvard Club Austin (pres. 1990-92), Harvard Club San Antonio, Phi Beta Kappa. Republican.

SPIRO, PETER M., legislative staff member; Legis. dir. for Rep. Tim Roemer, US House of Reps., Washington, 2000—02, 2002—03, Rep. Ciro Rodriguez, 2002, Rep. Rahm Emanuel, 2003—05, Rep. Timothy Bishop, 2005—06, chief of staff, 2007—. Office: Office of Congressman Tim Bishop 306 Cannon House Office Bldg Washington DC 20515 Office Phone: 202-225-8450, 202-225-3143. E-mail: pete.spiro@mail.house.gov.*

SPIRO, RICHARD GLENN, corporate financial executive; b. Bklyn., May 31, 1964; s. Eugene Howard and Linda Diane (Krebs) S.; m. Nancy Bess, July 5, 1987. AB in Econs. magna cum laude, Princeton U., 1986. Fin. analyst First Boston Corp., NYC, 1986-88; from assoc. to mng. dir., COO global ins. group, financial institutions group First Boston Corp. (now Credit Suisse First Boston), NYC, 1988—98; mng. dir., head US ins. investment banking, financial services group Lehman Brothers, 1998—99; mng. dir., head N. America Financial Institutions Group Citigroup Global Markets Inc., 1999—2008; exec. v.p., CFO Chubb Corp., 2008—. Mem. Univ. Cottage Club. Office: Chubb Corp 15 Mountain View Rd Warren NJ 07059*

SPIRO, ROBERT HARRY, JR., foundation and business executive, educator; b. Asheville, Dec. 5, 1920; s. Robert Harry and Eoline Peterson (Shaw) S.; m. Juanita T. Henderson, June 25, 2006; children by previous marriage: Robert Timothy, Elizabeth Susan, James Monroe. BS, Wheaton Coll., Ill., 1941; postgrad. Navy Supply Sch., Harvard U., 1943; postgrad., U. N.C., 1945-46; PhD, U. Edinburgh, Scotland, 1950; student, Union Theol. Sem., summers 1951-53; postdoctoral, Duke U., summer 1956; ScD (hon.), Fla. Inst. Tech. Assoc. prof. King Coll., Bristol, Tenn., 1946-50; prof. history Miss. Coll., 1950-57; pres. Blue Ridge Assembly, Black Mountain, NC, 1957-60; dean Coll. Liberal Arts Mercer U., prof. history, 1960-64; pres. Jacksonville U., Fla., 1964-79; under sec. of Army, 1980-81; cons. to bus., 1981-84, 86-99; nat. exec. dir. Res. Officers Assn. U.S., 1984-86; chmn. RHS Imprinted Products Inc., 1988-99; past bd. mgrs. Voyager Variable Annuity of Fla., 1972-79. V.p. Am. Security Coun. Found., 1991—99, chmn., 2002—06; pres. Nat. Security Caucus Found., 1997—2002; past pres. Fla. Assn. Colls. and Univs.; mem., past chmn. Ind. Colls. and Univs., 1964—79, chmn, 1967; sec.-treas. Assn. Urban Univs., 1968—76; past mem. Fla.-Columbia Ptnrs.; gen. chmn. Jacksonville Sesquicentennial Commn., 1970—72; mem. N.C. Tricentennial Commn., 1959—65; past mem. adv. coun. Robert A. Taft Inst. Govt., Inst. Internat. Edn. Editor (with D.F. Winkler and J.C. Reilly Jr.) Destroyer Squadron Two From Leyte Gulf Through Okinawa, 2002; contbr. articles to profl. publs. and encys. Trustee Southwestern Bapt. Theol. Sem., 1968—78; chmn. bd. Bapt. Coll. and Sem., Washington, 1989—2001. Ensign to lt. USNR, 1941—45, PTO, ret. rear adm. USNR, 1978. Decorated Palmes Academique (France); recipient Disting. Civilian Svc. award, Dept. of Army, 1981, Disting. Alumnus award, Navy Supply Corps Sch., 2000, Disting. Svc. award, Mil. Order Carabao, 2005; named U. Benefactor, U. Edinburgh, 2006. Mem. Navy League U.S. (former pres. Jacksonville coun.), Naval Res. Assn. (nat. adv. coun.), Res. Officers Assn. U.S. Naval Inst., Clan Munro Assn., Am. Legion, Kiwanis (pres. Clinton, Miss. 1956-57; pres. Georgetown, D.C. Club 1991-92), Phi Delta Kappa, Alpha Kappa Psi, Phi Alpha Theta, Phi Kappa Phi. Home: 904 Cherokee Rd Charlotte NC 28207 Home Phone: 704-376-1111. *Esse Quam Videre "To Be Rather than to Seem" is an eloquent apothegm I learned in high school Latin classes. For me it has been a demanding goal for daily living, a worthy aspiration for each task in life and a challenging vision of what I wish and ought to be.*

SPIRO, THOMAS GEORGE, chemistry professor; b. Aruba, Netherlands Antilles, Nov. 7, 1935; s. Andor and Ilona S.; m. Helen Handin, Aug. 21, 1959; children: Peter, Michael. BS, UCLA, 1956; PhD, MIT, 1960. Fulbright rschr. U. Copenhagen, Denmark, 1960-61; NIH fellow Royal Inst. Tech., Stockholm, 1962-63; research chemist Calif. Research Corp., LaHabra, 1961-62; mem. faculty Princeton U., 1963—, prof. chemistry, 1974—, head dept., 1979-88, Eugene Higgins prof., 1981—. Author: (with William M. Stigliani) Environmental Issues in Chemical Perspective, 1980, Chemistry of the Environment, 1996, 2002; contbr. articles to profl. jours. Recipient Bomem-Michelson award Bomem Corp., 1986; NATO sr. fellow, 1972, Guggenheim fellow, 1990. Fellow AAAS; mem. Am. Chem. Soc. (award for Disting. Svc. in Advancement of Inorganic Chemistry 2005, Biophys. Soc. Founders award 2006), Phi Beta Kappa, Sigma Xi. Office: Princeton U Dept Chemistry Princeton NJ 08544-0001 E-mail: spiro@princeton.edu.

SPISAK, JOHN FRANCIS, corporation executive; b. Cleve., Mar. 27, 1950; s. Ernest Lawrence and Adele Marie (Chipko) S.; m. Barbara Ann Heisman, June 10, 1972; children: John Stefan, Theresa Rose. BS in Chemistry, Purdue U., 1972, BS in Biology with honors, 1972. Rsch. engr. Anaconda Minerals, Tucson, 1972-79; chief metallurgist Fed. Am. Uranium, Riverton, Wyo., 1979-80; v.p. ops. Anschutz Mining Corp., Denver, 1980-87; chmn. bd. dirs. Warrenton Refining (subs. of Anschutz Corp.), Denver, 1987-89; dir., owner BE&K/Terranext, Inc., Denver, 1989—; pres. Continental Supply, Woodland, Calif., 2003—; pres., CEO Precision Assessment Tech. Corp., Lone Tree, 2006—08; pres. Sola Rover Mobile Solar Energy Sys., Lone Tree, Colo., 2008—. Mem. Western States-U.S. Senate Coalition for Superfund Reform; CEO, Am. Purification Corp., Newport Beach, Calif., 1998-02, pres. Prosonic Corp., Marietta, Ohio, 2002-03; CEO, Exegesis, 2005-, mgmt. cons., exec. coach, 2003-06. Contbr. articles to profl. publs.; patentee sequential flotation of sulfide ores. Named One of Fifty Colo. Top Bus. Leaders, Colo. Assn. Commerce and Industry. Mem. AIME, Soc. Mining, Metallurgy and Exploration, Nat. Assn. Environ. Mgrs. (co-founder, bd. dirs. Washington chpt., co-chmn. govt. liaison and advocacy com.), Denver Petroleum Club, Elks. Republican. Roman Catholic. Avocations: classical piano, bicycling, model railroads. Home: 9384 Oakbrush Way Lone Tree CO 80124-3070 Office: Precision Assessment Tech Corp 9980 Park Meadows Dr Ste 112F Lone Tree CO 80124 Office Phone: 720-279-2392, 303-339-9638, 303-810-6602. Personal E-mail: tnxtceo@aol.com. Business E-Mail: john.spisak@solarover.com.

SPITLER, CAROLYN ELIZABETH, music educator; b. Rogersville, Tenn. d. Ivan Ralph and Oria Webb (Smith Maiden) Keys; m. Jerry Lee Spitler (div.); 1 child, Kimberly Dawn Wright. MusB, U. Cin., 1963, MusM, 1972. Pvt. practice, Cin., 1963—66; piano tchr. U. Cin., 1971—73, Oakland City U., Ind., asst. prof. music, 1974—87, assoc. prof. music, 1987—, pianist, organist, accompanist, 1973—; organist Good Shepherd United Methodist Ch., Oakland City, 1973—. Composer (piano composition): Noctourne Op.1, 1988. Named Tchr. of Yr., Oakland City Coll., 1981. Mem.: Phi Kappa Lambda, Mu Phi Epilson, Delta Kappa Gamma. Methodist. Avocations: walking, hiking, reading, cooking. Office: Oakland City Univ 138 N Lucretia St Oakland City IN 47660

SPITLER, KENNETH F., food products executive; b. 1949; BA in Philosophy, Univ. of Tulsa, 1971. With Sysco Corp, 1986—, exec. v.p. Dallas, 1986—92, pres. Detroit, 1992—95, pres., CEO Houston, 1995—2000, sr. v.p. operations, northeast region, 2000—02, exec. v.p., redistribution and northeast region, 2002—03, exec. v.p. food service operations, 2003—05; exec. v.p., pres. No. Am. food service ops. Sysco Corp., 2005—07, pres., COO, 2007—09, vice chmn., pres., COO, 2009—. Office: Sysco Corp 1395 Enclave Pkwy Houston TX 77077*

SPITZ, BARBARA SALOMON, artist; b. Chgo., Jan. 8, 1926; d. Fred B. and Sadie (Lorch) Salomon; m. Lawrence S. Spitz, Mar. 19, 1949; children— Thomas R., Linda J., Joanne L. Student, Art Inst. Chgo., 1942—43, R.I. Sch. Design, 1945; AB, Brown U., 1947. One-woman exhbns. include Benjamin Galleries, Chgo., 1971, 73, Kunsthaus Buhler, Stuttgart, Germany, 1973, Van Straaten Gallery, Chgo., 1976, 80, Elca London Studio, Montreal, Que., Can., 1977, Loyola U. Chgo., 1988, Schneider, Bluhm, Loeb gallery, Chgo., 1993, Newport Beach Pub. Lib., 2002, The Ctr. Gallery, 1994; group exhibitions include Am. Acad. Arts and Letters, Library of Congress traveling print exhbn., Tokyo Cen. Mus. Arts, Nat. Acad. Design, NYC, Pratt Graphic Ctr., Honolulu Acad. Arts, Wadsworth Atheneum, Nat. Aperture, 1986—, Laguna Art Mus., others; represented in permanent collections Phila. Mus. Art, DeCordova Mus., Okla. Art Ctr., Milw. Art Ctr., Los Angeles County Mus. Art, Art Inst. Chgo., Portland Mus. Art, Wadsworth Atheneum, med. arts programs UCLA, Block Mus./Northwestern U., Smart Mus./U. Chgo. Vice-chmn. Chgo. area Brown U. Bicentennial Drive; treas. Hearing and Speech Rehab. Ctr., Michael Reese Hosp., 1960; fine arts patron bd. Newport Harbor Art Mus. Mem. Print Club Phila., Boston Printmakers, Arts Club of Chgo., Soc. Am. Graphic Artists. Address: 1106 Somerset Ln Newport Beach CA 92660-5629 Personal E-mail: bsslss@mac.com, bsslss@gmail.com.

SPITZ, SEYMOUR JAMES, JR., retired fragrance company executive; b. Milw., Nov. 17, 1921; s. Seymour James and Marie (Spinette) S.; m. Elizabeth Taylor Parks, Feb. 7, 1948 (div. Aug. 1967); children: William Taylor, Elizabeth Seymour, Anne Bellin; m. Ellen C. Flynn, July 25, 1969; 1 dau., Ellen Christina. SB, MIT, 1943. With Newport Industries div. Heyden Newport Chem. Corp., Pensacola, Fla., 1946-65; asst. chief engr., 1955-57; asst. v.p., 1957-58; v.p. Newport Industries div. Heyden Newport Chem. Corp., 1959-60, exec. v.p., 1960-61, pres., 1961-65; v.p. parent co. Heyden Newport Chem. Corp., 1962-65, became group v.p., 1965; exec. v.p. Heyden Newport Chem. Corp. (renamed Tenneco Chems., Inc.), 1966; pres. Tenneco Chems., Inc., 1967-69; sr. v.p. parent co. Tenneco Inc.; pres. and dir. Internat. Flavors & Fragrances Inc., NYC, 1970-85. Mem. MIT Corp. Devel. Com., 1977-86; trustee Spence Sch., 1982-88, Savannah (Ga.) Symphony, 1990-95, 98, Telfair Mus. Art, Savannah, 1993-96; USN ENS-LCDR, 1943-46. Mem. Univ. Club (N.Y.C.), Larchmont Yacht Club (N.Y., trustee 1986-89), Landings Club, Oglethorpe Club (Savannah, bd. dirs. 1995-99). Home: 6 Brandenberry Rd Savannah GA 31411-2201 E-mail: sjstennis@bellsouth.net.

SPITZBERG, IRVING JOSEPH, JR., lawyer; b. Little Rock, Feb. 9, 1942; s. Irving Joseph and Marie Bettye (Seeman) S.; m. Roberta Frances Alprin, Aug. 21, 1966 (div. 1988); children: Edward Storm, David Adam; m. Virginia V. Thorndike, Dec. 24, 1988. BA, Columbia U., 1964; B.Phil., Oxford U., 1966; JD, Yale U., 1969. Bar: Calif. 1969, DC 1985, Va. 1995. Asst. prof. Pitzer Coll., Claremont, Calif., 1969-71; fellow Inst. Current World Affairs, NYC, 1971-74; vis. lectr. Brown U., Providence, 1973; assoc prof. SUNY, Buffalo, 1974-80, dean of coll., 1974-78; gen. sec. AAUP, Washington, 1980-84; exec. dir. Coun. for Liberal Learning of Assn. Am. Colls., Washington, 1985-89; pres. The Knowledge Co., Fairfax, Va., 1985-2001; ptnr. Spitzberg & Drew, Washington, 1990-92; of counsel Spirer & Goldberg, Washington, 1993—2006; pvt. practice, 1993—. Coord. Alvan Ikoku Coll., Nigeria, 1979-80; cons. Bd. Adult Edn., Kenya, 1973-74, Philander Smith Coll., Little Rock, 1978-80; co-dir. nat. study on campus life for Carnegie Found. for Advancement Teaching, 1989-90, pres. James House Found., 1988- Author and editor: Exchange of Expertise, 1978, Universities and the New International Order, 1979, Universities and the International Exchange of Knowledge, 1980; author: Campus Programs on Leadership, 1986, Racial Politics in Little Rock, 1987; co-author: (with Berdahl and Moodie), Quality and Access in Higher Education, 1991, (with Virginia Thorndike) Creating Community on College Campuses, 1992; polit. columnist Prince William Times, 2001-02. Founder Coalition for Ednl. Excellence, Western NY, 1978-80, Advocates for the Rural Crescent, Va., 1999-2002, Coun. Liberal Learning; founding mem. Alliance for Leadership Devel., Washington, 1985; counsel GASP, Pomona, Calif., 1969-71; Dem. Committeeman, Erie County, NY, 1978-80; founding pres. Internat. Found. for St. Catherine's Coll., Oxford, 1986-91; v.p. Sparks-Glencoe Cmty. Coun., 2004-05; pres. North County Preservation, Inc., 2004—; chair Internat. Quranic Ctr., 2006—; co-founder and coordinator, The Marie Award, Little Rock, AR, 2006-, program chair, Rotary Club of Hunt Valley, 2007-. Nat. winner Westinghouse Sci. Talent Search, 1960; Kellett scholar Trustees of Columbia U., 1964-66, fellow. Boston North County Projovation. Mem. Am. Immigration Lawyers Assn., Nat. Acad. Elder Law Attys., Washington Ethical Soc. (adj. leader 2002—), Ethical Culture Soc., Columbia Club, Yale Club (Washington), Rotary Internat, James Houck Found. (pres. 2008-), Internat. Quranic Ctr. (chair 2007-). Jewish. Avocation: internet radio. Office Phone: 410-357-5984. Personal E-mail: ijs@aol.com.

SPITZE, ROBERT GEORGE FREDERICK, agricultural studies educator; b. Berryville, Ark., Oct. 12, 1922; s. Wesley Henry and Nora Catherine (Stullken) Spitze; m. Hazel Cleo Taylor, Mar. 4, 1944; children: Glenna Dean, Ken Rollin. Student, Columbia U., 1944; BS (Sears Roebuck nat. fellow), U. Ark., 1947; PhD (Knapp research fellow), U. Wis., 1954. Instr. U. Wis., Madison, 1950; asst. prof. to prof. U. Tenn., Knoxville, 1951-60; prof. agrl. econs. U. Ill., Urbana, 1960-93. Vis. prof. Wye Coll., U. London, 1967-68; vis. research prof. policy U.S. Dept. Agr., Washington, 1975; vis. lectr. various univs., U.S. and Eng.; cons. Fed. Intermediate Credit Bank, 1958-59, Ill. Gen. Assembly Commn. on Revenue, 1963, Tex. A&M U., 1970, Am. Farm Bur. Fedn., Chgo., 1971, Ill. Gov.'s Commn. on Farm Income, 1972, Nat. Agrl. Research Policy Adv. Com., 1975, U.S. Dept. Agr. Econs. Research Service, 1976, Wharton Econometric Forecasting Inc., 1977, Nat. Rural Center, Washington, 1979-80, Nat. Public Policy Com., 1980, Okla. State U., 1986; mem. Ill. Gov.'s Council Econ. Advisers, 1974-76 Co-author: Food and Agricultural Policy, Economics and Politics, 1994; co-editor: Policy Rsch. Notes, 1975-92, Food, Agriculture, and Rural Policy into the Twenty-first Century, 1994, Agricultural and Food Policy: Issues and Alternatives for the 1990s, 1990; contbr. articles to profl. jours., chpts. to books Lt. USNR, 1943—47. Recipient Funk recognition award, 1973, Excellence in Teaching award U. Ill., 1977; co-recipient Outstanding Agr. Coll. Alumni award U. Ark., 1994, Outstanding Philanthropist Award Nat. Agrl. Alumni Devel. Assn., 2004 Mem. AAAS, Am. Econ. Assn., Am. Agrl. Econs. Assn. (Disting. Policy award 1981, Disting. Teaching award 1972, travel study grantee to France 1964), Internat. Assn. Agrl. Econs., Agrl. Econs. Soc. (U.K.), AAUP, Blue Key, Sigma Xi, Omicron Delta Kappa, Gamma Sigma Delta, Phi Eta Sigma, Alpha Zeta, Phi Sigma Office: U Ill Dept Agr Econ 1301 W Gregory Dr Dept Agr Urbana IL 61801-9015

SPITZER, ADRIAN, pediatrician, educator; b. Bucharest, Rumania, Dec. 21, 1927; came to U.S., 1963, naturalized, 1968; s. Osias and Sophia S. S.; m. Carole Zelter, Oct. 31, 1951; 1 son, Vlad. BS, Matei Basarab Lyceum, Bucharest, 1946; MD, Med. Sch. Bucharest, 1952. Diplomate: Am. Bd. Pediat., Am. Bd. Pediats./Nephrology. Intern White Plains (N.Y.) Hosp., 1964; resident Hosp. Med. Coll. Pa., 1965-66; postdoctoral fellow pediatric nephrology Albert Einstein Coll. Medicine, 1966-67; postdoctoral fellow in renal physiology Cornell U. Med. Sch., 1967-68; practice medicine specializing in pediatric nephrology Bronx, NY, 1968—; asst. prof. pediatrics Albert Einstein Coll. Medicine, 1968-72, assoc. prof., 1972-76, prof., 1976—, dir. div. nephrology, 1973-99; mem. staff Bronx Mcpl. Hosp. Ctr., Hosp. Albert Einstein Coll. Medicine/Montefore Med. Ctr.; mem. Medicine B Study sect.-NIH, 1976-80. Prof. C. Donders rotating chmn. U. Utrecht, The Netherlands, 1990-91; Christiansen vis. fellow St. Catherine's Coll.; vis. fellow dept. biochemistry Oxford U., 1981-82; coord. Internat. Study Kidney Disease in Children; chmn. organizing com. 1st-7th Internat. Workshop on Devel. Renal Physiology, 1980-98, pres., 2001; mem. renal adv. com. N.Y.C. Dept. Health; sci. adv. bd. rsch. and grant com. Nat. Kidney Found., 1982; chmn. pediatric nephrology bd. Am. Bd. Pediat., 1982-83. Mem. editorial bd.: Pediatric Nephrology, Seminars in Nephrology; assoc. editor: Pediatric Renal Disease, 1979, 2d edit., 1992; editor: The Kidney Development, 1982. NIH spl fellow, 1967; John E. Fogarty Sr. Internat. fellow, 1981-82; grantee NIH, N.Y. State Health Research Council, Nat. Kidney Found.; recipient Bela Schick medal for extraordinary achievements in acad. and clin. pediatrics; The Scientific Advancement award of the Internat. Pediatr. Nephrol. Assn. Mem.: Intersoc. Coun. for Kidney and Urinary Tract Rsch. (sec.-treas. 1984—89), Am. Pediat. Soc., Am. Acad. Pediat. (Henry L. Barnett award 2005), Soc. Pediatric Rsch., Am. Physiol. Soc., Am. Fedn. Clin. Rsch., Am. Soc. Pediatric Nephrology (coun. 1977—80, pres. 1981—82, Founder's award 2006), Am. Soc. Nephrology (com. on govtl. rels. 1999—2001). Office: Albert Einstein Coll Medicine Montefiore Med Ctr 111 E 210th St Bronx NY 10467-2401 Office Phone: 718-655-1120. Business E-Mail: spitzer@aecom.yu.edu.

SPITZER, BRUCE ALAN, education educator; b. Iowa City, June 5, 1962; m. Gail K. Jurgensen, June 27, 1998. BA, McPherson Coll., Kans., 1984; MA, Ft. Hays State U., Kans., 1993; EdD, Okla. State U., Stillwater, 2004. Tchr. Eureka Jr.-Sr. HS, Kans., 1984—89, Maur Hill Prep. Sch., Atchison, Kans., 1989—90; instr. Allen County CC, Iola, Kans., 1990—99; v.p. instrn. Teletraining Sys., Inc., Stillwater, 1999—2002; grad. tchg., rsch. asst. Okla. State U., Stillwater, 2002—04; asst. prof. instrnl. tech. Ind. U., South Bend, 2004—. Mem.: Assn. Ednl. Comm. and Tech. (divsn. pres. 2006—07). Office: Ind U South Bend 1700 Mishawaka Ave South Bend IN 46634-7111 Business E-Mail: baspitze@iusb.edu.

SPITZER, CARY REDFORD, avionics consultant, electrical engineer; b. New Hope, Va., July 31, 1937; s. Clyde Burke and Marion Jeanette (Redford) S.; m. Carrie Laura Ruth Logan, June 18, 1960; 1 child, Stiegel Logan (dec.). BSEE, Va. Poly. Inst. & State U., 1959; MS in Engring. Mgmt., George Washington U., 1970. Rsch. engr., engring. mgr. Langley Rsch Ctr., NASA, Hampton, Va., 1962-94; founder, pres. AvioniCon, Inc., 1993—. Lectr. UCLA, 1989—, George Washington U., 1994. Author: Viking Orbiter Views of Mars, 1981, Digital Avionics Systems, 1987, 2d edit., 1993, Avionics Handbook, 2000, Digital Avionics Handbook, 2007; contbr. articles to sci. publs. 1st lt. USAF, 1959-62. Recipient Volare award Airline Avionics Inst., 1988; named Va. Peninsula Engr. of Yr., 1993; recipient Digital Avionics award Am. Inst. of Aeronautics and Astronautics, 1994; nominated Collier Trophy, 1991. Fellow: IEEE (Centennial medal 1984, Millennium medal 2000), AIAA (assoc.); mem.: Aerospace and Electronic Systems Soc. of IEEE (pres. 1973—74, editor-in-chief Trans. 1996—99, chmn. IEEE-USA aerospace policy com. 1997—2000), Exch. Club (pres. Williamsburg 1985). Methodist. Avocations: kite flying, car mechanics. Home and Office: 3409 Foxridge Rd Williamsburg VA 23188-2499 Home Phone: 757-229-8296; Office Phone: 757-221-8031.

SPITZER, ELIOT LAURENCE, political science professor, former Governor of New York; b. Bronx, June 10, 1959; s. Bernard and Anne Spitzer; m. Silda Alice Wall, Oct. 17, 1987; children: Elyssa, Sarabeth, Jenna. BA, Princeton U., 1981; JD, Harvard U., 1984. Law clk. to Hon. Robert W. Sweet US Dist. Ct. (so. dist.) NY, NYC, 1984—85; assoc. Paul, Weiss, Rifkind, Wharton & Garrison, 1985—86, Skadden Arps

Slate Meagher & Flom, 1992—94; ptnr. Constantine & Ptnrs., NYC, 1994—98; asst. dist. atty. NYC, 1986—92, chief, Labor Racketeering unit, 1991—92; atty. gen. State of NY, Albany, 1999—2007, gov., 2007—08; columnist Slate.com, 2008—; adj. instr. polit. sci. CCNY, 2009—. Analyst, commentator on nat. news programs including NBC's Today Show, CNN's Burden of Proof, CNBC, Court TV; pro bono counsel NY State Commn. for Study of Youth Crime & Violence, 1993—94; resigned as governor of NY on Mar. 12, 2008, after reports of connection to a prostitution ring. Editor: Harvard Law Rev.; contbr. articles to newspapers and legal jours. Founder Ctr. for Cmty. Interest; co-founder Children for Children, 1996—. Recipient Paul H. Douglas Ethics in Govt. award, U. Ill., 2004, Jacob J. Javits Pub. Svc. award, Am. Psychiatric Assn., 2005; named Crusader of Yr., TIME mag., 2002; named one of The World's Most Influential People, 2005. Democrat. Jewish. Avocations: running, tennis.*

SPITZER, JOHN J., retired economics professor; b. Lake Placid, NY, Dec. 5, 1944; s. Eugene and Valerie Spitzer; m. Linda Kay Fitz Gerald; m. Tam Mackenzie (div.); m. Michele Perry (dec.); children: Tara M. Spitzer-List, Ian M. BA, Syracuse U., NY, 1966; MA, PhD, U. Pitts., 1971. Prof., economics SUNY Coll. Brockport, NY, 1971—2008. Contbr. articles to jours. Recipient Best Conf. Paper award, CFP Bd. Stds., 2000, Outstanding Fin. Planning Paper award, 2006, Am. Coll. Best Conf. Paper award, Acad. Fin. Svcs., 2002, Rsch. Recognition award, SUNY Rsch. Found., 2005, Chancellor's award, SUNY, 2006, award, Arthur N. Caple Found., 2008; Judges' grant, Janus Capital Group, 2006. Achievements include research in seminal work on box-cox transformations; ground breaking work on retirement withdrawal strategies; optimal age to begin taking social security, impact of required minimum distributions on retirement portfolio longevity. Avocation: bridge.

SPITZER, MARC LEE, commissioner, former state legislator; b. Pitts., Sept. 12, 1957; s. Richard A. and Edith (Brodie) S., m. Jacqueline Raub; 1 child, Bennett Alexander BA in History and Polit. Sci. summa cum laude, Dickinson Coll., 1979; JD cum laude, U. Mich., 1982. Bar: Ariz. 1982, U.S. Dist. Ct. Ariz. 1982, U.S. Tax Ct. 1982, U.S. Ct. Appeals (9th cir.) 1985. Dir. KPMG Peat Marwick, Phoenix, 1982—; mem. Ariz. State Senate from Dist. 18, Phoenix, 1992—2000, majority leader, 1997—2000; commr. Ariz. Corp. Commn., Phoenix, 2000—06, chmn., 2003—05; commr. Fed. Energy Regulatory Commn. (FERC), Washington, 2006—. Bd. dirs. Ariz. Acad., 1990; mem. devel. com. Dickinson Coll., 1985-86; dir. Arizonans for Cultural Devel.; vice-chmn. Ariz. 18th Dist., 1986—; alternate del. 1988 Rep. Nat. Conv. GOP; legal counsel Ariz. Rep. Party. Recipeint awards for legis. svc. from 32 non-profit orgns. Mem. ABA (vice-chmn., tax legis. sect.), State Bar Ariz. (cert. specialist taxation), Ariz. Tax Research Found. (bd. dirs. 1984—), Ariz. Tax Research Assn., Maricopa County Bar Assn., Phoenix 100 Rotary, Heritage Found., Ariz. Club, Phi Beta Kappa, Sigma Alpha Epsilon. Republican. Jewish. Avocations: fishing, prospecting, classical music, racquetball. Office: Fed Energy Regulatory Commn 888 First St NE Washington DC 20426*

SPITZER, TOBA, rabbi; MDiv, Reconstructionist Rabinnical Coll., 1997. Rabbi Congregation Dorshei Tzedek, West Newton, Mass. Named one of The Top 50 Rabbis in America, Newsweek Mag., 2007. Office: Congregation Dorshei Tzedek 60 Highland St West Newton MA 02465 Office Phone: 617-965-0330.

SPITZLI, DONALD HAWKES, JR., lawyer; b. Newark, Mar. 19, 1934; s. Donald Hawkes and Beatrice (Banister) S.; children: Donald Hawkes III, Peter Gilbert, Seth Armstrong. AB, Dartmouth Coll., 1956; LLB, U. Va., 1963. Bar: Va. 1963. Assoc. Willcox, Savage, Lawrence, Dickson & Spindle, Norfolk, Va., 1964-67, 68-70, ptnr., 1971-77; atty. Eastman Kodak Co., Rochester, N.Y., 1967-68; pres. Marine Hydraulics Internat., Inc., Chesapeake, Va., 1978-80; sole practice Virginia Beach, Va., 1980—. Owner Chieftain Motor Inn, Hanover, N.H., 1980-87. Comdr. USNR, 1956-70. Episcopalian. Office: 4460 Corporation Ln Ste 180 Virginia Beach VA 23462 Office Phone: 757-499-1191. Personal E-mail: airbuzzard24@aol.com.

SPITZNAGEL, JOHN KEITH, retired microbiologist, immunologist, physician; b. Peoria, Ill., Apr. 11, 1923; s. Elmer Florian and Anna S. (Kolb) S.; m. Anne Moulton Sirch, Feb. 2, 1947; children: John, Jean, Margaret, Elizabeth, Paul. BA, Columbia U., 1943, MD, 1946. Diplomate Nat. Bd. Med. Examiners, Am. Bd. Internal Medicine. Intern Johns Hopkins Hosp., Balt., 1946-47; resident in internal medicine Barnes Hosp., St. Louis, 1949-51; vis. investigator Rockefeller Inst., NYC, 1952-53, Nat. Inst. Med. Research, London, 1967-68; mem. faculty U. N.C., Chapel Hill, 1957-79, prof. microbiology and infectious diseases, prof. medicine, 1957-79; cons. N.C. Meml. Hosp., Chapel Hill, 1974-79; ad hoc adviser NIH, 1971—; prof. microbiology and immunology, chmn. dept. Emory U., Atlanta, 1979-93, prof. emeritus microbiology and immunology, 1993—, assoc. dean rsch., 1997-98; attending physician, vol. and co-founder Good Samaritan Health and Wellness Ctr., Jasper, Ga., 2002—, chmn. exec. bd., CEO, 2004—06. Mem. study sect. bacteriology and mycology NIH, 1975-79, 85-89, chmn., 1977-79. Editor: Infection and Immunity, 1970-80, Jour. Immunology, 1973-80, Jour. Reticuloendothelial Soc, 1973-80. Served with M.C. AUS, 1947-57. Recipient Research Career Devel. award USPHS, 1957-67, Disting. Service award Sch. Medicine U. N.C., Chapel Hill, 1987; USPHS postdoctoral fellow, 1968; USPHS and AEC grantee; lectureship named in his honor, Spitznagel Lectureship on Host Antimicrobial Def., Emory U., 1998. Fellow ACP, Infectious Disease Soc.; mem. AAAS (life), Am. Soc. Microbiology (div. group councilor 1977-79), Am. Assn. Immunologists, Reticuloendothelial Soc. (pres. 1982), Infectious Disease Soc., So. Soc. Clin. Rsch., Assn. Am. Med. Sch. Microbiology and Immunology Chmn. (pres. 1990-91), Sigma Xi. Achievements include research on cell biology of human neutrophil polymorphonuclear leukocytes, and oxygen ind. mechanisms of antimicrobial phagocytoses; first to demonstrate cationic antimicrobial proteins of polymorphonuclear leukocytes granules; co-discoverer of a cationic protein of polymorph granules with antimicrobial action and a powerful attractant for mononuclear phagocytes. Home: 95 Starcross Ln # 20804 Jasper GA 30143-7883 Office: 1510 Clifton Rd NE Atlanta GA 30322-4218 E-mail: spitzna@mac.com.

SPIVACK, BARNEY S., physician; b. NYC, Oct. 28, 1952; s. Irwin and Rosalind (Brensilber) S.; m. Robin Gail Oshman, Aug. 3, 1974; 1 child, Josh. BA, Bklyn. Coll., 1974; MD, Mt. Sinai Sch. Medicine, 1978. Diplomate in internal medicine, rheumatology and geriatric medicine Am. Bd. Internal Medicine. Dir. liaison rehab. Meml. Hosp. of R.I., Pawtucket, 1983-86; dir. geriatric assessment N.Y. Med. Coll., Valhalla, 1986-89; chief of medicine Hosp. for Spl. Care, New Britain, Conn., 1989-92; dir. geriatric medicine Norwalk (Conn.) Hosp., 1993-97, Stamford (Conn.) Health Sys., 1997—2003; dir. med. svcs. Wavery Ctr. Network, New Canaan, Conn., 2003—07; med. dir. Lifecare Inc., Shelton, Conn., 2007—; assoc. prof. Columbia U., NY, 2000—. Editor: Evaluation and Management of Gait Disorders, 1995. Bd. dir. Southwestern Conn. Agy. on Aging, Bridgeport, 1995-2003; pres. Conn. Geriatrics; del. White House Conf. on Aging, Washington, 1995. Fellow ACP, Alzheimers Assn. (bd. dir. 1996-2003). Avocations: gardening, travel. Office: Armstrong Rd Shelton CT 06484 Office Phone: 203-291-3409. Business E-Mail: bspivack@lifecare.com.

SPIVAK, ALVIN A., retired public relations executive; b. Phila., Nov. 30, 1927; s. Herman and Bella (Haimovitz) S.; m. Martha Barry, Dec. 21, 1964; 1 dau., Denise. BS, Temple U., 1949. With I.N.S., 1949-58, Senate reporter, also mem. gen. staff Washington, 1951-58; with U.P.I., 1958-67, White House reporter, 1960-67; pub. affairs dir. Nat. Adv. Commn. on Civil Disorders, 1967-68, Democratic Nat. Com., 1968-70; corp. pub. affairs dir. Gen. Dynamics Corp., 1970-94, ret., 1994. Served with USAAF, 1946-47. Mem. Mil. Order of Carabao, Nat. Press Club, Beta Gamma Sigma. Home: 5726 W 1st Sq SW Vero Beach FL 32968-2256

SPIVAK, JOAN CAROL, communications executive; b. Phila., May 12, 1950; d. Jack and Evelyn Lee (Copelman) S.; m. John D. Goldman, May 17, 1980; children: Jesse, Marcus. AB, Barnard Coll., 1972; M of Health Scis., Johns Hopkins U., 1980. Freelance writer, NYC, 1980-84; project dir. Impact Med. Communication, NYC, 1984-87; exec. v.p., gen. mgr. health and sci. strategies Edelman Worldwide, NYC, 1987—2002; pres. Prime Medica, Inc., 2002—07; prin. Spivak Consulting Group, 2007—. Co-author: (pamphlet) Lead: New Perspectives on an Old Problem, 1978; contbr. The Book of Health, 1981, articles to profl. jours. Bd. dirs. May O'Donnell Dance Co., N.Y.C., 1983-85, Chamber Ballet U.S.A., N.Y.C., 1985-87, Nat. Child Labor Commn., 1991-2000, Cases, 1995-2001, Learning Through an Expanded Arts Program, 2004—. Mem. N.Y. Acad. Sci. Democrat. Jewish. Avocations: pottery, boating. Personal E-mail: joan.spivak@gmail.com.

SPIVAK, MAURICE SIDNEY, civil engineer, consultant; b. Milford, Mass., Jan. 5, 1926; s. Phillip None and Esther Sarah Spivak; m. Annette Charlotte Mann; children: Michelle Melinger, Jonah, Myra Taylor. BS, The Citadel, Charleston, SC, 1950; MS, W. Va. U., Mogantown, 1955; PhD (hon.), U.of Berkley, Southhill, Mich. Registered Profl. Engr., Wis., 1976. Biochemical asst. Mass. Gen. Hosp., Boston, 1950—53; Biochemist Worcester Found., Shrewsbury, Mass., 1955—56; chem. engr. U.S.Army, Springfield, Mass., 1956—67; project engr. U.S.Army Arsenal, Edgewood, Md., 1967—73; chief project mgmt. engring. U.S. Army Corps of Engrs., Norfolk, Va., 1973—86; project mgr. Air bases Island, 1979. Cons. U.S. Army Corps of Engrs., Norfolk, Va., 1986—99. Author: (Engineering Papers) Published in Govt. and Jour.Biolog. Chemistry, 1960 (Numerous awards, 1977). Direct commr. USNR; First V.P. B'rith Sholom, Norfolk, Va. Pvt. First Class US Army, 1944—46, European Theater. Decorated Bronze Star Medal US Army, Combat Infantry badge; recipient Several Civilian Awards, Springfield Armory, 1956-1966, Numerous Awards, Edgewood Arsenal, 1967-1973, US Army Corps of Engineers, 1973-1986; named Outstanding Person 20th Century, 1998; named one of 500 People of Influence, 1999; fellow, Worcester Found., 1955, W. Va. U., 1955. Mem.: ASCE. Home: 821 Jennings St Virginia Beach VA 23464 Personal E-mail: MSpivak650@aol.com.

SPIVEY, BRUCE E., ophthalmologist, educator, health facility administrator; b. Cedar Rapids, Iowa, Aug. 29, 1934; s. William Loranzy and Grace Loretta (Barber) S.; children: Lisa, Eric; m. Patti Amanda Birge, Dec. 20, 1987. BA, Coe Coll., 1956; MD, U. Iowa, 1959, MS, 1964; MEd, U. Ill., 1969; DSc (hon.), Coe Coll., 1978. Diplomate Am. Bd. Ophthalmology (fellow, bd. dirs. 1975-83, chmn. oral exam 1976-81). Asst. prof. U. Iowa Coll. Medicine, Iowa City, 1966, assoc. prof., 1968—71; dean Sch. Med. Scis. U. Pacific, San Francisco, 1971—76; prof., chmn. dept. ophthalmology Pacific Med. Ctr. (now Calif. Pacific Med. Ctr.), San Francisco, 1971—87; pres., CEO, dir. Calif. Pacific Med. Ctr., San Francisco, 1976—91; exec. v.p., CEO Am. Acad. Ophthalmology, San Francisco, 1977—93; pres., CEO Calif. Healthcare Sys., Bay area, 1986—92; CEO Northwestern Healthcare Network, Chgo., 1992—97, Columbia Cornell Care, NYC, 1997—2000, Columbia Cornell Network Physicians, NYC, 1998—2000. Bd. dirs. Reliance Group Holdings Inc., NYC; trustee, bd. dirs., sec. bd. MedEx, Balt., 1999—; v.p. Am. Bd. Med. Spltys., 1978—80, pres., 1980—82, Coun. Med. Splty. Socs., 2000—02, 1975—2008, dep. exec. v.p., 2002—08; chmn. bd. dirs. Vol. Hosps. of Am.-No. Calif., 1985—87, nat. bd. dirs., 1991—96; nat. adv. coun. NEI/NIH, 1987—92; spl. med. adv. group Dept. Vets Affairs, 1987—93; trustee, bd. dirs., sec. bd. Ophthal. Mut. Ins. Co., 1988—2007; trustee, sec. bd. PrimeSight, San Francisco, 1996—99. Contbr. over 120 articles to profl. jours.; inventor instruments for eye surgery. Bd. dirs. Pacific Vision Found., San Francisco, 1978—, U.S.-China Ednl. Inst., 1979—; trustee Coe Coll., 1985—, Found. AAO, 1981—, Internat. Coun. Ophthalmology, 1985—, Helen Keller Internat., 1999—; trustee Medbiquitous, 2000-07, chmn, 2001—07. Served to capt. U.S. Army, 1964-66, 85th Duke Hosp., Vietnam, 1965-66. Decorated Bronze Star; recipient Emile Javal Gold medal Internat. Contact Lens Council, San Francisco, 1982, Gradle medal Pan-Am. Assn. Ophthalmol., Disting. Alumni award U. Iowa, 2003, others. Fellow ACS, Am. Acad. Ophthalmology (Disting. Svc. award 1972, Sr. Honor award 1986, Guest of Honor 1996, Lifetime Achievement award, 2002, Internat. Blindness Prevention award, 2007); mem. AMA, Am. Ophthal. Soc. (Howe medal 1993, bd. dirs. 1986-91, pres. 1994-95), Academia Ophthal. Internat. (Bernardo Streiff Gold medal 2002), Soc. Med. Adminstrs. (pres. 1999-2001), Internat. Congress Ophthalmology (sec.-gen. 1978-82), Internat. Coun. Ophthalmology (sec.-gen. 1994—2006, trustee 1985—, pres. 2006—, Jules Francois Gold medal 2006, Sir John Wilson award 2007, Jose Rizal Internat. medal 2009), Pacific-Union Club, Chevy Chase Club, Knickerbocker Club, Cosmos Club, Asia Pacific Acad. Ophthalmalogy. Presbyterian. Office: 945 Green St San Francisco CA 94133 Business E-Mail: bruce@spivey.org.

SPIVEY, DONALD, history professor; AB in History, U. Ill., Urbana-Champaign, 1971, MA in History, 1972; PhD in History, U. Calif., Davis, 1976. Rsch. asst. dept. elem. edn. U. Ill., 1971—72; tchg. asst. dept. history U. Calif., Davis, 1972—74, lectr. in history, 1975—76; music instr. Sacramento, 1972—74; asst. prof. history Wright State U., Dayton, Ohio, 1976—79; assoc. prof. history U. Conn., 1979—85, prof. history, 1985—93, dir. grad. studies dept. history, 1987—89, founding dir. Inst. African-Am. Studies, 1989—93; prof. history U. Miami, Coral Gables, Fla., 1993—, chair dept. history, 1993—98, assoc. dir. Ctr. for Rsch. on Sport in Soc., 1997—. Vis. asst. prof. history U. Mich., Ann Arbor, 1978—79; presenter in field; mem. exec. v.p. and provost search com. U. Miami, 2004—; co-dir. African-Am. History Summer Inst. for Miami-Dade Tchrs., 1999—2004; mem. exec. bd. Ctr. for Rsch. on Sport in Soc., 1998—; chair Prologue Hist. Soc.; hist. advisor Dade County African-Am. Tchrs. for Curriculum Reform. Author: Schooling for the New Slavery: Black Industrial Education, 1868-1915, 1978, The Politics of Miseducation: The Booker Washington Institute of Liberia, 1929-1984, 1986, Fire From the Soul: A History of the African-American Struggle, 2003; contbg. editor: Union and the Black Musician: The Narrative of William Everett Samuels and Chicago Local 208, 1984, Sport in America: New Historical Perspectives, 1985; contbr. articles to profl. jours., chapters to books. Developer, host Grooving in the Grove Jazz Series; mem. Historic Overtown Restoration Comm.; mem., host Miami Com. to Select Outstanding Local History Tchr.; bd. dirs. Wolfson Media History Ctr., 1993—94. Recipient Tchg. cert. of appreciation, Omega Psi Phi, 1997, cert. of appreciation, Dade County Sch. Bd., Fla., 1997, Twelve Good Men Cmty. Svc. award, Ronald McDonald Ho., Miami, 1998, Excellence in Tchg. award, U. Miami, 2002. Mem.: Conn. Acad. Arts and Scis., Phi Beta Kappa, Phi Kappa Phi. Office: Dept History U Miami PO Box 248107 Coral Gables FL 33124-4662

SPIVEY, KAREN, nursing educator; BSN, Med. Coll. Ga., Augusta, 1971; MSN, Albany State U., Ga., 1992. Registered nurse lic., Ga., 1971, Tenn., 2003. RN Bulloch Meml. Hosp., Statesboro, Ga., 1971—73, Dorminy Med. Ctr., Fitzgerald, Ga., 1974—84, Pub. Health Home Health, Fitzgerald, 1996—2005; asst. prof., assoc. degree nursing program Abraham Baldwin Agrl. Coll., Tifton, Ga., 1984—2002; instr., assoc. degree nursing program Northwestern Tech. Coll., Rock Spring, Ga., 2002—. Office: Northwestern Tech Coll 265 Bicentennial Trail Rock Spring GA 30739 Business E-Mail: kspivey@northwesterntech.edu.

SPLANE, RICHARD BEVERLEY, social work educator; b. Calgary, Alta., Can., Sept. 25, 1916; s. Alfred William and Clara Jane (Allyn) S.; m. Verna Marie Huffman, Feb. 22, 1971. BA, McMaster U., 1940, LLD (hon.), 1990; cert. social sci. and adminstrn., London Sch. Econs., 1947; MA, U. Toronto, 1948, MSW, 1951, PhD, 1961, LLD (hon.), 2005, Wilfrid Laurier U., 1988, U. B.C., 1996. Exec. dir. Children's Aid Soc., Cornwall, Ont., Canada, 1948—50; with Health and Welfare Can., Ottawa, 1952—72, exec. asst. to dep. min. nat. welfare, 1959—60, dir. unemployment assistance, 1960—62, dir. gen. welfare assistance and svcs., 1960—70, asst. dep. min. social allowances and svcs., 1970—72; vis. prof. U. Alta., Edmonton, 1972—73; prof. social policy Sch. Social Work, U. B.C., Vancouver, 1973—82. Cons. Govt. Can., Govt. Alta., UNICEF. Author: The Development of Social Welfare in Ontario, 1965; (with Verna Huffman Splane) Chief Nursing Officers in National Ministries of Health, 1994, 75 Years of Community Service to Canada: Canadian Council on Social Development, 1920-1995, George Davidson Social Policy and Public Policy Exemplar, 2003 Served with RCAF, 1942-45. Recipient Centennial medal Govt. Can., 1967, Charles E. Hendry award U. Toronto, 1981, Commemorative medal for 125th anniversary of Confedn. of Can., 1992, Disting. Svc. award Internat. Coun. on Social Welfare, 1996, Queen's Golden Jubilee medal, 2002. Mem. Can. Assn. Social Workers (Outstanding Nat. Svc. award 1985, Touzel award 2002, Queens Golden medal 2002), Can. Inst. Pub. Adminstrn., Can. Hist. Assn., Can. Coun. on Social Devel. (Lifetime Achievement award 1995), Internat. Assn. Schs. Social Work, Internat. Confs. Social Devel. (prof. emeritus U. BC 1991-), World Federalists Can., UN Assn. Can. (bd. dirs. Vancouver br.), Vancouver Club, Officer Order Can. Mem. United Ch. Can.

SPLETE, ALLEN PETERJOHN, educational association administrator, educator; b. Carthage, NY, June 24, 1938; s. Howard Henry and Minnie Bertha (Peterjohn) S.; m. Marilyn Lois Detweiler, June 18, 1966; children: Heidi, Michael. BA, St. Lawrence U., 1960; MA with distinction, Colgate U., 1962; PhD, Syracuse U., 1968; LHD, Campbellsville Coll., 1990; LLD, Davis and Elkins Coll., 1990; LHD, Mt. Union Coll., 1992, St. Thomas Aquinas Coll., 1992, U. Indpls., 1994, Juniata Coll., 1994, Hastings Coll., 1994; EdD, Marywood Coll., 1995; LHD, Holy Family Coll., 1996, Wesley Coll., 1996, Bluffton Coll., 2003, Millikin U., 2007, St. Lawrence U., 2009. Adminstrv. asst. to v.p. acad. affairs Syracuse U., NY, 1965—68, assoc. dean, exec. asst. to provost, 1968—70; v.p. for acad. planning St. Lawrence U., Canton, NY, 1970-82; pres. Westminster Coll., New Wilmington, Pa., 1982-85; exec. v.p. Coun. Ind. Colls., Washington, 1985-86, pres., 1986-2000; dir., pres. Consulting Svc., 2002—05; pres. emeritus Coun. Ind. Colls., Washington, 2000—. Dir. Nat. Prepaid Tuition Plan, 1988-91; cons. York Coll., Pa., 1974; planning and rsch. com. NY State Com. on Ind. Colls. and Univs., 1975-82; statewide higher edn. adv. com. NY State Senate Com. on Higher Edn., 1979-82; nat. adv. bd. Flaming Rainbow U., 1989-96; adv. bd. Assn. Gov. Bds. Presdl. Search Consultation Svc., 1987-94, Academic Search Consultation Svc., 1989—, mem. Harvard Sem. for new pres. adv. bd., 1990—; bd. dirs. Tchr. Edn. Accreditation Coun., 1998—2006, chair, 2001—06, chair emeritus 2006- ; oversight and rev. com. leadership and orgnl. devel. program United Negro Coll. Fund, 1991-96, SCT adv. coun., 1996-2001; adv. bd. Eric Nat., 1996-03, Boyer Ctr. for Advanced Studies, 1998-2005; UAW/Ford U. Help Steering Com., 1997-01; exec. bd. Project Pericles, 1999-05 (nat. adv. bd. 2005-), CIC Pres. Consulting Svc., 2003-05, designated Fulbright Senior Specialist 2006-. Co-author: Frederic Remington-Selected Letters, 1988, A Good Place To Work: Sourcebook for the Academic Workplace, 1991, Presidential Transitions in Private Colleges, 2005; editor: (with others) Confs. on Adirondack Park, 1972-82, Can.-Am. Relations, 1974-75, Presidential Essays-Success Stories, 2000, Boats and Boating on Cranberry Lake, 2009; contbr. articles to profl. jours. Chmn. planning bd. Village of Canton, 1974-81; elder Neelsville Presbyn. Ch., 1986-89; trustee Adirondack Conservancy, Wilsboro, NY, 1980-82; trustee Millikin U., 2000-06; mem. adv. bd. Sage Scholars, 2000-06, mem. nat. bd., 2006-. Served to 1st lt. US Army, 1960-62. Recipient Alumni citation, St. Lawrence U., 1987, Algernon Sydney Sullivan award, 1997, CIC Acad. Leadership award, 2000, Henry D. Paley award, Nat. Assn. Ind. Colls. and Univs., 2001, Partnership award, Assn. Presbyn. Colls. and Univs., 2000; grantee, John Ben Snow Found., 1981. Mem. Pa. Assn. Colls and Univs. (govt. rels. com. 1983-85), Mid. States Assn. (team chmn. com. on higher edn. 1976-78, 81), Assn. Am. Colls. (project rev. cons. 1981-82), Soc. Educators and Scholars (bd. editors), Assn. Am. Colls. (pres. adv. com. 1977-78, reviewer Quill project 1978-79), St. Lawrence County Hist. Assn. (pres. 1977-82), Frederic Remington Mus. Assn., Beta Theta Pi (v.p. 1980-83). Republican. Avocations: sports, gardening, travel, poetry, classical music. Home: 10821 Longmeadow Dr Damascus MD 20872-2240 Office: Coun Ind Colls 1 Dupont Cir NW Ste 320 Washington DC 20036-1137 Office Phone: 301-253-1274. Personal E-mail: amsplete@yahoo.com.

SPLINTER, MICHAEL R., manufacturing executive; BEE, U. Wis., Madison, 1972, MEE, 1974. Gen. mgr., exec. v.p. Intel Corp., Santa Clara, Calif., 1984—96; v.p. and asst. Gen. mgr. Tech. and Mfg. Group, Intel Corp., Santa Clara, Calif., 1996—98, v.p. and Gen. mgr., 1998—99, sr. v.p. and Gen. mgr., 1999—2001, exec. v.p. and Gen. mgr., 2001, exec. v.p. and dir., Sales and Mktg. group, 2001—03; pres. and CEO Applied Materials, Inc, Santa Clara, Calif., 2003—09, chmn., pres., CEO, 2009—. Mem. Computer Sys. Policy Project; bd. dir. Semiconductor Equipment and Materials Intern., Silicon Valley Leadership Group. Recipient Intern. Partnership Award, Calif.-Israel C. of C., Disting. Alumni Award, U. Wis.; named to, Jr. Achievement Hall of Fame. Mem.: Governors' Coun. of World Econ. Forum, Applied Materials (bd. dir. 2003). Office: Applied Materials Inc 3050 Bowers Ave Santa Clara CA 95054*

SPLINTER, WILLIAM ELDON, agricultural engineering educator; b. North Platte, Nebr., Nov. 24, 1925; s. William John and Minnie (Calhoun) Splinter; m. Eleanor Love Peterson, Jan. 10, 1952 (dec. Jan. 6, 1999); children: Kathryn Love, William John, Karen Ann, Robert Marvin; m. Elizabeth Butters Calhoun, Feb. 9, 2002. BS in Agrl. Engring., U. Nebr., 1950; MS in Agrl. Engring., Mich. State U., 1951,

PhD in Agrl. Engring., 1955. Instr. agrl. engring. Mich. State U., East Lansing, 1953-54; assoc. prof. biology and agrl. engring. N.C. State U., Raleigh, 1954-60, prof. biology and agrl. engring., 1960-68; head agrl. engring. dept. U. Nebr., Lincoln, 1968—88, vice chancellor rsch., 1988—93; interim dean Coll. Engring. & Tech. U. Nebr., 1994—95, 2001—02; interim dir. Nebr. State Mus., 2002—. Cons. engr.; exec. bd. Am. Assn. Engring. Socs.; hon. prof. Shengyang (People's Republic of China) Agrl. U. Contbr. articles to tech. jours.; patentee in field. Vol. dir. L.F. Larsen Tractor Mus. Served with USNR, 1946-51. Recipient Massey Ferguson Gold medal, 1978, John Deere Gold medal, 1995, Disting. Svc. award Kiwanis, 1994, George Howard-Loiuse Pound award, 2001; named to Nebr. Hall of Agrl. Achievement; named Disting. Alumni, U. Nebr., Lincoln, 2000, Mich. State U., 2005; named U. Nebr. Splinter Rsch. Lab. in his honor, 2004. Fellow AAAS, NSPE, Am. Soc. Agrl. Engrs. (pres., adminstrv. council, found. pres., Presdl. citation 1999); mem. Nat. Acad. Engring., Soc. Automotive Engrs., Am. Soc. Engring. Edn., Sigma Xi, Sigma Tau, Sigma Pi Sigma, Pi Mu Epsilon, Gamma Sigma Delta, Phi Kappa Phi, Beta Sigma Psi. Home: 4801 Bridle Ln Lincoln NE 68516-3436 Office: U Nebr Lincoln PO Box 830833 Lincoln NE 68583-0833 Office Phone: 402-472-8389. Business E-Mail: wsplinter1@unl.edu.

SPODAK, MICHAEL KENNETH, forensic psychiatrist; b. Bklyn., Nov. 5, 1944; s. Harry and Betty (Rahn) S.; children: Lisa Beth, Brett David. BS, Union Coll., 1966; MD, SUNY-Syracuse, 1970. Diplomate: Nat. Bd. Med. Examiners, Am. Bd. Neurology and Psychiatry. Intern Mary Imogene Bassett Hosp., Cooperstown, NY, 1970-71; resident John Hopkins Hosp., Balt., 1974-77; practice medicine specializing in civil and criminal forensic psychiatry Towson, Md., 1977—; chief dept. psychiatry Balt. County Gen. Hosp., Randallstown, 1978-85; mem. staff Clifton T. Perkins Hosp. Ctr., Jessup, Md., 1977-92; clin. asst. prof. psychiatry U. Md. Hosp., Balt., 1983-97; psychiat. cons. Bur. Disability Ins., Social Security Adminstrn., Workmen's compensation Commn., Balt., 1981—; dir. community forensic services Mental Hygiene Adminstrn., Md., 1982-92; faculty Nat. Jud. Coll., 1988—. Mem. Md. Task Force on Somatic Therapies Contbr. numerous articles on forensic psychiatry to profl. jours., chpt. to book. Served with M.C. USN, 1972-74. Mem. Am. Acad. Psychiatry and Law, Am. Psychiat. Assn., Md. Psychiat. Soc. (chmn. peer rev. com. 2001), Md. Med. Soc. (chmn. occupational health com. 1983-90), Baltimore County Med. Soc. Office: 26 W Pennsylvania Ave Towson MD 21204-5001 Office Phone: 410-337-0343. E-mail: mkspodak@yahoo.com.

SPODEK, BERNARD, early childhood educator; b. Bklyn., Sept. 17, 1931; s. David and Esther (Lebenbaum) S.; m. Prudence Debb, June 21, 1957; children: Esther Yin-ling, Jonathan Chou. BA, Bklyn. Coll., 1952; MA, Columbia U., 1955, EdD, 1962. Cert. early childhood edn. tchr., N.Y. Tchr. Beth Hayeled Sch., NYC, 1952-56, N.Y. City Pub. Schs., Bklyn., 1956-57, Early Childhood Ctr., Bklyn. Coll., 1957-60; asst. prof. elem. edn. U. Wis.-Milw., 1961-65; assoc. prof. early childhood edn. U. Ill., Champaign, 1965-68, prof. dept. curriculum and instrn., 1968-97, dir. dept. grad. programs, 1986-87, chair dept., 1987-89, dir. hons. program, Coll. Edn., 1984-86, mem. faculty Bur. Ednl. Rsch., 1981-85, prof. emeritus, 1997—; adv. prof. Hong Kong Inst. of Edn., 1999-2001. Dir. insts. Nat. Def. Edn. Act, 1965-67, dir. experienced tchr. fellowship program, 1967-69, co-dir. program for tchr. trainers in early childhood edn., 1969-74; vis. prof. Western Wash. State U., 1974, U. Wis., Madison, 1980, Kobe Shinwa Women's U., Japan, 2004, 07; vis. scholar Sch. Early Childhood Studies, Brisbane (Australia) Coll. Advanced Edn., Delissa Inst. Early Childhood Studies, S. Australia Coll. Advanced Edn., 1985, Beijing Normal U., Nanjing Normal U., East China Normal U., Shangai, People's Republic China, 1986; rsch. fellow Kobe U., Japan, 1996; adj. prof. Queensland (Australia) U. Tech., 2000. Author or co-author: (with others) A Black Studies Curriculum for Early Childhood Education, 1972, 2d edit., 1976, Teaching in the Early Years, 1972, 3d edit., 1985, Early Childhood Education, 1973, Studies in Open Education, 1975 (Japanese trans.), Early Childhood Education: Issues and Perspectives, 1977, (with Nir-Janiv and Steg) International Perspectives on Early Childhood Education, 1982 (Hebrew trans.), with Saracho and Lee (Mainstreaming Young Children, 1984, (with Saracho and Davis) Foundations of Early Childhood Education, 1987, 2d edit. (Japanese trans.), 1991, Right from the Start, 1994 (Chinese, Portuguese and Korean translations), Dealing with Individual Differences in the Early Childhood Classroom, 1994; editor: Handbook of Research in Early Childhood Education, 1982, rev. edit., 2005, Today's Kindergarten, 1986; (with Saracho and Peters) Professionalism and the Early Childhood Practitioner, 1988; (with Saracho) Early Childhood Teacher Education, 1990, Issues in Early Childhood Curriculum, 1991, Educationally Appropriate Kindergarten Practices, 1991, Issues in Childcare, 1992, Handbook of Research on the Education of Young Children (Portuguese tranls.), 1993, Language and Literacy in Early Childhood Education, 1993, Issues in Early Childhood Educational Evaluation and Assessment, 1996, Multiple Perspectives on Play in Early Childhood Education, 1998, Contemporary Perspectives in Early Childhood Curriculum, 2002, Contemporary Perspectives on Literacy in Early Childhood Education, 2002, Contemporary Perspectives on Play in Early Childhood Education, 2003, Studying Teachers in Early Childhood Settings, 2003, Contemporary Perspectives on Language Policy and Literacy Instruction, 2004, Contemporary Perspectives on Families, Communities, and Schools for Young Children, 2005, International Perspectives on Research in Early Childhood Education, 2005, Handbook of Research on the Education of Young Children, 2d edit., 2006, Contemporary Perspectives on Socialization and Social Development in Early Childhood Education, 2007, Contemporary Perspectives on Social Learning in Early Childhood Education, 2007, Contemporary Perspective on Mathematics in Early Childhood Education, 2008, Contemporary Perspectives on Science in Early Childhood Education, 2008; (with Safford and Saracho) Early Childhood Special Education, 1994; (with Garcia, McLaughlin & Saracho) Meeting the Challenge of Cultural and Linguistic Diversity, 1995; (with Saracho and Pellegrini) Issues in Early Childhood Educational Research, 1998, others; series editor Yearbook in Early Childhood Education, early childhood edn. publs., 1990-00; series co-editor: Contemporary Perspectives in Early Childhood Education, 2002—; guest editor Studies in Ednl. Evaluation, 1982, Early Education and Child Development, 1995; also contbr. chpts to books, articles to profl. jours. Mem. Am. Ednl. Rsch. Assn. (chair early childhood and child devel. spl. interest group 1983-84, publs. com. 1984-86), Nat. Assn. Edn. Young Children (sec. 1965-68, bd. govs. 1968-72, pres. 1976-78, editl. adv. bd. 1972-76, book rev. editor, 1972-74, cons. editor, 1985-87 Young Children jour., tchr. edn. commn. 1981-88, chair commn. on appropriate edn. 4-5 yr. old children, 1984-85, cons. editor Early Childhood Rsch. Quar. 1987-90), Nat. Soc. for Study of Edn. (1972 yearbook com., Asia-Pacific edn. rev.), Pacific Early Childhood Edn. Rsch. Assn. (pres. 2000-08). Home Phone: 217-352-1482. Business E-Mail: b-spodek@illinois.edu.

SPOELSTRA, ERIK, professional basketball coach; b. Evanston, Ill., Nov. 1, 1970; s. Jon and Lisa Spoelstra. Degree in comm., U. Portland, 1992. Player, coach Tus Herten, Germany; video coord. Miami Heat, 1995—97, asst. coach, video coord., 1997—99, asst. coach, advance scout, 1999—2001, asst. coach, dir. scouting, 2001—08, head coach, 2008—. Head, individual player devel. program Miami Heat, summer league coach, 2005—07. Office: Miami Heat 601 Biscayne Blvd Miami FL 33132

SPOERRY, ROBERT F., manufacturing executive; b. 1955; B Mech. Engring., Fed. Inst. Tech., Zurich Switzerland; MBA, U. Chgo. Mgmt. positions with Mettler-Toledo Internat., 1983—87, head. indsl. & retail (Europe), 1987—93, pres., CEO, 1993—98, chmn., pres., CEO, 1998—2007, exec. chmn., 2008—. Bd. dirs. Mettler-Toledo Internat., 1996—, Phonak Group, Sonova Holding AG. Bd. dir. Swiss-Am. C. of C. Office: Mettler-Toledo Internat 1900 Polaris Pkwy Columbus OH 43240 Office Phone: 614-438-4511.

SPOFFORD, SALLY (HYSLOP), artist; b. NYC, Aug. 20, 1929; d. George Hall and Esther (McNaull) Hyslop; m. Gavin Spofford, Mar. 11, 1950 (dec. Jan. 1976); children: Lizabeth Spofford Smith, Leslie Spofford Russell. Student, The China Inst., NYC, 1949, The Art Students League, 1950; BA with high honors, Swarthmore Coll., 1952. Instr. Somerset Art Assn., Peapack, N.J., 1978-95, Hunterdon Mus. Art, Clinton, N.J., 1985—; adv. bd., lectr. Apollo Muses, Inc., Gladstone, N.J.; trustee Artshowcase, Inc. One-woman shows include Riverside Studio, Pottersville, NJ, 1985, Morris Mus., Morristown, NJ 1989, Schering-Plough Gallery, Madison, NJ, 1989, Phoenix Gallery, NYC, 1990, Robin Hutchins Gallery, Maplewood, NJ, 1992, Berlex Labs. Corp. Office, Wayne, NJ, 1992, Hunterdon Mus. Art, Clinton, 1993, 2003, Newark Acad., Livingston, NJ, 1997, Simon Gallery, Morristown, 2004, 2007; exhibited in group shows at Hickory, NC Mus., 1983, Purdue U., 1983, Monmouth, NJ, 1984, Nabisco Brands Gallery, East Hanover, NJ, 1985, 89, Hunterdon Mus. Art, 1988, 93, 99, Schering-Plough Gallery, Madison, 1988, Morris Mus., Morristown, 1989, Montclair, NJ State U., 1995, Williams Gallery, Princeton, NJ, 1997, Monmouth Mus., Lincroft, NJ, 1998, Newark Acad., Livingston, 2000, Bristol-Myers Squibb Gallery, Princeton, NJ, 2005; represented in permanent collections NJ State Mus., Trenton, Newark Mus., Morris Mus., Morristown. Painting residency fellow Vt. Studio Ctr., 1992. Mem. Assoc. Artists N.J. (pres. 1985-87), N.J. Watercolor Soc., Federated Art Assns. of N.J. (panel mem. 1985, demonstrator 1991). Home: PO Box 443 Bernardsville NJ 07924-0443 Office Phone: 908-766-1219.

SPOGLI, RONALD PAUL, private equity form executive, former ambassador; b. L.A., 1948; m. Georgia Beth Caudle; 2 children. AB in Hist., Stanford U., Calif., 1970; MBA, Harvard U., 1975. V.p. corp. fin. dept. Dean Witter Reynolds, Inc., L.A., 1978—82, mng. dir. investment banking divsn.; co-founder, ptnr. Freeman Spogli & Co., L.A., 1983—; US amb. to Italy US Dept. State, Rome, 2005—09, US amb. to San Marino, 2006—09. Lead rschr. Stanford U. Labor Migration Project, Milan. Bd. dirs. (presdl. appointee) J. William Fulbright Fgn. Scholarship Bd., 2002—. Recipient J. William Fulbright Fgn. Scholarship, 2002. Republican. Office: Freeman Spogli & Co 11100 Santa Monica Blvd Ste 1900 Los Angeles CA 90025*

SPOHN, DOROTHY M., retired elementary school educator; b. Bloomington, Ind., Dec. 31, 1929; d. Charles L. and Martha V. (Staley) Mc Conville; m. Charles L. Spohn, Sept. 23,1949; children: Charles David, Steven Michael. BA, Wichita State U., 1973; MEd, Miami U., 1978. Cert. tchr. Ohio. Tchr. Ross Local Sch. Dist., Hamilton, Ohio, until 1995. Marth Holden Jennings Found. scholar, 1986; recipient Southwestern Ohio Spl. Edn. cert. of recognition, 1987, Golden Apple Achievement award Ashland Oil Co., 1990. Mem. AAUW, NEA, NSTA, Nat. Assn. Gifted Children, Ohio Assn. Gifted Children, Ohio Edn. Assn., Ross Edn. Assn. Home: 8407 Barnesburg Rd Cincinnati OH 45247-3551

SPOHN, HERBERT EMIL, psychologist; b. Berlin, June 10, 1923; s. Herbert F. and Bertha S.; m. Billie M. Powell, July 28, 1973; children: Jessica, Madeleine. BSS., CCNY, 1949; PhD, Columbia U., 1955. Research psychologist VA Hosp., Montrose, NY, 1955-60, chief research sect., 1960-64; sr. research psychologist Menninger Found., Topeka, 1965-80, dir. hosp. research, 1979-94, dir. research dept., 1981-94; ret., prof. emeritus for rsch., 1994—. Mem. mental health small grant com. NIMH, 1972-76, mem. treatment assessment rev. com., 1983-86, chmn. 1986-87. Author: (with Gardner Murphy) Encounter with Reality, 1968; assoc. editor: Schizophrenia Bull, 1970-87, 91—; contbr. articles to profl. jours. Served with AUS, World War II. USPHS grantee, 1964— Fellow Am. Psychopath. Assn.; mem. AAAS, N.Y. Acad. Sci., Soc. Psychopath. Research, Phi Beta Kappa, Sigma Xi. Office: 1906 SW Village Dr Topeka KS 66604-3714 E-mail: hspohn@prodigy.net.

SPOHN, NOR RAE, computer company executive; married; 2 children. BS in Computer Sci., Iowa State U., Calif., 1980; MEE, Stanford U. R&D engr. Hewlett-Packard Co., 1980, R&D mgr. LaserJet Divsn., 1998—2002, v.p., gen. mgr. Personal LaserJet Solutions, 2002—07, sr. v.p. LaserJet Printing Bus., 2007—. Mem. Gov.'s Sci. & Tech. Adv. Coun., Idaho, 2006—. Chair Idaho Sci., Math. and Tech. Coalition; bd. mem. Treasure Vallet Math. & Sci. Ctr.; bd. adv. Sch. Engring. Boise State U. Named to Women in Tech. Internat. Hall of Fame, 2006. Office: Hewlett Packard Co Personal LaserJet Solutions Divsn 3000 Hanover St Palo Alto CA 94304-1185

SPOHN, WILLIAM GIDEON, JR., mathematician, retired musician; b. Lancaster, Pa., Mar. 8, 1923; s. William Gideon and Inza Mae (Huber) S.; m. Alice Liane Bailey, Sept. 13, 1946 (div.); children: Susan Jeannine Grochowina (dec.), William Gideon III (dec.), Peter Jonathan, Kathleen Anne Precht, Mary Louise; m. Evelyn Walsh Moreland, June 15, 1963 (div. Oct. 1978); m. Claire Louise Burgstahler, Dec. 19, 1987 (div. Sept. 1999). BA, St. Johns Coll., 1947; MA, U. Calif., Berkeley, 1950; PhD, U. Pa., 1962. Instr. math. Temple U., Phila., 1952-54, U. Del., Newark, 1954-56; mathematician Aberdeen Proving Ground, Md., 1954-55; instr. math. Bowling Green (Ohio) State U., 1956-59; mathematician, sr. staff Johns Hopkins U. Applied Physics Lab., Laurel, Md., 1959-84; singer, prodr. Spohn Music Co., Columbia, Md., 1981-99. Contbr. articles to profl. jours. Served to lt. USNR, 1943-46, PTO. Johns Hopkins U. Applied Physics Lab. fellow, 1966-67. Mem. Math. Assn. Am. Home: 1 Heritage Farm Dr Mount Airy MD 21771-5783

SPOKANE, ROBERT BRUCE, biophysical chemist; b. Cleve., Aug. 5, 1952; s. Herbert Norman and Marjorie Ellen (Firsten) S.; m. Linda Carol Wright, June 20, 1976; children: Lea, Hannah, Tara. BS in Chemistry, Ohio U., 1975; MS in Biophys. Chemistry, U. Colo., 1978, PhD in Biophys. Chemistry, 1981. Cert. full cave diver. Tchg. asst. dept. chemistry U. Colo., Boulder, 1975-77, rsch. asst. dept. chemistry, 1977-81; staff scientist Procter & Gamble Co., Cin., 1981-84; rsch. scientist dept. neurophysiology Children's Hosp., Cin., 1984-90; sr. scientist, product mgr. YSI Co., Yellow Springs, Ohio, 1990—2005; sr. rsch. scientist U. Dayton, Ohio, 2006—. Cons. Synthetic Blood Internat., Yellow Springs, 1992. Contbr. articles to profl. jours. Rescuer, treas. Boulder Emergency Squad, 1980; rescue diver Kitty Hawk Scuba, Dayton, Ohio, 1992. Recipient Merck Index award Ohio U., 1975. Mem. Am. Chem. Soc., N.Y. Acad. Sci., Am. Physiol. Soc., Nat. Speleological Soc. (cave diving sect.), Sigma Xi. Achievements include research in implantable glucose sensors; oxygen tonometer for peritoneal oxygen measurements; interferant removal system for biosensors for methanol, ethanol, glutamate, and glutamine, optical carbon dioxide sensor, water chemistry in submerged caves. Home: 1715 Garry Dr Bellbrook OH 45305-1362 Office: UDRI 300 Collose Pk Dayton OH 45469-0181 Office Phone: 937-767-7241. Business E-Mail: rspokane@ysi.com.

SPOLAN, HARMON SAMUEL, lawyer; b. Phila., Dec. 12, 1935; s. Jay and Edythe (Greenberg) S.; m. Betty Jane Evnitz, Mar. 30, 1958; children: Michael, Suzanne. AB, Temple U., 1957, LLB, 1959; postgrad., Oxford U., 1966. Bar: Pa. 1960. Ptnr. Ravetz & Shuchman, Phila., 1960-68, Blair & Co., NYC, 1968-72; v.p. Butcher & Singer, Phila., 1972-74; pres. Capital First Corp., Phila., 1974-75, State Nat. Bank, Rockville, Md., 1975-78, Jefferson Bank, Phila., 1978-99; pres., bd. dirs. JeffBanks, Inc., Phila., 1986-99; sr. mem. Cozen O'Connor, Phila., 1999—2007, of counsel, 2007—. Lectr. law U. Pa., Phila., 1964-68. Author: Federal Aids to Financing, 1970; contbr. articles to profl. jours. Former chmn. bd. Huntingdon Hosp., Willow Grove, Pa., 1982—89; bd. dirs. YMHA, Phila., 1978—95, Anti-Defamation League, 1982. Named Man of Yr., Nat. Assn. Women Bus. Owners, 1978, Disting. Alumnus, Central H.S., 1975. Mem. ABA, Phila. Bar Assn., Coleman Cable Inc. (bd. mem, 2007-), Atlas America. Inc.(bd. mem, 2006-) Democrat. Jewish. Office: 1900 Market St Philadelphia PA 19103-3527 Home Phone: 215-985-0260. Business E-Mail: hspolan@cozen.com.

SPOMER, PENNY SUE, elementary school educator; d. Pete and Pat Tuckness; m. Vernon Lee Spomer, June 29, 1974; children: Nicole Lea Lopez, Leslie Ann Buddecke. BA, Mesa State Coll., Grand Junction, Colo., 1991; M in Tech. in Edn., Lesley Coll., 2000. Sixth grade tchr. Orchard Mesa Mid. Sch., Grand Junction, 1993—. Mem.: Delta Kappa Gamma (assoc.; 2nd v.p. 2004). Business E-Mail: xfile@mesa.k12.co.us.

SPONG, DONALD A., physicist; s. Clarence R. Spong and Mildred Atchison; m. Janet E. Swift, May 23, 1981; 1 child, Kate E. Swift-Spong. PhD, U. Mich., Ann Arbor, 1975. Sr. scientist Oak Ridge Nat. Lab., Tenn., 1975—. Vis. prof. Nat. Inst. Fusion Scis., Japan, 2007. Contbr. scientific papers. Vol. builder Habitat Humanity, Oak Ridge, 1990—2008. Recipient Martin Marietta Author of Yr. award, 1994. Mem.: Sigma Xi, Phi Eta Sigma, Am. Phys. Soc. (local arrangements coord. 1988), Phi Kappa Phi. Achievements include research in development and physics studies of a compact quasi-poloidal stellarator; development of gyrofluid closure models for energetic particle driven alfven instabilities; moments method analysis of plasma flow shearing in 3D toroidal configurations; computational modeling of runaway electrons in tokamaks; development of models of alfven instabilities in stellarators. Avocations: sailing, hiking, travel, scuba diving, skiing.

SPONG, DOUGLAS K., public relations executive; B in English, Iowa State U. Sr. v.p., mng. dir. and bd. dirs. Colle & McVoy Pub. Rels.; co-founder, mng. ptnr., pres. pub. rels. divsn. Carmichael Lynch Spong, Mpls., 1990—; mng. ptnr. Carmichael Lynch, 2009—. Founding mem. Coun. of Pub. Rels. Firms, NYC, 1998; past. dir. and treas. Mem.: Pub. Rels. Soc. America (past pres., chair honors and awards com., mem. Counselor's Acad.). Office: Carmichael Lynch 110 N 5th St Minneapolis MN 55403-1603 Office Phone: 612-375-8555. Business E-Mail: doug.spong@clynch.com.*

SPONG, JOHN SHELBY, retired bishop, writer, columnist; b. Charlotte, NC, June 16, 1931; s. John Shelby and Doolie Boyce (Griffith) S.; m. Joan Lydia Ketner, Sept. 5, 1952 (dec. 1988); children: Ellen Elizabeth, Mary Katharine, Jaquelin Ketner; m. Christine Mary Bridger, Jan. 1, 1990. AB, U. N.C., 1952; M.Div., Va. Theol. Sem., 1955; D.D., St. Paul's Coll., 1976, Va. Theol. Sem., 1977; DHL (hon.), Muhlenburg Coll., 1998, Holmes Inst. Chgo., 2003, Lehigh U., 2006, U. NC, 2006. Ordained to ministry Episcopal Ch., 1955, bishop, 1976; rector St. Joseph's Ch., Durham, NC, 1955-57, Calvary Ch., Tarboro, NC, 1957-65, St. John's Ch., Lynchburg, Va., 1965-69, St. Paul's Ch., Richmond, Va., 1969-76; bishop Diocese of Newark, 1976-2000, ret., 2000. Mem. governing body Nat. Episc. Ch., 1973-76; vis. lectr., Harvard U. Div. Sch., 2000, U. Pacific, Stockton, Calif., 2003, Drew U., 2008; mem. faculty Grad. Theol. Union, Berkeley, Calif., 1997, 99, 2001, 03, 05, 07. Author: Honest Prayer, 1973, This Hebrew Lord, 1974, Dialogue--In Search of Jewish-Christian Understanding, 1975, Christpower, 1976, The Living Commandments, 1977, The Easter Moment, 1980, Into the Whirlwind: The Future of the Church, 1983, Beyond Moralism, 1986, Survival and Consciousness, 1987, Living in Sin? A Bishop Rethinks Human Sexuality, 1988, Rescuing the Bible from Fundamentalism--A Biship Rethinks the Meaning of Scripture, 1991, Born of a Woman, 1992, Resurrection: Myth or Reality?, 1994, Liberating the Gospels, Reading the Bible with Jewish Eyes, 1996, Why Christianity Must Change or Die, 1998, Here I Stand: My Struggle for a Christianity of Integrity, Love and Equality, 2000, A New Christianity for a New World, 2001, The Sins of Scripture-Exploring the Bible's Texts of Hate to Discover The God of Love, 2005, Jesus for Non Religious, 2007, Eternal Life: A New Vision: Beyond Religion, Beyond Theism, Beyond Heaven and Hell, 2009; columnist Beliefnet.com, 2000—02, Waterfront Media, 2002—. Elected Quartercentury Scholar Emmanuel Coll., Cambridge, Eng., 1992, named Humanist of Yr., 1999, William Belden Noble lectr. Harvard U., 2000. Mem.: Rotary. Episcopalian. Home: 24 Puddingstone Rd Morris Plains NJ 07950-1114

SPONZILLI, EDWARD GEORGE, lawyer; b. Newark, Mar. 30, 1948; s. Edward James and Dorothy Maria (Murillo) Sponzilli. BA in History with high honors, Rutgers U., 1971, JD, 1975; summer diploma, Cath. Inst. of Paris, 1971; MA, Columbia U., 1972. Bar: N.J. 1975, U.S. Dist. Ct. N.J. 1975, U.S. Ct. Appeals (3d cir.) 1976, U.S. Supreme Ct. 1979, D.C. 1979, N.Y. 1981, U.S. Ct. Appeals (2d cir.) 1992, U.S. Dist. Ct. (so. dist.) N.Y. 1991, U.S. Dist. Ct. (ea. dist.) N.Y. 1991, US Dist. Ct. (we. dist.) NY 2009. Law clk. to judge U.S. Dist. Ct. NJ, Newark, 1975—77; assoc. Pitney, Hardin & Kipp, Morristown, NJ, 1975—81, Dunn, Pashman, Sponzilli, Swick & Finnerty (formerly Cummins, Dunn & Pashman), Hackensack, NJ, 1981—, ptnr., 1984—95, Norris, McLaughlin & Marcus, P.A., 1995—. Adj. prof. Rutgers U., New Brunswick, NJ, 1980—81, 1994, 98, mcpl. pros., 1981—2007, mem. Jessup Internat. Law Moot Ct. Team, 1975, coach Mock Trial Team, 1994—97; counsel Judo of NJ Inc., Cranford, 1983—; judge law sch. moot ct. competition Seton Hall, 1977—79, 1981, 81, 86; cert. civil trial atty. NJ Supreme Ct., 1997—; mem. faculty Nat. Inst. Trial Advocacy, 1995—; faculty N.J. Atty. Gens. Trial Advocacy Inst., 2002—. Contbr. articles to profl. jours. Active Rutgers U. Found., 1987—; bench bar media com. NJ Supreme Ct., 2007—. Recipient Nancy Higgenson Dorr award, Rutgers U., 1971, Disting. Svc. award, Animals Need You-Kindness Corp., NJ, 1981, Client Protection award, NJ Supreme Ct. Fund for Client Protection, 1999, Professionalism award, Trial Attys. NJ, 2008; named Superlawyer, NJ Mag., 2005—09; named one of Best Lawyers, 2007—09; Henry Rutgers scholar. Fellow: ABA (trial practice com. of litigation sect. 2008), Am. Inns Ct. (master, pres. 2000—01); mem.: ATLA, NYC Inns Ct., NYC Bar Assn., NY State Bar Assn., Assn. Fed. Bar NJ, NJ Mcpl. Prosecutors Assn., NJ Criminal Def. Assn., NJ

State Ct. (mediator, fed. arbitrator), Nat. Assn. Coll. and Univ. Attys., NJ Def. Assn., Middlesex County Bar Assn., Essex County Bar Assn., Bergen County Bar Assn., Trial Attys. NJ (trustee 1987—), NJ Trial Lawyers Assn., NJ State Bar Assn. (higher edn. com.), Columbia Grad. Faculties Alumni Assn., Scarlet R Round Table Alumni Assn., Rutgers U. Law Sch. Alumni Assn. (nominating com. 1982, program dir. 1982, treas. 1991—92, sec. 1992—93, v.p. 1993—94, pres. 1994—95, exec. counsel, alumni fedn. rep.), Phi Alpha Delta, Kappa Sigma (sec. 1978—79, alumnus advisor 1978—99, v.p. 1979—82, pres. 1982—86, dist. grand master 1986—2000, pres. 1994—2001, chmn. nat. legal commn. 1995—97, trustee Gamma Upsilon chpt., Steven Alonso Jackson award 1999), Phi Beta Kappa. Home: 37 Brookside Ave Caldwell NJ 07006-5603 Office: Norris McLaughlin & Marcus PA 721 Rt 202-206 PO Box 5933 Bridgewater NJ 08807 Office Phone: 908-252-4166. Business E-Mail: egsponzilli@nmmlaw.com.

SPOON, ALAN GARY, venture capital company executive; b. Detroit, June 4, 1951; s. Harry and Mildred (Rudman) S.; m. Terri Alper, June 3, 1975; children: Ryan, Leigh, Randi. BS, MS, MIT, 1973; JD, Harvard U., 1976. Cons. The Boston Cons. Group, 1976-79, mgr., 1979-81, v.p., 1981, The Washington Post Co., 1982-84; v.p., contr. Washington Post, 1985-86, v.p. mktg., 1986-87; v.p. fin., CFO The Washington Post Co., 1987-89; pres. Newsweek mag., 1989-91; COO The Washington Post Co., 1991-2000, pres., 1993-2000; mng. gen. ptnr. Polaris Venture Ptnrs., Waltham, Mass., 2000—. Dir. Info. Industry Assn., Washington, 1982-83, 88-89; bd. dirs. Danaher Corp. Washington, Interactive Corp., N.Y.C.; regent Smithsonian Instn., Washington; mem. corp. MIT. Bd. dirs. Norwood Sch., 1989-93, chmn., 1993-95; bd. dirs. Smithsonian Nat. Mus. Natural History, Washington, 1994-99; trustee WETA-Pub. Broadcasting, 1986-92. Recipient award for scholarship and athletics Ea. Coll. Athletic Conf. and MIT, 1973. Office: Polaris Venture Partners 1000 Winter St Ste 3350 Waltham MA 02451-1476

SPOONER, DAVID M., federal agency administrator, lawyer; BA, U. Va., 1991; JD, Coll. William and Mary, 1994. Legal counsel to Rep. Wes Cooley US Ho. of Reps, Washington, comm. dir. Com. on Agr., assoc. Com. on Rules; adminstrv. asst. Office of Rep. Sue Myrick, US Ho. of Reps, Washington, press sec., legis. dir.; transition coord. Office of US Trade Rep. Exec. Office of the Pres., Washington, spl. textile negotiator Office of US Trade Rep., 2002—05; asst. sec. import adminstrn. Internat. Trade Adminstrn. US Dept. Commerce, Washington, 2005—. Office: US Dept Commerce Herbert Clark Hoover Bldg 1401 Constitution Ave NW Washington DC 20230 Office Phone: 202-482-1780. Office Fax: 202-482-0947.*

SPOONER, DONNA, management consultant; b. DeLand, Fla. d. Michael and Ruth Elizabeth Linkovich. BS, Fla. State U., 1971, MPA, 1993, PhD in Pub. Adminstrn. and Policy, 2001. Budget analyst Dept. Adminstrn./Exec. Office of Gov. State of Fla., Tallahassee, 1977-80, spl. projects adminstr./acting chief, Bur. of Employee Cert., 1980-81, sr. govtl. analyst Exec. Office of Gov., 1981-85, pub. and legis. affairs dir. Dept. Adminstrn., 1985-87, asst. dir. Gov.'s Drug and Crime Policy Office, 1987-90; statewide planning coord. alcohol, drug abuse, mental health Fla. Dept. Health and Rehab. Svcs., Tallahassee, 1990-95; owner Spooner Energy Assocs., Tallahassee, 1996—2000; dir., founder Ctr. for Policy and Mgmt. Strategies, Tallahassee, 2001—; co-founder, co-dir. CE Studies LLC, Tallahassee, 2005—. Mem. Am. Soc. Pub. Adminstrn., S.E. Evaluation Assn., Capital Women's Network, Pi Alpha Alpha. Avocations: reading, hiking, dance. Office: Ctr for Policy and Mgmt Studies PO Box 14595 Tallahassee FL 32317 also: Continuas Edn Studies LLC PO Box 12337 Tallahassee FL 32317

SPOONER, SHARON NAU, pediatric ophthalmologist; b. Melrose, Mass., Apr. 15, 1952; BA in Molecular Biology, San Diego State Coll., 1972, San Jose State U., Calif., 1975; MD, UCLA Sch. Medicine, 1980. Cert. in ophthalmology 1986. Internship in internal medicine Hosp. the Good Samaritan, LA, 1980—81; residency in ophthalmology UCLA Jules Stein Eye Inst., 1981—84, fellowship in pediatric ophthalmology, 1984—86, hosp. appointment, clin. instr.; pvt. practice in pediatric ophthalmology and strabismus surgery Santa Monica, Calif. Grantee Rosalind Alcott fellowship, 1984. Mem.: AMA, Am. Acad. Ophthalmology, Am. Assn. Pediatric Ophthalmology and Strabismus. Office: 2222 Santa Monica Blvd Ste 401 Santa Monica CA 90404 Office Phone: 310-453-0471. Office Fax: 310-453-0473. Business E-Mail: info@sharonspoonermd.com.

SPOOR, WILLIAM HOWARD, food products executive; b. Pueblo, Colo., Jan. 16, 1923; s. Charles Hinchman and Doris Field (Slaughter) S.; m. Janet Spain, Sept. 23, 1950; children: Melanie G., Cynthia F., William Lincoln. BA, Dartmouth Coll., 1949; postgrad., Denver U., 1949, Stanford U., 1965. Asst. sales mgr. N.Y. Export divsn. Pillsbury Co., 1949-53; mgr. N.Y. office Pillsbury Co., 1953-62, v.p. export divsn. Mpls., 1962-68, v.p., gen. mgr. internat. ops., 1968-73, CEO, 1973-85, also bd. dirs., chmn. exec. com., 1987, pres., CEO, 1988, past chmn. bd. dirs. Bd. dirs. Coleman Co. Mem. regional export expansion coun. Dept. Commerce, 1966-74; bd. dirs. exec. Coun. Fgn. Diplomats, 1976-78; mem. bd. visitors Nelson A. Rockefeller Ctr., Dartmouth Coll., 1992-95; Minn. Orchestral Assn., United Negro Coll. Fund, 1973-75; chmn. Capitol City Renaissance Task Force, 1985; trustee Mpls. Found., 1985-92; mem. sr. campaign cabinet Carlson Com. U. Minn., 1985; mem. corps. rels. com. Nature Conservancy, 1985; mem. Nat. Cambodia Crisis Com., pres. pvt. sector Dept. Transp. task force, 1982, pres. pvt. sector survey on cost control, 1983; chmn. YWCA Tribute to Womwn in Internat. Industry. 2d lt. inf. U.S. Army, 1943-46. Recipient Golden Plate award, Am. Acad. Achievement, Disting. Bus. Leadership award, St. Cloud State U., Miss. Valley World Trade award, Outstanding Achievement award, Dartmouth Coll., Horatio Alger award, 1986, Medal of Merit, U.S. Savs. Bond Program; honored with William H. Spoor Dialogues on Leadership, Dartmouth Coll., honored Fair Player Minn. Women's Polit. Caucus, 1989. Mem.: Nat. Fgn. Trade Coun., Grocery Mfrs. Am. (treas. 1973—84), Minn. Bus. Partnership, Minn. Hist. Soc. (mem. exec. com. 1983, bd. dirs.), Mpls. Club (bd. govs. 1985, pres. 1986), Old Baldy Club, Woodhill Country Club, River Club NYC, The Country Club Salt Lake City, Alta Club, Phi Beta Kappa. Home: 1173 Oak Forest Rd Salt Lake City UT 84103 Office: 4900 IDS Ctr Minneapolis MN 55402 Home Phone: 801-521-2525; Office Phone: 612-330-4621.

SPORE, KEITH KENT, newspaper executive; b. Milw., May 29, 1942; s. G. Keith and Evelyn A. (Morgan) S.; divorced; children: Bradley, Julie, Justine; m. Kathy Stokebrand. BS in Journalism, U. Wis., Milw., 1967. City editor Milw. Sentinel, 1977-81; asst. mng. editor/news, 1981-89; mng. editor Milw. Jour. Sentinel, 1989-91, editor, 1991-95, editl. page editor, 1995, pres., 1995—, pub., 1996—2004. Author: (novels) The Hell Masters, 1977, Death of a Scavenger, 1980. With U.S. Army, 1961-64. Recipient Freedom of Info. award Soc. Profl. Journalists, 1995; named Mass Comms. Alumnus of Yr., U. Wis.-Milw., 1994. Mem. Greater Milw. Com. Office: Milw Jour Sentinel PO Box 661 Milwaukee WI 53201-0661 E-mail: kspore@onwis.com.

SPORER, SCOTT M., orthopedist, surgeon; b. Davenport, Iowa, June 3, 1971; m. Alissa Lynn Swearingen, June 29, 1996; children: Andrew Daniel children: Emma Kathryn, Claire Elizabeth. BS in Biomed. Engring., U. Iowa, Iowa City, 1993; MD, U. Iowa Coll. Medicine, 1997; MS in Clin. Outcomes Rsch., Dartmouth Coll., Hanover, NH, 2001. Diplomate Am. Acad. Orthopaedic Surgery, cert. Am. Bd. Orthopaedic Surgery, 2005, lic. Ill. Resident Dartmouth Hitchcock Med. Ctr., 1997—2002; resident in children's orthopaedic surgery Conn. Children's Med. Ctr., 1999—2000; fellow in orthopaedic adult reconstruction Rush Presbyn. St. Luke's Med. Ctr., Chgo., 2002—03; staff mem. Rush U. Med. Ctr., 2002—, asst. prof. orthopaedic surgery, Midwest Orthopaedics, 2003—; staff mem. Ctrl. Dupage Hosp., Winfield, Ill., 2002—, Oak Park Hosp., Ill., 2003—. Contbr. articles to profl. jours., chapters to books. Recipient James Kary award, outstanding orthopaedic rsch. Fellow: Assn. Arthritic Hip and Knee Surgery; mem.: Mid-America Orthopaedic Assn. Office: Midwest Orthopaedics at Rush ASP Ste 505 25 North Winfield Rd Winfield IL 60190 Office Phone: 630-682-5653. Office Fax: 630-682-8946.*

SPORN, AARON ADOLPH, physician, educator; b. NYC, Nov. 5, 1953; s. Herbert and Eunice (Aron) S.; m. Beverly Sporn; children: Hunter, Melanie. BS, SUNY, Stony Brook, 1974; MD, Columbia U., 1978. Diplomate Am. Bd. Orthopaedic Surgery. Intern. gen. surgery Roosevelt Hosp., NYC, 1978-79, resident gen. surgery, 1979-80; resident, chief resident in orthopaedic surgery NYU and Bellevue Hosp., NYC, 1980-83; fellow Midwest Inst. for Orthopaedics, Cin., 1983-84; v.p. medical affairs Inst. for Medicine in Sports, Trenton, NJ, 1984-85; clin. sr. instr. Hahnemann U. Med. Sch., Phila., 1986—; 1991clin. instr. Rutgers U. Med. Sch., New Brunswick, NJ, 1986—91; chief, dept. orthopaedic surgery Robert Wood Johnson U. Hosp., Hamilton, 1994—2004, vice chmn., dept. surgery, 1993—95, chmn. dept. surgery, 1995—98, chmn. surg. peer review com., chmn. operating room com. Vis. clin. fellow Columbia U., N.Y.C., 1978-80, teaching asst. NYU, N.Y.C., 1982-83; com. mem. Arthroscopy Bd. N.Am. Exam Com., 1989-90; cons. N.J. State Police, Trenton, 1987-92; fundraising com. orthopaedics wing Hamilton Hosp., Trenton, 1989. Contbr. articles to profl. jours. Ind. Rsch. Project grantee NIMH, 1975, 88. Fellow Am. Acad. Orthopaedic Surgery, Arthroscopy Bd. N.Am.; mem. Phi Beta Kappa. Office: Med Arts Bldg 8 Quakerbridge Plz Hamilton NJ 08619-1255

SPORTY, LAWRENCE DOUGLAS, psychiatrist; b. June 17, 1943; BA in Chemistry and Biology, Queens Coll., CUNY, 1964; MD, SUNY, Bklyn., 1968. Diplomate Am. Bd. Psychiatry and Neurology. Attending psychiatrist SUNY, Bklyn., 1972—74; adminstrv. and clin. dir. South Beach Psychol. Ctr., NY, 1972—74, chief of svc. NY, 1974—75; asst. clin. prof. SUNY-Downstate Med. Ctr., Bklyn., 1975—76; med. dir. Met. State Hosp., Norwalk, Calif., 1978—79; assoc. prof. clin. psychiatry U. So. Calif., LA, 1978—79, chief adult in-patient svcs., 1979; acting chmn. dept. psychiatry U. Calif.-Irvine Med. Ctr., Orange, 1979—82, vice chmn. clin. svcs., 1982—87, assoc. clin. prof., 1979, clin. prof., 1979—83, prof. clin. psychiatry, 1983—. Cons., lectr. in field. Contbr. articles to profl. jours. Fellow: Am. Psychiat. Assn. (disting. life); mem.: So. Calif. Psychiat. Soc. (exec. coun. 1982—84), Alpha Omega Alpha. Office: 2021 E 4th St Ste 118 Santa Ana CA 92705 Office Phone: 714-285-0870.

SPOSET, BARBARA ANN, secondary school educator; b. Cleve., Oct. 14, 1947; m. Raymond Wilbur Sposet, Aug. 19, 1972; 1 child, Michael Samuel. BA, Kent State U., 1968; MEd, Millersville State U., 1974; PhD, Kent State U., 1997. Cert. tchr., prin., asst. supt., Ohio. Tchr. and dept. chair Brooklyn (Ohio) City Schs., 1968—2000; asst. to assoc. prof. edn. Notre Dame Coll., 2000—05; assoc. prof., mid. childhood coord. Baldwin-Wallace Coll., 2005—. Instr. Kent State U., 1996-1999; instr. edn. Walsh U., Ohio, 1996-2007. Recipient Disting. Faculty award, Notre Dame Coll.; Rockefeller Found. fellow, 1987; Jennings scholar, 1997; Jennings Tchr. grantee, 1988. Mem. ASCD, Ohio Mid. Sch. Assn. Home: 18175 Trailside Pl Cleveland OH 44136-4247 Office Phone: 440-826-8173. E-mail: bspost@bw.edu.

SPOTTSWOOD, LYDIA CAROL, nurse, health facility administrator; b. NYC, May 6, 1951; d. Rudolph Messerschmidt and Eleanor Schlesinger; m. Paul Gregory Spottswood, Feb. 17, 1989; children: Mark Philip, Jayne Alexander, Erin Lenore. BS in Nursing, U. Va., Charlottesville, 1972. RN Va., Colo., D.C. Head nurse operating room U. Va. Hosp., Charlottesville, Va., 1974—77; nurse Children's Hosp., Washington, 1978—79, Wurzburg Army Med. Hosp., Germany, 1979—80; mem. city coun. City of Kenosha, Wis., 1990—98; dir. New Start Cmty. Health Ctr. (now Kenosha Cmty. Health Ctr.), Wis., 1994—95; mem. bd. U. Wis. Benevolent Found., 2000—. State and regional bd. mem. Area Health Edn. Ctr. Sys., Wis., 1996—2000; columnist Kenosha News, Wis., 2001—02. Past chair 1st Dist. Dem. Party Wis., congl. cand., 1996—98; mem. First Presbyn. Ch., Kenosha, Wis. Recipient Congl. Svc. Recognition award, Rep. Peter Barca, 1996, Svc. award, Kenosha County Med. Soc., 1996; grantee, HHS, 1994. Avocations: skiing, horseback riding, interior decorating, travel.

SPRADLEY, GAREY B., philosopher, educator, rancher, theologian; b. Corpus Christi, Tex., Jan. 27, 1945; s. H.B. and Berniece W. S.; m. Judy A., Dec. 20, 1975; children: Paul, Laurel, David. BBA, U. Tex., 1967, JD with high honors, 1971; MDiv with highest honors, Southwestern Sem., Ft. Worth, 1983; PhD, Syracuse U., 1990. Law clk. U.S. Ct. Appeals, Jackson, Miss., 1971-72; assoc. Butler & Binion, Houston, 1972-78; prof. Grove City (Pa.) Coll., 1991—; assoc. prof., chair phil. dept. U. Houston Law Ctr., 1978-83. Elder Grove City Alliance Ch., 1993-97, 99-2000; mgr. Grove City Little League, 1993-96. Mem.: Evangel. Polit. Scholars Soc., Assn. Polit. Theory, Evang. Philos. Soc., Soc. Christian Philosophers, Soc. Philosophy Religion. Avocations: reading, investing. Office: Grove City Coll Dept Philosophy 100 Campus Dr Grove City PA 16127-2101 Home Phone: 724-748-3363; Office Phone: 724-458-2196. Business E-Mail: gbspradley@gcc.edu.

SPRADLEY, PAMELA CLAIRE, art educator; b. Amarillo, Feb. 23, 1955; d. Leon Herman and Winifred Claire Skidgel; 1 child, Jordan Leon. BSE in art and Spanish, U. Ctrl. Ark., 1980; MA in Adult Edn., U. Ark., Little Rock, 2007; MEd, 2007. Cert. tchr. Art tchr. Smith Mid. Sch., Killeen, Tex., 1983—84; Spanish tchr. Killeen HS, 1984—85, Northwood Jr. HS, 1987—88; art, Spanish tchr. North Little Rock Pub. Sch., 1985—87, Rose Bud Pub. Schs., 1989—2005, art edn., Spanish instr. 7-12, 2005—. Avocations: drawing, painting, printmaking. Home: 3000 John Harden Dr #142 Jacksonville AR 72076 Office: Rose Bud Pub Schs 124 Sch Rd Rose Bud AR 72137 Office Phone: 501-556-5152. Personal E-mail: pspradley@aol.com.

SPRADLIN, PATRICIA C., literature and language professor; m. Rod Spradlin; 1 child, Andrew. MA in English and Humanities, Marshall U., Huntington, W.Va., 1987. Asst. prof. Shawnee U., Portsmouth, Ohio, 2002—. Dir. Ohio Writing Inst., Portsmouth, Ohio, 2004—. Grant, Ohio Bd. Regents, 2003—. Office: Shawnee State Univ Second St Portsmouth OH 45662

SPRADLIN, SHANE M., lawyer, automotive executive; Assoc. Latham & Watkins, NYC, 1995—99, Washington, 1995—99; corp. counsel Nextel Comm., Reston, Va., 1999—2003, Penske Automotive Group, 2003—07, corp. sec., 2004—, sr. v.p., gen. counsel, 2007—. Office: Penske Automotive Group 2555 Telegraph Rd Bloomfield Hills MI 48302-0954 Office Phone: 248-648-2560.*

SPRAGG, GREGG E., retail executive; Student, N.C. State U. Exec. v.p. mktg. and ops. Finast Foods Stores, Cleve.; exec. v.p. ops. Bi Lo Supermarkets, Greenville, SC; regional v.p. ops. Sam's Club divsn. Wal Mart Stores, Inc., 1998—2001, exec. v.p. ops. Sam's Club divsn., 2001—05, exec. v.p. merchandising, replenishment Sam's Club divsn., 2005—. Office: Wal-Mart Stores Inc 608 SW Eighth St Bentonville AR 72716-6297*

SPRAGGINS, JOHNNIE DAVID, sociology and cultural studies educator; b. Opelika, Ala., Oct. 13, 1954; s. John David and Alma Jean McCormick Spraggins; 1 child, Jada Ruth. BA, Auburn U., 1978, MA, 1988, U. Mich., 1993, PhD, 1995. Rsch. assoc. Auburn U., 1981-90; prof. Madonna U., U. Mich.-Ann Arbor, 1990—96; prof. sociology Asian divsn. U. Md., Tokyo, 1996—99; prof. Randolph-Macon Coll., Ashland, Va., 1999—2001; asst. prof. Our Lady of the Lake U., San Antonio, 2001—06; mem. faculty dept. sociology U. Tex., San Antonio, 2006—. Advisor Woman's Studies Coun., Randolph-Macon Coll., 1999—; vis. asst. prof. SUNY, Geneseo; vis. asst. prof. Asian divsn. U. Md., Sagamihara-shi, Japan; prof. Kitasato U., Sagamihara-shi, Kanagawa-ken, 1996-98. Contbr. articles to profl. jours. Mem. Ctr. for Rsch. on Social Orgn., Am. Sociological Assn., Soc. Applied Sociology. Democrat. Buddhist. Avocations: gardening, travel. E-mail: johnnie.spraggins@utsa.edu.

SPRAGUE, CATHY L., secondary school educator; b. Waukegan, Ill., Dec. 2, 1955; d. Birch Lyle and Carol Kay Smith; children: Cathryn Jae, Cristopher Birch Glen. M, Marietta Coll., Ohio, 1998. Tchr. Ft. Frye Local Schs., Beverly, Ohio, 1982—. Dir.: over 100 different plays and musicals. Pres. Ft. Frye Tchrs. Assn., 1990—93. Recipient Disting. HS Tchr. award, Miami U., 2001; named Ohio Sch. Bds. Assn. Tchr. of Yr., Southeast Region; nominee Ohio Sch. Bds. Assn. and DDE Tchr. of Yr., 2007—08. Mem.: Ednl. Theater Assn. (hon.). Home: PO Box 374 Beverly OH 45715 Office: Fort Frye High School PO Box 1089 Beverly OH 45715 Personal E-mail: ff_csprague@seovec.org.

SPRAGUE, CHARLES W., lawyer, finance company executive; b. Orange, NJ, Nov. 14, 1949; BA cum laude, Yale U., 1971; MBA, JD, NYU, 1975. Bar: NY 1976, DC 1993, Wis. Atty. Sullivan & Cromwell, 1975—83, Reboul MacMurray, 1983—92, Sprague & Coultas, 1992—94; exec. v.p., gen. counsel, sec. Fiserv, Inc., Brookfield, Wis., 1994—, chief admin. officer, 1999—. Mem.: ABA, Wis. State Bar Assn., DC Bar Assn., Internat. Bar Assn. Office: Fiserv Inc PO Box 979 255 Fiserv Dr Brookfield WI 53045 Office Phone: 262-879-5000.

SPRAGUE, CHARLES WARREN, geologist; b. Berlin, Nov. 29, 1955; s. Kenneth Manchester and Ingrid Emma Marie Sprague; m. Penni Marie O'Brien, May 2, 1998; 1 child, Charles Wilfred. BS, U. of Fla., 1978—80, MS, 1980—83. Professional Geoscientist Tex., 2003, Professional Geologist Tenn., 1990. Geologist Chevron USA, Inc., New Orleans, 1983—85; geologist/lead geologist Groundwater Tech., Inc., Mandeville, La., 1989—92; project geologist/hydrogeologist Fugro-McClelland (SW), Inc., Dallas, 1992—93; project/sr. hydrogeologist Law Engring. and Environ. Services, Inc., Dallas, 1993—96; sr. hydrogeologist LCA Environ., Inc., Dallas, 1996—98; v.p.ops. Dougherty Sprague Environ., Inc., Richardson, Tex., 1998—. Bd. mem. Ellison Miles Geotechnology Inst. Earth Sci. Tchr. Enhancement Adv. Bd., Farmers Branch, Tex., 1999—2000; student/boy scout trainer and/or advisor Ellison Miles Geotechnology Inst. Cmty. Outreach Program, Farmers Branch, Tex., 2001—09, environ. geology focus group, 2006—09. Commr. Planning and Zoning Commn., Sachse, Tex., 2000—06; judge Dallas Morning News Regional Sci. Fair, 1995—2009; leadership sachse class no. 1 Econ. Devel. Corp./Sachse C. of C., 2005; leadership sachse application com. Sachse C. of C., 2006—07. Mem.: Sons Union Vet. Civil War (E.E. Ellsworth camp mem.), Gen. Soc. Mayflower Descendants, Soc. Am. Mil. Engineers, Assn. Engring. Geologists, Nat. Ground Water Assn., Geol. Soc. Am., Tex. Assn. Profl. Geoscientists (bd. dirs. 2001—04, pres. 2002—03), Tex Soc. the Nat. Soc. the Sons the Am. Revolution (1st v.p. Plano, Tex. chpt.), Norton Hist. Soc., Leadership Sachse Class 1. Avocations: gourmet cooking, genealogy. Office: 3902 Indistrial St Rowlett TX 75088 Office Fax: 972-412-8633. E-mail: cwsprague@dsei.com.

SPRAGUE, EDWARD AUCHINCLOSS, retired professional society administrator, economist; b. NYC, Oct. 9, 1932; s. Irvin Auchincloss and Maude Browning (Fisher) Sprague; m. Patricia Ivy Cannon, Apr. 27, 1957; children: James Edward, Elizabeth Mary, Jennifer Ann. BA, Princeton U., 1954; MA, NYU, 1961. Rsch. analyst NJ State C. of C., Newark, 1957-59; assoc. economist F.W. Dodge Corp., NYC, 1959-62; economist Lehman Bros., NYC, 1962-67; v.p. Nat. Assn. Mfrs., NYC, Washington, 1967-77; dir. tax policy Tax Found., Washington, 1977-82, sr. v.p., 1985-89; exec. dir. Tax Exec. Inst., 1982-85; v.p., exec. dir. Tax Coun., 1979-82, 86-91, cons., 1991-92, Employers Coun. Flexible Compensation, Washington, 1992-93; ret., 1993. Editor: Building Business, 1961—62, Tax. Exec., 1983—85. With US Army, 1955—57. Republican. Home: 16 Matthew Dr Brunswick ME 04011

SPRAGUE, ESTHER SPARKS, art history educator; b. Washington, Sept. 18, 1932; d. Aaron Milliman and Heien Yvonne Singer; m. Philip Allcock Sprague, 1999; m. Morton Jay Sparks, 1952; children: Victoria Regina, Amy Hannah. BA, U. Chgo., Ill., 1951; MA, Northwestern U., Evanston Ill., 1968, PhD, 1971. Curatorial asst. Art Inst. Chgo., 1970—85, guest curator, 1985—86; gallery dir. W.Graham Arader III Gallery, Chgo., 1986—94; adj. asst. prof. Valparaiso U., Ind., 1994—2007, U. Miss., Oxford, 1995—2009; adj. faculty Northwestern U., Chgo., 2005—09. Dir. Print Council America, 1975—78; mem. Bd. Trustees, Lakeview Museum, Ill., 1962—66, Senate Monmouth Coll., Ill., 1974—78, Art Adv. Beloit Coll., Wis., 1979—83. Mem. Ill. Arts Council, 1965—70; reviewer Nat. Endowment, Washington, 1981—2000; adv. com. mem. Ctr. Study Southern Culture, U. Miss., 1996—99. Travel grant, Nat. Endowment Arts, 1979, Rsch. grant, Henry Luce Fund, NY, 1982. Mem.: Assn. Historians Am. Art, Arts Club Chgo. Avocations: reading, sewing, travel.

SPRAGUE, JOHN LOUIS, management consultant; b. Boston, 1930; s. Robert Chapman and Florence Antoinette (van Zelm) S.; m. Mary-Jane Whitney, June 19, 1952; children: John Louis, William Whitney, Catherine van Zelm, David Hyatt. AB, Princeton, 1952; PhD, Stanford, 1959. With Sprague Electric Co., North Adams, Mass., 1959-87, co-dir. engring. labs., sr. v.p. engring., 1964-65, v.p. research and devel., 1965-66, sr. v.p. semi-condr. div., 1967-76, pres., 1976-87, chief exec. officer, 1981-87; pres. John L. Sprague Assocs. Inc., 1988—2003; self-employed, 2003—. Bd. dirs. MRA Labs., Inc., Calif. Micro Devices. Chmn. Williamstown United Fund-ARC Campaign, 1961; trustee

Pine Cobble Sch., 1978, Middlesex Sch., 1994-96. Lt. (j.g.) USNR, 1952-55. Mem. IEEE, Electrochem. Soc., Am. Chem. Soc., Sci. Research Soc. Am., Confrerie des Chevaliers du Tastevin, Confrerie de la Chaine des Rotisseurs, Princeton Club (N.Y.C.), Sigma Xi, Phi Lambda Upsilon. Home: 175 Bee Hill Rd Williamstown MA 01267-2703 Office Phone: 413-743-9454. E-mail: beehilljon@aol.com.

SPRAGUE, RAYMOND, music educator; b. Yonkers, NY, Nov. 28, 1947; s. Raymond Arthur and Rosemary (Lockwood) S.; m. Kathleen Jane Turner, May 30, 1981. BA in Music, Williams Coll., Williamstown, Mass., 1969; MMus, U.N.Mex., 1973; DMA, U. Colo., 1979. Tchr. cert. music/choral-gen. k-12 Ind., 1985. Instr. Albuquerque Acad., 1969-71; grad. asst. U. N.Mex., Aubuquerque, 1972-73; instr., grad. asst. U. Colo., Boulder, 1973-77; dir. music King of Glory Luth. Ch., Arvada, Colo., 1974-77; asst. prof., dir. choral activities St. Mary's Coll., South Bend, Ind., 1977-84; assoc. prof., dir. choral activities U. New Orleans, 1985-95, prof., 1995—99; dir. music St. Charles Ave. Bapt. Ch., New Orleans, 1986-91; artistic dir., conductor La. Vocal Arts Chorale, New Orleans, 1992—99; prof. and dir. choral activities Davidson (NC) Coll., 1999—, chmn. music dept., 2000—06. Clinician, adjudicator, guest conductor high sch. and colls. Musical debut Carnegie Hall, 1999, Return Engagement, 2006; Mus. and book reviewer The Choral Jour., 1977—; editor Treble Choir Music, 1985—; articles to profl. jours. Mem. Am. Choral Dirs. Assn. (state pres. La. chpt. 1989, state pres. Ind. choral dirs. 1983), Chorus Am., Coll. Music Soc, Nat. Collegiate Cho Orgn. Episcopalian. Avocations: hiking, camping, fishing, golf, sports. Office: Davidson Coll Dept Music PO Box 7131 Davidson NC 28035 Office Phone: 704-894-2591. Business E-Mail: rasprague@davidson.edu.

SPRAGUE, VICKI L., educational consultant; d. Harry and Evelyn Jones; m. Robert Sprague, 1971; children: Shona Christy, Lia Meehan. BS in Elem. Edn., Kent State U., Ohio, 1973, M in Edn., Curriculum and Instrn., 1978. Cert. tchr. Ohio. Tchr. Elyria City Schs., 1973—2003; ednl. cons. Northcoast Ednl. Cons., Ltd., Bay Village, Ohio, 2004—; sch. improvement instrnl. coach Ohio Dept. Edn., Columbus, 2004—. Chair Ohio Resource Ctr. for Math., Sci., and Reading, Columbus, 2000—03; writing team Ohio Educators Stds. Bd., Columbus, Ohio Content Stds. for Math. and Sci., Columbus, Ohio Math. Acad. Program; mem. Ohio Com. Practitioners, Columbus, 2002—05; bd. examiners Nat. Coun. for the Accreditation Tchrs. Edn., Ohio; adj. prof. Baldwin-Wallace Coll., Berea, Ohio, Lorain County CC, Elyria; math specialist Mentor Exempted Village Schs., Ohio; assessment adminstr. Nat. Assessment Ednl. Progress. Eisenhower grant, Miami U., Ohio, 1997, Kent State U., 1999. Mem.: NEA (life; del. to representive assembly 1976—2006), Nat. Coun. Tchrs. Math., NE Ohio Edn. Assn. (del. to rep. assembly 1976—2006), Ohio Edn. Assn. (life; del. to representive assembly 1976—2006, exec. com. 2000—06). Avocations: reading, hiking, kayaking. Office: Northcoast Ednl Cons Ltd 27131 Lake Rd Bay Village OH 44140

SPRAGUE, WILLIAM WALLACE, JR., retired food company executive; b. Savannah, Ga., Nov. 11, 1926; s. William Wallace and Mary (Crowther) S.; m. Elizabeth Louise Carr, Oct. 3, 1953; children: Courtney, Lauren Duane, William Wallace III, Elizabeth Louise BSME, Yale U., 1950. With Savannah Foods & Industries, Inc., 1952-94, ret., 1994, sec., 1961-62, v.p., 1962-72, pres., chief exec. officer, 1972-92, chmn. bd. dirs., CEO, 1993-94, also bd. dirs., 1999, chmn. emeritus, 1998—. Bd. dirs., pres. Adeline Sugar Factory Co., Ltd., Savannah, Coastal Mgmt. Corp., Savannah. Trustee Savannah Bus. Group; chmn. emeritus Youth Futures Authority, Savannah. With USN, 1945-46. Named Sugar Man of Yr. and recipient Dyer Meml. award B.W. Dyer & Co., 1985; named Industrialist of Yr. Internat. Mgmt. Coun., 1988. Mem. World Sugar Rsch. Orgn. (chmn. 1982-85), The Sugar Assn. (bd. dirs.),Carolina Plantation Soc., St. Andrews Soc., Oglethorpe Club, Century Club (Savannah). Office: Sprague Enterprises PO Box 1313 Savannah GA 31402-1313

SPRAKER, JOHN STEPHEN, mathematician, educator; b. Charlottesville, Va., Apr. 6, 1960; s. Harold Stephen and Betty Jean (Conley) S. BS, Middle Tenn. State U., 1982; MA, Ind. U., 1984, PhD, 1987. Asst. prof. Western Ky. U., Bowling Green, 1987—. Contbr. articles to Transactions of Am. Math. Soc., Proceedings of Am. Math. Soc. Mem. Nat. Coun Tchrs. of Math., Am. Math. Soc., Math. Assn. Am., Sigma Xi Sci. Rsch. Soc., Nat. Rifle Assn., Optimist Club., So. Ky. Choral Soc. Lutheran. Avocations: target shooting, singing, church activities. Home: 33 Chaney Way Bowling Green KY 42104-0350 Office: Western Ky # U Bowling Green KY 42101

SPRANG, MILTON LEROY, obstetrician, gynecologist, educator; b. Chgo., Jan. 15, 1944; s. Eugene and Carmella (Bruno) S.; m. Sandra Lee Karabelas, July 16, 1966; children: David, Christina, Michael. Student, St. Mary's Coll., 1962-65; MD, Loyola U., 1969. Diplomate Am. Bd. Ob-gyn; Nat. Bd. Med. Examiners; CME accreditation. Intern St. Francis Hosp., Evanston, Ill., 1969-70, resident, 1972-75, sr. attending physician, 1985—; assoc. attending phsycian Evanston Hosp., 1975-79, attending physician, 1980-84, sr. attending physician, 1985—, v.p. med. staff, 1990-91, pres.-elect, 1991-92, pres., 1992-93; also bd. dirs., 1991-94; sec. exec. com. Evanston Hosp., 1993-94; chmn. ob-gyn Cook County Grad. Sch. Medicine, Chgo., 1983-91. Instr. Northwestern U. Med. Sch., Chgo., 1975-78, asst. prof., 1984-95, assoc. prof., 1995-04, prof., 2004—; pres. Northwestern Healthcare Network Physician Leadership, 1994; lectr. acad. and civic groups Ob-Gyn. Nat. Ctr. Advanced Med. Edn., 1991—; bd. dirs. Ill. Found. Med. Rev.; bd. trustees Ill. State Ins. Svcs., 1992—, chair, 1998-00, chair rates and res., 2002—; bd. govs. Ill. State Med. Inter-Inst. Exch., 1987-92; adv. bd. practicing physicians Sec. Health and Human Svc. and Ctr. for Medicare Svcs., 2005—, Ctrs. Medicare and Medicaid. Editor: Profl. Staff News, 1992-93; chmn. editorial bd. Jour. Chgo. Medicine, 1986-91; contbr. articles to profl. jours. Bd. dirs. Am. Cancer Soc., chmn. profl. edn. com. North Shore unit, 1982-85; bd. dirs. Chgo. Community Info. Network, 1994-95; mem. Nat. Rep. Congrl. Com., 1981—, Ill. Med. Polit. Action Com.; bd. advisors Nat. Youth Leadership Forum on Medicine, Chgo., 1998—; trustee Midwest Ctr. Women's Healthcare, 2002—, pres. and chmn. bd. trustees, 2002—; adv. patients and med. profession. With USN, 1970-72. Fellow: ACOG (chmn. Ill. sect. 1975—76), ACS, Inst. Medicine Chgo.; mem.: AMA (com. to select pub. mem. 2003—, Physician Recognition award 1977, 1980, 1983), Gt. Lakes States Coalition of Dels. to AMA (chmn. 2003—), Orgn. State Med. Assn. Presidents (steering com. 2003—06, sec. 2006—, v.p. 2007, pres. 2008—09), Chgo. Found. Med. Care (med. care evaluation and edn. com. 1980—83, nominating com. 1980—84, practice guidelines com. 1984), Ednl. and Scientific Found. (bd. dirs. 1994—98), Chgo. Med. Soc. (adv. com. advt. stds. 1978—84, physician's rev. com. 1980—85, trustee ins. bd. 1982—, nominating com. 1985—, treas. 1986—89, chmn. fin. com. 1986—89, trustee 1986—92, sec. 1989—90, pres.-elect 1990—91, chmn. bd. trustees 1990—91, pres. 1991—92, chmn. ethical rels. com. 1994—), Ill. Med. Soc. (del. to AMA 1987—, govt. affairs com. 1988—, chmn. reference com. 1989, chmn. fin. com. 1992—94, sec.-treas. 1994—96, chmn. bd. trustees 1996—98, chmn. bylaws com. 1998—99, pres. 2000—01, vice speaker HOD 2007—09), Physician Benefit Trust (chmn. fin. com. 1993—2004, chmn. and pres. 2004—). Roman Catholic. Avocations: reading, swimming. Home: 4442 Concord Ln Skokie IL 60076-2606 Office: AGSO 1000 Central St Evanston IL 60201-1777 Home Phone: 847-677-5890; Office Phone: 847-869-3300. E-mail: sprangml@aol.com.

SPRATLAN, LEWIS, composer, educator; b. Miami, Sept. 5, 1940; m. Melinda Spratlan. BA, Yale U., 1962, MusM, 1965. Faculty mem. Pa. State U., 1967—70, Amherst Coll., Mass., 1970—, prof. music. Mass., 1980—, chmn. music dept. Mass., 1977—94. Composer: Missa Brevis, 1965, Cantate Domine, 1968, Serenade for 6 instruments, 1970, Moonsong, 1970, Two Pieces for orch., 1971, Woodwind quintet, 1971, Fantasy, 1973, Ben Jonson Songs, 1974, Coils for ensemble, 1980, String Quartet, 1982, When Crows Gather, 1986, Hung Monophonies, 1990, Night Music, 1991, In Memorian, 1993, A Barred Owl, 1994, Concertino, 1994, Psalm 42, 1996, Apollo and Daphne Variations, Vocalise with Duck, 1998, Sojourner, 2000, Life is a Dream, 2000 (Pulitzer prize for music, 2000), Mayflies, 2000, Of Time and the Seasons, 2001, Peeves, 2001, (chamber opera) Earthrise, 2002, Zoom, 2003, The Manatees at Blue Springs, 2003, Streaming, 2004, Mega-Ditty, 2004, Piccolosophy, 2005, Wonderer, 2005, Shadow, 2006, Concerto for Saxophone and Orchestra, 2006, Wink (Chamber Opera), 2007, Elephant Rocks, 2008. Guggenheim fellowship, NEA fellowship, Mass. Artists Found. fellowship, MacDowell fellowship. Office: Music Dept Amherst Coll PO Box 5000 Amherst MA 01002-5000 Office Phone: 413-542-5811. Business E-Mail: mlspratlan@amherst.edu.

SPRATT, JOHN MCKEE, JR., United States Representative from South Carolina, lawyer; b. Charlotte, NC, Nov. 1, 1942; s. John McKee and Jane Love (Bratton) Spratt; m. Jane Stacy, May 31, 1968; children: Susan Elizabeth, Sarah Stacy, Catherine Bratton. AB, Davidson Coll., NC, 1964; MA, Corpus Christi Coll., Oxford U., 1966; LL.B., Yale U., 1969. Ops. analyst Office Asst. Sec. US Dept. Def., 1969-71; ptnr. Spratt, McKeown & Spratt, York, SC, 1971-82; pres. Spratt Ins. Agy., Ft. Mill, SC, 1973-82, Bank of Ft. Mill, SC, 1973-82; mem. US Congress from 5th SC Dist., 1983—; ranking mem. US House Budget Com., 1997—2006, chmn., 2007—; mem. US House Armed Services Com.; vice chair US House Democratic Policy Com., 1994—96. Chmn. bd. visitors Winthrop Coll., Rock Hill, SC, 1976; bd. visitors Davidson Coll., 1978—80; bd. dirs. Piedmont Legal Svcs., Inc., 1978—82; chmn. bd. trustees Divine Saviour Hosp., York, 1980—82. Positions up to capt. JAGC US Army, 1969—71. Decorated Meritorious Svc. medal US Army. Mem.: ABA, SC Bar Assn. Democrat. Presbyterian. Office: US Congress 1401 Longworth Ho Office Bldg Washington DC 20515-4005 Office Phone: 202-225-5501.*

SPRATT, RANDALL N., healthcare services and information technology executive; BS in Biology, U. Utah. Various exec. positions to COO Advanced Lab. Systems; joined McKesson Corp., 1986, sr. v.p. imaging, tech. and bus. process improvement, 2000—03, chief process officer MPT (McKesson Provider Technologies) Alpharetta, Ga., 2003—05, exec. v.p. chief info. officer San Francisco, 2005—, chief tech. officer, 2009—. Office: McKesson Corpn 1 Post St San Francisco CA 94104 Office Phone: 415-983-8300. Business E-Mail: randall.spratt@mckesson.com.*

SPRAWLS, PERRY, biomedical engineer, educator; b. Williston, SC, Mar. 2, 1934; s. Perry and Neva Sprawls; m. Charlotte Edith Williams, Dec. 16, 1961; 1 child, Charles Perry. BS, Clemson U., SC, 1956, MS, 1961, PhD, 1968. Cert. profl. engr., Ga., 1974, Am. Bd. Clin. Engring., 1978; in diagnostic physics Am. Bd. Radiology, 1974, Am. Bd. Med. Physics, 1991, in magnetic resonance physics 2000. Faculty Emory U., Atlanta, 1960—2005, prof. emeritus, 2005—; dir. Sprawls Ednl. Found., Montreat, NC, 1990—. Co-dir., coll. med. physics Internat. Ctr. Theoretical Physics, Trieste, Italy, 1988—. Author: (textbook) Physical Principles of Medical Imaging, Magnetic Resonance Imaging, Principles, Methods, and Techniques, The Physical Principles of Medical Imaging - Chinese Language Edition, Principles of Radiography for Technologists, The Physics and Instrumentation of Nuclear Medicine, The Physical Principles of Diagnostic Radiology. Pres. Asheville Lyric Opera, NC, 2005—06. 1st lt. Signal Corp US Army, 1957—58. Recipient Harold Johns medal, Internat. Orgn. Med. Physics, 2003. Fellow: Am. Coll. Radiology, Am. Assn. Physicists Medicine (Achievement award 1989); mem.: IEEE (vice chair, wnc sect. 2008, Meritorious Achievement award 2006), Radiol. Soc. North Am. Democrat. Baptist. Avocations: scuba diving, photography, hiking. Office: Sprawls Ednl Found 130 Kanawha Dr Montreat NC 28757 Business E-Mail: sprawls@emory.edu.

SPRAY, PAUL ELLSWORTH, retired surgeon; b. Wilkinsburg, Pa., Apr. 9, 1921; s. Lester E. and Phoebe Gertrude (Hull) S.; m. Mary Louise Conover, Nov. 28, 1943; children: David C., Thomas L., Mary Lynn (Mrs. Thomas Branham). BS, U. Pitts., 1942; MD, George Washington U., Washington, DC, 1944; MS, U. Minn., 1950. Diplomate Am. Bd. Orthop. Surgery. Intern U.S. Marine Hosp., SI, 1944-45; resident Mayo Found., Rochester, Minn., 1945-46, 48-50; practice medicine specializing in orthop. surgery Oak Ridge, Tenn., 1950-98; ret., 1998; vol. physician Knoxville Interfaith Clinic, 1998—2008. Mem. active staff Oak Ridge Hosp., 1950-98, hon. staff, 98-; courtesy staff Harriman Hosp., Tenn., ret., 1998; vol. vis. cons. CARE Medico, Jordan, 1959, Nigeria, 1962, 65, Algeria, 1963, Afghanistan, 1970, Bangladesh, 1975, 77, 79, Peru, 1980, U. Ghana, 1982; AMA vol. physician, Vietnam, 1967, 72; vis. assoc. prof. U. Nairobi, 1973; mem. tchg. team Internat. Coll. Surgeons to Peru, 1979, 84; vis. prof. orthop. surgery U. Khartoum, 1976; hon. prof. San Luis Gonzaga U., Ica, Peru, 1979; AmDoc vol. cons. U. Biafra Tchg. Hosp., 1969; vis. prof. Mayo Clinic, 1988; sec. orthops. overseas divsn. CARE Medico, 1971-76, sec. Medico adv. bd., 1974-76, vice chmn., 1976, chmn., 1977-79, v.p. CARE, Inc., 1977-79, pub. mem. CARE bd. dirs., 1980-90, mem. bd. overseers, 1991-99; chmn. Orthops. Overseas, Inc., 1982-86, treas., 1986-88, emeritus mem., 1994; mem. U.S. organizing com. 1st Internat. Acad. Symposium on Orthops., Tianjin, China, 1983; mem. CUPP Internat. Adv. Coun., 1986-99; invited guest spkr. Japan Orthop. Assn., 1994; mem. curriculum com. Oak Ridge Inst. Continual Learning, 1999-2007; bd. dirs. MMC Oak Ridge Found., chmn., 2003-04, emeritus, 2007. Mem. editl. bd. Contemporary Orthopedics, 1984-96. Pres. Anderson County Health Coun., 1976—77, v.p., 1975, hon. bd. dirs.; pres. health commn. Coun. So. Mountains, 1958—65, sec., bd. dirs., 1965—66; Tenn. pres. UN Assn., 1966—67; vice-chmn. bd. Camelot Care Ctr., Tenn., 1979—82, chmn. Tenn., 1982—86; hon. mem. World Orthopedic Concern, 1990; with del. to Vietnam People to People, citizen amb. to Vietnam, 1993; del. to Oak Ridge's Sister City, Obninsk, Russia Obninsk, Russia, 1993; trustee Vietnam Am. Scholarship Fund, 1992—95; Rotary vol. orthopaedic surgeon Kikuyu Hosp. Rehab. Ctr. of East Africa Presbyn. Ch., 1998; vol. Habitat for Humanity, 2004; bd. dirs. Meth. Hosp. Oak Ridge Found., 2000—, chmn., 2003—04, emeritus, 2007; bd. dirs. Hope of East Tenn., 2002—06, Clinch River Home Health Assn., 2005—08. Capt. USMC, 1946—48. Recipient Svc. to Mankind award, Serotoma, 1967, Humanitarian award, Lions Club, 1968, Freedom Citation, Sertoma, 1978, award, Amb. Goodwill Lions Club, 1979, Medico Disting. Svc. award, 1990, 1st Ann. Vocat. Svc. award, Oak Ridge Rotary, 1979, Tech. Comm. award, East Tenn. chpt. Soc. for Tech. Comm., 1983, Individual Achievement award, Meth. Med. Ctr. of Oak Ridge, 1991, Humanitarian award, Orthopaedics Overseas, 1992, Biographic Exhibit recognition, Mus. Appalachia Hall of Fame, Norris, Tenn.; named to Anderson County Hall of Fame for Philanthropy, 2007; fellow Melvin Jones fellow, Lions Club, 1993. Fellow Internat. Coll. Surgeons (Tenn. regent 1976-80, bd. councilors 1980-84, hon. chmn. bd. trustees 1981-83, trustee 1983-84, v.p. US sect. 1982-83, mem. surg. teams com. 1983-90, Humanitarian award 1992); mem. AMA (Humanitarian Svc. award 1967, 72), Sociètè International Chirugie Orthopèdique et de Traumuatologie, So. Orthop. Assn., Western Pacific Orthop. Assn., Am. Fracture Assn., Am. Acad. Orthop. Surgeons (mem. com. on injuries 1980-86), Tenn. Med. Assn. (com. on emergency med. svcs. 1978-97), Peru Acad. Surgery (corr.), Peruvian Soc. Orthop. Surgery and Traumatology (corr.), Clin. Orthop. Soc., Mid-Am. Orthop. Soc., Rotary Club (Oak Ridge chpt., chmn. cmty. and world svc. com. 2000-04, Paul Harris fellow). Home: 507 Delaware Ave Oak Ridge TN 37830-3902 Home Phone: 865-483-9936. Home Fax: 865-483-8657. Personal E-mail: spray507@aol.com.

SPRAYREGEN, JAMES H.M., lawyer, former diversified financial services company executive; b. Dec. 2, 1959; BA cum laude, U. Mich., 1982; JD cum laude, U. Ill., 1985. Bar: Ill. 1985, NY 1985, US Dist. Ct. (no. dist. Ill.) 1985, US Dist. Ct. (ea. dist. Wis.) 1988, US Dist. Ct. (so. & ea. dists. NY) 1992, US Dist. Ct. (we. dist Mich.) 1992, US Dist Ct. (dist. Ariz.) 1992, US Dist. Ct. (dist. Del.) 1992. Atty. Lord, Bissell & Brook, 1985—89, Rudnick & Wolfe, 1989—90; ptnr., mem. firm mgmt. com. Kirkland & Ellis LLP, Chgo., 1990—2006, 2008—; mng. dir. investment banking divsn. The Goldman Sachs Group, Inc., NYC, 2006—08. Co-chmn. Internat. Com. Am. Bankruptcy Inst., bd. dir.; Chicago region bd. dir. Anti-Defamation League; vice chmn. Chicago region Am. Com. Weizman Inst. Sci. Named Top Debtor Lawyer by active assignments, Deal's Bankruptcy Insider newsletter, 2004; named one of 12 Dealmakers of Yr., Am. Lawyer, 2004, 45 Under Forty: Rising Stars Pvt. Bar, 2003. Mem.: Seventh Circuit Bar Assn. (Ill. chmn. Comml. Bankruptcy Law & Procedure), Chicago Bar Assn., Ill. Bar Assn., Comml. Law League Am., ABA. Office: Kirkland & Ellis LLP 200 E Randolph Dr Chicago IL 60601 E-mail: jsprayregen@kirland.com.*

SPREAT, SUSAN ROGERS, veterinarian; b. Wilkes-Barne, Pa., July 10, 1952; d. Lewis L. and Betty Whitenight Rogers; m. Scott Spreat; 1 child, Gracie Anne Whitenight. BS, Dickinson Coll., Carlisle, Pa., 1974; MS, Drexel U., Phila., 1979; VMD, U. Pa., Phila., 1983. Lic. vet. NJ. Microbiologist Schering Plough Inc., Cream Ridge; owner, vet. Veterinary Clinic Imlaystown, Allentown, 2005—. Contbr. articles to profl. jours.; prodr.: (TV series) Pet Peeves, Homeless Tails. Mem. Upper Freehold Twp. Environ. Com., 1980. Mem.: NJ Vet. Med. Assn. (editor of newsletter), Am. Vet. Med. Assn., Phi Zeta. Office: Imlaystown Veterinary Clinic 3 Imlaystown-Hishtstown Rd Allentown NJ 08501

SPRECHER, JEFFREY C., commodities exchange executive; b. 1955; BSChemE, U. Wis., Madison; MBA, Pepperdine U., Malibu, Calif. Pres. Western Power Grp., Inc.; owner Continental Power Exch., 1997—2000; founder, CEO Intercontinental Exch. (ICE), Atlanta, 2000—, chmn. bd., 2002—. Bd. dirs. NY Bd. Trade, 2007—. Named a Top Entrepreneur, Bus. Week mag., 2002; named one of five finalists, CEO of the Year, Marketwatch, 2006. Mem.: U.S. Commodity Futures Trading Commn. Global Market Adv. Com., Energy Security Leadership Coun. Office: Intercontinental Exch 2100 RiverEdge Pky Ste 500 Atlanta GA 30328*

SPRECHER, BARON WILLIAM GUNTHER, pianist, composer, conductor, diplomat; b. Saarbrucken, Germany, Jan. 20, 1924; arrived in U.S., 1952; s. Wolf and Karoline (Jung) Sprecher; m. Blossom Tag, Aug. 6, 1952. Studied piano with Prof. Wittels, Tel Aviv; studied piano with Madame Vengerova, NYC; studied composition with Paul Ben-Haim, Tel Aviv, studied conducting with Georg Singer; degree (hon.), Inst. Vocal Arts, 1957; D in Philosophy Music (hon.), World U. Roundtable, 1988; Mus D (hon.), London Inst. Applied Rsch., 1991, DFA, HHD, London Inst. Applied Rsch., 1993; Mus D (hon.), Australian Inst. Coord. Rsch., 1991; diploma, Gran Premio Am., 1990, Paladino del Tricolore, 1990; D Musicology, Somerset U.; D Music (hon.), Atlantic Southeastern U.; Diploma, Acad. Argentina de Diplomacia; Assoc. (hon.), Inst. Affairs Internat., Paris, 1993; DD (hon.), The Christian Congregation; rerum politicarum LittD (hon.), U. Aeterna Lucina Vitama, 1991; LittD (hon.), Eng., 1994; PhD (hon.), Germany, 1994. Korrepetitor Israel Folk Opera, Tel-Aviv, 1940-43; piano soloist Israel Philharm. Orch., Tel-Aviv, 1946-48; music dir. Temple Anshe Chesed, NYC, 1966—69, Temple Sholom, Greenwich, Conn., 1976—82; pres., music dir. Bronx Philharm., NYC, 1971-83; music dir. Sta. WEVD, NYC, 1969-85; asst. pianist accompanying Lotte Lenya, Richard Tucker, Jan Peerce, Itzhak Perlman, Jan Kiepura, Ilona Massey; prof. Inst. Hautes Etudes Economiques et Sociales; senator Lord Sprecher House Internat. Intellectuals, Acad. MIDI, Paris. Rsch. prof. Alliance Universelle Paix Connaissance, Paris, 1991; prof. Haute Ecole de Recherche, Inst. des Hautes Etudes Economiques et Sociales; mem. coun. Inst. de Documentation et D'Etudes Europeennes; dep. mem., diplomat Internat. State Parliament; dep. mem. assembly Internat. Parliament for Safety and Peace. Composer: (song book) Yinglish, piano soloist 1st performance of Gershwin's Concerto in F in Israel; composer Piano Sonata, 1945, Jerusalem Concerto for Piano and Orch., 1967, (TV) Great is Thy Faith, 1970; pianist-condr. 24 record albums; mem. The First Piano Quartet (Acad. award nomination, Peabody award). Consul Sovereign State Aeterna Lucina for State and City of NY; comdr. fgn. rels. Island Du Caricom, 1995; diplomat World Jewish Congress; senator Coun. of States for Protection of Life and Human Rights, Palermo, Italy; del. at large Rep. Presdl. Task Force, nat. rep. senatorial com.; active Nat. Com. to Preserve Social Security and Medicare, Ctr. for Am. Values, Sr. Coalition, Common Cause; founding sponsor Disabled Vets. Life Meml. Gold Medal Merit Soc., Washington, 2004; Reagan Presdl. Libr. supporter USS Ronald Reagan, Air Force One. Decorated noble knight Noble House of Amena, knight order Knight Templars of Jerusalem, knight comdr. Lofsensis Ursinius Order, baron Order of Bohemian Crown, comdr. Order of Golden Lance (Australia), Capt. Légion de L'Aigle Mer, Baron of Montsalvat, knight Holy Grail, count San Ciriaco, comdr. fgn. rels. Island du Caricom, 1995, Sen Maison Internat. Des Intellectuels, Sen European Parliament, Internat. Parliament for Safety and Peace, diplomat World Jewish Congress, Laird-Lord of Camster, Caithness, Scotland, 1995; recipient Diplomatic medal Internat. Parliament for Safety and Peace, 1995, Gold Cross of Honour, Albert Schweitzer Soc. Austria, Albert Einstein medal, Circulo Nobiliario Caballeros U., 1992, Swan Knight (Chevalier du Cygne), Order of the Swan, Congl. Order of Merit, 2006; named Knight of Yr., Internat. Writers and Artists Assn., 1995; recipient Medal of Merit, Rep. Presdl. Task Force, 1998, Noble Conquistador, Internat. Chivalric Order of the Knights of Justice, Music and Humanity award, 2003, Hall of Fame Music and Humanity award ABI, 2003, Disting. Leader Gold medal, 2003, Rep. Senatorial Gold medal of Freedom, 2004; Ronald Reagan Ranch Trailblazer, Name on Freedom Wall, Rep. Presidential Task Force (Life), name on Wall of Freedom, Rep. Ctr., Washington, Cert. of

Appreciation, Pres. Bush and V.P. Dick Cheney, others. Fellow United Writers' Assn. India; mem. ASCAP, Maison Internat. des Intellectuels, Internat. Parliament for Safety and Peace, World Parliament Confedn. of Chivalry (Grand Coun.), World Acad. Assn. of the Universe (life), Bronx Philharm. Symphony Soc., Inc. (founder, pres.), Internat. Platform Assn., Am. Fedn. Musicians, Robert Stolz Soc. Gt. Britain, World Univ. Roundtable (trustee, founder), Internat. Cultural Corr. Inst., Circulo Nobiliario de los Caballeros Universales (grandmaster U.S.), Lègion de L'Aigle de Mer (capt.), USA United Srs. Assn. Inc., Order the Templars (knight, count San Ciriaco). Avocations: walking, music, coin collecting/numismatics, antique coptic ethiopian crosses.

SPREEN, THOMAS H., agricultural studies educator; b. Muncie, Ind., Dec. 24, 1950; s. Edward H. and Florence M. Spreen; m. L. Hobbs, Jan. 29, 1972; children: John F., Thomas Luke. PhD, Purdue U., West Lafayette, Ind., 1977. Cert. in leadership development ESCOP ACOP, 1994. Prof. Food & Resource Econ., U. Fla., Gainesville, 1987—, chair, 2002—08. Cons. Food and Agrl. Orgn., Rome, 1996—99. Author: (textbook) Applied Mathematical Programming. Recipient Lifetime Achievement award, Southern Agr. Econ. Assoc. Mem.: Applied Agrl. Economics Assn. Home: 1011 SW 112th St Gainesville FL 32607 Office: Food and Resource Economics Univ Fla PO Box 110240 Gainesville FL 32611 Office Phone: 352-392-1826 Ext. 209. Office Fax: 352-392-8634. Business E-Mail: tspreen@ufl.edu.

SPRIESTER, REBECCA GROEN, librarian; d. Calvin and Anna Wilhemina Groen; m. Fred Russell Spriester, June 27, 1986; m. Norvin John Noteboom, June 6, 1970 (div. May 30, 1986); children: Anna Nicole Noteboom, Heather Day Noteboom. BA, Northwestern Coll., Orange City, IA, 1972; MA, U. SD, Vermillion, 1978. Media cons. Aea 4 Sioux Ctr., Iowa, 1978—87; instrnl. svcs. Aea 3, Cylinder, Iowa, 1987—93; coll. libr. Iowa Lakes C.C., Estherville, 1993—96; dist. dir. libraries Iowa Valley C.C. Dist., Marshalltown, 1996—. Independent. Home: 20516 S Sandpiper Dr Spirit Lake IA 51360 Personal E-mail: rebeccaspriester@yahoo.com.

SPRIESTERSBACH, DUANE CARYL, academic administrator, speech pathology/audiology services professional, educator; b. Pine Island, Minn., Sept. 5, 1916; s. Merle Lee and Esther Lucille (Stucky) Spriestersbach; m. Bette Rae Bartell, Aug. 31, 1946; children: Michael Lee, Ann. BEd, Winona State Tchrs. Coll., 1939; MA, U. Iowa, 1940, PhD, 1948. Asst. dir. pers. rels. Pacific Portland Cement Co., San Francisco, 1946-47; prof. speech pathology U. Iowa, Iowa City, 1948-89, prof. emeritus, 1989—, dean. Grad. Coll., v.p. ednl. devel. and rsch., 1965-89, v. pres. and dean emeritus, 1989—, acting pres., 1981-82; v.p. ops. Breakthrough, Inc., Oakdale, Iowa, 1993-94; freelance cons., 1994—2006. Com. mem. Nat. Inst. Neurol. Disease and Blindess; chmn. dental tng. com. Nat. Inst. Dental Rsch., 1967—72, chmn. spl. grants rev., 1978—82; chmn. bd. dirs. Midwest Univs. Cons. Internat. Activities, Columbus, 1978—87. Author: (book) Psychosocial Aspects of Cleft Palate, 1973; author: (with others) Diagnostic Methods in Speech Pathology, 1978; co-editor: Cleft Palate and Communication, 1968, Diagnosis in Speech Language Pathology, rev. edit., 1999, The Way It Was: The University of Iowa 1964-1989, 1999. Pres. Iowa City Cmty. Theater, 1964, 1977, 1983. Served to lt. col. US Army, 1941—46, ETO. Decorated Bronze Star; fellow Nat. Inst. Dental Rsch., 1971. Fellow: AAAS; mem.: Midwestern Assn. Grad. Schs. (chmn. 1979—80), Am. Cleft Palate Assn. (pres. 1961—62, disting. svc. award), Am. Speech and Hearing Assn. (pres. 1965, honor award), Assn. Grad. Schs. (pres. 1979—80), Cosmos Clug (Washington), Mortar Bd., Sigma Xi. Home: 2 Longview Knoll NE Iowa City IA 52240-9148 Office: Univ Iowa M212 Oakdale Hall Iowa City IA 52242-5000 Home Phone: 319-351-8756; Office Phone: 319-335-4012. Business E-Mail: duane-spriestersbach@uiowa.edu.

SPRINCE, LEILA JOY, retired librarian; b. Toronto, Ont., Can., July 10, 1936; came to U.S., 1981; d. Harry and Anna Helen Caller; children: Alan Rosenthal, Joel Rosenthal; m. Arnold Joel Sprince, Feb. 16, 1982 BA, U. Toronto, 1957, B of Edn., 1962; MA, U. South Fla., 1987. Cert. tchr., Ont. Ballet dancer Volkoff Can. Ballet, Toronto, 1953-54; tchr. h.s. North York Bd. Edn., Toronto, 1958-60; libr. Broward County Libr. Sys., Plantation, Fla., 1987-88, 91-93, Margate, Fla., 1988-91, head youth svcs. Coconut Creek, Fla., 1996—2001; ret., 2001. Advisor Omnigraphics Pub., Detroit, 1993—; cons. Gale/U*X*L* Pubs., N.Y.C., 1996—; state facilitator summer programs State Libr. Fla., 1993. Contbr. articles to profl. jours. Mem. nat. children and youth membership orgns. outreach com. ALA/ALSC, 2001—; mem. adv. bd. Broward County Libr., 2006—. Mem. ALA (Best Books for Young Adult Cmty. spkr. 1989, 90), Fla. Libr. Assn. (spkr.), B'nai B'rith Women (fin. sec. 1983, pres. 1984, 85), Phi Kappa Phi, Beta Phi Mu. Democrat. Jewish. Avocations: music/dance, computers, travel, history. Home Phone: 954-741-3288. Personal E-mail: ajsprince@aol.com.

SPRING, ANITA, anthropologist, educator; d. Samuel and Elsie Spring; 1 child, Ben Hansen. BA, U. Calif., Berkeley, 1963; MA, San Francisco State U., 1966, Cornell U., Ithaca, NY, 1967, PhD, 1976. Diplomate US Dept. State, 1979. Rschr. NIMH, Zambezi, Zambia, Chavuma, Zambia, 1970—72, Human Latation Ctr., Zambezi, Chavuma, 1979; social scientist, Design Agrl. U. USAID, Yaonde, Cameroon, 1980, chief party Lilongwe, Malawi, 1981—83, cons. Mogodishu, Somalia, 1987, social scientist, RONCO Mbabene, Swaziland, 1993, team leader Nairobi, Kenya, 1996, cons., gender assessment, Widtech Asmara, Eritrea, 2002, cons., democracy and governance, Mgmt. Sys. Internat. Addis Ababa, Ethiopia, 2004; cons. US Congress, Office Tech. Assessment, Washington, 1984—87, with Gabarone, Botswana, 1987, evaulation mem. Harare, Zimbabwe, 1987; dir., women agr. U. Fla., Gainesville, 1984—86, prof., 1993—2009; chief, women agrl. prodn. and rural devel. svc. FAO UN, Rome, 1988—92; project dir. GTZ, German Aid Agy., Awassa, Ethiopia, 1996, FAO, Castries, Saint Lucia, 2000, North-South Ctr., Black River, Kingston, Jamaica, 1994—95. Assoc. dean U. Fla., Gainesville, 1985—88; guest lectr. U. Asmara, 2002. Author: (book) Women Farmers and Commercial Ventures: Increasing Food Security in Developing Countries, Agricultural Development and Gender Issues in Malawi; co-editor (with W. Susan Poats & Marianne Schmink): Gender Issues and Farming Systems Research and Extension; co-editor: (with Rita Gallin) Women Creating Wealth: Transforming Economic Development.; co-editor: (with Judith Hoch-Smith) Women in Ritual and Symbolic Roles, 1979; contbr. articles to 61 profl. jours., chapters to books. Chair, urban design strategies City Beautification Bd., Gainesville, Fla., 1993—2008; founder Worldwide Digital Libr. Collection Women and Devel., U. Fla. Libr., Gainesville, 2008—. Grantee Fulbright fellowship, US Govt. Agy., Ethiopia, 1996; Rsch. Scholars grant, Ctr. African Studies, 1993, 2003, Internat. Bus. Rsch. grant, Ctr. Internat. Bus. Edn. and Rsch., 2001—03, Rsch. grant, U. Fla., 2003—05. Fellow: Soc. Applied Anthropopology, Culture and Agr. (pres. 2008—), Am. Anthrop. Assn. (pres. culture and agr. 2008—); mem.: Com. Ethics, Am. Anthrop. Assn. (chair 2006—07), Assn. Farming Sys. Rsch. and Ext., African Studies Assn. Achievements include research in success for women in agriculture and business; discovery of best techniques to help women achieve food security; new focus on China in Africa entrepreneurs and agriculture.

SPRING, BONNIE JOAN, preventive medicine professor; b. Hackensack, NJ, Oct. 9, 1949; d. John Edwin and Sonja Joan (Litwinowich) S. BA, Bucknell U., 1971; MA, Harvard U., 1975, PhD, 1977. Diplomate Am. Bd. Health Psychology, Am. Bd. Profl. Psychology; lic. psychologist, Mass., Ill. Rsch. scientist Biometrics Rsch., NYC, 1975-78; instr. psychology Harvard U., Cambridge, Mass., 1977, asst. prof., 1977-82, assoc. prof., 1982-84; prof. psychology Tex. Tech U., Lubbock, 1984-88, dir. clin. tng., 1986-88; prof. U. Health Scis.-Chgo. Med. Sch., 1988-98, U. Ill., Chgo., 1998—2005; prof. preventive medicine, psychology, psychiatry, dir. behavioral medicine, co-dir. cancer prevention Feinberg Sch. Medicine, Northwestern U., Chgo., 2005—. Lectr. psychiatry Columbia Coll. Physicians and Surgeons, NYC, 1979-86; vis. lectr. nutrition MIT, Cambridge, 1979-80; staff psychologist Mass. Mental Health, Boston, 1981-84; rsch. assoc. prof. psychiatry U. Md. Med. Sch., Balt., 1984-90. Author: Psychology, 1988; editor: Attentin in Schizophrenia, 1979, Psychopharmacology, 1986-95; mem. editl. bd. Jour. Social and Clin. Psychology, 1985—, Psychopharmacology, 1995-2000, Jour. Cons. and Clin. Psychology, 1996-, Health Psychology, 2005-08. Panel mem. com. on nat. needs for behavioral rsch. pers. Inst. Medicine, NAS, Washington, 1984086; panel mem. nat. plan for rsch. on schizophrenia NIMH, 1987; mem. behavioral medicine study sect. NIH, 1994-98. Nutrition grantee Ctr. for Brain Scis., 1980-81, Ford Found., 1981-82, VA, 1989—, schizophrenia grantee NIMH, 1980-84, grantee NIH, 1995—. Fellow APA, Am. Psychol. Soc., Soc. for Behavioral Medicine (pres. 2007-), Acad. Behavioral Medicine Rsch. Am. Coll. Neuropsychopharmacology. Avocation: travel. Office Phone: 312-908-2293. Business E-Mail: bspring@northwestern.edu.

SPRINGATE, JAMES EDWARD, pediatrician; b. Cleve., Aug. 10, 1954; s. Daniel and Garnett Springate; m. Laura Marino, Apr. 21, 1981; children: Beth, Kathrine. BA, Harvard U., 1976; MD, Johns Hopkins, 1981. Diplomate Am. Bd. Pediat., 1989, Am. Bd. Pediat. Nephrology, 1991. Resident The Children's Hosp. of Buffalo, 1981—84; attending physician Women & Children's Hosp. Buffalo, Ohio, 1987—; prof. pediats. SUNY, Buffalo, 1995—2003. Contbr. articles to profl. jours. Mem.: Soc. for Pediat. Rsch., Internat. Pediatric Transplant Soc., Am. Physiology Soc., Am. Acad. Pediat. Home: 251 Old Lyme Dr Amherst NY 14221 Office: Women & Childrens Hosp Buffalo 219 Bryant St Buffalo NY 14222 E-mail: jspringate@upa.chob.edu.

SPRINGER, CHARLES EDWARD, retired judge; b. Reno, Feb. 20, 1928; s. Edwin and Rose Mary Cecelia (Kelly) S.; m. Jacqueline Sirkegian, Mar. 17, 1951; 1 dau., Kelli Ann. BA, U. Nev., Reno, 1950; LLB, Georgetown U., 1953; LLM, U. Va., 1984; student Grad. Program for Am. Judges, Oriel Coll., Oxford U., Eng., 1984. Bar: Nev. 1953, U.S. Dist. Ct. Nev. 1953, D.C. 1954, U.S. Supreme Ct. 1962. Pvt. practice law, Reno, 1953-80; atty. gen. State of Nev., 1962, legis. legal adv. to gov., 1958-62; legis. bill drafter Nev. Legislature, 1955-57; mem. faculty Nat. Coll. Juvenile Justice, Reno, 1978—; juvenile master 2d Jud. Dist. Nev., 1973-80; justice Nev. Suprem Ct., Carson City, 1981—99; vice-chief justice Nev. Supreme Ct., Carson City, 1987, chief justice, 1998-99, ret., 1999. Mem. Jud. Selection Commn., 1981, 98, Nev. Supreme Ct. Gender Bias Task Force, 1981—; trustee Nat. Coun. Juvenile and Family Ct. Judges, 1983—; mem. faculty McGeorge Sch. Law, U. Nev., Reno, 1982—; mem. Nev. Commn. for Women, 1991-95. With AUS, 1945-47. Recipient Outstanding Contbn. to Juvenile Justice award Nat. Coun. Juvenile and Family Ct. Judges, 1989, Midby-Byron Disting. Leadership award U. Nev., 1988. Mem. ABA, Am. Judicature Soc., Am. Trial Lawyers Assn., Phi Kappa Phi. Home: 1001 Dartmouth Dr Reno NV 89509 Office: Nev Supreme Ct Capitol Complex 201 S Carson St Carson City NV 89701-4702

SPRINGER, DAVID WILLIAM, dean, social sciences educator; b. NYC, Sept. 1, 1968; s. Paul David and Elizabeth Springer; m. Sarah Eagle Smith, Dec. 8, 2001; 1 child, Aidan David. BA, Fla. State U., 1990, MSW, 1992, PhD, 1997. LCSW Tex., ACSW. Clin. social worker Univ. Behavioral Ctr., Orlando, Fla., 1992—94; rsch. assoc. Fla. State U., Tallahassee, 1994—97; asst. prof. U. Tex., Austin, 1997—2000, assoc. prof., 2000—02, assoc. dean, 2002—, assoc. dean, disting. tchg. prof., 2005—. Author: Substance Abuse Treatment for Criminal Offenders, 2003, Handbook of Forensic Mental Health with Victims and Offenders, 2007. Fundraiser Leukemia and Lymphoma Soc., Austin, 2000; bd. dirs. Austin Child Guidance Ctr., 1998—2003, Great Wall China Adoption, 2007—. Recipient Outstanding Grad. Tchg. award, U. Tex. at Austin, 2003; named to Acad. Disting. Tchrs., 2005, Who'w Who in Social Scis. Higher Edn., 2004. Mem.: NASW, Tex. Assn. Social Work Deans and Dirs. (pres. 2005—07), Coun. Social Work Edn., Soc. Social Work and Rsch. Democrat. Avocations: guitar, photography, camping, hiking, surfing. Office: U Tex at Austin Sch Social Work Austin TX 78712 Office Fax: 512-471-7268. Business E-Mail: dwspringer@austin.utexas.edu.

SPRINGER, DEBRA ANN, psychologist; d. William V. and Joyce B. Waryck; m. Don Christopher Springer; children: Kaleb Christopher, Anna Elizabeth. PhD, Penn State U., U. Pk., Pa., 1997. Cert. in sch. psychology Dept. Edn., Pa., 1991. Sch. psychologist Applachia IU 8, Ebensburg, Pa., 1991—99, Hollidaysburg Area Sch. Dist., Pa., 1999—. CCD teacher St. Michael's Cath. Ch., Hollidaysburg, 2007—09. Mem.: NASP, ASPP, Penn State Alumni Assn.

SPRINGER, DOUGLAS HYDE, retired food products executive, lawyer; b. Englewood, NJ, Jan. 31, 1927; s. Arthur Hyde and Melicent Katherine (Messenger) S.; m. Virginia Helen Chouinard, Nov. 23, 1949; children: Susan Compton, Debora Lee. Student, Wesleyan U., 1944-45; AB, Yale U., 1947; LLB, Columbia U., 1950. Bar: N.Y. 1950. Atty. Port of N.Y. Authority, 1950-52; legal counsel Worthington Corp., Harrison, N.J., 1953-61, asst. sec., 1956-61; asst. counsel Campbell Soup Co., Camden, N.J., 1961-65, asst. sec., 1965, spl. assignments, 1966, dir. spl. studies, corp. planning, 1966-69, dir. corp. planning frozen foods, 1969-70, asst. treas., 1970-71, treas., 1971-73, v.p. fin. planning, 1973-75, v.p., controller, 1975-78, v.p., treas., 1978-88, v.p. investment mgmt., 1988-90. Trustee Meml. Health Alliance, 1981—99; trustee, treas. Virtua Health Hosp., 2000—06, Virtua Health Found., 2003—08; mem. adv. bd. Pa. Liberty Mut. Ins. Co., 1971—88; Ea. regional adv. bd. Arkwright-Boston Mfrs. Mut. Ins. Co., 1985—90; exec. sec. Gov.'s Interstate Adv. Com., 1966; asst. to mem. Pres.'s Commn. on Postal Orgn., 1967—68; spl. asst. to chmn. South Jersey Port Corp., 1969—71; mem. NJ Econ. Devel. Coun., 1972—76; mem. adv. coun. Tax Found., 1980—89. Trustee Nat. Food Processors Assn. Retirement Plan and Trust Indenture Fund, 1976—89, Perkins Ctr. for Arts, 1979—88, Ind. Coll. Fund NJ, 1982—88, The Estaugh, 2004—; mem. exec. bd., v.p. fin. Camden County coun. Boy Scouts Am., 1978—90; bd. dirs. YMCA of Burlington County, 1995—2007, sec., 2000—07, Yale Alumni Fund, 1996—2002, exec. com., 1998—2002. With USNR, 1944—46. Mem. Nat. Assn. Corp. Treas. (bd. dirs. 1982-88), Phila. Treas. Club, Internat. Bus. Forum (bd. dirs. 1980-88), Phi Nu Theta, Phi Delta Phi, N.J. Soc. Pa. (pres. 1992-93, treas. 1994—). Clubs: Yale (Phila., N.Y.C.); Nassau (Princeton, N.J.), Laurel Creek (Mt. Laurel, N.J.), Y's Men's Club (v.p., 1992-94, pres., 1994-95). Home: 670 Medford Leas Medford NJ 08055

SPRINGER, FLOYD LADEAN, architect; b. Goodrich, ND, Feb. 1, 1922; s. George Roy Springer and Louise Baumbach; m. Dorothy Mae Shepard (dec. Sept. 1995); children: Debra Louise, Tami June. Student, U. Denver, 1948-51; BS in Archtl. Engring., U. Colo., 1952; postgrad., U. Wash., 1953-54, U. Utah, Portland, Oreg., 1980. Apprentice to arch. Gilbert R. Horton AIA, 1946-48; job capt. Robert Hall and Ira Cummings, Archs., 1956-57; mem. archtl. staff Austin Co., 1964, Naramore, Bain, Brady and Johanson, 1965, Roland Terry and Assocs., 1967, John Graham & Co., 1967-68; mem. various archtl. firms Wash. and Alaska, 1952-69; prin. Floyd Springer/Arch., Seattle, 1969—. Arch. numerous pvt. comml. and residential projects, 1969—; corp. mem., emeritus Am. Inst. of Arch. Contbr. articles to profl. jours. Cpl. inf. U.S. Army, 1941-44, PTO. Decorated Silver Star. Mem.: AIA (emeritus), Pacesetters Club, Masons. Presbyterian. Avocations: photography, ballroom dancing, leaded art glass, painting, writing, poetry. Home and Office: 18548 60th Ave NE Kenmore WA 98028-8725

SPRINGER, GEORGE STEPHEN, mechanical engineering educator; b. Budapest, Hungary, Dec. 12, 1933; came to U.S., 1959; s. Joseph and Susan (Grausz) S.; m. Susan Martha Flory, Sept. 15, 1963; children: Elizabeth Anne, Mary Katherine. B in Engring., U. Sydney, Australia, 1959; M in Engring., Yale U., 1960, MSc in Engring., 1961, PhD, 1962; D (hon.), Tech. U. Budapest, 2000, U. Sydney, 2007. Registered profl. engr., Mass. Asst. prof. mech. engring. MIT, Cambridge, 1962-67; prof. mech. engring. U. Mich., Ann Arbor, 1967-83; Paul Pigott prof. Stanford (Calif.) U., 1983—, chmn. dept. aeronautics and astronautics, 1990—2001. Author: Erosion by Liquid Impact, 1975; co-author, co-editor 14 books; contbr. over 200 articles to scholarly and profl. jours. Recipient Pub. Svc. Group Achievement award, NASA, 1988, Medal of Excellence in Composite Materials U. Del., 1999. Fellow AIAA (Engr. of Yr. 1995, Structures Structural Dynamics and Materials award 2000), ASME (Worcester Reed Warner medal 1994), Soc. Advancement Materials and Process Engring. (Delmonte award 1991); mem. Am. Phys. Soc., Soc. Automotive Engrs. (Ralph Teetor award 1978), NAE, Hungarian Nat. Acad. Sci. (fgn. mem.), Am. Soc. Composites (Outstanding Rschr. award 1997). Achievements include patents in field. Office: Stanford U Dept Aeronautics & Astronautics Stanford CA 94305 Office Phone: 650-723-4135. Business E-Mail: gspringer@stanford.edu.

SPRINGER, JOHN KELLEY, hospital administrator; b. Salem, Ohio, May 11, 1931; s. Wilbur Johnson and Nellie Marie (Kelley) S.; m. Jane Lee Parsons, Oct. 13, 1956; children: Kelley Lynn, Dana Lee, Susan Elizabeth, Nellie Jane. AB, Dartmouth Coll., 1953; MHA, U. Mich., 1960; LLD (hon.), Briarwood Coll., 1991. Adminstrv. resident Mary Hitchcock Meml. Hosp., Hanover, NH, 1959-60, asst. adminstr., 1960-64, assoc. adminstr., 1964-69, adminstr. for ops., 1969-71; assoc. exec. dir. Hartford (Conn.) Hosp., 1971-73, exec. dir., 1974-76, pres., 1977-87, vice chmn., CEO, 1987-89, vice chmn., 1989—92; pres., CEO Conn. Health Sys., 1986—96. Bd. dirs. Hartford Mut. Fund; pres. Combined Hosps. Alcoholism Program, Inc., 1972—75; chmn. Capital Area Health Consortium, 1987—90; lectr. Sch. Pub. Health Yale U., 1975. Deacon 1st Ch. of Christ Congl., West Hartford, 1975-79; bd. dirs. Urban League Greater Hartford, 1973-76, Hartford Sem. Found., Greater Hartford chpt. ARC, vice-chmn., 1978-80; trustee New London (N.H.) Hosp., 2003, Dartmouth Hitchcock Alliance; bd. visitors Rockefeller Ctr., Dartmouth Coll., pres. Dartmouth Class 1953, 2008-. Capt. USMC, 1953-58; col. USMCR, ret. Mem.: Lake Sunapee Vis. Nurse Assn. (bd. dirs. 2003—04), Greater Hartford C. of C. (bd. dirs. 1980—82), Am. Hosp. Assn. (coun. on fin. 1975—78, del.-at-large 1979—80, chmn. 1981—86, bd. trustees 1992—94, award of honor 1996), Conn. Hosp. Assn. (chmn. bd. trustees 1982—83), New Eng. Hosp. Assembly (pres. 1972), Am. Coll. Healthcare Execs., Harbour Ridge Yacht and Country Club, Lake Sunapee Yacht Club, Lake Sunapee Country Club, Twilight Club, Hartford Golf Club, Hartford Club. Home: 27 Birch Point Lane Sunapee NH 03782-2600

SPRINGER, KARL, school system administrator; b. Hollywood, Calif., Sept. 27, 1948; m. Catherine Springer, 1972; children: Andrea, Nathan. BA in Edn., Calif. State U., Chico, 1970, tchg. cert., 1971; EdM, Northeastern State U., Tahlequah, Okla., 1980. Track & cross-country coach Butte Coll., Oroville, Calif., 1970—71; supr. Container Corp. of America, Santa Clara, Calif.; 1974—77; tchr. Muskogee Pub. Schs., 1977—84; spl. edn. tchr. Norman Pub. Schs., Okla., 1984—89, asst. dir. spl. svcs. Okla., 1989—95; asst. supt. Chickasha Pub. Schs., Okla., 1995—2000; supt. Mustang Pub. Schs., Yukon, Okla., 2000—08, Oklahoma City Pub. Schs., 2008—. Bd. dirs. Mustang C. of C., 2001. Lt. USMC, 1971—74, capt. res. USMC, 1974—77, served up to col. (ret.) USAR, 1977—2002. Named Dist. 14 Coop. Coun. for Okla. Sch. Adminstrn. Ctrl. Adminstr. of Yr., 2006. Office: Oklahoma City Pub Schs 900 N Klein Oklahoma City OK 73106 Office Phone: 405-587-0000.*

SPRINGER, MARLENE, retired academic administrator; b. Murfreesboro, Tenn., Nov. 16, 1937; d. Foster V. and Josephine Jones; children: Ann Springer, Rebecca Springer. BA in English and Bus. Adminstrn., Centre Coll., 1959; MA in Am. Lit., Ind. U., 1963, PhD in English Lit., 1969. Chair English dept. U. Mo., Kansas City, 1980-81, acting assoc. dean grad. sch., 1982; Am. Coun. of Edn. Adminstrn. fellow U. Kans., Lawrence, 1982-83; dean grad. sch. U. Mo., Kansas City, 1983-84, assoc. vice chancellor acad. affairs & grad. studies, 1985-89; vice chancellor acad. affairs East Carolina U., Greenville, NC, 1989-94; pres. Coll. Staten Island, CUNY, 1994—2007. Author: Edith Wharton and Kate Chopin: A Reference Guide, 1976; What Manner of Woman: Essays, 1977, Thomas Hardy's Use of Allusion, 1983, Plains Woman: The Diary of Martha Farnsworth, 1986 (Choice award 1986), Ethan Frome: A Nightmare of Need, 1993. Huntington Libr. fellow, 1988. Mem.: Coun. Grad. Schs. (chair 1986—88), Assn. Tchr. Educators (chair 1992), Acad. Leadership Acad. (exec. com. 1992—94), Am. Assn. State Colls. and Univs., Am. Coun. on Edn. (profl. devel. com. 1991—; invited participant Nat. Forum 1984, bd. dirs. 2001—). Business E-Mail: springer@mail.csi.cuny.edu.

SPRINGER, PAUL DAVID, lawyer, film company executive; b. NYC, Apr. 27, 1942; s. William W. and Alma (Markowitz) S.; m. Mariann Frankfurt, Aug. 16, 1964; children: Rob, Will. BA, U. Bridgeport, 1963; JD, Bklyn. Law Sch., 1967. Bar: N.Y. 1968, U.S. Dist. Ct. (so. and ea. dists.) N.Y. 1968, U.S. Ct. Appeals (2d cir.) 1970, U.S. Supreme Ct. 1973, Calif. 1989. Assoc. Johnson & Tannenbaum, NYC, 1968—70; assoc. counsel Columbia Pictures, NYC, 1970, Paramount Pictures, NYC, 1970—79, v.p., theatrical distbn. counsel, 1979—85, sr. v.p., chief resident counsel East Coast, 1985—87, sr. v.p., asst. gen. counsel LA, 1987—. Bar: N.Y. 1968, U.S. Dist. Ct. (so. and ea. dists.) N.Y. 1968, U.S. Ct. Appeals (2d cir.) 1970, U.S. Supreme Ct. 1973, Calif. 1989. Trustee West Cunningham Park Civic Assn., Fresh Meadows, N.Y., 1978—. Mem. ABA, Assn. of Bar of City of N.Y., L.A. Copyright Soc., Acad. Motion Picture Arts and Scis., Motion Picture Pioneers. Office Phone: 323-956-8408. Business E-Mail: paul_springer@paramount.com.

SPRINGER, ROBERT DALE, retired air force officer, consultant, lecturer; b. Millheim, Pa., Jan. 17, 1933; s. Simon Peter and Ruth Olive (McCool); m. Bonnie Joan Brubaker, Aug. 30, 1953; children: Robert Dale Jr., Debra K. Springer Miller, Curtis A., Michele L. Becker, Tania. BA in Social Sci., George Washington U., 1964, MS in Internat. Affairs, 1969. Cert. command pilot. Commd. 2d lt. USAF; advanced through grades to lt. gen.; comdr. 435th Tactical Airlift Wing, Rhein-Main Air Base, Federal Republic Germany, 1978-80, 322d Airlift Divsn., Ramstein Air Base, Federal Republic Germany, 1980-81, Air Force Manpower and Pers. Ctr., Randolph AFB, Tex., 1982-84, 21 A.F., McGuire AFB, NJ, 1984-85; insp. gen. USAF, Washington, 1985-87; with DCS-pers. Mil. Airlift Command, Scott AFB, Ill., 1981-82, vice comdr.-in-chief, 1987-88; ret., 1988; pres. bsone, Inc., 1999—, NovaLogic Sys., 1999—2007. Media cons., lectr., 1989—; dir. Air Force Commissary Svc., San Antonio, 1982-84, Army-Air Force Exch. Svc., Dallas, 1982-84; chmn. bd. dirs. Air Force Welfare Bd., San Antonio, 1982-84; mem. adv. bd. First Bank, 1997-; bd. dirs. NovaLogic, Inc., 1999-2009. Founding exec. dir Air Force Meml. Found., 1992-96, pres. 1996-98, vice chmn., 1998—2007; trustee Aerospace Edn. Found., 1992-94, The Falcon Found., 1996-2008; dir. NC Military Found., 2006-: active Air Force Meml. Adv. Com., 2007- Mem. Air Force Assn. (Presdl. Citation 1984), Airlift-Tanker Assn. (life mem., sr. v.p. 1989-94), Arnold Air Soc. (exec. dir. 1990-93, trustee 1993-2001), Ret. Officers Assn. (life), Daedalians (life), Masons (33 deg.). Lutheran. Avocations: golf, reading. Office Phone: 910-235-0490. Personal E-mail: bsone@nc.rr.com.

SPRINGER, SALLY PEARL, university administrator; b. Bklyn., Mar. 19, 1947; d. Nathaniel Margulies and Fanny (Schoen) S.; m. Hakon Hope; children: Erik Jacob Hope, Mollie Liv Hope. BS, Bklyn. Coll., 1967; PhD, Stanford U., 1971. Postdoctoral fellow Stanford U. Med. Sch., Calif., 1971-73; asst. prof. SUNY, Stony Brook, 1973-78, assoc. provost, 1981-85, assoc. prof., 1978-87; exec. asst. to chancellor U. Calif., Davis, 1987-92, asst. chancellor, 1982-2001, assoc. chancellor, 2001—07, assoc. chancellor emerita, 2007—. Author: (with others) Left Brain, Right Brain, 1981 (Am. Psychol. Found. Disting. Contbr. award 1981), 5th rev. edit., 1998, How to Succeed in College, 1982, Admission Matters: What Students and Parents Need to Know About Getting Into College, 2nd rev. edit., 2009; contbr. articles to profl. jours Mem. Internat. Neuropsychol. Soc., Psychonomic Soc. Office: 501 Citadel Dr Davis CA 95616 Home Phone: 530-756-3990; Office Phone: 530-400-5346.

SPRINGER, TIMOTHY ALAN, health researcher, immunology educator; b. Ft. Benning, Ga., Feb. 23, 1948; BA in Biochemistry, U. Calif., Berkeley, 1971; PhD in Biochemistry & Molecular Biology, Harvard U., 1976. NIH rsch. fellow U. Cambridge (Eng.)/MRC Lab. Molecular Biology, 1976-77; asst. prof. Med. Sch., Harvard U., 1977-83, assoc. prof., 1983-89, Latham family prof., 1989—. Chief lab. membrane immunochemistry Dana-Farber Cancer Inst., Boston, 1981-88; v.p. Ctr. Blood Rsch. Inst. Biomed. Rsch., Boston, 1988—; organizer Juan March Found. Workshop, Madrid, 1991. Assoc. editor Jour. Immunology, 1981-85; adv. editor Jour. Exptl. Medicine, 1981-85; mem. editl. bd. Hybridoma, 1981-, Jour. Clin. Immunology, 1988-92, Cellular Immunology, 1988-93, Cell Regulation, 1989-92, New Biologist, 1989—; contbr. numerous articles to profl. jours. NIH grantee, 1988, basic Rsch. prize, Am. Heart Assn., 1993, William B. Coley Medal for Disting. Rsch. in Fundamental Immunology, Cancer Rsch. Inst., 1995, Marie T. Bonazinga award for Excellence in Leukocyte Biology Rsch, Society for Leukocyte Biology, 1995, Crafoord prize, 2004. Mem. Am. Assn. Immunologists, Reticuloendothelial Soc. (membership chair 1986—, chair 1989), Am. Soc. Biol. Chemists, Am. Assn. Immunologists (block chmn. macrophages and natural killer cells 1985-86), Am. Assn. Pathologists, Nat. Acad. Scis. (chair biophysics and computational biology sect. 29 2004-), Am. Acad. Arts and Sciences, Phi Beta Kappa. Achievements include mapping a different group of adhesion molecules in the cell membrane of the blood cells, termed integrins. Office: Ctr for Blood Rsch Inst for Biomedical Rsch Harvard Med Sch Warren Alpert Bldg Rm251 200 Longwood Ave Boston MA 02115 Office Fax: 617-278-3200, 617-278-3232. Business E-Mail: springer@cbr.med.harvard.edu.

SPRINGER, WILMA MARIE, retired elementary school educator; b. Goshen, Ind., Jan. 13, 1933; d. Noah A. and Laura D. (Miller) Kaufman; m. Walter Frederick Springer, May 25, 1957; children: Anita Daniel, Timothy, Mark. BA, Goshen Coll., 1956; MS, Bradley U., 1960. Tchr. Topeka Elem. Sch., Ind., 1956—57, Metamora Grade Sch., Ill., 1957—59, Bellflower Unified Sch. Dist., Calif., 1960—61, 1968—2001, Lindstrom Elem. Sch., 1970—89, Jefferson Elem. Sch., Bellflower, 1989—92, Woodruff Elem., 1992—93, Williams Elem. Sch., Lakewood, Calif., 1993—96, Baxter Elem. Sch., Bellflower, 1996—2001; ret., 2001. Chmn. gifted and talented edn. Lindstrom Elem. Sch., Lakewood, 1986—89, Jefferson Elem. Sch., Bellflower, 1989—91, Baxter Elem., 1996—2001; stage mgr. Hour of Power TV Crystal Cathedral, 1983—; mem. program quality rev. team State of Calif., 1989—91; mem. adv. bd. Weekly Reader, 1989—96; adminstrn. coord. Nat. Assement Educational Progress Nat. Report Card, 2009. Contbr. articles to profl. jours. Active sch. bd. campaign, 1984, Bellflower City Coun., 1988, state senator and assemblyman campaigns, 1986-87; petition circulator various state initiatives, 1987-88; bd. dirs. Women's Ministries of Crystal Cathedral, Garden Grove, Calif., 1978-88; educator del. People to People Ambassadors Program, South Africa, 2003, Russia, 2004. Instructional Improvement Program grantee State of Calif., 1986-87; recipient Recognition award Regional Ednl. TV Adv. Coun., 1986, Cathedral Star award Women's Ministries of Crystal Cathedral, 1985. Mem.: AAUW, NEA (del. nat. conv. 1986, 1987, 1990, 1992, 1993, 1994, 1995), Nat. Assesment Ednl. Progress Nation's Report Card, Calif. Tchrs. Assn. (del. 1986, 1994), Bellflower Edn. Assn. (elem. dir. 1986—88, treas. 1988—89, v.p. 1989—91, pres. 1991—95), Toastmasters (Founder's Dist. Gov. 2001—02, Presidential Citation award, Calagary, Alberta 2008, Disting. Toastmaster, Disting. Dist.), Delta Kappa Gamma. Republican. Mem. Reformed Churches of Am. Avocations: quilting, painting. Home: 3180 Marna Ave Long Beach CA 90808-3246 Personal E-mail: wmspr@aol.com.

SPRINGER-SCOTT, GLADYS LORRAINE, retired educator, consultant; b. NYC, May 14, 1930; d. James Alexander and Gladys Isobel (Evelyn) Springer; m. George A. Scott, II, May 21, 1959; children Celeste Lorraine, George A. III, BA, Goddard Coll., 1972; MS, Bank Street Coll. Edn., 1976; postgrad. U. Mass., 1984. Dir. edn. NYC Bd. Edn., Bklyn., 1972-74, ednl. adminstr., NYC, 1983-2002; edn. dir. CUNY, Bklyn., 1976-81; exec. dir. East Harlem Community Devel. Agy., NYC, 1981-83; tchr. Irvington House, Irvington, NY, 1956-60, Abbott House, Irvington, 1960-65; tchr., dir. East Side House Settlement, South Bronx, NY, 1966-72. Mem. Head Start Policy Council, NYC, 1981; founder Bridge Apts. Nursery, NYC, 1962; mem. NFO edn. com. Recipient numerous awards for competitive voice concerts, 1945-47; Cary fellow Bank Street Coll. Edn., NYC, 1974-76. Mem. Assn. Black Women Higher Edn., Phi Delta Kappa.

SPRINGFIELD, DEMPSEY STEWART, physician, educator; b. Feb. 21, 1945; AB, Emory U., 1967; MD, U. Fla., 1971. Diplomate Am. Bd. Orthopaedic Surgery. Intern in surgery U. Ala., Birmingham, 1971-72; resident in orthopaedic surgery U. Fla., Gainesville, 1972-76, assoc. prof. Coll. Medicine, 1978-87, Harvard Med. Sch., Boston, 1987-96; prof., chair Mt. Sinai Sch. Medicine, NYC, 1996—. Co-editor: Surgery for Bone and Soft-Tissue Tumor, 1998. Home: 5 E 98th St # 1188 New York NY 10029-6501 Office: Mt Sinai Sch Medicine Dept Orthopedics 5th and 100th St New York NY 10029 Office Phone: 212-241-8311. Business E-Mail: dempsey.springfield@mssn.edu.

SPRINGFIELD, JAMES FRANCIS, retired lawyer, banker; b. Memphis, Nov. 5, 1929; s. C.L. and Mildred (White) S.; m. Shirley Burdick, June 1, 1951 (div.); children: Sidney, Susan, James Francis; m. Nancy Hardwick Ragan, Feb. 8, 1987 (dec. Jan. 1988); m. Donna Thomas Moore, Feb. 22, 1989. BA with distinction in econs., Rhodes Coll., 1951; LLB, U. Memphis, 1960. Bar: Tenn. 1960. With Union Planters Nat. Bank, Memphis, 1951-94, exec. v.p., sr. trust officer, head trust dept., 1968-85, gen. counsel, sec. bd., 1985-94; sec. bd., exec. v.p., gen. counsel Union Planters Corp., 1985-94; ret., 1994. Adv. bd. Memphis Alzheimer's Assn., 1999-2001; president's coun. Rhodes Coll., Memphis, chmn., 1991-92, internat. chmn. ann. fund, 1995-96; chmn. bd. trustees So. Coll. Optometry, 1978-80; trustee Plough Found., Memphis Conf. United Meth. Ch. Found., 1978-85, U. Tenn. Med. Units Found., 1975-82, MidSouth Pub. Comm. Found., 1985-87, 98-2007, sec. bd., 2002-07; chmn. fin. com. Hutchinson Sch.; sec. bd. trustees Vision Edn. Found., 1977-78; bd. regents Tenn. Trust Sch., chmn., 1977; mem. pres.'s adv. coun. Lambuth Coll., 1982-85; exec. bd. Chickasaw coun. Boy Scouts Am., 1983-87; bd. visitors Memphis State U. Cecil C. Humphreys Sch. Law, treas. Balmoral Civic Club, 1967-68; pres., bd. dir. Village of Bailey Station Homeowners Assn., Inc., 2000-01; dir. Shoreline Towers Condominium Assn. Inc., 2004-06. Lt. (j.g.) USNR, 1951-54. Mem. Tenn. Bar Assn. (chmn. interprofl. rels. com. 1976), Memphis and Shelby County Bar assn. (chmn. moral fitness com. 1972), Tenn. Bankers Assn. (chmn. legis.com. trust div. 1976-77, treas. 1972-73, pres. 1976-77, bd. dir. 1976-77), Bank Adminstrn. Inst. (chmn. trust commn. 1981-82), Estate Planning Coun. Memphis (pres. 1973-74), Sigma Nu (div. comdr. 1967-68, treas., bd. dir. House Corp. 1966-81), Omicron Delta Kappa (Rhodes Coll. chpt., pres. ODK Assocs. 2002-03). Republican. Home: 1692 Village Ridge Rd Collierville TN 38017-9793 Personal E-mail: jimmyspringfield@msn.com.

SPRINGMAN, RICHARD ARTHUR, mechanical engineer, director; b. Phila., Jan. 11, 1947; s. Eugene Robert and Alice Harris Springman; children: Jenny E. Perin, Lindsay R. Kunis. B in Mech. Engring., Ohio State U., Columbus, 1970, MS in Mech. Engring., 1972. Registered profl. engr., Ohio, 1975. Engr. tng., dept. highways Ohio, Marietta, 1966—67; prodn. technician Shell Chem. Co., Belpre, Ohio, 1968; engr., mining & metals Div. Union Carbide Corp., Marietta, 1969—72; instr. North Am. Heating & Air Conditioning Wholesalers Home Study Inst., Columbus, 1971—80; prof., dept. mech. engring. U. Toledo, 1979—86, chmn., dept. mech. engring., 1986—87, asst. chmn. dept. mech. engring., 1986—88, mech. engring. tech. program dir., dept. mech. engring., 1996—2000; dean undergraduate studies U. Toledo Coll. Engring., 1988—95, dir. student support, dept. mech. engring., 2000—. Cons. Midwest Environ. Rsch. Corp., Columbus, 1971—79, Robert H. Fuller Assocs., Columbus, 1979—80, Systems Engring. Assocs., Columbus, 1979—88. Contbr. scientific papers. Mem. & elder Covenant United Presbyn. Ch., Toledo, 1980—2005. Recipient Dr. Robert Schlembach award, U. Toledo Office Admissions, 1994, Svc. Recognition award, U. Toledo Coll. Engring., 1995, Outstanding Tchr. award, 2002. Master: Triangle Frat. (alumni bd. 2005—08); mem.: NSPE, Ohio Soc. Profl. Engrs. (Outstanding Engring. Educator award 2008), Toledo Soc. Profl. Engrs. (pres. 2005—07), Sigma Xi, Pi Tau Sigma Mech. Engring. Honor Soc. (hon.; chpt. advisor 1988—94). Office: Univ Toledo 2801 W Bancroft St MS #402 Toledo OH 43606 Office Fax: 419-530-3068. Business E-Mail: richard.springman@utoledo.edu.

SPRINGSTEEN, BRUCE (BRUCE FREDERICK JOSEPH SPRINGSTEEN), musician, singer; b. Freehold, NJ, Sept. 23, 1949; s. Douglas and Adele Springsteen; m. Julianne Phillips, May 13, 1985 (div. 1989); m. Patti Scialfa, June 8, 1991; children: Evan James, Jessica Rae, Sam Ryan. Student, Ocean County CC, 1967. Playing & performing with The E-Street Band, 1972—89, 1995, 1999—. Musician: (albums with The E Street Band) Greetings from Asbury Park, 1973, The Wild, The Innocent and the E-Street Shuffle, 1973, Born to Run, 1975 (Gold Record award, 1975), Darkness on the Edge of Town, 1978, The River, 1980, Born in the U.S.A., 1984 (Best Pop/Rock Album of Yr., Downbeat Readers Poll, 1984), Bruce Springsteen and the E-Street Band Live/1975-85, 1986, Tunnel of Love, 1987, Chimes of Freedom, 1988, Bruce Springsteen's Greatest Hits, 1995, Tracks, 1998, 18 Tracks, 1999, Live in New York City, 2001, The Rising, 2002 (Grammy award best male rock vocal performance, 2003, Grammy award best rock song, 2003, Grammy award best rock album, 2003), The Essential Bruce Springsteen, 2003, Bruce Springsteen & The E-Street Band: Hammersmith Odeon, London '75, 2006, Magic, 2007, Bruce Springsteen and The E Street Band's Greatest Hits, 2009, Working on a Dream, 2009, (solo albums) Nebraska, 1982, Human Touch, 1992, Lucky Town, 1992, The Ghost of Tom Joad, 1995, In Concert/MTV Unplugged, 1997, Devils and Dust, 2005 (Grammy award, Best Solo Rock Vocal Performance, 2006), We Shall Overcome: The Pete Seeger Sessions, 2006 (Grammy award, Best Traditional Folk Album, 2007), (songs) Streets of Philadelphia, 1994 (Golden Globe award for Best Original Song in a Film, 1994, Acad. award for best original song in a film, 1994, MTV Best Video from a Film award, 1994, Grammy, Song of Yr., 1994), Dead Man Walking, 1996 (Acad. award nominee for best original song in a film, 1996), Disorder in the House, 2002 (Grammy award, Best Rock Performance By A Duo Or Group With Vocal, 2003), Once Upon a Time in the West, 2007 (Grammy award, Best Rock Instrumental Performance, 2008), Radio Nowhere, 2007 (2 Grammy awards: Best Rock Song, Best Solo Rock Vocal Peformance, 2008), The Wrestler, 2008 (Critic's Choice award for Best Song, Broadcast Film Critics Assn., 2009, Golden Globe award for Best Original Song for Motion Picture, Hollywood Fgn. Press Assn., 2009), Girls in Their Summer Clothes (Grammy award for Best Rock Song, 2009); appears on: (albums by Rumble Doll) Rumble Doll with Patti Scialfa, 1993, (albums by Warren Zevon) The Wind, 2003, (albums by Ennio Morricone) We All Love Ennio Morricone, 2007; appeared in (documentaries) No Nukes, 1980, Sun City: Artists United Against Apartheid, 1986, Chuck Berry Hail! Hail! Rock 'n' Roll, 1987, The History of Rock 'N' Roll, 1995, Bruce Springsteen and the E Street Band: Live in New York City, 2001, Bruce Springsteen and The E Street Band: Live in Barcelona, 2003, Bruce Springsteen & The Sessions Band: Live in Dublin, 2007, appeared in, exec. prodr. Wings for Wheels: The Making of Born to Run, 2005 (Grammy award for Best Long Form Music Video, 2007). Recipient Grammy award for best male rock vocalist, 1984, 1987, 1994; named one of The 100 Most Influential People in the World, TIME mag., 2008; named to The Rock & Roll Hall of Fame, 1999, The Songwriters Hall of Fame, 1999, NJ Hall of Fame, 2007. Office: c/o Barbara Carr Creative Artists Agy LLC 2000 Ave of the Stars Los Angeles CA 90067 Office Phone: 424-288-2000.*

SPRINKLE, MARTHA CLARE, elementary school educator; b. Tehachapi, Calif., Oct. 17, 1944; d. William Foote and Mildred Sprinkle; BA, U. Calif., Santa Barbara, 1966; MA in Orgn. Mgmt., U. Phoenix, 2000. Cert. tchr. Calif., water aerobics instr. 1986. Tchr. Muroc Unified Sch. Dist., Edwards, Calif., 1966—71, Elk Hills Sch., Tupman, Calif., 1971—79, Tehachapi Valley Recreation and Pks., 1979—2007, So. Kern Unified Sch., Rosamond, Calif., 1984—2003. Planning commr. City of Tehachapi, Calif., 1984—2007, Tehachapi Unified Sch., Facilities Use Com., 2008—. Home: PO Box 667 Tehachapi CA 93581 Personal E-mail: mcsprink@yahoo.com.

SPRINTHALL, NORMAN ARTHUR, psychology educator; b. Attleboro, Mass., Aug. 19, 1931; s. William Archie and Edith Jarvis (Clark) S.; m. Barbara Weller (div. 1974); children: Douglas, Jayne, Carolyn; m. Lois May Thies. AB magna cum laude, Brown U., 1954, MA, 1959; EdD, Harvard U., 1963. Dir. fin. aid Brown U., 1955-60; asst. prof., then asso. prof. psychology, program chmn. counseling Harvard U., 1963-72; mem. faculty U. Minn., Mpls., 1972-82, prof. ednl. psychology, 1973-82, program chmn. counseling, 1972-74; prof. psychology, head counselor edn. program N.C. State U., Raleigh, 1982-87, prof., counselor, 1987-95, prof. emeritus, 1995—. Co-dir. Ethical Reasoning Project in Pub. Adminstrn., U.S. and Poland, 1993-95, Russia, 1998-99. Author: Educational Psychology: Readings, 1969, Guidance for Human Growth, 1971, Educational Psychology: A Developmental Approach, 7th edit., 1998, Value Development as the Aim of Education, 2d edit., 1981, Adolescent Psychology: A Developmental View, 1984, 2d rev. edit., 1988, 3d edit., 1995; co-author: Stewart-Sprinthall Management Survey (SSMS) Ethics and Public Administration, others; mem. editl. bd. profl. jours. Bd. dirs. Josephson Inst. Advancement of Ethics, 1986-90, mem. bd. advisors Character Counts Coalition, 1994—2004. Co-recipient Kuhmerker Career Rsch. award, Assn. Moral Edn., 2005. Fellow APA (Disting. Sr. Contbr. award); mem. Phi Beta Kappa. E-mail: nlsprint@aol.com.

SPRITZER, RALPH SIMON, lawyer, educator; b. NYC, Apr. 27, 1917; s. Harry and Stella (Theuman) S.; m. Lorraine Nelson, Dec. 23, 1950 (dec. Sept., 2008); children: Ronald, Pamela. BS, Columbia U., 1937, LL.B., 1940. Bar: N.Y. bar 1941, U.S. Supreme Ct. bar 1950. Atty. Office Alien Property, Dept. Justice, 1946-51; anti-trust div. Dept. Justice, 1951-54, Office Solicitor Gen., 1954-61; gen. counsel FPC, 1961-62; 1st asst. to solicitor gen. U.S., 1962-68; prof. law U. Pa., Phila., 1968-86, Ariz. State U., Tempe, 1986—; gen. counsel AAUP, 1983-84. Adj. prof. law George Wasington U., 1967; cons. Adminstrv. Conf. U.S., Ford Found., Pa. Gov.'s Justice Commn. Served with AUS, 1941-46. Recipient Superior Service award Dept. Justice, 1960; Tom C. Clark award Fed. Bar. Assn., 1968 Mem. Am. Law Inst. Office: Ariz State Univ Coll Law Tempe AZ 85287 Home: 7017 S Priest Dr Apt 2017 Tempe AZ 85283-6013 Home Phone: 480-456-8862; Office Phone: 480-965-7419.

SPROAT, EDWARD F., III, (WARD SPROAT), federal agency administrator; b. Sept. 12, 1951; With Gas Cooled Reactor Assocs., La Jolla, Calif.; mgr.-nuc. group bus. unit, mgr. projects Limerick Engring. Station PECO Energy, sect. mgr. computer engring., mgr. elec. engring. nuc. generation br., dir. quality mgmt. Phila. Electric, 1991—94, dir. engring. PECO Nuc., dir. engring and maintenance Limerick Nuc. Generating Station, dir. strategic programs PECO Nuc.; v.p. internat. projects Exelon Generation, bd. dirs., COO Board of Pebble Bed Modular Reactor Pty. Ltd. South Africa, 2002; mng. ptnr. McNeill, Sproat & Assocs., LLC, Berwyn, Pa.; dir. Office Civilian Radioactive Waste Mgmt. US Dept. Energy, Washington, 2006—. Office: US Dept Energy 1000 Independence Ave SW Washington DC 20585*

SPROAT, RUTH C., retired director, consultant; b. Lake Forest, Ill., Aug. 22, 1930; d. Christian Peter and Anna Elsa Christensen; m. Robert M. Volpe (div.); m. John Gerald Sproat, Mar. 18, 1967; 1 stepchild, Barbara Jeanne. BA in History, Lake Forest Coll., 1952; MA in History, Northwestern U., 1962. Registrar, admissions counselor Lake Forest Coll., 1948—68, dir. alumni affairs, 1972—74; dir. Master's Degree Program, asst. to pres. Lake Forest Coll. Grad. Sch. Mgmt., 1968—70, asst. to pres., 1971—72; dir. higher edn. SC Ednl. TV Network, Columbia, 1974—80, asst. dir. programming, exec. prodr., prodr., 1980—82, dir. higher edn., project dir., prodr., exec. prodr., 1982—87, asst. to pres. for devel. Satellite Ednl. Resources Consortium, 1988—92, exec. staff, dir. planning, grants and rsch., project dir., exec. prodr., 1992—97, cons. and asst. to pres., 2000—02; dir. devel. U. SC, Columbia, 1997—99; ret., 2002; cons. in field, 2002—. V.p. S.C. chpt. Am. Women in Radio and TV, 1983; co-prodr. with Am. Film Inst. Am. TV and Video Festival, India, 1985, prodr., presenter, India, 1986—91. Project dir., grant writer: (PBS TV series) Voices and Visions; U.S. project dir. Spaceship Earth; coordinating prodr. Cinematic Eye (Day Time Emmy award). Mentor to devel. staff Columbia Mus. Art, 2002. Recipient Alumni Disting. Svc. citation, Lake Forest Coll., 1987. Mem.: Hist. Columbia Found., Ill. Assn. Coll. Registrars and Admissions Officers (hon.; pres. 1965), Am. Assn. Collegiate Registrars and Admissions Officers (hon.; sec. 1966—68), Riverbanks Zoo Soc., Friends of U. S.C. Sch. Music (sec. 2001—03, dir. publicity for ann. fundraiser 2002—03, 2003—04, v.p. 2005—), State Mus. S.C., Sierra Club. Democrat. Avocations: gardening, writing, photography, travel. Home: 1686 Woodlake Dr Columbia SC 29206 E-mail: rcsproat@sc.rr.com.

SPROGER, CHARLES EDMUND, retired lawyer; b. Chgo., Feb. 18, 1933; s. William and Minnette (Weiss) Sproger. BA (David Himmelblau scholar), Northwestern U., 1954, JD, 1957. Bar: Ill. 1957. Assoc. Ehrlich & Cohn, 1958-63, Ehrlich, Bundesen, Friedman & Ross, 1963-72; partner Ehrlich, Bundesen, Broecker & Sproger, 1972-77; pvt. practice, 1977—2000; ret., 2000. Mem. adv. com. curriculum Ill. Inst. Continuing Legal Edn., Chgo., 1976—90; v.p. Mediation Coun. of Ill., 1986-87; arbitration panelist for Cir. Ct. Cook County, 1990—. Editor: Family Lawyer, 1962-63; contbr. articles to legal publs. Mediator Pastoral Psychotherapy Inst., 1982-86, vol. Coun. for Jewish Elderly, Chgo., 2002-. Recipient Vol. of Yr. award, Coun. for Jewish Elderly, 2004. Fellow Am. Acad. Matrimonial Lawyers (bd. examiners 1972-86, chmn. Law Day U.S.A. 1975); mem. ABA, Ill. Bar Assn. (chmn. coun. family law 1970-71), Chgo. Bar Assn. (matrimonial law com. 1958-2000), Am. Arbitration Assn. (divorce mediation com. 1983-92), Decalogue Soc., U. Mich. Club Chgo. (pres. 1988-89, bd. dirs. 1987-2004), Phi Alpha Delta. Address: 2800 W Birchwood Ave Chicago IL 60645-1218

SPROLE, FRANK ARNOTT, retired pharmaceutical executive, lawyer; b. Bklyn., Sept. 13, 1918; s. Frank Newland and Eleanor Arnott (Greenberg) S.; m. Sarah Louise Knapp, Sept. 23, 1944; children: Wendy Sprole Bangs, Frank J., Anne Sprole Mauk, Jonathan K., Sarah Sprole Obregon. BA, Yale U., 1942; LLB, Columbia U., 1949. Bar: N.Y. 1949. Assoc. firm Winthrop Stimson, Putnam & Roberts, NYC, 1949-50; atty. Bristol-Myers Co., NYC, 1950-52, asst. sec., 1952-55, sec., 1955-67, v.p., 1965-73, sr. v.p., 1973-77, vice-chmn. bd., 1977-84; ret.,

1984. Officer Proprietary Assn., Washington, 1978-84; dir., officer Knapp Fund, N.Y.C., 1960-93. Pres. bd. trustees Hotchkiss Sch., Lakeville, Conn., 1980-85; trustee Internat. Inst. Rural Reconstrn., N.Y.C., and Manila, 1983-87. Lt. comdr. USNR, 1942-45, PTO. Mem. Assn. of Bar of City of N.Y., Yale Club of N.Y.C., Wee Burn Country Club, Bohemian Club, John's Island Club, Riomar Country Club, Oak Harbor Club. Republican. Episcopalian. Home: 394 Mansfield Ave Darien CT 06820-2112

SPROLES, DARREN LEE, professional football player; b. Waterloo, Iowa, June 20, 1983; s. Annette. B in Speech Pathology, Kans. State U., Manhattan, 2004. Running back San Diego Chargers, 2005—. Recipient Ed Block Courage award, 2007; named Spl. Teams Player of Yr., San Diego Chargers, 2008; named to Am. Football Conf. Pro Bowl Team (2d Alt.), NFL, 2007, 2008. Office: San Diego Chargers PO Box 609609 San Diego CA 92160-9609*

SPROUL, HARVEY LEONARD, lawyer; b. Williamsburg, Ky., Oct. 8, 1933; s. Harvey Lafayette and Ruth (Renfro) S.; m. Sylvia Ann Moulton, May 31, 1958; children: Daniel Harvey, Susan Rebecca Sproul Brown, Jane Anne Sproul Luttrell, Lyda Bentley Sproul Beane. BSBA, U. Tenn., 1955, JD, 1957. Bar: Tenn. 1957, U.S. Dist. Ct. (ea. dist.) Tenn. 1957, U.S. Supreme Ct. 1960, U.S. Ct. Appeals (6th cir.) 1972. Assoc. Dannel & Fowler, Lenoir City, Tenn., 1961-62; ptnr. Dannel & Sproul, Lenoir City, 1962-65; judge County of Loudon, Tenn., 1966-74; ptnr. Sproul & Harvey, Lenoir City, 1979-82, Sproul & Hinton, Lenoir City, 1988—. Prin. Harvey L. Sproul, Lenoir City, 1974-79, 82-88; vice-chair Tenn. Adv. Comm. for Local Planning, 1971-74; atty. Lenoir Bd. Edn., 1980-90; county atty. Loudon County, 1982-2007; staff judge adv. 125th ARCOM/USAR, Nashville, 1986-89. Pres. Lenoir City Jaycees, 1966-67, Lenoir City Rotary, 1970, Lenoir City C. of C., 1980-82, Loudon County C. of C., 1993, bd. dirs., 1988-; organizing chmn. East Tenn. Devel. Dist., 1966-68, Tellico Planning Coun., 1966-74, Loudon County Visitors Bur., 1989-91, Knoxville HS Alumni Assn., 1993-95; bd. dirs. Loudon County Econ. Devel. Agy., 1990-, Nine Counties One Vision, 2000-05, Good Samaritan Ctr., 2003-05, Loudon County Edn. Found., 2005-, Loudon County United Way, 2006-, bd. chair., 2008-; bd. trustees Roane State CC, 2001-. Ret. col. JAGC USAR. Recipient Robert E. Gonia Regional Leadership award, 2002; named Tenn.'s Outstanding Young Man, Tenn. Jaycees, 1967, Man of Yr., Loudon County C. of C., 1989. Mem. ABA, Tenn. Bar Assn., Tenn. County Attys. Assn. (pres. 1997-98), Loudon County Bar Assn., Tenn. Coun. Sch. Bd. Attys. (v.p.), Tenn. County Judges Assn. (v.p. 1972-74), Omicron Delta Kappa, Kappa Sigma, Phi Delta Phi, Delta Sigma Phi. Democrat. Methodist. Avocation: tennis. Office: Sproul & Hinton 205 E Broadway St Lenoir City TN 37771-2911 Personal E-mail: hlsproul@charter.net.

SPROUL, JOAN HEENEY, retired elementary school educator; b. Johnstown, Pa., July 17, 1932; d. James L. and Grace M. (Dunn) Heeney; m. Robert Sproul, July 31, 1957 (dec.); 1 child, Mary Claire. BS, Clarion U., 1954; MA, George Wash. U., 1963; postgrad., U. Va., 1966-88. Cert. tchr., Va. Kindergarten tchr. Jefferson Sch., Warren, Pa., 1954-55; primary grades tchr. Alexandria (Va.) Pub. Schs., 1955-64; elem. tchr. Fairfax County Schs., Springfield, Va., 1965-97; math. lead tchr. West Springfield (Va.) Sch., 1987-97, ret., 1997. Contbr. (with others) Virginia History, 1988. Advisor Springfield Young Organists Assn., 1971-83; mem. Fairfax County Dem. Com., 1988-94, West Springfield Civic Assn., 1965—, Women's Aux. Fairfax Co. Salvation Army. Grantee Impact II, 1985-86. Mem. AAUW, NEA, Nat. Fedn. Bus. and Profl. Women (pres., dir., dist. VIII 1984—, Woman of Yr. 1985, 88), Delta Kappa Gamma (2d v.p. Va. chpt. 1963—), Phi Delta Kappa, Sigma Sigma Sigma. Episcopalian. Avocations: reading, music, gardening, fashion design. Home: # 124 1881 Harvest Dr Winchester VA 22601

SPROUL, JOHN ALLAN, retired utilities executive; b. Oakland, Calif., Mar. 28, 1924; s. Robert Gordon and Ida Amelia (Wittschen) S.; m. Marjorie Ann Hauck, June 20, 1945; children: John Allan, Malcolm J., Richard O., Catherine E. AB, U. Calif., Berkeley, 1947, LL.B., 1949. Bar: Calif. 1950. Atty. Pacific Gas & Electric Co., San Francisco, 1949-52, 56-62, sr. atty., 1962-70, asst. gen. counsel, 1970-71, v.p. gas supply, 1971-76, sr. v.p., 1976-77, exec. v.p., 1977-89; ret.; gen. counsel Pacific Gas Transmission Co., 1970-73, v.p., 1973-79, chmn. bd., 1979-89, also bd. dirs. Atty. Johnson & Stanton, San Francisco, 1952-56. Bd. dirs. emeritus Hastings Coll. Law. Served to 1st lt. USAAF, 1943-46. Mem. Calif. Bar Assn. (inactive), Pacific Coast Gas Assn., Pacific-Union Club, Orinda Country Club. Home: 8413 Buckingham Dr El Cerrito CA 94530-2531 Office: Pacific Gas & Electric Co Mail Code B26 PO Box 770000 San Francisco CA 94177-0001 also: Pacific Gas & Electric Co 77 Beale St Rm 2680 San Francisco CA 94105-1814 Office Phone: 415-973-2693. Personal E-mail: johnsproul@comcast.net.

SPROUL, SARAH LEE, conductor, musician, educator; b. NJ, Mar. 16, 1976; d. George and Sandra Lee Sproul. MusB, So. Meth. U., 1998, MusM, 2000. Cert. Tex. Bd. Edn. Orch. dir. Forestwood Mid. Sch., Flower Mound, Tex., 2000—; condr. Lone Star Youth Orch., Las Colinas, 2001—; asst. condr. Las Colinas Symphony Orch., 2001—, Garland (Tex.) Symphony Orch., 2001—, Symphony Arlington, Tex., 2001—; orch. dir. Shadow Ridge Mid. Sch., Flower Mound, Tex., 2005—. Recipient Don Nobles Meml. award, Meadows Sch. Arts, So. Meth. U., 1999, Sigma Alpha Iota award, 1999; Meadows Artistic scholar, 1994—98, Algur H. Meadows Grad. Conducting and Tchg. fellow, 1998—2000. Mem.: ASPCA, Tex. Music Edn. Assn., Am. Symphony Orch. League (guardian), Condr.'s Guild. Avocation: music. Personal E-mail: sproulsl@lisd.net.

SPROULE, JAMES MICHAEL, communications educator, writer; b. Dayton, Ohio, Feb. 8, 1949; s. John Harper and Katherine Veronica Sproule; m. Betty Ann Mathis, Mar. 3, 1973; children: John Harold, Kevin William. BA, MA, Ohio State U., Columbus, 1971, PhD, 1973. Asst. prof. U. of Tex. of Permian Basin, Odessa, 1973—77; assoc. prof. Ind. U. S.E., New Albany, 1977—86; vis. lectr. U. of Calif., Berkeley, 1986—87; prof., dir. Bowling Green (Ohio) State U., 2001—04; prof. St. Louis U., 2004—08, dean, 2004—06; prof. San Jose (Calif.) State U., 1987—2001, prof. emeritus, 2001—. Author: (book) The Rhetoric of Western Thought, Propaganda and Democracy, Channels of Propaganda, Speechmaking, Communication Today, Argument: Language and Its Influence. Recipient Golden Anniversary Monograph award, Nat. Comm. Assn., 1988; fellow, NEH, 1983. Mem.: Western States Comm. Assn., Internat. Soc. for the History of Rhetoric, Author's Guild, Nat. Comm. Assn. (pres. 2007). Home: 110 7th St Pacific Grove CA 93950-2907

SPROULE, MICHAEL E., insurance company executive; b. Toronto, Can. m. Doreen Sproule; 3 children. BA in Math, Physics, U. Toronto, MBA in Fin., Mktg. Cons. Tillinghast; various positions MetLife; former sr. v.p., CFO Alper Holdings USA, Inc., NYC; exec. v.p., CFO AmerUs Group; sr. v.p. New York Life, 1999—2001, 2002—03, acting CFO, 2001, CFO, 2002—, exec. v.p., 2003—. Fellow: Soc. Actuaries; mem.: Am. Acad. Actuaries. Office: New York Life 51 Madison Ave New York NY 10010*

SPROULL, ROBERT FLETCHER, research and development company executive; b. Ithaca, NY, June 6, 1947; s. Robert L. and Mary L. Sproull; m. Lee Sonastine, June 26, 1971; 1 child, Katherine. AB in Physics, Harvard U., 1968; MS in Computer Sci., Stanford U., 1970, PhD in Computer Sci., 1977. Mem. rsch. staff Xerox Palo Alto Rsch. Ctr., 1973—77; asst. prof. Carnegie Mellon U., Pitts., 1977-80, assoc. prof., 1980-83; v.p. Sutherland, Sproull & Assoc., Pitts., 1980-90, Sun Microsystems Lab., Burlington, Mass., 1990—2006, fellow, 1990—, interim dir., 2000—06, dir., 2006—. Venture ptnr. Advanced Tech. Ventures, 1981—2008; mem. tech. adv. coun. R. F. Donnelley & Sons, Chgo., 1981—89; mem. adv. com. NSF, Washington, 1990—97; bd. dirs. Alphatech, Inc., 2000—04. Co-author: (book) Principles of Interactive Computer Graphics, 1979, Logical Effort: Designing Fast CMOS Circuits (The Morgan Kaufmann Series in Computer Architecture and Design). Mem. sci. adv. bd. USAF, 1997—99. Sr. asst. health svcs. officer USPHS, 1970—72. Fellow: Am. Acad. Arts & Scis.; mem.: AAAS, NAE (councillor 2006—). Achievements include patents in field. Office: SUN Microsysystem Lab ubur02-311 35 Network Dr Burlington MA 01803-2757 Home Phone: 617-964-7793; Office Phone: 781-442-0353. Personal E-mail: bob.sproull@sun.com.

SPROULL, ROBERT LAMB, retired academic administrator, physicist, director; b. Lacon, Ill., Aug. 16, 1918; s. John Steele and Chloe Velma (Lamb) S.; m. Mary Louise Knickerbocker, June 27, 1942; children: Robert F., Nancy M. Sproull Highbarger. AB, Cornell U., 1940, PhD, 1943; LLD (hon.), Nazareth Coll., 1983; DMusic (hon.), New Eng. Conservatory, 1997. Research physicist RCA labs., 1943-46; faculty Cornell U., 1946-63, 65-68, prof. physics, 1956-63, dir. lab. atomic and solid state physics, 1959-60, dir. materials sci. center, 1960-63, v.p. for acad. affairs, 1965-68; dir. Advanced Research Projects Agy., Dept. Def., Washington, 1963-65; v.p., provost U. Rochester, NY, 1968-70, pres., 1970-84, pres. emeritus, 1984—. Prin. physicist Oak Ridge Nat. Lab., 1952; physicist European Rsch. Assoc., Brussels, 1958-59; lectr. NATO, 1958-59; pres. Environ. Literacy Coun., 1997-99, chmn. 1999—; past bd. dirs., John Wiley & Sons, Charles River Labs., United Technols. Corp., Xerox Corp., Bausch & Lomb; mem. sci. adv. com. GM Corp., 1971-80, chmn., 1973-80; mem. Def. Sci. Bd., 1966-70, chmn., 1968-70; mem. Naval Rsch. Adv. Com., 1974-76, Sloan Commn. Higher Edn., 1977-79, N.Y. Regents Commn. Higher Edn., 1992-93. Author: Modern Physics, 1956, A Scientist's Tools for Business, 1997; Editor: Jour. Applied Physics, 1954-57. Trustee Deep Springs Coll., 1967—75, 1983—87, Cornell U., 1972—77. Ctr. for Advanced Study in Behavioral Scis. fellow, 1973; Meritorious Civilian Svc. medal Sec. of Def., 1970. Fellow Am. Acad. Arts and Scis.; mem. Telluride Assn. (pres. 1945-47), Inst. of Def. Analysis (trustee 1984-92). Home: 6 Eliot Circle Pittsford NY 14534 Personal E-mail: lambspr@aol.com.

SPRUANCE, HALSEY, museum director; b. Wilmington, Del. Grad., U. Del., 1986; MA, Am. U. Illustration asst., Traveler Mag. Nat. Geog. Soc., pub. rels. coord., TV divsn., pub. affairs specialist; pub. rels. dir. Brandywine Conservancy, Chadds Ford, Pa., 1997—2007; exec. dir. Del. Mus. Natural History, Wilmington, 2007—. Office: Del Mus Natural History 4840 Kennett Pike PO Box 3937 Wilmington DE 19807-0937 Office Phone: 302-658-9111. Business E-Mail: hspruance@delmnh.org.

SPRUCE, SARA ELIZABETH, education educator; b. Kansas City, Kans., Dec. 6, 1943; d. Fletcher Clarke and Irene Lillian (Holloway) S. BS, Ea. Nazarene Coll., Quincy, 1967; MA in Edn., Ball State U., 1969; advanced cert. in edn., U. Ill., 1976, EdD, 1979. Elem. tchr. Quincy (Mass.) Pub. Schs., 1967-68, Marion (Ind.) Pub. Schs., 1969-75; prof. edn. Olivet Nazarene U., Bourbonnais, Ill., 1979—, faculty mem., 2009—. Presenter (workshop presentations) IL Reading Conf., 2002—09. Mem. Internat. Reading Assn., Ill. Reading Assn., Two Rivers Reading Coun., Ill. Assn. for Tchr. Edn., Orgn. Tchr. Educators in Reading, Delta Kappa Gamma, Kappa Delta Pi (sponsor Nu Beta chpt., Disting. Dissertation award 1980), Phi Kappa Phi, Phi Delta Kappa. Office: Olivet Nazarene Univ Dept Edn 1 University Ave Bourbonnais IL 60914-2345 Office Phone: 815-939-5139.

SPRUCH, GRACE MARMOR, physics professor; b. NYC, Nov. 19, 1926; d. Isadore and Mollie (Pogel) Marmor; m. Larry Spruch, Jan. 8, 1950. BA, Bklyn. Coll., 1947; MS, U. Pa., 1949; PhD, NYU, 1955. Assoc. rsch. scientist NYU, NYC, 1955-56, 58-63, 1965-67, rsch. scientist, 1968—69; instr. The Cooper Union, NYC, 1957-58; vis. assoc. prof. Rutgers U., Newark, 1964-65, assoc. prof., 1969-75, prof., 1975—. Sci. sec. Internat. Conf. Luminescence, NYC, 1961; hon. rsch. assoc. in applied sci. Harvard U., Cambridge, Mass., 1977-78; hon. assoc. Nieman Found. for Journalism, Harvard U., Cambridge, 1977-78; mem. interview team China US Physics Examination and Application Program, 1985, 86. Author: Such Agreeable Friends, 1983, Squirrels at my Window, 2000; co-author: The Ubiquitous Atom, 1974, 21 Astounding Science Quizzes, 1982; co-editor: Luminescence of Organic and Inorganic Materials, 1962; translator: (M. Françon) Holography, 1974; co-translator: (R. Jungk) The Big Machine, 1968; contbg. editor Internat. Sci. and Tech. Mag., 1955-60; referee Am. Jour. Physics, 1973—; contbr. articles to profl. jour. Recipient Lifetime Achievement award Bklyn. Coll. Alumni Assn., 2002; fellow AAUW, Oxford (Eng.) U., 1963-64, Ctr. for Energy and Environ. Studies, Princeton U., 1981, Ctr. for Tech. Studies, NJ Inst. for Tech., 1986-87; scholar NY State Regents, Bklyn. Coll., NYC, 1943-47; Humanities grantee Dept. Higher Edn., NJ, 1989-90. Mem. ACLU, Am. Phys. Soc., Phi Beta Kappa (chpt. pres. 1978-82), Sigma Xi, Sigma Pi Sigma, Pi Delta Epsilon (hon.). Avocations: listening to music, tennis, swimming, hiking, animals. Home: 14 E 8th St New York NY 10003-5917 Office: Rutgers Univ Physics Dept 101 Warren St Newark NJ 07102-1811 Home Phone: 212-777-9398; Office Phone: 973-353-5428. Business E-Mail: spruch@andromeda.rutgers.edu.

SPRUILL, LOUISE ELAM, retired mathematics educator; b. Mecklenburg County, Va., Aug. 17, 1918; d. William Llewellyn and Lillie Clayton (Puryear) Elam; m. Jacob Sipe Fleming, Aug. 12, 1941 (dec. Nov. 1957); children: James Sipe Fleming, William Patrick Fleming (dec. May 1952); m. Edward Muse Spruill, Nov. 6, 1968; 1 stepdaughter, Florence Spruill Mackie. BA, East Carolina U., 1939, MA, 1961. cert. secondary tchr. Tchr. Washington County Bd. Edn., Plymouth, NC, 1957—69. Chmn. math. dept. Plymouth High Sch., 1965-69; treas. Washington County Hosp. Aux., 1991-93, v.p., 1993-95. Active Plymouth City Coun., 1980-87; trustee Pettigrew Regional Libr., 1983-88; mem. Washington County Libr. Bd., 1983-92, chmn., 1985-88; mem. Bd. of Adjustments, Plymouth, 1989-2001; sec. vestry Grace Ch., 1981-84, vestry, 1981-84, 95-98; pres. Fortnightly Lit. Club, Chase City, Va., 1978-79. Named Outstanding Woman in Washington County, Washington County Coun. on Status of Women, 1988. Mem. NC Ret. Sch. Pers., Washington County Hist. Soc. (bd. dirs. 1987-2001), Delta Kappa Gamma (v.p. chpt. 1968-70, corr. sec. chpt. 1986-88). Democrat. Episcopalian.

SPRUILL, W. MURRAY, lawyer; b. Columbia, NC, Mar. 24, 1954; BS in Biology, E. Carolina U., 1976; PhD in Genetics, Molecular Biology, NC State U., 1981; JD, George Washington U., 1992. Bar: Va. 1992, NC 1996, registered: US Patent and Trademark Off. Sr. atty. Ciba-Geigy Corp.; patent examiner US Patent and Trademark Office, Washington; ptnr., chmn., biotech., pharmaceutical patent group, Research Triangle Alston & Bird LLP, Raleigh, NC. Frequent lectr. and author on biotech. and pharmaceutical patent law. Office: Alston & Bird LLP Ste 600 3201 Beechleaf Ct Raleigh NC 27604-1062 Office Phone: 919-862-2202. Office Fax: 919-862-2260. Business E-Mail: murray.spruill@alston.com.

SPRUNGER, KEITH L., historian, educator; b. Berne, Ind., Mar. 16, 1935; s. Arley and Lillian (Mettler) S.; m. Aldine Mary Slagell, June 13, 1959; children: David, Mary, Philip. BA, Wheaton Coll., 1957; MA, U. Ill., 1958, PhD, 1963. Tchr. Berne (Ind.) High Sch., 1958-60; Oswald H. Wedel prof. history Bethel Coll., N. Newton, Kans., 1963—2001. Author: Dutch Puritanism, 1982, The Learned Doctor William Ames, 1972, Voices Against War, 1973, Auction Catalogue of The Library of William Ames, 1988, Trumpets From The Tower, 1994, Campus, Congregation, and Community, 1997. Mem. Newton Historic Preservation Commn.; bd. dirs. Germantown Mennonite Historic Trust. Recipient Harbison award Danforth Found., 1972; fellow Social Sci. Rsch. Coun., 1969, Am. Coun. Learned Soc. fellow, 1976, Huntington Libr. fellow, 1982, 90; grantee Am. Philos. Soc., 1967, 1969, 83, The Netherlands Orgn. for Advancement of Pure Rsch., 1983. Fellow Pilgrim Soc.; mem. AAUP, Am. Hist. Assn., Am. Soc. Ch. History (coun. 1974-76), Conf. on Faith and History, Dutch Mennonite Hist. Cir. Mennonite. Avocation: book and postcard collecting. Home: 2412 Clg Ave North Newton KS 67117 Office: Bethel Coll 300 E 27th St North Newton KS 67117 Office Phone: 316-283-2500. Business E-Mail: sprunger@bethelks.edu.

SPRY, LESLIE ALLEN, nephrologist, director; b. Lexington, Nebr., May 26, 1951; s. Don Horton and Hulda Bertha Spry; m. Denise Jean Thielfoldt, June 25, 1977; children: Eric John, Nicole Ruth. MD, U. Nebr., Omaha, 1977. Intern Internal Medicine, U. Nebr. Affiliated Hosp., Omaha, 1977—80, residency, 1977—80; physician St. Louis U. Sch. Medicine, 1982—87, Lincoln Nephrology & Hypertension, 1987—. Med. dir. Dialysis Ctr. Lincoln, 1987—; chmn. Nat. Kidney Found., Pub. Policy Com., NYC, 2007—; pres. Nebr. Med. Assn., Lincoln, 2008—. Chmn. Commn. on Legislation and Govtl. Affairs, Nebr. Med. Assn., Lincoln, Nebr., 1996—2007. Recipient Pub. Health Recognition award, Lincoln Lancaster County Health Dept., 1999, Disting. Vol. Svc. award, Nat. Kidney Found. Nebr., 2007. Fellow: ACP, Am. Soc. Nephrology; mem.: AMA (del. 1987—2008), Internat. Soc. Nephrology, Nebr. Med. Assn. (pres. 2008—). Democrat. Lutheran. Avocations: racquetball, skiing. Office: Lincoln Nephrology & Hypertension 7441 O St Lincoln NE 68510 Office Fax: 402-484-5630.

SPUDICH, JOHN LEE, biochemist, molecular biologist, chemistry professor; PhD, Univ. Calif., Berkeley. Jane Coffin Childs Postdoctoral Fellow Harvard Univ.; prof., dept. biochemistry, molecular biology, microbiology and molecular genetics Univ. Tex. Houston Med. Sch., 1991—, and Robert A. Welch disting. chair in chemistry, 2002—, also dir., Ctr. for Membrane Biology, 2002—. Recipient Merit award, Nat. Inst. Gen. Med. Sci., NIH, 2003. Fellow: Am. Acad. Arts & Scis.; mem.: Am. Soc. Photobiology (past. pres.). Office: UT Houston Med Sch PO Box 20708 Houston TX 77225 Office Phone: 713-500-5473. Office Fax: 713-500-0545. Business E-Mail: John.L.Spudich@uth.tmc.edu.

SPUNGIN, CHARLOTTE ISABELLE, retired secondary school educator, writer; b. Providence, June 12, 1929; d. Abraham Spungin and Golde Morrison. BA, U. RI, 1951; MEd, U. Fla., 1966; EdS, Nova Southeastern U., Davie, Fla., 1981. Tchr., head dept. social sci. South Broward HS, Hollywood, Fla., 1962-90. Cons. Fla. Atlantic U., Boca Raton, 1985-90, U. Miami, Fla., 1980-90, Broward County Sch. Dist., Ft. Lauderdale, Fla., 1990-96; tchr. trainer Fla. Performance Measurement Sys.; instr. psychology and sociology Broward CC Co-author: (books) (with N. Tallent) Psychology: Understanding Ourselves and Others, 1977, (with H. Besner) Gay and Lesbian Students: Understanding Their Needs, 1995, Training for Professionals Who Work with Gays and Lesbians in Educational and Workplace Settings, 1997, (curriculum guides) Creativity with Bill Moyers, 1984, World of Difference, 1987, Holocaust Curriculum Guide for the State of Florida, 1990, The Holocaust Remembered, 1986, (monograph) Southeast Asian Monograph on Comparative Educational School Systems: Singapore, Malaysia and the Indonesian Islands, 1971. Cons., bd. dirs. Holocaust Documentation Ctr., North Miami, Fla., 1985-90; bd. dirs. Fla. Coun. for Social Studies, Orlando and Tallahassee, 1979-85. Recipient Spirit of Excellence award Miami Herald, 1985, Skretting award Fla. Coun. for Social Studies, Wilma Simmons Golden Svc. award, 1985, Outstanding Svc. in Mental Health award Fla. divsn. Nat. Assn. Mental Health, Woman of Yr. in Edn. award Women in Comm., 1990; Fulbright fellow, 1970, 76; scholar NSF, 1965. Mem. APA, ASCD, Nat. Coun. on Social Studies, Fla. Coun. for Social Studies, Phi Delta Kappa, Phi Alpha Theta. Democrat. Jewish. Avocations: travel, writing, reading. Office: PO Box 8833 Fort Lauderdale FL 33310-8833 Office Phone: 954-566-8288. Personal E-mail: spunbar@comcast.net.

SPUR, GÜNTER, engineering educator; b. Brunswick, Germany, Oct. 28, 1928; s. Wenzel and Martha (Held) S.; m. Maria Alberts. Student, Tech. U., Brunswick, Germany, 1948-54, DEng, 1960; degree (hon.), Catholic U., Leuven, Belgium, 1983, Tech. U. Chemnitz, 1986, Tech. U. Prague, 1991, Tech. U. Stankin, 1993, Beijing Inst. Technology, 1994, Tongji U., 1994, Tech. U. Cottbus, 1996, Tech. U. Berlin, 1998, U. Dortmund, 2000. Sci. asst. Tech. U., Berlin, 1956, prof. machine tool and prodn. tech., 1965—97. Recipient M. Eugene Merchant Mfg. medal, ASME, 1992, Sci. prize, German Technion Soc. Mem.: NAE USA, SME (hon.), Chinese Acad. Engring., Royal Acad. Engring. Gt. Britain, Swedish Acad. Engring., Internat. Rsch. Assn. Mechanic Prodn. Tech. (Schlesinger prize 2000), Assn. German Engrs. (chmn. Berlin dist., hon. ring, hon. medal, Grashof medal, Helmholtz medal 2006), Rotary Club. Home: Richard Strauss St 20 14193 Berlin Germany Office: Tech U Berlin Fraunhofer Inst for Production 10587 Berlin Germany Home Phone: 0049 0 30 826 4875; Office Phone: 0049 30 39006166. Business E-Mail: spur@ipk.fhg.de. E-mail: profspur@aol.com.

SPURGEON, DENNIS RAY, federal agency administrator, former manufacturing executive; b. Lake City, Iowa, Oct. 21, 1943; s. Merle Donald and Dorothy (Gidel) S.; m. Carrol Ann Malanoski, Feb. 19, 1966; children: Dennis Jr., Scott, Kimberly. BS, U.S. Naval Acad., 1965; SM in Nuclear Engring., MIT, 1969. Regional mgr. Gen. Atomic Co., Washington, 1973-75, exec. asst. to pres. San Diego, 1975-76; asst. dir. U.S. Energy Rsch. and Devel. Adminstrn., Washington, 1976-77; v.p. UNC Naval Products Div., Montville, Conn., 1977-78; pres. UNC Nuclear Industries, Richland, Wash., 1978-80; group v.p. UNC Inc., Falls Church, Va., 1980-85; chmn., CEO Swift Group LLC, Potomac, Md.; exec. v.p., COO USEC, Inc., 2001—03; asst. sec. for nuclear energy US Dept. Energy, Washington, 2006—. Chmn. Normco Contractors Inc., Morgan City, La., 1985—, NGS Enterprises Inc., Morgan City, 1985—. With USN, 1965-73. Office: US Dept Energy Forrestal Bldg 1000 Independence Ave SW Washington DC 20585*

SPURGEON, JIM D., dentist; DDS, U. Oklahoma. Cosmetic dentist Smile Solutions, Norman, Okla. Vol. dentist D-dent program, C.A.R.E. Mem.: ADA, Ctrl. Okla. Dental Assn., Am. Acad. Gen. Dentistry, US Dental Inst., Okla. Dental Assn., Am. Acad. Cosmetic Dentistry. Office: Smile Solutions 550 24th Ave SW Norman OK 73069 Office Phone: 405-364-7385. Office Fax: 405-447-8888.

SPURGEON, SARA LOUISE, literature and language professor; b. Topeka, Kans., Jan. 20, 1964; d. Leland Martin Spurgeon and Colleen June Spurgeon nee Ihla; m. Gregory Paul Roberts, Aug. 6, 1995; children: Seth Eugene Spurgeon Roberts, Ian Martin Spurgeon Roberts. BA, Coll. St. Catherine, St. Paul, 1987; MA, U. New Mex., Albuquerque, 1993; PhD, U. Ariz., Tucson, 2000. Vis. asst. prof. U. Ariz., 2000—05; assoc. prof. Tex. Tech. U., Lubbock, 2005—. Mem. Editl. Bd. Jour., Western Am. Lit., 2003—, Exec. Coun., Western Lit. Assn., 2005—, Adv. Bd., Western Writers Series, 2005—. Contbr. articles to profl. jours. Mem.: Assn. Study Lit. Environment, Modern Lang. Assn. Liberal. Avocations: running, hiking. Office: Tex Tech Univ Dept English ms 43091 Lubbock TX 79409 Business E-Mail: sara.spurgeon@ttu.edu.

SPURLOCK, MORGAN, television producer, film producer; b. Parkersburg, W.Va., Nov. 7, 1970; m. Alexandra Jamieson, May 3, 2006; 1 child, Laken James. BFA, NYU, 1993. Prodr.: (TV series) I Bet You Will, 2002; exec. prodr.: 30 Days, 2005—; (films) Class Act, 2006, Chalk, 2006, The Third Wave, 2007; prodr.: What Would Jesus Buy?, 2007; prodr., dir., writer: Super Size Me, 2004; Where in the World is Osama Bin Laden?, 2008; actor: Drive-Thru, 2006; author: Don't Eat This Book: Fast Food and the Supersizing of America, 2006. Mem.: ACLU.

SPURR, STEPHEN JOSIAH, economics professor; s. Robert Anton and Elizabeth Snider Spurr; m. Laura Wesley, Mar. 13, 1971; children: Nathaniel Wesley, Josiah Hopkins. JD, U. Mich., Ann Arbor, 1969; LLM in Taxation, NY U., NYC, 1972; PhD, U. Chgo., 1985. Vis. asst. prof. Carnegie-Mellon U., Pitts., 1985—87; prof., economics Wayne State U., Detroit, 1987—. Author: (book) Economic Foundations of Law; contbr. articles to profl. jours. Mem.: Am. Law and Economics Assn. Liberal. Unitarian Universalist. Office: Wayne State Univ 656 W Kirby Detroit MI 48202 Office Fax: 313-577-9564; Home Fax: 313-331-0244. Business E-Mail: sspurr@wayne.edu.

SPURRIER, STEVE (STEVEN ORR SPURRIER), college football coach; b. Miami Beach, Fla., Apr. 20, 1945; s. John Graham and Marjorie Spurrier; m. Jerrie Spurrier. Grad., U. Fla. Quarterback San Francisco 49'ers, 1967-75, Tampa Bay Buccaneers, 1976; quarterbacks coach U. Fla. Gators, 1978, Ga. Tech. Yellow Jackets, 1979; asst. coach Duke U. Blue Devils, 1980—82; head coach Tampa Bay Bandits, US Football League, 1983—85, Duke U. Blue Devils, 1987—89, U. Fla. Gators, Gainesville, 1990—2001, Wash. Redskins, 2002—03, U. South Carolina Gamecocks, Columbia, 2005—. Recipient Heisman trophy, 1966; named Atlantic Coast Conf. Coach of Yr., 1988, 1989, Southeastern Conf. Coach of Yr., 1990, 1991, 1994, 1995, 1996, 2005; named to Hall of Fame, U. Fla., Athletic Hall of Fame, Gator Football Ring of Honor, 2006. Mem.: Alpha Tau Omega. Achievements include being the only coach in Southeastern Conference history and one of only three coaches in major college history to lead a team to 12 consecutive seasons of nine or more wins (1990-2001); being the only coach in Southeastern Conference history to win eight conference games in a season for four straight years (1993-96); being the only coach in Southeastern Conference history and one of only two coaches in major college history to lead a team to six straight seasons of 10 or more wins (1993-1998). Office: Rex Enright Athletic Center 1300 Rosewood Drive Columbia SC 29208

SPYERS-DURAN, PETER, librarian, educator; b. Budapest, Hungary, Jan. 26, 1932; came to U.S., 1956, naturalized, 1964; s. Alfred and Maria (Almasi-Balogh) S-D; m. Jane F. Cumber, Mar. 21, 1964; children: Kimberly, Hilary, Peter. Certificate, Free U. Budapest, 1955; MA in L.S, U. Chgo., 1960; Ed.D., Nova S Ea. U., 1975. Profl. asst. libr. adminstrn. div. ALA, Chgo., 1961-62; assoc. dir. librs., assoc. prof. U. Wis., 1962-67; dir. librs., prof. Western Mich. U., 1967-70; dir. librs., prof. libr. sci. Fla. Atlantic U., 1970-76; dir. libr. Calif. State U., Long Beach, 1976-83; prof. libr. and info. sci., dir. libr. Wayne State U., Detroit, 1983-86, dean, prof. libr. and info. sci. program, 1986-95, dean and prof. emeritus, 1995—; cons. Spyers-Duran Assocs., 1995—; acting univ. libr. Nova Southeastern U., Ft. Lauderdale, Fla., 1996-97. Vis. prof. State U. N.Y. at Geneseo, summers 1969-70; cons. publs., libr. and info. scis.-related enterprises; chmn. bd. internat. confs., 1970—. Author: Moving Library Materials, 1965, Public Libraries - A Comparative Survey of Basic Fringe Benefits, 1967; editor: Approval and Gathering Plans in Academic Libraries, 1969, Advances in Understanding Approval Plans in Academic Libraries, 1970, Economics of Approval Plans in Research Libraries, 1972, Management Problems in Serials Work, 1973, Prediction of Resource Needs, 1975, Requiem for the Card Catalog: Management Issues in Automated Cataloging, 1979, Shaping Library Collections for the 1980's, 1981, Austerity Management in Academic Libraries, 1984, Financing Information Systems, 1985, Issues in Academic Libraries, 1985; mem. editorial bd. Jour. of Library Adminstration, 1989-95. Mem. Kalamazoo County Library Bd., 1969-70; Bd. dirs. United Fund. Reciient G. Flint Purdy award for outstanding contbns. Wayne State U., 1999. Mem. ALA, Mich. Libr. Assn., Internat. Fed. Libr. Assns., Assn. Info. Sci., Fla. Libr. Assn., Calif. Libr. Assn., Fla. Assn. Community Colls., Boca Raton C. of C., U. Chgo. Grad. Libr. Sch. Alumni Club (pres. 1973-75), Solinet Mich. Libr. Consortium (founder charter bd. mem. 1973—, bd. dirs. 1973-76), Detroit Area Libr. Network (pres. bd. dirs. 1985-95), Mich. Ctr. for Book (pres. 1988-89), Am. Soc. Info. Sci., Assn. Libr. and Info. Sci. Edn., Sago Point Homeowners Assn. (pres., bd. dirs. 2001-05), Bayou Club Cmty. Assn. (pres., bd. dirs. 2005—). Home: 7295 Maidencane Ct Largo FL 33777-4900 Office: Wayne State Univ Librs Detroit MI 48202 Business E-Mail: spyers-duran@wayne.edu, ae8249@wayne.edu.

SPYKER, LEOLA EDITH, missionary; b. Wallace, Mich., Mar. 15, 1925; d. Oscar Eugene Anderson and Edith Ragnhild Nelson; m. George Spyker, Feb. 16, 1951 (div. June 1967); children: Marilyn Joy, John George, Thomas Oscar, Sandra Lee. AA, N. Park U., Chgo., 1944; BA, Bob Jones U., Greenville, SC, 1947; postgrad. in Counseling, Seattle Pacific U., Seattle, Wash., 1969—70. Cert. in ESL Upton Coll., Pasadena, Calif., 1961, in French and Italian, Academia Uruapan, Michoacan, Mex. 1965, in Secondary Edn. Mich., Wis., Wash., Tex. Instr. King's Garden Sch., Seattle, 1969—71; lectr. Seminario El Calvario, El Carmen, Nuevo Leon, Mexico, 1971—74, 1977—80; lectr. in missionary outreach, anthropology, history, comparative religions Inst. Misionera Morelia, Michoacan, 1983—92; prof. U. Michoacan, Uruapan, Michoacan, Mexico, 1975—77, Mexico, 1982—84. Founder, dir. Casa Hogar La Esperanza, Uruapan, Michoacán, Mexico; conf. spkr. Vida Abundante, Morelia, Mexico, 1980—2003; coord. student groups to Honduras, Cuba, Nicaragua and Spain, 1995, 99, 2002; Spanish translator internat. conf. for Billy Graham, Amsterdam, 1996; worker refugee rehab. and outreach, Honduras, Nicaragua, 84, Honduras, Nicaragua, 86. Contbr. 40 articles to mission publs. Avocations: painting, travel, reading, ornithology. Home: PO Box 2050 2021 Harvey Dr Mcallen TX 78501 Office Phone: 956-682-6774. Personal E-mail: leolas@juno.com.

SQENZ, SYLVIA, counseling administrator; b. Chgo., June 17, 1960; d. Zeferino Sáenz and Maria Delua; m. Valentine Espiricueta, July 26, 1986; 1 child, Valentine Espiricueta IV. BS in Edn. magna cum laude, Pan Am. U., Edinburg, Tex., 1983; MS in Edn., Counseling, Guidance, U. North Tex., Denton, 1990. Cert. counselor Tex., tchr. Tex., lic. brain gym instr. 2008. Bilingual tchr. Mission Sch. Dist., Tex., Austin Ind. Sch. Dist., Tex., Irving Ind. Sch. Dist., Tex.; tchr. Spanish Mesquite Ind. Sch. Dist., Tex.; binlingual psychotherapist MHMR, Dallas, Galaxy Ctr., Garland, Tex.; elem. sch. counselor Grand Prairie Ind. Sch. Dist., Tex., Arlington Ind. Sch. Dist., Tex. Whole brain tutor, Dallas, Ft. Worth, 1998—; lectr. in field; bilingual storyteller Arlington Pub. Libr., 2002. Singer, songwriter: CD After the Rain Comes the Sun, 2003; author: Positive Choices, 1996, Teach to Reach, 2002, Choosing to Learn to Climb, 2002. Internat. singer, songwriter. Recipient 2d pl. singer/songwriter, Festival de la Cancion, 2004, Song of Yr., 2005, Honorable Mention Billboard award, 2008; finalist, Festival Cancion Latin Am., Calif., 2003, Christian/faith, UK Internat. Song Competition, 2007, Christian gospel, Song of Yr., 2007, 6th Pl., Am. Idol Underground, 2007, Internat. Song of Yr., 2008. Mem.: ASCAP, LA Music Network, Ft. Worth Songwriters Assn. Home: 2205 Walterbury Pl Arlington TX 76013 Office Phone: 682-365-2894. Personal E-mail: espiricuetasylvia@hotmail.com, sylviaads88@gmail.com.

SQUATRITO, DOMINIC J., judge; BA, Wesleyan U., 1961; JD, Yale U., 1965. Sr. judge US Dist. Ct. Conn., 1994—. Fulbright scholar, U. Florence, Italy, 1962. Office: US Dist Court 450 Main St 1st Fl Ste 108 Hartford CT 06103-3010 Office Phone: 860-240-3873.

SQUERI, LAWRENCE, history professor; b. NYC, July 13, 1942; s. Louis Squeri and Mary Marchini; m. Rosemarie Butler, Dec. 29, 1974; 1 child, Nicholas. BA, Fordham U., NYC, 1964; MA, Columbia U., NYC, 1965, Temple U., Phila., 1986; PhD, U. Pa., Phila., 1976. Prof. history Cheyney U., Pa., 1970—88, East Stroudsburg U., Pa., 1988—. Author: (book) Better in the Poconos: The Story of Pennsylvania's Vacationland, Pride and Promise: A Centennial History of East Stroudsburg University. Roman Catholic. Avocations: walking, reading, travel. Home: 122 N 5th St Stroudsburg PA 18360 Office: East Stroudsburg Univ 200 Prospect St East Stroudsburg PA 18301 Personal E-mail: lawrencesqueri@yahoo.com.

SQUERI, STEPHEN, diversified financial services company executive; BS, MBA, Manhattan Coll. Cons. Arthur Andersen & Co., 1981—85; mgmt. positions Am. Express, NYC, 1985—2000, pres. establishment services, U.S. & Canada, 2000—01, pres. global comml. card group, 2002—05, exec. v.p., CIO, 2005—. Office: Am Express Am Express Tower World Fin Ctr 200 Vesey St New York NY 10285*

SQUIBB, JOHN R., history professor; s. John W. and Veneta C. Squibb; m. Mary L. Rios, Oct. 15, 1994; children: Bradley T., Tanya M. Pounds, Tanum L. Smith, Teresa L. Bryant. PhD in History, U. Wis., Madison, 1992. Prof. Lincoln Land C.C., Springfield, Ill., 1970—2007, U. Ill., Springfield, 1973—2006. Divsn. chair social scis. Lincoln Land C.C., Springfield, 1976—91. Bd. dirs. Springfield Urban League, Ill., 1980—86; reviewer Nat. Social Sci. Assn., San Diego, 1990—94. Recipient Tchg. Excellence award, U. Tex. Austin, 1990, Bd. Trustees award, Lincoln Land C.C., 1996, Pearson Master Tchr. award, Lincoln Land C.C. Found., 2002; fellow, NEH, 1976, 1980, 1982. Baptist. Achievements include curriculum design and creation of courses such as Vietnam War, African-American History, and various problems courses. Avocations: travel, reading. Office Phone: 217-786-2287.

SQUIBB, SAMUEL DEXTER, chemistry professor; b. Limestone, Tenn., June 20, 1931; s. Benjamin Bowman and Lou Pearl S.; m. JoAnn Kyker, Dec. 15, 1951; children: Sandra Lavanne, Kevin Dexter. BS, E. Tenn. State U., 1952; PhD, U. Fla., 1956. Assoc. prof., dir. chemistry Western Carolina U., Cullowhee, NC, 1956-60; asst. prof., dir. chemistry Eckerd Coll., St. Petersburg, Fla., 1960-63, assoc. prof., 1963-64; prof. chemistry U. N.C., Asheville, 1964-94, prof. emeritus, 1994—, chmn. dept., 1964-94. Vis. prof. U. NC, Chapel Hill, 1976-81, 83-87, 92-95, Clemson U., SC, 1982; cons. So. Assn. Colls. and Schs., State of W.Va. Author: Experimental Organic Chemistry, 1972, Understanding Chemistry One, 1979, rev. 1990, Two, 1981, rev. 1991, Three, 1981, rev. 1992, Four, 1981, rev. 1992, Five, 1981, rev. 1989, Six, 1984, Chemistry One, 1976, rev. 1987, Two, 1980, rev. 1990, Experimental Chemistry One, 1976, rev. 1988, Two, 1981, rev. 1991; contbr. articles to profl. jours. Mem. Grose United Meth. Ch. Disting. Tchr. award U. N.C.-Asheville, 1983; S.D. Squibb Disting. Chemistry Lectureship U. N.C., Asheville, established 1997; named to We. Carolina Fedn. Square and Round Dancing Hall of Fame, 2001; recipient Pres.'s Svc. award, Folk, Round and Square Dancing Fedn. N.C., 2001. Fellow Am. Inst. Chemists (life, nat. publs. bd. 1988-92); mem. Am. Chem. Soc. (Charles H. Stone award Carolina Piedmont sect. 1979, Disting. Chemist award Western Carolinas sect. 1993, chmn. Tampa Bay subsect. 1963, Western Carolina sect. 1981, editor Periodic News Western Carolina sect. 1980-2007), NC Inst. Chemists (pres. 1977-79, sec. 1975-77, 85-91, Disting. Chemist award 1986), Skyland Twirlers Square Dance Club, Silver Spurs Advanced Square Dance Club, Jerry's Kids Advanced Square Dance Club, Skylarks Round Dance Club, Phi Beta Kappa.

SQUIER, DAVID LOUIS, manufacturing executive; b. Buffalo, Oct. 30, 1945; s. Clayton L. and Ruth H. Squier; m. Sue Sampson, Aug. 12, 1967; children: Jennifer, Allison. BS in Mech. Engring., Lehigh U., 1967; MBA, Wharton Sch., U. Pa., 1971. With mfg. mgmt. program GE, various cities, 1967-70; mgr. corp. planning Howmet Corp., Greenwich, Conn., 1971-73, mgr. corp. and bus. planning Muskegon, Mich., 1973-75, plant mgr. Hampton, Va., 1976-78, gen. mgr. Wichita Falls, Tex., 1979-82, v.p. Greenwich, 1983-87, sr. v.p., 1987-89, exec. v.p., 1989-91, COO, 1991-92, pres., CEO, 1992-2000, also bd. dirs., advisor, 2000—. Mem. rev. and prioritization bd. Iacocca Inst., Bethlehem, Pa., 1990—. Office: Howmet Corp 1 Misco Dr C Whitehall MI 49461-1755

SQUIER, JACK LESLIE, sculptor, retired art educator; b. Dixon, Ill., Feb. 27, 1927; s. Leslie Lee and Ruth (Barnes) S.; m. Jane Bugg, June 9, 1950. Student, Oberlin Coll., Ohio, 1945—46; BS, Ind. U., Bloomington, 1950; M.F.A., Cornell U., Ithaca, NY, 1952. Instr. Cornell U., 1952, asst. prof. art, 1958—61, assoc. prof., 1961—65, prof. art, 1965—2005, prof. emeritus, 2005—. Designer Howell Pottery Co., N.Y.C., 1953; account exec. Jamian Advt. Co., N.Y.C., 1954-58; asst. prof. U. Calif., Berkeley, 1960; mem. Internat. Assn. Art, UNESCO, 1964-72, mem. exec. com., 1966-69, v.p., 1969-72 One-man shows include Alan Gallery, N.Y.C., 1956, 59, 62, 64, White Mus., Cornell U., 1959, 68, Instituto de Arte Contemporaneo, Lima, Peru, 1963, Landau-Alan Gallery, N.Y.C., 1966, 69, Herbert F. Johnson Mus., Cornell Univ. (retrospective of work, 1953-93); exhibited in group shows at Mus. Modern Art, N.Y.C., 1957, Whitney Mus., N.Y.C., 1952, 54, 56, 58, 62, 67, 78, Hirshhorn Mus., Washington, 1978, Mus. Fine Arts, Boston, 1958, Chgo. Art Inst., 1960, Brussel's Worlds Fair, 1956, competition, Auschwitz, Poland, 1957, Albright-Knox Mus., Buffalo, 1968, Claude Bernard Gallery, Paris, 1957, Hanover Gallery, London, 1958; represented in permanent collections Mus. Modern Art, N.Y.C., Whitney Mus. Art, Hirshhorn Mus., Instituto de Arte Contemporaneo, Everson Mus., Syracuse, N.Y., Stanford U. Mus., St. Lawrence U. Mus., SUNY at Potsdam, Ithaca Coll., Johnson Mus. at Cornell U., Houston Mus., Hamilton Coll. Mus., Hood Mus.-Dartmouth (N.H.) U., Castellani Mus., Niagara U., N.Y., Fogg Mus., Harvard U., Cambridge; bronze garden piece at Fogg Mus./Harvard U., Conn. Conservancy; retrospective exhbn. Herbert F. Johnson Mus. Cornell U., 1993; work pub. in various, books, mags., newspapers, slide collections, catalogs. Served with AC USN, 1945-47.

SQUIRE, ANNE MARGUERITE, retired humanities educator; b. Amherstburg, Ont., Can., Oct. 17, 1920; d. Alexander Samuel and Coral Marguerite Park; m. William Robert Squire, June 24, 1943; children: Frances, Laura, Margaret. BA, Carleton U., Ottawa, 1972, BA with honors, 1974, MA, 1975; LLD (hon.), Carleton U., 1988; DD (hon.), United Theol. Coll., 1979, Queen's U., 1985. Cert. tchr., Ont. Adj. prof. Carleton U., 1975-82; sec. div. ministry personnel and edn. United Ch. Can., Toronto, 1982-85, moderator, 1986-88; ret., 1988. Author curriculum materials, 1959—; contbr. articles to profl. jours. Mem. bd. mgmt. St. Andrew's Coll., Saskatoon, Sask., 1982, Queens Theol. Coll., Kingston, Ont., 1999-2005; founding mem. Muslim-Christian Dialogue Group; patron MultiFaith Housing Initiative; hon. advisor Can. Ctr. for Progressive Christianity. Recipient Senate medal Carleton U., 1972. Mem. Can. Research Inst. for Advancement Women, Delta Kappa Gamma (pres. 1978-79). Mem. United Ch. Can. Office: 731 Weston Dr Ottawa ON Canada K1G 1W1 E-mail: a.squire@sympatico.ca.

SQUIRE, LARRY RYAN, neuroscientist, psychologist, educator; b. Cherokee, Iowa, May 4, 1941; s. Harold Walter and Jean (Ryan) S.; children: Ryan, Luke, Charls, Caroline. BA, Oberlin Coll., 1963; PhD in Psychology, MIT, 1968; postgrad., Albert Einstein Med. Coll., 1968-70. With U. Calif. San Diego (UCSD), 1970—, prof., 1981—; rsch. career scientist VA Med. Ctr., San Diego, 1980—; mem. faculty U. Calif. Irvine Ctr. Neurobiology of Learning & Memory, 1981—. Lectr. in field. Editor, author: Memory and Brain, 1987; co-author: Memory: From Mind to Molecules, 1999; editor Behavioral Neuroscience, 1990-95; mem. editl. adv. bd. numerous profl. jours.; contbr. articles to profl. jours., chpts. to books. Recipient Charles A. Dana Award for Pioneering Achievements in Health and Education, 1993, Disting. Sci. Contbn. award APA, Lashley prize Am. Philosophical Soc., McGovern award AAAS; William James fellow Am. Psychol. Soc. Mem. Nat. Acad. Scis., Am. Acad. Arts and Scis., Soc. Neurosci. (pres. 1994), Am. Philos. Soc., Inst. Medicine. Office: UCSD SDVAMC 3350 La Jolla Village Dr San Diego CA 92161 Office Fax: 858-552-7457. E-mail: lsquire@ucsd.edu.

SQUIRE, MOLLY ANN, organizational psychologist; b. Highland Park, Mich., Aug. 18; d. George Edward and Dorothy Laura (Molteni) Squirrell; m. Arthur Bruce Hanson, June 23, 1990; 1 child, Mark Arthur Hanson. AA, NYU, 1978; BS cum laude, U. LaVerne, 1980; MA, Claremont Grad. U., Calif., 1982; PhD, Pacific-Western U., 1991. Cert. cons. to mgmt. Health svcs. adminstr. health care delivery orgns., 1978-82; nat. dir. Huntington's Disease Rsch. Project, Calif., 1981-82; CEO Claremont Mgmt. Cons. (now Squire Trainers), LA, Calif., 1982—. Past statis. analyst to pres. LA City Coll.; past part-time instr. LA Trade Tech.; part-time instr. Glendale CC, 1994—96. Founding editor LASER; editor: BEACON newsletter, 1989—96; past editor Benezet Gazette, past editor yearbook So. Calif. Com. to Combat Huntington's Disease; contbr. articles to profl. jours. Lt. 78th Fraser Highland Regiment San Juan Capistrano Bn. Decorated Knight Templar of Jerusalem, Internat. br. Netherlands; recipient Cert. Appreciation, City of Ukiah, Calif., 1984, We. Square Dance Assn., 1986, Am. Heart Assn., 1990, So. Calif. Skeptics, 1987, Pacific Bell, 1990, Achievement award, No. Am. Women's Inner Circle, 1991, Cert. Appreciation, LA City Coll., 1995, Clan MacKenzie Soc. So. Calif., 1996, Award of Merit, BSA Dist., 2008; named Woman of Magic scholarship, 1997—; named a Krauthamer & Squire 'Thelma & Louise' Women's Scholarship, LA City Coll., 1993—; fellow, Claremont Grad. Sch., 1980—82. Mem.: ASTD, Soc. Indsl. and Orgnl. Psychologists, Nat. Bur. Cert. Cons., Assn. Psychol. Type, Pacific Coast Assn. Magicians (golden cir.), Soc. Am. Magicians (life Zinger award, Cert. Appreciation, Merit award 1991, 1994, Best Character Act 1994, Peller Meml. trophy 1994), Internat. Brotherhood Magicians (past pres. #254, sec., Best Mentalist trophy 1987, Cert. Appreciation, Blackstone Floating Ring), Arthurian Soc. Arthuret UK (life), Mensa (life; past proctor). Achievements include patents for bus. and health care products. Office: PO Box 41633 Los Angeles CA 90041-0633 Personal E-mail: 3hansons@sbcglobal.net.

SQUIRE, WALTER CHARLES, lawyer; b. NYC, Aug. 5, 1945; s. Sidney and Helen (Friedman) S.; m. Sara Jane Abamson; children: Harrison, Russell, Zachary, Andrew. BA, Yale U., 1967; JD, Columbia U., 1971. Bar: N.Y. 1971, U.S. Dist. Ct. (so. and ea. dists.) N.Y. 1975, U.S. Ct. Appeals (2d cir.) 1974, U.S. Supreme Ct. 1977. Ptnr. Jones Hirsch Connors & Bull P.C., NYC, 1986-98, Jacobson, Mermelstein & Squire, LLP, NYC, 1998—; prin. Squire & Co., LLC, NYC, 1998—. Bd. govs. Arthritis Found. N.Y., Inc., 1993-99; bd. dirs. MedicAlert Found., N.Y., 1990-99. Mem. ABA, N.Y. State Bar Assn., Assn. of Bar of City of N.Y., Internat. Bar Assn., Licensing Execs. Soc., Chartered Inst. Arbitrators (London), Am. Arbitration Assn. (arbitrator 1975-2000, mediator 1993—), Am. Acad. Hosp. Attys., Risk Ins. Mgmt. Soc. (lectr. 1983-84), AIDA Reinsurance & Ins. Arbitration Soc. (cert.). Office: Jacobson Mermelstein et al 52 Vanderbilt Ave New York NY 10017-3808 Office Phone: 212-697-1420. Business E-Mail: walter@jmslegal.com.

SQUIRES, ARTHUR MORTON, chemical engineer, educator; b. Neodesha, Kans., Mar. 21, 1916; s. Charles Loren and Vera Amber (Moore) S. AB with distinction in Chemistry, U. Mo., 1938; PhD, Cornell U., 1947. Design engr. M.W. Kellogg Co., NYC, 1942-46; asst. dir. process devel. Hydrocarbon Research, Inc., NYC, 1946-51, dir. process devel., 1951-59; cons. chem. process industries NYC, 1959-67; prof. chem. engring. CUNY, 1967-74, disting. prof., 1974-76, chmn. dept. chem. engring., 1970-73; Vilbrandt prof. chem. engring. Va. Poly. Inst. and State U., Blacksburg, 1976-82, disting. prof., 1978-86, disting. prof. emeritus, 1986—. Author: The Tender Ship, 1986; editor: (with D.A. Berkowitz) Power Generation and Environmental Change, 1971; contbr. articles to profl. jours.; patentee in field Mem. N.Y. Pro Musica, 1953-60 Fellow Am. Acad. Arts and Scis., AAAS; mem. ASME, NAE, AIChE (inst. lectr.), Am. Chem. Soc. (Henry H. Storch award 1973), Internat. Soc. for Human Ethology, Human Behavior and Evolution Soc., Sigma Xi, Tau Beta Pi Avocation: performing medieval and renaissance music. Home: 2710 Quincy Ct Blacksburg VA 24060-4124 Office: Va Poly Inst and State U Dept Chem Engring Blacksburg VA 24061 Home Phone: 540-951-8369. Business E-Mail: verasqu@vt.edu.

SQUIRES, JAMES A., rail transportation executive; Atty. Norfolk So. Corp., Va., 1992, sr. gen. counsel, 2002—03, v.p. law, 2003—04, sr. v.p. law, 2004—06, sr. v.p. fin. planning, 2006—07, exec. v.p. fin., 2007—, CFO, 2007—. Office: Norfolk So Corp Three Commercial Pl Norfolk VA 23510-2191 Office Phone: 757-629-2680.

SQUIRES, JOHN, publishing executive; b. Pocatelllo, Idaho; BA, U. Washington, 1981. Asst. circulation director People mag., 1989—92; consumer mktg. dir. Entertainment Weekly & Sports Illus. mags., 1992—96; pres. Entertainment Weekly, 1998—2002; sr. v.p. consumer mktg. Time Inc., NYC, 1996—98, pres., sports & leisure grp., 2004—05, co-COO, 2005, pres. Sports Illus., exec. v.p., 2002—. Bd. dirs. Audit Bur. Circulations, 2001—. Named to Direct Mktg. Assn. Circulation Coun. Circulation Hall of Fame, 2003. Mem.: Mag. Publishers America (treas. 2007—). Office: Sports Illustrated 1271 Ave of Americas New York NY 10020-1300 Office Phone: 212-522-5600.*

SQUIRES, KATHLEEN ELAINE, internal medicine educator; b. Sydney, May 24, 1953; came to U.S., 1965; d. Samuel Arthur and Jean (Calder) S.; m. Matthew H. Carabasi, Apr. 5, 1952. BA in Classics, Princeton U., 1974; MD, Med. Coll. Pa., 1981. Diplomate Am. Bd. Internal Medicine, Am. Bd. Infectious Diseases. Intern ob-gyn., internal medicine Med. Coll. of Pa., 1981-82, resident internal medicine, 1982-84, chief resident, 1984-85; fellowship infectious diseases Cornell Med. Coll., 1985-88; asst. prof. medicine Cornell U. Med. Coll., NYC, 1988—. Contbr. articles and abstracts to med. jours. Mem. AMA, ACP, Am. Fedn. Clin. Rsch., Am. Soc. Internal Medicine, Med. Soc. State N.Y., Infectious Diseases Soc. of Am., Alpha Omega Alpha.

SQUIRES, NINA GRACE, artist; b. Point Fortin, Trinidad and Tobago, Mar. 25, 1929; came to U.S., 1986; d. Oswald De Freitas and Maude Rebecca (Bowen) Callender; m. George William Lamming, Mar. 29, 1950 (div. Apr. 1961); children: Gordon William, Natasha Anna Lamming-Lee; m. Cecil Noel Squires, Feb. 23, 1963; children: Ian Patrick, Richard St. Clair. Entrance to Brit. Libr. Assn., Ea. Caribbean Libr. Sch., Port of Spain, Trinidad, 1949; student in art, Hammersmith Sch., London, 1954, Ctrl. Sch. Arts and Crafts, 1954, Montgomery Coll., Takoma Park, Md., 1992-93. Libr. asst., cataloger Trinidad Pub. Libr., Port of Spain, 1949-51; clerical asst. High Commn. for India, London, 1952-54; libr. dir. U.S. Info. Svc. and State Dept., Port of Spain, 1955-65, specialist cultural affairs, ednl. cons., 1965-85; receptionist various depts. U. Miami, Fla., 1986-91; assistance info. mgr. EPA, Nat. Caucus and Ctr. on Black Aged, Inc., Washington, 1993—2001. Owner, dir. Nina's Art Gallery, Port of Spain, 1962-63. One-woman shows include Nat. Mus. and Art Gallery, Trinidad and Tobago, 1975, The Art Mart Gallery, Diego Martin, Trinidad, 1987, Takoma Park Pub. Libr., Md., 1993, Orgn. Am. States, Washington, 1998; exhibited in group shows Commonwealth Art Inst., London, 1962, Scotland, 1974, Inst. Cultura Hispanic, Madrid, 1963, Sao Paulo Bienal, Brazil, 1963, 73, 75, Carifesta, Guyana, 1972, Jamaica, 1976, Barbados, 1981, Museo de Bellas Artes de Caracas, Venezuela, 1977, Clark Humanities Mus., Calif., 1986, Paxtutent Art League, Md., 1994, Dundalk Gallery, Md., 1996, Smithsonian's Anacostia Mus., 1999, IADB, Washington, 2002, Art Soc. Trinidad & Tobago, 2006, Art Trinidad & Tobago, Wash., Around the World Open House, Coppin State U., Balt., Westworth Studio, Balt., 2007; work documented in Internat. Rev. African Am. Art, Hampton U., 1989, 98; represented in Nat. Mus. & Others, permanent collections Trinidad and Tobago Govt., U. W.I., Trinidad Hilton Hotel, Dictionary of Caribbean Biography, 1969-70, numerous others. Judge Trinidad Carnival Celebrations, Port of Spain, 1957-84; mem. project for arts, Washington, 1997; vol. Bapt. Hosp., Miami, 1991, Montgomery Pub. Schs., 1992-93, S.W. Pub. Libr., Washington, 1993-95. Recipient 2d place prize UN Ednl. Sci. and Cultural Orgn., Port of Spain, 1972. Mem. Trinidad Art Soc., Smithsonian Instn. (nat. assoc.). Episcopalian. Avocations: reading, music, sports. Personal E-mail: ninagrace29@yahoo.com.

SQUIRES, RICHARD FELT, research scientist; b. Sparta, Mich., Jan. 15, 1933; s. Monas Nathan and Dorothy Lois (Felt) S.; m. Else Saederup, 1 child, Iben. BS, Mich. State U., 1958; postgrad., Calif. Inst. Tech., 1958-61. Rsch. biochemist Pasadena Found. for Med. Rsch., 1961-62; chief biochemistry sect. rsch. dept. A/S Ferrosan, Soeborg, Denmark, 1963-78; neurochemistry group leader CNS Biology sect. Lederle Labs. div. Am. Cyanamid Co., Pearl River, NY, 1978-79; prin. rsch. scientist The Nathan S. Kline Inst. for Psychiat. Rsch., Orangeburg, NY, 1979-2000, ret., 2000. Contbr. over 85 articles to profl. jours.; patentee in field. Nat. Inst. Neurol. and Communication Disorders and Stroke grantee, 1981-84. Mem. Soc. Neurosci., Collegium Internat. Neuro-Psychopharmacologicum, Internat. Soc. Neurochemistry, Am. Soc. Neurochemistry, Am. Soc. Biochemistry and Molecular Biology, Am. Soc. Pharmacology and Exptl. Therapeutics. Home: 861 Laugenour Ct Woodland CA 95776-4911 Personal E-mail: else_dick@hotmail.com.

SQUIRES, WILLIAM RANDOLPH, III, lawyer; b. Providence, Sept. 6, 1947; s. William Randolph and Mary Louise (Gress) S.; children: Shannon, William R. IV, Mayre Elisabeth, James Robert. BA in Econs., Stanford U., 1969; JD, U. Tex., 1972. Bar: Wash. 1973, U.S. Dist. Ct. (we. dist.) Wash. 1973, U.S. Dist. Ct. (ea. dist.) Wash. 1976, U.S. Ct. Appeals (9th cir.) 1976, U.S. Supreme Ct. 1976, U.S. Ct. Fed. Claims 1982. Assoc. Oles, Morrison, Rinker, Stanislaw & Ashbaugh, Seattle, 1973-78; ptnr., chmn. litig. group Davis Wright Tremaine, Seattle, 1978-97; mem. Summit Law Group, Seattle, 1997—2007, chmn., 2005—07; of counsel Corr Cronin Michelson Baumgardner & Preece, Seattle, 2007—. Fellow Am. Coll. Trial Lawyers; mem. ABA, Internat. Bar Assn., Wash. State Bar Assn., King County Bar Assn., Wash. Athletic Club, Rainier Club (Seattle). Episcopalian. Office: Corr Cronin Michelson Baumgardner and Preece 1001 Fourth Ave Ste 3900 Seattle WA 98154 Home: 1622 35th Ave Seattle WA 98122-3411 Office Phone: 206-652-8658. Business E-Mail: rsquires@corrcronin.com.

SREENIVAS, MYTHELI, history professor; BA, Yale U., New Haven; PhD, U. Pa., Phila. Asst. prof. Ohio State U., 2005—. Author: (book) Wives, Widows, and Concubines: The Conjugal Family Ideal in Colonial India (Joseph W. Elder prize, Indian Social Scis., 2006).

SRERE, BENSON M(ORTIMER), communications executive, consultant; b. Rock Island, Ill., Aug. 13, 1928; s. Jacob H. and Margaret (Weinstein) S.; m. Betty Ann Cerruti, June 20, 1957; children: David Benson, Anne Michele, Peter John. BA magna cum laude, U. So. Calif., 1949. Newsman U.P., LA, 1948-56; assoc. editor Good Housekeeping mag., NYC, 1956-59, sr. editor, 1959-67, asst. mng. editor, dir. spl. publs. div., 1967-68, mng. editor, 1968-72, exec. editor, v.p., 1972-75, v.p., editorial dir., 1975-76; v.p., gen. mgr. King Features Syndicate, 1976-81; v.p. Hearst Metrotone News, 1976-81; exec. asst. to pres. Hearst Corp., 1981—, v.p., 1983-94. Dir. Hearst/ABC Video Svcs., Hearst/ABC Viacom Entertainment Svcs., A&E Cable Network, Lifetime Cable Network, 1980-94. Trustee Optometric Center of NY Found., 1978-79. Served with U.S. Army, 1950-52. Mem. Soc. Profl. Journalists, Phi Beta Kappa, Phi Kappa Phi, Phi Eta Sigma. Home: 11 Lafayette Ct Greenwich CT 06830-5324

SRICHAI-PARSIA, MONVADI BARBARA, cardiologist, educator; d. Prakob and Marasri Srichai; m. Sam S. Parsia; children: Dominic Parsia, Zachary Parsia. BS, MIT, Cambridge, 1992; MD, Johns Hopkins Sch. Medicine, Balt., 1996. Cert. Am. Bd. Internal Medicine, 1999, in cardiovascular disease 2002, Am. Soc. Nuc. Cardiology, 2004, Nat. Bd. Echocardiography, 2005. Asst. prof. NY U. Sch. Medicine, 2004—. Co-dir. Advanced Cardiovasc. Imaging Fellowship, NYC, 2007—. Fellow: Am. Coll. Cardiology; mem.: Working Group Cardiovasc. Magnetic Resonance ESC, Soc. Cardiovasc. Magnetic Resonance, Soc. Cardiovasc. Computed Tomography, Am. Heart Assn. (Melvin Judkins Young Investigator award 2004, Scientist Devel. award 2005—). Office: NY Univ Sch Medicine 530 First Ave HCC-C48 New York NY 10016 Business E-Mail: srichai@alum.mit.edu.

SRIDHAR, NIGAMANTH, engineering educator; b. Chennai, Tamil Nadu, India, Oct. 13, 1976; s. Sridharan Devarajan and Mythili Sridharan; m. Divya Sridhar, June 4, 2004. PhD, Ohio State U., Columbus, 2004. Asst. prof. Cleve. State U., 2004—. Recipient Career award, NSF, 2008—. Mem.: Assn. Computing Machinery. Office: Cleveland State Univ 1960 E24th St SH 332 Cleveland OH 44115

SRIDHARAN, ARVIND, engineer; s. Sridharan Krishnaswamy Akkor and Pankajavalli Sridharan. BTech, Indian Inst. Tech., Chennai, 1999; MS, U. Notre Dame, Ind., 2001, PhD, 2005. Sr. asst. engr. Seagate Tech., Longmont, Colo., 2005—07, staff engr., 2007—. Contbr. articles to profl. jours., chapters to books. Fellowship, Dept. Math., U. Notre Dame, 2003—04. Mem.: IEEE. Business E-Mail: arvind.sridharan@seagate.com.

SRIHARI, VINOD HIREMAGALUR, psychiatrist; b. Madras, Tamil Nadu, India, Aug. 26, 1972; s. H. N. and Vidya Srihari; m. Shipra Bunjun, Aug. 8, 2001; 1 child, Karun. MD, U. Rochester, NY, 1998. Diplomate Am. Bd. Psychiatry and Neurology, 2005. Asst. prof. Yale U. Sch. Medicine, New Haven, 2005—08. Office: Yale Univ Sch of Medicine 34 Park St CMHC New Haven CT 06519

SRIKRISHNAN, THAMARAPU, cancer research scientist, biophysicist; b. Tirupathi, India, Aug. 2, 1943; came to U.S., 1974; d. T.V. Desikachary and T. Chellammal; m. Mythili Srikrishnan, Aug. 26, 1971; children: Ananth, Bharath. Diploma in French, Madras U., India, 1962, diploma in German, 1961; M. in Physics, Presidency Coll., Madras, 1964; PhD in Biophysics, U. Madras, 1969. Jr. rsch. fellow U. Madras, 1964-65, sr. rsch. fellow, 1966-68, postdoctoral fellow, 1968-70, U. Bern (Switzerland), 1971-73, Swiss Fed. Inst. Tech., Zurich, Switzerland, 1973-74; asst. rsch. prof. SUNY, Buffalo, 1982—; prof. Niagara U., Niagara Falls, N.Y., 1985—. Contbr. chpts. to Biomolecular Stereodynamics, 1981, Conformation in Biology, 1982, Molecular Structure of Biological Activity, 1981; contbr. numerous articles and abstracts to profl. jours. Recipient Proficiency Prize in physics Vivekananda Coll., Madras, 1961. Mem. AAAS, Am. Crystallographic Assn., N.Y. Acad. Sci., Biophys. Soc., Am. Chem. Soc. Hindu. Achievements include research on intercalation of water molecules between nucleic acid bases and their geometry, on the characterization of some Cyclolentane Dimers synthesized. Office: Roswell Park Cancer Inst 666 Elm St Buffalo NY 14263-0001

SRIKUMAR, RAMAKRISHNAN, microbiologist, researcher; arrived in Can., 1984, naturalized, 1989; BSc, Concordia U., Montreal, Can., 1988; PhD, McGill U., Montreal, Can., 1995. Postdoctoral fellow Queen's U., Kingston, Ont., Canada, 1996—2001; scientist Targanta Therapeutics Inc, St-Laurent, Que., Canada, 2002—05, Allergan, Irvine, Calif., 2005—. Contbr. articles to profl. jours. Recipient Vector Labs. Young Investigator award, Am. Soc. Microbiology, 2000; Postdoctoral fellowship, Natural Scis. and Engring. Rsch. Coun. Can., 1996—98, Can. Insts. Health Rsch., 1998—99, Kinsmen fellowship, Can. Cystic Fibrosis Found., 1998—99, Indsl. Rsch. fellowship, Natural Scis. and Engring. Rsch. Coun. Can., 2003—05. Mem.: Parenteral Drug Assn., Am. Chem. Soc., Am. Soc. Microbiology (Vector Labs. Young Investigator award 2000). Achievements include diverse experience in antibacterial research in both academic and industrial settings; research in bacterial efflux-mediated multidrug resistance; bacterial physiology including membrane permeability; microbiological safety of pharmaceutical products. Home: 16 Gretchen Ct Aliso Viejo CA 92656 Business E-Mail: srikumar_ramakrishnan@allergan.com.

SRINIVASA, NARAYAN, research scientist; s. Solamalai Appan Srinivasan; m. Bharati Manda, May 27, 2005; children: Vikram Prasad, Nisha, Nikita. PhD, U. Fla., Gainesville, 1994. Fellow Beckman Inst. Advanced Sci. & Tech., Urbana, Ill., 1994—97; mem. tech. staff HRL Labs. LLC, Malibu, Calif., 1998—2000, scientist, 2000—. Contbr. articles to numerous profl. jours. Donor St. Jude's Children's Hosp., Ohio, 2005—; blood donor ARC, Thousand Oaks, Calif. Recipient fellowship, Beckman Inst., U. Ill., 1994—97, HRL New Inventor award, HRL Labs. LLC, 1999, HRL Disting. award, 1999—2003, 2005—06. Mem.: IEEE, Internat. Neural Network Soc. Achievements include patents in field. Office: HRL Labs LLC 3011 Malibu Canyon Rd Malibu CA 90265 Business E-Mail: nsrinivasa@hrl.com.

SRINIVASA, VEMURU R., engineering educator, researcher; arrived in U.S., 1986; s. Prabhakara R. and Nirmala Vemuru; m. Lakshmi G. Gali, July 12, 1965; children: Lekha S. Vemuru, Priyanka S. Vemuru. BSEE, Indian Inst. Tech., Madras, India, 1984, MSEE, 1986; PhD, U. Toledo, 1991. Asst. prof. City Coll., CUNY, NYC, 1991—2001. Cons. Anadigics, Inc, Warren, NJ, 1996—2001. Home: 25969 Wood Creek Ct Perrysburg OH 43551 Office: Ohio Northern University Dept ECE & CS 525 S Main St Ada OH 45810 Office Fax: 419-772-2404. Business E-Mail: s-vemuru@onu.edu.

SRINIVASAGUPTA, DEEPAK, chemical engineer, researcher; s. Ranganayaki Sanji and Srinivasa Gupta Aravela. Bachelor of Tech. with honors, Indian Inst. Tech., Kharagpur, West Bengal, 1998; MS, Washington U., St. Louis, 2001, DSc, 2002. Cert. in lab. safety, U. South Fla., Tampa, 2003, in cleanroom safety, U. South Fla., Tampa, 2003, in high pressure gas cylinder safety, U. South Fla., Tampa, 2003, in personal protection equipment, U. South Fla., Tampa, 2003, in hazard comm., U. South Fla., Tampa, 2004, in workers compensation for suprs., U. South Fla., Tampa, 2004, in solid edge fundamentals, Pella Corp., 2005. Engr. Bhoruka Gases Ltd., Bangalore, Karnataka, India, 1997; testing engr. Aspen Tech. Inc., Cambridge, Mass., 2000; grad. rsch. and tchg. asst. Wash. U., Saint Louis, Mo., 1998—2002; post-doctoral rsch. assoc. U. South Fla., Tampa, 2003—04, vis. rsch. asst. prof., 2004; sr. composite process engr. Pella Corp., Murray, Ky., 2004—. Lectr. in field. Author: (literary column) International Policy for the 21st Century, Do Appearances Matter, Judicial Activism: Self-serving and Ill-thought?; contbr. articles to profl. jours. Mentor Upward Bound, Murray, Ky., 2005; webmaster Grad. Professsional Coun., Wash. U., Saint Louis, Mo., 1999—2000; web designer Dept. Chem. Engring., Wash. U., Saint Louis, 1999—2000. Recipient Best Hall Coun. Mem. award, Indian Inst. Tech., 1995-1996, Prem Internat. Award, AVOPA, 1998; fellow, Dept. Chem. Engring., Wash. U., 1998-2000, Boeing McDonnell Found., Wash. U., 2000-2002; Nat. Talent Search Scholarship, Govt. of India, 1992-1998. Mem.: Am. Chem. Soc., IEEE, AIChE (AIChE Process Devel. Division's Student Paper Award 2004), Am. Radio Relay League, World Wildlife Fund, Murray State U. Amateur Radio Club (assoc.), Mensa, Tau Beta Pi, Sigma Xi (life). Achievements include invention of time-stamped model predictive control algorithm; research in sensor fault detection. E-mail: deepu134@gmail.com.

SRINIVASAN, ASHA, music educator, composer; d. Venkataraman and Lalitha Srinivasan; m. Andrew Cole, July 2, 2006. MusB, Goucher Coll., Balt., 2001; MusM in Theory Pedagogy, Johns Hopkins U., Balt., 2003, MusM in Computer Composition, 2004; MusD, U. Md., Coll. Pk., 2008. Lectr., music theory, peabody conservatory Johns Hopkins U.; instr., theory Peabody Prep. Music, Balt., 2002—05; instr., electronic music Balt. Sch. Arts, 2003—05; adj. faculty, electronic music Loyola Coll., Balt., 2004; instr., music theory U. Md., 2005; adj. faculty, music theory Goucher Coll., 2007—08; asst. prof. music Lawrence U., Appleton, Wis., 2008—. Composer: By the River Near Savathi (BMI's 1st Ann. Women, 2006), Kalpitha (Walsum Competition prize, 2006), Alone Dancing (2nd prize, 2004), Falling:Samsaaram, Bapu. Recipient Marvin Perry award, Goucher Coll., 1997—2001, Doris Sirkis Himelfarb 36 Endowed prize, 2001, Ruth Blaustein Rosenberg prize, Peabody Conservatory Music, 1998; Career Devel. grant, 2002—04. Mem.: Am. Composers Forum, Soc. Composers Inc., Soc. Electro-Acoustic Music (US), Pi Kappa Lambda, Phi Beta Kappa. Business E-Mail: asha.srinivasan@lawrence.edu.

SRINIVASAN, AVINASH, science educator; b. Kolar Gold Fields, Karnataka, India, June 2, 1977; s. Srinivasan Saragoor Venkatsubbaiah and Nagamani Srinivasan; m. Archana Gupta, May 6, 2005. BS in Engring., U. Mysore, India, 1999; MS in Computer Sci., Pace U., NYC, 2003; D, Fla. Atlantic U., Boca Raton, 2008. Grad. tech. trainee Reva Electric Car Co. Pvt. Ltd., Bangalore, Karnataka, 1999—2000; rsch. exec. Feed Back Bus. Consulting Svcs. Pvt. Ltd., Bangalore, 2000—01; grad. asst. Pace U., Pleasantville, NY, 2001—03; tchg. asst. adj. instr. rsch. asst. Fla. Atlantic U., Boca Raton, 2004—08; rsch. asst. Motorola Inc., Plantation, Fla., 2006—08; asst. prof. computer forensics Bloomsburg U. Pa., 2008—. Contbr. articles to profl. jours. Active mem. Sri Sathya Sai Orgn., USA, 2004—. Mem.: IEEE. Office: Bloomsburg Univ Penn 227 Ben Franklin Hall 400 E 2nd St Bloomsburg PA 17815 Office Fax: 570-389-3599. Business E-Mail: avinash@bloomu.edu.

SRINIVASAN, GANESAN, molecular biologist, educator; b. Thanjavur, Tamil Nadu, India, June 11, 1958; came to the U.S., 1982; s. Srinivasan Subramaniam and Jayalakshmi Srinivasan; m. Chandra Rajagopalan, July 7, 1985. BS in Chemistry, U. Madras, India, 1978, MS in Biochemistry, 1981; PhD, U. Md., 1986. Jr. rsch. fellow Protein Rsch. Unit Loyola Coll., Madras, 1981-82; teaching asst. U. Md., Baltimore County, 1982-86, postdoctoral fellow Balt., 1986-87, U. Tex. Med. Br., Galveston, 1988-90, asst. prof., 1991—. Contbr. articles to profl. jours. Grantee Am. Heart Assn., 1991-93. Mem. Endocrine Soc., Sigma Xi. Hindu. Avocations: politics, photography, tennis, philosophy, astrology. Office: U Tex Med Br 607 Basic Science Bldg Galveston TX 77555-0001

SRINIVASAN, RAGHAVAN, engineering educator; b. Villupuram, India, Mar. 16, 1967; s. Raghavan and Varija (Krishnamachari) R.; m. Srimathy Gopalan, Nov. 7, 1994. B Tech., Indian Inst. Technology, Madras, 1988; MS, U. Va., 1991; PhD, U. Calif., Davis, 1996. Engr.-in-tng., Calif. Rsch. asst. U. Va., Charlottesville, 1988-90; rsch. engr. Inst. Transp. Studies/Univ. Calif., Davis, 1990-96; asst. prof. Dowling Coll., Oakdale, N.Y., 1996—. Mem. com. Transp. Rsch. Bd., Washington, 1997—; participant and presenter in field at profl. confs. Contbg. author: Ergonomics and Safety of Intelligent Driver Interfaces, 1997; contbr. articles to profl. jours. U.S. Transp. fellow Transp. Ctr. U. Calif. and U.S. Dept. Transp., 1990-92. Mem. Soc. Automotive Engrs., Human Factors and Ergonomics Soc. (assoc.), Inst. Transp. Engrs. (assoc.), Am. Soc. Civil Engrs. (assoc.). Achievements include being a lead rsch. engr. in $1 million project to evaluate in-vehicle ino. systems; conducted one of the earliest studies to evaluate head-up route guidance displays in cars, detailed rsch. on problems of older drivers at intersections; principal investigator on evaluation of graduated driver licensing system in New Jersey, and study of traffic flow and safety impacts of 55 mph and 65 mph speed limits; co-investigator project to evaluate economic impact of investment in transportation infrastructure. Office: Dowling Coll Sch of Avia & Transp Oakdale NY 11769

SRINIVASAN, RANGASWAMY, chemical physicist; b. Madras, India, Feb. 28, 1929; came to U.S., 1953; s. K. Rangaswamy. BSc with honors, Madras U., India, 1949; PhD, U. So. Calif., 1956. Mgr., rsch. T.J. Watson Rsch. Ctr. IBM, Yorktown Heights, NY, 1961-90; chief exec. officer UV Tech Assocs., Ossining, NY, 1990—. Vis. rsch. prof. chemistry Ohio State U., Columbus, 1966-67, Wellman Lab., Mass. Gen. Hosp., Boston, 1987-89, Columbia-Presbyn. Med. Ctr., N.Y.C., 1984-90. Editor: (books) Organic Photochemical Syntheses, Vol. 1., 1972, Vol. 2, 1976; contbr. over 200 articles to profl. jours. Guggenheim fellow, 1966; recipient award for creative invention Am. Chem. Soc., 1997, Essalen award for chemistry in the pub. interest, 1997, prize Rank Found., 2009. Fellow AAAS, Am. Physical Soc. (Biol. Physics prize 1998), NY Acad. Scis., Am. Soc. Laser Medicine and Surgery; mem. Nat. Acad. Engring. (Inventor's Hall of Fame 2002), Am. Inst. Physics (Indsl. Applications prize 2003), Optical Soc. Am. (Wood prize 2004). Achievements include invention of Ablative Photodecomposition, a laser technique for removal of microscopic thickness of organic matter such as plastics (of use in microelectronics) or tissue (of use in LASIK eye surgery).

SRINIVASAN, RENGASWAMY, research scientist; s. Narayanaswamy and Rajalakshmi Rengaswamy; m. Uma Mahalakshmi Ramachandran; children: Lakshminarayan (Ram), Shyam. PhD, Indian Inst. Sci., 1978. Rsch. assoc. Georgetown U., Washington, 1983—87; profl. staff scientist Applied Physics Lab. Johns Hopkins U., Laurel, Md., 1987—. Lectr. Indian Inst. Tech., Bombay, 1978—83. Recipient Inventor of Yr., Office Tech. Transfer, Applied Physics Lab., Johns Hopkins U., 2008. Mem.: Electrochem. Soc. Home: 3616 Chateau Ridge Dr Ellicott City MD 21042-4814 Office: Applied Physics Lab 11100 Johns Hopkins Rd Laurel MD 20723-6099

SRINIVASAN, SOUNDARARAJAN, engineer, researcher; s. Ramanuja Soundararaja and Lakshmi Srinivasan. BS in Engring., U. Madras, Chennai, Tamil Nadu, 1999; PhD, Ohio State U., Columbus, 2006. Engr. projects Eurotherm Del India Ltd., Chennai, 1999—2000; grad. rsch. assoc. Ohio State U., 2001—06; rsch. engr. Robert Bosch LLC, Pittsburgh, 2006—. Contbr. articles to profl. jours. Grad. fellow, Ohio State U., 2000, Travel grant, NSF, 2004. Mem.: IEEE, Internat. Speech Comm. Assn. (founding mem. 2005—06). Office: Robert Bosch LLC 2 NorthShore Ctr Ste 320 Pittsburgh PA 15212

SRINIVASAN, SRI, lawyer; AB with honors, Stanford U., Calif., 1989; MBA, Stanford U. Bus. Sch., 1995; JD, Stanford U. Law Sch., 1995. Bar: DC. Law clk. Hon. Sandra Day O'Connor US Supreme Ct., Washington; law clk. Hon. J. Harvie Wilkinson III US Ct. Appeals (4th cir.); Bristow fellow Office of the Solicitor Gen., Washington, 2002—07; ptnr. appellate & complex litig., hiring ptnr. O'Melveny & Myers LLP, Washington, 2007—. Contbr. articles to profl. jours. Recipient Award for Excellence in Furthering the Interests US Nat. Security, US Atty. Gen., 2003, Award for Excellence, Sec. of Def., 2005; named one of 50 Most Influential Minority Lawyers in America, Nat. Law Jour., 2008. Office: O'Melveney & Myers LLP 1625 Eye St NW Washington DC 20006 Office Phone: 202-383-5232. Office Fax: 202-383-5414. Business E-Mail: ssrinivasan@omm.com.*

SRINIVASAN, VEDANTH, engineer; s. Srinivasan Rajagopalan and Sucheta Srinivasan. PhD, U. Ky., Lexington, 2006. Multiphase devel. engr. AVL Powertrain Engring. Inc, Plymouth, Mich., 2007—. Travel fellowship, Internat. Conf. Liquid Atomization & Spray Sys., 2006. Mem.: Indian Student Assn. (pres. 2003—04). Achievements include patents pending for devices for atomizing liquids; research in numerical simulation of liquid jet breakup using VOF methods.

SRINIVASAN, VENKATARAMAN, marketing and management educator; b. Pudukkottai, Tamil Nadu, India, June 5, 1944; came to U.S., 1968; s. Annaswamy and Jambagalakshmi Venkataraman; m. Sitalakshmi Subrahmanyam, June 30, 1972; children: Ramesh, Mahesh. B Tech., Indian Inst. Tech., Madras, India, 1966; MS, Carnegie-Mellon U., 1970, PhD, 1971. Asst. engr. Larsen & Toubro, Bombay, 1966-68; asst. prof. mgmt. and mktg. U. Rochester, NY, 1971-73, assoc. prof. NY, 1973-74, Stanford (Calif.) U., 1974-76, prof., 1976-82, dir. PhD program in bus., 1982-85, Ernest C. Arbuckle prof. mktg. and mgmt. sci., 1982—2003, Adams disting. prof. mgmt., 2003—; mktg. area coord. Stanford U., 1976—78, 1988—93, 2000—03. Mem. bd. acad. trustees Mktg. Sci. Inst., 2004—; cons. in field. Mem. editl. bd. Jour. Mktg. Rsch., 1988—, Mktg. Sci., 1980—, Mgmt. Sci., 1974-91; contbr. articles to profl. jours. Fellow INFORMS Soc. Mktg. Sci.; mem. Am. Mktg. Assn., Inst. Ops. Rsch./Mgmt. Scis. Hindu. Avocation: classical music.

SRINIVASARAGHAVAN, JAGANNATHAN, forensic psychiatrist; b. May 13, 1950; naturalized U.S. citizen; MD, Thanjavur Med. Coll./U. Madras, 1974. Diplomate in psychiatry and forensic psychiatry Am. Bd. Psychiatry and Neurology. Rotating intern Thanjavur Med. Coll. Affiliated Hosps., 1973-74; resident in internal medicine Madras Med. Coll. and Govt. Gen. Hosp., 1974-77; resident in psychiatry U. Health Scis./Chgo. Med. Sch. Affiliated Hosps., 1977-80; chief resident St. Mary of Nazareth Hosp., Chgo., 1979-80; staff psychiatrist VA Med. Ctr., North Chicago, Ill., 1981-86, ECT unit dir., 1990-94; acting chief psychiatry, 1993; various positions including chief psychiatry svc. VA Med. Ctr., Canandaigua, N.Y., 1994-98; med. dir. Clyde L. Choate Mental Health and Devel. Ctr., Anna, Ill., 1998—; clin. assoc. prof. psychiatry U. Rochester, N.Y., 1994-98; prof. and chief, divsn. cmty. and public psychiatry So. Ill. U. Sch. Medicine, 1998—. Contbr. articles to Comprehensive Psychiatry, Violence and Victims, others. Recipient numerous awards and commendations. Fellow: Am. Psychiat. Assn. (pres. Caucus Asian Am. Psychiatrists 1999—2002, rep. 2002—, pres.-elect 2003, disting. fellow); mem.: India Assn. So. Ill. (v.p. 1999—2000, nominee, pres.-elect 2003), India Med. Assn., Am. Assn. Psychiatrists from India, Indo-Am. Psychiat. Assn. (life; treas. 1994—96, sec. 1996—98, pres.-elect 1998—2000, pres. 2000—03), Internat. Acad. Law and Mental Health, Am. Acad. Psychiatry and the Law (counselor, chair internat. rels. com.), Ill. Psychiat. Soc. (downstate councilor 2001—). Office: Clyde L Choat MH and Devel Ctr 1000 N Main St Anna IL 62906-1652 Office Phone: 618-833-5161 2221. Personal E-mail: jagran@gmail.com. Business E-Mail: jvan@dhs.state.il.us.

SRIVASTAVA, ALOK M., research scientist; b. Mumbai, Aug. 23, 1960; s. C. M. and Leela Srivastava; m. Maria T. Sobieraj. PhD, Poly. U. NY, Bklyn., 1989. Prin. scientist GE Global Rsch., Niskayuna, NY, 1989—. Achievements include patents in field. Office: GE GRC 1 Rsch Cir Niskayuna NY 12309 Business E-Mail: srivastava@crd.ge.com.

SRIVASTAVA, AMITABH, computer software company executive; BSEE, Indean Inst. Tech., Kanpur, 1979; MS in Computer Sci., Penn. State U., 1984. Rschr. Tex. Instruments Inc., Dallas, 1984—91; with Digital Equipment Corp. Western Rsch. Labs, Palo Alto, Calif., 1991; chief tech. officer, v.p. engring. Tracepoint Tech. Inc.; with Microsoft Rsch., 1997—2003, sr. rschr., 1997, disting. engr., 2001; founder, dir. Programmer Productivity Rsch. Ctr., 1999—2003, Ctr. Software Excellence, 2003—; corp. v.p. Windows core operating sys. devel. Microsoft Corp., 2003—07, corp. v.p. Cloud infrastructure services, 2007—09, sr. v.p. Windows Azure, 2009—. Recipient Disting. Alumnus award, Indian Inst. Tech., Kanpur, 2004, Outstanding Engring. Alumnus award, Penn. State U., 2004; named Disting. Engr., Microsoft Corp., 2001. Achievements include development of OM, ATOM and SCOOPS software systems; Vulcan binary transformation system. Office: Microsoft Corp 1 Microsoft Way Redmond WA 98052-6399*

SRIVASTAVA, ASHOK NARAIN, computer scientist, consultant; s. Jagdish Narain and Usha Srivastava; m. Lynn Clare Waelde. PhD, U. Colo., Boulder, 1996. Sr. cons. IBM, San Jose, Calif., 1996—2000; sr. dir. Blue Martini Software, San Mateo, Calif., 2000—02; leader intelligent data understanding group Rsch. Inst. Advanced Computer Sci., Moffett Field, Calif., 2002—04; dep. tech. area, mgr. NASA Ames Rsch. Ctr., Moffett Field, 2004—. Program mgr. vulnerability discovery from distributed databases NASA, Moffett Field, 2004—06. Editor: (jour. special issue) Data Mining in Fin. Acharya SGRY, Boulder, 2001—06. Recipient Golden Cir. award, IBM, 1996, Profl. Svcs. award, Blue Martini Software, 2001, Performance award, Rsch. Inst. Advanced Computer Sci., 2003, Disting. Achievement award, NASA, 2005, Group Achievement award, 2005. Mem.: IEEE. Achievements include patents for attributing forecasts to specific variables: a new method to understand why forecasts are made using nearest neighbor methods; symbol extraction from time series: a new method to convert time series into symbolic representations; patents pending for system and method for comparing populations of entities: a method to compare arbitrary groups of entities using naive Naïve Bayes methods; COLAP database and interactive visualization: a method to develop clickstream online analytical processing cubes with automatic clickstream pattern recognition; research in text mining, data mining, and machine learning. Office: NASA Ames Rsch Ctr Intelligent Systems Divsn Moffett Field CA 94035

SRIVASTAVA, RADHEY SHYAM, research scientist; b. Bahadurganj, India, June 7, 1931; s. Umeshwar Prasad and Ganesha Devi; m. Vijay Laxmi, Feb. 12, 1959; children: Suneeta, Sanjay, Sangita. BSc, Lucknow U., India, 1951, MSc, 1953, cert. in French, 1957, PhD, 1963. Rsch. fellow, lectr. Lucknow U., India, 1954-56, 56-57; jr. sci. officer Def. Sci. Lab., New Delhi, 1958-61, sr. sci. officer, 1961-71, prin. sci. officer, 1971-80; chief sci. officer Def. Sci. Ctr., New Delhi, 1980-91; pvt. rschr., 1991—. Rsch. fellow Royal Soc. London, Imperial Coll. Sci. and Tech., 1965; vis. scientist MRL, Melbourne, Australia, 1983, Inst. Aerospace Studies, Toronto, Can., 1980, Chiba U., 1991; vis. prof. Ernst Mach Inst., Freiburg, Germany, 1995, Tohoku U., Sendai, Japan, 2000, Chiba (Japan) U., 2000, Tokyo Denki U., 2001, Aachen U., Germany, 2002; organizing com. winter sch. in physiol. fluid dynamics, 1975. Author: Turbulence (Pipe Flows), 1977, Interaction of Shock Waves, 1994; contbr. to profl. publ. Mem. gen. body Welfare Assn., New Delhi, 1985—. Grantee Def. Rsch. Can., 1980, USAF, 1980, Min. Def., New Delhi, 1983, Min. Edn. Japan, Chiba, 1991; recipient 20th Century award for Achievement (medal) Eng., 1998, Millennium medal of hon. USA, 2000, Vijay Ratan medal, India, 2005, Rajiv Gandhi Excellence award, 2006, Bharat Jyoti award, India, 2008, Rashtriya Samman Puraskar, Gold medal, India, 2008, Lifetime Achievement award and Gold medal, India, 2008; named to Rising Personalities India, 2006. Fellow: NAS India, United Writers' Assn. India; mem.: Indian Sci. Congress, Bharat Ganita Parishad (life), Sci. Officer's Assn. Hindu. Achievements include development of Srivastava's theory. Avocations: music, movies, sports. Home and Office: A 3/260 Janakpuri New Delhi 110058 India Home Phone: 00911125500381. Personal E-mail: rssuncle@yahoo.co.uk.

SRIVASTAVA, ROHIT, real estate company executive, researcher; b. New Delhi, Nov. 25, 1970; s. Shanker and Usha Suhail; m. Shweta Srivastav; children: Ayoush, Prithvi. BArch, Manipal Inst. Tech., India, 1993; MSRED in Real Estate Fin., MIT, Cambridge, 2003. Registered Coun. Architecture, 2000. Project arch. Design Plus, New Delhi, 1993—95; project mgr. Plan India Group, New Delhi, 1995—2001; rsch. asst. MIT, 2002—03; assoc. Trepp LLC, NYC, 2004, Gramercy Capital Corp., NYC, 2004—06, Credit Suisse, NYC, 2006—. Consulting Design Plus, 1993—95; consulting directorship Plan India Group, 1995—2001. Recipient first prize, Mauritius Supreme Ct., 1999, prize for Design Victoria Hosp., Ministry Pub. Infrastructure, Govt. Mauritius, 2000. Mem.: Urban Land Inst. (assoc.), Royal Inst. Chartered Surveyors (assoc.). Achievements include research in commercial mortgage backed securities study for defaults of loans. Office: Credit Suisse Eleven Madison Ave New York NY 10010 Home: 244 W 101st St Apt 3C New York NY 10025-8413 Personal E-mail: rohits@alum.mit.edu. Business E-Mail: rohit.srivastava@credit-suisse.com.

SRIVASTAVA, VINOD K., research scientist, educator; s. Keshari L. and Roopmati Srivastava; m. Poonam Srivastava, July 1, 1987; 1 child, Rahul. PhD in Chemistry, Awadh U., Faizabad, India, 1986. Postdoc. rsch. assoc. Wash. State U., Pullman, 1986—88; rsch. scientist Tex. A&M U., Coll. Sta., 1999—2008, rsch. asst. prof., 2008—. Achievements include research in alcohol effects on female puberty. Business E-Mail: vsrivastava@cvm.tamu.edu.

SRIVATSAN, TIRUMALAI SRINIVAS, engineering educator; s. Srinivas Raghavachari Tirumalai and Radha Srinivas; m. Jayashree Krishnaswamy; children: Sitara, Santosh. BS in Mech. Engring., Bangalore U., India, 1980; MS, Ga. Inst. Tech., Atlanta, 1981, PhD in Mech. Engring., 1984. Assoc. prof. U. Akron, Ohio, 1992—97, prof., 1997—. Recipient Outstanding Rsch. award, ALCOA Found., 1991, Louis Hill award, Coll. Engring., U. Akron, 2006; named Outstanding Young Alumnus, Ga. Inst. Tech., 1996, Outstanding Rsch. Faculty, Coll. Engring., U. Akron, 1997. Fellow: ASME (mem., chair com. 1981—2008), Am. Soc. Materials Internat. (chair 1984—2008, internat. exch. lectr. 1988). Achievements include research in materials processing, materials characterization, failure analysis, mechanical behavior, composite materials, fracture mechanics and fatigue analysis, mechanical design, nano-materials and nano-structure. Office: Univ Akron Dept Mech Engring Akron OH 44325-3903 Office Fax: 330-972-6027. Business E-Mail: tss1@uakron.edu.

SROCK, MARLENE, elementary school educator; b. Wells, Minn., 1951; BS in Elem Edn., Saint Cloud State Univ., 1973; MS in Elem Edn., Minot State Univ. Named ND Tchr. of Yr., 2007. Office: Bel Air Elem Sch 501 25 St NW Minot ND 58703 Business E-Mail: m.srock@sendit.nodak.edu.

SRULOWITZ, MARVIN, lawyer; BA, AA, Yeshiva U., 1969; JD, NYU, 1972. Bar: N.Y. 1973, U.S. Dist. Ct. (ea. and so. dists.) N.Y. 1973, U.S. Ct. Appeals (2d cir.) 1974, U.S. Ct. Internat. Trade 1976, U.S. Supreme Ct. 1976. Assoc. Delson & Gordon, NYC, 1972-77, Mayer Nussbaum Katz & Baker, P.C., NYC, 1977-80; sole practice NYC, 1981—. Mem. New York County Lawyers Assn., Am. Arbitration Assn. Office: 16 E 34th St 16th Fl New York NY 10016-4359 Office Phone: 212-686-1224. Office Fax: 212-532-3206. Business E-Mail: marvinlaw@aol.com.

SSEMAKULA, MUKASA EMMANUEL, engineering educator; b. Banda, Buganda, Uganda, May 13, 1958; s. Emmanuel Yawe Lulika and Eseza Nanfuka; m. Cleophas Nampoza; children: Adorabelle Kyaterekera Namigadde, Gonza Albert Lulika, Asiimwe Teresa Najjuma, Kizito Matthias Katende. BSc, U. Manchester, Eng., 1980, MSc, 1981, PhD, 1984. Rsch. engr. Delta Computer Aided Engring. Ltd., Birmingham, England, 1984—85; vis. asst. prof. U. Md., Coll. Pk., 1985—86, asst. prof., 1986—92; assoc. prof. Wayne State U., Detroit, 1993—. Contbr. chapters to books, articles to profl. jours. (Dr. Nam P. Suh Best Paper award, 1997). Founder and webmaster Buganda Home Page, Canton, Mich., 1995—2008; active parishioner Resurrection Parish, Canton, 1995—2008; promoting eucharistic devotion on a statewide basis Real Presence Assn. Mich., Canton, 2007—08. Recipient Excellence in Tchg. award, Wayne State U. Coll. Engring., 2005; ORS scholarship, Com. Vice-Chancellors UK Univs., 1981—84, grant, NSF, 2002—04, 2008—. Mem.: ASME, Am. Soc. Engring. Edn., Soc. Mfg. Engrs. (grant 2005—07). Roman Catholic. Office: Wayne State Univ Engring Tech Divsn 4855 Fourth St Detroit MI 48202

SSTANKEY, JOHN T., telecommunications industry executive; b. Calif. m. Shari sStankey; 3 children. B in Fin., Loyola Marymount U., LA, 1985; MBA, UCLA, 1991. Exec. dir. advanced comm. network, local wholesale ops. Pacific Bell, 1985—98; v.p. industry markets SBC Comm. Inc., 1998—2000, pres. industry markets, 2000—02, pres., CEO SBC Southwestern Bell, 2002—03, sr. exec. v.p., chief tech. officer, 2003—06, AT&T Inc., 2006—07, grp. pres. ops. support, 2007, grp. pres. telecomm. ops., 2007—. Named one of Premier 100 IT Leaders, Computerworld, 2006, Top 25 Chief Tech. Officers, InfoWorld mag., 2006. Office: AT&T Inc 175 E Houston St San Antonio TX 78205*

STAAB, DIANE D., lawyer; BA, CUNY Hunter Coll., 1977; JD, Yeshiva U., 1980. Bar: N.Y. 1981. Assoc. atty. Hall, McNicol, Hamilton & Clark, 1980-84, Patterson, Belknap, Webb & Tyler, 1984-87; corp. counsel Internat. Paper Co., 1987—95; v.p., gen. counsel, corp. ethics/environ. compliance officer Ariz. Chem., Panama City, 1996—2001; gen. counsel Internat. Paper Europe, 2001—. Mem. ABA (mem. bus. law sect. fed. ref. of securities com. 1988-2001, vice-chmn. com. on corp. & bus. legis. subcom. on corp. governance 1992-98), Assn. of the Bar of the City of N.Y. (mem. spl. com. on election law 1987-89, mem. corp. law com. 1989-92, sec. com. on corp. law dept. 1992-93). Office: Internat Paper 400 Atlantic St Stamford CT 06921 Office Phone: 32 02 774 1254.

STAAB, THOMAS ROBERT, consumer product company financial executive; b. Beaver Falls, Pa., Apr. 23, 1942; s. Henry Louis and Margaret Constance (Clarke) S.; m. Angela Maria Simon, Aug. 6, 1965; children: Thomas II, Jennifer, Thea. BBA, U. Pitts., 1964, MBA, 1965. CPA, Pa. Sr. audit mgr. Price Waterhouse & Co., Pitts., 1970-77; practice fellow Fin. Acctg. Standards Bd., Stamford, Conn., 1978-80; dir. corp. acctg. and taxes Fieldcrest Cannon Inc., Eden, NC, 1981-84, asst. contr., 1985, contr., 1986-91, v.p. fin., 1992-93, CFO, 1994-97; bd. dirs., sr. v.p., CFO Lorillard Inc., Greensboro, NC, 1998—2008; sr. v.p. chief acctg. officer, 2009—. Served to lt. USN, 1966-70. Mem. AICPA, Pa. Inst. CPAs. Independent. Roman Catholic. Home: 3726 NC # 65 Reidsville NC 27320 Office: Lorillard Inc PO Box 10529 714 Green Valley Rd Greensboro NC 27404-0529

STAAL, ERIC, professional hockey player; b. Thunder Bay, Ont., Can., Oct. 29, 1984; s. Henry and Linda Staal; m. Tanya VandenBroeke, Aug. 3, 2007. Center Carolina Hurricanes, 2003—. Recipient NHL All-Star Game, 2009; named MVP, NHL All-Star Game, 2008; named to NHL YoungStars Game, 2004, NHL All-Star Game, 2007, 2008, Second All-Star Team, NHL, 2006. Achievements include being a member of Stanley Cup Champion Carolina Hurricanes, 2006. Office: Carolina Hurricanes RBC Ctr2 1400 Edwards Mill Rd Raleigh NC 27607*

STAAL, JORDAN, professional hockey player; b. Thunder Bay, Ont., Can., Sept. 10, 1988; s. Henry and Linda Staal. Center Pitts. Penguins, 2006—. Named to NHL YoungStars Game, 2007, All-Rookie Team, NHL, 2007. Achievements include being the youngest player in NHL history to score two shorthanded goals in one game and the youngest player to score on a penalty shot, 2006; being the youngest player in NHL history to score a hat trick, 2007; being a member of Stanley Cup Champion Pittsburgh Penguins, 2009. Office: Pittsburgh Penguins 66 Mario Lemieux Pl Pittsburgh PA 15219

STAATS, ARTHUR W., psychology professor; b. Jan. 17, 1924; BA in Psychology, UCLA, 1949, MA in Psychology, 1953, PhD in Gen. Exptl. and Clin. Psychology, 1956. Psychologist UCLA Counseling Ctr., Los Angeles, 1950-53; clin. trainee VA Hosps., Los Angeles, 1953-55; instr. psychology Ariz. State U., Tempe, 1955-56, asst. prof., 1956-58, assoc. prof., 1958-60, prof., 1960-64; NSF faculty fellow U. London, 1961-62; vis. prof. U. Calif., Berkeley, 1964-65; prof. ednl. psychology and research U. Wis. Research and Devel. Ctr. Cognitive Learning, Madison, 1965-67; vis. prof. U. Hawaii, Honolulu, 1966-67, prof. psychology and ednl. psychology, 1967—. Author Complex Human Behavior, 1963, Learning, Language and Cognition, 1968, Child Learning, Intelligence, and Personality: A Behavioral Interaction Approach, 1971, Social Behaviorism, 1975, Psychology's Crisis of Disunity: Philosophy and Method for a Unified Science, 1983, Behavior and Personality: Psychological Behaviorism, 1996; editor Human Learning, 1964, Current Issues in Theoretical Psychology, 1987, Annals of Theoretical Psychology, Vol. 5, 1987; contbr. over 80 articles to profl. jours. and 61 chpts. to books; editl. bd. 9 Am. and internat. jours. Named in his honor, Arthur W. Staats Unifying Psychology lectr. (annually); named one of 20 People Who Changed Childhood, CHILD, 2006. Fellow AAAS, Am. Psychol. Soc., APA (gen. psychology divsn., exptl. psychology divsn., devel. psychology divsn., personality and social psychology divs., clin. psychology divsn., ednl. psychology divsn., theoretical and philos. psychology divsn., exptl. analysis of behavior divsn.); mem. Sociedad Interamericana de Psicologia, Psychonomic Soc., Assn. Latinoamericana del Analisis y Modificacion del Comportamiento, Soc. for Exptl. Social Psychology. Achievements include invention of timeout for children. Home: 1460 Kamole St Honolulu HI 96821-1422 Office: U Hawaii Dept Psychology Honolulu HI 96822 Home Phone: 808-373-4630; Office Phone: 808-377-3195, 8083773184. Business E-Mail: staats@aloha.com.

STAATS, DEAN ROY, retired reinsurance executive; b. Somerville, NJ, Sept. 18, 1924; s. Roy Theodore and Mabel Ellen (Rhodes) S.; m. Marilyn Ann Hockenbury, 1947 (div. 1956; 1 child, Barry Clinton; m. Marilyn Lee Truitt, Dec. 16, 1961 B.Sc., Brown U., 1946, MA, 1948. Asst. actuary N.Am. Reassurance Co., NYC, 1959-67, data processing officer, 1967-69, v.p., actuary, 1969-71, sr. v.p., 1971-84, exec. v.p., 1984-86; pres., dir. NARe Life Mgmt. Co., NYC, 1985-86; rep. Life Ins. Guaranty Corp, 1977-86; U.S. mgr. Can. Reassurance Co., 1984-86; cons. actuary, 1986-89. Served to lt. (j.g.), USN, 1943-46, PTO Fellow Soc. Actuaries; mem. Am. Acad. Actuaries N.Y. Jr. Actuaries Club (pres. 1960-61), Soc. Actuaries (reins. adminstrn. com. 1984-85) Clubs: Anchor and Saber (pres. 1959-60). Republican. Avocations: art, tennis, gardening, travel. Home and Office: 3 Post Run Newtown Square PA 19073-3014 Home Phone: 610-356-5236; Office Phone: 610-356-5236.

STAATS, ELMER BOYD, foundation executive, former government official; b. Richfield, Kans., June 6, 1914; s. Wesley F. and Maude (Goodall) S.; m. Margaret S. Rich, Sept. 14, 1940; children: David Rich, Deborah Rich Staats Sanders, Catharine Rich Staats Taubman. AB, McPherson Coll., Kans., 1935, LLD (hon.), 1966; MA, U. Kans., 1936; PhD, U. Minn., 1939; D. in Pub. Service (hon.), George Washington U., 1971; D. in Adminstrn. (hon.), U. S.D., 1973; LLD (hon.), Duke U., 1975, Nova U., 1976, U. Pa., 1981, Lycoming Coll., 1982; LHD (hon.), Ohio State U., 1982. Research asst. Kans. Legis. Council, 1936; teaching asst. U. Minn., 1936-38; staff Pub. Adminstrn. Service, Chgo., 1937-38; staff mem. U.S. Bur. Budget, Exec. Office Pres., 1939-47, asst. to dir., 1947, asst. dir. charge legis. reference, 1947-49, exec. asst. dir., 1949-50, dep. dir., 1950-53, 58-66; comptroller gen. U.S. Washington, 1966-81; pres. Harry S. Truman Scholarship Found., 1981-84, chmn., 1984—, now chmn. emeritus. Bd. dirs. rsch. dir. Marshall Field & Co., Chgo., 1953; exec. dir. ops. coord. bd., Nat. Security Coun., 1953-58; professorial lectr. pub. adminstrn. George Washington U., 1944-49; mem. bd. visitors Nat. Def. U., 1981-90; mem. vis. com. John F. Kennedy Sch. Govt., Harvard U., 1974-80, Grad. Sch. Mgmt., UCLA, 1976—; mem. Com. on Pub. Policy Studies U. Chgo., 1976—; trustee Nat. Inst. Pub. Affairs, 1969-77; mem. Conf. Bd., 1966; mem. dir.'s adv. coun. Met. Life Ins. Co., 1985-94, emeritus mem., 1994—; dir. Computer Data Systems, Inc., 1981—; bd. advisors Alexander Proudfoot & Co., 1981-85; mem. pub. rev. bd. Arthur Andersen & Co., 1981-91; bd. dirs. Air Products and Chems., 1981-85, Met. Life Ins. Co., 1981-85, Nat. Intergroup Inc. (formerly Nat. Steel Corp.), 1981-86; chmn. congl. panel on social security orgn., 1983-84; mem. nat. commn. on pub. svc., 1987-90; mem. commn. to rev. honor code of West Point U.S. Mil. Acad., 1988-89; mem. Govt. Acctg. Standards Bd., 1984-90; chmn. Fed. Acctg. Standards Adv. Bd., 1991-96. Author: Personnel Standards in the Social Security Program, 1939; contbr. to: Am. Polit. Sci. Rev. Trustee Am. U., 1969-81; trustee McPherson Coll., 1969-79, mem. bd. trustees and research and policy com., com. for econ. devel., 1981—; bd. govs. Internat. Orgn. of Supreme Audit Instns., 1969-80; trustee Kerr Found., 1981—; bd. dirs. George C. Marshall Found., 1984—. Recipient Rockefeller Pub. Service award, 1961, Alumni achievement award U.

Minn., 1964, Disting. Service citation U. Kans., 1966, Warner D. Stockberger Achievement award, 1973, Abraham O. Smoot Pub. Service award Brigham Young U., 1975, Person of Yr. award Washington chpt. Inst. Internal Auditors, 1975, Thurston award Inst. Internal Auditors, 1988, medal of honor Am. Inst. CPAs, 1980, Engr. of Yr. award San Fernando Valley Engrs. Council, 1980, Presdl. Citizens medal, 1981, Hubert Humphrey medal, 1981, Pub. Service Achievement award Common Cause, 1981; fed. exec. award Evaluation Research Soc., 1980; named to Acctg. Hall of Fame, 1981; fellow Brookings Instn., 1938-39. Mem. Nat. Acad. Pub. Adminstrn., Assn. Govt. Accountants, Am. Acad. Polit. and Social Sci. (dir. 1966-92), Am. Soc. Public Adminstrn. (pres. Washington 1948-49, nat. coun. 1958-65, nat. pres. 1961-62), Am. Mgmt. Assns. (gen. mgmt. coun. 1966-85, trustee 1981-85), Cosmos Club (Washington), Chevy Chase (Md.), Phi Beta Kappa, Pi Sigma Alpha, Beta Gamma Sigma, Alpha Kappa Psi. Methodist. Office: Harry S Truman Scholarship Found 712 Jackson Pl NW Washington DC 20006-4901

STAATS, THOMAS ELWYN, neuropsychologist; s. Percy Anderson and Julia (Bourmorck) S.; m. Debra R.; children: Lauren Malu, Kara Kristyn, Stacy Rhnea, Ronald Derek. BA cum laude, Emory U., 1970; MA, U. Ala., 1972, PhD, 1974; postgrad., U. Tex., Tyler, 1992. Diplomate Am. Bd. Profl. Disability Cons.; lic. psychologist. Dir., chief psychologist Caddo Parish Diagnostic Ctr., Shreveport, La., 1974-81; exec. dir. Doctors Psychol. Ctr., Shreveport, 1979-91, Comprehensive Assessments, 1991—. Cons. to Charter Forest Hosp., 1989-2000, Shreveport Impairment and Disability Evaluation Ctr., 1993—; clin. assoc. prof. psychology La. State U., Shreveport, 1977-1990; clin. assoc. prof. psychiatry La. State U. Sch. Medicine, Shreveport, 1980-92, 2003—; neuropsychol. cons. to dept. psychiatry, 1992-2002; mem. faculty Am. Acad. Disability Evaluating Physicians, 1986—, Health South Impairment Evaluation Lectr. Series, 1998—. Author: Manual for the Stress Vector Analysis Test Series, 1983, The Doctors Guide to Instant Stress Relief, 1987, Stress Management and Relaxation Training System Handbook; contbr. articles to profl. jours. and popular mags. Mem. Gov.'s Com. of 1000, La., 1979. Recipient AADEP award, 1991; Grad. Rsch. Coun. fellow, 1974. Fellow Am. Inst. Stress; mem. APA, Nat. Acad. Neuropsychology, Nat. Register of Health Svc. Providers. Episcopalian. Avocations: scuba diving, gun collecting, camping, boating, paintball competition. Home: 4 Beaux Rivages Dr Shreveport LA 71106 Office: Comprehensive Assessments Inc 4300 Youree Dr Ste 200 Shreveport LA 71105 Office Phone: 318-861-0194. Personal E-mail: drtomstaats@bellsouth.net.

STABEL, JUDITH R., microbiologist; b. Buzzards Bay, Mass., Oct. 25, 1957; d. Taylor and Dorothy T. Reffett; m. Timothy A. Reinhardt, July 24, 2004; 1 child, Meredith T. BS, U. Ky., Lexington, 1981, MS, 1983; PhD, NC State U., Raleigh, 1987. Supervisory rsch. microbiologist USDA-ARS-Nat. Animal Disease Ctr., Ames, Iowa, 1991—, postdoc. rsch. assoc. Contbr. articles to profl. jours. Recipient Midwest Area Early Career Scientist of Yr., USDA-ARS, 1996, Outstanding Alumni award, U. Ky. Coll. Agr., 2008; grantee, Dairy Mgmt. Assn., 2000—02, USDA-NRICREES, 2004—07, USDA-National Rsch. Inst., USDA-NRICGP. Mem.: Internat. Assn. Paratuberculosis (US bd. mem. 2002—08), US Animal Health Johne's Com. (sci. adv. subcom. chair 2001—08), Am. Vet. Immunologists Assn., Internat. Dairy Fedn. (task force mem. 2000—08), Am. Dairy Sci. Assn. (com. chair 2004—07), Gamma Sigma Delta, Alpha Zeta Frat. Conservative. Roman Catholic. Achievements include invention of immortalization of bovine macrophage cell line; development of real-time PCR assay. Avocations: travel, crafts, cooking. Home: 3121 Sycamore Rd Ames IA 50014 Office: USDA-ARS-Nat Animal Disease Ctr 2300 Dayton Rd Ames IA 50010 Office Fax: 515-663-7458. Personal E-mail: johnes2@mchsi.com. Business E-Mail: judy.stabel@ars.usda.gov.

STABENOW, DEBORAH ANN, United States Senator from Michigan, former congresswoman; b. Gladwin, Mich., Apr. 29, 1950; d. Robert Lee and Anna Merle (Hallmark) Greer; m. Dennis Stabenow (div. 1990); children: children: Todd Dennis, Michelle Deborah. m. Tom Athans, Feb. 16, 2003; 1 stepdaughter, Gina BS magna cum laude, Mich. State U., 1972, MSW magna cum laude, 1975. With spl. svcs. Lansing (Mich.) Sch. Dist., 1972-73; county commr. Ingham County, Mason, Mich., 1975-78; state rep. State of Mich., Lansing, 1979—91, state senator, 1991—94; mem. 103rd-106th Congress from Mich. 8th dist. U.S. Ho. Reps., 1997—2001; US Senator from Mich., 2001—. Founder Ingham County Women's Commn.; co-founder Council Against Domestic Assault. Recipient Service to Children award Council for Prevention of Child Abuse and Neglect, 1983, Disting. Service to Mich. Families award Mich. Council Family Relations, 1983, Outstanding Leadership award Nat. Council Community Mental Health Ctrs., 1983, Snyder-Kok award Mental Health Assn. Mich., Awareness Leader of Yr. award Awareness Communications Team Developmentally Disabled, 1984, Communicator of Yr. award Woman in Communications, 1984, Lawmaker of Yr. award Nat. Child Support Enforcement Assn., 1985, Disting. Service award Lansing Jaycees, 1985, Disting. Service in Govt. award Retarded Citizens of Mich., 1986, Cmty. award Mich. Mental Health, 1988, Boxing Glove award Nat. Com. to Preserve Social Security and Medicare, 1999, Home Health Hero Nat. Assn. for Home Care, 1999, Friend of Farm Bur. Mich. Farm Bur., 1999, Leadership award Nat. Coun. of Space Grant Dirs., 1998, Outstanding Achievement Nat. Farmers Union, 1998, Legislator of Yr. award Nat. Multiple Sclerosis Soc., 1992, Assn. for Children's Mental Health, 1991, Mich. Assn. of Vol. Adminstrs., 1989, Citizens Alliance to Uphold Spl. Edn., 1989, Recognition award State 4-H Alumni, 1991, Public. Elected Ofcl. award Nat. Assn. Social Workers, 2004, Congressional Support for Sci. award Inst. Food Technologists, 2004, Cmty. Health Defender award Nat. Assn. Cmty. Health Centers, 2005; named One of Ten Outstanding Young Ams. Jaycees, 1986. Mem. NAACP, Nat. Assn. Social Workers, Lansing Regional C. of C., Delta Kappa Gamma. Democrat. Meth. Office: US Senate 702 Hart Senate Office Bldg Washington DC 20510 also: District Office Ste 100 221 W Lake Lansing Rd East Lansing MI 48823-8661 Office Phone: 202-224-4822, 517-203-1760. Office Fax: 202-228-0325, 517-203-1778. E-mail: senator@stabenow.senate.gov.*

STABILE, BRUCE EDWARD, surgeon; b. Monterey Park, California, Apr. 14, 1944; s. Edward Emilio and Angela (Tramantozzi) S.; m. Caroline Graston, Sept. 18, 1967; children: Jessica, Drew. BA, UCLA, 1966; MD, U. Calif., San Francisco, 1970. Diplomate Am. Bd. Surgery. From assoc. prof. to prof. vice chmn. dept. surgery Sch. Medicine U. Calif., San Diego, 1985—93; from asst. prof. to assoc. prof. Sch. Medicine UCLA, 1977—85, vice chmn. dept. surgery Sch. Medicine, 1993—. Chmn. dept. surgery Harbor UCLA Med. Ctr., Torrance, 1993—, acting med. dir., 1997-98; interim assoc. dean UCLA Sch. Medicine, 1997-98; med. expert Med. Bd. Calif., 1980—; bd. dirs. Am. Bd. Surgery, 1998-2004. Mem. editl. bd.: Jour. Surg. Rsch., 1993—97, Archives of Surgery, 1991—2004. Fellow, ACS (gov. 2001-07, pres. So. Calif. chpt. 2005-06), Am. Surg. Assn.; mem. Soc. Univ. Surgeons, Assn. Acad. Surgery, Am. Gastroenterol. Assn., San Diego Soc. Gen. Surgeons (pres. 1992-93), L.A. Surg. Soc. (pres. 2000-01), Pacific Coast Surg. Assn. (pres. 2007-08). Office: Harbor U Calif at L A Med Ctr 1000 W Carson St Torrance CA 90502-2004 Office Phone: 310-222-2701. Business E-Mail: bstabile@ucla.edu.

STABILE, PATRICE CHRISTINE, mathematics educator; b. Bronx, Aug. 19, 1956; d. Herman and Dolores Hansen; m. Stephen Lawrence Stabile, Aug. 11, 1979; children: Kristen Patrice, Robert Lawrence. BA, Iona Coll., New Rochelle, NY, 1978; MA, We. Conn. State U., Danbury, 2006. Math tchr. Msgr. Scanlan H.S., Bronx, NY, 1978—84, Wappingers Jr. H.S., Wappingers Falls, NY, 2001—. Substitute tchr. Wappingers Ctrl. Sch. Dist., NY, 1998—2001. Pres. Oak Grove PTA, Poughkeepsie, NY, 1993—97; cheerleading coach Wappingers Pop Warner, Wappingers Falls, NY, 2001—06, Wappingers Jr. High, 2006—. Named Rotary Club Tchr. of the Yr., Rotary Club, 2005. Home: 66 Helen Dr Wappingers Falls NY 12590 Office: Wappingers Junior High School 30 Major Macdonald Way Wappingers Falls NY 12590-3740 Office Fax: 845-298-5156. Personal E-mail: btm819@msn.com.

STABLER, LEWIS VASTINE, JR., lawyer; b. Greenville, Ala., Nov. 5, 1936; s. Lewis Vastine and Dorothy Daisy Stabler; m. Monteray Scott, Sept. 5, 1958; children: Dorothy Monteray Scott, Andrew Vastine, Monteray Scott Smith, Margaret Langston. BA, Vanderbilt U., 1958; JD with distinction, U. Mich., 1961. Bar: Ala. 1961. Assoc. Cabaniss & Johnston, Birmingham, Ala., 1961-67; assoc. prof. law U. Ala., 1967-70; ptnr. Cabaniss, Johnston, Gardner, Dumas & O'Neal (and predecessor firms), Birmingham, 1970-91, Walston, Stabler, Wells, Anderson and Bains, Birmingham, 1991-97; pvt. practice, Birmingham, 1997—. Mem. com. of 100 Candler Sch. Theology, Emory U. Bd. editors: Mich. Law Rev, 1960-61. Fellow Am. Bar Found. (life); mem. Am. Law Inst. (life), Ala. Law Inst. (mem. coun., dir. 1968-70), ABA, Ala. Bar Assn., FINICA (arbitrator), Birmingham Bar Assn., Am. Assn. R.R. Trial Counsel, Order of Coif. Methodist (cert. lay speaker). Clubs: Country of Birmingham, Rotary. Home: 3538 Victoria Rd Birmingham AL 35223-1404 Office: PO Box 53-1161 Birmingham AL 35253-1161 Office Phone: 205-970-4990. Personal E-mail: vstabler@gmail.com.

STABLER, SCOTT LAWRENCE, historian, educator; s. Carl L and Barbara L Stabler. Phd, Ariz. State U., 2004. Grad. instr. Ariz. State U., Tempe, Ariz., 1999—; rsch. fellow Papers of Abraham Lincoln, Springfield, Ill., 2003—03. Sunday sch. tchr. Gilbert United Meth., Gilbert, Ariz., 2003—04. Grantee Rsch. grantee, Carlisle Mil. Libr., 2003. Mem.: Orgn. of Am. Historians. Personal E-mail: stabler9@yahoo.com.

STABREIT, IMMO FRIEDRICH HELMUT, diplomat; b. Rathenow, Germany, Jan. 24, 1933; s. Kurt and Johanna Maria (Groeger) S.; m. Barbara Philippi, Aug. 1, 1962; children: Eberhard, Felix, Sophie Charlotte. BA, Princeton U., 1953; First Law Exam., Free U. Berlin, Germany, 1957; Second Law Exam., U. Heidelberg, Germany, 1961, LLD, 1963. With Fgn. Ministry, Bonn, Germany, 1962, German Embassy, Moscow, Russia, 1962-63; with divsn. Russian affairs Fgn. Ministry, Bonn, 1964-66; first and second sec. German Embassy, Moscow, Russia, 1966-71; dep. dir. divsn. Russian affairs Fgn. Ministry, Bonn, 1971-74; with Ctr. Internat. Affairs, Harvard U., 1974-75; head divsn. fgn. rels. Internat. Energy Agy., Paris, France, 1975-78; head divsn. European polit. affairs Fgn. Ministry, Bonn, 1978-83; head directorate fgn. and devel. policy Fed. Chancellery, Bonn, 1983-87; amb. German Embassy, Pretoria, Cape Town, South Africa, 1987-92, Washington, 1992-95, Paris, France, 1995-98; exec. v.p. German Soc. Fgn. Affairs, Berlin, Germany, 1998—2001. Recipient Commendatore del Orden de merito de la Republica Italiana, 1978, Commandeur de l'Ordre de Merite de la République Francaise, 1987, Rechtsritter of the Order of St. John, 1988, Grand Officer of the Order of Good Hope Republic of South Africa, 1992, Comdr. de la Légion d'Honneur de la République Française, 1996, Comdrs. Cross of the Order of Merit of the Fed. Republic of Germany, 1997; named Diplomat of Yr., World Affairs Coun., 1994. Mem. Phi Beta Kappa. Avocations: tennis, squash. Home: Wundt Str 18 14059 Berlin Germany

STABY, DOROTHY LOUISE, elementary school educator; b. Washington, July 26, 1932; d. Charles Pemberton and Eleanor (Thompson) Sheffield; m. Jack Bradford Staby, Oct. 27, 1956; children: John Bradford, Robert Stanford, Mary Katherine. BS in Edn. with honors, James Madison U., 1954; MA, State U. Iowa, 1955; postgrad., Columbia U., 1957, Bklyn. Coll., 1957, SUNY, New Paltz, 1962, SUNY, Binghamton, 1993. Cert. elem., health and phys. edn. tchr., N.Y. Tchr. phys. edn. Garden City (N.Y.) High Sch., 1955-58; substitute tchr.1st-12th grades Amityville Sch., Capaigue Sch., Massapeque Sch., LI, N.Y., 1958-63; tchr. 1st and 2d grades St. Patricks Elem. Sch., Owego, N.Y., 1969-70; tchr. 5th grade Glenwood Elem. Sch., Vestal, N.Y., 1970-83; tchr. 2d grade Clayton Ave. Elem. Sch., Vestal, NY, 1983—97. Head, counselor Coll. Settlement Farm Camp, Willow Grove, Pa., 1954-55; instr. Iowa City Recreation Dept., 1955; counselor Garden City Recreation Dept., 1956-57, Country Day Camp, Plainedge, N.Y., 1960-62; tchr. computer Vestal Schs., 1983-87, Vestal Recreation Dept., Vestal, 1989-90, health tchr. Vestal H.S., 1988. Reading vol. Clayton Ave Elem. Sch., 1997—2007. State U. Iowa scholar, 1954-55. Mem. NEA, AAUW, N.Y. Edn. Assn., Vestal Ret. Tchrs. Assn. Democrat. Methodist. Avocations: computers, reading, sports. Home: 700 Hickory Dr Aliquippa PA 15001

STACEY, JAMES ALLEN, retired judge; b. Norwalk, Ohio, Dec. 26, 1925; s. James Calvin and Glenna (Cleveland) S.; m. Marlyn Frederick, Aug. 21, 1948; children: James A. Jr., Libble M. Romigh, Lorrie Stacey Singler, David F., CamAllison Shenigo, Tricia Stacey Berger. Student, Bucknell U., 1943—44, Ohio Wesleyan U., 1944—46, U. N.C., 1944—45; JD, Cleveland-Marshall Law Sch., 1951. Bar: Ohio 1952, U.S. Dist. Ct. (no. dist.) Ohio 1955. Ptnr. McGory & Stacey, Sandusky, Ohio, 1954—56; assoc. Steinemann & Zieher, Sandusky, Ohio, 1956—60; ptnr. Work, Stacey & Moyer, 1960—67; judge Sandusky Mcpl. Ct., 1967—95, ret., 1995. Mem. Ohio State Traffic Law Com., 1969-95, chmn., 1978-82. Mem. Sandusky Jaycees, 1952-62, Erie-Ottawa Mental Health Bd., 1968-87, Ex-Offenders for Help Bd., 1975-81; bd. dirs. Camp Fire Girls, 1956-60, L.E.A.D.S., 1984-86, Sandusky C. of C., 1984-86. Served with USNR, 1943-46. Mem. Ohio State Bar Assn., Ohio Mcpl. Judges Assn. (exec. bd. 1970-80), Am. Judicature Soc., Am. Judges Assn., Erie County Bar Assn., Amvets (life), Beta Theta Pi, Sandusky Exch. Club (bd. dirs. 1999-2004), Car Coddlers Ohio (life mem.), Am. Legion, Elks, Eagles Club. Republican. Presbyterian. Home: 1407 Julianne Cir Sandusky OH 44870-7032

STACEY, WESTON MONROE, JR., nuclear engineer, physicist, educator; b. Birmingham, Ala., July 23, 1937; s. Weston Monroe and Dorothy (Toole) S.; m. Penny Smith; children: Helen Lee, Weston Monroe III, Lucia Katherine. BS in Physics, Ga. Inst. Tech., 1959, MS in Nuc. Sci., 1963; PhD in Nuc. Engring., MIT, 1966. Nuc. engr. Knolls Atomic Power Lab., Schenectady, NY, 1962-64, 66-69; assoc. dir. applied physics divsn. and dir. fusion program Argonne Nat. Lab., Chgo., 1969-77; Callaway Regents prof. Ga. Inst. Tech., Atlanta, 1977—. Author: Modal Approximation in Reactor Physics, 1967, Space-Time Nuclear Reactor Kinetics, 1969, Variational Methods in Nuclear Reactor Physics, 1972, Fusion Plasma Analysis, 1981, Fusion, 1984, 2nd edit., 2009, Nuclear Reactor Physics, 2001, 2d edit., 2007, Fusion Plasma Physics, 2005; contbr. 270 articles to profl. jours. Recipient Cert. Appreciation Dept. Energy, 1981, 88, Disting. Assoc. award Dept. Energy, 1990, Rsch. award Sigma Xi, 1998; Disting. Career award Fusion Plasma Assn., 2009. Fellow: Am. Nuc. Soc. (bd. dirs. 1974—77, Outstanding Achievement award 1981, 1996, Seaborg medal 2001, Wigner award 2003), Am. Phys. Soc.; mem.: AAAS, Am. Soc. Engring. Edn. Office: Ga Inst Tech Nuclear Engring Dept 0425 Atlanta GA 30332-0425 Office Phone: 404-894-3714. Business E-Mail: weston.stacey@nre.gatech.edu.

STACHEL, JOHN JAY, physicist, researcher; b. NYC, Mar. 29, 1928; s. Jacob Abraham and Bertha Z. Stachel; m. Evelyn Lenore Wassermann, Feb. 8, 1953; children: Robert, Laura, Deborah. BS, CCNY, 1956; MS, Stevens Inst. Tech., 1959, PhD, 1962. Instr. physics Lehigh U., Bethlehem, Pa., 1959-61; instr. physics U. Pitts., 1961-62, research assoc., 1962-64; asst. prof. physics Boston U., 1964-69, assoc. prof., 1969-72, prof., 1972-96; dir. Ctr. for Einstein Studies, Boston U., 1985—, prof. emeritus, 1996—. Vis. rsch. assoc. Inst. Theoretical Physics, Warsaw, 1962; vis. prof. King's Coll., U. London, 1970-71, U. Paris, 1990-91, Max Planck Inst. History of Sci., Berlin, 1994—, Calif. Inst. Tech., 1998; vis. sr. rsch. fellow Dept. Physics, Princeton U., 1977-84; rsch. assoc. U. Calif., Berkeley, 1994; master mind lectr. British Acad., 2005; lectr. Smithsonian Inst. Ann. Dibner Lecture, 2005, Wartofsky Meml. Lecture, City U. NY, 2005. Author: Einstein from B to Z, 2002; editor: Selected Papers Leon Rosenfeld, 1979, Foundations of Space-Time Theories, 1977, Einstein Studies, 1989—, Collected Papers of Albert Einstein, 1977-88, Einstein's Miraculous Year, 1998, 2d edit., 2005. Office: Boston U Ctr Enstein Studies 745 Commonwealth Ave Rm 505 Boston MA 02215-1401 Home Phone: 617-734-9684. Business E-Mail: stachel@bu.edu.

STACK, EDWARD W., retail executive; Mdse. mgr., store mgr., pres. Dick's Sporting Goods Inc., Pitts., 1977—84, chmn., CEO, 1984—. Office: Dick's Sporting Goods Inc RIDC Park W 300 Industry Dr Pittsburgh PA 15275

STACK, EDWARD WILLIAM, diversified financial services company executive; b. Rockville Centre, NY, Feb. 1, 1935; s. Edward Henry and Helen Margaret (Leitner) S.; m. Christina Carol Hunt, Aug. 19, 1967; children: Amy Alison, Kimberly Anne, Suzanne Gail. BBA, Pace U., 1956; LLD (hon.), Hartwick Coll., 1982; LHD (hon.), Pace U., 1991, L.I. U., 1994. With Clark Estates, Inc., NYC, 1956-2000, pres., bd. dirs., 1990-2000. Trustee NY State Hist. Assn., Cooperstown, 1975—2002, Mary Imogene Bassett Hosp., 1973—; vice chmn. NY State Trooper Found.; bd. chair Soc. Family Svcs., Glen Cove, NY; emeritus trustee Hartwick Coll., Oneonta, NY; sec. Nat. Baseball Hall of Fame and Mus., Inc., Cooperstown, 1961—77, pres., chmn., 1977—93, chmn., 1993—2000, dir., 1977—; chmn. adv. bd. Salvation Army Nassau County; hon. mem. adv. bd. Salvation Army Greater NY, NYC; v.p. Mental Health Assn., Nassau County, NY; mem. adv. bd. Ctr. Family Life, Bklyn.; trustee United Meth. Ch., Sea Cliff, NY; bd. dirs. Farmers' Mus., Inc., Cooperstown, The Clark Found., NYC; hon. dir. United Meth. City Soc. Mem. Mohican Club (Cooperstown, NY). Independent. Home: 25 Waverly St Glen Head NY 11545-1004 Personal E-mail: ewstack@aol.com.

STACK, FRANK HUNTINGTON, painter, retired art educator; b. Houston, Oct. 31, 1937; s. Maurice Z. and Norma Rose (Huntington) S.; m. Mildred Roberta Powell, June 12, 1959; children: Joan Elaine, Robert Huntington. BFA, U. Tex., 1959; postgrad., Sch. Art Inst. Chgo., 1960-61; MA, U. Wyo., 1963. Assoc. art editor Houston Chronicle, 1959-60; instr. U. Mo., Columbia, 1963-69, prof. art, 1969-95, Catherine P. Middlebush prof. humanities, 1995-2000, prof. emeritus, 2000—. Mem. regional adv. bd. Mo. Arts Coun., Columbia, 1979-80; mem. exec. bd. U. Mo. Art and Archaeology Mus., Columbia, 1981-84; chmn. art dept. U. Mo., Columbia, 1981-83; mem. pers. com. U. Mo. Columbia Arts and Sci. Coll., Columbia, 1976-80; vis. artist W.Va. Arts Coun. and Exxon, Shepherd Coll., Shepherdstown, W.Va., 1983. Artist, author: (cartoons) The New Adventures of Jesus, 1963-95, The New Adventures of Jesus: The Second Coming, 2007, (book of cartoons) Dorman's Doggie, 1990, Les Novvelle Aventures De Jesus (French Translation), 2008; illustrator artist: (graphic novel) Our Cancer Year, 1994 (Best Graphic Novel Harvey award 1995), Naked Glory: erotic art of Frank Stack. 1997, The Bard Must Die (Harvey award Best Graphics Story, 1995); artist traveling exhibit Watercolors by Frank Stack, 1977-79; editor: (collection of comic strips) Alley Oop, 3 vols. 1946-47, 47-48, 48-49, 1990, 93, 95 (nominated Best Reprint 1991, 94, 96), Alley Oop mag., 1997—; mem. dv. bd. Jour. Cartoon and Comic Art, 1984—; contbg. writer The Comics Jour., 1989—; author: (novels) Les Aventures de Jesus, 2008. Mem. mus. rev. bd. U. Mo., Nouvelles 4 Campus Sys., Columbia, 1989. With US Army, 1960—62. Recipient Rsch. Grants, U. Mo. Rsch. Coun., Columbia, 1969, 85, 93, 98, Gov.'s Arts awards Artist of Yr. Mo. Arts Coun., St. Louis, 1986. Mem. Kans. Watercolor Soc. (awards 1992, 96), Columbia Art League (adv. bd. 1978-82), Mo. Watercolor Soc. (award 2003). Avocations: historical research, art history, newspaper comics of 1930's and 40's, collector of master prints. Home: 409 Thilly Ave Columbia MO 65203-3458 Office Phone: 573-442-3009. Personal E-mail: frankstack@gmail.com. Business E-Mail: stackf@missouri.edu.

STACK, GARY EDWARD, medical educator; b. Cheverly, Md., Nov. 18, 1953; s. Edward Henry and Virginia Alice Stack; m. Maria Nenita Calleja, Nov. 26, 1975; children: Matthew, Kathryn. BS, U. Md., 1975; PhD, U. Wis., 1983; MD, Johns Hopkins U., 1984. Cert. clin. pathology Am. Bd. Pathology, blood banking and immunohematology Am. Bd. Pathology. Resident in internal medicine Yale-New Haven Hosp., 1987—90, clin. fellow transfusion medicine dept. lab. medicine, 1990—91; instr. dept. lab. medicine Yale U. Sch. Medicine, New Haven, 1991—92; chief pathology and lab. medicine svc. VA Conn. Healthcare Sys., West Haven, 1992—. Asst. prof. dept. lab. medicine Yale U. Sch. Medicine, New Haven, 1992—2001, assoc. prof. dept. lab. medicine, 2001—; mem. med. adv. bd. Conn. Red Cross, Farmington, Conn., 1992—; insp. Coll. Am. Pathologists, 1992—; lectr. in field. Co-author: Practical Guide to Transfusion Medicine, 2001; contbr. chapters to books, articles to profl. jours. Fellow, Rockefeller Found., 1984—86; rsch. fellow, NIH, 1985—87. Mem.: Am. Soc. for Apheresis, Am. Assn. Clin. Chemists, Am. Assn. Blood Banks. Achievements include discovery of pro-inflammatory cytokines in liquid portion of blood components; development of technique for mapping functional domains of estrogen receptor; model for mechanism of estrogen stimulation of cell proliferation. Office: Yale New Haven Hosp Dept Lab Medicine 20 York St New Haven CT 06504 Business E-Mail: gary.stack@yale.edu.

STACK, GEOFFREY LAWRENCE, real estate developer; b. Trinidad, Brit. West Indies, Sept. 16, 1943; s. Gerald Francis and V. Louise (Bell) S.; m. Victoria Hammack, 1970 (div. 1986); 1 child, Kathryn; m. Nancy J. Haarer, Apr. 19, 1987; children: Alexandra, Natalie. BA, Georgetown U., 1965; MBA, U. Pa., 1972. Dir. acquisitions J.H. Snyder Co., LA, 1972-75; from project mgr. to exec. v.p. Richards West, Newport Beach, Calif., 1975-77; pres. Regis Homes Corp., Newport

Beach, 1977-93; mng. dir. Sares-Regis Group, Irvine, Calif., 1993—. Bd. dirs. Calif. Housing Coun., Sacramento, Tejon Ranch Co. Bd. dirs. Nat. Multihousing Coun., 1987—89; bd. regents Georgetown U., 2009; trustee Cystinosis Rsch. Found., 2006, Urban Land Inst. Capt. USMC, 1967—70. Decorated 2 Bronze Stars, 21 Air medals, Navy Commendation medal, Purple Heart, Combat Action Ribbon. Mem. Young Pres. Orgn., Big Canyon Country Club, Pacific Club, Olympic Club, Calif. Pacific Union Club. Democrat. Roman Catholic. Office: SARES REGIS Group 18802 Bardeen Ave Irvine CA 92612-1521 Office Phone: 949-756-5959. Business E-Mail: jstack@sares-regis.com.

STACK, GEORGE JOSEPH, philosopher, writer; b. NYC; m. Mary K. Di Maria, 1997; children: Diane, Christopher, stepchildren: Jena, Shelley. BA, Pace U., 1960; MA, Pa. State U., 1962, PhD, 1964. Instr. humanities Pa. State U., 1962-63; instr. philosophy L.I. U., 1963-64, asst. prof., 1964-67, SUNY, Brockport, 1967-68, asso. prof., 1968-70, prof., chmn., 1970-77, 1985—94, prof., 1994—95, prof. emeritus, 1995—, also advisor Center for Philosophic Exchange, 1970-82. Author: Berkeley's Analysis of Perception, 1970, reprinted, 1991, On Kierkegaard: Philosophical Fragments, 1976, Kierkegaard's Existential Ethics, 1977;: 2d edit., 1992, Japanese transl., 1985, Sartre's Philosophy of Social Existence, 1978, reprinted, 1992, Lange and Nietzsche, 1983, Japanese translation, 2006, Nietzsche and Emerson, 1992, Nietzche's Anthropic Circle, 2005; contbg. author Nietzsche and Modern German Thought, 1991, Emerson/Nietzsche, 1998, The Emerson Enigma, 2003; contbg. author: Ralph Waldo Emerson Bicentenary Appraisals, 2006; contbr. numerous articles and reviews to profl. jours. Office: PO Box 92 Grapevine TX 76099-0092

STACK, JIM, professional sports team executive; Grad., Northwestern U., 1983. Draft pick Houston Rockets, 1983; profl. basketball player Belgium, Israel and France, 1983—88; scout Chgo. Bulls, 1988—89, spl. asst. to v.p. basketball ops., 1989—96, asst. v.p. basketball ops., 1996—2000; asst. coach Ind. Pacers, 2000—03; advanced scout NY Knicks, 2003—04; gen. mgr. Minn. Timberwolves, 2004—. Office: Minn Timberwolves 600 First Ave N Minneapolis MN 55403*

STACK, PAUL FRANCIS, lawyer; b. Chgo., July 21, 1946; s. Frank Louis and Dorothy Louise Stack; m. Nea Waterman, July 8, 1972; children: Nea Elizabeth, Sera Waterman. BS, U. Ariz., 1968; JD, Georgetown U., 1971. Bar: Ill. 1971, U.S. Ct. Claims 1975, U.S. Tax Ct. 1974, U.S. Ct. Internat. Trade 1977, U.S. Supreme Ct. 1975. Law clk. U.S. Dist. Ct., Chgo., 1971-72; asst. U.S. atty. No. Dist. Ill., Chgo., 1972-75; mng. dir. Stack Chtd., Chgo., 1976—. Bd. dirs. Riverside (Ill.) Pub. Libr., 1977-83, Suburban Libr. Sys., Burr Ridge, Ill., 1979-82; mem. Mayor's ad hoc adv. com. on Ctrl. Libr., Chgo., Ill., 1987-88; mem. bd. edn. Twp. H.S. Dist. 208, Riverside, Ill., 1989-97; pres. Village of Riverside, Ill., 1997-2001; mem. exec. com. Chgo. Area Transp. Study, 1999-2001. Mem. Chgo. Zool. Soc. (gov. 1980—, planned giving adv. com. 1996-99), Chgo. Bar Assn., Union League Club of Chgo. (bd. dirs. 1986-89). Home: 238 N Delaplaine Rd Riverside IL 60546-2035 Office: 140 S Dearborn St Ste 411 Chicago IL 60603-5201

STACK, SEAN M., metal products executive; BS in Bus. Adminstrn., U. Notre Dame. V.p. ABN AMRO Bank; asst. treas. Splty. Foods Corp., Deerfield, Ill., 1996, v.p., treas., 1996—2000, Noveon, Inc., Cleve., 2001—04, Commonwealth Industries, Inc., Louisville, 2004; sr. v.p., treas. corp. devel. Aleris Internat., Inc., Beachwood, Ohio, 2005—06; exec. v.p., CFO Aleris Internat. Europe, 2006—07, Aleris Internat., Inc., Beachwood, Ohio, 2007—09, exec. v.p. corp. devel. and strategy, 2008—09, exec. v.p, CFO, 2009—. Office: Aleris Internat Inc 25825 Science Park Dr Ste 400 Beachwood OH 44122 Office Phone: 216-910-3400.*

STACK, STEPHEN S., manufacturing executive; b. DuPont, Pa., Apr. 25, 1934; s. Steve and Sophie (Baranowski) Stasenko; m. Lois Sims Agnew, May 25, 1996. BSME, Case Western Res. U., 1956; postgrad., Syracuse Univ. registered profl engr., Ill. Mech. engr. Kaiser Aluminum, Erie, Pa., 1956-58; instr. Gannon Univ., Erie, Pa., 1958-60, Syracuse U., NY, 1960-61; engrg. supr. A.O. Smith Corp., Erie and Los Angeles, 1961-66; gen. mgr. Am. Elec. Fusion, Chgo., 1966-67; mgr.new products Maremont Corp., Chgo., 1967-69; dir. market planning Gulf and Western Ind., Bellwood, Ill., 1969-71; mgmt. and fin. cons. Stack & Assocs., Chgo., 1971-76; founder, pres. Seamcraft, Inc., Chgo., 1976—. Mem. Ill. Legis. Small Bus. Conf., 1980, Gov.'s Small Bus. Adv. Commn., 1984-94, Ill. State House Conf. on Small Bus., 1984, 86, 99; chmn. West Cell Svcs., 1988-2000; chmn., founder Bridge Pers. Svcs. Corp., 1989—; vice pres., founder Ind. Bus. Assn. Ill., 1993-94; small bus. adv. coun. Fed. Res. Bank Chgo., 1989-91, Nat. Fedn. Ind. Bus., 1980—, mem. Ill. State. Leadership Coun. 1999-, del. White House Conf. on Small Bus., 1986, Nat. Small Bus. Attitudes Rsch. Panel, 1987-2009, pres. Chgo. Marine Heritage Soc., 1999-2009, mem. Navy League of US, 1991—, del. Congl. Small Bus. Summit, 1998, 2000, 02, 04, 06; with Ill. Small Bus. Leadership Coun., 2000—. Treas. Sem. Townhouse Assn., 1993-94; active Lincoln Park Conservation Assn., Sheffield Neighbors Assn.; mem. adv. coun., DePaul U. Coll. Commerce, 2000—, mem. planning com. Cathedral Prep HS, Erie, Pa, 2007. Recipient Am. Legion award, 1948, Case Western Res. U. Honor key, 1956, Eagle Scout award, 1949. Mem. Ill. Mfrs. Assn. (bd. dirs. 1986-98, vice chmn. 1995-98), Small Mfrs. Action Couns. (vice chmn. 1986-87, chmn. 1988-89), Mfrs. Polit. Action Com. (exec. com. 1987-98, vice chmn. 1993-95, chmn. 1995-98), Am. Mgmt. Assn., Pres. Assn., Blue Key, Beta Theta Pi, Theta Thau, Pi Delta Epsilon. Chgo. Yacht Club, East Bank Club, Fullerton Tennis Club (pres. 1971-79, treas. 1979-83, bd. dirs. 1983-86), Lake Shore Ski Club (v.p. 1982, 91), Lincoln Park Tennis Assn. Patentee in liquid control and metering fields. Office: 932 W Dakin St Chicago IL 60613-2922

STACK, STEVEN J., emergency physician; m. Tracie Stack; 1 child. Grad. magna cum laude, Coll. of the Holy Cross; MD, Ohio State U. Med. dir. Emergency Dept. Baptist Meml. Hosp., Memphis; chair, med. dir. Dept. Emergency Medicine St. Joseph Hosp. East, Lexington, Ky. Henry Bean Scholar. Mem.: AMA (bd. trustees 2006—, chair Compensation Com. & Health Information Tech. Adv. Group), Ohio State Med. Assn., Tenn. Coll. Emergency Physicians, Nat. Emergency Medicine Polit. Action Com., Emergency Medicine Residents' Assn. Office: St Joseph Hosp East Dept Emergency Medicine 150 N Eagle Creek Dr Lexington KY 40509 Office Phone: 859-967-5176. Office Fax: 859-967-5784.*

STACKELBERG, JOHN RODERICK, history professor; b. Munich, May 8, 1935; came to U.S., 1946; s. Curt Freiherr and Ellen (Biddle) von Stackelberg; m. Steffi Heuss, Oct. 10, 1965 (div. Apr. 1983); m. Sally Winkle, Mar. 30, 1991; children: Katherine Ellen, Nicholas Olaf, Emmet Winkle. AB, Harvard U., 1956; MA, U. Vt., 1972; PhD, U. Mass., 1974. Reading instr. Baldridge Reading Svcs., Greenwich, Conn., 1957-62; lang. tchr. Hartnackschule, Berlin, 1963-67; English and social studies tchr. Lake Region Union High Sch., Orleans, Vt., 1967-70; lectr. history San Diego State U., 1974-76; asst. prof. history U. Oreg., Eugene, 1976-77, U. S.D., Vermillion, 1977-78, Gonzaga U., Spokane, Wash., 1978-81, assoc. prof. history, 1981-88, prof. history, 1988—, Powers prof. of humanities, 1997—2004. Author: Idealism Debased, 1981, Hitler's Germany: Origins, Interpretations, Legacies, 1999, 2nd edit., 2009, (with Sally A. Winkle) The Nazi Germany Sourcebook: An Anthology of Texts, 2002, The Routledge Companion to Nazi Germany, 2007; contbr. articles to profl. jours. Pres. Spokane chpt. UN Assn., 1986-90. With U.S. Army, 1958-60. Leadership Devel. fellow Ford Found., 1969-70. Avocations: chess, tennis. Home: 530 W 24th Ave Spokane WA 99203 Office: Gonzaga U Dept History Spokane WA 99258-0001 Office Phone: 509-747-2077. Personal E-mail: rodstackelberg@comcast.net.

STACKHOUSE, DANIEL J., science educator; s. Kenneth A. and Marcia Stackhouse. BA, Washington and Lee U., Lexington, Va., 1998; MS, Nova Southeastern U., Fort Lauderdale, Fl., 2006. Cert. Nat. Bd. Profl. Tchg. Standards, 2008. Sci. tchr. Nova HS, Davie, Fla., 2003—; sci. prof. Broward Coll., Davie, Fla., 2008—. Named Best Overall Tchr., Nova HS Students, 2004—05. Office: Nova HS 3600 College Ave Davie FL 33314 Personal E-mail: danstackhouse1@aol.com.

STACKHOUSE, MAX LYNN, religious studies educator; b. Ft. Wayne, Ind., July 29, 1935; s. C. Dale and Naomi Elizabeth (Graham) S.; m. N. Jean Hostetler, Aug. 19, 1959; children: Dale Emil, David Graham, Sara Elizabeth. BA, De Pauw U., Greencastle, Ind., 1957; cert., Nijenrode U., Breukelen, The Netherlands, 1958; MDiv, Harvard U., Cambridge, Mass., 1961, PhD, 1965; DLitt (hon.), DePauw U., 1994. Ordained to ministry United Ch. of Christ, 1961. Lectr. Harvard Divinity Sch., Cambridge, Mass., 1964-66; asst. prof. Andover-Newton Theol. Sch., Mass., 1966-69, assoc. prof. Mass., 1969-73, prof. Mass., 1973-78, Herbert Gezork prof. Mass., 1978-93; Stephen Colwell prof. Princeton Theol. Sem., NJ, 1993—2004, Rimmer and Ruth de Vries prof. theology and pub. life NJ, 2004—06, prof. emeritus, 2007—. Frederick disting. vis. prof. De Pauw U., 2007, vis. prof. United Theol. Coll., Bangalore, India, 1973, 76, 82, 87, 00, Pacific Theol. Coll., Suva, Fiji, 1982, Das Sprachenkonvikt, East Berlin, 1983; pres. joint doctoral program Boston Coll. and Andover Newton Theol. Sch., 1988-89, chmn. rels. and soc. dept., 1975-93; dir. Kuyper Ctr. Pub. Theology, 1994-06; pres. Berkshire Inst. Theology and Arts, 1991—; vis. prof. Pts. Grad. da Eschala Superior de Tech. Inst. da UNISINOS, Sao Leapoldo, Brazil, 2008. Author: Creeds, Society and Human Rights, 1984, Public Theology and Political Economy, 1987, Apologia, 1988 (Best Booklist Internat. Bull. Missiology 1988), On Moral Business, 1994, Christian Ethics in a Global Era, 1996, Covenant and Committments, 1998, God and Globalization, vol. 1, 2000, vol. 2, 2001, vol. 3, 2002, vol. 4, 2007; author, editor 22 books; mem. editl. bd. Jour. Religious Ethics, Christian Century, Jour. Polit. Theology; contbr. articles to profl. jours. Investigation team Am. Com. Human Rights, Philippines, 1984; pres. James Luther Adams Found., 1987-93; exec. sec. Am. Com. Higher Edn. in India, 1986-91. Rsch. grantee Ctr. for Urban Studies, Harvard U., 1965-66, Assn. Theol. Schs., 1986-87, Lilly Endowment, Indpls., 1989, 91, Pew Charitable Trusts, 1993, 98; recipient Outstanding Alumnus award DePauw U., 1988. Fellow Soc. Sci. Study Religion (bd. dirs. 1980-84), Soc. Values in Higher Edn.; mem. NAACP, Amnesty Internat., Soc. Christian Ethics (past pres., past exec. sec.), Am. Theol. Soc. (pres. 2008-09), Stockbridge Club. Democrat.

STACKLEY, SEAN JOSEPH, civilian military employee; BS in Mech. Engring., with distinction, US Naval Acad., 1979; MS in Mech./Ocean Engring., MIT. Cert. profl. engr. Commonwealth Va., 1994. Surface warfare officer to engring. duty officer, engring. and combat sys. aboard USS John Young USN, prodn. officer USS Arleigh Burke, prog. mgr. LPD 17, 2001—05; profl. staff mem. Senate Armed Services Com.; asst. sec. rsch., devel. & acquisition Dept. Navy, US Dept. Def., 2008—. Office: US Navy 1000 Navy Pentagon Rm 4E739 Washington DC 20350*

STACOM, DARCY A., real estate company executive; d. Matthew and Claire Stacom; m. Chris Kraus. Degree in Mktg., Lehigh U., 1980. Lic. comml. real estate agent. Capital markets intermediary Cushman & Wakefield, Inc., NYC, 1980; exec v.p. Cushman Wakefield, Inc., NYC, 2000—02; exec v.p., ptnr. investment properties institutional grp. CB Richard Ellis, 2002—. Bd. dirs. Comml. Real Estate Women NY, mem. adv. com. Mem. adv. coun. Acad. Woman Achievers of YWCA; fundraiser United Way; mem. women's bd. Madison Sq. Boys & Girls Clubs, 1999—. Named one of The 100 Most Influential Women in NYC Bus., Crain's NY Bus., 2007. Mem.: Real Estate Bd. of NY (bd. govs. 2001—). Office: CB Richard Ellis Group Inc 200 Park Ave New York NY 10166

STACOM, TARA IRENE, real estate company executive; d. Matthew J. and Claire P. Stacom; m. Paul Allan Nussbaum, June 8, 1985. BS in Fin., Lehigh U., Pa., 1980. Broker to exec. v.p. Cushman & Wakefield, Inc., NYC, 1980—2005, bd. dirs., 2003—, vice chmn., 2005—. Mem. ethics com. Real Estate Bd. NY, bd. dirs. comml. brokerage divsn.; bd. dirs. WX (NY Women Execs. in Real Estate), 2004—; dir. Realty Found. NY, 2004—. Dir.'s Cir. mem. Girls, Inc.; bd. trustees Lehigh U., Pa. Named one of The 100 Most Influential Women in NYC Bus., Crain's NY Bus., 2007. Achievements include becoming Cushman & Wakefield's top-producing broker in 2004, the first woman to accomplish this at the company. Office: Cushman & Wakefield 51 W 52nd St New York NY 10019-6178 Office Phone: 212-841-7843. E-mail: tara.stacom@cushwake.com.

STACY, DENNIS WILLIAM, architect; b. Council Bluffs, Iowa, Sept. 22, 1945; s. William L. and Mildred Glee (Carlsen) S.; m. Judy Annette Long, Dec. 28, 1968; 1 child: Stephanie. BArch, Iowa State U., 1969; postgrad., U. Nebr., 1972. Registered arch., Iowa, Tex., Colo., Mo., Nat. Coun. Architectural Registration Bds. Cert.; registered interior designer Tex. Designer Troy & Stalder Archs., Omaha, 1967, Archs. Assocs., Des Moines, 1968-69, Logsdon & Voelter Archs., Temple, Tex., 1970; project arch. Roger Schutte & Assocs., Omaha, 1972-73; arch., assoc. Robert H. Burgin & Assocs., Council Bluffs, 1973-75, Neil Astle & Assocs., Omaha, 1975-78; owner, prin. Dennis W. Stacy, AIA, Arch., Glenwood, Iowa, 1978-81; pres. Stacy Archs., Inc., Dallas, 1981—2001, Stacy Archtl. Studio, PLLC, 2002—. Mem. organizing com. symposium Tex. A&M U., 1991—2008. Archtl. works include: Davies Amphitheater, 1980, Addison Nat. Bank Bldg., 1985, Villa Roma, 1988, C.U. Performing Arts Ctr., 1989, Mercedes-Benz Distbn. Ctr., 1987, Dallas Chpt. AIA Offices, 1990, Janadria Festival Arena, 1994, Physicians Consultants Clinic, 1994, Horizon Pain Mgmt. Ctr., 1995, Rheumatology Assoc. Clinic, 1996, Addison Nat. Br. Bank, 1996, Cummins So. Plains Distbn., Fabrication and Corp. Offices Ctr., 1998, Arthur Murray Dance Studios, 2001, 06, Tatum Residence, 2001, Big Glee Office Plz., 2006; co-author Guide to Dallas Architecture, 1999, Transformations-The Architects, Buildings and Events That Shaped Dallas Architecture, 2008. Mem. City of Dallas Urban Design Adv. Com., 1992-96, chmn., 1995-96; dir. Greater Dallas Planning Coun., 1997-05; chmn. Glenwood Zoning Bd. Adjustment, 1979-81; chmn. Mills County Plant Iowa Program, 1979-81; mem. S.W. Iowa Citizen's Adv. Com., Iowa State Dept. Transp., 1977-81; regional screening chmn. Am. Field Svc. Internat./Intercultural Programs, 1974-79, Iowa-Nebr. rep., 1978-80. With U.S. Army, 1969-71. Decorated Nat. Def. Svc. medal, Vietnam Svc. medal, Vietnam Campaign medal, Army Commendation medal, Disting. Alumnus Design Achievement award Iowa State U., 1999. Fellow AIA (chmn. nat. conv. 2000, Iowa Design Honor award 1981, Dallas AIA commendation awards 1990, 92, 95-98, 2007 (2), Citation of Honor award 1991-92, 96, 2001, 08, Dallas Design awards 1991 (2), 96-97, Tex. Design Honor award 1992, Dallas AIA Firm of Yr. award 1992, Nat. Presdl. Citation 2000, Dallas commr. design 1991, chmn. Dallas design awards 1992, pres. Dallas AIA 1996), Tex. Soc. Archs. (environ. resource com. 1994-95, chmn., Tex. arch. pub. com., 1992-98, chmn. 1997, 98), Nat. Coun. Archtl. Registration Bds., Iowa State U. Adv. Coun. (1997-2000, 05-07, chmn. 1999-2000). Home and Office: 4148 Cobblers Ln Dallas TX 75287-6725 Office Phone: 972-250-1909. Personal E-mail: dstacyarch@aol.com.

STACY, MARK ALLEN, neurologist; b. Cape Girardeau, Mo., May 4, 1959; s. Billy Wayn and Jane Cooper S.; m. Tina Estrada, June 26, 1982; children: Bryan, Andrea. BS, S.E. Mo. State, 1981; MD, U. Mo., 1986. Diplomate Am. Bd. Neurology. and Psychiatry. Intern in internal medicine St. Mary's Hosp., St. Louis, 1986-87; resident in neurology Hahnemann U., Phila., 1987-90, chief resident, 1989-90, clin. instr., 1989-90; asst. prof. neurology U. Mo., 1991-96, dir. Parkinson's Disease Clinic and Movement Disorders Ctr., 1992-96; neurologist Barrow Neurol. Inst., St. Joseph's Hosp., 1996, dir. Muhammad Ali Parkinson Rsch. Ctr., 1997; assoc. prof. neurology, dir. movement disorders prog. Duke U., Durham, NC, dir. Neurology Clin. Rsch. Ctr. Cons. neurology Harry S. Truman Meml. Vet. Hosp., 1991-96; adv. bd. DuPont Pharma, 1996—, Athena Pharm., 1997—, SmithKline Beecham, 1999, Elan Pharm., 1999; assoc. med. dir. Nat. Parkinson Found., 1997—; mem. Dystonia Study Group, 1996—, Parkinson Study Group, 1997—, WeMove, LME, adv. com., 1998—. Author: (chpt.) Current Pediatric Therapy, Vol. 16, 1999; co-author: (chpt.) Current Therapy in Neurologic Disease-3, 1990, Pathology of the Aging Nervous System, 1991, Neurobehavioral Aspects of Parkinson's Disease, 1992, Movement and Allied Disorders in Childhood, 1995, Adult Neurology, 1997, Textbook of Clinical Neurology, 1998; ed.: The Handbook of Dystonia; mem. editl. bd. Neurology Network Commentary, 1996—, Movement Disorders, 1997—; editl. bd. Southern Medical Jour. ad hoc reviewer, 1999—; contbr. articles to profl. jours. Mem. counseling staff Mo. Boys State, 1979—, dean of counselors, 1993—, bd. dirs., 1993—; mem. adv. bd. Physician's Home Health & Hospice Network, 1993-95, WE Move, 1998—; advisor Greater Mo. Tourette Syndrome Chpt., 1991-96, Am. Parkinson's Disease Assn., Columbia, Mo., 1992-96, bd. dirs. Fight Night Found., 1999—, Dystonia Med. Rsch. Found., 1993-96, Multiple Sclerosis Inst., 1993-96, Benign Essential Blepharospasm Found., 1997—; bd. deacons First Bapt. Ch., Columbia, 1995-96; mem. Internation Congress of Parkinsons Disease. 1999. Recipient Outstanding Young Alumni award S.E. Mo. State U., 1995, Caregivers award Nat. Parkinson Found.; Movement Disorders fellow Baylor Coll. Medicine, 1990-91; grantee DuPont Pharma, 1992, 93, Childrens Miracle Network Telethon, 1993, Sandoz Pharm., 1993, Berlex Pharm., 1994, Allergan, Inc., 1995-96, MDS Harris and Scherer DDS, 1997, Eli Lilly Pharm., 1997-98, Amgen, Inc., 1997, 98, Smith Kline Beecham, 1998—, NIH, 1998—, Pentech Pharm., Inc., 1999, Teva Pharm. USA, 1999, Roberts Pharm., 1999, others. Mem. Am. Acad. Neurology (movement disorders sect. 1995—, liaison com. 1995—), Movement Disorders Soc., Ariz. State Med. Assn., Maricopa County Med. Soc. Office: DUMC 3333 Durham NC 27710 Office Phone: 919-668-7600, 919-668-2493. Office Fax: 919-681-4935.*

STADE, GEORGE GUSTAV, humanities educator; b. NYC, Nov. 25, 1933; s. Kurt Herman and Eva Bergit (Aronson) S.; m. Dorothy Louise Fletcher, Dec. 16, 1957; children: Bjorn, Eric, Nancy, Kirsten. BA, St. Lawrence U., 1955; MA, Columbia U., 1958, PhD, 1965. Tchr. Collegiate Sch., NYC, 1957-58; instr. Bernard Baruch Sch. Bus., NYC, 1958-59, Bklyn. Poly. Inst., 1959-60, Rutgers U.-Newark, 1960-62, Columbia U., NYC, 1962, asst. prof., 1965, assoc. prof., 1968, prof. English, 1971—. Cons. in field. Author: Robert Graves, 1967, Confessions of a Lady-Killer, 1979, Sex and Violence, a Love Story, 2005, Love is War, 2006, Equipment for Living, 2008; editor: European Writers, Selected Letters of E.E. Cummings, 1968, Six Modern British Writers, 1974, Six Contemporary British Writers, 1976, European Writers: Selected Authors, 1992, British Writers Supplement II, 1992, British Writers Supplement III, 1995, British Writers Supplement IV, 1997; cons. editl. dir.: Barnes and Nobles Classics; contbr. articles to profl. jours. Mem. PEN, NY Book Critics Circle, Popular Culture Assn., MLA Home: 430 W 116th St New York NY 10027-7220 Office: Columbia U 604 Philosophy Hall New York NY 10027 Office Phone: 212-854-6410. Business E-Mail: ggs3@columbia.edu.

STADELMAN, WILLIAM RALPH, chemicals executive; b. Ont., Can., July 18, 1919; s. John Joseph and Lillian (Trachsell) S.; m. Jean MacLaren, Nov. 2, 1951; 1 child, Mary Laren. BASc, U. Toronto, 1941; MBA, U. Pa., 1949. Chief process engr. Can. Synthetic Rubber, Ltd., 1943-47; lectr. mktg. U. Pa., 1948-49; asst. to mgr. Pa. Salt Mfg. Co., 1950; sec.-treas. Ont. Research Found., Mississauga, 1950-64, pres., 1964-84, WRS Assocs., 1984—; dir., sr. exec. Inst. Chem. Sci. and Tech., 1985-89. Dir. Med. Tech. Investment Corp. Fellow World Acad. Art and Sci.; mem. Assn. Profl. Engrs. Ont., Innovation Mgmt. Assn. Can., Bd. Trade Met. Toronto, Club of Rome, Caledon Ski Club. Home Phone: 416-443-0185.

STADELMANN, WAYNE KARL, plastic surgeon; b. Milw., Wis., July 17, 1964; MD (with honors), U. Chgo.-Pritzker Sch. Medicine, 1990. Cert. Am. Bd. Plastic Surgery. Intern, gen. surgery U. Chgo. Hosp. & Clinics, 1990—91, resident, gen. surgery, 1991—94; resident, plastic surgery South Fla. Coll. Medicine, Tampa, Fla., 1994—97; joined staff Concord Hosp., NH, 2003—, New London Hosp., 2005—; private practice Stadelmann Plastic Surgery, PC, NH. Named one of Top Doctor, NH Mag. Mem.: Phi Beta Kappa. Office: Stadelmann Plastic Surgery PC 248 Pleasant St Ste 201 Pillsbury Bldg Concord NH 03301 Office Phone: 603-224-5200. Office Fax: 603-224-5091.

STADLER, EVA MARIA, literature and language professor; d. Ernest and Else Stadler; m. Richard A. Brooks, Dec. 22, 1957. BA, Barnard Coll., NYC; PhD, Columbia U., NYC, 1967. Chair, divsn. humanities Fordham Coll. Lincoln Ctr., NYC, 1973—79, dir. media studies program, 1988—95, dir. lit. studies program, 2000—03, assoc. prof. English, comparative lit. and media studies. Contbr. articles to profl. jours. Achievements include research in French and francophone film. Home: 2 Washington Sq Village - Apt 5A New York NY 10012 Office: Fordham Univ 113 W 60 St Rm 422 New York NY 10023 Office Fax: 212-636-7878. Business E-Mail: estadler@fordham.edu.

STADLER, SELISE MCNEILL, laboratory and x-ray technician, medical assistant; b. Portsmouth, Va., Dec. 27, 1960; d. William M. and Jorja Lee (Rigg) Gaidos; m. Stephen Michael McNeill, Feb. 29, 1988 (div. July 1993); 1 child, Stephen Michael Jr.; m. David Robert Stadler, June 15, 1996. Cert. chiropractic asst., Practice Mgmt. Assn., 1983; student, Tarrant County Coll., 2000—01. Cert. limited radiologic technologist, instr. cert. World Modeling Assn. Chiropractic asst. Dr. Brad Hayes, DC, Tulsa, Okla., 1982-84; adminstrv. asst. Dr. Wallace Gauntner, MD, Pitts., 1984; traffic mgr., office mgr. WVBS-AM/FM, Wilmington, NC, 1985-87; med. asst. Dr. J. Bailey Bland, DC, Wilmington, 1988-90; therapy/radiology supr. Dr. Roy L. Creasy Jr., DC, Wilmington, 1990-91; med. asst., radiologist Westside Clinic, Dallas, 1991-94; model, exec. instr. Aleksandra's Prodns., Ft. Worth, 1994-96; med. asst., radiologist Dr. Wayne R. English Jr., DO, Ft. Worth, 1994-2000; lab/x-ray technician, med. asst. Care Now, Ft. Worth, 2001—02; x-ray/bone scan technician Kaner Med. Group, Bedford, Tex., 2001—02; med. asst., x-ray tech. Premier Orthopedics, Dr. Craig Saunders, MD and Dr. Marvin Van Hal, MD, 2002—07; x-ray tech., med. asst. HEB Bone & Joint Surgeons, Dr. Daniel Foster & Dr. Frank Swords, 2007—. Author published poetry. Vol. Holy Family Cath. Ch., Ft. Worth, 1997-99. Recipient Employee Excellence award, Aleksandra's Prodns., 1996. Mem. Tex. Soc. Radiologic Technologists (cert. in CPR and automated external defibrillation program), Am. Soc. Radiologic Technologists, Fort Worth Astronomy Club. Episcopalian. Avocations: scuba diving, tennis, rollerblading, equestrian, photography. Home Phone: 817-238-9317; Office Phone: 817-540-1185.

STADTHERR, MARK A., chemical engineer, educator; b. Austin, Minn. BChE in Chem. Engring., U. Minn., Mpls., 1972; PhD in Chem. Engring., U. Wis., Madison, 1976. Faculty U. Ill., Urbana-Champaign, 1976-95; chem. engring. faculty U. Notre Dame, Ind., 1996—. Lectr. in field. Contbr. articles to profl. jours. Recipient Xerox award for engring. rsch., 1982, Computing in Chem. Engring. award AIChE, 1998; named GTE Emerging scholar lectr. U. Notre Dame, 1986. Mem.: ASEE, SIAM, ACS, AICHE (chair Computing and Sys. Tech. Divsn. 2002—03). Achievements include research on advanced computational strategies for process engineering, application of interval analysis to chemical engineering problems, environmentally conscious process design, ecological modeling. Office: Dept Chem Engring Univ Notre Dame Notre Dame IN 46556 Business E-Mail: markst@nd.edu.

STADTLER, WALTER EDWARD, diplomat; b. NYC, Apr. 4, 1936; s. Walter Henry and Paula (Nagl) S.; m. Maida Maria Macdonald, Mar. 4, 1937; children: Fiona, Walter Jr., Catriona. Student, Sorbonne U., Paris, 1955-56; AB, Fordham U., 1957; postgrad., Columbia U., 1957-58. With Dept. State, 1962—94; vice consul Am. Consulate, Southampton, Eng., 1962-63; third sec. Am. Embassy, London, 1963-64, econ. officer, second sec. Bonn, Fed. Republic of Germany, 1966-69; personnel officer Dept. State, Washington, 1966-69; second sec. Am. Embassy, Pretoria, South Africa, 1969-72, charge' d'affaires then dep. chief of mission, 1982-85, first sec. Addis Ababa, Ethiopia, 1972-75, Stockholm, 1975-78; European affairs advisor U.S. Mission UN, NYC, 1978; mem. Royal Coll. Def. Studies, London, 1979; counselor Am. Embassy, Bonn, Fed. Republic of Germany, 1980-82; mem. Sr. Seminar, Washington, 1985-86; ambassador Am. Embassy, Cotonou, Benin, 1986-90; v.p. Nat. Def. U., Ft. McNair; sr. fellow Office of the Sec. of Def., 1992—94; U.S. mem. Internat. Def. Adv. Bd. for the Baltic Republics, 1995—2000; prof. and dir., program on peacekeeping policy George Mason U., Fairfax, Va., 1995—2000; bd. chair Geodata Systems, Inc., 1999—2007. Pres. Nat. Def. U. Found., 2008—; bd. mem. Coop. Housing Found.; mem. Coun. on Standards for Internat. Edn. Travel; councillor Atlantic Coun. of the U.S. Served to capt. U.S. Army, 1958-62. Mem. Am. Fgn. Service Assn., Army and Navy Club. Roman Catholic. Avocations: music, travel, fgn. policy and polit. mil. hist. Office: 7063 Wyndale St NW Washington DC 20015-1428 Office Phone: 202-685-2215. E-mail: stadtlerw@nduf.org.

STADTMAN, THRESSA CAMPBELL, biochemist; b. Sterling, NY, Feb. 12, 1920; d. Earl and Bessie (Waldron) Campbell; m. Earl Reece Stadtman, Oct. 19, 1943. BS, Cornell U., 1940, MS, 1942; PhD, U. Calif., Berkeley, 1949. Rsch. assoc. U. Calif., Berkeley, 1942-47, Harvard U. Med. Sch., Boston, 1949-50; biochemist Nat. Heart, Lung and Blood Inst. NIH, USPHS, HHS, Bethesda, Md., 1950—. Mem. Burroughs-Wellcome Fund Toxicology Adv. Commn., 1994-97; pres. Internat. Soc. Vitamins and Related BioFactors, 1998-2001. Editor Jour. Biol. Chemistry, Archives Biochemistry and Biophysics, Molecular and Cellular Biochemistry; editor-in-chief Bio Factors, 1991-95; contbr. articles on amino acid metabolism, methane biosynthesis, vitamin B12 biochemistry, selenium biochemistry to profl. jours. Helen Haye Whitney fellow Oxford U., Eng., 1954-55; Rockefeller Found. grantee U. Munich, 1959-60; recipient Rose award, 1987, Klaus Schwarz medal, 1988, Life Achievement Women in Sci. award L'Oreal-UNESCO, 2000, Bertrand medal and prize Assn. European Trace Elements and Metals in Biology and Medicine, Venice, 2001, Lifetime Achievement award, Oxygen Club Greater Washington, 2007. Mem. NAS, Am. Soc. Microbiology, Biochem. Soc., Soc. Am. Biochemists, Am. Chem. Soc., Am. Acad. Arts and Scis., Sigma Delta Epsilon (hon.). Home: 16907 Redland Rd Derwood MD 20855-1954 Office Phone: 301-496-3002. Business E-Mail: tc.stadtman@nih.gov.

STADTMAUER, DAVID, judge; b. Bklyn., Dec. 16, 1934; s. Simon Asher and Bertha G. (Kamelhar) S.; m. Catherine Shoshana Gottesman, Nov. 21, 1965; children: Marc, Steven, Jeffrey, Karen. LLB, N.Y. Law Sch., 1960; LLM, NYU, 1977. Bar: N.Y. 1961. Ptnr. Fuss, Geller & Stadtmauer, NYC, 1964-65; law sec. Civil Ct., NYC, 1965-68, Supreme Ct., New York County, 1969-72; mem. N.Y.C. Civil Svc. Com., 1972-73; judge Civil Ct., City of N.Y., 1974-88; acting justice Supreme Ct., State of N.Y., Bronx, 1980-88, justice, 1989—. Adj. prof. Hofstra U., Hempstead, N.Y., 1979-94; mem. jud. faculty Advanced Practice Inst., Law Sch., Hofstra U., 1978-79. Contbr. articles to profl. jour. Mem. Cmty. Bd. 12, N.Y.C., 1969-75; mem. Nat. Jewish Commn. on Law and Pub. Affairs, 1970-75; bd. dirs. Palisades Gardens Found., Palisades, N.Y., 1975—. Mem. Assn. of Bar of City of N.Y., N.Y. State Trial Lawyers Assn., Yeshiva U. Alumni Assn., Bronx County Bar Assn. Office: Supreme Ct State of NY 265 E 161st St Bronx NY 10451-2937 Office Phone: 718-618-3666. Business E-Mail: dstadt@courts.state.ny.us.

STADTMUELLER, JOSEPH PETER, federal judge; b. Oshkosh, Wis., Jan. 28, 1942; s. Joseph Francis and Irene Mary (Kilp) S.; m. Mary Ellen Brady, Sept. 5, 1970; children: Jeremy, Sarah. BS in Bus. Adminstrn., Marquette U., 1964, JD, 1967. Bar: Wis. 1967, U.S. Supreme Ct. 1980. With Kluwin, Dunphy, Hankin and McNulty, 1968-69; asst. U.S. atty. Dept. Justice, Milw., 1969-74, 1st. asst. U.S. atty., 1974-75; with Stepke, Kossow, Trebon and Stadtmueller, Milw., 1975-76; asst. U.S. atty. Dept. Justice, 1977-78, dep. U.S. atty., 1978-81, U.S. atty., 1981-87; judge U.S. Dist. Ct. (ea. dist.) Wis., Milw., 1987—, chief judge, 1995—2002. Mem. 7th Cir. Jud. Coun., 1995—2002. Recipient Spl. Commendation award Atty. Gen. U.S., 1974, 80. Mem. ABA, State Bar Wis. (bd. govs. 1979-83, exec. com. 1982-83), Am. Law Inst., Fed. Judges Assn. (bd. dirs. 1995—, sec. 2001--). Clubs: University (Milw.). Republican. Roman Catholic. Office: 471 US Courthouse 517 E Wisconsin Ave Milwaukee WI 53202-4500

STAEHELIN, LUCAS ANDREW, cell biology professor emeritus; b. Sydney, Feb. 10, 1939; came to U.S., 1969; s. Lucas Eduard and Isobel (Malloch) S.; m. Margrit Weibel, Sept. 17, 1965; children: Daniel Thomas, Philip Roland, Marcel Felix. Dipl. Natw., Swiss Fed. Inst. Tech., Zurich, 1963, PhD in Biology, 1966. Research scientist N.Z. Dept. Sci. and Indsl. Research, 1966-69; research fellow in cell biology Harvard U., Cambridge, Mass., 1969-70; asst. prof. cell biology U. Colo., Boulder, 1970-73, assoc. prof., 1973-79, prof., 1979—2007, prof. emeritus, 2007—. Vis. prof. U. Freiburg, 1978, Swiss Fed. Inst. Tech., 1984, 92, U. Melbourne, Australia, 1998; mem. cellular biology and physiology study sect. NIH, Bethesda, Md., 1980-84; mem. DOE panel on rsch. directions for the energy bioscis., 1988, 92; mem. NSF adv. panel for cellular orgn., 1994-96; mem. plant biology panel NASA; mem. adv. bd. BioEnergy Sci. Ctr., Oak Ridge, Teen., 2008-. Editl. bd. Jour. Cell Biology, 1977-81, European Jour. Cell Biology, 1981-90, Plant Physiology, 1986-92, Plant Jour., 1991-97, Biology of the Cell, 1996-99, Planta, 2003—, Current Opion in Plant Biology, 2003-2007; editor: (with C.J. Antzen) Encyclopedia of Plant Physiology, Vol. 19, Photosynthesis III, 1986; contbr. numerous articles to sci. jours. Recipient Humboldt award Humboldt Found., 1978, Sci. Tchr. award U. Colo., 1984, Outstanding Faculty award U. Colo.-Boulder Parents Assn., 2001, Highly Cited Rschr. ISI, 2004, Haselkorn Scholar award, U. Chgo., 2006; grantee NIH, 1971-2006, USDA, 1994-2005, NASA, 1997-2006; hon. sr. fellow U. Melbourne, Australia, 1998, Am. Assn. Adv. Sci., 2005. Fellow Am Soc. Plant Biologists; mem. AAAS, Am. Soc. Cell Biology, German Acad. Natural Scis. Leopoldina, Bio Energy Sci.(Sci. Adv bd., 2007-). Home: 2855 Dover Dr Boulder CO 80305-5305 Office: Dept Molecular Cell U Colo 347 UCB Boulder CO 80309-0347 Office Phone: 303-492-8843. E-mail: staeheli@colorado.edu.

STAEHLE, ROBERT L., foundation executive; b. Rochester, NY, Apr. 22, 1955; s. Henry Carl and Isabel Montgomery S. BS in Aero. and Astronautic Engring., Purdue U., 1977. Prin. investigator Skylab Expt. ED-31 (bacteria aboard Skylab), NASA/Marshall Space Flight Center, Huntsville, Ala., 1972-74, student trainee engring., 1974-77; sci. observation analyst Caltech/Jet Propulsion Lab., Pasadena, Calif., 1977-78, engr. advanced projects group, 1978-83, mem. tech. staff system integration sect. of Space Sta., 1983-87, mem. tech. staff and space sta., user ops. team leader, 1987-88; from tech. mgr. to dep. mgr. various positions Jet Propulsion Lab., Pasadena, Calif., 1988—2007; asst. mgr. Advanced Concepts Instruments and Data Sys. Divsn., 2007—. Prin. founder, pres. World Space Found., South Pasadena, Calif., 1979—; founding dir. So. Calif. Space Bus. Roundtable, 1987-95; bd. dirs. Altadena Foothills Conservancy, 2000—. Co-author: Project Solar Sail, New Am. Libr., 1990; contbr. articles to profl. jours. Mem. Cmty. Leaders Adv. Bd. for Irvine Scholars, Occidental Coll., L.A., 1996-97; bd. dirs. Caltech Y, 1987-93. Nat. Space Club Goddard scholar, 1977; Charles A. Lindbergh Fund grantee, 1986. Fellow Brit. Interplanetary Soc.; mem. Tau Beta Pi, Sigma Gamma Tau. Avocations: photography, hiking, mountain biking. Office: Jet Propulsion Lab Pasadena CA 91109 Business E-Mail: robert.l.staehle@jpl.nasa.gov.

STAELIN, DAVID HUDSON, electrical engineering educator, consultant; b. Toledo, May 25, 1938; s. Carl Gustav and Margaret E. (Hudson) S.; m. Ellen Mahoney, June 16, 1962; children: Carl H., Katharine E., Paul H. SB, MIT, 1960, SM, 1961, ScD in Elec. Engring., 1965. Instr. elec. engring. MIT, Cambridge, 1965, asst. prof., 1965—69, assoc. prof., 1969—76, prof., 1976—, asst. dir. Lincoln Lab. Lexington, 1990—2001. Vis. asst. scientist Nat. Radio Astronomy Obs., Charlottesville, Va., 1968-69; cons. Jet Propulsion Lab., Pasadena, Calif., 1969, Wellesley, Mass., 1965—; dir. Environ. Rsch. and Tech., Inc., Concord, Mass., 1969-78; co-founder, chmn. PictureTel Corp., Peabody, Mass., 1984-87; mem. com. on radio frequency requirements for rsch., NAS, Washington, 1980-86, chmn. 1983-86; chmn. advanced microwave sounder working group NASA, Washington, 1981-82, mem. space applications adv. com., 1983-86; mem. adv. com. info. tech. Pres. U.S., Washington, D.C., 2003-05. Co-author: Made in America, 1989, Electromagnetic Waves, 1994; contbr. articles to profl. jours. Fellow: IEEE, AAAS; mem.: Am. Geophys. Union, Am. Meteorl. Soc., Internat. Union for Radio Sci. Achievements include patents for grinding and polishing sheet glass, display of dynamic images, ribbon-beam cathode ray tube. Office: MIT Rm 26-341 Cambridge MA 02139

STAELIN, EARL HUDSON, lawyer; b. Toledo, Apr. 24, 1940; s. Carl Gustav and Margaret E. (Hudson) S.; m. Carol Jane Keeney, Mar. 24, 1973 (div. 1995); 1 child, Vijay Hudson. BA, Yale U., 1962; LLB, U. Mich., 1966. Bar: Ohio 1966, Tex. 1982, Colo. 1998, US Dist. Ct. (we. dist.) Tex. 1988, US Ct. Appeals (5th cir.) 1994. Assoc. atty. Marshall, Melhorn, Toledo, 1966-69; pvt. practice Toledo, 1969; lectr. law U. Toledo Coll. Law, 1971-72; staff atty. Toledo Legal Aid Soc., 1969-71, dir., 1971-76, sr. staff atty., 1977-81; pvt. practice cons. nutrition Austin, Tex., 1981—82, Denver, 2001—05; staff atty. City of Austin Law Dept., 1982-86; pvt. practice Law Ofcs. of Earl H. Staelin, Austin and Aurora, Colo., 1986—2004; ptnr. Onsager Staelin & Guyerson LLC, Denver, 2004—. Presenter in field. Contbr. articles to profl. jours. Pres. Toledo Coun. on World Affairs, 1971-76; co-organizer Conferences on Nutrition and Crime, Austin, 1982, San Antonio, 1983. Mem. Colo. Bar Assn., State Bar Tex., Humanists Colo. (bd. mem. 2001-, pres. 2007). Democrat. Unitarian Universalist. Office: Ste 1401 1873 S Bellaire St Denver CO 80222 Mailing: 7982 S Cedar St Littleton CO 80120 Office Phone: 303-512-1123. E-mail: estaelin@comcast.net.

STAELIN, RICHARD, business administration educator; b. Larchmont, NY, Aug. 3, 1939; s. Richard Carl and Dorothy (Potts) S.; m. Julie Ann Fischer, Aug. 24, 1963; children: Adam, Kate. BSME, U. Mich., 1961, BS in Math., 1962, MBA, 1963, PhD, 1969. Market planner IBM, Harrison, NY, 1963-66; prof. Carnegie-Mellon U., Pitts., 1969-82; Edward and Rose Donnell prof. Duke U., Durham, NC, 1982—, assoc. dean faculty affairs, 1982-91, assoc. dean exec. edn., 2000—02, dep. dean, 2002—04; exec. dir. Teradata CRM Ctr., 2004—; mng. dir. GEMBA, 1995-97; exec. dir. Mktg. Sci. Inst., Cambridge, Mass., 1991-93. Vis. prof. Australian Grad. Sch., Kensington, 1980—81. Author: Consumer Protection Legislation and the U.S. Food Industry, 1980; mem. editl. bd. Jour. Mktg. Rsch., 1974-82, Jour. Consumer Rsch., 1976-87; area editor Mktg. Sci., 1983-88; editor-in-chief Mktg. Sci., 1995-97. Mem. Pitts. Exec. Bd.; treas. Pitts. Arts and Crafts Ctr., 1976-79; bd. dirs. Dispute Settlement Ctr., Chapel Hill, NC, Bio Electronics, Frederick, Md., 2005—; bd. vis. drama dept. Duke U., 1990-96. Recipient Best Mktg. Paper award Inst. Mgmt. Sci., 1985, NCNB Faculty award 1990, AMA/Irwin Disting. Mktg. Educators award, 1996, O'Dell award JMR, 1998, Manyard award, 2006; HEW grantee, 1972-74, NSF grantee, 1973-79. Mem.: INFORMS Soc. Marketing Sci. (pres. elect 2006—07), INFORMS (pres. 2008—), Assn. Consumer Rsch., Am. Mktg. Assn. (Converse award 2000). Office: Fuqua Sch of Bus Science Dr Rm 339 Durham NC 27706-2597 Home Phone: 919-382-9977; Office Phone: 919-660-7824. E-mail: rick@staelin.com.

STAFF, JOEL V., energy executive; b. 1944; BA, U. Tex., Austin, 1967; MBA, Tex. A&M U., Kingsville, 1971. Various fin. and gen. mgmt. positions Baker Hughes, Inc., 1976—93; chmn., pres., CEO Nat.-Oilwell Inc., 1993—2001, exec. chmn., 2001—02; chmn., CEO Reliant Energy, Inc., Houston, 2003—07, non-exec. chmn., 2007—. Bd. dirs. Reliant Energy, Inc., 2002—, Nat. Oilwell, Inc., Ensco Internat., Inc.; adv. dir. King Chapman & Broussard; devel. bd. U. Tex. Health Sci. Ctr., Houston. Adv. dir. Boys and Girls Club, Houston. Office: Reliant Energy Exec Offices PO Box 2286 Houston TX 77252-2286

STAFFIER, PAMELA MOORMAN, psychologist; b. Passaic, NJ, Dec. 7, 1942; d. Wynant Clair and Jeannette Frances (Rentzsch) Moorman; m. John Staffier, Jr., Apr. 5, 1975; children: M. Anthony, C. Matthew. BA, Bucknell U., 1964; MA in Psychology, Assumption Coll., Worcester, Mass., 1970, CAGS, 1977; PhD, Union U., 1978. Psychologist Westboro (Mass.) State Hosp., 1965, prin. psychologist, dir. program planning & devel., 1973—76; rsch. psychologist Wrentham (Mass.) State Sch., 1966, Cushing Hosp., Framingham, Mass., 1967; prin. psychologist, dir. program planning & devel. Grafton (Mass.) State Hosp., 1967—72; dir. Staffier Clinic, 1978—2008; clin. dir. Moriarty Mental Health Clinic, 1975—78. Mem.: APA, Nat. Register Health Svc. Providers Psychology, Mass. Psychol. Assn., Am. Psychol. Practitioners Assn. (founding mem.). Achievements include research in state hospital closings; biochemical basis of schizophrenia. Home: 68 Adams St Westborough MA 01581 Office: 45 Lyman St Westborough MA 01581-1464 Office Phone: 508-366-2300.

STAFFORD, DONALD GENE, chemistry professor; b. Valliant, Okla., Oct. 9, 1930; s. Otto Lewis and Rose Lavelle (Osterdock) S.; m. Jane Wright, July 5, 1951; children: Michael Royce, Robert Gene, Joel Dan. BS, U. Okla., 1957, PhD, 1969; MS, Okla. State U., 1961. Prof. sci. edn. East Cen. U., Ada, Okla., 1961-73, prof. chemistry, 1973—. Adj. prof. U. Okla., Norman, 1970—. Author: The Improvement of Science in Oklahoma (7-12), 1970, Guidelines and Successful Practices in Elementary Edn, 1970, Wings for a Dinosaur, 1972, Early Childhood Resource Book, 1972, Teaching Science in the Elementary School, 1973, 3d edit., 1979, Teaching Science in the Secondary School, 1973, Research, Teaching, and Learning with the Piaget Model, 1976, Investigations in Physical Science, 1976, The Learning Science Program K-6 (7 children's books and 7 tchr.'s guides), 1976, TOP, The Oklahoma Project, Chemistry, 1987, The Learning Cycle, 1988, The Lost City of Balee, A Novel for Young Teenagers, 2000, Don's Rhymes, A Book of Poetry, 2000. Served with AUS, 1948-53. Mem. Am. Chem. Soc., Nat. Sci. Tchrs. Assn., Okla. Sci. Tchrs. (pres. 1973-74, 78-79), Sigma Xi. Home: 2202 Fullview Dr Ada OK 74820-4436 Personal E-mail: donjane@cableone.net.

STAFFORD, FRANK PETER, JR., economics professor, consultant; b. Chgo., Sept. 17, 1940; s. Frank Peter and Ida Gustava (Tormala) S.; m. Lilian Elisabeth Lundin, Aug. 8, 1964; children: Craig Peter, Jennifer Elisabeth, Christine Anna BA, Northwestern U., 1962; MBA, U. Chgo., 1964, PhD, 1968. Asst. prof. econs. U. Mich., 1966-71, assoc. prof., 1971-73, 74-75, prof., 1976—, chmn. dept. econs., 1980—, rsch. scientist Inst. Social Rsch., 1995—, chair budget study com., 1995—, assoc. dir. Inst. for Social Rsch., 2000—. Vis. assoc. prof. Grad. Sch. Bus.-Stanford U., 1973-74; spl. asst. for econ. affairs U.S. Dept. Labor, Washington, 1975-76; vis. prof. dept. econs. U. Saarlandes, Fed. Republic Germany, 1986; faculty rsch. assoc. Inst. Social Rsch., Ann Arbor, 1979—; vis. scholar Indsl. Inst. for Econs. and Social Rsch., Stockholm, 1979, 83, 90, Worklife Study Ctr., Stockholm, 1988, 90; Tinbergen Found. prof. U. Amsterdam, 1992, 94; panel mem. Social Sci. Rsch. Coun., N.Y.C., 1979—; rsch. assoc. Nat. Bur. Econ. Rsch., Cambridge, Mass., 1983—; prof. econs. Tinbsrgne Found. U. Amsterdam, 1992; vis. scholar U. Stockholm, 1994. Author, editor: Time Use Goods and Well Being, 1986, Studies in Labor Market Behavior: Sweden and the United States, 1981; mem. editorial bd.: Am. Econ. Rev., 1976-78; contbr. articles to profl. jours. Dir. Panel Study of Income Dynamics, 1995—. Grantee NSF, 1973, 80, 95—, 2002—, NICHD, 1995—, Nat. Ins. on Aging, 1999—. Mem. Am. Econs. Assn. Home: 3535 Daleview Dr Ann Arbor MI 48105-9686 Office: U Mich Dept Econs Lorch Hall Rm 312 Ann Arbor MI 48105 Office Phone: 734-936-0323. Business E-Mail: fstaffor@umich.edu.

STAFFORD, JAMES FRANCIS CARDINAL, cardinal, archbishop; b. Balt., July 26, 1932; s. F. Emmett and Mary Dorothy Stafford. Student, Loyola Coll., Balt., 1950—52; BA, St. Mary's Sem., Balt., 1954; STB, STL, Gregorian U., Rome, 1958; MSW, Cath. U., 1964; postgrad., Rutgers U., 1963, St. Mary's Sem. and Univ., Balt., 1973—75. Ordained priest Archdiocese of Balt., 1957; Spiritual moderator Ladies of Charity Ch., Balt., 1966—76; spiritual moderator Soc. St. Vincent de Paul, Balt., 1965—76; urban vicar Archdiocese of Balt., 1966—76; ordained bishop, 1976; aux. bishop, vicar gen. Archdiocese of Balt., 1976—82; bishop Diocese of Memphis, 1982—86; archbishop Archdiocese of Denver, 1986—96; pres. Pontifical Coun. Laity, 1996—2003; elevated to cardinal, 1998; cardinal-deacon Gesu Bon Pastore alla Montagnola, 1998—2008; major penitentiary Apostolic Penitentiary, Rome, 2003—09, major penitentiary emeritus, 2009—; cardinal-priest S. Pietro in Montorio, 2008—. Archdiocesan liaison Md. Cath. Conf., Balt., 1975—78; Oriental Orthodox/Roman Cath. cons. Nat. Cath. Conf. Bishops, 1977—85, com. on doctrine, 1978—82, chmn. ecumenical and interreligious affairs com., 1987—90; co-chmn. bilateral dialogue Roman Cath./World Meth. Coun., 1977—86; co-chmn. U.S. Roman Cath.-Luth. Dialogue, 1986—; chmn. Bishops' com. marriage and family life U.S. Cath. Conf., 1978—84; mem. gen. Synod Bishops, Vatican City, 1980. Contbr. articles to profl. jours. Trustee Good Samaritan Hosp., Balt., 1973—77, Cath. U. Am., 1990—, Blue Cross of Md., Inc., 1973—76, Balt. Urban Coalition, 1970—75; trustee, chmn. St. Thomas Theol. Sem., 1987—; bd. dirs. Assn. Cath. Charities, Balt., 1966—76, U. Md. Sch. Social Work and Planning, 1973—76. Recipient Father Kelly Alumni award, Loyola H.S., 1978, Alumni Laureate, Loyola Coll., 1979. Mem.: Oriental Orthodox Roman Cath. Consultation, World Meth. Conf. Roman Cath. Dialogue (co-chmn. 1977—86), Congregation for Doctrine of Faith, Luth. Roman Cath. Dialogue, Nat. Conf. Cath. Bishops. Roman Catholic. Office: Major Penitentiary Apostolic Penitentiary 00120 Vatican City Italy Home Phone: 3906 69887203; Office Phone: 0669887625. Business E-Mail: vati877@apostpnt.va.*

STAFFORD, MATT (JOHN MATTHEW STAFFORD), professional football player; b. Tampa, Fla., Feb. 7, 1988; s. John and Margaret. Student in speech comm., U. Ga., Athens, 2006—09. Quarterback Detroit Lions, 2009—. Named Offensive MVP, Chick-fil-A Bowl, 2006, MVP, Capital One Bowl, 2009. Achievements include being the first overall pick in the NFL Draft, 2009. Office: Detroit Lions Inc 222 Republic Dr Allen Park MI 48101*

STAFFORD, WILLIAM HENRY, JR., federal judge; b. Masury, Ohio, May 11, 1931; s. William Henry and Frieda Gertrude (Nau) S.; m. Nancy Marie Helman, July 11, 1959; children: William Henry III, Donald Helman, David Harrold. BS, Temple U., 1953, LL.B., 1956; JD, 1968. Bar: Fla. 1961, U.S. Ct. Appeals (5th cir.) 1969, U.S. Supreme Ct. 1970. Assoc. firm Robinson & Roark, Pensacola, 1961-64; individual practice law Pensacola, 1964-67; state atty., 1967-69; U.S. atty., 1969-75; U.S. dist. judge U.S. Dist. Ct. for No. Dist. Fla., Tallahassee, 1975—, chief judge, 1981-93, sr. judge, 1996—, Fgn. Intelligence Surveillance Ct., 1996—2003. Instr. Pensacola Jr. Coll., 1964, 68; mem. judicial council U.S. Ct. Appeals (11th cir.), 1986-89; apptd. com. on intercircuit assignments, 1987-92, subcom. on fed. jurisdiction, 1983-87; adj. prof. Fla. State U. Coll. Law, 1992-97. Lt. (j.g.) USN, 1957-60. Mem. Fla. Bar (mem. numerous coms., bench/bar commn. 1991-92, bench/bar implementation commn. 1993), Dist. Judges Assn. 11th Cir. (pres. 1984-85), State Fed. Judicial Council Fla., William H. Stafford Am. Inn Ct., Tallahassee Bar Assn., Tallahassee Inn (founding pres. 1989-91), Mason (33d degree), Sigma Phi Epsilon, Phi Delta Phi. Republican. Episcopalian. Office Phone: 850-521-3617.

STAGAMAN, DAVID JOHN, priest, theology educator; b. Cin., July 29, 1935; s. Harry Terstage and Elinora (Willenbrink) Stagaman. AB, Loyola U., Chgo., 1958; PhL, West Baden Coll., 1960; MA, Loyola U., Chgo., 1967; STL, Bellarmine Sch. Theology, 1967; Docteur en Théologie, Institut Catholique, Paris, 1975. Ordained priest Roman Catholic Ch., 1966; tchr. math. St. Xavier HS, Cin., 1960—63; lectr. theology Loyola U., Chgo., 1968; asst. prof., assoc. prof. systematic theology Jesuit Sch. Theology, Berkeley, Calif., 1972—, dean, 1987—. Am. Theology Schs. fellow, 1978—79. Mem.: Cath. Theol. Soc. America (chair ecclesiology seminar 1983—84), Am. Acad. Religion. Democrat. Roman Catholic. Office: Jesuit Sch Theology 1735 Le Roy Ave Berkeley CA 94709-1193

STAGEBERG, ROGER V., lawyer; B in Math. with distinction, U. Minn., 1963, JD cum laude, 1966; MA in History and Theology, Luther Seminary, 2006. Assoc. Mackall, Crounse & Moore, Mpls., 1966-70, ptnr., 1970-86; shareholder and officer Lommen, Abdo, Cole, King & Stageberg, P.A., Mpls., 1986—. Co-chmn. joint legal svcs. funding com. Minn. Supreme Ct., 1995-96. Mem. U. Minn. Law Rev. Bd. dirs. Mpls. Legal Aid Soc., 1970-2003, treas., 1973, pres., 1977, dir. of fund, 1980—, chmn. of fund, 1998-2000; chmn. bd. trustees Colonial Ch. of Edina, 1975, chmn. congregation, 1976, pres. found., 1978; officer, trustee Mpls. Found, 1983-88. Mem. Minn. State Bar Assn. (numerous offices and coms., pres. 1994), Hennepin County Bar Assn. (chmn. securities law sect. 1979, chmn. attys. referral svc. com. 1980, sec. 1980, treas. 1981, pres. 1983), Order of Coif. Office: Lommen Abdo Cole King & Stageberg PA 80 S 8th St Ste 2000 Minneapolis MN 55402-2119 Home Phone: 612-378-3001; Office Phone: 612-336-9335. Business E-Mail: roger@lommen.com.

STAGEMAN, JAMES HENRY, physician; s. James Henry and Celia Thelma Stageman; m. Sandra Sue Campbell, Apr. 29, 2005; children: James Henry, Rachel Elizabeth Skaff, Matthew Allen, Jill Marie Campbell, Andrea Rodriguez. BS in Naval Sci., US Naval Acad., Annapolis, Md., 1963; MD, U. Nebr., Coll. Medicine, Omaha, 1974. Diplomate Am. Bd. Family Medicine, 1977. Pvt. practice, Colville, Wash., 1977—85; faculty Dept. Family Medicine, U. Nebr. Med. Ctr., 1985—, program dir. residency tng., 1988—2004; asst. dean grad. med. edn. U. Nebr. Med. Ctr., Coll. Medicine, 2005—. Lt. USN, 1963—69. Decorated Bronze Star (V) USN, Navy Commendation medal (V). Mem.: VFW, Am. Acad. Family Physicians, Alpha Omega Alpha Nebr. Independent. Avocation: exercise. Office: Univ Nebr Med Ctr 985524 Nebr Med Ctr Omaha NE 68198-5524 Office Fax: 402-559-9232. Business E-Mail: jstagema@unmc.edu.

STAGG, ENID, educational consultant; d. Irving and Rose Okun; m. Barry Stagg, Nov. 26, 1977; children: Ashley, Matthew. At, Bklyn. Coll., 1973—77; BA, Calif. State U., Northridge, 1980; postgrad. in Admin., Grand Canyon U., 2005—06; MS, Walden U., Minn., 2006. Cert. multiple subjects credential Calif., All Kinds of Minds Tng., LA, 2002, English lang. devel./specially designed academic instrn. in English LA Office Edn., 2002. Educator Ctr. for Early Edn., West Hollywood, Calif., 1981—84; educator, staff developer Las Virgenes Unified Sch. Dist., Calabasas, Calif., 1986—. Ednl. cons. Saban Entertainment, LA, 1997—98, WNET-TV-"Cyberchase", NYC, 2001—05; adj. prof. grad. sch. edn. Pepperdine U., Malibu, Calif., 2007. Author: (children's book) Land of Equals, 2000. Recipient Presdl. Award for Excellence in Math. Tchg., NSF, 1998, Outstanding Math Educator award, Am. Electronics Assn., 1998; named Outstanding Math Educator, Ventura County Math Coun., 1997, Tchr. of Yr., Las Virgenes Unified Sch. Dist., 2000, Exceptional Educator of Yr., 2006. Mem.: Calif. Math Coun. (Outstanding Math Educator 1997), Soc. Elem. Presdl. Awardees, Calif. Presdl. Awardees in Math., Nat. Coun. Tchrs. Math. Avocations: reading, writing. Office: Willow Elementary 29026 Laro Dr Agoura Hills CA 91301 Office Fax: 818-706-0159. Personal E-mail: pizzamath@aol.com.

STAGGERS, KERMIT LEMOYNE, II, history and political science professor, state legislator, municipal official; b. Washington, Pa., Nov. 2, 1947; s. Kermit LeMoyne and Christine Ruby (Scherich) S.; m. June Ann Wenda, Aug. 22, 1970; children: Ayn Kristen Staggers Bird, Kyle Lee Staggers. BS, U. Idaho, 1969, MA, 1975; PhD, Claremont Grad. U., 1986. Cert. in theol. studies Sioux Falls Seminary, 2009. Instr. history Troy (Ala.) State U., 1975-76, U. Idaho, Moscow, 1977, Northwestern Coll., Orange City, Iowa, 1979-80, Coll. Lake County, Grayslake, Ill., 1981-82; lectr. history Chapman Univ., Orange, Calif., 1979, U. Md.-Europe, Heidelberg, Germany, 1988-89; vis. instr. history Trinity Internat. U., Deerfield, Ill., 1980; adj. instr. history U. St. Francis, Joliet, Ill., 1982; prof. history and polit. sci. U. Sioux Falls (S.D.), 1982—; mem. S.D. Senate, Pierre, 1995—2002, Sioux Falls City Coun., 2002—. Lectr. Diplomatic Acad. Ukrainian Fgn. Ministry and Nat. U. Kiev-Mohyla Acad., 2001; expert analyst on polit. and social issues for local radio and TV. Contbr. articles to profl. jours. Chair Senate Transp. Com., 1997-99; bd. dirs. Siouxland Heritage Museums, Sioux Falls, 2006—. Capt. USAF, 1970-76. Recipient Guardian Small Bus. award Nat. Fedn. Ind. Bus., 1996; Malone Faculty fellow, 1993. Mem. Great Plains Polit. Sci Assn. (pres. 2000-01), Federalist Soc., Fulbright Assn., Hist. Soc., Kiwanis, Phi Alpha Theta, Phi Kappa Phi. Republican. Avocations: book collecting, travel. Home: 616 E Wiswall Pl Sioux Falls SD 57105-2030 Office: U Sioux Falls Dept History/Polit Sci 1101 W 22nd St Sioux Falls SD 57105-1699 Home Phone: 605-332-0357; Office Phone: 605-331-6754. Business E-Mail: kermit.staggers@usiouxfalls.edu.

STAGGERS, MARY E., minister; b. Rocky Mount, NC, Sept. 28, 1923; d. John and Emma Jane White; m. Calvin Staggers, Jr., May 18, 1938; children: Luther, Gervis, Earlie Mae, Curtis, Herbert, Betty Joann, Yvonne. BA, Coll. New Rochelle, 1983; M in Profl. Studies, N.Y. Theol. Sem., 1985; M in Humanities, Ctr. Humanities N.Y., 1985; D of Theology of Bible, Internat. Sem. Fla., 1990; DD, Balt. Coll. Bible, 1988. Pastor Holy Redeemer Bapt. Ch., Bklyn., 1961—. Family therapist Beth Israel Hosp., NYC, 1980—98; min. N.Y.C. World's Fair. Author: It's Seed Time, 1999, The Spirit Supercedes Nature, 2003. Liaison N.Y.C. Cmty. Bd. Dist. 16; v.p. Women's Nat. Evang. and Missionary Conf., 1996—2001; pres. World Conf. Gospel Explosion, 1994—, United Ladies Ministers Counsel, 1978—99; pres. Ea. N.Y. br. Women's Nat. Evang. and Missionary Conf., 1997—2001; pres. Mother's Bd. Cedar Grove Bapt. Ch., 1940—51. Mem.: N.Y.C. Clergy Conf., Ea. Bapt. Conf., So. Bapt. Conf., Nat. Bapt. Conf. Democrat. Avocations: cooking, reading, writing. Office Phone: 718-816-5181.

STAGGS, SUSAN HETTIE, medical educator; BS, PharmD, U. Tenn., Memphis. Cert. pharmacotherapy specialist Bd. Pharm. Specialties, 2007. Asst. prof. clin. U. Iowa Coll. Pharmacy, Iowa City, 2006—. Mem.: Am. Assn. Colls. Pharmacy, Am. Coll. Clin. Pharmacy, Am. Pharmacists Assn. Office: Univ Iowa Coll Pharmacy 115 S Grand Ave S413 PHAR Iowa City IA 52242-1112

STAGGS, THOMAS O., entertainment company executive; Mgr. strategic planning Walt Disney Co., Burbank, Calif., 1990—94, v.p. planning & development, 1995—97, exec. v.p., CFO, 1998—99, sr. exec. v.p., CFO, 2000—. Office: Walt Disney Co 500 S Buena Vista St Burbank CA 91521-0006 Office Phone: 818-560-1000.*

STAGLIN, GAREN KENT, computer services company executive, venture capitalist; b. Lincoln, Nebr., Dec. 22, 1944; s. Ramon and Darlene (Guilliams) S.; m. Sharalyn King, June 8, 1968; children: Brandon Kent, Shannon King. BS in Engring. with honors, UCLA, 1966; MBA, Stanford U., 1968. Assoc. Carr Mgmt. Co., NYC, 1971-75; v.p. Crocker Nat. Bank, San Francisco, 1975-76; dir. fin. Itel Corp., San Francisco, 1976-77, pres. ins. services divsn., 1977-79; corp. v.p., gen. mgr. ADP Automotive Svcs. Group, San Ramon, Calif., 1978-91; chmn., CEO Safelite Glass Corp., Columbus, Ohio, 1991-97, chmn., 1998-2000; owner Staglin Family Vineyard, Rutherford, Calif., 1985—; pres., CEO eOne Global L.L.C., Napa, Calif., 2000—05; sr. advisor FT Capital, San Francisco, 2005—, Irving Place Pvt. Equity, NYC. Bd. dir. Certive Corp., Specialized Bicycle Corp., Global Document Solutions, Inc., ExL Svcs., Inc., Free Run Techs., Bottomline techs. Bd. dir. Peralta Hosp. Cancer Inst., 1977-78, Berkeley Repertory Theatre, 1979-85, Nat. Alliance for Rsch. Schizophrenia & Depression, 2000-2008; trustee Justin Sienna HS, Napa, Calif., 1995-20; chmn. major gifts program East Bay region Stanford U., Calif., 1989-92; mem. adv. bd. Stanford Bus. Sch., 1995-2000; judge Cambridge Bus. Sch., 2004-; chmn. 75th anniversary campaign Stanford Grad. Sch. Bus., 1998-00; capital campaign UCLA Coll. Letters Sci., 2004-07; pres. bd. trustees Am. Ctr. Wine, Food and Arts, Napa, Calif., 1998-03;founder Music Festival Mental Health, 1994-. Lt. USN, 1968—71. Recipient Gold Spike award, Stanford U., 2000, Honors Fellow award, UCLA, 2006. Mem. Stanford Assocs. (bd. govs. 1985-92), World Pres. Orgn., Internat. Inst. Soc. (bd. govs. 1985-92), Nappa Valley Vintners Assn. Democrat. Lutheran. Home: PO Box 680 1570 Bella Oaks Ln Rutherford CA 94573 Office Phone: 707-280-5374. Business E-Mail: garen.staglin@staglinfamily.com.

STAGNARO-GREEN, ALEX, medical educator; MD, Mt. Sinai Sch. Medicine, 1983; MHPE, U. Ill., Chgo., 2005. Dean student affairs & med. edn. Mt. Sinai Sch. Medicine, acting chmn. dept. med. edn.; prof. obstetrics, gynecology & women's health NJ Med. Sch., assoc. dean for curriculum & faculty devel., sr. assoc. dean for edn.; sr. assoc. dean academic affairs Touro U. Coll. Medicine. Mem.: Assn. Am. Med. Coll., Nat. Bd. Med. Examiners, Acad. Med. Educators (chmn.). Office: Touro University College of Medicine 19 Main St Hackensack NJ 07601 Office Phone: 201-883-9320 ext. 2010. E-mail: alex.stagnaro-green@touro.edu.*

STAHL, FRANK LUDWIG, civil engineer; b. Fuerth, Germany; came to U.S., 1946, naturalized, 1949; s. Leo E. and Anna (Regensburger) S.; m. Edith Cosmann, Aug. 31, 1947; children: David, Robert. BSCE, Tech. Inst. Zurich, Switzerland, 1945. With Ammann & Whitney, Cons. Engrs., NYC, 1946-93, project engr., 1955-67, assoc., 1968-76, sr. assoc., 1977-81, chief engr. Transp. div., 1982-93; pvt. cons., 1994—. Expert in field. Prin. works include Verrazano-Narrows Bridge, Throgs Neck Bridge, Walt Whitman Bridge, improvements to Golden Gate Bridge, rehab. of Williamsburg Bridge, N.Y.C., Royal Gorge Bridge, Colo., Interstate-10 Deck Tunnel, Phoenix; author: Cable Corrosion in Bridges and Other Structures; co-author: Golden Gate Bridge, Report of the Chief Engineer to the Board of Directors, Vol. II; contbr. articles to profl. jours. on bridge design and constrn. Recipient Gold award The James F. Lincoln Arc Welding Found., 1986, John A. Roebling medal Internat. Bridge Conf., 1992. Fellow ASCE (Thomas Fitch Rowland prize 1967, Innovation in Civil Engring. award of mert 1983, Metro. Civil Engr. of Yr. award 1987, Roebling award 1990), ASTM (vice chmn. com. A-1 on steel, stainless steel and related alloys 1978-83, chmn. steel reinforce-subcom. 1971-82, award of merit 1982); mem. Am. Inst. Steel Constrn. (Prize Bridge award 1986), Engring. Found. (rsch. coun. on structural connections), Internat. Assn. Bridge and Structural Engring., Internat. Bridge Tunnel and Turnpike Assn. Home: 20911 28th Rd Flushing NY 11360-2412 Personal E-mail: bridgfrank@aol.com.

STAHL, JACK LELAND, real estate company executive; b. Lincoln, Ill., June 28, 1934; s. Edwin R. and Edna M. (Burns) S.; m. Carol Anne Townsend, June 23, 1956; children: Cheryl, Nancy, Kellea BS in Edn., U. N.Mex., 1957. Tchr. Albuquerque Pub. Schs., 1956-59; pres. House Finders, Inc., Albuquerque, 1959-65; v.p. N.Mex. Savs. & Loan Assn., Albuquerque, 1965-67; chmn. bd. Hooten-Stahl, Inc., Albuquerque, 1967-77; mem. N.Mex. Ho. of Reps., 1969-70; pres. The Jack Stahl Co., Albuquerque, 1977—; mem. N.Mex. Senate, 1981-86; lt. gov. State of N.Mex., 1987-90. Mem. exec. bd. Gr. S.W. Coun. Boy Scouts Am, 1982-89; bd. dirs. BBB N. Mex., 1968-82, pres. 1975-76; trustee Univ Heights. Hosp.,1980-85; vice chmn. N. Mex. Bd. Fin., 1987-90, N. Mex. Cmty. Devel. Coun., 1987-90; bd. dirs. Ctr. for Entrepreneurship and Econ. Devel., 1994-96; mem. Gov.'s Bus. Adv. Coun., 1995-97. Named Realtor of Yr., Albuquerque Bd. Realtors, 1972. Mem. Nat. Assn. Realtors, Nat. Homebuilders Assn., N.Mex. Amigos, 20-30 Club (pres. 1963-64), Rotary. Republican. Methodist. Office: 1911 Wyoming Blvd NE Albuquerque NM 87112-2865 Office Phone: 505-292-6635.

STAHL, LADDIE L., engineering company executive; b. Terre Haute, Ind., Dec. 23, 1921; s. Edgar Allen and Martha (Llewellyn) S.; m. Thelma Mae Beasley, Dec. 11, 1942; children: Stephanie, Laddie L., Craig. BSCE, Purdue U., 1942; MS in Engring., Johns Hopkins U., 1950. With GE, 1954-90, mgr. planning and resources, electronics sci. and engring., corp. research and devel. Schenectady, NY, 1974-76, mgr. electronics systems programs ops., elec. sci. and engring., 1976-84, mgr. spl. programs and project devel. operation, 1984-90; dir. tech. transfer program Data Storage Systems Ctr. Carnegie Mellon U., Pitts., 1990—. Chmn. adv. group US Army Electronics Command, 1971-74; mem. US Army Sci. Bd., 1978-87; cons. in field. Contbr. articles to profl. publs. Mem. alumni bd. dirs. Purdue U., 1979-82. Served with U.S. Army, 1942-54, ETO; maj. gen. Res. (ret.), 1954-77. Decorated DSM, Legion of Merit. Mem. AIAA (sr.), IEEE (life), Am. Def. Preparedness Assn., Army and Navy Club (Washington), Tau Beta Pi, Chi Epsilon. Home: 29 Fairway Ln Rexford NY 12148-1213 Office: Carnegie Mellon U Data Storage Sys Ctr ECE Dept 5000 Forbes Ave Pittsburgh PA 15213-3815

STAHL, LESLEY RENE, news correspondent; b. Lynn, Mass., Dec. 16, 1941; d. Louis and Dorothy J. (Tishler) Stahl; m. Aaron Latham, 1977; 1 child, Taylor. BA cum laude, Wheaton Coll., Norton, Mass., 1963; LHD (hon.), Colgate U., Hamilton, NY, 2008, Loyola Coll., Md., 2008. Asst. to speechwriter NYC Mayor's Office, 1966—67; rschr. NY Election unit CBS News, 1967—68; rschr. London-Huntley Brinkley Report, NBC News, 1969; prodr., reporter WHDH-TV, Boston, 1970—72; news corr. CBS News, Washington, 1972—; co-anchor CBS Morning News, 1977—79; White House corr. CBS News, 1979-91; moderator Face the Nation, 1983-91; anchor America Tonight, 1990—91; co-editor, corr. CBS News, 60 Minutes, 1991—; host 48 Hours Investigates, 2002—04. Author: (memoir) Reporting Live, 1999; TV appearances include: Murphy Brown, 1993, 1995; Frasier, 1997. Trustee Wheaton Coll. Recipient Tex. Headliners award, 1973, Dennis Kauff Journalism award for lifetime achievement in news profession, 1990, Matrix Award for Broadcasting, NY Women in Comm. Inc., 1993, Fred Friendly First Amendment award, Quinnipiac Coll., 1996, Edward R. Murrow award for overall excellence in TV reporting, Radio & TV News Dir.'s Assn., 1996; named Best White House Corr., Washington Journalism Rev., 1991; named to Broadcasting Mag. Hall of Fame, 1992. Office: CBS Broadcasting Inc 51 W 52nd St New York NY 10019*

STAHL, NICK, actor; b. Harlingen, Tex., Dec. 5, 1979; Actor: (TV miniseries) Seasons of Love, 1999; (TV series) Carnivàle, 2003—05; (TV films) Stranger at My Door, 1991, Woman with a Past, 1992, Incident in a Small Town, 1994, Blue River, 1995, My Son Is Innocent, 1996, Wasted, 2002; (films) The Man Without a Face, 1993, Safe Passage, 1994, Tall Tale, 1995, Eye of God, 1997, Disturbing Behavior, 1998, Soundman, 1998, The Thin Red Line, 1998, All Forgotten, 2000, Sunset Strip, 2000, In the Bedroom, 2001, The Sleepy Time Gal, 2001, Bully, 2001, Taboo, 2002, Bookies, 2003, Terminator 3: Rise of the Machines, 2003, Twist, 2003, Sin City, 2005, The Night of the White Pants, 2006, How to Rob a Bank, 2007, Quid Pro Quo, 2008, Sleepwalking, 2008. Office: c/o 1 Management 9000 Sunset Blvd Ste 1550 Los Angeles CA 90069

STAHL, NORMAN A., literature and language professor, department chairman; b. San Francisco, Apr. 21, 1949; AA, City Coll. San Francisco, 1969; BA, San Francisco State U., 1971, MA, 1976; PhD, U. Pitts., 1983. Rsch. assoc. U. Pitts., 1980-82; asst. prof. divsn. devel. studies Ga. State U., Atlanta, 1982-87; assoc. prof. dept. curriculum & instrn. No. Ill. U., DeKalb, 1987-93, prof., chair dept. curriculum & instrn., 1994-99, chair dept. literacy edn., 1999—. Author: Teaching Developmental Reading, 2003; contbr. articles to profl. jours. Pres. DeKalb Edn. Found., 1999—2001. Recipient Disting. Rsch. award Coll. Reading and Learning Assn., 1990, NY. Coll. Learning Skills Assn., 1996; Am. Coun. Devel. Edn. Assns. fellow, 2006. Mem. Coll. Reading Assn. (pres. 1991-92, treas. 1985-88), Internat. Reading Assn. (pres. history reading spl. interest group 1992-94), Am. Reading Forum (chair bd. dirs. 1996-97), Nat. Reading Conf. (historian 1998-2003, bd. dir. 2003-05, v.p. 2005-06, pres. elect 2006-07, pres. 2007-08). Office: No Ill U Dept Literacy Edn Dekalb IL 60115 Office Phone: 815-753-9032. Business E-Mail: stahl@niu.edu.

STAHL, NORMAN H., federal judge; b. Manchester, NH, 1931; BA, Tufts U., 1952; LLB, Harvard U., 1955. Law clk. to Hon. John V. Spalding Mass. Supreme Ct., 1955—56; assoc. Devine, Millimet, Stahl & Branch, Manchester, NH, 1956—59, ptnr., 1959—90; judge US Dist. Ct. (NH dist.), 1990—92, US Ct. Appeals (1st cir.), Concord, NH, 1992—, sr. judge, 2001—. Del to Rep. Nat. Conv., 1988. Mem.: N.H. Bar Assn. Office: US Courthouse Ste 8730 1 Courthouse Way Boston MA 02210*

STAHL, RICHARD G. C., journalist, editor; b. Chgo., Feb. 22, 1934; m. Gladys C. Weisbecker; 1 child, Laura Ann. Student, Northwestern U., U. Ill., Chgo. Editor Railway Purchases and Stores Mag., Chgo., 1960-63; editor pub. rels. dept. Sears Roebuck & Co., Chgo., 1963-68; dir pub. rels. dept. St. Joseph's Hosp. Med. Ctr., Phoenix, 1968-72; v.p. pub. rels. Consultation Svcs., Inc., Phoenix, 1972-73; creative dir. Don Jackson and Assoc., Phoenix, 1973; editor, pub. rels. mgr. Maricopa County Med. Soc., Phoenix, 1974-76; sr. editor Ariz. Hwys. mag., Phoenix, 1977-99; ret., 1999. Regional editor: (travel guides) Budget Travel, 1985, USA, 1986, Arizona, 1986; free-lance writer and editor. Mem. Soc. Profl. Journalists. Avocation: woodworking. Office: Ariz Hwys Mag 2039 W Lewis Ave Phoenix AZ 85009-2819 *Personal philosophy: Follow your dream and fulfill your potentialities.*

STAHL, RICHARD SHELDON, surgeon; b. Chattanooga, Tenn., Dec. 8, 1950; s. Paul and Alena S. BA in Physics, Emory U., 1972; MD, Vanderbilt U., 1976; MBA, U. New Haven, 1994. Diplomate Nat. Bd. Med. Examiners, Am. Bd. Surgery, Am. Bd. Plastic Surgery. Intern, asst. resident dept. surgery Yale U. Sch. Medicine, New Haven, 1976-80, chief resident, 1980-81; resident plastic and reconstructive surgery Emory U. Sch. Medicine, 1981-82, chief resident, 1982-83; instr. surgery Yale U. Sch. Medicine, 1980-81, asst. prof. plastic surgery, 1983-89, assoc. prof. plastic surgery, 1989-90, assoc. clin. prof. plastic surgery, 1991-95, clin. prof. plastic surgery, 1995—, attending physician Yale Vascular Ctr., 1986-90, chmn. telemedicine com., 1998—2001; attending physician dept. surgery Yale-New Haven Hosp., 1980-81, 83—, asst. med. dir. surgery emergency svcs., 1983-90, attending physician surg. ICU, 1986-88, dir. internat. ops. dept. surgery, 1995—99, assoc. chief dept. surgery, 1994—2006, exec. dir., perioperative svc., 2002—06, v.p., ambulatory svcs., 2006—; attending physician Hosp. St. Raphael, 1983—; ptnr., pvt. practice Thoracic Healing Solutions, Guilford, Conn. Founding co-dir. Yale Breast Care Ctr., 1989-90; cons. physicians assoc. surg. residency program Yale U.-Norwalk Hosp., 1978-81; resident surgeon Hospital Albert Schweitzer, Deschapelles, Haiti, 1980; med. mgmt. cons. Yale-New Haven Health Sys., 1997-98; program dir. of clin. telemedicine of NASA Comml. Space Ctr. at yale, 1997-2008; spkr. in field. Sports reporter The Chattanooga Times, 1967-69; contbr. over 40 articles to profl. jours. Pres. Kingswood Homeowner's Assn., 1987-93; mem. Charter Oak Bassett Hound Club, 1981-90. Recipient Rsch. grant Charles W. Ohse Fund, Rsch. grant Smith Kline and French Labs., Rsch. grant Kendall Co.; named one of Top Doctors in NY Met. area, NY mag., 2007, Redbook, McCall's. Fellow Am. Coll. Surgeons (mem. Conn. chpt.); mem. Am. Coll. Health Care Execs., AMA, Am. Assn. Plastic Surgeons, Am. Soc. Plastic and Reconstructive Surgeons, Am. Coll. Physician Execs., Am. Coll. Med. Quality, Am. Burn Assn., Soc. for Critical Care Medicine, New Eng. Soc. Plastic and Reconstructive Surgeons (v.p. 1998-99, pres. 1999-2000), New Haven County Med. Soc., Conn. Soc. Am. Bd. Surgeons, Conn. State Med. Soc. Office: Ambulatory Svcs Divsn #5B 60 Temple St New Haven CT 06510 also: 5 Durham Rd Guilford CT 06437 Office Phone: 203-458-4440.

STAHL, SANDRA MICHELLE, communications executive; b. NYC, Feb. 5, 1962; d. Irwin and Rae Stahl; m. Jeremy Dan Jacob, June 5, 1988; children: Sophie Isabel Jacob, Jesse Reuben Jacob, Jack Benjamin Jacob. BA, CUNY, 1983. Sr. v.p. Ruder Finn, NYC, 1983—92, mng. dir., global healthcare, 1993—94, exec. v.p., 1995—97; v.p., mktg. comm. CDx Labs., Suffern, NY, 1999—2003; prin. Jacobstahl Inc., NYC, 2003—. Contbr. articles to profl. jours. Dir. Freedom From Fear, NYC, 1996—2007. Recipient Svc. award, Cancer Care. Avocations: reading, soccer, travel, cooking. Office: Jacobstahl Inc New York NY 10065 Personal E-mail: jacobstahl@aol.com.

STAHLMAN, MILDRED THORNTON, pediatrician, pathologist, educator, researcher; b. Nashville, July 31, 1922; d. James Geddes and Mildred (Thornton) Stahlman. AB, Vanderbilt U., 1943, MD, 1946; MD (hon.), U. Goteborg, Sweden, 1973, U. Nancy, France, 1982. Diplomate Am. Bd. Pediat., Am. Bd. Neonatology. Intern Boston Children's Hosp., 1947—48; resident Vanderbilt Univ. Hosp., 1948—49; fellow Royal Caroline Inst. Medicine, Sweden, 1949—50; cardiac resident La Rabida Sanitarium, Chgo., 1951; instr. pediat. Vanderbilt U., Nashville, 1951—58, instr. physiology, 1954—60, asst. prof. pediat., 1959—64, asst. prof. physiology, 1960—62, assoc. prof. pediat., 1964—70, prof., 1970—, prof. pathology, 1982—, Harvie Branscomb Disting. prof., 1984, dir. divsn. neonatology, 1961—89, prof. pediat. and pathology. Editor: Respiratory Distress Syndromes, 1989; contbr. over 175 articles to profl. publs., chpts. to books. Recipient Apgar award, Am. Acad. Pediat., 1987; grantee NIH, 1954—. Mem.: AAAS, Inst. Medicine NAS, Royal Swedish Acad. Scis., So. Soc. Pediatric Rsch. (pres. 1961—62), Am. Physiology Soc., Soc. Pediatric Rsch., Am. Pediatric Soc. (pres. 1984, John Howland award 1996). Episcopalian. Home: 538 Beech Creek Rd S Brentwood TN 37027-3421 Office: Vanderbilt Univ Med Ctr 2215 B Garland Ave 1125 MRB IV LH Nashville TN 37232-0656 E-mail: mildred.stahlman@vanderbilt.edu.

STAHOVICH, MARCIA, nurse; m. Joseph Stahovich; children: Tracy Lee, Brian Joseph. ADN, Palomar Coll., San Marcos, Calif., 1986. CCRN, AACN, San Diego, 1989. RN mechnical assist device coord. Sharp Meml. Hosp., San Diego, 2001—. Mem.: San Diego AACN (pres. 2005—07, Outstanding Local Mem. SDAACN 2007). Office: Sharp Meml Hosp 7901 Frost St San Diego CA 92123 Office Fax: 858-939-3812.

STAHR, CELIA SUZANNE, art historian, educator; d. Carl Wolfgang and Illene Louise Stahr; m. Gary Allen Lee, May 21, 2000; 1 child, Mei Lin Miriam Lee-Stahr. BA, San Francisco State U., 1980, MA, 1989; PhD, U. Iowa, Iowa City, 1997. Adj. prof. San Francisco State U., 1997—2007, Sonoma State U., Cotati, Calif., 1998—99, Coll. Marin, Calif., 1999—2000, Calif. Coll. Arts, Oakland, 1999—2003, San Francisco Art Inst., 2004—05, U. San Francisco XARTS, 2004—. Affiliated scholar Inst. for Women & Gender, Stanford U., 2000—02; presenter in field. Contbr. essays to books, articles to profl. pubs. Vol. Women's Resource & Action Ctr., Iowa City, 1991—95; active Women Against Racism, 1994—95; vol. Rape Victim Advocacy, Iowa City, 1995. Grantee Schumacher scholarship, U. Iowa, 1996, Seashore Dissertation fellowship, 1996, USA Rsch. grant, 1996. Mem.: Coll. Art Assn. Avocations: tai chi, salsa dance. Office: The U San Francisco XARTS 2130 Fulto St San Francisco CA 94117-1080 Personal E-mail: CeliaStahr@aol.com.

STAI, DEBORAH, biology professor, director; b. Rochester, Minn., Feb. 4, 1952; d. Harry Stanley Stai and Marion Beatrice Berg. BS in Biology, U. Minn., Mankato, 1974; BS in Med. Tech., U. Minn., 1978, MA in Microbiology, 1980; PhD in Clin. Microbiology, Union Inst., Cin., 1989. Cert. in secondary tchg. State Minn. Med. technologist Mercy Hosp., Cedar Rapids, Iowa, 1977—78, microbiology instr., 1979—81; enzyme rsch. technologist Mayo Clinic, Rochester, Minn., 1978—79; instr. biology, med. tech. Ark. Coll., Batesville, 1981—84; assoc. prof. clin. lab. sci. Ferris State U., Big Rapids, Mich., 1984—90; clin. instr. microbiology, immunology U. Wis., Madison, 1990—91; biology prof. Lake Superior State U., Saulte Sainte, Mich., 1991—. Cons. Analytab Products Inc., Plainview, NY, 1987—88. Contbr. articles to profl. jours. Bd. mem. Red Cross, Battesville, 1981—84; cons. Local Health Dept., Saulte Sainte, Mich., 1994—; with LSSU Found., Saulte Sainte, Mich., 1996—. Recipient Disting. Tchr. award, Lake Superior State U., 2003. Mem.: Am. Soc. Microbiology (twin br. 1991—), Mich. Soc. Clin. Lab. Sci. (pres. 1994—), Am. Soc. Clin. Lab. Sci., Mich. Assn. Clin. Lab. Sci. (bd. mem. 2005—). Democrat. Lutheran. Avocations: tennis, golf, swimming. Office: Lake Superior Univ 650 W Easteraay Ave Sault Sainte Marie MI 49783 Office Phone: 906-635-2806. Office Fax: 906-635-2244. Business E-Mail: dstai@issu.edu.

STAINBACK, SUSAN BRAY, professor emeritus; b. Balt., May 22, 1947; d. William Devaugh and Cleo Margaret (Selig) Bray. BS, Radford Coll., 1968; MEd, U. Va., 1971, EdD, 1973. Prof. excel Atlantic U., Fla., 1979—80; Matthew J. Gujlielmo Endowed Chair dept. spl. edn. Calif. State U., LA, 1988-89; prof. U. Northern Iowa, Cedar Falls, 1974—98. Author numerous books; contbr. chapters to books, articles to profl. jours., over 200 publs. Achievements include research in career focus on equity and inclusion issues in disability studies. Home: 65 Rippling Waters Rd Blairsville GA 30512-8015

STAINES, DAVID MCKENZIE, language educator; b. Toronto, Aug. 8, 1946; s. Ralph McKenzie and Mary Rita (Hayes) S. BA, U. Toronto, 1967; AM, Harvard U., 1968, PhD, 1973. Asst. prof. English Harvard U., Cambridge, Mass., 1973-78, vis. assoc. prof., summers 1980, 82; assoc. prof. English U. Ottawa, Ont., 1978-85, prof. Ont., 1985—, vice-dean faculty of Arts Ont., 1994-95, dean faculty of arts Ont., 1995—2003. Author: Tennyson's Camelot, 1982, Beyond the Provinces: Literary Canada at Century's End, 1995; contbr. articles to profl. jours.; editor: The Canadian Imagination, 1977, The Forty-ninth and Other Parallels, 1986, Margaret Laurence: Critical Reflections, 2001, The Letters of Stephen Leacock, 2006; editor Jour. Can. Poetry, 1984—; gen. editor New Can. Libr., 1988—; translator The Complete Romances of Chrétien de Troyes, 1990; co-editor Elements of Literature, 1987, 90, 04, 09, The Short Story in English, 1991, Northrop Frye on Canada, 2003, Marshall McLuhan's Understanding Me, 2003. Recipient Lorne Pierce medal, 1998; Ind. study fellow NEH, London, 1977-78, fellow Huntington Libr., San Marino, Calif., 1979. Fellow Royal Soc. Can.; mem. Medieval Acad. Am. (chmn. com. on ctrs. and regional assn. 1981-87), MLA, Internat. Arthurian Soc., Assn. Can. Univ. Tchrs. English. Roman Catholic. Avocations: theater, bridge. Home: 222 Clemow Ave Ottawa ON Canada K1S 2B6 Business E-Mail: dstaines@uottawa.ca.

STAINES, GAIL M., academic administrator; BA, MLS, U. Buffalo, PhD in Higher Edn. Adminstrn. Assoc. prof. Niagara CC, Sanborn, NY, 1988—98; exec. dir. Western NY Libr. Resources Coun., 1998—2006; asst. provost St. Louis U., Mo., 2006—. Vis. prof. School of Informatics, SUNY, Buffalo, 1990—. Named one of Movers and Shakers, Libr. Jour., 2004. Mem.: ALA, Libr. Adminstrn. and Mgmt. Assn., Assn. Coll. and Rsch. Librs., Beta Phi Mu. Office: Saint Louis U Pius XII Meml Libr 3650 Lindell Blvd Saint Louis MO 63108 E-mail: gstaines@slu.edu.

STAINROOK, HARRY RICHARD, photographer, retired bank executive; b. Phila., Jan. 11, 1937; s. Millward M. and Janet Stainrook; m. Judith Anne, May 21, 1966; children: Jennifer, Eric. BA, Rutgers U., 1970. Mgr. bank ops. First Pa. Bank, Phila., 1956-61, asst. v.p. br. dept., 1964-73, v.p., mgr. London office, 1973-75, v.p. internat. dept., 1975-78, sr. v.p. comml. group, 1978-81, exec. v.p., trust and investments, 1981-85; exec. v.p. trust and investments Mfrs. and Traders Trust Co., Buffalo, 1985-97, ret., 1997; prin., owner Harry Stainrook, Ltd., NYC, 2006—. Exhibitions include Art Dialogue Gallery, Buffalo, 2006, 2008, Collectors Gallery, Albright Knox Art Mus., 2009, Stedman Gallery, Rutgers U., Camden, NJ, 2007—08, Landmark Gallery, NYC, 2008, 2009. Past chmn., bd. dirs. Greater Buffalo Opera Co.; past pres. Buffalo Philharm. Orch., Acad. Vocal Arts, Phila. With US Army, 1961—64. Mem. Western NY Artists Group, World Future Soc., Inst. Noetic Scis., Saturn Club. Lutheran. Home: 150 Columbus Ave Apt 4A New York NY 10023-5964 Home Phone: 212-769-0202.

STAIR, THOMAS OSBORNE, physician, educator; b. Richmond, Va., Jan. 10, 1950; s. Frederick Rogers Jr. and Martha (Osborne) S.; m. Lucy Caldwell, Dec. 28, 1973; children: Rebecca Caldwell, Peter Caldwell. AB, U. N.C., 1971; MD, Harvard U., 1975. Diplomate Am. Bd. Emergency Medicine (examiner 1982-88). Residency dir. emergency dept. Georgetown U. Sch. Medicine, Washington, 1979-85, asst. dir. emergency dept., 1979-89, asst. dean for continuing med. edn., 1985-89, chair dept. emergency medicine, 1989-95; prof. U. Md., Balt., 1995-98; assoc. prof. Harvard Med. Sch., 1998—; attending emergency physician Brigham and Women's Hosp., Boston, 1998—. Co-author: Common Simple Emergencies, 1985, Emergency Medicine, 1997, Minor Emergencies, 1999. Recipient Excellence in Teaching award Emergency Medicine Residents Assn., 1986. Fellow Am. Coll. Emergency Physicians, Am. Med. Informatics Assn., Am. Acad. Emergency Medicine; mem. Soc. Acad. Emergency Medicine. Home: 46 Woodcliff Rd Newton MA 02461-1825 Office: 75 Francis St Boston MA 02115-6110 Home Phone: 617-928-3375; Office Phone: 617-732-5640. Business E-Mail: tstair@partners.org.

STAIRS, DENIS WINFIELD, political science professor, department chairman; b. Halifax, NS, Can., Sept. 6, 1939; s. Henry Gerald and Freda (Winfield) S.; m. Valerie Downing Street, Aug. 10, 1963 (div. Dec. 1986); children: Robert Woodliffe, Christopher Winfield; m. Jennifer Smith, July 18, 1987. BA, Dalhousie U., 1961, Oxford U., 1964, MA, 1968; PhD, U. Toronto, 1969. Asst. prof. dept. polit. sci. Dalhousie U., 1966-70, assoc. prof., 1970-75, dir. Centre Fgn. Policy Studies, 1971-75, prof. polit. sci., 1975—, McCulloch prof., 1995—2005, chmn. dept., 1980-85, v.p. acad. and rsch., 1988-93; prof. emeritus, 2005—. Bd. dirs. Atlantic Coun. Can., 1979—, Inst. Rsch. Pub. Policy, 1989-97, 98-06; mem. coun. Social Sci. and Humanities Rsch. Coun. Can., 1981-87; mem. rsch. coun. Can. Inst. Advanced Rsch., 1986-97; bd. dirs. Orgn. for Study of Nat. History of Can., 1995-98; bd. vis. Can. Forces Coll., 2002—, chair, 2006—; fellow, mem. adv. com. Can. Def. and Fgn. Affairs Inst., 2002-, chair, 2008-. Author: The Diplomacy of Constraint: Canada, the Korean War, and the United States, 1974; editl. bd. Internat. Jour., 1997—. Rhodes scholar, 1961; J.W. Dafoe postgrad. fellow internat. studies, 1965-66; Can. Coun. leave fellow, 1972-73; Social Scis. and Humanities Rsch. Coun. Can. leave fellow, 1979-80; recipient Disting. Writing award, Marcel Cadieux, 2000, 2003. Fellow Royal Soc. Can., Order of Can. (officer 2006-); mem. Can. Polit. Sci. Assn. (pres.), Can. Inst. Internat. Affairs, Internat. Studies Assn. Clubs: Royal N.S. Yacht Squadron, Pearson Peacekeeping Ctr. (bd. dirs. 2007-). Office: Dalhousie U Dept Polit Sci Halifax NS Canada B3H 4H6 Office Phone: 902-494-2396.

STAIVISKY, JEANNE LOUISE, counselor, alcohol/drug abuse services professional; b. Hughesville, Pa., Dec. 30, 1947; d. Charolotte Bowen and John Staivisky. AA in Psychology, Palm Beach Jr. Coll., 1981; BS in Gen. Psychology, Nova U., 1984, MS in Sci. in Counseling Psychology, 1987. Lic. profl. counselor Ill., 2003, nat. cert. psychologist Psychology Profl. Bd., 2000, lic. mental health counselor Ind., 1999, cert. Nat. Bd. Cert. Counselors, 1996, Am. Acad. Health Providers Addictive Disorders, 1995, lic. marraige and family therapist Washington, 2009. Program mgr., counselor Hugs Not Drugs Treatment Program, Boca Raton, Fla., 1987—87; clin. supr., counselor The Starting Pl., Hollywood, Fla., 1987—89; counselor, clin. supr. Adolescent Substance Abuse Counseling Svc., Kaiserslautern and Hanau, Army Military Bases, Germany, 1987—89, clin. supr., counselor Kaiserslauter and Hanau, 1989—97, counselor, acting clin. supr. Camp Zama, 1997—2002, counselor Schofield Barracks/Wahiawa, Hawaii, 2002—05, Army Substance Abuse Program, Ft. Campbell, Ky., 2005—08; alcohol & drug counselor Army Substance Abuse Program Schofield Barracks, Hawaii, 2008—. Cons. Crisis Intervention Team, Kaiserslauter; sponsor Teen Peer Facilitator Programs, Kaiserslautern; chair Character Edn. Program in Schools, Camp Zama, Japan, 2000—02; team mem. Camp Zama HS Crisis Intervention Team, 1997—2002; yean mem. WMS Crisis Intervention Team Wheeler Army Airfield Middle School, 2002—; youth 2 youth group Youth 2 Youth Internat. Group Camp Zama, 1998—2002; sponsor S.A.D.D., Kaiserslautern and Camp Zama, 1987—2002; chairperson Jorney Into Adulthood for Teens Risk, 1996—97; sponsor ASACS Role Model Club, Wheeler Army Air Base/WMS, Hawaii, 2002—05; sponsor educating parents teen issues Teen Panel, Schofiield Barracks/Wahiawa, 2002—05; counselor Army Substance Abuse Program, counselor psychol. series 180 GS-11, 2005—. Author: Looking For The Pot of Gold at The End of The Rainbow, poems; contbr. articles to profl. jours. Sponsoring mem. So. Law Poverty-Wall of Tolerance Civil Rights, Alabama, Ga., 2004—07. Mem.: APA, Nat. Assn. Master Psychologists, Nat. Alcohol and Drug Abuse Counselors, Tenn. Alcohol and Drug Abuse Counselors, Am. Mental Health Counselors, Am. Assn. Counseling. Achievements include 1990 letter of Commendation from Gerneral Crosbie E. Saint; SAIC 1990 Environmental Achievement Award for Single Superior Performance; 1997 415th Base Support Battalion Community Coin; SAIC 2000 Founders Award; Y2Y group nominated to represnt the Army in the first DoD Youth Alcohol and Drug Awareness Program Award; 2002 Legendary Service Award for the Army Military Community in Hawaii. Avocations: needlecrafts, stamp'in up-making cards, designing clothes, collecting poreclain dolls from all over the world. Personal E-mail: jeanne123047@yahoo.com.

STAKE, PETER, artist, educator; BFA, Ariz. State U.; MFA, Calif. State U., Long Beach. Chmn. art & art hist. dept. Skidmore Coll., Saratoga Springs, Calif. Exhibitions include, Ctr. Art & Design, U. Wales Inst. Bd. trustees Hyde Collection. Office: Skidmore College- Art Dept 815 North Broadway Sasselin 200 Saratoga Springs NY 12866 Office Phone: 518-580-5032. E-mail: pskake@skidmore.edu.

STAKIAS, G. MICHAEL, private equity; b. Norfolk, Va., Feb. 2, 1950; s. George and Gloria Stakias. BA, William & Mary, 1972; JD, Thomas M. Cooley Law Sch, 1976; LLM, NYU, 1977. Bar: Mich., 1976, D.C. 1980, Pa. 1980, N.Y. 1994. Atty. U.S. SEC, Washington, 1977-80; ptnr. Blank, Rome, Comisky & McCauley, Phila., 1980-98, chmn. bus. and corp. dept., 1996-98; pres., ptnr., CEO Liberty Ptnrs., LP, NYC, 1998—2009. Bd. dirs. Thomas M. Cooley Law Sch., Lansing, Mich., 1988—. Mem. Patrons Found Office: Liberty Partners LP Floor 34 1370 Ave of the Americas New York NY 10019-4602 Business E-Mail: mstakias@libertypartners.com.

STAL, SAMUEL, plastic surgeon, educator; b. Chgo., June 29, 1950; s. Morris Stal; m. Linda Mae Sparks, Sept. 13, 1982; children: Brian Jeffery, David Randal, Drew Nathaniel. MD, Loyola, chgo., 1975. Cert. plastic surgeon Tex., 1983. Prof. plastic surgery Baylor Coll. Medicine, Houston, 1981—; prof., 2008—; chief plastic surgery, 2008—. Office: Baylor Coll Medicine 6701 Fannin Mc610 Houston TX 77030 Personal E-mail: sstal@msn.com. Business E-Mail: sxstal@texaschildrenshospital.org.

STALCUP, JOE ALAN, retired lawyer, dean; b. Hooker, Okla., Feb. 13, 1931; s. Herbert I. and Ruby (Gantt) S.; m. Nancy Jo Vaughn, Sept. 3, 1950; children: Melinda, Sondra Jo, Cheri Ann. BBA cum laude, So. Methodist U., 1951, JD magna cum laude, 1959, M.Th. magna cum laude, 1978. Bar: Tex. 1959. Tchr. Dallas Ind. Sch. Dist., 1951-57; assoc. atty. firm Locke, Purnell, Boren, Laney & Neely, Dallas, 1959-66; assoc. atty., partner firm Geary, Brice & Lewis, Dallas, 1966-67; founder, sr. partner firm Stalcup, Johnson, Meyers & Miller (and predecessor firm), Dallas, 1968-75; dean Sch. Theology for the Laity, 1978—80, 1992—96, 2003—06. Pres. Dallas County Young Democrats, 1952-54; Bd. dirs., mem. exec. com. N. Tex. Christian Communications Commn., 1972-78; bd. dirs., v.p. Greater Dallas Council Chs., 1972-75; bd. dirs., chmn. Christian Ch. Found., 1976-84, 86-91, Christian Bd. Publ., 1991-98. Mem. ABA, Tex. Bar Assn., Dallas Bar Assn., Am. Judicature Soc., Phi Alpha Delta. Mem. Disciples of Christ (minister). Home and Office: 7528 Benedict Dr Dallas TX 75214-1903

STALEY, AIRICA, biologist; d. Becky A. Bauer-Page and April A. Miller (Stepmother), Douglas S. Page (Stepfather); m. Eric L. Fleischmann, June 26, 1999; children: Aidan O. Fleischmann, Errol A. Fleischmann. BS in Zoology, U. Idaho, Moscow, 1997; MS in Raptor Biology, Boise State U., Idaho, 2003. Lab. technician Conservation & Rsch. Ctr., Nat. Zool. Pk., Smithsonian Instn., Front Royal, Va., 1997—99; rsch. asst. Colo. State U., Fort Collins, 2001—06. Feild asst. Peregrine Fund, Boise, 1997; field asst. USFWS, Front Royal, 1998; rsch. field asst. Boise State U., 2000; vol. Rocky Mountain Raptor Program, Fort Collins, Idaho, 2001—02. Contbr. articles to profl. jour. Named to Dean's List, U. Idaho, 1992, 1997, Boise State U., 2001. Democrat. Avocations: photography, gardening. Personal E-mail: airicas@hotmail.com.

STALEY, DAWN MICHELLE, women's college basketball coach, retired professional basketball player; b. Phila., May 4, 1970; d. Estelle. Grad., U. Va., 1992. Profl. basketball player Brazil, France, Italy, Spain, Richmond Rage, ABL, 1996—98, Charlotte Sting, 1999—2005, Houston Comets, 2005—06; ret., 2006; head women's basketball coach Temple U. Owls, 2000—08, U. SC Gamecocks, 2008—. Mem. US Women's Sr. Nat. Basketball Team, 1989—2004, asst. coach, 2008. Founder Dawn Staley Found. Recipient Spectrum Award, ARC, 1998, Entrepreneurial Spirit Award, WNBA, 1999, Sportsmanship Award, 1999, Woman One award, 2005; named USA Basketball Female Athlete of Yr., 1994, 2004, MVP, Goodwill Games, 1994, Phila. Big Five Coach of Yr., 2002, Atlantic 10 Coach of Yr., 2004, 2005; named to First Team All-ABL, 1997, WNBA All-Star Team, 2001, 2002, 2003. Achievements include being a member of US Women's Basketball Olympic gold medal team, Atlanta, 1996, Sydney, 2000, Athens, 2004; having her number retired at U. Va; being the first women in professional basketball history to record 1,000 career assists; serving as Olympic Flag bearer, Athens Olympic Games, 2004. Office: U SC c/o Dept Athletics Roost Bldg B 1322 Heyward St Columbia SC 29208 Office Phone: 803-777-5204. Office Fax: 803-777-2967.*

STALEY, JES (JAMES EDWARD STALEY), diversified financial services company executive; b. 1956; BS in Economics, Bowdoin Coll., 1979. Joined J.P. Morgan & Co. Inc., 1979, with Latin Am. dept. Sao Paulo, Brazil, 1980—89, head Pvt. Bank, 1999—2001; CEO J.P. Morgan Asset Mgmt., mem. exec. com. J.P. Morgan Chase & Co., 2001—. Bd. trustees Bowdoin Coll., 2007—. Office: JP Morgan Chase & Co 245 Park Ave New York NY 10167-2070*

STALEY, KENNETH BERNARD, civil engineer; b. Dec. 31, 1948; s. Kinzy and Bernice Florence (Williams) S.; m. Sheila Ruth Keeys, Apr. 26, 1975; children: Tabbatha, Christina, Harrison. ThM, Villanova U., 1971, MA, 1976, DD, 1978. Registerd profl. engr.; ordained to ministry Bapt. Ch., 1978. Cost estimator Joseph A. McCollum Inc., Marlton, N.J., 1967-69; expeditor R. V. Rulon Inc., Riverton, N.J., 1971; field engr. United Engrs., Phila., 1971-72; civil engr., v.p., dir. Kinzy Staley & Sons, Inc., Phila., 1972—. Vol. Aid Sickle Cell Anemia, 1974, Mendenhall Ministries, Miss.; asst. pastor Christian Stronghold Bapt. Ch., Phila., 1978—; bd. dirs. Christian R&D, Phila., Germantown Cmty. Devel., Phila.; bd. advisors Manna Bible Inst., Phila.; trustee Ctr. Urban Theol. Studies, Conservative Bapt. Sem., Phila. Prison Sys. Mem. Nat. Soc. Profl. Engrs., Assn. Cost Engrs., Am. Arbitration Assn., Am. Ceramic Soc., Am. Concrete Inst., Phila. Engrs. Club, Alpha Phi Alpha. Democrat. Home: 1130 Lakeside Ave Philadelphia PA 19126-2308

STALEY, MICHAEL, legislative staff member; Field dep. for Rep. Spencer Bachus, US House of Reps., 2004—07, legis. dir., 2007, chief of staff, 2007—. Office: Office on Congressman Spencer Bachus 2246 Rayburn House Office Bldg Washington DC 20515-0106 Office Phone: 202-225-4921. Office Fax: 202-225-2082. E-mail: michael.staley@mail.house.gov.*

STALEY, THOMAS FABIAN, literature and language professor, museum director; b. Pitts., Aug. 13, 1935; s. Fabian Richard and Mary (McNulty) S.; m. Carolyn O'Brien, Sept. 3; children: Thomas Fabian, Caroline Ann, Mary Elizabeth, Timothy X. AB, BS, Regis Coll., 1957; MA, U. Tulsa, 1958; PhD, U. Pitts., 1962; D.H.L., Regis Coll. Asst. prof. English Rollins Coll., 1961-62; mem. faculty U. Tulsa, 1962-88, prof. English, 1969-88, dean Grad. Sch., 1969, dean Coll. Arts and Scis., 1981-83, provost, v.p. acad. affairs, 1983-88, McFarlin prof. modern lit., 1988; prof. English, dir. Ransom Humanities Rsch. Ctr. U. Tex., Austin, 1988—, Chancellor's Centennial prof. of the Book, 1989—92, Harry Huntt Ransom chair liberal arts, 1992—. Fulbright prof., Italy, 1966-67; Fulbright lectr., 1971; Danforth assoc., 1962-67; chmn. Internat. James Joyce Symposium; dir. Grad. Inst. Modern Letters, 1970-81. Author: James Joyce Today, 1966, James Joyce's Portrait of the Artist, 1968, Italo Svevo: Essays on His Work, 1969, (with H.J. Mooney) The Shapeless God: Essays on the Modern Novel, 1968, (with B. Benstock) Approaches to Ulysses: Ten Essays, 1970, Approaches to Joyce's Portrait: Ten Essays, Jean Rhys: A Critical Study; editor: Il Punto Su Joyce, 1973, Dorothy Richardson, Ulysses: Fifty Years, 1974, Twentieth-Century Women Novelists, 1982, British Novelists, 1890-1929, Traditionalists, Dictionary of Lit. Biography, Vols. 34, 36, 70, 77, An Annotated Critical Bibliography of James Joyce, 1989, Joyce Studies: An Annual edit., 1990-2003, Studies in Modern Literature Series, 1990—, Reflections on James Joyce: Stuart Gilbert's Paris Journal, 1993, Writing the Lives of Writers, 1998, James Joyce Quar., 1963-89; adv. editor Twentieth-Century Lit., 1966—, Jean Rhys Rev., 1986—; bd. dirs. Eighteenth-Century Short Title Catalogue/North America, 1990; mem. editl. bd. Tulsa Studies in Women's Literature, Jour. Modern Lit., 1989—, Mailer Rev., 2007—; contbr. articles to profl. jours. Bd. dirs. Tulsa Arts Coun., 1969-76, NCCJ, 1979—, Christopher Isherwood Found.; pres. James Joyce Found., 1968-72; chmn. bd. Undercroft Montessori Sch., 1968-70, Marquette Sch., 1969-70; bd. dirs. Cascia Hall Prep. Sch.; chmn. disting. authors com. Tulsa Libr. Trust, 1984; mem. bd. commrs. Tulsa City-County Libr., chmn., 1980-82; mem. adv. coun. Tex. Inst. for Humanities; trustee Regis U., 1992—; bd. dirs. Libr. of Am., 1994—, Harlick Trust, 1994—; mem. symposium com. Lyndon Baines Johnson Presdl. Libr., 1993—; mem. AFI Dallas Internat. Film Festival Bd., 2006—. Recipient Am. Council Learned

Socs. award, 1969, 80 Mem. MLA, Internat. Assn. Univ. Profs. English, Anglo-Irish Studies Assn., Am. Com. for Irish Studies, Assn. Internat. de Bibliophilie, James Joyce Soc., Hopkins Soc., Tex. Philos. Soc. (bd. dirs. 1991—), Internat. James Joyce Found. (hon. trustee), LBJ Centennial Hist. Soc., US Tennis Assn., Tulsa Tennis Club, Westwood Country Club, The Athenaeum Club (London), Grolier Club (N.Y.), Edgecomb Tennis Club (Kennebunk, Maine), Tarry House, Phi Beta Kappa. Business E-Mail: TFS@mail.utexas.edu.

STALHEIM-SMITH, ANN, biology educator; b. Garretson, SD, Oct. 19, 1936; d. Oliver Theodore and O'dessa Beldina (Olson) Stalheim; m. Christopher Carlisle Smith, Aug. 24, 1960; children: Heather, Andrea, Jamie. BS, Augustana Coll., Sioux Falls, SD, 1958; MS, U. Colo., 1960; PhD, No. Ariz. U., 1982. Teaching asst. Augustana Coll., 1955-58; teaching fellow U. Colo., Boulder, 1958-59, rsch. asst., 1959-60; instr. Pacific Luth. U., Tacoma, 1960-61, Fisk U., Nashville, 1967, Kans. State U., Manahattan, 1970-86, asst. prof. biology, 1986-94, assoc. prof., 1994—2003, emeritus prof., 2003—. Mem. grant rev. panel NSF, Washington, 1979, 81, 91; textbook reviewer Harper & Row Pub., West Pub., Saunders, others, 1975-87. Author: (with Greg K. Fitch) Understanding Human Anatomy and Physiology, 1993; contbr. articles to profl. jours. Grantee NSF, 1979-81, 90—, Howard Hughes Found., 1992—. Mem. AAAS, Am. Soc. Zoologists, Sigma Xi. Democrat. Lutheran. Home: 1328 Fremont St Manhattan KS 66502-4001 Home Phone: 785-539-6918. Personal E-mail: stalheim@ksu.edu.

STALKER, JACQUELINE D'AOUST, academic administrator, educator; b. Penetang, Ont., Can., Oct. 16, 1933; d. Phillip and Rose (Eaton) D'Aoust; m. Robert Stalker (dec. Nov. 2007); children: Patricia, Lynn, Roberta. Teaching cert., U. Ottawa, 1952; tchr. music, Royal Toronto Conservatory Music, 1952; teaching cert., Lakeshore Tchrs. Coll., 1958; BEd with honors, U. Manitoba, 1977, MEd, 1979; EdD, Nova U., 1985. Cert. tchr. Ont., Man., Can. Adminstr., tchr., prin. various schs., Ont. and Que., 1952-65; area commr. Girl Guides of Can., throughout Europe, 1965-69; administr., tchr. Algonquin Community Coll., Ottawa, Ont., 1970-74; tchr., program devel. Frontenac County Bd. Edn., Kingston, Ont., 1974-75; lectr., faculty advisor dept. curriculum, edn. U. Man., Can., 1977-79; lectr. U. Winnipeg, Man., Can., 1977-79; cons. colls. div. Man. Dept. Edn., 1980-81, sr. cons. programming br., 1981-84, sr. cons. post secondary, adult and continuing edn. div., 1985-88, dir. post secondary career devel. br. and adult and continuing edn. br., 1989; asst. prof. higher edn., coord. grad. program in higher edn. U. Man., 1989-92, assoc. prof., coord. grad. program in higher edn., 1992-95. Cons. lectures, seminars, workshops throughout Can. Contbr. articles to profl. jours.; mng. editor Can. Jour. of Higher Edn., 1989-93. Mem. U. Man. Senate, 1976-81, 86-89, bd. govs., 1979-82; Can. rep. Internat. Youth Conf., Garmisch, Fed. Republic of Germany, 1968; vol. Can. Cancer Soc.; mem. Assn. RN Accreditation Coun., 1980-85; chair Child Care Accreditation Com., Man., 1983-90; chair Task Force Post-Secondary Accessibility, Man., 1983; vol. United Way Planning and Allocations; provincial dir., mem. nat. bd. Can. Congress for Learning Opportunities for Women. Recipient award for enhancing the outreach activities of the univ. U. Man., 1994. Mem. U. Man. Alumni Assn., Women's Legal Edn. and Action Fund, Retired Tchrs. Assn. Man.

STALL, ALAN DAVID, manufacturing executive; arrived in US, 1982, naturalized; s. Joel and Evelyn (Schwartz) S.; m. Carol I. Johnston; children: Jeffrey, Jennifer, Michael, Timothy. BSME, U. Sask., 1973; MBA, Lewis U., 1986. Registered profl. engr., Ont. Devel. engr. DuPont Can., North Bay, Ont., 1973-76; project engr. Union Carbide Corp. Can., Lindsay, 1976-79, engring. mgr., 1979-82; mgr. shirring rsch. Union Carbide Corp., Chgo., 1982-85; dir. engring. tech. Viskase Corp., Chgo., 1985-90, v.p. engring., 1990-95; gen. mgr. Kuko Corp., Gross-Gerau, Germany, 1995-98; pres. Films Casings Tech. Inc., Woodridge, Ill., 1996—; gen. mgr. Alfacel Inc., Woodridge, 1998—; v.p. Teepak de Mex., 2003—; CEO Stratek Plastics, Wallingford, Conn., 2006—. Patentee breathable plastic, shirring apparatus, sausage stuffing machine, cellulose casings, cellulose regeneration. Rotary bus. exchange fellow, London, 1982. Mem. Engring. Inst. Can., Can. Soc. Mech. Engrs., Soc. Plastics Engrs., Assn. Profl. Engrs., Ont., Am. Mensa, Can. Club Chgo. Home: 23W540 James Way Naperville IL 60540-9552 Personal E-mail: astall@msn.com.

STALL, JOHN A., energy executive; Sr. v.p. nuc. divsn. FPL Group Inc., exec. v.p., nuc. divsn., v.p., nuc. engring, 2000—01, v.p., nuc. divsn., 2007, pres., nuc. divsn., chief nuc. officer, 2009—; sr. v.p., nuc. divsn. Fla. Power & Light Co., 2001, exec. v.p., nuc. divsn., 2008—. Office: FPL Group Inc 700 Universe Boulevard North Palm Beach FL 33408 Office Phone: 561-694-4000. Office Fax: 561-694-4999.

STALL, ROBERT, geriatrician; b. Bronx, NY, May 11, 1957; SBEE, MIT, Cambridge, Mass., 1979; MD, UB Sch. Medicine & Biomed. Sci., Buffalo, 1983. Diplomate geriatrics Am. Bd. Internal Medicine, 2008. Pres., ceo Stall Geriat. LLC, Tonawanda, NY, 1993—. Tive Cmty. Health Found. Ctrl. & Western NY, Buffalo. Recipient Med. Dirs. award, Ctr. Hospice & Palliative Care, 2000, Disting. Svc. award, Lions Club Lancaster, NY, 2004, Social Impact Award, AARP NY, 2008. Office: Stall Geriatrics LLC 350 Greenhaven Ter Tonawanda NY 14150 Business E-Mail: drstall@stallgeriatrics.com.

STALL, WILLIAM M., weed scientist, educator; b. Apr. 14, 1944; BS, Ohio State U., 1967; MS, U. Fla., 1969, PhD, 1973. Ext. agt. Dade County Cooperative Ext. Svc., 1974-80; assoc. prof. U. Fla., Gainesville, 1980-85, prof., 1985—; prof. emeritus, 2009—. Author chpts. to books; contbr. articles to profl. jours. Mem. Am. Soc. Hort. Scis. (chmn. weed sci. and IPM working group 1986, Extension Edn. Aids award, 1994, 2000), Weed Sci. Soc. Am. (mem. minor use com. 1991-94, Outstanding Ext. award 1995), Fla. State Hort. Soc. (dir.-at-large 1977, v.p. vegetable sect. 1983), Fla. Weed Sci. Soc. (dir. 1985-89, pres. 1994-95, Outstanding Weed Scientist award, 2000), Fla. Fruit and Vegetable Assoc. (Outstanding Rsch. award, 2001). Office: U Fla Hort Scis Dept Inst Food and Agrl Scis PO Box 110690 Gainesville FL 32611-0690

STALLARD, DONNA, art educator; b. Louisville, Mar. 24, 1965; d. Donald and Mary Stallard. BFA, Ind. U. SE, New Albany, 1988; MA in Art, U. Dallas, Irving, Tex., 1992, MFA, 1994. Vis. lectr. fine arts Ind. U. SE, 2005, lectr. fine arts, 2005—. Adj. prof. North Lake Coll., Irving, 1999—2004. Solo exhbns., Last 10 Years: Print Constructions, Mixed-Media Constructions. Mem. Mary Anderson Ctr. Arts, Mt. St. Francis, Ind., 2005—06. Mem.: So. Graphics Coun., Mid-America Print Coun. Office: Ind Univ SE 4201 Grant Line Rd New Albany IN 47150 Business E-Mail: dstallar@ius.edu.

STALLER, JOHN EDWARD, archaeologist, anthropologist, educator; b. Grosseraming, Austria, Jan. 28, 1951; s. John Staller and Elizabeth; m. Margaret Mary Tentler, Jan. 20, 1973. BA, Roosevelt U., Chgo., 1981; MA, So. Meth. U., Dallas, 1990, PhD, 1994. Rsch. assoc. The Field Mus., Chgo., 1999—. Bd. dirs. Fulbright Assn., Chgo., 1999—; adj. prof. Loyola U., Chgo., 1996, Roosevelt U., 2000; vis. asst. prof. U. Ill., Chgo., 1999—2000; vis. faculty in Summer Inst. MIT Workshop, 2001; vis. lectr. Northeastern Ill. U., 2003; vis. asst. prof. U. Ky., 2005—06. Editor (senior editor): Histories of Maize: Multidisciplinary Approaches to the Prehistory, Biogeography, Domestication, and Evolution of Maize; contbr. articles to profl. jours. Fulbright scholar, 1988—89, 1989, 2007. Mem.: World Archtl. Congress, Soc. Am. Archaeology, Fulbright Assn., Inst. Andean Studies, Am. Anthrop. Assn. Office: The Field Museum Dept of Anthropology 1400 S Lake Shore Dr Chicago IL 60605

STALLINGS, CHARLES HENRY, retired physicist; b. Durham, NC, Dec. 28, 1941; s. Henry Harroll and Dorothy (Powers) S.; m. Elizabeth Bright, Sept. 4, 1965; children: Deborah, Sharon. BS, N.C. State U., 1963, MS, 1964; PhD, U. Wis., 1970. Sr. physicist Physics Internat. Co. (now Maxwell Physics Internat.), San Leandro, Calif., 1970-73, dep. dept. mgr., 1974-76, dept. mgr., 1976-79, dir. satellite x-ray test facility office, 1979-81, dir. bus. devel., 1981-83, v.p., dir. rsch. devel., v.p., gen. mgr., 1983—2001; ret., 2001. Contbr. articles to tech. jours. Mem. Gen. Plan Rev. Com., Pleasanton, Calif., 1983. Mem. Am. Phys. Soc., IEEE (mem. pulsed power sci. and tech. com. 1996—, chmn. 12th internat. pulsed power conf. 1999), Def. Sci. Bd. Task Force, 2003-05. Home: 3608 Fieldview Ct Pleasanton CA 94588

STALLINGS, CHARLES KENDALL, music educator, composer; b. Cape Girardeau, Mo., June 20, 1940; s. Tharon Eugene and Tylene (Kendall) S.; m. Johann Candiano, Aug. 22, 1964; 1 child, Laura Ann. BA, Washington U., St. Louis, 1962, MA, 1964, PhD, 1969; spl. study, Teylers Mus., The Netherlands, 1972, Calif. Inst. Arts, 1974. Instr. music Webster U., St. Louis, 1967-69, asst. prof., 1969-73, assoc. prof., 1973-91, prof., 1991—98, prof. emeritus, 1998—. Advisor Synchronia, music ensemble, St. Louis, 1986-99. Composer: Exchanges I, 1965, minimovement, 1970, Gas Light Square: A Requiem Celebration, 1974, Collins Mix, 1980, Figures and Grounds, 1985, Synchronicity, 1992, Dr. John's Contrapunctus, 1999, The Fire Sermon, 2002, Mr. Ives's Rounds, 2006, Synchronicity Redux, 2008-09. Mem. ASCAP. Office: Webster U 470 E Lockwood Ave Saint Louis MO 63119-3194 Office Phone: 314-968-7032. E-mail: k-j-stallings@sbcglobal.net.

STALLINGS, KEVIN, men's college basketball coach; m. Lisa Stallings; children: Jacob, Alexa, Jordyn. B in Bus. Mgmt., Purdue U., West Lafayette, Ind., 1982, M, 1985. Asst. coach Purdue U. Boilermakers, 1983—88, U. Kans. Jayhawks, 1989—94; head basketball coach Ill. State U. Redbirds, 1994—99, Vanderbilt U. Commodores, 1999—. Named Coach of Yr., Southeastern Conf., 2007. Office: Vanderbilt U Athletics McGugin Ctr 2601 Jess Neely Dr Nashville TN 37212 Office Phone: 615-343-8482.*

STALLINGS, RONALD DENIS, lawyer; b. Evansville, Ind., Feb. 22, 1943; s. Denis and Gertrude (Tong) S.; m. Vicki Lee Chandler, Aug. 21, 1965; children: Courtnay, Claire, Ryan. B in Indsl. Engring., Ga. Inst. Tech., 1965; LLB, U. Va., 1968. Bar: Ga. 1968. Assoc. Powell, Goldstein, Frazer & Murphy LLP, Atlanta, 1968—75, ptnr., 1976—2000, co-counsel, 2001—05; exec. v.p., gen. counsel, corp. sec. Reliance Fin. Corp. and Reliance Trust Co., Atlanta, 2001—. Co-author: Georgia Corporate Forms, 1988. Mem. ABA, Ga. Bar Assn., Atlanta Bar Assn., Nat. Assn. Bond Lawyers, Am. Soc. Corp. Secs., Phoenix Soc. Atlanta (trustee 1987-93). Roman Catholic. Home: 4601 Polo Ln NW Atlanta GA 30339-5345 Office: Reliance Trust Co 500 Northpark Ste 400 1100 Abernathy Rd NE Atlanta GA 30328-5646 Business E-Mail: rstallings@relico.com.

STALLINGS, TOMMY RAY, legislative staff member; BS, MBA, Tex. Christian U., Ft. Worth. Pres. Mirage Spring Water Co., 1991—93; ops. mgr. Brinks Home Security, 1994—98; quality assurance analyst Radio Shack, 1998—2001; rsch. asst., Senator George Allen US Senate, Washington, 2001—02, legis. asst., Senator George Allen, 2002; legis. asst., Rep. Trent Franks US House of Reps., 2003—05, chief of staff to Rep. Trent Franks, 2005—. Republican. Office: 2435 Rayburn House Office Bldg Washington DC 20515 Office Phone: 202-225-4576. Office Fax: 202-225-6328. Business E-Mail: tom.stallings@mail.house.gov.*

STALLMAN, DONALD LEE, environmental executive; b. Rochester, NY, Feb. 20, 1930; s. William F. and Clara Elizabeth (Boulle) S.; (dec. Nov. 9, 2007); stepchildren: Nancy, Terri, Jeff. Student, Hobart Coll., Geneva, NY, 1948-49, U. Rochester, 1953-54. V.p. Kolstad Assocs., Inc., Rochester, NY, 1954—2002; pres. Water Treatment Assocs., Latham, NY, 1975—, KB Fabrications, Latham, 1977—. Chmn. bd. Water Treatment Assocs.; vice chmn. bd. KB Fabrications; adv. bd., pres. Bruner Corp., Milw., 1982-83. Designer Chock-o-Lette Spl. Aircraft Wheel Chock, 1978, Water Treatment Skid for Oil Field Applications, 1980; inventor in field. Cons. Capital Dist. Planning Commn., Albany, 1980-81. With U.S. Army, 1951-53. Decorated Bronze Star medal, Silver Star medal, Purple Hearts (2). Mem. Am. Soc. Plumbing Engrs., Quiet Birdman Soc., Sigma Chi. Republican. Roman Catholic. Avocations: flying, boating, golf. Office: Water Treatment Assocs PO Box 367 Latham NY 12110-0367 Home: 16 Hillcrest Rd Latham NY 12110-4133 Home (Winter): 111 Royal Pk Dr 4H Oakland Park FL 33309 Home Phone: 518-785-3457; Office Phone: 518-785-5654. Personal E-mail: alboff@aol.com, alb@aol.com.

STALLMAN, KURT, composer, educator; AM, Harvard U., 1997, PhD, 1999. Mem. faculty Boston Conservatory; mem. faculty, founder computer music studio Longy Sch. Music, Cambridge, Mass.; asst. prof. music Harvard U., 1999—2002; assoc. dir. Harvard U. Studios for Electro-Acoustic Composition, 1999—2002; asst. prof. music composition Shepherd Sch. Music, Rice U., Houston, 2002—, Lynette S. Autrey chair music, dir. REMLABS. Mem. Composers in Red Sneakers, Boston, 2001—03, Musiqa, Houston. Fellow John Simon Guggenheim Meml. Found., 2008, AAAL, 2009. Mem.: Soc. Electro-Acoustic Music US (bd. dirs. 2005—, editor SEAMUS newsletter 2005—). Office: Rice U Shepherd Sch Music 2811 Alice Pratt Brown Hall 610 Main St Houston TX 77005-1892 Office Phone: 713-348-8387. E-mail: stallman@rice.edu, kurt@trigonmusic.com.*

STALLMAN, RICHARD MATTHEW, software developer; b. NYC, 1953; BA in Physics, Harvard U., Cambridge, Mass., 1974; PhD (hon.), Royal Inst. Tech., Stockholm, 1996, U. Glasgow, Scotland, 2001, Free U., Brussels, 2003, U. Nacional de Salta, Argentina, 2004, U. Pavia, Italy, 2007, U. Los Angelos de Chimbote, Peru, 2007, U. Nacional Trujillo, 2008, Lakehead U., Can., 2009. Software developer MIT, Cambridge, 1971-83. Chief GNUisance, GNU Project, 1984—; founder, pres. Free Software Found., Boston, 1985—; hon. prof. U. Nacional de Ingeniería de Perú, 2003, U. Inca Garcilaso de la Vega, 2007. Author: Free Software, Free Society, 2002; (software) EMACS, 1975, GNU EMACS, 1984, GNU C Compiler, 1988, GNU General Public License, 1989, GNU GPL Version 3, 2007. Bd. dirs. League Programming Freedom, 1989-95, pres., 1989-92. Recipient Grace Hopper award Assn. Computing, 1990, MacArthur prize fellowship MacArthur Found., 1990, Pioneer award Electronic Frontier Found., 1998, Yuri Rubinski Insight Found. award, 1999, Takeda prize for social/econ. betterment, 2001, Fondazione Pistoletto prize, 2005, Extremadura Free Knowledge prize, 2007. Mem.: NAE, Am. Acad. Arts and Scis. Avocations: Balkan folk dance, Balinese and Javanese Gamelan music, reading. Office: Free Software Found 51 Franklin St 5th Fl Boston MA 02111 Office Phone: 617-542-5942.

STALLMEYER, JAMES EDWARD, engineering educator; b. Covington, Ky., Aug. 11, 1926; s. Joseph Julius and Anna Catherine (Scheper) S.; m. Mary Katherine Davenport, Apr. 11, 1953; children: Cynthia Marie, James Duncan, Michael John, Catherine Ann, John Charles, Gregory Edward. BS, U. Ill., 1947, MS, 1949, PhD, 1953. Jr. engr. So. Ry. System, 1947; research asst. U. Ill., Urbana, 1947-49, research asso., 1951-52, asst. prof. civil engring, 1952-57, assoc. prof., 1957-60, prof., 1960-91, prof. emeritus, 1991—. Cons. on structural problems various indsl. and govt. agys. Author: (with E.H. Gaylord Jr.), Design of Steel Structures; editor: (with E.H. Gaylord Jr.) Structural Engineering Handbook; contbr. to Shock and Vibration Handbook. Served with USN, 1944-46. Standard Oil fellow, 1949-51; recipient Adams meml. award, 1964, Everitt award for teaching excellence, 1981 Mem. ASCE, Am. Concrete Inst., Am. Ry. Engring. Assn., ASTM, Am. Welding Soc., Am. Soc. Metals, Soc. Exptl. Stress Analysis, Scabbard and Blade, Sigma Xi, Chi Epsilon, Sigma Tau, Tau Beta Pi, Phi Kappa Phi. Clubs: KC. Republican. Roman Catholic. Office: Newmark Civil Engring 205 N Mathews Ave Urbana IL 61801-2350 Business E-Mail: jestall26@gmail.com.

STALLONE, GEORGE R., neurophysiologist; b. Camden, NJ, Aug. 22, 1963; s. George Ralph and Rose Marie Anne Stallone. BS in Zoology, U. Md., 1989; D of Chiropractic, We. States Chirpractic Coll., 1994; postgrad. in clin. neurology, Logan Coll. Chiropractic, 1998. Cert. intraoperative neurophysiologic monitoring. Resident Triad Family Health, Hanover, Pa., 1995—96; intern Banister Chiropractic, Jacksonville, Fla., 1996—97; chiropractor pvt. practice, Nephi, Utah, 1998—2003; intraoperative neurophysiologist Teaneck, NJ, 2004—. Instr., rschr. Triad Family Health, 1995—96; rschr., lectr. Mind/Body Inst., Jacksonville, 1996—97. Sec. Ch. Men's Group, Mona, Utah, 2000—01. Mem.: Am. Soc. Electrophysiologists, Masons. Avocations: flying, scuba diving, skiing, martial arts. Home: PO BOX 4 Harrisonville NJ 08039-0004 E-mail: stallone@nebonet.com.

STALLONE, SYLVESTER GARDENZIO, actor, film director, scriptwriter, producer; b. NYC, July 6, 1946; s. Frank and Jacquline (Labofish) Stallone; m. Sasha Czack, Dec. 28, 1974 (div. Feb. 14, 1985); children: Sage, Seth; m. Brigitte Nielsen, Dec. 15, 1985 (div. July 13, 1987); m. Jennifer Flavin, May 17, 1997; children: Sophia, Sistine, Scarlet. Student, Am. Coll. of Switzerland, 1965-67, U. Miami, 1967-69. Actor: (films) The Party at Kitty and Stud's, 1970, No Place to Hide, 1970, The Prisoner of Second Avenue, 1975, Capone, 1975, Death Race 2000, 1975, Farewell, My Lovely, 1975, Cannonball!, 1976, Nighthawks, 1981, Victory, 1981, Lock Up, 1989, Tango & Cash, 1989, Oscar, 1991, Stop! Or My Mom Will Shoot, 1992, Demolition Man, 1993, The Specialist, 1994, Judge Dredd, 1995, Assassins, 1995, Daylight, 1996, The Good Life, 1997, Cop Land, 1997, An Alan Smithee Film: Burn Hollywood Burn, 1998, (voice) Antz, 1998, Get Carter, 2000, D-Tox, 2002, Avenging Angelo, 2002, Shade, 2003, Spy Kids 3-D: Game Over, 2003; writer, actor (films) The Lord's of Flatbush, 1974, Rocky, 1976, F.I.S.T, 1978, First Blood, 1982, Rhinestone, 1984, Rambo: First Blood Part II, 1985, Cobra, 1986, Over the Top, 1987, Rambo III, 1988, Rocky V, 1980, Cliffhanger, 1993, dir., writer, actor Paradise Alley, 1978, Rocky II, 1979, Rocky III, 1982, Rocky IV, 1985, Rocky Balboa, 2006, prodr., dir., writer, actor Staying Alive, 1983, Rambo, 2008; prodr.: (films) Heart of a Champion: The Ray Mancini Story, 1985; prodr., writer, actor (films) Driven, 2001, exec. prodr., writer Father Lefty, 2002; actor(guest appearances): (TV series) Police Story, 1975, Kojak, 1975, Liberty's Kids: Est. 1776, 2002, Las Vegas, 2005; prodr.: The Contender, 2005, The Contender Rematch: Mora vs. Manfredo, 2005; author: Sly Moves: My Proven Program to Lose Weight, Build Strength, Gain Will Power, and Live Your Dream, 2005. Recipient Star of Yr. award, 1977, Artistic Achievement award, Nat. Italian Am. Found., 1991, Order of Arts and Letters, French Ministry, 1992, Caesar award for Career Achievement, 1992; named Show West Actor of Yr., 1979. Mem.: SAG, Dirs. Guild, Writers Guild, Stuntmans Assn. (hon.). Achievements include being nominated for two Oscars (acting and writing) in same year (1976); occurred for only 3d time in history. *Once in one's life, for one mortal moment, one must make a grab for immortality; if not, one has not lived.*

STALLWORTH, CHARLES DEROTHA, JR., psychologist; b. Riderwood, Ala., July 4, 1940; s. Charles D. and Annie (Horn) S. BS, Tenn. State U., Nashville, 1963, MS, 1966; postgrad., Calif. Sch. Profl. Psychology, 1977-79, U. South Ala., Mobile, 1967, Tuskegee Inst., 1968, U. Ky., Lexington, 1980; PhD in Psychology, Internat. Coll., 1983; cert. in mental disability law, N.Y. Law Sch., 2001. Diplomate Am. Bd. Psychotherapy, Am. Psychotherapy Assn., Am. Coll. Mental Health Practitioners, Am. Coll., Forensic Counselors, Acad. Cert. Neurotherapists. Psychiat. asst. Hubbard Hosp., Nashville, 1964-66; counselor, tchr. North Ctrl. H.S., Chatom, Ala., 1966-68; tchr. Washington County H.S., 1968—70; supr. adult edn. Washington County Bd. Edn., Chatom, 1968-70; dir. counseling ctr. Albany State Coll., Ga., 1970—91; pvt. practice, 1993—. Mem. staff Auburn U., summer 1969; counselor Spl. Svc. program Albany State Coll., 1992-93; cons. Peace Corps, 1979-81; dep. dir. gen. Internat. Biographical Ctr., Cambridge, Eng., 2004-. Contbr. articles to profl. jours. Bd. dirs. Dougherty County CODAC, Inc., Albany, 1973-77; hon. mem. Ga. Sheriff's Assn, citizen amb. People to People Internat., Kansas City, Mo. Recipient Eagle Scout award, Boy Scout America, 1955, Internat. Poet of Merit award, Internat. Soc. Poets, 2003, Internat. Peace prize, United Cultural Consortium, 2002, Poet of Merit award, 2002—04, 2006, 2008; named Oracle of the Arrow, Boy Scout America, 1957, Most Admiral Man of Decade, Bd. Internat. Rsch., Am. Biog. Inst., 1990, Most Admired Man of Decade, Am. Biog. Inst., Decade of 90's, 1992, Shield of Valor, 1992; named to Hall of Fame, 1985; grantee, HEW, 1970—77, US Office Edn., 1972. Mem. APA, Am. Psychotherapy Assn., Nat. Assn. Cognitive-Behavioral Therapists, Nat. Assn. Forensic. Counselors, Alpha Phi Alpha. Democrat. Baptist. Achievements include research on impact of affective domain on learning outcomes and on application of cognitive therapies as a means of controlling negative effects. Home: 805 E 4th Ave Albany GA 31705-1203

STALLWORTH, MONICA LAVAUGHN, geriatrician; b. Savannah, Ga., July 29, 1952; d. William D. and Betty Lou Stallworth; m. Robert J. Kolimas, Oct. 17, 1955; 1 child, Catherine. BS in Biology, St. Mary's Coll., Notre Dame, Inc., 1974; MA in Biology and Health Edn., Ball State U., 1975; MD, Mayo Med. Sch., 1980. Diplomate Am. Bd. Family Practice; cert. Am. Bd. Hospice and Palliative Medicine; bd. cert. Geriatric Medicine. Family practitioner MacGregor Med. Assn., Houston, 1983-97; asst. prof. family medicine Georgetown U. Sch. Medicine, Washington, 1997—; geriatrician Washington Home and Hospice, 1998-99; dir. geriatric assessment clinic Georgetown Family Practice Residency, Md., 1999—. Dir. home care program Georgetown Residency Family Practice, 1998—. Recipient Civic Svc. award City of West University Place, 1994, Svc. award Rotary Club, 1994, 95. Bd. dirs.

Newcomers Club, Houston, 1995-97, Rotary Club, Tex., 1995-97, U. Tex.; chmn. Innunization Project, Houston, 1995-97; mem. pres. adv. coun. SMC. Fellow Am. Acad. Family Practice; mem. Am. Geriatric Soc. (bd. dirs. D.C. chpt. 1998—). Avocations: ice skating, reading. E-mail: lavonnie_20002@yahoo.com.

STALLWORTH, STANLEY B., lawyer; b. 1963; BS summa cum laude, Ala. Agrl. and Mech. U., 1985; JD, U. Wis., 1990. Bar: Ala. 1990, Ill. 1990, Wis. 1990. Joined Sidley Austin Brown & Wood, Chgo., 1990—, now ptnr. real estate practice, and co-chmn. com. on racial and ethnic diversity. Articles editor Univ. Wis. Multi-Cultural Law Jour., 1989—90. Bd. trustees Univ. Wis. Law Alumni Assn.; chmn. bd. trustees Chgo. Acad. for Arts. Mem.: Chgo. Coun. of Lawyers (bd. dir.), Nat. Bar Assn., ABA, Cook County Bar Assn. (past mem. exec. bd. dir.). Office: Sidley Austin Brown Wood 1 S Dearborn St Ste 900 Chicago IL 60603-2310 Office Phone: 312-853-4715. Office Fax: 312-853-7036. Business E-Mail: sstallworth@sidley.com.

STALNAKER, JUDITH ANN, education educator; b. San Diego, Sept. 3, 1942; d. Harold Willard and Dorothy Ione (Maxwell) Growcock; m. Archie LaVern Stalnaker, Aug. 31, 1963; children: Dena Lyn Garcia, Keri Leigh Hale. BA, teaching credential, Calif. State U., San Diego, 1973; MA, reading specialist credential, San Diego State U., 1985. Cert. tchr., reading specialist. Tchr. El Centro Sch. Dist., Calif., 1976—98; prof. San Diego State U., Calexico, Calif., 1987—89; ret. Presenter critical thinking skills, Imperial County, Calif., 1986, El Centro, 1986, English/lang. arts framework, El Centro, 1989. Mem. Young Democrats, San Diego, 1962-63; mem. McKinley Sch. PTA, 1969-75, pres., 1971-72. Mem. AAUW, Imperial County Reading Coun. (v.p. 1988-89), Internat. Reading Assn., Lang. Arts Leadership Team, Jr. Women's 10,000 Club (pres. 1971-72), Calif. Fedn. Women's Clubs (jr. mem. De Anza dist., v.p. 1972-73, Calif. Jr. Citizen of Yr. 1972), Del Rio Ladies Golf Assn. (officer, 1998-02, Pres. Cup winner, 2005), B.P.O Elks El Centro (officer, 1999-02, chmn., vet. affairs nat. hon., 2003). Lutheran. Avocations: world travel, reading, golf.

STALOFF, ARNOLD FRED, financial services executive; b. Dover, NJ, Dec. 12, 1944; s. William and Ida (Greenberg) S.; m. Sharon Marcia Teplitsky, June 10, 1967; children: Kimberly, Lindsay. BBA, U. Miami, 1967. Statistician U.S. Census Bur., Washington, 1967-68; fin. analyst SEC, Washington, 1968-71; sr. v.p. Phila. Stock Exch., 1971-78; v.p. Securities Industry Automation Corp., NYC, 1978-80; pres. Fin. Automation Corp., Phila., 1980-83, Phila. Bd. Trade, 1983-89; pres., CEO Commodity Exch., Inc. (COMEX), NYC, 1989-90; CEO Bloom Staloff Corp., Phila., 1991—2003; chmn. SFB Market Sys., Inc., 2005—07. Bd. dirs. Lehman Bros. Fin. Products, Inc., 1994-2008, Shiner Internat., Inc., Aqfeed, Inc., Deer Consumer Products, Smart Heat, Inc.; bd. govs. Phila. Stock Exch., 1991-97. Bd. dirs. Variety Club for Handicapped Children, Phila., 1987-92; mem. adv. bd. Phila. Internat. Airport, 1988—; mem. U. Miami Pres.'s Cir. Mem. Nat. Futures Assn. (bd. dirs. 1987-90). Avocations: fly fishing, golf, skiing. Office Phone: 856-853-1800. Business E-Mail: staloff@staloff.com.

STALTER, ANN MARIE, nursing educator; d. Donald F. and Mary Ann Stalter; m. Mark S. Justice, Dec. 26, 1987; children: Amber N. Justice, William Seth Justice, Megan Elizabeth Justice. PhD, Ohio State U., Columbus, 2008. Interim, dir. nurses Acad. Health Svcs., Dayton, Ohio, 1985—99; clin. instr. Wright State U., Dayton, 1998—. Zoning bd. Beavercreek Twp., Ohio, 2007—. Recipient MNRS Hon. Poster award, 2005. Conservative. Roman Catholic. Office: Wright State Univ CONH 3640 Col Glenn HWY Dayton OH 45435 Business E-Mail: ann.stalter@wright.edu.

STALZER, FRANK JOSEPH, electronics company executive; b. Oceanside, NY, May 8, 1957; s. Erwin and Emma Stalzer; m. Jennifer Ann Nuzzi, Aug. 17, 1980 (div.); children: Frank Jr., Angela Marie, Jenna; m. Maria Stalzer; children: Andrew, Victoria. BS in Polit. Sci., Pub. Adminstrn., NY Inst. Tech., 1980; postgrad., LI U.; attended gen. mgmt. program, Harvard U. Bus. Sch. With support services dept. FBI, NYC, 1977-80; police officer Port Authority NY, NJ, NYC, 1980-81; sales adminstr. Peerless Radio Corp., Lynbrook, NY, 1981-83, sales mgr., 1983-85, mgr. domestic sales, 1985-87, dir. sales; regional v.p. Richey Electronics; v.p., gen. mgr. Arrow Electronics; pres. Astrex Electronics. Committeeman Nassau County Rep. Com., Westbury, NY; LI coord. Congressman Jack Kemp's Primary Campaign, 1988. Republican. Roman Catholic. Office: Astrex Electronics 205 Express St Plainview NY 11803 Office Phone: 516-433-1700. Office Fax: 516-433-1796.

STAM, DAVID HARRY, librarian; b. Paterson, NJ, July 11, 1935; s. Jacob and Deana B. (Bowman) S.; m. Deirdre Corcoran, May 15, 1963; children: Julian, Wendell, Kathryn. AB, Wheaton Coll., 1955; postgrad., New Coll., U. Edinburgh, 1955-56; MLS, Rutgers U., 1962; postgrad., CUNY, 1963-64; PhD, Northwestern U., 1978. Asst. editor library publs., reference librarian, manuscript cataloguer New York Pub. Library, 1959-64; librarian Marlboro (Vt.) Coll., 1964-67; head tech. services dept. Newberry Library, Chgo., 1967-71, assoc. librarian, 1969-73; librarian Milton S. Eisenhower Library, Johns Hopkins U., Balt., 1973-78; Andrew W. Mellon dir. rsch. libraries N.Y. Pub. Library, NYC, 1978-86; Univ. librarian Syracuse U., 1986-98, Univ. librarian emeritus, 1998—, sr. scholar, history dept., 1998—. Trustee Gladys K. Delmas Found. Author: Wordsworthian Criticism, 1974, International Dictionary of Library Histories, 2001; co-author (with Rissa Yachnin): Turgenev in English: A Checklist of Works by and about Him, 1960; co-author: (with Deirdre C. Stam) Books on Ice, 2005; contbr. articles to profl. jours. Bd. dirs. Chamber Music Am., NY, Served with USNR, 1956-58. Brit. Acad. Overseas fellow, 1975, Brit. Libr. fellow, 1995-96. Mem.: American Trust for British Library, Am. Antiquarian Soc., Keats-Shelley Assn. Am. (bd. dirs.), Grolier Club (N.Y.C.), Princeton Club N.Y. Office: Syracuse U History Dept Eggers Hall Syracuse NY 13244 E-mail: dhstam@syr.edu.

ST-AMAND, PIERRE, geophysicist; b. Tacoma, Wash., Feb. 4, 1920; s. Cyrias Z. and Mable (Berg) St. A.; m. Marie Pöss, Dec. 5, 1945; children: Gene, Barbara, Denali, David. BS in Physics, U. Alaska, 1948; MS in Geophysics, Calif. Inst. Tech., 1951, PhD in Geophysics and Geology, 1953; Dr. honoris causa, U. De Los Altos, Tepatitlan, Mex., 1992. Cert. in spl. congressional regulation Kevin McCorth. Asst. dir. Geophys. Lab., U. Alaska, also head ionospheric and seismologic investigations, 1946-49; physicist U.S. Naval Ordnance Test Sta., China Lake, Calif., 1950-54, head optics br., 1955-58; head earth and planetary sci. div. U.S. Ordnance Test Sta., 1961-78, cons. to tech. dir., head spl. projects office, 1978-88; fgn. service with ICA as prof. geol. and geophys. Sch. Earth Scis., U. Chile, 1958-60; originator theory rotational displacement Pacific Ocean Basin. Pres. Saint-Amand Sci. Services; adj. prof. McKay Sch. Mines, U. Nev., U. N.D.; v.p., dir. Covillea Corp.; v.p., dir. tech. Mueta1 Corp.; cons. World Bank, Calif. Div. Water Resources, Am. Potash & Chem. Co., OAS; mem. U.S. Army airways comms. sys., Alaska and Can., 1942-46; cons. Mexican, Chilean, Argentine, Philipines, Can., Rhodesian govts.; mem. Calif. Gov.'s Com. Geol. Hazards; mem. com. magnetic instruments Internat. Union Geodesy and Geophys., 1954-59, Disaster Preparation Commn. for L.A.; charter mem. Sr. Exec. Svc.; led drought relief expdns., India, The Philippines, Mex., Okinawa, Japan; rep. fed. emergency com. for LA (Calif.), USN. Adv. bd. GeoScience News; contbr. 100 articles to scientific jours. Chmn. bd. dirs. Ridgecrest Regional Hosp.; chmn. bd. dirs. Indian Wells Valley Airport Dist.; pres., dir. Indian Wells Valley Water Dist.; v.p. bd. dirs. Kern County Acad. Decathlon; mem. water resources bd. Kern County. Decorated knight Mark Twain, Mark Twain Jour.; recipient cert. of merit OSRD, 1945, cert. of merit USAAF, 1946, letter of commendation USAAF, 1948, Spl. award Philippine Air Force, 1969, Diploma de Honor Sociedad Geologica de Chile, Disting. Civilian Svc. medal USN, 1968, L.T.E. Thompson medal, 1973, Thunderbird award Weather Modification Assn., 1974, Disting. Pub. Svc. award Fed. Exec. Inst., 1976, Meritorious Svc. medal USN, 1988, Disting. Alumnus award U. Alaska, 1990; Fulbright rsch. fellow France, 1954-55, Lifetime AChievement award. Fellow AAAS, Geol. Soc. Am., Earthquake Engr. Rsch. Inst.; mem. Am. Geophys. Union, Weather Modification Assn., Am. Seismol. Soc., Sister Cities (Ridgecrest-Tepatitlan) Assn. (pres.), Rotary (past pres., Paul Harris fellow), Footprinters Internat. (mem. grand bd., pres.), Sigma Xi. Achievements include patents in photometric instrument, weather and ordnance devices, pvt. pilot multi-engine-instruments; identified Denali: Fairweather Faults in Alaska and Canada, Atacama Fault in Chile. Home and Office: 1748 W Las Flores Ave Ridgecrest CA 93555-8635 Home Phone: 760-375-0481; Office Phone: 760-375-0481. Personal E-mail: st-amand@ridgecrest.ca.us.

STAMAS, STEPHEN, not-for-profit administrator; b. Salem, Mass., Apr. 26, 1931; s. Theodore and Georgia (Fotopulos) S.; m. Elaine Heidi Zervas, Apr. 24, 1955; children: Heidi, Theodore. AB, Harvard, 1953, PhD, 1957; B.Phil. (Rhodes scholar), Oxford U., 1955. Budget examiner Bur. Budget, Washington, 1957-59; loan officer Devel. Loan Fund, Washington, 1959-60; mgr. internat. divsn. treasurer's dept. Standard Oil Co. (NJ), NYC, 1960-63, dep. European fin. rep. London, 1963-64, chief economist NYC, 1969-70, dep. mgr. pub. affairs dept., 1971; govt. rels. mgr. Esso Europe, 1964-67; petroleum planning mgr. Esso Internat., 1967-68; dep. asst. sec. for fin. policy Dept. Commerce, Washington, 1968-69; v.p., pub. affairs Exxon Corp., NYC, 1973-86; pres. Wallace Funds, NYC, 1986-87, NY Philharm., 1984-89, chmn., 1989-96. Trustee, pres. Am. Ditchley Found.; trustee emeritus Rockefeller U.; chmn. Am. Assembly, Columbia U., Marlboro Sch. Music; mem. bd. overseers Harvard Coll., 1979-85; bd. dirs. NY Philharm.-Symphony Soc.; bd. dirs. emeritus Lincoln Ctr. for the Performing Arts; bd. dirs. The Greenwall Found., Seacor SMIT, Inc.; co-chmn. Am. Trust for Brit. Libr. Fellow Am. Acad. Arts & Scis.; mem. Am. Assocs. Royal Acad., Coun. Fgn. Rels., Acad. Polit. Sci., Am. Coun. on Germany, Scarsdale Golf Club (NY), Phi Beta Kappa. Clubs: Harvard (NYC), Century Assn. (NYC), Manursing Island (Rye, NY). Home: 325 Evandale Rd Scarsdale NY 10583-1505 E-mail: astolatz@aol.com.

STAMBAUGH, ARMSTRONG A., JR., restaurant and hotel executive; b. Cleve., Nov. 1, 1920; s. Armstrong Alexander and Beatrice (Snyder) S.; m. Janet Turley Marting, July 26, 1943 (div. 1958); children: Susan Reed (Mrs. Roy H. Beaton, Jr.), Sally Russell (Mrs. Michael H. Huber), Elizabeth Renshaw (Mrs. Michael C. Warr); m. Aagot Hinrichsen Cain, June 10, 1972. BA, Dartmouth Coll., 1942; Indsl. Adminstr., Harvard U., 1943, MBA, 1946. Research asst., then instr. bus. adminstrn. Harvard Grad. Sch. Bus. Adminstrn., 1946-48; with Gulf Oil Corp., 1948-66, coord. sales devel. mktg. hdqrs. Houston, 1962-63, v.p. Eastern marketing region Phila., 1963-66; exec. v.p. adminstrn. Howard Johnson Co., Inc., 1966-70, exec. v.p. ops. and adminstrn., 1970-79, exec. v.p., asst. to pres., 1979-81, dir., 1969-81; operator, developer food and lodging facilities, 1981-98. Pres. trustees Fox Chapel Country Day Sch., Pitts., 1955-57; div. vice chmn. Boston United Fund, 1961; bd. dirs. Houston Internat. Trade and Travel Fair, 1962-63, World Affairs Coun. Phila., 1964-65; dir. Phila. C. of C., 1964, 65, 66; bd. overseers Hanover Inn, Dartmouth Coll., 1979-85, chmn., 1984-85; trustee Old Sturbridge Village, Mass., 1979-01. Served to lt. (j.g.) USNR, 1943-46. Mem. Pine Valley Golf Club (N.J.), Weston Golf Club (Mass.), Edgartown Golf Club (Mass.), Boston Skating Club, Vineyard Haven Yacht Club (Mass.), Paradise Valley Country Club (Ariz.), Delta Tau Delta. Home (Winter): 6845 N Rocking Rd Scottsdale AZ 85250

STAMBAUGH, LARRY G., strategic business consultant; b. Topeka, Feb. 1, 1947; s. Merle J. and Eileen M. (Denslow) S.; m. Sallie M. Underwood, Jan. 18, 1969 (div. Oct. 1981); children: Matt, Julie; m. Suzanne Van Slyke, May 14, 1982 (div. Oct. 2006); children: Todd, Scott, Andy; m. Pamela Truax, Oct. 27, 2007. BBA, Washburn U., 1969. CPA, Kans. Mgr. KPMG Peat, Marwick, Mitchell Co., Kansas City, Mo., 1969-76; co-owner Automotive Investment & Devel. Co., Olathe, Kans., 1976-82; EVP, CFO CNB Fin. Corp., Kansas City, Kans., 1983—90; CFO ABC Labs., Columbia, Mo., 1990, chmn., pres., CEO, 1990-92, Maxim Pharms., San Diego, 1993—2006; prin. Apercu Cons., 2006—, pres., 2007—08; CEO Calando Pharmaceuticals, 2007; chmn., pres., CEO CryoPort, Inc., 2009—; chmn to bd. dir. Ridge Diagnostics Inc., 2007; bd. dir. Elixir Industries, 2007—08, Ecodog, 2008—, Assure Controls, 2008—09. Bd. dirs. BioCom, Eco Dog Inc., 2008-; mem. adv. bd. U. Calif. San Diego Rady Sch. Bus. Chmn. bd. dirs. Forum for Corp. Dirs., 1996-99. Recipient Dir. of Yr. award, Forum for Corp. Dirs., 2002, 2006—07, Jim Mcgraw Disting. award, 2008. Mem. Am. Mgmt. Assn., Nat. Assn. Corp. Dirs. (Jim McGraw award 2008). Avocations: photography, golf. Home: 645 Front St 314 San Diego CA 92101 Office Phone: 858-531-9201. Personal E-mail: lgstambaugh@gmail.com.

STAMELMAN, RICHARD HOWARD, French and humanities educator; b. Newark, Mar. 7, 1942; s. Louis Robert and Golda (Senzer) S.; children: Emily, Gibson, Jeremy White. BA, Hamilton Coll.; PhD, Duke U. Asst. prof. French and humanities Wesleyan U., Middletown, Conn., 1967-74, assoc. prof., 1974-79, prof., 1979-93, William R. Kenan Jr. prof. humanities, 1983-92, dean humanities, 1986-89, dir. Ctr. for the Humanities, 1976-82, dir. humanities devel., 1982-85; dir. Weston Ctr. for Fgn. Langs., Lits. and Cultures Williams Coll., Williamstown, Mass., 1992-97, prof. Romance langs., comp. lit., 1992—2007; chmn. dept. French and Italian U. Colo., Boulder, 1991-92; vis. prof. comp. lit. Dartmouth Coll., 2007—09; exec. dir. Kenneth & Harle Montgomery Endowment Dartmouth Coll., 2008—. Organizer study group Ecrire le Livre: Autour d'Edmond Jabès, Cerisy-la-Salle, France, 1987; co-dir. Edouard Morot-Sir Summer Inst. for French Cultural Studies, Hanover, NH, 1994. Author: The Drama of Self in Guillaume Apollinaire's Alcools, 1976, Claude Garache: Prints, 1965-85, 1985, Lost Beyond Telling: Representations of Death and Absence in Modern French Poetry, 1990, Perfume: Joy, Obsession, Scandal, Sin A Cultural History of Frangrance from 1750 to the Present, 2006; editor: Contemporary French Poetry, Studies in 20th Century Literature, 1989, Ecrire le Livre: Autour d'Edmond Jabès, 1989, Italian transl., 1991, French Poetry since the War, L'Esprit Créateur, 1992; editor, prin. translator: The Lure and the Truth of Painting, Selected Essays by Yves Bonnefoy, 1995; translator: The Grapes of Zeuxis and Other Fables by Yves Bonnefoy, 1987, Once More the Grapes of Zeuxis by Yves Bonnefoy, 1989, The Last Grapes of Zeuxis by Yves Bonnefoy, 1993, Transmorphoses by Yves Bonnefoy, 1998; mem. editl. bd. French Forum; contbr. articles to profl. jours. Recipient Chevalier dans l'ordre des Palmes Académiques award French Govt., 1993; NEH fellow, 1973, John Simon Guggenheim Meml. Found. fellow, 1999; Am. Council Learned Socs. grantee, 1983 Mem. MLA (regional del. 1987-90, mem. program com. 1996-99), Societe Francaise des Parfumeurs. Home: PO Box 1624 Norwich VT 05055 Business E-Mail: richard.h.stamelman@dartmouth.edu.

STAMEY, THOMAS ALEXANDER, urologist, educator; b. Rutherfordton, NC, Apr. 26, 1928; s. Owen and Virginia (Link) S.; m. Kathryn Simmons Dec. 1, 1973; children: Fred M., Charline, Thomas A. III, Allison, Theron. BA, Vanderbilt U., 1948; MD, Johns Hopkins U., 1952. Diplomate Am. Bd. Urology. Intern, then resident Johns Hopkins Hosp., 1952-56; asst. prof. urology Johns Hopkins U. Sch. Medicine, Balt., 1958-60, assoc. prof., 1960-61; assoc. prof., chmn. divsn. urology Stanford U., Calif., 1961-64, assoc. prof., 1964-90, prof., 0191—, chmn. dept., 1964-95. Author: Renovascular Hypertension, 1967, Pathogenesis and Treatment of Urinary Tract Infections, 1980, Urinalysis and Urinary Sediment: A Practical Guide for the Health Science Professional, 1985; editor: Campbell's Urology, edits. 4-6, 1978-92, Monographs in Urology, 1980-99. Capt. M.C., USAF, 1956-58. Recipient Sheen award ACS, 1990, Ferdinand C. Valentine award N.Y. Acad. Medicine, 1991. Mem. Am. Urol. Assn. (Ramon Guiteras award 1995, John K. Lattimer award 2000, Eugene Fuller Triennial Prostate award 2001), Am. Surg. Assn. (sr.), Inst. Medicine of NAS. Avocations: fishing, astronomy. Office: Stanford U Med Ctr Dept Urology S 287 300 Pasteur Dr Stanford CA 94305-5118 Home Phone: 650-851-3100. Business E-Mail: tstamey@stanford.edu.

STAMKOS, STEVEN, professional hockey player; b. Markham, Ont., Can., Feb. 7, 1990; Center Tampa Bay Lightning, 2008—. Named to NHL YoungStars Game, 2009. Achievements include being the first overall draft pick in NHL entry draft, 2008. Office: Tampa Bay Lightning Hockey Club St Pete Times Forum 401 Channelside Dr Tampa FL 33602*

STAMLER, JEREMIAH, medical professor, researcher; b. NYC, Oct. 27, 1919; s. George and Rose (Baras) Stamler; m. Rose Steinberg, 1942; 1 child, Paul J. AB, Columbia U., NYC, 1940; MD, SUNY, Bklyn., 1943. Cert. specialist in clin. nutrition. Intern LI Coll. Medicine, Kings County Hosp., Bklyn., 1944, fellow pathology, 1947; rsch. fellow cardiovasc. dept. Med. Research Inst., Michael Reese Hosp., Chgo., 1948, rsch. assoc., 1949-55, asst. dir. dept., 1955-58; dir. heart disease control prog. Chgo. Bd. Health, 1958-74, dir. chronic disease control divsn., 1961-63, dir. adult health & aging divsn., 1963-74; assoc. dept. medicine Northwestern U. Feinberg Sch. Medicine, Evanston, Ill., 1958-59, asst. prof., 1959—65, assoc. prof., 1965-71, prof., dept. cmty. health & preventive medicine, 1972—90, chair dept., 1972—86, Harry W. Dingman prof. cardiology, 1973—90, prof. emeritus, 1990—, founder Master in Pub. Health prog. Exec. dir. Chgo. Health Rsch. Found., 1963—72; cons. medicine St. Joseph Hosp., Chgo., 1964—, Rush-Presbyn.-St. Luke's Hosp., Chgo., 1966—, vis. prof. internal medicine, 1972—; attending physician Northwestern Meml. Hosp., 1973—89, chmn. dept. cmty. health & preventive medicine, 1973—85; profl. lectr. dept. medicine U. Chgo. Pritzker Sch. Medicine. Author: (with L. N. Katz) Experimental Atheroscleroses, 1953, (with A. Blakeslee) Your Heart Has Nine Lives-Nine Steps to Heart Health, 1963, Four Keys to a Healthy Heart, 1976; co-author: Nutrition and Atherosclerosis, 1958, Epidemiology of Hypertension, 1967, Lectures on Preventive Cardiology, 1967; contbr. articles to profl. jours., chapters to books. Served in US Army, 1944—46. Recipient Howard W. Blakeslee award, 1964, Albert & Mary Lasker Med. Journalism award, 1965, Conrad Elvehjem award, Wis. Med. Soc., 1967, Albert Lasker Spl. Svc. award, 1980, Donald Reid medal, London Sch. Hygiene & Tropical Medicine/Royal Coll. Physicians, 1988, John Jay award, Columbia U., 1990; named to Nutrition Hall of Fame, Ctr. for Sci. in Pub. Interest. Fellow: AAAS, Am. Pub. Health Assn. (John M. Snow award 1986), Am. Coll. Cardiology (Disting. Svc. award 1985); mem.: Chgo. Inst. Medicine (Coleman award 1987), Internat. Soc. & Fedn. Cardiology (chmn. sci. bd., mem. exec. com.), Chgo. Acad. Scis., Chgo. Nutrition Assn., Am. Inst. Nutrition, Soc. Exptl. Biology & Medicine (sec. Ill. chpt.), Diabetes Assn. Greater Chgo., Ill. Acad. Scis., Ill. Pub. Health Assn. (mem. exec. com.), Chgo. Heart Assn. (Coeur d'Or award 1979, Gold Heart award 1992), Ctrl. Soc. Clin. Rsch., Middle States Pub. Health Assn., Assn. Clin. Scientists, Am. Soc. Study Arteriosclerosis (past bd. dirs., past chmn. prog. com., past sec.-treas.), Am. Soc. Clin. Nutrition, Am. Soc. Clin. Investigation, Am. Physiol. Soc., Am. Heart Assn. (bd. dirs., past vice-chmn. exec. com., fellow coun. arteriosclerosis, chmn. coun epidemiology & prevention, Outstanding Efforts in Heart Rsch. award 1964, Merit award 1967, Svc. award 1981, Disting. Rsch. Achievement award 1981, Achievement award 1987), Am. Fedn. Clin. Rsch., Phi Beta Kappa. Office: Northwestern U Feinberg Sch Dept Preventative Medicine 680 N Lake Shore Dr Ste 1102 Chicago IL 60611 Office Phone: 312-908-7914.*

STAMM, ALAN, lawyer; b. Galesburg, Ill., Nov. 22, 1931; s. Gustave Frederick and Miriam (Simon) S.; m. Shelley Lynn Ramage, Mar. 19, 1978; 1 child, Lucinda Anne. Student, Universidad Nacional de Mex., summer 1950; AB, Yale U., 1952; JD, Harvard U., 1957. Bar: Calif. 1957, U.S. Supreme Ct. 1963. Assoc. Thelen Reid, Brown Raysman & Steiner LLP, San Francisco, 1957—60; staff atty. Litton Industries Inc., Beverly Hills, Calif., 1960-66, asst. sec., 1963-66; sec., gen. counsel Internat. Rectifier Corp., LA, 1966-69, v.p., 1968-69; v.p., gen. counsel Republic Corp., LA, 1969-71, bd. dirs., 1970-71; v.p., gen. counsel Sat. Rev. Industries, NYC, 1971-72, Mattel Inc., Hawthorne, Calif., 1972-74, staff cons., 1974-75; of counsel Long & Levit, LA, 1975-82, O'Donnell & Gordon, LA, 1983-87, Hedges, Powe & Caldwell, LA, 1988-90; pvt. practice LA, 1990—. Judge pro tem Mcpl. Ct. LA Jud. Dist., 1977—, LA Superior Ct. 1989—; arbitrator Fin. Industry Regulatory Authority, Nat. Assn. Securities Dealers, 1981—, NYSE, 1994-2007. Founding trustee Ctr. for Law in Pub. Interest; former trustee Marlborough Sch., LA; former mem. bd. govs. Century City Hosp., LA; counsel bus. and profl. com. LA Philharm.; mem. bd. dirs. Yale Alumni Fund. Lt. j.g. USNR, 1952—54, ret. lt. comdr. USNR. Mem. ABA, State Bar of Calif., LA Bar Assn., Harvard Law Sch. Assn., LA County Art Mus., Am. Arbitration Assn. (nat. panel arbitrators 1968—), Sierra Club (life), Nat. Assn. Yale Alumni (former bd. govs.), Yale Club of So. Calif. (mem. dir.), Harvard Club of So. Calif., Phi Beta Kappa. Home: 422 Denslow Ave Los Angeles CA 90049-3507 Office: 1950 Pelham Ave Unit 1 Los Angeles CA 90025-5835

STAMM, BARBARA MARIE ANDERSON, elementary school educator, interior designer; b. Oakland, Calif., June 11, 1937; d. Reuben Anders Anderson and Helen Frances (Westphal) Sjogren-Anderson; m. George F. Stamm, July 26, 1959; children: George Anders, Anne-Marie. AA, U. Calif., Berkeley, 1957, BA, 1959. Tchr. Antioch Unified Sch. Dist., Calif., 1959—62, 1966—68, 1976—95; interior designer San Francisco Bay Area, 1975—. Author: (classroom trial) People v. Mission Mouse, 1987; dir.: (choral reading) T.S. Eliot's Cats, 1992. Pres. Delta Meml. Hosp. Aux., Antioch, 1970; bd. trustees Delta Meml. Hosp. Bd., Antioch, 1973; v.p. Citizens for Responsible Active Waterfront Design and Devel., Antioch, 1987. Republican. Lutheran. Avocations: travel, gardening, reading, cooking. Home: 501 B St Antioch CA 94509-1202 Personal E-mail: bstamm501@aol.com.

STAMM, BRAD, economics professor; Prof. economics Cornerstone U., Grand Rapids, Mich., 1999—.

STAMM, CAROL ANN, obstetrician, gynecologist; b. Denver, Aug. 8, 1959; d. Robert L. and Mary Ellen Stamm. BA in Biology cum laude, U. Colo., 1981; MD with honors, U. Colo., Denver, 1991. Diplomate Am. Bd. Ob-Gyn; cert. in elem. tchg. U. Colo., 1986. Bilingual elem. tchr. Denver Pub. Schs., 1986—87; intern in ob-gyn U. Colo. Sch. Medicine, Denver, 1991—92, resident in ob-gyn, 1992—95, asst. prof., 1997—2003; staff ob-gyn, asst. prof. Denver Health Med. Ctr., 1995—2003; dir. women's health rotation Colo. Health Found. (formerly High St. Primary Care Clinic), Denver, 2003—, asst. prof. clin. medicine, 2003—, dir. women's svcs., 2004—. Mem. Patient and Family Edn. Work Group, 1996—97; mem. ob-gyn edn. com. U. Colo. Health Scis. Ctr., 1997—2003; dir. ob-gyn Grand Rounds, 1997—2001; provider design team Lifetime Clin. Record Project, 1998—2001; alt. mem. Colo. Multiple Instl. Rev. Bd., 1998—2003; presenter in field. Co-author: (book) Management of High-Risk Pregnancy, 4th edit., 1999, Medical Care of the Pregnant Patient, 2000, The Female Athlete, 2002, Contemporary Therapy in Obstetrics and Gynecology, 2002; contbr. articles to profl. jours.; peer reviewer Jour. Obstetrics and Gynecology, 1999—, Am. Jour. Obstetrics and Gynecology, 1999—. Recipient Richard Whitehead award, Phi Rho Sigma, 1989; grantee, March of Dimes, 2000—01; Trust fellow, Am. Cancer Soc. Brooks, 1988, Acad. Enrichment grantee, U. Colo. Health Scis. Ctr., 1993—95, NIH subcontract grantee, U. Pitts., 2000—03, NIH grantee, IBBEX, 2002. Fellow: ACOG (History fellow 2006); mem.: N.Am. Menopause Soc, Golden Key, Phi Beta Kappa (mem. mortar bd.). Avocations: reading, running, pilates, symphony, opera. Home: 155 S Jackson St Unit C Denver CO 80209 Office: Colorado Health Found 1801 High St Denver CO 80218 Office Phone: 303-869-2158. Business E-Mail: cstamm@coloradohealth.org.

STAMOOLIS, JAMES JOHN, academic administrator, educator; s. James Peter and Evangeline K. Stamoolis; m. Evelyn Carol Nilsson, June 3, 1967; children: John James, Joel James, Joshua James. BS in Indsl. Engring., Lehigh U., 1967; MDiv, Trinity Evang. Div. Sch., Deerfield, Ill., 1970, ThM, 1971; ThD, U. Stellenbosch, South Africa, 1980. Ordained to ministry Bapt. Gen. Conf., 1977. Regional dir. Students Christian Assn. of South Africa, Cape Town, Cape Province, 1978—80; theol. sec. Internat. Fellowship of Evang. Students, London, 1981—89; grad. dean Wheaton Coll., Ill., 1989—98; exec. dir. theol. commn. World Evang. Fellowship, Wheaton, Ill., 1998—2001; pres./CEO, Wycliffe Seed Co., Santa Ana, Calif., 2002—02; pres. Mgmt. Cons. Assocs., Wheaton, Ill., 2003—05; sr. v.p. for acad. affairs, dean of Coll. and Grad. Sch., Trinity Internat. U., Deerfield, Ill., 2005—07; ednl. cons. author speaker, 2007—. Trustee No. Bapt. Theol. Sem., Lombard, Ill., 1997—2006. Author: (book) Eastern Orthodox Mission Theology Today; editor: Three Views on Eastern Orthodoxy and Evangelicalism; contbr. articles to profl. jours. Mem.: Am. Acad. of Religion, Internat. Assn. of Mission Studies, Am. Soc. of Missiology (pres. 2000—01). Home Phone: 847-726-2620. Personal E-mail: jstamoolis@cs.com.

STAMOS, JOHN, actor; b. Orange County, Calif., Aug. 19, 1963; s. Bill and Loretta Stamos; m. Rebecca Romijn, Sept. 19, 1998 (div. Mar. 1, 2005). Drummer with various bands. Actor: (TV series) General Hospital, 1982-84 (Emmy award, 2 Soap Opera Digest awards), Dreams, 1984, You Again?, 1986-87, Full House, 1987-95, ER, 2005-09, (TV movies) Daughter of the Streets, 1990, Captive, 1991, The Disappearance of Christina, 1993, Fatal Vows: The Alexandra O'Hara Story, 1996, A Match Made in Heaven, 1997, Sealed with a Kiss, 1999, How to Marry a Billionaire: A Christmas Tale, 2000, Fortunate Son, 2000, The Reagans, 2003, Wedding Wars, 2006, A Raisin in the Sun, 2008; (films) Never Too Young to Die, 1986, Born to Ride, 1991, Private Parts, 1998, The Marriage Fool, 1998, Dropping Out, 2000, Party Monster, 2003, I Am Stamos, 2004; actor, assoc. prodr. (films) My Best Friend's Wife, 2001, actor, prodr. (TV series) Theives, Jake in Progress, 2005; exec. prodr. (TV series) Virgin Chronicles, 2002, (TV films) The Beach Boys: An American Family, 2000; TV appearances include Hangin' with Mr. Cooper, 1992, Tales from the Crypt, 1993, Step by Step, 1994, Baywatch, 1995, Clone High, 2003, Friends, 2003. Recipient Youth in Film award. Mem. AFTRA, Child Help U.S.A. (nat. spokesperson). Office: William Morris Agy care Les Stollman 151 El Camino Dr Beverly Hills CA 90212-2775

STAMP, FREDERICK PFARR, JR., federal judge; b. Wheeling, W.Va., July 24, 1934; s. Frederick P. Sr. and Louise (Aul) S.; m. Joan A. Corson, Sept. 20, 1975; children: Frederick Andrew, Joan Elizabeth. BA, Washington and Lee U., 1956; LLB, U. Richmond, 1959, LLD (hon.), 2006. Bar: W.Va. 1959, Va. 1959, Pa. 1986, U.S. Supreme Ct. 1973, U.S. Ct. Appeals (4th cir.) 1962, U.S. Dist. Ct. (no. dist.) W.Va. 1960, U.S. Dist. Ct. (so. dist.) W.Va. 1975, U.S. Dist. Ct. (we. dist.) Pa., U.S. Tax Ct. 1973, W.Va. Supreme Ct. Appeals 1966, Va. Supreme Ct. Appeals 1959. Assoc., then ptnr. Schrader, Stamp, Byrd, Byrum & Companion and predecessor firms, Wheeling, 1960-90; judge US Dist. Ct. (no. dist.) W.Va., Wheeling, 1990-94, 2001—06, chief judge, 1994—2001, sr. judge, 2006—. Mem. ho. of dels. W.Va. Legislature, Charleston, 1966-70. Mem. W.Va. Bd. Regents, Charleston, 1970-77; trustee Linsly Sch., Wheeling, 1977—, U. Richmond, 1997—. Fellow Am. Bar Found., Am. Coll. Trial Lawyers; mem. W.Va. Bar Assn. (pres. 1981-82), W.Va. Commn. on Uniform State Laws, Nat. Conf. Commrs. on Uniform State Laws. Office: US Dist Ct PO Box 791 12th and Chapline Sts Wheeling WV 26003

STAMP, TERENCE HENRY, actor; b. London, July 22, 1938; s. Thomas and Ethel Esther (Perrott) S. ArtsD, U. East London, 1993. Actor: (films) include Billy Budd (Oscar nomination, Golden Globe award), 1960; Term of Trial, 1962, The Collector (Cannes Best Actor award), 1964, Alfie, 1964, Modesty Blaise, 1966, Far From the Madding Crowd, 1966, Poor Cow, 1967, Blue, 1967, Tales of Mystery, 1967, Theorem, 1968, The Mind of Mr. Soames, 1969, A Season in Hell, 1971, Hu-man, 1975, The Divine Creature, 1976, Black-OUt, 1977, Striptease, 1977, Meetings With Remarkable Men, 1978, Superman, 1978, Superman II, 1979, I Love You, I Love You Not, 1979, Death in the Vatican, 1980, Monster Island, 1981, The Bloody Chamber, 1982, The Company of Wolves, 1984, The Hit, 1984, Link, 1985, Hud, 1986, Legal Eagles, 1986, The Sicilian, 1987, Wall Street, 1987, Alien Nation, 1988, Young Guns, 1988, Genuine Risk, 1990, Beltenebros, 1991, Prince of Shadows, 1991, The Real McCoy, 1993, The Adventures of Priscilla, Queen of The Desert, 1994, Mindbender, 1995, Tire a Part, 1997, Bliss, 1997, The Bitter End, 1997, Tiré à part, 1997, Love Walked In, 1998, Kiss the Sky, 1999, The Limey, 1999, Star Wars: Episode I-The Phantom Menace, 1999, Bowfinger, 1999, Red Planet, 2000, My Wife Is an Actress, 2001, Revelation, 2001, Full Frontal, 2002, My Boss's Daughter, 2003, The Kiss, 2003, The Haunted Mansion, 2003, Dead Fish, 2004, Elektra, 2005, September Dawn, 2006, These Foolish Things, 2006, Get Smart, 2008, Wanted, 2008, Yes Man, 2008, Valkyrie, 2008; (TV films) The Thief of Baghdad, 1978, Deadly Recruits, 1986, Cold War Killers, 1986, The Alamut Ambush, 1986; (TV series) Chessgame, 1983, The Hunger, 1997-98; TV appearances include Smallville, 2003, 04, Static Shock, 2003; (plays) Dracula, The Lady From the Sea; author: Stamp Alan, 1987, Coming Attractions, 1988, Double Feature, 1989, The Night, 1992. Mem. Brook's Club (London), Manchester. Office: IFA 8730 W Sunset Blvd Ste 490 Los Angeles CA 90069-2248*

STAMPER, JOHN W., architecture educator, academic administrator; b. Mishawaka, Ind., Dec. 18, 1950; s. Clay V. and Hazel M. Stamper; m. Erika Pistorius, June 28, 1986; 1 child, Alessandra Marie. Mar., U. Ill., Champaign-Urbana, 1973—75; MA, Williams Coll., Williamstown, Mass., 1975—77; PhD, Northwestern U., Evanston, Ill., 1981—85. Lic. architect, Ill., 1981. Prof. U. Notre Dame, Ind., 1984—, assoc. dean, 2004—. Author: (scholarly books) The Architecture of Roman Temples: The Republic to the Middle Empire, Chicago's North Michigan Avenue: Planning and Development, 1900-1930. Com. mem. Mayor's Civic Alliance, South Bend, Ind., 2003—06. Grantee Fontainebleau Traveling Fellowship, U. Ill., Dept. Architecture, 1974. Mem.: AIA, Soc. Archtl. Historians. Democrat-Npl. Roman Catholic. Achievements include proposing a radically new reconstruction of the Temple of Capitoline Jupiter in Rome. Avocations: travel, photography. Home: 228 N Esther St South Bend IN 46617 Office: Univ Notre Dame Sch Architecture Notre Dame IN 46556 Office Fax: 574-631-8486; Home Fax: 574-631-8486. Business E-Mail: stamper.1@nd.edu.

STAMPER, ROBERT LEWIS, ophthalmologist, educator; b. NYC, July 27, 1939; m. Naomi T. Belson, June 23, 1963; children: Juliet, Marjorie, Alison. BA, Cornell U., 1961; MD, SUNY-Downstate, 1965. Diplomate Am. Bd. Ophthalmology (assoc. examiner 1976-92, bd. dirs. 1992-99). Intern Mt. Sinai Hosp., NYC, 1965-66; resident in ophthalmology Washington U.-Barnes Hosp., St. Louis, 1968-71; Nat. Eye Inst.-NIH fellow dept. ophthalmology Washington U., St. Louis, 1971-72, from instr. ophthalmology to asst. prof. dept. ophthalmology, 1971-72; asst. prof. dept. ophthalmology Pacific Presbyn. Med. Ctr., San Francisco, 1972-76, assoc. prof. ophthalmology, 1976-87; chmn. dept. ophthalmology Calif. Pacific Med. Ctr. (formerly Pacific Presbyn. Med. Ctr.), San Francisco, 1987-96; vice-chmn. dept. ophthalmology U. Calif., San Francisco, 1999—2003, prof. clin. ophthalmology, dir. glaucoma, 1999—. Asst. opthalmologist Barnes Hosp., St. Louis, 1971-72, Harkness Hosp., San Francisco, 1973-74; dir. ophthalmic photography and fluorescin angiography, dept. ophthalmology Washington U., St. Louis, 1969-72; dir. resident tng. Pacific Presbyn. Med. Ctr., 1972-89, dir. glaucoma svc., vice-chmn. dept. ophthalmology, 1974-87; chief ophthalmology svc. Highland Hosp., Oakland, Calif., 1974-76; clin. instr. dept. ophthalmology U. Calif., San Francisco, 1974-77, prof. clin. ophthalmology, 1998—; clin. asst. prof. ophthalmology U. Calif., Berkeley, 1974-78, asst. clin. prof. ophthalmology, 1978-85; sr. rsch. assoc. Smith-Kettlewell Inst. Visual Scis., San Francisco, 1972-89; project co-dir. ophthalmic curriculum for med. students Nat. Libr. Medicine, 1973-75; commr. Joint Commn. on Allied Health Pers. in Ophthalmology, 1975-87, bd. dirs., 1978-88, sec., 1980, v.p., 1982-83, pres., 1984-85; provisional asst. chief dept. ophthalmology Mt. Zion Hosp., San Francisco, 1976-87, assoc. chief dept. ophthalmology, 1982-86; ophthalmic cons. Ft. Ord, Calif., 1976-1984, Oakland Naval Hosp., 1978-83; instr. Stanford U., Calif., 1977—1992; glaucoma cons. U. Calif., Davis, 1978-84; vis. lectr. dept. ophthalmology Hadassah Hebrew U. Med. Ctr., Jerusalem, 1978, Oxford U. Eye Hosp., Eng., 1986; ind. med. examiner State of Calif., 1979—; mem. appeals hearing panel Accreditation Coun. for Grad. Med. Edn., 1986-93, mem. residency rev. com. for ophthalmology, 1993-98; mem. provisional courtesy staff Peralta Hosp., Oakland, 1988-92; mem. ophthalmic devices adv. panel USFDA, 1989-92; presenter, lectr. in field. Co-author: Update in Glaucoma, 2004, 2d edit., 2006; editor Ophthalmology Clinics of North Am., 1988-2004, 06; mem. editl. adv. com. Ophthalmology, 1982-89, mem. editl. bd., 1983-94; co-author: Becker and Shaffer's Diagnosis and Management of the Glaucomas, 7th edit., 1999, 8th edit., 2009; co-editor Essentials in Ophthalmology: Glaucoma, 2007, 2009; contbr. articles to profl. jours. Chmn. bd. Agy. Jewish Edn., Oakland, 1986-89; bd. dirs. Jewish Fedn. Greater East Bay, Oakland, 1992-94; bd. dirs. Found. Glaucoma Rsch.; mem. glaucoma adv. com. Nat. Soc. to Prevent Blindness, 1981-2004; mem. Am. Diabetes Assn. Surgeon USPHS, 1966-68. Recipient Self-Instrnl. Material in Ophthalmology award Nat. Soc. for Performance and Instrn., 1975, Honor award Am. Acad. Ophthalmology, 1982, Sr. Honor award, 1992, lifetime Achievement award, 2008, Am. Acad. Ophthalmology, 2008, Statesmanship award Joint Commn. on Allied Health Pers. in Ophthalmology, 1989, Disting. Alumnus award Wash. U. Sch. Medicine, 2004; named Troutman Master Tchr. in Ophthalmology, 2000; Regents scholar NY State, 1961, scholar NY State, 1965; Blalock fellow UCLA Sch. Medicine, 1961, Fight for Sight fellow Dept. Ophthalmology NY Hosp. and Cornell Med. Ctr., 1962, 63, 64. Fellow Am. Acad. Ophthalmology and Otolaryngology (rep. to joint commn. on allied health pers., faculty home study course sect. X, chmn. sect. VIII 1983-85, bd. councilors, editl. adv. com. Opthalmology jour. 1982-89, editl. bd. Ophthalmology jour. 1983-94, and many others), ACS; mem. AMA (Physician's Recognition award 1989), Am. Ophthalmologic Soc., Assn. for Rsch. in Vision and Ophthalmology, Calif. Med. Assn. (asst. sec. sect. ophthalmology, chmn., sci. bd. rep. adv. panel on ophthalmology 1985-91), Nat. Soc. Prevent Blindness (mem. glaucoma adv. com. 1981-2004), No. Calif. Soc. Prevent Blindness (bd. dirs. 1986—, pres.-elect 2006—, pres. 2008-), Calif. Assn. Ophthalmology, Pan Am. Ophthal. (bd. dirs. 1992—), Soc., NY Acad. Scis., Las Vegas Ophthal. Soc. (hon.), Am. Glaucoma Soc. (v.p. 1997-99, pres. 1999-2000), Glaucoma Rsch. Found. (bd. dirs.). Office: Dept Opht UCSF Med Ctr 8 Koret Way San Francisco CA 94143-0730 Business E-Mail: stamperr@vision.ucsf.edu.

STAMPFLI, LEONARD THOMAS, music educator, department chairman; s. Leonard Thomas and Eleanor E. Stampfli; m. Carla J. Kuper, Apr. 23, 1982; children: Matthew Thomas, Christopher J., Catherine Jean, Jonathan Thomas. MusB, Tex. Tech U., Lubbock, 1976, MusM, 1979; PhD in Music Edn., U. Okla., Norman, 1994. Cert. tchr. Tex., 1983. Piano lab tchr. Dunbar H.S., Lubbock, Tex., 1980—90; asst. prof. music Milligan Coll., Johnson City, Tenn., 1994—2000; chair music dept. Greenville Coll., Ill., 2000—, assoc. prof. music, 2000—. Composer: (keyboard orchestra arrangement) Also Sprach Zarathustra, Black is the Color of My True Love's Hair, (keyboard orchestral work) Moonlight Sonata for Orchestra, Fantasy on a Theme of Yankee Doodle, Arrangement of Amazing Grace, (songs) All American Rag. Bd. dir. Bond Cound Academic Found., Greenville, Ill., 2007—. Mem.: Phi Kappa Phi Honor Soc. Republican. Baptist. Avocations: woodworking, swimming, flying. Office: Greenville Coll 315 E College Ave Greenville IL 62246 Business E-Mail: tom.stampfli@greenville.edu.

STAMPLEY, STEPHEN M., legislative staff member; Staff mem., Rep. Roger Wicker US House of Reps., Washington, legis. correspondent, systems adminstr., Rep. Henry Brown, Jr., 2002—03, comm. dir. to Rep. Rob Wittman, 2008—. Republican. Office: 1318 Longworth House Office Bldg Washington DC 20515 Office Phone: 202-225-4261. Office Fax: 202-225-4382.*

STAMPS, LEIGHTON ELDERKIN, psychology educator; b. Pitts., Mar. 10, 1947; s. Ranzie Washington and Florence Elderkin (Cromlish) S.; children: Jason, Lauren, Christopher, Justin. BA in Econs., Westminster Coll., 1969; MA in Psychology, W.VA. U., 1972, PhD, 1974. Lic. psychologist, La.; From asst. prof. to prof. psychology U. New Orleans, 1974—, chmn. dept., 1982-84, 2003-07, prof. Belmont Abbey Coll. 2007-.; pvt. practice psychology, La., 1978—. Contbr. articles to profl. jours. Mem. APA, La. Psychol. Assn. (chmn. sci. affairs com. 1984). Office: Belmont Abbey Coll Dept Psychology Belmont NC 28012 Home: 2004 Gladelynn Ct Belmont NC 28012

STAMSTA, JEAN F., artist; b. Sheboygan, Wis., Nov. 2, 1936; d. Herbert R. and Lucile Caroline (Malwitz) Nagel; m. Duane R. Stamsta, Aug. 18, 1956; children: Marc, David. BS, BA, U. Wis., 1958. Guest curator Milw. Art Mus., 1986; resident artist Leighton Artist Colony, Banff, Alta., Can., 1987. One-woman shows include Am. Craft Mus., N.Y.C., 1971, Winona (Minn.) State U., 1986, Lawrence U., Appleton, Wis., 1990, Walkers Point Ctr. Arts, Milw., 1990, U. Wis. Ctr., Sheboygan, 1998, Wis. Luth. Coll., Milw., 1999, Carroll Coll., Waukesha, Wis., 2006, exhibited in group shows at Cleve. Mus. Art, 1977, Milw. Art Mus., 1986, 1988, Nat. Air and Space Mus., Smithsonian Instn., Washington, 1986, Madison (Wis.) Art Ctr., 1987, 1990, Paper Press Gallery, Chgo., 1988, North Arts Ctr., Atlanta, 1990, Dairy Barn Cultural Arts Ctr., Athens, Ohio, 1991, Paper Arts Festival, Appleton, 1992, Fine Arts Mus., Budapest, Hungary, 1992, Tilburg Textile Mus., Netherlands, 1993, U. Wis. Union Gallery, 1994, Holland Area Arts Coun. Gallery, U. Mich., Ann Arbor, 1996, Charles Allis Art Mus., Milw., 1996, Bergstrom-Mahler Mus., Neenah, Wis., 1998, Wis. Mus. atr, Wis., 2000, 2007—08, Three Rivers Arts Festival, Pitts., 2001, U. Wis. Alumni Assn., Milw., 2002, Racine (Wis.) Art Mus., 2003, 2005, 2008, Rochester Art Ctr., 2004, David Barnett Gallery, Milw, Wis., 2009. Fellow Craftsman fellow, NEA, 1974. Avocations: swimming, travel. Home: 9313 Center Oak Rd Hartland WI 53029 E-mail: jstamsta@aol.com.

STANCELL, ARNOLD FRANCIS, chemical engineering educator, retired oil industry executive; b. NYC, Nov. 16, 1936; s. Francis and Maria (Lucas) S.; m. Constance Newton, Apr. 21, 1973; 1 child, Christine. BChemE magna cum laude, CCNY, 1958; ScD, MIT, Cambridge, 1962. Lic. profl. engr., NY, Conn. Rsch. scientist, rsch. mgr. Mobil Oil Corp., Edison, NJ, 1962—72, chem. planning assoc., mgr. NYC, 1973—75, v.p. chem. divsn. Macedon, NY, 1976—79, mgr. corp. planning NYC, 1980—81, regional exec. mktg. and refining London, 1982—84, planning v.p. mktg. and refining NYC, 1985—86, v.p. U.S. exploration and prodn. Fairfax, Va., 1987—88, v.p. internat. exploration and producing, 1989—93; prof. chem. engring. Ga. Inst. Tech., Atlanta, 1994—2001, endowed chair prof. chem. engring., 2001—. Vis. prof. MIT, Cambridge, 1970, 1998, adv. bd., 1976—; adv. bd. CCNY, 1990—, Carnegie Mellon U., 1999— Contbg. author: Polymer Science and Materials, 1971; contbr. articles to Jour. Applied Polymer Sci., AIChE Symposia Series, Jour. Macromolecular Sci. Recipient Profl. Achievement award, Nat. Orgn. Black Chemists and Chem. Engrs., 1975, Career Achievement award CCNY, 1993, Townsend Harris medal, 2009. Fellow AIChE (Chem. Engring. Practice award 1997, One of One Hundred Chem. Engrs. of Modern Era, 1940-); mem. Nat. Acad. Engring. Governing Coun., Tau Beta Pi. Achievements include research in management and growth of large domestic and international businesses in chemicals, oil and natural gas; patents for petrochemical and polymer processes and plasma processes at surfaces. Business E-Mail: arnold.stancell@chbe.gatech.edu.

STANCEU, TIMOTHY CHARLES, federal judge; b. Canton, Ohio, July 31, 1951; AB, Colgate U., 1973; JD, Georgetown U., 1979. Bar: DC 1980. Environ. protection specialist US EPA, Washington, 1974-82; spl. asst. to asst sec. US Dept. Treasury, Washington, 1982-85, dep. dir. Office Trade and Tariff Affairs, 1985-89; atty. Hogan & Hartson, Washington, 1990—2003; judge US Ct. Internat. Trade, NYC, 2003—. Republican. Office: US Ct Internat Trade One Federal Plz New York NY 10278-0001*

STANCZAK, JULIAN, artist, educator; b. Borownica, Poland, Nov. 5, 1928; came to U.S., 1950, naturalized, 1957; s. Victor and Elizabeth (Cwynar) S.; m. Barbara M. Meerpohl, June 10, 1963; children: Danuta M., Christopher. B.F.A., Cleve. Inst. Art., 1954; M.F.A., Yale U., 1956. Tchr. Art Acad. Cin., 1957-64, Cleve. Inst. Art, 1965—. One-man shows include Dayton Art Inst., 1964, Martha Jackson Gallery, N.Y.C., 1964, 65, 68, 71, 72, 75, 77, 79, Miami U., Oxford, Ohio, 1965, Feingarten Galleries, Los Angeles, 1966, Kent State U., 1968, Dartmouth, 1968, Akron (Ohio) Art Inst., 1969, Cleve. Inst. Art, 1971, London Arts Gallery, 1971, Cin. Art Mus., 1972, 80, Corcoran Gallery Art, Washington, 1972, Canton (Ohio) Art Inst., 1974, Pollack Gallery, Toronto, 1975, Ohio State U., 1976, IMF and CARE, Washington, 1978, Butler Inst. Am. Art, Youngstown, Ohio, 1980, Nat. Mus., Warsaw, Poland, 1981, Alice Simsar Gallery, Ann Arbor, Mich., 1982, 88, New Gallery, Cleve., 1983, Charles Foley Gallery, Columbus, Ohio, 1984, 88, Walker Gallery, Chgo., 1986, Carl Solway Gallery, Cin., Jane Haslem Gallery, Washington, 1986, Standard Oil Co. Hdqrs., Cleve., 1987, Alice Simsar Gallery, Ann Arbor, Mich., Boca Raton Mus. Art, Fla., 1989, Carl Solway Gallery, Cin., Charles Foley Gallery, Columbus, Ohio, Ctr. for Contemporary Art, Cleve., 1990; one man retrospective David Anderson Gallery, Buffalo, N.Y., Dennos Mus.,Traverse City, Mich., Butler Inst. of Am. Art., Youngstown, Ohio, 2000, /Columbus Mus. of Art, 2001, Ashville Mus. of Art, N.,C., 2001, Lowe Art Mus Univ. Miami, Fla., 2001; many others; exhibited in group shows: Mus. Modern Art, N.Y.C., 1965, Albright Knox Art Gallery, Buffalo, 1965, 68, Detroit Art Inst., 1965, Larry Alrich Mus., 1965, U. Ill., 1965, Gallery Moos, Toronto, 1965, Kranert Art Mus., Urbana, Ill., 1965, San Francisco Mus. Art, 1965, Flint (Mich.) Inst. Art, 1966, Carnegie Inst., Pitts., 1967, Japan Cultural Forum, 1967, Smithsonian Instn., Washington, 1967, 69, 85, Dept. State, Washington, 1968, Cin. Art Mus., 1968, 83, Del. Art Ctr., 1970, Seibu, Tokyo, 1971, Mansfield (Ohio) Art Ctr., 1973, Butler Art Inst., Youngstown, Ohio, 1973, Minn. Art Mus., Mpls., 1973, Akron Art Inst., 1975, Indpls. Mus. Art, 1976, Bklyn. Mus. Art, 1976, 80, Cleve. Mus. Art, 1976, 77, 83, Memphis Acad. Art, 1981, Nat. Gallery Art, 1981, 85, Hirshhorn Mus. Art, 1981, Montclair Art Mus., N.J., 1982, Art Acad. Cin., 1986, Embassies Travelling Exhbn., Madrid, 1987, Warsaw, Poland, 1991; represented in permanent collections: Nat. Mus. Am. Art, Albright Knox Art Gallery, Larry Aldrich Mus., Mus. Modern Art, Dayton Art Inst., Hirshhorn Mus., Washington, Butler Inst. Am. Art, Youngstown, Ohio, Rufino Tomajo Mus., Mex., Cleve. Art Assn., Milw. Art Inst., Canton (Ohio) Art Inst., USIA, N.Y.C., Balt. Mus. Art, San Francisco Mus. Art, Herron Mus. Art, Indpls., Okla. Art Ctr., Oklahoma City, Pa. Acad. Fine Arts, Phila., Carnegie Inst., Pitts., Cleve. Mus. Art, Cin. Art Mus., Tulsa Mus. Fine Arts, Columbus (Ohio) Art Mus., Akron Art Inst., Corcoran Art Mus., Nat. Gallery, Washington, Lowe Art Mus., Coral Gables, Fla., Contemporary Art Mus., Houston, Winnipeg Fine Arts Ctr., Man., Can., Dracket Fine Art Collection, Cin., Kalamazoo Inst. Arts, Worcester Art Mus., Phoenix Art Mus., Indpls. Mus. Art, Wasserman Devel. Corp., Cambridge, Dartmouth Coll., Hanover, N.H., Etzold Sammlung, Cologne, Fed. Republic Germany, Johnson & Johnson Fine Art Collection, Conn., Nelson Rockefeller Collection, N.Y., Chase

Manhattan Bank, N.Y., Mus. Fine Arts, Los Angeles, Newport Harbor Mus., Newport Beach, Calif., N.Y. State U. at Buffalo; mus. collections include Aldrich Mus. Comtemporary Art, ridgefield, Conn., Akron Art Inst., Ohio, Asheville Mus. Art, Asheville, N.C., Albright Knox Art Gallery, Buffalo, Ball State U. Mus. Art, Muncie, Ind., Balt. Mus. Art, Boca Raton, Fla., Butler Inst. Am. Art, Youngstown, Ohio, Canton Art Inst., Ohio, Carnegie Inst., Pitts., Mus. Modern Art; others; represented in permanent collections at Air Products & Chems., Alcoa, Am. greetings, Cleve., Ameritrust Bank, Cleve., David Anderson Collection, Buffalo, Am. Republic Ins. Co., Des Moines, Atlantic ridgefield Com., N.Y., The Art Collection First Nat. Bank Chgo., Balt. Gas & Electric, Balt., Bank N.Y.; others; monographs include Gene Baro Corcoran Gallery Art, Washington, Rudolf Arnheim, Harry Rand, Robert Bertholf, Poetry and Rare Book Collection, SUNY Buffalo, 20 Tectronic Images and Poetry Barbara Stanczak Clev., (color and form Vibrations of Geometrical Space) Dennos Mus. ctr. Northwestern Mich. Coll., Traverse City, Mich. Recipient 1st prize Dayton Art Inst., 1964; recipient Butler Inst. Am. Art award, 1966, Cleve. Fine Arts prize, 1970, Ohio Arts Council award, 1972, Best of Show award Internat. Platform Assn., 1973-76 Mem. Abstract Artists Am., Internat. Platform Assn. Achievements include being a pioneer in optical art. Address: 6229 Cabrini Ln Seven Hills OH 44131-2848 Business E-Mail: bstanczak@gate.cia.edu.

STANDARD, KENNETH G., lawyer; b. Sept. 4, 1936; AB, Harvard Coll., 1958; LLB, Harvard Law Sch., 1962; LLM, NYU, 1971. Bar: US Ct. Appeals (2nd Cir.), US Dist. Ct. (Ea. Dist. NY), US Dist. Ct. (So. Dist. NY). Staff atty., divsn. counsel Bristol-Myers Co., v.p., sr. divsn. counsel, 1967—84; dir. Office Legal Svcs. NYC Sch. Sys., 1985—89; asst/ gen. counsel labor rels. Environ. and Benefits Plans ConEd, NYC, 1989—2000; spl. counsel labor and employment practice group Morgan Lewis & Bockius LLP, 2000—04; ptnr. Epstein Becker & Green PC, 2004—. Named one of 100 Most Powerful Minority Bus. Leaders in N.Y., Crain's N.Y. Bus., 2003. Mem.: ABA, Vis. Nurse Svc. NY (bd. mem. 1990—), NYC Bar Assn., NY State Bar Assn. (treas. 2003, pres. 2004), Harvard Club (v.p. 1997—99, pres. 1999—2002). Office: Epstein Becker & Green PC 250 Park Ave New York NY 10177 Office Phone: 212-351-4500. Office Fax: 212-661-0989.

STANDBERRY, HERMAN LEE, school system administrator, educational consultant, corporate executive; b. Oran, Mo., Feb. 22, 1945; s. Willie Standberry and Bettie Mae (Thompson) Standberry-Taylor; m. Barbara Irene Palmer, July 1, 1942; children: Donna, Debra, Nina, Miriam, Miranda, Gretchen, Charles, Mary, Dwayne, Helena, Regina, Lakesha. BS, So. Ill. U., 1968; MA, Newport U., 1981, LHD (hon.), 1990; EdD, Walden U., 1992; DMin, Am. Christian Coll. and Sem., 1997; MEd, Ind. Wesleyan U., 1997. Cert. supt., gen. adminstr., curriculum, tchr., sch. counselor; approved profl. devel. provider Ill. State Bd. Edn. and Ill. State Tchr. Cert. Bd. Tchr. Community H.S. Dist. 428, Blue Island, Ill., 1968-70; exec. dir., dep. dir. program planner, HeadStart dir. Kane County Coun. for Econ. Opportunity, Batavia, Ill., 1970—75; case mgr., youth supr., educator State of Ill., Dept. Pub. Aid., Dept. Corrections, Chgo., Joliet and St. Charles, Ill., 1975—85; adminstrv. asst. to prin. Bloom High Sch. Dist. 206, Chicago Heights, Ill., 1993—94; asst. prin. Rogers High Sch., Michigan City, Ind., 1994-95; prin. Mich. City (Ind.) Area Alternative H.S., 1999—2000; chmn. bd./CEO Dr. Herman Standberry and Assocs., 2001—; interim supt. LaPorte Cmty. Schs., asst. supt. personnel, asst. supt. curriculum-instruction; prof. curriculum instruction Indiana Wesleyn U., 1997—2005; supt. United Ednl. Cultural Acad., 2000, principal, supt., 2000—. Chmn. bd. dirs. Greater Chgo. Coun. of Religious Orgns., 1985-89; mem. George Bush's Rep. Presdl. Task Force, Washington, 1989; nominated mem. U.S. Rep. Senatorial Inner Cir., Washington, 1989; hon. chmn., Bus. Advisory Coun. Rep. Nat. Advisory Coun.; faculty advisor, mentor, Indiana Wesleyan U.; NCATE Accreditation, Indiana Wesleyan U., Valpraiso U, pub. safety dir. South Suburban Mayers & Mgrs., 1993-94. Author (curriculum) Business Law I & II, 1968, Career Counseling and Survival, 1978, Accelerated Learning, 1993, Recovery from Academic Deficiency, 2000, Pastoral Counseling and Organizational Compliance, 2005. Bd. dirs. United Way, Elgin, Ill, 1972, City of Elgin-Fremont Youth Orgn., 1971-72; host agy. rep. Dept. Human Svcs., Chgo., 1985-90; sustaining mem. Ill. Rep. Party, Springfield, 1989; host agy. Percy Julian High Sch., Chgo., 1989-90, 2000—, Ill. Dept. Pub. Aid, Chgo., 1987. Recipient NBC 5/Chgo. and AT&T Jefferson award; grantee Ill. Dept. Pub. Aid, 1984-87, hon. award Christian World Affairs Conf., 1985-86. Mem. Internat. Assn. Police and Community Rel. Officers, United Evangelistic Consulting Assn. (chmn. bd. dirs., pres. 1999-), Assn. Christian Schs. Internat. Administrator, 2005, Internat. Assn. Christian Sch. Bds., 2005, S Suburban Ministeral Conf., 2006, Phi Beta Lamda. Avocation: hunting. Office: United Evangelistic Consulting Assn 1242 W 103rd St Chicago IL 60643-2361 Home Phone: 708-757-6510, 773-238-0059; Office Phone: 773-238-2707. Personal E-mail: drstandberry@yahoo.com.

STANDISH, JOHN SPENCER, textile manufacturing company executive; b. Albany, NY, Apr. 17, 1925; s. John Carver and Florence (Spencer) S.; m. Elaine Joan Ritchie, Oct. 20, 1962 (div. 1984); children: John Carver, Christine Louise; m. Patricia Hunter, Nov. 9, 1985. BS, MIT, 1945. Asst. to prodn. mgr. Forstmann Woolen Co., Passaic, NJ, 1945-52; various positions Albany Internat. Corp., 1952-72, v.p., 1972-74, exec. v.p., 1974-76, vice chmn., 1976-84, chmn., 1984-98, also bd. dirs., 1958-98, chmn. emeritus, 1998—. Bd. dirs. Albany chpt. ARC, 1966-92, chpt. chmn., 1971-74, bd. govs., Washington, 1980-86; bd. dirs. United Way Northeastern N.Y., Albany, 1980-97, pres., 1984-85; trustee Albany Med. Coll. and Ctr., 1984-93, Siena Coll., Loudonville, N.Y., 1987-2003; chmn. U. Albany Fund, 1982-87, 89-92; pres. U. Albany Found., 1992-98. Sgt. U.S. Army, 1946-47. Mem.: Ft. Orange Club, Schuyler Meadows Country Club, John's Island Club (Fla.). Republican. Episcopalian. Avocations: bridge, tennis, golf. Home: 395 Llwyd's Ln Vero Beach FL 32963

STANDISH, WILLIAM LLOYD, judge; b. Pitts., Feb. 16, 1930; s. William Lloyd and Eleanor (McCargo) S.; m. Marguerite Oliver, June 12, 1963; children: Baird M., N. Graham, James H., Constance S. BA, Yale U., 1953; LLB, U. Va., 1956. Bar: Pa. 1957, U.S. Supreme Ct. 1967. Assoc. Reed, Smith, Shaw & McClay, Pitts., 1957—63, ptnr., 1963—80; judge Ct. Common Pleas Allegheny County, Pitts., 1980—87, U.S. Dist. Ct. (we. dist.) Pa., Pitts., 1987—. Solicitor Edgeworth Borough Sch. Dist., 1963-66. Bd. dirs. Sewickley (Pa.) Cmty. Ctr., 1981-83, Staunton Farms Found., mem., 1984-2002, trustee, 1984-92; corporator Sewickley Cemetery, 1971-87; trustee Mary and Alexander Laughlin Children's Ctr., 1972-90, Leukemia Soc. Am., 1978-80, We. Pa. chpt., 1972-80, We. Pa. Sch. Deaf, 1983—, YMCA of Sewickley, 1996—; bd. dirs. Pitts. Theol. Sem., 2001—. Recipient Pres. award, Leukemia Soc. Am., 1980. Mem. ABA, Pa. Bar Assn., Allegheny County Bar Assn., Am. Judicature Soc., Acad. Trial Lawyers Allegheny County (treas. 1977-78, bd. dirs. 1979-80), Am. Inn of Ct. (Pitts. chpt. 1993—). Office: US Dist Ct 6170 US Post Office & Ct House 700 Grant St Pittsburgh PA 15219-1906 Office Phone: 412-208-7430. Business E-Mail: Judge_William_Standish@pawd.uscourts.gov.

STANDLEY, JOHN T., retail executive; married; 2 children. BS in Acctg., Pepperdine U. Audit mgr. retail and fin. industry groups Arthur Andersen LLP, LA; v.p. fin. Food 4 Less Supermarkets, Inc., Compton, Calif., 1991—94; sr. v.p. admin. Smith's Food & Drug, Salt Lake City; CFO Smitty's Supervalu Inc., Phoenix; sr. v.p., CFO Ralphs Grocery Co., 1996—98, Fred Meyer, Inc., Portland, Oreg., 1998—99; exec. v.p., CFO Fleming Co. Inc., Oklahoma City, 1999, Rite Aid Corp., Camp Hill, Pa., 1999—2002, sr. exec. v.p., chief adminstrv. officer, 2002, CFO, 2003—05; CEO Pathmark Stores, Inc., 2005—08; pres., COO Rite Aid Corp., Camp Hill, Pa., 2008—. Office: Rite Aid Corp 30 Hunter Lane Camp Hill PA 17011

STANDLEY-BURT, NANCY VILMA, retired psychologist, educator; b. Chgo., Aug. 6, 1934; d. Joseph and Anna (Tichna) Pav; m. Fred L. Standley, Sept. 8, 1956 (div. Mar. 1982); m. Jesse W. Burt, Dec. 18, 1982. BS, Northwestern U., 1957; MA, MacMurray Coll., Jacksonville, Ill., 1960; PhD, Fla. State U., 1969. Cert. sch. psychologist and counselor; nat. cert. counselor; lic. psychologist, Fla. Tchr. English Niles Twp. HS, Skokie, Ill., 1957-59; counselor, psychologist Maine Twp. HS, Pk. Ridge, Ill., 1960-63; instr. English Fla. State U., Tallahassee, 1963-65, asst. prof., 1965-70; assoc. prof. Fla. A&M U., Tallahassee, 1970-75, prof., 1975—2001, dir. career devel. ctr., 1973-75, dir. tchr. edn. ctr., 1982-92; adj. prof. Ctr. for Bib. Studies, 2002; prof. emeritus Fla. A&M U., Tallahassee, 2002—. Adj. prof. Tallahassee Ctr. for Bibl. Studies, 2002. Author: (with Fred Standley) James Baldwin: A Reference Guide, 1979, Critical Essays: James Baldwin, 1984; contbr. articles to profl. jours. and monographs. Named Fla. A&M U. Educator of the Century; Danforth Found. Assoc. award, 1969, 74; Salley Eckert Stevenson scholar, 1955-57. Mem. ACA, So. Assn. Counselor Edn., Fla. Counseling Assn., Fla. Assn. Counselor Edn., Big Bend Counseling (past pres.), Leon Mental Health Assn., Assn. for Counselor Edn. and Supervision, Psi Chi. Democrat. Methodist. Home: 2466 Thornton Rd Tallahassee FL 32308-6020 Home Phone: 850-877-7731. Personal E-mail: nvburt@aol.com.

STANDRIDGE, CHARLES ROBERT, engineering educator, consultant; b. St. Louis, Aug. 19, 1953; s. Robert Lee and Lois Claire (Held) S.; m. Marcia Dorothy Brown, July 13, 1985. BS in Computer Sci., Washington U., 1974; MS in Indsl. Engring., Purdue U., 1977, PhD, 1978. Asst. prof. U. Iowa, Iowa City, 1978-82; sr. sys. cons. Pritsker Corp., West Lafayette, Ind., 1982-89; pvt. practice Lubbock, Tex., 1989-90; assoc. prof. Fla. A&M U./Fla. State U. Joint Coll. Engring., Tallahassee, 1990—. Guest lectr. NSF, Repubic of China, 1988; cons. Cubic Western Data, San Diego, 1990, Shell Devel. Co., Houston, 1992. Author: Tess: The Extended Simulation Support System, 1986, Modeling and Analysis of Manufacturing Systems, 1994. Treas. Luth. Social Svcs. of North Fla., Tallahassee, 1993-94, Univ. Luth. Ctr., Tallahassee, 1993-94. Named Indsl. Engring. Prof. of Yr., Tau Beta Pi, 1993. Avocations: travel, softball. Office: PO Box 2175 Tallahassee FL 32316-2175

STANEK, ALAN EDWARD, retired music educator, performing arts association administrator; b. Longmont, Colo., July 3, 1939; s. Edward Thomas and Mary Rose Stanek; m. Janette Elizabeth Swanson, Aug. 23, 1963; children: Michael Alan, Karen Leigh. MusB Edn., U. Colo., 1961; MusM, Eastman Sch. Music, 1965; DMusArts, U. Mich., 1974. Dir. instrumental music Ainsworth Pub. Sch., Nebr., 1961-64, Cozad Pub. Sch., Nebr., 1965-67; asst. prof. music Hastings Coll., Nebr., 1967-76; prof., chmn. music dept. Idaho State U., Pocatello, 1976-2001, ret., 2001. Contbr., editor, reviewer profl. jours. including The Clarinet, Idaho Music Notes, Nebr. Music Educator. Mem. Music Educators Nat. Conf., Idaho Music Educators Assn. (chmn. higher edn. 1978-86, 97-98, pres. 1988-90, chair state solo contest 1990-92), Internat. Clarinet Assn. (sec. 1978-84, v.p. 1986-88, pres. 1996-98, historian 2002—), Coll. Music Soc., Nat. Assn. Coll. Wind and Percussion Instrs. (chmn. Idaho 1978-88), Nat. Assn. Schs. Music (sec. N.W. region 1979-82, vis. evaluator 1990—2002, chair N.W. region 1991-94), Rotary (pres. Gate City chpt. 1994-95). Business E-Mail: stanalan@isu.edu.

STANFIELD-MADDOX, ELIZABETH, language educator, writer, translator, library advocate; b. Jacksonville, Fla., Aug. 9, 1930; d. Thomas William and Mattie Olene (Padgett) Poplin; m. William Thomas Stanfield, June 30, 1956; children: C. Freeman, William Thomas III; m. Houston Noble Maddox, June 26, 2004. BA in English magna cum laude, U. N.C., Greensboro, 1952; MA, Emory U., 1966. Tchr. fgn. langs. Atlanta City Schs., 1952—57, Fulton County H.S., 1963—65; instr. Spanish Ga. State U., Atlanta, 1968—78, asst. prof., 1978—95, asst. prof. emerita, 1995—. Lectr. Learning Resources Ctr., 1975—95, Spkrs. Bur., 1979—95, Elderhostel, 1990—93, so. culture and living, 1992—95; cons. Internat. Bus. Coun. Inst. Internat. Cons. Directory, 1984; coll. supr. student tchrs. Ga. State Dept. Edn.; adv. coun. Internat. Quarterly. Author: From Plantation to Peachtree: A Century and a Half of Atlanta Classic Homes, 1987, Insight Guides: Old South, 1996; contbg. author: The University Bookman, 1984; translator: Carolina Coronado's, My Cousin Angela, 1995; contbr. articles to profl. jours. and mags. Founder New Hanover County Libr. Found., NC, 2006; donor Friends of New Hanover County Pub. Libr., NC, 2006; mem. adv. bd. New Hanover County Pub. Libr., 2002—08, centennial com., 2006, pres., 2007—08. Fellow, AAUW, 1964—65. Mem.: SAMLA, DAR, AAUP, AAUW, Carteret Writers Assn., So. Assn. Women Historians, N.C. Libr. Assn., Am. Lit. Translators Assn. (conf. coord. 1993, sec.-treas. 1994), Atlanta Assn. Interpreters and Translators (bd. dir. 1985—95, chair accreditations 1986—95), 19th Century Studies Assn., Am. Assn. Tchrs. Spanish and Portuguese (pres. Ga. chpt. 1979—81), Smithsonian, Nat. Trust Hist. Preservation, United Daus. Confederacy, Phi Sigma Iota, Sigma Delta Pi, Omicron Delta Kappa, Phi Beta Kappa. Mem. Ch. Of Christ. Office: 2912 Park Ave Wilmington NC 28403

STANFILL, DENNIS CAROTHERS, corporate financial executive; b. Centerville, Tenn., Apr. 1, 1927; s. Sam Broome and Hattie (Carothers) S.; m. Therese Olivieri, June 29, 1951; children: Francesca, Dennis Carothers. BS, U.S. Naval Acad., 1949; MA (Rhodes scholar), Oxford U., 1953; LHD (hon.), U. S.C. Corporate finance specialist Lehman Bros., NYC, 1959-65; v.p. finance Times Mirror Co., Los Angeles, 1965-69; exec. v.p. 20th Century-Fox Film Corp., 1969-71, pres., 1971, chmn. bd., chief exec. officer, 1971-81; pres. Stanfill, Bowen & Co., 1981-90; chmn. bd. dirs., chief exec. officer AME, Inc., 1990-91; co-chmn., co-CEO Metro-Goldwyn-Mayer, Inc., 1992-93; sr. advisor Credit Lyonnais, 1993-95; pres. Dennis Stanfill Co., 1995—. Trustee Calif. Inst. Tech. Served to lt. USN, 1949-59; politico-mil. policy div. Office Chief Naval Ops., 1956-59.

STANFORD, JOSEPH STEPHEN, diplomat, lawyer, educator; b. Montreal, Que., Can., May 7, 1934; s. Walter Albert and Geraldine (O'Loghlin) S.; m. Agnes Mabelle Walker, Nov. 16, 1957; children: Kevin, Karen, Michael. BA, U. Montreal, 1953; LLB, U. Alta., Edmonton, Can., 1956. Bar: Alta. 1957; called to Queen's Counsel 1984. Mem. Greenan, Cooney & Stanford, Calgary, Alta., Canada, 1957-60; joined Fgn. Svc., Dept. External Affairs, Govt. of Can., 1960; amb. to Israel Tel Aviv, 1979-82; also Can. high commr. to Cyprus; asst. dep. min. for Africa and Mid. East Dept. External Affairs, Ottawa, Ont., 1983-85, asst. dep. min. for Europe, 1985-87, assoc. undersec. of state for external affairs, 1987-88; dep. solicitor gen. Govt. of Can., Ottawa, 1988-93; ret., 1994; sr fellow, conflict mgr. Canadian Center Mgmt. Devel., Ottawa, 1993-96; assoc., bd. dirs. Conflict Mgmt. Group, Cambridge, Mass., 1994—97, 2002—04, chmn. bd. dirs., 1997-99. Cons. Conflict Mgmt. Group, Cambridge, Mass., 1994—97. Contbr. articles on internat. law, fgn. investment and conflict resolution to profl. jours. Roman Catholic. Avocations: canoeing, skiing. Home: 58 Amberwood Cres Ottawa ON Canada K2E 7C3 Home Phone: 613-226-2334; Office Phone: 613-226-1328. Personal E-mail: joseph.stanford066@sympatico.ca.

STANG, PETER JOHN, organic chemist; b. Nürnberg, Germany, Nov. 17, 1941; came to U.S., 1956; s. John Stang and Margaret Stang Pollman; m. Christine Schirmer, 1969; children: Antonia, Alexandra. BS, DePaul U., Chgo., 1963; PhD, U. Calif., Berkeley, 1966; degree (hon.), Moscow State Lomonossov U., 1992, Russian Acad. Scis., 1992. Instr. Princeton (N.J.) U., 1967-68; from asst. to assoc. prof. U. Utah, Salt Lake City, 1969-79, prof., 1979-92, Disting. prof. chemistry, 1992—. Co-author: Organic Spectroscopy, 1971; author: (with others) Vinyl Cations, 1979; editor: (with F. Diederich) Modern Acetylene Chemistry, 1995, Metal Catalyzed Cross Coupling Reactions, 1998, (with Z. Rappaport) Dicoordinated Carbocations, 1997; editor-in-chief Jour. Organic Chemsitry, 2000-01; contbr. numerous articles to sci. publs. Recipient Humboldt-Forschungspreis, 1977, Linus Pauling medal, 2006; JSPS fellow, 1985; Fulbright-Hays sr. scholar, 1988. Fellow AAAS; mem. NAS, Am. Acad. Arts and Scis., Am. Chem. Soc. (assoc. editor jour. 1982-99, editor 2002-, George A. Olah award in hydrocarbon chemistry 2003, award for creative rsch. and applications iodine chemistry, 2007), Chinese Acad. Scis. (fgn. mem.), Hungarian Academy of Sciences(fgn. mem.). Office: U Utah Dept Chemistry 315 South 1400 East Salt Lake City UT 84112-0850 Office Phone: 801-581-8329. E-mail: stang@chemistry.utah.edu.

STANG, ROLF KRISTIAN, vocalist, educator, actor, advertising executive, writer; b. Rockford, Ill., Sept. 19, 1939; s. Trygve Ingvald and Kirsten (Anfinsen-Kristiansen) S. BA, Augustana Coll., 1961; MA, Columbia U., 1963; performance/repertoire cert., opera div., Musikhochschule, Hamburg, Germany, 1964. Vocal soloist Christoph-Weber-Barock Ensemble, Hamburg, 1965-67; German and music faculty Coll. of White Plains, N.Y., 1968-73; sec. Internat. Percy Grainger Soc., White Plains, N.Y., 1974-79, pres., 1979—. Music critic Norwegian Am. Weekly, NYC, 1970—; advt. exec. The Frank Vos Co AS/VP, 1973-83; lectr., recital Songs of Frederick Delius, Cambridge U., 1984—; multimedia lectr. on career of Wagnerian singer Kirsten Flagstad, 1995—; lectr. on English composer Frederick Delius, 1966—. Translator Songs of Grieg, Collected Works of Grieg, 1993; composer (for solo voice, chorus and orch.) Backward Tracings--A Tallahassee Triptych, 1974; (for soprano, chorus) Train Window Thoughts; (for chorus/6 instruments) Hymns in Praise of Night/Nietzschean Nocturnes; Coach Lied/Romanse Art Song and opera rep. (Am., English, German, Norwegian, Swedish) 1968—; concert vocalist numerous states and countries, 1963—; author, actor touring with one-man play on Norwegian composer Edvard Grieg, US, Norway, Eng., 1993—; Millennium characterization of Viking-age voyager Icelander Leif Eriksson, 2000—; touring as Danish author Hans Christian Andersen, 1994—, as Askeladden telling Norwegian fairytales and singing traditional songs, 1995—; author one-man show, portrayer Henrik Ibsen--The Quiet Eye of the Hurricane, 2006-. Vol. Norwegian Seamen's Ch., NYC, 1968-, Cath. Ctr. for Deaf, N.Y.C., 1975-79, Children to the Beach program, N.Y.C., 1978-83, Reaching Out to the Homeless, N.Y.C., 1988—. Decorated knight (Norway), St. Olav medal King Harald V of Norway, 1997; named to Scandinavian-Am. Hall of Fame, 1998; recipient Leif Eriksson citation, 2000. Mem. SAG, Am. Choral Dirs. Assn. (life), Nordmanns Forbundet/Norsemen's Fedn. (hon., life), Delius Assn. of Fla. (life), Delius Soc. of Great Britain, Sons of Norway Internat., Delius Soc. of Phila. (life), Am.-Scandinavian Soc. of N.Y., Soc. for Advancement of Scandinavian Studies (life), Edvard Grieg Soc. Great Britain (hon., life). Lutheran. Avocations: furniture making, gardening, promoting Nordic culture and music. Home: The Monks Cell 29 W 65th St New York NY 10023-6640 E-mail: rolf_k_stang@hotmail.com.

STANGE, JAMES HENRY, architect; b. Davenport, Iowa, May 25, 1930; s. Henry Claus and Norma (Ballhorn) S.; m. Mary Suanne Peterson, Dec. 12, 1954; children: Wade Weston, Drew Dayton, Grant Owen. BArch, Iowa State U., 1954. Registered architect, Iowa, Nebr., Kans., Mo., Okla. Designer Davis & Wilson, Lincoln, Nebr., 1954-62, v.p., 1962-68; v.p., sec. Davis, Fenton, Stange, Darling, Lincoln, Nebr., 1977-92, pres., 1976—93, chmn., 1978—94. Mem. State Bd. Examiners for Engrs. and Architects, 1989-92, chmn. region V NCARB, 1991. Prin. works include Dorsey Labs., 1960, East H.S., Lincoln, 1966, Lincoln Gen. Hosp., 1967, Lincoln Airport Terminal, Sq. D Mfg. Plant, Lincoln, Bryan Meml. Hosp. (masterplans and additions), 1970, 80, 90, Bryan Ambulatory Care Ctr. Med. Office Bldg., Same Day Surgery Conf. Ctr., Parking Garage, 1993-95, Nebr. Wesleyan Theatre, Lincoln, Hasting (Nebr.) YMCA, various structures U. Nebr., Lincoln, ctr. and br. offices Am. Charter Fed. Savs. & Loan, UNL Love Appn, 1980, Old Pather Hall, 1982, Lincoln South East HS (addition), 1984, U. Nebr. Animal Sci. Bldg., 1987, Beadle Ctr., UNL, 1991, Carriage Park Parking Garage, 1995. V.p. Nebr. Jazz Orch., 1995, 2000—, pres., 1997, Nebr. Art Assn. Bd., 1996—99; deacon 1st Presbyn. Ch., 1960, chmn. bd. trustees, 1968—90, elder, 1972—, 1997—99, chmn. property com., 1998—2000, found. bd. trustees, 2005—; bd. dirs. Capitol Assn. Retarded Citizens, 1968—72, 1994—, pres., 1970; chmn. United Way Campaign, 1986, chmn. bd., 1988; chmn. endowment com. Bryan Hosp. Found., 1988—90; bd. dirs. Delta Dental, 1987—92, Downtown Lincoln Assn., 1975—94, mem. steering com., 1989, pres., 1979; mem. mayor's com. Study Downtown Redevel., 1989, pub. bldg. commn., masterplan rev. com., 1994; bd. dirs. Bryan Lincoln Gen. Hosp. Found.; pres. Lincoln Ctr. Assn., 1979. Recipient Honor award Conf. on Religious Architecture-First Plymouth Ch. Addition, 1969, also numerous state and nat. awards from archtl. orgns.; inducted into Hall of Fame, Iowa H.S. Athletic Assn., 2001. Mem. AIA (Nebr. bd. dirs. 1964-65, treas. 1965, sec. 1966, v.p. 1967, pres. Nebr. 1968, mem. com. on architecture for health 1980-94, Regional Design award 1976, 88, 96), Am. Assn. Health Planners, Interfaith Forum on Religion, Art, Architecture, Lincoln C. of C. (bd. dirs. 1982), Exec. Club (pres. 1972), Crucible Club, 12 Club, Hillcrest Country Club (pres. 1977), Lincoln U. Club (sec. 1992, bd. dirs. 1991-97, pres. 1995, 96, teammates mentor 2000—). Avocations: travel, photography, golf. Home: 3545 Calvert St Lincoln NE 68506-5744 Office: Davis Design 211 N 14th St Lincoln NE 68508-1616 Personal E-mail: jh3545@aol.com.

STANGER, JOHN GOODMAN, literature and language professor, archivist; b. Chgo., 1940; s. Julius John and Rosamond Fixmer Stanger; m. Carol Jean Lenling, June 27, 1965; children: John, Jeanne, Jennifer. BA, Ill. Coll., Jacksonville, 1961; MA, Concordia U., River Forest, Ill., 1967. Cert. D.T.E. Ill., 1969. Tchr. English and history Sch. Dist. 89, Maywood, Ill., 1966—2000; instr. English Triton Coll., River Grove, 1968—77; instr. reading Concordia U., River Forest, 1977—79, instr. English, 1999, Morton Coll., Cicero, 2000—01, Wright Coll., Chgo.,

2000—01; prof. English Elmhurst Coll., 2001—. History fair sponsor Melrose Pk. Sch., Ill., 1990—2000, supr. student tchrs. history, 1986—97, sponsor sch. newspaper, 1975—91. Editor: English: Argumentation, 2003, English Composition I, 2004, English, 2006, Argumentation II, 2006, Writing Across the Curriculum, 2007; columnist: Wednesday Jour., 2007—. Mem. econ. com. Village of Oak Park, Ill., 1983; archivist Grace Luth. Ch., River Forest, 2004—; mem. reunion planning com. Oak Park-River Forest HS, 2005—07. Capt. Ill. Nat. Guard, 1964—65. Mem.: ROMEOS, Soc. Am. Archivists, Kappa Delta Pi, Alpha Phi Sigma, Pi Gamma Mu, Phi Alpha Theta. Lutheran. Avocations: reading, sports, writing. Office: Elmhurst Coll 190 Prospect Ave Elmhurst IL 60126-3296 Home: 727 Gunderson Ave Oak Park IL 60304 Office Phone: 630-617-3475. Business E-Mail: stangerj@elmhurst.edu.

STANGL, WALTER DAVID, science educator; b. Bethlehem, Pa., Apr. 9, 1949; s. David Frank and Esther Margaret Stangl; m. Ann Middlebrook, Apr. 1, 1972; children: Deborah Ann Belletto, Rebecca Lynn. BA, MS, PhD, Lehigh U., Bethlehem, 1974; MDiv, Denver Sem., Littleton, Colo., 1984. Assoc. prof. Gordon Coll., Wenham, Mass., 1975—80; asst. prof. Colo. Christian U., Lakewood, 1980—84; assoc. prof., dean scis. Biola U., La Mirada, Calif., 1984—. Office: Biola Univ 13800 Biola Ave La Mirada CA 90639 Business E-Mail: walt.stangl@biola.edu.

STANHAUS, JAMES STEVEN, lawyer; b. Evergreen Park, Ill., Oct. 22, 1945; s. Wilfrid Xavier and Mary (Komanecky) S.; m. Naomi Evelyn Miller, June 27, 1971; 1 child, Heather. AB magna cum laude, Georgetown U., 1966; JD magna cum laude, Harvard U., 1970. Bar: Ill. 1970, U.S. Dist. Ct. (no. dist.) Ill. 1970. Assoc. Mayer, Brown, LLP, Chgo., 1971—76, ptnr., 1977—2005, sr. counsel, 2005—. Mem. ABA, Ill. Bar Assn., Chgo. Bar Assn., Chgo. Coun. Lawyers, Chgo. Estate Planning Coun., Met. Club, Phi Beta Kappa. Avocations: computers, tennis. Office: Mayer Brown LLP 71 S Wacker Dr Ste 3300 Chicago IL 60606-4637 Office Phone: 312-701-7135. Business E-Mail: jstanhaus@mayerbrown.com.

STANISH, HEIDI, science educator; b. Charlottetown, PEI, Can., Mar. 28, 1971; BPE, Acadia U., Wolfville, NS, 1992; MS, Dalhousie U., Halifax, NS, 1995; PhD, Oreg. State U., Corvallis, 1998. Asst. prof. St. Francis Xavier U., Antigonish, NS, Canada, 1999—2004, U. Mass., Boston, 2004—, adj. asst. prof. Worcester, 2007—. Office: Univ Mass Boston 100 Morrissey Blvd Boston MA 02125 Office Fax: 617-287-7504. Business E-Mail: heidi.stanish@umb.edu.

STANISLAO, JOSEPH, engineering educator, consultant; b. Manchester, Conn., Nov. 21, 1928; s. Eduardo and Rose (Zaccaro) S.; m. Bettie Chloe Carter, Sept. 6, 1960. BS, Tex. Tech. U., Lubbock, 1957; MS, Pa. State U., Univ. Park, 1959; DSc in Industrial Engring, Columbia U., NYC, 1970. Registered profl. engr., Mass., Mont. Asst. engr. Naval Ordnance Research, University Park, Pa., 1958-59; asst. prof. NC State U., Raleigh, 1959-61; dir. rsch. Darlington Fabrics Corp., Pawtucket, RI, 1961-62; from asst. prof. to prof. U. RI, Kingston, 1962-71; prof., chmn. dept. Cleve. State U., 1971-75; prof., dean ND State U., Fargo, 1975-94, acting v.p. agrl. affairs, 1983-85; asst. to pres. N.D. State U., Fargo, 1983—, dir. Engring. Computer Ctr., 1984—, prof. emeritus indsl. engring. and mgmt. Fargo, 1994—; pres. XOX Corp., 1984-90; chmn. bd., CEO ATSCO, 1989-94, chief engr., 1993—; prof. emeritus ND State U., 1994. Adj. prof. Mont. State U., 1994—, dir. indsl. and mgmt. engring. program, 1996—, mfg. rsch., sponsored by Nat. Sci. Found. 1997—; pres., CEO J&B Inc., 1996—2006; v.p., co-owner, bd. dirs. D.T.&J., Inc., Fargo, ND, 1999-2006, London, 1999—; v.p. engring. Roll-A-Ramp, Rolla-A-Latter, and Rolla-A-conveyor, 2000-05; cons. to healthcare sys., 1999-2005. Contbr. chpts. to books, articles to profl. jours. Served to sgt. USMC, 1948-51. Recipient Sigma Xi award, 1968; Order of the Iron Ring award N.D. State U., 1972, Econ. Devel. award, 1991; named Best Tchr., Alpha Pi Mu, 2005; USAF recognition award, 1979, ROTC appreciation award, 1982. Mem. Am. Inst. Indsl. Engrs. (sr.; v.p. 1964-65), ASME, Order of the Engr., Am. Soc. Engring. Edn. (campus coord. 1979-81), Acad. Indsl. Engrs. Tex. Tech U., Lions, Elks, Am. Legion, Phi Kappa Phi, Tau Beta Pi (advisor 1978-79). Roman Catholic. Achievements include patents for pump apparatus, pump fluid housing, roll-conveyer, vertical lift, gas-less engine, and handicap loading dock; roll-a-ramp; invention of Telescopic Sliding Ramp, Thermal-Brick. Avocations: pool, billiards. Home: 8 Park Plaza Dr Bozeman MT 59715-9343 Office: Mont State U M&IE Dept 304 Roberts Hall Bozeman MT 59717-3800 Office Phone: 406-994-5943. Personal E-mail: bstanislao2314@msn.com. Business E-Mail: jstanslo@ie.montana.edu.

STANISLAUS, MATHY V., federal agency administrator, environmental lawyer, chemical engineer; b. Sri Lanka, 1962; BS in Chem. Engring.; JD, U. Chgo., 1988. Bar: NY, NJ. Sr. environ. assoc. Environ. Dept. Huber Lawrence & Abell; sr. environ. assoc. EPA, asst. regional counsel NY Region II Offices, former mem. Nat. Environ. Justice Adv. Coun. (NEJAC), Waste and Facility Siting Subcommittee, chair Waste Transfer Station Workgroup, asst. adminstr. for solid waste & emergency response, 2009—; CEO Allegiance Resources Corp., North Plainfield, NJ; co-founder, co-dir. New Ptnrs. for Cmty. Revitalization, NYC. Founding bd. mem. NYC Environ. Justice Alliance, Inc. Office: EPA Ariel Rios Bldg 1200 Pennsylvania Ave, NW Washington DC 20460*

STANIUNAS HOPPER, JODI ANN, graphics designer, educator; d. Alexander A. and Kathleen M. Staniunas; m. Christopher L. Hopper. MFA in Advt. & Design, Marywood U., Scranton PA, 2004. Art dir. WQLN, Erie, Pa., 1989—91; graphic designer Nat. Pub. Radio, Wash., DC, 1991—95; designer Will Design For Food, Erie, Pa., 1995—2007; asst. profs. art, graphic design Mercyhurst Coll., Erie, 1997—. Bd. mem. Erie Advt. Club, 2004—06. Recipient Numerous Gold & Silver awards, Erie Advt. Club Addy, 1989—91, 1998, 1999, 2003. Mem.: Ad Fedn. NWPA (bd. mem. 2004—06). Avocations: crafts, travel. Office: Mercyhurst Coll 501 E 38th St Erie PA 16546 Personal E-mail: jstaniunashopper@mercyhurst.edu.

STANKEVITZ, DIANE LYNN, athletic trainer; b. West Covina, Calif., May 7, 1963; d. Richard Joseph Stankevitz and Geraldine Ann Vezzuso. BS, UCLA, 1996; MS, Calif. State U., Long Beach, 1998. Cert. athletic trainer Nat. Athletic Trainer's Assn., 2000, strength and conditioning specialist NSCA, 1999, MT L.A. County Dept. of Health, 1998. Athletic trainer East L.A. Coll., Monterey Park, Calif., 2000—, instr., 2000—, Rio Hondo Coll., Whittier, Calif., 2001—. Prodr.(stand-up comedienne): (comedy) The Comedy Train. Scholarship fundraiser The Comedy Train, West Covina, Calif., 2001. Recipient Faculty Appreciation award, Student Body of Rio Hondo Coll., 2004. Mem.: Nat. Strength and Conditioning Assn. (assoc.), Nat. Athletic Trainer's Assn. (assoc.), Phi Kappa Phi (life). Home: 1818 Sam Diego St West Covina CA 91790 Office: East Los Angeles College 1301 Avenida Cesar Chavez Monterey Park CA 91754 Office Fax: 323-265-8909. E-mail: distanky@hotmail.com.

STANKEY, JOHN T., telecommunications industry executive; BA in Fin., Loyola Marymount U., 1985; MBA, UCLA, 1991. V.p. industry markets SBC Telecommunications, 1998; joined Pacific Bell, 1985, exec. dir. advanced comm. network; pres. industry markets SBC Southwest, 2000, pres., CEO, 2001; pres. bus. comm. svcs. SBC Southwestern Bell, 2001; sr. exec. v.p., chief info. officer SBC Comm., Inc.; sr. exec. v.p., chief tech. officer AT&T Inc., 2004, group pres. ops. support, group pres. telcom ops., 2007—, pres., CEO AT&T Ops., Inc., 2008—. Office: AT&T Inc 175 E Houston St PO Box 2933 San Antonio TX 78299*

STANKIEWICZ, ANDRZEJ JERZY, physician, biochemistry educator; b. Lidzbark, Poland, Sept. 28, 1948; arrived in US, 1981; s. Wincenty and Zofia (Plawgo) S. MD, Med. Sch., Gdansk, Poland, 1972, PhD, 1976. Asst. prof. Med. Sch., Gdansk, 1972—77, adj. prof., lectr., 1978—81; rsch. fellow Harvard U. Med. Sch., Boston, 1981—84; resident Brown U. Sch. Medicine, Providence, 1984—87, fellow in oncology, 1987—90; pvt. practice Providence, 1990—. Contbr. articles to profl. jours. Fellow Internat. Union Biochemistry; mem. ACP, Societas Scientiarum Gedanensis. Roman Catholic. Achievements include evolution of adenine metabolizing systems, rare abnomalities of blood coagulation interactions between hemostasis and complement system. Office: St Josephs Hosp 200 High Service Ave North Providence RI 02904-5113 Office Phone: 401-456-3064.

STANKO, JOSEPH C., lawyer, lobbyist; b. Stamford, Conn., Nov. 27, 1961; BA in Econs., Boston U., 1984, JD, 1989. Bar: Mass. 1989, DC 1992. Analyst House Rules and Natural Resources Com. State House, Boston, 1984—86; assoc. Hale and Dorr, Washington, 1989—91, Beveridge & Diamond, Washington, 1991—97; counsel Com. on Energy and Commerce US Ho. of Reps., Washington, 1997—2003; ptnr., head govt. rels. Hunton & Williams LLP, Washington, 2003—. Mem.: ABA, DC Bar Assn. Office: Hunton & Williams LLP 1900 K St NW Washington DC 20006 Office Phone: 202-955-1529. Office Fax: 202-778-2201. E-mail: jstanko@hunton.com.*

STANKOVICH, ALLA (TSYKALO), research scientist; b. Volgograd, Russia, Nov. 5, 1981; MA, Moscow Lomonosov State U., 2004; PhD in Internat. Rels., Diplomatic Academy, 2006. Quality auditor TVV Academy, Moscow, 2006; environ. mgmt. specialist, 2006; chief specialist Gazprom, 2005—07; sr. rschr. Diplomatic Acad. Ministry of Foreign Affairs, 2005—08. Co-author: (book) A Civil Soc. Russia & Globalization, 2005, Globalization at the Beginning of the XXI Century, 2005; author: Italy: Yesterday and Today, 2009. Mem.: Internat. Fed. Jouranist. Avocation: politics. Business E-Mail: 4ugun09@mail.ru.

STANKUNAS, EDWARD JOSEPH, banker; m. Lillian A. Stankunas, June 12, 1971; children: Kimberly A., Alison M. BBA, U. Miami, Coral Gables, 1969. Cert. mortgage banker, Mortgage Bankers America, 1988. Faculty, bus.-tech. North Lake Coll., Irving, Tex., 2002—08; sr. loan officer PrimeLending, Dallas, 2006—. Pres. Dallas Mortgage Bankers, 1996—96. Fund raiser North Collin County Habitat Humanity, McKinney, Tex., 2005—08. Sgt. US Army, 1969—71, Ft. Hood, Tex. Mem.: KC (grand knight 1999—2000). Office: PrimeLending 17000 Dallas Pky # 103 Dallas TX 75248 Business E-Mail: estankunas@primelending.com.

STANLEY, BRUCE MCLAREN, SR., lawyer; b. Cleve., May 13, 1948; s. Willard Cyrus and Isabel (Anderson) S.; m. Pamela Soderholm, June 23, 1984; children: Bruce McLaren, Willard Charles. BA with high honors, Coll. William and Mary, 1970; JD, U. Va., 1974. Bar: Fla. 1974, U.S. Dist. Ct. (so. dist.) Fla. 1974, U.S. Dist. Ct. (mid. dist. Fla., U.S. Ct. Appeals (5th cir.) 1975, U.S. Ct. Appeals (11th cir.) 1982, U.S. Supreme Ct. 1978; diplomate Nat. Bd. Trial Advocacy. Assoc. Bradford, Williams, McKay, Kimbrell, Hamann & Jennings, Miami, Fla., 1974-79; ptnr. Blackwell, Walker, Gray, Powers, Flick & Hoehl, Miami, 1979-85, Henderson, Franklin, Starnes & Holt, Ft. Myers, Fla., 1985—, shareholder, 1989—. Mem. ABA, Fla. Bar Assn. (cert. in trial civil law 1984), Dade County Bar Assn. (bd. dirs. 1982-85), Lee County Bar Assn., Internat. Assn. Def. Counsel. Avocation: commercial pilot. Home: 2506 Mcgregor Blvd Fort Myers FL 33901-5828 Office: Henderson Franklin Starnes & Holt PO Box 280 Fort Myers FL 33902-0280 E-mail: bruce.stanley@henlaw.com.

STANLEY, CAROL JONES, academic administrator, educator; b. Durham, NC; BS, NC Ctrl. U., Durham, 1969; MS, NC Ctrl. U., 1975; spl. student, U. NC, Greensboro, 1987-90; student, Duke U., 2006. Master's G teaching cert. Instr. Fayetteville State U., NC, 1975-76, adj. instr., 1986-89; instr. Durham Tech. CC, 1977; sec. to outpatient bus. office mgr. Duke U. Med. Ctr., 1977—78; sec. speech and lang. pathology NCCU, 1979—81; adminstrv. sec., adj. instr., rsch. asst. NC Ctrl. U., 1989, asst. dir. recruitment, 1994—; admissions, discharge coord., emergency dept. adminstrn. Duke U. Med. Ctr., Durham, 1991—97, fin. care coord., 1997—. Vol. pres. USA Read Am. Program, 1981-82; vol. tchr. for Vietnamese children Immaculation Cath. Sch., 1982-83; asst. dir. recruitment NC Ctrl. U. Sch. Law, 1993—. With Atomonic Energy Comm., Washington, 1996—97; alter soc. co-coord. Holy Cross Cath. Ch. Recipient Outstanding Customer Svc. Gold stars, Duke U. Med. Ctr. Mem. ASCD, Nat. Bus. Edn. Assn., Delta Sigma Theta (scholarship 1989). Home: Po Box 3048 Durham NC 27715-3048

STANLEY, DAVID JOHN, research and development company executive; b. Camp Lejeune, NC, Mar. 8, 1951; s. Herbert Nelson Stanley and Mildred Bennet Davis; m. Judy Jennifer Mattie, June 13, 1998 (div. Nov. 28, 2006); children: Kristin E. Patrie, Jennifer M. Chambers, Caralissa Caprice Mattie-Stanley, Siteris Olyssa Mattie-Stanley. Attended, Aberdeen HS, Md., 1970. Cert. explosive ordnance disposal US Army, 1971. Cons. Ordnance Cons., Pueblo, 1991; ammunition insp. Dir. Logistics, 1991—93, logistics, 1994—96; mil. logistics instr. B & T Svcs., Fort Carson, Colo., 1999—2005; pres., CEO, founder Pikes Peak Cargo Secure, Inc., Colo. Springs, 2002—; exec. v.p., founder Invention Venture, Inc., Denver, 2005—. Equity mem. Strap Inventions, LLC, Container System Inventions, LLC, Compact Container Systems Inventions, LLC, Shelter Systems Inventions, LLC. Chief warrant officer three US Army, 1970—91, many US locations, Germany, Korea, explosive ordnance disposal technician US Army, 1971—80, conventional ammunition technician US Army, 1980—91. Decorated MSM, ARCOM, NDSM, Overseas, EOD, German Silver EIC US Army. Mem.: Rocky Mt. Inventors Assn. (assoc.). Independent. Bapt. Achievements include patents for cargo tie-down system; patents pending for cargo securement devices; trademark variable all terrain tiedown systems; development of shelter systems for the military; container systems for the military. Avocations: travel, reading. Office: Pikes Peak Cargo Secure Inc 4740 Forge Rd Ste 112 Colorado Springs CO 80907 Office Fax: 719-538-5935; Home Fax: 719-538-5935. Personal E-mail: vatts@comcast.net. Business E-Mail: david.stanley@ppcsinc.com.

STANLEY, EDWARD ALEXANDER, geologist, paleontologist, researcher, retired director, forensic specialist; b. NYC, Apr. 7, 1929; s. Frank and Elizabeth (Wolf) S.; m. Elizabeth Ann Allison, June 7, 1958 (dec. May 5, 2009); children: Karen (dec.), Scott. BS, Rutgers U., 1954; MS, Pa. State U., 1956, PhD, 1960. Rsch. geologist Amoco Petroleum Co., Tulsa, Okla., 1960-62; prof. U. Del., 1962-64, U. Ga., 1964-77; assoc. dean rsch., chmn. geology dept. Indiana (Pa.) U., 1977-81; supr. biostratigraphy Phillips Petroleum Co., Bartlesvill, Okla., 1981-86; dir., comdg. officer NYC Police Dept. Crime Lab., 1986—94; pvt. practice, 1994—2008; ret., 2008. Cons. in field. Contbr. articles to profl. jours. Served to sgt. U.S. Army Air Corps/USAF, 1947—50. Grantee NSF, 1965-68, 74, Rsch. grant Office Water Resources, 1965-68; NAS exch. prof. Soviet Union, 1968-69, 73; invited guest Moscow Police Dept. Forensic Labs., 1990; invited speaker FBI Internat. Symposium on Forensic Trace Evidence, 1991, 98; recipient Commemorative medal of the lab. Dept. Botany, Jozsef Attilla U., Szeged, Hungary, 2000, Millenium medal, 2000. Fellow: AAAS, Geol. Soc. Am.; mem.: Am. Soc. Crime Lab. Dirs., Am. Acad. Forensic Sci., Sigma Xi. Presbyterian. Avocations: photography, music, firearms. Home: 578 Myrtle Ct Harrisburg PA 17112-2255 Personal E-mail: eas.aquila7@verizon.net.

STANLEY, ELIZABETH G., legislative staff member; Press sec., Rep. Nita Lowey US House of Reps., Washington, 2001—04, comm. dir., Rep. Nita Lowey, 2004—05, asst., appropriations com., 2005—, chief of staff to Rep. Nita Lowey, 2005—. Democrat. Office: 2329 Rayburn House Office Bldg Washington DC 20515 Office Phone: 202-225-6506. Office Fax: 202-225-0546.*

STANLEY, ELIZABETH KATHRYN, music educator; d. Betty Liskey; m. Carl Robert Liskey, June 24, 1977; 1 child, Franklin Stanley Carl. MA in Music Vocal Performance, Calif. State U., Hayward, 1982. Prof. William Jessup U., Rocklin, Calif., 1996—, founding dept. chair, 1996—. Mem.: MENC, Am. Choral Dirs. Assn. Office: William Jessup Univ 333 Sunset Rocklin CA 95765 Office Fax: 916-577-2260. Business E-Mail: lstanley@jessup.edu.

STANLEY, GREGORY V., art educator; b. Norfolk, Va., Dec. 6, 1956; s. Leonard B. and Sarah V. Stanley; m. Kerry L. Farrell, Aug. 2, 1980; children: Kathryn V., Caroline D. BFA, MICA, Balt., 1978; MFA, Towson U., Md., 2005. Prin. GVStanley & Assocs., Balt., 1982—91; designer BGE, Balt., 1991—99; prin. GVStanley Design, Towson, 2002—; assitant prof. art Stevenson U., Md., 2004—. Fine arts and graphic design, Publ. And Exhibitions. Faculty Devel. grant, Stevenson U., 2008—. Mem.: AIGA (student adv. 2005). Avocations: movies, photography, hiking, gardening, travel. Office: Stevenson Univ 1525 Greenspring Valley Rd Stevenson MD 21153-0641 Personal E-mail: greg@gvstanleydesign.com. Business E-Mail: gstanley@stevenson.edu.

STANLEY, HARRIETT LARI, state legislator; b. Arlington County, Va., Mar. 30, 1950; d. E. L. and Mariana T. Stanley. AB, Coll. William and Mary, 1972; MS with honors, Boston U., 1974; MBA, Harvard U., 1982. NASD registered. Asst. to dir. Close-up Found., Washington, 1974-76; spokesman Boston Edison Co., 1976-79; asst. dir. Mass. Energy Office, Boston, 1979-80, Smith Barney, Harris Upham & Co., NYC, 1983-87; v.p. Prudential-Bache Capital Funding, NYC, 1987-90; mng. prin. The Hadley Group, Boston, 1990-94; mem. 2nd Essex Dist. Mass. House of Reps., Boston, 1995—, vice chmn. ways & means com., 1997-2001, chair health care com., 2001—. Mem. Town Dem. Com., Merrimac, Mass., 1989—; mem. Town Fin. Com., Merrimac, 1990, vice chmn., 1990-92, town treas., 1992-95; mem. William and Mary Soc. of Alumni, 1984-90, treas., 1986-88, exec. com., 1988—, v.p., 1989. Mem. Publicity Club Boston (bd. dirs., pres. 1979-80, Bellringer award 1978). Catholic. Avocation: competitive equestrian activities. Office: State House Rm 236 Boston MA 02133 Office Phone: 617-722-2430. Business E-Mail: Rep.HarriettStanley@hou.state.ma.us.*

STANLEY, HARRY EUGENE, physicist, researcher; b. Norman, Okla., Mar. 28, 1941; s. Harry Eugene and Ruth S.; m. Idahlia (Dessauer), June 2, 1967 (dec. Mar. 2003); children: Jannah, Michael, Rachel. BA in Physics, Wesleyan U., 1962; postgrad., U. Cologne, Germany, 1962—63; PhD in Physics, Harvard U., 1967; PhD (hon.), Bar Ilan U., Ramat Gan, Israel, 1994, Roland Eötvös U., Budapest, Hungary, 1997, U. Liege, 2001, U. Dortmund, 2001, U. Wroclaw, 2004, Northwestern U., 2009. NSF pre-doctoral rsch. fellow Harvard U., Mass., 1963—67; mem. staff Lincoln lab. MIT, Cambridge, 1967—68, asst. prof. physics, 1969—71, assoc. prof., 1971—73; Miller rsch. fellow U. Calif., Berkeley, 1968—69; Hermann von Helmholtz assoc. prof. health sci. and tech. Health Sci. and Tech. Program Harvard U., MIT, 1973—76; vis. prof. Osaka U., Japan, 1975; prof. physics, physiology Sch. Medicine, dir. ctr. polymer studies Boston U., 1976. Joliot-Curie vis. prof. Ecole Superieure de Physique et Chimie, Paris, 1979; vis. prof. Peking U., 1981, Seoul Nat. U., 1982; hon. prof. U. Pavia; 30th Ann. Saha Meml. Lecture, 1992; Sigma Xi nat. lectr., 2002-03; dir. NATO Advanced Study Inst., Cargese, Corisca, 1985, 88, 90, IUPAP Internat. Conf. on Thermodynamics and Statis. Mechanics, 1986, Enrico Fermi Sch., Varenna, Italy, 1996, 2003, Gordon Rsch. Conf. on Water and Aqueous Solutions, 1998, NATO advanced rsch. workshop, 1999, 2001; cons. Sandia Nat. Lab., 1983-94, Dowell Schlumberger Co., 1982-92, Elscint Co., 1983-85; nat. co-chmn. Com. of Concerned Scientists, 1974-76; Disting. prof. U. Paris, 2004. Author: Introduction to Phase Transitions and Critical Phenomena, 1971, From Newton to Mandelbrot: A Primer in Theoretical Physics, 1990, Fractal Forms, 1991, Fractal Concepts in Surface Growth, 1995, Cours de physique, 1999, Introduction to Econophysics: Correlations and Complexity in Finance, 2000; editor: Biomedical Physics and Biomaterials Science, 1972, Cooperative Phenomena Near Phase Transitions, 1973, On Growth and Form: Fractal and Non-Fractal Patterns in Physics, 1985, Statis. Physics, 1986, Random Fluctuation and Pattern Growth, 1988, Correlations and Connectivity: Geometric Aspects of Physics, Chemistry and Biology, 1990, Fractals in Science, 1994, Disordered Materials and Interfaces, 1996, Physics of Complex Systems, 1997, Statis. Mechanics in the Physical Biological and Social Sciences, 1997, Application of Statis. Mechanics to Practical Problems, 1999, Structure and Function of Biological Systems under Extreme Conditions, 2002, Statis. Physics, 2000, Statis. Mechanics: From Rigorous Results to Applications, 2000, Scaling in Disordered Systems, 2002, New Kinds of Phase Transitions, 2002; editor Physica A., 1988—. Recipient Choice award, Am. Assn. Book Pubs., 1972, Macdonald award, 1986, Venture Rsch. award, Brit. Petroleum, 1989, Mass. Prof. of Yr. award, Coun. Advancement and Support of Edn., 1992, Floyd K. Richtmyer prize, 1997, Turnbull prize, 1998, Memory Ride prize, 2001, NSF Disting. Tchr. Scholar prize, 2001, Nicholson medal, 2003, Boltzmann medal, 2004, Teresiana medal, 2004, Julius Edgar Lilienfeld prize, 2008; Nat. Merit scholar, Wesleyan U., 1962, Fulbright scholar, U. Cologne, 1962—63, John Simon Guggenheim Meml. fellow, 1979—80. Fellow AAAS, NAS, Am. Phys. Soc. (chmn. New Eng. sect. 1982-83, Centennial lectr. 1999); mem. NAS (non-linear sci. panel), Hungarian Phys. Soc. (hon.), Brazilian Acad. Sci. (hon.). Office: Boston U Ctr for Polymer Studies Boston MA 02215 Home: 1501 Beacon St Apt 1401 Brookline MA 02446 Home Phone: 857-891-1941; Office Phone: 617-353-2617. Business E-Mail: hes@bu.edu. *The greatest joy of my prof. life is to share in the excitement of learning something new, however minor about the workings of nature. The greatest joy of my personal life is to be able to imagine that I've* *done my very best to meet the needs of my family and my co-workers. The greatest obstacle to happiness is the persistent feeling that it is impossible to find that tortuous path whereby both joys may occasionally be experienced.*

STANLEY, HEIDI B., bank executive; b. 1956; m. Ron Stanley. Grad., Wash. State U., 1979. With IBM, San Francisco, Tucson; joined Sterling Savings Bank, Spokane, Wash., 1985, exec. v.p. Corp. Adminstrn., vice chair, COO, 2003—07, pres., CEO, 2007—. Vice chmn. Am.'s Cmty. Banker's Membership Com.; mem. Govt. Affairs Steering Com.; bd. govs. WSU Found., chmn. planning com. Named one of 25 Most Powerful Women in Banking, US Banker, 2006, 2007. Mem.: Wash. State U. Alumni Assn., Spokane C. of C. (bd. mem.). Avocation: golf. Office: Sterling Savings Bank 111 N Wall St Spokane WA 99201

STANLEY, HELEN CAMILLE, composer, musician; b. Tampa, Fla. d. Edward and Lucy Gage (Crehore) S.; widowed; 1 child, Helen Marjorie. MusB, Cin. Conservatory Music, 1951; MusM, Fla. State U., 1954; BS, Muskingum Coll., 1961. Instr. music and fine arts Jacksonville (Fla.) U., 1962-67; instr. music in communications Jones Coll., Jacksonville, 1965-66; composer, condr. St. Paul's by-the-Sea, Jacksonville Beach, Fla., 1976; composer-in-residence, pianist Fla. Contemporary Ensemble, Jacksonville, 1986; ind. composer, lectr., pianist, 1963—. Cons. Beaches Fine Arts Series, Neptune Beach, Fla., 1973—. Composer Rhapsody for Electronic Tape and Orchestra, 1972 (Composition Commn. award), Allegro, Passacaglia, Sonata for trombone and piano, various instrumental and vocal works, Evocation I for piano; orchestral works on CD include: Fanfare for Orchestra (Warsaw Nat. Philharmonic Orch. and Owensboro Symphony), 1994, Passacaglia (St. Petersburg Philharmonic), Concerto Romantico, Prague, 1997, Fanfare for Orchestra (All American Celebration by Owensboro Symphony), 1999; composer website theme music The Living Music Found.; composer Dorian Diversion in Functional Chromaticism, 2003, Phrygiana for Piano, 2005, Concerto Romantico, 2006, Public Lecturing on background of my recorded music, 2007-, Aeolus for Piano, 2009. Mem. Soc. Mayflower Descs., 1987—. Recipient Pogner Music Composition award, Cin., 1950, C. Hugo Ensemble Composition award, Cin., 1951, Anthem Descant award St. Paul's by-the-Sea, 1980, Art Ventures Fund award, 1992, Jacksonville Comty. Found. award, 1994; named Outstanding Achievements Classical Music, Jacksonville, 1997. Mem. ASCAP, Am. Music Ctr., Am. Keyboard Artists, Performing Arts Directory, Pi Kappa Lambda. Avocations: art, walking, dance. Address: 1768 Emory Cir S Jacksonville FL 32207-7707 Home and Studio: Aladdin Farm 12047 Aladdin Rd Jacksonville FL 32223-3201 Office Phone: 904-268-5475. E-mail: hscomposer@aol.com.

STANLEY, HUGH MONROE, JR., lawyer; b. Ft. Lewis, Wash., Oct. 25, 1944; s. Hugh Monroe Sr. and Rita (McHugh) S.; m. Patricia Page, Aug. 17, 1968; children: Allison Michelle, Matthew Monroe, Trevor Marshall. BA magna cum laude, U. Dayton, 1966; JD, Georgetown U., 1969. Bar: Ohio 1969, U.S. Ct. Appeals (6th cir.) 1983, U.S. Supreme Ct. 1979. Assoc. Arter & Hadden, Cleve., 1969-76, ptnr., 1976—2003, chmn. litigation dept., 1983-96; ptnr. Tucker Ellis & West LLP, 2003—. Fellow Am. Bar Found., Bar Assn. Greater Cleve., Am. Coll. Trial Lawyers, Internat. Acad. Trial Lawyers, Internat. Soc. Barristers, Nat. Assn. R.R. Trial Counsel; mem. ABA, Fed. Bar Assn., Def. Rsch. Inst., Cleve. Assn. Civil Trial Attys., Ohio Assn. Civil Trial Attys. Republican. Roman Catholic. Avocation: reading. Office: Tucker Ellis & West 1150 Huntington Bldg 925 Euclid Ave Ste 1100 Cleveland OH 44115-1475 Home Phone: 440-338-6920; Office Phone: 216-696-3934. Business E-Mail: hstanley@tuckerellis.com.

STANLEY, JAMES CHARLES, vascular surgeon; b. Detroit, Sept. 18, 1938; s. Joseph Dean and Jeannette Estelle Stanley; m. Nancy Marion Norville, Aug. 5, 1961; children: Timothy James, Jeffrey John. MD, U. Mich., Ann Arbor, 1964. Diplomate in vascular surgery Am. Bd. Surgery, Phila., 1983. Handleman prof. surgery U. Mich. Med. Sch., Ann Arbor, 2005—, dir., cardiovasc. ctr., 2008—. Contbr. articles to profl. jours., chapters to books. Vice chmn. U. Musical Soc., Ann Arbor, 2003—. Capt., m.c. US Army, 1965—67, Fort Sam Houston, San Antonio. Fellow: Royal Coll. Surgeons (hon.); mem.: Royal Australasian Coll. Surgeon, Sect. Vascular Surgery, Nat. Academy Medicine Columbia, Soc. Vascular Surgery (pres. 1996—97). Episcopalian. Achievements include research in Aortic, cerebrovascular and renal disease. Avocations: classical music, jazz. Office: Univ Michigan 1500 East Med Ctr Dr Ann Arbor MI 48109

STANLEY, JASON, education educator; b. Syracuse, NY, Oct. 12, 1969; s. Manfred Intrator and Sara Stanley, Mary Breya Stanley (Stepmother) and William Rivera (Stepfather); m. Njeri Thande, Aug. 18, 2001. BA, SUNY at Stony Brook, 1990; PhD, MIT, Cambridge, 1995. Lectr. U. Coll., Oxford, England; asst. prof. philosophy Cornell U., Ithaca, NY, 1995—2000; assoc. prof. philosophy U. Mich., Ann Arbor, 2000—04; prof. dept. philosophy Rutgers U., New Brunswick, NJ, 2004—. Author: Knowledge and Practical Interests, 2005, Language in Context, 2007; editor: Stanford Encyclopedia of Philosophy, 2002—; mem. editl. bd. Philosopher's Imprint, 2002—, assoc. editor Nous, 2004—. Recipient H. Lee Dennison Valedictorian, SUNY at Stony Brook, 1990; Vis. Fellow, New Coll., Oxford U., 2003, Australian Nat. U., 2003. Jewish. Avocation: blogging. Office: Rutgers U Dep Philosophy 26 Nichol Rd New Brunswick NJ 08901 Personal E-mail: jasoncs@rci.rutgers.edu.

STANLEY, JEAN-DANIEL, geoarchaeologist; b. Metz, France, Apr. 14, 1934; came to US, 1941, naturalized, 1946; s. Paul Emile and Madeleine (Simon) Streisguth; m. Adrienne N. Ellis, Mar. 5, 1988; children: Marc Michel, Eric Paul, Brian Northrop, Natalie Anne, Susan N. B.Sc., Cornell U., 1956; M.Sc., Brown U., 1958; D.Sc., U. Grenoble, France, 1961. Rsch. geologist French Petroleum Inst., Paris, 1958-61; asst. to dir. US Waterways Expt. Sta., Vicksburg, Miss., 1961-63; asst. prof. geology Ottawa U., Ont., Canada, 1963-64; rsch. assoc. prof. Dalhousie U., Halifax, NS, Canada, 1964-66; sr. scientist, oceanographer, dir. Geoarchaeology-Global Change Program, NMNH Smithsonian Instn., Washington, 1966—; adj. prof. U. Québec, 1992—2001. Cons. to govts. Mediterranean countries; sci. expert Internat. Ct. Justice, 1981—. Author: book, Geoarchaeology: Underwater Archaeology in the Canopic Region Egypt; Editor: New Concepts of Continental Margin Sedimentation, 1969, Mediterranean Sea: A Natural Sedimentation Laboratory, 1972, Marine Sediment Transport and Environmental Management, 1976, Sedimentation in Submarine Canyons, Fans and Trenches, 1978, The Shelfbreak: A Critical Interface on Continental Margins, 1983, Geological Evolution of the Mediterranean Basin, 1985, Nile Delta, A Geological Excursion, 1997;Geoarcheology, 2007; contbr. chpts to books, articles to profl. jours. Bd. dirs. Geoarchaeology and World Deltas Programs. Served to capt. C.E., US Army, 1961-63. Recipient médaille Alpes Maritimes, France, 1976, F.P. Shepard medal Soc. for Sedimentary Geology, 1990, Gold Trident medal Italian Acad., 1998; named Hon. Prof., East China U., 1995; grantee in field. Fellow Geol. Soc. Am., AAAS, Geol. Soc. Belgium; mem. Internat. Assn. Sedimentologists, Am. Assn. Petroleum Geologists, Soc. Econ. Paleontologists and Mineralogists, Geol. Soc. Washington, Cosmos Club (Washington), Sigma Xi. Clubs: Cosmos (Washington). Office: Smithsonian Instn E205 Nl Mus Natural History Washington DC 20013-7012

STANLEY, JOHN SLUSARSKI, art museum administrator; b. Saginaw, Mich., July 23, 1956; s. Dale Stanley and Leona Emily (Sowuleski) Slusarski; m. Ellen Marie Forrester, Oct. 4, 1980; 1 child, Kathleen Page. BBA, U. Toledo, 1979; MBA, Bowling Green State U., 1988. Asst. comptroller Toledo Mus. Art, 1982-84, asst. to dir., 1984-88, asst. dir., 1986-88, dep. dir. for ops., asst. sec., treas., 1988-95; COO, dep. dir. programs and services Mus. Fine Arts, Boston, 1995—2008; dep. dir. Whitney Mus. Am. Art, NYC, 2008—. Bd. dirs. Boston-Fenway Program, 1995—. Bd. dirs. Toledo Cultural Arts Ctr., 1989-95, UpTown Assn., Toledo, 1985-90; mem. cmty. coll. bd. advisors U. Toledo, 1986-95. Mem. Ohio Mus. Assn. (bd. dirs. 1986-88), Intermus. Conservation Assn. (trustee 1993), Assn. Am. Mus, (participant mus. assessment program 1988—), Assn. Investment Mgmt. and Rsch., Beta Gamma Sigma. Office: Whitney Mus Am Art 945 Madison Ave New York NY 10021*

STANLEY, KENNETH, statistician, educator; s. Earl and Marie Stanley; m. Cheryl Stanley; children: Jon, Matthew, Michael. BA in Math., Alfred U., NY, 1969; MA in Math., Bucknell U., Lewisburg, Pa., 1970; PhD in Stats., U. Fla., Gainesville, 1974. Scientist WHO, Geneva, 1982—90; exe. dir. ctr. biostats. & AIDS rsch. Harvard U., Boston, faculty mem. dept. biostats. & stats., 1990—. Contbr. articles to profl. publs. Recipient Distinction award, Dean Undergrad. Academic Programs Harvard U., 2007. Achievements include design of current standard therapy for children with HIV disease.

STANLEY, MARGARET KING, performing arts administrator; b. San Antonio, Dec. 11, 1929; d. Creston Alexander and Margaret (Haymore) King; children: Torrey Margaret, Jean Cullen. Student, Mary Baldwin Coll., 1948-50; BA, U. Tex., Austin, 1952; MA, U. Incarnate Word, 1959. Cert. elem. tchr. Tex. Elem. tchr. San Antonio Ind. Sch. Dist., 1953-54, 55-56, Arlington County Schs., Va., 1954-55, Ft. Sam Houston Schs., San Antonio, 1956—58; art and art history tchr. St. Pius X Sch., San Antonio, 1959-60; originator, founding chairwoman Student Music Fair, San Antonio, 1963; English tchr. Trinity U., 1963-65; designer-mfr., owner CrisStan Clothes, Inc., San Antonio, 1967-73; founder, exec. dir. San Antonio Performing Arts Assn., 1976-92; founding chmn. Joffrey Workshop, San Antonio, 1979; radio host On Stage with Margaret Stanley Sta. KTRU-FM, San Antonio, 1983-98. Founder MKS Designs, 2002. Orginator with the Joffrey Ballet Jamboree, 1984. Mem. Met. Opera Nat. Coun., 1969—80; founder Arts Coun. San Antonio, 1962, v.p., 1975, Originator Symphony Belles Program, 1972; pres. San Antonio Symphony League, 1971—74; v.p., founder San Antonio Opera Guild, 1974—, pres., 2002—05; bd. govs. Artists Alliance San Antonio, 1982; founder San Antonio Early Music Festival, 1990—92; artistic advisor, dir. presentation, dir. devel. San Antonio Symphony, 1992—94; founding organizer Musica San Antonio, 1997—98; v.p. Instnl. Devel. Carver Cultural Ctr., 1998—2000; adv. bd. Hertzberg Circus Collection, San Antonio Dance Umbrella, Houston Early Music, Morgan-Scott Ballet, Hot Springs Mus. Festival; pres. Univ. Roundtable, 1995—97. Recipient Outstanding Tchr. award, Arlington County Sch. Dist., 1954, Emily Smith award for outstanding alumni, Mary Baldwin Coll., 1973, Today's Woman award, San Antonio Light Newspaper, 1980, Woman of the Yr. in Arts award, San Antonio Express News, 1983, Erasmus medal, Dutch Consulate, 1992, Mary Baldwin Sesquicentennial medallion, 1992, Opera Guild Founder's award, 2000, Vol. Achievement award, Opera Vols. Internat., 2005, Music Support award, Cactus Pear Festival, 2006; named to Women's Hall of Fame, San Antonio, 1984, Disting. Alumnae, St. Mary's Hall, 1990; Tchg. fellow, Trinity U., San Antonio, 1964—66. Mem.: Opera Guild (v.p. edn. 2006—09), S.W. Performing Arts Presenters (chmn. 1988—92), Battle Flowers Assn., Jr. League San Antonio (Vol. Extraodinaire 2001), Women in Comm. (Headliner award 1982), Assn. Performing Arts Presenters (award for commn.of Jamboree 1984), Internat. Soc. for Performing Arts (hon.; regional rep. 1982—85, bd. dirs. 1991—97). Avocations: travel, reading, cooking, music, dance.

STANLEY, PAUL, physics professor; PhD in Physics, Oreg. State U., Corvallis, 1995. Head sci. St. Bede's Coll., Savusavu, Fiji, 1987—92; chair math and physics Calif. Luth. U., Thousand Oaks, 1997—2001; chair physics Beloit Coll., Wis., 2003—, dobson endowed prof. physics, 2006—; dir., physics team AAPT, 2007—. Sci. panelist Calif. Commn. tchg. Credentialing, Sacramento, 2000—04. Vol. Peace Co, Fiji, 1985—89. Recipient Prof. of Yr., Calif. Luth. U., 2002.

STANLEY, RACHEL H. R., oceanographer; b. Boston, Jan. 21, 1979; d. H. Eugene and Idahlia Stanley; m. Dwight Kennedy Brown, Sept. 17, 2006; 1 child, Idahlia Lily Clarissa Brown. BS, MIT, Cambridge, 2000; PhD, Woods Hole Oceanog. Instn., 2007. Postdoc. fellow Princeton U., NJ, 2007—. Contbr. scientific papers. Recipient Excellence in Analytical Chemistry, Am. Chem. Soc., 2000; fellow, NOAA Global and Climate Change, 2007—; Hess fellow, Princeton U., 2007—, Nat. Def. Sci. and Engring. fellowship, Dept. Def., 2001—03, Fulbright fellow, Fulbright Commn., 2000—01. Mem.: Am. Geophys. Union, Phi Beta Kappa. Achievements include research in marine biogeochemistry and air-sea gas exchange. Office: Woods Hole Oceanog Inst 266 Woods Hole Rd Woods Hole MA 02543 Business E-Mail: rstanley@whoi.edu.

STANLEY, RICHARD HOLT, consulting engineer; b. Muscatine, Iowa, Oct. 20, 1932; s. Claude Maxwell and Elizabeth Mabel (Holthues) S.; m. Mary Jo Kennedy, Dec. 20, 1953; children: Lynne Elizabeth, Sarah Catherine, Joseph Holt. BSEE, BSME, Iowa State U., 1955; MS in Sanitary Engring., U. Iowa, 1963. Registered profl. engr., Iowa. With Stanley Cons. Inc., Muscatine, Iowa, 1955—, bd. dirs., pres., 1971-87, chmn., 1984—2008, chmn. emeritus, 2008—. Vice chmn. HNI Corp., 1979-05; chmn Nat. Constrn. Industry Coun., 1978, Com. Fed. Procurement Archtl.-Engring. Svcs., 1979; pres. Ea. Iowa CC, Bettendorf, 1966-68; mem. indsl. adv. coun. Iowa State U. Coll. Engring., Ames, 1969-97, chmn., 1979-81. Contbr. articles to profl. jours. Bd. dirs. N.E.-Midwest Inst., 1989-95, treas., 1991-93, chmn., 1993-95; bd. dirs. Stanley Found., 1956—, pres., 1984—2007, chmn., 1995—; bd. dirs. Muscatine Health Support Found., pres., 1984—; bd. dirs. Muscatine United Way, 1969-75, Iowa State U. Meml. Union, 1968-83, U. Dubuque, Iowa, 1977-93, Inst. Social and Econ. Devel., 1992-2001, Unity Healthcare, 1999-2005, chmn. 1999-2002; bd. govs. Iowa State U. Found., 1982-96. Recipient Young Alumnus award Iowa State U. Alumni Assn., 1966, Disting. Svc. award Muscatine Jaycees, 1967, Profl. Achievement citation Coll. Engring., Iowa State U., 1977, Anson Marston medal Iowa State U., 1991, Harry S. Truman disting. svc. award Am. Assn. C.C., 1998; Disting. Alumni Achievement award U. Iowa Alumni Assn., 1999, award for Citizen Diplomacy, Nat. Coun. for Internat. Visitors, 2000, Hoover medal, 2001, Order of Knoll Cardinal and Gold award Iowa State U., 2004; named Sr. Engr. of Yr., Joint Engring. Com. Quint Cities, 1973; named to Disting. Engring. Alumni Acad., U. Iowa, 1998; named to Muscatine H.S. Hall of Honor, 2000. Fellow ASCE, Am. Coun. Engring. Cos. (chmn. 1976-77, Cmty. Svc. award 1997, Disting. Award of Merit 1998), Iowa Acad. Sci.; mem. IEEE (sr.), ASME, Am. Soc. Engring. Edn., Nat. Soc. Profl. Engrs. (award 2009), Am. Coun. Engring. Cos. Iowa (pres. 1967), Iowa Engring. Soc. (pres. 1973-74, John Dunlap-Sherman Woodward award 1967, Disting. Svc. award 1980, Voice of Engr. award 1987, Herbert Hoover Centennial award 1989), Muscatine C. of C. (pres. 1972-73), C. of C. of U.S. (constrn. action coun. 1976-91), Rotary, Tau Beta Pi, Phi Kappa Phi, Pi Tau Sigma, Eta Kappa Nu. Presbyterian (elder). Home: 516 Hogan Ct Muscatine IA 52761-2740 Office: Stanley Cons Inc Stanley Bldg Muscatine IA 52761

STANLEY, ROBERT ANTHONY, artist, educator; b. Defuniac Springs, Fla., Mar. 10, 1942; m. Jane Tumosa, May 11, 1973; children: Daiva, Thomas, Daniel. BA cum laude, U. Dayton, 1964; MS, Pratt Inst., NYC, 1969. Dir. art program Upward Bound project Earlham Coll., Richmond, Ind., 1967-68; lectr. art dept. U. Dayton, Ohio, 1967-68; asst. prof. art and humanities Harrisburg C.C., Pa., 1969-71; prof. art Oakton Coll., Des Plaines, Ill., 1971—2002, prof. emeritus, 2002—. Mem. com. League for Humanities Study Grant, Des Plaines, 1988-89; assoc. dir. Inst. for Environ. Response, NYC, 1968-70; Bd. dirs. So. Shore Art Assn., 2005; presenter League for Innovation Conf., 1994, Mid-Am. Art Conf., 1997. Author: Exploring the Film, 1968 (Maxi award 1969), (interactive multimedia) VisLang, 1994; contbr. articles to profl. jours.; shows include William Penn Mus., Harrisburg, Pa., New Horizons in Art Chgo., 1974, Internat. All on Paper, Buffalo, 1979, Zaner Gallery, Rochester, N.Y., 1983, Joy Horwich Gallery, Chgo., 1988, 95, U. Oreg., Portland, 1991, Atrium Gallery, NYC, 1991, Shelter Gallery, Chgo., 1992, Matrix Gallery, Chgo., Museé d'Art Contemporain, Chamalieres, France, 1994, 97, Blank Arts Ctr., Michigan City, Ind., 1997, No. Ind. Ctr. Visual and Performing Arts, Munster, Ind., 1998, Contemporary Art Ctr., Peoria, Ill., 1999, Gov.'s Mansion, Indpls., 1998, Vichy, FR, 2000, Blank Art Ctr., M.C., Ind., 2001, Koehnline Gallery, Des Plaines, Ill., 2002, 59th Salon NIAA, Munster, 2002, Exhbn. Am. Art, Chgo., 2003, Gallery Artists, Chgo., 2003, Gallery 415, Chgo., 2003, 18th Ann. Exhibit, Lubeznik Ctr. Arts, M.C., 2003, Midwest Mus. Art, 2004, Columbia Coll., Chgo., 2005, Evanston Art Ctr., 2005, Zhon B Ctr., Chgo., 2006, Phoenix, NYC, 2007, Hyde Park Art Ctr., Chgo., 2008, Brauer Mus., Valparaiso, Ind. 2008; solo exhibits Chesterton Art Ctr., 2004, Lubeznik Ctr. Arts, 2007, France Wayne Mus., Ind., Koehnline Mus., Des Plaines. Bd. dirs. Kloempken Prairie Restoration, Des Plaines, 1987-89, Brickton Art Ctr., 1998—. Grantee OCC Ednl. Found., 1989; recipient 2d Place Paragon award for video Nat. Coun. Cmty. Rels., 1985, 1st place Gold award for graphics Art Ctr. Show, Dayton Art Inst., 1969, award of merit Internat. Works on Paper, 1979, Prix de la Ville de Vichy Chamalieres Triennial, 1997, Merit award Chesteron Ind. Regl. 2000; named Top 100, World Digital Art, 2001, ArtComp Merit award, 2004, Ind. Arts Commn. grant, 2005. Personal E-mail: robert@robertstanleyart.com.

STANLEY, SAMUEL LEONARD, JR., academic administrator, medical educator; b. Seattle; m. Ellen Li. BA in Biological Scis., Coll. of Univ. of Chgo., 1976; MD, Harvard U., 1980. Tchg. asst. biology Coll. of Univ. of Chgo., 1976; intern Mass. Gen. Hosp., Boston, 1980—81, resident, 1981—83; fellow infectious diseases Washington U. Sch. Medicine, St. Louis, 1983—84, Pfizer fellow microbiology and immunology, 1985—88, instr. medicine, 1987—88, asst. prof. Divsn. Infectious Diseases, 1988, asst. prof. Dept. Molecular Microbiology, 1989, assoc. prof., 1994—2004, prof., 2004—09, assoc. prof. Dept. Medicine, 1993—99, prof., 1999—2009, dir. Midwest Regional Ctr. of Excellence for Biodefense and Emerging Infectious Diseases Rsch., 2003—09, vice chancellor rsch., 2006—09; attending physician internal medicine and infectious diseases Barnes-Jewish Hosp., St. Louis, 1987—2009; pres. Stony Brook U. (SUNY at Stony Brook), 2009—. Chief med. cons. BarnesCare Travelers Clinic, 1990—; bd. dirs. Ctr. Emerging Technologies, 2006; bd. mem. Rsch. Alliance of Mo., 2006, St. Louis Ctr. of Excellence, Mo. Life Scis. Trust Fund, 2007; bd. trustees St. Louis Acad. Sci., 2006; mem. Blue Ribbon Panel on the New England Infectious Diseases Rsch. Lab. NIH, 2008—, mem. Nat. Adv. Allergy & Infectious Diseases Coun., 2008—; mem. Emerging Tech. and Rsch. Adv. Com. US Dept. Commerce, 2008—; spkr. in field. Contbr. articles to profl. jours. Mem.: Am. Soc. Clin. Investigation, Infectious Disease Soc. America, Am. Soc. Microbiology, Am. Fedn. Clin. Rsch., Am. Soc. Tropical Medicine and Hygiene, Infectious Disease Soc. of America, Am. Coll. Physicians. Office: Stony Brook U Office of Pres 310 Administration Bldg Stony Brook NY 11794-0701 E-mail: Samuel.Stanley@stonybrook.edu.*

STANLEY, SCOTT, JR., editor; b. Kansas City, July 11, 1938; s. Winfield Scott and Irene Mae (Flint) S.; m. Janice Johns, Aug. 30, 1959 (dec. July 1992); children: Leslie, Scott, Margaret; m. Cynthia Ward, Dec. 30, 1995; 1 child, Elizabeth. BA, Earlham Coll., 1960. Mng. editor Am. Opinion mag., Boston, 1961-85; editor Rev. of The News mag., Boston, 1965-85; editor-in-chief Conservative Digest, Washington, 1985-88, Am. Press Internat., Washington, 1987—; pres. USA Tech., 1991-92; mng. editor Nutrition and Healing, 1994-2000; dep. editor Insight on the News, Washington, 1995—2005. Mem. nat. bd. dirs. Young Ams. for Freedom, 1960-62; public speaker and univ. lectr., 1962— Keynote speaker Am. Party Nat. Conv., 1976; pres. Ams. Legal Def. Fund, 1977—; bd. govs. Council for Nat. Policy, 1981—; bd. dirs. Free Congress Polit. Action Com., 1985-88, bd. trustees, Conservative Caucus Found., 2006—; pres. Scott Stanley Real Estate Trust, 1988— Recipient award of merit Young Ams. for Freedom, Freedom award Nat. Congress for Freedom. Mem.: Nat. Press Club. Episcopalian. Personal E-mail: cwardstanley@cox.net.

STANLEY, SHIRLEY DAVIS, artist; b. Mt. Vernon, NY, Dec. 5, 1929; d. Walter Thompson and Elsie Viola (Lumpp) Davis; m. Charles B. Coble Jr., June 11, 1951 (div. 1968); children: Jennifer Susan Farmer, Charles B. Coble III; m. Marvin M. Stanley, Dec. 18, 1983 (dec.). BA in Home Econs. and Gen. Sci., Greensboro Coll., 1951; grad., Real Estate Inst., 1962. Tchr. Dryher HS, Columbia, SC, 1951-52, Haw River Sch., NC, 1954—56, Alexander Wilson Sch., Graham, NC, 1957-58; guest essayist for news Mebane Enterprise, NC, 1955-56; pres. Shirley, Inc., Burlington, NC, 1962—2004. One woman show Art Gallery Originals, Winston-Salem, 1976, Olive Garden Gallery, 21st Century Gallery, Williamsburg, Va., galleries in Fla., NC Bd. dirs. Girl Scouts Am. Kings Daus., Burlington, 1961, Williamsburg Libr. Found., 1997—; life mem. Rep. Inner Cir., Washington, 1990—; active Salvation Army; com. mem. York County Rep. Party, 1995; vol. disaster & blood banks ARC, 1990—; founding mem. Am. Air Force Mus.; bd. dirs. William Burg Libr. Found., 1997—; pres. Burlington Coun. Garden Clubs, 1955-56. Recipient Rep. Medal of Freedom, 1994, 2002, 2003. Mem. AAUW, Am. Watercolor Soc. (assoc.), Va. Watercolor Soc., Sierra Club, Williamsburg Bibliophiles, Raleigh Tavern Soc. Colonial Williamsburg, Christopher Wren Soc., Williamsburg C. of C., Williamsburg Photography Soc., Mil. Officers Assn. (life), Waterman's Assn., Army-Navy Country Club. Episcopalian. Avocations: travel, gardening, writing, dance, reading. Home: 103 Little John Rd Williamsburg VA 23185-4907 also: 1953 Shirley Dr Burlington NC 27215-4831

STANLEY, STEVEN MITCHELL, paleontologist, educator; b. Detroit, Nov. 2, 1941; s. William Thomas and Mildred Elizabeth (Baker) S.; m. E. Ellen Reynolds, Dec. 28, 2005. AB with highest honors, Princeton U., 1963; PhD, Yale U., 1968. Asst. prof. U. Rochester, 1967-69; asst. prof. paleobiology Johns Hopkins U., 1969-71, assoc. prof., 1971-74, prof., 1974—2005, chmn. dept. Earth and planetary Scis., 1987-88, chmn. MS program in environ. scis. and policy, 1993—2005; rsch. prof. U. Hawaii, 2005. Assoc. in rsch. Smithsonian Instn., 1972—; mem. bd. earth scis. NRC, 1985—, vice chmn., 1988, mem. bd. earth scis. resources, 1988-88, com. on solid earth scis., exec. and steering com., 1988, 2004—, com. on geoscis., environ, and resources, 1990-96. Author: Relation of Shell Form to Life Habits in the Bivalvia, 1970, (with D.M. Raup) Principles of Paleontology, 1971, Macroevolution: Pattern and Process, 1979, The New Evolutionary Timetable: Fossils, Genes, and the Origin of species, 1981, Earth and Life Through Time, 1986, Extinction, 1987, Exploring Earth and Life Through Time, 1992, Children of the Ice Age: How a Global Catastrophe Allowed Humans to Evolve, 1996, Earth System History, 1999; mem. editl. bd. Am. Jour. Sci., 1975—, Paleobiology, 1975-82, 88—, Evolutionary Theory, 1973—. Recipient Outstanding Paper award Jour. Paleontology, 1968, Allan C. Davis medal Md. Acad. Scis., 1973, Outstanding Tech. Paper award Washington Geol. Soc., 1986, Bownocker medal Ohio State U., 1997; Guggenheim fellow, 1981 Fellow NAS (Mary Clark Thompson Medal, 2006), Am. Acad. Arts and Scis., Geol. Soc. Am. (chmn. Penrose com. 1978, councilor 2002—); mem. Paleontol. Soc. (councilor 1976-77, sr. councilor 1991-93, pres. 1993-94, Charles Schuchert award 1977, medal 2007), Soc. for Study Evolution (councilor 1982-84), Am. Geophys. Union (pub. affairs com.), Paleontol. Rsch. Inst., Am. Geol. Inst. (mem. exec. com. 1996-99, pres. 2001—), Nat. Assn. Geosci. Tchrs. (James H. Shea award, 2004), Soc. Sedimentary Geology (Twenhofel medal 2008). Business E-Mail: stevenst@hawaii.edu.

STANLEY, TIM, information technology executive; BS in Engring., U. Wash.; degree in Internat. Bus. and Tech. Mgmt., Thunderbird U., Ariz. State U. With Intel Corp., Optima/KPMG, Innova Tech, Kimberly-Clark Corp.; v.p. info. sys. Nat. Airlines, chief info. officer; ptnr. USWeb (now marchFIRST); v.p., info. tech. devel. Harrah's Entertainment, Las Vegas, 2001—03, sr. v.p., chief info. officer, 2003—. With USAF. Named one of the Top 25 Unsung Heroes of the Internet, Interactive Week Mag., Top 25 Chief Tech. Officers, InfoWorld mag., 2006. Office: Harrahs Entertainment Inc One Harrahs Ct Las Vegas NV 89119

STANSBERRY, JAMES WESLEY, air force officer; b. Grafton, W.Va., Dec. 29, 1927; s. William Adrian and Phyllis Gay (Robinson) S.; m. Audrey Mildred Heinz, May 7, 1950; children: Nora G., Amy G. Stansberry Goodhand, Lisa Porten. BS, U.S. Mil. Acad., 1949; MBA with hons., Air Force Inst. Tech., 1956. Advanced through grades from pvt. to lt. gen. USAF; chief prodn. (Kawasaki Gifu Contract Facility), Gifu, Japan, 1956-57; dep. asst. to Sec. of Def. for atomic energy Washington, 1970-71; dep. dir. procurement policy U.S. Air Force, 1972-73; dep. chief staff contracting and mfg. (Hdqrs. Air Force Systems Command), Andrews AFB, Md., 1977-81; comdr. Electronic Systems Div. Hanscom AFB, Mass., 1981-84; pres. Stansberry Assocs. Inc., 1984—. Bd. dirs. Griffon Corp., Triton. Decorated DSM with oak leaf cluster, Legion of Merit with oak leaf cluster; named Disting. grad. Lancaster (N.Y.) H.S., award, Wall St. Jour., 1956, Mervin E. Gross award, USAF, 1956. Mem.: Order of Sword. Methodist. Home: 1217 Alliance Dr Apt 136 Virginia Beach VA 23454-7412 Home Phone: 757-716-2804; Office Phone: 757-716-2804. Personal E-mail: us49@aol.com. *The real secrets are enthusiasm, competence and good luck; and it helps immensely to marry a good woman. Work and persistence define us, accomodating various levels of talent and intelligence. Work and persistence prevail, buttressed by discipline and determination, and supported by a good sense of humor.*

STANSBRY, MICHAEL DAVID, set designer, educator; b. Wadsworth, Ohio, Sept. 26, 1950; s. David Honor and Mary Lois Stansbery; m. JaNae Ottosen, Aug. 6, 2002; children: M'Linda Karen Stansbery, Graham Michael Stansbery. MDiv, Andover Newton Theol. Sem., Mass., 1978. Theatre designer & dir., 1972—; theartre dept. chair, prof. theatre Pikes Peak CC, Colo. Springs, 1987—; tech. theatre instr. U. Colo., Colo. Springs, 2006—; resident scenic designer Theatreworks, Colo. Springs, 2006—. Home: 101 Panorama Pl Manitou Springs CO 80829 Office: Univ of Colo POBox 7150 Colorado Springs CO 80933-7150 Office Fax: 719-262-3677. Personal E-mail: msmasquers@earthlink.net. Business E-Mail: mstansbe@uccs.edu.

STANSBURY, RICK, men's college basketball coach; b. Dec. 23, 1958; s. Robert and Norma Stansbury; m. Meo Mellen; children: Issac, Noah, Luke. B in Bus., Phys. Edn., Campbellsville Coll., Ky., 1982; M in Bus. Edn., Cumberland Coll., Williamsburg, Ky. Student asst. coach Campbellsville Coll. Tigers, 1982—83; grad. asst. Cumberland Coll. Patriots, 1983—84; asst. coach, recruiting coord. Austin Peay State U. Governors, Clarksville, Tenn., 1984—90; asst. coach Miss. State U. Bulldogs, 1990—94, assoc. head coach, 1994—98, head basketball coach, 1998—. Organizing com. vol. Coaches Care, 2005; vol. Camp Rising Sun, Columbus, Miss. Recipient Disting. Alumni award, Campbellsville Alumni Assn., 1999; named to Campbellsville U. Athletic Hall of Fame, 2003. Office: Miss State U Athletic Dept PO Box 5327 Mississippi State MS 39762 Office Phone: 662-325-3800.*

STANSELL, LELAND EDWIN, JR., lawyer, mediator, educator; b. Central, SC, July 13, 1934; s. Leland Edwin and Hettie Katherine (Hollis) S.; children: James Leland, Susan. BS, Fla. So. Coll., 1957; LLB, U. Miami, Fla., 1961, JD, 1968. Bar: Fla. 1961; cert. civil mediator Fla. Supreme Ct., U.S. Dist. Ct. Fla. Assoc. Wicker & Smith, Miami, 1961-62, ptnr., 1962-75; pvt. practice, Miami, 1975-99, Leland E. Stansell, Jr., P.A., Miami, 1995—. Chmn. Appellate Jud. Nominating Com., Dade County (Fla.), 1983-87; mem. adv. com. Am. Arbitration Assn., 1975-90. Served with U.S. Army, 1957. Mem. ABA (ho. of dels. 1982-86), Fla. Bar (bd. govs. 1966-70, 70-80), Dade County Bar Assn. (dir. 1969-72, exec. com. 1974-75, pres. 1975-76), U. Miami Law Alumni Assn. (dir., officer, pres. 1968-69), Fla. Criminal Def. Attys. Assn. (treas. 1964-66), Am. Judicature Soc., Am. Bd. Trial Advs., Internat. Assn. Def. Counsel, Fla. Acad. Profl. Mediators, Fedn. Ins. Counsel, Miami Beach Rod and Reel Club (pres.), Coral Reef Yacht Club, Miami City Club, Ocean Reef Yacht Club, Delta Theta Phi (pres. Miami alumni chpt. 1966, regional dir. 1968.

STANSELL, RONALD BRUCE, retired investment banker; b. Hammond, Ind., Apr. 9, 1945; s. Herman Bruce and Helen Rose Stansell; children: Kelsey, Kymberlie. BA, Wittenberg U., 1967; MA, Miami U., Oxford, Ohio, 1969. Investment officer First Nat. Bank, Chgo., 1969-73; mgr. investments Chrysler Corp., Detroit, 1973; asst. v.p. A.G. Becker, Chgo., 1973-76; v.p. Blyth Eastman Dillon, Chgo., 1976-79, Dean Witter Reynolds Inc., Chgo., 1979-82, First Boston Corp., 1982-88; sr. v.p. Prudential-Bache Securities, Chgo., 1988-90; ptnr. William Blair & Co., 1991-99; pres. Oakmont of Carolina, 1999—2001. Mem. Mettawa (Ill.) Zoning Bd., 1978-80; treas. Village of Mettawa, 1977-78, trustee, 1980-91. With USMCR, 1968-74. Mem. Bond Club Chgo., Investment Analyst Soc., Fixed Income Group, Grandfather Golf Club, Forest Creek Golf Club, Belfair Golf Club, Berkeley Hall Club, Old Chatham Club, Diamond Creek Golf Club, Univ. Club.

STANSFIELD, CHARLES W., educational administrator; m. Charlene Rivera, Sept. 6, 1989. BA in Spanish, Fla. State U., 1968, MA in Fgn. Lang. Edn., 1969, MS in Teaching English as Second Lang., 1970, PhD in Fgn. and Second Lang. Edn., 1973. Tchr. English, Centro Colombo-Americano, Bogota, Colombia, 1966; 2jr. high sch. tchr. Spanish Fla. State U. Demonstration Sch., 1968-69; instr. Spanish, U. Colo., Boulder, 1970-73, asst. prof., 1973-80, assoc. prof., 1980-81; assoc. program dir. lang. programs Ednl. Testing Svc., Princeton, NJ, 1981-86; dir. fgn. lang. edn. and testing div. Ctr. for Applied Linguistics, Washington, 1986-94, dir. ERIC Clearinghouse Lang. and Linguistics, 1986-94; pres. Second Lang. Testing, Inc., Bethesda, Md., 1994—. Dir. Peace Corps Tng. Ctr., Managua, Nicaragua, 1978; mem. exec. com. Joint Nat. Com. Langs., 1988—93; conf. coord. Interagy. Lang. Roundtable Invitational Symposium Lang. Aptitude Testing, Rosslyn, Va., 1988; mem. adv. bd. Nat. Fgn. Lang. Resources Ctr. U. Hawaii, 1991—93; presenter in field. Author: Cuademo de ejercicios, 1976, rev. edit., 1981; author: (with others) Multiple-Choice Close Items and the Test of English as a Foreign Language, 1988; co-author: Manual de laboratorio, 2d rev. edit., 1981, The Test of Spoken English as a Measure of Communicative Ability in the Health Professions, Validation and Standard Setting, 1983; co-editor: Second Languag Proficiency Assessment: Current Issues, 1988, Language Aptitude Reconsidered, 1990; contbr. articles to profl. jours. Named Outstanding Alumnus, Fla. State U., 1994; Colo. Congress Fgn. Lang. Tchrs. scholar, 1981. Mem.: Colo. Tchrs. English Spkrs. Other Langs. (Gladys Doty award 1987), Washington Area Tchrs. English Spkrs. Other Langs., Tchrs. English Spkrs. Other Langs., Internat. Lang. Testing Assn. (pres. 1992—93), Nat. Coun. Measurement Edn., Nat. Assn. Bilingual Edn., Internat. Assn. Applied Linguistics, Am. Ednl. Rsch. Assn., Am. Coun. Tchg. Fgn. Langs. (Paul Pinsleur award 1984), Am. Assn. Tchrs. Spanish and Portuguese (life). Office: 6135 Executive Blvd Rockville MD 20852-3437 Office Phone: 301-231-6046. Business E-Mail: cstansfield@2lti.com.

STANSKY, PETER DAVID LYMAN, historian, writer, retired professor; b. NYC, Jan. 18, 1932; s. Lyman and Ruth (Macow) Stansky. BA, Yale U., 1953, King's Coll., Cambridge U., Eng., 1955, MA, 1959; PhD, Harvard U., 1961; DL (hon.), Wittenberg U., 1984. Tchg. fellow history and lit. Harvard U., 1957-61, from instr. to asst. prof. history, 1961-68; assoc. prof. Stanford (Calif.) U., 1968-73, prof., 1973-74, Frances and Charles Field prof., 1974—2004, Frances and Charles Field prof. emeritus, 2004—, chmn. dept. history, 1975-78, 79-82, 89-90, assoc. dean humanities and scis., 1985-88. Chmn. publs. com. Conf. Brit. Studies, 1970—78; vis. fellow Wesleyan Ctr. Humanities, Middletown, 1972; pres. Pacific Coast Conf. Brit. Studies, 1974—76, N.Am. Conf. Brit. Studies, 1983—85; vis. fellow All Soul's Coll. Oxford (Eng.) U., 1979, vis. fellow St. Catherine's Coll., 83. Author: Ambitions and Strategies, 1964, England Since 1867, 1973, Gladstone, 1979, William Morris, 1983, Redesigning the World, 1985, On or About December 1910, 1996, Another Book that Never Was, 1998, From William Morris to Sergeant Pepper, 1999, Sassoon: The Worlds of Philip and Sybil, 2003, The First Day of the Blitz, 2007; co-author: Journey to the Frontier, 1966, The Unknown Orwell, 1972, Orwell: The Transformation, 1979, London's Burning, 1994. Guggenheim fellow, 1966—67, 1973—74, Am. Coun. Learned Socs. fellow, 1978—79, NEH fellow, 1983, 1998—99, Royal Hist. Soc. fellow, Ctr. Advanced Study Behavioral Scis., 1988—89. Fellow: Am. Acad. Arts and Scis. (coun. 1994—98, 2002—05); mem.: AAUP, Century Assn., William Morris Soc., Victorian Soc., Conf. Brit. Studies, Am. Hist. Assn. Home: 375 Pinehill Rd Hillsborough CA 94010-6612 Office: Stanford U Dept History Stanford CA 94305-2024 Office Phone: 650-723-2663. Business E-Mail: stansky@stanford.edu.

STANTON, ANDREW, animator, film director, film producer, scriptwriter; b. Boston, Dec. 3, 1965; married; 2 children. Grad., Calif. Inst. Arts, 1987. Animator Pixar (now Disney Pixar), 1990—. Writer, prodr., animator, dir. (films) A Story, 1987, animator Luxo Jr. in 'Surprise' and 'Light & Heavy', 1991, writer, voice, story artist Toy Story, 1995 (Best Individual Achievement: Writing Annie Awards, 1996), writer, voice, story artist, co-dir. A Bug's Life, 1998, writer, voice Toy Story 2, 1999 (Outstanding Individual Achievement for Writing in an Animated Feature Prodn. Annie Awards, 2000), writer, exec. prodr. Monsters, Inc., 2001 (Best Feature Film Brit. Acad. Film and TV Arts Award, 2002), writer, voice, dir. Finding Nemo, 2003 (Hollywood Film award for Animation, 2003, Outstanding Writing in an Animated Feature Prodn. Annie Awards, 2004, Outstanding Directing in an Animated Feature Prodn. Annie Awards, 2004, Oscar for Best Animated Feature, 2004), voice The Incredibles, 2004, Cars, 2006, exec. prodr. Ratatouille, 2007 (Christopher award for Feature Films, 2008), Presto, 2008, writer, dir. WALL-E, 2008 (Best Animated Feature Film, Golden Globe award, Hollywood Fgn. Press Assn., 2009, Best Animated Film, Brit. Acad. Film and TV Arts, 2009, Acad. award for Best Animated Feature Film, 2009), writer (TV series) Mighty Mouse, the New Adventures, 1987. Recipient Animator Dir. of Yr., ShoWest, 2004. Office: Pixar Animation Studios 1200 Park Ave Emeryville CA 94608

STANTON, DONALD SHELDON, retired academic administrator; b. Balt., June 8, 1932; s. Kenneth Gladstone and Dorothy Erma (Hetrick) S.; m. Barbara Mae Hoot, June 25, 1955; children: Dale Richard, Debra Carol, Diane Karen. AB, Western Md. Coll., 1953; Litt.D., Oglethorpe U., 1999; LLD, Western Md. Coll., 1981; MDiv magna cum laude, Wesley Theol. Sem., 1956; MA, Am. U., 1960; Ed.D., U. Va., 1965; L.H.D., Columbia Coll., 1979; Litt.D., Albion Coll., 1983. Ordained to ministry United Methodist Ch., 1956; pastor Balt. and Va. confs. United Meth. Ch., 1953-59; dir. Richmond (Va.) Area Wesley Found., 1959-63; chaplain, dean of students Greensboro Coll., 1963-65; chaplain Wofford Coll., 1965-69; dir. office coll. services United Meth. Div. Higher Edn., Nashville, 1969-75; v.p. for devel. Wesleyan Coll., 1975-78; pres. Adrian Coll., 1978-88, Oglethorpe U., Atlanta, 1988-99, pres. emeritus, 1999—; interim pres. Haywood Cmty. Coll., 2005—06. Adminstr., prof. European internat. ednl. programs, summers 1960, 69-71, 73; chmn. pres.'s assn. Mich. Intercollegiate Athletic Assn., 1986-87. Contbr. articles, revs. to profl. publs. in U.S., Japan, Argentina, chpts. to books; editor: Faculty Forum, 1972-74; bass-baritone soloist. Bd. dirs. Toledo Symphony, 1980-83, Lewanee County Jr. Achievement, 1980-83, Found. Ind. Higher Edn., 1996-99, Nat. Conf. for Cmty. and Justice, Atlanta Region, Atlanta Area coun. Boy Scouts Am.; chair bd. trustees U. Ctr. Ga., 1994-96; chair So. Collegiate Athletic Conf., 1994-95. Adminstrn. bldg. at Adrian Coll. named in honor of Stanton and his wife, 1988. Mem. Am. Assn. Univ. Adminstrs. (bd. dirs. 1990-93), Ga. Assn. Colls. (pres. 1992), Soc. Wesley (Disting. Alumni Recognition award 1988), Ga. Found. for Ind. Colls. (vice chair 1992), Nat. Assn. Ind. Colls. and Univs. (past mem. pub. rels. com.), Assn. Pvt. Colls. and Univs. Ga. (treas. 1996-97), Lake Juneburka Assembly (bd. dir. 2008-), Rotary, Omicron Delta Kappa, Order of Omega, Tau Kappa Epsilon, Psi Chi, Phi Eta Sigma. Home: 312 Tillman Rd Lake Junaluska NC 28745-9779 Personal E-mail: stantons2@earthlink.net.

STANTON, GREGORY HOWARD, lawyer, educator; b. Delta, Colo., June 25, 1946; s. Howard Earl and Alison May (White) S.; m. Mary Ellen Munsche, June 23, 1973; children: Elizabeth Chantana, Theodore Saroun. BA, Oberlin Coll., 1968; MA, U. Chgo., 1973, PhD, 1986; MTS, Harvard Div. Sch., 1974; JD, Yale U., 1982. Bar: Wis. 1982, U.S. Dist. Ct. (ea. and we. dists.) Wis. 1982, U.S. Ct. Appeals (9th cir.) 1982, Va. 1988. Legis. aide U.S. Senate, Washington, 1967; vol. U.S. Peace Corps, Abidjan, Ivory Coast, 1969-71; lect. U. Chgo., 1975; Fulbright fellow, dept. anthropology Abidjan, 1975-77; rsch. fellow Indian Law Inst., New Delhi, 1978-79; field dir. Ch. World Svc., Phnom Penh, Cambodia, 1980; law clk. U.S. Ct. Appeals (9th cir.), Portland, 1982-83; assoc. Foley & Lardner, Milw., 1983-85; asst. prof. law Washington & Lee U., Lexington, Va., 1985-91; asst. prof. justice, law and society Am. U., Washington, 1991—. Cons. on law USIA, Rwanda, 1988-89; vis. prof. law U. Swaziland, 1989-90; legal advisor Rukh Kiev, Ukraine, 1990-91. Contbr. articles to profl. jours. Vice pres. Internat. Alert, London and L.A., 1988—; elder Lexington Presbyn. Ch., 1988-91. NSF fellow, 1975; Social Sci. Rsch. Coun. grantee, 1975; Woodrow Wilson fellow, 1968, Fulbright fellow, 1989. Fellow Am. Anthrop. Assn.; mem. Law and Society Assn., Am. Soc. Internat. Law. Avocations: photography, filmmaking, poetry writing, piano. Office: Am U Sch Pub Affairs 4400 Massachusetts Ave NW Washington DC 20016-8001

STANTON, JOHN JEFFREY, editor, director, journalist, government agency administrator, educator; b. Wichita Falls, Tex., July 19, 1956; s. John Joseph Jr. and Joan (Marley) S.; m. Scylla Maria Silva, Jan. 6, 1981; 1 child, Damien Kristian. BS in Pub. Adminstrn. and Bus. Adminstrn., Nichols Coll., 1978; M in Pub. Adminstrn., U. Detroit, 1980. Rsch. asst. Am. Enterprise Inst., Washington, 1977; rep. aide R.I. Ho. of Reps., Providence, 1977-78; mng. editor Am. Politics, Washington, 1982, assoc. editor, 1983, corp. advisor, 1984, sr. editor, 1985-87; editor, govt. programs mgr. ENTEK, Alexandria, Va., 1988-90; govt. programs dir., cons. Tuckerman Group, Springfield, Va., 1991; analyst, writer Nat. Security Issues, Arlington, Va., 1991—; program dir. TeleStrategies, McLean, Va., 1991-93; Washington corr., mem. editl. bd. Tech. Transfer Jour., 1994-98; editor Tech. Transfer Newsletter; asst. to pres., info. transfer specialist Am. Def. Preparedness Assn., Arlington, 1994-97; contbg. writer Nat. Def. Mag., 1996—2004; adminstrn. dir. Nat. Def. Indsl. Assn., Arlington, 1997—2004; Washington corr. Australian Def. Mag., 1998-99; editor Voice of the Indsl. Base NDIA, 1998—2000; tchr., adminstr. St. Stephens & Agnes, 2005—; rsch. assoc. Rsch. Inst. for European and Am. Studies, 2006—; mem. Triangle Inst. for Security Studies, 2007—, Internat. Inst. Strategic Studies. Creator, co-host (radio) Power Breakfast, Sta. WNTR, Washington, 1987, Am. Politics Radio, 1987; commentator WAMU-NPR, WBAL, KPFA, Am. Talk Live, NYC, Radio 101, Croatia, Radio Adelaide, KCMO, Kansas City, WNTR, WAMU, WBAC, Balt.; campaign mgr. Madsen for Congress, 8th dist., Va., 2004; polit.-mil. analyst CBS News, CNN, ABC, 2001—. Co-author: America's Nightmare, 2003; author: A Power But Not Super, 2004, Talking Politics with God and the Devil in Washington, DC, 2007; contbr. articles to profl. jours., popular mags. Polit. campaign cons. to Glenn Tenney, 1992—; commr. Arlington Little League Baseball, 1993, coach 1997—; mentor Arlington County Ct. Sys., 1997; varsity football coach Wakefield H.S., Arlington, Va., 1998-2002, St. Stephen's Agnes, 2003—. Recipient Doers Honoree The Washington Times, 1988. Mem.: NDIA (life). Avocation: coaching youth sports programs. Office: St Skephens St Agnes 1000Sp Skphenn Rd Alexandria VA 22304 Personal E-mail: cioran123@yahoo.com. Business E-Mail: jstanton@sssas.org.

STANTON, KAMILLE STONE, literature and language professor; m. Robert David Stanton. BA in English with honors, U. Houston, 1998; MA in English: Renaissance to Enlightenment Lit., U. Coll. London, 2000; PhD in English, U. Leeds, Eng., 2006. Asst. prof. Savannah State U., Ga., 2006—. Office: Savannah State Univ Liberal Arts Dept Box 20029 Savannah GA 31404

STANTON, LOUIS LEE, federal judge; b. NYC, Oct. 1, 1927; s. Louis Lee and Helen Parsons (La Fétra) S.; m. Berit Eleonora Rask; children: L. Lee, Susan Helen Benedict, Gordon R., Fredrik S. BA, Yale U., 1950; JD, U. Va., 1955. Assoc. Davis Polk Wardwell Sunderland & Kiendl, NYC, 1955-66, Carter, Ledyard & Milburn, NYC, 1966-67, ptnr., 1967-85; judge U.S. Dist. Ct. (So. Dist.), NY, 1985—96, sr. judge NY, 1996—. Served to 1st lt. USMCR, 1950-52. Fellow Am. Coll. Trial Lawyers, N.Y. Bar Found.; mem. Va. Bar Assn.

STANTON, MATT, lobbyist, beverage company executive; Lobbyist Distilled Spirits Coun. of US, Allied Domecq Spirits & Wine N.Am., 2003—05; corp. affairs dir. Jim Beam Brands Worldwide, 2005—; v.p. corp. affairs Beam Global Spirits & Wine, Inc. Office: Beam Global Spirits & Wine, Inc 1301 K St NW, #250W Washington DC 20005 Office Phone: 202-962-0551.*

STANTON, MORRIS DUNCAN, psychologist, researcher, dean; b. Lockport, NY; *Descended from: Emperor Charlemagne, El Cid, William the Conqueror, over 50 other kings and a ruling queen in European countries (France, England/Scotland, Spain, Portugal), 36 American colonists (arriving 1623—1641), Rhode Island Colony's first Governor, Canada's first female medical school graduate, two other country doctors, four judges, three clergy, 12 American military officers, a civil engineer who helped build the Panama Canal, artists, writers, and many teachers. Blood relatives include: King Richard the Lion-Heart, Queen Elizabeth I, 20 other European kings/ruling queens (three in Italy), Sir Francis Drake, England's Poet Laureate John Dryden, five U.S. Presidents (Washington, Grant, Garfield, Cleveland, F.D.R.), Plymouth Colony's Governor Winslow, three other governors, New England's first licensed physician, Gen. Moses Cleaveland, Commodore Oliver Perry, Samuel F.B. Morse, Lincoln's Secretary of War Edwin M. Stanton, Susan B. Anthony, portraitist/abolition activist Edwin W. Goodwin, Elizabeth Cady Stanton's husband Henry B. Stanton (an award-winning anti-slavery journalist, attorney, Massachusetts/New York state senator, and political lecturer), three judges, three registered nurses, two superintendents of schools.* BA in Psychology, Alfred U., 1962; MA in Clin. Psychology, George Washington U., 1964; PhD in Clin. and Cmty. Psychology, U. Md., 1968. Lic. psychologist NY, Ky., bd. cert. diplomate in clin. psychology Am. Bd. Profl. Psychology, bd. cert. diplomate in family psychology Am. Bd. Profl. Psychology, approved supr. Am. Assn. Marriage Family Therapy, cert. in treatment of alcohol and other psychoactive substance abuse disorders APA. Commd. 2d lt. US Army, 1962, advanced through grades to capt., 1966; intern Walter Reed Gen. Hosp., Washington, 1966—67, dir. psychology tng., 1971—72; chief psychologist Ft. Dix, NJ, 1968—69, 98th Med. Detachment Vietnam, 1969—70, Ft. Meade, Md., 1970—71; lectr. U. Md., 1969—72; from asst. prof. to assoc. prof. psychology in psychiatry U. Pa. Sch. Medicine, Phila., 1972—83; assoc. clin. dir. Penn Psychiatry Phila. Gen. Hosp., 1972—74; dir. addicts and families prog. Phila. Child Guidance Clinic, 1974—83; dir. family therapy tng. program Drug Dependence Treatment Ctr., Phila. VA Med. Ctr., 1974—79; faculty mem. family therapy tng. ctr. Phila. Child Guidance Clinic, 1977—83; tchg. faculty Family Inst. of Phila., 1977—83; instr. Wilmington Med. Ctr., Del., 1978—79; dir. rsch. Phila. Child Guidance Clinic, Pa., 1982—83; prof., psychiatry (psychology) U. Rochester Sch. Medicine and Dentistry, 1983—97; dir. div. family programs, dept. psychiatry U. Rochester Med. Ctr., 1983—93; dir. rsch. div. family programs, dept. of psychiatry U. of Rochester Med. Ctr., 1993—97; prof., dean Sch. Profl. Psychology and Social Work Spalding U., Louisville, 1997—99, v.p., acad. rsch., 1999, prof. emeritus psychology, 1999—. Vis. scholar Fulbright Found., USIA, Argentina, 1991; cons. White House Office of Drug Abuse Policy, 1977—81, USIA, 1987—96, Inst. Medicine Nat. Acad. Scis., 1988, 1991—92; chair, mem. various rev. comms., task forces, site visit teams NIDA, NIMH, NIAAA, 1975—; mem. 16 editl. bds., including Am. Jour. Drug Alcohol Abuse, Family Process, Psychosocial Stress, 1980—; bd Family Process Press, NYC, 1982—99; spkr., presenter invited lectrs., workshops in 27 countries. *Conducted an anonymous survey of drug use among 2,372 Army personnel in Vietnam which, via testimony before the U.S. Senate Special Subcommittee on Alcoholism and Narcotics, received considerable attention in the national media. Consultant/advisory board member to over 90 government agencies, universities, medical centers, and organizations across five continents. Published reviews of the outcome studies on family and couples therapy for drug and alcohol abuse (1997 meta-analysis, 2005 review), and the methods for getting reluctant substance abusers to enter treatment or self-help (2004).* Contbr. more than 150 works to sci., profl. publs.; author: monographs and books in field, 1968—. Mem. dept. del. task group on alcoholism The Pentagon, Washington, 1971—72; ad hoc com. mem. special action office on drug abuse policy The White House, Washington, 1974; mem. advisory group family therapy prevention rsch. project Nat. Inst. Drug Abuse, 1981—82; chair, moderator family rsch. conf. Alcohol, Drug Abuse and Mental Health Adminstrn., 1981; cons. Family Health Plan, 1985—88; cons., sponsor, supr. Fulbright Commn., 1987—92. Decorated Bronze Star Medal; recipient Plaque of Appreciation, Found. for Parents in Action (Argentina), 1991, Shield of Police of Salta Province (Argentina), 1991, Cert. of Appreciation for Svc. on Mayor's Drug, Alcohol Planning Com., City of Louisville, 1998; named to Hall of Fame, Schenectady City Sch. Dist., 2008; grantee, NIH (NIDA/NIAAA), 1974—84, 1995—; Ann. Disting. fellow, Pikes Peak Mental Health Ctr., 1980. Fellow: APA (Pres. Citation 2001), Acad. Family Psychology, Nat. Coun. Family Rels. (Award Appreciation for dedication to the enhancement of family life 1988, Recognition cert. for longstanding svc. 1988, Legacy Circle award 1999), Am. Assoc. Marriage and Family Therapy (Outstanding Rsch. Contbn. in Marital and Family Therapy 1980, Cumulative Contbn. Family Therapy Rsch. award 2003, Ky. Divsn. award of Appreciation 2004); mem.: Internat. Family Therapy Assn., Am. Family Therapy Acad. (chair alcohol and drug interest group 1982—87, Disting. Contbn. Family Systems Rsch. 1997), Associacion Sistemica de Buenos Aires (hon.), South African Inst. Marital and Family Therapy (hon.). Office: The Morton Center 1028 Barret Ave Louisville KY 40204

STANTON, PATRICK MICHAEL, lawyer; b. Phila., Sept. 8, 1947; s. Edward Joseph and Helen Marie (Coghlan) S.; m. Kathleen Ann Fama, Aug. 22, 1970; children: Cheryl Marie, Susan Elizabeth. BS in History, St. Joseph's U., 1969; JD, U. Va., 1972; MBA, Fairleigh Dickinson, 1984. Bar: Ohio 1972 (inactive), N.J. 1982, N.Y. 1985, U.S. Dist. Ct. (so. dist.) Ohio 1972, U.S. Dist. Ct. (ea. dist.) N.J. 1982, U.S. Dist. Ct. (so. dist.) N.Y. 1984. Assoc. Taft, Stettinius & Hollister, Cin., 1972—80; labor counsel Union Camp Corp., Wayne, NJ, 1980—83; dir. labor rels., equal employment opportunity programs W.R. Grace & Co., NYC, 1983—86; of counsel Shanley & Fisher, P.C., Morristown, NJ, 1986—89, ptnr., chmn. labor and employment group, 1989—95; dir. Stanton, Hughes, Diana, Cerra, Mariani & Margello, P.C., Morristown, 1995—2003; atty., shareholder Ogletree, Deakins, Nash, Smoak & Stewart, P.C., Morristown, 2004—. Adj. prof. bus. law Fairleigh Dickinson U. 1984-92; pres. Sidney Reitman employment law Am. Inn. Ct., 1997-2001. Pres., bd. dirs. N.Y. State Adv. Coun. on Employment Law, Inc., N.Y.C., 1985-86. Named one of Best Lawyers in Am., 1989—, Top 100 Lawyers in NJ, 2008—09; fellow, Coll. Labor Employment Lawyers; DuPont scholar, U. Va., 1970—72. Fellow: Coll. Labor Employment Lawyers; mem. ABA, N.J. State Bar Assn. (exec. com. labor employment law sect. 1989—, rec. sec. 1995-97, treas. 1997-99, 2d vice chair 1999-2001, 1st vice chair 2001-03, chair 2003-05, immediate past chmn. 2005-07), Phi Alpha Theta, Delta Mu Delta. Roman Catholic. Office: Ogletree Deakins Nash Smoak & Stewart PC 10 Madison Ave Ste 402 Morristown NJ 07960-7303 Home: 2 Hamilton Rd Apt 4m Morristown NJ 07960-5342 Office Phone: 973-656-1600. Office Fax: 973-656-1611. Business E-Mail: patrick.stanton@ogletreedeakins.com.

STANTON, PAUL E., JR., academic administrator; b. Atlanta; m. Nancy Stanton; children: Eric, Ryan, Shelley. BS in Chemistry, Emory U., 1965; MD, Med. Coll. Ga., 1969. Gen. and vascular surgery resident, 1969—75; gen. and vascular surgeon, instr. Ga. Bapt. Med. Ctr., Atlanta; chief, divsn. peripheral vascular surgery East Tenn. State U. Coll. Medicine, Johnson City, 1985—86, chmn., dept. surgery, 1986—88, interim dean, Coll. Medicine, and v.p. divsn. health scis., 1988—89, dean of medicine, v.p. health affairs, 1989—97, pres., 1997—. Office: Office of Pres / East Tenn State U PO Box 70734 206 Dosset Hall Lake St Johnson City TN 37614 Office Phone: 423-439-4211. E-mail: stantonp@etsu.edu.

STANTON, ROBERT ALAN, orthopaedic surgeon; b. NYC, June 28, 1946; s. Jay and Shirley (Rader) S.; m. Debby Ellen Beach, June 16, 1973; 1 child, Jim. BA, Williams Coll., 1968; MD, Coll. Physicians and Surgeons, 1972. Intern Columbia-Presbyn. Med. Ctr., NYC, 1972-73, resident in surgery, 1973-74; resident in orthopaedics Yale U., 1974-77; chmn., dir. Orthopedic Specialty Group, P.C., Fairfield, Conn., 1981—; clin. instr., orthopaedics, rehabilitation Yale Univ. Med. Sch. Chmn. Alumni Fund of Williams Coll., Williamstown, Mass., 1993-96; bd. dirs. Bridgeport Hosp. Found., 1988-95; bd. investors Bridgeport Hosp., 1995-2007. Edward John Noble Found. fellow Columbia U., 1969-70. Fellow ACS, Am. Acad. Orthop. Surgeons; mem. Am. Orthop. Soc. Sports Medicine (pres.-elect), Arthrascopy Assn. N.Am., Internat. Soc. for Arthroscopy, Knee Surgery and Orthop. Sports Medicine, Williams Club N.Y., Nantucket Yacht Club, Fairfield County Hunt Club (pres.), Internat. Polo Club (Palm Beach), Aiken Polo Club, Green Boundary Club (Aiken, SC), Wharf Rat Club, Nantucket Anglers Club. Avocations: skiing, polo, tennis, running, gardening. Office: Orthopaedic Specialty Group PC 75 Kings Highway Cutoff Fairfield CT 06824-5340 Office Phone: 203-337-2600.

STANTON, ROBERT JAMES, JR., geologist, educator; b. LA, June 17, 1931; s. Robert James and Audrey (Franke) S.; m. Patricia Ann Burns, Sept. 13, 1953; children: John, Carol. BS, Calif. Inst. Tech., 1953, PhD, 1960; MA, Harvard U., 1956. Research geologist Shell Devel. Co., Houston, 1959-67; mem. faculty Tex. A&M U., 1967—, prof. geology, 1972-86, Ray C. Fish prof. geology, 1986-98, head dept., 1979-83, prof. geology emeritus, 1998—. Vis. prof. U. Nuremburg-Erlangen, Germany, 1984; rsch. assoc. invertebrate paleontology Natural History Mus. L.A. County, 2000-. Co-author: Paleoecology: Principles and Applications, 1981, 2d edit., 1990. Served with AUS, 1953-55. Fellow Geol. Soc. Am.; mem. Internat. Paleontol. Union, Paleontol. Soc., Paleontol. Research Inst., Soc. Econ. Paleontologists and Mineralogists (Outstanding Paper award 1970), Sigma Xi, Tau Beta Pi. Home: 2297 Valleyfield Ave Thousand Oaks CA 91360 Office: Nat Hist Mus LA County Dept Invertebrate Paleontol 900 Exposition Blvd Los Angeles CA 90007 Home Phone: 805-493-1517. Personal E-mail: starton.robertj@gmail.com.

STANTON, ROGER D., lawyer; b. Oct. 4, 1938; s. George W. and Helen V. (Peterson) S.; m. Judith L. Duncan, Jan. 27, 1962; children: Jeffrey B., Brady D. (dec.), Todd A. AB, U. Kans., 1960, JD, 1963. Bar: Kans. 1963, U.S. Dist. Ct. Kans. 1963, U.S. Ct. Appeals (10th cir.) 1972, U.S. Supreme Ct. 1973. Assoc. Stanley, Schroeder, Weeks, Thomas & Lysaught, Kansas City, 1963—68; ptnr. Weeks, Thomas & Lysaught, Kansas City, 1969—81, also bd. dirs., chmn. exec. com., 1981-82; ptnr. Stinson, Mag & Fizzell, Kansas City, 1983-96, chmn. products practice group, also bd. dirs., 1993-95; ptnr. litig. practice Berkowitz Stanton Brandt Williams & Shaw LLP, Prairie Village, Kans., 1997—2005; pvt. practice Overland Pk., Kans., 2005—. Chmn. bd. editors Jour. Kans. Bar Assn., 1975-83; contbr. articles to profl. jours. Active Boy Scouts Am., 1973-79; pres. YMCA Youth Football Club, 1980-82; co-chmn. Civil Justice Reform Act com. Dist. of Kans., 1991-95; bd. dirs. Kans. Appleseed Found., 2000—. Fellow: Am. Bar Found., Am. Coll. Trial Lawyers (state SRSC Com. 1983—88, state chmn. 1984—86, state SRSC Com. 2001—02); mem.: Hist. Soc. Tenth Cir. (bd.dirs. 2005—), Earl O'Conner Inn of Ct. (founding mem. 1991—), Kans. Assn. Def. Counsel (pres. 1977—78), Johnson County Bar Assn. (pres. elect, chmn. bench, bd. dirs., pres. elect), Johnson County Bar Found. (pres., trustee), Kans. Bar Assn. (Pres.'s award 1982), Def. Rsch. Inst. (state co-chmn. 1979—90, Exceptional Performance award 1979), Internat. Assn. Def. Counsel, U. Kans. Kansas City Alumni (bd. dirs. 2001—), U. Kans. Sch. Law Alumni Assn. (bd. dirs. 1975—76, 1985—86), Phi Delta Phi. Office: Ste 500 Bldg 51 9393 W 110th St Overland Park KS 66210 Office Phone: 913-451-6958. Business E-Mail: rstanton@stanton-law.com.

STANTON, RUSS W., editor-in-chief; b. 1958; married; 3 children. BS, Calif. State U., 1981. Bus. reporter Visalia Times-Delta; with San Bernardino County Sun, Riverside Press-Enterprise, Orange County Register; Orange county bus. reporter LA Times, 1997—98, Orange county bus. editor, 1998—2000, asst. bus. editor, 2000—01, sr. tech. editor, 2001—02, dep. bus. editor, 2002—05, bus. editor, 2005—07, innovation editor, 2007—08, editor, 2008—. Fellow Herbert J. Davenport Econ. Prog., U. Mo. Office: LA Times 202 W 1st St Los Angeles CA 90012 E-mail: russ.stanton@latimes.com.*

STANTON, SANDRA SUNQUIST, consultant, educator; b. Morris, Minn., Nov. 4, 1946; d. Herbert Charles and Marie C. Sunquist; m. Robert David Stanton, Apr. 15, 1967; children; Dawn, Jennifer, Heidi. BA, U. Wis., Eau Claire, 1968; MS, U. Wis., Stout, 1980. Cert. tchr., Wis.; cert. counselor, Wis.; cert. elem. adminstr., Wis.; cert. curriculum dir., Wis., Nat. Cert. Counselor, N.C.C., 1984—. Counselor, tchr. Bitburg Am. Dependent Sch., Bitburg AFB, West Germany, 1968-70; sch. counselor Osseo-Fairchild (Wis.) Sch. Dist., 1981-89, Eau Claire Area Pub. Schs., 1989—2004; CEO Connections of the Heart, LLC, 2004—. Project dir. Osseo-Fairchild Devel. Guidance Curriculum K-12, 1985-89; cons. Coop. Edn. Soc. Agy. 10, Chippewa Falls, Wis., 1986-89; final rev. team Wis. Devel. Guidance Model, Madison, 1987; mem. Eau Claire Edn. for Employment coun., 1989-93, Sch. to Work coun., 1993—; mem. Young-Am. Partnership com., 1995—; group leader Applied Acads., 1996—; mem. Brain Rsch. Awareness Integration Network, 2000-; sch. counselor Kunming Internat. Acad., China, 2004; year range to sch. counselor 1981-2004; Health Ed Network Profl. seminar presenter, 2008-; freelance writer 2001-; U-W Stout Sch. Edn. Adv. Bd. mem., 2008-. Contbr. chpts. to books, articles to profl. jours. Pres. bd. dirs. telephone counseling svc. T-A-P Line, Eau Claire, 1982-84; mem. Wis. Tchr.'s Forum. Wis. Dept. Pub. Inst. Project grantee, 1985-89, 87, alcohol and drug abuse project mini grantee, 1991. Mem. NEA, ASCD, Am. Sch. Counselor Assn., Wis. Sch. Counselors Assn. (elem. v.p. 1991-92, chair profl. recognition 1992—, pres. 1997-98, spkr.). Avocations: music, photography, walking, golf, writing. Home: E4520 Woodfield Rd Eau Claire WI 54701-8566 Office Phone: 715-878-4867. Personal E-mail: sandi@ourbrainbuddies.com.

STANTON, SYLVIA DOUCET, artist, gallery owner; b. New Orleans, Sept. 21, 1935; d. Clifton Leo Sr. and Maria Delbert (Alfonso Swiber) Doucet; m. Robert Elmer Stanton, Jan. 3, 1953; children: Robert, Sylvia, Barbara, Richard, Laura, Cheri. Grad. high sch., New Orleans, 1952. Real estate agt. Century 21, Slidell, La., 1982-88; ptnr. Doucet's Jewelry, Slidell, 1969-82; owner Plantation Antiques, Slidell, 1974-88, Magnolia Plantation, Slidell, 1988-97, Doucet-Stanton Ltd., Slidell, 1988-97, Gallery at Milbrook, Picayune, Miss., 2001—05. Appraiser jewelry, antiques, real estate, 1969—; artist, painter, 1950—. Exhibitions include Montserrat Gallery, N.Y.C., Caboose Gallery, Long Beach, Miss., Agora Gallery, NYC, Saatchi Gallery, London, Maggie May's—Off The Coast, Nashville, Maggie May's in Bay, St. Louis, Represented in permanent collections City of New Orleans, exhibitions include Art Ctr., Foley, Ala. Founder Le cotillion, Slidell, 1975; founding chmn. Pres. Coun. of Le Cotillion, 1987. Recieved title of nobility Countess De Miron Delbert, Greece, 1988. Mem.: Allied Artists of Am., New Orleans Art Assn., Inner Wheel (dist chmn. 6840 1990—91, founding pres. Slidell 1989), World Trade Ctr., Albuquerque Art League, Bayou Liberty Garden Club (sec. 1988—), Picayune Garden Club, Ozone Camellia Club. Republican. Roman Catholic. Avocations: art, antiques, gardening, interior decorating. Home: 615 E Lakeshore Dr Carriere MS 39426 Home Phone: 601-798-0002. Personal E-mail: stanfam2@bellsouth.net.

STANTON, WILLIAM ANTHONY, diplomat; b. Jersey City, Jan. 17, 1947; s. Harold Arthur Stanton and Armen Katherine Kharajian; m. Karen Clark Stanton, Sept. 14, 1984; children: Katherine Ruth, Elizabeth Armen. BA, Fordham U., 1968; MA, U. N.C., 1970, PhD, 1978. Fgn. svc. officer, 1978—; consular Embassy Beirut, 1979—81; staff asst. Sec. NE S Asian Affairs, 1982—83; polit. officer U.S. Embassy, Beijing, 1987-90; sr. tng. Hoover Instn., Stanford, Calif., 1990-91; polit.-mil. affairs officer U.S. Embassy, Islamabad, Pakistan, 1991-93; spl. asst. for East Asian affairs Office Under Sec. for Polit. Affairs, U.S. Dept. State, Washington, 1993-94; dep. dir. office Chinese and Mongolian affairs U.S. Dept. State, Washington, 1994-95; min. counselor for polit. affairs U.S. Embassy, Beijing, 1995-98; sr. seminar U.S. Dept. State, Washington, 1998-99, dir. Office of UN Polit. Affairs, 1999-2001, dir. Office of Egyptian and No. African Affairs, 2001—03; dep. chief of mission, US Embassy in Canberra US Dept. State, Washington, 2003, chargé d'affaires ad interim, US Embassy in Canberra, 2005—06; dep. chief of mission US Embassy, Seoul, Republic of Korea, 2006—. Mem. Am. Fgn. Svc. Assn., Phi Beta Kappa. Office: US Embassy Seoul Unit Number 15550 APO AP 96205-5550 E-mail: stantonwa@state.gov.

STANTON, WILLIAM JOHN, JR., marketing educator, author; b. Chgo., Dec. 15, 1919; s. William John and Winifred (McGann) S.; m. Imma Mair, Sept. 14, 1978; children by previous marriage: Kathleen Louise, William John III. BS, Ill. Inst. Tech., 1940; MBA, Northwestern U., 1941, PhD, 1948; D (hon.), Cath. U. Santo Domingo, Dominican Republic, 2003. Mgmt. trainee Sears Roebuck & Co., 1940-41; instr. U. Ala., 1941-44; auditor Olan Mills Portrait Studios, Chattanooga, 1944-46; asst. prof., asso. prof. U. Wash., 1948-55; prof. U. Colo., Boulder, 1955-90; prof. emeritus, 1990—; head mktg. dept. U. Colo., 1955-71, acting dean, 1963-64; assoc. dean U. Colo. (Sch. Bus.), 1964-67; ret. Author: Economic Aspects of Recreation in Alaska, 1953; author: (with others) Challenge of Business, 1975; author: (with M. Etzel and B. Walker) Marketing, 14th edit., 2007, Marketing, Spanish, Chinese, Portuguese, Indonesian and Korean transl., 2003; author: (with R. Varaldo) Italian edit., 2d edit., 1989; author: (with others) South African edit., 1992; author: (with M.S. Sommers and J.G. Barnes) Canadian edit., Fundamentals of Marketing, 11th edit., 2004; author: (with K. Miller and R. Layton) Australian edit., 4th edit., 2000; author: (with Rosann Spiro and G.A. Rich) Management of a Sales Force, 12th edit., Spanish, Portuguese, Chinese, and Russian transl., 2007; contbr. articles to profl. jour. Mem. Am. Mktg. Assn., Mktg. Educators Assn., Beta Gamma Sigma. Roman Catholic. Home: 1445 Sierra Dr Boulder CO 80302-7846 Home Phone: 303-443-3300.

STANTON-HICKS, MICHAEL D'ARCY, anesthesiologist, pain medicine specialist; b. Adelaide, Australia, June 3, 1931; arrived in U.S., 1972; s. Cedric Stanton-Hicks and Florence (Haggett) Perrin; m. Kristina Litsmark, Aug. 4, 1969 (div. Aug. 1984); children: Erik Michael, Leif Neal; m. Ursula Koch, Aug. 27, 1985. MB, BChir, Adelaide U., 1962; Dr. med., U. Dusseldorf, 1984. Bd. equivalent Am. Bd. Anesthesiology; diplomate Am. Bd. Pain Medicine, Interventional Pain Practice, 2002. Intern Queen Elizabeth Hosp., Adelaide, 1961-62, tutor, staff anesthesiologist, 1970-72; resident Royal Postgrad. Med. Sch., London and Lasarettet Köping, 1966-68; asst. dir. anesthesiology intensive care Södersjükhuset, Stockholm, 1968-69; instr. anesthesiology U. Wash. Med. Sch., Seattle, 1969-70, asst. prof., 1972-75; prof., chmn. dept. U. Mass. Med. Sch., Worcester, 1975-83; prof. U. Colo. Health Scis. Ctr., Denver, 1983-86, vice chmn. dept., 1983-85, acting chmn., 1985-86; prof., dir. pain clinic and rsch. Johannes Gutenberg U., Mainz, Germany, 1986-88, prof., 1986—97; dir. pain mgmt. ctr. Cleve. Clinic Found., 1988-98, vice chmn. pain mgmt. and rsch. divsn. anesthesia, 1998—; prof. Lerner Coll. Medicine, Case Western Res. U., Cleve., 2004—; staff physician Shaker Pediat. Pain Program, 2008—; with Dept. Functional Neurosurgery, 2009—. Med. examiner Indsl. Commn. Ohio; mem. Ohio Pain Adv. Com., Dept. Health; mem. liaison com. med. bd. Ohio Pain Com.; advisor Am. Acad. Disability Evaluating Physicians, 2000-02; appt. to gov.'s task force on compassionate care, Dept. of Health, Ohio; bd. dirs. World Inst. Pain; sci. advisor Reflex Sympathetic Dystrophy Assn., 2006. Author, editor Regional Anesthesia: Advances and Selected Topics, 1978, (with Boas) Chronic Low Back Pain, 1982; author, editor: (with Wilson and Harden) CRPS: Current Diagnosis and Therapy, 2005; co-author: (with Raj and Nolte) Illustrated Manual of Regional Anesthesia, 1988 (Most Beautiful Book of Yr. award Frankfurt, Fed. Republic Germany Pubs. Book Conv., 1989), (with Janig and Boas) Reflex Sympathetic Dystrophy, 1989, (with Janig) Reflex Sympathetic Dystrophy: A Reappraisal, 1996; author: Pain and Sympathetic Nervous System, 1989; exec. editor Pain Practice Jour., 2001—, sect. editor Complex Regional Pain Syndrome, 2002, mem. editl. bd. Pain Physician, 2002—. Squadron leader res. Royal Australian Air Force, 1962-65. Named Scientist of Yr. Am. Herschel Soc., 1991-92; recipient Disting. Scientist award Reflex Sympathetic Dystrophy Assn., 2002, Disting. Svc. award European Soc. Regional Anesthesia, 2003, Lifetime Achievement award, Am. Soc. Interventional Pain Physicians, 2007; Australian Univs. Commn. mature age scholar, 1953-60. Fellow Royal Coll. Surgeons (faculty anesthetists), Royal Coll. Anesthetists, Am. Acad. Pain Medicine, Interventional Pain Practice; mem. Internat. Assn. Study Pain (chmn. spl. interest group pain and sympathetic nervous sys. 1990-2008), World Inst. Pain (bd. dirs. 1995—), Am. Soc. Regional Anesthesia (bd. dirs. 1979-91, pres. 1989-90, Disting. Svc. award, 1998), Assn. Anesthetists Gt. Britain and Ireland, Ohio State Med. Assn., Cleve. Acad. Medicine, Am. Acad. Med. Infrared Imaging (bd. dirs. 1991-95, pres. 1994-95, William Hobbins Rsch. award 1993), Am. Acad. Disability Evaluating Physicians (adv. com. mem. complex regional pain syndrome 2000—02), Am. Pain Soc., Am. Acad. Pain Medicine, Am. Neuromodulation Soc. (pres. 1994-98, bd. dirs. 1998-2000), Reflex Sympathetic Dystrophy Assn. (sci. adv. bd. 2000-05), Am. Soc. Interventional Pain Practice (Lifetime Achievement award 2007), Army-Navy-Air Force Club. Republican. Anglican. Avocations: skiing, photography, travel, flying. Home: 11405 Clearfield Lane Chardon OH 44024 Office: Cleve Clinic Found 9500 Euclid Ave Cleveland OH 44195-0001 Office Phone: 216-445-9559. Business E-Mail: stantom@ccf.org.

STANTURF, JOHN ALVIN, IV, soil scientist, researcher; b. Monterey, Calif., Feb. 16, 1948; s. Jack Alvin and Mabel (Zirk) S.; m. Barbara Clowers, Aug. 12, 1966 (div. July 1973); children: Colleen, Jeremy (dec.); m. Eileen Sullivan, June 12, 1977. BS, Mont. State U., 1974; MS, Cornell U., 1979, PhD, 1983. Cert. profl. soil scientist. Asst. soil scientist Dept. Natural Resources, Helena, Mont., 1974; research asst. Ctr. Environ. Research, Ithaca, N.Y., 1975-77; postdoctoral fellow Technion-Israel Inst. Tech., Haifa, 1982-83; research forester U.S. Forest Service, Warren, Pa., 1983-85; dir. Allegheny Research Devel. Ctr., Bradford, Pa., 1985-89;, 1985-89; assoc. dir. Pa. Hardwoods Devel. Coun., University Park, 1989-90; rsch. scientist Union Camp, Savannah, Ga., 1990-92; project leader U.S. Forest Svc., Stoneville, Miss., 1992—. Adj. prof. Auburn U., 1994—, Miss. State U., 1994—; edtl. adv. bd. Forest Ecology and Mgmt.; chair consortium for rsch. Southern Forested Wetlands, 1994—. Author: (with others) Conservation and Management Tidal Wetlands Southeast Asia, 1987; (software) Nutrient Cycling, 1979; author, tech. editor (film) Soil Taxonomy, 1982; contbr. articles to profl. jours. Recipient Program of Yr. award Mont. Broadcasting Assn., 1971; fellow German Acad. Exchange Svc., Munich, Fed. Republic of Germany, 1976, Lady Davis fellow, Technion, Haifa, 1982. Mem. Soil Sci. Soc. Am., Soc. Am. Foresters, Internat. Soc. Tropical Foresters, Soc. Wetland Scientists, Coun. on Forest Engring., So. Hardwood Forest Group. Democrat. Baptist. Avocations: furniture making and restoration, photography, gardening. Office: So Hardwood Lab PO Box 227 Stoneville MS 38776-0227

STANUTZ, DONALD J., chemicals executive; Various sr. positions Texaco Chem. Co.; with Huntsman Corp., 1994—, exec. v.p. polyurethanes, PO and performance chems., 1999—2000, exec. v.p. global sales and mktg., 2000—01, exec. v.p., COO Huntsman LLC, 2001—04, divsn. pres. performance products, 2004—. Office: Huntsman Corp 500 Huntsman Way Salt Lake City UT 84108 Office Phone: 801-584-5700.

STAPLES, DONALD EDWARD, radio, film and television educator; b. NYC, Apr. 15, 1934; s. Edward Daniel and Ethlyne Babcock Staples; m. Diane Staunton, June 2, 1956 (div. July 1980); children: Douglas Arthur, Daniel Charles; m. Kristen Petersen, Nov. 26, 1982; stepchildren: Julia Lynn Smith, Susan Smith Milner. BS in Speech, Northwestern U., 1955; MA in Cinema, U. So. Calif., 1959; PhD, Northwestern U., 1967. Instr. So. Ill. U., Carbondale, 1959-63; lectr. Northwestern U., Evanston, Ill., 1963-65; asst. prof. Ohio State U., Columbus, 1965-68, assoc. prof., 1968-69; prof. NYU, NYC, 1969-79, Vassar Coll., Poughkeepsie, N.Y., 1972-74, U. North Tex., Denton, 1979—2004, prof.

emeritus, 2004—. Author, editor: American Cinema, 3d edit., 1991; co-author: Film Encounter, 1973; contbr. articles, film revs. to profl. jours. Mem. Greater Denton Arts Coun., 1980—, Denton Cmty. Theatre, 1980—; bd. dirs. Nat. Mus. Comms., Irving, Tex., 1983-93; juror film festivals, 1969—; mem. adv. bd. Arts and Humanities Citation Index, Phila., 1979—. Lt. (j.g.) USN, 1955-57. Univ. scholar U. So. Calif., 1957-59, Northwestern U., 1963-65; Danforth Found. assoc., 1968-85. Mem. SAG, Soc. for Cinema Studies (pres. 1974-75), Univ. Film and Video Assn. (pres. 1975-77, life mem.), Internat. Congress of Schs. of Film and TV (v.p. 1982-86), Univ. Film and Video Found. (trustee emeritus), Dallas Corinthian Yacht Club (bd. dirs. 1995-98). Methodist. Avocations: sailing, golf. Home: 2901 Montecito Dr Denton TX 76205-8513 Office: U North Tex Dept Radio/TV/Film Denton TX 76203 Personal E-mail: dkstaples2@verizon.net.

STAPLES, GEORGE MCDADE, Director, Fgn Serv, United States Department State, former ambassador; b. 1947; m. Jo Ann; 1 child, Catherine. BA, U. So. Calif., 1970; MS, Ctrl. Mich. U. With U.S. Fgn. Svc., El Salvador, Uruguay, Equatorial Guinea, Bahamas, Zimbabwe, 1961-81, sr. Turkey desk officer Bur. European Affairs Washington, sr. watch officer State's Ops. Ctr., dep. chief of mission Bahrain; US amb. to Rwanda US Dept. State, Kigali, Rwanda, 1999—2001, US amb. to Equatorial Guinea & Cameroon, 2001—04; nat. security affairs fellow Hoover Instn., Stanford U., 1995-96; polit. advisor to Supreme Allied Comdr. NATO, Brussels, 2004—06; dir. US Fgn. Svc. US Dept. State, Washington, 2006—, dir. human resources, 2006—. Officer USAF, 1970-78. Office: US Dept State Harry S Truman Bldg 2201 C St NW Rm 6218 Washington DC 20520 E-mail: rwandaamb@yahoo.com.

STAPLES, HEIDI L, poet, writer; b. Dade County, Fla., Dec. 12, 1971; d. Jeaniene Eddye Cole and Robert Wesley Kitchen; m. John V. Staples, May 16, 2004. PhD in English Lit. and Creative Writing, U. Ga., 2003. Edn. assoc. Planned Parenthood, Syracuse, 1994—95; writing instr. Syracuse U., 1996—98; tefl instr. The Lang. Ho., Prague, Czech Republic, 1998—99; asst. to the editors Ga. Rev., Athens, 2002—03; writing instr. U. Ga., 2002—03; part-time faculty Syracuse U., NY, 2003—. Co-founder and co-editor Parakeet, Syracuse, NY, 2003—05; asst. editor Verse, Athens, Ga., 2001—03; asst. coord. Helen Lanier Speaker's Series, Chaired Series of the UGA English Dept., Athens, Ga., 2001—03; asst. editor Salt Hill, Syracuse, 1997—98, poetry editor, 1995—97. Founder and moderator Grad. Student Reading Series, Athens, Ga., 2002—03; judge Ga. Scholastic Assn., Athens, Ga., 2001; mentor Syracuse Mentor and Youth in Learning Program, 1995—98; hotline counselor Athens Rape Crisis Line, Ga., 1992—93. Scholar Grad. Sch. scholarship, Syracuse U., 1995—98; Grad. assistantship, U. of Ga., 2002—03, Tchg. assistantship, 2000—02, Summer Rsch. grant, Syracuse U., 1996, fellowship, 1995—96. Mem.: PEN, Assoc. Writing Programs. D-Liberal. Avocations: baking, piano, canoeing. Office: Syracuse Univ 240 Hbc Syracuse NY 13210 Home: 34 New Haven Mauritioustown Rosslare Strand Ireland Personal E-mail: hlkitche@syr.edu.

STAPLES, LOLA ROEBUCK, healthcare educator; d. Enos Wood and Frances Mary Sloane; m. James Staples; children: Stephen Craig Roebuck Jr., Tracy Lynette Roebuck, Duane Anthony. BS, Am. U., DC, 1976; MS, Bowie State U., Md., 1990. Cert. in project mgmt. Villanova U., 2004. Computer programmer, analyst Dept. Health and Human Svcs., Food and Drug Adminstrn., Rockville, Md., 1976—80; commd. officer US Pub. Health Svc., Rockville, Md., 1980—2004, computer sys. analyst, programmer, 1985—89, health svcs. officer, sr. staffing officer, 1989—92; pub. health analyst Health and Human Svcs., Pub. Health Svc., Maternal and Child Health, Rockville, 1992—95; program devel. coord. HHS, Pub. Health Svc., Maternal and Child Health, Rockville, 1994—95; computer sys. analyst Health and Human Svcs., Pub. Health Svc., Medicare and Medicaid Svcs., Balt., 1997—2005; adj. prof. Bowie State U., Md., 1999—. Chair Bus. and Profl. Women's Club, Landover, Md., 1988—92. Decorated PHS Achievement medal US Pub. Health Svc., Surgeon Gens. Exemplary Svc. award, Crisis Response Svc. award, Commendation medal, Spl. Assignment award; recipient Equal Opportunity Achievement award, Dept. Health and Human Svcs., 1989, Administrator's Achievement award, Ctrs. Medicare and Medicaid Svcs., 2001; named Women of Yr., Govt. Md., 1988. Mem.: Health Care Execs. (life), Alpha Kappa Alpha. Roman Catholic. Achievements include development of Lincoln Park after school program. Avocation: travel. Office: Bowie State Univ 14000 Jerico Park Rd BGS Rm 3326 Bowie MD 20715-9465 Personal E-mail: lstaples1@msn.com. Business E-Mail: lstaples@bowiestate.edu.

STAPLES, LYLE NEWTON, lawyer; b. Radford, Va., Feb. 16, 1945; s. Lester Lyle and Velma Jean (King) S.; m. Christie Mercedes Carr, Feb. 1, 1971; children: Scott Andrew, John Randolph, Brian Matthew, Melissa Ann. BA, U. Md., 1967, JD, 1972; LLM in Taxation, Georgetown U., 1977. Bar: Md. 1973, U.S. Supreme Ct. 1978, U.S. Tax Ct. 1981, U.S. Dist. Ct. Md. 1981, U.S. Ct. Appeals (4th cir.) 1981. Tax law specialist IRS, Washington, 1972-77; assoc. Hessey & Hessey, Balt., 1978-82, Rosenstock, Burgee & Welty, Frederick, Md., 1982-84; sole practice Hampstead, Md., 1984-91; mem. firm Johnson, Parker & Hess, Westminster, Md., 1991-96; pvt. practice Westminster, 1996—. Vis. asst. prof. Towson (Md.) State U., 1981—82. Treas., bd. dirs. Literacy Coun. of Carroll County, Inc., 1993-98. Served with U.S. Army, 1968-69, Vietnam. Mem. ABA, Md. Bar Assn., Fin. Planning Assn., Carroll County C. of C. Democrat. Methodist. Home: 813 Clearview Ave Hampstead MD 21074-2325 Office: Ste 210 79 E Main St Westminster MD 21157-5026 Office Phone: 410-840-2000. E-mail: lstaples@infionline.net.

STAPLES, MAVIS, singer; b. Chgo., 1940; d. Roebuck "Pops" and Oceloa S. Singer Staple Singers, 1951—; represented by United, 1954, Vee Jay Label, 1956, CBS/Epic, 1964, Stax, 1968, Curtom, 1975. Opened for Prince's overseas tour, 1990; provided back-up vocals for Ray Charles, Kenny Loggins, Marty Stuart and others. Albums include Mavis Staples, 1969, Only for the Lonely, 1970, A Piece of the Action, 1977, Mavis Staples, 1984, Time Waits for No One, 1989, The Voice, 1993, Spirituals & Gospel: Dedicated to Mahalia Jackson, 1996, Have a Little Faith, 2004, We'll Never Turn Back, 2007, Live: Hope at the Hideout, 2008. Single "Uncloudy Day" reached number one on gospel charts; single "I'll Take you There" reached number one on gospel and rythym and blues charts, 1993. Office: c/o 525 Worldwide Music PO Box 957 Salem MA 01970 also: c/o The Rosebud Agy PO Box 170429 San Francisco CA 94117*

STAPLES, NATHAN CHARLES, biology professor; s. Oliver Samuel and Brunette Darling Staples; m. Michelle Kathleen Androvich, May 10, 1997; children: Sarah Noelle, Matthew Stephen. BS in Biology, Loyola Marymount U., LA, 1993; degree in Biochemistry, Loyola Marymount U., 1993; PhD in Molecular, Cellular & Devel. Biology, U. Calif., Santa Barbara, 2002. Lectr. Life Scis., U. Calif., Santa Barbara, 2000—04; assoc. prof., biol. scis. Cañada Coll., Redwood City, Calif., 2004—. Rsch. fellow Industry Initiatives Sci. & Math Edn. & Genencor Internat., Inc., Palo Alto, Calif., 2006. Vol. Queen Apostles Ch., San Jose, Calif., 2008. Mem.: Barbershop Harmony Soc. (bd. mem. 1999—2004, Rookie of Yr. 1998), Alpha Sigma Nu, Sigma Xi, Nat. Sci. Rsch. Soc. Roman Cath. Avocations: singing, art, basketball, bicycling. Office: Cañada Coll 4200 Farm Hill Blvd Santa Clara CA 95051

STAPLETON, BEVERLY COOPER, aerospace executive; b. Birmingham, Ala., June 4, 1933; d. Herston MacAger and Virginia (Averyt) Cooper; m. John Parker Stapleton, Aug. 31, 1959 (div. July 1981); children: Lisa Karen, Lawrence Cooper BBA magna cum laude, U. Miami, 1954; MA, U. Ala., 1960. Tchr. Miami Beach H.S. Dade County Pub. Schs., Fla., 1956—59; mem. behavior R & D program U. Ala., Tuscaloosa, 1959—61; contracts adminstr. Houghton Mifflin Co., Palo Alto, Calif., 1974—78; Calif. sales rep. Prentice-Hall Inc., San Jose, 1978; contract adminstr., cost analyst United Techs., Sunnyvale, Calif., 1978—82; mgr. contract adminstrn. Echo Sci. Corp., Mountain View, Calif., 1982; contracts mgr. Lockheed Martin Corp. Missiles & Space, Sunnyvale, 1982—98; ret., 1998. Instr. master's program in contracts and material mgmt. St. Mary's Coll., Moraga, Calif., 1984—86; mem. adv. bd. grad. program in contracts and acquisition mgmt. Golden Gate U., San Francisco, 1984—85; contracts mgr. Hubble Space Telescope Program, 1983—85. Fellow polit. sci. U. Ala., 1954-55; recipient Women of Achievement award Santa Clara County Commn. on Status of Women, 1985 Fellow Nat. Contract Mgmt. Assn. (cert., pres. San Francisco area chpt. 1984-85, nat. coun. fellows 1983—, nat. exec. com. 1986-88, nat. bd. dirs. 1985-86, 97-98, nat. v.p. 1987-88), Mgmt. Assn. (treas. Chem. Systems divsn., 1981), Beta Gamma Sigma, Delta Delta Delta Democrat. Presbyterian.

STAPLETON, CRAIG ROBERTS, former ambassador; b. Kansas City, Mo. m. Dorothy Walker, 1971; children: Walker, Wendy Reyes. BA magna cum laude, Harvard U., 1967, MBA. Real estate exec., pres. Marsh and McLennan Real Estate Advs., Inc., NYC, 1982—2001; US amb. to Czech Republic US Dept. State, Prague, 2001—03, US amb. to France and Monaco Paris, 2005—09. Ptnr. Tex. Rangers, 1989—98; chmn. Conn. State Re-Election Campaign George W. Bush, 2004; bd. dirs. Allegheny Properties, Metro PCS, TB Woods and Winston Ptnrs. Former bd. dirs. Peace Corps; pres. Vaclav Havel Found.; trustee Brunswick Sch., Greenwich, Conn.; vis. com., other coms. Harvard U. Recipient Jan Masaryk Medal for Svc. to Czech Republic.*

STAPLETON, F. BRUDER, pediatric nephrologist, academic administrator; b. Lawrence, Kans., Dec. 19, 1946; s. Harold Jack and Hazel Maria Stapleton; m. Barbara R. Stapleton, Sept. 16, 1969; children: Hillary J., F. Reed. BA, U. Kans., 1968, MD, 1972. Cert. Am. Bd. Pediat., in pediatric nephrology. Residency U. Kans. Med. Ctr., Kansas City, fellowship; residency U. Wash. Sch. Medicine, Seattle, Ford/Morgan Prof. and Chair, dept. pediat., 1996—; prof. pediat. U. Tenn. Coll. Medicine, Memphis, 1979—89; pediatrician Children's Hosp. Buffalo, 1989—96; chair dept. pediat. SUNY, 1989—96; pediatrician-in-chief Children's Hosp. and Med. Ctr., Seattle, 1996—, sr. v.p., chief academic officer, dir., dept. medicine. Contbr. articles to profl. jours.; founding editor-in-chief: Jour. Watch Pediat. and Adolescent Medicine, 2002—. Bd. dirs. Seattle Cancer Care Alliance, Ronald McDonald Children's Home, Buffalo, 1993—95, Seattle, 2000—. Lt. comdr. USN, 1977—79. Fellow pediatric nephrology, U. Kans., Kansas City, 1974—77. Mem.: Am. Bd. Pediat. (bd. dirs. 1998—2004, chair subspecialties com.), Am. Soc. Pediatric Nephrology (pres. 1995—96), Assn. Med. Sch. Dept. Chairs (pres. 2005—07), Internat. Pediatric Nephrology Assn. (treas. 2001—04). Home: 4693 NE 89th St Seattle WA 98115 Office: Childrens Hosp Dept Pediatrics CH-65 4800 Sand Point Way NE T-0211 Seattle WA 98105 Business E-Mail: bruder.stapleton@seattlechildrens.org. E-mail: bstaplet@u.washington.edu.

STAPLETON, HARVEY JAMES, physics professor; b. Kalamazoo, Dec. 22, 1934; s. Herbert James and Viola Delia (Early) S.; m. Joan Eilleen Sylvander, June 22, 1957; children: Patricia Lynne, Susan Joan, Jeffrey Denis. BS, U. Mich., 1957; PhD, U. Calif., Berkeley, 1961. Faculty physics U. Ill., Urbana, 1961—, prof., 1969-95, prof. emeritus, 1995—, assoc. dean Grad. Coll., 1980-95, assoc. vice chancellor for rsch., 1987-95; interim dean Grad. Coll., 1992; interim vice chancellor for rsch. U. Ill., 1992. Alfred P. Sloan fellow, 1962-64 Contbr. articles to profl. jours. Fellow Am. Phys. Soc.; mem. Phi Beta Kappa, Sigma Xi, Phi Sigma Kappa, Phi Kappa Phi, Phi Eta Sigma. Roman Catholic. Home: 3806 Gulf Of Mexico Dr Unit 310 Longboat Key FL 34228-2733 Personal E-mail: hjstapleton@comcast.net.

STAPLETON, JAMES FRANCIS, lawyer; b. Bridgeport, Conn., June 30, 1932; s. James M. and Lucy V. (Moran) S.; m. Margaret M. Daly, July 13, 1957; children: James F., Mark T., Paul and Kathleen. BSS, Fairfield U., 1954; LLB, Boston Coll., 1957; LLM, Georgetown U., 1958. Bar: Conn. 1957, U.S. Dist. Ct. (ea. and so. dists.) N.Y. 1979, U.S. Ct. Appeals (2d cir.) 1966, U.S. Dist. Ct. Conn. 1961, Mass. 1957, U.S. Supreme Ct. 1965. Atty., Appellate Sect., Antitrust Divsn. U.S. Dept. Justice, 1957-58; assoc., ptnr. Marsh, Day & Calhoun, Bridgeport, 1958-73; city atty. City of Bridgeport, 1971-73; legis. counsel Conn. Bankers Assn., 1971-73; judge Conn. Superior Ct., 1973-78; chmn. Criminal Justice Commn. State of Conn., 1991-95; ptnr. Day, Berry & Howard, Stamford, Conn., 1978—2002, of coun., 2003—. Active Bridgeport Bd. Edn., 1960—69. Fellow Am. Bar Found., Am. Coll. Trial Lawyers (chmn. state com. 1994-96, regent 1996-2000), Coll. Comml. Arbitrators; mem. ABA (ho. of dels. 1984-88), Am. Bd. Trial Advocates, Conn. Bar Assn. (bd. govs., ho. of dels., v.p., pres.), Fed. Bar Coun. Found. for 2d Cir. (v.p., chmn.). Home: 6 Winding Way Trumbull CT 06611 Office: Day Pitney LLP One Audubon St New Haven CT 06511 Personal E-mail: jfstapleton@daypitney.com.

STAPLETON, JAMES HALL, retired statistician, educator; b. Royal Oak, Mich., Feb. 8, 1931; s. James Leo and Dorothy May (Hall) S.; m. Alicia M. Brown, Apr. 3, 1963; children: James, Lara, Sara. BA, Eastern Mich. U., 1952; MS, Purdue U., 1954, PhD, 1957. Statistician Gen. Electric Co., 1957-58; asst. prof. stats. and probability Mich. State U., East Lansing, 1958-63, assoc. prof., 1963-72, prof., 1972—2007, chmn. dept., 1968-75, grad. dir., 1987—2006. Cons. Gen. Telephone Co. of Ind.; vis. prof. U. Philippines, 1978-79 Mem. USS-Mich. Swim Com., AAU, 1976-84, chmn., 1976-78; mem. Mich. AAU Exec. Bd., 1976-81. NSF fellow, 1966-67 Mem. Inst. Math. Stats., Am. Statis. Assn. Office: Mich State U Dept Statistics East Lansing MI 48823 Office Phone: 517-355-9678. E-mail: stapleton@stt.msu.edu, staplet5@aol.com.

STAPLETON, JEAN, journalism educator; b. Albuquerque, June 24, 1942; d. James L. and Mary (Behrman) S.; m. John Clegg, Apr. 15, 1965 (dec. Sept. 1972); m. Richard Bright, Jan. 13, 1973 (div. 1985); children: Lynn, Paul Bright; m. William Walter Farran, Nov. 9, 1996. BA, U. N.Mex., 1964; MS in Journalism, Northwestern U., 1968. Reporter Glenview (Ill.) Announcements, 1967-68, Angeles Mesa News Advertiser, LA, 1968-69, City News Svc., Radio News West, LA, 1969-71; press sec. polit. campaign, 1972; instr. journalism East L.A. Coll., 1973-75, prof., dept. chair, 1975—. Author: Equal Marriage, 1975, Equal Dating, 1979. Recipient Lifetime Achievement award, Journalism Edn. Coalition, 2006. Mem. NOW (pres. LA chpt. 1973-74), Soc. Profl. Journalists, LA Poets and Writers Collective. Democrat. Methodist. Home: 3232 Philo St Los Angeles CA 90064-4719 Office: East LA Coll 1301 Avenida Cesar Chavez Monterey Park CA 91754-6001 Office Phone: 323-265-8875. Business E-Mail: staplej@elac.edu.

STAPLETON, KATHARINE HALL (KATIE STAPLETON), commentator, writer; m. Benjamin Franklin Stapleton; children: Benjamin Franklin III, Craig Roberts, Katharine Hall. BA, Vassar Coll., 1941. Prodr., writer, host Cooking with Katie Sta. KOA, 1979—89. Author: Denver Delicious, 1980, 3d edit., 1983, High Notes, 1985. Chmn. women's divsn. United Fund, 1955-56; founder, chmn. Denver Debutante Ball, 1955, 56; hon. chmn. Nat. Travelers Aid Assn., 1952-56; commr. Denver Centennial Authority, 1958-60; trustee Washington Cathedral, regional v.p., 1967-73; trustee Colo. Women's Coll., 1975-80; sole trustee Harmes C. Fishback Found., 1989-; hon. chmn. Le Bal à Versailles, 2000-07, Rocky Mountain Planned Parenthood Campaign, 2007. Decorated Chevalier de L'Etoile Noire (France), officer comdr. Confrerie des Chevaliers du tastevin; recipient People-to-People citations, 1960, 66, Beautiful Activist award, Colo.-Wyo. Restaurant Assn. award, 1981, Humanitarian of Yr. award Arthritis Found., 1995, Arts award Colo. Symphony, 1998; Outstanding Vol. Fundraiser, Nat. Philanthropy Day, 1995, Outstanding Alumna, Barstow Sch., 2003, Girl Scout award, 2006., Jr. League Denver Founders award, 2009 Mem. Denver Country Club. Republican. Episcopalian. Home: 8 Village Rd Cherry Hills Village CO 80113-4908 E-mail: kties@aol.com.

STAPLETON, WALTER KING, federal judge; b. Cuthbert, Ga., June 2, 1934; s. Theodore Newton and Elizabeth Grantland (King) Stapleton; m. Georgianna Duross Stapleton; children: Russell K., Theodore N., Teryl J. BA, Princeton, 1956; LLB, Harvard, 1959; LLM, U. Va., 1984. Bar: Del. Assoc. Morris, Nichols, Arsht & Tunnell, Wilmington, Del., 1959—65; dep. atty. gen. State of Del., 1963—64; ptnr. Morris, Nichols, Arsht & Tunnell, 1966—70; judge US Dist. Ct., Wilmington, Del., 1970—85, chief judge, 1983—85; judge US Ct. Appeals (3d cir.), 1985—99, sr. judge, 1999—. Mem. Jud. Conf. US, 1984—85. Bd. dirs. Am. Bapt. Chs., 1978. Mem.: ABA, Del. Bar Assn., Am. Jud. Soc. Baptist. Office: US Ct Appeals Lockbox 33 5323 Fedl Bldg 844 N King St Wilmington DE 19801-3519*

STAPP, DAN ERNEST, retired lawyer, utilities executive; b. New Orleans, July 1, 1934; s. James Frank Stapp Jr. and Marguerite Edna (Joubert) Stapp; m. Barbara Allan Wilmot, June 10, 1961; children: Marguerite Wilmot(dec.), Mary Darby, Paul Wilmot(dec.), James Andrew. BBA, Loyola U., New Orleans, 1955, LL.B., 1957. Bar: La. 1957. With New Orleans Pub. Service Inc., 1958-68, asst. to v.p., 1965-68; with Entergy Svcs. (formerly MSU System Svcs. Inc.), New Orleans, 1968-92; v.p., sec., asst. treas. Entergy Svcs., 1968-80, sr. v.p., 1980-92. Sec. System Fuels, Inc., New Orleans, 1972-92, Entergy Corp. (formerly Middle South Utilities, Inc.), New Orleans, 1974-92, Systems Entergy Resources, Inc., Jackson, Miss., 1974-91, Electec, Inc., 1984-91, Entergy Ops., Inc., 1990-91, Entergy Power, Inc., 1990-92. Trustee Mercy Hosp., New Orleans, 1973-80, pres., 1975, chmn. bd. devel., 1971-72; mem. pres.'s coun. Loyola U., 1975-85, chmn., 1980-82; adv. coun. Coll. Bus. Adminstrn., 1969-70; mem. adv. bd. Asso. Cath. Charities, 1979-82; gen. chmn. United Way Greater New Orleans, 1978, trustee, 1978-84; mem. exec. bd. New Orleans Area coun. Boy Scouts Am., 1980-85, pres., 1984-85. 2d lt. AUS, 1957. Mem. La. Bar Assn., New Orleans Country Club, Blue Key (past chpt. pres.), Alpha Sigma Nu, Delta Theta Phi. Republican. Roman Catholic. Home: 19415 Kelly Wood Ct Baton Rouge LA 70809

STAPP, HENRY PIERCE, physicist; b. Cleve., Mar. 23, 1928; s. Sarah Reeves Clapp Shupe Stapp and Davis Pierce Shupe; m. Olivia Brewer Stapp, Jan. 29, 1965; 1 child, Henry Pierce Shupe Stapp IV. PhD in Physics, U. Calif., Berkeley, 1956. Theoretical physicist Lawrence Berkeley Nat. Lab., Calif., 1952—. Author: (book) Quantum Dualism: an Alternative to Materialism, Philosophy of Mind and the Problem of Free Will in the Light of Quantum Mechanics, Mindful Universe: Quantum Mechanics and the Participating Observer., Mind, Matter, and Quantum Mechanics. Recipient Albert Einstein award, UNESCO, 1979. Office: Lawrence Berkeley Nat Lab Univ Calif Berkeley CA 94720

STAPP, JOSHUA PAUL, computer engineer; s. Philip Stapp and Karen Elizabeth Kaucher; m. Melissa Ann Tiseo, Aug. 6, 2004; children: Riley Charles, Grace Elizabeth. BS, NJ. Inst. Tech., Newark, 2003; MS in Engring., Stevens Inst. Tech., Hoboken, NJ, 2006. Cert. level III r&d engr.; sys planner, US Dept. Def., Picatinny Arsenal, NJ, 2008. Computer engr. US Dept. Def., 2003—. Cons. Stapp Techs. LLC, Belvidere, NJ, 2008—. Personal E-mail: stapptech@gmail.com.

STAPRANS, ARMAND, electronics executive; b. Riga, Latvia, Feb. 28, 1931; s. Theodore and Elvira (Ulmanis) S.; m. Vija Spalvins, Sept. 25, 1955; children: Silvija, Armin, Erik. Student, Willamette U., 1949-52; BSEE, U. Calif., Berkeley, 1954, MSEE, 1955, PhDEE, 1959. Rsch. asst. dept. elec. engring. U. Calif., 1955-57; engr. microwave tube div. Varian Assocs., Palo Alto, Calif., 1957-60, engring. mgr., 1960-68, ops. mgr., 1978-78, 86-89, chief engr., 1978-86, gen. mgr. coupled cavity tube divsn., 1989-92, v.p., 1990-95; gen. mgr. microwave power tube products, 1992-95; pres. microwave power tube products divsn. Comms. and Power Inds., Palo Alto, Calif., 1995-98; mgmt. cons., 1999—. Contbr. articles to profl. jours., chpt. to book; patentee microwave tubes field. Fellow IEEE (electron device adminstrv. com. 1983-88). Home: 445 Knoll Dr Los Altos CA 94024-4732 Office: Comm & Power Inds M S B 100 Microwave Power Tube Prod Divsn PO Box 50750 Palo Alto CA 94303-0665 Home Phone: 650-948-9521.

STAR, ALEXANDER, chemist, educator; b. Almaty, Kazakhstan, May 8, 1971; s. Victor Star and Regina Koritny-Star; m. Angela Goldman, Aug. 13, 1992; children: David, Michelle. BSc in Chemistry, Tel Aviv U., 1994, PhD in Chemistry, 2000. Postdoctoral assoc. UCLA, Calif., 2002; sr. scientist Nanomix Inc., Emeryville, Calif., 2002—05; asst. prof. U. of Pitts., Pitts., 2005—. Cons. Nanomix Inc., Emeryville, Calif., 2005—07. Contbr. articles to profl. jours. Recipient Intel award, Intel, 1998; grantee, NSF, 2003—04, 2007—, DOE, 2003, EPA, 2003; fellow Buchmann Doctoral fellow, Buchmann Fund, 1996—99; scholar Schwarz Meml. Grad. scholar, Schwarz Fund, 1997. Mem.: Israel Chem. Soc., Materials Rsch. Soc., Am. Chem. Soc. Achievements include patents for carbon nanotube sensors; research in chemistry of carbon nanotubes; development of industrial gas nantechnological sensors; invention of medical breath and bio-nanoelectronic sensors; patents pending for fabrication of nanosensor arrays. Office: University of Pittsburgh 219 Parkman Ave Pittsburgh PA 15260 Office Fax: 412-624-4027. Business E-Mail: astar@pitt.edu.

STARBUCK, WILLIAM HAYNES, business management educator; b. Portland, Ind., Sept. 20, 1934; AB in Physics, Harvard Coll., 1956; MS in Indsl. Adminstrn., Carnegie Inst. Tech., 1959, PhD in Indsl. Adminstrn., 1964; PhD (hon.), U. Stockholm, 1995, U. Paris, 2004, Paul Cezanne U., 2006. Instr. indsl. mgmt. and econs. Purdue U., West Lafayette, Ind., 1960-64, from asst. prof. to assoc. prof. adminstrv. scis. and econs., 1964-67; prof. adminstrn. Grad. Sch. Bus. and Pub.

Adminstrn. Cornell U., 1967-71, prof. sociology Coll. Arts and Scis., 1968-71; sr. rsch. fellow Internat. Inst. Mgmt., Berlin, 1971—74; Helfaer prof. bus. adminstrn. U. Wis., Milw., 1974-84; ITT prof. creative mgmt. NYU, NYC, 1985—2005, prof. emeritus, 2005—; prof. in residence U. Oreg., 2005—. Vis. assoc. prof. social rels. Johns Hopkins U., 1966—67; vis. prof. adminstrn. London Grad. Sch. Bus. Studies, 1970—71; chmn. Coll. on Orgn., Inst. Mgmt. Scis., 1973—74; rsch. prof. U. Wis., Milw., 1974—75; vis. prof. Norwegian Sch. Econs. and Bus. Adminstrn., Bergen, 1977—78, Stockholm Sch. Econs., U. Gothenburg, Sweden, 1977—78, U. Versailles, 1998, U. Canterbury, 1999, 2007, U. Paris IX, 1999, U. Oreg., 1999, U. Aix-Marseilles, 2000, 03, 06, U. Oxford, 2004, 09, ESSEC, 2006—08, U. S. Fla., 2008—; dir. doctoral program Grad. Sch. Bus. Adminstrn., NYU, 1985—89; mem. rsch. adv. com. USAF Pers. Rsch. Lab., 1966—69. Mem. editl. bd. Adminstrv. Sci. Quar., 1966—68, 1982—85, Jour. Applied Social Psychology, 1970—78, Jour. Mgmt. Studies, 1978—, Scandinavian Jour. Mgmt., 1984—, Jour. Behavioral Econs./Jour. Socioecons., 1988—, Brit. Jour. Mgmt., 1989—2008, Acctg. Mgmt. and Info. Techs., 1989—2000, Jour. Mgmt. Inquiry, 1991—, Organization, 1993—, Asian Case Rsch. Jour., 1997—, Internat. Jour. Mgmt. Revs., 1998—, Info. and Orgn., 2001-; editor: Adminstrv. Sci. Quar., 1968—71, The Programmer's Corner, ICON, 1984—85; contbr. articles to profl. jours. Fulbright Rsch. fellow London Bus. Sch., 1970-71, U. Gothenburg, 1977-78; recipient Disting. Scholarly Contbns. awards Acad. Mgmt., 2005; named Disting. scholar Western Acad. Mgmt., 2009. Fellow: APA, Soc. Indsl. Orgnl. Psychology, Brit. Acad. Mgmt., Am. Psychol. Soc., Acad. Mgmt. (bd. govs. 1991—99, v.p. 1994—97, pres. 1997—98, editl. bd. Acad. Mgmt. Rev. 1981—86, Disting. Scholarly Contbns. award 2005); mem.: NSF (adv. panel rsch. mgmt. improvement program 1974), Coun. Internat. Exch. Scholars (adv. screening com. for Sr. Fulbright awards in bus. mgmt. 1981—83, chmn. 1983—84). Office: Lindquist Coll Bus U Oreg Eugene OR 97403 Office Phone: 541-346-0751. Business E-Mail: starbuck@uoregon.edu.

STARCHER, DIANA L., bank executive; BA in Bus Adminstrn., W.Va. U., Morgantown. Various positions in ops. mgmt. Wells Fargo & Co., exec. v.p., dir. customer svc., sales, and ops., 2005—. Former pres., mem. bd. dirs. Houston Business Forum; former bd. mem. Electronic Check Clearing House Org., Payment Solutions Network, Banker's Clearinghouse, Fed. Res. Wholesale Payment Systems; bd. dirs. Identity Theft Assistance Corp.; bd. govs. The Doctor's Co. Active United Way, Am. Conservatory Theatre, San Francisco. Named one of 25 Women to Watch, US Banker, 2007, 2008. Office: Wells Fargo & Co 420 Montgomery St San Francisco CA 94104 Office Phone: 415-396-4000.*

STARCHMAN, DALE EDWARD, medical educator; b. Wallace, Idaho, Apr. 16, 1941; s. Hubert V. and Lottie M. (Alford) Starchman; m. Erlinda Socrates Starchman, Dec. 13, 1969; children: Ann, Cindy, Julie, Mark. Student, Rockhurst Coll., 1959—61; BS in Physics, Pitts. State U., 1963; MS in Radiation Biophysics, U. Kans., 1965, PhD in Radiation Biophysics, 1968. Cert. Radiol. Physicist, Health Physicist, Med. Physicist. Chief health physicist IIT Rsch. Inst., Chgo., 1968—71; radiol. physicist Mercy Hosp. Inst. of Radiation Therapy, Chgo., 1968—71; prof., head radiation biophysics Northeast Ohio U. Coll. of Medicine, Rootstown, 1971—; pres. Med. Physics Svcs., Inc., Canton, Ohio, 1971—. Author: (with Wayne R. Hedrick and David L. Hykes) Ultrasound Physics and Instrumentation, 4th edit., 2005; contbr. numerous articles in profl. jours., chpts. in books, monographs. Fellow Am. Coll. Radiology; mem. Am. Assn. Physicists in Medicine (bd. mem. at large 1984-86, pres. Penn-Ohio chpt. 1975-76, rec. sec. midwest chpt. 1970, edn. coun. 1980-83, chmn. Am. assn. med. dosimetrists task group 1976-78, physics curriculum diagnostic residents task group 2003—, numerous other coms. 1975-83), Health Physics Soc. (chmn. summer sch. sub. com. 1977-78), Radiol. Soc. N.Am. (assoc. scis. com. 1976-86, task force chmn. 1983-86), Sigma Xi, Kappa Mu Epsilon. Achievements include research areas including selection, quality assurance and acceptance testing of diagnostic x-ray units, design of radiology facilities; effects of tissue inhomogeneities on electron therapy, radiation atrophy in bone, large field therapy swing technique, polymer dosimetry, photon spectra through thick shields, fetal effects, ultrasound, mammography. Office: 5942 Easy Pace Cir NW Canton OH 44718-2216

STARCK, CHRISTIAN WALTER, law educator; b. Breslau, Germany, Jan. 9, 1937; s. Walter and Ruth (Hubrich) S.; m. Brigitte Edelmann, Aug. 31, 1965; children: Annette, Johannes, Marie-Christine. Student, U. Kiel, 1957, U. Freiburg, 1958-59; Dr. iur., U. Würzburg, 1963, Habil., 1969. Clk. Fed. Constl. Ct., 1964-67; govt. ofcl., 1968-69; lectr. U. Würzburg, 1969-71; prof. pub. law U. Göttingen, Germany, 1971; prof. emeritus, 2005—; rector U. Göttingen, 1976-77; judge Constl. Ct. Lower Saxony, Germany, 1991—2006; pres. Acad. Scis., Gottingen, 1982—2008. Vis. prof. U. Paris-Sorbonne, 1987, U. Nanjing, 1989; mem. TV bd. Zweites Deutsches Fernsehen, 1978-92; pres. TV bd. ARTE, 1991-2000. Author: Der Gesetzesbegriff des Grundgesetzes, 1970, Spanish edit., 1979, Das Bundesverfassungsgericht im politischen Prozess, 1976, Japanese edit., 1978, Der demokratische Verfassungsstaat, 1995, La Constitution, cadre et mesure du droit, 1994, Praxis der Verfassungs auslegung, 1994, vol. II, 2006, Grundgesetz Kommentar, 5th edit., 3 vols., 2005, Freiheit und Institutionen, 2002, Verfassungen, 2009; editor: Studien und Materialien zur Verfassungsgerichtsbarkeit, 1973—; co-editor: Juristenzeitung, 1978—2006; contbr. over 300 articles to law jours. and festschriften, —. Fellow, Inst. for Advanced Study, Berlin, 1990—91. Mem. Internat. Assn. Constl. Law (exec. com. 1981-2004, hon. pres. 2004-), Assn. German Profs. Pub. Law (exec. com. 1988-89, pres. 1998-99), German Assn. Comparative Law (exec. com. 1986-2009), Soc. Juris Publici Europaei (pres. 2003-07, hon. pres. 2007-). Home: Schlegelweg 10 D-37075 Göttingen Germany Office: Theaterstr 7 Göttingen D37033 Germany Personal E-mail: cstarck@gwdg.de.

STARER, BRIAN DOUGLAS, lawyer; b. Utica, NY, 1945; BS, U.S. Merchant Marine Acad., 1967; JD, Union U., 1972. Bar: NY 1972, US Dist. Ct. (no., so. and ea. dists.) NY, US Ct. Appeals (2nd, 3rd and 5th cirs.) 1973, US Ct. Appeals (9th cir.) 1976, US Supreme Ct. 1977, US Ct. Internat. Trade 1977, US Ct. Customs and Patent Appeals 1980. Mem. Haight Gardner Holland & Knight, NYC; ptnr., maritime law, dir., mem. mgmt. com. Holland & Knight, NYC, 1997—. Mng. editor Albany Law Rev., 1971-72; contbr. articles to profl. jours. Named to Internat. Maritime Hall of Fame, 2002. Mem. ABA, Maritime Law Assn. US, Internat. Bar Assn., NY State Bar Assn. Office: Squire, Sanders & Dempsey LLP 1095 Avenue of the Americas, 31st Fl New York NY 10036 Business E-Mail: brian.starer@hklaw.com.

STARFIELD, BARBARA HELEN, pediatrician, educator; b. Bklyn., Dec. 18, 1932; d. Martin and Eva (Illions) Starfield; m. Neil A. Holtzman, June 12, 1955; children: Robert, Jon, Steven, Deborah. AB, Swarthmore Coll., 1954; MD, SUNY, 1959; MPH, Johns Hopkins U., 1963. Tchg. asst. in anatomy Downstate Med. Ctr., NYC, 1955—57; intern in pediat. Johns Hopkins U., 1959—60, resident, 1960—62, dir. pediatric med. care clinic, 1963—66, dir. cmty. staff comprehensive child care project, 1966—67, dir. pediatric clin. scholars program, 1971—76, prof. health policy, joint appointment in pediat., 1975—, disting. univ. prof., 1994—. Mem. Nat. Com. Vital Stats., 1994—2002; cons. DHHS; mem. nat. adv. coun. Agy. for Health Care Policy and Rsch., 1990—94; adv. subcom. on Health Systems and Svcs. Rsch. Pan Am. Health Orgn., 1988—92, 1995—; cons. Health Care Fin. Adminstrn., 1980—. Editl. bd. Med. Care, 1977—79, Pediat., 1977—82, Internat. Jour. Health Svcs., 1978—, Med. Care Rev., 1980—84, Health Svc. Rsch., 1996—, assoc. editor Ann. Rev. Pub. Health, 1996—2001; contbr. articles to profl. jours. Recipient Dave Luckman Meml. award, 1958, HEW Career Devel. award, 1970—75, Disting. Investigator award, Assn. Health Svcs. Rsch., 1995, 1st Primary Care Achievement award, Pew Charitable Trust Fund, 1994, 1st Ann. Rsch. award, Ambulatory Pediatric Assn., 1990, Baxter prize, 2004. Fellow: Am. Acad. Pediat.; mem.: APHA (Martha May Eliot award 1995), Internat. Soc. for Equity in Health (pres. 2000—02), Ambulatory Pediatric Assn. (pres. 1980), Internat. Epidemiologic Assn., Soc. Pediatric Rsch., Inst. Medicine of NAS (governing coun. 1981—83), Alpha Omega Alpha, Sigma Xi. Office: Johns Hopkins Sch Hygiene 624 N Broadway Baltimore MD 21205-1900 Business E-Mail: bstarfie@jhsph.edu.

STARGATT, BRUCE M., lawyer; b. NYC, July 8, 1930; s. Sydney S. and Janet (Feldman) S.; m. Barbara Hirschfield, Aug. 21, 1954; children: Linda, Daniel, Deborah. AB, U. Vt., 1951; LLB, Yale U., 1954. Bar: Del. 1955, N.Y. 1955, D.C. 1956. Assoc. Arnold Fortas & Porter, Washington, 1954; ptnr. Young, Conaway, Stargatt & Taylor, Wilmington, Del., 1956—, now of counsel. Lawyer chmn. Del. Appellate Ct. Handbook comm., 1984—95; chmn. Del. Supreme Ct. Rules Lawyers Adv. Comm., 1986—93. 1st Lt. USAF, 1954—56. Recipient Herbert Harley award Am. Judicature Soc., 1993. Fellow Am. Bar Found., Am. Coll. Trial Lawyers; mem. ABA (ho. of dels., bd. gov. 2003-2006), Am. Law Inst., Del. State Bar Assn. (pres. 1981-82, 1st State Disting. Svc. award 1992), Del. Bar Found. (pres. 1995-2000). Office: Young Conaway Stargatt & Taylor 17th Fl 1000 West St PO Box 391 Wilmington DE 19899-0391

STARING, GRAYDON SHAW, lawyer; b. Deansboro, NY, Apr. 9, 1923; s. William Luther and Eleanor Mary (Shaw) S.; m. Joyce Lydia Allum-Poon, Sept. 1, 1949; children: Diana Hilary Agnes, Christopher Paul Norman. AB, Hamilton Coll., 1947; JD, U. Calif., Berkeley, 1951. Bar: Calif. 1952, U.S. Supreme Ct. 1958. Atty. Office Gen. Counsel, Navy Dept., San Francisco, 1952-53; atty. admiralty and shipping sect. U.S. Dept. Justice, San Francisco, 1953-60; assoc. Lillick & Charles (now Nixon Peabody), San Francisco, 1960-64, ptnr., 1965—88, of counsel, 1989—. Titulary mem. Internat. Maritime Com.; bd. dirs. Marine Exch. at San Francisco, 1984-88, pres. 1986-88; instr. pub. speaking Hamilton Coll., 1947-48; adj. prof. Hastings Coll. Law, 1996-97, Boalt Hall, U. Calif., 1999. Author: Law of Reinsurance, 1993; assoc. editor Am. Maritime Cases, 1966-92, editor, 1992-2008; contbr. articles to legal jours. Mem. San Francisco Lawyers Com. for Urban Affairs, 1972-90; bd. dirs. Legal Aid Soc., San Francisco, 1974-90, v.p., 1975-80, pres., 1980-82. With USN, 1943-46, comdr. USNR. Fellow Am. Bar Found., Am. Coll. Trial Lawyers; mem. ABA (chmn. maritime ins. com. 1975-76, mem. standing com. admiralty law 1976-82, 86-90, chmn. 1990, ho. dels. 1986-90), Fed. Bar Assn. (pres. San Francisco chpt. 1968), Bar Assn. San Francisco (sec. 1972, treas. 1973), Calif. Acad. Appellate Lawyers, Maritime Law Assn. U.S. (exec. com. 1977-88, v.p. 1980-84, pres. 1984-86), Brit.-Am. C. of C. (bd. dirs. 1987-2001), Tulane Admiralty Inst. (permanent adv. bd.), Assocs. Maritime Mus. Libr. (dir. 1990-2001, pres. 1992-94). Office: Nixon Peabody LLP 1 Embarcadero Ctr Fl 18 San Francisco CA 94111-3900 Home Phone: 510-540-7722; Office Phone: 415-984-8310. Personal E-mail: Starlaw@att.net. Business E-Mail: gstaring@nixonpeabody.com. *"How small, of all that human hearts endure,/That part which laws or kings can cause or cure!".*

STARK, BRUCE GUNSTEN, artist; b. Queens, NY, Feb. 17, 1933; s. Richard M. and Karen (Gunsten) S.; m. Joan Patricia Lauer, Nov. 19, 1960; children: Robert, Ronald. Student, Sch. Visual Arts, NYC, 1955-58. Artist, cartoonist NY Daily News, NYC, 1961—82. One-man shows Art Inst., Pitts., 1968, U. Kutztown, Pa., 1970, N.Y. Bank for Savs., N.Y.C., 1971; group shows Nat. Art Mus. Sport, N.Y.C., 1971; represented in permanent collections Everett Dirksen Library, L.D. Johnson Library, Baseball Hall Fame, Cooperstown, N.Y., Basketball Hall Fame, Mass. Served with USN, 1952-54. Recipient Nat. Cartoonist Soc.'s Rueben Catagory awards for sports, 1966, 75, spl. features, 1968; Page One award for best sports cartoon, 1970, 73 N.Y.C., 71; 3d, 4th, 6th prizes Internat. Salon de Caricatures Montreal, 1966, 68, 69; Most Outstanding Achievement award Sch. Visual Arts, 1982 Achievements include having original cartoons requested by Pres. Nixon, Johnson; 1st color cartoon appearing on front page of N.Y. Daily News. Home: 3139 Stonewater Dr Lakeland FL 33803-2572 *My goals, ideas, principles and standards of conduct are all helpfully outlined for me by God in His holy word— the Bible. I really need no other source. Whatever success has come to me, I think, is because of this, and what God has done for me, through His Son, Jesus Christ.*

STARK, DENNIS EDWIN, private investor, retired bank executive and university administrator; b. Springfield, Ill., Dec. 24, 1937; s. Edwin C. and Ida (Fentem) S. BS, Ill. Wesleyan U., 1959; Sanxay fellow practical ethics, Princeton U., 1959-60; MBA, Harvard U., 1962. Adminstrv. asst. to chmn. bd. Industrial Valley Bank, Phila., 1962-64; fin. analyst E.I. DuPont de Nemours, Wilmington, Del., 1964-65; asst. treas. Old Stone Bank, Providence, 1965-68, treas., 1968-71; sr. v.p., treas., sec. Old Stone Bank and Old Stone Corp., Providence, 1971-76; exec. v.p., chief fin. officer Old Stone Corp., Old Stone Bank, 1976-86, Dime Bank, NYC, 1986-88; ptnr. Bank Mgmt. Ptnrs., NYC, 1988-90; sr. v.p., CFO, corp. sec. Cen Fed Bank, Pasadena, Calif., 1990-92; exec. v.p., CFO, corp. sec. Ea. Bank, Lynn, Mass., 1992-96; ptnr. Fin. Mgmt. Ptnrs., Pawtucket, RI, 1996-99; v.p. bus. and fin., CFO U. R.I., Kingston, 1999—2003; bank dir., exec. v.p., CFO, corp. sec. Ind. Bank, East Greenwich, RI, 2003—05; ret., 2005. Bd. dirs. Preservation Soc. Pawtucket; hon. trustee, past chmn. Preserve R.I.; bd. dir., pres. Elizabeth Johnson Pawtucket History Rsch. Ctr.; pres. elect Friends of the Brown Librs.; bd. dirs. Gilbert Stwart Mus.; co-chmn. Endowment And Investment Com. Chorus of Westerly; vestry, treas. St. Martins Episcopal Ch., Providence; mem. exec. coun. Episcopal Ch.; mem. investment com. Episcopal Ch. USA; bd. dirs. fin. com., co-chmn. strategic planning com. R.I. Philharm.; bd. trustees, chmn. Audit Com., Episcopal Div. Sch.; bd. dirs., chmn. devel. com. R.I. Hist. Soc., mem. fin. com., chmn., strategic planning com.; bd. trustees Mus. Primitive Art and Culture, Fin. Com. Mem. Fin. Execs. Inst. (treas.), Harvard Bus. Sch. Assn. Southeastern, New England, Hist. Dist. Com., Pawtucket, Acacia (co-founder Ill. Wesleyan U. chpt.), Providence Art Club, Hope Club, Univ. Club (R.I.), Harvard Club (N.Y.C.), Agawam Hunt, Dunes Club, Brown Faculty Club, U. R.I. Univ. Club (treas.). Episcopalian. Avocations: stamp collecting/philately, coin collecting/numismatics. Home (Summer): 41 Courtway St Narragansett RI 02882-3610 E-mail: destark@cox.net.

STARK, DIANA, public relations executive; b. NYC, July 01; d. Benjamin and Sara (Zelasny) S. BA, Hunter Coll. Promotion mgr. TV Guide mag., NYC, 1950-61, Show Bus. Illustrated, NYC, 1961-62; broadcast specialist Young & Rubicam, NYC, 1962-69; pres. Stark Comms. Inc., NYC, 1969-76; pub. svc. publicity account exec. Y & R E, NYC, 1976-77; pres. Stark Comms. Internat., NYC, 1978—. Pub. rels. workshop leader Chgo. Econ. Devel. Corp., 1973-76; cons. to Asahi Shimbun for English Language Newsletter. 1991-92, columnist Host mag., 1960-65; writer, producer programs for women's TV shows, 1962—. Book developer Ellis Island: The First Experience With Liberty, 1991; the executive television workshop: Media Training 1985-91, promotion for The Perot Legacy: A New Political Party By Pat Benjamins Published December 2007, illuminus Publisher Choice Co-ord. We Have Arrived, Portraits at Ellis Island, Augustus Sherman Photographs, 1902-24. Mem. NATAS (trustee 1974-78, publicity com., chmn., chpt. gov. 1972-76, 82-86, 87-91, editor N.Y. TV Directory 1987-90). Home Phone: 212-582-5619; Office Phone: 212-582-5619. Office Fax: 212-765-3670. Business E-Mail: dstarkny@aol.com.

STARK, FORTNEY HILLMAN (PETE STARK), United States Representative from California; b. Milw., Nov. 11, 1931; s. Fortney Hillman and Dorothy M. (Mueller) Stark; m. Deborah Roderick; children: Hannah Marie, Andrew Peter; children: Jeffrey Peter, Beatrice Ann, Thekla Brumder, Sarah Gallun, Fortney Hillman III. BS in Engring., MIT, 1953; MBA, U. Calif. Berkeley, 1960. Teaching asst. MIT, Cambridge, 1953-54; prin. Skaife & Co., Berkeley, Calif., 1957-61; founder Beacon Savs. & Loan Assn., Antioch, Calif., 1961; pres., founder Security Nat. Bank, Walnut Creek, Calif., 1963-72; mem. US Congress from 13th (formerly 9th) Calif. dist., 1973—, mem. ways and means com., formerly chmn., now ranking minority mem. health subcom., mem. joint com. taxation. Del. Dem. State Ctr. Com.; bd. trustees Calif. Dem. Coun.; mem. Progressive Caucus. Bd. dirs., former chmn. Starr King Sch. Ministry; past bd. dirs. Common Cause; past bd. mem. Housing Devel. Corp., Coun. Civic Unity. Capt. USAF, 1955—57. Mem.: Delta Kappa Epsilon. Democrat. Unitarian Universalist. Office: US Ho Reps 239 Cannon Ho Office Bldg Washington DC 20515-0513 Office Phone: 202-225-5065.*

STARK, JOAN SCISM, education educator; b. Hudson, NY, Jan. 6, 1937; d. Ormonde F. and Myrtle Margaret (Kirkey) S.; m. William L. Stark, June 28, 1958 (dec.); children: Eugene William, Susan Elizabeth, Linda Anne, Ellen Scism; m. Malcolm A. Lowther, Jan. 31, 1981. BS, Syracuse U., 1957; MA (Hoadly fellow), Columbia U., 1960; Ed.D., SUNY, Albany, 1971. Tchr. Ossining (N.Y.) High Sch., 1957-59; free-lance editor Holt, Rinehart & Winston, Harcourt, Brace & World, 1960-70; lectr. Ulster County Community Coll., Stone Ridge, NY, 1968-70; asst. dean Goucher Coll., Balt., 1970-73, asso. dean, 1973-74; assoc. prof., chmn. dept. higher postsecondary edn. Syracuse (N.Y.) U., 1974-78; dean Sch. Edn. U. Mich., Ann Arbor, 1978-83, prof., 1983-2001, prof. and dean emeritus, 2001—; dir. Nat. Ctr. for Improving Postsecondary Teaching and Learning, 1986—91. Editor: Rev. of Higher Edn., 1991-96; contbr. articles to various publs. Leader Girl Scouts U.S.A., Cub Scouts Am.; coach girls Little League; dist. officer PTA, intermittently, 1968-80; mem. adv. com. Gerald R. Ford Library, U. Mich., 1980-83; trustee Kalamazoo Coll., 1979-85; mem. exec. com. Inst. Social Research, U. Mich., 1979-81; bd. dirs. Mich. Assn. Colls. Tchr. Edn., 1979-81. Mem. Am. Assn. for Higher Edn., Am. Ednl. Rsch. Assn. (Div. J. Rsch. award 1998), Assn. Study Higher Edn. (dir. 1977-79, v.p. 1983, pres. 1984, Rsch. Achievement award 1992, svc. award 1998, Disting. Career award 1999), Assn. Innovation Higher Edn. (nat. chmn. 1974-75), Assn. Instl. Rsch. (disting. mem., Sidney Suslow award 1999), Assn. Colls. and Schs. Edn. State Univs. and Land Grant Colls. (dir. 1981-83), Acctg. Edn. Change Commn., Phi Beta Kappa, Phi Kappa Phi, Sigma Pi Sigma, Eta Pi Upsilon, Lambda Sigma Sigma, Phi Delta Kappa, Pi Lambda Theta.

STARK, MARTIN J., international management consultant; b. NYC, May 29, 1941; s. Nathan and Lola (Belmont) S.; m. Shigemi Matsumoto, Apr. 27, 1967. AA, Glendale Coll., 1960; BA, Calif. State U., 1966; postgrad., San Fernando Valley Coll. Law, 1967—70. Prodn. control supr. Indsl. Electronic Engrs., Van Nuys, Calif., 1967—69, sys. analyst, 1969—71, internat. sales mgr., 1971—73; sales rep. Columbia Artists Mgmt., Inc., NYC, 1973—78, sales mgr., 1978—79, v.p. bus. affairs, and mgr. data processing, 1979—82; dir. corp. affairs Kolmar-Luth Entertainment, Inc., NYC, 1982—84; pres. Oryx & Corp., NYC, 1984—85; exec. v.p. Asco Aerospace Products, Inc., El Segundo, Calif., 1985—87, Internat. Engine Parts, Inc., Chatsworth, Calif., 1987—92; pres. Stark & Assocs., Northridge, Calif., 1985—91; owner Mail Boxes Etc., 1992—2008. Lectr. Calif. State U., Long Beach, U. So. Calif., Chapman U.; cons. City of N.Y., Memory Data Software, IEPO, Inc.; advisor Thornton Protégé Program Thornton Sch. Music U. So. Calif.; bd. dirs. Holy Cross Hosp.; mentor Thornton Sch. Music, U. So. Calif. Mem.: Calabas C. of C., Classical Singer's Assn., Delta Upsilon. Avocations: sports cars, antiques, travel. Office: 18342 Chatham Ln Northridge CA 91326-3603 Personal E-mail: mbe1047@aol.com, starkconsultancy@aol.com.

STARK, NELLIE MAY, forester, ecologist, educator; b. Norwich, Conn., Nov. 20, 1933; d. Theodore Benjamin and Dorothy Josephine (Pendleton) Beetham; m. Oscar Elder Stark, Oct. 1962 (dec.). BA, Conn. Coll., 1956; AM, Duke U., 1958, PhD, 1962. Botanist Exptl. Sta., U.S. Forest Svc., Old Strawberry, Calif., 1958-66; botanist, ecologist Desert Rsch. Inst., Reno, 1966-72; prof. forest ecology Sch. Forestry, U. Mont., Missoula, 1972-92; pvt. cons. Philomath, Oreg. Pres. Camas Analytical Lab., Inc., Missoula, 1987—92. Author: Will Your Family Survive the 21st Century, 1997, Memories of Wren, Oregon, 1998, So You Want to Build a Little Log Cabin in the Woods, 2002, Thirteen Days of Christmas, 2005, Midshipman Randel, 2009, Humble Launching, 2009; contbr. articles to profl. jours. Named Disting. Dau. Norwich, Conn., 1985; recipient Conn. award Conn. Coll., 1986, 54 grants. Mem. Ecol. Soc. Am. (chair ethics com. 1974, 76), Soc. Am. Foresters (taskforce 1987-88).

STARK, PATRICIA ANN, psychologist; b. Ames, Iowa, Apr. 21, 1937; d. Keith C. and Mary L. (Johnston) Moore. BS, So. Ill. U., Edwardsville, 1970, MS, 1972; PhD, St. Louis U., 1976. Counselor to alcoholics Bapt. Rescue Mission, East St. Louis, Ill., 1969; rschr. alcoholics Gateway Rehab. Ctr., East St. Louis, 1972; psychologist intern Henry-Stark Counties Spl. Edn. Dist. and Galesburg State Rsch. Hosp., Ill., 1972—73; instr. Lewis and Clark C.C., Godfrey, Ill., 1973—76, asst. prof., 1976—84, assoc. prof., 1994, coord. child care svcs., 1974—84; mem. staff dept. psychiatry Meml. Hosp., St. Elizabeth's Hosp., 1979—2001; supr. students interns, 1974—94. Dir. child and family svc. Collinsville Counseling Ctr., 1977-82; clin. dir., owner Empas-Complete Family Psychol. and Hypnosis Svcs., Collinsville, 1982—; cons. cmty. agys., 1974—; mem. adv. bd. Madison County Coun. on Alcoholism and Drug Dependency, 1977-80. Mem. APA, Ill. Psychol. Assn., Midwestern Psychol. Assn., Am. Soc. Clin. Hypnosis, Internat. Soc. Hypnosis. Office: 2802 Maryville Rd Maryville IL 62062 Office Phone: 618-345-6632.

STARK, PAUL, small business owner; b. Phoenix; m. Jane Stark; children: Kristina, Sarah. BBA in Acctg., U. Wis., Milw.; MA in Bus. Taxation, U. Minn. CPA. Customer svc. rep. nat. constrn. co.; accountant CPA firm; founder constrn. co., Eau Claire, Wis., 2003—. Mem., usher,

Eucharistic min. Immaculate Conception Cath. Ch. Mem.: Nat. Assn. Realtor's, Wis. Realtor's Assn., Realtor's Assn. Northwestern Wis., Nat. Home Builder's Assn., Wis. Home Builder's Assn., Chippewa Valley Home Builder's Assn. Republican. Mailing: PO Box 3172 Eau Claire WI 54702

STARK, S. DANIEL, JR., casino and gaming resort company executive; b. Port Hueneme, Calif., Mar. 26, 1953; s. S. Daniel and Eloise Marie (Fisher) S.; m. Pauline Laube Finley, June 7, 1997; 1 child, Kaitlyn Elizabeth. BS, Calif. Poly. U., Pomona, 1981; cert. in exec. mgmt., Claremont Grad. U., 1989, MA in Mgmt., 1992. Driver-guide San Diego Wild Animal Pk./Zool. Soc. San Diego, Escondido, Calif., 1974—76; attractions host Disneyland divsn. The Walt Disney Co., Anaheim, Calif., 1976—80, mgmt. intern, 1981, supr. ops., 0981—1982, area supr. ops., dept. mgr., 1982—87; mgmt. cons. S.D. Stark, Jr., Las Vegas, 1985—2000; dir. mktg. Ramada Express Hotel & Casino, Laughlin, Nev., 1988—89; exec. dir. San Bernardino Conv. and Visitors Bur., Calif., 1989—98; pres., CEO Panama City Beach Conv. & Visitors Bur., 1998—99; exec. dir. Bay County Tourist Devel. Coun., Fla., 1998—99; dir. corp. mktg. Boyd Gaming Corp., Las Vegas, 1999—2005, v.p. corp. mktg., 2006—. Part-time instr. mgmt. and mktg. So. Calif. campus U. Phoenix, 1997-98, Nev. campus, 1999—, area chair for mktg., 2001-04; cons. Hemmeter Devel. Corp., Honolulu, 1985, Calif. Authority Racing Fairs, Sacramento, 1987-88, USIA for Latvian Ministry Transp., tourism divsn., 1992, U.S. Bur. Land Mgmt., tourism mgmt. project U. Alaska Fairbanks Sch. Mgmt.; adj. prof. Sch. Bus. and Pub. Adminstrn., Calif. State U., San Bernardino, 1992-93; participant USAF Air War Coll. Nat. Security Forum Maxwell AFB, Ala., 2009. Bd. dirs. Leadership So. Calif., 1993-98, grad. pub. affairs tng., 1993; congl. appointee del. White House Conf. on Travel and Tourism, 1995; mem. regional econ. strategies consortium So. Calif. Assn. Govts., 1996-98; mem. Visit Fla. Mktg. Com., 1998-99; bd. dirs. Fla. Assn. Conv. and Visitors Burs., 1998-99, Speedway Childrens Charities Las Vegas Chpt., 1999—, treas., 2000-01, chmn., 2001-2002; v.p. Cops Helping Kids, 2002-2003, pres., 2003-04; mem. spl. events com. Las Vegas Centennial Commn.; bd. trustees Crime Stoppers of Nev., Inc., 2004—. Recipient World Champion Trail Horse award Am. Jr. Quarter Horse Assn., 1972, resolution Calif. Assembly, 1989, 98, San Bernardino County Bd. Suprs., 1989, City of San Bernardino Mayor and Coun., 1989, 98, Calif. Senate, 1989, 98, Calif. Tourism award for Best Spl. Event-Rt. 66 Rendezvous, 1997, Rt. 66 Rendezvous Founder's award San Bernardino Conv. and Visitors Bur., 2004; selected as one of 1991 Up and Coming Young Bus. Leaders in San Bernardino County; named one of Inland Empire Bus. All Stars, 1991. Fellow USAF Air War Coll. (MaxwellAFB, Ala.) (nat. security forum 2009); mem. U.S. Equestrian Fedn. (life), Am. Quarter Horse Assn (life), Assn. Conv. and Visitors Burs. (cert. comm., conv. mktg., tourism mktg.), Pub. Rels. Soc. Am. (bd. dirs. Calif. Inland Empire chpt. 1990-95, Polaris award 1997), Calif. and Nev. Festivals and Events Assn. (pres. 1997-98, bd. dirs. 1994-98, 2002—), Inland Empire Tourism Coun. (bd. dirs. 1996-98, exec. com. 1996-98, treas. 1997-98), Calif. Travel Industry Assn., Tourism Assn. So. Calif. (bd. dirs. 1990-95, vice chair 1992-95), Western Assn. Convs. and Vis. Bur. (chmn. Calif. coun. 1992-94), E Clampus Vitus Inc. (bd. proctors 2005—, sec. treas 2006-07, v.p. 2007-08, pres. 2008-09), FarmHouse Fraternity (internat. bd. dirs. 1986-94, v.p. 1990-92, Snyder Alumni award 1984). Avocations: boating, fishing, films, equestrian competition. Office: Boyd Gaming Corp 6465 S Rainbow Blvd Las Vegas NV 89118-3215

STARK, WALTER J., ophthalmologist, educator; s. Walter Stark and Lucy Anderson; m. Carey Pauline Allen, July 25, 1964; children: Heather Anne Anderson, Walter Jackson Jr.; 1 child, Melissa Lea Lilley. MD, U. Okla. Sch. Medicine, 1967. Assoc. prof. ophthalmology Johns Hopkins U., Wilmer Eye Inst., Balt., 1976—82, prof. ophthalmology, 1982—. Fellowship dir. Johns Hopkins U.; med. dir. Md. Eye Bank, 1987—; dir. Tissue Banks Internat., Md., 1987—. Office: Johns Hopkins Univ Wilmer Eye Inst 600 N Wolfe St Maumenee 327 Baltimore MD 21287 Office Fax: 410-614-9172.

STARKE, HAROLD EUGENE, JR., lawyer; b. Richmond, Va., Aug. 1, 1944; BA, Randolph-Macon Coll., Ashland, Va., 1967; JD, U. Richmond, 1971; LLM in Taxation, NYU, 1973. Bar: Va. 1971, DC 1981. Ptnr. Troutman Sanders LLP, Richmond. Adj. prof. law Wash. and Lee Law Sch. Editor U. Richmond Law Rev., 1970-71. Bd. trustees Randolph-Macon Coll., 1983-85, 95-97, 99—. Fellow Am. Coll. Tax Counsel, Am. Bar Found.; mem. ABA (taxation sect.), Va. State Bar (chmn. taxation sect. 1985-86), DC Bar, Richmond Estate Planning Coun., McNeill Honor Soc., Phi Delta Phi. Office: Troutman Sanders LLP Troutman Sanders Bldg 1001 Haxall Point PO Box 1122 Richmond VA 23218-1122 Office Phone: 804-697-1287.

STARKEY, BOB (ROBERT G. STARKEY), women's college basketball coach; b. Sept. 7, 1959; m. Sherie Hayslett. Asst. coach Winfield HS, W.Va. Coll., 1984—87, Poca HS, W.Va.; asst. coach women's basketball Marshall U., Huntington, W.Va., 1988—89; asst. coach men's basketball La. State U., 1990—96, adminstrv. asst. men's and women's basketball, 1996—97, asst. coach women's basketball, 1998—2007, acting head coach women's basketball, 2007, assoc. head coach, 2007—. Office: La State Univ Womens Basketball Athletics Dept PO Box 25095 Baton Rouge LA 70894-5095 Office Phone: 225-578-6643. E-mail: rstarke@lsu.edu.*

STARKEY, RUSSELL BRUCE, JR., energy executive; b. Lumberport, W.Va., July 20, 1942; s. Russell Bruce and Dorotha Mable (Field) S.; m. Joan McClellan, May 27, 1966; children: Christine, Pamela, Joanne. BS, Miami U., Oxford, Ohio, 1964; grad. student, U. New Haven, 1972—73, N.C. State U., 1974—75; postgrad., U.S. Navy Schs., 1964—66, postgrad., 1968. From sr. engr., nuc. generation sect. to prin. engr. Carolina Power & Light Co., Raleigh, NC, 1973—75; supr. quality assurance, supt. tech. and administrn. Brunswick Steam Electric Plant, Southport, NC, 1975—77; plant mgr. H. B. Robinson Steam Electric Plant, Hartsville, SC, 1977—83; mgr. environ. svcs. Carolina Power & Light Co., Raleigh, 1984—85, mgr. nuc. safety and environ. svcs. dept., 1985—88; mgr. Brunswick Nuc. Project Dept., 1988—89, v.p., 1989—92, v.p. Nuc. Svc. Dept., 1992—93; exec. v.p. energy mgmt. divsn. Hesco, Inc., 1993; from dir. indsl. electrotech. lab. to v.p. gen. tech. mgr. Advanced Energy Corp., 1993—97; cons. U.S. Enrichment Corp., Paducah, Ky., 1997—98, tng. mgr., 1998—2001, plant gen. mgr., 2001—05, v.p. ops., 2005—08; v.p. Am. Centrifuge project, 2008—. With USN, 1964-73. Named Hon. Ky. Col. Mem.: Am. Nuc. Soc. Office: 6903 Rockledge Dr Bethesda MD 20817 Home: PO Box 189 Oxford OH 45056-0189

STARKMAN, GARY LEE, lawyer; b. Chgo., Sept. 2, 1946; s. Oscar and Sara (Ordman) Starkman. AB, U. Ill., 1968; JD cum laude, Northwestern U., 1971. Bar: Ill. 1971, U.S. Dist. Ct. (no. dist.) Ill. 1972, U.S. Ct. Appeals (7th cir.) 1972, U.S. Supreme Ct. 1974, Trial Bar U.S. Dist. Ct. (no. dist.) Ill. 1982, U.S. Ct. Appeals (3d cir.) 1984, U.S. Ct. Appeals (D.C. cir.) 1984. Asst. U.S. Atty. No. Dist. Ill., 1971-75; gen. counsel, dir. rsch. Citizens for Thompson Campaign Com., 1975-77; counsel to Gov. of Ill., 1977-81; admissions com. U.S. Dist. Ct. (no. dist.) Ill., 1982-90; ptnr. Ross & Hardies, Chgo., 1990—2003, McGuire Woods LLP, Chgo., 2003—. Co-author: (textbook) Cases and Comments on Criminal Procedure, 1974, 6th edit., 2008; contbr. articles to profl. jours.; reviewer in field. Chmn. state agys. divsn. Jewish United Fund Met. Chgo., 1978-81; chmn. Ill. Racing Bd., 1991-96; bd. dirs. Internat. Assn. Racing Commn., 1992-94; cmty. adv. bd. Jr. League Chgo., 1979-83. Recipient John Marshall award for appellate litigation, Atty. Gen. U.S., 1974, Nat. Svc. award, Tau Epsilon Pi, 1968; named one of Ten Outstanding Young Citizens, Chgo. Jr. C. of C., 1978. Mem.: ABA (litigation sect.), Chgo. Bar Assn. (constl. law com.), Decalogue Soc., Northwestern U. Law Alumni Assn. Office: McGuire Woods LLP 77 W Walker Dr Ste 4100 Chicago IL 60601-1681 Office Phone: 312-750-2785. Business E-Mail: gstarkman@mcguirewoods.com.

STARKS, DANIEL J., medical technology and services executive; BA, Shimer Coll., Waukegan, Ill.; JD magna cum laude, U. Minn. Law Sch., 1979. Comml. litigation atty. Nichols, Starks, Carruthers and Kaster, 1979—85; gen. counsel to pres., CEO Daig Corp. (bought by St. Jude Medical Inc.), 1985—96; pres., CEO, Daig Corp. St. Jude Medical Inc., St. Paul, 1996—98, dir., 1996—, pres., CEO Cardiac Rhythm Mgmt. div., 1998—2001, pres., COO, 2001—04, chmn., pres., CEO, 2004—. Bd. dir. Urologix Inc. Office: St Jude Medical Inc 1 Lillehei Plz Saint Paul MN 55117-9913*

STARKS, FRED WILLIAM, chemicals executive; b. Millford, Ill., Aug. 16, 1921; s. Otis Earl and Evelyn Viola Starks; m. Minnie Jane Reynolds, Sept. 4, 1946; children: David F., Steven J., Daniel J. BS, U. Ill., 1943, MS, 1947; PhD, U. Nebr., 1950. Supr. US Rubber Co., Torrance, Calif., 1943—44, DuPont, Niagara Falls, NY, 1950—57; pres. Starks Assocs., Inc., Buffalo, 1957—89, chmn., 1989—. Spl. lectr. U. Buffalo, 1959—63. Lt. (j.g.) USNR, 1944—46. Avery fellow, 1948—49, USPHS fellow, 1949—50. Mem.: Am. Inst. Chemists, NY Acad. Sci., Am. Chem. Soc., Chemists Club, Buffalo Club, Cosmos, Sigma Xi. Achievements include patents in field. Office: Starks Assocs Inc 1280 Niagara St Buffalo NY 14213-1592 Office Phone: 716-886-1700.

STARKS, VENESSA G., retired elementary school educator; BS in Elem. Edn., Western Ky. U., Bowling Green, 1977, MA in Elem. Edn., 1982, Rank I cert., 1990. Title I, regular classroom tchr. Barnes Elem. Sch., Franklin, Ky., 1978—79, Franklin Elem. Sch., 1979—2006; substitute tchr. Warren County, Bowling Green, 2006—. Mem. usher bd. Loving Chapel Bapt. Ch. Recipient Outstanding Svc. recognition, Modern Woodman of Am., 1992; named Outstanding Tchr., Franklin Lions Club, 1991. Mem.: Simpson County Ret. Tchrs. Home: 1290 Sportsman Lake Rd Franklin KY 42134

STARKWEATHER, FREDERICK THOMAS, retired data processing executive; b. Sioux City, Iowa, Feb. 24, 1933; s. Fred Ervin and Gertrude Faye (Madden) S.; m. Margot Glassen, Nov. 19, 1959; children: Thomas Frederick, Jerry Russell, Michael Glassen. BA in Math. and Physics, U. Nebr., Omaha, 1955. Mathematician Flight Determination Lab., White Sands Missile Range, N.Mex., 1955-56; supervisory mathematician Analysis & Computation, White Sands Missile Range, 1956-81; chief data scis. divsn. Nat. Range Ops., White Sands Missile Range, 1981—93; co-owner B and T Managed Care, LLC, 2001—; owner The Spotlight Restaurant, 2002—. Nat. coun. rep. Am. Def. Preparedness Assn., Washington, 1980-93; pres. White Sands Pioneer Group, White Sands Missile Range, 1983-86; bd. dirs. Assn. U.S. Army, Washington. Author hist. and geneal. books; contbr. book revs. and articles to newspapers and mags. Chmn. El Paso City Planning Commn., Tex., 1980-84; bd. dirs. El Paso County Hist. Soc., 1983-87; active El Paso County Hist. Commn., 1983-2000. With USAR, 1955-63. Recipient Profl. Secs. Internat. Exec. of Yr. award, 1987, Conquistador award City of El Paso, 1980; named Disting. Alumnus U. Nebr., Omaha, 1985; named to Hon. Order of St. Barbara U.S. Field Arty. Assn., 1988; cited for svcs. to mankind El Paso chpt. Sertoma, 1985. Mem. Fed. Mgrs. Assn. (bd. dirs.), Freedom Found. at Valley Forge (pres. El Paso chpt., George Washington Hon. medal 1982), El Paso C. of C. (assoc. dir. 1984-92, bd. dirs.), Toastmasters (dist. gov. 1970-71), Masons, Tau Kappa Epsilon (Hall of Fame 1986). Avocations: coin collecting/numismatics, genealogy, books, weaponry. Home Phone: 915-449-5082.

STARLING, DAVID L., rail transportation executive; Mgmt. positions in rail ops. St. Louis San Francisco RR, Burlington Northern, 1971—84; gen. mgr. & v.p. In-Terminal Services Mi-Jack Products, 1984—88; mng. dir., Chgo. & So. region Am. President Lines, 1988—93, mng. dir. Philippines, 1993—94, mng. dir. Hong Kong-China region, & v.p. Ctrl. Asia, 1995—99; pres., gen. dir. Panama Canal Railway Co., 1999—2008; pres., COO Kans. City Southern Industries, 2008—; pres., CEO Kans. City So. Railway Co., 2008—. Mailing: Kans City Southern PO Box 219335 Kansas City MO 64121-9335

STARLING, RANDALL CARSON, cardiologist, educator; b. Pitts., Pa., Aug. 1, 1951; BS, MPH, U. Pitts.; MD, Temple U., 1981. Cert. Internal Medicine, Cardiovascular Disease, Bd. Med. Examiners. Intern U. Pitts. Med. Ctr., Pa., resident, internal medicine Pa., 1981—85, chief med. resident Pa., instr. medicine Pa., med. dir., cardiac transplant program Pa.; fellow, cardiology Ohio State U. Hospitals, Columbus, 1985—88, staff; asst. to assoc. prof., medicine Ohio State U., Columbus, med. dir., Cardiac Transplant Program; staff cardiologist, cardiovascular disease Cleve. Clinic, Ohio, 1995—, dir., heart transplant med. svcs. Ohio, 1995, sect. head, heart failure and cardiac transplant medicine Ohio, staff physician, Multi-Organ Transplant Ctr. Ohio, med. dir., Kaufman Ctr. for Heart Failure Ohio. Contbr. articles to profl. jours.; editl. bd. mem. Jour. Am. Coll. Cardiology, reviewer, editl. cons. for numerous jours.; editor: (chapter) Heart Failure in the Am. Coll. Cardiology Self-Assessment Program; editl. cons. 20/20, CNN Heroes In Medicine & PBS Specials. Fellow: Am. Coll. Cardiology; mem.: Internat. Soc. for Heart and Lung Transplantation, Heart Failure Soc. Am., Am. Soc. Transplantation, Am. Heart Assn. (mem. Coun. on Clin. Cardiology), Alpha Omega Alpha. Office: Cleveland Clinic Mail Stop F25 9500 Euclid Ave Cleveland OH 44195 Office Phone: 216-444-2268.

STARLING, VIRGINIA R., music educator, consultant; b. Loraine, Tex., Apr. 26, 1929; d. Lawrence Livingston and Ruth Cleo (Martin) Trott; widowed; children: Catherine, Caroline, Randall. B of Music Edn., Mary Hardin Baylor U., 1950; MusM, 1976; BS in Psychology, Coll. of Southwest, 1989. Choir dir. Methodist Ch., Belton, TX, 1949-50; music instr. Monahans (Tex.) Pub. Schs., 1950-52, Lovington (N.Mex.) Pub. Schs., 1952-54, N.M. Jr. Coll., Hobbs, 1976-79; pvt. sch. music tchr. Hobbs, N.M., 1987-93; ch. organist, pvt. tchr. Lovington, Hobbs, N.M., 1952-99; ch. organist, cons. Cloudcroft, N.Mex., 1999—2005. Bd. dirs. Cloudcroft Dance Acad. Soloist: (CD) Enduring Devotion; composer piano solos for children, Just For You, 2000; concert performances in Hobbs, N. Mex., Carnegie Hall. Bd. dirs. Southwest Symphony. Mem. Music Tchrs. Nat. Assn., Profl. Music Tchrs. of N.Mex. (bd. dirs.), Lea County Music Forum, Sigma Alpha Iota. Baptist. Avocations: gardening, travel, history, music. Home: 3003 North Houston Hobbs NM 88240

STARNES, EARL MAXWELL, retired urban and regional planner, architect, educator; b. Winter Haven, Fla., Sept. 14, 1926; s. Thomas Lowe and Kathryn Maxwell (Gates) Starnes; m. Dorothy Jean Prather, Aug. 21, 1949; children: Tom, Will, Janet, Patricia. Student, Fla. So. Coll., 1946—48; BArch cum laude, U. Fla., 1951; MS in Urban and Regional Planning, Fla. State U., 1973, PhD, 1977. Registered arch., Fla. Assoc. Courtney Stewart, Ft. Lauderdale, Fla., 1951-52, William Bigoney, Ft. Lauderdale, 1952-53, William T. Vaughn, Ft. Lauderdale, 1953, Alfred B. Parker, Miami, Fla., 1953-55, Rufus Nims, Miami, 1955-57; ptnr. Starnes & Rentscher, Miami, 1957-63, Starnes, Rentscher & Assocs., Miami, 1963-71; dir. divsn. mass transp. Fla. Dept. Transp., Tallahassee, 1971-72; dir. divsn. state planning Fla. Dept. Adminstrn., 1972-75; engaged in rsch. and cons. svc. Tallahassee, 1975; prof., chmn. urban and regional planning Coll. Architecture U. Fla., Gainesville, 1976-88, prof. urban and regional plan coord., doctoral studies, 1989-93, prof. emeritus, 1993—. Instr. architecture U. Miami, 1953; adj. asst. prof. dept. urban and regional planning Coll. Social Scis., Fla. State U., 1971—74; mem. adv. panel B8-15 Nat. Coop. Hwy. Rsch. Program, Transp. Rsch. Bd., NRC-Nat. Acad. Scis., 1974—; mem. adv. bd. Pub. Tech., Inc., 1974—; mem. N. Ctrl. Fla. Regional Planning Com., 1980—85, Fla. Substate Dist. Com., 1985—87; co-chmn. Joint Liaison Com. Divsn. Responsibility Urban Svcs., Dade County, Fla., 1965—71; chmn. joint policy com. U. Miami-Dade County Jackson Med. Ctr., 1966—71; chmn. Cape Fla. State Pk. Adv. Coun., 1966—69, Dade County Landscape Ordinance Study Com., 1967—70, S. Fla. Everglades Area Planning Coun., 1969—71; vis. lectr. Calif. Poly. State U., San Luis Obispo, 1988—89; cons. Urban Planning Fla. and Caribbean. Prin. works include 1st Unitarian Ch., Miami; co-author: Growth Management, 1992, Rural Sustainability in America, 1996; co-author: (with Richard Rubino) History of Planning in Florida, 2008; contbr. articles to profl. jours., chapters to books. Active Nat. Task Force Natural Resources and Land Use Info. and Tech., 1973—74, Cape Fla. Acquisition Com., 1966, South Dade Mental Health Soc., 1967—68, Dade County Downtown Govtl. Ctr. Com., 1967—71, Miami Downtown Devel. Authority, 1970, Gov.'s Task Force Resource Mgmt., 1971—72, Fla. Gov.'s Commn. Property Rights, 1993—94, Fla. Greenway's Commn., 1991—93, Fla. Greenway Coordinating Coun., 1998—99; bd. dirs., chmn. retirement and compensation com. State Assn. County Commrs., 1968—71; mem. Alachua County Budget Study Com., 1978, Fla. Land Use Adv. Com. Phosphate Lands, 1978—80, Suwanee River Water Mgmt. Bd., 1982—87, 1991—98, chmn., 1987—88, Fla. Inst. Phosphate Rsch., 1984—87; bd. dirs. 1000 Friends Fla., 1986—2003; mem. gov.'s adv. commn. coastal mgmt., 1997; county commr. Dist. 7 Dade County, 1964—71; vice mayor, 1964, 1968. With USCG, 1944—46. Fellow: AIA (urban design com. 1976—80), Assn. Collegiate Schs. Planning (bd. dirs. 1986—88), Nat. Inst. Bldg. Scis. (steering com. for rsch. 1979—80), Am. Inst. Cert. Planners, Gargoyle Soc.; mem.: Phi Kappa Phi. Democrat. Unitarian Universalist. Office: PO Box 234 Cedar Key FL 32625-0234 Personal E-mail: estarnes@inetw2.net, earldorothy@bellsouth.net.

STARNES, KATIE GERARD, retired community health nurse; b. Corpus Christi, Tex., Mar. 3, 1940; d. James Robert Gerard and Lillie Myrtle Henderson-Gerard; m. Lawrence Edwin Starnes, June 30, 1962; children: Nelvia LaVoy Starnes-Terrell, Ann Starnes-Adams, Nina Faye. BSN, Prairie View A&M, Tex., 1963; MSN Cmty. Health Focus in Adminstrn./Mgmt., Tex. Womens U., Denton/Houston, 1978. Cert. in gerontology nursing, ANA, 2008, in Anger Mgmt., 2008. Staff charge nurse Hermann Hosp., Tex. Med. Ctr., Houston, 1964—67; staff and nurse supr. Vis. Nurse Assn., Houston, 1967—69, patient care mgr., 1969—74, br. office mgr. Rosenberg, Tex., 1978—83; dir. nursing/patient care facilitator United Home Health, Houston, 1976—78; auditing specialist Blue Cross/Blue Shield Medicare Intermediary, Dallas, 1983—84; home care nurse mgr. Houston Veterans Affairs Med. Ctr., Houston, 1985—2002, spinal cord home care, 1994—2002, intermediate care nurse mgr., 2001—02; home care cons., svc. edn, 2002—. Bd. dirs. United Home Health, Houston, 1976—79, Planned Parenthood, Fort Bend County, Tex., 1979—83; sub-com. chairperson ARC, Fort Bend County Chpt., Houston, 1978—85; chairperson disaster nursing svcs. ARC, Houston Chpt., 1985—87, mem., 2002—; organizer, bd. dirs. Ft. Bend County Health Coun., Richmond/Rosenburg, 1980—84; home care cons. Greater Houston Health Care, 1985; organizer, co-leader caregivers support group Houston Vet. Med. Ctr., Hosp. Based Home Care, 1987—2002; adj. clin. prof. U. Tex. Health Sci. Ctr., Houston, 1987—2005; adj. clin. prof., adv. bd. Alvin Jr. Coll., Tex., 1990—2002; profl. nurse std. bd. Houston Vet. Affairs Med. Ctr. Nursing Svc., 1988—2002; co-leader, vol. Alzheimer's Assn., 1988; mem. Gero-Education Com., Huffington Ctr. Aging, Baylor Coll. Medicine, Houston, 1996—2002; nursing cons. In-svc. Edn., 2002—. Active vol. Am. Heart Assn., Alzheimer's Disease Assn., Am. Red Cross Greater Houston Chpt.; instr., CPR & babysitting courses Tchg., Edn., Enrichment, Recreation, Outreach Ctr., bd. mem. & mentorship program, chair, fundraising & health svcs. com.; sec. Nurse Alumni Prairie View A&M U.; leader Alzheimers Support Group; mem., edn. com. Am. Orgn. Nurse Execs., 1995. Recipient Nat. Sec.'s award, VSN 16, Houston VAMC, 1999; named one of Top Twenty Nurses, Growth of Profession, Tex. Nurses Assn. Dist. 9, 1992. Mem.: AARP, Black Nurses Assn., Fed. Employees Assn. (assoc.), Prairie View A&M Nurse Alumni Assn. (life; sec.), Alzheimer's Assn., A. Phillip Randolph Assn., Jack and Jill America, Inc. (charter mem. and past pres. Fort Bend Co. chpt.), Sigma Theta Tau, Eta Delta Chpt. (assoc.), Delta Sigma Theta Sorority, Inc. (Houston Met. Chpt.) (life; chair youth acad. & GEMS 2009—). Church Of Christ. Avocations: writing, travel, community involvement. Home: 15031 Chaseridge Dr Missouri City TX 77489 Personal E-mail: k.gerard-starnes@sbcglobal.net.

STARNES, SOFIA MOLINA, writer, editor; b. Manila, Philippines, Dec. 10, 1952; arrived in US, 1986, naturalized, 1989; d. Antonio M. Molina and Carmen Gómez-Arnau; m. William H. Starnes, Jr., Mar. 4, 1986. BA in English Philology, U. Complutense, Madrid, 1975; MA in English Philology, U. Complutense, 1976. Tchr. English Colegio Manzanares, Madrid, 1970—72, Colegio Rodríguez Sopeña, Madrid, 1973—83, Centro Profesional Sopeña, Madrid, 1980—84, head studies, 1982—84; instr. English Berlitz Sch. Langs., Madrid, 1984—86; freelance writer and manuscript editor Williamsburg, Va., 1986—. Assoc. editor Eve's Legacy, NYC, 1987—89; poetry columnist Christianity and the Arts (on-line), Chgo., 1999—2001; jury panel mem. Va. Commn. Arts, Richmond, 2001; manuscript editor Creative Writing Critiques, Williamsburg, Va., 1995—; poetry judge Christopher Newport U. Writers Conf., Newport News, Va.; poetry editor Anglican Theol. Rev., 2007—; up write series poet Lock Haven U., 2008. Author: more than 160 pub. poems, The Soul's Landscape, 2002, A Commerce of Moments, 2003, Corpus Homini, 2008; contbr. essays to Christianity and the Arts, Christianity and Lit. Liturgical min. St. Bede Cath. Ch., Williamsburg. Recipient Rainer Maria Rilke Poetry award, Internat. Tng. Sys., Calif., 1997, Aldrich Poetry award, Aldrich Mus. Contemporary Art, Ridgefield, Mass., 2001, Editor's prize, 2001, Transcontinental Poetry prize, Pavement Saw Press, 2001, Editor's Choice Marlboro Poetry award, Marlboro Rev., Vt., 2002, Honor Book award, Libr. Va., Richmond, 2003, Whitebird Poetry Series prize, Wings Press, San Antonio, 2008, Christianity and Literature Poetry prize, Conf. on Christianity and Lit., Calif.; named Disting. scholar, Union Coll. Ky.,

2009; Poetry fellowship, Va. Commn. for Arts, 2000. Mem.: Hon. Order Ky. Colonels, Legacy Soc. Union Coll., Acad. Am. Poets, Poetry Soc. Va. (poetry judge), Va. Writers Club (2d v.p. 1997—98, poetry judge 2005, Outstanding Poetry Achievement award 2006), Conf. on Christianity and Lit. (Poetry prize 2004), Ut Prosim Soc., Va. Tech. Roman Catholic. Avocations: travel, needlecrafts, creative cuisine. Home: 4951 Burnley Dr Williamsburg VA 23188-8806 Personal E-mail: smstarnes@cox.net.

STARNES, WILLIAM HERBERT, JR., chemist, educator; b. Knoxville, Tenn., Dec. 2, 1934; s. William Herbert and Edna Margaret (Osborne) Starnes; m. Maria Sofia Molina, Mar. 4, 1986. Attended, Union Coll., Ky., 1950—52; BS with honors, Va. Poly. Inst., Blacksburg, 1955; PhD, Ga. Inst. Tech., Atlanta, 1960. Rsch. chemist Esso Rsch. & Engring. Co., Baytown, Tex., 1960—62, sr. rsch. chemist, 1962—64, polymer additives sect. head, 1964—65, rsch. specialist, 1965—67, rsch. assoc., 1967—71; instr. and rsch. assoc. dept. chemistry U. Tex., Austin, 1971—73; mem. tech. staff AT&T Bell Labs., Murray Hill, NJ, 1973—85; prof. chemistry Poly. U., Bklyn., 1985—89, head dept. chemistry and life scis., 1985—88, assoc. dir. polymer durability ctr., 1987—89; Floyd Dewey Gottwald Sr. prof. chemistry Coll. William and Mary, Williamsburg, Va., 1989—2006, Floyd Dewey Gottwald Sr. prof. chemistry emeritus, 2006—, prof. applied sci., 1990—2006. Invited lectr. several fgn. countries and U.S.; ofcl. guest USSR Acad. Scis., 1990, Russian Acad. Scis., 1992; disting. vis. prof. Beijing Inst. Tech., 1996; vis. scientist Tex. Acad. Scis., 1964—67; mem. bd. doctoral thesis examiners Indian Inst. Tech., New Delhi, 1988, McGill U., Montreal, 1989, MacQuarie U., Sydney, 1991, McMaster U., Hamilton, Canada, 1994; panelist, reviewer NSF Acad. Rsch. Facilities Modernization Program, 1990; channel program mentor U. Cairo, 1994—95; mem. opinion leader panel Wall St. Jour., 1995—; charter mem. dept. chemistry adv. coun. Va. Poly. Inst. and State U., 1998—; sci. advisor European Multinational Environ. Rsch. Project on PVC in Soil and Landfills, 1995—99; cons. numerous indsl. cos., govtl. and pvt. agys.; course dir. continuing edn. Editor-in-chief: Jour. Vinyl and Additive Tech., 1998—, mem. adv. bd., bd. reviewers: Jour. Vinyl Tech., 1981—83, mem. editl. bd.: Jour. Chem. and Biochem. Kinetics, 1992—, Polymer Degradation and Stability, 1997—, Internat. Jour. Coatings Sci., 2001—, The Chemist, 2003—; contbr. chapters to books, articles to profl. jours. Recipient Profl. Progress award, Soc. Profl. Chemists and Engrs., 1968, Disting. Tech. Staff award, AT&T Bell Labs., 1982, Polymer Sci. Pioneer award, Polymer News, 1988, Honor Scroll award, N.J. Inst. Chemists, 1989, Excellence in Innovation award, Hampton Rds. Tech. Coun., 2004; named honoree Plastics History and Artifacts Program, Plastics Pioneers Assn., 2001, Disting. Alumni Scholar, Union Coll., 2009, Hon. Order of Ky. Cols., 2009; named to Southwest Va. Walk of Fame, 2008; grantee, NSF, 1989—, Nat. Bur. Stds. Ctr. Fire Rsch., Internat. Copper Rsch. Assn., Va. Ctr. Innovative Tech., GenCorp Found., several indsl. cos.; fellow, NSF, 1958—60. Fellow: AAAS (Project 2061 1985—86, chmn. chemistry subpanel 1985—86, mem. panel on phys. scis. and engring. 1985—86), Soc. Plastics Engrs. (thesis advisor nat. award of vinyl plastics divsn. 1996, 1998, nat. publs. com. 1998—2001, 2006—, Best Student Paper Advisor nat. award vinyl plastics divsn. 2007, hon. grantee), NY Acad. Scis., Am. Inst. Chemists (life); mem.: Legacy Soc., Union Coll., Soc. Chem. Industry, Va. Acad. Sci., Am. Chem. Soc. (bd. dirs. southeastern Tex. sect. 1970, spkrs. bur. divsn. polymer chemistry 1976—, mem.-at-large exec. com. Va. sect. 1995), N.Am. Thermal Analysis Soc., Ut Prosim Soc. Va. Tech., Phi Lambda Upsilon (pres. Va. Poly. Inst. chpt. 1954—55), Sigma Xi (M. A. Ferst award Ga. Inst. Tech. chpt. 1960), Phi Kappa Phi (life). Achievements include patents in field; invention of ester thiol stabilization technology for poly(vinyl chloride); research in degradation, stabilization, flammability, microstructures and polymerization mechanisms of synthetic polymers, especially poly(vinyl chloride); free radical chemistry; carbon-13 nuclear magnetic resonance and organic synthesis; subspecialities include organic chemistry, polymer chemistry. Office: Coll William and Mary Dept Chemistry PO Box 8795 Williamsburg VA 23187-8795 Business E-Mail: whstar@wm.edu.

STAROBIN, LESLIE ANN, art educator; d. Oscar Ephraim Starobin and Ruth Rosen Singer; m. Shlomo Segev, Oct. 7, 1990; children: Ori Benjamin-Reuven Segev, Tamar Shirit Segev. BA, Hampshire Coll., Amherst, Mass., 1977; MFA, San Francisco Art Inst., 1982. Prof. Framingham State Coll., Mass., 1986—. Exhibition, The Last Address, Danforth (Hadassah Brandeis Inst. Rsch. award, 2007); photographer (exhibition) Shadows Across the Promised Land, Oregon, montage and photography Visual Montages-Of Past and Future, photographer Childhood: Notes and Letters (Nat. Endowment, 1984), photography Dead Sea Bathers, Worcester Art Mus. Sch. (Kinnicutt award, 1988), photographer Dancers' Feet, Duke U. Art Mus. (Honorarium, 1990), Photographs by Leslie Starobin, Smith Coll. Mus. Art. Vol. Polit. Orgns., Needham, Mass., 2008; vol. advisor to art curriculum Rashi Sch., Newton, Mass., 2000—06. Mem.: Photographic Resource Ctr. Office: Framingham State Coll 100 State St Framingham MA 01701 Personal E-mail: leslie@starobinartworks.com. Business E-Mail: lstarobin@framingham.edu.

STAROBIN, MICHAEL, composer, orchestrator; m. Hannah Starobin; children: Joshua, Samuel. Orchestrator (Broadway plays) Sunday in the Park with George, 1984 (Drama Desk award for Outstanding Orchestration, 1984), The Mystery of Edwin Drood, 1985, Sunday in the Park with George, 1994, Rags, 1986, Romance/Romance, 1988, Carrie, 1988, Legs Diamond, 1988, Once on This Island, 1990, Guys & Dolls, 1992, Falsettos, 1992, Face Value, 1993, A Christmas Carol, 1994, Beauty and the Beast, 1994, King David, 1997, The Adventures of Tom Sawyer, 2001, Assassins, 2004 (Tony award for Best Orchestrations, 2004), Drama Desk award for Best Orchestrations, 2004), The 25th Annual Putnam County Spelling Bee, 2005, Dr. Seuss' How the Grinch Stole Christmas!, 2006, The Little Mermaid, 2008, Next to Normal, 2009 (Tony award for Best Orchestration, 2009), numerous off-Broadway/regional plays, (films) Beauty and the Beast, 1991, Aladdin, 1992, Life with Mikey, 1993, Addams Family Values, 1993, Pocahontas, 1995, The Hunchback of Notre Dame, 1996, Hercules, 1997, In & Out, 1997, Beauty and the Beast: The Enchanted Christmas, 1997, Chicago, 2002, (TV films) Rodgers & Hammerstein's Cinderella, 1997, South Pacific, 2001, A Christmas Carol, 2004, Once Upon a Mattress, 2005; composer: Ringling Bros., Barnum & Bailey Circus, 1999, 2000, 2003, 2005, (TV miniseries) Freedom: A Story of Us, 2003. Recipient LA Drama Critic's award, 1985. Office: 134 Croton Ave Mount Kisco NY 10549 E-mail: michael@starobin.com.*

STAROBIN, NANCY, photographer; b. Washington, Feb. 14, 1955; d. Sam Starobin and Rita Sternberg. Student, Hamilton Sch. Photography, 1980—82, Santa Monica Cmty. Coll., 1986—87. Photographer Howard County Times, Ellicot City, Md., 1974—75, Columbia Flier, 1975—76; ofcl. photographer United Way Ctrl. Md., 1976—78; stringer AP, UPI, L.A. Daily News, LA, 1983—90; owner Nancy Starobin Photo, Columbia, Md., 1974—2008, LA, 1974—2008. N.Y. Times, L.A. Times, Horse Illustrated, Capitol Records, Wilhelmina West, Car Craft, Ins. Inst. for Hwy. Safety, Petersen's Photographic, Photographer's Market, Santa Monica Weekend Outlook, and others. Vol. George McGovern Campaign, Washington, 1972. Home: PO Box 1893 Glendora CA 91740

STAROSELSKY, ALEXANDER, mechanical engineer, materials scientist; 3 children. ScD, Russian Acad. Sci., Moscow, 1991; PhD, MIT, 1997. Vis. scientist Courant Inst. of Math. Scis., NYU, 1993; staff scientist United Techs. Rsch. Ctr., East Hartford, Conn., 1997—2004, Pratt and Whitney, 2004—. Adj. prof. Hartford U., Conn., 1998—2006, Rensselaer Poly. Inst., 2007—. Contbr. articles to profl. jours. Grantee NASA, 2000—02, Office of Naval Rsch., 2001—07, USAF, 2006—. Fellow: NY. Acad. Sci.; mem.: ASME, Soc. for Computational Engring. and Sci. Achievements include patents in field; research in fracture: thermal-mechanical fatigue, mechanics of advanced alloys; large deformation plasticity; surfactant assisted fracture; acoustics, vibration; mass transport in non-saturated porous media. Office: Pratt and Whitney 400 Main St MS 165-16 East Hartford CT 06108 Personal E-mail: starosel@alum.mit.edu. Business E-Mail: alexander.staroselsky@pw.utc.com.

STARR, ALBERT, thoracic surgeon, educator, research scientist; b. NYC, June 1, 1926; MD, Columbia Coll. Physicians & Surgeons, 1949; HHD, Lewis and Clark Coll., 1968; PhD (hon.), U. London, 1986. Cert. Surgery, Thoracic Surgery. Intern John Hopkins Hosp., Balt., 1949—50; resident Bellevue Hosp. & Presbyn. Hosp., 1950—57; asst. in surgery Columbia U., 1957; hosp. appointment Heart Inst., St Vincent, Portland, Oreg.; prof. surgery, head heart surgery prog. Oreg. Health Sci. U., 1957—64; pediatric staff mem. Starr-Wood Children's Cardiac Ctr.; med. dir. Providence Heart and Vascular Inst., Portland, Oreg., 1964—; dir., Bioscience R&D Providence Health Sys., Oreg.; chair holder Albert Starr Academic Ctr. for Cardiac Surgery, Oreg. Recipient Oreg. Heart Assn. award for Scientific Achievement, 1964, Modern Medicine award, 1971, Golden Plate award, Am. Acad. Achievement, 1973, Internat. Heart Pioneer award, Societe de Chirurgie Thoracique Cardio-Vasculaire de Langue Francaise, 2000; co-recipient (with Alain Carpentier) Lasker-DeBakey Clin. Med. Rsch. award, Lasker Found., 2007. Mem.: ACS (chmn. thoracic adv. bd.), Am. Coll. Chest Physicians (past trustee), Western Thoracic Surgical Assn., Assn. Thoracic and Cardiovascular Surgeons of Asia, Soc. U. Surgeons, Soc. Thoracic Surgeons (pres. 1985—86), Pan Pacific Surgical Assn., Internat. Cardiovascular Soc., Am. Surgical Assn., AMA, Am. Coll. Cardiology (Disting. Scientist award 1988), Am. Assn. for Thoracic Surgery (past coun. mem.), Pan Hellenic Surgical Soc. (hon.). Achievements include co-inventing of the first artificial heart valve, successfully implanted in 1960; joined Dr. Alain Carpentier in Paris for one of the world's first computer-assisted robotic surgeries in 1998. Home: Starr Wood Cardiac Group Svcs 9155 SW Barnes Rd #240 Portland OR 97225 Office Phone: 503-297-1419. Office Fax: 503-296-4027.*

STARR, DAVID, editor, publisher; b. NYC, Aug. 1, 1922; s. Aaron and Helen (Simon) S.; m. Marjorie Giffen, Aug. 3, 1943; children: Pamela, Peter. BA, Queens Coll., 1942. Reporter, rewriteman L.I. Daily Press, 1942-50; exec. editor Nassau Daily Rev. Star, 1950-53; asst. editor Newark Star-Ledger, 1954-56; asso. editor L.I. Press, 1953-54, 56-62, mng. editor, 1962-69, editor, 1969-77; sr. editor Newhouse Newspapers, 1971—; pub. Springfield Republican, 1977-99, pres., 1999—. Pres. Springfield Ctrl., Inc., 1978-88, chmn., 1989-95. Trustee Nassau C.C., SUNY, 1959-66; bd. dirs. Springfield Libr. and Mus. Assn., chmn., 1988-90; mem. Mass. Cultural Coun., 1980—; bd. dirs. Am. Arts Alliance, 1988-92, chmn., 1989-92. Mem. Am. Soc. Newspaper Editors, Am. Newspaper Pubs. Assn. Office: The Republican Co 1860 Main St Springfield MA 01103-1000 E-mail: dstarr@repub.com.

STARR, DOROTHY ANNE, retired psychiatrist; b. NYC, July 17, 1922; d. James Edward and Eileen Lillian (Gorman) S.; m. Charles O. Olsen, Aug. 29 1953; children: Margrete, Therese, Sara, Marie. BS, NYU, 1943; MD, SUNY, 1950. Intern St. Johns Episcopal Hosp., Bklyn., 1950-51; resident in ob-gyn St. Albans Naval Hosp., N.Y., 1951-52; resident psychiatrist Bethesda (Md.) Naval Hosp., 1953-54, St. Elizabeth's Hosp., Washington, 1954-56; pvt. practice psychiatry Washington, 1957—2004. Chief adult mental health Dept. Pub. Health, Washington, 1960-64; cons. St. Elizabeth's Hosp., Washington, 1965-73; physician mem. Mental Health Commn., Washington, 1969-73;/ asst. clin. prof. Georgetown U., Washington, 1975-81; assy. rep. Am. Psychiatric Assn., 1981-87, asys. recorder, 1987-88; bd. dirs. Nat. Capital Underwriters, Inc., Washington, 1980-97, Legal Resources Fund, Washington, 1982-84; psychiat. cons. Christ House Health Care for the Homeless, 1995-2005. With U.S. Army, 1943-45, USN, 1950-54. Mem. AMA (mem. adv. panel on women in medicine 1989-91, chmn. adv. panel 1991-92), Am. Med. Women's Assn., Washington Psychiatry Soc. (mem. coun. 1965-67, 71-72, asst. del. 1981-87, sec. 1972-73), Med. Soc. D.C. (pres. 1980, mem. exec. bd. 1974-92, chmn. exec. bd. 1981, alt. del. 1983-87, del. 1988-92), Am. Psychiat. Assn. (fellow, recorder assembly 1987-88). Home: 700 New Hampshire Ave Nw Washington DC 20037-2407

STARR, ISIDORE, law educator; b. Bklyn., Nov. 24, 1911; BA, CCNY, 1932; LLB, St. John's U., Jamaica, NY, 1936; MA, Columbia U., 1939; JSD, Bklyn. Law Sch., 1942; PhD, New Sch. Social Rsch., 1957. Bar: NY 1937. Tchr. various high schs., NYC, 1934-61; from assoc. prof. to prof. edn. Queen's Coll., 1961-75, prof. emeritus, 1975—. Dir. Inst. on Law-Related Edn., Lincoln-Filene Ctr., Tufts U., 1963, Law Studies Inst., NYC, 1974; adv. on Our Living Bill of Rights Film Series (6 films) Ency. Brit. Ednl. Corp.; mem. Ariz. Ctr. for Law-Related Edn.; coun. on pub. legal edn. State of Wash., 2001—; cons. in field. Author: The Lost Generation of Prince Edward County, 1968, The Gideon Case, 1968, The Feiner Case, 1968, The Mapp Case, 1968, The Supreme Court and Contemporary Issues, 1968, Human Rights in the United States, 1969, The American Judicial System, 1972, The Idea of Liberty, 1978, Justice: Due Process of Law, 1981; co-editor Living American Documents, 1971, (with John Hope Franklin) The Negro in 20th Century America, 1967. Bd. dirs. Phi Alpha Delta Juvenile Justice Program, 1981—. 1st lt. U.S. Army, 1943-46. John Hay fellow, 1952-53; recipient Army Commendation medal, 1946, Outstanding Citizen award Philip Morris Cos., 1992. Mem. ABA (hon. chair adv. commn. on Youth Edn. for Citizenship, Isidore Starr award for Spl. Achievment in Law Studies, Leon Jaworski award 1989), Nat. Coun. Social Studies (past pres.), Washington Coun. Pub. Legal Edn., Phi Beta Kappa, Phi Alpha Delta (cert. of appreciation 1981). Home: 12501 Greenwood Ave N Apt C406 Seattle WA 98133-8000

STARR, JUDSON WILMARTH, lawyer; b. Boulder, Colo., July 18, 1945; s. Wilmarth Holt and Eva Jones Starr; 1 child, Alexander. BA, Washington and Jefferson Coll., 1968; JD, Georgetown U., 1975. Bar: D.C. 1975, Va. 1978. Staff Office of the Adminstr. U.S. EPA, Washington, 1972—73; asst. editor Environ. Law Inst., Washington, 1973—75; assoc. Price Grove, Washington, 1975—78; dir. environ. crimes unit Dept. Justice, Washington, 1982—87; chief environ. crimes sect., 1987—88; ptnr., Environ., Corp. Def. & White Collar practices Venable LLP, Washington, 1988—. Adv. mem. U.S. Sentencing Commn. on Corp. Sentencing; co-chair Ann. Am. Law Inst.-ABA Conf. on Environ. Crimes; chair Environ. Crimes Subcom. Bus.; mem. adv. bd. Corp. Counsel Inst., Georgetown Univ.; mem. adv. panel criminal law Am. Law Inst. of ABA. Contbr. articles to profl. jours.; editor: Georgetown Rev. Law & Pub. Interest; co-author: Environmental Crimes Deskbook, 1995, Environmental Criminal Liability: Avoiding & Defending Enforcement Actions, 1995, Chamber of Shipping of America's Environmental Criminal Liability in the United States: A Handbook for the Marine Industry, 2000; author: The Knock on the Door: Preparing for and Responding to a Criminal Investigation, 1999. Founding mem., pres. Bethesda (Md.)/Chevy Chase Baseball League, 1995—99. Capt. US Army, 1968—70. Decorated Bronze Star; named a Top Washington Lawyer, Washingtonian Mag., 2004, 2007; named one of Nation's Top White Collar Crime Experts, Nat. Law Jour., Corp. Counsel's Best Lawyers, Criminal Def. Law, 2004; named to Best Lawyers in Am., 2003—04, 2005—06, 2006—07, Chambers US, Am. Leading Lawyers Bus., 2004—07. Mem.: Barristers. Avocations: baseball, golf, sailing. Office: Venable LLP 575 7th St NW Washington DC 20004 Office Phone: 202-344-4886. Office Fax: 202-344-8300. Business E-Mail: jwstarr@venable.com.

STARR, KENNETH WINSTON, dean, law educator, lawyer; b. Vernon, Tex., July 21, 1946; s. W. D. and Vannie Maude (Trimble) Starr; m. Alice Jean Mendell, Aug. 23, 1970; children: Randall Postley, Carolyn Marie, Cynthia Anne. BA, George Washington U., 1968; MA, Brown U., 1969; JD, Duke U., 1973; LLD (hon.), Hampden Sydney Coll., 1992, Shenandoah U., 1993, John Marshall Coll. Law, 1993, Pepperdine U., 1996. Bar: Calif. 1973, D.C. 1979, Va. 1979. Law clk. to Judge David Dyer U.S. Ct. Appeals (5th cir.), Miami, Fla., 1973—74; assoc. Gibson, Dunn & Crutcher, Los Angeles, 1974—75; law clk. to Chief Justice Warren E. Burger U.S. Supreme Ct., Washington, 1975—77; assoc., ptnr. Gibson, Dunn & Crutcher, Washington, 1977—81; counselor to atty gen. of U.S. Dept. Justice, Washington, 1981—83; judge U.S. Ct. Appeals (D.C. circuit), Washington, 1983—89; solicitor gen. US Dept. Justice, Washington, 1989—93; ptnr. Kirkland & Ellis LLP, Washington, 1993—2005, of counsel LA, 2005—; ind. counsel for Whitewater, 1994—99; Duane and Kelly Roberts Dean and Dean, prof. law Pepperdine U. Sch. of Law, Malibu, Calif., 2004—. Author: First Among Equals: The Supreme Court in American Life, 2002; contbr. articles to legal jours. Legal advisor CAB transition team office of pres.-elect, 1980—81, SEC transition team, 1980—81; bd. adv. Duke Law Jour. Recipient Disting. Alumni awards, George Washington U., Duke U., Atty. Gen.'s award for disting. svc., 1993, Am. Values award, U.S. Indsl. Coun. Ednl. Found., 1993; named one of 75 Best Lawyers In Washington, Washingtonian survey mag., 2002. Fellow: Am. Bar Found. (jud. fellows com., jud. conf. com. on bicentennial of U.S. constn.); mem.: ABA, Am. Inns of Court, Va. Bar Assn., D.C. Bar Assn., Calif. Bar Assn., Supreme Ct. Hist. Soc., Inst. Jud. Adminstrn. (pres.), Am. Judicature Soc., Am. Law Inst., Phi Delta Phi (Hughes chpt. Man of Yr. 1973), Order of Coif. Republican. Office: Pepperdine U Sch of Law 24255 Pacific Coast Hwy Malibu CA 90263 Fax: 310-506-4266. Business E-Mail: ken.starr@pepperdine.edu.*

STARR, KEVIN, librarian, educator; b. San Francisco, Sept. 3, 1940; m. Sheila Gordon, June 10, 1963; children: Marian, Jessica. BA, U. San Francisco, 1962; MA, Harvard U., 1965, PhD, 1969; MLS, U. Calif., Berkeley, 1974; postgrad., Ch. Div. Sch. Pacific, Berkeley, 1983-84. From asst. to assoc. prof. Am. lit. Harvard U., Cambridge, Mass., 1969-74; city libr. San Francisco, 1973-76; prin. Kevin Starr Assocs., San Francisco, 1983-85; prof. comm. arts U. San Francisco, 1981-89; prof. Sch. Planning and Devel. U. So. Calif., 1989—98, univ. prof., 1998—; state libr. Calif., 1994—2004; state libr. emeritus, 2004—. Allston Burr sr. tutor Eliot House Harvard U., Cambridge, 1970-73; cons. Beyl and Boyd, Inc., San Francisco, 1979-83; sr. cons. Hill and Knowlton USA, San Francisco, 1983-84; vis. assoc. prof. English U. Calif., Berkely, 1974, vis. lectr. polit. sci., 1976, lectr. librarianship, 1978; adj. prof. humanities San Francisco State U., 1975-76; Regent's lectr. polit. sci. U. Calif., Riverside, 1977; adj. prof. English Santa Clara (Calif.) U., 1977-78; vis. prof. history U. Calif., Davis, 1985-86; vis. scholar, media fellow Hoover Inst., 1986-88; vis. fellow Ctr. Humanistic Studies, Claremont McKenna Coll., 1987; faculty master Embassy Residential Coll., 1990-94. Sr. editor New West Mag., 1977; vatican corr. Hearst Newspapers, Rome, 1978; columnist Examiner, San Francisco, 1977-83; contbng. editor L.A. Times, 1994—; contbr. articles to profl. jours., chpts. to books; auth. Americans and the California Dream, 1850-1915, 1973, Inventing the Dream: California Through the Progressive Era, 1985, Material Dreams: Southern California Through the 1920s, 1990, Endangered Dreams: The Great Depression in California, 1996, The Dream Endures: California Enters the 1940s, 1997, Embattled Dreams: California in War and Peace, 1940-1950, 2002, Coast of Dreams: California on the Edge, 1990-2003, 2004, California: A History, 2005. Exec. aide to mayor San Francisco, 1973; bd. trustees Am. Issues Forum, 1975-76, Calif. Hist. Soc., 1992—; co-chmn. sister city com., San Francisco and Sydney, Australia, 1981-86; advisor Jr. League San Francisco, 1982-84; canidate San Francisco Bd. Suprs., 1984; councilor Am. Antiquarian Soc., 1996—; mem. Calif. Coun. Humanities, 1996—; regent Cathedral St. Mary Assumption, San Francisco, 1996—. Lt. German Army, 1962-64. Recipient Nat. Humanities Medal, NEH, 2006. Mem.: Calif. Historical Soc., Calif. Coun. Humanities, Am. Antiquarian Soc. Office: Univ So Calif SOS 175 Los Angeles CA 90089

STARR, KIMBERLY ANN, assistant principal, school system administrator; d. Lauren J. Holcomb and Carol A. Rood; m. Edwin E. Starr, Apr. 15, 1989; children: Zachary R., Bethany A. BA, U. Mary Hardin-Baylor, Belton, Tex., 1992; MS, U. Ctrl. Ark., Conway, 2006. Cert. educator 1-6 Ark. Dept. Edn., 2000, spl. edn. Pre-K-12 Ark. Dept. Edn., 2000, ESL Pre-K-12 Ark. Dept. Edn., 2000, adminstr. P-8 Ark. Dept. Edn., 2006. Educator Ft. Worth Ind. Sch. Dist., 1993—97, 1st Presbyn. Presch., Arlington, Tex., 1997—99; coord. Conway Pub. Schs., 2000—07; asst. prin. Florence Mattison Internat. Elem. Sch. for Conway Pub. Schs., 2007—. Com. mem. CAPCA Head Start, Conway, 2002—04. Grantee William F. Goodling Even Start, US Dept. Edn., 2001—, Schs. 21st Century, Yale U., 2003—05, Ark. Better Chance for Sch. Success, Ark. HHS, 2004—. Mem.: Ark. Assn. Elem. Sch. Prins., Ark. Assn. Curriculum and Instrnl. Adminstrs., Ark. Early Childhood Assn., Ark. Assn. Ednl. Adminstrs., So. Early Childhood Assn. Presbyterian. Avocations: reading, travel.

STARR, MARTIN KENNETH, management educator; b. NYC, May 21, 1927; s. Harry and Melanie (Krauss) S.; m. Polly Exner, Apr. 3, 1955; children: Christopher Herschel, Loren Michael. BS, MIT, 1948; MS, Columbia U., 1951, PhD, 1953. Ptnr., dir. M.K. Starr Assocs., 1956-61; prof. mgmt. sci. Columbia U., NYC, 1961-96, dir. Ctr. for the Study of Ops., 1980-95, dir. Ctr. for Enterprise Mgmt., 1995-96, vice dean Grad. Sch. Bus., 1974-75; Disting. prof. ops. mgmt. Crummer Grad. Sch. Bus. Rollins Coll., Winter Park, Fla., 1996—2003, prof. emeritus, 2003—, dir. Ctr. for Enterprise Mgmt., 1996—2001; prof. emeritus Columbia U., 1996—. Lectr. in field; cons. in field. Author: (with David W. Miller) The Structure of Human Decisions, 1967, (with David W. Miller) Inventory Control-Theory and Practice, 1972, Product Design and Decision Theory, 1963, (with David W. Miller) Executive Decisions and Operations Research, 2d edit., 1969, Systems Management of Operations, 1971, Management: A Modern Approach, 1971, Production Management: Systems and Synthesis, 2d edit., 1972, (with Irving Stein) The Practice of Management Science, 1976, Operations Management, 1978, (with David G. Dannebring) Management Science: An Introduction, 1981, (with Earl K. Bowen) Statistics for Business and Economics, 1982, (with Marion Sobol) Statistics for Business and Economics: An Action Learning Approach, 1983, Managing Production and Operations, 1989, Global Corporate Alliances and the Competitive Edge, 1991, (with Marion Sobol) Introduction to Statistics for Executives, 1993, Operations Management: A Systems Approach, 1996, CD-text rev., 2000, Production and Operations Management, 2004, 2nd edit., 2008, Foundations of Production and Operations Management, 2006, Executive Readings in Management Science, 1965, (with Milan Zeleny) Multiple Criteria Decision Making, 1977; editor: Global Competitiveness: Getting the U.S. Back on Track, 1988; editor-in-chief Mgmt. Sci., 1967-82; mem. editl. bd. Behavioral Sci., 1970-2002, Internat. Jour. Flexible Mfg. Sys., 1989—; mem. editl. adv. bd. Jour. Ops. Mgmt., 1983-2009; editl. adviser Operational Rsch. Quar., 1970-85; cons. editor: Columbia Jour. World Business: Focus: Decision Making, fall, 1977, Quantitative Methods in Mgmt.; contbr. articles to profl. jours. Fellow Inst. for Ops. Rsch. and the Mgmt. Scis., Inst. Mgmt. Scis. (pres. 1974-75), Prodn. and Ops. Mgmt. Soc. (pres.-elect 1994—, pres. 1995, past pres., bd. dirs. 1996—, chair Coun. of Pres. 1999—); mem. Beta Gamma Sigma. Achievements include having an annual award for practitioner excellence in operations named in his honor by the Production and Operations Management Society. Home: 100 S Interlachen Ave #304 Winter Park FL 32789-4450 Office: Rollins Coll 120 Crummer Grad Sch Bus Winter Park FL 32789 Office Phone: 407-212-1118. Business E-Mail: starr@columbia.edu. *The ability to manage complex systems, to maximize societal benefits under conditions of economic stability and physical security has become the most pressing requirement in the vicennial period 2010-2029. Remarkable growth of global systems interdependencies has occurred since 2000. Because these connections were not understood naive financial engineering led to a worldwide economic crisis. To set things right requires systemic intelligence of global connections. Management science uses the systems approach to combine art and logic to create transitions that have significant social benefit. If is properly used the impact of systems-oriented management science can help to avoid chaos and disasters. The goal is to make life in the 21st century better than ever for the entire world community.*

STARR, MICHAEL, lawyer; b. NYC, July 20, 1948; s. Harry and Gertrude (Spitz) S.; m. Marsha Talan, Sept. 5,1982; children: Rachel Talan, Garret Matthew. BA summa cum laude, SUNY, Binghamton, 1970; PhD in Philosophy, U. Mich., 1976; JD, Yale U., New Haven, Conn., 1979. Bar: NY 1980, US Dist. Ct. (so. and ea. dists.) NY 1981, US Ct. Appeals (DC cir.) 1980, US Ct. Appeals (2d cir.) 2000, US Supreme Ct. 1986. Law clk. to judge Abner J. Mikva US Ct. Appeals (DC cir.), Washington, 1979—80; assoc. Kaye, Scholer, Fierman, Hays & Handler, NYC, 1980—88; of counsel Parker, Chapin, Flattau & Klimpl LLP, NYC, 1988—97; ptnr. Hogan & Hartson LLP, NYC, 1997—. Bd. arbitrators Nat. Assn. Securities Dealers, 1995-03; mem. human resources com. NYC Partnership & C. of C., 1990-98; bd. dirs. Ct. Apptd. Spl. Advs., NYC, 1982-2000; mediator US Ct. (ea. dist.) NY, 1992—. Editor Yale Law Jour., 1978-79; editl. bd. Employment Law Strategist, The Corporate Counsellor; employment law columnist Nat. Law Jour., 1998—; contbr. articles to profl. publs. Woodrow Wilson fellow, 1970. Fellow Coll. Labor and Employment Lawyers; mem. ABA (labor and employment law sect., internat. labor law com.), Internat. Soc. Labor Law, Fed. Bar Coun., Assn. of Bar of City of NY (US in global economy select com. 1995-00, labor and employment law com. 1989-92, civil rights com. 1985-88, children and the law com. 1984-85), Coun. NY Law Assocs. (bd. dirs. 1982-86), Second Cir. Pro Bono Panel Civil Appeals. Office: Hogan & Hartson LLP 875 3rd Ave New York NY 10022-6225 Home Phone: 212-249-5021; Office Phone: 212-918-3000. Business E-Mail: mstarr@hhlaw.com.

STARR, ROSS MARC, economist, educator; b. Oak Ridge, Nov. 14, 1945; s. Chauncey and Doris E. S.; m. Susan S. Strauss, July 2, 1967; children: Daniel, Diana. BS, Stanford U., 1966, PhD, 1972. Cons. Rand Corp., summers 1966, 67, Western Mgmt. Sci. Inst., Grad. Sch. Mgmt., UCLA, summers 1967, 71; Cowles Found. staff rsch. economist Yale U., New Haven, 1970, faculty, 1970-74, assoc. prof. econs., 1974, U. Calif., Davis, 1975-76, prof. econs., 1976-80, San Diego, 1980—, chmn. dept., 1987-90. Vis. lectr. London Sch. Econs., 1973-74, Peoples U. China, Beijing, 1987; vis. scholar U. Calif., Berkeley, 1978-80, vis. prof., 1997; vis. prof. European U. Inst. Florence, Italy, 2007. Author: General Equilibrium Theory: An Introduction, 1997; co-editor: Essays in Honor of Kenneth J. Arrow, 1986: v.1, Social Choice and Public Decision Making, v.2, Equilibrium Analysis, v.3, Uncertainty, Information and Communication; editor: Gen. Equilibrium Models of Monetary Economies, 1989; contbr. articles to profl. jours. NDEA fellow, 1966-69, Yale jr. faculty fellow, 1973-74, Guggenheim fellow, 1978-79; NSF grant, 1979-81, 83-85. Office: U Calif San Diego Dept Econs 0508 9500 Gilman Dr La Jolla CA 92093-0508 Home Phone: 858-455-1630; Office Phone: 858-534-3879. Business E-Mail: rstarr@ucsd.edu.

STARR, STEPHEN, restaurant owner; Grad., Temple U., 1977. Owner Grand Mom Minnie's, Phila.; owner cabaret, comedy club Stars, Phila.; owner Ripley Music Hall, Phila., The Concert Co. (acquired by Electric Factory Concerts in 1990), Phila., Shake, Burger and Roll, Phila., The Bank, Phila., Cafe Republic, Phila.; founder, owner Starr Restaurant Org., Phila., 1995—, Continental Restaurant and Martini Bar, Phila., 1995—, Buddakan, Phila., Tangerine, Phila., Pod, Phila., Alma de Cuba, Phila., Morimoto, Phila., Jones, Phila., Angelina, Phila., El Vez, Phila., Striped Bass, Phila., Washington Square, Phila., Barclay Prime, Phila., Morimoto, NYC, 2006—, Buddakan, NYC, 2006—. Named Restaurateur of the Year, Bon Appetit mag., 2005. Office: Starr Restaurant Org 134 Market St Philadelphia PA 19106 Office Phone: 215-923-4835.

STARR, STEVEN DAWSON, photographer; b. Albuquerque, Sept. 6, 1944; s. Richard Vernon and Carol (Harley) S.; m. Marilynne Sue Anderson, Aug. 6, 1965; 1 child, Stephen Richard. Student, Antioch Coll., 1962-63, Bethel Coll., 1963-64; BA, San Jose State Coll., 1967. Photographer San Jose Mercury-News, Calif., 1966-67; photographer, picture editor A.P., 1968-73; audiovisual producer Starr Productions, Inc., Coral Gables, Fla., 1974-85; photographer Picture Group Agy., 1986-88, Saba Press, NYC, 1988—2000, Corbis, 2000—; writer Cltristian Ministry Pub., 2002—, photo journalist, 2002. Recipient Pulitzer prize for spot news photography, 1970, Nat. Headliners award, 1970, George Polk Meml. award, 1970, Pictures of Year hon. mention, 1970

STARRETT, FREDERICK KENT, lawyer; b. Lincoln, Nebr., May 23, 1947; s. Clyde Frederick and Helen Virginia (Meyers) Starrett; m. Linda Lee Jensen, Jan. 19, 1969; children: Courtney, Kathryn, Scott. BA, U. Nebr., 1969; JD, Creighton U., 1976. Bar: Nebr 1976, Kans 1977, US Dist Ct Nebr 1976, US Dist Ct Kans 1977, US Ct Appeals (8th and 10th cirs) 1983, Mo 1987, US Dist Ct (we dit) Mo 1987, US Supreme Ct 1993, US Ct Appeals 9th cirs. 2009. Pvt. practice law, Gt. Bend, Kans., 1976-77, Topeka, 1977-86; with Miller, Bash & Starrett, P.C., Kans. City, Mo., 1986-90; ptnr. Lathrop Norquist & Miller, 1990-91, Lathrop and Norquist, Overland Pk., Kans., 1991-95, Lathrop & Gage L.C., Overland Pk., 1996—2008, Lathrop & Gage L.L.P., Overland Pk., 2009—. Judicial nominating commr 10th Judicial Dist, 2000—04. Lt (jg) USNR, 1969—72. Named one of, Mo./Kans. Super Lawyers, 2006. Mem.: ABA, Litigation Counsel Am., Kans. Assn. of Defense Counsel, Mo. Orgn. Def. Lawyers, Def. Rsch. Inst. (state rep. Kans. 1998—2001, bd. dirs. 2002—05), Am. Bd. Trial Advs. (pres. Kans. chpt. 1997), Kans. Bar Assn. (pres. litig. sect. 1985—86), Civitan Club (pres. 1985—86, Disting. Pres. award 1985—86). Democrat. Presbyterian. Avocations: aviation, scuba diving, sailing. Office: Lathrop & Gage LLP 10851 Mastin Blvd Bldg 82 Ste 1000 Shawnee Mission KS 66210-1669 Home Phone: 913-469-8271; Office Phone: 913-451-5140. Business E-Mail: fstarrett@lathropgage.com.

STARRS, JAMES EDWARD, retired law and forensics educator, consultant; b. Bklyn., July 30, 1930; s. George Thomas and Mildred Agatha (Dobbins) S.; m. Barbara Alice Smyth, Sept. 6, 1954; children: Mary Alice, Monica, James, Charles, Liam, Barbara, Siobhan, Gregory, William. BA, LLB, St. John's U., Bklyn., 1958; LLM, NYU, 1959. Bar: N.Y. 1958, D.C. 1966, U.S. Ct. Mil. Appeals 1959, U.S. Dist. Ct. (so. and ea. dists.) N.Y. 1960. Assoc. Lawless & Lynch, NYC, 1958; tchg. fellow Rutgers U., Newark, 1959-60; asst. prof. law DePaul U., Chgo., 1960-64; assoc. prof. law George Washington U., Washington, 1964-67, prof. law, 1967—, prof. forensic scis., 1975—, David B. Weaver rsch. prof. law, 2005; ret., 2007. Cons. Nat. Commn. Reform Fed. Criminal Laws, Washington, 1968, Cellmark Diagnostics, Germantown, Md., 1987—, Time-Life Books, 1993; participant re-evaluation sci. evidence and trial of Bruno Richard Hauptmann for Lindbergh murder, 1983; participant reporting sci. re-analysis of firearms evidence in Sacco and Vanzetti trial, 1986; project dir. Alfred G. Packer Victims Exhumation Project, 1989, A Blaze of Bullets: A Sci. Investigation into the Deaths of Senator Huey Long and Dr. Carl Austin Weiss, 1991, Meriwether Lewis Exhumation Project, 1992—, Frank R. Olson Exhumation Project, 1994, Jesse W. James Exhumation Project, 1995, Samuel Washington-Harewood Excavations, 1999, The Boston Strangler Re-Investigation, 2000, The Exhumation of Carl E. Williams, Sr., 2001, The Exhumation of Samuel Swan, 2002, The Gettysburg Excavations, Pa., 2002—; prin. investigator Exhuymation of Harry Houdini, 2007; Snider lectr. U. Toronto, 1999, Boston Strangler Re-Investigation, 2000, Mutter Lectr. Coll. of Physicians, Phila., 2003; lectr. Royal Coll. Edinburgh, 2004, Frost lectr. W. Va. Med. Sch., 2007. Author: A Voice for the Dead, 2005; co-author: (with Moenssens and Inbau) Scientific Evidence in Criminal Cases, 1986, (with Moenssens, Inbau and Henderson) Scientific Evidence in Civil and Criminal Cases, 1996, (with Katherine Ramsland)A Voice for the Death, The Literary Cyclist,; editor: The Noiseless Tenor, 1982, The Literary Cyclist, 1997, The Mysterious Death of Meriwether Lewis; co-editor: (review) Scientific Sleuthing, 1976—; mem. editl. bd. Jour. Forensic Sci., 1980-98, Encyclopedia of Forensic Sciences; contbr. articles to profl. jours. Sgt. U.S. Army, 1950-53, Korea. Recipient Vidocq Soc. award, 1993; Ford Found. fellow, 1963; vis. scholar in residence USMC, 1984. Fellow Am. Acad. Forensic Sci. (chmn. jurisprudence sect. 1984, 1994, 1995, bd. dirs. 1986-89, 98-2001, chmn. AAFS Lastword Soc., 2006-, Jurisprudence Sect. award 1988, Disting. fellow 1996); mem. ABA, Mid-Atlantic Assn. Forensic Sci. (emeritus), Am. Assn. Justice, Internat. Soc. Forensic Sci. (chmn. jurisprudence sect. 1988), Internat. Assn. for Identification, Geol. Soc. Am. Roman Catholic. Home: 8602 Clydesdale Rd Springfield VA 22151-1301 Office Phone: 571-276-8158. Business E-Mail: jstarrs@law.gww.edu.

STARRY, DONN ALBERT, retired aerospace corporate executive, retired military officer; b. NYC, May 31, 1925; s. Don Albert and Edith (Sortor) S.; m. Leatrice Hope Gibbs, June 15, 1948; children: Michael, Paul, Melissa, Melanie. BS, U.S. Mil. Acad., 1948; MS in Internat. Affairs, George Washington U., 1966. Commd. 2d lt. U.S. Army, 1948, advanced through grades to gen., 1977; svc. in Europe, Korea and Vietnam; comdr. 11th armored cavalry rgt. Vietnam, Cambodia, 1969-70; assigned Dept. Army Staff, 1970-72; comdr. Armor Center and Ft. Knox, Ky., 1973-76, V Corps, Europe, 1976-77; comdr. Tng. and Doctrine Command Ft. Monroe, Va., 1977-81; comdr. in chief U.S. Readiness Command, 1981-83, ret., 1983; v.p. mission analysis and tech. affairs Ford Aerospace and Communications Corp., Detroit, 1983-84, v.p., gen. mgr. space missions group, 1984-86; exec. v.p. Ford Aerospace Corp., Arlington, Va., 1987-90; spl. asst. to pres. BDM Internat., McLean, Va., 1988-90. Chmn. bd. Maxwell Techs. Inc., San Diego, 1995-97, Universal Voltronics, Brookfield, Conn., 1998-2007; author, lectr., counselor to govt. and industry. Mem. Def. Sci. Bd., 1985—93, Order of Aaron and Hur, Friends of Fifth of May; mem. bd. Eisenhower Found., 1995—; chmn. bd. U.S. Cavalry Meml. Found., 1995—2003; mem. bd. Army Hist. Found., 2000—; mem. Army Sci. Bd., 2002—. Decorated Def. D.S.M., Army D.S.M. with oak leaf cluster, Silver Star, Bronze Star with V, Soldier's medal, Purple Heart, Legion of Merit with 2 oak leaf clusters, French Ordre Nationale du Merite, German Knight Commdr.'s Cross of Order of Merit with Badge and Star, Disting. Flying Cross, Air Medal with 9 oak leaf clusters; named to U.S. Army Ft. Leavenworth Command and Gen. Staff Coll. Hall of Fame, 1993; recipient Gold medal The Order of St. George; named to Joint Forces Staff Coll. Hall of Fame, 2006, Internat. Comdrs. Wall, The Armor Ctr., Ft. Knox, 2006, Castle Meml. award West Point Soc. DC, 2009, named Disting. Grad. USMA West Point, 2009. Mem.: Assn. U.S. Army, U.S. Armor Assn. Episcopalian. Address: 3003 Downing St Williamsburg VA 23185 Personal E-mail: dastarry@cox.net.

STARYK, STEVEN SAM, violinist, concertmaster, educator; b. Toronto, Ont., Can., Apr. 28, 1932; s. Peter and Mary Staryk; m. Ida Elisabeth Busch, May 17, 1963; 1 child, Natalie. Student, Royal Conservatory of Music, Toronto, 1942-48, Harbord Collegiate Inst., 1945-48; LittD (hon.), York U., Toronto, 1980. Soloist, concertmaster CBC-Radio Can., Toronto, 1951-55, Royal Philharmonic Orch., London, 1956-59; 1st concertmaster, tchr. Concertgebouw Orch. and Amsterdam Conservatory, 1960-63; concertmaster Chgo. Symphony Orch., 1963-67; prof. of violin Oberlin (Ohio) Coll. Conservatory, 1968-72, Acad. of Music, Vancouver, B.C., Canada, 1972-75, Royal Conservatory of Music, Toronto, 1975-87; concertmaster Toronto Symphony, 1982-87; prof. of violin, chair string div. U. Wash. Sch. Music, Seattle, 1987-97, prof. emeritus, 1997—. Faculty music U. Toronto, 1980-87; vis. prof. U. Victoria, 1972, U. Ottawa, 1975, Northwestern U., 1965-66; founding mem. Quartet Can., 1975-80. Soloist, recitalist, N.Am., Europe and the Far East; recording artist on EMI-HMV, CBC, Everest, Orion, other labels; biography (by Thane Lewis) Fiddling with Life, 2000. Recipient 2 Arts awards Can. Coun., Ottawa, 1968, 75, Queen's Silver Jubilee medal Govt. of Can., Toronto, Shevchenko medal, Winnipeg, Man., Can.; biography "Fiddling with Life" by T. Lewis and S. Staryk, 2002; named Officer of the Order of Canada, Ottawa, 2007; Fellow Royal Conservatory Music, Toronto, 2008 Office: U Wash Sch Music Mail Stop DN-10 PO Box 353450 Seattle WA 98195-3450 Home: 242 Broadway Ave Toronto ON M4P 1V9 Canada Home Phone: 416-932-0159; Office Phone: 206-543-1201.

STARZINGER, VINCENT EVANS, political scientist, educator; b. Des Moines, Jan. 12, 1929; s. Vincent and Genevieve (Evans) Starzinger; m. Mildred Hippee Hill, June 16, 1953; children: Page Hill, Evans. AB summa cum laude, Harvard U., 1950, LLB, 1954, PhD, 1959; AM (hon.), Dartmouth Coll., 1968. Bar: Iowa 1954. Practice with firm Bannister, Carpenter, Ahlers & Cooney, Des Moines, 1954; tchg. fellow, instr. govt. Harvard U., 1957—60; mem. faculty dept. govt. Dartmouth U., 1960—94, chmn. dept. govt., 1972—77, 1983—85, Joel Parker prof. law polit. sci., 1976—94, prof. emeritus, 1994—. Author: Middlingness: Juste Millieu Political Theory in England and France, 1815-48, 1965, republished as The Politics of the Center, 1991; contbr. articles to profl. jours. With US Army, 1955—56. Recipient award, Am. Philos. Soc.; fellow, Earhart Found., 1970—71; Sheldon Traveling fellow, 1950—51, Social Sci. Rsch. Coun. fellow, 1958—59, Faculty fellow, Dartmouth U., 1963—64. Mem.: ABA, Iowa Bar Assn., Am. Polit. Sci. Assn., Cambridge (Mass.) Boat Club, Am. Alpine Club, Phi Beta Kappa. Home: Elm St Norwich VT 05055 Office: PO Box 981 Hanover NH 03755-0981 Home Phone: 802-649-1590; Office Phone: 603-643-6016.

STARZL, THOMAS EARL, physician, educator; b. Le Mars, Iowa, Mar. 11, 1926; s. Roman F. and Anna Laura (Fitzgerald) S.; m. Barbara Brothers, Nov. 27, 1954 (div.); children: Timothy, Rebecca, Thomas; m. Joy D. Conger, Aug. 1, 1981. BA in Biology, Westminster Coll., Fulton, Mo., 1947, DSc (hon.), 1965; MA in Anatomy, Northwestern U., Chgo., 1950, MD with distinction, 1952, PhD in Neurophysiology, 1952; DSc (hon.), N.Y. Med. Coll., 1970, Westmar Coll., 1974, Med. Coll. Wis., 1981, Northwestern U., 1982, Bucknell U., 1985, Muhlenberg Coll., 1985, Mt. Sinai Sch. Medicine, 1988; MD (hon.), U. Louvain, Belgium, 1985, U. Genova, 1988, U. Rennes, 1988; LLD (hon.), U. Wyo., 1971; LHD (hon.), LaRoche Coll., 1988. Intern Johns Hopkins U. Hosp., Balt., 1952-53, fellow, surg., 1953-54, resident, 1955-56; mem. faculty Northwestern U. Med. Sch., Evanston, Ill., 1958-61; assoc. prof. surgery U. Colo. Med. Sch., Denver, 1962-80, prof. surgery, 1964-80, chmn. dept. surgery, 1972-80; prof. surgery U. Pitts. Sch. Med., 1981—; dir. U. Pitts. Transplantation Inst., 1991—96; dir. emeritus U. Pitts. Transplantation Inst. (now called the Thomas E. Starzl Transplantation Inst.), 1996—. Mem. staff Presbyn. Univ. Hosp., Univ. Hosp., Children's Hosp. of Pitts., Pitts. VA Hosp; spkr. in field. Author: Experience in Renal Transplantation, 1964, Experience in Hepatic Transplantation, 1969, (autobiography) The Puzzle People: Memoirs of a Transplant Surgeon, 1992; mem. of several editl. bds.; contbr. articles to profl. jours. Recipient award Westminster Coll., 1965, Achievement award Lund U., 1965, Eppinger award Soc. Internat. de Chirurgie, 1965, Eppinger prize, Freiburg, 1970, William S. Middleton award for outstanding research in VA system, 1968, Merit award Northwestern U., 1969, Disting. Achievement award Modern Medicine, 1969, Creative Council award U. Colo., 1971, Colo. Man of Yr. award, 1967, Brookdale award in Medicine, AMA Bd. Trustees and Brookdale Found., 1974, David M. Hume Meml. award Nat. Kidney Found., 1978, Pitts. Man of Yr. award, 1981, Bigelow medal, Boston Surgical Soc., the City of Medicine award, Disting. Svc. award, Am. Liver Found., 1991, Willam Beaumont prize, Am. Gastroenterological Assn., Peter Medawar prize, Transplant Soc., Jacobson Innovation award, Am. Coll. Surgeons, 1998 Lannelongue Internat. medal, Nat. Acad. Surgery, France, 2001 King Faisal Internat. prize for Medicine, Nat. Medal of Science for Biol. Sciences, 2004; Markle scholar, 1958. Fellow ACS (Sheen award 1982), Am. Acad. Arts and Scis.; mem. Soc. Univ. Surgeons, Soc. Vascular Surgery, Am. Surg. Assn., Internat. Transplantation Soc.(past pres.), Deutsche Gesellschaft für Chirurgie, founding pres., Am. Soc. of Transplant Surgeons and Transplant Recipients Internat. Orgn., Nat. French Acad. Medicine, and numerous others. Achievements include performing transplantation on dogs, 1958-1960; the world's first liver transplant in 1963; the performing six baboon kidney transplants in 1963 and 1964; first successful liver transplant in 1967; the world's first chimpanzee liver transplant in three children between 1969 and 1974; first multiple organ transplant in 1983; the first heart and liver transplant in 1984; announcing the first-time use of a new, more effective anti-rejection agent, FK506 (tacrlimus) in 1989, approved for clinical use by FDA in 1994; made medical history with team in 1992 and 1993, when surgeons performed two baboon-to-human liver transplants; established chimerism theory in 1992; most cited scientist in clinical medicine in 1999. Office: Thomas E Starzl Transplant Inst Ste 729 Montefiore Hosp 3459 Fifth Ave Pittsburgh PA 15213-3403 Office Phone: 412-624-0112.*

STASEK, LORRAINE ANNE, elementary school educator; b. East Chicago, Ind., July 12, 1932; m. Charles R. Stasek; children: Diane, Charles, John Charles, Ruthanne. AA in Social Work, 1976; BA in Sociology, Calumet Coll., 1978, BS in Elem. Edn., 1980; BA in Theology, Cal Coll., 1984; M Elem. Edn., Purdue U., Hammond, Ind., 1990. Lic. life elem. tchr., Ind. Substitute tchr. East Chicago Pub. Sch. System, Ind.; tchr. Ind. Harbor Cath. Elem. Sch., East Chicago. Task force Grand Cal, bd. pres., citizen of yr. award. Leadership roles Roman Cath. Ch.; mem. Citizens in Action, Operation Hope Inc.(pres.). Recipient Silver Beaver medal Boy Scouts Am., St. Anne medal Cath. Diocese of Gary, Vol. in Action award State of Ind., Hoosier Environ. Coun. award. Mem.: ASCD, NSTA, Save Dunes Coun., Coalition for a Clean Environment.

STASHENKO, VETALEY, anatomist, educator; s. Maria Stashenko; m. Galina Stashenko; children: Ruslan, Yaroslav, Darina. PhD (hon.), Nat. Agrl. U., Kiev, 1984. Cert. dr. naturopathy Ala., 1998. Assoc. prof. Nat. Agrl. U., 1980—94; prof. Palm Beach Coll., 2006—; prof. biology South U., 2006—. Dir. Am. Apitherapy Soc., Fla., 2002—. Dir. editl. com. AAS, 2004—. Mem.: Am. Assn. Profl. Agriculturists, Am. Entomological Soc. Home and Office: HMF Inc 11384 41 Ct N West Palm Beach FL 33411 Home Phone: 561-239-4848. Business E-Mail: vse@bellsouth.net.

STASHOWER, DANIEL MEYER, writer; b. Cleve., Sept. 21, 1960; s. David L. and Sally (Weiss) S.; m. Alison Corbett, May 18, 1996; 2 children. BA, Northwestern U., 1982; MFA, Columbia U., 1984. Magician, 1978—; author, 1986—. Author: The Ectoplasmic Man, 1985, Elephants in the Distance, 1989, Teller of Tales: The Life of Arthur Conan Doyle, 1999 (Edgar award 2000), The Dime Museum Murders, 1999, The Floating Lady Murder, 2000, The Houdini Specter, 2001, The Boy Genius and the Mogul, 2002, The Beautiful Cigar Girl, 2006; co-author: Arthur Conan Doyle: A Life in Letters, 2007 (Edgar award for best critical/biog. book 2008). Raymond Chandler Fulbright fellow, 1992-93. Business E-Mail: daniel@stashower.com.

STASNEY, C. RICHARD, otolaryngologist, director; s. Homer R. and Eska Gage Stasney; m. Susan Pitzer Pitzer, June 8, 1968; children: Kathryn Stasney Childers, Elizabeth Stasney Moriarty, W. Spencer. BA, Yale U., New Haven, 1965; MD, Baylor Coll. Medicine, Houston, 1969. Diplomate Am. Bd. Otolaryngology, 1974. Dir. Tex. Voice Ctr., Houston, 1977—; chmn. Ctr. Performing Arts Medicine, Houston, 2001—. Contbr. articles to profl. jours. Bd. mem. Tex. State Bd. Med. Examiners, Austin, 1987—93, Mus. Health & Med. Sci., Houston, 2001—06. Lt. comdr. USN, Oakland. Recipient Physician of yr., Houston Acad. Communicative Disorders, 1998, Disting. Surgeon of Yr., Assn. Oper. Rm. Nurses, 2006; named one of America's Top Physicians, Consumer's

Rsch. Coun. Am., 2001—09. Achievements include research in medical problems Of performing artists. Office: Tex Voice Ctr 6550 Fannin Ste 2001 Houston TX 77030 Office Fax: 713-796-2349.

STASSEN, JOHN HENRY, lawyer; b. Joliet, Ill., Mar. 22, 1943; s. John H. and Florence C. (McCarthy) S.; m. Sara A. Gaw, July 6, 1968; children: John C., David A. BS, Northwestern U., 1965, JD, Harvard U., 1968. Bar: Ill. 1968. Assoc. Kirkland & Ellis, LLP, Chgo., 1968, 73-76, ptnr. 1977-2009. Contbr. articles to legal jours. Mem. bd. govs. Northwestern U. Libr., chmn., 2003-07; bd. dirs. Landmarks Preservation Coun. Ill., chmn., 2001-03. Lt. comdr., JAGC, USNR, 1969-79. Mem. ABA (past chmn. com. on futures regulation), Ill. Bar Assn., Chgo. Bar Assn., Phila. Soc. Home: 16346 Timber Ln New Buffalo MI 49117 Home Phone: 269-469-6197. Business E-Mail: jstassen@mac.com.

STASSUN, KEIVAN GUADALUPE, astronomer, educator; b. LA; s. Norman Richard and Luisa Stassun; m. Justine Clotfelter, Oct. 2, 2004; 1 child, James Guadalupe. BA, U. Calif., Berkeley, 1994; PhD, U. Wis., Madison, 2000. NASA hubble postdoc. fellow U. Wis., 2001—03; prof. astronomy Vanderbilt U., Nashville, 2003—. Grantee Career award, NSF, 2004; Dissertation fellowship, Ford Found., 1999, Cottrell scholarship, Rsch. Corp., 2006. Mem.: Am. Astron. Soc. Office: Vanderbilt Univ VU Sta B 1807 Nashville TN 37235 Business E-Mail: keivan.stassun@vanderbilt.edu.

STASTNY, PETER, medical educator; b. Prague, Czech Republic, Mar. 22, 1931; s. Viktor Stastny and Margarete Mosberg; m. Maruja Infante, Dec. 14, 1959; children: Paul, Victor, Cesar. MD, San Marcos U., Lima, Peru, 1957. Cert. Physician Tex., 1964. Asst. resident medicine Parkland Meml. Hosp., Dallas, 1963—64; fellow, rheumatic diseases unit UT Southwestern Med. Ctr., Dallas, 1960—63, instr., internal medicine, 1964—65, asst. prof. internal medicine, 1965—71, assoc. prof., 1971—77, dir., transplantation immunology divsn., 1970—, prof. internal medicine, 1977—. Veterans adminstrn. clin. investigator VA, Dallas; bd. mem. United Network for Organ Sharing (UNOS), Dallas, 1995—97; guest editor Human Immunology, Dallas, 2004—05. Dir., trustee Folk Art & Crafts Found., Heath, Tex., 1999—. Recipient Master Am. Coll. Rheumatology award, 1997, Pemberton Meml. Lecture award, 1977, Paul I. Terasaki Clin. Sci. award, 2008. Mem.: Am. Coll. Rheumatology (arthritis found. fellow 1965—68), Clin. Immunology Soc., Am. Soc. Transplant Physicians, Am. Soc. Histocompatibility & Immunogenetics (pres. 1995—96, Terasaki Clin. Sci. award 2008), Transplantation Soc., Am. Assn. Immunologists, Am. Soc. Clin. Investigation. Achievements include discovery of Association of HLA-DR4 with Rheumatoid Arthritis susceptibility; HLA antigens in Peruvian mummies; Antibodies against MICA antigens in kidney transplantation; Endothelial specific antigens in organ transplantation; Mismatching for MICA alleles associated with acute graft-versus-host disease in bone marrow transplant recipients. Avocation: photography. Office: UT Southwestern Med Ctr 5323 Harry Hines Blvd Dallas TX 75390-8886

STASZESKY, FRANCIS MYRON, electric power industry executive, consultant; b. Wilmington, Del., Apr. 16, 1918; s. Frank J. and Ruth (Jones) S.; m. Barbara F. Kearney, May 30, 1943; children: Francis Myron, John B., Barbara J., Faith A., Paul D. BSME, MIT, 1943; MSME, Mass. Inst. Tech., 1943. Mech. engr. Union Oil Co. Calif., LA, 1943-45; with E.I. duPont de Nemours Co., Wilmington, Del., 1946-48; joined Boston Edison Co., 1948, supervising engr. design and constrn., 1948-57, supt. engring. and constrn. dept., 1957-64, v.p., asst. to pres., 1964-67, exec. v.p., 1967-79, pres., chief operating officer, 1979-83; cons., 1983—; dir. Boston Edison Co., 1968-83. Fellow ASME (life); mem. IEEE (sr., life), Nat. Acad. Engring., Engring. Soc. New Eng. (pres. 1961-62). Address: 60 Champlain Cir Plymouth MA 02360

STATE, MATTHEW W., cell biologist, neuroscientist, educator; BA, Stanford U., 1984, MD, 1991; PhD, Yale U., 2001. Dir. program on neurogenetics Yale Sch. Medicine, co-dir. med. genomics program, assoc. prof. child psychiatry & genetics. Office: Child Study Center 230 South Frontage Rd PO Box 207900 New Haven CT 06520-7900 Office Phone: 203-785-4659. Office Fax: 203-785-7560. E-mail: matthew.state@yale.edu.*

STATES, J. CHRISTOPHER, molecular biology educator, researcher; b. Albany, NY, Oct. 22, 1952; s. Jonathon C. and Ninfa F. (Scorzari) S.; m. Germaine Russo, Apr. 26, 1980; children: Gregory, Vanessa. BS Biochemistry, SUNY, Buffalo, 1974; PhD Pathology and Molecular Biology, Albany Med. Coll., 1980. Rsch. asst. Albany Med. Coll., 1974-75; postdoctoral fellow U. Calgary, Alberta, Can., 1980-84; rsch. scholar Children's Hosp. Rsch. Found., Cin., 1984-86, asst. prof., 1986-88, Wayne State U., Detroit, 1988-97, assoc. prof., 1997—. Reviewer Nat. Sci. and Engring. Rsch. Coun., Ottawa, Can., 1993; program dir. rsch. apprentice program, Wayne State U., 1989—; reviewer Toxicology and Applied Pharmacology, 1994—, DNA and Cell Biology, 1993—, Biotechs., 1996—, Drug Metabolism & Disposition, 1996—. Contbr. articles to profl. jours.; patentee in field. Recipient N.Y. State Regents scholarship, 1970-74, postdoctoral fellowship Alberta Heritage Med. Rsch. Found., Edmonton, Can., 1980-84; rsch. grantee Nat. Cancer Inst., Bethesda, Md., 1988-94, Nat. Inst. Environ. Health Scis., Research Triangle Park, 1997—. Mem. Internat. Soc. for Study of Xenobiotics. Office: Wayne State U 2727 2nd Ave Detroit MI 48201-2671

STATHAM, JASON, actor; b. London, Sept. 12, 1972; Former Olympic diver British Nat. Diving Team. Actor: (films) Lock, Stock and Two Smoking Barrels, 1998, Snatch, 2000, Turn It Up, 2000, Ghosts of Mars, 2001, The One, 2001, Mean Machine, 2001, The Transporter, 2002, The Italian Job, 2003, Collateral, 2004, Cellular, 2004, Transporter II, 2005, London, 2005, Revolver, 2005, Chaos, 2006, The Pink Panther, 2006, Crank, 2006, War, 2007, In the Name of the King: A Dungeon Siege Tale, 2008, The Bank Job, 2008, Death Race, 2008, Transporter 3, 2008, Crank: High Voltage, 2009. Office: Creative Artists Agency 2000 Avenue Of The Stars Los Angeles CA 90067-4700*

STATHOS, LIFTERIA K., retired educational association administrator; b. Hartford, Conn. d. Peter Karlames and Nota Politis; Student, Hart Sch. Music Hillyer Coll. (now U. Hartford), Conn., 1950—60; AA with honors, Tunxis CC, Farmington, Conn., 1971; BA, BS, Ctrl. Conn. State U., New Britain, 1980, MA, 1982; PhD, U. Conn., Storrs, 1984. Edn. sec. Bur. Pupil Pers. and Spl. Edn. Svcs., State Dept. Edn., Hartford, 1959—69, edn. acct., 1969—80, edn. adminstr., 1980—89; ret. Co-chmn. St. George Ch. Libr., New Britain; New Britain Gen. Hosp. Aux.; mem. planning com. Hospice of Greater New Britain; founder ch. libr. St. George Ch., New Britain, 1993—; mem. Organized Srs. St. George Ch.-Still Going Strong, 1985—. Mem.: AAUW, Daus. Penelope (life), New Britain Indsl. Mus., Ladies Philoptochos Soc. (bd. dirs., former pres., v.p., sec., treas.), New Britain Mus. Am. Art, Coll. Club New Britain (mem. scholarship com. 1989). Republican. Greek Orthodox. Avocations: piano, stamp collecting/philately, gardening, cooking, reading. Home: 40 Knollwood Dr New Britain CT 06052-1123

STATKUS, DARYL ANNE, literature and language professor; M, Assumption Coll., Worcester, Mass., 1972. Assoc. prof. English Becker Coll., Mass., 1979—. Treas. Becker Faculty Fedn. Tchrs., Leicester, Mass., 1985. Maj. USCG, 1970—72, Boston, MA. Mem.: Am. Fedn. Tchr., Nat. Coun. Tchrs. English. Avocations: fishing, travel, gardening. Home: PO Box 261 Leicester MA 01524 Office: Becker Coll 964 Main St Leicester MA 01524 Business E-Mail: daryl.statkus@becker.edu.

STATLER, IRVING CARL, aerospace engineer; b. Buffalo, Nov. 23, 1923; s. Samuel William and Sarah (Strauss) S.; m. Renee Roll, Aug. 23, 1953; children: William Scott, Thomas Stuart BS in Aero. Engring., U. Mich., 1945, BS in Engring. Math., 1945; PhD, Calif. Inst. Tech., 1956. Research engr. flight research dept. Cornell Aero. Lab., Inc., Buffalo, 1946-53, prin. engr. flight research dept., 1956-57, asst. head aeromechanics dept., 1957-63, head applied mechanics dept., 1963-70, sr. staff scientist aeroscis. div., 1970-71; research scientist U.S. Army Air Mobility Research and Devel. Lab., Moffett Field, Calif., 1971-73, dir. Aeromechanics Lab., 1973-85, dir. AGARD, 1985-88; sr. staff scientist NASA Ames Rsch. Ctr., 1988-92, chief Human Factors Rsch. Divsn., 1992—2008, assoc. emeritus, 2008—. Research scientist research analysis group Jet Propulsion Lab., Pasadena, Calif., 1953-55; chmn. flight mechanics panel adv. group aerospace research and devel. NATO, 1974-76; lectr. U. Buffalo, Millard-Fillmore Coll., Buffalo, 1957-58 Served with USAAF, 1945-46 Fellow AIAA (Internat. Cooperation in Space Sci. medal 1992), AAAS, German Aerospace Soc., Royal Aero Soc.; mem. Am. Helicoptor Soc., Sigma Xi. Home: 1362 Cuernavaca Circulo Mountain View CA 94040-3571 Office: NASA Ames Rsch Ctr MS 262-4 Moffett Field CA 94035 Home Phone: 650-966-1364. E-mail: irving.c.statler@nasa.gov.

STATNIKOV, EFIM SMULEVICH, physicist, researcher; d. Shmuel Moshkovich Statnikov and Liya Boruhovna Chudnovskaya; m. Liubov Dmitrievna Bogdanova, Mar. 10, 1960; children: Mayya Efimovna Kundzich, Itta Efimovna Statnikova. PhD, Tech. U., Brjansk, Russia, 1959. Cert. Physicist in engring., Russian Acoustical Acad., 1982. V.p. Applied Ultrasonics, Irondale, Ala., 1999—. Office: Applied Ultrasonics 5871 Old Leeds Rd Ste 201 Irondale AL 35210 Office Fax: 205-951-7750. Business E-Mail: estatnikov@appliedultrasonics.com.

STATON, JOSEPH L., marine biologist, educator; married. PhD, U. La., Lafayette, 1992. Postdoc. fellow Smithsonian Marine Sta., Fort Pierce, Fla., 1992—93; NSF postdoc. fellow U. Mich., Ann Arbor, 1993—94; NASA postdoc. fellow UCLA, 1995—97; rsch. fellow Harvard U., Cambridge, Mass., 1997—98; rschr. USC, Columbia, 1998—2003; assoc. prof. USCB, Bluffton, 2003—. Mem.: Internat. Brotherhood Magicians. Office: USCB 1 University Blvd Bluffton SC 29909 Business E-Mail: jstaton@uscb.edu.

STAUB, CAROL ANNE, artist; b. Milford, Del., Jan. 30, 1948; d. Charles Edward and Isabelle Gill; m. William Edward Staub, July 23, 1977; children: William Knapp, Denise Casalino. Instr., Port St. Lucie, Fla., 2003, Elliott Mus., Stuart, Fla., 2004, 05, 06, 07, Somerset Art Assn., Bedminster, NJ, 2006, 07. One-woman shows include Town of South Palm Beach, Fla., 2005, Mark's In The Park, Boca Raton, Fla., 2007, Palm Beach Gardens City Hall, 2007, Garden of Art, 2007, Palm Beach Gardens, 2007, Lineart Gallery, Barcelona, 2008, Miarte Gallery, Coral Gables, Fla., 2008, Represented in permanent collections U. Fla., Ft. Pierce, Fla., Elliott Mus. Art, Stuart, Fla., Arcolle, Sergines, France, Museo De Collage, Mexico, Assn. Promotion Social Artetica, Rome, Italy, Country Arts Found., Ingram, Tex., Real Tart Gallery, Taranaki, New Zealand; contbr. articles to newspapers; numerous group shows including most recently, exhibited in group shows at Somerset Art Assn., Pluckemin, NJ, 2006, Cornell Mus. Art, Delray Beach, Fla., 2006, Vero Beach Mus. Art, Fla., 2006, Morris Pub. Libr., Whippany, NJ, 2006, Elliott Mus., Stuart, Fla., 2006, 2007, Coral Springs Mus. Art, Fla., 2007, Boca Raton Mus. Art Artist's Guild, Boca Raton, Fla., 2007, Vero Beach Mus. Art, Fla., 2007, Cornell Mus. Art, Delray Beach, Fla., 2007, Anniston Mus. Nat. History, Ala., 2007, A.E. Backus Mus., Ft. Pierce, Fla., 2007, Somerset Art Assn., Pluckemin, NJ, 2007, exhibitions include Internat. Soc. Exptl. Artists, San Diego, 2009, Catharine Lorrilard Wolfe Art Club, NYC, 2009, Boca Raton Mus. Art, Fla., 2009, Nat. Arts Club, NYC, 2009, Coral Springs Mus. Art, Fla., 2009. Recipient 1st Pl., The Artist's Mag., 2007, Merit award, A.E. Bean Backus Mus., 2005, award, Nat. Collage Soc., 2005, Best in Show award, Somerset Art Assn., 2006, Ana Drobnies award, San Diego Watercolor Soc., 2004, East West Arts Frames award, 2005, numerous others, hon. mention, Best Abstract Design award, Creative Catalyst Productions, 2006, 1st Pl., Watercolor Magic Mag., 2007, Boca Raton Mus. Art Artist's Guild, 2009, Artist Mag. All Media Online Competition, 2009; finalist, The Artist's Mag., 2002, Artist's Mag., 2006. Mem.: Coral Spring Museum Art (3rd Place), Watercolor Soc. Ala. (assoc. past pres. award 2006), The Fla. Watercolor Soc. (assoc.), The Palm Beach Watercolor Soc., Fla. (assoc.), Exptl. Artists Am. (assoc.), The Nat. Watercolor Soc. (assoc.), The Nat. Collage Soc. (assoc. award 2005, cash award 2006), The Am. Watercolor Soc. (assoc.), The Internat. Soc. Exptl. Artists (assoc. Am. Frame award 2006), Soc. Layerists Multi-Media (life), Am. Juried Art Salon (life Master Class Plus 2007), Vero Beach Museum and Art Club (life 1st Place 2008), Boca Raton Museum Art Artists Guild (life), Watercolor Art Soc. (life), Catharine Lorillard Wolfe Art Club (life), Vero Beach Mus. Art Artist's Guild (life), San Diego Watercolor Soc. (life Ana Drobnies award 2004, East West Arts and Frames award 2005), NJ Watercolor Soc. (life Excellence award 2005, Beall Rodgers Meml. award 2005, Nicholas Reale Meml. award 2006), Women In The Visual Arts (life), Garden State Watercolor Soc. (life Am. Frame award 2005), Internat. Soc. Acrylic Painters (life Savoir-Faire award 2006), The Nat. Assn. Women Artists (life; bd. dirs., treas. Fla. chpt., merit award 2005), Allied Artists Am. (life), The Boca Raton Mus. Art Artists Guild (life 3rd Place 2008), Catharine Lorillars Wolfe Art Club (life). Avocations: cooking, golf, bowling, reading, photography. Home (Summer): 531 Elizabeth Ave Somerset NJ 08873 Home (Winter): 10316 Crosby Place Saint Lucie West FL 34986 Home Fax: 772-466-2982. Personal E-mail: carolcando@aol.com.

STAUB, W. ARTHUR, health care products executive; b. Detroit, Dec. 25, 1923; s. Edward Elmer and Emma Josephine (Fleury) S.; m. Alla Elizabeth Edwards, June 26, 1948; children: James Randall, Sally Ann, David Scott. BS, Dartmouth Coll., 1944; MD, Temple U., 1947. Intern Muhlenberg Hosp., Plainfield, NJ, 1947-48; resident in pediatrics Abington (Pa.) Meml. Hosp., 1950-51; practice medicine specializing in pediatrics Westfield (N.J.) Med. Group, 1948-63; assoc. med. dir. Ciba Pharm. Co., Summit, NJ, 1963-66; med. dir., v.p. life sci. div. Becton-Dickinson and Co., Rutherford, NJ, 1966-70; v.p. med. affairs C. R. Bard Co., Murray Hill, NJ, 1970-88, also bd. dirs. Bd. dirs. Crestmont Fed. Savs. and Loan Assn., Edison, N.J., Colonial Trust Nat. Bank, North Palm Beach, Fla.; cons. Children's Specialized Hosp., Westfield, 1948-88, Overlook Hosp., Summit, 1948-88. Contbr. articles to profl. jours. Deacon Presbyn. Ch., Westfield, 1959—. Ensign USNR, 1944—50, to capt. USAF, 1950—53. Fellow Am. Coll. Physician Execs.; mem. AAAS, Assn. Advancement Med. Instrumentation, Health Industry Mfrs. Assn. (chmn. med. and sci. steering com.). Clubs: Echo Lake Country (Westfield) (bd. trustees 1984-88); Lost Tree (North Palm Beach, Fla., bd. govs. 1989-94, sec. 1989-94); Skytop (Pa.). Republican. Presbyterian. Avocations: golf, physical fitness, reading, sailing, travel. Home: 3330 Devonshire Way Palm Beach Gardens FL 33418 E-mail: DoctorWAS@aol.com.

STAUBER, MARILYN JEAN, retired elementary and secondary school educator; b. Duluth, Minn., Feb. 5, 1938; d. Harold Milton and Dorothy Florence (Thompson) Froehlich; children: Kenneth D. and James H. Atkinson; m. Lawrence B. Stauber Sr., Jan. 11, 1991 (dec.). BS in Edn., U. Minn., Duluth, 1969, MEd in Math., 1977. Cert. elem. and secondary reading tchr., remedial reading specialist, devel. reading tchr., reading cons. Sec. div. vocat. rehab. State Minn., Duluth, 1956-59; sec. Travelers Ins. Co., Duluth, 1962-66; lead tchr. Title 1 reading and math. Proctor, Minn., 1969-98; ret. Singer: (songs) North Shore Sound Barbershop. Mem. choirs and Choral Soc. John Duss Music, chairperson Outreach, Forbes Meth. Ch., proctor; treas. Eastern Star; sec. North Shore Sounds, Admin. Coun. Forbes, sec. UMW Forbes. Mem. NEA, VFW, Internat. Reading Assn., Nat. Reading Assn., Minn. Arrowhead Reading Coun., Elem. Coun. (pres. 1983-84, 86-87), Proctor Fedn. Tchrs. (recert. com. 1980—, treas. 1981-86), Proctor Edn. Assn. (chairperson recert. com.), Am. Legion, Euclid Ea. Star(treas.), Phi Delta Kappa, Military Assn. America. Home: 6713 Grand Lake Rd Saginaw MN 55779-9782

STAUBER-JOHNSON, ELIZABETH JANE, retired elementary school educator; b. Duluth, Minn., Apr. 7, 1950; d. Edward James and Kathleen Mary (LeBlanc) Stauber; m. A(lden) Ronald Johnson, July 26, 1975; children: Todd Alden, Heidi Ann, Dean Edward, Shane Ronald. BS summa cum laude, Coll. St. Scholastica, 1972; MEd summa cum laude, U. Minn., Duluth, 1982; PhD in Curriculum/Instrn. Elem. Math. Edn., U. Minn., 1996. Cert. tchr., Minn. Tchr. Ind. Sch. Dist. 709/Duluth Pub. Schs., 1972-88; tchr. elem. math. Nettleton Math./Sci./Computer Magnet Sch., Duluth, 1988-93; asst. prof. math. edn. U. Wis., Superior, 1993-97; ret., 1997. Pres. Equine Allies, Inc., 2004—; trainer Success Understanding Math. Project, Des Moines, gender-ethnic excellence student achievement GESA, 1991—; instr. tchr. Family Math., Mpls., 1988—; mem. project for reforming and improving math. edn. com. Minn. Dept. Edn., math. framework team, 1992—; com. mem. Gov.'s Nat. Sci. Found. Statewide Systemic Initiative, 1991—, Coll. of St. Scholastica Ctr. for Promotion of Underrepresented in Sci., 1990—; desegregation adv. com. Duluth Schs., 1987—; initiative com. Gov.'s Nat. Sci. Found.; team mem. Minn. Dept. Edn. Math. Frameworks; presenter in field Trustee Coll. St. Scholastica, Duluth, chair acad. affairs; trustee com., excentive com., chair student affairs com., bd. dirs. Marshal Coll. Prep. Sch., 2003—, v.p., 2004—; pres. Equine Allies, Inc., 2004—; bd. dirs. Marshall Sch., Duluth, 2004—, v.p., 2005—. Mem. Minn. Coun. Tchrs. Math., Nat. Assn. Tchrs. Math., Minn. Reading Assn., Arrowhead Reading Coun. (bd. dirs. 1984—, pres. 1988-89), Assn. Childhood Edn. (pres. Duluth chpt. 1980-81, state bd. dirs. 1982-83), Phi Kappa Phi, Alpha Delta Kappa (pres. 1982-84), Phi Delta Kappa. Avocations: reading, children's pop-up books, orchid collecting/growing, showing and breeding quarter horses. Home: 2400 Minnesota Ave Duluth MN 55802-2518

STAUBITZ, ARTHUR FREDERICK, retired lawyer, health products executive; b. Omaha, Mar. 14, 1939; s. Herbert Frederick Staubitz and Barbara Eileen (Dallas) Alderson; m. Linda Medora Miller, Aug. 18, 1962; children: Michael, Melissa, Peter. AB cum laude, Wesleyan U., Middletown, Conn., 1961; JD cum laude, U. Pa., 1964. Bar: Ill. 1964, U.S. Dist. Ct. (no. dist.) Ill. 1964, U.S. Ct. Appeals (7th cir.) 1964, Pa. 1972. Assoc. Sidley & Austin, Chgo., 1964-71; sr. internat. atty., asst. gen. counsel, dir. Japanese ops. Sperry Univac, Blue Bell, Pa., 1971-78; from asst. to assoc. to dep. gen. counsel Baxter Internat. Inc., Deerfield, Ill., 1978—85, v.p., dep. gen. counsel, 1985—90; v.p. Baxter Diagnostics, 1990—91; sr. v.p., sec., gen. counsel Amgen, Inc., Thousand Oaks, Calif., 1991—92; v.p., gen. mgr. Ventures Group Baxter World Trade Corp., Deerfield, Ill., 1992—93; v.p., sec., gen. counsel Baxter Internat. Inc., Deerfield, 1993, sr. v.p., gen. counsel, 1993—97, sr. v.p. portfolio strategy, 1997—98; ret., 1998. Mem. Planning Commn., Springfield Twp., Montgomery County, Pa., 1973-74, mem. Zoning Hearing Bd., 1974-78; bd. dirs. Twp. H.S. Dist. 113, Deerfield and Highland Park, Ill., 1983-91, pres., 1989-91; trustee Food and Drug Law Inst., 1991-92, 93-96, Carthage Coll., Kenosha, Wis., 1996—, exec. com., 1999—2007; bd. dirs. Music of the Baroque, 1994-2001, vice-chmn., Ariz. Opera, 2008-. Episcopalian. Home: 6251 E Placita Aspecto Tucson AZ 85750 Home Phone: 520-529-2331. Personal E-mail: staubitz@msn.com.

STAUBUS, GEORGE JOSEPH, finance educator; b. Brunswick, Mo., Apr. 26, 1926; s. George Washington and Florence Lidwina (Pittman) S.; m. Sarah Mayer, Apr. 11, 1949; children: Lindsay, Martin, Paul, Janette. BS, U. Mo., 1947; MBA, U. Chgo., 1949, PhD, 1954. C.P.A., Ill. Instr. U. Buffalo, 1947-49, U. Chgo., 1950-52; asst. prof. then prof. acctg. U. Calif.-Berkeley, from 1952, now Michael N. Chetkovich prof. emeritus. Vis. prof. NYU, 1965, London Bus. Sch., 1966-67, U. Kans., 1969-70; Erskine lectr. U. Canterbury, New Zealand, 1972, 91. Author: A Theory of Accounting to Investors, 1961, Activity Costing and Input-Output Accounting, 1971, Making Accounting Decisions, 1977, An Accounting Concept of Revenue, 1980, Activity Costing for Decisions, 1988, Economic Influences on the Development of Accounting in Firms, 1996, The Decision-Usefulness Theory of Accounting: A Limited History, 2000. Served with USN, 1944-46. Recipient Disting. prof. Calif. Soc. C.P.A.s, 1981 Mem. Am. Acctg. Assn. (disting. internat. lectr. 1982), AICPA, Fin. Execs. Inst. Office: UC Berkeley Haas Sch Bus Berkeley CA 94720-0001 Business E-Mail: staubus@haas.berkeley.edu.

STAUDENMEIER, WILLIAM JOHN, JR., sociology professor; b. Wilmington, Del., Oct. 28, 1950; s. William John and Virginia Arlene Staudenmeier; m. Elizabeth Robin Medina, May 28, 1978; children: William Francis, Thomas Maxim. BS, U.S. Mil. Acad., West Point, NY, 1972; MA in Mgmt. and Human Rels., Webster Coll., St. Louis, Mo., 1978; PhD in Sociology, Washington U., St. Louis, Mo., 1985. Chief drug and alcohol edn. and rehab. Travis AFB, Fairfield, Calif., 1972—75; chief drug/alcohol abuse control Clark AFB, Angeles, Philippines, 1975—76, Hdqs. Mil. Airlift Command, Scott AFB, Ill., 1976—78; acting asst. prof. sociology Drake U., Des Moines, 1985—87; asst. prof. sociology Eureka Coll., Ill., 1987—90, assoc. prof. sociology, 1990—95, prof. sociology, 1995—, v.p. acad. affairs, dean, 2005—06. Divsn. chair social scis. and bus. divsn. Eureka Coll., 1991—94; manuscript referee jours., 1987—2005; instr. cmty. orgn. sect. Nat. Alcoholism Tng. Program for Profls., St. Louis, 1976—78; cons. and instr. alcohol studies cert. program, employee assistance program Continuing Edn. Washington U., St. Louis, 1980—84; cons. Harbor Ho., St. Louis, 1983—84; cons. employee assistance edn. and rsch. program Sch. of Indsl. and Labor Rels., Cornell U., Ithaca, NY, 1987; cons. medicalization of substance abuse treatment in the workplace Inst. for Behavioral Rsch., U. of Ga., Athens, 1987; faculty rep. to bd. of trustees Eureka Coll., 1988—90, chair coll. strategic planning, 1989—91, founder, dir., faculty colloquia series, 1988—94; vis. scientist U. Edinburgh, 1994; vis. fellow Sch. Indsl. and Labor Rels., Cornell U., NY, 1992. V.p. Eureka Area United Way, 1989—91; charter chpt. faculty adviser Eureka Coll. Nat. Charter Campus Chpt. of Habitat for Humanity, 1988—92; bd. dirs. Solano County Mental Health Adv. Bd., Vallejo, Calif., 1974—75. Capt. USAF, 1972—78. Recipient PhD tuition scholarship, Washington U., 1980—85, Helen B. Cleaver Disting. Tchg. award, Eureka Coll., 1989—90; named pioneering EAP practioner for oral history project, Prof. Harrison M. Trice, Cornell U., 1987, Dean's Lectr., Office of the Dean, Eureka Coll., 1988, 1995; fellow, Nat. Inst. on Alcohol Abuse and Alcoholism, 1979—80. Mem.: Kettil Bruun Soc. for Social and Epidemiol. Rsch. on Alcohol, Midwest Sociol. Soc. (soc. bd. of dirs. 2004—06, sec. 1999—2001), Ill. Sociol. Assn. (governing bd. 1995—2001, pres. 1998—99), Alpha Chi (life). Achievements include helping pioneer early social actions drug/alcohol education/rehabilitation in the USAF. Avocations: hiking, reading, chess, soccer. Office: Eureka Coll 300 E College Ave Eureka IL 61530

STAUDERMAN, ALBERT PHILIP, JR., media production consultant; b. Englewood, NJ, Dec. 14, 1936; s. Albert Philip Stauderman and Martha Louise (Dodd) Williamson; m. Helen MacKenzie Layton, Dec. 27, 1958; children: Elizabeth, Sarah, Edward (Ted). BSc, Syracuse U., 1958. Audio-visual prodn. supr. Luth. Ch. in Am., Phila., 1960-64; TV comml. prodn. supr. Procter & Gamble, Cin., 1964-71, assoc. mgr., 1971-82; dir. advt. prodn. Richardson-Vicks, Wilton, Conn., 1982-85; chmn., CEO Bird Bonette Stauderman Inc., Westport, Conn., 1985—; co-chmn., dir. Bird Bonette Stauderman Europe Ltd., London, 1996-2000, chmn., dir., 2000—, founder Sao Paulo, Brazil, 2001—, Sydney, 2006—. Pres. Dikaia Found., Inc., 1995—2001. Author: TV Commercial Production Cost Trends, 1985, 2d. edit., 1986; writer, dir. various pub. svc. TV Commls., 1970-82; actor Golden Age TV programs, 1949-56. Commr. Wilton (Conn.) various land use Commns., 1988—; founding pres. Syracuse U. Newhouse Sch. Alumni Assn., 1985—87; pres. congregation and coun. St. Michael's Luth. Ch., New Canaan, Conn., 1999—2001. Recipient Alumni Svc. award Syracuse U., 1981. Mem. Sprite Island Yacht Club (chmn. race com. 1993-98), Minute Man Yacht Club, Sloane Club (London), Williams Club (NYC), Delta Upsilon. Republican. Office Phone: 203-454-8781.

STAUDERMAN, BRUCE FORD, advertising executive, writer; b. Jersey City, Mar. 17, 1919; b. Herbert Henry and Helen Ann (Jacobus) S.; m. Claude Dorsenne, Mar. 23; 1946. Student, Syracuse U., 1936-38, TV Workshop, NYC, 1949-50, Sch. TV Technique, 1950. V.p. TV, radio, films Meldrum & Fewsmith, Inc., Cleve., 1954-62, exec. v.p., chmn. plans bd., exec. creative dir., 1973-79; v.p., creative dir. Ogilvy & Mather, NYC, 1962-69, Kenyon & Eckhardt, Inc., NYC, 1979-83, Barnhart & Co., Denver, 1983-84; pres. Stauderman Advt., 1984—; v.p., creative dir. Mktg. Resources Group, 1985-88. Dir. TV, Intermarco-Elvinger (advt. co.), Paris, 1969-73; TV cons. gov., Ohio, 1958; mem. coun., judge C.L.I.O. Festival, 1960—; chmn. Paris jury, 1969-73; jury mem. Internat. Advt. Film Festival, Cannes, Venice, 1976— Author: The England Book, 2006; radio, TV program writer: House of Mystery, The Big Story, Columbia Workshop, 1946-51; writer, producer, dir., WXEL-TV, Cleve., 1951-54. Mem. men's com. Cleve. Playhouse, 1958-62; chmn. TV com. Cleve. United Fund, 1958-59. Served from pvt. to 2d lt. AUS, 1941-46; to 1st lt. N.G. Essex Troop AUS, 1948-50. Mem. Am. Assn. Advt. Agys. (TV and radio adminstrs. com. 1958-62), Am. Fedn. TV and Radio Artists, Naval Club (London). Home: 31400 Fairview Rd Orange Village OH 44022 Home Phone: 440-542-0325. Personal E-mail: bfswriter@aol.com.

STAUDOHAR, PAUL DAVID, economics professor, labor arbitrator; b. Duluth, Minn., Dec. 3, 1940; s. Matthew Paul Staudohar and Patricia Constance Landell. BA, U. Minn., 1962; MBA, U. So. Calif., LA, 1966, MA, 1968, PhD, 1969. Adminstrv. officer United Calif. Bank, LA, 1964—66; instr. econ. U. So. Calif., LA, 1967—69; asst. prof. bus. adminstrn. Calif. State U., Hayward, 1969—72, assoc. prof. bus. adminstrn., 1972, prof. bus. adminstrn., 1977—2007, prof. emeritus, 2007—. Pres. Internat. Assn. of Sports Economists, France, 1999—2002; bd. editors Jour. of Collective Negotiations, 1978—, Jour. Individual Employment Rights, 1992—2008; co-founder Jour. of Sports Econs., bd. editors, 2000—. Author: Labor Econ. and Indsl. Rels., 1994, Playing for Dollars, 1996; author, editor: Diamond Mines: Baseball and Labor, 2000, More Sports Best Short Stories, 2004, The Best Dog Stories, 2007, Murder Short and Sweet: Classic Stories, 2008, mem. editl. adv. bd.: Wolters Kluwer Law & Bus., 2007—08; co-editor: Proceedings of the Sixty-First Annual Meeting, 2009. Recipient disting. svc. award, Omicron Delta Epsilon, 1981. Mem.: Am. Arbitration Assn., Am. Econ. Assn., Nat. Acad. Arbitrators, Beta Gamma Sigma (hon.). Office: Calif State U East Bay 25800 Carlos Bee Blvd Hayward CA 94542 Office Phone: 510-885-3080.

STAUFFER, ERIC P., lawyer; b. Tucson, Feb. 1, 1948; s. Robert D. and Jeanne E. (Catlin) S.; m. Jane F. Snyder, Aug. 2, 1969; children: Curtis Austen, Marcus Elias, Laura Afton. BA, New Coll. of Fla., 1969; JD, Yale U., 1972. Bar: Ariz. 1972, Maine 1974, D.C. 1979. Spl. asst. to gov., fed. state coord. State of Maine, 1973-75; Maine alt. New England Regional Commn., 1973-75; gen. counsel Maine State Housing Auth., 1976-77; adminstrv. asst. to chmn. Dem. Nat. Com., 1977-78; mem. Preti, Flaherty, Beliveau & Pachios, PLLP, Portland, Maine, 1978—. Bd. dirs. Jr. Achievement Maine, Inc., 1995-98; pres. Goodwill Industries No. New Eng., 1981-82, bd. dirs., 1979-93, 1999-2005. Fellow Am. Coll. Mortgage Attys.; mem. Am. Health Lawyers Assn., Maine State Bar Assn., Ariz. State Bar, DC Bar, Maine Real Estate Devel. Assn. (bd. dirs. 1991—, Pub. Svc. award 1992, Founder's award 2002, Vol. of Yr. 2007), Maine Bar Found. (bd. dirs. 2007-, mem. exec. com. 2008-09, treas. 2009-). Office: Preti Flaherty Beliveau & Pachios PLLP PO Box 9546 One City Ctr Portland ME 04112-9546 Home Phone: 207-774-2461; Office Phone: 207-791-3000. Business E-Mail: estauffe@preti.com.

STAUFFER, GEORGE B., dean, musician, historian, consultant; b. Hershey, Pa., Feb. 18, 1947; s. Howard Hamilton and Elizabeth Boyer Stauffer; 1 child, Matthew. BA, Dartmouth Coll., Hanover, NH, 1969; MA, Bryn Mawr Coll., Pa., 1971; PhD, Columbia U., NYC, 1978. Adj. asst. prof. Yeshiva U., NYC, 1978—79; asst. to prof. music CUNY, NYC, 1979—2000; dean, prof. music Mason Gross Sch. Arts, Rutgers U., New Brunswick, NJ, 2000—. U. organist, chapel music dir. Columbia U., 1977—99; bd. trustees Keewaydin Found., Salisbury, Vt., 1981—2000. Author: (books) The Organ Preludes of J.S. Bach, 1980, Bach: The Mass in B-Minor, 1997; co-author: Organ Technique: Modern & Early, 2002; editor: J.S. Bach as Organist, 1986, The World Of Baroque Music, 2006; gen. editor: Yale Music Masterworks Series, 2002—. Fellowship, Guggenheim Found., NYC, 1985—86, Fulbright Commn., DC, 1999—2000, Am. Coun. Learned Societies, NYC, 1999—2000. Mem.: Coll. Music Soc., Am. Bach Soc. (adv. bd. mem. 2000—, pres. 1996—2000), Am. Musicological Soc. Avocation: canoeing. Home: 1050 George St 16M New Brunswick NJ 08901 Office: Office of Dean Mason Gross Sch 33 Livingston Ave New Brunswick NJ 08901 Office Phone: 732-932-9360. Business E-Mail: stauffer@masongross.rutgers.edu.

STAUFFER, JEFFERY DEAN, education educator; s. Lt Col Ivery Dean and Jeanne Francis Stauffer; m. Chalaine Dee Miller, Dec. 8, 1969; children: Michon Dee Olivas, Justin Dean. M in Pub. Adminstrn., Ball State U., Zaragoza, Spain, 1972; M in Edn. Admin, Calif. Luth. U., Thousand Oaks, 1977; EdD, U. La Verne, 1982. Prof. dept. chair Ventura Coll., Calif., 1974—; core faculty masters program Antioch U., Santa Barbara, 1994—. Bus. adv. group Ventura Coll., Calif., 2000—08. Capt. USAF, 1969—74, Kansas and Spain. Recipient Nat. Transit Innovation award, 1995; UCLA fellowship, 1995, Faculty Study Coun. Internat. Edn. grant, Ventura Coll. Found., 2008. Mem.: Alpha Beta Gamma (faculty advisor 1976—2008). Avocations: travel, swimming, hiking. Office: Ventura Coll 4667 Telegraph Rd Ventura CA 93003

STAUFFER, JOHN WILLIAM, cultural historian; b. Lincoln, Nebr. s. William Albert and Jean Stanley Stauffer; m. Deborah Cunningham; 1 child, Erik Isaiah. MALS in Humanities, Wesleyan U., 1991; MA in Am. Studies, Purdue U., 1993; PhD in Am. Studies, Yale U., 1999. Asst. prof. Harvard U., Cambridge, Mass., 1999-2001, assoc. prof., 2001—03, prof., 2003—. Spkr. in field. Author: The Black Hearts of Men, 2002 (Frederick Douglass Book prize 2002, Lincoln prize, 2d pl. winner, 2003), The Meteor of War: The John Brown Story, 2004; editor: My Bondage and My Freedom, 2003, The Works of James McCune Smith, 2006, Prophets of Protest, 2006, The Problem of Evil, 2007, The Parallel Lives of Frederick Douglass and Abraham Lincoln, 2008, The State of Jones, 2009. Newhouse fellow in writing Yale U., 1996-97, Rsch. fellow, 1994-95, History and Am. Studies Rsch. fellow, 1996, Charlotte Newcombe fellow Woodrow Wilson Nat. Fellowship Found., 1997-98; grantee NEH, 1999; recipient Ralph Henry Gabriel prize, 1999, Jan Thaddeus Tchg. award Harvard U., 2002, Frederick Douglass Book prize, 2002, Avery Craven pize, 2003, Lincoln prize, 2003, Everett Mendelsohn Excellence in Mentoring award, 2005, Walter Channing Cabot fellowship, 2009-. Mem. Soc. for Values in Higher Edn., Orgn. of Am. Historians (presenter 1998), Am. Studies Assn. (Ralph Henry Gabriel prize 1999), Daguerreian Soc., Phi Kappa Phi. Avocations: photography, tennis, ballet, dance (jazz). Office: Harvard U Dept English Barker Ctr 12 Quincy St Cambridge MA 02138-3804 Home: 1 Amory Pl Cambridge MA 02139 Home Phone: 617-642-7108; Office Phone: 617-864-4508. Business E-Mail: stauffer@fas.harvard.edu.

STAUFFER, PHILIP HENRY, hydrogeologist; m. Elizabeth Marie Allen, June 21, 2008; 1 child, Denali Toliver Allen. PhD, U. Calif., Santa Cruz, 1999. Hydrogeologist Los Alamos Nat. Lab., N.Mex., 2000—. Cons. CRDF, Alexandria, Va., 2005—. Contbr. articles to profl. jours. Schlanger Ocean Drilling fellowship, NSF, 1997. Mem.: Geol. Soc. America, Am. Geophys. Union. Green Party. Office: Los Alamos Nat Labr Mail Stop T-003 Los Alamos NM 87545 Office Phone: 505-665-4638. Business E-Mail: stauffer@lanl.gov.

STAUFFER, RONALD EUGENE, lawyer, physicist; b. Hempstead, NY, Jan. 22, 1949; s. Hiram Eugene and Florence Marie S.; m. Vicki Lynn Hartman, June 12, 1973; children: Eric Alan, Craig Aaron, Darren Adam. SB, MIT, 1970; JD magna cum laude, Harvard U., 1973. Bar: D.C. 1973, U.S. Ct. Mil. Appeals 1976, U.S. Tax Ct. 1979. Ptnr. Hogan & Hartson, Washington, 1977-87, Sonnenschein Nath & Rosenthal, Washington, 1988—2004; founder Lake Anna Inst. Theoretical Physics, 2005—, chair, 2005—. Contbr. articles to profl. publs. Capt. U.S. Army, 1970-77. Mem. ABA (chair TIPS Employee Benefits Com. 1977-2004), D.C. Bar Assn., Tau Beta Pi, Sigma Gamma Tau. Avocations: running, water-skiing. Home and Office: Lake Anna Inst Theoretical Physics 149 Acorn Cir Mineral VA 23117-4703

STAUFFER, THOMAS GEORGE, retired hotel executive; b. Akron, Ohio, Mar. 4, 1932; s. Caldwell E. and Rose C. (Ortscheidt) S.; m. Lois Campsey, June 18, 1960. BS, Case Western Res. U., 1954. Cert. hotel adminstr. Pres. Renaissance Hotels Internat. (Ams.), 1954-98; ret., 1998. Trustee Cleve. Bot. Garden. Recipient Legion of Honor, Order of DeMolay. Mem. Am. Hotel and Motel Assn., Urban Land Inst., Nat. Restaurant Assn. (past dir.), Rolling Rock Club, Lakewood Country Club, Masons, Scottish Rite, Sigma Chi (Significant Sigma Chi). Home: 19 Warwick Ln Cleveland OH 44116-2305 Personal E-mail: lcstgs@cox.net.

STAUFFER, THOMAS MICHAEL, university president; b. Harrisburg, Pa., Dec. 5, 1941; s. John Nisley and Louise Lee Stauffer; children: Amity Juliet, Courtney Amanda, Winston Thomas; m. Susie Heller; stepchildren: Lauren Heller, Adam Heller, Elizabeth Stinson. BA cum laude, Wittenberg U., Ohio, 1963; Cert. in E. European Politics, Freie U. Berlin, 1964; MA, PhD, Josef Korbel Sch. Internat. Studies, U. Denver, 1973; Doctorate (hon.), Jackson State U., 2002. Dir. office leadership devel., v.p., external rels. Am. Coun. on Edn., 1972—82; pres., prof. pub. policy U. Houston-Clear Lake, 1982—91; spl. asst. to adminstr. NASA, 1991—92; pres., prof. pub. policy and internat. rels. Golden Gate U., 1992—99; mng. ptnr. Global Consultation and Family Bus. Internat., 1985—; CEO Young Pres. Orgn. Internat., 1999—2001; exec. dir. Lincoln Ctr. for Internat. Mgmt. Ethics; prof. global bus. Thunderbird Sch. Global Mgmt., 2003—05; pres., CEO, prof. mgmt. Am. U. Afghanistan, Kabul, 2006—09. Exec. sec. Fedn. Assn. of Acad. Health Care Profls.; chmn. task force Am. Coun. Edn.; exec. dir. Bus. Higher Edn. Forum, Nat. Com. Higher Edn. Issues, 1975—82; bd. dirs. Am. U. Afghanistan Found. Contbr. chpts. to books and articles to profl. jours. and newspapers. Chair, nat. bd. Challenger Ctr. for Space Sci. Edn.; chair Ctr. for Advanced Space Studies; com. advanced tech. Tex. Econ. Devel.; chmn. Houston Com. on Econ. Diversification Planning, Houston World Trade Ctr. Task Force; chmn. com. advanced tech. Clear Lake Area Econ. Devel. Found.; co-chair Tex. Sci. and Tech. Coun.; pres. St. John Hosp.; co-chair San Francisco World Trade Assn.; chair San Francisco Consortium on Higher Edn., San Francisco Mayor's Blue Ribbon Com. on Econ. Devel.; mem. steering com. Silicon Valley Mfrs. Group; bd. dirs. San Francisco C. of C., San Francisco YMCA, Acad. of Art U.; lectr. George Washington U., Regis U. Oceania Cruise Line. Recipient Disting. Alumni award Joseph Korbel Sch. Internat. Studies U. Denver, 1989, Tex. Senate Resolution of Commendation, 1991, Challenger Ctr. Nat. award, 1990, ACE Fellow Anniversary award, 1990, 05, Leadership HS Do the Right Thing award, 1998; Am. Coun. on Edn. fellow in acad. adminstrn., 1971-72, Ford Found. and Social Sci. Found. fellow, 1963-68, sr. fellow Am. Leadership Forum. Mem.: Cosmos Club, Washington, DC. Home: 3080 Coombsville Rd Napa CA 94558 Office Phone: 415-516-8767. Office Fax: 707-255-4999. Business E-Mail: globalcosultation@gmail.com.

STAUFFER, WILLIAM MOYER, medical educator, director; b. Utah, Sept. 29, 1965; s. William and Ruth Stauffer; m. Carol Lunderberg, June 19, 1993; children: Jacob, Maxwell. BA, St. Olaf Coll., Northfield, Minn., 1988; MS in Pub. Health, U. Colo. Health Scis. Ctr., Denver, 1992; MD, U. Minn., Mpls., 1995; Diploma in Tropical Medicine and Hygiene, Johns Hopkins U., Baltimore, 1999. Diplomate in internal medicine Am. Bd. Internal Medicine, 1999, cert. in infectious diseases Am. Bd. Internal Medicine, 2008, pediatrician Am. Acad. Pediat., 1999, Am. Acad. Pediat., 2004. Faculty dept. internal medicine, pediat. and infectious diseases Health Ptnrs., St. Paul, 1999—, geosentinal site dir., 2001—; assoc. prof. to assoc. co-dir. global health resident tng. program dept. medicine U. Minn., 2005—, adj. faculty sch. pub. health, 2005—, course dir. UMN/CDC global health course, 2005—; tech. cons. divsn. global migration & quarantine Ctrs. Disease Control and Prevention, Atlanta, 2006—. Editor: (book) Immigrant Medicine; prodr.(medical cons.): (film) If We Knew Their Stories; contbr. articles to numerous profl. jours. Vol. physician, Arusha, Tanzania, 2005—; bd. dirs. Peru Health Share, Mpls., 1991—93. Recipient Ctr. Edn. Tchg. award, U. Minn., 2006, Cmty. Health Commitment award, Minn. Hosp. Assn., 2006, Top US Travel Physicians, Conde Nast Traveller Mag., 2007; fellowship, Johns Hopkins Ctr. Advanced Internat. Studies, 2006. Mem.: Am. Soc. Tropical Medicine and Hygiene (pres. clin. com. 2008—, cert. clin. tropical medicine & travel medicine 1999). Achievements include research in health, malaria, neglected tropical disease and medical education research. Office: Univ Mpls 420 Del St SE Minneapolis MN 55455 Office Fax: 612-625-4410. Business E-Mail: stauf005@umn.edu.

STAUSBOLL, ANNE, pension fund administrator; b. 1956; BA in English, Oberlin Coll., Ohio; JD, U. Calif. Davis Sch. Law. With legal office Calif. Pub. Employees' Retirement Sys. (CalPERS), Sacramento, 1993—97, dep. gen. counsel, 1997—99, asst. exec. officer investment ops., 2004—08, interim chief investment officer, 2008—09, CEO, 2009—; gen. counsel Calif. State Treas. Phil Angelides, Sacramento, 1999—2000, chief dep. treas., 2000—04. Mem. Ceres Bd.; governing bd. UN Principles for Responsible Investment; adv. bd. Toigo Found. Named one of Top 20 Nonbank Women in Fin., US Banker, 2007, 2008. Mem.: Order of the Coif. Office: Calif Pub Employees' Retirement Sys - CalPERS Lincoln Plz N 400 Q St Sacramento CA 95811 Office Phone: 916-795-3829.*

STAVE, ANNA M., education educator; d. Edward LeMaster and Anna Rea Montedonico. BA, St. Louis U., 1965; MFA, Ohio U., Athens, 1967; MS, Syracuse U., NY, 1984, PhD, 1991. Cert. English and speech tchr. NY. English 12th grade honors, 9th grade drama Highland Pk. HS, Mich., 1967—69; youth theatre dir. Karamu Theatre, Cleve., 1969—72, Salt City Playhouse, Syracuse, 1972—73; youth dir. YWCA, Syracuse, 1973—75; assoc. prof. English, drama Onondaga CC, Syracuse, 1975—83; grad. asst. divsn. study tchg. Syracuse U., 1984—87, lectr. divsn. study tchg., 1990—91, 1988—89; lectr. English dept. SUNY, Cortland, 1987—88, assoc. prof. Oneonta, 1991—. Dir.: (plays), 1969—83; contbr. articles to profl. publs.; co-author (with Alison Black): A Comprehensive Guide to Readers, 2007—; co-author: Enhancing Fluency and Comprehension in Middle School and Beyond, —. Mem.: NY State English Coun. (Educator Excellence 2001), Am. Ednl. Rsch. Assn., Nat. Coun. Tchrs. English, Internat. Reading Assn.

STAVERT, ALEXANDER BRUCE, archbishop; b. Montreal, Apr. 1, 1940; s. R. Ewart and Kathleen H. (Rosamond) S.; m. Diana Greig, June 26, 1982; children: Kathleen, Rosamond, Timothy. Student, Lower Can. Coll., Montreal, 1957; BA, Bishop's U., Lennoxville Sherbrooke, Can., 1961, DCL (hon.), 2007; STB, U. Toronto, Ont., Can., 1964, ThM, 1976, DD (hon.), 1986. Ordained to ministry Anglican Ch. as deacon, 1964, as priest, 1965. With Mission of Schefferville, Que., 1964-69; fellow, tutor in div. Trinity Coll., U. Toronto, 1969-70, chaplain, 1970-76; with St. Clement's Mission East, St. Paul's River, Que., 1976-81; chaplain Champlain Regional Coll., Bishop's U., 1981-84; dean, rector St. Alban's Cathedral, Prince Albert, Sask., Canada, 1984-91; consecrated bishop Anglican Diocese of Que., Quebec, 1991—; metropolitan Province of Can., 2004—; archbishop Quebec, 2004—. Address: Diocese of Que 31 rue des Jardins Quebec City PQ Canada G1R 4L6 Office Phone: 418-692-3858. Business E-Mail: archbishop@quebec.anglican.ca.

STAVISKY, TOBY ANN, state legislator; b. NYC; m. Leonard Stavisky, 1964 (dec. 1999); 1 child, Evan. BA, Syracuse U.; MA, Hunter Coll., Queens Coll. Actuarial dept. Ins. Co.; social studies tchr. NYC Pub. High Schs.; dist. mgr. NE Queens 1980 Census; mem. Dist. 16 NY State Senate, Albany, 1999—, asst. minority whip Dist. 16, 2003—. Mem. legis. coms. fin., transp., tourism, recreation and sports devel. N.Y. State Sen. 16th Dist., ranking minority mem. higher edn. com., mem. aging com., mem. civil svc. and pensions com., mem. edn. com. Founder North Flushing Sr. Ctr., bd. dirs.; trustee Whitestone Hebrew Ctr. Recipient Claire Shulman award, Top 10 Women in Bus., 2004, award, Neurol. Impaired Brain Injured Children, 2002, Counseling, Admissions and Fin. Aid Legis. Consortium, 2003, Flushing C. of C. and Bus. Assn., Taiwanese Assn. Am., CUNY, Korean-Am. Assn. Flushing; named Worthy Woman of Forest Hills. Democrat. Office: Dist Office 144-36 Willets Point Blvd Flushing NY 11387 also: Capitol Office Rm 509 Legislative Office Bldg Albany NY 12247 Office Phone: 718-445-0004, 518-455-3461. Office Fax: 718-445-8398, 518-426-6857. Business E-Mail: stavisky@senate.state.ny.us.*

STAVITSKY, ABRAM BENJAMIN, immunologist, educator; b. Newark, May 14, 1919; s. Nathan and Ida (Novak) S.; m. Ruth Bernice Okney, Dec. 6, 1942; children: Ellen Barbara, Gail Beth. AB, U. Mich., 1939, MS, 1940; PhD, U. Minn., 1943; VMD, U. Pa., 1946. Research fellow Calif. Inst. Tech., 1946-47; faculty Case Western Res. U., 1947—, prof. microbiology, 1962—, prof. molecular biology and microbiology, 1983—89; emeritus, 1989; mem. expert com. immunochemistry WHO, 1963-83; mem. microbiology fellowship com. NIH, 1963-66; mem. microbiology test com. Nat. Bd. Med. Examiners, 1970-73; chmn. microbiology test com. Nat. Bd. Podiatry Examiners, 1978-82; adj. staff in pathobiology Lerner Rsch. Inst., Cleve. Clinic Found., 2006—. Mem. editl. bd. Jour. Immunological Methods, 1979-88, Immunopharmacology, 1983-96. Vice pres. Ludlow Community Assn., 1964-66. Fellow AAAS; mem. Am. Assn. Immunologists, Am. Soc. Microbiology, Sigma Xi. Home: 14604 Onaway Rd Shaker Heights OH 44120-2845 Office: 2119 Abington Rd Cleveland OH 44106-2333 Home Phone: 216-752-8631. Business E-Mail: abs7@case.edu.

STAVRIDIS, JIM (JAMES GEORGE STAVRIDIS), career military officer; b. West Palm Beach, Fla., Feb. 15, 1955; s. Paul George and Shirley Anne Stavridis; m. Laura Elizabeth Hall, May 28, 1981; children: Christina Anne, Julia Elizabeth. BS, U.S. Naval Acad., Annapolis, Md., 1972; PhD, Tufts U., 1983, MA in Law & Diplomacy, 1984; Disting. grad., Nat. War Coll., 1992. Commd. ensign USN, advanced through grades to adm., 2006; commdg. officer USS Barry, Norfolk, Va., 1993—96; comdr. Destroyer Squadron 21, San Diego, 1997—98; exec. asst. to sec. USN, Washington, 1998—2000, dir. navy ops. group, 2000—02; comdr. USS Enterprise Carrier Strike Group, 2002—04, Cruiser Destroyer Group 12, Mayport, Fla., 2002—04; sr. mil. asst. to sec. US Dept. Def., Washington, 2004—06; comdr. US So. Command (USSOUTHCOM), Miami, 2006—09, US European Command (USEUCOM), Stuttgart, Germany, 2009—; supreme allied comdr. NATO, Europe (SACEUR), Brussels, 2009—. Author: Division Officer's Guide, Watch Officer's Guide, Command at Sea; contbr. articles to profl. jours. Decorated Def. Superior Svc. medal, Legion of Merit, Meritorious Svc. medal, Navy Commendation medal, Navy Achievement medal; recipient Adm. Arleigh Burke award, Newport Navy League award, John Paul Jones award for Inspirational Leadership, Navy League. Office: US European Command (USEUCOM) Unit 30400 Patch Barracks APO AE 09131 Vaihingen Germany also: NATO Blvd Leopold III 1110 Brussels Belgium*

STAVROPOULOS, ROSE MARY GRANT, community activist, volunteer; b. Decatur, Ill. d. Walter Edwin and Ora Lenore (Kepler) Grant; m. Stan Stavropoulos; children: Becky Ann Stavropoulos Betian, Stephanie Diane. BS, Ea. Ill. U. Cert. elem. edn. Tchr. 2nd grade Garfield Sch., Decatur; bd. dirs. Wilmot Sch. Bd. PTA, Deerfield, Moraine Girl Scout Coun., Deerfield, also bd. dirs.; chmn. Human Rels. Commn., Deerfield; mem. sr. citizen adv. com. Deerfield Park Dist.; pres. Lake County (Ill.) LWV; chmn. Deerfield Village Caucus; pres. Caring For Others, Inc., Deerfield, Deerfield Area LWV; bd. mem., pres. Deerfield Area United Way, pres. Mem. Deerfield Village Caucus Adv. Coun. Recipient Deerfield Human Rels. Humanitarian award, Lerner Life's Citizen of Month. Mem. Deerfield Area Hist. Soc., Highland Park Hosp. Aux, Legacy at Bryant Ranch Home Assn. (bd. dirs., treas., sec.), Delta Zeta. Home: 23959 Sanctuary Pkwy Yorba Linda CA 92887 Personal E-mail: jjjjgrandma@aol.com.

STAVROPOULOS, WILLIAM S., retired chemical company executive; b. Bridgehampton, NY, May 12, 1939; m. Linda Stavropoulos; children: S. William, Angela D. BS in Pharm. Chemistry, Fordham U.; PhD in Medicinal Chemistry, U. Washington; LLD (hon.), Northwood U., 1998. Rsch. chemist in pharm. rsch. Dow Chem. Co., Midland, Mich., 1967, rsch. chemist for diagnostics product rsch., 1970, rsch. mgr. diagnostics product rsch., 1973, bus. mgr. diagnostics product rsch., 1976, bus. mgr. polyolefins, 1977, dir. mktg. plastics dept., 1979; comml. v.p. Dow Chem. Co. Latin Am., Coral Gables, Fla., 1980; pres. Dow Latin Am., 1984; comml. v.p., basics and hydrocarbons Dow Chem. Co. U.S.A., Midland, Mich., 1985-87, group v.p., 1987-90; pres. Dow U.S.A., 1990; v.p. The Dow Chem. Co., 1990, sr. v.p., 1991, pres., COO, 1993—95, CEO, 1995—2000, 2002—04, chmn., 2001—06. Bd. dirs. Dow Corning Corp., The Dow Chem. Co., Marion Merrel Dow Inc., BellSouth Corp., Chem. Financial Corp., Maersk Inc., NCR Corp.; trustee, Fidelity Group of Funds; bd. Am Enterprise Inst. Public Policy Rsch.; CEO Essex Chem Corp, 1988-92. Recipient Ellis Island Medal of Honor, 1998, Man of the Year award, Hellenic Am. C. of C., 2000, Palladium Medal award, Societe de Chimie Industrielle, 2001, Annual Bus. Mgmt. award, Society of Plastic Engineers, 2003. Mem.: Society of Chem. Industry (Chem. Industry Medal award 2003).

STAWICKI, STANISLAW PETER, surgeon, medical researcher; s. Leslaw Jozef Stawicki and Ludmila Stawicka; m. Tram Le Stawicki, July 11, 1998; children: Joseph, Theresa. BA in biology, U. of Louisville, 1994—97, MD, 1997—2001. Clin. rsch. coord. Neurosurgical Group of Greater Louisville, Louisville, 1995—2001; resident physician in gen. surgery St Luke's Hosp., Bethlehem, Pa., 2001—06; fellow in traumatology and surg. critical care U. Pa., 2006—. Contbr. articles to profl. jours. Recipient Sci. Exhibits award for Excellence, Ky. Med. Assn., 1997; U. Louisville Sch. Medicine Dean's Academic scholarship, U. of Louisville, 1997, fellowship, Univ. Pa. Hosp. Trauma and Critical Care Surgery, 2006—. Mem.: ACS. R-Liberal. Avocations: classical music, physics, cosmology. Office: Ohio State U Med Ctr N-717 410 West 10th Ave Columbus OH 43210 Personal E-mail: stawicki_ace@yahoo.com.

STAY, BARBARA, zoologist, educator; b. Cleve., Aug. 31, 1926; d. Theron David and Florence (Finley) S. AB, Vassar Coll., 1947; MA, Radcliffe Coll., 1949, PhD, 1953. Entomologist Army Research Center, Natick, Mass., 1954-60; vis. asst. prof. Pomona Coll., 1960; asst. prof. biology U. Pa., 1961-67; asso. prof. zoology U. Iowa, Iowa City, 1967-77, prof., 1977—, prof. emeritus, 2008. Fulbright fellow to Australia, 1953; Lalor fellow Harvard U., 1960 Fellow AAAS, Entomol. Soc. Am.; mem. Soc. Comparative and Integrative Biology, Am. Inst. Biol. Scis., Am. Soc. Cell Biology, Iowa Acad. Scis., Sigma Xi. Office: Univ Iowa Dept Biology Iowa City IA 52242 Home Phone: 319-351-5036. E-mail: barbara-stay@uiowa.edu.

STAYIN, RANDOLPH JOHN, lawyer; b. Cin., Oct. 30, 1942; s. Jack and Viola (Tomin) S.; children: Gregory S., Todd R., Elizabeth J. BA, Dartmouth Coll., 1964; JD, U. Cin., 1967. Bar: Ohio 1967, U.S. Dist. Ct. (so. dist.) Ohio 1968, U.S. Dist. Ct. D.C. 1977, U.S. Ct. Appeals (6th cir.) 1968, U.S. Ct. Appeals (fed. cir.) 1986, U.S. Supreme Ct. 1974, U.S. Ct. Appeals (D.C. cir.) 1976, U.S. Ct. Internat. Trade, 1985. Assoc. Frost & Jacobs, Cin., 1967-72; exec. asst., dir. of legislation U.S. Sen. Robert Taft, Jr., Washington, 1973-74, chief of staff, 1975-76; assoc. Taft, Stettinius & Hollister, Washington, 1977, ptnr., 1978-88, Barnes & Thornburg, Washington, 1988—. Mem. adv. coun. U.S. and FGN. Comml. Svc., U.S. Dept. Commerce. Chmn., mem. numerous coms., chmn., worker campaigns for local politicians Rep. Party state and local orgns.; mem. Citizens to Save WCET-TV, 1967-72, Fine Arts Fund, 1970-72, Cancer Soc., 1970-72; chmn. agy. rels. com. Hamilton County Mental Health and Mental Retardation Bd., 1969-71, vice chmn., 1971, chmn., 1971-72; v.p. Recreation Commn., City of Cin., 1970-72; mem. funds mgmt. com. Westwood 1st Presbyn. Ch., 1968, v.p., 1969, pres., 1970, trustee, 1970, elder, 1971-72; bd. dirs. Evans Mill Pond Owners Assn., v.p., 1986, pres., 1987; chmn. Washington Nat. Cathedral Fund Com., mem. devel. com.; co-chair 1907 Soc. Mem.: ABA (sect. on internat. law and practice, vice chmn.com.on nat. legislation 1977—79, internat. sect., anti-trust sect.), D. C. Bar Assn. (com. on internat. law), Internat. Bar Assn., Am. Soc. Assn. Execs. (legal sect., internat. sect.). Avocations: theater, tennis, skiing, travel, boating. Office: Barnes & Thornburg 750 17th St NW Ste 900 Washington DC 20006-2225 Office Phone: 202-289-1313. Personal E-mail: rstayin@btlaw.com.

STAYNER, LESLIE THOMAS, epidemiologist; b. Nyack, NY, Mar. 7, 1951; s. George S. Stayner and Eva (Mora) Shiffman; m. Monica M. Stayner, June 8, 1971; 1 child, Tanya. BA, U. Mass., 1977; MSc, Harvard U., 1980; PhD, U. N.C., Chapel Hill, 1989. Epidemiologist Nat. Inst. for Occupl. Safety and Health, Cin., 1981-88, supr. epidemiologist, 1988-89, sr. epidemiologist, 1989-91, asst. dir. for risk assessment, 1991—95, chief risk evaluation br., 1995—2002; dir., epidemiology & biostats. Sch. Pub. Health, U. Ill., Chgo., 2002—. Editl. cons. Am. Jour. Epidemiology; lectr. on occupl. epidemiology in U.S. and internat. univs. Contbr. articles to profl. jours. including Am. Jour. Pub. Health, Am. Jour. Ind. Medicine, Am. Jour Epidemiology, Scandinavian Jour. Work and Environment, Epidemiology, among others. Mem. APHA, Soc. for Epidemiologic Rsch., Soc. for Risk Analysis. Avocations: photography, biking, tennis. Office: Divsn Epidemiology & Biostats HC 923 R 1603 W Taylor St Chicago IL 60612-4394

STAYTON, THOMAS GEORGE, lawyer; b. Rochester, Minn., May 1, 1948; m. Barbara Joan Feck, Aug. 8, 1970; children: Ryan, Megan. BS, Miami U., Oxford, Ohio, 1970; JD, U. Mich., 1973. Bar: Ind. 1973, U.S. Dist. Ct. (so. dist.) Ind. 1973, U.S. Ct. Appeals (7th cir.) 1977. Ptnr. Baker & Daniels, Indpls., 1973—. Sustaining mem. Product Liability Adv. Coun. Recipient Sagamore of the Wabash Gov. of Ind., 1988. Mem. ABA, Ind. State Bar Assn., Indpls. Bar Assn. Office: Baker & Daniels 300 N Meridian St Ste 2700 Indianapolis IN 46204-1782 Home Phone: 317-733-0516; Office Phone: 317-237-1260. E-mail: tstayton@bakerd.com.

STAYTON, WILLIAM RALPH, psychologist, educator; b. Kelso, Wash., Dec. 25, 1933; s. Ralph Willard and Marguerite (Hunter) S.; m. Kathleen Boucher, Sept. 4, 1954; children: Mark, John, Cheryl, Paul. BA, U. Redlands, 1956; MDiv, Andover Newton Theol. Sem., 1960; ThD, Boston U., 1967; PhD, Inst. Advanced Study of Human Sexuality, 2002. Ordained to ministry Am. Bapt. Ch., 1959. Assoc. min. 1st Bapt. Ch. in Newton, Mass., 1956-61; min. 1st Bapt. Ch., Gloucester, Mass., 1961-68; chaplain New Eng. Bapt. Hosp., Boston, 1968-71; asst. prof. U. Pa. Sch. Medicine, Phila., 1971—78; adj. assoc. prof. U. Pa. Grad. Sch. Edn., Phila., lectr., faculty, 1982—2004; asst. prof. Jefferson Med. Coll./Thomas Jefferson U., 1978-83; marriage and family therapist Wm R. Stayton & Assocs., Ltd., P.C., Phila., 1978—. Mem. faculty La Salle U., Phila., 1983-2002; prof. and coord., human sexuality program Widener U., Chester, Pa., 1999-2006, prof./scholar-in-residence, 2006—; exec. dir. Ctr. for Sexuality and Religion, 2006-08; prof. sexuality & religion Morehouse Sch. Medicine, Interdenominational Theol. Ctr., Atlanta, 2008-. Editor spl. issue Topics in Clin. Nursing, 1980; contbr. articles to profl. jours., chpts. to books. Pres. Cmty. Svcs. for Human Growth, Paoli, Pa., 1989-91, bd. dirs., 1981-97. Named Man of Yr., B'nai B'rith, Gloucester, Mass., 1968; recipient Outstanding Svc. award Community Svcs. for Human Growth, 1990, Richard J. Cross award U. Medicine and Dentistry N.J., 1997, Dean's award Sch Human Svc. Professions Widener U., 2002, Tchr. Excellence award Kappa Delta Pi, 2006. Mem. APA, Am. Assn. Marriage and Family Therapists, Am. Assn. Sex Educators, Counselors and Therapists (bd. dirs. 1982-86, 88-90, chmn. dist. VI 1982-86, pres. 1996-98, Outstanding Svc. award 1978-87, Disting. Svc. award 2000, Profl. Standard of Excellence award 2006), Sex Info. and Edn. Coun. U.S. (pres. 1985-87, sec. 1990-92), Soc. for Sci. Study Sex (chmn. ann. meeting 1983), Pa. Assn. Marriage and Family Therapists (continuing edn. com. 1985-90), Planned Parenthood Southeastern Pa. (bd. dirs. 1999—2006, 1st vice chmn. 2001-04, chmn. 2004-06), Phi Kappa Phi. Democrat. Home: 226 Highlands Ridge Pl SE Smyrna GA 30082 Office: Morehouse Sch Medicine 720 Westview Dr SW Ste 233 Atlanta GA 30310-1495 Office Phone: 404-752-1704. Office Fax: 404-756-8958. Business E-Mail: wstayton@msm.edu.

STEAD, JAMES JOSEPH, JR., securities company executive; b. Chgo., Sept. 13, 1930; s. James Joseph and Irene (Jennings) S.; m. Edith Pearson, Feb. 13, 1954; children: James, Diane, Robert, Caroline. BS, DePaul U., 1957, MBA, 1959. Asst. sec. C. F. Childs & Co., Chgo., 1957-62; exec. v.p., sec. Koenig, Keating & Stead, Inc., Chgo., 1962-66; 2d v.p., mgr. midwest mcpl. bond dept. Hayden, Stone Inc., Chgo., 1966-69; sr. v.p., nat. sales mgr. Ill. Co. Inc., 1969-70; mgr. instl. sales dept. Reynolds and Co., Chgo., 1970-72; partner Edwards & Hanly, 1972-74; v.p., instnl. sales mgr. Paine, Webber, Jackson & Curtis, 1974-76; v.p., regional instl. sales mgr. Reynolds Securities, Inc., 1976-78; sr. v.p., regional mgr. Oppenheimer & Co., Inc., 1978-88; sr. v.p., regional mgr. fixed income Tucker Anthony, 1988—; instr. Mcpl. Bond Sch., Chgo., 1967—. With AUS, 1951-53. Mem. Security Traders Assn. Chgo., Nat. Security Traders Assn., Am. Mgmt. Assn., Mcpl. Fin. Forum Washington. Clubs: Execs., Union League, Mcpl. Bond, Bond (Chgo.); Olympia Fields Country (Ill.); Wall Street (N.Y.C.). Home: 1005 Hickory Ridge Ct Frankfort IL 60423-2114 Office: 1 S Wacker Dr Chicago IL 60606-4614 Office Phone: 312-853-2820 ext. 118.

STEADMAN, DAVID ROSSLYN AYTON, corporate financial executive, director; b. Wembley, Eng., June 7, 1937; came to U.S., 1980; s. Eric and Iris Sina (Smith) S.; m. Beryl Ellen Giles, Jan. 5, 1963 (div.); children: Michael, Christopher, Timothy; m. Sharon Ruatto, Apr. 9, 2001 B.Sc. in Engring. with honors, City U., London, 1960. Mng. dir. Cossor Electronics, Harlow, England, 1974-78; chmn. EMI med. Electronics, London, 1978-80; pres. Raytheon Data Systems, Norwood Mass., 1980—84, Raytheon Ventures, Lexington, 1985-87; chmn., CEO GCA Corp., Andover, Mass., 1987-88; pres. Atlantic Mgmt. Assocs., Inc., Bedford, NH, 1988—; chmn. Brookwood Cos., Inc., 1989—2007, Visibility, Inc., 1996-2000, CEO, 1999-2000; chmn. Visaer, Inc., 2000—05, Telequip Corp., 2000—06. Chmn. Tech/Ops-Sevcon, Inc.; bd. dirs. Aavid Thermal Techs., Inc., Sterling Constrn. Co. Inc. Fellow Instn. Elec. Engrs. (U.K.); mem. Inst. Mgmt. (U.K.; companion), Inst. Mech. Engrs. (U.K.). Avocations: music, sailing. Office: Atlantic Mgmt Assocs Inc PO Box 10670 Bedford NH 03110 Personal E-mail: drsteadman@aol.com.

STEADMAN, DAVID WILTON, retired museum director, deacon; b. Honolulu, Oct. 24, 1936; s. Alva Edgar and Martha (Cooke) S.; m. Kathleen Carroll Reilly, Aug. 1, 1964; children: Alexander Carroll, Kate Montague. BA, Harvard U., Cambridge, Mass., 1960, MAT., 1961; MA, U. Calif.-Berkeley, 1966; PhD, Princeton U., NJ, 1974; M Theol. Studies, Ch. Divinity Sch. of Pacific, 2002. Ordained deacon Episcopal Ch., 2004. Lectr. Frick Collection, NYC, 1970-71; asst. dir., acting dir., assoc. dir. Princeton U. Art Mus., 1971-73; dir. galleries Claremont Colls., Calif., 1974-80; art cons. Archtl. Digest, LA, 1974-77; rsch. curator Norton Simon Mus., Pasadena, Calif., 1977-80; dir. Chrysler Mus., Norfolk, Va., 1980-89, Toledo Mus. Art, Ohio, 1989-99; ret., 2000. Author: Graphic Art of Francisco Goya, 1975, Works on Paper 1900-1960, 1977, Abraham van Diepenbeeck, 1982. Trustee Phillips Collection, Washington, Norton Simon Mus., Pasadena. Chester Dale fellow Nat. Gallery Art, Washington, 1969-70 Episcopalian. Personal E-mail: punto31157@aol.com.

STEADMAN, JOHN MONTAGUE, Senior Judge, DC Court of Appeals; b. Honolulu, Aug. 8, 1930; s. Alva Edgar and Martha (Cooke) S.; m. Alison Storer Lunt, Apr. 8, 1961; children: Catharine N., Juliette M., Eric C. Grad., Phillips Acad., Andover, Mass., 1948; BA summa cum laude, Yale U., 1952; LLB magna cum laude, Harvard U., 1955. Bar: D.C. 1955, Calif. 1956, U.S. Supreme Ct. 1964, Hawaii 1977. Assoc. Pillsbury, Madison & Sutro, San Francisco, 1956-63; atty. US Dept. Justice, 1963-64; dep. under sec. for internat. affairs US Army, 1964-65; spl. asst. to sec. & dep. sec. US Dept. Def., 1965-68; gen. counsel USAF, 1968-70; vis. prof. law U. Pa. Law Sch., 1970-72; prof. law Georgetown U. Law Ctr., Washington, 1972-85, assoc. dean, 1979-84; assoc. judge DC Ct. Appeals, 1985—2004, sr. judge, 2004—. Instr. Lincoln Law Sch., San Francisco, 1961-62, San Francisco Law Sch., 1962-63; vis. prof. U. Mich. Sch. Law, 1976, U. Hawaii Sch. Law, 1977; of counsel firm Pillsbury, Madison & Sutro, Washington, 1979-85 Editor: Harvard Law Rev, 1953-55. Sinclair-Kennedy Traveling fellow, 1955-56 Mem. Am. Law Inst., Cosmos Club, Phi Beta Kappa, Delta Sigma Rho, Zeta Psi. Episcopalian. Office: DC Ct Appeals 430 E St NW Washington DC 20001 Office Phone: 202-879-2765. Business E-Mail: jsteadman@dcappeals.gov.*

STEADMAN, STEPHEN GEOFFREY, physicist; b. Rochester, NY, June 28, 1942; s. Luville T. and Elizabeth (Genung) S.; m. Brigitte M. Kreuzer, Aug. 1, 1975; children: Claudia, Mark, William. BS, U. Rochester, 1964; MS, Rutgers U., 1966, PhD, 1969. Asst. Univ. Freiburg, Germany, 1971-72; vis. scientist Univ. Erlangen-Nürnberg, Erlangen, Germany, 1969-71; sr. rsch. assoc. MIT, Cambridge, 1972-74, asst. prof., 1975-79, assoc. prof., 1979-82, sr. rsch. scientist, 1982-98, asst. dir. sci. adminstrn. lab. nuc. sci., 2004—06, assoc. dir., 2006—; guest scientist Max Planck Inst., Heidelberg, Germany, 1974-75, program mgr., 1998—2001; sr. nuc. physics advisor US Dept. Energy, Washington, 2001—04. Program dir. nuc. physics NSF, Arlington, Va., 1994—97; E866 co-spokesman Brookhaven Nat. Lab., Upton, NY, 1992—98. Contbr. articles to profl. jours. Watertown provincial guard, 1998—; mem. Arsenal Reuse Com., Watertown, Mass., 1992—97. Fellow: Am. Phys. Soc.; mem.: AAAS. Episcopalian. Avocations: piano, tropical fish. Office: MIT Lab for Nuclear Sci RM 26-505 Cambridge MA 02139 Home Phone: 617-926-4139; Office Phone: 617-258-8678.

STEAMER, ROBERT JULIUS, political science professor; b. Rochester, NY, Oct. 14, 1920; s. William August and Lotte (Becker) S.; m. Jean Worden, Apr. 12, 1947; children: Gregg Robert, James Worden. BA in Social Sci., Bucknell U., 1947; MA in Polit. Sci., U. Va., 1952; PhD, Cornell U., 1954; postgrad. law, Oxford U., Eng., 1968-69. Asst. prof. Oglethorpe U., 1952-55, U. Mass., 1955-56; assoc. prof. La. State U., 1956-62; prof. polit. sci., chmn. dept. Lake Forest (Ill.) Coll., 1962-72; prof. U. Mass., Boston, 1972-88, dean Coll. II, 1974-76, vice chancellor for acad. affairs, provost, 1976-79. Vis. summer prof. Tulane U., 1958, Cornell U., 1960, UCLA, 1965; staff cons. La. sect. U.S. Commn. Civil Rights, 1961 Author: The Constitution: Cases and Comments, 1959, The Supreme Court in Crisis, 1971, The Supreme Court: Constitutional Revision and the New Strict Constructionism, 1973, Chief Justice: Leadership and the Supreme Court, 1986; sr. co-author: American Constitutional Law: Cases and Commentary, 1991; contbr. articles to profl. jours. Served with USAAF, 1942-46. Recipient Gt. Tchr. award Lake Forest Coll., 1965; Lilly Found. Research award, 1967; Major Research award Project 87, 1981; hon. research fellow U. Exeter, Eng., 1981 Mem. Am. Polit. Sci. Assn., Midwest Polit. Sci. Assn. (v.p. 1970-71), New Eng. Polit. Sci. Assn. (pres. 1979-80) Home: 1 Sinclair Dr Apt 101 Pittsford NY 14534-1735 Office Phone: 585-248-1388.

STEARLEY, ROBERT JAY, retired packaging company executive; b. Brazil, Ind., Sept. 6, 1929; s. Melvin George and Hila Mona (Bolin) S.; m. Helen Louise Dellacca, Nov. 25, 1950; children: Rhonda Jo, Robert Thomas. BS in Mech. Engring., Rose Hulman Inst. Tech., 1957; postgrad., Harvard U., 1979. Gen. mgr. Poly Tech Corp., Mpls., 1961-63; gen. mgr. plastics Gt. Plains Bag Corp., Stamford, Conn., 1963-66, v.p., 1966-71, v.p. ops., 1971-75, pres., 1975-84, dir., 1966-84; v.p. Jefferson Smurfit Corp., Alton, Ill., 1984—. Mem. Paper Shipping Sack Mfg. Assn. (dir. 1980-82), Am. Legion Clubs: Norwood Hills Country (St. Louis). Lodges: Elks. Republican. Methodist. Home: 2 Country Estates Pl Saint Louis MO 63131-3411

STEARNS, CLIFFORD BUNDY, United States Representative from Florida; b. Washington, Apr. 16, 1941; s. Clifford Robert and Emily Elizabeth (Newlin) Stearns; m. Joan Bette Moore, 1973; children: Douglas Moore, Clifford Bundy Jr., Scott Newlin. Grad., US Air Force ROTC; BSEE, George Washington U., 1963; student, UCLA. Mgr. Control Data Sys., Inc., LA, 1967-69; sr. contract adminstr. CBS, Inc., Stamford, Conn., 1969; account exec. Kutola Advt. Agy., Greenwich, Conn., 1970-71, Images 70/Wilson Haight Welch, Inc., Greenwich, 1971-72; pres., motel mgr. Stearns House, Inc., Silver Springs, Fla., 1972—88; mem. US Congress from 6th Fla. dist., 1989—, dep. leader vets. affairs com., mem. energy & commerce com., chair vets.' health subcom., 1997—2000, chmn. commerce, trade & consumer protection subcom., 2001—07. Motel owner, Hatfield, Mass., 1972—77; broker Silver Springs Real Estate, Fla., 1981—88; mem. Tourist Devel. Coun., Asthma Awareness Caucus, Am. Quarter Horse Caucus, Congl. Cystic Fibrosis Caucus, Congl. Chronic Obstructive Pulmonary Disease Caucus, Rep. Policy Com., Nat. Guard & Reserve Components Caucus, Marion County/Ocala Energy Task Force, Congl. Coalition Adoption; co-chair Congl. Horse Caucus; co-founder, co-chair Congl. Chronic Obstructive Pulmonary Disease Caucus, US Air Force Caucus. Pres. Toastmaster Club, LA, 1962; bd. dirs. Boys Club Ocala, 1980—84; trustee, vice chmn. Monroe Regional Hosp., Ocala, Fla., 1984—89. Capt. USAF, 1963—67. Mem.: Marion County Motel Assn. (pres. 1979), Fla. Assn. Realtors, Am. Assn. Realtors, Fla. Hotel/Motel Assn., Am. Hotel/Motel Assn., Marion C. of C. (bd. dirs. 1987—), Kiwanis Club (pres. Ocala club 1984). Republican. Presbyterian. Avocations: basketball, swimming, computers. Office: US House of Reps 2370 Rayburn House Office Bldg Washington DC 20515-0906 also: 115 SE 25th Ave Ocala FL 34471-9179 Office Phone: 352-351-8777.*

STEARNS, FRANK WARREN, lawyer; b. Washington, July 20, 1949; s. Robert Maynard and Ermyntrude (Vaiden) S.; m. Judith Anne Ketcheson, Sept. 7, 1974; children: Frank W. Jr., Brian S., Joe G. BA, Washington & Lee, 1971; JD with honors, George Washington U., 1974. Bar: Washington DC 1975, Va. 1980, Supreme Ct. Va., U.S. Dist. Ct. (DC 1975, ea. dist. Va.), U.S. Ct. Appeals (DC cir. 1975, 4th cir. 1985), U.S. Supreme Ct. Law clk. Superior Ct. D.C., Washington, 1974-75; asst. corp. counsel Office of the Corp. Counsel, Washington, 1975-79; asst. county atty. County Atty's Office, Fairfax County, Va., 1979-80; mng. ptnr. Wilkes Artis P.C., Fairfax, Va., 1984-2001; ptnr., Real Estate, State & Local Govt., Communications practices Venable LLP, Vienna, Va., 2001—. Bd. dirs. No. Va. Bldg. Industry Assn., 1987-94; trustee Greater Washington Bd. Trade-P.A.C., 1987-2003; chmn. tech. adv. com. NVBIA, Loudoun, Va., 1986-90, mem. Econ. Devel. Commn. Arlington County, Va. Coun. Excellence in Govt., Washington, 1989—98; Commr. Arlington County Econ. Devel. Commn., Arlington, Va., 1987—91. Mem. ABA, Va. State Bar Assn., Va. Trial Lawyers Assn., DC Bar Assn., Fairfax County Bar Assn., Barristers, Counsellors, Fairfax C. of C. (PAC trustee 2003—). Avocations: tennis, golf. Office: Venable LLP Ste 300 8010 Towers Crescent Dr Vienna VA 22182 Office Phone: 703-760-1956. Office Fax: 703-821-8949. Business E-Mail: fwstearns@venable.com.

STEARNS, MARILYN TARPY, music educator; b. Peoria, Ill., Aug. 3, 1936; d. Roger Maynard Tarpy and Nellie Mae Livingston; m. Gordon Woodburn Stearns, June 13, 1958; children: Gordon Schuyler, Jennifer Maye, William Livingston. Student, Ohio Wesleyan U., 1954—56; BA, Mt. Holyoke Coll., 1958; MA, Goddard Coll., 1988. Instr. piano, vocal pvt. practice, 1959—; substitute tchr. Portslade Schs. C.C., England, 1973—75; owner Grain Weaving, Inc., Springfield, Vt., 1976—85; tchr. Head Start, 1977—78; instr. spl. edn., 1980—81; mission/stewardship cons. Vt. Conf. of United Ch. of Christ, 1982—90; soprano soloist, 1954—; adminstrv. asst. Epilepsy Found. Greater Chgo., 1991; tchr., adminstr., devel. officer Stechman Studio Music, Chgo., 1991—95, Oak Park, 1991—95; tutor voice, piano, music literacy pvt. practice, Chgo., 1995—98, Oak Park, 1995—98. Performed numerous recitals; soloist, oratorio works with choirs throughout New Eng. & Va.; soloist Vt. Symphony Orch.; mem. Sounds of Joy Choristers, Burlington Oriana Singers, Vt. Chamber Singers, Arts Acad. Chorale of Shenandoah U. Author: Sunday's Child, 1978, (workbook) The Art of Grain Weaving, 1978, A Handbook on Our Churches, 1990; editor: Don't Throw it Away, Through A Glass Darkly, Children's Sermons for Young Stewards, Reflections on Tithing, Simply Christmas - Good Stewardship, Stewards of History, Stewardship Lenten Devotions, A Church Treasurer's Handbook; author: (poetry) Internat. Lib. Poetry, 2007, 2009, Noble House, 2009. Trustee Vt. Hist. Soc., Montpelier, 1983—90; bd. dirs. Epilepsy Found. Vt., Rutland, 1979—83; vol. Archeol. dig, Ill., 2001; vol. tchr. Global Vol., Poland, 2007; pres. Vt. Conf. United Ch. Christ, 1985; corp. mem. Bd. Homeland Ministries, United Ch. Christ; mem. nominating com. United Ch. Christ, 1985—89. Recipient Recognized Outstanding

Svc., Free Med. Clinic, 2006, Accomplishment cert., Internat. Lib. Poetry. Independent. Avocations: archaeology, poetry, travel, art, reading, music. Home Phone: 540-665-2823. Personal E-mail: gmstearns@aol.com.

STEARNS, NEELE EDWARD, JR., investment company executive; b. Chgo., Apr. 2, 1936; s. Neele Edward Sr. and Grace (Kessler) S.; m. Bonnie Ann Evans; children: Katherine Stearns Sprenger, Kendra Stearns Drozd. BA magna cum laude, Carleton Coll., 1958; MBA with distinction, Harvard U., 1960. Audit staff Arthur Andersen Co., 1962-66, audit mgr., 1966-67; asst. gen. mgr. internat. divsn. Imperial-Eastman Corp., 1967-68; asst. treas. Allied Products Corp., 1968-69, treas., 1969-72; v.p. Henry Crown (Ill.) and Co., 1972-75, v.p., controller, 1975-79; exec. v.p., COO Henry Crown and Co., 1979—86; pres., CEO, CC Industries, Inc., Chgo., 1986-95; chmn. exec. com. Barnes Internat., Inc., Northbrook, Ill., 1996-99; chmn. Wallace Computer Svcs., Inc., 2000, Fin. Investments Corp., Chgo., 2001—. Bd. dir. Merge Healthcare, Inc., Navicure, Inc., Schwarz Supply Source Inc. Life trustee Evanston Northwestern Healthcare; bd. dir. Presbyn. Homes. Mem. Comml. Club Chgo., Econ. Club Chgo., Country Club Fla., Chgo. Club, Old Elm Club, Skokie Country Club, Phi Beta Kappa. Office: Fin Investments Corp 50 East Washington St Ste 400 Chicago IL 60602 Office Phone: 312-494-4513. Business E-Mail: nstearns@fic-cep.com.

STEARNS, ROBERT LELAND, curator; b. LA, Aug. 28, 1947; s. Edward Van Buren and Harriett Ann (Hauck) S.; m. Sheri Roseanne Lucas, Oct. 2, 1982 (div. 1994); children: Marissa Hauck, Caroline Lucas. Student, U. Calif., San Diego, 1965-68, BFA, 1970; student, Calif. Poly. State U., San Luis Obispo, 1968. Asst. dir. Paula Cooper Gallery, NYC, 1970-72; prodn. asst. Avalanche Mag., NYC, 1972; dir. Kitchen Ctr. for Video/Music, NYC, 1972-77, Contemporary Arts Ctr., Cin., 1977-82; dir. performing arts Walker Art Ctr., Mpls., 1982-88; dir. Wexner Ctr. for Arts, Columbus, Ohio, 1988-92; mem. Wexner Ctr. Found., Columbus, 1990-92; dir. Stearns & Assocs./Contemporary Exhbn. Svcs., Columbus, Ohio, 1992—2000; sr. prgm. dir. Arts Midwest, Mpls., 1998—2005; cons. curator Franklin Park Conservatory, Columbus, Ohio, 2005—09, Bellevue Arts Mus., Wash., 2008—09; project mgr. Pelm Springs Art Mus., 2009—. Adj. prof. dept. art, assoc. dean Coll. Art, Ohio State U., Columbus, 1988-92; lectr. Sch. of the Art Inst. Chgo., 2002; cons. McKnight Found., St. Paul, 1978, Jerome Found., 1978-79; chmn. Artists TV Workshop, N.Y.C., 1976-77; bd. dirs., chmn. Minn. Dance Alliance, Mpls., 1983-88; bd. dirs. Haleakala, Inc., N.Y.C.; mem. various panels Nat. Endowment for Arts, Washington, 1977-91; mem. pub. arts policy Greater Columbus Arts Coun., 1988-90; adv. coun. Bklyn. Acad. Music, 1982-84, Houston Grand Opera, 1991-93; fundraising cons. Art for Life Columbus AIDS Task Force, 2000-2006; mem. Advocacy Com. Ballet Met, Columbus, 2003-2006; mem. db. dirs. Architecture and Design Coun. Palm Springs Atr Mus., 2008-, Laquinta Arts Found., 2008-, Coachella Valley Art Alliance, 2008-; chair leadership coun., ArtsOasis, 2008-. Author, editor: Robert Wilson: Theater of Images, 1980, Photography and Beyond in Japan, 1995; author: Mexico Now: Point of Departure, 1997, Robert Wilson: Scenografie e Installazioni, 1997, Illusions of Eden: Visions of the American Heartland, 2000, Aspirations: Toward a Future in the Middle East, 2001, The View from Here: Recent Pictures from Central Europe and the American Midwest, 2002, Russel Wright: Living with Good Design, 2006, Bending Nature, 2008; editor: Dimensions of Black, 1970; exec. editor: Breakthroughs: Avant Garde Art in Europe and America 1950-1990, 1991; author and editor numerous catalogues. Mem. gov.'s residence com. State of Ohio, 2004—06. Decorated chevalier Order of Arts and Letters (France); Travel grantee Jerome Found., 1986, Japan Found., 1991, Can. Cultural Ministry, 2004. Office: 2218 N Sunshine cir Palm Springs CA 92264 E-mail: arts2020@aol.com.

STEARNS, STEWART WARREN, charitable association executive; b. Denver, Apr. 8, 1947; s. Vinton H. and Marjorie L. (Tedro) S.; m. Marjorie L. Fuller, Jan. 25, 1969; children: Theresa Lyn, Gregory Robert. BS, Ea. N.Mex. U., 1970; MA, No. Ill. U., 1973; postgrad., SUNY, Albany, 1974—. Mng. editor Studies in Linguistics, DeKalb, Ill., 1972-73; instr. No. Ill. U., DeKalb, 1972-73; cons. AID, Guatemala, 1973-74; instr. Skidmore Coll., Saratoga Springs, N.Y., 1975; OAS fellow Guatemala, 1976-77; asst. dir. Chaves County Cmty. Action Program, Roswell, N.Mex., 1977-78; exec. dir. United Way Chaves County, Roswell, 1978-83, Levi Strauss Found., Dallas, 1983-85, Cmty. Trust Met. Tarrant County, Ft. Worth, 1985-88; pres., CEO, Cmty. Found., Sarasota County, 1989—. NDEA fellow, Dallas, 1970-71. Office Phone: 941-955-3000. Business E-Mail: stewart@cfsarasota.org.

STEARNS, SUSAN TRACEY, lighting design company executive, lawyer; b. Seattle, Oct. 28, 1957; d. Arthur Thomas and Roberta Jane (Arrowood) S.; m. Ross Alan De Alessi, Aug. 11, 1990; 1 child, Chase Arthur. AA, Stephens Coll., 1977, BA, 1979; JD, U. Wash., Seattle, 1990. Bar: Calif. 1990, U.S. Ct. Appeals (9th cir.) 1990, U.S. Dist. Ct. (no. dist.) Calif 1990, U.S. Dist. Ct. (we. dist.) Wash. 1991, Wash. 1991. TV news prodr. KOMO, Seattle, 1980-86; atty. Brobeck, Phleger & Harrison, San Francisco, 1990-92; pres. Ross De Alessi Lighting Design, Seattle, 1993—. Author periodicals in field. Alumnae Assn. Coun. Stephens Coll., Columbia, Mo., 1995—. Named Nat. Order of Barristers, U. Washington, Seattle, 1990. Mem. ABA (mem. state labor and employment law subcom.), Wash. State Bar Assn. (mem. bench-bar-press com.), State Bar Calif., King County Bar Assn., Bar Assn.San Francisco, Wash. Athletic Club. Avocations: travel, dance. Office: Ross De Alessi Lighting Des 2330 Magnolia Blvd W Seattle WA 98199-3813

STEBBINS, BARRY STEVEN, educational technologist; b. Dayton, Feb. 10, 1949; s. Joy Edward and Dorothy Irene Stebbins; m. Cynthia Kaye Shoutd, Dec. 22, 1973; children: Christopher, Jenna. BS in Edn., Ohio State U., Columbus, 1971, ME in Edn., 1976. Cert. tchr. Ohio. Sci. tchr. Roosevelt Jr. HS, Columbus, 1971—77; vocat. coord. Wedgewood Jr. HS, Columbus, 1978—79, West HS, Columbus, 1979—86, sci. tchr., 1986—97; edn. technologist Columbus Pub. Schs., 1997—. Lead sci. tchr. Apple Classrooms of Tomorrow Columbus Pub. Schs., 1986—97, virtual hs lead tchr., 2004—06; mem. adv. bd. Tech. Corps Ohio, Columbus, 1999—2005; master examiner US Judo Assn., Colorado Springs, 2000—; sys. adminstrn. Blackboard; webmaster Columbus Learning Interchange Cmty. Author: (book) Microsoft Press-Multimedia, 1988; contbr. articles to mags. Recipient Lazarus Writing award, Columbus Pub. Schs., 1989; named Tchr. of Yr., Sigma Xi. Mem.: Midori Judo Club (head instr. 2004—), Phi Kappa Phi. Home: 3728 Cypress Creek Dr Columbus OH 43228 Office: Columbus Pub Schs 737 E Hudson St Columbus OH 43211 Personal E-mail: colbarry@aol.com.

STEBBINS, DONALD J., car parts manufacturing company executive; BS in Fin., Miami U., Ohio; MBA, U. Mich. With Citibank, Bankers Trust Co.; v.p., treas., asst. sec. Lear Corp., Southfield, Mich., 1992, sr. v.p., CFO, treas., 1997, pres., COO Americas, pres., COO Europe, Asia and Africa; pres., COO Visteon Corp., Belleville, Mich., 2005—08, pres., CEO, 2008, chmn., pres., CEO, 2008—. Office: Visteon Corp One Village Center Dr Belleville MI 48111*

STEBBINS, GREGORY KELLOGG, foundation executive; b. Lafayette, Ind., Jan. 10, 1951; s. Albert Kellogg and Nancy Ruth (Osborn) S. BS in Data Processing, Calif. Poly., Pomona, 1974; MBA, U. So. Calif., 1976; EdD, Pepperdine U., 1985. Pres. Insight U., 2008—, bd. dirs. pres., 2008. Mem.: APA, Sigma Xi. Avocations: flying, scuba diving, photography. Office: PeopleSavvy 944 Princeton Dr Marina Del Rey CA 90292

STEBBINS, PAUL H., energy executive; b. 1965; 3 children. BA Govt., Georgetown Univ., 1979. Bunker broker Gary Bunkering Services, Inc.; with Trans-Tec Services, 1985, World Fuel Services Corp., 1995—, sr. vice-pres, 1995—97, exec. vice-pres., 1997—2000, pres. and COO, 2000—02, chmn. and CEO, 2002—. Planning coord. Internat. Energy Corp. Office: World Fuel Services Ste 400 9800 NW 41st St Miami FL 33178

STEBBINS, ROBERT ALAN, sociology educator; b. Rhinelander, Wis., June 22, 1938; s. William Nelson and Dorothy May (Guy) S.; m. Karin Yvonne Olson, Jan. 11, 1964; children: Paul, Lisa, Christi. BA, Macalester Coll., 1961; MA, U. Minn., 1962, PhD, 1964. Assoc. prof. Presbyterian Coll., Clinton, SC, 1964-65; assoc. prof.to prof. Meml. U. Nfld., St. John's, Canada, 1965-73; prof. U. Tex.-Arlington, 1973-76; prof. sociology U. Calgary, Alta., Canada, 1976-99, faculty prof. social scis. Alta., 2000—, dept. head Alta., 1976-82; head dept. sociology and anthropology Meml. U. Nfld., 1968-71. Author: Commitment to Deviance, 1971, The Disorderly Classroom: Its Physical and Temporal Conditions, 1974, Teachers and Meaning, 1975, Amateurs, 1979, The Magician, 1984, Sociology: The Study of Society, 2d edit., 1990, Canadian Football: The View from the Helmet, 1987, Deviance: Tolerable Differences, 1988, The Laugh-Makers: Stand-Up Comedy as Art, Business, and Life-Style, 1990, Amateurs, Professionals and Serious Leisure, 1992; co-editor: Fieldwork Experience, 1980, The Sociology of Deviance, 1982, Experiencing Fieldwork, 1991, Career, Culture, and Social Psychology in a Variety Art, 1993, Predicaments: Moral Difficulty in Everyday Life, 1993, The Franco-Calgarians: French Language, Leisure and Linguistic Lifestyle in an Anglophone City, 1994, The Connoisseur's New Orleans, 1995, The Barbershop Singer: Inside the Social World of a Musical Hobby, 1996, Tolerable Differences: Living with Deviance, 2d edit., 1996; After Work: The Search for an Optimal Leisure Lifestyle, 1998, The Urban Francophone Volunteer: Searching for Personal Meaning and Community Growth in a Linguistic Minority, 1998, The French Enigma: Survival and Development of Canada's Francophone Societies, 2000, Exploratory Research in the Social Sciences, 2001, New Directions in the Theory and Research of Serions Leisure, 2001, The Organizational Basis of Leisure Participation: A Motivational Exploration, 2002, Francophonie et langue dans un monde diverse en évolution: contacts interlinguistiques socioculturels, 2003, Volunteering as Leisure/Leisure as Volunteering: An International Assessment, 2004, Between Work and Leisure: A Study of the Common Ground of Two Separate Worlds, 2004, Challenging Mountain Nature: Risk, Motive, and Lifestyle in Three Hobbyist Sports, 2005, Serious Leisure: A Perspective for our Own Time, 2007, A Dictionary of Nonprofit Terms and Concepts, 2006, The Pivotal Role of Leisure Education: Finding Personal Fulfillment in This Century, 2007, Personal Decisions in the Public Square: Beyond Problem Solving into a Positive Sociology, 2009, Leisureand Consumption Common Ground, Seperate Worlds, 2009. Pres. St. John's Orch., 1967-68; mem. Dallas Civic Symphony, 1973-76, Orch. Soc. of Calgary, 1978-97. Can. Coun. Sabbatical Leave fellow, 1972-72, Calgary Inst. for Humanities fellow, 1987-88, Killam resident fellow, 1990; NEH summer stipend, 1976; Acad. Leisure Scis. fellow, 1996—, Royal Soc. Can. fellow, 1999—. Mem. Leisure Studies Assn., Can. Sociology and Anthropology Assn. (pres. 1988-89), Internat. Sociol. Assn., Assn. for Can. Studies, World Leisure and Recreation Assn. (bd. dirs. 1997-2002), Social Sci. Fedn. Can. (pres. 1991-92), Can. Assn. for Leisure Studies (v.p. 1993-96). Home: 144 Edgemont Estates Dr NW Calgary AB Canada T3A 2M3 Office: U Calgary Dept Sociology 2500 University Dr NW Calgary AB Canada T2N 1N4 Office Phone: 403-220-5827. E-mail: stebbins@ucalgary.ca.

STEBEL, MICHAEL DAVID, marketing professional, consultant; b. NYC, June 8, 1953; s. Bernard and Arlene Stebel; m. Beth Roberts, Mar. 5, 2006; children: Jacob Alan, Meryl Ann. BA, Hofstra U., Hempstead, NY, 1976. Dir. mktg. AT&T Global Info. Solutions, Hauppauge, NY, 1992—94; exec. v.p. corp. strategy Boundless Technologies, Hauppauge, 1994—99; pres. Boca Rsch., Boca Raton, Fla., 1999—2001; chief mktg. officer Ener1, Inc., Boca Raton, 2001—03; CEO TVR Comm., Woodside, NY, 2003—06; pres. Nexentra Tech. Mktg., LLC, Delray Beach, Fla., 2006—. Cons. in field. Named to Pres.'s Club, AT&T Global Info. Solutions, 1994. Mem.: Nat. Assn. Photoshop Profls., Am. Mktg. Assn. Office Fax: 954-697-0306. Business E-Mail: mike@nexentra.com.

STEBENNE, DAVID LAWLER, historian, educator; b. Providence, July 4, 1960; s. William Joseph Stebenne and Regina Marie Perkins. BA, Yale U., 1982; JD, MA, Columbia U., 1986, PhD, 1991. Lectr. history dept. Yale U., New Haven, 1991-93; asst. prof. Ohio State U., Columbus, 1993-97, assoc. prof., 1997—. Mem. at large ROTC program subcom., U.S. Dept. Army, Washington, 1997-2001. Author: Arthur J. Goldberg: New Deal Liberal, 1996, Modern Republican: Arthur Larson and the Eisebhe over Years, 2006; Co-Author(with Joseph Mitchell) New City Upon A Hill: A History of Columbia, 2007 Whiting Found. fellow, 1989-90. Mem. Md. Bar Assn., Yale U. Club of Ctrl. Ohio. Office: Ohio State U Dept History 106 Dulles Hall 230 W 17th Ave Columbus OH 43210-1361

STEBICH, STEPHANIE A., museum director; b. Germany; BA in Art History, Columbia U.; MA, NYU. Cert. in non-profit mgmt. Case Western Res. U. Intern Guggenheim Mus.; asst. Am. Fedn. of Arts, Assn. Art Mus. Dirs.; exec. asst. to dir. Bklyn. Mus.; asst. dir. Cleve. Mus. Art, 1995—2001, Mpls. Inst. Arts, 2001—05; exec. dir. Tacoma Art Mus., 2005—. Avocation: golf. Office: Tacoma Art Mus 1701 Pacific Ave Tacoma WA 98402 Office Phone: 253-272-4258. Office Fax: 253-627-1898.

STEC, JOHN ZYGMUNT, retired real estate company officer; b. Stalowawola, Poland, Jan. 21, 1925; Came to U.S.A. 1947. s. Valenty and Maria (Madej) S. m. Wanda G. Baca, Oct. 13, 1956; children: David, Maria, Monica. Student, Poland, 1941-44, Kent State U., Ohio, 1965-66, student, 1966-67. Cert. Master of Corporate Real Estate. With The Singer Co., Cleve., 1952-54, dis. mgr., 1954-60, sales supr., 1960-67, dir. real estate Detroit and Chgo., 1967-73; v.p. Fabri Center of Am., Beachwood, Ohio, 1973—; sr. v.p. real estate Fabri-Centers of Am., Inc., Beachwood, Ohio, 1987—2005, spl. counsel to pres., 2005—; ret., 2005. Cons. in field. With U.S. Army, 1950-52. Mem. Nat. Assoc. of Corporate Real Estate (speaker, organizer 1974-77, audit Com. 1977-79, bd. dirs. 1970-82, Outstanding Achievement award 1982). Chagrin Valley Club. Repulican. Roman Catholic. Avocations: swimming, hiking, reading. Home: 725 Sagewood Dr Chagrin Falls OH 44023-6733 Office: Coventry Investment Real Estate Advisors 8401 Chagrin Rd Ste 1 Chagrin Falls OH 44023 Office Phone: 440-708-0439. Business E-Mail: jstec@coventryadvisors.com. *Personal philosophy: Think success and you'll be successful. Perseverence of any goal leads to achievement. Learning is knowledge. Knowledge is the most powerful key that leads to greatness and opens any door.*

STECCATO, CARL L., lawyer; b. Bronx, NY, Mar. 18, 1954; BA, York Coll., CUNY; JD, NY Law Sch., 1985. Bar: NY 1987, NJ 1987, US Dist. Ct. So., Ea., No. & We. Districts NY, US Supreme Ct. Ptnr. Wilson, Elser, Moskowitz, Edelman & Dicker LLP, White Plains, NYC. Contbr. articles to profl. jours. Mem.: Am. Corporate Counsel Assn., Am. Boat Yacht Coun., NY State Bar Assn. Tort Sect., Propane Gas Def. Assn., Nat. Fire Protection Assn., US Supreme Ct. Office: Wilson Elser Moskowitz Edelman & Dicker LLP 3 Gannett Dr White Plains NY 10604 Office Phone: 914-323-7000 ext. 4269. Office Fax: 914-323-7001. Business E-Mail: steccatoc@wemed.com.

STECHER, ESTA E., lawyer, investment company executive; b. Mpls., Apr. 3, 1957; BA summa cum laude, U. Minn., 1979; JD, Columbia U., 1982. Bar: N.Y. 1983. Ptnr. Sullivan & Cromwell, 1982—94; gen. counsel, mng. dir. Tax dept. Goldman, Sachs & Co., NYC, 1994—2000, gen. counsel, co-head legal dept., 2000—. Trustee Columbia Univ. Mem.: ABA, Assn. Bar City of New York, N.Y. Bar Assn. Office: Goldman Sachs and Co Legal Dept 1 New York Plz 37th Fl New York NY 10004 Office Phone: 212-902-3490. Office Fax: 212-902-3876.*

STECHER, JOE W., prosecutor; b. Fremont, Nebr., 1952; BA, Wayne State Coll., 1974; JD, U. Nebr. Coll. Law, 1984. County atty. Dodge County, Nebr., 1999—2002; asst. US atty. Dist. Nebr. US Dept. Justice, 2002—06, acting US atty., 2006—07, US atty. Dist. Nebr., 2007—. Dir. Neb. County Attorney's Assn., 1996—2002. Recipient Dir. award, US Atty's Office Nebr., 2005. Office: US Atty First Nat Bank Bldg 1620 Dodge St Ste 1400 Omaha NE 68102 Office Fax: 402-661-3082, 402-661-3700.

STECHER, KENNETH W., financial corporation executive; With Inter-Ocean Life Ins. Co. (acquired by Cin. Fin. Corp.); joined Cincinnati Fin. Corp., Fairfield, Ohio, 1973—, sr. v.p., treas., co. sec., 1997—2008, CFO, 2001—08, CEO, 2008—. Office: 6200 S Gilmore Rd Fairfield OH 45014-5141

STECHER, PAULINE, painter, educator; b. Bklyn. d. Helen Solomon; m. Bernard Stecher, Aug. 20, 1950; children: Martin Alan, David Joseph. Attended, pvt. studio instrn. with Paul Puzinas, NYC, 1961—63. Oil painting instr., Bellerose, Bellerose Village, Little Neck, New Hyde Park, NY, 1965—85. Judge, lecture demonstrator American Pen Women, Floral Park Art League, Flushing Art League, Ind. Art Soc., Island Art Guild, Rockville Ctr. Art Club, Tri-County Artists, Queens Alliance Artists, Suburban Art League, 1978—. Exhibitions include Newington-Cropsey Found. Gallery Art, Hastings-on-Hudson, NY, Westchester County Ctr., NY, Salmagundi Club, NYC, Nat. Arts Club, Nassau County Mus. Art, Roslyn, NY, various galleries, Long Island's East End, Boca Raton and Naples, Fla.; painting reproduced in Literary Cyclist by Prof. James E. Starrs, 1997; contbr. articles and paintings to Grumbacher's Palette Talk magazine, 1983, as featured tchr., 1987, in cover, 1990. Fellow: Hudson Valley Art Assn. (Isabel Steinschneider Meml. award 1991, First prize Dumond Meml. award Best Light and Atmospheric Effect 1998, Spradling Meml. award 2000, Georgie Read Barton Meml. award 2002, First place Still-life Jane Peterson Meml. award 2004); mem.: Nat. Art League (Gold medal 1973), Art. League Nassau County (Coun. Am. Artists Soc. Painting award 1993), Am. Artists Profl. League (bd. dirs. 1985—2002, Dirs. award 1991, John R. Grabach Meml. award 1994, Helen De Cozen award 1997, Pres.'s award 1998, 2001, Raymond Chow Meml. award 2006, Alden Bryan Meml. award 2007, William P. Lawrence Meml. award 2008). Avocation: painting. Home: 80-30 250th St Bellerose NY 11426 Personal E-mail: pauline.stecher@worldnet.att.net.

STECKE, KATHRYN ELIZABETH, operations management educator; b. Neponset, Mass., June 28, 1950; d. Joseph P. and Elizabeth C. (Konig) S. BS in Math., Boston State U., 1972; MS in Applied Math., Purdue U., 1974, MS in Indsl. Engring., 1977, PhD in Indsl. Engring., 1981. Teaching asst. dept. math. Purdue U., West Lafayette, Ind., 1972-75, rsch. asst. Sch. Indsl. Engring., 1975-79, instr. Sch. Indsl. Engring., 1980, asst. prof. Sch. Indsl. Engring., 1981; asst. prof. policy and control Grad. Sch. Bus. Adminstrn. U. Mich., Ann Arbor, 1981-85, assoc. prof. ops. mgmt. Grad. Sch. Bus. Adminstrn., 1985-95, Jack D. Sparks/Whirlpool Corp. Rsch. Prof. Bus. Adminstrn., 1995—. Rsch. assoc. Ctr. Études et Recherches de Toulouse, Dept. Études et Recherches en Automatique, France, 1984, COMAU, Automation div., Turin, Italy, 1987-88, Fraunhofer Inst., Stuttgart, Germany, 1990; vis. prof. transp. rsch. dept. GM Rsch. Labs., 1985—; speaker, presenter in field. Editor-in-chief: Internat. Jour. Flexible Mfg. Sys., 1986—; assoc. editor mfg. issues Large Scale Sys., 1985-87, INFORS, 1988—, automated mfg. sys. issues Annals of Ops. Rsch., 1990; editor: (with Rajan Suri) Annals of Ops. Rsch. Vol. 3, 1985, Vol. 15, 1988; spl. deptl. editor: Mgmt. Sci. Vol. 34, 1988; area editor: Jour. Prodn. and Ops. Mgmt., 1989—; series editor: CIMware Ltd., 1990—; mem. several editl. and editl. rev. bds.; contbr. articles, papers to profl. jours. Rsch. grantee Ford Motor Co., 1982, 83, 84, NSF initiation grantee, 1984-87, NSF grantee, 1992-96; Alexander von Humboldt fellow, 1989-90. Mem. ASME, Prodn. and Ops. Mgmt. Soc. (program coms. 1991, 92, 93), Soc. Mfg. Engrs. (speaker Machining Sys. Clinic 1989), Am. Inst. for Decision Scis. (session chair 1988-94), Inst. Indsl. Engrs., Math. Programming Soc., Ops. Rsch. Soc. Am. (nominating com. 1989, sec.-treas. computer sci. tech. sect. 1983-84), Inst. Mgmt. Scis. (program chair 1989, 95, session chair and spkr. 1984, 86, 89, 91, 93, 94, 96, 97, cluster chair 1989, 91—). Office: U Mich Grad Sch Bus Adminstrn Ann Arbor MI 48109-1234

STECKEL, JULIE RASKIN, psychotherapist, lecturer, consultant; b. LA, Jan. 3, 1940; d. Edward M. and Selma (Romm-Rosby) Raskin; m. Richard Jay Steckel, June 16, 1960; children: Jan Marie, David Matthew. BA, UCLA, 1960, MSW, 1975; MA in Teaching., Harvard U., 1961. Lic. clin. social worker; Bd. Cert. Diplomate in Clin. Social Work, in archeology UCLA. Music tchr., Los Angeles, Beverly Hills and Santa Monica, Calif., 1968-70; psychol. cons. BMA Dialysis Units, Torrance, Calif., 1976—2008; pvt. practice Santa Monica, Calif., 1976—2008, Santa Barbara, Calif., 1975—. Affiliate staff Del Amo Hosp., Torrance, 1983-90; lectr., cons. UCLA Dental Sch., 1984—; lectr. social welfare UCLA Grad. Sch., 1985-90. Mem. editl. bd. Comtemporary Dialysis and Nephrology Jour.; contbr. articles to jours. Bd. dirs. Palisades Dem. Hdqrs., Pacific Palisades, Calif., 1972; credentials currier Dem. Conv., Miami, Fla., 1972; mem. LA Women's Commn. Task Force on Child Abuse, 1990—. Fellow Soc. Clin. Social Workers, Nat. Acad. Traumatic Stress; mem. Nat. Assn. Social Workers, Acad. Psychosomatic Medicine. Home and Office: 1126 Bel Air Dr Santa Barbara CA 93105-4642 Office Phone: 805-898-1044. Personal E-mail: listenr2@cox.net.

STECKER, MICHAEL S., interventional radiologist; s. Enid M. and Arthur Stecker; m. Jennifer A. Deaton, June 14, 1992; children: Maxwell S., Morrissa S. BS, Wright State U., Dayton, Ohio, 1988; MD, SUNY, Stony Brook, 1992. Diplomate in diagnostic radiology bd. Cert. Am. Bd. Radiology, 1988, in vascular and interventional radiology CAQ 2002, diplomate in med. Nat. Bd. Med. Examiners, 1993. Surgery resident Mary Imogene Bassett Hosp., Cooperstown, NY, 1992—94; radiology resident Nassau County Med. Ctr., East Meadow, NY, 1994—98, radiology chief resident, 1997—98; vascular and interventional radiology fellow U. Iowa Hosps. and Clinics, Iowa City, 1998—99; attending physician Ind. U. Radiology Assocs., Indpls., 1999—2005; asst. prof. Ind. U. Sch. Medicine, Indpls., 1999—2005; attending physician Brigham and Women's Hosp., Boston, 2005—, interventional radiology inventory mgr., 2007—; asst. prof. Harvard Med. Sch., Boston, 2005—. Interventional radiology site dir. Veteran's Adminstrn. Med. Ctr., Indpls., 1999—2005; assoc. editor CME, Jour. Vascular & Internat. Radiology, 2009—. Recipient Eagle Scout, Boy Scouts Am., 1982, Disting. Reviewer, Jour. Vascular and Interventional Radiology, 1999, 2000, 2006. Mem.: AMA (Physician's Recognition awards 1995—), New England Soc. Interventional Radiology (pres. 2006—07, sec. 2006—08, treas. 2006—), Am. Heart Assn., Soc. Interventional Radiology, Am. Roentgen Ray Soc., Radiol. Soc. N.Am., Am. Coll. Radiology, Tau Beta Pi, Beta Theta Pi. Office: Brigham and Women's Hosp 75 Francis St Boston MA 02115

STECKLER, CHARLES N., theater educator; b. NYC, May 4, 1945; s. Mildred and Samuel Steckler; m. Janet (Ginger) Ertz; 1 child, Matthew P. BA, Queens Coll., CUNY, 1968; MFA, Yale U., Sch. Drama, New Haven, Conn., 1971. Prof. theatre, resident designer Union Coll. Dept. Theater and Dance, Schenectady, NY, 1071—. Exhibitions include Bricoleur Bricolage, exhibitions include retrospective Charles Steckler-:Stage Design. Office: Union Coll Dept Theater and Dance 807 Union St Schenectady NY 12308 Business E-Mail: stecklec@union.edu.

STECKLER, LARRY, publishing executive, writer; b. Bklyn., Nov. 3, 1933; s. Morris and Ida (Beekman) S.; m. Catherine Coccozza, June 6, 1959 (div. June 1999); children: Gail Denise, Glenn Eric, Kerri Lynn, Adria Lauren; m. Lorraine Mary Rubsamen, Oct. 16, 1999. Student, CCNY, 1951; degree in Grad. Realtor's Inst., Parkstate Inst., 2007. Lic. realtor Ariz., 2005, cert. E-Pro Nat. Assn. Realtors. Assoc. editor Radio-Electronics mag., NYC, 1957-62, editor, 1967-85; pub., editor-in-chief Radio Electronics mag., NYC, 1985-92; electronics editor Popular Mechanics mag., NYC, 1962-65; assoc. editor Electronic Products mag., Garden City, NY, 1965-67, Electro-Tech., 1967; editl. dir. Merchandising 2-Way Radio mag., NYC, 1975-77; v.p., dir. Gernsback Publs., NYC, 1975-84, pres., dir., 1984—2003; pub., editl. dir. Spl. Projects mag., 1980-84, Radio-Electronics Ann., 1982-84; pub., editor-in-chief Hands-On Electronics, 1984-88, Computer Digest, 1985-90, Experimenters Handbook, 1986-96, Modern Short Stories, 1987-90, Video/Stereo Digest, 1989-91, Popular Electronics Mag., 1988-99, GIZMO, 1988-99, Hobbyists Handbook, 1989-96, Sci. Probe! mag., 1989-93, StoryMasters, 1989—2001, Electronics Shopper, 1990-99, Electronics Market Ctr., 1991-99, Electronics Now Mag., 1992-99, Radio Craft, 1993-96, Poptronix Handbook, 1996—2003; pres. Claggk, Inc., 1986—2003, Silicon Chip, 1993-94, Sci. Probe Inc., 1989-93, Poptronix Inc., 1997—2005, Ariz., 2005—; realtor Long Realty Co., Tucson, 2005—. Mem. electronics adv. bd. Bd. Coop. Ednl. Svcs., Nassau County, NY, 1975—77; pres. Electronics Industry Hall of Fame, 1985—2001; bd. dirs. Pub. Hall of Fame, 1987—89. Pub., editor-in-chief Poptronics, 2000-03, Poptronics Shopper, 2000-03, PC Tech, 2000-03; co-editor The Shofar, 1998-2002; contbr. articles to profl. jours., popular mags.; author Hugo Gernsback, A Man Well Ahead of His Time, 2007. Bd. dirs. Nassau County coun. Camp Fire Girls, 1971-72; 1st v.p. bd. dirs. Temple Beth Am, Las Vegas, 1998-2002 pres. 2001-02; apptd. bd. adjusters, Marana, Ariz., 2005—; apptd. sec.-treas. Dove Mt. Civic Assn., Marana, 2005—; appt. adv. bd. Citizens Park, Marana, 2007—, chair, 2007—; mem. adv. commn. Dove Mountain Preserve, 2008-. With US Army, 1953—56. Recipient Coop. award Nat. Alliance TV and Electronic Svcs. Assns., 1974, 75; inducted into Electronics Industry Hall of Fame, 1985; ISCET Gov's. award, 1998, FESA Pres. award, 1998. Mem.: IEEE, RTA CART Com., Grad. Registrate Inst., Dore Mountain Clinic (group sec. 2006—), Marana Pks. & Recreation Dep. (chair adv. bd. 2007—), Marana C. of C., LA Press, Soc. Profl. Journalists, Internat. Performing Magicians (exec. dir.), Internat. Underwater Explorers Soc., Am. Mgmt. Assn., Nat. Electronics Sales and Svc. Dealers Assn. (rec. sec. NY State 1976—78, treas. 1991—94, Man of Yr. award 1975, 1985, M.L. Finneyberg Excellence award 1994), Internat. Soc. Cert. electronic Technicians (chmn. 1974—76, 1979—81, dir.-at-large 1991—93, rep. to NESDA bd. 1991—93, chmn. 1993—95, Region 9 dir. 1995—97, chmn. 1999—2001, Chmn.'s award 1985), Am. Soc. Bus. Press Editors (sr.), Radio Club Am. Home: 12317 N Fallen Shadows Dr Marana AZ 85658 Office: Long Realty Co 12080 N Dove Mountain Blvd Ste 100 Marana AZ 85653 Home Phone: 520-572-8144; Office Phone: 520-918-5761. Personal E-mail: lartronics@aol.com, larrysteckler@aol.com. *Do not be afraid to try the unaccepted. Do not be afraid to do the undesirable. Do what you enjoy...do it well...and after it is done...never regret having done it...only regret what you have not yet done.*

STECKLER, PHYLLIS BETTY, business owner; b. NYC; d. Irwin H. and Bertha (Fellner) Schwartzbard; m. Stuart J. Steckler (div.); children: Randall, Sharon. BA, Hunter Coll.; MA, NYU. Editl. dir. R.R. Bowker Co., NYC, Crowell Collier Macmillan Info. Pub. Co., NYC, Holt Rinehart & Winston Info. Systems, NYC; pres., CEO Oryx Press, Scottsdale, Ariz., 1973-76, Phoenix, 1976—2000, Zephyr Info., Phoenix, 2001—06; publ. cons., 2001—; ptnr. It's All About Time, Concierge's Consulting Firm, 2007—. Adj. prof. mktg. scholarly publs. Grad. History dept., Ariz. State U., Tempe; mem. dean's coun. Coll. of Extended Edn., Ariz. State U., Phoenix; mem. adv. coun. Republic Bank Ariz., NA. Past chmn. Info. Industry Assn.; past chair Ariz. Ctr. for the Book; past pres. Contemporary Forum of Phoenix Art Mus.; founding mem. Nat. Edn. Network, U.S. Dept. Edn.; past pres. Friends of the Libr., U.S.A.; mem. Ariz. Women's Forum; bd. dirs. Ariz. region Com. for the Weizmann Inst. Sci.; mem. order coun. Republic Bank, Ariz.; mem. Young Arts Ariz. Bd. Recipient Women Who Make a Difference award The Internat. Women's Forum, 1995, Excellence in Pub. award Ariz. Book Pub. Assn., 1997, The Pub. History Program Ariz. State U. Founding Friend award, 2000; elected to Hunter Coll. Hall of Fame. Mem.: ALA, Ariz. Libr. Assn., Univ. Club of Phoenix. Home and Office: 6446 N 28th St Phoenix AZ 85016-8946 Business E-Mail: pbs@iaat.net.

STECKO, PAUL T., packaging company executive; With Internat. Paper Co.; pres., CEO Tenneco Packing, 1993-96, COO, 1997-98, pres., COO, 1998-99; CEO, chmn. bd. Packaging Corp. of Am., Lake Forest, Ill., 1999—. Bd. dirs. Tenneco, Am. Forest and Paper Assn., State Farm Mut. Ins. Co. Office: Packaging Corp of Am 1900 W Field Ct Lake Forest IL 60045-4828

STEDMAN, VICTORIA, economics professor; d. James Stedman and Mary Tarbox-Stedman; children: Michael Nally, Daniel Nally. MS in Economics, U. RI, Kingstown, 1997. Prof. economics CC RI, Newport, 1996—, Bryant U., Smithfield, RI, 1999—, U. RI, 2008—. Home: 79 Conanicus Rd Narragansett RI 02882

STEED, PATRICIA L., literature and language professor; d. William G. Steed and Margaret Morris. PhD, Tex. Woman's U., Denton, 1988. Prof. dept. english Northwestern Okla. State U., Alva, 1988—. Contbr. articles to numerous publs. Home: 612 Linden St Alva OK 73717

STEED, THERESA JEAN, manufacturing executive; b. Grapeland, Tex., Mar. 10, 1932; d. Robert Tresband and Alma Inez (Denson) Bobbitt; m. Jarvis Lacy Steed, July 8, 1950; children: Judy Karen, Pamela Kay, Kim Lacy. Grad., Elliott Bus. Sch., Houston, 1949; BMus. Edn., So. Coll. Fine Arts, Houston, 1956; postgrad., U. Tex., 1961, Sul Ross U., Alpine, Tex., 1962, U. Wis., 1962; M Rhymes (hon.), Duke U., 1961. Exec. sec. various cos., Houston, 1950—57; tchr. elem. sch. Rosenburg Ind. Sch. Dist., Tex., 1957—; tchr. kindergarten/music edn. Sonora Ind. Sch. Dist., Tex., 1959—65; tchr. elem. sch. Houston Ind. Sch. Dist., 1965—67, Conroe Ind. Sch. Dist., Tex., 1968—70; co-founder, co-owner Steed Tile & Mfg. Co., Conroe, 1965—. Author: Audio-Visual Curriculums for Music Education: Kindergarten Through Eighth Grade, 1962 Mem. Dem. Nat. Com., Washington, 1993—, Dem. Senatorial Campaign Com., Washington, 1996—, Nat. Senatorial Com., 2000-07. Recipient Presdl. Letter of Commendation, Excellence in Field of Edn., Pres. Lyndon B. Johnson, 1968—70, Am. Order of Ednl. Merit. Mem.: IBC, Eng. (dir.), World Congress Arts Sci. and Comm. (ambassador), Soverign Order Knights of Justice (UK), Am.'s Nat. World War II Mus. (charter), Nat. Women's History Mus. (charter), Nat. Trust for Hist. Preservation, Women in Constrn. (charter) (reporter 1970—75, publicity chmn.), Order Ea. Star (assoc. matron 1963), Nat. Federated Music Clubs Am., Pilot Club, Delta Kappa Gamma (publicity chmn. 1962—65). Methodist. Achievements include one of several American ambassadors to the world forum. Avocations: cooking, gardening, politicking. Home: 452 Lexington Ct Conroe TX 77302-3050 Personal E-mail: quechick007@yahoo.com.

STEEDMAN, DORIA LYNNE SILBERBERG, foundation administrator; b. LA; d. Mendel B. and Dorothy H. (Howell) Silberberg; m. Richard Cantey Steedman, Feb. 19, 1966; 1 child, Alexandra Loren. BA summa cum laude, UCLA. Producer EUE/Screen Gems, NYC, 1963-66, Jack Tinker & Ptnrs., NYC, 1966-68, Telpac Mgmt., NYC, 1968-72; v.p. broadcast prodn. Geer DuBois Advt., NYC, 1973-78, account mgr., dir. ops., 1979-92; exec. v.p., creative dir. Partnership for a Drug-Free America, NYC, 1992—. Bd. dirs. Friends of the Earth. Recipient Andy award Art Dirs. Club, 1968, 71; named one of 100 Best and Brightest Women in Advt., Advt. Age mag.; named Advt. Woman of Yr., 1996. Mem. Advt. Women N.Y. (pres. 1993-95), Advt. Women N.Y. Found. (pres. 1995-97), Phi Beta Kappa. Office: Partnership for a Drug-Free Am 405 Lexington Ave New York NY 10174-0002 Business E-Mail: doria_steedman@drugfree.org.

STEEFEL, DAVID SIMON, lawyer; b. Mpls., June 27, 1951; s. Lawrence D. Jr. and Marion (Charlson) S.; m. Mary Ann Moody, May 24, 1981; children: Emily, Daniel, Katherine. BA, Carleton Coll., 1973; JD, U. Colo., 1978. Bar: Colo. 1978, U.S. Dist. Ct. Colo. 1978, U.S. Ct. Appeals (10th cir.) 1978. Assoc. Gorsuch, Kirgis, Denver, 1978-80, Holme Roberts & Owen, Denver, 1980-84, ptnr., 1984—, litig. practice group leader, 1999—2006. Instr. U. Colo. Law Sch., Boulder, 1978, 91. Home: 1300 Green Oaks Dr Littleton CO 80121-1331 Office: Holme Roberts & Owen 1700 Lincoln St Ste 4100 Denver CO 80203-4541 Home Phone: 303-347-2913; Office Phone: 303-866-0348. Business E-Mail: david.steefel@hro.com.

STEEG, MOISE S., JR., lawyer; b. New Orleans, July 25, 1916; s. Moise S. and Carrie (Gutmann) S.; m. Marion B., Sept. 14, 1943 (dec.); children: Barbara Steeg Midlo, Marion, Robert M.; m. Melba Law, Nov. 29, 1969. LLB, Tulane U., 1937. Bar: La. 1937, U.S. Dist. Ct. (ea. dist.) La. 1939, U.S. Ct. Appeals (5th cir.) 1946, U.S. Supreme Ct. 1950, U.S. Ct. Appeals (11th cir.) 1981. Practice, New Orleans, 1937—; assoc. Rittenberg & Rittenberg, 1937-38; sole practice, 1938-46; founder Gertler & Steeg, 1946-48, Steeg & Morrison, 1948-50, Marcus & Steeg, 1950-54, Steeg & Shushan, 1954-71; sr. ptnr. The Steeg Law Firm, LLC, 1972—. Bd. dirs. Loyola U., chmn., 1979—, mem. search com. for dean Coll. Law; chmn., founder New Orleans Hist. Dist. and Landmarks Com.; bd. dirs. chmn. bd. New Orleans Mus. Art, 1980; bd. overseers Hebrew Union Coll.; bd. dirs. Delgado Jr. Coll., New Orleans Symphony; founder, dir. New Orleans Ednl. and Rsch. Corp.; bd. dirs. Louise Davis Sch. for Retarded Children, Touro Infirmary, 1963-69; mem. Ochsner Found. Hosp. Bd., 1985—; bd. visitors Trinity Episcopal Sch., 1989—; organizer, sec. New Orleans Bus. Coun., 1986; pres. Temple Sinai, 1966-67; chmn. Anti-Defamation League, Jewish Cmty. Ctr., chmn. Aquarium Drive, Aquarium of Ams.; local counsel Nat. Dem. Party, 1966. Served to capt. USAF, 1942-46. Recipient Brotherhood Award, NCCJ, 1980, Disting. Alumnus award Tulane Law Sch., 1991, Isidore Newman Sch., Svc. award Newcomb Coll. Soc., Cmty. Svc. award New Orleans Bar Assn. Times-Picayune Loving Cup, 2004, Contbn. to Arts award Mayor, 2004; Mem. Paul Tulane Honor Soc. Home: One River Place 3 Poydras St New Orleans LA 70130-1665 Office: 201 Saint Charles Ave Ste 3201 New Orleans LA 70170-1032 Office Phone: 504-582-1199. Business E-Mail: msteeg@steeglaw.com.

STEEL, DANIELLE (DANIELLE FERNANDE DOMINIQUE SCHUELEIN-STEEL), author; b. NYC, Aug. 14, 1947; d. John and Norma Schuelein-Steel; m. Claude-Eric Lazard (div.); m. Danny Zugelder (div.); m. William Toth (div.); m. John Traina, 1981 (div.); m. Tom Perkins (div.); 9 children. Student, Parsons Sch. Design, NYU. Vice pres. pub. relations and new bus. Supergirls Ltd., NYC, 1968-71; copywriter Grey Advt., San Francisco, 1973-74; founder Steel Gallery of Contemporary Art, San Francisco, 2003—. Author: (novels) Going Home, 1973, Passion's Promise, 1977, Now And Forever, 1978, The Promise, 1978, Golden Moments, 1979, Season Of Passion, 1980, Summer's End, 1980, The Ring, 1980, Palomino, 1981, To Love Again, 1981, Remembrance, 1981, Loving, 1981, Once In A Lifetime, 1982, Crossings, 1982, A Perfect Stranger, 1983, Thurston House, 1983, Changes, 1983, Full Circle, 1984, Family Album, 1985, Secrets, 1985, Wanderlust, 1986, Fine Things, 1987, Kaleidoscope, 1987, Zoya, 1988, Star, 1989, Daddy, 1989, Message From Nam, 1990, Heartbeat, 1991, No Greater Love, 1991, Jewels, 1992, Mixed Blessings, 1992, Vanished, 1993, Accident, 1994, The Gift, 1994, Wings, 1994, Lightning, 1995, Five Days In Paris, 1995, Malice, 1996, Silent Honor, 1996, The Ranch, 1997, Special Delivery, 1997, The Ghost, 1998, The Long Road Home, 1998, The Klone and I, 1998, His Bright Light, 1998, Mirror Image, 1998, Bittersweet, 1999, Granny Dan, 1999, Irresistible Forces, 1999, The Wedding, 2000, The House On Hope Street, 2000, Journey, 2000, Lone Eagle, 2001, Leap Of Faith, 2001, The Kiss, 2001, The Cottage, 2002, Sunset in St. Tropez, 2002, Answered Prayers, 2002, Dating Game, 2003, Johnny Angel, 2003, Safe Harbour, 2003, Ransom, 2004, Second Chance, 2004, Echoes, 2004, Impossible, 2005, Miracle, 2005, Toxic Bachelors, 2005, The House, 2006, Coming Out, 2006, H.R.H, 2006, Bungalow 2, 2007, Amazing Grace, 2007, Honor Thyself, 2008, Rogue, 2008, A Good Woman, 2008, One Day at a Time, 2009, (children's books) Martha's New Daddy, 1989, Max and the Babysitter, 1989, Martha's Best Friend, 1989, Max's Daddy Goes to the Hospital, 1989, Max's New Baby, 1989, Martha's New School, 1989, Max Runs Away, 1990, Martha's New Puppy, 1990, Max and Grandma and Grampa Winky, 1991, Martha and Hilary and the Stranger, 1991, Freddie's Trip, 1992, Freddie's First Night Away, 1992, Freddie and the Doctor, 1992, Freddie's Accident, 1992. Decorated Chevalier of Ordre des Arts et des Lettres France. Office: care Dell Publishing 1540 Broadway New York NY 10036-4039 Home: PO Box 470130 San Francisco CA 94147-0130*

STEEL, DUNCAN GREGORY, engineering educator; b. Cleve., Jan. 11, 1951; s. Robert John and Mildred (Graham) S.; children: Adam, Benjamin. BA, U. N.C., 1972; MS, U. Mich., 1975, PhD, 1976. Physicist Exxon Rsch. and Engring., Linden, NJ, 1977-78, Hughes Rsch. Labs., Malibu, Calif., 1975-85; prof. EECS, physics, biophysics U. Mich., Ann Arbor, 1985—; sr. rsch. scientist Inst. Gerontology Sch. Medicine, U. Mich., Ann Arbor, 1986—, sr. rsch. scientist biophys. rsch. divsn., 1992—2007, area chair optical scis., dir. optical scis. lab., 1989—2007, chair biophysics, 2007—08, Robert J. Hiller prof., 2005—, Peter S. Fuss prof., 2001—05, prof. biophysics, 2009—. Topical editor Jour. Optical Soc., Washington, 1986—92. Contbr. articles to profl. jours. Guggenheim fellow, 1999. Fellow IEEE, Optical Soc. Am., Am. Phys. Soc. Achievements include development of first phase conjugate laser; first high resolution nonlinear laser spectroscopy of semiconductor heterostructures; research in of collision induced resonances in atoms; low noise (below the standard quantum limit) room temperature semiconductor lasers; of first demonstration of coherence optical control and wave function engineering in quantum dots; of first demonstration of wave function engineering; first deimonstration quantum entanglement in a single quantum dot; demonstration of in vitro tryptophan phosphorescence for studies of protein structure in solution; discovery of of structural annealing in proteins during protein folding. Office: U Mich Physics Dept 500 E University Ave Ann Arbor MI 48109-1120 Home: 11516 Waters Rd Chelsea MI 48118-9615 Home Phone: 734-433-9034. Business E-Mail: dst@umich.edu.

STEEL, GEORGE ROBERT, opera company director; b. Md., 1966; m. Sarah Brook Fels, Oct. 5, 2002. Grad., Yale U., New Haven, 1994; student, Am. Conservatory Music. Mng. prodr. Tisch Ctr. for Arts/92nd St. YW-YMHA, NYC; exec. dir. Miller Theatre, Columbia U., NYC, 1997—2008; gen. dir. Dallas Opera, 2008—09; gen. mgr., artistic dir. NYC Opera, 2009—. Founder, condr. Gotham City Orchestra, Vox Vocal Ensemble. Composer: What is American Music, Africa in America. Mem. French-Am. Cultural Exch., 2003—06; mem. Young Leaders Forum, Nat. Com. US-China Rels., 2005—07. Recipient Trailblazer Award, Am. Music Ctr., 2003, ASCAP-Chamber Music America (CMA) Award for Adventurous Programming of Contemporary Music, 2002, 2005, ASCAP Concert Music Award, 2003. Office: NYC Opera NY State Theater at Lincoln Ctr New York NY 10023*

STEEL, ROBERT KING, bank executive, former federal agency administrator; b. Aug. 3, 1951; m. Gillian Steel; 3 children. BA in History & Polit. Sci., Duke U., 1973; MBA, U. Chgo., 1984. Joined Goldman Sachs Group, Inc., 1976, head equities divsn. Europe NYC, 1988—94, head instnl. equities U.S., 1994—98, co-head equities divsn., 1998—2001, head equities divsn., 2001—02, vice chmn., 2002—04, adv. dir., non-exec. chmn., securities divsn., 2004—06; sr. fellow, Ctr. Bus. & Govt. John F. Kennedy Sch. Govt., Harvard U., Cambridge, Mass., 2004—06; under sec. for domestic fin. US Dept. Treasury, Washington, 2006—08; pres., CEO Wachovia Corp., Charlotte, NC, 2008—. Bd. dirs. Wachovia Corp., 2008—. Chmn. bd. trustees Duke Univ. Mem.: NYSE (mem. various coms.), Securities Industry Assn. (bd. dirs.). Office: Wachovia Corp 1 Wachovia Ctr Charlotte NC 28288*

STEEL, VIRGINIA (GINNY STEEL), university librarian; BA, U. Rochester; MLS, U. Chgo. Libr. Ariz. State U. Librs., Tempe; head Social Scis. and Humanities Libr., head Access Svcs. Dept., acting asst. univ. libr. pub. svcs. U. Calif., San Diego, 1988—97; assoc. dir. pub. svcs. MIT, Cambridge, 1997—2001; dir. librs. Wash. State U., Pullman, 2001—05; univ. libr. U. Calif., Santa Cruz, 2005—. Office: U Calif Santa Cruz Univ Libr 320 McHenry Libr 1156 High St Santa Cruz CA 95064 Office Phone: 831-459-2076. E-mail: vsteel@ucsc.edu.

STEELE, ANA MERCEDES, retired federal agency administrator; b. Jan. 18, 1939; d. Sydney and Mercedes (Hernandez) S.; m. John Hunter Clark, June 2, 1979. AB magna cum laude, Marywood Coll., 1958. Actress, 1959-64; sec. Nat. Endowment for Arts, Washington, 1965-67, dir. budget and rsch., 1968-75, dir. planning, 1976-78, dir. program coordination, sr. exec. svc., 1979-81, assoc. dep. chmn. programs, dir. program coordination, 1982-93, acting chmn., acting sr. dep. chmn., 1993, sr. dep. chmn., sr. exec. svc., 1993-96, dep. chmn. mgmt. and budget, sr. exec. svc., 1996-98; ret., 1998. Guest lectr. George Washington U., 1987; trustee Marywood Coll., 1989-96, Marywood U., 1997-98. Author, editor report: History of the National Council on the Arts and National Endowment for the Arts During the Johnson Administration, 1968; editor: Museums USA (Fed. Design Coun. award of Excellence 1975), 1974, National Endowment Arts, 1965-85: A Brief Chronology of Federal Involvement in the Arts, 1985. Former reader Rec. for the Blind, N.Y.C.; former tutor Future for Jimmy, Washington; judge Helen Hayes Awards, 2003-06. Named Disting. Grad. in Field of Arts, Marywood Coll., 1976; recipient Sustained Superior Performance award Nat. Endowment for Arts, 1980, Disting. Svc. award, 1983-85, 89, 92, 96, Presdl. medal Marywood U., 2000; named to Disting. Alumnae Hall of Fame, Ursuline Acad., 2001. Mem. Actors' Equity Assn., Screen Actors Guild, Delta Epsilon Sigma, Kappa Gamma Pi. Home: 2475 Virginia Ave NW Apt 604 Washington DC 20037-2639

STEELE, (MARGARET) ANITA MARTIN, law librarian, educator; b. Haines City, Fla., Dec. 30, 1927; d. Emmett Edward and Esther Majulia (Phifer) Martin; m. Thomas Dinsmore Steele, June 10, 1947 (div. 1969); children: Linda Frances, Roger Dinsmore, Thomas Garrick, Carolyn Ann; m. James E. Beaver, Mar. 1980 (dec. Feb. 1996). BA, Radcliffe Coll., 1948; JD, U. Va., 1971; M in Law Librarianship, U. Wash., 1972. Asst. prof. law U. Puget Sound, Tacoma, 1972—74, assoc. prof. law, 1974—79, prof. law, 1979—94, dir. law libr., 1972—94; prof. law, dir. law libr. Seattle U., Tacoma, 1994—98, prof. law emeritus, 1998—. Author: (book) Martin and Carmichael Descendants in Ga., 1811-1994, 1994; contbr. articles to profl. jours.; mem. editorial adv. bds.: various law book pubs. Treas. Congl. Campaign Orgn., Tacoma, 1978, 1980. Mem.: DAR, Colonial Dames XVII Century. Republican. Home: 4434 Pheasant Ridge Rd Condo # 303 Roanoke VA 24014-5280 E-mail: ams145@cox.net.

STEELE, C. WILLIAM, scouting organization administrator; b. Dayton, Ohio, Oct. 17, 1948; s. Charles William Sr. and Helen Jolly Steele; children: Brian, Audrey. BS, Ind. U., 1973. Profl. scouter Boy Scouts Am., San Antonio, 1980-96; dir. Rels. & Nat. Eagle Scout Assn., Irving, Tex., 2001—. Author: Yochib: The River Cave, 1985, Huautla: Thirty

Years in One of the World's Deepest Caves, 2009. Fellow Explorers Club. Avocation: speleology. Office: 1325 W Walnut Hill Ln Irving TX 78038 Office Phone: 972-580-2436.

STEELE, CARL LAVERN, academic administrator; b. Patoka, Ill., Aug. 22, 1934; s. Boyd Alfa and Effie Jane (Corson) S.; m. Lula Irene Saliba, June 11, 1961; children: Jeffrey Van, Gregory Michael, Douglas Alan. BEd, So. Ill. U., 1956, MEd, 1960; MLS, No. Ill. U., 1971. Tchr. Shawneetown (Ill.) Community High. Sch., 1956-57; GED instr. U.S. Army, Ft. Hood, Tex. and Ulm, Fed. Republic of Germany, 1957-59; tchr. Forrest-Strawn-Wing Unit Dist., Forrest, Ill., 1959-61, Richwoods Community High Sch., Peoria, Ill., 1961-66; asst. dir. instructional materials Sauk Valley Coll., Dixon, Ill., 1966-68; dir. Ednl. Resources Ctr., Rock Valley Coll., Rockford, Ill., 1968-93; ret., 1993. Part-time traffic safety instr. Rock Valley Coll., 1992—2006. Asst. World Record sec. Nat. Fresh Water Fishing Hall of Fame, Hayward, Wisc., 1977-79. Served with U.S. Army, 1957-59. Democrat. Presbyterian. Avocations: fishing, travel, reading, woodworking, gardening. Home: 5758 Weymouth Dr Rockford IL 61114-5569 Personal E-mail: lsteele@steele.com.

STEELE, CHARLES, JR., retired civil rights association executive, former state legislator; b. Tuscaloosa, Ala., Aug. 3, 1946; m. Cathelean Annette; children: LeKeisha, Charla. Student, Miss. Valley State, Oakland U.; BA, Am. Internat. U.; LHD (hon.), Stillman Coll.; Ph.D (hon.), Am. Internat. U. Co-owner Van Hoose and Steele Funeral Home; mem. Tuscaloosa City Coun., Ala. State Senate from Dist. 24, Montgomery, 1995—2004; pres., CEO So. Christian Leadership Conf. (SCLC), Atlanta, 2004—09, cons., 2009—. Mem. Local Legis. No. 1 Com., Fiscal Responsibility and Accountability Com., Fin. and Taxation Gen. Fund Com., Fin. and Taxation Edn. Com., Agr. and Forestry Com., Health and Human Resources Com., Oil and Gas subcom. Commerce, Transp., and Utilities Com., Indsl. Devel. and Recruitment Com., Small Bus. and Rural Devel. Com., Constitution, Campaign Fin., Ethics, and Elections Com., Postsecondary and Higher Edn. subcom. Edn. Com., Law Enforcement and Victims Rights subcom., Violence in Schs. subcom. Judiciary Com.; chairperson Rural Devel. subcom. Small Bus. and Rural Devel. Com., Mental Health subcom. Health and Human Resources Com. Named one of Most Influential Black Americans, Ebony mag., 2006. Mem. Nat. Assn. Funeral Dirs. and Morticians, Ala. Funeral Dirs. and Morticians Assn. Democrat. Baptist. Avocations: walking, reading.*

STEELE, CHARLES GLEN, retired accountant; b. Faulkton, SD, July 24, 1925; s. Clifford D. and Emily O. (Hanson) S.; m. Shirley June Ferguson, Nov. 9, 1947; children: Richard Alan (dec.), Deborah Ann Steele Most (dec.). BBA, Golden Gate U., San Francisco, 1951, MBA, 1962. With Deloitte Haskins & Sells, 1951-86, partner, 1963-86, partner charge Chgo. office, 1973-76, partner charge personnel and adminstrn. NYC, 1976-78, chmn., chief exec. officer, 1978-86. Instr. evening program Golden Gate U., 1952-58. Served with USNR, 1943-48, aircraft carrier fighter pilot, 1946-48. Recipient Elijah Watts Sells Gold medal for highest grade in U.S. for C.P.A. exam., 1951 Mem. AICPA. Home: 7831 Rush Rose Dr Unit 124 Carlsbad CA 92009-6843

STEELE, CHARLES RICHARD, biomedical and mechanical engineering educator; b. Royal, Iowa, Aug. 15, 1933; married, 1969; 4 children. BS, Tex. A&M U., 1956; PhD in Applied Mechanics, Stanford U., 1960; PhD (hon.), Zaporozhye State U., Ukraine, 1997. Engring. specialist aircraft structure Chance-Vought Aircraft, Dallas, 1959-60; rsch. scientist shell theory Lockheed Rsch. Lab., Palo Alto, 1960-66; assoc. prof. Stanford (Calif.) U., 1966-71, prof. applied mechanics, 1971—. Lectr. U. Calif., Berkeley, 1964-65; vis. prof. Swiss Fed. Inst. Technology, Zurich, 1971-72, U. Luleá, Sweden, 1982, Chung Kung U., Taiwan, 1985, U. Cape Town, South Africa, spring 1993, U. Trento, Italy, fall 1999; tech. dir. Shelltech Assoc. Editor-in-chief: Internat. Jour. Solids Structures, 1985—2005, Jour. Mechanics of Materials and Structures, 2005-. Recipient NIH Claude Pepper award, 1988, Humboldt award, 1994; named Eminent Academician Ukrainian Acad., 1998. Fellow ASME (chmn. exec. com. applied mechanics divsn. 1983-84, Warner T. Koiter medal 1999), Am. Acad. Mechanics (pres. 1989-90); mem. AIAA, NAE, Acoustical Soc. Am. Achievements include research in asymptotic analysis in mechanics; thin shell theory; mechanics of the inner ear; noninvasive determination of bone stiffness; and morphology of plants. Office: Stanford Univ Divsn Mechanics and Computation Durand Bldg 355A Stanford CA 94305-4040

STEELE, CLAUDE MASON, academic administrator, psychology professor; b. Chgo., Jan. 1, 1946; s. Shelby and Ruth (Hootman) Steele; married, Aug. 27, 1967; children: Jory, Claude Benjamin. BA in Psychology, Hiram Coll., 1967; MA in Social Psychology, Ohio State U., 1969, PhD in Social Psychology, minor in Statistical Psychology, 1971; PhD (hon.), Yale U., 2002, Princeton U., 2003. Asst. prof. U. Utah, Salt Lake City, 1971-73; from asst. to prof. U. Washington, Seattle, 1978-87, prof. psychology, 1985—87; prof. U. Mich., Ann Arbor, 1987-91, rsch. scientist Inst. Social Rsch., 1989—91; prof. psychology Stanford U., Calif., 1991—2009, fellow Ctr. Advanced Study in Behavioral Sciences, 1994—95, chmn. Dept. Psychology, 1997—2000, Lucie Stern prof. social sciences, 1997—2009, co-dir. Ctr. Comparative Studies in Race and Ethnicity, 1999—2002, dir. Ctr. Comparative Studies in Race and Ethnicity, 2002—09, dir. Ctr. for Advanced Study in the Behavioral Scis.; provost, prof. psychology Columbia U., NYC, 2009—. Mem. psychosocial rsch. study sect. Nat. Inst. Alcohol Abuse and Alcoholism, 1984—88; mem. rev. panel and mental health rsch. edn. rev. panel Nat. Inst. Mental Health, 1979—83. Assoc. editor Personality and Social Psychology Bull., 1984—87, consulting editor Jour. of Social Issues, 1983—90, Jour. Personality and Social Psychology, 1990—, Attitudes and Social Cognition, 1990—, Psychol. Rev., 1990—, Motivation and Emotion, 1990—, Basic and Applied Social Psychology, 1990—, Jour. Exptl. Social Psychology, 1990—. Mem. King County Alcoholism and Drug Abuse Adminstrv. Bd., 1980—85. Recipient numerous rsch. grants. Fellow: Am. Psychol. Assn. (Cattell Fellowship), Am. Psychol. Soc. (bd. dirs. 1991—96, William James Fellow award 2000, Gordon Allport Prize); mem.: NAS, Nat. Acad. Edn., Am. Acad. Arts and Scis., Soc. Personality and Social Psychology (pres. 2002—03, Donald Campbell award 2001), Soc. Exptl. Social Psychology (sec.-treas. 1987—88, chmn. 1988—89). Home: 562 Junipero Serra Blvd Stanford CA 94305-8442 Office: Columbia U / Office of Provost 205 Low Memorial Library, Mail Code 4313 535 W 116th St New York NY 10027 Office Phone: 212-854-2404. E-mail: cs2816@columbia.edu.*

STEELE, ELISA ANNE, Internet company executive, marketing professional; b. 1966; BS, U. NH Whittemore Sch. Bus. & Econs., 1988; MBA, San Francisco State U. Sch. Bus., 1990. Gen. mgr. bus. svcs. AT&T Inc., 1991—99; mktg. exec., v.p. Sun Microsystems, Inc., 1999—2004; sr. v.p. corp. mktg. NetApp Inc., 2005—09; chief mktg. officer Yahoo! Inc., 2009—. Named a Woman to Watch, Advt. Age, 2009. Office: Yahoo Inc 701 First Ave Sunnyvale CA 94089 Office Phone: 408-349-3300. Office Fax: 408-349-3301.*

STEELE, ERNEST CLYDE, retired insurance company executive; b. Corbin, Ky., May 11, 1925; s. J. Fred and Leona (McFarland) S.; m. Cora Jones, June 17, 1944 (dec. Nov. 1988); children: Gerald R., David. P.; m. Helen LeCoultre, July 7, 1990 (dec. Jan. 2007). BS with honors, U. Ky., 1948, MS, 1950. Asst. actuary Peninsular Life Ins. Co., Jacksonville, Fla., 1950-54; actuary Pioneer Life & Casualty Co., Gadsden, Ala., 1955; v.p., actuary Guaranty Savs. Life Ins. Co., Montgomery, Ala., 1956-57; exec. v.p., actuary Am. Investment Life Ins. Co., Nashville, 1958-59; pres., actuary Appalachian Nat. Life Ins. Co., Knoxville, Tenn., 1959-67; sr. v.p., chief investment officer, ops. analyst Coastal States Life Ins. Co., Atlanta, 1968-71, exec. v.p., dir., 1971-74, pres., dir., 1974-79; pres. Occidental Life Ins. Co. of N.C., 1979-85, chmn., 1986-88; pres., dir. Peninsular Life Ins. Co., 1981-83, chmn., 1986-88; exec. v.p. investments MCM Corp., 1985-88; ret., 1988. Past pres. Ga. Assn. Life Inst. Cos., 1976-77. Past pres. Gt. Smoky Mountain Coun. Boy Scouts Am., 1965—66. Served to 2d lt. US Army, 1943—45. Fellow Life Mgmt. Inst.; mem. Life Office Mgmt. Assn. (past chmn. bd.), Am. Coun. Life Ins. (past dir.), U. Ky. Alumni Assn. (past bd. dirs.), Am. Acad. Actuaries, Pi Mu Epsilon, Order Ky. Colonels(hon.) Republican. Baptist. Home: 103 Newell Village Cir Seymour TN 37865-5931 Personal E-mail: erneststeele@bellsouth.net. *My success in life is measured by the success of those with whom I have been associated.*

STEELE, GLENN DANIEL, JR., oncologist, healthcare system executive; b. Balt., June 23, 1944; m. Diana; 1 child, Joshua; m. Lisa; children: Kirsten, Lara. AB magna cum laude, Harvard Coll., 1966; MD, NYU, 1970; PhD, Lund U., Sweden, 1975. Intern, then resident Med. Ctr. U. Colo., Denver, 1970-76; fellow NIH in immunology Univ. Lund, Sweden, 1973-75; asst. surgeon Sidney Farber Cancer Inst., Boston, 1976-78; cons. surgeon Boston Hosp. for Women, 1977-80; clin. assoc. surgical oncology Sidney Farber Cancer Inst., 1978-79; jr. assoc. in surgery Peter Bent Brigham Hosp., Boston, 1976-82; instr. surgery Med. Sch. Harvard, Boston, 1976-78; asst. prof. surgery Med. Sch. Harvard Coll., 1978-81; asst. physician surgical oncology Sidney Farber Cancer Inst., 1979-82; assoc. prof. surgery Med. Sch. Harvard Coll., 1981-84; surgeon Brigham & Women's Hosp., 1982-84; assoc. physician surgical oncology Dana-Farber Cancer Inst., 1982-84, physician surg. oncology, 1984-95; chmn. dept. surgery, deaconess Harvard Surg. Svc. New England Deaconess Hosp., Boston, 1985-95; William V. McDermott prof. surgery Med. Sch. Harvard Coll., 1985-95; prof. Univ. Chgo., 1995—2001, dean biological scis. divsn. and Pritzker Sch. Medicine, 1995—2001, v.p. medical affairs Pritzker Sch. Medicine, 1995—2001; pres, CEO Geisinger Health System, Danville, Pa., 2001—; chair. Am. Bd. Surgery, Phila., 1999—. Assoc. editor Jour. Clin. Oncology, 1986—, Jour. Hepatobiliary-Pancreatic Surgery, 1993—; mem. editl. bd. Annals of Surgery, Annals of Surg. Oncology, Brit. Jour. Surgery, Surgery, Surg. Oncology; contbr. numerous articles to profl. jours. Recipient NIH fellow 1973-75, Am. Cancer Soc. fellow 1972-73, 76-79, various other rsch. grants. Fellow ACS (chmn. patient care and rsch. com. commn. on cancer 1989-91, mem. bd. govs. 1991-95, chmn. commn. on cancer 1991-93, mem. exec. com. commn. on cancer 1992-93); mem. Am. Assn. Immunologists, Am. Bd. Surgery (dir. 1993-98, vice-chmn. 1998—), Ill. Surg. Soc., Am. Bd. Med. Specialties, Am. Soc. Clin. Oncology, Am. Surg. Assn., Assn. Program Dirs. in Surgery, Assn. for Surg. Edn., Internat. Fedn. Surg. Colls., Internat. Surg. Group, Soc. Surg. Oncology (treas. 1994-97, v.p. 1997, pres. 1999-2000), Inst. of Medicine of NAS, others. Office: Geisinger Health System 100 North Academy Ave Danville PA 17822

STEELE, HOWARD LOUCKS, economic development consultant, author; b. Pitts., Jan. 27, 1929; s. Howard Bennington and Ruby Alberta (Loucks) S.; m. Sally E. Funk, June 6, 1952 (div. 1977); children: John F., David A., Patricia A.; m. Jane R. Cornelius, July 30, 1977 (div. 1996); 1 child, Jennifer L.; m. Elaine Haddock, Aug. 23, 1997. BS, Washington and Lee U., 1950; MS, Pa. State U., 1952; PhD, U. Ky., 1962. Sales mgr. Greenville (Pa.) Dairy Co., 1952-56; owner H.L. Steele Bulk Milk Hauling, Greenville, 1955-60; asst. prof. Clemson (S.C.) U., 1956-57, assoc. prof., 1957-64, Ohio State U., Columbus, 1964-71; with Fgn. Agrl. Svc./Internat. Coop. and Devel. U.S., Dept. Agr., Washington, 1971-97; ret.; econ. devel. cons., 1997—. Project mgr. AID, Guatemala, 1976-77, Bolivia, 1977-80, Honduras, 1980-82, Sri Lanka, 1982-84, Bur. L.Am. and Caribbean USAID, Washington, 1984-88, office of the dir. tech. assistance divsn., 1988-90, with office of dep. adminstr., 1990-97; USDA liaison officer Inter-Am. Inst. Coop. in Agr., 1993-97; instr. U. Md., College Park, 1974-76; vis. prof. U. Sao Paulo, Piracicaba, Brazil, 1964-66; ptnr. Kingwood Acres Farm, Rockwood, Pa., 1966-98. Author: Commercializacao Agricola, 1971, A 200 Year History of Some Descendents of the Pioneer James Steel of Castleblaney, Ireland and Mt. Pleasant, Pennsylvania, 1994, Your Tax Dollars at Work (I'd Rather Have Gone Business Class!), 1998, Food Soldier, 2002, Bushels and Bales: A Food Soldier in the Cold War, 2008; contbr. articles to profl. jours. Recipient Nat. Forensic Union award; named One of Outstanding Young Men U.S., U.S. Jaycees, 1965; cert. of merit Dept. Agr., 1975, 92. Mem.: SAR, Masons, Internat. Assn. Agrl. Economists, Am. Agrl. Econs. Assn., Shriners, Sigma Nu, Gamma Sigma Delta. Home: 5204 Holden St Fairfax VA 22032-3418 Office Phone: 703-978-4066. Personal E-mail: ehsteele@cox.net.

STEELE, JAMES EUGENE, retired school system administrator; b. South Norfolk, Va. s. James Edward and Blanche Eugenia (Munden) S. BS in Music Edn., Coll. William and Mary (now Old Dominion U.), Norfolk, Va., 1961; MEd in Ednl. Adminstrn. and Supervision, Temple U., Phila., 1972; EdD in Ednl. Adminstrn., Nova U., Ft. Lauderdale, Fla., 1976. Cert. tchr., Va. Piccoloist Va. Symphony Orch., 1951-73; dir. choral music Hampton City Schs., Va., 1960-65, supr. music, 1965—2003; ret., 2003. Guest flute soloist Music Tchrs. Assn., Great Britain, 1962. Dir. fine arts divsn. Hampton Assn. Arts Humanities, 1967—. Mem. NEA, Va. Edn. Assn., Hampton Edn. Assn., Va. Assn. Sch. Execs., Hampton Instrnl. Suprs. Assn., Tidewater Regional Suprs., Va. Assn. Sch. Curriculum Devel., Va. Music Suprs. Assn., Va. Music Educators Assn., Music Educators Nat. Conf., Va. Choral Dirs. Assn., Va. Band and Orch. Dirs. Assn., Va. String Tchrs. Assn. Home: 132 Fayton Ave Norfolk VA 23505-4428

STEELE, JAMES HARLAN, retired veterinarian; b. Chgo., Apr. 3, 1913; s. James Hahn and Lydia (Nordquist) S.; m. Aina Oberg, 1941 (dec. 1969); children: James Harlan, David, Michael; m. 1970 Maria-Brigitte Meyer. DVM, Mich. State Coll., 1941; MPH, Harvard U., 1942. With USPHS, 1943-71; advancing through grades to asst. surgeon gen. for vet. affairs and chief vet. officer; chief vet. pub. health activities Communicable Disease Center, Atlanta, 1947-71; prof. environ. health U. Tex. Sch. Pub. Health, Houston, 1971-83, prof. emeritus, 1983—. Cons. WHO, 1950-2005, Pan-Am. Health Orgn., 1945—, FAO, UN, 1960; vis. prof. Tex. A&M U., 1976—, all univ. prof., 1981-82; spkr. in field. Author: (with J. Arthur Myer) Bovine Tuberculosis Control in Man and Animals, 1969, 95, (with Charles Thoen), Mycobacterium Bovis Infections, revised edit., 2005, (with James Steele) Hendrik Stafseth and Public Health Veterinarians Ole Stalheim, 2005; editor-in-chief CRC Zoonoses Handbooks, 1979-84, cons. editor, 1994, 8 vols. transl. into Russian and Farsi, Bacterial & Viral Zoonoses, 2 vols. rev. by Beran; mem. editl. cons. bd. APHA Control Communicable Disease, 1960-2000, Merck Vet. Manual, 1955-2005; contbr. articles to profl. jours. and sects. to books on food hygiene and irradiation. Recipient Carlos Finlay medal Cuba Acad. Sci., 1952, Mich. State U. Centennial award, 1955, Mich. State U. Alumni award, 1958, USPHS Order of Merit, 1963, Karl F. Meyer Gold Head Cane award, 1966, Disting. Svc. award USPHS, 1971, Mich. State U. Coll. Vet. Medicine award, 1972, hon. mem. Epidemic Intelligence Svc., 1975, James Law lectr. Cornell U., 1983, Centennial award U. Pa., 1984, Am. Vet. Med. Assn. Internat. Vet. award, 1984, Pub. Svc. award, 1993; Disting. Svc. award Am. Vet. History Soc., 1995, James H. Steele award Ctr. for Disease Control, 1998, Disting. Alumni award Mich. State U., 2001, Calvin Schwabe Lifetime Achievement award, 2005, James McCallam award Mil. Surgeons, 2005, Surgeon Gen.'s medallion USPHS, 2005, Abraham Horowitz award, Pan American Edn. Health Org., Wash., 2006; named James H. Steele ann. lectr. in his honor U. Tex. Health Sci. Ctr., 1993, James H. Steele Epidemiology Professorship in his honor, 1996, James Steele Diseases in Nature, Tex. Health Dept., Austin, 2007. Fellow APHA (emeritus, 1984; Bronfman award 1971, Centennial award 1972), Am. Coll. Epidemiology (founding fellow, Life Time Merit award, 2009); mem. Am. Soc. Tropical Medicine (emeritus), Am. Coll. Vet. Preventive Medicine (founder, hon. diploma 1983, Pres.'s award 1994), Nat. Acad. Health Practiioners, World Vet. Epidemiology Soc. (founder, pres. 1971), Am. Vet. Epidemiology Soc. (pres. 1968-88), World Vet. Assn. (hon.), Philippines Vet. Med. Assn. (hon.), Peru Vet. Med. Assn. (hon.), Hellenic Vet. Soc. (Athens Greece, hon. diploma, 1977), U.S. Animal Health Assn. (life), U.S.-Mex. Pub. Health Assn. (hon., life, Border award 2003), Mil. Surgeons Assn. (hon. life), Infectious Disease Soc. Am. (emeritus), XXI World Vet. Congress, Athens (hon. Moscow, hon. diploma 1979), German Health Svc. (hon. diploma, 1988, Order of Merit 1993), Harvard U. Alumni Assn. (Alumni award 1998), Alpha Psi. Episcopalian. Home: 10722 Riverview Houston TX 77042-1121 Personal E-mail: drjameshsteele@comcast.net. *I have believed firmly throughout my career that I should share my knowledge and expertise with my fellow man, be he American or citizen of the world. Those of us who are more fortunate to be endowed with intellectual advantages have an even greater responsibility to share.*

STEELE, JOHN HYSLOP, marine scientist, oceanographic institute administrator; b. Edinburgh, Nov. 15, 1926; s. Adam and Annie H.; m. Margaret Evelyn Travis, Mar. 2, 1956; 1 son, Hugh. B.Sc., Univ. Coll., London U., 1946, D.Sc., 1964. Marine scientist Marine Lab., Aberdeen, Scotland, 1951-66, sr. prin. sci. officer, 1966-73, dep. dir., 1973-77; dir. Woods Hole Oceanographic Instn., Mass., 1977-89, pres. Mass., 1986-91. Mem. NAS/NRC Ocean Sci. Bd., 1978-88, chmn., 1986-88; mem. rsch. and exploration com. Nat. Geog. Soc.; mem. Arctic Rsch. Commn., 1988-92; trustee U. Corp. Atmospheric Rsch., 1987-91, Bermuda Biol. Sta., R.W. Johnson Found.; del. Internat. Coun. Exploration Sea; hon. prof. U. Aberdeen. Author: The Structure of Marine Ecosystems, 1974; Contbr. articles to profl. jours. Served with Brit. Royal Air Force, 1947-49. Recipient Alexander Agassiz medal Nat. Acad. Sci., 1973 Fellow Royal Soc. London, AAAS, Royal Soc. Edinburgh, Am. Acad. Arts and Scis. Home: PO Box 25 Woods Hole MA 02543-0025 Office: Woods Hole Oceanographic Inst Woods Hole MA 02543 E-mail: jsteele@whoi.edu.

STEELE, JUDITH MCCONNELL, writer; b. Lamar, Colo., Oct. 5, 1945; d. Taylor and Elva June (Buchtel) McC.; m. Richard M. Steele, Nov. 14, 1975. BA, Cornell Coll., 1967; MA, Northwestern U., 1972. Vol. Peace Corps, Sergipe, Brazil, 1968-70; translator office Project Hope, Rio Grande do Norte, Brazil, 1972; reporter, columnist The Idaho Statesman, Boise, 1978-93; freelance writer fiction, poetry Boise, 1993—. Chair young writers competition IJA Prodns., Boise, 1994, project dir. Fine Line Press, 2007-. Author: Stories From Home, 1989, More Stories From Home, 1993, (anthology) Family, 1998, Woven on the Wind, 2001; collaborative work with Sun Valley Ctr. Arts, 1999, Balance Dance Co., 2003, 09, Dance Forum, 2003; group exhibits with Chris Binion, 1998-99; poetry duet, 2000-2002. Mem. Snake River Writers, Log Cabin Literary Ctr., Acad. Am. Poets.

STEELE, KAREN DORN, journalist; b. Portland, Oreg., Oct. 27, 1943; d. Ronald and Margaret Elizabeth (Cates) Moxness; m. Charles Stuart Dorn, Oct. 30, 1965 (div. Oct. 1982); children: Trilby Constance Elizabeth Dorn, Blythe Estella Dorn; m. Richard Donald Steele, July 4, 1983. BA, Stanford U., 1965; MA, U. Calif., Berkeley, 1967. Prodr. Sta. KSPS-TV, Spokane, Wash., 1970—72, dir. news and pub. affairs, 1972—82; reporter Spokesman-Rev., Spokane, 1982—87, environ./spl. projects reporter, 1987—2005, investigative reporter, 2005—. Contbr. articles to sci. publs. (Olive Br. award NYU Ctr. War, Peace & The Media, 1989). Bd. dirs. Women Helping Women, Spokane, 1994; trustee St. George's Sch., Spokane, 1988-92. Mid-career fellow Stanford Knight Fellowship Program, 1986-87, Arms Control fellow Ctr. for Internat. Security and Arms Control, Stanford U., 1986-87; Japan Travel grant Japan Press Found., Tokyo, 1987, Rsch. grantee John D. and Catherine T. MacArthur Found., 1992; recipient Gerald Loeb award Anderson Sch. Mgmt. UCLA, 1995, George Polk award L.I. U., 1995, William Stokes award U. Mo., 1988, Nat. Headliner award, Excellence in Legal Journalism award Wash. State Bar Assn., 2000, Payne award U. Oreg., 2006; named to State Hall of Journalistic Achievement, Wash. State U., Pullman, 1995. Unitarian Universalist. Office: Spokesman Review 999 W Riverside Ave Spokane WA 99210-2160 Office Phone: 509-459-5462. Business E-Mail: karend@spokesman.com.

STEELE, KENNETH FRANKLIN, JR., hydrologist; b. Statesville, NC, Jan. 16, 1944; s. Kenneth Franklin and Ruth Virginia (Wilhelm) Steele; m. Sheila Kay Stumpf, Sept. 3, 1966 (dec.); children: Krista Robin, Celisa Anne; m. Beth Vaughan-Wrobel, Sept. 24, 2005. BS in Chemistry, U. N.C., 1966, PhD in Geology, 1971. Registered profl. geologist, Ark., registered hydrogeologist Am. Inst. Hydrology. From instr. to prof. geology U. Ark., Fayetteville, 1970—83, prof. emeritus, 2007, dir. Ark. Water Resources Ctr., 1988—2001, prof. emeritus, 2007. Mem. State Bd. Registration for Profl. Geologists, 1992-96, 2000-2004, chmn., 1996, 2002-03, vice chmn., 2001-02; cons. in field. Contbr. numerous articles to profl. jour., chpts. to books; editor: Animal Waste and the Land-Water Interface. Mem. Internat. Order St. Luke the Physician. Summer faculty fellow Oak Ridge Associated Univ., 1981, 83, 85. Mem. Nat. Ground-Water Assn., Internat. Assn. Hydrologists, Am. Inst Hydrology, Assn. Applied Geochemists, Soc. Environ. Geology & Health, Geol. Soc. Am. (regional bd. dir. 1980-82, 84-86), Am. Water Resources Assn. (bd. dirs. 1991-94), Ark. Ground Water Assn. (bd. dir. 1988-90, 93-95, v.p. 1991, pres. 1992), Nat. Assn. Water Inst. Dirs. (counselor 1990-93), Nat. Inst. Water Resources (bd. dir. 1998-2001). Achievements include research on the importance of rainstorms on ground and surface water chemistry in karstic terrain, nitrate and pesticide contamination of ground water, and evolution of ground water chemistry with emphasis on iron and arsenic. Office: U Ark Dept Geoscis 113 Ozark Hall U Ark Fayetteville AR 72701-4040 Home: PO Box 1065 Fayetteville AR 72702 Office Phone: 479-575-7937. Business E-Mail: ksteele@uark.edu.

STEELE, MARK A., pediatric ophthalmologist; b. NYC, May 12, 1960; MD, NYU, 1986. Cert. in ophthalmology 1991. Internship in medicine Lenox Hill Hosp., NYC, 1986—87, hosp. appointment; residency in ophthalmology NYU Med. Ctr., 1987—90, clin assoc. prof., dept. ophthalmology, dir., pediatric ophthalmology and strabismus divsn.; clin. fellowship in pediatric ophthalmology & stabismus Willis Eye Hosp., Phila., 1990—91; attending surgeon NY Eye & Ear Infirmary, NYC; founder Pediatric Ophthalmic Consultants, NYC. Former pres. Greater NY Soc. Pediatric Ophthalmology and Strabismus; complex strabismus cons. NYU Ctr. Craniofacial Anomalies. Contbr. articles to profl. jours. Named to America's Top Doctors, Castle and Connolly Med., Ltd., NY Metro Top Doctors, New York Mag. Office: Pediatric Ophthalmic Consultants 40 W 72nd St New York NY 10023 Office Phone: 212-981-9800. Office Fax: 212-981-9818.

STEELE, MICHAEL S., political organization administrator, former lieutenant governor; b. Oct. 19, 1958; m. Andrea Steele; children: Michael, Drew. Grad., Johns Hopkins U.; JD, Georgetown U., 1991; student, Augustinian Friars Sem. Pvt. law practice; assoc. internat. law firm Cleary, Gottlieb, Steen & Hamilton, Wash., DC, 1991—97; chmn. Rep. Ctrl. Com. for Prince George's County, Md., 1994—2000, Md. Republican Party, 2000—02; lt. gov. State of Md., Annapolis, 2003—07; ptnr. Dewey & LeBoeuf LLP, Washington, 2007—; chmn. GOPAC (Republican Polit. Action Committee), 2007—, Republican Nat. Com. (RNC), Washington, 2009—. Treas., advisor Michele Dyson for Congress, 1994. Host (hour long radio program) WOLB 1010AM, Balt., Md., appeared (numerous radio and TV programs including) Politically Incorrect with Bill Maher, Metro Talk, That Show With Those Black Guys, The Joe Madison Show, Extra, Capitol Sunday, BET Tonight; contbr. columns in newspapers including The Washington Times, The Washington Post, The Baltimore Sun, The Jour. Newspapers. Bd. visitors US Naval Acad., 2002; commr. Nat. Fed. Election Reform Commn.; mem. St. Mary's Cath. Ch., Landover Hills, Md. Named Md. State Republican Man of Yr., Man. of Yr., Ch. cmty., 1998; grantee Rodel Fellowship in Pub. Leadership, Aspen Inst., 2005—07. Mem.: NAACP (served blue ribbon panel on election reform, bd. dirs. hospice of nat. capital area, Prince George's County chpt.), Johns Hopkins U. (bd. trustees), Johns Hopkins Soc. Black Alumni, Term Limits Coalition (chmn. 2000), Truth iN Taxation Com. (hon. co-chmn. 1996), Republican Nat. Convention Phila., Pa. (del. 2000), Republican Nat. Convention San Diego, Calif. (alt. del. 1996), Md. State Minority Outreach Task Force (chmn. 1995—97), Md. State Republican Party Victory Campaigns, Prince George's County Md. Black Republican Coun., Republican Nat. Com. (mem. exec. com.), Knights of Columbus. Republican. Catholic. Office: Republican National Committee 310 First St SE Washington DC 20003 also: Dewey & LeBoeuf LLP 1101 New York Ave, NW Washington DC 20005-4213 Office Phone: 202-346-8027. Office Fax: 202-956-3282. E-mail: msteele@dl.com.*

STEELE, MILDRED ROMEDAHL, educator; b. Boone, Iowa, Jan. 13, 1924; d. Joe and Gladys Madeline (Bonebright/Cree) Romedahl; m. Otto Scott Steele Jr., Sept. 4, 1947; children: Martha Steele Knepper, John Joseph, Timothy Scott. BA, Simpson Coll., 1946; MA, Drake U., 1968; Edn. Specialist, U. Iowa, 1973, PhD, 1982. Instr. Des Moines Area Community Coll., Ankeny, 1972-73, Drake U., Des Moines, 1973, 77; coord. communication Cen. Coll., Pella, Iowa, 1977-90, emerita asst. prof. of English, 1990. Lectr. Iowa Humanities Bd., 1991—; lectr. in field. Co-author: 101 Voices and Guide, 1973; editor: An Iowa Soldier in World War I, 1993, 15 volumes Romedahl Family History (CD-ROMs), 1996; author numerous poems and contbr. numerous articles to profl. jours. Chmn. Higher Edn. and Campus Ministry, Iowa, 1984-88; vice chmn. adminstrv. coun. Pella United Meth. Ch., 1988—, chmn. bd. trustees, 1990-92, cons. to bldg. com.; bd. dirs., bd. fellows Sch. Religion U. Iowa, 1986-88. Recipient Alumni Achievement award Simpson Coll., 1991, Stars in Our Crown award, 1992. Mem. AAUW, Nat. Assn. Devel. Edn. (nat. sec. 1988-90, chmn. 1987-88, exec. bd., Outstanding Svc. award 1988, Nat. Rsch. award 1986, 95), Nat. Simpson Coll. Alumni Bd., Pella Iowa United Methodist Ch., Libr. Memory Otto Steele, 2008, Pi Lambda Theta, Sigma Tau Delta, Delta Delta Delta. Democrat. Office Phone: 402-315-3499.

STEELE, MYRON THOMAS, state supreme court chief justice; b. Taunton, Mass., July 28, 1945; s. Myron Thetus and Coleen Amelia (Polk) Steele; m. Beverly June Heaps, Feb. 4, 1967; children: Clayton Carter, Jenness Farnham. BA, U. Va., 1967, JD, 1970. Bar: Va. 1970, Del. 1970, U.S. Dist. Ct. Del. 1970, U.S. Ct. Appeals (3d cir.) 1974. Assoc. Prickett, Ward, Burt & Sanders, Dover, Del., 1970, 1973, ptnr., 1974; dep. atty. gen. State of Del., 1971—72; v.p., dir. Prickett, Jones, Elliott, Kristol & Schnee, Dover, 1974—88; assoc. judge Superior Ct., 1988—90, res. judge, 1990—94; vice chancellor Ct. Chancery, Del., 1994—2000; justice Del. Supreme Ct., 2000—, chief justice, 2004—. Mem. exec. com. Del. Democratic State Com., 1974—88; bd. dirs. Childrens Bur. Del., Del. News Coun.; chmn. Consumer Affairs Bd., 1974—88, Ctrl. Del. Health Care Corp., 1990—93. Served to 1st. lt. US Army, 1970, col. ret. Del. N.G., 1974—97. Mem.: ABA (mem. jud. liaison comml. and bus. litig. com., bus. sect.), Del-Vets, Commn. on Ct. 2000 (Del.), Kent County Bar Assn. (past pres.), Va. State Bar, Del. Bar Assn. (past v.p.), Kiwanis (past pres.), Rehoboth Beach Country Club, Wilmington Club, Masons. Episcopalian. Office: Del Supreme Ct Carvel State Office Bldg 820 N French St Fl 11 Wilmington DE 19801*

STEELE, RODNEY REDFEARN, judge; b. Selma, Ala., May 22, 1930; s. C. Parker and Miriam Lera (Redfearn) S.; m. Frances Marion Blair, Aug. 1, 1964; children: Marion Scott, Claudia Redfearn, Parker Blair. AB, U. Ala., 1950, MA, 1951; LLB, U. Mich., 1954. Bar: Ala. 1954, U.S. Dist. Ct. (mid. dist.) Ala. 1959, U.S. Ct. Appeals (5th cir., now 11th cir.) 1981. Law clk. Ala. Ct. Appeals, 1956-57; assoc. Knabe & Nachman, Montgomery, Ala., 1957-61; asst. U.S. atty. Dept. Justice, Montgomery, 1961-66; staff atty. So. Bell T&T Co., Atlanta, 1966-67; judge U.S. Bankruptcy Ct., Mid. dist. Ala., Montgomery, 1967—, chief judge, 1985-99; ret., 1999—. Served with U.S. Army, 1954-56, Korea. Mem. ABA, Ala. State Bar, Montgomery County Bar Assn. Democrat. Episcopalian. Home: 1227 Magnolia Curv Montgomery AL 36106-2136

STEELE, SHELBY, writer, educator; b. Chgo., 1946; s. Shelby Sr. and Ruth S. Grad., Coe Loll., 1968; M in Sociology, So. Ill. U., 1971; PhD in English, U. Utah, 1974. Prof. dept English Calif. State U., San Jose; Robert J. and Marion E. Oster sr. fellow Hoover Instn., Stanford, Calif., 1994—. Author: The Content of Our Character: A New Vision of Race in America, 1991 (Nat. Book Critics Circle award 1991), A Dream Deferred: The Second Betrayal of Black Freedom in America, 1998, White Guilt: How Blacks and Whites Together Destroyed the Promise of the Civil Rights Era, 2006, A Bound Man: Why We Are Excited About Obama and Why He Can't Win, 2007 (TV documentary) Seven Days in Bensonhurst (Emmy award, San Francisco Film Festival award); contbr. essays to profl. jours. Recipient Nat. Humanities Medal, 2004, Bradley prize, 2006. Mem.: Ctr. for New Am. Cmty. at Manhattan Inst. (nat. bd.), Univ. Accreditation Assn., Am. Acad. Liberal Edn. (nat. bd.), Nat. Assn. Scholars. Office: Hoover Inst Pub Affairs Stanford Univ Stanford CA 94305-6010

STEELE, VALERIE FAHNESTOCK, museum director, writer, educator; b. Boston, June 29, 1955; d. George S. and Valerie (Noel) S.; m. John Stephen Major, Aug. 25, 1979; 1 child, Stephen Nicholas. BA in History summa cum laude, Dartmouth Coll., 1978; MA, Yale U., 1980, PhD in Modern European Cultural and Intellectual History, 1983. Tchr. fashion history Fashion Inst. Tech. Sch. Grad. Studies, 1985—97; chief curator Mus. at the Fashion Inst. Tech., 1997—2003, acting dir., 2000—03, dir., 2003—. Bd. dirs. Costume Soc. Am., Internat. Assn. for Costume; chair, Fashion Walk of Fame selection com. Fashion Ctr. Bus. Improvement Dist. Author: Fashion and Eroticism, 1985, Paris Fashion, 1988, Women of Fashion, 1991, Fetish: Fashion, Sex & Power, 1996, Fifty Years of Fashion: New Look to Now, 1997, Shoes: A Lexicon of Style, 1999, The Red Dress, 2001, The Corset: A Cultural History, 2001, Fashion, Italian Style, 2003; founding editor: Fashion Theory: The Jour. of Dress, Body & Culture; editor: Men and Women: Dressing the Part, 1989; contbr. articles to profl. pubs. Recipient Iris Found. award for outstanding contbns. to decorative arts, Bard Grad. Ctr., 2002, Artistry of Fashion award, Am. Apparel and Footwear Assn., 2003. Mem. Phi Beta Kappa.

STEELE-GOETEMANN, JUDITH ANN, artist, gallery owner, educator; b. Gloucester, Mass., June 11, 1935; d. Owen Eldred Steele and Elizabeth Verna Lawson; m. Gordon George Goetemann, Dec. 27, 1958; children: Elisabeth, David, Mark, Christopher. AA, Sullins Coll., Bristol, Va., 1955; student, Boston Mus. Sch., 1956, Romano Sch. Art, Gloucester, 1954—55, Evanston Arts Ctr., Chgo., 1966—69; BA in Art and Secondary Edn., Coll. St. Benedict, St. Joseph, Minn., 1974. Instr. spl. art labs. Kennedy Sch., St. Joseph, Minn., 1972—73, tchr. grades 1-3, 1974—75; tchr. grades 9-12 Apollo H.S., St. Cloud, 1976—77; co-dir. European studies St. John's U., St. Joseph, 1983, 1988, 1989, Upper Mid-West Assn. Ind. Colls., St. Paul, 1983, 1984, 1988, 1990; bd. govs. Rockport Art Assoc., 2009. Adj. prof. art Coll. St. Benedict, St. Joseph, 1980—90, St. Johns U., Colleqeville, Minn.; lectr. in field. One-woman shows include St. John's U., 1976, 1989, Blaisdell Pl., Mpls., 1982, Coll. St. Benedict, 1984, 1991, Meridian Hotel, Boston, 1988, Hammond Castle, Gloucester, 1989, U. St. Thomas, 1995, exhibited in group shows at Marshall Field and Co. Gallery, Chgo., 1976, U. Minn., St. Paul, 1977, Augsburg Coll., 1978, Bergen County Mus., NJ, 1980, North Hennepin C.C., Bklyn. Pk., Minn., 1981—82, Women's Art Regional Minn., Mpls., 1982, BFM Gallery, NYC, 1983, 1985, Gallery 702, St. Cloud, 1993, Coll. St. Benedict/St. John's U., 1993, Rockport Art Assn., Mass., 1994 (Excellence in Watercolor award), Nat. Weavers Symposium, Mpls., 1994, exhibitions include Am. Craft Coun., Rhinebeck, NY, 1978, 1980, Notre Dame U., South Bend, Ind., 2005, Bryan Gallery, Rocky, Mass., 2005, 2006, Rocky Neck, 2005, Gloucester Stage Co., 2006, Art in Bloom, Boston Mus. Fine Arts, 2007, Sullins Coll., Bristol, Va., Boston Mus. Sch., others. Critic, juror various schs. and assns., 1976—2000; critic Oddessy of the Mind, St. Cloud, 1996—98; bd. govs. Rockport Art Assn., 2007, Rockport Art Assoc., Mass., 2008—09. Recipient Cerino Meml. prize, 1996, Harriet Wengenroth award, 1996, Cereno Meml. prize, 1997, G.O. Davis award, 1998, W.J. Hibbard Meml. award, 1999, Marguerite Pearson Gold medal, 2006, 2007, 2008, Joyce Pigeon Meml. award, 2008. Mem.: Cape Ann Artisans, Soc. Encouragement of Arts (charter mem.), Rocky Neck Art Colony (mem. exec. bd. 1995—2005). Democrat. Roman Catholic. Office: Goetemann Gallery 37 Rocky Neck Ave Gloucester MA 01930 Office Phone: 978-281-6128. Personal E-mail: goetemanngallery@verison.net.

STEELMAN, FRANK (FRANK SITLEY), lawyer; b. Watsonville, Calif., June 6, 1936; s. Frank S. Sr. and Blossom J. (Daugherty) S.; m. Diane Elaine Duke, June 27, 1960; children: Susan Butler, Robin Thurmond, Joan Bentley, David, Carol Pina. BA, Baylor U., 1958, LLB, 1962. Spl. agt. IRS, Houston, 1962-64, atty. for estate tax, 1964-68; trust officer First City Nat. Bank, Houston, 1968-71; sr. v.p., trust officer First Bank & Trust, Bryan, Tex., 1971-73; assoc. Goode, Skrivanek & Steelman, College Station, Tex., 1973-74; pvt. practice Bryan, 1974—. Vis. lectr. Tex. A&M U., College Station, 1974-75; mcpl. judge City of Bryan, 1986-88. Pres. Brazos Valley Estate Planning Coun., 1973-74, Am. Heart Assn., 1975-76; bd. dirs. Bryan Bus. Coun., 1988-2002, v.p. bd. dirs., 1998-99; bd. dirs. Bryan Devel. Found., 1994-97; mem. Bryan Zoning Bd. Adjustments, 1992-94; v.p. bd. dirs. Bryan Housing Authority, 2005—, commr., 2006—; deacon, mem. ch. choir, Sunday sch. tchr. So. Bapt. Ch. Mem. Rotary (bd. dirs. Bryan club 1973-74). Avocations: walking, golf. Office: 1810 Greenfield Plz Bryan TX 77802-3492 Office Phone: 979-260-9774. Personal E-mail: fssteelman@aol.com.

STEELMAN, SARA GERLING, retired art association administrator; b. Wichita, Kans., Apr. 24, 1946; d. Paul Henry and Amy (Gessner) Gerling; m. John Henry Steelman; 1 child, Amy. BS in Zoology, U. Chgo., 1967; PhD in Behavior Genetics, Stanford U., 1976. Instr. dept. psychology No. Ill. U., DeKalb, 1974-75; instr. Fullerton (Calif.) Jr. Coll., 1976-80; postdoctoral fellow dept. psychobiology U. Calif., Irvine, 1976-80; asst. prof. dept. biology Skidmore Coll., Saratoga Springs, NY, 1980-83; staff writer Saratogian, Saratoga Springs, 1983-86; contbg. writer Indiana Gazette, 1987-93; elected mem. Pa. Ho. of Reps., Harrisburg, 1991—2002; adminstr. Indiana Arts Coun., Indiana, Pa., 2002—06; ret. Contbr. articles to sci. publs. Co-chair com. women in politics Pitts. Inst. Politics, 1993—2002; bd. dirs. Adagio Health, Ind. Libr. Rsch. fellow, Nat. Inst. Aging, 1979—80. Mem.: LWV, AAUW (Notable Woman 1991), Common Cause (state chairperson), New Century Club (treas.). Democrat. Avocations: gardening, music, horseback riding.

STEEN, ELLEN, lawyer; b. Monroe, La., Feb. 26, 1966; d. Willie Hiram and Marilyn Buckley Steen; m. Robert McLean Greer, June 18, 2005; 1 child, Willie Marcus Greer. BA in Internat. Relations, Tulane U., New Orleans, 1984—88; JD, U. NC, Chapel Hill, 1988—91. Bar: NC 1991, US Ct. Appeals, DC 1994, US Ct. Appeals (9th cir.) 2001, US Ct. Appeals (7th and 10th cirs.) 2003, US Ct. Appeals (1st and 6th cir.) 2006, US Supreme Ct. 1998. Assoc. Morgan, Lewis & Bockius, DC, 1991—96; ptnr. Crowell & Moring, LLP, DC, 1996—. Mem.: ABA (sect. of environment, energy & resources, vice-chair agrl. mgmt. com. 2001—), DC Bar Assn. Office: Crowell & Moring LLP 1001 Pennsylvania Ave NW Washington DC 20004 Office Fax: 202-628-5116. Business E-Mail: esteen@crowell.com.

STEEN, JOHN THOMAS, JR., lawyer; b. San Antonio, Dec. 27, 1949; s. John Thomas and Nell (Donnell) S.; m. Ida Louise Clement, May 12, 1979; children: John T. III, Ida Louise Larkin, James Higbie Clement. AB cum laude, Princeton U., NJ, 1971; JD, U. Tex., 1974; Honor grad., US Army Mil. Police Sch., 1974. Bar: Tex. 1974, US Dist. Ct. (we. dist.) Tex. 1976, US Ct. Appeals (5th cir.) 1989. Assoc. Matthews & Branscomb, San Antonio, 1977—82; ptnr. Soules, Cliffe & Reed, San Antonio, 1982—83; sr. v.p., gen. counsel, dir. Commerce Savs. Assn., San Antonio, 1983—88; pvt. practice San Antonio, 1988—. Trustee San Antonio Acad., 1976-81, 87-93, chmn. bd., 1989-91, adv. coun., 1991—; v.p. Bexar County Easter Seal Soc., San Antonio, 1976-77; trustee, vice-chmn. San Antonio C.C. Dist., 1977-82; bd. dirs. Tex. Easter Seal Soc., Dallas, 1977-80, San Antonio Rsch. and Planning Coun., 1978-81, Cmty. Guidance Ctr., 1983-84, Accord Med. Found., 1987-92; vice-chmn. Leadership San Antonio, 1978-79; dir. Fiesta San Antonio Commn., 1982-83, 93-96, 98-2001, 2003—, v.p., 2004-06, pres. 2007-08; commr. Bexar County, San Antonio, 1982, Tex. Commn. on Economy and Efficiency in State Govt., 1985-89; adv. bd. Freeman Coliseum, 1985-91, chmn. bd. 1990-91; pres. San Antonio Performing Arts Assn., 1984-85; trustee World Affairs Coun. San Antonio, 1982—, chmn. bd., 1984-86, disting. leaders coun., 2009-; trustee United Way, San Antonio, 1985-92, Tex. Cavaliers Charitable Found., 1994-97, 2003-05, Austin Coll., 1996-2001; bd. dirs. Houston Livestock Show and Rodeo; adv. bd. U. Tex., San Antonio, 1987—, vice chmn., 2008-; exec. com. chancellor's coun. U. Tex. Sys., 2005—; active Pan-Tex. Assembly, 1985-2002; chmn. Tex. Alcoholic Beverage Commn., 2003-08, commr., 1998-2008; commr. Tex. Dept. Pub. Safety, 2008-; exec. com. Rep. Eagles, 2000-01; hon. dir. San Antonio Livestock Exposition, Inc.; bd. dirs. Fiesta Commn. Charitable Corp., 2004-09, chmn. and pres., 2007-08. 1st lt. USAR. Named Chevalier Confrérie de Chevaliers du Tastevin, Sous-Commanderie de So. Tex., 1994—; Philanthropy award, Tex. Assn. Against Sexual Assault, 2007. Fellow San Antonio Bar Found., Tex. Bar Found. (life); mem. Tex. Bar Assn., San Antonio Acad. Alumni Assn. (pres. 1976-77, Disting. Alamnus award 2009), Ivy Club (Princeton, NJ), San Antonio German Club (pres. 1982-83), Order of Alamo, Order of Cascaron, Tex. Cavaliers (bd. dirs. 1989-92, 94-97, comdr. 1994-95, King Antonio LXXIV 1996-97, Kings coun. 1997—, vice chmn. 2003-04, chmn. 2004-05), San Antonio Country Club (bd. govs. 1990-93, v.p. 1992-93), Argyle Club, Conopus Club (bd. dirs. 1989-90), Princeton Club San Antonio and South Tex. (pres. 1980-81), Maclean Soc. at Princeton U., Sons of Republic of Tex. (life), Phi Delta Phi. Republican. Presbyterian. Home: 601 Garraty Rd San Antonio TX 78209-6148 Office: 300 Convent St Ste 2440 San Antonio TX 78205-3722 Office Phone: 210-224-7700.

STEEN, LYNN ARTHUR, mathematician, educator; b. Chgo., Jan. 1, 1941; s. Sigvart J. and Margery (Mayer) S.; m. Mary Elizabeth Frost, July 7, 1940; children: Margaret, Catherine. BA, Luther Coll., 1961; PhD, MIT, 1965; DSc (hon.), Luther Coll., 1986, Wittenberg U., 1991, Concordia Coll., Minn., 1996. Prof. math. St. Olaf Coll., Northfield, Minn., 1965—2009. Vis. scholar Inst. Mittag-Leffler, Djursholm, Sweden, 1970-71; writing fellow Conf. Bd. Math. Sci., Washington, 1974-75; exec. dir. Math. Sci. Edn. Bd., Washington, 1992-95; spl. asst. to provost St. Olaf Coll. Author: Counterexamples in Topology, 1970, Everybody Counts, 1989; editor: Mathematics Today, 1978, On the Shoulders of Giants, 1990, Math. Mag., 1976-80, Why Numbers Count, 1997, Mathematics and Democracy, 2001, Achieving Quantitative Literacy, 2004, Math and Biology 2010, 2005; contbg. editor: Sci. News, 1976-82. NSF Sci. faculty fellow, 1970-71, Danforth Found. grad. fellow, 1961-65. Fellow AAAS (sec. math. sect. 1982-88); mem. Am. Math. Soc., Math. Assn. Am. (pres. 1985-86, Disting. Svc. award 1992), Coun. Sci. Soc. Pres. (chmn. 1989), Sigma Xi (Bd. Dirs. Spl. award 1989). Home: 716 Saint Olaf Ave Northfield MN 55057-1523 Office: St Olaf Coll Dept of Math Northfield MN 55057 E-mail: steen@stolaf.edu.

STEEN, PAUL JOSEPH, retired broadcasting executive; b. Williston, ND, July 4, 1932; s. Ernest B. and Inez (Ingebrigtson) S.; m. Judith Smith; children— Michael M., Melanie. BA, Pacific Luth. U., 1954; MS, Syracuse U., 1957. Producer, dir. Sta. KNTV, San Jose, Calif., 1957-58, Sta. KVIE, Sacramento, 1958-60; asst. prof. telecommunications Pacific Luth. U., Tacoma, 1960-67; dir. ops. Sta. KPBS San Diego State U., 1967-74; gen. mgr., 1974-93; prof. telecommunications and film, 1974-93; dir. univ. telecommunications. Co-chmn. Office of New Tech. Initiatives. Dir. (tel. program) Troubled Waters (winner Nat. Ednl. TV award of excellence 1970). With AUS. Named Danforth Assoc. Mem. Pacific Mountain Network (bd. dirs., chmn., bd. of govs. award 1993), NATAS, Assn. Calif. Pub. TV Stas. (pres.), San Diego County Sr. Golf Assn. (past pres.), Pi Kappa Delta. Home: 6068 Caminito De La Taza San Diego CA 92120-5323 Business E-Mail: psteen@mail.sdsu.edu.

STEENBURGEN, MARY, actress; b. Newport, Ark., Feb. 8, 1953; m. Malcolm McDowell, 1980 (div. 1990); children: Lilly, Charlie; m. Ted. Danson, Oct. 7, 1995. Student, Neighborhood Playhouse. Films: Goin' South, 1978, Time After Time, 1979, Melvin and Howard, 1980 (Academy award best supporting actress 1981), Ragtime, 1981, A Midsummer Night's Sex Comedy, 1982, Cross Creek, 1983, Romantic Comedy, 1983, One Magic Christmas, 1985, Dead of Winter, 1987, End of the Line, 1987 (also exec. prodr.), The Whales of August, 1987, Miss Firecracker, 1989, Parenthood, 1989, Back to the Future III, 1990, The Long Walk Home, 1990 (narrator), The Butcher's Wife, 1991, Philadelphia, 1993, What's Eating Gilbert Grape, 1993, Clifford, 1994, It Runs in the Family, 1994, Pontiac Moon, 1994, Powder, 1995, Nixon, 1995, My Family, 1995, The Grass Harp, 1995, About Sarah, 1995, Trumpet of the Swan (voice), 1999, Life as a House, 2001, I Am Sam, 2001, Sunshine State, 2002, Wish You Were Dead, 2002, Hope Springs, 2003, Casa de los babys, 2003, Elf, 2003, Marilyn Hotchkiss Ballroom Dancing & Charm School, 2005, Inland Empire, 2006, The Dead Girl, 2006, Elvis and Anabelle, 2007, Nobel Son, 2007, Numb, 2007, The Brave One, 2007, Honeydripper, 2007, Step Brothers, 2008, Four Christmases, 2008, The Proposal, 2009; appeared in Showtime TV's Faerie Tale Theatre prodn. of Little Red Riding Hood and (miniseries) Tender Is the Night, 1985, Gulliver's Travels, 1996;, (miniseries) Noah's Ark, 1999, Living with the Dead, 2002; TV series: Ink, 1996, Joan of Arcadia, 2003-; TV films: The Attic: The Hiding of Anne Frank, 1988, About Sarah, 1998, Picnic, 2000, Nobody's Baby, 2001, It Must Be Love, 2004, Capital City, 2004; theater appearances include: Holiday, Old Vic, London, 1987, Candida, Broadway, 1993. Nat. spokesperson Elizabeth Glaser Pediatric AIDS Found. Office: c/o The Gersh Agy 232 N Canon Dr Beverly Hills CA 90210*

STEEN-HINDERLIE, DIANE EVELYN, social worker, musician; b. Duluth, Minn., June 13, 1947; d. Julian Sem and Evelyn Synnove (Helgaas) Steen; m. John Peter Hinderlie, June 27, 1971 (div. Sept. 1987); children: Peder Donald, Erik Steen; m. John Richard Olson, July 21, 1989. BA in Asian Studies/Social Psychology cum laude, St. Olaf Coll., 1969; MusB, U. Minn. and other instns., 1991; postgrad., Hamline U., 1989—91. Lic. social worker, Minn.; cert. music tchr. Music Tchrs. Nat. Assn. Social worker child care licensing Hennepin County Welfare Dept., Mpls., 1970—73; mem. clergy team exch. program Luth. World Fedn., Göppingen, Germany, 1973—77; mem. clergy team, music dir. Jubilation Singers Bethel Luth. Ch., Rochester, Minn., 1978—83; mem. clergy team, music dir. youth choir First Luth. Ch., St. Louis Park, Minn., 1983—86; adminstr. Family Child Care facility, St. Louis Park, 1986—90; faculty, tchr. Stenson Suzuki Studios and Home Studio, St. Louis Park, 1988—92; small group leader, tchr. vol. Mt. Olive Ch., Children's Hosp., Mpls., 1993, 1996—98; workshop and children's ministry Augsburg Coll. Youth and Family Inst., Trinity Cong., 1998—; founding dir. Fair Pay Inst., Mpls., 1995—; trainer United for a Fair Economy, 1997—. Founder orgn. and curriculum Early Childhood Orgn. for Edn. with Singing, 1993—, co-leader German-Am. youth group exch., 1979-82; co-founder Family DayCare Cert. Program and Babygarten (B-12 edn.) classes, 1970-73; bd. dirs. Midwest Coun., Nat. Peace Inst. Found., Grinnell, Iowa, 1991; presenter in field.; root causes of violence action team Initiative for Violence-Free Families, 4th Jud. Dist. Minn., 1997—; cons. Concordia Lang. Villages, 2005—. Author: (tng.

manual) Mother Tongue Singing/Voice Method, 1988, (study packet) School Start Time/Teen Sleep Deprivation, 1996-97, A+=Baby Church School, 2002; rec. artist, mem. ensemble record/cassettes Nowell Sing We, 1986; performer Nordic Am. Psalmodikon Forbundet, 1997—. Vol. People of Faith Peacemakers, Feminists in Faith/ReImagining and Jewish Cmty. Rels. Coun., 1992-2003, Muslim-Christian Rels. Coun., Joint Religious Legis. Coalition, Bread for the World; founder People for Reforming Early Start Time for Teens Orgn., Mpls., 1993—; mem. steering com. Progressive Cmty. and FairVote, Minn., 1994-99; local host youth com. NAACP Conv., Mpls., 1995; vol. Common Cause, St. Paul and Washington; charter mem. US Holocaust Mus., 1993; co-founder antitorture com. Women Against Mil. Madness, 2005. Recipient appreciation plaque Christian Boy/Girl Scouts Germany; Svc. pin Am. Luth. Ch. Women; listed in Minn. Profiles, Minn. Hist. Soc. A Tribute to Outstanding Minn. Women by Marilyn Chelstrom, 2001; named Asset Builder of Month, St. Louis Park Children First Initiative, 1997; named to Honor Roll, Mendota Mdewakanton Dakota Cmty., 1999. Mem.: MADD, Minn. Music Tchrs. Assn. (first early childhood music chair 2001—03), Assn. Pre- and Perinatal Psychology and Health, Wash. Nat. Cathedral, Soc. for Psychol. Studies of Social Issues, Nat. Luth. Choir Acad., Suzuki Assn. Americas (study area co-organizer, editl. adviser), Internat. Suzuki Assn., Nat. Assn. Tchrs. Singing and VoiceCare Network, UN Assn., Sojourner Project, Inc., Am.'s Jr. Miss. Coun., World Wildlife Fund, Ctr. for Victims of Torture, Minn. Parenting Assn., Amnesty Internat., Nat. Peace Found., Germanic-Am. Inst., Sons of Norway (lodge trustee 1991—), Phi Beta Kappa, Am. Mensa. Green. Lutheran. Avocations: reading, political activism, concerts, travel, memory albums. Office: Fair Pay Inst PO Box 16031 Minneapolis MN 55416-0031

STEENLAND, DOUGLAS M., former air transportation executive; b. 1951; married; 2 children. BA in History, Calvin Coll., 1973; JD, George Washington U., 1976. Sr. ptnr. Verner, Liipfert, Bernhard, McPherson and Hand, Washington; v.p., dep. gen. counsel Northwest Airlines Corp., Eagan, Minn., 1991—94, sr. v.p., gen. counsel, 1994—98, exec. v.p., gen. counsel & alliances, 1998—99, exec. v.p., chief corp. officer, 1999—2001, pres., 2001—04, pres., CEO, 2004—08. Bd. dirs. Northwest Airlines Corp., 2001—08, MAIR Holdings, Inc., 2004—05, Delta Air Lines, Inc., 2008—, Chrysler Group LLC, 2009—, Am. Internat. Group, Inc. (AIG), 2009—. Bd. dirs. The Guthrie Theater, The Minn. Symphony Orch.; mem. Super Bowl XL-Detroit 2006 Host Com.*

STEENSGAARD, ANTHONY HARVEY, federal agency administrator; b. Rapid City, SD, Mar. 21, 1963; s. Harvey Hans and Dorothy Lorraine (Hansen) S. Student, Ft. Mead Vocat. Inst., 1974—75, U. SD, 1978—80, Anchorage CC, 1983—84; degree, US MC Res., Quantico, Va., 1984; BSCE, U. Alaska, 1985, BS in Petroleum Engring., 2006; student, Northwestern U., 1986; AAS in Indsl. Security, CC Air Force, 1989; BS in Criminal Justice, Wayland U., 1989; MS in Computer Systems Engring., U. Calif., San Diego, 1996; LLD in Criminal Law, Trinity Coll.-Oxford U., Eng., 2000, PhD in Computer Engring., 2000; BSc in Criminal Psychology, Rusland Coll., 2003. Lic. pilot, amateur radio operator; lic. sec. specialist Alaska, 1985; cert. hostage negotiator FBI, FBI Nat. Acad., Va., 1987; Fed. Air Marshal Sch., FAA; cert. Instr. Am. Soc. Protection Profls., 1986—, Unified Command System, 2007, fed. emergency mgmt. agy. level III incident comdr., Fed. Law Enforcement Tng. Ctr., Brunswick, 1987, security specialist, 2001—, info. security specialist, intelligence and surveillance profl., 2001—, dept. def. info. security mgr. and auditor, 1986; criminal investigator USAF, 1985-2008, investigator, Nat. Trans. Safety Bd., 1992-2008; US Border Patrol Acad., Class 227, Brunswick, Ga. Bookseller B. Dalton Bookseller, Rapid City, 1978—81, Anchorage, 1981—83; warehouseman Sears, Roebuck & Co., Anchorage, 1983—85; air res. technician Alaska Air N.G., Anchorage, 1985—88; agt., draftsman, engr., asst. intelligence officer US Border Patrol, El Centro, Calif., 1988—; mil. liaison Def.-Law Enforcement Assistance Program, 2004; spl. agt. Dept. Homeland Security, 2004—. Cons. US Navy Fighter Weapons Sch., 1994-98, fed. counter terrorism, 2001—, fed. info. warfare, 2001—, computer, 1994-2000, Euro-fighter Typhoon Project Simulator, 1996-1998, US Space Command, 1998-2001; spl. response team leader US Dept. Def. Counter Terrorism Task Force, LA, 1988-2003; spl. cons. Fed. Bur. Investigation, Hayward Field Office, Task Force 2, Calif., 1998-2003; instr. USN Jr. Res. Officers Tng. Program, Alaska, 1981-83; computer criminal investigator, 1999—; CEO Totalwarfare.com webzine, 1997—, Gunfighters.net, 1994-, Virtual Options, Internet Contract Agts., 2006-; founding assoc. Amazon.com.; technical support working group, technical support officer Dept. Homeland Security, 2002—; intelligence officer US Coast Guard Auxiliary, 2003-08; founding mem. US Dept. Homeland Security, 2003, founder VF-124 Gunfighters Flight Simulation Tng. & Design Team, fellow Tech. Entertainment Design, 2007. Author: Unit Security Manager's Guide Book, 1988, Space Fighter Tactics and Manuever, 2008. Vol. Spl. Olympics, Rapid City, 1981; pilot Civil Air Patrol, Rapid City, SD, 1980, navigator, observer Anchorage, 1981; mentor Municipality Anchorage Sch. Dist., 1983—84; mem. Alaska Peace Officer's Assn., 1986—89, Calif. Law Enforcement Officers Assn., 1989—96; sr. pilot Civil Air Patrol, Rapid City, 1996, pub. affairs officer, 1996—98, aerospace edn. officer, 1998—2000, wing dir. aerospace edn., 2000—04; aviator, aircraft navigator US Coast Guard Aux., 2003—08; umpire Little League Baseball, Elcentro, Calif., 1989—92; mem. Boy Scouts America, Order of Arrow, Crazy Horse Chpt., SD, 1976; competitor rifles, standing archery, track and field 29th Nat. Vets. Wheelchair Games; vol. US Senator George McGovern's Campaign, Rapid City, 1980, Senator Tom Daschle's Campaign, Rapid City, 1980. With USNR, 1980—81, with USMCR, 1981—85, with USAFR, 1985—98, with Operation Desert Shield, 1990, with Operation Desert Storm, 1991, with Operation Provide Comfort, 1991, with Operation Liberty Shield, 2002, with Operation Enduring Freedom, 2001—03, with USAR, 2001—05. Recipient Hon. Sci. award Bausch and Lomb, 1984, Alaska Air Nat. Guardsman of the Yr., 1986, 1987, commendation State of Alaska, 1987, 2d commendation, 1988, Brigadier Gen. Charles E. Yeager Aerospace Achievement award, 2000, Blanchard trophy, 1990, Afghanistan royal Oder Almara el Ala, 2003, Freedom Team Commendation, US Army, 2005, Svc. award, US Dept. Justice, named Alaska Nat. Guardsman of Yr., 1987. Fellow TED, 2007, N.Am. Acad. Arts and Sci.; mem. DAV (life), Am. Chem. Soc., US Cavalry Assn. (heritage mem.), HTML Writer's Guild, Am. Legion, Air Force Assn., VFW, Fraternal Order Eagles, SD Sheriff's Assn., Fraternal Order of Police, Nat. Border Patrol Coun., Virtual Geog. League, WWII Meml. Soc. (charter mem.), US Naval Inst., US Coast Guard Inst., Nat. D-Day Mus. Found., Nat. WWII Mus. (founding mem.), USMC Heritage Found. (founding mem.), Adventurer's Club, Paralyzed Vet. America (life), Am. Inst. Pub. Svc. (Jefferson award 2007), US Border Patrol Mus., Nat. Geographic Soc., Nat. Soc. Pershing Rifles, West River Electric Assn., Chugach Electric Assn., Pennington County (SD) (sheriff candidate), USA Para Olympic Team, Phi Beta Kappa. Avocations: reading, flight simulations, aviation, history, board games, bowling, languages. Office: US Border Patrol Dept Homeland Security 1300 Pennsylvania Ave NW Washington DC 20229 Office Phone: 202-344-1780. Personal E-mail: ahsteensgaard@juno.com.

STEEPLES, DOUGLAS WAYNE, retired university dean, consultant, researcher; b. Great Bend, Kans, Mar. 30, 1935; s. Marion Wayne and Dorothy Augusta (King) S.; children from previous marriage: Donald Bruce, John Douglas, Sheila Margaret; m. Christine Marie MacKinnes Webster, Dec. 8, 1990. BA summa cum laude, U. Redlands, 1957; MA, U.N.C., 1958, PhD, 1961; cert., Inst. Ednl. Mgmt., Harvard U., 1981. Asst. prof. history Calir. State U., North Ridge, 1961—64; prof. history Earlham Coll., Richmond, Ind., 1963-80; acad. v.p. Wartburg Coll., Waverly, Iowa, 1979-80; exec. v.p. Westminster Coll., Salt Lake City, 1980-83; provost Ohio U., Delaware, Ohio, 1983-85, acting pres., winter 1984; dean Coll. Liberal and Fine Arts, U. So. Colo., Pueblo, Colo., 1985-89; v.p. for acad. affairs Aurora U., Ill., 1989—93, v.p. acad. planning, 1993—94; dean, prof. history Coll. Liberal Arts, Mercer U., Macon, Ga., 1994-2000, ret., 2000; proctor, participant clin. practice program Mercer U. Med. Sch., Macon, 2005—. Cons. higher edn. mgmt.; cons., reader advanced placement program Ednl. Testing Svc., Princeton, NJ, 1976-93; cons., evaluator North Ctrl. Assn. Sch. and Coll., Chgo., 1985-1994; mem. Accreditation Rev. Commn., 1992-94; bd. dirs. Western Ind. Coll. Fund, Salt Lake City, 1980-83; bd. dirs. Am. Conf. Acad. Deans, 1995-2000, sec.-treas., 1998-99; trustee Econ. and Bus. Hist. Soc., 1995-2000, pres., 1998-99; bd. dirs. Associated New Am. Colls., 1994-00. Editor, contbg. author: Institutional Revival: Case Histories, 1986, Successful Strategic Planning: Case Studies, 1989, Mng. Change in Higher Ed., 1990, Treasure from the Painted Hills: Calico Calif., 1882-1907, 1999; (with David O. Whitten) Democracy in Desperation: The Depression in the 1890s, 1998 (Choice Mag. Acad. Book of Yr. award); editor John Randolph Spears, Illustrated Sketches of Death Valley, 2000, Advocate for Am. Enterprise: William Buck Dana and the Commercial and Fin. Chronicle, 1865-1910, 2001; assoc. editor Bus. Libr. Rev., 1996-2001; occational columnist for Macon Telegraph; contbr. over 50 articles to profl. jours.; contbr. over 100 book revs. Adv. bd. Pueblo Symphony Orch., 1987—89; allocations com. United Way, Richmond, 1976—79, Pueblo, 1988—89, Aurora, 1990—94; vol. in svc., spl. cons. to pres. Ho-Chunk Wis./ Winnebago Nation, 2001; mem. Mayor's Commn. on Restoration of Ft. Hawkins, Macon, Ga., 1997—; pipe maj. Mercer U. Pipes and Drums, 2002—06, pipe sgt., 2006—; chmn. Eagle Scouts Troop Com.; scoutmaster Eagle Scouts, dist. scout committeeman; neighborhood commr. wood badge Eagle Scouts Lurit Commr., 2008—; pres. Luth. Inter-parish Coun., Richmond, 1975—78; bd. dir. Soc. for Use and Preservation of Resources, Richmond, 1976—79. Scholar U. Redlands, Calif., 1953-57; Danforth fellow, 1957-61; Woodrow Wilson fellow, 1957-58; Found. for Econ. Edn. fellow in bus., 1963; Am. Philos. Soc. grantee, 1966 Mem. Am. Hist. Assn., Orgn. Am. Hist., So. Hist. Assn., Soc. for Values in Higher Edn., Sierra Club, Rotary (bd. dirs. 1983-84), Palaver Club, Phi Beta Kappa (senator united chpt. 1973-79, sec.-treas. mid-Ga. alumni assoc. 1996-2000, pres. 2003-04), Omicron Delta Kappa, Phi Kappa Phi, Alpha Mu Gamma. Republican. Avocations: mountain climbing, running, bagpiping. Office: 656 River North Blvd Macon GA 31211-6340 Office Phone: 478-750-1051. E-mail: douglassteeples@aol.com.

STEERE, ALLEN CARUTHERS, JR., physician, educator; b. Apr. 11, 1943; m. Margaret Mercer, 1969; children: Allen Caruthers III, Margaret Hamilton, Samuel Mercer, John Summers. BA, Columbia U., 1965, MD, 1969; DSc. (hon.), Indiana U., 1992, SUNY, 1997; DSc (hon.), Ohio Wesleyan U., 2008; M (hon.), Harvard Med. Sch., 2002. Diplomate Am. Bd. Internal Medicine; lic. rheumatologist, N.Y., Ga., Ct., Mass. Intern St. Luke's Hosp., NYC, 1969-70, asst., sr. resident, 1970-72, chief resident, instr. medicine, 1972-73; chief resident, instr. medicine Coll. Physicians and Surgeons Columbia U., NYC, 1972-73; clin. fellow in rheumatology Yale U., New Haven, 1975-77, asst. prof. medicine, epidemiology and pub. health, 1977-81, assoc. prof. medicine, 1981-87; prof. medicine, chief rheumatology and immunology New Eng. Med. Ctr. Tufts U., Boston, 1987—2002, Natalie V. & Milton O. Zucker prof. rheumatology/immunology, 1998—2002; prof. medicine Harvard Med. Sch., Boston, 2002—; dir. rheumatology Mass. Gen. Hosp., 2002—06, dir. clin. rsch. in rheumatology, 2006—. With USPHS, 1973-75. Recipient Citation for Elucidation of Lyme disease, Infectious Diseases Soc. Am., 1984, Ciba-Geigy Rheumatology prize, Internat. League Against Rheumatism, 1985, award for discovery of Lyme disease, Nat. Inst. Arthritis and Musculoskeletal Skin Diseases, 1988, Richard and Hinda Rosenthal award, ACP, 1990, Joseph Mather Smith prize, Coll. Physicians and Surgeons, Columbia U., 1990, Zucker Faculty prize, Tufts U., 1990, award for studies Lyme disease, Nat. Health Coun., 1990, Lee C. Howley Sr. prize, Arthritis Found., 1993, Gold medal, Albert Sabin Vaccine Inst., 1998, Astute Clinician award, NIH, 1999, award, Am. Lyme Disease Found., 2000, Columbia Coll. of Phys. and Surgeon's Alumni award for Disting. Acad. Accomplishment, 2001, Physician Achievement award, Artist Found.(Mass. Chapt.), 2006. Master Am. Coll. Rheumatology (Howard and Martha Holley rsch. prize in rheumatology 1995); mem. Am. Soc. Clin. Investigation, Am. Fedn. Clin. Rsch., Assn. Am. Physicians, Clin. Immunology Soc. Office: Mass Gen Hosp 55 Fruit St CNY 149/8301 Boston MA 02114

STEFANI, GWEN RENEE, singer; b. Anaheim, Calif., Oct. 3, 1969; d. Dennis and Patti Stefani; m. Gavin McGregor Rossdale, Sept. 14, 2002; children: Kingston James McGregor, Zuma Nesta Rock. Student, Calif. State U., Fullerton. Singer No Doubt, 1986—. Designer, creator fashion line L.A.M.B. (Love. Angel. Music. Baby.), 2004—; launched toy doll line (8 dolls) Love. Angel. Music. Baby. Fashion Dolls, 2006. Singer: (albums with No Doubt) No Doubt, 1992, Tragic Kingdom, 1995, Beacon Street Collection, 1995, Collector's Orange Crate, 1997, Return of Saturn, 2000, Rock Steady, 2001 (Grammy awards: Best Pop Performance By A Duo Or Group With Vocal for song "Hey Baby", 2002, Best Pop Performance By A Duo Or Group With Vocal for song "Underneath it All", 2003), The Singles 1992-2003, 2004, Everything In Time, 2005, (solo albums) Love, Angel, Music, Baby, 2004, The Sweet Escape, 2006, (songs) Just A Girl, Spiderwebs, Don't Speak, 1995, Simple Kind of Life, 2000, Hella Good, Hey Baby, Underneath It All, 2001, It's My Life, 2003 (MTV Video Music award Best Group Video, 2004, MTV Video Music award Best Pop Video, 2004), Hollaback Girl, 2005 (Billboard awards, Digital Song of Yr., 2005), (with Moby) South Side, 1999, (with eve) Let Me Blow Your Mind, 2001 (Grammy award, Best Rap/Song Collaboration, 2001); actor: (films) Zoolander, 2001, The Aviator, 2004, (voice only): (TV appearances) King of the Hill, 2001, (TV guest appearances) Saturday Night Live, 1996, 2001, Mad TV, 2000, Dawson's Creek, 2002. Recipient Best Choreography In a Video for Hollaback Girl, MTV Video Music Awards, 2005, Best Art Direction In a Video for What You Waiting For?, Favorite Female Artist, Am. Music Awards, 2005, New Artist of Yr., Billboard Music Awards, 2005, Best-Selling New Female Artist, World Music Awards, 2005; named Favorite Female Singer, People's Choice Awards, 2008; named one of The 100 Most Powerful Celebrities, Forbes.com, 2008. Office: c/o David Schiff Schiff Co 9465 Wilshire Blvd #480 Beverly Hills CA 90212

STEFANOVIC, MARGARETA, science educator; d. Predrag and Branislava Stefanovic. MS in Elec. Engring., U. So. Calif., LA, 2002, PhD in elec. Engring., 2005. Post doctoral rschr. U. So. Calif., 2005; asst. prof. U. Wyo., Laramie, 2005—. Contbr. articles to profl. jours. Charles L. Powell engring. doctoral fellowship, U. So. Calif., 2000—04. Mem.: IEEE. Achievements include research in control systems. Office: U of Wyo Dept 3295 1000 E University Ave Laramie WY 82071 Business E-Mail: mstefano@uwyo.edu.

STEFANSKI, EDWARD A., professional sports team executive; b. Mar. 23, 1954; m. Karen A. Stefanski; children: Edward Jr., Kevin, Matthew, David. Grad., U. Pa., 1976. Pres. Preferred Mortgages Corp.; head basketball coach Monsignor Bonner HS, Drexel Hill, Pa., 1979—83; color analyst Big Five Basketball, 1979—90; Atlantic 10 color analyst ESPN, 1988—99; dir. scouting NJ Nets, 1999—2003, sr. v.p. basketball ops., 2003—04, gen. mgr., 2004—07, Phila. 76ers, 2007—. Mailing: c/o Phila 76ers 1st Union Ctr Philadelphia PA 19148*

STEFANYSHYN-PIPER, HEIDEMARIE M., astronaut; b. St. Paul, Feb. 7, 1963; d. Michael and Adelheid Stefanyshyn; m. Glenn A. Piper; 1 child. BS in Mech. Engring., MIT, 1984, MS in Mech. Engring., 1985. Tng. as Navy basic diving officer and salvage officer Naval Diving and Salvage Tng. Ctr., Panama City, Fla.; several tours of duty as an engring. duty officer in area of ship repair and maintenance; underwater ship husbandry ops. officer for the supr. of salvage and diving Naval Sea Systems Command; astronaut, mission specialist NASA Johnson Space Ctr., 1996—. Crew mem., will perform spacewalks Space Shuttle Atlantis (STS-115), 2006; crew mem. STS-126 Endeavour Mission, 2008. Recipient Meritorious Svc. medal, Navy Commendation medal (2), Navy Achievement medal (2). Mem.: Am. Soc. Mech. Engineers. Achievements include being the first woman to be assigned as lead spacewalker for a shuttle flight on STS-126 mission in 2008. Avocations: scuba diving, swimming, running, rollerblading, ice skating. Office: Astronaut Office CB NASA Lyndon B Johnson Space Ctr Houston TX 77058*

STEFFEN, CAROLYN MCKINNIS, biology professor; m. Alan Deane Steffen (div.); children: Dewey Deane, Charlotte. BS, Appalachian State U., Boone, NC, 1966; MS, Mich. Technol. U., Houghton, 1974; PhD, Wayne State U., Detroit, 1985. Cert. in tchg. Appalachian State U., 1966. Biology tchr. Cochrane Jr. HS, Charlotte, NC, 1966—68, Am. Dependents, Def. Dept., Vicenza, Italy, 1968—71; biology prof. Schoolcraft Coll., Livonia, Mich., 1975—. Grad. tchg. asst. Mich. Technol. U., 1971—74. Author (with McGraw Hill): (collegiate book) Biology, A Basic Review; author: (with Kendall Hunt) Biology, The Study of Life; contbr. articles to profl. publs. Mem. Religion Kirk Hills, Bloomfield Hills, Mich., 2003—09. Recipient Presdl. award, Schoolcraft Coll., 1990; named Men's Golf Team Coach of Yr., MCCAA, 2002. Mem.: ASM, Christ Child Soc. Avocation: golf. Office: Schoolcraft Coll 18600 Haggerty Rd Livonia MI 48152 Business E-Mail: csteffen@schoolcraft.edu.

STEFFEN, JASON H., astrophysicist; b. Calif., May 15, 1975; s. David and Thail Steffen; m. Faith A. Kimball; children: James, Michael. BS in Physics and Math., Weber State U., Ogden, Utah, 2000; MS in Physics, U. Wash., Seattle, 2003, PhD in Physics, 2006. Embedded software engr. L-3 Comm., Salt Lake City, 2000—01; Brinson postdoc. fellow Fermilab Ctr. Particle Astrophysics, Batavia, Ill., 2006—. Mem.: Am. Astron. Soc. Mem. Lds Ch.

STEFFEN, LLOYD HOWARD, minister, religious studies educator; b. Racine, Wis., Nov. 27, 1951; s. Howard C. and Ruth L. (Rode) S.; m. Emmajane S. Finney, Feb. 14, 1981; children: Nathan, Samuel, William. BA, New Coll., 1973; MA, Andover Newton Theol. Sch., 1978; MDiv, Yale U., 1978; PhD, Brown U., 1984. Ordained to ministry United Ch. of Christ, 1983. Chaplain Northland Coll., Ashland, Wis., 1983-90, assoc. prof., 1982-90, Lehigh U., Bethlehem, Pa., 1990-97, chaplain, 1990—, prof., 1997—, chair dept. religion studies, 2000—06, dir., ctr. dialogue, ethics & spirituality, 2009—; co-dir. Mellon Global Citizenship, 2003—04. Mem. theol. com. Wis. Conf. United Ch. of Christ, Madison, 1985—87; mem. div. ch. and ministry NW assn. Wis. Conf., Eau Claire, 1987—90; mem. ecumenical commn. Penn N.E. Conf., 1994—96; mem. Common Ground, Bethlehem, Pa., 1994—97, chair, 1995—97; mem. ch. and ministry com. Pa. Northeast Conf., 1997—2000; mem. ethics com. St. Luke's Hosp., Bethlehem, Pa., 1998—; mem., sec., vice chair, bd. dirs. Religious Coalition for Reproductive Choice, 2002—; non-govtl. orgn. rep. UN, 2002—, sec., 2005—; 10th Curtis Lectr. Sacred Heart Univ., 1999; Frederick C. Wood Lectr. Cornell U., 2002; mem. instl. rev. bd. Haverford Coll., 2005—; Tiefel lectr. Coll. William & Mary, 2008. Author: Self-Deception and the Common Life, 1986, Life/Choice: The Theory of Just Abortion, 1994, Abortion: A Reader, 1996, Executing Justice: The Moral Meaning of the Death Penalty, 1998, 2d edit., 2006, The Demonic Turn: The Power of Religion to Inspire or Restrain Violence, 2003, Holy War, Just War: Exploring the Moral Meaning of Religious Violence, 2007; contbr. articles to profl. jours. Town supr. Town of La Pointe, Wis., 1984-87; bd. dirs. Justice Witness Ministries, United Ch. of Christ, 2006- Recipient 1st Pilgrim Press Church and Soc. Book award, 2001, NEH Inst. award, Harvard U., 1988, East-West Ctr., 1995, Mlking award Dedication and Commitment to Svc., Lehigh U., 2009; fellow, Brown U., 1982; faculty devel. grant, Northland Coll., 1986, faculty devel. grantee, 1990, Lehigh U., 1994, 1998, 2003, Travel grant, Ford Found., 2004, Mellon Global Citizenship grant, Japan, 2003. Mem. Soc. Christian Ethics, Am. Acad. Religion, Assocs. for Religion and Intellectual Life, Assn. for Coordination of Univ. Religious Affairs. Home: 1349 Woodland Cir Bethlehem PA 18017-1636 Office: Lehigh U Johnson Hall # 36 Bethlehem PA 18015 Office Phone: 610-758-3877. Business E-Mail: lhs1@lehigh.edu.

STEFFER, ROBERT WESLEY, clergyman; b. Spokane, Wash., June 24, 1934; s. Harold Wesley and Kathryne (Trumble) S.; m. Diane DeMoisey, Aug. 19, 1960; children: Erika Kirsten, Beauregard Gregory Robert. BA, Whitworth Coll., 1956; BD, Lexington Theol. Sem., 1959; MA, Ind. U., 1966, PhD, 1967. Ordained to ministry Christian Ch. (Disciples of Christ), 1959. Civilian dir. religious edn. U.S. Army Armor Ctr., Ft. Knox, Ky., 1960-64; assoc. regional min. Christian Ch. (Disciples of Christ), Oklahoma City, 1967-71; prof. Phillips U., Enid, Okla., 1971-76; fraternal worker div. overseas ministries Christian Ch. (Disciples of Christ), Barrow-in-Furness, Cumbria, Eng., 1976-79; Lilly vis. prof. religious edn. Christian Theol. Sem., Indpls., 1979-81; dir. edn. for mission Christian Ch. (Disciples of Christ), Indpls., 1981-87; exec. regional min. Christian Ch. (Disciples of Christ) in Can., Guelph, Ont., 1987-97; interim sr. minister Eureka (Ill.) Christian Ch., 1997-98; curator Cane Ridge Hist. Preservation Project, 1998—2006. Sec. Coll. Chs. of Christ in Can., Guelph, 1987-97. Editor Cane Ridge Bull., 1998-2006; contbr. articles to religious publs. and ency. Col., chaplain USAR ret., 1964—. Lilly Found. fellow in adult edn. Ind. U., 1964-66. Mem. Disciples of Christ Hist. Soc. (life, trustee 1990-94), Religious Edn. Assn. (bd. dirs. 1994-97), Conf. Regional Mins. and Moderators (2nd v.p.), Ch. Fin. Coun. (bd. dirs. 1995-96, exec. com. 1995), Phi Delta Kappa, Theta Phi. Democrat. Avocations: gardening, reading, travel, music. Office: 2708-65 Harbour Sq Toronto ON M5J 2L4 Canada Office Phone: 416-363-9609. E-mail: canerdgmtg@aol.com, steffer@sympatico.com.

STEFFY, MARION NANCY, state agency administrator; b. Fairport Harbor, Ohio, Sept. 23, 1937; d. Felix and Anna (Kosaber) Jackopin; 1 child, Christopher C. BA, Ohio State U., 1959; postgrad., Butler U., 1962-65, Ind. U., 1983. Exec. sec. Franklin County Mental Health Assn., Columbus, Ohio, 1959-61; caseworker Marion County Dept. Pub. Welfare, Indpls., 1961-63, supr., 1963-66, asst. chief supr., 1966-73; dir. divsn. pub. assistance Ind. Dept. Pub. Welfare, Indpls., 1973-77, asst. adminstr., 1977-85; regional adminstr. Adminstrn. Children and Families Ill. Dept. Health and Human Svcs., Chgo., 1985-98; nat. dir. Performance Initiative, 1998—. Lectr. Ball State U., Lockyear Coll., Ind. U. Grad. Sch. Social Work; mem. Ind. Devel. Disabilities Coun., 1979-81, Ind. Cmty. Svcs. Adv. Coun., 1978-81; Ind. Child Support Adv. Coun., 1976-82, Welfare Svc. League, 1968—; chmn. rules com. Ind. Health Facilities Coun., 1974-81; chmn. Lawrence Twp. Roundtable, 1983—; dir. Palette and Chisel Acad. Fine Arts, 2003. Mem. Nat. Assn. State Pub. Welfare Adminstrs., Am. Pub. Welfare Assn., Network of Women in Bus. Roman Catholic.

STEGENGA, JAMES JAY, senior compliance examiner; b. Berea, Ky., May 1, 1954; s. Preston Jay and Marcia J Stegenga. BA, Hope Coll., Holland, Mich., 1976; MA, U. So. Calif., LA, 1978; MBA, San Diego State U., 1982. Cert. regulatory compliance mgr. Inst. Cert. Bankers, Washington, 1999, bank examiner FDIC, 1990. Asst. examiner FDIC, Seattle, 1986—88, bank examiner Sacramento, 1990—98, sr. bank compliance examiner; sr. compliance examiner Roseville, 2008—. Mem.: Inst. Cert. Bankers (licentiate), Mensa. Mem. Reformed Church In America.

STEGER, CHARLES WILLIAM, academic administrator; b. Richmond, Va., June 16, 1947; s. Charles William and Virginia Belle (Garrett) S.; m. Janet Grey Baird, Sept. 13, 1969; children: Christopher B., David C. BArch, Va. Poly. Inst. & State U., 1970, MArch, 1971, PhD, 1978. Registered architect, Va. Project planner, architect Wiley & Wilson Inc., Lynchburg, Va., 1971-72, mgr. urban planning dept., 1973-74; dir. Environ. Design Consortium Inc., Blacksburg, Va., 1974-85; inst. grad. urban design program Coll. Architecture and Urban Studies, Va. Poly. Inst. and State U., Blacksburg, 1974-76, chmn. grad. urban design program, 1976-81; dean Coll. Architecture and Urban Studies, Va. Poly. Inst. and State U., Blacksburg, 1981-93; acting v.p. for pub. svc. Va. Poly. Inst. and State U., Blacksburg, 1990-93, v.p. for devel. and univ. rels., 1993-99; pres. Va. Tech. U., 2000—. Bd. dirs. Va. Found. Architecture, Richmond, Innovative Tech. Authority; mem. Gov.'s Secure Va. Tech. Initiative, 2001-02; mem. Gov.'s Va. Preparedness and Security Panel, 2001-02; bd. mem. Va. Advanced Shipbuilding and Carrier Integration Ctr., 2001-. Contbr. articles to jours. in field. Bd. dirs. Hollins Coll., Roanoke, Va., 1987-96, Boswil Found., Switzerland, 1986—, Ctr. in the Square, Roanoke, 1993-99; v.p. Va. Tech. Found., Inc., 1993-99; adv. coun. Va. Ctr. on Rural Devel., 1992—; commr. Govs. Commn. on Population Growth and Devel., Richmond, 1989-94; pres. Endowment Found. for We. Va. Found. for Arts and Scis. Fellow AIA (bd. dirs. ACSA Health Facilities Rsch. Program, Washington 1989—, ACSA Coun. on Arch. Rsch., 1987—); mem. Am. Planning Assn., Am. Inst. Cert. Planners, Commonwealth Club (Richmond, Va.), Shenandoah Club (Roanoke, Va.). Avocations: cattle farming, golf, canoeing. Office: Va Tech (0131) Office of Pres 210 Burruss Hall Blacksburg VA 24061 Office Phone: 540-231-6231.*

STEGLITZ, MARC H., museum administrator; b. Newark, Dec. 7, 1942; s. Jerome and Charlotte (Saba) Steglitz; m. Ilene G. Haas, June 7, 1964; children: Brian, JoAnne. BBA, U. Mich., 1964; MS, MIT, 1965. Sr. v.p., mgr. computer dept. Bankers Trust Co., NYC, 1976—84, sr. v.p. strategic planning, 1984; mng. dir. Credit Suisse First Boston, NYC; dep. dir. fin. & ops. Solomon R. Guggenheim Found., NYC, 2003—05, COO, 2005—, Solomon R. Guggenheim Mus., NYC, 2005—, interim dir., 2007—. Office: Guggenheim Mus 1071 5th Ave New York NY 10128-0173 Office Phone: 212-423-3500.

STEGMULLER, AGNES LEONORE, physical education educator; b. Phila., Jan. 24, 1923; d. George August and Agnes B. Stegmuller. BS in Edn., Temple U., Phila., 1945, MS in Edn., 1948; postgrad., Sorbonne U., Paris, 1954, Brigham Young U., Laie, Hawaii, Pa. State U. From tchr. to dept. head health and phys. edn. Sch. Dist. Phila., 1946—93; adj. prof. Temple U., Phila., 1993—. Pres. Dist. I Track Offcls., Abington, Pa., 2004—06. Vol. Spl. Olympics, Phila., March of Dimes, Pa.; mem. U.S. Women's Basketball Olympic Com., 1978—79; pres. Temple U. Coll. Health, Physical Edn., Recreation and Dance Alumni, 1998—99. Recipient Steoher award, Phila. Sch. Dist., 1986, Coach of Yr., Women's Sports Fedn., 1988, Pathfinder award, Am. Alliance Health, Physical Edn., Recreation and Dance, 1990, Conwell award, Temple U., 2000, Meritorious Svc. award, Pa. Interscholastic Athletic Assn., 2004; named Agnes L. Stegmuller scholarship in her honor, Temple U., 1994; named to Temple U. Hall of Fame, 1989, Pa. Sports Hall of Fame, 1999, Pa. Lacrosse Hall of Fame, 2002. Mem.: AAHPERD (Pa. liason), Pa. AAHPERD (v.p. 1988—92, girls sports chmn.), Delta Phi Kappa, Phi Delta Kappa. Home: 27 Jeffrey Rd Aldan PA 19018

STEH, BILL DRAGO, neuropsychologist; b. San Pedro, Calif., Oct. 22, 1971; s. Drago and Ann Steh; m. Kristi Lynn Wagner Steh, July 10, 1999; 1 child, Derek James Drago. BS in Biol. Psychology, U. Calif., 1993; PhD in Clin. Psychology/Neuropsychology, Calif. Sch. Profl. Psychology, 2000. Lic. psychologist Calif., 2002. Assoc., pvt. practice Neuroscience Associates, Inc., LA, 2001—; assoc. dir. clin. svcs. med. psychology assessment ctr. UCLA-Neuropsychatric Inst. and Hosp., 2003—. Adj. prof. Pepperdine U., Grad. Sch. Edn. and Psychology, Culver City, Calif., 2003—. Fellow, UCLA, Neuropsychiatric Inst. and Hosp., 2000—02; scholar, Calif. Sch. Profl. Psychology, Fresno, 1993—97. Mem.: APA, Internat. Neuropsychological Soc., Nat. Acad. Neuropsychology, Psi Chi. Avocations: baseball, exercise, weightlifting, music, backgammon. Office: UCLA-Neuropsychiatric Inst 760 Westwood Plz C8-734 Los Angeles CA 90095 E-mail: bsteh@mednet.ucla.edu.

STEHOUWER, DONALD J., neuroscientist; b. Grand Rapids, Mich., Nov. 26, 1951; s. William Stehouwer, Mildred Stehouwer (Stepmother); m. Beverly Ann Shankle, Mar. 7, 2001; 1 child, Veronica. PhD, Princeton U., NJ, 1978. Postdoc. fellow U. NC, Chapel Hill, 1978—82. Assoc. editor Devel. Psychobiology, 1995—2003; dir. Neurobehavioral and Cognitive Scis. Program, Gainesville, Fla., 2003—08. Contbr. scientific papers. Mem.: Internat. Soc. Devel. Psychobiology (treas. 1989—92), Soc. Neurosci. Achievements include research in vertebrate pedal locomotion in vitro; development of air-stepping model of locomotor. Office: Univ Fla Dept Psychology Gainesville FL 32611-2250 Office Fax: 352-392-7985. Business E-Mail: steh@ufl.edu.

STEHR, CHRISTIAN PETER, literature and language professor; s. Josef Paul and Lisbeth Agnes Stehr; m. Tamara Dawn Goesch; children: Sophia Lisbeth, Carsten Jens, Björn Christian. PhD, U. Oreg., Eugene, 1973. Prof. German lang. and lit. Oreg. State U., Corvallis, 1975—. Dir. internat. programs Oreg. Pub. Broadcasting, Portland, 1980—95. Exec. prodr. (PBS special TV series, movies) (Emmy Nomination, 1985, World Gold medal, NY Festivals, 1990, A & P award, PBS, World medal, NY Festivals & NEA award, 1995); prodr.: (movie) Luther. Recipient Officer's Cross of German Order of Merit, Pres., Fed. Republic Germany, 2002, Oreg. Fgn. Lang. Tchr. of Yr., Fgn. Lang. Coun. and Oreg. Assn. Fgn. Lang. Tchrs., 1975, Mayor's award, City Coun., Eugene, 1972, Top Prof. award, Mortar Bd. Sr. Scholastic Hon., Oreg. State U., 1995. Mem.: Am. Assn. Tchrs. German. Office: Oreg State Univ 228 Kidder Hall Corvallis OR 97331 Business E-Mail: cstehr@oregonstate.edu.

STEIB, JAMES TERRY, bishop; b. Vacherie, La., May 17, 1940; Ordained priest Soc. of Divine Word, 1967; ordained bishop, 1984; aux. bishop Archdiocese of St. Louis, Mo., 1984—93; bishop Diocese of Memphis, Tenn., 1993—. Roman Catholic. Office: Diocese of Memphis 5825 Shelby Oaks Dr PO Box 341669 Memphis TN 38184-1669 Office Phone: 901-373-1200. Office Fax: 901-373-1269.

STEIDLEY, JUAN DWAYNE, lawyer, judge; b. Claremore, Okla., Mar. 8, 1959; s. J.D. and Gwendolyn Ann (Barnes) S.; m. Teresa Ann Brim, July 31, 1987; 1 child, Terrence. BA, Okla. State U., 1981; JD, Tulsa U., 1984. Bar: Okla. 1985. Judge, 1999—. Mem. Ho. of Rep. Okla. Ho. of Reps., Oklahoma City, 1986-98; past chmn. Sequoyah Dist. Boy Scouts Am. Methodist. Home: 2710 Highwood Ct Claremore OK 74017-4872 Office: Rogers County Court House 219 S Miss Divs II Claremore OK 74017

STEIER, AUDREY KELLER, music educator; b. Newark; d. Solomon Charles and Tillie (Tomarin) Keller; m. Herbert Steier (dec.); children: Marcy Byer, Lisa Moore, David. BS in Music Edn., NYU, 1956; Hebrew cert. and religious edn., Hebrew Union Coll. Jewish Inst. Religion. Music tchr. Elizabeth Bd. Edn., NJ, 1956—57; religious sch. music tchr. Temple B'Nai Jesurun, Short Hills, NJ, 1957—80, pre-sch. dir., 1966—91, youth group adv., 1980—82; pre-sch. dir. Temple Has Shalom, Warren, NJ, 1992—97. Cons. Various Pre-Sch., Essex County, 1990. Mem.: Nat. Coun. Jewish Women (life; v.p. 1980—93). Avocations: knitting, needlecrafts, travel, reading. Home: 4200 Cleveland Lane Rockaway NJ 07866

STEIER, MICHAEL EDWARD, cardiac surgeon; b. NYC, Mar. 22, 1942; s. Philip and Gertrude S.; m. Christie Elizabeth Steier; children: Douglas (dec.), Lauren, Aubry, Erik. BA, Long Island U., 1964; MD, Univ. Health Scis., Chgo., 1968. Diplomate Am. Bd. Surgery, Am. Bd. Thoracic Surgery. Resident in gen. surgery St. Vincent's Hosp., NYC, 1969-73; resident in thoracic surgery Mayo Clinic, Rochester, Minn., 1973-75; cardiac surgeon SW Fla. Regional Med. Ctr., Ft. Myers, Fla., 1975—, Lee Meml. Hosp., Ft. Myers, 1975—, Cape Coral Hosp., Fla., 1977—, Naples Cmty. Hosp., Fla., 1996—; pres. Cardiac Surg. Assocs. West Fla., Ft. Myers; med. dir. Open Door Clinic of Addison County, 2005—. Chief surgery, SW Fla. Regional Med. Ctr., Ft. Myers, 1980-82, pres. med. staff, 1982; cons. Naples Cmty. Hosp., 1996—. Capt., USAR, 1969-78. Recipient Vt. Gov.'s award for svc., 2005, Middlebury Coll. medal for svc., 2007. Fellow ACS, Am. Coll. Chest Physicians, Am. Coll. Cardiology; mem. Soc. for Thoracic Surgeons, NY Acad. Scis., Cardiac Surg. Assn. SW Fla. (pres. 1993-99), Explorers Club. E-mail: steiers@comcast.net.

STEIGBIGEL, ROY THEODORE, epidemiologist, educator, research scientist; b. Bklyn., Nov. 23, 1941; s. Samuel and Lillian I. (Parker) S.; m. Julia Ann Enterline, June 10, 1967 (div. 1983), children: Keith D., Glenn N.; m. Sidonie Ann Morrison, Oct. 15, 1985; 1 child, Andrew M. BA, Carleton Coll., 1962; MD, U. Rochester, 1966. Diplomate Am. Bd. Internal Medicine, Am. Bd. Infectious Disease. Resident U. Rochester, NY, 1966-68, Stanford U., Palo Alto, Calif., 1970-71, fellow, 1971-73; from asst. to assoc. prof. U. Rochester, NY, 1973-83; prof. SUNY, Stony Brook, 1983—. Mem. adv. panels NIH, Bethesda, Md., 1985-87. Contbr. over 20 chpts. to books and over 100 articles to profl. jours. Served in USPHS, 1968-70. Fellow NIH, 1971-73, grantee, 1985—. Fellow ACP, Infectious Disease Soc. Am. Office: SUNY Stony Brook Sch Medicine Hsc T 15 080 Stony Brook NY 11794-8153 Office Phone: 631-444-3490. Business E-Mail: roy.steigbigel@stonybrook.edu.

STEIGER, JAMES HUBERT, psychology professor; s. Ernest and Mary Agnes Steiger; m. Juanita Jane Albers, Aug. 17, 1969; children: Andree Rebecca, Roberta Ann. BA, Cornell U., Ithaca, NY, 1970; MS, U. Okla., Norman, 1972; PhD, Purdue U., West Lafayette, Ind., 1976. Asst. prof. psychology U. BC, Vancouver, Canada, 1976—81, assoc. prof. psychology, 1981—88, prof. psychology, 1988—2003, Vanderbilt U., Nashville, 2003—; vis. prof. stats. U. South Africa, Pretoria, 1983. With US Army, 1968, Honolulu. Recipient Killam Rsch. prize, Killam Found., 1986—87. Mem.: APA (Samuel J. Messick prize 2007), Soc. Multivariate Exptl. Psychology (pres. 2005, Raymond B. Cattell award 1986), Psychometric Soc. Achievements include research in multivariate correlational methods. Office: Vanderbilt Univ 0552 GPC 230 Appleton Pl Nashville TN 37203-5721 Office Fax: 615-322-5514. Business E-Mail: james.h.steiger@vanderbilt.edu.

STEIGER, PAUL ERNEST, editor-in-chief, journalist; b. NYC, Aug. 15, 1942; s. Ernest and Mary Agnes (Walsh) Steiger; m. Heidi Brine, Nov. 23, 1985 (div.); children: Isabelle Amanda, William Ernest; m. Wendy Brandes, July 22, 2001; children from previous marriage: Erika Maren, Laura Arlene. BA in economics, Yale U., 1964. Staff reporter Wall Street Jour., San Francisco, 1966-68; staff writer LA Times, 1968-71, econ. corr. Washington, DC bur., 1971-78, bus. editor LA, 1978-83; asst. mng. editor Wall Street Jour., NYC, 1983-85, dep. mng. editor, 1985—91, mng. editor, 1991—2007, v.p., 1992—2007, editor-at-large, 2007; v.p. Dow Jones & Co., NYC, 2007; editor-in-chief, pres., CEO ProPublica, NYC, 2008—. Mem. Pulitzer Prize Bd., 1999—2007, chmn., 2007; rep., Dow Jones SmartMoney Bd., Wall Street Journal Mag., SmartMoney.com; chmn. Com. to Protect Journalists. Co-author (with John F. Lawrence): The 70's Crash and How to Survive It, 1970. Chmn. Com. to Protect Journalists, 2005—; trustee John S. & James L. Knight Found. Recipient John Hancock Award, 1971, G.M. Loeb Award, UCLA, 1971, 1974, 1978, George Beveridge Editor of Yr. Award, Nat. Press Found., 2001, Leadership Award, Am. Soc. Newspaper Editors, 2002, Columbia Journalism Award, Columbia U. Sch. Journalism, 2002, G.M. Loeb award for Lifetime Achievement, John E. Anderson Sch. Mgmt., UCLA, 2002, Decade of Excellence Award, World Leadership Forum, 2005, Mo. Honor medal for Disting. Svc. in Journalism, Mo. Sch. Journalism, 2005, Fourth Estate award, Nat. Press. Club, 2007; Poynter Fellow, Yale U., 2001—02. Office: ProPublica One Exchange Pl 55 Broadway 23rd Fl New York NY 10006*

STEIGER, WILLIAM R. (BILL STEIGER), federal agency administrator; BA history, Yale U., New Haven, CT; PhD Latin American History, U. Calif. LA. Edn. policy advisor to Gov. Tommy G. Thompson, Wis.; spl. asst. sec. internat. affairs U.S. Dept. Health and Human Services, 2001, dir. Office of Global Health Affairs, 2001—. U.S. mem. exec. bd. World Health Org.; pres. exec. com. Pam Am. Health Org.; alternative U.S. mem. bd. dirs. Global Fund to Fight HIV/AIDS, Tuberculosis and Malaria. Office: Dept of Health & Human Services 200 Independence Ave SW Rm 639 H Washington DC 20201 Office Phone: 202-690-6174. Office Fax: 202-690-7127.*

STEIGMAN, ANDREW L., academic dean; b. NYC, Aug. 30, 1933; s. Nathan and Sarah (Levine) S.; m. Meryl Fialka, June 20, 1959; children: Daria H., Jonathan S. AB summa cum laude, Princeton U., 1954; postgrad., London Sch. Econs., 1954-55, Am. U., Washington, 1958-60. Fgn. svc. officer Dept. State, various locations, 1958-69; first sec. Dept. State, U.S. Embassy, Paris, 1969-72, polit. counselor Lagos, Nigeria, 1972-75, U.S. ambassador to Gabon Libreville, Gabon, 1975-77; dir. nat. intelligence tasking office Intelligence Community Staff, Washington, 1978-80; dep. asst. sec. for personnel Dept. State, Washington, 1981-84; asst. dean/prof. internat. relations Georgetown U., Washington, 1985—, assoc. dean, 1996. Vis. fellow Woodrow Wilson Fellowship Found., Princeton, 1987-93; mem. edn. com. Atlantic Council, Washington, 1989-98. Author: The Foreign Service of the United States, 1985. With U.S. Army, 1955-57. Wilbur Carr award, U.S. Dept. State, 1985. Mem.: DACOR, Am. Fgn. Svc. Assn., Am. Hist. Assn. Office: Georgetown U Sfs Icc # 301 Washington DC 20057-0001 E-mail: steigman@georgetown.edu.

STEIGMANN, DAVID JOHN, professor; s. Axel John and Yolande G. Steigmann; life ptnr. Laura Lynn Feren; children: Benjamin David, Nicholas Daniel. PhD, Brown U., Providence, 1988. Prof. U. Alta., Edmonton, Alberta, Canada, 1988—96, U. Calif., Berkeley, 1996—. Office: Univ Calif 6133 Etcheverry Hall Berkeley CA 94720

STEIN, ADAM MATTHEW, military officer; b. West Palm Beach, Fla., Feb. 12, 1983; s. Lewis Michael and Bonita Robins Stein. BA in Polit. Sci., Duquesne U., Pitts., 2005; MBA, U. Pitts., 2007. Sr. fin. svcs. cons. PNC Bank, Pitts., 2004—05; commd. USN, Pitts., 2005; asst. store mgr. Tuesday Morning Inc., Allison Pk., 2006; asst. weapons officer USS Antietam, 2007—. Pres. student exec. bd. Katz Bus. Sch. U. Pitts., 2006—07; asst. weapons officer USS Antietam, 2007—. Recipient Dean's Outstanding Student Svc. award, Katz Grad. Sch. Bus., 2007; Navy Postgrad. scholar, USN, 2005. Democrat. Avocations: travel, reading, jogging, sports. Personal E-mail: amstein@gmail.com.

STEIN, ALEXANDER, psychoanalyst, consultant; b. Morristown, NJ, June 8, 1962; s. David Stein and Bascha Mon; m. Helayne Schiff, Sept. 9, 2000; children: Miles Schiff Stein, Oliver Schiff Stein. PhD, H. R. Rosenthal Coll. Psychoanalysis, Heed U., 2007. Lic. psychoanalyst Edn. Dept. State of NY, 2005. Psychoanalyst pvt. practice, NYC, 1998—; prin. Boswell Group LLC, NYC, 2007—; columnist, spl. feature writer Fortune Small Bus., Time Inc. Publ., NYC, 2007—. Dir. Mind and Music Project, 2004—; editl. bd. dirs. Psychoanalytic Rev., NYC, 2005—, Am. Imago, John Hopkins U. Press Publ., Balt., 2006—; guest faculty New Directions Psychoanalytic Thinking, Wash. Ctr. Psychoanalysis, Washington. Contbr. articles to numerous profl. jours. (Ernest Angel award, Nat. Psychol. Assn. Psychoanalysis, 1998), columns in newspapers. Cons., on-camera expert numerous media outlets. Mem.: Am. Psychoanalytic Assn. (NYC) (mem., com. pub. info. 2007), Nat. Psychol. Assn. Psychoanalysis (NYC) (mem., faculty, tng. and supervising analyst 2005—), Nat. Assn. Advancement Psychoanalysis (Gradiva award, Pub. Edn. Corp. World Assn. 2004). Avocations: reading, travel, cooking, bicycling. Office: 80 5th Ave New York NY 10011 Personal E-mail: astein@hoswellgroup.com. Business E-Mail: psykhe@att.net.

STEIN, ARTHUR OSCAR, retired pediatrician; b. Bklyn., Apr. 3, 1932; s. Irving I. and Sadie (Brander) S.; m. Judith Lenore Hurwitz, Aug. 27, 1955; children: Susan, Jeffrey, Benjamin. AB, Harvard U., 1953; MD, Tufts U., 1957; postgrad., U. Chgo., 1963—66; BFA, San Jose State U., 1998. Intern U. Chgo. Hosps., 1957-58, resident, 1958-59, NY Hosp.-Cornell U. Med. Ctr., 1959-61; pediatrician, 1963-70, Healthguard Med. Group, San Jose, Calif., 1970-72, Permanente Med. Group, San Jose, 1972-95; ret., 1995; owner Artform Photography, 2001—05. Instr. pediat. Cornell U. Med. Sch., 1960-61, U. Chgo. Sch. Medicine, 1963-66, asst. prof., 1966-70; tchg. asst. photography San Jose State U., 1995—. Author: (CD) The Sketch Class. V.p. Jewish congregation 1969-70, pres. 1972-73. Capt., M.C., AUS, 1961-63. USPHS Postdoctoral fellow, 1963-66. Fellow Am. Acad. Pediat., Santa Clara County Med. Assn., Calif. Med. Assn.; mem. Light and Shadow Camera Club (pres. San Jose 1978-80), Ctrl. Coast Counties Camera Club (v.p. 1980-81, pres. 1981-82), Santa Clara Camera Club (pres. 1991), Villages Camera Club (pres. 2007-08). Achievements include co-discovery (with Glyn Dawson) of genetic disease lactosylceramidosis. Home: 8656 Solera Dr San Jose CA 95135 E-mail: artform2@pacbell.net.

STEIN, BARRY EDWARD, medical educator; BA, CUNY, Queens, 1966, MA, 1969; PhD, CUNY, 1971. Prof. dept. physiology Med. Coll. Va.-Va. Commonwealth U., Richmond, 1982-94, affil. prof., 1994—; prof., chair dept. neurobiology and anatomy Wake Forest U Sch. Medicine, Winston-Salem, NC, 1994—. Bd. trustees The Gwendolyn Hardy Williams and Oliver Williams Found., Inc., 1992—; lectr. in field. Co-author: The Merging of the Senses, 1993; contbr. chpts. to books including The Cognitive Neurosciences, 1995, 99, Electrophysiology of Vision, 1991, The Development of Intersensory Perception: Comparative Perspectives, 1994, others; co-editor: The Handbook of Multisensory Processes, 2004; mem. editl. bd. Jour. Cognitive Neuroscience, The Behavioral and Brain Sciences; contbr. numerous articles to profl. pubs. including Jour. Neurophysiology, Jour. Neurosci., Sci., Jour. Comparative Neurology, others. Home: 1825 Georgia Ave Winston Salem NC 27104-3101 Office: Wake Forest Sch Medicine Med Ctr Blvd Winston Salem NC 27157-0001 Business E-Mail: bestein@wfubmc.edu.

STEIN, BEN (BENJAMIN JEREMY STEIN), television personality, writer, lawyer, economist; b. Washington, Nov. 25, 1944; s. Herbert and Mildred (Fishman) S.; m. Alexandra Denman, June 22, 1968 (div. 1974); m. Alexandra Denman, 1977; 1 child, Thomas. BA, Columbia U., 1966; LLB, Yale U., 1970. Bar: Conn. Trial lawyer FTC, Washington, 1970-72; speechwriter The White House, Washington, 1973-74; columnist Wall St. Jour., NYC, 1974-76; writer, commentator, columnist LA Herald-Examiner, 1978-87; TV personality Win Ben Stein's Money, Comedy Ctrl., 1997—2003; host Turn Ben Stein On, Comedy Ctrl., 1999—2001. Fin. cons. LAACO, Inc., LA; contbg. editor Am. Spectator, 1980—; law and econs. tchr. Pepperdine, Malibu, 1992—; adj. prof. Am. U., Washington, U. Calif. Santa Cruz; spokesperson Clear Eyes eye drops. Author: On The Brink, 1977, The View from Sunset Boulevard, 1978, DREEMZ, 1978, Moneypower, 1980, 'Ludes, 1981, Financial Passages, 1986, A License to Steal, 1992, Tommy and Me, 1999, How To Ruin Your Life, 2002, How to Ruin Your Love Life, 2003, How to Ruin Your Financial Life, 2004, How Succesful People Win: Using Bunkhouse Logic to Get What You Want in Live, 2006; co-author (with Phil DeMuth) Mechanical and Electrical Equipment for Buildings, 1999, Yes, You Can Time the Market!, 2003, Can America Survive? The Rage of the Left, the Truth, and What to Do about It, 2004, Yes, You Can Be a Successful Income Investor: Reaching for Yield in Today's Market, 2005, Yes, You Can Still Retire Comfortably: The Baby-Boom Retirement Crisis and How to Beat It, 2005, Yes, You Can Get a Financial

Life!: Your Lifetime Guide to Financial Planning, 2007, The Real Stars: In Today's America, Who Are the True Heroes?, 2007, How to Ruin the United States of America, 2008; author numerous articles on leveraged buy-outs and other fin. frauds for Barrons, 1984—; syndicated columnist King Features Syndicate; regular columnist LA Mag., NY Mag., E! Online, NY Times (Everybody's Money) SundayBusiness; contbr. Wash. Post, Wall St. Jour., CBS TV News; guest speaker on fin. Fox News Channel; co-creater: (TV series) Fernwood Tonight; actor: (films) The Wild Life, 1984, Ferris Bueller's Day Off, 1986, Planes, Trains, and Automobiles, 1987, Ghostbusters II, 1989, Soapdish, 1991, Honeymoon in Vegas, 1992, Dennis the Menace, 1993, My Girl 2, 1994, North, 1994, The Mask, 1994, Richie Rich, 1994, Miami Rhapsody, 1995, Casper, 1995; (TV series) The Wonder Years, 1988-91, (voice only) Animaniacs, 1993, Freakazoid, 1995, Earthworm Jim, 1995, The Mask, 1995, Bruno the Kid, 1996, The Secret Files of the SpyDogs, 1998; (TV films) Mastergate, 1992, The Day My Parents Ran Away, 1993, (voice only) Santa vs. the Snowman, 1997, Breakfast with Einstein, 1998; exec. prodr. Turn Ben Stein On, 1999; host: (TV series) Win Ben Stein's Money, 1997-2002 (Daytime Emmy award Outstanding Game Show Host, 1999); (TV appearances) Charles in Charge, 1987, 88, 90, MacGyver, 1991, Melrose Place, 1993, Full House, 1993, Hearts Afire, 1993, 94, Tales from the Crypt, 1995, Lois & Clark: The New Adventures of Superman, 1995, Married...With Children, 1995, The Marshal, 1995, (voice only) Duckman, 1996, 97, Seinfeld, 1997, Murphy Brown, 1997, Muppets Tonight!, 1998, (voice only) Rugrats, 1998, The Drew Carey Show, 2001, (voice only) The Adventures of Jimmy Neutron: Boy Genius, 2002, Family Guy, 2003, The Fairly Odd Parents, 2004; writer: (documentaries) Expelled: No Intelligence Allowed, 2008 Mem. Writers Guild Am., Screen Actors' Guild, Am. Fedn. TV and Radio Actors, Yale Club NYC, Friars, LA Athletic Club, Calif. Yacht Club, Morningside Country Club. Republican. Jewish. Office: 8787 Shoreham Dr West Hollywood CA 90069-2231 Office Phone: 310-652-9406. Personal E-mail: benstein@aol.com.

STEIN, BERNARD ALVIN, retail executive, consultant; b. Winnipeg, Can., June 4, 1923; s. Herman Louis and Rebecca (Harris) S.; m. Dorothy Lock, Jan. 1, 1942; 1 dau., Marilynn Stein Lakein. Vice-pres. food drug div. Giant Food, Inc., Washington, 1951-69; v.p., gen. mgr. Read Drug Stores, Balt., 1969-70; pres. Scotty Stores div. Sav-A-Stop, Jacksonville, Fla., 1970-71; pres., gen. mgr. Liberal Markets, Dayton, Ohio, 1971-72; pres. Pueblo Supermarkets, San Juan, P.R., 1972-74, Hills Supermarkets, Brentwood, NY, 1974-75, Allied Supermarkets, Detroit, 1976-78, Chatham Supermarkets, Detroit, 1978-81; CEO Network Assocs., Chgo., 1981-92; bus. cons. Balt., 1992—; pres. Jewelery Markdowns, Inc., 2003—. Pres. Jewelry website business, 2003—. Mem. Presdl. Com. for Emergency Food Controls, 1969; mem. scholarship com. Am. Indian Edn. Found., 2004—. Served with USAAF, 1943-45. Decorated Air medal. Home: 7902 Brynmor Ct # 104 Pikesville MD 21208-4351 Office Phone: 410-486-3099. Personal E-mail: bernie230@comcast.net, jewelrymd@comcast.net.

STEIN, CY AARON, oncologist, pharmacologist; b. NYC, Nov. 1, 1952; s. Herbert and Ruth (Schiffenbauer) S.; m. Myra Levine, Aug. 15, 1976; children: Allison, Lauren. BA magna cum laude, Brown U., 1974; PhD in Organic Chemistry, Stanford U., 1978; MD, Albert Einstein Coll. Medicine, 1982. Diplomate Am. Bd. Internal Medicine, 1986, Am. Bd. Oncology, 1987, lic. Md., NY. Intern N.Y. Hosp.-Cornell Med. Ctr., NYC, 1982-83, resident in internal medicine, 1983-85; clin. assoc. Nat. Cancer Inst., Bethesda, Md., 1985-88, sr. staff fellow, 1988-90; asst. prof. medicine and pharmacology Columbia U., Coll. of Physicians and Surgeons, NYC, 1990-93, Irving asst. prof. medicine and pharmacology, 1993-95, assoc. prof. medicine and pharmacology, 1996—2003; prof., medicine, urology and molecular pharmacology Med. Genitourinary Oncology, Bronx, NY; attending physician Montefiore Med. Ctr., Bronx, NY. Grant reviewer NIAID Nat. Coop. Drug Discovery Group-AIDS, 1993, NCI Nat. Coop. Drug Discovery Group, 1995, NCI Exptl. Therapeutics Study Sect., 1997; cons. chief med. officer, Tokai Pharm., Cambridge, Mass., Trilink Biotech., San Diego, Calif. Mem. editl. bd. Jour. of Therapeutic Biotechnology, Nucleic Acids Rsch.; co-editor: Antisense and Nucleic Acids, Drug Devel.; contbr. numerous articles to profl. jours. Recipient Clin. Career Devel. award Am. Cancer Soc., 1992-95; named one of Best Drs. NY Metro Area, 2004-09, Castle Connolly Med. Ltd., 2004-2009, NY Times Mag., 2008-2009, Most Preferred Oncologist Montefiore Med. Ctr., 2008, NY's Super Drs., NY Times Mag., 2008-09. Mem. Am. Soc. for Clin. Investigation, Am. Assn. for Cancer Rsch., Am. Soc. for Clin. Oncology, European Soc. Med. Oncology, Am. Soc. for Gene Therapy (Oligonucleotide Com. 2005-08), Salus Therapeutics (Salt Lake City) (bd. dirs. 2003), Cytogenix (Woodlands, Tex.) (bd. dirs. 2004-), Oligonucleotide Therapeutics Soc. (founder 2004, treas. 2004-08, ex-officer 2009) Alpha Omega Alpha. Achievements include development of medical genitourinary oncology program at Albert Einstein College of Medicine. Home: 11 Dolphin Rd New City NY 10956-6306 Office: Montefiore Med Ctr 111 E 210th St Bronx NY 10467 Home Fax: 718-652-4027. Personal E-mail: cstein@montefiore.org.

STEIN, DANIEL, hotel and resort operations executive; b. Cape Girardeau, Mo., Aug. 13, 1964; s. Oscar and Emma Laverne Stein; m. Alesia Kaye Jones, Feb. 14, 1983; children: Amanda Kaye, Daniel Andrew. Regional contr. Am. Skiing Co., Bethel, Maine, 1999—2001, Westgate Resorts, Orlando, Fla., 2001—03; corp. contr. Nantucket Island Resorts, Nantucket, Mass., 2003—05; dir. fin. Ginn Co./Resorts, Orlando, Fla., 2005—07; dir. of resorts Dune Mgmt., East Hampton, NY, 2007—09.

STEIN, DAVID ERIC, physicist, defense analyst, futurist, retired military officer; b. Jacksonville, Fla., Jan. 13, 1950; s. Stanley Wolfe and Dorothy Jean (Lilley) S. BS with high honors, U. Fla., 1971, postgrad., 1971-72, MS in Physics, 1977; grad., Air Command and Staff Coll., 1982, Naval War Coll., 1995, Air War Coll., 1996. Instr. dept. physics U. Fla., Gainesville, 1971-74, NSF rsch. asst., 1974-76; 1st lt. US Army, 1977—79; capt. USAF, 1979—87; transferred to USAF Reserve, 1987, maj., 1989—94, lt. col., 1994—99; with USAF HQ Air Force Systems Command, Andrews AFB, Md., 1992, Air Force Sci. adv. bd., 1994-95; project engr. advanced surveillance concepts Rome Air Devel. Ctr., 1979-81; field engr. radar systems test and evaluation Rome Air Devel. Ctr. and MIT Lincoln Lab., 1981-83; radar data and imagery analyst 6585th Test Group, Holloman AFB, N.Mex., 1983-87; elec. engr. specialist LTV Aircraft Products Group, 1987-90; fellow engr. Westinghouse Electric Corp., 1990-91; ops. rsch. analyst CSCI, 1992-94, Office of Asst. Sec. of Air Force, 1995, 96-97, Joint Staff, 1996, 98-99, Army Digitization Office, 1999-2000, CACI, 2000—03, Northrop Grumman Info. Tech., 2003—08. Adj. coll. faculty, 1982-84; short course instr. radar techs. George Washington U., 1991-97; adv. assoc. editor NATO Advanced Rsch. Workshop, Bad Windsheim, Germany, 1988; cons., 1994—. Editor-in-chief Applied Computational Electromagnetics Soc. Jour., 1987-93, FUTUREtakes, 2003-; assoc. sci. editor: Frontier Perspectives, 2000—09; contbr. articles to profl. jours.; patentee in field. Mem. exec. bd. dirs. Ctr. Frontier Scis., 2006—09; mem. adv. bd. Inst. Future Anne Arundel CC, 2008—. Recipient Disting. Svc. award Applied Computational Electromagnetics Soc., 1994; fellow Alpha Found.'s Inst. for Advanced Study, 2002-2004; J. Hillis Miller Meml. scholar U. Fla., Ford Found. fellow. Mem. Am. Phys. Soc., Am. Assn. Physics Tchrs., World Affairs Coun., World Future Soc., Army-Navy Club, Philos. Soc. Washington, Fla. Blue Key, Phi Beta Kappa, Sigma Pi Sigma, Omicron Delta Kappa, Phi Kappa Phi. Achievements include identification of atmospheric refractivity effects on low-altitude radar propagation, extended quantum-mech. computational technique to electromagnetic scattering, co-pioneered new acquisition sizing methodology for next-generation fighter aircraft; co-authored section of Defense Critical Technologies Plan for the Executive Office of the President; key advisor to Air Force Requirements Oversight Council; mem. U.S. delegation to NATO Y2K integrated process team; identified non-Y2K compliant NATO command and control systems and possible impact to interconnected U.S. systems; identified systems acquisition implications of alternative geostrategic futures, asymmetric-capable adversaries, new concepts in warfare, futuristic techs; co-pioneered modeling and simulation as a technology investment planning tool for an uncertain and rapidly changing national security environment. Home: PO Box 571433 Las Vegas NV 89157-1433 Office Phone: 202-452-5592, 202-263-1140. Business E-Mail: editorinchief@tvtunetukes.org.

STEIN, DAVID FRED, investment company executive; b. NYC, May 17, 1940; s. William Howard and Phoebe Louise (Hockstader) S.; m. Susan Vail Berresford, June 17, 1963 (div. 1970); 1 child, Jeremy Vail; m. Ellen Gail Cohen, Sept. 16, 1973; children: Katharine Ellen, Nicholas David. BA, Harvard U., 1962; MBA, Harvard Grad. Sch. Bus. Adminstrn., 1965. Assoc. Bache & Co., NYC, 1965-68; assoc., then gen. ptnr. Kuhn Loeb & Co., NYC, 1969-77; mng. dir. Lehman Brothers Kuhn Loeb, NYC, 1977-83, Shearson Lehman Am. Express, NYC, 1983-86; sr. exec. v.p., dir. Am. Express Bank, NYC, 1986-87; mng. dir. Shearson Lehman Hutton, NYC, 1987-89; mng. dir., mem. exec. com. The Stamford Co., NYC, 1989-90; mng. dir. J & W Seligman & Co., NYC, 1990-96, vice chmn., 1997—2008; co-chmn. Seligman Henderson Co., NYC, 1991-98. Bd. dirs. Griffin Land & Nurseries Inc. Trustee P.R. Traveling Theatre, NYC, 1970-72, Altro Health and Rehab. Ctr., Bronx, NY, 1975-82, Montefiore Med. Ctr., Bronx, 1990—, Montefiore Health Svcs., 2006—, Our Lady of Mercy Hosp., 2006—, Children's Aid Soc., 2000—; trustee Blythedale Children's Hosp., Valhalla, NY, 1977-2001, hon. trustee, 2001—; trustee Riverdale Country Sch., Bronx, 1988-2000, chmn. bd. trustees, 1997-2000, trustee emeritus, 2005—; active Coun. on Fgn. Rels. With U.S. Army, 1962-63. Mem. Nat. Assn. Security Dealers (internat. com. 1970-85), Century Country Club (Purchase, N.Y.), River Club (NYC), Harvard Club (NYC), Edgartown (Mass.) Yacht Club, Mill Reef Club (Antigua, Brit. V.I.), Chappaquiddick Beach Club (Edgartown), Reading Room Club (Edgartown). Democrat. Avocations: reading, sailing, bicycling, fishing, tennis. Home: 875 Park Ave New York NY 10021-0341

STEIN, DOUGLAS WARREN, lawyer; b. Albany, Jan. 11, 1971; s. Arthur A. and Zelda S. Stein; m. Deborah Stein, June 11, 1995; children: Miriam, Tamar. BS, U. Md., 1994; JD, Benjamin N. Cardozo Sch. Law, NY, 1997. Atty. Pierro & Assoc., LLC, Albany, 2003; ptnr. Barris, Sott, Denn & Driker, Detroit, 2003—08, Smith, Gambrell & Russell, Atlanta, 2008—. With SBM, Estates & Trust, Taxation State Bar MI, 2006—08; chair Bus. Investment Entities, LLC'S Partnerships, 2007—09. Contbr. articles to profl. jours. Recipient Mich. Rising Star, 2008; named Ga. Best Lawyer, Atlanta, 2009; named one of Best Lawyers in America, 2009. Mem.: State Bar NY, State Bar Mich., State Bar Mass., State Bar Ga. Office: Smith Gambrell & Russell LLP 1230 Peachtree St Northeast Ste 3100 Atlanta GA 30309

STEIN, ELEANOR BANKOFF, retired judge; b. NYC, Jan. 24, 1923; d. Jacob and Sarah Rashkin Bankoff; m. Frank S. Stein, May 27, 1947; children: Robert B., Joan Jenkins, William M. Student, Barnard Coll., 1940—42; BS in Econ., Columbia U., NYC, 1944; LLB, N.Y. U., NYC, 1949; grad., Ind. Jud. Coll., 1986. Bar: N.Y. 1950, Ind. 1976, U.S. Supreme Ct. 1980. Atty. Hillis & Button, Kokomo, Ind., 1975—76, Paul Hillis, 1976—78, Bayliff, Harrigan, 1978—80; judge Howard County Ct., 1981—89; ret., 1989. Co-referee Howard County Juvenile Ct., Kokomo, 1976—78. Mem. Rep. Women's Assn. Kokomo, 1980—; bd. dir. Kokomo Human Rels. Commn., Ind., 1967—70, Howard County Legal Aid Soc., 1976—80; bd. advisors St. Joseph Hosp., 1979—2000; bd. dir. Howard County Children's Ctr., 1993—98. Mem.: ABA, Howard County Bar Assn., Ind. Bar Assn., Nat. Assn. Women Judges, Ind. Jud. Assn., Am. Judicature Soc., Kokomo Country Club. Jewish. Home: 3204 Tally Ho Dr Kokomo IN 46902 Office Phone: 765-453-4706. Personal E-mail: eleanorbstein@aol.com.

STEIN, ELIAS M., mathematician, educator; b. Antwerp, Belgium, Jan. 13, 1931; arrived in US, 1941; s. Elkan and Chana (Goldman) S.; m. Elly Intrator, Mar. 21, 1959; children— Jeremy, Karen AB, U. Chgo., 1951, MA, 1953, PhD, 1955; degree (hon.), Peking U., 1988, U. Chgo., 1992. Instr. MIT, Cambridge, 1956-58; asst. prof., then assoc. prof. U. Chgo., 1958-63; mem. Inst. for Advanced Study, Princeton, N.J., 1962-63, 1984-85; prof. dept. math. Princeton U., N.J., 1963—, chmn. dept. math. N.J., 1968-70, N.J., 1985-87. Author: Singular Integrals and Differentiability Properties of Functions, 1970 (Am. Math. Soc. Steele prize 1984), Topics in Harmonic Analysis Related to the Littlewood-Paley Theory; co-author: (with G. Weiss) Introduction to Fourier Analysis on Euclidean Spaces, Harmonic Analysis, 1993; contbr. articles to profl. jours. NSF fellow, 1955-56, sr. post-doctoral fellow, 1962-63, 71-72; Sloan Found. fellow, 1961-63; Guggenheim Found. fellow, 1976-77, 1984-85, Wolf prize in math., Wolf Found., Israel, 1999, Nat. Medal of Sci., 2002. Mem. NAS, Am. Acad. Arts and Scis., Am. Math. Soc., Swedish Acad. of Scis. (Schock prize 1993). Home: 132 Dodds Ln Princeton NJ 08540-4106 Office: Princeton U Dept Math 802 Fine Hall Washintgon Rd Princeton NJ 08544-0001 Office Phone: 609-258-6463. Business E-Mail: stein@math.princeton.edu.

STEIN, ELLIOT, JR., business executive; b. St. Louis, Jan. 31, 1949; s. Elliot and Mary Ann (Bleiweiss) S.; m. Pamela Sztybel, Oct. 4, 1997. BA, Claremont McKenna Coll., 1971. Assoc. Lehman Bros., NYC, 1972-79; chmn. Caribbean Internat. News Corp., San Juan, 1985; ptnr. Commonwealth Capital Ptnrs., NYC, 1988—, mng. dir., Cloud Solutions LLC, Cohere Comm. Bd. dirs. Cloud Solutions LLC; adv. bd. Investigative Group Internat., 1998—. Bd. dirs. Apollo Investment Corp., 2004- Mem. Coun. on Fgn. Rels.; trustee Claremont Grad. U., 1980—, New Sch. U., 1990—. Office: Commonwealth Capital Ptnrs 509 Madison Ave Ste 604 New York NY 10022

STEIN, ERIC, retired law educator; b. Holice, Czechoslovakia, July 8, 1913; arrived in US, 1940, naturalized, 1943; s. Zikmund and Hermina (Zalud) Stein; m. Virginia Elizabeth Rhine, July 30, 1955. JUD, Charles U., Prague, Czechoslovakia, 1937; JD, U. Mich., 1942; Dr. honoris causa, Vrije U., Brussels, 1978, U. Libre, 1979, West-Bohemian U., Pilsen, Czech Republic, 1997. Bar: Ill. 1946, DC 1953. Practiced law, Prague, 1937; with State Dept. Bureau United Nations Internat. Orgn., 1946-55; acting dep. dir. Office UN Polit. Affairs, 1955; mem. faculty U. Mich. Law Sch., Ann Arbor, 1956, prof. internat. law and orgn., 1958-76, Hessel E. Yntema prof. law, 1976-83, emeritus prof., 1983—; co-dir. internat. legal studies, 1958-76; dir., 1976-81. Vis. prof. Stanford Law Sch., 1956, 77, Law Faculties, Stockholm, Uppsala, Lund, Sweden, 1969, Inst. Advanced Legal Studies U. London, London, 1975, U. Ariz., 1991, 92; lectr. Hague Acad. Internat. Law, 1971; vis. lectr. European U. Inst., Florence, Italy, 1983, Jean Monnet prof., 91; vis. lectr., Beijing, 86, Shanghai, 90, U. Tokyo, Kyoto, 1986, Coll. Europe Bruges, Madrid, 1985, U. Ponteficia, 1988, Inst. Pvt. & Comparative Law, Paris, 1988, Inst. Fgn. Pub. & Internat. Law Heidelberg Inst. Pvt. Comp. Law, Hamberg, Germany; Henry Morris lectr. Kent Coll. Law, Chgo., 1992; Jeanne Kiewit Taylor disting. vis. lectr. U. Ariz., 1993; adviser US del. UN Gen. Assembly, 1947—55; mem. adv. panel, cons. Bur. European Affairs, State Dept., 1966—73; cons. US rep. for trade negotiations, 1979; vice chmn. com. Atlantic studies Atlantic Inst., 1966—68; mem. adv. coun. Inst. European Studies Free U., Brussels, 1965—70; mem. US Com. Legal Edn. Exch. with China, 1983—91; lectr. Acad. European Law, Florence, 1990. Author (with others): American Enterprise in the European Common Market-A Legal Profile, vols I, II, 1960; author: (with H. K. Jacobson) Diplomats, Scientists and Politicians: The United States and the Nuclear Test Ban Negotiations, 1966 (U. Mich. Press Best Book of Yr. award); author: Harmonization of European Company Law: National Reform and Transnational Coordination, 1971, Impact of New Weapons Technology on International Law-Selected Aspects, 1971, Un Nuovo Diritto per l'Europa, 1991, Czecho/Slovakia: Ethnic Conflict, Constitutional Fissure, Negotiated Breakup, 1997, Czech translation, 2000, Thoughts from a Bridge: A Retrospective of Writings on New Europe and American Federalism, 2000 (U. Mich. Press Best Book of Yr. award); editor (with Peter Hay): Law and Institutions in the Atlantic Area, Readings, Cases and Problems, 1987; editor: (with Peter Hay and Michel Waelbrock) European Community Law and Institutions in Perspective, 1976; co-author, co-editor: Courts and Free Markets-Perspectives from the United States and Europe, 1982; bd. editors Am. Jour. Internat. Law, 1965—, mem. adv. bd. Common Market Law Rev., 1964—, Legal Issues of European Integration, 1974—, Rivista di Diritto Europeo, 1978—, Columbia Jour. E. European Law, 1994—; contbr. articles to profl. jours. Mem. Internat. Com. Revision Czechoslovak Constn., 1990—92. With US Army, 1943—46. Decorated Bronze Star, Order Italian Crown, Italian Mil. Cross; recipient Lifetime Achievement medal, Am. Soc. Comparative Law, 2004, Lifetime Contbn. prize, European Union Studies Assn., 2005, First Degree Outstanding Scholarly Achievement medal, Pres. Czech. Republic, 2001, Gold medal, Charles U., Prague, 2005; named Hon. Citizen of Hometown Holice, Czech. Republic, 2001, Eric Stein Collegiate Chair, U. Mich. Law Sch., 2007; fellow, Inst. Advanced Study, Berlin, 1984—85; Gugenheim fellow, 1962—63, Social Sci. Rsch. Coun. grantee, Rockefeller Found. scholar-in-residence, Bellagio, Italy, 1965, 1973, Alexander von Humboldt Stiftung grantee, 1982, Rsch. grantee, IREX, 1995. Mem.: ABA (co-chmn. European law com. 1982, mem. coun. sect. internat. law and practice 1983—84), Am. Jour. Internat. Law (bd.editors 1962—), Internat. Acad. Comparative Law, Brit. Inst. Internat. and Comparative Law, Am. Soc. Internat. Law (exec. coun. 1954—57, bd. rev. and devel. 1965—67, 1970—75, hon. v.p. 1982—2000), European Studies Assn., Coun. Fgn. Rels., Internat. Law Assn. Home: 2649 Heather Way Ann Arbor MI 48104-2850 Office Phone: 734-764-0541. E-mail: steine@umich.edu.

STEIN, FLORENCE TAUB, retired social worker; b. Bklyn. d. Isidor and Mary Marcus Taub; m. Milton Stein, June 23, 1949 (dec.); children: Susan D., Joseph L. BA, NY U., NYC, 1938; MS, Columbia U. Sch. Social Work, NYC, 1941. ACSW. Social worker Bklyn. Jewish Hosp., 1941—44, social work supr., 1944—46, Grace New Haven Hosp., 1946—48; social work cons. NY Dept. Health, NYC, 1948—51; dir. dept. social work Kingsbrook Hosp., Bklyn., 1951—55; assoc. dir. social work Maimonides Hosp., Bklyn., 1964—67; cons. staff edn. Mt. Sinai Hosp., NYC, 1967—69; asst. prof. social work Mt. Sinai Sch. Medicine, NYC, 1968—69; asst. dir. to assoc. dir. dept. social work Roosevelt Hosp., NYC, 1969—78; dir. dept. social work St. Luke's Roosevelt Hosp., NYC, 1978—82; social work cons. Columbia U. Sch. Social Work, NYC, 1982—87. Bd. mem. Jewish Family Svcs. South Middlesex County, 1986—2006; chair pers. practices Jewish Family Svcs. South Middlesex County, 2000—06, merger com. chair, 2004—06; bd. mem. Jewish Family and Vocat. Svcs., Middlesex, 2006—. Editor conf. proceedings; contbr. articles to profl. jours. Commr. Office on Aging Monroe Twp., NJ, 1997—; pres. Monroe Twp. Hadassah, NJ, 1988—90, Sisterhood Rossmoor Jewish Congregation; v.p. Southern NJ Region Hadassah, Neptune, 2001—03; bd. mem. Cancer Care, NYC, 1982—90. Recipient Outstanding Leadership as Pres., Met. NY Soc. Hosp. Social Work Dirs., 1978, honors as chair merger com., Jewish Family and Vocational Svcs., 2006, proclamation, NJ State Senate and Gen. Assembly, 2006; named Citizen of Yr., Kiwanis, 1991. Mem.: Soc. Social Work, Leadership in Health Care (pres. 1978, adminstr.), Nat. Assn. Social Workers (life). Democrat. Jewish. Avocations: bridge, dance, shuffleboard, reading, volunteering. Home: 604 A Tilton Way Monroe Township NJ 08831-2002 Home Phone: 609-655-8169. Personal E-mail: fmsj@verizon.net.

STEIN, FRANKLIN JOSEPH, music educator; b. Eau Claire, Wis., Mar. 26, 1945; s. Herbert Charles Stein and Gwenn Marie Lassek. BS in Secondary Edn., U. Wis., Eau Claire, 1968; BS in Computer Sci., Coleman Coll., La Mesa, Calif., 1989, MIS in Info. Sys., 1995. Cert. tchr. Wis. Biology, sci., Spanish tchr. Stanley-Boyd HS, Stanley, Wis., 1968-71; salesman Jerry's Hammond Organ & Piano Studios, Eau Claire, Wis., 1971—72; dept. mgr. Day Music Co., Eau Claire, 1973—74; store mgr. Tropic Waters Pet Store, Eau Claire, 1975-76, Thearle Music Co., San Diego, 1977—82; 6th grade tchr. St. Paul's Luth. Sch., Pacific Beach, Calif., 1977-78; profl. theatre organist Organ Power Pizza Restaurants, San Diego, 1977-85; store mgr. Organ Stop Inc., San Diego, 1982—89; computer programmer analyst Health Examinetics, Rancho Bernardo, Calif., 1989-91; clin. computer systems specialist SHARP Health Care, San Diego, 1991—97; systems programmer/clin. analyst U. Calif., San Diego, 1997—2002; counselor emotionally disturbed youth New Alternatives, Inc. Comprehensive Adolescent Treatment Ctr., San Diego, 2003—04. Profl. musician, 1965—. Author: Technician's Manual of Thermography, 1987, IDXrad User's Manual & Annual Updates, 1991-97; editor: Manual of Thermography, 1988. Music dir., organist, Miramar, Calif., 1996—2007; sponsor PLAN USA/Childreach, 2000—07. Recipient Silver medal Piano Performance Wis. Music Educators, 1962, 63, Cert. of Merit for Excellence in Sci., Wis. Jr. Acad. of Sci., 1963. Democrat. Buddhist. Avocations: classical music, reading, travel. Home and Office: 10227 Kamwood Pl San Diego CA 92126-5139 Personal E-mail: fjstein@msn.com.

STEIN, GARY S., lawyer, retired state supreme court justice; b. Newark, June 13, 1933; s. Morris J. and Mollie (Goldfarb) S.; m. Et Tilchin, July 1, 1956; children: Jill, Carrie, Michael, Terri, Jo AB, Duke U., 1954, LL.B. with distinction, 1956; D.H.L. (hon.), N.J. Inst. Tech., 1985. Bar: D.C. 1956, Ohio 1957, N.Y. 1958, N.J. 1963. Research asst. US Senate AntiTrust & Monopoly Subcom., Washington, 1955; assoc. Kramer, Marx, Greenlee & Backus, NYC, 1956-65; sole practice Paramus, NJ, 1966-72; ptnr. Stein & Kurland, Esquires, Paramus, NJ, 1972-82; dir. Gov.'s Office of Policy and Planning, Trenton, NJ, 1982-85; assoc. justice NJ Supreme Ct., Hackensack, 1985—2002; spl.

counsel Pashman Stein, Hackensack, 2002—; interim trustee Tropicana Casino & Resort, 2007—. Mcpl. atty., Paramus, 1967-71; counsel N.J. Election Law Revision Commn., 1970; atty. Bd. Adjustment, Teaneck, N.J., 1973-82 Mem. editl. bd. Duke Law Jour., 1954-56, assoc. editor, 1955-56. Mem. Dist. Ethics Com. for Bergen County, N.J., 1977-80, chmn. 1981. Served with U.S. Army, 1957-58, 61-62 Mem. ABA, N.J. State Bar Assn. (com. on state legislation 1973-79, chmn. 1973-76, jud. selection com. 1976-81, Constl. amendment com. 1977-79, court modernization com. 1976-79), Bergen County Bar Assn., Order of Coif. Jewish. Avocation: tennis. Office: Pashman Stein Ct Plaza South 21 Main St Hackensack NJ 07601 Office Phone: 201-488-8200. Business E-Mail: gstein@pashmanstein.com.

STEIN, HOWARD S., retired banker; b. NYC, Dec. 27, 1939; s. J. Zachary and Adele (Epstein) S. BA, U. Mich., 1961; MBA, Harvard U., 1963. Mem. treas.'s staff Gen. Motors Corp., NYC, 1963-69; dep. dir., dir. fiscal ops. Human Resources Adminstrn., City of N.Y., 1969-71, dep. adminstr., 1972-74, 1st dep. adminstr., 1974-78; asst. commr. Manpower and Career Devel. Agy., NYC, 1971-72; dep. commr. rent and housing maintenance Housing and Devel. Adminstrn., City of N.Y., 1972; v.p. Citicorp Credit Services Inc., NYC, 1979-86; sr. v.p. Citicorp Retail Services Inc., NYC, 1986-87; exec. dir. Landmark Mut. Funds Group of Citibank, N.A., NYC, 1987-88; v.p. br. banking sect. devel. div. Citibank NA, 1989-91, sr. credit officer worldwide securities svcs. div. Fin. Instns. Group NYC, 1991-94; group risk mgr. Global Transaction Svcs., NYC, 1995—2001, head operational risk mgmt., emerging markets and transaction svcs., 2002—03; mng. dir., head operational risk mgmt. Global Corp. and Investment Bank, 2003—04; ret., 2004—08; treas., bd. dirs. Ptnrs. of '63 (formerly Applecore Ptnrs.), 1999—2009; sr. advisor Fortent (formerly Searchpace Corp.), 2005—09; chmn. adv. com. Risk Bus., 2006—09; mem. bd. dirs. AIG Fed. Savings Bank, 2008—. Lectr. human resources policy Nova U., Ft. Lauderdale, Fla., 1973-74; field instr. adminstrn. specialization NYU Sch. Social Work, 1976-77; mem. risk mgmt. com. Participants Trust Co., 1995-99. Past Bd. dirs., chmn. program com. Vol. Urban Cons. Group, Inc.; past chmn. bd. dirs. Nova Inst; past treas., past pres., bd. dirs. Child Study Assn. Am./Wel-Met, Inc., 1963-85; past treas., bd. dirs. Career Center for Social Services Greater N.Y., Inc.; past treas., past pres. bd. dirs. Cavalier King Charles Spaniel Club U.S.A., Inc.; past bd. dirs., past sec. Child Welfare Info. Services; treas., bd. dirs., chmn. fin. com. WNYC Radio; bd. dirs. Senate Residence Owners Inc., New Goddard-Riverside Housing Devel. Fund Co., N.Y.C. Health and Hosps., Corp., 1976,; past bd. dirs. Homes for the Homeless; past mem. corp. Children's Mus., Boston; bd. dirs., treas., chair fin. com. Goddard Riverside Neighborhood House; trustee, chair fin. com. Pratt Inst.; treas., bd. dirs. Ptnrs. of '63, 1999—; past mem. Dept. Disciplinary com. Supreme Ct. State N.Y. Appellate Divsn. 1st Jud. Dept.; past mem. corp. adv. com. U. Mich., Coll. Lit., Sci and the Arts, treas.; bd. dirs. The Childrens' Cause for Cancer Advocacy, 2003—; mem. risk mgmt. adv. com., Fin. Svcs. Vol. Corp, 2006—. Recipient Vol. Svc. award, Pres. US, 2007, award. Mem.: Risk Mgmt. Assn. (co-chmn. operational risk coun. 2002—03, chair 2004, past mem. bd. and exec. com.), Inst. Internat. Fin. (mem. working group on operational risk 2001—04), Harvard (N.Y.C., past mem. admissions com.). Home: 1158 5th Ave New York NY 10029-6917 Personal E-mail: owardstein@gmail.com.

STEIN, JAMES HOWARD, medical educator, researcher; b. Milw., Aug. 17, 1964; Bachelor's degree with honors, U. Wis.; MD, Yale U., 1990. Diplomate Am. Bd. Echocardiography in Comprehensive Adult Echocardiography, cert. Internal Medicine, 1993, Cardiovascular Disease, 1997. Intern, internal medicine U. Chgo. Pritzker Sch. Med. Ctr., 1990—91, resident, cardiology, 1991—93; fellow in cardiology Rush-Presbyterian-St. Luke Med. Ctr., Chgo., 1994—96; assoc. prof. cardiovascular medicine U. Wis. Med. Sch., Madison, Wis., 1996, prof. cardiovascular medicine, dir. Atherosclerosis Imaging Rsch. Prog., dir. preventive cardiology, assoc. dir. adult echocardiography. Dir., atherosclerosis imaging rsch. program U. Wis.; assoc. dir., preventative cardiology program U. Wis. Hosp. and Clinics, dir., vascular health screening program, dir., preventive cardiology; dir. Outpatient Cardiovascular Medicine Svcs.; assoc. dir. Adult Echocardiography Lab.; mem. Complications of HIV Therapy Subcommittee Rsch. Adv. Com., Adult AIDS Clin. Trial Group Divsn. AIDS, Nat. Inst. Allergy and Infectious Diseases; ad hoc reviewer for two NIH study sessions. Co-author: Am. Soc. Echocardiography Recommendations for Use Echocardiography in Clinical Trials; contbr. articles to peer-reviewed jours. Named one of Top Docs in Cardiology, Madison Mag., 2000—, 20 Best Cardiologists, Men's Health Mag., 2007, Women's Health Mag., 2008. Fellow: Am. Coll. Cardiology (co-chmn. ann. scientific sessions 2006, rep. to Nat. Cholesterol Edn. program, mem. clin. expert and consensus documents task force, W. Proctor Harvey Young Tchr. award for Excellence in Tchg. 2001); mem.: ACP, Am. Soc. Echocardiography (mem. Carotid IMT task force), Am. Heart Assn., Alpha Omega Alpha. Office: U Wis Dept Medicine Mail Code 3248 600 Highland Avenue Madison WI 53792-3248 Office Phone: 608-263-9648. Office Fax: 608-263-0405. Business E-Mail: jhs@medicine.wisc.edu.*

STEIN, JARED J., theater director, educator; s. Jerome and Sima Stein. BFA, Carnegie Mellon U., Pitts., 1995; MFA, UCLA, 2001. Gen. & artistic dir. Fourthworld Theatre Projects, NYC, 2003—; vis. faculty & guest dir. Southwestern U., Georgetown, Tex. Office: Fourthworld Theatre Projects 660 Riverside Dr Ste 4J New York NY 10031 Business E-Mail: jared@thefourthworldlab.org.

STEIN, JEREMY CHAIM, economics professor; b. Chgo., Oct. 17, 1960; s. Elias M. and Elly (Intrator) S.; m. Anne Louise Maasland, May 25, 1990. AB summa cum laude, Princeton U., 1983; PhD, MIT, 1986. Asst. prof. fin. Harvard Bus. Sch., Cambridge, Mass., 1986-89; sr. staff economist Coun. Econ. Advisers, Exec. Office of the Pres., Washington, 1989-90; assoc. prof. fin. MIT Sloan Sch. of Mgmt., Cambridge, 1990—93, prof. fin., 1993—94, J.C. Penney prof. mgmt., 1994—2000; prof. economics Harvard U., 2000—05, Moise Y. Safra prof. economics, 2005—. Staff economist Presdl. Task Force on Market Mechanisms, Washington, 1987-88; rsch. assoc. Nat. Bur. Econ. Rsch., 1992-; fin. adv. roundtable Fed. Reserve Bank of NY, 2006- Contbr. articles to profl. jours.; adv. editor Economics Letters, 1993-2002; editl. bd. Am. Econ. Review, 1993-96; assoc. editor Quarterly Jour. Economics, 1992-2006, Jour. Fin. Economics, 2000-06; co-editor Jour. Econ. Perspectives, 2007-. Recipient Merton Miller prize, 1996, Jensen prize, 1998, Excellence in Tchg. award, Sloan Sch., 1993-96, Alumni award, 1998, Fama-DFA prize, 2001, 2002, Brattle prize, 2002; grantee NSF, 1992-94, 1995-98, 1999-2002, 2002-07; grad. fellow, NSF, Washington, 1983-86; rsch. fellow, Harvard Bus. Sch., 1986-87, Marvin Bower fellow, 1999-2000; Batterymarch fellowship, 1991-92; vis. scholar, Fed. Reserve Bd., 1990. Fellow Am. Acad. Arts and Sciences; mem. Am. Econ. Assn. (bd. dirs., 2000-03, v.p., 2006, pres.-elect, 2007, pres., 2008), Am. Fin. Assn., Phi Beta Kappa. Office: Dept Economics Littauer 209 Harvard U Cambridge MA 02138 Office Phone: 617-496-6455. Office Fax: 617-496-7352. E-mail: jeremy_stein@harvard.edu.*

STEIN, JOEL, physiatrist; BS, Columbia U.; MD, Albert Einstein Coll. Medicine, 1986. Intern Montefiore Hosp., Bronx, NY, 1987, resident, 1989, Columbia-Presbyterian Medical Ctr., 1992; medical staff Spaulding Rehab. Hosp., Boston, 1992—2008, chief medical officer, 2000—08, medical dir. stroke rehab program; faculty mem. Harvard Medical Sch., 1993—2008; physiatrist-in-chief NewYork-Presbyterian Hosp., 2008—; Simon Baruch Prof., chair dept. rehab. medicine Columbia U. Coll. Physicians and Surgeons, 2008—; prof., chief rehab. medicine Weill Cornell Medical Coll., 2008—. Office: Rehab Medicine Associates Harkness Pavilion 180 Fort Washington Ave Ste 1-199 New York NY 10032 Office Phone: 212-305-3535.*

STEIN, JOHN C., lawyer; b. Flint, Mich., May 8, 1939; s. Joseph Aloyosius and Gertrude (Carlin) S.; m. Dorothea Ruel, Nov. 20, 1965; children: John Jr., Christian, Peter, Thea. BA, U. San Francisco, 1963; JD, U. Calif. Hastings, San Francisco, 1966; cert., Mil. Justice Sch., Newport, RI, 1968. Bar: Calif. 1966, U.S. Dist. Ct. (no., ctrl. and so. dists.) Calif. 1969. Dep. city atty. City of San Francisco, Office of City Atty., 1969-71; with The Boccardo Law Firm, San Jose, Calif., 1971—, mng. ptnr., 1981-99. Judge pro tem San Francisco County Superior Ct., 1978—, Santa Clara County Superior Ct., 1981—; lectr. U. Santa Clara Law Sch., 1985—, Hastings Coll. of Law, U. C. San Francisco. Bd. dirs. Katherine Delmar Burke Sch. Girls, San Francisco, 1988-92, Planning Orgn. for The Richmond, San Francisco, 1985-88. Capt. USMC, 1966-69. Fellow Am. Coll. Trial Lawyers; mem. ATLA, Consumer Attys. of Calif. (Trial Lawyer of Yr. San Jose), Am. Bd. Trial Advocates. Democrat. Roman Catholic. Avocations: golf, skiing, scuba diving. Office: Boccardo Law Firm 111 W Saint John St Ste 400 San Jose CA 95113-1107 Office Phone: 408-298-5678. Business E-Mail: jstein@boccardo.com.

STEIN, JULIE K., museum director, educator; BA, Western Mich. U., Kalamazoo, 1974; MA, U. Minn., Mpls., 1976, PhD, 1980. Asst. prof., dept. anthropology U. Wash., 1980—86, assoc. prof., dept. anthropology, 1986—94, prof., dept. anthropology, 1994—, prof., interdisciplinary grad. program in museology, 1996—; dir. Burke Mus. of Natural History and Culture, U. Wash., 2005—. Adj. asst. prof., Quaternary Rsch. Ctr. U. Wash., 1981—86, adj. assoc. prof., Quaternary Rsch. Ctr., 1986—94, adj. prof., Quaternary Rsch. Ctr., 1994—, assoc. chair, dept. anthropology, 1993—94, acting chair, dept. anthropology, 1994—95, divisional dean, Coll. Arts and Scis., 1999—2005; chair Wash. Archeol. Rsch. Ctr., 1986; adj. prof., dept. anthropology U. Tenn., 1998—2000; lectr. in field. Author: (books) Deciphering a Shell Midden, 1992, Exploring Coast Salish Prehistory: The Archaeology of San Juan Island, 2000, Vashon Island Archaeology: A View from Burton Acres Shell Midden, 2003; contbr. articles to profl. jours. Recipient Young Am. Women Scholars Recognition award, Am. Assn. Univ. Women Ednl. Found., 1983—84, Evergreen award, Wash. State, 1993, Hist. Preservation award for enhancing pub. edn., State Hist. Preservation Officer's, 1997, Alumni Achievement award, Western Mich. U., 2000, Disting. Tchg. award, U. Wash., 2005; named to Outstanding Alumni Acad., Western Mich. U., Dept. Geosciences, 2001. Mem.: Assn. Wash. Archaeology (v.p. 1995—96), Am. Assn. Mus., Soc. for Archeol. Sci., Geol. Soc. Am. (chair archeol. geology divsn. awards com. 1986—88, 2nd vice chair archeol. geology divsn. 1988—89, 1st vice chair archeol. geology divsn. 1989—90, chair archeol. geology divsn. 1990—91, Rip Rapp Archeol. Geology Divsn. award 1999), Soc. for Am. Archaeology (mem. publ. com. 1991—93, mem. exec. com. 1993—96, chair geoarchaeology spl. interest group 1998—99), Phi Beta Kappa. Office: Burke Mus of Natural History and Culture U Wash Box 35-3010 Seattle WA 98195 Office Phone: 206-543-2784. Business E-Mail: jkstein@u.washington.edu.

STEIN, KEITH LANCE, health system administrator; Diploma, Rensselaer Poly. Inst.; MD, Albany Med. Coll., 1980. Diplomate in anesthesiology and critical care medicine Am. Bd. Anesthesiology. Intern, resident, fellow U. Mass. Med. Ctr., 1980—85; chief med. officer, sr. v.p. Bapt. Health, Jacksonville, Fla., 1999—. Fellow: Am. Coll. Chest Physicians, Am. Coll. Critical Care Medicine. Office: Bapt Health 800 Prudential Dr Jacksonville FL 32207 Business E-Mail: keith.steinmd@bmcjax.com.

STEIN, KIRA D., psychiatrist; d. David H. and Vivien Y. Burt; m. Michel R. Stein, Aug. 18, 1996. BA in Polit. Sci., UCLA, 1991; MD, U. Rochester, NYC, 1997. Post-baccalaureate pre-med. cert. Bryn Mawr Coll., Pa., 1993, cert. in cognitive behavioral therapy UCLA Anxiety Disorders Clinic, 2000, in interpersonal psychotherapy UCLA Interpersonal Psychotherapy Clinic, 2001, in psychiatry Am. Bd. Psychiatry and Neurology, 2003, registered Drug Enforcement Agy., 1999. Intern internal medicine Huntington Meml. Hosp., LA, 1997—98; resident adult psychiatry program UCLA Neuropsychiatric Inst., 1998—2001, clin. instr., David Geffen Sch. Medicine, 2001—. Pvt. practice, Sherman Oaks, Calif., 2001—. Contbr. chapters to books, articles to profl. jours. Avocations: travel, camping, hiking, swimming, theater. Office: Ste 410 15300 Ventura Blvd Sherman Oaks CA 91403

STEIN, LAURA, lawyer, consumer products company executive; b. 1961; children: Amanda, Christopher. BA, Dartmouth Coll., 1983; JD, Harvard Law Sch., 1987; MA, Dartmouth Coll. Bar: Calif., 1987. Tracsactional corp. lawyer Morrison & Foerster, San Francisco; asst. gen. counsel, regulatory affairs The Clorox Co., Oakland, Calif., 1992—99; sr. v.p., gen. counsel H.J. Heinz Co., Pittsburgh, Pa., 2000—05, The Clorox Co., Oakland, Calif., 2005—. Dir. Franklin Resources, Inc. Mem.: Am. Soc. Corp. Sect., ABA (chmn. Commn. on Domestic Violence), Assn. Corp. Counsel (treas., mem. exec. com.), Calif. State Bar. Office: Clorox Co 1221 Broadway Oakland CA 94612-1888

STEIN, LAURENCE JAY, lawyer; b. West Hartford, Conn., Mar. 20, 1961; s. Milton and Selma (Roth) S.; m. Miriam Beth Siegel, Aug. 17, 1986. AB magna cum laude, Harvard Coll., 1982; JD, Stanford U., 1985. Bar: Ill. 1986, Calif. 1999. Clk. to Chief Judge Walter J. Cummings U.S. Ct. Appeals (7th cir.), Chgo., 1985-86; assoc. Latham & Watkins, Chgo., 1986-92, partner, 1993-97, LA, 1997—, global chmn. Tax Dept., 2000—. Recipient Urban A. Sontheimer award Stanford U., 1985, John Harvard Scholarships, Harvard Coll., 1979-82. Mem. ABA, Calif. Bar Assn., Order of the Coif, Phi Beta Kappa Avocation: golf. Office: Latham Watkins 355 S Grand Ave Los Angeles CA 90071-1560

STEIN, LAWRENCE V., lawyer; b. Newark, Feb. 10, 1950; AB cum laude, Columbia Coll., 1971; MA, Cornell U., 1974; JD magna cum laude, U. Pa. Law Sch., 1976. Atty. Arnold & Porter, 1976—84, ptnr., 1984—92; sr. v.p., gen. counsel, sec. Genetics Inst., 1992—97; sr. v.p., chief legal counsel Wyeth-Ayerst Global Pharms. and Genetics Inst., 1997—2001; sr. vp., dep. gen. counsel Wyeth, 2001—03, sr. v.p., gen. counsel, 2003—. Comment editor U. Penn Law Rev., 1975—76. Avocation: golf. Office: Wyeth 5 Giralda Farms Madison NJ 07940-0874 Office Phone: 973-660-6138. E-mail: steinl@wyeth.com.

STEIN, MARVIN, psychiatrist, historian; b. St. Louis, Dec. 8, 1923; s. Samuel G. and Dora (Kline) S.; m. Ann Hackman, May 5, 1950; children: Leslie, David, Lisa. BS, MD, Washington U., St. Louis, 1949; grad., Phila. Psychoanalytic Inst., 1959. Intern St. Louis City Hosp., 1949-50; asst. resident in psychiatry Barnes Hosp., St. Louis, 1950-51; fellow in psychiatry Hosp. U. Pa., 1953-55; asst. prof., then assoc. prof. psychiatry U. Pa. Med. Sch., 1956-63; prof. psychiatry Cornell U. Med. Sch., NYC, 1963-66; prof., chmn. dept. psychiatry SUNY Downstate Med. Ctr., Bklyn., 1966-71; chmn. dept. psychiatry Mt. Sinai Sch. Medicine, NYC, 1971-87, Esther and Joseph Klingenstein prof., 1971-94, Esther and Joseph Klingenstein prof. emeritus, 1994—. Mem. fellowships rev. panel NIMH, 1961-64, chmn. mental health extramural rsch. adv. com., 1968-71, chmn. rev. com. Mental Health Aspects of AIDS, 1988-90; mem. rsch. adv. com. VA, 1965-68, mem. rsch. svc. merit rev. bd. in behavioral sci., 1972-75; chmn. Mental Health Rsch. Career Award Com., 1963-67; chmn. bd. dirs. Founds. Fund for Rsch. in Psychiatry, 1967-70; mem. behavioral medicine study sect. NIH, 1981-83, geriatric rev. com., 1986-88. Contbr. articles on brain and behavior and immune function and history of psychiatry to med. and history jours. USPHS postdoctoral fellow, 1951-53; mental health career investigator, 1956-61; sr. fellow grantee, 1961-63. Mem. Am. Psychiat. Assn. (chmn. rsch. coun. 1981-84), N.Y. Acad. Medicine (Salmon com. 1984—), Alpha Omega Alpha. Home: 5700 Arlington Ave Bronx NY 10471-1503 Office: Mt Sinai Sch Medicine 1 Gustave L Levy Pl New York NY 10029-6500 Business E-Mail: marvin.stein@mssm.edu.

STEIN, MELVIN A., accountant; b. NYC, Sept. 7, 1932; s. William H. and Lillian (Goldberg) S.; m. Barbara Blumencranz, Dec. 17, 1955 (dec.); children: Susan, Karen; m. Marie Sacco, Nov. 1, 1992. BS, NYU, 1953. Pvt. practice acctg., Jericho, NY, 1961-75; pres. Stein & Stein, P.C., Hicksville, 1975-81, Stein, Stein & Feit, P.C., 1982—. Bd. dir. Stern Sch. Bus. N.Y. U., treas. bd. dir., 1991—92, v.p. bd. dir., 1995—, alumni bd. dir., mem. dean adv. coun., 2002—, pres. exec. forum, 2002—, dir. entrepreneurship conf., 2000—. Recipient NYU Alumni Meritorious Svc. award, 2005. Mem. AICPA, N.Y. State Soc. CPAs, N.J. Soc. CPAs, C.W. Post Tax Inst., NYU Club, Princeton Club, The Exec. Forum (pres.). Jewish. Home: 7 Ingleside Ln White Plains NY 10605-5009 Office: 1 Frederick Pl Hicksville NY 11801-4205 also: Buccaneer Mall St Thomas VI 00801 Office Phone: 516-938-2100. Personal E-mail: cpa35@aol.com.

STEIN, MILTON MICHAEL, retired lawyer; b. NYC, Sept. 18, 1936; s. Isidore and Sadie (Lefkowitz) S.; m. Jacqueline Martin, June 17, 1962; children: April, Alicia. AB, Columbia U., NYC, 1958, LLB, 1961. Bar: N.Y. 1962, Pa. 1971, U.S. Supreme Ct. 1971. Asst. dist. atty. N.Y. County, 1962-67; sr. counsel Nat. Commn. for Reform of Fed. Criminal Law, Washington, 1967-70; asst. dist. atty., chief of appeals City of Phila., 1970-73; asst. dir. Nat. Wire Tapping Commn., Washington, 1973-75; dir. D.C. Law Revision, Washington, 1975-77; spl. asst. HUD, Washington, 1977-79; asst. gen. counsel U.S. Commodity Futures Trading Commn., Washington, 1979-83; v.p. N.Y. Futures Exch., NYC, 1983-89, N.Y. Stock Exch., NYC, 1989—2005; ret., 2005; arbitrator, 2005—; adjudication com. COMEX, MYMEX, 2006—. Democrat. Jewish. Home: Hudson House PO Box 286 Ardsley On Hudson NY 10503-0286 Personal E-mail: thejamis@aol.com.

STEIN, MIRIAM, social worker, training services executive; b. Boston, Sept. 25, 1941; d. Ernest and Grete Hamburger; m. William Mark Stein, July 11, 1965; children: Adam, Amelle. MSW, Boston U., 1965. Lic. ind. clin. social worker Mass. Program dir. Mass. Human Services Coalition, Boston, 1978—82; free-lance journalist, 1980—; dir. comm. Mass. Immigrant and Refugee Advocacy Coalition, Boston, 1998—2001; advocacy and media trainer, cons. Stein Consulting, Arlington, Mass., 2001—; project dir. Coop. Met. Ministries, Newton, Mass., 2002—. Interfaith religious task force on welfare Campaign for Real Welfare Reform, Boston, 1994—96; mem. adv. bd. Office of Justice and Peace, Sisters of St. Joseph, Boston, 1994—2002; guest lectr. Sch. Social Work, Simmons Coll., 2003—; pres. Mass. Human Services Coalition, Boston, 2005—. Author: (memoir) To Trust The Future. Co-chair Vision 2020 Diversity Task Group, Arlington, Mass., 1994—2004; mem. Arlington Fair Housing Adv. Com., 1983—94. Recipient Citizen award, Arlington Fair Housing Adv. Com., 1998, Spl. award, Foster Kids' Caucus of the Mass. Legislature, 1998, MLK Jr. Cmty. Svc. award, 2003, Social Worker of the Yr., Nat. Assn. Social Workers, Mass. Chpt., 2006. Mem.: NASW (dir. of govtl. affairs Mass chpt. 1984—98, recognition award 1996). Jewish. Home: 17 Oak Knoll Arlington MA 02476 Office: Stein Consulting 17 Oak Knoll Arlington MA 02476 E-mail: miriam.stein@comcast.net.

STEIN, PAUL DAVID, cardiologist; b. Cin., Apr. 13, 1934; s. Simon and Sadie (Friedman) S.; m. Janet Louise Tucker, Aug. 14, 1966; children: Simon, Douglas, Rebecca. BS, U. Cin., 1955, MD, 1959. Intern Jewish Hosp., Cin., 1959-60, med. resident, 1961-62, Gorgas Hosp., C.Z., 1960-61; fellow in cardiology U. Cin., 1962-63, Mt. Sinai Hosp., NYC, 1963-64; rsch. fellow Harvard Med. Sch., Boston, 1964-66; asst. dir. cardiac catheterization lab. Baylor U. Med. Ctr., Dallas, 1966-67; asst. prof. medicine Creighton U., Omaha, 1967-69; assoc. prof. medicine U. Okla., Oklahoma City, 1969-73; prof. rsch. medicine U. Okla. Coll. Medicine, Oklahoma City, 1973-76; dir. cardiovascular rsch. Henry Ford Hosp., Detroit, 1976-94, med. dir. cardiovascular rehab., 1994-2000; dir. rsch. St. Joseph Mercy Oakland Hosp., Pontiac, Mich., 2000—04, dir. rsch. edn., 2005—; prof. medicine, Henry Ford Case Western Res. U., Cleve., 1994—2000; prof. medicine Wayne State U., Detroit, 2003—. Adj. prof. physics Oakland U., Rochester, Mich., 1985—Author: A Physical and Physiological Basis for the Interpretation of Cardiac Ausculation: Evaluations Based Primarily on Second Sound and Ejection Murmurs, 1981, Pulmonary Embolism, 1996, 2d edit., 2007; contbr. articles to profl. jours. Coun. on Clin. Cardiology fellow Am. Heart Assn., 1971, Coun. on Circulation fellow, 1972. Ret. capt. USAFR. Recipient Aristotle Gold medal, Aristotle U. Thessaloniki, 1993, Lifetime Achievement award, Am. Heart Assn., Mich. chpt., 2002, Plaque Recognition, St. Joseph Mercy Hosp., 2007; named to Hon. Order Ky. Cols., 1997. Master Fellow: Am. Coll. Chest Physicians (pres. 1993, medal recognition outstanding contbns. coll.); fellow ACP (Laureate award, Mich. chpt. 2003), ASME, Am. Coll. Cardiology, Am. Heart Assn. Office: St Joseph Mercy Oakland 44405 Woodward Ave Pontiac MI 48341-5023 Office Phone: 248-858-6772. Office Fax: 248-858-6974. Business E-Mail: steinp@trinity-health.org.

STEIN, PAULA JEAN ANNE BARTON, hotel real estate company executive, broker; b. Chgo., July 29, 1929; m. Marshall L. Stein; children: Guy G., George L.; guardian of Bradley Stein, Gregory Stein. BA, Lake Forest Coll., Ill., 1951; postgrad., Roosevelt U., Chgo., 1955—77, UCLA, 1978—79. Adminstrv. asst. publicity Kefauver for Pres., Chgo., 1951; adminstrv. asst. Wells Orgns., Chgo., 1952; rschr., writer Employers Assn. Am., Chgo., 1951-52; writer Woodworking Jobbers Assn., Chgo., 1953; cons. LA, 1978-80; pres., broker Steinvest, Inc., Chgo., 1980—; freelance writer, 1996—. Cons., hotels Nat. Diversified Svcs., Inc., Chgo., 1990—, Beach Hotel, Inc., Monterey, Calif., IBA Women's Adv. Bd., 1999; advocate for learning disorder solutions. Script for first TV bus. prog. on WGN-TV, 1951-52. Mem.

Ragdale Found., Lake Forest, Ill. IBA fellow, 1990. Mem. World Future Soc. (profl.), Sisters in Crime, Mystery Writers, So. Poverty Law Ctr., others. Avocations: painting, writing. Home and Office: Steinvest Inc 2291 Hybernia Dr Highland Park IL 60035-5509 Office Fax: 847-748-8349. Personal E-mail: steinvest@msn.com.

STEIN, RICHARD ALAN, cardiologist, educator; b. NYC, Apr. 7, 1942; BA, Columbia Coll., 1963; MD, NYU, 1967. Diplomate in internal medicine, cardiovascular diseases, geriatrics and sports medicine Am. Bd. Internal Medicine; lic. physician, N.Y., Conn.; lic. handler radioactive materials, N.Y.C. Intern, then resident in medicine Downstate Med. Ctr.-Kings County Hosp., Bklyn., 1967—69, cardiology fellow, 1972—74; chief resident in medicine Kings County Hosp., 1971—72, attending physician; prof. medicine, chief cardiology divsn. dept. medicine SUNY-Health Sci. Ctr., Bklyn., 1985—95; chief preventive and rehab. cardiology Lenox Hill Hosp., NYC, 1995—99; attending physician SUNY Hosp., Bklyn.; chief cardiology dept. Bklyn. Hosp. Ctr., 1999—2003; assoc. chair dept. medicine, chief medicine Beth Israel Hosp. - Singer Divsn., NYC, 2003—05; dir. preventive cardiology Beth Israel Med. Ctr., NYC, 2005—07, dir. Cardiology Fellowship Program, 2005—07; prof. medicine, dir. urban cardiology program NYU Sch. Medicine, NYC, 2007—. Mem. vis. faculty Yale-New Haven Hosp., 1982; dir. cardiology fellowship program Bklyn. VA Hosp., Brookdale Hosp., S.I. U. Hosp., 1985—95; dir. cardiac rehab. program 92d St. YM-YWHA, NYC; prof. clin. medicine Weill-Cornell Med. Ctr., 1999—2003, Albert Einstein Coll. Medicine, NYC, 2003—. Co-editor: Complementary and Alternative Medicine in Cardiovascular Disease, 2004; mem. editl. bd. Preventive Cardiology, Jour. Cmty. Health; sect. editor Heart Disease: A Jour. of Cardiovasc. Disease; editor: (textbook) Cardiovascular Alternative and Complementary Medicine, 2004, Outliving Heart Disease - Winning By the New Rules, 2006; contbr. chpt. to: Coronary Rehabilitation for the Practicing Physician, 1979, Sports Medicine for the Primary Care Physician, 1984, Anesthesia as Co-Existing Heart Disease, 1993, (with others) Diabetic Renal-Retinal Syndrome, 1980; contbr. articles to profl. jours. Maj. USAF, 1969-71. Recipient Acad. Career award, Preventive Cardiology Acad. award NIH, 1985-90. Fellow ACS, Am. Coll. Cardiology, Am. Coll. Chest Physicians, Am. Coll. Sports Medicine, N.Y. Cardiol. Soc. (bd. dirs.), N.Y. Acad. Medicine; mem. Am. Heart Assn. (fellow coun. on clin. cardiology, pres. Heritage affiliate, grantee in aid 1979-81), Assn. Profs. Cardiology, Am. Fedn. for Clin. Rsch., Sigma Xi. Office: Beth Israel Hosp 1st Ave and 16th St New York NY 10003 Office Phone: 212-420-4126, 212-263-7751. Personal E-mail: rastein@msn.com.

STEIN, ROBERT ALAN, electronics executive; b. Chgo., Oct. 18, 1930; s. Manfred and Mildred (Rosenfield) S.; m. Frances Roslyn Berger, Dec. 25, 1960; 1 dau., Marcia Beth. BA, U. Chgo., 1950, MBA, 1953. C.P.A., Ill. Sr. auditor Scovell, Wellington & Co., Chgo., 1955—63; supr. corp. acctg. Mack Trucks, Inc., Montvale, NJ, 1963—65; v.p. fin., treas. Lionel Corp., NYC, 1965—82; pres. ITI Electronics, Inc., Livingston, NJ, 1982—. With US Army, 1953—55. Mem. Am. Inst. CPAs. Personal E-mail: itielect@aol.com.

STEIN, ROBERT ALLEN, lawyer, educator, former legal association administrator; b. Mpls., Sept. 16, 1938; s. Lawrence E. and Agnes T. (Brynildson) S.; m. Sandra H. Stein; children: Linda Stein Routh, Laura Stein Conrad, Karin Stein O'Boyle. BS in Law, U. Minn., 1960, JD summa cum laude, 1961; LLD (hon.), Uppsala U., Sweden, 1993. Bar: Wis. 1961, Minn. 1967. Assoc. Foley, Sammond & Lardner, Milw., 1961-64; prof. U. Minn. Law Sch., 1964—94, dean, 1979-94, Everett Fraser prof. law, 2006—; assoc. dean U. Minn., 1976-77, v.p. adminstrn. and planning, 1978-80, faculty rep. men's intercollegiate athletics, 1981—94; of counsel Mullin, Weinberg & Daly, PA, Mpls., 1970-80, Gray Plant Mooty, Mpls., 1980-94, 2006—. Vis. prof. UCLA, 1969-70, U. Chgo., 1975-76; commr. Uniform State Laws Commn. Minn., 1973—; pres. Nat. Uniform Laws Com., 2009-, exec. comm., 1991—, sec., 1997-2005, chair scope and program comm., 2005-07, chair exec. com., 2007-09, v.p., 1991-93; pres. 2009-; acad. fellow Am. Coll. Trusts and Estates Counsel, 1975—; vis. scholar Am. Bar Found., Chgo., 1975-76; trustee Gt. No. Iron Ore Properties, 1982—, Uniform Laws Found., 1992-2008, chair, 2002-08; advisor Restatement of Law Second, Property, 1977—, Restatement of Law Trusts (Prudent Investor Rule), 1989-90, Restatement of Law Third, Trusts, 1993—; chmn. bd. dirs. Ednl. Credit Mgmt. Group, 1993-; bd. dirs. Fiduciary Counselling Inc., 1994-2008. Author: Stein on Probate, 1976, 4th edit., 2004, How to Study Law and Take Law Exams, 1996, Estate Planning Under the Tax Reform Act of 1976, 2d edit, 1978, In Pursuit of Excellence: A History of the University of Minnesota Law School, 1980, Law School Success in a Nutshell: A Guide to Studying Law and Taking Law School Exams, 2008, contbr. articles to profl. jours. Founding bd. dirs. Park Ridge Ctr., 1985-95; co-chair Gov.'s Task Force on Ctr. for Treatment of Torture Victims, 1985, bd. dirs., 1985-87. Fellow Am. Bar Found (bd. dirs. 1987-94), Am. Coll. Tax Counsel; mem. ABA (coun. sect. of legal edn. and admission to bar 1986-91, vice chairperson 1991-92, chair-elect 1992-93, chair 1993-94, exec. dir., COO 1994-2006), Internat. Acad. Estate and Trust Law (academician 1980-), Internat. Bar Assn. (profl. and pub. interest divsn. sec. 2004-06, vice chair 2006-08, chair 2009-), Am. Judicature Soc. (bd. dirs. 1984-88), Am. Law Inst. (coun. mem. 1987—, exec. com. 1993—2007, audit com. 2002-09, governance com. 2007-, investment com. mem. 2009-), Minn. Bar Assn. (bd. govs. 1979-94, exec. coun., probate and trust law sect. 1973-77), Hennepin County Bar Assn., U. Minn. Alumni Assn. (nat. pres. 2005-06). Office: U Minn Law Sch 229 19th Ave S Minneapolis MN 55455 Home Phone: 763-545-1701; Office Phone: 612-625-3047. Business E-Mail: stein@umn.edu.

STEIN, RONALD J., lawyer; b. NYC, 1935; AB, Columbia U., 1956; LLB cum laude, Harvard U., 1959; LLM, Georgetown U., 1962. Bar: NY 1959, DC 1959, Fla. 1975. Trusts and estates practice area Stroock & Stroock & Lavan LLP, NYC. Bd. dir. City Parks Found., NYC, 92nd St. YMCA, NYC. Bd. of editors Harvard Law Rev., 1958—59. Mem.: NY State Bar Assn., Assn. Bar City NY. Office: Stroock & Stroock & Lavan LLP 180 Maiden Ln New York NY 10038-4982 Office Phone: 212-806-6018. Office Fax: 212-806-9018. Business E-Mail: rstein@stroock.com.

STEIN, RUTH ELIZABETH KLEIN, physician; b. NYC, Nov. 2, 1941; d. Theodore and Mimi (Foges) Klein; m. H. David Stein, June 9, 1963; children: Lynn Andrea Stein Melnick, Sharon Lisa, Deborah Michelle. AB, Barnard Coll., NYC, 1962; MD, Albert Einstein Coll. Medicine, Bronx, NY, 1966. Diplomate Am. Bd. Pediat., Devel. Behavioral Pediat. Intern, then resident Bronx Mcpl. Hosp. Ctr., 1966—68; sr. resident, fellow; 1968instr. dept. pediats. George Washington U., Washington, 1968—70; with Albert Einstein Coll. of Medicine, Bronx, 1970—77, assoc. prof. pediats., 1977—83, prof., 1983—; vice-chmn. dept. pediats. Albert Einstein Coll., 1992—2002, dir. office of acad. affairs, dept. pediats., 1997—2002; pediatrician-in-chief, dir. pediats. Jacobi Med. Ctr. (formerly Bronx Mcpl. Hosp. Ctr.), 1992—97. Vis. prof. pub. health dept. epidemiology Yale U. Sch. Medicine, New Haven, 1986-87; scholar-in-residence United Hosp. Fund, NY, 1995-97; dir., prin. investigator Preventive Intervention Rsch. Ctr. for Child Health, NY, 1983-94, Nat. Child Health Assessment Planning Project, NY, Behavioral Pediatric Tng. Program, NY; dir. gen. pediatrics Pediat. Divsn., NY, 1992-97; apptd. to Montefiore Med. Ctr., North Ctrl. Bronx Hosp., Jacobi Med. Ctr.; bd. dirs. Ctr. for Child Health Rsch. of Am. Acad. Pediatrics, mem. exec. com., 1999-2004; co-chmn. com. on evaluation of child health 2002-04, NRC/Inst. Medicine, 1999-2005; bd. sci. advisors Nat. Inst. Arthritis and Musculoskelatal and Skin Diseases, 2005—; bd. sci. counselors Nat. Ctr. Health Stats. of CDC, 2006—; cons., Nat. Children's Study, Nat. Inst. Child Health & Human Devel., NIH, 2008-. Editor: Caring for Children with Chronic Illness: Issues and Strategies, 1989, Health Care for Children: What's Right, What's Wrong, What's Next, 1997; mem. editorial bd. Jour. Behavioral and Devel. Pediatrics, 1993-2006, Ambulatory Pediatrics, 1998-2005; contbr. articles to profl. jours. Fellow Am. Acad. Pediats.; mem. APHA, Am. Pediatric Soc., Soc. for Pediat. Rsch., Ambulatory Pediat. Assn. (bd. dirs. 1982-89, pres. 1987-88, rsch. award 1995, Ray Helfer award 1999), NY Acad. Medicine (chmn. NY forum on child health 2001-05), Soc. for Devel. and Behavioral Pediats., Alpha Omega Alpha. Jewish. Home: 91 Larchmont Ave Larchmont NY 10538-3748 Office: Albert Einstein Coll Med Montefiore Med Ctr Dept Pediat 111 E 210 St Bronx NY 10467-2804 Office Phone: 718-920-7932. Business E-Mail: rstein@aecom.yu.edu.

STEIN, SANDRA LOU, educational psychology professor emerita; b. Freeport, Ill., Oct. 6, 1942; d. William Kenneth and Marien Elizabeth Stein. BS, U. Wis., Madison, 1964; MS Edn., No. Ill. U., 1967, EdD, 1969. Tchr. English Rockford Sch. Dist., Ill., 1964—65; tchr. Russian Jefferson County Sch. Dist., Lakewood, Colo., 1965—66; asst. prof. edn. U. S.C., Columbia, 1969—71, No. Ill. U., DeKalb, 1971—72, Rider U., Lawrenceville, NJ, 1972—75, assoc. prof. edn., 1975—81; prof. edn. Rider Coll., Lawrenceville, 1981—2007, dept. chair, 1983—91, 2003—06; ret., 2007. Cons. on measurement and evaluation, women's edn., 1973—. Contbr. articles to ednl. publs Deacon Presbyn. Ch. Lawrenceville, 1984—87. Recipient Disting. Tchg. award Rider Coll. and Lindback Found., 1981 Mem. APA, AAUP (chpt. pres. 2000-01, negotiating team 2002, Outstanding Achievement award Rider Coll. chpt. 1988), Am. Ednl. Rsch. Assn., Phi Delta Kappa (chpt. pres. 1986-87, Svc. Key award 1991, faculty advisor 1994—99) Home: 70 Wiltshire Dr Lawrenceville NJ 08648-2585 E-mail: stein@rider.edu.

STEIN, SANDRA THERESE, pharmacist; b. Milw., Sept. 21, 1935; d. Harland Wheaton Stein and Sylvia Therese Perla. BS, U. Wis., Madison, 1960; PhD in Neotarian Philosophy, 1977, D of Nutripathy, 1988; LLB, Lasalle U., Chgo., 1991; D of Pharmacy, Broadmore U., Belize, 2000. Registered pharmacist Wis. Pharmacist mgr. Enterprise Pharmacy, Milw., 1968—83; pharmacy staff VA Hosp., North Chgo., 1983—88; pharmacist-in-charge Sentry Drugs, Milw., 1988—94, Durg Emporium, Greenfield, Wis., 1994—98; pharmacy staff Kohls Pharmacy, Milw., 1998—2003; relief pharmacist RPH On The Go, Milw., 1994—. Cons. Health Foods, Milw., 2000—. Avocations: reading, writing, movies, computers.

STEIN, STEPHEN, lawyer; b. Bklyn., Oct. 22, 1943; s. Alex and Rachel (Osbrach) S.; m. Anna Perett, Sept. 29, 2007; children: Sharyn, David, Katie Rachel. AB, NYU, 1964; JD, Bklyn. Law Sch., 1967. Bar: NY 1967, US Dist. Ct. (so. dist.) NY 1967, US Ct. Appeals (3rd cir.) 1973, Nev. 1974, US Ct. Appeals (9th cir.) 1974, US Supreme Ct. 1974, US Ct. Appeals (5th cir.) 1975, US Ct. Appeals (4th cir.) 1976, US Ct. Appeals (8th and 11th cirs.) 1982, US Ct. Appeals (6th cir.) 1987. Spl. atty. criminal div. US Dept. Justice, Phila., 1971-74; ptnr. Goodman, Stein & Chesnoff, Las Vegas, Nev., 1974—92, Stein & Rojas, Las Vegas, Nev. Pres. Temple Beth Am, Las Vegas, 1985-87. Lt. comdr. JAGC, USN, 1968-71. Named one of Best Criminal Defense Attys., Las Vegas Review-Jour., 1999. Mem. Nev. Trial Lawyers Assn. (bd. dirs. 1986-87). Democrat. Office: Stein & Rojas 520 S 4th St Las Vegas NV 89101 Office Phone: 702-384-5563. Personal E-mail: stephenstein.esr@yahoo.com.

STEIN, STEPHEN WILLIAM, lawyer; b. NYC, Apr. 12, 1937; s. Melvin S. and Cornelia (Jacobowitz) S.; m. Judith N., Jan. 22, 1966. AB, Princeton U., 1959; LLB, Columbia U., 1962; LLM, NYU, 1963. Bar: NY 1962. Assoc. White & Case, NYC, 1963-67; atty. advisor U.S. Agy. Internat. Devel., Washington, 1967-69, regional legal advisor Mission to India New Delhi, 1969-71, asst. gen. counsel Washington, 1971-73; assoc. ptnr. Delson & Gordon, NYC, 1973-87; ptnr. Kelley Drye & Warren, NYC, 1987—. U.S. exec. com. Indonesian Trade, Tourism & Investment Promotion Program, 1990-92; mem. U.S.-Indonesia Trade & Investment Adv. Com., 1989-92; vis. instr. Internat. Devel. Law Inst., 1993; lectr. Internat. Law Inst., Washington, 1984, 85; spkr. in field. Mem. ABA (mem. sect. internat. law, co-chair African law com. 1999-2002), Assn. Bar of City of N.Y. (mem. com. project fin. 1997-2003, mem. com. Asian affairs 1992—2004, former mem. others), Am. Indonesian C. of C. (bd. dirs. 1986—, pres. 1989-96). Home: 320 Central Park W New York NY 10025-7659 Office: Kelley Drye & Warren 101 Park Ave New York NY 10178-0062 Office Phone: 212-808-7794. Business E-Mail: sstein@kelleydrye.com.

STEIN, THOMAS HENRY, social sciences educator; b. Elmhurst, Ill., May 17, 1949; s. Peter Leonard and Marion Edith (Zirbel) S.; m. Alberta Piazza, July 10, 1971; 1 child, Heather. BA in Polit. Sci., Loyola U., Chgo., 1971; postgrad., Loyola U., 1972-76; MS in Edn., Pacific Western U., 1988, PhD in Edn., 1989. Cert. tchr., Ill. Budget analyst, dean global studies divsn. U.S. Dept. Def., Gt. Lakes Naval Sta., Ill., 1971—72; global studies dean, tchr. social sci., coach bowling, softball Mother Guerin High Sch., River Grove, Ill., 1972—; tchr. Highland Park (Ill.) High Sch., 1981-84. Instr. Franklin Park (Ill.) Park Dist., 1977—; tchr. Triton Coll., River Grove, 1990-91; evaluator Chgo. Met. History Fair, 1980-89; faculty adviser Scholastic, Inc., N.Y.C., 1990—; dir. Students Against Animal Cruelty, River Grove, 1991—; moderator Nat. Honor Soc., 1993—; adj. faculty St. Mary's U., 2003–. With Ill. N.G., 1971-77. Recipient Outstanding Achievement award Am. Express/Assn. Am. Geographers, 1989, Heart of the Sch. award for Peace and Justice, Archdiocese of Chgo. Fellow Acad. Polit. Sci.; mem. ASCD, Nat. Coun. Social Studies, Nat. Hist. Soc., Ctr. Study of the Presidency, Nat. Cath. Edn. Assn., Orgn. History Tchrs., Am. Polit. Sci. Assn. Democrat. Roman Catholic. Home: 3601 Emerson St Franklin Park IL 60131-1713 Office: Guerin Coll Prep HS 8001 W Belmont Ave River Grove IL 60171-1096 Office Phone: 708-453-6233 ext 91. Business E-Mail: tstein@guerinprep.org.

STEINBACH, LYNNE SUSAN, radiologist, educator; b. San Francisco, Dec. 28, 1953; d. Howard Lynne and Ilse (Rosengarten) S.; m. Eric Franklin Tepper, Aug. 14, 1977; 1 child, Mark Evan. Student, Vassar Coll.; BA, Stanford U., 1975; MD, Med. Coll. Pa., 1979. Cert. Am. Bd. Radiology, 1983. Intern Coll. Medicine and Dentistry N.J., Newark, 1979—80; resident radiology N.Y. Hosp.-Cornell Med. Ctr., NYC, 1980—83; fellow musculoskeletal radiology Hosp. Spl. Surgery Cornell Med. Ctr., NYC, 1983—84; asst. prof. radiology U. Calif., San Francisco, 1984—92, assoc. prof., 1992—98, prof., 1998—. Chief musculoskeletal imaging U. Calif. San Francisco, 1998—2007. Editor 4 books; contbr. articles 130 on radiology, chpts. on musculoskeletal radiology to profl. publs. Fellow Am. Coll. Radiology; mem. Internat. Skeletal Soc. (mem.-at-large 2002-03, asst. sec. 2003-04, bd. dirs., 2006-, sec., 2008-, Pres. medal, 1996), Internat. Soc. Mag. Res. Med. (bd. dirs., 2007-), San Francisco Radiol. Soc. (sec. treas. 1994, pres. 1996), Radiol. Soc. N.Am., Am. Assn. Women Radiologists (mem.-at-large 1987-88, sec. 1989-91, v.p. 1991-92, pres.-elect 1992-93, pres. 1993-94), Am. Roentgen Ray Soc., Assn. U. Radiologists, Soc. Skeletal Radiology. Avocations: swimming, travel, music, art. Home Phone: 415-388-7840. E-mail: lynne.steinbach@radiology.ucsf.edu.

STEINBACH, MEREDITH LYNN, writer, educator; b. Ames, Iowa, Mar. 18, 1949; d. Christopher Gene and Joy Janice (Johnson) Steinbach; m. Charles Ossian Hartman, May 5, 1979 (div. Dec. 1991); 1 child Zachary Steinbach Hartman BGS, U. Iowa, 1973, MFA, 1976. Teaching fellow U. Iowa, Iowa City, 1975-76; writer in residence Antioch Coll., Yellow Springs, Ohio, 1976-77; lectr. in fiction Northwestern U., Evanston, Ill., 1977-79; vis. asst. prof. U. Washington, 1979-82; Bunting fellow Harvard-Radcliffe, Cambridge, Mass., 1982-83; asst., assoc. prof. Brown U., Providence, R.I., 1983-97, prof. English, 1997—. Author: Zara, 1982, Here Lies the Water, 1990, Reliable Light, 1990, The Birth of the World As We Know It, Or, Teiresias, 1996, In the Realm of Which There Is No Sign, 1995. Recipient Pushcart prize Best of the Small Presses, 1976, R.I. award for Excellence in Lit., R.I. Coun. on Arts, 1986-87, O'Henry award for short story, 1990, creative writing fellow in fiction Nat. Endowment for Arts, 1978; Travel grant Thomas J. Watson Inst. for Internat. Study, France and Greece, 1993-94. Mem.: PEN, Assoc. Writing Programs, Amnesty Internat. Office: Brown U Dept of English Grad Program Literary Arts Box 1923 Providence RI 02912 E-mail: Meredith_Steinbach@Brown.edu.

STEINBACK, THOMAS R., business management educator; b. Evansville, Ind., May 17, 1950; s. Edward Oscar and Thelma Jean (Ellison) Steinback; m. Sherry Lynn Amos, Mar. 12, 1982; children: Lindsay Ann, Laura Jean, Chelsea Lynn. BA in Comm., Psychology and Religion, Amb. Coll., Eng., 1972; postgrad., Miss. State U., 1974—75; MBA, Syracuse U., 1980. Cert. office automation profl. 1987. Exec. trainee Ambascol Corp., England, 1970—72; coll. rep., field lectr. Ambassador Coll., Pasadena, Calif., 1972—77; mgr. employee and cmty. rels. Gen. Electric: HABD, Utica, NY, 1979—84; mgr. indsl. and profl. rels. Chgo. Pneumatic Tool Co., Utica, 1984—87; owner TRS Cons., 1987—93; corp. human resources payroll, dir. Moll Platicrafters LLP, 1993—94; corp. dir. human resources Hanson Industries, The ERTL Co., 1994—95; sr. assoc., bus. cons. Honkamp Krueger & Co. PC, HK Fin. Svcs., 1995—2003; CEO G&G Living Ctrs., G&G Found., 2003—06; pres., owner Advantage Bus. Cons., 2006—; asst. prof. entrepreneurship and small bus. devel. U. Wis., Platteville, 2007—. Cert. dir. FA-SHRM State Coun., 1996—2002. Mem. United Way Leadership Cir., 1944—2003. Recipient Grad. Alumni award, Syracuse U., 1980. Mem.: UWP Collegiate Entreprenews Orgn. (faculty adv.), Vis. Nurses Assn. (vice chair, sec., bd. dirs. 2004—07), Soc. for HR Mgrs. Personal E-mail: yankeefaninia@yahoo.com. Business E-Mail: steinbackt@uwplatt.cok.

STEINBAUGH, ROBERT P., management and finance educator; b. Mineral City, Ohio, Aug. 25, 1927; s. Paul W. and Blanche (Lechner) Steinbaugh; m. Carolyn Ann Gates, Nov. 24, 1967. BS, Ohio State U., 1950, MA, 1952, PhD, 1957. Instr. Miami U., Oxford, Ohio, 1953-55, Ohio State U., Columbus, 1955-57; asst. prof. mgmt. and fin. Ind. State U., Terre Haute, 1957-60, assoc. prof., 1960-63, prof. bus. adminstrn., 1963—. Mem. Acad. Mgmt., Am. Mgmt. Assn., Ohio State Alumni Assn., Beta Gamma Sigma, Delta Sigma Pi, Delta Pi Epsilon, Phi Delta Kappa, Phi Kappa Phi. Lodges: Rotary. Republican. Episcopalian. Home: 675 Woodlawn Ct Terre Haute IN 47803-4253

STEINBAUM, BERNICE, art dealer; b. Flushing, NY, Jan. 3, 1941; d. Julius Dov and Sarah (Lasker) Aptowitz; m. Harold Steinbaum; children: Jeremy, Sarah, Carrie. BA, Queens Coll., 1961; MA, Hofstra U., 1965; PhD in Art Edn., Columbia U., 1977. Tchr. Iowa Pub. Sch. System; assoc. prof. Drake U., Iowa; prof. Hofstra U., NYC; gallery dir. Bernice Steinbaum Gallery, NYC. Curator numerous exhbns. and traveling mus. shows; speaker in field; juror numerous art shows. Host: Art Time with Mrs. Steinbaum, Iowa; contbr. articles to profl. publs., mags., and newspapers; author: The Rocker, 1992. Named Woman of Yr. NOW, 1988. Office: Bernice Steinbaum Gallery 3550 N Miami Ave Miami FL 33127-3112 Office Phone: 305-573-2700. Personal E-mail: bernicefla@bellsouth.net.

STEINBAUM, ROBERT S., publishing executive, lawyer; b. Englewood, NJ, Oct. 13, 1951; s. Paul S. and Esther R. (Rosenberg) S.; m. Rosemary Konner, May 26, 1982; children: Marshall, Elliot. BA, Yale U., 1973; JD, Georgetown U., 1976. Bar: D.C. 1976, N.J. 1980, N.Y. 1982. Atty. Cole & Groner P.C., Washington, 1976—79; asst. U.S. atty. U.S. Atty.'s Office, Newark, 1979—84; atty. Scarpone & Edelson, Newark, 1984—87; pub. N.J. Law Jour., Newark, 1987—. Trustee N.J. Jewish News, Whippany, 1990-95, 96—, pres., 2002-04, Blood Ctr. N.J., East Orange, 1987-93, Leadership N.J., 1990; trustee Leadership Newark, 1997—, United Jewish Cmtys. MetroWest, N.J., 2002—, N.J. Vol. Lawyers for Arts, 2004-, JTA 2009-. Office: NJ Law Jour PO Box 20081 238 Mulberry St Newark NJ 07101-6081 Business E-Mail: robert.steinbaum@incisvemedia.com.

STEINBERG, ANDREW B., former federal agency administrator, lawyer; b. 1958; m. Roxann Steinberg; 2 children. BA magna cum laude, Princeton U., 1980; JD cum laude, Harvard Law Sch., 1984. Jud. law clk. to Hon. Richard A. Gadbois, Jr. US Dist. Ct., Calif.; assoc. Gibson, Dunn and Crutcher LLP, 1986—90; assoc. gen. counsel & sr. atty. for antitrust Am. Airlines, Inc., 1990—96; sr. v.p. to exec. v.p., gen. counsel, and sec. Sabre, Inc., 1996—2000; exec. v.p. adminstrn., gen. counsel & corp. sec. Travelocity.com, Inc., 2000—02; v.p., gen. counsel & corp. sec. Church & Dwight Co., Inc., 2002—03; chief counsel FAA, Washington, 2003—06; asst. sec. for aviation & internat. affairs US Dept Transp, Washington, 2006—08.

STEINBERG, ARNOLD (H. ARNOLD STEINBERG), academic administrator, former diversified financial services company executive; b. Montreal, Can., 1933; m. Blema Steinberg; children: Margot, Donna, Adam. BComm, McGill U., 1954, LLD (hon.), 2000; MBA, Harvard U., 1957. With Dominion Securities (now RBC Dominion Securities), Montreal, Canada; exec. v.p., CFO, dir. & mem. exec. com. Steinberg Inc., Montreal, Canada, 1958—89, chmn. Ivanhoe Inc.; prin. retail & investment banking, sr. officer Cleman Ludmer Steinberg Inc., Montreal, Canada, 1989—2009; chancellor McGill U., Montreal, Canada, 2009—. Former dir. Banque Nationale du Canada, Bell Canada Internat.; bd. dir. Almiria Capital Corp., Provigo Inc., Teleglobe Inc. Mem. Canada Coun., 1979—85, mem. exec. com., 1981—85; chmn. bd. gov. McGill U.-Montreal Children's Hosp. Rsch. Inst., 1972—91; mem. bd. gov. McGill U., 1980—90; chmn. interim bd. McGill U. Health Ctr., 1995—97, chmn. bd., 1997—2000; bd. mem. McGill U. Health Ctr. Found., 2000—; chmn. adv. bd. McGill U. Faculty of Medicine; chmn. Canada Health Infoway, 2003—. Recipient Order of Canada, 1993; named one of Top 200 Collectors, ARTnews Mag., 2004, 2005, 2006. Mem.: Order of Canada. Avocation: collector of modern & contemporary art. Office: McGill U / Office of Chancellor Rm 536, James Administration Bldg 845 Sherbrooke St W Montreal PQ H3A 2T5 Canada Office Phone: 514-398-1568. Office Fax: 514-398-4758.*

STEINBERG, ARTHUR JAY, lawyer; b. Bklyn., Sept. 25, 1955; s. Eugene and Estelle (Bzezensky) S.; m. Ninette Zavelson, Oct. 19, 1980; children: Jaclyn, Lauren, Alyx. BA in Econs. cum laude, Columbia Coll., 1976; JD, NYU, 1979. Bar: NY 1980, US Dist. Ct. (so., ea. and no. dists.) NY, US Cir. Ct. (2d cir.) 1986, US Cir. Ct. (4th cir.) 1991. With Kaye, Scholer LLP, NYC, 1979-87, ptnr., dept. co-chmn., 1988—2008, Kiny & Spaldiny LLP, 2008—. Recipient Order of the Coif. Mem. ABA, Am. Banks Inst., NYC Bar Assn. Democrat. Jewish. Office: Kiny & Spaldiny LLP 1185 Avenue of the America New York NY 10036 Office Phone: 212-556-2158. E-mail: asteinberg@kslaw.com.

STEINBERG, CRAIG RUSSELL, mediator; b. Buffalo, Dec. 19, 1973; life ptnr. Kenneth S. Rogalski. BA, SUNY, Buffalo, 1996; JD, Penn. State Sch.Law, Carlisle, 1997; MBA, Canisus Coll., Buffalo, 1999. Head del. UN, 1994—97; law clk. NYS Dept. Workmen's Compensation, 1997; tchg. asst. Buffalo State Coll., 1997—99; appeals officer NCAA, 1997—99; chief jud. clk. Amherst Town Ct., 1997—99; chief NASD, Boca Raton, Fla., 1999—2001; dep. policy dir. Janet Reno U.S. Atty. Gen., Wash., DC, 2002—03; mediator ARC Mediation, Jupiter, Fla., 2008—; igi Govt., DC, 2009—. Mem. Am. Bar Assoc., Wash., DC, 2007—, Internat. Bar Assn., 2007—; spl. envoy Internat. Criminal Ct., Hague, Netherlands, 2008—; mem. UN, 2008—, Intelligence & Nat. Security Alliance, DC, 2008—, Overseas Security Adv. Counsil, Wash., DC, 2008—, Am. Judges Assn., 2009—. Recipient Mediators award, Internat. Ct. Arbitration, 2008.

STEINBERG, DANIEL, biomedical scientist; b. Windsor, Ont., Can., July 21, 1922; came to US, 1922. s. Maxwell Robert and Bess (Krupp) S.; m. Sara Murdock, Nov. 30, 1946 (dec. July 1986); children: Jonathan Henry, Ann Ballard, David Ethan; m. Mary Ellen Stratthaus, Aug. 11, 1991; 1 stepchild: Katrin Seifert. BS with highest distinction, Wayne State U., Detroit, 1941, MD with highest distinction, 1944; PhD with distinction, Harvard U., Boston, 1951; MD (hon.), U. Gothenburg, Sweden, 1991. Intern Boston City Hosp., 1944-45; physician Detroit Receiving Hosp., 1945-46; instr. physiology Boston U. Sch. Medicine, 1947-48; joined USPHS, 1951, med. dir., 1959; research staff lab. cellular physiology and metabolism Nat. Heart Inst., 1951-53, chief sect. metabolism, 1956-61, chief of lab. metabolism, 1962-68; lectr. grad. program NIH, 1955, mem. sci. adv. com. ednl. activities, 1955-61, com. chmn., 1955-60; mem. metabolism study sect. USPHS, 1959-61; chmn. heart and lung research rev. com. B Nat. Heart, Lung and Blood Inst., 1977-79; vis. scientist Carlsberg Labs., Copenhagen, 1952-53, Nat. Inst. Med. Research, London, 1960-61, Rockefeller U., 1981; pres. Lipid Research Inc., 1961-64, adv. bd., 1964-73; prof. medicine Sch. Medicine, U. Calif., San Diego, 1968—2000, prof. emeritus, 2000—. Former editor Jour. Lipid Research; mem. editorial bd. Jour Clin. Investigation, 1969-74, Jour. Biol. Chemistry, 1980-84, Arteriosclerosis, 1980—; exec. editor Analytical Biochemistry, 1978-80; contbr. articles to profl. jours. Bd. dirs. Found. Advanced Edn. in Scis., 1959-68, pres., 1956-62, 65-67. Served to capt. M.C. AUS, World War II. Fellow, Am. Cancer Soc., 1950—51. Mem. Nat. Acad. Scis., AAAS, Am. Acad. Arts and Scis., Am. Heart Assn. (mem. exec. com. coun. on arteriosclerosis 1960-63, 65-73, chmn. coun. arteriosclerosis 1967-69), Fedn. Am. Scientists (exec. com. 1957-58), Am. Soc. Biol. Chemists, Am. Soc. Clin. Investigation, Assn. Am. Physicians, Am. Fedn. Clin. Rsch., Inst. Medicine, European Atherosclerosis Discussion Group, Alpha Omega Alpha. Home: 7742 Whitefield Pl La Jolla CA 92037-3810 Office: U Calif San Diego Dept Medicine 9500 Gilman Dr La Jolla CA 92093-0682 Personal E-mail: dsteinb1@san.rr.com. Business E-Mail: dsteinberg@ucsd.edu.

STEINBERG, DAVID JOEL, academic administrator, historian, educator; b. NYC, Apr. 5, 1937; s. Milton and Edith (Alpert) S.; m. Sally Levitt (div. Dec. 1986); children: Noah, Jonah; m. Joan Diamond, Aug. 28, 1987. BA magna cum laude, Harvard U., 1959, MA, 1963, PhD, 1964; LittD, Kyung Hee U., Seoul, Korea, 1989; LLD (hon), Keimyung U., Daegu, Korea. Prof. history U. Mich., 1964-73; exec. asst. to pres. Brandeis U., Waltham, Mass., 1973-77, v.p., univ. sec., 1977-83; pres. L.I. U., Brookville, NY, 1985—. Testified before Com. on Fgn. Affairs, U.S. Ho. of Reps., Fgn. Affairs Com. of U.S. Senate; cons. The Ford Found., UN Fund for Population Activities. Author: Philippine Collaboration in World War II, 1967 (Univ. Press award, 1969), The Philippines: A Singular and a Plural Place, 1982, 1987, Asia in Western and World History: A Guide for Tchg., 1993; co-author: The Emergence of Modern Southeast Asia: A New History, 2004, Religion and Religiosity in the Philippines and Indonesia: Essays on State, Society and Public Creeds, 2005. Chmn. Commn. Ind. Colls. and Univs.; past pres. Cambridge (Mass.) Ctr. for Adult Edn., chmn. L.I. Group; bd. trustee Nat. Commn. Coop. Edn. English Speaking Union Exch. scholar, Malvern Coll., NDEA scholar, Fulbright Found. exch. scholar. Mem. Coun. Fgn. Rels., Assn. Asian Studies (chmn. fin. com.), Harvard Club (N.Y.C.), Century Club (N.Y.C.). Democrat. Jewish. Office: LI Univ Off Pres 700 Northern Blvd Greenvale NY 11548-1320 Business E-Mail: pres@liu.edu.

STEINBERG, DEBRA BROWN, lawyer; b. Nashville, May 16, 1954; BA in Govt., Smith Coll., 1976; JD cum laude, Boston Coll., 1979. Bar: N.Y. 1980, U.S. Dist. Ct. (so. and ea. dists.) N.Y., 1981, U.S. Tax Ct., U.S. Ct. Appeals (2d cir.) 1987, U.S. Ct. Appeals (fed. cir.), U.S. Supreme Ct. 1994. Ptnr. Cadwalader, Wickersham and Taft LLP, NYC, 1990—, leader, pro bono representation of families of World Trade Ctr. victims, 2001. Adv., drafter N.Y. State's Sept. 11th Victims and Families Relief Act, 2002, Fed. Sept. 11th Family Humanitarian Relief and Patriotism Act. Recipient Achievement in Cmty. Leadership award, NYC, 2005, Medal of Honor award, Ellis Island, 2007; named a Pub. Svc. honoree, NY State Legis. Resolution, 2003. Mem.: NY State Bar Assn. (Pres. Pro Bono Svc. award 2003), NY County Lawyers Assn., ABA (pro bono com. 2008—, Pro Bono Publico award 2006), NY Women's Bar Assn. Office: Cadwalader Wickersham Taft LLP 1 World Financial Ctr New York NY 10281-1003 Office Phone: 212-504-6598. Business E-Mail: debra.steinberg@cwt.com.

STEINBERG, GARY K., neurosurgeon, educator; b. Bklyn., July 31, 1952; s. Robert J. and Shirley P. Steinberg; m. Sandra A. Garritano, Oct. 12, 1997; children: Jeff A., Elizabeth A. BS in Biology with honors, Yale U., New Haven, 1974; PhD, Stanford U., Calif., 1979, MD, 1980. Diplomate Nat. Bd. Med. Examiners, Calif., 1981, Am. Bd. Neurol. Surgeons, 1989. Chmn. dept. neurosurgery Stanford U., 1995—, Bernard and Ronni Lacroute-William Randolph Hearst prof. neurosurgery and neuroscis., 1997—, dir., Inst. Neuro-Innovation and Transl. Neuroscis., 2008—. Recipient Individual Nat. Rsch. Svc. award, NIH-NINCDS, 1984—85, Young Faculty award, Am. Assn. Neurol. Surgeons, 1988—89; named one of Top Doctors Am., Castle Connolly's, 2001—08, Best Doctors in Am., 2005—08, America's Top Surgeons, Consumer's Rsch. Coun. Am., 2008; grant, Stanford U. Sch. Medicine, 1975—80. Mem.: Phi Beta Kappa. Office: Stanford Univ Sch Medicine 300 Pasteur Dr Stanford CA 94305 Business E-Mail: gsteinberg@stanford.edu.

STEINBERG, HOWARD ELI, lawyer, diversified financial services company executive; b. NYC, Nov. 19, 1944; s. Herman and Anne Steinberg; m. Judith Ann Schucart, Jan. 28, 1968; children: Henry Robert, Kathryn Jill. AB, U. Pa., 1965; JD, Georgetown U., 1969. Bar: N.Y. 1970, U.S. Dist. Ct. (so. and ea. dists.) N.Y. 1973, U.S. Ct. Appeals (2d cir.) 1976. Assoc. Dewey, Ballantine, Bushby, Palmer & Wood, NYC, 1969-76, ptnr., 1977-83; exec. v.p., gen. counsel Reliance Group Holdings, Inc., NYC, 1983-2000, exec. v.p., chief corp. ops., 2000—01; exec. v.p., gen. counsel Prudential Securities, Inc., NYC, 2001—03, Prudential Equity Group, NYC, 2003—05; ptnr. McDermott Will & Emery LLP, NYC, 2005—. Chmn. N.Y. State Thruway Authority, 1996—99; dep. chmn. L.I. Power Authority, 1999—2009, acting chmn., 2009—. Editor: Georgetown Law Jour., 1968—69. Bd. dirs. Puerto Rican Legal Def. and Edn. Fund, Inc., 1993—95, Sheltering Arms Children's Svc., 1997—2005; bd. overseers U. Pa. Sch. Arts and Scis., 1989—2002; bd. regents Georgetown U., 1999—2005. Capt. JAGC USAR, 1972—74. Mem.: ABA, Securities Industry Assn. (co-chair, mem. fed. regulation com. 2001—05, mem. exec. com. compliance and legal divsn. 2001—05), Assn. Bar City of N.Y. (mem. com. scurities regulation 1984—87, mem. com. corp. law 1987—90, mem. com. fed. legis. 1990—93, chair ad hoc com. Senate Confirmation Process 1991—92), N.Y. State Bar Assn., Univ Club. Office: McDermott Will Emery 340 Madison Ave New York NY 10017 Office Phone: 212-547-5415. Business E-Mail: hsteinberg@mwe.com.

STEINBERG, JAMES BRAIDY, federal agency administrator; b. Boston, May 7, 1953; s. Herbert Steinberg; m. Sherburne Bradstreet Abbott, Oct. 1, 1994; adopted children: Jenna, Emma. BA, Harvard U., Cambridge, Mass., 1972; JD, Yale Law Sch., New Haven, 1987. Bar: DC. Spl. asst. to asst. sec. planning/evaluation US Dept. Health Edn. & Welfare, 1977; law clk. to Hon. David L. Bazelon US Ct. Appeals (DC Cir.), 1978—79; spl. asst. to asst. atty. gen. (civil divsn.) US Dept. Justice, 1979—80; minority counsel Labor & Human Resources Com. US Senate, 1981—83, prin. aide to senator Edward Kennedy Armed Svcs. Com., 1983—85; sr. fellow US strategic policy Internat. Inst. Strategic Studies, London, 1985—87; sr. dep. issues dir. fgn. policy/nat. def. Michael Dukakis Presdl. Campaign, 1988; sr. analyst RAND Corp., Santa Monica, Calif., 1989—93; dep. asst. sec. analysis Bur. Intelligence & Rsch. US Dept. State, Washington, 1993—94, chief of staff, dir. policy planning staff, 1994—96; dep. nat. security adv. to Pres. Bill Clinton NSC, 1996—2000; personal rep. to Pres. Bill Clinton G-8 summits The White House, 1998—99; v.p., dir. fgn. policy studies Brookings Instn., Washington, 2001—05; dean Lyndon B. Johnson Sch. Pub. Affairs, U. Tex., Austin, 2006—09; dep. sec. US Dept. State, Washington, 2009—. Mem. pres.'s coun. internat. activities Yale U.; bd. dirs. Pacific Coun. Internat. Policy. Author: An Ever Closer Union: European Integration and Its Implications for the Future of US-European Relations, 1993; co-author: Protecting the Homeland 2006/2007, 2006, Difficult Transitions: Foreign Policy Troubles at the Outset of Presidential Power, 2008; mem. editl. bd. The Washington Quarterly, mem. sci./security bd. Bulletin of Atomic Scientists', bd. advs. Yale Jour. Internat. Law; contbr. articles to profl. jours. Mem. sr. adv. coun. Next Generation Project The Am. Assembly, Columbia U. Mem.: Coun. Fgn. Rels. Democrat. Office: US Dept State 2201 C St NW Washington DC 20520*

STEINBERG, JAMES PAUL, infectious diseases physician, educator; b. Omaha, June 12, 1954; s. Maurice M. and Muriel Naomi (Frank) S.; m. Shari Chaya Wasser, May 22, 1994; children: Eva Rose, Jonathan Alexander. BA, Cornell U., 1976; MD, U. Nebr., 1979. Med. resident Emory U., Atlanta, 1979-83; infectious diseases fellow Northwestern U., Chgo., 1985-87, assoc. in medicine, 1987-89; asst. prof. medicine Emory U., Atlanta, 1989-96, assoc. prof. medicine, 1997, prof. medicine; hosp. epidemiologist Crawford Long Hosp., Atlanta, 1991—, assoc. chief of medicine, 1993—. Fellow Infectious Diseases Soc. Am.; mem. ACP, AAAS, Am. Soc. Microbiology, Soc. for Healthcare Epidemiology of Am., Infectious Diseases Soc. Ga. (pres. 1995—). Office: Emory U Hosp Midtown 550 Peachtree St NE Atlanta GA 30308 Office Phone: 404-686-8114. E-mail: james.steinberg@emory.edu.*

STEINBERG, JONATHAN S., cardiologist, educator; BA, Queens Coll., 1976; MD, Mt. Sinai Sch. Medicine, 1980. Diplomate Am. Bd. Internal Medicine with subspecialty cardiovasc. disease and clin. electrophysiology. Resident NYU Med Ctr., chief resident NY VA, 1981-84; fellow critical cardiology George Washington U. Med. Ctr., 1984-86; fellow electrophysiology Columbia Presbyn. Hosp., 1986-88; chief divsn. cardiology, dir. arrhythmia svc. St. Luke's-Roosevelt Hosp. Ctr. Prof. medicine Columbia U., Coll. Physicians and Surgeons. Office: St Lukes-Roosevelt Hosp Ctr 1111 Amsterdam Ave New York NY 10025-1716 Fax: 212-523-3915.

STEINBERG, LAURA, lawyer; b. Phila., Feb. 3, 1948; d. Leonard and Pearl (Zeid) S.; children: Seth, Adam, Bree. BA magna cum laude with honors, Bryn Mawr Coll., 1968; JD cum laude, Harvard U., 1972. Bar: Mass. 1972, U.S. Dist. Ct. Mass. 1972, U.S. Dist. Ct. R.I. 1974, U.S. Ct. Appeals (1st cir.) 1973, U.S. Ct. Appeals (10th and D.C. cirs.) 1986, U.S. Ct. Appeals (4th cir.) 1988, U.S. Claims Ct. 1979, U.S. Supreme Ct. 1988. Assoc. Sullivan & Worcester, Boston, 1972-79, ptnr., 1979—, mem. mgmt. com., 1988-2000, head litigation dept., 1987—99, chair complex bus. fiduciary litigation group, 2004—. Dir. Greater Boston Legal Svcs., 1987-90. Bd. dirs. Law Firm Resources Project, Boston, 1980-86, Lawyers Com. for Civil Rights Under Law, 1998—; pres. Peirce Extended Day Program, Inc., West Newton, Mass., 1983-86. Spl. career fellow U. Calif., Berkeley, 1968-69; Fulbright scholar, 1968. Mem. Boston Bar Assn. (vice-chmn. litigation sect. 1992-94, chmn. 1994-95). Avocations: reading, tennis. Office: Sullivan & Worcester LLP One Post Office Sq Ste 2100 Boston MA 02109-2129 Office Phone: 617-338-2800. E-mail: lsteinberg@sandw.com.

STEINBERG, LAWRENCE EDWARD, lawyer; b. Dallas, Nov. 25, 1935; s. Oscar J. and Pearl L. (Soloman) S.; children: Adam Joseph, Ilana Sara, Oliver David. BBA, U. Tex., 1958; JD, So. Meth. U., 1960. Bar: Tex. 1960. Since practiced in, Dallas; ptnr. firm Steinberg Soloman & Meer, 1971-88, Johnson & Steinberg, Dallas, 1988-93; chmn., CEO Eagle Equity, Inc., Dallas, 1991—; of counsel Jenkins & Gilchrist, Dallas, 1993—98; mem. US Commn. Preservation of America's Heritage Abroad, 2007—. Active program Dallas Ind. Sch. Dist., 1974-76; regional bd. chmn. Anti-Defamation League of B'nai Brith, 1974-77, nat. exec. com., 1977—, nat. law com., 1974-87; trustee Edna Gladney Home, 1975-92; v.p., trustee Shelton Sch., 1987-90; trustee Temple Emanu-El, 1992-94, 2008-, Dallas Jewish Cmty. Found., 1990-2001, 2005—; pres. U. Tex. Hillel Found., 2001-2003, mem. exec. com., 2001—; bd. dirs. Jewish Fedn. Greater Dallas, 1984-87, 91-94, Dallas Coun. on World Affairs, 1998-2007, Stephen Wise, Acad., 1998-2002, Dallas Holocaust Ctr., 1998—, Jewish Inst. Nat. Securities Affairs, 1999—, Dallas Furniture Bank, 2003—; v.p. Am. Jewish Commn., 2003-06; regional bd. chmn. Am. Israel Pub. Affairs Com., 1997-2001, nat. exec. com., 1998-2008; mem. Dallas Com. Fgn. Rels. 2d lt. U.S. Army, 1959-60. Mem. Honors Golf Club, Masons, Shriners, Zeta Beta Tau, Phi Delta Phi, Beta Gamma Sigma, Pi Tau Pi (nat. pres. 1964-66). Home: 10131 Hollow Way Rd Dallas TX 75229-6634 Office: 5430 LBJ Fwy Ste 1575 Dallas TX 75240 Office Phone: 972-770-2255.

STEINBERG, LEIGH WILLIAM, sports agent; b. LA, 1949; 3 children. BA in Polit. Sci., UCLA, 1970; JD, U. Calif., Berkeley, 1973. Founder, ptnr. Steinberg, Moorad & Dunn, 1975—99; CEO Assante Sports Mgmt. Group, 1999—2003; founder, ptnr. Steinberg, Tollner & Moon, Newport Beach, Calif., 2003—. Co-author (with Michael D'Orso): Winning with Integrity: Getting What You Want Without Selling Your Soul, 1998. Office: 660 Newport Ctr Dr Ste 1000 Newport Beach CA 92660

STEINBERG, MARVIN EDWARD, orthopaedic surgeon, educator; b. New Brunswick, NJ, Aug. 31, 1933; s. David and Fannie (Karshmer) S.; m. Delores Gusky White, Nov. 22, 1956; children: David, James, Susan, Julie. BA, Princeton U., 1954; MD, U. Pa., 1958; MA (status pro tem), U. Oxford, Eng., 1964. Cert. Am. Bd. Orthop. Surgery, re-cert.; lic. Pa., NJ. Asst. prof. orthop. surgery U. Pa., Phila., 1968-73, assoc. prof., 1973-80, vice chmn., 1977-2000, prof. orthop. surgery, 1980—2002, prof. orthop. surgery in medicine, 1988—2002, interim chmn., 1994-95, prof. emeritus, 2002—. Dir. Joint Reconstrn. Ctr., Hosp. U. of Pa., Phila., 1987-97; examiner Am. Bd. Orthop. Surgeons, Chgo., 1977-97. Editor, author: The Hip and Its Disorders, 1991, Revision Total Hip Arthroplasty, 1998; guest editor, author: Seminars in Arthroplasty, 1998; guest editor: Orthop. Clinics of N.Am., 1982, (jour.) Seminars in Arthroplasty, 1991, Techniques in Orthopaedics, 2008; editl. cons. Clin. Orthop. and Related Rsch., 1987; assoc. editor Jour. Bone & Joint Surgery, 1992-2000; contbr. numerous articles to jours. and textbooks. Named one of The Best Drs. in Phila., Phila. Mag., 1984, 87, 94, 96, Best Drs. in America, 1996-98, 2001-02; Fulbright scholar, U. Oxford, 1963-64; fellow Arthritis Found., U. Oxford, 1963-64. Fellow ACS, Am. Acad. Orthop. Surgeons; mem. AMA, Assn. for Acad. Surgery, Ea. Orthop. Assn. (pres. 1975-76), Orthop. Rsch. Soc., Internat. Soc. for Orthop. Surgery and Traumatology (sec.-treas. 1997-2000, chmn. elect 2000-02, chmn. 2002-04), Am. Orthop. Assn., Hip Soc., Girdlestone Soc., Assn. Rsch. Circulation Osseous, Lupus Found. Jewish. Avocations: travel, sailing, boating, photography. Home: 221 Winding Way Merion Station PA 19066-1217 Office: Hosp of U of Pa 3400 Spruce St Philadelphia PA 19104-4206 Office Phone: 215-349-3340. Business E-Mail: marvin.steinberg@uphs.upenn.edu.

STEINBERG, MEYER, chemical engineer; b. Phila., July 10, 1924; s. Jacob Louis and Freda Leah S.; m. Ruth Margot Elias, Dec. 24, 1950; children: David Martin, Jay Louis. BSChemE, Cooper Union, 1944; MSChemE, Bklyn. Poly. Inst., 1949. Registered profl. engr. N.Y. Jr. chem. engr. Manhattan dist., Kellex Corp., Oak Ridge, Los Alamos, 1944-46; asst. chem. engr. Deutsch & Loonam, 1947-50; chem. engr. Guggenheim Brothers, Mineola, NY, 1950-57; head process sci. div. Brookhaven Nat. Lab., Upton, NY, 1957—. Expert in fossil and nuclear energy; v.p. HCE LLC on coal conversion energy and environment. Author: (with Martin Hallman) Carbon Dioxide Greenhouse Gas Mitigation Technologies, 1999; contbr. articles to profl. jours. Served with AUS, 1944-46. Recipient IR-100 award, 1970; Wasson award Am. Concrete Inst., 1972, Engr. of Year award, 1985, Ind. award Quest, 1985, Greenman award, Internat. Energy Agy., London UK, IEA Greenhouse Program, 1996. Fellow Am. Nuclear Soc., Am. Inst. Chem. Engrs. (dir. L.I. sect.); mem. Am. Chem. Soc., AAAS, Am. Concrete Inst., Inst. Assos. Hydrogen Energy, Sigma Xi. Democrat. Jewish. Achievements include research on nuclear and fossil energy. Home: 15 Alderfield Ln Melville NY 11747-1724 Office: Brookhaven Nat Lab Upton NY 11973 Office Phone: 631-427-0768. Office Fax: 631-427-0590. Personal E-mail: mrsteinberg@verizon.net.

STEINBERG, MORTON M., lawyer; b. Chgo., Feb. 13, 1945; m. Miriam C. Bernstein, Aug. 25, 1974; children: Adam Michael, Shira Judith. AB with honors, U. Ill., 1967; JD, Northwestern U., 1971. Bar: Ill. 1971, DC 1994, Colo. 1995, NY, 2003, US Dist. Ct. (no. dist.) Ill. 1971, US Dist. Ct. Colo. 1998, US Ct. Appeals (7th cir.) 1971, US Supreme Ct. 1974. Assoc. Caffarelli & Wiczer, Chgo., 1971-73, Arnstein, Gluck, Lehr, Barron & Milligan, Chgo., 1974-76, ptnr., 1977-86, DLA Piper US LLP (and predecessor firms), 1986—. Spkr. in field. Sr. editor Jour. Criminal Law and Criminology, Northwestern U., 1969-71. Chmn. Chgo. region Leaders Tng. Fellowship, 1962-63; bd. dirs. Camp Ramah Wis., Inc., Chgo., 1974—, sr. v.p., 1992-94, pres. 1994-2003, chmn. bd. trustees, 2003-; bd. dirs., pres. Ramah Day Camp, Inc., Chgo., 2001-03; bd. dirs., v.p. Camp Ramah Wis. Endowment Corp., 1993-2003, pres. 2003-; bd. dirs. North Suburban Synagogue Beth-El, Highland Park, Ill., 1978—, corp. sec., 1983-87, pres., 1989-91, chmn. bd. trustees, 1991-93, trustee, 1991—; mem. Nat. Ramah Commn., Jewish Theol. Sem., 1987—, v.p., 1994-2003, pres., 2003-2007, chairman bd. trustees, 2007-; bd. dirs., pres. Nat. Ramah Endowment Corp., 2007-; bd. overseers Albert A. List Coll., 2004-08; mem. leadership coun. Conservative Judaism, 2004-2007; bd. dirs. MERCAZ USA 2006-, Found. Conservative Judaism in Israel, 1985-90; Midwest region bd. dirs. United Synagogue of Conservative Judaism, 1989-91, 94-2003; mem. editor's cir. Jewish Forward Newspaper, 1997-2000; trustee Am. Jewish Hist. Soc., 1998—; charter mem. US Holocaust Meml. Mus., 1992; pro bono counsel Frank Lloyd Wright Preservation Trust, Oak Park, Ill., 1996—; elected del. from US to 35th World Zionist Congress, Jerusalem, 2006; midwest region bd. govs. State Israel Bonds, 2007-. With 801st Gen. Hosp. USAR, 1969—75. Recipient Youth Leadership award Nat. Fedn. Jewish Men's Clubs, NYC, 1963; Merit cert. US Dist. Ct. Fed. Defender Program, Chgo., 1969, Pras Ramah, The Ramah award Nat. Ramah Commn., 2007; named Ill. Super Lawyer, Chgo. Mag., 2005-09. Mem. ABA, DC Bar, NY State Bar Assn., Ill. State Bar Assn., Chgo. Bar Assn., Profl. Assn. Diving Instrs. (cert. scuba open water diver 2005), Standard Club. Jewish. Home: 1320 Lincoln Ave S Highland Park IL 60035-3459 Office: DLA Piper US LLP Ste 1900 203 N La Salle St Chicago IL 60601-1225

STEINBERG, ROBERT PHILIP, lawyer; b. Danville, Ill., Apr. 4, 1931; s. Frederick Philip and Beulah Iona (Olmsted) S.; m. Doris Elizabeth Blank, May 10, 1958; children: Susan Elizabeth, Mary Louise. BA, DePauw U., 1953; LLB, N.Y. U., 1956. Bar: N.Y. 1956, Pa. 1959. Assoc. Shearman & Sterling, NYC, 1956, Drinker Biddle & Reath, Phila., 1958-65, ptnr., 1965-97, chmn., 1992-94, of counsel, 1997-98; ptnr. Commons & Commons LLP, Phila., 1998—2004, of counsel, 2004—. V.p. Germantown Hist. Soc., Phila., 1991-95, The Phila. Theatre Co., 1992-96; pres. E. Falls Cmty. Coun., 1997-2000. Mem. Phila. Bar Assn. (treas. 1970-72). Home: 3906 W Netherfield Rd Philadelphia PA 19129-1014 Office: Commons & Commons LLP 6377 Germantown Ave Philadelphia PA 19144 Office Phone: 215-849-4400. E-mail: psteinberg@commonslaw.com.

STEINBERG, ROBERTA GAIL, language educator; d. Melvyn Arthur and Jeannette Ostroff Steinberg; m. Avishai Shafrir, July 4, 1974; children: Doree Shafrir, Michael Shafrir, Karen Elana Shafrir. AB, U.

Mich., Ann Arbor, 1970; MEd, Harvard U., Cambridge, Mass., 1974. Cert. English tchr. Mass. Tutor Winsor Sch., Boston, 1987; prof. Mt. Ida Coll., Newton, Mass., 1988—; instr. MIT, Cambridge, 2008. Pres. MATSOL, 1992—93. Recipient Ronald Lettieri Outstanding Tchg. award, 2003. Mem.: Phi Beta Delta (pres. 2000—09). Democrat. Jewish. Avocations: swimming, reading. Office: Mt Ida Coll 777 Dedham St Newton MA 02130 Business E-Mail: rgsteinberg@mountida.edu.

STEINBERG, RUBIN, retired art educator, artist; b. Chgo., May 31, 1934; s. Louis Steinberg and Tanya Zelmanov; m. Marcia Kay Mann, 1960. B in Edn., Chgo. Tchrs. Coll., 1957; M in Edn., Roosevelt U., 1961; MFA, Art Inst. Chgo., 1968. Art tchr. Curie HS for the Performing and Creative Arts, Chgo., 1960—95. One-man shows include Bernard Horwich Jewish Cmty. Ctr., Chgo., 4 Arts Assocs., Evanston, Ill., One Ill. Ctr., Chgo., Monroe Gallery, Oak Park Libr., Park Forest Art Ctr., Northbrook Racquet Club # 2, Deerfield HS, Mayer Kaplan Jewish Cmty. Ctr., Skokie, Ill., Krochs & Brentanos, Chgo., Bonwit Teller, Suburban Fine Arts Ctr., Highland Park, Ill., A.R.C. Gallery, Chgo., Chgo. Cultural Ctr., Renaissance Ct., 2008, exhibited in group shows at Chgo. Soc. Artists Retrospective, 1983, Mus. Sci. and Industry, Chgo., Ill. State Mus., Springfield, So. Ohio Mus., Portsmouth, 1982, Oakbrook Invitational Crafts Exhbn., 1979—80, 1987—91, North Shore Art League, 1979, Chgo. Soc. Artists, 1977—, Am. Jewish Artists Club Exhbns., 1970—, 2006—08, Midwest Craft Festival, —, North Shore Art League, 1974—, 1978—, 1986, Art Inst. Chgo., 1968, 1973 (Mcpl. Art League award, 1973), Suburban Fine Arts Festeival, Highland Park (award for excellence, 1973), Old Orchard Art Festival, North Shore Art League, 1971—96, Gold Coast Assn., 1967—89, Mcpl. Art League (award for excellence, 1990), Blue Moon Gallery, Skokie, 1996, 2000, Balzekas Mus., Chgo., 1996, Loyola U., 1997, Taipei Fine Arts Mus., Taiwan, 1999, Time Life Bldg., Chgo., 1999, Spertus Mus., Represented in permanent collections So. Ohio Mus., Ill. State Mus., Spertus Mus. Judaica, Kraziai Mus. Contemporary Art, Lithuania, Sudler & Co., Chgo., McDonald's Corp., Oakbrook, Ill., Continental Bank, Chgo., Borg Warner, JJ Barrett, Inc. Comm., Slotowski Sausage Co., Malow Cordage Corp., Mt. Prospect, Ill., Morgan, Madison Steel Co., Skokie, Dance Fashions, Chgo., Aval Corp., P&R Mfg. Co., Lyric Opera Chgo., Peat, Marwick & Mitchell, Accts., Chgo., Marshall Field's Home Store, Schaumburg, Ill., Binney & Smith Co., Easton, Pa., Sanford Co., Bellwood, Ill., Sakura of Am., Hayward, Calif., Emily Oaks Nature Ctr., Skokie. Served with US Army, 1958—60. Address: 3127 W Jerome St Chicago IL 60645

STEINBERG, RUSSELL MAX, behavioral pediatrician, educator; b. Salinas, Calif., Aug. 18, 1941; s. Martin and Eve S. AB in Zoology, UCLA, 1963, MA in Zoology and Endocrinology, 1964, PhD in Zoology and Endocrinology with distinction, 1969; MD, Med. Coll. Ohio, Toledo, 1972. Diplomate Nat. Bd. Med. Examiners. Intern in pediatrics U. Calif. Irvine Affiliated Hosps., 1972—73, resident in pediatrics, 1973—74; chief resident in pediatrics then mem. staff Childrens Hosp. of Orange County and U. Calif. Irvine Affiliated Hosps.; fellow in behavioral pediatrics and learning disabilities UCLA, 1975-76; behavioral pediatrician Childrens Med. Group, Anaheim, Calif., 1976-79; physician in child devel. program Fairview Devel. Ctr., Costa Mesa, 1979—81, physician behavior adjustment program, 1981—2004, chief med. staff, 1985, 1994—95; asst. clin. prof. pediatrics U. Calif., Irvine, 1990—94. Adj. asst. prof. zoology UCLA, 1969, instr. pediatrics, 1976; adj. asst. prof. pharmacy, U. Toledo, 1970-71; vis. lectr. Tchr. Edn. U. Calif., Irvine, 1980-93; lectr. and presenter in field. Contbr. articles to profl. jours. Rsch. fellow Ford Found., 1966, US Pub. Health Svc., 1965-69. Mem. Am. Acad. Pediatrics (assoc.), Soc. Devel. and Behavioral Pediatrics, Orange County Pediatric Soc., Sigma Xi.

STEINBERG, SALME ELIZABETH HARJU, academic administrator, historian; b. NYC; d. Johan Edward and Jenny Lydia (Peltonen) Harju; m. Michael Stephen Steinberg, Sept. 15, 1963; children: William, Katharine Lovisa. BA, Hunter Coll., 1960; MA, CCNY, 1962; PhD, Johns Hopkins U., 1971. Lectr. history Goucher Coll., Towson, Md., 1971—72; asst. prof. history Northwestern U., Evanston, Ill., 1972—75; prof. Northeastern Ill. U., Chgo., 1975—83, chmn. dept., 1983—87, assoc. provost then acting provost, 1987—92, provost, v.p. for acad. affairs, 1992—95, pres., 1995—. Author: Reformer in the Marketplace: Edward W. Bok and The Ladies' Home Journal, 1979; contbr. articles to profl. jours. Recipient 14th Ann. award Appreciation, Asian Am. Coalition Chgo., 1997; named to, Hunter Coll. Hall of Fame, 1997; grantee, Danforth Found., 1967—68. Episcopalian. Avocations: opera, theater. Office: Northeastern Ill U Office of President 5500 N Saint Louis Ave Chicago IL 60625-4679

STEINBERG, STEPHEN, sociologist, educator, writer; PhD, U. Calif., Berkeley. Prof. Dept. Urban Studies Queens Coll.; prof. sociology Grad. Ctr., CUNY. Co-author: The Tenacity of Prejudice: Anti-Semitism in Contemporary America, 1969; co-author: (with Sharon Friedman) Writing and Thinking in the Social Sciences, 1989; author: The Ethnic Myth, 2001, Academic Melting Pot, 1977, Turning Back: The Retreat from Racial Justice in American Thought and Policy, 1995, 2001 (Oliver Cromwell Cox Award for Distinguished Anti-Racist Scholarship), Race Relations: A Critique, 2007. Office: Queens Coll Powdermaker 250H 65-30 Kissena Blvd Flushing NY 11367 Office Phone: 718-997-5130. E-mail: stephen.steinberg@qc.cuny.edu.

STEINBERGER, JACK, physicist, researcher; b. Bad Kissingen, Germany, May 25, 1921; came to U.S., 1935; s. Ludwig Lazarus and Berta (May) S.; m. Joan Beauregard, 1943, (div. 1962); children: Joseph, Richard Ned; m. Cynthia Eva Alff; children: Julia Karen, John Paul. BS in Chemistry, U. Chgo., 1942, PhD in Physics, 1948; degree (hon.), Ill. Inst. Tech., 1989, U. Glasgow, 1990, Dortmund U., 1990, Columbia U., 1990, U. Autonoma de Barcelona, Spain, 1992, U. Blaise Pascal, Clermont-Ferrand, France, 1995, U. Würzburg, 1997. Mem. Inst. for Advanced Study, Princeton, NJ, 1948-49; asst. U. Calif., Berkeley, 1949-50; prof. Columbia U., NYC, 1950-68, Higgins prof., 1968-72; staff mem. European Orgn. for Nuclear Research, Geneva, 1968-86, dir., 1969-72; prof. physics Scuola Normale, Pisa, Italy, 1986—. Pfc. U.S. Army, 1943-46. Co-recipient Nobel prize in physics, 1988; recipient Nat. Medal of Sci., 1988, Mateuzzi medal Societa Italiane delle Scienze, 1991; fellow Guggenheim Found., Sloan Found. Mem. Am. Acad. Arts and Scis., Heidelberg Acad. Scis., Academia Europea, Academia Nationale dei Lincei. Avocations: tennis, sailing. Home: 25 Chemin des Merles CH 1213 Onex Switzerland Office: European Ctr for Nuclear Rsch CH 1211 Geneva 23 Switzerland E-mail: jack.steinberger@cern.ch.*

STEINBOCK, BONNIE, philosophy educator; b. NYC, Feb. 6, 1947; d. Elmer Lincoln and Natalie (Bachrach) S.; m. Stuart Edward Dreyfus, 1970 (div. Feb. 1973); m. David Anthony Pratt, July 30, 1977; children: Nicholas, Sarah, Samuel Steinbock-Pratt. BA, Tufts U., 1968; PhD, U. Calif., Berkeley, 1974. Asst. prof. Coll. of Wooster, Ohio, 1974-77; asst. prof. dept. philosophy SUNY, Albany, 1977-85, assoc. prof., 1985-93, prof., 1993—, chmn. dept., 1991-94. Author: Life Before Birth: The Moral and Legal Status of Embryos and Fetuses, 1992; editor: Killing and Letting Die, 1980, (with Alastair Norcross), 2d edit., 1994, (with John Arras), Ethical Issues in Modern Medicine, 1995. Fellow Hastings Ctr. (v.p. 1991, 93, 94); mem. Nat. Adv. Bd. of Ethics in Reproduction (bd. dirs.). Democrat. Jewish. Office: SUNY Dept Philosophy Hu 257 Albany NY 12222-0001

STEINBOCK, JOHN THOMAS, bishop; b. LA, July 16, 1937; Student, LA Diocesan sems. Ordained priest Archdiocese of LA, Calif., 1963; ordained bishop, 1984; aux. bishop Diocese of Orange, 1984—87; bishop Diocese of Santa Rosa, 1987—91, Diocese of Fresno, 1991—. Roman Catholic. Office: Diocese of Fresno 1550 N Fresno St Fresno CA 93703-3788 Office Phone: 559-488-7400. Fax: 559-488-7464. E-mail: malanis@dioceseoffresno.org.

STEINBRENNER, GEORGE MICHAEL, III, professional baseball team and shipbuilding company executive; b. Rocky River, Ohio, July 4, 1930; s. Henry G. and Rita (Haley) Steinbrenner; m. Elizabeth Joan Zieg, May 12, 1956; children: Henry George III, Jennifer Lynn, Jessica Joan, Harold Zeig. BA, Williams Coll., 1952; postgrad., Ohio State U., 1954—55. Asst. football coach Northwestern U., 1955, Purdue U., 1956—57; treas. Kinsman Transit Co., Cleve., 1957—63; pres. Kinsman Marine Transit Co., Cleve., 1963—67, dir., 1965; pres., chmn. bd. Am. Ship Bldg. Co., Cleve., 1967—78, chmn. bd., 1978—; prin. owner NY Yankees, Bronx, 1973—90, 1993—2008, limited ptnr., 1990—93, chairperson, 2008—; owner Bay Harbor Inn, Tampa, Fla., 1988—. Bd. dirs. Gt. Lakes Internat. Corp., Gt. Lakes Assocs., Cin. Sheet Metal & Roofing Co., Nashville Bridge Co., Nederlander-Steinbrenner Prodns. Chmn. Olympic Overview Commn.; v.p. US Olympic Com., 1989; mem. Cleve. Little Hoover Com., group chmn., 1966; chmn. Cleve. Urban Coalition; vice chmn. Greater Cleve. Growth Corp., Greater Cleve. Jr. Olympic Found.; founder Silver Shield Found., NYC. 1st lt. USAF, 1952—54. Recipient Gen. Douglas MacArthur award, US Olympic Com., 2002; named Outstanding Young Man of Yr., Ohio Jr. C. of C., 1960, Cleve. Jr. C. of C., 1960, Chief Town Crier, Cleve., 1968, Man of Yr., Cleve. Press Club, 1968, New Yorker of Yr.; named one of The Most Influential People in the World of Sports, Bus. Week, 2007, 2008. Mem.: Greater Cleve. Growth Assn. (bd. dirs.). Avocation: owns racehorse Bellamy Road trained by Nick Zito. Office: NY Yankees Yankee Stadium E 161st St & River Ave Bronx NY 10451*

STEINBRENNER, HAL (HAROLD ZEIG STEINBRENNER), professional baseball team executive; b. Dec. 3, 1968; s. George Michael and Elizabeth Joan (Zieg) Steinbrenner; m. Christina L. Steinbrenner. BA, Williams Coll., 1991; MBA, U. Fla., 1994. Exec. v.p., treas., bd. mem. Yankee Global Enterprises LLC, chmn. bd., 2007—; gen. ptnr. NY Yankees, co-chmn., 2008—, prin. owner, 2008—; chmn., CEO Steinbrenner Hotel Properties. Mem. bd. dirs. Yankees Entertainment and Sports (YES) Network. Bd. dirs. Boys and Girls Club of Tampa Bay. Named one of Most Influential People in the World of Sports, Bus. Week, 2008, 25 Leaders Reshaping NY, Crain's NY mag., 2008. Office: NY Yankees Yankee Stadium E 161st St & River Ave Bronx NY 10451*

STEINDLER, WALTER G., retired lawyer; b. NYC, Dec. 2, 1927; s. Mortimer B. and Ray (Feingold) S.; m. Carol A. Halpin, June 28, 1969; children: Michael, Morty, Melissa, Amy, Ellen. BA, Queens Coll., 1950; JD, NYU, 1953. Bar: N.Y. 1953, U.S. Supreme Ct. 1965, U.S. Dist. Ct. (ea. dist.) N.Y. 1972, U.S. Dist. Ct. (so. dist.) 1974, U.S. Ct. Appeals (2d cir.) 1974. Ptnr. Borden Skidell Fleck & Steindler, Jamaica, NY, 1955-62; pvt. practice law Babylon, NY, 1962-67; town atty. Town of Babylon, 1967-69; asst. county atty. Suffolk County, NY, 1970-71; ptnr. Sarisohn, Carner, Steindler, Lebow, Braun & Castrovinci, Commack, NY, 1976-93; ret., 1993. Capt., judge adv. 2d area command N.Y. Guard, N.Y.C., 1965-70; guardian ad litem 20th Jud. Cir. Lee County, Fla., 1995-98. With US Army, 1946—47. Mem.: Free Sons Israel (pres. 1953), Masons. Office: 350 Veterans Memorial Hwy Commack NY 11725-4330 Office Phone: 631-543-7667. Personal E-mail: wgscas@charter.net.

STEINEMANN, THOMAS L., ophthalmologist, educator; MD, Med. Coll. Ohio, Toledo, 1985. Diplomate Am. Bd. Ophthalmology, 1990. Prof. ophthalmology Case Western Res. U., Cleve., 1999—; media corr. Am. Acad. Ophthalmology, San Francisco, 2003—09. Cons. US Food & Drug Adminstrn., Silver Spring, Md., 2006—. Contbr. articles to profl. jours. Dir. Contact Lens Assn. Ophthalmologists, St. Paul, 2004—09; cons. Cleve. Sight Ctr. Fellow: Am. Acad. Ophthalmolgy (councilor 2008—09, Secretariat award 2006, 2008). Achievements include patents for ophthalmic uses of activated protein c. Office: MetroHealth Med Ctr 2500 MetroHealth Dr Cleveland OH 44109-1998*

STEINER, DAVID MILTON, state official, school system administrator, former dean; BA, MA, Oxford U.; PhD, Harvard U. Assoc. prof. Sch. Edn. Boston U., chmn. Edn. Policy; dir. Arts Edn. Nat. Endowment of Arts, Washington, DC, 2004—05; Klara & Larry Silverstein dean Hunter Coll. Sch. Edn., CUNY, NYC, 2005—09; commr. edn. NY State Edn. Dept., 2009—; pres. Univ. of State of NY, 2009—. Vis. prof. Cambridge U.; sr. rsch. assoc. Mass. State Edn. Policy. Contbr. articles to profl. jours. Mem.: Clare Hall Coll. (life). Office: NY State Edn Dept 111 Education Bldg 89 Washington Ave Albany NY 12234 Office Phone: 518-474-5844. Office Fax: 518-473-4909.*

STEINER, DAVID P., waste management executive; BS in Acctg., La. State U., Baton Rouge, 1982; JD with honors, UCLA, 1986. Assoc. Gibson, Dunn & Crutcher, San Jose; ptnr. Phelps Dunbar, New Orleans; v.p., dep. gen. counsel Waste Mgmt., Inc., Houston, 2000—01, sr. v.p., gen. counsel, corp. sec., 2001—03, exec. v.p., CFO, 2003—04, CEO, 2004—. Mem.: ABA, Calif. Bar Assn., La. Bar Assn. Office: Waste Mgmt Inc 1001 Fannin St Ste 4000 Houston TX 77002 Office Phone: 713-512-6200.

STEINER, DONALD FREDERICK, biochemist, physician, educator; b. Lima, Ohio, July 15, 1930; s. Willis A. and Katherine (Hoegner) Steiner. BS in Chemistry and Zoology, U. Cin., 1952; MS in Biochemistry, U. Chgo., 1956, MD, 1956; DMS (hon.), U. Umea, Sweden, 1973, U. Ill., 1984, U. Uppsala, Sweden, 1993, Mt. Sinai Sch. Medicine, NYC, 1998. Intern King County Hosp., Seattle, 1956-57; USPHS postdoc. rsch. fellow, asst. medicine U. Wash. Med. Sch., 1957-60; faculty U. Chgo. Pritzker Sch. Medicine, 1960—, chmn. dept. biochemistry, 1973-79, A.N. Pritzker prof. biochemistry, molecular biology & medicine, 1985—. Sr. investigator Howard Hughes Med. Inst., Chevy Chase, Md., 1986—. Co-editor: The Endocrine Pancreas, 1972; contbr. articles to profl. jours. Recipient Lilly award, 1969, Ernst Oppenheimer award, 1970, Hans Christian Hagedorn medal, Steensen Meml. Hosp., Copenhagen, 1970, Gairdner award, Toronto, 1971, Diaz-Cristobal award, Internat. Diabetes Fedn., 1973, Passano award, 1979, Banting medal, Brit. Diabetes Assn., 1981, Wolf Found. prize in medicine, Israel, 1985, Frederick Conrad Koch award, Endocrine Soc., 1990. Mem.: NAS, AAAS, Am. Acad. Arts & Scis., Am. Diabetes Assn. (Albert Renold award 2007), Am. Philos. Soc., Am. Soc. Biochemists & Molecular Biologists, European Assn. Study Diabetes (hon.), Alpha Omega Alpha, Sigma Xi. Office: Pritzker Sch Medicine 5841 S Maryland Ave AMB N216 Chicago IL 60637 Office Phone: 773-702-1334. Office Fax: 773-702-4292. Business E-Mail: dfsteine@uchicago.edu.

STEINER, ELIZABETH, philosopher, psychologist, educator; b. St. Louis, Jan. 30, 1925; d. Anton Steiner and Walburga Rustige; m. George S. Maccia, Feb. 10, 1947. BS in Zoology, St. Louis U., 1946; grad. studies in Zoology, U. Kans., Lawrence, 1947; MEd in Biology and Edn., U. Mo., Columbia, 1949; MA in Philosophy and Psychology, U. Manitoba, Ft. Garry, Can., 1954; PhD in Philosophy, U. Southern Calif., LA, 1957. Tchg. asst. gen. chemistry and gen. zoology St. Louis U., 1945—46; instr. zoology U. Kans., 1947; tchr. phys. and biol. scis. Kanawha HS, Iowa, 1949—50; tchr.anatomy and microbiology LA City Coll., 1950—52; tchr. phys. and biol. scis. LA Sr. HS, 1951—52; instr. philosophy U. Manitoba, 1953—54; lectr. philosophy U. Southern Calif., 1956—57; asst. prof. philosophy Marietta Coll., Ohio, 1957—60; prof. philosophy of edn. Ohio State U., 1961—66; prof. philosophy U. Southwestern La., 1966—67; prof. philosophy of edn. and rsch. methodology Ind. U., Bloomington, 1967—90, prof. women's studies, 1973—90, honors prof., 1985—90, prof. emeritus, 1990—. Chemist Atlas Powder Co., Weldon Springs, Mo., 1943, Scullen Steel Co., St. Louis, 1947—48; microbiologist Wood Treating Chem. Co., St. Louis, 1947—48; vis. prof. grad. studies Ohio State U., 1959, rsch. assoc., 1960—61; vis. prof. psychology of edn. U. BC, Canada, 1960; vis. prof. philosophy of edn. UCLA, 1963; vis. prof. postgrad. studies Nat. U. Mex., Mexico City, 1981; Fulbright prof. philosophy of edn. Fed. U. Rio de Janeiro, 1981; vis. prof. U. Warsaw, U. Zagreb, Croatia, Hungarian Acad. Scis. Inst. Sociology, Czechoslovak Acad. Scis., 1984; rsch. coord. inst. child devel. and family life Ohio State U., 1960—61, co-dir. ednl. theory ctr., 1962—66, co-dir. social studies curriculum ctr., 1963—66; dir. ednl. inquiry methodology program Ind. U., 1973—76, dir. grad. studies in hist. philos. and comparative studies of edn., 1976—78, dir. nat. sci. found. project, 1979, dir. grad. studies in philosophy of edn., 1981—90; dir. overseas study program Hangzhou U., China, 1988; presenter in field. Author: (books) Women and Education, 1975, Education and American Culture, 1980, Educology of The Free, 1981, Methodology of Theory Building, 1987, others; contbr. numerous articles to profl. jours. Achievements include logical analysis of education as a field of study and so introduction of educology as its designation; application of logic as a critical tool in decision-making about the morality of human behavior; psychological analysis of the female professorial workspace in the US and throughout the world; development of women studies as part of the university curriculum.

STEINER, GEORGE (FRANCIS STEINER), author, educator; b. Paris, Apr. 23, 1929; s. Frederick George and Elsie (Franzos) S.; m. Zara Shakow, 1955; children: David Milton, Deborah Tarn. BA, U. Chgo., 1949; MA, Harvard U., 1950; PhD, Oxford U., 1955; DLitt (hon.), Trinity Coll., Dublin, 1996; LittD (hon.), Louvain U., 1980, Mount Holyoke Coll., 1983, Durham U., 1995; D honoris causa, U. Bristol, 1989; DLitt (hon.), U. Glasgow, 1990, U. Liége, 1990, U. Ulster, 1993, U. Durham, 1995, Kenyon Coll., 1996, U. Rome, 1998, U. Sorbonne, 1998, U. Salamanca, 2002, U. London, 2006, U. Bologna, 2006. Mem. staff Economist, London, 1952-56; mem. staff Inst. Advanced Study Princeton (N.Y.) U., NJ, 1956-58, Gauss lectr. NJ, 1959-60; Massey lectr., 1974; First Lord Weidenfeld prof. Comp. Lit. Oxford U., 1994—; Charles Eliot Norton prof. poetry Harvard U., 2001—. Cons. and lectr. in field; Maurice lectr. U. London, 1984, Leslie Stephen lectr. Cambridge U., 1985, W.P. Ker lectr. U. Glasgow, 1986; lectr. Page-Barbour Lectures U. Va., 1987, Gifford lectr., 1990; vis. prof. Coll. France, 1992; First Lord Weidenfield vis. prof. comparative lit., Oxford U., 1994—. Author: Tolstoy or Dostoevsky, 1958, The Death of Tragedy, 1960, Anno Domini, 1964, Language and Silence, 1967, Extraterritorial, 1971, In Bluebeard's Castle, 1971, The Sporting Scene: White Knights in Reykjavik, 1973, After Babel, 1975 (adapted for TV as The Tongues of Men, 1977), Heidegger, 1978, On Difficulty and Other Essays, 1978, The Portage to San Cristobal of A.H., 1981, Antigones, 1984, George Steiner: A Reader, 1984, Real Presences, 1989, Proofs and Three Parables, 1992, Homer in English, 1996, No Passion Spent, 1996, The Deeps of the Sea, 1996, Errata, An Examined Life, 1997, Grammars of Creation, 2001, Lessons of the Masters, 2003, My Unwritten Books, 2008, George Steiner at the New Yorker, 2009; editor: The Penguin Book of Modern Verse Translation, 1966, Homer: A Collection of Critical Essays (with Robert Flagles), 1962. Decorated chevalier de la Legion d'Honneur (France); Churchill Coll. fellow, 1961-; Hon. Royal Academician (London), Commandeur dans l'Ordre des Arts et des Lettres (Paris); hon. fellow Balliol Coll., Oxford, Eng., 1995, St. Anne's Coll., Oxford; Fulbright prof., 1958-69; recipient O. Henry Short Story award, 1958, Guggenheim fellowship, 1971-72, Zabel award Nat. Inst. Arts and Letters, U.S., 1970, King Albert medal Royal Belgian Acad., 1982, P.E.N. Internat. Fiction prize, 1993, Alfonoso Reyes prize Mexico, 2007; Faulkner Fiction grantee P.E.N., 1983; Le Prix du Souvenir, 1974, Truman Capite Lifetime award for Lit., 1999, Prince of Asturias prize in humanities, 2001, Ludwig-Börne prize, Germany, 2003; named Hon. Royal Academician, London. Fellow British Acad.; mem. Am. Acad. Arts and Scis. (hon.), English Assn. (pres. 1975), German Acad. Lit. (corr.). Office: Churchill Coll Cambridge England

STEINER, GREG, Internet company executive; BS in Fin., U. Ill., Urbana-Champaign, 1990. With Interstate Consolidation Svcs.; v.p. ops. Pacer Internat., Concord, Calif., 1990—99, NetFreight.com (now Cyntric), 1999—2000; pres., COO eHarmony.com, Pasadena, Calif., 2000—. Office: eHarmony PO Box 60157 Pasadena CA 91116 Office Phone: 626-795-4814.

STEINER, HEINZ, science professor, researcher; b. Birrwil, Aargau, Switzerland, July 1, 1956; Diploma, Swiss Fed. Inst. Tech., Zuerich, 1980; PhD, U. Duesseldorf, Germany, 1989. Postdoctoral rschr. NIMH, Bethesda, Md., 1990—95; rsch. asst. prof. U. Tenn. Coll. Medicine, Memphis, 1995—2000; assoc. prof. molecular and cellular pharmacology Rosalind Franklin U. Medicine & Sci./Chgo. Med. Sch., North Chgo., 2000—. Rsch. grant, NIH, 1998—. Business E-Mail: heinz.steiner@rosalindfranklin.edu.

STEINER, HENRY JACOB, law and human rights educator; b. Mt. Vernon, NY, June 14, 1930; s. Meier and Bluma (Henigson) S.; m. Pamela Pomerance, Aug. 1, 1982; stepchildren: Duff, Jacoba. BA magna cum laude, Harvard U., 1951, MA, 1955, LLB magna cum laude, 1955. Bar: N.Y. 1956, Mass. 1963. Law clk. to Hon. John M. Harlan U.S. Supreme Ct., 1957-58; assoc. Sullivan and Cromwell, NYC, 1958-62; asst. prof. sch. law Harvard U., Cambridge, Mass., 1962-65, prof., 1965—, Jeremiah Smith Jr. prof. law, 1986—2005; prof. emeritus, 2005—. Founder, dir. Law Sch. Human Rights Program, 1984—2005; chair univ. com. on human rights studies Harvard U., 1994—2002; bd. dirs. U. Middle East project, 1996—99, chair bd. dirs., 2000—07; vis. prof. Yale U., 1972—73, Stanford U., 1965; cons. AID, 1962—64, Ford Found., 1966—69. Co-author: (textbook) Transnational Legal Problems, 4th edit., 1994, Tort and Accident Law, 2d edit., 1989, International Human Rights in Context: Law, Politics, Morals, 3d edit., 2007; author: Moral Argument and Social Vision in the Courts, 1987, Diverse Partners: Non-Governmental Organizations in the Human Rights Movement, 1991; former devels. editor Harvard Law Rev.; contbr. articles to profl. jours. Avocation: photography. Office: Harvard U Law Sch Cambridge MA 02138 Home: 28 Madison St Cambridge MA 02138 Business E-Mail: hsteiner@law.harvard.edu.

STEINER, HENRY-YORK, English language and literature educator; b. Chgo., Mar. 12, 1932; s. Richard Morrow and Deborah (Lantz) S.; m. Margaret Gray, June 3, 1957 (div.); children: Anne Elizabeth, Edward Yagi, Riley Jane; m. Leonor Coleman Flores, Jan. 13, 1990. BA, Grinnell Coll., 1956; MA, Yale U., 1957; PhD, U. Oreg., 1963. Instr. Grinnell (Iowa) Coll., 1957-59, assoc. prof., assoc. dean faculty, 1964-68; instr. U. Oreg., Eugene, 1959-62; assoc. prof. Yankton (S.D.) Coll., 1959-62; dean undergrad. studies Ea. Wash. U., Cheney, 1968-77, prof. English, 1977—. Chmn. Wash. State Folklife Coun., Olympia, 1988-92. Editor: (autobiography) St. Peter & I, 1967, (anthology) 12 Poets, 1967; contbr. articles to profl. jours., including Internat. Edn. Chmn. Spokane (Wash.) Cmty. Action, 1971-76; bd. dirs. Expo '74, Spokane World's Fair, 1972-75; dir. 49 Degrees N. Ski Patrol, Chewelah, Wash., 1982-86, 97-2001; sect. chief Inland Empire Region Nat. Ski Patrol, Spokane, 1994-97, 01, dir. 2001--. Named Patroller of Yr., Inland Empire region Nat. Ski Patrol, 1998, Patrol Dir. of Yr., Pacific N.W. divsn., 1998; Fellow Yale U. and Ford Found., 1957. Mem. AAUP (sec. Wash. State coun. 1993-98), Nat. Ski Patrol (founding mem., Patroller Com., 2005—). Avocations: skiing, sailing, gardening. Home: 2627 W Gardner Ave Spokane WA 99201 Office: Ea Wash U Dept English Cheney WA 99004 Business E-Mail: hsteiner@mail.ewu.edu.

STEINER, HERBERT MAX, physics professor; b. Goeppingen, Germany, Dec. 8, 1927; came to U.S., 1939, naturalized, 1944; s. Albert and Martha (Epstein) S. BS, U. Calif., Berkeley, 1951, PhD, 1956. Physicist Lawrence Berkeley Lab., Berkeley, Calif., 1956—; mem. faculty U. Calif., Berkeley, 1958—, prof. physics, 1966-2000, prof. emeritus, 2000—, William H. McAdams prof. physics, chmn. dept., 1992-95; vis. scientist European Center Nuclear Research, 1960-61, 64, 68-69, 82-83, Max Planck Inst. Physics and Astrophysics, Munich, 1976-77; vis. prof. Japanese Soc. Promotion Sci., 1978. Vis. prof. physics U. Paris, 1989-90; vis. scientist Deutsches Electron Synchrotron Lab., 1995-96. Author articles in field. Served with AUS, 1946-47. Recipient Sr. Am. Scientist award Alexander von Humboldt Found., 1976-77; Guggenheim fellow, 1960-61 Fellow Am. Phys. Soc. Office: U Calif Berkeley Dept Physics 7300 Berkeley CA 94720-0001 Home Phone: 510-527-8692; Office Phone: 510-486-6805. Business E-Mail: steiner@lbl.gov.

STEINER, JOHN MICHAEL, sociologist, educator; b. Prague, Czech Republic, Aug. 3, 1925; arrived in US, 1953; s. Kurt John and Ilse (Ornstein) Steiner; 1 child, Ingmar Michael Augustus. BA, U. Melbourne, 1952; MA, U. Mo., 1955; PhD, U. Freiburg, 1968. Liaison officer United Relief and Rehab. Adminstrn. Mission, Prague, 1946—48; immigration officer Dept. Immigration, Canberra, Melbourne, Australia, 1949—52; indsl. therapist Hosp. No. 1, Fulton, Mo., 1955—56; lectr. speech U. Calif., Berkeley, 1956—59; rsch. social psychologist USAF, Wright-Patterson AFB, Ohio, 1959—61; rsch. assoc. Inst. World Civilization, Freiburg, Germany, 1963—64; vis. asst. prof. Dept. Criminology, 1964—65; prof. sociology Sonoma State U., Rohnert Park, Calif., 1968—92, sr. scholar in residence, 1993—, prof. emeritus, 1992—. Founding dir. Sonoma State Holocaust Studies Ctr., 1984—92. Author: Power Politics and Social Change in National Socialist Germany, 1975; author: (with Joel E. Dimsdale) Survivors, Victims, and Perpetrators Essays on the Nazi Holocaust, 1980; author: Craig, Haney, Curtis Banks and Philip Zimbardo, Das Stanford Gefängnis Experiment, 1984; contbr. articles to profl. jours., books, chpts. to books on polit. crime. Co-founder, v.p. Ams. Dem. Action, Berkeley, 1960. Recipient Disting. cross Svc. and Valor, Czech Republic, 1948, cert. recognition, Calif. State Assembly, 1994, Order of Merit, Pres. Germany, 2002; fellow, Fulbright Found., 1974—75, 1981—82; Alexander von Humboldt rsch. fellow, U. Freiburg, 1964—67, 1990. Mem.: Fulbright Assn., Czechoslovak Acad. Arts and Scis., Acad. Criminal Justice Scis., Alexander von Humbodt Assn., Am. Sociol. Assn., Alpha Pi Zeta. Democrat. Achievements include research in authoritarian personality based on SS (Nazi) perpetrators; role margin as the site of moral and social intelligence; case of Germany and national socialism; Hitler's exemptions from the Nuremberg Racial Laws; genocide, Holocaust and perpetrator studies on price-tag switching. Avocations: art, antiques, swimming, photography. Home: 65 Sotelo Way Novato CA 94945 Office: Sonoma State U Dept Sociology Rohnert Park CA 94928 Home Phone: 415-897-3184. Business E-Mail: john.steiner@sonoma.edu.

STEINER, JOSHUA LINDER, private equity firm executive; b. Washington, Oct. 17, 1965; s. Daniel and Prudence (Linder) S.; m. Antoinete Delruelle, Oct. 27, 1996. BA, Yale U., 1987; MS, Oxford U., 1990. Exec. asst. to pres. NY Pub. Libr., NYC, 1990-92; chief of staff to sec. US Dept. Treasury, Washington, 1993-95; v.p., mng. dir. Lazard Frères & Co. LLC, NYC, 1995—2000; mng. prin. Quadrangle Group LLC, NYC, 2000—, co-pres., 2009—. Bd. dirs. Grupo Corporativo Ono, 2005—, West Corp., 2006—. Bd. trustees Phillips Acad., Andover, Mass., 1991—, vice chmn. NY Pub. Libr.; adv. bd. Enterprise Found., N.Y.C., 1995—. Mem. Coun. Fgn. Rels. Office: Quadrangle Group LLC 375 Park Ave New York NY 10152

STEINER, KENNETH DONALD, bishop; b. David City, Nebr., Nov. 25, 1936; s. Lawrence Nicholas and Florine Marie (Pieters) Steiner. BA, Mt. Angel Sem., 1958; MDiv, St. Thomas Sem., 1962. Ordained priest Archdiocese of Portland, Oreg., 1962, aux. bishop, 1978—, vicar clergy, 1978—80, clergy personnel dir., 1978—80, vicar worship & ministry, 1979—81, vicar sr. & infirm priests, 2002—, interim adminstr., 1995—96, 1997; assoc. pastor St. Monica Parish, Coos Bay, Oreg., 1962—67, St. Mary's Cathedral, Portland, 1967—70, St. Stephen Parish, Portland, 1970—72; pastor Holy Name Parish, Coquille, 1972-76, St. Francis Ch., Roy, 1976—78, St. Mary's Ch., Corvallis, 1987—2000, St. John the Baptist Parish, Milwaukie, 2000—02, St. Edward Parish, North Plains, 2002—; adminstr. St. Mary Parish, Vernonia, 1976—78, St. Mary's Ch., Corvallis, 1986—87; ordained bishop, 1978. Bd. dirs. Oreg. Cath. Conf., Portland. Mem. bd. Martha & Mary Home, Poulsbo, Wash. Democrat. Roman Catholic. Office: Archdiocesan Pastoral Ctr 2838 E Burnside St Portland OR 97214

STEINER, ROBERT L., economist; b. Charlevoix, Mich., Aug. 12, 1923; s. Albert and Therese Steiner; m. Christine Johnson Steiner, Dec. 27, 1959; children: Therese, Carl; m. Joan Friedlander, June 25, 1949 (div. 1959). BA magna cum laude, Dartmouth Coll., Hanover, 1947; MA in Econ., Columbia U., NYC, 1948. V.p. to pres. Kenner Products Co., Cin., 1948—72; adj. prof. mktg. Coll. Bus. Adminstrn., U. Cin., 1974—78; staff econ. FTC Robert L. Steiner Consulting, Cin., 1973—2006; sr. rsch. fellow Am. Antitrust Inst., DC, 2004—. Dir., chair mktg. com. Toy Manufacturers America, NYC, 1966—67; dir. Clopay Corp., Cin., 1976—86, Wcet TV, Cin., 1975—78. Contbr. articles to profl. jours. Dir. Am. Coun. Judaism, Ponte Vedra, Fla., 2001—09; dir., pres. Robert Krohn Livingston Meml. Camp, Cin., 1950—70; dir., v.p. legislative action Charter Com., Cin., 1952—72; commr. Ohio Commn. Local Govt. Svc., Columbus, 1973—74. 1st lt. Navigator Army Air Force, 1942—45. Decorated Air medals 78th Air Force Eng. Mem.: U. Club Cin., Am. Mktg. Assn., Am. Economic Assn., Phi Beta Kappa. Avocations: fly fishing, tennis, squash, reading. Office Phone: 202-337-3537.

STEINER, ROBERT LISLE, retired language educator; b. Tehran, Iran, May 21, 1921; s. Robert Lisle and Lois (Foresman) S.; m. Margaret S. Sherrard, June 4, 1944; children: Patricia Jean, Robert Lisle III, William Sherrard, John Scott. BA, Wooster Coll., Ohio; MA, Columbia U., 1948. Cons. Commn. Chs. on Internat. Affairs, 1948-49; cultural attache Am. embassy, Iran, 1950-52; educationist U.S. Office Edn., 1952-54; program dir. Am. Friends of Mid. East, 1954-59; v.p. Vershire Co., Vt., 1959-62; dir. Peace Corps, Kabul, Afghanistan, 1962-66; regional dir. North Africa, Near East and South Asia, 1966-69; dir. Washington office Devel. & Resources Corp., 1969-70; dir. Ctr. for Cross-Cultural Tng. and Rsch., adviser to univ. pres. on internat. affairs U. Hawaii, Honolulu, 1971-72; dir., gen. mgr. Hawaii Pub. Broadcasting Authority, 1972-73; exec. dir. N.J. Edn. Consortium, Princeton, 1973-78; pres. InterLink Lang. Ctrs., Princeton, 1979-91, chmn., 1992—. Tchr. U. Kansas City, Mo., 1957, Bradford (Vt.) Acad., 1961; poultry cons. Mid. East Tech. U., Ankara, Turkey, 1963. Councilman, v.p. Shanks Village Assn., Orangeburg, N.Y., 1948; chmn. Kabul Sch. Bd., 1965. Served as pilot USNR, 1943-46. Mem. Princeton Mid. East Soc. (sec. 1986-88, treas. 1993-95). Democrat. Presbyterian. Home: 1898 Villa Ct Lancaster PA 17603-2386 Office: Interlink Lang Ctrs 1898 Villa Ct Lancaster PA 17603-2386

STEINER, RONALD LEE, lawyer, educator, director; b. Jeanette, Pa., May 5, 1960; s. John R. Steiner, Sr. and Ethel M. Steiner; m. Mariam Shirvani, June 26, 1993; children: Cameron, Darius. BA in English, Lafayette Coll., Easton, Pa., 1978—82; MA, U. Del., Newark, 1983—85; PhD in Polit. Sci., U. Minn., Mpls., 1985—93; JD, U. So. Calif., LA, 1995—98. Bar: Calif. 1998, US Dist. Ct. (ctrl. dist.), Calif. 1998, US Dist. Ct. (no. dist.), Calif. 2000, US Ct. Appeals (9th cir.) 1998. Asst. prof. polit. sci. Chapman U., Orange, Calif., 1993—98, assoc. prof. polit. sci., 2002—07, assoc. prof. law, dir. grad. studies; jud. extern to Hon. M. Vogel Calif. Ct. Appeal, LA, 1996; jud. clk. to Hon. F. Fernandez US Ct. Appeals, 9th Cir., Pasadena, Calif., 1998—99; assoc. Sidley, Austin, Brown & Wood, LLP, LA, 1999—2002. Dep. counsel Govs. Blue Ribbon Adv. Panel on Hate Groups, LA, 1999—2000; temp. dep. dist. atty., Orange, 2009; dir. legal studies Chapman U., 2002—07. Contbr. encyclopedias, treatise/practice guide; co-author (government report) Final Report of the Governor's Blue Ribbon Advisory Panel on Hate Groups. V.p. ACLU of Orange County, Costa Mesa, Calif., 1996. Recipient Order of Coif, U. So. Calif. Law Sch., 1998, Faculty Recognition award, Chapman U., 2005, Outstanding Tchr. award, Am. Polit. Sci. Assn., 2005, Faculty Mem. of Yr.award, Chapman U. Alumni Assn., 2006. Mem.: ABA, Southwestern Polit. Sci. Assn., We. Polit. Sci. Assn., Phi Alpha Delta (pre-law chpt. advisor 2003—06), Am. Polit. Sci. Assn. Office: Chapman Univ Sch Law 1 University Dr Orange CA 92866 Business E-Mail: steiner@chapman.edu.

STEINFELD, JEFFREY IRWIN, chemistry professor emeritus, writer; b. Bklyn., July 2, 1940; s. Paul and Ann (Ravin) S. B.Sc., MIT, 1962; PhD, Harvard U., 1965. Postdoctoral fellow U. Sheffield, Yorkshire, England, 1965-66; asst. prof. chemistry MIT, Cambridge, 1966-70, assoc. prof., 1970-79, prof., 1980—2007. Author: Molecules & Radiation, 1974; co-author: Chemical Kinetics and Dynamics, 1989, 2d edit., 1999; editor: Laser and Coherence Spectroscopy, 1977, Laser-Induced Chemical Processes, 1981; co-editor: Spectrochimica Acta, 1983-98; contbr. articles to profl. jours. Treas. Ward 2 Democratic Com., Cambridge, 1972-73 NSF fellow Harvard U., Cambridge, 1962-65; NSF fellow Sheffield U., 1965-66; Alfred P. Sloan Found. research fellow MIT, 1969-71; Guggenheim fellow, 1972-73 Fellow Am. Phys. Soc. Academia Everything Found. (ptnr. com.); mem. AAAS, Union Concerned Scientists, Fedn. Am. Scientists, Sigma Xi, Phi Lambda Upsilon. Jewish. Office: MIT Room 2-221 Cambridge MA 02139

STEINFELD, MANFRED, furniture manufacturing executive; b. Josbach, Germany, Apr. 29, 1924; s. Abraham and Paula (Katten) Steinfeld; m. Fern Goldman, Nov. 13, 1949; children: Michael, Paul, Jill. Student, U. Ill., 1942; BS in Commerce, Roosevelt U., 1948, LLH (hon.), 1997. Rsch. analyst State of Ill., 1948-50; v.p. Shelby Williams Industries, Inc., Chgo., 1954-63, pres., 1964-72, chmn. bd., 1973-96, chmn. exec. com., 1996—99. Bd. dirs. Amalgamated Trust & Savs. Bank; founder Daniel Paul Chairs LLC, 2004. Mem. adv. bd. Sch. Human Ecology U. Tenn., 1981—87, devel. coun., 1982—87; mem. adv. bd. dept. interior design Fla. Internat. U., 1981—85; life trustee Roosevelt U., Chgo.; past pres. Roosevelt U. Bus. Sch. Alumni Coun.; hon. governing mem. Art Inst. Chgo., mem. com. 20th century decorative art, life trustee, 2009, endowed gallery on 20th century deocrative art, 1984; established Manfred Steinfeld Sch. Hospitality Mgmt. Roosevelt U., 1988; endowed Fern and Manfred Steinfeld Chair Judaic Studies, U. Tenn., Knoxville, 1995; endowed Danny Cunniff Leukemia Rsch. Lab., Hadassah Hosp., Jerusalem; endowed profl. chair Weitzman Inst., Rehovot, Israel, 1993; mem. U. Tenn. Devel. Coun., 1985—2005; nat. vice chmn. Jewish United Fund, 1988—94, bd. dirs., 1987, 1997; chmn. bd. dirs. Jewish Fedn. Chgo., 1988—2000. Staff sgt. AUS, 1942—45, 1st lt. AUS, 1950—52. Decorated Bronze Star, Purple Heart; recipient Horatio Alger award of disting. Ams., 1981, Outstanding Bus. Leader award, Northwood Inst., 1983, Lifetime Achievement award, Hospitality Design Mag., 1999, Julius Rosenwald award, 2000; named Small Bus. Man of Yr., Ctrl. Region, 1967, Vol. of Yr., U. Tenn., 1995. Mem.: Horatio Alger Assn., Bocaire Country Club (Boca Raton, Fla.), Bryn Mawr Country Club (Chgo.), Std. Club (Chgo.), Beta Gamma Sigma. Home: 1300 N Lake Shore Dr Apt 34D Chicago IL 60610-5165 Personal E-mail: manfern@aol.com.

STEINFELD, PHILIP SHELDON, pediatrician; b. Bronx, Mar. 4, 1932; s. Samuel and Sarah (Frishman) S.; m. Ruth L. Hyman, Aug., 1961 (div. June 1977); children: Andrea, Melissa, David; m. Sherry Lynn Rubinroit, Jan. 15, 1978; 1 child, Sara. BS, Queens Coll., 1953; MD, U. Basle, Switzerland, 1960. Diplomate Am. Bd. Pediats., 1965. Rotating intern Kings County Hosp. Ctr., Bklyn., 1960-61; resident pediatrics Mt. Sinai Hosp., NYC, 1961-63, jr. clin. asst. pediatrics, 1963-65, sr. clin. asst., 1965—; attending pediatrician L.I. Jewish Hosp., 1968—, North Shore Univ. Hosp., 1970—; clin. instr. pediatrics Cornell U., NYC, 1986-90, clin. asst. prof. pediatrics, 1991—. Mem. adv. bd. TEMPO, Woodmere, N.Y., 1975-92, Five Town Adolescent Ctr., Woodmere, 1975-93. Fellow Am. Acad. Pediatrics. Office: 1573 Broadway Hewlett NY 11557-1428 Home Phone: 516-374-6356; Office Phone: 516-374-3322. Business E-Mail: philsteinfeld@pol.net.

STEINGLASS, PETER JOSEPH, psychiatrist, educator; b. NYC, Mar. 1, 1939; s. Sam and Bella Sarah (Bernstein) S.; m. Abbe Stahl, July 1, 1962; children: Matthew Aaron, Joanna Eowyn. AB, Union Coll., 1960; MD, Harvard U., 1965. Diplomate Am. Bd. Psychiatry and Neurology. Head clin. rsch. program Nat. Inst. Alcohol Abuse and Alcoholism, Washington, 1971-74; asst. prof. psychiatry George Washington U., Washington, 1974-77, assoc. prof. psychiatry, 1977-81, prof. psychiatry and behavioral sci., 1981-90; exec. dir. Ackerman Inst. for the Family, NYC, 1990—2004, pres., CEO, 2004—05, pres. emeritus, 2005—. Vis. prof. psychiatry Hebrew U., Jerusalem, 1981-82; clin. prof. psychiatry Cornell U. Med. Coll., 1993—. Author: The Alcoholic Family, 1987; contbr. articles to sci. publs. Lt. comdr. USPHS, 1969-71. Fellow Am. Psychiat. Assn., Am. Assn. Marriage and Family Therapy (cumulative contbn. award 1992), Assn. Clin. Psychosocial Rsch.; mem. Am. Family Therapy Acad. (charter, bd. dirs. 1987-89, v.p. 1989-91, Disting. Contbn. award 1987), Aesculapian Soc., Phi Beta Kappa. Democrat. Jewish. Avocations: photography, classical music. Office: Ackerman Inst for Family 149 E 78th St New York NY 10075 Office Phone: 212-481-1860. Business E-Mail: psteinglass@ackerman.org.

STEINHAFEL, GREGG WILLIAM, retail executive; b. Wis., 1955; m. Denise E. Steinhafel. BBA, Carroll Coll., 1977; MBA, Northwestern U., 1979. With Target Corp., Mpls., 1979—, sr. v.p., gen. mdse. mgr., 1987—94, exec. v.p. merchandising, 1994—99, pres. Target Stores, 1999—2008, pres., CEO, 2008—09, chmn., pres., CEO, 2009—. Bd. dirs. The Toro Co., 1999—, Target Corp., 2007—. Dir. Walker Art Ctr. Mem.: Retail Industry Leaders Assn., Tree House. Office: Target Corp 1000 Nicollet Mall Minneapolis MN 55403-2467*

STEINHARDT, ALICIA ANN, biology professor, director; M, UCSC, Santa Cruz, 1996. Biology instr. Hartnell CC, Salinas, Calif., 1996—, sci. activity dir., 2009—. Business E-Mail: asteinhardt@hartnell.edu.

STEINHARDT, MICHAEL H., diversified financial services company executive; b. Bklyn., 1940; s. Sol Frank Steinhardt; m. Judy Steinhardt; children: Jacob, Joshua, Kira. BS, U. Pa. Wharton Sch. Fin., 1960. Rsch. assoc.; staff writer; securities analyst; founding ptnr. Steinhardt Ptnrs. L.P., 1967—95; mng. mem. Steinhardt Mgmt. LLC, 1996—. Author: No Bull: My Life In and Out of the Markets, 2001. Chmn. Jewish Life Network/Steinhardt Found., NYC, 1994—, Jewish Media Renaissance, Birthright Israel; trustee & chmn. investment com. NYU, 1995—; trustee Brandeis U., Bklyn. Bot. Garden, Wildlife Conservation Soc., Mus. Jewish Heritage; mem. vis. com., dept. Greek & Roman art Met. Mus. Art, NYC. Recipient Medallion, U. Albany, 2004; named one of Top 200 Collectors, ARTnews Mag., 2003—08. Jewish. Avocation: collector of classical antiquities & modern art, especially drawings. Mailing: Jewish Life Network 10th Fl 6 E 39th St New York NY 10016

STEINHAUER, GILLIAN, lawyer; b. Aylesbury, Bucks, Eng., Oct. 6, 1938; d. Eric Frederick and Maisie Kathleen (Yeates) Pearson; m. Bruce William Steinhauer, Jan. 2, 1960; children: Alison (Humphrey) Eric, John, Elspeth. AB cum laude, Bryn Mawr Coll., Pa., 1959; JD cum laude, U. Mich., 1976. Bar: Tenn. 1998, U.S. Dist. Ct. (ea. dist.) Mich. 1976, U.S. Ct. Appeals (6th cir.) 1982; cert. sr. profl. in human resources SPHR. From assoc. to sr. ptnr. Miller, Canfield, Paddock & Stone, Detroit, 1976-92; dir. Commonwealth of Mass. Workers' Compensation Litigation Unit, Boston, 1992—2002; atty. U.S. Postal Svc., 2002—. Chancellor Cath. Ch. St. Paul, Detroit, 1976-83, 91; pres. bd. trustees Cath. Cmty. Svcs. Inc., 1989-92; bd. dirs. Spaulding for Children, 1991-92, Davenport House, 1992-96, chair 1995-96, vestry mem. St. Michael's Ch., Marblehead, Mass., 1994-97; chpt. mem. St. Mary's Cathedral, Memphis, 2005-2007 Mem. Mich. State Bar Found. (life), Fed. Jud. Conf. 6th Cir. (life). Home: 4010 S Galloway Dr Memphis TN 38111-6842

STEINHAUER, HEIDI MARIE, manufacturing engineer, educator; d. William and Dolores Marie Steinhauer; m. Raul Rumbaut, May 7, 2001. BS in Aircraft Engring., Embry Riddle Aero. U., Daytona Beach, Fla., 1993, MS in Sys. Engring., 2003; PhD candidate in Engring. Edn., Va. Tech, Blacksburg, 2008—. Mfg. documentation engr. Bomax Engring., Watertown, NY, 1993—95; mfg. design engr. Daytona Plastix, Daytona Beach, 1995—97; asst. prof. engring. Embry Riddle Aero. U., 1997—, advisor women's baja SAE team, 2005—, senator faculty senate, 2005—, mentor Coll. Engring. women's mentoring program, 2006—. Recipient Presdl. Diversity award, ABET, 2008. Mem.: CATIA Operators Exch. (mem. tech. edn. com. 2007—), Am. Soc. Educating Engrs., Soc. Automotive Engrs. Achievements include research in acedemic success of women engineers; retention of women engineers. Office: Embry Riddle Aero Univ 600 S Clyde Morris Blvd Daytona Beach FL 32114 Office Fax: 386-226-6747. Business E-Mail: steinhah@erau.edu.

STEINHAUER, JOSEFA MELISSA, biologist; b. NYC, Oct. 21, 1977; BS, Case Western Res. U., Cleve., 1999; MA, Columbia U., NYC, 2002, PhD, 2005, MPhil, 2002. Postdoc. rsch. fellow NYU Med. Ctr., NYC, 2005—. Recipient Peter Sajovic Meml. prize, Columbia U., 2006, Ruth L. Kirschstein Nat. Rsch. Svc. award, NIH, 2007—08, Ann. Drosophila Rsch. Conf. Hon. award, Genetics Soc. America, 2008.

STEINHAUER, SHERRI, professional golfer; b. Madison, Wis., Dec. 27, 1962; Student, U. Tex. Mem. Futures Tour, LPGA Tour, 1986—; mem. US Team Solheim Cup, 1994, 1998, 2000. Achievements include winning LPGA Tour events including du Maurier Ltd. Classic, 1992, Sprint Championship, 1994, Weetabix Women's British Open, 1998, 99, Japan Airlines Big Apple Classic, 1999, Sybase Classic Presented by Lincoln Mercury, Women's British Open, 2006, State Farm Classic, 2007; 4 LPGA career holes-in-one. Office: c/o LPGA 100 Internat Golf Dr Daytona Beach FL 32124-1092

STEINHAUS, JOHN EDWARD, retired anesthesiologist, educator; b. Omaha, Feb. 23, 1917; s. Emil F. and Pearl (Haynie) S.; m. Mila Jean Pinkerton, Feb. 21, 1943; children: Kathryn, Carolyn, Barbara, William, Elizabeth. BA, U. Neb., Lincoln, 1940, MA, 1941; MD, U. Wis., Madison, 1945, PhD, 1950. Diplomate Am. Bd. Anesthesiologists. Pvt. practice specializing in anesthesiology, Madison, Wis., 1951-58, Atlanta, 1958—; faculty U. Wis., 1951-58; mem. faculty Emory U., Atlanta, 1958—, prof. anesthesiology, 1959-87, prof. emeritus, 1987—, chmn. dept., 1959-85; chief anesthesiology service Grady Meml. Hosp., 1959-77, Emory U. Hosp., 1958-85; ret., 1987. Author: Medical Care Divided; contbr. articles to profl. jours. Past pres. Anesthesia Found. Mem. Am. Soc. Anesthesiologists (past pres., Disting. Service award 1982), So. Soc. Anesthesiologists (past pres.), AMA, AAAS, Assn. U. Anesthetists (past pres.), Anesthesiology History Assn. (past pres.), Soc. Pharm. Exptl. Therapeutics, Phi Beta Kappa, Sigma Xi, Alpha Omega Alpha. Home and Office: 836 Castle Falls Dr NE Atlanta GA 30329-4114 Home Phone: 404-636-5670.

STEINHAUS, RICHARD FREDERICK, criminologist, educator; b. Sheboygan, Wis., Aug. 12, 1942; s. Frederick Campbell and Amy Eloise Steinhaus; m. Patricia Louise Steinhaus, Aug. 7, 1971 (div. Oct. 31, 2003); children: Benjamin Campbell, Katherine Marie. BSc in Sociology and Psychology, Carroll Coll., Waukesha, Wis., 1965; MA in Sociology, Norhtern Ill. U., De Kalb, 1971. Non-resident program dir. St. lenard's Ho., Chgo., 1965—68; instr. sociology Bethel Coll., St. Paul, 1968—70; counselor Genesis Ho., Rockford, Ill., 1971—75; regional program dir. Ill. Dept Corrections, Carbondale, 1975—80; clin. svcs. supr. Graham Correctional Ctr., Hillsboro, 1980—99; instr. sociology Ill. CC Sys., 1983—99; chair dept. criminal justice Mt. Senario Coll., Ladysmith, Wis., 2000—02; prof. sociology, psychology and criminal justice N.Mex Jr. Coll., Hobbs, 2003—. Bd. mem. Mpls. Model City Mgmt. Bd., 1969—70; co-chair No. Ill. Drug Abuse Com., De Kalb, 1970—71; bd. mem. Criminal Justice Standards Planning Com., Carbondale, 1975—76; spkr. in field. Reviewer: McGraw Hill Pub. Co., 2007—; reviewer Pearson/Allyn Bacon Pub. Co., 2009—, Parentice Hall, Allyn & Bacon, 2009—; contbr. scientific papers to profl. pubs. and confs. Served on Meth. Ch. Adminstrv. Bd., Hillsboro, 1984—85, Crisis Line Adminstrv. Bd., Rockford, Ill., 1972—75. Mem.: Am. Correctional Assn., Midwest Sociol. Soc. Achievements include development of handbook for development and operation of a halfway house for parolees; research in the needs of elderly citizens living in Rockford, Illinois; misdemeanor offenders in Illinois Department of Corrections. Home: 1219 Zuni Hobbs NM 88240 Personal E-mail: rsteinhaus@nmjc.edu.

STEINHOFF, LYNNETTE KAY, special education educator; b. Viroqua, Wis., Sept. 10, 1970; d. Eugene F. and Nancy L. Steinhoff; children: Jacob M. Gilchrist, Tremayne J. BS in Sociology Psychology, U. Wis. La Crosse, 1999; MA in Leadership Edn., U. Colo., Colo. Springs, 2008, MA in Special Edn., 2003. Sr. lead tchr. bldg. lead Devereux Cleo Wallace Ctr., 1999—2003; spl. edn. tchr. Harrison Sch. Dist., 2003—07; interventionist Falcon Sch. Dist., 2007—. Home: 4358 Allesandro Dr Colorado Springs CO 80916 Office: Falcon Sch Dist #49 7545 Mohawk Rd Colorado Springs CO 80922 Business E-Mail: lsteinhoff@d49.org.

STEINHOFF, RAYMOND O(AKLEY), consulting geologist; b. Hart, Mich., Apr. 22, 1925; m. Anne M. Steinhoff, 1952; 1 child, Kirk O. BS, MS, So. Meth. U., 1948; PhD in Geology, Tex. A&M, 1965. Instr. geology Tex. A&M U., Coll. Sta., Tex., 1948-51; geologist Atlantic Rich., Wichita, Kans., 1951-53, Humble Oil and Refining Co., New Orleans, 1953-57; asst. prof. geology Tulane U., New Orleans, 1957-65, assoc. prof., 1965-70, chmn. dept., 1969-70; prof. and dept. head geology Stephen F. Austin State U., Nacogdoches, Tex., 1970-78; divsn. geologist Buttes, New Orleans, 1978-79; cons. geologist Graham, New Orleans, 1979-83. Cons. Trinexco, New Orleans, 1964-69. Sgt. US Army, 1944—46, WWII, 1st lt. USAF, 1952—53, Korea. Mem. New Orleans Geol. Soc. (emeritus), Phi Kappa Phi (emeritus).

STEINHORN, IRWIN HARRY, lawyer, corporate financial executive, educator; b. Dallas, Aug. 13, 1940; s. Raymond and Libby L. (Miller) Steinhorn; m. Deborah Kelley Steinhorn, Apr. 7, 2002; 1 child, Leslie Robin. BBA, U. Tex., 1961, LLB, 1964. Bar: Tex. 1964, U.S. Dist. Ct. (no. dist.) Tex. 1965, Okla. 1970, U.S. Dist. Ct. (we. dist.) Okla. 1972. Assoc. Oster & Kaufman, Dallas, 1964-67; ptnr. Parness, McQuire & Lewis, Dallas, 1967-70; sr. v.p., gen. counsel LSB Industries, Inc., Oklahoma City, 1970-87; v.p., gen. counsel USPCI, Inc., Oklahoma City, 1987-88; ptnr. Hastie & Steinhorn, Oklahoma City, 1988-95; sr. ptnr., dir. Conner & Winters, Okla. City, 1995—. Adj. prof. law Oklahoma City U. Sch. Law, 1979—; lectr. in field. Mem. adv. com. Okla. Securities Commn., 1986—; mem. exec. adv. bd. Oklahoma City U. Sch. Law, 2000—; bd. dirs. Okla. Venture Forum, 2000—. Served to capt. USAR, 1964-70. Mem.: ABA, Com. to Revise Okla. Bus. Corp. Act, Okla. Bar Assn. (bus. assn. sect., sec., treas. 1986—87, chmn. 1988—89), Tex. Bar Assn., Rotary, Phi Alpha Delta. Republican. Jewish. Home: 224 NW 18th St Oklahoma City OK 73103 Office: Conner & Winters One Leadership Sq 211 N Robinson Ave Ste 1700 Oklahoma City OK 73102-7136 Home Phone: 405-524-5621; Office Phone: 405-272-5711. Business E-Mail: isteinhorn@cwlaw.com.

STEINMAN, LISA MALINOWSKI, English literature educator, writer; b. Willimantic, Conn., Apr. 8, 1950; d. Zenon Stanislaus and Shirley Belle Malinowski; m. James A. Steinman, Apr. 1968 (div. 1980); m. James L. Shugrue, July 23, 1984. BA, Cornell U., 1971, MFA, 1973, PhD, 1976. Asst. prof. English Reed Coll., Portland, Oreg., 1976-82, assoc. prof., 1982-90, prof., 1990—, Kenan prof. English lit. and humanities, 1993—. Cons. NEH, Washington, 1984—85. Author: Lost Poems, 1976, Made in America, 1987, All That Comes to Light, 1989, A Book of Other Days, 1992, Ordinary Songs, 1996, Masters of Repetition, 1998, Carslaw's Sequences, 2003, Invitation to Poetry, 2008; editor: Hubbub Mag., 1983—; mem. editl. bd. PMLA, 2006—09, Williams Rev., 1991—, Stevens Jour., 1994—; contbr. articles to profl. jours. Fellow Danforth Found., 1971-75, NEH, 1983, 96, 2006, Oreg. Arts Commn., 1983, Nat. Endowment for Arts, 1984; Rockefeller Found. scholar, 1987-88; recipient Pablo Neruda award, 1987, Oreg. Inst. Lit. Arts award, 1993. Mem. MLA, Poets and Writers, PEN (N.W. chpt., co-founder, officer 1989-93). Home: 5344 SE 38th Ave Portland OR 97202-4208 Office: Reed Coll Dept English 3203 SE Woodstock Blvd Portland OR 97202-8138 Business E-Mail: lisa.steinman@reed.edu.

STEINMAN, RALPH M., medical educator; b. Montreal, Can., Jan. 14, 1943; m. Claudia Hoeffel; children: Adam, Alexis, Lesley. BSc with honors, McGill U., 1963; MD magna cum laude, Harvard Med. Sch., 1968; degree (hon.), U. Innsbruck, 1998, Free U., Brussels, 1999, Erlangen U. Intern and resident Mass. Gen. Hosp.; postdoctoral fellow, cellular physiology and immunology lab Rockefeller U., NYC, 1970—72, asst. prof., 1972—76, assoc. prof., 1976—88, prof., 1988—95, Henry G. Kunkel prof., 1995—, dir., Chris Brown Ctr. for Immunology and Immune Diseases, 1998—, head, cellular physiology and immunology lab.; sr. physician Rockefeller U. Hosp., NYC, 1995—. Scientific advisor Charles A. Dana Found., Campbell Family Inst. Breast Cancer Rsch., Toronto, Canada, M.D. Anderson Cancer for Immunology Rsch., Houston, RIKEN Ctr. for Allergy and Immunology Rsch., Yokohama, Japan, CHAVI Ctr. for HIV AIDS Vaccine Immunology, Durham, NC. Editor: Jour. Exptl. Medicine; adv. editor Human Immunology, Jour. Clin. Immunology, Jour. Immunological Methods, Proceedings NAS. Trustee Trudeau Inst., Saranac Lake, NY. Recipient Emil von Behring prize, 1996, Freidrich-Sasse prize, 1996, Rudolf Virchow medal, 1997, Max Planck award, 1998, Coley medal, 1998, Robert Koch prize, 1999, Gairdner Found. Internat. award, 2003, Mayor's award in Biol. & Med. Scis., NY Acad. Scis., 2004, Debrecen prize in Molecular Medicine, U. Debrecen, Hungary, 2007, Albert Lasker award for Basic Med. Rsch., Lasker Found., 2007. Fellow: Royal Soc. Edinburgh (corr.); mem.: NAS, Soc. Leukocyte Biology, Am. Assn. Immunologists, Am. Soc. Cell Biology, Am. Acad. Microbiologists, Am. Soc. Clin. Investigation, Inst. Medicine, Kunkel and Practitioner's Societies, Harvey. Achievements include discovery of dendritic cells, the preeminent component of the immune system that initiates and regulates the body's response to foreign antibodies. Office: Lab Cellular Physiology and Immunology Rockefeller Univ 1230 York Ave New York NY 10021 Office Phone: 212-327-8000. E-mail: steinma@rockefeller.edu.*

STEINMANN, ANDREW E., theology studies educator; b. Cin., May 29, 1954; s. Melvin Louis and Grace Marie (Masters) S.; m. Rebecca Ann Sizelove; children: Christopher, Jennifer. BSChemE, U. Cin., 1977; MDiv, Concordia Theol. Sem., Ft. Wayne, Ind., 1981; PhD, U. Mich., Ann Arbor, 1990. Assoc. pastor St. John Luth. Ch., Fraser, Mich., 1981—86; asst. prof. Concordia U., Ann Arbor, 1986—91, prof. theology and hebrew River Forest, Ill., 2000—; editor God's Word Nations Bible Soc., Fairview Pk., Ohio, 1991—94; staff pastor Luth. Home, Westlake, Ohio, 1995—2000. Contbr. articles to profl. jours. Mem., chair Walther Luth. HS, Melrose Pk., Ill., 2005—08. Mem. Soc. Bibl. Lit., Evang. Theol. Soc., Mich. Acad. Sci., Arts and Letters. Lutheran. Office: Concordia Univ 7400 Augusta St River Forest IL 60305 Business E-Mail: andrew.steinmann@cuchicago.edu.

STEINMANN, JOHN COLBURN, architect; b. Monroe, Wis., Oct. 24, 1941; s. John Wilbur and Irene Marie (Steil) S.; m. Susan Koslosky, Aug. 12, 1978 (div. July 1989); m. Genevieve Sim, Aug. 29, 1998. BArch, U. Ill., 1964; postgrad., Ill. Inst. Tech., 1970-71. Registered architect, Wash., Oreg., Calif., N.Mex., Ariz., Utah, Alaska, Wis., Ill., Hawaii. Project designer C.F. Murphy Assocs., Chgo., 1968-71, Steinmann Architects, Monticello, Wis., 1971-73; design chief, chief project architect State of Alaska, Juneau, 1973-78; project designer Mithun Assos., architects, Bellevue, Wash., 1978-80; owner, prin. John C. Steinmann Assos., Architect, Kirkland, Wash., 1980-94; supr. head facilities sect. divsn. fin. Dept. Edn. State of Alaska, Juneau, 1994-96; docs. mgr. Loschky Marquardt and Nesholm, Architects, Seattle, 1996-98; project mgr. Dept. Gen. Adminstrn. Divsn. Engring. and Archtl. Svsc., State of Wash., Olympia, 1998-99; project mgr. URS Architects, Seattle, 2000—04, RIM Architects, Honolulu, 2005—07, Architects Hawaii, Honolulu, 2007—. Bd. dirs. Storytell Internat.; lectr. Ill. Inst. Tech., 1971-72. Prin. works include Grant Park Music Bowl, Chgo., 1971, Menomonee Falls (Wis.) Med. Clinic, 1972, Hidden Valley Office Bldg., Bellevue, 1978, Kezner Office Bldg., Bellevue, 1979, The Pines at Sunriver, Oreg., 1980, also Phase II, 1984, Phase III, 1986, The Pines at Sunriver Lodge Bldg., 1986, 2d and Lenora highrise, Seattle, 1981, Bob Hope Cardiovascular Rsch. Inst. lab animal facility, Seattle, 1982, Wash. Ct., Bellevue, 1982, Anchorage Bus. Pk., 1982, Garden Townhouses, Anchorage, 1983, Vacation Internationale, Ltd. Corp. Hdqs., Bellevue, 1983, Vallarta Torres III, Puerto Vallarta, Mex., 1987, Torres Mazatlan (Mex.) II, 1988, Canterwood Townhouses, Gig Harbor Wash., 1988, Inn at Ceres (Calif.), 1989, Woodard Creek Inn, Olympia, Wash., 1989, Northgate Corp. Ctr., Seattle, 1990, Icicle Creek Hotel and Restaurant, Leavenworth, Wash., 1990, Bellingham (Wash.), Market Pl., 1990, Boeing Hot Gas Test Facility, Renton, Wash., 1991, Boeing Longacres Customer Svc. Tng. Ctr. Support Facilities, Renton, 1992, Boeing Comml. Airplane Group Hdqs., Renton, 1996, U. Wash./Cascade C.C., Bothell, 1999, Wash. State U., Pullman, Wash., Sea-Tac Airport Comm. Control Ctr., Seattle, 2000, McCarty, Internet Cafe and Residence Hall Renovation, U. Wash., Seattle, 2001, K'ima Med. Ctr. Dental Clinic, Hoopa, Calif., 2001, Sea-Tac Airport Flight Info. Mgmt. Sys., 2002; 600 Bed student housing, classroom, parking mixed use project, U. Idaho, Moscow, The Vegetable Bin, Seattle, 2004, Kona Coffee and Tea Plantation Visitors Ctr., Hawaii, 2006, Misawa Family Housing, Misawa, Japan, 2007, 1723 Kalakaua Mixed Use Condominium High Rise, Honolulu, 2008, 1830 Kapiolani Mixed Use Condominium High Rise, Honolulu, Laie Resort Hotel, Hawaii, 2009; also pvt. residences. Served to 1st lt. C.E., USAR, 1964-66, Vietnam. Decorated Bronze Star. Mem. AIA, Am. Mgmt. Assn., Nat. Coun. Archtl. Registration Bds., U. Wash. Yacht Club, Columbia Athletic Club, Alpha Rho Chi. Republican. Roman Catholic. Mailing: PO Box 2041 Honolulu HI 96805

STEINMETZ, RICHARD BIRD, JR., lawyer; b. Orange, NJ, Mar. 27, 1929; s. Richard Bird and Charlotte (Quinby) S.; m. Merriam Holly Miller, June 9, 1956; children: Richard Blair, Jonathan Bird, Edward Quinby. BA, Yale U., New Haven, Conn., 1950; JD, Harvard U., Cambridge, Mass., 1955. Bar: NY 1955. Assoc. Chadbourne and Parke, NYC, 1955-59; with Anaconda Co., NYC, 1959-79, v.p., gen. counsel, 1971-79; v.p. Colt Industries Inc., NYC, 1979-82; v.p., gen. counsel Pittston Co., Greenwich, Conn., 1982-84; exec. v.p. Case, Pomeroy and Co., NYC, 1984-94. Bd. dirs. Case, Pomeroy & Co., 1985-2008. Served to capt. USMC, 1950-52. Mem. ABA, Assn. of Gen. Counsel. Republican. Episcopalian. Home: 275C Park St New Canaan CT 06840-5739

STEINMETZ, WAYNE EDWARD, chemistry educator; b. Huron, Ohio, Feb. 16, 1945; s. Ralph Freeman and Helen Louise (Rossman) S. AB, Oberlin Coll., 1967; AM, Harvard U., 1968, PhD, 1973. Asst. prof. chemistry Pomona Coll., Claremont, Calif., 1973-79, assoc. prof., 1979-88, prof., 1988-91, Carnegie prof., 1991—2008, prof. emeritus, 2008—. Akademischer Gast (vis. prof.) Eidgenössische Technische Hochschule, Zurich, Switzerland, 1979-80, 86-87; cons. Abbott Labs., Abbott Park, Ill., 1993-94. Contbr. articles on spectroscopy, molecular modeling and molecular structure to profl. jours. Scoutmaster, dist. chmn., Woodbadge course dir. Old Baldy coun. Boy Scouts America, 1973-2003; vol. USFS. Fellow NSF, Woodrow Wilson Found.; recipient Dist. Merit award Boy Scouts Am., 1978, Silver Beaver award, Boy Scouts Am., 1993. Mem. AAUP, NRA, Am. Chem. Soc., Phi Beta Kappa (local sec.-treas. 1980-89, pres. 1995-96), Sigma Xi (local sec.). Democrat. Roman Catholic. Avocations: hiking, cross country skiing, choral singing. Home: 1081 W Cascade Pl Claremont CA 91711-2525 Office: Pomona Coll Dept Chemistry 645 N College Ave Claremont CA 91711-4412

STEINMEYER, ROBERT JAY, retired lawyer; b. Aug. 10, 1921; s. William F. and Willie (Davis) Steinmeyer; m. Susie (Levicki), Dec. 23, 1948; children: William Bruce, James Jay, Sharon Sue. BS, U. Nebr., 1943; post grad., Albany Law Sch., 1947—48; LLB, George Washington U., 1949. Bar: D.C. 1950, Calif. 1958. Devel. engr. G.E. Co., Schenectady, NY, 1943—46, patent atty., 1947—53, patent counsel, 1953—57, Beckman Instruments, Inc., Fullerton, Calif., 1957—63, resident counsel, 1963—71, v.p., legal, 1971—85, dir., 1984—85; sole practice Fullerton, Calif., 1985—86; of counsel Karon, Morrison, and Savikas Ltd., Fullerton, Calif., 1986—88; ret., 1988. Mem.: ABA, Assn. Corp. Patent Counsel (pres. 1975—76), Am. Patent Law Assn., Pi Mu Epsilon, Sigma Tau, Order of Coif. Home: 813 Morningside Dr Fullerton CA 92835 Personal E-mail: steinfull21@gmail.com.

STEINMILLER, JOHN F., professional sports team executive; b. Mt. Prospect, Ill. m. Corinne Steinmiller; children: John Henry, Mary Kate. V.p. bus. ops. Milw. Bucks, 1977—. Bd. dirs. Midwest Athletes Against Childhood Cancer Fund, Metro Milw. YMCA; mem. Milw. Conv. and Visitors Bur. VISIT Milw., Greater Milw. Com.; mem. bd. trustees Milw. Urban Day Sch. Recipient Contardi Commitment award Midwest Athletes Against Childhood Cancer Fund, 1991, Vol. of Yr. award YMCA, 1996. Office: Milw Bucks 1001 N Fourth St Milwaukee WI 53203-1314 Office Phone: 414-227-0500. E-mail: jsteinmiller@milwaukeebucks.com.*

STEINORTH, CHRISTINA ENNI, psychotherapist, author; m. Matthew E. Steinorth, Apr. 3, 1999. MA in Marriage and Family Therapy, Phillips Grad. Inst., 1995. Pvt. practice, Channel Islands, Calif., 2000—. Monthly columnist Inland Empire Mag., 2000—02; former newspaper advice columnist. Office: 3600 Harbor Blvd #228 Channel Islands CA 93035

STEINOUR, STEPHEN D., bank executive; married; 2 children. Grad. in Exec. Program, Stanford U.; degree in Econ., Gettysburg Coll. Various fin. mgmt. positions FDIC, 1980—83; mgmt. positions through exec. v.p. Bank of New England, 1983—91; divsn. exec. Recoll Mgmt. Fleet Fin. Group, 1991—92; exec. v.p., chief credit officer wholesale banking Citizens Fin. Group, 1992—96, exec. v.p. credit policy adminstrn., 1996—97, vice chmn., 1997—2001, vice chmn., CEO, Mid Atlantic region, 2001—05; chmn., CEO Citizens Bank Pa., 2001—05; vice chmn., CEO mid-states Citizens Fin. Group, 2005—06, pres., 2006—07, pres., CEO, 2007—08; mng. ptnr. Cross Harbor Capital Ptnrs., 2008—09; chmn., CEO, pres. Huntington Bancshares Inc., 2009—. Bd. dir. Huntington Bancshares Inc., Exelon Corp. Office: Huntington Bancshares Inc 41 South High St Huntington Center Columbus OH 43287 Office Phone: 614-480-8300, 614-480-3761.*

STEINS, JANET L., librarian, consultant; b. NYC, July 17, 1949; MS in Libr. Sci., Columbia U., NY, 1979; MA in Anthropology, NY U., 1990. Assoc. libr. tech. svcs. and collections Tozzer Libr., Harvard U., Cambridge, 1999—. Cons. Huntington Free Libr., Bronx, 2003—04; subject editor anthropology Assn. Coll. and Rsch. Librs., Middletown, Conn., 2008—. Author: (reference book) NY State Population; contbr. articles. Mem.: ALA, SUNY Librs. Assn. (pres. 1987—88), Am. Anthrop. Assn. Office: Tozzer Libr Harvard Univ 21 Divinity Ave Cambridge MA 02138 Home Phone: 617-628-1902; Office Phone: 617-495-2292. Business E-Mail: steins@fas.harvard.edu.

STEIN-SMITH, KATHLEEN, librarian, foreign language educator; b. Englewood, NJ; d. Frederick Albert Stein and Alice Mary Holland; m. Frederick Augustus Smith, May 5, 1984; children: Frederick Andrew, Sean Daniel, Patrick Edward. BA in French with honors, Montclair State Coll., NJ, 1972; BA in French avec grande distinction, U. Laval, Quebec, Can., 1972, MA in Linguistics, 1977; student, Middlebury Coll. Summer Lang. Inst., 1977, student, 1978; MS in Libr. Svc., Columbia U., NYC, 1979; MA in Learning Disabilities, Fairleigh Dickinson U., Teaneck, NJ, 1996; PhD student in Interdisciplinary Studies, Union Inst. & U., Cin., 2005—. Cert. French tchr. NJ, 1975, NY, 1977, Spanish tchr. NJ, 1975, NY, 1977, German tchr. NY, 1977, profl. libr. NJ, 1979, edn. media specialist NJ, 1984. Tchr. St. Mary's HS, Rutherford, NJ, 1975—77, North Arlington HS, NJ, 1977—78; reference libr. Mercy Coll., Dobbs Ferry, NY, 1979—81; libr. dir. West NY Pub. Libr., 1981—89; reference libr. Fairleigh Dickinson U., Teaneck, NJ, 1990—93, head periodicals dept. and computerized database svcs., 1993—2003, head periodicals dept., info. literacy coord., 2003—06, adj. faculty foreign langs. & related areas, 2004—, dir. pub. svcs., 2006—08, assoc. libr. & dir. pub. svcs., 2009—. Recipient Pillars award, Fairleigh Dickinson U., 2007. Mem.: ALA, NJ Global Educators, Assn. Coll. and Rsch. Librs., Am. Coun. Tchrs. Fgn. Langs., Am. Assn. Tchrs. French, Nat. Honor Soc., Phi Kappa Phi. Roman Catholic. Avocations: gardening, cooking. Office: Fairleigh Dickinson Univ Libr 1000 River Rd Teaneck NJ 07666

STEINWEG, KENNETH K., medical educator, department chairman; s. Donald H. and Lois Steinweg; m. Sue Byrd, Aug. 4, 1974; children: Emily A., Jessica Megan. MD, U. NC, Chapel Hill, 1975. Family medicine residency Womack Army Cmty. Hosp., Ft. Bragg, NC, 1975—78; dir., geriat. divsn. Brody Sch. Medicine, Greenville, NC, 1996—2007, interim chair & prof., dept. family medicine, 2008—. Col. Med. Corps, 1976—96. Decorated Legion Merit award US Army; Geriat. fellowship, Brody Sch. Medicine, 1986—87. Mem.: Am. Med. Dirs. Assn. (Columbia). Avocation: model trains. Office: Brody Sch Medicine 600 Moye Blvd Brody Sci Bldg Greenville NC 27858

STEITZ, JOAN ARGETSINGER, biochemistry professor; b. Mpls., Jan. 26, 1941; d. Glenn D. and Elaine (Magnusson) Argetsinger; m. Thomas A. Steitz, Aug. 20, 1966; 1 child, Jon. BS, Antioch Coll., 1963; PhD, Harvard U., 1967; DSc (hon.), Lawrence U., Appleton, Wis., 1981, Rochester U. Sch. Medicine, 1984, Mt. Sinai Sch. Medicine, 1989, Bates Coll., 1990, Trinity Coll., 1992, Harvard U., 1992, Brandeis U., 2002, Brown U., 2003, Princeton U., 2003, Watson Sch. Biol. Sciences, Cold Spring Harbor Lab., 2004. NSF postdoctoral fellow, Andorra, 1967—69; Jane Coffin Childs Meml. Fund Fellow, Divsn. Cell Biology Med. Rsch. Coun. Lab. Molecular Biology, Cambridge, England, 1967—70; asst. prof. molecular biophysics and biochemistry Yale U., New Haven, 1970-74, assoc. prof., molecular biophysics and biochemistry, 1974-78, prof., molecular biophysics and biochemistry, 1978—92, Henry Ford II prof. molecular biophysics and biochemistry, 1992—98, chmn. dept. molecular biophysics and biochemistry, 1996—99, dir. molecular genetics program Boyer Ctr. Molecular Medicine, Sterling prof. molecular biophysics and biochemistry, 1998—. Josiah Macy Scholar Max Planck Inst. fur Biophysikalische Chemie (Göttingen), Germany and Med. Coun. Ctr., Lab. of Molecular Biology, Cambridge, England, 1976—77; Fairchild Disting. Fellow Calif. Inst. Technology, Pasadena, Calif., 1984—85; investigator Howard Hughes Med. Inst, Yale Univ., 1986—; scientific dir. Jane Coffin Child Fund for Med. Rsch., 1991—2002; dir., molecular genetics program Boyer Center for Molecular Medicine; mem. vis. com. for biology divsn. Caltech, Calif. Inst. Technology, 1999—; mem. basic sciences scientific adv. bd. Fred Hutchinson Cancer Ctr., 2001—; mem. scientific adv. bd., biology divsn. Molecular Biology Dept., Princeton Univ., Max Planck Inst. for Biophysical Chemistry (Göttingen), 1999—; mem. Lasker Awards Jury, 2001—, Jury for L'Oréal UNESCO award, 2001—; mem. scientific adv. com. Sci. Found. Ireland, 2002—. Mem. editl. bd. Genes and Development, 1994—, assoc. editor RNA, 1994—, bd. reviewing editors Science, 2004—. Bd. overseers Harvard Univ., 2003—. Recipient Young Scientist award, Passano Found., 1975, Eli Lilly award in Biol. Chemistry, 1976, US Steel Found. award in Molecular Biology, 1982, Lee Hawley, Sr. award for Arthritis Rsch., 1983, Nat. Medal Sci., 1986, Radcliffe Grad. Soc. Medal for Disting. Achievement, 1987, Dickson Prize for Sci., Carnegie-Mellon U., 1988, Christopher Columbus Discovery Award in Biomed. Rsch., 1992, Rebecca Rice award for Disting. Achievement, Antioch Coll. Alumni Assn., 1993, Weizmann Women and Sci. Award, 1994, City of Medicine Award, 1996, Disting. Svc. award, Miami Bio/Technology Winter Symposium, 1996, Novartis Drew Award in Biomed. Rsch., 1999, UNESCO-L'Oreal Women in Sci. Award, 2001, Lewis S. Rosenstiel for Distinguished Work in Basic Medical Rsch. Award, 2002, FASEB Excellence in Sci. Award, 2003, Howard Taylor Ricketts Award, U. Chgo., 2004, Caledonian Rsch. Found. Prize Lectureship, Royal Soc. Edinburgh, 2004, The RNA Soc. Lifetime Achievement Award, 2004, E.B. Wilson medal, Am. Soc. Cell Biology, 2005, Gairdner Found. Internat. award, 2006, Rosalind E. Franklin award for Women in Sci., Nat. Cancer Inst., 2006; co-recipient (with Thomas R. Cech) Warren Triennial Prize, Mass. Gen. Hosp., 1989, Albany Med. Ctr. Prize in Medicine & Biomedical Rsch., 2008; named Fritz Lipmann Lectr., Am. Soc. for Biochemistry and Molecular Biology, 1989, 11th Ann. Keith Porter Lectr. on Cell Biology, Am. Soc. for Cell Biology, 1992. Fellow: AAAS, Am. Acad. Microbiology; mem.: NAS, Inst. Medicine, Academia Europaea, Japanese Biochemical Soc. (hon.), European Molecular Biology Orgn. (assoc.), Conn. Acad. Sciences and Engring., Am. Philos. Soc., Am. Acad. Arts and Sciences. Achievements include discovering and defining the function of small nuclear ribonucleoproteins in pre-messenger RNA which play a key role in recognizing and eliminating introns; research which has improved diagnosis and treatment of autoimmune diseases. Office: Molecular Biophysics and Biochemistry Dept Yale Univ PO Box 208024 333 Cedar St New Haven CT 06520-8024 Office Phone: 203-737-4418. Business E-Mail: joan.steitz@yale.edu.*

STEITZ, THOMAS A., science educator; b. 1940; BA, Lawrence U., 1962, DSc (hon.), 1981; PhD, Harvard U., 1966. Postdoctoral fellow, chemistry Harvard U., 1966—67; Jane Coffin Childs postdoctoral fellow Med. Rsch. Coun. Lab. Molecular Biology, Cambridge, England, 1967—70; with Yale U., New Haven, 1970—, Sterling Prof. Molecular Biophysics and Biochemistry; chemistry investigator Howard Hughes Med. Inst., 1986—. Vis. prof. U. Colo., Boulder, 1992—93. Contbr. articles to profl. jours. Recipient Pfizer award in Enzyme Chemistry, Am. Chemical Soc., 1980, Rosenstiel award for Disting. Work in Basic Med. Rsch., 2001, Newcomb Cleveland prize, AAAS, 2001, Lucia R. Briggs Disting. Achievement award, Lawrence U., Keio Med. Sci. prize, 2006, Gairdner Found. Internat. award, 2007; Macy Fellow, Göttingen, Germany, 1976—77, Fairchild Scholar, Calif. Inst. Tech., 1984—85. Fellow: Am. Acad. Arts & Scis.; mem.: NAS. Office: Yale U Dept Molecular Biophysics & Biochemistry Bass Center Room 418 PO Box 208114 266 Whitney Ave New Haven CT 06520-8114 Office Phone: 203-432-5619. Office Fax: 203-432-3282. Business E-Mail: peggy.eatherton@yale.edu.*

STELCK, CHARLES RICHARD, geology educator; b. Edmonton, Alta., Can., May 20, 1917; s. Robert Ferdinand and Florella Maud (Stanbury) S.; m. Frances Gertrude McDowell, Apr. 24, 1945; children: David, Brian, Leland, John (dec.). BSc, U. Alta., 1937, MSc, 1941, DSc (hon.), 2003; PhD, Stanford U., 1951. Registered profl. geologist Alta. Field geologist B.C. Dept. Mines, Victoria, Canada, 1939-41, Canol Project, Norman Wells, N.W.T., Canada, 1941-43, Imperial Oil Co., Calgary, Alta., 1943-49; from lectr. to prof. emeritus geology U. Alta., Edmonton, 1946—. Contbr. numerous articles principally on biostratigraphy of Cretaceous to sci. publs. Decorated officer Order of Can.; recipient Disting. Educator award Am. Assn. Petroleum Geologists, 2001, Queen's Golden Jubilee medal, 2002, Alberta Centenial medal, 2005; named to Can. Petroleum Hall Fame, 2005. Fellow Royal Soc. Can.; mem. Assn. Profl. Engrs., Geologists and Geophysicists Alta. (Centennial award 1979), Geol. Assn. Can. (Logan medal 1982), Geol. Soc. Am., Can. Soc. Petroleum Geologists (Douglas medal 1994, Stanley Slipper gold medal 2002), Order of Can. (officer 1997). Conservative. Office: U Alta Dept Earth & Atmospheric Scis Edmonton AB Canada T6G 2E3

STELLA, JOHN ANTHONY, financial executive; b. Jessup, Pa., Feb. 3, 1938; s. John Anthony and Alda (Parri) S.; m. Aurelia M. Arre, Feb. 20, 1965; children: John C., Matthew A., Krista R. BS, U. Detroit, 1960; MBA, NYU, 1965. Bus. evaluation cons. Allied Chem. Co., NYC, 1965-70; treas. Spinnerin Yarn Co., Hackensack, NJ, 1970-72, Penn-Dixie Cement Corp., NYC, 1972-74; v.p. finance Halecrest Co., 1974-76; treas. Rsch.-Cottrell, 1976-84, v.p., contr./treas., 1984-88; pres. John A. Stella & Assocs., Plainfield, NJ, 1988-91; sr. v.p. Investment Support Systems, Inc., Bloomfield, NJ, 1991-95. Pres. State Tax Auditing and Rsch., Inc., Bethlehem, 1993—2005. Served with AUS, 1960. Home: 1775 Arden Ln Bethlehem PA 18015-5829

STELLAR, ARTHUR WAYNE, school system administrator; b. Columbus, Ohio, Apr. 12, 1947; s. Fredrick and Bonnie Jean (Clark) S. BS, Ohio U., 1969, MA, 1970, PhD, 1973. Tchr. Athens City Schs., Ohio, 1969-71; curriculum coord., tchr. Belpre City Schs., Ohio, 1971-72; prin. elem. schs., head tchr. learning disabilities South-Western City Schs., Grove City, Ohio, 1972-76; dir. elem. edn. Beverly Pub. Schs., Mass., 1976-78; coord. spl. projects and systemwide planning Montgomery County Pub. Schs., Rockville, Md., 1978-80; asst. supt. Shaker Heights, Ohio, 1980-83; supt. schs. Mercer County Pub. Schs., Princeton, W.Va., 1983-85, Oklahoma City Pub. Schs., 1985-92, Cobb County, Ga., 1992-93, Kingston Sch. Dist., NY, 1996—2001; dep. supt. Boston Pub. Schs., 1993-95, acting supt., 1995-96; pres., CEO High/Scope Ednl. Rsch. Found., Ypsilanti, Mich., 2001—03; v.p., chief edn. officer Renaissance Learning, Madison, Wis., 2003—04; sr. assoc. Proact Search, Inc., Milw., 2004—09; rep. Docufide, Inc., LA, 2004—05, also adv. bd. dirs., 2004—05; supt. Taunton Pub. Schs., Mass., 2005—09. Mem. ednl. adv. bd. Tchrs. Support Network, 2004-08; adj. prof. Lesley Coll., Cambridge, Mass., 1976-78; adj. faculty Harvard U., 1992-93; assoc. Sch. Match, Ohio, 2004—09. Author: Educational Planning for Educational Success; Effective Schools Research: Practice and Promise; editor: Effective Instructional Management; cons. editor, book rev. editor Jour. Ednl. Pub. Rels.; mem. editl. bd. Jour. Curriculum & Supervision, Reading Today's Youth; contbr. articles to profl. jours. Mem. Urban Ctr. Ednl. Adv. Bd., US Dept. Edn. Urban Supt. Network, Coun. Great City Schs. Bd., Urban Edn. Clearing House Adv. com., U. Okla. Adminstrn. cert. program com., Cmty. Literacy Coun. Bd.; chmn. bd. dirs. Langston U.; bd. dirs. Oklahoma County chpt. ARC, Jr. Achievement Greater Oklahoma City Bd., Okla. State Fair Bd., Horace Mann League, 1993—, v.p. 2000-01, pres.-elect, 2001-02, pres. 2002-03, past pres. 2003-04, mem. found. com., 2003-05; v.p. Last Frontier Coun. Bd., v.p. NY State PTA, 1996-2000, Kingston chpt. Rip Van Winkle Coun.; v.p. Boy Scouts Am., 1996-2001, membership chmn., 1996-97; exec. bd. Nat. Dropout Prevention Ctr. Network, 1998-2008, chmn., 2003-07; curriculum com. NY State Coun. Sch. Supts., 1996-2001; bd. dirs. Friends Historic Kingston, 1996-2001, Friends Senate House, Kingston, 1996-2001, Project Contemporary Competitiveness Inc., 2005-09. Recipient Silver Beaver award, Boy Scouts Am., 1990, Amb. award, Horace Mann League, 1995—2009, Crystal Star Leadership award, NDPC/N, 2007, Disting. Svc. award, Pub. Edn. Mass., Tech. award, JFY Networks, 2008; named a Friend, Horace Mann League, 2006; named to Linden McKinley H.S. Acad. Hall of Fame, 2003; fellow, Charles Kettering Found. IDEA, 1976, 1978, 1980, NEH, Danforth Found., 1987—88. Mem. ASCD (life, exec. coun., pres. 1994-95, rev. coun. 1997-2002), Mich. ASCD, Mass. ASCD, Ohio ASCD, Okla. ASCD (Publ. award 1989), NY ASCD, Wis. ASCD, Internat. Soc. Ednl. Planning, Internat. Reading Assn. (govt. rels. com. 2003-04), Nat. Soc. Study Edn., Nat. Planning Assn., Nat. Assn. Gifted Children (life), Nat. Assn. Edn. Young Children (life), Nat. Coun. Tchrs. English (life), Music Educators Nat. Conf. (life), Nat. Orgn. Legal Problems Edn., Nat. Policy Bd. Ednl. Adminstrn., Am. Assn. Sch. Adminstrs. (life, Leadership for Learning award 1991, Dr. Effie Jones Humanitarian award 2007), Coll. Bd. Advanced Placement Spl. Recognition award 1991, Nat. Assn. Elem. Sch. Prins. (life), Am. Edn. Fin. Assn., Nat. Assn. Edn. Young Children (life), Nat. Sch. Pub. Rels. Assn. (Honor award 1991), Am. Mus. Natural Hist. (assoc.), Mass. Assn. for Sch. Supts., Mass. Assn. for Edn. of Young Children, Harvard U. Roundtable of Supts., Mass. Urban Supts., Nat. Sch. Pub. Rels. Assn., Taunton Area C. of C., World Coun. Curriculum and Instrn. (life, bd. dirs. N.Am. chpt. 1996-2000, pres. 2000-02), Coun. Basic Edn., Ohio Assn. Elem. Sch. Adminstrs., Buckeye Assn. Sch. Adminstrs., Ohio U. Coll. Edn. (disting. alumnus award 1991), Okla. Assn. Sch. Adminstrs., Mass. Assn. Sch. Adminstrs., Okla. Coalition Pub. Edn., Okla. Commn. Ednl. Leadership, Urban Area Supts. (Okla. br.), Ohio U. Alumni Assn. (nat. dir. 1975-78, pres. Ctrl. Ohio chpt. 1975-76, pres. Mass. chpt. 1976-78, life mem. trustees acad.), World Future Soc. (life) Greater Oklahoma City C. of C. (bd. dirs.), Okla. Heritage Assn., Heritage Hills Assn. (bd. dirs.), Victorian Soc. (New England chpt.), Nat. Eagle Scout Assn. (life), Aerospace Found. (hon. bd. dirs.), PLATO, Learning, Inc. (bd. dirs. 2000-03), Tchrs. Support Network (adv. bd. dirs. 2004-08), Am. Bus. Card Club, Coca Cola Collectors Club, Internat. Club, Mgmt. Consortium (bd. advisors),Fulbright Alumni Assn. (life), Tau Kappa Epsilon Alumni Assn. (regional officer Mass. 1976-78, named Alumni Nat. Hall of Fame 1986, Nat. Alumnus of Yr. 1993, Excellence in Edn. award 1993), Kappa Delta Pi (life; advisor Ctrl. Okla. chpt., nat. publs. com.), Phi Delta Kappa (life; mem. Fulbright tchr. and adminstr. exch. program to Mexico, 2009, mem. Fulbright tchr. and adminstr. exch. program to Brzil, 2009). Methodist. Office Phone: 508-922-6389. Personal E-mail: artstellar@yahoo.com. Business E-Mail: astellar@tauntonschools.org.

STELLATO, LOUIS EUGENE, lawyer; b. Bethlehem, Pa., 1950; BBA, U. Tex., 1972; JD, U. Pitts., 1977; LLM, Temple U., 1979. Bar: PA. 1977. With Touche Ross & Co., 1979-81; with tax dept. Sherwin-Williams Co., 1981-87, sr. corp. counsel, 1987-90, asst. secy., corp. dir. taxes, 1990-91, v.p., gen. counsel, sec., 1991—. Office: Sherwin Williams Co 101 Prospect Ave NW Cleveland OH 44115-1075 Office Phone: 216-566-2000.

STELLE, KELLOGG SHEFFIELD, physicist; b. Washington, Mar. 11, 1948; s. Charles Clarkson and Jane Elizabeth (Kellogg) S. AB, Harvard Coll., 1970; PhD, Brandeis U., 1977. Field observer Bartol Research Found., South Pole, Antarctica, 1970-72; lectr. math. King's Coll., U. London, Eng., 1977-78; sci. assoc. Cern, Geneva, 1980-81, 87, 97-98, 2007; rsch. fellow Imperial Coll., London, 1978-80, advanced fellow, 1982-87, lectr. then reader, 1987-95, prof. physics, 1995—, head theoretical physics group, 2002—07. Mem. Inst. Advanced Study, Princeton, N.J., 1986; vis. fellow Ecole Normale Supérieure, Paris, 1981-82; program dir. Inst. Henri Poincaré, Paris, 2000; vis. prof. Albert Einstein Inst., Potsdam, Germany, 2007-08. Editor Classical and Quantum Gravity, 1984-93; contbr. articles to profl. jours. Recipient Rsch. award, Alexander Von Humboldt Found., 2006. Fellow Inst. of Physics, Am. Phys. Soc.; mem. AAAS, Fedn. Am. Scientists. Office: Blackett Lab Imperial Coll Prince Consort Rd London SW7 2AZ England

STELLMACHER, JON MICHAEL, corporate financial executive; b. Green Bay, Wis., Feb. 25, 1956; s. Leroy Frederick and Helen Mae (Koss) S.; m. Rebecca Jean Hein, Aug. 20, 1976; children: James Michael, Paul Frederick, Abigail Joy. BBA with distinction, U. Wis., 1978. Underwriting clk. State Life Insur. Fund, Madison, Wis., 1977-78; actuarial student Aid Assn. for Luths., Appleton, Wis., 1978-79, actuarial asst., 1979-83, asst. actuary, 1983-85, assoc. actuary, 1985-87, 2nd v.p., actuary, 1987—97, v.p., 1997—99, sr. v.p., 1999—2002; exec. v.p. Thrivent Fin. for Luths., Appleton, 2002—05, exec. v.p., chief adminstrv. officer, 2005—08, sr. v.p., chief staff & adminstrn., 2008—. Chpt. reviewer Health Ins. Textbook, Soc. Actuaries, 1984-85; chmn. actuaries sect. Health Workshop Nat. Fraternal Congress Am., 1986, 88; mem. actuarial adv. com. Wis. Health Ins. Risk Sharing Pool, 1987—92; co-chmn. workshop, spring meeting Soc. Actuaries, 1989, 91, Loma Ins. Comm., 1999-2000. Acting pres., v.p. coun. 1st English Luth. Ch., Appleton, 1984; mission interpreter Am. Luth. Ch., Appleton area, 1985-87, Sunday Sch. tchr., 1984-2006, stewardship com., 1981-90, social concerns com. 1991-94, Elderly Housing Task Force, 1990-91, Benevolence Task Force, 1994; co-chair Capital Appeal, 2000; asst. den leader Cub Scouts, Boy Scouts Am., Appleton, 1989-91; asst. coach Appleton Soccer Club, 1990-93, Odyssey of the Mind, 1990-93; coach Appleton Park and Recreation Dept., 1990-98; vice chmn. Arthur Krempin Sch. Music and Art, 2003-04; bd. dirs. Appleton Boychoir, 1994-2008, chair, 1999-2008; bd. dirs. Appleton Med. Ctr. Found., 2000—, sec., 2001—; bd. dirs. United Way Fox Cities, 2001-08, co-chmn. campaign com., 2002, vice-chair, 2006, chair, 2007; mem. sr. adv. bd. Jr. Achievement, 2001—; bd. dirs. YMCA of the Fox Cities, 2002-08, vice-chair, 2006-07, co-chair capital campaign, 2006-07; bd. dirs. Fox Cities Performing Arts Ctr., 2003—, ThedaCare, 2006—, Wis. Mfrs. and Commerce, 2006-08; mem. Theda Care Quality Coun., 2003—, Cmty. Health Action Team, 2005—; co-chair Emergency Shelter Endowment Campaign, 2005-06; bd. regents Luther Coll., 2007—; co-chair Wisconsin's Econ. Success, 2007-; co-chair Project Promise Poverty Coalition, 2008-, Wis. Gov.'s. State Adv. Coun. Early Childhood Ednl. Care, 2008-. Fellow Soc. Actuaries; mem. Am. Acad. Actuaries. Office: Thrivent Fin for Luths 4321 N Ballard Rd Appleton WI 54919 Home: 3124 E Sandpiper Ln Appleton WI 54913-7771 Office Phone: 920-628-2002. Business E-Mail: jon.stellmacher@thrivent.com.

STELLWAGEN, ROBERT HARWOOD, biochemistry professor; s. Harwood John and Alma Dorothy S.; m. Joanne Kovacs, June 15, 1963; children: Robert Harwood, Alise Anne. AB, Harvard U., 1963; PhD, U. Calif., Berkeley, 1968. Staff fellow NIH, Bethesda, Md., 1968-69; postdoctoral scholar U. Calif., San Francisco, 1969-70; asst. prof. biochemistry, molecular biology U. So. Calif., LA, 1970-74, assoc. prof., 1974-80, prof., 1980—2008, chmn. dept., 1981-86, vice chmn. dept., 1993—2006, emeritus prof., 2008—. Vis. scientist Nat. Inst. for Med. Rsch., Mill Hill, Eng., 1979. Contbr. articles to profl. jours. Recipient Henderson prize Harvard U., 1963; NSF fellow, 1963-67; NIH grantee, 1971-84. Mem. Sierra Club, Phi Beta Kappa. Democrat. Office: U So Calif Keck Sch Medicine 1333 San Pablo St Los Angeles CA 90089-9151 Home Phone: 805-532-9986; Office Phone: 323-442-1149. Business E-Mail: stellwag@usc.edu.

STELPSTRA, WILLIAM JOHN, minister; b. Paterson, NJ, Nov. 1, 1934; s. Duke and Nellie (Stapert) S.; m. Anna Rizkovsky, Sept. 6, 1958; 1 child, Linda Mae. BA, Alma White Coll., 1957; B. of Religion, Zarephath Bible Sem., 1958. Ordained to ministry Pillar of Fire Ch., 1954. Pastor Pillar of Fire Ch., Little Falls, N.J., 1956-60; evangelist Wesleyan Meth. Ch., 1960-64; founder, dir. Bethel Children's Home, Paterson, N.J., 1964-71, Bethel Ranch Rehab. for Men, West Milford, N.J., 1971—; founder, pres. World for Christ Crusade, Inc., N.J., Fla., 1960—, dir. fgn. missions Haiti, Ghana, India, 1980—; adminstr. Fellowship House, Bloomfield, N.J., 1979—, Bright Side Manor, Teaneck, N.J., 1978—. Mem. Ocean Grove C. of C. Republican. Wesleyan Ch. Avocations: painting with oils, swimming, boating, travel, gardening. Home: 1005 Union Valley Rd West Milford NJ 07480-1220 Office Phone: 973-728-3267. Personal E-mail: revstelpstra@aol.com.

STELWAGON, JENNIFER COOPER, psychiatrist; b. Valdosta, Ga., Jan. 18, 1973; d. Michael Thomas and Margaret Ann (Sorensen) Cooper; m. William Mantz Stelwagon, Apr. 28, 2007; 1 child, William Cooper. BA magna cum laude, DePauw U., Greencastle, Ind., 1995; MD, Johns Hopkins U., Balt., 1999. Lic. physician NY, diplomate Am. Bd. Psychiatry and Neurology, Am. Bd. Addiction Psychiatry. Resident in psychiatry NY Presbyn. Hosp./Weill Cornell Med. Ctr./Payne Whitney Clinic, NYC, 1999—2003; fellow in addiction psychiatry Weill Med. Coll. of Cornell U., NYC, 2003—04; staff psychiatrist Bridge Back to Life, NYC, 2004—05, 2009—; pvt. practice psychiatry NYC, 2004—; med. dir. drug treatment Exponents, NYC, 2004—07. Clin. instr. psychiatry Weill Med. Coll. of Cornell U., 2006—; mem. adv. bd. David Dawes Nee II Found., 2007—. Ordained elder First Presbyn. Ch. NYC. Recipient Alumni award for resident tchg., Payne Whitney Clinic, 2003; named Career Directions Resident of the Yr., Pfizer Inc., 2002. Mem.: Presbyterian Church (ordained elder), David Dawes Nee II Found. (mem. adv. bd. 2007—), Am. Acad. Addiction Psychiatry, Am. Psychiat. Assn. Avocations: skiing, scuba diving. Office: 239 E 73d St Ste 1W-A New York NY 10021 Home: 1175 York Ave 7E New York NY 10065

STELZER, IRWIN MARK, economist; b. NYC, May 22, 1932; s. Abraham and Fanny (Dolgins) S.; m. Marian Faris Stuntz, 1981. BA cum laude, NYU, 1951, MA, 1952; PhD, Cornell U., 1954. Fin. analyst Econometric Inst., 1952; tchg. fellow Cornell U., 1953-54; instr. U. Conn., 1954-55; rschr. Twentieth Century Fund, 1953-55; economist W.J. Levy, Inc., 1955-56; sr. cons., v.p. Boni, Watkins, Jason & Co., Inc., 1956-61; rschr. Brookings Instn., 1956-57; pres. Nat. Econ. Rsch. Assocs., Inc., 1961-85, I.M. Stelzer Assocs. Inc., 1986—; dir. Energy and Environmental Ctr., Harvard U., 1987-90. Dir. econ. policy studies Am. Enterprise Inst., 1990-98; bd. dirs. Econs. Policy Inst., Oxford U.; dir. econ. policy studies Hudson Inst., 1998—; adv. coun. Electric Power Rsch. Inst.; adv. com. revision of rules of practice and procedure FERC; chmn. com. on adequate power supply FPC; bd. dirs. The Energy Adv. Group of the Keystone Ctr; mng. dir. Rothschild, Inc.; mem. trade and environment policy adv. com. US Trade Rep.; vis. fellow Nuffield Coll., Oxford U.; sr. rsch. fellow Smith Inst.; adv. bd. Am. Antitrust Inst.; vis. com. mem. Harris Sch. U. Chgo.; lectr. in field. Author: Selected Antitrust Cases: Landmark Decisions, 1955, The Antitrust Laws: A Primer, 1993, 4th edit., 2001, Neoconservatism, 2004, The New Capitalism, 2008, The NEOCON Reader, 2004; econ. columnist The Sunday Times, London, 1986—; contbg. editor The Weekly Standard; columnist Courier Mail, Australia; contbr. articles to econs. field. Mem. Mayor's Energy Policy Adv. Group for NYC; adv. panel Pres.'s Nat. Commn. for Rev. of Antitrust Laws and Procedures; mem. Gov.'s Adv. Panel on Telecom., bd. governing trustees Am. Ballet Theatre; bd. dirs. U.S. Nat. Com., World Energy Conf., Regulatory Policy Inst., Oxford U.; mem. Fed. Energy Regulatory Com. Task Force on Pipeline Competition; pres. appointee advisor to U.S. Trade Rep. Mem. Am. Econ. Assn., Reform Club, Cosmos Club, Phi Beta Kappa. Home: PO Box 1008 Aspen CO 81612-1008 Office: 1150 17th St NW Ste 502 Washington DC 20036 Home Phone: 202-797-9292; Office Phone: 202-777-3000. Personal E-mail: stelzer@aol.com.

STELZER, PATRICIA JACOBS, retired secondary school educator; b. Springfield, Ohio, Sept. 7, 1936; d. George Kenneth and Beatrice Snook Jacobs; m. James Glea Stelzer, May 12, 1956; children: Michael G., Samantha S. Moehn, James Todd. BS in Edn., Wright State U., 1973, MA in History, 1997. Reporter, features writer, columnist Springfield News-Sun, 1962—65; social studies tchr. Schaefer Jr. H.S., Springfield, 1975—77, 1978—81, South H.S., Springfield, 1977—78, 1981—2000; ret., 2000; chmn. social studies dept. South H.S., Springfield, 1991—2000. Adj. prof. history Clark State C.C., Springfield, 2001—08; ret., 2008; cons. Ohio test scholastic achievement State of Ohio Dept. Edn., Columbus, 1985—87; participant cert. assessment pilot program social studies program Nat. Bd. Profl. Tchg. Stds., 1998. Author (book): Dangerous Research, By George!, Deadly Research By George!. Pres. Springfield Civic Theater, 1984—85; performer, mem. pub. rels. com. Music-Stage Theater, Springfield, 1964—68, 1975; dir., choreographer Northwestern H.S. and South H.S., Springfield, 1977—91; advt. dir. Choral Arts Springfield, 2004—05. Lutheran. Avocations: golf, travel, theater, writing. Home: 6541 Troy Rd Springfield OH 45502

STELZER, PAUL, thoracic surgeon, educator; Attended, U. Nebr., Lincoln, 1964—65; BA summa cum laude, Abilene Christian U., 1968; MD, Columbia U., 1972. Diplomate Am. Bd. Surgery, Am. Bd. Thoracic Surgery. Intern, resident gen. surgery Roosevelt Hosp., NYC, 1972-77; resident cardiothoracic surgery NY Hosp.-Cornell Med. Ctr., 1979—81, staff cardiothoracic surgeon, asst. prof. surgery, 1981—85; chief thoracic surgery Okla. Meml. Hosp.; assoc. prof. surgery U. Okla. Health Scis. Ctr., Oklahoma City, 1985—89; staff cardiothoracic surgeon Lenox Hill Hospital, NYC, 1989—96; chief divsn. cardiothoracic surgery St. Luke's/Roosevelt Hosp. Ctr., 1999—2000; sr. cardiothoracic surgeon Beth Israel Med. Ctr., 1996—2007; co-dir. valve surgery Mt. Sinai Med. Ctr., 2007—. Office: Mt Sinai Hosp Dept Cardiothoracic Surgery 1190 Fifth Ave, Box 1028 New York NY 10029 Home Phone: 212-737-8103; Office Phone: 212-659-6871. Office Fax: 212-659-6818. Business E-Mail: pstelzer@bethisraelny.org. E-mail: Paul.Stelzer@mountsinai.org.

STEM, CARL HERBERT, business educator; b. Eagleville, Tenn., Jan. 30, 1935; s. Marion Ogilvie and Sara Elizabeth (Jones) Stem; m. Linda Marlene Wheeler, Dec. 28, 1963; children: Anna Elizabeth, Susan Kathleen, John Carl, David Leslie. BA, Vanderbilt U., Nashville, 1957; AM (Woodrow Wilson fellow, Harvard scholar), Harvard U., Cambridge, Mass., 1960, PhD, 1969. Internat. fin. economist, bd. govs. Fed. Res. System, Washington, 1963—70; from assoc. prof. to prof. econs. Tex. Tech. U., Lubbock, 1970—75; from assoc. prof. to prof. internat. fin. Tex. Tech U., Lubbock, 1970—2001; prof. emeritus Tex. Tech. U., Lubbock, 2001—; from chmn. fin., adminstr. grad. programs, exec. assoc. dean to dean Tex. Tech U. Rawls Coll. Bus. Adminstrn., Lubbock, 1971—97; dean emeritus Tex. Tech U. J. Rawls Coll. Bus. Adminstrn., Lubbock, 1997—. Sr. econ. adviser Office Fgn. Direct Investments, U.S. Dept. Commerce, Washington, 1973-74; cons. US Dept. Treasury, 1974-75; mem. faculty Grad. Sch. Credit and Fin. Mgmt., Lake Success, NY, 1974-87; adj. scholar Am. Enterprise Inst. Pub. Policy Rsch., Washington, 1974-88; treas. Mission Jour., Inc., 1969-88. Editor (with Makin and Logue): Eurocurrencies and The International Monetary System; contbr. articles to profl. jours. Trustee St. Mary Plains Hosp., Lubbock, Tex., 1987-92, chmn., 1992; v.p. Tex. Coun. Collegiate Edn. Bus., 1977-78, pres., 1978-79; mem. acad. adv. bd. United Arab Emirates U., Al Ain, 1996-03; mem. Coun. on Podiat. Med. Edn., Washington, 1998—; bd. visitors Abilene Christian U., 1998-2007; elder Broadway Ch. of Christ, Lubbock, 2001-04; elder Overland Pk. Ch. of Christ, Kans., 2007—. Capt. Security Agy. AUS, 1961-62. Fulbright scholar, U. Reading, Eng., 1957—58. Fellow Phi Beta Kappa; mem. Southwestern Bus. Adminstrn. Assn. (pres. 1982-83), Nat. Assn. for Bus. Econs., So. Bus. Adminstrn. Assn. (v.p. 1985-86, pres. 1986-87), Lubbock Econ. Coun. (pres. 1973), Am. Assembly Collegiate Schs. Bus. (stds. com. 1981-84, bd. dirs. 1993-96), Lubbock Club (bd. of dirs. 1983-1987, pres. 1986-87), Omicron Delta Kappa, Phi Kappa Phi, Beta Gamma Sigma, Tau Kappa Alpha, Phi Beta Kappa. Avocations: genealogy, history. Home: 12508 W 123rd St Overland Park KS 66213 Home Phone: 913-814-9911. Personal E-mail: cstem@sbcglobal.net. *Most important to me are the ever timely values of our Judeo-Christian heritage- faith in God and a deep appreciation for the inherent value of man. These values have underpinned my aspirations and sustained me through disappointments. They have generated the perseverance and continual hope so vital to me as I have worked for self-growth and to make a contribution to the institutions and people with which I have been associated in various periods of my life.*

STEMERMAN, DAVID H., radiologist; b. Elmira, NY, Aug. 2, 1966; BA, Emory U., 1988; MD, Boston U., 1992. Diplomate Nat. Bd. Med. Examiners; bd. cert. Am. Bd. Radiology. Intern Mass. Gen. Hosp.,

Boston, 1992-93; resident Temple U., Phila., 1993-97; fellow NYU, NYC, 1997-98; assoc. radiologist Abington Meml. Hosp., Pa., 1998-99, St. Joseph's Med. Ctr., 1999—2000, St. Barnabas Hosp., 2000—01; med. dir. Open High-Field MRI and CT, Westchester and Fordham Radiology. Office Fax: 914-833-9641.

STEMMLER, EDWARD JOSEPH, physician, retired health facility administrator, dean; b. Phila., Feb. 15, 1929; s. Edward C. and Josephine (Heitzmann) Stemmler; m. Joan C. Koster, Dec. 27, 1958; children: Elizabeth, Margaret, Edward C., Catherine, Joan. BA, La Salle Coll., Phila., 1950, ScD (hon.), 1983; MD, U. Pa., 1960; ScD (hon.), Ursinus Coll., 1977, Phila. Coll. Pharmacy and Sci., 1989; LHD (hon.), Rush U., 1986, Med. Coll. Pa., 1994; ScD (hon.), SUNY, Syracuse, 1994; ScD, Georgetown U., 1998. Diplomate Am. Bd. Internal Medicine. Intern U. Pa. Hosp., 1960—61, resident in internal medicine, 1961—63, fellow in cardiology, 1963—64, chief med. resident, 1964—65, chief med. outpatient dept., 1966—67; chief of medicine U. Pa. Med. Svc., VA Hosp., Phila., 1967—73; deans com. VA Hosp., 1974—88; instr. medicine grad. divsn. medicine U. Pa., 1964—66, NIH postdoctoral rsch. trainee, dept. physiology, grad. divsn. medicine, 1965—67, assoc. in medicine grad. divsn. medicine, 1966—67; assoc. in physiology Grad. Div. Medicine, 1967—72, from asst. prof. medicine to prof., 1967—91, Robert G. Dunlop prof., 1981—91, prof. emeritus, 1991—; assoc. dean Univ. Hosp. Sch. Medicine, 1973, assoc. dean student affairs, 1973—75, from acting dean to dean, 1974—88, dean emeritus, 1989—; exec. v.p. U. Pa. Med. Ctr., 1986—89, Assn. Am. Med. Colls., 1990—94, sr. adv. to pres., 1994—95. Nominating and ad hoc governance coms. Nat. Bd. Med. Examiners, 1985, exec. com., 1986—99, vice-chmn., 1987—89, treas., 1989—91, chmn., 1991—95; ednl. policy com. Nat. Fund for Med. Edn., 1975—77; deans com. VA Hosp., 1974—89; chmn. Pa. Deans Com., 1976—87, Mid-Ea. Regional Med. Libr. Svcs., 1978—81; adv. com. dept. medicine U. Ala., Birmingham, 1985—89; vis. com. Tufts U. Sch. Medicine, 1990—94, Med. U. S.C., 1990—99, U. Calif., Davis, 1993—2008. Contbr. articles to profl. jours. Trustee Dorothy Rider Pool Healthcare Trust, 1991—2000, Ursinus Coll., 1991—2006, Wintergreen Nature Found., 1996—2001, Saw Cmty. Found., 2000—04, AHC Cmty. Found., 2002—08; mem. oper. bd. U. Va. Med. Ctr., 2004—; chair Quality Soc. Com. Recipient Frederick A. Packard award, 1960, Albert Einstein Med. Ctr. staff award, 1960, Roche award, 1960, Disting. Svc. award, Nat. Bd. Med. Examiners, 1999. Master: ACP (treas., chmn. investment com. 1975—80, Laureate award Ea. Pa. region 1986, Disting. Svc. award); mem.: AMA, Am. Clin. and Climatological Soc. (pres. 1997—98), Coll. Physicians Phila. (bd. censors, coun. 1979—85, coun. 1990—92), Assn. Am. Med. Colls. (ad hoc external exam. rev. com. 1980—82, exec. coun., coun. of deans adminstrv. bd. 1980—85, chmn. 1983—85, nat. chmn.-elect 1985—86, chmn. assembly 1986—87), Inst. Medicine, Alpha Omega Alpha. Republican. Home: RR 1 Box 676 Roseland VA 22967-9209 Personal E-mail: ejstemmler@aol.com.

STEMPEL, GUIDO HERMANN, III, journalism educator; b. Bloomington, Ind., Aug. 13, 1928; s. Guido Hermann Jr. and Alice Margaret (Menninger) S.; m. Anne Elliott, Aug. 30, 1952; children: Ralph Warren, Carl William, Jane Louise. Student, Carnegie Tech., 1945-46; AB in Journalism, Ind. U., 1949, AM in Journalism, 1951; PhD in Mass Communication, U. Wis., 1954. Sports editor Frankfort (Ind.) Times, 1949-50; instr., asst. prof. Sch. Journalism, Pa. State U., University Park, 1955-57; from assoc. prof. to prof. Dept. Journalism, Cen. Mich. U., Mt. Pleasant, 1957-65; assoc. prof. Sch. Journalism, Ohio U., Athens, 1965-68, prof., 1968-82, Disting. prof., 1982—96, Disting. prof. emeritus, 1996—, dir., 1972-79, dir. Scripps Survey Rsch. Ctr., 2002—07. Meeman vis. disting. prof. U. Tenn., 1999; rsch. cons. Ohio Newspaper Assn., Columbus, 1985—; chmn. rsch. com. Coll. Media Advisors, 1963-69, 79-84; adv. bd. dept. comm. arts U. West Fla., 1987-00; survey coord. Scripps Howard News Svc., 1992—. Co-author: The Media in the 1984 and 1988 Presidential Campaigns, 1991; assoc. editor, Newspaper Rsch. Jour., 1992-2001; co-editor Web Jour. of Mass Comm. Rsch., 1997—; editor, co-author: The Practice of Political Communication, 1994; co-editor, co-author: Research Methods in Mass Communications, 1981, 2d edit., 1989, The Media in the 1984 and 1988 Presidential Campaigns, 1991, Historical Dictionary of Political Communication in the United States, 1999, Mass Communication Research and Theory, 2003; author: Media and Politics in America, 2003; editor: Journalism Quar., 1972-89; sr. rsch. editor Newspaper Research Jour., 2000—; contbr. articles to profl. jours. Mem. bd. visitors Def. Info. Sch., Ft. Meade, 1985-96. Recipient Chancellor's award, U. Wis., 1977, Francis Asbury award, West Ohio Meth. Conf., 2004, Harold C. Nelson award, U. Wis., 2004; named to Ctrl. Mich. Journalism Hall of Fame, 2004. Mem. Assn. for Edn. in Journalism and Mass Comm. (chmn. rsch. com. 1968-71; Eleanor Blum award 1989, Trayes Tchr. of Yr. 1997, Disting. Svc. award 1999, award for excellence in contbns. to journalism 2005, Paul Deutschmann award for excellence in rsch. 2007), Soc. Profl. Journalists, Rotary (pres. Athens unit 1984-85). Democrat. Methodist. Home: 7 Lamar Dr Athens OH 45701-3730 Office: Ohio Univ Sch of Journalism Athens OH 45701 Business E-Mail: stempel@ohio.edu.

STEMPEL, JOHN DALLAS, international studies educator; b. Easton, Pa., July 26, 1938; s. John Emmert and Mary Roberts (Farmer) S.; m. Nancy A. Dean, Feb. 11, 1961 (div. Jan. 1980); m. Susan Hodgetts, May 18, 1991; children: Amy, Alix, Jill. AB cum laude, Princeton U., 1960; MA with distinction, U. Calif., Berkeley, 1963, PhD, 1965. Jr. officer U.S. Embassy U.S. Fgn. Svc., Conakry, Guinea, 1966, acting dep. chief mission U.S. Embassy Bujumbura, Burundi, 1966-68, watch officer State Dept. Ops. Ctr. Washington, 1968-70, staff asst. to dep. sec. state, 1968-70, Ghana desk officer, 1970-72, polit.-econ. officer U.S. Embassy Lusaka, Zambia, 1972-74, from sr. internal polit. reporter to dep. chief sect. to acting polit. counselor U.S. Embassy Tehran, Iran, 1975-79; diplomat-in-residence, mem. faculty U.S. Naval Acad., Annapolis, Md., 1979-81; dir. ops. ctr. Dept. State U.S. Fgn. Svc., Washington, 1981-83, dir. Office Near East and South Asian Affairs Bur. Internat. Security Affairs Dept. Def., 1983-84; spl. asst. Persian Gulf affairs U.S. Dept. State, Washington, 1984-85; consul gen. U.S. Fgn. Svc., Madras, India, 1985-88; prof. internat. studies, assoc. dir. Patterson Sch. Diplomacy and Internat. Commerce U. Ky., Lexington, 1988-93, prof. internat. studies, dir. Patterson Sch. Diplomacy, 1993—2003, sr. prof. internat. studies Patterson Sch. Diplomacy, 2003—. Adj. prof. George Washington U., Washington, 1968-72, 80-85, Am. U., Washington, 1975; prof. Regional Coop. and Devel. Coll., Tehran, 1975-78; rsch. assoc. Mershon Ctr. Ohio State U., 1972; Mary Moody Northen chair prof. Va. Mil. Inst., 2005. Author: Inside the Iranian Revolution, 1981, Faith, Diplomacy and the International System, 2000, Common Sense and Foreign Policy, 2008; (monograph) Theory and Practice in Foreign Affairs: Why Two Worlds Seldom Meet, 1972; contbr. articles to profl. jours. Mem. bd. trustees Georgetown Coll., 2007—. With USN, 1960-62, lt. USNR, 1962-70. Mem. Internat. Studies Assn., N.Y. Coun. on Fgn. Rels. Avocations: tennis, reading, railroads, philosophy. Office: U Ky Patterson Sch Diplomacy Patterson Tower Rm 455 Lexington KY 40506-0027 Home Phone: 859-255-5356; Office Phone: 859-257-8261.

STEMPER, BRIAN D., biomedical engineer, educator; b. Fond du Lac, Wis., Oct. 30, 1974; s. Gerald A. and Judith M. Stemper; m. Julie M Rumpf, June 28, 2003. BS in Biomed. Engring., Milw. Sch. Engring., 1998; PhD, Marquette U., Milw., 2004. Biomed. rschr. Milw. Sch. Engring. Rapid Prototyping Ctr., 1996—98; tchg. asst. Marquette U., Milw., 1998—2000, rsch. asst., 2000—03; rsch. engr. dept. neurosurgery Med. Coll. Wis., Milw., 2003—04, assoc. prof. dept. neurosurgery, 2004—. Contbr. 40 articles in peer-reviewed jours. Bd. mem. Rocky Mountain Bioengring. Symposium, Inc. Recipient Best of Session, Rocky Mountain Bioengring. Symposium, 2000, Best Paper by a Young Rschr., Internat. IRCOBI Conf. Biomechanics of Impact, 2004. Mem.: Nat. Neurotrauma Soc., Soc. Automotive Engrs., Assn. for the Advancement of Automotive Medicine, ASME, Cervical Spine Rsch. Soc. R-Consevative. Roman Catholic. Office: Med Coll of Wis 9200 W Wisconsin Ave Milwaukee WI 53226 Business E-Mail: bstemper@mcw.edu.

STEMPSEY, WILLIAM EDWARD, medical philosopher; b. Albany, NY, Jan. 26, 1952; s. William Edward and Helen Theresa (Kuras) S. BS in Biology/Psychology magna cum laude, Boston Coll., 1974; MD, SUNY, Buffalo, 1978; AM in Philosophy, Loyola U., Chgo., 1988; MDiv, Jesuit Sch. Theology, Berkeley, Calif., 1991; STM in Moral Theology, Jesuit Sch. Theology, 1992; PhD in Philosophy, Georgetown U., 1996. Diplomate Nat. Bd. Med. Examiners; joined S.J., Roman Cath. Ch., 1982, ordained priest, 1992. Intern in anatomic pathology Boston City Hosp., 1978-79; resident in clin. pathology U. Hosp., Boston, 1980-82; resident in pediatric pathology Children's Hosp., Boston, 1984-85; teaching fellow Boston U. Sch. Medicine, 1981-82; clin. fellow in pathology Harvard Med. Sch., Boston, 1984-85; clin. scholar Ctr. for Clin. Bioethics, Georgetown U. Med. Ctr., 1995-96; assoc. prof. philosophy Coll. of the Holy Cross, Worcester, Mass., 1996—. Tchr. Claver Coll., Punda Gorda, Belize, 1983; hosp. min. Youville Hosp., Cambridge, 1983; mem. ethics com. St. Mary's Hosp. and Med. Ctr., San Francisco, 1989-92; mem. admissions com. Jesuit Sch. Theology, Berkeley, 1989-90; rsch. asst. for dir. Kennedy Inst. Ethics, Georgetown U., 1992-94; guest retreat dir. Mercy Ctr., Burlingame, Calif., 1990, 91; pastoral care min. Loyola Med. Ctr., Maywood, Ill., 1986-87, St. Francis Hosp., Evanston, Ill., 1987-88. Author: Disease and Diagnosis: Value-Dependent Realism, 1999, Elisha Bartlett's Philosophy of Medicine, 2005; contbr. articles to profl. publs. Vol. Shelter, Inc., Cambridge, Mass., 1982; mem. bioethics commn. Diocese of Worcester, Mass., 1997—; mem. ethics com. Fallon Clinic, Worcester, 1998—; mem. regional ethics com. Vis. Nurses Assn. Care Network, Worcester, 1998—. Mem. Am. Philos. Assn., Soc. for Health and Human Values, Kennedy Inst. Ethics, Hastings Ctr. (assoc.), Alpha Epsilon Delta. Avocations: music, piano, accordion, fishing. Office: Coll of the Holy Cross Dept Philosophy 1 College St Worcester MA 01610-2395

STENBERG, CARL W., III, public administration educator, dean; b. Pitts., July 8, 1943; s. Carl W. and Mildred (Baggs) S.; m. Kirstin D. Thompson; children: Erik Anders, Kerry Cathryn, Kaameran Baird. BA, Allegheny Coll., 1965; MPA, SUNY, Albany, 1966, PhD, 1970. Research asst. NY State Div. Budget, Albany, 1967; analyst, then sr. analyst US Adv. Commn. on Intergovtl. Relations, Washington, 1968-77, asst. dir. for policy implementation, 1977-83, acting exec. dir., 1982; exec. dir. Council of State Govts., Lexington, Ky., 1983-89; prof., dir. Weldon Cooper Ctr. for Pub. Svc. U. Va., Charlottesville, 1989-95, Disting. prof. pub. svc., 1991-95; prof., dean Yale Gordon Coll. Liberal Arts U. Balt., 1995—2003; prof. Sch. Govt. U. NC, Chapel Hill, 2003—, dir., pub. adminstrn. program, 2006—. Mem. Am. Part Program USIA, 1987; adj. prof. George Washington U., 1971, 81, Am. U., 1972-80, 82, U. Md., 1976, U. So. Calif., 1984-87; v.p. Bureaucrat Inc., Washington, 1973-77, mng. editor, 1973-77. Feature editor Pub. Mgmt. Forum Pub. Adminstrn. Rev., 1977-83, editor U. of Va. newsletter, 1994-95; co-editor-in-chief The Regionalist, 1997-2002. Pres. Reston Home Owners' Assn., Va., 1973-74; mem. U.S. del. Ad Hoc Group on Urban Problems, OECD, 1980-82. Vivien Stewart vis. fellow Cambridge U., Eng., 1980; recipient Disting. Alumni award Polit. Sci. Dept. Rockefeller Coll., 1985. Fellow: Nat. Acad. Pub. Adminstrn. (chair bd. dirs. 2002—04); mem.: Va. Alliance for Pub. Svc. (pres. 1991—92), Am. Soc. Pub. Adminstrn. (pres. 1990—91, Marshall E. Dimock award, Louis Brownlow award, Donald Stone award). Home: 301 Madera Ln Chapel Hill NC 27517-8356 Office: U NC Sch Govt CB # 3330 Knapp Bldg Chapel Hill NC 27599-3330 Office Phone: 919-962-2377. E-mail: stenberg@sog.unc.edu.

STENBERG, DONALD B., lawyer; b. David City, Nebr., Sept. 30, 1948; s. Eugene A. and Alice (Kasal) Stenberg; m. Susan K. Hoegemeyer, June 9, 1971; children: Julie A., Donald B. Jr., Joseph L., Abby E. BA, U. Nebr., 1970; MBA, Harvard U., 1974, JD cum laude, 1974. Bar: Nebr. 1974, U.S. Dist. Ct. Nebr. 1974, U.S. Ct. Appeals (fed. cir.) 1984, U.S. Ct. Claims 1989, U.S. Ct. Appeals (8th cir.) 1989, U.S. Supreme Ct. 1991. Assoc. Barlow, Watson & Johnson, Lincoln, Nebr., 1974—75; ptnr. Stenberg and Stenberg, Lincoln, 1976—78; legal counsel Gov. of Nebr., Lincoln, 1979—82; sr. prin. Erickson & Sederstrom, Lincoln, 1983—85, of counsel, 2003—; pvt. practice Lincoln, 1985—90; atty. gen. State of Nebr., Lincoln, 1991—2002. Mem.: Phi Beta Kappa. Republican. Office: Erickson & Sederstrom Regency Westpointe 10330 Regency Pkwy Dr Ste 100 Omaha NE 68114-3761 Office Phone: 402-390-7120. Business E-Mail: donstenberg@eslaw.com.

STENBIT, JOHN PAUL, former federal agency administrator; b. Oakland, Calif., June 1, 1940; s. Paul Charles and Antoinette (Inguglia) S.; m. Albertine Heederik, Aug. 19, 1966; children: Elisabeth Francesca, Antine Elaine. BS, Calif. Inst. Tech., 1961, MS, 1962; postgrad., Stanford U., 1981. Rsch. fellow Technische Hogesch., Eindhoven, The Netherlands, 1962-63, 65-67; engr. Aerospace Corp., El Segundo, Calif., 1962-68; prin. dep. dir. Office of Sec. US Dept. Def., Washington, 1973-77; engr. TRW, Redondo Beach, Calif., 1968—73, Fairfax, Va., 1977—2001; asst. sec. def. networks & info. integration (formerly command, control, comm. & intelligence) US Dept. Def., Washington, 2001—04. Mem. adv. bd. Dir. Naval Intelligence, Washington, 1982-91; mem. sci. adv. group Def. Communications Agy., Arlington, Va., 1989—; cons. Def. Sci. Bd., Washington; bd. trustees, The Mitre Corp.; bd. dirs., ViaSat, Inc., 2004-; bd. dirs., Cogent Systems, 2004-, Loral Space & Communications Inc., 2006-, Cryptek, Inc., 2008- Chmn. Internat. Children's Festival, Fairfax, 1991-92; mem., Defense Sci. Bd.; Naval Studies Bd.; bd. adv., Nat. Security Agency Mem., Sci. Adv. Group U.S. Strategic Command. Recipient medal for outstanding pub. svc. Sec. Def., 1977; Fulbright fellow, The Netherlands, 1962-63, Aerospace Corp., The Netherlands, 1965-67. Mem. NAE, AIAA, Security Affairs Support Assn. (bd. dirs. 1990—), Electronic Industries Assn. (bd. dirs. 1991—), Armed Forces Communications and Electronics Assn., Va. Bus. Coun., Korean-Am. Bus. Coun., Met. Club (Washington). Republican. Office: ViaSat Inc 6155 El Camino Real Carlsbad CA 92009 Office Phone: 760-476-2200. Office Fax: 760-929-3941.

STENCHEVER, MORTON ALBERT, obstetrician, gynecologist; b. Paterson, NJ, Jan. 25, 1931; s. Harold and Lena (Suresky) Stenchever; m. Diane Bilsky, June 19, 1955 (dec. 1999); children: Michael A., Marc R., Douglas A.; m. Luba Kane, Sept. 8, 2001. AB, NYU, 1951; MD, U. Buffalo, 1956. Diplomate Am. Bd. Ob-gyn., 1965, recertified 1986. Intern Mt. Sinai Hosp., 1956-57; resident obstetrics and gynecology Columbia-Presbyn. Med. Center, NYC, 1957-60; asst. prof., Oglebey research fellow Case-Western Res. U., Cleve., 1962-66, asso. prof. dept. reproductive biology, 1967-70, dir. Tissue Culture Lab., 1965-70, coordinator Phase II Med. Sch. program, 1969-70; prof., chmn. dept. obstetrics-gynecology U. Utah Med. Sch., Salt Lake City, 1970-77; prof. ob-gyn. U. Wash. Sch. Medicine, Seattle, 1977-98; prof. emeritus, 1998—; chmn. dept. U. Wash. Sch. Medicine, Seattle, 1977-96. Chmn. test com. for ob-gyn. Nat. Bd. Med. Examiners, 1979-82; cons. in urogynecology Fedn. Internat. for Gynecology & Obstetrics, 1998—. Author: Labor: Workbook in Obstetrics, 1968, Labor: Workbook in Obstetrics, 2d edit., 1993, Human Sexual Behavior: A Workbook in Reproductive Biology, 1970, Human Cytogenics: A Workbook in Reproductive Biology, 1973, Introductory Gynecology: A Workbook in Reproductive Biology, 1974; co-author: Comprehensive Gynecology, 1987, Comprehensive Gynecology, 4th edit., 2001, Caring for the Older Woman, 1991, Health Care for the Older Woman, 1996, Office Gynecology, 1992, Office Gynecology, 2d edit., 1996, Good Health, Great Sex After 40: A Woman's Guide, 1997; sr. editor: Atlas of Gynecology, 5 vols., 1997—99, assoc. editor: Ob-Gyn., 1986—2001, Ob-Gyn. Survey; editor: Clinical Updates in Women's Health Care, 2001—, ACOG Clin. Review, 2001—; mem. editl. bd.: Western Jour. Medicine; contbr. articles to profl. jours. Served to capt. USAF, 1960-62. Fellow Am. Coll. Obstetricians and Gynecologists (com. on residency edn. 1974-80, learning resource commn. 1980-86, vice chmn. 1982-83, chmn. prolog self-assessment program 1982-86, vice chair com. health care for the underserved women 1995-97), Am. Assn. Obstetricians and Gynecologists, Am. Gynecol. Soc., Am. Gyencol. and Obstetrical Soc., Pacific Coast Ob-Gyn. Soc.; mem. AAAS, AMA, Am. Bd. Ob-Gyn. (bd. dir. 1988-2004, v.p. 1990-92, treas. 1992-96, chmn. 1996-98, mem. resident rev. com. 1993-97, chmn. divsn. female pelvic medicine/reconstructive surgery), Assn. Profs. Gynecology and Obstetrics (chmn. steering com. teaching methods in ob-gyn. 1970-79, v.p. 1975-76, pres. 1983-84, v.p. Found. 1986-87, pres. Found. 1987-91), Pacific N.W. Ob-Gyn. Soc., Wash. State Med. Assn., Seattle Gynec. Soc. (v.p. 1981, pres.-elect 1982, pres. 1982-83), Am. Soc. Human Genetics, Ctrl. Assn. Ob-Gyn., Soc. Gynecologic Investigation, Wash. State Obstet. Soc., Tissue Culture Assn., N.Y. Acad. Sci., Utah Ob-Gyn. Soc., Utah Med. Assn., Teratology Soc., Am. Fertility Soc., Internat. Pelvic Floor Dysfunction Soc. Home: 8301 SE 83rd St Mercer Island WA 98040-5644 Office: Ob-Gyn 130 Knickerson St Ste 211 Seattle WA 98109 Office Phone: 206-286-1775. Business E-Mail: mstenchever@acog.org.

STENDAHL, BRITA KRISTINA, humanities and social studies educator; b. Stockholm, Jan. 10, 1925; came to U.S., 1954; d. Johan Victor and Ingeborg (Normann) Johnsson; m. Krister Stendahl, Sept. 7, 1946; children: Johan, Anna, Dan. Cand. Theology, Uppsala U., Sweden, 1949, cand. Philosophy, 1954, PhD (hon.), 1981. Hist. and lit. tchr. Gymnasium, Uppsala, Sweden, 1949-54; hist. and lit. tchr. extension program Harvard U., Cambridge, Mass., 1956-59, hist. and lit. tchr. freshman program, 1964-74; hist. and lit. tchr. seminar program Radcliffe Coll., Cambridge, 1976-84; cultural sec. Ch. of Sweden, Stockholm, 1984-88. Mem. Govt. Coun. for Coord. and Planning of Rsch., Stockholm, 1985-88. Author: (monographs) Søren Kierkegaard, 1976, The Force of Tradition, 1984, The Education of a Self-Made Woman, Fredrika Bremer, 1801-1865, 1994, (autobiography) Sabbatical Reflections, 1978; contbr. Multicultural Writers from Antiquity to 1945, 2002; book reviewer:, translator Swedish drama and poetry. Co-chair Fellowship in Israel for Arab-Jewish Youth, Boston, 1972-84, 88-95; bd. dirs. The Abraham Fund, N.Y.C., 1996-2006. Bunting fellow, Radcliffe Coll., Cambridge, Mass., 1961-63; assoc. fellow Henry A. Murray Ctr. at Radcliffe, 1981-82; recipient Myron B. Bloy award The Assn. for Religion and Intellectual Life, 1993. Mem. Arstasallskapet for Fredika Bremer-Studier (first chmn. 1985—89). Democrat. Lutheran. Avocations: walking, Tai Chi.

STENEHJEM, WAYNE KEVIN, state attorney general, lawyer; b. Mohall, ND, Feb. 5, 1953; s. Martin Edward and Marguerite Mae (Peg) (McMaster) Stenehjem; m. Tama Lou Smith, June 16, 1978 (div. Apr. 1984); l child, Andrew; m. Beth D. Bakke, June 30, 1995. AA, Bismarck Jr. Coll., ND, 1972; BA, U. ND, 1974, JD, 1977. Bar: N.D. 1977. Ptnr. Kuchera & Stenehjem, Grand Forks, ND, 1977—2000; spl. asst. atty. gen. State of ND, 1983—87, atty. gen., 2000—; mem. ND Indsl. Commn., 2001—; chair RAGA, 2001—02; mem. ND Ho. Reps., 1976—80, ND State Senate, 1980—2000, pres. pro tempore, 1998—99; bd. Univ. and Sch. Lands, 2001—. Chmn. Senate Com. on Social Svcs., 1985—86, Senate Com. on Judiciary, 1995—2000, Interim Legis. Judiciary Com., 1995—2000, Legis. Coun., 1995—2000; mem. Nat. Conf. Commrs. on Uniform State Laws, 1995—2000, Gov.'s Com. on Juvenile Justice. Exec. bd. dirs. No. Lights coun. Boy Scouts Am., 2005—; chmn. Dist. 42 Reps., Grand Forks, 1986—88; bd. dirs. Christus Rex Luth. Ch., pres., 1985—86; bd. dirs. no. lights coun. Boy Scouts Am., 2005—; bd. dirs. ND Spl. Olympics, 1985—89, Bismarck Mandan Big Bros. Big Sisters, 2001—. Recipient Excellence in County Govt. award, ND Assn. Counties, 1991, Love Without Fear award, Bismarck Abused Adult Resource Ctr., 2003, Lone Eagle award, ND Peace Officers Assn., 2005, Public Svc. award, Lignite Energy Coun., 2005; named Champion of People's Right to Know, Sigma Delta Chi, 1979, ND Friend of Psych., ND Psychol. Assn., 1990, Outstanding Young Man of ND, Jaycees, 1985, Scandinavian-Am. Hall of Fame, Norsk Høstfest, 2007. Mem.: Big Muddy Bar Assn., N.D. State Bar Assn. (Legis. Svc. award 1995). Republican. Home: 1216 Crestview Ln Bismarck ND 58501 Office: Office of the Atty Gen State Capitol Bldg 600 E Boulevard Ave Bismarck ND 58505-0040*

STENGEL, JAMES R., retired consumer products company executive; b. Lancaster, Pa., May 5, 1955; BA, Fraklin & Marshall Coll., 1977; MA, Pa. State U., 1983. With Time, Inc., 1977—81; brand asst. Duncan Hines RTS Cookies Proctor & Gamble Co., 1983, asst. brand mgr. Jif, 1984—86, brand mgr. Jif, 1986—89, assoc. advt. mgr., Jif, Duncan Hines, 1989—91, advt. mgr. Olestra, 1991—93, mktg. dir. US cosmetics products, 1993—95, gen. mgr. Europe, Middle East, Africa, 1995—99, v.p. Europe baby care, 1999—2000, v.p. global baby care strategic planning, mktg., new bus. devel., 2000—01, v.p., global mktg. officer, 2001—08, ret., 2008. Bd. trustees Chatfield Coll., St. Martin, Ohio, 1989—93, Bryn Mawr Sch., Balt., 1993—95, Cin. Ballet, 2001—, Seven Hills Sch., 2003—; chmn. Assn. Nat. Advts. Inc., 2004—06; bd. dirs. Motorola Inc., 2005—. Mem.: Heart Am. Found. (exec. adv. bd.).

STENGEL, RICHARD, editor; b. NYC, May 2, 1955; m. Mary Pfaff; children: Gabriel, Anton. BA magna cum laude, Princeton U., 1977; student in English and History, Christ Church Oxford U., 1981. Staff writer TIME mag., NYC, 1981—83, assoc. editor, 1984—88, sr. writer, essayist, contbr., 1989—, mng. editor TIME.com, 2000, culture editor, nat. editor, mng. editor, 2006—; pres., CEO Nat. Constitution Ctr., Phila., 2004—06. Ferris prof. journalism, instr. course Politics and the Press Princeton U., 1998—99; senior adviser, chief speechwriter presidential candidate Bill Bradley, 1999. Author: January Sun: One Day, Three Lives, a South African Town, 1990, You're Too Kind: A Brief History of Flattery, 2000; co-author (with Nelson Mandela): Long Walk to Freedom, 1993; co-prodr.: (documentaries) Mandela, 1995; writer (articles) The New Yorker, The New Republic, NY Times, and many other publications, TV commentator MSNBC, CNN. Rhodes Scholar. Office: TIME mag 1271 Ave of the Americas New York NY 10020*

STENGEL, ROBERT FRANK, engineering and applied science educator; b. Orange, NJ, Sept. 1, 1938; s. Frank John and Ruth Emma (Geidel) S.; m. Margaret Robertson Ewing, Apr. 8, 1961; children: Brooke Alexandra, Christopher Ewing. SB, MIT, 1960; MS in Engring., Princeton U., 1965, MA, 1966, PhD, 1968. Aerospace technologist NASA, Wallops Island, Va., 1960-63; tech. staff group leader C.S. Draper Lab., Cambridge, Mass., 1968-73, Analytic Scis. Corp., Reading, Mass., 1973-77; assoc. prof. Princeton (N.J.) U., 1977-82, prof. engring. and applied sci., 1982—, assoc. dean engring., 1994-97. Cons. GM, Warren, Mich., 1985-94; mem. com. strategic tech. U.S. Army NRC, 1989-92; vice chmn. Congl. Aero. Adv. Com., Washington, 1986-89; mem. com. on trans-atmospheric vehicles USAF Sci. Adv. Bd., 1984-85; mem. com. on low altitude wind shear and its hazard to aviation Nat. Rsch. Coun., 1983, Navy Theater Missile Defense com. NRC, 2000-01. Author: Stochastic Optimal Control: Theory and Application, 1986, reprinted as Optimal Control and Estimation, 1994, Flight Dynamics, 2004; N.Am. editor Cambridge Aerospace Series, 1993—98; contbr. over 200 tech. papers to profl. publs.; patentee wind probing device. Lt. USAF, 1960—63. Recipient Apollo Achievement award NASA, 1969, Cert. of Commendation, MIT, 1969, Excellence in Aviation award FAA, 1997, John R. Ragazzini Edn. award, AACC, 2002. Fellow IEEE, AIAA (Mechanics and Control of Flight award 2000); mem. Inst. Advanced Study. Home: 329 Prospect Ave Princeton NJ 08540-5330 Office: Princeton U D202 Engineering Quadrangle Princeton NJ 08544-0001 Office Phone: 609-258-5103. Office Fax: 609-258-6109. Business E-Mail: stengel@princeton.edu.

STENGEL, RONALD FRANCIS, management consultant; b. Lock Haven, Pa., Oct. 18, 1947; s. Elmer S. and Elizabeth (Heivley) S.; m. Margaret Linda Dezack, Aug. 23, 1969. BSME, U. Pa., 1969, MBA, 1976. Mfg. engr. Control Data Corp., Valley Forge, Pa., 1969-70; mgr. mfg. svcs. Knoll Internat., East Greenville, Pa., 1970-75; ptnr. mgmt. cons. Touche Ross & Co., Phila., 1976-85; pres. RF Stengel & Co. Inc., Valley Forge, 1985—. Office Phone: 610-296-8950.

STENHOLM, CHARLES WALTER, lobbyist, former congressman; b. Stamford, Tex., Oct. 26, 1938; m. Cynthia Ann Watson; children: Chris, Cary, Courtney Ann. Card., Tarleton State Jr. Coll., 1959; BS in Agrl. Edn., Tex. Tech U., 1961, MS in Agrl. Edn., 1962; LL.D. (hon.), McMurry Coll., 1983, Abilene Christian U., 1991. Farmer, Tex.; past pres. Rolling Plains Cotton Growers and Tex. Electric Coops.; mem. US Congress from 17th Tex. Dist., Washington, 1979—2005, mem. agrl. com.; sr. policy advisor Olsson Frank Weeda Terman Bode Matz PC. Co-chmn. Congl. Leaders United for a Balanced Budget. Active Bethel Luth. Ch., Ericksdahl, Tex.; charter trustee Cotton Producer Inst.; former mem. state Dem. exec. com. Recipient Gerald W. Thomas Outstanding Agriculturalist award Tex. Tech U., 1979, Am. Farmer Degree Future Farmers Am., 1979, Disting. Alumnus award Tarleton State U., 1979, Pres. Coun. award Tex. Future Farmers Am., 1981, Disting. Alumnus award Tex. Tech U., 1987, MORE Common Sense Sound Dollar awards, 1988, 90, Guardian of Small Bus. awards, 1980-92, Watchdogs of the Treasury awards, 1980-92, Legis. award Nat. Rural Health Assn., 1991, Disting. Svc. award Tex. Soc. Biomed. Rsch., 1993, Disting. Svc. award Tex. Med. Assn., 1993, Dr. Nathan Davis award AMA, 1993, Leadership in Advocacy for Children's Health award Nat. Assn. Children's Hosps., 1996, Meritorious Health Svc. award Nat. Assn. Cmty. Health Ctrs., 1997, Golden Plow award Am. Farm Bur. Fedn., 1988, 92, 96, Golden Triangle award Nat. The Nat. Farmers Union 1994, 2007, Thomas Jefferson award Food Distbn. Industry, 1994, 95, Progressive Fermer Man of Yr. award, 1993, Econ. Patriot award, 1997; named Legislator of Yr. Chem. Prodrs. and Distbrs. Assn., 1992, Man of Yr. Progressive Farmer, 1993, Cooperative Hall of Fame, 1998. Mem. Tex. State Soc. (Washington, past pres.), Tex. Breakfast Club (Washington, past pres.), Rolling Plains Cotton Growers (past pres.), Stamford C. of C. (past pres.). Democrat. Lutheran. Office: Olsson Frank Weeda Terman Bode Matz PC 1400 Sixteenth St, NW, Ste 400 Washington DC 20036 Office Phone: 202-518-6334. Office Fax: 202-234-1560.*

STENHOUSE, EVERETT RAY, clergy administrator; b. Minco, Okla., May 15, 1931; s. George E. and Jessie Loraine (Dean) S.; m. Alice Irene English, Aug. 22, 1948; children: Brenda Jones, Judy Lundberg, Stephen, Andrew. Student, U. Calif. Berkeley, U. Athens, 1969-71. Ordained to ministry Assemblies of God, 1955. Pastor Wayside Chapel, Bakersfield, Calif., 1955-59, Bethel Temple, Bakersfield, 1960-63; dist. dir. youth So. Calif. Dist. Assemblies of God, Costa Mesa, Calif., 1963-67; assoc. pastor 1st Assembly of God, San Diego, 1968-69; missionary Assemblies of God Fgn. Missions, Athens, Greece, 1969-73; pastor Bethany Ch., Alhambra, Calif., 1974-79; supt. So. Calif. Dist., Assemblies of God, Costa Mesa, 1979-85; asst. gen. supt. Gen. Coun. Assemblies of God, Springfield, Mo., 1986-94. Bd. adminstrn. Nat. Assn. Evangs., Wheaton, Ill., 1986-94, Pentecostal Fellowship of No. Am., Ont., Can., 1986-94; chmn., bd. dirs. Assemblies of God Theol. Sem., Springfield, 1991-94, Vanguard U., Costa Mesa, Calif., Ministers Benefit Assn., Springfield, 1986-94, chmn.; bd. mem. Evangel U., 1986-94. Contbr. articles to various mags. Mem. Assemblies Of God Ch. Home: 77696 Westbrook Ct Palm Desert CA 92211-0416 Personal E-mail: erevev@aol.com.

STENNETT, WILLIAM CLINTON (CLINT), state legislator, entrepreneur; b. Winona, Minn., Oct. 1, 1956; s. William Jessie and Carole Lee Stennett; m. Michelle Stennett. BA in Journalism, Idaho State U., 1979. Gen. mgr. Wood River Jour., Hailey, Idaho, 1979-85, pres., pub., 1985-87; pres. Sta. KSVT-TV, Ketchum, Idaho, Sta. KSKI-FM, Sun Valley, Idaho; mem. Idaho House of Reps., Boise, 1990-94; mem. Dist. 25 Idaho State Senate, Boise, 1996—, minority leader, 1996—. Recipient Gen. Excellence award, Idaho Newspaper Assn., 1985, 1986—87; named Legislator of Yr., Idaho Soil Conservation Dists., 1994, Idaho Wildlife Found., 1996, Idaho Assn. Recyclers, 2002, Idaho Profl. Firefighters Assn., 2002. Mem.: Idaho Broadcasters (bd. dirs.), Ketchum Sun Valley C. of C. (bd. dirs. 1990—95), Rotary. Democrat. Office: Dist 25 PO Box 475 Ketchum ID 83340 Office Phone: 208-726-8106. Business E-Mail: stennett@senate.idaho.gov.*

STENSON, WILLIAM FREDERICK, gastroenterologist; b. Rome, NY, Dec. 2, 1945; s. Frederick Vincent and Mary Catherine (Tucker) S.; m. Janet Marie Breaugh, Dec. 28, 1968; children: Catherine, Karen, Thomas. BS, Providence Coll., 1967; MD, Washington U., 1971. Diplomate Am. Bd. Internal Medicine and Gastroenterology. Intern Barnes Hosp., St. Louis, 1971—72, resident in medicine, 1972—73, resident medicine, 1975—76; chief gastroenterology Jewish Hosp. of St. Louis, 1981—98; assoc. prof. medicine Washington U., St. Louis, 1985—91, prof. medicine, 1991—. Co-author: Manual of Nutritional Therapeutics, 1st edit., 1983, 2d edit., 1988, 4th edit., 2002, 5th edit., 2008; editor: (book) Inflammatory Bowel Disease, 1991, Gastrointestinal Pharmacology, 1992. Maj. USAF, 1973-75. Named Nicholas V. Costrini Prof. Gastroenterology & Inflammatory Bowel Disease, 2007—. Office: Washington U Sch Medicine PO Box 8124 Saint Louis MO 63110 Office Phone: 314-362-8952.

STENSTROM, MICHAEL KNUDSON, civil engineering educator; b. Anderson, SC, Nov. 28, 1948; s. Edward Farnum and Virginia Frances (Garrett) S.; m. Linda Ann Moxley, Aug. 15, 1974 (div. Nov. 1976); m. Margaret Merle Allen, Jan. 13, 1977 (div. Apr. 1994). BSEE, Clemson U., 1971, MS in Environ. Engring., 1972, PhD in Environ. Engring., 1976. Registered profl. engr., Calif. Project mgr. Amoco Oil Co., Naperville, Ill., 1975—77; asst. prof. civil engring. UCLA, 1977—81, assoc. prof., 1981—84, prof., 1984—, dir. Engring. Computer Ctr., 1985—89, asst. dean, 1989—92, chair dept. civil engring., 1991—98, assoc. dean, 2001—03. Cons. in field. Contbr. articles to profl. jours. Chmn. sci. adv. bd. Heal-the-Bay, L.A., 1987-88. With USAF, 1969-70. Recipient numerous grants. Mem. ASCE (Walter L. Huber award 1989), Am. Acad. Environ. Engrs., Assn. Environ. Engring. Profs., Water Environ. Fedn. (Harrison Prescott Eddy medal 1992, Calif. EPA Water Quality Protection award, 2002, 05), Internat. Assn. on Water Quality, Am. Chem. Soc., Blue Key, Sigma Xi, Tau Beta Pi. Democrat. Avocations: photography, amateur radio. Home: 3032 Motor Ave Los Angeles CA 90064 Office: UCLA 5714 Boelter Hall Los Angeles CA 90095-1593 Office Phone: 310-825-1408. Business E-Mail: stenstro@seas.ucla.edu.

STENT, ANGELA E., political scientist, educator, director; b. London, Feb. 24, 1947; arrived in U.S., 1970; d. Ronald Walter and Gabriele Stent; m. Daniel H. Yergin, Aug. 10, 1975; children: Alexander Yergin, Rebecca Yergin. BA in Econs. and History with honors, Cambridge U., Eng., 1969; MSc with distinction, London Sch. Econs., 1970; AM in Soviet Studies, Harvard U., 1972, PhD in Govt., 1977. Assoc. prof. dept. govt. Georgetown U., Washington, 1983—, prof. dept. govt. and Sch. Fgn. Svc., 1998—, dir. Ctr. for Eurasian, Russian and East European Studies, 2001—; nat. intelligence officer for Russia and Eurasia, Nat. Intelligence Coun., Washington, 2004—06. Sr. policy advisor Office Policy Planning U.S. Dept. State, Washington, 1999—2001; adv. bd. mem. U.S.-Russia Bus. Coun., Women in Internat. Security, Am. Inst. for Contemporary German Studies. Author: From Embargo to Ostpolitik, 1981, Russia and Germany Reborn, 1999; contbr. articles to profl. jours. Mem.: Coun. Fg. Rels. N.Y., Cosmos Club. Office: Ctr for Eurasian Russian and East European Studies Georgetown Univ Washington DC 20057

STENTIFORD, BARRY MAXFIELD, education educator, military officer; b. Worcester, Mass., Nov. 11, 1964; s. Robert Edmond Stentiford and Janet Maxfield Hall; m. Vitida Sirisinha, Aug. 6, 2000. BS, Coll. Great Falls, Mont., 1990; MA, U. Mont., 1995; PhD, U. Ala., 1998. Assoc. prof. history Grambling State U., 1997—2008; assoc. prof. mil. history Sch. Advanced Mil. Studies, 2008; with Army Command & Gen. Staff Coll., 2009—. Author: The Am. Home Guard: The State Militia in the Twentieth Century, 2002; editor: Jim Crow Encyclopedia, 2008. Maj. USAR, 1985—. Mem.: Res. Officers Assn., Phi Alpha Theta. Avocations: writing, speaking Thai. Home: 27125 179th St Leavenworth KS 66048-7192 Office: 250 Gibbon Ave Fort Leavenworth KS 66027 Office Phone: 913-758-3287. Business E-Mail: barry.m.stentiford@us.army.mil.

STENWICK, MICHAEL WILLIAM, retired internist, geriatrician, consultant; b. Red Wing, Minn., Nov. 12, 1941; s. Vincent Ferdinand and Geraldine Frances (Veith) S.; m. Judith Ann Nelson, June 10, 1961; children: Scott Michael, Gregg William. BS cum laude, Hamline U., 1963; MD, U. Minn., 1969. Diplomate Am. Bd. Internal Medicine. Fellow dept. pharmacology U. Minn., Mpls., 1966-68; intern in internal medicine Northwestern Hosp., Mpls., 1969-70, resident in internal medicine, 1970-73; sr. internist internal medicine sect. Bloomington Lake Clinic, Mpls., 1973—2000; ret., 2000. Bd. dirs. Bloomington Lake Clinic, Mpls., pres. 1977, v.p. 1989-97, fin. com., 1987—, chmn. properties, 1984—, chmn. trustees profit sharing; med. adviser Kimberly Quality Care, St. Paul, 1990-94; internal medicine cons. Fairview Multiple Sclerosis Ctr. and Rehab. Unit, Mpls., 1986-91; informal adviser internal medicine sect. Minn. Relative Value Index, Mpls., 1971; mem. task force Riverside Med. Ctr., Mpls., 1988-91, chmn. critical care com., 1986-91, reviewer quality assurance subcom., 1989-90. Contbr. articles to profl. jours. Mem., co-organizer, 1st pres. Cyrus Barnum Soc., U. Minn. Med. Sch., Mpls.; bd. dirs. Signal Inn Beach and Racquetball Club, Sanibel Island, Fla., 1983-84, 89-98, Signal Inn Condominium Assn., Sanibel Island, 1983-84, 89-98; co-emcee Nursing Talent Show, Northwestern Hosp., Mpls., 1969; 1st med. dir. Beltrami Health Ctr., Mpls., 1970-72. Recipient scholarship Charles and Alora Allis Found., 1960-63, Walter Kenyon award, 1963, grant U. Minn., 1963; named to Wall Honor, Red Wing HS, 2005. Fellow ACP; mem. AMA, Am. Soc. Internal Medicine, Minn. Med. Assn., Hennepin County Med. Assn., Mpls. Soc. Internal Medicine, Minn. Acad. Medicine. Republican. Lutheran. Achievements include research in drug specificity that could be defined even in an alkylating agent; providing evidence for an active role of the choroid plexus in distributing and concentrating morphine in the brain. Office: Bloomington Lake Clinic 3017 Bloomington Ave Minneapolis MN 55407-1771

STENZEL, MARY FRANCIS, social worker; b. Milw., Apr. 9, 1960; d. Joseph Edward and Betty Josephine (Andracki) Gronowski; m. Paul Anthony Stenzel, Oct. 17, 1997. BSW, Marian Coll., 1982; MBA, Cardinal Stritch Coll. U., 1992. Sec., geriat. & disabled population social worker various Nursing Homes, 1983—84, geriatric social worker Milw., 1984—86; youth care specialist Child and Adolescent Treatment Ctr., Milw. County, 1988—94. Pres. Milw. Area Self Help, W. Milw., 1997—2007. Mem.: Milw. Area Self Help Group (v.p. 2007—), Brain Injury Assn. Wis. (Brain Injury Support Group mem. 1995—). Roman Catholic. Avocations: crafts, gardening, scrapbooks, woodworking. Home: 3115 W Plaza Dr Franklin WI 53132 Home Phone: 414-761-3186.

STEP, EUGENE LEE, retired pharmaceutical executive; b. Sioux City, Iowa, Feb. 19, 1929; s. Harry and Ann (Keiser) S.; m. Hannah Scheuermann, Dec. 27, 1953; children: Steven Harry, Michael David, Jonathan Allen. BA in Econs., U. Nebr., 1951; MS in Acctg. and Fin., U. Ill., 1952. With Eli Lilly Internat. Corp., London and Paris, 1964-69, dir. Elanco Internat. Indpls., 1969-70, v.p. marketing, 1970-72, v.p. Europe, 1972; v.p. mktg. Eli Lilly and Co., Indpls., 1972-73, pres. pharm. div., 1973-86, exec. v.p., 1986—. Bd. dirs. Cell-Genesys. 1st lt. U.S. Army, 1953-56. Mem. Pharm. Mfrs. Assn. (bd. dirs. 1980-92, chmn. 1989-90), Internat. Pharm. Mfrs. Assn. (pres. 1991-92). Home: PO Box 8997 Rancho Santa Fe CA 92067-8997 Office Phone: 858-759-8958.

STEPAN, FRANK QUINN, chemicals executive; b. Chgo., Oct. 24, 1937; s. Alfred Charles and Mary Louise (Quinn) S.; m. Jean Finn, Aug. 23, 1958; children: Jeanne, Frank Quinn, Todd, Jennifer, Lisa, Colleen, Alfred, Richard. AB, U. Notre Dame, 1959; MBA, U. Chgo., 1963. Salesman Indsl. Chems. div. Stepan Chem. Co., Northfield, Ill., 1961-63, mgr. internat. dept., 1964-66, v.p. corporate planning, 1967-69, v.p., gen. mgr., 1970-73, pres., 1973-84; pres., chmn., CEO Stepan Co., Northfield, Ill., 1984-99, chmn., CEO, 1999—2005, chmn., 2006—. Bd. dirs. Am. Chemistry Coun. Mem. liberal arts coun. Notre Dame U., South Bend, Ind., 1972—; bd. dirs. Big Shoulders, Chgo. 1st lt. AUS, 1959-61. Mem. Soap and Detergent Assn. (bd. dirs., exec. com., chmn.), Ill. Bus. Roundtable (policy com., sec.), Econ. Club Chgo., Exmoor Country Club, Bob O'Link Golf Club, Everglades Club, Sailfish Club Fla. Home: 200 Linden St Winnetka IL 60093-3862 Office: Stepan Co Edens & Winnetka Rds Northfield IL 60093

STEPAN, FRANK QUINN, JR., (F. QUINN STEPAN JR.), chemical company executive; b. 1960; married; 3 children. BA, U. Notre Dame, 1982; MBA, U. Chgo., 1988. With Monsanto Co., 1983—87, Stepan Co., Northfield, Ill., 1987—, v.p., gen. mgr. Surfactant dept., pres., 1999—2005, CEO, 2005—. Dir. Follett Corp.; bd. dirs. Am. Chem Coun. Office: Stepan Co 22 W Frontage Rd Northfield IL 60093 Office Phone: 847-446-7500, 847-501-2100.

ŠTĚPÁNEK, PETR, computer science educator; b. Pardubice, Czech Republic, Jan. 24, 1943; s. Otakar and Ludmila (Brabcová) Š.; m. Olga Burešová, Dec. 19, 1970; children: Kateřina Barbora. Promovany matematik, Charles U., Prague, 1965, RNDr, 1968, postgrad., 1973, DSc in Logic, 1991. Asst. prof. computer sci. Charles U., Prague, 1965-87, assoc. prof., 1987-98, prof., 1998—, mem. bd. grant agy., 2008—. Author: Mathematical Logic Set Theory, 1982. Mem. Fed. Assembly, Prague, 1992; chmn. Dist. Orgn. Civic Dem. Party, Prague, 1993-95. Rsch. grantee Ministry Edn., Prague, 1993, Czech Grant Agy., 2000-05, Prague, 1996—. Mem. Am. Math. Soc., Assn. Symbolic Logic, Assn. Logic Programming (hon.), Info. Soc. (Czech forum 2000—07). Mem. Civic Democratic party. Business E-Mail: petr.stepanek@mff.cuni.cz.

STEPANIAN, STEVEN ARVID, II, lawyer, financial consultant; b. Charleroi, Pa., Apr. 15, 1935; s. Steven A. and Edithmarion M. (McElligott) Stepanian; m. Pamela S. Abbey, Feb. 15, 1979. AB magna cum laude, U. Pitts., 1957; LLB, Harvard U., 1963. Bar: Pa. 1964, U.S. Supreme Ct. 1967. Assoc. Reed Smith, 1963—69, ptnr., 1970—78; pvt. practice Pitts., 1978—; ptnr., gen. counsel Marine Magnesium Co., 1988—, US Windforce, 1998—; gen. counsel Strategic Market Resources LLC, 2004—. Dir. NFL Alumni, 1982—89. Lt. USAF, 1957—69, maj. USAF, 1968—69. Mem.: ABA (chair sports law com.), Pa. Athletic Assn., Pa. Bar Assn., Univ. Club (past pres.), Duquesne Club. Democrat. Roman Catholic. Office: Gateway Towers Ste 4-G 320 Fr Duquesne Blvd Pittsburgh PA 15222-1103 Home: 20 KLM Gateway Towers 320 Ft Duquesne Blvd Pittsburgh PA 15222-1133 Office Phone: 412-281-0555. Business E-Mail: sastepanian@comcast.net.

STEPEHNSON, ANDREW J., urologist; MD, U. Western Ont., London, Can., 1997. Cert. urologist Royal Coll. Physicians and Surgeons Can., 2002. Attending staff Cleve. Clinic, 2006—. Recipient Merit award, Am. Soc. Clin. Oncology, 2003—06, Prostate Cancer Found. award, Soc. Urologic Oncology, 2005; named Tchr. of Yr., Glickman Urol. and Kidney Inst., Cleve. Clinic, 2008. Office: Cleve Clinic 9500 Euclid Ave Q10 Cleveland OH 44195-0001 Office Phone: 216-445-9628.

STEPENOFF, BONNIE MARIE, history professor; b. Allentown, Pa., July 18, 1949; d. Ernest W. and Nancy Owens Steckel; m. Jerald Sheldon Stepenoff, Feb. 14, 1986; m. Peter L. Wright, 1977 (div.); m. Francis M. Ryck, 1969 (div.); children: Samantha Marie Wright, Hannah Evelyn. BA, Ohio State U., Columbus, 1971; MA, U. Mo., Columbia, 1978, MA in Libr. Sci., 1981, PhD, 1992. Acquisitions specialist State Hist. Soc. Mo., Columbia, 1978—84; cultural resource preservationist Mo. Dept. Natural Resources, Jefferson City, 1984—92; prof. history SE Mo. State U., Cape Girardeau, 1993—. Author: Their Fathers' Daughters: Silk Mill Workers in Northeastern Pennsylvania, 1999, Thad Snow: A Life of Social Reform in the Missouri Bootheel, 2003, From French Community to Missouri Town: Ste. Genevieve in the Nineteenth Century, 2006, Big Spring Autumn, 2008, short stories, poems; contbr. articles to profl. jours. Active Mo. Adv. Coun. on Hist. Preservation, 2004. Recipient Book award, Mo. Conf. History, 2007; Sullivan fellow, Mus. Am. Textile History, 1991, Short-term Rsch. grantee, Hagley Mus. and Libr., 1991, William E. Foley fellowship, Mo. State Archives, 2007. Mem.: State Hist. Soc. Mo. (Best Article award 1991, Richard S. Brownlee grantee 1992, 1997, Mo. Conf. History Book award 2007). Office: Southeast Missouri State University One University Plaza Cape Girardeau MO 63701 Business E-Mail: bstepenoff@hotmail.com.

STEPHAN, ALEXANDER FRIEDRICH, German language and literature educator; b. Lüdenscheid, Fed. Republic Germany, Aug. 16, 1946; arrived in US, 1968; s. Eberhard and Ingeborg (Hörnig) S.; m. Halina Konopacka, Dec. 15, 1969; 1 child, Michael. MA, U. Mich., 1969; PhD, Princeton U., 1973. Instr. German Princeton (NJ) U., 1972-73; from asst. prof. to prof. German UCLA, 1973-85; prof. German U. Fla., Gainesville, 1985-2000, chmn., 1985-93; prof. German, Ohio Eminent scholar, sr. fellow Mershon Ctr., Ohio State U., 2000—. Author: Christa Wolf, 1976, Die deutsche Exilliteratur, 1979, Christa Wolf (Forschungsbericht), 1981, Max Frisch, 1983, Anna Seghers im Exil, 1993, Im Visier des FBI, 1995, paperback edit. 1998, English transl. Communazis, 2000, Anna Seghers: Das siebte Kreuz. Welt und Wirkung eines Romans, 1997; editor: Peter Weiss: Die Ästhetik des Widerstands, 1983, 3d edit., 1990, Exil. Literatur und die Künste, 1990, Exil-Studien, 1993—, Christa Wolf: The Author's Dimension, 1993, 2d edit., 1995, Themes and Structures, 1997, Uwe Johnson: Speculations about Jakob and Other Writings, 2000, Early 20th Century German Fiction, 2003, Anna Seghers, Die Entscheidung, 2003, Americanism and Anti-Americanism. The German Encounter with American Culture after 1945, 2004, Exile and Otherness: New Approaches to the Experience of the Nazi Refugees, 2005, The Americanization of Europe: Culture, Diplomacy, and Anti-Americanism After 1945, 2006; co-editor: Studies in GDR Culture and Society, 1981—90, Schreiben im Exil, 1985, The New Sufferings of Young Werther and Other Stories from the GDR, 1997, Rot=Braun? Brecht Dialog, 2000, Nationalsozialismus und Stalinismus bei Brecht und Zeitgenossen, 2000, Jeans, Rock und Vietnam. Amerikanische Kultur in der DDR, 2002, Refuge and Reality: Feuchtwanger and the European Emigres in California, 2005, Das Amerika der Autoren von Kafka bis, 2006, America On My Mind, 2006; co-prodr.: (TV films) Im Visier des FBI, 1995, Das FBI und Marlene Dietrich, 2000, Das FBI und Brechts Telephon, 2002, Exilanten und das OSS, 2002, Thomas Mann und der CIA, 2002. Grantee, NEH, 1974, 1984, 1997, Am. Coun. Learned Socs., 1976, 1977, 1984, Am. Philos. Soc., 1979, 1981, 1992, Humboldt Found., 1988, 1994, 1998—99, 2002—03, Guggenheim Found., 1989, German Acad. Exch. Svcs., 1993, 1997, Feuchtwanger Meml. Libr., 1998, Weichmann Stiftung, 1998, Transcoop/AvH, 2002—04; Fulbright Sr. Specialist, 2005—. Mem.: German PEN, German Assn. for Am. Studies, German Studies Assn., Internat. Anna Seghers Soc., Soc. Exile Studies. Office: Ohio State U Dept Germanic Lang Lit 498 Hagerty Columbus OH 43210-1340 Office Phone: 614-247-6068. Business E-Mail: stephan.30@osu.edu.

STEPHAN, JOHN, finance educator; m. Anne Schmutz, Dec. 16, 1978. PhD, Columbia U., NYC. Asst. prof. Fla. Atlantic U., Ft. Lauderdale, 2003—. Recipient Roethlisberger Meml. Award, Jour. of Mgmt. Edn.,

2003. Mem.: Acad. of Mgmt. Achievements include research in Published several scholarly articles in journals such as. Avocations: jazz, theater. Office: Florida Atlantic University Askew Twr 111 E Las Olas Blvd Fort Lauderdale FL 33065

STEPHAN, JOHN JASON, historian, educator; b. Chgo., Mar. 8, 1941; s. John Walter and Ruth (Walgreen) S.; m. Barbara Ann Brooks, June 22, 1963. BA, Harvard U., 1963, MA, 1964; PhD, U. London, 1969. Rsch. assoc. Social Sci. Ctr., Waseda U., Tokyo, 1969—70; mem. faculty U. Hawaii, Honolulu, 1970—, prof. history, 1977—2001, emeritus prof. history, 2001—, chmn. East Asian studies program, 1973—74, dir. program on Soviet Union in Pacific-Asia region, 1986—88. Rsch. prof. Japan Found.; fellow U. Hokkaido, 1976-77; vis. prof. Inst. of Far East, Moscow, 1982, Inst. Econ. Rsch., Khabarovsk, USSR, 1982-83, Stanford U., 1986, Kennan Inst. for Advanced Studies, 1987; adj. rsch. assoc. East-West Ctr., 1988-92; Sanwa disting. lectr. Tufts U. Fletcher Sch. Law and Diplomacy, 1989. Author: Sakhalin: A History, 1971, The Kuril Islands: Russo-Japanese Frontier in the Pacific, 1974, The Russian Fascists, 1978, Hawaii Under the Rising Sun, 1984, Soviet-American Horizons on the Pacific, 1986, The Russian Far East, 1994. Sr. assoc. mem. St. Antony's Coll., Oxford (Eng.) U., 1977; Bd. dirs. Library Internat. Relations, Chgo., 1976-87; Hawaii rep. U.S.-Japan Friendship Commn., 1980-83. Recipient Kenneth W. Baldridge prize Hawaii chpt. Phi Alpha Theta, 1996; Fulbright fellow, 1967-68; Asia Found. grantee, 1974. Mem. AAUP, Am. Hist. Assn., Am. Assn. Advancement Slavic Studies, Assn. Asian Studies, Authors Guild, Internat. House of Japan, Can. Hist. Assn. Home: 4334 Round Top Dr Honolulu HI 96822-5021 Office: U Hawaii Dept History 2530 Dole St Honolulu HI 96822-2303 Office Phone: 808-956-9600. Business E-Mail: stephan@hawaii.edu.

STEPHAN, KARL DAVID, electrical engineering educator; b. Fort Worth, Dec. 18, 1953; s. Adolph Ernest and Nancy Marie (Davis) S.; m. Pamela Louise Simons, Apr. 8, 1978. BS, Calif. Inst. Tech., 1976; M. Engring., Cornell U., 1977; PhD, U. Tex., 1983. Devel. engr. Motorola, Ft. Worth, 1977-79; radio-frequency engr. Sci.-Atlanta, Norcross, Ga., 1979-81; asst. prof. U. Mass., Amherst, 1983-89, assoc. prof., 1990—2000; asst. prof. Tex. State U., San Marcos, 2000—03, assoc. prof., 2003—. Cons. MIT Lincoln Labs., Lexington, Mass., 1989—, Millitech Inc., South Deerfield, Mass., 1990-93. Contbr. articles to profl. jours. Mem. IEEE (sr.). Achievements include patents for quasi-optical polarization-duplexed balanced mixer, quasi-optical transmission/reflection switch and millimeter-wave imaging system using the same. Office: Tex State Univ Dept Engring and Tech San Marcos TX 78666

STEPHAN, KENNETH C., state supreme court justice; b. Omaha, Oct. 8, 1946; m. Sharon Ross, Apr. 19, 1969; 3 children. BA, U. Nebr., 1968, JD with high distinction, 1972. Bar: Nebr. Atty. pvt. practice, 1973-97; judge Nebr. Supreme Ct., Lincoln, 1997—. With US Army, 1969—71. Mem.: Am. Coll. Trial Lawyers (jud. fellow). Office: Nebr Supreme Ct State Capitol Bldg Rm 2211 PO Box 98910 Lincoln NE 68509-8910 Office Phone: 402-471-3737. Business E-Mail: kenneth.stephan@nebraska.gov.*

STEPHAN, PAULA ELIZABETH, economics professor, academic administrator; b. Menomonie, Wis., Mar. 31, 1945; d. A. Stephen and Margaret (Shaffer) S.; m. William D. Amis, July 27, 1974; 1 child, David. BA, Grinnell Coll., 1967; MA, U. Mich., 1970, PhD, 1971. Asst. prof. econs. Ga. State U., Atlanta, 1971—76, assoc. prof. econs., 1976—81, prof. econs., 1981—, assoc. dean Andrew Young Sch., 1996—2001. Vis. scholar Sci. Ctr., Berlin, 1992, 93, 94; mem. com. on equal opportunities in Sci. NSF, 1999-2002; nat. adv. gen. med. scis. coun. NIH, 2006-; mem. adv. bd. SBE, 2001-2008; assoc. Nat. Bur. Economic Rsch, 2007-; mem. various coms. NRC. Author: Striking the Mother Lode in Science, 1992; contbr. over 50 articles to profl. jours. Mem. bd. dirs. Paideia Sch. Endowment, Atlanta, 1983—, chair, 1991-98. Grantee, Alfred P. Sloan Found., 1993—95, 1999, 2002, Andrew Mellon Found., 1995, 2000, 2006—, NSF, 1983—85, 1990—91, 2000—02, 2002—04, 2006—; Wertheim fellow, Harvard U., 2007. Avocations: reading, travel. Home: 2101 Black Fox Dr NE Atlanta GA 30345-4124 Office: Ga State Univ Andrew Young Sch Box 3992 Atlanta GA 30302-3992 Office Phone: 404-413-0160. Business E-Mail: pstephan@gsu.edu.

STEPHAN, ROBERT B., federal agency administrator; B in Polit. Sci., US Air Force Acad.; M in Internat. Rels., U. Belgrano, Buenos Aires, Johns Hopkins U. Dir. Interagency Incident Mgmt. Group; sr. dir. for critical infrastructure protection Exec. Office of Pres.; spl. asst. to sec. and dir. operational integration staff US Dept. Homeland Security, asst. sec. infrastructure program, 2005—. Comdr. spl. tactics squadrons USAF, joint battlestaff planner and mission comdr. USAF, Saudi Arabia. Office: US Dept Homeland Security 12th & C St SW Washington DC 20024*

STEPHAN, THOMAS, physicist, researcher; D, U. Heidelberg, Germany, 1989. Sr. rsch. assoc. U. Chgo., 2007—. Office: Univ Chgo 5734 S Ellis Ave Chicago IL 60637

STEPHANIC, BARBARA JEAN, art historian, writer, curator, researcher; b. LA, Sept. 1, 1937; d. Frank Cecil (Stepfather) and Ethel Louise Jones; m. Jeffery Lynn Stephanic, May 4, 1985; children: Deborah Louise Arnold, Lorraine Marie Ward, Charles Frank Ward. AA, Antelope Valley Coll., Lancaster, Calif., 1978; BA, George Washington U., Washington, 1981, MA, 1985; PhD, U. Md., College Park, 1997. Art history lectr. Montgomery Coll., Rockville, Md., 1986—87, No. Va. C.C., Alexandria, 1987—90; assoc. prof. art history Charles County C.C., La Plata, Md., 1990—97; prof. art history Coll. So. Md., La Plata, 1997—. Art history lectr. Georgetown U., Washington, 1990—97; curator Fine Arts Ctr. Gallery Coll. So. Md., La Plata, 1993—; adj. prof. Parsons Sch. Design and Smithsonian Instn., Washington, 1993—2000; study abroad lectr. Coll. So. Md., La Plata, 2003—; faculty cons. Ednl. Testing Svc., Princeton, NJ, 1993—2004; adj. prof. Am. U., Washington, 1995—96; academic advisor Parsons Sch. Design, Washington, 1996—97; mem. art adv. bd. U. Md. U. Coll., Adelphi, 2003—, vice chmn. art adv. bd., 2006—; guest lectr. in field. Contbr. exhibition catalogue; author: (exhibition catalogue) The Graphic Work of Joseph Pennell From the Permanent Collection of The George Washington University; contbr. exhibition catalogue; author: (exhibition catalogue) Dialogue in Color and Form: The Art of Joseph Holston, Dynamic Spaces: Abstract Form Within and Beyond the Landscape: Painting, Collage, and Assemblage by Larry Chappelear, Color in Freedom: Journey Along the Underground Railroad, Paintings and Graphics by Joseph Holston. Founding mem. Nat. Mus. Am. Indian, Washington, 2000—06; mentor Literacy Coun. No. Va., Alexandria, Va., 1998—2000; mem. Sewell-Belmont Ho., Washington, 2005—06. Recipient Faculty Svc. award, Coll. So. Md., 1996, 1999, Faculty Excellence award, Faculty Senate, Coll. So. Md., 1999, Nat. Inst. for Staff and Orgnl. Devel., C.C. Leadership Program, 2000; Outstanding Scholar in the Field of Humanities, Antelope Valley Coll., 1978, Outstanding Scholar, Alliance Francaises, 1978, Faculty Devel. grantee, Coll. So. Md., 2004, 2006. Mem.: Nat. Assn. U. Women, Assn. Historians Am. Art, Assn. Faculty for Advancement C.C. Tchg., Am. Studies Assn., Coll. Art Assn., C.C. Profs. Art and Art History (treas. 1999—2000), George Wash. U. Alumni (life), Literacy Coun. Am., Alliance Francaises (Outstanding Scholarship 1978), Phi Delta Gamma (Beta chpt., Scholastic Achievement award 1983, 1986). Office: College Southern Maryland 8730 Mitchell Rd La Plata MD 20646 Business E-Mail: barbaras@csmd.edu.

STEPHANOPOULOS, GEORGE ROBERT, political reporter; b. Fall River, Mass., Feb. 10, 1961; s. Robert and Nikki C. Stephanopolous; m. Alexandra Wentworth, Nov. 20, 2001; children: Elliott Anastasia, Harper Andrea. BA in Polit. Sci. summa cum laude, Columbia U., 1982; MA in Theology, Oxford U., 1986; LLD (hon.), St. John's U., 2007. Adminstrv. asst. to Rep. Edward Feighan US Congress, Washington; dep. comm. dir. Dukakis/Bentsen campaign, 1988; exec. floor mgr. to House Majority leader Dick Gephardt US Congress, Washington; dir. comm. Clinton/Gore campaign, Little Rock, 1992, The White House, Washington, 1992—96, sr. adv. to the Pres. for policy & strategy, 1993-96; vis. prof. polit. sci. Columbia U., NYC, 1997; contbr. & corr. ABC News, 1997—, chief Washington corr., 2005—; host This Week with George Stephanopoulos, 2002—. Author: All Too Human: A Political Education, 1999. Recipient Medal of Excellence, Columbia U., 1993; named Maverick, Details mag., 2007; Rhodes Scholar, Oxford U. Mem.: Phi Beta Kappa. Democrat. Greek Orthodox. Address: 1717 DeSales St NW Washington DC 20036*

STEPHEN, BERENS, artist, educator; MFA, Fla. State U., Tallahassee, 1977. Prof. art Chapman U., Orange, Calif., 1995—. Avocation: photography. Office: Chapman Univ 1 University dr Orange CA 92866

STEPHEN, JOHN ERLE, lawyer, consultant; b. Eagle Lake, Tex., Sept. 24, 1918; s. John Earnest and Vida Thrall (Klein) S.; m. Gloria Yzaguirre, May 16, 1942; children: Vida Leslie Stephen Renzi, John Lauro Kurt. LLB, JD, U. Tex., 1941; postdoctoral, Northwestern U., 1942, U.S. Naval Acad. Postgrad. Sch., Annapolis, 1944; cert. in internat. law, U.S. Naval War Coll., Newport, RI, 1945; cert. in advanced internat. law, U.S. Naval War Coll., 1967. Bar: Tex. 1946, FCC 1946, US Ct. Appeals (DC cir.) 1949, US Dept. Treasury 1947, US Tax Ct. 1953, US Supreme Ct. 1955, US Dist. Ct. DC 1956, US Ct. Appeals (2d cir.) 1959, Wash. 1963, Ohio, 1964, US Ct. Appeals (7th cir.) 1964, US Dist. Ct. (so. dist.) NY 1964, Ind. 1968, US Dist. Ct. (so. dist.) Fla. 1969, DC 1972, US Dist. Ct. (no. dist.) Ill. 1974, US Dist. Ct. (we. dist.) Wash. 1975, Mich. 1981, US Dist. Ct. (we. dist.) Mich. 1981, US Dist. Ct. (so. dist.) Tex. 1981. News editor Tex. Broadcasting Sys., 1937; grad. asst., instr. radio-TV broadcasting, co-founder Radio Hall U. Tex., 1938—41; dir. news and spl. events Capital Broadcasting Co., Inc. Sta. KTBC, Austin, Tex., 1941; gen. mgr., corp. counsel Sta. KOPY, Houston, 1946; gen. atty., exec. asst. to pres. Tex. Star Broadcasting Co. and affiliated cos., Houston, 1947-50; law ptnr. Hofheinz & Stephen, Houston, 1950—56; sr. v.p., gen. counsel TV Broadcasting Co. of Houston, Tex. Radio Corp., Gulf Coast Network, 1953—56; spl. counsel, exec. asst. Mayor, City of Houston, 1953—57; spl. counsel Houston C. of C., 1953—57; sr. v.p., gen. counsel Air Transp. Assn. Am., Washington, 1958-70; v.p., gen. counsel Amway Corp. and affiliated cos. (now Alticor, Inc.), Ada, Mich., 1971-82; counsellor, cons. Austin, Tex., 1983—. Radio, TV adv. Jack Wrather Prodns. Inc., Dallas, 1946—50, Beverly Hills, 1948—54, Mercury Films, Hollywood, Calif., 1948—52; chief protocol City of Houston, 1953—56; advisor Chancellors and Consulates Gen. of Mex., San Antonio, Houston, New Orleans, Washington, 1956—66, Aero. Radio, Inc., 1956—66, Zenith Pictures, Santurce, PR, 1967—69, Mobil Internat. Oil Co., South Am., 1971—72, US Econ. Stabilization Agy., 1972—75, co-chmn. industry task-force on term-limit pricing, 1972—75; chair, counsel aerospace industries joint com. navigable airspace worldwide Internat. Air Transport Assn., Montreal, London, 1961—72; appointed legal advisor US Interagy. Group on Internat. Aviation, Washington, 1958—69; exec. com. global airlines supersonic/high-capacity jets insurer Soc. Préparatoire pour Air Transport Ins., S.A., Zurich, 1967—70; atty. Gen. Creighton W. Abrams Jr., Comdr. US Mil. Assistance Command, Vietnam, Saigon/Washington, 1970—71; adv. bd. Jour. Air Law and Commerce, 1966—72; vis. lectr. Harvard Bus. Sch., Pacific Agribus. Conf., Southwestern Legal Found., Inter-Am. Aviation Law Conf., Inst. Aerospace Law, Indsl. Coll. of Armed Forces, Assn. of Bar City of NY, Chgo. Bar. Assn., Internat. Assn. Ins. Coun., Am. Women in Radio & TV, Radcliffe Coll., U. Houston; apptd. by Pres. of US legal advisor, del. US Diplomatic Dels. to Internat. Treaty Confs., Paris, London, Rome, Tokyo, Madrid, Bermuda, Guadalajara, Dakar, 1958—69, Internat. Air-Rte. Dels. to UK, France, Spain, Portugal, Belgium, The Netherlands, Japan, Rep. of Korea, Mex., Australia, Argentina, Soviet Union, and Brazil, 1958—69; legal advisor, del. US dels. to UN Specialized Orgns. Montreal, Geneva, Paris, Rome, 1964—71; US rep. Internat. Conf. on Aircraft Disturbance and Sonic Boom, London, 1966; hon. faculty, vis. lectr. sch. of law, sch. of bus. U. Miami, 1968—72; accredited corr. UN, NATO, Rep. and Dem. Nat. Convs.; exec. officer USNR Pub. Affairs Co. 8-7, 1950—57; cons. Edison Electric Inst. Task Force Nuc. Property Ins., 1972. Assoc. editor Air Laws and Treaties of the World (3 vols.), US editor Yearbook of Air and Space Law. Chief comm. and transp. group Harris County/Houston CD, 1952-56; chmn. legal com. Nat. Aircraft Noise Abatement Coun., Washington; mem. adv. bd. Mus. Fine Arts Houston, 1953-57, Battelle Meml. Inst., 1962-66; bd. dirs. Contemporary Arts Assn. and Mus., Houston, 1952-57; mem. exec. com. Tex. Transp. Inst., 1964-72; apptd. conferee Global Strategy Conf., US Naval War Coll., 1958. Comdr. USNR, ret. PTO and S.E. Asia, 1941-46, mem. staff Supreme Allied Comdr. Atlantic NATO, 1954. Recipient Jesse L. Lasky award RKO Pictures-CBS, Hollywood, Calif., 1939, H.J. Lutcher Stark prize U. Tex., 1939, 40, Walter Mack award PepsiCo, U. Tex., 1941, Internat. Rels. award Nouvelle Caledonie, Noumea, New Caledonia, 1943, Best US Pub. Svc. Broadcasts award CCNY, 1946, Arthur Freed award Freed-Eisemann Corp., 1946, First-FM (West) award Frequency Modulation Assn., Washington, 1947, Tex. State Network award mobile coverage Nat. Presdl. Convs., Phila., 1948, Chgo., 1952, Trusonic Wireless Microphone award Acad. Motion Picture Arts & Scis., Beverly Hills, 1951, Air Cargo Devel. award, Latin Am. Free Trade Assn., Mexico City, 1953, Frank White award, Mutual Broadcasting Sys., NY, 1953, H.M.S. SHEFFIELD citation Brit. Royal Navy U.S. Cruise, 1954, C.R. Smith Aviation Devel. award Am. Airlines, NY, 1955, Universal Internat./Interstate Theaters world premiere ceremonial award, Houston, 1955, award Latin Am. Free Trade Assn., Caracas, 1955, KLM Royal Dutch Airlines Super-Constellation Transatlantic award, Washington, 1956, Capt. Eddie Rickenbacker Air Transport Advancement award Eastern Air Lines, NY, 1956, Padre Alvarez award Boys Town Chorale Internat. Tour, Canavati Industries, Monterrey, 1957, Allied Rod & Gun Club Triple Crown trophy, Gander, Nfld., 1958, Iron Duke award No. Va. Lit. Soc., Arlington, 1962, Scandinavian Airlines Sys. Transpolar US-Africa Route, Johannesburg, 1967, Pres.'s Outstanding commendation internat. law U.S. Naval War Coll., Newport, 1967, IBM Corp. Exec. Computer Concepts prize, San Jose, Calif., 1976, M.Y. ENTERPRISE Cruise award Peter Island, Brit. V.I., 1978, Martha's Vineyard, Nantucket, 1979, Glacier Bay Cruise award M.V. MALIBU, Sitka, Alaska, 1980, 50 yr. Meritorious Practice award State Bar Tex., 1996. Mem.: ARC (lifeguards-water safety examiner), ABA (chmn. coun. sect. pub. utility, comms. and transp. law, standing com. on aero. law, chmn. sect. adminstrv. law aviation com.), FBA (DC chpt., exec. com. transp. coun., comm. coun.), State Bar Tex., Avatar Lit. Soc. (pres.), State Bar Mich. (emeritus), DC Bar, Houston Bar Assn., Am. Law Inst. (advisor Restatement (2d) of Torts), World Peace Through Law Ctr. Geneva (chmn. internat. aviation law com., advisor world air piracy and hijacking treaties), Fed. Comm. Bar Assn. (frequency modulation broadcasting com., tall-TV towers com.), Assn. ICC Practitioners, Am. Judicature Soc., Washington Fgn. Law Soc. (vis. lectr. 1967—68), Naval Submarine League, Naval War Coll. Found., Japanese Air Law Soc. (hon.), Venezuelan Air and Space Law Soc. (hon.), USS St. Paul (CA-73) Assn. (life), USS Pres. Adams APA-19 Assn. (hon.), Tex. Navy (Admiral), Flying Col., Internat. Club (Washington), Houston Polo Club, Nat. Aviation Club (Washington), Del Coronado Beach and Tennis Club (Calif.), Execs. Club (Houston), Lago Vista Polo Club (hon.), Boca Raton Beach and Tennis Club (Fla.), Breakfast Club (Houston), Saddle and Cycle Club (Chgo.), Lake Shore Club (Chgo.), Order Ky. Cols., Phi Eta Sigma, Delta Sigma Rho (pres. Tex. chpt. 1940). Home: 6904 Ligustrum Cv Austin TX 78750-8352 Personal E-mail: johnerle_stephen@yahoo.com.

STEPHEN, NINIAN MARTIN, judge; b. Oxford, Eng., June 15, 1923; s. Frederick and Barbara (Cruickshank) S.; m. Valery Mary Sinclair, June 4, 1949; children: Mary, Ann, Sarah, Jane, Elizabeth. LLB, U. Melbourne, 1949; LLD (hon.), U. Sydney, U. Melbourne, U. Griffith; DLitt (hon.), We. Australia U. Called to Victoria bar, 1952; created queen's counsel, 1966; judge Victorian Supreme Ct., 1970-72; justice High Ct. of Australia, 1972-82; U.K. privy councillor, 1979; gov.-gen. of Australia, 1982-89; amb. for the environ., 1989-92; chmn. Second Strand No. Ireland Talks, 1992; expert Group on Cambodia, 1998-99; mem. ethics commn. Internat. Olympic Com., 2000—. Chmn. Australian Libr. Coun., 1990—94, Blood and Blood Products Inquiry, 1999, Citizenship Coun., 1999, Internat. Labor Orgn. Report on Forced Labor, Myanmar, 2001. Served with Australian Army, 1941-46; judge internat. criminal tribunal former Yugoslavia, 1993-97. Decorated Knight of Garter, Knight, Order of Australia, Knight Grand Cross St. Michael & St. George, Knight Grand Cross Royal Victorian Order, Knight British Empire, Comdr. Légion d'Honneur, France, Knight St. John Jerusalem. Address: Flat 13/1 193 Domain Rd South Yarra VIC 3141 Australia Office Phone: 0396500266.

STEPHENS, ANNABEL KUYKENDALL, retired library and information scientist; b. New Albany, Miss., Apr. 17, 1947; d. Carl Hunter and Ruth Nell Stephens; life ptnr. Pat L. Dunbar. BA, Miss. State Coll.for Women, Columbus, 1968; MLS, George Peabody Coll., Nashville, 1970; DLS, Columbia U., NYC, 1988. Libr. Muscle Shoals Regional Libr., 1968—70, Memphis Pub. Libr., 1970—72, br. head, 1972—79; dir. Jennie Stephens Smith Pub. Libr., New Albany, Miss., 1982—83; assoc. prof. U. Ala. Sch. Libr. Info. Studies, Tuscaloosa, Ala., 1986—2007. Planning cons. Homewood Pub. Libr., Ala., 2006, Gardendale Pub. Libr., Ala., 2007. Contbr. articles to profl. jours.; author: Assessing the Public Library Planning Process, 1995, Public Library Collection Development in the Information Age, 1998. Bd. dir. W. Ala. AIDS Outreach, Tuscaloosa, 2003—07. Recipient Libr. of Yr. award, Phi Beta Mu, Ala. Chpt., 2004, Ruth Blackburn Cmty. Svc. award, 2004, Steven L. Mann award, Mystic Krewe of Druids, 2007, Knox Hagood award, Coll. Comm. and Info. Sci., 2007. Mem.: ALA (life), Reference User Svc. Assn., Pub. Libr. Assn., Assn. Libr. Info. Sci. Educators, Ala. Libr. Assn. (Humanitarian award 2002, Eminent Libr. award 2006, Lifetime Achievement award 2006). Presbyterian. Avocations: travel, reading, theater. Home: 11851 Grandview Dr Northport AL 35475

STEPHENS, B. CONSUELA, minister, consultant; b. Bklyn., May 12, 1947; d. Montiphus (Mortimer King) DeReyes and Bernadine Whitley. PhD Religion, Clayton Theol. Inst., 1983. Pastor Chenaniah Missionary Ch., Hollis, NY, 1986—. Cons. Chenaniah Missionary Ch., Hollis, United States, 1986—. Author: (book) Behold, I Shew You A Mystery, 1998. Dir. CASE Group, Inc., 2003—. Avocation: gardening. Home: 575 Mt Prospect Ave #8c Newark NJ 07104 Home Phone: 678-437-8637; Office Phone: 404-381-0558. E-mail: consuelastephens@yahoo.com.

STEPHENS, BART NELSON, former foreign service officer; b. Norfolk, Va., May 29, 1922; s. Bart Dannelly and Lura Lee (Cannon) S.; m. Barrett Krausz, Jan. 7, 1950; children: Tracey Rainier, Schuyler Barrett, Holly Cannon, Sinah Kendall Lee. AB, Duke, 1943; grad., USNR Midshipman Sch., Notre Dame, 1944; AM, Harvard, 1947. Divisional asst. Greece-Turkey-Iran sect., pub. affairs overseas program staff Dept. State, 1948-49; asst. pub. affairs officer Thessaloniki, Greece, 1950; asst. info. officer Athens, 1950-51; pub. affairs officer Patras, Greece, 1951-54 and, Thessaloniki, 1954; dir. Amerika Haus, Nuernberg, Germany, 1955-59; mem. cultural council City of Nuernberg, 1958-59; mgmt. analyst USIA, Washington, 1959-61; cultural attache Am. Embassy, Warsaw, Poland, 1963-65; dir. Am. Cultural Center, Saigon, Vietnam, 1967-68; 1st sec., regional projects officer Am. Embassy, Vienna, Austria, 1968-70; consul, pub. affairs officer Am. consulate gen. Stuttgart, Germany, 1970-73; area coordinator (Europe) USIA, Washington, 1973, seminar-conf. Programming officer, 1973-74; dep. dir. Office Internat. Arts Affairs, Dept. State, 1974-76; counselor cultural affairs officer Am. Embassy, Bangkok, 1977-82; counselor Sr. Fgn. Service. Contbr. articles to profl. jours. Vice chmn., bd. dirs. Thailand-U.S. Ednl. Found., 1977-82; bd. dirs. John F. Kennedy Found., Thailand, 1977-82, John E. Peurifoy Found., 1979-82, Lynchburg Symphony Orch., 1992-93; exec. sec. Eisenhower Exch. Fellowship Selection Com., Thailand, 1977-82; mem. winter forums com. Sweet Briar Coll., 1990-96. Lt. (j.g.) USNR, 1944-46, PTO. Decorated Bronze Star with combat V, Purple Heart.; recipient Meritorious Svc. award USIA, 1956, medal for civilian service in Vietnam, 1968, Civilian award U.S. European Command, 1973. Mem. Am. Fgn. Svc. Assn., Soc. Lees of Va., Siam Soc., Phi Beta Kappa, Omicron Delta Kappa, Phi Eta Sigma, Pi Kappa Phi. Home: 501 V E S Rd Apt C210 Lynchburg VA 24503 *Personal responsibility should be an essential principle for all of us, in the family, job and community. My 34 years in the U.S. Foreign Service gave me a wonderfully stimulating and rewarding career and a profound belief: the diplomatic service is America's first line of defense.*

STEPHENS, BOBBY GENE, college administrator, consultant; b. Glendale, SC, Mar. 8, 1935; s. Dewey and Bertha Cordelia (Mott) S.; m. Sandra Elizabeth White, June 27, 1957; children: Elaine, Ward, Todd, Adam. BS, Wofford Coll., Spartanburg, SC, 1957; MS, Clemson U., SC, 1961, PhD, 1964; LHD, MacMurray Coll., Jacksonville, Ill., 1987. Textile chemist Reeves Bros., Fairforest, SC, 1957-58; grad. asst. Clemson U., 1960-63; instr. chemistry Wofford Coll., Spartanburg, SC, 1963-64, asst. prof., 1964-67, assoc. prof., 1967-72, prof., v.p. acad. affairs, 1972-80; pres. MacMurray Coll., Jacksonville, Ill., 1980-86; v.p. research and enrollment Wofford Coll., Spartanburg, SC, 1986-91, v.p. sci. and tech., 1991—, prof. chemistry emeritus, 2000—. Project dir. Howard Hughes Med. Inst., 1992—; pres. BGS Cons.; cons. in field Contbr. articles to sci. jours.; inventor extractions with propylene carbonate, 1975; producer: TV series The Psychology of Interpersonal Behavior, 1974. Co-chmn. Daniel Morgan Restoration Com., 1986-88; vice chmn. Spartanburg County Pollution Control Authority, 1970-74;

bd. dirs. SC Lung Assn., Spartanburg, 1970-75; sect. maj. United Way, 1975-77; chair SC State Libr. Bd., 2004—. 1st lt. US Army, 1958-60. Recipient Jefferson award SC Acad. Sci., 1969; recipient 1st prize graphics div. 2d Edit. Art Contest, 1971, 2d and 3d prizes Lawson's Fork Creek Photography Contest, 1978, Alumni Disting. Svc. award Wofford Coll., 2001; USPHS grantee; NSF grantee Mem. Am. Chem. Soc. (chair Western Carolinas sect. 2003), Nat. Assn. Gifted Children, Assn. Ednl. Communications and Tech., Phi Beta Kappa. Methodist. Home: 460 S Fairview Ave Spartanburg SC 29302 Office: Wofford College 429 N Church St Spartanburg SC 29303-3663 Office Phone: 864-573-8844. Personal E-mail: bgsphd@bellsouth.net. Business E-Mail: stephensbg@wofford.edu.

STEPHENS, CAROLYN KING, retired literature and language professor; d. David Byron and Winifred Hamel King; m. John Alton Stephens, June 24, 1961; children: Allison King, John Webster, Matthew Douglas, Stephanie Caroline. BA in English & Drama, Milw.-Downer Coll., 1962; MBA, U. Wis.-Milw., 1980; PhD, Union Inst. Grad. Coll., Cin., 2000. Lic. in tchg. English, speech Wis. Dept. Pub. Instn., 1962, cert. in ESL WI Bd. Vocat., Tech., Adult Edn., 1970. Dir. cmty. rels. Cardinal Stritch Coll., Milw., 1975—80; dir. Telesis inst. Alverno Coll., Milw., 1980—81; gen. mgr. Ballet Found. Milw., 1981—84; dir. sales & mktg. Pers. Pool Temp. Svcs., 1984—86; pres. Pers. Devel. Employment & Staffing Svcs., 1986—88; dir. liberal arts & assoc. prof. English Concordia U. Wis., Mequon, 1989—2003. Coord. Com. Renovation Downer Bldgs., Milw., 1972—79; trustee Lawrence U., Appleton, Wis., 1984—87; sabbatical St. Andrews U., Fife, Scotland, 1996—96. Author: (play) Anonymous Canon. Co-chair cmty. action seminar Jr. League Milw., 1978—79; benefit performances music, dance United Performing Arts Fund; U. Sch. Milw., 1975—85; clk. session North Shore Presbyn. Ch., Shorewood, Wis., 2006—08. Mem.: Wis. Fellowship Poets, Sigma Tau Delta. Office: Concordia Univ Wis 12800 N Lake Shore Dr Mequon WI 53097

STEPHENS, DEBRA L., state supreme court justice; m. Craig Stephens, 1989; children: Lindsey, Bob. Grad. magna cum laude, Gonzaga U., Spokane, Wash., 1987; JD summa cum laude, Gonzaga U. Sch. Law, 1993. Comm. tchr., debate team coach Spokane Falls CC, 1987—88; asst. dean admissions Gonzaga U., 1988—90; staff atty., Hon. Fred L. Van Sickle US Dist. Ct. (ea. dist.), Wash., 1993—95; pvt. practice atty.; judge Wash. Ct. of Appeals, Divsn. Three; assoc. justice Wash. State Supreme Ct., 2008—. Adj. prof. Gonzaga U. Sch. Law, 1995—; mem. Appellate Ct. Edn. Com., Ct. Rules Com. Mem. fundraising cir. Sacred Heart Children's Found.; cmty. bd. advisor People for Environ. Action & Cmty. Health; undergrad. vol. Gonzaga U.; vol. supervising atty. Gonzaga U. Legal Assistance Clinic; deacon, elder Millwood Cmty. Presbyn. Ch.; bd. dirs. Orchard Prairie Sch. Dist. No. 123, Spokane Valley Rotary Club; trustee Wash. Jud. Coll. Avocations: skiing, golf. Office: Wash State Supreme Ct PO Box 40929 Olympia WA 98504-0929 Office Phone: 360-357-2049.*

STEPHENS, DONALD R(ICHARDS), investor; b. San Francisco, June 28, 1938; s. Donald Lewis and Anona Marie (O'Leary) S.; m. Christina Brinkman, Sept. 11, 1971 (div. 1996); m. Patricia Hamilton, Oct. 21, 2000; children: Lane B., Justin H., Nicholas W., Adam H. BS, U. So. Calif., 1961; JD, Hastings Coll., 1969. Pres. Campodonico & Stephens, San Francisco, 1963-65; pres., owner Union Investment Co., San Francisco, 1966-69; assoc. Law Offices of Louis O. Kelso, 1969-72; pres. D.R. Stephens & Co., San Francisco, 1972—; mng. ptnr. Stephens & Stephens, San Francisco, 1999—. Chmn., bd. dirs., CEO Bank of San Francisco Co., 1978-91; chmn., bd. dirs. N.Am. Trust REIT; bd. dirs. Am. Inst. for Fgn. Study, Charles Schwab Family of Funds Inc. Bd. dirs. Bay Area Coun.; trustee St. Francis Meml. Hosp., San Francisco, 1976-82; mem. policy adv. bd. U. Calif., 1985—. Mem. Urban Land Inst., World Bus. Coun., Bohemian Club, Reserve Palm Desert, Napa Valley Reserve. Republican. Presbyterian. Avocations: tennis, bridge. Business E-Mail: info@drstephens.com, drstephens@drstephens.com.

STEPHENS, EDWARD CARL, communications educator, writer; b. LA, July 27, 1924; s. Carl Edward and Helen Mildred (Kerner) S.; children: Edward, Sarah, Matthew. AB, Occidental Coll., 1947; MS, Northwestern U., 1955. Advt. exec. Dancer-Fitzgerald-Sample Inc., NYC, 1955-64; prof. Medill Sch. Journalism, Northwestern U., Evanston, Ill., 1964-76; prof., chmn. dept. advt. S.I. Newhouse Sch. Pub. Communications, Syracuse U., NY, 1976-80, dean, 1980—89; prof. comms. S.I. Newhouse Sch. Pub. Comms. Syracuse U., 1990-92, prof. emeritus, 1992—. Author: (novels) A Twist of Lemon, 1958, One More Summer, 1960, Blow Negative!, 1962, Roman Joy, 1965, A Turn in the Dark Wood, 1968, The Submariner, 1974, (nonfiction) Submarines, 1960. Mem. George Polk Awards Com. With USN, 1943-46, 1950-53. Capt. USNR (ret.). Decorated Purple Heart Mem. Am. Acad. Advt. (pres. 1976-77), Assn. Edn. Journalism and Mass Communication, The Army and Navy Club, Authors League, Century Club of Syracuse, Alpha Tau Omega. Episcopalian. Personal E-mail: stephens@dreamscape.com.

STEPHENS, ELISA, college president; d. Richard A. Stephens; married; 1 child. BA, Vassar Coll.; JD, U. San Francisco, 1985. Law clk. San Francisco Superior Ct., Calif., 1985—86; in-house counsel Cellular Holdings, Inc., 1987—88, Acad. of Art Coll., San Francisco, 1989—92, pres., 1992—. Contbg. editor Barclays Law Publishers, 1986—88. Bd. dirs. Am. Red Cross Bay Area Chpt., San Francisco Lyric Opera. Mem.: Royal Soc. Arts, Assn. Rewards for Coll. Scientists, Nob Hill Assn. (pres. 2003—05), San Francisco Jr. League, San Francisco Rotary Club, Univ. Club, Met. Club, San Francisco City Club, Young Pres. Orgn., Calif. Bar Assn. Office: 79 New Montgomery St 6th Fl San Francisco CA 94105-3410

STEPHENS, GRAEME LESLIE, meteorologist, educator; b. Ballart, Victoria, Australia, Jan. 1, 1952; s. Dudley William James and Thelma Joyce Stephens; m. Janice Lyn King, Feb. 3, 1973; children: Michael James, Philip John, Mark Graeme, Sara Kathleen. B in Physics and Meteorology (hon.), U. Melbourne, Victoria, Australia, 1973; PhD, U. Melbourne, 1977. Faculty U. Melbourne, Dept. Meteorology, 1977—84; rsch. scientist Commonwealth Sci. Indsl. Rsch. Orgn., 1977—79, sr. rsch. scientist, 1979—84; assoc. prof. Colo. State U., 1984—91, prof., 1991—2005, disting. prof., 2005—. Dir. Coop. Inst. Rsch. Atmosphere, Ft. Collins, 2008—. Author: (book) Remote sensing of the lower atmosphere: An introduction; contbr. articles to profl. jours., chapters to books. Recipient Internat. Radiation Commn. Gold medal, Internat. Assn. Meteorology & Atmospheric Scis., 2008, Atmospheric & Oceanog. Scis. Libr. edit. bd. mem., Kluwer Academic Publs., 1996—, Editor award, Monthly Weather Rev., 1981—83, Assoc. Editor award, Jour. Atmospheric Scis., 1984—89, 1989—94, Henry G. Houghton award, Am. Meteorol. Soc., 1990, Jule G. Charney award, 2005, Rotary Stellar award, NASA, 2008, Exceptional Pub. Svc. medal, 2008, Group Achievement award, 2008, Halliburton New Faculty Rsch. award, Colo. State U., 1986, Abell Faculty Rsch. award, 1993, U. Disting. Prof. award, 2005; fellowship, Am. Meteorol. Soc., 1994, Am. Geophys. Union, 2003, AAAS, 2006. Mem.: IEEE, Royal Meteorol. Soc., Am. Meteorol. Soc., Am. Geophys. Union. Achievements include first to introduce CloudSat satellite mission that has produced entirely new information about clouds. Office: Colo State Univ Dept Atmos Sci 1371 Campus Delivery Fort Collins CO 80523-1371 Office Fax: 970-491-8449. Business E-Mail: stephens@atmos.colostate.edu.

STEPHENS, GREGORY D., religious studies educator; s. Duane P. and Jennie D. Stephens; m. Dorothy J. Samson; children: Jeremy R., Jesse B., Melanie R., Darrell J., Shari M. Diploma in Pastoral Studies, U. Binghamton, NY, 1978; BRE, Bapt. Bible Coll. Pa., Clarks Summit, 1980; MDiv, Bapt. Bible Sch. Theology, Clarks Summit, 1984; attending, Bapt. Bible Sem., Clarks Summit, 1995, PhD, 2003; ThM, Capital Bible Sem., Lanham, Md., 2000; MEd, Columbia Internat. U., SC, 2001, Tenn. Temple U., Chattanooga, 2005. Cert. Taylor-Johnson Temperent Analysis, 1984, bible specialist Assoc. Ch. Sch. Internat., 2000; in premarital/marital Prepare-Enrich, supt. 2000, adminstr. Am. Assoc. Ch. Sch., 2000. Pastor Faith Bible Ch., Wappinger Falls, NY, 1984—90, Emerson Bible Ch., NJ, 1990—92; sr. pastor Captiol Bapt. Ch., Upper Marlboro, Md., 1992—2001; supt. Capitol Christian Acad., Upper Marlboro, 1992—2001; adj. prof. bible & theology Washington Bible Coll., Lanham, Md., 1995—2001; adj. prof. Capital Bible Sem., Lanham, 1997—2001; prof. nt & Greek Temple Bapt. Sem., Chattanooga, 2001—04, academic dean, 2004—, prof. bibl. langs. & lit. and discipleship, 2004—. Mem. Bibl. Archaeology Soc., 1984, Evang. Theol. Soc., 2001, Evang. Missiological Soc., 2005, Evang. Philos. Soc., 2005, Soc. Bibl. Lit., 2005. Office: Temple Baptist Sem Grad Div-TTU 1906 Union Ave Chattanooga TN 37404 Business E-Mail: gregory.stephens@tntemple.edu.

STEPHENS, JAMES T. (J.T. STEPEHENS), publishing executive; b. 1939; married. BA in Bus. Adminstrn., Yale U., 1961; MBA, Harvard U., 1964. With Ebsco Industries Inc., Birmingham, Ala., 1961—, asst. v.p., 1966-67, v.p., 1967-70, exec. v.p., 1970—71, pres., also bd. dirs., 1971—2005, chmn. Office: EBSCO Industries Inc 5724 Highway 280 E Birmingham AL 35242-6818 also: PO Box 1943 Birmingham AL 35201-1943

STEPHENS, JAY B., lawyer, defense technologies company executive; b. Akron, Iowa, Nov. 5, 1946; s. Lyle R. and Marie (Borchers) S.; m. Julie Stephens; children: Amanda, Jessica, Jay Jr., Alexandra BA magna cum laude, New Coll., Oxford, 1969, BA, 1969; JD cum laude, Harvard U., 1973. Bar: DC 1973, US Supreme Ct., 1979. Assoc. Wilmer, Cutler & Pickering, Washington, 1973-74; asst. spl. prosecutor Watergate Spl. Prosecution Force, Washington, 1974-75; assoc. gen. counsel Overseas Pvt. Investment Corp., Washington, 1976-77; asst. US atty. US Dept. Justice, Washington, 1977-81, spl. counsel to asst. atty. gen., 1981-83, dep. assoc. atty. gen., 1983-85, assoc. dep. atty. gen., 1985-86, US atty. DC Dist., 1988-93; dep. counsel to Pres. The White House, Washington, 1986-88; ptnr. Pillsbury, Madison & Sutro, Washington, 1993-97; v.p. and dep. gen. counsel Honeywell, Morristown, NJ, 1997—2001; assoc. atty. gen. US Dept. Justice, Washington, 2001—02; sr. v.p., gen. counsel, sec. Raytheon Co., Waltham, Mass., 2002—. Dir. New Eng. Legal Found. Contbr. articles to profl. jours. Knox fellow Oxford, Eng., 1968-69. Mem. DC Bar Assn., Asst. US Atty. Assn., Nat. Assn. Former US Attys. (dir.), Supreme Ct. Hist. Soc., Assoc. Gen. Counsel, Phi Beta Kappa. Office: Raytheon Co 870 Winter St Waltham MA 02451 Office Phone: 781-522-5096. Office Fax: 781-522-6471.

STEPHENS, JERRY WAYNE, librarian, director; b. Birmingham, Ala., Sept. 10, 1949; s. William Larkin and Odell (Kerr) S.; m. Lisa Brown, June 2, 1972; children: Jeramy Wayne, Elizabeth Ashley, John Larkin BS in Acctg., U. Ala.-Birmingham, 1974, MBA, 1976; M.L.S., U. Ala., 1977, PhD in Adminstrn. Higher Edn., 1982. Svc. mgr. Hammond Organ Studios, Birmingham, 1973-74; acct. Mervyn Sterne Libr., U. Ala., Birmingham, 1974-75, asst. to dir., 1975-76, asst. dir., 1976-85, libr., dir., 1985—; interim fiscal officer Univ. Coll. U. Ala., Birmingham, 1982, interim asst. v.p. for acad. affairs, 1989-91. Vice chmn. Network Acad. Librs., 1985-86, 95-96, chmn., 1986-88, 96, 2000-01; cons. Birmingham Pub. Libr., 1977—; cons. Southeastern Libr. Assn., Atlanta, 1979-80; bd. dirs. Southeastern Libr. Network, treas., 1992-93, chmn., 1993-94; mem. user's coun. Online Computer Libr. Ctr., 1997—, pres.-elect, 2000-01, pres., 2001-2002, bd. trustees, 2002—. Contbr. articles to profl. publs. Sponsored exec. United Way, Birmingham, 1978, sr. exec., 1982; foster parent Dept. Pensions and Securities, Birmingham, 1982-83; elder Homewood Cumberland Presbyn. Ch., Birmingham, 1982-84, 88-90. With USN, 1972-73 Named one of Outstanding Young Men Am., U.S. Jaycees, 1978, 79 Mem. ALA, SE Libr. Assn., Ala. Libr. Assn. (treas. 1977-78), Am. Mgmt. Assn. Avocations: camping, softball. Office: U Ala-Birmingham Mervyn H Sterne Libr 1530 3d Ave South Birmingham AL 35294-0014 Office Phone: 205-934-6360. E-mail: jerry@beowulf.mhsl.uab.edu, jerryws@uab.edu.

STEPHENS, KATHLEEN (D. KATHLEEN STEPHENS), United States Ambassador to South Korea; b. Tex. 1 child. BA in East Asian Studies, with honors, Prescott Coll., Ariz.; MA, Harvard U., Cambridge, Mass.; student, U. Hong Kong, 1972—73. Joined US Fgn. Svc., 1978; consular and pub. affairs officer US Dept. State, Guangzhou, China, 1980—82, chief internal polit. unit Seoul, Republic of Korea, 1984—87, prin. officer, the US Consulate Busan, Republic of Korea, 1987—89, polit. officer, US mission Belgrade, Zagreb, former Yugoslavia, 1989—92, sr. UK country officer Washington, 1992—94, dep. chief of mission, US Consul General Belfast, Northern Ireland, 1995—98, dep. chief of mission, US Embassy Lisbon, Portugal, 1998—2001, dir. Office Ecology & Terrestrial Conservation Washington, 2001—03, dep. asst. sec. for European & Eurasian Affairs Bosnia-Herzegovina, 2003—05, prin. dep. asst. sec., polit. advisor, Bur. East Asian & Pacific Affairs, 2005—08; US amb. to the Republic of Korea US State Dept., Seoul, 2008—; dir. European affairs NSC, Washington, 1994—95. Vol. Peace Corps, Republic of Korea, 1975—77. Office: DOS Amb 9600 Seoul Pl Washington DC 20521*

STEPHENS, LAURENCE DAVID, JR., linguist, investor, oil industry executive; b. Dallas, July 26, 1947; s. Laurence D. Sr. and Amy Belle (Schickram) S.; m. Susan Leigh Foutz, Apr. 16, 1988; 1 child, Laurence David III. MA, Stanford U., 1972, PhD, 1976. Cert. minerals mgr. Nat. Assn. Royalty Owners, 2003. Vis. fellow Yale U., New Haven, summer 1979; rsch. fellow U. SC, Columbia, 1980; asst. prof. U. NC, Chapel Hill, 1982-88, assoc. prof., 1989—; pres. Colgate Mgmt. Co., Inc., Dallas, 1997—; gen. ptnr. Moorman, Schickram & Stephens, Ltd., Dallas, 1997—; mgr. Stephens Resources, LLC, 2004—; v.p., mgr. 4025 Colgate LLC, 2004—05, 3712 Wentwood, LLC, 2004—05. Co-author: Two Studies in Latin Phonology, 1977, Language and Metre, 1984, The Prosody of Greek Speech, 1994, Discontinuous Syntax, 1999, Latin Word-Order: Structured Meaning and Information, 2006; editor ann. vol. L'Année Philologique, 1987-92; contbr. numerous articles to profl. jours. Mem. University Park Cmty. League, Park Cities Hist. Soc., Nat. Trust for Hist. Preservation, Washington, 1989—, The Dallas Symphony Assn. Ann. Fund, Metro. Opera Guild, N.Y.C., 1992—, Wythe County VA Hist. Soc., 1998—. Grantee L'Année Philologique, NEH, 1987-89, 89-91, 91-93. Mem. Am. Philol. Assn., Greek and Latin Linguistic Assn. (chmn. 1987-92), N.Y. Acad. Scis., Indogermanische Gesellschaft, Internat. Soc. Bibliographie Classique, Arabian Horse Assn., Nat. Assn. Royalty Owners, Sigma Xi. Achievements include discovery of language universal regularities concerning labiovelar phonemes, laws of palatalization, the law of catathesis in Greek (pitch lowering), and grammatical, semantic, pragmatic (information structure) regularities of discontinuous constituency and nonconfigurational syntactic structures in Greek and Latin; co-developer of Justeson-Stephens probability distribution for cognates between unrelated languages, Justeson-Stephens probability distribution of the numbers of vowels, consonants, and total phonological inventory size in the languages of the world; research on the law of the quantitative form of diachronic polysemy growth, semantic universals of aspect and modality, universals of writing systems and their evolution. Home: 2785 Turnpike Rd Lexington VA 24450 also: 3319 Greenbrier Dr Dallas TX 75225 Office: 30 Crossing Ln Ste 204 Lexington VA 24450 Office Phone: 540-463-3146. Personal E-mail: lsteph8694@aol.com.

STEPHENS, LEE-ANN WILLIAMS, elementary school educator; b. Cleve., July 9, 1962; d. Joseph Ernest Williams and Joan Lee (Campbell) Warren; m. Terry Brian Stephens, Sept. 21, 1985. BA in Internat. Studies, Miami U., 1984; postgrad., U. Mex., 1984; BS in Elem. Edn., U. Minn., 1989. Cert. elem. tchr., Minn. Asst. adult probation officer Alliance (Ohio) Mcpl. Courthouse, 1982-83; assoc. buyer Dayton Hudson Dept. Store Co., Mpls., 1985-88; elem. tchr. Dowling Pub. Sch., Mpls., 1989; now tchr. Park Spanish Immersion Sch., Minn. Math tutor African Am. Acad. for Accelerated Learning, Mpls., 1989—; coord. Mpls. Council Chs. Tutoring Program, 1988-89. Named Minn. Tchr. of Yr., 2007. Mem. ASCD, Nat. Coun. Tchrs. Math. Avocations: aerobics, bowling, reading. Office: Park Spanish Immersion Sch 6300 Walker St Minneapolis MN 55416

STEPHENS, LOREN M., publishing executive, writer, film producer; b. NYC, Mar. 8, 1944; d. Seymour and Carol Meyer; m. Dana Miyoshi; 1 child, Joshua. BA, Cornell U., Ithaca, NY, 1965; MA in Internat. Affairs, Columbia U., NYC, 1967. Editor Houghton Mifflin, Boston, 1969—71; assoc. Berg & Co./Mortgage Banker, Boston, 1971—73, sr. v.p., 1973—80; asst. v.p. Nat. Med. Enterprises, LA, 1980—82; prin. Stephens & Hyde, LA, 1982—84, One Step Prodns., Studio City, 1984—97; asst. devel. officer Anti Defamation League, LA, 1990—94, dir. devel., 1994—2000, dir. planned giving & endowments, 2000—05; dir. devel. U. Judaism, 2005—06. Pres. Write Wisdom, Inc.; founder, owner Provenance Press, 2000—. Exec. prodr.: (documentaries) Legacy of the Hollywood Black List, 1985 (Cine Gold Eagle, 1985), Sojourner Truth: Ain't I a Woman, 1987 (Golden Apple, 1987), Los Pastores (Cine Gold Eagle, 1997). Alice Stetton Fellow, Columbia U., 1967. Home: 847 S Bundy Dr Los Angeles CA 90049 Office Phone: 310-826-6217. Business E-Mail: loren@writewisdom.com.

STEPHENS, NORRIS LYNN, school librarian; b. Charleroi, Pa., Dec. 14, 1930; BFA, Carnegie-Mellon U., 1954, MFA, 1957; M in Sacred Music, Union Theol. Sem., NY, 1956; MLS, U. Pitts., 1966, PhD, 1968. Sales clk. Wagner-Bund Music Co., Pitts., 1957—62; assoc. organist E. Liberty Presbyn. Ch., Pitts., 1962—83, First Bapt. Ch., Pitts., 1983—98. Sr. libr. U. Pitts., 1966—98, adj. asst. prof., 1972—82. Co-author: Collected Editions, Historical Series and Sets-Monuments of Music, 1997; contbr. chapters to books, articles to profl. pubs., encys.; composer and arranger Organ, Handbells, Choirs. Grantee, NEH, 1984. Mem.: Am. Guild Organists, Am. Musicological Soc. (chpt. chair 1982—84), Internat. Music Libr. Assn., Music Libr. Assn. (chpt. chair 1982—84), Bibl. Archaeol. Soc., Charles Avison Soc. Avocations: gardening, model railroading, stamp collecting/philately, coin collecting/numismatics.

STEPHENS, NORVAL BLAIR, JR., marketing consultant; b. Chgo., Nov. 20, 1928; s. Norval Blair and Ethel Margaret (Lewis) S.; m. Diane Forst, Sept. 29, 1951; children: Jill E., John G., Sandra J. (dec.), Katherine B., James N. BA, DePauw U., 1951; MBA, U. Chgo., 1959. Asst. to v.p. ops. Walgreen Drug Co., Chgo., 1953-56; with Needham, Harper Worldwide (formerly Needham, Harper & Steers), Chgo., 1956-86, v.p., 1964-70, sr. v.p., 1970-72, exec. v.p. internat., 1972-74, exec. v.p., mng. dir. NYC, 1974-75; exec. v.p. Chgo. office Needham, Harper & Steers, 1975-82, exec. v.p. internat., 1982-86; also dir.; pres. Deltacom, NYC, 1971-76; pres. Norval Stephens Co., 1987—2000; exec. dir. Internat. Comms. Agy. Network, 1988-98; founder, dir., pres. Barrington Area Cmty. Found., 1998—. Trustee DePauw U., 1979—; dir. North Am. Interfraternity. Found., 2007—. Recipient Rector award DePauw U., 1976, Old Gold Goblet award for outstanding svc. DePauw U., 1994, Outstanding Greek Vol. award N.Am. Interfraternity Conf., 2001, Carol Beese award Barrington Area C. of C., 2004; named Young Man of Yr., Arlington Heights Jaycees, 1964, Barrington Area Citizen of Yr., 1999; named to Sr. Hall of Fame, Barrington, Ill., 2002. Mem. DePauw Alumni Assn. (pres. 1977-79), Phi Beta Kappa, Delta Tau Delta (bd. dirs. edn. found. 1987—, vice chmn. 1994-95, chmn. 1995—, 2d v.p. Arch chpt. 1988-90, 1st v.p. 1990-92, pres. 1992-94). Republican. Methodist. Home: 3400 Garlands Lane Barrington IL 60010 Personal E-mail: norval@norvalstephens.com. *I view my life not as a passage but a daily renewing challenge: to be better; to be a better father, husband, brother, son; to return each day an honest day's work; to bear witness to my beliefs and my faith; to serve my fellowman. I seek a whole life and a life of rewarding parts, each a lesson and an experience.*

STEPHENS, PHILIP JOHN, chemistry professor; b. West Bromwich, Eng., 1940; BA in Chemistry, Oxford U., 1962, DPhil in Chemistry, 1964. Asst. prof. chemistry U. Southern Calif., 1967—70, assoc. prof. chemistry, 1970, prof., 1976, chair, dept. chemistry, 1992—98. Vis. fellow Rsch. Sch. Chemistry, Australian Nat. U., Canberra, 1975; vis. prof. Kemisk Lab., U. Copenhagen, 1978; sr. vis. fellow U. East Anglia, Norwich, 1977; vis. prof. Lab. Optics Physics, Ecole Superieure Physics and Indsl. Chemistry, Paris, 1998, Lab. Spettroscopia Molecular U. Degli Studi, Firenze, Italy, 1999; Schatz lectr., dept. chemistry U. Va., 1999; lectr. VCD spectroscopy. Contbr. articles to jour. publs. Recipient John Simon Guggenheim fellowship, U. Sussex, Brighton, 1984; Alfred P. Sloan Rsch. fellowship, 1968. Achievements include research in fields of theoretical chemistry, molecular spectroscopy and bioinorganic chemistry. Office: Univ Southern Calif Chemistry Dept Los Angeles CA 90089-0482 Office Phone: 212-740-4119. Office Fax: 213-740-3972. Business E-Mail: pstephen@usc.edu.

STEPHENS, RACHEL DE-VORE, finance company executive, educator; b. Akron, Ohio, Feb. 18, 1954; d. William Wallace; m. Charles Richard Stephens; children: Kirk children: Reginald Louis Young Jr., Demetrius Azxandra Young. BA, Malone Coll., 1990; MA, U. Akron, Akron, Oh, 1997; PhD, Ctrl. State, Riverside, Calif., 1999; DD, Summit Bible Seminary. Account mgr. Goodyear Tire & Rubber Co, Akron, Ohio, 1973—2005. Author: (dessertation) Managing Workforce Diversity. Bd. mem. The Coming Together Project, Akron, Ohio, 1997—2002. Mem.: Alpha Kappa Alpha (v.p. 1996—). Office: Goodyear Tire & Rubber Co 1144 E Market St Akron OH 44316 Office Fax: 330-666-6280; Home Fax: 330-666-6280. Personal E-mail: ryoung2048@aol.com.

STEPHENS, RICHARD, aerospace transportation executive; BS in Math., U. So. Calif., 1974; MS in Computer Sci., Calif. State U., Fullerton, 1984. V.p., gen. mgr. Integrated Def. Sys. Homeland Security and Svcs. Boeing Co., Chgo., sr. v.p. Internal Svcs., pres. Shared Svcs. Grp., sr. v.p. Human Resources and Adminstrn., 2005—; mem. Boeing Exec. Coun. Vice chmn. Orange County Bus. Coun.; mem. Pvt. Sector Sr. Adv. Com. Dept. Homeland Security, 2003—; mem. Sec. of Edn.'s Commn. on Future of Edn., 2005. Officer USMC. Recipient Profl. of Yr. Award, Am. Indian Sci. & Engring. Soc., 2004, Gold. Silver Knight and Excellence in Leadership awards, Nat. Mgmt. Assn. Fellow: AIAA; mem.: Pala Band of Mission Indians (chmn. 1988—89). Office: Boeing Co 100 N Riverside Chicago IL 60606-1596 Office Phone: 312-544-2000.*

STEPHENS, ROBERT DAVID, environmental engineering executive; b. La Follette, Tenn., Nov. 8, 1949; s. Robert Oscar and Billie Jean (Maples) S.; m. Donna Jean Reece, July 11, 1970 (div. Apr. 1984), m. Mary Nasca, Sept. 2004; children: Jaclyn-Marie Svetlana, Robert Igor. BA in Biology, Berea Coll., Ky., 1971; postgrad., U. Cin., 1973-74. Cert. environ. assessor Fla., environ. trainer, registered environ. mgr., lic. environ. profl. Environ. specialist Ky. Dept. Health, Ludlow, 1971-74; project mgr. Pedco Environ. Specialists, Cin., 1974-77; environ. control mgr. Mobil Chem. Corp., Richmond, Va., 1978-84; v.p. Environ. Analysis Corp., Richmond, 1984-85; mgr. Environ. Rsch. and Tech. Group GSX Corp., Greensboro, N.C., 1985-86; mgr. regulatory affairs and cmty. rels. Internat. Tech. Corp., Knoxville, Tenn., 1986-88, mgr. environ. studies Tampa, Fla., 1988-90; gen. mgr. First Environment, Inc., Tampa, 1990-91; co-owner Bruder Stephens, Inc., Tampa, 1991—2004; pres. Environ. Evaluations Inc., 2004—. Faculty Fla. C. of C. Environ. Seminars, 1988—; adj. faculty U. Fla. Treeo Ctr., U. South Fla. Coll. Pub. Health; expert witness in environ. mgmt., sampling and analysis, environ. risk, indoor air quality, mold and mildew. Contbr. articles to profl. jours. Co-founder Berea Cmty. Theater, 1970; bd. dirs. So. Waste Info. Exch., Inc., 1998-2007. Mem. Fla. Bar Assn. (assoc., environ and land use sect.), Fla. Environ. Assessors Assn. (pres. 1996-97, bd. dirs. 1993—), Internat. Soc. Tech. & Environ. Profls. (exec. dir.), Va. Orchid Soc. (pres. 1980-85, del. World Orchid Congress, Miami 1984), Ridge Orchid Soc., Tampa Club (bd. dirs. 1999-2002), Outback Bowl (bd. dirs. 2001—). Republican. Avocations: horticulture, guitar. Home: PO Box 145 Mango FL 33550-0145 Office: 717 W Wheeler Rd Brandon FL 33510 Office Phone: 813-684-8049. Business E-Mail: robert@environmentalevaluations.com.

STEPHENS, ROBERT OREN, retired English language educator; b. Corpus Christi, Tex., Oct. 2, 1928; s. Joe Key, Sr., and Mary Emma (Robertson) S.; m. Carey Virginia Jones, Sept. 8, 1956; children: Nancy, Melissa, Robert Allan. Student Del Mar Coll., 1945-47; BA, Tex. Coll. Arts and Industries, 1949; MA, U. Tex., 1951, PhD, 1958. English tchr. Shiner (Tex.) High Sch., 1949-50; instr. English U. Tex.-Austin, 1958-61; asst. prof. English U. N.C.-Greensboro, 1961-66, assoc. prof., 1966-68, prof., 1968-94, chmn. dept., 1981-88, dir. grad. studies in English, 1967-81, prof. emeritus, 1994—; vis. asst. prof. English Appalachian State U., Boone, N.C., summer 1962, vis. assoc. prof., summer 1967. Author: Hemingway's Nonfiction: The Public Voice, 1968; Ernest Hemingway: The Critical Reception, 1977, The Family Saga in the South, 1995, That Time of Year, 2004; author articles on Ernest Hemingway, colonial Am. authors, Tex. Oil Folklore, George Washington Cable, Companion to So. Lit., others. Ruling elder Presbyterian Ch., Greensboro, 1965—. Served to lt. USNR, 1951-55. Coop. fellow in humanities, U. N.C.-Duke U., 1965-66. Mem. MLA, South Atlantic MLA, Soc. for Study of So. Lit., Southeastern Am. Studies Assn., Philol. Assn. of the Carolinas. Democrat. Presbyterian. Avocations: hiking; landscape gardening and design.

STEPHENS, SCOTT, art educator; BFA in Printmaking, Wash. U., St. Louis; studied grad. work, Sch. of Art Inst. Chgo.; MFA, U. Ala. Prof. fine art Montevallo U., 1983—. Exhibitions include Montgomery Mus. Fine Art, U. Montevallo, residencies, Centrum vor Grafiek Frans Masereel in Kasterlee, Belgium, Tamarind Summer Workshop in Traditional Lithography. Named U.S. Prof. Yr. State Ala., Carnegie Found. Advancement of Teaching, 2006; fellow So. Arts Fedn., NEA, Ala. State Coun. Arts. Office: Dept Arts U Montevallo Montevallo AL 35115

STEPHENS, SIDNEY DEE, human resources specialist, retired chemical manufacturing company executive; b. St. Joseph, Mo., Apr. 26, 1945; s. Lindsay Caldwell and Edith May (Thompson) S.; m. Ellen Marie Boeh, June 15, 1968 (div. 1973); m. Elizabeth Ann Harris, Sept. 22, 1973; 1 child, Laura Nicole. BS, Mo. Western State U., 1971; MA, U. Houston, 1980; advanced cert. employment law, Inst. Applied Mgmt. and Law, 1998. Cert. Stephen Covey programs facilitator, 1997. Assoc. urban planner Met. Planning Commn., St. Joseph, 1967-71; prodn. acctg. assoc. Quaker Oats Co., St. Joseph, 1971-72, office mgr., pers. rep. Rosemont, Ill., 1972-73, employee and cmty. rels. mgr. New Brunswick, NJ, 1973-75, Pasadena, Tex., 1975-80; mgmt. cons., Houston, 1981—; regional mgr. human resources Syngenta Crop Protection Inc., 2001—, ret., 2004—; pvt. advisor fin. adminstrn. Ross Estates Investments, Ltd., Houston, 2004—; pvt. mgmt. cons. Stephens & Stephens Ltd., 2006—. Contbr. articles to profl. jours. With USNR, 1963-65. Mem. ASTD, Nat. Soc. for Human Resources Mgmt., Houston Human Resources Mgmt. Assn. (cmty. and govtl. affairs com. 1984-85, 85-86). Republican. Methodist. Home and Office: 16446 Longvale Dr Houston TX 77059-5420 Office Phone: 281-488-8330. Fax: 281-488-8912. E-mail: elsid45@aol.com.

STEPHENS, STEPHANIC MICA, executive secretary, educator; b. Lubbock, Tex., Dec. 19, 1964; d. John Springer and Carolyn Joyce Stephens. BA, Tex. Tech. U., Lubbock, 1987, degree in Telecom., MA in Edn., 1992. Cert. tchr. in secondary English & spl. edn. Tex. English instr. Howard Coll., Lamesa, Tex., 1994—; substitute tchr. Lamesa I.S.D., 2002—, Wilson I.S.D., Tex., 2004—; sec. Stephen's Mgmt. Co., Borden County, Tex., 2007—. Lamesa campus rep. Howard Coll., Big Spring, Tex., 2007—, faculty senate sec., 2007; rep. QEP Oversight Com., Tex., 2008—. Contbr. columns in newspapers. Curch memorial sec. Mcmurry U., Abilene, Tex. Recipient O'Donnell Girl Scouts award, 1996—2009. Mem.: O'ponnel Study Club (pres. 2008—), Rho Lamda, Beta Theata Pi, Gamma Phi Beta (chmn.). Democrat. Methodist. Avocation: piano. Home: 1051 County Rd 124 Odonnell TX 79351 Business E-Mail: mica@poka.com.

STEPHENS, THOMAS G., automotive executive; b. 1948; BS in Mech. Engring., U. Mich., 1971. With General Motors Corp., Mich., 1969—; exptl. engr., staff project engr. GM Cadillac Motor Car Divsn., Detroit, 1971—80, supr. product engring., 1980—82, staff engr. emission, transmissions, 1982—85; sr. staff engr. transmission, powertrain controls GM Buick-Oldsmobile-Cadillac Powertrain Divsn., 1985—88; plant mgr. GM Buick-Oldsmobile-Cadillac Powertrain Livonia Engine Plant, 1988—90; dir. engring. GM Engine Divsn., 1990—91; dir. engine engring. GM Powertrain, 1991—93, engring. ops. gen. mgr. Pontiac, 1993—94; v.p., group dir. engring. ops. GM Truck Group., 1996—2000; v.p. Gen. Motors Corp., Detroit, 1994, v.p. vehicle integration, 2001, group. v.p. global powertrain, 2001—07, group v.p. global powertrain & quality, 2007—08, exec. v.p. global powertrain & quality, 2008—09, vice chmn. global product devel., 2009—. Mem.: NAE, U. Mich. Nat. Adv. Coun., Detroit Sci. Ctr. (bd. trustees). Office: General Motors Corp 300 Renaissance Ctr PO Box 300 Detroit MI 48265-3000*

STEPHENS, THOMAS M(ARON), education educator; b. Youngstown, Ohio, June 15, 1931; s. Thomas and Mary (Hanna) S.; m. Evelyn Kleshock, July 1, 1955. BS, Youngstown Coll., 1955; MEd, Kent State U., 1957; EdD, U. Pitts., 1966. Lic. psychologist, Ohio. Tchr. Warren (Ohio) public schs., 1955-57, Niles (Ohio) public schs., 1957-58; psychologist Montgomery County, Ohio, 1958-60; dir. gifted edn. Ohio Dept. Edn., Columbus, 1960-66; assoc. prof. edn. U. Pitts., 1966-70; prof. edn. Ohio State U., 1970—, chmn. dept. exceptional children, 1972-82, chmn. dept. human services edn., 1982-87, assoc. dean Coll. Edn., 1987-92, prof., 1987-92, prof. emeritus, 1992—; clin. prof. edn. U. Dayton, Ohio, 1993—; exec. dir. Sch. Study Coun. Ohio, Columbus, 1987—2007, exec. dir. emeritus, 2007—; pvt. practice, 2007—; newspaper columnist, 2008—. Mem. Higher Edn. Consortium for Spl. Edn., chmn., 1976-77; pub., pres. Cedars Press, Inc. Author: Directive Teaching of Children with Learning and Behavioral Handicaps, 2d edit, 1976, Implementing Behavioral Approaches in Elementary and Secondary Schools, 1975, Teaching Skills to Children with Learning and Behavioral Disorders, 1977, Teaching Children Basic Skills: A Curriculum Handbook, 1978, 2d edit., 1983, Social Skills In The Classroom, 1978, 2d edit., 1991, Teaching Mainstreamed Students, 1982, 2d edit., 1988, Social Behavior Assessment Scale, 1991; dir.: Jour. Sch. Psychology, 1965-75, 80—; exec. editor: The Directive Tchr.; assoc. editor: Spl. Edn. and Tchr. Edn., Techniques, Behavioral Disorders, Spl. Edn. and Remedial Edn.; contbr. articles to profl. jours. Named to Ohio State U. Coll. of Edn. Hall of Fame, 1999; U.S. Office of Edn. fellow, 1964-65. Mem. APA, NASP (charter), State Dirs. for Gifted (pres. 1962-63), Coun. for Exceptional Children (gov., Tchr. Educator of Yr. tchr. edn. divsn. 1985), Coun. Children with Behavioral Disorders (pres. 1972-73). Home: 551 E Cooke Rd Columbus OH 43214-2813 Office: Sch Study Coun of Ohio 2080 Citygate Dr Columbus OH 43219 Office Phone: 614-785-0481. Personal E-mail: tstephens@copper.net. Business E-Mail: tstephens@ssco.org.

STEPHENS, WALTER, language educator; b. Anniston, Ala., July 14, 1949; married. PhD in Comparative Lit., Cornell U., Ithaca, NY, 1975; Dottorato Ricerca, Scuola Normale Superiore Pisa, Italy, 1977. Asst. prof., Italian U. Wash., Seattle, 1981—83; prof., French and Italian Dartmouth Coll., Hanover, NH, 1983—99; prof., Italian studies Johns Hopkins U., Balt., 1999—. Mem.: Network Italian Scholars Abroad, Renaissance Soc. America. Office: Johns Hopkins Univ German and Romance Langs Dept Baltimore MD 21218-2687 Office Fax: 410-516-5358. Business E-Mail: walter.stephens@jhu.edu.

STEPHENS, WILLIAM A. (DEAN STEPHENS), computer consultant; b. NC, Mar. 30, 1945; BBA, Ga. State U., Atlanta. Sales mgr.; product mgr., advanced Internet technologies KLA Tencor; dir. mgmt. info. systems Allied Signal Corp., 1981—89; dir. systems devel. EMI Music, Inc., 1989—91; v.p. mgmt. info. systems Print Tech., Inc.; co-founder, CEO The Seminars Group; CFO First Commerce Mortgage; mng. ptnr. William Stephens & Associates, 1992—2001; founder, computer cons. ASL Computing, 2003—. Republican. Achievements include patents for word processing and Internet to bank network bridge technologies. Office: ASL Labs PO Box 325 Colerain NC 27924 Office Phone: 252-325-3125.

STEPHENS, WILLIAM OLEN, humanities educator, consultant; s. Mark Wheeler and Mary Irene Stephens; PhD, U. Pa., Phila., 1990. Asst. prof. philosophy Creighton U., Omaha, 1990—97, assoc. prof. philosophy, 1997—2005, assoc. prof. classical & near eastern studies, 1997—2005, prof. philosophy, 2005—, prof. classical & near eastern studies, 2005—. Editor: (anthology) The Person: Readings in Human Nature, (book) Stoic Ethics: Epictetus and Happiness as Freedom; translator: The Ethics of the Stoic Epictetus: An English translation. Recipient Tchg. Tomorrow award, Omicron Delta Kappa, Creighton U., 2005. Mem.: Am. Philos. Assn., Phi Sigma Tau, Eta Sigma Phi, Phi Beta Kappa. Progressive. Avocations: tennis, travel, chess. Office: Creighton Univ 2500 California Plz Omaha NE 68178 Office Fax: 402-280-3359. Business E-Mail: stphns@creighton.edu.

STEPHENSON, ALAN CLEMENTS, lawyer; b. Wilmington, NC, Nov. 7, 1944; s. Abram Clements and Ruth (Smith) Stephenson; m. Shannon Kennedy; children from previous marriage: Edward Taylor, Anne Baldwin. AB in Hist., U. N.C., 1967; JD, U. Va., 1970. Bar: NY 1971. Assoc. Cravath, Swaine & Moore, NYC, 1970-78, ptnr., 1978-88; mng. dir. Wasserstein, Perella and Co. Inc., NYC, 1988-92; ptnr., corp. Cravath, Swaine & Moore LLP, NYC, 1992—. Mem. external adv. bd. undergrad. honors program U. N.C., 1998—. Trustee Cold Spring Harbor Lab., 2003-. Morehead scholar, John M. Morehead Found., 1963. Mem.: NY State Bar Assn., Assn. of Bar of City of NY, Brook Club, Meadow Brook Club, Farmington Country Club, Links Club, Phi Beta Kappa. Office: Cravath Swaine & Moore LLP 825 8th Ave 47th Fl New York NY 10019-7475 Office Phone: 212-474-1400. Office Fax: 212-474-3700. Business E-Mail: astephenson@cravath.com.

STEPHENSON, ARTHUR EMMET, JR., investment company executive; b. Bastrop, La., Aug. 29, 1945; s. Arthur Emmet and Edith Louise Stephenson; m. Toni Lyn Edwards, June 17, 1967; 1 child, Tessa. BS in Fin. magna cum laude, La. State U., 1967; MBA (Ralph Thomas Sayles fellow), Harvard U., 1969. Chartered fin. analyst. Adminstrv. aide to U.S. Sen. Russell Long of La., Washington, 1966; security analyst Fidelity Funds, Boston, 1968; sr. ptnr. Stephenson Ventures; founder, chmn. Gen. Comm., Inc., Domain.Com Inc.; founder, chmn. bd. dirs. StarTek, Inc., 1987—2006. Bd. dirs. Danaher Corp., 1986—2008; founder Charter Bank and Trust, chmn., 1980—91; mem. adv. bd. First Berkshire Fund, 1984—2002, Capital Resources Ptnrs., L.P., 1987—2004; former pub. Law Enforcement Product News, Colo. Book, Pub. Safety Product News, 1990—98, Denver mag., Denver Bus. mag.; founder Stephenson Disaster Mgmt. Inst., La. State U.; bd. dean's adv. Bus. Sch. Harvard U., 2006—09. Del. White House conf., 1980; past. nat. trustee Nat. Symphony Orch., John F. Kennedy Ctr. Performing Arts, 1995—98; past mem. nat. steering com. Norman Rockwell Mus., Stockbridge, Mass.; past mem. Colo. Small bus. Coun.; past mem. assocs. coun. Templeton Coll., Oxford (Eng.) U. Recipient Hall of Fame award, Inc. mag., 1994, Albert Einstein Tech. medal, 1999; named to Hall of Distinction, Coll. Bus. Adminstrn., La. State U., 1999, La. State U., 2006. Mem.: Young Pres. Orgn. (chpt. chmn. 1992—93), Colo. Investment Advisors Assn. (treas., bd. dirs. 1975—76), World Pres.'s Orgn., Chief Execs. Orgn., Harvard U. Bus. Sch. Assn. (internat. pres. 1987—88), So. Calif. Harvard Bus. Sch. Club, Jonathan Club (L.A.), Thunderbird Country Club (Rancho Mirage, Calif.), Colo. Harvard Bus. Sch. Club (pres. 1980—81, chmn. 1981—82), Delta Sigma Pi, Kappa Sigma, Beta Gamma Sigma, Phi Kappa Phi, Omicron Delta Kappa. Office: 400 Nevada Way Boulder City NV 89005

STEPHENSON, BARBARA J., United States Ambassador to Panama; PhD in English Lit. Econ., polit. officer US Dept. State, Panama, polit. officer San Salvador, El Salvador, The Hague, Netherlands, polit., mil. officer South Africa, desk officer UK, spl. asst. to the under sec. for polit. affairs, consul gen., chief of mission Curacao, Netherlands Antilles, Aruba, 1998—2001, consul gen. Belfast, Northern Ireland, 2001—04, dir. planning, office the coordinator for reconstrn. and stabilization, dep. sr., advisor to the sec. and dep. coord. Iraq, US amb. to Panama Panama City, 2008—. Office: DOS Amb 9100 Panama City Pl Washington DC 20521-9100*

STEPHENSON, GARY VAN, aerospace engineer; b. Huron, SD, Mar. 25, 1958; s. Phillip Carlyle Stephenson and Barbara Jean (O'Leary) Yeager; m. Sandra Lynn Deault, June 4, 1977 (div. Feb. 1989); m. Nancy Watkins Gossett, July 19, 1991. BS in Physics, Mont. State U., Bozeman, 1983, BA in Philosophy, 1983. Mem. tech. staff Hughes Aircraft Co., El Segundo, Calif., 1983-86; sr. engr. ITT-Aerospace Optical Div., Ft. Wayne, Ind., 1986-88; electro-optics engr. Weyerhaeuser Co., Federal Way, Wash., 1988-89; systems engr. Hughes Aircraft Co., Seattle, 1989—97, The Boeing Co., Seattle, 1997—2006, Boeing Satellite Systems, El Segundo, Calif., 2007—. Pres. Seculine Consulting, Redondo Beach, Calif., 1989—. With US Army, 1976-79. Mem. Rainier Club, Sigma Pi Sigma. Democrat. Episcopalian. Achievements include patents in field. Avocations: skiing, bicycling, hiking. Mailing: PO Box 925 Redondo Beach CA 90277 Home: 411 S Gertruda Ave Redondo Beach CA 90277 Office: Boeing M/S W/S37/H374 PO Box 92919 Los Angeles CA 90009 Personal E-mail: seculine@gmail.com.

STEPHENSON, HERMAN HOWARD, retired banker; b. Wichita, Kans., July 15, 1929; s. Herman Horace and Edith May (Wayland) S.; m. Virginia Anne Ross, Dec. 24, 1950, (dec. March 2004); children: Ross Wayland, Neal Bevan, Jann Edith. BA, U. Mich., 1950; JD with distinction, U. Mo., Kansas City, 1958, LLD (hon.), 1993. Bar: Kans. 1958. With City Nat. Bank, Kansas City, Mo., 1952-54, City Bond & Mortgage Co., Kansas City, 1954-59, Bank of Hawaii, Honolulu, 1959-94, CEO, 1989-94, ret. chmn., 1994—. Bd. dirs. Friends of Cancer Rsch. Ctr. Hawaii. With US Army, 1950—52. Mem.: Pacific Forum/CSIS (bd. govs.), Navy League U.S., Waialae Country Club, Oahu Country Club, Eagle Bend Country Club, Rotary, Pi Eta Sigma, Kappa Sigma.

STEPHENSON, HUGH EDWARD, JR., retired surgeon; b. Columbia, Mo., June 1, 1922; s. Hugh Edward and Doris (Pryor) S.; m. Sarah Norfleet Dickinson, Aug. 15, 1964; children: Hugh Edward III, Ann Dunlop. AB, BS, U. Mo., Columbia, 1943; MD, Washington U., St. Louis, 1945. Diplomate Am. Bd. Surgery, Am. Bd. Thoracic Surgery. Mem. faculty U. Mo. Sch. Medicine, Columbia, 1953—; prof. surgery U. Mo. Hugh E. Stephenson Jr. Dept. Surgery, Columbia, 1956—, chmn. dept. surgery, 1956—60, chief div. gen. surgery, 1976—87, chief staff, 1982—94; John Growdon Disting. prof. surgery emeritus U. Mo. Sch. Medicine, Columbia, 1987—, interim dean, 1988—89, assoc. dean, 1989—92, dist. prof. surgery emeritus, 1993; curator U. Mo. System, 1996—. Pres. bd. curators U. Mo., 2000; Markle scholar acad. medicine, 1954-60. Author: Immediate Care of the Acutely Ill and Injured, 2d edit, 1974, Cardiac Arrest and Resuscitation, 4th edit., 1975, The Kicks That Count; Contbr. articles to profl. jours. Named one of Outstanding Young Men of Nation, Nat. Jr. C. of C., 1956, James IV Surg. Traveler Gt. Britain, 1962, Dist. Faculty award, 1989. Mem. ACS, AMA (del., chmn. coun. on med. edn. 1994-95, co-chmn. liaison com. on med. edn. 1995, pres. surgical caucus 1996, Stephenson Endowed chair of Surgery), Vascular Surgery Soc., Soc. Thoracic Surgeons, So. Thoracic Surgery Assn., So. Med. Assn. (coun., pres. 2001), Mo. Med. Assn. (chmn. jud. coun. 1986-, v.p. 1986-), Beta Theta Pi (trustees, pres. gen. frat. 1978-81) Baptist. Home: 5 Danforth Cir Columbia MO 65201-3509 Office: University of Missouri Hugh E Stephenson Jr Dept Surgery 1 Hospital Dr Columbia MO 65201-5276 Home Phone: 573-442-3834; Office Phone: 573-882-5645.

STEPHENSON, JANE CONNELL, artist, educator; b. Ruston, La., Feb. 23, 1932; m. Alvis Doyle Stephenson, June 28, 1957; children: John Thomas, Deborah Lynn, Mary Elizabeth, Ann Liddell. BA, La. Tech. U., 1953; degree in art edn., U. Colo., 1955. Art instr. Clarksdale (Miss.) Ind. Sch. Dist., Clarksdale; art tchr. Dallas Ind. Sch. Dist., 1955—58; designer Atelier Stephenson, Dallas, 1977—85; artist Artisan Studio, Dallas, 1989—99; asst., masters class in figure La. Tech. U., Ruston, 1989—95; faculty art North Lake Coll. Continuing Edn., Dallas, 1983—93; faculty art dept. Creative Art Ctr., Dallas, 2001—04. Leader drawing tours, The Netherlands, Belgium, France, 1992—96, 1998—99, Italy, 1999. Exhibitions include Found. Fighting Blindness, 1990—92, 1994, Irving Art Ctr., 1992, Goodrich Gallery, 2001, Art in the Metro Plex, Ft. Worth, Represented in permanent collections Miss. Art Mus., Jackson, Jackson Art Mus., Sr. Voice, 2004. Recipient Exxon Mobile Award of Excellence, Tex. Neighbors Exhibit, 2002; named one of Nation's Top 50 Experimental Artists, Artist Mag., 1991. Mem.: Irving Art Assn. (recipient over 150 awards in 200 nat. exhbns.; featured in article in Sr. Voice, 2004), Nat. Women's Mus. Washington, Nat. Watercolor Soc. Calif. (signature mem.), Watercolor Soc. Miss. (signature mem.), Watercolor Soc. La. (signature mem.), Watercolor Soc. Tex. (signature mem.), Okla. Watercolor Soc., Western Fedn. Watercolor Socs., Southwestern Art Soc. (signature mem., bd. dirs.), Tex. Visual Art Assn. (signature mem., bd. dirs., show chmn.). Avocations: travel, music, anthropology, gardening, reading. Home: 3524 Northaven Rd Dallas TX 75229 Home Phone: 214-357-4261; Office Phone: 469-766-1617. Personal E-mail: jane.stephenson@sbcglobal.net.

STEPHENSON, LARRY KIRK, geography educator, financial planner; b. Seattle, Sept. 22, 1944; s. Norman Eugene and Virginia Dare (Frost) S.; m. Margery Alsever, Aug. 15, 1992 (dec. Sept. 2006); children: Matthew Alan, Leah Anela. BS, Ariz. State U., 1966, MA, 1971; PhD, U. Cin., 1973. Manpower rsch. analyst Employment Security Commn. of Ariz., 1969-70; asst. prof. geography U. Hawaii, Hilo, 1973-76, assoc. prof., 1976-78, chmn. dept. geography, 1975-77; planner Ariz. Dept. Health Svcs., Phoenix, 1978-84; strategic planner City of Glendale, Ariz., 1984-92; pub. health analyst Gila River Indian Cmmty., Ariz., 1992-98, econ. devel. planner, 1998—2005; exec. dir. Eastern Ariz. Counties Orgn., 2006—. Vis. lectr. dept. geography Ariz. State U., 1978, adj. assoc. prof., 1979—; vis. assoc. prof. dept. geography, area devel. and urban planning U. Ariz., 1978; faculty U. Phoenix, 1979—; adj. prof. Golden Gate U., 1981—, Coll. St. Francis, 1982—; ptnr. Urban Rsch. Assocs., Phoenix, 1981—; faculty Troy State U., 1990-. Author: Statistics for Health Managers, 1981; co-author: Student Study Guide and Instructor's Manual to accompany Geography: A Modern Synthesis, 4 edits., 1975-83; editor: Kohala keia: Collected Expressions of a Community, 1977; contbr. articles to profl. jours., chpts. to textbooks. Active. Hawaii Island Health Planning Coun., 1974-78, Glendale Cmty. Colls. Pres.'s Coun., 1986-92. With US Army, 1966-68. NDEA fellow 1971-72. Mem. Am. Inst. Cert. Planners, Am Planning Assn., Assn. Am. Geographers, Ariz. Planning Assn. (pres. 1987—), SW Profl. Geog. Assn., Lambda Alpha, Gila County CC Dist. (Ariz.) (mem.

governing bd. 2004-). Unitarian Universalist. Home: HC 4 Box 28K Payson AZ 85541 Office: PO Box 2010 Payson AZ 85547 Office Phone: 928-972-5378. Personal E-mail: lstephe739@aol.com.

STEPHENSON, LINDA S., school librarian; b. Flint, Mich., July 26, 1946; d. Raymond E. Weber and Hilda Gillig; m. Jack P. Stephenson. BS in Edn., Ind. U., Bloomington, 1970, degree, 1974; M in Bibl. Studies, Dallas Theol. Sem., 1984; MLS, U. North Tex., Denton, 1987. Tchr. Maconaquah Sch. Corp., Bunker Hill, Ind., 1970—71, sch. libr., 1971—84; asst. libr. Dallas Bible Coll., 1984—86; reference libr. Dallas Bapt. U., 1987—. Mem.: Assn. Christian Librs. Baptist. Avocations: travel, reading, gardening. Office: Dallas Baptist Univ 3000 Mountain Creek Pky Dallas TX 75211 Office Fax: 214-333-5323. Business E-Mail: lindas@dbu.edu.

STEPHENSON, MASON WILLIAMS, lawyer; b. Atlanta, May 29, 1946; s. Donald Grier and Katherine Mason (Williams) S.; m. Linda Frances Partee, June 13, 1970; children: Andrew Mason, Walter Martin. AB cum laude, Davidson Coll., 1968; JD, U. Chgo., 1971. Bar: Ga. 1971, U.S. Dist. Ct. (no. dist.) Ga. 1985. Assoc. Alston, Miller & Gaines, Atlanta, 1971-76, ptnr., 1976-77, Trotter, Bondurant, Griffin, Miller & Hishon, Atlanta, 1977-82, Bondurant, Miller, Hishon & Stephenson, Atlanta, 1982-85, King & Spalding, LLP, Atlanta, 1985—, mng. ptnr. Atlanta office, 2001—. Fin. com. Atlanta Olympic Organizing Com., 1988—90. Mem. ABA (sect. bus. law, real property, probate and trust sect.), Am. Coll. Real Estate Lawyers, State Bar Ga. (exec. com., real property law sect. 1989-97, chair intangible rec. tax com. 1994-97), Atlanta Bar Assn. (chair real estate sect. 1981-82), Causeway Club, Capital City Club, Phi Beta Kappa, Phi Delta Phi. Avocations: boating, skiing, jogging. Office: King & Spalding LLP 1180 Peachtree St Atlanta GA 30309 Office Phone: 404-572-4600. Office Fax: 404-572-5100. Business E-Mail: mstephenson@kslaw.com.

STEPHENSON, MIMOSA SUMMERS, literature and language professor; b. Huntsburg, Ohio, Nov. 18, 1939; d. Philip Sidney Summers and Edna Elizabeth White; m. William Alva Stephenson, Apr. 2, 1988; m. Ronald Gene Schraer, May 29, 1968 (div. Dec. 8, 1983); children: Mimosa Schraer Flores, Amanda Schraer Lopez, Adam David Schraer. PhD, Tex. Technol. Coll., Lubbock, 1965. Lectr. Hong Kong Bapt. Coll., 1965—67; assoc. prof. William Jewell Coll., Liberty, Mo., 1967—73; prof. English U. Tex. Brownsville, 1973—. Fulbright lectr. Xiamen U., China, 2000—01. Contbr. articles to profl. jours. Missionary journeyman So. Bapt. Conv., Hong Kong, 1965—67. Recipient Chancellor's Outstanding Tchg. award, U. Tex. Sys., 1992, NISOD award, 2004; Nat. Def. fellowship, 1961—64. Mem.: Assn. Lit. Scholars and Critics, Nathaniel Hawthorne Soc., SW Conf. Christianity and Lit. (pres. 2004—05). Baptist. Office: Univ Texas Brownsville 80 Ft Brown Brownsville TX 78520 Office Fax: 956-882-7064. Personal E-mail: willsteph@aol.com. Business E-Mail: mimosa.stephenson@utb.edu.

STEPHENSON, NEAL TOWN, writer; b. Fort Meade, Md., Oct. 31, 1959; BA in Geography, Boston U., 1981. Author: (fiction) The Big U, 1984, Zodiac, 1988, Snow Crash, 1992, The Diamond Age, 1995 (Hugo Award for Best Novel, 1996), Cryptonomicon, 1999, Quicksilver, 2003 (Arthur C. Clarke award, 2004), The Confusion, 2004 (Locus award, 2005), The System of the World, 2005 (Prometheus award, Libertarian Futurist Soc., 2005, Locus award, 2005), Anathem, 2008 (Publishers Weekly bestseller); author: (under pseudonym Stephen Bury, with J. Frederick George) Interface, 1994, The Cobweb, 1996; author: (short stories) Spew, 1994, The Great Simoleon Caper, 1995, Jipi and the Paranoid Chip, 1997, others; contbr. numerous short stories, articles to mags. Mailing: c/o Darhansoff Verrill Feldman Lit Agy 236 W 26th St New York NY 10001 Office Phone: 917-305-1300. Office Fax: 917-305-1400.*

STEPHENSON, RANDALL L., telecommunications industry executive; b. Oklahoma City, Apr. 22, 1960; m. Lenise H. Stephenson. BS in Acctg., Ctrl. State U., Edmond, Okla., 1982; MS in Acctg., U. Okla., Norman. With Southwestern Bell Tel. Co., Oklahoma City, 1982, area mgr. corp. taxes, 1986—91, dist. mgr. fin. analysis, 1991—92; dir. fin. SBC Internat. SBC Comm., Inc., Mexico City, 1992—96, contr. San Antonio, 1996—97, v.p., contr., 1997, sr. exec. v.p., CFO, 2001—04; chmn. Cingular Wireless LLC, 2003—04; COO SBC Comm., Inc., 2004—05, AT&T Inc. (merger of SBC Comm. & AT&T Corp.), San Antonio, 2005—07, chmn., pres., CEO, 2007—. Bd. dirs. Cingular Wireless LLC, 2001—06, AT&T Inc., 2005—, Emerson Electric, 2006—; mem. audit com. H.E. Butt Grocery Co. Mem. nat. exec. bd. Boy Scouts Am.; mem. exec. com., audit com. United Way San Antonio; bd. mem. San Antonio Met. Missions Bd. Named one of 50 Who Matter Now, Business 2.0, 2007. Mem.: Okla. Soc. CPAs. Office: AT&T Inc 175 E Houston St PO Box 2933 San Antonio TX 78299-2933*

STEPHENSON, RICHARD ISMERT, lawyer; b. Augusta, Kans., Oct. 13, 1937; s. Paul Noble and Dorothy May (Ismert) S.; m. Mary Lynn Bryden, July 2, 1967 (div. 1973); 1 child, Richard William; m. Linda Cox, Apr. 5, 1976. BA, U. Kans., 1958; JD, U. Mich., 1965. Bar: Kans. 1965, U.S. Dist. Ct. Kans. 1965, U.S. Ct. Appeals (10th cir.) 1965. Assoc. Fleeson, Gooing, Coulson & Kitch, Wichita, Kans., 1965-72, ptnr., 1973-95; gen. counsel RAGE Inc. and Affiliated Cos., Wichita, 1995—. Lt. (j.g.) USNR, 1959-62. Recipient Hilden Gibson award, U. Kans., 1958. Mem. ABA (forum on franchising), Def. Rsch. Inst., Internat. Assn. Def. Counsel, Kans. Bar Assn., Wichita Bar Assn., Wichita Country Club, Pi Sigma Alpha, Beta Theta Pi. Avocations: golf, fishing. Home: 9203 Killarney Wichita KS 67206-4027 Office: RAGE Inc 1313 N Webb Rd Ste 200 Wichita KS 67206-4077 Office Phone: 316-634-1888. Business E-Mail: dick@rage-inc.com.

STEPHENSON, SHERRY MADELINE, trade economist; d. Joe Harrell and Bettie Beasley Stephenson; children: Matthew Hector Travis, Corinne Louise Madeline. MA, NYU, 1976; PhD, Grad. Inst. Internat. Studies, Geneva, 1987. Trade specialist UNCTAD, Geneva, 1978—80, GATT, Geneva, 1980—82; prin. adminstr. Trade Directorate OECD, Paris, 1983—91; advisor Ministry of Trade, Jakarta, Indonesia, 1992—95; prin. trade specialist Trade Unit OAS, Washington, 1995—2000, dep. dir. for trade, 2000—05, dir. dept. trade and competitiveness, 2006—, dir. instn. rels., 2008. Cons. Pacific Econ. Cooperation Coun., Singapore, 1993—2000, Asian Devel. Bank, Manila, 1993—96, World Bank, Washington, 1995—97, USAID, 1997—2000. Editor: (academic books) Services Trade in the Western Hemisphere, 2000, Services Trade Liberalization and Facilitation, 2002. Mem.: European Inst., Internat. Trade and Fin. Assn., Pacific Econ. Cooperation Coun., Inter-American Dialogue, Cosmos Club. Office: Orgn Am States 1889 F St NW Washington DC 20006 Office Phone: 202-458-3342. Business E-Mail: sstephenson@oas.org.

STEPHENSON, THOMAS A., publishing executive; b. SD; BS, Northern State U., Aberdeen, SD; MBA, U. Minn. With Knight Ridder Newspapers, 1975—97; sr. v.p. ops. & adminstrn. San Antonio Express-News, 1997, exec. v.p. & gen. mgr., pres. & pub., 2006—. Bd. dirs. United Way, San Antonio, Econ. Devel. Found, San Antonio, The Chamber, San Antonio. Mem.: Tex. Daily Newspaper Assn. (legis. affairs com.). Office: San Antonio Express-News 301 Ave E San Antonio TX 78205 Office Phone: 210-250-3710. E-mail: tstephen@express-news.net.*

STEPHENSON, THOMAS F., United States Ambassador to Portugal; b. Wilmington, Del. married; 4 children. AB in Econs., Harvard Coll., Cambridge, Mass.; MBA, Harvard Bus. Sch.; JD, Boston Coll. Law Sch. Securities analyst Fidelity Mgmt. Co.; founder Fidelity Ventures, pres., 1977—87; ptnr. Sequoia Capital, 1988—2007; US amb. to Portugal US Dept. State, Lisbon, 2007—. Mem. bd. overseers, exec. com. Harvard U., Stanford U. Hoover Instn.; bd. advisors Stanford Inst. Econ. Policy Rsch.; bd. dirs. Conservation Internat., Wilson Ctr. Coun.; corp. fund vice chmn. Kennedy Ctr.; bd. & com. mem. Tufts New Eng. Med. Ctr. Office: DOS Amb 5320 Lisbon Pl Washington DC 20521-5320*

STEPHENSON, TONI EDWARDS, publishing, internet domain communications and investment company executive; b. Bastrop, La., July 23, 1945; d. Sidney Crawford and Grace Erleene Little; m. Arthur Emmet Stephenson Jr., June 17, 1967; 1 child, Tessa Lyn. Grad. owner/pres. mgmt. program, Harvard Bus. Sch. Pres. dir. domain.com Inc.; pres., dir. Gen. Comm., Inc., Neveda; ptnr. Stephenson Ventures, 1977—. Past. pres. Children's Hosp. Assn. Vols.; past troop leader Girl Scouts Am.; past dir. Anchor Ctr. for Blind Children; past dir. bd. dean's advisors Harvard U. Bus. Sch.; past dir. The Children's Hosp., St. Joseph's Hosp., Cherry Creek H.S. Parent Tchr. Conf. Orgn. Mem.: DAR, Thunderbird Country Club, Delta Gamma. Business E-Mail: domainmaster@great.net.

STEPHENSON-BENNETT, MICHELLE ANNETTE, music educator; b. Hillsdale, Mich., Apr. 4, 1967; d. Robert Marcus and Carol Ann Stephenson. BMus, We. Mich. U., Kalamazoo, 1990, postgrad., 1994—2000; MusM, Oreg. State U., Corvallis, 2004. Cert. profl. tchr. Dir. band Edwardsburg Pub. Schs., Mich., 1990—94, Wayland Union Schs., Mich., 1994—. Past mem. sch. improvement com. Wayland Schs. Founder 7th Grade Drumming Cir., 2009. Recipient Disney Tchr. award, 2001; World Music grant, 2008—. Mem.: Mich. Edn. Assn., Mich. State Band and Orch. Assn. (state solo/ensemble adjudicator 2000—, officer dist. 10 2006—08, pres. mid. sch. solo and ensemble 2006—08, past officer dist. 6), We. Mich. U. Alumni Assn., Sigma Alpha Iota (mem. alumni, past officer). Avocations: motorcycling, gardening. Office: Wayland Union Schs 701 Wildcat Dr Wayland MI 49348 Personal E-mail: dubussi@yahoo.com.

STEPHENS-RICH, BARBARA E., minister, educator; Ordained minister 1975. Min. Califon United Meth. Ch., NJ, 1976—81, Trinity United Meth. Ch., Clifton, NJ, 1981—86, Salem United Meth. Ch., Sandusky, Ohio, 1990—91, Fairview United Meth. Ch., Niles, Ohio, 1991—95, First United Meth. Ch., Girard, Ohio, 1996—2001; chaplain Elyria United Meth. Home, Ohio, 1987—90; dir. religion and edn. Lakeside Assn., Ohio, 2001—06; min. Bloomville United Meth. Ch., Ohio, 2007, Columbus Ave. United Meth. Ch., Sandusky, 2007. Mem. bd. ordained min., No. NJ, 1977—84, ea. Ohio, 1992—2000; adj. faculty Drew Theological Sch., Madison, NJ, 1983—85. Author: Chicken Soup for the Single Parent and Soul, 2005. Avocations: reading, hiking, swimming, cross country skiing, travel. Personal E-mail: bstephensrich@aol.com.

STEPIEN, CAROL ANN, molecular geneticist, fisheries educator; b. Cleve., Apr. 21, 1958; d. Theodore John and Anna M. (Bowerman) Stepien. BS, Bowling Green U., 1979; MS, U. So. Calif., 1980, PhD, 1985. Lectr. U. San Diego, 1984-86; rsch. assoc. Hubbs Marine Research Inst., San Diego, 1985-86, NSF and Scripps Instn. Oceanography, La Jolla, Calif., 1986-88; Sloan postdoctoral fellowship in molecular evolution, 1989-91; rsch. assoc. NRC/Marine Fisheries/NOAA, 1991-92; asst. prof. molecular evolutionary biology Case Western Res. U., Cleve., 1992-2000; prof., dir. Gt. Lakes Environ. Genetics Lab. Cleve. State U., 2000—04; dir. Lake Erie Rsch. Ctr., Univ. Toledo, 2004—; prof. dept. earth, ecol. and environ. sci. U. Toledo, 2004—. Editor: (with Thomas D. Kocher) Molecular Systematics of Fishes, 1997; edit. bd. Molecular Phylogenetics and Evolution; assoc. editor Jour. of Great Lakes Rsch.; contbr. articles to profl. jours. NSF fellow, 1986-88; Lerner Marine grantee Am. Mus. Natural History, 1982-84. Mem. Am. Soc. Ichthyologists and Herpetologists (Best Paper 1983), Am. Fisheries Soc., Soc. for Study of Evolution, Soc. Systematic Biology. Avocations: scuba diving, underwater photography. Office: Lake Erie Ctr Univ Toledo 6200 Bayshore Rd Toledo OH 43618 Home Phone: 440-498-0329; Office Phone: 419-530-8360. Fax: 216-687-5393. Business E-Mail: carol.stepien@utoledo.edu.

STEPLETON, JAMES, composer; BA in Communication Arts, Mich. State U., East Lansing, 1963, MA in Philosophy, 1965; MusM, Ball State U., Muncie, Ind., 1973. Composer: (guitar) Serenade for Solo Guitar (Mario Castelnuovo award, 1975), (Operas) The Awakening, (voice and orchestra) Five Sonnets of Michelangelo. Recipient Margaret Jory Copying award, Am. Music Ctr., 2003; Hon. fellowship, Woodrow Wilson Found., 1963. Mem.: Am. Music Ctr. Office: Douglas Moore Fund Am Opera 30 W 26th St Ste 1001 New York NY 10010 Office Phone: 212-366-5260 40. Business E-Mail: douglasmoovefund@att.net.

STEPONAITIS, VINCAS PETRAS, archaeologist, anthropologist, educator; b. Boston, Aug. 10, 1953; s. Vincas and Elena (Povydis) S.; m. Laurie Cameron, Dec. 31, 1976; children: Elena Anne, Lillian Kazimiera. AB in Anthropology magna cum laude, Harvard U., 1974; MA in Anthropology, U. Mich., 1975, PhD in Anthropology, 1980. From lectr. to assoc. prof. dept. anthropology SUNY, Binghamton, 1979-87; assoc. prof. U. N.C., Chapel Hill, 1988-94, prof., 1995—, dir. Rsch. Labs. Archaeology, 1988—. Guest worker Nat. Bur. Stds., 1979; adj. lectr. dept. anthropology SUNY, Binghamton, 1979; lectr. and presenter in field. Author: Ceramics, Chronology, and Community Patterns, An Archaeological Study at Moundville, 1983, Archaeology of the Moundville Chiefdom, 1998, (CD-Rom) Excavating Occaneechi Town, 1998; editor Southeastern Archaeology, 1984-87; regional editor Investigations in Am. Archaeology, 1987-91; mem. editl. bd. Prehistory Press, 1990-97, Southern Cultures, 1992—, Am. Archaeology, 1996-2000; contbr. articles to profl. jours. Smithsonian Instn. fellow, 1978-79; grantee NSF, 1978-80, 83, 89-92, 94, 2000, 05, IMLS, 2003, Wenner-Gren Found., 1981, 86-88, Nat. Geographic Soc., 1987-88, Z. Smith Reynolds Found., 1992-94, Alcoa Found. 2005. Fellow Am. Anthrop. Assn.; mem. Soc. Am. Archaeology (Presdl. Recognition award 1993-94, exec. com. 1983-84, treas. 1992-94, pres. 1997-99), Archaeological Conservancy (bd. dirs. 2000—, chmn. 2003-07), NAGPRA (rev. com. 2004-09), Ctr. Maya Rsch. (bd. dirs. 2002-), Southeastern Archaeol. Conf. (editor 1984-87, pres. 1990-92), N.C. Archaeol. Soc. (exec. sec. 1988-91, sec. 1991-96), N.C. Archaeol. Coun. (exec. com. 1988-92), Archaeol. Soc. S.C., Ala. Archaeol. Soc., Miss. Archaeol. Soc., La. Archaeol. Soc. Office: U NC Rsch Labs Archaeology Alumni Bldg Cb 3120 Chapel Hill NC 27599-3120

STEPP, MARY ANN, medical educator; b. Lexington, Ky., Dec. 25, 1957; d. John R. Stepp and Brooks J. Moore; m. Jerry A. Bell; children: Christina M. Bell, Allison R. Bell. PhD, Boston U., Mass, 1985. Prof. GWU Med. Sch., Washington, 1990—2008. Office: GWU Med sch 2300 I St NW Washington DC 20037 Office Fax: 202-994-8885.

STEPTO, ROBERT BURNS, literature and language professor; b. Chgo., Oct. 28, 1945; s. Robert Charles and Ann Burns Stepto; m. Michele Anne Leiss, June 21, 1967; children: Gabriel Burns, Rafael Hawkins. BA, Trinity Coll. Hartford, 1966; PhD, Stanford U., Calif., 1974. Asst. prof. English Williams Coll., Williamstown, Mass.; asst. prof. English & African Am. Studies, Yale U., 1974—79, assoc. prof., 1979—83, prof., 1984—. Contbr. poetry to anthology. Recipient Alumni medal, Trinity Coll. Hartford, 1986, Alumni award, 1999, Robert Frost Chair award, Bread Loaf Sch. English, 1995, Frank & Eleanor Griffiths Chair award, 2007; named Best Am. Essays award, 1995—97; Grad. fellow, Woodrow Wilson Found., 1966—67, Rsch. fellowship, NEH, 1981—82, Sr. Faculty fellowship, Yale U., 1981—82. Avocations: travel, art, music. Office: Yale Univ 81 Wall St New Haven CT 06520-3388 Office Fax: 203-432-2102. Business E-Mail: robert.stepto@yale.edu.

STEPTOE, MARY LOU, lawyer; b. Washington, July 15, 1949; d. Philip Pendleton and Irene (Hellen) S.; m. Peter E. Carson, Sept. 1986; children: Elizabeth Maud, Julia Grace. BA, Occidental Coll., 1971; JD, U. Va., 1974. Bar: Va., 1974, Supreme Ct., 1987, D.C. 1996. Staff atty., Bur. of Competition FTC, Washington, 1974-79, atty. advisor to commr., 1979-86, exec. asst. to chmn., 1988-89, assoc. dir., Bur. of Competition, 1989-90, dep. dir., 1990-92, acting dir., 1992-95, dep. dir., 1995-96; ptnr. Skadden Arps Slate Meagher & Flom LLP, Washington. Office Phone: 202-371-7020. Business E-Mail: msteptoe@skadden.com.

STEPTOE, SONJA, legal firm administrator; b. Lutcher, La., June 16, 1960; d. Eldridge Willie and Rosa Jane Steptoe. BA in Econs., U. Mo., 1982, B in Journalism, 1982; JD, Duke U. Law Sch., 1985. Staff reporter Wall St. Jour., NYC, 1985—90; sr. editor Sports Illustrated, NYC, 1990—2001, People Mag., NYC, 2001—02; nat. corr. CNN Sports, NYC, 1999—2001; corr. HBO Sports, 1995—2001; sr. corr. Time Mag., LA, 2002—06, deputy news dir., 2006—07; client devel. mgr. O'Melveny & Myers LLP, LA, 2007—. Bd. visitors Duke Law Sch., Durham, NC, 2007—, Knight Commn. on Intercollegiate Athletics, 2008—; mem. U. Mo. Strategic Develop. Bd., 1988—. Co-author: (book) Guide to Women's Golf, 1993, A Kind of Grace" The Autobiography of the World's Greatest Female Athlete, 1997. Bd. mem. Alvin Ailey Dance Sch., NYC, 2001—02, Knight Commn. Intercollegiate Athletics, 2008—. Recipient Emmy award, Nat. Assn. TV Arts and Sci., 1998, Nat. Headliner award, Press Club of Atlantic City, 1999, Disting. Alumni award, U. Mo., Duke Law Sch. Young Alumni award, 1994, 2000. Mem.: ABA. Business E-Mail: ssteptoe@omm.com.

STERBA, JEFFRY E., energy executive; BA in Econ. summa cum laude, Washington Univ., St. Louis; post-grad study in Econ., Washington Univ., Univ. N.Mex. Various positions PNM (subs. PNM Resources), Albuquerque, 1977—98; exec. v.p. USEC, Md., 1998—2000; pres. PNM (subs. PNM Resources), Albuquerque, 2000; chmn., pres., CEO PNM Resources, Albuquerque, 2000—08, chmn., CEO, 2008—. Chmn. Edison Elec. Inst., 2007—, Elec. Power Rsch. Inst. Former campaign chmn. United Way Ctrl. N. Mex.; mem. Gov. Bus. Adv. Coun.; bd. dir. US C. of C.; co-chmn. Albuquerque Econ. Forum. Mem.: Mortar Board, Omicron Delta Kappa. Office: PNM Resources Alvarado Sq Albuquerque NM 87158-0001 Office Phone: 505-241-4568. Office Fax: 505-241-2368. Business E-Mail: jeff.sterba@pnmresources.com.*

STERLIN, SHRITA D., legislative staff member; Chief of staff to Assemblywoman Crystal D. Peoples NY State Assembly, Albany, NY; comm. dir. to Edolphus Towns US House of Reps., Washington. Mem.: Delta Sigma Theta. Democrat. Office: 2232 Rayburn House Office Bldg Washington DC 20515 Office Phone: 202-225-5936. Office Fax: 202-225-1018. Business E-Mail: shrita.sterlin@mail.house.gov.*

STERLING, ANNE D., not-for-profit developer; b. Evanston, Ill., Aug. 24, 1938; d. Theodore Craig and Barbara (Cox) Diller; m. Keir B. Sterling, Apr. 3, 1961; children: Duncan D., Warner S., Theodore C. BA in History, NYU, 1964. Editl. staff Columbia U. FORUM Quar. Jour., NYC, 1969; asst. editor Columbia U. Sch. Bus. Hermes Mag., NYC, 1970; assoc., rights and permissions Random House Pub., NYC, 1974, assoc., inst. human resources, 1975; writing asst. Robert K. Parker, Syndicated Columnist, 1975; notes editor Vassar Coll. Quar. Mag., Poughkeepsie, NY, 1977—80; cmty. editor Rhinebeck Gazette-Advertiser, NY, 1979—80; writing instr., BOCES program gifted children Poughkeepsie Pub. Schs., 1982—83. Chair selection com. Am. Field Svc. Fgn. Exch. Student Program, 1979—80; outreach parent Johns Hopkins U. Ctr. Talented Youth, 1986—88; pres. Bel Air Mid. Sch. PTA, Md., 1986—88; mem. Harford County Bd. Edn., Md., 1988—94, v.p., 1992—93; parent representative Phillips Acad., Andover, Mass., 1993—2007; pres. Harford County Bd. Edn., Md., 1993—94; exec. com. Friends of Boatwright Libr., U. Richmond, 1997—2000, 2004—; chair Va. Women's Network, 1998—2000; lobbyist Va. Women's Netrwork, 2000—02; mem. adv. bd. County of Henrico Pub. Libr., Va., 1998—; pres. Coll. Hills Civic Assn., Richmond, 1998—99, Coll. Hills Women's Club, Richmond, 1999; del. UN NGO Conf., NYC, 1999, 2001, 2003, 2007; dir. Internat. Assn. Torch Clubs, 2000—04, pres.-elect, 2004—06, pres., 2006—08; editor ALTA Voice, Am. Libr. Assn. Trustees and Advocates Divsn., 2003—05, pres.-elect, 2005—06, pres., 2006—07; del. UN conf. on the status of women; League Women Voters, US, 2004, nominating com., 2006—08; project team facilitator Leadership Met. Richmond, 2004, mem. programs com., 2007—08. Mem.: NOW, ACLU, AAUW (Va., v.p. pub. policy 2002—04), ALA, Va. Libr. Assn., World Affairs Coun. Greater Richmond, UN Assn., League Women Voters, Va. (legis. coord. 2005—, adminstr. Va. Gen. Assembly women's round table 2006—, 2nd. v.p. state bd. 2007—, sec., Richmond Met. Area 2008—), Va. Redistricting Coalition, Vassar Club Richmond. Episcopalian. Home: 7104 Wheeler Rd Richmond VA 23229 Office Phone: 804-304-4142. Office Fax: 804-285-9133. Personal E-mail: nimbleleap@aol.com.

STERLING, ARTHUR JAMES, retired legal assistant; b. Pineville, La., July 27, 1944; s. Leon Henry and Dorothy Mae Sterling; children: Hope, Monique, Heather. AA in Bus. Adminstrn., Compton CC, Calif., 1986; student in psychology, U. Southern Calif., LA, 1988—89; AA in Bus. Paralegal, Cerritos CC, Norwalk, Calif., 1994; PhD in Counseling, Progressive Univeral Life Ch., Sacramento, 2000. With U.S. Naval Weapons Sta., Seal Beach, Calif., 1979-83, Norwalk Superior Ct., 1991; law clk.; guidance counselor, 2000—02; ret., 2006. Dave Holt Meml scholar, K.T. Skula meml. scholar, Johnson Controls, Inc. Fund scholar, Amy Welch Meml. scholar. Mem. Soc. for Advancement of Mgmt. (pres.), Phi Beta Lambda (pres.), Associated Student Body (senator, pres.), The Oxford Club, The Highlander Club. Democrat. Avocations: computers, cooking, reading. Home: 4216 Carlin Ave #C Lynwood CA 90262-5278 Personal E-mail: drdoodlebug06@yahoo.com.

STERLING, DONALD T., real estate mogul, professional sports team owner; b. Chgo., 1934; m. Shelly Stein, 1957; 3 children. BA, Calif. State U., LA; JD, Southwestern U. Sch. Law, LA. Owner NBA LA (formerly San Diego) Clippers, 1981—, chmn. bd. Bd. govs. NBA. Founder Donald T. Sterling Charitable Found. Office: LA Clippers Staples Ctr 1111 S Figueroa St Ste 1100 Los Angeles CA 90015*

STERLING, KEIR BROOKS, historian, educator; b. NYC, Jan. 30, 1934; s. Henry Somers and Louise Noel (de Wetter) S.; m. Anne Cox Diller, Apr. 3, 1961; children: Duncan Diller, Warner Strong, Theodore Craig. BS, Columbia U., 1961, MA, 1963, profl. diploma, 1965, PhD, 1973. Asst. to dean Sch. Gen. Studies Columbia U., NYC, 1959-65; rsch. grantee England, 1965-66; adj. instr. history Pace U., NYC and Pleasantville, NY, 1966-71, from asst. adj. prof. to assoc. adj. prof., 1971-77, adj. prof., 1977-83; ordnance br. historian U.S. Army Ordnance Ctr. and Sch., Aberdeen Proving Ground, Md., 1983-94, Ft. Lee, Va., 1994-98; historian U.S. Army Combined Arms Support Command, Ft. Lee, 1998—2008; ind. historian, author, 2008—. Lectr. gen. counseling Bklyn. Coll., CUNY, 1967-68; asst. acad. dean, adj. asst. prof. history, coord. Am. studies program, dir. summer session Marymount Coll., Tarrytown, N.Y., 1968-71; asst. dean Rockland C.C., SUNY, Suffern, 1971-73; vis. prof. Mercy Coll., Westchester C.C., King's Coll., Nyack Coll., U. Wis., 1971, 75, 78-80, 83, Harford (Md.) C.C., 1987-94; instr. Army Logistics Mgmt. Coll., Ft. Lee, 1995—2008; co-project dir. Am. Ornithologists Union Centennial Hist., Project, 1976-89; cons. Arno Press, Inc., 1973-78, Coun. State Colls. of N.J., 1984-85, NSF, 1983—, Am. Trust for Brit. Libr., 1986-89; active Columbia U. Seminar on History and Philosophy of Sci., 1976-83; archivist, historian mem. steering com. sect. mammalogy Internat. Union Biol. Scis., 1985-2007; chair historian/archivist com. Internat. Fedn. Mammalogy, 2007-; judge Ann. Nat. History Day Competition U. Md., 1993-; grant reviewer Tchg. Am. History Program U.S. Dept. Edn., 2003-. Author: Last of the Naturalists: The Career of C. Hart Merriam, 1974, 77; editor: Notes on the Animals of North America (B.S. Barton), 1974; assoc. editor: Am. Nat. Biog., 1989-98; editor, contbr.: Natural Sciences in America, 1974, 68 vols., 1974, Biologists and Their World, 1978, 77 vols.; gen. editor, contbr.: The International History of Mammalogy, 1987—; sr. editor, contbr. (with R. Harmond, G. Cevasco, and L. Hammond) Biographical Dictionary of American and Canadian Naturalists and Environmentalists, 1997; contbg. author: Ground Warfare: An International Encyclopedia, 2002, Dictionary of Am. History, 3d edit., 2003, Encyclopedia of World Environmental History, 2003, Science in Uniform, Uniform in Science, 2007, Military Comm. Ancient Times to the 21st Century, 2007; editor, contbr. to numerous works in history, Am. natural scis., and Am. mil. history. Boy scout leader, Seattle, Ft. Devens, Mass., NYC, Tarrytown, NY, 1953—77; pres. Rhinebeck, NY Hist. Soc., 1982—83; co-v.p. Coll. Hills Civic Assn., Richmond, Va., 2006—07. With US Army, 1954—56. Grantee Theodore Roosevelt Meml. Fund, Am. Mus. Natural History, 1967, Nat. Geog. Soc., 1977, NSF/Am. Soc. Mammalogists, 1978, Pace U., 1980, 81, NSF, 1981-82, IREX, 1982; recipient Editor's Quill Award, Internat. Assn. of Torch Clubs, 2003. Mem.: History of Sci. Soc., Orgn. Am. Historians, Am. Hist. Assn., Assn. Bibliography of History (mem. coun. 1994—98), Am. Soc. Environ. History (sec., mem. governing bd., editor newsletter), Am. Ornithologists Union (co-chmn. centennial hist. com., mem. archives com., grantee 1976, 1977), Am. Soc. Mammalogists (mem. archives com., mem. 75th ann. com.), Phi Delta Kappa, Sigma Tau Delta, Phi Alpha Theta. Democrat. Episcopalian. Avocations: reading, travel. Home and Office: 7104 Wheeler Rd Richmond VA 23229-6939 Business E-Mail: kbs1934@cs.com.

STERLING, RICHARD LEROY, English and foreign language educator; b. Atlantic City, Feb. 18, 1941; s. Richard Leroy and Anne (Bass) S. BA, Am. U., 1968; MA, Cath. U., 1971; PhD, Howard U., 1990. Head Start tchr. DC Pub. Schs., summer 1968, tchr. French and English, adult and continuing edn., 1969-71, 76-83; instr. French Howard U., Washington, 1973-76, grad. tchg. asst., 1983-85, instr., lectr. in French, 1985-89; tchr. English Cmty.-Based Orgns., DC Pub. Schs., 1989-91; asst. prof. French and English Bowie (Md.) State U., 1991-97, assoc. prof. French, 1997—2008, dir. modern langs. program, 1997—, full prof. French, 2008—. Tchr. summer enrichment program for gifted children Sch. Edn., Howard U., summers 1985, 86; tchr. ESL, DC Pub. Schs., summer, 1989, 94; asst. coord. Humanities Immersion Program, Project Access for H.S. Students, Bowie State U., summer 1997-98; vice-chmn. World Centennial Conf.; French, Am. and Planetary Dimensions of Saint-John Perse, U. DC, 1987; mem. adv. coun. Northeast Conf. Tchg. Fgn. Langs; NAACP-ACT-SO competition humanities judge 1997-2000; adj. assoc. prof. English, Southeastern U., Washington, summer 1998-2008, adj. prof., 2008-; judge DC Pub. Schs. World Langs. Festival, 2001; presenter, book reviewer in field. Author: The Prose Works of Saint-John Perse: Towards an Understanding of His Poetry, 1994; contbg. editor MaComere Rev., 2003-07; contbr. articles to profl. jours. Active Assn. Democratique des Francais a L.Etranger, 1988—, Senegal friendship com. Office Cmty. and Ethnic Affairs, Prince George's County Govt., Md., 1993-94, Inst. for Haitian Cultural and Sci. Affairs, 1992-94, local arrangements com. Conf. Coll. Composition and Communication, Washington, 1995, Friends of the Corcoran, 1999; membership com. and outreach com. St. John's Ch., Washington, 1993, ch. growth com., 1995. With U.S. Army, 1964-66. Mem. MLA, Coll. Lang. Assn., Mid. Atlantic Writers Assn. (chmn. essay contest com. 1995-2000, bd. dirs. 2000-04), Samuel Beckett Soc., Societe des Professeurs Francais et Francophones d'Amerique, Zora Neale Hurston Soc., Am. Assn. Tchrs. French (sec.-treas. Washington chpt. 1986-90), Nat. Cathedral Assn., Coun. Internat. d'Etudes Francophones, Friends DC Superior Ct. (bd. dirs. 1996—), Univ. Club (Washington), Md. Fgn. Lang. Assn. (bd. dirs., 1997-2001, 03-06), Oxford Round Table (presenter), Am. Coun. on Tchg. Fgn. Langs., Alliance Francaise de Washington, DC, So. Poverty Law Ctr., Pi Delta Phi, Sigma Tau Delta. Democrat. Episcopalian. Avocations: classical music, history, travel, genealogy. Office: Bowie State U Dept English & Modern Langs Bowie MD 20715 Business E-Mail: rsterling@bowiestate.edu.

STERLING, ROBERT LEE, JR., investment company executive; b. Cleve., June 12, 1933; s. Robert Lee and Kathryn (Durell) S.; children from previous marriage: Robert Livingston, William Lee, Cameron Platt; m. Joyce Lanier Milner, June 4, 1994. Student, U. Edinburgh, Scotland, 1955; BA, Brown U., Providence, 1956; MBA, Columbia U., NYC, 1962. Corp. rsch. analyst Morgan Guaranty Trust, NYC, 1962-63; asst. comptr. Western Hemisphere CPC Internat., NYC, 1963—76; v.p. White, Weld & Co., Inc., NYC, 1976—78, Merrill Lynch Asset Mgmt., 1978-80, Wood, Struthers & Winthrop Mgmt. Corp., NYC, 1980-83; sr. v.p. Shearson Lehman Bros. Asset Mgmt., 1983-88; v.p., sr. portfolio mgr. Chase Manhattan Bank, 1988-93; exec. sr. v.p., sr. portfolio mgr. Melhado, Flynn & Assocs., Inc., NYC, 1993—2008; sr. portfolio mgr. HG Willington, 2008—. Mem. adv. bd. Mus. Modern Art, Oxford U., Eng.; trustee Soc. of the Four Arts, Palm Beach, Preservation Soc., Palm Beach, Game Coservancy, U.S. Mem. New Eng. Soc. (past pres., J.P. Morgan medal), St. Nicholas Soc., Pilgrims, NY State Soc. of Cin. (past pres.), St. Andrew's Soc., Univ. Club (NY), Everglades Club, Bath and Tennis Club (Palm Beach), Bathing Corp., Anabell's (London), Medow Club (Southamington), Alpha Delta Phi, Alpha Kappa Psi. Home: 200 Regent Park Palm Beach FL 33480 Office: HG Wellington 140 Broadway New York NY 10005 Home Phone: 561-655-3232; Office Phone: 212-288-1379.

STERLING, THOMAS W., metal products executive; B in Civil Engring., Vanderbilt U., Nashville; law degree, Samford U., Birmingham, Ala. Bar: Ala., Pa. Mgmt. trainee Fairfield Works US Steel, Ala., 1969, various positions in oper., pers. svcs. and comml. depts., 1969—75, asst. mgr. equal employment opportunity Employee Rels. Dept. Pitts., 1975, various employee rels. positions, v.p. employee rels., 1986, v.p. employee benefits, 1996, sr. v.p. human resources, 2003—04, sr. v.p. human resources & bus. svcs., 2004—07, sr. v.p. adminstrn., 2007—; v.p. labor rels., steel and related resources US Steel Group USX Corp., 1984—86; pres. Transtar, Inc. (now subs. of US Steel), 2000—03. US Steel rep. on bd. dirs. Maglev, Inc. Pres., bd. dirs. Greater Pitts. Coun. of Boy Scouts of Am.; bd. trustees Robert Morris U., Moon Twp., Pa.; chmn. bd. dirs. U. Pitts. Med. Ctr. Braddock; bd. dirs. U. Pitts. Med. Ctr. McKeesport, Heritage Health Found. Office: US Steel 600 Grant St Pittsburgh PA 15219-2800 Office Phone: 412-433-1121.

STERMER, DUGALD ROBERT, designer, writer, illustrator, consultant; b. LA, Dec. 17, 1936; s. Robert Newton and Mary (Blue) S.; children: Dugald, Megan, Chris, Colin, Crystal. BA, UCLA, 1960. Art dir., v.p. Ramparts mag., 1965-70; freelance designer, illustrator, writer, cons. San Francisco, 1970—; founder Pub. Interest Communications, San Francisco, 1974; chmn. illustration dept. Calif. Coll. Arts and Crafts, 1994—, disting. prof., 1994—. Bd. dirs. Am. Inst. Graphic Arts, Illustration Partnership Am.; mem. San Francisco Art Commn., 1997—. Cons. editor: Communication Arts mag., 1974-90; designer: Oceans mag., 1976-82; editor: The Environment, 1972, Vanishing Creatures, 1980; author: The Art of Revolution, 1970, Vanishing Creatures, 1980, Vanishing Flora, 1994, Birds and Bees, 1994; illustration exhbn. Calif. Acad. Scis., 1986; one-man show Jernigan Wicker Gallery, San Francisco, 1996 Mem. Grand Jury City and County San Francisco, 1989; bd. dirs. Delancey St. Found., 1990—. Recipient various medals, awards for design and illustration nat. and internat. competitions. Achievements include design of 1984 Olympic medals. Office: 600 The Embarcadero # 204 San Francisco CA 94107-2121 Office Phone: 415-777-0110. Business E-Mail: ds@dugaldstermer.com.

STERN, ALAN (SOL ALAN STERN), science administrator, astrophysicist, researcher; b. New Orleans, Nov. 22, 1957; s. Leonard Arthur and Joel Strauss (Sugar) Stern; m. Carole Ann Jones, Aug. 5, 1982; children: Sarah L., Kate E., Jordan. BS, U. Tex., 1978, MS in Aerospace Engring., 1980, BA, 1981, MS in Planetary Atmospheres, 1981; PhD in Astrophysics and Planetary Sci., U. Colo., 1989. Engr. NASA Johnson Space Ctr., Houston, 1979-80; systems engr. Martin Marietta Aerospace, Denver, 1982-83; spacecraft / instrument engr. Lab. for Atmospheric and Space Physics U. Colo., Boulder, 1983-86, rsch. assoc., 1989—90, asst. dir. Office of Space Sci. and Tech., 1986—87, asst. to v.p. for rsch., 1987—88, rsch. fellow Ctr. for Space & Geosciences Policy, 1989—91, rsch. assoc. Ctr. for Astrophysics and Space Astronomy, 1990—91, prof. adj. Astrophysical and Planetary Scis. Dept., 2002—; prin. scientist Space Science Dept. S.W. Rsch. Inst., 1991-92, sect. mgr., 1992—97, dept. dir., 1998—2005, exec. dir. Space Sci. and Engring. Div., 2004—07; assoc. adminstr. sci. mission directorate NASA, 2007—. Mem. lunar exploration sci. working group NASA, 1992—, discovery program sci. working group, 1989—90, chmn. Neptune/Pluto outer planet sci. working group, 1994—, project scientist Spartan-Halle spacecraft mission; prin. investigator Alice UV spectrometer in ESA/NASA Rosetta mission, Lunar Recon Orbiter Lyman-Alpha Mapping (LAMP) Experiment, Ralph Imager/IR Spectrometer on New Horizons, Alice UV Spectrometer on New Horizons, New Horizons Pluto-Kuiper Belt Mission. Author: The U.S. Space Program After Challenger, 1987, Pluto and Charon, 1997, The Exploration of Pluto, 1997, The Search for Extra-Solar Earthlike Planet: Techniques and Technology, 1997, Our Worlds, 1998, Our Universe, 2000, Worlds Beyond: The Thrill of Planetary Exploration as told by Leading Experts, 2003; editor: Geophysical Research Letters Special Issues, Pluto and the Moon, 1989, 1991; contbr. articles to profl. jours. Recipient Martin Marietta New Design Innovation award, 1983, Solar Max Repair Mission Recognition award, 1984, Hale-Bopp Sounding Rocket Campaign Grp. Achievement award, 2002, NASA, 1998, New Millennium Deep Space-1 Mission Grp. Achievement award, 2002, Rosetta Grp. Achievement award, 2005; named one of The World's Most Influential People, TIME mag., 2007; fellow Colo. Commn. Higher Edn., 1988—89. Mem.: AIAA, AAAS, Aircraft Owners & Pilots Assn., Am. Geophys. Union, Am. Astron. Soc., Internat. Astron. Union. Avocations: flying, scuba diving, photography, skiing, hiking, gardening, writing. Office: Sci Mission Directorate NASA 300 E St SW Washington DC 20546-0001 Office Phone: 303-546-9670, 202-358-3889. E-mail: astern@swri.edu, alan.stern@nasa.gov.

STERN, ANDREW L. (ANDY STERN), labor union administrator; b. West Orange, NJ, Nov. 22, 1950; m. Jane Perkins (div.); children: Matt, Cassie(dec.). BA in Edn. & Urban Planning, U. Pa., 1971. State social svc. worker, mem. Local 668 Svc. Employees Internat. Union (SEIU), 1973—80, mem. internat. exec. bd. Washington, 1980—, head orgn. field svc. programs, 1984—96, internat. pres., 1996—. Bd. dirs. AFL-CIO Housing and Bldg. Investment Trust, Medicare Rights Ctr., Aspen Inst., Broad Found., Inst. of Medicine. Author: A Country That Works: Getting America Back on Track, 2006. Chmn. Ctr. Cmty. & Corp. Ethics; bd. dirs. Rock the Vote. Mem.: Am. Hosp. Assn. (commn. on workforce for hosps. & health systems.), Nat. Acad. Social Ins. (bd. dirs.). Democrat. Office: SEIU 1800 Massachusetts Ave NW Washington DC 20036 Office Phone: 202-730-7000, 202-730-7162.*

STERN, ARTHUR PAUL, electronics executive; b. Budapest, Hungary, July 20, 1925; arrived in U.S., 1951; s. Leon and Bertha (Frankfurter) Stern; m. Edith M. Samuel; children: Daniel, Claude, Jacqueline. Diploma in Elec. Engring., Swiss Fed. Inst. Tech., Zurich, 1948; MSEE, Syracuse U., NY, 1956. Mgr. electronic devices and applications lab. GE, Syracuse, NY, 1957-61; dir. engring. Martin Marietta Corp., Balt., 1961-64; dir. ops. Bunker Ramo Corp., Canoga Park, Calif., 1964-66; v.p., gen. mgr. advanced products divsn. Magnavox, Torrance, Calif., 1966-79; pres. Magnavox Advanced Products and Systems Co., Torrance, 1980-90; vice chmn., bd. dirs. Magnavox Electronic Systems Co., Ft. Wayne, Ind., 1987—90; pres. Ea. Beverly Hills Corp., 1991—. Instr. GE Bus. Mgmt., 1955—57; non-resident staff mem. MIT, 1956—59; pres. Calif.-Israel C. of C., 1994—98, chmn. bd. dirs., 1998—2000; bd. dirs. Jewish Coun. Pub. Affairs, 1996—2002; mem. governing coun. Am.-Jewish Congress, 1997—98; v.p. Progressive Jewish Alliance, 1999—2004. Co-author: (book) Transistor Circuit Engineering, 1957, Handbook of Automation, Computation and Control, 1961; contbr. articles to profl. jours. Mem. adv. bd. dept. elec. engring. U. Calif., Santa Barbara, 1980—92; mem. Sch. Engring. Adv. and Devel. Coun. Calif. State U., Long Beach, 1985—90; chmn. bd. dirs. Calif. Humanitarian Found. for Holocaust Survivors, 2000—06; regional chair, bd. dirs. Ams. for Peace Now, 2002—; bd. dirs. So. Calif. Ams. for Dem. Action, 2000—; chmn. engring. divsn. United Jewish Appeal, Syracuse, 1955—57; bd. dirs. Bur. Jewish Edn., LA, 1995—, chmn. investment com., 2000—05; vice-chmn. Jewish Cmty. Rels. Com. of Jewish Fedn. of L.A., 1998—2003; bd. dirs. Jewish Fedn. Greater L.A., 2003—05. Recipient Justice-Tzedek award, Labor Zionist Alliance, 2001, Educating for Life award, Bur. Jewish Edn., 2004. Fellow: IEEE (pres. 1975, bd. dirs., officer 1970—77, guest editor spl. issue IEEE Trans. on Circuit Theory 1956, invited guest editor spl. issue Procs. IEEE on Integrated Electronics 1964, Centennial medal 1984, Millennium medal 2000, Haraden Pratt award 2001), AAAS; mem.: Sigma Xi, Eta Kappa Nu Assn. (eminent mem.). Achievements include patents in field.

STERN, CARL LEONARD, retired news correspondent, federal official, educator; b. NYC, Aug. 7, 1937; s. Hugo and Frances (Taft) S.; m. Joy Elizabeth Nathan, Nov. 27, 1960; children: Lawrence, Theodore. AB, Columbia U., 1958, MS, 1959; JD, Cleve. State U., 1966, JD (hon.), 1975, New Eng. Coll. Law, 1977. Bar: Ohio 1966, DC 1968, US Supreme Ct. 1969. Law corr. NBC News, Washington, 1967—93; dir. Office of Pub. Affairs U.S. Dept. Justice, Washington, 1993—96; Shapiro Prof. of Media and Pub. Affairs George Washington U., 1996—2008, prof. emritus, 2008—. Mem. editl. stds. rev. com. Pub. Broadcasting Svc., 2005; lectr. Nat. Jud. Coll.; adj. prof. George Washington U., Stanford U. Editl. bd. The Dist. Lawyer Mem. Dept. Transp. Task Force on Assistance to Families in Aviation Disasters, 1997; mem. nat. adv. coun., Cleve. Marshall Law Sch.; bd. dir. Hist. Soc., DC Cir. Adv. Bd. Collaboration on Govt. Sec., Washington Coll. Law, Am U. Recipient Peabody award, 1974, Emmy award, 1974, Gavel award, 1969, 74, Headliner Club award, 1991, Edmond J. Randolph award US Dept. Justice. Mem. ABA (vice chmn. criminal justice sect. com. on criminal justice and media, gov., forum com. on comm. law, working group intelligence requirements and criminal code reform, standing com. on strategic comm.), AFTRA (nat. exec. bd. 1984-86, first v.p. Washington, Balt. chpt. 1985-87) Home: 2956 Davenport St NW Washington DC 20008 Office: George Washington U #400 805 21st St NW Washington DC 20052 Home Phone: 202-362-0181. Personal E-mail: sterncarl@aol.com. Business E-Mail: cstern@gwu.edu.

STERN, CARL WILLIAM, JR., management consultant; b. San Francisco, Mar. 31, 1946; s. Carl William and Marjorie Aline (Gunst) S.; m. Karen Jaffe, Sept. 7, 1966 (div. Mar. 1972); 1 child, David; m. Holly Drick Hayes, Mar. 21, 1985; children: Kenneth, Matthew. BA, Harvard U., 1968; MBA, Stanford U., 1974. Cons. Boston Cons. Group, Inc., Menlo Park, Calif., 1974-77, mgr., 1977-78, London, 1978-80, v.p. Chgo., 1980-87, sr. v.p., 1987-97, pres., CEO, 1998—2003, co-chmn. bd., 2004—07, chmn. bd., 2007—. Lt. USNR, 1968-71. Office: Boston Consulting Group Inc 200 S Wacker Dr Ste 2700 Chicago IL 60606-5846

STERN, CLAUDIO DANIEL, medical educator, embryological researcher; b. Montevideo, Uruguay, Feb. 9, 1954; came to U.S., 1994; s. Erico and Trude Stern. BSc with honors, U. Sussex, 1975, DPhil, 1978; MA, U. Oxford, 1985, DSc, 1994. Asst. prof. anatomy dept. Cambridge (England) U., 1984-85; assoc. prof. dept. human anatomy U. Oxford (England), 1985-93; prof., chmn. dept. genetics and devel. Coll. Physicians and Surgeons Columbia U., NYC, 1994—2001; J Z Young Pro. U. Coll. London, 2001—, head dept. anatomy & developmental biology, 2001—07, head cell & developmental biology, 2007—. Contbr. articles to profl. jours.; mng. editor Mechanisms of Devel.; mem. editorial adv. bd. Devel.; mem. editorial bd. Internat. Jour. Devel. Biology, Cell. Rsch. fellow U. Coll. London, 1978-84, fellow Christ Ch. Coll., 1985-93. Office: University College London Gower St WC1E 6BT England*

STERN, DAVID JOEL, National Basketball Association commissioner; b. NYC, Sept. 22, 1942; s. William and Anna (Bronstein) Stern; m. Dianne Bock, Nov. 27, 1963; children: Andrew, Eric. BA, Rutgers U., 1963; LLB, Columbia U., 1966. Bar: N.Y. 1963. Assoc. Proskauer Rose Goetz & Mendelsohn, NYC, 1966—74, ptnr., 1974—78; gen. counsel NBA, NYC, 1978—80, exec. v.p. bus. & legal affairs, 1980—84, commr., 1984—. Mem. Martin Luther King Jr. Fed. Holiday Commn., 1988, White House Conf. for a Drug-Free Am., 1988; bd. dirs. NAACP, 1990—93, Thurgood Marshall Scholarship Fund, Mus. TV and Radio, Jazz at Lincoln Ctr.; trustee Beth Israel Med. Ctr., 1985—, Rutgers U. Found., 1987—; trustee, chair emeritus Columbia U., 1992—. Named one of Most Influential People in the World of Sports, Bus. Week, 2007, 2008; named to Internat. Jewish Sports Hall of Fame, 1998. Mem.: ABA, Assn. Bar City NY (chmn. com. on entertainment and sports 1983—86), NY State Bar Assn., Coun. on Fgn. Rels. Achievements include assisting in creation of NBA Entertainment Divsn. Office: NBA Olympic Tower 645 5th Ave Fl 10 New York NY 10022-5986*

STERN, DAVID MARK, dean, medical educator; b. Great Neck, NY; s. Robert and Florence Stern; m. Kathleen Shirley Stern; children: Eric David, Alan Robert. BS, Yale U., 1973; MD, Harvard U., 1978. Mem. faculty Coll. Physicians and Surgeons, Columbia U., NYC, 1983—2002, named Gerald & Janet Carrus Prof. of Surg. Sci., 1998, dir. Ctr. Vascular and Lung Pathobiology, dir. Juvenile Diabetes Rsch. Ctr.; dean sch. medicine, sr. v.p. clin. activities Med. Coll. Ga., Augusta, 2002—05, prof. medicine, physiology and grad. studies, 2002—05; Christian R. Holmes prof. medicine U. Cin. Coll. Medicine, 2005—, dean, 2005—, v.p. health affairs. Mem.: Am. Assn. Physicians, Am. Soc. Clin. Investigation. Office: U Cin Coll Medicine 231 Albert Sabin Way PO Box 670552 Cincinnati OH 45267-0552 Office Phone: 513-558-7334. Business E-Mail: dstern@mail.mcg.edu. E-mail: david.stern@uc.edu.*

STERN, DAVID R., retail executive; V.p. fin. planning and analysis Safeway, Inc., 1994—2002, sr. v.p. planning and bus. devel., 2002—. Office: Safeway Inc 5918 Stoneridge Mall Rd Pleasanton CA 94588 Office Phone: 925-467-3000. Office Fax: 925-467-3323.*

STERN, DONALD ALLAN, lawyer; b. NYC, Apr. 13, 1954; s. Robert and Florence S.; m. Antje Mewes, Sept. 14, 1989; children: Elizabeth, Robert. AB, Harvard U., 1976, JD, 1980. Assoc. Cleary, Gottlieb, Steen & Hamilton, NYC, 1980-88, ptnr., 1989—. Corp. trustee Jackson Lab., Bar Harbor, Maine, 1986-90, governing trustee, 1990—, chmn. bd., chmn. exec. com., chmn. compensation com., 2001-06, life trustee, 2006—; unit commr. Boy Scouts Am., Nassau County, N.Y., 1992—; commr.-at-large Village of Thomaston, 1998—. Office: Cleary Gottlieb Steen & Hamilton 1 Liberty Plz Fl 38 New York NY 10006-1470 Office Phone: 212-225-2640. E-mail: dstern@cgsh.com.

STERN, DONALD KENNETH, lawyer; BA, Hobart Coll., 1966; JD, Georgetown U., 1969; LLM, U. Pa., 1973. Intern Dist. Atty.'s Office, Mineola, NY, 1967, Citizen's Adv. Ctr., Washington, 1968; staff atty. Defender Assn. Phila., Cmty. Legal Svcs., Phila., 1969-71; adj. prof. law, supervising atty. Boston Coll. Law Sch., Boston Coll. Legal Assistance Bur., 1971-73, asst. prof. law, dir. clin. programs, supervising atty., 1973-75; asst. atty. gen., dir. atty. gen. clin. program, Mass. Atty. Gen.'s Office, Boston Coll. Law Sch., 1975-77, asst. prof. law, dir. atty. gen. clin. program, spl. asst. atty. gen., 1977-78, asst. atty. gen., dir. atty. gen. clin. program, 1978-79; chief govt. bur. Mass. Atty. Gen.'s Office,

1979-82; assoc. Hale and Dorr, Boston, 1982-85, jr. ptnr., 1985-87, sr. ptnr., 1987, 91-93, of counsel, 1990-91; chief legal counsel to Gov. Mass., 1987-90; U.S. atty. Dist. Mass., 1993—2001; ptnr. Bingham McCutchen, LLP, 2001—08; lectr. Harvard Law Sch., 2002—05. Office: Cooley Godward Kronish LLP 800 Boylston St Fl 46 Boston MA 02199 Office Phone: 617-937-2321.

STERN, EDWARD ABRAHAM, physics professor; b. Detroit, Sept. 19, 1930; s. Jacob Munich and Rose (Kravitz) S.; m. Sylvia Rita Sidell, Oct. 30, 1955; children: Hilary, Shari, Miri. BS, Calif. Tech., 1951, PhD, 1955. Post-doctoral fellow Calif. Tech., Pasadena, 1955-57; asst. prof. U. Md., College Park, 1957-61, assoc. prof., 1961-64, prof., 1964-65, U. Wash., Seattle, 1965—2000, emeritus, 2000—. Contbr. over 200 articles to profl. jours.; editor; three books. Recipient B. Warren award Am. Crystallography Assn., 1979, Outstanding Achievement award Internat. XAFS Soc., 2000; named Guggenheim fellow, Cambridge, Eng., 1963-64, NSF Sr. Post-doctoral fellow, Haifa, Israel, 1970-71, Fulbright fellow, Jerusalem, Israel, 1985-86. Fellow AAAS, Am. Physical Soc.; mem. Materials Rsch. Soc. Achievements include patent for x-ray focusing device; development of x-ray absorption fine structure technique; research on surface plasmons, nonlinear reflection from surfaces, electronic properties of alloys, structural phase transition; named Father of EXAFS. Office: U Wash Dept Physics PO Box 351560 Seattle WA 98195-1560 Home Phone: 206-525-2771; Office Phone: 206-543-2023. Business E-Mail: stern@phys.washington.edu.

STERN, ELIZABETH ESPIN, lawyer; b. Prince Georges County, Md., June 21, 1961; d. Cesar A. and M. Cecilia (Salvador) E.; m. Michael L. Stern, May 16, 1992; children: Alexander, David. BA magna cum laude, U. Va., 1983; JD, U. Va. Sch. Law, 1986. Bar: Va. 1986, U.S. Dist. Ct. (Ea. Dist.) Va., D.C. 1988, Supreme Ct. Va., U.S. Ct. Appeals, D.C. Cir. Ptnr. comml. immigration Pillsbury Winthrop Shaw Pittman LLP (formerly Shaw Pittman LLP), Washington, 1986—2005, ptnr. & head bus. immigration practice group, 2005; ptnr., head global migration and exec. transfers Baker & McKenzie LLP, Washington, 2005—. Spkr. in field. Recipient Martin Preis award, Vol. Bar Assn. D.C., 1992; named one of Top 30 lawyers in Washington, Washingtonian Mag., 2004, Top 10 Immigration Lawyers in DC, Legal Times, 2006, DC Super Lawyers, 2007. Fellow: ABA, Bar Assn. D.C. (chair immigration com.); mem.: U.S. C. of C., Internat. Sects. Am. Immigration Lawyers Assn., Soc. for Human Resources Mgmt., Immigration Tech. Assn. Am., D.C. Bar Assn. (internat. sec. 1986—, chair young lawyers sect. 1992—93, del. to ABA, Young Lawyer of Yr. 1994), Va. Bar Assn., Am. Immigration Lawyers Assn., Washington Internat. Trade Assn. Republican. Avocation: journalism. Office: Baker & McKenzie LLP 815 Connecticut Ave NW Washington DC 20006-4078 Office Phone: 202-452-7000. Business E-Mail: elizabeth.e.stern@bakernet.com.

STERN, FRITZ RICHARD, historian, educator; b. Breslau, Germany, Feb. 2, 1926; came to U.S., 1938, naturalized, 1947; s. Rudolf A. and Catherine (Brieger) S.; m. Margaret J. Bassett, Oct. 11, 1947 (div. 1992); children: Frederick P., Katherine Stern Brennan; m. Elisabeth Niebuhr Sifton, Jan. 1, 1996. BA, Columbia U., 1946, MA, 1948, PhD, 1953; DLitt (hon.), Oxford U., 1985; LLD (hon.), New Sch. for Social Rsch., 1997, Columbia U., 1998, U. Wroclaw, 2002; DHL, Princeton U., 2007; PhD European U. Viadrina (hon.), Frankfurt, 2006. Lectr., instr. Columbia U., 1946-51, faculty, 1953—, prof. history, 1963—, Seth Low prof. history, 1967-92, univ. prof., 1992-96, provost, 1980-83; acting asst. prof. Cornell U., 1951-53; univ. prof. emeritus Columbia U., 1997—; tchr. Free U. Berlin, 1954, Yale U., 1963; permanent vis. prof. U. Konstanz, West Germany, 1966—; sr. adviser U.S. Embassy, Bonn, 1993-94. Élie Halévy prof. U. Paris, spring 1979; Phi Beta Kappa vis. scholar, 1979-80; Tanner lectr. Yale, 1993. Author: The Politics of Cultural Despair, 1961, The Failure of Illiberalism-Essays in the Political Culture of Modern Germany, 1972, rev. edit., 1992, Gold and Iron: Bismarck, Bleichroeder and the Bldg. of the German Empire, 1977 (recipient Lionel Trilling award Columbia U.), Dreams and Delusions: The Drama of German History, 1987, rev. edit. 1999, Einstein's German World, 1999, Five Germanys I Have Known, 2006; editor: The Varieties of History, 1956, 71, (with L. Krieger) The Responsibility of Power, 1967; mem. editorial bd. Foreign Affairs, 1978-92; reviewer Fgn. Affairs, 1963-95; contbr. articles to profl. jours. Trustee German Marshall Fund, 1981-99, Aspen Inst. of Berlin, 1983—; senator Deutsche Nationalstiftung, 1994—; mem. Trilateral Commn., 1983-90. Decorated Officer's Cross Order of Merit Fed. Republic of Germany; fellow Center Advanced Behavioral Scis., 1957-58; fellow Social Sci. Research Council, 1960-61; fellow Am. Council Learned Socs., 1966-67; fellow Netherlands Inst. Advanced Study, 1972-73; mem. Nuffield Coll., Oxford, 1966-67, Inst. Advanced Study Princeton, 1969-70; Guggenheim fellow, 1969-70; Ford Found. grantee, 1976-77; vis. scholar Russell Sage Found., 1989, spring 1993; recipient Leopold-Lucas-prize Evang. Faculty U. Tübingen, 1984, Peace prize German Book Trade Frankfurt Book Fair, 1999, Bruno Snell medal U. Hamburg, 2002, Leo Baeck medal, NY, 2004, Nationalpreis, Berlin, 2005, award Jewish Mus., Berlin, 2007). Mem. Am. Hist. Assn., AAAS, Am. Philos. Soc., Coun. Fgn. Rels., Deutsche Akademie für Sprache und Dichtung (corr.), Berlin Brandenburgische Akademie der Wissenschaften (corr.), Orden Pour le Mérite, Germany, Phi Beta Kappa (senator-at-large 1973-78). Clubs: Century (N.Y.C.). Home: 15 Claremont Ave New York NY 10027-6802 E-mail: fs20@columbia.edu.

STERN, GARY HILTON, bank executive; b. San Luis Obispo, Calif., Nov. 3, 1944; s. Robert Earl and Joy Merdis (Shimon) Stern; m. Mary Katherine Nelson, Aug. 17, 1969; children: Matthew Stuart, Meredith Faulkner. AB, Washington U., St. Louis, 1967; MA, Rice U., Houston, 1970, PhD, 1972. Economist Fed. Res. Bank NY, NYC, 1970-73, mgr. domestic rsch., 1973-77; mgr. fixed income rsch. Loeb Rhoades, Hornblower, NYC, 1977-78; sr. economist A.G. Shilling & Co., NYC, 1978-81; sr. v.p. Fed. Res. Bank Mpls., 1982-85, CFO, 1983, pres., CEO, 1985—. Adj. asst. prof. Columbia U., NYC, 1976—79; adj. prof. NYU, 1980—82. Author: In the Name of Money, 1980. Trustee West Side Montessori Sch., NYC, 1978—79; bd. trustees Hamline U., Mpls. Coll. Art & Design; bd. dirs. Nat. Coun. Econ. Edn., N.W. Area Found., U. Minn. Carlson Sch. Mgmt. Bache & Co. scholar, 1963—67, NDEA scholar, 1969—70. Mem.: Mpls. Club (treas.). Office: Fed Res Bank Mpls 90 Hennepin Ave Minneapolis MN 55401 Office Phone: 612-204-5000.*

STERN, GEOFFREY, lawyer; b. Columbus, Ohio, Nov. 29, 1942; s. Leonard J. and Anastasia (Percin) S.; m. Barbara Feuer; children: Emily Staheli, Elizabeth Leskowyak; 3 stepchildren. Student, Williams Coll., 1960-63; BA cum laude, Ohio State U., 1965, JD summa cum laude, 1968. Bar: Ohio 1968. Assoc. Alexander, Ebinger, Holschuh & Fisher, Columbus, Ohio, 1968-72; ptnr. Folkerth, Calhoun, Webster & O'Brien, Columbus, Ohio, 1972-80, Arter & Hadden, Columbus, Ohio, 1980-93; disciplinary counsel Supreme Ct. of Ohio, 1993-97; counsel Kegler, Brown, Hill & Ritter, Columbus, 1997-2000, dir., 2000—. Nat. coordinating counsel for asbestos litigation Combustion Engring. Inc. and Basic, Inc., 1985-93; lectr. on legal ethics and profl. responsibility; mem. Spl. Commn. to Review Ohio Ethics Rules, 1995-98, Spl. Commn. on Legal Edn., 1995-98; mem. symposium on ethics and Chinese legal sys., Shanghai, 1998; keynote spkr. Faith and Law Symposium, 1999; spl. investigator Bd. Commrs. Character and Fitness Ohio Supreme Ct., 1998. Sr. editor Ohio State Law Jour. Pres. Bexley (Ohio) City Coun., 1977-80, mem., 1973-80, mem. Bexley Civil Svc. Commn., 1983-85; v.p., trustee Creative Living, Columbus, 1981-89, Ohio Citizens Com. for Arts, Columbus, 1982-88; mem. Nat. Def. Com. on Asbestos in Bldgs. Litigation, 1986-92; pub. mem. Ohio Optical Dispensers Bd., Columbus, 1978-82. Recipient Am. Jurisprudence Evidence award Ohio State U. Coll. Law, Verdict Top Attorneys, Best Lawyers in Am., Ohio Superlawyer. Fellow Am. Bar Found., Litigation Counsel America, Columbus Bar Found., Ohio State Bar Found.; mem. Ohio State Bar Assn. (com. on legal ethics and profl. conduct, sec., vice chmn., chmn.), Columbus Bar Assn. (profl. ethics com., Liberty Bell award for Cmty. and Profl. Svc.), Order of Coif, Phi Beta Kappa, Pi Sigma Alpha. Home: 278 Crossing Crk N Columbus OH 43230-6108 Office: Kegler Brown Hill & Ritter 65 E State St Ste 1800 Columbus OH 43215-4294 Office Phone: 614-462-5400. Business E-Mail: gstern@keglerbrown.com.

STERN, GERALD MANN, lawyer; b. Chgo., Apr. 5, 1937; s. Lloyd and Fannye (Wener) S.; m. Linda Stone, Dec. 20, 1969; children: Eric, Jesse, Maia. BS in Econs., U. Pa., 1958; LL.B. cum laude, Harvard, 1961. Bar: D.C. 1961, Calif. 1991, U.S. Supreme Ct. 1971. Trial atty. civil rights div. U.S. Dept. Justice, 1961-64; assoc. firm Arnold & Porter, Washington, 1964-68, ptnr., 1969-76; founding ptnr. Rogovin, Stern & Huge, Washington, 1976-81; exec. v.p., sr. gen. counsel Occidental Petroleum Corp., LA, 1981—92; spl. counsel fin. instn. fraud and health care fraud U.S. Dept. Justice, Washington, 1993-95; ind. legal cons. pvt. practice, Washington, 1995—; cons. Antitrust divsn. U.S. Dept. Justice, 1998—2001. Author: The Buffalo Creek Disaster, 1976, The Scotia Widows, 2008; co-author: Southern Justice, 1965, Outside the Law, 1997. Trustee Facing History and Ourselves, 1996. Home and Office: 3322 Newark St NW Washington DC 20008-3330 Office Phone: 202-253-2257, 202-362-2078. Fax: 202-364-2595. E-mail: GMS37@aol.com.

STERN, GUY, German language and literature educator, writer; b. Hildesheim, Germany, Jan. 14, 1922; came to U.S., 1937, naturalized, 1943; s. Julius and Hedwig (Silberberg) S.; m. Judith Owens, June 16, 1979 (dec. June 2003); 1 child, Mark; m. Susanna Pointek, May 16, 2006. BA in Romance Langs., Hofstra Coll., 1948; MA in Germanic Langs. with honors, Columbia U., 1950, PhD with honors, 1953; Dr. (hon.), Hofstra U., 1998. Grad. asst., then instr. Columbia U., 1948-55; asst. prof., then assoc. prof. Denison U., Granville, Ohio, 1955-63; prof. German, dept. head U. Cin., 1964-73, dean univ., 1973-76; prof., chmn. Germanic and Slavic dept. U. Md., College Park, 1976-78; v.p., provost Wayne State U., Detroit, 1978-80, disting. prof. German, 1980—2003. Guest prof. Goethe Inst., Freiburg U., summers 1963-66, 84, Frankfurt U., 1993, Leipzig U., 1997, Potsdam U., 1998, Munich U., 1999; adv. editor langs. and linguistics Dover Publs. Co-author: Brieflich Erzaehlt, 1956, Listen and Learn German, 1957, Say It in German, 1958, Uebung macht den Meister, 1959, An Invitation to German Poetry, 1960, Hints on Speaking German, 1961, Quick Change Pattern Drills, vol. I, 1962, vol. II, 1963, Hoer zu und Rat mit, 1964; author: Efraim Frisch: Zum Verstaendnis des Geistigen, 1964, War, Weimar and Literature, 1971, Alfred Neumann (anthology with biography), 1979, Literatur im Exil, 1989, Nazi Book Burning and the American Response, 1989; Literarische Kultur im Exil (essay collection), 1997, Fielding, Wieland, Goethe and the Rise of the Novel, 2003; editor: Konstellationen: Die besten Erzaehlungen des Neuen Merkur, 1964; co-editor: Nelly Sachs Ausgewaehlte Gedichte, 1968; assoc. editor: Lessing Yearbook, 1970-72, edit. bd. 1972—; sr. editor, 1979-81; co-editor (Kurt Weill) Auf dem Weg zum Weg der Verheissung; contbr. articles on 18th and 20th century German lit. to profl. jours., also chpts. to books; mem. editl. bd. CG, 1976. Bd. dirs. Kurt Weill Found., sec., 1990—; bd. dirs. Leo Baeck Inst., 1967—, mem. exec. bd., 1978—; bd. dirs., chair acad. adv. com. Holocaust Meml. Mus. Greater Detroit, dir. Inst. Righteous; co-founder, pres. Lessing Soc., 1975-77; mem. pub. bd. Aufbau, 1997-2000; exec. com. MLA, 2004-07. With AUS, 1942-45. Decorated Bronze Star; Fulbright Rsch. grantee U. Munich, 1961-63; recipient Order of Merit 1st Class, 1968, Friendship award, 1983, Germany, 1987, Grand Order of Merit, Festschrift in Honor of Guy Stern; Exile and Enlightment, 1987, Goethe medal, 1989, Presdl. award for Excellence in Tchg., 1992, Disting. Alumni award Hofstra U., 1993, Disting. Grad. Faculty award Wayne State U., 1998, Festschrift Hommage fur Guy Stern, Autobiographische Zeugnisse der Verfolgung, 2004-05, named Mentor of Year U. Mich., Dearborn, 2008. Mem. Am. Assn. Tchrs. German (pres. 1970-72, Disting. Germanist of Yr. 1985, hon. mem. 1989), AAUP, Internat. PEN Club, MLA, South Atlantic MLA, Soc. for Exile Studies (v.p. 1981—), Holocaust Meml. Ctr. (interim dir. 2008). Home: 6197 Forest Grv West Bloomfield MI 48322-1375 Office Phone: 313-577-3129. Personal E-mail: ad5422@gmail.com.

STERN, HAL, information technology executive; BS, Princeton U., NJ. Mem. rsch. staff massive memory project Princeton U.; mem. tech. staff Polygen Corp.; with Sun Microsystems, Inc., Santa Clara, Calif., 1991—, chief technologist NE US sales area, chief tech. officer Sun ONE (iPlanet) infrastructure products, chief arch. Sun profl. svcs., chief tech. officer Sun svcs., v.p., chief tech. officer software, 2005, sr. v.p. systems engring. Author: Managing NFS and NIS; contbg. editor: SunWorld Mag.; mem. editl. staff, adv. bd. JavaWorld mag. Office: Sun Microsystems Inc 4150 Network Cir Santa Clara CA 95054 Office Phone: 650-960-1300.

STERN, HAROLD PHILIP ELLIOTT, electrical engineer, director; b. San Diego, July 13, 1956; s. Morris Stern and Myrna Longenecker; m. Lee Elliott, June 21, 1999; 1 child, Dylan Elliott. BSEE, U. Tex., Austin, 1978; MSEE, U. Tex., Arlington, 1986, PhD, 1991. Sr. avionics sys. engr. Boeing Comml. Airplane Co., Seattle, 1980—83; sr. engr. ElectroCom Automation, Arlington, Tex., 1983—88; asst. prof. elec. engring. U. Ala., Tuscaloosa, 1991—98, assoc. prof. elec. and computer engring., 1998—2005; dir., Ingram sch. engring. Tex. State U., San Marcos, 2007—. Ind. cons. pvt. practice, San Marcos, Tex., 1988—. Author: (textbook) Communication Systems: Analysis and Design. Mem. Wimberly ISD Engring. Adv. Bd., Tex., 2008, Hays County ISD Engring. Adv. Bd., San Marcos, Tex., 2008. Recipient Outstanding Tchg. award, U. Ala. Alumni Assn., 2000; grantee, NSF, 2007. Mem.: IEEE. Liberal. Jewish. Office: Tex State Univ 601 University Dr San Marcos TX 78666

STERN, HOWARD ALLAN, radio personality, television show host; b. Jackson Heights, NY, Jan. 12, 1954; s. Ben and Rae S.; m. Alison Berns, June 4, 1978 (div. 2001); children: Emily Beth, Debra Jennifer, Ashley Jade; m. Beth Ostrosky, Oct. 3, 2008 BA in Comm., Boston U., 1976. Disc jockey Sta. WRNW, Briarcliff Manor, NY, 1976-78, Sta. WCCC, Hartford, Conn., 1978-79, Sta. WWWW, Detroit, 1979-80, Sta. WWDC, Washington, 1980-82, Sta. WNBC, NYC, 1982-85, Sta. WXRK, NYC, 1985—2005, numerous other markets, 1986—2005; disc jockey Howard Stern Show Sirius Satellite Radio, 2006—. Author: Private Parts, 1993, Miss America, 1995; TV shows include The Howard Stern Show (WOR-TV), 1990-92, The Howard Stern Interview (E!), 1992-93, The Howard Stern Show (E!), 1994-2005, Howard Stern on Demand, 2005-; actor (films) Private Parts, 1997; writer, exec. prodr., voice Doomsday, 2000; writer, exec. prodr. (TV series) Son of the Beach, 2000-02; recordings include 50 Ways To Rank Your Mother, 1982, Crucified by the FCC, 1991; pay-per-view spls./videos include: Howard Stern's Négligé and Underpants Party, U.S. Open Sores, Butt Bongo Fiesta, The Miss Howard Stern New Year's Eve Pageant. Libertarian candidate for gov. State of NY, 1994. Rest Stop on I-295 in NJ named in his honor, 1995, recipient Rave Awards, Wired Renegade, WIRED, 2005; named one of 100 Most Influential People, Time Mag., 2006, The 100 Most Powerful Celebrities, Forbes.com, 2008 Office: care Don Buchwald & Associates 10 E 44th St New York NY 10017-3601*

STERN, JAMES ANDREW, investment banker; b. NYC, Oct. 1, 1950; s. Arthur and Lenore (Oppenheimer) S.; m. Jane Yusem, April 13, 1975; children: Peter, David. BS, Tufts U., 1972; MBA, Harvard U., 1974. Assoc. Lehman Bros. Inc., NYC, 1974-79, v.p., 1979-82, mng. dir., 1982-94; chmn. The Cypress Group, NYC, 1994—. Bd. dirs. Lear Corp., Southfield, Mich., Affinia Group Inc., Cooper Standard, Inc. Trustee Tufts U., Medford, Mass., 1982-, chmn. bd. trustees 2003-, Jewish Mus., N.Y.C.; bd. dirs. Cystic Fibrosis Found. Mem. Quaker Ridge Golf Club (Scarsdale, NY), Beach Point Club (Mamaroneck, NY). Avocations: golf, reading. Office: The Cypress Group Inc 65 E 55th St New York NY 10022-3219 Office Phone: 212-705-0151. Business E-Mail: jstern@cypressgp.com.

STERN, JEAN, museum director; b. Casablanca, Morocco, Mar. 28, 1946; arrived in U.S., 1955, naturalized, 1962; s. Frederic and Sultana Stern; m. Linda Susan Stern, Jan. 18, 2004; m. Carol Elizabeth Adams (div.); children: Carrie Dona, Hannah Marie. BA History, Calif. State, Northridge, Calif., 1968; MA Art History, Calif. State, San Diego, Calif., 1972; post graduate, UCLA, LA. Instr. San Diego State Univ., San Diego, 1974—76; instr. art history Mesa Coll., San Diego, 1976; dir. Petersen Galleries, Beverly Hills, Calif., 1978—91; exec. dir. The Irvine Mus., Irvine, Calif., 1992—. Guest curator San Diego Mus. of Art, San Diego, 1976. Co-author: Enchanted Isle, 2003, California, This Golden Land, 2001; contbr. essays, articles pub. numerous to profl. jour. Mem.: Am. Assn. Mus., Calif. Art Club (Man of the Yr. 1998). Avocation: coin collecting/numismatics. Office: The Irvine Mus 18881 Von Karman #100 Irvine CA 92612 Office Phone: 949-476-0294.

STERN, JEFFREY ROSS, lawyer; s. Peter Marc and Joan Stern; m. Amelia Wong Stern; 1 child, Joshua. AB magna cum laude, Harvard Coll., Cambridge, Mass., 1990; JD, Va. Law Sch., Charlottesville, 1994. Bar: Conn. 1994, NY 1995. Assoc. Weil, Gotshal & Manges, NYC, 1994—97, Va. Law Rev., Articles Rev. bd. Educator, Latham & Watkins, NYC, 1997—2000; exec. dir. law dept. Morgan Stanley, NYC, 2000—. Contbr. articles to profl. jours. Mem.: Assn. Corp. Counsel (chair nat. info. tech., privacy & e-commn. CMTE 2008—), Securities Industry and Fin. Markets Assn. (working group co-head 2006—). Office: Morgan Stanley 1221 Ave of the Americas New York NY 10020

STERN, JOEL N.H., biochemist, researcher; s. Joel and Flora D. Stern. BS, Columbia U., NY, 1998; ALM, Harvard U., Cambridge, Mass., 2003, PhD, 2008. Tutors bd. biochem. scis., postdoc. rsch. scientist Harvard U., 2008—. Contbr. scientific papers. Democrat. Roman Catholic. Achievements include discovery of treatments for autoimmune diseases. Office: Harvard Univ 7 Divinity Ave Fairchild Bldg Rm 411 Cambridge MA 02138 Business E-Mail: jstern@fas.harvard.edu.

STERN, JOSEPH A., lawyer, former publishing executive; b. Cleve., Dec. 7, 1949; s. Arthur J. and Thelma (Arnold) S. BA, Yale U., 1972, JD, 1976. Assoc. Winthrop Stimson, NYC, 1976-79, Fried Frank Harris Shriver & Jacobson, NYC, London, 1979-84, ptnr., 1984—2005; gen. counsel, exec. v.p., corp. sec. Dow Jones & Co., 2005—07. Chmn., dir. Mex. Am. Legal Defense and Edn. Fund, L.A., 1991-95; dir. Am. Friend Chamber Music of Europe, N.Y.C., 1986—. Mem. ABA, City Bar N.Y., Am. Law Inst.

STERN, JUDITH SCHNEIDER, nutritionist, researcher, educator; b. Bklyn. d. Sidney and Lillian (Rosen) Schneider; m. Richard C. Stern; 1 child, Daniel Arthur. BS, Cornell U., 1964; MS, Harvard U. Sch. Pub. Health, 1966, ScD, 1970. Rsch. asst., dept. food sci. and nutrition MIT, Cambridge, 1964—65; rsch. assoc. dept. human behavior and metabolism The Rockefeller U., NYC, 1968—72, asst. prof. dept. human behavior and metabolism, 1972—74; contbg. editor Vogue Mag., Conde Nast Publs., NYC, 1974; asst. prof. nutrition U. Calif., Davis, 1975—77, assoc. prof. dept. nutrition, 1977—82, dir. food intake lab. group, 1980—2001, prof. dept. nutrition, 1982—, prof. divsn. endocrinology, clin. nutrition and vascular biology, 1988—, disting. prof., 2003—. Mem. editl. bd. Internat. Jour. Obesity, 1976-85, Appetite, 1990, Obesity Rsch., 1993—2002, Nutrition Today, 1999—. Bd. sci. advisors Am. Coun. Sci. and Health, 1980—; mem. U.S. Dept. Agr. Dietary Guidelines Adv. Com., 1983—85; mem. obesity task force NIDDK, 1996—2002; mem. expert com. U.S. Pharmacopeia Bioavailability and Nutrient Absorption, 2000—03; mem. adv. bd. USDA Nat. Agrl. Rsch. Ext., Edn. and Econs., 2000—03. Recipient Sec.'s Honor award USDA, 2004; NIH tng. grantee, 1979-2006. Fellow AAAS (mem. obesity task force), Am. Heart Assn.; mem. Am. Soc. Clin. Nutirition (pres. 1995-96), Am. Dietetic Assn., Am. Diabetes Assn., Am. Obesity Assn. (co-founder, v.p. 1995-2006), N.Am. Assn. for Study of Obesity (pres. 1992-93), Inst. Medicine of NAS, Inst. Food Technologists, Am. Soc. Nutrition Sci. (chair pub. info. com. 1992-94), Sigma Xi, Delta Omega. Office: U Calif Dept Nutrition 1 Shields Ave Davis CA 95616-5271 Office Phone: 530-752-6575. Business E-Mail: jsstern@ucdavis.edu.

STERN, JULIAN NATHANIEL, lawyer, pharmaceutical executive; b. NYC, Oct. 13, 1924; s. Mark James and Celia (Bluestone) Stern; m. Dorothy Bennett, Oct. 15, 1956; children: John Hiram, Michael Vaughn. BS, NYU, NYC, 1946; LLB, Yale U., New Haven, 1949. Bar: NY 1950, DC 1951, Calif. 1956. Ptnr. Heller Ehrman LLP, Menlo Park, Calif., 1960—2006; chmn. bd. dirs. Pherin Pharm. Inc., Redwood City, Calif., 2004—. Bd. dirs., corp. sec. FibroGen, Inc., South San Francisco, Calif., 1993—, DepoMed, Inc., Menlo Park, Calif., 1996—, Roxro Pharm., Inc., Menlo Park, 2001—. Contbr. articles to legal jours.; revising editor: Mertens Law of Taxation, 1955—56. Trustee Am. Cancer Soc., Calif., 1966—, chmn. Calif., 1988—89; pres. Alta Bates Hosp. Found., Berkeley, Calif., 1985—86; trustee, treas. U. Calif. Mus., Berkeley, 1970—72; trustee Gasser Found., 1993—; pres., trustee Williams Found., 2001—; chmn. Fedn. Dem. Clubs, Contra Costa, Calif., 1966—68. With US Army, 1943—46, ETO. Recipient St. George medal, Am. Cancer Soc., 1990. Avocation: tennis.

STERN, KENNETH P., former broadcast executive, information technology executive; b. 1963; BA in Internat. Sci., Haverford Coll., Pa.; JD, Yale U. Mgmt. and legal cons. Radio Free Europe/Radio Liberty, Munich and Prague; dep. gen. counsel Clinton/Gore Campaign, 1996; chief counsel 53rd Presdl. Inaugural Com.; sr. adv., cons. to dir., dir. affiliate rels., rsch. & media training US Internat. Broadcasting Bur., Washington, 1996—99; exec. v.p. Nat. Pub. Radio (NPR), 1999—2006,

CEO, 2006—08; bd. dirs. RegScan, Inc., Williamsport, Pa., 2008—. Recipient Harold Kurzman prize in Polit. Sci.; named a Maverick, Details mag., 2007. Mem.: Phi Beta Kappa.

STERN, LEO G., lawyer; b. Mpls., Apr. 10, 1945; s. Philip J. and June I. (Monasch) S.; m. Christine E. Lamb, June 29, 1968; children: Alison M., Zachary A. BA, U. Calif., Davis, 1967; JD cum laude, U. Minn., 1970. Bar: Minn. 1970, U.S. Dist. Ct. Minn. 1971, Calif. 1971, U.S. Ct. Appeals (6th, 7th and 8th cirs.) 1985, U.S. Supreme Ct. 1993, Wis. 1999; cert. mediator and arbitrator, Minn. Ptnr. Cox, King & Stern, Mpls., 1970-77, Wright, West & Diessner, Mpls., 1977-84, Fredrikson & Byron, P.A., Mpls., 1984—. Mem. Minn. Bar Assn. (governing coun. environ. and natural resources law sect. 1989-95, governing coun. litig. sect. 1995-99), Am. Arbitration Assn. (arbitrator, mediator), Nat. Arbitration Forum, Nat. Assn. Securities Dealers, Internat. Inst. Conflict Prevention and Resolution. Avocations: sailing, jogging. Home: 206 Central Ave S Wayzata MN 55391-1818 Office: Fredrikson & Byron PA 4000 US Bank Plz 200 S 6th St Minneapolis MN 55402 Home Phone: 952-476-2461; Office Phone: 612-492-7061. Business E-Mail: lstern@fredlaw.com.

STERN, LEONARD BERNARD, television and motion picture production company executive; b. NYC, Dec. 23, 1923; s. Max and Esther (Marton) S.; m. Gloria Jane Stroock, Aug. 12, 1956; children: Michael Stroock, Kate Jennifer. Student, NYU, 1944. Dir. TV, LA, 1946-53; writer, dir., producer Jackie Gleason Show/Honeymooners, Sergeant Bilko, Steve Allen Show NYC, 1953-60; founder Price-Stern-Sloan, LA, 1959-64, v.p., 1964-69, dir., 1969-80; pres. Heyday Prodns., LA, 1962-69, 75-97; v.p. Talent Assocs./Norton Simon, L.A. and NYC, 1965-75; pres. Tallfellow Prodns., LA, 1997—. Author: (with Roger Price) Mad Libs, 1958, What Not to Name the Baby, 1960, Dear Attila the Hun, 1985; (with Roger Price and Larry Sloan) The Baby Boomer Book of Names, 1985, (with Diane L. Robison) A Martian Wouldn't Say That, 1994; writer, dir.: (motion pictures) Just You and Me, Kid, 1979, Target, 1985, Missing Pieces, 1990; creator, writer, dir. 21 TV series, including Get Smart, McMillan and Wife and He and She, 1953-89; media editor Dialogue newsletter. Mem. adv. coun. Sch. of Arts, NYU; bd. dirs. Nat. Coun. for Families and TV, Inst. for Mental Health Initiatives. Recipient Peabody award U. Ga., Writers Guild award 1956, 66, Nat. Assn. TV Arts and Scis. award 1956, 66-67, Emmy award 1956, 1966. Mem. Writers Guild Am., Dirs. Guild Am., Caucus for Producers, Writers and Dirs. (co-chmn., Mem. of Yr award 1987, Disting. Svc. award 1987), Producers Guild Am. (pres.), Bd. Motion Picure and TV Fund Found. Office: Tallfellow Productions 9454 Wilshire Blvd Ste 550 Beverly Hills CA 90212-2905

STERN, LEONARD NORMAN, real estate developer, former pet supply manufacturing company executive; b. NYC, Mar. 28, 1938; s. Max and Hilda (Lowenthal) Stern; m. Judith Stern (div.); children: Emanuel Theodore, Edward Julius, Andrea Caroline; m. Allison Maher, 1987. BS cum laude, NYU, 1956, MBA, 1957; DHL (hon.), Yeshiva U., 1985; LLD (hon.), Fairleigh Dickinson, 1995. Formerly pres., dir., now chmn., CEO Hartz Group, Inc., 1959—, sold pet div., 1999; chmn., CEO Hartz Mountain Industries Inc., 1966—; founder Stern Pub., 1986—99; owner 667 Madison Ave., NYC, Tribeca Grand Hotel, NYC, SoHo Grand Hotel, NYC, Harmon Cove, Secaucus, NJ, Lincoln Harbor, Weehawken, NJ, Colgate Ctr., Jersey City, Journal Square, Jersey City. Mem. adv. bd. Chem. Bank, NYC, 1970-; active real estate constrn., devel. Bd. dirs. Manhattan Day Sch., Jewish Ctr., NYC; founder Albert Einstein Coll. Medicine, 1958; mem. NYC Holocaust Meml. Commn.; founder Homes for the Homeless, 1986-; trustee NYU, 1976-1996, former chmn. fin. com. Recipient Albert Gallatin medal, NYU; named Graduate and Undergraduate Schs. of Bus. The Leonard N. Stern Sch. Bus., 1984; named one of Forbes' Richest Americans, 1999—, World's Richest People, Forbes mag., 2001—. Office: Hartz Group 667 Madison Ave 26th Floor New York NY 10021

STERN, LOUIS WILLIAM, marketing educator, consultant; b. Boston, Sept. 19, 1935; s. Berthold Summerfield Stern and Gladys (Koch) Cohen; m. Rhona L. Grant; children: Beth Ida, Deborah Lynn. AB, Harvard U., 1957; MBA in Mktg, U. Pa., 1959; PhD in Mktg, Northwestern U., 1962. Mem. staff bus. research and consumer mktg. sects. Arthur D. Little, Inc., Cambridge, Mass., 1961-63; from asst. prof. bus. orgn. to prof. Ohio State U., Columbus, Ohio, 1963—70, prof. mktg., 1970—73; from prof. mktg. to A. Montgomery Ward prof. mktg. Northwestern U., 1973—83, John D. Gray disting. prof. mktg., 1983—2001, John D. Gray disting. prof. emeritus mktg., 2001—; on leave as exec. dir. Mktg. Sci. Inst., Cambridge, Mass., 1983-85; Thomas Henry Carroll Ford Found. vis. prof. Harvard U. Grad. Sch. Bus. Adminstrn., 1984-85; Dorinda and Mark Winkelman Disting. Scholar sr. fellow, co-dir. Jay H. Baker Retailing Initiative, The Wharton Sch., U. Pa., 2004—06; mem. bd. trustees Williston Northhampton Sch., Easthampton, Mass., 2006—; bd. dirs. Acad. Urban Sch. Leadership, Chgo., 2008—. Mem. staff Nat. Commn. on Food Mktg., Washington, 1965-66; vis. assoc. prof. bus. adminstrn. U. Calif., Berkeley, 1969-70; guest lectr. York U., U. Minn., U. Ky., UCLA, Ohio State U., U. N.C., Duke U., U. Wis., U. Pitts., U. Chgo., MIT, U. Mich., U. Pa., Cornell U., U. Mo., Norwegian Sch. Econs. and Bus. Adminstrn.; faculty assoc. Hernstein Inst., Vienna, Austria, 1976-77, Mgmt. Centre Europe, 1988-96; faculty assoc. Gemini Cons. Inc., Montvale, N.J., 1977-96, mem. midwest adv. bd., 1989-94; Xerox rsch. prof. Northwestern U., 1981-82; cons. to FTC, 1973, 80; vis. scholar U. Calif., Berkeley, 1997-2001; mem. faculty adv. bd. CSC Index, 1997-98; co-dir. Jay H. Baker Retailing Initiative Wharton Sch., U. Pa., 2004; bd. dirs., Acad. Urban Sch. Leadership, Chgo., 2007-. Author: Distribution Channels: Behavioral Dimensions, 1969, (with Frederick D. Sturdivant and others) Managerial Analysis in Marketing, 1970, Perspectives in Marketing Management, 1971, (with John R. Grabner, Jr.) Competition in the Marketplace, 1970, (with Anne T. Coughlan, Erin Anderson and Adel I. El-Ansary) Marketing Channels, 6th edit., 2001, (with Thomas L. Eovaldi) Legal Aspects of Marketing Strategy: Antitrust and Consumer Protection Issues, 1984; (with Adel I. El-Ansary and James R. Brown) Management in Marketing Channels, 1989; mem. editl. bd. Jour. Mktg. Rsch., 1976-82, Jour. Mktg., 1979-83, Mktg. Letters, 1988-94; contbr. articles to profl. jours. Mem. exec. com. Northwest Area Coun. on Human Rels., Columbus, 1971—72. Rsch. grantee Ohio State U., 1964-73, Mktg. Sci. Inst., 1976-77, 88-90, 92-94; recipient Harold H. Maynard award best article Jour. Mktg., 1980, Kellogg's Spl. Lifetime Achievement Award for Tchg. Excellence, 1999; named Mktg. Educator of Yr. Sales and Mktg. Execs. Internat., 1989, also Chgo. chpt. 1990, Outstanding Profl. of Yr. award, 1992, and named One of Top 6 Profs. in Kellogg Sch., Northwestern U., Grad. Mgmt. Assocs., 1984-94, (named 6 times Outstanding Prof. Exec. Masters Program), One of Top 12 Tchrs. in U.S., U.S. Bus. Schs., Bus. Week; named Dorinda and Mark Winkelman Disting. scholar, Sr. fellow Wharton Sch., U. Pa., 2004. Mem. AAUP, Am. Mktg. Assn. (mem. program com. educators conf. 1971, chmn. com. 1978, Paul D. Converse award 1986, Richard D. Irwin Disting. Mktg. Educator of Yr. 1994), Hellenic Inst. Mktg. (hon.), Beta Gamma Sigma. Home: Apt 1401 800 Elgin Rd Evanston IL 60201-5629 Office: Northwestern U Kellogg Sch Mgmt Dept Mktg Evanston IL 60208-2001 Home Phone: 847-866-8952; Office Phone: 847-491-2718. Business E-Mail: lwstern@kellogg.northwestern.edu.

STERN, MARCUS A., journalist; b. Washington; Grad., UCLA. With San Pedro News-Pilot, Calif., States News Svc., Washington; with Washington Bur. Copley News Svc., 1983—, news editor, Washington bur., 2000—. Recipient Eugene Katz award, Ctr. Immigration Studies, 1998, Edgar A. Poe award, White House Corrs. Assn., 2006, George Polk award for polit. reporting, 2006, Pulitzer Prize for nat. reporting, 2006. Office: Copley News Svc Washington Bur 1100 Nat Press Bldg Washington DC 20045 Business E-Mail: marcus.stern@copleydc.com.

STERN, MARGARET BASSETT, retired special education educator, author; b. Bklyn., June 6, 1920; d. Preston Rogers and Jeanne (Mordorf) Bassett; m. Fritz R. Stern Oct. 11, 1947 (div. Dec. 1992); children: Frederick Preston, Katherine Stern Brennan. BA, Wellesley Coll., 1942; MEd, Bank Street Coll. Edn., NYC, 1943, MEd, 1974. Propr. Castle Sch., NYC, 1944-51; dir. Mothers' Coop. Nursery Sch., Ithaca, N.Y., 1952-54; tchr. sci. and math. The Brearley Sch., NYC, 1956-57. Cons., lectr. Head Start, Tuskegee, Ala., 1964; cons. in math. The Gateway Sch., N.Y.C., 1967-90; spl. lectr. Columbia U. Tchrs. Coll., N.Y.C., 1990-94; condr. workshops in Eng., 1960-88. Author: (with Catherine Stern and Toni Gould) Structural Reading Program, Workbooks and Teachers Guides A through E, 1963, 3d edit., 1978, Structural Arithmetic Workbooks and Teachers Guides Grades 1-3, 1965, 2d edit., 1966, (with Stern) Children Discover Arithmetic, 1971, (with Gould) Spotlight on Phonics, Four Workbooks and Teachers Guides, 1980, Sound/Symbol Activities and Decoding Activities, 1980, 2d edit., 1994; Experimenting with Numbers, 1988, 2004, Structural Arithmetic, 1-3, 1992, 2006. Recipient award, Orton Dyslexia Soc. N.Y., 1989, Bank St. Coll. Edn., 1998. Mem.: Nat. Coun. Tchrs. Math., Internat. Dyslexia Assn. Home: 3204 River Crescent Dr Annapolis MD 21401 Business E-Mail: structuralarith@aol.com.

STERN, MARILYN, technical services, academic librarian; b. NYC; 2 children. MLS, C. W. Post Grad. Sch. Libr. Sci., Greenvale, NY, 1976. Info. specialist Marshe InfoSvcs. Inc., Roslyn, NY, 1977—84; libr. dir. NY Chiropractic Coll., Greenvale, 1985—91; tech. svcs. libr. US Mcht. Marine Acad., Kings Point, NY, 1991—. Mem.: Assn. Coll. & Rsch. Librs., NY Libr. Assn., Nassau County Libr. Assn. Office: US Merchant Marine Acad Steamboat Rd Kings Point NY 11024

STERN, MARILYN JEAN, special education educator; b. Akron, Ohio, Oct. 7, 1937; d. Walter Keith Pallage and Betty Jane Freeman-Pallage; m. Robert Stern, June 14, 1974 (dec.); children: John Daily, Anne Tunney, Jane Henault, Andrew Daily. BS in Elem. Edn., U. Akron, 1961, MS in Spl. Edn., 1978. Cert. in tchg. Ohio, 1974, Penn., 1963, in tchg. spl. edn. 1978. Tchr. Phila. Sch. Dist., 1963—64; spl. edn. tchr. Summit County Bd. Mental Health, Tallmadge, Ohio, 1974—78, Girard Sch. Dist., Pa., 1978—2004; spl. edn. Learning Disabilities tchr. NW Tri-County Intermediate Unit, Girard, 1978—88, county computer advisor edn. Erie County, Pa., 1988—90, ret., 2004. Computer cons. NW Tri-County Intermediate Unit, 1985—90; vol. reading tutor Neighborhood Network Program, Erie County, 2004—; presenter in field; leader spl. programs 4th grade level. Mem. Lake Erie Ballet Bd., Erie, Pa., 1980—92; polit. action chair Girard Fedn. Tchrs., 2000—04; past pres. Erie Reading Coun.; nominating chmn. Local Ridge Coun., act 48 hours chairperson, spl. projects chair; reader Erie Zoo. Mem.: Keystone State Reading Assn. (exec. bd. mem. 2003—), Internat. Reading Assn. (chair 2000—, del. to conf. 2005), Reading Tchrs. Orgn. (pres. 2003—05). Presbyterian. Avocations: reading, gardening, quilting, fiber arts, quilting. Home: 1420 Lord Rd Fairview PA 16415

STERN, MITCHELL, broadcast executive; B, U. Pa., 1976; MBA, U. Chgo., 1978. With CBS TV Stas. Divsn., 1978—86, dir. planning and adminstrn. WCBS-TV NYC, dir. planning and adminstrn. WBBM-TV Chgo., fin. analyst corp. office; v.p., CFO Fox TV Stas., LA, 1986—90, v.p., sta. mgr. KTTV-Fox 11, 1990—92, sr. v.p., 1990—92, exec. v.p., COO, 1992—93, pres., COO, 1993—98, chmn., CEO, 1998—2003, Twentieth TV, LA, 1998—2003; CEO DirecTV, 2003—05. Office: Fox TV Stas Inc 205 E 67th St New York NY 10021

STERN, MORT(IMER) P(HILLIP), communications educator, editor, reporter, consultant; b. New Haven, Feb. 20, 1926; s. Bernard and Louise Eleanor (Spiro) S.; m. Patricia Ruth Freeman, Jan. 10, 1946; children: Susan C., Margaret L. AB, U. Ark., 1947; MS, Columbia U., NYC, 1949; postgrad., Harvard U., Cambridge, Mass., 1954—55; PhD, U. Denver, 1969. Reporter S.W.-Am., Ft. Smith, Ark., 1946-47; night bur. mgr. UPI, Little Rock, 1947-48; reporter, polit. writer, state editor Ark. Gazette, Little Rock, 1949-51; reporter, rewrite man Denver Post, 1951-53, night city editor, 1953-54, asst. editor Rocky Mountain Empire sect., 1955-56, mng. editor, 1956-58, assoc. editor, 1958, editl. page editor, 1958-65, asst. to pub., 1965-70, editl. page editor, 1971-73; dean Sch. Pub. Comm. U. Ala., 1973-74; dean Sch. Journalism U. Colo., Boulder, 1974-77; lectr. journalism U. Denver, 1953-54, adj. prof., 1970, exec. dir. pub. affairs, 1977-78, exec. asst. to chancellor, 1978-84; prof., chmn. dept. journalism and mass communication U. No. Colo., Greeley, 1985-90. Atwood prof. journalism U. Alaska, Anchorage, 1981-82. With USAAF, 1944-45. Mem. Georgetown Bd. of Selectmen, 1997-99; mem. Georgetown Bd. Adjustment, 2001-07. Nieman fellow Harvard U., 1954-55; named Disting. Alumnus dept. journalism U. Ark., 1999; inducted to Fulbright Coll. Alumni Acad. U. Ark., 1999. Mem.: Georgetown Libr. Assn. (v.p. 1999, pres. 2001—04, bd. dirs.), Phi Beta Kappa, Sigma Delta Chi, Omicron Delta Kappa. Baptist. Home: PO Box 549 Georgetown CO 80444-0549

STERN, NATHALIE M., pediatrician; b. Tourcoing, France, Sept. 1, 1964; MD, Lille U. Medicine & Pharmacy, Nord, France, 1993. Diplomate Am. Bd. Pediat. Internship in pediat. NY Hosp. Cornell Med. Ctr., NYC, 1994—95, residency in pediat., 1995—97, attending physician, 1998, clin. instr. pediat., 1998, Lenox Hill Hosp., NYC, 1998; pediatrcian The Continuum Ctr. Health and Healing, NYC; pvt. practice in pediatric homeopathy France. Contbr. articles to profl. jours. Mem.: French Homeopathic Ednl. Ctr. Office: c/o The Continuum Ctr Health and Healing 245 Fifth Ave 2nd Fl New York NY 10016 Office Phone: 646-935-2220.

STERN, NOAH J., lawyer; b. Albany, NY, Apr. 26, 1971; BA, U. Calif. Berkeley, 1993; MA, Ind. U. Bloomington, 1996; JD, NY U. Sch. Law, 1999. Bar: Ohio 1999, US Tax Ct. Ptnr. Dinsmore & Shohl LLP, Cin. Mem., Bd. Trustee Adath Israel Synagogue. Named one of Ohio's Rising Stars, Super Lawyers, 2006, 2007. Mem.: Ohio State Bar Assn., Cin. Bar Assn. Office: Dinsmore & Shohl LLP 255 E Fifth St Ste 1900 Cincinnati OH 45202-4700 Office Phone: 513-977-8460. Office Fax: 513-977-8141.

STERN, PAULA, international trade consultant; b. Chgo., Mar. 31, 1945; d. Lloyd and Fan (Wener) Stern; m. Paul A. London; children: Gabriel Stern London, Genevieve Stern London. BA, Goucher Coll., 1967; MA in Middle Eastern Studies, Harvard U., 1969; MA in Internat. Affairs, Fletcher Sch. of Law and Diplomacy, 1970, MA in Law and Diplomacy, 1970, PhD, 1976; D Comml. Sci. (hon.), Babson Coll., 1985; LLD (hon.), Goucher Coll., 1985. From legis. asst. to sr. legis. asst. to US Sen. Gaylord Nelson US Senate, Washington, 1972—74, 1976; guest scholar Brookings Inst., Washington, 1975-76; policy analyst Pres. Carter-V.P. Mondale Transition Team, Washington, 1977-78; internat. affairs fellow Council on Fgn. Rels., Washington, 1977-78; commr. Internat. Trade Commn., Washington, 1978—87, chairwomen, 1984—86; sr. assoc. Carnegie Endowment for Internat. Peace, Washington, 1986-88; chairwomen The Stern Group, Inc., 1988—; sr. fellow Program Policy Inst., 1994—95. Howard W. Aikire chmn. internat. bus. and econs. Hamline U., 1994—2000; bd. dirs. Avon Products, Inc., 1997—, Hasbro, Inc., Rent-A-Center, Inc., 2009—; mem., sr. advisor U.S. trade policy coun. Competition Policy Inst., 1991—93; sr. fellow Progressive Policy Inst., 1994—95; pub. vice chairwoman Atlantic Coun. US; trustee Com. Econ. Devel.; mem. Inter-Am. Dialogue, Coun. Fgn. Rels., Bretton Woods Com.; mem. high level adv. group Global Subsidies Initiative Project; past co-chair Internat. Competition Adv. Com.; antitrust divsn. US Dept. Justice; past chmn. US Export-Import Bank; past mem. US Pres. Adv. Com. on Trade Policy and Negotiation. Author: Water's Edge--Domestic Politics and the Making of American Foreign Policy, 1979; contbr. articles to profl. jours. Mem. adv. coun. Columbia U. Sch. Social Work; bd. dirs. Carnegie Coun. Ethics and Internat. Affairs. Recipient Journalism award, Alicia Patterson Fund, 1971, Joseph Papp Award for Racial Harmony, Found. Ethnic Understanding, 2004. Democrat. Jewish. Avocations: sculpting, tennis, dance. Office: The Stern Group, Inc 3314 Ross Pl NW Washington DC 20008-3332 Office Phone: 202-966-7894. Office Fax: 202-966-7891. Business E-Mail: pstern@sterngroup.biz.

STERN, PHYLLIS NOERAGER, nursing educator; b. San Mateo, Calif., Sept. 2, 1925; d. Philip Julius and Grace Ann (Zoellen) Noerager; m. David Arthur Hungerford, May 20, 1949 (div. Sept. 1956); 1 child, Paula Ann; m. Milton Stern, July 5, 1960 (dec. Jan. 2001). AA, Coll. San Mateo, 1968; BS magna cum laude, San Francisco State U., 1970; MS, U. Calif., San Francisco, 1971, D of Nursing Sci., 1976; LLD (hon.), Dalhousie U., Can., 2003. Asst. prof. Calif. State U., Hayward, 1971-76, U. Calif., San Francisco, 1976-80; prof. Northwestern State U. La., Shreveport, 1980-82; prof., dir. Dalhousie U., Halifax, N.S., Can., 1983-87, prof., 1987-91; prof. emeritus Ind. U., Indpls., 1991-96, prof., 1996—. Editor, author: Women Health and Culture, 1986; editor: Childbirth and Childcare, 1988, Lesbian Health Care, 1991, Grounded Theory: The Second Generation, 2009; editor-in-chief: Health Care for Women Internat., 1983-2001; co-editor: (with R.S. Schreiber) Grounded Theory for Nurses (Am. Jour. Nursng Book of Yr. award 2001), 2001. Health educator Battered Women's Shelter, Indpls., Salvation Army, Indpls., 1994-96. Named Disting. Alumna U. Calif., San Francisco, 1995, named to Hall of Fame; rsch. grantee Ind. U., 1995; Glenn W. Irwin Jr. Rsch. scholar, 1999; recipient Lifetime Achievement award for contbns. to women's health internationally Internat. Soc. Qualitative Rschrs. Fellow Am. Acad. Nursing (mem. expert panel 1989-96, Living Legend 2008), Am. Acad. Practice Coun. (Disting. Practitioner 1992), Coun. Gen. Internat. on Women's Health Issues (co-founder 1984, coun. gen. emeritus 2002—, Biennial Phyllis Stern lectr. to Internat. Congress on Women's Health Issues 2004—), Sigma Theta Tau. Avocations: films, reading, walking, mentoring. Office: Ind U 1111 Middle Dr Indianapolis IN 46202-5243 Home Phone: 317-872-7363; Office Phone: 317-274-0032. Personal E-mail: pnstern@comcast.net. Business E-Mail: pstern@iupui.edu.

STERN, RICHARD DAVID, investment company executive; b. New Rochelle, NY, Nov. 5, 1936; s. Leo and Grace Marjorie S.; m. Phyllis Marlene Edelstein, Nov. 20, 1966; children: Marjorie Anne, Andrew Howard. AB, Princeton U., 1958; MBA, Harvard U., 1962. CFA. 1st v.p. Newburger, Loeb & Co., NYC, 1962-74, also bd. dirs., 1969-74; sr. investment officer Ctrl. Trust Co. (now known as PNC Bank), Cin., 1974—76, owner bus. valuation cons. co., 1976—78; v.p. Gt. Western Bank & Trust Co. (now Wells Fargo Bank), Phoenix, 1978-84; pres. Stern, Ludke & Co. (now Stellar Capital Mgmt. LLC.), Phoenix, 1984—, mng. mem., 2000—. Co-author: Air Cushion Vehicles, 1962. Trustee endourment trust Phoenix Chamber Music Soc., 1982-91; v.p., 1986-90, bd. dirs., 1982-91, 93-94; pres. Cen. Ariz. chpt. Arthritis Found., 1982-84, chmn. planned giving com., 1986-91, mem. nat. planned giving com., 1987-89; chmn. endowments and trusts com. Temple Beth Israel, Phoenix, 1980-83; dir., investment com. Endowment Found., Temple Solel, Paradise Valley, 1990-92; pres. Am. Jewish Com., Phoenix, 1983-84, bd. dirs., 1980-84, adv. bd., 1985-2005; Jewish Cmty. Found., Greater Phoenix, 2008-, mem. profl. adv. com. 2008-; bd. dirs. Asian Arts Coun., Phoenix Art Mus., 1987-93, v.p., 1989-90, pres., 1990-92; trustee Ariz. Theatre Co., 1990-97, mem. regional nominating com., 1995-97, chmn., 1995-96, asst. treas., 1996-97; grants award panelist Phoenix Office of Arts and Culture, 2002, 05. Mem. CFA Inst., Phoenix CFA Soc. (chmn. profl. conduct com. 1980-83, membership com. 1990-91, bd. dirs.), Anti-Defamation League (dir. Ctrl. Ariz. chpt. 1986—, exec. bd. 1989—, chair nominating com. 1990-94, 2001—, chair bd. devel. 1993-94, treas. 1994-2004, assoc. nat. commr. 1998—), Princeton Alumni Assn. No. Ariz. (alumni schs. com. 1992—, v.p. 2005—), Univ. Club Phoenix (bd. dirs. 1990-92, fin. com. 1990-91), Harvard Bus. Sch. Club Ariz. (bd. dirs. 1991—, pres. 1993-95), Clearwater Hills Improvement Assn. (dir. 2002-08, sec. 2006-08). Republican. Home: 7547 N Lakeside Ln Paradise Valley AZ 85253-2857 Office: 2200 E Camelback Rd Ste 130 Phoenix AZ 85016-3455 Business E-Mail: rstern@stellarmgt.com.

STERN, ROBERT, psychiatrist; b. Aug. 12, 1928; BS, Swiss Fed. Inst. Tech., Zurich, 1951; MS, Yale U., 1953, PhD, 1956; MD, Case Western Res. U., 1966. Diplomate Am. Bd. Psychiatry and Neurology; lic. physician, Conn. Asst. prof. chemistry Wesleyan U., Middletown, Conn., 1957—58, Conn. Coll., New London, 1959-60; supr. bio-organic chem. rsch. Arthur D. Little, Inc., Cambridge, Mass., 1960-62; vis. fellow medicine Mass. Gen. Hosp., 1964; rsch. assoc. biol. chemistry Harvard Med. sch., Boston, 1964, tchg. fellow psychiatry, 1967-68; intern medicine King County Hosp./U. Wash., Seattle, 1966-67; resident in psychiatry McLean Hosp., Belmont, Mass., 1967-68; jr./sr. asst. resident internal medicine Yale-New Haven Hosp., 1968-70, clin. fellow medicine, 1970-71; postdoctoral fellow psychiatry Yale U. Sch. Medicine, 1971-73, asst. clin. prof. psychiatry, 1974-86, assoc. clin. prof. psychiatry, 1986—; pvt. practice New Haven, 1973—. Cons. Child Guidance clinic of Southeastern Conn., New London, 1973-82; cons. CHAMPUS peer reviewer Qualidigm, Inc., Middletown, 1994—; lectr. in field. Contbr. articles to profl. jours. Fellow Am. Psychiat. Assn. (Disting. life fellow); mem. New Haven Individual Practice Assn. (co-chmn. psychiatry panel 1985-98, quality assurance com. 1989-98, bd. dirs. 1986-89), Conn. Psychiatry Soc. (councilor-at-large 2001—06, councilor 2000-01, pres. New Haven/Middlesex chpt. 1999-2000, treas. 1996-99). Conn. State Med. Soc., New Haven County Med. Assn. Office: 340 Whitney Ave New Haven CT 06511-2317 Office Phone: 203-562-9110.

STERN, ROBERT ARTHUR MORTON, architect, educator, writer; b. NYC, May 23, 1939; s. Sidney S. and Sonya (Cohen) Stern; m. Lynn G. Solinger, May 22, 1966 (div. 1977); 1 child, Nicholas S.G. BA, Columbia U., 1960; MArch, Yale U., 1965. Registered architect, Calif., Colo., Conn., Fla., Hawaii, Ill., Ind., Maine, Mass., Mich., NH, NJ, Ohio, SC, Tex., NY, DC, Ga. Program dir. Archtl. League NY, 1965-66; designer Office Richard Meier, Architect, NYC, 1966; cons. Small Parks Program, Dept. Parks, NYC, 1966-70; urban designer, asst. to asst. adminstr. housing and devel. adminstrn. NYC, 1967-70; ptnr. Robert A.M. Stern & John S. Hagmann, Architects, NYC, 1969-77; prin. Robert A.M. Stern, Architects, 1977-89, sr. ptnr., 1989—; dean Yale Sch. Arch., 1998—, J.M. Hoppin prof. arch., 2000—. Bd. dirs. Walt Disney Co., 1992-2003; cons. Eye on New York TV documentary, CBS-TV, 1966-67; mem. architecture com. Whitney Mus. Am. Art, 1970-76, adv. commn., archtl. sect. Venice Biennale, 1980; lectr. architecture Columbia U., 1970-72, asst. prof. 1973-77, assoc. prof., 1977-82, prof. 1982—; vis. fellow Inst. for Architecture and Urban Studies, 1974-76, trustee, 1983-85; dir. Temple Hoyne Buell Ctr. for Study Am. Architecture, 1984-88, dir. Hist. Preservation Program, 1991-98; vis. lectr. Yale U., 1972, 73; vis. critic R.I. Sch. Design, 1976, U. Pa., 1977, N.C. State U., Raleigh, 1978; William Henry Bishop vis. prof. architecture Yale U., fall 1978; editorial cons. Archtl. History Found., 1979-83. Author: New Directions in American Architecture, 1969, rev. edit., 1977, George Howe: Toward a Modern American Architecture, 1975, (with Deborah Nevins) The Architect's Eye, 1979, (with John M. Massengale) The Anglo-American Suburb, 1981, (with Thomas Catalano) Raymond Hood, 1982, East Hamptons Heritage, 1982, (with John M. Massengale and Gregory Gilmartin) New York 1900, 1983, Pride of Place, 1986, (with Gregory Gilmartin and Thomas Mellins) New York 1930, 1987, (with Raymond Gastil) Modern Classicism, 1988, The House That Bob Built, 1991, The American Houses of Robert A.M. Stern, 1991, (with Thomas Mellins and David Fishman) New York 1960, 1995, (with Thomas Mellins and David Fishman) New York 1880, 1999, (with David Fishman and Jacob Tilove) New York 2000, 2006. Mem. NYC Mayor's Task Force on Urban Design, 1966-67, architects selection com. NY Conv. Ctr., 1979; trustee Am. Fedn. Arts, 1967-79, Inst. for Architecture and Urban Studies, 1983-85; v.p. Cunningham Dance Found., 1969-73; bd. dirs. Preservation League NY, 1984—, Historic Landmarks Preservation Ctr., 1995—; trustee Nat. Bldg. Mus., 1999—, Trust for Historic Preservation, 2000—. Recipient John Jay award, Columbia Coll., 1991, Athena award, Congress for the New Urbanism, 2007, bd. dirs.' honor, Inst. Classical Architecture and Classical America, 2007, Vincent Scully Prize, Nat. Bldg. Mus., 2008. Fellow Am. Acad. Arts & Scis., AIA (bd. dirs. NY chpt. 1976-78, Disting. archtl. award, NY chpt., 1982, 1984, 1985, 1987, Nat. honor award, 1980, 1985, 1990, medal of honor, 1984), Soc. Archtl. Historians (bd. dirs. 1975-78), Archtl. League N.Y. (pres. 1973-77, exec. com. 1977—), NY State Assn. Architects (excellence in design cert., 1985), Am. Architecture Found. (bd. regents 1989-91), Skidmore, Owings and Merrill Found. (bd. dirs. 1984-90), Chgo. Inst. for Architecture and Urbanism (bd. dirs. 1990-93), Century Assn., Coffee House Club. Office: Robert AM Stern Architects LLP 460 W 34th St Fl 18 New York NY 10001-2320 also: Yale Sch Architecture 180 York St New Haven CT 06511-8924 Office Phone: 212-967-5100, 203-432-2279. Office Fax: 212-967-5588. E-mail: robert.a.m.stern@yale.edu.*

STERN, ROBERT D., publishing executive; b. NYC, Sept. 30, 1929; s. Morris and Jean (Gordon) S.; m. Natalie Greenberg, Sept. 5, 1952 (div. 1978); children: Mitchell, Bradley; m. Roslyne Paige, June 5, 1978. BA, Syracuse U., 1950; JD, NYU, 1953, LLM, 1958. Bar: N.Y. 1955, U.S. Dist. Ct. (D.C. cir.) 1953, U.S. Supreme Ct. 1967. Ptnr. Fink, Weinberger, Levin & Gottschalk, NYC, 1957-59, 1957—72; chmn. Rudor Consol. Industries, 1972—99, Dance Mag., Inc., 1985—2001, AGC/Sedgwick Inc., Princeton, NJ, 1990—2001. Bd. dirs. Ctr. for Graphic Comms. Mgmt. and Tech., NYU, N.Y.C., 1979—; chmn. bd. dirs. AGC Sedgwick, Princeton, N.J., Rudor Consol. Ind. Inc.; pub. Stern's Performing Arts Directory, 1989-98. Bd. dirs. YMCA, N.Y.C., 1987-90 Mem. ABA, N.Y. State Bar Assn., Sheldrake Yacht Club (Mamaroneck, N.Y.), Birchwood Country Club (Westport, Conn.). Avocations: tennis, skiing, sailing. Home: 1930 Broadway Apt 25C New York NY 10023-6946 Office Phone: 203-454-0752.

STERN, ROBERT JAMES, geologist, educator; b. Sacramento, Feb. 2, 1951; s. Robert Joseph Stern and Esther Juanita Weigel; m. Melissa Byer Fenton, Nov. 1950; children: Ryan Robert, Rebecca Lynn, Alexis Byer. BS, U. Calif., Davis, 1974; PhD, U. Calif., San Diego, 1979. Rsch. fellow Carnegie Inst. Washington, 1979-82; from asst. to assoc. to prof. U. Tex., Dallas, 1982—. Mem. editl. bd. Geology, Geologische Rundschau, 1982—; contbr. articles to profl. jours. NSF grantee, 1982—, NASA grantee, 1987—. Mem. Am. Geophys. Union, Geol. Soc. Am. Office: U Tex Geosci Dept PO Box 830688 Dept Richardson TX 75083-0688 Home: 4111 Gilbert Ave Apt 212 Dallas TX 75219-3829

STERN, ROBERT MORRIS, psychologist, gastroenterology researcher; b. NYC, June 18, 1937; s. Irving Dan and Nellie (Wachstetter) S.; m. Wilma Olch, June 19, 1960; children: Jessica Leigh, Alison Rachel. AB, Franklin and Marshall Coll., 1958; MS, Tufts U., 1960; PhD, Ind. U., 1963. Research assoc. dept. psychology Ind. U., 1963-65; asst. prof. psychology Pa. State U., 1965-68, assoc. prof., 1968-73, prof., 1973—2005, emeritus, 2005—, disting. prof., 1992—2005, head dept., 1978-87. Author (with W.J. Ray): Biofeedback, 1977; author: (with W.J. Ray and C.M. Davis) Psychophysiological Recording, 1980; author: (with K.L. Koch) Electrogastrography, 1985; author: (with W.J. Ray and K.S. Quigley) Psychophysiological Recording, 2nd edit., 2001; author: (with K.L. Koch) Handbook of Electrogastrography, 2004; contbr. articles. Recipient Nat. Media award Am. Psychol. Found., 1978 Mem. Am. Psychol. Soc., Aerospace Med. Assn., Soc. Psychophysiol. Rsch., Am. Gastroent. Assn., Internat. EGG Soc., Functional Brain-Gut Rsch. Assn., Internat. Brain-Gut Soc. Home: 1360 Greenwood Cir State College PA 16803-3232 Office: Pa State U Moore Bldg University Park PA 16802-3105 Home Phone: 814-238-7063. Business E-Mail: rs3@psu.edu.

STERN, ROBIN LAURI, medical physicist; b. Urbana, Ill., Mar. 12, 1959; d. Morris Stern and Myrna (Tanzer) Stern Longenecker; m. Donald Neil Bittner, May 20, 1989. BA in Physics and German Studies, Rice U., 1981; MS in Physics, U. Mich., 1983, PhD in Physics, 1987. Rsch. assoc. Duke U., Durham, N.C., 1987-89; postdoctoral rsch. fellow U. Mich., Ann Arbor, 1989-91; asst. prof. U. Calif.-Davis, San Francisco, 1992-98; assoc. prof. U. Calif., Davis, 1998—2004, prof., 2004—. Cons. Scanditronix, Inc., Livonia, Mich., 1991. Contbr. articles to jours. Rev. of Sci. Instruments, Magnetic Resonance Imaging, Med. Physics. Argonne Nat. Lab. grantee, 1985-86; Nat. Merit scholar, 1977-81. Fellow Am. Assn. Physicists in Medicine; mem. Am. Soc. Therapeutic Radiology and Oncology, Sigma Pi Sigma, Phi Beta Kappa. E-mail: robin.stern@ucdc.udavis.edu.

STERN, ROSLYNE PAIGE, magazine publisher; b. Chgo., May 26, 1926; d. Benjamin Gross and Clara (Sniderman) Roer; m. William E. Weber, May 3, 1944 (div. Mar. 1956); m. Richard S. Paige, June 28, 1958 (div. Apr. 1978); children: Sandra Weber (dec.), Barbara Paige Kaplan, Elizabeth Paige (dec.); m. Robert D. Stern, June 5, 1978. Cert., U. Chgo., 1945. Profl. model, singer, 1947-53; account exec. Interstate United, Chgo., 1955-58; sales mgr. Getting To Know You Internat., Great Neck, NY, 1963-71, exec. v.p., 1971-78; pub. After Dark Mag., NYC, 1978-82; assoc. pub. Dance Mag., NYC, 1978-85, pres., pub., 1985—2001, pres. emeritus, 2001—. Bd. dirs. Rudor Consol. Industries, Inc., N.Y.C., AGC/Sedgwick, Inc., Princeton, N.J. Founding pres. Dance Mag. Found., NYC, 1984-86 chair Dance Mag. awards, 1986-2004; life mem. nat. women's com. Brandeis U., Waltham, Mass., 1958—; bd. dirs. Westport Arts Ctr.; The Internation Com. for Dance Libr. of Israel. Recipient Disting. Svc. award Dance Notation Bur., 1996, Am. Coll. Dance Festival award, 1998, Pres.'s award Dance Masters of Am., Inc., 1998, Documents of Dance award Dance Library of Israel, 1999. Mem. Pub. Relations Soc. Am., LWV, Am. Theatre Wing, Nat. Arts Club. Democrat. Jewish. Avocations: dance, theater, opera, visual arts, travel. Home and Office: 1930 Broadway Ste 25C New York NY 10023 Personal E-mail: sterndance@aol.com.

STERN, SAMUEL ALAN, lawyer; b. Phila., Jan. 21, 1929; AB, U. Pa., 1949; LLB, Harvard U., 1952. Bar: Mass. 1952, D.C. 1958. Ptnr. Wilmer, Cutler & Pickering, Washington, 1962-88, Dickstein, Shapiro & Morin, Washington, 1988-92, Hills, Stern & Morley LLP, Washington, 1999—; pvt. practice law and bus. Washington and St. Petersburg, Russia, 1992-94, Washington, 1997-98; counsel Rogers & Wells, Washington, NYC, 1994-97. Vis. prof. law Harvard Law Sch., Cambridge, Mass., 1976; dir. Internat. Law Inst. Georgetown U., 1971—2004, adj. prof. law, 1979—92; asst. counsel Warren Commn., 1964; cons. UN, 1984—96; bd. dirs. Warp Cybertech Corp., Verihealth Internat., Pan-Asia Pictures, VeriPay, Target World Ltd., Commonwealth Shore Power, China Alarm Holdings LTD, Global Dataguard Inc., Precipia, Inc., RST Industries LLC, Exactus US Inc., BB Tech. Solutions LLC; lectr. profl. confs. on project fin., privatization, cross-border investment and alternative dispute resolution; arbitrator internat. comml. disputes. Contbr. articles to legal jours. Mem. ABA, Am. Law Inst., Internat. Bar Assn., D.C. Bar Assn. Home: 210 Lee Ct Alexandria VA 22314 Office: 1120 20th St NW North Bldg 2d Fl Washington DC 20036 Office Phone: 202-822-1638. Business E-Mail: sastern@hillsandstern.com.

STERN, SANDOR, film director, writer; b. Timmins, Ont., Can., July 13, 1936; s. Stephen Mendel and Ann (Gurevitch) S.; m. Marlene Greenstein, May 19, 1957 (div. 1976); children: Shawn, Mark, Adam, Jamie; m. Kandy Lea Cave, Jan. 26, 1980; children: Lauren, Seth. BA, U. Toronto, 1957, MD, 1961. Intern New Mount Sinai Hosp., Toronto, 1961-62; physician Toronto, Can., 1962-68; writer LA, 1968—; dir., 1974—. Writer (films) The Amityville Horror, 1978, Fastbreak, 1979 (NAACP Image award); writer, dir. (film) Pin, 1988, (TV films) Web of Deceit, 1990, Deception: A Mother's Secret, 1991, Dangerous Pursuit, 1989, John and Yoko, 1985, Muggable Mary: Street Cop, 1982, (TV miniseries) Woman on the Run: The Lawrencia Bembeneck Story, 1992-93; dir. (TV films) Glitz, 1988, Passions, 1984, Heart of a Child, 1993, The Stranger Beside Me, 1995, Gridlock, 1995, Badge of Betrayal, 1996, In My Sister's Shadow, 1997; co-writer, dir. (TV films) Jericho Fever, 1992, Duplicates, 1992, A Child's Cry for Help, 1994, (episodes for TV shows) Touched by an Angel, 1997, 98, 99, Promised Land, 1997, 98, 99, Early Edition, 2000, Leap Years, 2001. Mem. Writers Guild Am., Dirs. Guild Am., Producers Guild Am. Office: Jamson Prodns Inc 9472 Rembert Ln Beverly Hills CA 90210-1720 Personal E-mail: sandor.stren@att.net.

STERN, S(EESA) BEATRICE, executive secretary, medical/surgical nurse; b. Atlantic City, Feb. 13, 1919; d. Max and Gussie (Thierman) Rosen; m. Francis H. Stern, June 29, 1958 (dec. Feb. 1973); m. Bernard N. Abelson, Dec. 5, 1973 (div. Feb. 1992). AA, Miami-Dade C.C., Fla., 1982, AS in Nursing with honors, 1982; grad. with honors. RN Fla., NJ, Nev. Profl. dancer, 1928—32; sec. N.J. State Highway Dept., Trenton, 1938-41; columnist N.J. Herald, Trenton, 1939-41; sec. U.S. Army, various locations, 1941-46; legal sec. Gus Feuer, Atty. at Law, Miami, 1946-47; exec. sec. to pres. Pharms., Inc., NYC, 1947-58; med. sec. Phila., 1958-72; nurse Mt. Sinai Med. Ctr., Miami Beach, Fla., 1982-83, Atlantic City Med. Ctr., 1983-84. Vol. Hollywood Med. Ctr., 1992-96, Aventura Med. Ctr., 1992—; mem. Bd. Govs. Brith Sholom, 1970—. Mem. Brith Sholom Women (nat. pres. 1970-72), Four Chaplains Legion of Hon., Phi Theta Kappa. Achievements include competitive scholastic swimming with Olympic (1936) tryout 1934-36. Avocations: swimming, handcrafts, reading, crossword puzzles.

STERN, STEPHAN TIMOTHY, toxicologist, researcher; s. Timothy Land Stern and Barbara Ann Burns; m. Ann Marie Masters, Jan. 26, 2006. BS, U. Rochester, 1994; PhD, U. Conn., Storrs, 2001. Postdoc. fellow divsn. drug delivery and disposition U. NC, Sch. Pharmacy, Chapel Hill, 2001—04; toxicologist Nat. Cancer Inst., Frederick, Md., 2004—. Postdoc. fellow, Nat. Inst. Environ. Health and Safety, 2001—02. Mem.: Internat. Soc. Study Xenobiotics, Soc. Toxicology. Achievements include research in toxicology and pharmacology of nanotechnology drug delivery platforms. Office: Nat Cancer Inst Frederick MD 21702-1201

STERN, WALTER EUGENE, neurosurgeon, educator; b. Portland, Oreg., Jan. 1, 1920; s. Walter Eugene and Ida May (McCoy) S.; m. Elizabeth Naffziger, May 24, 1946; children: Geoffrey Alexander, Howard Christian, Eugenia Louise, Walter Eugene III. AB cum laude, U. Calif., MD, 1943. Diplomate Am. Bd. Neurol. Surgery (vice chmn. 1975-80). Surg. intern, asst. resident surgery and neurol. surgery U. Calif. Hosp., 1943-46, asst. resident neurol. surgery and neuropathology, 1948; clin. clk. Nat. Hosp. Paralyzed and Epileptic, London, 1948-49; Nat. Rsch. fellow med. sci. Johns Hopkins, Balt., 1949-50; asst. resident, resident U. Calif. Svc., 1951; clin. instr. U. Calif., 1951; asst. prof. neurosurgery UCLA, 1952-56, assoc. prof., 1956-59, prof., 1959—87, prof. emeritus, 1987—, chief divsn. neurosurgery, 1952-85, chmn. dept. surgery, 1981-87; NIH spl. fellow univ. lab. physiology Oxford (Eng.) U., 1961-62. Cons. neurosurgery Wadsworth VA Hosp. Former mem., chmn. editl. bd. Jour. Neurosurgery; contbr. articles to sci. jours., chpts. to books. Lt. to capt. M.C. AUS, 1946-48. Fellow ACS (sec.); mem. AMA, Am. Surg. Assn., Pacific Coast Surg. Assn., L.A. Surg. Soc. (pres. 1978), Am. Assn. Neurol. Surgeons (pres. 1979-80, Cushing medalist, 1992), James IV Assn. Surgeons, Western Neurosurg. Soc. (past pres.), Soc. Neurol. Surgeons (past pres., Disting. Svc. award 1999), Neurosurg. Soc. Am., Am. Neurol. Assn., Soc. Univ. Surgeons, Soc. Brit. Neurol. Surgeons (hon.), Calif. Assn. Neurol. Surgery (Disting. Svc. award 2004), Phi Beta Kappa, Sigma Xi, Alpha Omega Alpha. Episcopalian. Home: 435 Georgina Ave Santa Monica CA 90402-1909

STERN, WALTER PHILLIPS, investment company executive; b. NYC, Sept. 26, 1928; s. Leo and Marjorie (Phillips) S.; m. Elizabeth May, Feb. 12, 1958; children: Sarah May, William May, David May. AB, Williams Coll., 1950; MBA, Harvard U., 1952. With Lazard Freres & Co., NYC, 1953-54; assoc. Burnham & Co., Inc. (predecessor firm to Drexel Burnham Lambert Group, Inc.), NYC, 1954-60, ptnr., 1960-71, sr. exec. v.p., 1972-73; mng. dir. Ea. ops. Capital Rsch. Co., 1973-95; chmn. bd. New Perspective Fund, Inc., 1973—2003, chmn. emeritus, 2003—; chmn. Capital Internat. Inc., 1973—2002, vice-chmn., 2002—; sr. ptnr. Capital Group Inc., 2002—. Chmn. Europacific Growth Fund, Inc., 1984—99; chmn. bd. dirs. Emerging Markets Growth Fund Capital Group Internat., Inc., 1987—2004, chmn., 1984—2004, chmn. emeritus, 2005—; mem. Mcpl. Securities Rulemaking Bd., 1984—87; trustee Fin. Analysts Rsch. Found., 1975—2003; chmn. bd. trustees Hudson Inst., 1983—2007; instr. investment mgmt. and fin. NYU, 1956—62; mem. adv. bd. South African Growth Fund, 1996—2002, Hillhouse Capital Mgmt., 2006—, chmn. emeritys, 2007. Contbr. articles to profl. jours. Mem. Coun. Fgn. Rels.; chmn. fin. adv. com. Haddassah, Tel Aviv U., 1980-2007; dir. Am.-Israel Friendship League, 1996—; Rep. Jewish Coalition, 2005—; v.p., mem. exec. com. Washington Inst. Near East Policy; chmn. steering com. Freedom Trade with Israel; adv. bd., dir. Am. Committees on Fgn. Rels., 1998—; bd. visitors Monterrey Inst., 2001—; trustee The Jewish Pol. Ctr.; adv. bd. CFA Ctr. Fin. Mkt. Integrity, 2004— Mem. N.Y. Soc. Security Analysts (bd. dirs.), Fin. Analysts Fedn. (pres. 1971-72, bd. dirs.), Inst. Chartered Fin. Analysts (pres. 1976-77, bd. dirs.), Assn. Investment and Mgmt. Rsch. (bd. dirs., exec. com. 1990-92), Harvard Club, Econ. Club, Sunningdale Country Club, Calif. Club, Belle Meade County Club, Phi Beta Kappa. Jewish. Home: 450 Fort Hill Rd Scarsdale NY 10583-2413 Office: Capital Group Inc 630 5th Ave New York NY 10111-0100 also: Capital Group Inc 333 S Hope St Los Angeles CA 90071-1406 Office Phone: 212-581-5000. Business E-Mail: wps@capgroup.com.

STERN, WALTER WOLF, III, lawyer; b. Cin., Mar. 25, 1946; s. Walter W. Jr. and Harriet Louise Stern; (div.); 1 child, Rachael Louise. BA, Carthage Coll., 1969; JD, Marquette U., 1974. Bar: Wis. 1974, U.S. Dist. Ct. (ea. and we. dists.) Wis. 1974, U.S. Ct. Appeals (7th cir.) 1981, U.S. Supreme Ct. 1983, U.S. Dist. Ct. (no. dist.) Ill. 1999. Pvt. practice, Kenosha, Wis., 1974—83; sr. ptnr. Joling Rizzo Willems Stern & Burroughs, Kenosha, 1982-85, Caviali & Stern, 1985—91; pvt. practice Union Grove, Wis., 1991—2007; ret. Lectr. criminal law Carthage Coll., Kenosha, Wis., 1976-2005. Educator, Domestic Violence Project, Kenosha, 1983-94; hearing examiner Gen. Relief, Kenosha, 1990-95; candiate Cir. Judge, 2005. Fellow Am. Acad. Forensic Scis, Nat. Alliance Mentally Ill (adv. Kionosha br.). Avocations: fishing, hunting, jogging, reading, creative writing, fencing. Home and Office: Po Box 351 Kenosha WI 53141-0351 Office Phone: 262-880-0192. Personal E-mail: wstern1@wi.rr.com.

STERN, YAAKOV, neuroscientist; BA in psychology, Touro Coll., 1975; PhD, CUNY, 1983. Prof. Columbia U., NYC, 1996—; prof. clin. neuropsychology Taub Inst. Rsch. on Alzheimer's Disease and the Aging Brain and Gertrude H. Sergievsky Ctr., Columbia U. Coll. Physicians and Surgeons, NYC; leader cognitive neuroscience divsn., Gertrude H. Sergievsky Ctr. Columbia U. Coll. Physicians and Surgeons, NYC; dir. neuropsychology, Memory Disorders Clinic NY State Psychiat. Inst. Office: Taub Inst 630 W 168th St New York NY 10032 Office Phone: 212-342-1350. Office Fax: 212-342-1838. E-mail: ys11@columbia.edu.*

STERNBERG, BETTY J., school system administrator; b. NY, Jan. 30, 1950; d. Julius and Edith Jane (Meyer) Levin; m. Robert Jeffrey Sternberg, June 18, 1972 (div. Jan. 13, 1987); children: Seth, Sara. BA, Brandeis U., 1971; MA, Columbia U., 1972; PhD, Stanford U., 1978. Bur. chief Conn. Dept. Edn., Hartford, Conn., 1980-85, divsn. dir., 1985-92, assoc. commr., 1992—2003, commr., 2003—07; sch. supt. Greenwich Pub. Schools, Greenwich, Conn., 2007—. Cons. Nat. Bd. for Profl. Teaching Standards, Washington, 1992. Co-author: (textbook) Metric Multibase Mathematics, 1973, Attribute Acrobatics, 1973, People Pieces Primer, 1975; (textbook series) Math In Stride, 1987. Mem. bd. dirs. William Benton Mus. of Art U. Conn., 1989—; mem. adv. coun. Ctr. for Ednl. Excellence, 1992-93. Recipient Disting. Managerial Svc. award State of Conn., 1986. Mem. ASCD (sec. 1975-80), Conn. Assn. Suprs. of Curriculum Devel. Avocations: tennis, interior design, gardening. Office: Greenwich Pub Schools 290 Greenwich Ave Greenwich CT 06830

STERNBERG, HILGARD O'REILLY, geographer, educator; b. Rio de Janeiro, July 5, 1917; s. Bruno Ludwig and Johanna Mary O'Reilly (Begg) S.; m. Carolina da Silveira Lobo, July 28, 1942; children: Hilgard, Jr. Maria Inês (Mrs. Francis Anthony Mangiola), Ricardo, Leonel, Cristina (Mrs. David L. Rausch). Bacharel, U. do Brasil, 1940, Licenciado, 1941; PhD, La. State U., Baton Rouge, 1956; Docteur h.c., U. Toulouse, France, 1965. Asst. prof U. Brazil (now Fed. U. Rio de Janeiro), 1942—44, prof. geography, 1944—64, prof. emeritus, 1977—; dir. Ctr. Rsch. Geography of Brazil, U. Brazil, Rio de Janeiro, 1951—64; prof. geography U. Calif., Berkeley, 1964—88, prof. emeritus, 1988—. First v.p. Internat. Geog. Union, 1956-60; mem. com. research priorities in tropical biology NRC, 1977-80 Author articles, books in field. Decorated comdr. Nat. Order Merit, comdr. Order Rio Branco Nat., great cross Order Sci. Merit, Brazil; recipient Best Publ. award Nat. Coun. Geog. Edn., 1966. Fellow AAAS, Calif. Acad. Scis.; mem. Brazilian Acad. Scis., Deutsche Akademie der Naturforscher Leopoldina, Assn. de Géographes Français, Assn. Am. Geographers, Assn. de Geógrafos Brasileiros, Calif. Acad. Scis.; hon. mem. Soc. de Géographie (Paris), Gesellschaft für Erdkunde zu Berlin, Soc. Serbe de Géographie; hon. corr. mem. Royal Geog. Soc., Brazilian Hist. and Geog. Inst. (corr. mem.), Mato Grosso Hist. and Geog. Inst. Achievements research in geomorphology, settlement patterns, land-use in Amazonia, climatic variability in Amazonia, N.E. Brazil, West Central Brazil; environmental impact of development especially in tropics, geography of food, historical geography; geographic education. Home: 466 Michigan Ave Berkeley CA 94707-1738 Office Phone: 510-524-8542. Office Fax: 510-524-8542. E-mail: hilgard_or@berkeley.edu.

STERNBERG, PAUL WARREN, biologist, educator; b. Queens, NY, June 14, 1956; BA in Biology and Math., Hampshire Coll., 1978; PhD in Biology, MIT, 1984. Rsch. asst. U. Pa., 1977-78; postdoctoral fellow U. Calif., San Francisco, 1984-87; asst. prof. biology Calif. Inst. Tech., Pasadena, 1987-92, assoc. prof. biology Pasadena, 1992—. Asst. investigator Howard Hughes Med. Inst., 1989-92, assoc. investigator, 1992—; adj. asst. prof. dept. cell and neurobiology U. So. Calif. Sch. Medicine, 1989—. Contbr. articles, revs. to profl. publs., chpts. to books. Recipient Presl. Young Investigator award, NSF, 1988; named fellow Jane Coffin Childs Meml. Found. for Med. Rsch., 1984-85, Searle scholar, 1988-91. Fellow AAAS, Am. Acad. Arts & Sci.; mem. Am. Soc. Cell Biology, Genetics Soc. Am., Helminthological Soc. Washington, Soc. for Devel. Biology, Soc. Nematologists, Nat. Acad. Sci. Office: Calif Inst Tech Mail Code 156 # 29 Pasadena CA 91125-0001 Office Phone: 626-395-2181. Business E-Mail: pws@caltech.edu.

STERNBERG, ROBERT JEFFREY, dean, psychology professor, researcher; b. Newark, Dec. 8, 1949; s. Joseph Sternberg and Lillian Myriam (Politzer) Weingast; m. Karin Sternberg; children: Seth, Sara. BA summa cum laude, Yale U., 1972; PhD in Psychology, Stanford U., 1975; D honoris causa (hon.), Complutense U., Madrid, 1994, U. Cyprus, 2000, U. Paris, 2000, U. Leuven, Belgium, 2001, Constantine the Philosopher U., Nitra, Slovakia, 2004; DSc, U. Durham, Eng., 2006, St. Petersburg U., Russia, 2006, U. Tilburg, Netherlands, 2007, Ricardo Palma U., 2008, Eureka Coll., 2008, U. Conn., 2009. Mem. faculty dept.

psychology Yale U., New Haven, 1975—2005, asst. prof., 1975—80, assoc. prof., 1980—83, prof. psychology, 1983-86, dir. grad. studies, 1983—88, IBM prof. psychology and edn., 1986—, acting chmn. dept. psychology, 1992, dir. Yale Ctr. Psychology of Abilities, Competencies and Expertise, 2000—05, prof. Sch. Mgmt., 2005; dean Sch. Arts and Scis. Tufts U., Medford, Mass., 2005—, prof. psychology, 2006—; adj. prof. edn. U. Heidelberg, 2006—, hon. prof., 2007—; sr. scholar Ctr. for Pub. Leadership, Kennedy Sch. Govt., Harvard U., 2006—. Disting. assoc. Psychometrics Ctr., Cambridge, England, 2007—. Editor-in-chief Ency. of Human Intelligence, Psychol. Bull., 1991-96, Contemporary Psychology, 1999-2004; cons. editor Learning and Individual Differences, 1992—, Intelligence, 1977—, Devel. Rev., 1987-91, Jour. Personality and Social Psychology, 1989-91, Psychol. Rev., 1989-91; assoc. ed. Ann. Rev. of Psychology, 2008-; author: Intelligence, Information Processing and Analogical Reasoning, 1977, Beyond IQ, 1985, The Triarchic Mind, 1988, Metaphors of Mind, 1990, In Search of the Human Mind, 1995, 98, (with T. Lubart) Defying the Crowd, 1995, Successful Intelligence, 1997, Pathways to Psychology, 1997, Thinking Styles, 1997, Intelligence, Heredity and Environment, 1997, Love is a Story, 1998, Cupid's Arrow, 1998, Handbook of Intelligence, 2000, Psychology 101-1/2, 2002, Wisdom, Intelligence, and Creativity Synthesized, 2003; co-author (with Karin Sternberg): The Nature of Hate, 2008. Recipient award for Excellence Mensa Edn. and Rsch. Found., 1989, Disting. Lifetime Contbn. to Psychology Conn. Psychology Assn., 1999, Disting. Scientist and Scholar award Positive Psychology Network, 2002, Anton Jurovsky award, Slovak Psychol. Soc., 2004, Interam. Psychologist award Interam. Psychol. Soc., 2005, E. Paul Torrance award, 2006, Sir Francis Galton award Internat. Assn. Empirical Aesthetics, 2008; Guggenheim Found. fellow, 1985-86. Fellow AAAS, APA (bd. dirs. 2002-04, pres. 2003, past pres. divsns. 1, 10, 15, 24, trustee ins. trust 2004, McCandless Young Scientist award divsn. devel. psychology 1982, Disting. Sci. award for early career contbn. 1981, pres. 2003, Farnsworth award, Arthur W. Staats award, E.L. Thorndike award 2003, Arnheim award, 2005, Disting. Lifetime Contribution to Pub. U. Psychology award, 2008), East Psychol. Assn. (bd. dirs., pres. 2007—), Am. Psychol. Found. (trustee 2005—), Am. Acad. Arts and Scis., Am. Psychol. Soc., Soc. Exptl. Psychologists, Internat. Assn. Cognitive Edn. and Psychology (pres.-elect 2007—); mem. Am. Ednl. Rsch. Assn. (Rsch. Rev. award 1986, Outstanding Book award 1987, Sylvia Scribner award 1996, James McKeen Cattell award 1999), Soc. Multivariate Exptl. Psychology (Cattell award 1982), Nat. Assn. Gifted Children (Disting. Scholar award 1985, E. Paul Torrance award 2006), Phi Beta Kappa, Kappa Delta Pi (Laureate chpt. 2003). Achievements include theory of successful intelligence; balance theory of wisdom; theory of mental self; investment theory of creativity; triangular theory of love; duplex theory of hate. Avocations: exercise, travel, reading, cello. Office: Tufts U Office Dean Art and Scis Ballou Hall 3d Fl Medford MA 02155 Office Phone: 617-627-3864. Office Fax: 617-627-3703. Business E-Mail: robert.sternberg@tufts.edu.

STERNE, HEDDA, artist; b. Bucharest, Romania, Aug. 4, 1910; arrived in U.S., 1941; d. Simon and Eugenie (Wexler) Lidenberg; m. Frederick Sterne (div.). Solo exhibitions including ICL Gallery, East Hampton, NY, 1980, CDS Gallery, NYC, 1982, 84, 87, 90, 95, 98, 2000, 04, 06, Queens Mus., Flushing, NY, 1985, Philippe Briet Gallery, NYC, 1993, Bibliotheque Municipale, Ville de Caen, France, 1998, Krannert Art Mus, Urbana-Champaign, Ill., 2006, U. Va. Art Mus., Charlottesville, 2007, and others; group exhibitions including Guild Hall Mus., East Hampton, 1982, Penn Plaza, NYC, 1983, CDS Gallery, 1988, Pollock-Krasner House and Study Ctr., East Hampton, 1997, Arlene Bujese Gallery, East Hampton, 1997, Lawrence Gallery, Rosemont Coll., Pa., 1997, Centro Atlantico de Arte Moderno, Las Palmas de Gran Canaria, Spain, 1999, Ulmer Mus., Ulm, Germany, 2001, Musei Civici, Veneziani, Italy, 2002, and others; permanent collections include Whitney Mus. Am. Art, NYC, Met. Mus. Art, NYC, Mus. Modern Art, NYC, Am. Acad. Arts, NY, Ford Found, NY, Rockefeller Inst., NY, Albright-Knox Art Gallery, Buffalo, Everson Mus. Art, Syracuse, Art Mus. of Chgo., and numerous others. Recipient Contemporary Am. Painting Purchase award, U. Ill., 1949, 2d prize, Art Inst Chgo. Ann., 1957, 1st prize, Art Inst. Newport Ann., 1967, Childe Hassam Purchase award, Am. Acad. Arts and Letters, 1971, Hassam and Speicher Purchase Fund award, 1984; named to Ordre des Arts et des Lettres, Ambassador of France, NY, 1999; Fulbright fellow, 1963.

STERNER, FRANK MAURICE, manufacturing executive; b. Lafayette, Ind., Nov. 26, 1935; s. Raymond E. and Maudelene M. (Scipio) S.; m. Elsa Y. Rasmusson, June 29, 1958; children: Mark, Lisa. BS, Purdue U., 1958, MS, 1959, PhD, 1962. Sr. staff specialist Gen. Motors Inst., Flint, Mich., 1962-63; dir. personnel and orgnl. research Delco Electronics, Milw., 1963-66, dir. personnel devel. and research, 1966-68; partner Nourse & Sterner, Inc., Milw., 1968-69; pres., 1969-73; assoc. dean, prof. Krannert Grad. Sch. of Mgmt., Purdue U., West Lafayette, Ind., 1973-79; v.p. strategic mgmt. Johnson Controls, Inc., Milw., 1979-89; pres., chief exec. officer E.R. Wagner Mfg. Co., 1989—2008; pres., owner Ridgeway Devel. Inc., Milw., 1993—; pres. Sterner Family Found., 2008—. Bd. dirs. Ridgeway Devel. Inc., Greenheck Fan Corp. Home: 1440 E Standish Pl Milwaukee WI 53217-1958 Office: Bayshore Town Ctr 500 W Silver Spring Dr Ste K-200 Glendale WI 53217 Office Phone: 414-847-6314. Business E-Mail: fms@wi.rr.com.

STERNHEIMER, KAREN, sociologist, writer; d. Lee and Toby Sternheimer. PhD, U. Southern Calif., LA, 1998. Sociologist U. Southern Calif., 1998—, faculty fellow, 2008—. Author: (book) It's Not the Media: The Truth About Pop Culture's Influence on Children, Kids These Days: Facts and Fictions About Today's Youth, Connecting Popular Culture and Social Problems: Why Media Is Not the Answer, (textbook) Childhood in American Society: A Reader. Mem.: Pacific Sociol. Assn. (program chair 2006—07), Am. Sociol. Assn.

STERNLICHT, BARRY STUART, investment company executive, former hotel executive; b. Lake Success, NY, Nov. 27, 1960; m. Mimi Sternlicht; 3 children. BA magna cum laude, Brown U., 1982; MBA with distinction, Harvard U., 1986; PhD in bus. adminstrn. (hon.), Johnson & Wales. Pres., CEO Starwood Capital Group, LLC, Phoenix, 1991—2004; chmn., CEO Starwood Hotels and Resorts Trust, Phoenix, 1995—2004; CEO iStar Fin. Inc., 1996—97, chmn., 1996—2000, Starwood Hotels & Resorts Worldwide, Inc., White Plains, NY, 1997—2004, CEO, 1999—2004, exec. chmn., chief design officer, 2004—05; chmn., CEO Starwood Capital Group, Greenwich, Conn., 2005—. Bd. dirs. The Estée Lauder Companies Inc., 2004-, Starwood Fin. Trust, U.S. Franchise Systems and Comm.; bd. trustees Equity Residential Trust; mem. Urban Land Inst., Nat. Multi-Family Housing Coun, Young Presidents Org., World Travel & Tourism Council, Council for the U.S. and Italy. Bd. dirs. Com. to Encourage Corp. Philanthropy, Bus. Com. for the Arts, Inc., Channel 13/WNET, Nat. Leadership Advocacy Program for Juvenile Diabetes Rsch. Found. Internat., Kids in Crisis, Fairfield County Jr. Achievement, Ctr. for Christian-Jewish Understanding; bd. govs. NAREIT. Recipient Preston Robert Tisch Disting. Industry Leadership award, NYU Sch. Hospitality, Tourism & Travel Admin.; named Man of the Year, Juvenile Diabetes Rsch. Found. Internat. Office: Starwood Capital Group 591 W Putnam Ave Greenwich CT 06830 Office Phone: 203-422-7700. Office Fax: 203-422-7784.*

STERNLICHT, BENO, research and development company executive; b. Nowy Sacz, Poland; arrived in U.S., 1949, naturalized, 1950; s. Hugo Charles and Helena (Anisfeld) Sternlicht; m. Lisa Spilberg; children: Mark David, Eric Alan, Joshua Hugh, Aaron Jonathan. BSEE, Union Coll., Schenectady, NY, 1950; MS, Columbia U., 1951, PhD, 1954, DSc (hon.), 1970. Staff engr. Thermal Power Sys., gen. engring. lab. GE, 1951-54, specialist applied mechanics, 1954-58, cons. engr., 1958-61; co-founder, 1961; since chmn. bd., tech. dir. Mech. Tech., Inc., Latham, NY; pres. Benjosh Mgmt. Corp., NY, 1983, Ameast, NYC, 1981—; co-founder Arben Internat. LLC, NYC, 1994—. Dir. Small Diesels Ltd., India, New Ea. India Ltd., Plug Power LLC; pres. Vols. Internat. Tech. Assistance, 1965—71, chmn. bd. dirs., 1971—73; chmn. com. energy tech. and space propulsion NASA, 1969—72, mem. rsch. adv. coun., 1970—72; mem. Nat. Energy Task Force, 1981; bd. chmn. Comfortex Corp., 1995—; cons. to PRC, Israel, India. Author: numerous tech. articles on energy, tech., social and ednl. fields. Mem. AIPAC, World Jewish Congress, Jewish Fedn., ORT; chmn. Lisbon Charitable Trust; advisor on energy & innovation to Pres. Carter; advisor on energy and transp. to Pres. Reagan; advisor Pres. Bush. Fellow: ASME (Machine Design award 1966); mem.: AIAA, Am. Soc. Lubrication Engrs., Nat. Acad. Engring., Navy League, Sigma Xi, Tau Beta Pi. Achievements include patents in field. Address: 123 Partridge Run Schenectady NY 12309-1321 Office Phone: 718-376-0070. Personal E-mail: Lisben26@aol.com.

STERNLICHT, SANFORD, literature educator, writer; b. NYC, Sept. 20, 1931; s. Irving Stanley and Sylvia (Hilsenroth) S.; m. Dorothy Hilkert, June 4, 1956 (dec. 1977); children: David, Daniel. BS, SUNY, Oswego, 1953; MA, Colgate U., 1955; PhD, Syracuse U., 1962. Instr. SUNY, Oswego, 1959-60, asst. prof., 1960-62, prof. and dir. grad. studies in English, 1962-72, chmn. dept. theater, 1972-84; adj. prof. English Syracuse NY U., 1981—2007, prof. English, 2007—. Leverhulme vis. prof. English, U. York, Eng., 1965-66; Fulbright sr. specialist, vis. prof. English, U. Pecs, Hungary, 2004. Author: Gull's Way, 1961, The Blue Star Commodore, 1961, Love in Pompeii, 1967, John Webster's Imagery and the Webster Canon, 1972, John Masefield, 1977, McKinley's Bulldog, 1977 (Mil. Book Club award, Saturday Evening Post Book Club award), C.S. Forester, 1981, Padraic Colum, 1985; (with E.M. Jameson) The Black Devil of the Bayous, 1971; (with E.M. Jameson) U.S. F. Constellation: Yankee Racehorse, 1981, John Galsworthy, 1986, R.F. Delderfield, 1988, Stevie Smith, 1990, Stephen Spender, 1992, Siegfried Sassoon, 1993, All Things Herriot: James Herriot and His Peaceable Kingdom, 1995, Jean Rhys, 1997, A Reader's Guide to Modern Irish Drama, 1998, C.S. Forester and the Hornblower Saga, 1999, Chaim Potok: A Critical Companion, 2000, A Reader's Guide to Modern American Drama, 2002, A Student Companion to Elie Wiesel, 2003, A Reader's Guide to Modern British Drama, 2004, The Tenement Saga: The Lower East Side and Early Jewish American Writers, 2004, Masterpieces of Modern British and Irish Drama, 2005, Masterpieces of Jewish American Literature, 2007; editor: The Selected Short Stories of Padraic Colum, 1985, The Selected Plays of Padraic Colum, 1986, The Selected Poems of Padraic Colum, 1988, In Search of Stevie Smith, 1991, New Plays from the Abbey Theatre, 1993-1995, 96, 96-98, 99, 99-2001, 2003. Lt. (j.g.) USN, 1955-59, comdr. USNR, ret. Recipient New Poets award Writer mag., 1960, Chancellor's award SUNY, 1974; fellow Poetry Soc. Am., 1964; rsch. grantee SUNY, 1963-70; named Tchr. of Yr. Syracuse U., 1986. Mem. MLA, PEN. Democrat. Jewish. Home: 128 Dorset Rd Syracuse NY 13210-3048 Office: Syracuse U Dept English Syracuse NY 13244-0001 Home Phone: 315-472-5639; Office Phone: 315-443-9480. Business E-Mail: svsternl@syr.edu.

STERNMAN, JOEL W., lawyer; b. NYC, Oct. 20, 1943; s. Abraham and Sarah (Simon) S.; children: Mark S., Cheryl A.; m. Barbara E. Shiers, March 31, 1985; children: Matthew S., Julia S. AB, Dartmouth Coll., 1965; LLB, Yale U., 1968. Bar: N.Y. 1970, U.S. Dist. Ct. (so. and ea. dists.) N.Y. 1971, U.S. Ct. Appeals (2d cir.) 1972, U.S. Supreme Ct. 1984, U.S. Ct. Appeals (6th cir.) 1985, U.S. Ct. Appeals (9th cir.) 1994, U.S. Tax Ct. 1996, U.S. Dist. Ct. (ea. dist.) Mich. 1997. Law clk. to judge U.S. Dist. Ct., New Haven, 1968-69; assoc. Rosenman Colin Freund Lewis & Cohen, NYC, 1969-77; ptnr. Rosenman & Colin LLP, NYC, 1977—2002, Katten Muchin Rosenman LLP (formerly Katten Muchin Zavis Rosenman), 2002—. Editor Yale Law Jour., New Haven, 1966-68. Mem. Phi Beta Kappa. Office: Katten Muchin Rosenman LLP 575 Madison Ave New York NY 10022-2585 Home Phone: 914-723-0947; Office Phone: 212-940-7060. E-mail: j.sternman@kattenlaw.com.

STERNS, HARVEY LEONARD, psychologist, gerontologist; b. Waterville, Maine; s. Frederick James and Sarah (Hoos) S.; m. Ronni Susan Small, Nov. 14, 1964; children: Anthony Alexander, Randy Rose, George Herbert. Bachelor, Bard Coll., 1965; Master, SUNY, Buffalo, 1968; PhD, W.Va. U., 1971. Lic. psychologist. Prof. psychology U. Akron, Ohio, 1971—, dir. Inst. Life-Span Devel. and Gerontology Ohio, 1976—; rsch. prof. gerontology Northeastern Ohio Univs. Coll. Medicine and Pharmacy, Rootstown, 1978—. Prin. Creative Action Inc., Akron, 1988—. Editor: Gerontology in Higher Education: Perspectives and Issues, 1978, Gerontology in Higher Education: Building Institutional and Community Strength, 1979, Annual Review, Gevontology and Gervatrics:Gevontological and Gervatric Education vol.28, 2009; co-author: with Rothwell, W.J., Spokus, D. & Reaser, J.M. Working Longer: New Strategies for Managing, Training, and Retaining Older Workers New York: Am. Mgmt Assn., 2008, with Papalia, D.E., Feldman, R.D., & Camp C.J. Adult Development and Aging 3rd Edition, New York: McGraw-Hill, 2007; contbr. chpts. to books and articles to profl. jours. Bd. trustees Ohio Presbyn. Retirement Communities, Columbus, 1989-2000, Sumner Home, Akron, 2001-08; pres. Jewish Family Svcs., Akron, 1991-92, Mature Svcs., Inc., Akron, 1998-2005; chair City of Akron Sr. Citizens Adv. Commn., Akron, 1995-2003. Recipient award Andrus Found., 1976, 77, 78, award Dept. HEW, 1977-79, award Nat. Inst. Disability and Rehab. Rsch., 1992-2003, award Ohio Dept. Aging, 1993. Fellow APA (editor Adult Devel. and Aging News 1997-2002, pres. divsn. 20 Adult Devel. and Aging 2002-03), Am. Psychol. Soc., Assn. Gerontology in Higher Edn. (pres. 1983-84, Clark Tibbitts award 1994), Gerontol. Soc. Am., Ohio Acad. Sci. (v.p. psychology sect. 1973-74), Sigma Phi Omega (life, nat. pres. 1985-86). Democrat. Jewish. Avocations: sailing, old house restoration, old car restoration. Home: 680 N Portage Path Akron OH 44303 Office: Univ Akron Inst Li-Span Dev&Geron Arts & Scis Bldg Ste 340 Akron OH 44325-4307 Office Fax: 330-972-5174; Home Fax: 330-867-6899. Business E-Mail: hsterns@uakron.edu.

STERNS, WILLIAM S., III, lawyer; b. Wilkes Barre, Pa., Feb. 16, 1948; s. William S. Sterns, Jr. and Harriette B. Sterns; m. Wenke B. Thoman, May 1, 1999; children: William IV, Stefan, Olivia. BA, Colgate U., 1970; JD, NYU, 1977. Bar: NY 1978, Conn. 1991. Assoc. Casey Lane & Mittendorf, NYC, 1977—80; ptnr. Jones Hirsch, 1980—96; ptnr.,corp. securities and securities group Alston & Bird LLP, 1996—. Contbr. Abington Theatre, Manhattan Theatre; patron Dorset Play House, Internat. House. Mem.: Ekwanok Country Club, The River Club, Baltusrol Golf Club. Avocations: golf, tennis, skiing. Office: Alston & Bird LLP 90 Park Ave New York NY 10016 Office Phone: 212-210-9530. Office Fax: 212-210-9444. Business E-Mail: william.sterns@alston.com.

STERNSTEIN, ALLAN J., lawyer; b. Chgo., June 7, 1948; s. Milton and Celia (Kaganove) Sternstein; m. Miriam A. Dolgin, July 12, 1970 (div. July 1981); children: Jeffery A., Amy R.; m. Beverly A. Cook, Feb. 8, 1986 (div. 2004); 1 child, Julia S. BS, U. Ill., 1970; MS, U. Mich., 1972; JD, Loyola U. Sch. Law, Chgo., 1977. Bar: US Patent and Trademark Office 1974, Ill. 1977, US Dist. Ct. (no. dist.) Ill. 1977, US Dist. Ct. (no. dist.) Ohio 1977, US Dist. Ct. (ea. dist) Mich. 1986, US Dist. Ct. (we. dist.) Mich. 1990, US Ct. Customs and Patent Appeals 1978, US Ct. Appeals (7th cir.) 1979, US Ct. Appeals (Fed. cir.) 1982, US Dist. Ct. (ea. dist.) Wis. 2003, US Ct. Appeals (5th cir.) 2003, US Dist. Ct. (ea. dist.) Tex. 2007. Patent agt. Sunbeam Corp., Oak Brook, Ill., 1972—76; ptnr. Neuman, Williams, Anderson & Olson, Chgo., 1976—84; divsn. patent counsel Abbott Labs., North Chgo., Ill., 1984—87; ptnr. Brinks Hofer Gilson & Lione, Chgo., 1987—2005, mng. ptnr., 1996—99; ptnr., dir. IP and IP litigation Dykema Gossett, Chgo., 2005—. Adj. prof. law John Marshall Sch. Law, 1989—90, DePaul U. Sch. Law, 1990—92, U. Ill., 1992—; lectr. U. Victoria, Canada, 2002, 04, Oxford U., England, 2003. Co-author: Designing an Effective Intellectual Property Compliance Program; contbr. articles to profl. jours. Legal advisor Legal Aid Soc., Chgo., 1974—76, Pub. Defender's Office, Chgo., 1974. Mem.: ABA, Intellectual Property Owners Assn., Am. Intellectual Property Law Assn., Intellectual Property Law Assn. Chgo. (com. chmn. 1982), Chgo. Bar Assn., Phi Eta Sigma, Sigma Gamma Tau, Sigma Tau, Tau Beta Pi. Jewish. Office: Dykema Gossett 10 S Wacker Dr Ste 2300 Chicago IL 60606 Office Phone: 312-627-2143.

STERRETT, JAMES KELLEY, II, lawyer; b. St. Louis, Nov. 26, 1946; s. James Kelley and Anastasia Mary (Holzer) S.; 1 child, Brittany. AB, San Diego State U., 1968; JD, U. Calif., Berkeley, 1971; LLM, U. Pa., 1973. Bar: Calif. 1972, U.S. Dist. Ct. (so. dist.) Calif. 1972. From assoc. to ptnr. Gray, Cary, Ames & Frye, San Diego, 1972-83; ptnr. Lillick, McHose & Charles, San Diego, 1983-90, Pillsbury, Madison & Sutro, San Diego, 1991-96, Dostart Clapp Sterrett & Coveney, LLP, 1996-99; sole practice, 1999—. Contbr. articles to profl. jours. Bd. dirs. Holiday Bowl, San Diego, 1980—, Mus. Photog. Arts, San Diego, 1985-88, San Diego Internat. Sports Coun., 1980—, pres., 1990, chmn., 1992. Capt. USAFR, 1972. Fellow U. Pa. Ctr. Study Fin. Instns., 1971-72. Mem. ABA, Calif. Bar Assn., San Diego County Bar Assn. Clubs: Fairbanks Ranch Country (Rancho Santa Fe) (bd. dirs. 1985-87). Republican. Episcopalian. Avocations: golf, hiking, football.

STERRETT, SAMUEL BLACK, lawyer, former judge; b. Washington, Dec. 17, 1922; s. Henry Hatch Dent and Helen (Black) S.; m. Jeane McBride, Aug. 27, 1949; children: Samuel Black, Robin Dent, Douglas McBride. Student, St. Albans Sch., 1933-41; grad., US Mcht. Marine Acad., 1945, BS, 2004; BA, Amherst Coll., 1947; LLB, U. Va., 1950; LLM in Taxation, NYU, 1959. Bar: D.C. 1951, Va. 1950. Atty. Alvord & Alvord, Washington, 1950-56; trial atty. Office Regional Counsel, Internal Revenue Service, NYC, 1956-60; ptnr. Sullivan, Shea & Kenney, Washington, 1960-68; municipal cons. to office vice pres. U.S., 1965-68; judge U.S. Tax Ct., 1968-88, chief judge, 1985-88; ptnr. Myerson, Kuhn & Sterrett, Washington, 1988-89; of counsel Vinson & Elkins, Washington, 1990—2002; pvt. practice Washington, 2002—07, Chevy Chase, Md., 2007—09. Bd. mgrs. Chevy Chase Village, 1970-74, chmn., 1972-74; 1st v.p. bd. trustees, exec. com. Washington Hosp. Ctr., 1969-79, chmn. bd. trustees, 1979-84, trustee, 1999-2007; chmn. bd. trustees Washington Healthcare Corp., 1982-87; chmn. bd. trustees Medlantic Healthcare Group, 1987-89; mem. audit com. Medstar Health, 1990-2006; trustee Protestant Episcopal Cathedral Found., 1973-81, 99-2007, fin. com., 1998-2007, chmn., 1999-2006; governing bd. St. Albans Sch., 1977-81; trustee Louise Home, 1979-89. Wwith AUS, 1943, with U.S. Mcht. Marine, 1943-46. Fellow Am. Bar Found. (life); mem. ABA, D.C. Bar Assn., Am. Coll. Tax Counsel, Soc. of the Cincinnati, Coun. for Future, Am. Inns. of Ct., Chevy Chase Club (bd. govs. 1979-84, pres. 1984), Met. Club, Lawyers Club, Alibi Club, Alfalfa Club, Ch. of N.Y. Club, Beta Theta Pi. Episcopalian. Personal E-mail: sbsterrett@aol.com.

STERZER, FRED, research physicist; b. Vienna, Nov. 18, 1929; came to U.S., 1947, naturalized, 1952; s. Karl and Rosa (Trumer) S.; m. Betty Distel, Sept. 5, 1964 (dec.). BS in Physics, CCNY, 1951; MS in Physics, NYU, 1952, PhD in Physics, 1955. With RCA, 1954-87, RCA Labs., David Sarnoff Research Center, Princeton, NJ, 1956-87, dir. microwave tech. center, 1972-87; dir. microwave research lab. David Sarnoff Research Ctr., 1987-88; pres. MMTC, Inc., Princeton, 1988—. Herbert J. Kayser research prof., City Coll., CUNY, 1986-87. Contbr. numerous articles to profl. publs. Fellow IEEE; mem. Am. Phys. Soc., Nat. Acad. Engring., Sigma Xi, Phi Beta Kappa. Achievements include condr. research on optical components, microwave solid-state devices and circuits, med. microwave tech. Home: 4432 Province Line Rd Princeton NJ 08540-4368 Office: MMTC Inc 12 Roszel Rd Princeton NJ 08540-6234 Office Phone: 609-520-9699. Business E-Mail: sterzer@mmtc.com.

STETLER, LARRY D., geologist; b. Rapid City, SD, Dec. 2, 1956; s. Harold Lawrence and Alice Elaine (Kellum) S.; m. Jeanette Marie Gross, Aug. 6, 1988. BS in Geol. Engring., S.D. Sch. Mines and Tech., 1979, MS in Geol. Engring., 1989; PhD in Geology, Wash. State U., 1993. Field engr. Schlumberger, Williston, N.D., 1979-81, Casper, Wyo., 1983-86; fluids engr. Newpark Drilling Fluids, Casper, 1981-82; rsch. asst., teaching asst. S.D. Sch. Mines and Tech., Rapid City, 1987-89, Wash. State U., Pullman, 1989-92; rsch. scientist Northwest Coll. and Univ. Assn. for Sci., Pullman and Richland, Wash., 1990-92, Washington State U., Pullman, 1993—. Author lab. manuals on fluids engring.; contbr. articles to profl. publs. Grantee Battelle Meml. Inst., 1990, 92, Wash. State U., 1991. Mem. Am. Assn. Petroleum Geologists, Geol. Assn. Am., Soc. Sedimentary Geologists. Republican. Avocations: hunting, fishing, backpacking, travel, reading. Home: NW 435th Irving Pullman WA 99163 Office: Wash State U Biol Systems Engring Smith Hall Pullman WA 99164-6120

STETLER, RUSSELL DEARNLEY, JR., investigator; b. Phila., Jan. 15, 1945; s. Russell Dearnley and Martha Eleanor (Schultz) S. BA with honors in Philosophy, Haverford Coll., Pa., 1966; postgrad., New Sch. Social Rsch., 1966-67. Research asst. to Bertrand Russell, 1967; lectr. Hendon Coll., London, 1968-69; pres. Archetype, Inc., Berkeley, Calif., 1971-78; pub. Westworks, Berkeley, 1977-80; pvt. investigator, 1980-90; chief investigator Calif. Appellate Project, 1990-95; dir. of investigation and mitigation N.Y. State Capital Defender Office, NYC, 1995—2005; nat. mitigation coord. Office of the Fed. Pub. Defender, Oakland, Calif., 2005—. Cons., dir. Ramparts Press, Palo Alto, 1971-80; editorial cons. Internews, Berkeley, 1973-78; faculty Caribbean Sch., Ponce, P.R., 1978-80 Author: The Battle of Bogside, 1970; co-editor: The Assassinations: Dallas and Beyond, 1976. Research grantee Atlantic

Peace Found., 1969-70 Mem. Calif. Assn. Lic. Investigators, Nat. Assn. Legal Investigators, Calif. Soccer Referees Assn.-North (treas. Marin County chpt. 1982-90), Amigos de las Americas (pres. Marin chpt. 1985-88). Clubs: Mill Valley Soccer (dir. 1981), Albany-Berkeley Soccer (pres. 1977-78). Office: Office of the Fed Pub Defender 555 12th St Ste 650 Oakland CA 94607 E-mail: russell_stetler@fd.org.

STETLER-STEVENSON, MARYALICE, cytologist, director; d. Zieber Ralph and Margaret Antoinette Stetler; m. William George Stetler-Stevenson; 1 child, Margaret Georgina. MD, Northwestern U., Chgo., PhD, 1976. Diplomate in anatomic pathology Am. Bd. Pathology, 1990. Dir. flow cytometry lab. NIH, Nat. Cancer Inst., Bethesda, Md., 1989—. Past pres. Clin. Cytometry Soc., 2003—05. Mem.: Am. Soc. Clin. Pathology. Office: Nat Inst Health 10 Ctr Dr Bethesda MD 20892

STETSON, DANIEL EVERETT, museum director; b. Oneida, NY, Jan. 3, 1956; s. Robert Everett and Barbara Elizabeth (Gray) S.; m. Catherine Marie Smith; children: Kellee, Natalie, Philip. BA in Art History, Potsdam Coll. Arts and Scis., 1978; MFA in Museology, Syracuse U., 1981. Teaching asst. fine arts dept. Potsdam Coll. Arts and Scis., NY, 1977-78; grad. asst. Syracuse U. Art Collections, 1979-80; acting dir. Picker Art Gallery and Colgate U. Art Collections, Colgate U., Hamilton, NY, 1980-81; dir. Gallery of Art U. No. Iowa, Cedar Falls, 1981-87; dir. Davenport Mus. Art, Iowa, 1987-91; exec. dir. Austin Mus. Art (formerly Laguna Gloria Art Mus.), Tex., 1991-96, founding exec. dir., 1994; exec. dir. Polk Mus. Art, Lakeland, Fla., 1993—. Guest curator Joe and Emily Lowe Art Gallery, Syracuse U., 1980; mem. Inter Mus. Conservation Lab., Oberlin, 1987-91; mem. design adv. com. Iowa Capitol, Des Moines, 1989-91; panel cons. Arts Midwest/Affiliated States Art Assns. of Upper Midwest, Mpls., 1983, 88; bd. dirs. Iowa Arts Coalition, 1990-91; chair Tex. Commn. on the Arts Visual Arts Review Panel, 1994; mem. planning com. Tex. Assn. of Mus., 1994; mem. art in pub. pls. com. Austin Airport, 1995. Author/curator: (exhbn. catalog) José de Creeft (1884-1982), 1983, Contemporary Icons and Explorations, 1988, (exhbn. catalog) Philip Perlstein-Painting to Watercolors, 1983, Walter Dusenbery Classical Echoes, 1985, Jaune Quick-to-See Smith and George Longfish: Personal Symbols, 1986, Reuban Nakian: Leda and The Swan, 1983, Focus 1 Michael Boyd: Paintings, 1980, 89, Focus 2 Photo Image League, 1989, Focus 3 The Art of Haiti: A Sense of Wonder, 1989, Focus 6—Contemporary Devel. in Glass, 1990, Peter Dean: Landscapes of the Mind, 1981, Joseph Raffael, 1987, Born in Iowa-The Homecoming, 1986, Stieglitz and 40 Other Photographers—The Development of a Collection, 1991-92, New Works (Austin and Central Texas Artists), 1992, 94, Companions in Time: The Paintings of William Lester & Everett Spruce Catalogue Essay, 1993, Human Nature, Human Form Catalogue Essay, 1993, Sources and Collaborations: The Making of the Holocaust Project by Judy Chicago and Donald Woodman tour and catalog, 1994—, Bucking the Texan Myth-Scouting the Third Frontier, 1996. Bd. mem. arts coun. Cedar Arts Forum, Black Hawk County, Iowa, 1983-85; curriculum com. Leadership Investment for Tomorrow, Cedar Falls-Waterloo, Iowa, 1985-86; mem. adv. com. MBA Course of Study Styles and Strategies Non-Profit Orgns. St. Ambrose U., 1989-91, Austin BCA Arts Week Poster and Awards, 1993; mem. City of Austin Funding Process Rev. Com., 1992; Facilities Team Austin Comprehensive Arts Plan, 1991-93; mem. adv. panel Tex. Commn. Arts Visual Arts, 1993; field reviewer Inst. Mus. Svcs.-Gen. Operating Support Grant Field Reviewer, 1993; mem. arts com. Downtown Mgmt. Assn., 1995; mem. arts sub-com. Downtown Commn.; bd. dirs. Friends of the Libr., Lakeland, 1996—, Quality Improvement Coun. Harrison Arts Ctr., Lakeland, 1996—; participant Leadership Lakeland Class XV, 1997-98. Fellow N.E. Mus. Conf., Rochester, N.Y., 1979; grantee Iowa Arts Coun., Tex. Commn. Arts, NEA advancement program grant phase I & II, 1993-95; recipient mus. scholarship Am. Law Inst. ABA, Atlanta, Phila., 1984, 93. Mem. Am. Assn. Mus., Midwest Mus. Conf., Iowa Mus. Assn. (chair steering com. exhbn. workshop 1984-86, legis. action com. and indemnification com. 1981-90, bd. dirs. 1983-85), Tex. Assn. Mus. (program com., resources sharing com., 1992-94, Art Mus. Affinity group) Davenport Rotary (cultural affairs com. 1987-91), Fla. Art Mus. Dirs. Assn. (bd. dirs. 1997—), Fla. Assn. Museums (accreditation peer reviewer 1997—), Southeast Mus. Assn. Avocations: books, music, bike riding, visual world and media. Home: 5564 Highlands Vista Cir Lakeland FL 33813-5217 Office: Polk Mus Art 800 E Palmetto Lakeland FL 33801-5529 Office Phone: 868-688-7743. E-mail: DEStetson@PolkMuseumofArt.org.

STETSON, JANE WATSON, political organization administrator; m. E. William Stetson. Dem. activist, fundraiser, Vt.; nat. fin. chair Dem. Nat. Com., Washington, 2009—. Democrat. Office: Dem Nat Com 430 S Capitol St SE Washington DC 20003*

STETSON, ROBERT FRANCIS, retired metallurgist; b. NYC, Oct. 20, 1928; s. Ralph Jerome and Margaret Mary Stetson; m. Rita Marie Jubach, Dec. 30, 1950 (dec. May 31, 1994); 1 child, Barbara A.; m. Mary Jane McKinney, June 10, 1999. Cert. in Metallurgy, Pa. State U., 1955. ICET A NSPE. Lab. technologist, insp. Babcock & Wilcox Co., Beaver Falls, Pa., 1949—58; tech. specialist materials sci. Gen. Atomics, San Diego, 1958—86, cons., 1986—98; ret., 1998; cons. NASA Marshall Space Flight Ctr., Huntsville, Ala., 2002—07. With AC US Army, 1946—47, ETO. Recipient Nat. Engring. Assocs. Achievement award, Am. Soc. Metals, 1979, James F. Lincoln Arc Welding Found. award, 1979. Fellow: Am. Soc. Metals Internat. (exec. bd. San Diego chpt. 1964—96, chmn. San Diego chpt. 1972—73). Achievements include patents for plasma orifice tip. Avocation: genealogy.

STETTER, KARL OTTO, microbiologist, educator; b. Munich, July 16, 1941; s. Josef and Elisabeth (Huebner) S.; m. Heidi Zahradnik, Dec. 20, 1969; children: Sabine, Florian, Claudia. Abitur, Staatl. Luitpold-Oberrealschule, Munich, 1960; diploma in Biology, Tech. U., Munich, 1969, D (hon.), 1973, Ludwig-Maximilians U., 1977. Asst. Ludwig-Maximilians U., 1969-73; post doctoral fellow Max-Planck Inst. Biochemistry, Martinsried, Germany, 1974-75; asst. lectr. Ludwig-Maximilians U., 1975-77, lectr., 1977-80; prof. microbiology U. Regensburg, Germany, 1980—; vis. prof., faculty UCLA, 1989—; co-founder Diversa Corp., San Diego, 1994. Dir. Inst. Microbiology U. Regensburg, Germany, 1980. Mem. editl. bd.: Systematic and Applied Microbiology, Extremophiles. Recipient Deutsche Ges. Hygiene award U. Microbiology, 1985, Gottfried-Wilhelm-Leibniz-Preis Deutsche Forschungsgemeinschaft, Germany, 1988, medal Lectr. The Internat. Inst. Biotech., London, 1994, Bergey medal, 1999, Leeuwenhoek medal, 2003. Fellow Am. Acad. Microbiology; mem. Am. Soc. Microbiology, Deutsche Akademie der Naturforscher Leopoldina, Royal Netherlands Acad. Arts and Scis., Bayerische Akademie der Wissenschaften, Vereinigung f. Allg. U. Angew. Mikrobiologie, Deutsche Gesellschaft f. Hygiene und Mikrobiologie, Gesellschaft Deutscher Naturforscher und Ärzte, Gesellschaft Deutscher Chemiker, Gesellschaft f. Biologische Chemie, The Internat. Inst. Biotech. Avocations: life sciences, orchid cultivation. Office: U Regensburg Abt Mikrobiologie Universitätsstrasse 31 D-93053 Regensburg Germany Office Phone: 499419431821. Business E-Mail: karl.stetter@biologie.uni-regensburg.de.

STETTLER, STEPHEN F., performing company executive; b. Phila., May 1, 1952; s. Wallace Frederick and Catherine Sue (Brill) S. AB summa cum laude, Kenyon Coll., 1974; MFA in Directing, Cath. U. Am., 1982; MLitt in Theatre, Lincoln Coll., Oxford, Eng., 1983. Dir. dramatics Westminster Sch., Simsbury, Conn., 1975-80; acting coach Hartke Conservatory Cath. U., Washington, 1982; chair drama dept. St. Albans and Nat. Cathedral Schs., Washington, 1980-84; dir., instr. acting Nat. Theatre Inst. O'Neill Theater Ctr., Waterford, Conn., 1984-93; artistic dir. TNT/New Theatre Bklyn., 1985-90; producing dir. Weston (Vt.) Playhouse, 1988—. Lit. asst. Arena Stage Co., Washington, 1983-84; site evaluator theatres Nat. Endowment for Arts, Washington, 1990—; panelist Vt. Coun. Arts, Montpelier, Vt., NEA, Washington, D.C.; mem. capital grants com. N.Y.C. Dept. Cultural Affairs; guest instr. directing Teatret Vart, Norway. Dir.: Who's Afraid of Virginia Woolf?, Dancing at Lughnasa, Animal Fair, Rough Crossing, Nora, Donkeys' Years, Floyd Collins (Moss Hart award for best prodn. in New Eng.), Sweeney Todd, Six Degrees of Separation, A Midsummer Night's Dream (Best Play award Folger Shakespeare Libr. competition). Mem. Phi Beta Kappa. Office: Weston Playhouse 703 Main St Weston VT 05161 Business E-Mail: sstettler@westonplayhouse.org.

STETTNER, EDWARD A., political science professor; b. NYC, Feb. 18, 1940; s. Frederick Albert and Celia Carolyn S.; m. Laura Gagliardi, July 17, 1966; children: Victoria, Jeffrey, Thomas. BA, Brown U., 1962; MA, Princeton U., 1964, PhD, 1968. Lectr. polit. sci. Rutgers U., New Brunswick, N.J., 1965-66; instr. polit. sci. Wellesley (Mass.) Coll., 1966—68, asst. prof. polit. sci., 1968—74, assoc. prof., 1974—80, prof. polit. sci., 1980-95, Ralph Emerson and Alice Freeman Palmer prof. polit. sci., 1995—2008, assoc. dean of the coll., 1977-86, dean of the faculty, 1986—88, prof. emeritus, 2008—. Trustee Mount Ida Coll., Newton, Mass., 2000—. Author: Shaping Modern Liberalism: Herbert Croly and Progressive Thought, 1993; editor: Perspectives on Europe, 1970. Mem. AAUP (mem. nat. coun. 1970-73, pres. Mass. State Conf. 1975-77), Am. Polit. Sci. Assn., New Eng. Polit. Sci. Assn., Phi Beta Kappa. Home: 67 Carriage Hill Cir Southborough MA 01772 Office: Wellesley College 106 Central St Wellesley MA 02481 Business E-Mail: estettner@wellesley.edu.

STETZ, MELBA DEL CARMEN, psychologist; BA in Clin. Psychology, U. Sacred Heart, San Juan, 1986, BA in Psychology Minors, 1992; MS with honors, Carlos Albizu U., San Juan, 1994, PhD in Indsl. and Orgnl. Psychology, 1999. Lic. rsch. psychologist. Indsl. & orgnl. psychologist Psychometric Corp., PR; phys. therapist & med. legal asst. Phys. Therapy Inst., PR, 1984—86; nursing asst., home health aide Sherwood Ter. Nursing Home, Washington, 1987; orthop. specialist 8th Evacuation Hosp., Ft. Ord, Calif., 1988—90; platoon leader-2nd lt. C Co. 192nd Support Bn. Prang, 1991—93; mil. sci. officer Lincoln Mil. Acad., PR, 1993; asst. rsch. psychologist Carlos Albizu U., San Juan, 1994—95; med. plans officer-2nd lt. US Army, Panama, 1996; med. logistician-1st lt. 424th Med. Logistics Bn., NJ, 1997—99; pers. rsch. psychologist US Office Pers. Mgmt., Washington, 1999—2000; rsch. psychologist Walter Reed Army Inst. Rsch., Md., 2001—03; asst. dir. Rsch. Area Directorate Mil. Operational Rsch. Program, Ft. Detrick, Md., 2003—05; detachment comdr. & adj. maj. US Army Aero-med. Rsch. Lab., Ft. Rucker, Ala., 2005—06, chief, combat stress rsch., 2006—07; med. ops. officer Multi-Nat. Corps and Forces, Iraq, 2008; rsch. dir., psychology dept. Tripler Army Med. Ctr., Hawaii, 2008—. Contbr. numerous sci. papers to profl. jours. Decorated German Armed Forces Proficiency badge, Army Achievement medal, Army Res. Commendation medal, Overseas Svc. Ribbon, Nat. Def. Svc. medal, Army Svc. Ribbon, Armed Force Res. medal, NCO Devel. Proft. Ribbon; recipient Arthur W. Melton award, Iraq Campaign medal, Aviation badge, Parachutist badge, Meritorious Svc. medal. Business E-Mail: melba.stetz@us.army.mil.

STEUBEN, NORTON LESLIE, lawyer, educator; b. Milw., Feb. 14, 1936; s. Benjamin and Ria (Beerman) S.; m. Judith Ann Dickens, June 21, 1958; children: Sara Ann, Marc Nelson. AB, U. Mich., 1958, JD with distinction, 1961. Bar: N.Y. 1962, Colo. 1975. Assoc., then ptnr. Hodgson, Russ, Andrews, Woods & Goodyear, Buffalo, 1961-68; mem. faculty U. Colo. Law Sch., Boulder, 1968—2002, prof. law, 1974—2002, Nicholas Rosenbaum prof., 1997—2002, Nicholas Rosenbaum prof. emeritus, 2002—; of counsel Ireland, Stapleton, Pryor & Pascoe, Denver, 1980-97, 1999—2004. Lectr. Law Sch., SUNY, Buffalo, 1961-68; officer Buffalo-Niagara Indsl. Devel. Corp., 1963-68, Buffalo Opportunities Devel. Corp., 1966-68; vis prof. law U. Puget Sound. Sch. Law, 1992-93; resident tax policy advisor to the govt. of Ukraine, Treas. Dept., 1997-99. Author: Cases and Materials on Real Estate Planning, 1974, 4th edit., 2006; co-author: Problems in the Fundamentals of Federal Income Taxation, 1985, 3d edit. 1994, Problems in the Federal Income Taxation of Business Enterprises, 1985, 3d edit., 1996; co-editor: Bittker, Fundamentals of Federal Income Taxation, 1983; editor Jour. Affordable Housing & Cmty. Devel. Law, 1994-97; contbr. articles to profl. jours. Mem. Boulder Human Rights Commn., 1969-74, chmn., 1972-74; mem. Boulder Landlord-Tenant Com., 1973-74; trustee Boulder Open Space Bd., 1976-81, vice chmn., 1978-79, chmn., 1979-81; trustee Congregation Har Ha-Shem, Boulder, 1978-79, v.p., 1979-81, pres., 1982-84; mem. Boulder Housing Authority, 1982-89, vice chmn., 1984-85, chmn., 1985-88; mem. advocacy and pub. policy com. Am. Tinnitus Assn., 2002—, Cmty. Adv. Panel Roche Colo., 2004-; mem. Boulder County Aging Svcs. Found., 2005—08, Boulder Housing Counselors, 2007—09; bd. mem. Boulder Chorale, 2008-, Taxaide, AARP Tax Aide, 2008-; v.p. U. Colo. Ret. Faculty Assn., 2008-; vol. Atty. Boulder County Legal Svc., 2008-. Recipient S.I. Goldberg award Alpha Epsilon Pi, 1957, Disting. Svc. to Community award Buffalo Area C. of C., 1966, John W. Reed award U. Colo. Law Sch., 1970, Calhoun Cmty. Svc. award, 2005; Teaching Recognition award U. Colo.-Boulder, 1972, Teaching Excellence award, 1982; Commendation for Exceptional Assistance to Govt. of Ukraine, 1999; Presdl. Tchg. scholar U. Colo., 1989, Fulbright scholar, Ukraine, 2003-04. Mem. ABA, N.Y. State Bar Assn., Colo. Bar Assn., Boulder County Bar Assn., Am. Law Inst., AAUP, Scribes (officer, editor Scrivener 1975-76, dir. 1979-82), Barristers Soc., Order of Coif, Tau Epsilon Rho. Democrat. Home: 845 8th St Boulder CO 80302-7408 Office: 700C Wolf Law Boulder CO 80309 Home Phone: 303-447-1581; Office Phone: 303-492-7963. E-mail: norton.steuben@colorado.edu.

STEUER, MICHAEL, mathematics professor; b. NYC, Mar. 6, 1944; s. Joseph and Frieda Steuer; m. Sharon Arlene Cohen, June 25, 1967; children: David Howard, Deborah Malka Kotz. BS, CUNY, 1964; MA, U. Pa., Phila., 1966; PhD, Adelphi U., 1977. Prof. math. Nassau C.C., Garden City, NY, 1966—, asst. dept. chair, 1983—. Chair academic senate Nassau C.C., Garden City, 1989—93, Garden City, 2005—09; pres. faculty coun. cmty. colleges SUNY, Albany, 1995—97. Co-author: (textbook) Logic and Set Theory, 1983, 2004, 2006, 2009. Bd. dirs. Commack Jewish Ctr., NY, 1976—2005. Recipient Outstanding Svc. award, NY State Assn. Two Yr. Colleges, 1994, Faculty Disting. Achievement award, Nassau C.C., 1995. Mem.: Math. Assn. Am., NY State Math. Assn. Two Yr. Colleges (treas., bd. mem. 1970—76), Am. Math. Assn. Two Yr. Colleges (Outstanding Svc, Math. Edn. award 1976). Office: Nassau CC One Education Dr Garden City NY 11530 Business E-Mail: michael.steuer@ncc.edu.

STEUER, RICHARD MARC, lawyer; b. Bklyn., June 19, 1948; s. Harold and Gertrude (Vengar) S.; m. Audrey P. Forchheimer, Sept. 9, 1973; children: Hilary, Jeremy. BA, Hofstra U., 1970; JD, Columbia U., 1973. Bar: NY 1974, US Dist. Ct. (ea. and so. dists.) NY 1974, US Ct. Appeals (2d cir.) 1974, US Supreme Ct. 1979, US Dist. Ct. (no. dist.) NY 1984, US Dist. Ct. (we. dist.) NY 1997, US Ct. Appeals (3d cir.) 1987, US Ct. Appeals (5th cir.) 1995, US Ct. Appeals (10th cir.) 2003, US Ct. Appeals (fed. cir.), 2004. Ptnr. Kaye Scholer LLP, NYC, 1973—2002, chair antitrust practice group, 1996—2002; ptnr. Mayer Brown LLP, NYC, 2002—. Adj. assoc. prof. law NYU, 1985; adj. prof. law St. John's U., 2003; lectr. in field; neutral evaluator U.S. Dist. Ct. Ea. Dist., N.Y, 1994-96. Author: A Guide to Marketing Law: Law and Business Inc., 1986; contbr. articles to profl. jours. Fellow: Am. Bar Found.; mem.: ABA (editl. bd. antitrust devel. vol. 1984—86, vice-chmn. program com. 1988—91, coun. sect. antitrust law 1993—96, chmn. pubis. com. 1996—98, editl. chmn. Antitrust mag. 1998—2001, coun. sect. antitrust law 2001—04, comms. officer 2004—05, sec. 2004—05, ho. of dels. 2005—08, com. officer 2008—09, vice chair 2009—), Assn. Bar City N.Y. (chmn. antitrust and trade regulation 1995—98, antitrust and trade regulation, internat. trade, lectures and CLE coms). Office: Mayer Brown LLP 1675 Broadway New York NY 10019-5820 Office Phone: 212-506-2530. Business E-Mail: rsteuer@mayerbrown.com.

STEUERT, DOUGLAS MICHAEL, engineering and construction management company executive; b. Oklahoma City, May 21, 1948; s. Douglas Anselm and Geraldine (Sparks) S.; m. Nancy Elizabeth Ridd, Aug. 22, 1970. BS in Physics, Carnegie-Mellon U., Pitts., 1971, MS in Indsl. Mgmt. Staff asst. TRW, Inc., Cleve., 1971-73, mgr. fin. rsch. and analysis, 1973-75, dir. fin. US, 1975-76, dir. fin. Europe Frankfurt, Germany, 1976-79, asst. treas. internat. Cleve., 1979-81, sr. fin. dir. automotive worldwide sector, 1981-84, contr. valve divsn., 1984-86; v.p., treas. GenCorp Inc., Ohio, 1986-87, v.p. fin. and planning Ohio, 1987-90, v.p, CFO, treas. Ohio, 1990-94, sr. v.p., CFO Ohio, 1994—99, Litton Industries, Inc., 1999—2001, Fluor Corp., Calif., 2001—. Dir. Weyerhaeuser Co., 2004—. Dir. Mental Health Assn. Summit County, 1993; mem. coun. on fin. Grad. Sch. Indsl. Adminstrn., Carnegie-Mellon U., 1994—. Mem. Fin. Execs. Inst. (nat. chpt., NE Ohio chpt.), Mfrs. Alliance for Productivity and Innovation, Conf. Bd. Coun. of CFOs, Leadership Akron, Alumni Assn. Carnegie-Mellon U. Office: Fluor Enterprises 3 Polaris Way Aliso Viejo CA 92698 Office Phone: 949-349-2000. Office Fax: 949-349-2585.

STEVCEVA, LILJANA, medical educator, researcher; d. Risto Vitanov and Galaba Vitanova; m. Jovica Stevcev, Dec. 24, 1981; children: Ilija Stevcev, Risto Stevcev. MD magna cum laude, U. Kiril i Metodi, Skopje, Macedonia, 1981; PhD in Med. Scis., Australian Nat. U., Canberra, Australia, 1998. Lic. Min. Health, 1984. Med. officer br. virology Divsn. Microbiology and Infectious Diseases Nat. Inst. Allergy and Infectious Diseases, NIH; postdoc. fellow Md. U. Inst. Human Virology, 1993—; assoc. prof. immunology and microbiology Paul L. Foster Sch. Medicine, Tex. Tech Health Scis. Ctr., El Paso, Tex., 2007—; vis. acad. infectious diseases Mass. Gen. Hosp., Boston, Harvard Med. Sch., Boston, 2005—; asst. in virology, instr. medicine, infectious diseases Mass. Gen. Hosp. and Harvard Med. Sch., 2000—. Grant reviewer Ont. HIV Treatment Network, Toronto, Canada, 2004—, S.African AIDS Vaccine Initiative, South Africa, 2005—; abstract reviewer XVI Internat. AIDS Conf., Toronto, 2006; cons. Schlesinger Assoc. NJ, NJ, 2007—, Med. Rsch. Coun., South Africa, 2007—; grant reviewer Nat. Health Lab. Svcs., South Africa, 2007—; abstract reviewer 4th IAS Conf. on HIV Pathogenesis, Treatment and Prevention, Sydney, 2007; cons. Min. Health, Singapore, XVII Internat. AIDS Conf., Mexico City, 2008. Reviewer (jours.) Jour. Vaccine, 2004—, Jour. Reproductive Immunology, 2004—, Jour. Virology, 2000—, Jour. Nature Medicine, 2000, Advanced Drug Delivery Reviews, 2001—, Med. Sci. Monitor, 2001—, Trends in Microbiology, 2002—, Jour. Infectious Diseases, 2007—; contbr. articles to profl. jours. Liaison officer Am. Field Svc., Columbia, Md., 2004—05, host parent, 2002—03; vol. Red Cross, Macedonia, 1981—90. Recipient Travel award, Australian Soc. Med. Rsch., 1994, Young Investigator award, Soc. Mucosal Immunology, 2002, 14th Conf. Retroviruses and Opportunistic Infections, 2007; grantee, NIH, 2005; Fogarty fellow, Nat. Cancer Inst., NIH, 1998—, Internat. Rsch. fellow, NIH, 2000. Home: 18 Walnutwood Ct Germantown MD 20874 Personal E-mail: liljana@hotmail.com.

STEVENS, ANNE L., metal products executive, retired automotive executive; b. Reading, Pa., Dec. 1948; BS in mechanical & materials engring., Drexel U., 1980; Grad. Level Business student, Rutgers U; PhD (hon.), Ctrl. Mich. U. With Exxon Corp.; mktg. specialist plastic products divsn. Ford Motor Co., 1990—92, mgr., Quality Services Dept., 1992—95, mfr. mgr., Automotive Components Divsn., 1995, Plant mgr., Automotive Components Div. Enfield, England, 1995—97, asst. vehicle line dir., Ford Automotive Operations Dunton, England, 1997—99, dir., Manufacturing Business Office, N. Am., 1999—2000, v.p. N. Am. Assembly Ops., 2000—01, v.p. N. Am. Vehicle Ops., 2001—03, group v.p., Canada, Mexico, and S. Am., 2003—05, exec. v.p., COO, The Americas, 2005—06; chmn., CEO, pres. Carpenter Tech. Corp., Wyomissing, Pa., 2006—. Bd. dirs. Lockheed Martin Corp., 2002—, Coun. Americas; bd. trustees Drexel U.; trustee Women's Automotive Assn. Internat.; mem. advisory bd. Mexico Inst., Woodrow Wilson Internat. Ctr. for Scholars; mem. exec. advisory bd. Juran Ctr. for Leadership in Quality, U. Minn. Recipient Shingo Leadership award, 2000, Circle of Distinction award, Drexel U. Coll. Engring., 2001, Eli Whitney award, Soc. Mfg. Engineers, 2003; named one of Most Powerful Women in Bus., Fortune mag., 2005. Mem.: NAE. Home: 1635 Museum Rd Wyomissing PA 19610-2828

STEVENS, ART, public relations executive; b. NYC, July 17, 1935; m. Eva Sandberg, Mar. 19, 1972. BA, CCNY, 1957. Pub. relations dir. Prentice Hall, Inc., Englewood Cliffs, NJ; account exec. William L. Safire Public Relations Inc., NYC, 1966-69, v.p., 1967-68, pres., 1968-69, Lobsenz-Stevens Inc., NYC, 1970—99; instr. Fairleigh Dickinson U.; chmn. & CEO Publicis Dialog, NYC, 1999—2002; mng. ptnr. Stevens Gould Pincus., LLC, 2003—. Weekly humor commentator WINK-TV, Ft. Myers, Fla.; cons. in field. Author: The Persuasion Explosion, 1985, Sanibel Shell Shocked, 1992; weekly columnist Sanibel-Captiva (Fla.) Islander; contbr. articles to profl. jours. Bd. dirs. United Way of Putnam County, N.Y.; trustee Gotthelf Lupus Rsch. Inst. Inducted City Coll. N.Y. Comms. Alumni Hall Fame, 2001. Mem.: Public Relations Soc. Am. (sec. 2003, pres. N.Y. chpt. 2006, nat. bd., pub. rels. com., chair-elect tri-state dist., exec. com., chmn. eligibility com., counselors acad. sect.), Publicity Club N.Y. (Disting. Svc. award 1969), Gipsy Trail (pres., chmn. Carmel, N.Y.). Office Phone: 732-748-8583. Personal E-mail: artstevens@att.net. *Life is not an accident. The events in one's life are not accidents either. When I look back at what I have done and the lives that have been interwined with mine, it's as though it's all been scripted by a higher power.*

STEVENS, BERTON LOUIS, JR., data-processing executive; b. Chgo., Apr. 4, 1951; s. Berton Louis Sr. and Mary Cover (Kochavaris) S.; m. Janet Alene Madenberg, May 20, 1990. Student, Ill. Inst. Tech., Chgo., 1969-73. Systems and applications programmer Judge & Dolph, Ltd., Elk Grove Village, Ill., 1978-91, mgr. data processing, 1991-99; bus. sys. coord. Meml. Med. Ctr., Inc., 2000-2001, lead sys. analyst, 2001—02; svc. ctr. mgr. Siemens Health Sys., 2002—04; mgr. applications Province Healthcare, Las Cruces, N.Mex., 2004—06; dir. MIS LifePoint Hosps., Las Cruces, N.Mex., 2006—. Instr. Adler Planetarium and Astron. Mus., Chgo., 1980-86; dir. Desert Moon Observatory #448. Editor and author newsletter Bert's Bull., 1987-90; editor newsletter No. Lights, 1990-98; columnist Starry Dome, 2004- Recipient Regional award North Ctrl. Region Astron. League, 1989. Mem. Nat. Assn. Sys. Programmers, Internat. Occulation Timing Assn. (sec. 1975-78), Chgo. Computer Soc., Chgo. Astron. Soc. (pres. 1977, 80, 84), Racine Astron. Soc. (pres. 1979), Astron. League (exec. sec. 1993-95, webmaster 1995-02), Desert Moon Observatory (dir.), Astron. Soc. Las Cruces (pres, 2001, 2007). Personal E-mail: bstevens@zianet.com. Business E-Mail: Berton.Stevens@lpnt.net.

STEVENS, BRAD K., men's college basketball coach; m. Tracy Stevens; 1 child, Brady. BA in Econs., DePauw U., Greencastle, Ind., 1999. Mktg. assoc. Eli Lilly and Co., Indpls.; coord. basketball ops. Butler U., Indpls., 2000—01, asst. coach, 2001—07, head coach, 2007—. Named Coach of Yr., Horizon League, 2009. Office: Butler Mens Basketball 510 W 49th St Indianapolis IN 46208 Office Phone: 317-940-9897. E-mail: bksteven@butler.edu.*

STEVENS, CHERITA WYMAN, social sciences educator, writer; b. Erick, Okla., Jan. 12, 1938; d. Forrest Clarence and Wilma Peter Wyman; m. Paul Donald Stevens, May 30, 1958 (div. Nov. 10, 1978); children: Paul McDonald, Mark Liu. BA in Social Sci., Phillips U., 1961; MA in Sch. Law and Fin., Calif. State U., LA, 1976. Gen. secondary credential, grades 7-14 & adult 1976, life credential in gen. secondary, grades 7-14 and adult Calif. Credential Commn., 1987, in gen. adminstrv. svcs., prin. v.p., coord. credential K-12 and adult LA, 1998, cert. in ESL UCLA. Classroom tchr. grades 7-9 South Pasadena (Calif.) Unified, 1966—74; assoc. regional pastor Disciples of Christ, Pacific Southwest, 1976—82; computer store owner Claremont (Calif.) Computer, 1982—87; tchr., prin., grant writer Cabrillo Unified Sch. Dist., Half Moon Bay, Calif., 1987—97; ESL computer lab. media instr. Chapman Edn. Ctr., Garden Grove, Calif., 1997—2009. Legis. intern Calif. State Assembly, Sacramento, 1978—80; NASD registered rep. Primerica Life-Citigroup, Orange, Calif., 2000—09; grant reviewer U.S. Dept. Edn., Washington, 2002; presenter in field; grant writer Calif. Dept. Edn./Joint Partnership Training Act, Half Moon Bay, 1996. Editor: Direction Newspaper, 1976—82; author: (software) Apartment Maintenance, 1988, Grants Tracking, 1989, Financial Management, 1991, Curriculum and Lesson Plans for the Independent Learning Lab, 1995; designer, lesson plan builder: OTAN Website, 2002—09; contributor KOCE (PBS) Schoolhouse Video Project, 2004; contbr. articles to newspapers and mag.;, author of poems, Banking for ESL, 2005, US History for ESL, 2006. Mem. Ams. for Dem. Action, Pasadena, 1963—80; civil rights activist, 1960—69; organizer first Martin Luther King Jr. celebration in U.S. LA, 1972; active 1st Christian Ch., Orange, Pasadena, Calif., 1963—2009. Mem.: Calif. Tchrs. English to Spkrs. Other Langs., Assn. Calif. Sch. Adminstrs. (site rep. 1993—97, state presenter 2005—09, state workshop presenter). Avocations: golf, photography, genealogy. Home: 401 W La Veta Ave #220 Orange CA 92866-2649 Personal E-mail: cheri1066@msn.com.

STEVENS, CHRISTOPHER WILLIAMS, lawyer; BA, Hampden-Sydney Coll., Va., 1992; JD, U. Richmond, Va., 1997. Bar: Va. 1997, U.S. Dist. Ct. (we. dist.) Va. 1997. Assoc. Cranwell & Moore, Roanoke, Va., 1997—98, Wooten & Hart, Roanoke, 1998—2003, Wood Rogers PLC, Roanoke, 2003—; vol., 2000; bd. dirs., 2008—. Co-author: Insurance Law in Virginia, 2002. Chmn. Light-the-Night walk Leukemia-Lymphoma Soc., Roanoke, 2005—06; bd. dirs. YMCA, Roanoke, 2004—06. Mem.: Roanoke Bar Assn., Def. Rsch. Inst., Va. Assn. Def. Attys. Office: Woods Rogers PLC 10 S Jefferson St Roanoke VA 24014 Office Phone: 540-983-7600. Office Fax: 540-983-7711.

STEVENS, DAVID ALEC, medical educator; b. NYC, June 3, 1940; m. Julie Anne Teece, Aug. 15, 1964; children: Joseph John, Emily Beth Stevens Marsh. BA, Cornell U., Ithaca, NY, 1960; MD, U. Rochester, NY, 1965. Diplomate Nat. Bd. Med. Examiners, Am. Bd. Internal Medicine and Infectious Diseases; med. lic. Wis., Calif. Intern, asst. resident dept. medicine U. Wis. Hosps., Madison, 1965-67; rsch. assoc. Nat. Cancer Inst., Bethesda, Md., 1967-69; resident dept. medicine UCLA Med Ctr., 1969-70; fellow divsn. infectious diseases, dept. medicine Stanford U., Calif., 1970—72, asst. prof. divsn. infectious diseases dept. medicine, 1972—78, assoc. prof. divsn. infectious diseases, dept. medicine, 1978—85, prof., 1985—, assoc. chief divsn. infectious diseases, 1992—2003; epidemiologist Santa Clara County-Valley Med. Ctr., San Jose, Calif., 1972—, assoc. chief dept. medicine, 1972—, chief divsn. infectious diseases, 1972—. Co-dir. microbiology lab. Santa Clara Valley Med. Ctr., 1972—; prin. investigator Infectious Diseases Rsch. Lab., Calif. Inst. Med. Rsch., San Jose, 1973—, bd. regents, 1978-90, 92—, sec.-treas., 1979-81, sci. dir. coun., 1986-88, pres., 1992—, Internat. Agy. Rsch. Cancer, WHO, Lyon, France, 1976; mycology ref. lab. Pub. Health Lab. Svcs. Dept. Microbiology, U. London, 1979; dir. clin. labs. Calif. Inst. Med. Rsch., 1980—; co-dir. AIDS program Santa Clara Valley Med. Ctr., 1986-88, assoc. dir., 1988-98; lectr. fourth ann. O.J. Farness lecture, U. Ariz., Tucson, 1999; Ian Murray Meml. lectr. British Soc. Mycopathology, Canterbury, Eng., 1985; spl. lectr. fourth ann. Japanese Soc. Med. Mycopathology, Chiba, 1996, Focus on Fungal Infections 17, San Diego, 2007; keynote spkr. Focus on Fungus Infections 13, Maui, Hawaii, 2003, 3rd Advances Against Aspergillosis, Miami Beach, 2008. Author: (with others) Coccidioidomycosis, 1980; mem. editl. bd. various profl. jours.; contbr. articles to profl. jours, chpt. to books. With USPHS, 1967-69. Recipient Charles Smith Meml. award, Coccidioidomycosis Study Group, 2006. Fellow ACP, Am. Soc. Microbiology (chair mycology 1992-93, divsn. lectr. mycology ann. gen. meeting 2001), Infectious Diseases Soc. Am., Am. Acad. Microbiology; mem. AMA, AAUP, AAAS, Am. Fedn. Clin. Rsch., Am. Soc. Clin. Investigation, Fedn. Am. Scientists, Med. Mycology Soc. Ams. (Rhoda Benham medal 1999), Calif. Med. Assn., Western Assn. Physicians, Santa Clara County Med. Soc. (Outstanding Achievement in Medicine award 2003), Internat. Soc. Human and Animal Mycology (clin. mycology com. 1985-91, Lucille Georg medal 2006). Achievements include patents for antigenic preparation and diagnostic method for identification of Nocardia infections; use of synthetic molecules to stimulate leukocytes; topical therapy with collectins. Avocations: jazz, running, philately. Office: Santa Clara Valley Med Ctr 751 S Bascom Ave San Jose CA 95128-2699

STEVENS, DAVID H., federal agency administrator; b. NYC; BA, U. Colo., Boulder, 1983. With World Savings Bank, 1983, group sr. v.p., nat. sales mgr. mortgage divsn.; exec. v.p. single family bus. Freddie Mac (Fed. Home Loan Mortgage Corp.), 1999; exec. v.p., nat. wholesale mgr. Wells Fargo Home Mortgage, 2006; v.p. mortgage, title, & ins. divsn. Long & Foster Companies, 2006—08, pres., COO, 2008—09; asst. sec. for housing, commr. Fed. Housing Authority (FHA) US Dept. Housing & Urban Devel. (HUD), Washington, 2009—. Founding exec. sponsor Women's Mortgage Industry Network. Office: FHA US Dept Housing & Urban Devel (HUD) 451 7th St SW Washington DC 20410 Office Phone: 202-708-1112.*

STEVENS, DIANA LYNN, elementary school educator; b. Waterloo, Iowa, Dec. 12, 1950; d. Marcus Henry and Clarissa Ann (Funk) Carr; m. Paul John Stevens; 1 child, Drew Spencer. BS, Mid Am. Nazarene Coll. (now Mid-Am. Nazarene U.), Olathe, Kans., 1973; M in Liberal Arts, Baker U., Baldwin, Kans., 1989. Elem. tchr. Olathe (Kans.) Sch. Dist. #233, 1975—. Artwork appeared in traveling exhibit ARC/Nat. Art Edn. Assn., 1968, Delta Kappa Gamma Bull., 2001. Olathe Sch. Dist. Action grantee, 1996-97, Summer Reading grantee Olathe Pub. Schs., 2007; recipient Excellence in Edn. award Olathe Pub. Schs. Found., 2002,; recipient Reading grantee 2008. Mem. NEA, Kans. Edn. Assn., Olathe Edn. Assn. (social com. Olathe chpt.), Coll. Ch. of the Nazarene, Delta Kappa Gamma (profl. affairs com. mem., chpt. membership chair 2006-, Excellence in Edn. award 2002), Beta Omega (membership chair, 2d v.p. 2006-). Avocations: portrait art, reading, walking. Home: 217 S Montclaire Dr Olathe KS 66061-3828

STEVENS, DONALD KING, retired aeronautical engineer, consultant; b. Danville, Ill., Oct. 27, 1920; s. Douglas Franklin and Ida Harriet (King) S.; m. Adele Carman de Werff, July 11, 1942; children: Charles August, Anne Louise, Alice Jeanne Stevens Kay. BS in Ceramic Engrng. with high honors, U. Ill., 1942; MS in Aeros. and Guided Missiles, U. So. Calif., 1949; grad., U.S. Army Command and Gen. Staff Coll., 1957, U.S. Army War Coll., 1962. Staff mem. Ill. State Geol. Survey, 1938—40; air defense officer (434th AAA Bn) in England, Algeria. Tunisia, Italy, 1942—44; regimental staff officer 473d Infantry Regiment, Italy, 1945; commd. 2d lt. US Army, 1942; ceramic engr. Harbison-Walker Refractories Co., Pitts., 1945—46; rsch. and analysis directorate antiaircraft and guided missiles br. The Arty. Sch. US Army, Ft. Bliss, Tex., 1949—52, asst. S-3 1st GM Brigade, 1953, commdr. 2d battalion 1st guided missile group, 1954—56, mem. weapons sys. evaluation group Office Sec. Def. Washington, 1957—61, chief J2 plans br. UN command/US Forces Korea, 1962—63, advanced through grades to col., 1963, comdr. Niagara-Buffalo def. 31st arty. brigade Lockport, NY, 1963—65, chief air def. and nuc. br. war plans divsn. Dept. Army Washington, 1965—67, dir. US ballistic missile def. studies DEPEX and X-66 for Sec. Def., 1965—66, chief strategic forces divsn. office dep. chief of staff mil. ops., 1967—69, chief J5 spl. weapons plans U.S. European command Germany, 1969—72, ret., 1972. Co-authored layout of McGregor Range, N.Mex, as guided missile firing range, 1955; guest lectr. U.S. Mil. Acad., 1958-59; mem. Study Group Army Air Def. Sys. for the 1970's, The AADS-70 Study in 1964 defined requirements for SAM-D, later named 'Patriot' 1964; cons. US Army Concepts Analysis Agy., Bethesda, Md., 1973-95; cons. on strategy Lulejian & Assocs., Inc., 1974-75; cons. nuc. policy and plans to Office Asst. Sec. of Def., 1975-80, 84-93; cons. Sci. Applications, Inc., 1976-78. Contbr. articles to profl. jours. Asst. camp dir. Piankeshaw Area coun. Boy Scouts Am., 1937; mem. chancel choir, elder First Christian Ch., Falls Church, Va., 1957-61, 65-69, 72-2002, elder emeritus 2004-; elder, trustee Presbyn. Ch., Niagara Falls, NY, 1963-65. Decorated DSM, Legion of Merit, Bronze Star, Order of St. Barbara. Mem. Am. Ceramic Soc., Assn. U.S. Army, U. Ill. Alumni Assn., U. So. Calif. Alumni Assn., Rotary, Keramos, Niagara Falls Country Club, Ill. Club (Washington), Terrapin Club, Sigma Xi, Sigma Tau, Tau Beta Pi, Phi Kappa Phi, Alpha Phi Omega. Disciples Of Christ. Achievements include pioneer in tactics and deployment plans for Army surface-to-air missiles. Address: 5916 5th St N Arlington VA 22203-1010 Personal E-mail: donaldksteven@verizon.net. Business E-Mail: dkstevens@starpower.net.

STEVENS, DWIGHT MARLYN, educational administrator; b. Wheeler, Wis., May 13, 1933; s. Clifford and Alva Orpha (Follensbee) S.; children: Patricia Lee Stevens Vanden Heuvel, Jacqueline Ann Stevens Barnett, Cynthia May Stevens Manthey, Robert Louis Stevens. BS, Eau Claire State U., Wis., 1957; MS, U. Wis., 1959, PhD, 1972. High sch. speech tchr., Ft. Atkinson, Wis., 1957-61; high sch. prin. Oostburg, Wis., 1961-64; prin. Arrowhead High Sch., Hartland, Wis., 1964-66; dist. adminstr. Arrowhead Sch. Dist., 1966-73; dep. state supt. Wis. Dept. Pub. Instrn., Madison, 1973-81; supt. schs. Stevens Point, Wis., 1982-93; faculty U. Wis.-Whitewater, 1971, U. Wis.-Superior, 1985, U. Wis.-Stevens Point, 1988-92, 93—, adj. prof., 1992-99. Author: (with Eye, Netzer and Benson) Strategies for Instructional Management, 1980. Dir. Ford Found., Cmty. Planning Project for Chippewa Indians, 1970-71, Nat. Validation Team, Title III, Elementary Secondary Edn. Act; cons. HEW Workshops on Innovation, Eagle River, Wis.; chmn. Wis. sch. dist. adminstrn., 1992; bd. dirs. St. Michaels Hosp., Stevens Point, chmn. bd., 1997—; bd. dirs. Stevens Point YMCA, 1998; internat. referee World Taekwondo Fedn. Internat.; 8th dan chang Moo Kwan, 8th dan Han Moo Kwan, 7th dan Kukkiwon, N.S.A. pres. won do kwan Internat. Taekwondo; owner Stevens Tackwondo Acad.; vice chmn. bd. suprs. Portage County, 1998-2006; chmn. County Parks Commn., 1998-99, County Pers. Commn., 1998-99; pres. Ctrl. C.W.A. Airport Bd., 2004-06; pres. Stevens Point Area Sch. Bd., 2006-. With U.S. Army, 1953-55. Recipient Outstanding Citizenship award Waukesha County, Wis., 1974; Ford fellow John Hay Fellowship in Humanities, Williams Coll., 1963; Kettering fellow Nat. Seminar on Innovation, Honolulu, summer 1967, Outstanding Adminstrv. Practitioner award U. Wis.-Stevens Point, 1991; Disting. Alumni award U. Wis., Eau Claire, 1980. Mem. Cen. Wis. C. of C. (pres. 1986-87), Acad. Letters and Scis. (v.p. 1987—, pres. 1988-90), Phi Delta Kappa (v.p. 1985-87), Pi Kappa Delta. Home: 3323 Echo Dells Ave Stevens Point WI 54481-5118 Home Phone: 715-341-5271.

STEVENS, ELISABETH GOSS (MRS. ROBERT SCHLEUSSNER JR.), writer, graphic artist; b. Rome, NY, Aug. 11, 1929; d. George May and Elisabeth (Stryker) Stevens; m. Robert Schleussner, Jr., Mar. 12, 1966 (dec. 1977); 1 child, Laura Stevens Forné. BA, Wellesley Coll., 1951; MA with high honors, Columbia U., 1956. Editl. assoc. Art News Mag., 1964-65; art critic and reporter Washington Post, Washington, 1965-66; freelance art critic and reporter Balt., 1966—; contbg. art critic Wall Street Jour., NYC, 1969-72; art critic Trenton (NJ) Times, 1974-77; art and architecture critic The Balt. Sun, 1978-86; critic-at-large srqradio.com, 2004—; art correspondent Sarasota Herald Tribune, 2005—07; contbg. writer The Senses mag., 2007. Author: Elisabeth Stevens' Guide to Baltimore's Inner Harbor, 1981, Fire and Water: Six Short Stories, 1982, Children of Dust: Portraits and Preludes, 1985, Horse and Cart: Stories from the Country, 1990, The Night Lover: Art & Poetry, 1995, In Foreign Parts, 1997, Household Words, 1999, 2d edit., 2000, Eranos, 2000, Cherry Pie & Other Stories, 2001, Long Trail Winding: New & Collected Upstate Stories, 2008, 10 Large Etchings, 2008, Ragbag, 2009, numerous poems; contbr. articles short stories to jours., newspapers and popular mags.; one-woman shows include Coll. Notre Dame of Md., 1997, Galerie Francoise, Lutherville, Md., 2000, Kirkland Libr., Clinton, NY, 2007, Sarasota Art Ctr., Sarasota, Fla., 2008, Utica Pub. Libr., Utica, NY, 2008, exhibited in group shows at Corcoran Gallery of Art, Washington, Towson State U., Balt., Atelier A/E, NYC, Stephen Gang Gallery, Govt. Ho., Annapolis, U. Minn., Morris, Cooperstown Art Assn., NY, Armory Art Ctr., West Palm Beach, Fla., Venice Art Ctr., Fla., Ft. Meyers Alliance for the Art, Katharine Butler Gallery, Sarasota, Fla., 2004, Combined Talents: Fla. Internat., Tallahassee, 2005, Mus. Fine Arts, Tallahassee, 2005, Silvermine Guild Arts Ctr., Wilton, Conn., 2006, N.Mex. Printmakers, Santa Fe, 2006—07, Kirkland Libr., Clinton, NY, 2007, Old Print Shop, NYC, Binghamton U. Art Mus., 2008; contributing arts writer: Sarasotas, Arts and Culture Mag., 2006—07. Recipient A.D. Emmart award for journalism, 1980, Critical Writing citation Balt.-Washington Newspaper Guild, 1980, fiction awards Md. Poetry Rev., 1992, 93, 94, 2d prize Lite Circle, 1994, 1st prize in fiction Lite Circle, 1995, 96, Balt. Writers Alliance Play Writing Contest award, 1994; art critics' fellow NEA, 1973-74, fellow MacDowell Colony, 1981, Va. Ctr. for Creative Arts, 1982-85, 88-90, 92, 93, 95, 97, 2000, 07, Ragdale Found., 1984, 89, Yaddo, 1991, Villa Montalvo, 1995; Work-in-Progress grantee for poetry Md. Art Coun., 1986, Creative Devel. grantee for short fiction collection Balt. Mayor's Com. on Art and Culture, 1986. Mem. Coll. Art Assn., Authors Guild, Soc. Am. Graphic Artists, Women Contemporary Artists Sarasota. Home: Bards Castle 5353 Creekside Trail Sarasota FL 34243

STEVENS, ERIC R., automotive executive; b. Balt., Dec. 28, 1955; BA with honors, Acadia U., Wolfville, NS, Can., 1977; M in Internat. Affairs, Queen's U., Kingston, Ont., Can., 1979. Various positions in material mgmt., quality, and mfg. Gen. Motors Can., Oshawa, Ont., 1978—86, fin. staff, 1986—88, joint venture assignment, Gen. Motors-Suzuki Ingersoll, 1988—91; dir. quality and reliability Opel España, Zaragoza, Spain, 1991—93; pres. Opel Eisenach, 1993—97, exec. dir. lean mfg. Zurich, Switzerland, 1997—2000; plant mgr., Oshawa car assembly plant Gen. Motors Corp., 2000, exec. dir. mfg. engrng. Warren, Mich., 2000—04; exec. dir. mfg. Gen. Motors Europe, Zurich, Switzerland, 2004—06, v.p. mfg., 2006—. Office: Gen Motors Europe Walchestrasse 27 8006 Zurich Switzerland*

STEVENS, GEORGE RICHARD, business consultant, public information officer; b. Chgo., Sept. 6, 1932; s. George and Irene (Kaczmarek) S.; m. Jeanne E. Sowden, Aug. 2, 1957; children: Stacey, Samantha, Pamela. BS with honors, Northwestern U., 1954. CPA, Ill. With Arthur Andersen & Co., 1954-78, mng. ptnr. Brussels, 1957—71, ptnr. Chgo., 1971-78; pres. Daubert Industries, Oak Brook, Ill., 1978-80, G.R. Stevens Group, 1981—; founder, pres. Stevens Ctr. for Pub. Policy Studies, 1981—. Commr. Ill. Ednl. Facilities Authority, 1989-04. Commr. Ill. State Scholarship Commn., 1981-87; vice chmn. Ill. Ind. Higher Edn. Loan Authority, 1982-88. Home and Office: 22615 N Las Lomas Ln Sun City West AZ 85375-2022

STEVENS, GLADSTONE TAYLOR, JR., retired industrial engineer, retired educator; b. Brockton, Mass., Dec. 16, 1930; s. Gladstone Taylor and Blanche Ruth S.; m. Jane A. Crouch, July 20, 1953; children—Robert, Bartlett. BSM.E., U. Okla., 1956; MSM.E., Case Inst. Tech., 1962; PhD in Indsl. Engrng, Okla. State U., 1966. Registered profl. engr., Tex., Okla. Project engr. E.I. duPont, Orange, Tex., 1956-59; research engr. Thompson-Ramo-Wooldridge, Cleve., 1960-62; asst. prof. mech. and indsl. engrng. Lamar U., Beaumont, Tex., 1962-64; asst. prof. to asso. prof. indsl. engrng. Okla. State U., Stillwater, 1966-75; prof., chmn. dept. indsl. engrng. U. Tex., Arlington, 1975-98; ret., 1998. Author: (with J.E. Shamblin) Operations Research: A Fundamental Approach, 1974, Economic and Financial Analysis of Capital Investments, 1993; Engineering Economy, 1983. Served with AUS, 1948-52. Recipient E.L. Grant award, 1974, AMOCO Teaching award, 1979, Wellington award, 1992. Fellow Am. Inst. Indsl. Engrs.; mem. Sigma Xi, Alpha Pi Mu (nat. pres.), Tau Beta Pi, Sigma Tau, Omicron Delta Kappa. Home: 2501 Spanish Trl Apt 212 Arlington TX 76016-1410

STEVENS, GLENN H., lawyer; Grad., Johns Hopkins U.; JD, NYU. Positions in legal dept. US West Inc., 1979—92; atty. pvt. practice, 1992—94; v.p., gen. counsel, sec. Maxtor Corp., Milpitas, Calif., 1994—2001, sr. v.p., gen. counsel, sec., 2001; spl. counsel Stevens, Littman, Biddison, Tharp & Weinberg, LLC, Boulder, Colo., 2005—. Mem.: Nebr. State Bar Assn., Colo. Bar Assn. Office: Stevens, Littman, Biddison, Tharp & Weinberg, LLC 250 Arapahoe, Ste 301 Boulder CO 80302 Office Phone: 303-443-6690. Office Fax: 303-449-9349. E-mail: glenn@slb-llc.com.

STEVENS, HELEN JEAN, music educator; b. Nevada, Iowa, July 11, 1934; d. Paul Ellison and Helen Margaret (Ives) Stevens. MusB, U. So. Calif., 1956. Cert. secondary music tchr. Calif. Tchr. San Francisco Sch. Dist., 1956-58; prin. oboist Marin Symphony Orch., San Rafael, Calif., 1956-94, Santa Rosa (Calif.) Symphony, 1956-86; tchr. Santa Venetia Mid. Sch., San Rafael, 1958-83; asst. prof. music Sonoma State Coll., Rohnert Park, Calif., 1963-76; tchr. Davidson Mid. Sch., San Rafael, 1984-89; pvt. tchr. oboe. Oboist Evenings on the Roof Series, LA, 1953—56, Debut TV Show, LA, 1954—56, Carmel (Calif.) Bach Festival, 1954—82; prin. oboist Light Opera Curren Theatre, San Francisco, 1966—67, Marin Opera Co., San Rafael, 1980—84. Leader Sonoma County 4-H Guide Dog Project Guide Dogs for Blind, Inc., 1974—87; organist, choir dir. Korean Meth. Ch., LA, 1953—56; music dir. United Meth. Ch., St. James, Mo., 2002—. Recipient Svc. award, PTA, 1974, Golden Bell award, Marin County Office Edn., 1984, Continuing Svc. award, Calif. Congress Parents, Tchrs. and Students, Inc., 1989; named Outstanding Tchr., Marin Edn. Found., 1986. Avocations: computers, animals. Home: 14713 State Rt BB Saint James MO 65559 E-mail: stevfam@fidnet.com.

STEVENS, HERBERT FRANCIS, lawyer, educator; b. Phila., Nov. 19, 1948; s. Herbert F. and Lois Marie (Kenna) S.; m. Jane Pickard, 1994; children: Sarah, Ben. SB, MIT, 1970; JD, Catholic U. Am., 1974; ML in Tax, Georgetown U, 1983. Bar: D.C., 1975; U.S. Supreme Ct., 1980. Law clk Md. Ct. of Spl. Appeals, 1974-75; with Morgan, Lewis & Bockius, Washington, 1975-78, Lane & Edson, P.C., Washington, 1979-89, Kelley Drye & Warren, Washington, 1989-93, Nixon Peabody LLP, Washington, 1993—; adj. prof. Georgetown U. Law Ctr., 1983-98. Spkr. in field. Editor: Real Estate Aspects of the 1984 Tax Law, 1984; author: Real Estate Taxation: A Practitioner's Guide, 1986, Developer's Guide to Low Income Housing Tax Credit, 4th edit., 2000. Bd. dirs. Nat. Fund for U.S. Botanic Garden, 2000—06, exec. com.; bd. dirs. Ctr. Mental Health, 1992—2005. Mem. ABA, D.C. Bar Assn. Presbyterian. Home: 8301 Hackamore Dr Potomac MD 20854-3877 Office: Nixon Peabody LLP 401 9th St NW Washington DC 20004-2128 Business E-Mail: hstevens@nixonpeabody.com.

STEVENS, JAMES HERVEY, JR., retired financial planner; b. Balt., June 22, 1944; s. James H. and Hilda (Pearce) S.; m. Patricia Carol Donohue, Aug. 27, 1967 (div. Mar. 1983); children: James III, Carol; m. Lisa Gay Landrum, Apr. 29, 1984. BA, Duke U., 1966; MS in Fin. Scis., Am. Coll., Bryn Mawr, Pa., 1981. CLU; ChFC; CFP; registered health underwriter. Supr. New Eng. Life, Overland Park, Kans., 1969-75, agt., 1969—; v.p., treas. Creative Planning, Inc., Overland Park, 1980-95; pres. Hokanson, Lehman & Stevens, Inc., Overland Park, 1982-95;

founder, chmn. Wings Over Mid-Am., Inc., 1995-97, chmn. emeritus, 1997—; chmn. Air Care Alliance, 1997—; chmn. emeritus Wings Over Mid-Am., Inc., 1997—; founder, chmn. legacy fund Angel Flight Ctrl., Inc., Kansas City, Mo. Contbg. editor monthly tax topics Kansas City Bus. Jour.; contbg. editor Pvt. Pilot Mag.; contbr. articles to profl. jours. Bd. dirs. Mo. divsn. Am. Cancer Soc., Kans. and Mo., 1982-84, Ctrl. United Meth. Ch., Kansas City, Mo., 1990-92, North Cross United Meth., 1991—; bd. dirs. Apple Valley Homes Assn., Overland Park, 1990—, pres. 1992; co-founder Kansas City Friends of Gilda's. Recipient Outstanding Young Man award, 1977; named one of Top 200 Fin. Advisors, Money Mag., 1987, Boss of Yr., Kansas City LICOMA, 1983. Mem. Kansas City Life Underwriters (pres. 1980-82, Herbert A. Hedges award 1987), Kansas City CLU & ChFC Soc. (pres. 1981-83), Mo. Life Underwriters (pres. 1984-86), Am. Soc. CLU & ChFC (vice chmn., bd. dirs.). Republican. Avocations: model railroading, collecting post-war "lionel", airline transport pilot, instrument flight instr. Home: 5200 W 98th Ter Shawnee Mission KS 66207-3221 Office: Angel Fly Ctrl Inc 10 Richards Rd Kansas City MO 64113 E-mail: jstevens10@gmail.com.

STEVENS, JEFF A., oil industry executive; m. Sharon Stevens. V.p. supply & mktg. Phoenix Fuel, 1993—97; sr. v.p. supply & mktg. Giant Industries, 1997—2000; exec. v.p. Western Refining Co., El Paso, Tex., 2000—08, exec. v.p., COO, 2008—09, pres., COO, 2009—. Office: Western Refining Co 6500 Trowbridge Dr El Paso TX 79905*

STEVENS, JOANN A., textile, political leader, author, minister; b. Snow Hill, NC, May 15, 1957; d. Moses Lee and Annie Iola Artis; m. Willard Ray Stevens, Apr. 3, 1993; children: Thyais Artis, Jorel, Shakira. Student, Wayne C.C., Goldsboro, NC, 1983; student in criminal justice, Lenoir C.C., Kinston, NC, 1984. Ordained elder Bapt. Ch., 1983; cert. substance abuse counselor N.C., 1986, Min. Inst. Shaw Divinity Sch., 1987, protective intervention Caswell Ctr., Dept. Human Resource, 1988, Safety E.I. Dupont, 1989. Founder, owner JoAnn's Christian Supply, Bibile and Bookstore, Snow Hill, NC, 1989—93; founder, counselor Spectrum's Substance Abuse, N/A, A/A Group, Snow Hill, NC, 1991—94; founder Rosenwald Ctr. Cultural Enrichment, 2001—; co-founder Power of Prayer Bible Inst. and Sem., 2002—04. Incorporator Spectrum for Living, Snow Hill, NC, 1990—93; assoc. pastor Cry Out Loud Ministries, 2006—; presenter in field. Author: The Holy Spirit, Is He a Stranger in Your House?, 1997 (1999), Could it Be I'm Chosen? (Fear, Peer Pressure, Rejection), 1999; host (TV Show) Appearances on various morning TV shows., 2002—03; singer: You Can Love Again, 1985; author: Fear, Peer Pressure Rejection- Could it be I'm Chosen. Policy coun. chair person Greene Lamp Headstart Inc., Kinston, NC; v.p. Greene County Interfaith Vols., Snow Hill, NC, 1999—2001; host Parad in Honor Local Africa. Am. Heroes, 2004; cert. grantwriter HUD; press sec. Com. To Elect Don Davis for Mayor, Snow Hill, NC, 2002; sec. Snow Hill Dem. Party, Snow Hill, NC; asst. regional chmn. Dem. Get Out to Vote Campaign, 2002; coord. ticket sales Mal Williams Gospel World Tour, Germany, 1996; bd. dirs. Legal Aide, NC, 2002—. Recipient Cert. of Achievement, Goshen Rubber Co., 1984, Cert. of Award, Snow Hill Primary Sch., 1985, Cert. of Appreciation, State of NC, Dept. of Correction & Human Resources, 1985 -1986, Award of Merit, East Carolina U. Sch. of Medicine / Project Concern Internat., 1988 - 1990, Cert. of Recognition, Self Image Bldg. Program, 1989, Letter of Appreciation, First Lady Hillary Rodham Clinton, 1998, Letter of Recognition, N.C. Gen. Assembly - Marian McLawhorn 9th Dist., 1999 -2001, Friends of Project Head Start award, 1999, cert. of Excellence, N.C. Hist. Preservation Office, 2003; Nat. Trust Diversity scholar, 2004. Mem.: N.C. Ctr. for Non Profit Gifts In Kind Internat., Nat. Trust. for Hist. Preservation, Greene County Arts & Hist. Soc. (bd. dirs. 2001—03, neighborhood affairs com., vice chmn. hist. commn. 2002—03). Achievements include initiated process of Nat. Register Nomination for Snow Hill Colored, Greene Co. Sch; partnering with Vocational Rehabilitation to open first transitional house in Greene County, NC; Established Rosenwald Center, counties first community development corporation. Avocations: travel, reading, counseling, research, history. Home: PO Box 343 Snow Hill NC 28580 Home Phone: 252-560-6221; Office Phone: 252-747-4912. Personal E-mail: rcenter@earthlink.net.

STEVENS, JOHN, professional hockey coach, retired professional hockey player; b. Campbellton, NB, Can., May 4, 1966; m. Stacy Stevens; children: John, Nolan. Defenseman Hershey Bears, 1984—90, Phila. Flyers, 1986—88, Springfield Indians, 1990—96, Hartford Whalers, 1990—94, Phila. Phantoms, 1996—99, asst. coach, 1999—2000, head coach, 2000—06; asst. coach Phila. Flyers, 2006, head coach, 2006—. Named Coach of Yr., The Hockey News, 2008. Office: Phila Flyers Wachovia Ctr 3601 S Broad St Philadelphia PA 19148-5250

STEVENS, JOHN A., classicist, educator; s. Jack A. and Katherine V. Stevens; m. Karen M. Gilloon, 1988; 3 children. BA in Classics, MA in Classics, U. Iowa; PhD in Classical Studies, Duke U. Vis. asst. prof. NY U., NYC, 1992—93; assoc. prof., classics East Carolina U., Greenville, NC, 1993—, dir., classical studies & gt. books, 2003—. Contbr. articles. Recipient Lowden prize, U. Iowa, 1985, 1986, Outstanding Tchg. U. award, East Carolina U., 2004. Mem.: Classical Assn. Mid. West and South, Soc. Ancient Greek Philosophy, Am. Philol Assn., Vergilian Soc. Office: E Carolina Univ Classical Studies Dept FLL Bate 3324 Greenville NC 27858-4353

STEVENS, JOHN PAUL, United States supreme court justice; b. Chgo., Apr. 20, 1920; s. Ernest James and Elizabeth (Street) Stevens; m. Elizabeth Jane Sheeren, June 7, 1942 (div. 1979); children: John Joseph(dec.), Kathryn Stevens Jedlicka, Elizabeth Jane Stevens Sesemann, Susan Roberta Stevens Mullen; m. Maryan Mulholland Simon, Dec. 1979. AB, U. Chgo., 1941; JD magna cum laude, Northwestern U., 1947. Bar: Ill. 1949. Practiced in, Chgo.; law clk. to Justice Wiley B. Rutledge US Supreme Ct., Washington, 1947—48; assoc. Poppenhusen, Johnston, Thompson & Raymond, 1949—52; assoc. counsel, sub-com. on study monopoly power, com. on judiciary US House Reps., Washington, 1951—52; ptnr. Rothschild, Stevens, Barry & Myers, 1952—70; judge US Ct. Appeals (7th circuit), Chgo., 1970—75; assoc. justice US Supreme Ct., Washington, 1975—. Lectr. anti-trust law Northwestern U. Sch. Law, 1953—54, U. Chgo. Law Sch., 1955—58; mem. Atty. Gen.'s Nat. Com. to Study Anti-Trust Laws, 1953—55; chief counsel to commn. investgating the judgment of People v. Isaacs Ill. Supreme Ct., 1969; appellate judge seminar NYU Sch. Law, 1972. Contbr. articles to profl. jours. With USNR, 1942—45. Decorated Bronze Star. Fellow: American Acad. Arts & Sciemces; mem.: American Law Inst., Fed. Bar Assn., Ill. Bar Assn., American Bar Assn., Chgo. Bar Assn. (2d v.p. 1970), Order of Coif, Phi Delta Phi, Psi Upsilon, Phi Beta Kappa. Office: US Supreme Ct One First St NE Washington DC 20543*

STEVENS, JONATHAN J., information technology executive; BS in Computer Info. Systems Mgmt., U. Dayton, Ohio. Cons. Microsoft Consulting Svcs.; regional tech. dir. Avanade Inc., Seattle; v.p. info. tech. CDW Corp., Vernon Hills, Ill., 2001—02, v.p., chief info. officer, mem. exec. com., 2002, v.p. internat., 2005—06, sr. v.p., chief info. officer, 2007—. Bd. dir. IT Resource Ctr. Office: CDW Corp 200 N Milwaukee Ave Vernon Hills IL 60061

STEVENS, JOSEPH CHARLES, psychology professor; b. Grand Rapids, Mich., Feb. 28, 1929; s. Joseph, Jr. and Anne Katheryn Stevens. AB, Calvin Coll., Grand Rapids, 1950; MA, Mich. State U., 1953; PhD, Harvard U., 1957. Instr., asst. prof. psychology Harvard U., 1957-66; fellow emeritus John B. Pierce Found. Lab., sr. rsch. scientist Yale U., 1966—. Cons. in field. Author: Laboratory Experiments in Psychology, 1965; co-editor: Sensation and Measurement, 1974; mem. editl. bds. profl. jours.; contbr. numerous articles to profl. jours. Grantee NSF; Grantee NIH, Air Force Office Sci. Rsch. Fellow AAAS, Am. Psychol. Soc., NY Acad. Scis.; mem. Acoustical Soc. Am., Optical Soc. Am., Soc. Neuroscience, Ea. Psychol. Assn., Gerontol. Soc. Am. Office: 290 Congress Ave New Haven CT 06519-1403 Business E-Mail: jstevens@jbpierce.org.

STEVENS, JUDY A., epidemiologist; PhD in epidemiology, Emory U. With Nat. Ctr. Injury Prevention and Control, CDC, Atlanta, 1996—, sr. epidemiologist, divsn. unintentional injury prevention. Office: CDC NCIPC MS F-63 4770 Buford Hwy NE Atlanta GA 30341-3717*

STEVENS, KENNETH ALLEN, retired defense department worker; b. Exeter, NH, June 21, 1933; s. Albert Howard and Helen Susan (Sewall) S. BA, U. N.H., 1961. With Dept. Def., 1961-88. Mem. Howard County Election Rev. Commn., Md., 1975-76, Howard County Dem. Ctrl. Com., 1990-94, Howard County Charter Rev. Commn., 2003-04; bd. dirs. Columbia Dem. Club, Md., 1988-90; vol. Office Human Rights, Howard County, 1989-2001; steering com., Democracy for Howard County, 2005- Staff sgt. USAF, 1953—57. Recipient Cmty. Svc. award, Howard County Human Rights Commn., 1992. Mem. ACLU (coord. Howard County chpt. 1988-98). Democrat. Avocations: computer games, crossword puzzles.

STEVENS, KENNETH NOBLE, electrical engineer, educator; b. Toronto, Ont., Can., Mar. 23, 1924; arrived in U.S., 1948, naturalized, 1962; s. Cyril George and Catherine (Noble) Stevens; m. Phyllis Fletcher, Jan. 19, 1957 (div. 1979); children: Rebecca, Andrea, Michael Hugh, John Noble; m. Sharon Manuel, Jan. 14, 1994; children: Kendra Wenyu Manuel, Mackenzie Yin Ying Manuel. BASc., U. Toronto, 1945, MASc., 1948; Sc.D., MIT, 1952. Instr. U. Toronto, 1946—48; faculty MIT, Cambridge, 1948—, prof. elec. engring., 1963—, Clarence J. LeBel prof., 1977—. Vis. fellow Royal INst. Tech., Stockholm, 1962—63; cons. to industry, 1952—; vis. prof. phonetics U. Coll., London, 1969—70; mem. Nat. Adv. Coun. on Neurol. and Communicative Disorders and Stroke, NIH, 1982—86. Author (with A.G. Bose): Introductory Network Theory; author: Acoustic Phonetics, 1998; contbr. articles to profl. jours. Trustee Buckingham Browne and Nichols Sch., 1974—80. Recipient Quintana award, Voice Found., 1992, medal, European Speech Comm. Assn., 1995, Nat. Medal of Sci., 1999; fellow, Guggenheim, 1962. Fellow: IEEE (James L. Flanagan Speech and Audio Processing award 2004), Am. Acad. Arts and Scis., Acoustical Soc. Am. (exec. com. 1963—66, v.p. 1971—72, pres.-elect 1975—76, pres. 1976—77, Gold medal 1995); mem.: NAE, NAS. Office: MIT 77 Massachusetts Ave Cambridge MA 02139-4307 Home: 15298 SE Oregon Tr Dr Clackamas OR 97015

STEVENS, KENNETH T., retail executive; b. 1952; Grad., DePauw U., 1974; student, U. Redlands; MBA, U. So. Calif. Former ptnr. McKinsey & Co., Inc.; former sr. v.p. and treas. Pepsico; exec. v.p. mktg. Taco Bell divsn. of Pepsico, 1993—94, pres. and COO, 1994—97; chmn. and CEO Banc One Retail Group, 1997—2000; pres. and COO inChord Comm., 2001—02; exec. v.p. and COO Bath & Body Works divsn. of Ltd. Brands, Inc., 2002—03, pres., 2003—04; CEO Express (subs. Limited Brands), 2004—06; exec. v.p., CFO Limited Brands, Inc., 2006; pres., COO,sec., treas. Tween Brands, Inc., 2007—, also bd. dir., 2007—. Bd. mem. Spartan Stores, 2002—. Office: Tween Brand Inc 8323 Walton Pkwy New Albany OH 43054-9522

STEVENS, LAWRENCE EDWARD, ecologist, curator; b. Cleve., Nov. 11, 1951; PhD, Northern Ariz. U., Flagstaff, 1989. Sr. ecologist Grand Canyon Wildlands Coun. Inc., Flagstaff, 1999—; curator Mus. Northern Ariz., Flagstaff, 2005—. Conservation rep. Glen Canyon Dam Adaptive Mgmt. Work Group, FACA, Salt Lake City, 2003—. Author: (book) Colorado River, North American Springs Ecology; contbr. articles to sci. jours. Home: PO Box 1315 Flagstaff AZ 86002 Office: Mus Northern Ariz 3101 N Ft Valley Rd Flagstaff AZ 86001 Office Fax: 928-779-1527. Personal E-mail: farvana@aol.com.

STEVENS, LORETTA MARIE, special education educator; b. Bethpage, NY, Nov. 26, 1955; d. Hamilton Thomas and Evelyn Barbara Pendergast; m. Louis C. Stevens, Apr. 2, 1987 (dec.); children: Erin Michelle Cook, Megan Colleen Oneill. BS, Shenandoah U., Winchester, Va., 1995; MEd, James Madison U., Harrisonburg, Va., 1997; M of Ednl. Adminstrn., Shenandoah U., Winchester, Va., 2005. Cert. elem. edn. tchr. Va., 1995, spl. edn. tchr. Va., 1997, ednl. adminstr. Va., 2005. Learning disabilities specialist Warren County Pub. Schs., Front Royal, Va., 1995—2004, ednl. diagnostician, 2004—06, supr. spl. edn., 2006—. Lead tchr. for learning disabilities Warren County Pub. Schs., Front Royal, Va., 1996—2004, spl. edn. dept. chairperson, 1997—2004; individual edn. plan coord. Warren County Pub. Schools, Front Royal, Va., 1999—; mentor new spl. educators Old Dominion U., Newport News, Va., 1997—. Pres. PTA, Manassas Park, Va., 1986—89; mem./advisor 4-H Club, Warren County, Va., 2002—04; dir. children's choir St. John the Bapt. Cath. Ch., Front Royal, Va., 1989—93, dir. adult modern music choir, 1993—98. Mem.: ASCD, Va. Coun. Spl. Edn. Adminstrs., Internat. Coun. Learning Disabilities, Therapeutic Riding Assn., Internat. Reading Assn., Learning Disabilities Assn., Coun. for Exceptional Children (Professionall Recognized Spl. Educator 200-2005). Achievements include development of Educational program to improve learning for students who are slow learners. Avocations: horseback riding, hiking. Office: Warren County Public Schs 210 N Commerce Ave Front Royal VA 22630

STEVENS, LORI ANN LABEAU, public librarian, administrator; b. Yakima, Wash., Dec. 31, 1959; d. Raymond L. and Irene A. LaBeau; m. Mark D. Stevens, Apr. 24, 1981; children: Elisabeth A., Jared S., Mark D., Jonathan R. BMus, Brigham Young U., 1983; MLS, Emporia State U., 1999. Pub. svcs.- media ref. libr. Orem Pub. Libr., Utah, 1991—99; media instrn. libr. Utah Valley State Coll., Orem, 1999—2007; asst. dir. pub. svcs. Orem Pub. Libr., 2007—. Contbr. chapters to books. Chair libr. adv. commn. City of Orem, 2002. Recipient Merit award, Utah Humanities Coun., 2001, Trustees award Excellence, Utah Valley State Coll. Bd. Trustees, 2002. Mem.: ALA (assoc.; chair 2001—05), Video Round Table ALA (assoc.; program chair 2004), Music Libr. Assn., Mountain Plains Chpt. (assoc.; mem. at large 2002—03), Utah Libr. Assn. (assoc.; mem. at large 2002—05, Spl. Recognition award 2005), Music Libr. Assn. (assoc.; chair film music roundtable 2005—). Mem. Lds Ch. Avocations: singing, piano, hiking, travel, gardening. Home Fax: 801-863-7065. E-mail: lastevens@orem.org.

STEVENS, LYDIA HASTINGS, community volunteer; b. Highland Park, Ill., Aug. 2, 1918; d. Rolland T.R. and Ruth Shotwell (Beebe) Hastings; m. George Cooke Stevens, Nov. 2, 1940; children: Lydia Stevens Gustin, Priscilla Stevens Goldfarb, Frederick S., Elizabeth Stevens MacLeod, George H., Ruth Stevens Stellard. BA, Vassar Coll., 1939. State rep. 151st Dist. of Conn., Greenwich, 1988-92. Cons. Nat. Exec. Svc. Corps, N.Y.C., 1985. Pres. Greenwich YWCA, 1971-74, Greenwich Housing Coalition, 1982-86; v.p. planning Greenwich United Way, 1973-76; sr. warden Greenwich Christ Episcopal Ch., 1981-86; chmn. rev. commn. Episcopal Diocese of Conn., 1985-87; bd. dirs. Greenwich Libr., 1985-93; chmn. Greenwich Commn. Aging, 1986-88; pres., bd. dirs. Greenwich Broadcasting Corp., 1977-79; bd. dirs. Fairfield County Cmty. Found., 1992, United Way of Greenwich, Save the Sound, 1996—, League Conservation Voters Conn., 1999. Recipient Golden Rule award J.C. Penney, 1987, President's award Greenwich YWCA, 1992, Brava award, 1994, Conn. Assn. for Human Svc. Dirs. award, 1992, Spirit Greenrid award YWCA; named Layperson of Yr., Coun. Chs. and Synagogues, 1995. Republican. Episcopalian. Avocations: sailing, organic gardening. Home: 125 West Ln Guilford CT 06437-3230

STEVENS, MARTIN BRIAN, publisher; b. NYC, Dec. 29, 1957; s. David Robert and Shirley Stevens. Grad. high sch. Advt. artist Unitron Pubs., NYC, 1977, Westchester Publs., Elmsford, 1978; founder, CEO The Composing Rm., NYC, 1979—83; pub. Retailers Forum, Centerport, 1981—, Swap Meet mag., 1990—; founder, CEO Forum Pub. Co., 1981—. Pub. 8 bus. directories; rep. 6 bus. book pubs.; founder Rodeo Dr. Limousine Svc., 1990—93, Mercedes-Benz Limousine Svc., 1990—93; founder, CEO Party Fun House, Inc., 2004—. Named Top Mail Order Dealer, Nat. Mail Dealers Counsel, 1978. Mem. Mail Order Bus. Bd. (pres. 1978-80), Better Bus. Bur., Nat. Assn. Self-Employed, Nat. Assn. Desktop Pub., L.I. Assn., Can. Direct Mail Assn. Avocations: weight training, reading. Office: Forum Pub Co 383 E Main St Centerport NY 11721-1538

STEVENS, MAY, artist; b. Boston, June 9, 1924; d. Ralph Stanley and Alice Margaret (Dick) S.; m. Rudolf Baranik, June 5, 1948; 1 child, Steven. BFA, Mass. Coll. Art, 1946; postgrad., Academie Julian, Paris, 1948-49, Art Students League, 1948. Mem. faculty Sch. Visual Arts, NYC, 1964-96, Skowhegan Sch. Painting and Sculpture, 1992, Vt. Studio Ctr., 1997, 2005, Santa Fe Art Inst., 2000, 2003. Lectr. Royal Coll. Art, London, 1981, U. Wis.-Racine, 1973, Coll. Art Assn., Washington, 1975; sole juror Am. Drawing Biennial, Coll. William and Mary, Williamsburg, Va., 2000; lectr. Coll. Santa Fe, 1998, Santa Fe Art Inst., 2003. One-woman shows include Terry Dintenfass Gallery, NYC, 1971, Cornell U., 1973, Douglass Coll., Rutgers U., 1974, Lerner-Heller Gallery, NYC, 1975, 76, 78, 81, Clark U., 1982, Boston U. Art Gallery, 1984, Frederick S. Wight Gallery, UCLA, 1985, U. Md., College Park, 1985, Real Art Ways, Hartford, Conn., 1988, New Mus. Contemporary Art, 1988, Orchard Gallery, Derry, No. Ireland, 1988, Kenyon Coll., Gambier, Ohio, 1988, Greenville County Art Mus., SC, 1991, Herter Gallery, U. Mass., Amherst, 1991, U. Colo., Boulder, 1993, U. N.Mex., Albuquerque, 1996, Mary Ryan Gallery, NYC, 1996-97, 99, 2001, 03, 05, 07, Mus. Fine Arts, Boston, 1999, LewAllen Contemporary, Santa Fe, 1998, Minn. Inst. Art, 2005, Nat. Mus. Women in the Arts, Washington, 2005, Springfield Art Mus., Mo., 2006; exhibited in group shows at Santa Fe Art Inst., 2002, Mus. Fine Art, Santa Fe, 2002, Guild Hall, East Hampton, NY, 2002, Hobart & William Smith Colls., 2002, We. Wash. U. Bellingham, 2002, UBS Paine Webber Art Gallery, NYC, 2002, Deutsche Bank, NYC, 2002, Bass Mus. Art, Miami Beach, Fla., 2002, Bklyn. Mus., 2003, Nat. Mus. Women in the Arts, Washington, 2003, Danese Gallery, NYC, 2003, Tamarind Inst., Albuquerque, N.Mex., 2004, Harwood Mus., Taos, N.Mex., 2004, Ctr. Contemporary Arts Warehouse, Santa Fe, N.Mex., 2004, Nat. Acad. Design, NYC, 2004, Evo Gallery, Santa Fe, 2005, Mason Gross Sch. Arts, Rutgers U., New Brunswick, NJ, 2006, others; represented in permanent collections: Met. Mus. Art, NYC, Mus. Modern Art, NYC, Moca, LA, San Francisco Mus. Art, New Mus. Contemporary Art, Whitney Mus., Bklyn. Mus., Herbert F. Johnson Mus., Cornell U., Mus. Fine Arts Boston, De Cordova Mus., Lincoln, Mass., Harwood Mus., Taos, N.Mex., Joslyn Art Mus., Omaha, Nat. Mus. Women in Arts, Washington, Minn. Inst. Art, Mpls., Springfield Mus. Art, Mo., Mcnhy Art Mus., San Antonio, Tex., McCormick Pl. Ctr. Art Coll., Chgo., Jacksonville Art Mus., Fla., Cleve. Mus. Art, Ill., U. Miami, Fla.; contbr. articles to various mags. Recipient Childe Hassam Purchase awards Nat. Inst. Arts and Letters, 1968, 69, 75, N.Y. State Coun. on Arts award, 1974, Disting. Alumna award Mass. Coll. Art, 1997, Disting. Artist award Coll. Art Assn., 2001, Edwin Palmer Meml. prize NAD, 2004; Andy Warhol Found. grantee for project space Headlands Ctr. for Arts, Sausalito, Calif., 2001; MacDowell Colony fellow, 1971, 72, 74, 75, 81, 82, 84, Bunting Inst. fellow Radcliffe Coll., 1988-89; Line Assn. grantee for artists books, 1978; grantee NEA, 1983, Guggenheim, 1986; honoree Women's Caucus for Art, 1990. Mem.: NAT, Coll. Art Assn.

STEVENS, MURIEL KAUIMAEOLE LEE, retired elementary school educator; b. Hana, Hawaii, May 29, 1942; d. Charles Pohaku and Violet Leimamo (Wahihako) Lee; m. James Gary Stevens, 1964 (div. 1976); 1 child, James Todd (dec.). AS, Ch. Coll. Hawaii, 1962; BS in Edn., Brigham Young U., 1964; postgrad., U. Utah, 1969, U. Hawaii, 1974—. Cert. and lic. elem. tchr., Hawaii. 1st grade tchr. Woodstock Elem. Sch., Salt Lake City, 1965-69; kindergarten-1st grade team tchr. Ewa (Hawaii) Elem. Sch., 1971-78; tchr. Honowai Elem. Sch., Waipahu, Hawaii, 1978—99, Hana Elem.-HS, 1999—2006, ret., 2006. Aerospace tchr., coord. after sch. improvement program Honowai Elem. Sch., 1991, 95; mem. Citizen Amb. Program, Spokane, 1987-95; participant Tchr. in Space program NASA, 1985-86. Spiritual living tchr. LDS Ch., Kaneohe, 1994, choir mem., 1992-94, sem. tchr., single adult rep. Waipahu II ward, 1996; tchr. and music leader LDS Primary at Hana Branch, 1999-2001; amb. People to People Internat., Spokane, Wash., 1987-95. With CAP, 1985-95. Recipient Aerospace Edn. Achievement award Aux. USAF CAP, 1985. Mem. ASCD, Hawaii Parent, Tchr., Student Assn., NEA, Hawaii State Tchrs. Assn., Wilson Ctr. Assocs., Acad. Polit. Sci., World Aerospace Edn. Orgn. Republican. Avocations: hula dancing, swimming, sewing, baking, arts and crafts. Home: PO Box 879 Hana HI 96713-0879

STEVENS, PAUL SCHOTT, lawyer; b. New Orleans, Nov. 19, 1952; s. Miles Gordon and Rosemary Louise (Schott) S.; m. Joyce Lynn Pilz, Aug. 18, 1979; Paul Schott Jr., Alexander Holmes, Andrew Colby, Carl Bernard. BA magna cum laude, Yale U., 1974; JD, U. Va., 1978. Bar: D.C. 1979, U.S. Dist. Ct. D.C. 1979, U.S. Ct. Appeals (D.C. cir.) 1979, U.S. Ct. Appeals (fed. cir.) 1983, U.S. Supreme Ct. 1982. Assoc., prin. Dickstein, Shapiro & Morin, Washington, 1978-85, ptnr., 1989-93; dep. dir., gen. counsel Pres.'s Blue Ribbon Commn. on Def. Mgmt., Washington, 1985-86; legal adviser NSC, Washington, 1987, exec. sec., 1987-89; spl. asst. to Pres. for nat. security affairs The White House, Washington, 1987-89; exec. asst. to Sec. of Defense, Washington, 1989; sr. v.p., gen. counsel Investment Co. Inst., Washington, 1993-97; sr. v.p., gen. counsel Mut. Funds and Internat. Enterprise, Charles Schwab & Co., Inc., San Francisco, 1997-99; ptnr. Dechert LLP, Washington, 1999—2004; pres., CEO Investment Co. Inst., 2004—. Bd. dirs. ICI

Mut. Ins. Co. 2004-; lectr. law Washington Coll. Law, Am. U., Washington, 1980-83; trustee M.G. Stevens Corp., New Orleans, 1978—; quality of markets com. NASDAQ Stock Market, Inc., 1997, investment cos. com. NASD Regulation, Inc., 1999; adv. bd. Ctr. Banking and Fin. Law, Boston U., 1996-2007. Author: U.S. Armed Forces and Homeland Defense: The Legal Framework, 2001. Chmn. bd. dirs. Student Conservation Assn., Charlestown, N.H., 1986-87, bd. dirs., 1985-91, 94-96, sec., gen. counsel, 1991-93; mem. fin. coun. Cath. Diocese of Arlington, 2006—; mem. Life Guard Soc. of Mt. Vernon, 2005-, mem. bd. trustees, Yale Libr. Assoc., 2006—; mem. libr. devel. coun., Yale U., 2007—. Recipient medal for disting. pub. svc. Dept. Def., 1989; Bates fellow Yale U., 1973, Scholar of House, 1973-74, Rotary Internat. Found. grad. fellow, 1978, U.S.-Japan Leadership fellow Japan Soc., 1989-90, assoc. fellow Saybrook Coll., Yale U., 1993—. Mem.: ABA (chmn. standing com. law and nat. security 1995—98), Fed. Bar Assn., Coun. Fgn. Rels., Federalist Soc., DC Bar Assn., Soc. of Sons of the Am. Revolution, Soc. of Mayflower Descendants, Soc. War 1812, Jamestowne Soc., Cosmos Club, Elizabethan Club, Yale Club, Met. Club. Republican. Roman Catholic. Office: Investment Co Inst 1401 H St NW Washington DC 20005 Business E-Mail: paul.stevens@ici.org.

STEVENS, REBECCA ANN, sociologist, educator; b. Bedford, Ohio, Dec. 15, 1957; d. Lawrence Raymond and Sophia Francis Stevens; m. Timothy Brian Corley. D. U. Akron, Akron, 1991. Dept. chair prof. Mt. Union Coll., Alliance, 1996—. Donor Wigs for Kids, Cleve., 1996. Recipient Gt. Tchr. award, Mt. Union Coll., 2001. Mem.: ACJS.

STEVENS, RICHARD THOMAS, neuroscientist, researcher; b. Middletown, Conn., June 7, 1948; s. John Wilford and Mary Agnus (Shannon) Stevens; m. Joan Marie Corcoran, Sept. 5, 1970; children: Laura Marie, Craig William, Kevin Thomas. MS, SUNY Environ. Sci. and Forestry, Syracuse, 1974. Lt. col. USAR; principle rsch. scientist SUNY Upstate Med. U., 1974—. Contbr. articles to profl. jours. Leader Boy Scout America, Liverpool, NY, 1992—2001. Grant, NIH, 2003—, NICHHD. Mem.: Soc. for Neurosci. Liberal. Roman Catholic. Avocations: travel, photography, astronomy, golf, genealogy. Home: 7630 Harvest Home Pl Liverpool NY 13088 Office: SUNY Upstate Medical Univ 750 East Adams St Syracuse NY 13210 Business E-Mail: stevensr@upstate.edu.

STEVENS, RICHARD YATES, state legislator; b. Raleigh, NC, Dec. 12, 1948; s. Floyd L. and Luna (Yates) Stevens; m. Jere Ann Gilmore, Sept. 13, 1980; children: Charles Andrew, Katherine Elizabeth. BA in Polit. Sci., U. N.C., 1970, JD, 1974, MPA, 1978. Bar: N.C. 1974. Asst. dean men U. NC, Chapel Hill, 1970-71, asst. residence dir., 1971-75, asst. Office Student Affairs, 1973-75, adj. prof., pub. adminstrn., 2008—; pvt. practice Chapel Hill, NC, 1974-76; adminstrv. asst. City of Durham, NC, 1975-76, budget officer, 1976-78, dir. adminstrn., 1978-79, dir. fin. and program devel., 1979-80; from asst. county mgr. to county mgr. Wake County, NC, 1980—2000; mem. Dist. 17 NC State Senate, 2003—. Coord. NC State Govt. Intern Program, Inst. Govt., 1971; adj. prof. polit. sci. NC State U., 1980, 92, 94; sr. budget advisor NC Gov.'s Transition Team, 2000—01. Bd. visitors U. N.C., Chapel Hill, 1991—95, trustee, 1995—2003, chmn., 1997—99; chmn. bd. dirs. U. N.C. Endowment Fund, 1997—99; chmn. U. N.C. Found., 1997—99. Mem.: ASPA (Nat. Pub. Svc. award 2000), NC Mus. Natural Scis. Soc. (bd. dirs. 1987—88, treas. 1988—89, pres.-elect 1989—90, pres. 1990—91), NC City-County Mgmt. Assn. (bd. dirs. 1991—92, 2d v.p. 1997—98, 1st v.p. 1999—99, pres. 1999—2000), NC Bar, Nat. Assn. County Adminstrs. (bd. dirs. 1989—92), Internat. City-County Mgmt. Assn. (life), Yates Mill Assn. (bd. dirs. 2001—07), Cary Acad. (bd. dirs.), U. NC Gen. Alumni Assn. (dir. 1978—80, 1983—88, treas. 1988—98, chmn.-elect 1999—2000, chmn. 2000—01, Disting. Svc. medal 1994), U. NC Pub. Adminstrn. Alumni Assn. (pres. 1977—79, dir. 1982—84, Disting. Pub. Svc. award 1998), Carolina Club (vice chmn. 1993—94, chmn. 1994—98, 2002—). Republican. Home: 132 Lochwood Dr W Cary NC 27518 Office: NC Senate 300 N Salisbury St Rm 406 Raleigh NC 27603-5925 Home Phone: 919-851-0228; Office Phone: 919-733-5653.

STEVENS, ROBERT BOCKING, lawyer; b. UK, June 8, 1933; naturalized, 1971; s. John Skevington and Enid Dorothy (Bocking) S.; m. Katherine Booth, Dec. 23, 1985; 1 child, Robin; children by previous marriage: Carey, Richard. BA, Oxford U., 1955, BCL, 1956, MA, 1959, DCL, 1984; LLM, Yale U., New Haven, Conn., 1958; LLD (hon.), NY Law Sch., 1984, Villanova U., Pa., 1985, U. Pa., Phila., 1987; DLitt. (hon.), Haverford Coll., Pa., 1991. Bencher, Gray's Inn, 1999. Barrister-at-law, London, 1956; tutor in law Keble Coll. Oxford U., 1958-59; asst. prof. law Yale U., 1959-61, assoc. prof., 1961-65, prof., 1965-76; provost, prof. law and history Tulane U., 1976-78; pres. Haverford Coll., 1978-87; chancellor, prof. history U. Calif., Santa Cruz, 1987-91; counsel Covington and Burling, Washington and London, 1991—; master Pembroke Coll., Oxford, 1993-2001; mem. Essex Court Chambers, 1966—; sr. rsch. fellow U. Coll., London, 2001—06. Vis. prof. U. Tex., 1961, U. East Africa, 1962, London Sch. Econs., 1963, Stanford U., 1966, Brookings Instn., 1967-68, U. Coll. London, 1991-94, U. Hong Kong, 1998, Yale U., 1999, George Washington U., 2003, Cardozo Law Sch., 2004; cons. UN, HEW, US Dept. State; hon. fellow, Keble Coll., Oxford U., 1985, Pembroke Coll., Oxford U., 2001. Author: The Restrictive Practices Court, 1965, Lawyers and the Courts, 1967, In Search of Justice, 1968, Income Security, 1970, Welfare Medicine in America, 1974, Law and Politics, 1978, The Law School, 1983, The Independence of the Judiciary, 1993, The English Judges, 2002, 2d edit., 2005, From University to Uni, 2004, 2d edit., 2005. Chair Marshall Memorial Commn., 1994—2001, Sulgrave Manor, 2001—06; mem. Nat. Humanities Coun., 1982—86. Grantee, Rockefeller Found., 1962—64, Ford Found., 1962—64, 1973—74, Nuffield Found., 1975; fellow, Russell Sage Found., 1967—68, Cromwell Found., 2005;, NEH, 1973—74, 2005. Office: Covington and Burling 265 Strand London WC2R 1BH England Home: 19 Burgess Mead Oxford OX2 6XP England Office Phone: 44-20-7067-2213. Business E-Mail: rstevens@cov.com.

STEVENS, ROBERT DAVID, librarian, educator; b. Nashua, NH, Aug. 11, 1921; s. David Philip and Ruth (Ackley) S.; m. Helen Medora Conrad, Jan. 16, 1943 (dec. Oct. 28, 2006) m. Margaret J. Oueye, Mar. 22, 2009; children: Ruth Wilson Robertson, Hope Conrad. AB magna cum laude, Syracuse U., 1942; BS in L.S. with honors, Columbia, 1947; MA, Am. U., 1955, PhD, 1965. Employed Libr. Congress, Washington, 1947-64, coord. pub. law, 480 programs, 1962-64; dir. Libr. East West Ctr., Honolulu, 1964-65; dean Grad. Sch. Library Studies U. Hawaii, 1966-75; chief cataloging div. Copyright Office, 1975-80, coordinator copyright collections, 1980; lectr. grad. Sch. Libr. Studies, U. Hawaii, 1981-91; vol. Kaui Hist. Soc. Libr. and Archives, 2001—08; chief exec. officer Molesworth Inst. West, Inc., 1984-91, chmn., 1991-96. Fulbright lectr. U. Indonesia, 1971; US del. Intergovtl. Conf. Planning Nat. Libraries Infrastructures, 1974 Author: Role of the Library of Congress in International Exchange of Government Publications, 1955, Toshokan Kyoryoku, 1970, Documents of International Organizations, 1974, Japanese and US Research Libraries at the Turning Point, 1977, Short History of the School of Library and Information Studies, 1991; contbr. articles to profl. publs. Served to lt. USNR, 1943-46, res. 47-68. Mem. Hawaii Library Assn. (pres. 1966-67), ALA (mem. council 1967-70, mem. US, Japan adv. com. 1972-79, chmn. 1974-76, Rlms policy and rsch. com. 1977-81), Assocs. U. Hawaii Library (vice chmn. 1981-84), Japan Library Assn., Hui Dui, Phi Beta Kappa. Clubs: 15 (Honolulu). Democrat. Home: 1111 Alvarado Ave A208 Davis CA 95616 Business E-Mail: robertds@hawaii.edu.

STEVENS, ROBERT J., aerospace transportation executive; b. McKeesport, Pa. BS summa cum laude, Slippery Rock U., 1976; grad., Dept. Def. Sys. Mgmt. Coll.; M in Engring. and Mgmt., Polytechnic U. N.Y.; M in Bus., Columbia U. With Fairchild Republic Co.; gen. mgr. to v.p., CFO Loral Sys. Manufacturing Co. (acquired by Lockheed Martin), 1987—93; exec. v.p., sr. v.p., CFO, air traffic mgmt. Lockheed Martin, 1993—96; pres., air traffic mgmt. Lookheed Martin, 1996—98; pres., COO energy and environ. bus Lockheed Martin, 1998—99, v.p. strategic devel. Bethesda, Md., 1998—99, exec. v.p., CFO, 1999—2001, pres., COO, 2000—04, pres., CEO, 2004—, chmn., 2005—. Commr. Commn. Future of US Aerospace Industry, 2001—02; chmn., bd. dirs. Sandia Corp.; presiding dir., bd. dirs. Monsanto Co., 2002—; assoc. fellow Am. Inst. Aeronautics and Astronautics; mem., internat. adv. bd British-American Business Coun. Served USMC. Recipient Disting. Alumni award, Slippery Rock Univ., 2003, Exec. Yr., Nat. Mgmt. Assn., 2004; fellow Fairchild Fellowship, Am. Aeronautical Soc. Fellow: Am. Astronautical Soc.; mem.: Aerospace Industries Assn. (mem. exec. com.).*

STEVENS, ROBERT JAY, magazine editor; b. Detroit, July 25, 1945; s. Jay Benjamin and Louise Ann (Beyreuther) S.; m. Dahlia Jean Conger, Aug. 15, 1970; children— Sandra Lee, Julie Ann. Student, Huron Coll., SD, 1963-66, Wayne State U., 1968-71. Sr. staff writer Automotive News, Detroit, 1968-71; editor Excavating Contractor mag., Cummins Pub. Co., Oak Park, Mich., 1971-78, Chevrolet's Pro Jour., Sandy Corp., Southfield, Mich., 1978—79, Cars and Parts mag., Cars and Parts Corvette mag. Amos Press, Sidney, Ohio, 1979—; truck editor Automotive Design & Devel. mag., 1971-78. Lectr., speaker in field. Contbr. articles to profl. jours.; author: numerous poems. Served with AUS, 1966-68, Vietnam. Decorated Air medal, Bronze star, Commendation medal; recipient Alphomega Publs. award, 1965—, Robert F. Boger Meml. award for outstanding constrn. journalism, 1975, U.L.C.C. nat. editl. award, Am. Pub. Works Assn., 1978, Moto award for outstanding automotive journalism, Internat. Automotive Media Conf., 1997, 1998, 1999, 2000, 2001, Internal. Automotive Media Conf., 2002, Best of Divsn. award, Internat. Automotive Media Conf., 2001, Folio mag. Editl. Excellence award, 2001. Mem. Antique Automobile Club Am. (Lifetime Achievement award 2005.) Republican. Presbyterian. Home: 653 Ridgeway Dr Sidney OH 45365-3432 Office: PO Box 482 911 Vandemark Rd Sidney OH 45365 E-mail: bstevens@carsandparts.com.

STEVENS, ROBERTA A., librarian; BA, MLS, SUNY Buffalo; MA in English, SUNY Binghamton. Assoc. dir. tech. ops. Fairfax County Pub. Libr., Va., 1981—85; customer svcs. officer, cataloging distbn. svc. Libr. of Congress, Washington, 1985—89, spl. asst. to assoc. libr. cultural affairs, 1990—95, spl. asst. to dir. nat. svcs, libr. svcs., 1995—2000, bicentennial prog. mgr., 2000—02, outreach projects & partnerships officer, 2002—. Bicentennial prog. mgr. Libr. of Congress, 2000; project mgr. Nat. Book Festival, 2001—. Mem.: ALA (coun. mem. 2001—, com. on legis. 2001—, mem. exec. bd. 2006—). Office: Libr of Congress 101 Independence Ave SE Washington DC 20540-1400 Office Phone: 202-707-1550. Office Fax: 202-707-0312. Business E-Mail: rste@loc.gov.*

STEVENS, RON A., lawyer, advocate, surveyor; b. Indpls., Sept. 4, 1945; s. Granville Thomas and Charlotte May (Wheeler) S.; m. Judy Rohde, June 15, 1968; children: Samuel Thomas, Alison Elizabeth. BA, Okla. State U.; JD with honors, Ill. Inst. Tech., 1976. Bar: Ill. 1976. Staff atty. Legal Assistance Found. Chgo., 1976-79; staff atty., dir. housing agenda Bus. and Profl. People for Pub. Interest, Chgo., 1979-81; chief housing divsn. Office of Cook County State's Atty., Chgo., 1981-82; campaign coord. north lakefront Washington for Mayor, Chgo., 1982-83; program officer The Joyce Found., Chgo., 1983-86; pres. Citizens for a Better Environment, Chgo., 1986-89; pres., CEO United Way Santa Fe County, 1989—2003; dir. cmty. impact svcs. United Way Am., 2003—06; pres. ChangeWays LLC, 2006—. Adv. bd. state support ctr. on environ. hazards Nat. Ctr. for Policy Alternatives, Washington, 1987-89; chair Local Bd. EFSP, 1989—, Santa Fe Affordable Housing Roundtable, 1992-97; chair Exec. Leadership Coun. for Cmty. Schs, 1998—; bd. dirs. No. N.Mex. Grantmakers Assn., v.p., 1999, pres., 2000. Mem. bldg. code enforcement com. Mayor's Transition Team Housing Task Force, Chgo., 1983, steering com. Chgo. Ethics Project, 1986-88; founder, chmn. Progressive Chgo. Area Network, 1981-84; bd. dirs. Uptown Recycling Sta., Chgo., 1987-89; mem. South Ctrl. Regional Coun., United Way of Am., 1993-98. Mem. Chgo. Coun. Lawyers (chmn. housing com. 1978-81, bd. govs. 1981-83, bd. dirs. Fund for Justice, 1986-88), Chgo. Area Runners Assn. (founder, v.p. 1977-81). Home and Office: 7006 Stone Mill Pl Alexandria VA 22306-1329

STEVENS, ROSEMARY ANNE, medicine and public health historian, artist; b. Bourne, Eng. came to U.S., 1961, naturalized, 1968; d. William Edward and Mary Agnes (Tricks) Wallace; m. Robert B. Stevens, Jan. 28, 1961 (div. 1983); children: Carey, Richard; m. Jack D. Barchas, Aug. 9, 1994. BA, Oxford U., Eng., 1957; Diploma in Social Adminstrn., Manchester U., Eng., 1959; MPH, Yale U., 1963, PhD, 1968; LHD (hon.), Hahnemann U., 1988; DSc (hon.), Northeastern Ohio U. Coll. Medicine, 1995; DSc, Rutgers U., 1995. Various hosp. adminstrv. positions, Eng., 1959-61; rsch. assoc. Med. Sch. Yale U., 1962-68, asst. prof. Med. Sch., 1968-71, assoc. prof. Med. Sch., 1971-74, prof. pub. health Med. Sch., 1974-76; master Jonathan Edwards Coll., 1974-75; prof. dept. health systems mgmt. and polit. sci. Tulane U., New Orleans, 1976-78, chmn. dept. health systems mgmt., 1977-78; prof. history and sociology of sci. U. Pa., Phila., 1979—2002, chmn. dept., 1980-83, 86-91, UPS Found. prof., 1990-91, dean Sch. Arts and Scis., Thomas S. Gates prof., 1991-96, Stanley I. Sheerr prof., 1997—2001, prof. emeritus, 2002—. Prof. emeritus U. Pa., Phila., 2002-; vis. lectr. Johns Hopkins U., 1967-68; guest scholar Brookings Instn., Washington, 1967-68; acad. visitor London Sch. Econs., 1962-64, 1973-74; DeWitt Wallace disting. scholar social medicine and pub. policy, dept. psychiatry Weill Cornell Med. Coll., 2005—. Author: Medical Practice in Modern England: The Impact of Specialization and State Medicine, 1966, new edit., 2003, American Medicine and the Public Interest, 1971, rev. edit., 1998, In Sickness and in Wealth: American Hospitals in the Twentieth Century, 1989, rev. edit., 1999, (with others) Foreign Trained Physicians and American Medicine, 1972, Welfare Medicine in America, 1974, new edit., 2003, Alien-Doctors: Foreign Medical Graduates in American Hospitals, 1978, The Public-Private Health Care State, 2007; editor: (with others) History and Health Policy in the United States: Putting the Past Back In. Bd. dirs. Milbank Meml. Fund. Rockefeller Humanities fellow, 1982-83, Guggenheim fellow, 1984-85; Bellagio Study and Conf. scholar, 1984; recipient Frohlich medal Royal Soc. Medicine, London, 1986, Baxter Found. prize distinction in health svcs. rsch., 1990, James A. Hamilton Book award Am. Coll. Healthcare Execs. best book, 1990, Welch medal distinction in history of medicine Am. Assn. History Medicine, 1990, Arthur Viseltear award history pub. health Am. Pub. Health Assn., 1990, Nicholas E. Davies award Piedmont Hosp., Atlanta, 1997, Investigator award in health policy rsch. Robert Wood Johnson Found., 1998-2003, Carlson award for extraordinary contbns. to history of medicine Cornell U., Weill Med. Coll, 2000., Lifetime Achievement award Am. Assn. History Medicine, 2002. Fellow Am. Acad. Arts and Scis.; mem. AAAS (chmn. sect. history and philosophy of sci., 2002-03), Inst. Medicine of Nat. Acad. Sci., Am. Sociol. Assn., Am. Assn. for History of Medicine, Coll. Physicians Phila. Home: 500 E 77th St Apt 419 New York NY 10162 Business E-Mail: ras2023@med.cornell.edu.

STEVENS, ROY W., sales and marketing executive; b. Ottumwa, Iowa, Oct. 28, 1924; s. Manley O. and Ruth (Worrell) S.; m. Donna R. Borman, June 7, 1952 (dec. Jan. 1973); children: Katharine Anne Stevens Dillon, Thomas W., John M.; m. Beth A. Murphy, Apr. 20, 1974; children: Carrie Theresa Hamilton, Elizabeth Mary Crough. BSc, U. Iowa, 1948. With Coca-Cola Co., 1948-54, Gen. Foods Corp., 1954-67; exec. v.p. Riviana Foods, Houston, 1967-73; v.p. mktg. Hiram Walker Inc., Detroit, 1973-75, pres., 1975-80, Maidstone Wine & Spirits Inc., LA, 1980-91, Kahlua Group (Allied Domecq), 1987-91; exec. v.p. The Century Coun., Los Angeles, 1991-98. Bd. dirs., past chmn. Detroit Met. YMCA; bd. dirs. L.A. Met. YMCA. Lt. (j.g.) USN, 1943-46. Mem. Jonathan Club, Sigma Alpha Epsilon. Episcopalian. Home: 1444 S Marengo Ave Pasadena CA 91106-4228

STEVENS, ROY W., microbiologist, researcher, photographer; BS, SUNY, Albany, 1956, MS, 1958; PhD, Albany Med. Coll., 1965. Diplomate Am. Bd. Med. Microbiology, cert. emeritus Am. Bd. Med. Microbiology, 2002. Rsch. scientist Wadsworth Ctr., N.Y. State Dept. Health, Albany, 1967—70, assoc. rsch. scientist, 1970—73, prin. rsch. scientist, 1973—79, dir. lab. diagnostic immunology, 1979—85, dir. retrovirology and immunology lab., 1985—91; adj. prof. microbiology and immunology Albany Med. Coll., 1982—92; assoc. prof. sch. pub. health State Univ. N.Y., Albany, 1988—98; pres. Bio-med. Resource Group, Albany, 1991—2001. Trustee Bender Sci., Albany, 1986-98; chair Bender Sci. Ltd. Cmty. Found., Albany, 2002—; mem. libr. devel. com. U. at Albany, 2001—, chair 2003-06. Fellow Am. Acad. Microbiology (emeritus 2002), Assn. Med. Lab. Immunologists (pres. 1989), Am. Soc. Microbiology (chmn. clin. and diagnostic immunology divsn. 1997-98), Nat. Assn. Photoshop Profls. Office: White Photography PO Box 12393 Albany NY 12212 Home: 507 Acre Dr Schenectady NY 12303-5226

STEVENS, SCOTT, retired professional hockey player; b. Kitchener, Ont., Canada, Apr. 1, 1964; m. Donna Stevens; children: Kaitlin, Ryan, Kara. Defenseman Washington Capitals, 1982—90, St. Louis Blues, 1990—91, NJ Devils, 1991—2005, capt., 1992—2005, spl. assignment coach, 2005—. Played in NHL All-Star Game, 1985, 89, 91-94, 96; named to NHL All-Rookie Team, 1982-83, Sporting News All-Star Second Team, 1987-88, NHL All-Star First Team, 1987-88, 93-94, 2004, NHL All-Star Second Team, 1991-92, Sporting News All-Star First Team, 1993-94; recipient Conn Smythe Trophy, 2000; set NHL record for games played by a defensemen. Achievements include being a member of Stanley Cup Champion New Jersey Devils, 1995, 2000, 2003; setting NHL record for games played by a defensemen; having his number, 4, retired by New Jersey Devils, 2006; being inducted into the Hockey Hall of Fame, 2007. Office: c/o NJ Devils Prudential Ctr 165 Mulberry St Newark NJ 07102

STEVENS, SHANE, novelist; s. John and Caroline (Royale) S. MA, Columbia U. Mem. numerous writers confs. including Bread Loaf, Santa Barbara Writers Conf. Author: Go Down Dead, Way Uptown in Another World, Dead City, Rat Pack, By Reason of Insanity, The Anvil Chorus; (as J.W. Rider) Jersey Tomatoes (Best Novel award), Hot Tickets; contbr. articles to pubs. including N.Y. Times, Life, Washington Post; screenwriter: By Reason of Insanity, The Me Nobody Knows. Mem. Authors Guild, Writers Guild Am.

STEVENS, SHARON COX, lawyer; b. 1948; m. Michael Callahan. BA, Washington State Univ.; JD, McGeorge Sch. Law. Bar: Oreg. 1977. Ptnr. Callahan & Stevens, Keizer, Oreg. Mem.: ABA (bd. govs. 2004—07). Office: Callahan & Stevens 5845 Shoreview Lane N PO Box 20937 Keizer OR 97307-0937 also: Callahan & Stevens 156 Chemawa Rd N Salem OR 97303-5356 Office Phone: 503-240-4133.

STEVENS, SHEILA MAUREEN, retired teachers union administrator; b. Glendale, Calif., Nov. 1, 1942; d. Richard Chase and Sheila Mary (Beatty) Flynn; m. Jan Whitney Stevens, Sept. 12, 1964; children: Ian Whitney, Bevin Michelle. AA in Liberal Arts, Monterey Peninsula Coll., Calif., 1963; BA in Anthropology, Calif. State U., Long Beach, 1969; postgrad. studies in Edn., U. Guam, 1976-77. Tchr. U.S. Trust Territory of the Pacific, Koror, Palau Island, 1968-72, Kolonia, Ponape Island, 1972-76, Dept. Edn., Agana, Guam, 1976-79; newspaper editor Pacific Daily News (Gannett), Agana, 1979-83; comm. dir. Guam Fedn. of Tchrs., Agana, 1983-84, exec. dir., 1984-85, Alaska Fedn. Tchrs., Anchorage, 1985-87; labor rels. specialist N.Y. State United Tchrs., Watertown, 1987-93, regional staff dir. Potsdam, 1993—2003; ret., 2003. Mem. Gov.'s Blue Ribbon Panel on Edn., Agana, Guam, 1983-85; leadership devel. coord. Am. Fedn. Tchrs., Washington, 1983—; trainer positive negotiations program Situation Mgmt. Sys., Hanover, Mass., 1988—. Author, editor: Pacific Daily News, 1981-83 (Guam Press Club awards 1981, 82, 83); contbr. articles to mag. and jours. Mem. task force on labor policy, com. on self determination, Govt. of Guam, Agana, 1984-85, Adult Basic Edn. Planning Com., 1985; mem. labor studies adv. bd., Anchorage, Alaska, 1989, regional compact coalition N.Y. State Edn. Dept., Albany, 1994; del. NY State Labor Religion Coalition; pres. Friends of the Cape Vincent Pub. Libr., 2008—. Named Friend of Edn., Carthage (N.Y.) Tchrs. Assn., 1990. Mem. NOW, ACLU, ASCD, AAUW, Am. Fedn. Tchrs. Comm. Assn. (Best Editorial award 1984), Indsl. Rels. Rsch. Assn. Democrat. Methodist. Avocations: travel, reading, free-lance writing, cross country skiing. Personal E-mail: seawings49@hotmail.com.

STEVENS, SIMON, healthcare company executive; m. Maggie Thurer; 1 child, Samuel. Attended, Oxford U., Strathclyde U., Columbia U. Health policy dir. to prime min. Govt. of The UK; pres. internat. bus. in Europe, Asia and the Americas UnitedHealth Group Inc., CEO Ovations, 2006—09, exec. v.p., 2009—, pres. Global Health, 2009—. Vis. prof. London Sch. Econs. Office: UnitedHealth Group PO Box 1459 Minneapolis MN 55440-1459 Office Phone: 800-328-5979.*

STEVENS, STANLEY DAVID, historian, researcher, retired librarian, archivist; b. San Francisco, Nov. 10, 1933; s. David Franklin and Ellen Myrtle (Wixson) S.; m. Carli Ann Lewis, Sept. 3, 1960; adopted children: Alexander Lewis, Nikolas Harriman, Brooke Cayton Stevens. BA, San Jose State U., Calif., 1959. Conf. officer polit. and security com. 14th Gen. Assembly, UN, NYC, 1959; map libr. U. Calif., Santa Cruz, 1965-93, ret., 1993, coord. Hihn-Younger Archive, Univ. Libr., 1994—.

Mem. Cartographic Users Adv. Coun., 1976-86, chmn., 1982-86; presenter in field; adj. prof. libr. sci. San Jose State U., 1989, 91. Author: Index to Guinn's Biographical Record of Santa Cruz, San Benito, Monterey and San Luis Obispo Counties, Catalog of aerial photos by Fairchild Aerial Surveys, Inc. now in the collections of the Dept. Geography, UCLA, 1982, Correspondence of Charles B. Younger Sr. and Charles B. Younger Jr., Santa Cruz, California Attorneys and Counsellors at Law, vols. 1-13, 1996—, indexed edit. Santa Cruz County, Calif., 1997, Index to Personal Names, Portraits & Illustrations Appearing in California City, County & Regional Histories 1867-1910, 2005; editor: Santa Cruz County History Jour., 1994-96, 98; co-author: 2009, Index to Sidewalk Companion to Santa Cruz Architecture, 3d edit., 2005; co-author: A Legal History of Santa Cruz County: an account of the local bench and bar through the end of the Twentieth Century, 2006, Index to Morton Marcus, Striking Through The Masks, 2008, The Rowland Website & The Content of the Leon Rowland Collection, 2006, Index to Lime Kiln Legacies: The History of the Lime Industry in Santa Cruz County, 2007, Index to Santa Cruz County History Jour., 2009, Index to Great Register of Voters, Santa Cruz County, 1866-1875, 2009, others; prodn. editor: Index to Boulder Creek Mountain Echo, 1896-1916, 1999; contbr. articles to profl. jours. and Map Collections Mem. adv. com. archaeol. program Cabrillo Coll., Aptos, Calif., 1985—; bd. dirs. Santa Cruz County Hist. Soc., 1985-94, chmn. publs. com., 1985-96, mem. programs adv. coun., 1994-95; mem. Santa Cruz Orgn. for Progress and Euthenics, 1987—; bd. dirs. Friends of U. Calif.-Santa Cruz Libr., 1994-97; founding mem. Rschr. Anonymous, Santa Cruz, 1993—; mem. U. Calif.-Santa Cruz Emeriti Group, sec.-treas. 1996—; mem. collections adv. com. Santa Cruz City Mus. Natural History, 1995—; mem. hist. publs. com. Mus. Art and History, 2000—, chmn., 2006—; vol. Spl. Collections, Univ. Libr., U. Calif., Santa Cruz, 1994—. With U.S. Army, 1954-56. Recipient honors award geography and map divsn. for outstanding achievement in map librarianship Spl. Librs. Assn., 1981, cert. of commendation Santa Cruz Hist. Soc., 1986, appreciation cert. for svcs. Assn. Info. and Image Mgmt., 1989, Proclamation of Honor, Santa Cruz County Bd. Suprs., 1998, Historian of Yr. award History Forum of Santa Cruz Mus. of Art and History, 2001; grantee Librs. Assn. U. Calif., 1981-82, Rsch. grantee Office of Pres., U. Calif., 1985-86. Mem. ALA (publs. com. Map and Geography Round Table 1985-86, editl. bd. Meridian 1989-2000, honors award Map and Geography Round Table 1992), ACLU (chmn. bd. dirs. Santa Cruz County chpt. 1962-68, bd. dirs. No. Calif. br. 1973-76), Western Assn. Map Librs. (hon. life, founding pres. 1967-68, treas. 1968-89, editor Info. Bull. 1969-84, Exec. Com. award 1984, Stanley D. Stevens Hon. Map presented at 30th anniversary meeting 1997, Calif. Hist. Soc., Calif. Map Soc., Pajaro Valley Hist. Assn., Santa Cruz County Geneal. Soc., Capitola Hist. Soc., El Paso de Robles Hist. Soc. (life). Democrat. Avocations: researching local history, listening to jazz and classical music. Home: 231 13th Ave Santa Cruz CA 95062-4831 Office: U Calif Dean E McHenry Libr Santa Cruz CA 95064 Business E-Mail: sstevens@library.ucsc.edu.

STEVENS, STANLEY M., lawyer; b. Dec. 21, 1948; m. Kristin Stevens. BA, U. Mo., Columbia, 1970; JD, U. Chgo., 1973. Bar: Ga. 1973, US Dist. Ct. No. Dist. Ga. 1974, Ill. 1976, US. Dist. Ct. No. Dist. Ill. 1977, Fla. 1987, US Dist. Ct. Mid. Dist. Fla. 1987. Exec. v.p., chief legal counsel, sec. Equity Office Properties Trust, Chgo., 1996—2007; ptnr. Sidley Austin LLP, Chgo., 2007—. Office: Sidley Austin LLP One S Dearborn Chicago IL 60603

STEVENS, STEVE J., lawyer; s. Jerry G. Speigelman and Susan C. Varon. BA, Loyola U., 1976; MA in Bus. & Mgmt., U. Redlands, 1982; JD, Drake U. Law Sch., 1988; tchr. edn. cert., Chapman U., 1999. Bar: S.D. 1992, Calif. 1998, D.C. 1998; lic. pvt. detective. Paralegal Hughes, Hubbard, Reed, LA, 1980—83, State Bar Calif., LA, 1989—90; criminal def. atty. Earl Carter & Assocs., Glendale, Calif., 2000—. Judge pro tem L.A. Superior Ct., various cts. in Los Angeles County. Author: (book) Access to the Courts, 1982. Mem.: ABA, Calif. Assn. Lic. Investigators, LA County Bar Assn. Roman Catholic. Avocations: reading, swimming, dance. Office: Earl Carter & Assocs 715 N Central #216 Glendale CA 91203 also: 468 Camdenon Ste 289I Beverly Hills CA 90210 Office Phone: 310-860-5694. Office Fax: 310-207-0109.

STEVENS, SUSAN SELTENREICH CIRILLO, special education educator; b. Rockville Centre, NY, Apr. 16, 1962; d. Richard Paul and Estelle Duboise Seltenreich; m. John Stafford Cirillo (div.); children: Adam Cirillo, Jeremy Cirillo, Nicholas Cirillo; m. Peter Stevens, Oct. 4, 2003 (div.). AS in Early Childhood Edn., SUNY, Farmingdale, 1982; BS in Edn., SUNY, Geneseo, 1986; MEd, U. North Tex., 1992. Cert. lay min. United Meth. Ch. of N.Y., local lay min. United Meth. Ch. of N.Y.; spl. edn. tchr. N.Y., tchr. nursery, kindergarten, grades 1-6 N.Y., spl. edn. tchr. K-12 Wash., tchr. ESL Wash., elem. edn. tchr. Wash., early childhood educator Wash., spl. edn. tchr. Tex., tchr. ESL Tex., elem. edn. tchr. Tex., kindergarten tchr. Tex. Spl. edn. tchr. United Cerebral Palsy of Queens, Jamaica, NY, 1987—88; elem. and ESL educator Herbert Marcus Elem. Sch., Dallas Ind. Sch. Dist., 1988—92, spl. edn. educator Hillcrest H.S., 1994—96; enrichment educator The Huntington Learning Ctr., Issaquah, Wash., 1999—2000; spl. edn. educator Beaver Lake Mid. Sch., Issaquah Sch. Dist., 2000—02; spl. edn. educator Silas Wood 6th Grade Ctr., South Huntington Union Free Sch. Dist., Huntington Sta., NY, 2000—. Author: (poetry) Mellie the Muskrat, 2004. Lay min., mem. edn. com., Sunday sch. educator, children's sermon min. Dix Hills (N.Y.) United Meth. Ch., 2002—05; Sunday sch. educator Faith United Meth. Ch., Issaquah, 2000—02, St. John's Luth. Ch., Columbia, Md., 1996—98; Sunday sch. educator, mem. worship and music coun. Preston Meadow Luth. Ch., Plano, Tex., 1988—96. Fellow ednl. grantee, South Huntington Parent Tchr. Ctr., 2004. Mem.: Coun. Exceptional Children (assoc.). Avocations: poetry, travel. Home: 3 Wexford St Huntington NY 11743 Office: Silas Wood 6th Grade Ctr 23 Harding Pl Huntington Station NY 11746 Personal E-mail: susanc001@msn.com. E-mail: sstevens@shufsd.org.

STEVENS, TED (THEODORE FULTON STEVENS), former United States Senator from Alaska; b. Indpls., Nov. 18, 1923; s. George A. and Gertrude (Chancellor) S.; m. Ann Mary Cherrington, Mar. 29, 1952 (dec. 1978); children: Susan B., Elizabeth H., Walter C., Theodore Fulton, Ben A.; m. Catherine Chandler, 1980; 1 child, Lily Irene. BA, U. Calif. at Los Angeles, 1947; LL.B., Harvard U., 1950. Bar: Calif., Alaska, D.C., U.S. Supreme Ct. bars. Atty. Northcutt Ely, Washington, 1950—52, Collins & Clasby, Fairbanks, Alaska, 1953; U.S. atty. Dist. Alaska US Dept. Justice, Fairbanks, 1953-56; legis. counsel US Dept. Interior, Washington, 1956—57, asst to sec., 1958—59, solicitor, 1960; ptnr. Stevens & Roderick, Anchorage, 1961—63, Stevens & Stringer, Anchorage, 1964, Stevens, Savage, Holland, Erwin & Edwards, Anchorage, 1964—65, Stevens & Holland, Anchorage, 1966—68; mem. Alaska Ho. of Reps., 1965-68, majority leader, speaker pro tem, 1967-68; US Senator from Alaska, 1968—2009; minority whip, 1977—81; majority whip, 1981—85; pres. pro tempore, 2003—07; chmn. appropriations com., 1997—2001, 2003—05, commerce, sci., & transp. com., 2005—07, vice chmn., 2007—09. Served in USAF, 1943—46. Decorated Disting. Flying Cross, Air medal with Cluster, Yuan Hai Medal Chinese Nationalist Govt., China-Burma-India Ribbion; recipient Alaska 49'er, Alaska Press Club, 1963, Disting. Svc. Award, UCLA, 1971, Man of Yr. Award, Nat. Fisheries Inst., 1975; named Alaskan of Yr., 1974. Mem. ABA, Alaska Bar Assn., Calif. Bar Assn., D.C. Bar Assn., Am. Legion, VFW. Lodges: Rotary, Pioneers of Alaska, Igloo #4. Republican. Episcopalian.*

STEVENS, THELMA KAPLAN, artist, educator; b. NYC, Dec. 4, 1932; d. Nathan and Shirley (Laufer) Kaplan; m. Jay P. Stevens, Mar. 17, 1956; children: Wendy, Andrew BS, Pratt Inst., 1954; MS, Queens Coll., 1959; PhD, Fordham U., 1980. Tchr. art pub. schs., NY, 1954—88; instr. Grad. Sch. Fordham U., NYC, 1979; pres. Isis Gallery Ltd., Searingtown, NY, 1982—. Pres. Reunions to Remember, Manhasset, NY, 1996—. Co-author: Super Sculpture, 1974; contbr. numerous articles to profl. jours Mem. Internat. Soc. Edn. Thru Art (N.Y. state rep. 1989—), U.S. Soc. for Edn. Thru Art, N.Y. State Art Tchrs. Assn., Nat. Art Edn. Assn. (dir. ea. region U.S. and Can. secondary art edn. 1986-89, N.Y. State Art Educator of Yr. 1983), James Madison H.S. Alumni Assn. (pres. 1995-2004, bd. dirs.) Avocations: travel, reading, cooking, theater. Studio: Reunions to Remember 565 Plandome Rd # 130 Manhasset NY 11030 Office Phone: 516-944-2240.

STEVENS, WARREN, actor; b. Clark's Summit, Pa., Nov. 2, 1919; s. Albert Clifford and Helen Dodd (Blakeslee) S.; m. Barbara Helen Fletcher, Sept. 9, 1969; children— Adam Fletcher, Matthew Dodd; 1 son by previous marriage, Laurence Blakeslee. Student, U.S. Naval Acad., 1939-40. Appeared on: New York stage in Gallileo, 1947, Sundown Beach, 1948, Smile of the World, 1949, Detective Story, 1949; appeared in numerous motion pictures, since 1950, including, Barefoot Contessa, Forbidden Planet; appeared on: numerous television shows, including Richard Boone Rep. With USN, 1937-40; with USAAF, 1942-46. Mem. Actors Studio.

STEVENS, WILBUR HUNT, accountant; b. Spencer, Ind., June 20, 1918; s. John Vosburgh and Isabelle Jane (Strawser) S.; m. Maxine Dodge Stevens, Sept. 28, 1941; children: Linda Maxine Piffero, Deborah Anne Augello. BS, MBA, U. Calif., Berkeley, 1949. CPA, Calif.; cert. fraud examiner, fin. svcs. auditor. Staff acct. McLaren, Goode, West & Co., San Francisco, 1949-52; mng. ptnr. Wilbur H. Stevens & Co., Salinas, Calif., 1952-70; regional ptnr. Fox & Co., CPAs, Salinas, 1970-73, nat. dir. banking practice Denver, 1973-80; pres., chmn. Wilbur H. Stevens, CPA, PC, Salinas, 1980-94; chmn. Stevens, Sloan & Shah, CPAs, 1994—. Adj. prof. acctg. U. Denver, 1975-78; faculty mem. Assemblies for Bank Dirs., So. Meth. U., Dallas, 1976-81, Nat. Banking Sch., U. Va., Charlottesville, 1979-87; chmn., dir. Valley Nat. Bank, 1963-71, Pacific Ag Credit, Inc., 1997—, Pacific Valley Bank, 2002-05; dir. World Travel, Inc.; v.p., dir. Dirs. Coun. Ind. Banks, Global Uplift, Inc.; mem. bus. adv. coun. NRCC. Editor Issues in CPA Practice, 1975; contbr. articles to profl. jours. Capt. AUS, 1942-53. Decorated Bronze Star, Burma Star, UK, China Victory medal; Frank G. Drum fellow U. Calif., Berkeley, 1949. Fellow Am. Bd. Forensic Acctg.; mem. AICPA (v.p. 1971), Am. Acctg. Assn., Am. Assembly Collegiate Schs. Bus. (accreditation coun. 1975-78, 81-84), Nat. Assn. State Bds. Accountancy (pres. 1976-77, strategic initiatives com. 1997-99), Inst. Internal Auditors (fin. svcs. group), Am. Acad. Cert. Consultants and Experts, Calif. Soc. CPAs (pres. 1968-69, Disting. Svc. award 1988), Acctg. Rsch. Assn. (pres. 1973-75), Acad. Acctg. Historians, Assn. Cert. Fraud Examiners, Am. Coll. Forensic Examiners, Ctrl. Calif. Past Masters Assn. (pres. 1998), Burma Star Assn., CBI Vets. Assn., 14 AF Assn., Hump Pilots Assn., Salinas C. of C. (pres. 1960), Commonwealth Club Calif., Masons (master 1992, 97, Hiram award 1998, grand lodge com. taxation), Knight Templar (comdr. 2000), Royal Arch (high priest 1998, grand chpt. inspector 1999-2000), Cryptic Masons (illus. master 2000), Fedn. Knight Masons Am., Knight of York (Cross of Honor), Allied Masonic Degrees (sov. master 2001 York Rite Coll.), Royal Order Scotland, 32 degree Scottish Rite, Nat. Sojourners (pres. Monterey Bay chpt. 1996), Heroes of '76 (comdr. John C. Fremont chpt. 1996-97), Fed. for Collingwood Libr. and Mus., Red Cross of Constantine, Salinas High Twelve Club (pres. 1995), Philalethes Soc., QCCC, London, Rotary (dist. gov. 1983, chmn. internat. fellowship CPAs 1994-96, Paul Harris fellow 1973), Phi Beta Kappa, Beta Gamma Sigma (v.p. 1949), Beta Alpha Psi. Republican. Methodist. Home: 38 Santa Ana Dr Salinas CA 93901-4136 Office: 975 W Alisal St Ste D Salinas CA 93901-1148

STEVENS, WILLIAM GRANT (GRANT STEVENS), plastic surgeon; b. Orange, Calif., Nov. 13, 1953; s. William Raymond Stevens and Donna Lynn (Stabbert) Watson; m. Sheri Diane Eagle, Aug. 13, 1977; 1 child, Catherine Eagle. BS in Psychology, U. Oreg., 1976; MD, Washington U. Med. Sch., St. Louis, 1980. Lic. Calif., 1981, Idaho, 1994, diplomate Nat. Bd. Med. Examiners, 1981, Am. Bd. Plastic Surgery, 1989. Intern Harbor UCLA Med. Ctr., Torrance, 1980-81, resident, 1981-83; hand surgery fellow Washington U. Sch. Medicine, St. Louis, 1983-84, fellow plastic surgery, 1984-85, chief resident, 1985-86; med. dir. Marina Plastic Surgery Associates (Marina Outpatient Surgery Ctr.), Marina del Rey, 1988—; med. dir. hand therapy svcs. Washington Hosp., 1988—93; chmn. dept. surgery, mem. med. exec. com. Daniel Freeman Marina Hosp., Marina del Rey, Calif., 1989—96, assoc. med. dir. Marina Breast Ctr., 1991—92, physician advisor, Skin Care POD, 1995—98. Attending cons. surgeon, plastic surgery sect. UCLA, Olive View Med. Ctr., 1992, UCLA, Wadsworth Vet. Adminstrn., 1992—2000; clin. prof. Liposuction U.; clin. instr., dept. surgery, divsn. plastic & reconstructive surgery UCLA Sch. Medicine; assoc. clin. prof., dept. surgery, divsn. plastic & reconstructive surgery U. So. Calif. Sch. Medicine; plastic surgery expert cons. Med. Bd. Calif., 1988—, mem., 11th dist. med. quality review com., 1990—94; clin. evaluator Dow-Corning M.S.I. Breast Implant, 1991—93; mentor clin. investigator adj. gel mammary study, 1992—; mentor investigator, saline mammary prosthesis prospective study, 1992—; facility inspector Am. Assn. for Accreditation Ambulatory Plastic Surgical Facilities, Inc., 1992—; McGhan clin. investigator adj. gel mammary study, 1998—; mentor clin. investigator adj. gel mammary study, 1998—; ebdotine endoscope brow investigator, 2001—; Silimed clin. investigator cohesive gel mammary implant study, 2003—; vis. plastic surgery professorships U. Herlev Hosp., Copenhagen, 1998, U. Switzerland, Luzon, Switzerland, 1997, Loma Linda U., 1997, U. So. Calif., 2002; lectr. in field; presenter in field; clin. investigator for several studies. Mem. editl. bd. Wounds: A Compendium of Clin. Rsch. & Practice, 1988, mem. editl. adv. bd. Plastic Surgery Products, 1998—2006, Cosmetic Surgery Times, 1998—2006, frequent TV appearances include Personal Story, TLC, Hard Copy, Plastic Surgery Before & After, Discovery Health, The Perfect Cut, frequently featured in The Argonaut, Glamour, LA Times Mag., Plastic Surgery News, Longevity, LA Times, LA Mag., Daily Breeze, Cosmetic Plastic Surgery Times, Cosmetic Plastic Surgery Mag., Cosmetic Surgery Mag.; contbr. articles to profl. journals. Pres. Native Sons of the Golden West, Santa Monica, 1989—; active Boys and Girls Club Marina Del Rey; plastic surgeon Ice Dog Hockey Team, 1995-98 Recipient Kovitz sr. prize in Surgery, 1980, County of LA Commendation, 1996, Disting. Svc. Citation, Med. Bd. Calif., 1984, cert. of tribute, City of LA, 1996, GTE Cmty. Spirit award, 1996, cert. of recognition, Calif. State Assembly, 1997, cert. of Spl. Congl. Recognition, 1997, cert. of recognition, Calif. State Senate, 1997; Louis & Dorothy Kovitz fellowship in Surg. Rsch., 1979. Fellow: Am. Soc. for Laser Medicine & Surgery, Internat. Coll. Surgeons, ACS; mem.: AMA (Physician Recognition award, Physician Recognition award), Calif. Soc. Plastic Surgeons, Inc. (mem. legis. com. 1992—96, med. bd. Calif., liaison com. 1992—93), Internat. Soc. Aesthetic Plastic Surgery, Internat. Confederation for Plastic, Reconstructive and Aesthetic Surgery, LA County Med. Assn., ACS, Southern Calif. ch., Calif. Med. Assn. (adv. panel on plastic surgery sect. asst. sec. 1991—92, adv. panel on plastic surgery sect. sec. 1992—93, adv. panel on plastic surgery chmn. 1993—94, past chmn., adv. panel), Lipoplasty Soc. N.Am., Barnes Hosp. Plastic Surg. Soc., Plastic Surgery Ednl. Found., LA Society of Plastic Surgeons, Inc., Am. Soc. for Aesthetic Plastic Surgery, Inc., Am. Soc. Plastic Surgeons, Am. Soc. Plastic & Reconstructive Surgeons, Inc. (young plastic surgeons com. 1991—93, CPT com. 1992—93, practice devel. com. 1992—93, govt. rels. com. 1992—95), Phi Beta Kappa. Republican. Office: 4644 Lincoln Blvd Ste 552 Marina Del Rey CA 90292 Office Phone: 866-588-7507.*

STEVENS, YVETTE MARIE See KHAN, CHAKA

STEVENSON, ADLAI EWING, III, lawyer, former United States Senator, Illinois; b. Chgo., Oct. 10, 1930; s. Adlai Ewing and Ellen (Borden) S.; m. Nancy L. Anderson, June 25, 1955; children: Adlai Ewing IV, Lucy W., Katherine R., Warwick L. Grad., Milton Acad., 1948; AB, Harvard U., 1952, LL.B., 1957. Bar: Ill. 1957, D.C. 1977. Law clk. Ill. Supreme Ct., 1957-58; assoc. Mayer, Brown & Platt, Chgo., 1958-66, ptnr., 1966-67, 81-83, of counsel, 1983-91; treas. State of Ill., 1967-70; U.S. senator from Ill., 1970-81; chmn. SC&M Internat. Ltd., Chgo., 1991-95, pres., 1995-98, chmn. bd., 1998—; co-chmn. Huamei Capital Co., Inc., 2005—08. Mem. Ill. Ho. of Reps., 1965-67; Dem. candidate for gov. of Ill., 1982, 86. Capt. USMCR, 1952-54. Office: 2117 N Fremont St Chicago IL 60614 Office Phone: 773-281-3578.

STEVENSON, AMANDA (SANDY STEVENS), librettist, composer, songwriter; b. Bklyn., Oct. 24, 1943; d. Haakon and Grace Svendsen. Cert. Nat. Bur. Document Examiners. Composer, librettist, Nellie Bly, Victorine, (screenplay) The Last Assignment Mem. Actors Equity Assn., BMI, Songwriters Guild. Democrat. Avocations: chess, art history, songwriting. Home and Office: 35-43 84th St Apt 327 Jackson Heights NY 11372 Office Phone: 718-429-5998. Personal E-mail: lyricist@mindspring.com.

STEVENSON, BEN, performing company executive; b. Portsmouth, Eng., Apr. 4, 1936; arrived in U.S., 1968; s. Benjamin John and Florence May (Gundry) S.; m. Joan Toastivine, Jan. 6, 1968. Grad., Arts Ednl. Sch., London, 1955. Artistic dir. Harkness Ballet Youth Dancers, 1968—71, Chgo. Ballet, 1974—75, Houston Ballet, 1973—2003, artistic dir. emeritus, 2003—; co-dir. Nat. Ballet, Washington, 1971—74; artistic dir. Tex. Ballet Theater, 2003—. Mem. dance panel Tex. Commn. Arts, 1977; guest tchr. Am. Ballet Theatre, Joffrey Ballet, Royal Ballet, London, Beijing Dance Acad. Dancer Theatre Arts Ballet, London, 1952-54, Sadler's Wells Theatre Ballet, 1955-56, Royal Ballet, 1956-60, London Festival Ballet, 1960-62; appearances in Wedding in Paris, 1954-55, Music Man, London, 1962-63, Half a Sixpence, also, Boys in Syracuse, London, 1964; prin. dancer, ballet master, London Festival Ballet, 1964-68; prin. ballets choreographed include Three Faces of Eve, 1965, Cast Out, 1966, Sleeping Beauty (full length), 1967, 71, 76, 78, Fervor, 1968, Three Preludes, 1968, Forbidden, 1969, Cinderella (full length), 1969, 71, 73, 74, 76, Bartok Concerto, 1970, Nutcracker (full length), 1972, 76, Symphonetta, 1972, Courant, 1973, Swan Lake (full length), 1977, L, 1978, Britten Pas de Deux, 1979, Four Last Songs, 1979, Space City, 1980, Peer Gynt (full length), 1981, Zheng Ban Qiao, 1982, The Prince of Pagodas, 1986 Recipient 1st prize London Choreographic competitions, 1965, 66, 67, modern ballet choreography Internat. Ballet Competition, Varna, Bulgaria, 1972, Gold medal for choreography Internat. Ballet Competition, 1982, Dance mag. award, 2000; named Order of Brit. Empire, 1999. Asso. mem. Royal Acad. Dancing (Adeline Genee Gold medal 1955) Office: Tex Ballet Theatre 6845 Green Oaks Rd Fort Worth TX 76116 Office Phone: 817-763-0207 817-763-0207. E-mail: bstevenson@texasbalettheater.org.*

STEVENSON, BRADFORD ALLEN, management consultant; s. James Richard and Sara Jean Stevenson; m. Sarah Alaine Powers, Aug. 8, 2001; children: Paige Anne, Braden Allen. BS in Criminal Justice, So. Ill. U.; MBA, So. Ill. U., Albuquerque, 2007. Cert. program enhancement instr. TWD N.Mex, 2006. COO Exec. Intelligence Svcs., Inc, Albuquerque, 1990—2004, Trans-World Dynamics, LLC, Albuquerque, 2004—. Bus. coach TWD Ind., Albuquerque, 1991—2007. Contbr. articles to profl. jours. Staff sgt. spl. forces US Army, 1984—90. Decorated Combat Inf. badge US Army, Jungle Expert award. Home: PO Box 82066 Albuquerque NM 87198 Office: Trans-World Dynamic LLC, PO Box 82512 Albuquerque NM 87198 Personal E-mail: brad@thepowerofthanks.com. Business E-Mail: brad@transworldynamics.com.

STEVENSON, DAVID WAYNE, municipal official; b. Commerce, Tex., Aug. 9, 1957; s. Billy Wayne Stevenson and Constance Marie-Essary Underwood; m. Tami Gail Thomas; children: James David, Ashlei Gail Jones, John Thomas, Amber Michelle. Degree in acctg., Tyler Comml. Coll., 1976. Office mgr. Fountain & Holdredge CPA, Athens, Tex., 1976—78; brakeman Union Pacific RR, Mineola, Tex., 1978—86; firefighter City of Mineola, 1986—94, city sec., 1994—. Firefighting instr. Tex. A&M, College Station; mem. homeland security adv. bd. East Tex. Coun. of Govts., Kilgore, 2003—; mem. adv. bd. Nat. Coun. Readiness and Preparedness, Washington, 2005—. Chief Mineola Vol. Fire Dept., 1997—. Named Mineola Man of Yr., Mineola C. of C., 1997, Mineola Firefighter of Yr., Mineola Fire Dept., 1990, 1994; named to Leadership Mineola, C. of C., 1997. Mem.: Tex. State Fireman's and Fire Marshal's Assn., Wood County Fire Chiefs Assn. (pres. 1998—99), Kiwanis (pres. 1997). Methodist. Avocations: hunting, golf, reading. Office: City of Mineola 300 Greenville Ave Mineola TX 75773 Home: 316 County Rd 2460 Mineola TX 75773-6824 Office Phone: 903-569-6183. Business E-Mail: dstevenson@mineola.com.

STEVENSON, DEBORAH L., government official, educator; BA summa cum laude, George Mason U., Virginia; attended, Yale & Oxford U. Govt. ofcl. US Dept. Justice, 1974—. Filmed as figure skater Learning Channel, 1999, ice skating choreographer USA, Switzerland, 1972—2006;, translator numerous articles; contbr. articles. Mem. bd. and com. chair Symphony Orch. League Alexandria, 2005—07; mem. adv. bd. English-Speaking Union, 2007—; chpt. v.p., state historian Ladies Ancient Order of Hibernians, Va., 1999—2001; vol. NYC Ballet, 1994—96, US Open Golf Championships, 1993—97, Shakespeare Theatre Co., Washington, 1998—2007, Folger Shakespeare Theatre, Washington, 1998—2007, Arlington Symphony Orch., Va., 2001—05, Kennedy Ctr., Washington, 2006—08; dir. Lasley Music Scholarship Competition, 2007, Books as Envoys Program, 2009, English in Action Program, Washington, 2007—08; vol. NYC Opera, 1994—98; vol. numerous other orgns.; bd. mem. Parades Coms., Alexandria, Va., 2000—01. Recipient numerous awards, Dept. Justice, Dept. Def., Pres.'s Vol. Lifetime Svc. award, US Figure Skating Assn., Atty. Gen. Vol. Svc. awards, Phi Theta Kappa, various faculty awards, Nat. Slavic Honor

Soc.; fellow, Royal Soc. Arts; fellowship awards, English-Speaking Union, London. Mem.: Oxford Univ. Soc., Royal Overseas League, World Affairs Coun., Am. Translators Assn., Royal Inst. Internat. Affairs. Personal E-mail: deblstevenson@gmualumni.org.

STEVENSON, DENISE L., diversified financial services company executive, realtor, consultant; b. Washington, Sept. 18, 1946; d. Pierre and Alice (Mardrus) D'Auga; m. Walter Henry Stevenson, Oct. 17, 1970 (div. 1990). AA, Montgomery Coll., 1967; BA in Econs./Bus. Mgmt., N.C. State U., 1983; cert. legal asst., Meredith Coll., 1989; cert. in mgmt., Fin. Women Internat., 1990. Lic. ins. agt.; accredited buyer rep. Nat. Assn. of Realtors, grad. Realtor Inst., srs. real estate specialist, e-PRO Coun. of Residential Spleciaists, cert. new home specialist. Savs. counselor Perpetual Bldg. Assn. (now Crestar Bank), Washington, 1968—70; regional asst. v.p. 1st Fed. Savs. (now RBC Bank, Rocky Mount), NC, 1971—83; pres., owner Diversified Learning Svcs., Raleigh, 1983—; pres., treas. Daily Life Svcs., Inc., 1994—99; realtor and broker Prudential York Simpson Underwood Realty, 2002—. Instr. Inst. Fin. Edn., Raleigh, 1983—89, Am. Inst. Banking, 1986. Mem. Am. Bus. Women's Assn. (Woman of Yr. 1982), Fin. Women Internat. (cert. leader 1987, Mem. of Yr. award 1992, N.C. Woman of Yr. 1992), Laurel Hills Women's Club (pres. 1974-75, Raleigh), Omicron Delta Epsilon. Avocation: fishing. Office: Diversified Learning Svcs PO Box 33231 Raleigh NC 27636-3231

STEVENSON, DOUGLASS EDWARD, entomologist, toxicologist; b. Salt Lake City, Sept. 30, 1943; s. Claudius Edward and Marie Douglass Stevenson; m. Susan Claudia Enslow, Apr. 27, 1974; children: Cynthia Marie, Linda Susan, Jane Amanda, Kathryn Claudia. BS, Brigham Young U., Provo, Utah, 1971; PhD, Tex. A&M U., Coll. Sta., 2004. Bd. cert. entomologist Entomol. Soc. America, 2009. Rsch. technician, dept. zoology & entomology Brigham Young U., Provo, Utah, 1968—71; inf. platoon leader US Army, Ft. Benning, Ga., 1971—72, capt., 1972—85; entomologist Utah Coop. Ext. Svc., County Ext., Provo, 1973—75, Utah Dept. Agr. Divsn. Agr. Inspection, Provo, 1974—75, Intermountain Farmers Assn., Salt Lake City, field agronomist, 1975—84; divsn. mgr. Snake River Chems., UAP, Con-Agra Corp., Orem, Utah, 1984—86; biologist US EPA, Washington, 1987—88; ext. agt., IPM Tex. Agrl. Ext. Svc., Ft. Stockton, 1988—93; ext. assoc. ret. Tex. AgriLife Ext., Coll. Sta., 1993—2006; missionary Ch. LDS, San Jose, Costa Rica. Chmn. facilities com. Entomol. Soc. Am. Pacific Br., Coll. Pk., Md., 1983—84; entomologist Internat. Cotton Pest Work Group, Mex. City, 1988—2006; entomologist cons. Concep Corp. & Hoechst Internat. SA, Cali, Colombia, 1993, cons., GMBH, Lima, Peru, 93; cons. USDA Fgn. Agr. Svc. CAFTA Program, San Salvador, El Salvador, 2006, US Dept. State, Guatemala Food Program, Solola, Guatemala, 2006; co-dir., prin. investigator USDA Fgn. Agr. Svc., USAID Hurricane Mitch Recovery Program, Tegucigalpa, Honduras, 2000—02, Managua, Nicaragua, 2000—02. Contbr. articles to numerous profl. publs. Mem.: Entomol. Soc. America (Nat. Champion, Linnean Games, Tex. A&M Team 2002). Mem. Lds Ch. Achievements include first to application of statistical and mathematical processes in the development of insect population and physiological time models using data collected in the field when laboratory methods were not possible. Home: 340 W 400 N Payson UT 84651-1411 Office: Tex AgriLife Ext Agronomy Rd College Station TX 77843-2488 Personal E-mail: d-stevenson@tamu.edu.

STEVENSON, EARL, communications executive, entrepreneur; s. Jacobus Johannes Gerhardus and Dorothy May Stevenson; m. Sherry-Lynn Gagnon; children: Brandon, Dylan, Hunter, Chad, Cheyenne, Destiny, Sierra. ITIL Cisco, Kukkiwon. Mgr., network ops. Sprint, Reston, Va., 1999—2002, regional support mgr., 2002—; chair, moderator Connect2Can., Washington, DC, 2006—, Ky. Good Citizenship, Frankfort, 2007—. Actor: (films) Nightmare on Elm Street, 1983, ABC PrimeTime Special, 1983, KTLA TV, 1983; (TV miniseries) Capitol, 1985. Admiral Tex. Navy, 2009; hon. chmn. Rep. Nat. Com., Washington, 2007—08; appointee Presdl. Bus. Commn., 2008; hon. aide-de-camp to Ky. Gov., 2008—; mem. Donald Trump for Governors Commn. Ky. Gov. on Donald Trump, 2008. With USMC, 1978—84, admiral Tex. Navy, 2009, hon. col. Ala. State Militia, 2009, col. Aide de Camp, 2009, Tenn. Recipient Mayor's Cert. Appreciation, LA, Cert. Appreciation, Pres. Ronald Reagan, Pres. George Bush, 2009, Cert. Recognition, Calif. State Senate, Sacramento, Gov. Calif, Sacramento, Congl. Order Merit, US Nat. Rep. Congl. Com.; named Ky. Col., Ky Gov. Steven Beshear, 2007, hon. aide-de-camp, Hon. Texan, Tex. Gov., 2009, Hon. Tennesseean, Gov. Tenn., 2009, Tenn. Amb. Goodwill, 2009, Ala. Col., Ala. Gov. Bob Riley, 2009; named to Order of Long Leaf Pine with rank of Amb. Extraordinary, Gov. NC, 2009; nominee Order of Brit. Empire, Her Majesty the Queen. Mem.: SAG, AFTRA, Acad. TV Arts, Hon. Order Ky. Cols., Mensa. Avocations: Tae Kwon Do (5th Dan Black Belt), surfing, rugby, travel, politics.

STEVENSON, EDWARD WARD, retired otolaryngologist, surgeon; b. Chester, SC, Jan. 9, 1926; s. Thomas M. and Annie Lou (Ward) S.; m. Dorothy Giles, Sept. 2, 1947; children: Sally Anne Stevenson Yeilding, Laura Stevenson Healy, Nancy Stevenson Shoneberger(dec.), Molly Stevenson Walker. B in Medicine, Duke U., 1945; MD, U. Md., Balt., 1949. Intern Bapt. Meml. Hosp., Memphis, 1949-50; resident Med. Coll. Va. Hosp., Richmond, 1953-55; fellow Ochsner Found. Hosp., New Orleans, 1955-56; staff otolaryngologist Ochsner Clinic, 1956-57; pvt. practice Birmingham, 1957-60, 65-94, 1965—94; instr., clin. asst. prof. surgery U. Ala., 1957-94; pvt. practice Decatur, 1960-65; ret., 1994. Faculty Tulane U. Sch. Medicine, 1956-57; staff Bapt. Med. Ctr. Montclair, Birmingham, vice chmn. 2007. Contbr. articles to profl. jours. Bd. dirs. So. Mus. Flight, Birmingham, 1989—, Ala. Aviation Hall Fame, chmn., bd. dirs., 2003—, vice-chmn. 2006—; pres. Birmingham Aero Club, 1996; bd. dirs., past pres. Birmingham-Jefferson Mus. History, 2008 Lt. M.C. USNR, 1949—53. Mem. AMA, ACS, Am. Laryngol., Rhinol. and Otol. Soc. (sec.- treas. so. sect. 1990-93, v.p. so. sect. 1993-94), Am. Soc. Head and Neck Surgery, Am. Acad. Otolaryn., Jefferson County Med. Soc., Ala. Otolaryn. Soc. (founder, pres. 1971), Med. Assn. State Ala., Morgan County Med. Soc. (pres. 1964-65), Tri-State Otolaryn. Assembly (co-founder), Birmngham Otolaryn. Soc. (pres. 1984), Newcomen Soc., Birmingham-Jefferson Hist. Soc. (pres. 2007-09), Birmingham Downtown Rotary Club, Sons Revolution, Alb., Newcomen Soc. Alb., United Flying Octogenerians. Methodist. Avocations: aerobatic flying, world travel. Home: 400 Univ Pk Dr Apt 194 Birmingham AL 35209 E-mail: edstevenson@charter.net.

STEVENSON, GARTH, social sciences educator; b. Montreal, Que., Can., Apr. 7, 1943; s. Andrew Archibald Stevenson and Ruth Graham (Scott) Swinton; m. Carol Barbara Krell, Aug. 10, 1968 (div. 1983); children: Colin, Fiona, Moira; m. Yvonne Brown, Aug. 5, 1983 (separated 2005); 1 child, Jacqueline. BA, McGill U., Montreal, 1963, MA, 1965; PhD, Princeton U., 1971. Asst. prof. Carleton U., Ottawa, Ont., 1968—76, assoc. prof., 1976—78, U. Alberta, Edmonton, Alberta, Canada, 1978—82, prof., 1982—87, Brock U., St. Catharines, Ont., Canada, 1987—, chmn. dept. polit. sci., 2003—06. Vis. prof. Duke U., Durham, NC, 1992—93. Author: The Politics of Canada's Airlines, 1987, Ex Uno Plures, 1993, Community Besieged, 1999, Parallel Paths, 2006. Candidate in Canadian Gen. Election New Democratic Party, Edmonton North, Alberta, 1984. Mem.: World Soc. for Protection of Animals, United Nations Assn. in Can., Canadian Railroad Hist. Assn., Amnesty Internat. Canadian Civil Liberties Assn., Internat. Polit. Sci. Assn., Canadian Polit. Sci. Assn. (bd. dirs. 1998—2000), Am. Polit. Sci. Assn. Anglican Ch. Of Canada. Office: Brock U 500 Glenridge Ave Saint Catharines ON Canada L2S 3A1 Address: Brock U Polit Sci Dept PO Box 1600 Lewiston NY 14092-5000 Office Phone: 905-688-5550. Business E-Mail: stevensn@brocku.ca.

STEVENSON, HOWARD HIGGINBOTHAM, business educator; b. Salt Lake City, June 27, 1941; s. Ralph Shields and Dorothy Dee (Higginbotham) S.; m. Fredericka O'Connell; children: William, Charles, Andrew. BS, Stanford U., 1963; MBA, Harvard U., 1965, DBA, 1969. Asst. prof. Harvard U., Cambridge, Mass., 1968—78, prof., 1982—, sr. assoc. dean for fin. adminstrn., 1991-94, sr. assoc. dean external rels., 2000—04, sr. assoc. provost resources and planning, 2004—05, vice provost resources and planning, 2005—06; sr. assoc. dean, dir. bus. pub. Harvard Bus. Sch., Boston, 2006—. Faculty chair, owner, pres., mgr. Program Exec. Edn., 1998—2000; chmn. publs. rev. bd. Harvard Bus. Sch. Press, 1999—2000; faculty chmn. Latin. Am. Adv. Bd., 1999—2001; v.p. Simmons Assocs., Boston, 1970—71; v.p. fin. adminstrn. Preco Corp., West Springfield, Mass., 1978—81; bd. dirs. Landmark Comms. Inc., Norfolk, Va., 1989—2008, Camp Dresser and McKee Inc., Cambridge, The Baupost Group, Inc., Boston, Commonwealth Capital Ptnrs., Boston; vice-chmn. Nat. Pub. Radio, Washington, 2007—08, chmn., 2008—. Co-author: Policy Formation and Administration, 1984, New Business Ventures and the Entrepreneur, 1985, 89, 94, 99, 6th edit., 2007, Entrepreneurial Ventures, 1992, 2d edit., 1999, Do Lunch or Be Lunch: The Power of Predictability in Creating Your Future, 1997, (with David Amis) Winning Angels: The Seven Fundamentals of Early Stage Investing, 2001, (with David Amis) Winning Angels: Mentors in a Network of Success, 2003, (with Laura Nash) Just Enough: Tools for Creating Success in Your Work and Life, 2004, (with Eileen Shapiro) Make Your Own Luck, 2005, (with Jane Wei-Skillern, James Austin, Herman Leonard) Entrepreneurship in the Social Sector, 2007. Trustee Rural Land Found., Lincoln, Mass., 1973-78, Boston Ballet, 1991-2004, Nat. Pub. Radio Dir. 2004-; chair Investment Com. 2008-, Suffield Land Conservancy, Conn., 1978-82; dir. Sudbury Valley Trustees, 1991-2004, pres. bd. trustees, 1996-2000; trustee, dir. Nat. Pub. Radio Found., 1998-, Mass. Chpt. Nature Conservancy, trustee, Mt. Auburn Hosp., 2006-, fin. com., Care Group, Inc., 2006-. IBM Nat. Merit scholar, 1959; Ford Found. fellow, 1965. Mem. Fin. Execs. Inst., Acad. Mgmt., Harvard Club (N.Y.C.). Office: Harvard Bus Sch Rock Center 314 Soldiers Field Boston MA 02163

STEVENSON, JAMES LARAWAY, engineering company executive, electronics, computer and communications engineer, educator; b. Detroit, Oct. 25, 1938; s. Joseph Morley and Kittie Harriet (Laraway) S.; m. Jeanie Lorraine Minkstein, Aug. 7, 1965; children: Amy Jean, Brian Morley. AAS in Electronics Engring., Joint Armed Forces Staff Coll., 1958; BSEE in Electronics Engring., MIT, 1960, MSEE in Electronics Engring., 1962; DSc in Electronics and Computer Engring., Buxton U., 1994. Cert. in acctg. and fin. for owners and managers, Mich. State U. Grad. Sch. Bus. Adminstrn., 1986; Master Radio and Telecom. engr. with Master Endorsements in Radiating and Non-Radiating Catagegories, Internat. Assn. Radio, Telecomm., Electromagnetics Inc., DataShaping Certified; 1st class cert. competency Associated Pub. Safety Comm. Officers, Inc., lic. 1st class FCC Commercial Radiotelephone, 1964. With USN Mercury Space Project, 1957-63, Office of Naval Rsch. (Naval Rsch. Lab. and Flight Test Ctr., Patuxent River Naval Air Sta. MD/Argonne Nat. Lab.), DC, 1962—63, London, 1962—63; engr. Sta. WBCM-FM, Bay City, Mich., 1964-65; chief engr. Sta. WCRM, Clare, Mich., 1965-66, Sta. WSMA, Marine City, Mich., 1966; engr. Sta. WWJ-AM-FM-TV, Detroit, 1966-79; owner, mgr. Twin Oaks Comms. Engring. now Twin Oaks Comms. Engring. P.C.), North Branch, Mich., 1972—. Charter pilot, flight and ground instr. G. B. DuPont Co., Almont Marlette Aviation Inc., 1977-82; expert legal witness, 1968—; corp. edn. dean's adv. coun. Colls. Bus. Adminstr., Sci., Engring. and Tech., Saginaw Valley State U., 1997—; curriculum adv. com. ITT Tech. Inst., Canton, Mich., 2002—; mem. Intern. Engring. Consortium, 2005-; cons. in field. Mem. editl. advisory panel: eWeek Mag., 2004; contbr. articles to profl. jours. Jury foreman, Lapeer County Circuit Ct, 1974; sr. divsn. judge Detroit Met. Sci. and Engring. Fair, 1975—, Mich. State Sci. and Engring. Fair, 2000—; spl. awards judge Intel Internat. Sci. and Engring. Fair, Detroit, 2000; search and rescue pilot, mission comdr., capt. Mich. wing CAP, 1961-81; cubmaster Boy Scouts Am., North Branch, 1983-85; hon. state chmn. bus. adv. coun. Rep. Congl. Com., 2002—. With USN, 1957—63. Recipient appreciation award CAP, 1980, North Branch Area Schs., 1985, Century award Boy Scouts Am., 1984, Chairman's award, Saginaw Valley Engrg. Coun., 1991, 2001, Intl. Scientist of Yr. award, IBC, Cambridge, 2002. Mem. AIAA, IEEE (life sr. mem., Comm. Soc., Circuits and Systems Soc., Computer Societychmn. N.E. Mich. sect. 1987-88, 1995-2006, bd. dirs. 1984—), NSPE, Am. Soc. for Engring. Edn. (profl. mem.), Internat. Assn. Radio, Telecom., Electromagnetics (master mem.), Am. Inst. Physics (assoc.), Mich. Soc. Profl. Engrs. (flint chpt.), Network and Sys. Profls. Assn., Saginaw Valley Engring. Coun. (chmn. 1990-91, 2000-01, sec.-treas. 1992-95, Outstanding Leadership award 1991, 2001), Engring. Soc. Detroit (profl.), Profl. Activities Coun. Engrs. (chmn. U.S. activities bd. 1985—), Network and Systems Profls. Assn., Nat. Pilots Assn. (sr. pilot citation, Safe Pilot award 1978), Aircraft Owners and Pilots Assn., Network and Systems Profls. Assn., North Br. C. of C. (charter), Tri-County Econs. Club, Am. Legion, (vice-commander North Br. club 2001-02), Lions (sec. North Br. club 1985-90, pres. 1990-91), Radio Club Am., Tri-County Econs. Club, Sigma Alpha Epsilon (Order of Minerva honoree), Assn. Computing Machinery (profl. mem.). Conservative. Methodist. Achievements include first to establish an FCC licensed amateur radio repeater for the state of Michigan, 1968. Avocations: computers, amateur radio, flying, photography. Office: Twin Oaks Comms Engring PC 2465 Johnson Mill Rd PO Box 340 North Branch MI 48461-0340 Office Phone: 810-688-2633. Personal E-mail: stepthe8@aol.com. Business E-Mail: j.stevenson@ieee.org.

STEVENSON, JOAN CATHARINE, anthropologist, educator; b. Richland, Wash., Jan. 22, 1951; d. Robert Louis and Viola Miller Stevenson; m. Phillip Mark Everson, July 31, 1982; children: Robert Ward Everson, John Harley Everson. BA, U. Wash., Seattle, 1973; MA, U. Wis., Milw., 1975, PhD, 1978. Prof., anthropology Western Wash. U., Bellingham, 1979—, with, expert witness human remains, 1979—2008. Contbr. articles to profl. jours. Fellow: Am. Assn. Anthrop. Genetics (v.p. & pres. 2002—04), Human Biology Assn. (book rev. jour. editor 1998—), Am. Assn. Phys. Anthropologists (assoc. jour. editor 2008—). Office: Dept Anthropology Western Wash Univ 516 High St Bellingham WA 98225-9083 Office Fax: 360-650-7668. Business E-Mail: joan.stevenson@wwu.edu.

STEVENSON, JOSIAH, IV, management consultant; b. Jamaica, NY, Oct. 4, 1935; s. Josiah and Ruth Lillian (Leech) S.; m. Jane Margaret Kupfer, Sept. 1, 1957; children: Josiah V., Todd Sander. AB, Dartmouth Coll., 1957; MBA, Amos Tuck Sch. Bus., 1958. Instr. U. Md.-Far East, 1959—61; account supr. Benton & Bowles, Inc., NYC, 1961—66; group product mgr., gen. mgr. Japan Chesebrough-Pond's Inc., Greenwich, Conn., 1967—77; dir. devel. Dartmouth Coll., 1977—84, Boston Symphony Orch., 1984—95; v.p. Curtis Inst. Music, Phila., 1995—2003; mng. ptnr. Dover Stevenson & Assocs., 1987—. Trustee, Opera North, v.p. With USAF, 1958—61. Mem. US C. of C., Assn. Fund Raising Profls. (Mass. chpt. bd. dirs., v.p. 1993-95, Greater Phila. chpt. bd. dirs., v.p. fin. 1996-2003), Dartmouth Club, Tokyo Lawn Tennis Club, Yale-Dartmouth Club (NYC), Badminton and Tennis Club (Boston), Pinchurst Country Club. Episcopalian. Home: 6 Squires Ln Pinehurst NC 28374-6866 Home Phone: 910-420-2596. Personal E-mail: jstevensoniv@nc.rr.com.

STEVENSON, JOYCE R.L., retired psychologist; d. Harry W. and Rosetta P. Lambertson; m. William J. Stevenson, Aug. 30, 1957 (dec. 2006); children: Cathy A. Hansell, Jeffrey L. BA in Law Justice, Glassboro State Coll., NJ, 1979, MA in Sch. Psychology, 1985. Cert. sch. psychologist NJ, 1992. Sr. probation officer Camden County Probation Dept., NJ, 1976—89; sch. psychologist Gloucester County Spl. Svc. Sch. Dist., Sewell, NJ, 1991—92, Edgewood Sch. HS, Sicklerville, NJ, 1992—94; chairperson and child study team sch. psychologist Vineland Bd. Edn., NJ, 1994—2003; ret., 2003. Hist. costume maker. Contbr. scientific papers. Jud. vol. Gloucester County Visionage. Mem.: MENSA, DAR (treas.), Colonial Dames Seventeenth Century, Swedish Colonial Soc. Avocations: genealogy, tai chi. Personal E-mail: joycerls@verizon.net.

STEVENSON, LAURA CAROLINE, writer, educator; b. Ann Arbor, Mich., Sept. 8, 1946; d. Charles Leslie and Louise Ellen (Destler) S.; m. Michael William O'Connell, Sept. 27, 1969 (div. July 1981); children: Katharine O'Connell, Margaret O'Connell; m. Franklin D. Reeve, Dec. 22, 1997. AB with highest honors, U. Mich., 1968; MPhil, Yale U., 1971, PhD, 1974. Lectr. history U. Calif., Santa Barbara, 1970-71; prof. humanities Bradford Coll., Haverhill, Mass., 1980-83, Marlboro (Vt.) Coll., 1986—. Author: Praise and Paradox, 1984, 2d edit., 2002, Happily After All, 1990, The Island and the Ring, 1991, All the King's Horses, 2001, A Castle in the Window, 2003. Recipient Grant-in-Aid, Am. Coun. Learned Socs., 1975; Andrew W. Mellon Faculty fellow Harvard U., 1982-83, Rsch. fellow NEH, 1996-97. Mem.: Windham County Farm Bur., Vt. Natural Resources Coun., Authors Guild, Royal Oak Found., Assn. Late-Deafened Adults, Beatrix Potter Soc., Phi Beta Kappa. Soc. Of Friends. Avocations: gardening, farming. Home: PO Box 14 Wilmington VT 05363-0014 Office: Marlboro Coll Dept Humanities Marlboro VT 05344 Home Phone: 802-464-3712; Office Phone: 802-258-9285. Business E-Mail: lsteve@marlboro.edu.

STEVENSON, LYNNE W. (LYNNE LESLIE WARNER STEVENSON), cardiologist, educator; b. Joplin, Mo., June 15, 1954; AB summa cum laude, Princeton U., 1975; MD, Stanford U., 1979. Cert. Internal Medicine, 1982, Cardiovascular Disease, 1985. Intern Stanford U. Hosp., Calif., 1979—80; resident UCLA Ctr. for Health Scis., 1980—82, fellow cardiology, 1982—84, attending staff physician, 1984—93; med. dir. Heart Transplantation Program UCLA Med. Ctr., 1983—93, dir. UCLA Heart Failure Program, 1983—88, dir. Ahmanson-UCLA Cardiomyopathy Ctr., 1988—93; physician Brigham and Women's Hosp., Boston, 1993—, clin. dir. Cardiomyopathy and Heart Failure Program, 1993—, supr. 12ACT (Advanced Cardiomyopathy Therapies) Nursing Unit, 1994—, cardiology rep. Heart Failure Divsn. Mgmt. Devel. Team, 1998—2002, cons., 2002—. Adj. instr. cardiology UCLA Sch. Medicine, 1984—85, adj. asst. prof., 1985—87, asst. prof. medicine in residence, 1987—90, asst. prof. medicine, 1990—91, assoc. prof., 1991—93, Harvard Med. Sch., Boston, 1993—94, prof., 1994—; mem. Review Com. Clin. Programs of Cardiac Transplantation Health Care Financing Adminstrn., 1994—. Guest editor Jour. Am. Coll. Cardiology, 1992—, Am. Heart Jour.; contbr. articles to med. jours. Recipient Eugene Braunwald Tchg. Award, 1998. Fellow: Am. Heart Assn., Am. Coll. Cardiology; mem.: US Transplant Cardiology Rsch. Database Group (exec. com. mem.), Am. Coll. Physicians, Am. Fedn. Clin. Rsch., Internat. Soc. Heart and Lung Transplantation. Office: Brigham and Women's Hosp Cardiovascular Divsn 75 Francis St, PBB-1 Boston MA 02115 Office Phone: 617-732-7141. Office Fax: 617-278-6931. E-mail: lstevenson@partners.org.

STEVENSON, MARSHALL FIELD, JR., history professor; m. Lynda Ward, Dec. 19, 1982; children: Kellye Lynae Stevenson-Crape, Marshall Field III, Lyndsay. Attended, Oakwood Coll. U., Huntsville, Ala., 1978; BA, U. Cin., Ohio., 1980; PhD, U. Mich., Ann Arbor, 1988. Asst. prof. Ohio State U., Columbus, 1988—97; dean Dillard U., New Orleans, 1999—, prof. history, 1999—. External on-site reviewer Southern Assn. Coll. Contbr. chapters to books. Vice-chair La. State Police Commn., Baton Rouge, 2001—08. Postdoc. fellowship, Carter G. Woodson Inst., U. Va., 1992—93. Mem.: ASALH, Am. Assn. Coll. and U., Pi Gamma Mu, Omicron Delta Kappa. Adventist. Avocations: physical culture, reading, Fashion. Personal E-mail: mstevenson@dillard.edu.

STEVENSON, MICHAEL KEITH, elementary school educator; b. Columbus, Jan. 3, 1963; s. John Barnt and Elaine Elizabeth Stevenson; m. Cynthia Ann Paulson, Nov. 10, 1990; children: Dustin, Devin, Dylan. BS in Edn., U. Wis., LaCrosse, 1986; MS in Kinesiology, U. Nev., Las Vegas, 1994. Phys. edn. tchr. Clark County Pub. Schs., Las Vegas, 1986—95, 1998—, Orange County Pub. Schs., Orlando, Fla., 1995—98. Youth coach City of Henderson Parks and Recreation, Nev., 2000—. Recipient Disting. Educator award, Clark County Sch. Dist., 2001; named Coach of Yr., City of Henderson Parks and Recreation, 2004, Nat. Coach of Yr., Nat. Youth Sports Coaches Assn., 2005. Avocations: sports, woodworking.

STEVENSON, ROBERT EDWIN, microbiologist, consultant; b. Columbus, Ohio, Dec. 2, 1926; s. Arthur Edwin and Mary Lucille (Beman) Stevenson. BS, Ohio State U., 1947, MS, 1950, PhD, 1954. Cert. Am. Bd. Microbiology. Virologist USPHS, Cin., 1954-58; head cell culture sect., Tissue Bank U.S. Naval Med. Sch., Bethesda, Md., 1958-60; head cell culture and tissue material sect. Nat. Cancer Inst., Bethesda, 1960-63, chief viral carcinogenesis br., 1963-67; mgr. biolog. scis., corp. devel. dept. Union Carbide Corp., Tarrytown, NY, 1967-72; v.p., gen. mgr., Frederick (Md.) div. Litton Bionetics, 1972-80; dir. Am. Type Culture Collection, Rockville, Md., 1980-93; dir. emeritus, 1993. Dir. Large Scale Biology, Inc., Rockville, 1984-90; cons. Am. Assn. Tissue Banks, 1999—; chmn. biotech. adv. com. Dept. Commerce, Washington, 1985-93; lectr. Yale U. Coll. Med., 2006. With USNR, 1944—45. Recipient Hyatt award, AATB, 2004. Mem. Tissue Culture Assn. (pres. 1988-90), World Fedn. Culture Collections, U.S. Fedn. Culture Collections (pres. 1988-90), Am. Soc. Micrbiology, Cosmos Club (Washington). Avocations: painting, cross country skiing. Home: 27 Evart's Ln Madison CT 06443-2564 Office Phone: 703-827-9582. Personal E-mail: adobebob@aol.com.

STEVENSON, ROBERT MURRELL, music educator; b. Melrose, N.Mex., July 3, 1916; s. Robert Emory and Ada (Ross) S. AB, U. Tex., El Paso, 1936; grad., Juilliard Grad. Sch. Music, 1938; MusM, Yale, 1939; PhD, U. Rochester, 1942; STB cum laude, Harvard U., 1943; BLitt, Oxford U., Eng.; Th.M., Princeton Theol. Sem.; DMus honoris causa, Cath. U. Am., 1991; LHD honoris causa, Ill. Wesleyan U., 1992; LittD honoris causa, Universidade Nova de Lisboa, 1993. Instr. music U. Tex., 1941-43, 46; faculty Westminster Choir Coll., Princeton, NJ, 1946-49; faculty rsch. lectr. UCLA, 1981, mem. faculty to prof. music, 1949—. Vis. asst. prof. Columbia, 1955-56; vis. prof. Ind. U., Bloomington, 1959-60, U. Chile, 1965-66, Northwestern U., Chgo., 1976, U. Granada, 1992; adj. prof. Cath. U. Am., 1991—; cons. UNESCO, 1977; Louis Charles Elson lectr. Libr. of Congress, Washington, 1969; inaugural prof. musicology Nat. U. Mex., 1996; spkr. Dumbarton Oaks Pre-Columbian Music Workshop, 1998, Internat. Colonial Music Congress, Lima, Peru, 2000; lectr. Tureck Bach Rsch. Found., Oxford U., 2000; hon. prof. Conservatorio Nacional, Peru, 2000, Real Conservatorio Superior, Madrid, 1991-2003; hon. lectr. Royal Conservatory, Madrid, 2004; keynote spkr. Morales Colloquium, Oxford U., 2004. Author: Music in Mexico, 1952, Patterns of Protestant Church Music, 1953, La musica en la catedral de Sevilla, 1954, 85, Music Before the Classic Era, 1955, Shakespeare's Religious Frontier, 1958, The Music of Peru, 1959, Juan Bermudo, 1960, Spanish Music in the Age of Columbus, 1960, Spanish Cathedral Music in the Golden Age, 1961, La musica colonial en Colombia, 1964, Protestant Church Music in America, 1966, Music in Aztec and Inca Territory, 1968, Renaissance and Baroque Musical Sources in the Americas, 1970, Music in El Paso, 1970, Philosophies of American Music History, 1970, Written Sources for Indian Music Until 1882, 1972, Christmas Music From Baroque Mexico, 1974, Foundations of New World Opera, 1973, Seventeenth Century Villancicos, 1974, Latin American Colonial Music Anthology, 1975, Vilancicos Portugueses, 1976, Josquin in the Music of Spain and Portugal, 1977, American Musical Scholarship, Parker to Thayer, 1978, Liszt at Madrid and Lisbon, 1980, Wagner's Latin American Outreach, 1983, Spanish Musical Impact Beyond the Pyrenees, 1250-1500, 1985, La Música en las catedrales españolas del Siglo de Oro, 1993; contbg. editor: Handbook Latin Am. Studies, 1976—; editor Inter-Am. Music Rev., 1978—; contbr. to New Grove Dictionary of Music and Musicians, 17 other internat. encys. Decorated Army Commendation ribbon, 1946; fellow Folger Shakespeare Library, 1950, Ford Found., 1953-54, Gulbenkian Found., 1966, 81, Guggenheim Found., 1962, NEH, 1974, Comité Conjunto Hispano-Norteamericano (Madrid), 1989; recipient Fulbright rsch. awards, 1958-59, 64, 70-71, 88-89, Carnegie Found. tchg. award, 1955-56, Gabriela Mistral award OAS, 1985, Heitor Villa Lobos Jury award OAS, 1988, OAS medal, 1986, Cert. Merit Mexican Consulate San Bernardino, Calif., 1987, Silver medal Spanish Ministry Culture, 1989, Gold medal Real Conservatorio Superior, 1994, 97, 1st Lifetime Achievement award Sonneck Soc., 1999, All-Calif. Constantine Penunzio award, 2004. Mem. Real Academia de Bellas Artes (hon.), Hispanic Soc. Am., Am. Liszt Soc. (cons. editor), Heterofonia (cons. editor), Brazilian Musicol. Soc. (hon.), Portuguese Musicol. Soc. (hon.), Argentinian Musicol. Soc. (hon.), Venezuelan Musicol. Soc. (hon.), Am. Musicol. Soc. (hon.), Orden Andrés Bello, Primera Clase, Venezuela, 1992. Avocation: playing piano. Office: UCLA Dept Music 405 Hilgard Ave Los Angeles CA 90095-9000 Business E-Mail: info@ericdilauro.com.

STEVENSON, WILLIAM ALEXANDER, retired justice of Supreme Court of Canada; b. Edmonton, Alta., Can., May 7, 1934; s. Alexander Lindsay and Eileen Harriet (Burns) S.; m. Patricia Ann Stevenson; children: Catherine, Kevin, Vivian, James. BA, U. Alta., Edmonton, 1956, LLB, 1957; LLD (hon.), U. Alta., 1992. Called to Alta. bar, 1958. Ptnr. Hurlburt Reynolds Stevenson & Agrios, Edmonton, 1957-68; prof. U. Alta., 1968-70; ptnr. Reynolds Stevenson & Agrios, Edmonton, 1970-75; judge Dist. Ct. Alta., Edmonton, 1975-79; justice Ct. of Queens Bench Alta., Edmonton, 1979-80, Ct. of Appeal Alta., Edmonton, 1980-90, Supreme Ct. Can., Ottawa, Ont., 1990-92. Officer Order of Can., 1997. Co-author: Civil Procedure Guide, 1995. Mem. Can. Bar Assn., Can. Inst. for Adminstrn. Justice (pres. 1983-85, hon. dir.), Nat. Jud. Inst. (hon. dir.), Legal Archives Soc. Alta (hon. dir.). Home: 7 Laurier Pl Edmonton AB Canada T5R 5P4 E-mail: wmstevenson@shaw.ca.

STEVENSON, ZOLLIE JULIUS, JR., former school system and government agency administrator, consultant; b. Greensboro, NC, Apr. 6, 1953; s. Zollie and Cletus (Jackson) S. BA in Psychology, U. NC, Asheville, 1975; MS in Edn. and Counseling, NC A&T State U., 1977; PhD in Ednl. Psychology, U. NC, 1984. Asst. to dean of students U. NC, Asheville, 1976-78, lectr. in psychology, 1977-78; regional coord. of rsch. and testing NC Dept. Pub. Instrn., Raleigh, 1984-86; asst. prof. East Carolina Univ., Camp LeJeune, NC, 1984-85; sr. rsch. assoc. DC Pub. Schs., Washington, 1986-89, dir. rsch. and evaluation br., 1989-92, exec. asst. for adminstrn., chief of staff Ctr. Systemic Ednl. Change, 1994; evaluation specialist divsn. adolescent and sch. health Ctrs. for Disease Control and Prevention, Atlanta, 1993-94; dir. rsch., assessment, and evaluation Balt. City Pub. Schs.; co-state team leader Title I US Dept. Edn.; group leader, standards, assessment and accountability Student Achievement and Sch. Accountability Programs, US Dept. Edn., dep. dir., acting dir., dir., 2008—; dep. dir. ops. NSF Urban Systemic Initiative grant. Adj. asst. prof. George Washington U., 1987-88, U. NC, Asheville, East Carolina U., U. Md., Bowie State U.; cons. McKenzie Group, Washington, 1988; mem. adv. bd. Jour. Negro Edn., Washington, 1991, DC AIDS Edn. Task Force, 1989, Ctr. Ednl. Change, Washington, 1992. Contbr. articles to profl. jours. Mem. Am. Ednl. Rsch. Assn., Assn. for Supervision and Curriculum and Devel., Phi Delta Kappa, Alpha Phi Alpha, Psi Chi. Episcopalian. Office: Office of Elementary and Secondary Edn 400 Maryland Ave SW Washington DC 20202

STEVER, HORTON GUYFORD, aerospace scientist, engineer, educator, consultant; b. Corning, NY, Oct. 24, 1916; s. Ralph Raymond and Alma (Matt) Stever; m. Louise Risley Floyd, June 29, 1946; children: Horton Guyford, Sarah, Margarette, Roy. AB, Colgate U., 1938, ScD (hon.), 1958; PhD, Calif. Inst. Tech., 1941; LLD, U. Pitts., 1966, Lehigh U., 1967, Allegheny Coll., 1968, Ill. Inst. Tech., 1975; DSc, Northwestern U., 1966, Waynesburg Coll., 1967, U. Mo., 1975, Clark U., 1976, Bates Coll., 1977; DH, Seton Hill Coll., 1968; D.Engring., Washington and Jefferson Coll., 1969, Widener Coll., Poly. Inst. N.Y., 1972, Villanova U., 1973, U. Notre Dame, 1974; DPS, George Washington U., 1981. Staff radiation lab. MIT, Cambridge, Mass., 1941—42, asst. prof., 1946—51, assoc. prof. aero. engring., 1951—56, prof. aero. and astro., 1956—65, head depts. mech. engring., naval architecture, marine engring., 1961—65, assoc. dean engring., 1956—59, exec. officer guided missiles program, 1946—48; chief scientist USAF, 1955—56; pres. Carnegie-Mellon U., Pitts., 1965—72; dir. NSF, Washington, 1972—76; sci. adviser, chmn. Fed. Council Sci. and Tech., 1973—76; dir. Office Sci. and Tech. Policy, sci. and tech. adviser to Pres., 1976—77, sci. cons., corp. trustee, 1977—. Secretariat guided missiles com. Joint Chiefs of Staff, 1945; sci. liaison officer London Mission, OSRD, 1942—45; guided missiles tech. evaluation group Rsch. and Devel. Bd., 1946—48; sci. adv. bd. to chief of staff USAF, 1947—69, chmn., 1962—69; steering com. tech. adv panel on aeros. Dept. Def., 1956—62; chmn. spl. com. space tech. NASA, chmn. rsch. adv. com. missile and spacecraft aerodynamics, 1959—65; mem. Nat. Sci. Bd., 1970—72, ex-officio, chmn. exec. com., 1972—75; mem. Def. Sci. Bd., 1962—68; adv. panel U.S. Ho. Reps. Com. Sci. and Astronautics, 1959—72; mem. Pres.'s Commn. on Patent System, 1965—67; chmn. U.S.-USSR Joint Commn. Sci. and Tech. Cooperation, 1973—77, Fed. Council Arts and Humanities, 1972—76; Pres. com. Nat. Sci. medal, 1973—77. Author: Flight, 1965, In War and Peace: My Life in Sci and Tech, 2002; contbr. articles to profl. jours. Past trustee Colgate U., Shady Side Acad., Sarah Mellon Scaife Found., Buckingham Sch; trustee Univ. Rsch Assn., 1977—, pres., 1982—85; trustee Woods Hole Oceanographic Inst., 1980—, Sci. Svc., 1982—, Univ. Corp. for Atmospheric Rsch., 1980—83; bd. dirs. Saudi Arabia Nat. Ctr. for Sci. and Tech., 1978—81; bd. govs. U.S. Israel Binat. Sci. Found., 1972—76, chmn., 1972—73; mem. Carnegie Commn. on Sci., Tech. and Govt., 1988—93. Recipient Pres.'s Cert. of Merit, 1948, Exceptional Civilian Svc. award, USAF, 1956, Scott Gold medal, Am. Ordinance Assn., 1960, Disting. Pub. Svc. medal, award, Dept. Def., 1969, NASA, 1988, Nat. Medal of Sci., 1991. Fellow: AAAS, AIAA (hon.; pres. 1960—62), Am. Phys. Soc., Royal Soc. Arts, Am. Philos. Soc., Am. Acad. Arts and Scis., Royal Aero. Soc.; mem.: NAE (chmn. aero. and space engring. bd. 1967—69, fgn. sec. 1984—88), NAS (chmn. assembly engring. 1979—83, chmn. policy divsn. 1995—97), Royal Acad. of Engring. of Great Britain (fgn. mem.), Acad. Engring. of Japan (fgn. mem.), Cosmos Club, Phi Beta Kappa, Tau Beta Pi, Sigma Gamma Tau, Sigma Xi. Episcopalian.

STEVES, GALE C., marketing professional, writer, editor-in-chief, publishing executive; b. Mineola, NY, Dec. 20, 1942; d. William Harry and Ruth (May) Steves; m. David B. Stocker, Mar. 31, 1972 (div. Apr. 1978); m. Philip L. Perrone, Aug. 14, 1983. BS, Cornell U., 1964; MA, NYU, 1966. Editl. asst. Ladies Home Jour., NYC, 1966-69; seafood consumer specialist U.S. Dept. Commerce, NYC, 1969-73; editor food Homelife mag., NYC, 1973-74; editor food and equipment Co-Ed mag., NYC, 1974-76, Am. Home mag., NYC, 1976-78; editor kitchen design and equipment Woman's Day mag., NYC, 1979-83; editor-in-chief Woman's Day Spls., NYC, 1983-91; v.p., editor-in-chief Home Mag. Group, NYC, 1991—2001; pres. Open House Prodns., NYC, 2001—03, 2005—; v.p., editl. dir., pub. AMI Mini Mags. Group, NYC, 2003—05. Bd. dirs. Les Dames d'Escoffier, Coun. Sr. Ctrs. and Svcs. N.Y.C., Catskill Ctr. Cons. and Econ. Devel. Author: Game Cookery, 1974, The International Cook, 1980, Creative Microwave Cooking, 1981; author: (with Lee M. Elman) Country Weekend Cooking, Home Magazine's Best Little Houses, 1998; mem. editl. bd. Sr. Summary, N.Y.C., 1982—88. Co-chmn. Alder Lake Restoration Soc.; chmn. alumni adv. bd. Coll. Human Ecology, Cornell U., 1993—97, mem. univ. coun., 1996—2000, mem. pres.'s coun. Cornell Women; mem. adv. bd. Cornell Plantations, 1998—2005; bd. mem. Catskill Ctr. Conservation and Econ. Devel. Mem.: Garden Writers Assn. Am., Am. Soc. Mag. Editors, Internat. Furnishings and Design Assn., Acad. Women Achievers YWCA N.Y.C. Address: 185 West End Ave Ste 26C New York NY 10023-5551

STEVES KEISER, SUSAN, bank executive; 2 children. English, journalism tchr., Tex.; writer Tex. Commerce; exec. v.p., global securities & trust services LaSalle Bank Corp. (now Bank of America), Chgo. Co-chair Ill. Arts Alliance Found.; bd. mgrs. YMCA Met. Chgo.; bd. trustees Chgo. Botanic Garden; com. mem. United Way Tocqueville Soc. Named one of 25 Women to Watch, US Banker, 2007. Office: LaSalle Bank Corp 135 S LaSalle St Chicago IL 60603 Office Phone: 312-904-2000.

STEW, (MARK STEWART), musician; b. Calif., 1961; Founder The Negro Problem, 1995; co-founder STEW afro-baroque cabaret, 2000. Musician: (albums) Guest Host, 2000 (Album of Yr., Entertainment Weekly), The Naked Dutch Painter, 2002 (Album of Yr., Entertainment Weekly), Something Deeper Than These Changes, 2003, (with The Negro Problem) Post Minstrel Syndrome, 1997, Joys and Concerns, 1999, Welcome Black, 2002; author, co-composer (plays) Passing Strange, 2004, (Broadway plays), 2008 (NY Drama Critics' Cir. Best Musical, 2008, Drama Desk awards for Outstanding Musical, Outstanding Music, and Outstanding Lyrics, 2008, Obie awards for Best New Theater Piece and Best Ensemble, 2008, Tony award for Best Book of a Musical, 2008). Office: c/o William Craver PARADIGM 360 Park Ave S 16th Fl New York NY 10010 E-mail: tnp@negroproblem.com, stewoffice@gmail.com.

STEWARD, DAVID L., technology company executive; b. Clinton, Mo. m. Thelma Steward; children: David, Kimberly. BS, Ctrl. Mo. State U., 1973. Various sales and mktg. positions Wagner Elec., Mo. Pacific Railroad, Fed. Express; founder, chmn. World Wide Tech., Maryland Heights, Mo., 1990—. Bd. dir. St. Louis Cmty. Coll. Found., Civic Progress of St. Louis, St. Louis Regional Chamber and Growth Assn., Mo. Tech. Corp., First Banks, Inc., St. Louis Sci. Ctr., United Way of Greater St. Louis Bd., Greater St. Louis Area Coun. of Boy Scouts of Am., Harris-Stowe State Coll. African-Am. Bus. Leadership Coun., RCGA, Barnes-Jewish Hosp.; chaired (with wife) United Way's 2000 African-American Leadership Giving Initiative. Named 14th Best Am. Entrepreneur, Success Mag., 1998, Minority Small Bus. Person of Yr., Small Bus. Adminstrn., 1997—98, Entrepreneur of Yr. in Tech., Ernst & Young, 1998, #1 African-Am.-Owned Bus. in US, Black Enterprise Mag., 2000; named to Small Bus. Adminstrn. Hall of Fame, 2001, Power 150, Ebony mag., 2008. Office: World Wide Technology 60 Weldon Pkwy Maryland Heights MO 63043-3237

STEWARD, JAMES CHRISTEN, museum director, educator; BA, U. Va., 1981; PhD, Oxford U., Eng., 1992. Chief curator U. Calif., Berkeley, 1992—98; dir. U. Mich. Mus. Art, Ann Arbor, 1998—. Cons., Ann Arbor, 1988—2005. Author: (book and exhbn. catalogue) The New Child: British Art and the Origins of Modern Childhood, 1995, The Mask of Venice, 1996, When Time Began to Rant and Rage: Figurative Art from 20th-Century Ireland, 1998, The Photographs of Ernestine Ruben (Photography Book of Yr., Ind. Pubs. Assn., 2001), The Collections of the Romanovs: European Art from the State Hermitage Museum, St. Petersburg, 2003, Betye Saar: Extending the Frozen Moment, 2005. Exhbn. grantee, Nat. Endowment for the Arts, project grantee, Samuel H. Kress Found., Brit. Coun., Overseas Student scholar, Oxford U., 1988—91. Mem.: Am. Assn. Museums, Coll. Art Assn., Mich. Museums Assn. (v.p. 2001—05), Assn. Art Mus. Dirs., The Walpole Soc., Rotary. Democrat. Avocations: equestrian sports, book collecting, antiques. Office: U Mich Mus Art 525 S State St Ann Arbor MI 48109 Office Fax: 734-764-3731. E-mail: jsteward@umich.edu.

STEWARD, LARRY G., agricultural studies educator, consultant; b. Columbus, Ohio, July 12, 1943; s. Harold E. and Ruth C. Steward; m. DeAnna M. Mason, July 10, 1971; children: Lin A., Dennis E., Kristina S. Humiston, Michael G. BS in Agr., Ohio State U., Columbus, 1966; MS in Agr., Va. Poly. Inst. & State U., Blacksburg, 1995. Dir. of grounds U. Va., Charlottesville, 1970—87; adj. instr. Va. Cmty. Colls., Charlottesville, Chesapeake, Goochland, 1975—99; owner Land Stewards of N.Am., Troy, Va., 1986—2001; assoc. prof., horticulture techs. Ohio State U., Wooster, Ohio, 1999—. Cons. Landstewards, Wooster, Ohio, 1999—, US Forest Svc., 2008. Contbr. articles to profl. jours.; author: (reference CD) Eastern United States Fire Performance Plant Selector. Deacon 1st Presbyn. Ch., Charlottesville, Va., 1985—88, St. Peter's United Christian Ch., Apple Creek, Ohio, 2005—08, elder, 2009—; red cross vol. Red Cross, Wooster, Ohio, 2006—08. Recipient Honorarium Tree Planting award, U. Va., 2003. Mem.: Internat. Soc. Arboriculture, Ohio Landscape and Nursery Assn. (assoc.), Profl. Landscape Assn. (life; dir. 1993—95). Protestant. Avocations: camping, bicycling, model trains. Home: 685 Robinson Rd Wooster OH 44691 Office: Ohio State Univ Agr Tech Inst 1328 Dover Rd Wooster OH 44691 Office Phone: 330-287-1265. Office Fax: 330-287-1333. Business E-Mail: steward.31@osu.edu, landsteward@sssnet.com.

STEWART, ALBERT ELISHA, safety engineer, engineering executive; b. Urbana, Mo., Dec. 20, 1927; s. Albert E. and Maurine (Lighter) S.; m. Elizabeth O. Tice, May 31, 1958 (div.); children: Sheryl E., Mical A. BA, U. Kans., 1949; MS, U. Mo., 1958, MBA, 1970; PhD, Western States U., 1984. Cert. safety engr., cert. indsl. hygenist. Sales engr. Kaiser Aluminum and Chem. Co., Toledo, 1949-56; tchr. Kansas City (Mo.) Pub. Schs., 1959-65; indsl. hygienist Bendix Corp., Kansas City, 1960-65; safety adminstr. Gulf R&D, Merriam, Kans., 1968-71; sr. indsl. hygienist USDOL-OSHA, Kansas City, 1971-77; pres. Stewart Indsl. Hygiene, Kansas City, 1977—. Adj. prof. Cen. Mo. State U. Mem. Boy Scouts Am. With U.S. Army, 1950-53. Fellow AIHA; mem. Am. Indsl. Hygiene Assn., Am. Chem. Soc., Am. Acad. Indsl. Hygiene, Am. Soc. Safety Engrs., Am. Welding Soc., Nat. Mgmt. Assn., Nat. Sci. Tchrs. Assn., Adminstrv. Govt. Soc., DAV, ARC, Alpha Chi Sigma. Episcopalian. Avocations: fishing, golf, travel.

STEWART, ALEC THOMPSON, physicist, educator; b. Windthorst, Sask., Can., June 18, 1925; s. Arthur and Nelly Blye (Thompson) Stewart; m. Alta Aileen Kennedy, Aug. 4, 1960 (dec. Sept. 2000); children: A. James Kennedy, Hugh D., Duncan R.; m. Annabel C. Wenzel, Apr. 21, 2004. BSc, Dalhousie U., Halifax, NS, Can., 1946, MSc, 1949; PhD, Cambridge U., Eng., 1952; LLD, Dalhousie U., Halifax, NS, Can., 1986. Research officer Atomic Energy Can., Chalk River, Ont., Canada, 1952-57; assoc. prof. Dalhousie U., Halifax, 1957-60; assoc. prof. to prof. U. N.C., Chapel Hill, 1960-68; head physics Queen's U., Kingston, Ont., 1968-74, prof. physics, 1968-90, prof. physics emeritus, 1990—. Vis. prof. various univs., Can., Europe, Japan, China, Hong Kong; founder, chmn. internat. adv. com. series positron confs. Author: 2 books; contbr. over 100 articles to profl. jours. Dir. Can. Olympic Tng. Regatta Kingston, 1976—82, Marine Mus. Great Lakes, Kingston, 1988—94. Decorated officer Order of Can., 2001; recipient CAP medal for achievement in physics, 1992, Canada 125 medal, 1992, Queen Elizabeth II Golden Jubilee medal 2002. Fellow Am. Phys. Soc., Royal Soc. Can. (pres. Acad. Sci. 1984-87), Japan Soc. for Promotion Sci.; mem. Can. Assn. Physicists (pres., other offices 1970-74). Achievements include research in solid state physics, behavior of phonons, electrons, positrons and postronium in crystals and liquids, positron annihilation, nuclear reactor safety, possible hazards of power frequency electric and magnetic fields, emergency measures following a nuclear accident, state of nuclear technology in Canada. Office: Queens U Dept Physics Kingston ON Canada K7L 3N6

STEWART, ANNE MATSUMOTO, language educator; married. MA, Cornell U., Ithaca, NY, 1986. Japanese lectr. U. Hawaii, Honolulu, 1980—84, Cornell U., 1984—86, Waseda U., Tokyo, 1992—97; guest lectr., REX program Tokyo U. Fgn. Studies, 1990—2004; japanese instr. Bellevue Coll., Wash., 2008—. Author: (book) Power Japanese: All about Katakana, Kodansha's Katakana Workbook, Kodansha's Hiragana Workbook; contbr. articles. Mem.: Am. Coun. Tchg. Fgn. Langs., Nat. Coun. Japanese Lang. Tchrs., Wash. Assn. Tchrs. Japanese, Assn. Tchrs. Japanese. Office: Bellevue Coll 3000 Landerholm Cir SE Bellevue WA 98007-6484

STEWART, ANNE WILLIAMS, historian, writer, researcher; b. New Haven, Oct. 13, 1933; d. Howard Dudley and Minnie Victoria (Rattelsdorfer) Williams; m. Kenneth Neal Stewart (div. Oct. 1985); children: Elizabeth Anne Stewart-Marshall, Kenneth Neal Jr., David Bradley (dec.). BA, Allegheny Coll., Meadville, Pa., 1955. Coord. hist. sites survey Crawford County Planning, Meadville, 1976-80; chmn. hist. sites survey Meadville Redevel. Authority, 1980-83; program coord. Crawford County Hist. Soc., Meadville, 1981-88; bd. dirs. Meadville Bicentennial, 1986-88; dir. Academy Theater restoration Meadville Redevel. Authority, 1988-90; gen. reporter Meadville Tribune, 1990-92; grantsman Meadville Redevel. Authority, 1991—2000; adminstr. The Col. Inc., Drake Well Mus., Titusville, Pa., 1992-95. Historian, advisor Meadville Main St., 1986—90; historian Meadville Comprehensive Plan, 1992—93. Author: John A. Mather: Legacy of Pennsylvania's Oil Region Photographer, 1995, A Concise History of Meadville, 1995, 4th edit., 2002; author: (with Jonathan Miller Design) Meadville: Heart of the French Creek Valley, 1997; author: (with William B. Moore) Images of America, Meadville, 2001; editor: A Guide to City and County, 1972, Meadville: Yesterday and Today, 1976, Gentle Giants: Stories of Ballooning, 1992, George Washington's French Creek Trip, 1999, (newsletters) The Oilfield Barker, 1993—96, Market Square Messenger, 1996—99, Crawford County History, 2001—09; contbr. articles to mags.; editor: John Brown: From the Record, 1999, Erie: Jour. of Erie Studies, 2002; author (with Steven Utz): Meadville Architectural Heritage, 2005. Planning commr. Crawford County, Meadville, 1971—95, City of Meadville, 2000—03; bd. dirs. Meadville Area Meml., 1983—95; chmn. bd. dirs. Health Svcs. Inc. Crawford County, 1976—81; coord. Meadville Area Coalition; chair The Founders Forum, 1997—99. Mem.: Pa. Planning Assn. (bd. dirs. 1974—80), Crawford County Hist. Soc. (bd. dirs. 2003—09), Woman's Lit. Club (lectr.). Avocations: travel, research, textile crafts. Office: 443 Byllesby Ave Meadville PA 16335-1411 Business E-Mail: byllesby@zoominternet.net, cchresearch@zoominternet.net.

STEWART, ANNETTE, retired judge; b. Paris, Tex., Jan. 1, 1928; d. Ray Bryan and Mary Christene (Plumer) Stewart. BA, U. Tex., Austin, 1949; MEd, U. Tex., 1952; LLB summa cum laude, So. Meth. U., 1966. Bar: Tex. 1966. Assoc. Parnass, McGuire & Handy, 1966-67; ct. reporter Ct. Domestic Rels., Dallas, 1957-66, 67-74, judge, 1975-77, 301st Dist. Ct., Dallas, 1977-83, 305th Dist. Ct., 1985-86, Ct. Appeals, Dallas, 1983-84, 86-92, sr. judge, 1993—2008. Fellow Tex. Bar Found.; mem. State Bar Tex., Tex. Bar Found., Dallas Bar Assn., P.E.O., Phi Beta Kappa. Democrat. Presbyterian.

STEWART, ARDEN RUTH, retired automotive executive; d. Oliver Shaw and Helen (Neitzel) Stewart; children: Mark, Todd. BA, Baldwin Wallace Coll., 1952. Trainee GM, Cleve., 1952—57; tchr. Elyria City Bd. Edn., Ohio, 1967—85; pres., CEO AAR, Inc., Cleve., 1984—2005. Pres. Elyria Schs. PTA, 1967; treas. Homeowners Assn., North Ridgeville, Ohio, 1988-89; mem. adv. com. bus. and tech. Cuyahoga CC Recipient Weatherhead 100 award Case Western Res. U., 1990, 91, 92, 93, 94, 95. Mem.: Navy League US, PGA Nat. Mem. Club. Republican. Episcopalian. Avocations: music, scuba diving, dance, piano, computers. Home: 32889 Brownstone Ln PO Box 39359 North Ridgeville OH 44039-0359 also: 37 Princewood Ln PO Box 33599 Palm Beach Gardens FL 33420-3599 Personal E-mail: arden9201@aol.com.

STEWART, BILL, college football coach; b. New Martinsville, W.Va., 1952; m. Karen Stewart; 1 child, Blaine. BE, Fairmont State U., 1975; M in Health and Phys. Edn., W.Va. U., 1977. Asst. coach Sistersville HS, 1975, Salem Coll., 1977—78, NC U., 1979, 1985—87, Marshall U.,

1980, William & Mary Coll., 1981—83, USN Acad., 1984, Ariz. State U., 1988—89, USAF Acad., 1990—93; head coach Va. Mil. Inst. Keydets, 1994—96; offensive line coach Montreal Alouettes (Can. Football League), 1998; offensive coord. Winnipeg Blue Bombers (Can. Football League), 1999; quarterbacks and asst. coach W.Va. U. Mountaineers, 2000—07, interim head coach, 2007, head coach, 2008—. Office: c/o WVa U Mountaineers Intercollegiate Athletics PO Box 0877 Morgantown WV 26507 Office Phone: 304-293-4194.*

STEWART, CARL E., federal judge; b. Shreveport, La., 1950; BA magna cum laude, Dillard U., 1971; JD, Loyola U., New Orleans, 1974. Atty. Piper & Brown, Shreveport, La., 1977—78; staff atty. La. Atty. Gen. Office, Shreveport, 1978—79; asst. US atty. Office US Atty. (we. dist.) La., Shreveport, 1979—83; prin. Stewart & Dixon, Shreveport, 1983—85; spl. asst. dist. atty., asst. prosecutor City of Shreveport, 1983—85; judge La. Dist. Ct., 1985—91, La. Ct. Appeals (2d cir.), 1991—94, US Ct. Appeals (5th cir.), 1994—. Bd. trustees Cmty. Found. Shreveport-Bossier, Shreveport, La., 1994—2004, Am. Inns. Ct. Found.; chmn. nat. search com. Boy Scouts Am. Capt. JAGC other, 1974—77, Ft. Sam Houston, Tex. Recipient Am. Silver Buffalo awrd, Boy Scouts Am., 2002. Mem.: La. State Bar Assn. (bench/bar liaison com.), La. Conf. Ct. Appeal Judges, Black Lawyers Assn. Shreveport-Bossier, Am. Inns of Ct. (Harry Booth/Henry Politz chpt. Shreveport), Nat. Bar Assn., Omega Psi Phi (Rho Omega chpt.). Office: US Ct Appeals 5th Cir 300 Fannin St Ste 2299 Shreveport LA 71101-3124 Home Phone: 318-636-4829; Office Phone: 318-676-3765.*

STEWART, CHARLES HAINES, political science educator; b. Winder, Ga., Mar. 31, 1958; s. Charlie Haines Stewart and Joan (Chastain) VanderBurg; m. Kathryn M. Hess, Sept. 10, 1983. BA, Emory U., 1979; AM, Stanford U., 1982, PhD, 1985. Asst. prof. MIT, Cambridge, Mass., 1985-89, assoc. prof. dept. polit. sci., 1989—; Cecil and Ida Green Career Devel. assoc. prof., nat. fellow Hoover Inst., Stanford, Calif., 1989-90. Author: Budget Reform Politics, 1989; columnist Toray World Confidential Report, Tokyo, 1988—; contbr. articles to profl. jours. Mem., sec. Commn. on the Status and Role of Women in the United Meth. Ch., Evanston, Ill., 1989-91. Mem. Am. Polit. Sci. Assn., Am. Econs. Assn., Midwest Polit. Sci. Assn., So. Polit. Sci. Assn. Democrat. Avocations: wine, baseball, travel. Office: MIT Dept Polit Sci Cambridge MA 02139

STEWART, CHARLES LESLIE, lawyer; b. Fayetteville, Ark., Aug. 12, 1919; s. Charles Leslie and Ruth (Want) Stewart; m. Edalee Esther Gastrock, Aug. 30, 1941; children: William Paul, Thomas Alan, Katherine Jean, Robert Edward. AB, U. Ill., 1940; MA, La. State U., 1941; student, George Washington U. Law Sch., 1944-45; JD, U. Chgo., 1947. Bar: Ill., 2005, U.S. Supreme Ct. 1954. Economist Dept. Agr., Tenant Purchase Divsn., 1941—42; adminstrv. asst. OPA, Food Rationing Divsn., 1942-43, Bd. Econ. Warfare, Blockade and Supply Br., 1943; exec. dir. Chgo. divsn. ACLU, 1946—47; assoc. Mayer, Brown, LLP, Chgo., 1947-55, ptnr., 1956-67, 70-71, resident ptnr. charge European office, Paris, 1967-70; v.p., gen. counsel Hart Schaffner & Marx, Chgo., 1971-73, v.p., sec., gen. counsel, 1974-83, Hartmarx Corp., Chgo., 1983-84, v.p., sec., sr. counsel, 1984, of counsel legal dept., 1985-89; arbitrator Mandatory Arbitration Program Cir. Ct., Cook County, Ill., 1990—2005. Mem. Am. Law Inst., 1983-90. Mem. Glencoe (Ill.) Bd. Edn., 1965-66; mem. planning com. Corp. Counsel Inst., Northwestern U. Sch. Law and Ill. Inst. Continuing Legal Edn., 1978-84, vice-chmn., 1983, chmn., 1984; mem. Glencoe Union Ch. Served with Rsch. and Analysis Br., OSS, AUS, 1943-45., sec. projects com., 1944-45. Mem. ABA, Ill. State Bar Assn., Chgo. Bar Assn. (com. devel. of law 1977-91, vice chmn. 1984-85, chmn. 1985-86, corp. law com. 1981-91, corp. law depts. com. 1981-83, sr. lawyers com. 1987-92), Am. Soc. Corp. Secs. (adv. com. Chgo. regional group 1978-83, vice chmn. 1979-80, chmn. 1980-81, nat. dir. 1981-84, exec. com. 1983-84, corp. practices com. 1982-87, assoc. mem. 1986-91), Delta Phi. Avocations: genealogy, history, stamp collecting/philately.

STEWART, CONNIE WARD, retired academic administrator; b. Athens, Ga., Nov. 19, 1938; d. Fred Tendal and Elsie (Janes) Ward; m. D.G. Stewart, 1960 (div. 1967); 1 daughter, Sheri Mann Stewart; 2 grandsons, Tendal Mann and Royce Mann; m. Nick Vista, Apr. 16, 1982. AB in Journalism, U. Ga., Athens, 1959, MA, 1968; postgrad., George Washington U., Washington, 1979; cert. in ednl. mgmt., Harvard U., Cambridge, Mass., 1985. Cert. elem. and secondary tchr., Ga. Promotion-pub. rels. staff Sta. WSB-TV, Atlanta, 1959—61; assoc. dir. Ga. Scholarship Commn., Atlanta, 1967; faculty U. Ga. Journalism Sch., Athens, 1967—70; dir. orientation U. Ga., Athens, 1970—71; project mgr. Planned Mgmt. Corp., Tampa, Fla., 1976—77; dir. policy comm., mem., Carter-Mondale adminstrn. HEW, Washington, 1977—79; orgnl. staff U.S. Dept. Edn., Washington, 1979; v.p. Mich. State U., East Lansing, 1980—87; assoc. v.p. Emory U., Atlanta, 1987—93; ret., 1994. Dir. Cmty. Forum on Children and Families Ga. State U., 1995; mil. acad. screening com. Office U.S. Senator Donald Riegle, Lansing, Mich., 1984-86. Editor, columnist Oconee Enterprise, 1971-72. Steering com. Carter for Pres. Campaign, Fla., 1975—76; exec. com. Mich. Sesquicentennial Celebratoin, 1985—87; mem. Ga. Scholarship Commn., 1965—67, Ga. Motion Picture-TV Adv. Bd., 1972—76, Ga. Gov.'s Commn. on Edn., 1965—67, Mich. Film and TV Coun., 1984—86; exec. com. Comm. Coun., The Atlanta Project, 1992—94; vol. mentor in pub. schs. Success-by-Six program, 1993—96; trainer vols. United Way, 1993—96, Big Bros./Bis Sisters Teach One program, 1997—99; docent Carter Presdl. Libr./Mus., 1998—; bd. councilors Carter Presdl. Ctr., 2005—; bd. dirs. Olympic Acad., 1987—88, Atlanta Olympics Organizing Com. for Olympic Games, 1991—93. Recipient Outstanding Alumna award Henry W. Grady Coll. of Journalism and Mass Communications, U. Ga., 1993, hon. alumnus award Mich. State U., 1987; disting. svc. award Ga. Edn. Advancement Coun., 1990. Mem. Coun. for Advancement and Support Edn., Nat. Assn. State Univs. and Land Grant Colls. (univ. rels. coun. 1984-87), Atlanta C. of C. (Forward Atlanta 1989), Soc. Profl. Journalists, Nat. Press Club (Washington), Pub. Rels. Soc. Am., Phi Beta Kappa (v.p. Mich. State U. chpt. 1986, pres. 1987), Phi Kappa Phi, Sigma Delta Chi, Theta Sigma Phi, Di Gamma Kappa, Zeta Tau Alpha. Democrat. Avocations: travel, reading, poetry. Home: 2848 Warrington Close Tucker GA 30084-2598 E-mail: cstew1119@aol.com.

STEWART, DAVID JAMES, oncologist, educator; m. Lesley Gayle Carruthers, 2002. MD, Queen's U., Kingston, Ont., 1974. Faculty assoc. and instr. U. Tex. M.D. Anderson Hosp. and Tumor Inst., Houston, 1978—79, asst. prof. and asst. internist dept. devel. therapeutics, 1979—80; med. oncologist and clin. asst. prof. of medicine Ottawa Regional Cancer Ctr. and U. of Ottawa, Ont., Canada, 1980—84, med. oncologist and prof. of medicine, cellular and molecular medicine (pharmacology), 1988—2003, med. oncologist and assoc. prof. of medicine and pharmacology, 1984—88; chief of the divsn. of med. oncology Ottawa Civic Hosp., Canada, 1989—99; oncologist U. Tex. M.D. Anderson Cancer Ctr., Houston, 2003—, prof. medicine, 2003—, chief exptl. therapeutics dept. thoracic/head and neck med. oncology, 2003—06, dep. chair dept. thoracic/head and neck med. oncology, 2006—. Contbr. over 500 articles and abstracts to profl. jours., chapters to books. Mem.: Am. Assn. for Cancer Rsch., Am. Soc. of Clin. Oncology. Achievements include research in anticancer agents, mechanisms of resistance to chemotherapy, methods of overcoming resistance and lung cancer. Avocations: running, skiing, hiking. Office: UT MD Anderson Cancer Center 1515 Holcombe Blvd Houston TX 77030 Personal E-mail: dstewart@mdanderson.org.

STEWART, DAVID MARSHALL, librarian; b. Nashville, Aug. 1, 1916; s. David and Mary (Marshall) Stewart; m. Gladys Carroll, June 9, 1947; 1 child, James Marshall. BA, Bethel Coll., 1938; BSLS, George Peabody Coll., 1939. Circulation asst. Vanderbilt U. Library, 1938-39; county librarian Ark. Library Commn., 1939-40; Tenn. supr. WPA library service projects, 1940-42; librarian Memphis State U., 1942-46; spl. asst. to chief card div. Library of Congress, Washington, 1947; librarian CIA, Washington, 1948-60; chief librarian Nashville Pub. Library, 1960-85; Instr. Peabody Library Sch., 1966-80. Bd. dirs. Coun. Cmty. Agys., Nashville, Friends Chamber Music, Nashville, Travelers Aid, Nashville; v.p. bd. Mid.-E. Tenn. Arthritis Found. Served to lt. comdr. USNR, 1942—46. Mem.: ALA, Pub. Libr. Assn. Am. (chmn. stds. com. 1964—65, pres. 1966—67), Southeastern Libr. Assn., Tenn. Libr. Assn. (chmn. legis. com. 1961—65, v.p. 1965, pres. 1966, Honor award 1983), Alumni Assn. Bethel Coll. (dir., Disting. Alumni award 1992), Coffe House Club (Nashville), Kiwanis. Democrat. Mem. United Meth. Ch. Home: 6342 Torrington Rd Nashville TN 37205-3157

STEWART, DAVID PENTLAND, lawyer, educator; b. Milw., Dec. 24, 1943; s. James Pentland and Frederica (Stockwell) S.; children from previous marriage: Jason, Jonathan; m. Jennifer Kilmer, June 21, 1986; children: Daniel, Mary Elizabeth. AB, Princeton U., 1966; JD, MA, Yale U., 1971; LLM, N.Y.U., 1975. Bar: N.Y. 1972, U.S. Dist. Ct. (ea. and so. dists.) N.Y. 1973, U.S. Ct. Appeals (2d cir.) 1973, D.C. 1976. Assoc. Donovan, Leisure, Newton & Irvine, NYC, 1971-76; atty. adviser, office of legal adviser U.S. Dept. State, Washington, 1976-82, asst. legal adviser, 1982—2008; vis. prof. law Georgetown U. Law Ctr., 2008—. Adj. prof. law Georgetown U., Washington, 1984-2008, Am. U., Washington, 1985-86, Johns Hopkins U. Sch. Advanced Internat. Studies, 2000—; vis. lectr. Sch. Law U. Va., 1993-96, Nat. Law Ctr., George Washington U., 1993-99; elected mem. Inter-Am. Juridical Com., 2008. Co-editor: (ann. vols.) Digest of United States Practice in International Law, 1989—2005; contbr. articles to profl. jours. Served to maj. USAR, 1970-87. Mem. ABA, Am. Law Inst., Am. Soc. Internat. Law., Internat. Law Assn., Internat. Bar Assn., Inter-America Bar Assn. Office: Georgetown Univ Law Ctr 600 NJ Ave NW Washington DC 20001 Office Phone: 202-662-9927. Business E-Mail: stewartd@law.georgetown.edu.

STEWART, DAVID WITHERINGTON, business consultant; b. Marion, Ind., Feb. 9, 1939; s. Edgar Allen Jr. and Faye Maxine (Cummings); m. Ruth Ada Valk, Aug. 26, 1961, (div.); m. Annette Louise Witherington, Dec. 17, 1962 (dec. Aug. 1999); children: Edna (dec.), Geoffrey. BS in Physics, U. Fla., Gainesville, 1959. Sr. engr. Atlas Gen. Dynamics/Convair, Cape Canaveral, Fla., 1959—63; lead engr. Gemini-Titan Martin Canaveral, Cape Canaveral, 1963—66; lead engr. Sprint Martin-Orlando, Orlando, Fla., 1966—67; lead engr. Apollo Rockwell Internat., Kennedy Space Center, Fla., 1967—74, lead engr. avionics, 1975—78, prime system integ. engr. shuttle, 1978—79, supr. orbiter software, 1979—81, project mgr. software, 1982—84, project mgr. design, 1984—85, project mgr. adv. programs, 1985—89, mgr. adv. program, 1989—91, project mgr. adv. program and bus. devel., 1991—92, program devel. mgr. Fla. ops. space sys. divsn., 1992—96; owner, pres. L&D Consulting, Titusville, Fla., 1996—; owner, gen. mgr. Coreopsis Publs., 2004—. Author: Edie and the Gobie, 1966. Pres. North Brevard Environ. Action Com., Titusville, 1970-73; chmn. Marine Resources Coun. East Fla., 1996-97, 2000—02; pres.-elect Space Coast Devel. Commn., 1995-96; sec. Space Coast Grant Profls. Network, 1997-99; pres. Brevard Adult Literacy Vols., Inc., 2000—04; vol., treas. Brevard Humanity Ctr., Inc, 2000—. Mem. Inst. Cert. Profl. Mgrs. (cert. mgr.), Am. Cons. League (accredited profl. cons.). Republican. Unitarian Universalist. Mailing: PO Box 5869 Titusville FL 32783-5869 Personal E-mail: david@davidwstewart.com.

STEWART, DENISE MARGARET, ESL educator, consultant; d. Maurice Jean and Frederica Stewart; m. Eugene W. Cross, Dec. 19, 1998; m. Nashat Shafik Ghali, Aug. 24, 1975 (div. Nov. 8, 1987); children: Renee Frederica Ghali, Michael Denis Ghali. BA, Hunter Coll., 1972; MA, NYU, 1978. Adult ESL instr. Hudson Valley Opportunities Industrialization Ctr., Beacon, NY, 1978—81; ESL lectr. SUNY, New Paltz, 1981—87; ESL tchr. LA Unified Sch. Dist., 1988—98; English lang. devel. tchr. Willow Glen HS, San Jose, Calif., 1998—. Lang. devel. specialist, cross lang. acquisition devel. trainer, bilingual tchr. tng. plan LA Unified Sch. Dist., 1990—98; adj. prof. U. San Diego, 2002—; trainer Calif. Tchrs. Assn., Burlingame, 1998—2002; scorer "Respect a Child, Respect a Tchr." program Calif. Tchrs. Assn., West Edn., San Francisco, 1998—2002; instr. Profl. Devel. Inst., Chapman U., Fullerton, Calif., 2000—; Crosscultural Lang. and Academic Devel. trainer Santa Clara County Office Edn., San Jose, 2000—; ednl. cons. Lang. Acquisition Consultants in Edn., Santa Rosa, Calif., 2003—; ELL tchr. support adviser Williow Glen HS, SJ, Calif., 2008—, cons. ELL tchr. pres., 2008—; presenter in field. Mem.: TESOL, Calif. Assn. Bilingual Educators, Nat. Assn. Bilingual Educators. Democrat. Roman Catholic. Home: 473 School St Fremont CA 94536 Office: Willow Glen HS 2001 Cottle Ave San Jose CA 95125 Home Phone: 510-894-4038; Office Phone: 510-882-6819. Personal E-mail: dmcyberteacher@gmail.com.

STEWART, DONALD GEORGE, musician, composer, music industry executive; b. Sterling, Ill., Jan. 8, 1935; s. Donald Balmer and Elinore Maud (Denison) S.; m. Susan Ann Trainer, June 13, 1963 (div. 1979); 1 child, Elizabeth Ann. MusB, Ind. U., 1960; postgrad., Manhattan Sch., 1960-62; student, Sch. of Jazz, 1958-60; studied with Roy Harris, Bernhard Heiden, Gunther Schuller. 2d clarinetist Birmingham (Ala.) Symphony, 1954-56, Fla. Symphony, Orlando, 1963; musician with numerous jazz groups including Ornette Coleman, David Baker, Sammy Davis, 1957-65; woodwind player Orch. USA, NYC, 1963-65; libr. Harkness Ballet, NYC, 1967-72; founder, clarinetist Boehm Quintette, NYC, 1968-88; music asst. N.Y. State Coun. on the Arts, NYC, 1972-75; freelance copyist NYC, 1958-88; founder, pres. Trillenium Music Co., 1986—, clarinetist, saxophonist, 1958—; pres. Opera North, Norwich, Vt., 1987-89; musician Sarasota Jazz Ensemble and Sarasota Pops, 2005—; bd. mem. Vt. Symphony Orch., 1990—96, Sarasota Pops, 2008—. Founder, treas. Chamber Music Am., N.Y.C., 1977-81; panelist Vt. Coun. on the Arts, 1976-78. Composer Piccolo Concerto, 1973, August Lions for Youth Orch., 1978, Song of Arion, 1985 (2d prize Am. Harp Soc.), First Blue Symphony, 1988, Book of Sliding Things, 1989, Green Mountain Christmas Card (opera), 1995, Never Seek to Tell Thy Love (voice and ensemble), 1998, Duo for Violin and Cello, 1999, Flute Quartet, 2003, Third Symphony, 2005, Wind Quintet #3 (Period Pieces with NooGlu), 2007, Metric Measures, 2008; others; transcriber wind chamber music; composer, arranger for G. Schirmer, Boosey and Hawkes, Carl Fischer, Trillenium Music Co.; recs. for Columbia, Orion, New World, Margun and Marlboro, 1964—; participant Marlboro Festival, Vt., 1966-68, Berkshire Festival, Mass., summer 1965, 68. Vt. Coun. on the Arts fellow, 1985, Nat. Endowment for Arts grant, 1978—. Mem. ASCAP, Am. Fedn. Musicians, Am. Soc. Music Copyists (bd. dirs. 1970-87, treas. 1984-87), Music Pub.'s Assn. Democrat. Congregationalist. Office: Trillenium Music Co PO Box 51059 Sarasota FL 34232-0329 Office Phone: 941-377-7375. Office Fax: 941-377-9043. Business E-Mail: don@trillmusic.com.

STEWART, DONALD M., college president; b. Chgo., July 8, 1938; m. Isabel Carter Johnston; children: Jay Ashton, Carter Mitchell. BA, Grinnell Coll., 1959; MA, Yale U., 1962; MPA, Harvard U., 1969, postgrad., 1975. Asst. to rep. for West Africa Ford Found., 1962-64, program asst. Mid. East Africa Project, 1964-66, asst. rep. Cairo, asst. for North Africa, 1966-67; program officer Mid. East Africa Program, 1968-70; exec. asst. to pres. U. Pa., 1970-72; researcher Ford Found. Study Award, Washington, 1972-73; dir. Community Leadership Seminar Program, 1973-74, Continuing Edn., 1973-74, Higher Edn. Research, 1973-74; instr. City Planning and Pub. Policy Analysis, 1973-74; pres. Spelman Coll., 1976-87, Coll. Bd., NYC, 1987—99; sr. program officer, spl. adv. to pres. Carnegie Corp., NYC, 1999—2000; pres., CEO Chgo. Cmty. Trust, 2000—05. Bd. dirs. Bankers Life of Iowa Ins. Co., Nat. Bank of Ga., vis. prof. Harris Sch. Pub. Policy Studies, Univ. Chgo. Pres., treas. Atlanta Symphony Orch.; trustee, mem. adv. council of pres., mem. governing bd. Grinnell Coll.; mem. Council on Fgn. Relations; bd. dirs. Com. forEcon. Devel.; pres. Com. on Arts and Humanities; trustee Atlanta Botanical Gardens; mem. research com. Ind. Sector Adv. Com. Fellow Am. Acad. Arts & Scis.; mem. Nat. Acad. Pub. Adminstrn. (bd. dirs.). Office: Harris Sch Pub Policy Studies Univ Chgo 1155 East 60th St Chicago IL 60637

STEWART, DORIS MAE, biology professor; b. Sandsprings, Mont., Dec. 12, 1927; d. Virgil E. and Violet M. (Weaver) S.; m. Felix Loren Powell, Oct. 8, 1956; children: Leslie, Loren. BS, Coll. Puget Sound, 1948, MS, 1949; PhD, U. Wash., 1953. Instr. U. Mont., Missoula, 1954-56, asst. prof., 1956-57, U. Puget Sound, Tacoma, 1957-58; head sci. dept. Am. Kiz Lisesi, Istanbul, Turkey, 1958-62; rsch. asst. prof. U. Wash., Seattle, 1963-67, rsch. assoc. prof., 1967-68; assoc. prof. Cen. Mich. U., Mt. Pleasant, 1970-72, U. Balt., 1973-81, prof., 1981-95, prof. emeritus, 1995—. Contbr. numerous articles to profl. jours. Mem. Am. Physiol. Soc., Sigma Xi. Home: 1103 Frederick Rd Baltimore MD 21228-5032

STEWART, DOROTHY K., librarian; b. Bristol, Conn., Sept. 28, 1928; d. Robert and Anna Esther (Schwirtz) Konopask; m. David Benjamin Stewart, Sept. 27, 1952 (div. Nov. 1979); children: Douglas Neil, Diane Alison. BA in Romance Langs. and Lit. cum laude, Boston U., 1950; MSLS, Cath. U. Am., Washington, DC, 1959. Children's libr. Brookline Pub. Libr., Mass., 1953-55, Takoma Park Libr., Md., 1955-57; reference libr. US Geol. Survey, 1961; libr. Washington Internat. Sch., 1979-80, Office Sea Grant NOAA, Rockville, Md., 1980-82; info. specialist Life Ring, Inc., Silver Spring, Md., 1983-84; pub. svc. libr. Urban Inst., Washington, 1984-85; user svcs. coord. ERIC Clearinghouse on Tchg. and Tchr. Edn., Washington, 1985-97; ret., 1997. Active, past pres. PTA, Rockville, Md., 1973-78; chmn., mem. com. adv. com. Potomac Libr., 1975-85; vol. English Conversation Club, 2005-. Mem. Capital PC User Group, French lang. clubs, Phi Beta Kappa, Beta Phi Mu. Democrat. Avocations: travel, hiking, birding, computers. Personal E-mail: dkstewart24@comcast.net.

STEWART, E(DWARD) NICHOLSON, investment management executive; b. Bronxville, NY, Sept. 28, 1940; s. Edward Nicholson and Helen (Davis) S.; m. Mary Patricia Hunter, Aug. 8, 1964; children: Pamela S. Burke, Wendy S. Leary. Student, Hamilton Coll., 1959-62; BA, New Sch. Social Rsch., 1965. Dir. membership Investment Co. Inst., NYC, 1968; v.p. Lord, Abbett & Co., NYC, 1969-74; pres. Trevor Stewart Burton & Jacobsen Inc., NYC, 1974-95, CEO, 1990—2004, chmn., 1995—. Pres., bd. dirs. Robert Hampton Tapp Found., 1993—. Co-founder, editor Hackley Rev., 1963-68. Trustee Hackley Sch., 1971-87, treas., 1972-87, v.p. 1980-87; pres. Hackley Alumni Assn., Inc., 1967-69. Mem. Naval War Coll. Found. (life), Nat. Def. Indsl. Assn. (life), Union League Club (bd. govs. 1985-87, 95-97, vice-chmn. 1987, pres. 1989-90), Sleepy Hollow Country Club (bd. govs. 1993-96, sec. 1995, 2001-2003, asst. sec. 2000, v.p. 2003-2004, pres. 2005-06), Econ. Club N.Y., The 200 Club (bd. dirs.), Delta Kappa Epsilon. Republican. Office: 405 Lexington Ave Ste 4700 New York NY 10174

STEWART, ELIZABETH ANNELLA, gynecologist, researcher; b. Atlanta, Apr. 24, 1959; married. BA molecular biology magna cum laude, Vanderbilt U., 1980; MD, Harvard U., 1985. Cert. Nat. Bd. Med. Examiners 1986, Mass. License Registration 1988, Am. Bd. Ob-Gyn. 1993, diplomate in ob-gyn. and reproductive endocrinology Am. Bd. Ob-gyn., 1995, cert. Am. Bd. Ob-Gyn., Annual Recertification 2003. Intern Obstetrics & Gynecology, Magee Women's Hosp., Pitts., 1985—86; resident Obstetrics & Gynecology, Brigham & Women's Hosp., 1986—89, fellow, Reproductive Endocrinology Boston, 1990—92; clin. dir., Ctr. Uterine Fibroids, Brigham and Women's Hosp., Boston, 1998—; asst. prof. ob-gyn and reproductive biology Harvard Med. Sch., 1995—2003, assoc. prof., 2003—; assoc. ob-gyn. Brigham and Women's Hosp., Boston, 1989—; asst. gynecologist Mass. General Hosp., Boston, 1989—90; assoc. in ob-gyn. Mass. Inst. Tech. Med. Dept., Cambridge, 1989—90; clinical dir., Ctr. for Uterine Fibroids Brigham and Women's Hosp., 1998—; assoc. gynecologist Faulkner Hosp., Boston, 2005—. Rsch. asst., Dept. of Surgery Vanderbilt U. Sch. of Medicine, 1981, summer fellow, Diabetes Ctr., 82; clinical assoc. Nat. Institutes of Health (NIH), Clinical Elective in Endocrinology and Metabolism, 1984; med. dir., Quality Assurance Com. Fertility and Endocrinology Unit, Brigham and Women's Hosp., Boston, 1993—95; assoc. dir., Lab. of Cell Biology, Dept. of Obstetrics, Gynecology and Reproductive Biology Brigham and Women's Hosp., Harvard Med. Sch., 1995—99; cons., Reproductive Sciences Program U. Mich., 2000; visiting prof. of ob-gyn. Kuwait U., Kuwait, 2000; cons. for Women's Health Care Emirates Palomar Med. Tech. Services, Abu Dhabi, United Arab Emirates, 2000; assoc. dir., Reproductive Endocrinology Fellowship Program Brigham and Women's Hosp., 2002—04; ad hoc mem. Bd. of Sci. Counselors, Review of Epidemiology Br. Nat. Inst. of Environ. Health Sciences, Nat. Institutes of Health, 2005. Recipient First Prize, Boston Fertility Soc. Prize Paper Competition, 1991, Berlex Scholar Award, 1993, First Prize, Boston Obstetrical Soc. Prize Paper Competition, 1994, Second Prize, Boston Fertility Soc. Prize Paper Competition, 1996, Partners in Excellence Award, Partners HealthCare System, 1996, Bear and Eagle Feather Mentoring Award, Four Directions Summer Rsch. Program, Harvard Med. Sch., 2000, Partners in Excellence Award, Partner's Health Care System, 2000, Residency Teaching Award in Reproductive Endocrinology, Brigham and Women's Hospital, 2004, Leadership Award for Clinical Innovation, Brigham and Women's Physician's Org., 2004. Fellow: Am. Coll. Ob-Gyn.; mem.: Soc. for Gynecologic Investigation, Soc. of Reproductive Endocrinologists, Am. Soc. for Reproductive Medicine, Mortar Bd. Hon. Soc., Phi Beta Kappa. Achievements include U.S. Patent 6440445: Methods and Compounds for Treatment of Abnormal Uterine Bleeding. Office: Brigham and Women's Hosp 75 Francis St Boston MA 02115 Office Phone: 617-732-4285. Office Fax: 617-566-7752. Business E-Mail: eastewart@partners.org.

STEWART, ELLEN D., theater producer; Former fashion designer; founder, dir. La Mama Exptl. Theatre Club, NYC, 1961—. Vis. prof. Inst. Drama, Republic of Korea. Prodr. innovative theatre, including Antigone, a part of SEVEN: Seven Greek Plays in Repertory; dir., most recently Perseus, Great Jones Rep. Co.; active in internet theatre exch. Recipient Margo Jones award, 1969, MacArthur Genius award, Les Kurbas award disting. svc. to art and culture, Ukraine, Order of Sacred Treasure Gold Rays with Rossette, Emperor Japan, 1994, Human Rights award, Philippines, Praemium Imperiale prize, Japan Art Assn., 2007; named Officer Ordre des Arts et Lettres, Republic France; named to Theatre Hall of Fame, 1993. Mem.: Seoul Internat. Theatre Inst. Office: La MaMa ETC 74A E 4th St New York NY 10003-8903 Office Phone: 212-254-6468. Business E-Mail: lamama@lamama.org.

STEWART, GEOFFREY S., lawyer; b. Kansas City, Mo., Oct. 21, 1951; s. Gordon D. and Patricia S. Stewart; m. Marybeth Boyle, July 28, 1979; children: John, Elisabeth Cameron. AB, AM, Brown U., 1973; JD, Harvard U., 1976. Bar: NY, DC, US ct of appeal (1st, 4th, 6th, 9th, 11th, dc & fed. cirs.), various dists. cts., US Supreme Ct. Assoc. Davis, Polk & Wardwell, NYC, 1976-79, Washington, 1980-81; spl. counsel Dept. Justice, Washington, 1981-82, dep. asst. atty. gen., 1983; assoc. Hale & Dorr, Washington, 1985-86, ptnr., 1986, Jones Day, NYC. Assoc. counsel Iran arms sales/contra diversion Office of Ind. Counsel, Wash., 1987-90. Contbr. articles to profl. jour. Mem. ABA, DC Bar Assn. Editor Harvard Jour. on Legis. Office: Jones Day 222 E 41st St New York NY 10017 Office Phone: 212-326-3939, 212-326-7877. Office Fax: 212-755-7306. Business E-Mail: gstewart@jonesday.com.

STEWART, GEORGIANA LICCIONE, writer; b. Mount Vernon, NY, May 18, 1943; d. Arthur Alfred and Grace Marie (Zuzzolo) Liccione; m. William Lawrence Stewart, July 18, 1975. BA, Columbia U., 1971; MA, Columbia Tchr.'s Coll., NYC, 1973; MAT, Manhattanville Coll., 1973. Author, cons. Kimbo Ednl., Long Branch, NJ, 1970—; spl. edn. tchr. Bronxville (N.Y.) H.S., 1989—. Cons. NAEYC, SACUS, 1975-89, Pres.'s Coun. on Physical Fitness, 1979-81. Author: (69 children's musical activity records and books including) Adaptive Motor Learning, 1982, Bean Bag Activities, 1983, Preschool Aerobic Fun, 1989, Children of the World, 1991, ulticultural Rhythm Stick Fun, 1992, Toddlerific, 1993, World of Parachute Play, 1997, Children's Folk Dances, 1998, Moving with Mozart, 1999 (Early Childhood Dir.'s Choice award NAEYC), Nursery Rhyme Time, 2000, Cool Aerobics for Kids, 2001, Musical Scarves, 2002, Circle Time, 2004. Recipient Student Advocacy Overcoming the Odds award, 1997. Mem. AAHPERD, Nat. Assn. for Edn. of Young Children, So. Assn. for Children Under Six, Faculty Dance Educators Am., Assn. for Retarded Citizens, Columbia Club, Women's Nat. Rep. Club. Avocations: Heatsong music and art therapy program, organizing local benefit programs. Home: 81 Pondfield Rd # 328 Bronxville NY 10708-3818 Office: Kimbo Ednl PO Box 477 Long Branch NJ 07740-0477

STEWART, GILBERT WRIGHT, computer science educator; b. Washington, Oct. 1, 1940; s. Gilbert Wright and Ruth (Blount) S.; m. Mary Lynn Tharp, 1964; children: Michael, Laura; m. Astrid Schmidt-Nielsen, Apr. 29, 1978. AB, U. Tenn., 1962, PhD, 1968. Programmer Union Carbide Nuclear Co., Oak Ridge, 1959-62, 63-64, 65-68, computer div. Gen. Electric Co., Phoenix, 1964-68; asst. prof., assoc. prof. U. Tex.-Austin, 1968-72; assoc. prof. Carnegie-Mellon U., Pitts., 1972-74, U. Md., College Park, 1974-76, prof. Computer Sci. Dept.; prof. computer sci. Carnegie-Mellon U., 1976—; cons. Argonne Nat. Lab., Ill., 1974—, Nat. Bur. Standards, Gaithersburg, Md., 1979—; dir. Lab. Parallel Computation U. Md., 1983. Author: Introduction to Matrix Computations, 1974; co-author: (with Dougarra, Bunch and Moler) LINPACK Users' Guide, (with I.G. Sun) Matrix Perturbation Theory; translator: Gauss's Theoria Combinations. Woodrow Wilson fellow, 1962; NSF grantee, 1983 Mem. NAE, Soc. Indsl. and Applied Math., Am. Math. Assn., Am. Statis. Assn. Democrat. Office: U Md Dept Computer Sci College Park MD 20742-0001 Office Phone: 301-405-2681, 301-405-6707. E-mail: stewart@cs.umd.edu.

STEWART, GORDON CURRAN, retired insurance institute executive; b. Chgo., July 22, 1939; s. Henry Stewart and Evangeline (Williams) Bolton; m. Elizabeth Knorr, June 19, 1965 (div. 1968); m. Zanne Early, Dec. 20, 1995; 1 child, Katarina Guadalupe Hadley. BA, Oberlin Coll., 1960; MA, U. Chgo., 1962; student, U. Vienna, Austria, 1963; MFA, Yale U., 1967. Instr. Amherst Coll., Mass., 1967-68; dir. Bus. Comm. for Arts, NYC, 1969-71; exec. asst. Mayor of NYC, 1971-73; dir., writer NYC, LA, UK, 1973-78; dep. chief speechwriter President of US, Washington, 1978-81; instr. Bus. and Govt. Acad. forums, U.S. and fgn. countries, 1981-82; v.p. AMSE, NYC, 1982-89; exec. v.p. Ins. Info. Inst., NYC, 1989-91, pres., 1991—2006; ret.; pres. Mind Inc., Garrison, NY, 2006—. Cons. Am. Bus. Conf., Washington, 1982-89, Internat. Commn. for Ctrl. Am., Washington, 1986-88, Coun. on Competitiveness, Washington, 1987-88, Def. Sci. Bd., Washington, 1988-89; pres., CEO Mind, Inc., 2007-. Writer films: The Store, 1978, Joey, 1978, Gallery, 1978; dir. (play) The Elephant Man (1st US prodn.), 1977, Jesse, 1975, Cowboy Mouth, 1976, Sleep, 1977, (films) The Blazers, 1975; condr. Beggar's Opera, 1969, West Side Story, 1970. Dir. NY Urban Coalition, NYC, 1984-88; dir. policy Samuels for Gov., NY, 1974; speechwriter numerous dem. campaigns, 1974-81; mem. fin. coun. Dem. Nat. Com., 1984-88; mem. adv. coun. Dem. Leadership Coun., 1984-90. Woodrow Wilson fellow Woodrow Wilson Found., 1961. Mem. Writers Guild Am. (west), Judson Welliver Soc. of Chief Presdl. Speechwriters (sec.-treas.), Coun. Fgn. Rels., Century Assn., Phi Beta Kappa, Yale Club. Avocations: politics, music.

STEWART, GWENDOLYN JOHNS, music educator; b. Winston-Salem, NC, Feb. 11, 1926; d. Island Lemuel Johns and Vandelia Trumilla Perry-Johns; m. Jason Hawkins, Sr. (dec.); 1 child, Jason Hawkins Jr.; m. George Sturgis (dec.); 1 child, Daryl Sturgis; m. Robert H. Stewart, Jan. 20, 1979 (dec.). Student, Spelman Coll., 1943—46, Juilliard Sch. Music, 1947; BS in Edn., Winston-Salem Tchrs. Coll., 1950; postgrad., A & T State U., Greensboro, NC, 1955. Tchr. Pub. Sch. Sys., Gastonia, NC, 1951—57, Mooresville, NC, 1957—61, Forsyth County Pub. Sch. Sys., Winston-Salem, 1961—65; owner-oper. Jack & Jill Kindergarten #2, Winston-Salem, 1965—68; dir. chancel choir Friendship Bapt. Ch., Winston-Salem, 1961—79; pianist, organist, dir. Grace Presbyn. Ch. USA, Winston-Salem, 1997—; pianist, organist Gen. Bapt. State Conv. N.C., Winston-Salem, 1982—86, dir. music, 1986—90. Chmn. music dept. Shiloh Bapt. Ch., Winston-Salem, 1997—2002. Author: The Gwen Johns Basic Music Guide, 2000, Bells Alive Book One, 2003, composer song collection; contbr. poetry to anthologies. Avocations: sewing, cooking. Home: 2795 Bethabara Rd Winston Salem NC 27106-9604 E-mail: gjstewart12@triad.rr.com.

STEWART, GWENDOLYN M., elementary school educator; b. San Francisco, Dec. 13, 1954; d. James Calhoun and Annette Marie Miller; m. Stephen Michael Stewart, Jan. 1, 2000; children: Alicia Marie Rozario, Alexander Rozario Jr. BA, U. San Francisco, 1977; M in pub. admin., Coll. of Notre Dame, 1989; D in edn., U. San Francisco, 1995. Vice principal San Lorenzo (Calif.) Unified Sch. Dist., 1992—93; tchr. Martin Luther King Jr. Mid. Sch., Madera, Calif., 1993—2001; adj. faculty Merced Cmty. Coll., Merced, Calif., 1994—98; mentor tchr. Martin Luther King Jr. Mid. Sch., Madera, Calif., 1999—2000; principal Fresno Unified Alternative Edn., Fresno, Calif., 2000—01; tchr. Westside Intermediate Sch., Los Banos, Calif., 2001—04; English tchr. Los Banos (Calif.) HS, 2004—. Grant writing cons. self employed, Madera, Calif., 1992—; summer sch. principal Los Banos HS, 2006. Author: An Analysis of New Teacher Introduction Program in Madera Unified School District, 1995. Recipient Cmty. Svc. award, Martin Luther King Jr. Sch., 1991, Distg. Tchr. award, Madera Unified Sch. Dist. Com., 1994. Mem.: The Link, Inc., Fresno Cpt. (recording sec. 2004—05), Nat. Soc. of Philathropy, Madera County Food Bank (recording sec. 1999—2005). Avocations: writing poetry, exercise, reading, jazz. Office Phone: 559-474-6341.

STEWART, HENRY R., library director; b. Wilmington, Del., Apr. 16, 1944; s. Henry R. and Elizabeth P. Stewart; m. Margaret J. Adams, Mar. 14, 1977; 1 child, Margaret Elizabeth. BA, Cornell Coll., Mt. Vernon. Iowa, 1966; MS in Libr. Svc., U. Denver, Colo., 1967; PhD, Ind. U., Bloomington, Ind., 1972. Audiovisual and reference libr. Cornell Coll., 1967—69; asst. prof. U. Ala., Tuscaloosa, 1972—77; vis. dept. chair librarianship Tasmanian Coll. Advanced Edn., Hobart, Australia, 1976—76; assoc. dean, mgmt. and pub. svcs, Old Dominion U. Libr., Norfolk, Va., 1977—84; dir. William Allen White Libr., Emporia State U., Kans., 1984—96; dean U. Libr., Troy U., Ala., 1996—. Recipient Contbn. award, Kans. Libr. Assn, Coll. and U. Sect., 1996; fellowship, US Office Edn., 1969—72. Mem.: Ala. Libr. Assn. (pres. 2001—02). Office: Troy Univ Libr 501 University Ave Troy AL 36082 Business E-Mail: hstewart@troy.edu.

STEWART, HOWARD L., engineering educator; s. Howard and Ida M. Stewart; m. Frances R. Reynolds, Sept. 10, 1988; children: Craig H., Karen C., Karla C., Melissa D. Primus, Jeremiah Primus III. BSME, Calif. State U., LA, 1963, MSEE, 1972; M in Engring., U. Calif., LA, 1973. Design engr. sect. head Gen. Dynamics Corp., Pomona, Calif., 1963—81; sr. tech. specialist engring. mgr. Aerojet Corp., Azusa, Calif., 1981—87; dir. product design engring. Northrop Grumman Corp., Anaheim, Calif., 1987—91, dir. engring. & mfg. Hawthorne, Calif., 1991—97, dir. engring. Rolling Meadows, Ill., 1997—2001; adj. prof., math & engring. Chaffey CC, Rancho Cucamonga, Calif., 2004—. Office: Chaffey CC 5885 Haven Ave Rancho Cucamonga CA 91737-3002 Business E-Mail: howard.stewart@chaffey.edu.

STEWART, JOAN HINDE, academic administrator; b. NYC, Aug. 11, 1944; d. Wade and Dorothy (Ronning) H.; m. Philip Robert Stewart, Jan. 31, 1970; children: Anna Faye, Justin. Student, Université Laval Summer Sch, Quebec, 1963, Middlebury Coll. Summer Sch., 1964-65; BA summa cum laude, St. Joseph's Coll., 1965; student, Salzburg Summer Sch., Austria, 1966; MPhil, Yale U., 1969, PhD, 1970. Tchg. assoc. French Yale U., New Haven, 1967—69, acting instr. French, 1969—70; instr. French Wellseley Coll., 1970—71, asst. prof. French, 1971—72, NC State U., Raleigh, 1973—77, assoc. prof. French, 1977—81, prof. French, 1981—99, asst. head dept. fgn. langs. and lits., 1978—82, asst. dean rsch. and grad. programs, 1983—85, acting head dept. fgn. langs. and lits., 1984—85, head dept. fgn. langs. and lit., 1985—97; prof., dean liberal arts U. SC, 1999—2003; prof. French, pres. Hamilton Coll., Clinton, NY, 2003—. Author: The Novels of Mme Riccoboni, 1976, Colette, 1983, 1996, Gynographs: French Novels by Women of the Late Eighteenth Century, 1993; editor: Mme Riccoboni's Lettres de Mistriss Fanni Butlerd, 1979; co-editor: Isabelle de Charrière's Lettres de Mistriss Henley, 1993, Marie Riccoboni's Histoire d'Ernestine, 1998. Chmn. N.C. Humanities Coun., 1988-89. Fellow Camargo Found., Cassis, France, 1979, Nat. Humanities Ctr., 1982-83, (sr.) ctr. for humanities Wesleyan U., 1990; NEH summer seminar fellowship, Princeton U., 1980; NEH fellowship Coll. Tchrs. and Ind. Scholars, 1990-91, 1994-95; fellow Ctr. d'Etude du XVIII Siecle, U. Paul Valery, Montpellier, France, 1995, Liguria Study Ctr. for the Arts and Scis., Bogliasco, Italy, 1997, Beinecke Rare Book and Manuscript Libr., Yale U., 1997; stipend younger humanists NEH, 1973; travel grantee ACLS, 1983; travel to collections grantee NEH, 1984; vis. scholar European Humanities Rsch. Ctr., Oxford U., 1995. Mem. AAUP, MLA, Am. Assn. Tchrs. French. Office: Hamilton Coll Pres Office 198 College Hill Rd Clinton NY 13323 Office Phone: 315-859-4104. E-mail: jstewart@hamilton.edu.

STEWART, JOHN HARGER, music educator; b. Cleve., Mar. 31, 1940; s. Cecil Tooker and Marian (Harger) S.; m. Julia Wallace, Aug. 14, 1977; children: Barbara, Cecily Bronwen. BA, Yale U., 1962; MA, Brown U., 1972; cert., New Eng. Conservatory, 1965. With various operas including Santa Fe Opera, N.Y.C. Opera, Met. Opera, U.S. and Europe, 1965—; lectr. Mt. Holyoke Coll., South Hadley, Mass., 1988-90; dir. vocal activities Washington U., St. Louis, 1990—, dir. Friends of Music. Office: Dept Music Washington U Campus Box 1030 One Brookings Dr Saint Louis MO 63130-4899 Home Phone: 314-533-0665; Office Phone: 314-935-5597. Business E-Mail: jstewart@wustl.edu.

STEWART, JOHN MILLER, psychologist, educator; b. Bradford, Pa., Sept. 27, 1938; s. James A. and Virginia G. (Essington) S.; m. Sharon Stewart, Sept. 7, 1963; 1 child, David Dylan. Student, U. Birmingham, Eng., 1969; PhD in Psychobiology, Bowling Green State U., 1971. NIMH postdoctoral fellow Jackson Lab., Bar Harbor, Maine, 1971-75; staff fellow NIMH, Bethesda, Md., 1975-77; clin. asst. prof. U. Md., Balt., 1978-79; co-founder, chief rsch. and evaluation Regional Inst. for Children, Rockville, Md., 1980-88; clin. assoc. prof. Georgetown U., Washington, 1983-92; assoc. faculty Johns Hopkins U., Balt., 1986-92; prof., chair dept. psychology Northland Coll., Ashland, Wis., 1992—2005, dir. Wolf Rsch. Team, 1992—, emeritus prof. psychology, 2005—. Mem. Bd. Sci. Integrity, State of Md., Balt., 1990-92, mem. Instnl. Rev. Bd., 1986-92; mem. Wolf Monitoring Team, State of Wis., Madison, 1992-2002. Contbr. chpts. to books, numerous articles to sci. jours. Pres. bd. dirs. Frederick County Librs., Frederick, Md., 1982-88, New Horizons North, Ashland, 1993-98, Chequameque Humane Assn., Ashland, 2001-05; trustee Washburn (Wis.) Edn. Found., 1998-2000; scoutmaster Boy Scouts Am. Recipient Outstanding Tchg. award, Outstanding Scholarship award, Disting. Svc. award Northland Coll.; fellow NCI, NSF, NICHD, NATO, 1963-71; grantee W.T. Grant Found., NIMH, NICHD, NATO, 1968-80. Fellow Internat. Soc. for Rsch. on Aggression (charter); mem. APA, AAUP, Animal Behavior Soc., Union of Concerned Scientists, Am. Psychol. Soc., Psi Chi. Achievements include being a recognized expert in the development of social behavior in domestic dogs and wolves in the wild. Office: PO Box 393 Washburn WI 54891-0373 Business E-Mail: jstewart@ncis.net.

STEWART, JOHN MURRAY, bank executive; b. Summit, NJ, Apr. 2, 1943; s. Robert John Stewart and Mary Catherine Grabhorn; m. Sandra Meyers Frazier, 1966 (div. 1997); children: Jennifer Bricar Crone, Catherine Dorothy Lochead; m. Rebecca Marie Mellen, July 10, 1998. BA, U. Va., Charlottesville, 1965; MBA, NYU, 1983. Trust officer, v.p. Bankers Trust Co., NYC, 1965-82, Morgan Guaranty Trust Co., NYC, 1982-83; mgr., pres., dir. Morgan Trust Co. Fla., Palm Beach, 1983-89; pres., dir. Bankers Trust Co. Fla., 1989-93; founder, pres. pvt. capital group SunTrust Bank, Orlando, Fla., 1993-96; pres., dir. Harris Trust/Bank of Montreal, West Palm Beach, 1996—2001; contbg. writer Cannon Fin. Inst., 2004—; sr. trust advisor Wachovia Bank, 2006—. Campaign chmn. Palm Beach Cmty. Chest, 1985, 1986; exec. com. Tampa Bay and Palm Beach County Local Initiatives Support Corp.; mem. planned giving coun. U. Va., 1997—, pres. alumni club, 1990—98; vestryman Bethesda By the Sea Ch., Palm Beach, 1986—89, 1992—94, treas., 1986—87, Cathedral Ch. of St. Luke, Orlando, 1996; bd. dirs. Orlando Opera Co., 1994—96, Palm Beach Opera Co., 1996—2001. Mem. Fla. Bankers Assn. (chmn. trust bus. devel. com. 1989, planning commn., chmn. trust legis. com. 1990), NY State Bankers Assn. (mem. trust bus. devel. com. 1978-82), NY Yacht Club (NYC), St. Petersburg Yacht Club, Monmouth Boat Club (Red Bank, NJ), SAR (pres. Palm Beach chpt. 1997-98, 2009-). Home: 1049 Pinellas Bayway S Tierra Verde FL 33715 Office Phone: 561-313-4444. Personal E-mail: uva1965@msn.com.

STEWART, JOHN NORMAN, scenic artist; b. San Bernadino, Calif., May 2, 1940; s. John T. and Rachel (Powell) S.; m. Judith Kay Coleman, Sept. 1959 (div. 1961); 1 child, Pamela Joy Perrini; m. Barbara Lyn Perlman, Feb. 6, 1966; 1 child, Dawn Sheryl; m. Valerie Anne DeRenzo, Dec. 9, 2001 Student, Chouinard Art Inst., 1958—60, Art Ctr., LA, 1966. Ind. artist. sculptor, scenic artist, 1958—2002; artist Cottonwood, Calif., 2002—. Muralist Hilton Hotels, Reno, 1993—94; artist Disney Studios (WED), Glendale, Calif., 1981—83; scenic artist Universal Studios, North Hollywood, Calif., 1976—81; free lance artist Self Employed, Sun Valley, Calif., 1966—76. Scenic and portrait artist (films) Smokey and the Bandit parts I and II, Blues Brothers, Extremities, Xanadu, Harvest Home, Saint Elmo's Fire, Vibes, E. T.-The Extraterrestrial, Love at First Bite, Poltergeist, Bachelor Party, One From the Heart, Ghostbusters, Space Balls, Karate Kid, Starman, Bonfire of the Vanities, 1990, Naked Gun 2 1/2, 1991, Addams Family The Movie, 1991, Public Eye, Johnnie Zombie, Addams Family 2, Deep Space Nine, Murder She Wrote, George of the Jungle, Home Alone 3, Men in Black, Notorious, (TV shows) Tonight Show, Grammy Awards Show, 1987, All in the Family, Soul Train, Wheel of Fortune, Osmonds, Battlestar Gallactica, V, Bionic Woman, Dinosaurs, Dark Shadows, (TV commls.) Krispy Krunchies, Pepsi, McDonalds, Unical, Coke, (film promotionals) Airport '77, Beau Geste, The Sting, 7% Solution, Swashbuckler, Paramount Pictures Logo; artist: (watercolor) Mechanica; paintings and sculptures represented in pvt. collections including Richard Nixon, Barry Goldwater, John Wayne, Milton Perlman, Herschel Bernardi; exhibitions include Gallery Hawaii, Copenhagen Galleri, Space Gallery, Emerson Gallery, La Jolla Fine Arts Gallery, Lakeland (Ohio) Coll.; author: Changing Patterns Computer Graphics Program for Atari-800, 1981, computer illustrations for Hilton Hotels, 20th Century Fox TV, Besure Corp.; portrait artist for Bette Davis, James Brolin, Norman Lloyd, Ben Cross, Henry Winkler, Ricardo Monteblan, Marty Feldman, Elton John; murals Walt Disney, Hilton Hotel Reno (Nev.); prodr. (CD-ROMs) The Art of John N. Stewart, 1996, The Stewart Collection, 1995-96, (web site) The Art of John N. Stewart, 1996; composer: Peruvian Suite, 1992-97, Piano Abstract, 1994-98. Mem. L.A. Art Assn. Chouinard scholar Glendale (Calif.) Art Assn., 1958. Mem. Nat. Watercolor Soc., IATSE (v.p. scenic and title artists 1989-92), Order of DeMolay, Calif. Art Club. Republican. Mem. Foursquare Ch. Avocations: piano, computers, photography, enjoying nature. Home and Office: 19700 Sweet Brier Pl Cottonwood CA 96022 Personal E-mail: john@jstewart.com.

STEWART, JOHN TODD, economist, consultant; AB, Stanford U., 1961; MA, Tufts U., 1962, MALD, 1970. With Am. Fgn. Svc., 1962-98; U.S. amb. to Republic of Moldova, 1995-98; dep. head U.S. diplomatic missions to Can., Costa Rica and Jamaica; dir. office maritime and land transport Dept. of State, Washington; dir. GATT affairs Pres.'s Spl. Rep. for Trade Negotiations; dep. dir. Inst. Internat. Econs., Washington, 1998—2002; diplomat-in-residence Am. U., 2003—04. Vis. fellow Inst. Internat. Econs., 2002—. Home and Office: PO Box 3200 Sun Valley ID 83353 Office Phone: 208-622-7343. E-mail: todd.stewart@stanfordalumni.org.

STEWART, JOHN WRAY BLACK, college dean; b. Coleraine, Northern Ireland, Jan. 16, 1936; s. John Wray and Margaret Reid (Black) S.; m. Felicity Ann Patricia Poole, Aug. 7, 1965; children: J.W. Matthew, Hannah Louise. BSc with honors, Queen's U., Belfast, Northern Ireland, 1958, BSA with honors, 1959, PhD, 1963, DSc, 1988. Registered profl. agrologist. Sci. officer chem. rsch. divsn. Ministry of Agr., Belfast, 1959-64; asst. prof. soil sci. dept. U. Sask., Saskatoon, Canada, 1966-71, assoc. prof., 1971-76, prof., 1976-81, dir. Sask. Inst. Pedology, 1981-89, dean Coll. Agr., 1989-99, prof. emeritus, 1999—, dean emeritus, 1999—, interim dir. Inter-Am. Inst. for Global Change Rsch., 2002, 2005. Tech. expert, cons. FAO/IAEA, U.N.D.P., Vienna, 1971, Vienna, 1974—75; mem. program com. Can. Global Change, 1985—98; sec.-gen. Sci. Com. on Problems of Environ., Paris, 1988—92, pres., 1992—95, editor-in-chief, 1999—2006; cons. UNESCO, Paris, 1990; trustee Internat. Inst. Tropical Agr., Nigeria, 1991—97; chair sci. adv. com. Inter-Am. Inst. for Global Change Rsch., 1994—2001. Contbr. articles to profl. publs., chapters to books. Fellow: Can. Soc. Soil Sci., Berlin Inst. Advanced Study, Soil Sci. Soc. Am., Am. Soc. Agronomy, Agrl. Inst. Can.; mem.: Internat. Assn. Agrl. Sci. and Tech. Devel. (bureau mem. 2005—08), Internat. Soc. Soil Sci., Brit. Soc. Soil Sci. Avocations: golf, tennis. Personal E-mail: stew9250@telus.net.

STEWART, JON (JONATHAN STEWART LEIBOWITZ), television personality, comedian; b. NYC, Nov. 28, 1962; m. Tracy McShane, 2000; children: Nathan Thomas, Maggie Rose. BS in Psychology, Coll. William and Mary, 1984. Actor: (TV films) Since You've Been Gone, 1998; (films) Mixed Nuts, 1994, Wishful Thinking, 1997, Half Baked, 1998, The Faculty, 1998, Playing by Heart, 1998, Big Daddy, 1999, The Office Party, 2000, Jay and Silent Bob Strike Back, 2001, Death to Smoochy, 2002, (voice only) Doogal, 2006; host: (TV series) Short Attention Span Theater, 1989; You Wrote It, You Watch It, 1992; The Daily Show, 1999— (Emmy award Outstanding Variety, Music or Comedy Series, 2004); (TV special) The Daily Show with Jon Stewart: Indecision 2000 (Emmy award, 2001, George F. Peabody award, 2001); The Daily Show with Jon Stewart: Indecision 2004 (George F. Peabody award, 2005); exec. prodr., writer: (TV series) The Daily Show, 1996— (Primetime Emmy for Outstanding Variety, Music or Comedy Series, Acad. TV Arts and Scis., 2007, 2008); writer, host The Jon Stewart Show, 1993; writer (TV series) The Sweet Life, 1989; exec. prodr.: (TV series) The Colbert Report, 2005— (Prodr. of Yr. award in Live Entertainment/Competition, Prodrs. Guild America, 2009); author: (book) Naked Pictures of Famous People, 1998; co-author (with Ben Karlin and David Javerbaum): The Daily Show With Jon Stewart Presents America (The Book): A Citizen's Guide to Democracy Inaction,

2004 (Book of the Year, Publishers Weekly, 2004, Quills award for best humor book, best audio book, 2005, Thurber Prize for American Humor, 2005). Recipient George F. Peabody award, 2005; named one of Time Mag. 100 Most Influential People, 2005, The 100 Most Powerful Celebrities, Forbes.com, 2008. Office: The Daily Show 604R W 52nd St New York NY 10019-5013*

STEWART, JULIA A., food service executive; m. Jon Greenawalt (div.); 2 children. BA in Communications, San Diego State U., 1977. Regional mktg. dir. Carl's Jr. Restaurant, 1978—80; regional mktg. mgr. Burger King Corp., 1980—84; mktg. dir. Spoons Grill & Bar Stuart Anderson's Black Angus/Cattle Co. Restaurants, 1985, mktg. v.p., 1986—91; western region v.p. operations Taco Bell Yum! Brands, 1991, nat. v.p. franchise, license Taco Bell, 1997—98; pres. domestic div. Applebee's Internat., Inc., 1998—2001; pres, COO Internat. House Pancakes (IHOP), 2001—07, CEO, 2002—07, chmn., 2006—07; chmn., CEO DineEquity, Inc. (Applebee's Neighborhood Grill and Bar and IHOP restaurants), 2007—. Bd. dirs. Avery Denison, Town Hall, LA, Women's Franchise and Distbn. Forum; mem. Elliott Inst. Leadership Coun.; bd. visitors UCLA Anderson Sch. Mgmt.; trustee Calif. Sci. Ctr. Found. Named one of Top 50 Women in Food Svc., Nation's Restaurant, 50 Most Powerful Women in Bus., Fortune mag., 2007. Mem.: Nat. Restaurant Assn. (pres. mktg. executives group), Calif. Restaurant Assn. (exec. bd. mem.), Women's Foodservice Forum (past pres., founding mem.). Avocations: cooking, skiing. Office: DineEquity Inc 450 N Brand Blvd Glendale CA 91203-1903*

STEWART, J.W., energy executive, lawyer; b. Mar. 2, 1944; BSEE, Univ. Tex., Arlington, 1966; JD, Univ. Houston, 1973. V.p. legal, sec. Hughes Tool Co.; chmn., pres., CEO BJ Services, Houston, 1990—. Office: BJ Services 5500 N W Ctrl Dr Houston TX 77092 Mailing: BJ Services PO Box 4442 Houston TX 77210-4442

STEWART, KAREN BREVARD, federal agency administrator, former ambassador; b. Fla., 1951; BA in Astronomy and Econs., Wellesley Coll., Mass.; student, U. Va.; MS in Nat. Security Strategy, Nat. War Coll., Nat. Def. U., Washington, 1998. Joined Fgn. Svc. US Dept. State, 1977, various overseas assignments in Colombo, Sri Lanka, Vientiane, Laos, Udorn, Thailand, Islamabad, Pakistan, and Bangkok, dep. chief of mission Minsk, Belarus, internat. rels. officer, Office Fisheries Affairs Washington, econ. officer, Office Energy Consuming Countries, econ./comml. desk officer, Office Israel & Arab-Israeli Affairs, dir. Office of Ukraine, Moldova, and Belarus Affairs, US amb. to Belarus, 2006—08, prin. dep. asst. sec., Bur. Democracy, Human Rights & Labor, 2008—. Recipient Meritorious and Superior Honor awards, US Dept. State, Diplomacy for Freedom award, 2007. Office: US Dept State 2201 C St NW Washington DC 20520*

STEWART, KENDALL, city councilman, podiatrist; BS, CCNY; DPM, NY Coll. Podiatric Med. City councilman Dist. 45 NY City Coun., 2002—. Chmn. Immigration com. NY City Coun. Mem. APHA, Podiatric Med. Assn., Med. Panel of Local Union 1199, Caribbean America C. of C., Borokeete USA, Sunjets Club, Caricom East 56 St. Rummy Assn., Rugby Domino Club; sponsor, Little Rascals Soccer Club, Hairoon Soccer Club; bd. mem., Caribbean America Sports and Cult Youth Movement, All Fours Alliance of America. Democrat. Office: Dist Off 1694 Flatbush Ave Brooklyn NY 11210 also: 250 Broadway, 18 Floor New York NY 10007 Office Phone: 718-951-8177, 212-788-6859. Office Fax: 718-951-8191. Business E-Mail: stewart@council.nyc.ny.us.*

STEWART, KENT KALLAM, analytical biochemistry educator; b. Omaha, Sept. 5, 1934; s. George Franklin and Grace S.; m. Margaret Reiber, June 10, 1956; children: Elizabeth, Cynthia, Richard, Robert. Student, U. Chgo., 1951-53; AB, U. Calif., Berkeley, 1956; PhD, Fla. State U., 1965. Guest investigator Rockefeller U., NYC, 1965-67, research assoc., 1967-68, asst. prof., 1968-69; research chemist U.S. Dept. Agr., Beltsville, Md., 1970-75, lab. chief Nutrient Composition Lab., 1975-82; prof., head dept. food sci. and tech. Va. Poly. Inst. and State U., Blacksburg, 1982-85, prof. biochemistry, anaerobic microbiology, food sci./tech., 1985—96, prof. emeritus of biochemistry; adj. prof. dept. chemistry and biochemistry U. Tex., Austin, 1996—2004. Editor Jour. Food Composition and Analysis, 1987-97, also 3 books; contbr. articles to profl. jours., co-author book; patentee in field. Capt. USMCR, 1956-59. Fellow AAAS, Inst. Food Technologist. Home: 3900 Glengarry Dr Austin TX 78731-3812 Office Phone: 512-458-1072. E-mail: stewart.kent@gmail.com.

STEWART, KRISTEN JAYMES, actress; b. LA, Apr. 9, 1990; d. John Stewart. Actress (films) The Safety of Objects, 2001, Panic Room, 2002, Cold Creek Manor, 2003, Catch That Kid, 2004, Undertow, 2004, Fierce People, 2005, Zathura: A Space Adventure, 2005, In the Land of Women, 2007, The Messengers, 2007, The Cake Eaters, 2007, Into the Wild, 2007, Cutlass, 2007, Yellow Handkerchief, 2008, What Just Happened?, 2008, Jumper, 2008, Twilight, 2008 (Best Female Performance, MTV Movie Awards, 2009, Best Kiss, MTV Movie Awards, 2009, Choice Movie Actress: Drama, Teen Choice Awards', 2009, Choice Movie Liplock, Teen Choice Awards, 2009), Adventureland, 2009. Named to 30 Under 30 list, Entertainment Weekly, 2008. Office: c/o The Gersh Agy 232 N Canon Dr Beverly Hills CA 90210*

STEWART, LUCILLE MARIE, retired special education coordinator, educator; b. Pitts., Feb. 24; d. William H. and Edna (Hoffman) S. BEd, Duquesne U.; MEd, U. Pitts.; postgrad., Columbia U., U. Calif., Calif. State U. Cert. elem. and secondary tchr., spl. edn. tchr., supr., adminstr. Tchr., group leader mentally retarded Ednl. Alliance, NYC, 1950—53; tchr. Lincoln State Sch., Ill., 1953; tchr., program leader, sec. Edn. Alliance, NYC, 1954-58; tchr. mentally retarded Ramapo Ctrl. Sch. Dist., Spring Valley, NY, 1958-60, tchr. seriously emotionally disturbed, 1960-64, supr. presch. program for educationally disadvantaged, 1965-67; program dir. Pomona Camp for Retarded, NY, summers 1960-63; tchr. mentally retarded Stockton Sch., San Diego, 1964-65; tchr. mentally retarded sch. Cathedral City Sch., 1967-78; program specialist spl. edn. Palm Springs Unified Sch. Dist., Calif., 1978-95, prin. elem. summer schs., 1971-72; prin.-tchr. Summer Extended Sch. for Spl. Students, summer 1979-99; tchr. Primary EMR sch., San Diego, Pre Sch. Summer, 1965, Stockton Elementary, San Diego. Exec. com. U. Calif. Extension, area adv. com.; spl. edn. surrogate parent Palm Springs Unified Sch. Dist. Vol. Palm Springs Unified Dist. HS Alternative Program, 2001—. Named to Educator's Hall of Fame, Riverside Ch., 2008. Mem. NEA, AAUW, ASCD, Calif. Adminstrs. Spl. Edn., Coun. Exceptional Children (adminstrn. divsn., early childhood-learning handicap divsns.), Am. Assn. Childhood Edn., Autism Soc., Coachella Valley, Learning Disabilities Assn., Desert Theater League, Alpha Kappa Alpha, Phi Delta Kappa, Delta Kappa Gamma.

STEWART, LYNNE F., former lawyer; b. Bklyn., Oct. 8, 1939; d. John and Irene Feltham. BA in Polit. Sci., Wagner Coll., 1961; M in Libr. Sci., Pratt U., 1964; JD, Rutgers U., 1975. Bar: NJ 1975, NY 1976. Mem.: Nat. Lawyers Guild. Office: The Lynne Stewart Def Com 350 Broadway Ste 700 New York NY 10013 Office Phone: 212-625-9696. *Convicted of conspiracy, providing material support to terrorists, & defrauding the US government, Feb. 10, 2005; sentenced to 28 months in prison, Oct. 16, 2006; disbarred from practicing law, April 25, 2007.*

STEWART, MARTHA KOSTYRA, entrepreneur, lecturer, author; b. Jersey City, Aug. 3, 1941; d. Edward and Martha (Ruszkowski) Kostyra; m. Andy Stewart, July 1, 1961 (div. 1990); 1 child, Alexis Gilbert. BA European History and Archtl. History, Barnard Coll. Former model; former stockbroker NYC; former profl. caterer; mag. owner, editor-in-chief Martha Stewart Living, 1990—97; CEO Martha Stewart Living Omnimedia, 1997—2003, chief creative officer, 2003—04, chmn., 1997—2004, founding editl. dir., 2004—. Lifestyle cons. for K-Mart Corp., 1987; bd. dirs., NYSE, 2002-04. Host (TV show) Martha Stewart Living, 1993-2004, The Apprentice: Martha Stewart, 2005, (TV talk show) Martha 2005-; Author: (with Elizabeth Hawes) Entertaining, 1982, Weddings, 1987; Martha Stewart Hors d'Oeurvres: The Creation and Presentation of Fabulous Finger Food, 1984, Martha Stewart's Pies and Tarts, 1985, Martha Stewart's Quick Cook Menus: Fifty-two Meals You Can Make in Under an Hour, 1988, The Wedding Planner, 1988, Martha Stewart's Gardening: Month by Month, 1991, Martha Stewart's New Old House: Restoration, Renovation, Decoration, 1992, Martha Stewart's Christmas, 1993, Martha Stewart's Menus for Entertaining, 1994, Holidays, 1994, Good Things: The Best of Martha Stewart Living, 1997, Four Seasons of Great Menus to Make Every Day, 1997, Hors D'Oeuvres Handbook, 1999, The Best of Martha Stewart Living: Weddings, 1999, The Barefoot Contessa Cookbook: Secrets from the East Hampton Specialty Food Store for Simple Food and Party Platters You Can Make at Home, 1999, (with Ina Garten) Favorite Comfort Food, 1999, The Martha Stewart Living Cookbook, 2000, Halloween: The Best of Martha Stewart Living, 2001, Classic Crafts and Recipes Inspired by the Songs of Christmas, 2002, Martha Stewart Living 2003, Recipes, 2002, Simple Home Solutions, 2004, The Martha Rules, 2005, Martha Stewart's Baking Handbook, 2005, Martha Stewart's Homekeeping Handbook: The Essential Guide to Caring for Everything in Your Home, 2006; contbr. (magazine) Blueprint: Design Your Life, 2006-; appeared in semi-monthly cooking segment on Today Show; syndicated columnist, NY Times. Named one of World's 100 Most Influential People, Time Mag., 2005, 50 Most Powerful Women in Bus., Fortune mag., 2006. Office: 10 Saugatuck Ave Westport CT 06880-5720 also: care Susan Magrino Agy 40 W 57th St Fl 31 New York NY 10019-4001

STEWART, MARY TOMLINSON, science educator, researcher; b. San Francisco, Aug. 27, 1944; d. John Reid and Evelyn Tomlinson; children: David Christophere, Mary Cameron. BA, Goddard Coll., 1966; MLS, U. Okla., 1990; MS in Math. and Sci. Edn., U. Tulsa, 1996. Tchr. Hyde Park (Vt.) Elem., 1966—78, Marlow (Okla.) Elem., 1978—84, Monte Casino Elem., Tulsa, 1984—88; tchr. gifted Emerson Elem., Tulsa, 1988—93; adminstr. sci. Okla State Dept. Edn., Okla. City., 1993—96, Tulsa Pub. Schs., 1996—2002; rsch. assoc. U. Tulsa, 2002—. Co-author: Fossils to Fuel, 1995, Petro Active, 1998. DKG, PEO, Tulsa; bd. mem. Okla. Sci. Tchrs. Assn., 1989—2002, pres., 1996—97, convention presenter. Recipient Jack Renner award, Okla. Sci. Tchrs. Assn., 1998; named Support Person of Yr., Tulsa Pub. Schs., 2001. Mem.: Nat. Coun. Tchrs. Math. (presenter), Okla. Coun. Tchrs. Math. (presenter), Tulsa Coun. Tchrs. Math. (bd. mem. 1991—93, presenter), Nat. Sci. Tchrs. Assn. (conv. chair 1990—99, review bd. sci. tchrs. 1994—96, convention presenter), Coalition for Advancement Sci. (pres., v.p., bd. mem. 1995—2008). Democrat. Unitaria. Avocations: reading, travel. Home: 4638 S Quincy Pl Tulsa OK 74105 Office: Univ Tulsa 800S Tucker Dr Tulsa OK 74104 Office Phone: 918-631-3519. Business E-Mail: mary-stewart@utulsa.edu.

STEWART, MELBOURNE GEORGE, JR., physicist, researcher; b. Detroit, Sept. 30, 1927; s. Melbourne George and Ottilie (Tuholke) S.; m. Charlotte L. Ford, Jan. 23, 1954; children— Jill K., John H., Kevin G. AB, U. Mich., 1949, MS, 1950, PhD, 1955. Research assoc. dept. physics AEC, Ames Lab., Iowa State U., 1955-56, asst. prof., 1956-62, assoc. prof., 1962-63; prof. Wayne State U., Detroit, 1963-94, prof. emeritus, 1994—, chmn. dept. physics, 1963-73, assoc. provost for faculty relations, 1973-86; hon. research fellow Univ. Coll., London, 1986-87,93. Editorial bd.: Wayne State U. Press, 1969-73. Served with AUS, 1946-47. Mem. Am. Phys. Soc., AAAS, Sigma Xi, Phi Beta Kappa. Office: Dept Physics Wayne State U Detroit MI 48202 Business E-Mail: stewart@physics.wayne.edu.

STEWART, MICHAEL GLENN, otolaryngologist, educator; b. Bowling Green, Ky., Sept. 17, 1962; s. Michael Joseph and Barbara (Weisser) S. B in Engring. summa cum laude, Vanderbilt U., 1984; MD, Johns Hopkins U., 1988; MPH, U. Tex., 1996; Gen. Surgery, Baylor Coll. Medicine, 1990, Otolaryngology, 1994. Diplomate Am. Bd. Otolaryngology. Asst. prof. Baylor Coll. Medicine, Houston, 1994-99, assoc. prof., 1999—2005, dir. residency edn. dept. otolaryngology, 1996—2005, asst. dean clin. affairs, 1998-2000, gen. dir. affil. med. svc., 1999—2005, assoc. dean clin. affairs, 2000—05; prof., chmn. Dept. Otorhinolaryngology Weill Cornell Med. Coll., NYC, 2005—; otorhinolaryngologist-in-chief NY Presbyn. Hosp., 2005—. Chief otolaryngology Ben Taub Gen. Hosp., 1994-2005; chmn. med. bd. Harris County Hosp. Dist., Houston, 1999-2000; sr. examiner Am. Bd. Otolaryngology, 2007-08, dir. 2008-, edtl. bd. mem. ENToday, dir. Am. Bd. Otolarygology, 2008- Editor Rev. Head and Neck, 1994—; reviewer Archive Otolaryngology-Head and Neck, 1997—, Jour. Trauma, 1998—, Otolaryngology-Head and Neck Surgery, 1998—, Cancer, 2001—; assoc. editor, mem. editl. bd. Am. Jour. Rhinology, 2003—; mem. editl. bd. Archives of Otolaryngology-Head and Neck Surgery, 2005—. Recipient Outstanding Clin. Rsch. award Kelsey-Seybold Found., 1992, 93, Houston Disting. Surgeon award Assn. Perioperative Nurses, 2005. Fellow: ACS, Am. Rhinologic Soc., Am. Laryngol., Rhinol. and Otol. Soc., Am. Acad. Otolaryngology Head and Neck Surgery (chair rsch. adv. bd. 2008—, Disting. Svc. award 2004); mem.: Triological Soc., Assn. Acad. Depts. Otolaryngology (pres.-elect), Soc. Univ. Otolaryngologists (pres. 2007—08). Office Phone: 646-962-4777. Business E-Mail: mgs2002@med.cornell.edu.

STEWART, MURRAY BAKER, retired lawyer; b. Muskogee, Okla., May 16, 1931; s. Francis and Fannie Penelope (Murray) S.; m. Roseanna Furgason; children: Melinda, Jeffrey, Cheryl. BA, U. Okla., 1953, JD, 1955; postgrad., Georgetown U., 1958-59. Bar: Okla. 1955; CLU, ChFC. Judge adv. U.S. Army, 1955-59; ptnr. Stewart & Stewart, Tulsa and Muskogee, Okla., 1955, 62-72; asst. v.p. First Nat. Bank and Trust Co. of Tulsa, 1959-62, 77-78; mem. Hutchins, Stewart, Stewart & Elmore, Tulsa, 1972-77; atty. cons. advanced underwriting Metlife Ins. Co., NYC, 1978-94; assoc. Metlife Securities, Inc., SEC Registered Investment Advisors, 1984-94; of counsel Brumley & Bishop, Tulsa, 1997-99; ret., 1999. Cons. on Am. Indian books; lectr. in field. Contbr. articles to profl. and hist. jours.; prodr. texts and videos on history, investment and bus. Fellow Life Mgmt. Inst.; mem. Okla. Bar Assn., Sons Confederate Vets. (judge advocate Army of Trans-Mississippi 1998-2000, Okla. divsn. 2008-), Civil War Roundtable Tulsa, Sons Union Vets. Civil War.

STEWART, PAMELA L., lawyer; b. Bogalusa, La., Mar. 13, 1953; d. James Adrian and Patricia Lynn (Wood) Lloyd; m. Steven Bernard Stewart, Aug. 31, 1974 (div. July 1980); 1 child, Christopher. BA, U. New Orleans, 1986; JD, U. Houston, 1990. Cert. debtor educator Coalition Consumer Bankruptcy Edn., lic. realtor Tex. Intern La. Supreme Ct., New Orleans, 1984, Councilman Bryan Wagner, New Orleans, 1984—85; legal asst. Clann, Bell & Murphy, Houston, 1988—89, Tejas Gas Corp., Houston, 1989—90; atty. Law Offices of Pamela L. Stewart, Houston, 1991—; vice chair NRC Cinco Ranch Property Owners Assn., 2007—; sec. Bankruptcy Law Network, 2007—; bd. dirs. Nat. Assn. Consumer Bankrupt Attys., 2008—. Spkr. in field; spkr. People's Law Sch., 2007—, State Bar Tex. Advanced Consumer Bankruptcy Law, 2007—. Editor in chief (book) Credit Scores and Consumer Reports, Evan Hendricks, 3rd edit., 2008. Bd. dirs. Alliance for Good Govt., New Orleans, 1983-84, NACBA, 2008-, Attention Deficit Hyperactivity Disorder Assn. Tex., 1989-90; vol. Houston Vol. Lawyers Program, Houston, 1992—; bd. dirs. West Lane Place Civic Assn., sec., 2001-2003, v.p., 2003-07, block captain, 2002—07; mem. com. Lawyers Against Waste, Habitat for Humanity; apptd. Harris County Appraisal Rev. Bd.; vice chair Tex. State Bar Bankruptcy Section Ch. 13 Survey Com.; editor-in-chief Credit Scores, Credit Reports by Evan Mendricks, 2008, co-chair NRC-Cinco Ronch POA, 2007- Innsbruck scholar, U. New Orleans, 1985. Fellow Inst. Politics, Houston Bar Found.; mem. ABA, Tax Freedom Inst., Nat. Assn. Consumer Bankruptcy Attys.(bd. dirs. 2008-), Houston Bar Assn. (com. mem. bankruptcy sect.), Katy Bar Assn. (3d v.p. 1997-98), Houston Assn. Debtors Attys. (pres. 1996-98, 2006—), Upper Kirby Dist. Optimist Club (v.p. 2000-01, pres. 2001-02), Feng Shui Guild, Feng Shui Basics (pres.), Nat. Assn. Consumer Advs., NRC Cinco Ranch Property Owners Assn.(vice-chair 2007-). Methodist. Avocations: music, cooking, swimming, politics. Office: 4635 SW Fwy Ste 610 Houston TX 77027 also: 5606 N Navarro 200 Victoria TX 77904 Office Phone: 713-622-3893, 361-576-1779. Personal E-mail: plsatty@swbell.net.

STEWART, PATRICIA CARRY, foundation administrator; b. Bklyn., May 19, 1928; d. William J. and Eleanor (Murphy) Carry; m. Charles Thorp Stewart, May 30, 1976. Student, U. Paris, 1948—49; BA, Cornell U., 1950. Fgn. corr. Irving Trust Co., NYC, 1950-51; with Janeway Rsch. Co., NYC, 1951-60, sec., treas., 1955-60; with Buckner & Co. and successor firms, NYC, 1961-73, ptnr., 1962-70, v.p., treas., 1970-71, pres., treas., 1971-73, Knight, Carry, Bliss & Co., Inc., NYC, 1971-73, G. Tsai & Co., Inc., 1973; v.p. Edna McConnell Clark Found. Inc., 1974-92; bd. dirs. Trans World Airlines, 1973—95, F. W. Woolworth Co., 1973—75, Continental Corp., 1974—95, Borden Inc. Morton, 1974—96, Norwich/Bankers Trust, 1978—81, CVS Corp., 1986—98. Dir. Cmty. Found. Palm Beach and Martin Counties, 1993-2001, chair, 1998, 2000; allied mem. N.Y. Stock Exch., 1962-73; past mem. nominating com. Am. Stock Exch., N.Y. Stock Exch., N.Y.C. Fin. Svcs. Corp.; dir. emeritus, past chmn. Investor Responsibility Rsch. Ctr. Trustee emerita, vice chair Cornell U., mem. bd. life overseers Cornell Med. Coll.; mem. vis. com. Grad. Sch Bus., Harvard U., 1974-80; bd. dirs. NOW Legal Def. and Edn. Fund, 1984-92, Women in Founds./Corp. Philanthropy, 1980-86; v.p. fin. com. Women's Forum, 1982-90; vice chmn. CUNY, 1976-80; bd. dirs. United Way of Tri-State, 1977-81, Inst. for Edn. and Rsch. on Women and Work; voting mem. Blue Cross and Blue Shield Greater N.Y., 1975-82; trustee N.Y. State 4-H Found., 1970-76, Intenrt. Inst. Rural Reconstrn., 1974-79; mem. N.Y.C. panel White House Fellows, 1976-78; mem. bus. adv. coun. The Hosp. Chaplaincy. Recipient Elizabeth Cutter Morrow award YWCA, 1977, Catalyst award Women Dirs. in Corps., 1978, Trustee medal CUNY, 1983, Acomplishment award Wings Club N.Y. 1984, Women's Funding Coalition Innovators for Women$hare award, 1986, Banking Industry Achievement award Nat. Assn. Bank Women, 1987, Cert. Disting. Accomplishments Barnard Coll., 1989; named to YWCA Acad. Women Achievers. Mem. Fin. Women's Assn. N.Y., Country Club of Fla. (bd. dirs.), Univ. Club (N.Y.C), Gullane Golf Club (Scotland), North Berwick Golf Club (Scotland), Dunbar Golf Club (Scotland), St. Andrews Club (Delray Beach, Fla.), Phi Beta Phi. Home and Office: 2613 N Ocean Blvd Delray Beach FL 33483-7367

STEWART, PATRICIA DIANE, psychologist; b. Clemson, SC, Dec. 29, 1948; d. Gustavus Hoffmeyer and Juanita Stewart; m. Sam Harrelson, Aug. 10, 1982; children: Jeremy Ryan Harrelson, Hillary Stewart Harrelson. BA, U. Ga., Athens, 1971; MEd, Francis Marion U., Florence, Johnsonville, SC, 1981, MS, 1987; EdD, SC Sate U., Orangeburg, 2007. Cert. psycho ednl. specialist SC Labor Licensing, 2000, Nationally Cert. Sch. Psychologist, 2000. Guidance counselor Johnsonville Mid. Sch., SC, 1980—90; psychologist Florence Sch. Dist. Five, 1985—90, Horry County Sch., Conway, SC, 1991—. Youth dir. Johnsonville United Meth. Ch., 2001—08. Mem.: NASP, SC Assn. Sch. Psychologists (Columbia) (bd. mem. 1998—2008). Methodist. Avocation: travel. Home: 171 B Atlantic Ave Pawleys Island SC 29585 Office: Horry County Sch PO Box 260005 Conway SC 29527

STEWART, PATRICK, actor; b. Mirfield, Eng., July 13, 1940; s. Alfred and Gladys (Barraclough) S.; m. Sheila Falconer, Mar. 3, 1966 (div. 1990); 2 children; m. Wendy Neuss, Aug. 25, 2000 (div. 2003). Trained, Bristol Old Vic Theatre Sch. Actor: (theatre) Treasure Island (UK, debut), 1959, (US) A Midsummer Night's Dream (Broadway debut), 1970, A Christmas Carol, 1991, 92, 94, Macbeth, West End, 2007, Broadway, 2008, Hamlet, Royal Shakespeare Co., 2008 (Laurence Olivier award for best supporting actor, 2009); (TV series) Star Trek: The Next Generation, 1987-94, Eleventh Hour, 2006, (narrator) High Spirits with the Ghostman, 2005, (mini series) Fall of Eagles, 1974, I, Claudius, 1977, Tinker, Sailor, Soldier, Spy, 1979, Maybury, 1981, Smiley's People, 1982, Playing Shakespeare, 1983, When the Lion Roars, 1992, (voice) 500 Nations, 1995, Mysterious Island, 2005, (TV movies) The Gathering Storm, 1974, Anthony and Cleopatra, 1974 (Olivier award best supporting actor), North and South, 1975, The Madness, 1976, Hamlet, Prince of Denmark, 1980, Little Lord Fauntleroy, 1980, John Paul II, 1984, The Devil's Disciple, 1987, Death Train, 1993, In Search of Dr. Seuss, 1994, (also co-prodr.) The Canterville Ghost, 1996, Moby Dick, 1997, Safe House, 1998, (voice) Animal Farm, 1999, (also exec. prodr.) A Christmas Carol, 1999, (also exec. prodr.) King of Texas, 2002, The Lion in Winter, 2003; host on Saturday Night Live, 1994, (films) Hennessy, 1975, Hedda, 1975, Excalibur, 1981, The Plague Dogs (voice) 1982, Dune, 1984, Uindii, 1984, Lifeforce, 1985, Code Name: Emerald, 1985, Wild Geese II, 1985, The Doctor and the Devils, 1985, Lady Jane, 1986, L.A. Story, 1991, Robin Hood: Men in Tights, 1993, Gunmen, 1994, Star Trek: Generations, 1994, The Pagemaster, 1994 (voice), Jeffrey, 1995, Let It Me Be (aka Love Dance), 1995, Star Trek: First Contact, 1996, Conspiracy Theory, 1997, Safe House, 1997, Dad Savage, 1997, Master Minds, 1997, (voice) Prince of Egypt, 1998, X-Men, 2000, (voice) Jimmy Neutron: Boy Genius, 2001, Star Trek: Nemesis, 2002, X-Men 2, 2003, (voice) Back to Gaya, 2004, Steamboy, 2004, The Game of Their Lives, 2005, (voice) Chicken Little, 2005, X-Men: The Last Stand, 2006, TMNT, 2007, (voice) Earth, 2007; assoc. prodr. Star Trek IX: Insurrection, 1998; assoc. artist with Royal Shakespeare Co., 1967—; recording: Prokofiev: Peter and the Wolf

(Grammy award best spoken word album for children 1996). Recipient Sir John Gielgud award, Nat. Arts Club, 2008. Office: William Morris Agy 151 El Camino Dr Beverly Hills CA 90212*

STEWART, PAUL ARTHUR, pharmaceutical company executive; b. Greensburg, Ind., Sept. 28, 1955; s. John Arthur and Alberta Jeannette (Densford) S.; m. Susan Rhodes, Dec. 20, 1975; children: John Rhodes, Daniel Robbins. BS, Purdue U., 1976; MBA, Harvard U., 1987. Grad. asst. Purdue U., West Lafayette, Ind., 1977; asst. treas. Stewart Seeds Inc., Greensburg, 1997-82, sec., treas., 1982-84; cons. The Boston Cons. Group Inc., Chgo., 1986; founder, owner PASCO Group, mgmt. and computer cons., aircraft leasing, 1979-87; mgr. bus. planning agrichems. Eli Lilly & Co., Indpls., 1987-88, dist. sales mgr. agrichems., 1989-90, tech. acquisition mgr. med. devices and diagnostics divsn., 1990-92; dir. mktg. info. and bus. devel. IVAC Corp. subs. Eli Lilly & Co., 1992-94, advisor corp. fin. and investment banking, 1994-96; mgr. global bus. devel. (animal health) Eli Lilly & Co., 1996—. Author: (nonfiction) A Harvard MBA's Advice to His Sons, 2005. Mem. Greensburg-Decatur County Bd. Airport Commrs., 1980-85, pres., 1980-81, 83; mem. Decatur County Data Processing Bd., 1982-85; deacon 2d Presbyn. Ch. Indpls., 1991-92, elder, 1996-99; bd. dirs. Friends of Nat. Inst. Nursing Rsch., NIH, 1995-98, Park Tudor Sch., Indpls., 1997-2003. Mem.: Indpls. Legal Aid Soc. (bd. dirs. 2004—), Harvard Bus. Sch. Alumni Assn. (bd. dirs. 1999—2003, v.p. 2001—03), Alpha Gamma Rho. Republican. Presbyterian. Office: Eli Lilly & Co Lilly Corp Ctr Indianapolis IN 46285-0001 Office Phone: 317-277-6120. Personal E-mail: pstewart@mba1987.hbs.edu.

STEWART, PRISCILLA ANN MABIE, art historian, educator; b. Iowa City, Sept. 21, 1926; d. Edward Charles and Grace Frances (Chase) Mabie; m. Thomas Wilson Stewart, Aug. 28, 1949 (dec. Mar. 1996). BA, U. Iowa, 1948; MA, U. South Fla., 1971; EdS, Fla. Atlantic U., 1983. Coord. elem. art Manatee County, Fla., 1953-59; prof. art history dept. fine and performing arts, intercultural humanities, founder photography Manatee CC, Bradenton, Fla., 1959—, State Coll. Fla., 2009—. Organizer, dir. Pelican Perch Wild Bird Hosp., Bradenton, 1953-85; participant Women's Archives U. Iowa Librs. Apptd. charter mem. of adv. bd. to dean of Liberal Arts, U. Iowa, 1999—2009. Mem. AAUP, Pres.'s Club U. Iowa, Fla. Assn. CCs, Sarasota-Manatee Phi Beta Kappa Assn. (pres. 1984-86), Phi Beta Kappa, Alpha Xi Delta, Phi Kappa Phi. Episcopalian. Home: 2705 Riverview Blvd Bradenton FL 34205-4335 Office: State Coll Fla Manatee Sarasota Dept Fine and Performing Arts 5840 26th St W Bradenton FL 34207-3522 Home Phone: 941-749-1853; Office Phone: 941-752-5548. Business E-Mail: stewarp@scf.edu.

STEWART, RICHARD DONALD, internist, educator, writer; b. Lakeland, Fla., Dec. 26, 1926; s. LeRoy Hepburn and Zoa Irene (Hachet) S.; m. Mary Leeuw, June 14, 1952; children: R. Scot, Gregory D., Mary E. AB, U. Mich., 1951, MD, 1955, MPH, 1962; MA, U. Wis. Milw., 1979; PhD in English, U. Wis., Milw., 1997. Diplomate Am. Bd. Internal Medicine, Am. Bd. Med. Toxicology, Acad. Toxicol. Scis. Intern Saginaw (Mich.) Gen. Hosp., 1955-56; resident in internal medicine U. Mich. Med. Ctr., Ann Arbor, 1959-62; dir. med. rsch. sect. Dow Chem. Co., Midland, Mich., 1962-66; staff physician Midland Hosp., 1962-66; assoc. prof. preventive medicine Med. Coll. Wis., Milw., 1966-68, prof., chmn. dept. environ. medicine, 1968—78, prof. emergency med., 1989—91, adj. prof. dept. pharmacology and toxicology, 1978—. Cons. Children's Hosp. Wis., 1989-93, Internal Medicine St. Mary's Hosp., Racine, Wis., 1983-93; prof., dir. med. toxicology fellowship Dept. Emergency Medicine Milw. Regional Med. Ctr., 1989-91; sr. attending staff, 1967-90; staff Internal Medicine St. Luke's Hosp., Racine, 1983-93; med. dir. Poison Control Ctr. Southeastern Wis., 1989-93; corp. med. advisor S.C. Johnson & Son, Inc., Racine, 1971-78, corp. med. dir., 1978-89. Author: (med. biography) Leper Priest of Molokai, 2000. Mem. adv. med. staff Milw. Fire Dept., 1975—. Cadet USAF, 1945-46. Fellow ACP, Am. Coll. Occupl. Medicine, Am. Acad. Clin. Toxicology, Acad. Toxicological Scis.; mem. AMA, Soc. Toxicology, Wis. State Med. Soc., Racine Acad. Medicine, Rotary Internat., Phi Theta Kappa, Phi Kappa Phi, Sigma Tau Delta. Achievements include invention of medical devices including the hollow fiber artificial kidney and capillary artificial lung; being leader of team that performed first human dialyses with the Hollow Fiber Artificial Kidney, beginning Aug.4, 1967. This artificial kidney is universally used for long-term dialysis. Avocations: hiking, literature, creative writing. Home and Office: 5337 Wind Point Rd Racine WI 53402-2322 Office Phone: 262-639-6483.

STEWART, RICHARD DOW, science educator; m. Kathleen Marie Collins, Oct. 6, 1979; children: Alena Kitty, Alexander Philip, Meredith Laura, Maureen Dow. BS, US Mcht. Marine Acad., Kings Point, NY, 1973; MS, U. Wisconsin-Green Bay, 1982; PhD, Rennsselar Poly. Inst., Troy, NY, 1997. Cert. Steam & Motor Vessels US Coast Guard, 1979, STCW 1995, 2002, in transp. & logistics AM. Soc. Transp. & Logistics, 2002. Seaman Sailors Union Pacific, San Francisco, 1967—68; prof. & rsch. dir. U. Wis. Superior, 1999—. Mcht. marine officer Gulf Oil Corp., Phila, 1973—79; capt. USNR, Washington, 1973—2003; mcht. marine officer Inter Ocean, 1980—82, Inter Ocean Transport, Phila, 1980—82; master Titan Nav., 1982—86; fleet mgr. Falcon Carriers, Houston, 1986—87; dept. head & prof. US Mcht. Marine Acad., Kings Point, midshipman, 1969—73, prof. & dept. head, 1987—99. Office: Univ Wis Superior Erlanson Hall 5 Superior WI 54880

STEWART, RICHARD EDWIN, insurance consulting company executive; b. Washington, Nov. 4, 1933; s. Irvin and Florence Elsie (Dezendorf) S.; m. Barbara Lewis Dickson, Oct. 29, 1993. BA, W.Va. U., 1955; BA (Rhodes scholar), Oxford U., Eng., 1957, MA, 1961; JD, Harvard, 1959. Bar: N.Y. 1960. Assoc. Royall, Koegel & Rogers, NYC, 1960-63; asst. counsel to Gov. of N.Y., 1963-64, 1st asst. counsel, 1965-66; supr. ins. N.Y. State Ins. Dept., 1967-70; sr. v.p., gen. counsel First Nat. City Bank, NYC, 1971-72; sr. v.p., dir. Chubb & Son Inc., NYC, 1973-81; sr. v.p. Chubb Corp., NYC, 1973-81, CFO, 1974-81; gov. N.Y. Ins. Exch., NYC, 1979-81; chmn. Stewart Econs., Inc., NYC, 1981-90, Chapel Hill, NC, 1990—2005, San Francisco, 2005—. Mem. adv. com. HUD, 1968-72; mem. Adminstrv. Conf. U.S., 1970-74; bd. dirs. Am. Arbitration Assn., 1970-80; mem. UN panel experts on Transnational Bank failure, 1991. Co-author: Automobile Insurance-...For Whose Benefit?, 1970, Watergate: Implications for Responsible Government, 1974, Medical Malpractice, 1977, Managing Insurer Insolvency, 1988, Insurance Insolvency Guarantees, 1990, A Brief History of Underwriting Cycles, 1991, Niche Insurance Companies, 1997, Information Technology and Insurance Agent Licensing, 1998, The Loss of the Certainty Effect, 2002, Managing Insurer Insolvency, 2003; author: Reason and Regulation, 1972, Insurance and Insurance Regulation, 1980, Arbitration and Insurance without the Common Law, 2004, The Attorney General, the SEC and the Commissioners of Insurance, 2007. Trustee Coll. Ins., N.Y., 1970-78, Am. Coll. Life Underwriters, 1990-93; mem. Mayor's Com. on Taxi Regulation, 1979-82, ABA Com. to Improve Liability Ins. System, 1989; mem. panel experts on transnat. bank failure UN, 1991; mem. spl. panel U.S. Senate Com. on Presdl. Campaign Practice, 1974. Served with AUS, 1959. Mem. Nat. Acad. Pub. Adminstrn., Nat. Acad. Social Ins., Cosmos Club of Washington, Century Club of N.Y.C., Phi Beta Kappa Assn. Home and Office: 550 Davis St Unit 29 San Francisco CA 94111 Business E-Mail: res@stewarteconomics.com.

STEWART, RICHARD WILLIAMS, lawyer; b. Harrisburg, Pa., Aug. 21, 1948; s. Alexander H. and M. Winifred (Williams) S.; m. Mary A. Simmonds, June 7, 1975; 1 child, Anne W. AB cum laude, Franklin and Marshall Coll., 1970; JD, Duke U., 1973. Bar: Pa. 1973, U.S. Dist. Ct. (mid. dist.) Pa. 1975, U.S. Tax Ct. 1984. Assoc. Stone & Sajer, New Cumberland, Pa., 1973-77; ptnr. Stone, Sajer & Stewart, New Cumberland, 1977-87, Johnson, Duffie, Stewart & Weidner, Lemoyne, Pa., 1987—. Solicitor West Shore Sch. Dist., Lemoyne, Pa., 1977-93, No. York County Sch. Dist., Dillsburg, Pa., 1984—2008, Pa. Bd. Law Examiners 2008-, Camp Hill Sch. Dist., 1986—, Fairview Twp., 1987-98; v.p. Cedar Cliff Abstract Agy., 1980-87; v.p. Secured Land Transfers, Inc., Camp Hill, Pa., 1985-2000, pres., 2000-05; pres. Lawyers Realty LLC, 2006—. Chmn. Cumberland County Rep. Com., 1981-84; mem. Rep. State Com. Pa., 1990—. Mem. ABA, Pa. Bar Assn. (house of dels. 2004-), Cumberland County Bar Assn. (pres.2004), Supreme Ct. of Pa. (disciplinary bd. 1998—, vice chmn. 2003, chmn. 2004), Ctrl. Pa. Estate Planning Coun. (bd. dirs. 1983-85), Pa. Sch. Solicitors Assn. (pres. 1995), Rotary (bd. dirs. West Shore, Harrisburg). Presbyterian. Home: 1811 Warren St New Cumberland PA 17070-1148 Office: 301 Market St Lemoyne PA 17043-1628 Office Phone: 717-761-4540.

STEWART, RITA JOAN, academic administrator; b. Muncie, Ind., June 6, 1945; d. John Marion and Crystalee Masterson; children: Jon Lewis, Robert Forrest. BS, Ball State U., 1967, MA, 1974. Tchr. Blue River H.S., Mt. Summit, Ind., 1968-69, Sunnyside Elem. Sch., New Castle, Ind., 1967-68; copywriter, announcer Sta. WTIM, Taylorville, Ill., 1974-75; dir. Kitselman Conf. Ctr. Ball State U., Muncie, Ind., 1978-2000, dir. conf. and spl. events, 2000—. Contbr. articles to profl. jours. Precinct committeewoman Henry County Dem. Party, New Castle, Ind., 1969-70; precinct chmn. March of Dimes, New Castle, Ind., 1974-75; chmn. edn. com. West Viwe Sch. Coun., Muncie, 1987-88; sec., bd. dirs. PAL Club, Muncie, 1988-93; pres., bd. dirs. Altrusa Club Found., Muncie, 1997-98, v.p., 2001-01, pres., 2002. Mem.: AAUW (v.p. 1984—85), Ind. Conf. Dirs. Assn., Assn. Collegiate Conf. and Event Dirs. Internat. (dir. region 8 1999—2000, pres. elect 2006—07, pres. 2008—, internat. bd. dirs., Mentor Yr. award 2004), Altrusa Club of Muncie (pres. 2002—03), Kappa Delta Pi (Disting. Svc. award 1995). Methodist. Office: Ball State U Confs and Spl Events Muncie IN 47306 Home: # 1-203 4501 N Wheeling Ave Muncie IN 47304-1277 Office Phone: 765-285-1396. Office Fax: 765-285-5457. Business E-Mail: rstewart@bsu.edu.

STEWART, ROBERT D., JR., lawyer; b. Manchester, NH, Mar. 26, 1942; s. Robert Desbrow Stewart and Ruth E. Burgess; m. Patricia Ann Byrne, Dec. 3, 1966; children: Kimberly Anne Bishop, Robert III, Deborah Kaye Lestina. BA, U. Okla., 1966, JD, 1971. Bar: Okla., US Supreme Ct. 1981. Assoc. Horsley, Epton & Culp, Wewoka, Okla., 1972-73, ptnr., 1973-79; gen. counsel Okla. Corp. Commn., Oklahoma City, 1979-82; atty. Okla. Gas and Electric Co., Oklahoma City, 1982—2003; of counsel Rainey, Ross, Rice & Binns, Oklahoma City, 2003—. Instr. U. Okla. Continuing Legal Edn., Norman, Okla., 1977-79, Coll. of Law, 1982; instr. elec. utility execs. Okla. City U., People's Republic China, 1996—2001. Lt. Col. US Army, 1966—90, ret. US Army, 2002. Office: 735 First Nat Ctr West Oklahoma City OK 73102 Office Phone: 405-235-1356. E-mail: stewarrd@oge.com.

STEWART, ROBERT S., construction executive; B, MBA, U. Wash. With Weyerhaeuser Co., 1977—2000; sr. v.p. strategic planning and mktg. Centex Corp., Dallas, 2000—05, sr. v.p. strategy and corp. devel., 2005—. Bd. dirs. Tex. Bus. and Edn. Coalition. Office: Centex Corp PO Box 199000 Dallas TX 75219-9000 Office Phone: 214-981-5000. Office Fax: 214-981-6859.

STEWART, ROD (RODERICK DAVID STEWART), singer; b. North London, Eng., Jan. 10, 1945; m. Alana Collins, Apr. 6, 1979 (div. 1984); children: Kimberly, Sean; child with Kelly Emberg: Ruby Rachel; m. Rachel Hunter, Dec. 15, 1990 (div. Nov. 2, 2006); children: Renée, Liam; m. Penny Lancaster, June 16, 2007; 1 child, Alistair Wallace Lead singer Jimmy Powell and the Five Dimensions, 1963, The Hoochie Coochie Men, 1964—65, Soul Agents, 1965—66, Shotgun Express, 1966, The Jeff Beck Group, 1968—69, The Faces, 1969—75; solo artist, 1969—. Singer: albums (with The Jeff Beck Group) Truth, 1968, Beck-Ola, 1969; (with The Faces) The First Step, 1970, Long Player, 1971, A Nod Is As Good as a Wink...To a Blind Horse, 1971, Ooh La La, 1973, Coast to Coast/Overture & Beginners, 1974, Snakes and Ladders: The Best of The Faces, 1975, The Best of the Faces, 1977, Good Boys...When They're Asleep, 199, Five Guys Walk Into a Bar..., 2004; (solo albums) An Old Raincoat Won't Ever Let You Down, 1969, Gasoline Alley, 1970, Every Picture Tells a Story, 1971, Never a Dull Moment, 1972, Sing it Again Rod, 1973, Smiler, 1974, Atlantic Crossing, 1975, The Best of Rod Stewart, 1976, The Best of Rod Stewart Vol. II, 1976, A Night on the Town, 1976, Foot Loose & Fancy Free, 1976, Blondes Have More Fun, 1978, Greatest Hits Vol. I, 1979, Foolish Behaviour, 1980, Tonight I'm Yours, 1981, Absolutely Live, 1981, Camouflage, 1984, (with Jeff Beck) Get Workin', 1985, Out of Order, 1988, Storyteller: The Complete Anthology 1964-1990, 1990, Downtown Train, 1990, Vagabond Heart, 1991, You Wear It Well, 1992, The Mercury Anthology, 1992, Once In A Blue Moon Vintage, 1993, Ridin High, The Rod Stewart Album, Unplugged...And Seated, 1993 (Grammy nomination, Best Pop Male Vocal for "Have I Told You Lately"), Spanner in the Works, 1995, Handbags and Gladrags, 1996, When We Were the New Boys, 1998, Human, 2001, It Had to Be You...The Great American Songbook, 2002, As Time Goes By...The Great American Songbook, Vol.:II, 2003, Stardust...The Great American Songbook, Vol.:III, 2004, Thanks for the Memory: The Great American Songbook, Vol. 4, 2005, Ain't That Loving You Baby, 2005, Gold, 2005, Still the Same...Great Rock Classics of Our Time, 2006; performer: (films) Rod Stewart - The Best of Rod Stewart, Rod Stewart and The Faces - The Final Concert, 1974, Rod Stewart and Faces, 1975, Rod Stewart Live at Los Angeles Forum, 1980, Rod Stewart-Tonight He's Yours, short and long versions, 1981, The Rod Stewart Concert Video, 1984, Rod Stewart -Storyteller 1984-91, 1991, Rod Stewart - Vagabond Heart; composer (films) Night at the Roxbury, 1998, Almost Famous, 2000, About Schmidt, 2002 and several others; performer Olympic Torch Concert Live, 2004 and several others. Named Rock Star of Year Rolling Stone mag., 1971; recipient British Rock and Pop Lifetime Achievement award, 1992, named an Honorary Knight Commander of the Most Excellent Order of the British Empire by Queen Elizabeth II, 2007; inducted into the Rock & Roll Hall of Fame, 1994. Office: Warner Bros Records 3300 Warner Blvd Burbank CA 91505-4694

STEWART, ROD, retired literature and language professor; b. San Angelo, Tex., Sept. 30, 1946; s. Hollis Lee and Lois Marie Stewart. MA, U. Tex. Permian Basin, Odessa, 1982. Cert. in tchg. Tex. Edn. Agy., 1969. AP sr. English tchr. Ector County Ind. Sch. Dist., Odessa, 1998—2007; adj. English lectr. U. Tex. Permian Basin, 2007—. With US Army, 1967—68, Ft. Polk, La.

STEWART, S. EVELYN, child psychiatrist, researcher; d. Terry and Miriam Stewart; children: Emanuelle Grace, Gabrielle Simone. BS in Chemistry, Dalhousie U., Can., 1991, BA in Comparative Religion, 1991, Degree in Med., 1996. Diplomate in Psychiatry Royal Coll. Physicians Surgeons Can., 2002. Rsch. fellow Harvard U., Boston, 2002—05; instr. psychiatry Mass. Gen. Hosp., Harvard Med. Sch., Boston, 2005—07; asst. prof. Mass. Gen. Hosp., Harvard U., Boston, 2007—. Dir. rsch. obsessive, compulsive disorder inst. McLean Hosp., Belmont, Mass., 2005—; dir. ocd pgy3 residency tchg. module Mass. Gen. Hosp., Boston, 2005—, pediatric psychopharmacologist, 2005—, ocd and related disorders clin. psychiatrist, 2005—; faculty mem. Psychiat. and Neurodevelopmental Genetics Unit, 2007—. Fellow Rsch. Fellowship, McLean Hosp., 2003—04, Early Investigator Postgraduate Fellowship, Can. Institutes of Health Rsch., 2002—03. Mem.: Can. Psychiat. Assn., Am. Acad. Child Adolescent Psychiatry, AMA, Can. Acad. Child Adolescent Psychiatry. Avocation: running. Business E-Mail: stewart@pngu.mgh.harvard.edu.

STEWART, SANDRA KAY, music educator; b. New Albany, Ind., Dec. 24, 1947; d. Dale F. and June V. (Martin) Byrne; m. William Lee Stewart, June 25, 1971. B Music Edn., Ind. U., 1969; MusM, Norfolk State U., 1992; D Mus. Arts, U. S.C., 1995. Cert. vocal music tchr., N.Y., Mo.; nat. cert., state cert. piano tchr. Vocal music tchr., choral dir. Ritenour Sch. Dist., St. Louis, 1969-75, Sch. Dist. # 54, Chgo., 1975-76, Waverly (N.Y.) Jr./Sr. H.S., 1977-78, Clarence (N.Y.) H.S., 1978-82; piano instr., show choir dir. Inst. Fine Arts, Reading, Pa., 1982-85; piano accompanist Berks Grand Opera Co., Reading, Pa., 1982-85, Va. Opera Co., Norfolk, 1986, Old Dominion U., 1986—92, U. S.C., Columbia, 1992-95, Jacksonville Masterworks Sr. Chorale, 1996-99, Bolles Sr. H.S., 1996-98, Pinewood Presbyn. Ch., 1996-98; piano and music theory instr. Acad. of Music, Virginia Beach, Va., 1986-91, 2002—03; piano instr., choral dir., vocal jazz dir., accompanist Jacksonville (Fla.) U., 1995—2000; chair vocal music dept. Douglas Anderson Sch. of Arts, 1998—2000; prof. music U. North Fla., Jacksonville, 2000—. Editor: Florida Music Teacher, 1999-2000; contbr. articles to profl. publs. Mem. Virginia Beach Pops Orch., 1989-91; founder, dir. North Fla. Piano Camp, 2000-2009. Recipient Fla. First Lady's Art Scholar award, 2000. Mem. AAUW (numerous offices 1975—), Am. Choral Dirs. Assn., Coll. Music Soc., Nat. Piano Found., Music Educators Nat. Conf., Nat. Guild Piano Tchrs., Music Tchrs. Nat. Assn., Delius Assn. Fla. (bd. dirs. 1997-99), Phi Kappa Lambda, Mu Phi Epsilon, Delta Kappa Gamma Soc. Internat., TRI-M Music Honor Soc, Jacksville Music Tchrs. Assn.(vice pres.2007-09, pres. 2009-). Home: 4782 Harpers Ferry Ln Jacksonville FL 32257-4544 Office: U North Fla 1 UNF Dr S Jacksonville FL 32224

STEWART, SANDRA KAY, dean; d. Walter and Vivian Kupchik; children: Kelly Murphy, Kerry Peterson. BS, Ky. Wesleyan Coll., Owensboro, 1966; MS, Ind. State U., Terre Haute, 1986. Lic. life tchg. State Ind., 1986. Life sci. prof. Vincennes U., Ind., 1983—2008, chair, life sci. dept., 2004—07, dean instrn. Indpls., 2009—; reviewer Pearson Pub., San Francisco, 1998—2008, cons., 1998—2008. Contbr. articles to profl. jours. (Excellence Tchg. award, 2003). Exec. bd. dirs., sec. Knox County Chpt. ARC, Vincennes, 1980—95. Faculty fellow, Vincennes U., 2002. Mem.: Human Anatomy & Physiology Soc. (chair, tech. com. 1998—2001). Methodist. Avocations: travel, golf. Office: Vincennes Univ BDU 1155 S High Sch Rd Indianapolis IN 46214 Business E-Mail: sstewart@vinu.edu.

STEWART, SHIRLEY S., retired elementary school educator; b. Adams Run, SC, Oct. 17, 1939; d. Herbert and Ella (Harris) Simmons; children: Charlette, Kieshea. BS Edn., Carlin U., Orangeburg, SC. Tchr. Minnie Huge Elem. Sch., Hollywood, SC, Farm Sch. for Farmworkers Families, Ravanal, SC, Baptist Elem. Sch., SC. Adminstr. grants USDA, Charleston, SC, 1990—. Author: (book) Young Girl Struggling for Protection, 2009. Cmty. activist Salvation Army, Charleston, SC, 1988—; vol. helper to seniors in need of help Adams Run; cmty. organizer Mt. Nebo AMF Ch., Adams Run, SC, 1963—; Missionary Mt. Nebo AME Ch. Avocations: reading, cooking, acting. Office: PO Box 11 5065 Hwy 174 Adams Run SC 29426

STEWART, SUE S., lawyer; b. Oct. 9, 1942; d. Fraizer McVale and Carolyn Eliabeth (Hunt) S.; m. Arthur L. Stern, III, July 31, 1965 (div.); m. children: Anne, Mark Alan; m. John A. Ciampa, Sept. 1, 1985 (div.); m. Stephen L. Raymond (dec.). BA, Wellesley Coll., 1964; postgrad., Harvard U. Law Sch., 1964-65; JD, Georgetown U., 1967. Bar: N.Y. 1968. Clk. to judges Juvenile Ct., Washington, 1967-68; mem. Nixon, Hargrave, Devans & Doyle (now Nixon Peabody LLP), Rochester, NY, 1968-74, ptnr., 1975—2001, mng. ptnr., 1998—2001, ret., 2001; sr. v.p., gen. counsel U. Rochester, 2003—. Lectr. in field; trustee Found. of Monroe County (N.Y.) Bar, 1976-78; v.p. & Gen. Counsel Univ. Rochester, NY, 2003-. Author: Charitable Giving and Solicitation. Sec., dir. United Cmty. Chest of Greater Rochester, 1973-87, 1992-; trustee, sec. Internat. Mus. Photography at George Eastman House, Rochester, 1974-97, 2000-03, Genesee Country Mus., Mumford, N.Y., 1976-2002; bd. dirs. Ctr. for Govtl. Rsch., 1990-97; trustee, chmn. United Neighborhood Ctr. of Greater Rochester Found., 1991-2003; trustee, chmn. exec. com. Nat. Ctr. Edn. and Economy, 1997-; dir. Canandaigua Nat. Bank, NY, 2000-. Mem. ABA (chmn. task force on charitable giving, exempt orgns. com. tax sect. 1981-2003), N.Y. State Bar (exec. com. tax sect. 1974-76, chmn. com. exempt orgns. 1975-76), Monroe County Bar Assn. (trustee 1974-75), BNA Portfolio, Pvt. Found. Distbns. (Athena award 2000, de Tocqueville award 2003). Office: Office of Counsel 266 Wallis Hall PO Box 270040 Rochester NY 14627-0040 Office Phone: 585-273-2167.

STEWART, TERRY, museum administrator; b. Daphne, Ala. BA, Rutgers U., 1969; MBA, Cornell U., 1972, JD, 1974. Officer Conn. Bank & Trust Co., 1974—79; v.p. bus. devel. to gen. mgr. strategic planning and bus. devel. Continental Group, Inc., 1979—84; v.p. bus. devel. Combustion Engring., Inc., 1984—89; joined Marvel Entertainment Group, 1989, pres., COO to vice chmn.; now pres., CEO Rock and Roll Hall of Fame and Mus., Cleve. Bd. mem. US Com. for UNICEF, Nat. Com. for Prevention of Child Abuse, Chgo., Rhythm & Blues Found., City Parks Found., NYC, Cleve. Convention & Visitors Bur. Named Mktg. Exec. of Yr., CNBC, 1991. Office: Rock and Roll Hall of Fame and Mus 1100 Rock and Roll Blvd Cleveland OH 44114 Office Phone: 216-781-7625.

STEWART, THOMAS CLIFFORD, investment company executive; b. Portland, Oreg., Oct. 25, 1950; s. Jack Fry Stewart and Naomi June Gedney Cuyler; m. Susan Elizabeth Sample; children: Andrew, Tommy, MacKenzie, Cortny. Student, U. Gothenburg, Sweden, 1971; BS, U. Oreg., 1974; MBA, UCLA, 1982. Exec. dir. Morgan Stanley & Co.,

NYC, 1982—90; pres. Cort MacKenzie & Co., Portland, 1990—2003; dir. Acrymed, Lake Oswego, Oreg., 1995-96, Morley Fin. Svcs., Lake Oswego, Oreg., 1995-97; prin. Andrew Thomas & Co. L.L.L., 2003—. Dir. NCAA Leadership Adv. Bd., 2003—. Contbr. articles to profl. jours. Trustee U. Oreg. Found., 1994-2004; bd. dirs. Oreg. Air and Space Mus., 2001-05; chmn. U. Oreg. Pres.'s Assn., 1997-99; mem. exec. com. Lundquist Coll. of Bus., Univ. Oregon, 1998-2001, 03-05, bd. advisors Coll. Bus., U. Oreg., 1990—, mem. athletic dept. bd. advisors, 1998-2005; Oreg. State Commn. on Higher Bus. Edn., 1992-94; mem. leadership coun. U. Oreg., 1995-99; bd. dirs. Lake Oswego Sch. Found., 1996-2000; treas. adv. cabinet State of Oreg., 1993-94; adv. bd. Sec. of Navy Nat. Naval Res. Policy Bd., Washington, 1987-89; mem. edn. specification com. Eugene 4J, Oreg., 2001-04. Comdr. USN, 1974-80, USNR, 1980-91. Decorated Air medal, Navy Commendation for Valor; Baker scholar, 1981. Mem. Naval Res. Assn. (Jr. Officer of Yr. 1988), U.S. Navy League, ROA, Am. Legion, VFW, Beta Gamma Sigma, Beta Alpha Psi, Alpha Mu Alpha, Skull & Dagger.

STEWART, TIMOTHY GLEN, organist; b. Atlanta, Sept. 18, 1960; s. Glen A. Stewart and Carol Ann Hicks; m. Melodee Beth Adams, Sept. 6, 1986. BS in Chemistry, Ga. State U., Atlanta, Ga., 1982; MS in Metallurgy, Ga. Inst. of Tech., Atlanta, Ga., 1985; PhD in Ednl. Psychology, Ga. State U., Atlanta, Ga., 1992. Chemistry lab asst. DeKalb Coll., Decatur, Ga., 1978—79; organist/asst. choir dir. Tucker Christian Ch., Tucker, Ga., 1981—88; metallurgy lab instr. Ga. Tech, Atlanta, 1983—84; chemistry/math instr. DeKalb Coll., Decatur, Ga., 1986—88; organist Indian Creek Bapt. Ch., Stone Mountain, Ga., 1988—91; owner/operator Stewart Musical Svcs., Loganville, Ga., 1991—; dir. music ministries/organist Westminster Presbyn. Ch., Snellville, Ga., 1992—93; organist First Bapt. Ch., Avondale Estates, Ga., 1995—; v.p. Miller Pipe Organ Svcs., Inc., Buford, Ga., 1995—2002; organist Two Tuners Music Ministry, Loganville, 2006—. Author: The Elemental Book of Facts, 1982; musician: (recordings) Christmas Music for Everyone, 1987, Music from Roswell United Methodist Church, 2002. Mem.: Planetary Soc., Am. Guild of Organists. Achievements include development of Advanced MIDI organ voice module. Avocations: genealogy, classic television, chemistry, extrabiblical studies, astronomy. Personal E-mail: tgstewart@earthlink.net.

STEWART, TONY (ANTHONY WAYNE STEWART), professional race car driver; b. Columbus, Ind., May 20, 1971; s. Nelson Stewart and Pam Boas. Race car driver NASCAR Joe Gibbs Racing, 1999—2008, Stewart-Haas Racing, 2009—; owner World of Outlaws, Eldora Speedway, Rossburg, Ohio, 2004—; co-owner Paducah Internat. Raceway, Ky., Macon Speedway, Ill. 1st pl. Exide NASCAR Select Batteries 400 Richmond Internat. Raceway, 1999, 1st pl. Pontiac Excitement 400, 2001, 02; 1st pl. Checker Auto Parts/Dura Lube 500 Phoenix Internat. Raceway, 1999; 1st pl. Pennzoil 400 Homestead-Miami Speedway, 1999, 2000; 1st pl. MBNA Platinum 400 Dover Internat. Speedway, 2000, 1st pl. MBNA.com 400, 00; 1st pl. Kmart 400 Mich. Internat. Speedway, 2000; 1st pl. thatlook.com 300 NH Internat. Speedway, 2000, 1st pl. New Eng. 300, 05; 1st pl. NAPA Autocare 500 Martinsville Speedway, 2000, 1st pl. DirecTV 500, 06; 1st pl. Dodge/Save Mart 350 Infineon Raceway, 2001, 05; 1st pl. Sharpie 500 Bristol Motor Speedway, 2001; 1st pl. MBNA Am. 500 Atlanta Motor Speedway, 2002, 1st pl. Bass Pro Shops 500, 06; 1st pl. Sirius at the Glen Watkins Glen Internat. Raceway, 2002, 04, 05, 1st pl. Centurion Boats at the Glen, 07, 09; 1st pl. Pocono 500 Pocono Raceway, 2003, 09; 1st pl. UAW-GM Quality 500 Lowe's Motor Speedway, 2003, 1st pl. NASCAR Sprint All-Star Race, 09; 1st pl. Tropicana 400 Chicagoland Speedway, 2004, 1st pl. USG Sheetrock 400, 07; 1st pl. Pepsi 400 Daytona Internat. Speedway, 2005, 06, 1st pl. Coke Zero 400, 09; 1st pl. Allstate 400 at The Brickyard Indpls. Motor Speedway, 2005, 07; 1st pl. Banquet 400 Kans. Speedway, 2006; 1st pl. Dickies 500 Tex. Motor Speedway, 2006; 1st pl. Amp Energy 500 Talladega Superspeedway, 2008. Founder Tony Stewart Found., 2003. Recipient ESPY award for best driver, 2006; named NASCAR Winston Cup Champion, 2002, NASCAR Nextel Cup Champion, 2005, NASCAR Nationwide Series Champion, 2009; named one of The Most Influential People in the World of Sports, Bus. Week, 2007. Mailing: Tony Stewart Found 5644 W 74th St Indianapolis IN 46278 Office: Stewart-Haas Racing 6001 Haas Way Kannapolis NC 28081 Office Phone: 704-652-4227.*

STEWART, VERLINDSEY LAQUETTA, accounting educator; b. Birmingham, Ala., Dec. 27, 1965; d. Nathan Jr. and Shirley Ruth Brown; m. Kelvin Lorenzo Stewart I, June 22, 1991 (div. Feb. 1999); 1 child, Kelvin Lorenzo II. BS in Acctg., Ala. A&M U., Normal, 1988, MS in Bus. Edn., 1995, AA Cert. in Bus. Edn., 1997; EdD in Higher Edn. Leadership, Nova Southeastern U., Ft. Lauderdale, Fla., 2004. Cert. tchr. bus. 7-12 Ala. Jr. acct. Childress Acctg., Huntsville, Ala., 1990-93; acctg. clk. Appeal Beauty Salon, Huntsville, 1988-94; receptionist Coop. Ext., Normal, Ala., 1992-94; grad. asst. Ala. A&M U., Normal, 1995; student tchr. J.O. Johnson H.S., Huntsville, Ala., 1995; acctg. instr. J.F. Drake State Tech., Huntsville, 1996—. Cons. Jr. Achievement, Huntsville, 1995—96. Post-reviewer: (book) College Accounting 9th, 1999 (Honorarium 1999). Vol. Habitat for Humanity, Huntsville, 1995-97; vol. asst. leader Girl Scouts North Ala., Huntsville, 1995-96. Recipient Adminstrv. Acad. award Rust Coll., 1999, Emerging Leaders Sch. award Ala. Edn. Assn., 1994, Ala. Master Tchr. Seminar, 2001. Mem. Nat. Bus. Edn., Ea. Star Mitzpah Ctr., Phi Beta Lambda (adviser 1998—), Delta Sigma Theta. Democrat. Baptist. Avocations: aerobics, weightlifting, reading, jazz. Office: JF Drake State Tech Coll 3421 Meridian St N Huntsville AL 35811-1544 Personal E-mail: vbdst28@aol.com.

STEWART, WILLIAM C., medical researcher, director; s. Robert Bell and Margaret (Hollifield) S.; m. Jeanette Adams, Aug. 29, 1981. MD, Southwestern Med. Sch., Dallas, 1981. Diplomate Am. Bd. Ophthalmology. Founder, med. dir. Pharm. Rsch. Network, LLC, Dallas, 1996—; founder, cons. Pharm. Rsch. Corp., Dallas, 1996—. Cons., lectr. Pharm. Cos. Author: Clinical Practice of Glaucoma, 1990; contbr. over 300 articles to sci. jours. Founder Teleios Inc., Charleston, SC, 2000. Recipient Jr. Instr. award, Am. Acad. Ophthalmology. Fellow Am. Acad. Ophthalmology; mem. Am. Glaucoma Soc., S.C. Ophthalmology Soc., Phi Beta Kappa. Christian Ch. Office: Pharm Rsch Network LLC 5430 LBJ Freeway Ste 1200 Dallas TX 75240 Office Fax: 800-980-0718. Business E-Mail: info@prnorb.com.

STEWART, WILLIAM JAMES, cardiologist; b. Cleve., Aug. 17, 1951; s. James B. and Virginia Stewart; m. Denise Elizabeth Balk, Dec. 30, 1972; children: Emily, Travis. AB in Biology cum laude, Harvard U., 1973; MD, U. Cin., 1977. Diplomate Am. Bd. Internal Medicine with subspecialty in cardiovascular disease; lic. physician, Ohio. Intern/resident U. Mich. Affiliated Hosps., Ann Arbor, 1977-80; clin. fellow dept. cardiology Boston U. Hosp., 1980-82; clin./rsch. fellow Cardiac Ultrasound Lab. Mass. Gen. Hosp./Harvard Med. Sch., Boston, 1982-84; staff physician Cleve. Clinic, 1984—, dir. Echo Lab, 1992—. Clin. assoc. in medicine Boston U., 1980-82; rsch. fellow in medicine Harvard Med. Sch., 1982-84; asst. prof. medicine Ohio State U., Cleve. Clinic Health Scis. Campus, 1992-94, assoc. prof., 1995—. Contbr. numerous articles and abstracts to profl. jours., chpts. to books; reviewer Circulation, Jour. Am. Coll. Cardiology, Jour. Am. Soc. Echocardiography, Echocardiography, Am. Heart Jour., Am. Jour. Cardology, Brit. Heart Jour., Annals of Thoracic Surgery, Jour. Thoracic and Cardiovascular Surgery, Am. Jour. Cardiac Imaging; editl. bd. Echocardiography, 1992-96, Jour. Am. Soc. Echocardiography, 1991—. Christian youth leader. Fellow Am. Coll. Cardiology (Ohio chpt. adv. expert team in echocardiography 1995—), chmn. task force tng. in echocardiography 1994, mem. echocardiography com. 1991-96); mem. Am. Heart Assn. (mem. edn. com. N.E. Ohio chpt. 1985-88), Am. Soc. Echocardiography (chmn. com. on echocardiography in emergency medicine 1997, chmn. sci. sessions 1996, abstract chmn. sci. sessions 1994, mem. physicians' edn. and tng. com. 1993—, abstract vice chmn. 1993, bd. dirs. 1989-92), Internat. Soc. Ultrasound in Cardiac Surgery (pres. 1994—), Greater Cleve. Soc. Echocardiography (founder, bd. dirs. 1985—). Episcopalian. Avocations: jogging, sailing, skiing, music. Office: Cleveland Clinic Found Dept Cardiology F-15 9500 Euclid Ave Dept Cleveland OH 44195-0002

STEWART SIMPSON, DONNAMAY ANGELA, interior designer; b. Mandeville, Jamaica, W.I., Dec. 31, 1965; d. Ermine Stewart and Mary Ester Stewart Bromfield; m. Everton Seymour Simpson (div.); 1 child, Dimitre Andre Simpson. Student, Miami Dade C.C., 1986. Sec. Jamaica Transformer Co., 1986—87; secretarial clk. Pat Thompson Constrn. Co., Jamaica, 1987—89; ops. mgr. Blaise Trust, Mandeville, Jamaica, 1989, Nat. Car Rental, Mandeville, Jamaica, 1989—90; sec., accounts clk. Simpsons Wholesale Co., Elizabeth, Jamaica, 1990—91; ops. mgr. Simpson Supermarket, Elizabeth, Jamaica, 1991—94, Wesley Plz., Mandeville, Jamaica, 1995—97; owner Angelique Enterprises, Miramar, Fla., 1997—; fgn. exch. teller Ft. Lauderdale Internat. Airport, 1999—2001. Songwriter: Hill Top Records, 2006, Amerecord. Interior decorator, stage performer Perfect Praise Sch. Dance, Fla., 2002; conf. spkr. Women's Empowerment Conf. Believers and Achievers Internat., 1998. Mem.: Reagan Ranch Found., Paralyzed Vets. Am., USO, U.S. Navy Meml., Internat. Poetry Soc. Avocations: dance, writing, design, motivational speaking. Home: 1980 SW 103d Terr Miramar FL 33025 Office: Angelique Enterprises 1980 SW 103d Terr Miramar FL 33025 Office Phone: 954-295-8694, 1877-962-7771 ext. 295. Personal E-mail: donnamay01@yahoo.com. E-mail: Dimitre01@aol.com.

STEYER, THOMAS FAHR, hedge fund manager; b. 1957; s. Roy H. and Marnie (Fahr) Steyer; m. Kathryn Taylor, Aug. 16, 1986; 4 children. BA in Econs. and Polit. Sci., summa cum laude, Yale U., 1979; MBA, Stanford Grad. Sch. Bus., Calif., 1983. Fin. analyst mergers & acquisitions dept. Morgan Stanley & Co.; assoc. risk arbitrage dept. Goldman, Sachs & Co.; founder, sr. mng. ptnr. Farallon Capital Mgmt. LLC, San Francisco, 1986—; mng. dir. Hellman & Friedman LLC, San Francisco, 1986—. Bd. dirs CapitalSource, Chevy Chase, Md. Dir. Californians for Fair Election Reform, 2007—. Fellow: Am. Acad. Arts & Scis.; mem.: Phi Beta Kappa. Office: Farallon Capital Mgmt One Maritime Pz Ste 2100 San Francisco CA 94111 also: Hellman & Friedman LLC One Maritime Plz 12th Fl San Francisco CA 94111 Business E-Mail: tsteyer@faralloncapital.com.*

STIBBE, AUSTIN JULE, retired accountant; b. St. Paul, Mar. 29, 1930; s. Austin Julius and Agnes Dorothea (Delaney) S.; m. Mary Elizabeth King, May 29, 1952; children: Anne Marie, Craig Jule, David King, Karen Lee. BSB in Acctg., U. Minn., 1952. CPA, Minn., Wis. Tax acct. Ernst & Ernst, Mpls., 1955-60; corp. tax mgr. EcoLab, Inc., St. Paul, 1960-65; audit mgr. Coopers & Lybrand, Mpls., 1965-74; v.p. Wilkerson, Guthmann & Johnson, Ltd., St. Paul, 1974-93, of counsel, 1993—2006; ret., 2006. Exec. officer Twin Cities Squadron, U.S. Naval Sea Cadet Corps, Mpls., 1974-80; bd. dirs., treas., mem. Twin Cities coun. Navy League, 1970—, pres., 1979-81, treas., 1975-79, 81-91; mem. adv. coun. to dept. acctg. U. Minn., Mpls., 1983-86; bd. dirs., chmn. audit com. St. Paul Area Coun. Chs., 1985-87; mem. adv. bd. Headwaters Sec., 1987-88; mem. fin. reporting com. United Way St. Paul Area, 1981-93, mem. audit com., 1991-93; dist. commr. staff Indianhead coun. Boy Scouts Am., 1962-65. Lt. USN, 1952-55. Mem. Minn. Soc. CPAs (life), U.S. Naval Inst. (life), Belle Taine Lake Assn. (dir. 1995-2001, treas. 1996-2001), Hubbard County COLA Print Com., 1995-98, Friends of Heritage, 1996—, Hubbard County Works of Improvement (steering com. 2001), VFW (life), Am. Legion, Heritage Campus (bd. mem., 2007-). Presbyterian. Avocations: music, boating, history. Home: PO Box 41 Nevis MN 56467-0041 E-mail: austib30@msn.com.

STIBBE, CRAIG JULE, engineer; b. St. Paul, Apr. 2, 1956; s. Austin Jule and Mary Elizabeth Stibbe; m. Jane Marie Denery, May 9, 1981; children: Matthew Jule, Kevin Lowell, Aileen Marie. Cert. Chief A Stationary Engr., Minn., 1986, Class D Water Operator, Minn., 2004. Engr. Mid-America Dairymen, Inc., Farmington, Minn., 1981—84, Am. Hoist and Derrick, St. Paul, 1984—85, Jacob Schmidt Brewing Co., 1985—88, NW Airlines, 1989—2005, Packaging Corp. Am., Mpls., 2006—, Regions Hosp., St. Paul, 2007—. Boiler technician third class USN, 1976—80. Mem.: Mensa. Home: 20060 Akin Rd Farmington MN 55024 Office: Regions Hosp 640 Jackson St Saint Paul MN 55101 Business E-Mail: cjstibbe@charter.net.

STICCA, ROBERT P., surgeon; b. Carlisle, Pa., May 8, 1954; m. Celeste Adele LaFlamme; children: Jonathan Albert, Katherine Rose. AA, Springfield Tech, 1976; BA, U. N.H., 1979; MD, U. Conn., 1984. Oncology surgeon Upstate Surg. Specialists, Greenville, S.C., 1993—; assoc. dir. surg. edn. Greenville Hosp. Sys., 1993—, med. dir./adminstr. Cancer Treatment Ctr., 1996—. Contbr. articles to profl. jours. Vol. physician Greenville Free Med. Clinic, 1994—; Upstate Race for the Cure dir. Susan B. Komen Found., 1995, adv. coun. mem., 1995—, chmn., 1998; mem. hospice profl. adv. com. Greenville Hosp. Sys., 1996. Maj. USAF, 1982-91. Conn. Grad. Student scholar U. Conn. Health Ctr. Assn., 1980, Hartford County Med. Assn. scholar, 1980, 83, U. Conn. Sch. Medicine scholar, 1982, 83, Mosby scholar, 1984. Fellow ACS; mem. AMA, Am. Coll. Physician Execs., Am. Soc. Clin. Oncology, Mass. Med. Soc., S.C. Med. Soc., S.C. Oncology Soc., Soc. Surg. Oncology, Southeastern Surg. Congress, Assn. Program Dirs. Surgery, Greenville County Med. Soc., Roswell Park Surg. Soc., Soc. Gastrointestinal Endoscopic Surgeons, Phi Beta Kappa, Alpha Epsilon Delta. Roman Catholic. Home: 5863 Pinehurst Ct Grand Forks ND 58201-2813

STICE, DWAYNE LEE, broadcasting company executive, professional organist; b. Paducah, Ky., Aug. 10, 1956; s. Freeman D. and Dorris Olive (Lee) S. AA, Paducah Community Coll., 1976; BS, Murray State U., 1977; MS, Southern Ill. U., 1983. Lic. funeral dir., Ky. Dir. Johnson-Lambert Funeral Home, Calvert City, Ky., 1974-81; gen. mgr. Paducah Area Transit System, 1980-92; pres. Sta. WCCK-FM, Stice Comm., Inc., Calvert City, 1990—2001; human resources, programming WPSD-TV, Paducah, Ky., 2001—. Adj. bus. instr. Paducah Community Coll., 1979-91, Lindsey Wilson Coll., Columbia, Ky., 1991; adj. reporter CBS Radio Network, 1997-2000; cons. in field. Contbr. articles to profl. jours. Mem. Calvert Area Devel. Assn.; transp. com. Purchase Area Devel. Dist.; organist St. Matthew by the Lake Luth. Ch., 1986-2007, Calvert City United Meth. Ch., 2004—. Outstanding grantee Ky. Transp. Cabinet, 1985, 86. Mem. Ky. Pub. Transit Assn. (pres. 1988-91), Ky. Broadcasters Assn. (bd. dirs. 1997-2000), Marshall C. of C. (bd. dirs., vice chmn. govt. affairs 1998), Paducah C.C. Alumni Assn. (pres. 1983), Hon. Order Ky. Cols., Travelers Protective Assn. (pres. Paducah chpt. 1989-90), Nashville Area UMC (Com. on Episcopacy 2008-), Lions, Masons (master Calvert City 1984), Shriners, Order Ea. Star, Phi Kappa Phi, Phi Theta Kappa Rivera Owners Assn. Methodist. Avocations: travel, baseball, antique clocks, automobiles, hiking. Office: WPSD-TV 100 TV Ln Paducah KY 42003 E-mail: ky4202956@yahoo.com.

STICE, JAMES EDWARD, chemical engineer, educator; b. Fayetteville, Ark., Sept. 19, 1928; s. F. Fenner and Charlotte (Anderson) S.; m. Patricia Ann Stroner, Sept. 22, 1951 (dec.); children: Susan Emily, James Clayton; m. Betty B. Gowdy, Aug. 3, 1996. BS, U. Ark., 1949; MS, Ill. Inst. Tech., 1952, PhD, 1963. Registered profl. engr., Ark. Process engr. Visking Corp., North Little Rock, Ark., 1951-53; chem. engr. Thurston Chem. Co. div. W.R. Grace & Co., Joplin, Mo., 1953-54; asst. prof. chem. engring. U. Ark., 1954-57, from assoc. prof. to prof., 1962-68; instr. chem. engring. Ill. Inst. Tech., Chgo., 1957-62; dir. Bur. Engring. Teaching, assoc. prof. chem. engring. U. Tex., Austin, 1968-73, prof. engring. edn. in chem. engring., 1973-85, T. Brockett Hudson prof. chem. engring., 1985-90, Bob R. Dorsey prof. engring., 1990-96, dir. Ctr. for Teaching Effectiveness, 1973-89; dir. Effective Teaching Inst. U. Tex. System, summer 1970; prof. emeritus, 1996—. Vis. prof. U. Iberoamericana, Mexico City, summer 1977; disting. vis. prof., H.T. Person chair engring. U. Wyo., Laramie, 1996; summer cons. E.I. duPont de Nemours & Co., Inc., Savannah River Plant, Aiken, S.C., 1955, Humble Oil & Refining Co., Baytown, Tex., 1956, Universal Oil Products Co., Des Plaines, Ill., 1957, 58, Phillips Petroleum Co., Bartlesville, Okla., 1963, Ethyl Corp., Baton Rouge, 1965, U. Wis., Eau Claire, 1970-97; vis. scholar in NSF and Am. Soc. for Engring. Edn. programs to improve engring./sci. tech. at various univs. Author: (with B.S. Swanson) Electronic Analog Computer Primer, 1965, Computadoras Analogicas Electronicas, 1971, Expansion of Keller Plan Instruction in Engineering and Selected Other Disciplines, 1975, Developing Critical Thinking and Problem-Solving Abilities, 1987. Recipient Jour. award, Instrument Soc. Am., 1966, Outstanding Engring. Advisor award, U. Tex., 1993, Gen. Dynamics award for excellence in engring. tchg., 1980, Disting. Alumni award, U. Ark. Coll. Engring., 2006, Profl. Achievement award, Ill. Inst. Tech., 2006; named Outstanding Chem. Engring. prof., U. Tex., 1977, 1979, 1988, 1991, 1993, 1996, Disting. Alumnus, U. Ark., 1995; tchg. fellow, Friar Soc., 1993—94. Fellow Am. Soc. Engring. Edn. (life; elected dir. 1983-85, chmn. chem. engring. div. 1988-89, bd. dirs. 1990-92, v.p. 1991-92, Western Electric Fund award for excellence in engring. tchg. 1981, Chester F. Carlson award for innovation in engring. tchg. 1984, Donald Marlowe award for leadership in engring. edn. 1999, Lifetime Achievement award in chem. engring. 2002); mem. AIChE, Ark. Acad. Chem. Engrs., bd. dirs., 2005-07, U. Tex. Ret. Faculty-Staff Assn. (pres. 2000-01), Scabbard and Blade, Scholia (pres. 1989-90), Sigma Xi, Delta Sigma, Sigma Chi, Phi Eta Sigma, Pi Mu Epsilon, Alpha Chi Sigma, Tau Beta Pi, Omicron Delta Kappa, Phi Lambda Upsilon, Phi Kappa Phi. Home: 4205 N Hills Dr Austin TX 78731-2827 Home Phone: 512-794-8046.

STICH, ROBERTA LYNN, not-for-profit fundraiser, social worker; b. NYC, May 23, 1948; d. Melvin Harold Stich and Shirley Pearl Kaplan-Stich. Student, U. Rochester, 1965—67; BA, Bklyn. Coll., 1970; MSW, Hunter Coll., 1972; postgrad., Stanford Law Sch., 1980—85. Lic. master social worker N.Y. Legal asst. Howard Deutsch Atty. at Law, NYC, 1977—80, Donald Lindover Atty. at Law, NYC, 1982; rsch. asst. sociology dept. Stanford (Calif.) U., 1986—87; rsch. asst. Merit Co., Jerusalem, 1989—91; fundraiser Nat. Symphony Orch. Assn., Washington, 1991—95, Nat. Rep. Senatorial Com., Washington, 1995—97, Nat. Capital Teleservices, LLC, Washington, 1997—. Telephone solicitor Nat. Children's Ctr. Value Village Project Inc., Beltsville, Md., 1992—. Mem. Smithsonian Instn., Washington, 1996—, Phillips Collection, 2005, U.S. Holocaust Mus., Washington, 2000—, Rep. Nat. Com., 2002—. Mem.: Nat. Trust Historic Preservation, Stanford Alumni Assn. (life). Republican. Jewish. Avocations: surfing the Internet, cassettes and videos, casino gambling, travel, fashion. Home: Apt 208 1255 New Hampshire Ave NW Washington DC 20036 Office: CAPTEL 300 5th St NE Washington DC 20002 Office Phone: 202-547-4614. E-mail: robersti@aol.com.

STICKEL, FREDERICK A., publishing executive; b. Weehawken, NJ, Nov. 18, 1921; s. Fred and Eva (Madigan) S.; m. Margaret A. Dunne, Dec. 4, 1943; children: Fred A., Patrick F., Daisy E., Geoffrey M., James E., Bridget A. Student, Georgetown U., 1939-42; BS, St. Peter's Coll., 1943. Advt. salesperson Jersey Observer daily, Hoboken, NJ, 1945-51; retail advt. salesperson Jersey Jour., Jersey City, 1951-55, advt. dir., 1955-66, pub., 1966-67; gen. mgr. Oregonian Pub. Co., Portland, Oreg., 1967-72, pres., 1972-86, pub., 1975—. Bd. regents U. Portland; adv. bd. Portland State U., St. Vincent's Hosp.; bd. dirs. Portland Rose Festival Assn., United Way Oreg.; chmn. Portland Citizens Crime Commn. Capt. USMC, 1942-45. Mem. Assn. for Portland Progress (dir.), Portland C. of C. (dir.), Oreg. Newspaper Pubs. Assn. (past pres.), Pacific N.W. Newspaper Assn. (past pres.), Newspaper Assn. Am., University Club, Multnomah Athletic Waverley Country Club, Arlington Club, Rotary. Office: Oregonian Pub Co 1320 SW Broadway Portland OR 97201-3499 Office Phone: 503-221-8140. Office Fax: 503-294-4175.*

STICKLER, DANIEL LEE, health care management consultant; b. Fairmont, W.Va., Jan. 4, 1938; s. Elmer Daniel and Ruby Lee (Ball) S.; m. Donna Lou Johnson, Apr. 16, 1960; children— Dwight Lorne, Dwayne Lee, Douglas Lynn BS in Civil Engring., W.Va. U., 1960; M.P.H. in Health Adminstrn., U. Pitts., 1970. Registered profl. engr., Tex. Asst. dir. Presbyn.-Univ. Hosp., Pitts., 1970-71, assoc. dir., 1971-72, adminstr., chief operating officer, 1972-76, exec. dir., chief exec. officer, 1976-83, pres., chief exec. officer, 1983-86; pres., CEO, The Cedars Med. Ctr., Miami, Fla., 1986-91; pres. DLS Assocs., Inc., Miami, 1991-95; sr. v.p. The Hunter Group, 1996—. Adj. assoc. prof. Grad. Sch. Pub. Health, U. Pitts., 1976-86. Fellow Am. Coll. Hosp. Adminstrn.; mem. Palmaire Country Club (bd. gov. mem.). Methodist. Avocations: golf, gardening. Home and Office: 5803 Fairwoods Cir Sarasota FL 34243-3821 Business E-Mail: dstickle@tampabay.rr.com.

STICKLER, GUNNAR BRYNOLF, pediatrician; b. Peterskirchen, Germany, June 13, 1925; came to U.S., 1951, naturalized, 1958; s. Fritz and Astrid (Wennerberg) S.; m. Duci M. Kronenbitter, Aug. 30, 1956; children: Katarina Anna, George David. MD, U. Munich, Germany, 1949; PhD, U. Minn., Mpls., 1957. Diplomate Am. Bd. Pediatrics, ofcl. examiner and mem., 1965-95. Resident in clin. pathology Krankenhaus III Orden, Munich, 1950; resident in pathology U. Munich, 1950-51; intern Mountainside Hosp., Montclair, NJ, 1951-52; fellow in pediatrics Mayo Grad. Sch., Rochester, Minn., 1953-56; sr. cancer research scientist Roswell Park Meml. Inst., Buffalo, 1956-57; asst. to staff Mayo Clinic, Rochester, 1957-58, cons. in pediatrics, 1959-89, head sect. pediatrics, 1969-74; prof. pediatrics, chmn. dept. pediatrics Mayo Clinic and Mayo Med. Sch., 1974-80. Mem. test com. III Nat. Bd. Med. Examiners, 1973-75; vis. prof. at various univs and instns., including U. Dusseldorf (Germany) and U. Munich, 1971, Pahlavi U., Iran, 1975, Olga Hosp., Stuttgart, Germany, 1978, Martin Luther King Hosp., Los

Angeles, 1979, U. Man., 1981; mem. emeritus staff Mayo Clinic, 1989. Mem. editl. bd. Clin. Pediatrics, 1968-76, 79-97, European Jour. Pediatrics, 1976-84, Pediatrics, 1983-89; contbr. more than 290 articles to med. publs. Active parent support groups in field of cyclic vomiting syndrome; life pres. Stickler Syndrome support group, 1997—. Recipient Humanitarian award Chgo. region chpt. Nat. Found. Ileitis and Colitis, 1978, award for excellence of subject matter and presentation So. Minn. Med. Assn., 1978 Mem. Am. Acad. Pediatrics (Disting. Svc. award Minn. chpt. 1999), Soc. Pediatric Rsch., Am. Pediatric Soc., Nat. Coun. Reliable Health Info., Midwest Soc. Pediatric Rsch. (coun. 1967-69, pres. 1970-71, Founders award 1996), N.W. Pediatric Soc. (pres. 1973-74) Achievements include description of hereditary progressive arthropthalmopathy in 1965, now called Stickler syndrome; and the treatment otitis media, hypophosphatemic rickets, renal disease; research in areas of parents' fears and the need of routine physical examinations in adolescents, and the excesses of alternative medicine. Office: Mayo Clinic Emeritus Ctr Rochester MN 55905

STICKLER, RICHARD E., federal agency administrator; b. W.Va., 1944; BS in Gen. Engring., Fairmont State U., W.Va., 1968. Cert. mine safety profl. Internat. Soc. Mine Safety. With Bethenergy Mines, Bethlehem, Pa., 1996—97, various positions including coal miner, capt. mine rescue team, shift foreman, supt., mine mgr.; with Performance Coal Co., Charleston, W.Va.; dir. Pa. Bur. Deep Mine Safety, 1997—2003; asst. sec. mine safety & health adminstrn. US Dept. Labor, 2006—. Office: US Dept Labor 1100 Wilson Blvd Arlington VA 22209-3939*

STICKLER, STEPHEN H., photographer; Founder, photographer RecCenter Studio LLC, Echo Park, LA. Photographer (books) Korn: Life Is Peachy, 1997; contbr. photographs to Revolver mag., Man Outdoors, Stuff mag., Christian Sci. Monitor, Spin, Dallas Observer, others; photographer (albums) Classic American Songbook, Andre Previn, 1992, American Caesar, Iggy Pop, 1993, Lemonade and Brownies, Sugar Ray, 1995, A.D.I.D.A.S., KORN, 1997, Act Your Age, Home Grown, 1998, Can't Get There From Here, Great White, 1999, Breadline EP, Megadeth, 2000, California Crossing, Fu Manchu, 2001, In The Pursuit of Leisure, Sugar Ray, 2003, Best of Sugar Ray, 2005, The Right To Bare Arms, Larry the Cable Guy, 2005, others. V.p. Echo Park C. of C., 2007—. Studio: 1161 Logan St Los Angeles CA 90026 Address: 748 E Kensington Rd Los Angeles CA 90026-4427 Office Phone: 213-413-9302. Business E-Mail: mail@stephenstickler.com.

STICKNEY, JESSICA, former state legislator; b. Duluth, Minn., May 16, 1929; d. Ralph Emerson and Claudia Alice (Cox) Page; m. Edwin Levi Stickney, June 17, 1951; children: Claudia, Laura, Jeffrey. BA, Macalester Coll., St. Paul, Minn., 1951; PhD (hon), Rocky Mtn. Coll., Billings, Mont., 1986. Rep. State of Mont., 1989-92. Mem. Gov.'s Commn. on Post-Sec. Edn., Mont., 1973-75. Mem. Sch. Bd. Trustees, Miles City, Mont., 1968-74; mem., chmn. zoning bd., Miles City, 1975-89; mem. Govt. Study Commn., Miles City, 1974-76, United Ch. Christ Bd. Homeland Ministries, 1975-81; chmn., conf. moderator United Ch. Christ Bd. Mont.-Northern Wyo. Conf., 1980-82; chmn. Town Meeting on the Arts, Mont., 1980; mem., chmn. Miles Community Coll. Bd., 1975-89, chmn. 1978-80. Recipient Disting. Citizen's award, Macalester Coll., 2006. Mem. Mont. Arts Coun. (chmn. 1982-85), Western States Arts Found. (vice chmn. 1984), Nat. Assembly State Arts Agys. (bd. dirs. 1982-88), AAUW (pres. 1964-66). Democrat. Avocations: writing, sewing, painting, reading.

STICKNEY, JOHN MOORE, lawyer; b. Cleve., Apr. 8, 1926; s. Isaac Moore and Alicia Margaret (Burns) S.; m. Elfriede von Rebenstock, Oct. 4, 1958; children: Michaela B., Alicia J., Thomas M. AB, Western Res. U., 1948, LLB, 1951. Bar: Ohio 1952. Sole practice, Cleve., 1952-79; ptnr. Burgess, Steck, Andrews & Stickney, Cleve., 1979-88, of counsel Weston, Hurd, Fallon, Paisley & Howley, Cleve., 1988-90, sole practice, 1990-95; Stickney & Stickney, 1996-; pres. Scranton-Averell, Inc., Cleve., 1979—. Trustee Cleve. Music Sch. Settlement, 1967-95, Salzedo Sch. Harp, Cleve., 1962-04, Bishop Brown Fund, Cleve., 1981-06, Flats Oxbow Assn., Lake Erie Sci. & Nature Ctr., 1996-06, also pres., 1970-72; co-trustee Margaret & Edwin Griffiths Trusts, Cleve., 1968—. Served with USNR, 1945-46. Mem. ABA, Ohio State Bar Assn., Cleve. Bar Assn., Hermit Club (Cleve.), Rowfant Club (Cleve.). Republican. Episcopalian. Office Phone: 216-241-0140. Business E-Mail: stickeylaw@sbeglobal.net.

STIEBING, WILLIAM HENRY, JR., retired history professor; b. New Orleans, Dec. 21, 1940; s. William Henry and Eunice Sophie Stiebing; m. Ann Erma Thompson, Sept. 11, 1965; 1 child, Kimberly Ann Heston. BA, U. New Orleans, 1962; PhD, U. Pa., 1970. Instr. history U. New Orleans, 1967—70, asst. prof. history, 1970—73, assoc. prof. history, 1973—85, prof. history, 1985—2001, Seraphia D. Leyda tchg. prof. history, 2001—05. Staff mem. excavations Archaeological Expdn., U. Pa. Mus., Tell Es-Sa'idiyeh, Jordan, 1965; coord. European history U. New Orleans, 1974—83; pottery supr. excavations Archaeological Expdn., U. Pa. Mus., Sarafand, Lebanon, 1974. Author: (scholarly book) Ancient Astronauts, Cosmic Collisions and Other Popular Theories About Man's Past, 1984, Out of the Desert?: Archaeology and the Exodus/Conquest Narratives, 1989 (Named one of Choice Mag.'s Outstanding Acad. Books, 1990), Uncovering the Past: A History of Archaeology, 1993, Ancient Near Eastern History and Culture, 2003, 2008. Bd. dirs., v.p., pres., treas. Salem United Ch. of Christ, New Orleans, 1970—2005. Recipient Disting. Faculty award, La. State U. Alumni Fedn., 1985, Career award for Excellence in Rsch., U. New Orleans Alumni Assn., 2003; NDEA fellow, U. Pa., 1962—65. Mem.: Soc. Bibl. Lit., Archaeol. Inst. Am. (sec. New Orleans chpt. 1983—88), Am. Hist. Assn. Mem. Protestant Episcopal Ch. Avocation: travel. Home Fax: 501-767-3636.

STIEF, LOUIS JOHN, chemist; b. Pottsville, Pa., July 26, 1933; s. Louis Norman and Dorothy Elizabeth (Bassler) S.; m. Kathleen J. Talbot, Nov. 30, 1963 (div. 1980); children: Andrew, Lorraine. BA, La Salle Coll., 1955; PhD, Catholic U. Am., 1960. Nat. Acad. Scis.-NRC postdoctoral rsch. assoc. Nat. Bur. Standards, Washington, 1960-61; NATO postdoctoral fellow, ind. researcher chemistry dept. Sheffield (Eng.) U., 1961-63; sr. scientist, sr. chemist Melpar, Inc., Falls Church, Va., 1963-68; NAS-NRC sr. postdoctoral rsch. assoc. NASA/Goddard Space Flight Ctr., Greenbelt, Md., 1968-69, astrophysicist, 1969-76, head br. astrochemistry, 1976-90, sr. scientist, 1990—2004, emeritus scientist, 2004—. Research: numerous publs., especially in Jour. Chem. Physics and Jour. Phys. Chemistry. Recipient Alumni Achievement award Cath. U. Am., 1985; NASA fellow Queen Mary Coll., U. London, 1981-82 Fellow: Washington Acad. Sci.; mem.: Am. Astron. Soc. (divsn. planetary sci.), Royal Soc. Chemistry, Am. Chem. Soc. (Hillebrand prize Chem. Soc. Washington 2002), Sigma Xi.

STIEFEL, ETHAN, dancer, performing company executive, dean; b. Tyrone, Pa. s. Alan and Mima Stiefel. Studies with Mikhail Baryshnikov, Sch. Classical Ballet, 1987; student, Fordham U., 1995—. From mem. to prin. dancer NY City Ballet, 1989-95, prin. dancer, 1995-96, Am. Ballet Theatre, NYC, 1997—; artistic dir. Stiefel and Stars, 2002—, Stiefel and Students, 2004—06; prin. dancer, artistic assoc. Kings of the Dance, 2006—; dean of dance NC Sch. Arts, 2007—. With Zurich Ballet, 1992-93; guest artist NYC Ballet, 1998-99, Atlanta Ballet, 1999, Royal Ballet, 1999-2007. Dancer prin. roles include Le Corsaire, Romeo & Juliet, Giselle, Les Patineurs, Onegin, Swan Lake, Theme and Variations, Raymonda, Don Quixote, A Midsummer Night's Dream, La Bayadere, The Dream, The Four Temperaments, Apollo, Stars and Stripes, Harlequinade, Tarantella, Tchaikovsky Pas de Deux, Chaconne, Prodigal Son, La Fille Mal Gardee, The Nutcracker, Robbins' ballets Dances at a Gathering, West Side Story Suite, The Goldberg Variations, The Cage, Quiet City, Martins' ballets Fearful Symmetries, Ash, Tchaikovsky Pas de Quatre, The Sleeping Beauty, King of the Dance, Tharp Ballets Known by Heart, Manon, Percussion IV, Push Comes to Shove, In The Upper Room, others; appeared in PBS TV prodn. Le Corsaire, 1999, Born to be Wild, 2002, The Dream, 2004; artistic dir. Stiefel & Stars, 2001—, artistic dir Performance Project, 2004; guest artist Teatro Colon, 1999, Hamburg Ballet, 2000, Kirov Ballet, 2001, 04, Verona, Italy, 2003, Washington Opera, 2003, Budapest Opera, 2003, others; starring role: (film) Center Stage, 2000, Center Stage: Turn it Up, 2008. Recipient Silver medal, Prix de Lausanne, 1989, Statue award, Princess Grace Found., 1999, Dance Mag. award, 2008; emerging dance artist grantee, Princess Grace Found. USA, 1991-92 Office: care Peter S Diggins Assoc 133 W 71st St Ste 8-B New York NY 10023 Office Phone: 212-874-4534. Personal E-mail: festspiel@aol.com.

STIEG, PHILIP, neurosurgeon; b. Milw., July 30, 1952; BS, U. Wis., Madison, 1974; PhD in anatomy and neuroscience, Albany Med. Coll., Union U., 1980; MD, Med. Coll. Wis., 1983. Intern, resident U. Tex. Southwestern Med. Sch., Dallas, 1983—84, chief resident, 1988—89; fellow Karolinska Inst., Stockholm, 1987—88; instr. surgery Harvard Med. Sch., Boston, 1989—92, assoc. neurosurgery, 1989—, asst. prof. surgery, 1992—96, assoc. prof. surgery, 1996—; prof., chmn. neurological surgery Weill Cornell Med. Coll., NYC, 2000—; neurosurgeon-in-chief NY-Presbyn. Hosp., NYC, 2000—. Mem. Mem. Sloan Kettering Cancer Ctr., NYC, 2007—. Recipient Time, Feeling and Focus award, Am. Heart Assn., 1999, The Best Doctors in New York, NY Mag., 2008; named one of The Best Doctors, Boston Mag., 1997, The Best Doctors in New York, NY Mag., 2001—03, 2007. Fellow: ACS, NY Acad. Medicine, N.Am. Skull Base Soc.; mem.: AAAS, AMA, Med. Soc. of the State of NY, NY Soc. Neurosurgery (sec./treas. 2004, pres. 2006), Am. Acad. Neurological Surgery, Neurological Soc. America, Nat. Stroke Assn., Soc. U. Neurosurgeons (v.p. 1999—2000, pres. 2001—04), Am. Assn. Neurological Surgeons, Soc. for Neuroscience, Boston Soc. Neurology and Psychiatry, Am. Heart Assn., Am. Cleft-Palate-Craniofacial Assn., NY Acad. Sciences, New England Neurosurgical Soc., Congress of Neurological Surgeons, Boston Stroke Soc. Office: Starr Pavilion 651 525 E 68th St New York NY 10065 Office Phone: 212-746-4684. Office Fax: 212-746-6607.*

STIEHL, WALTER DAN, research scientist; s. Walter Alan and Elaine Stiehl; m. Lindsay Stiehl. BS in Mech. Engring., MIT, Cambridge, Mass., 2003; BS in Brain and Cognitive Scis., MIT, 2003, SM in Media Arts and Scis., 2005. Urop MIT Media Lab, Synthetic Characters Group, Cambridge, 1998—2001, MIT Media Lab, Personal Robots Group, 2001—03, rsch. asst., 2003—. Pres. St. Anthony Assn. Boston, Cambridge, 2005. Recipient Best Paper award, IEEE, 2005; Rsch. grant, NSF, 2005. Mem.: IEEE, Assn. Computing Machinery. Achievements include patents pending for interactive systems employing robotic companions; invention of huggable robot. Home: 48 Puritan Rd Somerville MA 02145 Office: MIT Media Lab 20 Ames St E15-468 Cambridge MA 02139 Personal E-mail: wdstiehl@alum.mit.edu. Business E-Mail: wdstiehl@media.mit.edu.

STIEHM, E. RICHARD, pediatrician, educator; b. Milw., Jan. 22, 1933; s. Reuben Harold and Marie Dueno S.; m. Judith Hicks, July 12, 1958; children: Jamie Elizabeth, Carrie Eleanor, Meredith Ellen. BS, U. Wis., 1954, MD, 1957. Diplomate Am. Bd. Pediat., Am. Bd. Allergy and Clin. Immunology (bd. dirs. 1977-83), Am. Bd. Diagnostic Lab. Immunology. Intern Phila. Gen. Hosp., 1957-58; fellow in physiol. chemistry U. Wis., 1959-61, asst. prof. pediat., 1965—68, assoc. prof., 1968—69; med. officer USNR, Johnsville, Pa., 1961-63; resident in pediat. Babies Hosp., NYC, 1963-65; rsch. fellow in pediat. immunology U. Calif., San Francisco, 1965-68; assoc. prof. UCLA, 1969—72, chief divsn. immunology, allergy and rheumatology, 1969—2003, prof., 1972—, assoc. dir. Ctr. for Interdisciplinary Rsch. in Immunologic Diseases, 1981-82, co-dir. Cystic Fibrosis Ctr., 1988—95, vice chair acad. affairs dept. pediat., 1989—99; vis. scientist metabolism br. Nat. Cancer Inst., Bethesda, Md., 1982-88. Vis. prof. Yale U., Mayo Clinic, U. Cin., Great Ormond St. Hosp., U.K., U. Wis.; bd. sci. dirs. Immune Deficiency Found., 1981—, Eczema Found., 1988—, Pediat. AIDS Found., 1989-99; task force on pediatric allergy NIH, 1977; mem. gen. clin. rsch. ctr. study sect. NIH, 1978-82, 84-88; adv. com. Hartford Fellowship, 1984-88; co-dir. LA Pediatric AIDS Consortium, 1988—. Editor: Immunologic Disorders in Infants and Children, 1972, 80, 89, 96, 2004; Am. editor: Pediatric Rsch., 1984-89; assoc. editor: Pediat. Update, 2003-; mem. editl. bd. Pediat., 1972-78, Pediat. in Rev., 1978-81, Jour. Allergy and Clin. Immunology, 1976-80, Jour. Clin. Immunology, 1985-89, Jour. Asthma Pediatric Allergy and Immunology, 1987-91, Am. Jour. Diseases of Children, 1987-97, Contemporary Pediat., 1991-96, Am. Jour. Clin. Nutrition, 1992-97; contbr. articles to profl. jours. Commr. HHS Commn. on Childhood Vaccines, 1988-90; mem. clin. rsch. adv. com. Nat. Found. March of Dimes, 1992-97, 2004-09. Recipient Career Devel. award Nat. Inst. Allergy and Infectious Diseases, 1967-69, E. Mead Johnson award for Pediat. Rsch., 1974, Alumni Citation award U. Wis. Med. Sch., 1988, Lifetime Achievement award Immune Deficiency Found., 1995, Med. Sci. award UCLA Med. Alumni, 1999, Disting. Alumni award Babies and Children's Hosp. Alumni Assn., N.Y., 1999, Abbott Labs. award, Clin. and Diagnostic Immunology Am. Soc. Microbiology, 2007; Markle scholar, 1967-72. Fellow AAAS; mem. Am. Assn. Immunologists, Western Soc. Pediat. Rsch. (coun. 1977-80, pres. 1983, Ross Rsch. award 1971), Soc. Pediat. Rsch., Am. Pediat. Soc., Am. Acad. Allergy, Asthma and Clin. Immunology, Am. Acad. Pediat. (infectious diseases com. 1971-77), Am. Soc. Clin. Investigation, Clin. Immunology Soc., Phi Beta Kappa, Alpha Omega Alpha. Office: UCLA Dept Peds Divsn Immunology 10833 Le Conte Ave Los Angeles CA 90095-3075 Office Phone: 310-825-6481. Business E-Mail: estiehm@mednet.ucla.edu.

STIEHM, JUDITH HICKS, political scientist; b. Madison, Wis., Oct. 9, 1935; d. Stratton Elson and Eleanor Spencer (Kilbourn) Hicks; m. E. Richard Stiehm, July 12, 1958; children: Jamie Elizabeth, Carrie Eleanor, Meredith Ellen. Student, Oberlin Coll., 1953; BA in E. Asian Studies, U. Wis., 1957; MA in Am. History, Temple U., 1961; PhD in Polit. Theory, Columbia U., 1969. Dir. resident hons. program U. So. Calif., LA, 1970-73, asst. prof., 1970-74, assoc. prof., 1974-83, dir. program for study of women and men in soc., 1975-81, prof. polit. sci., 1983, vice provost, 1984-87; provost Fla. Internat. U., Miami, 1987-91, prof. polit. sci., 1987—. Vis. prof. U. Wis., 1994, U.S. Army Peacekeeping Inst., U.S. Army War Coll., 1995-96, U.S. Army Strategic Studies Inst., U.S. Army War Coll., 1996, U. So. Calif., 2002-; lectr. U. Wis., Madison, 1966-69, UCLA, 1969-70; vis. lectr. San Francisco State U., 1965-66; affiliate NAS Project, 1981-82; cons. UN Div. for the Advancement of Women, Calif. Elected Women, Dept. HEW, AAUW, LWV L.A., UN Lessons Learned Unit, Dept. Peacekeeping Ops. Author: Nonviolent Power: Active and Passive Resistance in America, 1972, Bring Me Men and Women..., 1981, Arms and the Enlisted Woman, 1989, The U.S. Army War College: Military Education in a Democracy, 2002, Champions for Peace: Women Winners of the Nobel Peace Prize, 2006; editor: The Frontiers of Knowledge, 1976, Women and Men's Wars, 1983, Women's Views of the Political World of Men, 1984, It's Our Military, Too!, 1996; mem. editorial bd. Western Polit. Quar., 1972-75, Signs, 1981-84, Women and Politics, 1986-88, 2000-. Mem. Calif. Postsecondary Edn. Commn., 1978, Calif. Adv. Coun. on Vocat. Edn., 1978-82, Def. Adv. Com. on Women in Svcs., 1979-82; bd. dirs. So. Calif. and Miami chpts. ACLU. Named Woman of Yr., Santa Monica YWCA, 1981; recipient Outstanding Civilian Svc. medal U.S. Army, 1996, U. Wis. Disting Alumni award, 2006. Mem. Am. Polit. Sci. Assn. (exec. coun. 1989, sec. 2000, Frank Goodnow award, 2008), Western Polit. Sci. Assn. (pres. 1986), Women's Caucus Polit. Sci. (pres. 1996-97), Nat. Council for Research on Women (exec. council 1982), Council on Fgn. Relations, Phi Beta Kappa, Phi Kappa Phi (Victoria Schuck Book award 1990). Avocations: tennis, skiing, stained glass. Home: 434 24th St Santa Monica CA 90402-3102 Personal E-mail: stiehmj@fiu.edu.

STIENSTRA, STEPHANI ANN, editor, writer; b. Baytown, Tex., Aug. 6, 1955; d. Herbert Howard and Janice Faye (Stowe) Cruickshank; m. George Keyston III, Oct. 8, 1983 (div. Mar. 1997); children: Jeremy George, Kristopher Samuel; m. Thomas Frank Stienstra, Dec. 4, 1998. AA with honors, Merced Coll., Calif., 1975; BA in Journalism with distinction, San Jose State U., 1976. Reporter Fresno (Calif.) Bee, 1974-75; reporter, photographer Merced (Calif.) Sun-Star, 1974-77; pub. info. officer Fresno City Coll., 1977—80; dir. comms. Aerojet Tactical Sys. Co., Sacramento, 1980—83; co-owner, v.p. Keyco Landscape Contractor Inc., Loomis, Calif., 1984—96; co-owner Stienstra Outdoor Books, Inc., 2003—. Co-author (with Tom Stienstra): (book) Northern California Cabins and Cottages, 2002 (Hon. Mention Book award Outdoor Writers Assn. Calif., 2002), Washington Camping, 2002. Co-coord. Aerojet United Way Campaign, 1981; Aerojet Tactical Sys. Co. coord. West Coast Nat. Derby Rallies, 1981-83; co-founder, pres. Calif. Lion Awareness. Mem.: Internat. Assn. Bus. Communicators (dir. Sacramento chpt. 1983), Citrus Heights C. of C. (v.p. 1983). Office: PO Box 151 Mount Shasta CA 96067-0151 Personal E-mail: stienstra@jps.net.

STIERMAN, DONALD JOHN, geophysicist, educator; s. Laverne and Esther Stierman; m. Linda Lee Donar, Jan. 16, 1970; children: Peggy, Daniel, Robert, Michael. BS in Physics, SUNY, Brockport, 1969; MS in Geophysics, PhD in Geophysics, Stanford U., Palo Alto, CA, 1977. Vol. Peace Corps, Tegucigalpa, Honduras, 1969—72; asst. prof. geophysics U. Calif., Riverside, 1977—84; geophysicist (part-time, wae) U.S. Geol. Survey, Menlo Park, 1984—88; asst.,assoc. prof. geophysics U. Toledo, 1984—. Fulbright scholar/rschr., U.S. State Dept. Mem.: Archaeological Inst. America, Am. Geophys. Union, Seismol. Soc. America, Soc. Exploration Geophysicists, Geol. Soc. America. Roman Catholic. Avocations: gardening, music, cooking. Office: DES Univ Toledo MS 604 2801 W Bancroft Toledo OH 43606 Office Fax: 419-530-4421. Business E-Mail: dstierm@utnet.utoledo.edu.

STIFELMAN, MICHAEL D., surgeon, director; b. Newark, May 7, 1967; s. Frank Louis and Susan Rhee Stifelman; m. Jill D. Zimmerman, Aug. 22, 1993; children: Stephanie Chloe, Jake Matthew, Noah Samuel. Med. Doctorate, Albert Einstein Coll. Medicine, Bronx, NY, 1993. Chief urology svc. NYU Langone Med. Ctr., dir. robotic surgery, 2008—. Contbr. scientific papers to numerous profl. jours. Mem.: Am. Urol. Assn. Achievements include research in robotic surgery of kidney and ureter. Office: NYU Langone Med Ctr 150 E 32nd St New York NY 10016 Office Phone: 6468256325. Office Fax: 6468256397.

STIFF, LINDA E., federal agency administrator; b. Feb. 18, 1952; BA, Rollins Coll. Revenue agent IRS, US Dept. Treasury, Jacksonville, Fla., 1980, sr. adv. to wage and investment commr., COO & commr. Washington, dir. compliance Wage and Investment Divsn., dep. commr. Small Bus./Self-Employed Divsn., dep. commr. ops. support, 2006—07, dep. commr. services & enforcement, 2007—, acting commr., 2007—08. Office: IRS 1111 Constitution Ave NW Washington DC 20224-0002*

STIFF, PATRICK JOSEPH, internist, hematologist, oncologist, educator; b. Toledo, Nov. 27, 1950; BS, U. Toledo, 1972; MD, Loyola U., 1975. Intern Cleve. Clinic, 1975-76, resident in medicine, 1976-78; fellow in hematology and oncology Meml. Sloan-Kettering Med. Ctr., NYC, 1978-81; asst. prof. medicine Sch. Medicine So. Ill. U., 1981-86; asst. prof. medicine Loyola U. Med. Ctr., Maywood, Ill., 1986-92; assoc. prof. medicine Loyola U. Med. Ctr.-Stritch Sch. Medicine, Maywood, Ill., 1992-96; prof. medicine and pathology Loyola U. Med. Ctr., Maywood, Ill., 1996—, dir. Cardinal Bernardin Cancer Ctr., 2003—, dir. divsn. hematology and oncology, 2003—. Chair transplant subcom. Ill. State Med. Adv. Com., 1999—. Mem. Internat. Soc. Exptl. Hematology, Internat. Soc. Hematotherapy and Graft Engrs., S.W. Oncology Group, Am. Soc. Clin. Oncology, Am. Soc. Hematology. Office: Loyola Univ Med Ctr 2160 S 1st Ave Maywood IL 60153-3304 Office Phone: 708-327-3148. Business E-Mail: pstiff@lumc.edu.

STIFF, ROBERT MARTIN, newspaper editor; b. Detroit, Aug. 25, 1931; s. Martin L. and Gladys (Mathews) S.; m. Cindy Rose, Aug. 30, 1980; children: David Alan, Amy Anne, Kirsten Marie. BA in Radio and Journalism, Ohio State U., 1953. All-Am. sports editor Ohio State U., Daily Lantern, 1952—53; reporter, bur. chief, city editor Painesville Telegraph, Ohio, 1953-61; deskman, asst. city editor, sports editor, city editor, day editor, state editor, asst. mng. editor St. Petersburg Times, Fla., 1961-67; editor St. Petersburg Evening Ind., 1967-84; dir. St. Petersburg Times Pub. Co., 1969-84; exec. editor, v.p. Tallahassee Democrat, 1985-91; pres. Bob Stiff & Assocs., Tallahassee, 1991-95; exec. editor JMT Assocs., 1991—92, 1994—95; mng. editor About Fla., 1991-94; editor Lexington (NC) Dispatch, 1995—2006. Mem. Pulitzer Prize Jury, 1982-83; dir. devel. and pub. rels. Fla. Taxwatch Inc., 1992-94; bd. dirs. NC AP News Coun., 1995-2001, v.p., 1997-99, pres., 1999-2000; pres. Empty Stocking Fund, 1995-2006. Bd. dirs. Cancer Svcs. Davidson County, 1996—2004, NC Open Govt. Coalition, 2004—06, U. NC, Chapel Hill, Sch. Journalism Found., 2004—06; pres. Capital Press Assn., 1998—2001; bd. dirs. NC Daily Newspaper Assn., 1995—2006, v.p., 1998—99, pres., 1999—2000. Mem.: Nat. Coun. Editl. Writers, NC Press Assn. (bd. dirs. 1999—2000, 2002—05), AP Mng. Editors Assn., Fla. Bar Found. (bd. dirs. 1990—92), Fla. Soc. Newspaper Editors (pres. 1975—76, dir. 1971—84, 1990—93), Am. Soc. Newspaper Editors Found. (bd. dirs., treas. 1986—90), Am. Soc. Newspaper Editors (dir. 1981—87), AP Assn. Fla. (pres. 1970—71), Lexington Kiwanis (bd. dirs. 1996—2000, 2003—06), Sigma Delta Chi (pres. West Coast chpt. 1970—71). Personal E-mail: bobstiffela@aol.com.

STIFFLER, ERMA DELORES, minister, pastoral counselor, retired elementary school educator; b. Blairsville, Pa., June 26, 1942; d. Harry Reuben and Dorothy Velma (Buterbaugh) Berenbrok; m. Charles Harry Stiffler, July 15, 1966; children: Barbara Wojichowski, Dee-ann Bollinger, Crissy, Rebecca Stewart. BS in Edn. cum laude, Indiana State Coll., Pa., 1964; MTh, Christian Bible Coll., 1999, ThD, 2000; Bible diploma, Liberty U., 1996; pvt. investigator diploma, Harcourt Learning Direct, 2000; student, Ctr. Bibl. Counseling, 2001, student, 2003, Ctr. Bibl. Counselling, 2007. Ordained min. Gospel Revelation, Inc., 2001; cert. pastoral counselor Internat. Bd. Christian Counselor, 2008. Elem. tchr. Armstrong County Sch. Dist., Elderton, Pa., 1964—67, Purchase Line Sch. Dist., Commodore, Pa., 1968—70; pastor, founder Lighthouse Gospel Revelation Fellowship, Blairsville, Pa., 1995—. Intercessory prayer Breakthrough Internat., Lincoln, Va., 1997—; vol. Prison Fellowship Ministries, Washington, 1999—2000; outreach person Lighthouse Neighborhood Prayer Movement, Edina, Minn. and Blairsville, 1999—; prayer Mastermedia Internat., Redlands, Calif., 2001—03. Contbr. articles to mags. Contact person Nat. Day of Prayer, Blairsville, Pa.; active PTA, Blairsville; col. March of Dimes, Heart Assn.; spkr. cmty. luminary svc. Blairsville, Pa., 2003; Bible studies tchr., youth group leader, tchr., Sunday sch. supt., 1966—; vol. Blairsville Sch. Dist., Burrell Township Pub. Libr., Blacklick, Pa., 2007—; former tchr. Child Evangelism Fellowship, Indiana County, Pa.; former christian edn. dir. Missionary Alliance Ch., Blairsville. Mem.: Am. Assn. Christian Counselors, Kappa Delta Pi. Republican. Avocations: collecting old books, collecting figuerines, reading, walking. Home: 216 N Walnut St Blairsville PA 15717 Office: Lighthouse Gospel Revelation Fellowship Blairsville PA 15717 Office Phone: 724-459-0390.

STIFFLER, JACK JUSTIN, electrical engineer; b. Mitchellville, Iowa, May 22, 1934; s. John Justin and Helen Irene (Roorda) S.; m. Ardis Ann Ackerman, Aug. 21, 1955; 1 child, Julia Alise; m. Sally Voris Burns, Apr. 20, 1989. AB magna cum laude in Physics, Harvard U., Cambridge, Mass., 1956; MSEE, Calif. Inst. Tech., Pasadena, 1957, PhD, 1962; postgrad., U. Paris, 1957-58. Engr. Hughes Aircraft Corp., Culver City, Calif., 1956-57; mem. tech. staff Jet Propulsion Lab., Pasadena, Calif., 1959-67; cons. scientist Raytheon Corp., Sudbury, Mass., 1967-81; co-founder, exec. v.p. Sequoia Systems, Inc., Marlborough, Mass., 1981—97; co-founder, CTO Reliable Tech., Inc., 1998—; cons., 1997—. Lectr. Calif. Inst. Tech., U. So. Calif., UCLA, Northeastern U. Author: Theory of Synchronous Communications, 1971; contbr. chpts. to books, articles to profl. jours. Fellow: IEEE; mem.: Woods Hole Oceanographic Inst. (hon.), Sigma Xi, Phi Beta Kappa. Office Phone: 508-353-5611. Personal E-mail: stiffler@capecod.net.

STIFLER, WILLIAM L., JR., literature and language professor; s. William L. and Thelma J. Stifler; m. Judy L. Carter, July 28, 2007; m. Kathy Miller, Jan. 26, 1974 (div. Mar. 0, 2006); children: Natalie Baker, Wm. Brant, April, Benjamin. BA, Tenn. Temple U., Chattanooga, 1976; MRE, Temple Bapt. Theol. Sem., Chattanooga, 1981; MA in Writing, U. Tenn., Chattanooga, 1991. Assoc. prof. Chattanooga State Tech. CC, 1992—. Office: Chattanooga State Tech CC 4501 Amnicola Hwy Chattanooga TN 37406-1097 Business E-Mail: bill.stifler@chattanoogastate.edu.

STIGGALL, CORIN J., musician; b. Santa Clara, Calif., Aug. 18, 1967; s. James L. Stiggall and Lynne Muccigrosso. AA, De Anza coll., Calif., 1991; B, New Eng. Conservatory Music, Boston, 1994. Bassist New Eng. Chamber Orch., Boston, 1991—93; music tchr. NYC, 1994—2008. Recipient award, Internat. Assn. Jazz Educators, Boston, 1994. Mem.: Screen Actor's Guild, Internat. Soc. Bassists.

STIGLER, STEPHEN MACK, statistician, educator; b. Mpls., Aug. 10, 1941; s. George Joseph and Margaret (Mack) S.; m. Virginia Lee, June 27,1964; children: Andrew, Geoffrey, Margaret, Elizabeth. BA, Carleton Coll., 1963, DSc (hon.), 2005; PhD, U. Calif., Berkeley, 1967. Asst. prof. U. Wis., Madison, 1967-71, assoc. prof., 1971-75, prof., 1975-79, U. Chgo., 1979—, chmn. dept., 1986—92, 2005—, Ernest DeWitt Burton Disting. Svc. prof., 1992—. Trustee Ctr. Advanced Study in the Behavioral Scis., Stanford, Calif., 1986-92, 93-99, 2000-06, chmn., 1995-99, 2002-06; trustee JSTOR, 1998-2009, trustee Ithaka, 2009-. Author: The History of Statistics, 1986, Statistics on the Table, 1999; contbr. articles to jours. in field. Recipient Rsch. award Humboldt Found., 2005; Guggenheim Found. fellow, 1976-77; Ctr. for Advanced Study in Behavioral Scis. fellow, 1978-79. Fellow: AAAS, Royal Statis. Soc. (Fisher lectr. 1986, campion lectr. 2009), Am. Statis. Assn. (editor Jour. 1979—82), Inst. Math. Stats. (Neyman lectr. 1988, pres. 1993—94, LeCam lectr. 2006), Am. Acad. Arts and Scis. (mem. coun. 1995—99); mem.: Am. Philos. Soc., Brit. Soc. for History Sci., History of Sci. Soc., Bernoulli Soc., Statis. Soc. Can., Internat. Statis. Inst. (mem. coun. 1999—2001, pres. 2003—05), Quadrangle Club, Phi Beta Kappa, Sigma Xi. Office: U Chgo Dept Statistics 5734 S University Ave Chicago IL 60637-1514 Office Phone: 773-702-8328. Business E-Mail: stigler@uchicago.edu.

STIGLIANO, JOSE MARIA, information technology executive, computer scientist; b. Buenos Aires, Dec. 9, 1953; s. Jose and Yvonne Suzanne (Engel) S.; m. Daniela Saida Farinelli, Dec. 14, 1988; children: Veronica Maria, Carolina Maria, Jose Nicolas. Cert. in electronics, L.A. Huergo Tech. Coll., 1973; BSBA, Am. U., 1990; MS in Mgmt., Boston U., 1992; BS in Mgmt. Info. Systems, U. of State of N.Y., 1996; MSc in Computer Sci., Boston U., 1997. Programmer Ministry of Justice, Buenos Aires, 1973-76; analyst, programmer CTC Svc. Bur., Buenos Aires, 1976-77; systems analyst Aurora S.A., Buenos Aires, 1977-78; computer systems officer Internat. Fund Agrl. Devel. UN, Rome, 1981-88; info. tech.coord. Internat. Fund Agrl. Devel. of U.N., Rome, 1988—2005, dir. info. tech. divsn., 2006—. Lectr. U. Del Salvador, Buenos Aires, 1975—77; cons. in field. Contbg. author: Encyclopedia of Information Systems, 2002; inventor in field. Recipient IFAD Merit award, 1988, IFAD Svc. award, 1990. Mem. IEEE, IEEE Computer Soc., Assn. Computing Machinery, Boston U. Gen. Alumni Assn., Argentine Soc. for Informatics and Ops. Rsch. Avocations: music, bass guitar. Office: Internat Fund Agrl Devel 44 Via Paolo Di Dono Rome 00142 Italy Personal E-mail: j.stigliano@computer.org. Business E-Mail: j.stigliano@ifad.org.

STIGLITZ, JOSEPH EUGENE, economics professor, former federal official; b. Gary, Ind., Feb. 9, 1943; s. Nathaniel David and Charlotte (Fishman) Stiglitz; m. Anya Schiffrin, Oct. 29, 2004; children from previous marriage: Siobhan, Michael, Edward, Julia. BA, Amherst Coll., Mass, 1964; DHL, Amherst Coll., 1974; PhD in Econs., MIT, 1966; MA (hon.), Yale U., 1970; D in Econs. (hon.), U. Leuven, 1994. Asst. prof. economics MIT, 1966—67; asst. prof. Cowles Found., Yale U., New Haven, 1967—68, assoc. prof., 1968—70, prof., 1970—74; vis. fellow St. Catherine's Coll., Oxford, England, 1973—74; Joan Kenney professorship Stanford U., 1974—76, prof. economics & sr. fellow, Hoover Inst., 1988—2001; Oskar Morgenstern dist. fellow Inst. Advanced Studies Math., Princeton, NJ, 1978—79; Drummond prof. polit. economy Oxford U., England, 1976—79; prof. econs. Princeton U., 1979—88; mem. Coun. Econ. Advisors, Exec. Office of the Pres., Washington, 1993—97, chmn., 1995—97; sr. v.p., chief economist The World Bank, Washington, 1995—2000; sr. fellow Brookings Inst., Washington, 2000; Stern visiting prof. Columbia U., 2000, prof. exec. MBA programs; prof. economics & fin. Columbia U. Grad. Sch. of Bus., Dept. of Econ. and Sch. of Internat. and Public Affairs, 2001—; chmn. Columbia U. Com. Global Thought; chair Brooks World Poverty Inst., U. Manchester, England, 2005. Tapp rsch. fellow Gonville and Caius Coll., Cambridge, England, 1966—70; vis. prof. dept. econs. U. Canterbury, Christchurch, New Zealand, 1967; sr. rsch. fellow social sci. divsn. Inst. for Devel. Studies U. Coll. Nairobi, 1969—71; cons. World Bank, State of Alaska, Seneca Indian Nation, Bell Comm. Rsch. Editor: Jour. Econ. Perspectives, 1986—93; Am. editor: Rev. of Econ. Studies, 1968—76, assoc. editor: Am. Econ. Rev., 1968—76, Energy Econs., Managerial and Decision Econs., mem. editl. bd.: World Bank Econ. Rev.; author: Whither Socialism?, 1996, Frontiers of Development Economics: The Future in Perspective, 2000, New Ideas About Old Age Security: Toward Sustainable Pension Systems in the 21st Century, 2001, Globalization and Its Discontents, 2002, The Rebel Within: Joseph Stiglitz and the World Bank, 2002, The Roaring Nineties, 2003; co-author (with C.E. Walsh): Principles of Macroeconomics, 2002, Economics, 2002; co-author: (with R. K. Sah) Peasants Versus City-Dwellers: Taxation and the Burden of Economic Development, 2002; co-author: (with B. Greenwald) Towards a New Paradigm in Monetary Economics, 2003; co-author: (with Andrew Charlton) Fair Trade For All: How Trade Can Promote Development (Initiative for Policy Dialogue Series), 2006; co-author: (with Linda J. Bilmes) The Three Trillion Dollar War: The True Cost of the Iraq Conflict, 2008. Recipient John Bates Clark award, Am. Econ. Assn., 1979, Internat. prize, Accademia Lincei, 1988, Union des Assurances de Paris prize, 1989, Rechtenwald Prize, Germany, 1998, Nobel Prize in Economics, 2001; named a Guggenheim Fellow, 1969—70. Fellow: Inst. for Policy Rsch. (sr. 1991—93), Brit. Acad. (corr.); mem.: NAS (fellow, 1988), Econometric Soc., Am. Acad. Arts and Scis.(fellow, 1983), Am. Econ. Assn. (exec. com. 1982—84, v.p. 1985). Office: Columbia U Uris Hall Rm 814 3022 Broadway New York NY 10027 E-mail: jes322@columbia.edu.*

STIKA, RICHARD F., bishop; b. St. Louis, Mo., July 4, 1957; BS, Univ. St. Louis; MA, Cardinal Glennan Coll.; MDiv, Kenrick Sem. Ordained priest Archdiocese of St. Louis, Mo., 1985; parochial vicar Mary Queen of Peace parish, Webster Groves, Mo., 1986—91, St. Paul parish, Fenton, Mo., 1991—92; spiritual dir., assoc. dir. vocations CYO Archdiocese of St. Louis, 1991—94; parochial vicar Cathedral parish, St. Louis, 1992—94; chancellor Archdiocese of St. Louis, 1994—2004, sec. to archbishop & master of ceremonies, 1994—97, vicar gen. & vicar for religious, 1997—2004, coord. of the Papal visit, 1998—99, vicar for priests, 2002—05, vicar for child & youth protection, 2004—09; pastor Church of the Annunziata parish, Ladue, Mo., 2004—09; ordained bishop, 2009; bishop Diocese of Knoxville, Tenn., 2009—. Roman Catholic. Mailing: Diocese of Knoxville PO Box 11127 Knoxville TN 37939-1127 Office: Diocese of Knoxville The Chancery 805 Northshore Dr SW Knoxville TN 37939 Office Phone: 865-584-3307. Office Fax: 865-584-7538.*

STILES, BEVERLY LYNN, sociologist, educator; b. Middletown, Ohio, June 10, 1960; d. James Francis Stiles and Stella Mae Cantrell; children: Maria Lynn Ifcic-Tahmahkera, Angela Marie Ifcic-Goven. PhD, Tex. A & M U., Coll. Sta., 1999. Sociology prof. Midwestern State U., Wichita Falls, Tex., 1999—. Contbr. articles to profl. jours. Mem. First Step Inc., Wichita Falls, 2008, Wichita Falls Adult Literacy Coun., Tex., 2006. Ryan White grant, North Ctrl. Tex. HIV Planning Coun., 2007—08. Mem.: Southwestern Social Sci. Assn. (elections chair, sect. organizer, discussant).

STILES, RENEE A., hospital administrator, educator; BS, Ithaca Coll., NY, 1983; MS, Cornell U., NY, 1987; PhD, U. Mich., Ann Arbor, 1997. Asst. prof. Vanderbilt U. Sch. Medicine, Nashvillle, Tenn., 2001—, dir. quality measurement & rsch., 2008—. Office: Vanderbilt Univ Med Ctr 1112 22nd Ave S Rm B-131 Nashville TN 37232-7220

STILES, THOMAS BEVERIDGE, II, retired investment company executive; b. Easton, Pa., Oct. 4, 1940; s. Ezra Martin and Vivien (de Fay) S.; m. Elaine Ann Patyk, July 2, 1966 (div. Oct. 1980); children: Thomas Beveridge III, Jonathan Ezra; m. Barbara Toll Alexander, Mar. 7, 1981. BA, Yale U., 1963; MBA, Harvard U., 1968. V.p. Laird, Inc., NYC, 1968-73; sr. v.p., dir. Smith Barney Harris Upham and Co., Inc., NYC, 1973-82; exec. v.p., dir. E.F. Hutton & Co. Inc., NYC, 1982-87; chmn., CEO Shearson Lehman Advisors Asset Mgmt. Co., NYC, 1988-90, 99—, Bernstein Macaulay, NYC, 1988-90; CEO, chmn. Greenwich Street Advisors, NYC, 1990-97; mng. dir. Smith, Barney, Inc., NYC, 1993-99, retired, 1999—. Chmn. bd. dirs., pres. Cedar Lawn Cemetery, Paterson, NJ, 1973—. Bd. dirs. Sanford C. BErnstein Fund, 2003—. 1st lt. M.I., US Army, 1963-66. Fellow Fin. Analysts Fedn.; mem. NY Soc. Security Analysts, El Niguel Country Club (Calif.). Republican. Presbyterian. Avocations: political science, tennis, swimming.

STILL, CHARLES HENRY, SR., lawyer; b. Lubbock, Tex., Sept. 22, 1942; s. Charles Alphonso and Henri Sue S.; m. Frances Eugenia Odell, Apr. 29, 1967; children: Charles Henry Jr., Kathryn Elizabeth. BBA in Acctg., Tex. Tech. U., 1965; JD with honors, U. Tex., 1968. Bar: Tex. 1968. Assoc. Fulbright & Jaworski, Houston, 1968-75, ptnr., 1975—, head corp. dept., 1984-99, mem. exec. com., 1992-99. Speaker numerous confs. and meetings; bd. dirs. Oyo Geospace Corp. Comment editor Tex. Law Rev., 1967-68. Bd. dirs. St. Luke's Episcopal Hosp., Houston, 1991—, Catalyst Found., Houston, 1992—; mem. vestry Christ Ch. Cathedral, Houston, 1981-84, sr. warden, 1983, chancellor, 1986-2002. Fellow Am. Bar Found., Tex. Bar Found., Houston Bar Found.; mem. ABA (bus. law sect. 1968—, corp. laws com. 1983-89, fed. regulation of securities com. 1976—, com. on legal opinions 1989—, law firms com. 1990—, chmn. 1998-2000, ethics 2000 task force 1999-2002, multiple disciplinary practice task force 1998—, profl. conduct com. 2002—), Am. Law Inst., State Bar Tex. (chmn. bus. law sect. 1984-85, mem. coun. 1982-86, chmn. securities law com. 1981-83, Forest Club, Petroleum Club, Order of Coif, Phi Delta Phi, Phi Kappa Phi, Gamma Phi Beta, Beta Alpha Psi, Phi Delta Theta, Phi Eta Sigma. Avocations: hunting, reading. Office: Fulbright & Jaworski 1301 Mckinney St Ste 5100 Houston TX 77010-3095 Home: 16 Pine Briar Cir Houston TX 77056-1113

STILL, CHARLES NEAL, retired neurologist, medical educator, consultant; b. Richmond, Va., Apr. 15, 1929; s. Charles Wright and Ruth (Kemp) S.; m. Dorothy Lee Varn, Dec. 27, 1958; children: Charles Herbert, Carl Nelson, Sara Alice. BS in Chemistry, Clemson U., 1949; MS in Biochemistry, Purdue U., 1951; MD, Med. U. SC, 1959; MA in Religion, Luth. Theol. So. Sem., Columbia, SC, 2007. Diplomate Am. Bd. Psychiatry and Neurology. Instr. chemistry Clemson (S.C.) U., 1951-52; rotating intern U. Chgo. Clinics, 1959-60; neurology fellow Sch. Medicine Johns Hopkins U., Balt., 1960-63; resident in neurology Johns Hopkins-Balt. City Hosp., 1960-63; NIH rsch. fellow Harvard U.-McLean Hosp., Belmont, Mass., 1963-65; chief neurology svcs. William S. Hall. Psychiat. Inst., Columbia, S.C., 1965-81, assoc. dir. gen. psychiatry and neurology, 1989-92; dir. C. M. Tucker Human Resources Ctr., Columbia, 1981-88; clin. prof. neuropsychiatry USC Sch. Medicine, Columbia, S.C., 1981-88, prof. neuropsychiatry, 1989—2004, clin. prof. neuropsychiatry and behavioral sci. Sch. Medicine, 2004; ret., 2004. Instr. chemistry U.S. Mil. Acad., West Point, N.Y., 1953-55; assoc. clin. prof. neurology Med. U. S.C., Charleston, 1973-92; assoc. prof. neuropsychiatry U. S.C. Sch. Medicine, Columbia, 1976-78, prof. neuropsychiatry, 1978-81. Author: (with others) Handbook of Clinical Neurology, 1976, Neurologic Clinics, 1984, Movement Disorders, 1986; editor The Recorder Columbia Med. Soc., 1991-2003, editor emeritus, 2003—; mem. editl. bd. Jour. S.C. Med. Assn., 1980-2006, Jour. Applied Gerontology, 1983-88; contbr. articles to profl. jours. Chmn. grants rev. bd. S.C. Dept. Mental Health, Columbia, 1973-78; mem. exec. bd. Alzheimer's Assn. Columbia, 1985-93, pres. Mid-State chpt. Alzheimer's Assn., 1991-92; med. dir. Alzheimer's Disease Registry, Columbia, 1989-92, Alzheimer's Daycare Ctr., Columbia, 1989-92; mem. Gov.'s Adv. Coun. to Alzheimer's Disease and Related Disorders Resource Coordination Ctr., 1995-99. 1st lt. U.S. Army, 1952-55. Fellow: Am. Geriatrics Soc. (emeritus), Am. Acad. Neurology (emeritus), Gerontol. Soc. Am. (emeritus), Am. Inst. Chemists (life); mem.: AMA (life), Am. Chem. Soc. (emeritus). Baptist. Avocations: writing, photography. Home: 2 Culpepper Cir Columbia SC 29209-2234 Personal E-mail: cndstill@aol.com.

STILL, HOMER IBSON, information technology executive; b. Tulsa, Oct. 3, 1945; children: Walter D., Sarisa D., Joshua H., Homer Isaac, Quillie Mae Elisabeth. Student in Bus. Mgmt. and Programming, Tulsa Jr. Coll.; AA in Liberal Arts and Sci., Okla. Mil. Acad., Claremore, 1965; BS in Indsl. and Managerial Psychology, Okla. State U., Stillwater, 1969, BA in History, 1969. Cert. project mgmt. specialist, instr., cons. IBM Southwestern Region, planning and estimating specialist, instr., cons. IBM Southwestern Region. Sr. EDP systems engr., computer security mgr. Am. Airlines, Inc., 1974—82; sr. cons. Trans World Airlines, 1982—87; adv. system engr., account mgr., bus. analyst, program/project mgmt. cons., worldwide bus. cons., sr. ptnr. IBM, 1987—93; chief operating and info. officer, exec. v.p. Genesis Industries, Inc., 1994—95; computer and operations cons., 1995—98; sr. mgr., program mgr. Sabre Inc., 1998—2001; security screener Dept. Homeland Security, 2002—03; sr. program and project mgr. Capital One Auto Fin., 2003—04; flow team mem., mem. exec. mentoring program Target Corp., 2005—06; master program mgr. Capitol One Finance, 2005—06. Active reserve US Army, 1967—70, infantry officer, capt., brevet col., dep. commdg. officer Presidio of San Francisco US Army, 1970—73, Vietnam, active reserve US Army, 1974—79, 95th Infantry Divsn., Tulsa. Recipient SAR medal for outstanding cadet, Okla. Mil. Acad., 1965. Mem.: MENSA, Phi Theta Kappa. Conservative. Baptist. Avocations: fishing, hunting, reading, travel. Personal E-mail: homerstill@hotmail.com.

STILLER, BEN, actor, television producer; b. NYC, Nov. 30, 1965; s. Jerry Stiller and Anne Meara. m. Christine Taylor, May 13, 2000, children: Ella Olivia, Quinlin Dempsey. Student, UCLA. Actor: (theatre) The House of Blue Leaves, 1985, This Is How It Goes, 2005; (films) Hot Pursuit, 1987, Empire of the Sun, 1987, Fresh Horses, 1988, Next of Kin, 1988, That's Adequate, 1989, Elvis Stories, 1989, Stella, 1990, Highway to Hell, 1992, Reality Bites, 1994, Heavyweights, 1995, Happy Gilmore, 1996, Flirting With Disaster, 1996, Zero Effect, 1998, There's Something About Mary, 1998, Your Friends and Neighbors, 1998, Permanent Midnight, 1998, Nobody Knows Anything, 1998, The Suburbans, 1999, McClintock's Peach, 1999, Black and White, 1999, Mystery Men, 1999, The Independent, 2000, Keeping the Faith, 2000, Meet the Parents, 2000, The Royal Tannenbaums, 2001, Orange County, 2002, Duplex, 2003, Nobody Knows Anything, 2003, Along Came Polly, 2004, Envy, 2004, Meet the Fockers, 2004, Madagascar (voice), 2005, Danny Roane: First Time Director, 2006, School for Scoundrels, 2006, Night at the Museum, 2006, The Heartbreak Kid, 2007, (voice) Madagascar: Escape 2 Africa, 2008, Night at the Museum: Battle of the Smithsonian, 2009, actor, dir. Reality Bites, 1994, The Cable Guy, 1996, Zoolander, 2001, actor, prodr. Dodgeball: A True Underdog Story, 2004, actor, exec. prodr. Starksy & Hutch, 2004, Tenacious D: The Pick of Destiny, 2006, prodr.: Blades of Glory, 2007, writer, dir., actor Tropic Thunder, 2008; TV appearances include Kate McShane, 1975, Kate & Allie, 1986, Miami Vice, 1987, The Ben Stiller Show (also writer, dir.)(Emmy award for writing), 1992-93, Frasier, 1993, Duckman, 1995, Friends, 1997, Saturday Night Live, 1998, 2000, Freaks and Geeks, 2000, The Simpsons (voice), 2002, Undeclared, 2002, The King of Queens, 2002, Curb Your Enthusiasm, 2004, King of the Hill (voice), 2004, Arrested Development, 2004, 05; co-editor (with Marla Hamburg Kennedy) Looking at Los Angeles. Recipient Moving Image Salute, Mus. Moving Image, 2008, Generation award, MTV Movie Awards, 2009; named Man of Yr., Hasty Pudding Theatricals, Harvard U., 2007; named one of 50 Most Powerful People in Hollywood, Premiere mag., 2005, The 100 Most Powerful Celebrities, Forbes.com, 2007, 2008, 50 Smartest People in Hollywood, Entertainment Weekly, 2007.*

STILLER, JENNIFER A., lawyer; b. Washington, May 4, 1948; d. Ralph Sophian and Joy (Dancis) Stiller. AB in Econs. and History, U. Mich., 1970; JD, NYU, 1973. Bar: Pa. 1973, U.S. Dist. Ct. (mid. dist.) Pa. 1977, U.S. Supreme Ct. 1978, U.S. Dist. Ct. (ea. dist.) Pa. 1983, U.S. Ct. Appeals (3rd cir.) 1983, U.S. Ct. Appeals (D.C. cir.), 1996. Dep. atty. gen. Pa. Dept. Justice, Harrisburg, 1973-75, Pa. Dept. Health, Harrisburg, 1975-78; sr. staff atty. Am. Hosp. Assn., Chgo., 1978-80, mgr., dept. fed. law, 1980-81; gen. counsel Ill. Health Fin. Authority, 1981-82; sr. assoc. Berriman & Schwartz, King of Prussia, Pa., 1983-85, Wolf, Block, Schorr & Solis-Cohen, Phila., 1985-88, Montgomery, McCracken, Walker & Rhoads, LLP, Phila., 1988-90; ptnr. Montgomery, McCracken, Walker & Rhoads, Phila., 1990-2000, chair health law group, 1991-2000; sr. counsel Tenet Healthcare Corp., Phila., 2000-2001; pvt. practice Haverford, Pa., 2001—. Contbr. articles to profl. jours. Fellow Am. Health Lawyers Assn. (bd. dirs. 1997-2003, exec. com. 2002-03); mem. ABA (gov. com. Health Law Forum 1994-95), Pa. Bar Assn., Phila. Bar Assn., Health Care Mgrs. Assn. Avocations: gardening, bicycling, hiking, music. Office: Law Office Jennifer A Stiller 625 Haydock Ln Haverford PA 19041-1207 Home Phone: 610-649-9817; Office Phone: 610-642-3366. Business E-Mail: stiller@healthregs.com.

STILLER, SHALE DAVID, lawyer, educator; b. Rochester, NY, Feb. 23, 1935; s. Maurice Aaron and Dorothy (Salitan) S.; m. Ellen M. Heller; children: Lewis B., Michael J., Kenneth R.; stepchildren: William Heller, Lawrence Heller. BA, Hamilton Coll., 1954; LLB, Yale U., 1957; MLA, Johns Hopkins U., 1977. Bar: Md. 1957. Ptnr. corp. and securities, tax, trusts and estates practices DLA Piper, Balt., 1992—. Lectr. U. Md. Law Sch., 1963—. Contbr. articles to profl. jours. Trustee Johns Hopkins U., Assn. Jewish Charities, Bar-in-Law U.; trustee, vice chmn. Johns Hopkins Hosp. and Sch. Medicine; pres. The Harry and Jeanette Weinberg Found., Leonard & Helen Stulman Found., Charles Crane Family Found.; bd. mem. Bright Star Found., Shelter Found., Hittman Family Found.; mem. adv. bd. Tax Mgmt., 1972-93; chmn. Jud. Nominating Commn., Balt., 1979-83; officer, bd. dirs. Park Sch., 1973-79, pres., 1982-86; pres. Jewish Family Agy., 1972-74. Mem. ABA, Am. Law Inst., Am. Coll. Tax Counsel, Am. Coll. Trust and Estate

Counsel, Order of Coif. Democrat. Jewish. Home Phone: 410-435-2526; Office Phone: 410-654-6835, 410-654-4900. Business E-Mail: sstiller@theweinbergfoundation.org, shale.stiller@dlapiper.com. E-mail: sstiller@dlapiper.com.

STILLING, MARK, psychologist, professional football coach; b. Woodstock, Ill., Apr. 3, 1974; s. Ted Alger and Jean Ellen Stilling; m. Jami Joy Vielehr, July 4, 2003; 1 child, Jaden Flanagan. SSP, Ill. State U., Normal, 1999. Sch. psychologist Schaumburg HS, Ill., 1999—, head football coach, 2005—. Office: Schaumburg HS 1100 W Schaumburg Rd Schaumburg IL 60194

STILLINGER, JACK CLIFFORD, language educator; b. Chgo., Feb. 16, 1931; s. Clifford Benjamin and Ruth Evangeline (Hertzler) S.; m. Shirley Louise Van Wormer, Aug. 30, 1952; children: Thomas Clifford, Robert William, Susan, Mary; m. Nina Zippin Baym, May 21, 1971. BA, U. Tex., 1953; MA, Northwestern U., 1954; PhD, Harvard U., 1958. Teaching fellow in English Harvard U., 1955-58; asst. prof. U. Ill., Urbana, 1958-61, assoc. prof., 1961-64, prof. English, 1964—; permanent mem. Center for Advanced Study, 1970—. Author: The Early Draft of John Stuart Mill's Autobiography, 1961, Anthony Munday's Zelauto, 1963, Wordsworth: Selected Poems and Prefaces, 1965, The Letters of Charles Armitage Brown, 1966, Twentieth Century Interpretations of Keats's Odes, 1968, Mill: Autobiography and Other Writings, 1969, The Hoodwinking of Madeline and Other Essays on Keats's Poems, 1971, The Texts of Keats's Poems, 1974, The Poems of John Keats, 1978, Mill: Autobiography and Literary Essays, 1981, John Keats: Complete Poems, 1982, Norton Anthology of English Literature, 1986, 8th edit., 2006, John Keats: Poetry Manuscripts at Harvard, 1990, Multiple Authorship and the Myth of Solitary Genius, 1991, Coleridge and Textual Instability, 1994, Reading The Eve of St. Agnes, 1999, Romantic Complexity, 2006, Nina and the Balloon, 2008; editor Jour. English and Germanic Philology, 1961-72. Nat. Woodrow Wilson fellow, Northwestern U., 1954, Guggenheim fellow, 1964—65. Fellow AAAS; mem. MLA, Keats-Shelley Assn. Am. (bd. dirs., editorial bd. Jour., Disting. Scholar award 1986), Byron Soc., Phi Beta Kappa. Home: 806 W Indiana Ave Urbana IL 61801-4838 Business E-Mail: jstill@illinois.edu.

STILLMAN, BRUCE, molecular biologist; b. Melbourne, Australia, Oct. 16, 1953; came to US, 1979; s. Graham and Jessie (England) S.; m. Grace Begley, Mar. 21, 1981; children: Keith, Jessica. BSc with honors, U. Sydney, 1975; PhD, Australian Nat. U., 1979. Staff investigator Cold Spring Harbor Lab., NY, 1981-83, sr. staff investigator, 1984-85, sr. scientist, 1985-90, asst. dir., 1990-93, dir. cancer ctr., 1992—, dir., 1994—2003, pres., CEO, 2003—. Contbr. scientific papers to profl. publs. Apptd. to Order of Australia, 1999; Rita Allen Found. scholar, 1981-85; Cancer Rsch. fellow Damon Runyon-Walter Winchell, 1979-80, Alfred P. Sloane, Jr., GM Cancer Rsch. Found., 2004, Am. Cancer Soc. Basic Sci. award, Soc. Surgical Oncology, 2006, Curtin medal, Australian Nat. U., 2007. Fellow Royal Soc. London, Am. Acad. Arts and Scis.; mem. NAS, AAAS, Am. Soc. Microbiology, Am. Soc. Biochem. and Molecular Biology, Am. Assn. Cancer Rsch., NAS. Office: Cold Spring Harbor Lab PO Box 100 Cold Spring Harbor NY 11724-0100

STILLMAN, CHARLES ALLEN, lawyer; b. Bklyn., Sept. 8, 1937; s. Max and Anne (Parness) Stillman; m. Marilyn Norma Radezky, Aug. 30, 1959; children: Nina, Robert, Jay. BA, NYU, 1958, JD, 1962. Bar: NY 1962. Law clk. to Hon. Irving R. Kaufman US Ct. Appeald 2d cir., 1959—62; asst. US atty. US Dist. Ct. so. dist. NY, 1962—66; assoc. Phillips, Nizer, Benjamin, Krim & Ballon1966, 1966—68, Louis, Bender, Esquire, 1968—69; ptnr. Botein Hays Sklar & Herzberg, NYC, 1969—72; pvt. practice, 1972—77; ptnr. Stillman, Friedman & Shechtman, 1977—. Mem. Lawyers Com. on the Criminal Justice Act, 1977—86; adj. assoc. prof. trial advocacy Fordham U., 1978—85; hearing officer for environ. protection hearings NY Conv. Ctr.; mem. spl. investigation Roosevely Island Tramway Accident, 1981—82; chmn. lawyers divsn. Am. Friend Hebrew U. Trustee NYC Sch. Constrn. Authority, 2000—03. Recipient Torch of Learning award, lawyers divsn. Am. Friends of Hebrew U., 1984, Human Rels. award, Anti-Defamation League, 1993, Louis Dembitz Brandeis Disting. Legal Svc. medal, Brandeis U., 1997, Milton S. Gould Oustanding Advocacy award, Office of Appellate Defender, 1999, Robert M. Morgenthau award, Police Athletic League, 2003. Mem.: ABA, Internat. Acad. Trial Lawyers, Am. Coll. Trial Lawyers (coun. mem.), NY Coun. Def. Lawyers (dir. 1987—92, Norman S. Ostrow award 1992), NY State Bar Assn., NY County Lawyers Assn., NYC Bar Assn. Office: Stillman Friedman & Shechtman PC 425 Park Ave New York NY 10022 E-mail: cstillman@stillmanfriedman.com.

STILLMAN, CORY, professional hockey player; b. Peterborough, Ont., Can., Dec. 20, 1973; m. Mara Stillman; children: Riley, Madison, Chase. Left wing Calgary Flames, 1995—2001, St. Louis Blues, 2001—03, Tampa Bay Lightning, 2003—04, Carolina Hurricanes, 2005—08, Ottawa Senators, 2008, Fla. Panthers, 2008—. Achievements include being a member of Stanley Cup Champion Tampa Bay Lightning, 2004, Carolina Hurricanes, 2006. Office: Fla Panthers One Panther Parkway Sunrise FL 33323

STILLMAN, ELINOR HADLEY, retired lawyer; b. Kansas City, Mo., Oct. 12, 1938; d. Hugh Gordon and Freda (Brooks) Hadley; m. Richard C. Stillman, June 25, 1965 (div. Apr. 1975). BA, U. Kans., 1960; MA, Yale U., 1961; JD, George Washington U., 1972. Bar: D.C. 1973, U.S. Supreme Ct. 1976. Lectr. in English CUNY, 1963-65; asst. editor Stanford (Calif.) U. Press., 1967-69; law clk. to judge U.S. Dist. Ct. D.C., Washington, 1972-73; appellate atty. NLRB, Washington, 1973-78; asst. to solicitor gen. U.S. Dept. Justice, Washington, 1978-82; supr. appellate atty. NLRB, Washington, 1982-86, chief counsel to mem. bd., 1986-88, 94-00, chief counsel to chmn. bd., 1988-94; ret., 2000. Mem.: D.C. Bar Assn., Order of Coif, Phi Beta Kappa. Democrat.

STILLMAN, MARGARET (PEGGY STILLMAN), library director; m. Peter R. Stillman; children: Lindsay H. and Walker H. Forehand. BA in Edn., U. Richmond, 1973; MA in Edn., Va. Commonwealth U., 1974; MLS, U. Md., 1977. Children's libr. to dir. Chesapeake Pub. Libr. Sys., Va., 1975-85, dir., 1985—; acting asst. city mgr. City of Chesapeake, 1999—2002. Chmn. bd. Libr. Va., chmn. bldg. com. Chmn. State Adult Literacy Initiative, 1989-95; mem. Govs. Rural Econ. Devel. Task Force, 1990-92, U. Va. Continuing Edn. Ctr. Coun., 1990-94; bd. dirs. United Way Hampton Rds., 1995—, Vol. Hampton Rds., 1996-98, Va. Stage Co., 1979-85 (v.p. 1981-82), Colonial Girl Scouts, 1993-95, Cultural Alliance, 1985-91, Tidewater Red Cross, 1980-83. Recipient Outstanding Young Career Woman of Va. award, 1978; named Outstanding Profl. Woman, 1993, Woman of Yr., Hampton Roads C. of C., Women's Divsn., 2003, First Citizen of Chesapeake, Chesapeake Rotary Club, 2005; named one of Strong, Smart, and Bold Women of SW Hampton Roads, 2000. Mem. Pub. Libr. Assn. (bd. dirs. 1997-98, chmn. leadership devel. com. 1997, mem. pres.'s 2000 com.), Libr. Va. Found. (bd. dirs. 1996—), WHRO Found. (bd. dirs. 1997—), ALA (mem. awards com., mem. advancement for literacy award com., mem. adult lifelong learning com.). Office: Chesapeake Pub Libr Sys 298 Cedar Rd Chesapeake VA 23322-5598 E-mail: stillman@chesapeake.lib.va.us.

STILLMAN, MICHAEL ALLEN, dermatologist; b. NYC, Apr. 12, 1943; s. Aaron and Anne (Turansky) S.; m. Susan Fuchs, July 8, 1973; children: Julie, Jeremy. BA, Clark U., 1963; MD, SUNY, 1967. Diplomate Am. Acad. Dermatology. Med. intern Maimonides Hosp., Bklyn., 1967—68; dermatology resident NYU Med. Ctr. and Bellevue Hosp., NYC, 1970—73; pvt. practice Mt. Kisco, NY, 1973—. Cons. dermatology U.S. Mil. Acad., West Point, N.Y., 1973-75 Contbr. essays and articles to profl. jours. and newspapers Bd. trustees South Salem (NY) Libr., 1990-98; boys varsity tennis coach John Jay H.S., Katonah, NY, 1996. Capt. USAF, 1968-70, Vietnam Decorated Combat Inf. badge Fellow Am. Soc. Dermatol. Surgeons, Am. Acad. Dermatology; mem. N.Y. State Med. Soc., Noah Worcester Dermatology Soc Avocations: tennis, jogging, writing. Home: 33 Mead St Waccabuc NY 10597-1107 Office: Mt Kisco Med Group 111 Bedford Rd Katonah NY 10536 Office Phone: 914-232-3135.

STILLMAN, NINA GIDDEN, lawyer; b. NYC, Apr. 3, 1948; d. Melvin and Joyce Audrey (Gidden) S. AB with distinction, Smith Coll., 1970; JD cum laude, Northwestern U., 1973. Bar: Ill. 1973, US Dist. Ct. (no. dist.) Ill. 1973, US Dist. Ct. (ea. dist.) Wis. 1979, US Dist. Ct. (no. dist. trial bar) Ill. 1983, US Ct. Appeals (7th cir.) 1974, US Supreme Ct. 1981, US Dist. Ct. (ctrl. dist.) Ill. 1994, US Dist. Ct. (ea. dist.) Tex., 1996, US Dist. Ct. (Colo.), 1999, US Dist. Ct. (ND) 2002. Assoc. Vedder, Price, Kaufman & Kammholz, Chgo., 1973-79, ptnr., 1980—2004, Morgan, Lewis and Bockius, LLP, Chgo., 2004—. Adv. bd. occupational health and safety tng. program U. Mich., Ann Arbor, 1980-83; adj. faculty Inst. Human Resources and Indsl. Rels., Loyola U., Chgo., 1983-86, bd. advisors, 1986-93. Author: (with others) Women, Work, and Health: Challenge to Corporate Policy, 1979, Occupational Health Law: A Guide for Industry, 1981, Employment Discrimination, 1981, Personnel Management: Labor Relations, 1981, Occupational Safety and Health Law, 1988; contbg. author: Occupational Medicine: State of the Art Reviews, 1996; contbr. articles to profl. jours. Legal advisor, v.p. Planned Parenthood Assn. Chgo., 1979—81; sec. jr. governing bd. Chgo. Symphony Orch., 1983; trustee Merit Sch. Music, 2000—, vice chmn. bd. trustees, 2001—03; bd. dirs. Jewish United Fund/Jewish Fedn. Met. Chgo., 2008—; dean's law bd. Northwestern U. Sch. Law, 1997—. Recipient Svc. award Northwestern U., 1994. Mem.: ABA (occupl. safety and health law com. 1978—), Human Resources Mgmt. Assn. Chgo. (bd. dirs. 1986—88, officer), Am. Inns of Ct. (v.p. Wigmore chpt. 1988—89), Chgo. Bar Assn. (chmn. labor and employment law com. 1986—87), Northwestern U. Sch. Law Alumni Assn. (pres. 1991—92), Univ. Club Chgo. (bd. dirs. 1988—2001, sec. 1999—2000, v.p. 2000—01), Econ. Club Chgo., Lawyers Club, Smith Coll. Club Chgo. (pres. 1972). Avocations: travel, reading, the arts, collecting art. Office: Morgan Lewis and Bockius LLP 77 W Wacker Dr Ste 500 Chicago IL 60601 Office Phone: 312-324-1150. Business E-Mail: nstillman@morganlewis.com.

STILLWAGON, GARY BOULDIN, radiation oncologist; b. Memphis, Dec. 30, 1951; s. Jack Wright and Ida Jean (Bouldin) S.; m. Jan. 20, 1979. BS in Physics, Ga. Inst. Tech., 1974, MS in Nuclear Engring., 1975, PhD, 1978; MD, U. Tenn., 1983. Diplomate Nat. Bd. Med. Examiners, Am. Bd. Radiology in Radiation Oncology; cert. FLEX, 1983. Med. physicist Meth. Hosp., Memphis, 1974; rsch. asst. Ga. Inst. Tech., Atlanta, 1975-78; radiation safety officer, physicist VA Med. Ctr., Memphis, 1978-80, cons. radiation safety, 1980-83; fellow in radiation oncology Johns Hopkins U. and Hosp., Balt., 1983-87; asst. prof. oncology and radiology Johns Hopkins U. Sch. Medicine, Balt., 1987—; pres. house staff John Hopkins Hosp., 1986—87. Vis. rschr. radiobiology lab. U. Utah, 1978; com. mem., site visitor, radiation therapy oncology group, coop. group Nat. Cancer Inst., 1989—; cons. in field. Contbr. articles to profl. jours. Boy Scouts Am., Bapt. Ch. Dept. of Energy fellow, 1976-78, Clin. fellow Am. Cancer Soc., 1986-87. Fellow Am. Coll. Radiology; mem. Health Physics Soc., Am. Assn. Physicists in Medicine, Am. Soc. Therapeutic Radiology and Oncology, Am. Soc. Clin. Oncology, Sigma Xi. Republican. Home: 655 River Chase Rdg NW Atlanta GA 30328-3568 Office: 1000 Johnson Ferry Rd Atlanta GA 30342

STILLWELL, R. NEWCOMB, lawyer; b. Oct. 2, 1956; AB magna cum laude, Princeton Univ., 1979; JD cum laude, Harvard Univ., 1984. Bar: Mass. 1984. Assoc. Ropes & Gray, Boston, 1984—93, ptnr. corp. dept., 1993—, former co-leader private equity practice group. Former lectr. Harvard Law Sch. Former bd. dir. Hotchkiss Sch.; chmn. Volunteers of Am. of Mass.; bd. dirs. Godles Groups Inc. Office: Ropes & Gray 1 International Pl Boston MA 02110-2624 Office Phone: 617-951-7316. Office Fax: 617-951-7050. Business E-Mail: newcomb.stillwell@ropesgray.com.

STILLWELL, WALTER BROOKS, III, lawyer; b. July 30, 1946; s. Walter Brooks Jr. and Selpha T. (Everson) S.; m. Carolyn E. Laws, Dec. 20, 1992; children: Walter, Haviland. BA cum laude, Wake Forest U., 1968; JD, U. Ga., 1971. Bar: Ga. 1971, U.S. Dist. Ct. (so. dist.) Ga. 1971, U.S. Ct. Appeals (D.C. cir.) 1976, U.S. Ct. Appeals (11th cir.) 1981, U.S. Dist. Ct. (no. dist. 1996) Ga., U.S. Supreme Ct., 1977. Assoc. Hunter, Maclean, Exley & Dunn, P.C., Savannah, Ga., 1971-74, ptnr., 1974—; dir. First Nat. Bank, 2002—. Dir. Savannah (Ga.) Econ. Devel. Authority, 2008- Alderman City of Savannah, 1974-92, mayor-pro-tem, 1990-92; chmn. Chatham County Bd. Elections, 1999-2002. Mem. State Bar of Ga. (real property sect., exec. com. 1986-93, chmn. 1992), Am. Coll. Real Estate Lawyers, Savannah Bar Assn. (pres. 1999-2000). Office: Hunter Maclean Exley & Dunn PC 200 E Saint Julian St Savannah GA 31401-2700

STILWELL, WILLIAM EARLE, III, psychology educator, retired military officer; b. Cin., Ohio, July 28, 1936; s. William Earle Jr. and Frances (Hunt) S.; m. Doris Ann Nowak; children: Jane Belen Stilwell Angel, William Earle IV. AB, Dartmouth Coll., Hanover, NH, 1958; MS, San Jose State U., Calif., 1966; PhD, Stanford U., Calif., 1969. Lic. counseling psychologist, Ky., 2006; cert. profl. qualification in psychology Assn. State of Provincial Psychology Bds. Transp. engr. Hiller Aircraft, 1958—59; rsch. assoc. Am. Inst. Rsch., Palo Alto, Calif., 1967-69; prof. psychology U. Ky., Lexington, 1969—2006; prof. emeritus, 2006; cons. accreditation and internet U. Ky., Coll. Edn., 2006—. V.p. Ednl. Skills Devel., Lexington, 1969-85. Author: Psychology for Teachers and Students, 1981; mem. editl. bd. Counsel Edn. and Supervision, 1980-87; contbr. numerous (25) articles to profl. jour., chpts. to books. Assigned to patron nine, USNR, 1960—63, active res. in Alameda, Calif., Washington area, 1965—83, exec. officer, 1979—82; webmaster Coll. Edn., 1995—. Recipient Nat. Def. and Armed Forces Res. with cluster, Tchr. Who Makes a Difference award, UK Coll. Edn., 1998, 2002, Svc. award, Coun. Univ. Depts. Clin. Psychology, 1998, Study Web Academic Excellence award, 1999, 2000, Web Homework Spot award, 2000, Svc. award, Coun. Dirs. of Sch. Psychology Programs, 2004, Coun. Counseling Psychology Tng. program, 2001; Henry Stites Barker fellow, U. Ky. Mem. APA (life), Coun. Counseling Psychology Tng. Programs (Svc. award 2001), Am. Ednl. Rsch. Assn. (v.p. 1980-82), Ky. Psychol. Assn., Ky. Sch. Counseling Assn. (v.p. 1979-80, 81-82), Ohio Soc. of the Colonial Wars, Hon. Order Ky. Cols., Res. Officers Assn. US (life), Stanford Alumni Assn. (life). Achievements include kentucky department of education inaugeral Stilwell award for personal dedication and outstanding service in educational technology to the teachers and children of the Commonwealth 2008. Avocation: fishing in ontario. Home: 1919 Williamsburg Rd Lexington KY 40504-3013 Address: WES IV PO Box 4382 Midway KY 40347 Home Phone: 859-278-7086; Office Phone: 859-257-5997. Business E-Mail: westil3@uky.edu.

STIMAC, JOHN ANTHONY, small business owner, poet, cartoonist, inventor; b. Kansas City, Kans., Nov. 12, 1946; s. Max George and Lola Mae Stimac; m. Sherry Lynn Stimac, Apr. 30, 1965 (dec. Sept. 24, 2005); children: Mary Ann, John Anthony, Christopher John. Union painter Local 43, Leavenworth, Kans., 1973—79; owner Heritage Painting Co., Kansas City, Kans., 1979—85, J-Duncan's Painting Co., Kingsville, Mo., 1985—2001, John Stimac Painting Co., Kingsville, 2001—. Cartoons, Highlights for Children, 1983; contbr. poems to books and jours. With US Army, 1963—65. Recipient Editors Choice awards, Internat. Libr. of Poetry, 2001—02. Mem.: Soc. of Poets (Lifetime Mem. award 2005). Achievements include invention of inventive systems minor images. Avocations: guitar, instrumental music. Home and Office: 13 NW 1621 Rd Kingsville MO 64061 Office Phone: 816-682-5075.

STIMMEL, BARRY, cardiologist, internist, dean, educator; b. Bklyn., Oct. 8, 1939; s. Abraham and Mabel (Bovit) S.; m. Barbara Barovick, June 6, 1970; children: Alexander, Matthew. BS, Bklyn. Coll., 1960; MD, SUNY, Bklyn., 1964. Diplomate: Nat. Bd. Med. Examiners, Am. Bd. Internal Medicine. Resident Mt. Sinai Hosp., NYC, 1964—65; asst. dean admissions and student affairs Mt. Sinai Sch. Medicine, CUNY, 1970—71, assoc. dean, 1971—81, asst. prof. medicine, 1972—75, assoc. prof., 1975—83, prof. medicine and med. edn., 1984—, assoc. dean acad. affairs, 1975—81, assoc. attending physician, 1975—83, acting chmn. dept. med. edn., 1979—94, dean admissions, acad. affairs and student affairs, 1981—94, dean grad. med. edn., 1994—2008, attending physician, 1984—, Katherine and Clifford Goldsmith prof. medicine (cardiology), 1998—, dean emeritus, med. edn., 2008—, Ombudsman Sch., 2008—. Mem. com. planning, priorities and evaluation N.Y. Met. Regional Med. Program, 1971-73; adv. com. Nat. Ctr. Urban Problems CUNY, 1970-71; adv. com. methadone maintenance Office of Drug Abuse Svcs. State N.Y., 1976-79; sci. adv. bd. Nat. Coun. Drug Abuse, 1978-84, N.Y. State Bd. Profl. Med. Conduct, 1983-97; bd. dirs. Am. Soc. Addiction Medicine, N.Y. State Coun. on Grad. Med. Edn., Greater N.Y. Hosp. Assn. Task Force on Health Manpower. Author: Heroin Dependency: Medical Social and Economic Aspects, 1975, Cardiovascular Effects Mood Altering Drugs, 1979, Pain, Analgesia, Addiction, 1984, Ambulatory Care, 1983, The Facts about Drug Use, 1993, Drugs Abuse and Social Policy in America: The War That Must Be Won, 1996, Pain and Its Relief Without Addiction, 1997, Alcoholism, Drug Addiction and the Road to Recovery: Life on the Edge, 2002; editor Advances in Alcohol and Substance Abuse, 1980-91, Jour. Addictive Diseases, 1991—; assoc. editor Am. Jour. Drug and Alcohol Abuse, 1979-85; contbr. chpts. to books, articles to profl. jours. With M.C. USNR, 1965—67. Mem. AAUP, Am. Assn. Physicians Assts. (adv. bd. 1972-73), Am. Assn. Higher Edn., Soc. Study of Addiction to Alcohol and Other Drugs, Assn. Med. Edn. and Rsch. Substance Abuse, Inst. Study of Drug Addiction, Am., N.Y. heart assns., Am., N.Y. State socs. internal medicine, Soc. Internal Medicine County of N.Y. (dir.), Am. Coll. Cardiology, Greater N.Y. Coalition on Drug Abuse, NYS Coun. on Grad. Medical Edn., N.Y. Acad. Medicine, Nat. Coun. Alcoholism, Rsch. Soc. on Alcoholism, Am. Edn]. Research Assn., Am. Fedn. Clin. Rsch., Am. Soc. Addiction Medicine (hon. bd. mem. 2007-08). Office: Mt Sinai Sch Med 5 E 98th St Fl 3 New York NY 10029-6501 Office Phone: 212-241-6694. E-mail: barry.stimmel@mssm.edu.

STIMPERT, MICHAEL ALAN, retired agricultural products company executive; b. Madisonville, La., Aug. 21, 1944; s. Warren Eugene and Louisa (Beale) S.; m. Kim Kathleen Agee, Apr. 17, 1970 (div. 1985); 1 child, Kelly Kathleen; m. Helen Marie Evans, June 27, 1987; children: Katherine Helen, Michael Adam. Student, Washburn U., 1962-64, U. Copenhagen, 1964; BA, Western Res. U., 1967; MBA, Harvard U., 1974. Asst. to group v.p. Gold Kist Inc., Atlanta, 1974, mgr. internat. div., 1975-80, dir. spl. markets and staff services, 1980-81, group v.p., 1982-86; v.p. ops. and govt. affairs Golden Peanut Co., Atlanta, 1986-89; exec. v.p., 1989-95; sr. v.p. Gold Kist Inc., Atlanta, 1996—2007. Chmn. bd. dirs. Sunpower, Inc., Athens, Ohio, 2000-2008, Fundatropicos, Turrialba, Costa Rica, pres. Treas. Tropics Found., Atlanta. Lt. (j.g.) USN, 1967-72, Vietnam. Mem. Assn. for Corp. Growth, Japan-Am. Soc. Ga., Harvard Bus. Sch. Club Atlanta, Cherokee Town and Country Club., Buckhead Rotary Club. Democrat. Roman Catholic.

STIMPSON, CATHARINE ROSALIND, literature educator, writer; b. Bellingham, Wash., June 4, 1936; d. Edward Keown and Catharine (Watts) Stimpson. AB, Bryn Mawr Coll., 1958; BA, MA, Cambridge U., Eng., 1960; PhD, Columbia U., 1967. Mem. faculty Barnard Coll., NYC, 1963—80; prof. English, dean of grad. sch., vice provost grad. edn. Rutgers U., New Brunswick, NJ, 1980—92, univ. prof., 1991—; chmn. bd. scholars Ms. Mag., NYC, 1981—92; dir. fellows program MacArthur Found., 1994—97; univ. prof., dean Grad. Sch. Arts and Sci. NYU, NYC, 1998—. Author: Class Notes, 1979, Where the Meanings Are, 1988; editor: Signs: Jour. Women in Culture and Soc., 1974—81, Women in Culture and Society book series, 1981; contbr. Change Mag., 1992—93. Chmn. N.Y. Coun. Humanites, 1984—87, Nat. Coun. Rsch. on Women, 1984—89; trustee Bates Coll., 1990—2007; pres. Assn. Grad. Schs., 2000—01; bd. dir. Stephens Coll., Columbia, Mo., 1982—85, Legal Def. and Edn. Fund, 1991—96. Fellow, Woodrow Wilson Found., 1958, Nat. Humanities Inst., 1975—76; Fulbright fellow, 1958—60, Rockefeller Humanities fellow, 1983—84. Mem.: PBS (bd. dirs. 1994—2000), NOW, PEN, MLA (exec. coun., chmn. acad. freedom com., 1st v.p., pres. 1990). Democrat. Home: 29 Washington Sq W Apt 15C New York NY 10011-9199 Office: NYU 6 Washington Sq N New York NY 10003-6668 Office Phone: 212-998-8040. Business E-Mail: catharine.stimpson@nyu.edu.

STIMPSON, JIM P., medical educator; BA in Sociology, U. Nebr., Lincoln, 1996, MA in Sociology, 2000, PhD in Sociology, 2004. Postdoctoral fellow U. Tex. Med. Br., Galveston, 2004—06; asst. prof. U. North Tex. Health Sci. Ctr., Ft. Worth, 2006—. Contbr. articles to profl. jours. Fellow, Nat. Inst. Aging, 2004—06; Rosa Peterson Acad. scholar, U. Nebr., 1996, Scholastic Sociology Rsch. fellow, 1999. Mem.: Gerontological Soc. Am., Am. Sociological Assn., Am. Pub. Health Assn.

STINE, R. L. (ROBERT LAWRENCE STINE), children's book author; b. Columbus, Ohio, Oct. 8, 1943; s. Lewis and Anne (Feinstein) S.; m. Jane Waldhorn, June 22, 1969; 1 child: Matthew. BA, Ohio State U., 1965. Assoc. editor Jr. Scholastic, NYC, 1969-71; editor Search,

NYC, 1972-75, Barnas, NYC, 1972-83, Maniac, NYC, 1984-85. Author: The Time Raider, 1982, The Golden Sword of Dragonwalk, 1983, Horrors of the Haunted Musuem, 1984, Instant Millionaire, 1984, Through the Forest of Twisted Dreams, 1984, Indiana Jones and the Curse of Horror Island, 1984, Indiana Jones and the Giants of the Silver Tower, 1984, Indiana Jones and the Cult of the Mummy's Crypt, 1985, The Badlands of Hark, 1985, The Invaders of Hark, 1985, Demons of the Deep, 1985, Challenge of the Wolf Knight, 1985, Conquest of the Time Master, 1985, Cavern of the Phantoms, 1986, Operation: Deadly Decoy, 1986, Mystery of the Imposter, 1986, Blind Date, 1986, Twisted, 1986, The Baby-Sitter, 1989, Phone Calls, 1990, Curtains, 1991, Broken Date, 1991, Baby-Sitter II, 1991, Beach House, 1992, Dead Girlfriend, 1993, Halloween Night, 1993, Hitchhiker, 1993, Be Careful What You Wish For, 1993, Baby-Sitter III, 1993, Call Waiting, 1994, The Beast, 1994; (series) Fear Street, New Fear Street, Fear Street Super-Chillers, Fear Street Saga, Fear Street Cheerleaders, Fear Street Seniors, Fear Park, 99 Fear Street, Cataluna Chronicles, The House of Evil, Thrillers, Space Cadets, Goosebumps, Goosebumps Series 2000, Give Yourself Goosebumps, Rotten School, Goosebumps Horrorland; (as Jovial Bob Stine) The Absurdly Silly Encyclopaedia and Flyswater, 1978, How to Be Funny: An Extremely Silly Guidebook, 1978, The Complete Book of Nerds, 1979, The Dynamite Do-It-Yourself Pen Pal Kit, 1980, Dynamite's Funny Book of the Sad Facts of Life, 1980, Going out! Going Steady! Going Bananas!, 1980, The Pigs' Book of World Records, 1980, The Sick of Being Sick Book, 1980, Bananas Look at TV, 1981, The Beast Handbook, 1981, The Cool Kids' Guide to Summer Camp, 1981, Ghastly Gnomes, 1981, Don't Stand in the Soup, 1982, Bored with Being Bored!: How to Beat the Boredom Blahs, 1982, Blips! The First Book of Video Game Funnies, 1983, Everything You Need to Survive: Brothers and Sisters, 1983, Everything You Need to Survive: First Dates, 1983, Everything You Need to Survive: Homework, 1983, Everything You Need to Survive: Money Problems, 1983, Jovial Bob's Computer Joke Book, 1985, Miami Mice, 1986, One Hundred and One Silly Monster Jokes, 1986, The Doggons Dog Joke Book, 1986, Mostly Ghostly: Who Let the Ghosts Out?, 2004; (as Eric Affabee) G.I. Joe and the Everglades Swamp Terror, 1986, Attack of the King, 1986; (as Zachary Blue) The Petrova Twist, 1987, The Jet Fighter Trap, 1987. Recipient Champion of Reading award, Free Pub. Libr. Phila., 2002, Silver Bullet award, Thriller Writers of America, 2007. Achievements include #1 best-selling children's book series author, Guinness Book of World Records, 2003. Office: c/o Parachute Press Ste 500 322 8th Ave New York NY 10001

STINEHART, WILLIAM, JR., retired lawyer; b. LA, Dec. 15, 1943; s. William Sr. and Martha T. S.; m. Patricia Kidney, June 22, 1968; children: Jacqueline Elaine, William III. BA with distinction, Stanford U., 1966; LLB, UCLA, 1969. Bar: Calif. 1970, US Dist. Ct. (cen. dist.) Calif. 1970. Assoc. Gibson, Dunn & Crutcher LLP, LA, 1969-76, ptnr. tax dept., 1977—; ret., 2005. Bd. dir. Tribune Co. Trustee Harvard Westlake Sch., N. Hollywood, 1983-89, SW Mus., 1986-89. Mem. LA County Bar Assn., Order of Coif, LA Country Club, Beach Club of Santa Monica, Calif., LA Tennis Club. Republican. Episcopalian. Office: Gibson Dunn & Crutcher LLP 1043 Roscomare Rd Los Angeles CA 90077-2227 Office Phone: 310-552-8557. Office Fax: 310-552-7027. Business E-Mail: wstinehart@gbsondunn.com.

STING, (GORDON MATTHEW SUMNER), musician, songwriter, actor; b. Newcastle Upon Tyne, Eng., Oct. 2, 1951; s. Ernest Matthew and Audrey (Cowell) Sumner; m. Frances Eleanor Tomelty, May 1, 1976 (div. Mar. 1984); children: Joseph, Fuschia Katherine; m. Trudie Styler, Aug. 22, 1992; children: Brigette, Michael, Jake, Eliot, Paulina, Giacomo Luke. Grad., Warwick U., Coventry, Eng.; doctorate (hon.), Northumbria U., 1992; degree (hon.), Berklee Coll. Music, Boston, 1994. Schoolmaster, Newcastle Upon Tyne, Eng., 1975-77; songwriter, singer, bass player with rock group The Police, 1977-86; mng. dir. Kaliedescope Cameras, London, from 1982; singer, songwriter, 1986—. Albums (with The Police) Outlandos D'Amour, 1978, Reggatta De Blanc, 1979, Zenyatta Mondatta, 1980, Ghost in the Machine, 1981, Synchronicity, 1983, singles Every Breath You Take, 1986; appearance: (Broadway plays) Three Penny Opera, 1989; solo (albums) The Dream of the Blue Turtles, 1985, Bring On The Night, 1986, Nothing Like the Sun, 1987, The Soul Cages, 1991, Ten Summoner's Tales, 1993 (Grammy award, Best Long Form Music Video, 1994), Demolition Man, soundtrack, 1993, Mercury Falling, 1996, Brand New Day, 1999, Sacred Love, 2003 (Grammy award, Best Pop Collaboration With Vocals for song "Whenever I Say Your Name" with Mary J. Blige, 2003), appeared (films) Quadrophenia, 1979, The Secret Policeman's Other Ball, 1981, Brimstone and Treacle, 1982, Dune, The Bride, Plenty, 1985, Julia and Julia, 1987, Stormy Monday, 1988, Resident Alien, 1990, The Grotesque, 1995, Lock, Stock and Two Smoking Barrels, 1998; actor(voice): (films) Bee Movie, 2007; voice artist (TV series) Captain Planet and the Planeteers, 1990—92, rec. soundtracks (films) Brimstone and Treacle, Party, Party, The Secret Policeman's Other Ball, 1982, The Emperor's New Groove, 2000. Recipient 15 Grammy awards with The Police and as solo artist, 13 BMI awards, 4 Brit awards, Downbeat mag. Readers' Poll Pop/Rock Musician of Yr. award, 1989, Downbeat mag. Readers' Poll Pop/Rock group award, 1989, Internat. Rock award for Video Legend, 1991, Star on the Hollywood Walk of Fame, 2000, Golden Globe award Kate and Leopold, 2001; named Favorite Reunion Tour, People's Choice Awards, 2008; named to Rock and Roll Hall of Fame (The Police), 2003. Mem.: Rainforest Found. (co-founder), Amnesty Internat., Performing Rights Soc. also: Firstars 3520 Hayden Ave Culver City CA 90232-2413 also: A & M Records Inc 70 Universal City Plz Universal City CA 91608-1011 Office: KSM 826 Broadway Fl 4 New York NY 10003-4826

STINNETT, HESTER, art school administrator, educator; BFA, Hartford Art Sch.; MFA, Tyler Sch. Art, Phila. Lectr. U. of Arts, Phila., 1982-85, Bryn Mawr (Pa.) Coll., 1985-86; asst. prof. Tyler Sch. Art Temple U., Phila., 1986—; assoc. dean Tyler Sch. Art, Phila., 1992—. Vis. artist Pa. Acad. Fine Arts, Phila., 1984-85. Author: Water-Base Screenprinting, 1988; exhibited in group show Dolan/Maxwell Gallery, 1988; prodr. Electrical Matter, 1989-92; dir. Contemporary Viewpoints, 1987-89. Office: Tyler Sch Arts Temple U 7725 Penrose Ave Elkins Park PA 19027 Office Fax: 215-782-2799. Business E-Mail: hester.stinnett@temple.edu.

STINNETT, MARK ALLAN, lawyer; b. Jackson, Miss., Sept. 15, 1955; s. Allan J. and Joan (Mouser) S.; m. Carol Fowler, Sept. 5, 1992; children: Michelle, Michael. BA in Polit. Sci. with honors, Tex. Tech U., 1977; JD with honors, U. Tex., 1980. Bar: Tex. 1980, Colo., 2008, US Dist. Ct. (no. and ea. dists.) Tex. 1981, Southern Dist. Tex., 2009, Colo., 2009, US Ct. Appeals (5th cir.) 1993, (10th cir.) 2009, US Supreme Ct. 2006. Founding ptnr., mng. ptnr. Stinnett Thiebaud & Remington L.L.P., Dallas, 2000—; shareholder Cowles & Thompson, Dallas, 1986—2000. Mem. Boy Scouts Am. Nat. Coun.; chmn. outdoor actitivs com. Philmont Ranch Com., chmn. program & risk mgmt. task force. Fellow Tex. Bar Found., Dallas (Tex.) Bar Found.; mem. ABA, Am. Bd. Trial Advocates, Am. Inns of Ct., Am. Coll. Legal Medicine, Colo. Bar Assn., Am. Health Lawyers Assn., Am. Soc. Healthcare Risk Mgmt., Colo. Def. Lawyers Assn., State Bar of Tex., Dallas Bar Assn., Tex. Assn. Def. Counsel, Dallas Assn. Def. Counsel, Def. Rsch. Inst., El Paso County Bar Assn., Inns Ct. (barrister Dallas chpt. 1988-91), Tex. Ctr. Legal Ethics and Professionalism, Nat. Eagle Scout Assn., Philmont Staff Assn. (pres. 1994-98, editor High Country mag. 1998—2008). Avocations: backpacking, hiking, military history, writing. Home: 3801 Sonoran Dr Colorado Springs CO 80922 Office: Stinnett Thiebaud & Remington LLP 1445 Ross Ave Ste 4800 Dallas TX 75202-2702 Office Phone: 214-954-2200. Business E-Mail: mstinnett@strlaw.net.

STINNETT, TERRANCE LLOYD, lawyer; b. Oakland, Calif., July 22, 1940; s. Lloyd Monroe and Gertrude (Hyman) S. BS, Stanford U., 1962; JD magna cum laude, U. Santa Clara, 1969. Bar: Calif. 1970, U.S. Dist. Ct. (no. dist.) Calif. 1970, U.S. Dist. Ct. (ea. ctrl. and so. dists) Calif. 1975, U.S. Ct. Appeals (9th cir.) 1970, U.S. Supreme Ct. 1975. Law clk. to judge Calif. Ct. Appeals, San Francisco, 1969-70; assoc. Hyman, Rhodes & Aylward, Fremont, Calif., 1970-71, Glicksberg, Kushner & Goldberg, San Francisco, 1972-77; mem. Goldberg, Stinnett Meyers & Davis, San Francisco, 1977—2006; gen. counsel Fremont Bank, Fremont Bancorp., 2007—, sec., 2007—. Bd. dirs. Fremont Bancorp, Fremont Bank, 1990-, vice-chmn. bd., 1998-2000; sch. law bd. visitors Santa Clara U., 1995-, bd. fellows, 2009-. Mem. ABA, Calif. State Bar Assn., Bar Assn. San Francisco (chmn. bench bar liaison com. for U.S. Bankruptcy Ct., No. Dist. of Calif. 1997). Republican. Roman Catholic. Home: 131 Alamo Hills Ct Alamo CA 94507-2243 Office: Fremont Bank 39150 Fremont Blvd Fremont CA 94538 Office Phone: 510-505-5335. Business E-Mail: terrance.stinnett@fremontbank.com.

STINSMUEHLEN-AMEND, SUSAN, artist; b. Balt., Nov. 5, 1948; d. William I. and Geraldine S. (Dodds) Hamilton; m. Richard E. Amend, Nov. 27, 1987; children: Jason Stinsmuehlen, Wyatt Amend. Student, Hood Coll., U. Tex. Designer, owner Renaissance Glass Co., Austin, 1973-87; artist, glass, paint and mixed media dba Impresa, Inc., L.A. and Ojai, Calif., 1987—. Mem. Art in Pub. Places Panel, Austin, 1986-87; cons. Nat. Endowment for the Arts, Washington, 1986, 87, Cmty. Redevel. Agy., L.A., 1990-92; artist trustee Am. Craft Coun., 1988-92; lectr., lead artist Hollywood Blvd. Streetscape Team, Hollywood, Calif., 1991-94; lead artist Canoga Park, Calif., Pedestrianscape and Madrid Theater Project, City of L.A., 1996-2000; mem. Arts Commn., Ojai, Calif., 2000—; mem. Hollywood Art and Design Adv. Panel, 1994-2003; lead artist Canoga Pk., Calif., 1996-2000; guest lectr., artist Puchuck Glass Sch., 1980-92, 94-95, 97, 2005, 2008, R.I. Sch. Design, 1980, 2006, Mass. Coll. Art, 1980, 2006, Dallas Mus. Art, 1981, Japanese Glass Conf., 1985, Calif. Coll. Arts, Oakland, 1985, 89, Australian Glass Conf., 1987, Penland Sch. Craft, N.C., 1996; artist-in-residence Pilchuck Glass Sch., Wash., 2006, Mus. Glass, Tacoma, 2006; artist archive project Focus on the Masters, 2007, Ventura, Calif.; educator in field. One-woman shows include Mattingly Baker Gallery, Dallas, 1984, Kurland Summers Gallery, L.A., 1985, 88, 90, 92, Traver Sutton Gallery, Seattle, 1986, Habatat Galleries, Detroit, 1991, The Nest Gallery, Ojai, Calif., 1997, The Glass Gallery, Bethesda, Md., 2000, Carnegie Mus. Art, Oxnard, Calif., 2004, Sandy Carson Gallery, Denver, 2005, D&A Fine Arts, L.A., 2005, 07, Coll. the Sequoias Art Gallery, Visalia, Calif., 2006; exhibited in group shows at Whatcom Mus., Bellingham, Wash., 1992, 94, Finegood Art Gallery, West Hills, Calif., 1993-94, Miller Gallery, N.Y.C., 1994, The Wignall Mus., Chaffey Coll., Rancho Cucamonga, Calif., 1995, Traver Gallery, Seattle, 1995, Smithsonian Inst. Travelling Exhbn., 1999, Muckenthaler Cultural Arts Ctr., Calif., 1999, Loveland (Colo.) Mus. Gallery, 1998, 99, Fresno Art Mus., 1998, SOFA Chgo., 1998, Santa Cruz Mus. Art and History, 1999, Smithsonian Inst., 1998-2000, L.A. County Mus. Art, 1999, Orange County Mus. Art, 1999, L.A. Mcpl. Art Gallery, 2003, Reynolds Gallery, Richmond, Va., 2003, Nathan Larramendy Gallery, 2004, Ojai Valley Mus., 2003-07, San Francisco Mus. Craft & Design, 2005, L.A. Mcpl.Art Gallery, 2005, Beatrice Wood Ctr. Arts, 2005-07, William Traver Gallery, Seattle, 2006, 07, 08, Robert V. Fullerton Art Mus., San Bernandino, 2007—, Ctr. Contemporary Printmaking, Norwalk, 2008, others, Palos Verdes Art Ctr., Calif.; represented in permanent collection Am. Airlines, Dallas, Renwick Gallery Nat. Mus. Art, Washington, The Jewish Mus., N.Y.C., The Corning (N.Y.) Mus. Glass, Detroit Inst. Arts, Leigh Yawkey Woodson Mus., Wausau, Wis., Oakland (Calif.) Mus., Wagga Wagga City Art Gallery, NSW, Australia, Nishida Mus., Toyoma, Japan, Pilchuck Glass Ctr., Stanwood, Wash., Mus. Art & Design, N.Y.C., L.A. (Calif.) County Mus. Art, Radisson Hotel, Austin, AT&T, Dallas, AT&T, N.Y.C., Marshall Fields Corp. Collection, Chgo., City of L.A., Mus. Am. Art/Smithsonian Instn., Carnegie Art Mus., Mus. Glass, Tacoma, Wash., Ojai Valley Cmty. Hosp., others plus numerous pvt. collections. Nat. Endowment for the Arts grantee, Washington, 1982, 88; Hauberg fellowship Pilchuck Glass Sch., 2001, Libensky award for achievement in field of glass, 2007. Mem. Glass Art Soc. (hon. life; bd. dirs. 1982-86, pres. 1984-86), Mus. Contemporary Art (L.A.), L.A. County Mus. Avocations: gardening, swimming, walking, hiking, golf. E-mail: impresa@pobox.com.

STINSON, ALAN LYNN, insurance company executive; b. 1945; BA, U. Tex., 1968. CPA. Ptnr. Deloitte & Touche LLP, 1980—94; exec. v.p., CFO Alamo Title Holding Co., 1994—98; exec. v.p. fin. ops. Fidelity Nat. Fin., Inc., Jacksonville, Fla., 1998—99, exec. v.p., CFO, 1999—2006, exec. v.p., CFO, COO, 2006, exec. v.p., COO, 2006—07, CEO, 2007—. Mem.: Am. Inst. CPAs. Office: Fidelity Nat Fin Inc 601 Riverside Ave Jacksonville FL 32204-2950

STINSON, JOHN JEROME, literature and language professor; b. Bklyn., Sept. 30, 1940; s. John Oliver Stinson and Josephine Cecilia McGovern; m. Dianne Ellen Posthumus, July 5, 1969; children: Gregory John, Matthew Lawrence. BA, St. John's U., Bklyn., 1962; MA, St. John's U., Jamaica, NY, 1963; PhD, NYU, 1971. Lectr. English Bklyn Coll., 1964—65; instr. to prof English SUNY, Fredonia, 1965, assoc. chair, English, 2000—04, chair, English dept., 2004—05. Author: (books) Anthony Burgess Revisited, V. S. Pritchett: A Study of the Short Fiction. Liberal. Avocations: travel, football, genealogy. Home: 59 Cottage St Fredonia NY 14063 Office: SUNY Fredonia 280 Central Ave Fredonia NY 14063 Office Phone: 716-673-3587. Business E-Mail: stinson@fredonia.edu.

STINSON, KENNETH E., construction and mining company executive; b. Chgo., May 24, 1946; BS in Civil Engring., U. Notre Dame; MS in Civil Engring., Stanford U. Pres. Kiewit Constrn. Grp. Inc., Omaha, 1992—96, chmn., 1993—96; pres. Peter Kiewit Sons' Inc., Omaha, 1997—2000, chmn., 1997—, CEO, 1998—2004. Bd. dirs. ConAgra Foods, Inc., Omaha, 1996—, Valmont Industries, Inc., Omaha, 1996—. Recipient Outstanding Projects and Leaders awards, ASCE, 2003, Star of Courage award, Nebr. Med. Ctr., 2005. Mem.: NAE. Office: Kiewit Corp 3555 Farnam St Omaha NE 68131 Office Phone: 402-342-2052. Office Fax: 402-271-2939.

STINSON, MARY FLORENCE, retired nursing educator; b. Wheeling, W.Va., Feb. 11, 1931; d. Rolland Francis and Mary Angela (Voellinger) Kellogg; m. Charles Walter Stinson, Feb. 12, 1955; children: Kenneth Charles, Karen Marie Wiberg, Kathryn Anne Kartye. BSN, Coll. Mt. St. Joseph, 1953, postgrad., 1983; MEd, Xavier U., Cin., 1967; postgrad., U. Cin., 1981. Staff nurse contagious disease ward Cin. Gen. Hosp., 1953-54, asst. head nurse med. and polio wards, 1955, acting head nurse, clin. instr., 1955-56; instr. St. Francis Hosp. Sch. Practical Nursing, Cin., 1956-57, Good Samaritan Hosp. Sch. Nursing, Cin., 1957—66; instr. refresher courses for nurses Cin. Bd. Edn. and Ohio State Nurses Assn. Dist. 8, 1967—70; coord. sch. health office Coll. Mt. St. Joseph, Ohio, 1969-72, instr. dept. nursing, 1974-79, asst. prof., 1979-89; RN assessor pre-admission screening sys. providing options & resources today Coun. on Aging Southwestern Ohio, 1989-90, quality assurance coord. pre-admission screen sys. providing options & resources today program, 1990-93, quality assurance supr. pre-admission screen sys. providing options & resources today and elderly svcs. programs, 1993-94; quality assurance mgr. Coun. Aging Southwestern Ohio, 1995-2000; ret., 2000. Staff nurse St. Francis/St. George Hosp., Cin., 1988-89; vol. ombudsman Pro Srs. of S.W. Ohio, 2005—. Charter mem. Adoptive Parents Assn. St. Joseph Infant and Maternity Home, 1966—70; women's com. for performing arts series Coll. Mt. St. Joseph; chmn. by-law com. Coll. Mt. St. Joseph Nursing Honor Soc., 1996—98; active St. Antoninus Rosary Altar and Sch. Soc., 1973—84, St. Antoninus Athletic Club, com. chmn., 1969—70; bd. dirs. Coll. Mt. St. Joseph Alumni Assn., 1982—84, sec., 1968—69, v.p., 1969—70, pres., 1970—71, chmn. revision of constn., 1976—77; homecoming chmn. Coll. Mt. St. Joseph, 1970, co-chmn., 1977, co-chair com. to celebrate 75 years of nursing edn., 2001—02; mem. com. to plan 50th ann. of graduation Coll. Mt. St. Joseph Alumni Assn., 2003. Mem. River Squares Club (v.p. 1967), Sigma Theta Tau (charter Omicron Omicron chpt. 1998—), St. Antonious Adult Social Group (pres. 2005-08). Democrat. Roman Catholic. Home: 5549 Cleander Dr Cincinnati OH 45238-4266

STINSON, SARA, anthropologist, educator; b. Waterloo, Iowa, Aug. 29, 1952; d. Harry Theodore and Jean Magee Stinson; m. Warren Richard DeBoer, July 5, 1986. AB, Bryn Mawr Coll., Pa., 1973; MA, U. Mich., Ann Arbor, 1975, PhD, 1978. Asst., assoc. prof. anthropology Queens Coll., Flushing, NY, 1978—. Editor: (book) Human Biology: An Evolutionary and Biocultural Approach; contbr. articles to profl. jours. Fellow: Human Biology Assn., AAAS; mem.: Am. Assn. Phys. Anthropologists (editor), Am. Anthrop. Assn. (pres., biol. anthropology sect. 2000—02). Office: Queens Coll 6530 Kissena Blvd Flushing NY 11367 Business E-Mail: sara.stinson@qc.cuny.edu.

STINTON, DALE A., real estate association executive; m. Maryann Stinton; children: Brad, Ashley, Greg. BS, Western Ill. U.; MBA, DePaul U., 1982. CPA; cert. mgmt. acct., assn. exec., Realtor assn. cert. exec. With fin. dept. Nat. Assn. of Realtors, 1981—91, CFO, 1991—98, acting CEO, exec. v.p., 1996, CFO, chief info. officer, 1998—2005, CEO, exec. v.p., 2005—. Bd. dirs. RE FormsNet, Real Estate Bus. Technologies, Realtors Info. Network, Realtors Relief Found., Sentrilock LLC. Avocations: gardening, literature, movies. Office: Nat Assn Realtors 430 N Michigan Ave Chicago IL 60611-4087 Office Phone: 800-874-6500.

STIPANOVICH, JOHN MCKAGER (MAC STIPANOVICH), lobbyist, lawyer; b. Ocala, Fla., Nov. 26, 1948; BA with honors, U. Fla., 1972; JD with high honors, U. Fla. Levin Coll. Law, 1974. Bar: Fla. 1975. Dir. numerous mayoral/gov. campaigns Fla. rep. Bob Martinez, Tallahassee, Tampa, 1979—90; chief of staff to Gov. Bob Martinez Tallahassee, 1987—91; sr. adv. Jeb Bush for Gov. Campaign, Tallahassee, 1993—94; practicing atty., shareholder Fowler White Boggs PA, Tallahassee. Named one of Fla. Super Lawyer, 2006—08, The Best Lawyers in America, 2007—09. Mem.: ABA, Fla. Bar Assn. Republican. Office: Fowler White Boggs PA 101 N Monroe St Ste 1090 Tallahassee FL 32301 Office Phone: 850-681-0411. Office Fax: 850-681-6036. Business E-Mail: mckager@fowlerwhite.com.*

STIPE, MICHAEL, musician, film producer; b. Decatur, Ga., Jan. 4, 1960; Student, U. Ga. Singer R.E.M., 1980—; owner C-OO. Albums (with R.E.M.) Chronic Town, 1982, Murmur, 1983 (Rolling Stone Critics Poll Best Album of Yr., 1983), Reckoning, 1984, Fables of the Revolution, 1985, Life's Rich Pageant, 1986, Dead Letter Office, 1987, Document, 1987, Eponymous, 1988, Green, 1989, Out of Time, 1991 (Grammy award, Best Alternative Music Performance, 1992), Automatic for the People, 1992 (4 Grammy nominations, 1992), Monster, 1994, Songs That Are Live (4 song CD), 1995, New Adventures in Hi-Fi, 1996, Up, 1998, Reveal, 2001, In Time: The Best of R.E.M., 2003, Around the Sun, 2004, Live, 2007, Accelerate, 2008, songs (with R.E.M.) Orange Crush (MTV Video Music award, Best Post Modern Video, 1989), Losing My Religion (6 MTV Video Music awards, 1991, Best Group Pop Vocal Performance, Best Short Form Music Video, Grammy Awards, 1992), Everybody Hurts (4 MTV Video Music awards, 1994), guest artist with 10,000 Maniacs, 1987, Indigo Girls, 1989, soundtrack (films) Man on the Moon, 1999; prodr.: (films) Being John Malkovich, 1999, Saved!, 2004, (TV films) Olive, the Other Reindeer, 1999, Stranger Inside, 2001; exec. prodr.: (films) Velvet Goldmine, 1998, Spring Forward, 1999, Our Song, 2000, Thirteen Conversations About One Thing, 2001, Everyday People, 2004, Johnny Berlin, 2005. Recipient Top Modern Rock Artist award, Top World Album award, Billboard Music Awards, 1991, Best Internat. Group award, Brit Awards, 1992, 1993, 1995, Video Vanguard award, MTV Video Music Awards, 1995; named Rolling Stone Critics Poll Best New Group, 1983, Rolling Stone Group Artist of Yr., 1992, Rolling Stone Male Vocalist of Yr., 1992; named one of Top Newsmakers of Yr., Out mag., 1998; named to Rock & Roll Hall of Fame, with R.E.M., 2007. Office: Single Cell Pictures 1016 N Palm Ave West Hollywood CA 90069 also: c/o William Morris Agy 1 William Morris Pl Beverly Hills CA 90212 Office Phone: 310-360-7600. Office Fax: 310-360-7011.

STIPETIC, WERNER See HERZOG, WERNER

STIPHO, HUDA D., dentist, educator; d. Daoud Kattan and Victoria Ashoo; m. A. S. Stipho, Oct. 7, 1974; children: Sally B., Sarah. BDS, Baghdad U., Iraq, 1967; DMS, U. Wales Welsh Nat. Sch. Medicine, Dental Sch., Cardiff, 1977. Cert. Bd. Dental Examiner, Commonwealth Mass. Asst. prof. Tufts U. Sch. Dental Medicine, Boston, 1999—2005, assoc. prof., 2005—. Assoc. prof. King Saud U., Coll. Dentistry, Riyadh, Saudi Arabia, 1978—99. Independent. Roman Catholic. Achievements include research in laboratory and clinical studies on acquired pellicale and dental plaque formation and accumulation. Avocation: travel. Home: 30 Greenwood Rd Hopkinton MA 01748 Office: One Kneeland St Boston MA 02111

STIREWALT, JOHN NEWMAN, coal company executive; b. Springfield, Ill., July 14, 1931; s. Newman Claude and Genevieve (Henton) S.; m. Joan Marie McCarthy, Dec. 26, 1957; children: Genevieve, Janice, James, Christopher. AB, U. Miami, 1953; grad. execs. program, Carnegie Mellun U., 1978. Salesman Kaiser Aluminum, Indpls., 1957-63; dist. sales mgr. Consol. Coal, Detroit, 1963-67, Cleve., 1967-73, gen. sales mgr. Detroit, 1973-76, asst. v.p., 1976-79; v.p. mktg. Youghiogheny and Ohio Coal Co., St. Clairsville, 1979-81; v.p. mktg. Crown Coal and Coke Co. Pitts., 1981-85, Arch Mineral, 1985-90; sr. v.p. Crown Coal & Coke Co., 1990—. Exec. reservist U.S. Dept. Interior emergency solid fuels adminstrn., 1971, U.S. Energy Dept., 1991-97. Chmn. coun. Cub Scouts, Highland, Mich., 1976; mem. Mich. Energy Task Force,

1966; pres. bd. trustees Wheeling Country Day Sch., 1980-84; trustee Wheeling Symphony; bd. dirs. Teen Challenge for New Life Inc. Served with U.S. Army, 1954-56. Mem.: Vinyard Christian Fellowship, Ft. Henry Club, Symposiarchs, Wheeling Country Club, Sigma Chi. Home: 130 Spring Hill Ln Wheeling WV 26003-7746 Office: Crown Coal and Coke Co Pittsburgh PA 15220 Home Phone: 304-336-7888; Office Phone: 412-920-1908.

STIRITZ, MARETTE MCCAULEY, English language educator, consultant; b. Center Point, Ark., Dec. 9, 1931; d. Edrie Delos and Lucyle Virginia (Dautrieve) McCauley; m. Charles Wayne Jackson, July 1, 1950 (dec. June 1986); children: Charles, Retta, Shelia; m. John David Stiritz, Dec. 3, 1992. BSE, Ark. State U., 1962; MA, U. Ark., 1965, PhA, 1986. Tchr. elem. Plum Bayou (Ark.) Pub. Schs., 1950—52; tchr. Laura Connor H.S., Augusta, Ark., 1955-59, Swifton (Ark.) Elem. Sch., 1959-60, Swifton H.S., 1962-63; prof. English So. Ark. U., Magnolia, 1965-78, U. Cen. Ark., Conway, 1978—96; cons., 1996—. Cons. high schs., Conway, Morrilton, Vilonia, 1983—, Ark. Dept. Edn., Little Rock, 1982, 84; lectr. U. Chile, Santiago, 1989, Moscow Pedagogical U., 1991, 92, Academica Inst. Chileno-Norteamericano, Santiago, 1994; speaker 8th Bi-ann. Conf. Profs. Fgn. Langs., Chile, 1992, 9th Conf., Chile, 1994. Author: A Grammar for All Seasons, 1996, Using Language Effectively, 1996; editor: What the American Children Like to Read, 1995, Study Guide Russian Schs., 2000; contbr. articles to profl. jours.; book reviewer Ark. Elem. Coun., 1980—. Del. Faulkner County Dems., Conway, 1984; exec. sec., founder Columbia Tchrs. Eng., Magnolia, 1974-78. Mem. Ark. Coun. Tchrs. English (pres. 1979-80, bd. dirs. 1989-93), Ark. Philol. Assn., Nat. Coun. Tchrs. English, Ark. Coll. Tchrs. English (pres. 1992-93), Conway Rotary Internat. Breakfast Club (charter), Conway Shakespeare Club (v.p. 2005-06, pres. 2006-2008, parliamentarian 2008-), Alpha Chi (region II v.p. 1992-93. Democrat. Methodist. Office Phone: 501-329-5048. Personal E-mail: JorMStiritz@conwaycorp.net.

STIRLING, JAMES PAULMAN, investment banker; b. Chgo., Mar. 30, 1941; s. Louis James and Beverly L. (Paulman) S.; m. Ellen Adair Foster, June 6, 1970; children— Elizabeth Ginevra, Diana Leslie, Alexandra Curtiss. AB, Princeton U., 1963; MBA, Stanford U., 1965. CFA. Vice pres. corp. fin. Kidder, Peabody & Co. (now UBS), NYC and Chgo., 1965-71, 84-86, sr. v.p. corp. fin., 1987—; asst. to sec. U.S. Dept. Commerce, Washington, 1976-77; sr. advisor & chmn. midwest adv. bd. UBS Investment Bank, 2004—. Chmn. bd. Northwestern Meml. Mgmt. Corp., Chgo., 1989—; trustee Northwestern Meml. Hosp., Chgo., 1985—. Pres. jr. bd. Chgo. Symphony, 1968—70; mem. exec. coun. Chgo. Metropolis 2020; trustee Chgo. Symphony, 1970—75, Tchrs. Acad. for Math. Sci., 1991—95. Mem. CFA Soc. Chgo. (bd. dirs.), CFA Leadership Coun. (chmn.), Bond Club Chgo., Nat. Econ. Hon. Soc., Chicago Club, Racquet Club (Chgo.), Onwentsia Club (Lake Forest, Ill.). Office: UBS Tower One N Wacker Dr Ste 2500 Chicago IL 60606-4302

STITH, LAURA DENVIR, state supreme court judge; b. St. Louis, Oct. 30, 1953; m. Donald George Scott; children: Lisa, Rebecca, Cynthia. BA magna cum laude, Tufts U., 1975; JD magna cum laude, Georgetown U., 1978. Law clk. to Hon. Robert E. Seiler, Mo. Supreme Ct., 1978—79; assoc. Shook, Hardy & Bacon, Kansas City, Mo., 1979—84, ptnr., 1984—94; judge. Mo. Ct. Appeals (we. dist.), 1994—2001; judge Mo. Supreme Ct., 2001—, chief justice, 2007—09. Speaker Mo. New Judges Sch. Author: articles on appellate practice, products liability and civil procedure. Tutor, mentor Operation Breakthrough, St. Vincent's Sch.; founding dir., mem. Lawyers Encouraging Academic Performance. Mem.: Assn. Women Lawyers of Greater Kansas City (speaker, past pres.), Mo. Bar Assn., Kansas City Metropolitan Bar Assn. Office: Supreme Ct Mo PO Box 150 Jefferson City MO 65102*

STITH-CABRANES, KATE, law educator; b. St. Louis, Mar. 16, 1951; d. Richard Taylor and Ann Carter (See) Stith; m. Jeffrey Leonard Pressman, Dec. 23, 1970 (dec. Mar. 1977); m. José Alberto Cabranes, Sept. 15, 1984; children: Alejo, Benjamin José; stepchildren: Jennifer, Amy. BA, Dartmouth Coll., 1973; MPP, J.F.K. Sch. of Govt., 1977; JD, Harvard U., 1977. Bar: D.C. 1979. Law clk. to Judge Carl McGowan US Ct. of Appeals, Washington, 1977-78; law clk. to Justice Byron White US Supreme Ct., Washington, 1978-79; staff economist Coun. of Econ. Advisers, Washington, 1979-80; spl. asst. Dept. of Justice, Washington, 1980-81, asst. U.S. atty. NYC, 1981-84; assoc. prof. Yale Law Sch., New Haven, 1985-90, prof. of law, 1990—97, Lafayette S. Foster prof. law, 1998—, dep. dean, 1999—2001, 2003—04, acting dean, 2009; mem. adv com. Fed. Rules of Criminal Procedure, 1995—2001. Mem. Permanent Commn. on the Status of Women, State of Conn., Hartford, 1990-96. Author: (with José A. Cabranes) Fear of Judging: Sentencing Guidelines in the Federal Courts, 1998 (Cert. of Merit ABA); contbr. articles on criminal law and constl. law to profl. jours. Trustee Dartmouth Coll., Hanover, N.H., 1989-2000, Women's Campaign Sch., 1994—, Fed. Bar Found., 1998-2004. Mem. Am. Law Inst., Coun. Fgn. Rels., Conn. Bar Found. (bd. dirs. 1987—, chair 1999-2002). Office: Yale Law Sch PO Box 208215 New Haven CT 06520-8215 E-mail: kate.stith@yale.edu.

STITLE, STEPHEN A., bank executive; B in Econs. and Polit. Sci., Ind. U., JD cum laude. Bar: US Supreme Ct., US Dist. Ct. (so. dist. Ind.), Ind., Washington. Corp. v.p., bd. dirs., mem. mgmt. and policy coms. Eli Lilly and Co.; chmn. Ind. bank Nat. City Corp., 1995, chmn., pres., CEO Nat. City Bank Ind., corp. exec. v.p., pres. Ind. Banking, 1999—. Bd. dirs. Ctrl. Ind. Corp. Partnership, Ctr. Leadership Devel., Indpls. C. of C., US Auto Club, Sagamore Inst. Policy Rsch., Ind. C. of C. Bd. dirs. Ind. U. Found., Heart Ctr. Ind., YMCA, Greater Indpls. Progress Com., Pacers Basketball Corp. Found., Simon Youth Found. Office: Nat City Corp 101 W Washington St Indianapolis IN 46255 Office Phone: 317-267-7900.

STITT, MARI LEIPPER, poet; b. Salem, Ohio, May 1, 1923; d. Robert and Myrtle (Cost) Leipper; m. Rodney Dean Stitt, Apr. 22, 1944; children: Dana Lovelace, Rodney D. Jr. BA in Music, San Diego State U., 1946; MA in Human Rels., Calif. Western U., 1966. Dir. religious edn. Ctrl. Congl. Ch., 1941-50; tchr. sociology San Diego Evening Coll., 1966-84; writer poetry, 1984—. Green Party. Episcopalian. Achievements include research in religion of the 20th century through personal history interviews. Home: The Academy Village 7761 S Vivaldi Ct Tucson AZ 85747-9632 Personal E-mail: marilstitt@cox.net. *Did we miss the point? Somehow the stories of the Garden of Eden, Cain and Abel, and the Tower of Babel seemed so simple—take only what you need, care for your brother, stay with your own kind. After all our pious ponderings, why don't we get it?.*

STITTICH, ELEANOR MARYANN, retired nursing educator; b. Blawnox, Pa. d. Joseph John and Mary T. Stittich. BS in Nursing Ed., U. Pitts., 1951, M.Litt., 1954; postgrad., Johns Hopkins U., 1958-60, Humphrey's Sch. Law, Fresno, Calif., 1973-74. Staff nurse Sinai Hosp., Balt., 1947, U. Hosps., Cleve., 1947-48; staff nurse, clin. instr. St. Francis Med. Ctr., Pitts., 1948-51, med.-surg. instr., 1951-56; lectr. fundamentals, asst. in charge fundamentals U. Mich. Sch. Nursing, Ann Arbor, 1956-57; assoc. dir. nursing edn. Sinai Hosp. Sch. Nursing, Balt., 1957-64; prof. dept. nursing Calif. State U., Fresno, 1964—92; trustee NSM, 1986—94; ret., 1992; guest prof. emeritus. Western region cons. Neuman Systems Model, 1986—; prof. emerita, Calif. Nurses Assn., 1993; trustee, exec. com., 1988-94; rschr. program for RN, Calif. State U., Fresno, 1982, programs for BSN degree students, 1988, mem. steering com. Ctrl. Calif. Ctr. for Excellence in Nursing, 2006-. Author: (with others) Neuman Systems Model, 1989, 95. Educator program planning Alpha Tau Delta, 1975; mem. Cen. Valley chpt. Am. Heart Assn., Fresno, 1978-87, chairperson, 1982-85; mem., chairperson Cen. Valley Cancer Soc., Fresno, 1980-86; chairperson, vol. hospice com. St. Agnes Med. Ctr., Fresno, 1978-80, task force for pastoral care, hospice com., 1978-79; mem. exec. com. regional med. program UCLA, 1977-82. Scholar Sinai Hosp. Sch. Nursing, Balt., 1947; recipient Cert. of Merit, Am. Heart Assn., 1986, Meritorious Performance & Profl. Promise award, 1987, 90, Nurse of Yr. award Calif. Nurses Assn., 1991; named to Calif. State U. Sch. Edn. Wall of Fame, Fresno, 1999; named to Nursing Hall of Fame, 2005. Mem. AACN (bd. dirs. 1979-90, pres. 1982-83, corr. sec. 1984-86), Sigma Theta Tau (faculty advisor, bd. dirs., pres.-elect Mu Nu chpt. 1991-92, pres. 1992-94, parliamentarian 1994-96), Delta Kappa Gamma (Eta Tau chpt., Chi state 1991-95, chair legis. com. 1992-93). Roman Catholic. Avocations: swimming, golf, painting, gardening.

STIVER, JAMES FREDERICK, retired pharmacist, health physicist, administrator, scientist; b. Elkhart, Ind., Jan. 27, 1943; s. Melvin Hugh and Pauline Anna (Schrock) S.; m. Joan Louise Trindle, Aug. 14, 1965; children: Gregory James, Richard Frederick, Kristin Louise, Elizabeth Ann. BS in Pharmacy and Pharm. Scis., Purdue U., 1966, MS, 1968, PhD, 1970. Lic. pharmacist, Ind., N.D. From asst. prof. to assoc. prof., radiol. safety officer ND State U., Fargo, 1969—76; radiation safety officer KMS Fusion Inc., Ann Arbor, Mich., 1976—80; mgr., pharmacist Kroger Sav-On Pharmacy Co., Elkhart, Ind., 1980—81; pharmacist Elkhart Gen. Hosp., 1981; environ. regulatory affairs adminstr. Upjohn Co., Kalamazoo, 1981—88, patent liaison scientist, 1988—92, sr. patent liaison scientist, 1992—94; pharmacist, asst. mgr. Judd Drugs, Elkhart, 1994—95; pharmacist Meijer Pharmacy, Goshen, Ind., 1995—99; pharmacist, asst. mgr. Wal-Mart Pharmacy, Elkhart, 1999—2000, mgr., 2000, K-Mart Pharmacy, Elkhart, 2000—02, Plymouth, Ind., 2002—04, K-Mart North, 2004—08, pharmacist, 2004—08; ret., 2008. Cons., lectr. Contbr. articles, abstracts to publs. Named to Hon. Fellow Am. Inst. Chemists; mem. Am. Pharm. Assn., Am. Chem. Soc., Health Physics Soc., Internat. Radiation Protection Assn., Ind. Pharmacists Assn., N.D. Pharm. Assn., Order Ky. Cols., Kappa Psi, Rho Chi, Phi Lambda Upsilon, Sigma Xi. Home: 505 Skyview Dr Middlebury IN 46540-9427

STIVERS, LAURA A., religious studies educator; b. Long Beach, Calif., July 17, 1965; PhD, Grad. Theol. Union, Berkeley, 2000. Assoc. prof. Pfeiffer U., Misenheimer, NC, 2000—. Co-author: (book) Justice in a Global Economy: Strategies for Home, Community, and World (Choice Libr. award, 2007). Home: PO Box 42 Misenheimer NC 28109 Office: Pfeiffer Univ PO Box 960 Misenheimer NC 28109 Business E-Mail: laura.stivers@pfeiffer.edu.

STIVERS, STEVE, state legislator; BA in Econs., Internat. Rels., Ohio State U., Columbus, 1989, MBA, 1996. Lic. trader; v.p. govt. rels. Bank One; mem., dist. 16 Ohio State Senate, 2003—, vice-chair judiciary, civil justice com., mem. hwy. and transp., judiciary-criminal justice, and state and local govt. and vets. affairs coms. Pres. Dikaia Found., 1992—96; bd. dirs. Contemporary Am. Theatre Co., 1997—; bd. dirs., trustee Alvis House, 1997—; mem. Ohio Pub. Works Commn., 2000—03, Ohio Pub. Expenditures Coun., 2001—03. Vol. Big Brothers/Big Sisters, 2000—; mem. Columbus Urban League, 2001—03; bd. mem. Prevent Blindness Ohio, 2004—. Lt. col. Ohio Army Nat. Guard, 1985—, Iraq, Kuwait, Qatar, Djibouti. Recipient Watchdog the Treasury award, United Conservatives Ohio, 2005—06, Legislator of Yr., Ohio Advocates Mental Health, 2006. Mem.: Ohio Nat. Guard Officers Assn., Columbus Athletic Club. Republican. Office: Senate Bldg Rm 134 First Fl Columbus OH 43215 Office Phone: 614-466-7662. Business E-Mail: sd16@mailr.sen.state.oh.us.

STIVERS, TENILLE MARIE, psychology educator; b. Boise, Idaho, Sept. 30, 1981; d. Gary W. and Linda L. Stivers. BA, Nyack Coll., NY, 2003; MEd, U. Idaho, Boise, 2006; EdS, U. Idaho, 2008. Sch. psychologist Jerome Sch. Dist., Idaho, 2007—, sch. counselor, 2007—.

STOAKS, RALPH DUVAL, entomologist, educator, retired biotechnologist; b. Greenville, Miss., Apr. 8, 1935; s. Benjamin Duval and Joyce Fay (Neal),m. Roberts J. Upfold, 1959 (div. 1968); 1 child, Kent Duval; m. Carolyn Jeanne Bush, Dec. 29, 1977. BA in Biology, McMurry Coll., Abilene, Tex., 1958; M in Biol. Scis., U. Okla., 1967; PhD in Entomology, N.D. State U., 1975. Rsch. entomologist Bishop Mus. Natural History, Honolulu, 1978; urban entomologist, salesperson Orkin Pest Control, West Des Moines, Iowa, 1978-79; plant protection and quarantine officer USDA, Animal & Plant Health Inspection Svc., Plant Protection and Quarantine, San Diego, 1980—88, regional biotechnologist Sacramento, 1988—95, regional program mgr. biotech. and biol. control, 1996—2004; sr. regional biotechnologist USDA, Animal & Plant Health Inspection Svc., Biotech. Regulatory Svcs., We. Region, Ft. Collins, Colo., 2004—08; ret., 2008; vis. scientist, dept. bioagrl. scis. & pest mgmt. Colo. State U., Ft. Collins, 2008—; vis. scientist, bioagrl. dept. C.P. Gillette Mus. Arthropod Diversity, Colo. State U. Contbr. numerous articles to profl. jours. and books. With U.S. Army N.G., 1959-64, vol. Entomol Advisor, Fort Collings. Recipient Hammer award Vice Pres. Al Gore, 1997, USDA Honor award, Biotech. Regulatory Response Team, 2003; NSF rsch. grantee U. Okla., 1960, 62, 66, N.D. State U., 1968; NIH rsch. fellow Bishop Mus., 1978. Mem. AAAS, Entomol. Soc. Am. (bd. cert. gen. entomologist), Am. Registry of Profl. Entomologists (bd. dirs. North Calif. br. 1989-91), Great Plains Natural Sci. Soc. (life), N.Am. Bethnological Soc., Xerces Soc. Home: 2231 Silver Trails Dr Fort Collins CO 80526-6415 Personal E-mail: rdstoaks@comcast.net.

STOB, MARTIN, retired physiology educator; b. Chgo., Feb. 20, 1926; s. Cornelius and Theodora (Sluis) S BS, Purdue U., 1949, MS, 1951, PhD, 1953. Mem. faculty Purdue U., Lafayette, Ind., 1953—, assoc. prof. animal scis., 1958-63, prof., 1963-92; ret., 1992. Contbr. articles to profl. jours. Patentee prodn. of fermentation estrogen Served with USN, 1944-46; ETO, PTO Name Best Tchr. Sch. Agr., 1970, Best Counselor Sch. Agr., 1977, Best Counselor Purdue U., 1977 Fellow AAAS Episcopalian. Home: 6218 W Rd 75 N West Lafayette IN 47906

STOBAUGH, ROBERT BLAIR, professor emeritus; b. McGehee, Ark., Oct. 15, 1927; s. Robert B. and Helen (Parris) S.; m. Beverly Ann Parker, Oct. 18, 1947 (dec. 1990); children: Blair, Susan, William (dec.), Clay; m. June Gray Milton, Dec. 7, 1991. BS in Chem. Engring., La. State U., 1947; DBA, Harvard Bus. Sch., 1968. Refinery engr. Exxon Corp., Baton Rouge and Venezuela, 1947-52; engring. mgr. Caltex Oil Co., NY, Bahrain, London, 1952-59; mgr. econ. evaluation Monsanto Co., Houston, 1959-65; lectr. Harvard Bus. Sch., Boston, 1967-70, assoc. prof., 1970-71, prof., 1972-83, Charles E. Wilson prof., 1984-96, Charles E. Wilson prof. emeritus, 1996—, chmn. doctoral programs, 1984-89, dir. energy project, 1972-83, chmn. tech. and ops. mgmt. area, 1981-83. Bd. dirs. 11 cos.; adj. prof. mgmt. Rice U., 2002-06. Co-author: Money in the Multinational Enterprise, 1973, Energy Future (best-seller list N.Y. Times and Time mag.), 1979, How To Build an Effective Small-Company Board, 1996; author: Nine Investments Abroad and Their Impact at Home, 1976, Innovation and Competition, 1988; co-editor: Technology Crossing Borders, 1984; contbr. articles to profl. jours. Mem. bd. advisors Inst. Estudios Superiores de la Empresa, Barcelona, Spain, 1973-80; co-chmn. The Dumbarton Oaks Symposium on Energy Efficiency, Washington, 1979; bd. dirs. Alliance to Save Energy, Washington, 1979-94; expert testimony Congress 19 times; adv. cabinet-level depts. White House and UN; trustee French Libr. and Cultural Ctr., Boston, 1995-2004, Houston Firefighters' Relief and Retirement Fund, 2006—. Recipient Disting. Svc. award Harvard Bus. Sch., 2001; named to Hall of Distinction, La. State U., 1987. Fellow Acad. Internat. Bus. (pres. 1979-80), Coun. on Fgn. Rels., Am. Econ. Assn., Nat. Assn. Corp. Dirs. (bd. dirs. 1996-2005, vice-chmn. blue rimmon commn.), Forest Club (Houston) Episcopalian. Office: Harvard Bus Sch Soldiers Field Rd Boston MA 02163-1317 Office Phone: 617-495-6841.

STOBB, MARY JEAN, retired association administrator; b. Winnipeg, Man., Can., Oct. 16, 1934; came to U.S., 1955; d. Rudolph Edwin and Milla Elida (Corneliussen) Rasmussen; m. Gordon Wesley Stobb, June 14, 1958; children: Barbara Jean, David Gordon, William Eric. BS in Home Econs., U. Man., 1955. Cert. home economist. County home agt. U. Minn. at Stearns County, St. Cloud, 1955-58, U. Minn. at Mille Lacs County, Milaca, 1962-67; pvt. practice home economist Little Falls, Minn., 1967-71; interviewer Mid-Continent Surveys, Inc., Mpls., 1971-78, Rsch. Triangle Inst., Inc., Research Triangle Park, NC, 1976-78; dir. nutrition Region V Elderly Nutrition Program, Little Falls, Minn., 1978-80; dist. dir. Minn. unit Green Thumb, Inc., Wadena, Minn., 1980—89, mgr. field ops., 1989—95; field ops. coord. Green Thumb, Inc. (now Experience Works, Inc.), Minn., 1995—2003, ret., 2003. Key leader Riverwood Ramblers 4-H Club, Little Falls, 1968—70, 1971—79; county clothing leader Morrison County, Little Falls, 1974—75; chair adv. com. North Ctrl. Minn. Coun. on Aging, 2003—05, Ctrl. Minn. Coun. Aging, 2006—; commr. Little Falls Housing and Devel. Authority, 2005—, vice chair, 2008—; mem. adv. bd. Morrison County Interfaith Hospitality Network, 2004—06; pres. United Ch. Women's Assn., Little Falls, 1977—79; lay leader First United Ch., 2003—05, outreach chair, 1976—78, fin. chair, 1987—93, chair mission and ministry com., 1996—2002, 2007—08, choir mem., 1975—, treas., 2008—, pastoral search com. mem., 2008—09. Named 4-H Leader of Yr. Morrison County 4-H Leaders, 1974. Mem.: Minn. Home Econs. Assn. (dist. pres. 1969—71, chmn. home economists in homemaking 1972—73, by-laws chair 1977—78, del. 1981, 1982, dist. pres. 1986—87), Am. Assn. Family and Consumer Scientists (dist. pres. 1986—87), Internat. Fedn. Home Economists, Morrison County Interfaith Hospitality Network (host coord. 2005—), Mid-Sota Home Economists in Homemaking Club (Little Falls) (pres.). Methodist. Avocations: singing, gardening, walking. Home: 17861 Riverwood Dr Little Falls MN 56345 E-mail: maryjeans@charter.net.

STOBBS, RICHARD D. (DICK STOBBS), protective services official; b. Colerain, Ohio; s. Donald and Edna Stobbs; m. Jo Ann Stobbs; 4 children. Attended, Ohio U., Belmont; BBA, Ohio U., Athens; MA in Adminstrn., Ctrl. Mich. U., Mt. Pleasant, 1995. Cert. law enforcement instr. Laborer, carbon setter Ormet Corp.; supr., hot strip mill Wheeling-Pitts. Steel; sheriff Belmont County, Ohio; fed. official Dept. Justice, Washington. Legis. com. Buckeye State Sheriff's Assn. Firefighter, emergency squad mem. Colerain Vol. Fire Co.; life mem. Republican Nat. Com. Specialist 11th Armored Cavalry Regiment US Army, Vietnam. Decorated Bronze Star, Army Commendation Medal, Purple Heart Medal, Good Conduct Medal, Vietnam Svc. Medal, Vietnam Campaign Medal, Nat. Def. Svc. Medal; recipient Contbns. to Law Enforcement award, US Atty. Gen. Ed Meese. Mem.: VFW Post 8848 (life), NRA (life), Am. Soc. Indsl. Security, Belmont County Farm Bur., Ohio Gun Collectors (life), Rotary Internat., Columbus and St. Clairsville Jaycees, Am. Legion Post 38, 11th Armored Cav. Vets. Vietnam and Cambodia (life), Disabled Am. Vets. Post 117 (life). Republican. Mailing: 72311 Colerain Mt Pleasant Rd Dillonvale OH 43917

STOBER, WILLIAM JOHN, II, economics professor; b. Boston, Mar. 24, 1933; s. Ralph William and Marjorie Cairncross (Duthie) S.; m. Jeannine Lynn Defries, Sept. 10, 1955. B.Sc., Washington and Lee U., 1955; MA, Duke U., 1957, PhD, 1965. Instr., then asst. prof. econs. N.C. State U., Raleigh, 1959-65; asst. prof., then asso. prof. La. State U., 1965-69, acting head dept. econs., 1968-69; mem. faculty U. Ky., 1969—, prof. econs., 1974-97, chmn. dept., 1979-86, 90-95, dir. grad. studies, 1979-86, prof. emeritus, 1997—. Mem. Beta Gamma Sigma. Democrat. Home: 516 Mundys Lndg Versailles KY 40383-9468

STOBO, JOHN DAVID, academic administrator, physician; b. Somerville, Mass., Sept. 1, 1941; BA, Dartmouth Coll., 1963; MD, SUNY, Buffalo, 1968. Intern Osler Med. Services, Johns Hopkins, Balt., 1968-69, asst. med. resident, 1969-70, chief med. resident, 1972-73; research assoc. NIH, Bethesda, 1970-72; asst. prof. Mayo Clinic and Research Found., Rochester, Minn., 1973-76; assoc. prof. Moffitt Hosp., San Francisco, 1976-82, prof., head section rheumatology, clin. immunology, 1982-85; William Osler prof. medicine, chmn. dept. medicine John Hopkins Hosp. and Univ., Balt., 1985-94, vice dean clin. sci., assoc. v.p. medicine, 1994—97; v.p. Johns Hopkins Health System, Balt., 1994—97; chmn., CEO Johns Hopkins Healthcare LLC, Balt.; pres. U. Tex. Med. Br., Galveston, 1997—. Mem. transp. and immunobiology adv. com. NIAID, 1976—81; vice chmn. rsch. com. Arthritis Found., 1982—84, chmn. rsch. com., 1984—86, sr. investigator, 1974—77; mem. bd. sci. counselors Nat. Cancer Inst., 1982—; mem. sci. adv. bd. exec. com. Lupus Rsch. Inst.; mem. rsch. adv. bd. DuPont Co., 1987—94. Mem. editl. bd.: Jour. Immunology, 1981—86, Jour. Lab. and Clin. Investigation, 1977—82, Arthritis and Rheumatism, 1980—85, Jour. Reticuloendothelial Soc., 1982—84, Jour. Clin. Investigation, 1981—86, Jour. Clin. Immunology, 1982—87, Jour. Molecular and Cellular Immunology, 1984—86, Rheumatology Internat., 1984—86, Jour. Immunology, 1875—1987; contbr. numerous articles to profl. jours. Recipient Merck award, 1967, Maimonides Med. Soc. award, 1968. Fellow: ACP, Am. Clin. and Climatol. Assn.; mem.: AAAS, Assn. Profs. Medicine (sec.-treas. 1991—92, pres. 1994—95), Am. Soc. Clin. Investigation, Am. Fedn. Clin. Rsch., Assn. Am. Physicians, Am. Assn. Immunologists, Am. Rheumatism Assn. (sec., treas., 1st v.p. 1985—89), Am. Coll. Rheumatology (pres. 1989—90), Inst. Medicine, Md. Soc. Internal Medicine, Interurban Clin. Club, Balt. City Med. Soc., Alpha Omega Alpha. Office: U Texas Med Br Pres Office 301 University Blvd Galveston TX 77555-5302

STOCK, CARL WILLIAM, geology educator; b. Oceanside, NY, May 5, 1945; s. William Everett and Catherine Virginia (Narvesen) S.; m. Judith Anne Burry-Stock, 1993. BA in Biology, Hartwick Coll., Oneonta, NY, 1967; MA in Geology, SUNY, Binghamton, 1974; PhD, U.

N.C., 1977. Vis. instr. N.C. State U., Raleigh, 1975; instr. geology U. Ala., Tuscaloosa, 1976-77, asst. prof., 1977-84, assoc. prof., 1984—90, prof., 1990—2008, prof. emeritus, 2008—. Contbr. articles to profl. jours. With U.S. Army, 1969-71, Vietnam. Grantee NSF, 1984-86, Nat. Acad. Scis., 1994, 97-99, Petroleum Rsch. Fund, 1998-2001, Dept. Energy, 1998-2000. Mem. Paleontological Soc. (chmn. southeastern sect. 1982, tech. editor Jour. Paleontology 1992-93, sec. 1999-2004, patron), SEPM Soc. Sedimentary Geology, Palaeontological Assn., Paleontological Rsch. Instn., Geol. Soc. Am.; fellow. Internat. Assn. Study Fossil Cnidaria and Porifera (councilor 1988-95), Sigma Xi (chpt. pres. 1986-87). Avocations: gardening, reading, photography, exercise. Business E-Mail: cstock@geo.ua.edu.

STOCK, E. LEE, ophthalmologist, consultant; b. Pitts. s. Stock; m. Stock. MD, U. Mich., Ann Arbor. Prof. ophthalmology Eye Inst., Milw., 1999—2006; corneal surgeon Cornea Cons., SC, Grafton, Wis., 2006—. Contbr. articles to profl. jour. Mem.: Contact Lens Assn. Ophthalmologists (chair, internat. affairs 2008—). Home: 630 Shady Ridge Ct Grafton WI 53024 Office: Cornea Cons SC 630 Shady Ridge Ct Grafton WI 53024 Home Fax: 414-921-4919. Business E-Mail: corneaconsultant@gmail.com.

STOCK, RICHARD JOHN, cardiologist; b. Newark, Feb. 19, 1923; s. Archie Frank and Marie (Lergenmiller) S.; m. Eleanor Marguerite Schwarz, Sept. 1, 1945; children: Hilary Ann, Alan Constable; m. Martha Rusk Sutphen, Nov. 27, 2007. BS, Yale U., 1944; MD, Columbia U., 1947. Diplomate Am. Bd. Internal Medicine. Intern Presbyn. Hosp., NYC, 1947-48, resident in internal medicine, 1948-49, trainee Nat. Heart Inst., 1949-50; asst. physician in cardiology Columbia U. Hosp., NYC, 1949-50, asst. physician in medicine, 1951-61, asst. attending physician, 1961-64, assoc. attending physician, 1981—, attending physician; vis. fellow Nat. Heart Inst. Coll. Physicians and Surgeons Columbia U., NYC, 1949-50, asst. in medicine, 1951-56, instr. medicine, 1956-61, assoc. in medicine, 1961-64, asst. clin. prof., 1964-71, assoc. clin. prof., 1971-81, clin. prof., 1981-97, clin. prof. emeritus, spl. lectr., 1997—. Clin. prof. emeritus, spl. lectr. Coll. Physicians and Surgeons Columbia U., N.Y.C., 1997—. Author: Columbia Presbyterian Therapeutic Talks, 1963, 2nd edit., 1964; contbr. articles to profl. jours. Bd. dirs. N.Y. Heart Assn., 1979-85, mem. dir.'s coun., 1985—. Recipient Conspicuous Svc. medal Columbia U. Alumni Fedn., 1976; Richard J. Stock Professorship in dept. of medicine Columbia U., endowed, 1986. Fellow Am. Coll. Cardiology; mem. P & S Alumni Assn. (mem. admissions com. 1973-79, 81—, treas. 1973-81, mem. exec. com. 1973—, chmn. Alumni Day 1971-75, pres.-elect 1981-83, pres. 1983-85, chmn. capital campaign 1985—, Silver medal 1975, Gold medal 2004). Avocations: sculpture, music, skiing, tennis. Home: 155 E 72d St New York NY 10021-4371 Office: 755 Park Ave New York NY 10021-4255 E-mail: saggsodder@yahoo.com.

STOCK, STUART CHASE, lawyer; b. St. Louis, July 19, 1946; s. Sheldon Harry and Muriel Cecil (Lovejoy) Stock; m. Judith Ann Stewart, July 18, 1970; 1 child, Frederick Chase. BS in Engring., with highest distinction, Purdue U., 1968; JD magna cum laude, Harvard U., 1971. Bar: Mo. 1971, Ind. 1973, DC 1974. Law clk. to Chief Judge Henry J. Friendly U.S. Ct. Appeals 2d cir., New York, 1971-72; law clk. to Justice Thurgood Marshall U.S. Supreme Ct., Washington, 1972-73; assoc. Covington & Burling, Washington, 1974-78, ptnr., 1978—, chmn. of firm, exec. com., chmn. mgmt. com. Lectr. law U. Va., Charlottesville, 1987—90. Mem.: Am. Law Inst. Office: Covington & Burling PO Box 7566 1201 Pennsylvania Ave NW Washington DC 20044 Business E-Mail: sstock@cov.com.

STOCK, WENDY, physician, educator; m. James Baird, Oct. 14, 1984; children: Andrew Baird, Julia Stock Baird. MD, Rush Med. Sch., Chgo., 1985. Prof. medicine U. Chgo., 2000—. Editl. bd. mem. Blood Jour. Recipient SCOR award, Leukemia and Lymphoma Soc. America. Mem.: Am. Soc. Hematology.

STOCK, WILLIAM AUGUST, lawyer; b. Wakefield, RI, 1968; 3 children. BA, U. St. Thomas, St. Paul, Minn., 1990; JD, U. Minn., Mpls., 1993. Bar: Pa. 1993, NJ 1993. Assoc., ptnr. Dechert LLP, Phila., 1993—2003; ptnr. Klasko, Rulon, Stock & Seltzer, LLP, Phila., 2004—. Office: Klasko Rulon Stock & Seltzer LLP 1800 John F Kennedy Blvd Suite 1700 Philadelphia PA 19103 Office Fax: 215-825-8699. Business E-Mail: wstock@klaskolaw.com.

STOCKARD, JAMES ALFRED, lawyer; b. Lake Dallas, Tex., Aug. 4, 1935; s. Clifford Raymond and Thelma Gladys (Gotcher) S.; m. Mary Sue Hogan, Aug. 17, 1956; children— Bruce Anthony, James Alfred, Paul Andrew. BA with honors, N. Tex. State U., Denton, 1956; LLB magna cum laude, So. Methodist U., 1959. Bar: Tex. 1959. Pvt. practice, Dallas, 1959-62; with Employers Casualty Co., Dallas, 1962-65; v.p. Southland Life Ins. Co., Dallas, 1965-77, sr. v.p., gen. counsel, dir., 1977-87; exec. v.p., gen. counsel, sec. Southland Fin. Corp., Dallas, 1978-87; dir. Tex. Life, Accident, Health and Hosp. Svc. Ins. Guaranty Assn., 1978-84, chmn. bd., 1980-84; ptnr. Butler & Binion, Dallas, 1987-2000; pvt. practice Dallas, 2000—; counsel Employers Gen. Ins. Group, Inc., 1994—2006. Bd. dirs. Ins. Systems Am., Atlanta; pres., bd. dirs. Dallas County Mcpl. Utility Dist. 1, Irving, Tex.; gen. counsel, bd. dirs. Lone Star Life Ins. Co., 1988-99. Contbr. legal jours. Mem. exec. com., precinct chmn. Dallas County Dem. Com., 1971. Mem.: ABA, Tex. Bar Assn., Dallas Bar Assn., Assn. Life Ins. Counsel. Methodist. Home: 3607 Asbury St Dallas TX 75205-1848 Personal E-mail: jastockard@sbcglobal.net.

STOCKBAUER, ROGER LEWIS, retired physicist, researcher; b. Victoria, Tex., Feb. 3, 1944; s. Fred Ferdinand and Elizabeth (Nitschman) S.; m. Catherine Pauline Jones, June 10, 1972; children: Robbin Renee, Kathryn Elizabeth, Marc Daniel. BA, Rice U., 1966; MS, U. Chgo., 1968, PhD, 1973. Rsch. assoc. U. Chgo., 1972-73; rsch. physicist Nat. Inst. Stds. and Tech., Gaithersburg, Md., 1973-89; prof. physics La. State U., Baton Rouge, 1989—2005; ret., 2004. Editor: High Tc Superconducting Thin Films, 1990; contbr. articles to profl. jours. Recipient Silver medal US Dept. Commerce, 1983; NRC fellow, 1973-75. Fellow Am. Phys. Soc., Am. Vacuum Soc.; mem. AAAS, AAUP, Materials Rsch. Soc., Sigma Xi. Personal E-mail: rlstockbauer@mac.com.

STOCKBURGER, JEAN DAWSON, lawyer; b. Scottsboro, Ala., Feb. 4, 1936; d. Joseph Mathis Scott and Mary Frances (Alley) Dawson; m. John Calvin Stockburger, Mar. 23, 1963; children: John Scott, Mary Staci, Christopher Sean. Student, Gulf Park Coll., 1954-55; BA, Auburn U., 1958; M in Social Work, Tulane U., 1962; JD, U. Ark., Little Rock, 1979. Bar: Ark. 1979, U.S. Dist. Ct. (ea. dist.) Ark. 1980. Assoc. Mitchell, Williams, Selig, Gates & Woodyard and predecessor, Little Rock, 1979-85, ptnr., 1985-94, of counsel, 1994—. Bd. dirs., sec. Cen. Ark. Estate Coun., Little Rock, 1984—85, 2d v.p., 1985—86, pres., 1987—88. Assoc. editor: U. Ark. Law Rev., 1978—79. Bd. dirs. Little Rock Cmty. Mental Health Ctr., 1994—, v.p., 1996—99, pres., 1999—2001; bd. dirs. Sr. Citizens Activities Today, Little Rock, 1983—88, treas., 1986—88; bd. dirs. Vol. Orgn. for Ctrl. Ark. Legal Svcs., 1986—91, sec., 1987—88, chmn., 1989—91, H.I.R.E. Inc., 1994—2001. Mem. ABA, Ark. Bar Assn. (chmn. probate and trust law sect. 1986-88), Pulaski County Bar Assn. (bd. dirs. 1994-97), Ark. Bar Found., Am. Coll. Trust and Estate Counsel. Democrat. Methodist. Office: Mitchell Williams Selig Gates & Woodyard 425 W Capitol Ave Ste 1800 Little Rock AR 72201-3525 Home Phone: 501-661-0791; Office Phone: 501-688-8818. Business E-Mail: jstockburger@mwlaw.com.

STOCKDALE, CHRISTOPHER, physics professor; PhD in Physics, U. Okla., Norman, 2001. Postdoc. fellow Naval Rsch. Lab., Washington, 2001—03; asst. prof. physics Marquette U., Milw., 2003—. Mem.: Am. Astron. Soc. Office: Marquette Univ Physics Dept Wehr Physics #380 PO Box 1881 Milwaukee WI 53201-1881 Business E-Mail: chris.stockdale@mu.edu.

STOCKDALE, NANCY L., historian, educator; life ptnr. Carter McBeath. PhD, U. Calif., Santa Barbara, 2000. Asst. prof., mid. eastern history U. Ctrl. Fla., Orlando, 2001—06, U. North Tex., Denton, 2006—. Contbr. articles to profl. jours. Mem.: Am. Hist. Assn., Mid. East Studies Assn. N.Am.

STOCKDALE, STEWART A., data processing company executive; b. 1961; BBA in Mktg., U. Denver. Brand mgmt. Procter & Gamble, American Express, Citibank; sr. v.p. global mktg. and product mgmt. MasterCard Internat.; exec. v.p., chief mktg. officer Conseco, Inc.; chief mktg. officer Simon Property Group, Inc. (SPG), 2002—08; pres. Simon Brand Ventures (SBV), 2002—08; exec. v.p., pres. US & Can. Western Union Co., Englewood, Colo., 2008—. Named #2 Mktg. Exec. of Yr., Fin. Svc. Mktg., 2000; nominee Marketer of Yr., Direct Marketing Assn., 2002. Office: Western Union Co 12500 E Belford Ave Englewood CO 80112

STOCKER, ARTHUR FREDERICK, classics educator; b. Bethlehem, Pa., Jan. 24, 1914; s. Harry Emilius and Alice (Stratton) S.; m. Marian West, July 16, 1968. AB summa cum laude, Williams Coll., 1934; A.M., Harvard U., 1935, PhD, 1939. Instr. Greek Bates Coll., 1941—42; asst. prof. classics U. Va., 1946—52, assoc. prof. Va., 1952—60, prof. Va., 1960—84, prof. emeritus Va., 1984—, chmn. dept. Va., 1955-63, 68-78, assoc. dean Grad. Sch. Arts and Scis. Va., 1962—66; vis. asst. prof. classics U. Chgo., summer 1951. Editor: (with others) Servianorum in Vergilii Carmina Commentariorum Editio Harvardiana, Vol. II, 1946, Vol. III, 1965; assoc. editor: Classical Outlook. Served with USAAF, 1942-46, with USAAFR and USAFR, 1946-1974, ret. col., USAF. Sheldon Traveling fellow, Harvard U., 1940—41. Mem. Va. Classical Assn. (pres. 1949-52), Mid. West and South Classical Assn. (pres. So. sect. 1960-62, pres. 1970-71), Nat. Huguenot Soc. (pres. gen. 1989-91), Am. Philol. Assn., Mediaeval Acad. Am., Poetry Soc. Va. (pres. 1966-69), Soc. Colonial Wars in the State of Va., SAR (chpt. pres. 1972, 91), Huguenot Soc. Va. (pres. 1981-83), Raven Soc. (Raven award 1977), Phi Beta Kappa, Omicron Delta Kappa, Sons Am. Revolution, Sons Revolution. Republican. Presbyterian (elder). Clubs: Masons, Colonnade (Charlottesville, Va.), Farmington Country (Charlottesville, Va.), Commonwealth (Richmond, Va.), Army and Navy (Washington). Home: 250 Pantops Mountain Rd Charlottesville VA 22911-8682

STOCKER, CHRISTINE MARIE, language educator; b. Detroit, Oct. 14, 1946; d. Norman Robert and Verna Mary. BA in English, U. Windsor, Ont., Can., 1968; MA in Comparative Lit., U. Mich., Ann Arbor, 1969; cert. in Paralegal, Oakland C.C., 1993. Designer and copywriter Inst. Continuing Legal Edn., Ann Arbor, Mich., 1968—70; mgr. Donaldson Lufkin and Jenerette, NYC, 1980—82; cons. Warner Comms., NYC, 1982—83; assoc. prof. Madonna U., Livonia, Mich., 1986; pvt. practice tutor lang. Farmington Hills, Mich., 1994—. Tchr. ESL Lang. Ctr. Internat., Southfield, Mich., 1997—2000; assoc. prof. Oakland C.C., Farmington Hills, Mich., 2000, tutor, 2004—05; assoc. prof. St. Mary's Coll., Ave Maria U., Orchard Lake, Mich., 2002. Author: Human Life Internat.; prodr., editor: radio series, 1986—88; promotions, editor St. Gabriel Media, 1987—94 (The Fatima Movie Emmy award); reader: Reading for the Blind, 2006—07; contbr. articles to profl. jours.; dir.: (pro-life) Cable TV Programs. Mem.: Mensa, Human Life Internat. (vol.), Mystical Rose Soc. (founder 1988—, contbr. articles to newsletter).

STOCKHOLDER, JESSICA, sculptor; b. Seattle, 1959; BFA, Univ. Victoria, 1982; MFA, Yale Univ., New Haven, Conn., 1985. Instr., dept. Sculpture NYU, 1992, Bard Coll., 1993; prof., dir. grad. studies in sculpture Yale U., 1999—. One-woman shows include, Renaissance Soc., U. Chgo., 1991, Weatherspoon Gallery, U. NC, 1994, Jay Gorney Modern Art, NYC, 1995, 1997, Dia Ctr. Arts, NYC, 1995, Galerie Nathalie Obadia, Paris, 1995, 1998, 2001, 2004, White Cube, London, 1998, Gorney Bravin + Lee, NYC, 2001, 2003, Rice U. Art Gallery, Houston, 2004, P.S.1 Contemporary Art Ctr., NYC, 2006, 1301 PE, LA, 2007, one-woman shows include retrospective Kissing the Wall, U. Houston, Weatherspoon Art Gallery, and Blaffer Art Gallery, 2004—06, exhibited in group shows at Making a Clean Edge, P.S.1 Contemporary Art Ctr., 1989, Contingent Realms, Whitney Mus. Am. Art at Equitable Ctr., 1990, Whitney Biennial, Whitney Mus. Am. Art, NYC, 1991, 2004, Heart, Mind, Body, Soul: Am. Art in the 1990s, 1997, As Long As It Lasts, Witte de With, Rotterdam, 1992, Simply Made in America, Aldrich Mus. Contemporary Art, Conn., 1993, Biennial Exhbn. Contemporary Am. Painting, Corcoran Gallery Art, Washington, 1996, What I Did On My Summer Vacation, White Columns, NYC, 1996, Colorflex, Apex Art, NYC, 1997, Pop/Abstraction, Pa. Acad. Fine Arts, Phila., 1998, Now and Later, Yale U. Art Gallery, 1998, Objective Color, 2001, SiteLines, Addison Gallery Am. Art, Andover, Mass., 2002, Under Pressure, Cooper Union Sch. Art, NYC, 2003, Ann. Invitational Exhbn. Contemporary Am. Art, Nat. Acad. Mus., NYC, 2004, Conn. Contemporary, Wadsworth Atheneum, Hartford, 2007. Recipient Lucelia Artist award, Smithsonian Am. Art Mus., 2007; grantee NEA award for Sculpture, 1988, NY Found. Arts grant in Painting, 1989; fellow Guggenheim Found., 1996. Office: c/o Blaffer Gallery 120 Fine Arts Building Univ Houston Houston TX 77204

STOCKLI, MARTIN PETER, physics educator; b. Solothurn, Switzerland, June 30, 1949; came to U.S., 1980; s. Hans J. and Lydia (Schumacher) S.; m. Dionisia M. Trigo, Nov. 19, 1983. Diploma in physics, Swiss Fed. Inst. Tech., Zurich, 1974, PhD, 1978. Rsch. assoc. Swiss Fed. Inst. Tech., 1978-80, Western Mich. U., Kalamazoo, 1980-81, Kans. State U., Manhattan, 1981-86, assoc. scientist, 1986-89, asst. rsch. prof. physics, 1989-95, assoc. rsch. prof., 1995-97, assoc. prof., 1997—. Vis. scientist Inst. Nucler Physics, Paris, 1984; cons. Inst. Kernphysik, Frankfurt, Germany, 1984, 87. Contbr. articles to profl. jours. Mem. Am. Phys. Soc., Am. Vacuum Soc. Achievements include design and construction of first U.S. cryogenic electron beam ion source to produce fully stripped argon nuclei. Office: Kansas State Univ Dept Physics Cardwell Hall Manhattan KS 66506-2604

STOCKMAL, HENRY F., JR., retired principal; b. Derby, Conn., Apr. 24, 1942; s. Henry F. and Helen T. (Filip) S.; m. Elizabeth G. Bachman, Apr. 22, 1967; children: Gregory F., Edward J. BS, So. Conn. State Coll., 1964; MA, Fairfield U., Conn., 1968; cert. adv. study (6th yr. cert.), Fairfield U., 1972. Tchr. Fairfield pub. schs., Conn., 1964-89; asst. prin. Greenwich pub. schs., Conn., 1989-91; prin. Andover Elem. Sch., Conn., Chester Elem Sch., Chester, Conn.; ednl. cons. Regional Sch. District#4, Conn. Dept. Edn. Assessor Beginning Educator Support Tng. Program and Trainer of State Assessors, 1988—. Adminstr. sr. div. Dist. 4 Little League Baseball, New Haven, 1984-89. Gen. Electric grantee, 1984, 85. Mem. NEA, ASCD, Nat. Assn. Elem. Sch. Prins., Conn. Edn. Assn. (treas. 1975-78, bd. dirs.), Elem. and Mid. Sch. Prins. Assn. Roman Catholic. Avocations: astronomy, sports, sports card collection. Home: 112A Lake Rd Columbia CT 06237-1319

STOCKMAN, DAVID ALAN, investment banker, former US Representative from Michigan; b. Ft. Hood, Tex., Nov. 10, 1946; s. Allen and Carol (Bartz) S. BA in Am. History cum laude, Mich. State U., East Lansing, 1968; postgrad., Harvard U. Div. Sch., 1968—70. Spl. asst. to Rep. John Anderson US Congress, 1970-72, exec. dir. Republican Conf., 1972-75; mem. US Congress from 4th Mich. Dist., 1977—81; chmn. Rep. Econ. Policy Task Force, 1977-81; dir., Office Mgmt. & Budget Exec. Office of the Pres., Washington, 1981-85; mng. dir. Salomon Bros., NYC, 1985-88; sr. mng. dir. The Blackstone Group, NYC, 1988-99; founder Heartland Indsl. Ptnrs., 1999—; CEO Collins & Aikman, Southfield, Mich., 2003—05. Mem. Nat. Commn. on Air Quality, 1978. Author: The Triumph of Politics: Why the Reagan Revolution Failed, 1986. Fellow, Inst. Politics, 1974. Mem. Coun. on Fgn. Rels. Office: Heartland Indsl Ptnrs 55 Railroad Ave Greenwich CT 06830 Home Phone: 203-661-0007; Office Phone: 203-861-2622. Business E-Mail: david.stockman@heartlandpartners.com.*

STOCKMAN, JAMES ANTHONY, III, pediatrician; b. Phila., 1943; MD, Jefferson Med. Coll., 1969. Diplomate Am. Bd. Pediat. Intern Childrens Hosp. Pa., 1969—70, resident in pediat., 1970—72; fellow in pediatric hematology/oncology SUNY, Syracuse, 1972—74; now clin. prof. Duke U.; also with U. N.C., Chapel Hill. Mem.: American Bd. Pediatrics (pres. 2009). Office: Office of the Pres Am Bd Pediatrics 111 Silver Cedar Ct Chapel Hill NC 27514-1512 Office Phone: 919-929-0461.*

STOCKMAN, JENNIFER BLEI, political organization administrator; b. Phila., Dec. 5, 1954; d. William Harry and Florence (Sussberg) Blei; m. David. A. Stockman, Nov. 10, 1983; children: Rachel, Victoria. BS, U. Md., 1976; MBA in Fin., George Washington U., 1983. Systems engr. IBM Corp., Washington, 1976-78, mktg. rep., 1978-81, staff mktg. mgr., 1981-83; dir. tech. trade Sears World Trade, Washington, 1983-84, v.p. tech. investment, 1984-85; founder Stockman & Associates Inc., Greenwich, Conn., 1985, past pres., CEO. Co-chair Rep. Majority for Choice (formerly Rep. Pro-Choice Coalition); bd. mem. WISH List. Pres. Solomon R. Guggenheim Mus., NYC, 2003—; phography com. MOMA; co-chair Bruce Mus. Council; nat. adv. bd. Aspen Art Mus. Recipient Heart of Greenwich, YMCA; named Republican Woman of Year award, Conn. Women's Forum. Republican. Avocations: tennis, swimming, children. Office: Republican Majority For Choice 1660 L St NW Ste 609 Washington DC 20036-5676 Home: 1850 Henry Cowgill Rd Camden Wyoming DE 19934 Business E-Mail: jbstockman@aol.com.

STOCKMAN, KATHLEEN HELEN, elementary school educator; b. Hazleton, Pa., Aug. 29, 1954; d. John and Mildred Ann (Rick) Polak; m. Martin F. Stockman, Aug. 27, 1977; children: Martin Andrew, Alexander John. AA, Northampton C.C., Bethlehem, Pa., 1974; BA, Moravian Coll., Bethlehem, 1977; permanent cert., Lehigh U., Bethlehem, 1985. Permanent tchg. cert. Pa., 1985. Elem. tchr. Christ the King Sch., Whitehall, Pa., 1979—. Group facilitator Rainbows Program, Whitehall, Pa. Named Tchr. of Week, Local Radio Show; nominee Disney Tchr. of Yr., 2006. Mem.: Nat. Cath. Educators Assn. Roman Catholic. Avocations: travel, music, reading, gardening. Home: 3212 Highfield Dr Bethlehem PA 18020 Office: Christ the King School 22 S 5th St Coplay PA 18037 E-mail: katkas@aol.com.

STOCKMEYER, NORMAN OTTO, law educator, consultant; b. Detroit, May 24, 1938; s. Norman O. and Lillian R. (Hitchman) S.; m. Marcia E. Rudman, Oct. 1, 1966; children: Claire, Kathleen, Mary Frances. AB, Obelin Coll., 1960; JD, U. Mich., 1963. Bar: MIch. 1963, U.S. Ct. Appeals (6th cir.) 1964, U.S. Supreme Ct. 1974. Legis. grad. fellow Mich. State U., 1963; legal counsel Senate Judiciary Com., Mich. Legislature, 1964; law clk. Mich. Ct. Appeals, 1965, commr., 1966-68, rsch. dir., 1969-76; assoc. prof. law Thomas M. Cooley Law Sch., 1977-78, prof., 1978—. Vis. prof. Mercer U. Sch. Law, 1986, Calif. Western Sch. Law, 1993; lectr. Mich. Judicial Inst., 1995. Editor Mich. Law of Damages, 1989; contbr. numerous articles to state and nat. legal jours. Named one of 88 Greats, Lansing State Jour., 1988. Fellow Am. Bar Found. (life); mem. ABA (chmn. Mich. membership 1972-73, ho. of dels. 1988-92, editl. bd. Compleat Lawyer 1990-99), Nat. Conf. Bar Founds. (trustee 1985-90, sec. 1988-89), Mich. State Bar Found. (pres. 1982-85, trustee 1971-92), State Bar Mich. (chmn. Young Lawyers sect. 1971-72, rep. assembly 1972-79, bd. commrs. 1985-93), Ingham County Bar Assn. (bd. dirs. 1981-85), Mich. Assn. Professions (bd. dirs. 1981-84, Profl. of Yr. 1988), Thomas M. Cooley Legal Authors Soc. (pres. 1982-83), Scribes (bd. dirs. 1994—, pres. 2005-2007), Delta Theta Phi (dean Christiancy Senate 1962, Outstanding Prof. 1984). Address: PO Box 13038 Lansing MI 48901-3038 Home Phone: 517-339-2246; Office Phone: 517-371-5140 ext. 2727. Business E-Mail: stockmen@cooley.edu.

STOCKS, RUNDELL KINGSLEY, management, construction, education and general consultant; b. Kokstad, South Africa, Feb. 14, 1925; s. Gerald Restall and Edith Hannah (Duffy) S.; m. Janet Alma Parish, Mar. 23, 1949 (dec. 1964); 1 child, Virginia Anne Stocks Garde. Grad., Kingswood Coll., Grahamstown, South Africa, 1942. Chmn., mng. dir. Stocks Constrn., Port Alfred, South Africa, 1946-57; tech. clk. Vecor Ltd., Vanderbijlpark, South Africa, 1957-60; gen. mgr. F.A. Poole Group, Pretoria, South Africa, 1960-64; dir. gen. mgr. Stocks Group, Pretoria, South Africa, 1964-75; Pretoria dir. Eastern Province Bldg Soc., 1970-86; chmn. non exec. Habitech Group, Pretoria, 1975-85; chmn. Gem Valley Estates (Pty) Ltd., 1969—; external examiner U. Pretoria, 1970—2000. Mem. bldg. rsch. adv. com. Coun. for Sci. and Indsl. Rsch., 1972-88, nat. exec. com. Bldg. Industries Fedn. South Africa, exec. com. Master Builders Assn. of Pretoria, mgmt. com. Nat. Devel. Fund for Bldg. Industry, mem. South African affiliate Internat. Com. on Tall Bldgs. With South African Navy, 1943-46. Fellow Chartered Mgmt. Inst., Chartered Inst. Bldg. (hon., pres. 1977-78); mem. South African Inst. Mgmt. (hon. life), South African Inst. Pers. Mgmt. Christian Scientist. Home and Office: 19 Stocks Ave Stocksvillage Port Alfred 6170 South Africa Office Phone: 046-624-1677.

STOCKS, WILLIAM L., federal judge; Bar: N.C. Chief bankruptcy judge for mid. dist. N.C. U.S. Bankruptcy Ct., Greensboro, 1993—. Office: US Bankruptcy Ct 101 S Edgeworth St Greensboro NC 27401-2219 Office Phone: 336-358-4080.

STOCKSTILL, DAVID H., musician, research historian, lecturer; b. New Orleans, July 24, 1937; s. David H. and Doris (Fleming) Stockstill. BS, U. South Miss., Hattiesburg, 1964, MEd, 1972. Tchr. Hancock County Schs., Bay St. Louis, Miss., 1964—91; pipe organist Bay St. Presbyn. Ch., Hattiesburg, 1994—. Textbook selection com. Miss. Pub. Schs., 1985—91, accreditation com., 1985—91. Rschr., composer, pub. (various monographs);, performer concerts in various churches, synagogues, universities and theaters. Bd.dirs. Picayune Main St. Inc., Miss., 1995—2006; chmn. hist. com., 1995—2005; former officer Am. Guild Organists; elder Presbyn. Ch. Am. Named Citizen of Yr., Picayune C. of C., 2004. Mem.: Am. Harp Soc. (past pres. La. Chpt.), Picayune Main St., Inc., Organ Hist. Soc., Railroad Hist. Soc. Republican. Presbyn. Avocations: reading, photography, architecture. Home: 605 S Curran Ave Picayune MS 39466 Office: Bay St Presbyn Ch 204 Short Bay St Hattiesburg MS 39402 Home Phone: 301-310-4554; Office Phone: 601-798-3129. Personal E-mail: dhstill@bellsouth.net.

STOCKTON, DAVID A., lawyer; BA, Emory U., 1978; JD with honors, U. NC, Chapel Hill, 1982. Bar: Ga. 1982. Ptnr. Corp. Group Kilpatrick Stockton LLP, Atlanta. Editor (review): UNC Ch. Law. Mem.: ABA (mem. Fed. Regulation of Securities sub-com.), Atlanta Bar Assn., State Bar of Ga. (chmn. Bus. Law Sect.), Order of the Coif. Office: Kilpatrick Stockton LLP Ste 2800 1100 Peachtree St Atlanta GA 30309 Office Phone: 404-815-6500. Office Fax: 404-541-3402. E-mail: DStockton@KilpatrickStockton.com.

STOCKTON, DMITRI LYSANDER, diversified financial services company executive; b. 1964; m. Renee Stockton; 2 children. BS in Acctg., NC A&T State U., 1986. With Arthur Anderson; joined fin. mgmt. program GE, 1987; mem. audit staff GE Capital; project mgr. GE Comml. Real Estate, 1991—94, mng. dir., 1994—97; chief risk officer GE Mortgage Corp., 1997—99; sr. v.p mktg. & bus. devel. GE Mortgage Insurance, 1999—2001; CEO GE Capital Bank, Switzerland, 2001—04; pres., CEO Ctrl. & Eastern Europe GE Money, 2005—09; pres., CEO global banking GE Capital, 2009—; sr. v.p. GE, 2009—. Second dep. supervisory bd. Bank BPH; spkr. in field. Recipient Bus. Achievement award, Betta Gamma Sigma, 2007. Office: General Electric Co 3135 Easton Tpk Fairfield CT 06828-0001*

STOCKTON, PAUL NOBLE, federal agency administrator; b. 1954; m. Christin Anne Englert, Nov. 26, 1988. B, Dartmouth Coll., Hanover, NH, 1976; PhD in Govt., Harvard U., 1986. Legis. asst. to representative Daniel Patrick Moynihan US Senate, 1986—89; rsch. assoc. Internat. Inst. Strategic Studies, London; postdoc. fellow Ctr. Internat. Security & Cooperation, Stanford U., Calif., 1989—90, sr. rsch. scholar, 2006—09; asst. prof. dept. nat. security affairs Naval Postgrad. Sch., Monterey, Calif., 1990, dir. Ctr. Civil-Mil. Rels., 1995—2000, founder, acting dean Sch. Internat. Grad. Studies, 2000—01, assoc. provost, 2001, dir. Ctr. Homeland Def. & Security, 2002—06; asst. sec. (homeland def. & America's security affairs) US Dept. Def., Washington, 2009—. Co-editor: Reconstituting America's Defense: America's New National Security Strategy, 1992; mem. editl. bd. (quarterly jour.) Homeland Security Affairs, 2005—, rsch. pub. in Polit. Sci. Quarterly, Internat. Security, Strategic Survey; contbr. chapters to books. Office: US Dept Def 1400 Def Pentagon Washington DC 20301 Office Phone: 703-545-6700.*

STOCKWELL, LINDA M., principal; b. Mpls., Oct. 8, 1948; d. Irving Gordon and Neomie Lillian Reishus; m. David Lewis Stockwell, Dec. 20, 1969 (div.); children: Joel David, Jaime Lynn O'Brien. BA in Elem. Edn., Augsburg Coll., 1970; MS in Curriculum and Supervision, No. Ill. U., 1985. Cert. elem. sch. tchr. 1-6, elem. sch. prin. Minn. Dept. Edn. Elem. sch. tchr. Bloomington Pub. Schs., Minn., 1970—72, Menominee Cath. Ctrl. Schs., Menominee, Mich., 1974—76, Valley View Pub. Schs., Romeoville, Ill., 1981—85, curriculum coord., 1985—88, assoc. prin., 1988—92; elem. sch. prin. Rochester Pub. Schs., Minn., 1992—2009. Com. mem. Gloria Dei Luth. Ch., Rochester, Minn., 1998—2005. Recipient Ofcl. Core Knowledge Sch., Core Knowledge Found., 2000-2005, NCLB Blue Ribbon Sch., US Dept Edn., 2007. Mem.: Rochester Elem. Sch. Prins. Assn. (pres., v.p., sec.), Nat. Assn. Elem. Sch. Prins., ASCD. Home: 605 29th St NW Rochester MN 55901 Office: Washington Elem School 1200 11th Ave NW Rochester MN 55901 Office Phone: 507-328-3800. Business E-Mail: listockwell@rochester.k12.mn.us.

STOCKWELL, MARY ELIZABETH, history professor; PhD, U. Toledo, Ohio, 1984. Prof. and dept. chair Lourdes Coll., Sylvania, Ohio, 1996—. Author: (history book) Woodrow Wilson: The Last Romantic, A Journey through Maine, Massachusetts, Our Home (Golden Lamp Best Book award, 2005), The Ohio Adventure. Recipient Faculty Excellence award, Lourdes Coll., 2001, 2006. Achievements include research in Gilder-Lehrman research fellowship. Office: Lourdes Coll 6832 Convent Blvd Sylvania OH 43560 Business E-Mail: mstockwe@lourdes.edu.

STOCKWELL, ROBERT PAUL, linguist, educator; b. Oklahoma City, June 12, 1925; s. Benjamin P. and Anna (Cunningham) S.; m. Lucy Louisa Floyd, Aug. 29, 1946; 1 child, Paul Witten; m. Donka Minkova, Jan. 13, 2005. BA, U. Va., 1946, MA, 1949, PhD, 1952. Instr. English, Oklahoma City U., 1946-48; mem. linguistics staff Sch. Langs., Fgn. Service Inst., State Dept., 1952-56; mem. faculty UCLA, 1956-94, prof. English, 1962-66, prof. linguistics, 1966—94, chmn. dept., 1966-73, 80-84, prof. emeritus, 1994—. Mem. com. lang. programs Am. Coun. Learned Socs., 1965-69 Author: (with J.D. Bowen) Patterns of Spanish Pronunciation, 1960, Sounds of English and Spanish, 1965, (with J. D. Bowen, J.W. Martin) The Grammatical Structures of English and Spanish, 1965, The Major Syntactic Structures of English, 1973, (with P.M. Schachter, B.H. Partee) Foundations of Syntactic Theory, 1977, Workbook in Syntactic Theory and Analysis, 1977, (with Donka Minkova) English Words: History and Structure, 2001; also numerous articles.; editor: (with R.S.K. Macaulay) Linguistic Change and Generative Theory, 1972, (with Donka Minkova) Studies in the History of the English Language: A Millennial Perspective, 2003; assoc. editor: Lang., 1973-79, Festschrift: Rhetorica, Phonologica, Syntactica: A Festchrift for Robert P. Stockwell, 1988. Served with USNR, 1943-45. Am. Coun. Learned Socs. fellow, 1963-64. Mem. Linguistic Soc. Am. (exec. com. 1965-68), Philol. Assn. Great Britain. Home: 1929 Manning Ave #301 Los Angeles CA 90025 Office: UCLA Linguistics Dept Los Angeles CA 90095 Business E-Mail: stockwel@ucla.edu.

STODDARD, ANDREW T., legislative staff member; Staff asst., Rep. Nancy Pelosi US House of Reps., Washington, 2004, press asst., Rep. Nancy Pelosi, 2005—08, dep. chief of staff, comm. dir. to Rep. Dina Titus, 2009—. Democrat. Office: 319 Cannon House Office Bldg Washington DC 20515 Office Phone: 202-225-3252. Office Fax: 202-225-2185.*

STODDARD, ANNE MAHER, biostatistician, researcher, educator; b. Rochester, NY, Mar. 26, 1946; d. Robert Williamson and Mary Jane Gunter Maher; m. Sanford I. Roth; children: Joshua Forrest, Nathan Edward. AB, Hollins Coll., Roanoke, VA, 1964—68; MS, Harvard Sch. of Pub. Health, Boston, MA, 1971—73, ScD, 1973—78. Instr. in pub. health U. Mass., Amherst, 1977—78, asst. prof. pub. health, 1978—89, assoc. prof. pub. health, 1989—2003, assoc. prof. emerita, 2003—; sr. rsch. scientist New England Rsch. Inst., Watertown, Mass., 2003; dir. Ctr. for Statis. Analysis and Rsch., 2004—. Dir. UMASS/ Baystate Ctr. for Rsch. and Edn. in Women's Health, Amherst, Mass., 1997—2003; adj. lectr. Harvard Sch. of Pub. Health, Boston, 1997—2007; vis. scientist Dana Farber Cancer Inst., Boston, 2001—02. Fulbright Sr. Specialists grantee, 2004—05. Office: NERI 9 Galen St Watertown MA 02472 E-mail: astoddard@neriscience.com.

STODDARD, GLENN MCDONALD, lawyer; b. Washington, Feb. 18, 1958; BS, U. Wis., Stevens Point, 1980; MS, U. Wis., Madison, 1984, JD, 1994. Bar: Wis. 1995, U.S. Dist. Ct. (ea. and we. dists.) Wis. 1995, 7th Ct., US Ct. of App., 2002. Assoc. code adminstr. Washburn County, Shell Lake, Wis., 1980-81; assoc. planner Manitowoc County, Wis., 1981-82; legis. aide Wis. Legis., Madison, 1983-85; asst. dir. Gov.'s Commn. on Agr., Madison, 1985; exec. dir. Wis. Land Cons. Assn., Madison, 1985-89; dir. govt. affairs Wis. Farmers Union, Chippewa Falls, 1989-92; law clk. U. Wis. Legal Asst. Program, Madison, Wis., summer 1993, Wis. Dept. Justice, Madison, Wis., summer 1994; ptnr./shareholder Garvey & Stoddard, S.C., Madison, Wis., 1995—2005; pvt. practice, 2005—. Author: Essentials of Forestry, 4th edit., 1987. Chmn. Wis. Environ. Decade, Inc., Madison, 1991-92. Named Outstanding Citizen Adv., Ctr. for Pub. Rep., Madison, 1991, Environ. Adv. of Yr., Wis. Clean Water Action Coun., 2005, Wis. Super Lawyer, 2006, Good Citizen award, Sierra Club, 2007. Mem.: ABA, Wis. Assn. for Justice, Environ. Law Inst., Am. Assn. for Justice, State Bar Wis. Avocations: outdoor sports, Karate, tai chi, reading. Office: Glenn M Stoddard Atty at Law 130 S Barstow St Ste 2C Eau Claire WI 54701 Office Phone: 715-852-0345. E-mail: glennstoddard@gmail.com.

STODDARD, PETER HAWKINS, education educator, consultant; b. Biloxi, Miss., June 10, 1949; s. Richard Williams Stoddard and Winifred Gertrude Hawkins; 1 child, Matthew Richard. BA, Hiram Coll., 1967—71; MSW, San Francisco State U., 1979—81; PhD, Case Western Res. U., 1981—83. Reporter Charlotte Observer, NC, 1971—73; transp. mgr. Jesica/Gunne Sax, Ltd., San Francisco, 1973—74; news editor Alameda Times Star, Calif., 1975—77; social worker San Francisco Welfare Dept., 1977—79; aid to the mayor City of San Francisco, 1979—81; prof. of social work Moorhead State U., Moorhead, Minn., 1983—84, U. of Tenn. Grad. Social Work Sch., Knoxville, 1984—88, Austin Peay State U., Clarksville, Tenn., 1988—. Dir. Ctr. for Social Rsch./ Coun. of Cmty. Services, Nashville, 1986—89; founder and exec. dir. Montgomery County Coun. of Cmty. Services, Clarksville, 1993—94; founder and dir. APSU Cmty. Outreach Partnership Ctr., Clarksville, 1992—96, Vol. Ctr. of Clarksville, Tenn., 1995—96; co-founder Family Guidance Ctr., Clarksville. Author: (book) An Atlas of Montgomery County, Tennessee; contbr. articles to profl. jours. Bd. mem. Nat. Assn. of Planning Councils, Dallas; governor's task force on social svc. block grants State of Tenn., 1996—97; task force mem. Governor's Task Force on Manpower Needs in Mental Health, Nashville, 1987—89, SF Mayor's Task Force on Housing Needs, San Francisco, 1980—81; sec. and bd. mem. Red River Improvement Corp., Clarksville, Tenn.; pres. Cmty. Services Orgn., Clarksville, Tenn., 1993—96, AAUP Austin Peay State U. Chpt., Clarksville, Tenn., 2000—03. Grantee Austin Peay State U. Tower grant, Austin Peay State U., 1989; fellow NIMH fellowship, NIMH, 1981—82. Mem.: Austin Peay State U. Faculty Senate (senator 1998—2002), Coun. on Social Work Edn. Accreditation Com. (licentiate; u. accreditation team insp. 1998—2003), AAUP (life; chpt. pres. 2000—03). Democrat-Npl. Unitarian Universalist. Office: Austin Peay State Univversity College St Clarksville TN 37040 Personal E-mail: stoddardp@apsu.edu.

STODDARD, ROBERT H., geography educator; b. Auburn, Nebr., Aug. 29, 1928; s. Hugh P. and Nainie L. (Robertson) S.; m. Sally E. Salisbury, Dec. 10, 1955; children: Martha, Andrew R., Hugh A. BA, Nebr. Wesleyan, Lincoln, 1950; MA, U. Nebr., 1960; PhD, U. Iowa, 1966. Instr. Nebr. Wesleyan, 1961-63, asst. prof., 1963-67, U. Nebr., Lincoln, 1967-71, assoc. prof., 1971-81, prof., 1981—2001. Vis. prof. Tribhuvan U., Kathmandu, Nepal, 1975-76, U. Colombo, Sri Lanka, 1986; inst. instr. Okla. State U., Stillwater, 1966; TV instr. Nebr. Ednl. TV Higher Edn., Lincoln, 1969; instr. Career Opportunity Program, Lincoln, 1973; dir. Geog. Edn. of Nebr., Lincoln, 1989-95. Author: Field Techniques, 1982; 1st author: Human Geography, 1986, 2d edit., 1989; editor and contbr.: Sacred Places, 1997. Mem. subcom. Lincoln-Lancaster Planning Com., 1974-78. Recipient Robert Stoddard award for Svc., Geography of Religion and Belief Systems, 2005. Mem. Assn. Am. Geographers, Nat. Coun. for Geog. Edn. (Disting. Tchg. Achievement award 1992). Democrat. Unitarian Universalist. Office: Univ Nebr Geog Program Lincoln NE 68583-6996 Business E-Mail: rstoddard1@unl.edu.

STODDARD, ROGER ELIOT, scholar; b. Boston, Dec. 2, 1935; s. Merton Edgar and Helen (Bonney) S.; m. Helen Louise Heckel, May 24, 1958; children: Alison Louise, Christopher Paine AB, Brown U., 1957. Asst. curator Harris Coll. Am. Poetry and Plays, Brown U., Providence, 1961-63, curator, 1963-65; asst. to librarian Harvard U. Houghton Library, Cambridge, Mass., 1958-61, asst. librarian, 1965-69, assoc. librarian, 1969-85, sr. curator, 1995—2004; curator rare books Harvard Coll. Library, Cambridge, Mass., 1985—2004; lectr. English Harvard U., Cambridge, Mass., 1984-86, sr. lectr., 1986—2004, assoc., 2004—. Faculty mem. Columbia U. Rare Book Sch., N.Y.C., 1984-85; sec. Friends of Harvard Coll. Libr., Cambridge, Mass., 1983-98. Author: Catalogue of Books & Pamphlets Unrecorded in Wegelin's Early American Poetry, 1969, The Houghton Library 1942-82, 1982, Poet & Printer in Colonial & Federal America, 1983, The Parkman Dexter Howe Library, part 1: Early New England Books, 1983, Marks in Books, Illustrated and Explained, 1985 (N.E. Book Show award, 1986, Am. Libr. Assn. award, 1987), Put a Resolute Hart to a Steep Hill: William Gowans Antiquary and Bookseller, 1990; editor: A Glance at Private Libraries, 1991, Edmond Jabès in Bibliography, 1998, 2001, John Laurent, Maine Painter: An Annotated Register of Paintings, Prints and Drawings, 2000, Julien Offray de La Mettrie, 1709-1751: A Bibliographical Inventory, 2001, A Library-Keeper's Business: Essays, 2002, Abundant Bibliophiles: Hubbard Winslow Bryant on the Private Libraries of Portland 1863-1864, 2004, Andrée Chedid, A Bibliography, 2006, Jacques-Charles Brunet, Le Grand Bibliographe, 2007, B.H.B. in Retrospect, Am. Trust for Brit. Libr., 2007, A Long Good bye to Library Service, 2008; contbr. articles to profl. jours. Mem. Records and Archives Com., Concord, Mass., 1985-87; bd. dirs. Louisa May Alcott Meml. Assn., Concord, 1983—2004. Huntington Library fellow, San Marino, Calif., 1978, 2005; W.F. Milton fellow Harvard U. Med. Sch., Boston, 1978-80; D.W. Bryant fellow Harvard U., 1992. Mem. Bibliog. Soc. Am. (coun. mem. 1982-88), Bibliography of Am. Lit. (supervisory com. chmn. 1982-91, pres. 1996-2000), Am. Antiquarian Soc. (coun. mem. 1989-93), Assn. Internat. de Bibliophilie, Baxter Soc. Portland, Colonial Soc. Mass. (corr. sec. 1993-97), Bibliog. Soc. London (hon. sec. for Am. 1992—), Bibliog. Soc. Va., Grolier Club (N.Y.C.), Harvard Club (N.Y.C.), Club of Odd Vols. Boston (exec. com. 1985-87), Soc. of Printers Boston, Phi Beta Kappa. Home: 9 Birchwood Ln Lincoln MA 01773-4907 Office: Harvard Univ Barker Ctr 12 Quincy St Cambridge MA 02138-6502

STODDARD, STEPHEN DAVIDSON, ceramics engineer, retired state senator; b. Everett, Wash., Feb. 8, 1925; s. Albert and Mary Louise (Billings) S.; m. Joann Elizabeth Burt, June 18, 1949 (dec. Oct. 1993); children: Dorcas Ann, Stephanie Kay; m. Barbara L. Seitz, Feb. 18, 1995. Student, Tacoma Coll., Wash., 1944, Conn. Coll., New London, 1946; BS, U. Ill., Urbana, 1950. Asst. prodn. supr., asst. ceramic engr. Coors Porcelain Co., Golden, Colo., 1950-52; ceramics-powder metallurgy sect. leader Los Alamos (N.Mex.) Sci. Lab., U. Calif., 1952-82; pres., treas. Materials Tech. Assocs., Inc., 1978-94; cons. Ceramic Age Mag., 1958-60; Cons. Nuclear Applications for Ceramic Materials, 1958-60; Jury commr. Los Alamos County, 1969; justice of peace, 1956-62; mem. Los Alamos Sch. Adv. Council, 1966; mcpl. judge Los Alamos, 1976—77; chmn. Los Alamos Ordinance Rev. Com., 1958; Mem. Republican County and State Central Com., 1955—; county commr. Los Alamos, N.Mex., 1966-68; mem. Los Alamos County Planning Commn., 1962-63, N.Mex. Senate, 1980-92. Bd. dir. Los Alamos Econ. Devel. Corp., 1982-99, U. N.Mex. Los Alamos Found.; mem. Los Alamos Pub. Sch. Found., 2006-, vice chmn., 2007-. Patentee in field. Bd. dirs. Los Amigos de Valles Caldera, 2006—; mem. Los Alamos Cmty.; vestryman Episcop. Ch., 1999—2002; emeritus mem. Los Amigos de Valles Caldera, 2007—, bd. mem. & vice pres., 2008—; bd. dirs. Sangre de Cristo coun. Girl Scouts U.S.A., 1965—71; N.Mex. chpt. Nature Conservancy, 1988—97, v.p., 1993—94, disting. trustee, 2001; bd. dirs. Southwestern Assn. on Indian Affairs, Inc., 1987—91, chmn., 2000—02; chmn. bd. dirs. Los Alamos Vis. Nurses, 1995—2004, 2006—; chmn. Gov.'s Commn. in Nat. and Cmty. Svc., 2001, Los Alamos County 50th Anniversary Com., 1998—99; trustee, vice chmn. Valles Caldera Nat. Preserve, 2000—02; mem. Los Alamos Edn. Group, 1995—. With AUS, 1943—46. Decorated Bronze Star, Purple Heart, Combat Infantry Badge; recipient disting. alumni award U. Ill. Coll. Engring., 1986, Leopold Conservation award N.Mex. Nature Conservancy, 1988, Cmty. Svc. award. Fellow Am. Inst. Chemists, Am. Ceramic Soc. (treas. 1972-74, pres. 1976-77, disting. life 1984); mem. Nat. Inst. Ceramic Engrs. (PACE award 1965, Greaves Walker award 1984), Am. Soc. Metals, N.Mex. Soc. Profl. Engrs. (Ingeniero Veterano de Neuvo Mejico award 1992), Los Alamos C. of C. (citizen of yr. award 1992, Living Treasure of Los Alamos 2000), Valles Caldera Nat. Preserve(v.p. 2001-02), Los Alamos Pub. Sch. Found.(v.p. 2004-07), Masons, Shriners (pres. 1994-95), Elks (dist. dep. grand exalted ruler 1968-69), Los Alamos Golf Assn. (dir. 1964-66), Am. Legion (nat. legis. coun. 1992-94), Kiwanis (pres. 1964, lt. gov. 1968-69), Sigma Xi, Alpha Tau Omega. Episcopalian. Home: 4557 Trinity Dr Los Alamos NM 87544-1862 E-mail: sbstoddard@msn.com.

STODDART, J(AMES) FRASER, chemistry professor, researcher; b. Edinburgh, May 24, 1942; widowed; 2 children. BSc, Edinburgh U., Scotland, 1964; PhD, Edinburgh U., 1966, DSc, 1980; DSc (hon.), Birmingham U., 2005, U. Twente, 2006; DSc, U. Sheffield, 2008, Trinity Coll. Dublin, 2009. Postgrad. student U. Edinburgh, Scotland, 1964-66; NRC postdoctoral fellow Queen's U., Kingston, Ont., Canada, 1967-70; Imperial Chem. Industries rsch. fellow U. Sheffield, England, 1970, lectr. in Chemistry, 1970—82, reader in Chemistry, 1982—91; sci. rsch. coun. sr. vis. fellow UCLA, 1978; rschr. ICI Corp. Lab., Runcorn, England, 1978-81; prof. Org. Chem. Birmingham U., England, 1990-97, hon. prof. chemistry, 1997—2002, chair organic chemistry, 1990, head Sch. Chem., 1993-97; Saul Winstein chair, organic chemistry UCLA, 1997—2003, Fred Kavil Chair Nanosystems Sciences, 2003—07; acting co-dir. Calif. NanoSystems Inst., 2002—03, bd. dir., 2000, dir., 2003—07; prof. chemistry, dir. Ctr. for Chemistry of Integrated Sys. Northwestern U., Evanston, Ill., 2008—. Vis. prof. Tex. A&M U., 1980, Messina U., Italy, 1985-87, Ecole Nationale Supérieure de Chemie de Mulhouse, 1987; invited lectr. in supramolecular and macromolecular sci.; hon. prof. East China U. Sci. and Tech. in Shanghai, 2005; Carnegie Centenary vis. professorship, U. Scotland, 2005; mem. scientific adv. bd. Ctr. for Nanoscale Sci. and Tech., Rice U. Mem. editl. adv. bd. Crystal Growth and Design, Journal Organic Chemistry, Organic Letters; mem. internat. adv. bd. Collection of Czechoslovak Chem. Communications, Angewandte Chemie; mem. editl. bd. Chemistry-A European Jour., Organic Letters; editor Royal Society of Chemistry Series of Monographs on Supramolecular Chemistry; contbr. a significant number of articles to profl. jours. Recipient Hope prize 1964, RSC Perkin Divsn. Career award 1980, 81, 82, Internat. Izatt-Christensen award in macrocyclic chemistry, 1993, Chaire Bruylants award, U. Louvaine-La-Neuve, Belgium, 1994, Adolf Steinhofer Found. award, 1995, Nagoya Gold Medal award in organic chemistry, 2004, Mack Meml. award, Ohio State U., 2006. Fusion award, U. Nev., 2006, King Faisal Internat. prize Sci. King Faisal Found., Tetrahedron prize for creativity in organic chemistry, 2007, Feynman prize for nanotech., 2007, Albert Einstein award of sci., 2007; Leverhulme rsch. fellow, 1988-89, Humboldt Fellowship, 1998; named Alumnus of Yr., U. Endinburgh, 2005, Knight Bachelor, 2007. Fellow Royal Soc. Edinburgh (hon.), Royal Soc. Chem., German Acad. Natural Scis., AAAS, Sci. Divsn. Royal Netherlands Acad. Arts and Sciences, Royal Soc. (London) (Davy medal, 2008); mem. Chem. Soc.(Carbohydrate Chemistry award, 1978), Am. Chem. Soc. (Arthur C. Cope Scholar award, 1999, Arthur C. Cope award, 2008). Achievements include being co-creator of the world's densest memory circuit in 2007. Office: Northwestern U Dept Chemistry 2145 Sheridan Rd, #K148 Evanston IL 60208-3113 Office Phone: 847-491-3793. Office Fax: 847-491-1009. Business E-Mail: stoddart@northwestern.edu.

STODDART, VERONICA GOULD, travel editor; b. Bogotá, Colombia, Nov. 1, 1948; d. Juan Benedict Gould and Rose Arlene (Wall) Rodman; married (div. Jan. 1995); children: Shauna Irene, Kyra Theresa, Kristin Anna. BA, Wellesley Coll., 1970. Stringer Time-Life News Svc., Niamey, Niger, West Africa, 1970-71; rsch. asst. Harvard U., Cambridge, Mass., 1971-72; publs. asst. Ptnrs. of the Americas, Washington, 1973-74; assoc. editor Americas Mag., OAS, Washington, 1974-82, travel and art editor, 1982-85; contract editor Nat. Geographic Soc., Washington, 1985-86; editor-in-chief Caribbean Travel & Life, Inc., Silver Spring, Md., 1986-97; contbg. editor Capital Style, Washington, 1988; former leisure travel editor USA Today, dep, mng. editor travel. Guest faculty mem. SATW Inst. for Travel Writing and Photography, 2006, now faculty mem.; spkr. in field. Recipient Publishing Excellence award, Mag. Week, 1991, Marcia Vickery-Wallace award for Excellence in Travel Journalism, 1996, Westin award, N.Am. Travel Journalists Assn., 1996. Mem. Am. Soc. Mag. Editors, Soc. Am. Travel Writers (Ben Carruthers award 1986, Lowell Thomas award 1984, 88, 89, 90, 91, 92, 93), Soc. Profl. Journalists. Avocations: travel, collecting folk art, photography. Office: USA Today 7950 Jones Branch Dr Mc Lean VA 22108

STODOLA, MARK ALLEN, Mayor, Little Rock, Arkansas, former prosecutor; b. Mpls., May 18, 1949; s. Robert Allen and Elizabeth (Abeler); m. Jo Ellen Stodola; children: Allison, Robert, John Mark. BA in Journalism and Polit. Sci., U. Iowa, 1971; JD, U. Ark., 1974. Bar: Ark. 1974, US Dist. Ct. (we. and ea. dists.) Ark. 1975, US Ct. Appeals (8th cir.). Assoc. Givens & Buzbee, Little Rock, 1974-75; dep. pub. defender Pulaski County, Little Rock, 1975-76; pub. defender City of North Little Rock, Ark., 1976-85; ptnr. Stodola & Smith, North Little Rock, 1976-85; city atty. City of Little Rock, Ark., 1985—90, prosecuting atty., 1990—96, mayor, 2007—. Instr. criminal justice U. Ark., Little Rock, 1976—85; lectr. in Argentina & Russia Nat. Dist. Atty. Assn. Mem. exec. com. Dem. State Com., Little Rock, 1976—, Dem. Nat. Com., Washington, 1981—83; nat. pres. Young Dems. Am., Washington, 1981—83; vol. Big Brothers & Big Sisters; bd. mem. Ark. Repertory Theatre; pres. Quapaw Quarter Assn., Hist. Preservation Alliance of Ark.; mem. Heights Neighborhood Assn. 2nd lt. USAFR, 1969—74. Mem.: Internat. Mcpl. Lawyers Assn. (former chmn.), Ark. City Atty. Assn. (former pres.), Ark. Pros. Atty. Assn. (former pres.), Nat. Dist. Attys. Assn. (former v.p.), Am. Trial Lawyers Assn., Nat. Inst. Mcpl. Law Officers, Pulaski Bar Assn. (Lawyer's award 1981), Ark. Bar Assn., ABA, Rotary. Avocations: rugby, hist. preservation. Office: City Hall 500 W Makham Rm 203 Little Rock AR 72201 Home Phone: 501-666-6630; Office Phone: 501-371-4510, 501-371-4791. Office Fax: 501-371-4498. Business E-Mail: mayor@littlerock.org, mstodola@castlaw.com.

STOEBE, THOMAS GAINES, materials science educator; b. Upland, Calif., Apr. 26, 1939; s. Wallace Theodore and Martha Thomas (Gaines) S.; m. Jessica Rae Trout, June 20, 1959 (div. Jan. 1981); children: Brian, Paul, Diane; m. Janet Eleanor Dumm, Aug. 7, 1982. BS, Stanford U., 1961, MS, 1963, PhD, 1965. Instr. Imperial Coll., London, Eng., 1965-66; from asst. to assoc. prof. U. Wash., Seattle, 1966-75, prof., 1975—2001, assoc. dean, 1982-87, chmn. dept. materials sci. and engring., 1987-96, prof. emeritus, 2001—. Vis. prof. U. Sao Paulo, Brazil, 1972-73; fellow USAF Materials Lab., Wright-Patterson AFB, Ohio, 1975; dir. materials and mfg. Wash. Tech. Ctr., 1992-2001, pres. Materials Edn. Assoc., 2001-. Patentee direct response dosimeter system; contbr. numerous tech. articles to profl. jours. Bd. dirs. Wash. Math., Engring., Sci. Achievement Program, Seattle, 1984-94. Spl. fellow Atomic Energy Commn. Fellow Am. Soc. for Metals Internat. (chmn. found. bd. 2004-06, George Roberts award 2006); mem. Am. Soc. Engring. Edn. (Young Faculty award 1972, Western Electric award 1977), Materials Rsch. Soc., Metall. Soc. (chmn. No. Pacific sect. 1973), Am. Ceramic Soc. Home: 1004 Commercial Ave #136 Anacortes WA 98221 Office Phone: 425-890-4652. Personal E-mail: tgstoebe@earthlink.net. Business E-Mail: stoebe@u.washington.edu.

STOEBUCK, WILLIAM BREES, law educator; b. Wichita, Mar. 18, 1929; s. William Douglas and Donice Beth (Brees) S.; m. Mary Virginia Fields, Dec. 24, 1951; children: Elizabeth, Catherine, Caroline. BA, Wichita State U., 1951; MA, Ind. U., 1953; JD, U. Wash., 1959; SJD, Harvard U., 1973. Bar: Wash. 1959, US Supreme Ct. 1967. Pvt. practice, Seattle, 1959—64; asst. prof. law U. Denver, 1964—67; assoc. prof. U. Wash., Seattle, 1967—70, prof., 1970—95, Judson Falknor prof., 1995—99, prof. emeritus, 1999—; of counsel Karr, Tuttle, Campbell, Seattle, 1988—. Vis. prof. Hastings Coll. Law, 1987, Wash. & Lee U., 1979—80; guest lectr. U. Tubingen, 1996; spkr., cons. in field. Author: Washington Real Estate: Property Law, 1995, 2d edit., 2004, Washington Real Estate: Transactions, 1995, 2d edit., 2004, Basic Property Law, 1989, Law of Property, 1984, 3d edit., 2000, Nontrespassory Takings, 1977, Contemporary Property, 1996, 3d edit., 2008; contbr. articles to profl. jours. Bd. dirs. Cascade Symphony Orch., 1978-83, Forest Park Libr., 1975-80; ch. elder, congregational pres.; mem. City Lake Forest Pk. Planning Commn., 2008-. 1st lt. USAF, 1951—56. Mem. Pacific Real Estate Inst., Am. Coll. Real Estate Lawyers, Wash. State Bar Assn., Assn. Am. Law Schs., Order of Coif, Seattle Yacht Club. Republican. Presbyterian. Avocations: baroque music, boating, history. Home: 3515 NE 158th Pl Lk Forest Park WA 98155-6649 Office: Sch Law Univ Washington William H Gates Hall Seattle WA 98195-3020 Home Phone: 206-362-1621; Office Phone: 206-543-4917. Business E-Mail: stoebuck@u.washington.edu.

STOECKEL, LUKE EDWARD, psychologist, researcher; s. James and Susan Buck Stoeckel. AB, Harvard Coll., Cambridge, Mass., 2001; attending, U. Ala., Birmingham, 2003—. Clin. fellow psychology Harvard Med. Sch. Mass. Gen. Hosp., Boston, 2008—. Recipient Rsch. Tng. award, NIH, 2007, Travel award, 2008, Dean's Outstanding Grad. Student award, UAB, 2008; fellow Merit fellowship, 2006. Mem.: Soc. Neurosci., Orgn. Human Brain Mapping, Psi Chi.

STOECKER, DAVID THOMAS, retired banker; b. St. Louis, June 8, 1939; s. John Garth and Marie (Zahler) S.; m. Ann E. Conrad, Aug. 18, 1962; children— Lisa Ann, Susan Jane. BS, Ind. U., 1963. Sr. v.p. comml. loans Mercantile Trust Co. N.Am., St. Louis, 1965-80; pres. Gravois-Merc. Bank, St. Louis, 1980-87; pres., chief exec. officer Bank of South County, St. Louis, 1987-95; chmn. bd., CEO Ctrl. West End Bank, St. Louis, 1996—2006; ret., 2006. Served to 1st lt. AUS, 1963—65. Mem.: Robert Morris Assocs. (pres. St. Louis 1980), Sunset Country Club. Presbyterian. Office: 415 Debaliviere Saint Louis MO 63112

STOECKER, WILLIAM VAN, physician, computer scientist; b. St. Louis, Mar. 18, 1946; s. William Clayton and Mary Eugenia (Gaunt) S.; m. Ruth Carl, May 21, 1977; children: Charles, Will, John. BS, Calif. Inst. Tech., 1968; MS, UCLA, 1970; MD, U. Mo., Columbia, 1977. Adj. asst. prof. computer sci. U. Mo., Rolla, 1985—; v.p. Sulzberger Inst., Schaumburg, Ill., 1994—. Editor: Computer Apple Dermatology, 1993; inventor liquid lance. Cubmaster Cub Scouts Am., Rolla, 1989—. Me. Internat. Soc. Digital Imaging (pres. 1995-97). Office: 1100 W 10th St Rolla MO 65401-2937

STOELINGA, MARK THEODORE, meteorologist, educator; s. Jack Matthew and Corry Stoelinga; m. Amy Marie Locatelli, July 6, 1991; children: Anna Elizabeth, Luke James Matthew. BS, U. Ill., Urbana, 1987; PhD, U. Wash., Seattle, 1993. Post-doc. rsch. assoc. Pa. State U., Univ. Park, 1993—94; vis. scientist Nat. Ctr. Atmospheric Rsch., Boulder, Colo., 1994—95; rsch. meteorologist U. Wash., Seattle, 1995—2002, rsch. prof., 2002—. Instr. Seattle Maritime Acad., 1998. Contbr. to profl. jours. Mem.: Am. Meteorol. Soc. (Editor's Award 2006). Roman Catholic. Achievements include design of RIP software package. Avocation: travel. Home: 3835 37th Ave SW Seattle WA 98126 Office: Univ Wash Box 351640 Seattle WA 98195

STOELTJE, BEVERLY JUNE, liberal studies educator; b. Rotan, Tex., Apr. 1, 1940; d. Roger Caswell and Laura Inez (Kennedy) Smith; children: Gretchen, Rachael; m. Richard Bauman, Nov. 26, 1977; children: Mark, Andrew. BA, U. Tex., 1961, MA, 1975, PhD, 1979. Asst. prof. English U. Tex., Austin, 1983-86; assoc. prof. anthropology, folklore/ethnomusicology Ind. U., Bloomington, 1986—2008, mem. Am. studies faculty, 1986—, mem. African studies faculty, 1989—; prof., anthropology, folklore/ethnomusicology Indiana U., 2008—. Cons. S.W. Ednl. Devel. Lab., Austin, 1976, Tex. Women's History Project, San Antonio, 1981; dir. Folk Arts Survey Tex., Austin, 1977, 78; dir. USIA linkage performance Ind. U. and U. Ghana, 1989-93; assoc. dir. Ind. Ctr. Global Change World Peace, 1994-95. Author: Children's Handclaps, 1979; editor: (with C.B. Cohen and R. Wilk) Beauty Queens on the Global Stage, 1996; editor (essay collection) Feminist Revision in Folklore Studies, 1988, Women, Language, and Law in Africa, 2002; contbr. articles to profl. jours. and chpts. in books. Fulbright rsch. fellow Ghana, 1989-90; grantee Tex. Commn. for Humanities, 1980; Weatherhead scholar Sch. Am. Rsch., 1997-98. Mem. African Studies Assn., Am. Folklore Soc. (exec. bd. 1981-84), Am. Anthropol. Assn., Law and Soc. Office: Dept Anthropology Student Bldg Ind U Bloomington IN 47405 Business E-Mail: stoeltje@indiana.edu.

STOERI, WILLIAM R., lawyer; b. 1955; BA in History and Phil. summa cum laude, Kalamazoo Coll., 1978; student, U. Erlangen, Nurenberg, Germany, 1978—79; JD, Yale U., 1982. Bar: Minn. 1982. Law clerk, Hon. Diana E. Murphy US Dist. Ct., Minn. Dist., 1982—84; assoc. Dorsey & Whitney LLP, Mpls., 1984—89, ptnr., trial dept., 1990—, and co-chair, profl. malpractice group. Mem.: Phi Beta Kappa. Office: Dorsey & Whitney LLP Ste 1500 50 S Sixth St Minneapolis MN 55402-1498 Office Phone: 612-343-7942. Office Fax: 612-340-8800. Business E-Mail: stoeri.bill@dorsey.com.

STOESSINGER, JOHN GEORGE, political science professor; b. Vienna, Oct. 14, 1927; arrived in US, 1947; s. Oscar and Irene Stoessinger; m. Carolyn Stoessinger, 1966 (div. 1985); children: Richard Victor (dec.), Anna. BA, Grinnell Coll., 1950, LLB (hon.), 1970; MA, Harvard U., 1952, PhD, 1954; LLB (hon.), Am. Coll. in Switzerland, Leysin, 1981; LHD (hon.), Drury U., 2007. Prof. polit. scis. CUNY, NYC, 1957-83; dir. polit. affairs divsn. UN, NYC, 1967-74; disting. prof. internat. affairs Trinity U., San Antonio, 1983-2000; disting. prof. global diplomacy U. San Diego, 2000—. Teaching fellow Harvard U., Cambridge, Mass., 1952-54; asst. prof. polit. sci. Wellesley Coll., Mass., 1954-56; vis. prof. internat. affairs Columbia U., NYC, 1963-67, Princeton U., NJ, 1978. Author: The Might of Nations, 1962, 10th edit., 2000 (Bancroft prize 1963), Nations at Dawn, 1979, 6th edit., 1996, Henry Kissinger, 1979, Why Nations Go To War, 1983, 10th edit., 2007. Active UNA-USA, NY, 1960—. Mem. Coun. on Fgn. Rels. (book rev. editor Fgn. Affairs 1968-78). Jewish. Avocation: classical music. Office: U San Diego 5998 Alcala Park San Diego CA 92110 Home: 1337 Neptune Ave Encinitas CA 92024 Office Phone: 760-632-8682. Personal E-mail: johngstoessinger@cox.net.

STOFF, MICHAEL B., history professor; b. NYC, May 12, 1947; s. Laurence Wallace and Jean Stoff; m. Raquel Schuster, Aug. 2, 2008; children: Molly, Benjamin, Deborah Herr, Ilana Herr, David Herr. PhD, Yale Universtiy, New Haven, 1977. Assoc. prof. history U. Tex., Austin, 1979—. Dir. Plan II Honors Program, U. Tex., 2006—. Author: (monograph) Oil, War, and American Security; co-author: (textbook) Nation of Nations: A Narrative History of the American Republic; co-editor: (documentary narrative) The Manhattan Project: A Documentary Introduction to the Atomic Age, (series) The Oxford New Narratives in American History; co-author: (textbook) America, A History of Our Nation, The American Nation. With US Army, 1970, Long Island, New York. Decorated Army Commendation Medal US Army; recipient Friars Centennial Tchg. award, Friars Soc., U. Tex., 1996, Silver Spurs Tchg. Excellence Award, U. Tex., 2000, Acad. Disting. Tchrs., 2002, Disting. Lectr., Orgn. Am. Historians, 2008. Office: History Dept Univ Tex 1 Univ Sta (B-7000) Austin TX 78712 Business E-Mail: mbstoff@mail.utexas.edu.

STOFFEL, PAUL T., investment company executive; m. Gayle Stoffel. MBA, Harvard Bus. Sch. Various positions to bd. dirs. Centex Corp.; chmn. Triple S Capital Corp., Paul Stoffel Investments. Bd. dirs. Holly Corpn., Dallas, 2001—. Co-founder Gayle and Paul Stoffel Found.; bd. mem. Dallas Symphony Orch., Southwestern Med. Found., Zale Lipshy Hosp., St. Paul U. Hosp.; bd. dirs. Dallas Symphony Assn., Dallas Symphony Found. Named one of Top 200 Collectors, ARTnews mag., 2005—08. Mailing: 5949 Sherry Ln Ste 1465 Dallas TX 75225

STOFFEL, ROBERT E., delivery service executive; B in Bus. Mgmt., U. Ill. Joined UPS, Atlanta, Guam, 1975, ops. mgr., indsl. engring. mgr., v.p. quality, v.p. transp. process mgr., sr. v.p., COO logistics group, 2000—02, pres. supply chain solutions, 2002—03, sr. v.p. supply chain group. mem. mgmt. com., 2004—. Office: UPS 55 Glendale Pky Atlanta GA 30328*

STOFFEL, SHELLEY L., library media specialist; BA, Rosary Hill, Buffalo, NY, 1975; MLS, SUNY, Buffalo, 1977. Cert. sch. libr. media specialist SUNY, 1977, pub. libr. State of NY, 1977. Libr. media specialist Buffalo Pub. Schs., 1976—80; part-time libr. I Buffalo and Erie County Pub. Librs., 1977—2004; libr. media specialist William St. Sch., Lancaster, NY, 2003—. Active preschool and toddler time story hours Elma, Lancaster, Depew Librs., Buffalo, 1985—2004; Battle of the Books coach Elma Pub. Libr., NY, 1998—2004; storyteller Iroquois Boys and Girls' Club, Elma, 2000—04. Author: Titanic Survivor, 2005—06, Life in a Castle: Magical or Not, 2005—06, Fairy Tales, 2006—07, Its Not Greck to Me, 2007—08, Give Peace A Chance: World Peace Conf, 2008—09. Dir. music Vacation Bible Sch. Marilla Meth. Ch., NY, 1988—2005. Grantee, Lancaster Ctrl. Schs., 2005, 2005, 2006; grants, 2007, 5 mini grants, Lang. Sch. Mem.: NY Libr. Assn., Sch. Librs. Assn. Western NY, Kappa Delta Pi (life), Lambda Iota Tau (life), Delta Epsilon Sigma (life), Phi Beta Mu (life). Methodist. Avocations: quilting, reading, sewing, singing, crafts. Office: William Street School Media Center 5201 William St Lancaster NY 14086 Office Phone: 716-686-3815. Business E-Mail: sstoffel@lancaster.wnyric.org.

STOFFEL, VIRGINIA CARROLL, occupational therapist, educator; d. Thomas Pershing and Gertrude Carroll; m. Robert Stoffel, May 28, 1977; children: Brian Carroll, Eric Carroll, Adam Carroll. Ph.D. in Leadership Advancement Learning and Svc., Cardinal Stritch U., Fox Point, Wis., 2007. Cert. occupl. therapist State Wis., 2009. Occupl. therapist to mgr. DePaul Hosp., Milw., 1978—90; assoc. prof. U. Wis.-Milw., chair, grad. coord., 1987—. V.p. Am. Occupl. Therapy Assn., Bethesda, Md., 2009. Chair bd. Mental Health Am. Wis., 2006—08. Fellow: Am. Occupl. Therapy. Office: Univ Wis-Milw PO Box 413 Milwaukee WI 53201 Office Phone: 414-229-5583. Business E-Mail: stoffelv@uwm.edu.

STOFFER, DAVID STEWART, mathematics and statistics educator, research, consultant; b. Bklyn., June 21, 1950; s. Benjamin and Rose (Mendeloff) S.; m. Janice Singh, June 28, 1980; 1 child, Matthew Mohon. B.A., San Diego State U., 1975; Ph.D., U. Calif.-Davis, 1982. Asst. prof. math. and stats. U. Pitts., 1982—; statis. cons. Western Psychiat. Inst. and Clinic, Pitts., 1984—. Recipient Research award Earle C. Anthony Fund U. Calif., 1980-81; Faculty of Arts and Scis. U. Pitts. grantee, 1983. Mem. Am. Statis. Assn., Inst. Math. Stats., Ctr. Multivariate Analysis. Jewish. Avocation: guitar. Office: U Pitts Dept Math and Stats Pittsburgh PA 15260

STOFFLE, CARLA JOY, university library dean; b. Pueblo, Colo., June 19, 1943; d. Samuel Bernard and Virginia Irene (Berry) Hayden; m. Richard William Stoffle, June 12, 1964; children: Brent William, Kami Ann. AA, So. Colo. State Coll., Pueblo, 1963; BA, U. Colo., 1965; MLS, U. Ky., 1969; postgrad., U. Wis., 1980. Head govt. publ. dept. John G. Crabbe Library, Eastern Ky. U., Richmond, 1969-72; from head pub. svcs. to asst. chancellor edn. svcs. U. Wis. Parkside Libr., Kenosha, 1972—85; dep. dir. U. Mich. Libr., Ann Arbor, 1986—91; prof. libr. sci. U. Ariz., Tucson, 1991—, dean librs. and Ctr. for Creative Photography, 1991—, acting dir. Sch. Info. Resources and Libr. Sci., 1999—2001. Adv. bd. Bowker Librs., NY, 1985—90; bd. dirs. Trejo Foster Found., 2000—; state adv. com. Ariz. State Dept. of Libr. Archives and Pub. Records, 2000—; adv. com. U. Mich. Sch. Libr. Sci., 1986—92, OCLC Rsch. Librs., 1995—2000. Co-author: Administration of Government Documents Collection, 1974, Materials and Method for History Research, 1979, Materials and Methods for Political Science Research, 1979; mem. editl. bd. The Collection Bldg., 1978—95, The Bottom Line, 1989—95, Internet and Higher Edn., 1998—99, The Univ. Ariz. Press, 1992—. Vol. Peace Corps, Barbados, West Indies, 1965—67; mem. bd. Pima County Pub. Libr., 2004—; mem. bd. libr. examiners Ariz. State Libr. Recipient Pres.'s award, Ariz. Ednl. Media Assn., 1993, YWCA Tucson Outstanding Woman of 1992: A Woman on the Move award, 1992, Ariz. Libr. of Yr. award, 2000, Dir.'s award for Outstanding Svc., Sch. Info. Resources Libr. Sci., 2006; named Outstanding Alumnus, Coll. Libr. and Info. Sci., U. Ky., 1989. Mem.: ALA (councilor 1983—93, exec. bd. dirs. 1985—93, treas. 1988—93, endowment trustee 1988—93, endowment campaign com. 1989—93, pres. adv. com. 1993—96, legis. com. 1994—96, nominations com. 1997, Lippincott award com. 1997, spectrum scholarship com. 1998—2002, endowment trustee 2001—, chair com. accreditation 2002—04, libr. and outreach svcs. adv. com. 1997-99, chair 1997-98, Miriam Dudley Bibliographic Instrn. Libr. of Yr. award 1991, Acad. Rsch. Libr. of Yr. 1992, Elizabeth Futas Catalyst for Change award 2002, Equality award 2003, Loleta Fyan award Jury 2003—04), Greater Western Libr. Alliance (incoming chair 2006—), Ctr. Rsch. Librs. (budget and fin. com. 1994—2001, exec. com., bd. dirs. 1998—, treas. 1999—2000, vice chair, bd. dirs. 2001—03, chair, bd. dirs. 2003), Ariz. State Libr. Assn., Assn. Coll. Rsch. Librs. (bd. dirs. 1978—84, mem. exec. com. 1981—84, pres. 1982—83, planning com. 1993—95, chair nat. conf. planning com. 1995—97), Assn. Rsch. Librs. (com. stats. and measurement 1994—2003, bd. dirs. 1997—2001, mem. steering com. Scholarly Pub. and Acad. Resource Coalition 1998—2001, mem. govt. documents digitization project work group 2004—, bd. dirs. info. policies com. 2004—). Office: U Arizona Main Libr 1510 E University Blvd Tucson AZ 85721-0055 Office Phone: 520-621-2101. E-mail: stofflec@u.library.arizona.edu.

STOHL, SHARON ALINE, art therapist; b. Alameda, Calif., June 29, 1951; d. Richard LeRoy Stohl and Jacqueline Louise McGrew; children: Sean Parish, Jamison Shepherd, Allison Pepper Smith. AA in Gen. Studies, Reedley Coll., 1988; B Liberal Arts, Calif. State U., Fresno, 1992; MA in Art Therapy, MA in Marriage and Family Therapy, Notre Dame de Namur U., 1995. Clin. therapist Atascadero (Calif.) State Hosp. for Criminally Insane, 1996—98, Juvenile Assessment Ctr., Wasilla, Alaska, 2000—01, Vols. Am., Anchorage, 2001—02; clin. therapist long-term treatment ctr. North Star Behavioral Health Sys., Anchorage, 2002—. Mural, art bldg. Deedley Coll., 1988, exhibited in group shows at Deedley Fiesta Art Show, 1988. Clin. art therapist Green Rehab. Hosp., Pacifica, Calif., 1994; vol. therapist with rehab. patients, elderly, AIDS patients; mem. Pink Ladies Breast Cancer Survival Support Group, 2004—. Mem.: Alpha Gamma Sigma. Roman Catholic. Avocations: travel, painting, reading. Office: North Star Residential Treatment Ctr 1650 S Bragon Anchorage AK 99508 E-mail: sallysgt@aol.com.

STOHLMAN, CONNIE SUZANNE, neonatal intensive care unit nurse, obstetrical gynecological nurse; b. Tucson, Sept. 27, 1960; d. Irvin Wendell and Betty Jo (Stewart) Holmes; m. Bruce R. Stohlman, Sept. 14, 1991. BSN, Bishop Clarkson Coll. Nursing, 1987; BA, U. Nebr., 1982; cert. med. asst., Omaha Coll. Health Careers, 1983. Primary nurse I U. Md. Med. System, Balt., 1987-90; staff nurse ob-gyn and neonatal ICU Creighton U. Med. Ctr., Omaha, 1990. Mem. quality assurance task force U. Md. Med. System, 1987-90; mem. quality assurance com. St. Joseph Hosp., 1992-96. Named to Outstanding Young Women of Am., 1986.

STOIBER, CARLTON RAY, nuclear law consultant, freelance/self-employed cartoonist; b. Vallejo, Calif., July 5, 1942; s. Raymond F. and Grace Stoiber; m. Susanne Alexander, Sept. 10, 1966. BA summa cum laude, U. Colo., 1964, JD, 1969; LLM, U. London, 1975; diploma cum laude, Hague Acad. Internat. Law, 1975. Bar: Colo. 1969, DC 1970, US Supreme Ct. 1973. Atty. US Dept. Justice, Washington, 1969-71, dir. Office of Indian Rights, 1972-74; asst. gen. counsel US NRC, Washington, 1975-80, US Arms Control and Disarmament Agy., Washington, 1980-81; dir. Office Nuclear Export Control US Dept. State, Washington, 1981-85, dir. Office Nuclear Non-Proliferation Policy, 1988-91, dir. Office Nuclear Tech. and Safeguards, 1991-93; counselor US Mission to UN Agys., Vienna, 1985-88; dir. Internat. Programs USNRC, 1993-99; cons., lectr. Internat. Sch. Nuc. Law U., Mont Pellier, France, 2001—; cartoonist Issues in Sci. & Tech., 2000—. Rhodes scholar, 1964, Norlin award for disting. achievement U. Colo., 1994. Mem. Am. Soc. Internat. Law, Internat. Nuc. Law Assn., Am. Assn.; Editl. Cartoonists, Phi Beta Kappa. Avocations: mountain climbing, birding. Personal E-mail: crstoiber@earthlink.net.

STOIBER, KAREN CALLAN, psychologist, educator; b. Milw. d. James Henry and Dolores B. Callan; m. Gregory Robert Stoiber; children: Lucas Callan, Leah Callan, Zachary Callan, Andrew Callan. PhD, U. Wis., Madison, 1988. Prof. U. Wis., Milw., 1992—, sch. psychology tng. dir., 2007—. Project dir. Exemplary Model of Early Reading Growth and Excellence, Milw., 2004—. Contbr. articles to profl. jour. Early Reading First grant, US Dept. Edn., 2004, 2007. Mem.: NASP (assoc. editor 2007—08), APA (v.p. divsn. 16 social, responsibility, ethics, & ethnic minority 2006—). Democrat. Roman Catholic. Avocations: yoga, exercise, travel. Office: Univ Wis-Milw Ednl Psych 2400 E Hartford Ave Milwaukee WI 53211 Office Fax: 414-229-4939. Business E-Mail: kstoiber@uwm.edu.

STOIBER, SUSANNE A., health science association administrator; m. Carlton R. Stoiber. BA, MPA, U. Colo.; MSc, London Sch. Econs. Principal analyst for health care fin. programs Congressional Budget Office; adminstr. of clinical research Nat. Inst. of Health; dir. divsn. soc. and econ. studies NRC US Dept. HHS, 1990-94, dep. asst. sec. for health, planning and evaluation, 1979, 1995—96, dep. asst. sec. for health, health promotion and disease prevention, 1996, dep. asst. sec. for planning and evaluation, program sys., 1997—98; exec. officer Inst. Medicine, 1998—2007; prin. Striba Health Policy, LLC, Washington. Spkr. in field. Contbr. several articles to profl. jours. Recipient Secretary's Disting. Svc. award, 1979, 1981, 1997, Dirs. award, NIH, 1985, Presdl. Rank Award for lifetime achievement in Senior Exec. Svc., 1998. Office Phone: 202-966-7793. E-mail: s.stoiber@earthlink.net.

STOJAKOVIC, DEJAN, metallurgist, researcher; b. Subotica, Vojvodina, Serbia, Apr. 13, 1974; s. Milan and Ljubica Stojakovic; m. Angelina Stojakovic; 1 child, Filip. BS, U. Novi Sad, Serbia, 2000; PhD,

Drexel U., Phila., 2008. Tchg. and rsch. asst. U. Novi Sad, Vojvodina, Serbia and Montenegro, 2000—03; tchg. and rsch. asst. lab mgr. Drexel U., Phila., 2003—08; R & D scientist Williams Advanced Materials, Brewster, NY, 2008—. Exhibitions include Improvement of Magnetic Properties in Iron-Silicon Electrical Steel for Highly Efficient AC Motors (Best Poster award, 2005); author: (book) A Multistep Processing of Fe-Si Steel: Recovery of Preferred Texture and Optimum Grain Size. Recipient Excellence in Tchg. award, Drexel U., 2006, Excellence in Sci. award, Am. Assn. Advanced Sci., 2007, Rsch. Travel award, Office Grad. Studies, Drexel U., 2007. Mem.: Materials Advantage (TMS, ASM Internat., AIST, ACerS). Achievements include development of a multistage processing for recovery of preferred texture and optimum grain size in electrical steel. Home: 137 Deer Hill Ave Danbury CT 06810 Office: Williams Advanced Materials 42 Mt Ebo Rd S Brewster NY 10509 Personal E-mail: dejan@drexel.edu.

STOJAKOVIC, PEJA, professional basketball player; b. Slavoska Pozega, Croatia, June 9, 1977; s. Miodrag and Branka Stojakovic. Profl. basketball player YUBA League Crvena Zvezda Beograd, 1992—94, PAOK Thessaloniki, Greece, 1994—98; draft pick Sacramento Kings, 1996, forward, 1998—2006, Ind. Pacers, 2006, New Orleans Hornets, 2006—. Founder Peja Stojakovic Children's Found. Named to Western Conf. All-Star Team, NBA, 2002—04. Achievements include leading the NBA in free throw percentage (.927) and 3-point field goals (240), 2003-04. Office: New Orleans Hornets 1250 Poydras St Fl 19 New Orleans LA 70113*

STOJKOVIC, DEJAN B., physicist, educator; b. Vranje, Serbia-Montenegro, Feb. 4, 1971; arrived in US, 1997; s. Borivoje and Borka Stojkovic; m. Andrijana Stojkovic, May 5, 1998; children: Dejana, Natalia. BSc, U. Belgrade, 1994, MSc, 1997; PhD, Case Western Res. U., Cleve., 2001. Killam Meml. postdoctoral fellow U. Alta., Edmonton, Canada, 2001—03; Mich. Ctr. Theoretical Physics postdoctoral fellow U. Mich., Ann Arbor, 2003—05; asst. prof. Case Western Res. U., 2005—, Dept. Physics, SUNY, Buffalo. Recipient Spl. award, City Coun., Vranje, 2002, Astor award, Oxford U.; fellow Serbian (Yugoslav) Ministry of Sci.; scholar Case Western Res. U., 1997—2001. Achievements include research in theoretical physics (cosmology, particle physics, gravity, field theory, extra dimensions, topological defects). Avocations: philosophy, swimming, travel. Office: Dept Physics SUNY Buffalo NY 14260 Business E-Mail: dbs3@case.edu, DS77@buffalo.edu.

STOJKOVIC, DUSAN, lawyer; b. Zemun, Yugoslavia, Apr. 26, 1976; s. Sava and Dragica (Filip) Stojkovic. BA, Bernard M. Baruch Coll., 1997; JD, Harvard Law Sch., 2000. Bar: NY 2001. Assoc. LeBoeuf, Lamb, Greene & MacRae, L.L.P., NYC, 2000—05, Simmons & Simmons, London, 2005—. Mem. Sierra Club, NYC, 1995—2004. Belle Zeller scholar, CUNY, 1996. Avocations: travel, writing on-line film reviews, rock concerts. Office Fax: 011-44-20-7628-2070. Business E-Mail: dusan.stojkovic@simmons-simmons.com.

STOKER, DAVID ALLEN, plastic surgeon; b. Miami, Fla., July 6, 1969; BA/BS in Biology and Polit. Sci. (grad. with honors), Stanford U., 1991; MD, U. Calif. Sch. Medicine, San Francisco, 1995. Diplomate Am. Bd. Plastic Surgery, lic. Calif. and NY. Intern, plastic surgery NYU Med. Ctr., 1995—96, resident, general surgery, 1996—99, resident, plastic surgery, Inst. Reconstructive Plastic Surgery, 1999—2000, chief resident, plastic surgery, Inst. Reconstructive Plastic Surgery, 2000—01; med. staff St. Johns Health Ctr., Santa Monica, Calif., 2001—, UCLA Med. Ctr., Calif., 2001—, Centinela Hosp. Med. Ctr., 2001—, Marina Outpatient Surgery Ctr., 2001—, Daniel Freeman Marina Hosp., 2001—; plastic surgeon in private practice Marina Plastic Surgery Associates, Marina Del Ray, Calif., 2001—; clin. asst. prof. surgery Keck Sch. Medicine, U. So. Calif., 2006—. Teaches course: Liposuction: Comprehensive and Integrated Am. Soc. Plastic Surgeons, 2006, Am. Soc. for Aesthetic Plastic Surgery, 2007; rsch. experience at various institutions, 1985—2006; presenter in field. Contbr. articles to profl. jours.; author: (textbook) Chpt. on Liposuction and Body Contouring; plastic surgery expert Dr. Phil, featured on Learning Channel and Discovery Health Channel. Recipient 1st Place, Plastic Surgery Educational Found., 1993, British Journal Surgery award, 1999; named one of Top Plastic Surgeons in the nation with spl. mention about experience in liposuction, tummy tucks and breast surgery, NY Times, NY Times Style Mag., 2005; Howard Hughes Med. Inst. Major Grant for Undergrad. Rsch., 1991. Fellow: Am. Coll. Surgeons; mem.: Am. Soc. for Anesthetic Plastic Surgery, Am. Soc. Plastic Surgeons, Alpha Omega. Achievements include being nationally recognized for research in power-assisted liposuctionand anatomy of the facial nerve as it relates to facelifts; pioneering research with power-assisted liposuction, the safest and most effective lipoplasty method available, contributed to a major advance in the field of body contouring. Office: 4644 Lincoln Blvd Ste 552 Marina Del Rey CA 90292 Office Phone: 310-827-2653. Office Fax: 310-823-1984.*

STOKER, TAMMY EDWARDS, toxicologist, researcher; d. Glen and Gerry Edwards; m. Barry Lee Stoker, July 28, 1990; children: Eric Camoron, Travis Reid. BS, MS, PhD, NC State U., Raleigh, NC, 1998. Sr. scientist ManTech Environ., Durham, NC, 1988—95; rsch. biologist US EPA, Rsch. Triangle Pk., NC, 1995—. Contbr. articles to profl. jours. Mem.: SSR, Soc. Toxicology (Best Paper award 1999). Achievements include discovery of several new endocrine disruptors in the environment. Office: US Environ Protection Agy Md-72 Research Triangle Park NC 27711 Business E-Mail: stoker.tammy@epa.gov.

STOKES, ANNE DOROTHY, retired educational association administrator; b. Elyria, Ohio, Nov. 29, 1928; d. Edgar Pier and Dorothy Anne (Day) Gates; m. Kenneth Irving Stokes, June 30, 1951 (dec.); children: Alan, Randall, Bradley, Harlan. BA, Oberlin Coll., Ohio, 1950; MEd, U. Fla., 1970, EdS, 1974, EdD, 1977. Cert. K-12 tchr., Minn.; cert. parent educator. Kdg. tchr. Elyria Pub. Schs., 1950-51, Hamden (Conn.) Pub. Schs., 1951-53; owner, tchr. Lads N Lassies Kdg., Glen Ellyn, Ill., 1961-65; trainer, cons. Head Start, Bradford and Putnam Cty., Fla., 1968-69; instr. U. Fla., Gainesville, 1968-72, curriculum developer, 1972-73; edn. dir. Palmer King Day Care, Gainesville, 1971-72; interim prof. U. Minn., Mpls., 1977-78, Concordia Coll., St. Paul, 1986; coord. early childhood family edn. St. Louis Park (Minn.) Schs., 1979-96, ret., 1996. Sec. evaluation com. Minn. State Family Edn. Resources of Minn., Dept. Edn., 1986-99; cons., spkr. schs. and chs.; bd. dirs. Bell Nursery Sch. Project, Gainesville, 1970-73; mem. ethics com. Minn. Coun. of Family Rels., 1991-99. Author: The Thinking Parent, 1993, Career Education Manual for Teachers and Supervisors, 1976; contbr. articles to profl. jours. Informal lobbyist Early Childhood Family Edn., Minn. State Capitol; spkr., workshop leader Adult Faith Resources, 1996-2000; ind. cons. parent edn., 2000—. Career Growth fellowship Bush Found. U. Minn., 1983; fellowship U. Fla., 1969. Mem. ASCD, Assn. for Childhood Edn. Internat., Minn. Coun. on Family Rels., Nat. Assn. for Edn. of Young Children, Phi Kappa Phi, Pi Lambda Theta. Mem. United Ch. of Christ. Avocations: writing, travel, painting. Home: 787 Plymouth Rd Claremont CA 91711-4249

STOKES, HARVEY J., musician, educator, composer; s. Jesse and Shirley Stokes; m. Charlotte West, July 4, 1981; children: Serena, Janaya, Jeffrey Joseph. MusB in Music Theory and Composition, East Carolina U., Greenville, NC, 1979; MusM in Music Composition, U. Ga., Athens, 1981; PhD in Music Theory and Composition, Mich. State U., East Lansing, 1989. Asst. prof. Miami U., Oxford, Ohio, 1987—90; prof. music Hampton U., Va., 1990—. Devel. com. for the advanced placement in music theory exam. The Coll. Bd./Ednl. Testing Svc., New York, NY, 2001—04; adj. prof. music Coll. William and Mary, Williamsburg, Va., 2004; sr. lectr. IV Christopher Newport U., Newport News. Author: Compositional Language in the Oratorio The Second Act: The Composer as Analyst, A Selected Annotated Bibliography on Italian Serial Composers; composer: Oboe Concerto No. 3, Piano Sonata No. 2, Sonata for Viola and Piano, Ethnic Impressions for Two Saxophones and Piano, Concerto No. 2 for Oboe and Strings, Piano Sonata No. 1, Sonata for Violoncello and Piano, Sonata for Violin and Piano, Dominion Fragments for Mezzo Soprano, Clarinet and Piano, Symphony No. 4 to Jesse for Orchestra, Symphony No. 3 For the End of Time for Winds and Percussion, Sonata for Flute and Piano, In Memoriam S. C. A. for Symphony Band and SATB Chorus, Lyric Symphony for Orchestra (1st prize-Lancaster Summer Arts Festival/Orchestral Composition Contest, 1983), Short Symphony for Orchestra, Three Psalm Fragments for Soprano and Clarinet, Music for 12 Trumpets, Values and Proposals No. 6 (1st prize-New Eng. Conservatory New Works Competition, 1983), Sonata for Horn and Piano, The Triumphant Men, String Quartet No. 4, String Quartet No. 3, String Quartet No. 2, String Quartet No. 1, Quintet No. 3 for Winds,Trio Expressive for flute, clarinet & piano, Quintet No. 4 for Winds Clarinet Concerto. V.p. Va. Beach Symphony. Recipient Billy Taylor Music Merit award, Jackie Robinson Found., 1981; grantee, ASCAP Found., 1980.

STOKES, LINDA BAER, elementary school educator; b. Chelsea, Mass., Apr. 28, 1961; d. Henry Allen and Carolyn Myers Baer; m. Jeffrey Scott Stokes, Mar. 9, 1998; children: Jessica, Kelsey. BS, Tex. Christian U., Ft. Worth, 1983. Content master tchr. Pine Tree Intermediate Sch., Longview, Tex., 1992—93; 4th grade tchr. Pine Tree Ind. Sch. Dist., Longview, 1993—98, Lewisville Ind. Sch. Dist., Flower Mount, Tex., 1998—99, 5th grade tchr., 2001—. Recipient award, Fulbright Meml. Fund, 2002. Mem.: Internat. Reading Assn. Methodist. Avocations: travel, reading, running, scrapbooks, beading. Office: Lewisville Ind Sch Dist Vickery Elem Sch 3301 Wager Rd Flower Mound TX 75028 Home: 729 Tartan Trail Highland Village TX 75077 Office Phone: 469-713-5969. Business E-Mail: stokeslb@lisd.net.

STOKES, LOUIS, lawyer, former congressman; b. Cleve., Feb. 23, 1925; s. Charles and Louise (Stone) S.; m. Jeanette Francis, Aug. 21, 1960; children: Shelley, Louis C., Angela, Lorene. Student, Case We. Res. U., 1946—48; JD, Cleve. Marshall Law Sch., 1953; 26 hon. doctorate degrees, 1953—2001. Bar: Ohio 1953. Mem. 91st-105th Congresses from 11th (formerly 21st) Ohio dist., Washington, 1969—99; sr. counsel Squire, Sanders and Dempsey, Washington, 1999—. Former chmn. appropriations subcom. on VA, HUD and Ind. Agys.; Disting. vis. prof. Mandel Sch. Applied Social Scis. Case We. Res. U., 1999—. Served with AUS, 1943-46. Decorated Congl. DSM; recipient numerous awards for civic activities including Disting. Svc. award Cleve. br. NAACP; Certificate of Appreciation U.S. Commn. on Civil Rights. Mem. ABA, ACLU, Cuyahoga County Bar Assn., Cleve. Bar Assn., Urban League, Am. Legion, Masons, Kappa Alpha Psi. Democrat. Office: Squire Sanders & Dempsey Key Tower Bldg Cleveland OH 44114 Office Phone: 202-626-6697. Business E-Mail: lstokes@ssd.com.

STOKES, MACK BOYD (MARION), bishop; b. Wonsan, Korea, Dec. 21, 1911; arrived in U.S., 1929; s. Marion Boyd and Florence Pauline (Davis) Stokes; m. Ada Rose Yow, June 19, 1942; children: Marion Boyd III, Arch Yow, Elsie Pauline. Student, Seoul Fgn. High Sch., Korea; AB, Asbury Coll., 1932; BD, Duke, 1935; postgrad., Boston U. Sch. Theol., 1935-37, Harvard, 1936-37; PhD, Boston U., 1940; LLD, Lambuth U., Jackson, Tenn., 1963; DD, Millsaps Coll., 1974. Resident fellow systematic theology Boston U., 1936-38, Bowne fellow in philosophy, 1938-39; ordained to ministry Meth. Ch., deacon, 1938, elder, 1940; vis. prof. philosophy and religion Ill. Wesleyan U., 1940-41; prof. Christian doctrine Candler Sch. Theology, Emory U., 1941-56, asso. dean, Parker prof. systematic theology, 1956-72, chmn. exec. com. div. of religion of grad. sch., 1956-72; acting dean Candler Sch. Theology, Emory U. (Candler Sch.), 1968-69; bishop-in-residence Peachtree Rd. United Meth. Ch. Atlanta, 1988—. Faculty mem. Inst. Theol. Studies Oxford U., 1958; del. Meth. Ecumenical Conf., 1947, 52, 61, 71, Holston, Gen. confs., S.E. Jurisdictional Conf., 1956, 60, 64, 68, 72; chmn. com. ministry Gen. Conf. Meth. Ch., 1960; nat. com. Nature Unity We Seek, 1956—; mem. gen. com. ecumenical affairs theol. study com. United Meth. Ch., 1968—72, com. on Cath.-Meth. rels., 1969—, bishop, 1972—. Author: (book) Major Methodist Beliefs, 1956, Major Methodist Beliefs, rev. 15th edit., 1990, The Evangelism of Jesus, 1960, The Epic of Revelation, 1961, Our Methodist Heritage, 1963, Crencas Fundamentals Dos Methodistas, 1964, Study Guide on the Teachings of Jesus, 1970, The Bible and Modern Doubt, 1970, Major United Methodist Beliefs, 1971, Major United Methodist Beliefs, Korean transl., 1977, Major United Methodist Beliefs, rev. with added study guide, 1998, The Holy Spirit and Christian Experience, 1975, The Holy Spirit and Christian Experience, Korean transl., 1985, Twelve Dialogues on John's Gospel, 1975, Jesus, The Master-Evangel, 1978, Can God See the Inside of an Apple?, 1979, Questions Asked by United Methodists, Philippine transl., 1980, The Bible in the Wesleyan Heritage, 1981, Respuestas A Preguntas Que Hacen Los Metodistas Unidos, 1983, The Holy Spirit in the Wesleyan Heritage, 1985, The Holy Spirit in the Wesleyan Heritage, Spanish transl., 1992, The Holy Spirit in the Wesleyan Heritage, Korean transl., 1992, Scriptural Holiness of the United Methodist Christian, 1988, Talking with God: A Guide of Prayer, 1989, Theology for Preaching, 1994, Questions and Answers about Life and Faith, 2000, Person-to-Parson, 2007. Trustee Emory U., Millsaps Coll., Rust Coll., Wood Jr. Coll. Methodist. Home: Unit EPH2C 13597 Perdido Key Dr Pensacola FL 32507-2659 *Faith in God and basic trust in people. Knowing the direction in which to go, and moving with divine assistance toward it with persistence, resourcefulness, imagination and patience.*

STOKES, PATRICK T., brewery company executive; b. Washington, Aug. 11, 1942; m. Anna-Kristina Stokes. BS, Boston Coll., 1964; MBA, Columbia U., 1966. Fin. analyst Shell Oil Co., 1966-67; v.p. materials acquisitions Anheuser-Busch Cos., Inc., St. Louis, 1979-81, v.p., group exec., 1981—86; COO Campbell Taggart Inc. (subs. Anheuser-Busch Cos. Inc.), Dallas, 1986-90, CEO, 1990—2002; sr. exec. v.p. Anheuser-Busch Cos., Inc., St. Louis, 2000—02, pres., CEO, 2002—06, chmn., 2006—, Anheuser-Busch Internat. Inc, 1999—. Bd. dirs. Anheuser-Busch Cos. Inc., 2000—. Served to 1st lt. U.S. Army, 1967-69. Recipient Award of Excellence in Commerce, Boston Coll. Alumni Assn., 1991. Office: Anheuser-Busch Companies Inc 1 Busch Place Saint Louis MO 63118-1852

STOKES, RICHARD FRANCIS, lawyer; b. Teaneck, NJ, Jan. 7, 1946; s. Edwin Matthew and Norma S. (Bonn) Stokes; m. Sally Scott Stokes, Mar. 28, 1970; children: Sarah S., Richard Hunter. BA, Colgate U., 1967; JD, Duke U., 1970. Bar: Del. 1970, US Dist. Ct. Del. 1970, Del. Superior Ct. 1999. Law clk. Superior Ct., Wilmington, Del., 1970; ptnr. Tunnell & Raysor, Georgetown, Del., 1978—96; counsel Beebe Hosp., Lewes, 1983—95; with Del. Ct. Common Pleas, 1996—99; judge Superior Ct., Del., 1999—. Elder Rehoboth Beach Presbyn. Ch., Del., 1983—; mem. Abraham Lincoln Bicentennial Commn.; chmn. Sussex County Dem. Exec. Com., 1986—88. Capt. USAF, 1971—75. Mem.: Inn Ct. (pres. 2006—08), Terry Carey America, Rotary Club (sec. 1983). Home: 137 E Side Dr Rehoboth Beach DE 19971-1311 Home Phone: 302-226-7861; Office Phone: 302-856-5264. Business E-Mail: richard.stokes@state.de.us.

STOKES, SUSAN C., political science professor; AB in Anthropology magna cum laude, Harvard-Radcliffe, 1981; MA in Anthropology, Stanford U., 1985, MA in Polit. Sci., 1986, PhD in Polit. Sci., 1988. Asst. prof. polit. sci. U. Washington, 1988—91, U. Chgo., 1991—96, assoc. prof., polit. sci., 1996—2000; dir. Chgo. Ctr. on Democracy, 1995—2005; John S. Saden prof. polit. sci. Yale U., 2005—, dir., Yale Program on Democracy, 2005—. Dir. grad. studies U. Chgo., 1997—2000, grad. placement dir., 2001—02; invited lectr. in field. Contbr. articles to profl. jours.; author: Cultures in Conflict: Social Movements and the State in Peru, 1995, Mandates and Democracy: Neoliberalism by Surprise in Latin America, 2001 (Mattei Dogan award for the best comparative book of the yr., Soc. for Comparative Rsch., 2002, Best Book award, Comparative Democratization Sect., Am. Polit. Sci. Assn., 2003); co-author (with Matthew Cleary): Democracy and the Culture of Skepticism: Political Trust in Argentina and Mexico, 2006; editor: Public Support for Economic Reforms in New Democracies, 2001; co-editor (with Adam Przeworski and Bernard Manin): Democracy, Accountability, and Representation, 1999; referee for several jours., assoc. editor, comparative politics series Cambridge U. Press, 2001—, editl. bd. mem. Politics and Society, 1993—2000; contbr. chapters to books; manuscript reviewer NSF, American Political Science Review, Comparative Political Studies, Comparative Politics, Latin American Research Review, World Politics. NSF Grad. Studies Fellowship, 1982—85, Soc. Sci. Rsch. Coun.-MacArthur Fellowship in Internat. Peace and Security, 1990—94, Am. Philos. Soc. Sabbatical Fellowship, 1999—2000, John Simon Guggenheim Meml. Found. Fellowship, 2003—04. Fellow: Am. Acad. Arts & Scis.; mem.: Soc. for Comparative Rsch. (mem. selection com., Dogan Book prize 2004), Latin Am. Studies Assn., Am. Polit. Sci. Assn. (comparative politics sect. pres. selection com. 1996—97, Gabriel A. Almond award com. 1997—98, program chair, developing areas sub-sect., ann. mtgs. 2000, mem. comparative politics exec. com. 2003—05, program co-chair, ann. mtgs. 2005), Estudios sobre Violencia (Argentina) (exec. com. mem. 2004—). Office: Yale U Dept Polit Sci 124 Prospect St PO Box 208301 New Haven CT 06520-8301 also: Yale U Dept Polit Sci 8 Prospect Pl Rm 107 New Haven CT 06520 Office Phone: 203-432-6098. Business E-Mail: susan.stokes@yale.edu.

STOKOE, KENNETH H., II, civil engineer, educator; BSCE, U. Mich., 1966, MSCE, 1967, PhD, 1972. Instr. Univ. Mich., 1971; asst. prof. Univ. Mass., 1972—73, Univ. Tex., Austin, 1973—78, assoc. prof., 1978—83, prof. civil engring., 1983—85, Brunswick Abernathy Regents prof., 1985—97, Cockrell Family Regents Chair, 1997—99, Jennie C. and Milton T. Graves chair in engring., 2000—. Contbr. articles to prof. jours. Mem.: Nat. Acad. Engring., Am. Soc. Civil Engineers, Am. Soc. Nondestructive Testing, Am. Soc. Testing & Materials, Earthquake Engring. Rsch. Inst., Internat. Soc. Soil Mech. & Geotechnical Engring., Seismological Soc. Am., Soc. Exploration Geophysicists, Transp. Rsch. Bd., Soc. Profl. Engineers. Office: U Tex at Austin Dept Archl and Environ Engring 1 Univeristy Sta C1792 Austin TX 78712-0280

STOLAR, CHARLES J.H., pediatrician, surgeon, educator; BA cum laude, Washington U., St. Louis, 1970; MD, Georgetown U., 1974. Cert. Am. Bd. Surgery Gen. Surgery, 1982, Pediat. Surgery, 1986. Instr. biology Washington U., St. Louis, 1969—70; intern U. Ill. Hosp., Chgo., 1974—75, asst. resident, 1975—79, chief resident, 1979—80; pediat. surgery clin. fellow, rsch. assoc. Children's Hosp. Nat. Med. Ctr., George Washington U., Washington, 1976—77, 1980—82, instr. surgery, 1980—82, asst. attending Divsn. Pediat. Surgery, 1982—89; staff mem. Babies & Children's Hosp. of NY, NYC, 1982—; assoc. attending surgeon Divsn. Pediat. Surgery Morgan Stanley Children's Hosp. of NY-Presbyn., 1982—89, dir. Ctr. Extracorporeal Membrane Oxygenation, 1982—, surgeon-in-chief, 1982—, chief Divsn. Pediat. Surgery, 2000—, assoc. dir. Fellowship Training Program in pediat. surgery., co-dir. Ctr. for Prenatal Pediatrics, 2002—; asst. prof. divsn. pediat. surgery Columbia U. Coll. Physicians & Surgeons, 1982—89, assoc. prof., 1989—93, Rudolph N. Schullinger, MD, prof. surgery and pediats., 2000—. Disting. overseas lectr. Chilean Assn. Pediatric Surgery, 1995; William Kiesewetter meml. lectr. U. Pitts., Pittsburgh Children's Hosp., 1997; Arvin I. Philippart, invited lectr. Children's Hosp., Detroit; vis. prof., keynote spkr. Royal Coll.Surgeons of Thailand, 1998; vis. prof. Alder Hey Children's Hosp., Liverpool, England, 1999, U. Minn., 1999; cons. surgeon Wildlife Conservation Society, 1999—2002. Contbr. articles to profl. jours. Recipient Ray and Joan Kroc Award for Academic Surgery, U. Ill., 1980, Physician of Yr. Award, Pediat. Cancer Found., Scout of Yr. Award, Boy Scouts of Am., 2005; named Disting. Overseas Lecturer, Chilean Assn. of Pediat. Surgery, 1995; grantee NIH Training Grant Award, 1976—77. Mem.: AAAS, Am. Acad. Pediat., Am. Coll. Surgeons, Am. Heart Assn.-Cardiopulmonary Coun., Am. Pediat. Soc., Am. Pediat. Surgical Assn., Am. Soc. Artificial Internal Organs, Am. Soc. Clin. Oncology, Am. Soc. for Parenteral & Enteral Nutrition, Am. Surgical Assn., Assn. Academic Surgery, British Assn. Pediat. Surgeons, Extracorporeal Life Support Orgn., NY Acad. Scis., NY Soc. Pediat. Surgery, Societe Internat. De Chirugie, Soc. Pediat. Rsch., Soc. Univ. Surgeons. Office: Morgan Stanley Children's Hosp of NY-Presbyn Babies & Children's Hosp N Rm 212 3959 Broadway New York NY 10032 Office Phone: 212-305-2305. Office Fax: 212-305-5971. E-mail: cjs3@columbia.edu.

STOLARIK, M. MARK, history professor; b. St. Martin, Slovak Republic, Apr. 22, 1943; s. Imrich and Margita (Vavro) S.; m. Anne Helene Ivanco, June 15, 1968; children: Roman Andrej, Matthew Mark. BA, U. Ottawa, 1965, MA, 1967; PhD, U. Minn., 1974. Ast. prof. history Cleve. State U., 1972-76; hist. rschr. Nat. Mus. of Man, Ottawa, Ont., Canada, 1977-78; pres. Balch Inst. for Ethnic Studies, Phila., 1979-91; prof. history, chair dept. Slovak history and culture U. Ottawa, 1992—. Cons. Harvard Ency. Ethnic Groups, Cambridge, Mass., 1976-80; advisor State Hist. Records Bd., Harrisburg, Pa., 1982-91; cons. Ency. Canada's Peoples, 1991—99. Author: film documentary Vianoce-Slovak Christmas, 1978 (2d prize 1979), Slovaks in Bethlehem, Pa., 1985, The Slovak Experience, 1870-1918, 1989. Mem. Pa. adv. com. to U.S. Commn. on Civil Rights, 1985-91. Lehigh U. fellow, 1976. Mem. 1st Cath. Slovak Union, Nat. Slovak Soc., Can. Slovak League (pres. 1994-99). Roman Catholic. Home Phone: 613-825-6015; Office Phone: 613-562-5800 x1286. Business E-Mail: stolarik@uottawa.ca.

STOLBERG, SHERYL GAY, journalist; b. NYC, Nov. 18, 1961; d. Irving and Marcia Dawn (Papier) S. BA, U. Va., 1983. Reporter Providence Jour. Bulletin, 1983-87, L.A. Times, 1987-97; sci. & med. corr. NY Times, Washington, 1997—2002, congl. corr., 2002—06, White House corr., 2006—. Recipient Unity award Lincoln U., 1987. Office: NY Times Wash Bur 7th Fl 1627 I St NW Washington DC 20006-4007

STOLBERG, VICTOR, educator; Asst. prof. & counselor Essex County Coll., Newark, 1987—. Contbr. articles to profl. jours. V.p. Friends Newark Pub. Libr., 2008—. Mem.: Internat. Coalition Addiction Studies Educators (bd. mem. 2007—). Office: Essex County Coll 303 Univ Ave Newark NJ 07102 Business E-Mail: stolberg@essex.edu.

STOLIER, ALAN J., surgeon; BS, La. State U., New Orleans, Md, 1970. Cert. Am. Bd. Surgery, 1977. Breast surgeon Tulane U., New Orleans, 1977—.

STOLL, NEAL RICHARD, lawyer; b. Phila., Nov. 7, 1948; s. Mervin Stoll and Goldie Louise (Serody) Stoll Wilf; m. Linda G. Seligman, May 25, 1972; children: Meredith Anne, Alexis Blythe. BA in History with distinction, Pa. State U., 1970; JD, Fordham U., 1973. Bar: N.Y. 1974, U.S. Dist. Ct. (ea. dist.) N.Y. 1974, U.S. Ct. Appeals (2d cir.) 1974, U.S. Ct. Appeals (11th cir.) 1982, U.S. Dist. Ct. (ea. dist.) Mich. 1983, U.S. Dist. Ct. (so. dist.) N.Y. 1974, U.S. Supreme Ct. 1986. Assoc. Skadden, Arps, Slate, Meagher & Flom, LLP, NYC, 1973-81, mem., 1981—. Lectr. Practicing Law-Inst., N.Y.C. Author: (with others) Aquisitions Under the Hart Scott Rodino Antitrust Improvements Act, 1980, 88, 2008; contbr. articles to profl. pubs. Mem. Assn. Bar City of N.Y. (mem. trade regulation com. 1983-85), ABA, N.Y. State Bar Assn. Democrat. Office: Skadden Arps Slate Four Times Sq New York NY 10036-6522 Office Phone: 212-735-3660. Business E-Mail: neal.stoll@skadden.com.

STOLL, RICHARD GILES, lawyer; b. Phila., Oct. 2, 1946; s. Richard Giles and Mary Margaret (Zeigler) S.; m. Susan Jane Nicewonger, June 15, 1968; children: Richard Giles III, Christian Hayes. BA magna cum laude, Westminster Coll., 1968; JD, Georgetown U., 1971. Bar: DC 1971, US Dist. Ct. DC 1971, US Ct. Appeals DC 1971, US Ct. Appeals (4th cir.) 1977. Assoc. Arent, Fox, Kintner, Plotkin & Kahn, Washington, 1971-73; atty. Office of Gen. Counsel EPA, Washington, 1973-77, asst. gen. counsel, 1977-81; dep. gen. counsel Chem. Mfrs. Assn., Washington, 1981-84; ptnr. Freedman, Levy, Kroll & Simonds, Washington, 1984-2001, Foley & Lardner, Washington, 2001—. Instr. environ. law and policy U. Va., Charlottesville, 1981-90. Co-author: Handbook on Environmental Law, 1987, 88, 89, 91, Practical Guide to Environment Law, 1987; contbr. articles to profl. jours.; moderator, panelist legal ednl. TV broadcasts and tapes ABA and Am. Law Inst. Elder Georgetown Presbyn. Ch.; bd. dirs., mem. exec. com. Georgetown Ministry Ctr., 2004-06, pres. 2006—09; bd. dirs. Westminster Ingleside Found., Washington, 2004—. Capt., USAR, 1968-76. Recipient Alumni Achievement award Westminster Coll., 1998. Mem. ABA (sect. environment, energy and resources, chmn. water quality com. 1980-82, hazardous waste com. 1983-85, coun. mem. 1985-88, sect. chmn. 1990-91, sect. adminstrv. law co-chmn. rulemaking com. 2004-06, chmn. sponsorship com. 2004-07, mem. coun. 2005—08), Washington Golf and Country Club, Cosmos Club. Avocations: piano, golf, music composition. Office: Foley & Lardner 3000 K St NW Washington DC 20007 Business E-Mail: rstoll@foley.com.

STOLLE, RUSSELL ROBERT, chemicals executive; b. Houston; BA, Valparaiso U., Ind., 1984; JD with honors, U. Tex., 1987. Bar: Tex. 1987, US Patent and Trademark Office 1988. Intern Tex. Supreme Ct., Austin, Tex., 1987; assoc. Baker & Botts, Houston, 1987-89; patent atty. Texaco Inc., Austin, 1990-94; chief patent and licensing counsel Huntsman Corp., Austin, 1994—2000, v.p., chief tech. counsel, 2000—02, v.p., dep. gen. counsel, 2002—06, sr. v.p. global pub. affairs and comm., 2006—. Mem. Am. Intellectual Property Law Assn., Licensing Execs. Soc., Austin Intellectual Property Law Assn. Office: Huntsman Corp 10003 Woodloch Forest Dr The Woodlands TX 77380 Office Phone: 281-719-6000.

STOLLER, CLAUDE, architect; b. NYC, Dec. 2, 1921; s. Max and Esther (Zisblatt) S.; m. Anna Maria Oldenburg, June 5, 1946 (div. Oct. 1972); children: Jacob, Dorothea, Elizabeth; m. Rosemary Raymond Lax, Sept. 22, 1978. Student, Black Mountain Coll., NC, 1942; M.Arch., Harvard U., 1949. Architect Architects Collaborative, Cambridge, Mass., after 1949, Shepley, Bulfinch, Richardson & Abbot, Boston, 1951; co-founder, partner firm Marquis & Stoller, San Francisco, 1956; pvt. practice architecture NYC and San Francisco, 1974-78; founder, partner Stoller/Partners, Berkeley, Calif., 1978, Stoller, Knoerr Archs., 1988-95. Mem. faculty Washington U., St. Louis, 1955-56; mem. faculty U. Calif., Berkeley, 1957-91, prof. architecture, 1968-92, acting chmn. dept., 1965-66, chair grad. studies, 1984-91, prof. emeritus, 1991—; mem. Berkeley Campus Design Rev. Bd., 1985-91, chmn., 1992-93; commr. Calif. Bd. Archtl. Examiners, 1980-90, mem. exam. com., 1985-88; mem. diocesan commn. arch. Episcopal Diocese Calif., 1961-98; vis. arch. Nat. Design Inst., Ahmedabad, India, 1963; planning commr. City of Mill Valley, 1961-66, Marin County Planning Commn., 1966-67; mem. pub. adv. panel archtl. svcs. GSA, 1969-71; citizens urban design adv. com. City of Oakland, Calif., 1968; vis. com. nat. archtl. accrediting bd. U. Minn. and U. Wis., Milw., 1971; coun. Harvard Grad. Sch. Design Assn., 1976-77; mem. design rev. com. The Sea Ranch, Calif., 1990-2002. Prin. works include St. Francis Sq. Coop. Apts., San Francisco, 1961, Pub. Housing for Elderly, San Francisco, 1974, Learning Resources Bldg, U. Calif., Santa Barbara, 1975, Menorah Park Housing for Elderly, San Francisco, 1979, San Jose State U. Student Housing Project, 1984, Delta Airlines Terminal, San Francisco Internat. Airport, 1988. Served with AUS, 1943-46. Recipient numerous awards including AIA Honor awards, 1963, 64, AIA Bay Region Honor award, 1974, Concrete Reinforced Steel Inst. award, 1976, AIA award, 1976, CADA Site I Solar Housing award Sacramento, Calif., 1980, State of Calif. Affordable Housing award, 1981, PG&E Suntherm award, 1981, San Francisco Housing Authority award, 1983, Orchid award City of Oakland, 1989, Citation for achievement and svc. U. Calif., Berkeley, 1991, Design award Berkeley Design Advocates. Fellow AIA. Home: 2816 Derby St Berkeley CA 94705-1325 Home Phone: 510-843-7214. Business E-Mail: stoller@berkeley.edu.

STOLLER, MARSHALL, urologist, educator; b. Calif. Cert. physician Am. Urol. Assn. Prof., vice chmn. U. Calif., San Francisco, 1987—. Fellow: ACS. Achievements include patents in field. Office: Univ Calif San Francisco 400 Parnassus Ave A-610 San Francisco CA 94143-0738

STOLLERMAN, GENE HOWARD, internist, educator; b. NYC, Dec. 6, 1920; s. Maurice William and Sarah Dorothy (Mezz) S.; m. Corynne Miller, Jan. 21, 1945 (dec. Mar. 1997); children: Lee Denise Stollerman Meyburg, Anne Barbara Stollerman DiZio, John Eliot; m. Vita Mark, Nov. 9, 1997. AB summa cum laude, Dartmouth Coll., 1941; MD, Columbia U., 1944. Diplomate Am. Bd. Internal Medicine. Clin. tng. Mt. Sinai Hosp., NYC, 1944-46, chief med. resident, 1948; Dazian research fellow microbiology NYU Med. Sch., 1949-50, mem. dept. medicine, 1951-55; med. dir. Irvington House for Cardiac Children, 1951-55; prin. investigator Sackett Found. Research in Rheumatic Diseases, 1955-64; asst. prof. medicine Northwestern U., 1955-57, assoc. prof., 1957-61, prof. medicine, 1961-65; prof., chmn. dept. medicine U. Tenn., 1965-81, Goodman prof., 1977-81; physician-in-chief City of Memphis Hosps., 1965-81; prof. medicine Boston U. Sch. Medicine, 1981-95, prof. pub. health, 1991-95, prof. medicine and pub. health emeritus, 1996—. Chief sect. gen. internal medicine Univ. Hosp., Boston U. Med. Ctr., 1983-86; Disting. physician VA Med. Ctr., Bedford, Mass., 1986-89; assoc. chief of staff Geriatrics and Extended Care, 1989-92; clin. dir. Bedford div. Geriatric Rsch., Ednl. and Clin. Ctr., 1989-92; dir. VA Health Svcs. Rsch. Field, 1990-93; chmn. research career program com. NIAMD-NIH, 1967-70; mem. commn. streptococcal and staphylococcal diseases U.S. Armed Forces Epidemiol. Bd., 1956-74; adv. bd. immunization practices Center for Disease Control, 1968-71; expert adv. panel cardiovascular disease WHO, 1966—; mem. Am. Bd. Internal Medicine, 1967-73, chmn. cert. exam. com., 1969-73, mem. exec. com., 1971-73; chmn. Panel on Bacterial Vaccines, FDA, 1973-80; mem. nat. adv. council Nat. Inst. Allergy and Infectious Diseases, NIH, 1978-82; mem. Dept. Health & Human Services nat. vaccine adv. com. Editor-in-chief Advances in Internal Medicine, 1968-93, Jour. Am. Geriatric Soc., 1984-88; co-editor Hosp. Practice, 1990—, editor, 1998—; contbr. chpts. to Braunwald's Textbook of Cardiology, Harrison's Textbook of Medicine, Cecil & Loeb Textbook of Medicine, others; contbr. articles to profl. jours. Served as capt. M.C., AUS, 1946-48. Recipient Bicentennial award in internal medicine Columbia U., 1967, Disting. Alumnus award Mt. Sinai Hosp., 1989, Thewlis award Am. Geriatric Soc., 1990, Mentor award Infectious Disease Soc. Am., 2004. Master ACP (bd. regents 1978, v.p. 1984, Bruce medal for preventive medicine 1985), Am. Coll. Rheumatology; mem. Am. Heart Assn. (mem. exec. com., pres. coun. on rheumatic fever and congenital disease 1965-67), Am. Fedn. Clin. Rsch., Am. Rheumatism Assn., Am. Soc. Clin. Investigation, Cen. Soc. Clin. Rsch. (v.p. 1973-74, pres. 1974-75), Assn. Profs. Medicine (pres. 1975-76), Am. Assn. Immunologists, Assn. Am. Physicians, Infectious Disease Soc. Am. (coun. 1968-70), Phi Beta Kappa, Alpha Omega Alpha. Personal E-mail: gstollerman@valley.net.

STOLLEY, PAUL DAVID, medical educator, researcher; b. Pawling, NY, June 17, 1937; s. Herman and Rosalie (Chertock) Stolley; m. Jo Ann Goldenberg, June 13, 1959; children: Jonathan, Dorie, Anna. BA, Lafayette Coll., 1957; MD, Cornell U., 1962; MPH, Johns Hopkins U., 1968; MA (hon.), U. Pa., 1976. Diplomate Am. Coll. Preventive Medicine, Am. Coll. Epidemiology. Intern U. Wis. Med. Ctr., 1962—63, resident in medicine, 1963—64; med. officer USPHS, Washington, 1964—67; asst. prof. Johns Hopkins Sch. Pub. Health, Balt., 1968—71, assoc. prof., 1971—76; Herbert C. Rorer prof. medicine U. Pa. Sch. Medicine, Phila., 1976—91; prof. dept. epidemiology U. Md. Sch. Medicine, Balt., 1991—2002; staff epidemiologist Public Citizen Health Rsch. Group, 2002—04. Co-author: Foundations of Epidemiology, 3d edit., 1995, Epidemiology: Investigating Disease, 1995 (Am. Med. Writers Assn. award, 1996); contbg. author: Case-Control Studies, 1982, mem. editl. bd.: New Eng. Jour. Medicine, 1989—93, Millbank Quar., Health and Soc., 1986—, assoc. editor: Clin. Pharmacology and Therapeutics, 1987—93; contbr. articles to med. jours. Charter mem. Physicians for Social Responsibility, 1961—. Lt. comdr. USPHS, 1964—67. Fellow: ACP; mem.: Johns Hopkins Soc. Scholars, Internat. Epidemiol. Assn. (treas. 1982—84), Am. Epidemiol. Soc. (pres. 1994—), Soc. Epidemiol. Rsch. (pres. 1982—84), Inst. Medicine of NAS, Am. Coll. Epidemiology (pres. 1987—89). Office Phone: 410-706-3610. Personal E-mail: pstolley@aol.com, pstolley@yahoo.com.

STOLLEY, RICHARD BROCKWAY, journalist; b. Peoria, Ill., Oct. 3, 1928; s. George Brockway and Stella (Sherman) S.; m. Anne Elizabeth Shawber, Oct. 2, 1954 (div. 1981); children: Lisa Anne, Susan Hope, Melinda Ruth, Martha Brockway; m. Lise Jane Hilboldt, 1997. BS in Journalism, Northwestern U., 1952, MS, 1953; LLD, Villa Maria Coll., 1976, Hartwick Coll., 2005. Sports editor Pekin (Ill.) Daily Times, 1944-46; reporter Chgo. Sun-Times, 1953; mem. staff weekly Life mag., 1953-73, bur. chief Los Angeles, 1961-64, Washington, 1964-68, sr. editor Europe, 1968-70, asst. mng. editor NYC, 1971-73; mng. editor monthly Life mag., NYC, 1982-86; founding mng. editor People mag., NYC, 1974-82, Picture Week mag., NYC, 1985-86; dir. spl. projects Time Inc., NYC, 1987-89; editl. dir. Time Inc. Time Warner Inc., NYC, 1989-93, sr. editl. adviser, 1993—. Author: Sinatra: An Intimate Portrait of a Very Good Year, 2002; introd. to Leigh A. Wiener, Marilyn: A Hollywood Farewell: The Death and Funeral of Marilyn Monroe, 1990, Foreword To Life: The Platinum Anniversary Collection, 2006, American Photojournalism, 2009; editor People Celebrates People: The Best of 20 Unforgettable Years, 1994, rev. edit., 1996, Life: Our Century in Pictures, 1999, Life: Century of Change, America in Pictures, 1900-2000, 2000, LIFE: World War 2, 2001; exec. prodr. (TV) Extra, 1995-96; editl. cons. Our American Century series Time-Life Books, 1998-99. Bd. govs. Nat. Parkinson Found., Miami, Fla., Lensic Performing Arts Ctr., Santa Fe, N.Mex. With USN, 1946-48. Recipient Alumni merit award Northwestern U., 1977, Alumni medal Northwestern U., 1994, Henry Johnson Fisher award for lifetime achievement in mag. pub., 1997, Mag. Profl. of Yr. award Assn. for Edn. in Journalism and Mass Comm., 2002; inducted into Am. Soc. Magazine Editors' Hall of Fame, 1996, Hall of Achievement Medill Sch. Journalism Northwestern U., 1997. Mem. Am. Soc. Mag. Editors (pres. 1982-84), Nat. Press Club, Overseas Press Club (pres. 2004-06), Century Assn., Sigma Delta Chi. Home: 1243 Canyon Rd Santa Fe NM 87501

STOLOV, WALTER CHARLES, medicine physiatrist, educator; b. NYC, Jan. 6, 1928; s. Arthur and Rose F. (Gordon) S.; m. Anita Carvel Noodelman, Aug. 9, 1953; children: Nancy, Amy, Lynne. BS in Physics, CCNY, 1948; MA in Physics, U. Minn., 1951, MD, 1956. Diplomate Am. Bd. Phys. Med. and Rehab., Am. Bd. Electrodiagnostic Medicine. Physicist U.S. Naval Gun Factory, Nat. Bur. Stds., Washington, 1948-49; teaching and rsch. asst. U. Minn., Mpls., 1950-54; from instr. to assoc. prof. U. Wash., Seattle, 1960-70, prof., 1970-99, prof. emeritus, 1999—, also chmn., 1987-99, prof. emeritus, 1999—. Editl. bd. Archives Phys. Medicine and Rehab., 1967-78, Muscle and Nerve, 1983-89, 92-95; cons. Social Security Adminstrn., Seattle, 1975—; sec. Am. Bd. Electrodiagnostic Medicine, 1995—. Co-editor: Handbook of Severe Disability, 1981; contbr. articles to profl. jours. Surgeon USPHS, 1956-57. Recipient Townsend Harris medal CCNY, 1990. Fellow: AAAS, Am. Heart Assn.; mem.: Am. Spinal Cord Injry Assn., Am. Assn. Electrodiagnostic Medicine (pres. 1987—88, Lifetime Achievement award 2001), Assn. Acad. Physiatrists, Am. Congress Rehab. Medicine (Essay award 1959), Am. Acad. Phys. Medicine and Rehab. (Disting. Clinician award 1987). Avocations: dance, singing. Office: U Wash Box 356490 1959 NE Pacific St Seattle WA 98195-0001 Office Phone: 206-543-7065.

STOLPIN, WILLIAM ROGER, printmaker; b. Flint, Mich., June 25, 1942; s. William and Dorothy Florence (Mitchell) S.; m. Kathleen Diane Poyner, Aug. 14, 1970; children: Krishna Ann, James Mitchell. BME, Kettering U., 1965; AA, Charles Stewart Mott C.C., Flint, 1978; postgrad., Ea. Mich. U., 1992. Jr. reliability engr. GM Corp., Flint, 1968—76, sr. reliability engr., 1976—80, supr. quality control, 1980—83, mgr. product assurance, 1983—89, asst. staff engr. Warren, Mich., 1990—93; printmaker, print pub. Flint, 1969—80; printmaker, print pub., co-founder DAS Print Co., Holly, Mich., 1980—; art faculty Flint Inst. Arts, Mich., 2006—. Resident artist Robert T. Longway Planetarium, Flint, 1975—2008. Author: Printmaker: (lithograph) ...And the Santa Maria, 1969 (Smithsonian permanent collection 1973), (serigraph) One Giant Leap For Mankind, 1970 (Smithsonian permanent collection 1973), numerous pub. serigraphs, lithographs, intaglio prints and woodcuts, 1969—. Grant reviewer Oakland County Office Arts Culture & Film, 2008-09, grant reviewerGreater Flint Arts Coun., 1989-90, 2000-02, v.p., 1973-74, programming and planning, 1988, mktg. and pub. rels., 1999-2007, bd. dirs., 1999-2007; pres. Buckham Fine Arts Project, Flint, 1993-94, bd. dirs., 1993-2000; bd. dirs. Whaley Hist. House, Flint, 1997-2000; adv. com. U. Mich. Flint Art Gallery, 1997-2000, Shiawassee Arts Coun., 1999-2000, Alma Coll., 1999-2001; accessions and collections com. Flint Inst. Arts, 2000—, art sch. com., 2007; grant reviewer Oakland County Office Arts, Culture and Film, 2002—, commd. print Cmty. Found. Greater Flint, 2008. Recipient 1st in Graphics award Internat. Platform Assn., 1969, Koegler Meml. award Left Bank Gallery, 1991, 1st in Overall Attitude, Mich. Renaissance Festival, 1998, 99, 1st prize all media award Left Bank Gallery, 1998, Purchase prize Saginaw Art Mus., 1994, 98, hon. mention Ann Arbor Art Ctr., 2003, 04, 1st prize Flint (Mich.) Art Fair, 2004, Third prize 2006, Honorable Mention, 2009; Fed. Design and Art in Transp. grantee, 2002, 2nd prize Festival of the Masters, Walt Disney World, 2007. Mem. AAAS, AIAA, Internat. Assn. for Astron. Arts, Am. Soc. for Quality, Nat. Stereoscopic Assn., Soc. Automotive Engrs., Soc. Am. Graphic Artists, Flint Artist's Market, Detroit Artist's Market, Assn. Sci. Fiction and Fantasy Artists, Am. Color Print Soc., Mid Am. Print Coun., Internat. Ctr. for the Print, Wood Engravers Network, Guild Artists and Artisans. Avocations: directing community theater, participant in michigan renaissance festival, stereoscopic imaging. Studio: DAS Print Co 12201 Gage Rd Holly MI 48442-8339 Personal E-mail: bill@stolpinart.com.

STOLT, WILBUR A., library director; MA, U. Ill., Urbana-Champaign, 1978, MLS, 1979. Archivist U. Wis.-Milw., 1979—82, asst. dir. pub. svcs., 1982—86; dir. pub. svcs. U. Okla., Norman, 1986—2000; dir. librs. U. ND, Grand Forks, 2000—. Contbr. articles to profl. jours. Office: Univ ND 3051 University Ave Stop 9000 Grand Forks ND 58202-9000 Business E-Mail: wilburstolt@mail.und.edu.

STOLTZ, JOE, federal official; BS in Acctg., Pa. State U., 1972. CPA 1979. With Gen. Acctg. Office; audit staff mem. Fed. Election Commn., Washington, 1975, dep. dir. audit divsn., acting staff dir., 2002—. Office: Fed Election Commn 999 E St NW Washington DC 20463 Office Phone: 202-694-1007. Business E-Mail: director@fec.gov.*

STOLTZMAN, RICHARD LESLIE, clarinetist; b. Omaha, July 12, 1942; s. Leslie Harvey and Dorothy Marilyn (Spohn) S.; m. Lucy Jean Chapman, June 6, 1976 (div. Nov. 20, 2007); children: Peter John, Margaret Anne. MusB summa cum laude, Ohio State U., 1964; MusM magna cum laude, Yale U., 1967; postgrad., Columbia U. Tchrs. Coll., 1967-70. Mem. faculty Calif. Inst. Arts, 1970-75, New Eng. Conservatory, 1996. Western regional dir. Young Audiences, Inc., 1972-74, mem. nat. bd. Appeared in concerts throughout U.S., Europe, Japan, Hong Kong, Australia, 1976—; rec. artist, 1974—; debut LaScala, Milan, 1981, Carnegie Hall, N.Y.C., 1982; appeared in world premiere of Einar Englund concerto Helsinki Festival, 1991, Toru Takemitsu concerto (Fantasma/Cantos) Wales BBC, 1991, U.S. premiere of Lukas Foss concerto L.A. Philharm. Orch., 1991, Copland concert, 1993 (Emmy award for best performing arts video 1993), world premiere of Leonard Bernstein sonata for clarinet and orch. Pacific Music Festival, Sapporo, Japan, 1994, world premiere of Steven Hartke concerto PBS, Tenn., 2001, world premiere of William Thomas McKinley concerto 9 Shades of Lament, Boston Civic Orch., 2001, of Einojuhani Rautavaara Concerto, Nat. Symphony, Carnegie Hall, 2002. Recipient Horatio Parker award Yale U., 1966, Avery Fisher prize, 1977, Martha Baird Rockefeller award, 1973, Grammy award, 1983, 95, Avery Fisher artist award, 1986, Disting. Alumnus award Ohio State U., 1990, Sanford medal Yale U., 2005. Home: 6 Lincolnshire Way Winchester MA 01890-3048 Office: 121 West 27th St Ste 703 New York NY 10001-6213 Office Phone: 212-581-5197. Business E-Mail: info@franksalomon.com. *Be mindful of the breath. It gives life to the sound which sends music to the soul.*

STOLZBERG, MARK ELLIOTT, psychologist; b. NYC, Apr. 30, 1944; s. Seymour and Ruth (Petesky) S.; m. Marilyn Goldberg, Mar. 18, 1972; children: Susan Beth, David Jonathan, Daniel Jason. BA, Hofstra U., Hempstead, NY, 1966, PhD; MA in Exptl. Psychology, C.W. Post Coll., Greenvale, NY, 1970; postgrad. in clin. psychology, SUNY, Albany, 1973. Diplomate in clin. psychology Am. Bd. Profl. Psychology. Intern in clin. psychology Maimonides Hosp., Bklyn., 1972-73; pres. Stolzberg Rsch., LLC, Stony Brook, NY, 1976—. Adj. lectr. Bklyn. Coll., 1973; faculty Coll. Optometry, SUNY, 1985-86; cons. psychologist in numerous clinical and business settings, 1994—. Contbr. articles to profl. jours. Co-pres. North Shore SEPTA, 1999-2001; founder, past pres. Ind. Practitioners Geropsychology. Grad. fellow C.W. Post Coll., 1968-70, SUNY, Albany, 1970-72, N.Y. State War Svc. scholar; recipient Disting. Achievement award for Rsch. Mem. NY State Psychol. Assn. (adult devel. & aging divsn. 2004), Aircraft Owners and Pilots Assn., Nat. Aeronautics Assn. Achievements include two US transcontinental speed records for piston-engine aircraft. Home and Office: 6759 Shamrock Trail Boynton Beach FL 33437

STOLZENBURG, MARIBETH, research scientist; d. Carl and Faye Stolzenburg; m. Thomas C. Marshall, 1996. BS in Atmospheric Sci., SUNY, Albany, 1989; MS in Meteorology, U. Okla., Norman, 1993, PhD in Meteorology, 1996. Rsch. asst. SUNY Albany, Rsch. Found. NY, 1988—90; grad. rsch. asst. U. Okla., Coop. Inst. Mesoscale Meteorol. Studies, Norman, 1990—96; postdoc. rsch. asst. U. Miss., 1996—2000, rsch. asst. prof., 2000—, assoc. dir. rsch., 2002—06. Editl. adv. bd., Eos transactions AGU Am. Geophys. Union, Washington, 2001—; sec to treas. Beta Miss. Chpt. Phi Beta Kappa, 2001—08; with, selection com., editor's choice atmospheric & sapce electricity Am. Geophys. Union, Washington, 2006—. Contbr. articles to profl. jours. Patricia Roberts Harris fellowship, US Dept. Edn., U. Okla., 1990, grant, NSF, 1996—. Mem.: European Geosciences Union, Am. Meteorol. Soc., Am. Geophys. Union, Phi Beta Kappa (Beta of Miss. Chpt.). Office: Univ Mississippi Dept Physics and Astronomy University MS 38677 Office Fax: 662-915-5045. Business E-Mail: mstolzen@phy.olemiss.edu.

STOMBLER, ROBIN, health science association administrator; BA, U. SC. Dir. ops. US Rep. Rick Boucher, Washington, 1983—87; sr. Washington assoc. ACS, 1988—94; v.p., govt. affairs, dir. Am. Soc. Clin. Pathology, Washington, 1994—2003; pres. Auburn Health Strategies, LLC, Arlington, Va., 2003—. Health task force co-chair, historian, pub. rels. co-chair, leader Women Govt. Rels., Inc., Washington, 1990—98; bd. dirs. Leader Found., Washington, 1994—95, Internat. Registry Pathology, Silver Spring, Md., 2006—, Women's Health Va., Charlottesville, 2007—; instr. George Wash. U., Wash. Representatives Program, Washington, 1996; sr. scholar, Dept. Health Policy Jefferson Med. Coll., Phila., 2006—07. Contbr. articles to profl. jours. Chair Arlington Sch. Bd. Adv. Com. Social Studies, Va., 1985—91; vice-chair Arlington Tenant-Landlord Commn., 1986—92; cmty. affairs, mktg. com. mem. Arlington Hosp., 1995—96; campaign mgr. Va. State Senate Re-election Campaign, 1987—91; chair Arlington Com. 100, 1995—96; visionwalk team leader Found. Fighting Blindness, Balt., 2006. Recipient Cert. of Appreciation, Inst. Quality Lab. Medicine, 2005, Walk Visionary award, Found. Fighting Blindness, 2006. Achievements include co-founder Medicine and Health Executives Group. Office: Auburn Health Strategies LLC 4622 S 28th Rd Ste D Arlington VA 22206

STOMFAY-STITZ, ALINE MARIA, education educator; b. Newark; d. Adolph and Irene (Badowska) Wegrocki; m. Emery Stomfay-Stitz (dec.); children: Peter, John, Robert. BA, Barnard Coll., NYC; MA, Case We. Res. U., Cleve.; EdD, No. Ill. U., DeKalb, 1984. Asst. prof. Coll. St Scholastica, Duluth, Minn., 1984—85, St. Leo Coll., Fla., 1985—87, Nicholls State U., Thibodaux, La., 1989—91; assoc. prof. edn. Christopher Newport U., Newport News, Va., 1991—96. Vis. prof., assoc. prof. edn. U. No. Fla., Jacksonville, 1996-2003; assoc. editor Joun. Early Childhood Tchr. Edn. Author: Peace Education in America 1828-1990, 1993; online newsletter editor Peace Edn., 1998-2006; assoc. editor Jour. Early Childhood Tchr. Edn., 1998-2008; contbr. chpts. to books, articles to profl. jours. Mem.: Internat. Peace Rsch. Assn., Nat. Assn. for Early Childhood Tchr. Educators, Am. Ednl. Rsch. Assn. (SIG exec. coun.). Business E-Mail: astomfay@unf.edu.

STONE, ALAN JAY, retired academic administrator; b. Ft. Dodge, Iowa, Oct. 15, 1942; s. Hubert H. and Bernice A. (Tilton) S.; m. Jonieta J. Smith; 1 child, Kirsten K. Stone Morlock. BA, Morningside Coll., Sioux City, Iowa, 1964, HD, 2001; MA, U. Iowa, Iowa City, 1966; MTh, U. Chgo., 1968, DMin, 1970; PhD (hon.), Kyonggi U., Korea, 1985; LLD, Stillman Coll., Tuscaloosa, Ala., 1991, Sogong U., Korea, 1992, Alma Coll., Mich., 2001. Admissions counselor Morningside Coll., Sioux City, Iowa, 1964-66; dir. admissions, asso. prof. history George Williams Coll., Downers Grove, Ill., 1969-73; v.p. coll. relations Hood Coll., Frederick, Md., 1973-75; v.p. devel. and fin. affairs W.Va. Wesleyan Coll., Buckhannon, 1975-77; dir. devel. U. Maine, 1977-78; pres. Aurora U., Ill., 1978-88, Alma Coll., 1988-2000; pres., CEO Alzheimer's Assn., Chgo., 2001—02; ret., 2002; lectr. for cruises. Home: 28897 N 94th Pl Scottsdale AZ 85262 Personal E-mail: thestones3@cox.net.

STONE, ALAN JOHN, manufacturing and real estate company executive; b. Dansville, NY, Sept. 9, 1940; s. Guthrie Boyd and Doris Irene (Wolfanger) S.; m. Sandra Barber, Aug. 22, 1964; children: Teri, Timothy, Michael. BSME, Rochester Inst. Tech., 1963; MBA, U. Pitts., 1964. Engrng. aide Xerox Corp., Webster, N.Y., 1960-63; gen. mgr. mech. component divsn. Stone Conveyor Co., Inc., Honeoye, N.Y., 1964-67, v.p. sales, 1968; co-founder, CEO Stone Constrn. Equipment Inc., Honeoye, 1969-86, also cons., bd. dirs., 1969—; founder, pres. Canandaigua Apts. Inc., NY, 1967—83; pres. Wildtrak, Inc., 1983—; founder, gen. ptnr. Stone Properties, 1986—2002; mng. mem. Stone Family Properties, LLC, 2002—. Dir., co-founder Baker Rental Svc., Inc., 1973-75; met. adv. bd. Chase Lincoln Bank, 1981-84; co-founder, dir. Royal Lines Ltd., 1989-91; v.p. Naples Biol. Rsch. Sta. Inc., 1996-98; bd. dirs. Canandaigua Nat. Bank & Trust Co., 1986-, chmn. 1994-2004; co-founder, ptnr. Storage Assocs., 1996-2001; mem., City Mini Storage, LLC, 2001—, mng. mem., 2001-04. Patentee in field. Mem. Town of Richmond (N.Y.) Planning Bd., 1970-75, chmn., 1970-71; mem. Honeoye Ctrl. Sch. Bd. Edn., 1971-76, pres., 1974-75; com. chmn. pack 10 Boy Scouts Am., 1975-78; mem. Ontario County Overall Econ. Devel. Com., 1976-81; bd. dirs. F.F. Thompson Hosp., 1987-91; chmn. fin. com. United Meth. Ch., Allens Hill, 1995—2001; trustee Honeoye Pub. Libr., 1998-2003. Mem. Honeoye C. of C., Constrn. Industry Mfrs. Assn. (exec. mem. bus. challenges coun. 1980-83), Honeoye Valley Assn. (dir. 1991-95, treas. 1993-95), Griswold and Cast Iron Collectors Assn. (treas. 1994-96, chmn. fin. com. 1996-2002), Honeoye Area Hist. Soc. (bicentennial com. 1989), Grand Slam Club, Safari Club Internat., Found. N.Am. Wild Sheep. Methodist.

STONE, ALLAN DAVID, retired economics professor; b. Joliet, Ill., Jan. 9, 1937; s. William E. and Leona V. (Frieh) S.; m. Peggy J. Carter, Jan. 11, 1958; children: David, Richard. BA, Beloit Coll., 1961; MA, U. Okla., 1964, PhD, 1973. Asst. prof. econs. U. Tex., El Paso, 1963-65; instr. econs. Wartburg Coll., Waverly, Iowa, 1965-66; asst. prof. econs. Oklahoma City U., 1966-72; prof. econs. Mo. State U., Springfield, 1972—2001, dept. head, 1985—87, emeritus prof., 2001—. Served with U.S. Army, 1956-58. NSF grantee. Mem. Am. Econ. Assn., Mo. Coun. Econ. Edn. (bd. dirs. 1977-80), Phi Beta Kappa, Phi Kappa Phi. Home: 820 E Cherokee St Springfield MO 65807-2708 Home Phone: 417-887-1311. Personal E-mail: astone@emailthstones.com.

STONE, ANN ELIZABETH, marketing agency executive, entrepreneur, volunteer, consultant; b. Bridgeport, Conn., Aug. 9, 1952; d. Jack Reginald and Edith Pauline (Christiansen) Wesche; m. Roger J. Stone, June 15, 1974 (div. Dec. 1990). BA in History and Comm., George Washington U., 1974; postgrad. in Corp. Fin., Wharton Sch. Bus., Washington, 1982. Mktg. mgr. Human Events, Washington, 1974—76; v.p. polit. div. The Viguerie Co., Falls Church, Va., 1976—82; chmn. Capstone Lists, Alexandria, Va., 1983—; vice chmn. George Washington Nat. Bank, Alexandria, 1988—90; ptnr. Weintraub-Stone Direct, Inc., Woodland Hills, Calif., 1991—93; pres. The Stone Group Inc. (formerly Ann E.W. Stone & Assocs.), Alexandria, 1982—. Lectr. Am. U., Washington, 1978—; contract specialist trainer US State Dept., 1999—; bd. dirs. Action Products Internat. Inc., 2003—; spkr. in field. Co-host (TV show) The Alexandria Forum, TV appearances Larry King Live, Lehrer News Hour, Good Morning Am., Politically Incorrect, others; contbr. columns in newspapers including the NY Times, Hartford Courant, others, articles to profl. jours. Pres.'s exec. global adv. bd. European/Am. Women's Coun., 2003; chair emeritus Empowered Women Internat.; arbiter Va. Bar Assn.; trustee apptd. by gov. Va. Hist. Preservation Found.; chmn. DC Young Reps., Washington, 1975—77; fin. dir. Alexandria Rep. Party, 1989—92; chmn., foundr Reps. for Choice, Alexandria, 1989—; Republican candidate for mayor Alexandria, 1991; bd. dirs. Campaigns and Elections Mag., Washington, 1987—, Am. Heart Assn., 1990—, chmn. Alexandria Chpt., 1993—94; founding dir., bd. dirs. Nat. Womens History Mus., 1996—; bd. dirs. The Washington Ctr., Response mag., Influence mag.; bd. dir. The Campagna Ctr., 1995—2000, Assn. Direct Mktg. Agencies, 1998—99, Am. Assn. Polit. Cons., 1999—2000. Recipient Leadership in Edn. award, Am. U., 2007; named one of Women Who Changed Politics in Am., Campaigns and Elections mag., 1992. Mem. Direct Mktg. Assn. Washington, Washington Renaissance Women (bd. dirs. 1985—), Alexandria C. of C. (bd. dirs. 1988-92), Alexandria Soc. for Preservation of Black Heritage, Animal Welfare League, Alexandria Seaport Fedn. (past bd. dirs.), Assn. Ky. Cols. Republican. Lutheran. Achievements include development of women's organizations designed to give women skills and knowledge necessary for them to take advantage of opportunities presented to them and to achieve social justice. Avocations: reading, travel, historical renovation, rock collecting, music. Office: 205 S Whiting St 250 Alexandria VA 22304 Office Phone: 703-370-8282. Personal E-mail: tsgrp@aol.com.

STONE, ANTOINETTE R., lawyer; children: Matthew T., Lily B. BA, Brown U., Providence, 1968; M in Urban Planning, Wayne State U., Detroit, 1973; JD, Temple U., Phila., 1976. Bar: Pa. 1976. Enforcement atty. EPA, Phila., 1976—78; asst. US atty. US Atty.'s Office, Phila., 1978—82; assoc. to ptnr. Fox Rothschild LLP, Phila., 1982—90; shareholder Buchanan Ingersoll & Rooney PC, Phila., 1990—2007; ptnr. Brown Stone Nimeroff LLC, Phila., 2007—. Mem.: Pa. Bar Assn., Phila. Bar Assn. Office: Brown Stone Nimeroff LLC 1818 Market St Ste 2300 Philadelphia PA 19103 Office Phone: 267-861-5333.

STONE, ARTHUR A., psychologist, researcher; b. NYC, Oct. 30, 1951; s. Arthur J. and Julita M. Stone; m. Joan E Broderick; children: Danielle, Martina. PhD, Stony Brook U., 1978. Lic. psychologist N.Y. Disting. prof., vice chmn. dept. psychiatry SUNY at Stony Brook, 1978—. Editor-in-chief Health Psychology, 2000—04, Annals of Behavioral Medicine, —. Grantee, NSF, NIH. Fellow: Soc. of Behavioral Medicine (exec. com.), APA, Acad. of Behavioral Medicine Rsch. (exec. com., pres. 2000—01). Office: SUNY Dept Psychiatry Putnam Hall South Campus Stony Brook NY 11794-8790 Home: 166 Jonathan Ln Westhampton NY 11977-1029 Office Fax: 631-632-3165. Business E-Mail: arthur.stone@sunysb.edu.

STONE, BERNARD LEONARD, alderman, vice mayor; b. Chgo., Nov. 24, 1927; s. Sidney and Rebecca (Spinka) S.; m. Lois D. Falk, Aug. 28, 1949 (dec. 1995); children: Holly (dec.), Robin, Jay, Ilana, Lori. JD, John Marshall Law Sch., 1952. Claims adjuster State Farm Mutual Automobile Ins. Co., 1952—54; pvt. practice atty., 1955—71; asst. chief dep. sheriff Cook County, Ill., 1971—73; alderman, 50th ward Chgo. City Coun., 1973—; vice mayor City of Chgo., 1998—. Chmn. bldgs. com. Chgo. City Coun. Del. North Town Cmty. Coun., 1963—, bd. dirs.; zoning chmn. Hood Ave. Civic Improvement Assn., 1954-58; dist. leader Am. Cancer Soc., 1959; bd. dirs. Congregation Ezras Israel, 1958—, Bernard Horwich Jewish Cmty. Ctr., 1974-78, Assoc. Talmud Torahs, 1983—, Chgo. Assn. Retarded Citizens, 1979—; bd. govs. Bonds for Israel, 1972—; past campaign chmn. govt. agys. div. Jewish United Fund, 1978-79; commr. Northeastern Ill. Planning Commn., 1977-83; mem. Cook County Commn. on Criminal Justice, 1977-82. Recipient Svc. award, Chgo. & Cook County Criminal Justice Commn., 1982, Pub. Svc. award, Assn. Talmud Torahs, 1982, Spl. Recognition award, Landmark Preservation Coun., 1983, Svc. award, Northeastern Ill. Planning Commn., 1983, Jerusalem award, 1996; named Man of Yr., Shomrin Soc., Ill, 1974. Mem. Ill. Bar Assn., Decalogue Soc. Lawyers, Am. Legion, Westridge C. of C., B'nai B'rith (1st pres. Jacob M. Arvey Pub. Svc. Lodge), Jewish War Vets. (past state judge adv., post comdr.). Jewish. Office: 6199 N Lincoln Ave Chicago IL 60659 also: City Hall 121 N La Salle St Rm 200 Chicago IL 60602 Office Phone: 773-764-5050, 312-744-6855. Business E-Mail: bstone@cityofchicago.org.

STONE, BERNELL KENNETH, finance educator; b. Salt Lake City, Jan. 16, 1942; s. Warren Kenneth and Clara Corina Stone; m. Anna Tueller Tueller, July 2, 1996; children: Emma Tueller, Karine Kenna, Jared K.C.; m. Sandra Lelia Sellew, June 9, 1964 (div. Aug. 0, 1991). BS, Duke U., Durham, NC, 1964; MS, U. Wis., Madison, 1966; PhD, MIT, Cambridge, Mass., 1969. Instr., tchg. fellow U. Wis., Madison, 1965—66; pres. and founder Codon Computer Utilities, Boston, 1967—70; instr. MIT, Cambridge, 1967—68; prof. Cornell U., Ithaca, NY, 1970—76; Mills B. ln. prof. banking and fin. Ga. Inst. Tech., Atlanta, 1976—88; adj. scholar Heritage Found., Washington, 1978—88; Harold R. Slver prof. fin. Brigham Young U., Provo, Utah, 1986—; exec. dir. founding Assn. Fin. Profls. (formerly Nat. Corp. Cash Mgmt. Assn.), 1980—82; sr. economist SEC, Washington, 2003—04. Assoc. editor Fin. Mgmt., Tampa, Fla., 1973—81, Jour. Fin. and Quantitative Analysis, Seattle, 1974—83; founding editor Jour. Cash Mgmt., Atlanta, 1980—84; editor and principle writer NCCMA Newes Letter, Atlanta, 1980—83; principle instr. and co-founder Cash Mgmt. Acad., Atlanta, 1982—88; editl. bd. Advances Working Capital Rsch., NYC, 1986—. EDI Forum, Chgo. Author: (book) Risk, Return, and Equilibrium, Financing the Energy Industry, Petroleum Divestiture and the Use and Misuse of Business Segment Financial Statistics, One to Get Ready: How to Prepare your Company for E.D.I., Corporate Cash Management: Survey and Synthesis. Recipient Winner, Fin. Mgmt. Assn., 1971—72, 1974, 1998, Cash Mgr. of Yr., Cash Mgmt. Inst., 1986. Mem.: Fin. Mgmt. Assn. (dir. 1983—64), Am. Fin. Assn. Mem. Lds Ch. Avocations: weightlifting, fishing, skiing. Home: 4681 Windsor Dr Provo UT 84604 Office: Brigham Young Univ 626 Tnrb Provo UT 84602 Office Fax: 801-422-0108. Business E-Mail: bernell_stone@byu.edu.

STONE, BRIAN, engineering educator; b. Atlanta, Aug. 19, 1970; s. Brian Stone and Betsey Beach; m. Elizabeth C. Chandler, May 25, 1996; children: Brian Wesley, William Lewis. MEM, Duke U., Durham, NC, 1996; PhD, Ga. Inst. Tech., Atlanta, 2001. Asst. prof. U. Wis. Madison, 2001—05; assoc. prof. Ga. Inst. Tech., 2005—. Sci. Rsch. grant, US EPA, 2005—08.

STONE, CHRISTIAN DIAZ, medical educator; b. Santiago, Chile, Nov. 24, 1968; s. Sergio and Maria Stone; children: Lorencio Park, Josefina Lucia. MD, U. Calif., Irvine, MPH, 1995. Diplomate Am. Bd. Internal Medicine, 1995. Asst. prof. medicine Wash. U., Saint Louis, Mo., 2002—07, assoc. prof. medicine, 2008—. Achievements include research in inflammatory bowel disease. Office: Wash Univ 660 S Euclid CB 8124 Saint Louis MO 63110

STONE, DONALD RAYMOND, lawyer; b. Madison, Wis., Mar. 6, 1938; s. Donald Meredith and June Dorothy (Graffenberger) S.; m. Dorothy Tetzlaff, June 23, 1962; children: Randall, Brian. BS in Physics, U. Wis., 1960, JD, 1963. Bar: Minn. 1963, D.C. 1987, U.S. Supreme Ct. 1987. Patent atty. Honeywell, Inc., Mpls., 1963-66; patent atty. firm Burd, MacEachron, Braddock, Bartz & Schwartz, Mpls., 1966-68; with Medtronic, Inc., Mpls., 1968-87, v.p., then sr. v.p. product assurance and regulation, 1973-77, sr. v.p., sec., gen. counsel, 1977-80, sr. v.p., 1980-85, v.p., 1985-87; ptnr., mem. Burditt, Bowles & Radzius, Chartered, Washington, 1987-90; ptnr. McKenna & Cuneo, L.L.P., Washington, 1990-2001, Kirkpatrick & Lockhart LLP, Washington, 2001—03, of counsel, 2003; ret., 2003. Condr. seminars, 1974—. Contbr. articles to profl. jours. Bd. dirs., 1st v.p. East Side Neighborhood Services, Inc., Mpls., 1976-80; bd. dirs. Guthrie Theater Found., 1979-85; mem. allocations com. United Way Mpls., 1979-86, chmn. allocations com., 1985, bd. dirs. 1985-86; mem. Citizens League of Twin Cities, 1965-86. Mem. ABA, D.C. Bar Assn., Fed. Bar Assn., Hennepin County Bar Assn., Am. Soc. Quality, Am. Intellectual Property Law Assn., Advanced Med. Tech. Assn. (past chmn. legal and regulatory sect., std. sect., 1975-87), Nat. Elec. Mfrs. Assn. (past chmn. med. electronics sect., 1970-76), Minn. State Bar Assn., Minn. Intellectual Property Law Assn. (past sec.), Minn. Corp. Counsel Assn., Order of Coif, Phi Delta Phi, Kappa Sigma. Episcopalian.

STONE, EDMUND CRISPEN, III, banker; b. Charleston, W.Va., Nov. 29, 1942; s. Edmund C. and Sallie Ragland (Thornhill); S.; m. Annette Margarethe Isaksen, Nov. 26, 1965 (div.); 1 child, Kristine Margarethe; m. Barbara J. Sarff, June 15, 2000. BS, U.S. Mil. Acad., 1964; MBA, U. Va., 1972. V.p. Wachovia Bank, Winston-Salem, N.C., 1972-81; exec. v.p. First Am. Corp., Nashville, from 1981; vice chmn. First Am. Nat. Bank Nashville, 1988; exec. v.p. Regions Fin. Corp. (formerly First Ala. Bancshares, Inc.), Birmingham, 1988—2005; chief credit officer First Nat. of Nebr. Inc.; ret. Contbg. author: The International Banking Handbook, 1983. Mem. export policy task force U.S. C. of C., 1980-81. With inf. U.S. Army, 1964-70, Vietnam, Iran. Decorated Bronze Star (Valor) with oak leaf cluster, Vietnamese Cross of Gallantry, others; hon. mem. Imperial Iranian Spl. Forces, 1968. Mem. Assn. of Grads. U.S. Mil. Acad. (trustee 1992-93, 98-2001, 2001—08). Republican. Avocations: golf, sailing, hunting, fishing. E-mail: cstone@fnni.com.

STONE, EDWARD C., physicist, researcher; b. Knoxville, Iowa, Jan. 23, 1936; s. Edward Carroll and Ferne Elizabeth (Baber) Stone; m. Alice Trabue Wickliffe, Aug. 4, 1962; children: Susan, Janet. AA, Burlington Jr. Coll., 1956; MS, U. Chgo., 1959, PhD, 1964, DSc (hon.), 1992, Washington U., St. Louis, 1992, Harvard U., 1992, U. So. Calif., 1998. From rsch. fellow in physics to prof. Calif. Inst. Tech., Pasadena, Calif., 1964—94, Voyager project scientist, 1972—, chmn. divsn. physics, math. and astron., 1983—88, v.p., 1988—2001, dir. jet propulsion lab., 1991—2001, David Morrisroe prof. physics, 1994—, mem. Draper Lab., 2001, vice provost for spl. projects, 2004—. Cons. Office of Space Sci., NASA, 1969—85, adv. com. outer planets, 1972—73; high energy astrophysics mgmt. oper. working group NASA, 1976—84, cosmic ray program working group, 1980—82, outer planets working group, 1981—82, solar sys. exploration com., 1981—82, U. rels. study group, 1983; exec. com. Com. on Space Rsch. Interdisciplinary Sci. Commn., 1982—86; com. on space astronomy and astrophysics Space Sci. Bd., 1979—82, steering group study on maj. directions for space sci., 1984—85; mem. Space Sci. Bd., NRC, 1982—85; commn. on phys. sci., math. and resources NRC, 1986—89; adv. com. vis. sr. scientist program NASA/Jet Propulsion Labs., 1986—90; com. on space policy NAS/NAE, 1988—89; chmn., chief sci. advisor The Astronomers, KCET, 1989—91; chmn. adv. panel NAS/WQED TV program "Sail on, Voyager!", 1989—90; v.p. COSPAR Bur., 2001—. Mem. editl. bd. Space Sci. Instrumentation, 1975—81, Space Sci. Rev., 1982—85, Astrophysics and Space Sci., 1982—, Sci. mag. Bd. dir. W.M. Keck Found., 1994—. Recipient medal for exceptional sci. achievement, NASA, 1980, Am. Edn. award, 1981, DSM, 1981, 1998, 2001, Dryden award, 1983, Disting. Pub. Svc. medal, 1985, Outstanding Leadership medal, 1986, 1995, Achievement award, Soc. for Tech. Comm., 1984, Space Achievement award, AIAA, 1986, Oppenheimer Mem. Lecture Aviation Week and Space Tech. Aerospace Laureate, 1989, Sci. Man of Yr. award, ARCS Found., 1991, Nat. Medal of Sci., 1991, Golden Plate award, Am. Acad. Achievement, 1992, COSPAR award, 1992, LeRoy Randle Grumman medal, 1992, Disting. Pub. Svc. award, Aviation/Space Writers Assn., 1993, Internat. von Karman Wings award, 1996, Space Flight Award, Am. Astron. Soc., 1997, Alumni award, S.E. C.C., Burlington, Iowa, 1997, CEO of Yr. award, ARC, 1998, Allan D. Emil Meml. award, Internat. Astronautical Fedn., 1999, Carl Sagan award, Am. Astronautical Soc. and Planetary Soc., 1999, Prof. Achievement award, Alumni, U. Chgo., 2002, Nat. Award for Op., Assn. for Unmanned Sys., Nat. Medal of Sci., Pres. Bush; named an asteroid Edward C. Stone in his honor, 1996; named to Hall of Fame, Aviation Week and Space Tech., 1997, Hall of Honor, Burlington Comm., 1999; fellow Sloan Found., 1971—73. Fellow: AAAS (award 1993), AIAA (assoc.; Calif. coun. sci. and tech. 1996—2001, Space Sci. award 1984, von Karman lectureship in astronautics 1999), Internat. Astron. Union, Am. Geophys. Union, Am. Phys. Soc. (exec. com. 1974—76, chmn. cosmic physics divsn. 1979—80); mem.: NAS, Sci. Edit. Bd., Comm. of Phys. Sci., Math., and Applications, NRC, Am. Philos. Soc., Calif. Assn. Rsch. in Astronomy (bd. dirs., vice-chmn. 1986—88, vice-chmn. 1986—2003, bd. dirs., vice-chmn. 1991—94, chmn. bd. dirs. 1994—97, bd. dirs., vice-chmn. 1997—2000, chmn. bd. dirs. 2000—03), Royal Aero. Soc., Nat. Space Club (bd. govs., Sci. award 1990), Astron. Soc. Pacific, Am. Philos. Soc. (Magellanic award 1992), Am. Astron. Soc. (divsn. planetary sci. com. 1981—84, Space Flight award 1997), Internat. Acad. Astronautics (trustee 1989—2001, v.p. 2001—). Office: Calif Inst Tech Space Radiation Lab M/C 220-47 Pasadena CA 91125 Office Phone: 626-395-8321. Business E-Mail: ecs@srl.caltech.edu.

STONE, EDWARD HARRIS, II, landscape architect; b. Lanesboro, Pa., Aug. 28, 1933; s. Frank Addison and Beth Lee (Brennan) S.; m. Diane Gertrude Berg, June 11, 1955; children: Randel Harris, Deborah Dee. BS, SUNY, 1955. Landscape architect Harmon, O'Donnell & Henninger, Denver, 1955-56, U.S. Forest Service, Colo., 1958-61; regional landscape architect Alaska, 1961-64; regional landscape architect, Colo., 1964—65; chief landscape architect U.S. Forest Service, U.S. Dept. Agr., Washington, 1965—79, asst. dir. for recreation, 1979-85; ret., 1985; with C-3 Co., Bowie, Md., 1986—. Founder Edward H. Stone, Clockmaker, Bowie, Md., 1989—. Exhibitions include The White House, Washington, Md. Hist. Soc. With US Army, 1956—58. Recipient Arthur S. Flemming award for outstanding fed. govt. service U.S. Jr. C. of C., 1969 Fellow Am. Soc. Landscape Architects (pres. 1975-76); mem. Sigma Lambda Alpha (hon.) Home and Office: 13200 Forest Dr Bowie MD 20715-4390

STONE, EDWARD HERMAN, lawyer; b. July 20, 1939; s. Sidney and Ruth Stone; m. Penni G. Gray (dec. 1990); children: Andrew, Matthew; m. Elaine Ornitz, Dec. 22, 1995. BS in Acctg., U. Ill., 1961; JD, John Marshall Law Sch., 1967. Bar: Ill. 1967, Calif. 1970, cert.: Calif. (specialist probate, estate planning, and trust law), registered: Martindale Hubbell Preeminent Lawyer Aence 1993. With IRS, 1963—71; assoc. Eilers, Baranger, Myers & Smith, 1971—72; pvt. practice Newport Beach, Calif., 1972—88, Santa Ana, Calif., 1988—89; mem. Davis, Samuelson, Goldberg & Blakely (formerly Cohen, Stokke & Davis), Santa Ana, 1984—88; ptnr. Edward H. Stone A Law Corp., Irvine, Calif., 1990—. Instr. income and estate taxes Western States U. Sch. Law, 1971—72; temporary judge Orange County Superior Ct.; panel mem. Orange County Superior Ct. Arbitration, Mediation, Early Neutral Evaluation, 2008; mediator tax cases in appeals IRS ADR, 2000—; moderator, spkr. CEB on Trust and Probate Litig., 1999, 2001, 04, 05, CEB on Postmortem & Post Death Planning, 2002, 04, 07, CEB on Death, Debts, Taxes, Claims Against Decedant, 2009. Contbr. articles to profl. jours. Pres. Jewish Family Svcs. Orange County, 1975; v.p., bd. dirs. Jewish Fedn. Orange County, 1985—88; bd. dirs. Heritage Points Orange County, 1992—95, Eastbluff Homeowners Cmty. Assn., Newport Beach, 1980—82, pres., 1981—82. Named one of Southern Calif. Super Lawyers, 2009. Mem.: Orange County Bar Assn. (vice-chmn. estate planning probate and trust law sect. 1976—77, chmn. sect. 1977—78, instr. Probate Clinic 1980, chairperson ADR com. 1996, spkr. in substantive law, dir. 1977—82, past chmn. profl. edn. coun., chmn.del. real property and probate sect, chmn. del. real property and probate sect. state bar conv. 1992—), Phi Alpha Delta (pres. alumni chpt. 1975—76). Office Phone: 949-833-7708. Business E-Mail: edstonelawoffice@sbcglobal.net.

STONE, F. L. PETER, lawyer; b. Wilmington, Del., Feb. 24, 1935; s. Linton and Lorinda (Hamlin) S.; m. Therese Louise Hannon, Apr. 7, 1969; 1 child, Lisa Judith. AB, Dartmouth Coll, 1957; LLB, Harvard U., 1960. Bar: Del. Supreme Ct. 1960, U.S. Ct. Appeals (3d cir.) 1964, U.S. Supreme Ct. 1965, U.S. Ct. Appeals (fed. cir.) 1983. Assoc. Connolly, Bove & Lodge, Wilmington, 1960-64; dep. atty. gen. State of Del., Wilmington, 1965-66; atty. Del. Gen. Assembly, Dover, 1967-68; counsel Gov. Del., Dover, 1969; U.S. atty. Dist. of Del., Wilmington, 1969-72; ptnr. Connolly, Bove, Lodge, & Hutz, Wilmington, 1972-97; counsel Trzuskowski, Kipp, Kelleher & Pearce, Wilmington, 1997—98, 2001—02; dep. atty. gen., counsel to ins. dept. State of Del., 1998-2001; dep. commr. Del. Ins. Dept., 2002—05. Mem. Del. Agy. to Reduce Crime, 1969-72, Del. Organized Crime Commn., 1970-72, State Drug Abuse Coun., 1990-93, State Judicial Nominating Commn., 1991-93, State Coun. Corrections, 1992-99; co-founder, adj. prof. criminal justice progra, West Chester (Pa.) U., 1975-79; chmn. Gov.'s Harness Racing Investigation Com., 1977, Del. Jai Alai Commn., 1977-78, Del. Govs. Corrections Task Force, 1986-88. Contbr. articles to profl. jours. Chmn. UN Day, Del., 1989; mem. Del. Gov.'s Task Force on Prison Security, 1994—95; trustee Leukemia Soc. Am., NYC, 1972—74, Marywood Coll., Scranton, Pa., 1974—79, Ursuline Acad., Wilmington, 1974—80; bd. dirs. Boys and Girls Club Del., 1997—, Seamen's Ctr., Port of Wilmington, 2001—; Rep. candidate for atty. gen. Del., 1990; mem. Rep. exec. com. Wilmington region, 1991—2000; chmn. re-election campaign Del. Ins. Commr., 1996. Mem. Port of Wilmington Maritime Soc. (bd. dirs., chair 1998-2000), Wilmington Country Club, Rehoboth Beach Country Club, Lincoln Club Del. (pres. 1994), Wilmington Rotary (bd. dirs. 1995-97), Nat. Assn. Former U.S. Attys. (bd. dirs. 1995-98). Roman Catholic. Avocations: hiking, tennis, golf, music, mountain climbing. Office: PO Box 4161 Greenville DE 19807 Home Phone: 610-388-0902. *My major accomplishment has been establishing and maintaining a close relationship with my family, first and foremost, regardless of what activities and accomplishments were pursued in my professional, political and community life.*

STONE, FLORENCE SMITH, film presenter, festival producer, consultant; b. Balt., June 15, 1938; d. Howard Chandler and Mary (Burnam) Smith; m. Roger David Stone; 1 child, Leslie Burnam. BA, Vassar Coll., 1960; cert. Inst. Arts Adminstrn., Harvard U., 1978. Asst. to v.p. for pub. rels. Transam. Corp., San Francisco, 1962—64; newsletter editor U.S. Embassy, Rio de Janeiro, 1964—66; coord. cmty. rels. Am. Mus. Natural History, NYC, 1970—79, coord. spl. progrm, 1977—84; dir. Washington Office Earthwatch, 1985—90; ind. cons. to mus. and ednl. orgns. Washington, 1990—; pres. Environ. Film Festival, Washington, 1993—. Co-chmn. Margaret Mead Film Festival, 1977-84. Trustee, Environ. Film Festival, 2007-, The Textile Mus., Washington, 1994-08, Laura Boulton Found., N.Y.C., 1980-99, Mus. of the Hudson Highlands, Cornwall-on-Hudson, N.Y., 1974-96; mem. adv. com. Margaret Mead Film Festival, N.Y.C., 1992—; active Trees for Georgetown Com., Washington, 1990—. Mem.: Textile Soc., Women in Film and Video, Ind. Film and Video Assn., Internat. Documentary Assn., Cosmos Club, Cosmopolitan Club, Georgetown Garden Club. Democrat. Avocations: textiles, films, trees, performing arts, outdoor activities. Office: Environ Film Festival 1228 1/2 31st St NW Washington DC 20007-3402 Office Phone: 202-342-2564. Business E-Mail: flo@envirofilmfest.org.

STONE, FRED MICHAEL, lawyer; b. Bklyn., Jan. 20, 1943; s. Nathan and Rose (Silverman) Stone; m. Bonnie B. Dobkin, Aug. 14, 1965; children: Jonathan, Jennifer. AB cum laude, Bklyn. Coll., 1964; JD, Harvard U., 1967; LLM, NYU, 1971. Bar: N.Y. 1968. Assoc. Cadwalader, Wickersham & Taft, NYC, 1967-69; asst. gen. counsel Standard & Poor's/Intercapital, Inc., NYC, 1969-71; v.p., gen. counsel Neuwirth Funds, 1971-73, Mocatta Metals Corp., NYC, 1973-76; sr. v.p., gen. counsel Am. Stock Exch., Inc., NYC, 1976-86; exec. v.p., gen. counsel Jamie Securities Co., Caronan Ptnrs., NYC, 1986-88; sr. v.p., gen. counsel, sec. M.D. Sass Assocs., Inc., NYC, 1989-2000; chmn. exec. com. Amex Commodities Exch., 1980-81; dir. Am. Gold Coin Exch., Inc., 1981-85; exec. v.p., dir. Revere Copper and Brass, Inc., 1986-88; dir. Ea. Electric Motor Co., Inc., 1987-88; mng. dir. Chase & M.D. Sass Ptnrs., 1998-2000; sr. mng. dir., exec. counsel Millennium Ptnrs., L.P., NYC, 2000—. Ofcl. advisor drafting com. to Revise Uniform Securities Act Nat. Conf. Uniform State Law Commrs., 1981—85; sec., treas. steering com. Taxaple Mcpl. Bondholders Protective Com., 1990—95; lectr. in field. Mem. Manalapan (N.J.) Twp. Zoning Bd. Adjustment, 1975—86, 2000—03, chmn., 2001—02; mem. N.J. regional adv. com. Anti-Defamation League of B'nai B'rith, 1991—; vice chmn. Manalapan Dem. Com., 1988—96; Dem. candidate Manalapan Twp. Com., 1989, 1993. Mem.: ABA (subcom. pvt. investment entities 1994—), Nat. Futures Assn. (mem. nominating com. 1986—88), Nat. Assn. Securities Dealers (arbitrator 1986—2005), Assn. Bar City of N.Y. (mem. chorus), Harvard U. Law Sch. Assn. Democrat. Jewish. Home: 15 Kingsley Dr Manalapan NJ 07726-3134 Personal E-mail: fred.stone@mlp.com.

STONE, GAYNELL, museum director, educator; d. Arthur Adrian Stone and Madelyn May Fisher; m. Gerald Stanley Levine; children: Andrew, Toby. AA, Del Mar Coll., Corpus Christi, Tex., 1948; BS, Tex. Woman's U., Denton, 1951; MLS, Stony Brook U., NY, 1976, MA in Anthropology, 1978, PhD, 1987. Mus. dir. Suffolk County Archaeolog. Assn., Stony Brook, 1983—. Bd. dirs. Native Am., Hauppauge, NY; adj. prof. Suffolk County CC, Selden, 1985—; spkr. in field. Contbr. articles to profl. jours. Pres., founder Suffolk County Early Childhood Assn., 1962—70, Long Island Studies Coun., 1984. Recipient Founders award, Suffolk Early Childhood Edn. Coun., 1977, Suffolk County Heritage award, 1979, award, LI Social Studies Coun., 1992, NY Archaeol. Coun. Founder, 2009, Oakley Cert. of Merit, Assn. Gravestone Studies, award, 2009; named Woman of Distinction, 1st Legis Dist., 2004; nominee NY State Senator Woman of Distinction, 2005; grantee, NSF, 1983. Fellow: Suffolk County Archaeolog. Assn. (pres., treas., rec. sec. 1972—); mem.: Soc. Hist. Archaeology, Coun. N.E. Hist. Archaeology. Avocations: reading, travel, gardening. Home: 2332 N Wading River Rd Wading River NY 11792 Office: SCAA PO Box 1542 Stony Brook NY 11790

STONE, GERALD LEE, university administrator, educator, psychologist; b. Glendale, Calif., Aug. 25, 1941; s. Jack Charles and Edith Bernice (Alexander) S.; m. Chery Ann Montgomery, Sept. 6, 1963; children: Corbin Lee, Carrie LeeAnn. BA, UCLA, 1963; BD, Princeton Theol. Sem., 1966; MA, Mich. State U., 1970, PhD, 1972. Licensed psychologist. From asst. prof. to assoc. prof. psychology U. Western Ont., Can., 1972-79; from assoc. prof. to prof. U. Iowa, Iowa City, 1979—, dir. counseling service, 1985—. Cons. Iowa Med. and Classification Ctr., Iowa City, 1984—. Author: Cognitive/Behavioral Approach to Counseling Psychology, 1980, Counseling Psychology: Perspectives and Functions, 1986; editor: The Counseling Psychologist, 1991—; contbr. over 60 articles to profl. jours. Old Gold fellow U. Iowa, 1980, 81; recipient 10 grants in field. Fellow APA (sect. divsn. 17 1981-84); mem. Am. Ednl. Rsch. Assn. (sec. 1981-83), Am. Coll. Pers. Assn., Counseling Psychology Tng. Coun. (program chmn. 1984-85). Democrat. Presbyterian. Avocations: reading, movies, sports. Office: U Iowa U Counseling Svc Westland Iowa City IA 52240

STONE, ISSAC (BIZ STONE), application developer, consultant; m. Livia Stone. Student, Northeastern U., U. Mass. Designer Little, Brown and Co., 1994—97; creative dir. Xanga, Inc., 1999—2001; sr. specialist Google, Inc., 2003—05; dir. cmty. Odeo, Inc., 2005—06; co-founder Obvious Corp. (spun off Twitter, Inc.), 2006, Twitter, Inc., Calif., 2007, creative dir. Calif., 2007—. Advisor to start-ups such as Fluther.com, Trazzler.com (also co-founder), Plinky.com, Justgive.org. Author: Blogging: Genius Strategies for Instant Web Content, 2002, Who Let the Blogs Out?, 2004. Named one of The World's Most Influential People, TIME mag., 2009. Office: Twitter Inc 539 Bryant St Ste 402 San Francisco CA 94107*

STONE, JACQUELYN ELOIS, lawyer; b. Williamsburg, Va., Jan. 7, 1958; d. William Thomas and Sara Elizabeth (Cumber) Stone. BA in Am. Govt., U.Va., 1980; JD, Harvard U., 1985. Bar: Va. 1985. Legis. asst. US Ho. of Reps., Washington, 1980-82; assoc. McGuire, Woods, Battle & Boothe, LLP (now McGuireWoods LLP), Richmond, Va., 1985—94, ptnr., 1994—, mem. bd. partners, firmwide hiring ptnr. & recruiting com. chair, mem. diversity com. Bd. mem. Arts Coun. of Richmond, past pres.; bd. mem. Jr. Achievement of Ctrl. Richmond, Richmond Eye & Ear Hosp., Venture Richmond, asst. sec.; exec. com. mem. Va. Performing Arts Found.; mem. local adv. com. Local Initiatives Support Corp.; bd. mem. Va. Commn. for the Arts. Recipient Outstanding Woman Award, YWCA, 2000, Women of Achievement award, Met. Richmond Women's Bar Assn., 2005, Themis award, DuPont Women's Lawyer Network, 2005. Mem.: ABA (mem. bus. law sect. 1985—), Am. Immigration Lawyers Assn., Old Dominion Bar Assn. (mem. exec. com. 1990—92), Va. Bar Assn. (exec. com. young lawyers sect. 1988—90, chmn. membership com. 1988—90), Va. State Bar. Baptist. Avocation: travel. Office: McGuireWoods LLP One James Ctr 901 E Cary St Richmond VA 23219-4030 Office Phone: 804-775-1046. Office Fax: 804-698-2183. Business E-Mail: jstone@mcguirewoods.com.

STONE, JAMES HOWARD, management consultant; b. Chgo., Mar. 4, 1939; s. Jerome H. and Evelyn Gertrude (Teitelbaum) S.; divorced; children: Margaret Elisa, Emily Anne, Phoebe Jane. AB cum laude, Harvard U., 1960; MBA, Harvard Bus. Sch., 1962. Cert. mgmt. cons., 1977. From staff analyst to exec. com. Stone Container Corp., Chgo., 1962—83, former exec. and audit coms., 1983—96; founder, owner, CEO, pres. Stone Mgmt. Corp., Chgo., 1969—; dir. privately-owned beverage mfr. Sheridan Beverage Co., Chgo., 1989—96; dir. privately-owned distributor and fabricator metals and metal products Fullerton Metals Co., Northbrook, Ill., 1993—98; pres. JEMP, Inc., Chgo., 2002—. Mem. strategic alliance Boston Cons. Group, 1990—; trustee, sec., exec. com. Roosevelt U., Chgo., 1983—, exec. com. edn. alliance, 1994—; co-chmn. commn. fgn. and domestic affairs Northwestern U., Evanston, Ill., 1981-85, bus. plan judge Kellogg Grad. Sch. Mgmt., 1994—; mem. vis. com. libr., lectr. U. Chgo., 1980—, The Chgo. Com., 1986—, Mid-Am. Com., Chgo., 1993-98; bd. overseers, lectr. IIT Stuart Sch. Bus., 1993—; bd. dirs. Cinema Chgo./Chgo. Film, Festival, Pilgrim Chamber Players, pres.; past pres., regional dir. Chgo. chpt. Inst. Mgmt. Cons.; past dir. Chgo. Roundtable Coun. Logistics Mgmt.; past pres., dir. Harvard Bus. Harvard Bus. Sch. Club Chgo. Contbr. articles in various trade jours. Mem. Chgo. Coun. Fgn. Rels., 1967, bd. dirs., 1974-78; bd. dirs., mem. exec. com. NCCJ, Chgo., 1985, presiding co-chmn., 1990-97; trustee Hadley Sch. Blind, Winnetka, Ill., 1985-96, chmn. planning com., 1989-96, Hadley life trustee, 1996—; vice chmn. fin. com. North Shore Congregation Israel, 1995-98; bd. dirs. Suzuki-Orff Sch., 1997-03; pres. Pilgrim Chamber Players, 2002—; former presiding co-chair Chgo. region Nat. Conf. Christians and Jews; sec., trustee, mem. exec. com. Roosevelt U.; mem. Chgo. Alliance Com.; life trustee Hadley Sch. for the Blind; vis. com. libr., patron U. Chgo.; with Northwestern U. Asher Sch. Psychiatry, Med. Sch.; bd. overseers Ill. Inst. Tech. Stuart Sch. Bus.; pres.'s cir., former dir. Chgo. Coun. Fgn. Rels.; advisor DCFS; mem. JVS Duman Loan Com.; dir. Blue Gargoyle, Little City Found.; past vice chmn. fin. com. North Shore Congregation Israel. Recipient Spirit of Life award, 2003. Mem. Coun. Logistics Mgmt. (dir. Roundtable-Chgo. 1990-94, lectr. Northwestern U. Ill. Inst. Tech.), The Exec. Club Chgo., Econs. Club Chgo., Harvard Club Chgo. (dir. 1995—), Harvard Bus. Sch. Club Chgo. (dir. 1992—, pres. 1997-99), Traffic Club Chgo., Std. Club, Northmoor Country Club, Mid-Day Club, The Casino Club, MidAm. Club, Arts Club, Juvenile Protective Assn. (trustee 1999—, dir.), The East Bank Club, Little City Found. Avocations: reading, golf, travel, writing. Office Phone: 312-236-0800. Business E-Mail: stonem@stonemgnt.com.

STONE, JAMES LELAND, surgical neurologist, educator; b. Chgo., July 20, 1948; s. Sol and Anne (Mandal) S.; m. Michelle Seiden, Dec. 25, 1975; children: Jasmine, Jett BA, U. Wis., 1970; MD, St. Louis U., 1974. Diplomate Am. Bd. Neurol. Surgery, Am. Bd. Psychiatry and Neurology, Am. Bd. Clin. Neurophysiology and Electroencephalography. Intern Cook County Hosp., Chgo., 1974—75; resident neurosurgery U. Ill., Chgo., 1975—80, fellow clin. neurophysiology, 1984—85, resident neurology, 1987—88, prof. neurosurgery, 1993—; chmn. neurosurgery Cook County Hosp., Chgo., 1987—2004, attending neurosurgeon, 1980—, clin. neurophysiologist, 1985—, neurologist, 1988—; prof. neurosurgery and neurology U. of Ill., Chgo., 2003. Fellow ACS; mem. Am. Acad. Neurology, Am. Assn. Neurol. Surgeons, Am. EEG Soc., Soc. Neurol. Surgeons Home: 730 Sheridan Rd Evanston IL 60202-2502 Office: Univ Ill Chgo Dept Neurology 912 S Wood St 4th Floor Chicago IL 60612 Office Phone: 312-996-4842.

STONE, JAMES MERRILL, lawyer; b. Columbus, Ohio, Mar. 7, 1952; s. Irving Joseph and Dessie (Flauhaus) S. m. Winifred Ann Storkan, Apr. 11, 1981; children: Jennifer Elizabeth, Jeffrey Joseph. BA, Ohio State U., 1976; JD summa cum laude, Cleve. State U., 1986. Bar: Ohio 1986, U.S. Dist. Ct. Ohio 1986, U.S. Ct. Appeals (6th cir.) 1986. Tech. dir. Karamu House, Cleve., 1974-77; pres., gen. mgr. Merrill Stone Assocs., Inc., Cleve., 1977-83; ptnr. McDonald, Hopkins, Burke and Haber Co. LPA, Cleve., 1986—2006; ptnr., resident mgr. Jackson Lewis LLP, 2006—. Contbr. articles to profl. publs. Awards com. chairperson U.S. Inst. Theatre Tech., Cleve., 1984-89; bd. dirs. Cleve. Pops Orch., 2004-; Deacon Solon Cmty. Ch., Ohio. Frew scholar Cleve. State U., 1986. Mem. ABA, Cleve. Bar Assn., Soc. Human Resource Mgmt., Delta Theta Phi (Jaeger award 1984), Union Club. Home: 32638 Haver Hill Dr Solon OH 44139-1913 Office: Jackson Lewis LLP Pk Ctr Plz J Ste 400 6100 Oak Tree Blvd Cleveland OH 44131 Home Phone: 440-349-0974; Office Phone: 216-750-0407. Business E-Mail: james.stone@jacksonlewis.com.

STONE, JED, lawyer; b. Chgo., Sept. 30, 1949; s. William P. and Bernice (Birenhotz) Stone; children: Meghan Elizabeth, Allison Leigh, Benjamin William. BA with honors, Lake Forest Coll., 1971; JD, Chgo. U., 1975. Bar: Ill. 1976, Wis. 1984, Ill. (US Dist. Ct. (no. dist.)) 1976, (US Ct. Appeals (7th cir.)) 1983, (US Ct. Appeals (5th cir.)) 1985, (US Ct. Appeals (11th cir.)) 1986, (US Supreme Ct.) 1984, (US Dist. Ct. (cen. dist.) Ill.) 1988, cert.: (criminal trial adv.), diplomate: Nat. Bd. Trial Advocacy 1984. Staff atty. Lawyer's Com. Civil Rights Under Law and Land of Lincoln Legal Aid, Cairo, Ill., 1975; sr. staff atty. Prairie State Legal Svcs., Waukegan, Ill., 1975—77; ptnr. The Law Offices of Jed Stone, Ltd., Chgo.; lectr. Ill. Inst. Continuing Legal Edn., Ill. State Bar Assn. Law Edn. Series; mem. faculty Nat. Criminal Def. Coll., Macon, Ga., 1994—95; vis. lectr. Russian Acad. of Law & Sci., St. Petersburg, Russia, 1995; pres., bd. dirs. Prairie State Legal Svcs., Inc., 1982—84; bd. dirs. Lake County Urban League, Waukegan, 1981—; bd. mem. alumni bd. gov.'s. Lake Forest Coll., Ill., 1981—87; treas., pres., 1994—95; bd. dirs. Ill. Attys. Criminal Justice. Co-author: Defending Illinois Criminal Cases, 1988; author: Illinois Criminal Defence Motions, 1993. Mem.: NY State Defender Assn. (faculty defender inst.), Lake County Bar Assn. (chmn. criminal law sect. 1983—86), Ill. Attys. Criminal Justice (bd. dirs. 1986—), Nat. Assn. Criminal Def. Lawyers (various coms.), Ill. Coalition Against the Death Penalty (pres. 1995), Urban League (life), NAACP (life). Democrat. Jewish. Office: Stone & Associates LLC 415 Washington St Ste 107 Waukegan IL 60085 E-mail: jstone@jedstone.com.

STONE, JEREMY JUDAH, professional society administrator; b. NYC, Nov. 23, 1935; s. I.F. and Esther (Roisman) S.; m. Betty Jane Yannet, June 16, 1957. BS magna cum laude, Swarthmore Coll., 1957, LL.D. (hon.), 1985; PhD, Stanford U., 1960. Research mathematician Stanford Research Inst., 1960-62; mem. profl. staff Hudson Inst., Croton-on-Hudson, 1962-64; research asso., arms control and disarmament Harvard Ctr. Internat. Affairs, 1964-66; asst. prof. math., lectr. polit. sci. Pomona Coll., Claremont, Calif., 1966-68; pres. Fedn. Am. Scientists, Washington, 1970-2000, Catalytic Diplomacy, 1999—. Author: Containing the Arms Race; Some Concrete Proposals, 1966, Strategic Persuasion, 1967, "Every Man Should Try." Adventures of a Public Interest Activist, 1999. Recipient award for pub. svc. Forum on Physics and Soc., Am. Phys. Soc., 1979, Fedn. of Am. Scientists Pub. Svc. award, 1994; Social Sci. Rsch. Coun. fellow in econs. Stanford U., 1968-69, Coun. Fgn. Rels. internat. affairs fellow, 1969-70. Mem. Coun. Fgn. Rels., Internat. Inst. Strategic Studies, Phi Beta Kappa. Home and Office: 5615 Warwick Pl Bethesda MD 20815-5503 E-mail: Jstone@catalyticdiplomacy.org.

STONE, JIN, language educator; PhD, U. Minn., Mpls. Tchg. specialist U. Minn., 2000—. Vis. prof. Macalester Coll., St. Paul, 2002—. Contbr. articles to profl. jours. Mem.: MLA. Achievements include research in Asian American literature, and in Chinese language. Business E-Mail: jin@macalester.edu.

STONE, JONATHAN FRANCIS, biology professor; s. Richard Edward and Rita Mae Stone; m. Joanne Heiselman, July 28, 1985; children: Alexander Christian, Katherine Ann. BS in Natural Scis., U. Akron, Ohio, 1985; BS in Human Biology, Nat. U. Health Scis., Lombard, Ill., D in Chiropractic, 1988. Diplomate Nat. Bd. Chiropractic Examiners, 1985. Physician, Lees burg, 1992—2001; asst. prof. Kent State U., 2002—. Pres. Ctrl. Fla. Chiropractic Soc., Orlando, 1995—96. Recipient Outstanding Tchg. award, Kent State U., 2008, Vol. of Yr. award, ARC Fla., 1999. Libertarian.

STONE, JOSS (JOSCELYN EVE STOKER), singer; b. Dover, Eng., Apr. 11, 1987; d. Richard and Wendy Stoker. Winning contestant Jr. Star for a Night, BBC TV talent show, 2002; former back-up singer for Britney Spears. Spokeswoman The Gap, 2005. Singer: (albums) The Soul Sessions, 2003, Mind Body & Soul, 2004 (Capital Award, London's favourite UK album, 2005), Introducing Joss Stone, 2007, (songs) Family Affair (Grammy award for Best Group Vocal R&B Performance, 2007); actor: (films) Eragon, 2006. Recipient Brit Award best British female solo artist, 2005, Brit Award best British urban act, 2005, Grammy Nomination best new artist, 2005, Grammy Nomination best female pop vocal performance, 2005, Grammy Nomination best pop vocal performance, 2005.

STONE, LARRY DEAN, consumer products company executive; b. North Wilkesboro, NC, July 18, 1951; s. Clyde D. and Irene (Mamess) Stone; m. Diane Adams, Aug. 23, 1969; children: Larry Jr., Chris. Student in bus., Wilkes Community Coll., Wilkesboro, NC, 1971. With mailroom and printshop Lowe's Cos., Inc., North Wilkesboro, 1969-70, area gen. mgr., 1986-89; office trainee Lowe's of Hickory, NC, 1970-71; office and credit mgr. Lowe's of Raleigh, NC, 1971-75, sales mgr. NC, 1975-78; store mgr. Lowe's of Cary, NC, 1978-83, Lowe's of North Wilkesboro, 1983-86; v.p. store merchandising Lowe's Cos., North Wilkesboro, 1989-92, v.p. merchandising, 1992-95, sr. v.p. sales opers., 1995-96, exec. v.p. store opers., 1996, sr. exec. v.p. store opers., 2003—05, sr. exec. v.p. merchandising and mktg., 2005—06, pres., COO, 2006—. Bd. dir. North Wilkesboro Mchts. Assn., 1985, North Wilkesboro Homebuilders Assn., 1985. With US Army, 1970—76. Mem.: Rotary (treas. North Wilkesboro chpt. 1982-84), Elks. Republican. Baptist. Avocations: golf, swimming. Office: Lowe's Cos Inc PO Box 1111 North Wilkesboro NC 28656*

STONE, MARLA SUSAN, history professor; b. Huntington, NY, Apr. 18, 1960; d. Nelson and Dolores Stone; m. Scott Thomas Johnson, Mar. 11, 2001; 1 child, Claudia Johnson Stone. BA, Pomona Coll., Claremont, Calif., 1982; MA, Princeton U., NJ, PhD, 1990. Lectr. Princeton U., 1990—93; prof. history Occidental Coll., LA, 1994—. Contbr. numerous essay collection (Rome prize, 1996). Founding bd. mem. Jews Against Genocide, NYC, 1994—2000; bd. mem. ACLU, LA, 2004—08. Office: Occidental Coll 1600 Campus Rd Los Angeles CA 90041

STONE, MARVIN JULES, hematologist, oncologist, educator; b. Columbus, Ohio, Aug. 3, 1937; s. Roy J. and Lillian (Bedwinek) S.; m. Jill Feinstein, June 29, 1958; children: Nancy Lillian, Robert Howard. Student, Ohio State U., 1955-58; SM in Pathology, U. Chgo., 1962, MD with honors, 1963. Diplomate Am. Bd. Internal Medicine, (Hematology, Med. Oncology). Intern ward med. svc. Barnes Hosp., St. Louis, 1963-64, asst. resident, 1964-65; clin. assoc. arthritis and rheumatism br. Nat. Inst. Arthritis and Metabolic Diseases, NIH, Bethesda, Md., 1965-68; resident in medicine, ACP scholar Parkland Meml. Hosp., Dallas, 1968-69; fellow in hematology-oncology, dept. internal medicine U. Tex. Southwestern Med. Sch., Dallas, 1969-70, instr. dept. internal medicine, 1970-71, asst. prof., 1971-73, assoc. prof., 1974-76, clin. prof., 1976—, chmn. bioethics com., 1979-81; mem. faculty & steering com. Immunology Grad. Program, Grad. Sch. Biomed. Scis., U. Tex. Health Sci. Ctr., Dallas, 1975, adj. mem., 1976—2008; dir. oncology med. edn., quality & safety, assoc. dir. Cancer Ctr., 2008—. Dir. Charles A. Sammons Cancer Ctr., chief oncology, dir. immunology, co-dir. divsn. hematology-oncology, attending physician Baylor U. Med. Ctr., Dallas, 1976—; v.p. med. staff Parkland Meml. Hosp., Dallas, 1982, dir. Oncology Med. Edn. Quality and Safety, 2008-, assoc. dir., Baylor Charles A. Sammon Cancer Ctr. Contbr. chpts. to books, articles to profl. jours. Chmn. com. patient-aid Greater Dallas/Ft. Worth chpt. Leukemia Soc. Am., 1971-76, chmn. med. adv. com., 1978-80, bd. dirs., 1971-80; mem. v.p. Dallas unit Am. Cancer Soc., 1977-78, pres., 1978—; mem. adv. bd. Baylor U. Med. Ctr. Found., Marvin J. Stone Libr., Baylor Inst. Immunology Rsch., 1999. With USPHS, 1965-68. Recipient Wings of Eagles award, Baylor Health Care Sys., 2001, Disting. Svc. award, U. Chgo., 2002, Lifetime Achievement award, Internat. Soc. Study of Waldenstrom's Macroglobulinemia, 2004. Master ACP (gov. No. Tex. 1993-97, laureate Tex. chpt. 2000); fellow Royal Soc. Medicine (London); mem. AMA, Am. Assn. Immunologists, Am. Soc. Hematology, Internat. Soc. Hematology, Coun. Thrombosis, Am. Heart Assn. (established investigator 1970-75), Am. Soc. Clin. Oncology (edn. com. 2002-05, career devel. com. 2002-05), Am. Osler Soc. (bd. govs. 1997-2000, 2005—, v.p. 2001-03, pres. 2003-04), Am. Assn. for Cancer Rsch., So. Soc. Clin. Investigation, Tex. Med. Assn., Dallas County Med. Soc., Clin. Immunology Soc., Phi Beta Kappa, Sigma Xi, Alpha Omega Alpha. Office: Baylor U Med Ctr Charles A Sammons Cancer Ctr 3500 Gaston Ave Dallas TX 75246-2096 Business E-Mail: marvins@baylorhealth.edu.

STONE, MEREDITH JEAN, academic administrator; b. Bryan, Tex., Mar. 26, 1979; d. Lonnie Edward and Judy Ondrasek Hare; m. James Christopher Stone, Dec. 11, 1999; children: Hallie Elizabeth, Kinsey Abigail. BA, Hardin-Simmons U., Abilene, Tex., 2001; MA, Hardin-Simmons U., 2006; PhD student, Brite Divinity Sch. Grad. asst. Hardin-Simmons U., 2002—06, adj. prof., 2006—07. Contbr. bible study curriculum, articles to profl. jours. Treas. Comanche County Food Pantry, Comanche, Tex., 2003—05. Recipient Nat. Merit Scholar Hon. award, Bryan HS, 1997, All-American Team award, NCAA, 1998, 1999, 2001, Freshman of Yr., 1998, Baker Book Home award, Logsdon Sch. Theology, 2001, Aubrey W. Smith award, 2006; Leadership scholarship, Coop. Bapt. Fellowship, 2005—06. Mem.: Bapt. Women Ministry. Office: Logsdon Seminary Hardin-Simmons Univ Box 16235 Abilene TX 79698 Business E-Mail: mstone@hsutx.edu.

STONE, MERRILL BRENT, lawyer; b. Jersey City, Aug. 16, 1951; s. Leonard and Claire (Orlean) S.; m. Geri Ellen Satkin, Nov. 24, 1976; children: Jacqueline Blair, Erica Lauren. AB summa cum laude, Rutgers U., 1973; JD, Columbia U., 1976. Bar: N.J. 1976, N.Y. 1977, Fla. 1981, U.S. Dist. Ct. N.J. 1976, U.S. Dist. Ct. (so. dist.) N.Y. 1977, U.S. Dist. Ct. (so. dist.) Fla. 1983. Assoc. Kelley Drye & Warren, NYC, 1976-84, resident Miami, 1983-85, ptnr. NYC, 1985—, mng. ptnr., 1992—2003. Editor: (comments section) Columbia Human Rights Law Rev., N.Y.C., 1975-76. Trustee Greater Miami C. of C., 1984-85. Named Harlan Fiske Stone Scholar, Columbia Law Sch., N.Y.C., 1975-76. Mem. ABA (bus. bankruptcy com. sect. on bus. law, banking law com.), Fla. Bar Assn., Club 101, Phi Beta Kappa, Pi Sigma Alpha, Soc. Corp. Secs. & Governance Profls., Inst. Internat. Bankers, Securities Transfer Assn., Inc. (legal com. mem.) Office: Kelley Drye & Warren LLP 101 Park Ave New York NY 10178-0002 Office Phone: 212-808-7543. Business E-Mail: mstone@kelleydrye.com.

STONE, MICHAEL HOWARD, psychiatry educator; b. Syracuse, NY, Oct. 27, 1933; s. Moses Howard and Corinne (Gittleman) S.; m. Clarice Joan Kestenbaum, (div. 1979); children: David, John; m. Beth Janine Eichstaedt. BA, Cornell U., 1954, MD, 1958. Diplomate Am. Bd. Psychiatry and Neurology. Residency in psychiatry Columbia Coll. of Physicians & Surgeons, NYC, 1963-66; asst. prof. psychiatry Columbia Coll. Physicians and Surgeons, NYC, 1973-77; assoc. prof. Cornell Med. Coll., NYC, 1977-80; prof. psychiatry U. Conn., Farmington, 1980-84; clin. dir. U. Conn. Dept. Psychiatry, Farmington, 1980-84; prof. clin. psychiatry Mt. Sinai Sch. Medicine, NYC, 1984-85, Cornell Med. Coll., NYC, 1985-88, Columbia Coll. Physicians and Surgeons, NYC, 1988—; dir. research Middletown Psychiat. Ctr., NY. Visiting prof. psychiatry Albert Einstein Med. Ctr., NYC, 1987—; lectr. in field, 1987-; prof. clin. psychiatry Columbia Coll. Physicians and Surgeons. Author: The Borderline Syndromes, 1980, The Fate of Borderline Patients, 1990; editor: Borderline Disorders, 1981, Treating Schizophrenic Patients, 1983, Essential Papers on Borderline, 1985, Personality Disorders: Treatable and Untreatable, 2006, The Anatomy of Evil, 2009; host (TV show) Most Evil, 2006-07, (radio show) Sanfrancisco Phil Hendric, 2009; contbr. over 200 articles to profl. jours. Patron Metropolitan Opera. Recipient Hematology Fellowship NIH, 1961-63. Fellow Am. Psychiat. Assn.; mem. Am. Pschopathol. Assn., Am. Coll. Psychiatrists, Musica Sacra (bd. mem.) Republican. Jewish. Avocations: piano, collecting rare books, languages. Home and Office: 225 Central Park W New York NY 10024-6027 Office Phone: 212-758-2000. Personal E-mail: mhstonemd@yahoo.com.

STONE, NEIL JOSEPH, cardiologist, educator; b. Chgo., Jewish, Dec. 17, 1944; s. Milton J. and Margery Stone; m. Karla Saxon, May 4, 1975; children: Scott, Adam, Lauren. BS in Medicine, Northwestern U., 1966, MD with honors (summa cum laude), 1968. Diplomate Am. Bd. Internal Medicine, Am. Bd. Cardiovascular Diseases, Am. Bd. Clin. Lipidology. Intern to resident Peter Bent Brigham Hosp. at Harvard U. (now Brigham and Women's Hosp.), Boston, 1968—70; staff assoc. Nat. Heart, Lung, Blood Inst., NIH, Bethesda, Md., 1970—73; chief resident Northwestern Meml. Hosp., Chgo., 1973—74, adj. staff, 1975—76, assoc. attending staff, 1976—81, attending staff, 1981—, internist, cardiologist, lipidologist, 1975—, med. dir. Vascular Ctr., Bluhm Cardiovascular Inst., 2005—, Suzanne and Milton Davidson Disting. Physician, 2006—; fellow cardiology Feinberg Sch. Medicine, Northwestern U., Chgo., 1974—75, asst. prof., 1975—80, assoc. prof. medicine, 1981—96, prof. clin. medicine, cardiology, 1996—. Lectr. Cook County Grad. Sch., Chgo., 1976—; mem. NHLBI adult treatment guidelines panels, ATP I, III Nat. Cholesterol Edn. Program, 1986—87; mem. NHLBI Clin. Guidelines Leadership Group for Cardiovascular Risk Reduction; co-chmn. ATP IV guidelines com. Author: Fat Chance, 1980; co-author: Cholesterol: Your Guide for a Healthy Heart, 1993; co-author: (with Conrad Blum) Management of Lipids in Clinical Practice, 6th edit., 2006; contbr. articles to med. jours.; participated in the writing groups that published Am. Heart Assn. Guidelines for Primary Prevention of Cardiovascular Disease and Stroke, 2002, writing group mem. for revision 2004 Evidence-Based Guidelines for Cardiovascular Disease Prevention in Women for Am. Heart Assn. Coun. on Nutrition, Physical Activity, and Metabolism., writing group mem. Am. Heart Assn./Am. Dental Assn. Statement on Primary Prevention of CVD in Diabetes, assoc. editor Am. Heart Assn. Learning Library as editor for Metabolic Syndrome and Lipid Community Websites, Journal of Clinical Lipidology. Recipient Award of Yr., Chgo. Dietetic Assn., 1978, Teaching Attending of Yr. award, Northwestern Med. Sch., 1979, Jacques Smith Disting. Physician in Medicine award, 1993, NJ Healthcare Found. Humanism in Medicine award, Feinberg Sch. Medicine, Northwestern U., 2002. Master: ACP (Outstanding Vol. Clin. Tchr. award 2001); fellow: Inst. Medicine, Coun. Clin. Cardiology, Am. Coll. Cardiology, Am. Heart Assn. (mem. Couns. Arteriosclerosis and Clin. Cardiology, mem-at-large Coun. on Nutrition, Physical Activity and Metabolism, past chmn. nutrition com. and clin. affairs com., mem. expert panel on population and prevention sci., chair, com. on clin. lipidology, lipoprotein metabolism and thrombosis); mem.: Nat. Lipid Assn. (first pres. Midwest Lipid Assn. Chap., bd. dirs.), Am. Soc. Internal Medicine, Am. Fedn. Clin. Rsch., Chgo. Heart Assn. (nutrition sub com.), Northwestern Med. Sch. Alumni Coun. (pres. 1981—83). Avocations: golf, stamp collecting/philately. Office: 211 E Chicago Ave Ste 1050 Chicago IL 60611 Address: Feinberg Sch Med Northwestern U 303 E Chicago Ave Chicago IL 60611-3008 Office Phone: 312-944-6677. Office Fax: 312-944-3346. E-mail: n-stone@northwestern.edu.

STONE, OLIVER, film director, producer, scriptwriter; b. NYC, Sept. 15, 1946; s. Louis and Jacqueline (Goddet) S.; m. Najwa Sarkis May 22, 1971 (div. 1977); m. Elizabeth Stone June 6, 1981 (div. 1993); 2 children. Student, Yale U., 1965; BFA, NYU Film Sch., 1971. Tchr., Cholon, Vietnam, 1965-66; wiper U.S. Mcht. Marine, 1966; taxi driver NYC, 1971. Screenwriter: Midnight Express, 1978 (Acad. award for screenplay, Writers Guild Am. for screenplay), Evita, 1996; screenwriter, dir.: Seizure, 1974 The Hand, 1981, (with John Milius) Conan, the Barbarian, 1982 (writer), Scarface, 1983, (writer with Michael Cimino) Year of the Dragon, 1985, (writer with David Lee Henry) 8 Million Ways to Die, 1986; dir., writer (with Richard Boyle) Salvador, 1986, Platoon, 1986 (Acad. award for best dir., Dirs. Guild award, British Acad. award),(documenatary) Looking for Fidel, 2004; co-writer, dir.: Wall Street, 1987, Talk Radio, 1988, The Doors, 1991, Any Given Sunday, 1999; screenwriter, prodr., dir.: Born on the Fourth of July, 1989 (Acad. award for best dir. 1990), Heaven & Earth, 1993, Comandante, 2003, Looking for Fidel, 2004, Alexander, 2004, World Trade Center (Hollywood Dir. of the Yr. Hollywood Awards, 2006), 2006; co-writer, prodr., dir.: JFK, 1991, Natural Born Killers, 1994, Nixon, 1995 (Acad. award nominee for best screenplay with Stephen J. Rivele and Christopher Wilkinson 1996); prodr.: Love, Death, 1972, Sugar Cookies, 1973, Reversal of Fortune, 1991, South Central, 1992, Zebrahead, 1992, The Joy Luck Club, 1993, The New Age, 1994, The People vs. Larry Flynt, 1996, Savior, 1998, The Corruptor, 1999, (TV mini-series) Wild Palms, 1993; exec. prodr. The Iron Mze, 1991, Freeway, 1996, Killer: A Journal of Murder, 1996, Indictment: The McMartin Trial, 1995 (Emmy award), Cold Around the Heart, 1997, The Last Days of Kennedy and King, 1998, The Day Reagan was Shot, 2003; dir. only (short film) Last Year in Viet Nam, 1971, Mad Man of Martinique, 1979, U-Turn, 1992, Persona Non Grata, 2003, (films) W., 2008; film appearances include The Battle of Lover's Return, 1971, The Hand, 1981, Platoon, 1986, Wall Street, 1987, Born on the Fourth of July, 1989, The Doors, 1991, Nixon (voice only), 1995, Any Given Sunday, 1999. Served with U.S. Army, 1967-68. Decorated Purple Heart with oak leaf cluster, Bronze Star; Lifetime Achievement award, Stockholm Internat. Film Festival, 2004. Mem. Writers Guild Am., Dirs. Guild Am., Acad. Motion Picture Arts and Scis.

STONE, PETER HOWARD, cardiologist, educator; b. NYC, Mar. 31, 1948; s. Harvey and Ronnie (Eilenberg) S.; m. Lisa Vosburgh, May 6, 1984; children: Emily, Michael, Benjamin. BA, Princeton U., 1970; MD, Cornell U., 1974. Intern in internal medicine San Francisco Gen. Hosp., 1974-75; resident in internal medicine U. Calif., San Francisco, 1975-77; cardiology fellow Pacific Med. Ctr., San Francisco, 1977-79; rsch. fellow in medicine Peter Bent Brigham Hosp., Boston, 1979-80; instr. in medicine Harvard Med. Sch., Boston, 1979-83, asst. prof. medicine, 1983-91; assoc. prof. medicine, 1991—; assoc. dir. Samuel A. Levine cardiac unit Brigham and Women's Hosp., Boston, 1982-93; co-dir. Samuel A. Levine cardiac unit Brigham and Women's Hosp., Boston, 1993—, dir. clin. trials, cardiovascular div., 1991—. Dir. Clin. Trials Ctr. Brigham & Women's Hosp., 1995—. Fellow Am. Coll. Cardiology, Am. Heart Assn. (coun. on clin. cardiology). Office: Brigham & Women's Hosp Cardiovascular Div 75 Francis St Boston MA 02115-6106

STONE, PRECIOUS, communications educator; BA, Yale U., New Haven; MA, U. NC, Chapel Hill; MFA, U. NC Greensboro. Media coord. Discovery Comm., Md.; asst. prof. CCBC, Balt., 2000—. Dir.(co-prodr., writer): (video) The African Textile Collection of Mrs. Mattye Reed (Bronze Apple award, 1996), (prodr., writer) Racing, The Study, Across the Atlantic, (theatrical prodns.) The Colored Museum, The Children's Hour, Las Meninas. Office: CC Balt City 7201 Rossville Blvd E329 Baltimore MD 21237

STONE, RICHARD ALAN, medical educator; b. Cambridge, Mass., Nov. 21, 1945; s. Jack David and Abigail Stone; children: Chelsea, Jordan, Lisa, Caroline. BA, Brown U., Providence, 1964; attended, Columbia U., NY, 1966; MD, Tufts U., Boston, 1970. Cert. Nat. Bd. Med. Examiners, 1971, diplomate Am. Bd. Internal Medicine, 1973, Am. Bd. Nephrology, 1976, lic. Calif., 1975. Intern medicine Montefiore Hosp., Bronx, 1970—71, asst. resident medicine, 1971—72; fellow nephrology Duke U. Med. Ctr. Dept Biochemistry, Durham, NC, 1972—74; asst. prof. medicine U. Calif. Sch. Medicine, La Jolla, 1974—78, assoc. prof. medicine, 1978—79; dir. Vets. Adminstrn. Hosp. Hemodialysis Unit, San Diego, 1974—79; chmn. nephrology section. Eisenhower Med. Ctr., Rancho Mirage, Calif., 1979—, chmn. dept. medicine, 1982—84, sr. attending physician, 1985—; ASH specialist clin. hypertension, 1999—. Contbr. over 100 articles to profl. jours. Mem.: Riverside County Heart Assn., Internat. Soc. Nephrology, Am. Soc. Artificial Internal Organs, Southern Calif. Kidney Found., Nat. Kidney Found., Am. Assn. Advancement Scis., Am. Heart Assn., Am. Fed. Clin. Rsch., Am. Soc. Nephrology. Office: Eisenhower Medical Ctr 39000 Bob Hope Dr Ste 316 Rancho Mirage CA 92270-3221 Office Phone: 760-568-0383.

STONE, RICHARD JAMES, lawyer; b. Apr. 30, 1945; s. Milton M. and Ruth Jean (Manaster) S.; m. Lee Lawrence, Sept. 1, 1979; children: Robert Allyn, Katherine Jenney, Grant Lawrence. BA in Econs., U. Chgo., 1967; JD, UCLA, 1970. Bar: Calif. 1971, Oreg. 1994, D.C., 2000, Wash. State, 2004. Assoc. O'Melveny & Myers, LA, 1971-77; dep. asst. gen. counsel US Dept. Def., Washington, 1978-79; asst. to sec. US Dept. Energy, Washington, 1979-80; counsel Sidley & Austin, LA, 1981, ptnr., 1982-88; ptnr., head litig. dept. Milbank, Tweed, Hadley & McCloy, LA, 1988-94; mng. ptnr. Zelle & Larson, LLP, LA, 1994-97; counsel Ball Janik LLP, Portland, Oreg., 1998—2006, ptnr., 2007—. Adj. prof. law Lewis and Clark Northwestern Sch. Law, 1998—99; lawyer rep. 9th Cir. Jud. Conf., 1998—99; mem. legal ethics com. Oreg. State Bar, 2002—03, com. on spl. rules, 2002—03. Editor (editor-in-chief): (profl. jourl.) UCLA Law Rev., 1970; contbr. articles to profl. jours. Dir. Legal Aid Found., L.A., 1991—99, officer, 1994—98, pres., 1997—98; dir. Portland City United Soccer Club, 1999—2000, classic coach, 2002—04; gen. counsel and staff dir. Study of L.A. Civil Disturbance for Bd. Police Commrs., 1992; mem. vestry St. Aidan's Episcopal Ch., 1990—93, 1997—98, sr. warden, 1998; mem. pub. sector task force State Senate Select Com. on Long Range Policy Planning, Calif., 1985—86; mem. Oreg. Pub. Health Adv. Bd., 2008—; mem. adv. panel Coun. Energy Resource Tribes, 1981-85;, 1981—85; U.S. del. Micronesian Polit. Status Negotiations, 1978-79, 1978—79. With U.S. Mil. Acad. at West Point Oreg. Field Force, 2003—. Recipient Amos Alonzo Stagg medal and Howell Murray Alumni medal U. Chgo., 1967; honoree Nat. Conf. Black Mayors, 1980; recipient spl. citation for outstanding performance Sec. Dept. Energy, 1981. Fellow Am. Bar Found.; mem. ABA, Fed. Bar Assn., Calif. Bar Assn., Oreg. Bar Assn., Wash. Bar Assn., L.A. County Bar Assn. (trustee 1986-88), D.C. Bar Assn., Assn. Bus. Trial Lawyers, Multnomah County Bar Assn., Phi Gamma Delta. Home: 3675 NW Gordon St Portland OR 97210-1285 Office: Ball Janik LLP 101 SW Main St 11th Fl Portland OR 97204-3228 Office Phone: 503-228-2525. Business E-Mail: rstone@bjllp.com, rstone@balljanik.com.

STONE, RICHIE EUGENE, engineering educator; s. Bobby Eugene and Peggy Stone; m. Mitzi Diane Camp; children: Tyler Richard, Hannah Elizabeth. A in Drafting and Design Tech., NW Ala. State Tech. Coll., Hamilton, 1985; AAS, Bevill State CC, Phil Campbell, Ala., 1991; BSc, Athens State, Ala., 1996. Drafter Franklin Mfg., Russellville, Ala., 1985—90; drafting instr. Bevill State CC, Hamilton, 1990—.

STONE, ROGER DAVID, environmentalist; b. NYC, Aug. 4, 1934; s. Patrick William and Kathleen Mary Stone; married; 1 child. BA in English, Yale U., 1955. Asst. to pub. Time Mag., 1959-61, corr., news bur. chief San Francisco, Rio, Paris, 1961-68; asst. to pres. Time Inc., NYC, 1968-70; v.p. internat. dept. Chase Manhattan Bank, NYC, 1970-74; pres. Ctr. for Inter-Am. Rels., NYC, 1975-82; v.p. World Wildlife Fund, 1982-86, sr. fellow, 1986-90; vis. fellow, cons. on environ. issues Coun. on Fgn. Rels., 1990-92; vice chmn. ECO Inc., Washington, 1992-96; pres. Sustainable Devel. Inst., Washington, 1993—. Vis. lectr. Yale Ctr. Internat. and Area Studies, 1994-95; mem. external adv. bd. Yale Inst. Biospheric Studies. Author: Dreams of Amazonia, 1985, The Voyage of the Sanderling, 1990, Wildlands and Human Needs, 1991, The Nature of Development: Reports from the Rural Tropics on the Quest for Sustainable Economic Growth, 1992, Fair Tide: Sailing Toward Long Island's Future, 1996, Tropical Forests and the Human Spirit = Journeys to the Brink of Hope, 2001; guest editor: Am. Prospect, 2007—; contbr. chpts. to books, Warrington Monthly, 2008; contbr. articles to Time, Life, Life en Espanol, Fgn. Affairs, N.Y. Times, Internat. Herald Tribune, Christian Sci. Monitor, Harvard Bus. Rev., USA Today Mag., Cruising World, Conservation Found. Letter, the American Prospect, others. Bd. dirs. Astrolabe, Inc.; v.p. Armand G. Erpf Fund, Sotterley Found.; sec. St. Mary's River Watershed Assn.; former bd. dirs. U. Andes Found.; former bd. dirs. and exec. com. World Wildlife Fund-U.S., Ctr. for Inter-Am. Rels., Ams. Found., Accion Internat., Arts Internat., others. Lt. (j.g.) USN, 1956-59. Mem.: Century Assn. Democrat. Episcopalian. Avocation: sailing. Home: 1527 30th St Nw # B-32 Washington DC 20007 Office Phone: 202-338-1017. Fax: 202-337-9639. E-mail: susdev@igc.org.

STONE, SANDRA SMITH, sociologist, academic administrator, researcher; b. Chgo., Oct. 16, 1954; d. John Lawrence and Bernice (Pickett) Smith; m. Scott Lukens, 1973 (div. 1977); m. Charles M. Huguley, Oct. 17, 1982 (div. 1988); 1 child, Bailey Anne; m. Anthony V. Stone, Aug. 4, 1990; 1 stepchild, Adam Maraman. BA, U. West Ga., 1976, MA, 1978; PhD, Emory U., 1993. Cert. mediator, AACSB Freeman Sch. Bus., Tulane U., 2009. Social worker Carroll County Early Childhood Ctr., Carrollton, GA., 1977, Clayton Gen. Hosp., Riverdale, Ga., 1978-80; caseworker Fulton County Dept. Family and Children Svcs., Atlanta, 1981; caseworker prin. Cobb County Dept. Family and Children Svcs., Marietta, Ga., 1981-82; children's program supr. Coun. on Battered Women, Atlanta, 1982-83; sr. rsch. assoc. Ctrs. Disease Control/Ga. Dept. Human Resources, Atlanta, 1985-87; cons. Ctrs. Disease Control, Atlanta, 1987-88; rsch. assoc. Police Exec. Rsch. Forum, Washington, 1988-90; exec. dir. Rsch. Atlanta, 1990-91; sr. rsch. assoc. Emory U. Sch. Pub. Health, Atlanta, 1991-92; dir. planning & Rsch. Ga. Dept. Children & Youth Svcs., Atlanta, 1992-96; asst. prof. to prof. U. West Ga., Carrollton, 1996—2006, assoc. v.p. acad. affairs, 2002—06, acting v.p. acad. affairs, 2006; vice chancellor academic planning and programs Bd. Regents U. Sys. Ga., 2007—08, vice chancellor, spl. initiative, 2008—09; interim dir. Southern Poly. State U. Applied Rsch. Ctr., 2008—09; acting v.p. academic affairs U. West Ga., 2009—. Instr., Emory U., Atlanta, 1984-89; drug policy adviser Mayor's Office, City of Atlanta, 1989-90; grant application reviewer Nat. Ctr. Child Abuse and Neglect, Washington, Ga. Dept. Human Resources, Atlanta, Ctrs. Diseases Ctrl., Atlanta; cons. Coun. for Children, Atlanta, 1987, mem. Nat. Implementation Com. Am. Democracy Project. Contbr. articles, reports to profl. publs. Mem. DeKalb County Task Force on Child Care, Decatur, Ga., 1984, DeKalb County Task Force on Infant Mortality, Decatur, 1985-89, DeKalb County Task Force on AIDS, Decatur, 1987-88; assessor City of Atlanta Fire Chief Assessment Ctr., 1990; vol. United Way; mem. Criminal Justice Coord. Com., 1992-96; mem. statewide Task Force on Violence and Schs., 1993-95; profl. adv. coun. Mission New Hope, 1994-98; mem. nat. adv. bd. Juveniles Taken Into Custody Project, 1994-97; cons. family connection project Haralson County, 1997-2004; chair adv. bd. Ga. Dept. Juvenile Justice, Carroll County Ct. Svcs. Office, 1999-2001; bd. mem. Ga. Coun. Econ. Edn., 2007-, Possible Woman Found. Internat., 2008-. Mem. LWV, Ga. Coun. Child Abuse, Planned Parenthood, Am. Sociol. Assn., Am. Soc. Criminology, Ga. Sociol. Assn., Am. Pub. Health Assn., Am. Assn. State Coll. and U. (Am. Democracy Project, 2007-), So. Adv. Coun. (edn. testing svcs., 2007-), Adv. Coun. Early Learning Ctr., Kennesaw State U., Acad. Criminal Justice Scis., Sociol. Practice Assn., So. Criminal Justice Assn., Phi Kappa Phi, Alpha Kappa Delta. Democrat. Avocations: movies, theater, concerts, crafts, yoga. Home: 2078 Amberwood Way NE Atlanta GA 30345-3904 Office: Univ West Ga 1601 Maple St Carrollton GA 30118 Office Phone: 678-915-3266. Personal E-mail: sstone101654@aol.com. Business E-Mail: sstone@spsu.edu.

STONE, SHARON, actress; b. Meadville, Pa., Mar. 10, 1958; d. Joe and Dorothy S; m. George Englund Jr. (div.); m. Michael Greenburg, Aug. 18, 1984 (div. Jan. 20, 1987); m. Phil Bronstein, Feb. 14, 1998 (div. Jan. 29, 2004); 3 adopted sons, Roan Joseph, Laird Vonne, Quinn Kelly. Diploma in Creative Writing and Fine Arts, Edinboro State U. Model Eileen Ford Modeling Agy.; owner Chaos prodn. co. Actress (films) Stardust Memories, 1980, Deadly Blessing, 1981, Irreconcilable Differences, 1984, King Solomon's Mines, 1985, Allan Quatermain and the Lost City of Gold, 1986, Cold Steel, 1987, Police Academy 4: Citizens on Patrol, 1987, Action Jackson, 1988, Above the Law, 1988, Beyond the Stars, 1989 (Personal Choice award), Total Recall, 1990, Year of the Gun, 1991, Diary of a Hitman, 1991, He Said/She Said, 1991, Scissors, 1991, Basic Instinct, 1991, Where Sleeping Dogs Lie, 1992, Last Action Hero, 1993, Sliver, 1993, Intersection, 1994, The Specialist, 1994, (also co-prodr.) The Quick and the Dead, 1995 (also co-prodr.), Casino, 1995 (Golden Globe award for best actress in film 1996, Acad. award nominee for best actress 1996), Diabolique, 1996, Last Dance, 1996, Sphere, 1998, The Mighty, 1998 (Golden Global nominee), Antz, 1998 (voice), Gloria, 1999, The Muse, 1999, Simpatico, 1999, Beautiful Joe, 2000, Picking Up the Pieces, 2000, Cold Creek Manor, 2003, Cold Creek Manor, 2003, Catwoman, 2004, Jiminy Glick in La La Wood, 2004, A Different Loyalty, 2004, Broken Flowers, 2005, Alpha Dog, 2006, Basic Instinct 2, 2006, Bobby, 2006; TV appearances include Not Just Another Affair, 1982, Bay City Blues, 1983, Calendar Girl Murders, 1984, The Vegas Strip Wars, 1984, War and Remembrance, 1988, Tears in the Rain, 1988, (guest) The Larry Sanders Show, 1994, Big Guns Talk: The Story of the Western (tv spl.), 1997; narrator: Harlow: The Blond Bombshell, 1993, If These Walls Could Talk 2, 2000, Harold and the Purple Crayon, 2001, Cold Creek Manor, 2003. Chmn. Campaign for AIDS Rsch. amfAR, The Found. for AIDS Rsch., 2005—, global fundraising chmn., 2007—.

STONE, STEVEN MICHAEL, sports announcer, former baseball player; b. Euclid, Ohio, July 14, 1947; BS in Edn., Kent State U., 1969. Pitcher San Francisco Giants, 1971-72, Chgo. White Sox, 1973, Chgo. Cubs, 1974-76, Chgo. White Sox, 1977-78, Balt. Orioles, 1979—81;

color commentator, Chgo. Cubs WGN Continental Broadcasting Co., Chgo., 1983—2000, 2003—04; baseball analyst WSCR Radio, Chgo., 2005—, commentator, White Sox, 2008—. Restaurant owner, Scottsdale, Ariz. Co-author (with Barry Rozner): (book) Where's Harry?, 1999. Recipient Cy Young award, 1980; named Am. League Pitcher of Yr., The Sporting News, 1980; named to Am. League All-Star Team, 1980. Achievements include leading the American League in wins (25) during the 1980 season. Office: WSCR Radio 455 N Cityfront Plaza Dr Chicago IL 60611 Office Phone: 312-245-6000.

STONE, STUART LEE MORRISON, librarian, language educator; b. St. Louis, June 4, 1949; s. Norwood Lee Stone and Antoinette Aubouchon Engle. BS in Edn., The U. Mo., 1971; M of Libr. and Info. Sci., The Cath. U. Am., 1979, post-MLS, 1980—82. Cert. secondary edn. U. Mo., 1971, English as a fgn. lang. tchr. The Cambridge Sch., Ltd., London, 1982. Quadri-lingual rsch. asst. The Inter-Am. Def. Coll. / OAS, Washington, 1972—75; tchr. French, Spanish, & history The Wash. Ethical Soc. H.S., 1975—77; sr. staff asst. The U.S. Ho. Subcom. Postal Pers. and Modernization, 1980—82; tchr. English and Am. history The Am. Lang. Inst., Lisbon, Portugal, 1982—86; asst. libr. IMF, Washington, 1986—87; sr. cataloger, Portuguese-French-Spanish-Gaelic Libr. Congress, 1987—2002, recommending officer Scots-Gaelic, 1997—, sr. acquisitions specialist Europe and L.Am., 2000—, founder, coord. Scots Gaelic Lang. Table, 2004—. Instr. beginning and intermediate Scots-Gaelic Am. Gaelic Soc., Alexandria, Va., 1999—; mem. planning com. US Nat. Mod, 2006—. Translator (seminar instr. / U. Sao Paulo): (international library online networking) Training Manual / MARC Name Authorities; author: (ednl. discussion kit) Inauguration: An American Beginning (Presdl. Inaugural Com. award, 1981). Ward rep. bldgs. and grounds com. Fairlington Villages, Arlington, Va., 2003—06. With US Army, 1972—75. Decorated Joint Svc. Commendation medal Sec. Def. Pentagon. Fellow: Soc. Antiquaries Scotland; mem.: Libr. Congress Profl. Assn. (profl. assoc.), Am. Gaelic Soc. (newsletter editor asst. 1997—2000, Gaelic instr. 1997—), Am. Legion. Home: 3079 S Buchanan St C-2 Arlington VA 22206 Business E-Mail: ssto@loc.gov.

STONE, SUSAN A., lawyer; b. 1961; BA summa cum laude, Yale U., 1983; JD cum laude, Harvard U., 1987. Bar: Calif. 1987, U.S. Dist. Ct. (no. dist.) Calif. 1987, U.S. Ct. Appeals (9th cir.) 1987, U.S. Dist. Ct. (ctrl. dist.) Calif. 1988, Ill. 1990, U.S. Dist. Ct. (no. dist.) Ill. 1990, U.S. Ct. Appeals (7th cir.) 1990. Asst. U.S. atty. U.S. Dept. Justice, LA; law clk. to Judge William J. Orrick, U.S. Dist. Ct. for No. Dist. Calif.; ptnr. Sidley & Austin LLP, Chgo., 2001—, co-chair ins., reins. practice; and co-chair practice devel. com. Sidley Austin Brown & Wood, Chgo. Former adj. prof. trial practice DePaul U. Coll. Law, Chgo. Named one of Top Young Litigators Under 40, Ill. Legal Times, One of 40 Attorneys Under 40, Chgo. Lawyer. Mem. ABA, Ill. Bar Assn., Calif. State Bar, Phi Beta Kappa. Office: Sidley Austin Brown Wood 1 S Dearborn St Ste 900 Chicago IL 60603-2310 Office Phone: 312-853-2177. Fax: 312-853-7036. E-mail: sstone@sidley.com.

STONE, SUSAN FOSTER, mental health services professional; b. Salem, Mass., Mar. 15, 1954; d. Bruce and Carolyn (Foster) Hoitt; m. Norman Michael Stone, May 18, 1981; children: Brittany, Forrest. Student, U. York, Eng., 1974-75; BA in Psychology, Colby Coll., 1976; MS in Clin. Psychology, Abilene Christian U., 1979; PhD in Clin. Psychology, Calif. Sch. Profl. Psychology, 1985. Lic. psychologist, Calif. Mem. emergency response team Simi (Calif.) Dept. Police, 1980-81; cons. Children's Hosp. L.A., 1984-85; postdoctoral fellow Neuropsychiat. Inst. UCLA, 1985-86; clin. dir. Santa Clarita (Calif.) Child and Family Devel. Ctr., 1987-94, dir. tng., 1994-95. Cons. L.A. County Adoptions, 1985-88; expert witness L.A. Superior Ct., 1987—, State Funded Early Mental Health Initiatives, 1994; assisted in drafting congl. managed health care proposal, 1995; presenter in field. Mem. adv. coun. L.A. Foster Parent Assn., 1989-91. Office Juvenile Justice Systems grantee Spl. Children's Ctr., 1990, L.A. Regional Ctr. grantee, 1990. Mem.: APA. Office: 23504 Lyons Ave Ste 304 Newhall CA 91321-5776

STONE, SUSAN RIDGAWAY, marketing educator; b. Coronado, Calif., Oct. 30, 1950; d. Lester Jay and Marguerite Ridgaway (King) Stone; 1 child, Benjamin. AB, Wilson Coll., 1977; MBA, Shippensburg U., 1980; DBA, George Washington U., 1992. Prof. mgmt. and mktg. Shippensburg U., Pa., 1983—; dir. mktg. VSP Wastewater Tech., Gettysburg, Pa., 1982; pres. Ridgaway Rose Internat., Inc., 1999—; vis. lectr. U. Warsaw, Poland. Mktg. cons. Svcs. Unltd., Gettysburg, 1975—; lectr. in field. Author: (with Stephen J. Holoviak) Managing Human Productivity: People are Your Best Investment, 1987, 2nd printing 1991; contbr. articles to profl. jours. Recipient Excellence in Tchg. award, Corning Found., 1993, Outstanding Svc. award, 1994, 2002, Sprint Tchg. Excellence award, 1998, Orrston Bank Tchg. Excellence award, 2001, Panhellenic Coun. Tchg. award, 1999, Martin Babinec Outstanding Adv. award, 2003, tchg. award, Alpha Kappa Psi, 2008; fellow John L. Grove Rsch. fellow, 2002. Mem.: DAR, NOW, Am. Mktg. Assn., Acad. Mktg. Sci., Survivors, Inc., Nat. Hist. Trust, Adams County Literacy Coun., Mensa, Kappa Kappa Gamma, Beta Gamma Sigma. Democrat. Episcopalian. Avocations: gardening, writing, sailing. Office Phone: 717-477-1697. Business E-Mail: srston@ship.edu.

STONE, SYLVIA, voice educator, singer; d. Louie Moses Stone and Lettie Irene Snider; m. Ludwig Boder, July 14, 1974; m. Edward Corwin White, Aug. 26, 1959 (div. 1966); 1 child, Valerie Letitia White. AA, Stephens Coll., Columbia, Mo., 1955; MusB, Eastman Sch. Music, Rochester, NY, 1958, MusM, 1959; postgrad., Staatliche Hochschule für Musik, Stuttgart, 1964. Cert. in voice and opera Eastman Sch. Music, 1959. Guest artist Chautauqua Opera Assn., Chautauqua, NY, 1957—59, St. Louis Opera, St. Louis, Ill., 1959, Rochester Opera Under Stars, NY, 1960, Städtische Bühnen Heidelberg, Heidelberg, 1972, Bühnen der Stadt Kiel, Kiel, Germany, 1972, Operettenhaus Hamburg, Germany, 1973—76, Theater des Westens, Berlin, Saxony, Germany, 1975, Städtische Bühnen Freiburg, Germany, 1976—77, Landestheater Flensburg, Germany, 1977—78, Operagezellschap Forum Enschede, Enschede, Netherlands, 1977—78, Freilicht Basel, Switzerland, 1978, Schweizer Tournee Theater, Switzerland, 1978, Staatstheater Stuttgart, Germany; leading mezzo-soprano Bühnen der Hansestadt Lübeck, Freie Hansestadt, Germany, 1965—69, Städtische Bühnen Krefeld-Mönchenbladbach, Krefeld, Germany, 1969—73; assoc. prof. voice U. Ill., Urbana, 1981—91, advisor grad. students voice, 1983—, prof. voice, 1992—, prof. French diction singers, 1992—, prof. German diction singers, 1997—; artistic dir. Scuola Italia Summer Program Young Opera Singers, Urbania, Marche, 2004—. Cons. Komische-Kammer-Oper-München, Humbach, Bayern, Germany, 1996—2003; adjudicator Schs. Leopoldskron Competition Singers, Salzburg, Austria, 1998—2006; masterclass presenter clinician Austrian-Am.-Mozart-Academy, Salzburg, Austria, 1997—99, voice tchr., 1999—2007. Mem.: Nat. Assn. of Teachers of Singing.

STONE, VAN COURTRIGHT, not-for-profit developer; b. Deland, Fla., June 22, 1946; s. Wilfred Arthur and Catherine Louise Stone; m. Nancy M. Stone, July 19, 1969 (div. 1989); 1 child, Edana A. Stone Neundorf; m. Lisa L. Stone, Dec. 22, 1990; children: Melisa A., Wesley Alan. BA, Wichita State U., 1968; JD, Washburn U., 1974. Exec. v.p., officer S.W. State Bank, Topeka, Kans., 1974-81; pres. Nat. Bank of Andover, Kans., 1985-87; corp. atty. various corps., 1987-91; COO Gerber Bus. Devel. Corp., Petaluma, Calif., 1991-94; exec. dir. Lions of Ill. Found., Sycamore, 1995—. Bd. dirs. Ill. Sch. for the Visually Impaired, Jacksonville, Ill. Eye Fund, Chgo., mng. dir. Lions of Ill. Endowment Fund, 1995—; pres., N.Am. Conf. of Lions Founds., 2000-06, UIC Eye Fund. bd. dirs. Author: (newsletter) Lions Share, 1995—; contbr. articles to profl. jours. Capt. U.S. Army, 1968-71. Decorated 3 Bronze Stars; recipient Presl. medal of honor Ill. Coll. of Optimetry, 1999, Meritorious Svc. award Deicke Ctr., 1999; Lions Ill. Found. fellow Laureate, 2002. Mem. VFW (life), No. Aurora Lions Club, Lions Club Internat. (Melvin Jones fellow), Andover C. of C. (pres. 1986), Phi Sigma Rho, Tau Kappa Alpha, Phi Alpha Delta. Republican. Methodist. Avocations: golf, running, bridge, writing, bowling. Office: Lions Ill Found 2814 Dekalb Ave Sycamore IL 60178-3117 Home Phone: 630-262-8304; Office Phone: 815-756-5633 227.

STONE, VOYE LYNNE, women's health nurse practitioner; b. Grandfield, Okla., Apr. 17, 1941; d. Clint Voy and Mattie Evelyn (Averyt) Wynn; m. Don Dale Stone, Dec. 19, 1964; children: Melinda Anne Stone Phelps, Tari Elisabeth Stone Newhouse. Student, Bapt. Hosp. Sch. Nursing, Oklahoma City, 1965; diploma in nursing, U. Okla., Oklahoma City, 1965; BS, St. Joseph's Coll., North Windham, Maine, 1985; grad. women health care nursing program, U. Tex., Dallas, 1990; MS, U. Okla., 1996. Cert. women's health nurse; cert. legal nurse cons. Dietary cons. Frederick Meml. Hosp., 1967; pub. health nurse Dept. Health, State of Okla., Frederick, 1985; insvc. educator Frederick Meml. Hosp.; women's health nurse practitioner Dept. Health, State of Okla., Oklahoma City, 1990. Vol., unit pres. Am. Cancer Soc.; vol. ARC; pres. adv. coun. 4-H Club; pres. local PTA. Named one of Outstanding Young Women of Am., 1970. Mem. AWHONN, Am. Acad. Nurse Practitioners, ANA, Okla. State Nurses Assn., Okla. Pub. Health Assn., Okla. Mental Health Assn., PEO, Beta Sigma Phi (various offices, Girl of Yr. 1976, 77, 78), Sigma Theta Tau, Phi Kappa Phi, First United Methodist Ch. Home: 21918 CR EW 184 Frederick OK 73542-9721

STONE, WILLIAM EDWARD, academic administrator, consultant; b. Peoria, Ill., Aug. 13, 1945; s. Dean Proctor and Katherine (Jamison) S.; m. Deborah Ann Duncan; children: Jennifer, Allison, Molly. AB, Stanford U., 1967, MBA, 1969. Asst. dean Stanford U., 1969—71, asst. to pres., 1971—77; exec. dir. Stanford Alumni Assn., 1977—90, pres., CEO, 1990—98; pres., dir. Stanford Alumni Assn. divsn. Stanford U., 1998—2001, Stanford Sierra Programs LLC, South Lake Tahoe, Calif., 1998—2001, Alpine Chalet, Inc., Alpine Meadows, Calif., 1987—2001; pres.-emeritus Stanford Alumni Assn. Stanford U., 2001—, cons. in ednl. advancement, 2001—; prin. eAdvancement Consortium, 2001—. Dir. Coun. Alumni Assn. Execs., 1989-93, v.p., 1990-91, pres., 1991-92; trustee Coun. for Advancement and Support of Edn., 1988-91; bd. dirs. Univ. ProNet, Inc., chmn., 1990-92, sec. 1996-00. Bd. dirs. North County YMCA, 1975-76; bd. dirs., chmn. nominating com. faculty club Stanford U., 1979-81; trustee Watkins Discretionary Fund, 1979-82; mem. cmty. adv. bd. Resource Ctr. Women; dir. Stanford Hist. Soc., 2002—, v.p., 2003-06, pres., 2006-2008, past pres., 2008- Recipient K.M. Cuthbertson award Stanford U., 1987, Tribute award Coun. for Advancement and Support of Edn., 1991, Steuben Apple award, 2002, Stanford Assocs. award of merit, 2005. Mem.: Stanford Assocs., Stanford Faculty Club. Home: 1061 Cathcart Way Stanford CA 94305-1048 Office Phone: 650-494-6959. Business E-Mail: stone@eadvancement.org.

STONECIPHER, DAVID A., insurance company executive; b. 1941; m. Nancy Berend; 4 children. Degree, Vanderbilt U., 1962; M Agrl. Sci., Ga. State U., 1967. With Life Ins. Co. Ga., Altanta, 1967-92, sr. v.p., actuary Atlanta, 1978—84, exec. v.p., 1984—89, pres., COO, 1989—91, CEO, 1991—92, Southland Life Ins. Co, Altanta, 1991—92; CEO elect Jefferson-Pilot Corp., Greensboro, NC, 1992; pres., CEO Jefferson Pilot Corp., Greensboro, NC, 1993—2004, Jefferson-Pilot Life Ins. Co., 1993—2004; chmn. Jefferson-Pilot Corp., Greensboro, NC, 1998—2004, non-exec. chmn., 2005—06. Bd. dir. Bassett Furniture Industries, Inc., McKenney's Corp., Internat. Home Furnishings Ctr., Inc., Fin. Services Roundtable, Lincoln Nat. Corp., Phila., 2006—. Bd. dirs. McCallie Sch. Served US Army, 1962—64. Fellow, Soc. of Actuaries, 1970. Mem.: Am. Acad. Actuaries, Soc. Actuaries, Am. Coun. Life Insureres (past chmn.). Office: Lincoln Nat Corp Ctr Sq W Tower Ste 3900 1500 Market St Philadelphia PA 19102-2112

STONEHILL, ERIC, lawyer; b. Rochester, NY, Feb. 27, 1950; BA with distinction, Northwestern U., 1970; JD, Cornell U., 1973, MBA, 1981, cert. hosp. and health svc. adminstrn., 1981. Bar: N.Y. 1974, D.C. 1981, U.S. Dist. Ct. (we. dist.) N.Y. 1974, U.S. Dist. Ct. (no. dist.) N.Y. 1976. Assoc. Harris Beach PLLC, Rochester, 1973—81, ptnr., 1982—; mng. dir. Health and Human Svcs., HB Solutions LLC, 2007—. Adj. instr. Rochester Inst. Tech., 1990-92. Contbr. articles to profl. jours. Bd. dirs. Rochester Eye and Human Parts Bank, 1983-91, 92-2001, pres., 1987-90. Mem. Am. Health Lawyers Assn., N.Y. State Bar Assn. (mem. health law sect.), D.C. Bar Assn., Monroe County Bar Assn., Sloan Alumni Assn., Phi Beta Kappa. Office: Harris Beach PLLC 99 Garnsey Rd Pittsford NY 14534 Office Phone: 585-419-8641.

STONEHOUSE, JAMES ADAM, lawyer; b. Alameda, Calif., Nov. 10, 1937; s. Maurice Adam and Edna Sigrid (Thuesen) S.; m. Marilyn Jean Kotkas, Aug. 6, 1966; children: Julie Aileen, Stephen Adam. AB, U. Calif., Berkeley, 1961; JD, U. Calif., San Francisco, 1965. Bar: Calif. 1966; cert. specialist probate, estate planning and trust law. Assoc. Hall, Henry, Oliver & McReavy, San Francisco, 1966-71; ptnr. Whitney Hanson & Stonehouse, Alameda, 1971-77; pvt. practice Alameda, 1977-79; ptnr. Stonehouse & Silva, Alameda, 1979—2005. Judge adv. Alameda coun. Navy League, 1978-98. Founding dir. Alameda Clara Barton Found., 1977-80; mem. Oakland (Calif.) Marathon-Exec. Com., 1979; mem. exec. bd. Alameda coun. Boy Scouts Am., 1979—, pres., 1986-88, area III endowment chair, 1996—; trustee Golden Gate Scouting, 1986-95, treas., 1989-91, v.p., 1991-92, pres., 1993-95, v.p. area III western region, 1990-95, 98-, bd. dirs. western region, 1991—, Alameda (Calif.) Boy Scouts Found., 2003—; bd. dirs. Lincoln Child Ctr. Found., 1981-87, 94-98, pres., 1983-85; pres. Robert L. Lippert Found., 1990—; mem. sch. bd. St. Joseph Notre Dame, 1994-2000, pres., 1997-2000, chmn. Old Alamedan, 2008- Recipient Lord Baden-Powell Merit award Boy Scouts Am., 1988, Silver Beaver award, 1991, Silver Antelope award, 1999, Citizen of Yr. award City of Alameda, 1999, McLaughlin award, 2004; named Boss of Yr., Alameda Jaycees, 1977; Coro Found. fellow, 1961-62, Old Alamedan of Yr., 2003. Mem. ABA, Alameda County Bar Assn. (vice chmn. com. office econs. 1977-78), Commonwealth Club, Rotary (dir. 1976-78, trustee Alameda Rotary Found. 1991—, treas. 1994-98, pres. 1998-2000), Rotary District 5170 Far(asst. govs.2009-), Elks (past exalted ruler, all state officer 1975-76, all dist. officer 1975-77, 78-79), Sequoyah Country Club, Alameda Club (pres. 2007-2008) Republican. Roman Catholic. Home: 2990 Northwood Dr Alameda CA 94501-1606 Office: Stonehouse & Silva 1301 Marina Village Parkway Ste 330 Alameda CA 94501-5870

STONEMAN, MARK L., lawyer; b. Cleve., Jan. 11, 1971; s. Dean L. and Diana G. Stoneman; m. Jill L. Stoneman, June 24, 2000; children: William J., Nathaniel D. BS in Bus. Adminstrn., U. Mo., Columbia, 1993, JD, 1996; master degree in Accountancy, U. Mo., St. Louis, 2002. Lic.: Mo. 1996, Ill. 1997. Assoc. Armstrong Teasdale LLP, St. Louis, 1996—2004, ptnr., 2004—. Contbr. chapters to books. Tchg. vol. Jr. Achievement, St. Louis, 2004; bd. mem. Metro Theater Co., St. Louis, 2001—04. Recipient Order of the Coif, U. Mo., 1996, Fred L. Howard award for Excellence in Appellate Advocacy, 1996, Pacioli award, 2002; scholar Lynn and Peggy Ewing Scholar, U. Mo. Law Sch. Found., 1994-95, Curator's Scholar, U. Mo., 1994-95, Mary Fiser Meml. Scholar, 1994-95, Law Rev. Fellows Scholar, 1995-96. Mem.: Phi Kappa Phi, Mo. Law Rev. Office: Armstrong Teasdale LLP One Metropolitan Sq Ste 2600 Saint Louis MO 63102 Office Fax: 314-621-5065. Business E-Mail: mstoneman@armstrongteasdale.com.

STONER, HARRY DAVID-FOXE, science educator; b. Minot, ND, Mar. 13, 1958; s. Harry and Norma Stoner; m. Denise Margaret Curran, Sept. 12, 1992; children: Joshua David-Amadeus, Christian Gabriel-Dante, Claire Jean Anaiis, Hannah Marie Curran, David-Michael Elijah. MS, U. Pacific, Stockton, Calif., 1992. Tchr. San Joaquin Delta Coll., Stockton, 1996—. Mem.: CTA. Conservative. Roman Catholic. Avocations: fishing, woodworking, reading. Office: San Joaquin Delta Coll 5151 Pacific Ave Stockton CA 95207

STONER, JOHN RICHARD, federal agency administrator; b. Ypsilanti, Mich., May 11, 1958; s. Richard P. and Marjorie G. Stoner; m. Diane Leslie Snow. BA in Govt., Lawrence U., 1981, B in Music Edn., 1981; MS in Mgmt., U. Md., 2004, MBA, 2005. Staff asst. Senator Robert Kasten Jr., Washington, 1981-82; staff assoc. Wis. Office Fed.-State Rels., Washington, 1982-83; intergovtl. rels. officer U.S. Dept. Transp., Washington, 1983-86, congl. rels. officer, 1989-91; dir. Office of Program and Policy Support, Rsch. and Spl. Programs Adminstrn., Dept. Transp., Washington, 1991-93; exec. dir. Republican Nat. Lawyers Assn., 1993-97; rep. Primerica Fin. Svcs., 1993-97, mortgage banker, 1998—; state govt. rels. mgr. Am. Trucking Assn., Inc., Alexandria, Va., 1986-88; researcher George Bush for Pres. Com., 1988; staff asst. Office of Pres.-Elect, Washington, 1988-89; state dir. The Century Coun., Washington, 2000—03. Admissions contact Washington area Lawrence U., 1986-87; softball team mgr. Montgomery County Recreation League. Recipient Eagle Scout award Boy Scouts Am., 1972; Mortar Bd. scholar, 1980; Senate Rep. Policy Com. Legis. fellow, 1993-96. Republican. Mem. Ch. of Christ, Scientist. Avocations: water-skiing, organ. Home: 10409 Brunswick Ave Silver Spring MD 20902-4845 Office: The Century Coun 2345 Crystal Dr Ste 910 Arlington VA 22202-4817

STONESIFER, PATTY (PATRICIA Q. STONESIFER), former foundation administrator; b. Indpls., 1956; m. Michael Kinsley; 2 children from previous marriage. BA in Gen. Studies, Ind. U., 1982, LHD, 2007; D of Pub. Svc. (hon.), Tufts U., Medford, Mass., 2009. Editor-in-chief Que Corp., Indpls.; sr. mgr. Microsoft Press, 1988-89; gen. mgr. Microsoft Can., 1989-90; gen. mgr., then v.p. product support ops. consumer divsn. Microsoft Corp., Redmond, Wash., 1990-93, sr. v.p. interactive media divsn., 1993—96; chairwoman, pres. Gates Learning Found., 1997—99; pres., co-chair, CEO Bill & Melinda Gates Found., Seattle, 1997—2008, sr. adv. to trustees, 2008—; bd. regents Smithsonian Inst., Washington, 2001—, chairwoman, 2009—. Mem. US delegation to UN Gen. Assembly Spl. Session on AIDS; bd. dirs. Amazon.com, 1997—, Viacom Inc., 2000—05, CBS Corp.; founding bd. mem. Acad. Interactive Arts & Scis. Named one of The 25 Most Influential People in America, TIME mag., 1996. Democrat. Office: Office of Regents Smithsonian Inst PO Box 37012 SI Bldg Rm 153 MRC 050 Washington DC 20013-7012*

STONE-STREETT, NANCY HARRINGTON, painter, printmaker, educator; b. Helena, Mont., Oct. 8, 1948; d. Harvey Harrington and Borghild Stone; m. Douglas A. Streett, Feb. 5, 1994; m. Ben Chovanak (div.); 1 child, Harvey Harrington Chovanak. BA in Art, Mont. State U., 1985; MFA in Painting and Drawing, U. Mont., 1987. Dir. Beall Park Art Ctr., Bozeman, Mont., 1994—96; instr. Miss. Delta CC, Moorhead, Miss., 1999—, faculty mem. instr., 1999—; adj. faculty Delta State U., 2000—, adj. staff, 2006—. Tchr. Share-Mont. Arts Coun. Program, Helena, 1975—80. Recipient Miss. Humanities Tchr. award, Miss. Humanities Coun., 2005. Democrat. Episcopalian. Home: 2193 Carol Greenville MS 38703 Office: Miss Delta CC Art Dept Moorhead MS 38761

STONG, ROGER ALAN, lawyer; b. Chgo., May 2, 1962; s. Robert Evert and Therese (Countess Raczynski) Stong; m. Phyllis Ann Hoffman, Apr. 9, 1994; 1 child, Heather Nicole Ross. BA, U. Va., 1983; JD, Ind. U., 1985; MBA, U. Okla., 1986. Bar: Okla. 1986, U.S. Dist. Ct. (we. dist. Okla.) 1991. Assoc. Crowe & Dunlevy, Oklahoma City, 1986—93, dir., shareholder, 1993—, pres., 2008—. Fellow: Okla. Bar Found.; mem.: ABA, Okla. County Bar Assn., Okla. Bar Assn. (chair Bus. and Corp. Law sect. 2002—03), Okla. Lawyers for Children (asst. sec. 1998—), Okla. State C. of C. (bd. dirs. 2006—), U. Va. Alumni Assn., U. Okla. Alumni Assn., Ind. U. Alumni Assn., Okla. Hist. Soc. Republican. Roman Cath. Office: Crowe & Dunlevy 20 N Broadway Oklahoma City OK 73102 Home: 1508 Bedford Dr Nichols Hills OK 73116 Office Phone: 405-235-7700. Office Fax: 405-272-5255. Business E-Mail: stongr@crowedunlevy.com.

ST-ONGE, DENIS ALDERIC, geologist, research scientist, educator; b. Ste-Agathe, Man., Can., May 11, 1929; s. Adolphe and Jeanne M (Ritchot) St-Onge; m. Jeanne Marie Behaegel, Jan. 7, 1955; children: Marc R, Nicole J M. BA, Coll. St-Boniface, 1951; Lic. Sci., U. Louvain, Belgium, 1957, DSc, 1962; DSc (hon.), U. Man., 1990. Research scientist Geol. Survey, Ottawa, Ont., Canada, 1958-68, sect. head, 1982-85; chief sub. div. Quaternary Geology, 1985-87, dir. terrain scis. div., 1987-91, sci. advisor Polar Continental Shelf Project, 1991-97; prof. geography U. Ottawa, 1968-82, chmn. geography, 1974-77, vice dean grad. studies, 1977-80, prof. emeritus, 1998—, bd. govs., 2000—; scientist emeritus Geol. Survey Can., 1997—. Chmn. bd. dirs. Fluxnet Can., 2002—07, Cases, 2003—07. Author: (book) Geomorphologie Ellef-Ringnes Island, 1965, Quaternary Geology, Inman River Region, N.W.T. Canada, 1995; contbr. articles to profl jours. Pres Ont Francophone PTA, 1967—69. Decorated Officer Order of Can; recipient medal, Queen Elizabeth II, 1979, Commemorative medal, Govt. of Can., 1992, Medal of Honor, Univ Liege, Belgium, 1980, medal, A Cailleux, 1991, Can 125, 1992, Royal Scottish Geog, Soc, 1994, Golden Jubilee medal, Queen Elizabeth II, 2002. Fellow: Explorers Club (internat. fellow 2005), Arctic Inst. N.Am., Geol. Assn. Can. (pres. 1984—85, J. W. Ambrose medal 2001), Royal Can. Geog. Soc. (bd. dirs. 1980—2001, pres. 1992—98, chmn. Partnership Group Sci. Engrs. 1999—2001, Camsell medal 2005, 75th Ann. medallion 2005); mem.: Can. Geosci. Coun. (pres. 1996—97), Assn. Quebecoise pour l'etude du Quaternaire (hon.), Can. Quaternary Assn., Internat. Union Quaternary Rsch. (hon.), Can. Assn. Geographers (pres. 1979—80, Award Svc. to Profession 2000). Avocations: swimming, skiing, photography. Office: Geolog

Survey of Canada 601 Booth St Ottawa ON Canada K1A OE8 Home: 1188 Agincourt Rd Ottawa ON Canada K2C 2H9 Office Phone: 613-947-1652. Business E-Mail: dstonge@nrcan.gc.ca.

STOOKESBERRY, DENISE, musician, educator; d. Sylvester and Gladys Sauer; m. David Stookesberry, Nov. 18, 1989; children: John H. Kilper, Katherine M. MusM in Voice Performance, Washington U., St. Louis, 1994. Cert. K-12 music tchr. Mo. Pvt. practice voice tchr., St. Louis, 1990—; choral dir. Duchesne HS, St. Charles, Mo., 1984—89, St. Charles HS, 2000—04; music dept. chmn. symphony chorus sect. John Burroughs Sch., St. Louis, 2005—, choral dir., 2005—; voice tchr. Washington U., 1994—2000. Singer: Union Ave. Opera, 1978, 1979, Opera Theater St. Louis, 1996, Ohio Light Opera, 1997, (Madame Butterfly) Pensacola Opera, 1998, (recital) 20th Century Works, 2000; soloist, choir dir.: Temple Israel, 1995—, soloist: St. Louis Symphony Orchestra, 1996. Founder Opera Unltd. Recipient Friends of Music award, Wash. U., 1993; scholar, St. Louis U., 1975—79; Music Tech. grantee, St. Charles Sch. Dist., 2003. Mem.: Am. Choral Dirs. Assn. (assoc.), Music Educators Nat. Conf. (assoc.), Nat. Assn. Tchrs. Singing (assoc.; dist. treas. 1997—2000, 2007). Achievements include being a semi-finalist in the International Opera Singer's Competition, 1994, 1995. Avocation: hiking. Home: 12551 Merrick Dr Saint Louis MO 63146 Office: John Burroughs Sch 755 S Price Rd Saint Louis MO 63124 Business E-Mail: dstook@jburroughs.org.

STOOKSBURY, WILLIAM CLAUDE, minister; b. Knoxville, Tenn., June 6, 1947; s. William Claude and Vera Faye (Hudman) S.; m. Mary Jayne Moyer, Mar. 21, 1970; 1 child, William David. BS, U. Tenn., Chattanooga, 1980; MDiv, Vanderbilt U., 1987; PhD (hon.), Pennington U., 2001. Ordained to ministry Bapt. Ch., 1978; ordinations transfered to Unithed Meth. Ch., 1988. Min. of visitation 1st Bapt. Ch., Chattanooga, 1975-78; pastor Beacon Bapt. Ch., Rossville, Ga., 1978-80; asst. min. Ea. Pkwy. Bapt. Ch., Louisville, 1980-81; pastor 1st Bapt. Ch., Fisherville, Ky., 1981-84, Baker's Grove Bapt. Ch., Mt. Juliet, Tenn., 1984-86, Fairgarden United Meth. Ch., Sevierville, Tenn., 1988-92, Lonsdale United Meth. Ch., Knoxville, 1992—2000, St. Luke's United Meth. Ch., Knoxville, 2000—05; sr. pastor 2nd United Meth. Ch., Knoxville, 2005—09; bd. missions Holston Conf. United Meth. Ch. Design team urban ministry Holston Conf., Meth. Ch., Knoxville, 1992. Mem. search com. dean of human svcs. U. Tenn., Chattanooga, 1980; co-chair area II, Campbellsville Coll. Fund-raising, Ky., 1983; mem. steering com. Tenn. Alliance Strong Cmtys., Nashville, 1989—; charter mem. Ams. for Change, Washignton, 1993—; mem. nat. steering com. Clinton/Gore '96 Campaign. Named one of Outstanding Young Men of Am., Outstanding Young Assn., 1982, Dyer scholarship Vanderbilt Div., 1986. Mem. Am. Acad. Religion, Long Run Bapt. Assn. (chair asn. message com. 1984, com. to study ordination 1982, exec. bd. dirs. 1981-84), People for the Am. Way, The Interfaith Alliance, Internat. Platform Assn. Democrat. Avocation: reading. Home: 885 General George Patton Rd Nashville TN 37221-2574

STOOPLER, MARK BENJAMIN, physician; b. NYC, Sept. 29, 1950; s. Alex and Blanche Sylvia (Kappel) S.; m. Lynn Sara Fruchter, Jan. 10, 1982; children: David Andrew, Emily Rachel, Jesse Bryan. BS, Tulane U., 1971; MD, Cornell U., 1975. Diplomate Am. Bd. Internal Medicine, Am. Bd. Oncology. Intern and resident in internal medicine North Shore U. Hosp., Manhasset, N.Y., 1975-78, Meml. Sloan-Kettering Cancer Ctr., NYC, 1975-78, asst. chief resident in medicine, 1978, fellow in med. oncology, 1978-80; asst. attending physician Presbyn. Hosp., NYC, 1980-93, assoc. attending physician, 1993—; asst. clin. prof. medicine Columbia U. Coll. of Physicians and Surgeons, NYC, 1980-93; assoc. clin. prof. medicine, 1993—. Contbr. articles to profl. jours. Named one of Am.'s Top Drs. Castle Connolly Guide, 2003-08, Best Drs. NY Mag., 2006-09; Tulane U. scholar, 1970-71. Fellow ACP; mem. Am. Soc. of Clin. Oncology, Am. Fedn. for Clin. Research, Internat. Assn. for the Study of Lung Cancer, Phi Beta Kappa. Office: Columbia-Presbyn Med Ctr 161 Fort Washington Ave New York NY 10032-3713 Office Phone: 212-305-8230.

STOOPS, BOB, college football coach; b. Youngstown, Ohio, Sept. 9, 1960; BS, Univ. Iowa, 1983. Grad. asst. coach U. Iowa Hawkeyes, 1983—84, vol. coach, 1985—87; asst. coach Kent State U. Golden Flashes, 1988; defensive backs coach Kans. State U. Wildcats, 1989—90, co-defensive coord., 1991—95; def. coord., asst. head coach U. Fla. Gators, 1996—98; head football coach U. Okla. Sooners, 1998—. Recipient Paul "Bear" Bryant award, Nat. Sportscasters & Sportswriters Assn., 2000, George Munger award, Maxwell Football Club, 2000; named Bear Bryant Nat. Coach of Yr., 2000, Coach of Yr., AP, 2000, Eddie Robinson/FWAA Coach of Yr., 2000, Woody Hayes Nat. Coach of Yr., 2000, 2003, Nat. Coach Yr., Am. Heart Assn., 2000, Football News, 2000, Walter Camp awards, 2000, 2003, Big 12 Coach Yr., 2000, 2003, Dallas Morning News, 2004, 2006, Region IV Coach of Yr., AFCA, 2003, Bobby Dodd Nat. Coach of Yr., 2003. Achievements include coaching the University of Oklahoma Sooners to the BCS National Championship, 2000. Office: Univ Okla Football 180 W Brooks St Norman OK 73019*

STOOPS, JAMES KING, biochemistry researcher; b. Charleston, W.Va., Sept. 15, 1937; s. William Nelson and Mary Alice (Duncan) S.; m. Pamela Ann Moore, Aug. 18, 1962; children: Timothy, Mary. BS, Duke U., 1960; PhD, Northwestern U., 1966. Instr. Baylor Coll. of Medicine, Houston, 1971-75, asst. prof., 1975-83, assoc. prof., 1983-90, U. Tex. Health Sci. Ctr. Med. Sch., Houston, 1990—; adj. assoc. prof. Baylor Coll. of Medicine, Houston, 1990-98, prof., 1998—. Contbr. articles to profl. jours. Grantee NIH, 1990, 91, 94. Mem. AAAS, Am. Chem. Soc., Am. Soc. for Biochemistry and Molecular Biology. Presbyterian. Achievements include contbn. to understanding of structure-function relationships of the enzymes involved in lipid metabolism; determination of three-dimensional structures of human alpha-2-macroglobulins, pyruvate dehydrogenase Cam kinases and the fatty acid synthase which indicate how these macromolecules function. Home: 10310 Cliffwood Dr Houston TX 77035-3610 Office: U Tex Health Sci Ctr 6431 Fannin St Houston TX 77030-1501 Office Phone: 713-500-5345. Business E-Mail: james.k.stoops@uth.tmc.edu.

STOOPS, MIKE, college football coach; b. Youngstown, Ohio, Dec. 31, 1961; m. Nicole Stoops; children: Payton, Colton. Grad., U. Iowa, Iowa City, 1986. Defensive back Chgo. Bears, Pitts. Gladiators, Arena Football League; grad. asst. coach U. Iowa Hawkeyes, 1986—87, vol. coach, 1988—91; defensive ends coach Kansas State U. Wildcats, 1992—95, co-defensive coord., 1996—97, asst. head coach, 1998; assoc. head coach U. Okla. Sooners, 1999—2003; head coach U. Ariz. Wildcats, 2004—. Named First Team All-Am., UPI, 1984, First Team All-Conf., Big 10 Conf., 1983, 1984; finalist Asst. Coach of Yr., Am. Football Coaches Assn., 2001. Office: Univ Ariz Athletics McKale Ctr 1 National Championship Dr PO Box 210096 Tucson AZ 85721

STOOPS, ROSA MARIA, language educator; d. Luis Octavio De Mendoza Estrada and Rosa Maria Cervantes Lopez; 1 child, John. PhD, U. Ala., Tuscaloosa, 2005. Asst. prof. Spanish and French U. Montevallo, Ala., 2005—. Contbr. articles to profl. jour. Mem.: MLA, South Atlantic Modern Assn., Renaissance Soc. Am. Home: 67 Coeur d'Alene Montevallo AL 35115 Office: Univ Montevallo Station 6410 Montevallo AL 35115 Business E-Mail: stoopsrm@montevallo.edu.

STOPPARD, TOM (TOMAS STRAUSSLER), playwright; b. Zlin, Czechoslovakia, July 3, 1937; arrived in Eng., 1946; s. Eugene and Martha Stoppard Straussler, Kenneth Stoppard (Stepfather); m. Jose Ingle, 1965 (div. 1972); 2 children; m. Miriam Moore-Robinson, 1972 (div. 1992); 2 children. MLitt (hon.), U. Bristol, Eng., 1979, Brunel U., 1979, U. Sussex, 1980. Journalist Western Daily Press, Bristol, Eng., 1954-58, Evening World, Bristol, 1958-60; free-lance reporter, 1960-63. Bd. dir. Royal Nat. Theatre, London, 1989—. Author: (plays) The Gamblers, 1965, Rosencrantz and Guildenstern Are Dead, 1966 (Plays and Players Best Play award 1967, Best Play Tony award 1968), Enter a Free Man, 1968, The Real Inspector Hound, 1968, Albert's Bridge, 1969 (Prix Italia 1968), If You're Glad I'll Be Frank, 1969, After Magritte, 1970, Dogg's Our Pet, 1971, Jumpers, 1972 (Evening Standard Best Play award 1972, Plays and Players Best Play award 1972), Travesties, 1974 (Evening Standard Best Play award 1974, Best Play Tony award 1976), Dirty Linen and New-Found-Land, 1976, Every Good Boy Deserves Favor, 1974, Night and Day, 1978 (Evening Standard Best Play award 1978), Dogg's Hamlet, Cahoot's Macbeth, 1979, The Real Thing, 1982 (Evening Standard Best Play award 1982, Best Play Tony award 1984, Best Fgn. Play Tony award 1984), Hapgood, 1988, Artist Descending a Staircase, 1988, Arcadia, 1993 (Evening Standard Best Play award 1993, Oliver award 1994), Indian Ink, 1995, Invention of Love, 1997 (Evening Standard Best Play award 1997), The Coast of Utopia (trilogy), 2002 (Drama Desk award outstanding play 2007, Tony award best play, 2007), Rock 'n' Roll, 2006 (Evening Standard Best Play award, 2006); (play adaptations) Tango by Slawomir Mrozek, 1966, The House of Bernarda Alba by Federico Garcia Lorca, 1973, Undiscovered Country (based on Das Weite Land by Arthur Schnitzler), 1979, On the Razzle (based on Einen Jux will er sich machen by Johann Nestroy), 1981, Rough Crossing (based on The Play's the Thing by Ferenc Molnar), 1984, Dalliance (based on Liebelei by Arthur Schnitzler), 1986, Henry IV (Pirandello), 2003, Heroes (trans. Gérald Sibleyras), 2005, Ivanov (Chekhov), 2008; (radio plays) The Dissolution of Dominic Boot, 1964, M is for Moon Among Other Things, 1964, If You're Glad I'll Be Frank, 1966, Albert's Bridge, 1967, Where Are They Now?, 1970, Artist Descending A Staircase, 1972, The Dog It Was That Died, 1982, In the Native State, 1991; (radio serial episodes) The Dales, 1964, A Student's Diary, 1965; (screenplays) The Romantic Englishwoman, 1975, Despair, 1978, The Human Factor, 1980, (with Terry Gilliam and Charles McKeown) Brazil, 1985 (Best Screenplay Acad. award nominee 1985, Best Screenplay L.A. Critics Circle award 1985), Empire of the Sun, 1987, The Russia House, 1990; (author, dir.) Rosencrantz and Guildenstern Are Dead, 1990 (Grand prize Venice Film Festival 1990), Billy Bathgate, 1991, (with Marc Norman) Shakespeare in Love, 1998 (Golden Globe award and Oscar best screenplay), Enigma, 2001; (teleplays) A Walk on the Water, 1963, A Separate Peace, 1966, Teeth, 1967, Another Moon Called Earth, 1967, Neutral Ground, 1968, The Engagement (based on his radio play The Dissolution of Dominic Boot), 1970, One Pair of Eyes, 1972, (with Clive Exton) Boundaries, 1975, Three Men in a Boat, 1975, Professional Foul, 1977, Squaring the Circle: Poland 1980-81, 1985; (translator) Largo Desolato by Vaclav Havel, 1987; (novel) Lord Malquist and Mr. Moon, 1966; contbr. short stories to Introduction 2, 1964. Active Amnesty Internat., Com. Against Psychiatric Abuse, Index on Censorship. Decorated Knight Comdr. Order Brit. Empire; recipient John Whiting award, Arts Coun. Great Britain, 1967, Evening Standard Most Promising Playwright Drama award, 1972, Shakespeare prize, Hamburg, Germany, 1979; named one of The 100 Most Influential People in the World, TIME mag., 2008; grantee Ford Found., 1964. Fellow: Royal Soc. Literature. Office: United Agents Ltd London England

STOPPELMAN, JEREMY, Internet company executive, entrepreneur; b. Arlington, Va., 1978; BS in computer engring., U. Ill., 1999; student, Harvard Bus. Sch., 2003—04. With @Home Networks, X.com, Confinity; v.p. engring. PayPal, 2002—03; co-founder & CEO Yelp Inc., San Francisco, 2004—. Office: Yelp Inc 706 Mission St Fl 7 San Francisco CA 94103-3167 E-mail: info@yelp.com.

STORCH, ARTHUR, theater director; s. Sam and Bessie (Goldner) S.; children: Max Darrow, Alexander English, Bess Martin. BA, New Sch. Social Research, 1949. Actor in Broadway prodns. End as a Man, 1953, Time Limit, 1955, Girls of Summer, 1956, Look Homeward, Angel, 1957, Night Circus, 1958, The Long Dream, 1960, The Best Man, 1961; motion pictures The Strange One, 1956, Girls of the Night, 1959, The Exorcist, 1974; dir. off-Broadway Two by Saroyan, 1961, Three by Three, 1962, Talking to You (London debut), 1962, The Typists and the Tiger, 1963, The Owl and the Pussycat, 1964, The Impossible Years, 1965, The Local Stigmatic, 1970, Under the Weather, 1965, Golden Rainbow, 1967, The Chinese and Dr. Fish, 1969, Promenade All, 1970, 42 Seconds from Broadway, 1973, Tribute, 1978, Twice Around the Park, 1982, Clarence, 1986; Of Mice and Men, 1988; dir. nat. tour The King and I, 1989; dir. Syracuse Stage Waiting for Lefty, Noon, Of Mice and Men, 1974, 75, La Ronde, The Butterfingers Angel. Mornings at Seven, Dynamo, 1975-76, A Quality of Mercy, The Seagull, 1976-77, 1976-77, Love Letters on Blue Paper, End of the Beginning, 1977-78, Loved, 1978, Naked, 1979, The Comedy of Errors, 1980, The Impromptu of Outremont, 1982, The Double Bass, 1984, Arms and the Man, Handy Dandy, Cyrano de Bergerac, Romeo and Juliet, 1986, Of Mice and Men, NYC, 1987, Fugue, 1988, Seven By Beckett, 1988, Look Homeward Angel, Wait Unitl Dark, Dangerous Corner, 1990, A Walk in the Woods, 1989, Finding Donis Ann, 1990, Androcles and the Lion, 1991; Lend Me a Tenor, 1992; Awake and Sing, 1993; dir., actor Love Letters, 1992. Founder, producing artistic dir. Syracuse Stage; chmn. drama dept. Syracuse U., 1974-92, Arthur Storch Theatre, 1992; artistic dir. Berkshire Theatre Festival, Stockbridge, Mass., 1995-98. Home: 400 W 43d St Apt 13A New York NY 10036 Home Phone: 212-967-5442. Personal E-mail: arthurstorch@yahoo.com.

STORCH, GERALD L. (JERRY STORCH), retail executive; b. 1956; m. Jacquie Storch; 5 children. BA cum laude, Harvard U., 1978, MBA with hons., 1981, JD magna cum laude, 1982. Ptnr. McKinsey & Co., Boston, 1982—93; sr. v.p. strategic planning Dayton Hudson Corp., Mpls., 1993—98; pres. fin. services & new bus. Target Corp., Mpls., 1999—2001, vice chmn., 2001—05; chmn., CEO Toys R Us, Inc., Wayne, NJ, 2006—. Office: Toys R Us Inc 1 Geoffrey Way Wayne NJ 07470

STORDAHL, ANN M., retail executive; BS, NYU, 1975. Nurse's aide; sr. v.p., gen. mgr. Magnin-Bullocks Wilshire, LA, 1989; v.p., divisional mdse. mgr. Neiman Marcus Stores, Dallas, 1992—95, sr. v.p., divisional mdse. mgr., 1995—2004, exec. v.p. women's apparel, 2004—. Office: Neiman Marcus Group Inc One Marcus Sq 1618 Main St Dallas TX 75201

STORER, MARYRUTH, law librarian; b. Portland, Oreg., 1953; d. Joseph and Carol Storer; m. David Bailey, 1981; children: Sarah, Allison. BA in History, Portland State U., 1974; JD, U. Oreg., 1977; M in Law Librarianship, U. Wash., 1978. Bar: Oreg. 1978. Assoc. law libr. U. Tenn., Knoxville, 1978-79; law libr. O'Melveny & Myers, LA, 1979-88; dir. Orange County Pub. Law Libr., Santa Ana, Calif., 1988—. Mem. Am. Assn. Law Librs. (exec. bd. 1999-2002), So. Calif. Assn. Law Librs. (pres. 1986-87), Coun. Calif. County Law Librs. (sec./treas. 1990-94, pres. 1994-96), Arroyo Sero Libr. Network (chair 2000-03). Democrat. Episcopalian. Office: Orange County Public Law Library 515 N Flower St Santa Ana CA 92703-2304 Office Phone: 714-834-3002.

STORER, THOMAS W., medical educator; b. Oakland, Calif., Jan. 14, 1947; s. Irene P. Storer; m. Paula M. Storer, Sept. 9, 1978; children: Siegrun A., Lindsey A. PhD, U. Utah, Salt Lake City, 1979. Prof. kinesiology El Camino Coll., Torrance, Calif., 1970—; adj. prof. medicine David Geffen Sch. Medicine U. Calif., LA, 2001—, Boston U. Sch. Medicine, 2004—. Sci. adv. group HealtheTech, Inc, Golden, Colo., 2001—06; sci. expert panel BioMarin Pharms., Novato, Calif., 2003—05; sci. adv. bd. GTx Pharms., Memphis, 2004—; cons. Amgen, Merck, Wyeth, Ascend Phams. Cos. Contbr. articles to profl. jours. Mem., health adv. bd. Beach Cities Health Dist., Redondo Beach, Calif., 1999—2003. Recipient Svc. award., Am. Heart Assn., 1992; named Disting. Prof., El Camino Coll., 1998. Mem.: Endocrine Soc., Nat. Strength and Conditioning Assn., Am. Coll. Sports Medicine. Avocations: exercise, writing, travel.

STOREY, JAMES MOORFIELD, lawyer; b. Boston, Apr. 12, 1931; s. Charles Moorfield and Susan Jameson (Sweetser) S.; m. Adair Miller, Aug. 28, 1954 (div. 1973); children: Barbara Sessums Storey McGrath, Mary Sweetser Storey Meley (dec.), Susan Adair Storey Frank, Eliza Allison Tebo Storey Anderson, Alice Leovy Storey Wille (dec.); m. Isabelle Helene Boeschenstein, May 17, 1973. AB, Harvard U., 1953, LL.B., 1956. Bar: Mass. 1956. Atty. SEC, Washington, 1956-57, legal asst. to chmn., 1957-59; assoc. Gaston, Snow, Motley & Holt, Boston, 1959-62; ptnr. Gaston, Snow, Motley & Holt (name changed to Gaston Snow & Ely Bartlett), Boston, 1962-87, Dechert Price & Rhoads, Boston, 1987-94, ret., 1994, profl. trustee, corp. dir., 1994—. Trustee Mt. Auburn Cemetery, Cambridge, Mass., 1980-. Co-author: Mutual Fund Law Handbook, 1998, The Uneasy Chaperone, 2000. Mem. ABA, Boston Bar Assn., Tavern Club Boston (pres. 1985-87), Century Assn. of N.Y. Unitarian Universalist. Home: ISI Tremont St Apt 189 Boston MA 02111 Home Phone: 617-426-0282; Office Phone: 617-728-0429. Personal E-mail: jandistorey@worldnet.att.net.

STOREY, KENNETH BRUCE, biology professor; b. Taber, Alta., Can., Oct. 23, 1949; s. Arthur George and Madeleine Una (Mawhinney) S.; m. Janet Margaret Collicutt, June 6, 1975; children: Jennifer, Kathryn. BSc with honors, U. Calgary, Alta., 1971; PhD, U. B.C., Vancouver, Can., 1974. Asst. prof. Duke U., Durham, NC, 1975-79; assoc. prof. Carleton U., Ottawa, Ont., Canada, 1979-85, prof., 1985—, Can. Rsch. chair, 2001—. Chair. Can. rsch. molecular physiology, Canada; adj. prof. in botany and zoology Stellenbosch U., South Africa; lectr. in field. Editor Cell and Molecular Responses to Stress, Functional Metabolism; mem. editl. bd. Jour. Comparative Physiology, 1995—, Jour. Thermal Biology, 2007-; contbr. over 510 articles to profl. jours. Recipient E.W.R. Steacie award Nat. Sci. and Engring. Rsch. Coun. Can., 1984-86, Killam Sr. Rsch. fellowship, 1993-95, Disting. Alumni award, U. Calgary, 2007. Fellow AAAS, Royal Soc. Can.; mem. Can. Biochem. Soc. (Ayerst award 1989), Can. Soc. Zoology, Soc. Cryobiology. Avocations: movies, music, renaissance art. Office: Carleton U Dept Biology 1125 Colonel By Drive Ottawa ON Canada K1S 5B6 Office Phone: 613-520-3678. Business E-Mail: kenneth_storey@carleton.ca.

STOREY, MIMI ELLIS, lawyer; b. Rochester, Minn., Oct. 19, 1959; d. F. Henry Ellis, Jr. and Elizabeth Watson Blanchard; m. Charles Mills Storey, June 17, 1989; children: Armide de Saulles, Charles Moorfield. BA, Brown U., Providence, 1981; JD, U. Va., Charlottesville, 1987; MBA, U. Va., 1987. Bar: Mass. 1987. Assoc. Palmer & Dodge, Boston, 1987—89, Dechert LLP, Phila., 1989—91; dir. Atari Inc., Beverly, Mass., 2001—05; assoc. Nutter McClennen & Fish LLP, Boston, 2005—09; asst. gen. counsel Fresenius Med. Care N.Am., 2009—. Mng. editor Va. Jour. Internat. Law. Dir. Essex County Greenbelt Assn., Essex, Mass., 1997—2008; corp. trustee The Trustees of Reservations, Beverly, Mass., 1997—. Mem. Boston Bar Assn.,Women in Tech. Internat. Avocations: lit., travel, history. Home: 143 John Wise Ave Essex MA 01929 Office: Fresenius Med Care NAm 920 Winter St Waltham MA 02451 Home Phone: 978-768-6300; Office Phone: 781-699-9175. Personal E-mail: mimistorey@gmail.com. Business E-Mail: mimi.storey@fnc-na.com.

STOREY, NORMAN C., lawyer; b. Miami, Fla., Oct. 11, 1943; BA cum laude, Loyola-Marymount U., LA, 1965; JD, U. Ariz., 1968. Bar: Ariz. 1968. Law clk. to Hon. James A. Walsh U.S. Dist. Ct. Ariz.; ptnr. Squire, Sanders & Dempsey, L.L.P., Phoenix. Fin. Coun. Diocese Phoenix Cath. Ch.; mem. Mens Art Coun. Phoenix Art Mus. Mem.: State Bar Ariz. Office: 40 N Central Ave Ste 2700 Phoenix AZ 85004-4498 Business E-Mail: nstorey@ssd.com.

STORIE, ERIC DUANE, science administrator; b. Lenoir, NC, May 20, 1954; s. Clarence Lee and Daisy Puett Storie; children: Kathryn Elizabeth, Erin Christine. MS in Biology, U. NC, Charlotte, 1983. Dir. environ. tech. Roanoke-Chowan C.C., Ahoskie, NC, 1992—2003; dir. biotech. Coll. of The Albemarle, Elizabeth City, NC, 2003—. Mem. com. on anti-bioterrorism curricula NC Dept. of C.C.s, Raleigh, 2002—03. Mem. Union Concerned Scientists, 2003. Mem.: Am. Inst. Biol. Scis., Human Anatomy and Physiology Soc. Avocations: hiking, bicycling. Office: Coll of The Albemarle 1208 N Road St Elizabeth City NC 27909 Office Fax: 252-335-2011. E-mail: estorie@albemarle.edu.

STORIE, MELANIE, history professor; b. Grand Forks, ND, July 15, 1969; d. Charles William and Evelyn Louise Greer; m. Billy Storie, May 30, 1992; children: Joshua Lawrence, Emilee Hope. MA, East Tenn. State U., Johnson City, 1994. Cert. secondary edn. tchr. State of Tenn., 1991. History instr. Apex Learning Inc., Seattle, 2000—, East Tenn. State U., 2002—. Seasonal historian Sycamore Shoals State Pk., Elizabethton, Tenn., 1994—95. Mem.: Am. Hist. Assn., East Tenn. Hist. Assn. Home: 611 Westwood Dr Elizabethton TN 37643 Office: East Tenn State Univ PO 70672 Johnson City TN 37615 Business E-Mail: storiem@mail.etsu.edu.

STORIN, MATTHEW VICTOR, retired editor; b. Springfield, Mass., Dec. 24, 1942; s. Harry Francis and Blanche Marie S.; m. Keiko Takita, Aug. 1, 1975; 1 child, Kenyatta; children by previous marriage: Karen, Aimee, Sean. BA, U. Notre Dame, 1964. Reporter Springfield Daily News, 1964-65, Griffin-Larrabee News Bur., Washington, 1965-69; Washington corr., city editor, Asian corr., nat. editor, asst. mng. editor, dep. mng. editor, mng. editor Boston Globe, 1969-85; dep. mng. editor U.S. News & World Report, Washington, 1985-86; editor, sr. v.p. Chgo. Sun-Times, 1986-87; editor The Maine Times, Topsham, 1988-89; mng. editor N.Y. Daily News, 1989-91, exec. editor, 1991-92, Boston Globe, 1992-93, editor, 1993—2001; assoc. v.p., prof. Am. studies U. Notre

Dame, 2002—06, adj. prof. Am. studies, 2006—. Recipient Disting. Polit. Reporting award Am. Assn. Polit. Sci., 1969, Yankee Quill award New Eng. Chpt. Sigma Delta Chi, 1997, Hon. Dr. of Laws, U. Notre Dame, 2006. Home: 1741 W North Shore Dr South Bend IN 46617 Office Phone: 574-631-0477. E-mail: mstorin@nd.edu.

STORING, PAUL EDWARD, retired foreign service officer; b. Ames, Iowa, Oct. 24, 1929; s. James Alvin and Edith Nora (Ryg) S.; children: Mimi Storing Harlan, Felice Storing Kite. Student, U Oslo, Norway, 1950-51; BA, Allegheny Coll., 1952; MA with honors, Colgate U., 1956; postgrad., U. Wis., Madison, 1955-59. Fgn. service officer Dept. State, Washington, Mex. and Scandinavia, 1960-80; spl. asst. U.S. Sect. Internat. Boundary and Water Commn. U.S. And Mex., Washington, 1980-99; ret. Contbr. articles to profl. jours. Served to cpl. U.S. Army, 1953-55 Fellow U. Wis., 1957-58; Fulbright fellow U. Oslo, 1959-60 Mem. Am. Fgn. Svc. Assn., Fulbright Assn., Phi Beta Kappa, Delta Tau Delta (pres. Alpha chpt. 1949-50). Baptist. Avocations: music, photography, travel. Home: 9006 Opera Alley Manassas VA 20110 E-mail: storingpe@netscape.net.

STORK, DONALD ARTHUR, advertising executive; b. Walsh, Ill., June 17, 1939; s. Arthur William and Katherine Frances (Young) S.; m. Joanna Gentry, June 9, 1962; 1 child, Brian Wesley. BS, So. Ill. U., 1961; postgrad., St. Louis U., 1968—69. With Naegele Outdoor Advt., Mpls. and St. Louis, 1961—63; acct. exec. Richard C. Lynch Advg., 1963—64; media exec. Gardner Advt. Co., 1964—69; v.p. mktg. Advanswers Media/Programming, 1975—79; pres. Advanswers divsn. Wells/BDDP, NYC, 1979—98; pres. Advanswers unit Omnicom, St. Louis, 1998—2002, pres. PHD unit, 2002—04; ret., 2004. Corp. devel. coun. St. Louis Art Mus., 1999—2005, Southern Ill. U.; steering com. mem. Sch. Comm. Deans Coun. Capt. Mo. Air N.G., 1961—67. Recipient Journalism Alumnus of Yr. award So. Ill. U., Alumni Achievement award. Mem. St. Louis Advtsg. Club, Mensa (bd. dir. 2009), Mo. Athletic Club (bd. govs. 2009), MAC Bd. Govs., St. Clair Country Club (bd. dirs. 2001), Alpha Delta Sigma (Aid to Advtg. Edn. award). Home: 27 Symonds Dr Belleville IL 62223-1905 Office: Media Mgmt Inc 14755 N Outer Forty Dr Chesterfield MO 63017 Office Phone: 314-910-0373. Personal E-mail: dastork@sbcglobal.net.

STORK, GILBERT, chemistry professor; b. Brussels, Dec. 31, 1921; s. Jacques and Simone (Weil) Stork; m. Winifred Stewart, June 9, 1944 (dec. May 1992); children: Diana, Linda, Janet, Philip. BS, U. Fla., 1942; PhD, U. Wis., 1945; DSc (hon.), Lawrence Coll., 1961, U. Paris, 1979, U. Rochester, 1982, Emory U., 1988, Columbia U., 1993, U. Wis., 1997. Sr. rsch. chemist Lakeside Labs., 1945—46; instr. chemistry Harvard U., 1946—48, asst. prof., 1948—53; assoc. prof. Columbia U., NYC, 1953—55, prof., 1955—67, Eugene Higgins prof., 1967—92, prof. emeritus, 1992—, chmn. dept., 1973—76. Lectr. and cons. in field; chmn. Gordon Steroid Conf., 1958—59. Recipient Baekeland medal, 1961, Harrison Howe award, 1962, Edward Curtis Franklin Meml. award, Stanford, 1966, Gold medal, Synthetic Chems. Mfrs. Assn., 1971, Nebr. award, 1973, Roussel prize in steroid chemistry, 1978, Edgar Fahs Smith award, 1982, Nat. Medal of Sci., 1982, Linus Pauling award, 1983, Tetrahedron prize, 1985, Remsen award, 1986, Cliff S. Hamilton award, 1986, Mony Ferst award, Sigma Xi, 1987, George Kenner award, 1992, Robert Robinson award, 1992, Chem. Pioneer award, Am. Inst. Chemists, 1992, Welch Found. award in chemistry, 1993, Allan R. Day award, 1994, Wolf prize in chemistry, Wolf Found., Israel, 1996, Phila. Chemists Club award, 1998, Ryoji Noyori award, Soc. Synthetic Organic Chemistry Japan, 2003, Eminent Scientists award, Japanese Soc. for the Promotion Sci., 2005; fellow, Guggenheim, 1959. Fellow: NAS (award in chem. sci. 1982), Am. Philos. Soc., Am. Acad. Arts and Scis., Royal Soc., French Acad. Scis., Royal Soc. Chemistry (Barton Gold medal 2002); mem.: Am. Chem. Soc. (chmn. organic chemistry divsn. 1967, award in pure chemistry 1957, award for creative work in synthetic organic chemistry 1967, Nichols medal 1980, Arthur C. Cope award 1980, Willard Gibbs medal 1982, Roger Adams award in organic chemistry 1991, Herbert C. Brown award in organic chemistry 2005), Chem. Soc. Japan (hon.), Pharm. Soc. Japan (hon.), Chemists Club (hon.). Home: 188 Chestnut St Englewood Cliffs NJ 07632-1908 Office: Columbia U Dept Chemistry Chandler Hall New York NY 10027 Home Phone: 201-871-4032; Office Phone: 212-854-2178. Business E-Mail: gjs8@columbia.edu.

STORK, TRAVIS LANE, emergency physician; b. Fort Collins, Colo., Mar. 9, 1972; Grad. magna cum laude, Duke U.; MD with honors, U. Va. Resident Vanderbilt U., Nashville; faulty physician Emergency Dept. Vanderbilt Med. Ctr., Nashville; host The Doctors, 2008—. Co-author: Don't Be That Girl: A Guide to Finding the Confident, Rational Girl Within, 2008. Avocations: hiking, kayaking. Office: Dept Emergency Medicine 1313 21st Ave S 703 Oxford House Nashville TN 37232-4700*

STORK, VERA LEE, retired elementary school educator; b. Galveston, Tex., Dec. 21, 1942; d. Leslie Don and Ethel F. (Wakefield) Ward; m. Jack E. Stork; children: James Ward, Melissa Gayle. BS in Edn., Southwest Tex. State U., 1965; MEd, Sam Houston State U., 1974. Counselor's cert. U. Houston Clear Lake. Tchr. Port Isable (Tex.) Sch. Dist., 1965-67, Galveston Sch. Dist., 1974—; counselor Rosenberg Elem. Sch., Galveston, Tex., Boliver Elem. Sch., Galveston, 1995—2000; ret., 2000. Life mem. Tex. State PTA; first v.p. Rosenberg Sch. PTA, Galveston; active Galveston Hist. Soc., 1986-87, Galveston Hospice Group, 1986-87; mem. Leon County Rep. Women, 2000—; chmn. Neighbors Helping Neighbors, Hilltop Lakes, 2004-06; Hilltop Lakes Beautification Com., 2000—; mem. Hilltop Lakes Aux. Scholarship Com., 2005—, chairperson, 2006; pres. Hilltop Lakes Chapel Aux., 2007-08. Mem. AAUW (treas. 1978-79), LWV, Am. Field Service (pres. 1982-84), Assn. Tex. Profl. Women (bldg. rep.), Delta Kappa Gamma (project com., ceremonies com. Omicron chpt. 1975—). Beta Sigma Phi (Beta Kappa Mu chpt., 2002—, pres., 2003-04, 08-09), Red Hat Soc. (La Chapequx chpt., 2004—), Hilltop Dr. (pres. 2009). Episcopalian. Home: PO Box 1158 Normangee TX 77871-1158

STORM, CHRISTOPHER, music educator; b. Huron, SD, Mar. 18, 1978; s. Warren Walter and Ellen Fae Storm. MusB, SD State U., 2000; MusM, U. SD, 2006. Cert. tchr. SD, Iowa. Min. of music Congl. United Ch. of Christ, Huron, SD, 1998—2000; substitute music tchr. Sioux Falls Sch. Dist., 2000—01; choral dir. / gen. music tchr. Parkston Sch. Dist., SD, 2001—02; asst. dir. of choral activities Sioux City Bishop Heelan H.S., 2002—04, dir. choral activities, 2004—. Vocalist SD Symphony Chorus, 1998—2001; counselor SD Honors Choir, 2001—. Mem.: Music Tchrs. Nat. Assn., Nat. Assn. for Music Edn., Am. Choral Dir. Assn., Phi Kappa Phi, Mortar Bd. (life). Office: V J Angela Stutt Cath HS 3131 S 156 th St Omaha NE 68130 Home: 9735 Adamas Plz 2 Omaha NE 68127 Home Phone: 712-259-1160; Office Phone: 402-333-0818. Personal E-mail: chris.j.storm@gmail.com. E-mail: stormc@bishopheelan.org.

STORM, J. RENI, nurse, consultant; d. Edmund Francis and M. Helen (Saltzmann) Corrado; m. John A. Storm, Feb. 14, 1970 (div. Sept. 1990); 1 child, Kierston L Storm-Dubois. AAS in Nursing cum laude, Dutchess C.C., Poughkeepsie, NY, 1978; BS in Health Care Cmty., SUNY, New Paltz, 1987; workshop, Scottsdale Sch. for Artists, 2001; MA in Legal and Ethical Studies, U. Balt., 2003. RN NY. Clin. nurse III St. Vincent Hosp., Santa Fe, 1992—. Cmty. edn., mental health players NY State Psychiat. Ctr., Poughkeepsie, 1984—86; pvt. practice consulting legal nurse, Santa Fe, 2003—06; surveyor Accreditation Assn. for Ambulatory Health Care, Inc., 2006. Contbg. editor: (novel) Seas Raging, White Horse Flying; contbg. costume designer The Jungle Book, N.Mex. Ballet, creator (coloring book); exhibitions include 1st Nat. Bank Santa Fe, Limner Gallery, NYC, Santa Fe Soc. Artists, Kiva Gallery; actor: (debut) Inherit the Wind, Agatha Christie's Spider Web (Critical acclaim reviews, 1990); polit. cartoon strip, Udo. Mem. Santa Fe Coun. on Internat. Rels., N.Mex., 2002—03; mem., educator Cmty. Mental Health Players, Poughkeepsie, NY, 1984—86; tutor for cmty. immigrants Literacy Vols., Santa Fe, 2001—02; mem. founding group Santa Fe Living Wage Network, 2003—; rehab. group leader for stroke patients Santa Fe Care Nursing Home, 1999—2000; pres., bd. dirs. Mid Hudson Kennel Club, 1986—88; sponsor World Vision, Rhinebeck, NY, 1989—99; nursing, health care advisor KSK Buddhist Ctr., Santa Fe, 2001—03; AKC judges edn. coord. Mastiff Club Am., Rhinebeck, NY, 1986—88; pres. Dutchess County SPCA, Poughkeepsie, NY, 1986—88; v.p. Santa Fe Soc. Artists, 1997—98. Recipient Cmty. Svc. award for Devel. Contbn., Dutchess County SPCA Bd. Dirs., 1988; scholar, Union Plus, 2002. Mem.: Legal Nurse Consultants (Puget Sound chpt.), Am. Assn. Legal Nurse Cons. Achievements include development of long range plan for community project/Dutchess County SPCA. Avocations: world travel and cultures, cartooning, painting, writing, public speaking.

STÖRMER, HORST LUDWIG, physicist, educator; b. Frankfurt-Main, Fed. Republic Germany, Apr. 6, 1949; arrived in U.S., 1977; s. Karl-Ludwig and Marie (Ihrig) S.; m. Dominique A. Parchet, 1982. Studied Physics, JW Goethe Univ.; PhD, U. Stuttgart, 1977. From tech. staff to dir. phys. rsch. lab. AT&T Bell Labs., Murray Hill, NJ, 1977—97; I. I. Rabi prof. physics and prof. applied physics Columbia U., NYC, 1998—. Adj. physics dir. Lucent Tech., 1997—. Decorated Officier de la Legion d'Honneur France, Grosses Verdienstkreuz Mit Stern Germany; recipient Otto Klung prize, 1985, Benjamin Franklin medal in physics, 1998, Nobel prize in Physics, 1998, N.Y.C. Mayor's award for excellence in sci. and tech., 2000; fellow Bell Labs., 1983. Fellow: NAS, Am. Acad. Arts and Scis., Am. Phys. Soc. (Buckley prize 1984). Achievements include development of modulation doping, a method for making extremely high mobility two dimensional electron systems in semiconductors. Office: Columbia U Dept Physics MC 5206 538 W 120th St New York NY 10027-6601 also: Lucent Technologies 700 Mountain Ave New Providence NJ 07974-1208

STORMES, JOHN MAX, systems analyst; b. Manila, Oct. 7, 1927; s. Max Clifford and Janet (Heldring) S.; m. Takako Sanae, July 29, 1955; children: Janet Kazuko, Alan Osamu. BS, San Diego State U., 1950; BA, U. So. Calif., 1957, MA, 1967. Cert. secondary and community coll. tchr., sr. profl. human resources. Editing supr. Lockheed Propulsion Co., Redlands, Calif., 1957-61; proposals supr. Rockwell Internat., Downey, Calif., 1961-62; publs. dir. Arthur D. Little, Inc., Santa Monica, Calif., 1962-63; publs. coord. Rockwell Internat., Downey, 1963-68; project dir. Gen. Behavioral Systems, Inc., Torrance, Calif., 1969-73; tng. and comm. cons. Media Rsch. Assocs., Santa Cruz, Calif., 1973—; instrl. design supr. So. Calif. Gas Co., LA, 1985-2001; adj. assoc. prof. Alliant U., Alhambra, Calif., 2001—02. Lectr. Calif. State U., Northridge, 1991-2003; tng. cons. Nat. Ednl. Media, Chatsworth, Calif., 1966-81, comm. cons. Opinion Rsch. Calif., Long Beach, 1974-. Co-author: TV Communications Systems For Business and Industry, 1970; contbg. author: ASTD's In Action series of casebooks, 1996-99. Curriculum adv. bd. communications dept. Calif. State U., Fullerton, 1964-78. Sgt. U.S. Army, 1953-55, Japan. Mem. Soc. Tech. Communication (sr. mem., 2nd v.p. Orange County chpt. 1962-63), Internat. Soc. Performance and Instruction (v.p. L.A. chpt. 1989, pres. 1990). Democrat. Episcopalian. Avocations: photography, sailing. Home and Office: 136 Alamo Ave Santa Cruz CA 95060 Home Phone: 831-427-1558. Personal E-mail: jmstormes@comcast.net.

STORMONT, RICHARD MANSFIELD, hotel executive; b. Chgo., Apr. 4, 1936; s. Daniel Lytle and E. Mildred (Milligan) S.; m. Virginia Louellen Walters, Nov. 21, 1959; children: Stacy Lee Freeman, Richard Mansfield, John Frederick. BS, Cornell U., 1958. Cert. hosp. adminstrn.; cert. hosps. industry profl. Food cost analyst, sales rep. Edgewater Beach Hotel, Chgo., 1957-58; asst. sales mgr. Marriott Hotels, Inc., Washington, 1962-64, dir. sales Atlanta, 1964-68, resident mgr., 1969-71; gen. mgr. Marriott Hotel, Dallas, 1971-73, Phila., 1973-74, Atlanta, 1974-79; pres. Hardin Mgmt. Co., 1979-80; v.p. Marriott Franchise div. Marriott Corp., Washington, 1980-83, v.p. ops. Courtyard by Marriott, 1981-83; pres. The Stormont Cos. Inc., 1984—2004; chmn. Stormont Trice Corp., 1993-2000, Stormont Noble Devel. LLC, 2004—06; pres. The Stormont Cos., LLC, 2004—. Pres. Atlanta Conv. and Visitors Burs., 1975-76, vice chmn. bd., 1976-77, chmn., 1998-99, chmn. bd. exec. com., 1998-2000; trustee Young Harris Coll.; bd. dirs. Better Bus. Bur.; exec. com. Ctrl. Atlanta Progress, 1979-80; exec. coun. Boy Scouts Am.; bd. dirs., chmn. tourism divsn. Ga. Dept. Industry, Trade and Tourism, 1999-2001; chmn. bd. trustees Lenbrook Square Found., Inc., 2007—; chmn. bd. dirs. Atlanta St. Patricks Day Found., 2005-06. Paul Harris fellow Rotary Internat., 2006-07; recipient Disting. Salesman of Yr. award Marriott, 1967, Obi T. Brewer award for Decade of Outstanding Svc., 1979, Atlanta Hospitality Hall of Fame award, 2006. Mem. Sales and Mktg. Execs. (exec. v.p. 1969-70, pres. Atlanta 1970-71), Am. Hotel-Motel Assn. (exec. com., bd. dirs. 1993-95, Most Valuable Vol. Ga. 1999), Ga. Hospitality and Travel Assn. (founder 1975, bd. dir., pres. 1989-90, chmn. bd. 1991-92, Hotelier of Yr. award 1977, Hall of Fame 2001), Ga. Bus. and Industry Assn. (bd. dirs.), Atlanta Hotel Assn. (pres. 1976), So. Innkeepers Assn., Atlanta C. of C. (v.p. 1978-79), Gwinnett C. of C. (bd. dirs.), Cornell Soc. Hotelmen (pres. Ga. chpt. 1976, regional v.p. 1989-91), Cornell U. Hotel Soc. (SE Hotelier of Yr.), Rotary (Atlanta, bd. dirs. 1999-2007, pres. 2007—), Rotary Club Atlanta (pres. 2007-08, chmn. bd. 2008-09). Home and Office: 2980 Nancy Creek Rd NW Atlanta GA 30327-2000 E-mail: dstormont@bellsouth.net.

STORMS, CLIFFORD BEEKMAN, lawyer; b. Mount Vernon, NY, July 18, 1932; s. Harold Beekman and Gene (Pertak) S.; m. Barbara H. Grave, 1955 (div. 1975); m. Valeria N. Parker, July 12, 1975; children: Catherine Storms Fischer, Clifford Beekman. BA magna cum laude, Amherst Coll., 1954; LLB, Yale U., 1957. Bar: N.Y. 1957. Assoc. Breed, Abbott & Morgan, NYC, 1957—64; with CPC Internat., Inc., Englewood Cliffs, NJ, 1964—97, v.p. legal affairs, 1973—75, v.p., gen. counsel, 1975—88, sr. v.p., gen. counsel, 1988—97, atty. alternate dispute resolution, corp. dir., 1997—; bd. dirs. Corn Products Internat. Inc., 1997—2005; pvt. practice Greenwich, Conn., 1997—. Bd. dirs. Atlantic Legal Found., Indian Harbor Yacht Club; mem. Conn. Alternate Dispute Resolution panel Ctr. Pub. Resources. Trustee emeritus Food and Drug Law Inst. Mem. ABA (com. of corp. gen. counsel), Am. Arbitration Assn. (panel arbitrators large complex case program), Assn. Gen. Counsel (pres. 1992-94), NYC Bar Assn. (sec., com. on corp. law depts. 1979-81), Phi Beta Kappa. Office: 19 Burying Hill Rd Greenwich CT 06831-2604 Personal E-mail: cbstorms@aol.com.

STORRER, WILLIAM ALLIN, theater educator, consultant; b. Highland Park, Mich., Mar. 22, 1936; s. Fredrick Ray and Margaret Ann (Pitts) S.; m. Carol A. Tuthill, Nov. 6, 1964 (div. June 1969); 1 child, Kirsten; m. Patricia Alice Whalley, Dec. 30, 1976. Student, Albion Coll., 1954-56; AB in Engring. Scis., Harvard U., 1959; MFA in Theatre Arts, Boston U., 1962; PhD in Comparative Arts, Ohio U., 1968. Electronics engr. Raytheon Co., Wayland, Mass., 1958-60; tech. dir. small stage Boston Arts Festival, 1961, 62; dir. dramatics Melrose HS, Mass., 1962—63; dir. playhouse and repertory theatre, instr. drama-speech Hofstra U., 1963-66, instr. opera, 1965; asst. prof. theatre, dir. univ. theatre, U. Toledo, 1968-69; assoc. prof. theatre and film, dir. Southampton Coll., LI U., 1969—73; asst. prof. cinema studies and still photography Ithaca Coll., NY, 1973—76; assoc. prof. media arts U. SC, Columbia, 1976—82; pres. MINDaLIVE Creative Mind Enhancement, Newark, 1980—. Assoc. prof. theater and speech World Campus Afloat, Chapman Coll., 1972; edn. media specialist Newark Bd. Edn., 1990-94, Linden Bd. Edn., 1994-95, Harrison Bd. Edn., 1995-96, Rosa Parks Fine and Performing Arts HS, Paterson, NJ, 1996-2004, dir. Storrer/Storre/Storer Family Inst., vis. prof. U. Tex., 2004-. Author: The Architecture of Frank Lloyd Wright, A Complete Catalog, 1974, 4th edit. 2007, The Frank Lloyd Wright Companion, 1993, 2d edit., 2006; contbr. articles to popular mags. and profl. jours. Grantee Graham Found. for Advanced Studies in Fine Arts, 1987, 94. Home: Frankfort MI 49635-1121 Office: PO Box 1121 Frankfort MI 49635 Office Phone: 231-352-9343.

STORRS, ALEXANDER DAVID, astronomer; b. Idaho Falls, Idaho, May 30, 1960; s. Charles Lysander and Betty Lou (Wood) S.; m. Jean Elizabeth Seitzer, Nov. 4, 1989; 1 child, Matthew. BS, MIT, 1982; MS, U. Hawaii, 1985, PhD, 1987. Postdoctoral fellow NASA/Goddard Space Flight Ctr., Greenbelt, Md., 1987-89, U. Tex., Austin, 1989-91; assoc. scientist Space Telescope Sci. Inst., Balt., 1991—. Mem. AAAS, Am. Astron. Soc. (divsn. planetary scis.), Smithsonian Air and Space Mus. Office: Space Telescope Sci Inst 3700 San Martin Dr Baltimore MD 21218-2464

STORY, JOAN H., lawyer; b. Parsons, Kans., Feb. 7, 1944; AB, Occidental Coll., 1965; MA, UCLA, 1968; JD, U. Calif., Davis, 1977. Bar: Calif. 1977. Ptnr., mem. exec. com. Sheppard, Mullin, Richter & Hampton LLP, San Francisco. Co-chair Calif. adv. bd. Trust for Pub. Land. Volume editor U. Calif. at Davis Law Rev., 1976-77. Mem. alumni bd. govs. Occidental Coll., 1982-85. Mem.: Practicing Law Inst. (real estate law adv. com.), Am. Coll. Real Estate Lawyers, Bar Assn. San Francisco, State Bar Calif. (mem. real property law sect.), U. Calif. Davis Law Sch. Alumni Assn. (bd. dirs.), Lambda Alpha. Office: Sheppard, Mullin, Richter & Hampton LLP 17 Fl Four Embarcadero Ctr San Francisco CA 94111 Office Phone: 415-774-3211. Office Fax: 415-434-3947. E-mail: jstory@sheppardmullin.com.

STORY, JOYCE ANN, retired language educator; PhD, Ind. U., Bloomington. Faculty Glendale CC, Ariz., 1990—2008.

STORY, JULIE ANN, language educator; b. Muncy, Pa., Aug. 6, 1959; d. Phillip Mason Story and Mary Lee Peters. BA in English, Lock Haven U., 1982; MA in English, Ind. U. Pa., 1984. Assoc. dir. undergraduate writing ctr., lectr. English Pa. State U., U. Pk., 1987—2003; English instr. Juniata Coll., Huntingdon, Pa., 1987—89; dir. writing ctr., writing specialist Lock Haven U., Pa., 1998, 2003—. Internship coord. writing ctr. Pa. State U., University Park; cons. in field; faculty advisor Dangling Modifier. Mem. Pa. State Commn. for Women, University Park. Grantee, Ctr. Excellence Learning and Tchg., 2001. Mem.: Nat. Coun. Tchrs. English, Conf. Coll. Composition Comm., Ctrl. Pa. Writing Ctrs. Assn. (bd. dirs.), Nat. Conf. Peer Tutoring in Writing (adv. bd.), Mid-Atlantic Writing Ctrs. Assn. (bd. dirs.), Internat. Writing Ctrs. Assn., Phi Kappa Phi, Sigma Tau Delta. Democrat. Avocations: gardening, walking, photography, reading, movies. Home: 33 Julia Dr Lock Haven PA 17745 Office: Lock Haven Univ Pa 115 Russell Hall Lock Haven PA 17745 Business E-Mail: jstory@lhup.edu.

STORY, SUSAN N., utilities executive; b. 1960; B in Indsl. Engring., Auburn U., Ala.; MBA, U. Ala., Birmingham. Nuc. power plant engr. Southern Co., 1982, dir. human resources, v.p. real estate and corp. svcs., v.p. supply chain mgmt., exec. v.p. engring. and constrn. svcs. Southern Co. Generation and Energy Mktg., pres., CEO Gulf Power, 2003—. Mem. exec. coun. Fla. Coun. of 100; bd. trustees Fla. Chamber Found., US Naval Aviation Mus. Found.; chmn. Enterprise Fla. Tech. Innovation and Entrepreneurship Coun.; chair Auburn Alumni Engring. Coun.; vice chair bd. dirs. Enterprise Fla., Inc., 2005—07; bd. dirs. Fla. Coun. of 100, Fla. C. of C., Gt. NW Econ. Devel. Coun., Fla., Pensacola Area C. of C., Assn. Edison Illuminating Cos., Edison Electric Inst. CEO Com., Southeastern Electric Exch. CEO Com., Fla. Electric Reliability Coordinating Coun.; bd. mem. Ala. Engring. Hall of Fame. Recipient Presdl. Achievement award, Sacred Heart Hosp., 2004, Women Breaking the Corp. Glass Ceiling award, Women's Bus. Ctr., 2004, Woman of Distinction award, Girl Scouts, Outstanding Engring. Alumnus award, Auburn U. Coll. Engring., Leaders and Legends award for Environ. Leadership, 2006, Ethics in Bus. award, U. West Fla. and Combined Rotary Clubs of Pensacola region, 2006, Internat. Women's Day award, World Trade Ctr. Miami, 2007; named Fla. Econ. Devel. Vol. of Yr., So. Econ. Devel. Coun., 2005, Bus. Leader of Yr., Pensacola Area C. of C., 2007; named one of Top 10 Women in Bus., Birmingham Bus. Jour., 2002. Office: Gulf Power Co One Energy Pl Pensacola FL 32520*

STORY, TIMOTHY KEVIN (TIM STORY), film director; b. LA, Mar. 13, 1970; married; 1 child. Grad., U. Southern Calif. Dir.: (films) One of Us Tripped, 1997, Barbershop, 2002, Taxi, 2004, Fantastic Four, 2005, Fantastic Four: Rise of the Silver Surfer, 2007; dir., co-editor, writer (films) The Firing Squad, 1999, writer Urban Menace, 1999; prodr.: (films) First Sunday, 2008; prodr., dir.: (TV series) Standoff, 2006; The 12th Man, 2006. Named to Power 150, Ebony mag., 2008.

STOSSEL, THOMAS PETER, medical educator, researcher, director; b. Chgo., Sept. 10, 1941; m. Kerry Maguire, 1997. AB, Princeton U., NJ, 1963; MD, Harvard U., Cambridge, Mass., 1967; MD (hon.), U. Linkoping, Sweden, 1989, U. Geneva, 2004. Diplomate Am. Bd. Internal Medicine. Ho. staff medicine Mass. Gen. Hosp., Boston, 1967-69, chief hematology-oncology, 1976-90; staff assoc. NIH, Bethesda, Md., 1967-71; fellow to sr. assoc. Med. Ctr. Children's Hosp., Boston, 1971-76; prof. medicine Harvard Med. Sch., Boston, 1982—; chief divsn. exptl. medicine Brigham Women's Hosp., Boston, 1991—97, co-dir. hematology divsn., 1998—2006, dir. translational medicine div., 2006—; sr. fellow Manhattan Inst. Policy Rsch., 2008—. Sci. bd. Biogen Corp., 1987—2002, Dyax Corp., 1996—2002; clin. rsch. prof. Am. Cancer Soc., 1987—; bd. dirs. Zymequest, Inc., Critical Biologics Corp. Author (with B. Babior): (book) 2d edit., 1984, Hematology, A Pathophysiological Approach, 1994; editor (with R.

Handin and S. Lux): Blood, Principles & Practice of Hematology, 1995, 2d edit., 2003; contbr. articles to profl. jours. Bd. dirs. Am. Coun. Sci. and Health, 2006—. Lt. comdr. USPHS, 1969—71. Mem.: NAS, Am. Acad. Arts and Scis., Assn. Am. Physicians, Am. Soc. Hematology (pres. 1997, Damashek prize 1983, Thomas prize 1993), Am. Soc. Clin. Investigation (pres. 1987), Inst. Medicine (Lasker awards Jury). Achievements include patents in field. Office: Brigham & Womens Hosp Karp 625 1 Blackfan Cir Boston MA 02115 Home Phone: 617-489-1299; Office Phone: 617-355-9001. Business E-Mail: tstossel@partners.org.

STOTLAR, DOUGLAS W., transportation executive; b. Newbury, Ohio; BS, Ohio State Univ. Freight ops. supr. through regional mgr. Con-Way Transp. Svcs., Ann Arbor, Mich., 1985—96, v.p., gen mgr. Con-Way NOW, 1996—99, exec. v.p. ops., 1999—2002, exec. v.p., COO, 2002—04, pres., CEO, 2004—05, Con-Way Inc. (formerly CNF Inc.), San Mateo, Calif., 2005—. V.p., mem. exec. com. Am. Trucking Assn.; bd. dir. Am. Transp. Rsch. Inst. Office: Con-Way Inc 2855 Campus Dr Ste 300 San Mateo CA 94403-2512

STOTLER, ALICEMARIE HUBER, federal judge; b. Alhambra, Calif., May 29, 1942; d. James R. and Loretta M. Huber; m. James Allen Stotler, Sept. 11, 1971. BA, U. So. Calif., 1964, JD, 1967. Bar: Calif. 1967, U.S. Dist. Ct. (no. dist.) Calif. 1967, U.S. Dist. Ct. (ctrl. dist.) Calif. 1973, U.S. Supreme Ct. 1976; cert. criminal law specialist. Dep. Orange County Dist. Attys. Office, 1967-73; mem. Stotler & Stotler, Santa Ana, Calif., 1973-76, 83-84; judge Orange County Mcpl. Ct., 1976-78, Orange County Superior Ct., 1978-83, U.S. Dist. Ct. (ctrl. dist.) Calif., LA, 1984—. Assoc. dean Calif. Trial Judges Coll., 1982; lectr., panelist, numerous orgns.; standing com. on rules of practice and procedure U.S. Jud. Conf., 1991-98, chair, 1993-98; chair 9th cir. Pub. Info. and Cmty. Outreach, 2000-04; mem. exec. com. 9th Cir. Jud. Conf., 1989-93, Fed. State Jud. Coun., 1989-98, jury com., 1990-92, planning com. for Nat. Conf. on Fed.-State Jud. Relationships, Orlando, 1991-92, planning com. for We. Regional Conf. on State-Fed. Jud. Relationships, Stevens, Wash., 1992-93; chair dist. ct. symposium and jury utilization Ctrl. Dist. Calif., 1985, chair atty. liaison, 1989-90, chair U.S. Constn. Bicentennial com., 1986-91, chair magistrate judge com., 1992-93; mem. State Adv. Group on Juvenile Justice and Delinquency Prevention, 1983-84, Bd. Legal Specializations Criminal Law Adv. Commn., 1983-84, victim/witness adv. com. Office Criminal Justice Planning, 1980-83, U. So. Calif. Bd. Councilors, 1993-2001; active team in tng. Leukemia Soc. Am., 1993, 95, 97, 2000; legion lex bd. dirs. U. So. Calif. Sch. Law Support Group, 1981-83. Winner Hale Moot Ct. Competition, State of Calif., 1967; named Judge of Yr., Orange County Trial Lawyers Assn., 1978, Most Outstanding Judge Orange County Bus. Litig. Sect., 1990. Mem. ABA (jud. adminstrn. divsn. and litig. sect. 1984—, nat. conf. fed. trial judges com. on legis. affairs 1990-91), Am. Law Inst., Am. Judicature Soc., Fed. Judges Assn. (bd. dirs. 1989-92), Nat. Assn. Women Judges, U.S. Supreme Ct. Hist. Soc., Ninth Cir. Dist. Judges Assn., Calif. Supreme Ct. Hist. Soc., Orange County Bar Assn. (mem. numerous coms., Franklin G. West award 1984), Calif. Judges Assn. (mem. com. on jud. coll. 1978-80, com. on civil law and procedure 1980-82, Dean's coll. curriculum commn. 1981), Calif. Judges Found. Office: Ronald Reagan Fed Bldg & Courthouse 411 W 4th St Santa Ana CA 92701-4500

STOTO, MICHAEL A., statistician, epidemiologist; b. Jersey City, Jan. 4, 1954; s. Benjamin M. and Irene R. Stoto; m. Rosemary Chalk, May 25, 1948; children: Anna, Benjamin. AB with high honors, Princeton U., 1975; AM, Harvard U., 1977, PhD, 1979. Asst. prof. pub. policy Harvard U., Cambridge, Mass., 1979—83, assoc. prof., 1984—87; dep. dir. Divsn. Health Promotion and Disease Prevention NAS, Washington, 1983—84, 1987—98, sr. staff officer, 1983—98; prof. epidemiology and biostatistics George Washington U., Washington, 1998—2001; sr. statis. scientist RAND, Arlington, Va., 2001—. Adj. prof. biostatistics Harvard U., Boston, 1997—. Author: Data for Decisions: Information Strategies for Policy Makers, 1982; editor: Healthy People 2000: Citizens Chart the Course, Veterans and Agent Orange: Health Effects of Herbicides Used in Vietnam, HIV and the Blood Supply: An Analysis of Crisis Decision-marking, Healthy Communities: New Partnerships for the Future of Public Health, Improving Health in the Community: A Role for Performance Monitoring, Reducing the Odds: Preventing Perinatal Transmission of HIV in the United States, No Time to Lose: Getting More from HIV Prevention; contbr. articles to profl. jours. Fellow, NSF, 1975—78. Mem.: APHA (chair stats. sect. 2002—03), Am. Statis. Assn. (pres. Boston chpt. 1981—82), Am. Coll. Epidemiology. Democrat. Roman Catholic. Office: RAND 1200 S Hayes St Arlington VA 22202 Office Phone: 703-413-1100 x 5472. E-mail: mstoto@hsph.harvard.edu.

STOTSKY, ADAM, communications executive; b. 1969; BA, Western Va. U., 1991. Sr. account mgr. Fallon McElligott, Mpls., NYC; v.p. mktg. Travel Channel Discovery Comm.; sr. v.p. J. Walter Thompson Worldwide's Entertainment Practice; v.p brand mktg. Sci-Fi Channel NBC Universal, Inc., 2001—07, exec. v.p. global brand strategy and market devel. Sci-Fi Channel, 2007—08, pres. entertainment mktg., 2008—. Named one of 40 Executives Under 40, Multichannel News, 2006. Office: NBC Universal Inc Hdqs 30 Rockefeller Plz New York NY 10112 Office Phone: 212-664-4444. Office Fax: 212-664-4085. Business E-Mail: adam.stotsky@nbcuni.com.

STOTT, BRIAN, software company executive, consultant; b. Eccles, Eng., Aug. 5, 1941; came to U.S., 1983; s. Harold and Mary (Stephens) S.; m. Patricia Ann Farrar, Dec. 3, 1983. BSc, Manchester U., 1962, MSc, 1963, PhD, 1971. Asst. prof. Mid. East Tech. U., Ankara, Turkey, 1965—68; lectr. Inst. Sci. and Tech., U. Manchester, England, 1968—74; assoc. prof. U. Waterloo, Ont., Canada, 1974—76; cons. Electric Energy Rsch. Ctr. Brazil, Rio de Janeiro, 1976—83; prof. Ariz. State U., Tempe, 1983—84; chmn. Power Computer Applications Corp., Mesa, Ariz., 1984—2000; pres. Stott Inc. Cons. in field. Contbr. numerous articles to rsch. publs. Fellow IEEE (Millennium medal); mem. NAE. Home and Office: 10222E Southwind Lane #1004 Scottsdale AZ 85262 Business E-Mail: brianstott@ieee.org.

STOTT, GRADY BERNELL, lawyer; b. Bailey, NC, Sept. 19, 1921; s. William Willard and Zettie Harriett (Bissette) S.; m. Mays Beal, May 9, 1952; children: Sue J., Caroline Beal. AB, Duke U., 1947, JD, 1952. Bar: N.C. 1952. Dist. atty. 27th Jud. Dist., Gastonia, NC, 1957-62; partner firm Stott, Hollowell, Palmer & Windham, Gastonia, 1960—. Served with USMC, 1943-48. Fellow Am. Bar Found., Am. Coll. Trial Lawyers; mem. N.C. State Bar (pres. 1978-79), Am. Bar Assn. (del. 1980), N.C. Bar Assn., Assn. Ins. Attys. Clubs: Masons. Democrat. Methodist. Office: 401 E Franklin Blvd Gastonia NC 28054-7152 Office Phone: 704-864-3425. Personal E-mail: gbs@shpw.com.

STOTT, PETER WALTER, investment company executive; b. Spokane, Wash., May 26, 1944; s. Walter Joseph and Rellalee (Gray) S.; m. Julie L. Neupert, Oct. 12, 1996; 1 child, Preston. Student, Portland State U., 1962-63, 65-68, U. Americas, Mexico City, 1964-65. Founder, bd. chmn. emeritus Market Transport Ltd., Portland, Oreg., 1969—2006; pres. Columbia Investments, Ltd., Portland, 2005—; vice chmn., CEO, prin. ScanlanKemperBard Cos., Portland, 2005—. Pres., CEO, prin. Crown Pacific, 1988-2004; bd. dir. Con-Way Inc. Mem. cabinet Bldg. Our Future Campaign; trustee Portland Art Mus.; founding bd. dir. Crater Lake Nat. Park Trust; bd. dir. Portland State U. Found. With USAR, 1966-72. Mem. Nat. Football Found. and Hall of Fame, Oreg. Sports Hall of Fame (lifetime), Stop Oreg. Litter and Vandalism (founders' circle), Arlington Club, Mazamas Club, Multnomah Athletic Club, Univ. Club, Waverley Country Club, Valley Club. Republican. Roman Catholic. Office: Columbia Investments Ltd Ste 2600 1211 SW Fifth Ave Portland OR 97204 Business E-Mail: pstott@skbcos.com.

STOTT, TERRI JEUAN, residential services director; b. Ft. Lee, Va., Nov. 7, 1965; d. Terry and Gwendolyn Gilliam; m. Eric Lawrence Stott, Sept. 18, 1992. BSW cum laude, Norfolk State U., 1988; MSW, Howard U., 1990. Cert. brief solution focused psychotherapy Am. Hypnosis Tng. Acad. Grad. asst. office of assoc. dean Howard U., Washington, 1988—90; intern mental health therapist Arlington Mental Health Ctr., Va., 1988—90; relief counselor Prince William County Group Home for Boys, Va., 1988—91, counselor, 1991—92, asst. mgr., 1992—97; acting asst. mgr. Judge Patrick Molinari Juvenile Shelter, Manassas, Va., 1997—98, supr. shelter home, 1998—2006, Residential Svcs. Dir., Manassas, 2007—; youth residential adminstr. Judge Patrick Molinari Juvenile Shelter, Manassas, Va., 2006—07, residential svcs. dir., 2007. Cons., trainer Dept. Social Svcs., Manassas, 1992—, coun. on quality, 1999—; affiliate field instr. faculty Va. Commonwealth U., Richmond, 1996-97; field program adv. com. George Mason U., Fairfax, Va., 1998—. Recipient Dale City Multicultural Scholar Fund 18th Ann. Achievement award Outstanding Pub. Svc. 2002, Suggested Artist award, 2005; Semifinalist award, 2007; named one of Double Outstanding Young Women of Am., 1988; Child Welfare grantee Norfolk State U., 1987; finalist Internat. Song of Yr. contest, 2004 Mem. Greater No. Va. Nat. Alumni Assn. (Millennium Leaders Excellence award 2000), Pi Sigma Delta (sec. 1989-90), Alpha Delta Mu Avocations: songwriting, reading, music, travel, fashion.

STOTT, THOMAS EDWARD, JR., retired engineering executive; b. Beverly, Mass., May 14, 1923; s. Thomas Edward and Mildred (Ayers) S.; m. Mary Elizabeth Authelet, Feb. 26, 1944; children: Pamela, Randi, Wendy, Thomas E., Diana. BS, Tufts U., 1945. Design engr. Bethlehem Steel, Quincy, Mass., 1956-59, project engr., 1959-64, sr. engr. basic ship design, 1960-63, project coordinator, 1963-64; pres. Stal-Laval, Inc., Elmsford, N.Y., 1964-84, Thomas Stott & Co., Cummaquid, Mass., 1984-88; ret., 1988. Bd. dirs. Friends of Prisoners, Inc., 1990-05; deacon West Parish Barnstable, Mass., 1994-96, 2002-04, moderator, 1996-99. With USNR, 1944-46. Decorated (4) WWII medals with 5 combat stars, Combat ribbon. Fellow ASME (chmn. marine com., chmn. gas turbine div. exec. com., chmn. nat. nominating com., exec. sec. gas turbine div., Centennial medal 1980, R. Tom Sawyer award 1981, Dedicated Svc. award 1989), Soc. Naval Architects and Marine Engrs. Independent. Home: 51 Kates Path Yarmouth Port MA 02675-1448 Home Phone: 508-362-9633. Personal E-mail: tstott7668@aol.com.

STOTTER, HARRY SHELTON, banker, lawyer; b. NYC, Aug. 28, 1928; s. Jack and Adele Stotter; m. Marilyn H. Knight, Nov. 7, 1954; children: Jeffrey Craig, Cheryl dee. Student, L.I. U., 1948-49; JD, St. John's U., 1952; postgrad., NYU Law Sch., 1956-57. Bar: N.Y. 1952, N.J. 1974, U.S. Supreme Ct. 1983. Pvt. practice in, NYC, 1952-53, 54-56; atty. U.S. Dept. Def., 1953; with trust div. Bank of N.Y., 1956-63; exec. v.p., sr. mgmt. com. Summit Bank (now Bank of Am.), NJ, 1963-84; exec. v.p. Chase Manhattan Bank, NYC, 1984-94; dir., vice chmn. Chase Manhattan Trust Co. Fla., Palm Beach, Fla., 1984-87; pvt. trust and estates law practice NJ, 1974-2000; former mem. probate com. N.J. Supreme Ct. Jud. Conf. Mem. N.Y.C. and Bergen County estate planning couns.; former pres. Bergen County coun. Girl Scouts Am.; bd. dirs., pres., chief exec. officer Bergen County United Way; treas. 2d Century Fund, Hackensack Hosp.; bd. dirs. Holy Name Hosp., Teaneck, N.J. With USN, World War II; brig. gen. Army N.G. Mem. ABA (co-chmn. nat. conf. lawyers and corp. trustees 1991-93), Am. Bankers Assn. (chmn. trust counsel com. 1991-93), N.Y. Bar Assn., N.J. Bar Assn., N.Y. County Lawyers Assn., Bergen County Bar Assn. (former trustee, former chmn. probate and estate planning com.), Fed. Bar Assn., NY Mil. Assn. US, Nat. Guard Assn.

STOTTER, LAWRENCE HENRY, lawyer; b. Cleve., Sept. 24, 1929; s. Oscar and Bertha (Lieb) S.; m. Ruth Rapoport, June 30, 1957; children: Daniel, Jennifer, Steven. BBA, Ohio State U., 1956, LLB, 1958, JD, 1967. Bar: Calif. 1960, U.S. Supreme Ct. 1973, U.S. Tax Ct. 1976. Pvt. practice, San Francisco, 1963—; ptnr. Stotter and Coats, San Francisco, 1981-97; sole practitioner, 1997—; mem. faculty Nat. Judicial Coll.; mem. Calif. Family Law Adv. Commn., 1979-80. Editor in chief: Am. Bar Family Advocate mag, 1977-82; TV appearances on Phil Donahue Show, Good Morning America. Pres. Tamalpais Conservation Club, Marin County, Calif.; U.S. State Dept. del. Hague Conf. Pvt. Internat. Law, 1979-80; legal adv. White House Conf. on Families, 1980—. Served with AUS, 1950-53. Mem. ABA (past chmn. family law sect.), Am. Acad. Matrimonial Lawyers (past nat. v.p.), Calif. State Bar (past chmn. family law sect.), San Francisco Bar Assn. (past chmn. family law sect.), Calif. Trial Lawyers Assn. (past chmn. family law sect.) Home and Office: 2244 Vistazo St E Belvedere Tiburon CA 94920-1970 Office Phone: 415-435-3568. Personal E-mail: lhstotter@aol.com.

STOTTER, RUTH, retired college program director; b. Madison, Wis., July 26, 1936; d. Louis Marvin and Jeanne (Michael) Rapoport; m. Lawrence Henry Stotter, June 30, 1957; children: Daniel, Jennifer, Steven. BA, Ohio State U., 1958; MA, Stanford U., 1959; teaching cert., U. Calif., Berkeley, 1961; MA, Sonoma State U., 1984. Lifetime instr. credential (anthropology) Calif. Community Coll., lifetime teaching credentials (K-14) Calif. Bd. Edn. Freelance storyteller and workshop leader, 1974—; resident storyteller Renaissance Pleasure Faire, Novato, Calif., 1979-83, 85; assoc. prof. extended edn. dept. Sonoma State U., Rohnert Park, Calif., 1980, 89—; producer, host radio program KUSF-FM, San Francisco, 1982-88; instr., cert. in storytelling program Dominican Coll. Acad. for Profl. Devel., San Rafael, Calif., 1984-86, dir., cert. in storytelling program, 1986—95; ret. Apptd. cons. Puppeteers of Am., 1989; performing artist Youth-in-Arts, San Rafael, 1989-90; featured performer Mariposa (Calif.) Festival, 1990, Cambria, 1993, Edmonton and Lethbridge, Can., 1994. Author: (book) Little Acorns, 1976, rev. edit., 1993, About Story, 1994, Golden Axe, 1998, You're On, 2000, More About Story, 2002, Smiles!, 2005, A Loop of String: String Stories and Stunts, 2009; (calendar) The Storyteller's Calendar, 1988-98; contbr. to books Family Storytelling Handbook, 1987, Joining In, 1988, Jack in Two Worlds, 1993, Tell the World, 2007, American Folklore: An Encyclopedia, 1998, Archetypes and Motifs in Folklore and Literature, 2005, Holiday Stories All Year Round, 2008, Storytelling:An Encyclopedia of Mythology & Folklore(Sharpe Reference, 2008), Tell the World: Storytelling Across Language Barriers 2007; prodr., narrator (audio cassettes) Tales from California History, 1989, The West, 2001, 2007; contbr. numerous articles on storytelling to jours. and mags. Recipient Performance grant Alaska Arts Coun., Anchorage, 1980. Recipient Keables chair English, Iolani Sch., Honolulu, 1999, Reading the World award, U. San Francisco, 2004. Mem. Am. Folklore Soc. (panelist annual meetings, 1985, 87, 93), Calif. Folklore Soc. (panelist annual meetings, 1980, 86, 90). Avocations: hiking, kayaking, travel. Home: 2244 Vistazo St E Tiburon CA 94920-1970 Personal E-mail: speakingout2@comcast.net, r.stotter@comcast.net.

STOTTLEMYER, DAVID LEE, federal official; b. Waynesboro, Pa., June 1, 1935; s. Omar Samuel and Miriam (Noll) S.; m. Jane Ann Hembree, Aug. 26, 1961; children: Todd Andrew, Kristen Elizabeth, Kathryn Ann. AB, Miami U., Oxford, Ohio, 1959; M. Pub. and Internat. Affairs (NDEA fellow), U. Pitts., 1964, also postgrad. Program and budget analyst Exec. Office of Pres., Office of Mgmt. and Budget, Washington, 1964-69; sr. mgmt. officer UN, NYC, 1969-70; adviser internat. orgn. affairs US Mission to UN, NYC, 1971-72, counsellor internat. orgn. affairs, 1973-75, counsellor UN resources mgmt., 1976-77; also mem. U.S. del. 26th-31st gen. assemblies, mem. UN Com. on Contbns., 1971; mem. UN Adv. Com. on Adminstrv. and Budgetary Questions, 1973-77; dir. policy mgmt. staff Bur. Internat. Orgn. Affairs, US Dept. State, Washington, 1977-80, exec. asst. to asst. sec. of state for internat. orgn. affairs, 1980; mem. staff Office of Vice-Pres., Washington, 1981-83; dir. adminstrv. mgmt. service UN, NYC, 1984-85; exec. asst., dir. Office of Under-Sec.-Gen. for Adminstrn. and Mgmt., UN, NYC, 1986-87; pvt. practice as cons., 1987-90; dir. industry rels. NASA, Washington, 1990-91, dir. office nat. svc., 1992-93; retired, 1993; cons. pvt. practice, 1993—. Served with AUS, 1953-56. Recipient Superior Honor award State Dept., 1975 Mem. Am. Fgn. Svc. Assn. Home and Office: 12363 Grantley Ct Lake Ridge VA 22192 Office Phone: 703-967-0216. Personal E-mail: davestot@comcast.net.

STOTTLEMYER, TODD A., business association executive; BA, Coll. William and Mary; JD cum laude, Georgetown U., 1991. Corp. v.p. BDM Internat. Inc.; exec. v.p., CFO, chief adminstrv. officer BTG Inc.; mng. dir. McGuireWoods Capital Group; pres. McGuireWoods Cons.; CEO Apogen Technologies; pres., CEO Nat. Fedn. Ind. Bus., Washington, 2006—. Mem. Profl. Svcs. Coun.; vice chmn. bd. dirs. No. Va. Tech. Coun. Bd. dirs. Fairfax County C. of C., Am. Red Cross of Nat. Capital Region, INOVA Health System Foundation. Mem.: Phi Beta Kappa. Home: Nat Fedn Ind Bus 1201 F St NW Ste 200 Washington DC 20004

STOTZKY, GUENTHER, microbiologist, educator; b. Leipzig, Germany, May 24, 1931; arrived in US, 1939; s. Moritz Stotzky and Erna (Angres) Kester; m. Kayla Baker, Mar. 17, 1958; children: Jay, Martha, Deborah. BS, Calif. Poly. State U., 1952; MS, Ohio State U., 1954, PhD, 1956. Spl. sci. employee Argonne Nat. Lab. USAEC, Lemont, Ill., 1955; rsch. assoc. dept. botany U. Mich., Ann Arbor, 1956-58; head soil microbiology Ctrl. Rsch. Labs. United Fruit Co., Norwood, Mass., 1958-63; chmn., microbiologist Kitchawan Rsch. Labs. Bklyn. Botanic Garden, Ossining, NY, 1963-68; assoc. prof. dept. biology NYU, 1967-70, prof. dept. biology, 1970—2008, chmn. dept. biology, 1970-77, prof. emeritus, 2008—. Editor: Soil Biochemistry, 1990-2000; series editor Marcel Dekker, Inc., 1986-92; contbr. over 300 articles to profl. jours., chpts. to books. With USCG, 1957. Recipient Selman A. Waksman Hon. Lecture award Theobald Smith Soc., 1989, Honored Alumnus of Yr. award Calif. Poly. State U., 1992, fellowship Japanese Soc. for Promotion of Sci., 1996; named Disting. Vis. Scientist, U.S. EPA, 1986-89. Fellow AAAS, Am. Soc. Agronomy, Soil Sci. Soc. Am., Internat. Union Pure and Applied Chemistry, Internat. Symposia on Environ. Biogeochemistry; mem. Am. Acad. Microbiology, Am. Soc. Microbiology (Fisher Co. award for applied and environ. microbiology 1990, Excellence in Tchg. award N.Y.C. br. 1994). Jewish. Avocations: gardening, reading, music. Office: NYU Dept Biology 1009 Silver Ctr New York NY 10003 Home: PO Box 411 East Marion NY 11939 Office Phone: 212-998-8268. Business E-Mail: gs5@nyu.edu.

STOUCK, JERRY, lawyer; b. Washington, Mar. 24, 1955; s. Alex and Eileen Marion (Tepper) S.; m. Mindy A. Buren, Feb. 18, 1984; children: Danielle, David, Rachel. BA magna cum laude, Wesleyan U., 1977; JD, NYU, 1980. Bar: US Dist. Ct. DC 1981, US Ct. Fed. Claims 1981, DC Ct. Appeals, 1981, Md. Ct. Appeals 1983, US Ct. Appeals (4th cir.) 1983, US Dist. Ct. Md. 1985, US Ct. Appeals (fed. cir.) 1992, US Supreme Ct. 1993, US Ct. Appeals (DC cir.) 1997. Law clk. to Hon. Pettine US Dist. Ct. RI, 1980-81; assoc. McKenna, Conner & Cuneo, Washington, 1981-83, Shulman, Rogers, Gandel, Rockville, Md., 1984-87, Spriggs & Hollingsworth, Washington, 1983-84, 87-89, ptnr., 1989—2005; shareholder Greenberg Traurig, LLP, Washington, 2005—. Mem. Phi Beta Kappa. Office: Greenberg Traurig LLP 2101 L St NW Washington DC 20037 Office Phone: 202-331-3173. Business E-Mail: stouckj@gtlaw.com.

STOUDAMIRE, DAMON LAMON, professional basketball coach, retired professional basketball player; b. Portland, Oreg., Sept. 3, 1973; s. Willie Stoudamire and Liz Washington. Student, U. Ariz. Drafted Toronto Raptors, 1995, point guard, 1995—98, Portland Trail Blazers, 1998—2005, Memphis Grizzlies, 2005—08, asst. coach, 2009—; point guard San Antonio Spurs, 2008. Co-recipient Pac-10 Player of Yr., NCAA, 1995; named Schick NBA Rookie of Yr., 1996, Rookie All-Star Game MVP, 1996. Office: Memphis Grizzlies 191 Beale St Memphis TN 38103*

STOUDEMIRE, AMARE CARSARES, professional basketball player; b. Lake Wales, Fla., Nov. 16, 1982; Player Phoenix Suns, 2002—. Mem. US Olympic Basketball Team, Athens, Greece, 2004. Named McDonald's All-Am., 2002, NBA Rookie of Yr., 2003, MVP, Rookie Challenge, 2004; named to NBA All-Rookie First Team, 2003, All-NBA First Team, 2007, Western Conf. All-Star Team, NBA, 2005, 2007—09. Office: c/o Phoenix Suns 201 E Jefferson St Phoenix AZ 85004*

STOUDER, ROBIN RENEE, academic administrator, realtor; b. Ft. Wayne, Ind., May 22, 1962; d. Sharenne Diane Rachel; life ptnr. Barbara Carol Daughter. AS, Ind. Inst. Tech., Ft. Wayne, 1991; BS, Manchester Coll., Ind., 1984; MS, Purdue U., West Lafayette, Ind., 1987. Cert. in real estate Minn., 2006. Dir. weekend coll. U. St. Francis, Ft. Wayne, 1992—98; dir. profl. curriculum Coll. Pharmacy, U. Minn., Mpls., 1998—. Realtor Exit Realty Imagine, Edina, Minn., 2006—. Named Super Real Estate Agt. of Yr., Twin Cities Bus. Jour. and Mpls. St Paul Mag., 2008. Office: Coll Pharmacy Univ Minn 308 Harvard St SE WDH 5-120 Minneapolis MN 55455 Office Phone: 952-230-9458. Business E-Mail: stoud001@umn.edu.

STOUDT, EMILY LAWS, geologist, educator; b. Columbus, Ohio, Apr. 5, 1943; BA in geology, Ohio State U., Columbus, 1966; MS in geology, La. State U., Baton Rouge, 1968; PhD in geology, Ohio State U., Columbus, 1975. Rsch. geologist Getty-Texaco Oil Co., Houston & Midland, 1975—2001; coll. prof. geology U. Tex. Permian Basin, Odessa, 2002—. Pres. Permian Basin Section-SEPM, Midland, Tex., 2001—02. Recipient Best Poster Award, Nat. Am. Assn. Petroleum Geologists, 1979, West Tex. Geol. Soc., 2004. Mem.: Permian Basin

Section-SEPM (life). Home: 5513 Ridgemont Midland TX 79707 Office: Univ Texas Permian Basin 4901 E Univ Blvd Odessa TX 79762 Personal E-mail: stoudel@suddenlink.net. Business E-Mail: stoudt_e@utpb.edu.

STOUDT, GARY SCOTT, mathematics professor; b. Allentown, Pa., Dec. 29, 1963; s. Richard and Mildred Stoudt; m. Patricia Bland, June 1, 2006; children: Sara, Scott. PhD in Math., Lehigh U., Bethlehem, Pa., 1991. Prof. math. Ind. U., Pa., 1991—, chairperson math. dept., 2003—07, acting dean coll. natural sciences and math., 2008. Mem.: Sigma Xi, Can. Soc. History and Philosophy Math., Math. Assn. Am., Am. Math. Soc., Sigma Chi. Office: Math Dept 210 S Tenth St Indiana PA 15705 Business E-Mail: gsstoudt@iup.edu.

STOUFFER, GEORGE ANDREW, cardiologist, educator; b. Oct. 4, 1958; s. George A. and Anne K. S.; m. Margaret E. Edmondson, June 23, 1990. BSME, Bucknell U., Lewisburg, Pa., 1980; MD, U. Md., Baltimore, 1987. Assoc. prof. U. Tex. Med. Branch, Galveston, 1995—; clin. instr. U. Va. Health Sci. Ctr., Charlottesville, 1994-95. Contbr. articles to profl. jours. Recipient Jr. Facualty award, Am. Federation Med. Rsch., Washington, D.C., 1999, Cardiovascular Rsch. award, Astra-Merck, Lake Tahoe, N.V., 1998, honorable mention Young Investigator award, Am. Coll. Cardiology, Anaheim, Calif., 1997, Rsch. award, Am. Heart Assn., 1996. Fellow Am. Coll. Cardiology. Office: UNC Div Cardiology 99 Manning Drive Chapel Hill NC 27599-7075 Office Fax: 919-966-6955. E-mail: stouffer@aol.net.

STOUFFER, RONALD JAY, meteorologist; b. Hershey, Pa., Feb. 3, 1954; s. Jay Lester and Mary Catherine Stouffer; m. Patricia Leah Hilliard, Aug. 21, 1976; children: Matthew Jay, Rebecca J., Laura Ruth. BS, Pa. State U., 1976, MS, 1977. Rsch. meteorologist Geophys. Fluid Dynamics Lab., Princeton, N.J., 1977—. Mem. steering group Global Coupled Models, 1990-95, CLIVAR NEG II com. World Climate Rsch. Program, Geneva, 1995-96, WCRP Working Group on Coupled Modeling, 1996—. Co-author: (chpt.) Climate Change 1995: The Science of Climate Change, 1995. Recipient Disting. Authorship award NOAA, 1990, 95, Administrator's award, 1996, Norbert Gerbier-Mumm Internat. award, 1998. Mem. Am. Meteorol. Soc., Am. Geophys. Union. Achievements include use of coupled ocean-atmosphere models to study climate. Office: Geophys Fluid Dynamics Lab PO Box 303 Princeton NJ 08542-0303

STOUP, ARTHUR HARRY, lawyer; b. Kansas City, Mo., Aug. 30, 1925; s. Isadore and Dorothy (Rankle) S.; m. Kathryn Jolliff, July 30, 1948; children: David C., Daniel P., Rebecca Ann, Deborah E. Student, Kansas City Jr. Coll., Mo. 1942-43; BA, U. Kansas City, 1950; JD, U. Mo., Kansas City, 1950. Bar: Mo. 1950, D.C. 1979, U.S. Dist. Ct. (we. dist.) Mo., U.S. Dist. Ct. Kans., U.S. Dist. Ct. Ariz. Pvt. practice law, Kansas City, 1950—. Chmn. U.S. Jud. Merit Selection Com. for Western Dist. Mo., 1981. Chmn. com. to rev. continuing edn. U. Mo., 1978—79; mem. dean search com. U. Mo. Law Sch., Kansas City, Mo., 1979, 1994—95; trustee U. Mo.-Kansas City Law Found., 1972—, pres., 1979—82; trustee U. Mo., Kansas City, 1979—2001, hon. trustee, 2001—. With USNR, 1942—46. Recipient Alumni Achievement award, U. Mo., Kansas City, 1975, Law Found. Svc. award, U. Mo.-Kansas City Law Found., 1987, Lifetime Achievement award, 2002. Fellow Internat. Soc. Barristers (state mem. chmn.), Am. Bar Found. (life mem.); mem. ABA (ho. dels. 1976-80), Kansas City Met. Bar Assn. (pres. 1966-67, Dean of Trial Bar award 1991, mem. exec. com. 1965-68, 2003-04), Mo. Bar (bd. govs. 1967-76, v.p. 1972-73, pres. elect 1973-74, pres. 1974-75), Mo. Assn. Trial Attys. (sustaining), Assn. Trial Lawyers Am. (sustaining), So. Conf. Bar Pres.'s (life), Mobar Research Inc. (pres. 1978-86), Phi Alpha Delta Alumni (justice Kansas City area alumni 1955-56). Lodges: Optimists (pres. Ward Pkwy. 1961-62, lt. gov. Mo. dist. internat. 1963-64), Sertoma, B'nai B'rith. Home: 9002 Western Hills Dr Kansas City MO 64114-3566 Office: Palace Bldg Ste 230 1150 Grand Blvd Kansas City MO 64106-2317 Home Phone: 816-363-0970; Office Phone: 816-474-0707. Office Fax: 816-474-0714.

STOUT, JANET E., microbiologist, director; d. Graydon T. and Florence M. Stout. PhD, Grad. Sch. Pub. Health U. Pitts., 1997. Microbiologist Va. Med. Ctr., Pitts., 1983—2006; dir. Spl. Pathogens Lab., Pitts., 2007—; asst. prof. U. Pitts. Bd. mem. Uptown Ptnrs., Pitts., 2007—08. Named Water Technologist of Yr., Assn. Water Technologies, 1999; Rsch. grant, EPA, 2001—05. Achievements include first to link legionella bacteria in hospital drinking water. Office: Spl Pathogens Lab 1401 Forbes Ave Ste 209 Pittsburgh PA 15219 Office Fax: 412-281-7445. Business E-Mail: jstout@specialpathogenslab.com.

STOUT, JEFFREY LEE, religious studies educator; b. Trenton, NJ, Sept. 11, 1950; m. Sally Jane Starkey, June 2, 1973; children: Suzannah Elizabeth, Noah Jonathan, Samuel Livingston. AB magna cum laude et cum honoribus in religious studies, Brown U., 1972; PhD in religion, Princeton U., 1976. Instr. religion Princeton U., 1975—76, Melancthon Jacobus instr. religion, 1976—77, asst. prof. religion, 1977—83, assoc. prof. religion, 1983—88, prof. religion, 1988—, Andrew W. Mellon prof. humanities, 1989—92, chair, dept. religion, 1992—99, acting chair, dept. religion, 2002—03. Author: The Flight from Authority: Religion, Morality, and the Quest for Autonomy, 1981, Ethics After Babel: The Languages of Morals and Their Discontents, 1988 (Am. Acad. Religion award for Excellence, 1989), Democracy and Tradition, 2004 (Am. Acad. Religion award for Excellence, 2004); co-editor (with Robert MacSwain): Grammar and Grace: Reformulations of Aquinas and Wittgenstein, 2004. Fellow Am. Coun. Learned Societies, 1979—80; Harvey A. Baker fellow, 1972—75. Fellow: Am. Acad. Arts and Sciences; mem.: Soc. Christian Ethics, Am. Acad. Religion (pres. 2007), Phi Beta Kappa. Office: Dept Religion Rm 241 Seventy-Nine Hall Princeton U Princeton NJ 08544-1006 Office Phone: 609-258-4485. Office Fax: 609-258-2346. E-mail: stout@princeton.edu.

STOUT, MAYE ALMA, retired secondary school educator; b. Reliance, SD, Mar. 3, 1920; d. Jesse Wilbur and Susie Maude (Fletcher) Moulton; m. Dennis William Stout, Jan. 6, 1943; children: Perry Wilbur, David Jay. BA, Dakota Wesleyan U., Mitchell, SD, 1969. Tchr. Rural Lyman County Sch., Iona, SD, 1939—42, Oacoma, SD, Reliance, SD, 1944-45, Vivian Pub. Sch., SD, 1942, Reliance Cons. Dist., 1945-46, 49-51, Ft. Pierre Ind. Sch. Dist., SD, 1954—67, Kadoka Ind. Sch., SD, 1967—82; ret. Asst. editor: Jackson/Washabaugh County History 2, 1989; contbr. articles to books and publs. Vol. bingo Kadoka Care Ctr., 1982-2005, vol. Veterans and Meml. Day svcs., 1987-2004; pres. Kadoka Cmty. Betterment Assn., 1987; vol. Meals for Elderly; Sunday sch. tchr. asst.; tchr. 55 Alive, 1991-93; pres. Pierre/Ft. Pierre ACEI; tchr. Sunday sch. 5th grade 1st United Meth. Ch., 1953-67; deliverer meals to the elderly Mem. Am. Legion Aux. (dist. pres. 1985-89, chmn. com. Dept. Fgn. Rels. 1990-91, dept. chmn. constitution and by-laws com. 1992-93). Republican. Methodist. Avocations: reading, crocheting, travel. Address: PO Box 231 Kadoka SD 57543-0231 E-mail: mastout@gwtc.net.

STOUT, NANCY ANN, health science association administrator, director; b. Phila, Jan. 15, 1955; d. Benjamin Mortimer Stout and Ann Stout Walters; m. William Douglas Hostetler, Feb. 15, 1992. EdD, WV U., Morgantown, 1985. Dir., divsn. safety rsch. Nat. Inst. Occupl. Safety and Health, Ctrs. Disease Control and Prevention, Morgantown, 1997—. Achievements include research in Occupational injury surveillance and prevention. Office: Niosh Cdc 1095 Willowdale Rd Morgantown WV 26505

STOUT, NEIL RALPH, retired history educator; b. Marietta, Ohio, Aug. 12, 1932; s. Ralph Plumly and Carrie Baker Stout; m. Marilyn Blumenstiel, Sept. 8, 1956; children: Hilary Ann, Peter Neil. BA, Harvard U., 1954; MS, U. Wis., 1958, PhD, 1961. Asst. prof. Tex. A&M U., Hist. Dept., College Station, 1961—64; prof. U. Vt., Hist. Dept., Burlington, Vt., 1964—2000, prof. emeritus, 2000—. Editor Vt. Hist. Soc., Montpelier, 1993—94; pres. New Eng. Hist. Assn., Worcester, Mass., 1979—80. Author: Royal Navy in America, 1760-1775, 1973, The Perfect Crisis, 1976, The History Student's Vade Mecum (4 editions)Paper Delivered at IMEHA, 2008. Historian Vt. State Hist. Preservation Adv. Coun., Montpelier, 1990—94, Green Mountain Hash House Harriers; trustee Fletcher Free Libr., 2005—07; v.p. Friends of Fletcher Free Libr., Burlington, Vt., 2001—09, pres., 2009—; vestry mem. Cathedral Ch. St. Paul, Burlington, Vt., 2006—09, chair, buildings and grounds, 2006—, archivist, 2005—, jr. warden, 2007—08, sr. warden, 2008—09. With US Army, 1954—56, France. Mem.: Green Mountain Club. Home: 129 Robinson Pkwy Burlington VT 05401 Personal E-mail: nrs@burlingtontelecom.net.

STOUT, SHARON SPARKES, elementary school educator, counselor; d. Thomas and Frances Sparkes; m. Marvin Stout (div.); children: Franchesca Stout Jorgensen, Megan Stout Farias. BS in Edn., Ga. So. U., 1971, MEd, 1973; Cert. Advanced Grad. Studies, Fitchburg State Coll., 1983. Lic. mental health counselor Mass., marriage and family therapist Mass.; ednl. psychologist Mass., rehab. therapist Mass., cert. prin., reading tchr., elem. tchr., spl. edn. tchr., sch. psychometrist Ga. Spl. edn. tchr. Bulloch County Schs., Statesboro, Ga., 1971—73; learning disability specialist Screven County Schs., Sylvania, Ga., 1973—75; spl. edn. tchr. Harwich (Mass.) Pub. Schs., 1975—77, Eastham (Mass.) Elem. Sch., 1977—78; elem. sch. tchr. Chatham (Mass.) Pub. Schools, 1978—86, counselor, 1986—, devel., coord. caring for each student and bully prevention program, 2001—. Founder, dir. Cape Cod Learning Ctr., Harwich, 1980—87. Edn. chmn. Jr. Women's Club, Harwich, 1975—77; co-president Harwich Parent, Tchr. and Friends Orgn., Harwich, 1977—78; v.p. Cape Cod chpt. Mass. Assn. for Children with Learning Disabilities. Grantee, Dept. of Justice, 2001—03, Mass. Dept. Edn., 2003—06. Office: Chatham Pub Schs 147 Depot Rd Chatham MA 02633 Personal E-mail: capecod2000@comcast.net. Business E-Mail: sstout@chatham.k12.ma.us.

STOUT, WILLIAM E., science educator; s. James J. Stout; m. Vicki A. Debroux, July 14, 1984; children: Jennifer A., Timothy M., Matthew C. BS, Marquette U., Milw., 1984; MS, U. Wis., Stevens Point, 1995; PhD, U. Wis., Madison, 2004. Sci. tchr. Milw. Pub. Sch., Milw., 1984—93, Oconomowoc Area Sch. Dist., Wis., 1993—. Contbr. articles to profl. jours. Mem.: NEA, Wilson Ornithol. Soc., Raptor Rsch. Found., Cooper Ornithol. Soc., Assn. Field Ornithologists, Am. Ornithologist's Union, Wis. Edn. Assn. Coun., Wis. Soc. Ornithology, Wildlife Soc. Office: Oconomowoc High Sch 641 E Forest St Oconomowoc WI 53066 Business E-Mail: bill.stout@mail.oasd.k12.wi.us.

STOUTE, STEPHEN, marketing executive, entrepreneur; Talent exec. RCA Records; pres. urban music Sony Music Entertainment; pres. urban music, exec. v.p. Interscope Geffen A&M Records; co-founder mktg./advt. firm PASS, NYC, 2000; founder, CEO Translation Consultation & Brand Imaging, NYC, 2003—; co-founder Translation Advt., 2008—. Prodr.: several major motion picture soundtracks. Devel. several minority recruitment campaigns FDNY, NYC Police Dept.; co-chmn. NYC Fresh Air Fund, 2003; co-founder, bd. dirs. Found. Advancement of Women Now. Recipient Humanitarian award, FDNY, 2004, Am. Music award (for Wild Wild West movie soundtrack); named to Advt. Hall of Achievement, Am. Advt. Fedn., 2008. Office: Translation Consultation & Brand Imaging 145 W 45th St 12th Fl New York NY 10036 Office Phone: 212-299-5505. Office Fax: 212-299-5513.*

STOVALL, FRANCES MIDDAGH, journalist, preservationist; b. Lawrenceville, Ill., Dec. 7, 1921; d. John Judy and Rebecca (Fowler) Middagh; m. Jack N. Stovall, Aug. 16, 1941 (dec. 2004; children: Richard Middagh Stovall, Frances Tshudy, John Fowler Stovall, Susan Calvert G. Carter. Student, McMurry Coll., 1938-41. Woman's Page editor Odessa (Tex.) News Times, 1937-40; reporter Abilene (Tex.) Reporter News, 1938-41. Author: Clear Springs and Limestone Ledges, A History of San Marcos and Hays County, 1986; editor: San Marcos Bicentennial Cookbook, 1976, Cottage Kitchen Cookbook, 1983, Cottage Kitchen, Second Helping, 1986, Twenty Years In Cottage Kitchen, 1996, Historical Markers in Hays County, 2005-06; columnist San Marcos Daily Record, 1986-2007. Founder Heritage Assn. San Marcos, 1975, bd. dirs., 1975-2006, hon. life mem., 1989—; chmn. City of San Marcos Bicentennial Commn., 1972-76, Hays County Hist. Commn., 1987-2006; initiator Main St. in San Marcos, 1989; founder Preservation Assocs., Inc., 1986, Friends of Hays County Hist. Commn., 1990-2007. Named Woman of Yr. Beta Sigma Phi, San Marcos, 1976, 96, Vol. of Yr., Rotary Club San Marcos, 1995; recipient Tex. award for hist. preservation Tex. Hist. Commn., Austin, 1990, John Ben Shepperd Leadership award Tex. Hist. Commn., Austin, 1991, Lifetime Achievement award Tex. Hist. Commn., Austin, 1993; Preservation award named in her honor, 1999, The Frances Stovall Collection within the San Marcos City libr. dedicated in her honor, 2001. Mem. DAR, Nat. Trust for Hist. Preservation, Tex. Hist. Found., Tex. State Hist. Assn., Spring Lake Garden Club, Magna Charta Dames. Avocation: history. Home: 1104 Debbie Ct San Marcos TX 78666-3100

STOVALL, JERRY COLEMAN, insurance company executive; b. Houston, July 31, 1936; s. Clifford Coleman and Maxine (Lands) S.; m. Elsie Hostetter, June 20, 1959; 1 child, Brent Allen. BBA, U. Houston, 1968. Adminstr. home office Am. Gen. Life, Houston, 1955-63, agt., agy. mgr., 1963-66, agy. mgr., regional dir. agys., regional v.p., 1969-74; sr. brokerage cons. Conn. Gen. Life, Houston, 1966-69; sr. v.p., dir. mktg. Capitol Life Inst. Co., Denver, 1974-78; v.p., dir. mktg. Integon Life Ins. Corp., Winston-Salem, N.C., 1978-81; pres. Life of Mid-Am. Ins. Co., Topeka, 1981-85, Victory Life Ins. Co., Topeka, 1981-85, chmn., pres., chief exec. officer, 1981-87; pres., retired chief exec officer Integon Life Ins. Co., Winston-Salem, N.C., 1987-91; pres. Lamar Life Ins. Co., 1992-95, ret., 1995; pres., CEO Am. Pub. Holding Inc., 1996-2000, ret., 2000. Bd. dirs., vice-chmn., Ga. Internat. Life; vice-chmn. Mktg. One Inc., bd. dirs. Boy Scout Miss., 1987-91, Bank Topeka, Kans., 1981-87, Firstcitizens Bank, NC, 1987-91, adv. bd., Internat. Assn. Fin. Planners, 1975-78. Bd. dirs. Jr. Achievement Miss., Inc.; bd. trustees Miss. Bapt. Found. With U.S. Army, 1955-57. Mem. Nat. Assn. Life Cos., Nat. Assn. Life Underwriters, Am. Soc. CLUs (Gold Key soc.), Am. Coun. Life Ins., Exec. Round Table (chmn. 1995), The Country Club of Jackson. Home: 1406 Mossycup Ln Livingston TX 77351-3074

STOVER, ANNETTE BIRGIT, advertising and public relations executive; b. Wilhelmshaven, Fed. Republic Germany, Oct. 29, 1964; arrived in US, 1986; d. Joachim Karl and Rosemarie Else (Jordan) Stover; m. Richard Thomas Feiner, Dec. 31, 1986. Diploma in Polit. Sci., Paris, 1985; diploma in Advt. and Pub. Rels., Hochschule Der Künste, Berlin, 1986. Account exec. MDC SA, Paris, 1982-85, Dorland GmbH, Berlin, 1985-86; with Scali, McCabe, Sloves (acquired by Lowe Worldwide), JWT, Morgan Anderson Cons., Euro RSCG Worldwide, NYC, 1997—, chief of staff, COO, 2006—. Contbr. articles to profl. jours. Mgr. Berlin Play Actors, 1985—86. Named a Woman to Watch, Advt. Age, 2008. Mem.: Assn. Des Droits De L'Homme (France). Office: 350 Hudson St New York NY 10014-4413 Office Phone: 212-886-2000. Office Fax: 212-886-2016. Business E-Mail: annette.stover@eurorscg.com.*

STOVER, BRIAN ALLAN, advertising executive, marketing professional; b. Syracuse, NY, Aug. 12, 1947; s. David Reuben and Helen Rose (Smith) Stover; m. Fredda Ann Berkowitz, Oct. 12, 1980; children: Pamela Lynn, Amy Beth. BS in Mktg. and Advt., Syracuse U., 1968. Advt. producer Zayre Corp., Framingham, Mass., 1969-73; v.p. accounts Recruitment Advt. Inc., Boston, 1973-74; dir. advt. Superior Distbg. Co. Inc., Boston, 1974-76; pres. BGM Mktg., Inc., Syracuse, 1976-82, Oakmont Advt., Inc., Fayetteville, NY, 1982-87; pres., CEO Invincible Roofing Sys., Inc., Largo, Fla., 1987-94; pres. Invincible Assocs., Inc., 1987—2005, Teddy Bear Mktg. Co. Inc., 2004—, Brian Stover Group, Inc., 2005—. Pres. Clark/Kent Cons., Inc., 1991—93, Pub. Direct Svcs., Inc., 1992—, Invincible Mktg. Group, Seminole, Fla., Invincible Sys., Inc.; cons. GE, Syracuse, NY, 1968, Contemproary Talent, Nashville, 1984—92, Dread Beat Records, Nashville; advt. instr. Ctrl. Cities Bus. Inst., 1986; mktg. instr. Bd. Continuing Edn. Svcs., 1987. Author: Handbook Guide for Retail Advertising, 1974; columnist: The Sales Heretic, Fla. Roofing and Sheet Metal Contractors Assn., 2004—. Recipient Drummer award, Cahners Pub. Co., 1975, 3 Telly awards, 1987, 5 Silver Microphone awards, 1987, 7 Merit awards, Syracuse Ad Club, 1987, Steven's Gold Eagle award, 2002, Steven's Platinum Eagle award, 2003, 2004. Mem.: Constrn. Fin. Mgrs. Assn., Bayou Club. Jewish. Avocations: golf, tennis, music, reading. Office: Teddy Bear Mktg 13220 Belcher Rd Ste 4 Largo FL 33773 Office Phone: 727-424-1777. Personal E-mail: stofield@aol.com.

STOVER, CARL FREDERICK, foundation executive; b. Pasadena, Calif., Sept. 29, 1930; s. Carl Joseph and Margarete (Müller) S.; m. Catherine Swanson, Sept. 3, 1954; children: Matthew Joseph, Mary Margaret Stover Marker, Claire Ellen Stover Herrell; m. Jacqueline Kast, Sept. 7, 1973. BA magna cum laude, Stanford U., 1951, MA, 1954. Instr. polit. sci. Stanford U., 1953-55; fiscal mgmt. officer Office Sec. Dept. Agr., 1955-57; assoc. dir. conf. program pub. affairs Brookings Instn., 1957-59, sr. staff govtl. studies, 1960; fellow Center Study Democratic Instns., Santa Barbara, Calif., 1960-62; asst. to chmn. bd. editors Ency. Brit., 1960-62; sr. polit. scientist Stanford Research Inst., 1962-64; dir. pub. affairs fellowship program Stanford U., 1962-64; pres. Nat. Inst. Pub. Affairs, Washington, 1964-70, Nat. Com. U.S.-China Relations, 1971-72; pres., dir. Federalism Seventy-Six, Washington, 1972-74; dir. cultural resources devel. Nat. Endowment Arts, 1974-78; pres., dir. Cultural Resources, Inc., Washington, 1978-85; bd. dirs. H.E.A.R. Found., 1976-86, treas., 1976-80, pres., 1980-86. Bd. dirs. Ctr. for World Lit., pres., 1987-90, chmn., 1990-92; pvt. profl. cons., 1970—; scholar-in-residence Nat. Acad. Pub. Adminstrn., 1980-82; cons. in field. Author: The Government of Science, 1962, The Technological Order, 1963; Founding editor: Jour. Law and Edn., 1971-73; pub. Delos mag., 1987-92. Treas. Nat. Com. U.S.-China Rels., 1966-71, 82-87, 89-94, bd. dirs., 1966-74, 79-98, dir. emeritus, 1998—; bd. dirs. Coord. Coun. Lit. Mags., 1966-68, H.E.A.R. Found., 1976-86, treas., 1976-80; trustee Inst. of Nations, 1972-76, Nat. Inst. Pub. Affairs, 1967-71, Kinesis Ltd., 1972-78; vol. Nat. Exec. Svc. Corps, 1984-89; mem. Fellowship of Reconciliation Fellow AAAS, Phi Beta Kappa (hon. lectr. 1972-87); mem. Am. Soc. Pub. Adminstrn., Fedn. Am. Scientists, Soc. Internat. Devel., Jordan Soc. (dir. 1982-84), Nat. Acad. Pub. Adminstrn. (hon.), Internat. Soc. Panetics (pres. 1991-95, chmn. 1995-98, chmn. emeritus 1999—2009, bd. govs. 1991—2009, founding mem. 1991—). Democrat. Presbyterian. Home: 3142 Gracefield Rd Apt 102 Silver Spring MD 20904 E-mail: carlfstover@aol.com.

STOVER, DAVID S., science educator; married, M, U. Dayton, Ohio. Prof. Sinclair CC, Dayton, 1990—. Contbr. scientific papers. Vice flotilla comdr. USCG Aux., Dayton, divsn. pub. edn. officer, asst. dist. officer, 2007—; v.p. Dayton Blue Hawks Hockey Team, 2000—08. Office: Sinclair CC 444 W 3rd St Dayton OH 45402 Business E-Mail: david.stover@sinclair.edu, david.stov@sinclair.edu.

STOVER, ELLEN L., federal agency administrator, health scientist; b. Bklyn., Nov. 21, 1950; d. Ralph and Charlotte (Tulchin) Simon; m. Alan B. Stover, June 3, 1973; children: Elena Randall Simon, Randall Alan Simon, Samantha Anne Simon. BA with honors, U. Wis., 1972; PhD, Catholic U., Washington, 1978. Cons. Nat. Inst. Mental Health (NIMH), Rockville, Md., 1972-74, exec. sec. drug abuse rsch. review com., 1974-76, spl. asst. to assoc. dir. extramural programs, 1976-77, chief small grants program, 1977-79, asst. then acting chief rsch. resources br., 1980-85, dep. dir. Divsn. Basic Scis., 1985-88, dir. office AIDS, 1988—, dir. Divsn. Mental Disorders, Behavioral Rsch. & AIDS (DMDBA), 1997—. Dir. divsn. AIDS, health, behavior NIMH. Recipient Superior Svc. award, USPHS, 1992, 1993, NIH Dir.'s award, 1996, Presdl. Rank award, 2001. Mem.: APA. Avocations: gardening, dance. Office: NIMH DAHBR 6001 Executive Blvd Rm 6217 MSC 9621 Bethesda MD 20892-0001 Office Phone: 301-443-9700. Business E-Mail: estover@mail.nih.gov.*

STOVER, JILL S., school librarian, writer; BA in History, Ohio State U., 2001; MS in Libr. Sci., U. NC, 2004; student in Mktg., Va. Commonwealth U., Richmond, 2005—. Undergraduate svcs. libr. James Branch Cabell Libr. Va. Commonwealth U. Contbr. articles to profl. publs. Mem.: ALA, Reference and User Svcs. Assn., Assn. Coll. and Rsch. Librs., Phi Beta Kappa. Office: Va Commonwealth U Librs 901 Park Ave PO Box 842033 Richmond VA 23284-2033 Office Phone: 804-828-8964. E-mail: jsstover@vcu.edu.

STOVER, MILES RONALD, management consultant; b. Glendale, Calif., Dec. 23, 1948; s. Robert Miles and Alberta Mae (Walker) S.; m. Cynthia McNeil, Jan. 25, 1975; children: Christopher, Matthew. BS, U. So. Calif., 1974; MBA, Pepperdine U., 1979; PhD, Kennedy Western U., 2005. Cert. fraud examiner; cert. turnaround profl.; cert. profl. cons.; cert. mgmt. cons.; cert. confidentiality officer; cert. insolvency advisor. V.p., gen. mgr., CFO Johnson Controls Inc., LA, 1974-82; gen. mgr. MG Products Inc., San Diego, 1982-84; exec. v.p., gen. mgr. ICU Med. Inc., Mission Viejo, 1984-86; v.p., COO B.P. John Inc., Santa Ana, Calif., 1986-88; gen. mgr. MG Products Inc., San Diego, 1988-90; pres. Lucks Co., Kent, Wash., 1991-96, also bd. dirs.; prin. Crossroads LLC, 1998—2002; pres. Turnaround, Inc., 1996—98, 2002—. Cons. Turnaround Mgmt. Assn., Tacoma, 1990. With USN, 1967-71. Decorated Gallantry Cross USN; recipient award for Productivity US Senate, 1978, Congl. medal of Distinction Nat. Rep. Congl. Com.; named Businessman of Yr. Wash., 2006, Campaign medal NAM, Vietnum Svc. medal, Vietnum Campaign medal, USN. Mem. Inst. Mgmt. Cons., Turnaround Mgmt. Assn., Am. Bankruptcy Inst., Nat. Assn. Corp. Dirs., Assn. Cert. Fraud Examiners, Assn. Insolvency and Restructuring Advisors, Inst. Mgmt. Accts., Mensa. Republican. Methodist. Home: 3415 A St NW Gig Harbor WA 98335-7843 Home Phone: 253-851-7687; Office Phone: 253-857-6730, 253-857-6730, 253-857-6730. Business E-Mail: mstover@turnaround-inc.com.

STOVER, RICHARD L., investor; b. Uniontown, Pa., Oct. 11, 1942; s. Louis John and Sarah Virginia Stover; m. Dorothea Gerber Stover, June 19, 1965; children: Kristin Stover Matheny, Douglas Richard. BSBA, The Pa. State U., 1965. Sr. v.p. Mellon Fin. Corp., Pitts., 1969—89; exec. v.p. Bank of New Eng. Corp., Boston, 1989—91; exec. v.p. and chief credit officer Equimark Corp., Pittsburgh, Pa., 1991—93; mng. dir. GE Capital Corp., Stamford, Conn., 1993—94; founder and prin. Stover & Assocs., Wexford, Pa., 1994—96; founder and mng. dir. ARC Capital, Pittsburgh, Pa., 1995—96; pres. First Western Bancorp, Inc., New Castle, Pa., 1996—99; mng. prin. Birchmere Capital, Wexford, Pa., 2000—. Dir. SAFAS Corp., Clifton, NJ, 1995—, Bliley Technologies, Inc., Erie, Pa., 1999—, Ductmate Industries, Inc., Charleroi, Pa., 2004—. Bd. dirs. Inst. for Transfusion Medicine, Pitts., 1978; chmn. bd. suprs. Marshall Twp., Wexford, Pa., 1995—2001; chmn. WQED Multimedia, Pitts., 2002. Lt. USN, 1965—69. Mem.: Bonita Bay Club, Treesdales Golf and Country Club, The Duquesne Club. Avocations: golf, travel, exercise, history. Office: Birchmere Capital 5000 Stonewood Dr Ste 220 Wexford PA 15090 Office Fax: 724-940-2383.

STOW, GEORGE, history professor; b. Camden, NJ, Mar. 17, 1940; s. George Buckley and Elizabeth Furlong Stow; m. Susan Margaret Maynes; children: Meredith Anne, Jonathan Buckley. BA, Lehigh U., Bethlehem, Pa., 1967; MA, U. So. Calif., LA, 1968; PhD, U. Ill., Urbana, 1972. Prof. history La Salle U., Phila., 1972—2008. Author: (book) Historia Vitae et Regni Ricardi Secundi; contbr. articles to profl. jours. Sgt. US Army, 1959—62. Recipient Phi Beta Kappa award, Phi Beta Kappa Am., 1968; Woodrow Wilson Dissertation Fellowship, Woodrow Wilson Found., 1970—71. Fellow: Royal Hist. Soc.; mem.: Mediaeval Acad. Am. Avocations: squash, baroque music. Office: La Salle Univ 1900 W Olney Philadelphia PA 19141 Business E-Mail: stow@lasalle.edu.

STOWE, ZACHARY NEIL, psychiatrist, researcher; MD, U. Tex. Med. Branch, Galveston. Resident in psychiatry Duke U. Med. Ctr.; fellow in psychopharmacology Emory U. Sch. Medicine, prof. dept. psychiatry & behavioral sciences, 1992—, asst. prof. dept. gynecology & obstetrics, 1998—, founder & dir., Women's Mental Health Program. Recipient Young Investigator award, Nat. Depressive & Manic Depressive Assn. Mem.: Nat. Inst. Health, Nat. Alliance Mentally Ill, Am. Psychiatric Assn. (SmithKline Beecham Young Faculty award). Office: Emory University School of Medicine Emory Clinic Bldg B 1365 Clifton Rd NE Ste 6100 Atlanta GA 30322 Office Phone: 404-778-2524. Office Fax: 404-778-2535. E-mail: wmhp@emory.edu, zstowe@emory.edu.*

STOWELL, CHRISTOPHER R., performing company executive, choreographer, retired dancer; b. NYC, June 8, 1966; s. Kent and Francia (Russell) S. Student, Pacific N.W. Ballet Sch., 1979-84, Sch. Am. Ballet, 1984-85. Entered corps de ballet San Francisco Ballet, 1986, promoted to soloist, 1987, prin., 1990—2001; freelance choreographer for ballet and opera cos., 2001—; ballet master Balanchine Trust, 2001—; artistic dir. Oreg. Ballet Theater, 2003—. Guest artist Ballet Met, Ohio, Pacific N.W. Ballet, Seattle, and with Jean Charles Gil, Marseilles, France, Asami Maki Ballet, Tokyo. Created leading roles in Handel-A Celebration, Con Brio, The Sleeping Beauty, New Sleep, Connotations, Pulcinella, Meistens Mozart; other roles include Calcium Light Night, Rubies, The Sons of Horus, The Four Temperaments, Hearts, Tarantella, Flower Festival, La Fille Mal Garde, Haffner Symphony, Forgotten Land, The End, Agon, In the Middle Somewhat Elevated, Le Quattro Stagioni, Swan Lake, Job, Company B, Tchaikousky Pas de Deux, Maelstrom, Mercutio in Romeo and Juliet, The Dance House, Stars and Stripes, Ballo Della Regina, Drink to me Only With Thine Eyes, Pacific; performed in Reykjavik Arts Festival, Iceland, 1990, San Francisco Ballet at the Paris Opera Garnier, 1994, Bolshoi Theatre, Moscow, 1998. Avocations: cooking, reading, camping. Office: Oreg Ballet Theatre 818 SE 6th Ave Portland OR 97214*

STOWELL, KENT, retired ballet director; b. Rexburg, Idaho, Aug. 8, 1939; s. Harold Bowman and Maxine (Hudson) S.; m. Francia Marie Russell, Nov. 19, 1965; children: Christopher, Darren, Ethan. Student, San Francisco Ballet Sch., Sch. Am. Ballet; LHD (hon.), Seattle U., 2003, PhD (hon.), 2004. Lead dancer San Francisco Ballet, 1957—62, NYC Ballet, 1962—68; ballet dir., ballet master Frankfurt (Fed. Republic Germany) Opera Ballet, 1973—77; artistic dir. Pacific NW Ballet, Seattle, 1977—2005. Prof. dance Ind. U., Bloomington, 1969-70; bd. dirs. Sch. of Am. Ballet, Dance/USA, Washington, 1986—; bd. dirs. Sch. of Am. Ballet, NYC, 1981—; mem. Goodwill Games Arts Com., Seattle, 1987—; chmn. dance panel NEA, 1981-85. Grantee NEA, 1980, 85; fellow NEA, 1979. Choreographer: Silver Lining, Cinderella, Carmina Burana, Coppelia, Time & Ebb, Faurè Requiem, Hail to the Conquering Hero, Firebird, Over the Waves, Nutcracker, The Tragedy of Romeo and Juliet, Delicate Balance, Swan Lake, Time and Ebb, Through Interior Worlds, Quaternary, Orpheus. Recipient Arts Service award King County Arts Commn., 1985, Outstanding Contbn. to Pacific NW Ballet State of Was., 1987, Best Dance Co. award The Weekly Newspaper, Seattle, 1987, Gov. Arts award, 1988, Dance Mag. award, 1996, Lifetime Achievement award U. Utah, 2004, Lifetime Achievement in Arts award ArtsFund, 2004, award Seattle (Wash.) Ctr., 2004, Entrepreneur of Yr. award Ernst and Young, 2004, Mayor's Art award, 2004. Office: Pacific NW Ballet 301 Mercer St Seattle WA 98109-4600

STOWERS, CARLTON EUGENE, writer; b. Brownwood, Tex., Apr. 14, 1942; s. Ira Milton and Fay Eloise (Stephenson) S.; m. Patricia Ann Folks, Mar. 2, 1981; children: Anson, Ashley. Student, U. Tex., Austin, 1961-63. Sportswriter Abilene (Tex.) Reporter News, 1963-64; sports editor Roswell (N.Mex.) Daily Record, 1964-65; sportswriter Lubbock (Tex.) Avalanche Jour., 1965-67; sports editor Amarillo (Tex.) Globe News, 1967-72; reporter, columnist Dallas Morning News, 1972-81; freelance writer Cedar Hill, Tex., 1981—. Editor Dallas Cowboys Weekly, 1985-89. Author: The Randy Matson Story, 1971, Spirit, 1973; author: (with E.B. Hughes) Doc, 1976; author: (with Trent Jones) Where the Rainbows Wait, 1978; author: (with Wilbur Evans) Champions, 1978; author: The Overcomers, 1978; author: (with Roy Rogers and Dale Evans) Happy Trails, 1979; author: pub. softcover as Terlingua Teacher, 1982, 2005, The Unsinkable Titanic Thompson, 1982, softcover, 1988, Journey to Triumph, 1988, Partners in Blue: The 100-Year History of the Dallas Police Department, 1983; author: (with Billy Olson) Reaching Higher, 1984; author: The Dallas Cowboys: The First 25 Years, 1984, The Cowboy Chronicles, 1984; author: (ghosted for Pam Lontos) Don't Tell Me It's Impossible Until I've Already Done It, 1988; author: Careless Whispers, 1986 (Edgar Allan Poe award Mystery Writers Am.), The Cotton Bowl: The First 50 Years, 1986; author: (with Wiliam C. Dear) Please...Don't Kill Me: The True Story of the Milo Murder, 1989; author: (with Larry Wansley) The FBI Undercover: The True Story of Special Agent 'Mandrake', 1989; author: Innocence Lost, 1990, A Hero Named George, 1991, Hard Lessons, 1994, Open Secrets, 1994, Sins of the Son, 1995; author: (with Marcus Allen) Marcus, 1997; author: To the Last Breath, 1998 (Edgar Allan Poe award Mystery Writers Am.); author: (with Rev. Carroll Pickett) Within These Walls, 2002 (Violet Crown award, 2002, PEN S.W. Book award finalist, 2005); author: Scream at the Sky, 2003, Death in a Texas Desert, 2003, Where Dreams Die Hard, 2005, Oh, Brother How They Played the Game, 2007. Recipient numerous journalism awards. Mem.: Tex. Inst. Letters. Home: 1015 Randy Rd Cedar Hill TX 75104-3035 Office Phone: 972-291-4831. E-mail: cstowers1@att.net.

STOWERS, JAMES EVANS, JR., investment company executive; b. Kansas City, Mo., Jan. 10, 1924; s. James Evans Sr. and Laura (Smith) S.; m. Virginia Ann Glasscock, Feb. 4, 1954; children: Pamela, Kathleen, James Evans III, Linda. AB, U. Mo., 1946, BS in Medicine, 1947. Chmn. bd. Am. Century Investment Mgmt. Inc., Am. Century Cos., Inc.; Am. Century Group of Mutual Funds, Kansas City, 1958—. Author: Why Waste Your Money on Life Insurance, 1967, Principles of Financial Consulting, 1971, Yes, You Can...Achieve Financial Independence, 1992; co-author: (with Jack Jonathan) The Best is Yet to Be: A Story of Innovation, Generosity & Success, 2007 Co-founder, chmn. Stowers Inst. for Med. Rsch., Kansas City, 1995—. Capt. USAAF, 1943-45; with USAFR, 1945-57. Mem. Kansas City C. of C., Sigma Chi Republican. Office: Am Century Svcs 4500 Main St Kansas City MO 64111-1816

STOWMAN, DAVID L., lawyer; b. Rothsay, Minn., 1943; m. Judy Stowman; 4 children. BA, Moorehead State Univ.; JD, Univ. N.D. Co-founder NW Minn. Legal Services. Capt. USMC, 1965—69, Vietnam (1968-69). Named one of Minn. Top 25 Lawyers, Law & Politics mag., 2001. Mem.: ABA, Minn. State Bar Assn. (pres.-elect 2003, pres. 2004). Avocations: running, water-skiing. Office: Stowman Law Office PO Box 845 Detroit Lakes MN 56502-0845 also: Stowman Law Office 1100 W Lake Dr Detroit Lakes MN 56501 Office Phone: 218-847-5644.

STOYTCHEVA, LILIA STEFANOVA, concert pianist, educator; b. Sofia, Bulgaria, July 13, 1962; arrived in US, 1995, naturalized, 2005; d. Stefan Sotirov Stoytchev and Liliana Georgieva Sarafova. Studied with Liuba Entcheva, Bulgarian State Conservatory, M in Piano summa cum laude, 1987; M of Music summa cum laude, Winthrop U., Rock Hill, SC, 1997; DMA in Piano Performance, U. Iowa, Iowa City, 2005. Instr. piano Bulgarian State Conservatory, Sofia, 1988—92; asst. prof. piano Sofia's U. "Kliment Ohridski", 1988—90; prof. piano State Conservatory, Czech Republic, 1992—95; asst. prof. Ctrl. State U., Wilberforce, Ohio, 2003—06; assoc. prof. piano North Greenville U., Tigerville, SC, 2006—. Composer: 1300 Anniversary Bulgaria, 1981; musician (solo pianist): Symphony Orch. of the Bulgarian State Conservatory, 1987, Symphony Orch. of Biel/Bienne, 1992, The Jihoceske Chamber Orch. of South Bohemia, 1992, Acad. Symphony Orch., U. Iowa, 2002; musician: (pianist) Harper Hall, 2001, 2002, Clapp Hall, 2001, 2002, Rudolf Steiner House and St. Cyprianus Ch. Eng., 2001, Hancher Auditorium, 2002, Concert Hall at the Conservatory of Stravanger, 2002, Salle Munch at Ecole Normal de Musique, 2002, Schuster Ctr. for Performing Arts, 2004, Steinway Gala Concert, Hamlin Recital Hall, North Greenville U., 2006, Gunter Theater at Peace Ctr., 2007, Kennedy Ctr. Arts, Washington, DC, 2008. Recipient award, Nat. Composition Competition, Bulgaria, 1981, Internat. Piano Competition, Italy, 1988, John Simms award, 1998, 1999, 2001, award, Maia Quartet Competition, 2001; grantee, George Soros Found. Open Soc., Sofia, 1992, Met. Art. Coun., Greenville, SC, 2008; fellow Internat. Piano Master Classes with Norma Fisher, London, UK, 2001, Internat. Piano Master Classes with Nelson Delle-Vigne, John Perry, Phillippe Entremont and Einar Nokleberg, Paris, 2002; scholar Internat. Piano Master Classes with Rudolf Buchbinder and Victor Merzhanov, Switzerland, 1992, 1993, Walter Hautzig Piano Master Classes, S.C., 1995, 1996, Internat. Piano Workshop, Stavanger, Norway, 2002. Mem.: Studio of the Young Musician, Coll. Music Soc., Phi Kappa Phi. Avocations: travel, fine arts, languages. Personal E-mail: lstoytch@hotmail.com.

STOYTCHEVA, PETIA, economics professor; b. Yambol, Bulgaria, Sept. 17, 1977; d. Stoian Stoytchev and Nadegda Stoytcheva. BS, U. World and Nat. Economy, Sofia, Bulgaria, 2000; MS, PhD, La. State U., Baton Rouge, 2005. Asst. prof. Salisbury U., Md., 2006—08. Vis. asst. prof. St. Lawrence U., 2005—06. Personal E-mail: pstoyt1@gmail.com.

STRAATSMA, BRADLEY RALPH, ophthalmologist, educator; b. Grand Rapids, Mich., Dec. 29, 1927; s. Clarence Ralph and Lucretia Marie (Nicholson) S.; m. Ruth Campbell, June 16, 1951; children: Cary Ewing, Derek, Greer. Student, U. Mich., 1947; MD cum laude, Yale U., New Haven, Conn., 1951; DSc (hon.), Columbia U., NYC, 1984; JD cum laude, U. West LA, 2002. Diplomate Am. Bd. Ophthalmology (vice chmn. 1979, chmn. 1980). Intern New Haven Hosp., Yale U., 1951-52; resident in ophthalmology Columbia U., NYC, 1955-58; spl. clin. trainee Nat. Inst. Neurol. Diseases and Blindness, Bethesda, Md., 1958-59; assoc. prof. surgery/ophthalmology UCLA Sch. Medicine, 1959-63, chief div. ophthalmology, dept. surgery, 1959-68, prof. surgery/ophthalmology, 1963-68, prof. ophthalmology, 1968—2001, dir. Jules Stein Eye Inst., 1964-94, chmn. dept. ophthalmology, 1968-94, prof. emeritus, 2001—; ophthalmologist-in-chief UCLA Med. Ctr., 1968-94. Lectr. numerous univs. and profl. socs. 1971—; cons. to surgeon gen. USPHS, mem. Vision Research Tng. Com., Nat. Inst. Neurol. Diseases and Blindness, NIH, 1959-63, mem. neurol. and sensory disease program project com., 1964-68; chmn. Vision Rsch. Program Planning Com., Nat. Adv. Eye Coun., Nat. Eye Inst., NIH, 1973-75, 75-77, 85-89; mem. med. adv. bd. Internat. Eye Found., 1970-79; mem. adv. com. on basic clin. rsch. Nat. Soc. to Prevent Blindness, 1971-87; mem. med. adv. com. Fight for Sight, 1960-83; bd. dirs. So. Calif. Soc. to Prevent Blindness, 1967-77, Ophthalmic Pub. Co., 1975-93, v.p. 1990-93, Pan-Am. Ophthalmol. Found., 1985-95; chmn. sci. adv. bd. Ctr. for Partially Sighted, 1984-87; mem. nat. adv. panel Found. for Eye Rsch., Inc., 1984-94; mem. cons. com. Palestra Oftalmologica Panamericana, 1976-81; coord. com. Nat. Eye Health Edn. Program, 1989; mem. sci. adv. bd. Rsch. to Prevent Blindness, Inc., 1993—2003. Editor-in-chief Am. Jour. Ophthalmology, 1993-2002; mem. editorial bd. UCLA Forum in Med. Scis., 1974-82, Am. Jour. Ophthalmology, 1974-91, Am. Intra-Ocular Implant Soc. Jour., 1978-79, EYE-SAT Satellite-Relayed Profl. Edn. in Ophthalmology, 1982-86; mng. editor von Graefe's Archive for Clin. and Exptl. Ophthalmology, 1976-88; contbr. over 500 articles to med. jours. Trustee John Thomas Dye Sch., LA, 1967-72. Lt. USNR, 1952-54. Recipient William Warren Hoppin award NY Acad. Medicine, 1956, Univ. Service award UCLA Alumni Assn., 1982, Miguel Aleman Found. medal, 1992, Benjamin Boyd Humanitarian award Pan Am. Assn. Ophthalmology, 1991, Lucian Howe medal, Am. Ophthalmological Soc., 1992, Internat. Gold Medal award 3rd Singapore Nat. Eye Ctr. Internat. Meeting and 11th Internat. Meeting on Cataract, Implant, Microsurgery and Refractive Keratoplasty, 1998, award of merit in retinal rsch. Retina Rsch. Found., 2002, Jose Rizal gold medal Asia-Pacific Acad. Ophthalmology, 2003, Gold medal Barraquer Inst., 2005. Fellow Royal Australian and New Zealand Coll. Ophthalmologists (hon.); mem. Academia Ophthalmologica Internationales (pres. 1998-2002), Am. Acad. Ophthalmology (bd. councillors 1981, Life Achievement award 1999), Found. of Am. Acad. Ophthalmology (trustee 1989, chmn. bd. trustees 1989-92), Am. Acad. Ophthalmology and Otolaryngology (pres. 1977), Am. Soc. Cataract and Refractive Surgery, AMA (asst. sec. ophthalmology sect. 1962-63, sec. 1963-66, chmn. 1966-67, coun. 1970-74), Am. Ophthalmol. Soc. (coun. 1985-90, v.p. 1992, pres. 1993), Assn. Rsch. in Vision and Ophthalmology (Mildred Weisenfeld award 1991), Assn. U. Profs. of Ophthalmology (trustee 1969-75, pres.-elect 1973-74, pres. 1974-75), Assn. VA Ophthalmologists, Calif. Med. Assn. (mem. ophthalmology adv. panel 1972-94, chmn. 1974-79, sci. bd. 1973-79, ho. of dels. 1974, 77, 79), Chilean Soc. Ophthalmology (hon.), Columbian Soc. Ophthalmology (hon.), Glaucoma Soc. Internat. Congress of Ophthalmology (hon.), Heed Ophthalmic Found. (chmn., bd. dirs. 1990-98), Hellenic Ophthalmol. Soc. (hon.), Internat. Coun. Ophthalmology (bd. dirs. 1993-, Jules Francois medal 2002, Internat. Duke-Elder medal 2006), LA County Med. Assn., LA Soc. Ophthalmology, Pan-Am. Assn. Ophthalmology (coun. 1972—, pres. elect 1985-87, pres. 1987-89, Harry S. Gradle Tchg. award 2007), Peruvian Soc. Ophthalmology (hon.), Retina Soc., Barraquer Inst. Ophthalmology (pres. 1996-05), Academia Ophthalmol. Internat. (pres. 1998-02), Internat. Coun. Ophthalmology Found.(pres. 2002-08, dir. 2009-; Philip M. Corboy award 2005, Internat. Duke-Elder medal 2006, Middle East African Coun. Opthamology, Prince Abdul Aziz Ahmed Al-Saud Prevention of Blindness award, 2007), Internat. Coun. Opthamology (hon. life trustee, 2008-),The Jules Gonin Club. Republican. Presbyterian. Avocations: music, scuba diving. Home: 3031 Elvido Dr Los Angeles CA 90049-1107 Office: UCLA 100 Stein Plz Los Angeles CA 90095-7065 Office Phone: 310-825-5051. Business E-Mail: straatsma@jsei.ucla.edu.

STRACENER, DANIEL W., physicist; s. Wayne A. and Beverly R. Stracener; m. Joanne Lackey, Jan. 19, 1990; children: Daniel Reed, Wyatt Andrew. BS, McNeese State U., Lake Charles, LA, 1986; PhD, Wash. U., St. Louis, Mo., 1993. Task leader ISOL devel. Oak Rdige Nat. Lab., Tenn., 1993—. Vice chmn. Bd. Zoning Appeals, Roane County, Tenn., 1998. Recipient Outstanding Mentor award, US Dept. Energy, 2008. Office: Oak Ridge Nat Lab Bethel Valley Rd Oak Ridge TN 37830 Business E-Mail: 7dw@ornl.gov.

STRACK, HAROLD ARTHUR, retired electronics executive, military officer, financial consultant, musician, writer; b. San Francisco, Mar. 29, 1923; s. Harold Arthur and Catheryn Jenny (Johnsen) S.; m. Margaret Madeline Decker, July 31, 1945; children: Carolyn, Curtis, Tamara (dec.). Student, San Francisco Coll., 1941, Sacramento Coll., 1947, Sacramento State Coll., 1948, U. Md., 1962, Indsl. Coll. Armed Forces, 1963. Commd. 2d lt. USAAF, 1943; advanced through grades to brig. gen. USAF, 1970; comdr. 1st Radar Bomb Scoring Group Carswell AFB, Ft. Worth, 1956-59; vice comdr. 90th Strategic Missile Wing SAC Warren AFB, Cheyenne, Wyo., 1964; chief, strategic nuclear br., spl. studies group Joint Chiefs of Staff, 1965-67, dep. asst. to chmn. JCS for strategic arms negotiations, 1968; comdr. 90th Strategic Missile Wing SAC Warren AFB, Cheyenne, 1969-71; chief Studies, Analysis and Gaming Agy. Joint Chiefs Staff, Washington, 1972-74, ret., 1974; v.p., mgr. MX Peacekeeper Program v.p. strategic planning Northrop Electronics Divsn., Hawthorne, Calif., 1974-88; ret., 1988. 1st clarinetist, Cheyenne Symphony Orch., 1969-71. Mem. Cheyenne Frontier Days Com., 1970-71. Decorated D.S.M., Legion of Merit, D.F.C., Air medal, Purple Heart, Presdl. citation, Army, Air Force and Joint Svc. Commendation medals. Mem. Inst. Nav., Am. Def. Preparedness Assn., Air Force Assn., Aerospace Edn. Found., Am. Fedn. Musicians, Orde Pour le Merite, Cheyenne Frontier Days "Heels". Home: 707 James Ln Incline Village NV 89451-9612 *The precepts which have guided me recognize the dignity of the individual and human rights. I believe that living by the Golden Rule contributes to the quality of life by making us better and more useful citizens while favorably influencing others. Integrity, ideals, and high standards reinforce one's own character. While taking pride in accomplishment, show gratitude for opportunity and humility for success. Lead by example and always do your best. Service to humanity and country is the highest calling, and the satisfaction of a job well done, approbation, respect and true friendship are one's greatest rewards.*

STRADER, JAMES DAVID, lawyer; b. Pitts., June 30, 1940; s. James Lowell and Tyra Fredrika (Bjorn) S.; m. Ann Wallace, Feb. 8, 1964; children: James Jacob, Robert Benjamin. BA, Mich. State U., 1962; JD, U. Pitts., 1965. Bar: Pa. 1966, US Dist. Ct. (we. dist.) Pa. 1966, US Dist. Ct. (ea. dist.) Pa. 1973, US Dist. Ct. (mid. dist.) Pa. 1985, US Ct. Appeals (4th and 5th cirs.) 1977, US Ct. Appeals (3d and 11th cirs.) 1981, US Supreme Ct. 1982, W.Va. 1996. Assoc. Peacock, Keller & Yohe, Washington, 1967-68; atty. US Steel Corp., Pitts., 1968-77, gen. atty. worker's compensation, 1977-84; assoc. Caroselli, Spagnolli & Beachler, Pitts., 1984-87; ptnr. Dickie, McCamey & Chilcote, Pitts., 1987—. Bd. trustees Mt. Lebanon Pub. Libr., 2002—08, pres., 2004—05; del. Dem. Mid-Yr. Conv., 1974; mem. Dem. Nat. Platform Com., 1976; commr. Mt. Lebanon, Pa., 1974—78. Capt. US Army, 1965—67. Mem. ABA (sr. vice-chmn. worker's compensation com. 1978-94), Pa. Bar Assn. (chmn. worker's compensation law sect. 1994-95), Pa. Bar Inst. (bd. dirs. 2001-),State Bar W.Va., Allegheny County Bar Assn., Valley Brook Country Club. Democrat. Presbyterian. Office: Dickie McCamey & Chilcote 2 PPG Pl Ste 400 Pittsburgh PA 15222-5491 Home Phone: 412-343-2368; Office Phone: 412-392-5419. Business E-Mail: jstrader@dmclaw.com.

STRADLEY, WILLIAM JACKSON, lawyer; b. Houston, Oct. 27, 1939; s. Samuel and Mary Stradley; m. Emmalee H. Stradley, Apr. 16, 1960; children: Lisa D., William M. BS, U. Houston, 1964, JD, 1967. Bar: Tex. 1967, U.S. Dist. Ct. (so. dist.) Tex. 1967, U.S. Ct. Appeals (5th cir.) 1967, U.S. Supreme Ct. 1970, cert.: (civil trial law), Tex. Bd. Legal Specialization (personal injury trial law). Of counsel Mithoff Law Firm; mem. faculty trial advocacy course Law Sch. U. Houston, 1982. Pres. Police Adv. Com., 1981—84, sec., 1980—81; bd. dirs. Houston Coun. Human Rels., 1982—84; mem. adminstrv. bd. St. Luke's United Meth. Ch.; co-chair fed. judiciary appts. com. State Bar Tex., 1991, mem. cont. legal edn. com., 1991, adminstrn. justice com., spl. com. professionalism. Recipient Pub. Svc. award, Houston Police Dept., 1984; named one of Texas Super Lawyers, 2003, 2004, 2005, 2006, 2007, 2009. Mem.: Am. Assn. Justice, Assn. Trial Lawyers Am., Tex. Trial Lawyers Assn. (dir. emeritus, chmn. ethics com., by-laws com.), Houston Bar Assn. (chmn. tort and compensation sect. 1980—81, chmn. cont. legal edn. com., com. on professionalism), Houston Trial Lawyers Assn. (bd. dirs. 1980—82, v.p. 1983—84, pres. 1985—86), Am. Bd. Trial Advocates (pres., treas. 1980—82, v.p. Houston 1983—84), Houston Bar Found. (charter), The Houstonian Club, Houston Club. Office: 3450 One Allen Ctr Houston TX 77002 Home: 121 N Post Oak Ln #503 Houston TX 77024 Office Phone: 713-654-1122.

STRAHAN, MICHAEL ANTHONY, sportscaster, retired professional football player; b. Houston, Nov. 21, 1971; s. Gene and Louise Strahan; m. Wanda Hutchins, 1992 (div. 1996); children: Tanita, Michael Jr.; m. Jean Strahan, July 18, 1999 (div. July 20, 2006); children: Isabella,

Sophia. Grad. in bus. mgmt., Tex. Southern U., Houston, 1992. Defensive end NY Giants, 1993—2008; ret., 2008; studio analyst FOX NFL Sunday, 2008—. Co-author (with Jay Glazer): Inside the Helmet: Life as a Sunday Afternoon Warrior, 2007. Co-chair Meet the Giants Fundraisers. Named First Team All-American, 1992, NFL Defensive Player of Yr., 2001, NFL All-Pro, AP, 2003; named to NFL Pro-Bowl, 1997—99, 2001—03, 2005. Achievements include being the NY Giants franchise sacks leader (141.5); setting the NFL's single season sack record (22.5), 2001; being a member of Super Bowl XLII winning NY Giants, 2008. Office: c/o FOX Sports 1211 Avenue of the Americas New York NY 10036

STRAHLMAN, RICHARD SCOTT, pediatrician; s. Richard and Carol Ann Strahlman; m. Teresa Flores, May 11, 1996; children: John Wesley, Stephanie Leigh, Matthew Scott, Michael Allen. MD, Johns Hopkins U., Balt., 1978. Diplomate Am. Bd. Pediats. Instr. in pediats. Johns Hopkins U. Sch. of Medicine, Balt., 1985—; chief of pediats. Patuxent Med. Group, Columbia, Md., 1997—2004; pediatrician Columbia Med. Practice, Md., 2004—. Cons. in field, Columbia, 1995—. Author: (chpts. in med. textbooks) Primary Pediatric Care. Named Top Doc, Balt. Mag., 2002. Fellow: Am. Acad. Pediats. Office: Columbia Med Practice 5500 Knoll N Dr Columbia MD 21045 Office Fax: 410-964-6227.

STRAHM, MARY ELLEN, music educator; d. Edward Carey and Mary Margaret McBride; m. Shaun Robert Strahm, Feb. 16, 1976. MusB in Pipe Organ, Ohio U., Athens, 1971; MA in Music Edn., Ohio State U., Columbus, 1978. Elem. vocal music specialist Licking Valley Sch. Dist., Newark, Ohio, 1972—2003, St. Nicholas Sch., Zanesville, Ohio, 2003—06, Bishop Fenwick Sch., Zanesville, 2006—. Music dir. St. John's Luth. Ch., Evang. Luth. Ch. Am., Zanesville, 2000—. Vol. Eastside Food Pantry, Newark, 1988—98. Mem.: Friends and Alumni of Ohio U. Sch. Music (v.p. 1995—97, bd. dirs. 1990—99), Am. Guild Organists, Ohio Music Edn. Assn. (25-Yr. award 1998), Music Educators Nat. Conf. (assoc.). Democrat. Lutheran. Avocations: walking, reading, photography. Office: Bishop Fenwick Sch 1030 E Main St Zanesville OH 43701 Home: 3861 Litho Ln Zanesville OH 43701

STRAHM, SAMUEL EDWARD, retired veterinarian; b. Fairview, Kans., Feb. 9, 1936; s. Silas Tobias and Martha Mary (Beyer) S.; m. Barbara Jean Wenger, June 1, 1958; children: Gregory Lee, Bryan Scott, Andrea Marie Enloe. BS, DVM, Kansas State U., 1959. Owner Osage Animal Clinic Inc., Pawhuska, Okla., 1959—2007, pres., 1985—2007; ret., 2007. Bd. dirs. 1st Nat. Bank, Pawhuska, Okla.; bd. cons. Profl. Exam Svc., 1990-2000; adv. bd. USDA Users, 1991-95; adv. com. Pew Nat. Health Profession Vet. Medicine, 1991; state adv. coun. Okla. Coop. Extension Svcs., 2000—, chmn.-elect, 2000-01, chmn., 2001-07. Bd. dirs. Okla. Sch. Bd. Assn., 1977-98, 2d v.p., 1993, 1st v.p., 1994, pres., 1996; Okla. All-State Sch. Bd., 1993, Pawhuska Sch. Bd., 1974-98, 2001-06, pres., 2003-06; active Pawhuska Planning Commn., 1965-70, Okla. State U. Centennial Commn., Stillwater, 1986-91; bd. dirs. Nat. Sch. Bd. Assn., 1996-99, exec. com., 1997-99, western reg. chmn., 1996. Recipient Disting. Alumni award Coll. Vet. Medicine Kans. State U., 1994, Fairview HS, 2004, Outstanding Svc. award Nat. Sch. Bds. Assn., 1997, Disting. Svc. award Nat. Bd. Exam. Com., 2000, Friend of Yr. award Okla. Coop. Extension, 2002. Mem.: Acad. Vet. Consultants, AVMA (pres. 1989—90, coun. govt. affair 1992—98, coun. edn. 2003—06, AVMA award 1986), Am. Vet. Med. Found. (chmn. 1995—98, treas. 2004—), Am. Assn. Theriogenealogy, Am. Assn. Bovine Practitioners (Practitioner of Yr. award 2002), Am. Assn. Vet. State Bds., Am. Assn. Vet. Specialty Bd. (rep. coun. on edn.), Am. Assn. Food Hygiene Vets. (bd. dirs. 2000—06), Nat. Bd. Vet. Med. Examiners (Disting. Svc. award 2000), Okla. Vet. Med. Assn. (all offices 1959—, Veterinarian of Yr. 1990, Disting. Svc. award 1998), Kans. Vet. Med. Assn., Okla. Bd. Vet. Med. Examiners (pres.), Pawhuska C. of C. (pres. 1968), Toastmasters Club, Pawhuska Jaycees (all offices 1959—69). Republican. Baptist. Avocations: gardening, fishing, flying. Home: PO Box 1256 Pawhuska OK 74056-1256 Office: Osage Animal Clinic Inc PO Box 1209 Pawhuska OK 74056-1209

STRAIGHT, BILINDA, anthropologist, educator; b. Dayton, Ohio, Mar. 9, 1964; d. William Sylvester Straight and Michelle Miller; children: Jesse Allan Straight Farman, Jen Michael Straight Farman, Clare Rose Straight Holtzman, William S Straight Holtzman. PhD, U. Mich., Ann Arbor, 1997. Assoc. prof. Western Mich. U., Kalamazoo, 2000—. Contbr. scientific papers to profl. jours. (Fulbright award, IIE, 1992); author: (book) Women on the Verge of Home, Miracles and Extraordinary Experience in Northern Kenya; contbr. articles to profl. jours. Grant, NSF, 2004. Mem.: Brit. Inst. Eastern Africa, African Studies Assn., Soc. Humanistic Anthropology, Am. Anthrop. Assn. Mem. Soc. Of Friends. Avocations: poetry, photography. Office: Western Mich Univ 1001 Moore Hall Anthropology Kalamazoo MI 49008 Office Fax: 269-387-3970.

STRAIN, JAMES ARTHUR, lawyer; b. Alexandria, La., Oct. 11, 1944; s. William Joseph and Louise (Moore) S.; m. Cheryl Sue Williamson, Aug. 19, 1967; children: William Joseph, Gordon Richard, Elizabeth Parks. BS in Econs., Ind. U., 1966, JD, 1969. Bar: Ind. 1969, U.S. Dist. Ct. (so. dist.) Ind. 1969, U.S. Ct. Appeals (7th cir.) 1972, U.S. Supreme Ct. 1975, U.S. Ct. Appeals (5th cir.) 1978. Instr. Law Sch. Ind. U., Indpls., 1969-70; law clk. to Hon. John S. Hastings 7th Cir. Ct. Appeals, Chgo., 1970-71; assoc. Cahill, Gordon & Reindel, NYC, 1971-72; law clk. to Hon. William H. Rehnquist U.S. Supreme Ct., Washington, 1972-73; assoc. Barnes, Hickam, Pantzer & Boyd, Indpls., 1973-75; ptnr. Barnes, Hickam, Pantzer & Boyd (name changed to Barnes & Thornburg), 1976-96, Sommer Barnard, PC, Indpls., 1996—. Adj. asst. prof. law Ind. U. Sch. Law, 1986-92, 2003-07. Mem., bd. dirs. The Penrod Soc., Indpls., 1976—, Indpls. Symphonic Choir, 1988-91, Festival Music Soc., Indpls., 1990-96. Mem. 7th Cir. Bar Assn. (meetings chmn. Ind. chpt. 1979-88, portraits 1988-89, bd. govs. 1989—, 1st v.p. 1995, pres. 1996). Avocations: photography, music. Office: Taft Stettinius Hollister LLP Ste 3500 One Indiana Sq Indianapolis IN 46204 Home Phone: 317-686-1928; Office Phone: 317-713-3500. Business E-Mail: strain@taftlaw.com.

STRAIN, JAMES ELLSWORTH, pediatrician, educator, retired medical association administrator; b. Lincoln, Nebr., Apr. 23, 1923; s. Elmer Ellsworth and Tessa Elizabeth (Stevens) Strain; m. Ruby Lee Shepard; children: James A., John D., Janet M. Strain McKinney, Jeffrey Lee Phillips-Strain. AB, Phillips U., Enid, Okla., 1945; MD, U. Colo., Denver, 1947. Diplomate Am. Bd. Pediat. (examiner 1984-89, mem. 1989-93, emeritus mem. 1993—). Intern Mpls. Gen. Hosp., 1947—48; resident in pediat. Denver Children's Hosp., 1948—50, pres. med. staff, 1964, dir. genetic unit, 1982—86; pvt. practice specializing in pediat. Denver, 1950—86; exec. dir. Am. Acad. Pediat., Elk Grove Village, Ill., 1986—93, ret., 1993. Pres. med. bd. Colo. Gen. Hosp., 1969—70; clin. prof. pediat. U. Colo. Med. Ctr., 1969—86, 1993—, U. Chgo., 1987—93; mem. Colo. Med. Adv. Coun. for Title 19, 1968—75, chmn., 1968—71; mem. Task Force on Iowa Health Care Stds. Project, 1984—85; presenter numerous profl. confs. Editl. bd. Pediat. in Rev., reviewer Jour. Pediat.; contbr. articles to profl. publs. Mem. Colo. Commn. on Children and Youth, 1971—75; trustee Phillips U., 1974—. Capt. US Army, 1953—55. Recipient Disting. Alumnus award, Phillips U., 1974, Florence Sabin award, U. Colo., 1984, Excellence in Pub. Svc. award, U.S. Surgeon Gen., 1988, Abraham Jacobi award, AMA and Am. Acad. Pediat., 1994, James E. Strain Child Advocacy award established in his name, Denver Children's Hosp., 1983. Fellow: Am. Acad. Pediat. (Clifford Grulee award 1985); mem.: AMA, APHA, Inst. Medicine NAS, Ambulatory Pediatric Assn., Can. Pediatric Soc., Denver Med. Soc., Colo. Med. Soc., Alpha Omega Alpha. Republican. Mem. Christian Ch. (Disciples Of Christ). Avocations: fishing, sports, reading. Personal E-mail: jstrain121@aol.com.

STRAIT, GEORGE, musician; b. Poteet, Tex., May 18, 1952; m. Norma Strait; 1 child, George Bubba Jr. Degree in Agr., S.W. Tex. State U. Albums include Blue Clear Sky (Country Music Assn. Album of Yr. 1996), Strait Out of the Box (boxed set), Easy Come, Easy Go, Right or Wrong, Strait from the Heart, Strait Country, Does Ft. Worth Ever Cross Your Mind, 1985 (Country Music Assn. Album of Yr. 1985), Pure Country, 1986, No. 7, Something Special, 1986, Ocean Front Property, 1987, If You Aint Lovin' (You Aint Livin'), 1988, Beyond the Blue Neon, 1989, Livin' It Up, 1990, Ten Strait Hits, 1991, Chill of An Early Fall, 1991, Greatest Hits Volume I, II, Lead On, 1994, Strait Out of the Box, 1995, Blue Clear Sky, 1996 (Country Music Assn. Album of Yr. 1996), Carrying Your Love With Me, 1997 (Country Music Assn. Album of Yr. 1997), One Step at a Time, 1998 (Country Music assn. Album of Yr. 1998), Always Never the Same, 1999, Merry Christmas Wherever You Are, 1999, Latest Greatest Strait Greatest Hits, 2000, George Strait, 2000, The Road Less Traveled, 2001, 20th Century Masters, 2002, Honkytonkville, 2003, 50 Number Ones, 2004, Somewhere Down in Texas, 2005, It Just Comes Natural, 2006, (Single Record of Yr. & Song of Yr. awards for Give It Away, Acad. Country Music, 2007, Album of Yr., Country Music Assn., 2007), Live at Texas Stadium, 2007, George Strait 22 More Hits, 2007, Troubadour, 2008 (Album of Yr., County Music Assn., 2008, Best Country Album, Grammy Awards, 2009), other platinum albums; #1 country hits include Fool Hearted Memory, 1982, Amarillo By Morning, 1983, You Look So Good in Love, 1984, The Chair, 1986, Baby Blue, 1989, Beyond the Blue Moon, 1989, Baby's Gotten Good At Goodbye, 1989, Love Without End, Amen, 1990, I've Come to Expect It From You, 1990, Chill of An Early Fall, 1991, If I Know Me, 1991, The Big One, 1995, Good News Bad News (Due with Lee Ann Womack), 2005 (Country Music Assn. Musical Event of Yr. 2005), I Saw God Today, 2008 (Single of Yr., Country Music. Assn., 2008); (movie) Pure Country, 1992. Served with US Army until 1975. Named SRO Touring Artist of Yr., 1990; recipient Male Vocalist of Yr. award, Acad. Country Music, 1984, 1985, 1989, Entertainer of Yr. award, 1989, 1990, Male Vocalist of Yr. award, Country Music Assn., 1985, 1986, 1996, 1997, Entertainer of Yr. award, 1989, 1990, Top Country Vocalist award, Am. Music Awards, 1991, Tex Ritter Award for Pure Country, 1993, Voice of the Yr. award, ASCAP, 1995. Avocations: golf, skiing, fishing, hunting, Steer-roping.*

STRAIT, VIOLA EDWINA WASHINGTON, librarian; b. El Paso, Tex., Aug. 29, 1925; d. Leroy Wentworth and Viola Edwina (Wright) Washington; m. Freeman Adams, Mar. 6, 1943; 1 child, Norma Jean (Mrs. Louis Lee James); m. Clifford Moody, Jan. 8, 1950; 1 child, Viola Edwina III (Mrs. Paul M. Cunningham); m. Amos O. Strait, Dec. 9, 1972. Bus. cert., Tillotson Coll., 1946, BA, 1948; MS in Libr. Sci., U. So. Calif., 1954. Substitute tchr. El Paso Pub. Schs., 1948; sec., bookkeeper U.S.O.-YWCA, El Paso, 1948-50; libr. asst. Spl. Svcs. Libr., Ft. Bliss, Tex., 1950-53, libr., 1954-71; equal employment opportunity officer Ft. Bliss, 1971-72; dep. equal employment opportunity officer Long Beach (Calif.) Naval Shipyard, 1972-85; with Temp. Job Mart, Torrance, Calif., 1986-87; substitute tchr. Ysleta Ind. Sch. Dist., 1988-89; profl. libr. Eastwood Hts. Elem. Sch., 1989-90; sec. Shiloh Bapt. Ch., El Paso, 1991-92; br. mgr. El Paso Pub. Libr., 1992-96, retired, 1996. Host, prodr. (gospel music video with Viola Washington Strait), Time Warner TV, Cable Channel 15, 2003—04. Sec. Sunday sch. Bapt. Ch., 1956-66, 92-96, min. music, 1958-72, supr. young adult choir, 1966-72, pres. sr. choir, 1969-71; disc jockey Sta. KELP, El Paso, 1970-72; host radio show Sta. KTEP, U. Tex., El Paso, 1994-2004; hon. chmn. for ann. observance of Nat. Libr. Week, City of El Paso, 1970. Mem. ALA, Border Region Libr. Assn. (chmn. scholarship com. 1970), NAACP (sec. 1996), Alpha Kappa Alpha. Democrat. Baptist. Avocations: piano, reading. Home Phone: 915-857-3927. Personal E-mail: vstrait@att.net.

STRAIT, WILLIAM ROBERT, computer technician; b. Troy, NY, July 22, 1943; s. Ralph Ernest Strait and Ruth Edna Copping; m. Sandra Vada Sanborn, Aug. 10, 1994; children: Stefan Michael, Sean Eric. BS, Union Coll., 1965; MS, Northeastern U., Boston, 1967; PhD, Rensselaer Poly. Inst., 1975. Instr. Union Coll., Schenectady, NY, 1967—80; dir. MIS, OMRDD, Albany, NY, 1980—84; asst. dir. MIS, Nathan Kline Rsch. Inst., Orangeburg, NY, 1984—89; pres. Computer Solutions Ctr., Suffern, NY, 1989—90, Strait Consulting, Ocala, 2007—; v.p. Merritech, Tampa, Fla., 1990—91, SOS Techs., Tampa, 1991—92; sr. cons. Automation Rsch. Systems, Tampa, 1992—95; asst. dir. IT, U. South Fla., Tampa, 1995—2001; chief info. officer Ctr. Fla. C.C., Ocala, 2001—06. Bd. dirs. Fla. Assn. Ednl. Data Systems, Speede Com. (AACRAO), Washington. Founder, chair bd. Com. for Better Govt., Schenectady, NY, 1976—79; instr. Red Cross, Tampa, Fla., 1990—95. Mem.: Rotary (Tampa chpt. bd. dirs. 1993—97, Paul Harris fellow 1997), Sigma Xi. Avocations: jogging, bicycling, woodworking, stained glass. Home: 9643 SW 74th Ave Ocala FL 34476

STRAJA, SORIN RADU, chemical engineer, mathematician, computer programmer; b. Bucharest, Romania; s. Radu and Sonica Straja; m. Mihaela Cirstea, Mar. 26, 1982. MS, Poly. Inst., Bucharest, 1979, PhD, 1987. Chem. engr. Plastics Processing, Bucharest, 1979—81; rsch. and devel. cons. Chem. and Biochem. Energetics Inst., Bucharest, 1982—89; cons., vol. USDA, Washington, 1991—92; chemist U. Md., Balt., 1992—93; dir. occupl. health and safety dept. Temple U., Phila., 1993—95, asst. prof. stats., 1994—2001; v.p. Inst. Regulatory Sci., Columbia, Md., 1996—. Cons. Montgomery Investment Tech., Radnor, 1995—. Editor: Environmental International, 1993-99; contbg. editor: Technology, 1996—; contbr. numerous articles to profl. jours. Recipient Nicolae Teclu award Romanian Acad. Scis., 1983, Cert. Appreciation, USDA, 1992, Cert. Appreciation for Tchg., Temple U., 1999. Mem. AIChE, ACS. Avocations: history, geography. Home and Office: Inst Regulatory Sci 5406 Hildebrand ct Columbia MD 21044-1918 Office Phone: 410-997-6396.

STRAKA, ANGELINE C., broadcast executive; BS, MLS, U. Pitts.; JD cum laude, Duquesne U., Pitts. Spl. asst. US atty. US Atty.'s Office; with US Vets. Adminstrn., H.J. Heinz Co., Westinghouse Electric Corp.; v.p., dep. gen. counsel, sec. CBS Corp., 1992—2000; sr. v.p, gen. counsel, sec. Infinity Broadcasting Corp., 2000—01; with law dept. Viacom, 2001—05, v.p., assoc. gen. counsel, co-head corp. transactions & securities practice group, asst. sec., 2001—05; sr. v.p., dep. gen. counsel, sec. CBS Corp., 2006—. Mem.: Pa. Bar Assn., NY Bar Assn. Office: CBS Corp 51 W 52nd St New York NY 10019-6188 Office Phone: 212-975-4321.

STRAKA, LASZLO RICHARD, retired publishing consultant; b. Budapest, Hungary, June 22, 1934; came to U.S., 1950, naturalized, 1956; s. Richard J. and Elisabeth (Roeck) S.; m. Eva K. von Viczian, Jan. 20, 1962 (div. May 1981); children: Eva M., Monika E., Viktoria K. BA cum laude, NYU, 1959. Acct. Greatrex Ltd., NYC, 1952-53; pres. Maxwell Macmillan Internat. Pub. Group, NYC, 1991-92; with Pergamon Press, Inc., Elmsford, NY, 1954-90, v.p., 1964-68, exec. v.p., treas., 1968-74, pres., 1974-75, 80-88, chmn. bd., 1975-77, 88-90, vice chmn. bd., 1977-80, 88-89, also dir.; vice chmn. bd. Pergamon Books Ltd., Oxford, England, 1986-88; group v.p. Macmillan Inc., NYC, 1989-91; pub. cons. Alta Loma, Calif., 1992—2005; ret., 2005. Treas. Brit. Book Centre, Inc., N.Y.C., 1956-67; pres. Pergamon Holding Corp., 1981-86; chmn. bd. Microforms Internat., Inc., 1971-87. D. dirs., sec. Szechenyi Istvan Soc., N.Y.C., 1967-80, 89-93. Mem. Phi Beta Kappa. Home: 6405 Caledon Pl Alta Loma CA 91737 Home Phone: 909-912-4140. Personal E-mail: nagyapu100@yahoo.com.

STRALEY, TINA H., mathematics association director; b. NYC, Sept. 4, 1943; d. Abraham Sidney and Frances (Yankowitz) Handelman; m. William Forest Straley, June 1, 1967 (div. Oct. 1976); 1 child, Jessica Laura. BA with honors, Ga. State U., 1965, MS, 1966; PhD, Auburn U., Ala., 1971. Tchr. math. Miami Beach (Fla.) Sr. High Sch., 1966-67; instr. Spelman Coll., Atlanta, 1967-68, Auburn U., 1971-73; asst. prof. Kennesaw State Coll., Marietta, Ga., 1973-78, assoc. prof., 1979-84, prof., 1984-90, acting chair dept. math., 1987-88, chmn. dept. math., 1987-93, assoc. v.p. acad. affairs, 1995-98, dean grad. studies, 1996—, assoc. v.p. scholarship and grad. studies, 1998-2000; rsch. assoc. Emory U., Atlanta, 1978-79. Chair bd. of regents adv. com. on math. subjects, 1990-91. Contbr. articles to profl. jours. Originator state steering com. Futurescape Programs for High Sch. Girls, U. System and Ga. Dept. Edn., 1983-86. Recipient Salute to Women of Achievement award YWCA, Atlanta, 1985; grantee Kennesaw State Coll., 1980, AAUW, 1984-85, NSF, 1991-93, 98-01. Mem. AAUP, AAUW, Math. Assn. Am. (editor Southeastern Sect. newsletter, 1988-94, dept. rep. 1979-90, S.E sect. chair-elect, chair, past-chair 1994-98, editl. bd. MAA Notes 1992-99, editor 1996-99, coms. on math. edn. publs. and math. across the curriculum, exec. dir. 2000—), Am. Math. Soc., Assn. for Women in Math., Nat. Coun. Tchrs. Math., Phi Kappa Phi. Office: Math Assn Am 1529 18th St NW Washington DC 20036-1358

STRALING, PHILLIP FRANCIS, bishop emeritus; b. San Bernardino, Calif., Apr. 25, 1933; s. Sylvester J. and Florence E. (Robinson) Straling. BA, U. San Diego, 1963; MS in Child and Family Counseling, San Diego State U., 1971. Ordained priest Diocese of San Diego, 1959; mem. faculty St. John Acad., El Cajon, Calif., 1959—60, St. Therese Acad., San Diego, 1960—63; chaplain Newman Club, San Diego State U., 1960—72; mem. faculty St. Francis Sem., San Diego, 1972—76; pastor Holy Rosary Parish, San Bernardino, 1976—78; ordained bishop, 1978; bishop Diocese of San Bernardino, 1978—95; pub. Inland Cath. newspaper, 1979—95; bishop Diocese of Reno, 1995—2005, bishop emeritus Nev., 2005—. Bd. dirs. Calif. Assn. Cath. Campus Mins., 1960; exec. sec. Diocesan Synod II, 1972—76; Episcopal vicar San Bernardino Deanery, 1976—78. Mem.: Nat. Cath. Campus Ministries Assn. (bishop rep. 1992—98). Roman Catholic.

STRAMPEL, WILLIAM DERKEY, dean, medical educator; b. Saugatuck, Mich., Feb. 8, 1948; married; 3 children. BA, Hope Coll., 1970; DO, Chgo. Coll. Osteopathic Medicine, 1976. Intern Madigan Army Med. Ctr., Fort Lewis, Wash., 1976—77, resident in medicine, 1977—79; fellow in pulmonary disease Fitzsimons Army Med. Ctr., Aurora, 1980—82; staff internal medicine svc. and dir. intensive care 121 Evacuation Hosp., Seoul; pulmonary staff and dir. intensive care Fitzsimons Army Med. Ctr., Aurora, Colo.; divsn. surgeon First Infantry Divsn. Irwin Army Cmty. Hosp., Fort Riley, Kans., dep. comdr., dir. med. edn., Evans Army Cmty. Hosp., Fort Carson, Colo.; chief Quality Assurance Divsn., Dept. of Army, Office Surgeon Gen., 1991—94; dir. med. edn. Brooke Army Med. Ctr., 1994—96; comdr. Brooke Army Med. Ctr. and Great Plains Med. Command, 1996—97; dir. quality mgmt. Office Sec. Def.; chief med. officer Tricare Mgmt. Activity; spl. asst. for ops. and readiness to U.S. surgeon gen.; leader Mich. State U. Health Team; sr. assoc. dean Mich. State U. Coll. Osteo. Medicine, 1999—2002, prof. internal medicine, 2001—, acting dean, 2001—02, dean, 2002—. Served to col. US Army. Office: Mich State U Coll Osteo Medicine A308A E Free Hall East Lansing MI 48824-1316 Office Phone: 517-355-9616. Office Fax: 517-432-2125.*

STRANC, CATHLEEN L., music educator; d. George H. and Nancy L. Stranc. MusB in Bus., Southern Ill. U., 1982, MusB in Edn., 1984; MusM in Edn., VanderCook Coll. Music, Chgo., 1995. Cert. edn. Ill., 1984. Choral and instrumental music educator Jersey Cmty. Sch. Dist., Jerseyville, Ill., 1985—95; instrumental music educator Edwardsville (Ill.) Sch. Dist., 1995—. Guest condr. Madison County Band Festival, 2006. Recipient Outstanding Mid. Sch. Activity Sponsor award, Edwardsville Sch. Dist., 2005. Mem.: NEA, Madison County Band Dirs. Assn. (sec. 2002—), Ill. Grade Sch. Music Assn. (sec./treas. dist. 5 2005—), Ill. Edn. Assn. (region 45 elections com. chair 2000—), Edwardsville Edn. Assn. (sec. 1998—, Local Leadership award 2005), Ill. Music Educator Assn. (dist. 6 profl. devel. chair 2000—06), Women's Internat. Band Dirs. Assn. (life), Nat. Band Assn. (life), Phi Kappa Phi (life). Office: Edwardsville Cmty Sch Dist #7 #1 District Dr Edwardsville IL 62025 Home: 2540 Liberty Dr Maryville IL 62062 Personal E-mail: cstranc60@yahoo.com.

STRAND, CURT ROBERT, hotel executive; b. Vienna, Nov. 13, 1920; naturalized Am. citizen, 1943; m. Fleur Lillian Emanuel, June 14, 1946. BS, Cornell U., 1943. Supt. service Plaza, NYC, 1947-49; asst. to v.p. Hilton Hotels Corp., 1949-53; v.p. Hilton Internat. Co., NYC, 1953-64, exec. v.p., 1964-67, pres., chief exec. officer, 1967-86, chmn., 1986-87. Sr. v.p., dir. Trans World Air Lines, Inc.; lectr. Cornell U. Sch. Hotel Adminstrn., Ecole Superieure de Scis. Econs., Paris, NYU, Houston U.; sr. cons. Am. Express; mem. adv. panel com. Am. Hotel and Motel Assn.; dir. Sherry Netherland Corp.; mem. exec. com. Bd. Exec. Svc. Corps, Aspen. Mem. coun. Cornell U.; adv. bd. Aspen Found.; bd. govs. Snowmass Resort Assn., also pres.; fellow Aspen Inst. With Mil. Intelligence US Army, 1943—46. Mem. Cornell Soc. Hotelmen (Hotelier of Yr. 1986), Aspen Exec. Svc. Corps (mem. bd., v.p.), Snowmass Club. Home: PO Box 6359 Snowmass Village CO 81615

STRAND, FRED P., mathematics educator; b. ND; m. Donalee Strand. BS in Edn., Mayville State Univ., 1980. Math. tchr. Hatton (ND) H.S. Vol. St. John Luth. Ch. Named ND Tchr. of Yr., 2006. Luth. Office: Hatton High Sch 503 Fourth St Hatton ND 58240 Business E-Mail: fred.strand@sendit.nodak.edu.

STRAND, MARGARET N., lawyer; b. White Plains, NY, Apr. 27, 1946; BA, U. Rochester, 1968; MA, U. RI, 1971; JD, Coll. William and Mary, 1976. Bar: Va. 1976, DC 1977, US Supreme Ct. Chief, environ. def. sect. environ. and natural resources divsn. U.S. Dept. Justice, Washington, 1984—91; ptnr. Venable LLP, Washington. Lectr. George Washington U., 1993—2002; chair environ. law com. Transp. Rsch. Bd., Nat. Acad. Scis.; bd. dirs. Environ. Law Inst.; mem. editl. bd. Environ.

Law Reporter, Nat. Wetlands News. Author: Wetlands Deskbook, 1997; contbr. chapters to books, articles to profl. jours. Mem.: ABA. Office: Venable LLP 575 7th St NW Washington DC 20004 Office Phone: 202-344-4699. Office Fax: 202-344-8300. Business E-Mail: mnstrand@venable.com.

STRAND, MARK, poet; b. Summerside, PEI, Can., Apr. 11, 1934; came to U.S., 1938. s. Robert Joseph and Sonia (Apter) S.; m. Antonia Ratensky, Sept. 14, 1961 (div. June 1973); 1 dau., Jessica; m. Julia Rumsey Garretson, Mar. 15, 1976; 1 son, Thomas Summerfield. BA, Antioch Coll., 1957; BFA, Yale, 1959; MA, U. Iowa, 1962. Instr. English U. Iowa, 1962-65; asst. prof. Mt. Holyoke Coll., 1967; assoc. prof. Bklyn. Coll., 1971-72; Bain-Swiggett lectr. Princeton, 1973; Hurst prof. poetry Brandeis U., 1974-75; prof. U. Utah, 1981-93; U.S. poet laureate Library of Congress, Washington, 1990-91; prof. Johns Hopkins U., 1994—97; Andrew MacLeish disting. svc. prof. U. Chgo., 1997—. Fulbright lectr. U. Brazil, Rio de Janeiro, 1965-66; adj. assoc. prof. Columbia U., 1969-72; vis. prof. U. Wash., 1968, 70, U. Va., 1977, Wesleyan U., 1979, Harvard U., 1980; vis. lectr. Yale, 1969-70, U. Va., 1976, Calif. State U., Fresno, 1977, U. Calif., Irvine, 1979. Author: Sleeping with One Eye Open, 1964, Reasons for Moving, 1968, Darker, 1970, The Story of Our Lives, 1973 (Edgar Allan Poe award Acad. Am. Poets 1974), The Sargeantville Notebook, 1974, The Monument, 1978, Elegy for My Father, 1978, The Late Hour, 1978, Selected Poems, 1980, The Planet of Lost Things, 1982, The Night Book, 1983, Mr. and Mrs. Baby and Other Stories, 1985, Rembrandt Takes a Walk, 1986, William Bailey, 1987, The Continuous Life, 1990, Dark Harbor, 1993, Hopper, 1994, Blizzard of One, 2000 (Pulitzer Prize), Man and Camel, 2006; Editor: The Contemporary American Poets, 1968, New Poetry of Mexico, 1970, 18 Poems from Quechua, 1971, The Owl's Insomnia, 1973, The Best American Poetry 1991, The Golden Ecco Anthology, 1994; co-author: 89 Clouds, 1999; co-editor: Another Republic: Seventeen European and South American Writers, 1976, The Art of the Real, 1983, Traveling in the Family, 1987; translator: Souvenir of the Ancient World, 1976. Recipient award Am. Acad. and Inst. Arts and Letters, 1975, Utah Gov.'s award in arts, 1992, Bobbitt Nat. prize for poetry, 1992, Bollingen prize for poetry Yale Univ. Libr., 1993; Fulbright scholar in Italy, 1960-61; Ingram Merrill Found. grantee, 1966; Nat. Endowment for Arts grantee, 1967-68, 78-79, 86-87; Rockefeller Found. grantee, 1968-69; Guggenheim fellow, 1975-76; Acad. Am. Poets fellow, 1979; MacArthur Found. fellow, 1987; Pulitzer Prize in Poetry, Blizzard of One, 1999, Wallace Stevens prize, 2004. Fellow Acad. Am. Poets; mem. Am. Acad. and Inst. Arts and Letters. E-mail: ms3091@columbia.edu.

STRAND, ROGER GORDON, federal judge; b. Peekskill, NY, Apr. 28, 1934; s. Ernest Gordon Strand and Lisabeth Laurine (Phin) Steinmetz; m. Joan Williams, Nov. 25, 1961. AB, Hamilton Coll., 1955; LLB, Cornell U., 1961; grad., Nat. Coll. State Trial Judges, 1968. Bar: Ariz. 1961, U.S. Dist. Ct. Ariz. 1961, U.S. Supreme Ct. 1980. Assoc. Fennemore, Craig, Allen & McClennen, Phoenix, 1961-67; judge Ariz. Superior Ct., Phoenix, 1967-85, U.S. Dist. Ct. Ariz., Phoenix, 1985—2001, now sr. judge. Assoc. presiding judge Ariz. Superior Ct., 1971-85; lectr. Nat. Jud. Coll., Reno, 1978-87; mem. jud. conf. U.S. com. on info. tech., 1996-2002; mem. 9th Cir. Jud. Coun., 2004-2007 Past pres. cen. Ariz. chpt. Arthritis Found. Lt. USN, 1955-61. Mem. ABA, Ariz. Bar Assn., Maricopa County Bar Assn., Phi Delta Phi, Lodges: Rotary. Avocations: computer applications, golf, fishing. Home: 5825 N 3rd Ave Phoenix AZ 85013-1537 Office: Sandra Day O'Connor US Courthouse SPC 57 401 W Washington Phoenix AZ 85003-2156 Office Phone: 602-322-7550. Business E-Mail: roger_strand@azd.uscourts.gov.

STRAND, THERESA, educational consultant; b. NYC, Jan. 11, 1921; d. Louis and Anna Siegel; m. Peter Strand, June 17, 1944; 1 child, Robert Dennis. BA in Liberal Arts, CCNY Bklyn. Coll., 1942; MA in Fine Arts and Art Edn., Columbia U. Tchrs. Coll., NYC, 1946; PhD in Ednl. Evaluation and Rsch., Wayne State U., Detroit, 1975. Sr. profl. assoc. Ednl. Testing Svc., Evanston, Ill., Princeton, NJ, 1969—92; CEO Strand Consulting Svcs., Glenview, Ill., 1992—. Educator, evaluator, trainer, rschr., author, editor, cons. in field. Founding mem., mem. steering com. Assn. for Devel. Guidance of Adults, Wayne State U., Detroit, 1967—69; historian, archivist, coun. mem. Midwest Ednl. Rsch. Assn., Ill., 1994—2000. Mem.: Nat. Mus. Women in Arts, Wash., DC, Mus. Contemporary Art, Chgo., Block Mus. Art, Northwestern U., Evanston, Nat. Coun. Measurement in Edn., Am. Ednl. Rsch. Assn. Avocations: visual arts, theater, documentary films, computers.

STRANDBERG, MALCOM WOODROW PERSHING, physicist; b. Box Elder, Mont., Mar. 9, 1919; s. Malcom and Ingeborg (Riestad) S.; m. Harriet Elisabeth Bennett, Aug. 2, 1947 (dec.); children— Josiah R.W., Susan Abby, Elisabeth G., Malcom B. S.B., Harvard Coll., 1941; PhD, M.I.T., 1948. Research asso. M.I.T., Cambridge, 1941-48, asst. prof. physics, 1948-53, asso. prof., 1953-60, prof., 1960-88, prof. emeritus, 1988—. Author: Microwave Spectroscopy, 1954; patentee in field. Fellow Am. Phys. Soc., Am. Acad. Arts and Scis., IEEE, AAAS; mem. Am. Assn. Physics Tchrs. Episcopalian. Home: 82 Larchwood Dr Cambridge MA 02138-4639 Office: Mass Inst Tech 36-597 Cambridge MA 02139 Business E-Mail: mwpstr@mit.edu.

STRANG, RUTH HANCOCK, pediatrician, cardiologist, priest, educator; b. Bridgeport, Conn., Mar. 11, 1923; d. Robert H.W. and Ruth (Hancock) Strang. BA, Wellesley Coll., 1944, postgrad., 1944—45; MD, N.Y. Med. Coll., 1949; MDiv, Seabury We. Theol. Sem., 1993. Diplomate Am. Bd. Pediat.; ordained deacon Episc. Ch., 1993, priest Episc. Ch., 1994. Intern Flower and Fifth Ave. Hosp., NYC, 1949—50, resident in pediat., 1950—52; mem. faculty N.Y. Med. Coll., NYC, 1952—57; fellow cardiology Babies Hosp., NYC, 1956—57, Harriet Lane Cardiac Clinic, Johns Hopkins Hosp., Balt., 1957—59, Children's Hosp., Boston, 1959—62; mem. faculty U. Mich. Hosp., Ann Arbor, 1962—89, prof. pediat., 1970—89, prof. emeritus, 1989—; priest-in-charge St. Johns Episcopal Ch., Howell, Mich., 1994—. Dir. pediat. Wayne County Gen. Hosp., Westland, Mich, 1965-85; mem. staff U. Mich. Hosps., 1962-89; mem. med. adv. com. Wayne County chpt. Nat. Cystic Fibrosis Rsch. Found., 1966-80, chmn. med. adv. com. nat. found., Detroit, 1971-78; cons. cardiology Plymouth (Mich.) State Home and Tng. Sch., 1970-81; diocesan coun. Diocese Mich., 2003-05, mem. com. on nominations and elections Diocesan Conv., 2003, chmn. com., 2004. Author: Clinical Aspects of Operable Heart Disease, 1968; contbr. numerous articles to profl. jours. Mem. citizen's adv. coun. Juvenile Ct., Ann Arbor, 1968—76; mem. med. adv. bd. Ann Arbor Continuing Edn. Dept., 1968—77; v.p. Am. Heart Assn. Mich., 1989, pres., 1991; bd. dirs. Livingston Cmty. Hospice, 1995—99; bd. mgrs. Emrich Episcopal Retreat Ctr., 1998—2008; mem. Diocesan Com. for World Relief, Detroit, 1970—72; trustee Episcopal Med. Chaplaincy, Ann Arbor, 1971—96; mem. bishop's com. St. Aidan's Episc. Ch., 1966—69, sec., 1966—68, vestry, 1973—76, 1978—80, 1984—86, 1990—91, sr. warden, 1975—76, 1978, 1986, 1990; del. Episc. Diocesan Conv., 1980, 1991; mem. Congl. Life Circle Episcopal Diocese Mich., 1995—2001, mem. loans and grants com., 1995—99, mem. com. on reference ann. diocesan conv., 1995-98, chmn., 1996; mem. Diocese Mich. Clergy Family Project, 1996—98; co-dean Huron Valley area coun. Diocese Mich., 1998—2000; bd. trustees Ecumenical Theol. Sem., Detroit, 1996—2008, chair acad. affairs com., 2000—08; mem. Congl. Devel. Commn., 2001—03; bd. dirs. Livingston County Cath. Social Svcs., 2004—07. Recipient Alumnae Life Achievement award, Baldwin Sch., 2005, Disting. Svc. award, Ecumenical Theol. Sem., Detroit, 2008. Mem. AMA, Am. Acad. Pediat., Am. Coll. Cardiology, Mich. Med. Soc., Washtenaw County Med. Soc., N.Y. Acad. Medicine, Am. Heart Assn., Women's Rsch. Club (membership sec. 1966-67), Ambulatory Pediat. Assn., Am. Assn. Child Care in Hosps., Am. Assn. Med. Colls., Assn. Faculties of Pediat. Nurse Assn./Practitioners Programs (pres. 1978-81, exec. com. 1981-84), Episc. Clergy Assn. Mich., Northside Assn. Ministries (pres. 1975, 76, 79-80), Soc. Companions of Holy Cross. Home: 4500 E Huron River Dr Ann Arbor MI 48105-9335 E-mail: stjohns@saintjohnsepiscopalhowell.org.

STRANG, STEPHEN EDWARD, editor; b. Springfield, Mo., Jan. 31, 1951; s. A. Edward and Amy Alice (Farley) S.; m. Joy Darlene Ferrell, Aug. 19, 1972; children: Cameron Edward, Chandler Stephen. BS in Journalism, U. Fla., Gainesville, 1973; LittD (hon.), Lee U., Tex., 1995. Reporter Orlando Sentinel Star, Fla., 1973-76; editor Charisma mag. Calvary Assembly, Winter Pk., Fla., 1976-81; pres. Strang Comm. Co., Lake Mary, Fla., 1981—; owner Creation House Books, 1986, Christian Retailing mag., 1986, ChrismaLife Pubs., 1990—; founder, CEO Strang Comm. Co., Lake Mary, 1979—. Founding editor Charisma mag., 1975, (in Spanish) Vida Cristiana, 1996, Ministries Today mag., 1983; founding pub. CharismaLife Learning Resources, 1990, New Man mag., 1994; Author: Old Man, New Man, 2000. Mem. steering com. N.Am. Renewal Svcs. Com., 1985—; trustee Internat. Charismatic Bible Ministries, 1986—; pres. Christian Life Missions, 1991—; bd. dirs. World Relief, 2001—. Recipient First Pl. award Nat. Writing Championship, William Randolph Hearst Found., 1973, Alumnus of Distinction award U. Fla. Coll. Journalism and Comm., 1994, Industry of Yr. award for Seminole County, Fla., Econ. Devel. Commn. of Mid-Fla., 1994; Named one of the 25 Most Influential Evangelicals in America, Time Mag., 2005. Mem. Internat. Pentecostal Press Assn., Christian Booksellers Assn., Fla. Mag. Assn. (pres. 1979-80), Evang. Christian Pubs. Assn., Evang. Press Assn. Republican. Mem. Assemblies of God. Avocations: racquetball, golf. Office: Strang Comm Co 600 Rinehart Rd Lake Mary FL 32746-4898 E-mail: info@strang.com.

STRANGE, DONALD ERNEST, healthcare company executive; b. Ann Arbor, Mich., Aug. 13, 1944; s. Carl Britton and Donna Ernestine (Tenney) Strange; m. Lyn Marie Purdy, Aug. 3, 1968 (div. Mar. 2001); children: Laurel Lyn, Chadwick Donald. BA, Mich. State U., 1966, MBA, 1968. Asst. dir. Holland (Mich.) City Hosp., 1968-72, assoc. dir., 1972-74; exec. dir. Bascom Palmer Eye Inst./Anne Bates Leach Eye Hosp., U. Miami, Fla., 1974-77; v.p. strategic planning and rsch. Hosp. Corp. Am., Nashville, 1977-80, group v.p. Boston, 1980-82, regional v.p., 1982-87; chmn., chief exec. officer HCA Healthcare Can., Toronto, 1985-87; exec. v.p. Avon Products, Inc., NYC, 1987-89; chmn. Sigecom, Ltd., Greenwich, Conn., 1989-94, U.S. HomeCare Corp., 1990-91; exec. v.p., COO, dir. EPIC Healthcare Group, Dallas, 1991-93; chmn, CEO TransCare Corp., Dallas, 1993-95; chmn., CEO First New Eng. Dental Ctrs., Inc., Boston, 1996-98; pres., CEO Behavorial Healthcare Ptnrs., Inc., Quincy, Mass., 2000; sr. v.p. Bon Secours Health Sys. Inc., Mariottsville, Md., 2001—06, COO, 2006—08. Dir. Altoona (Pa.) Regional Health Sys., 2004—08, Bon Secours Cottage Health Sys., Grosse Pointe, Mich., 2002—07. Trustee Boston Ballet, 1998—2001, chmn. bd. overseers, 1999—2001. Mem. Harvard Club (Boston), Nat. Arts Club (N.Y.). Episcopalian. Personal E-mail: don413@mac.com.

STRANGE, HENRY HAZEN, judge; b. Oleary, PEI, Can., July 26, 1939; s. Henry Hazen and Marion Yvonne (Copp) S.; m. Heather Susan Carson, July 30, 1966; children: Elizabeth Marion, Jennifer Jody. BBA, U. N.B., Fredericton, 1961, BA, 1963, B in Civil Laws, 1964. Pvt. practice barrister, solicitor, N.B., 1964-66; spl. asst. to dir. of pub. rels. Centennial Commn., Ottawa, Ont., Canada, 1966-67; crown prosecutor Dept. Justice, Fredericton, N.B., 1967-71, dir. pub. prosecutions N.B., 1971-81; judge Provincial Ct., N.B., 1981—, chief judge N.B., 1987-97. Chmn. Can. Coun. Chief Judges, 1995. Apptd. as Queen's Counsel, N.B., 1977. Avocations: salmon fishing, sports. Home: 664 Woodstock Rd Fredericton NB Canada E3B 5N7 Office: Provincial Ct PO Box 6000 Fredericton NB Canada E3B 5H1 Home Phone: 506-459-4523; Office Phone: 506-459-4523. Personal E-mail: hazen.strange@gnb.ca.

STRANGE, SHARON LOUISE, special education educator, musician; d. William Ralph and Lizzie Mae (Longware) Strange. BA in Edn., Oakwood Coll., Ala., 1977; BA in Music Edn., Andrews U., Berrien Springs, Mich., 1976, BA in Organ Performance, 1978, MA in Music Edn. & Organ Performance, 1979; student, Trinity U., DC. Cert. elem. & secondary tchr. Ind., 1979, DC, 1981, Md., 2000. Tchr. Indpls. Pub. Sch. Sys., 1979—81; tchr., registrar Seventh-Day Adventist, Oakland, Calif., 1981—82, tchr. Allegheny E. Conf., 1982—87; music, spl. edn., tech. resource tchr. DC Pub. Sch. Sys., 1988—. Tech. resource cons. DC Pub. Schs., 2000—04; presenter in field. Author: (handbook) Ring Ye Into All the World, 1986, (instrl. book) Come All, Ring All-For Handbells, 1988; composer (song book) Sing for Joy, 1990. Resident harpist Providence Hosp. & Manage Care Ctrs., DC, 2000—, Md., 2000—; music therapist nursing care & rehab. ctrs., DC, 2000—, Md., 2000—; mem. Project Linus, DC, 2004—, Md., 2004—; facilitator, instr. Sr. Connection Providence Hosp., DC, 2004—; founder, dir. Children's Harp Ensemble, DC, Adult/Youth Harp Ensemble, DC. Recipient award, Adventist Musicians Guild, 2009. Mem.: Folk Harp Soc., Am. Guild English Handbell Ringers, Am. Guild Organist, Music Educators Nat. Conf., Am. Harp Soc., Knitters Guild Am. Avocations: knitting, crocheting, harp. Home and Office: 3704 Suitland Rd SE Washington DC 20020 Home Phone: 202-365-3033; Office Phone: 202-584-3309. Personal E-mail: docstrnge@aol.com.

STRANGES, ANTHONY NICHOLAS, science history educator; b. Niagara Falls, NY, Sept. 28, 1936; s. Victor Anthony and Maria Theresa (Serianni) S.; m. Sonya Michelene Rudy, Aug. 24, 1963; children: Krista, Kara. BS in Chemistry, Niagara U., 1958, MS in Chemistry, 1964; PhD in History of Sci., U. Wis., 1977. Secondary tchr. Notre Dame Coll. Sch., Welland, Ont., Can., 1959-63, Lewiston-Porter H.S., Youngstown, N.Y., 1963-69; prof. Tex. A&M U., College Station, 1977—. Author: Electrons and Valence, 1982; contbr. articles to profl. jours. Recipient Faculty Disting. award for Tchg. Assn. of Former Students, Tex. A&M U., 1987. Mem. Am. Hist. Assn., Can. Sci. and Tech. History Assn., Soc. for the History of Tech., Hist. of Sci. Soc. Democrat. Roman Catholic. Avocations: music, collecting stamps. Home: 1205 Barak Ln Bryan TX 77802-3202 Office: Tex A&M U Dept History College Station TX 77843-4236 Office Phone: 979-845-7151. Business E-Mail: a-stranges@tamu.edu.

STRANGFELD, JOHN R., JR., diversified financial services company executive; b. Dec. 27, 1953; m. Mary Kay Strangfeld. BBA, Susquehanna U., 1975; MBA, U. Va. Various mgmt. positions. Prudential Fin., Inc., 1977—89, chmn., PRICOA Capital Group Europe London, 1989—95, sr. mng. dir., The Pvt. Asset Mgmt. Group, 1995—98; CEO, Prudential Investment Mgmt. Prudential Ins. Co. Am., 1998—2002; chmn., CEO Prudential Securities, Inc., 2000—01; exec. v.p. Prudential Fin., Inc., 2001—02, vice chmn. investments & ins. divsn., 2002—07, chmn., pres., CEO, 2008—. Bd. mgrs. Wachovia Securities Fin. Holdings, LLC, 2003—; bd. dirs. Prudential Fin., Inc., 2008—. Vice chmn. bd. trustees Susquehanna U.; pres. bd. trustees Darden Found., U. Va. Office: Prudential Financial Inc 751 Broad St Newark NJ 07102-3777*

STRANGHOENER, LARRY W., corporate financial executive; BS, St. Olaf Coll., Northfield, Minn.; MBA, Northwestern U. CFA. Investment analyst Dain Bosworth, Mpls.; with Honeywell, Inc., 1983—99; dir. investor rels., dir. mktg./internat. sales Honeywell Centra, Germany, dir. corp. fin. planning/bus. analysis, asst. treas., 1992—93; v.p. fin. Honeywell Indsl. Automation and Control, Phoenix, 1993—96; v.p. bus. devel. Honeywell, Inc., Mpls., 1996—97, v.p., CFO, 1997-99; exec. v.p., CFO Techies.com, Edina, Minn., 2000—01, Thrivent Financial for Lutherans, Mpls., 2001—04, Mosaic Co., Plymouth, Minn., 2004—. Office: Mosaic Co Atria Corp Ctr 3033 Campus Dr Plymouth MN 55441

STRANGMAN, THOMAS, aerospace engineer; BS, U. Calif., Berkeley, 1968; MS, U. Conn., Storrs, 1971, PhD, 1978. Sr. materials engr. Pratt & Whitney, East Hartford, Conn., 1968—78; sr. prin. engr. Honeywell, Phoenix, 1978—. Author: (science fiction novel) Millennia Debt. Mem.: ASME, ASM, Am. Ceramic Soc. Achievements include invention of thermal barrier coatings for aircraft engines; development of environmental life prediction methods for metallic turbine airfoil coatings.

STRANIERE, ROBERT A., lawyer, restaurant owner; b. NYC, Mar. 28, 1941; m. Ruth Kaner; children: Geoffry, Pamela, Brett, Kenneth. BA cum laude, Wagner Coll., Staten Island, NY, 1962; JD, NYU, NYC, 1965, LLM, 1969. Sr. ptnr. Staniere Law Firm; mem. NY State Assembly, 1981—2005, asst. minority leader, 1995—2004, mem. ways and means com., environ. conservation com., rules com.; pvt. practice atty. NYC, 2005—; founder The New York City Hot Dog Co., NYC, 2005—. Advisor, cons. Internat. Rep. Inst., Macedonia, Romania; mem. exec. bd. Coun. State Govt., chmn. internat. com.; mem. exec. bd. Ea. Regional Coun. State Govts., Am. Legis. Exch.; active Nat. Coun. State Legislators; sr. advisor Ea. Trade Coun. Eagle scout Boy Scouts Am. Troop 18. Tank officer USAR. Recipient Torch of Liberty award, Anti-Defamation League of B'nai B'rith, Negev award, Alumni Achievement award, Wagner Coll., NY Ct. Officers Assn. award, Cmty. Svc. award, Asian-Am. Coalition SI; named Man of Yr., A Very Spl. Pl. Office: The New York City Hot Dog Co 105 Chambers St New York NY 10007

STRANTZ, NANCY JEAN, law educator, consultant; b. Calgary, Alta., Can., 1958; 1 child. LLB, U. Alta., 1981; JD, South Tex. Coll. Law, Houston, 1990; BA in Social Scis., U. N.D., Grand Forks, 1997. Bar: Alta. 1982. Articling lawyer Carma Developers Ltd., Calgary, 1981-82; barrister and solicitor Stewart & Stewart, Calgary, 1982-83; rsch. asst., author Can. Inst. Resources Law, U. Calgary, 1984-85; corp. counsel Chevron Can. Resources, 1985-90, Gulf Can. Resources, 1991-94, 98; asst. prof. U. N.D. Sch. Law, Grand Forks, 1994-97; contracts adminstr. Longview Fibre Co., 2005—07. Land and legal cons. N.J. Strantz Cons., Calgary, 1991-94, 1998, 2007-; adj. faculty U. Calgary, Mt. Royal Coll., So. Alta Inst. Tech., Calgary, 1991-94. Co-author: A Reference Guide to Hardrock Mining in Canada; contbr. articles to profl. jours. Trustee Rocky Mountain Mineral Law Found., 1994-97. Pvt. Can. Dept. Nat. Def., Naval Res., 1975. Recipient award and grants. Mem. Law Soc. Alta. Avocation: swimming.

STRASBAUGH, WAYNE RALPH, lawyer; b. Lancaster, Pa., July 20, 1948; s. Wayne Veily and Jane Irene (Marzolf) S.; m. Carol Lynne Taylor, June 8, 1974; children: Susan, Wayne T., Elizabeth. AB summa cum laude, Bowdoin Coll., 1970; AM in History, Harvard U., 1971, PhD in History, 1976, JD cum laude, 1979. Bar: Ohio 1979, Pa. 1983, U.S. Tax Ct. 1980, U.S. Ct. Fed. Claims 1980, U.S. Ct. Appeals (fed. cir.) 1982, U.S. Dist. Ct. (no. dist.) Ohio 1979, U.S. Dist. Ct. (ea. dist.) Pa. 1983. Assoc. Jones Day Reavis & Pogue, Cleve., 1979-82, Morgan Lewis & Bockius, Phila., 1982-84, Ballard Spahr Andrews & Ingersoll, LLP, Phila., 1984-88, ptnr., 1988—, chmn. tax group, 2001—. Mem. ABA (tax sect., chmn. com. 1992-94, 2007-09), Am. Coll. Tax Counsel (regent 2003-09)., Phila. Bar Assn. (tax sect., chmn. fed. tax com. 1992, coun. mem. 1995, sec.-treas. 1996, vice-chmn. 1997-98, chmn. 1999-2000). Episcopalian. Office: Ballard Spahr Andrews & Ingersoll LLP 1735 Market St Ste 5100 Philadelphia PA 19103-7599

STRASBURG, STEPHEN, professional baseball player; b. San Diego, July 20, 1988; s. Jim Strasburg and Kathleen Swett. Student in pub. adminstrn., San Diego State U., 2006—09. Pitcher Washington Nationals, 2009—. Pitcher, Team USA Haarlem Baseball Week Tournament, Netherlands, 2008, Internat. Univ. Sports Fedn. World Collegiate Championships, Czech Republic, 2008, Summer Olympic Games, Beijing, 2008. Recipient Bronze medal, baseball, Summer Olympic Games, Beijing, 2008, Golden Spikes award, USA Baseball, 2009; named 1st Team Consensus All-Am., 2008, Pitcher of Yr., Mountain West Conf., 2008. Achievements include being the first overall pick in Major League Baseball's amateur draft, 2009. Office: Washington Nationals 1500 S Capitol St SE Washington DC 20003*

STRASNICK, BARRY, otolaryngologist, health facility administrator, educator; b. Malden, Mass., Nov. 16, 1958; m. Victoria S. Strasnick; children: Evan, Ryan. BA in Biology summa cum laude, Boston U., 1980; MD, Baylor U., 1985. Diplomate Am. Bd. Otolaryngology. Intern Baylor Coll. Medicine, Houston, 1985—86, resident, 1986—87, UCLA Sch. Medicine, 1987—90; clin. prof. Vanderbilt U., 1991—92; from asst. prof. to assoc. prof. Ea. Va. Med. Sch., Norfolk, 1993—99, prof., 2000—, chmn., 1999—; dir. Hearing & Balance Ctr. DePaul Med. Ctr., Norfolk, 1993—; dir. pediatric otology divsn. Children's Hosp. King's Daus., Norfolk, 1993—. Co-author: (book) English Textbook of Otolaryngology, 1994, Ololaryngology, 1997, Pediatric Otolaryngology - H/N Surgery, 1998, The Ear: A Textbook of Otology, 2000. Chmn. Va. State Adv. Commn. Universal Newborn Hearing Screening, Richmond, 1998—; bd. dirs. Ear Ctr., Norfolk, 2000—. Fellow, Head/neck Surgery Found., 1997—. Fellow: Am. Acad. Otolaryngology; mem.: Norfolk Acad. Medicine, Tidewater Otolaryngology & Ophthalmology Soc., Va. Soc. Otolaryngologists (bd. dirs. 1997—), Va. Med. Soc. (Dr. Clarence A. Holland award 2001), Soc. Univ. Otolaryngologist. Office: Ea Va Med Sch 600 Gresnam Dr 1100 Norfolk VA 23507 Office Phone: 757-388-6200. Business E-Mail: strasnb@evms.edu.

STRASSBERG, BARBARA ESTHER, pediatrician, educator; b. Monticello, NY, 1946; d. Irving Strassberg; m. Harold Enten, Nov. 18, 1984. Grad. magna cum laude, Bklyn. Coll.; grad. cum laude, Upstate Med. Coll.; MD in Edn., SUNY Syracuse, 1981. Cert. in pediat. Am. Bd. Med. Specialties, 1986. Intern in pediat. NY Presbyn. Hosp., 1981—82, resident, 1982—84, St. Lukes Roosevelt Hosp., attending pediatrician; assoc. prof. clinical pediat. Columbia U. Coll. Physicians and Surgeons;

pediatrician Riverdale Pediat., NY. Named to America's Top Doctors, 2006. Office: Riverdale Pediat 2600 Netherland Ave Bronx NY 10463 Office Phone: 718-796-3580. Office Fax: 718-796-3987.

STRASSBURGER, JOHN ROBERT, academic administrator; b. Sheboygan, Wis., Apr. 6, 1942; s. J. Robert and Elizabeth (Mathewson) S.; m. Gertrude Hunter Mackie, Aug. 24, 1968; children: Sarah Electa, Gertrude Hunter. BA, Bates, 1964; Honours degree, Cambridge U., Eng., 1966; PhD, Princeton U., 1976. Faculty Hiram (Ohio) Coll., 1970-82; program officer NEH, Washington, 1982-84; prof. history, exec. v.p., dean Coll., Knox Coll., Galesburg, Ill., 1984-94; pres. Ursinus Coll., Collegeville, Pa., 1995—; CEO Philip & Muriel Berman Mus. Art at Ursinus Coll., Collegeville, Pa. Mem. commn. govt. rels. Am. Coun. Edn., 1997—. Contbr. articles to profl. jours. Bd. trustees Perkiomen Sch., 1997—. Mem. Am. Conf. Acad. Deans (chair 1990-91), Sunday Breakfast Club (Phila.). Office: Ursinus Coll Office of Pres PO Box 1000 Collegeville PA 19426-1000

STRASSER, GABOR, management consultant; b. Budapest, Hungary, May 22, 1929; s. Rezso and Theresa (Seiler) S.; m. Linda Casselman Pemble, Aug. 16, 1958 (div. 1976); children: Claire Margaret, Andrew John; m. Joka Verhoeff, Feb. 2, 1978; children: Steven Verhoeff, Tessa Christina. BCE, City Coll. N.Y., 1954; MS, U. Buffalo, 1959; PMD, Harvard, 1968; MDiv, Va. Theol. Sem., 1992. Research engr. Bell Aircraft Co., Buffalo, 1956-61; project leader Boeing Airplane Co., Seattle, 1961-62; dept. head Mitre Corp., Bedford, Mass., Washington, 1962-68; v.p. Urban Inst., Washington, 1968-69; tech. asst. to pres.'s sci. adviser White House, 1969-71, exec. sec. pres.'s sci. and tech. policy panel, 1970-71; dir. planning Battelle Meml. Inst., Columbus, Ohio, 1971-73; pres. Strasser Assocs., Inc., Washington, 1973-92. Author, editor: Science and Technology Policies-Yesterday, Today, Tomorrow, 1973; Contbr. articles to profl. jours. and theol. lit. Served to 1st lt., C.E. USAR. Recipient 1st nat. award Gravity Research Found., 1952 Home: 18525 Bear Creek Terrace Leesburg VA 20176-7424 Personal E-mail: gnmis@yahoo.com.

STRASSER, KURT ALBERT, law educator, researcher, author; b. Oak Ridge, Tenn., July 20, 1947; s. George Albert and Doris Maupin (Adams) S.; m. Jane Wyatt, Aug. 23, 1969; 1 child, Julia Wyatt. BA, Vanderbilt U., 1969, JD, 1972; LLM, Columbia U., 1979, JSD, 1986. Bar: Tenn. 1972, U.S. Dist. Ct. (mid. dist.) Tenn. 1972, Conn. 1986. Rsch. asst. Inst. Govt, U. NC, Chapel Hill, NC, 1971; assoc. Neal & Harwell, Nashville, 1972-74; asst. prof. Mercer U. Law Sch., Macon, Ga., 1974—77, assoc. prof., 1977—80, prof., 1980—81, U. Conn. Law Sch., Hartford, 1981—98, assoc. dean acad. affairs, 1996—99, Phillip I. Blumberg Prof. Law, 1999—, interim dean, 2006—07. Vis. prof. Exeter U., Exeter, England, 1984, 1991, Free U. of Berlin, 2003; Gilhuis prof., Tilburg U., 2008 Co-auuthor: Regulating Utilities with Management Incentives, 1989, Blumberg On Corporate Groups, 2nd edit.,Aspen, 2005. Mem. ABA, Environ. Law Inst. Democrat. Avocation: sailing. Home: 93 State St Wethersfield CT 06109-1851 Office: University Connecticut Law School 65 Elizabeth St Hartford CT 06105-2290 E-mail: kurt.strasser@law.ucoun.edu.*

STRASSER, RUDOLF, law educator; b. Steyr, Austria, Feb. 9, 1923; s. Josef and Rosa Strasser; m. Margarethe Strasser; children: Helmuth, Klaus; m. 2d. Ilse Prischl, Dec. 23, 1969; 1 child, Thomas. LLD, U. Graz; LLD (hon.), U. Salzburg, 1988. Ofcl., dir. Bd. of Workers and Staff, Linz, Austria, 1949-67; mgr. Legal Dept. and Child Care Dept., Linz, 1949-67; adj. prof. law faculty U. Vienna, 1964; prof. law Acad. Soc. and Econ. Scis., Linz, 1965-75, Johannes-Kepler U., Linz, 1975-93. Bd. dirs. Voest-Alpine AG, Linz, 1959—2001; hon. pres. bd. dirs. Vost-Alpine Stahl AG, Linz, 2001—; bd. dirs. Bauhutte Leitl GesmbH, Linz; pres. bd. dirs. Inst. for Labor Law and Social Law, Linz; cons. Wissenschaft, Forschung und Kunst, Vienna, 1975—88; mgr. Rsch. Inst. for Univ. Law, Linz, 1980—2000, Inst. for Bus. Partnerships, Linz, 1973—; dir. steering adv. com. Inst. for Savs. Banks, Linz, 1975—96; dir. Inst. for Communal Scis., Linz, 1970—87. Author: Die Betriebsratswahl, 1953, Die Betriebsvereinbarung n. osterr.udt. Recht, 1957, Der Immaterielle Schaden im osterr. Recht, 1964, Kollektivvertrag und Verfass, 1964, Die Beendigung d. Ges.n. burgerl. Recht, 1969, Arbeitsrecht II, 1976, 2004, Betriebspension und Gleischbehandlung, 1991, Kommentar Ablien G, 2001, Kommentar Ablien verlen G, 2002; co-author: Komm.z.Betr.rategesetz, 1961, Die Universitat als auton. Lehr-u., Forsch.unternehmen, 1968, Der Arbeitskampf, 1972, Kurzkomm.z.Arb.verfass.gesetz, 1974, Osterr.Hochschulr., 1986, Labor-Law and Industrial Relations in Austria, 1992, Kommentar z. AktienG., 1993; contbr. articles to jours. and newspapers. Mem. Social Dem. Party. Roman Catholic. Avocations: skiing, golf. Home: Hebenstreitrasse 11 A 4020 Linz Austria Office: Johannes-Kepler U Altenbergerstrasse 69 4040 Linz Austria Home Phone: 2468257; Office Phone: 0043732 2468-8270.

STRASSER, WILLIAM CARL, JR., retired college president, educator; b. Washington, Feb. 4, 1930; s. William Carl and Minnie Elizabeth (Saxton) S.; m. Jeanne Carol Peake, Sept. 17, 1954 (div.); children: Sheryl Lynn, Keith Edward, Robert Carl; m. Jane Ann Gunn, Nov. 25, 1978. BA with first honors, U. Md., 1952, MA, 1954; PhD, 1961; Carnegie postdoctoral fellow in coll. adminstrn, U. Mich., 1961-62. High sch. tchr., Cin. and Balt., 1955-57; v.p. W.C. Strasser Co., Inc., 1957-59; pub. info. specialist Balt. County (Md.) Pub. Schs., 1960-61; asst. dean, asst. prof. Sch. Edn., State U. N.Y. at Buffalo, 1962-64; rsch. asst. U.S. Office Edn., 1959-60, specialist ednl. adminstrn., 1964-65; asst. dir. profl. personnel Montgomery County (Md.) Pub. Schs., 1965-66; acting pres., exec. dean Montgomery Community Coll., Rockville, Md., 1966-67, pres., 1967-79, prof., 1978-86, pres. emeritus, prof. emeritus, 1986—. Vis. scholar U. Calif., Berkeley, 1977-79; vice pres. Md. Council Community Coll. Presidents, 1971-72, 75-77; pres., v.p. Jr. Coll. Council Middle Atlantic States, 1969-72; founder Council Chief Exec. Adminstrs., 1973-75; mem. exec. com. Pres.'s Acad., 1975-77; mem. Gov.'s Adv. Council, Md. Higher Edn. Facilities, 1977-79; Del. UNESCO Conf. on Africa, 1961; participant 50th Anniversary Conf. Fgn. Policy Assn. U.S., 1968; mem. Congl. Internship Adv. Com., 1969-78; chmn. Montgomery County Community White Ho. Conf. on Aging, 1971; cons. Middle States Assn. Colls. and Secondary Schs., 1975— Author: For The Community: Continuing General Education, 1979, A College For a Community, 1988, Strasser-Moxley: An American Family and Its Ancestors, 1997, Saxton-Rea: An American Family and Its Ancestors, 1999; co-author: Dual Enrollment in Public and Non-Public Schools, 1965; contbr. poetry and articles to jours. Served with AUS, 1954-55. Recipient Gov. Md. Cert. Disting. Citizenship, 1979; Danforth Found. study grantee, 1972; Ford Found. grantee, 1974-75; Silver medallion for Outstanding Service, Bd. Trustees of Montgomery Coll., 1986, Alumni award as Oustanding Leader in Pub. Edn., U. Md., 2005, Disting. Alumnus, Coll. Edn. U. Md., 2006. Mem. Am. Assn. Jr. Colls. (chmn. nat. commn. on instrn. 1969-71, mem. nat. assembly 1973, founder Pres. Acad. 1973-77), AAUP, Am. Assn. Higher Edn., Am. Mgmt. Assns., Nat. Soc. Sons and Daus. of the Pilgrims, Montgomery County C. of C. (Disting. Svc. award 1979), Rotary, Phi Kappa Phi, Omicron Delta Kappa, Pi Delta Epsilon, Phi Eta Sigma, Phi Delta Kappa. Democrat. Unitarian-Universalist. Home: 946 Comstock Dr Shepherdstown WV 25443-9570

STRASSFIELD, CHRISTINA MOSSAIDES, museum director, chief curator; d. Paul and Melika Mossaides; m. Paul Joseph Strassfield, July 9, 1983; children: Zoe Paula, Joseph Daniel, Peter Mossaides. BA with honors in Art History and Anthropology, CUNY, 1980; MA, Queens Coll., CUNY, Flushing, 1985. Libr. Photography and Slide Libr., Met. Mus. Art, 1985—87; assoc. curator, registrar Guild Hall Mus., East Hampton, NY, 1987—90, curator, 1990—96, 2002—; freelance art cons./curator, 1996—2002. Adj. assoc. prof. art history Southampton Coll. LI Univ., 1989—93. Art com. bd. mem. LongHouse Found., East Hampton. Mem.: ArtTable, LI Mus. Assn. (mem. exec. bd. 1990), Visual Resources Assn., Coll. Art Assn., Am. Assn. Mus. Office: Guild Hall Museum 158 Main St East Hampton NY 11937 Office Fax: 631-324-2722. Business E-Mail: museum@guildhall.org.

STRASSLER, MARC A., lawyer, retail executive; b. 1948; m. Meryl Strassler. BA, Bklyn. Coll., CUNY; JD, George Washington U. Bar: 1973. Joined Pathmark Stores Inc., Carteret, NJ, 1974, v.p., gen. counsel, sec., sr. v.p., gen. counsel, sec., 1998—2007; exec. v.p., gen. counsel, sec. Rite Aid Corp., 2009—. Office: Rite Aid Corp 30 Hunter Lane Camp Hill PA 17001 Office Phone: 732-499-3000.*

STRASSMANN, JOAN ELIZABETH, evolutionary biologist; b. Washington, May 6, 1953; d. Wolfgang Paul and Elizabeth Marsh (Fanck) S.; m. David Charles Queller, Jan. 2, 1988; children: Anna Strassmann Mueller, Daniel Strassmann Mueller, Philip Strassmann Queller. BS with distinction and honors in Zoology, U. Mich., 1974; PhD, U. Tex., Austin, 1979. NSF postdoctoral fellow U. Tex., Austin, 1979—80; asst. prof., biology dept. Rice U., Houston, 1980-85, assoc. prof., 1985-93, prof., 1993—, chair, ecology and evolutionary biology dept., 2003—, Harry C. & Olga K. Wiess prof. ecology and evolutionary biology, 2005—. Field experience U. Mich. Biol. Station, 1972—73, Costa Rica, 1974, Tex., 1976—, Venezuela, 1988—2001, Brazil, 1996—2000, Italy, 1997—, So. Appalachians, 2000—; spkr. in field. Contbr. articles to Science, Nature; editl. bd. mem. Animal Behavior, 1995-97, Insectes Sociaux, 2000-2006, American Naturalist, 2000-03, Ecology Letters, 2004-07, BMC Evolutionary Biology, 2005-, Journal Evolutionary Biology, 2005-, Ecology, Ethology, and Evolution 2006-John Simon Guggenheim Meml. Fellow, 2004. Fellow: AAAS, Animal Behavior Soc., Am. Acad. Arts & Scis.; mem.: Cambridge Entomological Soc., Houston Philos. Soc., Nat. Assn. Biology Teachers, Nat. Ctr. for Sci. Edn., Internat. Soc. Hymenopterists, Internat. Union for the Study Social Insects (pres., N.Am. sect. 2001), Am. Soc. Microbiologists, Internat. Soc. for Behavioral Ecology, Soc. for the Study Evolution (councilor 2002—04), Am. Soc. Naturalists, Associazione Italiana per to Studio degli Artopodi Sociali e Presociali (hon.), Phi Kappa Phi, Sigma XI. Achievements include research in society of temperate and tropical wasps. Office: Rice U Dept Ecology and Evolutionary Biology MS 170 133E Anderson Biology Lab 6100 Main St Houston TX 77005-1892 Office Phone: 713-348-4922. Office Fax: 713-348-5232. Business E-Mail: strassm@rice.edu.

STRASSNER, HOWARD TAFT, JR., obstetrician, educator; b. Tulsa, Okla., Dec. 2, 1948; BA in Biochemistry, U. Chgo., 1970, MD, 1974. Diplomate Am. Bd. Ob-gyn. Intern Columbia Presbyn. Med. Ctr., NYC, 1974, resident ob-gyn., 1974—78; fellow maternal fetal medicine L.A. County-U. So. Calif. Med. Ctr., 1978—80; physician, dir. sect. maternal fetal medicine Rush U. Med. Ctr., Chgo., 1980—, co-dir. Rush Perinatal Ctr. John M. Simpson prof., chmn. Rush U. Med. Ctr., Chgo. Office: Rush Med Ctr 1653 W Congress Pkwy Chicago IL 60612 Office Phone: 312-942-6678. Business E-Mail: howard.t.strassner@rush.edu.

STRATEN, ROLAND, retired protective services company executive; b. NYC, 1941; m. Susan Straten, 1969; 3 children. BS in Mech. Engring., Duke U., Durham, NC; MBA, Dartmouth Coll. Tuck Sch. Bus., Hanover, NH. Lic. profl engr., elec. contractor; cert. fire protection contractor. Sales engr. Foxboro Corp., NYC; fin. assoc. Union Camp Corp., Wayne, NJ; pres., CEO Associated Fire Protection, Paterson, NJ, 1971—2007; ret., 2007. Officer Fire Protection Engrs., NJ Chpt.; pres. NJ Assn. Fire Equipment Distributors; commr. NJ Fire Commn.; mem. tech. com. Fires Suppressions System Assn.; bd. mem. NJ Fire Equipment Adv. Coun., NJ Hotel and Multiple Dwelling Health and Safety Bd. Scoutmaster Boy Scout Troop 13; mem. Paterson Edn. Fund; chmn. Paterson C. of C., Paterson Econ. Devel. Corp., Meml. Day Nursery; vice-chmn. Montclair Redevel. Agency. Lt. USN, USS PYRO, Vietnam. Mem.: Paterson Rotary Club. Republican. Mailing: PO Box 43254 Montclair NJ 07043 Office Phone: 973-333-5415. Business E-Mail: RStraten@RolandStraten.com.

STRATHAIRN, DAVID, actor; b. San Francisco, Calif., Jan. 26, 1949; m. Logan Goodman; 2 children. Attended, Williams Coll., Ringling Bros. Clown Coll. Numerous stage appearances including: I'm Not Rappaport, Salonika, A Lie of the Mind, The Birthday Party, Danton's Death, Mountain Language, L'Atelier, A Moon for the Misbegotten, Temptation, Conversations in Tusculum, 2008; Actor (films) Return of the Secaucus Seven, 1980, Lovesick, 1983, Silkwood, 1983, The Brother From Another Planet, 1984, Iceman, 1984, Enormous Changes at the Last Minute, 1985, When Nature Calls, 1985, At Close Range, 1986, Matewan, 1987, Eight Men Out, 1988, Stars and Bars, 1988, Dominick and Eugene, 1988, Call Me, 1988, The Feud, 1989, Memphis Belle, 1990, City of Hope, 1991, Big Girls Don't Cry...They Get Even, 1992, Bob Roberts, 1992, Shadows and Fog, 1992, A League of Their Own, 1992, Sneakers, 1992, Passion Fish, 1992, April One, 1993, Lost in Yonkers, 1993, The Firm, 1993, A Dangerous Woman, 1993, The River Wild, 1994, Dolores Claiborne, 1995, Losing Isaiah, 1995, Home for the Holidays, 1995, Mother Night, 1996, Beyond the Call, 1996, Song of Hiawatha, 1997, The Climb, 1997, Bad Manners, 1997, L.A. Confidential, 1997, With Friends Like These..., 1998, Simon Birch, 1998, Meschugge, 1998, A Small Miracle, 1998, A Midsummer Night's Dream, 1999, A Map of the World, 1999, Limbo, 1999, Harrison's Flowers, 2000, A Good Baby, 2000, The Victim, 2001, Ball in the House, 2001, Speakeasy, 2002, Blue Car, 2002, The Root, 2003, Twisted, 2004, Heavens Fall, 2005, Missing in America, 2005, Good Night, and Good Luck (Coppa Volpi award for Best Actor, Venice Film Festival), 2005, The Notorious Bettie Page, 2005, Steel Toes, 2006, The Shovel, 2006, Heavens Fall, 2006, We Are Marshall, 2006, Matters of Life and Death, 2007, Fracture, 2007, The Bourne Ultimatum, 2007, My Blueberry Nights, 2007, The Spiderwick Chronicles, 2008, Cold Souls, 2009; (TV films) Broken Vows, 1985, The Feud, 1989, Wiseguy, 1990, Heat Wave, 1990, Judgment, 1990, Without Warning: The James Brady Story, 1991, Lethal Innocence, 1991, O Pioneers!, 1992, The American Clock, 1993, Beyond the Call, 1996, In the Gloaming, 1997, Evidence of Blood, 1998, Freedom Song, 2000, The Miracle Worker, 2000, Lathe of Heaven, 2002, Master Spy: The Robert Hanssen Story, 2002, Paradise, 2004; (TV series) Another World, 1987, The Days and Nights of Molly Dodd, 1988-90, Big Apple, 2001; (TV appearances) Miami Vice, 1985, Spense: For Hire, 1987, The Equalizer, 1988, Day One, 1989, Wiseguy, 1990, Big Apple, 2001, The Sopranos, 2004

STRATHE, MARLENE I., academic administrator; BS, Iowa State U., MS in Counseling Psychology, PhD in Ednl. Rsch. and Measurement; EdS in Ednl. Psychology, U. No. Iowa, 1973. Faculty mem., assoc. dean Coll. Edn., asst. v.p. academic affairs U. No. Iowa; provost U. ND, 1993—98; provost, v.p. academic affairs U. No. Colo., 1998—2003; provost, sr. v.p. Okla. State U., Stillwater, 2003—, interim sys. CEO, pres., 2007—08. Exec. com. mem. Higher Learning Commn. Bd. Trustees. Contbr. articles to profl. jours. Recipient Fulbright Award, 1995, Virgil Lagomarcino Award for Excellence in Edn., Iowa State U. Office: Okla State U 101 Whitehurst Stillwater OK 74078 Office Phone: 405-744-5627. E-mail: marlene.strathe@okstate.edu.

STRATHERN, JEFFREY N., medical researcher; PhD, U. Oreg., 1977. Sr. staff mem. Yeast Genetics Lab. Cold Spring Harbor Lab.; joined ABL-Basic Rsch. Program Nat. Cancer Inst., NIH, Frederick, 1984, joined Divsn. Basic Sciences (now Ctr. Cancer Rsch.), 1999, now chief Gene Regulation and Chromosome Biology Lab., Ctr. Cancer Rsch., also head Genome Recombination and Regulation Sect. Office: Gene Regulation and Chromosome Biology Lab Nat Cancer Inst at Frederick PO Box B Bldg 539 Rm 152 Frederick MD 21701-1201 Office Phone: 301-846-1274. Office Fax: 301-846-6911. E-mail: strather@mail.ncifcrf.gov, strathej@mail.nih.gov.*

STRATIGOS, WILLIAM NARGE, computer company executive; b. Huntington, NY, Mar. 14, 1946; s. Narge G. and Portia R. (Kleros) Stratigos; m. Deborah Feller, Jan. 4, 1981; children: Stephanie, Elena. BA in Biology cum laude, NYU, 1972, DDS, 1977. Lic. dentist N.Y. Mgr. div. Med. Ctr. NYU, NYC, 1966-74; mng. ptnr., dentist Stratigos et al, NYC, 1978-88; pres. Sigma Imaging Sys. Inc., NYC, 1988-95; also bd. dirs. Sigma Imaging Sys., Inc., NYC; v.p. Wang Software, N.Y., Inc., NYC, 1995-97, Eastman Software, Inc., NYC, 1997; v.p., bd. dirs. R2K, Inc., NYC, 1997—; pres. Comfidex Corp., NYC, 1998—. Bd. dirs. Animal Med. Ctr., 1997—2007. Author: (book) Hot Spot, 1993. Fellow: NYU Acad. Oral Rehab.; mem.: First Dist. Dental Soc., Dental Soc. State of N.Y., Assn. Image & Info. Mgmt. Internat. (bd. dirs., treas. exec. com., chmn. accreditation com.), Omicron Kappa Upsilon. Greek Orthodox. Achievements include patents in field. Avocations: writing, chess, bowling. Office: Comfidex Corp 304 E Main St Centerport NY 11721 Personal E-mail: wstratigos@aol.com.

STRATON, JOHN CHARLES, JR., investment banker; b. Warwick, NY, Apr. 18, 1932; s. John Charles and Helen (Sanford) S.; m. Sally M. Strawhand (div. Mar. 1970); children: John Charles III, Sara; m. Marion S. Holder, Feb. 18, 1974 (div. Mar. 1997); 1 child, Ashley Holder Straton; m. Donna S. DeCoursey, June 24, 1998. BA, U. Va., 1954. With Jas. H. Oliphant and Co., NYC, 1956—, gen. ptnr., 1962—, 1st v.p., 1972-75; v.p. Spencer Trask & Co., Inc., NYC, 1975-77, Hornblower, Weeks, Noyes & Trask, NYC, 1977-78, Loeb Rhoades, Hornblower & Co., 1978-79, Shearson Loeb Rhoades, 1979-81; v.p., fin. cons. Shearson Lehman Bros., NYC, 1981-93; sr. v.p. Smith Barney, NYC, 1993—, Saloman Smith Barney, NYC, 1997—, Smith Barney, NYC, 2004—09. Assessor Village of Tuxedo Park, N.Y., 1963-70, Morgan Stanley Smith Barney, 2009. Vestryman St. Mary's, Tuxedo, N.Y. Served to maj. AUS, 1954-56; ret. Mem. U. Va. Alumni Assn. N.Y. (pres., treas. 1973-90), Mil. Order Fgn. Wars (comdr. 1981-86, treas. 1986—), Pilgrims of U.S., Am. Legion, Tuxedo Park Club, Sigma Phi Epsilon. Home: 2 Ledge Rd Tuxedo Park NY 10987 Office: 450 Lexington Ave New York NY 10017

STRATT, RICHARD MARK, chemistry researcher, educator; b. Phila., Feb. 21, 1954; s. Stanford Lloyd and Florence Clair (Sussman) S. SB in Chemistry, MIT, 1975; PhD, U. Calif., Berkeley, 1979. Postdoctoral rsch. assoc. U. Ill., Champaign, 1979-80; NSF postdoctoral rsch. assoc., 1980; asst. prof. chemistry Brown U., Providence, 1981-85, assoc. prof., 1986-88, prof., 1988—, dept. chair, 1996—99, Harrison S. Kravis prof., 1999—2000, Newport Rogers prof. chemistry, 2004—, prof. physics, 2006—. Mem. editl. bd. Jour. Chem. Physics, 2002-04, Molecular Physics, 2003-06; mem. adv. bd. Jour. Phys. Chemistry, 1999-07; contbr. articles to profl. jours. Alfred P. Sloan fellow, 1985-89; Fulbright scholar Oxford U., 1991-92. Fellow Am. Phys. Soc.; mem. Am. Chem. Soc. (chmn.-elect theoretical chem. subdivsn. 1997-98, chair 1998-99, program chair phys. chem. divsn. 2000-01, chair 2001-02), Sigma Xi, Phi Lambda Upsilon. Office: Brown U Dept Chemistry Providence RI 02912-0001 Office Phone: 401-863-3418. Business E-Mail: Richard_Stratt@brown.edu.

STRATTON, EVELYN LUNDBERG, state supreme court justice; b. Bangkok, Feb. 25, 1953; came to US, 1971 (parents Am. citizens); d. Elmer John and Corrine Sylvia (Henricksen) Sahlberg; m. John A. Lundberg III; children: Luke Andrew, Tyler John. Student, LeTourneau Coll., Longview, Tex.; AA, U. Fla., 1973; BA, U. Akron, Ohio, 1976; JD, Ohio State U., 1978. Bar: Ohio 1979, US Dist. Ct. (so. dist.) Ohio 1979, US Ct. Appeals (6th cir.) 1983. Assoc. Hamilton, Kramer, Myers & Cheek, Columbus, Ohio, 1979-85; ptnr. Wesp, Osterkamp & Stratton, 1985-88; judge Franklin County Ct. Common Pleas, 1989-96; justice Ohio Supreme Ct., Columbus, 1996—. Vis. prof. Nat. Jud. Coll., Reno, 1997—. Contbr. articles to profl. jours. Trustee Ohio affiliate Nat. Soc. to Prevent Blindness, 1989—, bd. dirs., trustee Columbus Coun. World Affairs, 1990-99, chmn. bd. dirs., 1999—; bd. dirs., trustee Dave Thomas Adoption Found., 1996—, ArChSafe Found., 1997—; mem. women's bd. Zephyrus League Cen. Ohio Lung Assn., 1989—; mem. Alliance Women Cmty. Corrections, 1993—. Recipient Svc. commendation, Ohio House of Reps., 1984, Scholar of Life award, St. Joseph's Orphanage, 1998, Ellis Island Medal of Honor, NYC, 2008. Mem. ABA, ATLA, Columbus Bar Assn. (bd. govs. 1984-88, 90—, lectr.), Ohio Bar Assn. (jud. adminstrv. and legal reform com., coun. dels. 1992-96, Ohio Cmty. Corrections Orgn. (trustee 1995—), Columbus Bar Found. (trustee 1986-91, officer, sec. 1986-87, v.p. 1987-88), Am. Inns of Ct., Women Lawyers Franklin County, Phi Alpha Delta (pres. 1982-83). Office: Ohio Supreme Ct 65 S Front St Columbus OH 43215*

STRATTON, JOHN ALFRED, electrical engineer, educator; b. Rochester, NY, Sept. 12, 1941; s. Burton Elbridge and Alice Adele (Howie) Stratton; m. Lois Averett; children: Thomas C., Linda S. Palmer, Ann-Marie Giannosa. AAS, Rochester Inst. Technology, 1962, BS, 1964; MSEE, Rensselaer Poly. Inst., Troy, NY, 1966. Profl. engr. Sys. planning engr. NY State Elec. & Gas, Binghamton, 1966—69; asst. prof. Alfred State Coll., NY, 1969—71; from prof. elec. engring. tech. to chair dept., assoc. dean Rochester Inst. Tech., 1971—99, chair mfg. & mech. engring. technology, pckg. sci., 1999—2003, prof. elec./mech. engring., 2003—08, prof. emeritus, 2008. Cons. in field. Past pres. Classis Rochester Reformed Ch. Am., sr. mem. Mem. IEEE (sr.), Inst. Power Engring. Soc., Am. Soc. Engring. Edn. (chair zone 1), ABET TAC Commns. Avocation: riding trains. Home: 43 Queensway Rd Rochester NY 14623-4627 Home Phone: 585-334-7315. Business E-Mail: jasite@rit.edu.

STRATTON, JOHN G., telecommunications industry executive, marketing professional; V.p. merchandising Jersey Camera; dir. retail sales & ops., v.p. mktg., pres. Phila. region Bell Atlantic Mobile, 1993—2000; pres. NW area Verizon Wireless, 2000—01, v.p., chief mktg. officer,

2001—07; exec. v.p., chief mktg. officer Verizon Comm., NYC, 2007—. Named a Power Player, Advt. Age, 2008. Office: Verizon Comm 1095 Ave of the Americas New York NY 10036*

STRATTON, MARGARET ANNE, minister; b. Concordia, Kans., Oct. 10, 1948; d. Charles Edward and Marie Teresa Kier; m. Mick Stratton, June 9, 1973; children: James, Grace. BS Home Econs., Kans. State U., 1973; M Theology, Caribbean Comty. Ministerial Acad., Orlando, Fla., 1994; MDiv, So. Meth. U., 2000. Ordained elder United Meth. Ch., 2003. Pastor United Meth. Diamond Hill Parish and Mission, Ft. Worth, 2000—06, Robinson Dr. United Meth. Ch., Waco, Tex., 2006—. Chmn. Task Force on Hunger, Ctrl. Tex. Conf.; mem. Hispanic com.; mem. Confessing Movement United Meth. Ch.; clergy leadership initiative Tex. Meth. Found.; bd. dirs. Johnson Hill Children's Program, Eutaw, Ala., 1993—95. Recipient grants in field. Mem.: Christian Friendds of Israel Am., Confession Movement, Battalion of Deborah, Lifewatch, Nat. Assn. United Meth. Evangelists. Avocation: wood sculpting and carving. Office: 2801 Robinson Dr Waco TX 76706 Home: 5001 Stadium Dr Fort Worth TX 76133 Home Phone: 817-923-8777; Office Phone: 254-662-3155. Business E-Mail: margaretstratton@sbcglobal.net.

STRATTON, MARIANN, retired military nursing executive; b. Houston, Apr. 6, 1945; d. Max Millard and Beatrice Agnes (Roemer) S.; m. Lawrence Mallory Stickney, nov. 15, 1977 (dec.). BSN, BA in English, Sacred Heart Dominican Coll., 1966; MA in Mgmt., Webster Coll., 1977; MSN, U. Va., 1981. Cert. adult nurse practitioner. Ensign USN, 1966, advanced through grades to rear adm., 1991; patient care coord. Naval Regional Med. Ctr., Charleston, SC, 1981-83; nurse corps plans officer Naval Med. Command, Washington, 1983-86; dir. nursing svcs. U.S. Naval Hosp., Naples, Italy, 1986-89, Naval Hosp., San Diego, 1989-91; chief pers. mgmt. Bur. Medicine & Surgery, Washington, 1991-94; dir. USN Nurse Corps, Washington, 1991-94; ret. USN, 1994. Decorated Disting. Svc. medal, Meritorious Svc. medal with two stars, Naval Achievement medal, Navy Commendation medal. Mem. Interagy. Inst. Fed. Health Care Execs., Am. Volksporting Assn., Tex. Wanders, U. Va. Raven Soc., Fiber Artists San Antonio.

STRATTON, PAMELA, gynecologist; b. Goshen, NY, Aug. 27, 1954; d. Paul Joseph and Carolyn Clark Stratton; m. Edson Gardner Case, June 14, 2008; 1 child, Eric Stratton Cheskin. MD, NY Med. Coll., Valhalla, 1981. Diplomate Am. Bd. Ob-Gyn., 1988. Capt. USPHS, Bethesda, Md., 1986—2008; staff clinician Nat. Naval Med. Ctr., Bethesda, 1986—89; spl. asst. obstetrics, pediat., adolenscent and maternal AIDS br. NICHD, NIH, Bethesda, 1989—93, spl. asst. gynecology and clin. rsch., contraceptive devel. br., 1993, spl. asst. gynecology and clin. rsch., intramural program, 1997—99, chief, gynecology consult svc., intramural program, 1997—. Recipient Merit award, NIH, 2002, Outstanding Svc. medal, Commd. Corps., USPHS, 2007; named Physician Profl. Adv. Group, Rschr. of Yr., 2008. Mem.: Am. Coll. Ob-Gyn. Achievements include designed and oversaw the study ACTG 076 in which Zidovudine was found to interrupt mother to child transmission of HIV; research in agenda for spermicides and condoms to interrupt HIV transmission; clinical trials network for contraception; genital graft versus host disease after stem cell transplantation; clinical trial of raloxifene which shortened the time to return of pain in women with endometriosis. Avocation: singing. Office: RBMB NICHD NIH 10 Center Dr Bldg 10 Rm 1-3140 Bethesda MD 20892-1109 Business E-Mail: ps79c@nih.gov.

STRATTON, PAULINE A., retired elementary school educator, alderman; b. Chgo., Feb. 18, 1946; d. Sam Costa and Helene (Lazaris) Stavrakas; m. George William Stratton, June 25, 1967; children: Gina Marie, Paul Kevin. B of Edn., Nat. Coll. Edn., 1967. Cert. tchr. grades K-9. Primary tchr. Worth (Ill.) Sch. Dist. # 127, 1967-70, substitute tchr., 1970-91, North Palos Sch. Dist. # 117, Palos Hills/Hickory Hills, Ill., 1976-87; alderman 2d ward City of Palos Hills, 1987—. Mem. lay adv. bd. SW Coop. Spl. Edn., Ill., South Met. Assn. Mem. sch. bd. North Palos Sch. Dist. # 117, Hickory Hills, 1983-91; vol., bd. dirs. Am. Cancer Soc.; vol. Diabetes Assn., Easter Seals, March of Dimes, Miseracordia, former Sunday Sch. Tchr., choir mem. Named an Honored Guest, Greek Am. Parade, 2001; named to Wall of Honor as Grand Pres., Maids of Athens, US, Can. Mem. Ill. Congress Parents and Tchrs. (cert. hon. life mem.), Maids of Athena (past grand pres.). Greek Orthodox. Avocations: walking, helping people. Home: 10315 S Alta Dr Palos Hills IL 60465-1705 Office: City of Palos Hills 10335 S Roberts Rd Palos Hills IL 60465-1929 Office Phone: 708-598-3400.

STRATTON, ROBERT, retired electronics executive; b. Vienna, Aug. 14, 1928; came to U.S., 1959, naturalized, 1966; s. Kenneth Kurt and Eugenie (Schwatzer) S.; m. Elfriede Karlberger, Jan. 11, 1980; children: David Alexander, Valerie Pam. B.Sc. in Physics, Manchester U., 1949, PhD in Theoretical Physics, 1952. Rsch. physicist Met. Vickers Elec. Co., Manchester, Eng., 1952-59; with Tex. Instruments, Inc., Dallas, 1959-94, dir. physics rsch. lab., 1963-71, assoc. dir. cen. rsch. labs., 1971-72, dir. semiconductor R & D, 1972-75, dir. cen. rsch. labs., 1975-77, asst. v.p., dir. cen. rsch. labs., 1977-82, v.p. corp. staff, dir. cen. rsch. labs., 1982-94; dir. Indsl. Outreach Elec. Materials Sci. Tech. Ctr., dir. Engring. and Tech. Inst., U. Tex., Austin, 1994-96. Contbr. articles to profl. jours. Bd. dirs. Indsl. Rsch. Inst., 1985-88, Coun. on Superconductivity for Am. Competitiveness, 1987-90; adv. bd. dirs. Tex. Ctr. for Superconductivity, 1989-2000. Fellow IEEE, Inst. Physics (U.K.), Am. Phys. Soc.; mem. NAE. Personal E-mail: rstratton@tx.rr.com.

STRATTON, SALLY G. (SARA), retired school system administrator; b. Huntingdon, Pa., Feb. 19, 1937; d. E. Richeard Grove and Miriam May Strait; m. Lewis Palmer Stratton, June 18, 1960 (div. Oct. 1987); children: Laurie Beth, Stephanie Jo. BA in Elem. Edn., Juniata Coll., 1959; MS in Early Childhood Adminstrn., Southeastern Nova U., 1987; postgrad., U. Maine, Fla. State U., Furman U. 1st grade tchr. Tyrone (Pa.) Sch. Dist., 1959-60, Veazie Sch. Dist., Orono, Maine, 1960-61, Waculla County Sch. Dist., Sopchoppy, Fla., 1961-62, Leon County Sch. Dist., Tallahassee, 1962-67; substitute tchr. Greenville (SC) County Schs., 1968-69; presch. tchr. First Bapt. Ch., Travelers Rest, SC, 1971-74; dir., head tchr., co-founder Furman U. Child Devel. Ctr., Greenville, SC, 1974-98; dir. residential life SC Gov. Sch. for Arts, Greenville, 1984—98; dir. student svcs. SC Gov.'s Sch. Arts and Humanities, 1998—2002. Co-author: Student Handbook for Newly Created Gov. School for Arts and Humanities, 1999. Sec. Red Sunset Corp., Greenville, 1994—2006; founding mem. 1st Internat. Assn. for Univ. Women in Russia, 1991; bd. dirs. Greenville County Child Care Assn., 1990—2003. Mem. AAUW (chair ednl. found., treas., pres. 1989-91, recipient Named Gift award 1998, 2000), Greenville County Childcare Assn. (bd. dirs. 1988—), S.C. Assn. for Children Under Six, PTA (co-pres., treas., membership chair, adv. coun.). Baptist. Avocations: travel, interior decorating, reading, choir, sports. Home: 607 Half Mile Way Greenville SC 29609-1577

STRATTON, TIMOTHY PATRICK, pharmacy educator; b. Santa Rosa, Calif., Apr. 5, 1957; s. Robert Arthur and Carol Lee (St. Clair) S.; m. Suzanne Wasilczuk, Apr. 1, 1989. AS in Pre-Pharmacy, Santa Rosa Jr. Coll., Calif., 1977; BS in Pharmacy, Idaho State U., 1980; MS in Hosp. Pharmacy, U. Ariz., 1982, PhD in Pharmacy Adminstrn., 1986. Pharmacist lic. Ariz., Calif., Alaska. Tchg. asst. U. Ariz. Coll. Pharmacy, Tucson, 1980-85; staff pharmacist Tucson (Ariz.) Med. Ctr., 1982-84, White's Pharmacy, Sitka, Alaska, 1985-89; dir. pharm. svcs. Sitka (Alaska) Cmty. Hosp., 1985-89; asst. prof. pharm. adminstrn. U. B.C., Vancouver, 1989-93, U. Mont. Sch. Pharm., Missoula, 1993-96; assoc. prof. pharmacy adminstrn. U. Mont. Sch. Pharmacy, Missoula, 1996—. Cons. pharmacist Wrangell (Alaska) Hosp., 1987-89; rsch. cons. B.C. Pharmacy Assn., Vancouver, 1989-93, B.C. Coll. Pharmacists, Vancouver, 1989-93. Contbr. articles to profl. jours. United Way campaigner U. B.C., Vancouver, 1992-93, Missoula, 1994. Mem. Am. Assn. Colls. Pharm. (chair soc. adminstrn. sci. sect. 1998-99), Am. Pharm. Assn., Mont. Pharm. Assn. (legis. com. mem. 1995), Missoula Model Railroad Club (pres. 1995-96). Democrat. Unitarian Universalist. Avocations: model railroading, marimbist, hiking, skiing, softball. Office: Univ Montana Sch Pharmacy Missoula MT 59812-0001 Home: 5619 London Rd Duluth MN 55804-2516

STRATTON, WALTER LOVE, lawyer; b. Greenwich, Conn., Sept. 21, 1926; s. John McKee and June (Love) Stratton; m. DeAnna Weinheimer, Oct. 1, 1994; children from previous marriage: John, Michael, Peter(dec.), Lucinda. Student, Williams Coll., 1943; AB, Yale U., 1948; LLB, Harvard U., 1951. Bar: N.Y. 1952. Assoc. Casey, Lane & Mittendorf, NYC, 1951-53, Donovan, Leisure, Newton & Irvine, NYC, 1956—62, ptnr., 1963-84, Gibson, Dunn & Crutcher, 1984-93, Andrews Kurth, NYC, 1993-95; of counsel Andrews Kurth, NYC, 1996—2006. Asst. U.S. atty. N.Y., NYC, 1953—56; lectr. Practising Law Inst. With USNR, 1945—46. Fellow: Am. Coll. Trial Lawyers; mem.: ABA, N.Y. State Bar Assn., Fed. Bar Coun., Greenwich Riding and Trails Assn., Colo. Arlberg Club, Indian Harbor Yacht Club. Home Phone: 203-869-8294. Business E-Mail: wlstratton@msn.com.

STRATTON, WAYNE THOMAS, lawyer; b. Topeka, Dec. 16, 1933; s. Thomas Martin and Hazel Mae (Johnson) S.; m. Janet Crews; children: Wayne Thomas Jr., Kimberly, Marcus, Michael. AB, Washburn U., 1955, JD, 1958. Bar: Kans. 1958, U.S. Dist. Ct. Kans. 1958, U.S. Ct. Appeals (10th cir.) 1963, U.S. Supreme Ct. 1969. Assoc. Ascough, Bausch, Johnson & Stratton, Topeka, 1960-61; ptnr. Goodell, Stratton, Edmonds, Palmer and predecessors, Topeka, 1961—2006, of counsel, 2007—. Contbr. articles to profl. jours. Mem. Topeka Bd. Edn., 1973-77; mem. bd. regents Washburn U., Topeka, 1977-81. Lt. USAF, 1958-60, capt. Res. Recipient Disting. Svc. award Kansas Med. Soc., Topeka, 1986, Disting. Svc. award Washburn Law Sch. Assn., 1996, W.M. Kahrs Lifetime Achivement award, 2007. Fellow Am. Coll. Trial Lawyers, Am. Bar Found., KS. Bar Found., Kans. Assn. Def. Counsel (pres. 1985-86), Topeka Bar Assn. (pres. 1984-85, Warren W. Shaw Disting. Svc. award 2003). Republican. Congregationalist. Avocation: golf. Home: 948 SW Woodbridge Ct Topeka KS 66606-4600 Office Phone: 785-233-0593. Business E-Mail: wstratton@goodellstrattonlaw.com.

STRATTON-GONZALEZ, SANDRA, dance educator, administrator; b. Frankfurt, Germany, July 27, 1953; d. John Alan Stratton and Janet May Thorpe, Norman Thorpe (Stepfather); m. Jojo Gonzalez, June 14, 1992; children: Maya S Gonzalez, Zoe Ray Stratton, Samantha Alana Stratton. MA, Empire State Coll., 2008. Teacher of Dance NYS Dept. of Edn., 1999. Artistic and exec. dir. Soundance Repertory Co., NY, 1984—99; dance specialist PS 372, Bklyn., 1999—. Founding co-chair NYC Dance Educators, 2001—04; prodr. Regional 'Day of Dance', Bklyn., 2003—. Prodr.: (concert dance) NYC Dance Educators' Student Dance Festival; prodr.: (modern dance works) A Place In Line, 1999, (modern dance) Kalawang, 1997; prodr.: (Soundance Repertory Co.) Annual Choreographer Showcase, (dance concerts) Annual NYC Season, Soundance Repertory Company; co-author: Dance Education for Diverse Learners. Chair, staff Parish rels. com. Park Slope United Meth. Ch.; mem. Bklyn. Parents for Peace, 2004—08. Recipient BAXten award, Bklyn. Arts Exch., 2001; Arts in Edn. for Soundance, Inc. grant, NYS Coun. for the Arts, 1989—99, Arts Edn. Partnership award for PS 372, Ctr. for Arts Edn., 2000—02, Arts Edn. and Performance for Soundance Inc., NYC Dept. of Cultural Affairs, 1990—99. Mem.: NYC Dance Educators (exec. com.), Nat. Dance Edn. Orgn. (assoc.), Dance and The Child Internat. (assoc.). D-Liberal. Methodist. Avocation: camping.

STRAUB, CHESTER JOHN, federal judge; b. Bklyn., May 12, 1937; s. Chester and Ann (Majewski) Straub; m. Patricia Morrissey; children: Chester, Michael, Christopher, Robert. AB, St. Peter's Coll., 1958; JD, U. Va., 1961. Bar: N.Y. 1962, U.S. Dist. Ct. (so. and ea. dists.) N.Y. 1963, U.S. Ct. Appeals (2d cir.) 1967, U.S. Supreme Ct. 1978. Assoc. Willkie Farr & Gallagher, NYC, 1963—71, ptnr., 1971—98; mem. NY State Assembly, 1967—72, NY State Senate, 1973—75, Dem. Nat. Com., 1976—80; judge US Ct. Appeals (2d cir.), 1998—, sr. judge, 2008—. Past mediator U.S. Dist. Ct. (so. dist.) N.Y.; neutral evaluator U.S. Dist. Ct. (ea. dist.) N.Y.; chmn. jud. screening com. State of N.Y., 1988—94, first dept. jud. screening com., 1983—94, Senator Moynihan's jud. selection com., 1976—98. With US Army, 1961—63. Mem.: ABA, Assn. of Bar of City of N.Y.C., N.Y. State Bar Assn. Office: US Ct Appeals 2530 US Courthouse 500 Pearl St New York NY 10007*

STRAUB, PETER FRANCIS, novelist; b. Milw., Mar. 2, 1943; s. Gordon Anthony and Elvena (Nilsestuen) S.; m. Susan Bitker, Aug. 27, 1966; children: Benjamin Bitker, Emma Sydney Valli. BA, U. Wis., 1965; MA, Columbia U., NYC, 1966. English tchr. Univ. Sch., Milw., 1966-68. Bd. dirs. U. Wis. Author: Marriages, 1973, Julia, 1975, If You Could See Me Now, 1977, Ghost Story, 1979, Shadowland, 1980, Floating Dragon, 1983, Leeson Park and Belsize Square, 1984, Wild Animals, 1984, Blue Rose, 1985, Koko, 1988, Mystery, 1989, Houses Without Doors, 1990, Mrs. God, 1991, The Throat, 1993, The Hellfire Club, 1996, Mr. X, 1999, Pork Pie Hat, 1999, Magic Terror, 2000, Lost Boy Lost Girl, 2003, In the Night Room, 2004, Sides, 2007, 5 Stories, 2007, A Special Place, 2009, (with Stephen King) The Talisman, 1984, Black House, 2001; editor: Peter Straub's Ghosts, 1995, Conjunctions #39, 2002, Library of America H.P. Lovecraft Tales, 2005, Poe's Children, 2008, Library of America, American Fantastic Tales, 2009. Bd. dir. Fence, Conjunctions, Am. Poetry Rev., Poets & Writers. Recipient Brit. Fantasy award, August Derleth award, 1983, World Fantasy awards World Fantasy Conv., 1989, 93, World Horror Assn. awards, 1993, 98, 99, 2000, 03, 04, Grand Master award World Horror Conv., 1997, award Internat. Horror Guild, 1999, 2003, Writers award, Barnes & Noble Writers, 2008; sponsor Peter Straub Disting. Lectureship on Popular Culture, U. Wis. Mem. PEN, Horror Writers Assn. (life; Achievement award, 2006), Century Assn. Avocations: jazz, opera, classical music. Personal E-mail: pstraub@nyc.rr.com.

STRAUB, PETER THORNTON, lawyer; b. St. Louis, Mar. 27, 1939; s. Ralph H. and Mary Louise (Thornton) S.; m. Wendy B. Cubbage, Dec. 29, 1964; children: Karl Thornton, Philip Hamilton, Ellen Elizabeth. AB, Washington and Lee U., 1961, LLB, 1964. Bar: Mo. 1964, Va. 1964, US Dist. Ct. (ea. dist.) Mo. 1967, US Circuit Ct. Appeals (8th cir.) 1969, US Supreme Ct. 1970. US Circuit Ct. Appeals (DC cir.) 1971, Ct. Mil. Appeals 1970, US Tax Ct. 1971, US Bankruptcy Ct. 1991. Assoc. Evans & Dixon, St. Louis, 1966-68; asst. pub. defender St. Louis County, St. Louis, 1968-69; asst. US Atty. St. Louis, 1969-71; trial atty. internal security div. Dept. Justice, Washington, 1971-72, atty.-adviser office of dep. atty. gen., 1972-73, dir. office criminal justice, spl. asst. to atty. gen., 1974; minority counsel com. on judiciary US Ho. of Reps., Washington, 1973-74; gen. counsel SSS, Washington, 1974-76; pvt. practice Law Offices of Peter T. Straub, Alexandria, Va., 1976—. Pres., gov. bd. Alexandria Cmty. Mental Health Ctr., 1982—95; mem. No. Va. Estate Planning Coun., 1981—; pres.'s coun. Trinity Coll., Washington, 1980—87; adv. bd. Am. Heart Assn., Alexandria, 1991—92, Salvation Army, Alexandria, 1991—, v.p., 1994—96, chmn., 1997—99, Alexandria Cmty. Shelter Adv. Bd., 1995—97; Va. escheat atty. City of Alexandria, 1994—2002; dist. chmn. Boy Scouts Am., 1998—2001, risk mgmt. com. Nat. Capital Area coun., 2006—; adv. bd. Hospice No. Va., 2000—; mem. Econ. Opportunity Commn. City of Alexandria, 2006—; bd. dirs. Friends of the Washington and Old Dominion Trail, 2002—, Parc East Condominium, 1990—, sec., 1992—2006; bd. dirs. Sigma Nu Ednl. Found., Inc., 2000—08; charter mem. bd. dirs. Alexandria Country Day Sch., 1983—90. With US Army, 1964—66, capt. USAR, 1966—72. Recipient certificate of award Dept. Justice, 1970, certificate of appreciation Law Enforcement Assistance Adminstrn. Dept. Justice, 1974, Silver Beaver award Boy Scouts Am., Washington, 1987, Collins award Alexandria Coun. Persons with Disabilities, 1993, Cmty. Svc. award Am. Indian Alliance, 1995. Mem.: FBA, ABA, Nat. Acad. Elder Law Attys., Va. Trial Lawyers Assn., Alexandria Bar Assn., Mo. Bar Assn., Bar Assn. Met. St. Louis, Va. State Bar Assn., Optimists (bd. dirs., pres. Alexandria chpt. 1984, lt. gov. Nat. Capitol Va. Dist. 1987—89, treas. 1999—2001), Nat. Eagle Scout Assn., Sigma Nu. Republican. Congregationalist. Avocations: scouting, reading, bicycling. Office: 1225 Martha Custis Dr # 103 Alexandria VA 22302-2040 Office Phone: 703-820-3600. Office Fax: 703-820-8602. Business E-Mail: pstraub@straublawoffices.com.

STRAUB, SUNNY L., retired elementary school educator; b. Quincy, Ill., Aug. 19, 1950; d. Leonard Emery and Billie Louise Straub. BS in Elem. Edn., So. Ill. U., Carbondale, 1972; MS, Western Ill. U., Macomb, 1979. Cert. tchr. Ill., Mo., edn. adminstr. Truman State U., 1989. Tchr. Chpt. 1 reading Quincy Pub. Schs., Ill., 1974—81, tchr, reading, 1981—85, subject area leader/reading, 1981—91; dean of students Quincy Jr. HS, Ill., 1985—91, literacy tchr., 1991—2005, English dept. chairperson, 1991—2005, ret., 2005, 2005. Tutor Woodland Home, Quincy, Ill., 1975—76; presenter Nat. Coun. Tchrs. of English, Ill. Reading Coun.; GED tchr. Quincy Pub. Schs., Ill., 1977—78, dir. Quincy conf., 1980—81, right to read coord., 1984—85; study skills program coord. Quincy Jr. H.S., Ill., 1986—90, north ctrl. evaluation coord., 1987—89, sch. improvement team leader, 1993—2005; workshop presenter, instr., lectr.; curriculum alignment leader. Election judge, Quincy, Ill., 2006; co-founder Kids First Coalition. Mem.: Ill. Assn. Ret. Tchrs., Quincy Fedn. of Ret. Tchrs. Achievements include development of curriculum for reading comprehension; literacy block initiative; integrated content study skills program. Avocations: reading, volunteer, pursuit of learning, political campaigning, mentoring. Home: 5020 Lake Ridge Dr Quincy IL 62305 Personal E-mail: sunni@adams.net.

STRAUB, TERRENCE D., metal products executive; BBA, Ind. U., Bloomington; M in Internat. Pub. Policy, Johns Hopkins Sch. Advanced Internat. Study. Spl. asst. congl. affairs to Pres. Jimmy Carter White House, Washington, 1977—81; mgr. govtl. affairs US Steel, Washington, 1981, dir. govtl. affairs, gen. mgr. govtl. affairs Steel & Diversified Businesses, gen. mgr. govtl. affairs Energy, v.p. govtl. affairs USX Corp., 1991, mem. corp. policy com., 1996, sr. v.p. pub. policy & govtl. affairs, 2003—, mem. corp. mgmt. com., 2004. Mem. Industry Sector Adv. Com.; chmn. Coun. US Prodrs. Am. Iron and Steel Inst.; chmn. oper. com. Steel Alliance; lectr. Am. U., George Washington U., Conn. Coll., Harvard U. Inst. Politics at Kennedy Sch. Govt. Mem. adv. com. Export-Import Bank; vice chmn. Ctr. Nat. Policy; mem. adv. bd. Manna Inc., Washington; mem. Fed. City Coun., Washington Econ. Club. Office: US Steel 600 Grant St Pittsburgh PA 15219-2800 Office Phone: 412-433-1121.

STRAUCH, BERISH, plastic surgeon, hand and cosmetic surgeon; b. NYC, Sept. 19, 1933; m. Rena (Feuerstein), June 12, 1955; children: Robert, Laurie. BS, Columbia U., 1955, MD, 1959. Diplomate Am. Bd. Surgery, Am. Bd. Plastic Surgery, qualification in hand surgery. Intern Bellevue Hosp., NYC, 1959—60; resident gen. surgery Montefiore Med. Ctr., Bronx, NY, 1960—64; hand surgery fellow Roosvelt Hosp., NYC, 1961; resident plastic surgery Stanford U., Palo Alto, Calif., 1966—67, chief resident, 1967—68; asst. prof. plastic surgery Albert Einstein Coll. Medicine, Bronx, NY, 1968—76, assoc. prof., 1976—81; chief plastic surgery svc. Montefiore Med. Ctr. and Albert Einstein Coll. Medicine, Bronx, NY, 1978—87; prof. plastic surgery Albert Einstein Coll. Medicine and Montefiore Med. Ctr., Bronx, NY, 1981—; acting chmn. dept. plastic surgery Montefiore Med. Ctr. and Albert Einstein Coll. Medicine, Bronx, NY, 1987—89, chmn., 1989—2008. Instr. Stanford U., 1967-68; vis. plastic surgeon Sing Sing Prison, N.Y., 1968-75; pres. World Soc. Reconstructive Microsurgery, 2007—,mktg. cons. Berish Strauch Ltd., 2009-. Co-author: (with others) Atlas of Microvascular Surgery: Anatomy and Operative Approaches, 1993 (Best Healt Sci. Book, Doody's Rating Svc. 1993), 2nd edit., 2006; co-editor: Textbook on Microsurgery, 1976, (with others) Grabb's Encyclopedia of Flaps, 3 vols., 1990, (Outstanding Publ. in Clin. Medicine, Assn. Am. Pub. 1990), 2d edit. 1997, 3d edit. 2008, Anatomy of the Hand and the Surgical Implications, 2005; contbr. articles to profl. journals. and 20 chpts. to sci. books; assoc. editor Plastic and Reconstructive Surgery, 1982-88; founder, editor-in-chief Jour. Reconstructive Microsurgery, 1984—2008,Mktg. editor JRM, 2008-. Capt. Med. Corp. U.S. Army, 1964-66, Mem. AAAS, ACS, Am. Soc. for Reconstructive Microsurgery (founder, past sec., treas., pres., chmn. Founder's Lectr. 1988), Am. Assn. Plastic Surgeons, Internat. Soc. Reconstructive Microsurgery (chmn. founding coun. 1983-84, pres. 1984-85). Med. Soc. State of N.Y., Am. Trauma Soc. (founding mem.), N.Y. Acad. Sci., Am. Soc. for Peripheral Nerve Surgery (pres. 1993-94), World Soc. Reconstruction Microsurgery (pres. 2008-), Rhinoplasty Soc. (pres. 2008) and others. Home Phone: 914-967-9019; Office Phone: 914-282-4987. Business E-Mail: bstrauch@montefiore.org.

STRAUCH, EDWARD HUGO, writer, retired literature and language professor; b. Chgo., June 18, 1925; s. Moritz Franz and Ida (Pfeffer) Strauch; 1 child; 2 children. Diplôme Supérieur, Sorbonne U., Paris, 1950; BA in English and French, Calif. State U., LA, 1958, MA in English and Edn., 1961; PhD in Comparative Lit., Ind. U., Bloomington, 1969. Cert. instr. Calif. Dir. humanities program Nasson Coll., Caen, France, 1966—70; assoc. prof. English U. Guam, Mangilao, 1971—75; vis. prof. English Pahlavi U., Shiraz, Iran, 1975—76; writer multimedia English Free U., Teheran, 1976—77; prof. English Mohammed V U., Rabat, Morocco, 1977—78; head English dept. U. Maiduguri, Nigeria, 1979—86; assoc. prof. English U. Guam, Mangilao, 1987—95; ret., 1995. Author: How Nature Taught Man to Know, Imagine and Reason, 1995, Beyond Literary Theory: Literature as a Search for the Meaning of Human Destiny, 2001, The Creative Conscience as Human Destiny, 2004. Home: U Guam PO Box 5256 Mangilao GU 96923

STRAUCH, ERIC DAVID, surgeon; b. Washington, Dec. 13, 1964; s. Saul and Judith Strauch; m. Cecilia Anne Callahan, May 3, 1997; children: Jacob Connor, Julia Erin, Jessica, Jessica Caitlin, Jenna Kayley. MD, U. Md., Balt., 1988. Cert. in gen. surgery Am. Bd. Surgery, 1996, pediat. surgeon Am. Bd. Surgery, 1998. Pediat. surgeon U. Md. Sch. Medicine, 1996—. Office: Univ Md Sch Medicin 22 S Greene St Baltimore MD 21201

STRAUCH, KATINA PARTHEMOS, college librarian, publishing executive; m. Bruce Strauch; children: Raymond, Ileana. MLS, U. NC-Chapel Hill. Head libr., collection dept. Coll. Charleston Librs., SC; founder, dir. Charleston Conf., 1980—; founder, editor Against the Grain, 1989—. Chair bd. Charleston Report, 1996—, Charleston Advisor, 1999—; bd. dirs. Inst. Mus. & Libr. Svc., 2004—. Author: Legal and Ethical Issues in Acquisitions, 1990. Recipient Disting. Alumnus award, U. NC-Chapel Hill Sch. Libr. and Info. Sci., 1992, SC Outstanding Libr. award, 1996. Mem.: ALA, Reference and User Svcs. Assn. (Louis Shores-Greenwood Pub. Group award 2007), Assn. Libr. Collections and Tech. Svcs. (Leadership in Libr. Acquisitions award 1997). Office: Coll Charleston Librs 66 George St Charleston SC 29424 also: Charleston Info Group LLC MSC 98 The Citadel Charleston SC 29409 Office Phone: 843-953-8020, 843-953-8020. Office Fax: 843-953-8019. Personal E-mail: kstrauch@comcast.net, katina.strauch@gmail.com. Business E-Mail: strauchk@cofc.edu.

STRAUCHEN, JAMES ARTHUR, medical educator, pathologist; b. NYC, July 11, 1948; s. Murray and Helen Strauchen; m. Vivienne Sari Gold, May 27, 1972; children: Jennifer Mia, Katherine Sinead. BA magna cum laude, Columbia Coll., NYC, 1968; MD with honors, NY U., NYC, 1972. Diplomate Am. Bd. Pathology, 1978, cert. hematology Am. Bd. Pathology, 1981, diplomate Am. Bd. Internal Medicine, 1975, cert. med. oncology Am. Bd. Internal Medicine, 1977, hematology Am. Bd. Internal Medicine, 1978. Asst. prof. pathology Stanford U., Sch. Medicine, Palo Alto, Calif., 1978—81; assoc. prof. pathology U. Rochester, Sch. Medicine, NY, 1982—83; prof. pathology and neoplastic diseases Mt. Sinai Sch. Medicine, NYC, 1983—, vice chair dept. pathology, 2005—. Pres. NY Cancer Soc., NYC, 2006—07. Lt. comdr. USPHS, 1974—78. Mem.: Soc. for Study of Blood, NY Path. Soc., Arkadi M. Rywlin Pathology Club, Assn. Dirs. Anatomic and Surg. Pathology, Am. Soc. Hematology (assoc.), Phi Beta Kappa, Alpha Omega Alpha (pres. 1971—72). Office: Mt Sinai Sch Medicine 1 Gustave Levy Pl New York NY 10029 Office Phone: 212-241-9142. Office Fax: 212-289-2899. Business E-Mail: james.strauchen@mssm.edu.

STRAUGHAN, WILLIAM THOMAS, structural engineering consultant, educator; b. Shreveport, La., Aug. 2, 1936; s. William Eugene and Sara Chloetilde (Harrell) S.; m. Rubie Ann Barnes, Aug. 20, 1957; children: Donna Ann, Sara Arlene, Eugene Thomas. BS, MIT, 1959; MS, U. Tex., 1986; PhD, Tex. Tech. U., 1990. Registered profl. engr., Fla., Ill., Iowa., La., Tex., Wash. Project engr. Gen. Dynamics Corp., Chgo., 1959—60; chief project, design engr. Gen. Foods Corp., Kankakee, Ill., 1960—64; mgr. plant engring. Std. Brands Inc., Clinton, Iowa, 1964—66; regional mgr. Air Products & Chems., Inc., Creighton, Pa., 1966—68; gen. mgr. Skyline Corp., Harrisburg, NC, 1968—70; cons. Charlotte, NC, 1970—72; dir. engring. and Fla. ops. Zimmer Homes Corp., Pompano Beach, 1972—73; v.p. engring. and mfg. Nobility Homes, Inc., Ocala, Fla., 1973—78, Moduline Internat., Inc., Lacey, Wash., 1978—85; rsch. engr. U. Tex., Austin, 1985—86; lectr., rschr. Tex. Tech. U., Lubbock, 1987—90; assoc. prof. U. New Orleans, 1990—92; asst. prof. dept. civil engring. La. Tech. U., Ruston, 1992—98. Tchr. 30 different courses, 1987—; adj. prof. Coll. Engring., La. Tech. U., 2001-05, vis. prof., 2005-; cons. in field, Dubach, La., 1992—; condr. workshops in field; apptd. spokesman Mfrd. Housing Industry before U.S. Congress. Contbr. articles to numerous profl. jours. Vol. engring. svcs. Lubbock Fire Safety House, 1990; judge sci. fair Ben Franklin H.S., New Orleans, 1990. Recipient T.L. James Svc. award La. Tech. U., 1994; grantee Urban Waste Mgmt. and Rsch. Ctr., New Orleans, 1991, Shell Devel. Co., 1993, La. Edn. Quality Support Fund, Insituform Techs., Inc., Trenchless Tech. Ctr., PABCO, Inc., InLiner USA, Inc., 1995, others; numerous grants in field. Mem. ASME (life), ASCE (Student chpt. Tchr. of Yr. award 1995, 98, 2009), Nat. Coun. Structural Engrs. Assns., Structural Engrs. Assn. La., Phi Kappa Phi, Sigma Xi, Chi Epsilon. Avocations: flying, skiing, motorcycling, camping, reading. Home: 199 Sellers Rd Dubach LA 71235-3218 Personal E-mail: drtomstraughan@msn.com.

STRAUMAN, TIMOTHY J., psychology professor, department chairman; b. Nov. 5, 1956; m. Janice Johnstone; children: Anne Jacqueline, Katherine Janice. BA in Psychology and Comm., magna cum laude, Duquesne U., Pitts., 1978; MA in Psychology and Human Devel., U. Chgo., 1979; PhD in Clin. and Social/Personality Psychology, NYU, 1987. Lic. clin. psychologist NC. Rsch. asst. stress and illness project Dept. Behavioral Sci. U. Chgo., 1978—79; sr. clin. data coord. Lederle Laboratories, Pearl River, NY, 1980—82, clin. rsch. cons., 1982—84; adj. faculty mem. Dept. Social Sciences Rockland CC, Suffern, NY, 1981—83; sr. systems analyst ORI Inc., Bethesda, Md., 1983; tchg. asst. Dept. Psychology NYU, 1982—84, statistical cons. clin. and devel. area groups Dept. Psychology, 1983—86; rsch. asst. Anxiety Disorders Clinic NY State Psychiatric Inst., 1984—87; asst. prof. clin. psychology area group Dept. Psychology U. Wis., Madison, 1987—92, assoc. prof. Depts. Psychology and Psychiatry, 1992—2000, dir. psychology tng. Dept. Psychiatry, 1992—2000, co-dir. depression treatment program, 1994—2000; prof. Dept. Psychology & Neurosci., Dept. Psychiatry and Behavioral Sci. Duke U., Durham, NC, 2000—, chmn. Dept. Psychology & Neurosci., 2002—. Crisis intervention svc. Rockland Cmty. Coll. Mental Health Ctr., Pomona, NY, 1980—82; clin. psychology intern Albert Einstein Med. Coll., Montefiore Med. Ctr., Bronx, NY, 1986—87; pvt. practice Mental Health Resources, Madison, Wis., 1988—92; clin. asst. prof. Ctr. for Affective Disorders Dept. Psychiatry U. Wis., Madison, 1990—92. Mem. editl. bd. Jour. Abnormal Psychology, 1998—, Jour. Personality and Social Psychology, 2002—, Personality and Social Psychology Bulletin, 2002—, Psychology Rev., 2003—, Self and Identity, 2002—, Jour. of Personality, 1991—98, assoc. editor, 1994—97. Fellow: Acad. Cognitive Therapy; mem.: Beck Inst. Cognitive Therapy and Rsch. (Van Ameringen fellow), Soc. Rsch. in Psychopathology, Soc. Psychotherapy Rsch., Am. Assn. for Behavior Therapy, Soc. Experimental Social Psychology, Soc. for Sci. of Clin. Psychology, Am. Assn. for Applied and Preventive Psychology, Am. Psychological Soc., APA, Acad. Psychological Clin. Sci. (co-chmn. internship com. 1998—2001, chmn. membership com. 2003—, treas. 2004—). Office: Dept Psychology & Neurosci Box 90086 Duke Univ 9 Flowers Dr Durham NC 27708 Office Phone: 919-660-5709. Office Fax: 919-660-5726. E-mail: tjstraum@duke.edu.*

STRAUS, DAVID A., architectural firm executive; b. Medford, Oreg., 1943; m. Sherry Straus; 2 children. BArch, U. Oreg., 1967. Registered architect, Oreg. Founding ptnr. Skelton, Straus & Seibert, Medford, 1989—. Mem Oreg Transp Comn, Rogue Valley Area Comn Transp. Past pres Medford Arts Comn, Arts Coun Southern Oreg; coach Rogue Valley Soccer Asn; leader Boy Scouts Am; bd dirs, past pres Schneider Mus Art SOSC; bd dirs Medford YMCA, Rogue Valley Art Asn. Lt USNR, Vietnam. Mem.: AIA (pres. so. Oreg. chpt.), Archit Found Oreg (past bd. dirs.), Medford/Jackson County CofC (past bd. dirs., Mem of the Yr 2000), Univ Oreg Alumni Asn, Oreg Club Southern Oreg (past pres.), Univ Club Medford (past pres.), Rotary. Office: Skelton Straus & Seibert Arch 26 Hawthorne St Medford OR 97504-7114 Office Phone: 541-779-4363. Business E-Mail: dstraus@sssarchitects.com.

STRAUS, DAVID CONRAD, microbiologist, educator; b. Evansville, Ind., Apr. 27, 1947; s. Leo and Jeanne Catherine (Cummings) S.; m. Janet Helen Debelak, Sept. 13, 1975 (div. Oct. 1986). BS in Biology, Wright State U., 1969; PhD in Microbiology, Loyola U., 1974; postdoctoral studies, U. Cinn., 1975. Instr. microbiology Ill. Coll. Podiatric Medicine, Chgo., 1972-73, Univ. Tex. Health Sci. Ctr., San Antonio, 1975-76, asst. prof. microbiology, 1976-81; assoc. prof. microbiology Tex. Tech. Univ. Health Sci. Ctr., Lubbock, 1981-95; prof. microbiology Tex. Tech. U. Health Sci. Ctr., Lubbock, 1995—. Author: Medical Microbiology and Sick Building Syndrome, 1985; editor: Sick Building Syndrome, Advances in Applied Microbiology, vol. 55, 2004 Pres. People for Animal Welfare, Lubbock, 1989-91. Mem. Am. Soc. for Microbiology (Tex. br.), Am. Acad. Microbiology, Sigma Xi. Avocations: sports, running, weightlifting, hiking. Home: 7605 Saratoga Ave Lubbock TX 79424-0720 Office: Tex Tech Univ HSC 4th And Indiana Lubbock TX 79430-0001 Office Phone: 806-743-2523. Business E-Mail: david.straus@ttuhsc.edu.

STRAUS, FRANCIS HOWE, pathologist, educator; b. Chgo., Mar. 16, 1932; s. Francis Howe and Elizabeth (Kales) S.; m. Helen Lorna Puttkammer, June 11, 1955; children: Francis H., Helen E., Christopher M., Michael W. AB, Harvard Coll., 1953; MD, U. Chgo., 1957, MS, 1964. Intern U. Chgo. Hosp., 1957—58; resident dept. pathology U. Chgo., 1958—60, resident, 1960—62, USPH fellow, 1958—60, chief resident, 1962—63, instr. dept. pathology, 1962—65, asst. prof., 1965—71, assoc. prof., 1971—78, prof., 1978—2003, prof. emeritus, 2003—. Author: Hyperparathyroidism, 1973, Essentials of Surgical Pathology, 1974. Chmn. profl. edn. com. Ill. divsn. Am. Cancer Soc., 1980-88, v.p., 1984-88, pres., 1988-90, nat. del., bd. dirs., 1988-92; mem. Inst. of Medicine of Chgo., 1969—, Ill. Comm. on Continuing Med. Edn., 1984-86; bd. dirs. S.E. Chgo. Commn., Chgo., 1985; pres. Beaumont Emergency Operating Rm. Bd., Mackinac Island, Mich., 1985-2002. Fellow Am. Cancer Soc., 1962-63, clin. fellow, 1965-68. Mem. Chgo. Pathology Soc., Am. Soc. Investigative Pathology, Internat. Acad. Pathology, Am. Soc. Exptl. Pathologists, Chgo. Lit. Club, Cliffdwellers Club, Sigma Xi, Alpha Omega Alpha (hon.) Avocations: gardening, travel, boating, music, art. Office: U Chgo Dept Pathology 5841 S Maryland Ave Chicago IL 60637-1463 Business E-Mail: l-straus@uchicago.edu.

STRAUS, KATHLEEN NAGLER, academic administrator, educator; b. NYC, Dec. 3, 1923; d. Maurice and Mildred (Kohn) Nagler; m. Everet M. Straus, May 29, 1948 (dec. Nov. 1967); children: Peter R., Barbara L. BA in Econs., Hunter Coll., 1944; postgrad., Columbia U., 1944—45, Am. U., 1946—47, Wayne State U., 1976—78. Various positions, 1944—50, 1966; dep. dir. Model Neighborhood Agy., City of Detroit, 1968—70; dir. social svcs. Southeastern Mich. Coun. Govts., Detroit, 1970—74; staff coord. Edn. Task Force, Detroit, 1974—75; exec. dir. People and Responsible Orgns. for Detroit, 1975—76; staff dir. edn. com. Mich. Senate, Lansing, 1976—79; assoc. exec. dir. Mich. Assn. Sch. Bds., Lansing, 1979—86; dir. cmty. rels. and devel. Ctr. for Creative Studies, Detroit, 1986—87, pres., 1987—91; mem. Mich. Bd. Edn., 1992—, pres., 2003. Mem. Mich. Bd. for Pub. Jr. and C.C.s, Lansing, 1980-92, v.p., 1989, pres., 1991; cons. Met. Columbus (Ohio) Schs. Com., 1975-76; mem. steering com. Mich. Edn. Seminars, 1979-86; mem. Adv. Com. on Higher Edn. Needs in S.W. Mich., 1971-72, Ad Hoc Com. on Equal Access to Higher Edn., 1970-71, Citizens Action Com. on Sch. Fin. Contbr. articles to profl. jours. Active numerous civic orgns.; vice chmn. downtown br. Met. Detroit YWCA, 1970-74; bd. dirs. Citizens for Better Care, Inc., 1973-78; mem. edn. com. New Detroit, Inc., 1972—; trustee Detroit Sci. Ctr., Inc., 1975—; founder, pres. Mich. Tax Info. Coun., 1982—; v.p. bd. dirs. Univ. Cultural Ctr. Assn., 1986-91; trustee Comprehensive Health Planning Coun. Southeastern Mich., 1977-78; mem. Wayne County Art and History Commn., 1988; co-chmn. Nat. Arts Program, 1987-88; bd. dirs. North Ctrl. Regional Edn. Libr.; bd. dirs. North Ctrl. Regional Edn. Lab.; bd. mem. Midwest Regional Edn. Lab. Recipient Amity citation, Detroit, 1966, Disting. Cmty. Svc. award Am. Jewish Com., 1988, Common Coun., Detroit, 1976, resolution Mich. Ho. of Reps., 1986, Mich. Senate, 1988, Educator of Yr. Wayne State U., 1999, Disting. Warrior award Detroit Urban League, 2000; named to Mich. Edn. Hall of Fame, 1997; inducted into Mich. Women's Hall of Fame, 2000, Lifetime Achievement award Anti Defamation League, 2004, Multi Cultural Edn. award Nat. Conf. Cmty. and Justice, 2004, Lifetime Achievement award Communities in Schs., 2006. Mem.: LWV (pres. Detroit 1961—63), Alpha Chi Alpha. Democrat. Avocations: travel, theater, concerts. Office: State Bd Edn PO Box 30008 Lansing MI 48909-7508 Home: 8162 E Jefferson Ave # 5A Detroit MI 48214-2611 Office Phone: 517-373-3900. Business E-Mail: strausk@michigan.gov.

STRAUS, MURRAY ARNOLD, sociology educator; b. June 18, 1926; BA in Internat. Rels. with honors, U. Wis., 1948, MS in Sociology, 1949, PhD in Sociology, 1956. Instr. dept. econs. and sociology U. Wis. Extension Divsn., 1949; lectr. sociology U. Ceylon, Colombo, 1949-52; asst. prof. dept. sociology and rural sociology Wash. State U., 1954-57; asst. prof. U. Wis., 1957-59; assoc. prof. family sociology Cornell U., 1959-61; prof. Coll. Liberal Arts U. Minn., 1961-68, chairperson divsn. family social sci. Sch. Home Econs., 1961-64, prof. sociology, 1968—; founder, co-dir. family rsch. lab. U. N.H., Durham, 1975—. Cons. various orgns., including Ctr. for Measurement Devel. SUNY, Buffalo, 1969, Social Security Adminstrn., 1966, NSF, 1966, NAS, 1992-93, Ctrs. for Disease Control, 1994, others. Author: Beating the Devil Out of Them: Corporal Punishment in American Families, 1994, 2d edit., 2001; (with Arnold S. Linsky) Social Stress in the United States: Clues to Regional Patterns of Crime and Illness, 1986; (with Linsky and Ronet Bachman) Stress, Culture, and Aggression, 1995; (with Richard J. Gelles) Intimate Violence, 1988, Physical Violence in American Families: Risk Factors and Adaptations to Violence in 8,145 Families, 1990; (with Larry Baron) Four Theories of Rape in American Society: A State Level Analysis, 1989; editor or co-editor books in field; mem. editl. bd. Rural Sociology, 1964-69, Indian Sociol. Bull.; 1965-67, Internat. Jour. Sociology and Family, 1970-72, Univ. Press New England, 1977-79, Sage Family Studies Abstracts, 1979—, Violence, Aggression, Terrorism, 1986-88; asst. editor Sociol. Abstracts, 1957-59; assoc. editor Jour. Marriage and Family, 1964-69, Am. Sociol. Rev., 1968-69; founding editor Tchg. Sociology, 1973-76; adv. editor Jour. Family Psychology, 1987—; contbr. numerous articles to profl. publs., 1951—. With U.S. Army, 1944-46. Recipient Outstanding Contbns. award N.H. Psychol. Assn., 1993, Citizen of Yr. award NASW, 1994, award for career contbns. to child abuse rsch. Am. Profl. Soc. on Child Abuse, 1994, Charles Holmes Pettee medal U. N.H. Alumni Assn., 2000. Fellow AAAS (mem. coun. 1971-73); mem. APA (chairperson task force on corporal punishment 1992-94, mem. pres.'s task force on violence and family 1994), AAUP, Am. Sociol. Assn. (methodology, social psychology, and family sects., chair family sect. 1979-80, mem. coun. family sect. 1967-70, sec.-treas. methodology sect. 1966-69, 69-72, mem. nominations com. 1976, 77, mem. com. on coms. 1987-89, award for contbns. to tchg., sect. on undergrad. edn. 1979, Britt Found. prize for grad. student rsch. in social psychology 1953), Am. Soc. Criminology, Sociol. Rsch. Assn., Rural Sociol. Soc. (mem. coun. 1970-73), Nat. Coun. on Family Rels. (pres. 1972-73, bd. dirs. 1963-66, 67-70, chairperson rsch. divsn. 1969-70, chairperson bd. publs. 1967-69, gen. program chairperson 1972, Ernest W. Burgess award for outstanding contbns. to rsch. 1977), Acad. Criminal Justice Scis., Assn. for Asian Studies, Soc. for Study of Social Problems (pres. 1989-90, bd. dirs. 1983-85, chair publs. com. 1979-80, past chair family divsn.), Royal Asiatic Soc. (Ceylon br.), Internat. Sociol. Assn., Internat. Soc. Rsch. Aggression (mem. coun. 1980-82, 2005-08, Lifetime Achievement award, 2008), Ea. Sociol. Soc. (pres. 1990-91, v.p. 1976-78), Indian Sciol. Soc., Nat. Family Violence Legislature Resource Ctr. (Lifetime Achievement award, 2008). Office: Univ NH Family Rsch Lab 126 Horton SSC Durham NH 03824 Office Phone: 603-862-2594. E-mail: murray.straus@unh.edu.

STRAUS, ROBERT, behavioral sciences educator; b. New Haven, Jan. 9, 1923; s. Samuel Hirsh and Alma (Fleischner) Straus; m. Ruth Elisabeth Dawson, Sept. 8, 1945; children: Robert James, Carol Martin, Margaret Dawson, John William. BA, Yale U., 1943, MA, 1945, PhD, 1947. Asst. prof. Yale U., 1948—51, rsch. assoc. applied physiology, 1951—53; acting dir. Conn. Child Study and Treatment Home, New Haven, 1952—53; assoc. prof. preventive medicine SUNY Upstate Med. Ctr., 1953—56; prof. med. sociology U. Ky., Lexington, 1956—59, prof. dept. behavioral sci. Coll. Medicine, also chmn. dept., 1959—87; dir. for sci. devel. Med. Rsch. Inst. San Francisco, 1991—93. Vis. fellow Yale U., 1968—69; vis. prof. U. Calif., Berkeley, 1978, 86; sec. Com. Med. Sociology, 1955—57; chmn. Coop. Com. Study Alcoholism, 1961—63, Nat. Adv. Com. on Alcoholism, 1966—69; mem. Nat. Adv. Coun. on Alcohol Abuse and Alcoholism, 1984—87; trustee Med. Rsch. Inst. San Francisco, 1988—93; mem. Calif. Pacific Med. Ctr. Rsch. Coun., 1993. Author: Medical Care for Seamen, 1950; author: (with S.D. Bacon) Drinking in College, 1953; author: Alcohol and Society, 1973, Escape From Custody, 1974, A Medical School is Born, 1996; co-editor: Medicine and Society, 1963; mem. editl. bd.: Jour. Studies on Alcohol, 1950—2000. Pres. Bluegrass R.R. Mus., 1980. Mem.: Inst. Medicine NAS, Acad. Behavioral Medicine Rsch., Am. Pub. Health Assn. (lifetime achievement award sect. on alcohol, tobacco and other drugs 1993), Assn. Behavioral Scis. and Med. Edn. (pres. 1974), Am. Sociol. Assn. (chmn. med. sociology sect. 1967—68, Leo G. Reeder award Disting. Contbn. to Med. Sociology 1998), Sigma Xi, Phi Beta Kappa. Home: 656 Raintree Rd Lexington KY 40502-2874

STRAUSER, ROBERT WAYNE, lawyer; b. Little Rock, Aug. 28, 1943; s. Christopher Columbus and Opal (Orr) S.; m. Atha Maxine Tubbs, June 26, 1971 (div. 1991); children: Robert Benjamin, Ann Kathleen; m. Terri D. Seales, Oct. 17, 1998. BA, Davidson Coll., NC, 1965; postgrad., Vanderbilt U., Nashville, 1965-66; LLB, U. Tex., Austin, 1968. Bar: Tex. 1968, U.S. Ct. Mil. Appeals 1971. Staff atty. Tex. Legis. Coun., Austin, 1969-71; counsel Jud. Com., Tex. Ho. of Reps., Austin, 1971-73; chief counsel Jud. Com., Tex. Constl. Conv., Austin, 1974; exec. v.p. and legis. counsel Tex. Assn. Taxpayers, Austin, 1974-85; assoc. Baker Botts, LLP, Austin, 1985-87, ptnr., 1988—2008; pvt. practice, 2009—. Assoc. editor Tex. Internat. Law Jour., 1968. Mem. Tex. Ho. Speakers Econ. Devel. Com., Austin, 1986-87; life dir. McDonald Obs. Bd. Visitors, 1988-; bd. dirs. Tex. Assn. Bus. and C. of C., 2000-2002; mem. Dean's Roundtable, U. Tex. Law Sch.; bd. dirs. Austin Symphony Orch. Soc., 1985—, v.p., 1993-94, nominating com., 1998-2002. Capt. USNR, ret. Named Rising Star of Tex., Tex. Bus. Mag., 1983. Fellow Tex. Bar Found., Austin Bar Found.; mem. State Bar of Tex., Austin Bar Assn., Headliners Club (Austin). Office: 1005 Congress Ave Ste 1040 Austin TX 78701 Personal E-mail: robert.strauser@gmail.com.

STRAUSER, SUSAN PARKYN, performing arts educator, singer, professional soloist; d. Harold Mann and Helen Ruth (Knapp) Parkyn; m. George John Strauser; 1 child, Andrew. BS in Music Edn., West Chester U., Pa., 1964; MEd in Music, West Chester U., 1967; postgrad., Ind. U., 1976—80. Profl. singer, 1959—; prof. voice William Paterson U., Wayne, NJ, 1974—75; artistic dir. Vocal Arts Studio, Wallkill, NY, 1985—; voice seminar dir. Delaware Valley Opera, Narrowsburg, NY, 1985—86; prof. voice SUNY, Orange/Middletown, 1990—, voice program dir. Ulster/Stone Ridge, 2000—07; pvt. practice. Seminar presenter in field; artistic dir. Empire Artists of N.Y., Wallkill, 1992—; appeared with N.J. Symphony Orch., Hudson Valley Philharmonic Orch., West Chester Symphony, Ind. U. Philharm. and Opera Theatre; guest artist West Islip Symphony Orch. of L.I.; performances with opera and musical theatre cos. as well as in concert, oratorio and recital presentations include numerous leading roles; numerous appearances for cable TV Lunch N Listen series, Heroines-Women of the Musical Stage; profl. soloist Metro. NY area and East Coast; performance seminar presenter; lectr. in field. Contbr. articles to profl. jours.; Exhibited in group shows. Bd. dirs. Delaware Valley Opera, 1986. Recipient U.S. Congl. Citation in the Benjamin Gilman Congress, 1995, Theodore Presser Found. award, Westchester U., 1962, N.J. Opera Festival winner, Nat. Arion award. Avocation: genealogy. Home and Office: PO Box 412 37 DuBois St Wallkill NY 12589 Office Phone: 845-895-3959. Personal E-mail: parkyn@frontiernet.net.

STRAUSS, ALBRECHT BENNO, retired language educator, editor; b. Berlin, May 17, 1921; came to U.S., 1940; s. Bruno and Bertha (Badt) S.; m. Nancy Grace Barron, July 30, 1978; 1 child, Rebecca Ilse; stepchildren: Carolyn, Kathryn BA, Oberlin Coll., 1942; MA, Tulane U., 1948; PhD, Harvard U., 1956. Instr. English Brandeis U., 1951-52; teaching fellow gen. edn. Harvard U., 1952-55; instr. English Yale U., 1955-59; asst. prof. English U. Okla., Norman, 1959-60, U. N.C., Chapel Hill, 1960-64, assoc. prof., 1964-70, prof., 1970-91, prof. emeritus, 1991—; lectr. Duke Inst. for Learning in Retirement, 1993—2005. Editor Studies in Philology, 1974-80; sec. editorial com. Yale Edit. of Works of Samuel Johnson, 1975-2008; mem. editorial com. Ga. Edit. Works of Tobias Smollett, 1973-95; contbr. articles to lit. publs. Served with U.S. Army, 1942-46 Recipient Tanner Teaching award U. N.C., 1966; Fulbright fellow, Germany, 1983-84 Mem. MLA, South Atlantic MLA, Am. Soc. Eighteenth-Century Studies (pres. Southeastern group 1980-81), Johnsonians. Republican. Jewish. Home: 396 Lakeshore Ln Chapel Hill NC 27514-1728 Personal E-mail: strausshaus@mindspring.com.

STRAUSS, ARNOLD WILBUR, pediatrician, educator; b. Benton Harbor, Mich., Mar. 31, 1945; m. Patricia Tylisz, Mar. 14, 1970; children: Natasha Tanya, Lara Katyana. BA, Stanford U., 1966; MD, Washington U., St. Louis, Mo., 1970. Diplomate Am. Bd. Pediatrics. Resident in pediatrics St. Louis Childrens Hosp., St. Louis, 1970-72, fellow in pediatric cardiology, 1972-75; postdoctoral rsch. fellow Merck Sharp & Dohme Rsch. Labs., Rahway, NJ, 1975-77; asst. prof. pediatrics Washington U., St. Louis, 1977-79, asst. prof. biol. chemistry, 1977-80, assoc. prof. pediatrics, 1979-82, assoc. prof. biol. chemistry, 1980-82, dir. divsn. pediatric cardiology dept. pediatrics, 1981—2000, prof. pediatrics, 1982—2000, prof. biol. chemistry, 1983-89, prof. biochemistry and molecular physics, 1989-92, prof. molecular biology and pharmacology, 1992—2000, adj. prof. pediatrics, 2000—07; prof. molecular physiology and biophysics Vanderbilt U. Sch. Medicine, Nashville, 2000—07, James C. Overall prof. pediatrics, chair pediatrics, 2000—07, investigator, Kennedy Ctr. for Rsch. in Human Devel., 2000—07, investigator, human genetics prog., 2001—07, med. dir. Monroe Carell Jr. Children's Hosp., 2000—07; B.K. Rachford prof. and chair pediatrics U. Cin. Coll. Medicine, 2007—; med. dir., dir. rsch. found. Cin. Children's Hosp. Med. Ctr., 2007—. Investigator Am. Heart Assn., 1979-1984. Contbr. articles, chapters to books. NIH program grantee, 1989, prin. investigator, 1994; recipient E. Mead Johnson award for excellence in pediatric rsch., 1991, Alumni Faculty award, Washington U., 1995, Basic Sci. award, Am. Heart Assn., 2006. Fellow Am. Acad. Pediatrics; mem. AAAS, Inst. Medicine, Soc. for Pediatric Rsch. (mem. cardiovascular coun. 1987-90), Am. Coll. Cardiology (coun. Mo. chpt. 1992-94), Am. Heart Assn., Am. Soc. Clin. Investigation, Am. Pediatric Soc., Am. Assn. Physicians, Am. Physiol. Soc., Internat. Pediatric Rsch. Found. (trustee, sec. 1995—), Phi Beta Kappa, Alpha Omega Alpha. Roman Catholic. Office: Cin Childrens Hosp Med Ctr 3333 Burnet Ave Cincinnati OH 45229-3039 Office Phone: 513-636-2942. E-mail: arnold.strauss@cchmc.org.*

STRAUSS, BERNARD S., geneticist, educator; b. NYC, Apr. 18, 1927; s. Joseph and Kate (Silk) S.; m. Carol Maxine Dunham, Sept. 8, 1949; children: Leslie Joan Travis, David Wilson, Paul Leonard. BS, CCNY, 1947; PhD, Calif. Inst. Tech., 1950; postdoctoral fellow, U. Tex., 1950-52. Teaching asst. Calif. Inst. Tech., 1947-48; asst. prof. Syracuse U., 1952-56, assoc. prof., 1956-60; rsch. assoc. Brookhaven Nat. Lab., 1954-55; assoc. prof. U. Chgo., 1960, prof., 1965—2001, emeritus, 2001—, chmn. com. genetics, 1962-76, chmn. dept. microbiology, 1969-84, chmn. dept. molecular genetics and cell biology, 1984-85, dean basic scis., div. biol. scis., 1985-88. Vis. prof. U. Sydney, 1967, Hadassah Med. Sch., Hebrew U., Jerusalem, 1975, 81; mem. genetics tng. com. NIH, 1962-66, 70-73, mem. chem. pathology study sect., 1985-89. Served with U.S. Mcht. Marine, 1945-47. Fulbright, Guggenheim fellow Osaka U., Japan, 1958-59, Fogarty Sr. Internat. fellow NIH/Imperial Cancer Rsch. Fund, Eng., 1991. Fellow AAAS; mem. Am. Soc. Biochemistry & Molecular Biology, Am. Assn. Cancer Rsch., Genetics Soc. Am., Genetics Soc. Japan (hon.), Phi Beta Kappa. Home: 1700 E 56th St Apt 301 Chicago IL 60637-1933 Office Phone: 773-702-1628. E-mail: bs19@uchicago.edu.

STRAUSS, CAROLYN L., former broadcast executive; b. NYC, July 13, 1963; BA, Harvard U., 1985. Temp Documentaries Dept. HBO, 1986, asst. original programming, 1986—89, mgr. original programming, 1989—90, dir. original programming, 1990—94, v.p. original programming, 1994—99, sr. v.p. original programming, 1999—2002, exec. v.p. original programming, 2002—04, pres. entertainment, 2004—08. Named one of 100 Most Powerful Women in Entertainment, Hollywood Reporter, 2006, 2007. Office: HBO Entertainment 1100 Avenue of Americas New York NY 10036

STRAUSS, DAVID, political organization administrator, former legislative staff member; b. Fargo, ND, Apr. 2, 1950; BA in Polit. Sci. magna cum laude, Moorhead State U., Minn., 1973, BS in Secondary Edn. and Polit. Sci. magna cum laude, 1973. Exec. dir. ND Dem. Party, 1975-76; dir. ND Agrl. Stblzn. and Conservation Svc., 1977-81; adminstrv. asst., Senator Quentin Burdick US Senate, Washington, 1981-88, staff dir., Environment and Pub. Works Com., 1988-92, chief of staff to Senator Jocelyn Birch Burdick, 1992, chief of staff to Senator John Breaux, 1993; dep. chief of staff to Vice Pres. Al Gore Office of Vice Pres., Washington, 1993-97; exec. dir. Pension Benefit Guaranty Corp. (PBGC), Washington, 1997; chmn. Congressman Earl Pomeroy's Reelection Campaign, 2002, 2004, ND Dem.-NPL Com., Bismarck, 2005—. Vis. lectr. Ctr. Health Policy Rsch. and Ethics, George Mason U., Fairfax, Va., 2001—; lectr. Ctr. Study of Congress and the Presidency, Am. U., Washington. Eastman Kodak Congl. Fellow for Sr. Mgrs. in Govt. Program, John F. Kennedy Sch. Govt., Harvard U., 1992. Democrat. Office: ND Dem-NPL Com 1902 E Divide Ave Bismarck ND 58501 Office Phone: 701-255-0460. Office Fax: 701-255-7823.*

STRAUSS, ERIC JASON, orthopedist; b. New Hyde Pk., NY, Feb. 19, 1977; s. Howard Steven and Susan Strauss; m. Stacey Beth Koretsky, Oct. 15, 2005. BA, Emory U., Atlanta, 1999; MD, Weill Med. Coll. Cornell U., NYC, 2003. Lic. NY, 2005. Chief resident orthop. surgery NYU-Hosp. Joint Diseases, NYC, 2003—. Office: NYU-Hosp Joint Diseases 301 E 17th St New York NY 10003 Office Fax: 212-598-6096. Personal E-mail: ericstraussmd@gmail.com.

STRAUSS, GWEN B., writer, editor; b. Deschapelles, Haiti, May 19, 1963; d. Julian Max Strauss and Katie Cowles Nichols; m. Jody Gerard Jenkins, June 22, 1996; children: Noah Jenkins, Sophie Jenkins, Eliza Jenkins. BA in Poetry, Hampshire Coll., 1986; MA in Edn., Wheelock Coll., 1987. Tchg. asst. Park Sch., Boston, 1986—87; freelance writer France, 1990—2003; editl. asst. Frank Books, Paris, 1992; editor Design Press, Savannah, Ga., 2002—04; dir. French campus Savannah Coll. of Art and Design, Lacoste, France, 2005—. Editl. cons. So. Poetry Rev., Savannah, 2003. Author: (poetry book) Trail of Stones, 1989, (children's book) Night Shimmy, 1991; contbr. short stories and poetry to various lit. jours. Recipient hon. mention, Atlanta Rev., 2001; finalist Nat. Poetry Series, 1995, Allen Ginsburg Poetry prize, 2003. Mem.: Authors Guild, Amnesty Internat., Planned Parenthood. Democrat. Avocations: gardening, sailing. Office: SCAD Rue Basse 84480 Lacoste France Personal E-mail: gbs0885@aol.com. Business E-Mail: gstrauss@scad.edu.

STRAUSS, HERBERT LEOPOLD, chemistry professor; b. Aachen, Germany, Mar. 26, 1936; came to U.S., 1940, naturalized, 1946; s. Charles and Joan (Goldschmidt) S.; m. Carolyn North Cooper, Apr. 24, 1960; children: Michael Abram, Rebecca Anne, Ethan Edward. AB, Columbia U., 1957, MA, 1958, PhD, 1960; postgrad, Oxford U., 1960-61. Mem. faculty U. Calif., Berkeley, 1961—, prof. chemistry, 1973—2003, prof. grad. divsn., 2003—, vice chmn. dept. chemistry, 1975-81, 92-95, asst. dean. Coll. Chemistry, 1986-92, assoc. dean, 1995—2008. Vis. prof. Indian Inst. Tech., Kanpur, 1968-69, Fudan U., Shanghai, 1982, U. Tokyo, 1982, U. Paris du Nord, 1987; mem. IUPAC Commn. I.1, 1990-2005. Author: Quantum Mechanics, 1968; assoc. editor Ann. Rev. Phys. Chemistry, 1976-85, editor, 1985-2000. Recipient Bomen-Michaelson award Coblentz Soc., 1994, Ellis Lippincott award Optical Soc. Am., 1994, The Berkeley Citation, 2003, Faculty Svc. award, 2008; Alfred P. Sloan fellow, 1966-70. Fellow Am. Phys. Soc., AAAS; mem. Am. Chem. Soc., Sigma Xi, Phi Beta Kappa, Phi Lambda Upsilon. Achievements include research in elucidation of vibrational spectra associated with large amplitude molecular motion in gases, liquids and solids. Home: 2447 Prince St Berkeley CA 94705-2021 Office: U Calif Dept Chemistry Berkeley CA 94720-1420 Home Phone: 510-848-3522; Office Phone: 510-642-7114. Business E-Mail: hls@berkeley.edu.

STRAUSS, JEROME FRANK, III, medical researcher, educator; b. Chgo., May 2, 1947; s. Jerome Frank (Jr.) and Josephine (Newberger) Strauss; m. Catherine Blumlein, June 20, 1970; children: Jordan L., Elizabeth J. BA, Brown U., 1969; MD, U. Pa., 1974, PhD, 1975. Asst. prof. U. Pa. Sch. Medicine, Phila., 1976—83, assoc. prof., 1983—85, prof., 1985—, assoc. chair, 1987—, assoc. dean, 1990—98; Luigi Mastroianni jr. prof. and founding dir. Ctr. Rsch. on Women's Health and Reproduction, Phila., 1990—94; prof. Inst. Medicine NAS, 1994—; dean, exec. v.p. med. affairs, prof. ob-gyn. Va. Commonwealth U. Sch. Medicine, Richmond, 2005—. Biochem. endocrinology study sect. NIH, 1983—87, Nat. Adv. Child Health and Human Devel. Coun., 2002—06; chmn. population rsch. com. NICHHD, 1989—92; chair Reproductive Scientist of the Ams. Network, 1995—; dir. Ctr. Excellence in Women's Health, 1996—2002; co-chair Indo-U.S. Joint Working Grp. on Reproductive Sci. and Contraceptive Tech., 1999—; bd. dirs. Burroughs Wellcome Fund, 2003—; trustee Berlex Found., 2005—; Cheung Kong lectr., prof. Heilongjiang U. Chinese Medicine, 2006—08; clin. rsch. adv. com. NIEHS, 2009—. Editor: Lipoprotein and Cholesterol Metabolism in Sterodogenic Tissues, 1985, Current Topics in Membrane Research, 1987, Uterine and Embryonic Factors in Early Pregnancy, 1991, New Achievements in Research of Ovarian Function, 1995, Cell Death in Reproductive Physiology, 1997, Molecular Biology in Reproductive Medicine, 1999, Ovarian Function Research: Present and Future, 1999, Reproductive Medicine Molecular, Cellular and Genetic Fundamentals, 2002, New Frontiers in Contraceptive Research, 2004, Yen and Jaffe's Reproductive Endocrinology, 2004, Preterm Birth, 2007, Steroids jour., 1993—; assoc. editor Ency. of Reproduction, 1998—, assoc. editor, mem. editl. bd. Jour. Lipid Rsch., 1982—90, corr. editor Jour. Steroid Biochem. and Molecular Biology, 1990—99, mem. editl. bd. Endocrinology, 1986—90, 1997—2000, Biology of Reprodn., 1986—90, 1999—2003, Jour. of Women's Health, 1991—, Jour. Soc. Gynecologic Investigation, 1993—, Placenta, 1995—98, Trends in Endocrinology and Metabolism, 1999—2008, Reference en Gynecologie Obstetrique, 1999—, Seminars in Reproductive Endocrinology, 2000—, Jour. Endocrinology, 2000—06, Human Reproduction Update, 2001—05, Science, 2004—, assoc. editor Molecular Human Reproduction, 2007—. Recipient Transatlantic medal, Brit. Endocrine Soc., 1998, Disting. Grad. award, U. Pa., 2005, NAS Inst. Medicine, 2005, Rectoral medal, U. Chile, 2009. Fellow: Internat. Acad. Human Reproduction; mem.: Perinatal Rsch. Soc., Am. Soc. for Reproductive Medicine, Soc. for Study of Reproduction (bd. dirs. 1989—91, Rsch. award 1992), Endocrine Soc., Soc. Gynecologic Investigation (pres. 2003, Pres.'s Achievement award 1990, Disting. Scientist award 2006). Home: 2808 Monument Ave Unit 3 Richmond VA 23221 Office: Va Commonwealth U Dean's Office Sch Medicine 1101 E Marshall St Rm 1-070 Richmond VA 23298 Business E-Mail: jfstrauss@vcu.edu.

STRAUSS, JEROME MANFRED, lawyer, bank executive; b. Milw., Nov. 7, 1934; s. Emanuel and Loraine (Goetz) S.; m. Susan Jean Kauffman, Dec. 30, 1967; children: Martha Lynn, Jared Lee, David Aaron. BA with honors, Ind. U., 1956; JD, NYU, 1959. Bar: Ind. 1959, Fla. 1996, U.S. Dist. Ct. (so. dist.) Ind. 1959, U.S. Tax Ct. 1965, U.S. Ct. Appeals (7th cir.) 1969. Lawyer Ice Miller Donadio & Ryan, Indpls., 1959—93, ptnr., 1969-93; sr. v.p. and regional trust mgr. Merrill Lynch Trust Co., 1993-95; with Mershon, Sawyer, Johnston, Dunwody & Cole, Miami, Palm Beach, Naples, 1995-96; established Wollman, Strauss & Assocs., P.A., 1997; founder Midwest Tax and Estate Planning Inst., Indpls., 1976—; law practitioner Naples, Fla.; counsel Grant, Fridkin Pearson Athan & Crown, Naples, Fla., 2008—. Co-author: Marital Deduction Trusts, 1963, Real Estate in an Estate, 1963, Durable Powers of Attorney, 1993; contbr. articles to profl. jours. Bd. dirs. Orton Soc., Indpls., 1970-72, Indpls., 1970-72, Indpls. Hebrew Congregation, 1979-85, Planned Giving Group of Ind., Indpls., 1988-95, Ind. Continuing Legal Edn. Forum, 1989-94; devel. com. Collier County, Fla. Cmty. Found., 1995-2002; mem. Planned Giving Com. of Lee County, Fla., 1995-2002, Fla. Planned Giving Coun., 1995—; estate planning coun. Naples, Fla., 1996—. Fulbright scholar, 1956. Fellow Am. Coll Trust and Estate Counsel (charitable com., estate and gift tax com. 1996-2001), Am. Coll. Tax Counsel; mem. ABA (vice-chmn. marital deduction com. real estate property, probate and trust sect. 1988-90), Internat. Acad. Estate and Trust Law (academician 1987—), Ind. State Bar Assn. (sec. 1979-80, chmn. probate, trust and real property sect. 1970-71), Ind. Estate Planning Coun. (pres. 1970-71), Fla. State Bar Assn., Internat. Assn. of Fin. Planners of S.W. Fla., Collier County Bar Assn. Home: 1056 Diamond Lake Cir Naples FL 34114-9211 Office: 5551 Ridgewood Dr Naples FL 34108 Office Phone: 239-293-8661. Business E-Mail: rv-atty@lawyer4u.com.

STRAUSS, JOHN, literature and language professor; BA, Franklin & Marshall Coll., Lancaster, Pa., 1977; MA, U. Pa., Phila., 1986. Tchr., English and German Upattinas Sch., Glenmoore, Pa., 1978—79; tchr., English dept. head Wyncote Acad., Pa., 1980—84; adj. instr. English Temple U. Ambler Campus, Pa., 1986—87, Rider Coll., Lawrenceville, NJ, 1986—88; English prof. Bucks County CC, Newtown, Pa., 1987—. Author: She's Misunderstood (Cultural Incentive grant, 1988). Nat. polit. com. Dem. Socialists Am., NYC, 1999—; editor Dem. Left, 1999—; exec. com. Greater Phila. Dem. Socialists Am., 1994—; editor Greater Phila. Dem. Left, Newtown, 1995—. Mem.: Bucks County CC Fedn. Tchrs. (corr. sec. 1994—99). Avocation: music. Office: Bucks County CC 275 Swamp Rd Newtown PA 18940 Business E-Mail: straussj@bucks.edu.

STRAUSS, JOHN STEAVEN, psychiatrist, educator; b. Cleve., Aug. 18, 1932; s. Walton and Augusta Strauss; children: Jeffrey, Sarah. BA, Swarthmore Coll., 1954; postgrad., Jean Piaget, Geneva, 1956—57; MD, Yale U., 1959; cert. cmty. psychiatry, Washington Sch. Psychiatry, 1966. Intern New Eng. Ctr. Hosp., Boston, 1959—60; resident medicine Boston City Hosp., 1960—61; resident psychiatry McLean/Beth Israel Hosps., Boston, 1961—64; clin. assoc. USPHS, Bethesda, Md., 1964—66; chief psychiat. assessment NIMH, Bethesda, 1968—72; collaborating investigator WHO, Bethesda, 1966—76, U.S. rep. to Program on Internat. Collaboration for Psychiat. Diagnosis, 1980—83; assoc. prof. psychiatry U. Rochester, NY, 1972—76, prof., 1976—77; prof. psychiatry Yale U., New Haven, 1977—98, prof. emeritus psychiatry, 1998—. Cons. Woodley House, Washington, 1966—72; bd. dirs. dept. psychiatry Ctr. Studies Prolonged Psychiat. Disorders Conn. Mental Health Ctr. Yale U. Med. Sch., 1985—98. Editor: The Psychotherapy of Schizophrenia, 1980; co-author: Schizophrenia, 1981. NIMH grantee, 1980—96. Fellow: Am. Psychiat. Assn. (cons. Task Force Nomenclature 1974—80, disting., disting. life fellow, Stanley Dean award 1980, Samuel G. Hibbs award 1983, Van Amerigen award 1988, Amin Loeb award 1990); mem.: Associé Etranger Société Médico-Psychologique, Soc. Life History Rsch. Psychopathology (chmn. 1975—76), Assn. Clin. Psychiatry Rsch. Home: 50 Burton St New Haven CT 06515-2116 Office: Yale U Sch Medicine Dept Psychiatry 34 Park St New Haven CT 06519-1109

STRAUSS, JON CALVERT, retired academic administrator; b. Chgo., Jan. 17, 1940; s. Charles E. and Alice C. (Woods) S.; m. Joan Helen Bailey, Sept. 19, 1959 (div. 1985); children: Susan, Stephanie; m. Jean Anne Sacconaghi, June 14, 1985; children: Kristoffer, Jonathon. BSEE, U. Wis., 1959; MS in Physics, U. Pitts., 1962; PhD in E.E., Carnegie Inst. Tech., 1965; LLD (hon.), U. Mass., 1996. Assoc. prof. computer sci., elec. engring. Carnegie Mellon U., Pitts., 1966-70; dir. computer ctr., prof. computer sci. Tech. U. Norway, Trondheim, Norway, 1970; vis. assoc. prof. elec. engring. U. Mich., Ann Arbor, 1971; assoc. prof. computer sci. Washington U., St. Louis, 1971-74, dir. computing facilities, 1971-73; dir. computing activities U. Pa., Phila., 1974-76, faculty master Stouffer Coll. House, 1978-80, prof. computer, info. scis., prof. decision sci. Wharton Sch., 1974-81, exec. dir. Univ. Budget, 1975-78, v.p. for budget, fin., 1978-81; prof. elec. engring. U. So. Calif., Los Angeles, 1981-85, sr. v.p. adminstrn., 1981-85; pres. Worcester Poly. Inst., Mass., 1985-94, pres. emeritus; v.p., chief fin. officer Howard Hughes Med. Inst., Chevy Chase, Md., 1994-97; pres. Harvey Mudd Coll., Claremont, Calif., 1997—2006, pres. emeritus, 2006—. Cons. Electronics Assocs., Inc., 1965, IBM Corp., 1960-64, Westinghouse Elec. Corp., 1959-60; bd. dirs. Transamerica Income Fund, Variable Ins. Fund, United Educators Ins., mem. NSF Nat. Sci. Bd., 2004-. Contbr. articles on computer systems and university mgmt. to profl. jours.; co-holder patent. Bd. dirs. Presbyn.-U. Pa. Med. Ctr., Phila., 1980-81, U. So. Calif. Kenneth Norris Jr. Cancer Hosp., L.A., 1981-85, Med. Ctr. of Ctrl. Mass., 1986-94, Worcester Acad., 1986-91, Mass. Biotech. Rsch. Inst., 1985-94. Mem. New. Eng. Assn. Schs. and Colls., Inc., Commn. on Instns. of Higher Edn., Nat. Collegiate Athletic Assn. (pres.'s commn. 1990-94). Avocations: hiking, running, swimming. Office: Harvey Mudd Coll Kingston Hall Rm 201 301 E 12th St Claremont CA 91711-5980 Office Fax: 909-321-8360. Business E-Mail: jon_strauss@hmc.edu.

STRAUSS, MICHAEL GEORGE, physics professor; b. Ft Worth, Tex., Dec. 31, 1958; s. Richard Lehman and Mary Strauss; married. BS, Biola U., La Mirada, Calif., 1981; PhD, U. Calif., LA, 1988. Rsch. assoc. U. Mass., Amherst, 1988—95; assoc. prof. physics U. Okla., Norman, 1995—. Assoc. dir. Okla. Ctr. High Energy Physics, Norman, 2004—. Apologist and spkr. Reasons to Believe, Pasadena, Calif., 1996—2008. Office: Univ OK 440 W Brooks Norman OK 73019 Business E-Mail: strauss@nhn.ou.edu.

STRAUSS, PAUL, Shadow Senator to US Congress from DC; b. NYC; m. Kathy Strauss; children: Abigail, Samantha. BA, Am. U.; JD, Wash. Coll. Law. Atty. Law Offices of Paul Strauss & Assocs., PC, 1993—; various locally elected govt. positions including at-large mem. of Dem. State Com. and chmn. of Dem. Party Statehood Com. Washington; chmn. to commr. Advisory Neighborhood Commn., 1986—96; DC shadow senator to US Congress Washington, 1997—. Legis. asst. council's com. on consumer and regulatory affairs, Washington; union organizer Hotel and Restaurant Employee's Local 25. Pres. NW Youth Alliance, Inc.; atty. mem., panel chmn. Bd. Real Property Assessment and Appeals, Washington. Mem.: Internat. Assn. Assessment Officers, African-Am. Coalition (hon. chmn.). Democrat. Office: John A Wilson Bldg 1350 Pennsylvania Ave, NW Washington DC 20004 Office Phone: 202-727-7890. Office Fax: 202-727-9672. E-mail: paulstrauss@aol.com.

STRAUSS, PETER, actor; b. Croton-on-Hudson, NY, Feb. 20, 1947; m. Rachel Ticotin Dec. 31, 1998; children: Justin, Tristen. Attended, Northwestern U. Actor: (Broadway plays) Einstein and the Polar Bear, 1981, (films) debut in Hail Hero, 1969, Soldier Blue, 1970, The Trial of the Catonsville Nine, The Last Tycoon, 1976, Spacehunter, 1983, Nick of Time, 1995, Keys to Tulsa, 1997, xXx: State of the Union, 2005; (TV fims) The Man Without a Country, 1973, The FBI Story: The FBI Vs. the Ku Klux Klan, 1975, Attack on Terror, 1975, Rich Man, Poor Man, 1976, Rich Man, Poor Man-Book II, 1976-77, Young Joe, the Forgotten Kennedy, 1978, The Jericho Mile, 1979 (Emmy award), Angel on My Shoulder, 1980, Masada, 1981, Tender is the Night, 1985, Kane and Abel, 1986, Under Siege, 1986, Penalty Phase, 1986, The Proud Men, 1987, Brotherhood of the Rose, 1989, Peter Gunn, 1989, 83 Hours Till Dawn, 1990, Flight of the Black Angel, 1991, Fugitive Among Us, 1992, Trial: The Price of Passion, 1992, Men Don't Tell, 1993, The Yearling, 1994, Texas Justice, 1995, In the Lake of the Woods, 1996, My Father's Shadow: The Sam Sheppard Story, 1998, Seasons of Love, 1998 (also exec. prodr.), Joan of Arc, 1999, A Father's Choice, 2000, Murder on the Orient Express, 2002, (TV series) Moloney, 1996, Body & Soul, 2002; exec. prodr: (films) Buster, 1988; actor, co-exec. prodr. (TV films) Heart of Steel, 1983; actor, prodr. A Whale for the Killing, 1981; TV guest appearances include Mary Tyler Moore, 1973, Hawaii Five-O, 1974, Barnaby Jones, 1974, (voice) Batman, 1994, (voice) Duckman, 1996, (voice) The Incredible Hulk, 1996, Strange Frequency, 2001, Law & Order, 2004.

STRAUSS, PETER L(ESTER), law educator; b. NYC, Feb. 26, 1940; s. Simon D. and Elaine Ruth (Mandle) S.; m. Joanna Burnstine, Oct. 1, 1964; children: Benjamin, Bethany. AB magna cum laude, Harvard U., 1961; LLB magna cum laude, Yale U., 1964. Bar: DC 1965, US Supreme Ct. 1968. Law clk. US Ct. Appeals DC Cir., 1964-65, US Supreme Ct., 1965-66; lectr. Halle Selassie U. Sch. Law, Addis Ababa, Ethiopia, 1966-68; asst. to solicitor gen. Dept. Justice, Washington, 1968-71; assoc. prof. law Columbia U., 1971-74, prof., 1974—, Betts prof., 1985—, vice-dean, 1996, 2001—02. Gen. counsel Nuclear Regulatory Commn., 1975-77, Adminstrv. Conf. U.S., 1984-95; Byrne vis. prof. Sch. Law Harvard U., Cambridge, Mass., 1994; bd. dirs. Ctr. for Computer Assisted Legal Instrn., 2002—. Mem. adv. bd. Lexis Electronic Author's Press, 1995-99; editor: SSRN Administrative Law Abstracts, 1997-2006; author: (with Abba Paulos translator) Fetha Negast: The Law of the Kings, 1968, 2008; (with others) Administrative Law Cases and Comments, 2003; Administrative Justice in the United States, 2002; Legal Methods: Understanding and Using Cases and Statutes, 2008; Administrative Law Stories, 2005; Legislation: Understanding and Using Statutes, 2006; contbr. articles to profl. jours. Recipient John Marshall prize Dept. Justice, 1970, Disting. Svc. award Nuclear Regulatory Commn., 1977, Cudahy prize, 2008. Mem. ABA (chair sect. administrv. law and regulatory practice 1992-93, Disting. Scholarship award 1988), Am. Law Inst. Office: Columbia U Law Sch 435 W 116th St New York NY 10027-7201 Home Phone: 914-478-3221; Office Phone: 212-854-2370. Business E-Mail: strauss@law.columbia.edu.

STRAUSS, RICKY, film company executive, producer; BA in English and Theater, cum laude, U. Vt. Advt. exec. Columbia Pictures Industries, Inc., 1988—97; mktg. cons., sr. v.p. prodn. Sony Pictures Entertainment, Inc.; mktg. cons. Revolution Studios; founder, pres. Ricochet Entertainment; pres. Participant Prodns., LLC, 2005—. Prodr.: (films) Grownups, 2001, Double Vision, 2002; exec. prodr.: The Sweetest Thing, 2002, Fast Food Nation, 2006, An Inconvenient Truth, 2006, The Visitor, 2007, Chicago 10, 2007. Past bd. dirs. Project Angel Food, LA; vice-chmn. The Trevor Project; mentor Project: Involved; hon. bd. mem. Teamworks charity. Named a Maverick, Details mag., 2008. Office: Participant Prodns LLC 335 N Maple Dr Ste 354 Beverly Hills CA 90210

STRAUSS, ROBERT PHILIP, economics professor; b. Cleve., May 11, 1944; s. Harry and Carrie S.; m. Celeste G. Meade, Jan. 11, 1980; children: Sarah Elizabeth, David Anthony, Elena Nicole. AB in Econs., U. Mich., 1966; MA, U. Wis., 1968, PhD in Econs., 1970. Fellow Inst. Research on Poverty, 1968-69; asst. prof. econs. U. N.C., Chapel Hill,

1969-73, assoc. prof., 1973-79; econ. policy fellow Brookings Instn., Washington, 1971-72; economist U.S. Congress Joint Com. Taxation, 1975-78; prof. econs. and pub. policy Carnegie-Mellon U., Pitts., 1979—, assoc. dean Sch. Urban and Pub. Affairs, 1981-83, dir. Ctr. for Pub. Fin. Mgmt., 1984-91; dir. research Pa. Tax Commn., 1979-81. Vis. prof. econs. and pub. policy U. Rochester, 1992-94. Mem. Pa. Local Tax Reform Commn., 1987; sec. faculty Carnegie-Mellon U., 1991-92. Recipient Exceptional Service award U.S. Treasury, 1972, Disting. Service award Pitts. Tax Execs. Inst., 1987, Georgescu Roegen award, 1998, Steven B. Gold award, Assn. Pub. Policy and Mgmt. Nat. Tax Assn. and Fedn. Tax Adminstrs., 2005; named to Alumni Hall of Fame, Cleveland Heights H.S., 2004; grantee NSF, U.S. Dept. Labor, U.S. Treasury, HUD, Social Security Adminstrn.; William C. Lincoln fellow, 2005-06, 06-07. Mem. Am. Econ. Assn., Econometric Soc., Nat. Tax Assn., Pub. Choice Soc., Assn. for Pub. Policy and Mgmt., Am. Soc. for Pub. Adminstrn., Nat. Tax Assn. (bd. dirs. 1995-98). Clubs: Cosmos. Home: 2307 Country Pl Export PA 15632-9059 Office: 5000 Forbes Ave Pittsburgh PA 15213-3890 Office Phone: 412-268-4798. E-mail: rpstrauss@gmail.com.

STRAUSS, ULRICH PAUL, chemist, educator; b. Frankfurt, Germany, Jan. 10, 1920; s. Richard and Marianne (Seligmann) S.; m. Esther Lipetz, June 20, 1943 (dec. Sept. 1949); children— Dorothy, David; m. Elaine Greenbaum, Nov. 23, 1950; children— Elizabeth, Evelyn. AB, Columbia U., 1941; PhD, Cornell U., 1944. Sterling fellow Yale U., 1946-48; faculty Rutgers U., New Brunswick, NJ, 1948—, prof. phys. chemistry, 1960-90, prof. emeritus, 1990—; also dir. Sch. Chemistry, 1965-71, chmn. dept. chemistry, 1974-80. Prof. emeritus Rutgers U., 1990—. Mem. editorial bd. Macromolecules, 1990-93; contbr. articles to profl. jours. Recipient Sci. achievement award Johnson Wax Co., 1986; NSF sr. fellow Nat. Center Sci. Research, Strasbourg, France, 1961-62; Guggenheim fellow U. Oxford, Eng., 1971-72 Fellow N.Y. Acad. Scis.; mem. Am. Chem. Soc. (chmn. phys. chemistry group N.J. sect. 1956, councillor 1961-72, honored by 1-day symposium at nat. meeting N.Y.C. 1986, Excellence in Edn. award N.J. sect. 1994). Home: 227 Lawrence Ave Highland Park NJ 08904-1837 Office: Rutgers U Dept Chemistry New Brunswick NJ 08903 Business E-Mail: strauss@rci.rutgers.edu.

STRAUSSLER, TOMAS See STOPPARD, TOM

STRAUSSMAN, JEFFREY, dean, political science professor; BA, Hofstra U.; MA, Hunter Coll.; PhD in Polit. Sci., CUNY, 1975. Tchr. Mich. State U.; joined faculty Syracuse U., 1979, chair Dept. Pub. Adminstrn., assoc. dean Maxwell Sch., Maxwell prof. of tchg. excellence, 1999; dean Rockefeller Coll. Pub. Affairs and Policy U. Albany, 2006—. Fulbright Scholar, Budapest U. Econ. Scis., 1992. Fellow: Nat. Acad. Pub. Adminstrn. Office: Rockefeller Coll of Pub Affairs and Policy 135 Western Ave Albany NY 12222 E-mail: jstraussman@albany.edu.*

STRAUTMANIS, MICHAEL (MICHAEL A. STRAUTMANIS), federal official; b. Chgo., 1969; s. Sandra Bradley-Strautmanis and Juris Strautmanis (Stepfather); m. Damona Strautmanis; 3 children. BS, U. Ill., 1991; JD, U. Ill. Coll. Law, 1994. Paralegal Sidley & Austin, Chgo.; complex litigation and employment law atty. Chgo.; chief of staff to the gen. counsel US Agency Internat. Devel. (USAID), Washington; legis. dir., counsel to Rep. Rod Blagojevich US Congress, Ill.; counsel for legis. Am. Assn. Justice; chief counsel, dep. chief of staff Senator Barack Obama, Washington; mem. Congl. rels. team Senator Barack Obama's Presdl. Campaign, chief counsel, dir. pub. liaison & intergovernmental affairs, 2008—09; chief of staff to the asst. to the pres. for intergovernmental rels., pub. liaison The White House, Washington, 2009—. Democrat. Office: The White House 1600 Pennsylvania Ave NW Washington DC 20500*

STRAWBRIDGE, WILLIAM J., healthcare educator; b. Cin., Mar. 17, 1940; s. Louis Fetta Strawbridge and Jane Whipple Hoffmann; m. Margaret I. Wallhagen, Aug. 16, 1986. MPH, U.Washington, Seattle, 1987, PhD, 1991. Rsch. dir. Seattle Urban League, 1974—76, Puget Sound Health Sys. Agence, Seattle, 1977—80, hosp. planning dir., 1981—84; sr. rsch. scientist Human Population Lab., Berkeley, Calif.; adj. prof. Inst. Health and Aging, San Francisco, 2008. Contbr. articles. Vol. Oxfam Am., Boston, 1985—91; philanthropic bd. mem. LITA, San Rafael, Calif., 1994—2008. Ltjg USN, 1964—68, Vietnam, San Diego. Recipient Exempleton award, Templeton Found., 1998. Mem.: Gerontol. Soc. Am. (Fellow 2004). Office: Inst Health and Aging 3333 CA St Ste 340 San Francisco CA 94118-0646 Business E-Mail: bill.strawbridge@ucsf.edu.

STRAWDERMAN, WILLIAM E., statistics educator; b. Westerly, RI, Apr. 25, 1941; s. Robert Lee and Alida Browning (Dow) S.; m. Susan Linda Grube; July 20, 1985; children: Robert Lee, William Edward, Heather Lynne. BS, U. R.I., 1963; MS, Cornell U., 1965, Rutgers U., 1967, PhD, 1969. Mem. tech. staff Bell Tel. Labs., Holmdel, NJ, 1965-67; vis. asst. prof. Stanford (Calif.) U., 1969-70; instr. Rutgers U., New Brunswick, NJ, 1967-69, prof. stats., 1970—. Contbr. more than 150 articles to profl. jours. Fellow: Inst. Math. Stats., Am. Statis. Assn. Office: Rutgers U Statistics Dept Hill Ctr-Busch Campus New Brunswick NJ 08903 Home Phone: 908-874-4357; Office Phone: 732-445-2697. Business E-Mail: straw@stat.rutgers.edu.

STRAWHECKER, PAUL JOSEPH, fundraising consultant; b. Oct. 31, 1947; s. John Leslie and Leone Francis (Kalamaja) Strawhecker; m. Margaret Ellen Baumann, Aug. 31, 1974; children: Risa Nicole, Ryan John. Student, St. Joseph's Sem., 1963-67, Blessed John Neumann Coll., 1968-68; BA, Creighton U., 1970, postgrad. Law Sch., 1971-73; MPA, U. Nebr., 1980. Advanced cert. fundraising exec. Assn. Fundraising Profls. Rsch. specialist mayor's office City of Omaha, 1970, spl. asst. to mayor, 1971, mgr. spl. programs, 1972-73; dir. spl. resources Father Flanagan's Boys Home, Boys Town, Nebr., 1974-81; v.p. for devel. Luth. Hosps. and Homes Soc. Am., Fargo, N.D., 1982-86; asst. adminstr. Sacred Heart Gen. Hosp., Eugene, Oreg., 1986-87; v.p. Northwood U., Midland, Mich., 1987-94; pres. Paul J. Strawhecker, Inc., Omaha, 1995—. Adj. prof. U. Nebr., Omaha, 1995—; treas. Credit Union, 1975; clk., treas., liaison officer Village of Boys Town, 1974-81; writer Am. Soc. Planning Ofcls.; past owner The Wooden Spoon Ltd., Omaha.; exec. com. Assn. Philanthropic Counsel. Author: Fund Raising, 1997, Capital Campaigns, 1998, Resource Development, 1999. Chmn. Met. Area Planning Agy. Coun. Ofcls. Goals Com. for Human Svcs., 1976; mem. Omaha/Douglas County Criminal Justice Commn., 1977-80; mem. adv. com. Douglas County Office on ChildrenYouth, Midland County Cmty. Corrections, 1991-92; bd. dirs. "Say Yes" to Youth, 1990-92; chmn. urban affairs com. Met. Area Planning Agy. Mem. Assn. Fundraising Profls. (cert., pres. ND area chpt., bd. dirs. 1994-95, pres. Mich. chpt. bd. dirs. 1987-90, pres. Nebr. chpt. bd. dirs. 1997-99, vice chair nat. bd. 1991, nat. found. bd. 2000—, bd. mem. chair 2007—, U.S.A. Found.), Nat. Assn. Hosp. Devel. (spkr. 1983), Internat. City Mgmt. Assn. (spkr. 1971), Multi Hosp. Devel. Assn. (pres. 1986), Leadership Midland (alumni and steering com. 1990-92), Phi Kappa Psi. Roman Catholic. Home: 3424 N 129th Cir Omaha NE 68164-4240 Office: Paul J Strawhecker Inc 4913 Dodge St Omaha NE 68132-2917 Home Phone: 402-493-8049; Office Phone: 402-556-5785. Business E-Mail: paul@pjstraw.com.

STRAWN, EVELYN RAE, artist; b. Kerman, Calif., Nov. 24, 1921; d. Cloy Ray and Florence Grace (Angell) Hudson; m. Virgil Hollis Strawn, Sept. 19, 1940; children: C.J., Randall, Michael, Reagan. BA, U. Redlands, 1966. Artist freelance, Grand Terrace, Calif., 1959—; probation officer San Bernadino (Calif.) County, 1966-89. Developed and directed Sch. Based Teen Programs, San Bernardino, 1967-75, Pregnancy Program for Teens to Continue Schooling, 1967-68. Author: Moncho the Mule Stories, Manchas Brave Ach, Moncho the Mule; exhibited paintings and sculptures in pvt. collections and galleries. Bd. dirs., pres. Sexual Assault Svcs., San Bernardino, 1980-84; pres. Women in Mgmt., Inland Empire, 1983; found. mem. City of Grand Terrace, 2005. Recipient Cert. of Commendation, San Bernardino County Probation Dept., 1989. Mem. Nat. Soc. DAR (regent San Bernardino chpt.), Mayflower Soc., Soroptimist Internat. of Riverside (bd. dirs. 1984). Avocations: reading, horiculture, dance.

STRAWN, MATTHEW N., political organization administrator; b. Iowa; m. Erin Strawn; 2 children. BA, U. Iowa, 1996; JD, Cath. U. America, 2003. Comm. dir. and sr. legis. asst. to Rep. Saxby Chambliss US House of Reps., Washington, legis. dir. to Rep. Michael J. Rogers, 2001—03, chief of staff to Rep. Michael J. Rogers, 2003—07; founding ptnr. Riverside Partners, Inc., Ankeny, Iowa; mgr. Nathan Strawn Farms, Inc., Iowa; prin., owner Iowa Barnstormers, Des Moines; chmn. Republican Party of Iowa, Des Moines, 2009—. Named one of 40 Under 40, The Hill. Republican. Office: Republican Party of Iowa 621 E 9th St Des Moines IA 50309 Office Phone: 515-282-8105. Office Fax: 515-282-9019. E-mail: mstrawn@iowagop.org.*

STRAWSER, JERRY R., dean; BBA in Acctg., Tex. A&M U., 1983, MS in Acctg., 1984, PhD in Acctg., 1985. CPA Tex., 1985. Asst. prof. La. State U., 1985—90, Arthur Andersen & Co. rsch. fellow, 1989—90; assoc. prof. Conn. Bauer Coll. Bus., U. Houston, 1990—97, assoc. dean academic and rsch. programs, 1995—99, prof. and Arthur Anderson & Co. alumni prof. acctg. and taxation, 1997—2001, interim dean, 1999—2001; dean Mays Bus. Sch., Tex. A&M U., 2001—, Devel. Coun. chair bus., 2001—, Leland/Weinke chair acctg., 2001, now KPMG chair acctg. Mem. editl. bd. Issues in Acctg. Edn., 1998—. Co-author: (books) Auditing Theory and Practice, 1985—2001, Managerial Accounting, 1990—2000, Auditing & Assurance Services, 2004. Recipient Outstanding Tchg. award, Alpha Kappa Psi, 1985, George W. Fair award for tchg. excellence, 1986, Melcher award for rsch. excellence, 1992, 1995, Master Tchg. award, NationsBank, 1994, Disting. Faculty award, Exec. MBA Alumni Assn., 2000; Arthur Andersen rsch. fellowship, 1989, Melcher tchg. fellow, 1991, Melcher svc. fellow, 1993. Mem.: Am. Assn. Acctg., Assn. to Advance Collegiate Schools of Bus. Office: Tex A&M U Mays Bus Sch 4113 TAMU 3003 Wehner College Station TX 77843-4113 Office Phone: 979-845-4711. Office Fax: 979-845-6639. Business E-Mail: jstrawser@tamu.edu.*

STRAYER, BARRY LEE, retired judge; b. Moose Jaw, Sask., Can., Aug. 13, 1932; s. Carl John and Nina Naomi Strayer; m. Eleanor Lorraine Staton, July 2, 1955; children: Alison Lee, Jonathan Mark, Colin James. BA, U. Sask., Can., 1953, LLB, 1955; BCL, Oxford U., Eng., 1957; SJD, Harvard U., 1966. Bar: Sask., 1959. Crown solicitor Gov. Sask., Regina, 1959-62; prof. law U. Sask., 1962-68; dir. constitutional rev. Gov. Can., Ottawa, 1968-72, dir. constitutional law, 1972-74, asst. dep. minister justice, 1974-83; judge trial divsn. Fed. Ct. Can., Ottawa, 1983-94; jud. mem. Competition Tribunal Can., Ottawa, 1986-93; judge Fed. Ct. Appeal of Can., 1994—2004; chief justice Ct. Martial Appeal Ct. of Can., 1994—2004. Sessional lectr. U. Ottawa, 1973-78; constitutional advisor Rep. Seychelles, 1979; adviser Hongkong Govt. Bill of Rights, 1989. Author: Judicial Review of Legislation, 1968, Canadian Constitution and the Courts, 1983, 3d edit., 1988; contbr. articles to profl. jours. Mem.: Larrimac Golf Club, Rideau Club. Home: 504 Queen Elizabeth Dr Ottawa ON Canada K1S 3N4

STRAYER, JACQUELINE F., manufacturing executive; b. 1954; BA in Economics & Polit. Sci., U. Conn., 1976; MPS, NYU; attended, London Sch. Econs. Assoc., comm. cons. Mercer Human Resource Consulting, NY, 1984—87; corp. comm. GE Capital Corp., 1987—93, United Technologies Corp., 1995—2004; v.p. corp. comm. Arrow Electronics, Inc., 2004—08, Johnson Controls, Inc., 2008—. Trustee WNET/WLIW; past chair Conn. Pub. Broadcasting. Recipient Points in Light Award, Gen. Colin Powell. Mem.: Conf. Bd. (mem. Comm. Strategy Coun., Best in Class Award), Arthur Page Soc. Office: Johnson Controls Inc 5757 N Green Bay Ave Milwaukee WI 53209*

STRAYER, SCOTT MERLE, medical educator; b. Gustine, Calif., Aug. 19, 1965; s. Richart L. and Louise Judith Strayer; m. Karen Denton Denton, Feb. 17, 1996; children: Denton Elizabeth, Riley Paige. MD, Va. Commonwealth U., Richmond, 1994; MPH, St. Louis U., Mo., 2002. Diplomate Am. Acad. Family Physicians, 1997. Asst. prof. US Air Force, St. Louis U., Belleville, Ill., 1997—2001, U. Va., Charlottesville, 2001—, assoc. prof., 2007—. Author: (book) Handhelds in Medicine; contbr. articles to profl. jours. Statewide chmn. tar wars program Med. Soc. Va., Richmond, 2002—04. With USAF, 2007—08, USUHS, Bethesda, Md. Decorated Meritorious Svc. medal USAF; named Physician of Yr., Microsoft, 2001, Outstanding Vol. of Yr., Med. Soc. Va., 2004; Rsch. grant, NIAAA, 2006, Nat. Cancer Inst., 2006, Nat. Inst. Drug Abuse, 2008. Fellow: Am. Acad. Family Physicians (Tar Wars Star award 1997—2001); mem.: Am. Assn. Primary Care Endoscopists (bd. dirs. 2007—). Achievements include research in first handheld computer smoking intervention tool; invention of handheld computer billing application, pocketbilling and computer credentialling application. Office: Univ VA Health System PO Box 800729 Charlottesville VA 22908

STREAR, JOSEPH D., public relations executive; b. NYC, Nov. 5, 1933; s. Morris and Betty (Birenbaum) S. BA, CCNY, 1955. Pres. AC&R Pub. Relations, Inc., NYC, 1972-82; mng. ptnr. Kanan, Corbin, Schupak & Aronow, Inc., NYC, 1982-84; pres. Strear, David & Mitchell, Inc., NYC, 1984-91; prin. Joseph Strear Pub. Rels., NYC, 1992—. 1st lt. U.S. Army, 1955-57. Mem. Pub. Rels. Soc. Am. Avocation: sports. Office: 408 W 57th St New York NY 10019-3053 Office Phone: 212-757-9214. Business E-Mail: joejer@nyc.rr.com.

STREATOR, EDWARD, retired diplomat, management consultant; b. NYC, Dec. 12, 1930; s. Edward James and Ella (Stout) S.; m. Priscilla Craig Kenney, Feb. 16, 1957; children: Edward James, III, Elinor Craig Garcia-Garcia, Abigail Merrill Squance. AB, Princeton U., 1952. Commd. fgn. svc. officer Dept. State, 1956; assigned ICA, 1956-58; 3d sec. embassy Addis Ababa, Ethiopia, 1958-60; 2d sec. embassy Lome Togo, 1960-62; intelligence rsch. specialist Office Rsch. and Analysis for Africa, Dept. State, Washington, 1962-63, staff asst. to sec. state, 1964-66, chief polit.-mil. affairs unit, 1966-67; dep. dir. polit.-mil. affairs, 1967-68; dep. dir. polit. affairs US Mission to NATO, 1968-69; dep. dir. Office NATO and Atlantic Polit.-Mil. Affairs, Dept. State, 1969-73; dir. office, 1973-75; dep. US permanent rep. to NATO, dep. chief US Mission to NATO, 1975-77; minister, dep. chief of mission Am. embassy, London, 1975-84; ambassador, US rep. OECD Paris, 1984-87. Bd. dirs. South Bank, 1991-99; chmn. New Atlantic Initiative, 1996-2000. US dels. NATO and OECD Ministerial Meetings, 1964, 66, 69-75, 85-87; mem. 10th SEATO Coun. Min. Meeting, 1965; 2d spl. Inter-Am. Conf., 1965, Conf. Security and Coop., Europe, 1973; mem. Coun., Royal United Svcs. Inst., 1987-92, vice patron, 1991—; exec. com. The Pilgrims, UK, 1988-90, Internat. Inst. Strategic Studies, 1988-99; gov. Ditchley Found., 1988-, English Speaking Union, 1988-94; pres. Am. C. of C., UK, 1988-94; chmn. European Coun. Am. C. of C., 1992-94; bd. dirs. Brit-Am. Arts Assn., 1987-99; dir. Brit. Mus. Natural History Internat. Found.; devel. com. Nat. Gallery, UK, 1991-95; adv. bd. Inst. US Studies-U. London, 1993-99; mem. founding coun. Oxford Inst. Am. Studies, 1989-2001; adv. com. Fulbright Commn., 1995-2001; pres., trustee Northcoate Parkinson Fund, 2004-07, Train Found., 2007-, mem. bd. overseers John C. Whitehead Sch. Diplomacy & Internat. Relation, 2009 Lt.(jg) USNR, 1952—56. Recipient Presdl. Meritorious Svc. award, 1986, Wilbur Carr award Dept. of State, 1987, Benjamin Franklin medal Royal Soc. Arts, 1992. Mem. Knickerbocker Club NY, Pilgrims NY, Met. Club Washington, Beefsteak Club, White's Club London, Mill Reef Club Antigua, Century Assn. NY. Episcopalian. Mailing: 535 Park Ave New York NY 10065-8198 Office Phone: 212-486-6688. Personal E-mail: estreator@nyc.rr.com.

STRECKER, DAVID EUGENE, lawyer; b. Carthage, Mo., Nov. 29, 1950; s. Eugene Albert and Erma Freida (Wood) S.; m. Katherine Ann Pugh; children: Charles David, Carrie Christina. BA, Westminster Coll., 1972; JD, Cornell U., 1975, M in Indsl. Labor Rels., 1976. Bar: NY 1976, Okla. 1981, US Dist. Ct. (no. dist.) NY 1976, US Dist. Ct. (ea. dist.) Okla. 1984, US Dist. Ct. (we. dist.) Okla. 2000, US Dist. Ct. (we. and ea. dists.) Ark. 2000, US Ct. Appeals (no. dist.) Okla. 1981, US Ct. Appeals (10th cir.) 1982, US Ct. Appeals (6th cir.) 1990, US Supreme Ct. 1991, US Dist. Ct. (ea. dist.) Tex. 2006. Assoc. Conner & Winters, Tulsa, 1980-85, ptnr., 1985-91, Shipley, Inhofe & Strecker, Tulsa, 1991-95, Strecker & Assocs. P.C., Tulsa, 1995—. Instr. paralegal program Tulsa Jr. Coll., 1985—, mem. adv. com., 1986-91; mem. Cornell Secondary Schs. Com., Tulsa, 1985—; instr. labor rels. Okla. State U., 1995—; master Am. Inns of Ct. Bd. dirs., v.p. Tulsa Sr. Svcs., 1988-91; mem. pers. com. Philbrook Art Mus. Capt. JAGC, U.S. Army, 1976-80. Mem. ABA, Okla. Bar Assn. (chmn. labor sect. 1990-91), Tulsa County Bar Assn. (continuing legal edn. com. 1981—), Soc. for Human Resource Mgmt., Tulsa Area Human Resources Assn. (gen. counsel 1989-2000, v.p. 1994-98, bd. dirs. family and children's svcs. 2000—04), Kappa Alpha. Democrat. Episcopalian. Avocations: jogging, golf. Home: 5112 E 107th St Tulsa OK 74137-7238 Office: Midcontinent Tower 401 S Boston Ste 2150 Tulsa OK 74103-4009 Home Phone: 918-298-4652; Office Phone: 918-582-1716. E-mail: destreck@juno.com, david.strecker@streckerlaborlaw.com.

STREEB, GORDON LEE, diplomat, economist; b. Windsor, Colo., Dec. 24, 1935; s. Gerhard O. and Amelia (Martin) S.; m. Alice Junette Thomas, Aug. 11, 1962; children: Kurt, Kent, Kerry-Lynn. BSBA, BSChemE, U. Colo., 1959; PhD in Econs., U. Minn., 1978. Fgn. service officer U.S. Dept. State, Berlin, 1963-65; vice consul Am. Consulate, Guadalajara, Mex., 1965-67; instr. econs. U. Minn., 1968; examiner Bd. Examiners, 1972-73; internat. economist for trade policy Bur. Econ. and Bus. Affairs, Washington, 1973-77; econ. counselor U.S. mission European Office of the UN and other internat. orgns., Geneva, 1977-80; exec. asst. to undersec. of state on econ. affairs Washington, 1980-81; dep. asst. sec. state for econ. and social affairs Bur. Internat. Orgn. Affairs, Washington, 1981-84; dep. chief mission Am. Embassy, New Delhi, 1984-88; sr. inspector Dept. State, Washington, 1988-90; amb. to Zambia Am. Embassy, Lusaka, 1990-93; diplomat-in-residence The Carter Ctr., Atlanta, 1994-95, assoc. exec. dir. peace program, 1995—2004; vis. prof. Emory U., Atlanta, 2004—. Mem. Coun. on Fgn. Rels.; mem. adv. bd. Engrs. Without Borders-USA. Home: 2680 Churchwell Ln Tucker GA 30084-2402 Business E-Mail: gstreeb@emory.edu.

STREEP, MERYL (MARY LOUISE STREEP), actress; b. Summit, NJ, June 22, 1949; d. Harry, Jr. and Mary W. Streep; m. Donald J. Grummer, Sept. 15, 1978; children: Henry, Mary Willa, Grace, Louisa. BA in Drama, Vassar Coll., 1971; MFA, Yale U., 1975, DFA (hon.), 1983, Dartmouth Coll., 1981. Co-founder Mothers & Others for a Livable Planet. Appeared with: Green Mountain Guild; actress: (Broadway plays) Trelawny of the Wells, 1975; (plays) 27 Wagons Full of Cotton (Theatre World award); A Memory of Two Mondays; Henry V; Secret Service; The Taming of the Shrew; Measure for Measure; The Cherry Orchard; Happy End; Wonderland; Taken in Marriage; Alice in Concert (Obie award, 1981); Mother Courage, 2006; (films) Julia, 1977; The Deer Hunter, 1978 (Best Supporting Actress award nat. Soc. film Critics, Acad. award nomination, 1978); Manhattan, 1979; The Seduction of Joe Tynan, 1979; Kramer vs. Kramer, 1979 (NY Film Critics' award, LA Film Critics' award, both for best actress, Golden Globe award, Acad. award for best supporting actress, 1980); The French Lieutenant's Woman, 1981 (LA Film Critics award for best actress, Brit. Acad. award, Golden Globe award for best actress, Acad. award nomination, 1982); Sophie's Choice, 1982 (Acad. award for best actress, LA Film Critics award for best actress, Golden Globe award for best actress, 1983); Still of the Night, 1982; Silkwood, 1983 (Acad. award nomination); Falling in Love, 1984; Plenty, 1985; Out of Africa, 1985 (Los Angeles Film Critics award for best actress, Golden Globe award, 1985); Heartburn, 1986; Ironweed, 1987 (Acad. award nomination); A Cry in the Dark, 1988 (named Best Actress NY Film Critics' Circle, Best Actress Cannes Film Festival, 1989, Acad. award nomination); She-Devil, 1989; Postcards From the Edge, 1990; Defending Your Life, 1991; Death Becomes Her, 1992; The House of Spirits, 1993; The River Wild, 1994; The Bridges of Madison County, 1995 (Acad. award nominee for best actress, 1996); Before and After, 1996; Marvin's Room, 1996; Dancing at Lugnasa, 1998; One True Thing, 1998; Music of the Heart, 1999 (Acad. award nominee for best actress); The Hours, 2002; Adaptation, 2002 (Southeastern Film Critics Assn. award for best supporting actress, 2002, Chgo. Film Critics Assn. award for best supporting actress, 2003, Golden Globe for best supporting actress, 2003); The Manchurian Candidate, 2004; Lemony Snicket's A Series of Unfortunate Events, 2004; Prime, 2005; A Prairie Home Companion, 2006 (Best Supporting Actress, Nat. Soc. Film Critics, 2007); The Devil Wears Prada, 2006 (Best Supporting Actress, Nat. Soc. Film Critics, 2007, Best Performance by an Actress in a Motion Picture-Musical or Comedy, Golden Globe awards, Hollywood Fgn. Press Assn., 2007); Dark Matter, 2007; Evening, 2007; Rendition, 2007; Lions for Lambs, 2007; Mamma Mia!, 2008; Doubt, 2008 (Best Actress Washington DC Area Film Critics Assn., 2008, 2008 Best Actress, Critics' Choice award, Broadcast Film Critics Assn., 2009, Outstanding Performance by a Female Actor in a Leading Role, SAG, 2009); Julie & Julia, 2009; (voice only) Rabbit Ears: The Tale of Peter Rabbit, 1987; Rabbit Ears: The Tale of Jeremy Fisher, 1987; The Tailor of Gloucester, 1988; Rabbit Ears: The Fisherman and His Wife, 1989; Chrysanthemum, 1999; Artificial Intelligence: AI, 2001; The Ant Bully, 2006; actress: (TV films) Secret

Service, 1977; The Deadliest Season, 1977; Uncommon Women and Others, 1979; Alice at the Palace, 1982; actress, exec. prodr. First Do No Harm, 1997; narrator The Velveteen Rabbit, 1984 (Emmy award Best Children's Rec.); A Vanishing Wilderness, 1990; actress: (TV miniseries) Holocaust, 1978 (Emmy award for Outstanding Lead Actress in a Mini-series, 1978); Angels in America, 2003 (Screen Actors Guild Award for best actress, Golden Globe for best actress, Emmy award Outstanding Lead Actress in a Mini-series or a movie, 2004). Recipient Mademoiselle award, 1976, Woman of Yr. award, B'nai Brith, 1979, Hasty Pudding Soc., Harvard U., 1980, Best Supporting Actress award, Nat. Bd. of Rev., 1979, Best Actress award, 1982, Star of Yr. award, Nat. Assn. Theater Owners, 1983, People's Choice award, 1983, 85, 86, 87, 1990, Women in Film Crystal award, 1998, Gotham award for Lifetime Achievement, 1999, Bette Davis Lifetime Achievement award, 1999, Lifetime Achievement award, Am. Film Inst., 2004, Dana Reeve HOPE award, Christopher and Dana Reeve Found., 2007, Marcos Aurelius Lifetime Achievement award, Rome Film Festival, 2009, most nominated actor ever for an Academy Award; named Officer, French Ordre des Arts et des Lettres, 2000; named one of The 100 Most Influential People in the World, TIME mag., 2006, 50 Smartest People in Hollywood, Entertainment Weekly, 2007; named to NJ Hall of Fame, 2007. Office: c/o 42 West 11400 W Olympic Blvd Los Angeles CA 90064*

STREET, HUSTON LOWELL, professional baseball player; b. Austin, Tex., Aug. 2, 1983; s. James, Janie. Attended, U. Tex., Austin, 2002—03. Relief pitcher Oakland Athletics, 2004—08, Colo. Rockies, 2008—. Named First-Team All-Conf., Big 12 Conf., 2002—03, First-Team All-Am., NCAA, 2003, Ctrl. Tex. Coll. Pitcher of Yr., 2003, USA Baseball Athlete of Yr., 2003, Am. League Rookie of Yr., Maj. League Baseball, 2005. Office: Colo Rockies 2001 Blake St Denver CO 80205*

STREET, JOHN CHARLES, linguistics educator; b. Chgo., Apr. 3, 1930; s. Charles Larrabee and Mary Louise (Rouse) S.; m. Eve Elizabeth Baker, June 4, 1975. BA, Yale, 1951, MA, 1952, PhD, 1955. Asst. prof. English Mich. State U., 1957-59; asst. prof. linguistics and Mongolian langs. Columbia, 1959-62; vis. asst. prof. linguistics U. Wash., 1962-63; assoc. prof. linguistics U. Wis., Madison, 1963-65, prof. linguistics, 1965-92, prof. emeritus Madison, 1992—. Author: The Language of the Secret History of the Mongols, 1957, Khalkha Structure, 1963, The Journal of Oliver Rouse, 1983, An Ellis Family of Devon and Newfoundland, 1994, A Genealogy of the Rouses of Devon, 2002. Research asso. Am. Council Learned Socs., 1959-62. Served with AUS, 1955-57.

STREET, JOHN FRANKLIN, former mayor; b. Norristown, Pa., Oct. 15, 1943; m. Naomi Street; children: Sharif, Rasida, Lateef, Akeem. BA in English, Oakwood Coll., 1966; JD, Temple U., 1975. Pvt. law practice, 1975—80; city councilman City of Phila., 1979-98, coun. pres., 1992-98, past chmn. licenses and inspections, approprations coms., chmn. Whole, Rules & Fiscal Stability, Intergovt. coop. com., 1992—; mem. Phila. Gas Commn., 1984-89, chmn., 1992—; mayor City of Phila., 2000—08. Named one of 100 Most Influential Black Americans, Ebony mag., 2006. Democrat. Avocations: running, bicycling.

STREET, PAUL SHIPLEY, lawyer; b. Klamath Falls, Oreg., Mar. 4, 1948; s. Leon Rex and Mary Rebecca (Shipley) S.; children: Adam, Blake. BA, Coll. Idaho, 1970; JD, U. Wash., 1973. Bar: Idaho 1973, U.S. Dist. Ct. Idaho 1973, Idaho Supreme Ct. 1973. Law clerk Idaho Supreme Ct., Boise, 1973-74; pres., mng. ptnr. Moffatt, Thomas, Barrett, Rock & Fields, Boise, 1974—99; sr. v.p., gen. counsel, corp. sec. Bldg. Materials Holding Co., San Francisco, 1999—, chief adminstrv. officer, 2001—. Sec. BMC West Corp., Boise. Co-author: Idaho Law Review, 1991, Digest of Environmental Law of Real Property, 1991. Pres. Coll. Idaho Alumni Assn., Caldwell, 1986, Am. Diabetes Assn., 1984—; formerly bd. dirs. First United Meth. Ch., Boise; chairperson United Way of Ada County, Boise, 1982-83. Mem. ABA (sec. mem. patent, trademark and copyright law; litigation, econs. law practice), Am. Soc. Med. Assn. Counsel, Am. Soc. Law and Medicine, Am. Arbitration Assn., Idaho State Bar (chmn. corp. and securities law sect. 1992-93), Boise Bar Assn., Boise Ins. Adjusters Assn., Real Estate Lawyers Assn., Boise Area C. of C. (vice chmn. 1991—). Avocation: bird hunting. Office: Bldg Materials Holding Corp Four Embarcadero Ctr Ste 3200 San Francisco CA 94111 Office Phone: 415-627-9100. Office Fax: 415-627-9119.

STREET, ROBERT, retired academic administrator, physicist; b. Wakefield, Eng., Dec. 16, 1920; s. Joe and Edith Elizabeth (Jones) S.; m. Joan Marjorie Bere, June 26, 1943; children: Alison Mary, Nicholas Robert. MSc, U. London, 1944, PhD, 1948, DSc, 1966; DSc (hon.), U. Western Australia, 1986, U. Sheffield, Eng., 1987. With Min. Supply, London, 1941-45; lectr. in physics U. Nottingham, Eng., 1945-54; sr. lectr. U. Sheffield, Eng., 1954-60; found. prof. Monash U., Australia, 1960-74; dir. Rsch. Sch. Phys. Sci. Australian Nat. U., Canberra, 1974-78; vice chancellor U. Western Australia, Perth, 1978-86, hon. sr. rsch. fellow, 1987—. Contbr. articles to profl. jours. Decorated officer Order of Australia. Fellow Australian Acad. Sci., Inst. Physics, Australian Inst. Physics; mem. Inst. Elec. Engrs., Weld Club (Perth). Home: 60 Temby Ave Kalamunda Western Australia 6076 Australia Office: U Western Australia 35 Stirling Hwy Crawley WA 6009 Australia Home Phone: +6189293 2978. Business E-Mail: street@physics.uwa.edu.au.

STREET, ROBERT LYNNWOOD, civil, mechanical and environmental engineer; b. Honolulu, Dec. 18, 1934; s. Evelyn Mansel and Dorothy Heather (Brook) S.; m. Norma Jeanette Ensminger, Feb. 6, 1959; children: Brian Clark (dec.), Deborah Lynne, Kimberley Anne. Student, USN ROTC Program, 1952-57; MS, Stanford U., 1957, PhD (NSF grad. fellow 1960-62), 1963. Mem. faculty Sch. Engring. Stanford U., 1962—2005, prof. civil engring., assoc. chmn. dept. Sch. Engring., 1970-72, chmn. dept. Sch. Engring., 1972-80, 94-95, prof. fluid mechanics and applied math. Sch. Engring., 1972—2004, founding dir. environ. fluid mechanics lab. Sch. Engring., 1985-91, assoc. dean rsch. Sch. Engring., 1971-83, vice provost acad. computing and info. sys., 1983-85, vice provost, dean rsch. and acad. info. sys., 1985-87, v.p. for info. resources, 1987-90, acting provost, 1987, v.p. librs. and info. resources, 1990-92, vice provost, dean of librs. and info. resources, 1992—94, William Alden and Martha Campbell prof. Sch. Engring., 1997—2004, prof. emeritus fluid mechanics, applied math, 2005. Vis. prof. U. Liverpool, Eng., 1970-71, Ctr. for Water Rsch., U. Western Australia, 1985; vis. prof. mech. engring. James Cook U., Australia, 1995; trustee Univ. Corp. Atmospheric Rsch., 1983-94, chmn. sci. programs evaluation com., 1981, treas. corp., 1985, vice chmn. bd., 1986, chmn. bd., 1987-91; bd. dirs., sec.-treas. UCAR Found., 1987-91, mem. rep., 2005-; bd. govs. Rsch. Libr. Group, 1990-91; chmn. Com. Preservation Rsch. Libr. Materials, Assn. Rsch. Librs., 1993; mem. higher edn. adv. bds. computer corps., 1983-94; mem. basic energy sci. adv. com. U.S. Dept. Energy, 1993-96; bd. dirs. Stanford U. Bookstore, Inc., 1993-98; cons. Design of Libr., Sch. Engring., Stanford U., 2007; bd. dir. Stanford Campus Residential Leaseholder, 2008-, chair, capital planning com., 2009-. With C.E.C., USN, 1957-60. Sr. postdoc. fellow Nat. Ctr. Atmospheric Rsch., 1978-79, faculty fellow, 2007; sr. Queen's fellow in marine sci., Australia, 1985; fellow N.E. Asia-U.S. Forum on Internat. Policy at Stanford U., 1985-89; named to Beverly Hills H.S. Hall of Fame, 2005. Fellow: AAAS; mem.: NAE (sect. 4 peer com. mem. 2006—09), ASME (R.T. Knapp award 1986), ASCE (chmn. publs. com. hydraulics divsn. 1978—80, disting. mem. 2009, Walter Huber prize 1972, Hilgard Hydraulic Engring. prize 2002, Rouse Hydraulic Engring. award 2005), Am. Meteorol. Soc., Oceanographic Soc., Am. Geophys. Union, Sigma Xi, Phi Beta Kappa, Tau Beta Pi. Office: Dept Civil and Environ Engring Stanford Univ Yang Yamazaki Environ & Energy Bldg MC 4020 473 Via Ortega Stanford CA 94305 Office Phone: 650-723-4969. Business E-Mail: street@stanford.edu.

STREET, TERRY M., artist, educator; b. Bklyn., Dec. 11, 1929; d. William George Nappenbach and Marie Virginia Caron; m. Norman Street, Oct. 11, 1962 (dec. Sept. 1979); children: Lesa, David. Student, Chinourd Art Sch., 1948, Art Students League, 1950—53, Am. Art Sch., 1953—54, NYU Inst. Fine Art, 1953—54, Nat. Acad. Design, 1953—58, Vrijy Acad., 1956. Cert. tchr. Calif. Instr. Traphagen Sch. Design, NY, 1959, Conejo Valley Adult Sch., Thousand Oaks, Calif., 1980—93; art dir. Dwight Sch. for Girls, NJ, 1960—62, Carden Conejo Sch., Calif., 1976—93; exhibit specialist Smithsonian, Wash., 1962—63; founder, dir. Burke Sch. Art, Va., 1968—70; art cons. for occupl. therapists Pediatric Rehabilitation, Poland, Slovakia, Hungary, 1988—90; founder, dir. Hawthorne Studio, Portland, Oreg., 1993—. Instr. St. Francis Svcs., Portland, 2000—. Exhibitions include Knickerbocker Art Guild, 1955, Allied Artists Nat. Acad. Design, NY, 1956, Smithsonian Art Inst., Wash., DC, 1964, Gallery 33, Portland, Oreg., 1997—98, Hawthorne Studio; illustrator: Problem Solving in Occupational Therapy; numerous pvt. collections. Cons. park and recreation Children's Art Festival, Calif.; charter mem. Nat. Women's Mus.; coun. mem. St. Francis Ch., Portland. Fogg Mus. of Haravard U. scholar, 1954, Louis Comfort Tiffany fellow, 1956. Mem.: Allied Artists, Oriental Art Soc., Oreg. Soc. Artists, Keizer Art Assn., Watercolor Soc. Oreg., Nat. Watercolor Soc. (assoc.), Northwest Watercolor Soc. (assoc.), Art Students League (life). Home and Office: Hawthorne Studio 3511 SE Francis St Portland OR 97202 E-mail: tstreetart@msn.com.

STREETEN, BARBARA WIARD, ophthalmologist, medical educator; b. Candia, NH, Mar. 3, 1925; d. Robert Campbell Wiard and Gertrude Sarah Matheson; m. David Henry Palmer Streeten, Aug. 2, 1952; children: Robert Duncan, Elizabeth Anne, John Palmer. AB magna cum laude, Tufts U., 1945, MD cum laude, 1950. Diplomate Am. Bd. Ophthalmology. Jr. resident in gen. pathology Mallory Inst., Boston City Hosp., 1951-52; fellow in ophthalmic pathology Mass. Eye and Ear Infirmary, Boston, 1952-53; resident in ophthalmology Wayne County Gen. Hosp., Eloise, Mich., 1953-56; from jr. to sr. clin. instr. ophthalmology U. Mich. Med. Sch., Ann Arbor, 1956-60; from asst. prof. to prof. ophthalmology SUNY Health Sci. Ctr. (now called SUNY Upstate Med. U.), Syracuse, 1964—, dir. eye pathology lab., 1966—; from asst. prof. to prof. pathology SUNY Health Sci. Ctr., Syracuse, 1968—. Contbr. more than 120 articles to profl. jours., chapters to books. Mem. vision study sect. Nat. Eye Inst., NIH, Bethesda, Md., 1977-80, mem. bd. sci. counselors, 1982-86; mem. editl. bd., mem. editl. adv. com. Ophthalmology jour., 1982-94; gen. editor Investigative Ophthalmology and Visual Sci., 1979-82, mem. editl. bd., 1987-92. Grantee Nat. Eye Inst., NIH, 1975—2002. Mem. Am. Assn. Ophthalmic Pathologists (charter, past pres., bd. dirs., Zimmerman medal 1997), Am. Acad. Ophthalmology (honor award 1990), Verhoeff Ophthalmic Pathology Soc. (past pres.), Assn. for Rsch. in Vision and Ophthalmology (past sect. chmn.), Internat. Soc. Ophthalmic Pathology (co-v.p. N.Am. 1990-92), Phi Beta Kappa, Alpha Omega Alpha. Episcopalian. Achievements include establishment of elastic system nature of the suspensory ligament of the ocular lens; ultrastructural and immunopathologic contributions to diseases of the ocular connective tissue matrix, particularly those related to cataract and glaucoma. Home: 334 Berkeley Dr Syracuse NY 13210-3000 Office: SUNY Upstate Med Univ WH Rm 2107 766 Irving Ave Syracuse NY 13210-1602

STREETER, CHRIS CONWAY, psychiatrist, educator; b. Pitts., Sept. 17, 1957; d. Joseph Thomas Conway and Marie Conway Hobart; children: Nathaniel Thayer, Lillian Conway. BS in Nutritional Sci. with highest honors, U. Wis., Madison, 1979; MD, Ohio State U., Columbus, 1984. Cert. in neurology Am. Bd. Psychiatry and Neurology, 1989, in psychiatry Am. Bd. Psychiatry and Neurology, 1993, qualifications in forensics Am. Bd. Psychiatry and Neurology, 1999, lic. Bd. Registration in Medicine, 2007, cert. in behavioral neurology and neuropsychiatry United Coun. Neurologic Spltys., 2008. Behavioral neurology fellow Boston U. Sch. Medicine, 1988—90, dir. functional neuroimaging for psychiatry, 1997—, asst. prof. psychiatry, 1997—2001, instn. rev. bd., 2000—06, asst. prof. psychiatry and neurology, 2001—, functional magnetic resonance imaging adv. com., 2004—, divsn. membership grad. med. scis., 2007—; consulting psychiatrist Braintree Hosp., Braintree, 1992—94; staff psychiatrist Boston Va. Healthcare Sys., 1992—2006; dir. traumatic brain injury unit Lemuel Shattuck Hosp., Boston, 1993—94; consultation liaison psychiatry svc. New Eng. Med. Ctr., Boston, 1993—97; asst. prof. psychiatry and neurology Tufts Med. Sch., Boston, 1994—99, instr. psychiatry, 1999—2006; rsch. assoc. Brain Imaging Ctr., McLean Hosp., Belmont, Mass., 1996—; staff psychaitrist Boston Med. Ctr., 1997—; lectr. psychiatry Harvard Med. Sch., Boston, 1999—, assoc. prof. psychiatry & neurology, 2009—. Contbr. articles to profl. jours. Mem.: Mass. Psychiat. Assn. (assoc.), Am. Psychiat. Assn. (assoc.). Achievements include discovery of yoga as being associated with an increase in the brain's primary inhibitory neurotransmitter; research in the use of magnetic resonance spectroscopy to measure brain gamma amino-butyric (GABA) in cocaine dependent individuals; the use of neuropsychological tests to identify treatment compliance; the use of functional imaging to identify changes in brain function related to pharmacologic challenge and family history of alcoholism. Office: Boston Univ Sch Medicine 85 E Newton St M912E Boston MA 02118 Office Fax: 617-638-8007. Business E-Mail: streeter@bu.edu.

STREETER, OSCAR EDWARD, JR., radiation oncologist; b. Roanoke, Va., May 20, 1955; s. Oscar Edward Sr. and Betty (Richardson) S.; m. Paulette Y. Saddler; 1 child, Rebecca. BS in Biology, USC; MD, Howard U., 1982. Diplomate Am. Bd. Med. Examiners. Intern U. Calif., Irvine, 1983-85; resident Howard U. Med. Ctr., Washington, 1986-89; resident tng. program dir. dept. radiation oncology U. So. Calif. Sch. Medicine, LA, 1990-94, asst. prof. radiation oncology, 1990-95, asst. prof. clin. radiation oncology, 1995-97, assoc. prof. clin. radiation oncology, 1997—; dept. radiation oncology chief physician LAC, U. So. Calif. Med. Ctr., 1992-94, U. So. Calif. Norris Cancer Ctr., 1994—. Chair cancer com. U. So. Calif. Sch. Medicine, LA, 1997, med. exec., 1995—, acad. tech. adv. com., 1997; mem. leadership coun. U. So. Calif. Cancer Ctr., 1995—. Contbr. articles to profl. jours. Chmn. NBLIC/Western Region, LA, 1995—; adv. bd. Wellness Com. Foothills, Pasadena, Calif., 1995—; bd. dirs. Real Men Cook Found., LA, 1993—, Women of Color Breast Cancer Survivors Project, L.A., 1995—; mem. Real Men Cook Found., 1994; mem. Maxine Waters-35th Dist. Com. Svc., Mem. of Congress; mem. health svcs. Office of Willie Brown Jr. Spkr. of Assembly 13 Dist. Grantee U. So. Calif., 1993, 93-96, U. Calif., 1993-95, Biotech. Comms., LA, 1995; named one of Top 100 Black Physicians in Am., Black Enterprise Mag., 2001; named to America's Top Doctors, 2001-06, Best Doctors in Am., 2003-06. Office: USC/Norris Comprehensive Cancer Ctr 1441 Eastlake Ave Los Angeles CA 90089-0112 Business E-Mail: ostreeter@aol.com.

STREETER, ROBERT DAVENPORT, electrical engineer, consultant; b. Springfield, Mass., Sept. 17, 1941; s. William Allen Streeter and Muriel Ethel Davenport; m. Carole Janet Riley, Mar. 21, 1970 (dec. Nov. 2004); children: John Riley, Susan Streeter Billian; m. Donna Jean Preston Smith, Feb. 18, 2006. B in Elec. Engring., Ohio State U., 1964; MSEE, Purdue U., 1968. Registered profl. engr., Ind. Engr. WBNS Radio-TV, Columbus, Ohio, 1961—64, Ohio State U. Rsch. Found., Columbus, 1962—64, The Magnavox Co., Fort Wayne, Ind., 1965—82; pres. A M Stereo, Inc., Fort Wayne, 1982—; engring. fellow Raytheon, Fort Wayne, 1985—2008. Contbr. articles to profl. jours. Mem.: IEEE, Eta Kappa Nu (life). Achievements include invention of AM stereo, microelectromechanical systems. Avocations: private pilot, amateur radio, bicycling, gardening. Home: 6111 Eagle Creek Dr Fort Wayne IN 46814-3213 Office: Raytheon 1010 Production Rd Fort Wayne IN 46808 Personal E-mail: r.streeter@ieee.org.

STREETMAN, JOHN WILLIAM, III, museum director; b. Marion, NC, Jan. 19, 1941; s. John William, Jr. and Emily Elaine (Carver) S.; children: Katherine Drake, Leah Farrior, Burgin Eaves. BA in English and Theatre History, Western Carolina U., 1963; cert. in Shakespeare studies, Lincoln Coll., Oxford (Eng.) U., 1963. Founding dir. Jewett Creative Arts Ctr., Berwick Acad., South Berwick, Maine, 1964-70; exec. dir. Polk Mus. Art, Lakeland, Fla., 1970-75; dir. Mus. Arts and Sci., Evansville, Ind., 1975—; chmn. mus. adv. panel Ind. Arts Commn., 1977-78. Mem. Am. Assn. Museums, Assn. Ind. Museums (bd. dirs.) Episcopalian. Office: Evansville Mus Arts History and Sci 411 SE Riverside Dr Evansville IN 47713-1037

STREISAND, BARBRA JOAN, singer, actress, film director; b. Bklyn., Apr. 24, 1942; d. Emanuel and Diana (Rosen) S.; m. Elliott Gould, Mar. 21, 1963 (div. July 9, 1971); 1 son, Jason Emanuel; m. James Brolin, July 1, 1998. Grad. high sch., Bklyn.; student, Yeshiva of Bklyn.; Doctorate of Arts and Humanities (hon.), Brandeis U., 1995. NY theatre debut Another Evening with Harry Stoones, 1961; appeared in Broadway musicals I Can Get It for You Wholesale, 1962, Funny Girl, 1964-65; motion pictures include Funny Girl, 1968, Hello Dolly, 1969, On a Clear Day You Can See Forever, 1970, The Owl and the Pussy Cat, 1970, What's Up Doc?, 1972, Up the Sandbox, 1972, The Way We Were, 1973, For Pete's Sake, 1974, Funny Lady, 1975, The Main Event, 1979, All Night Long, 1981, Nuts, 1987, Meet the Fockers, 2004; actor, prodr. (films): A Star is Born, 1976; prodr., dir., actor (films) Yentl, 1983, The Prince of Tides, 1991, The Mirror Has Two Faces, 1996 (ASCAP Award for score, 1996; exec. prodr.: (TV movies) Serving in Silence: The Margarethe Cammermeyer Story, 1995; (TV spls.) My Name is Barbra, 1965 (5 Emmy awards), Color Me Barbra, 1966, Barbra Streisand: The Concert, 1995 (Cable ACE award for best performance and for best direction, Two Emmy awards), Barbra Streisand: Timeless, 2001 (Emmy award); rec. artist on Columbia Records; (albums) People, 1965, My Name is Barbra, 1965, Color Me Barbra, 1966, Barbra Streisand: A Happening in Central Park, 1968, Barbra Streisand: One Voice, Stoney End, 1971, Barbra Joan Streisand, 1972, The Way We Were, 1974, A Star is Born, 1976, Superman, 1977, The Stars Salute Israel at 30, 1978, Wet, 1979, (with Barry Gibb) Guilty, 1980, Emotion, 1984, The Broadway Album, 1986, Til I Loved You, 1989; other albums include: A Collection: Greatest Hits, 1989, Just for the Record, 1991, Back to Broadway, 1993, Concert at the Forum, 1993, The Concert Recorded Live at Madison Square Garden, 1994, The Concert Highlights, 1995, Higher Ground, 1997, A Love Like Ours, 1999, Christmas Memories, 2001, The Essential Barbara Streisand, 2002, The Movie Album, 2003, Guilty Pleasures, 2005, Guilty Too, 2005, Nur das Beste, 2006, Live in Concert 2006, 2007. Recipient: Emmy award, CBS-TV spl. (My Name Is Barbra), 1964, Acad. award as best actress (Funny Girl), 1968, Golden Globe award (Funny Girl), 1969, co-recipient Acad. award for best song (Evergreen), 1976, Georgie award AGVA 1977, Grammy awards for best female pop vocalist, 1963, 64, 65, 77, 86, for best song writer (with Paul Williams), 1977, 2 Grammy nominations for Back to Broadway, 1994; Nat. Acad. of Recording Arts & Sciences Lifetime Achievement Award, 1994, Cecil B. Demille Lifetime Achievement Award, 2000, Life Achievement award, Am. Film Inst., 2001, Liberty & Justice Award, Rainbow/PUSH Coalition, 2001, Humanitarian award, Human Rights Campaign, 2004, Kennedy Ctr. Honors, John F. Kennedy Ctr. for the Performing Arts, 2008; Inducted into French Legion Of Honor, 2007 Office: Barbra Streisand c/o Martin Erlichman Assoc Inc 5670 Wilshire Blvd Ste 2400 Los Angeles CA 90036 also: Nigro Karlin Segal 10100 Santa Monica Blvd Ste 1300 Los Angeles CA 90067*

STREISAND, ROBERT L., thoracic surgeon; s. Max and Florence Streisand; children: Adam, Eve, Rachael, Danielle. BS, Trinity Coll., West Hartford, Conn., 1963; MD, SUNY, Bklyn., 1966. Intern SUNY-Downstate Med. Ctr.; resident Baylor Coll. Medicine, Houston, 1967—68, SUNY, 1968—73; chief thoracic surgery White Plains Hosp., NY, 1985—2000, St. Johns Hosp., Yonkers, NY, 2000—; sr. attending thoracic surgeon Laurence Hosp., Bronxville, NY, 2000—. Med. cons. Med. Mut. Liability Ins. Co., NYC, 1995—. Lt. col. USAF, 1973—75. Fellow: Soc. Thoracic Surgeons, Am. Coll. Surgeons. Avocations: skiing, scuba diving. Home: 4 Lyon Pl Ste Ll2 White Plains NY 10601-5415

STREIT, MARK, professional hockey player; b. Bern, Switzerland, Dec. 11, 1977; Defenseman ZSC Lions Zurich (Swiss Nationalliga A), Switzerland, 2001—05, Montreal Canadiens, 2005—08, NY Islanders, 2008—. Mem. Team Switzerland, Olympic Games, Salt Lake City, 2002, Torino, Italy, 06. Named to NHL All-Star Game, 2009. Office: NY Islanders Nassau Vets Meml Coliseum 1255 Hempstead Turnpike Uniondale NY 11553*

STREIT, MICHAEL J., state supreme court justice; b. Sheldon, Iowa, Apr. 14, 1950; married; 1 child. BA, U. Iowa, 1972; grad., U. San Diego Sch. Law, 1975. Cert.: (U.S. Ct. Appeals) 1996. Atty. priv. practice, 1975—83; asst. atty. Lucas County, 1975—79, atty., 1979—83; judge Iowa Dist. Ct., Fifth Judicial Dist., 1983—96, Iowa Ct. of Appeals, 1996—2001; justice Iowa Supreme Ct., 2001—. Mem. Iowa Supreme Ct. Education Advisory Com., Iowa Supreme Ct. Judicial Technology Com., Judges Assn. Education Com. Mem.: Iowa State Bar Assn., Blackstone Inn of Ct., Iowa Jud. Inst. Office: Iowa Supreme Ct Jud Branch Bldg 1111 E Ct Ave Des Moines IA 50319*

STREIT, MICHAEL K., aeronautical engineer, educator; b. Ill. married. MA in Ednl. Adminstrn., Govs. State U., U. Pk, Ill. Cert. in aviation maintenance technician FAA, 1978. Assoc. chmn. Lewis U., Romeoville, Ill., 1981—. Office: Lewis Univ One Univ Pkwy - Unit 282 Romeoville IL 60446 Business E-Mail: streitmi@lewisu.edu.

STREM, RYAN DAVID, educator; b. Upland, Calif., Jan. 11, 1981; s. Dave and Katie Strem; m. Mandy Hasley, July 17, 2004; 1 child, Natalie. M in Ed. Leadership, Nat. - Louis, Lake County Florida, 2008—.

Eckerds photo lab tech. Eckerds Drug Store, Mt. Dora, Fla., 2000—03; funeral home asst. Beyers Funeral Home, Umatilla, 2000—. Athletic dir. Umatilla Mid. Sch., 2006—. Named to Best Rookie Tchr. award, Umatilla Mid. Sch., 2006.

STREMLER, MARK ANDREW, engineering educator, researcher; b. Albion, Mich., Mar. 16, 1971; s. Harvey Dean and Patricia Carol Stremler; m. Charlotte Liann Wright, May 28, 1994; children: Madison Janaye, Kaylie Beth, Kolby Luke, Bryson Andrew. BS in Mech. Engring., Rose-Hulman Inst. Tech., Terre Haute, Indiana, 1993, BS in Math., 1993; MS in Theoretical and Applied Mechanics, U. Ill., Urbana-Champaign, 1995, PhD in Theoretical and Applied Mechanics, 1998. Rsch. assoc. U. Ill., Urbana, 1998—2000; asst. prof. Vanderbilt U., Nashville, 2000—06; assoc. prof. Va. Tech, Blacksburg, 2006—. Recipient Herman A. Moench Disting. Sr. Commendation, Rose-Hulman Inst. Tech., 1993, Royse award, 1993, John A. Logan award, 1993, James O. Smith Tchg. award, U. Ill., 1998, Stanley I. Weiss Outstanding Thesis award, 2000, Tau Beta Pi Tchr. of Yr., Vanderbilt U., 2002; Grad. fellowship, Office Naval Rsch., 1993—96, Young Investigator award, Army Rsch. Office, 2004—07. Office: Virginia Tech Mail Code 0219 Blacksburg VA 24061 Business E-Mail: mark.stremler@vt.edu.

STRENG, WILLIAM PAUL, lawyer, educator; b. Sterling, Ill., Oct. 17, 1937; s. William D. and Helen Marie (Conklen) S.; children: Sarah, John. BA, Wartburg Coll., 1959; JD, Northwestern U., 1962. Bar: Iowa 1962, Ill. 1962, Ohio 1964, Tex. 1975. Law clk. to U.S. circuit judge Lester L. Cecil, Cin., 1963-64; assoc. firm Taft, Stettinius & Hollister, Cin., 1964-70; atty.-advisor Office Sec. Tax Policy, Office Tax Legis. Counsel, Dept. Treasury, Washington, 1970-71; dep. gen. counsel Export-Import Bank U.S., Washington, 1971-73; prof. law Sch. Law, So. Methodist U., Dallas, 1973-80; vis. prof. Coll. Law Ohio State U., Columbus, 1977; ptnr. firm Bracewell & Patterson, Houston, 1980-85; Vinson & Elkins prof. of law U. Houston Law Ctr, 1985—. Vis. prof. Rice U., NYU Law Sch., 1990, U. Tex. Sch. Law, 2002, Yokohama (Japan) Nat. U., 2005; disting. vis. prof. U. Hong Kong Law Faculty, 1992; Fulbright prof. U. Stockholm Law Faculty, 1993; vis. fellow law faculty Victoria U., Wellington, New Zealand, 1996; vis. law lectr. U. Leiden, Netherlands, 1997, 98, 2000, 07, 09; cons. Bracewell & Patterson (now Bracewell & Giuliani), 1985—; lectr. various confs. Am. Law Inst., World Trade Inst., Practicing Law Inst., Internat. Fiscal Assn., ABA, Tex. State Bar. Author: International Business Transactions-Tax and Legal Handbook, 1978, Estate Planning, 1991, 2006, International Business Planning: Law and Taxation, 6 vols., 1982, Tax Planning for Retirement, 2001, revised edit., 2008, Doing Business in China, 1990, 1996, Federal Income Taxation of Corporations and Shareholders--Forms, 1995—2009, Choice of Entity, 1994, 1999, 2007, U.S. International Estate Planning, 1996, revised, 2006. Served with USMC, 1962. Lutheran. Home: 1903 Dunstan Rd Houston TX 77005-1619 Office: U Houston Law Ctr Houston TX 77204-6060 Home Phone: 713-529-4802; Office Phone: 713-743-2148. Business E-Mail: wstreng@uh.edu.

STRENGTH, CATHERINE BUSH, nursing educator; b. New Orleans, Dec. 7, 1955; d. Joseph Ernest Jr. and Patsy Ruth (Johnson) Bush; m. Steven Cole Strength, Aug. 18, 1984. BSN, Southeastern La. U., 1977; M of Nursing, La. State U., 1981. RN, La.; cert. med.-surg. nurse, clin. nurse specialist, instr. BLS. Nurse emergency rm. East Jefferson Gen. Hosp., Metairie, La., 1977—81; dir. edn. and tng. St. Jude Hosp., Kenner, La., 1982—85; asst. prof. Charity Hosp. Sch. Nursing/Delgado C.C., New Orleans, 1990—94; assoc. prof. Charity Hosp. Sch. Nursing, New Orleans, 1994—. Recipient Adult Svc. award, St. Martha Ch., Harvey, LA, 2009. Mem. Nat. League Nursing, Sigma Theta Tau (hon.), Epsilon Nu. Home: 3905 Lake Des Allemands Dr Harvey LA 70058-5502 Office: Charity Delgado Nursing Sch 450 S Claiborne Ave New Orleans LA 70112-1310 Office Phone: 504-571-1346. Business E-Mail: cstren@dcc.edu.

STRIANESE, MICHAEL T., communications systems company executive; b. Mar. 13, 1956; Grad., St. John's U. CPA. With Ernst & Young; dir. spl. projects Loral Skynet, 1991—96; v.p. & contr., C31 & systems integration ctr. Lockheed Martin Corp., 1996—97; v.p. fin., contr. L-3 Comm. Holdings Inc., NYC, 1997—2000, sr. v.p. fin., 2000—05, sr. v.p., CFO, 2005—06, interim CEO, 2006, pres., CEO, 2006—08, chmn., pres., CEO, 2008—. Bd. dirs. L-3 Communications, Inc., 2006—. Avocations: boating, skiing. Office: L-3 Comm Holdings Inc 600 Third Ave New York NY 10016 Office Phone: 212-697-1111. Office Fax: 212-867-5249.*

STRICHERZ, VINCENT C., journalist; b. Sioux Falls, SD, Nov. 11, 1952; s. Leo P. and Agnes Susan Fox Stricherz; m. Regina J. Hills, Feb. 25, 1984. BA in Polit. Sci. and Mass Comm., U. SD, Vermillion, 1977. News dir. KORN Radio, Mitchell, SD, 1978—79; city editor Daily Rep., Mitchell, 1979—81; reporter UPI, Lincoln, Nebr., 1981—82, bur. mgr., reporter Omaha, 1982—83; mng. editor Daily Sentry-News, Slidell, La., 1984; reporter, asst. city editor Indpls. Star, 1985—87; reporter, editor Seattle Times, 1988—90; freelance writer Seattle, 1991; city editor, reporter Jour.-Am./King County Jour., Bellevue, Wash., 1992—98; sci. writer media rels. U. Wash., Seattle, 1998—. Steering com. mem. Regional Pub. Info. Network, Seattle, 2001—08. Constrn. vol., pub. rels. vol. Habitat Humanity Seattle/South King County, Seattle, 2000—. Recipient 1st Place award, Soc. Profl. Journalists, 1994, Bronze medal, Coun. Advancement & Support Edn., 2002, 2005, Silver medal, 2006. Mem.: Nat. Assn. Sci. Writers. Independent. Roman Catholic. Avocations: history, music. Office: Univ Wash Box 351207 Seattle WA 98195-1207 Business E-Mail: vinces@u.washington.edu.

STRICK, JEREMY, curator, museum director; BA in History of Art with highest honors, U. Calif., Santa Cruz, 1977; postgrad., Harvard U. Asst. curator 20th Century art Nat. Gallery Art, Washington, 1986-89, assoc. curator 20th Century art, 1989-93, acting dept. dept. 20th Century art, 1992-93, curator Nat. Sculpture Garden project, 1989-93; curator modern art St. Louis Art Mus., 1993-96; Frances and Thomas Dittmer curator 20th Century painting and sculpture Art Inst. Chgo., 1996-99; dir. Mus. Contemporary Art, LA, 1999—. Curator N.Y. Interpreted: Joseph Stella and Alfred Stieglitz, Nat. Gallery Art, 1987, Milton Avery, 1990, Mark Rothko: The Spirit Myth, 1990-95, asst. curator A Century of Modern Sculpture: The Patsy and Raymond Nasher Collection, 1987, co-curator Twentieth-Century Art: Selections for the Tenth Anniversary of the East Building, 1987; curator Brice Marden: A Painting, Drawings, Prints, St. Louis Art Mus., 1993, Currents 58: Susan Crile—The Fires of War, 1994, Louise Bourgeois: The Personages 1946-1954, 1995, Currents 60: Jerald Ieans, 1994, Masterworks from Stuttgar: The Romantic Age in German Art, 1995, Currents 66: Michael Byron, 1996, Currents 67: Leonardo Drew, 1996; curator The Sublime Is Now: The Early Work of Barnett Newman, Walker Art Ctr., Mpls., Pace Gallery, N.Y.C., 1994; curator In the Light of Italy: Corot and Early Open-Air Painting, Nat. Gallery Art, Bklyn. Mus., St. Louis Art Mus., 1996; lectr., symposia participant and organizer, 1980—; juror Showhegan awards, 1995. Contbg. author: Works by Antoine-Louis Barye in the Collection of the Fogg Art Museum, Vol. IV, 1982; contbr. articles to exhbn. catalogs, newspapers, mags., ency. Instnl. fellow Samuel H. Kress Found., Paris, 1983-85, fellow Mrs. Giles Whiting Found., 1985-86. Office: Mus Contemporary Art Dept 20th Century Painting 250 S Grand Ave Los Angeles CA 90012-3021 Home: 261 N Bundy Dr Los Angeles CA 90049-2825 E-mail: jstrick@moca.org.

STRICKER, STEVE, professional golfer; b. Edgerton, Wis., Feb. 23, 1967; m. Nicki Stricker; 1 child, Bobbi Maria. Grad., U. Ill., 1990. Profl. golfer, 1990—. Mem. US team Alfred Dunhill Cup, 1996, Presidents Cup, 1996, 2007, Ryder Cup, 2008. Named PGA TOUR Comeback Player of Yr., 2006, 2007. Achievements include winning international events: Victoria Open, Canada, 1990; Canadian PGA Championship, 1993; winning PGA Tour events: Kemper Open, 1996; Motorola Western Open, 1996; Accenture Match Play Championship, 2001; The Barclays, 2007, Crowne Plaza Invitational at Colonial, John Deere Classic, 2009; being a member of the Ryder Cup winning US team, 2008. Office: PGA Tour 112 PGA Tour Blvd Ponte Vedra Beach FL 32082*

STRICKHOLM, JEAN, musician, company executive, retired elementary school educator; b. Madison, Wis., Oct. 27, 1933; d. Hulsey and Eloise May (Bocker) Cason; m. Harry Jean Cason Strickholm, June 30, 1956; children: Karen, Sally Tayeb, Douglas, Glenn. Student, Red Fox Music Camp, Marlboro, Mass., 1952—54; BS, U. Rochester, Rochester, NY, 1955; MS, Queens Coll., Flushing, NY, 1959. Cert. tchr. N.Y. Dept. Edn., 1955, elem. edn. K-12 N.J. Dept. Edn., 1969, tchr. social studies K-12 N.J. Dept. Edn., 1973. Tchr. Gt. Neck Pub. Schs., Gt. Neck, NY, 1955—58, Tenafly Pub. Schs., NJ, 1969—70, Englewood Pub. Schs., NJ, 1970—98, ret., 1998. Co-dir., mgr., fund raiser, performer All Seasons Chamber Players, Demarest, NJ, 1981—. Chmn. Bergen County Equal Opportunities Study Com., Hackensack, NJ, 1969—70; active Civil Rights Movement Bergen County, 1961—70. Recipient award, Bergen County Fair Housing Coun., 1961—70. Mem.: Chamber Music Am. (assoc.). Democrat. Avocations: swimming, gardening, reading.

STRICKLAND, ARVARH EUNICE, history professor; b. Hattiesburg, Miss., July 6, 1930; s. Eunice and Clotiel (Marshall) S.; m. Willie Pearl Elmore, June 17, 1951; children: Duane Arvarh, Bruce Elmore. BA, Tougaloo Coll., 1951; MA, U. Ill., 1953, PhD, 1962; LHD (hon.), Tougaloo Coll., 2007. Tchr. Hattiesburg Schs., 1951-52; instr. Tuskegee Inst., 1955-56; prin. supr. Madison County Schs., Canton, Miss., 1956-59; asst. prof. history Chgo. State U., 1962-65, assoc. prof. history, 1965-68, prof., 1968-69, U. Mo., Columbia, 1969-96, prof. emeritus, 1996—, chmn. dept. history, 1980-83, interim dir. black studies program, 1994-96, sr. faculty assoc., Office of V.P. acad. affairs, 1987-88, assoc. v.p. acad. affairs, 1989-91. Author: History of the Chicago Urban League, 1966, reprint, 2001, (with Reich and Biller) Building the United States, 1971, (with Reich) The Black American Experience to 1877, 1974, The Black American Experience since 1877, 1974; editor: Working with Carter G. Woodson, (with Lorenzo J. Greene) The Father of Black History: A Diary, 1928-1930, 1989, Selling Black History for Carter G. Woodson: A Diary, 1930-33, 1996, (with Robert E. Weems) The African American Experience: A Historiographical and Bibliographical Guide, 2000. Commr. Planning and Zoning, Columbia, Mo., 1977-80, Boone County Home Rule Charter, 1982, Mo. Peace Officers Standards and Tng. Commn., 1988-89; co-chmn. Mayors Com. to Commemorate Contbns. of Black Columbians, Columbia, 1981; mem. exec. subcom. Mayor's Ad Hoc Election '82 Com., 1982; bd. dirs. Harry S. Truman Library Inst., 1987-96, U. of Mo.-Columbia Health Sys., 2003—. Recipient Disting. Svc. award Ill. Hist. Soc., 1957, Byler Disting. Prof. award U. Mo., 1994, St. Louis Am.'s Educator of Yr. award, 1994, Disting. Faculty award U. Mo.-Columbia Alumni Assn., 1995, Tougaloo Coll. Alumni Hall of Fame, 1995, Alumni Achievement U. Ill. Coll. Liberal Arts and Scis., 1997, Disting. Svc. award State Hist. Soc. Mo., 1997. Mem. Orgn. Am. Historians, Am. Hist. Assn., Assn. Study Afro-Am. Life and History (Carter Godwin Woodson Scholars medallion 1999), So. Hist. Assn., State Hist. Soc. Mo. (Disting. Svc. award 1997), Boone County Hist. Soc. (bd. dirs. 1998-2002, 2d v.p. 1999, 1st v.p. 2000-02), Kiwanis, Alpha Phi Alpha, Phi Alpha Theta (internat. v.p. 1991-93, pres. 1994-95, chair adv. bd. 1996-97, Disting. Svc. award 1997, Columbia Values Diversity award, 2005). Democrat. Methodist. Home: 4100 Defoe Dr Columbia MO 65203-0252 Office: U Mo Dept History 101 Read Hall Columbia MO 65211-7500

STRICKLAND, BONNIE RUTH, psychologist, educator; b. Louisville, Nov. 24, 1936; d. Roy E. and Billie P. (Whitfield) S. BS, Ala. Coll., 1958; MS, Ohio State U., 1960, PhD (USPHS fellow), 1962. Diplomate: clin. psychology Am. Bd. Examiners in Profl. Psychology. From asst. to asso. prof. psychology Emory U., Atlanta, 1962—73, dean of women, 1964—67; prof. psychology U. Mass., Amherst, 1973—2003, prof. emeritus, 2003—, chmn. dept. psychology, 1976—77, 1978—82, assoc. to chancellor, 1983—84. Mem. adv. coun. NIMH, 1984-87; Sigma Xi nat. lectr., 1991-93. Adv. editor numerous psychology jours., acad. pub. houses; contbg. author texts personality theory.; contbr. of numerous articles on social personality and clin. psychology to profl. jours.; contbg. author of two citation classics. Recipient Outstanding Faculty award Emory U., 1968-69; Chancellor's medal disting. service U. Mass., 1983. Fellow APA (pres. divsn. clin. psychology 1983, pres. divsn. gen. psychology 2005, chmn. bd. profl. affairs 1980-83, chmn. policy and planning bd. 1983-85, pres. 1987, bd. dirs. 1986-87, Outstanding Leadership award 1992, Disting. Contbns. and Psychology in the Pub. Interest award 1999, Presdl. Citation 2001), Am. Psychol. Soc. (founder 1988, bd. dirs. 1989-93), New Eng. Psychol. Assn. (Disting. Contbns. award 2002), Am. Assn. Applied and Preventive Psychology (founder 1990, bd. dirs. 1990-94, pres. 1992-94). Home: 558 Federal St Belchertown MA 01007-9754 Office: U Mass Dept Psychology Amherst MA 01003-7710

STRICKLAND, CARRIE D, music educator; d. Johnnie W. and Carole M. Strickland. MusB, U. Southern Miss., Hattiesburg, 1997; MusM, West Va. U., Morgantown, 2000; PhD Musical Arts, U. Ga., Athens, 2004. Adj. prof. of horn Toccoa Falls Coll., Ga., 2001—02, Augusta State U., Ga., 2000—03; grad. tchg. asst. U. of Ga., Athens, 2000—03; third horn Mobile Symphony Orch., Ala., 2005—; co-prin. horn Philharm. Soc. NW Fla., Destin, Fla., 2007—; prin. horn Sinfonia Gulf Coast, Destin, Fla., 2007—; instr. high brass Jones County Jr. Coll., Ellisville, Miss., 2005—. Adv. bd. mem. SE Horn Workshop, 2006—. Recipient Theodore Presser award, U. Southern Miss., 1995, award, Music Teachers Nat. Assn., 1993, Director's Excellence award, U. Ga., 2004; grant, Fulbright Found. Norway, 2003—04, fellowship, Am. Scandinavian Found., 2003—04, Winner, Young Artists Competition, Miss. Symphony Orch., 1991. Mem.: Am. Fedn. Musicians, Coll. Music Soc., Internat. Horn Soc., Golden Key Nat. Honor Soc., Pi Kappa Lambda Music Honor Soc. Office: Jones County Jr Coll 900 S Court St Ellisville MS 39437 Personal E-mail: cdshorn@aol.com.

STRICKLAND, DELPHENE COVERSTON, judge; b. Ponca City, Okla. d. Harry Ethelbert and Mary Louise (Reed) Coverston; m. Thomas Whitney Strickland, Aug. 31, 1946; children: Mary Herrington, Thomas Whitney Jr., Strickland, Jr. BA, John B. Stetson U., 1944; JD, U. Fla., 1945; postgrad., Fla. State U., 1965-70, Nat. Jud. Coll., Reno, 1979-80. Bar: Fla. 1945, US Dist. Ct. (so. dist.) Fla. 1946, US Dist. Ct. (no. dist.) Tex. 1979, US Dist. Ct. Hawaii 1980, US Supreme Ct. 1980, US Ct. Appeals (11th cir.) 1983. Assoc. Rogers & Morris, Ft. Lauderdale, Fla., 1945-46, Clayton, Arnow, Johnson & Duncan, Gainesville, Fla., 1946-51; pvt. practice Delphene Strickland Law Offices, Gainesville, 1951-59; legal rsch. asst. Fla. Supreme Ct., Tallahassee, 1960-68, exec. asst., 1968-70, mem. legis. ref. com., 1970—72; gen. counsel Fla. Dept. Transp., 1972; adminstrv. law judge Tallahassee; ret., 1972—82; part time gen. practice DC Strickland, 2002—. Adj. prof. U. Fla., Gainesville, Fla. State U., Tallahassee; Fla. del. to 1983 11th Cir. Jud. Conf.; mem. Fla. Bd. Bar Examiners, 1970-, sr. mem. 1980-; sr. mem. Fla. Traffic Ct., 1970—; mem. efficiency com. Fla. Supreme Ct., 1984—; organizer, charter mem. Leon Safety Coun. Contbr. articles to law jours. Sunday sch. tchr. St. Paul United Meth. Ch., Tallahassee, 1970-2002, with Nat. Trust Historic Preservation Fellow ABA Judicial Div. Nat. Conf. Adminstrv. Law Judges; mem. ABA (chmn. nat. conf. adminstrv. law judges 1983-84, exec. coun. 1985—), Fla. Govt. Bar Assn. (past pres., Earnie Webb award 1988), Fla. Assn. Women Lawyers (past pres.), Tallahassee Women Lawyers Assn. (past pres., founder,), Nat. Assn. Women Lawyers (Fla. del., charter mem.), Nat. Assn. Women Judges (charter mem.), Am. Arbitration Assn., AAUW (past pres. Gainesville), Supreme Ct. Hist. Soc., Fla. Supreme Ct. Hist. Soc. (organizer, charter, trustee), Fla. Govt. Bar Assn. (organizer, charter, past pres.), Tallahassee Bar Assn., North Fla. Legal Svcs., DAR (state del. Tallahassee, 99th nat. congress Washington 1989—), Nat. Soc. Daughters of the Am. Revolution, Nat. Soc. US Daughters 1812, United Daughters of the Confederacy, The Nat. Soc. Colonial Dames XVII Century, Capital City Country Club, Am. Camellia Soc., Tallahassee Camellia Soc., Am. Rose Soc., Tallahassee Rose Soc., Thomasville Camellia Soc., Thomasville Rose Soc., Apalachee Audubon Soc., Saint Andrew Soc. (organizer, charter mem.), Appalachian Trail Conservancy, Continental Divide Trail Alliance, Inc., Zonta, Phi Alpha Delta. Home: 2802 Sterling Dr Tallahassee FL 32312-3030 Personal E-mail: delphinesjd@gmail.com.

STRICKLAND, DOROTHY, education educator; BS, Newark State Coll.; MA, PhD, NYU. Elem. sch. tchr. N.J. pub. sch. sys., reading cons., learning disabilities specialist; prof. edn. Rutgers U., New Brunswick, NJ, 1985—, Samuel DeWitt Proctor Prof. Edn., 2002—. Active in numerous state and nat. adv. bds. Author: Language Literacy and the Child, Process Reading and Writing: A Literature Based Approach, The Administration and Supervision of Reading Programs, Educating Black Children: America's Challenge, Family Storybook Reading, Listen Children: An Anthology of Black Literature, Families: An Anthology of Poetry for Young Children, Teaching Phonics Today, 1998, Beginning Reading and Writing, 2000, Supporting Struggling Readers and Writers, 2002, Preparing Our Teachers, 2002, Language Arts: Learning and Teaching, 2003, Learning About Print in Preschool Settings, 2004. Inducted into the Reading Hall of Fame, pres., 1997-98. Mem. Nat. Coun. Tchrs. English (Rewey Belle Inglis award for Outstanding Woman in English Education Annual Conv., rsch. award, Outstanding Educator in Lang. Arts award 1998), Internat. Reading Assn. (past pres., Outstanding Tchr. Educator of reading award). Home: 131 Coccio Dr West Orange NJ 07052-4121 Office: Rutgers U Dept Edn Grad Sch Edn New Brunswick NJ 08903

STRICKLAND, HUGH ALFRED, lawyer; b. Rockford, Ill., May 3, 1931; s. Hugh and Marie (Elmer) S.; m. Donna E. McDonald, Aug. 11, 1956; children: Amy Alice Drecler, Karen Ann Stricklamn. AB, Knox Coll., 1953; JD, Chgo. Kent Coll. Law, 1959. Bar: Ill. 1960. Partner firm McDonald, Strickland & Clough, Carrollton, Ill., 1961—; asst. atty. gen. Ill., 1960-67; spl. asst. gen. Ill., 1967-69; pres. McDonald Title Co. Mem. Greene County Welfare Svcs. Com., 1963—, Ill. Heart Assn., 1961-65; trustee Thomas H. Boyd Meml. Hosp., 1972-95; pres. Long Lake Assn. Vilas County, Inc., 2002—. With AUS, 1953-55. Recipient award for meritorious service Am. Heart Assn., 1964 Fellow Ill. Bar Found. (charter); mem. ABA, Ill. Bar Assn., Greene County Bar Assn. (past pres.), Southwestern Bar Assn. (past pres.), Ill. Def. Counsel, Am. Judicature Soc., Def. Rsch. Inst., Elks Club, Westlake Country Club (v.p. 1968-70, dir.), Big Sand Lake Country Club, Phi Delta Theta, Phi Delta Phi. Methodist. Home: 827 7th St Carrollton IL 62016-1421 Office: 524 N Main St PO Box 71 Carrollton IL 62016-1027 Home Phone: 217-942-6271; Office Phone: 217-942-3115. Business E-Mail: has3@irtc.net.

STRICKLAND, ROBERT LOUIS, retired retail executive; b. Florence, SC, Mar. 3, 1931; s. Franz M. and Hazel (Eaddy) S.; m. Elizabeth Ann Miller, Feb. 2, 1952; children: Cynthia Anne, Robert Edson. AB, U. N.C., 1952; MBA with distinction, Harvard U., 1957. Bd. dirs. Lowe's Cos., Inc., North Wilkesboro, NC, 1961—2000, sr. v.p., 1970—76, exec. v.p., 1976—78, chmn. bd., 1979—98, chmn. exec. com., 1988—98, mem. office of pres., 1970—78, chmn. emeritus, 1999; founder Sterling Advt., Ltd., 1966. V.p., mem. adminstrv. com. Lowe's Profit-Sharing Trust, 1961-87, chmn. ops. com., 1972-78; mgmt. com. Lowe's ESOP Plan, 1978-97; prior bd. dirs. Lowe's Cos., Wilkesboro, NC, T.Rowe Price Assocs., Balt., 1991-2001, Hannaford Bros. Co., Portland, Maine, Krispy Kreme Corp., Winston-Salem, NC, Wholesale Club, Indpls., Summit Comms., Atlanta; vice chair, bd. dirs. Revelstoke Co., Calgary, Can.; panelist investor rels. field, 1972-99; spkr., panelist employee stock ownership, 1978-2000; spkr. on investor rels., London, Edinburgh, Glasgow, Paris, Zurich, Frankfurt, Milan, Vienna, Singapore, Tokyo. Author: Lowe's Cybernetwork, 1969, Lowe's Living Legend, 1970, Ten Years of Growth, 1971, The Growth Continues, 1972, 73, 74, Lowe's Scoreboard, 1978; contbr. articles to profl. jours. Mem. NC Ho. of Reps., 1962-64, Rep. Senatorial Inner Circle, 1980-95; exec. com. NC Rep. Com., 1963-73; trustee U. NC, Chapel Hill, 1987-95, chmn. bd., 1991-93; dir., dep. chmn. Fed. Res. Bank of Richmond, 1996-98; com. on bus. laws and the economy NC, 1994-97; dir. US Coun. Better Bus. Burs., 1981-85; bd. dirs., v.p. Nat. Home Improvement Coun., 1972-76; bd. dirs. NC Sch. Arts Found., 1975-79, NC Bd. Natural and Econ. Resources, 1975-76; bd. dirs., govt. affairs com. Home Ctr. Inst., co-chmn. Home Ctr. to Israel Del., 1984; trustee, sec. bd. Wilkes CC, 1964-73; chmn., pres. bd. dirs. Do-It-Yourself Rsch. Inst., 1981-89; pres. Hardware Home Improvement Coun. City of Hope Nat. Med. Ctr., LA, 1987-89; co-founder Home Safety Coun., 1993. With USN, 1952—55, lt. res. USN, 1955—62. Named Wilkes County NC Young Man of Yr., Wilkes Jr. C. of C., 1962; recipient Bronze Oscar of Industry award Fin. World, 1969-74, 76-79, Silver Oscar of Industry award, 1970, 72-74, 76-79, Gold Oscar of Industry award as best of all industry, 1972, 87, Excellence award in corp. reporting Fin. Analysts Fedn., 1970, 72, 74, 81-82, cert. of Distinction Brand Names Found., 1970, Retailer of Yr. award, 1971, 73, Disting. Mcht. award, 1972, Spirit of Life award City of Hope, 1983, Free Enterprise Legend award Students Free Enterprise, 1994; named to Home Ctr. Hall of Fame, 1985, Golden Hammer Hall of Fame, 2007. Mem. Nat. Assn. Over-Counter Cos. (bd. advisers 1973-77), Newcomen Soc., Employee Stock Ownership Assn. (pres. 1983-85, chmn. 1985-87), James Madison Club, Federalist Soc., Forsyth Country Club, Piedmont City Club, Ponte Vedra Inn and Club (Fla.), Harvard Club (NY), Scabbard and Blade, Phi Beta Kappa, Pi Kappa Alpha.

Home: 226 N Stratford Rd Winston Salem NC 27104-3132 also: 721 5th Ave Apt GH New York NY 10022 Office: 2000 W 1st St Winston Salem NC 27104-4225 Home: 67 Ponte Vedra Blvd Ponte Vedra Beach FL 32082

STRICKLAND, SYLVIA RAYE, social worker; b. Grand Prarie, Tex., Feb. 21, 1945; d. Nathaniel and Flora Evelyn Strickland; m. Julian B. Angel, Oct. 6, 1973 (div. Apr. 1983); 1 child, Sarah Renee Angel. BSW, U. So. Colo., Pueblo, 1986; MSW, N.Mex. Highlands U., Las Vegas, N.Mex., 1987. Lic. psychotherapist 1998, cert. grief recovery specialist Grief Recovery Inst., 2005. Social worker Highland Park Nursing Home, Pueblo, 1988; social worker III El Paso County Social Svcs., Colorado Springs, Colo., 1988—89; resident svcs. coord. Villa Santa Maria, Colorado Springs, Colo., 1990—91, ballot initative circulator, 1992; social worker Medalion Health Ctr., Colorado Springs, 1993—99, coord. activities personal care unit, 1993—96, resident family rep., 1999—2007, Grief Workshops, 2007; cognitive stimulation clinician Memory Bridging, 2008. Vol. Hospice of Comforter, 1994—96, Pikes Peak Hospice, 2008; active St. Paul's Cath. Ch.; sec. Social Work Action Team, U. So. Colo., 1984—85. Recipient award, Rementis Health Group, MBR Pikes Peak Justice, Therapy Alzheimers. Mem.: Colo. Soc. Clin. Social Work (chmn. program 1999—), Assn. Rsch. and Enlightenment, SOS Investment Club. Avocations: choir, water colors, attending concerts, quilting. Home: PO Box 38123 Colorado Springs CO 80937-8123 Personal E-mail: sylrstr@yahoo.com.

STRICKLAND, TED, Governor of Ohio, former United States Representative from Ohio; b. Lucasville, Ohio, Aug. 4, 1941; s. Orville and Carrie Strickland; m. Frances Smith. BA in Hist., Asbury Coll., Wilmore, Ky., 1963; MDiv, Asbury Theol. Seminary, Wilmore, Ky., 1967; PhD in Counseling Psych., U. Ky., Lexington, 1980. Min.; dir. social svcs. Ky. Meth. Home; consulting psychologist So. Ohio Correctional Facility, 1985—92, 1994—96; asst. prof. psych. Shawnee State U., Portsmouth, Ohio, 1988—92, 1994—96; mem. US Congress from 6th Ohio dist., 1993—95, 1997—2007, mem. energy & commerce com., vets. affairs com., ranking minority mem. oversight and investigations subcommittee; gov. State of Ohio, Columbus, 2007—. Dem. nominee for Gov., Ohio, 2006. Co-recipient Outstanding Psychologist award, Nat. Alliance Mentally Ill, 2004. Mem.: Ohio Psychol. Assn., APA. Democrat. Methodist. Office: Office Gov Vern Riffe Ctr 77 S High St 30th Fl Columbus OH 43215-6117

STRICKLAND, THOMAS L., federal agency administrator, former insurance company executive; b. Houston, May 16, 1952; BA with honors, La. State U., 1974; JD with honors, U. Tex., Austin, 1977. Bar: Tex. 1977, Colo. 1979. Law clk. to Hon. Carl. O. Bue, Jr. US Dist. Ct. (so. dist.) Tex., 1977—79; dir. policy & rsch. to Gov. Richard D. Lamm State of Colo., Denver, 1982—84; ptnr. Brownstein Hyatt & Farber, Denver, 1984—99; US atty. Dist. Colo. US Dept. Justice, 1999—2001; ptnr. Hogan & Hartson LLP, Denver, 2003—07; exec. v.p., chief legal officer UnitedHealth Group, Mpls., 2007—09; chief of staff US Dept. Interior, Washington, 2009—, asst. sec. for fish, wildlife & parks, 2009—. Legal counsel Denver Metro C. of C.; commr. Colo. Transp. Commn., 1985—89, chmn., 1987—88, Metro. Transp. Develop. Commn., Colo., 1989—90. Dem. nominee U.S. Senate from Colo., 1996, 2002; founding bd. mem. Great Outdoors Colo.; bd. mem. Children's Hosp., Denver, Denver Pub. Schools Found. Mem.: ABA, Colo. Bar Assn., State Bar Tex., Denver Bar Assn., Omicron Delta Kappa. Democrat. Office: US Dept Interior 1849 C St NW Washington DC 20240*

STRICKLAND, WILLIAM JESSE, lawyer; b. Newport News, Va., Mar. 21, 1942; BSBA, U. Richmond, 1964, JD, 1969. Bar: Va. 1969, US Dist. Ct. Ea. Dist. Va., US Dist. Ct. We. Dist. Va., US Ct. Appeals 4th Cir., US Ct. Claims, US Tax Ct., Bar Brussels. Mem McGuire Woods LLP, Richmond, Va., 1969—, mng. ptnr., 1996—2007. Bd. dirs. Cableform Inc., Zion Crossroads, Va., Eimeldingen Corp., Indpls, Greater Richmond. Mem. exec. com. Va. Found. for Rsch. & Econ. Edn., Inc., bd. dirs. U. Richmond Law Sch. Found.; mem. coun. Va. Inst. Marine Sci.; founder Marine Corps Heritage Found.; bd. dirs. World Affairs Coun. Greater Richmond; chmn. Am. Club Brussels. Capt. USMC, 1964—67. Mem. ABA (com. on tax exempt fin.), Va. Bar Assn., Richmond Bar Assn., Nat. Assn. Bond Lawyers, Va. Govt. Fin. Officers Assn., Va. Local Govt. Attorneys Assn., Va. Bond Club. Office: McGuire Woods LLP One James Ctr 901 E Cary St Richmond VA 23219-4030 Office Phone: 804-775-4350. Office Fax: 804-698-2185. Business E-Mail: wstrickland@mcguirewoods.com.

STRICKLER, JEFFREY HAROLD, pediatrician; b. Mpls., Oct. 14, 1943; s. Jacob Harold and Helen Cecelia (Mitchell) S.; m. Karen Anne Stewart, June 18, 1966; children: Hans Stewart, Liesl Ann. BA, Carleton Coll., 1965; MD, U. Minn., 1969. Diplomate Am. Bd. Pediatrics. Resident in pediatrics Stanford U., Calif., 1969-73; pvt. practice Helena, Mont., 1975—2005; chief staff Shodair Children's Hosp., Helena, 1984-86; consulting ptnr. Strickler Enterprises, 2006—. Dir. maternal-child health Lewis and Clark County, Helena, 1978-88; chief of staff St. Peters Hosp., Helena, 1994-96; bd.chmn. Helena Health Alliance, 1996-99; founding mem., bd. dirs. Caring Found. Mont., 1992-2005; bd. mem. Intermountain Opera Assn., 2007-. Author: Big Sky Names, An Amble Through Western History and Ecology on the Roads, Streams, and Developments of Big Sky Montana, 2008. Mem. Mont. Gov.'s Task Force on Child Abuse, 1978-79; mem. steering com. Region VIII Child Abuse Prevention, Denver, 1979-82; bd. dirs. Helena Dist. 1 Sch. Bd., 1982-88, vice chmn., 1985-87. Maj. MC USAF, 1973—75. Fellow: Am. Acad. Pediatrics (vice chmn. Mont. chpt. 1981—84, chmn. 1984—87, mem. nat. nominating com. 1987—90, chmn. 1989—90, coun. on govt. affairs 1990—96, future of pediatric edn. II 1996—2000, Wyeth award 1987); mem.: Am. Bd. Pediatrics (PMCP-G practice performance com. 2001—), Rotary (youth exch. chmn. dist. 539 1984—88, pres. Helena 1988—89, polio plus chair dist. 5390 1996—, asst. gov. dist. 5390 2002—04, dist. gov. elect 2005—06, gov. 2006—07). Avocations: skiing, hiking. Home: PO Box 161815 2125 Yellowtail Rd Big Sky MT 59716-1815 Office Phone: 406-431-4331. Personal E-mail: j.strickler@3rivers.net.

STRICKLER, MATTHEW M., lawyer; b. Bryn Mawr, Pa., June 27, 1940; s. Charles S and Mary Webster (Cornman) S.; m. Margaret Renshaw, Sept. 3, 1966; children: Matthew David, Andrew Kellogg, Timothy Webster, Edward Charles. AB, Haverford Coll., 1962; JD, Harvard U., 1965. Bar: Pa. 1965, U.S. Supreme Ct. 1975. Assoc. Ballard, Spahr, Andrews & Ingersoll, Phila., 1965-74, ptnr., 1974—2002, sr. counsel, 2003—; dir. legal affairs Sch. Medicine Temple U., Phila., 2003—09. Adj. prof. Temple U. Sch. Law, Phila., 1993-2008. Editor: Representing Health Care Facilities, 1981. Bd. dirs. Phila. chpt. Girl Scouts Am., 1978-96, v.p., 1984-90, 94-96; bd. dirs. Kardon Inst. Arts, 2000—, treas., 2003-05, chmn., 2005—. Mem. Union League Phila., Pocono Lake Preserve. Home: 523 Timber Ln Devon PA 19333-1234 Office: 1735 Market St 51st Fl Philadelphia PA 19103 Office Phone: 215-864-8115. Business E-Mail: strickler@ballardspahr.com.

STRICKLIN, CYNTHIA J., middle school educator; b. Nashville, May 24, 1958; d. James Spencer and Elizabeth McElroy Deaton; m. David W. Stricklin, Apr. 24, 1982; children: Spencer, Heath. BA, David Lipscomb, Nashville, 1980; EdM, Tenn. State U., Nashville, 2000. With Met. Nashville Pub. Schs., Nashville, educator. Mem.: NEA, NIVAE, TEA, MNEA, Alpha Delta Kappa (historian 2006—). Mem. Christian Ch. Avocations: camping, gardening, crafts. Office: Gra-Mar Mid Sch 575 Joyce Ln Nashville TN 37216 Business E-Mail: cynthia.stricklin@mnps.org.

STRICKLING, LAWRENCE E. (LARRY STRICKLING), federal agency administrator; b. 1951; BS in Economics, U. Md., 1973; JD, Harvard Law Sch., 1976. Ptnr. Kirkland & Ellis LLP, Chgo.; v.p. for pub. policy Ameritech; assoc. gen. counsel, chief competition divsn. FCC, Washington, chief common carrier bur., 1998—2000; chief regulatory and chief compliance officer Broadwing Comm.; policy coord. Obama for America; asst. sec. for comm. & info. US Dept. Commerce, Washington, 2009—, adminstr. Nat. Telecom. & Info. Adminstrn. (NTIA), 2009—. With Allegiance Telecom, CoreExpress, Inc.; bd. dirs. Network Plus. Bd. visitors sch. pub. policy U. Md.; bd. trustees court theatre U. Chgo.; bd. dirs. Music of the Baroque, Chgo. Mem.: Phi Beta Kappa. Office: US Dept Commerce Herbert C Hoover Bldg (HCHB) 1401 Constitution Ave NW Washington DC 20230*

STRICKON, HARVEY ALAN, lawyer; b. Bklyn., Nov. 9, 1947; s. Milton and Norma (Goodhartz) S.; m. Linda Carol Meltzer, July 2, 1972; children: Joshua Andrew, Meredith Cindy, Erica Stacey. BBA, CCNY, 1968; JD, NYU, 1971. Bar: NY 1972, US Dist. Ct. (so. and ea. dists.) NY 1973, US Ct. Appeals (2d cir.) 1973, US Supreme Ct. 1975, US Dist. Ct. (no. dist.) NY 1980, US Dist. Ct. (we. dist.) NY 1981, US Dist. Ct. Ariz. 1991, US Dist. Ct. Conn., 1996, US Tax Ct. 2006. Law clk. U.S. Dist. Ct. (ea. dist.) N.Y., Bklyn., 1971-73; assoc. Moses & Singer, NYC, 1973-80; from assoc. to ptnr. Kaye, Scholer, Fierman, Hays & Handler, NYC, 1980-91; from ptnr. to counsel Paul, Hastings, Janofsky & Walker LLP, NYC, 1991—. Mem. complaint mediation panel, departmental disciplinary com. appellate div., 1st dept. Supreme Ct. State N.Y.; mem. mediation panel U.S. Dist. Ct. (ea. dist.) N.Y.; mem. mediation register U.S. Bankruptcy Ct. (so. and ea. dists.) N.Y. Co-author: Enforcing Judgments and Collecting Debts in New York, 1996. Mem. Nassau County Rep. Com., Great Neck, N.Y., 1982—; chmn. bd. dirs. Flushing Community Vol. Ambulance Corps. Inc., N.Y., 1981-86, vice chmn., 1987-92. Mem. ABA, N.Y. State Bar Assn., Assn. Bar City N.Y. (chmn. com. on profl. discipline and complaint mediation panel com. on profl. discipline), Am. Judicature Soc., Assn. Comml. Fin. Attys., N.Y. Law Inst., Bankruptcy Lawyers Bar Assn., (bd. govs. 1987-89, corr. sec. 1989—), Am. Bankruptcy Inst. Republican. Jewish. Home: 11 West Brook Rd Great Neck NY 11024-1219 Office: Paul Hastings Janofsky & Walker LLP 75 E 55th St New York NY 10022-3205 Office Phone: 212-318-6380. Personal E-mail: hastrick@optonline.net. Business E-Mail: harveystrickon@paulhastings.com.

STRID-CHADWICK, KAREN S., musician, educator; m. Larry Chadwick. MusM, U. Alaska, Fairbanks, 1991. Adj. instr. Anchorage CC, 1978—87; asst. prof. U. Alaska, Anchorage, 1988—94, assoc. prof., 1994—2003, prof. jazz studies, 2003—. State collegiate advisor Alaska Music Educators Assn., Anchorage, 1994—. Prodr.: (annual jazz festival) UAA Jazz Week; musician (jazz pianist): Karen Strid Quartet. Office: Univ Alaska Anchorage 3211 Providence Dr Anchorage AK 99508 Business E-Mail: afkss@uaa.alaska.edu.

STRIDER, MARJORIE VIRGINIA, artist, educator; b. Guthrie, Okla. d. Clifford R. and Marjorie E. (Schley) S. BFA, Kansas City Art Inst., 1962. Faculty Sch. Visual Arts, NYC, 1970-2001; artist-in-residence City U. Grad. Ctr. Mall, NYC, 1976, Fabric Workshop, Phila., 1978, Grassi Palace, Venice, Italy, 1978. One-woman shows include Pace Gallery, N.Y.C., 1963-64, Nancy Hoffman Gallery, N.Y.C., 1973-74, Weather Spoon Mus., U.N.C., Chapel Hill, 1974, City U. Grad. Center Mall, 1976, Clocktower, N.Y.C., 1976, Sculpture Center, N.Y.C., 1983, Steinbaum Gallery, N.Y.C., 1983, 84, Andre Zarre Gallery, 1993, 95, Outdoor Installation, N.Y.C., 1997, Selby Gallery, Ringling Sch. of Art, Sarasota, Fla., 1998, Neuberger Mus., Purchase, N.Y., 1999, Andre Zarre Gallery, 2008; exhibited in group shows at Sculpture Center, N.Y.C., 1981, Drawing Biennale, Lisbon, Portugal, 1981, Newark Mus., 1984, William Rockhill Nelson Mus., Kansas City, 1985, Danforth Mus., Framingham, Mass., 1987, Delahoyd Gallery, N.Y.C., 1992; represented in permanent collections Guggenheim Mus., N.Y.C., U. Colo., Boulder, Albright-Knox Mus., Buffalo, Des Moines Art Center, Storm King (N.Y.) Art Center, Larry Aldrich Mus., Ridgefield, Conn., City U. Grad. Center, N.Y.C., Hirschhorn Mus. and Sculpture Garden, Washington, Santa Fe (N. Mex.) Mus. of Art, also pvt. collections. Grantee Nat. Endowment for Arts, 1973, 80, Longview Found., 1974, Pollock-Krasner Found., 1990, Florsheim Art Fund, 1998, 2000; Va. Ctr. for Creative Arts fellow, 1974, 92, Millay Colony for Arts fellow, 1992, Yaddo Colony, 1996-97 Home Phone: 845-247-3659. Business E-Mail: m_strider@hvc.rr.com.

STRIDIRON, IVER ALLISON, former attorney general; b. St. Thomas, VI, May 29, 1945; m. Priscilla Blyden; 4 children. BA Lincoln U., 1969; JD, Howard U. Sch. of Law, 1974. Atty. U.S. Nuclear Regulatory Commn., U.S. Commn. on Civil Rights, Washington, 1974—77; pvt. practice St. Thomas, V.I., 1977—99; mem. V.I. Legis., 1981—83, 1985—89, pres., 1987—88; atty. gen. V.I., 1999—2004. Democrat.

STRIDSBERG, ALBERT BORDEN (PAUL BORDEN), advertising consultant, editor, educator; Copywriter Howard Swink Advt., Inc., Marion, Ohio, 1955-58; acct. supr. McCann-Erickson, Co., Brussels, 1958-60, J. Walter Thompson Co., Amsterdam, The Netherlands, 1960-63, asst. to internat. exec. v.p. NYC, 1963-67, internat. cons. spl. projects, acquisitions and diversifications, 1969-73; cons., coord. Internat. Markets Advt. Agy., Inc., NY and London, 1967-69; editor-in-chief Advt. World mag., NYC, 1975-77; lectr. in mktg. NYU, NYC, 1978-84; lectr. in advt. Marist Coll., Poughkeepsie, NY, 1984-94; U.S. features editor Media Internat. Mag., London, 1984-90; papers and memoirs Hartman Ctr., Duke U. Libr. Author: (books) Controversy Advertising, 1977; co-author (with Neelankavil): Effective Advertising Self Regulation, 1980. Office: Box 1846 Poughkeepsie NY 12601-0846 Home Phone: 845-485-5819; Office Phone: 845-485-5819. E-mail: realtoads@webtv.net.

STRIEBY, B. LORRAINE, artist; b. Morgantown, W.Va., Dec. 5, 1938; d. Charles Willis Ayer and Margaret Ann Ferko; m. Michael Strieby (dec.); children: Vicki Parzyk, Lisa Magistro, Lori Constantine, Ann; m. Stanley Veerin Gunn, Nov. 22, 2003. BA in Bus. Edn., Calif. State U., Northridge, 1976, secondary tchg. credential, 1977. Tchr. L.A. Unified Sch. Dist., 1978—81. Pres. Women Painters West, LA, 1995—97. Exhibitions include Art Concepts Gallery, Tacoma, 1997, Black Sheep Gallery, Hardwarden Castle, Wales, 1999, Westminster Gallery, London, 1999, S.E. La. U. Gallery, Hammond, 2000, Segreto Gallery, Santa Fe, 2002, Barlow Gallery, New Orleans, 2004, Mus. Making Music, Carlsbad, Calif., 2004, Williamson Art Gallery and Mus., Liverpool, Eng., 2004, Sotto South Gallery, Savannah, Ga., 2004—06, Barrie Holt Gallery, New Orleans, 2006, Charlevoix Street Gallery, Albuquerque, 2006, Adobe Ranch Gallery, Chatsworth, Calif. Various positions Rep. Women West Valley, LA, 1990—99. Recipient Golden Products award, Nat. Acrylic Painters Assn. Home: PO Box 4928 Chatsworth CA 91311 Office Phone: 818-261-3968. E-mail: adobeart818@earthlink.net.

STRIEDER, WILLIAM CHRISTIAN, chemical engineering educator, consultant; b. Erie, Pa., Jan. 19, 1938; s. William Anthony and Virginia Melva (Parmenter) S.; m. Mary (Watt); children: John, Katherine, Tracy, Joseph. BS, Pa. State U., 1960; PhD, Case Inst. Tech., 1963. Rsch. fellow U. Brussels, 1963-65, U. Minn., Mpls., 1965-66; prof. chem. engrng. U. Notre Dame, Ind., 1966—. Cons. Plastics Engrng. Co., Sheboygen, Wis., 1979, CTS Corp., Elkhart, Ind., 1985-87, Honeywell Corp., South Bend, Ind., 2001-04. Co-author: Variational Methods Applied to Problems in Diffusion and Reaction, 1973; co-editor: Diffusion and Convection in Porous Catalysts, 1988; contbr. over 90 articles to profl. jours. Mem. Mayor's Com. for South Bend Ethanol Plant, 1985-88. Grantee NSF, 1967-69, 77-79, 80-83, Air Force Sci. Rsch., 1977-79, Dept. Transp., 1981-84, 88-90, Ind. 21st Cent. Fund, 2001-04, Honeywell Found., 2001-06. Fellow Am. Soc. Engrng. Edn.; mem. AAUP, AFS, Am. Chem. Soc. (grantee 1985-88, 89-93, 93-95), Am. Inst. Chem. Engrs. (session chmn. 1982, 85, 87, 89, 91, 99), Am. Phys. Soc., Soc. Ind. Applied Math., Sigma Xi Hon. Soc Avocations: swimming, history, literature. Home Phone: 574-255-6870; Office Phone: 574-631-5648. Business E-Mail: William.C.Strieder.1@nd.edu, strieder.1@nd.edu.

STRIETER, FREDERICK JOHN, engineering executive; b. Davenport, Iowa, Sept. 14, 1934; s. Frederick Lawrence and Selma Alfreda (Godehn) S.; m. Ann Elin Aronson, Aug. 10, 1957; children: Susan Elizabeth, Nancy Elin. AB, Augustana Coll., 1956; PhD, U. Calif., Berkeley, 1960. Rsch. asst. Lawrence Radiation Lab, U. Calif., Berkeley, 1957-59; mem. tech. staff Tex. Instruments Inc., Dallas, 1959—75, engrng. mgr.; mgr. IC Pilot Line, 1975—82; dir. Sensor Lab Honeywell Inc., Richardson, Tex., 1982—95; gen. mgr. MicroElectronics Tech., Divsn. Eastman Kodak, 1995—97; adj. prof. elec. computer engrng. Tex A&M Univ, 1998—. Active bd. of regent Concordia Coll., Austin, 1967-75, chmn. 1968-75. Mem. IEEE, Electrochem. Soc. Inc. (treas. 1973-76, v.p. 1979-82, pres. 1982-83), Sigma Xi, Phi Beta Kappa Lutheran. Home: 7814 Fallmeadow Ln Dallas TX 75248-5328 Office: Honeywell Inc 830 E Arapaho Rd Richardson TX 75081-2241 also: Tex ASM Univ 313 Zachry College Station TX 77843-3128 Business E-Mail: strieter@ece.tamu.edu.

STRIGL, DENNIS F., telecommunications industry executive; b. Apr. 13, 1946; BBA, Canisius Coll.; MBA, Dickinson U. With NY Tel. Co., 1968, AT&T; pres. Ameritech Mobile Commn., 1984—89; v.p. product mgmt. network svcs. Bell Atlantic, 1989—91; pres., CEO Bell Atlantic Mobile and Bell Atlantic Global Wireless, 1991—97, Bell Atlantic Global Wireless, 1997—2000, Verizon Wireless Joint Venture, 2000—07; exec. v.p. Verizon Comm., Inc., Bedminster, NJ, 2000—07, pres., COO, 2007—. Bd. dir. Verizon Wireless, Anadigics Inc., PNC Fin. Services Grp., PNC Bank, Eastman Kodak Co., 2008—. Chmn. bd. trustees Canisius Coll. Recipient Cellular Industry Achievement award; named to Pinnacle Soc. for disting. alumni, Fairleigh Dickinson U. Mem.: Cellular Telecom. & Internet Assn. (chmn. bd. dirs. 1996—97). Office: Verizon Wireless 180 Washington Valley Rd Bedminster NJ 07921*

STRIKER, CECIL LEOPOLD, archaeologist, educator; b. Cin., July 15, 1932; s. Cecil and Delia (Workum) S.; m. Ute Stephan, Apr. 27, 1968. BA, Oberlin Coll., 1956; MA, NYU, 1960, PhD, 1968; MA (hon.), U. Pa., 1972. From instr. to asst. prof. Vassar Coll., 1962-68; assoc. prof. U. Pa., Phila., 1968-78, prof. history art, 1978—2006, chmn. dept. history of art, 1980-87, prof. emeritus, 2006—; field archaeologist Dumbarton Oaks Center for Byzantine Studies, 1966-80, fellow, 1972-73. Adj. prof. Sabanci U., 1999—; dir. survey and excavation, Myrelaion, Istanbul, 1965-66; co-dir. Kalenderhane Archaeol. Project, Istanbul, 1966-78, Aegean Dendrochronology Project, 1977-88; gen. archaeol. cons. Istanbul Metro and Bosphorus Tunnel Project, 1985-87; dir. Archtl. Dendrochronology Project, 1988—; cons. Integrated Study of Hagia Sophia Structure, 1991-95. Mem. editorial bd. Architectura: Zeitschrift für Geschichte der Architektur, 1986—. Adv. bd. Ctr. for Advanced Study in the Visual Arts, 1986-88, Samuel H. Kress Found. Art History Fellowship Program, 1986-87. With U.S. Army, 1954-57. Fulbright grant in Germany, 1960-62, NEH grant, 1985-86; art historian in residence Am. Acad. in Rome, 1973. Mem. Archaeol. Inst. Am., Coll. Art Assn., Am. Rsch. Inst. in Turkey (fellow 1965-66, pres. 1978-84, hon. dir. 2002—), Coun. Am. Overseas Rsch. Ctr. (chmn. 1980-84), Soc. Archtl. Historians, Turkish Studies Assn., U.S. Nat. Com. for Byzantine Studies, Koldewey Gesellschaft, German Archaeol. Inst. (corr.). Office Phone: 215-573-9702. Business E-Mail: cstriker@sas.upenn.edu.

STRIMBU, VICTOR, JR., lawyer; b. New Philadelphia, Ohio, Nov. 25, 1932; s. Victor and Veda (Stancu) S.; m. Kathryn May Schrote, Apr. 9, 1955 (dec. 1995); children: Victor Paul, Michael, Julie, Sue; m. Marjorie Bichsel, Oct. 23, 1999. BA, Heidelberg Coll., 1954; postgrad., Western Res. U., 1956-57; JD, COlumbia U., 1960. Bar: Ohio 1960, U.S. Supreme Ct. 1972. With Baker & Hostetler LLP, Cleve., 1960—, ptnr., 1970—. Bd. dirs. North Coast Health Ministry; mem. Bay Village (Ohio) Bd. Edn., 1976-84, pres., 1978-82; mem. Bay Village Planning Commn., 1967-69; life mem. Ohio PTA; mem. Greater Cleve. Growth Assn.; trustee New Cleve. Campaign, 1987-94—, North Coast Health Ministry, 1989-2001, Heidelberg Coll., 1996—; mem. indsl. rels. adv. com. Cleve. State U., 1979—, chmn., 1982,1999, vice chmn., 1998. With AUS, 1955-56. Mem. ABA, Ohio Bar Assn., Greater Cleve. Bar Assn., Ohio Newspaper Assn. (minority affairs com. 1987-90), Ct. of Nisi Prius Club. Republican. Presbyterian. Office: Baker & Hostetler LLP 3200 National City Ctr 1900 E 9th St Ste 3200 Cleveland OH 44114-3485 Office Phone: 216-621-0200.

STRINER, HERBERT EDWARD, economist; b. Jersey City, Aug. 16, 1922; s. Harry and Pearl (Strynar) S.; m. Erma Steinert, Dec. 9, 1943 (div. 1970); children: Richard Alan, Deborah Jane; m. Iona V. Meredith. AB, Rutgers U., 1947, MA, 1948; PhD (Maxwell fellow 1949-50), Syracuse U., 1951. Asst. prof. Syracuse U., 1951; economist Interior Dept., 1951-54; program dir. NSF, 1954-55, Nat. Planning Assn., 1955-57; sr. analyst Operations Research Office, Johns Hopkins, 1957-59; program dir. Brookings Inst., 1959-61, Stanford Research Inst., 1961-62; program devel. dir. Upjohn Inst., Washington, 1962-69; dean Coll. Continuing Edn. Am. U., Washington, 1969-72, dean Coll. Bus., 1974-81, prof. econs. and mgmt., 1981-89; cons. Los Alamos Nat. Lab., 1990-91; chief planning and policy NIH, 1972-73; pres. U. Research Corp., 1973-74; assoc. faculty mem. Johns Hopkins U., 1997. Chmn. bd. dirs. NetTalon Corp. Inc., 2002—04. Author: (book) Toward a Fundamental Program for the Training, Employment and Economic Equality of the American Indian, 1968, Continuing Education as a National Capital Investment, 1972, Regaining The Lead: Policies for Economic Growth, 1984; co-author: Spending and The US Economy, 3 vols., 1958, Local Impact of Foreign Trade, 1960, Civil Rights, Employment and the

Social Status of American Negros, 1966, Analysis of the Bituminous Coal Industry in Terms of Total Energy Supply and a Synthetic Oil Program, 1979; contbr. articles to profl. jours. Mem. rev. panel Pres.'s Cabinet Com. Juv. Delinquency, 1961-63, D.C. Youth Employment Com., 1963, Pres.'s Task Force Am. Indians, 1967, White House Conf. Aging, 1971; bd. dirs. Opportunities Industrialization Ctr., NAACP, Washington. Officer inf. U.S. Army, 1943-46. Decorated Breast Order of Yun Hui with Ribbon, World War II Govt. China. Home: 3158 Gracefield Rd # 416 Silver Spring MD 20904

STRINGER, C. VIVIAN (CHARLENE VIVIAN SRINGER), women's college basketball coach; b. Edenborn, Pa., Mar. 16, 1948; m. William D. Stringer (dec. 1992); children: David, Janine, Justin. BS in Health & Phys. Edn., Slippery Rock State Coll., 1970, MEd in Health & Phys. Edn., 1973. Head coach Cheyney State Coll. Lady Wolves, 1971—83, U. Iowa Hawkeyes, 1983—95, Rutgers U. Scarlet Knights, 1995—. Head coach US Select Team tour China, 1980, World U. Games, Kobe, Japan, 1985, World Championship Zone Qualification Tournament, Sao Paulo, Brazil, 1989, US Pan-Am. Games, Havana, Cuba, 1991; asst. coach US Olympic Team, 2004. Co-author (with Laura Tucker): To Rise and Give Hope: Standing Tall in the Face of Adversity, 2008. Recipient Phila. Sportswriters' Coach of Yr., 1980, 1981, NCAA Wade Trophy Women's Nat. Coach of Yr. award, 1982, Converse Women's Nat. Coach of Yr. award, 1988, Naismith Coll. Coach of Yr. award, 1993, Carol Eckman award, 1993, Lifetime Achievement award, Black Coaches Assn., 2004, Women of Yr. award, NJ Sports Writers' Assn., 2008; named Dist. V Coach of Yr., 1985, 1988, 1993, Big Ten Coach of Yr., 1991, 1993, Coll. Coach of Yr., Sports Illustrated, 1993, USA Today, 1993, Converse, 1993, LA Times, 1993, Black Coaches Assn., 1993, Big East Coach of Yr., 1998, 2005, Dist. I Coach of Yr., 1998, Coach of Yr., Met. Basketball Writers Assn., 1998—2000, 2005, Female Coach of Yr., Rainbow/PUSH Organization, 2000; named one of The 101 Most Influential Minorities in Sports, Sports Illustrated, 2003; named to Women's Basketball Hall of Fame, 2001, Naismith Meml. Basketball Hall of Fame, 2009. Mem. Amateur Basketball Assn. US (bd. dirs.). Achievements include 1st head coach (male or female) to lead 3 different schools to the NCAA Final Four; third coach in NCAA women's basketball history to reach 800 career wins, 2008. Office: Rutgers U Athletic Dept 83 Rockafeller Rd Piscataway NJ 08854-8053*

STRINGER, SIR HOWARD, electronics company executive; b. Cardiff, Wales, Feb. 19, 1942; arrived in U.S., 1965, naturalized, 1985; s. Harry and Marjorie Mary (Pook) Stringer; m. Jennifer Kinmond Patterson, July 29, 1978; children: David Ridley, Harriet Kinmond. BA, MA in Modern History, Oxford U., Eng., 1964; PhD (hon.), London Arts Inst., 2003, U. Glamorgan, 2005, Am. Film Inst., 2007. Prodr., dir. CBS News, NYC, 1973—76, pres., 1986—88, exec. v.p., 1984—86; exec. prodr. CBS Reports, 1976—81, CBS Evening News with Dan Rather, 1981—84; pres. CBS Broadcast Group, 1988—95; chmn., CEO Tele-TV, 1995—97; pres. Sony Corp. America, 1997—98, chmn., CEO, 1998—, Sony Corp., 2005—09, chmn., pres., CEO, 2009—. Bd. dirs. Sony Corp., 2000—. Chmn. bd. trustees Am. Film Inst.; bd. mem. Am. Theatre Wing, NY Presbyn. Hosp., Am. Friends of the British Mus., Corp. Leadership Com. Lincoln Ctr. for the Performing Arts; bd. trustee Paley Ctr. Media (formerly Mus. TV and Radio); bd. mem. Teach for Am., Carnegie Hall. Sgt. US Army, 1965—67, Vietnam. Decorated US Army Commendation medal for Meritorious Achievement for Svc. in Vietnam; recipient Dupont Journalism award, Columbia Journalism Sch., Columbia Sch., 1979, 1981, Overseas Press Club awards, 1974, 1979, 1982, IRTS Found. award, 1994, honored Uncommon Vision Media Industry, Museum Moving Image, 1994, First Amendment Leadership award, Radio and TV News Dirs. Found., 1996, Steven J. Ross Humanitarian award, UJA-Federation NY, 1999, highest award, Ctr. for Communications, 2000, award, Literary Partners, Pub. Svc. award, Phoenix House, 2002, award, NY Hall of Sci., 2003, Dinner Champions honoree, Nat. Multiple Sclerosis Soc., 2002, medal of Honor, St. George Soc., 2004, Disting. Svc. award honoree, Big Brothers Big Sisters NYC, 2005, Teach Am. Annual award, 2001, Disting. Leadership award, Internat. Emmy Founders, 2002—03, honored, Alliance Lupus Rsch., 2007, Visionary award, Paley Ctr. Media (formerly Mus. Radio and TV), 2007; named Hon. Fellow Merton Coll., Oxford, 2000, Knight Comdr. of the British Empire (KBE), Her Majesty Queen Elizabeth II, 1999, Hon. Fellow Welsh Coll. Music & Drama, 2001; named a Living Landmarks of NY, 2005; named one of The World's 100 Most Influential People, TIME mag., 2005; named to Broadcasting and Cable Hall of Fame, 1996, Royal TV Soc. Welsh Hall of Fame, Wales, 1999. Mem.: Coun. on Fgn. Rels. Office: Sony Corp of Am 550 Madison Ave New York NY 10022-3211 also: Sony Corp 1-7-1 Konan Minato ku Tokyo 108-0075 Japan

STRINGER, JOHN, retired materials scientist; b. Liverpool, Eng., July 14, 1934; came to U.S., 1977, naturalized, 1996; s. Gerald Hitchen and Isobel (Taylor) S.; m. Audrey Lancaster, Feb. 4, 1957; children: Helen Caroline, Rebecca Elizabeth. BS in Engring., U. Liverpool, 1955, PhD, 1958, D in Engring., 1974. Chartered engr., U.K. Lectr. Univ. Liverpool, England, 1957-63, prof. materials sci., 1966-77; fellow Battelle Columbus (Ohio) Labs., 1963-66; sr. project mgr. Electric Power Rsch. Inst., Palo Alto, Calif., 1977-81, sr. program mgr., 1981-87, dir. tech. support, 1987-91, dir. applied rsch., 1991-95, tech. exec. Applied Sci. and Tech., 1995-96, exec. tech. fellow, 1997—2004; ret. Chmn. Sci. and Tech. Edn., Merseyside, Liverpool, 1971-74; pres. Corrosion and Protection Assn., London, 1972; mem. Nat. Material Adv. Bd., 1992-95, basic energy scis. adv. com., U.S. Dept. Energy, 1992-98, chmn., 1996-98. Mem. editl. bd.: Oxidation of Metals Jour., 1971—; author: An Introduction to the Electron Theory of Solids, 1967; editor: (book) High Temperature Corrosion of Advanced Materials, 1989, Chlorine in Coal, 1991, Applied Chaos, 1992; contbr. over 350 articles to profl. jours. Recipient U.R. Evans award Inst. Corrosion, U.K., 1993, Campbell Meml. Lectr. of ASM Internat., 1995. Fellow AAAS, NACE Internat. (Willis Rodney Whitney award 2004), AIME, Inst. Energy, Royal Soc. Arts, Instn. Corrosion (hon.), ASM Internat. Office Phone: 650-365-2471. Personal E-mail: jstringer@izambard.com, johnstringer@comcast.net.

STRINGER, L. E. (DEAN), retired lawyer; b. Sayre, Okla., June 22, 1936; s. Rex Herman and Bessie (Morris) S.; m. Carol Ann Woodson, Aug. 31, 1963; children: Craig Woodson, Laura DeAnn. BA, Okla. State U., 1958; LLB, Harvard U., 1961. Bar: Okla. 1961, US Ct. Appeals (10th cir.) 1962, US Dist. Ct. (we. dist.) 1963, US Supreme Ct. 1972. Assoc. Crowe, Boxley, et al (now Crowe & Dunlevy), Oklahoma City, 1961—68, mem., dir., 1968—2000, chmn. bd., 1999—2000. Pres. Crowe & Dunlevy, P.C., 1979-81, chmn. litigation dept., 1987-2000, ret. 2000; bd. dirs. Okla. Inst. for Child Advocacy, 2003-07, v.p., 2004, pres.-elect, 2005, pres. 2006. Pres. Okla. State U. Alumni Assn., 1972-73; bd. regents Okla. State U. and A&M Colls., Stillwater, 1986-94, vice-chmn., 1989-90, chmn., 1990-91; chmn. Okla. State U. Found., Stillwater, 1982-85; pres. Friends of the Libr., Okla. State U., 2000—; bd. dirs. Okla. Heritage Assn., 1995-2000; pres. adv. com. Okla. State U./OKC, 1998—, chmn., 2000—; mem. regents edn. adv. com. Okla. State Regents for Higher Edn., 1995-2001; trustee Youth Svcs. Oklahoma County, Inc., 2001—, vice chmn. 2002-04, chmn. 2004-07. Maj. Okla. N.G., 1961-71. Recipient Disting. Alumnus award Okla. State U., 1979, Neil E. Bogan Professionalism award, Okla. Bar Assn., 2005, Jour. Record award Okla. County Bar Assn. & Jour. Record, 2009; inducted Hall of Fame Okla. State U. Alumni Assn, 1998. Fellow Am. Bar Found. (adv. rsch. com. 1996-2000); mem. Okla. Bar Assn. (Jour. Record Law Day award, 2009). Democrat. Methodist. Home: 325 NW 17th St Oklahoma City OK 73103-3424

STRINGER, SCOTT M., city official, former state legislator; b. NYC, Apr. 29, 1960; BA, John Jay Coll. Mem. NY State Assembly from Dist. 67, Albany, NY, 1992—2005, mem. Edn., Higher Edn., Housing, and Judiciary committees; borough pres. Manhattan, NY, 2006—. Dist. coord. NY State Assemblyman Jerrold Nadler. Mem.: NAACP, Nat. Women's Polit. Caucus, West Side Crime Prevention Program, NYC Americans for Dem. Action, Manhattan New Dem. Coalition. Democrat. Office: Office Manhattan Borough Pres 1 Centre St 19th Fl New York NY 10007*

STRINGER, WILLIAM JEREMY, university official; b. Oakland, Calif., Nov. 8, 1944; s. William Duane and Mildred May (Andrus) S.; m. Susan Lee Hildebrand; children: Shannon Lee, Kelly Erin, Courtney Elizabeth. BA in English, So. Meth. U., Dallas, 1966; MA in English, U. Wis., Madison, 1968, PhD in Ednl. Adminstrn., 1973. Dir. men's housing Southwestern U., Georgetown, Tex., 1968-69; asst. dir. housing U. Wis., Madison, 1969-73; dir. residential life, assoc. dean student life, adj. prof. Pacific Luth., Tacoma, 1973-78; dir. residential life U. So. Calif., 1978-79, asst. v.p., 1979-84, asst. prof. higher and post-secondary edn., 1980-84; v.p. student life Seattle U., 1984-89, v.p. student devel., 1989-92, assoc. provost, 1989-95, assoc. prof. edn., 1990—, chair ednl. leadership, 1994—97, chair strategic planning, 1997—2000, chair prof. studies, 2001—. Author: How to Survive as a Single Student, 1972, The Role of the Assistant in Higher Education, 1973. Bd. dirs. NW Area Luth. Social Svcs. of Wash. and Idaho, pres.-elect, 1989, pres., 1990-91; bd. dirs. Seattle Coalition Ednl. Equity; chair parents' coun. Pacific Luth. U., 2006-08. Recipient John Hubbard Leadership award, 1984; Danforth Found. grantee, 1976-77. Mem. AAUP, Nat. Assn. Student Pers. Adminstrs. (bd. dirs. region V 1985-97, 2009-, mem. editl. bd. Jour. 1995-2001, Disting. Svc. to Profession award 2000, faculty fellow 2002-07, chair 2005-07), Am. Coll. Pers. Assn., Phi Eta Sigma, Sigma Tau Delta, Phi Alpha Theta, Lambda Chi Alpha Lutheran. Home: 4553 169th Ave SE Bellevue WA 98006-6505 Office: Seattle U Dept Edn Seattle WA 98122 E-mail: stringer@seattleu.edu.

STRINGFELLOW, GERALD B., engineering educator; b. Salt Lake City, Apr. 26, 1942; s. Paul Bennion and Jean (Barton) S.; m. Barbara Farr, June 9, 1962; children: Anne, Heather, Michael. BS, U. Utah, 1964; PhD, Stanford U., 1968. Staff scientist Hewlett Packard Labs., Palo Alto, Calif., 1967-70, group mgr., 1970-80; disting. prof. elec. engring., materials sci. U. Utah, Salt Lake City, 1980—, chmn., 1994-98, adj. prof. physics, 1988—, dean Coll. Engring., 1998—2003. Cons. Tex. Instruments, Dallas, 1995-97, AT&T-Bell Labs., Holmdel, N.J., 1986-90, Brit. Telecom., London, 1989-92; editor-in-chief Phase Diagrams for Ceramics, Vol. IX. Author: Organometallic Vapor Phase Epitaxy, 1989, 2d edit., 1999; editor: Metal Organic Vapor Phase Epitaxy, 1986, 2004, American Crystal Growth, 1987, Alloy Semiconductor Physics and Electronics, 1989, Phase Equilibria Diagrams-Semiconductors and Chalcogenides, 1991, High Brightness LEDs, 1997; prin. editor Jour. Crystal Growth, 1998-2003; letters editor Jour. Electronic Materials, 1992-99; contbr. over 360 articles to profl. jours. Recipient U.S. Sr. Scientist award Alexander von Humboldt Soc., Bonn, Germany, 1979, Gov.'s Sci. Tech. medal State of Utah, 1997, John Bardeen award TMS, 2003; guest fellow Royal Soc., London, 1990. Fellow IEEE, Japan Soc. Promotion of Sci.; mem. Am. Phys. Soc., Electronic Materials Com. (pres. 1985-87), Nat. Acad. Engring. Achievements include pioneering development of organometallic vapor phase epitaxy, development of theories of thermodynamic properties of alloy semiconductors; discovery of phenomenon of compositional latching in alloy semiconductor layers grown by epitaxial techniques. Office: U Utah Dept ECE 3280 MEB Salt Lake City UT 84112-1109 Business E-Mail: stringfellow@coe.utah.edu.

STRINGFELLOW, MARY WILLINGHAM, mathematics educator; b. Bessemer, Ala., Nov. 26, 1946; m. Davey Stringfellow; children: Matthew Wade, David Brian, Bradley Mark. BS, U. Ala., Tuscaloosa, 1969; MA, U. Ala., Birmingham, 1977. Math. instr. Bessemer State Tech. Coll., 1990—2005, Lawson State CC, Bessemer, 2005—. Tchr., missions leader Pleasant Ridge Bapt., Hueytown, Ala., 1976—2009. Baptist. Home: 315 Florence St Hueytown AL 35023 Office: Lawson State CC 1100 9th St S Bessemer AL 35022 Personal E-mail: granmary60@bellsouth.net.

STRINGHAM, PHYLLIS JOAN, retired music educator; b. Grand Rapids, Mich., Jan. 30, 1931; d. Wilhelmina Johanna and Harry Newton Stringham. MusB, Calvin Coll., Grand Rapids, Mich., 1952; MusM, U. Mich., Ann Arbor, Mich., 1955. Organist Chatham (Va.) Hall Girls Sch., 1955—59; prof. of music Carroll Coll., Waukesha, Wis., 1959—2001. Owner and mgr. Phylllis Stringham Concert Mgmt., Waukesha, Wis., 1964—. Musician concert organist. Mem.: Am. Guild of Organists. Avocation: reading. Home: 1101 Belmont Dr Waukesha WI 53186 Office: Phyllis Stringham concert Mgt 1101 Belmont Dr Waukesha WI 53186 Business E-Mail: pstringh@sbcglobal.net.

STRITCH, ELAINE, singer, actress; b. Detroit, Feb. 2, 1925; d. George Joseph and Mildred (Jobe) S.; m. John M. Bay, Feb. 2, 1973 (dec. 1973). Student drama workshop, New Sch. for Social Research; studies in singing with Burt Knapp, Drama Workshop, from 1948. Appeared in Broadway prodns. Loco, 1946, Three Indelicate Ladies, 1947, Yes M'Lord, 1949, Pal Joey, 1962, On Your Toes, Bus Stop, 1955, Sail Away, 1961, Who's Afraid of Virginia Woolf?, 1962, 65, Wonderful Town, 1967, Private Lives, 1968, Company, 1970, 1993, also London prodn., 1972, Love Letters, 1990, Show Boat, 1994, A Delicate Balance, 1996 (Drama Desk award for Outstanding Featured Actress, 1996), Elaine Stritch At Liberty, 2002 (Outstanding Book of a Musical & Outstanding Solo Performance, Drama Desk Awards, 2002); off-Broadway prodns. include At Home at the Carlyle, 2005, 2006, Endgame, 2008; appeared in Follies in Concert, NYC, 1982; (films) The Scarlet Hour, 1956, Three Violent People, 1956, A Farewell to Arms, 1957, The Perfect Furlough, 1958, Who Killed Teddy Bear?, 1965, Pigeons, 1971, The Spiral Staircase, 1975, Providence, 1977, September, 1988, Cocoon II: The Return, 1988, Cadillac Man, 1990, Out to Sea, 1997, Screwed, 2000, Small Time Crooks, 2000, Autumn in New York, 2000, Monster-in-Law, 2005, Romance & Cigarettes, 2005; (TV series) My Sister Eileen, 1960-61, The Trials of O'Brien, 1965-66, (British) Two's Company, 1975-76, The Ellen Burstyn Show, 1987, Stranded, 1986, Life's a B*tch, 2003; (TV movies) Chance of a Lifetime, 1991, An Unexpected Life, 1998, Paradise, 2004; (TV miniseries) An Inconvenient Woman, 1991, Elaine Stritch: At Liberty, 2002 (Emmy award Outstanding Individual Performance in a Variety or Music Program, 2004, Drama Desk award, outstanding solo performance, Drama Desk award, outstanding book of a musical, Tony award for best solo musical performance HBO 1991); author: Am I Blue?: Living With Diabetes and, Dammit, Having Fun, 1984. Recipient Nightlife award, outstanding cabaret female vocalist in a major engagement, 2006, Creative Arts Primetime Emmy for Outstanding Guest Actress in Comedy Series, Acad. TV Arts and Scis., 2007.

STROBAUGH, TERENCE PHILIP, JR., molecular biologist, microbiologist; b. Altoona, Pa., Dec. 19, 1958; s. Terence Philip Strobaugh, Sr. and Lois Ann Strobaugh; m. Shelly L. Kamp, Aug. 3, 2007. BA in Psychology, Pa. State U., University Park, 1988, BS in Life Sci., 1992. Molecular biologist, microbiologist USDA, Agrl. Rsch. Svc., Ea. Regional Rsch. Ctr., Wyndmoor, Pa., 1994—. Presenter in field. Contbr. articles to profl. jours. Mentor Mentornet, San Jose, Calif., 2000—06; parish rep. Malvern Laymen's Retreat League, Pa., 1985—2006. Recipient Cert. of Merit for Outstanding Performance rating, USDA, 1997, Silver medal for Achievement in Recognition of Outstanding Pub. Svc., Fed. Exec. Bd. Excellence in Govt. Awards Program, 1999. Mem.: Nittany Lion Club, Suburban Cyclists Unlimited (ride coord. 2001—02, Most Improved Male Cyclist 2001), Internat. Soc. for Philos. Enquiry (assoc.). Roman Catholic. Avocations: bicycling, photography, genealogy, chess. Home: 1272 Quakertown Ave Pennsburg PA 18073 Office: USAD-ARS-ERRC 600 E Mermaid Ln Wyndmoor PA 19038 Office Fax: 215-233-6581; Home Fax: 215-541-4001. Personal E-mail: terence.strobaugh1989@psualum.com. Business E-Mail: terence.strobaugh@ars.usda.gov.

STROBEL, PAMELA B., former energy executive; b. Chgo., Sept. 9, 1952; BS highest honors, U. Ill., 1974, JD cum laude, 1977. Bar: Ill. 1977, U.S. Dist. (ctrl. and no. dists.) Ill. 1977, U.S. Ct. Appeals (7th cir.) 1981, U.S. Claims Ct. 1983, U.S. Ct. Appeals (fed. cir.) 1985. Ptnr. Sidley & Austin, Chgo., 1988-93; exec. v.p., gen. counsel Commonwealth Edison Co., Chgo., 1993—2000; exec. v.p. Exelon Corp., Chgo., 2000—03, exec. v.p., chief adminstrv. officer, 2003—05; pres. Exelon Energy Delivery Co., Chgo., 2000—05, vice-chair, 2000—01, CEO, vice-chair, 2001—02, chmn., CEO, 2002—03. Bd. dirs. State Farm Mutual Automobile Ins. Co., 2004—, Domtar Corp., 2007—, Illinois Tool Works Inc., 2008—. Chair Ravinia Festival, 2008, Civic Consulting Alliance; bd. mem. Joffrey Ballet, Ill. Network Charter Schools. Recipient Woman of Achievement award, Anti-Defamation League, 1997, Founder's award, Chgo. Bar Assn. Alliance for Women, 1997, Diversity 2000 award, Minority Corporate Counsel Assn., 2000, Luminary award, Girl Scouts Chgo., 2002, Award for Exec. Leadership, Assn. Prof. Fundraisers, 2003, Myra Bradwell award for Excellence in the Profession, Woman's Bar Assn. Ill., 2003, YWCA Metropolitan Chgo. Outstanding Achievement award in Bus.; named a Disting. Alumnae, U. Ill. Coll. of Law, 1996; named one of The 50 Most Powerful Women, Fortune mag., 2002; named to The Chgo. Women's Hall of Fame. Mem. Econ. Club Chgo., Comml. Club Chgo., Chgo. Network, Kappa Tau Alpha (staff 1975-77).*

STROBEL, RUSS M., gas industry executive, lawyer; b. NYC, May 2, 1952; BA, Northwestern U., 1974; JD magna cum laude, U. Ill., 1977. Bar: Ill. 1977. Ptnr. Jenner & Block, Chgo., Friedman & Koven; sr. v.p., gen. counsel, & sec. Nicor Inc., Naperville, Ill., 2000—02; pres. Nicor Gas, Naperville, Ill., 2002—, CEO, 2003—, chmn., 2005—; exec. v.p. Nicor Inc., Naperville, Ill., 2002, pres., 2002—05, chmn., pres., CEO, 2005—. Dir., mem. exec. com. Am. Gas Assn. Bd. dir. USO Ill.; mem. adv. com. Gene Siskel Film Ctr., Art Inst. Chgo. Mem.: Econ. Club Chgo., Comml. Club Chgo. (mem. civic com.), Order of the Coif. Office: Nicor Inc 1844 Ferry Rd Naperville IL 60563-9600

STROBER, JONATHAN BRET, neurologist, educator; b. NYC, June 1, 1966; s. Stephen Ira and Lisa Carol Strober; m. William David Holt, Oct. 30, 2008. BS, Cornell U., Ithaca, Ny, 1988; MD, Temple U. Med. Sch., Phila., 1992. Asst. clin. prof., neurology & pediat. UCSF, San Francisco, 1999—2007, assoc. clin. prof., 2007—. Mem.: Am. Acad. Neurology, Child Neurology Soc. Office: Univ California San Francisco 350 Parnassus Ave Ste 609 San Francisco CA 94143-0137 Business E-Mail: stroberj@neuropeds.ucsf.edu.

STROBER, MYRA HOFFENBERG, education educator, consultant; b. NYC, Mar. 28, 1941; d. Julius William Hoffenberg and Regina Scharer; m. Samuel Strober, June 23, 1963 (div. Dec. 1983); children: Jason M., Elizabeth A.; m. Jay M. Jackman, Oct. 21, 1990. BS in Indsl. Rels., Cornell U., 1962; MA in Econs., Tufts U., 1965; PhD in Econs., MIT, 1969. Lectr., asst. prof. dept. econs. U. Md., College Park, 1967-70; lectr. U. Calif., Berkeley, 1970-72; asst. prof. grad. sch. bus. Stanford (Calif.) U., 1972-86, assoc. prof. sch. edn., 1979-90, prof. edn., 1990—, assoc. dean acad. affairs, 1993-95, interim dean, 1994; program officer in higher edn. Atlantic Philanthropic Svcs., Ithaca, N.Y., 1998-2000. Organizer Stanford Bus. Conf. Women Mgmt., 1974; founding dir. ctr. rsch. women Stanford U., 1974-76, 79-84, dir. edn. policy inst., 1984-86, dean alumni coll., 1992, mem. policy and planning bd., 1992-93, chair program edn. adminstrn. and policy analysis, 1991-93, chair provost's com. recruitment and retention women faculty, 1992-93, chair faculty senate com. on coms., 1992-93; mem. adv. bd. State of Calif. Office Econ. Policy Planning and Rsch., 1978-80; mem. Coll. Bd. Com. Develop Advanced Placement Exam. Econs., 1987-88; faculty advisor Rutgers Women's Leadership Program, 1991-93. Author: (with others) Industrial Relations, 1972, 1990, Sex, Discrimination and the Division of Labor, 1975, Changing Roles of Men and Women, 1976, Women in the Labor Market, 1979, Educational Policy and Management: Sex Differentials, 1981, Women in the Workplace, 1982, Sex Segregation in the Workplace: Trends, Explanations, Remedies, 1984, The New Palgrave: A Dictionary of Economic Theory and Doctrine, 1987, Computer Chips and Paper Clips: Technology and Women's Employment, Vol. II, 1987, Gender in the Workplace, 1987, Challenge to Human Capital Theory: Implications for the HR Manager, American Economic Review, 1995, Rethinking Economics Through a Feminist Lens, Feminist Economics, 1995, Making and Correcting Errors in Economic Analyses: An Examination of Videotapes, (with Agnes M.K. Chan) the Road Winds Uphill All the Way: Gender, Work, and Family in the U.S. and Japan, 1999, (with Jay M. Jackman) Fear of Feedback, 2003, Children As a Public Good, 2004, Can Harvard Ever Play a Positive Role for Women in Higher Education?, 2005; editor (with Francine E. Gordon) Bringing Women Into Management, 1975, (with others) Women and Poverty, 1986, Industrial Relations, 1990, Challenges to Human Capitol Theory: Implications for HR Managers, 1995, (with Sanford M. Dornbusch) Feminism, Children and the New Families, 1988, Rethinking Economics Through a Feminist Lens, 1995, (with Agnes M.K. Chan) The Road Winds Uphill All The Way: Gender, Work and Family in the U.S. and Japan, 1999, (with Jay M. Jackman) Fear of Feedback, 2003, Application of Mainstream Economics Constructs to Education: A Feminist Analysis, 2003, Children as a Public Good, 2004, Feminist Economics: Implications for Education, 2005, Can Harvard Ever Play a Positive Role for Women in Higher Education, 2005; Habits of the Mind: Challenges for Multidisciplinarity, 2006; Faculty Salaries and Maximization of Prestige, 2007, (with Tatiana Melguizo); mem. bd. editors Signs: Jour. Women Culture and Soc., 1975-89, assoc. editor, 1980-85; mem. bd. editors Sage Ann. Rev. Women and Work, 1984—; mem. editorial adv. bd. U.S.-Japan Women's Jour., 1991—; assoc. editor Jour. Econ. Edn., 1991—; contbr. chpt. to book, articles to profl. jours.

Mem. rsch. adv. task force YWCA, 1989—; chair exec. bd. Stanford Hillel, 1990-92; bd. dirs. Resource Ctr. Women, Palo Alto, Calif., 1983-84; pres. bd. dirs. Kaider Found., Mountain View, Calif., 1990-96; bd. trustees Mills Coll., 2004—. Fellow Stanford U., 1975-77, Schiff House Resident fellow, 85-87. Mem.: NOW (bd. dirs. legal def. and edn. fund 1993—98), Ctr. Gender Equality (bd. dirs. 2000—), Internat. Assn. Feminist Econs. (assoc. editor Feminist Econs. 1994—, pres. 1997), Indsl. Rels. Rsch. Assn., Am. Ednl. Rsch. Assn., Am. Econ. Assn. (mem. com. status of women in profession 1972—75). Office: Stanford U School Edn Stanford CA 94305 Office Phone: 650-723-0387. Business E-Mail: myra.strober@stanford.edu.

STROBER, SAMUEL, immunologist, educator; b. NYC, May 8, 1940; s. Julius and Lee (Lander) S.; m. Linda Carol Higgins, July 6, 1991; children: William, Jesse; children from a previous marriage: Jason, Elizabeth. AB in Liberal Arts, Columbia U., 1961; MD magna cum laude, Harvard U., 1966. Intern Mass. Gen. Hosp., Boston, 1966-67; resident in internal medicine Stanford U. Hosp., Calif., 1970-71; rsch. fellow Peter Bent Brigham Hosp., Boston, 1962-63, 65-66, Oxford U., England, 1963-64; rsch. assoc. Lab. Cell Biology Nat. Cancer Inst. NIH, Bethesda, Md., 1967-70; instr. medicine Stanford U., 1971-72, asst. prof., 1972-78, assoc. prof. medicine, 1978-82, prof. medicine, 1982—, Diane Goldstone Meml. lectr., 1978-97, John Putnam Merrill Meml. lectr., chief div. immunology & rheumatology, 1978-97. Investigator Howard Hughes Med. Inst., Miami, Fla., 1976-81; chmn., bd. dirs. La Jolla Inst. for Allergy and Immunology; founder Dendreon, Inc. Assoc. editor: Jour. Immunology, 1981-84, Transplantation, 1981-85, 99—, Internat. Jour. Immunotherapy, 1985—, Transplant Immunology, 1992—, Biol. Bone Marrow Transplantation, 1999—; contbr. articles to profl. jours. Served with USPHS, 1967-70. Recipient Leon Reznick Meml. Rsch. prize, Harvard U., 1966. Mem. Am. Assn. Immunology, Am. Soc. Clin. Investigation, Am. Coll. Rheumatology, Transplantation Soc. (councilor 1986-89), Am. Soc. Tranplantation Physicians, Western Soc. Medicine, Am. Assn. Physicians, Clin. Immunology Soc. (pres. 1996), Alpha Omega. Office: Stanford U Sch Medicine 300 Pasteur Dr Palo Alto CA 94304-2203

STROCK, JAMES MARTIN, author, speaker, executive educator, sustainability leadership development; b. Austin, Tex., Aug. 19, 1956; s. James Martin Strock Sr. and Augusta (Tenney) Cumby. AB, Harvard U., 1977, JD, 1981; postgrad, New Coll. Oxford U., 1981—82. Bar: Colo. 1983. Tchg. asst. Harvard U., 1980—81; spl. cons. to majority leader U.S. Senate, Washington, 1982—83; spl. asst. to adminstr. EPA, Washington, 1983—85, asst. adminstr. for enforcement, 1989—91; spl. counsel U.S. Senate Com. on Environment and Pub. Works, Washington, 1985—86; assoc. Davis, Graham & Stubbs, Denver, 1986—88; acting dir., gen. counsel U.S. Office Pers. Mgmt., Washington, 1988—89; sec. for environ. protection State of Calif., Sacramento, 1991—97; prin. James Strock & Co., Scottsdale, Ariz., 1997—. Adj. prof. U. So. Calif., 1996-97; mem. Intergovtl. Policy Adv. Com., rep. U.S. Trade, 1991-97; mem. Calif. State Pers. Bd., 1998; guest prof. U. Konstanz, 1998; mem. Calif. State Personnel Bd., 1997-99; spkr. in field Author: Reagan on Leadership, 1998, Theodore Roosevelt on Leadership, 2001; contbr. articles to profl. jours. Capt. JAGC USAR, 1987—96. Recipient Ross Essay award ABA, 1985, Environ. Leadership award Calif. Environ. Bus. Coun., 1994, Fed. Republic Germany Friendship award, 1996; Environ. Soc. India fellow, 1997, commendation Calif. Dist. Attys. Assn., 1997 Mem. Coun. Fgn. Rels., Authors' Guild, Phi Beta Kappa. Republican. Office: Ste B-111-601 15029 N Thompson Peak Pky Scottsdale AZ 85260 Business E-Mail: jms@jamesstrock.com.

STROCK, ROBERT S., retired education educator; b. Sewickley, Pa., Oct. 19, 1921; s. Paul Blazier and Jessie Serene Strock. BS, Geneva Coll., 1947; EdM, Shippensburg U., 1964; postgrad., Colo. State U., 1965, U. Tenn., 1966, U. Miami, 1968, Ind. U., 1969. Cert. tchr. Dept. Pub. Instrn., Pa., Nat. Coun. Bus. Schs. Acctg. tchr. Duffs Iron City Coll., Pitts., 1947—50; stock control clk. H.H. Robertson Co., Inc., Ambridge, Pa., 1950—57; tchr. Baden (Pa.)-Economy Sch. Dist., 1957—67; asst. prof. Slippery Rock (Pa.) U., 1967—72; assoc. prof. Indiana U. Pa., 1972—99, prof. emeritus, 2002—. Dir. homecoming parades Indiana U. Pa., 1974—98, Geneva Coll., 2000, 05, 06. Mem. Indiana Boro Coun., 1991—94, Bd. Elections, Beaver, Pa., 2002—. Staff sgt. USAF, 1943—45. Recipient Outstanding Prof. award, Student Pa. State Edn. Assn., 1992, Patriotic Achievement award, Mil. Order of the World Wars Chpt. 200, 1993, Pres. medal of distinction, Indiana U. Pa., 1998, Disting. Svc. award, Alumni Assn. Geneva Coll., 2007. Mem.: 27th Air Transp. Group WWII, Friends of Nat. Parks Gettysburg, Nat. Trust Hist. Preservation, Beaver County Geneal. Soc., Beaver Heritage Soc. (trustee), CWPT History Channel Club (life), Am. Legion, Alpha Phi Omega, Delta Pi Epsilon (treas. chpt. 1973—76), Theta Xi. Republican. Methodist. Avocations: genealogy, travel, collecting miniature bottles, collecting postcards. Home: 222 Fourth St Beaver PA 15009 Home Phone: 724-770-0876.

STRODE, JOSEPH ARLIN, lawyer; b. DeWitt, Ark., Mar. 5, 1946; s. Thomas Joseph and Nora (Richardson) S.; m. Carolyn Taylor, Feb. 9, 1969; children: Tanya Briana, William Joseph. BSEE with honors, U. Ark., 1969; JD, So. Meth. U., 1972. Bar: Ark. 1972. Design engr. Tex. Instruments Inc., Dallas, 1969-70; patent agent Tex. Instruments, Dallas, 1970—72; assoc. Bridges, Young, Matthews, Drake, Pine Bluff, Ark., 1972-74, ptnr., 1975—. Chmn. Pine Bluff Airport Commn., 1993; bd. dirs. United Way Jefferson County, Pine Bluff, 1975-77, campaign chmn., 1983, pres., 1986, exec. com., 1983-87; bd. dirs. Leadership Pine Bluff, 1983-85. Mem. Ark. Bar Assn., Jefferson County Bar Assn. (pres. 1995), Pine Bluff C. of C. (dir. 1981, 84, 94, 97), Ark. Wildlife Fed. (dir. 1979-81), Jefferson County Wildlife Assn. (dir. 1973-80, pres. 1974-76), Kiwanis (lt. gov. Mo.-Ark. divsn. 1983-84, chmn. lt. govs. 1983-84), Order of Coif, Tau Beta Pi, Eta Kappa Nu. Home: 7600 Jay Lynn Ln Pine Bluff AR 71603-9387 Office: 315 E 8th Ave Pine Bluff AR 71601-5005 Office Phone: 870-534-5532. Business E-Mail: joestrode@bridgesplc.com.

STRODEL, ROBERT CARL, lawyer; b. Evanston, Ill., Aug. 12, 1930; s. Carl Frederick and Imogene (Board) S.; m. Mary Alice Shonkwiler, June 17, 1956; children: Julie Ann, Linda Lee, Sally Payson. BS, Northwestern U., 1952; JD, U. Mich., 1955. Bar: Ill. 1955, U.S. Supreme Ct. 1970; diplomate Am. Bd. Profl. Liability Attys.; cert. civil trial specialist Am. Bd. Trial Advocacy. Mem. firm Davis, Morgan & Witherell, Peoria, Ill., 1957—59; pvt. practice Peoria, 1959—69; prin. Strodel, Kingery & Durree Assoc., Peoria, Ill., 1969—92, Law Offices of Robert C. Strodel, Ltd., Peoria, 1992—; asst. state's atty. Peoria, 1960—61; instr. bus. law Bradley U., Peoria, 1961—62; lectr. Belli seminars, 1969—87. Mem. U.S. Presdl. Commn. German-Am. Tricentennial, 1983; lectr. in trial practice and med.-legal litigation. Author: Securing and Using Medical Evidence in Personal Injury and Health-Care Cases, 1988; contbr. articles to profl. jours. Gov. appointee Ill. Dangerous Drugs Adv. Coun., 1970-71; gen. chmn. Peoria-Tazewell Easter Seals, 1963, Cancer Crusade, 1970; pres. Peoria Civic Ballet, 1969-70; mem. Mayor's Commn. on Human Rels., 1962-64; chmn. City of Peoria Campaign Ethics Bd., 1975; chmn., builder City of Peoria Mil. Svcs. Meml. Plaza Project, 1998; Peoria County Rep. Sec., 1970-74; campaign chmn. Gov. Richard Ogilvie, Peoria County, 1972, Sen. Ralph Smith, 1970; treas. Michel for Congress, 1977-94, campaign coord., 1982; bd. dirs. Crippled Children's Ctr., 1964-65, Peoria Symphony Orch., 1964-68. Served with AUS, 1956-64. Decorated Officer's Cross of Order of Merit (Fed. Republic Germany); named Outstanding Young Man Peoria, Peoria Jr. C. of C., 1963. Mem. ATLA (bd. govs. 1987-96), ABA, Ill. Trial Lawyers Assn. (bd. mgrs. 1985—), Ill. Bar Assn. (Lincoln awards for legal writing 1961, 63, 65), Am. Inns of Ct. (charter master of bench, Lincoln Inn-Peoria, Ill.), Civil Justice Found. (pres., charter founder, trustee 1986-2002, Masons, Scottish Rite. Office Phone: 309-688-4105. *The pursuit of professional excellence has been a lifetime goal, coupled with contributions to public, political and civic affairs. He who takes from his community must also contribute to it.*

STROEVE, PIETER, chemical engineering researcher and educator; arrived in US, 1959, naturalized, 1965; Student, Contra Costa Coll., 1962-65; BSChemE, U. Calif., Berkeley, 1967; MSChemE, MIT, 1969, ScD, 1973. Postdoc. Weizmann Inst. Sci., Rehovot, Israel, 1973—74; asst. prof. U. Nijmegen, The Netherlands, 1974-77; sr. scientist Weizmann Inst. Sci., 1977; from asst. to assoc. prof. SUNY, Buffalo, 1977-81; assoc. prof. U. Calif., Davis, 1981-83, prof. dept. chem. engring. and material sci., 1983—; sabbatical U. Queensland, 1988, IBM Almaden Research Lab., 1988—89, MPI Poly. Rsch., 1996, WUR, 2003—04. Cons. Los Alamos (N.Mex.) Nat. Lab., 1983—86, Ames Nat. Lab., 1995—97, Procter and Gamble Co., 2003; vis. prof. Max-Planck Inst., Mainz, Germany, 1996; Frontis prof. nanotech. Wageningen U., Netherlands, 2003—04; co-dir. NSF Ctr. on Polymer Interfaces and Macromolecular Assemblies, Calif. Solar Collaborative; co-founder ATA Co.; founder Q1NanoSys., Bloosolar Cos.; reviewer NSF, Dept. Energy, USDA. Author, editor (books): Integrated Circuits, 1985, Biomedical Engineering, 1983; editor: Transport with Chemical Reaction, 1981, Molecular Engineering of Ultrathin Polymeric Films, 1987, Macromolecular Assemblies in Polymeric Systems, 1992; author: (book) Polymer-Layered Silicate and Silica Nanocomposites, 2005; contbr. more than 210 articles to sci. and engring. jours., over 210 seminars, posters and papers at nat. and internat. meetings. Recipient Tchg. award, U. Calif., Davis, 1984, 1990, 1991, 1995, 2006, 2d Pl. award Big Bang Bus. plan competition, 2005; grantee NSF, 1985, 1987—89, 1994—2002; P.J. Flory fellow, IBM Almaden Rsch. Ctr., 1988—89. Mem. Am. Inst. Chem. Engrs., Am. Chem. Soc. Avocations: painting, swimming, kayaking. Office: U Calif Davis Dept Chem Engring and Material Sci 1 Shields Ave Davis CA 95616 Office Phone: 530-752-0400, 530-752-8778. Business E-Mail: pstroeve@ucdavis.edu.

STROHECKER, LEON HARRY, JR., orthodontist; b. Schuylkill Haven, Pa., Aug. 14, 1932; s. Leon Harry and Anna (Fabian) S.; m. Juanita Mary Puyoou, Apr. 13, 1957; children: Sandra Lee Strohecker Beckett, Leon Harry III. Student, U. Pa., 1950-53, DDS, 1957, orthodontic cert., 1960. Bd. cert. Am. Bd. Orthodontics. Pres., pvt. practice, Lansdale, Pa., 1961—; dir. Face Head & Neck Pain and Trauma Ctr., Lansdale, 1987-99. Bd. dirs. Artman Home Retirement Ctr., Ambler; treas., bd. dirs. Valley Ctr. Mental Health Clinic, Lansdale, 1984—2002; guest lectr. in field. Pres. Lansdale Rotary Club, 1967-68; coun. mem. Trinity Luth. Ch., Lansdale, 1977-85, chmn. fin. com., 1980-85. Lt. (j.g.) USN, 1957-59. Recipient Spoke award, Jr. C. of C., 1963, Spark Plug award, 1963, Widsom award of Honor, Best Orthodontist vote, 2 Lansdale area newspapers, One Thousand Great Ams. award, Internat. Biographical Ctr., 2001, 2002; named Internat. Health Profl. of Yr., 2003. Mem. ADA, Internat. Acad. Head, Neck and Facial Pain, Internat. Coll. Cranio-Mandibular Orthopedics, Am. Acad. Pain Mgmt. (diplomate), Am. Assn. for Functional Orthodontics, Am. Profl. Practice Assn., Am. Soc. Dentistry for Children, Am. Acad. Oral Medicine, Am. Assn. Orthodontists, Am. Assn. Stomatologists, Am. Acad. Oral Medicine, Middle Atlantic Orthodontic Soc., Pa. Orthod ontic Soc., Phila. Orthodontic Soc., Pa. Dental Assn., Second Dist. Dental Assn., Montgomery-Bucks Dental Soc., Alpha Omega, Omicron Kappa Epsilon. Avocations: tennis, travel, bridge, water sports. Home: 1512 Cedar Hill Rd Ambler PA 19002-1406 Office: 456 E Hancock St Lansdale PA 19446-3803 Office Phone: 215-855-7717. Personal E-mail: lstroheckr@hotmail.com.

STROHMEYER, JOHN, writer, retired editor; b. Cascade, Wis., June 26, 1924; s. Louis A. and Anna Rose (Saladunas) S.; m. Nancy Jordan, Aug. 20, 1949 (dec. 2000); children: Mark, John, Sarah; m. Sylvia Ciernick Broady, Oct. 25, 2003. Student, Moravian Coll., 1941—43; AB, Muhlenberg Coll., 1947; MA in Journalism, Columbia U., 1948; LHD (hon.), Lehigh U., 1983. With Nazareth Item, Pa., 1940—41; night reporter Bethlehem Globe-Times, Pa., 1941—43, 1945—47; investigative reporter Providence Jour.-Bull., 1949—56; editor Bethlehem Globe-Times, 1956—64, v.p., 1961—84, dir., 1963—84. African-Am. journalism tchr. in Nairobi, Freetown, 1964; Atwood prof. journalism U. Alaska, Anchorage, 1987-88, writer-in-residence, 1989—; Clendinen Prof., U. S. Fla., 2001. Author: Crisis in Bethlehem: Big Steel's Struggle to Survive, 1986, Extreme Conditions: Big Oil and The Transformation of Alaska, 1993, Historic Anchorage, 2001. Lt. (j.g.) USNR, 1943-45. Pulitzer Traveling fellow, 1948; Nieman fellow, 1952-53; recipient Comenius award Moravian Coll., 1971; Pulitzer prize for editl. writing, 1972; Alicia Patterson Found. fellow, 1984, 85. Mem. Am. Soc. Newspaper Editors, Pa. Soc. Newspaper Editors (pres. 1964-66), Anchorage Racquet Club. Home (Summer): 6633 Lunar Dr Anchorage AK 99504-4550 E-mail: jstroh@gci.net.

STROIK, ADRIENNE LISBETH, dance educator; b. Des Moines, Apr. 28, 1977; d. David James William and Ann Lisbeth Proctor; m. Lance Andrew Stroik. BA in Theatre Arts Dance cum laude, U. Wis., Stevens Point, 2000; PhD Dance History and Theory, U. Calif., Riverside, 2007. Lectr. Calif. State U., Long Beach, 2007—; assoc. faculty Mt. San Jacinto Coll., Menifee Valley Campus, Calif., 2007—. Mentor Puente Project, San Jacinto, Calif., 2008—. Mellon fellowship, U. Calif., Riverside, 2006—07. Mem.: Congress on Rsch. Dance, Soc. Dance History Scholars. Avocations: cooking, movies. Personal E-mail: aproctor@verizon.net.

STROIK, MARILYN L., elementary school educator; b. South Milwaukee; d. Leo Andrew and Adalyn LeVerne Stroik. BS in Edn., U. Wis., Milw., 1977; MEd, Carthage Coll., Kenosha, Wis., 1989. Lic. reading specialist Wis. Tchr. St. Alexander Sch., Milw., 1977—81; tchr., minister edn. Grace Luth. Sch., Oak Creek, Wis., 1983—. Cons. student assistance team Grace Sch., 1998—, mem. crisis intervention team, 1998—; mem. manuscript rev. bd. Internat. Reading Assn., 2001—; presenter Wis. State Reading Assn., Luth. Edn. Assn., Wis. Geographic Alliance; mem. children's lit. com. Wis. State Reading Assn., 1999—2003. Author: (pamphlet) Learning and Literacy, 1999, (article) Luth. Edn. Jour., 2005. Coord. food and toy drive Luth. Ch. and Sch., Oak Creek, 1983—. Recipient Outstanding Wis. Educator, Wis. Dept. Pub. Instrn., 2000. Mem.: Mensa, Pi Lambda Theta, Phi Kappa Phi. Office: Grace Luth Sch 8537 S Pennsylvania Ave Oak Creek WI 53154

STROKE, HINKO HENRY, physicist, researcher; b. Zagreb, Croatia, June 16, 1927; came to U.S., 1943, naturalized, 1949; s. Elias and Edith (Mechner) S.; m. Norma Bilchick, Jan. 14, 1956; children: Ilana Lucy, Marija Tamar. BEE, N.J. Inst. Tech., 1949; MS, MIT, 1952, PhD, 1955. From rsch. asst. to rsch. assoc. Princeton (N.J.) U., 1954-57; rsch. staff lab. electronics, lectr. dept. physics MIT, 1957-63; assoc. prof. physics NYU, NYC, 1963-68, prof., 1968—. Dept. chmn. NYU, 1988-91; prof. associé. U. Paris, 1969-70, Ecole Normale Supérieure, 1976; vis. scientist Max Planck Inst. für Quantenoptik, Garching, U. Munich, 1977-78, 81-82, 93; cons. Atomic Instrument Co., MIT Sci. Translation Svc., Tech. Rsch. Group, Cambridge Air Force Rsch. Ctr., Am. Optical Corp., ITT Fed. Labs., NASA, others; mem. com. on line spectra of elements NAS-NRC, 1976-82; sci. assoc. CERN, Geneva, 1983—. Contbg. author: Nuclear Physics, 1963, Atomic Physics, 1969, Hyperfine Interactions in Excited Nuclei, 1971, Francis Bitter: Selected Papers, 1969, Atomic Physics 3, 1973, Nuclear Moments and Nuclear Structure, 1973, A Perspective of Physics, Vol. 1, 1977, Atomic Physics 8, 1983, Lasers in Atomic, Molecular, and Nuclear Physics, 1989—, Symposium on Probing Luminous and Dark Matter, 2000; editor: Comments on Atomic, Molecular and Optical Physics, The Physical Review-The First Hundred Years, Benjamin Bederson: Works, Comments and Legacies, Advances in Atomic, Molecular and Optical Physics, Vol. 51. Mem. Chorus Pro Musica, 1951—54, 1957—63, Münchener Bach-Chor, Munich, 1977—82, 1992; Choeur pro Arte Lausanne, 1983—2004; mem. Collegiate Chorale, NY, 1964—94, Dessoff Choirs, 1994—2007, Westchester Oratorio Soc., 2001—07, New Armsterdam Singers, 2007—. Recipient Sr. U.S. Scientist award Alexander von Humboldt Found., 1977; NATO sr. fellow in sci., 1975 Fellow AAAS, Am. Phys. Soc. (publs. oversight com. 1991-93), Optical Soc. Am.; mem. IEEE (life), European Phys. Soc., Soc. Française de Physique, Sigma Xi, Tau Beta Pi, Omicron Delta Kappa. Office: NYU Dept Physics 4 Washington Pl New York NY 10003-6621 Office Phone: 212-998-7679. Business E-Mail: henry.stroke@nyu.edu, henry.stroke@cern.ch.

STROKOFF, SANDRA L., lawyer; b. 1950; m. Jay Strokoff. BA summa cum laude, U. Pa., 1972; MA, Kings Coll. U. London; JD, U. Pa. Law Sch., 1975. Legis. counsel US House of Reps., 2009—. Lectr. & instr. legis. analysis & drafting George Washington U. Sch. Law. Author: Legislative Drafter's Desk Reference, 2008; performer (violinist): Prince George's Philharmonic Orchestra, Prince George's Philharmonic String Quartet. Office: US Congress 136 Cannon House Office Bldg Washington DC 20515*

STROLLA, CORY C., lawyer; b. Omaha, Jan. 1, 1973; s. Carmine and Susan Strolla. JD, Stetson Coll. Law, Gulfport, Fla., 1997. Bar: US Fed. Ct. (no., mid. so. dists.), Fla. 1997, cert.: Fla. Internat. U. US Transp. Intoxilyzer; intoxilyzer tech. operator. Asst. state atty. State Atty. Office, West Palm Beach, Fla., 1998—2000; assoc. Meldon and Barbarette PA, Gainesville, Fla., 2000—01; pvt. practice West Palm Beach, 2001—. Adj. prof. Palm Beach CC; judge youth ct. Palm Beach County, 1998—; trial team coach U. Fla., Gainesville, 2000; mem. law adv. coun. Stetson Coll. Law, Gulfport, 2006—, mem. alumni adv. bd.; lectr. in field. Contbr. articles to profl. jours. Past pres. Bus. Network Internat., West Palm Beach, Fla. Mem.: Fla. Bar Assn. (criminal law divsn.), Fla. Assn. Criminal Def. Lawyers, Nat. Assn. Criminal Def. Lawyers. Office: 2247 Palm Beach Lakes Blvd Ste 107 West Palm Beach FL 33409 Office Phone: 561-802-8987.

STROLLO, PATRICK J., JR., medical educator, researcher; BS, Wash. Coll., 1976; MS, Wagner Coll., 1977; MD, Uniformed Services U. Health Sciences, 1981. Intern internal medicine Wright Patterson Med. Ctr., 1982; resident internal medicine Wilford Hall USAF Med. Ctr., 1984, fellow pulmonary, 1985—87; assoc. prof. medicine U. Pittsburgh, clin. dir., sleep disorder program. Mem. Nat. Football League Cardiovascular Health Com. Recipient Air Force Achievement medal, 1985, Meritorious Svc. medal, 1993; named to Doctors in America, 2001—. Fellow: Am. Acad. Sleep Medicine (bd. dirs.), Am. Coll. Chest Physicians; mem.: Sleep Rsch. Soc., Am. Thoracic Soc. (chmn., planning com., respiratory neurobiology and sleep assembly), Am. Coll. Physicians. Office: 628 NW UPMC-Montefiore 3459 Fifth Ave Pittsburgh PA 15213 Office Phone: 412-692-2880. Office Fax: 412-692-2888. Business E-Mail: strollopj@upmc.edu.*

STROM, ARE, biologist; b. Oslo, Jan. 26, 1956; s. Ivar Ernst Eugene and Randi J. Strom; life ptnr. Dale Evans Blum. BS in Fisheries, U. Wash., Seattle, 1997, MS in Aquatic and Fishery Scis., 2003. Shellfish biologist Wash. Dept Fish and Wildlife, Brinnon, 2001—. Labor union mem. Wash. Assn. Fish and Wildlife Profls., Olympia, 2007—08. Grantee, Achievement Rewards Coll. Scientists Found., 1998. Mem.: Am. Geophys. Union. Achievements include development of method to extract paleo-climate data from shells of long-lived clams. Office: Wash Dept Fish and Wildlife 1000 Point Whitney Rd Brinnon WA 98320 Business E-Mail: stromas@dfw.wa.gov.

STROM, BRIAN LESLIE, internist, educator; b. NYC, Dec. 8, 1949; s. Martin and Edith (Singer) S.; m. Elaine Marilyn Moskowitz, June 4, 1978; children: Shayna Lee, Jordan Blair. BS, Yale U., 1971; MD, Johns Hopkins U., 1975; MPH, U. Calif., Berkeley, 1980. Diplomate Am. Bd. Internal Medicine, Am. Bd. Epidemiology. Intern in medicine U. Calif., San Francisco, 1975-76, resident in medicine, 1976-78, research fellow in clinical pharmacology, 1978-80; from asst. prof. to assoc. prof. medicine and pharmacology U. Pa., Phila., 1980-93, prof. medicine, 1993—, prof. biostatistics & epidemiology, 1995—. Adj. asst. prof. clin. pharmacy Phila. Coll. of Pharmacy and Sci., 1981-90, adj. assoc. prof., 1990-93, adj. prof., 1993—; mem. U. Pa. Cancer Ctr., 1981—; attending staff Hosp. U. Pa., 1980—, co-dir Clin. Epidemiology Unit, 1980-91, dir., 1991-2001; dir. Clin. Pharmacology Cons. Svc., 1981-82; dir. Ctr. for Clin. Epidemiology and Biostats., 1993—, chair dept. biostats. and epidemiology, 1995—; lectr. in field; George S. prod. pub. health and preventive medicine, 2002—; cons. CDC, 1981, Coun. for Internat. Orgn. of Med. Scis., Geneva, Switzerland, 1981-83, Office of Tech. Assessment, Congress of U.S., 1980-81, Aging Rev. Com., Nat. Inst. Aging, 1982, Ministry of Pub. Health, State of Kuwait, 1982, Royal Tropical Inst., Amsterdam, 1983, others. Editl. cons. Johns Hopkins U. Press, J.B. Lippincott; referee Annals of Internal Medicine, Archives of Internal Medicine, Clin. Pharmacology and Therapeutics, Digestive Diseases and Sci., Internat. Jour. Cardiology, Internat. Jour. Epidemiology, Jour. AMA, Jour. Gen. Internal Medicine, Med. Care, Primary Care Tech., Sci.; editor Pharmaepidemiology and Drug Safety; mem. editl. bd. 7 jours.; contbr. numerous articles to profl. jours. Nat. Acad. Scis. grantee, Rockefeller Found. grantee, NIH grantee, many others. Fellow ACP, Am. Coll. Epidemiology, Am. Epidemiology Soc.; mem. Am. Fedn. Med. Rsch., Am. Pub. Health Assn., Am. Soc. Clin. Pharmacology and Therapeutics, Am. Soc. Clin. Investigation, Am. Assn. Physicians, Internat. Soc. Pharmacoepidemiology, Internat. Epideliol. Assn., Soc. for Epidemiologic Rsch., Soc. Gen. Internal Medicine, Inst. Medicine, Inst. Medicine. Democrat. Jewish. Avocations: hiking, bicycling, camping, skiing. Home: 332 Hidden River Rd Narberth PA 19072-1111 Office Phone: 215-898-2368. Business E-Mail: bstrom@cceb.med.upenn.edu.

STROM, E. (DWIN) THOMAS, chemistry professor, researcher; b. Des Moines, Iowa, June 11, 1936; s. Edwin Lewis and Maria Kristina Strom; m. Charlotte Faye Williams, June 14, 1958; children: Laura Christine, Eric William. PhD, Iowa State U., Ames, 1964. Sr. rsch.

chemist Mobil Rsch. & Devel. Corp., Dallas, 1964—95; adj. prof. U. Tex., Arlington, 1996—. Editor: (chemistry mag.) The Southwest Retort (ACS Wilfred T. Doherty award, 1989). Councilor Am. Chem. Soc., Dallas, 2004—. 1st lt. Chem. Corps USAR, 1964—66, Natick, Mass. Fellow: Am. Chem. Soc. (inaugured group mem. 2009, divsn. history chemistry 2009—); mem.: Oak Cliff Lions Club. Conservative. Presbyterian. Achievements include patents for Oil Field Chemistry. Avocations: reading, piano. Office: Univ Texas Dept of Chemistry and Biochemistry Arlington TX 76019-0065 Office Fax: 817-272-3808.

STROM, J. PRESTON, JR., lawyer; b. May 21, 1959; s. Grace and J.P. Sr. S.; m. Donna Savoca, Oct. 5, 1985; children: Margaret, Caroline. BA, U. S.C., 1981, JD, 1984; Program for sr. exec., Harvard U., Cambridge, 1995. Bar: S.C. 1984, U.S. Dist. Ct. S.C., 1986, U.S. Ct. Appeals (4th cir.) 1986. Law clerk to Hon. Frank Eppes 13th cir. Judge, 1984—85; asst. solicitor 5th Jud. Cir., S.C., 1985-86; ptnr. Leventis, Strom & Wicker, 1986-88, Strom Law Firm, 1988-90, Bolt, Popowski, McCulloch & Strom, 1990-93; acting U.S. atty. Office U.S. Atty., S.C., 1993, U.S. atty. S.C., 1993-96; atty. Strom Law Firm, LLC, Columbia, S.C., 1996—; ptnr. Strom & Young, L.L.P., Columbia, SC. Chmn. Law Enforcement Coord. Com.; juvenile justice and child support enforcement subcom. U.S. Dept. Justice; active Atty. Gen. Adv. Com. Contbg. articals to profl. jour. Chmn. Juvenile Justice and Child Support Enforcement Subcom. (U S Dept. of Justice), 1993, SC Law Enforcement Coordinating Com., 1993. Recipient James Pickett Fellowship in Criminal Justice, 1993—95; named Who's Who in American Law, 1994. Mem. S.C. Bar, S.C. Trial Lawyers Assn., Richland County Bar Assn. (chmn. criminal law sect.), Criminal def. Lawyers Assn., 4th Cir. Judicial Conf. Nat. Assn., former U S attys. Nat. Crime Victim Bar Assn., SC Trial Lawyers Assn.legis. streering Com., 1993-1994, atty. gen. adv. com. U S Dept. of Justice, 1993-1994, pres. Kappa Sigma Fraternity, 1981. Office: Strom Law Firm, LLC Ste A 2110 Beltline Blvd Columbia SC 29204 Office Phone: 888-490-2847. Office Fax: 803-252-4801.

STROM, KRISTINA CHASE, writer, consultant; b. Schenectady, NY, Dec. 28, 1948; d. Raymond Olaf and Lois Moulton Strom; children: Kia Strom Kuresman, Kamala Strom Kuresman, Kimberly Strom Kuresman, Kara Strom Kuresman. PhD, Universal Life Sem. Lic. in ins. Ohio, 1996; ordained clergy Ohio, 1996, Minn., 1996. Asst. buyer, buyer Hess's Dept. Store, Allentown, Pa., 1968—69; educator Xavier U., New Orleans, 1970; columnist Denver Free Press, 1972; co-founder, owner New World Ctr. Bookshop and Foodshop, 1973—74; tchr. Beth Adam Religious Sch., Cin., 1981—88, art dir., 1987—89, prin., 1988—89; editor Beth Adam Newsletter, Cin., 1982—86; designer Del Favero Enterprises, Cin., 1984—90; store mgr. B. Dalton Books, Cin., 1990—91; systems operator TriStateOnline Greater Cin. Consortium Colls. and Univs., 1999, adminstr., 1999; pvt. practice Glendale, Ohio, 1968—; freelance artist, 1970—; design and bus. cons., 1985—. Columnist, staff writer Silent Messages, Cin., 1996—99; moderator Wells List, 1995—; owner, mgr. CelestialPerspectives.com, Cin., 1999—. Exhibitions include Mich. State U., 2003—04, Represented in permanent collections Millennium Challenge; author: Denim and Lace, An historical mystery of first love, timeless love, numerous poems; co-editor, contbr. From Eulogy to Joy, A Heartfelt Anthology, Feathered Star, 2003, Monkey Wrench New Quilts from an Old Favorite, 2004, Seven Sisters New Quilts from an Old Favorite, 2005, Goose River Anthology, 2007; contbr. articles to profl. jours. Pres. Kindervelt #17 Cin. Children's Hosp. Aux., 1983—85. Mem.: Smithsonian Nat. Mus. Am. Indian, Nat. Ctr. for Preservation of Medicinal Herbs, The Nature Conservancy, Nat. Audubon Soc., Am. Quilter's Soc., Sierra Club, Twilight Club Ctr. Evolutionary Ethics. Avocations: gardening, genealogy, book collecting, anthropology, archaeology. Home: 171 West Sharon Road Glendale OH 45246-4334 Personal E-mail: kristinastrom@celestialperspectives.com.

STROM, LELAND A., federal agency administrator; m. Twyla Strom; 3 children. A, Kishwaukee Coll., Malta, Ill.; attended, Northern Ill. U. Bd. mem. 1st Farm Credit Svcs., chmn.; mem. adv. coun. on agr., labor, and small bus. Fed. Reserve Bank, Chgo., 2000—06; mem. country mutual fund trust bd. Ill. Farm Bur.; mem. bd. dirs. Farm Credit System Ins. Corp., chmn., 2006; mem. bd. dirs. Farm Credit Adminstrn., 2006—08, chmn., CEO, 2008—. Mem. Restructuring Task Force of the Sixth Farm Credit Dist.; bd. mem. Northern F.S., Inc., AgriBank, FCB, Farm Credit Coun. Mem. State Young Farmer Com., 1981—85. Office: Farm Credit Administrn 1501 Farm Credit Dr Mc Lean VA 22102-5090*

STROM, LYLE ELMER, judge; b. Omaha, Jan. 6, 1925; s. Elmer T. and Eda (Hanisch) Strom; m. Regina Ann Kelly, July 31, 1950 (dec.); children: Mary Bess, Susan Frances(dec.), Amy Claire, Cassie A., David Kelly, Margaret Mary, Bryan Thomas. Student, U. Nebr., 1946-47; AB, Creighton U., 1950, JD cum laude, 1953. Bar: Nebr. 1953. Assoc. Fitzgerald, Brown, Leahy, Strom, Schorr & Barmettler and predecessor firm, Omaha, 1953-60, ptnr., 1960-63, gen. trial ptnr., 1963-85; judge U.S. Dist. Ct. Nebr., Omaha, 1985-87, chief judge, 1987-94, sr. judge, 1995—. Adj. prof. law Creighton U., 1959-95, clinical prof., 1996—; mem. com. pattern jury instrns. and practice and proc. Nebr. Supreme Ct., 1965-91; spl. legal counsel Omaha Charter Rev. Commn., 1973; chair gender fairness task force U.S. Ct. Appeals (8th cir.), 1993-97. Exec. com. Covered Wagon Coun. Boy Scouts Am., 1953—57, bd. trustees, exec. com. Mid-Am. Coun., 1988—; chmn. bd. trustees Marian H.S., 1969—71; mem. pres. coun. Creighton U., 1990—95. With U.S. Maritime Svc., 1943—46. Fellow Am. Coll. Trial Lawyers, Internat. Acad. Trial Lawyers; mem. Nebr. Bar Assn. (ho. of dels. 1978-81, exec. coun. 1981-87, pres. 1989-90), Nebr. Bar Found. (bd. trustees 1998—), Omaha Bar Assn. (pres. 1980-81), Am. Judicature Soc., Midwestern Assn. Amateur Athletic Union (pres. 1976-78), Rotary (pres. 1993-94), Alpha Sigma Nu (pres. alumni chpt. 1970-71). Republican. Roman Catholic. Office: US Dist Ct Roman Hruska Courthouse 111 S 18th Plz Ste 3190 Omaha NE 68102 Office Phone: 402-661-7320.

STROM, MILTON GARY, lawyer; b. Rochester, NY, Dec. 5, 1942; s. Harold and Dolly (Isaacson) S.; m. Barbara A. Simon, Jan. 18, 1975; children: Carolyn, Michael, Jonathan. BS in Econ., U. Pa., 1964; JD, Cornell U., 1967. Bar: N.Y. 1968, U.S. Dist. Ct. (W. dist.) N.Y. 1968, U.S. Ct. Claims 1969, U.S. Ct. Mil. Appeals 1969, U.S. Ct. Appeals (D.C. cir.) 1970, U.S. Supreme Ct. 1972, U.S. Dist. Ct. (so. dist.) N.Y. 1975. Atty. SEC, Washington, 1968-71; assoc. Skadden, Arps, Slate, Meagher & Flom, NYC, 1971-76, ptnr., 1977—2004, of counsel, 2004—. Served with USCGR, 1967-73. Mem. ABA, N.Y. State Bar Assn. (corp. law sect.), Assn. of Bar of City of N.Y., Internat. Bar Assn., Beach Point Club, Fenway Golf Club, Banyan Golf Club. Republican. Jewish. Avocations: tennis, skiing, golf. Office: Skadden Arps Slate Meagher & Flom 4 Times Sq Fl 42 New York NY 10036-6522 Office Phone: 212-735-2300. Business E-Mail: mstrom@skadden.com.

STROM, PARIS SCOTT, education educator; s. Robert D. Strom. BFA, Ariz. State U., 1991, MA, 1994, PhD in Ednl. Psychology, 1997. Cert. secondary tchr. Ariz., instr. CC Ariz. Ariz. State Bd. Dirs. Faculty Ariz. State U., Tempe, 1998—99, rsch. assoc. Office Parent Devel. Internat., 1990—2001, asst. dir., 2002—; tchr. Scottsdale Pub. Schs., 1997—99, Peoria Pub. Schs., Ariz., 1999—2001; assoc. prof. Coll. Edn. Auburn U., Ala., 2001—. Co-author: Teaching Through Play, Adolescent Guidance in Japan; contbr. articles to profl. jours. Recipient Gerald & Emily Leischuck Outstanding Tchg. award, Auburn U., 2005; grantee, Motorola, 2000—02, Nat. Adv. Coun., Auburn U., 2002—04. Mem.: Am. Assn. Behavioral and Social Scis., Am. Ednl. Rsch. Assn. Office: Auburn U 4036 Haley Ctr EFLT Auburn University AL 36849-5221 Business E-Mail: stromps@auburn.edu.

STROM, ROBERT DUANE, psychologist, educator; BS, Macalester Coll., St. Paul, Minn.; MA, U. Minn., Mpls.; PhD, U. Mich., Ann Arbor. Prof. U. Conn., Storrs, 1962—64, Ohio State U., Columbus, 1964—69, Ariz. State U., Tempe, 1969—. Author: (book) Teaching In The Slum School, 1965, Mental Health And Achievement, 1965, The Inner-City Classroom, 1966, Psychology For The Classroom, 1969, Experiences In Educational Psychology, 1970, Values And Human Development, 1972, Education For Affective Achievement, 1973, Parent And Child In Fiction, 1977, Parent And Child Development, 1978, Growing Through Play, 1981, Eductional Psychology, 1982, Human Development And Learning, 1989, Grandparent Education, 1991, Becoming A Better Grandparent, 1991, Achieving Grandparent Potential, 1992, (measurement instruments) Grandparent Strengths and Needs Inventory, 1993, Parent As a Teacher Inventory, 1995, Parent Success Indicator, 1998, Interpersonal Intelligence Inventory, 2002, Adolescents in the Internet Age, 2009, Teamwork Skills Inventory, 2009. Scholar, Fulbright Found., 1975, 1976, 1985. Office: Coll Education Arizona State Univ Tempe AZ 85287-0611 Office Phone: 480-965-4397. Business E-Mail: bob.strom@asu.edu.

STROM, VICTORIA, small business owner; m. James Vodden. Degree in Real Estate (hon.), Ariz. Sch. Bus., Scottsdale, 2004. Realtor Solutions Real Estate; owner Bringing Investors Together Llc, Scottsdale, 2007—. Bd. mem. Investment Affiliates Llc, Scottsdale.

STROMAN, SUSAN, choreographer, theater director; b. Wilmington, Del., Oct. 17, 1954; d. Charles and Frances Stroman; m. Mike Ockrent, 1996 (dec. Dec. 2, 1999); stepchildren: Ben, Natasha. Grad., U. Del. Choreographer Flora Roberts Inc. Dancer Chgo., 1977—78, Whoopee!, 1979, Richard III, 1980, Peter Pan, 1983, choreographer (off-Broadway) Broadway Babylon, 1984, Sayonara, 1987, Flora, the Red Menace, 1987, Shenandoah, 1988, Slasher, 1988, Rhythm Ranch, 1989, The Roar of the Greaspaint-The Smell of the Crowd, 1990, Gypsy, 1991, And the World Goes 'Round, 1991 (Outer Critics' Cir. award for choreography, 1991), A Christmas Carol, 1994, (Broadway plays) Crazy for You, 1992 (Tony award for best choreography, 1992, Drama Desk award for choreography, 1992, Outer Critics' Cir. award, 1992, Laurence Olivier award for choreography, 1993), Picnic, 1994, Show Boat, 1994 (Tony award for best choreography, 1995, Astaire award Theatre Devel. Fund, 1995), Big, 1996 (Tony nomination for best choreography, 1996), Oklahoma, 2002 (Laurence Olivier Award for choreography, 2002, Tony nomination for best choreography, 2002), (Operas) Don Giovanni, 1989, A Little Night Music, 1990, 100 in the Shade, 1992, (spl.) Liza Minnelli: Stepping Out at Radio City Music Hall, 1991 (Emmy nomination for choreography, 1993), (films) The Producers, 2005; choreographer, conceiver (Broadway plays) Steel Pier, 1997 (Tony nomination for best choreography, 1997), dir., choreographer The Music Man, 2000 (Tony nomination for best choreography, 2000, Tony nomination for best dir., 2000), dir., choreographer, conceiver Contact, 2000 (Tony award for best choreography, 2000, Lucille Lortel Award for outstanding direction, 2000, Tony nomination for best dir., 2000), dir., choreographer The Producers, 2001 (Tony award for best choreography, 2001, Tony award for best dir., 2001, Drama Desk Award for best dir. musical, 2001, Touring Broadway award, best direction, League Am. Theatres and Producers, 2005), dir., choreographer, conceiver Thou Shalt Not, 2001, dir., choreographer The Frogs, 2004, Young Frankenstein, 2007, dir., choreographer, conceiver Double Feature, 2004, co-conceiver Trading Places, Equity Libr. Theatre Informals, 1983, dir., co-conceiver (off-Broadway) Living Color, 1986, co-conceiver, choreographer (TV spl.) Sondheim-A Celebration at Carnegie Hall, 1992, asst. dir., asst. choreographer (Broadway plays) Musical Chairs, 1980; dir.(TV spl.): An Evening With the Boston Pops-A Tribute to Leonard Bernstein, 1989. Recipient Disting. Achievement in Musical Theatre Award, Drama League, 2001, Elan award, 2005. Address: Flora Roberts Agy Penhouse A 157 W 57th St New York NY 10019-2210

STROMBERG, CLIFFORD DOUGLAS, lawyer; b. NYC, June 1, 1949; s. George M. and Greta (Netzow) Stromberg; m. Ava S. Feiner, June 25, 1972; children: Kimberly, Eric. BA summa cum laude, Yale U., 1971; JD, Harvard U., 1974. Bar: NY 1975, DC 1975, US Dist. Ct. (so. and ea. dists.) NY 1975, US Ct. Appeals (DC cir.) 1975, US Ct. Appeals (2nd cir.) 1975, US Supreme Ct. 1980. Law clk. to judge U.S. Dist. Ct. (ea. dist.) N.Y., 1974-75; assoc. Arnold & Porter, Washington, 1975-78, 80-83; dep. exec. sec. HHS, Washington, 1978-80; cons. FTC, Washington, 1980; ptnr. Dorsey & Whitney, Washington, 1983-84, Hogan & Hartson, Washington, 1984—. Adj. asst. prof. emergency medicine George Washington U. Sch. Medicine, 1991-97. Co-author: Mental Health and Law: A System in Transition, 1975, Alternatives to the Hospital: Ambulatory Surgery Centers and Emergicenters, 1984, Entrepreneurial Health Care: How to Structure Successful New Ventures, 1985, The Psychologist's Legal Handbook, 1988, Access to Hospital Information: Problems and Strategies: 4 Frontiers of Health Services Management 3-33, 1987, Healthcare Provider Networks: Antitrust Issues and Practical Considerations in Devels. in Antitrust Law, 1990, Healthcare Credentialing: Implications for Academic Medical Centers, 1991; mem. editl. bd. Harvard Law Rev., 1972-73; editor in chief Healthspan: The Report of Health Business and Law, 1984-87; cons. editor: Managed Care Law Strategist, 1999-2002; contbr. articles to profl. jours. Bd. dirs. Nat. Children's Eye Care Found., Washington, 1985-87. Teaching fellow in govt. Harvard U., 1973-74. Fellow Am. Bar Found.; mem. ABA (chair working group health care reform 1993-96, state membership chmn. 1984, bd. dirs. forum com. health law 1987-90, adv. com. govt. affairs 1993-98, governing bd., individual rights and responsibilities sect., exec. coun., 1980-90, sec. 1984-87, chair-elect 1987-88, chair 1988-89, legal aid and indigent defendants com. 1982-87), Am. Health Lawyers Assn., Nat. Assn. Coll. and Univ. Attys., Phi Beta Kappa. Office: Hogan & Hartson 555 13th St NW Washington DC 20004-1161 Office Phone: 202-637-5699. Business E-Mail: cdstromberg@hhlaw.com.

STROMBERG, GREGORY, printing ink company executive; b. Milw., Feb. 10, 1948; s. Clifford Norman and Margaret Betty (Hoover) S.; m. Gail Elizabeth Steinbach, Aug. 22, 1970; children: Christopher, Brian, Ellen. BS, Marquette U., Milw., 1970; MBA, Jones Internat. U., 2006. Office contact salesman Continental Can Co., Milw., 1970-78; sales rep. Sun Chem. Co., Milw., 1978-82; v.p., gen. mgr. Acme Printing Ink Co., Milw., 1982—; exec. v.p. Can. ops. Acme Printing Ink Can. Ltd., 1985—, pres., 1990—, v.p. sales/mktg. metal divsn., 2000—; CEO, pres. Canned Water 4 Kids Inc. Bd. dirs. Can. Ops. Acme Inks of Can.; pres. Toobee Internat., Inc., Milw., 1981—; v.p., dir. mktg. and internat. sales INX Internat. Ink Co., 1991—. Author: Toobee Air Force Flight Training Manual, 1983. Advisor Milw. Jr. Achievement, 1974; sponsor Muscular Dystrophy, 1983; asst. mem. com. toys for Tots, Children's Hosp., Milw., 1983; active United Meth. Men. Mem. Internat. Metal Decorators Assn., Am. Mgmt. Assn. Internat., Am. Soc. Quality Control, Nat. Metal Decorators Assn., Nat. Assn. Printers and Lithographers, Nat. Assn. Printing Equipment and Suppliers, Exec. Agenda of Wis Home: N69w23448 Donna Dr Sussex WI 53089-3245 Office Phone: 414-438-4384. E-mail: mitze@execpc.com.

STROMBERG, JEAN WILBUR GLEASON, lawyer; b. St. Louis, Oct. 31, 1943; d. Ray Lyman and Martha (Bugbee) W.; m. Gerald Kermit Gleason, Aug. 28, 1966 (div. 1987); children: C. Blake, Peter Wilbur; m. Kurt Stromberg, Jan. 3, 1993; 1 child, Kristoffer Stromberg. BA, Wellesley Coll., 1965; JD cum laude, Harvard U., 1968. Bar: Calif. 1969, D.C. 1978. Assoc. Brobeck, Phleger & Harrison, San Francisco, 1969-72; spl. counsel to dir. div. corp. fin. SEC, Washington, 1972-76, assoc. dir. div. investment mgmt., 1976-78; of counsel Fulbright & Jaworski, Washington, 1978-80, ptnr., 1980-96; dir. fin. instns. and market issues GAO, Washington, 1996-97; cons. Washington, 1997—. Mem. adv. panel on legal issues GAO, 1992—96; mem. NASD select com. on NASDAQ, 1994—96; trustee AARP Intestment Program and AARP Scudder Mut. Funds, 1997—2000; bd. dirs. DWS Scudder Mut. Funds., 2000—, Svc. Source, Inc., 2002—, Mut. Fund Dirs. Forum. Dir. William and Flora Hewlett Found., 2000—; overseer Wellesley Ctrs. Women, 2003-07. Mem. ABA (chmn. subcom. on securities and banks, corp. laws com., bus. sect. 1982-93), D.C. Bar Assn. (chmn. steering com. bus. sect. 1982-84), FBA (chair exec. coun., securities com. 1993-95), Am. Bar Retirement Assn. (bd. dirs. 1986-90, 94-96), Phi Beta Kappa. Home and Office: 3816 Military Rd NW Washington DC 20015-2704

STROMBERG, ROSS ERNEST, lawyer; b. Arcata, Calif., May 5, 1940; s. Noah Anders and Anne Laura (Noyes) S.; m. Toni Nicholas, Dec. 16, 1961; m. Margaret Telonicher, Oct. 3, 1965; children: Kristin, Matthew, Gretchen, Erik. BS, Humboldt State U., 1962; JD, U. Calif., Berkeley, 1965. Bar: Calif. 1966, U.S. Dist. Ct. (no. dist.) Calif. 1966, U.S. Ct. Appeals (9th cir.) 1966. Assoc. Hanson Bridgett, San Francisco, 1965-70, ptnr., 1970-85, Epstein Becker Stromberg & Green, San Francisco, 1985-90, Jones Day, San Francisco, 1990—. Past chmn. Jones Day's Healthcare Specialized Industry Practice; pres. Stromberg Vineyards, Healdsburg, Calif., 2002—. Author: Economic Joint Venturing, 1985, Acquisition and Enhancement of Physician Practices, 1988. Pres. Am. Acad. Hosp. Attys. of Am. Host. Assn., Chgo., 1978; bd. dirs. Sutter Med. Ctr., Santa Rosa, 2001—, chair, 2003—; pres. East Bay AHEC, Oakland, Calif., 1984—87; bd. dirs. Am. Cancer Soc., Oakland, 1984—95, Wildflowers Inst., San Francisco, 1984—2008; chair Pediat. Dental Initiative of the North Coast, Healdsburg, Calif., 2004. Mem.: Am. Health Lawyers Assn. Democrat. Office: Jones Day 26th Fl 555 Calif St San Francisco CA 94104 Office Phone: 415-875-5724. Business E-Mail: restromberg@jonesday.com.

STROME, MARSHALL, otolaryngologist, educator; b. Lynn, Mass., Apr. 27, 1940; s. David and Rose (Cantor) S.; m. Deena Lazarov, Sept. 23, 1962; children: Scott Eric, Randall Alan. Degree, U. Mich., 1960, MD, 1964, MS, 1970. Resident in otolaryngology U. Mich., Ann Arbor, 1966-70; asst. prof. U. Conn., Hartford, 1971, Beth Israel-Harvard, Boston, 1972-77, chief otolaryngology, 1977-93; prof., chmn. otolaryngology Cleve. Clinic Found., 1993—97. Sr. surgeon Brigham & Women's Hosp., Boston, 1982-93; assoc. prof. harvard Med. Sch., Boston, 1989-93, Longwood ORL coord., 1982-90; mem. cons. bd. Xomed Treace Corp., Jacksonville, Fla., 1987-90; advisor SLT Laser Corp., Oaks, Pa., 1994—; dir. Great Comebacks, Gresham, Oreg.; prof. otolaryngology Cleve. Clinic Found. Health Scis. Ctr. Ohio State U., 1994; hon. guest, prin. spkr. Turkish Otolaryngol. Soc., 1997; Qgura lectr., 2000; mem. sci. adv. bd. Somnus Corp.; pres. Soc. Univ. Otolaryngologists, 2002—, pres. Am. Laryngol. Assn., 2007-08, featured lectr. Japan Head & Neck Soc., 2006, chmn., bd. dir. NY Head & Neck Inst., 2009. Mem. editl. bd. Harvard Health News Letter, 1976-85; author: Differential Diagnoses in Pediatric ORL, 1975; editor: Manual of Otolaryngology, 1985, Complications of Laser Surgery of the Head and Neck, 1986; transplanted 1st total human larynx, 1998-. Mem. fund raising com. Belmont Hill (Mass.) Sch., 1984. Capt. U.S. Army, 1965-71. Recipient Medal City of Paris, 1987, Sword of Saudi Arabia, 1991, Cert. of Appreciation, Ministry of Health-Singapore, 1995, Presdl. citation Coll. Physicians and Surgeons of Pakistan, Classic Telly award, 1999, Innovator award, Cleve. Clinic, 2005; named One of Best Doctors in Cleve., Cleve. Mag., 1995—, One of Best Drs. in Am., 1996—, Outstanding People of 20th Century, 1999, Medical Hero Guiness Book of World Records, 2000; recipient award of excellence Cleve. Clinic, 2005, Leica Visionary award, 2005, Excellence award Clevelaun Clinic, 2005; named Honored Lectr. Garnett Passii, Australia, 2008, Honored Guest Am. Broucho Esopmagological Assn., 2008, Western Sec. Triological Soc., 2009, Honored Featured Spkr. South Anniversary Celebration Symposium Pusan Otolaringological Dept., Korea, 2006, Featured Honored Lectr. Otolaryn. Headomech Soc., France, 2008, Blauchard Lectr, 2007; named one of Americas Top Drs., Pres. Castle Connolle Med. Ltd., 2006-, Cancer Castle Connolle, 2008, NY Mag., 2009. Mem.: Triological Soc. (v.p. 1990—91), Cartesian Soc. (pres. 1999), Soc. Univ. Otolaryngologists (pres. 2003, Leica-Visionary award 2005), Am. Soc. Head and Neck Surgery, Am. Acad. Otolaryngology (Honor award 1987, one of nine recognized for conbtn. to medicine in last 250 years 1999, Internat. Scientist of Yr, 2002), Am. Acad. Facial Plastic Reconstructive Surgery (Medallion of Honor 1989), U. Mich. Med. Ctr. Alumni Soc. (coord. New Eng. Fund. Raising 1992, chair bd. govs. 1992—93, Cleve. Clinic tchr. of yr. 2002). Achievements include performance first robotic laser resection of laryngeal malignance; development of weh euroscopic approach for laryngeal cancer, new surgical procedure for swalloning post neurological injure. Avocations: bicycling, skiing, sculling, sea kyacking, tennis. Office: 110 E 59th St, Ste 10A New York NY 10022

STROME, STEPHEN, former music distribution company executive; b. Lynn, Mass., June 20, 1945; s. David and Rose (Cantor) S.; m. Phyllis Ruth Fields, Jan. 14, 1967; children: Michael, Rochelle. BA, Hillsdale Coll., Mich., 1967; MBA, Wayne State U., 1968. Trainee KMart Corp., Detroit, 1968-69, mgr. work measurement Troy, Mich., 1970-73; mgr. tng., edn. Fruehauf Corp., Detroit, 1974-76, regional mgr. labor relations, 1976-78; dir. ops. Handleman Co., Clawson, Mich., 1978-80, account exec., 1980-82, v.p. computer software div. Troy, 1983-85, pres. computer software/video div., 1986-87, exec. v.p., 1987-89, exec. v.p., chief oper. officer, 1990, pres., CEO, 1991-2001, chmn., CEO, 2001—07, cons., 2007—. Office: Handleman Co 500 Kirts Blvd Troy MI 48084-4142

STROMINGER, JACK LEONARD, biochemist; b. NYC, Aug. 7, 1925; AB, Harvard U., 1944; MD, Yale U., 1948; DSc (hon.), Trinity Coll., Dublin, 1975, Washington U., 1988. From asst. prof. to prof. pharmacology sch. med. Washington U., St. Louis, 1955-61, prof. pharmacology and microbiology, 1961-64; prof. pharmacology and chem. microbiology med. sch. U. Wis., Madison, 1964-68; prof. biochemistry Harvard U., 1968-83, chmn. dept. biochemistry and molecular biology, 1970-73, Higgins prof. biochemistry, 1983—; head tumor virol. divsn. Dana-Farber Cancer Inst., Boston, 1977—. Recipient

John J. Abel award, 1960, Paul-Lewis Lab award, 1962, Rose Payne award Am. Soc. Histocompat. & Immunogen., 1986, Hoechst-Roussel award, 1990, Pasteur medal, 1990, Albert Lasker Award for Basic Med. Rsch., Lasker Found., 1995; named Passano Found. laureate, 1993. Mem. NAS (mem. inst. medicine, Microbiology award 1968, Selman Waxman award 1968), AAAS, Am. Soc. Biol. Chemists, Am. Soc. Pharmacology & Exptl. Therapeutics, Am. Assn. Immunologists, Am. Soc. Microbiologists, Am. Chem. Soc., Am. Acad. Arts & Sci., European Molecular Biol. Orgn., Sigma Xi. Address: Harvard U Dept Molecular & Cell Bio 7 Divinity Ave Cambridge MA 02138-2019 Office: Dana Farber Cancer Inst Dept Biochem 44 Binney St Boston MA 02115-6084 Office Phone: 617-495-2733, 617-632-3083. E-mail: jlstrom@fas.harvard.edu.*

STRONACH, CAREY ELLIOTT, physicist, researcher; b. Boston, Aug. 8, 1940; s. Ralph Howard and Frances Burns (Maynard) S.; m. Joan Alice Louise Venner, Aug. 20, 1966; children: John Maynard, Howard Stanley. BS, U. Richmond, Va., 1961; MS, U. Va., Charlottesville, 1963; PhD, Coll. William and Mary, Williamsburg, Va., 1976. Instr. physics Va. State U., Petersburg, 1965-66, asst. prof., 1966—76, assoc. prof., 1976—80, prof., 1980—2006, prof. emeritus, 2006—. Dir. Muon Spin Rotation Rsch. Program, 1977-2006, Superconducting Materials Rsch. Program, 1988-97, Nanostructured Materials Rsch. Program, 1997-2001, Galactic Cosmic Radiation Rsch. Program, 1993-97, U.S.-France Joint Muon Spin Rotation Rsch. Program, 1985-91, Magnetic Materials Lab. Devel. Program, 1999-2001; radiation safety officer; mem. Solid State Physics Rsch. Inst., 1983-87; founding dir. Ctr. Interactive Micromagnetics, 2001-06; vis. assoc. prof. U. Alta, 1978-79; guest scientist Brookhaven Nat. Lab.; organizing com. Internat. Symposium on the Electronic Structure and Properties of Hydrogen in Metals, 1982, Internat. Symposium on the Physics and Chemistry of Small Clusters, 1986, From Clusters to Crystals, 1991, Sci. and Tech. Atomically Engineered Materials, 1995, Internat. Symposium on Cluster and Nanostructure Interfaces, 1999, Internat. Symposium Clusters and Nano-Assemblies: From Physical to Life Sciences, 2003; sci. adv. com. European Workshop Spectroscopy of Subatomic Species in Non-Metallic Solids, 1985, govs. com. on Superconducting Supercollider, 1987; TV physics lectr., 1991-94; adv. com. Internat. Conf. Muon Spin Rotation, 1996-2005, chmn., 1999-2002; assoc. Va. Inst. Pub. Policy, 2004-; cons. Marco Polo Project AAAS, 2002—; leadership coun. So. Poverty Law Ctr. Contbr. articles to profl. jours.; playwright; editor of sci. textbooks, author: plays Magnola Aftershock Out Of Ct Settlement, Royal Colours The Battle of Doorn One Day In The Life of Martin Bormann, The Day is Ours, Snow Bound In Star Bucks. Internat. adv. com. on acad. freedom Bar Ilan U., Israel, 2005—; pres. Petersburg area chpt. Va. Coun. Human Rels., 1965—67; active Petersburg Commn. Cmty. Rels. Affairs, 1974—77; long-range transp. adv. com. City of Petersburg, 1994—98; steering com. Gilmore for Gov., 1997; active Dramatists Guild; sec. adv. coun. bds. and commns. Commonwealth Coun., 1998—2002; active Richmond Playwrights Forum, 1999—, Virginians for Warner, 2001; reviewer of rsch. proposals Nat. Sci. Found.; corr. sec. Petersburg Dem. Com., 1974—77, active, 1972—85, vice chmn., 1981—85. Fellow duPont Corp., 1961-63, NSF, 1971-72, NASA, 1976; recipient Patrick Henry award Va. Gov. James C. Gilmore III, 2001. Mem.: AAUP (chpt. pres. 1968—70), AAAS, Nat. Ctr. for Sci. Edn., Richmond Realists and Naturalists Assn., Air Force Assn., Internat. Soc. on Muon Spectroscopy (founding mem.), WWII Meml. Soc. (charter), NY Acad. Scis., Planetary Soc., High Speed Rail/Maglev Assn. (govt. rels. com. 1992—97, Maglev task force 1994—97), Va. Assn. Scholars (bd. govs. 1999—, pres. 2004—), Southeastern Univs. Rsch. Assn. (site sel. com. 1980—81, materials sci. com. 1983—86, trustee 1983—98, sci. and tech. com. 1986—88, rules com. 1988—92, edn. com. 1992—94, new projects com. 1994—95, Jefferson Lab. com. 1995—98), Va. Acad. Sci. (sec. astronomy, math. and physics sect 1983—84, chmn. 1984—85), Nat. Assn. Scholars, Am. Assn. Physics Tchrs., Am. Phys. Soc., Met. Opera Guild, Americans United Separation Ch. and State, The Churchill Ctr., Bertrand Russell Soc., Scholars for Peace in Mid. East, Tri-univ. Meson Facility Users Group, Richmond Area Free Thinkers, Coun. Secular Humanism (assoc.), Pi Mu Epsilon, Sigma Pi Sigma, Sigma Xi (chpt. sec. 1977—78, chpt. pres. 1980—84, 1987—88), Phi Beta Kappa. Achievements include co-devel. of low-energy muon beam line at the AGS of Brookhaven Nat. Lab.; rsch. in pion-nucleus interactions, heavy-ion reactions, muon spin rotation studies of high-temperature superconductors and related materials, fullerenes, heavy-fermion materials, ferromagnetic metals, metal hydrides, fatigue in metals and other materials; participation in the establishment of the Southeastern Universities Research Association and the Thomas Jefferson Nat. Accelerator Facility; discovery of formation of muonium and muonated radicals in Buckminsterfullerene; discovery of simultaneous high-temp. superconductivity and magnetic ordering in strontium yttrium ruthenate. Home: 2241 Buckner St Petersburg VA 23805-2207 Office Phone: 804-732-8993. Personal E-mail: cestronach@comcast.net.

STRONE, MICHAEL JONATHAN, real estate consultant, lawyer, art consultant; b. NYC, Feb. 26, 1953; s. Bernard William and Judith Semel (Sogg); m. Andrea Nan Acker, Jan. 27, 1979; children: Noah Gregory, Joshua Samuel. BA cum laude, Colby Coll., Waterville, Maine, 1974; JD, Fordham Law Sch., NYC, 1978. Bar: NJ 1978, NY 1979, Conn. 1988, US Ct. Appeals (2d and 3d cirs.) 1979, US Dist. Ct. (so. and ea. dists.) NY 1979, US Dist. Ct. NJ 1979. Assoc. Ratheim Hoffman et al, NYC, 1978-80, Botein Hays et al, NYC, 1980-84; v.p., assoc. gen. counsel, asst. sec. GE Investment Corp., Stamford, Conn., 1984—2001; v.p., gen. counsel real estate GE Asset Mgmt. Inc., 2002—03, sr. cons., 2002—; CEO Oracle Investment Advisors, LLC, 2002—, Oracle Fin., LLC, 2004—; prin. Kokoro Japanese Art Advisors, 2007—. Cons. First Am. Title Ins. Co., 2002—05, Title Assoc., 2004—06; v.p. Internat. Netsuke Soc., 2007—, chair internat. connection, 2009, bd. dirs., 2005—, Holm & Drath, 2005—, spl. counsel, 2005—07; prin. Kokoro Japanese Art Advisors, 2007—; judge Internat. Moot Competition, 2009; judge grand semifinal Moot Ct. Competition, Pace Law Sch., 2009. Columnist: Jour. Internat. Netsuke Soc., 2002—, mem. editl. bd.:, 2005—; contbr. articles to profl. jours. in field. Bd. dirs. NY chpt. Juvenile Diabetes Found., NYC, 1981-89, vice chmn., 1981-88; mem. fin. com. Juvenile Diabetes Found. Internat., 1981-86; asst. prin. bassist Westchester Symphony Orch., Scarsdale, NY, 1982-2000, pres., 1982-87, chmn. bd., 1982-90, exec. mng. dir., 1990-93; vice chmn. ann. dinner NCCJ, 1987; bd. dirs. Parkinson's Disease Found., 1989-96, v.p., 1990-96, chmn. merger com., 1991-96; bd. dirs. Parkinson's Action Network, 1994-98; founding mem., trustee lay cantor Congregation Sulam Yaakov, 2005-07; trustee Jewish Cmty. Ctr. of Harrison, 1996-2003, mem. ritual com., 1996-2004, chmn., 2000-03, chmn. alt. svcs. com., lay cantor, 1997-2005, 2007—; chmn. county United Way Campaign, Fairfield, Conn., 1999, bd. dirs., gen. coun. Harrison Little League, 2001—, coach, 1989-2005; bd. dirs., v.p., gen. counsel Mariners Hockey, Inc., 2003-04, v.p. adminstrn., 2004-05, exec. mng. dir., 2005-07; mem. zoning bd. appeals, Village of Harrison, 2003—; mem. bd. dirs. NY Gilbert & Sullivan Players, 2006-, mem. exec. com., 2006—; chmn. strategic task force, 2006-07, chmn. bd. and exec. com. 2007—, troupe mem., performer 2007-; coach Babe Ruth League, 2006—08, WBA, 2006—08, Sr. Little League, 2006—08, All-Star Team Coach, 2007; commr. fall baseball, NY Dist. 20 Little League 2007-, Jr. League and Sr. League, Dist. 20; asst. dist. adminstr. NY Dist. 20 little League, 2008-; cons. Trouper's Light Opera Co., 2008-; judge ABA Law Sch. Nat. Client Counseling Competition, 2008. Recipient Gerald I. Phillippe Dist. Cmty. Svc. award, Juvenile Diabetes Found., 1994, Lifetime Achievement award, Juvenile Diabetes Rsch. Found. Internat., 2003. Mem. ABA (chmn. pension plan investments 1989-91, chmn. asset mgmt. 1992-94, 95-97, significant legis. coms. 1985-92, chmn. subcom. on joint ventures 1988-90), Am. Coll. Real Estate Lawyers (com. professionalism 1994—, vice chmn. 1999-2000), Nat. Assn. Real Estate Investment Mgrs. (sr. legal officers adv. com. 1993-2003, ann. forum chair 1997), Colby Coll. Alumni Coun. (nominating com. 1994-97), Fordham Law Alumni Assn., Internat. Netsuke Soc. (bd. dirs. 2005—, v.p. 2007—, chair 2009 internat. convention com.). Republican. Jewish. Avocations: political memorabilia, sports memorabilia, antiquarian books, baseball coaching, Japanese art. Home: 10 Genesee Trail Harrison NY 10528-1802 Office: PO Box 6 Harrison NY 10528-0006 Office Phone: 914-899-9000. Office Fax: 914-835-8111; Home Fax: 914-835-7111. Personal E-mail: michael@strone.com, hakutaku@aol.com. Business E-Mail: mstrone@oracleinvest.com, kokoro@japanart.us, kokoro@asianart.us.

STRONG, ANNSLEY CHAPMAN, interior designer, volunteer; b. Paterson, NJ, July 18, 1947; d. Donald John and Margaret Brawley Chapman; m. George Gordon Strong, Jr., Nov. 30, 1974; children: George Gordon III, Courtney Chapman Strong Thomas, Meredith Annsley, Alexis Palmer. BA, Wheaton Coll., Norton, Mass., 1969. Cert. N.Y. Sch. Design, 1969, Interior Designers Guild, 1975. Pres. Strong Studio Designs, La Canada, Calif., 1984—. Treas., commr. AYSO Region 13, Pasadena, Calif., 1993—97; mem. Bishop Stevens Found. Bd., Pasadena, Calif., 1994—; co-founder La Canada Sports Coalition, 1996; chmn. bd. Hathaway Sycamores, Pasadena, Calif., 2007—; past chair Verdugo Hills Hosp. Found., 2008—; bd. chair Verdugo Hills Hosp., Glendale, 2008—. Recipient 20th Century award, Pasadena YMCA, 1990, Bill Carroll Lifetime Achievement award, Am. Youth Soccer Orgn., 2000. Republican. Avocations: painting, piano, Bridge, skiing, golf. Office Phone: 818-957-0086.

STRONG, B. JEAN, writer, publisher; b. Marion, Iowa, July 19, 1925; d. Walter Benjamin and Thelma Iris (Oliver) S. BA in Journalism, U. Iowa, 1951. Editor, mgr. Center Point (Iowa) Weekly, 1949-50; feature writer, photographer The Gazette, Cedar Rapids, Iowa, 1951-54; reporter, rschr. Time Inc./Life and Fortune mags., NYC, 1954-62; freelance writer, pub. Cedar Rapids, 1962-71; assoc. editor books divsn. Farm Jour., Phila., 1971-72; instr. newswriting Temple U., Phila., 1973; project dir. U.S. Ho. of Reps., Washington, 1973-75; rschr., media mgr. Time-Life Books, Alexandria, Va., 1978-86; writer and pub. self-employed, Ark., 1990—. Editor, pub. ann. periodical Iowa Illus., 1964-66; author, editor, pub. A Prairie Almanac 1839-1919, 1996; Voices From the Mid South, 2002; author: The Marion Library, 2005; co-author; compiler Never Say Never, The Walter B. Strong Family, 2008, transpose book, 2005, 2008. Mem. ctr. com., precinct organizer Linn County Reps., Cedar Rapids, 1964-68; youth chair Linn County ARC, 1968-69; chmn. residence com. YWCA, Cedar Rapids, 1968. Recipient Outstanding Sr. Woman of Yr. award Mortar Board/Omicron Delta Kappa, 1949. Avocations: reading, writing, walking, photography. Home: 1478 Niagara St Springdale AR 72762-0431 Office Phone: 479-751-5886. Business E-Mail: papublisher@aol.com.

STRONG, DAVID A., JR., history professor; b. Mayfield, Ky., Oct. 30, 1946; s. David Alton and Valcalo Strong; m. Gara Lynn McCarthy; 1 child, Heidi Leigh El barky. EdD, Memphis State U., Tenn., 1989. Chief warrant officer 4 US Army, Dyersburg, Tenn., 1969—2006; prof. coll. prep. studies and history Dyersburg State CC, Tenn., 1979—. Command food advisor 230th Area Support Group, Dyersburg, 1995—2006. Advisor Alpha Epsilon Alpha Phi Theta Kappa, Dyersburg, 1995—2008. Mem.: Alpha Tau Omega. Office: Dyersburg State CC 1510 Lake Rd Dyersburg TN 38024 Business E-Mail: strong@dscc.edu.

STRONG, DOUGLAS L., health facility administrator; MA, U. Pa., MBA in Health Care Adminstrn. Various positions U. Pa. Sch. Medicine; assoc. dean planning and ops. St. Louis U. Sch. Medicine; assoc. dean adminstrn. and fin. sch. medicine State U. NY Stony Brook; assoc. dean Pritzker Sch. medicine and biol. scis. divsn. U. Chgo.; assoc. v.p. health system fin. and strategy U. Mich. Health Sys., 1998—, interim CFO, 2002—04, COO, 2004; interim CEO U. Mich. Hosps. and Health Ctrs., 2005—06, CEO, 2006—. Office: Univ Mich Health Sys 1500 E Med Ctr Dr Ann Arbor MI 48109*

STRONG, GARY EUGENE, university librarian; b. Moscow, Idaho, June 26, 1944; s. Authur Dwight and Cleora Anna (Nirk) S.; m. Carolyn Jean Roetker, Mar. 14, 1970; children: Christopher Eric, Jennifer Rebecca. BS in Edn., U. Idaho, 1966; AMLS, U. Mich., 1967. Adminstrv. and reference asst. U. Idaho, 1963-66; extension libr. Latah County Free Libr., Moscow, 1966; head libr. Markeley Residence Libr. U. Mich., 1966-67; libr. dir. Lake Oswego Pub. Libr., Oreg., 1967-73, Everett Public Libr., Wash., 1973-76; assoc. dir. services Wash. State Libr., Olympia, 1976-79, dep. state libr., 1979-80; state librarian Calif. State Libr., Sacramento, 1980-94; dir. Queens Borough Pub. Libr., Jamaica, NY, 1994—2003; dir. emeritus Calif. State Library Found., 1994—2003; univ. libr. UCLA, 2003—. Adj. prof. Queens Coll. Grad. Sch. of Libr. and Info. Scis., 2000-03; chief exec. Calif. Libr. Svcs. Bd., 1980-94; founder, bd. dirs. Calif. State Libr. Found., 1982-94, Calif. Literary Campaign, 1984-94, Calif. Rsch. Bur., 1992; bd. dirs. No. Regional Libr. Bd., 1983-94, Queens Libr. Found., 1994-2003; mem. adv. bd. Ctr. for the Book in Libr. of Congress, 1983-86; mem. nat. adv. com. Libr. of Congress, 1987-89; chmn. adv. bd. Calif. Libr. Constrn. and Renovation Bond Act Bd., 1989-94; vis. lectr. Marylhurst Coll., Oreg., 1968, Oreg. Divsn. Continuing Edn., 1972, San Jose State U. Sch. Libr. Svc., 1990; mem. N.Y. State Adv. Coun. Librs., 1996-97; mem. chancellor's task force ednl. tech. and librs. CUNY, 1996-97; convenor Archons of the Colophan, 1997-98; regents adv. coun. librs. N.Y. State, 1999-2003; mem. various coms., UCLA; lectr. and cons. in field. Host, producer: cable TV Signatures Program, 1974-76, nationwide videoconfs. on illiteracy, censorship, 1985; author: On Reading-in the Year of the Reader, 1987, U.S. Patriot's Act: Protecting Patron's Rights, 2002; editor Calif. State Library Found. Bull., 1982-94 (H.W. Wilson Periodical award 1988), Western Americana in the Calif. State Library, 1986, On Reading-In the Year of the Reader, 1987, Chinatown Photographer: Louis J. Stellman, 1989, Local History Genealogical Resources, 1990, Literate America Emerging, 1991; curator Queens Libr. Gallery, 1998; contbr. articles to profl. jours.; editor, designer and pub. of various books. Bd. dirs., v.p. Pacific N.W. Bibliog. Ctr., 1977-80; bd. dirs. Thurston Mason County Mental Health Ctr., 1977-80, pres., 1979-80; bd. dirs. Coop. Library Agy. for Sys. and Svcs., 1980-94, vice chmn., 1981-84; bd. dirs. Sr. Svcs. Snohomish County, 1973-76, HISPANEX (Calif. Spanish lang. database), 1983-86; bd. govs. Snohomish County Hist. Assn., 1974-76; mem. psychiat. task force St. Peters Hosp., Olympia, 1979-80; co-founder Calif. Ctr. for the Book, bd. dirs., 1987-94; mem. adv. bd. Calif. State PTA, 1981-86, Gov.'s Tech. Conf., 1993-94; mem. adv. com. Sch. Libr. Sci., UCLA, 1991-94, Sch. Libr. and Info. Studies, U. Calif., Berkeley, 1991-94, Libr. Sch. Queens Coll., 1996-2003, libr. sch. St. John's U., 1996-98; mem. Oreg. Coun. Pub. Broadcasting, 1969-73, Calif. Adult Edn. Steering Com., 1988-94, N.Y. State Adv. Coun. on Librs., 1996-97; chmn. collaborative coun. Calif. State Literacy Resource Ctr., 1993-94; bd. dirs. Queens coun. Boy Scouts Am., 1994-2003; v.p. 100 Yr. Assn. N.Y., 1996-2003; mem. Chancellor's Task Force on Ednl. Tech. and Librs., CUNY, 1996-97; participant N.Y. Pub. Libr. Conf. of World Libr. Leaders, 1996; trustee Flushing Cemetery Assn., 1998-2003; mem. com. on intellectual property rights and the engring. info. infrastructure Nat. Rsch. Coun., 1998-2000; chair organizing com. China-U.S. Libr. Conf., 2001, 05; mem. info. tech. planning bd. UCLA, 2003—, mem. privacy and data protection adv. bd., 2004—, mem. accreditation steering com. Western Assn. Schs. and Colls., 2005—06; mem. libr. adv. com., Calif. Rare Book Sch., 2003—; mem. adv. com. Libr. Sch., San Jose State U., 2006—. Oreg. Libr. scholar, 1966; recipient Disting. Alumnus award U. Mich., 1984, Disting. Svc. award, Calif. Literacy Inc., 1985, Spl. Achievement award, Literacy Action, 1988, Assn. Specialized and Coop. Libr. Agys. Exceptional Achievement award 1992, Gov.'s award of Achievement, Govt. Tech. Conf., 1994, Advancement of Literacy award, Pub. Libr. Assn., 1994, John Cotton Dana award, Libr. Adminstrn. and Mgmt. Assn., 1994, Charlie Robinson award, Pub. Libr. Assn., 2002; named Libr. of Yr., Calif. Assn. Libr. Trustees and Commrs., 1994, Disting. Svc. award, Chinese Am. Libr. Assn., 1996, 21st Century Libr. award, Syracuse U., 2002, Knowledge Trust Honors award for edn., 2006; named Bus. Person of Yr., Queens C. of C., 2002. Mem.: ALA (legis. com. 1980—82, commn. on freedom and equality of access to info. 1983—86, legis. com. 1995—97, chair intellectual property subcom. 1995—98, chmn. conf. librs. Beijing 1996, rep. Internat. Fedn. of Libr. Assn. nat. organizing com. 1996—2001, intellectual property com. 1998—2001, chair China U.S. planning com. for chair U.S. libr. coop. conf. 2001, Fedn. of Libr. Assn. UN rep. 2001—03, chair China U.S. planning com. for chair U.S. libr. coop. conf. 2003, IFLA governing bd. 2004—07, Humphrey award for Internat. Librarianship 2003), Rsch. Librs. Group (chmn. programs coun. 2006—), Oakshire Computer Libr. Ctr. (program coun. chair rsch. librs. group 2006—), The Digital Dilemma, Assn. of Coll. and Rsch. Libraries, Assn. Specialized and Coop. Libr. Agys., Western Coun. State Librs. (pres. 1989—91), Chief Officers of State Libr. Agys. (pres. 1984—86), Calif. Libr. Assn. (govt. rels.com. 1980—94), Pacific N.W. Libr. Assn. (hon. life mem., pres. 1978—79), Oreg. Libr. Assn. (hon. life mem., pres. 1970—71), Assn. of Rsch. Librs. (mem. task force on rsch. tchg. and learning 2005—, mem. task force spl. collections 2007—), Libr. Adminstrn. and Mgmt. Assn. (bd. dis. 1980—88, pres. 1984—85), Am. Printing History Assn., Metro (bd. dirs. 1994—2003, treas. 1996—99, 1st v.p. 1999—2001), Queens County C. of C. (bd. dirs. 1996—2003, named Bus. Person of Yr. 2002), Jamaica Devel. Corp., Everett Area C. of C. (bd. dirs. 1974—76), Zamorano Club, The Typophiles, Guild of Book Workers, Grolier Club, The Book Collectors Club of L.A., Roxburghe Club, Sacramento Book Collectors Club, Book Club of Calif. Office: UCLA Libr Box 951575 Los Angeles CA 90095-1575 Office Phone: 310-825-1201. Business E-Mail: gstrong@library.ucla.edu.

STRONG, GEORGE GORDON, JR., lawyer, management consultant; b. Toledo, Apr. 19, 1947; s. George Gordon and Jean Boyd (McDougall) S.; m. Annsley Palmer Chapman, Nov. 30, 1974; children: George III, Courtney, Meredith, Alexis. BA, Yale U., 1969; MBA, Harvard U., 1971; JD, U. San Diego, 1974. Bar: Calif. 1974, U.S. Dist. Ct. (cen. dist.) Calif. 1974; CPA, Calif., Hawaii, cert. mgmt. cons. Contr. Vitredent Corp., Beverly Hills, Calif., 1974-76; sr. mgr. Price Waterhouse, LA, 1976-82, ptnr., 1987—2001, mng. ptnr. west region dispute analysis and corp. recovery, 1993—99, mem. policy bd., bd. dirs., 1995-98, mem. combination bd., 1997-98; bd. ptnrs., prin. Pricewaterhouse Coopers LLP, LA, 1998-2001, mem. global oversight bd., 1998—2001; exec. v.p., COO Internat. Customs Service, Long Beach, Calif., 1982-84; CFO Uniform Software Systems, Santa Monica, Calif., 1984-85; exec. v.p., COO Cipherlink Corp., 1986; pres. Woodleigh Lane, Inc., Flintridge, Calif., 1985-87; mng. dir., gen. counsel sec. and bd. mem. Cornerstone Rsch., 2002—. Chmn. bd. dirs. LA SPCA; treas. Andover Abbot Alumni Assn. Southern Calif.; chmn. bd. trustees Harvard Bus. Sch. Assn. So. Calif. Scholarship Fund. Mem. ABA, AICPA, Calif. State Bar, Calif. Soc. CPAs, Andover Abbott Alumni So. Calif. (bd. dirs., treas.), Inst. Mgmt. Cons., Harvard Bus. Sch. Alumni Assn. (bd. dirs. 1996-99), Harvard Bus. Sch. Assn. So. Calif. (chmn. bd. trustees scholarship fund 1992—, pres. 1988-89, dir. 1996-99, 2001-03, 06—), Harvard Club NY, Harvard Club Boston, Yale Club NY, Lincoln Club, Calif. Club, Olympic Club, Jonathan Club, Annandale Golf Club, Coral Beach and Tennis Club, Mid Ocean Golf Club, Royal Bermuda Yacht Club, Valley Hunt Club, Tuckers Point Golf Club (Bermuda), Park Meadows Country Club. Republican. Presbyterian. Avocations: golf, tennis, bridge. Home: 5455 Castle Knoll Rd La Canada Flintridge CA 91011-1319 Office: Cornerstone Research 633 W Fifth St 31st Fl Los Angeles CA 90071-3509 Personal E-mail: gstrong@cornerstone.com.

STRONG, JOHN DAVID, insurance company executive; b. Cortland, NY, Apr. 12, 1936; s. Harold A. and Helen H. Strong; m. Carolyn Dimmick, Oct. 26, 1957; children: John David, Suzanne. BS, Syracuse U., 1957; postgrad., Columbia U., 1980. With Kemper Group, 1957-90, Kemper Corp., 1990-96, Empire sales divsn. mgr., 1972-74, Fed. Kemper Ins. Co., 1974—93; CEO, 1988—93; chmn. bd. Kemper Corp., 1989-93; vice chmn. Millikin Assocs., 1993-96, chmn., 1996; exec. v.p., dir. Facilitators, Inc., 1995-98. Mem. adv. coun. Sch. Bus., Millikin U., 1975-79, 84—; bd. dirs. United Way of Decatur and Macon County, Ill., 1976-83, campaign chmn., 1978-79, pres. bd. dirs., 1979-81; pres. United Way of Ill., 1981-83; bd. dirs. DMH Commn. Svcs. Corp., 1985-97, chmn., 1988-90; bd. dirs. Decatur-Macon County Econ. Devel. Found., 1983-88, DMH Health Systems, 1987-94, Richland C.C. Found., 1987-90, Symphony Orch. Guild of Decatur, 1992-96, DMH Found., 1988-97; bd. dirs. Ill. Ednl. Devel. Found., 1983-90, pres., 1986-87; bd. dirs. Decatur Meml. Hosp., 1985-94, vice chmn., 1988, chmn., 1990-92; bd. dirs. Ctrl. Ill. Health Assocs., Inc., 1994, vice chmn., 1994-96; mem. steering com. Decatur Advantage, 1981-93, pres., 1988-93. Capt. USAR, 1958-69. Mem. Metro Decatur C. of C. (bd. dirs. 1977-80, chmn. 1983-84), Decatur Club (bd. dirs. 19080-83, pres. 1983), Country Club of Decatur (bd. dirs. 1993-99, pres. bd. 1995-97), Union League Club Chgo., Anvil Club, Alpha Kappa Psi. Personal E-mail: jack@strongs.net.

STRONG, JOHN OLIVER, plastic surgeon, educator; b. Montclair, NJ, Feb. 1, 1930; s. George Joseph and Olivia (LeBrun) S.; m. Helen Louise Vrooman, July 19, 1958 (dec. Mar. 1973); m. Deborah Sperberg, May 20, 1978; children: John Jr., Jean LeB., Andrew D. BS, Yale U., 1952; MD, U. Pa., 1957. Cert. vol. paleontologist Calif. Practice medicine specializing in plastic and reconstructive surgery, Santa Ana, Calif., 1964-97; asst. clin. prof. plastic and reconstructive surgery U. Calif., Irvine, 1970—. Chief of staff Western Med. Ctr., Santa Ana, 1996-97, interim chmn. bd., 1996-97, bd. dirs.; bd. dirs. United Western Med. Ctrs., Healthcare Found. Orange County, chmn.; vol. Anza Borrego Desert State Pk., steering com., 1998-2003. Vol. Anza -Borrego Desert State Pk. Fellow ACS; mem. Calif. Med. Assn. (chmn. sci. adv.

panel 1983-89), Calif. Soc. Plastic Surgeons (pres. 1991-92). Republican. Office: PO Box 94 Borrego Springs CA 92004-0094 Address: 511 Seaward Rd Corona Del Mar CA 92625-2600

STRONG, JOHN SCOTT, finance educator; b. Phila., Aug. 28, 1956; s. John S. and Thelma J. (Willard) S. BS, Washington & Lee U., 1978; M of Pub. Policy, Harvard U., 1981, PhD in Bus. Econs., 1986. Rsch. fellow Harvard U., Cambridge, Mass., 1983-85, 89-90, 93, vis. asst. prof. econs., 1989-90; prof. fin. Coll. William and Mary, Williamsburg, Va., 1985—. Cons. on econs. and fin. Republic of Indonesia, 1987-99, MITI, Japan, 1988-89, European Bank for Reconstruction and Devel., 1993-95, Govt. of Bolivia, 1994, Govt. of Russia, 1996, Govts. of Brazil, Argentina and Uruguay, 1997, Govt. of Peru, 1998, World Bank, 1997—, Inter-Am. Devel. Bank, 2002—, U.S. Dept. Transp., 1999-02. Author: Why Airplanes Crash: Aviation Safety in a Changing World, 1992, Moving to Market: Restructuring Transport in the Former Soviet Union, 1996, Managing the Skies, 2008; co-author 2 books on airline deregulation; contbr. articles to profl. jours. Fulbright scholar, 1978-79; grad. fellow NSF, 1979-82. Business E-Mail: john.strong@business.wm.edu.

STRONG, JOHN WILLIAM, lawyer, educator; b. Iowa City, Aug. 18, 1935; s. Frank Ransom and Gertrude Elizabeth (Way) S.; m. Margaret Waite Cleary, June 16, 1962; children— Frank Ransom, Benjamin Waite. BA, Yale U., 1957; JD, U. Ill., 1962; postgrad, U. N.C., 1966-67. Bar: Ill. 1963, Oreg. 1976. Assoc. firm LeForgee, Samuels, Miller, Schroeder & Jackson, Decatur, Ill., 1963-64; asst. prof. law U. Kans., 1964-66; assoc. prof. Duke U., 1966-69; prof. U. Oreg., 1969-75; legal counsel Oreg. Task Force on Med. Malpractice, 1976; prof. U. Nebr., 1977-84, dean, 1977-82, vice chancellor for acad. affairs, 1981-84; Rosenstiel Disting. prof. law U. Ariz., 1984-98, prof. emeritus, 1998—. Nat. sec.-treas. Order of the Coif, 1992-98; cons. Nat. Judicial Coll. Author: (with others) Handbook on Evidence, 5th edit., 1999. Served with U.S. Army, 1957-59. Mem. Ill. Bar Assn., Oreg. Bar Assn., ABA, Am. Law Inst., Phi Delta Phi. Independent. Congregationalist. Office: U Ariz Coll Law Tucson AZ 85721-0001 Home: PO Box 8063 Black Butte Ranch OR 97759 Business E-Mail: strong@law.arizona.edu.

STRONG, JUDITH ANN, retired chemist; b. June 19, 1941; d. Philip Furnald and Hilda Bernice (Hulbert) S. BS cum laude, SUNY, Albany, 1963; MA, Brandeis U., 1966, PhD, 1970. Asst. prof. chemistry Moorhead State U., Minn., 1969—73, assoc. prof., 1973—81, prof., 1981—, chmn. chemistry dept., 1984—86, dean social and natural scis., 1986—97, assoc. v.p. acad. affairs, 1997—2008; ret., 2008. Recipient Gov.'s Acts of Kindness Vol. award, 1997; fellow, NSF, 1965—67. Mem.: Minn. Acad. Sci., Assn. Women in Sci., Am. Chem. Soc., Soroptimist Internat. (gov. North Ctrl. region 2002—04, program coun. 2004—08, bd. dirs. 2008—), Sigma Xi. Home: 1209 12th St S Moorhead MN 56560-3707 E-mail: strong@mnstate.edu.

STRONG, MARCELLA LEE, music specialist, educator; b. East Liverpool, Ohio, Oct. 16, 1954; d. Carl and Ruth I. (White) Hinkle; m. David Lee Strong, Feb 19, 1977. BA magna cum laude, U. Toledo, 1976; MA in Early Childhood Edn., Kent State U., 1982. Cert. music, elem. tchr., Ohio. Music instr. Cardinal Local Schs., Parkman and Huntsburg, Ohio, 1977—. Choir dir. G.V. Nazarene Ch., Orwell, Ohio 1981-83; organist, mem. bd. deacons and stewardship com., sr. choir, jr. choir and ch. band dir. Huntsburg Congl. Ch., 1985—; mem., officer Orwell Farm Bur.; band dir. Kent State U. Coll. for Kids, 1995—. Mem. Cardinal Edn. Assn. (negotiator 1982, 84, 87, 90, 93, 96, 99, 2002, sec. 1983-84, treas. 1984-85, pres. 1985-86, 89-91, 1997-2002), Ohio Music Educators Assn., Kappa Delta Pi, Mu Phi Epsilon, Delta Kappa Gamma. Democrat. Avocations: spectator sports, travel, reading, chess, member international trivia team. Home: PO Box 370 78 Chaffee Dr Orwell OH 44076-0370 E-mail: dlsmls@yahoo.com.

STRONG, MARK TUTHILL, botanist; b. Washington, Feb. 20, 1954; s. Benjamin Booth and Dorothy Elizabeth (Reeks) S.; m. Carol Lynn Kelloff, Aug. 25, 1990; 1 child, Jennifer Lee. BA, George Mason U., 1985, MS, 1992, PhD in Environ. Sci., 2004. Rsch. asst. George Mason U., Fairfax, Va., 1981-90; field botanist Nature Conservancy, Arlington, Va., 1986-87; rsch. specialist U.S. Fish & Wildlife Svc., Arlington, 1987; field botanist Fairfax Planning Commn., 1988; mus. specialist, botany Smithsonian Instn., Washington, 1988—. Environ. cons., Bio-Hunters, Fairfax, 1981-88. Contbr. articles on Cyperaceae to profl. jours.; coord. Cyperaceae for Flora of the Guianas. Mem. So. Appalachian Bot. Soc. Achievements include discovery and documentation of rare species of plants in Virginia and Florida; description and classification of new species of Cyperaceae in the Neotropics. Office: Smithsonian Instn Dept Botany MRC 166 PO Box 37012 Washington DC 20013-7012 Home Phone: 703-644-1924; Office Phone: 202-633-0966. Business E-Mail: strongm@si.edu.

STRONG, PAMELA KAY, material and process engineer; b. Mesa, Ariz., Oct. 17, 1950; d. Wayland Thorton and Adele (Gaumer) S. BS in Organic Chemistry, Phila. Coll. Pharmacy and Sci., 1972; MS in Organic Chemistry, Bryn Mawr Coll., 1974. Cons. formulation, rsch. chemist Western Indsl. Enterprises, Phoenix, 1974-75; analytical chemist Henkel Corp., Hawthorne, Calif., 1975-80; mem. tech. staff, process engr. Radar div. Hughes Aircraft, El Segundo, Calif., 1980-83; sr. process engr. Irvine Sensors Corp., Costa Mesa, Calif., 1983; sr. advanced composite and composite quality engr. Aircraft Engine Bus. Group, GE, Albuquerque, 1983-85; Mantech engring. specialist sr., sr. quality assurance engr. Advanced Systems div. Northrop Corp., Pico Rivera, Calif., 1985-87; material and process engring. tech. specialist, lead engr. McDonnell Douglas Missile and Space Systems Co., Huntington Beach, Calif., 1987—97; assoc. tech. fellow, prin. engr., scientist Boeing Co. (merged with McDonnell Douglas), 1997—2007; sr. engring. specialist for systems engring. divsn. Aerospace Corp., LA, 2007—. Recipient GE Mfg. Tech. Excellence award, 1984, Boeing Performance award, 2002, Boeing Chief Tech Officer Profl. Excellence award, 2004, J. Cordell Breed Women's Leadership award, Soc. Automotive Engrs., 2005; Bryn Mawr Coll. scholar; NSF rsch. fellow, 1971. Fellow Am. Inst. Chemists, Royal Australian Tech. Inst., Soc. Advancement Materials and Process Engrs. (treas. 1984-85), Soc. Women Engrs. (life, Achievement award 2007); mem. AAAS, Am. Chem. Soc. (Petroleum Rsch. fellow 1971, Scholastic award 1972), Soc. Applied Spectroscopy (chairperson 1977-79, sec. 1979-81), Soc. Women Chemists, NAFE, Iota Sigma Pi. Office: Aerospace Corp PO Box 92957 Los Angeles CA 90009-2957

STRONG, VIRGINIA WILKERSON, freelance writer, former special education educator; b. Vernal, Utah, Mar. 19, 1935; d. Arbun C. and Mildred (Wyman) Wilkerson; m. David Smith, Oct. 6, 1950 (div. Jan. 1960); children: Anna Smith Blyton, Dorothy Smith Wolf, Wendell Lee Smith, Ava Smith Eatman, Karen Smith Ritter; m. Lawrence D. Strong, June 1961 (div. May 1973); children: Lawrence D. Jr., Jeffrey A. BA, U. Miss., 1970, MEd, 1972; PhD, Ohio U., 1985; cert. film, TV, and digital entertainment media, UCLA, 2006. Cert. elem. edn. tchr., spl. edn. K-12 tchr., ednl. adminstrn., 1991; cert screenwriter, UCLA, 1995. Rsch. asst. U. Miss., University, 1968-70, Utah State U., Logan, 1974-78; tchr. spl. edn. various schs., nr. Oxford, Miss., 1969-74; instr. spl. edn., project coord., rsch. asst. Ohio U., Athens, 1978-82; supr. spl. edn. Meigs County Bd. Edn., Pomeroy, Ohio, 1982-84; tchr. spl. edn., dept. chmn. L.A. Unified Sch. Dist., 1986-93, co-faciliator alcohol drug abuse, 1990-93; freelance writer, owner, mgr. Fenix Devel., Henderson, Calif., 1990—. Early childhood adv. Utah Bd. Edn., Salt Lake City, 1976, evaluator edn. programs, Salt Lake City and Logan, 1976-77; curriclum developer Meigs County, 1982-84; dir. gifted edn. workshop Ohio U., 1980; acting dir. edn., cons. North Miss. Retardation Ctr., Oxford, 1993-94; creative cons. student film Patience UCLA, 2005. Author: The Role of the Special Education Supervisor, 1985, (scene in dir. cinematographer edit.) Big, (screenplays) To See the Elephant, Dark Encounters; contbr. articles to newspapers. Elector Dem. Party, Logan, 1976; religious instr. LDS Ch., various locations, 1953-97. U.S. Dept. Edn. grantee Utah State U., 1976. Mem. ASCD, Kappa Delta Pi, Phi Delta Kappa. Avocations: genealogy, gemology, photography, history buff, travel.

STRONG, WENDI ELLEN, insurance company executive; BA in Psychology, U. North Tex., Denton, MA in Journalism. With Halt & Assocs., Dallas, Hill & Knowlton; dir. pub. rels. and advt. Rosewood Hotels and Resorts; dir. corp. comm. Kimberly-Clark Corp.; v.p. strategic comm. Assocs. First Capital Corp.; with USAA (United Svcs. Automobile Assn.), 2000—, v.p. corp. comm., sr. v.p. comm. programs, 2001, exec. v.p. corp. comm. Office: USAA 9800 Fredericksburg Rd San Antonio TX 78288 Office Phone: 210-498-8222. E-mail: wendi.strong@usaa.com.

STRONG-CUEVAS, ELIZABETH, sculptor; b. St. Germain en Laye, France, Jan. 22, 1929; Am. citizen; d. George and Margaret (Strong) de Cuevas; 1 child, Deborah Carmichael. BA, Vassar Coll., Poughkeepsie, NY, 1952. Instr. Arts Students' League, NYC; student John Hovannes. One-woman shows include Lee Ault Gallery, NYC, 1977-78, Tower Gallery, Southampton, NY, 1980, Iolas-Jackson Gallery, NYC, 1983, 85, Guild Hall Mus., East Hampton, NY, 1985, Benton Gallery, Southampton, NY, 1987, Kerr Gallery, NYC, 1988, Grounds for Sculpture, Hamilton, NJ, 1999, Island Weiss Gallery, NYC, 2004-05, 07, Vassar Coll., Poughkeepsie, NY, 2006, Island Weiss Gallery, NYC, 2007-08, Art 20 & Modernism, Pk. Ave. Armory, Island Weiss Gallery, 2008-, Works on Paper Pk. Ave. Armory, Island Weiss Gallery, 2009-; group shows include Guild Hall, East Hampton, 1980, 84, 98, Art Students League of NY, 1982, Bruce Mus., Greenwich, Conn., 1984, 85, Tower Gallery, NYC, 1984, Kouros Gallery, Ridgefield, Conn., 1985, Andre Zarre Gallery, NYC, 1985, Susan Blanchard Gallery, NYC, 1986, Ruth Vered Gallery, East Hampton, 1986-88, Benton Gallery, Southampton, 1987, 1990, Benson Gallery, Bridgehampton, NY, 1989, 99, Koln Art Fair, Germany, 1989, 1991, Feingarten Galleries, NYC, 1990, Marisa del Re Biennale III, 1993, IV, 1994, Parrish Mus., Southampton, 1994, Grounds for Sculpture, Hamilton, NJ, 1994-96, Shidoni, Tesuque, N.Mex., 1995-98, Barnard-Biderman Fine Art, Southampton, 1997, The Tolman Collection, Singapore, 1997-98, Earl McGrath Gallery, 1998, Bulgari, NY, 2000, Grounds for Sculpture, Hamilton, 2000, 02, Russian Am. Cultural Ctr., 2001, Clark Fine Art, Southampton, 2001, 2003, The Ross Sch., East Hampton, 2003, Island Weiss Gallery, NYU, 2004-08, Kouros Gallery, NYC, 2003, UBS Bank Gallery, 200F5, Ann Norton Sculpture Gardens, West Palm Beach, Fla., 2006, Island Weiss Gallery, NYC, 2008; represented in pvt. collections at Bruce Mus., Greenwich, Conn., Grounds for Sculpture, Hamilton, NJ Guild Hall Mus., Heckscher Mus., Huntington, Ann Norton Sculpture Garden, West Palm Beach, Fla., NY, East Hampton Garden, East Hampton, 1982, Park Ave. Ter., NY, 1997. Recipient First prize, Guild Hall, NY, 1985. Mem. Vassar Club (NY), Century Club Avocation: yoga. Personal E-mail: strongworks@sc-sculpture.com.

STRONGIN, JONATHAN DAVID, physician; b. Kingston, NY, June 19, 1951; s. Jack and Thelma (Kaufman) S.; m. Ellen Wells Seely, June 11, 1983; children: Jessica, Matthew. BA, Columbia Coll., 1973; PhD, MD, Columbia U., 1982. Diplomate Am. Bd. Internal Medicine, Am. Bd. Pulmonary Disease, Am. Bd. Critical Care Medicine. Intern, resident Cambridge (Mass.) Hosp., 1982-84; med. resident Beth Israel Hosp., Boston, 1984-85; pulmonary fellow Mass. Gen. Hosp., Boston, 1985-97; physician Pulmonary Assocs. of Greater Boston, 1994—96. Pres. med. staff Whidden Meml. Hosp., Everett, Mass., 1995-97; trustee Melrose Wakefield Health Care Corp., 1996-98; med. dir. respiratory care, pres. med. staff Cambridge Health Alliance. Fulbright scholar, 1976-77. Fellow Am. Coll. Physicians, Am. Coll. Chest Physicians. Avocation: running.

STRONG-TIDMAN, VIRGINIA ADELE, marketing professional; b. July 26, 1947; d. Alan Ballentine and Virginia Leona (Harris) Strong; m. John Fletcher Tidman, Sept. 23, 1978. BS, Albright Coll., Reading, Pa., 1969; postgrad., U. Pitts., 1970-73, U. Louisville, 1975-76. Exec. trainee Pomeroy's divsn. Allied Stores, Reading, 1969-70; mktg. rsch. analyst Heinz U.S.A., Pitts., 1970-74; new products mktg. mgr. Ky. Fried Chicken, Louisville, 1974-76; dir. Pitts. office M/A/R/C, 1976-79; assoc. rsch. dir. Henderson Advt., Inc., Greenville, SC, 1979-81; sr. v.p., dir. rsch. Bozell, Jacobs, Kenyon & Eckhardt, Inc., Dallas, 1981-86, sr. v.p., dir. rsch. and strategic planning Atlanta, 1986-88; sr. v.p., dir. mktg. svcs. Bozell, Inc., Atlanta, 1988-91; sr. v.p., mng. ptnr. Henderson Adv., Inc., 1991-95; prin. Ender-Ptnr., Inc., 1995-96; v.p. mktg. Booth Rsch. Svcs., Inc., 1996-98; COO Moore & Symons, Inc., 1998—2009; ret., 2009. Cons. mktg. rsch. Greenville Zool. Soc., 1981; adj. prof. So. Meth. U., 1984-85. Mem. Am. Mktg. Assn. (Effie award N.Y. chpt. 1982). Republican. Episcopalian. Home: 146 Northshores Dr Seneca SC 29672

STRONGWATER, ALLAN, orthopedist, director; children: Julie, David. MD, Rush U. Sch. Medicine, Chgo., 1978. Cert. Am. Bd. Orthop. Surgery, 1985. Chmn. orthoap. surgery and musculoskeletal svcs. Maimonides Med. Ctr., Bklyn., 1995—2006; dir. neuromuscular svc. NYU Hosp. Joint Diseases, NYC, 2006—; chief pediat. orthop. surgery St. Joseph's Children's Hosp., 2009—. Pres. Custom Computing Concepts, NYC, 1985. Contbr. scientific papers to med. pubs. Fellow: Pediatric Orthop. Soc. N.Am., Am. Acad. Orthop. Surgery. Achievements include design of medical management software. Office: NYU Hos Joint Diseases 301 E 17th St New York NY 10003 Office Phone: 973-754-2414.

STROOCK, DANIEL WYLER, mathematician, educator; b. NYC, Mar. 20, 1940; s. Alan Maxwell and Katherine (Wyler) S.; m. Lucy Barber, Nov. 21, 1962; children: Benjamin, Abraham. AB, Harvard Coll., 1962; PhD, Rockefeller U., 1966. Vis. mem. Courant Inst., N.Y. U., 1966-69, asst. prof., 1969-72; assoc. prof. math. U. Colo., Boulder, 1972-75, prof., 1975-84, chmn. dept. math, 1979-81; prof. math. MIT, Cambridge, Mass., 1984—, Simons prof., 2003—07; hon. fellow Swansea U., Wales, 2007—. Adj. prof. U. Colo., Beijing Normal U. Author: (with S.R.S. Vanadhan) Multidimensional Diffusion Processes, 1979, (with J.D. Deutschel) Large Deviations, 1989, Probability Theory, An Analytic View, 1993, An Introduction to the Analysis of Paths on a Rieman Manfold, 1999, Markov Processes from K. Ito's Perspective, 2003; editor Math. Zeitschrift, 1992-2000, Ill. Jour. Math., 1976-82, Transactions of Am. Math. Soc., 1974-80, Annals of Probability, 1988-93, Advances in Math., 1995—, Jour. Functional Analysis, 1994—; contbr. articles on probability theory to profl. jours. Guggenheim fellow, 1978-79 Mem. Am. Acad. Arts and Scis., Nat. Acad. Scis., Polish Acad. Arts & Scis. (fgn. mem.). Democrat. Jewish. Home: 55 Frost St Cambridge MA 02140-2247 Office: MIT Dept Math Cambridge MA 02139

STROOCK, MARK EDWIN, II, public relations company executive; b. NYC, Nov. 6, 1922; s. Irving Sylvan and Blanche (Loeb) S.; m. Hanna Marks Eiseman, June 24, 1945 (dec. May 2003); children— Mark E., Carolyn E. BA, Bard Coll., 1947. Reporter The New York Journal of Commerce, 1947-50; writer Barrons, NYC, 1950-51; mng. editor Fairchild Publ., NYC, 1952-53; bus. editor World Mag., NYC, 1953-54; contbg. editor Time Mag., NYC, 1954-56; with Young & Rubicam Inc., NYC, 1956-87, sr. v.p., dir. corp. rels., cons., 1987—. Bd. trustee N.Y. Urban League, 1971-78, Alvin Ailey Dance Theatre, N.Y.C., 1977-84, Friends of the Theatre Mus. City N.Y., 1977-85, Arts Horizons, N.Y.C., 1998—; vice-chmn. Covenant House, N.Y.C., 1978-90; exec. com., mktg. and communications com., assoc. nat. commr. Anti-Defamation League, 1992—. With U.S. Army, 1943-46. Democrat. Jewish. Home: 50 Park Ave Apt 11B New York NY 10016-3075 Office: Young & Rubicam Inc 285 Madison Ave New York NY 10017-6486

STROOCK, THOMAS FRANK, oil and gas company executive; b. NYC, Oct. 10, 1925; s. Samuel and Dorothy (Frank) S.; m. Marta Freyre de Andrade, June 19, 1949; children: Margaret, Sandra, Elizabeth, Anne. BA in Econs., Yale U., 1948; LLB (hon.), U. Wyo., 1995; PhD (hon.), Universidad del Valle, Guatemala, 2001. Landman Stanolind Oil & Gas Co., Tulsa, 1948-52; pres. Stroock Leasing Corp., Casper, Wyo., 1952-89, Alpha Exploration, Inc., 1980-89; ptnr. Stroock, Rogers & Dymond, Casper, 1960-82; dir. First Wyo. Bank, Casper, 1967-89; mem. Wyo. Senate, 1969-89, chmn. appropriations com., 1983-89, co-chmn. joint appropriations com., 1983-89, mem. mgmt. and audit com., pres., 1988-89; mem. steering com. Edn. Commn. of States; amb. to Guatemala Govt. of U.S., 1989-93; pres. Alpha Devel. Corp., 1992—; prof. pub. diplomacy U. Wyo., Laramie, 1993—2002, chmn. internat. adv. bd., 2001—. Dir. Wyo. Med. Ctr., 1996-2004. Rep. precinct committeeman, 1960-68; pres. Natrona County Sch. Bd., 1966, 69; pres. Wyo. State Sch. Bds. Assn., 1965-66; chmn. Casper Cmty. Recreation, 1955-60; chmn. Natrona County United Fund, 1963-64, Wyo. State Rep. Com., 1975-78, exec. com. 1954-60; del. Rep. Nat. Conv., 1956-76, 92; regional coord. campaign George Bush for pres., 1979-80, 87-88; chmn. Western States Rep. Chmn. Assn., 1977-78; chmn. Wyo. Higher Edn. Commn., 1969-71, Wyo. Health Access Task Force, 2003-04; mem. Nat. Petroleum Coun., 1972-77; chmn. trustees Sierra Madre Found. for Geol. Rsch., New Haven; chmn. Wyo. Nat. Gas Pipline Authority, 1987-88; bd. dirs. Ucross Found., Denver; mem. Nat. Pub. Lands Adv. Coun., 1981-85; trustee Nature Conservancy, 1993-2005; chmn. Wyo. Health Reform Commn., 1993-95, Universidad del Valle Found., Guatemala City, 1995-2000, trustee, 2000-2005. Sgt. USMC, 1943-46. Mem. Rocky Mountain Oil and Gas Assn., Petroleum Assn. Wyo., Kiwanis, Casper Country Club, Casper Petroleum Club, Yale Club N.Y. Republican. Unitarian Universalist. Home and Office: PO Box 2875 Casper WY 82602-2875 Office Phone: 307-234-8925.

STROPKI, JOHN M., JR., electric power industry executive; BS indsl. engring., Purdue Univ.; MBA, Ind. Univ. Sales trainee Lincoln Electric Holdings, 1972, dist. mgr., nat. sales mgr., 1992—94, exec. vice-pres., 1996, dir., 1998—, COO, 2003—04, CEO, 2003—04, chmn., pres., CEO, 2004—. Bd. dirs. The Sherwin-Williams Co., 2009—. Mem. Am. Lung Assn.; Juvenile Diabetes Research Found.; mem. bd. Greater Cleveland Growth Assn., Great Lakes Sci. Ctr. Mem.: Nat. Electrical Manufacturers Assn. (mem. bd. gov.), Gas & Welding Distbr. Assn., Manufacturers Alliance/MAPI (pres. coun.), Am. Welding Soc. (hon.). Office: Lincoln Electric Holdings 22801 St Clair Ave Cleveland OH 44117 Office Phone: 216-481-8100. Office Fax: 216-486-1751.*

STROSAKER, ROBYN HEATHER, pediatrician, educator; b. Oct. 28, 1973; MD, Case Western Reserve U., 2000. Cert. Am. Bd. Pediat., 2003. Resident in pediat. U. Hospitals Cleve., 2003—04, chief resident in pediat.; asst. prof. gen. acad. pediat. Case Western Reserve U., Cleve.; pediatrician Rainbow Babies & Children's Hosp., Cleve. Office: UH Rainbow Babies & Childrens Hosp 11100 Euclid Ave Cleveland OH 44106 Office Phone: 216-844-8260, 216-844-8716. Office Fax: 216-844-8444. Business E-Mail: robyn.breen@case.edu.

STROSCIO, MICHAEL ANTHONY, physicist, researcher; b. Winston-Salem, NC, June 1, 1949; s. Anthony and Norma Lee (Sidbury) S.; m. Mitra Dutta; children: Elizabeth de Clare, Charles Marshall Sidbury, Gautam Dutta. BS, U. N.C., 1970; MPhil in Physics, Yale U., 1972, PhD in Physics, 1974. Physicist Los Alamos Sci. Lab., N.Mex., 1975-78; sr. staff mem. Johns Hopkins U. Applied Physics Lab., Laurel, Md., 1978-80; prof. mgr. for electromagnetic research Air Force Office of Sci. Research, Washington, 1980-83; spl. asst. to research dir. Office of Under Sec. Def., Washington, 1982-83; policy analyst White House Office of Sci. and Tech. Policy, Washington, 1983-85; prof. dir. for microelectrons, prin. scientist U.S. Army Research Office, Research Triangle Park, NC, 1985—2001; adj. prof. depts. physics and elec. and computer engring. N.C. State U., Raleigh, 1985—; Richard and Loan Hill prof. depts. bioengring., elec. and computer engring., physics U. Ill., Chgo., 2001—, dir. grad. studies, 2002—04. Adj. prof. depts. elec. engring. and physics Duke U., Durham, 1986-2005, dept. physics U. Ill., Chgo., 2002—; vis. prof. dept. elec. engring. U. Va., Charlottesville, 1990-95, U. Md., College Park, 1996-97; mem. congrl. coun. Duke U. Chapel, 1989-91; lectr. UCLA, 1987, U. Mich., 1988; cons. U.S. Dept. Energy, Washington, 1985-90; vice-chmn. White House Panel on Sci. Comm., Washington, 1983-84; chmn. Dept. Def. Rsch. Instrumentation Com., Washington, 1982; assoc. mem. Adv. Group on Electron Devices, 1985-91, liaison Nat. Laser Users Facility, Rochester, N.Y., 1984; liaison Panel on Sci. Comm. and Nat. Security, NAS, 1982, Panel on Materials for High-Density Electron Packaging, 1987-90; U.S. Army liaison to JASON, 1991-2001; mem. U.S. Govt. coord. com. on Semicondr. Rsch. Corp., 1992-2001, Nat. Rsch. Coun. Bd. on Army Sci. and Tech., 2008-; reviewer Irish Sci. Found. Author: Positronium: A Review of the Theory, 1975, Onslow Families, 1977, Quantum Heterostructures: Microelectronics and Optoelectronics, 1999, Phonons in Nanostructures, 2001, Biological Nanostructures and Applications of Nanostructures in Biology, 2004, Introduction to Nanoelectronics, 2007; editor: Quantum-Based Electronic Devices and Systems, 1998, Advanced Semiconductor Lasers and Applications to Optoelectronics, 2000, Advanced Semiconductor Heterostructures, 2003; reviewer: Army Rsch. Office, US Dept. Energy, NSF, Office of Naval Rsch., Dept. Commerce and the Natural Scis., Engring. Rsch. Coun. Can., 1981—, Irish Sci. Found., 2003, referee jours., —; contbr. articles to profl. jours. Capt. USAF, 1974-75. Grantee Los Alamos Sci. Lab., 1977, Air Force Office Sci. Rsch., 2002—, Army Rsch. Office, 2003—, Def. Advanced Rsch. Projects Agy., 2002—, Dept. Homeland Security, Def. Threat Reduction Agy., NSF, SRC, 2004-06. Fellow AAAS, APS, IEEE (exec. com. for plasma sci. 1983—, Harry Diamond Meml. award 1998), Yale Sci. and Engring. Assn. (exec. bd. dirs. 1983—), Editorial Bd. of Proceedings of IEEE, 2008; mem. Nat. Geneal. Soc., Phi Beta Kappa, Nat. Rsch. Coun. Bd. on Army Sci. Tech, 2008-. Achievements include patents in field. Home:

2045 Central Ave Wilmette IL 60091-2383 Office: U Ill Dept Elec and Computer Engring MC154 851 S Morgan St Chicago IL 60607 Home Phone: 847-920-1479; Office Phone: 312-413-5968. Business E-Mail: stroscio@uic.edu, m.stroscio@gte.net.

STROSS, CYNTHIA, lawyer; b. Seattle, May 7, 1967; BA magna cum laude, Kenyon Coll., 1999; JD cum laude, phi beta kappa, Cornell Univ., 1994. Bar: Wash. 1994. Assoc. atty., litig., alternative dispute resolution Savitt & Bruce, LLP, Seattle. Recipient Wash. Rising Star, SuperLawyer Mag., 2005; named, 2006. Mem.: ABA, Wash. Bar Assn. Office: Savitt & Bruce LLP Puget Sound Plz Ste 1410 1325 Fourth Ave Seattle WA 98101

STROTE, JOEL RICHARD, lawyer; b. NYC, Apr. 19, 1939; s. Jack and Fortuna (Benezra) S.; children: Jared, Noah, Sebastian; m. Elisa Ballestas, Dec. 14, 1991. BA, U. Mich., 1960; JD, Northwestern U., 1963. Bar: N.Y. 1964, D.C. 1965, Calif. 1967, U.S. Dist. Ct. (cen. dist.) Calif. 1967, U.S. Supreme Ct. 1971, Nev., 2003. Assoc. Damman, Blank, Hirsh & Heming, NYC, 1964-65, ICC, Washington, 1965-66, Capitol Records, Hollywood, Calif., 1966-67; ptnr. Strote & Whitehouse, Beverly Hills, Calif., 1967-89; of counsel Selvin, Weiner & Ruben, Beverly Hills, Calif., 1989-94; ptnr. with Cohen, Strote & Young, 1992-94; sole practice law, 1994—. Judge pro tem L.A. County Mcpl. Ct., 1973—; probation monitor Calif. State Bar Ct., L.A., 1985-2005; pres., Wheda Found., Las Vegas, Nev., 1987-2005; bd. chmn. Tuesday's Child, L.A., 1989-91. Mem. Thousand Oaks Arts Commn., 1997-99. Cpl. USMC, 1963-64. Mem. Calif. State Bar Assn., L.A. County Bar Assn., L.A. Copyright Soc., Beverly Hills Bar Assn., Assn. Internat. Entertainment Lawyers, Internat. Fedn. of Festival Orgns. Democrat. Jewish. Avocations: swimming, bicycling, hiking, opera, travel. Office: 200 N Westlake Blvd Ste 204 Westlake Village CA 91392 Home Phone: 818-259-2939; Office Phone: 818-707-1923. Personal E-mail: joelstrote@verizon.net.

STROTHER, ALLEN, biochemical pharmacologist, researcher; b. Nolan County, Tex., Feb. 20, 1928; s. Henry Allen and Minnie Etta (Taylor) S.; m. Julia Ann Gutch, Feb. 7, 1957; children: Wesley Allen, Lori Ann. BS, Tex. Tech U., 1955; MS, U. Calif., 1957; PhD, Tex. A&M U., 1963. Rsch. asst. Tex. A&M, Coll. Sta., 1959-63; rsch. biochemist FDA, Washington, 1963-65; asst. prof. pharmacology Loma Linda (Calif.) U., 1965-70, assoc. prof., 1970-75, prof., 1975-95, retired, vol. faculty, 1995—, prof. emeritus Physiology and Pharmacology, 1997—. Cons. WHO, Geneva, 1982-86. Contbr. numerous articles to profl. jours.; chpt. to WHO Bull. Pilot CAP/USAF Search and Rescue San Bernardino, Calif., 1967-95; pilot examiner CAP Air Force Aux., Norton AFB, 1970-86. Named Investigator of Yr. Walter E. McPherson Soc., Loma Linda U., 1984, Basic Sci. Fellow of Yr., 1986, Outstanding Faculty Rschr. of Yr. award, 1997. Mem. Am. Soc. Pharmacology and Exptl. Therapeutics, Am. Chem. Soc., Xzenobiotic Soc. Avocations: flying, golf. Home: 74448 Nevada Cir E Palm Desert CA 92260-2269 Office: Loma Linda U Sch Medicine Dept Physiology and Pharmacology Loma Linda CA 92354

STROTHER, JAMES M., lawyer; b. 1951; BA, JD, Univ. Minn. Pvt. practice, Mpls.; asst. gen. counsel Norwest Corp. (now Wells Fargo Home Mortgage), 1986—98; gen. counsel Wells Fargo Home Mortgage, 1998—2001; dep. gen. counsel Wells Fargo & Co., San Francisco, 2001—03, exec. v.p., gen. counsel, 2004—. Office: Wells Fargo Retechs 333 Market St Fl 3 San Francisco CA 94105-2104*

STROTHER, JUDITH DIANNE BANKS, linguistics educator; b. Corpus Christi, Tex., Dec. 5, 1945; d. William Bailey and Thelma Elizabeth (Aull) Banks; m. Edwin Folk Strother, June 15, 1968. BS, U. S.C., 1968; MBA, Fla. Inst. Tech., 1976; MA, Antioch Internat. U., 1985. Sec., research asst. U. S.C., Columbia, 1964-68, supr. secretarial ctr., 1969-71; bus. instr. Stevens Career Coll., Tampa, Fla., 1972-73; instr., adminstrv. asst. U. Fla. spl. program for Cuban lawyers, Miami, 1974; adj. instr. Fla. Inst. Tech., Melbourne, 1974-78, ESL instr., 1979-84, prof., adminstrv. asst., 1974—, asst. prof., asst. dir., 1985—. Author: Research in Reading English as a Second Language, 1987, Kaleidoscope, 1988; tech. editor Independent Contractor mag., 1979—; contbr. articles to profl. jours. Vol. cons. Am. Field Service, Melbourne, 1981-83; speaker various civic and profl. orgns., Brevard County, Fla., 1985—. Mem. Internat. Tchrs. of English to Speakers of Other Langs. (Gulf Area chpt. Ednl. Travel grant, 1984, bd. dirs., 1988—), Internat. Assn. Tchrs. of English as Fgn. Lang., AAUW, Alpha Lambda Delta, Beta Gamma Sigma. Lodges: Zonta. Baptist. Avocations: travel, bridge, sewing, handcrafts, reading. Home: 505 W Pine Rd Melbourne FL 32904-2531 Office: Virtual Langs Inc 1700 N Dixie Hwy Ste 114 Boca Raton FL 33432-1808

STROTHER, PATRICK JOSEPH, public relations executive; b. St. Louis, Dec. 14, 1953; s. Arch Oscar Strother and Mary Margaret Boyle; m. Patricia Henning; children: Sara Ann, Ryan Joseph. BS with distinction, U. Minn., 1978; MBA, U. St. Thomas, St. Paul, 1982. V.p. investor rels. First Bank System, Mpls., 1983-90; pres. Cevette and Co. Advt. and Pub. Rels., Mpls., 1990-92; founder, pres. Strother Comms. Group Pub. Rels., Mpls., 1992—. Adj. prof. Coll. St. Thomas, St. Paul, 1984-86, Coll. St. Catherine, St. Paul, 1986-92, vis. assoc. prof., U. Minn. Sch. Journalism, 1999. Bd. dirs. Trade Acceptance Group, Ltd.; bd., Human Devel. and Edn., Coll. Univ. Minn. Mem. Pub. Rels. Soc. Am., Counselors Acad., Nat. Investor Rels. Inst., Minn. Guitar Soc. Avocations: 6 and 12 string guitars, studio recording, weightlifting, reading, bicycling, fine art collector. E-mail: pats@scgpr.com.

STROTHMAN, JAMES EDWARD, editor-in-chief; b. Pitts., Mar. 27, 1939; s. Edward Charles and Harriet Hope (Jones) S.; m. Eleanor Shawfield Jacobs, Sept. 9, 1961; children— Joseph, Jill, Stuart. BA in Journalism, Pa. State U., University Park, 1961. Asst. city editor, city hall reporter Williamsport Grit, Pa., 1961-64; with Miami Herald, Fla., 1964-67; aerospace writer AP, Cape Kennedy, Fla., 1967-69; reporter Los Angeles bur. Electronic News, 1969-71, sr. editor computer news sect., 1971-73, mng. editor, 1973; sr. info. rep. corp. hdqrs., then program adminstr. data processing divsn. hdqrs. IBM Corp., 1973-77, mgr. ea. area comm. data processing divsn., 1977-79, field comm. mgr. data processing divsn., 1979-81, mgr. comm. rsch. divsn., 1981; free-lance writer and cons. Strothman Assocs., 1981-82; editor-in-chief MIS Week, NYC, 1982-88; free-lance writer, cons., 1988-89; editor-in-chief Computer Pictures, Chappaqua, NY, 1989-94; news editor InTech Mag. and ISA On Line Instrument Soc. Am. (ISA), Research Triangle Park, NC, 1994-2000. Online editor, eCommerce Bus. Mag., 2000-01; assoc. editor InTech Mag., 2001-02; freelance writer, mktg. comm. cons., 2003—. Presbyterian.

STROTHMAN, WENDY JO, literary agent; b. Pitts., July 29, 1950; d. Walter Richard and Mary Ann Strothman; children: Andrew Richard, Margaret Ann; m. John P. Bishop, Aug. 27, 2005. Student, U. Chgo., 1979-80; AB, Brown U., 1972. Copywriter, mktg. U. Chgo. Press, 1973-76, editor, 1977-80, gen. editor, 1980-83, asst. dir., 1983; dir. Beacon Press, Boston, 1983-95; v.p., pub. adult, trade and reference Houghton-Mifflin, Boston, 1995-96, exec. v.p. trade and reference divsn., 1996—2002, lit. agent, 2003—. Trustee Brown U., 1990-96, Deerfield Acad., 2003—. Edtl. adv. bd. Scholarly Pub., 1993-94; bd. editors Brown Alumni Monthly, 1983-89; chmn., 1986-89. Bd. dirs. Editorial Project for Edn., trustee, 1987-91, 826 Boston, 2008-, treas., 1988-90. Fellow Brown U., 1997—08 Mem. Renaissance Soc. (bd. dirs. 1980-83), Assn. Am. Pubs. (Freedom to Read com.), Pubs. Lunch Club (N.Y.C.), PEN New Eng. (adv. bd.), Examiner Club, NacRe Reins. Corp. (bd. dirs.). Office: Six Beacne St Boston MA 02108

STROUCKEN, ALBERT P. L., consumer products company executive, former chemical company executive; b. July 9, 1947; Exec. v.p. industrial chemicals divsn. Bayer Corp., 1992—97; gen. mgr. inorganic chemicals divsn. Bayer AG, 1997—98; pres., CEO H.B. Fuller Co., St. Paul, 1998—2006, chmn., 1999—2006; chmn., CEO Owens-Illinois, Inc., Toledo, 2006—. Bd. dir. Baxter Internat., Owens Illinois. Bd. dir. Twin Cities United Way; chmn. Minn. Bus. for Early Learning. Office: Owens-Illinois Inc One SeaGate Toledo OH 43666

STROUD, JAMES STANLEY, retired lawyer; b. Wimbledon, ND, Jan. 26, 1915; s. Herbert Montgomery and Amanda Getchell (Longfellow) S.; m. Marjorie Marsh Hovey, Sept. 11, 1940; children: Jay Stanley, Steven Hovey. AB, Jamestown Coll., 1936; JD, U. Chgo., 1939. Bar: Ill. 1939, U.S. Supreme Ct. 1945, D.C. 1972. Counsel Ill. Mcpl. Code Commn., Chgo., 1939-40; bill drafter Ill. Legis. Ref. Bur., Springfield, 1941; ptnr.-in-charge Mayer, Brown Row & Maw LLP, Washington, 1972-80, ret., 1982. Bd. dirs. Chgo. Community Renewal Found., 1962-70; mem. adminstrv. bd. Nat. United Meth. Ch., Washington, 1982-84; coord. Extended Family Program, 1981-82. Capt. AUS, 1943-46. Home: Apt 5310 3300 Darby Rd Haverford PA 19041-1063

STROUD, JOHN FRED, JR., judge; b. Hope, Ark., Oct. 3, 1931; s. John Fred and Clarine (Steel) S.; m. Marietta Kimball, June 1, 1958; children: John Fred III, Ann Kimball, Tracy Steel. Student, Hendrix Coll., Conway, Ark., 1949-51; BA, U. Ark., 1959, LLB, 1960. Bar: Ark. 1959, Tex. 1988, US Supreme Ct. 1963, cert.: Ark. (mediator). Ptnr. Stroud & McClerkin, 1959-62; city atty. City of Texarkana, Ark., 1961; legis. asst. to US Senator John L. McClellan, 1962-63; ptnr. Smith, Stroud, McClerkin, Dunn & Nutter, 1963-79, 81-95; assoc. justice Ark. Supreme Ct., Little Rock, 1980; judge Ark. Ct. Appeals, Little Rock, 1996—2001, chief judge, 2001—04. Chmn. Texarkana Airport Authority, 1966-67, Texarkana United Way Campaign, 1988; pres. Caddo area coun. Boy Scouts Am., 1971-73; former trustee Ark. Nature Conservancy; former bd. dirs. Ark. Cmty. Found.; mem. adv. bd. Donald W. Reyonds Inst. On Aging, bd. United Math. found. of Ark.; former pres. Red River Valley Assn.; former commr. Red River Compact Commn.; past vice chmn. Ark. Water Code Study Commn.; chmn. bd., chmn. coun. ministries Meth. Ch. Lt. col. USAF, 1951-56, Res. ret. Recipient award of exceptional accomplishment Ark. State C. of C., 1972, 86, Silver Beaver and Disting. Eagle awards Boy Scouts Am., Joint Presdl. award of excellence Ark. Bar Assn. and Ark. Bar Found., 2007; named Outstanding Young Man of Texarkana, 1966, One of Five Outstanding Young Men of Ark., 1967, Outstanding Alumnus of U. Ark. Law Sch., 1980. Fellow Am. Bar Found. (chmn. Ark. chpt.); mem. ABA, Ark. Bar Assn. (chmn. exec. coun. 1979-80, pres. 1987-88, C.E. Ransick award of excellence 1990-91, Presdl. award of excellence and Charles L. Carpenter Meml. award 1997-98, Golden Gavel award 2006), Four States Area Estate Planning Coun. (past chmn.), State Bar Tex., Miller County Bar Assn. (past pres.), Texarkana Bar Assn. (pres. 1982-83), Ark. Bar Found. (chmn. 1974-75, chmn. trust com. 2003-06), Am. Coll. Trust and Estate Counsel (chmn. Ark. chpt. 1986-91), S.W. Ark. Bar Assn., N.E. Tex. Bar Assn., Assn. Atty.-Mediators, Texarkana C. of C. (pres. 1969, C.E. Palmer award 1979), U. Ark. Law Alumni Soc. (bd. dirs.), Texarkana Country Club (pres. 1990-92), Rotary (pres. Texarkana 1965-66) Avocations: tennis, golf, hunting, fishing. Office: 405 Walnut Texarkana AR 71854 Office Phone: 870-772-0718. Personal E-mail: jstroudadr@yahoo.com.

STROUD, PEGGY, secondary school educator; d. James and Margret Monk; m. M. Cole Elrod (div.). BS in Edn., U. Ctrl. Ark., Conway, 1977; MEd, Tex. Wesleyan U., Ft. Worth, 2002. Cert. tchr. Ark. Sub. tchr. Conway Pub. Schs., Ark., 1978—82; buyer Old Faculty House, Oklahoma City, 1982—85; buyer, R&D, TCBY, Little Rock, 1983—86; owner Hager's Jewelry Store, Conway, Ark., 1986—88; adminstrv. asst. to dir. Ark. Pks. and Tourism, Little Rock, 1988—91; tchr. Perry-Casa H.S., 1991—93, Heber Springs H.S., 1993—. Bd. dirs. Parents with Children with Disabilities, Conway, Ark. Bd. dirs., sec. Faulkner-Cleburne Regional Water Dist., Conway, Ark., 1985—91; mem. Faulkner County Reps., Conway, Ark., 1986—87; bd. dirs. First United Meth. Ch., Conway, Ark., 1988—90. Mem.: NEA, Ark. Ednl. Assn., Conway C. of C. Methodist. Avocations: arts and crafts, water sports. Office: Heber Springs HS 800 W Moore Heber Springs AR 72543

STROUD, RHODA M., elementary school educator; Tchr. Webster Magnet Elem. Sch., St. Paul. Apptd. mem. Minn. Bd. Edn. for State of Minn. Recipient State Tchr. of Yr. Elem. award Minn., 1992.

STROUD, ROBERT EDWARD, lawyer; b. Chester, SC, July 24, 1934; s. Coy Franklin and Leila (Caldwell) S.; m. Katherine C. Stroud, Apr. 8, 1961; children: Robert Gordon, Margaret Lathan. AB, Washington and Lee U., 1956, LLB, 1958. Bar: Va. 1959, U.S. Ct. Appeals (4th cir.) 1967, U.S. Tax Ct. 1959. Assoc. McGuire Woods, LLP, Charlottesville, Va., 1959-64; ptnr. McGuire Woods, LLP, Charlottesville, Va., 1964—2002, exec. com., 1978-89. Lectr. math. Washington and Lee U., Lexington, Va., 1957-59; lectr. bus. tax Grad. Bus. Sch., U. Va., Charlottesville, 1969-87, lectr. corp. taxation Law Sch., U. Va., Charlottesville, Va. 1985-91; lectr. to legal edn. insts., lectr. in corp. law Washington and Lee Law Sch., Lexington Va., 1984. Co-author: Buying, Selling and Merging Businesses, 1975; editor-in-chief Washington and Lee Law Rev., 1959; editor: Advising Small Business Clients, Vol. 1, 1978, 4th edit., 1994, Vol. 2, 1980, 3d edit., 1990; contbr. articles to profl. jours. Pres. Charlottesville Housing Found., 1968-73; mem. mgmt. coun. Montreat Conf. Ct., NC, 1974-77; trustee Presbyn. Found., 1972-73, Union Theol. Sem., Va., 1983-91; bd. dirs. Presbyn. Outlook Found., 1968-02, pres., 1985-88; mem. governing coun. Presbyn. Synod of the Virginias, 1973-78, moderator of coun., 1977-78, moderator of Synod, 1977-78; trustee, v.p. Va. Tax Found., 1984-95; adv. bd. Westminster Orgn. Concert Series, 1989-93; bd. dirs. Shannon Found. for Excellence in Pub. Edn., Charlottesville, 1996—; adv. bd. Ashlawn-Highland Summer Festival, 1989-03, pres., 1994-00; bd. dirs. Ash Lawn Opera Festival Found., 2003-05, gov. coun. Presbyn. Presbytery of the James, 1993-96, moderator of coun., 1995-96; moderator of presbytery, 1997; dir. Nat. Soc. Arts and Letters, Va. and NC chpt., 2005-08, treas., 2006-08. Capt. inf. US Army, 1958, with res. 1958-70. Recipient Outstanding Law Alumnus award, Lee Law Sch., 2008. Fellow Am. Bar Found., Va. Law Found.; mem. ABA, Am. Judicature Soc., Va. State Bar, Va. Bar Assn., Washington and Lee Sch. Assn. (Lexington, Va.) (governing coun. 1974-80, pres. 1979-80), Order of the Coif (hon.), Phi Delta Sigma, Omicron Delta Kappa, Phi Delta Phi. Democrat. Home: 345 Terrell Ct Charlottesville VA 22901-2171 Office: McGuire Woods LLP PO Box 1288 Charlottesville VA 22902-1288 E-mail: rstroud@mcguirewoodseueritus.com.

STROUD, ROBERT MICHAEL, biophysicist, educator, biotechnologist; b. Stockport, Eng., May 24, 1942; BA in Natural Sci., Cambridge U., Eng., 1964, MA in Natural Sci., 1968; MS in Crystallography, London U., 1965, PhD, 1968. Asst. prof. chemistry Calif. Inst. Tech., Pasadena, 1971-75, assoc. prof., 1975-77; prof. biochemistry, biophysics U. Calif., San Francisco, 1977—. Cons. NIH, 1976—, DeWitt Stetton lectr., 1984—. Editor Ann. Rev. Biophysics and Biomolecular Structure; mem. editorial bd. Protein Engring., Jour. Structural Biology; contbr. articles to profl. jours. Research grantee NIH, 1971—, NSF, 1971—. Fellow Royal Soc. Medicine, Am. Acad. Arts and Scis.; mem. NAS (elected mem.), UK Biophys. Soc., Am. Biophys. Soc. (pres. coun.), Fedn. Exptl. Biologists. Avocation: windsurfing. Business E-Mail: stroud@msg.ucsf.edu.

STROUP, DARRYL RAY, systems engineer; b. Denver, Aug. 5, 1953; s. Norman Glen and Darlene Edna (Porath) Stroup; m. Mary Meta Vensel, Dec. 9, 1972; children: Jared Norman, Caryn Meta Hill, Elizabeth Marie. BSEE cum laude, U. Utah, 1977; MSEE, Air Force Inst. Tech., Dayton, Ohio, 1981. Cert. sys. flight test engr., USN Test Pilot Sch., Md., 1986; Program Management Def. Sys. Mgmt. Coll., Va., 1991, Def. Acquisition Corps, Dept. Navy, 2006. Chief FB-111 AMP avionics test engr. USAF, McClellan AFB, Calif., 1985—86, chief B-2 offensive avionics test engr. Edwards AFB, Calif., 1986—89; chief advanced sys. br. Asst. Sec. of Air Force (Acquisition), Pentagon, DC, 1989—90; lead F-15 program element Fighter Divsn., Asst. Sec. of Air Force (Acquisition), Pentagon, 1990—92; mgr. avionics, nav., and precision targeting sys. Adroit Sys. Inc, Alexandria, Va., 1992—96; CNS ATM lead sys. integration engr. USN, Patuxent River, Md., 2003—07, EW advanced capabilities sys. team lead, 2007—08, ESM lead engr., 2008; head Aircraft Signature & Measurement Br., Atlantic Test Range, 2008—. Contbr. articles to profl. engring. jours.; spkr. in field. Rsch. asst. Program in Occupl. Therapy Wash. Sch. of Medicine, St Louis, Mo., 1998—99; rsch. design engr. Ctrl. Inst. for the Deaf, St Louis, Mo., 2000; vol. Luth. Family Assn. and Luth. Hour Ministries, St Louis, 1999—2003. Maj. USAF, 1972—92. Decorated Meritorious Svc. medal USAF, Air Force Commendation medal. Mem.: Forefather Swedish Colonial Soc. Lutheran - Missouri Synod. Avocations: genealogy, religious sociology. Office: USN NAWCAD Bldg 2272 Patuxent River MD 20670 Business E-Mail: darryl.stroup@navy.mil.

STROUP, JOHN S., high speed electronic industry executive; BS in Mechanical Engring., Northwestern U., 1988; MBA, U. of Calif. Berkeley, 1994. Field application engr. Compumotor Div., various mktg. mgmt. positions Parker Hannifin, 1988—96; v.p. gen. mgr. gen. motion control bus. Rockwell Automation, 1996—98; v.p. mktg., gen. mgr. Scientific Technologies, Inc., 1998—2000; v.p. bus. develop. motion group Danaher Corp., 2000, pres. Kollmorgen Indsl. and Comml. div., 2001, pres. Gen. Purpose Systems, 2001, group exec. Danaher Motion, 2003—05; pres., CEO Belden Inc., St. Louis, 2005—. Office: Belden CDT 7701 Forsyth Blvd Ste 800 Saint Louis MO 63105*

STROUP, KALA MAYS, former education commissioner, educational alliance administrator; BA in Speech and Drama, U. Kans., 1959, MS in Psychology, 1964, PhD in Speech Comm. and Human Rels., 1974; EdD (hon.), Mo. Western State Coll., 1996; LHD (hon.), Harris-Stowe State Coll., 2000. V.p. acad. affairs Emporia (Kans.) State U., 1978-83; pres. Murray State U., Ky., 1983-90, S.E. Mo. State U., Cape Girardeau, 1990-95, Am. Humanics, Kansas City, Mo., 2002—; commr. higher edn., mem. gov.'s cabinet State of Mo., Jefferson City, 1995—2002. Pres. Mo. Coun. on Pub. Higher Edn.; mem. pres.'s commn. NCAA; cons. Edn. Commn. of States Task Force on State Policy and Ind. Higher Edn.; adv. bd. NSF Directorate for Sci. Edn. Evaluation; adv. com. Dept. Health, Edn. and Welfare, chair edn. com.; citizen's adv. coun. on state of Women U. S. Dept. Labor, 1974-76. Mem. nat. exec. bd. Boy Scouts Am., nat. exploring com., former chair profl. devel. com., mem. profl. devel. com., exploring com., Young Am. awards com., 1986-87, north ctrl. region strategic planning com., bd. trustees, nat. mus. chair; mem. Gov.'s Coun. on Workforce Quality, State of Mo.; bd. dirs. Midwestern Higher Edn. Commn.; chair ACE Leadership Commn.; mem. bd. visitors Air U.; v.p. Missourians for Higher Edn.; bd. dirs. St. Francis Med. Ctr. Found., 1990-95, Cape Girardeau C. of C., 1990-95, U. Kans. Alumni Assn.; pres. Forum on Excellence, Carnegie Found.; adv. bd. World Trade Ctr., St. Louis, Svc. Mems. Opty. Colls., 1997—; mem. Mo. Higher Edn. Loan Authority, 1995—, depts. econ. devel. & agrl. Mo. Global Partnership, 1995—, Mo. Tng. & Employment Coun., 1995-2002, Concordia U. Sys. Advancement Cabinet, State Higher Edn. Exec. Officers, 1995—, mem. com. workforce edn. and tng., 1996; bd. govs. Heartland's Alliance Minority Participation, 1995-2002; chair, mem. workforce devel. com. NPEC coun. U.S. Office of Edn., 1997—; bd. dirs. Midwestern Higher Edn. Com. Distributed Learning Workshop, 1998-2002, Dept. Natural Resources Minority Scholarship Adv. Bd.; chair Show Me Results sub-cabinet Educated Missourians; mem. Pub. Policy Initiative Stakeholder Com., 1999—; mem. Coun. Higher Edn. transfer and pub. interest com.; mem. access/diversity com. State Higher Edn. Exec. Officers; trustee, mem. adv. coun. Assn. Governing Bds. of Univs. and Colls. Ctr. for Pub. Edn., 2000—. ACE fellow; recipient Alumni Honor Citation award U. Kans., Award Distinction Profl. Black Men's Club, S.E. Mo., 1990, Dist. Svc. to Edn. award Harris-Stowe State Coll., 1996; named to U. Kans. Womans Hall of Fame, Ohio Valley Conf. Hall of Fame, 1997. Mem. Am. Assn. State Colls. and Univs. (past bd. dirs., mem. Pres.'s Commn. on Tchr. Edn., Task Force on Labor Force Issues and Implications for the Curriculum), Mortar Board, Phi Beta Kappa, Omicron Delta Kappa, Phi Kappa Phi, Rotary (found. Ednl. awards com.). Office Phone: 816-561-6415.

STROUP, MICHAEL D., economics professor, dean; s. Richard L. Stroup and Sandra L. Dasenbrcck; m. Lori D. Taylor, Aug. 4, 1985; children: Sarah, Sean. BS in Economics, Mont. State U., Bozeman, 1986; MA in Economics, U. Wash., Seattle, 1989; PhD in Economics, Fla. State U., Tallahassee, 1993. Asst. prof. Naval Postgrad. Sch., Monterey, Calif., 1993—99; prof. economics Stephen F. Austin State U., Nacogdoches, Tex., 1999—. Office: Stephen F Austin State Univ PO Box 13004 SFA Sta Nacogdoches TX 75962 Office Fax: 936-468-1560. Business E-Mail: mstroup@sfasu.edu.

STROUP, RICHARD L., lawyer; b. Shelby, Ohio, May 17, 1948; BSME, Ohio Northern U., 1970; JD, U. Va., 1976. Bar: Va. 1976, DC 1977, lic.: US Ct. Appeals (Fed. Cir.) 1982, registered: US Patent & Trademark Office. Law clk. to Hon. Francis C. Brown Trial Divsn., US Ct. of Claims, 1976—77; patent examiner US Patent & Trademark Office; ptnr. Finnegan, Henderson, Farabow, Garrett & Dunner LLP, Washington, leader, Litig. Sect., mem. mgmt. com. Mem.: Internat. Trademark Assn., Am. Intellectual Property Law Assn., ABA, Va. Bar Assn., Bar Assn. DC, DC Bar Assn., Phi Kappa Phi, Tau Beta Pi. Office: Finnegan Henderson Farabow Garrett & Dunner LLP 901 New York Ave NW Washington DC 20001-3315 Office Phone: 202-408-4000. Office Fax: 202-408-4400. Business E-Mail: richard.stroup@finnegan.com.

STROUP, RICHARD LYNDELL, economist, educator, writer; b. Sunnyside, Wash., Jan. 3, 1943; s. Edgar Ivan and Inez Louise (Kellett) S.; m. Sandra Lee Price, Sept. 13, 1962 (div. Sept. 1981); children— Michael, Craig; m. Jane Bartlett Steidemann Shaw, Jan. 1, 1985; 1 child, David. Student, MIT, 1961-62; BA, MA, U. Wash., 1966, PhD in Econs., 1970. Asst. prof. econs. Mont. State U., Bozeman, 1969-74, assoc. prof. econs., 1974-78; dir. Office Policy Analysis, Dept. Interior, 1982-84; prof. econs. Mont. State U., 1978—2006, dept. head, 2003—06; pres. Polit. Economy Rsch. Inst., Raleigh, NC, 2007—. Sr. fellow Property and Environ. Rsch. Ctr., Bozeman, 1980-. Author: Eco-nomics, 2003; co-author: Natural Resources, 1983, Economics: Private and Public Choice, 11th edit., 2005, Basic Economics, 1993, What Everyone Should Know About Economics and Prosperity, 1993, Common Sense Economics, 2005; editor: Cutting Green Tape, 2000; also articles, 1972—; mem. editorial bd. Regulation, 1993—. Adj. scholar Cato Inst., 1993—. Mem. Am. Econ. Assn., Western Econ. Assn., So. Econ. Assn., Mont Pelerin Soc., Phila. Soc., Assn. Pvt. Enterprise Edn. (Hayeck Endowed chair econs. 2005). Episcopalian. Office: NCSU Econ 4102 Nelson Hall 2801 Founders Dr Raleigh NC 27695 Business E-Mail: rstroup@ncsu.edu.

STROUPE, HENRY SMITH, university dean; b. Alexis, NC, June 3, 1914; s. Stephen Morris and Augie (Lineberger) S.; m. Mary Elizabeth Denham, June 2, 1942; children— Stephen Denham, David Henry. Student, Mars Hill Jr. Coll., 1931-33; BS, Wake Forest Coll., 1935, MA, 1937; PhD, Duke U., 1942. Faculty Wake Forest U., Winston-Salem, N.C., 1937—, assoc. prof. history, 1949-54, prof., 1954-84, prof. emeritus, 1984—, chmn. dept. history, 1954-68, dir. evening classes, 1957-61, dir. div. grad. studies, 1961-67, dean grad. sch., 1967-84, dean emeritus, 1984—. Vis. prof. history Duke U., 1960. Author: The Religious Press in the South Atlantic States, 1802-1865: An Annotated Bibliography with Historical Introduction and Notes, 1956; Mem. editorial bd.: N.C. Hist. Rev, 1963-69. Mem. N.C. Civil War Centennial Commn., 1959-60. Served from ensign to lt. USNR, 1943-46. Recipient Christopher Crittenden award N.C. Lit. and Hist. Assn., 1982 Mem. NC Hist. Soc. (pres. 1965), NC Lit. and Hist. Assn. (pres. 1974), Phi Beta Kappa, Omicron Delta Kappa. Democrat. Baptist. Home: 2016 Faculty Dr Winston Salem NC 27106-5221

STROUSE, JEAN, writer, cultural organization administrator; b. LA, Sept. 10, 1945; d. Carl David and Louise (Friedberg) S. BA, Radcliffe Coll., 1967. Editl. asst. N.Y. Rev. of Books, 1967-69; freelance writer NYC, 1969-72; editor Pantheon Books, NYC, 1972-75; freelance writer NYC, 1975-79, 1983—2003; book critic Newsweek Mag., NYC, 1979-83; dir. Cullman Ctr. for Scholars and Writers N.Y. Pub. Libr., NYC, 2003—. Selection com. J.S. Guggenheim Found., N.Y.C., 1995-97, trustee, 1987-94, 2001—04, fellow, 1977, 86; exec. coun. Authors Guild; Ferris prof. journalism Princeton U., 1998; John J. Rhodes chair in Am. instns. and pub. policy Barrett Honors Coll., Ariz. State U., 2003. Author: Alice James, A Biography, 1980, Morgan American Financier, 1999; editor: Women & Analysis: Dialogues on Psychoanalytic Views of Femininity, 1974. Recipient Bancroft prize, Columbia U., 1981; fellow, NEH, 1976, 1992, John D. and Catherine T. MacArthur Found., 2002—06. Fellow, Am. Acad. Arts & Sci.; mem. Soc. Am. Historians (pres. 2001-02), Am Philos Soc, The Century Assn., Phi Beta Kappa (vis. scholar 1996-97).

STROUSTRUP, BJARNE, computer science and engineering professor; b. Aarhus, Denmark, 1950; m. Marian Stroustrup; children: Annemarie, Nicholas. Grad., U. Aarhus, 1975; PhD in Computer Sci., Cambridge U., 1979. Joined Computer Sci. Rsch. Ctr., Bell Telephone Labs., Murray Hill, NJ, 1979; mem. AT&T Bell Labs. Rsch., head Large-Scale Programming Rsch. Dept., mem. Info. and Sys. Software Rsch. Lab.; Coll. Engring. chair prof. computer sci. Tex. A&M U., College Station, Tex., 2002—; AT&T Fellow AT&T Labs. Author: The C++ Programming Language, 1985, 1991, 1997, 2000; contbr. articles to profl. jours. Recipient ACM Grace Murray Hopper award, 1993; named one of Am.'s twelve top young scientists, Fortune Mag., 1990. Fellow: IEEE (Computer Entrepreneur Award 2004), Computer Hall of Fame; mem.: NAE, Tex. Acad. of Medicine, Engring. and Sci., Sigma Xi (William Procter Prize for Scientific Achievement 2005). Achievements include designer and original implementer of C++ programming language. Avocations: hiking, running, music, travel. Office: Tex A&M U Dept Computer Sci TAMU 3112 College Station TX 77843-3112 also: AT&T Rsch 180 Park Ave Florham Park NJ 07932-0971 E-mail: bs@cs.tamu.edu.

STROUT, ELIZABETH, writer, educator; b. Portland, Maine, Jan. 6, 1956; B, Bates Coll., Lewiston, Maine; JD, Syracuse U. Coll. Law, NY, 1982. Cert. of Gerontology Syracuse Sch. Social Work, 1982. Faculty MFA program Queens U., Charlotte, NC. Tchr. Manhattan Cmty. Coll., NY, Bard Coll., NY, Warren Wilson Coll., NC; NEH prof. Colgate U., Hamilton, NY, 2007. Author: (novels) Amy and Isabelle, 1998 (LA Times Art Seidenbaum award for First Fiction, Chgo. Tribune Heartland prize, NY Times bestseller), Abide with Me, 2006, Olive Kitteridge, 2008 (Pulitzer prize for fiction, 2009); contbr. numerous short stories to mags. Mailing: c/o Random House 1745 Broadway New York NY 10019*

STROUTH, BARON HOWARD STEVEN, geologist, mining engineer; b. Frankfurt, Germany, Sept. 28, 1919; arrived in U.S., 1941; s. Baron Karl Siegfried and Ida (Morck) von Strauss; m. Penelope Ann Creamer-Osteen, Nov. 3, 1951. BSc, U. Sorbonne, 1939; PhD in Engring., Bretton Woods U., 1965; PhD in Engring. (hon.), Rochedale U., Can., 1970. Asst. mgr. Drexel Bros. Ltd., NYC, 1941—43; pres. Std. Mining, NYC, 1951-58, Stanleigh Uranium Mine, Toronto, Can., 1954-61; mng. dir. Norsul Oil and Mining Quito, Ecuador, 1961-71; dir., officer Mining and Oil Cos., various locations; founder, operator Stanleigh Uranium and Norsul Oil. Sr. trustee Weingueter Baron K. S. von Strauss, Erben Trust, Vaduz, 1954—. Translator: author Rilke The Cornet, 1960, A Window to the Morrow, 1963, A Sonata for Frankfurt, 1967, Cities of the Break of Dawn, 1988, Beauty is Forever, 1996. Maj. USAR, 1943-69, ret. Recipient Conspicuous Svc. Cross, Gov. Dewey, 1947, French, Czech, Cambodian decorations. Fellow Explorers Club; mem. Can. Inst. Mining Engrs. (life), Am. Inst. Mining Engrs. (sr.; Legion of Honor), St. James Club (London), Ontario Club Toronto. Achievements include patents for mining and oil processes. Avocations: collector, antique books, pre-colombian art, antique maps. Personal E-mail: naturespirites@yahoo.com.

STROYD, ARTHUR HEISTER, JR., lawyer; b. Pitts., Sept. 5, 1945; 1 child, Elizabeth. AB, Kenyon Coll., 1967; JD, U. Pitts., 1972. Bar: Pa. 1972, U.S. Dist. Ct. (we. dist.) Pa. 1972, U.S. Ct. Appeals (3d cir.) 1972. Law clk. to judge U.S. Ct. Appeals (3d cir.), Phila., 1972—75; with Reed, Smith, LLP, Pitts., 1975—2006, mng. ptnr., Allegheny Region, 1997—2001; ptnr. Del Sole Cavanaugh Stroyd, LLC, Pitts., 2007—. Mem. Nat. Adv. Coun. on Child Nutrition, U.S. Dept. Agriculture, 1984-85. Mem. Mt. Lebanon Zoning Hearing Bd., 1978-81; pres. bd. dirs. Mt. Lebanon Sch. dist., 1981-87; solicitor Allegheny County Rep. Com., 1988-95; pres. bd. dirs. Ctr. for Theatre Arts, Pitts., 1984-93; grad. Leadership Pitts., 1991-92; chair bd. dirs. Mt. Lebanon Hosp. Authority, 1993-01; bd. dirs. Neighborhood Legal Svcs. Assn., 1989-91, U. Pitts. Cancer Inst., 1993-2008; chair bd. dirs. Leadership Pitts. Inc., 2006—, Material Handling Industry Found., 2006—; mem. alumni coun. Kenyon Coll., 1996-00; bd. dirs. Edn. Policy and Issues Ctr., 2000-03. Lt. USNR, 1969-71, John Heinz History Ctr., 2000-09. Fellow Am. Coll. Trial Lawyers; mem. ABA, Pa. Bar Assn. (commn. for justice initiatives in Pa. 2004—), Allegheny County Bar Assn. (past pres., bd. govs., past chair civil litig. sect., past chmn. judiciary com.), Acad. Trial Lawyers (past pres., bd. govs.), mem. Pa. Supreme Ct. Civil Procedural Rules Com., Duquesne Club, Pitts. Golf Club, Hist. Soc. We. Pa. (bd. dirs. 2000-09). Episcopalian. Avocations: skiing, motorcycling, golf. Office: Del Sole Cavanaugh Stroyd LLC Ste 300 200 1st Ave Pittsburgh PA 15222 Office Phone: 412-261-2393. Business E-Mail: astroy@dscslaw.com.

STRUBBE, THOMAS R., insurance industry executive; b. Ft. Wayne, Ind., Mar. 30, 1940; s. Rudolph C. and Maverne E. (Wagoner) S.; children: Tracy Lynn, Patrick Thomas, Christina Lee. BS, Ind. U., 1962; JD, Tulane U., 1965. Bar: Ind. 1965, Ill. 1969. Atty. Lincoln Nat. Life Ins. Co., Ft. Wayne, Ind., 1965-66, asst. counsel, 1967-68; with Washington Nat. Corp., Evanston, Ill., 1968-90, counsel, 1968-73, gen. counsel, 1973-79, corp. sec., 1970-84, v.p., 1975-79, sr. v.p., 1979-83, exec. v.p., 1983-84, pres., 1984-90, also bd. dirs., mem. exec. com.; pres., CEO Osborn Labs. Inc., Olathe, Kans., 1990-98, Guarantee Res. Life Ins. Co., Chgo., 1998-99, also bd. dirs., ret., 2000. V.p., bd. dirs., exec. com. Chgo. chpt. Epilepsy Found. Am., 1975—79; trustee Glencoe Union Ch., Ill., 1984—87; Stephen leader Trinity Luth. Ch., Kans., 2003—08; bd. dirs. Assn. Retarded Citizens Ill., 1985—89, Northlight Theater, 1984—89. Lt. USNR, 1965—71. Lincoln Found. grantee, 1964. Mem. ABA, Assn. Life Ins. Counsel, Nat. Investor Rels. Inst., Am. Soc. Corp. Secs., Home Office Life Underwriters Assn., Ind. Bar Assn., Ill. Bar Assn., Skokie Country Club (Ill.), Shadow Glen Golf Club (Kans.), Hallbrook Country Club (Kans.), Hideaway Beach Club (Fla.), Rotary, VFW, Lambda Chi Alpha, Delta Sigma Pi. Home (Summer): 9210 Oak Valley Dr De Soto KS 66018-7994 Home (Winter): 6000 Royal Marco Way Unit 350 Marco Island FL 34145 Personal E-mail: tomstrubbe@yahoo.com.

STRUBE, JUERGEN F., chemical company executive; b. Bochum, Germany, 1939; Studied law, Freiburg, Geneva, Munich; JD, 1967. Joined fin. dept. BASF Aktiengesellschaft, 1969, head Glasurit do Brasil, 1980, pres. Brazil regional div., 1982, appt. bd. exec. dirs., 1985, mem. bd. exec. dirs. Germany, 1988—90, chmn. bd. exec. dirs., 1990—2003, chmn. supr. bd., 2003—. Bd. mem. Allianz Lebensversicherungs-AG, 1990—, Hochtief AG, 1996—, Commerzbank AG, 1998—, Hapag-Lloyd AG, 1998—, Linde AG, 2000—, Bayerische Motoren Werke Aktiengesellschaft, Bertelsmann AG, Fuchs Petrolub. Recipient Centenary Medallion, Soc. Chem. Industry, 1999, Order of Merit, 1st Class, Fed. Rep. Germany, 2000, John J. McCloy Award, 2001; named honored dignitary, U. Md., 1995, honored mem., Mannheim U., Germany, 1998. Mem.: German Sci. Found., Transatlantic Bus. Dialogue (bd. mem. 1995—, chmn. bd. 1995—96, dep. chmn. 1998—), AGCI (bd. mem. 1990—, chmn. bd. 1996—97), Rhineland-Palantine Future Initiative Inst. (bd. mem. 1992—, chmn. bd. 1992—98). Office: BASF Aktiengesellschaft Carl-Bosch Strasse 38 67056 Ludwigshafen Germany

STRUBEL, RICHARD PERRY, Internet company executive; b. Evanston, Ill., Aug. 10, 1939; s. Arthur Raymond and Martha (Smith) S.; m. Linda Jane Freeman, Aug. 25, 1961 (div. 1974); children: Douglas Arthur, Craig Tollerton; m. Ella Doyle G'sell, Oct. 23, 1976. BA, Williams Coll., 1962; MBA, Harvard U., 1964. Assoc. Fry Cons., Chgo., 1964-66, mng. prin., 1966-68; with N.W. Industries, Inc., Chgo., 1968-83, v.p. corp. devel., 1969-73, group v.p., 1973-79, exec. v.p., 1979-83, pres., 1983; chmn. bd., pres. Buckingham Corp., NYC, 1972-73; pres., chief exec. officer Microdot Inc., Chgo., 1983-94; mng. dir. Tandem Ptnrs. Inc., Chgo., 1990-99; with UNext Inc., Deerfield, Ill., 1999—2008, pres., COO, 1999—2004, vice chmn., dir., 2004—08. Chmn. bd. trustee Mut. Funds of The No. Trust Co., Chgo., and bd. trustee of various mutual funds of Goldman Sachs Asset Mgmt., N.Y.C.; bd. dirs. Gildan Activewear, Inc., Montreal, Que., Can. Trustee U. Chgo.; mem. visiting com. Divinity Sch., U. Chgo. Mem. Casino Club, Chicago Club, Comml. Club, Racquet Club of Chicago, Commonwealth Club, Econ. Club. Presbyterian.

STRUBLE, THELMA PAULINE, elementary school educator; b. Caldwell, Kans., Jan. 16, 1934; d. Edwin Clarence and Edna Dorothy (Lungren) Johnson; m. LaVern Lee Nuse, Dec. 28, 1958 (dec. 1981); children: Dale Alan, Derald Leroy, Danita Rae; m. Gene Struble, Aug. 11, 1991. BA, Southwestern Coll., Winfield, Kans., 1957; MA, Northwestern Coll., Alva, Okla., 1974. Tchr. pub. schs., Goddard, Kans., 1953—61, Caldwell pub. schs., Kans., 1970—96. Conductor workshops/seminars in field. Mem. Internat. Reading Assn. (pres., v.p., coord., state coord. Dist. 4), Caldwell Tchrs. Assn., Kans. Edn. Assn., Kans. State Coll. Assn., 4-H Club (cmty. and project leader), United Meth. Women Orgn. (pres.), Caldwell Care Network (organizer, tutor after sch. program, chmn. after sch. program, vol. hosp., pres., v.p., coord., state coord. dist. 4) Republican. Methodist. Avocations: reading, bread making, nutrition, sewing. Home: 111 S Osage St Caldwell KS 67022-1644

STRUBLE, WAYNE T., legislative staff member; Chief of staff US House Budget Com., Washington, 2001; prof. staff mem. US Senate Homeland Security and Govtl. Affairs Com., Washington, 2001; chief of staff for Rep. David Hobson, US House of Reps., Washington, 2001—09, Rep. Steve Austria, Washington, 2009—; asst. US House Appropriations Com., 2007—08. Office: Office of Congressman Steve Austria 1641 Longworth House Office Bldg Washington DC 20515 Office Phone: 202-225-4324, 202-225-1984. E-mail: wayne.struble@mail.house.gov.*

STRUELENS, MICHEL MAURICE JOSEPH GEORGES, political science professor, consultant; b. Brussels, Mar. 10, 1928; m. Godelieve De Wilde, Aug. 2, 1949; children: Alain, Patricia, Brigitte, Bernard, Jean Paul (dec.). BA, Coll. St. Pierre, Brussels, 1944; MA, Antwerp U., Belgium, 1949; PhD, Am. U., Washington, 1968. Insp. econ. affairs Congo Govt., Leopoldville, 1950-54, chief insp. econ. affairs, 1954-55, dep. commr. transp., 1955-57; dir. Info. and Public Relations Office for Congo, Brussels, 1957-58, Congo Tourism Pavillion, Internat. World's Fair, Brussels, 1958-59; dir. gen. Belgian Congo and Ruanda Urundi Tourist Office, Congo, 1959; chmn. African Commn. Internat. Union Ofcl. Travel Orgns., Geneva, 1959-60; ofcl. Katanga rep. in U.S., NYC, 1960-63; dir. gen. Internat. Inst. for African Affairs in Can., 1963-64; spl. asst. to prime minister Democratic Republic Congo, fgn. affairs minister, adviser to Congo UN del., adviser Congo embassy Washington, NYC, 1964-66; dir. Eurafrica, Consultants on Fgn. Affairs, Washington, 1966—; prof. polit. sci., French, internat. bus. Am. U., 1968-93; prof. emeritus, 1993; dir. Ctr. Rsch and Documentation on European Community Am. U., 1971—, chmn. faculty rels. com., 1986-87, chmn. grad. studies com., SIS, 1989-90; dir. E.C. Inst. in Europe, 1978-93, U. Antwerp Exchange Program, 1979-83. Dir. EPSCI/ESSEC (France) Exchange Program, 1980-84, chmn. internat. bus. dept., 1980-84; dir. exchange program Bus. Sch. of Poly., U. Madrid, 1981-84; investment adviser, 1977—; adminstr. French Parish, 1974-75, Ctr. Studies on Internat. Relations, 1987-96, Econs. and Bus., La Rochelle, France, 1987-96; exec. v.p. Eglise St. Louis Corp., French-Speaking Union, Washington, 1974-75; mgr. by agreement with European Communities, European Documentation Ctr. (CERDEC), accessing by satellite EC Data Banks, 1985— and providing through WCL Libr. of Am. U., On Line Pub. Access Cataloging, 1991—. Author: (with Inforcongo) Congo Belge et Ruanda-Urundi, 1958; monograph Le Canada à l'Heure de l'Afrique, 1964; The United Nations in the Congo - or ONUC and International Politics, 1976. Recipient Internat. Union Ofcl. Travel Orgns. Poster award Brussels, 1958, Etoile de Service en Argent King of Belgium, 1956; chevalier de l'Ordre Royal du Lion, 1957; Faculty award for outstanding contbn. to acad. program devel. Coll. Bus. Adminstrn., Am. U., 1979; Faculty award for outstanding teaching, 1980, 82, 84; Faculty award for outstanding service to Am. U., 1981 Mem. Golden Key, Phi Sigma Alpha. Clubs: Cosmos (Washington) (Emeritus nominee); Bukavu Royal Sports (founder 1950, pres. 1951-54, hon. pres. 1957) (Congo). Lodges: Rotary. Home: 1374 Woodside Dr Mc Lean VA 22102-1536 Office: Am U 4400 Mass Ave NW Washington DC 20016-8071 *"Ad Augusta per Angusta". Using Latin, French writer Victor Hugo said it all! Nothing comes easy and "success," a very personal perception indeed, requires a great deal of luck, perseverance and hard work. True success, though, is directly related to the pursuit of happiness, which in turn is a state of mind. If and when I reach eternity, I'll then be able to tell how successful I was during my passage on earth.*

STRUHL, KEVIN, molecular biologist, educator; b. NYC, Sept. 2, 1952; s. Joseph and Harriet (Schachter) Struhl; m. Marjorie A. Oettinger, June 4, 1989. BS, MS, MIT, 1974; PhD, Stanford U., 1979; MA, Harvard U., 1989. Asst. prof. Harvard Med. Sch., Boston, 1982-86, assoc. prof., 1986-89, prof., 1989-91, David Wesley Gaiser prof. biol. chemistry and molecular pharmacology, 1991—. Scientific adv. bd. Pharmagenics, Inc., Allendale, N.J., 1989—, Scriptech, Cambridge, Mass., 1993—. Jane Coffin Childs fellow, 1980; Searle scholar, 1983; recipient award in Microbiology Eli Lilly, 1990. Fellow: Am. Acad. Arts & Scis. Office: Harvard Med Sch Dept Biological Chemistry & Molecular Pharmacology 240 Longwood Ave Bldg C2 Rm 315 Boston MA 02115-5701 Office Phone: 617-432-2104. Office Fax: 617-432-2529. Business E-Mail: kevin@hms.harvard.edu.

STRUHL, THEODORE ROOSEVELT, surgeon; b. NYC, Jan. 5, 1917; s. Samuel and Florence (Kossoy) S.; m. Ruth Brand, Oct. 19, 1941; children: Karsten, Wendy. BA, NYU, 1936; MS, 1938; MD, NY Med. Coll., 1942; MS in Surg., 1947; grad., Juliard Conservatory of Music, 1933. Dipl. Am. Bd. Abdominal Surg., Am. Bd. Surg.; spl. expert Agy. Health Care Adminstrn., Bd. Medicine, Fla. Int. Queens Gen. Hosp., Jamaica, NY, 1942-43; res. VA Hosp., Newington, CT, 1947-48, Cumberland Med. Ctr., Brooklyn, NY, 1948-51; prac. med. specializing in surg. Miami, FL, 1951—; staff mem. Mt. Sinai Med. Ctr., Miami Beach, FL, Jackson Meml. Hosp., Cedars of Lebanon Health Care Ctr., Variety Chldrns. Hosp., South Shore Hosp., Miami Beach, FL, Victoria Hosp.; former instr. in anatomy L.I. Coll. Med., NY; instr. in surg., instr. in anatomy and surg. anatomy U. Miami; instr. in surg. anatomy and surg. Mt. Sinai Med. Ctr. Mem. adv. ARC of Dade County, Fla.; chief med. examiner Miami Beach Boxing Commn.; med. adv. World Martial Arts, Judo and Karate; mem. Am. Bd. Quality Assurance and Utilization Rev. Physicians; formerly instr. in diving med. Underwater Demolition Team Sch., U.S. Navy, Key West, Fla.; spl. expert Bd. of Medicine of the State of Fla.; lectr., instr. in scuba diving, diving med.; lectr. med. and surg., cancer, artificial respiration, anatomy, hypnosis, boxing, weight lifting, judo, skin and scuba diving, swimming, water skiing; spl. expert AHCA Bd. Medicine, State of Fla., Agy. for Health Care Adminstrn. Contbr. articles to profl. jours. Active ARC, 1936—, now bd. dirs., chmn. safety svcs. ARC of Dade County, bd. trustees; instr./trainer in CPR, instr. in advanced cardiac life support Am. Heart Assn.; former mem. N.Y. div. Olympic Wrestling Com. Served to maj. M.C., combat surgeon U.S. Army, World War II; ETO. Fellow ACS, Internat. Coll. of Surgeons (vice-regent Fla.), Am. Coll. Angiology, Internat. Acad. Proctology; mem. AMA, So. Med. Assn., Fla. Med. Assn., Dade County Med. Assn., Israeli Med. Assn., Fla. Assn. Gen. Surgeons (charter), Med. Hypnosis Assn. Dade County Med. Assn., Israeli Med. Assn., Fla. Assn. Gen. Surgeons (charter), Med. Hypnosis Assn. Dade County (past pres.), Am. Coll. Angiology, Pan Am. Med. Assn., Am. Soc. Abdominal Surgeons, Am. Soc. Contemporary Med. and Surg., Med. Aspects of Atomic Explosion, Assn. Mil. Surgeons U.S., Am. Coll. Sports Med., Fla. Bar Ass. (appointed bd. govs. 1990-94, mem. unlicensed practice of law 1997—, mem. pub. info. com. 1997—, grievance com.), Dade County Bar Assn. (mem. grievance com. 1987-90, 94-97), Commodore Longfellow Soc., Miami Beach Power Squadron (charter), Am. Canoe Assn., Am. White Water Assn., Underwater Med. Soc., Photog. Soc. Am., Contin. Hon. Soc. of N.Y. Med. Coll., Phi Delta Epsilon (past pres. chpt.). Democrat. Jewish. Avocations: judo (3rd degree black belt), karate (black belt, 4th degree). Home and Office: 5066 N E 2 Ave Apt 611 Miami FL 33137

STRUKOFF, RUDOLF STEPHEN, retired music educator; b. Rostov, Don, Russia, July 18, 1935; came to U.S., 1951; s. Stephen and Olga (Flemming) S.; m. Donna Lee Hill, May 31, 1959; children: Rudolf Stephen, Jr., Robbin Stanley, Regan Stuart. B Music Edn., Andrews U., 1960; studied with Roger Wagner and Robert Shaw, 1960—62; MusM, Mich. State U., 1964, PhD in Music, 1970. Instr. music Mich. State U., East Lansing, 1963-65; asst. prof. Ind. State U., Terre Haute, 1966-69; assoc. prof. Andrews U., Berrien Springs, Mich., 1969-76; prof. music Gov's. State U., Univ. Park, Ill., 1977-97. Chorus master Ill. Philharm. Chorus, Park Forest, Ill., 1982-84; music dir. Univ. Cmty. Chorale, Univ. Park, Ill., 1978-96, Chamber Orch., Univ. Park, 1978-96. Composer: The Greatest of These, 1970, Childhood Sketches, 1973; singer (opera) Attila by Verdi, 1979; condr. Christmas Oratorio by Saint-Saens, 1986, Stabat Mater by Rossini, 1988, German Requiem by Brahms, 1989, Requiem by Mozart, 1990, Mass in C by Beethoven, 1991, Mass in E Flat by Schubert, 1992, Requiem in C Minor by Cherubini, 1993, Cathedral Series, Joliet, Ill., Mass in B Flat by Haydn, St. Liborius, Steger, Ill., 1994, Symphony #2 (Hymn of Praise), Temple Anshe Sholom, 1994, Olympia Fields, Ill., Requiem by Mozart, St. Liborius, Steger, Ill., 1995, Messiah by Handel, Ctr. for Performing Arts, University Park, Ill., 1995, Concert Overture and Requiem by Cherubini, 1996; rec. artist (CD) How Great Thou Art, 2003, My Native Land, 2003. Lectr. Lyric Opera, Chgo., 1979-89, Libr. Lectr. Series, Park Forest, 1982, Career Days, Chgo., 1982-97, Symposium on Soviet Russia, Univ. Park, 1985, Ill. Philharmonic Workshop Series, 1991-96. Mem. ASCAP, Chgo. Singing Tchrs. Guild (pres. 1984-86, 91-93, bd. dirs. 1986-96), Am. Choral Dirs. Assn., Nat. Assn. Tchrs. Singing, Nat. Assn. Schs. Music, Pi Kappa Lambda. Avocations: antiques, golf, reading. Personal E-mail: strukoff@comcast.net.

STRULL, GENE, technology consultant, retired manufacturing executive; b. Chgo., May 15, 1929; s. Albert and Helen (Wolf) S.; m. Joyce Landsbaum, July 6, 1952; children— David Jay, Brian Lee. BSEE, Purdue U., 1951; MS, Northwestern U., 1952, PhD in Elec. Engring, 1954. With Westinghouse Electric Corp., Pitts., later Balt., 1954-93, supervisory engr., adv. engr., mgr. solid state tech.-aerospace, 1958-68, mgr. sci. and tech. systems devel. div., mgr. advanced tech. labs., 1968-78, dep. gen. mgr. systems devel. div., 1979-81, gen. mgr. advanced tech. div., 1981-93, exec. dir. tech., 1987-93. Cons. Army Sci. Bd., 1979-83, NRC-NAS, 1980-82, Def. Sci. Bd., 1981-83, NSF, 1992—; cons. NASA, 1967-87, com. chmn., 1976-78; adv. com. panel USNR, 1989. Contbg. author: Integrated Electronic Systems, 1970, Integrated Circuit Technology, 1967; contbr. articles to profl. jours.; patentee in field. Gene Strull Tech. Ctr. at Westinghouse Electric Corp. Advanced Tech. Labs. named in his honor, Balt., 1993; named Outstanding Elec. Engr. award Purdue U., 1994. Fellow IEEE (life, Govt. Industry Svc. award 1987, Frederik Philips award 1991); mem. Md. Acad. Scis. (chmn. 1978-80). Home: One Gristmill Ct # 606 Baltimore MD 21208

STRUM, BRIAN J., real estate company officer; b. Bklyn., Nov. 27, 1939; s. Max J. and Beatrix (Galitzky) S.; m. Mickey Weiss, Nov. 19, 1966; children: Ira, Howard, Beth. BA, Bklyn. Coll., 1960; LLB, NYU, 1963. Bar: N.Y. 1964, N.J. 1969; CLU; counselor of real estate. Atty. Gilbert, Segall and Young, NYC, 1963-65; assoc. res. atty. Prudential Ins. Co. Am., NYC, 1965-67, various positions, law dept., 1967-75, v.p. real estate investments, 1975-86; chmn. Prudential Property Co., Newark, 1986—94; CEO Prudential Realty Group, Newark, 1992-94; Silverstein chair of real estate devel. NYU, 1995-98. Pres., trustee Prudential Realty Trust, 1985-94; mem. adv. bd. Chgo. Title & Trust Co., N.Y.C., 1982-96. Editor: Financing Real Estate in the Inflationary Eighties, 1981; contbr. articles to profl. jours. With USAR, 1963-69. Recipient Disting. Cmty. Svc. award Brandeis U., 1983, Urban Leadership award NYU, 1990, Good Scout award N.Y.C. coun. Boy Scouts Am., 1991, Nat. Achievement awrd D.A.R.E. Am., 1993. Fellow Anglo Am. Real Property Inst. (charter); mem. ABA (chmn. real property, probate and trust law sects. 1984-85), N.Y. State Bar Assn. (chmn. real property sect. 1975-76), Urban Land Inst. (coun. mem.), Am. Coll. Real Estate Lawyers (charter), Am. Soc. Real Estate Counselors. Home: 435 Pine Ln Haworth NJ 07641-1308 Office Phone: 201-384-1400. Personal E-mail: mstrum77@aol.com.

STRUM, JAY GERSON, retired lawyer; b. NYC, July 6, 1938; s. John and Dorothy (Chaikind) S.; m. Patricia Ann Burtis, Jan. 25, 1969; children: Daniel, Jennifer. BA in polit. sci. magna cum laude, CCNY, 1959; LLB, Harvard U., 1962. Bar: N.Y. 1963, U.S. Dist. Ct. (so. and ea. dists.) N.Y. 1963, U.S. Ct. Appeals (2d cir.) 1965, U.S. Supreme Ct. 1979. Ptnr. SEC, NYC, 1963-65, Coon, Dubow, Kleinberg & Strum, 1965-67; assoc. Kaye, Scholer, Fierman, Hays & Handler, 1967-70; ptnr. Kaye, Scholer LLP, 1971—2006. Mem. ABA, Assn. of Bar of City of N.Y., Harvard Club (N.Y.C.), Phi Beta Kappa, Ibis Golf and Country Club.

STRUM, PHILIPPA, political science professor, researcher; b. NYC, Dec. 14, 1938; d. Joseph B. and Ida P. Strum; 1 child, David Strum Weiss. BA, Brandeis U., 1959; MEd, Harvard U., 1960; PhD, New Sch. for Social Rsch., 1964. From instr. to assoc. prof. Rutgers U., Newark, 1964-72; vis. prof. Barnard Coll., NYC, 1978-79; vis. scholar NYU, NYC, 1982-83; prof. polit. sci. CUNY, NYC, 1972-99, prof. polit. sci. emeritus, 1999—; dir. U.S. Studies Woodrow Wilson Internat. Ctr. for Scholars, 2001—08, sr. scholar, 2008—. Vis. prof. constl. law Wayne State U., 2000—01; sr. Fulbright lectr. Bosphorus U., Istanbul, 1995. Author: The Supreme Court and "Political Questions", 1974, Brandeis: Justice for the People, 1984, 1984, Brandeis: Beyond Progressivism., 1993, Privacy: The Debate in the U.S. Since 1945, 1998, When the Nazis Came to Skokie, 1999, Women in the Barracks, 2002. Bd. dirs. ACLU, N.Y.C., 1979—; pres. Am.-Israeli Civil Liberties Coalition, N.Y.C., 1981-91. Guggenheim Found. rsch. fellow, 1986-87, ACLS rsch. fellow, 1980-81; Fulbright Exch. Program tchg. fellow, Istanbul, 1995; Woodrow Wilson Internat. Ctr. for Scholars rsch. fellow, 1997-98. Avocations: travel, music. Office: Wilson Center 1300 Pennsylvania Ave NW Washington DC 20004-3027 Business E-Mail: philippa.strum@wilsoncenter.org.

STRUNK, BRIAN L., medical educator; b. Coatesville, Pa., July 21, 1945; married. MD, Harvard, 1971. Cert. ACC, 1976. Assoc. clin. prof. U. Calif. San Francisco Med Sch., 1976—. Office: CAMSF 2 Bon Air Rd Larkspur CA 94939

STRUNK, ORLO CHRISTOPHER, JR., psychology professor; b. Pen Argyl, Pa., Apr. 14, 1925; s. Orlo Christopher and Katherine Elizabeth (Glasser) S.; m. Mary Louise Reynolds, July 3, 1947; children: Laura Louise, John Christopher. Certificate, Churchman Bus. Coll., Easton, Pa., 1948; AB, W. Va. Wesleyan Coll., Buckhannon, 1953; S.T.B., Boston U., 1955, PhD, 1957. Exec. sec. Inst. Pastoral Care, Mass. Gen. Hosp., 1955-57; grad. asst. Boston U., 1955-57, instr. psychology of religion, 1956; instr. Boston U. (Sch. Theology), 1957-58, 62; assoc. prof. psychology W. Va. Wesleyan Coll., 1957-60, dean, prof. psychology, 1959-69; prof. psychology of religion Boston U., 1969-86; also faculty counselor, supr. Albert V. Danielsen Inst. Part-time faculty Webster U., 1994—; pastoral psychotherapist The Coastal Samaritan Ctr., Myrtle Beach, S.C., 1986—2003; assoc. dir., staff psychologist Ecumenical Counseling Svc., Inc., Melrose, Mass.; rsch. cons. Religion in Edn. Found., Calif. Author: Readings in the Psychology of Religion, 1959, Religion: A Psychological Interpretaton, 1962, Mature Religion: A Psychological Study, 1965, The Choice Called Atheism, 1969, The Psychology of Religion, 1971, Dynamic Interpersonalism for Ministry, 1973, The Secret Self, 1976, Privacy: Experience, Understanding, Expression, 1983, three-Two Count, 2005, An Ever-Fixed Mark, 2007, Satan's Angels, 2009; mng. editor: Jour. Pastoral Care and Counseling, 1979-2007, mng. editor emeritus, 2009. Served with USAAF, 1943-46. Decorated Air medal with five oak leaf clusters. Fellow Am. Psychol. Assn.; mem. W.Va. Assn. Acad. Deans (pres.) Methodist (elder). Home: 1068 Harbor Dr SW Calabash NC 28467-2300 Office Phone: 910-579-5084. Personal E-mail: glass@atmc.net. *It is my conviction that life is a mystery to be lived more than it is a problem to be solved. As such, I have tried to develop a style of life which permits me to be open to a wide range of experiences guided by a simple principle which requires me to do battle with all those conditions which disrupt my and others freedom to live an authentic life of openness and continuous growth. The central principle guiding the openness to life is found in the spirit of Jesus Christ which includes love of Self, others, and my God. The task of working out these abstractions in a concrete manner is difficult and mysterious - but never, never dull.*

STRUNK, ROBERT CHARLES, physician; b. Evanston, Ill., May 29, 1942; s. Norman Wesley and Marion Mildred (Ree) S.; m. Juanita; children: Christopher Robert, Alix Elizabeth. BA in Chemistry, Northwestern U., 1964, MS in Biochemistry, 1968, MD, 1968. Lic. MD, Ariz., Colo., Mass., Mo. Resident in pediatrics Cin. Children's Hosp., 1968-70; pediatrician Newport (R.I.) Naval Hosp., 1970-72; rsch. fellow in pediatrics Harvard Med. Sch., Boston, 1972-74; asst. prof. pediatrics U. Ariz. Health Sci. Ctr., Tucson, 1974-78; dir. clin. svcs. Nat. Jewish Ctr. for Immunology and Respiratory Med., Denver, 1978-87; sabbatical leave Boston Children's Hosp., 1984-85; dir. divsn. allergy and pulmonary medicine Children's Hosp., St. Louis, 1987-98; pediatrician Barnes and Allied Hosp., St. Louis, 1987—; prof. pediatrics Washington U. Sch. Medicine, St. Louis, 1987—, Strominger prof., 2002—. Recipient Allergic Disease Acad. award Nat. Inst. Allergy and Infectious Disease of NIH. Mem. Am. Acad. Allergy and Immunology, Am. Thoracic Soc. Office: Washington U Sch Med Dept Pediatrics 1 Childrens Pl Saint Louis MO 63110-1002

STRUNZ, KAI, research scientist, educator; arrived in US, 2002; MS, Saarland U., Saarbruecken, Germany, 1996, PhD summa cum laude, 2001. Rsch. asst. Brunel U., London, 1995—97; engr. R&D Electricite de France, Paris, 1997—2002; asst. prof. U. Wash., Seattle, 2002—. Mem. editl. bd. IEEE Transactions on Power Electronics, 2006—, IET Renewable Power Generation, 2007—. Mem. editl. bd.: IET Renewable Power Generation, 2007—. Sgt. German Armed Forces, 1986—88. Recipient Best Master Degree in Saarland award, German Soc. Elec. and Electronic Engrs., 1996, Dr. Eduard Martin prize, Saarland U., 2002, Outstanding Tchg. award, Dept. Elec. Engring., U. of Wash., 2004; grantee CAREER award, NSF, 2003. Mem.: IEEE (mem. editl. bd. Transactions on Power Electronics 2006—), Internat. Assn. Hydrogen Energy. Achievements include research in multiscale modeling and simulation of electric networks; Stochastic modeling and simulation of electric networks; optimization of electric network design and operation.

STRUP, STEPHEN EDWARD, urologist, educator; s. Roger Dean and Shirlee Anne Strup; m. Sue Henrie Henrie, June 4, 1988; children: Spencer Henrie, Sydney Elizabeth. BA, DePauw U., Greencastle, Ind., 1984; MD, Ind. U. Sch. Medicine, Indpls., 1988. Diplomate Am. Bd. Urology, 1998. Fellow urologic oncology Nat. Cancer Inst., NIH, Bethesda, Md., 1994—96; resident surgery-urology Thomas Jefferson U., Phila., 1988—94, asst. prof. urology, 1996—2003; assoc. prof. urology U. Ky., Lexington, 2003—07, prof. and chief urology, 2007—. Mem.: Soc. Pelvic Surgeons, Am. Urol. Assn. Office: Univ Kentucky 800 Rose St MS-283 Lexington KY 40536

STRUPECK, C. DAVID, accounting educator; b. Chgo., Oct. 14, 1948; s. Carl L. and Viola B. Strupeck; m. Jeanne E. Strupeck (dec. Dec. 6, 2006); children: Benjamin Joseph, Joy Marie Swedeen, Samuel David. BS in bus., Quincy Coll., Ill., 1971; MBA, Southern Ill. U., Carbondale, 1974, PhD, 1981. Asst prof. acctg. U. Nortre Dame, Ind., 1983—85; assoc. prof acctg. Kent State U., Ohio, 1985—89, Bradley U., Peoria, Ill., 1989—93, Ind. U. Northwest, Gray, 1993—. Pres. Acad. Bus. Discipline, Mich., 1999—. Contbr. articles to profl. jours. Office: Ind Univ Northwest 3400 Broadway Gary IN 46408

STRUTHERS, MARGO S., lawyer; BA, Carleton Coll., 1972; JD cum laude, U. Minn., 1976. Atty., shareholder Moss & Barnett, P.A. and predecessor firms, Mpls., 1976-93; ptnr. Oppenheimer Wolff & Donnelly, LLP, Mpls., 1993—. Mem. Am. Health Lawyers Assn., Minn. State Bar Assn. (bus. law sect., former chair nonprofit com., former chair and former mem. governing coun. health law sect.). Office: Oppenheimer Wolff & Donnelly LLP Plaza VII 45 S 7th St Ste 3300 Minneapolis MN 55402-1614 Office Phone: 612-607-7427, 612-607-7000. Business E-Mail: mstruthers@oppenheimer.com.

STRUTHERS, RIC (RICHARD K. STRUTHERS), bank executive; b. 1956; m. Sharon Struthers; children: Corrie, Brice, Ryan. BA in Bus. Mgmt., Pa. State U. Smeal Coll. Bus., 1977; Grad., U. Va. Retail Sch. Banking. Mgr. consumer banking divsn. Md. Nat. Bank, 1978; founding mem. mgmt. team, pres., exec. v.p. MBNA Corp., Newark, Del., 1982—2006; exec. vice-chmn. MBNA America Bank MBNA Mktg. Svcs. Inc., Wilmington, Del., 2003—06; card svcs. ops. exec. Bank of America Corp., Wilmington, 2006—07, N.Am. card svcs. exec., 2007—08, consumer credit risk exec., 2008, pres. global card services, 2009—. Exec. sponsor Hispanic/Latino Orgn. Leadership & Advancement; co-chair capital campaign Del. Nature Soc.; bd. vis., past chmn. Pa. State U. Smeal Coll. Bus.; bd. dirs. The Second Mile, Pa., Emmaus House, Newark, Del. Recipient Disting. Alumni award, Pa. State U. Smeal Coll. Bus., 2002; named an Alumni Fellow, 1998. Mem.: Del. State C. of C. (exec. com.). Office: Bank of America Corp 1100 N King St Wilmington DE 19884 Office Phone: 302-453-9930. Office Fax: 403-294-3260.

STRUTIN, MILLARD DESMOND, surgeon; b. Bklyn., Nov. 15, 1954; s. Frederick and Estelle (Brodzansky) S.; children: William, Benjamin, Collin, Sarah, Lisa Marie. BS in Biology, St. John's U., Queens, NY, 1976; MD, U. Rome, Italy, 1981. Diplomate Am. Bd. Surgery with added qualifications in surgical critical care, 2008. Resident in surgery U. Medicine and Dentistry, Newark, 1981-86; pvt. practice surgery Randolph, N.J., 1988—; attending in gen. surgery Dover (N.J.) Gen. Hosp., 1987-91, St. Clares Hosp., Denville, N.J., 1988—; assoc. attending Morristown Meml. Hosp.; gen. surg., 2008. Fellow ACS (assoc.), Am. Soc. Abdominal Surgeons; mem. AAAS. Office: NW Surg Assocs 121 Center Grove Rd Randolph NJ 07869-4453 Personal E-mail: dtutu54@aol.com.

STRUVE, GUY MILLER, lawyer; b. Wilmington, Del., Jan. 5, 1943; s. William Scott and Elizabeth Bliss (Miller) S.; m. Marcia Mayo Hill, Sept. 20, 1986; children: Andrew Hardenbrook, Catherine Tolstoy, Frank Leroy Hill, Guy Miller, Beverly Marcia Wise Hill (dec.), Elena Wise Struve-Hill. AB summa cum laude, Yale U., 1963; LLB magna cum laude, Harvard U., 1966. Bar: NY 1967, DC 1986, US Dist. Ct. (so. dist.) NY 1970, US Dist. Ct. (ea. dist.) NY 1973, US Dist. Ct. (no. dist.) Calif. 1979, US Dist. Ct. DC 1987, US Dist. Ct. (we. dist.) NY 1991, US Dist. Ct. (no. dist.) NY 2000, US Ct. Appeals (2d cir.) 1969, US Ct. Appeals (DC cir.) 1973, US Ct. Appeals (8th cir.) 1976, US Ct. Appeals (9th cir.) 1979, US Supreme Ct. 1971. Law clk. Hon. J. Edward Lumbard, Chief Judge United States Ct. Appeals for 2d Circuit, 1966-67; assoc. Davis Polk & Wardwell, NYC, 1967-72, ptnr., 1973—, Ind. Counsel's Office, 1987-94. Mem. ABA, NY State Bar Assn., Assn. Bar City NY (chmn. com. antitrust and trade regulation, 1983-86, chmn. com. fed. cts. 1998-2001), Am. Law Inst, Civil War Preservation Trust (trustee). Office: Davis Polk & Wardwell 450 Lexington Ave Fl 30 New York NY 10017-3982 Office Phone: 212-450-4192. E-mail: guy.struve@davispolk.com.

STRUYK, RAYMOND JAY, economist; b. Ann Arbor, Mich., Sept. 5, 1944; s. Jack Howard and Margaret Hazel (McGarry) S.; m. Joan M. Klaski, June 15, 1968 (div. Sept. 1980); children: Pieter, Zachary; m. Jill Davis Khadduri, Sept. 24, 1983 (div. Jan. 1992); m. Anke Mertesdorf, Nov. 8, 1999. BA, Quincy Coll., 1965; MA, Washington U., 1967, PhD, 1968. Mem. staff urban studies group Nat. Bur. Econ. Rsch., NYC, 1968-72; vis. asst. prof. econs. Rice U., Houston, 1971-72; mem. staff Housing Studies Group, Urban Inst., Washington, 1972-74; dep. asst. sec. for rsch. Office of Policy Devel. and Rsch., HUD, Washington, 1977-79; sr. rsch. assoc. Urban Inst., Washington, 1979-83, dir. internat. activities, 1983—92; resident Cons. Russian Fedn., 1992—98, Cons. Germany, 2003—06, Cons. Egypt, 2006—07; sr. fellow NORC, 2007—. Cons. to Republic of Korea, 1975-76, 80, Republic of Indonesia, 1988-89; editor: J Am. Planning Assn., 1978-85, Review of Urban and Regional Development Studies 1898-, J of Housing Economics, 2000-, uropean J of Housing Policy, 2004-; bd. mem. Inst. Urban Economics, Moscow, 1995-, Legal Policy Rsch. Ctr., Almalty, 2008-. Author: Housing Finance: New and Old Models in Central Europe, 2006, Policy Analysis for Effective Development, 2006, Managing Think Tanks, 2006; contbr. articles to profl. jours. Lt. US Army, 1969-71, Vietnam. Mem. Am. Econ. Assn., Cosmos Club. Democrat. Office: NORC 4350 East-West Highway Bethesda MD 20814 Business E-Mail: struyk-ray@norc.org.

STRYCHALSKI, ELIZABETH ARLENE, nanotechnologist, physicist, researcher; b. Dunkirk, NY, Jan. 10, 1980; d. James and Irene Strychalski. Grad. rsch. asst. Cornell U., Ithaca, NY, 2003—. Home: 5170 W Shorewood Dr Dunkirk NY 14048 Business E-Mail: eas58@cornell.edu.

STRYKER, JOAN COPELAND, retired obstetrician, gynecologist, educator; b. Swayzee, Ind., Apr. 17, 1918; d. Kenneth Bayard and Elsie Weser Copeland; m. Walter Stryker (dec.); children: Sara Gill, Peter, David; m. Dawson James Lewis. BS, U. Ill., Urbana, 1939; MD, U. Ill., Chgo., 1943. Resident U. Mich., Ann Arbor, 1943—46, fellow, 1946—47; asst. prof. Wayne State U., Detroit, 1965—85, prof., 1985—2001, prof. emeritus, 2001—. Chief menopausal clinic Hutzel Hosp., Detroit, 1992—2001. Chief investigator (book) Addicted Neonatals. Med. dir. Planned Parenthood, Detroit, 1965—70, treas., 1970; staff mem. WHO, 1958—61. Recipient Disting. Svc. award, Wayne State U. Sch. Medicine, 1988, Pathfinders award in medicine, 1991; named Tchr. of Yr., 1990. Mem.: ACOG (pres., Cmty. Svc. award, Gynecologist of Yr. 1994), Am. Menopausal Soc., Alpha Omega Alpha, Sigma Xi. Avocations: sailing, skiing. Home: 9784 Hawthorne Glen Dr Grosse Ile MI 48138

STRYKER, RICHARD RIPLEY, JR., museum director; b. Anchorage, Aug. 7, 1948; s. Richard Ripley Sr. and Rogene (Garvin) S.; m. Catherine Connell, Aug. 23, 1970; children: Amanda Connell, Alan Connell, Julia Connell. BA in History, Austin Coll., 1971; MA in Am. History, U. Del., 1976. Curator Hist. Soc. of Del., Wilmington, 1976-79; asst. dir. Grand Rapids Pub. Mus., Mich., 1979-85; dir. Corpus Christi Mus. Sci and History, Tex., 1985—. Author articles, manuals, guides in field. Mem. legis. adv. com. to state rep., Del., 1977; mem. Greater Wilmington Area Devel. Council, 1978. Mem. Am. Assn. Museums, Am. Assn. State and Local History, Mus. Assn. South Tex. (pres. 1987-88), Navy League. Republican. Episcopalian. Avocation: golf. Office Phone: 512-883-2862. E-mail: ricks@cctexas.com.

STRYKER, ROBIN, social sciences educator; b. Bloomington, Ind., June 19, 1953; d. Sheldon and Alyce Stryker; m. Scott R. Eliason. BA summa cum laude in Sociology, Smith Coll., Northampton, Mass., 1975; MS, U. Wis., Madison, 1977, PhD, 1986. Asst. to prof. sociology U. Iowa, Iowa City, 1986—2000; prof. sociology, law U. Minn., Mpls., 2000—08, scholar Coll. Liberal Arts, 2004—07; prof. sociology, law U. Ariz., Tucson, 2008—. Scholar residence Max Planck Inst. Study Soc., Cologne, Germany, 1999; jean monnet fellow Robert Schuman Ctr., European U. Inst., Florence, Italy, 2001—02; pres. Soc. Advancement Socio-Economics, Paris, 2001—02; guggenheim fellow John Simon Guggenheim Found., New York, NY, 2008—. Recipient Founder's prize, Soc. Advancement Socio-Economics, 1997; Jean Monnet fellowship, Robert Schuman Ctr., European U. Inst., 2001—02, fellowship, John Simon Guggenheim Found., 2008. Mem.: NSF (law, social sci. adv. 2008—), Am. Sociol. Assn. (chair, theory sect. 2005—06, coun. mem. 2007—, Barrington Moore prize 1997).

STRYKER, SHELDON, sociologist, educator; b. St. Paul, May 26, 1924; s. Max and Rose (Moskevitz) S.; m. Alyce Shirley Agranoff, Sept. 7, 1947; children: Robin Sue, Jeffrey, David, Michael, Mark. BA summa cum laude, U. Minn., 1948, MA, 1950, PhD, 1955. Mem. faculty Ind. U., 1951—, prof. sociology, 1964—, disting. prof. sociology, 1985—2002, disting. prof. emeritus, 2002—; dir. Inst. Social Rsch., 1965—70, 1989—94, chmn. dept. sociology, 1969—75; co-dir. Ctr. Social Rsch., 1989—94. Cons. in field; mem. social scis. research rev. com. NIMH, 1974-79, chmn., 1976-79, mem. research scientist devel. award com., 1981-85 Editor: Sociometry, 1966-69, Rose Monograph Series of Am. Sociol. Assn., 1971-73, Am. Sociol. Rev., 1982-85; assoc. editor: Social Problems, 1957-59; author books, monographs, articles, chpts. in books. Served with AUS, 1943-46. Fellow Social Sci. Research Council, 1959-60, Ctr. Advanced Behavioral Scis., 1986-87; Fulbright research scholar Italy, 1966-67. Mem. Am. Sociol. Assn. (nat. coun. 1965-67, 80-81, chmn. social psychology sect. 1978-79, chmn. publs. com. 1991-93, Cooley-Mead award, W.E.B. DuBois Career Disting. Scholarship award, 2009), Soc. for the Study of Symbolic Interaction (George Herbert Mead award for lifetime scholarship 2000), Ohio Valley Sociol. Soc. (coun. 1965-67), North Ctrl. Sociol. Assn. (pres. 1978-79), Sociol. Rsch. Assn. (coun. 1978-84, pres. 1983-84), Phi Beta Kappa, Internat. Soc. Self and Identity (Lifetime Career award, 2006).

STRYKER, STEVEN CHARLES, lawyer; b. Omaha, Oct. 26, 1944; s. James M. and Jean G. (Grannis) S.; m. Gina; children: Ryan, Kevin, Gerrit, Courtney. BS, U. Iowa, 1967, JD with distinction, 1969; postgrad. studies, Northwestern U. Grad. Sch. Bus, 1969-70, DePaul U., 1971. Bar: Iowa 1969, Tex. 1986; CPA Ill., Iowa. Sr. tax acct. Arthur Young & Co., Chgo., 1969-72; fed. tax mgr. Massey Ferguson, Des Moines, 1972-74; fed., state tax mgr. FMC Corp., Chgo., 1974-78; gen. tax atty. Shell Oil Co., Houston, 1978-81, asst. gen. tax counsel, 1981-83, gen. mgr., 1983-86, v.p., gen. tax counsel, 1986—2000; pvt. practice Houston, 2000—. Mem. ABA, AICPA, Tex. Bar Assn., Tax Execs. Inst. Home and Office: 2117 Del Monte Houston TX 77019

STUART, ALICE MELISSA, lawyer; b. NYC, Apr. 7, 1957; d. John Marberger and Marjorie Louise (Browne) S. BA, Ohio State U., 1977; JD, U. Chgo., 1980; LLM, NYU, 1982. Bar: NY 1981, Ohio 1982, Fla. 1994, US Dist. Ct. (so. dist.) Ohio, 1983, US Dist. Ct. (so. and ea. dists.) NY 1985. Assoc. Schwartz, Shapiro, Kelm & Warren, Columbus, Ohio, 1982-84, Paul, Weiss, Rifkind, Wharton & Garrison, NYC, 1984-85, Kassel, Neuwirth & Geiger, NYC, 1985-86, Phillips, Nizer, Benjamin, Krim & Ballon, NYC, 1987—92; pvt. practice NYC, 1992—98; atty. Dewey & LeBoeuf, LLP, NYC, 1998—. Adj. prof. So. Coll., Orlando, Fla., 1997-98. Surrogate Speakers' Bur. Reagan-Bush Campaign, NYC, 1984; mem. Lawyers for Bush-Quayle Campaign, NYC, 1988. Mem. ABA, NY State Bar Assn., Winston Churchill Meml. Libr. Soc., Jr. League, Soc. Mayflower Descs. (bd. dirs. NY chpt. 2002-07, counselor NY chpt. 2002-07), Jamestowne Soc. (life), New Eng. Soc. (bd. dirs. 2007-), Huguenot Soc. (bd. dirs. 2007—), Women's Nat. Rep. Club (bd. dirs. 2004—), Phi Beta Kappa, Phi Kappa Phi, Alpha Lambda Delta. Republican. Business E-Mail: astuart@deweyleboeuf.com.

STUART, BRAD, professional hockey player; b. Rocky Mountain House, Alta., Can., Nov. 16, 1979; m. Melissa Stuart; children: Jake, Logan Michael. Defenseman San Jose Sharks, 1999—2005, Boston Bruins, 2005—07, LA Kings, 2007—08, Detroit Red Wings, 2008—.

Recipient All-Rookie Team, NHL, 2000. Achievements include being a member of Stanley Cup Champion Detroit Red Wings, 2008. Office: Detroit Red Wings Joe Louis Arena 600 Civic Center Dr Detroit MI 48226

STUART, CAROLE, publishing executive; b. NYC, Feb. 22, 1941; d. Frank and Sally (Stern) Rose: m. Lyle Stuart, Feb. 4, 1982(dec. June 24, 2006); 1 child, Jennifer Susan Livingston. Student, Bklyn. Coll. Pub. Lyle Stuart, Inc., Secaucus, NJ; assoc. pub. Carol Pub. Group, NYC; pub. Barricade Books, Inc., NYC. Author: Why Was I Adopted?, To Turn You On, 39 Sex Fantasies for Women; author: (with Claire Ciliotta) Why Am I Going to the Hospital?; author: I'll Never Be Fat Again, How To Lose 5 Pounds Fast, The Thank You Book. Mem.: Authors Guild, Women's Media Group, Wine and Food Soc. N.Y. Home: 1530 Palisade Ave Apt 6L Fort Lee NJ 07024-5402 Office: Barricade Books Ste 308A 185 Bridge Plz N Fort Lee NJ 02024

STUART, CHARLES EDWARD, electrical engineer, oceanographer; b. Durham, NC, Feb. 9, 1942; s. Charles Edward and Wilma Kelly Stuart; m. Margaret Ann Robinson, Jan. 9, 1982; children: Marjorie Kelly, Heather Alison BSEE, Duke U., 1963. Engr. Westinghouse Electric Corp., Balt., 1963—65; sr. engr. Booz Allen Hamilton, Chevy Chase, Md., 1966—68; rsch. dir. B-K Dynamics Inc., Huntsville, Ala., 1969—78; oceanographer Office of Naval Rsch., Arlington, Va., 1979—84; dir. Maritime Sys. Office Advanced Rsch. Projects Agy., Arlington, 1985—98; with def. programs US Dept. Energy, Washington, 1998—99; pres. Competitive Enterprise Solutions, LLC, Arlington, 2000—. Contbr. articles to profl. jours. Recipient Am. Def. Preparedness Assn. Bushnell award career contbns. undersea warfare, 1996 Mem. IEEE (sr., ad. com. 1991-93), Assn. Unmanned Vehicle Systems (trustee 1989-93) Methodist. Achievements include rsch. in antisubmarine warfare, cybersecurity and unmanned undersea vehicle technology. Office: Competitive Enterprise Solutions LLC PO Box 567 Slidell LA 70458 Office Phone: 985-290-9261. Business E-Mail: cstuart@cesllc.com.

STUART, DABNEY, poet, language educator; b. Richmond, Va., Nov. 4, 1937; s. Walker Dabney Jr. and Martha (vonSchilling) S.; m. Sandra Westcott, Jan. 20, 1983; children: Martha, Nathan vonSchilling, Darren Wynne. AB, Davidson Coll., 1960; AM, Harvard U., 1962. Instr. Coll. William and Mary, Williamsburg, Va., 1961-65; prof. English Washington and Lee U., Lexington, Va., 1965—2002, S. Blount Mason Jr. prof. English, 1991—2002. Vis. prof. Middlebury (Vt.) Coll., 1968-69, Ohio U., Athens, 1975, U. Va., Charlottesville, 1981-83. Author: The Diving Bell, 1966, A Particular Place, 1969, The Other Hand, 1974, Friends of Yours, Friends of Mine, 1974, Round and Round, 1976, Nabokov: The Dimensions of Parody, 1978, Rockbridge Poems, 1981, Common Ground, 1982, Don't Look Back, 1987, Narcissus Dreaming, 1990, Sweet Lucy Wine, 1992, Light Years: New and Selected Poems, 1994, Second Sight: Poems for Paintings by Carroll Cloar, 1996, Long Gone, 1996, The Way to Cobbs Creek, 1997, Settlers, 1999, Strains of the Old Man, 1999, No Visible Means of Support, 2001, The Man Who Loves Cezanne, 2003, Family Preserve, 2005, Tables, 2009. Recipient Dylan Thomas prize Poetry Soc. Am., 1965, Gov.'s award State of Va., 1979, Libr. Va. Poetry award, 2006; NEA lit. fellow, 1975, 82, Guggenheim fellow, 1987-88, Individual Artist fellow Va. Commn. for Arts, 1995, resident fellow Rockefeller Study and Conf. Ctr., Bellagio, Italy, 2000. Avocations: food, travel, painting. Home: 30 Edmondson Ave Lexington VA 24450-1904

STUART, GERARD WILLIAM, JR., investment company executive, alderman, city official; b. Yuba City, Calif., July 28, 1939; s. Gerard William and Geneva Bernice (Stuke) S.; m. Lenore Frances Lorona, 1981. Student, Yuba Jr. Coll., 1957-59, Chico State Coll., 1959-60; AB, U. Calif., Davis, 1962; MLS, U. Calif., Berkeley, 1963. Rare book libr. Cornell U., 1964-68; bibliographer scholarly collections Huntington Libr., San Marino, Calif., 1968-73, head acquisitions libr., 1973-75; sec.-treas., dir. Ravenstree Corp., 1969-80, pres, chmn. bd., 1980—, William Penn Ltd., 1981—. Councilman City of Yuma, 1992-96, deputy mayor, 1995; bd. dirs Ariz. Humanities Coun., 1993-99, Yuma Libr. Found., 1997, chmn., 1997-98, 99-2001, 05—. Lilly fellow Ind. U., 1964-63. Mem. Bibliog. Soc. Am., Rolls-Royce Owners Club, Grolier Club (N.Y.C.), Zamorano Club (L.A.), Phi Beta Kappa, Alpha Gamma Sigma, Phi Kappa Phi.

STUART, JEFFREY L., mathematics professor, consultant; m. Susan Stuart. BA in Math. & Physics, Pomona Coll., Claremont, Calif., 1980; MS in Math., PhD in Math., U. Wis., Madison, 1986. Vis. asst. prof. math. No. Ill. U., DeKalb, 1986—87; prof. math. U. So. Miss., Hattiesburg, 1987—2001, Pacific Luth. U., Tacoma, 2001—. Recipient K.T. Tang Faculty Excellence in Rsch. award, Pacific Luth. U., 2004—05, Faculty Excellence in Tchg. award, U. So. Missisippi, 2000, Disting. Tchg. award, Miss.-La. Sect. Math. Assn. Am., 2000. Mem.: Soc. Indsl. and Applied Math., Math. Assn. Am., Am. Statis. Assn. (v.p. Miss. chpt. 2000—01), Internat. Linear Algebra Soc. (sec.-treas. 2000—09), Phi Beta Kappa. Office: Math Dept Pacific Lutheran Univ Tacoma WA 98447 Business E-Mail: jeffrey.stuart@plu.edu.

STUART, JILL, apparel designer; m. Ron Curtis, 1986; children: Morgan, Chloe, Sophie. Student, RI Sch. of Design. Sold jewelry and handbag designs Bloomingdales, NYC; founded accessory line Jill Stuart, NYC, founded women's wear line, 1993—, launched intimate apparel, eyewear, denim and footwear lines, 2000—. Office: Jill Stuart Offices 550 7th Ave New York NY 10018 Office Phone: 212-921-2600.*

STUART, JOSEPH MARTIN, art museum administrator; b. Seminole, Okla., Nov. 9, 1932; s. Arch William and Lillian (Lindsey) S.; BFA in Art, U. N.Mex., 1959, MA in Art, 1962; m. Signe Margaret Nelson, June 18, 1960; 1 dau., Lise Nelson Stuart. Dir., Roswell (N.Mex.) Museum and Art Center, 1960-62; curator U. Oreg. Mus. Art, 1962-63; dir. Boise (Idaho) Gallery Art, 1964-68, Salt Lake (City) Art Ctr., 1968-71, S.D. Art Mus., Brookings, 1971-93; prof. art S.D. State U., 1971-93; represented in permanent collections: South Dakota Art Museum, Civic Fine Arts Ctr., Sioux Falls, S.D., Coll. Idaho, Eureka Coll., Salt Lake Art Ctr., Sioux City (Iowa) Art Ctr., U. N.Mex. Art Mus., West Tex. State U. With USN, 1951-55. Mem. Phi Kappa Phi. Unitarian. Author: Index of South Dakota Artists, 1974; Art of South Dakota, 1974, Harvey Dunn: Son of the Middle border, 1984, Art for a New Century, 1989; The Legacy of South Dakota Art, 1990; author numerous exhbn. catalogs. Office Phone: 505-466-6625.

STUART, JOSHUA M., biology professor; married. PhD, Stanford U., Calif., 2004. Asst. prof. U. Calif., Santa Cruz, 2003—. Fellowship, Alfred P. Sloan Found., 2005—. Office: Univ Calif Santa Cruz 1156 High St Mail Stop SOE2 Santa Cruz CA 95064 Business E-Mail: jstuart@soe.ucsc.edu.

STUART, LYN (JACQUELINE LYN STUART), state supreme court justice; b. Atmore, Ala., Sept. 23, 1955; m. George Stuart; children: Tucker, Shepard, Kelly. BA in Sociology and Edn., Auburn U., 1977; JD, U. Ala., 1980. Asst. atty. gen. State of Ala.; exec. asst. to commr. and spl. asst. atty. gen. Ala. Dept. Corrections; asst. dist. atty. Baldwin County; dist. judge, 1989—97; judge Ala. Cir. Ct., 1997—2001; assoc. justice Ala. Supreme Ct., 2001—. Faculty advisor Nat. Judicial Coll., Reno; former pres. Ala. Council of Juvenile & Family Ct. Judges; pres. Blue Ridge Inst. for Juvenile & Family Ct. Judges, 2002. Former pres. Heritage Junior Women's Club, Bay Minette Kiwanis Club, Jubilee Woman's Club; bd. mem. Ala. Federation of Women's Clubs. Republican. Office: Ala Supreme Ct 300 Dexter Ave Rm 3-215 Montgomery AL 36104-3741 Office Phone: 334-229-0626. Business E-Mail: lstuart@appellate.state.al.us.*

STUART, NANCY RUBIN (NANCY ZIMMAN STETSON), journalist, author, television producer; b. Boston, Nov. 25, 1944; d. Stuart Wendell and Ethel (Rabinovitz) Zimman; m. William W. Stetson, Apr. 28, 2001; children: Elisabeth, Jessica. BA, Tufts U., 1966; MA in Teaching, Brown U., 1967; PhD (hon.), Mt. Vernon Coll., 1995. Playwright, dir. Equity Library Theatre, Roundabout, Joseph Jefferson and St. Clement's theaters, N.Y.C., 1971-74; freelance reporter Westchester-Gannett newspapers and mags., 1975-77, N.Y. Times, NYC, 1977—. Faculty affiliate Bush Ctr. in Child Devel., Yale U., New Haven, 1981-86; mem. Westchester County Women's Adv. Bd., chair, 1988; bd. dirs. Women Writing Women's Lives Seminar; mem. faculty SUNY, Purchase, 1994-95, Fordham U., N.Y.C., 1996-99. Author: The New Suburban Women, Beyond Myth and Motherhood, 1982, The Mother Mirror: How a Generation of Women is Changing Motherhood in America, 1984, Isabella of Castile: The First Renaissance Queen, 1991, American Empress: The Life and Times of Marjorie Merriweather Post, 1995, Club Dance: The Show, The Steps, The Spirit of Country, 1998, The Reluctant Spiritualist: The Life at Maggie Fox, 2005, The Muse of the Revolution: The Secret Pen of Mercy Otis Warren and the Founding of a Nation, 2008; writer, assoc. prodr: TV series America's Castles for A&E Network, 1996—99 (Telly award, 1999, Telly award (3), 2001, Writing Communicator award, 1999), The Gold Coast for The Grand Tour A & E TV, 1997, writer prodr., prodr.: TV series Restore America, 1999; writer prodr., prodr. (TV series) Restore America, 2001 (3 Telly awards); writer/assoc. prodr.: TV series Eccentrics, 1999 (Crystal award, Telly award), The N.Y. Times, 1977—, writer: New England Quarterly; writer Baltimore Sun, American History Magazine; contbg. editor: Parents mag., 1987—91,: McCalls, Savvy, Travel & Leisure, Ladies Home Jour., 1980—92; theater critic: Stamford Advocate, 1994—96; co-prodr.:. Recipient Washington Irving award Westchester Libr. Assn., 1993, Telly award finalist, 2001; Am. Antiquarian Soc. fellow, 2005; Time, Inc.-Bread Loaf Writers' Colony scholar, 1979. Fellow MacDowell Colony; mem. Author's Guild, Am. Soc. Journalists and Authors (Author of Yr. award 1992, hon. mention oustanding book award, gen. nonfiction 2006, Hist. Window House Book award 2009), PEN, Nat. Arts Club. Avocations: skiing, sailing, ballet, classical music, dance. Personal E-mail: thewriteway@aol.com.

STUART, ROBERT, container manufacturing executive; b. Oak Park, Ill., Aug. 3, 1921; s. Robert S. and Marie (Vavra) Solinsky; m. Lillian C. Kondelik, Dec. 5, 1962 (dec. May 1978); m. Lila Winterhoff Peters, May 21, 1982, (dec., Dec. 07). BS, U. Ill., Chgo., 1943, LLD, 1982. Sec.-treas., gen. mgr. Warren Metal Decorating Co., 1947-49; asst. to gen. mgr. Cans, Inc., 1950-52; asst. to v.p., then v.p. Nat. Can Corp., Chgo., 1953-59, exec. v.p., 1959-63, pres., 1963-69, chief exec., 1966-69, chmn. bd., CEO, 1969-73, chmn. bd., 1973-83, chmn. fin. com., 1983, mem. corp. devel. com., until 1986, chmn. emeritus, 1986—. Past pres., bd. dirs. Corp. Responsibility Group of Greater Chgo. Past pres., bd. dirs. Chgo. Crime Commn.; past dir. Nat. Crime Prevention Coun.; founding chmn. Nat. Minority Supplier Devel. Coun., 1972-73, Lloyd Morey Scholarship Fund: Freedoms Found. at Valley Forge, past trustee; past mem. adv. bd. Salvation Army, Broader Urban Involvement and Leadership Devel.; chmn. emeritus World Federalist Assn.; past bd. dirs., past moderator Millard Congl. Ch.; past pres. Ctrl. Ch. Chgo.; chmn. emeritus Assn. to Unite the Democracies. Capt. AUS, 1943-46. Mem.: Rotary (past pres. Chgo. club, past dist. gov.), Little Ship Club (London), Yacht Club, Chgo. Club, Masons (32d degree, Red Cross of Constantine), Alpha Kappa Lambda (past nat. pres.). Home and Office: 233 SW 43d Ter Cape Coral FL 33914

STUART, ROBERT KENNETH, internist, hematologist, oncologist, educator; b. Baton Rouge, July 6, 1948; s. Walter Bynum and Rita Bess (Kleinpeter) S.; m. Gail Elaine Wiscarz, June 12, 1971 (div. Dec. 1988); children: R. Morgan, Elaine C.; m. F. Charlene Gates, Nov. 2, 1991. BS, Georgetown U., 1970; MD, Johns Hopkins U., Balt., 1974. Diplomate Am. Bd. Internal Medicine. Resident in medicine Johns Hopkins Hosp., Balt., 1974-76, oncology fellow Oncology Ctr., 1976-78; rsch. fellow Sloan-Kettering Inst., NYC, 1978-79; asst. prof. Johns Hopkins U., Balt., 1979-84, assoc. prof., 1984-85; prof. medicine Med. U. S.C., Charleston, 1985—; assoc. dir. Hollings Cancer Ctr., Charleston, 1993-97; chmn. dept. oncology King Faisal Specialist Hosp and Rsch. Ctr., Riyadh, Saudi Arabia, 1997-2001; prof. medicine Med.U. S.C., Charleston, 2001—. Bd. dirs. Aplastic Anemia Found., Balt., 1982-93, med. adv. bd., 1993-98; mem. nat. team Tour of Hope, 2004. Recipient Champions Advocacy award, Am. Soc. Hematology, 2004, Partners in Progress award, Leukemia and Lymphoma Soc., 2004, Physician Healthcare Hero award, Charleston Regional Bus. Jour., 2007; named one of Best Dr. Am., 2007. Democrat. Roman Catholic. Office: Medical Univ of South Carolina 171 Ashley Ave Charleston SC 29425-0100 E-mail: stuartrk@musc.edu.

STUART, SANDI, lobbyist; BA, U. NC. Legis. dir. to Rep. Bob Matsui US Ho. of Reps., legis. asst. to Rep. Vic Fazio, assoc. staff budget com., chief of staff to Rep. Vic Fazio, assoc. staff appropriations com.; asst. sec. def. for legis. affairs US Dept. Defense; sr. ptnr. Clark & Weinstock, Washington. Pres. America's Trust. Bd. dirs. Calif. State Soc.; adv. bd. US Merchant Marine Acad. Office: Clark & Weinstock 601 13th St, NW Ste 410 Washington DC 20005 Office Phone: 202-261-4000.*

STUART, SHERRY BLANCHARD, artist; b. Newport, Ark., Feb. 19, 1941; d. Walter Thomas Blanchard and Eathel Gladys Faulkner; m. Michael John Scholl, 1963 (div. 1970); 1 child, Aaron John Scholl; m. Roy Otto Stuart, Oct. 5, 1973; 1 child, Ross. BFA, Mpls. Coll. Art and Design, 1964. Designer logos. Exhibited in group shows at Bennington Ctr. for the Arts, 1999, Ariz. Hist. Mus./Joan Cawley Gallery, 1998, Merrill Johnson Gallery, Denver, 2001, Desert Caballeros Western Mus., 2001, Hilligoss Galleries, Chgo., 2002, Nita Stewart Haley Libr. and History Ctr./Elieb Biek Art Mus., 2002, Am. Artists Profl. League, N.Y.C., 2002, Nichols Fine Art Gallery, Taos, N.Mex., 2003, Ky. Horse Park, Lexington, 2003, Breckenridge Fine Arts Ctr., 2003, Harness Tracks of Am. 26th Ann. Art Show and Auction, Lexington, 2003, Stewart Gallery, 2004, Phoenix Civic Ctr. Plaza, 2004, Phippen Mus., 2004, Howard/Mandville Gallery, Kirkland, Wash., 2004, Norby Gallery, Cave Creek, Ariz., 2004, Mus. of the S.W., 2004, Open Range Gallery, Scottsdale, Ariz., 2008, numerous other group shows, juried and invitational, one-woman shows include Gold Nugget Art Gallery, Wickenburg, Ariz., 2003, Cowgirl Up: Desert Caballeros Western Mus. (Best Show award, 2008). Recipient People's Choice award, Am. Acad. Women Artists, 1999, 2d Ann. Western ARt Classic, Mpls., 1985, 1st place and Best of Show, Minnetonka Ctr. Arts, 1979, Award of Excellence, Chinese Artists Assn. N.Am., 2003, numerous other 1st and 2d place awards various exhbns., juried shows. Mem.: Western Artists of Am., Am. Plains Artists (signature mem.), Oil Painters of Am. (signature mem.), Am. Acad. Women Artists (signature mem.), Creative Women of Pinnacle Peak (founding mem.). Republican. Avocations: antiques, photography, cooking, golf, horseback riding. Business E-Mail: whoswho@sherryblanchardstuart.com.

STUART, WALTER BYNUM, III, retired banker; b. Baton Rouge, Oct. 5, 1922; s. Walter Bynum and Rosa (Gauthreaux) S.; m. Rita Kleinpeter, May 20, 1944; children: Walter Bynum IV, Robert, Douglas, Ronald, Scott. BS, La. State U., 1943. Adminstrv. mgr. Kaiser Aluminum & Chem. Corp., 1946-63; v.p. First Nat. Bank Commerce, New Orleans, 1963-65, sr. v.p., 1965, exec. v.p., 1965-73; vice chmn. bd., dir. 1st Nat. Bank Commerce, New Orleans, 1973-78; exec. v.p. 1st Commerce Corp., New Orleans, 1972-73, pres., 1973-75, vice-chmn. bd., 1975-78, dir., 1973-78; pres. Am. Bank & Trust Co., Lafayette, La., 1978-86, cons., ret., 1986. Assoc. dir., mem. faculty Sch. Banking La. State U., 1973-75, dir., 1975-78; mem. Faculty Assemblies for Bank Dirs. Campaign group chmn. industry com., mem. United Fund for Greater New Orleans Area, 1974; mem. research com. Pub. Affairs Research Council La., 1973-76, v.p., trustee, 1973-76; bd. dirs. Bur. Govtl. Research, 1973-77, Council Better La., 1975—; pres. New Orleans Indsl. Devel. Bd., 1973-75. Served to lt. (j.g.) USNR, 1943-46. Mem. C. of C. of Greater New Orleans Area (v.p. 1973-75, bd. dirs.), Am. Bankers Assn., La. Bankers Assn. (pres. 1977), Am. Mgmt. Assn., Kappa Alpha, Delta Sigma Pi, Beta Gamma Sigma. Democrat. Roman Catholic. Home: 10100 Hillview Dr Apt 2109 Pensacola FL 32514-5481 *Recognizing that life is the experiencing of reality, and that reality is simply a continuing series of problems, I long ago decided that I would treat a problem as an opportunity. Every incident of difficulty has always invited my intense interest as a challenge, and my thoughts have been immediately marshalled for positive effort. My life has been most rewarding because I believe that "a problem is an opportunity!".*

STUBBE, RAY WILLIAM, minister, writer; b. Milw., Aug. 15, 1938; s. Clarence Arnold and Ruby Otillie (Mueller) Stubbe. BA, St. Olaf Coll., 1962; MDiv, Northwestern Luth. Theol. Sem., 1965; postgrad., U. Chgo., 1967. Ordained to ministry Evang. Luth. Ch. Am., 1965. Mission devel. bd. Am. missions Luth Ch. in Am., Oak Creek, Wis., 1965-66; organizer, pastor All Saints Luth Ch., Oak Creek, 1966-67; enlisted USN, 1955; commd. ensign USNR, 1963, advanced through grades to lt., comdr. chaplain corps, 1971; augmented to USN, 1971; chaplain, 1967-85; ret. USN, 1985. Interviews on national televised programs including Vietnam: A Soldier's Story, 1998, War Stories With Oliver North: Khe Sanh, 2001, Atmospheres: War and Weather, 2002, R. Lee Ermey's Mail Call: Back to Vietnam, 2005, Inside: The Vietnam War, 2008. Author: Inside Force Recon, 1989, Khe Sanh Chaplain, 1970, Paddles, Parachutes, Patrols, 1979, Aarugha, 1989, Valley of Decision, 1991, The Final Formation, 1995, Khe Sanh and the Mongol Prince, 2002, Battalion of Kings, 2005, revised edit., 2008, B5-T8 in 48 QXD: The Secret Official History of the North Vietnamese Army of the Siege at Khe Sanh, Vietnam, Spring, 1968, 2006, numerous poems; editor: Khe Sanh Veteran/Red Clay, 1996—98; contbr. articles to profl. jours. Founder, pres. emeritus Khe Sanh Vets., Inc., 1988—; spkr. numerous vet. assemblies; chaplain Wis. Vietnam Vets., Milw., 1984—, 3d Marine Divsn. Assn., 1988. Decorated Bronze Star with combat V; recipient Legion of Honor award, Chapel Four Chaplains. Mem.: DAV (life), VFW (life), Soc. Bibucol Lt., 3rd Recon Assn. (life), Mil. Chaplains Assn. of USA (life), Wis. Acad. Scis., Arts and Letters (life), Spl. Ops. Assn. (life), 3d Marine Divsn. Assn. (life), Spl. Forces Assn. (life), Force Reconnaissance Assn. (life), Mil. Chaplains Assn. (life), Marine Corps Hist. Found. (life), Mil. Officers Assn. Am. (life), Wis. Vietnam Vets. (life), Vietnam Vets. Am. (life), Pi Kappa Delta. Lutheran. Avocation: boxing. Home: 8766 Parkview Ct Wauwatosa WI 53226-2729 *The most powerful Words of God have always been communicated to me by the occasional people encountered in life's pathways. These are the quiet ones whose very being reflect possibilities of being the image of God we all are; living Words of God who make us know we are free, forgiven, loved, blessed with value and future; heroes, who at great risk and pain to themselves, transform negatives into positives; great, good people who empty themselves into servants and incarnate love into all human conditions. When the vision they offer becomes life's task of who to become, all of life becomes a gift of everdeepening wells which nourish everything living with the deep underground stream, which is God.*

STUBBS, GERALD, biochemist, educator; b. Hobart, Australia, May 9, 1947; came to the US, 1976; m. Rebecca Lynn Harris; children: Andrew, Tamsin, Anneliese, Rachel. BSc, Australian Nat. U., 1968; DPhil, U. Oxford, 1972. Sci. asst. Max Planck Inst., Heidelberg, Germany, 1973-76; rsch. assoc. Brandeis U., Waltham, Mass., 1976-83; asst. prof. Vanderbilt U., Nashville, 1983-87, assoc. prof., 1987-90, prof., 1990—. Contbr. articles to profl. jour. Achievements include determination of molecular structure of tobacco mosaic virus. Office Phone: 615-322-2018. Business E-Mail: gerald.stubbs@vanderbilt.edu.

STUBBS, KENDON LEE, retired librarian; b. Washington, Apr. 6, 1938; s. Donald and Rosalee S.; m. Patricia Townsend, June 3, 1961; children: Christopher, Peter, Timothy. BA, St. John's Coll., Annapolis, Md., 1960; MA, U. Va., 1964; MS, Columbia U., 1965. Sr. asst. in manuscripts U. Va. Libr., Charlottesville, 1965, reference libr., 1966-76, acting acquisitions libr., 1967-68, assoc. univ. libr., 1976-87, assoc. univ. libr. for pub. svcs., 1987-92, acting univ. libr., 1993, assoc. univ. libr., 1994-98, dep. univ. libr., 1998—2003, ret., 2003. Cons. US Dept. Edn., Washington, 1982—84. Author: Quantitative Criteria for Academic Research Libraries, 1984; editor: Cumulated Assn. Research Libraries Statistics, 1981, Rsch. Libr. Statistics, 1990, ARL Statistics, 1992-95, Japanese Text Initiative on World Wide Web, 1995-2003; contbr. articles on library stats., rsch. to profl. publs., Internet. Mem. Assn. of Rsch. Librs. (mem. stats. com., vis. program officer 1995-97), Bibliog. Soc. U. Va. (pres. 1975-78, v.p. 1978-99).

STUBBS, LU, sculptor, educator; b. NYC, Aug. 16, 1925; d. Thomas Benedetti and Clara Benvenuto; m. Harold L. Stubbs, Nov. 16, 1945; children: Susan Lee, Mahi Swan. Grad. highest honors, Sch. Boston Mus. Fine Arts, 1963, grad., 1964. Art cert. L'Accademia di Belle Arti, Perugia, Italy, 1971. Tchg. grad. asst. Mus. Sch., Boston, 1963—64, Boston Ctr. Edn., 1964—76, Milton Acad., Mass., 1967—68, Boston U., 1976—77. Bronze sculpture, Three Women, Bookline Mass., 1975, Deborah Sampson Revolutionary War Heroine, Sharon, Mass., 1989, Foxtale Family, Children's Libr., Foxboro, Mass., 2000, Pregnant Woman II, Cooley Dickinson Hosp., Northampton, 2001, Mary Lyon, Mt. Holyoke Coll., South Hadley, Mass., 2006, Happy Frog, Northampton, Mass., 2008. Vol. Svc. Net., Northampton, Mass., 2000—; mem. Arts Coun., Northampton, Mass., 2005—07. Grantee, Nat. Endowment Arts and Humanites, 1977, Browne Fund, Boston, 1987. Fellow: Nat. Sculpture Soc.; mem.: New Eng. Sculptor's Assn., Sharon Creative Arts Assn. Avocations: gardening, creative writing.

STUBBS, WILLIAM W., interior designer; b. Gonzales, Tex. Attended, Internat. Inst. Design, Washington, DC. Owner, pres., designer William W. Stubbs & Assocs., Houston, 1987—. Author: I Hate Red, You're Fired! The Colorful Life of an Interior Designer, 2004; host (TV series) A Moment of Luxury, 2008—. Recipient Houston Chronicle & Am. Soc. Interior Design award, Prizm award, Great Houston Builders Assn., Golden Nugget - Best in the West award, Champion of Literacy award; named one of 100 World's Top Designers and Architects, Archtl. Digest. Mem.: Internat. Interior Design Assn. (Outstanding Design award). Office: WIlliam W Stubbs & Assocs 7745 San Felipe Ste 205 Houston TX 77063 Office Phone: 713-780-7772. Office Fax: 713-977-1151. Business E-Mail: Bill.Stubbs@wwstubbs.com.*

STUBER, CHARLES WILLIAM, retired genetics educator, researcher, director; b. St. Michael, Nebr., Sept. 19, 1931; s. Harvey John and Minnie Augusta (Wilks) S.; m. Marilyn Martha Cook, May 28, 1953; 1 child, Charles William Jr. BS, U. Nebr., 1952, MS, 1961; PhD, N.C. State U., 1965. Vet., agrl. instr. Broken Bow HS, 1956-59; rsch. asst. U. Nebr., Lincoln, 1959-61; rsch. geneticist Agrl. Rsch. Svc., USDA, Raleigh, NC, 1962-75, supervisory rsrch. geneticist, rsch. leader, 1975-98, collaborator, 1998—; prof. genetics & crop sci. NC State U., Raleigh, 1975-98, prof. emeritus, 1998—, dir. Ctr. Plant Breeding and Applied Plant Genomics, 2006—. Assoc. editor Crop Sci. Jour., 1979-82, tech. editor, 1984-86, editor, 1987-89; contbr. over 200 articles to profl. jour., chpt. to books. Chmn. coun. on ministries and numerous offices Highland United Meth Ch., Raleigh. Lt. USN, 1952-56. Named Outstanding Sci. of Yr., USDA-ARS, 1989; recipient Genetics and Plant Breeding award Nat. Coun. Comml. Plant Breeders, 1995, Award of Merit, U. Nebr. Alumni Assn., 1997; inductee USDA-Agrl. Rsch. Svc. Sci. Hall of Fame, 1999; Vol. 45 of MAYDICA dedicated to Charles W. Stuber, 2000. Fellow: Crop Sci. Soc. Am. (editor-in-chief 1987—91, pres. 1992—93, Crop Sci. Rsch. award 1995, DeKalb Genetics Crop Sci. Disting. Career award 1999), Fellow Am. Soc. Agronomy (pres. 2002); mem.: Am. Genetic Assn. (sec. 1984—86), Genetics Soc. Am., Phi Kappa Phi, Sigma Xi. Avocations: windsurfing, water-skiing. Home: 1800 Manuel St Raleigh NC 27612-5510 Office: NC State U NC Agril Res Svc 4124 Williams Hall Raleigh NC 27695-7620 Office Phone: 919-515-5834. Office Fax: 919-515-7959. Personal E-mail: cstuber2@aol.com.

STÜBGEN, JOERG-PATRICK, neurologist; b. Tripoli, Libya, Sept. 7, 1959; s. Fritz Hans Georg and Marie-Louise Hildegard Stübgen; m. Dana Annenberg; 1 child, Charlotte. MD, U. Pretoria, South Africa, 1983. Diplomate Am. Bd. Psychiatry and Neurology. Intern Grey's Hosp., Pietermaritzburg, South Africa; neurology resident U. Pretoria, South Africa, 1984—89, neuromuscular fellow, asst. prof. dept. neurology, 1990—91, assoc. prof., 1991—92; asst. prof. Cornell U., NYC, 1995—99, assoc. prof. dept. neurology, 2000—08, prof. clin. neurology, 2008—. Contbr. articles to profl. jours., chapters to books. Named one of Best Doctors in Am., 2003—04, America's Top Physicians, Consumer's Rsch. Coun. Am., 2005, Top Doctors N.Y. Metro Area, Castle Connelly Med. Ltd., 2006. Fellow: South Africa Coll. Medicine, Am. Bd. Electrodiagnostic Medicine, Royal Coll. Physicians and Surgeons Can., Coll. Physicians South Africa, Am. Assn. Electro-Diagnostic Medicine; mem.: AMA, Am. Neurological Assn., Med. Soc. State N.Y., N.Y. Med. Soc., Am. Acad. Neurology. Lutheran. Avocations: road running, travel. Office: Cornell Univ Med College 525 E 68th St New York NY 10021 Home Phone: 212-288-5047; Office Phone: 212-746-2334. Business E-Mail: pstuebge@med.cornell.edu.

STUCKER, BRENT, science educator; PhD, Tex. A&M U., Coll. Sta. Prof. U. RI, Kingston, 1997—2002; vis. prof. VTT Tech. Rsch. Ctr., Helsinki, Finland, 2008—. Contbr. articles to profl. jour. Office: Utah State Univ 4130 Old Main Hill Mech & Aero Engr Logan UT 84322-4130 Business E-Mail: brent.stucker@usu.edu.

STUCKER, FRED JOSEPH, otolaryngology educator; b. Chgo., Oct. 17, 1934; m. Debbie Stucker. MD, U. Mich., 1961. Diplomate Am. Bd. Otolaryngology. Intern USN Hosp., San Diego, 1961-62, resident in surgery Oakland, Calif., 1965-66, resident in otolaryngology, 1966-69; fellow in facial plastic and reconstructive surgery Am. Acad. Plastic and Reconstructive Surgery, Detroit, 1974; prof. otolaryngology, chmn. dept. La. State U., Shreveport; mem. staff Schumpert Med. Ctr., Shreveport. Officer M.C., USN, 1961-69. Fellow Am. Acad. Facial Plastic and Reconstructive Surgery, Am. Soc. Head and Heck Surgery; mem. ACS (bd. govs.), AMA, Am. Rhinologic Soc. (sec. 1996—), Triologic Soc. Office: La State U Med Ctr PO Box 33932 1501 Kings Hwy Shreveport LA 71103-4228

STUCKEY, ELLEN MAE, music educator; d. Charles Franklin and Mary Dolores Hershberger; m. Joseph Bruce Stuckey, Jr., June 9, 1979; children: Laura L., Aaron N. BS in Music Edn., West Chester U., 1977; MEd in Music Edn., Pa. State U., 1981. Cert. music tchr. Pa. Dept. Edn. Music tchr. K-5 Everett (Pa.) Area Sch. Dist., 1977—82; pvt. music tchr. Martinsburg, 1982—; tchr. jr./sr. high vocal/gen. music Hollidaysburg (Pa.) Area Sch. Dist., 1988—89; music tchr. K-5 No. Bedford County Sch. Dist., Loysburg, Pa., 1990—. Dir. adult choir 1st Bapt. Ch. Altoona, Pa., 1977—87, Martinsburg Grace Brethren Ch., 1989—2006. Composer, lyricist: songs Hail to You, O Northern Bedford, 1995, composer, co-author: mus. drama The Ark of Faith, 2003, composer, prodr., lyricist: musical CD Fence!, 2007; contbr. articles to profl. mags. Founder Aaron N. Stuckey Meml. Found.; dir. luminary svc. Am. Cancer Soc., Martinsburg, 2002, 2003; mistress of ceremonies Little Miss pageant Roaring Spring (Pa.) Lions Club, 1996, 1997, 1998. Mem.: Pa. State Educator's Assn., Nat. Guild Piano Tchrs., Am. Choral Dirs. Assn., Pa. Music Educators Assn. Republican. Grace Brethren. Avocations: gardening, photography, songwriting. Office: No Bedford County Sch Dist 217 NBC Dr Loysburg PA 16659 Home: 438 Brookfield Ln Martinsburg PA 16662

STUCKI, MARGARET ELIZABETH, painter, writer; b. West New York, NJ, Jan. 9, 1928; d. William Eugene and Elise (Hohl) Stucki. BA in Philosophy, Barnard Coll., 1949; MA in Fine Art, Columbia U., 1959; postgrad., Art Students League N.Y.C., 1949-51; ABD, NYU, 1961; PhD, Freedom U., Orlando, Fla., 1975. Prof. art Hartwick Coll., NY, 1962-72. One-woman shows include Wichita Art Assn., Kans., 1967, Swiss Ctr., N.Y.C., 1975, Capitol Bldg., Augusta, Maine, 1978, U.S. Senate, Washington, 1987, Idaho TV 8, 1998, Idaho State U. Women's Art Show, 2000, exhibitions include Treasure Valley Juried Exhbn., Boise State U., 1998, prin. works include oil painting The Crucifixion, Temple Bapt. Ch., Tallahassee, portraits; author: The Revolutionary Mission of Modern Art or Crud and Other Essays on Art, 1973, War on Light: The Destruction of the Image of God in Man Through Modern Art, 1975, Eco-Elegia: Elegies in Ecology, 1981, Gullible's Travels: An Educational Tax Exempt Trip Around the World in a Hot Air Balloon, 1987, October: A Thoreaunal, 2002, Margaret Stucki: A Pictorial Autobiography of the Swiss-American Artist (1928—), 2004, Croak: USSR-USA Top Secret Weather Control Tesla-Tech, 2005. Pub. spkr. Rorschach Soc. Projective Techniques, London, 1968, 3d Internat. Congress Social Psychiatry, Zagreb, Yugoslavia, 1970, Women for Constl. Gov., Washington, 1975, nat. convs., Boston, 1977, West Palm Beach, Fla., 1988, Rotary Club, Farmington, Maine, 1979. Recipient 4 awards for photography, 1951, 1961, 1997, 1999, Poetry prize, Swiss Civic Cultural Soc., 1983; grantee, Rsch. Coun., Finger Lakes, N.Y., 1967. Home: 1050 E Center St Pocatello ID 83201-5201

STUCKY, SCOTT WALLACE, federal judge, lawyer; b. Hutchinson, Kans., Jan. 11, 1948; s. Joe Edward and Emma Clara (Graber) S.; m. Jean Elsie Seibert, Aug. 18, 1973; children: Mary-Clare, Joseph. BA summa cum laude, Wichita State U., 1970; JD, Harvard U., 1973; MA, Trinity U., 1980; LLM with high honors, George Washington U., 1983; postgrad., Nat. War Coll., 1993. Bar: Kans. 1973, US Dist. Ct. Kans. 1973, US Ct. Appeals (10th circuit) 1973, US Ct. Mil. Appeals 1974, US Supreme Ct. 1976, DC 1979, US Ct. Appeals (DC circuit) 1979. Assoc. Ginsburg, Feldman & Bress, Washington, 1978-82; chief docketing and svc. br. Nuclear Regulatory Commn., Washington, 1982-83; legis. counsel USAF, Washington, 1983-96; gen. counsel US Senate Armed Services Com., 1996—2001, prin. minority counsel, 2001—03, gen. counsel, 2003—06; judge US Ct. Appeals for the Armed Forces, Washington, 2006—. Lectr. bus. law Maria Regina Coll., Syracuse, NY, 1977; congrl. fellow Office Senator John Warner, 1986; res. judge advocate USAF Reserve, Washington, 1982-2003; col. Appellate Mil. Judge, USAF Ct. Criminal Appeals, 1991-95, 97-98, 2001-03; sr. reservist USAF Judiciary, 1995-97, Air Reserve Pers. Ctr., 1998-99, Air Force Legal Svcs. Agy., 1999-2001. Contbr. articles to profl. jours. Capt. USAF, 1973-78. Decorated Legion of Merit, Air Force Meritorious Svc. medal with two oak leaf clusters. Mem. Fed. Bar Assn., Judge Advocates Assn. (bd. dirs. 1984-88), Reserve Officers Assn., Wichita State U. Alumni Assn. (pres. chpt. 1981-86, nat. bd. dirs. 1986-92), Adoption Svc. Info. Agy. (bd. dirs. 1998-2002, 04-07), Army and Navy Club (Washington), Mil. Order of Loyal Legion US (state comdr. and recorder 1984-92, nat. treas. 1987-89, nat. vice comdr. 1989-93, nat. comdr.-in-chief 1993-95), Sons of Union Vets Civil War (chpt. vice comdr. 1986-88), Phi Delta Phi, Phi Alpha Theta, Phi Kappa Phi, Omicron Delta Kappa (bd. dirs. 2006-), Sigma Phi Epsilon. Republican. Episcopalian. Office: US Ct Appeals for the Armed Forces 450 E St NW Washington DC 20442*

STUCKY, STEVEN (EDWARD), composer, conductor; b. Hutchinson, Kans., Nov. 7, 1949; s. Victor Eugene and Louise Doris (Trautwein) Stucky; m. Melissa Jane Whitehead, Aug. 22, 1970; children: Maura Catharine, Matthew Steven. MusB, Baylor U., 1971; MFA, Cornell U., 1973, DMA, 1978. Vis. asst. prof. Lawrence U., Appleton, Wis., 1978-80; prof. Cornell U., Ithaca, NY, 1980—, chmn. dept. music, 1992-97; vis. prof. Eastman Sch. of Music, 2001—02; Ernest Bloch vis. prof. U. Calif., Berkeley, 2003. Composer-in-residence L.A. Philharm. Orch., 1988-2009, Am. Acad. Rome, 2006. Author: Lutoslawski and His Music, 1981 (Deems Taylor award ASCAP 1982); composer: Sappho Fragments, 1982, Voyages, 1984, Boston Fancies, 1985, Dreamwaltzes, 1986, Concerto for orch., 1987, Son et Lumière, 1988, Angelus, 1990, Impromptus, 1991, Four Poems of A.R. Ammons, 1992, Ancora, 1994, Double Flute Cto., 1994, Fanfares and Arias, 1994, Pinturas de Tamayo, 1995, Music for Saxophones and Strings, 1996, Cradle Songs, 1997, Concerto Mediterraneo, 1998, Ad Parnassum, 1998, American Muse, 1999, Nell'ombra, nella luce, 2000, Etudes, 2000, Partita-Pastorale, after J.S.B., 2000, Concerto for Percussion and Wind Orchestra, 2001, Skylarks, 2001, Colburn Variations, 2002, Whispers, 2002, Album Leaves, 2002, Spirit Voices, 2003, Jeu de timbres, 2003, Second Concerto for Orchestra, 2003 (Pulitzer Prize for music, 2005), To Whom I Said Farewell, 2003, Sonate en forme de préludes, 2004, Piano Quartet, 2005, Three New Motets, 2005, Radical Light, 2007, August 4, 1964, 2008, Rhapsodies, 2008; received commn. from Nat. Endowment for Arts, 1982, Koussevitzky Found., 1991, Meet the Composer, 1995, 2004. Bd. advisors Barlow Endowment, 1993-97; bd. dirs. MacDowell Colony, 1993-95, Koussevitzky Found., 2006—, Am. Acad. in Rome, 2006-, Am. Music Ctr., 2008-. Fellow Guggenheim Found., Nat. Endowment for the Arts, Bogliasco Found., Goddard Lieberson fellow Am. Acad. Arts and Letters. Fellow: Am. Acad. Arts and Scis.; mem.: AAAL. Office: care Philip Wilder 21C Media Group 162 56th St Ste 506 New York NY 10019 Office Phone: 212-245-2110 ext. 205. Personal E-mail: stevenstucky@mac.com.

STUDDARD, (CHRISTOPHER) RUBEN, singer; b. Birmingham, Ala., July 14, 1978; s. Kevin Studdard Sr. and Emily Studdard; m. Surata Zuri, June 28, 2008. Graduated, Ala. A&M U., 2000. Singer, jazz and soul band Just a Few Cats; singer, gospel group God's Gift. Backup singer: American Idol: The Search for a Superstar, 2002; singer, 2003 (named American Idol, 2003), (single) Flying Without Wings, 2003, (albums) Soulful, 2003, I Need an Angel, 2004, The Return, 2006; singer: (with various artists) American Idol Season 2: All Time, 2003; cameo Scooby Doo 2: Monsters Unleashed, 2004; nominee commentator: I Wanna Thank My Mama: The BET Awards 2004 Nomination Special; performer: American Idol Tour, 9th Annual Walk of Fame Honoring Aretha Franklin, 2003, Fromage, 2003, American Idol Christmas, 2003, 3rd Annual BET Awards, 2003, Good Morning America, 2004; guest appearances Oprah Winfrey Show, 2003, 2004, Making the Video, Ruben Studdard: Flying Without Wings, 2003, American Juniors, 2003, Sharon Osbourne Show, 2003, Late Show with David Letterman, 2004, The Ellen DeGeneres Show, 2004, Mad TV, 2004, One on One, 2004, Jimmy Kimmel Live, 2004. Nominee Grammy award for best male vocal R&B performance. He was nicknamed the 'Velvet Teddy Bear' by the legendary soulful diva Gladys Knight. During the competition he acknowledged his home town of Birmingham, Alabama by wearing a t-shirt adorned with the city area code "205." The state declared March 11 'Ruben Studdard Day'. Office: J Records 745 5th Ave New York NY 10151 Office Phone: 646-840-5600.

STUDDS, COLIN EASTMAN, ecologist, researcher; b. Buffalo, Aug. 26, 1972; s. Colin Auld and Mary Lou Studds. BA, Brown U., Providence, 1997; MS, U. Rhode Island, South Kingstown, RI, 2001; PhD, U. Maryland, Coll. Pk. Md., 2008. Rsch. scientist Smithsonian Environ. Rsch. Ctr., Edgewater, Md., 2001—02; postdoctoral rschr. Smithsonian Migratory Bird Ctr., Washington, 2008. Contbr. scientific papers. Mem.: Am. Ornithologists Union. Home: 707 Jefferson St NW Washington DC 20011 Office: Smithsonian Migratory Bird Ctr 3001 Connecticut Ave NW Washington DC 20008 Business E-Mail: studdsc@si.edu.

STUDEBAKER, FORREST E., history educator; b. Saranac, NY, Feb. 2, 1941; s. Marion S. Boisvert and Esther D. Studebaker. BA, U. Md. U. Coll., Coll. Pk., 1968, MA with distinction, 1970; PhD, U. London, 1978. Adj. lectr. U. Md., Coll. Pk., 1980—85, grad. prof., 1993—97, adj. prof., Monterey Inst. Internat. Studies, Calif., 1988—90, prof., 1989—91, Clinton CC, Plattsburgh, NY, 1998—. Petty officer USN, 1958—66, human resources mgr., 1971—75, San Diego, 1977—79, Naval Ship R&D Ctr., Carderock, Md., 1967—71, USAR, Stuttgart, Baden-Wurtenburg, Germany, 1979—85, US Nat. Govt., Monterey, 1985—88. Contbr. articles to profl. jour.

STUDER, WILLIAM ALLEN, security consultant, retired military officer; b. Chgo., July 27, 1939; s. William Gotlieb and Annette Elizabeth (Bruzek) S.; m. Donna Barnes Bray, Dec. 26, 1961; children: Scott, Shannon. BS in Indsl. Mgmt., Ga. Tech., 1962; MS in Guidance and Counseling, Troy State U., 1975, MS in Mgmt., 1978; graduate, Air War Coll., Maxwell AFB, Ala., 1981, Air Command and Staff Coll., 1975. Commd. 2d lt. USAF, 1961, advanced through grades to maj. gen., 1989; legis. liaison U.S. Senate, Washington, 1981-83; dir. fighter ops./tng. USAF Hdqrs. Europe, Ramstein AB, Fed. Republic Germany, 1983-84; vice comdr. 10th Tactical Reconnaissance Wing RAF USAF, Alconbury, Eng., 1984-85, comdr. 10th Tactical Reconnaissance Wing RAF, 1985-86, comdr. 81st Tactical Fighter Wing RAF Bentwaters, Eng., 1986-87, comdr. 316th Air Div/Kaiserslautern Ramstein AB, Fed. Republic Germany, 1987-88, vice comdr. 12th Air Force/U.S. So. Command Bergstrom AFB, Tex., 1988-90, comdr. 13th Air Force Clark AFB, The Philippines, 1990-91; dir. ops. CENTCOM/J-3, MacDill AFB, Fla., 1992-94; ret. USAF, 1994; dir. pub. safety dept. Hillsborough County, Tampa, Fla., 1994—2005, emergency preparedness cons., 2005—; pres. Studer & Assoc., Tampa. Decorated D.S.M., Legion of Merit with oak leaf cluster, DFC with three oak leaf clusters, Bronze Star, Air medal with 35 oak leaf clusters; Legion of Honor, Bronze Cross medal (The Philippines). Mem. Daedalians, Quiet Birdmen, Rotary. Avocations: golf, reading, hiking. Home: 5309 Bayshore Blvd Tampa FL 33611 Office: Studer & Assoc Tampa FL 33611 Office Phone: 813-758-5106. Personal E-mail: studerdm@verizon.net.

STUDER, WILLIAM JOSEPH, library director; b. Whiting, Ind., Oct. 1, 1936; s. Victor E. and Sarah G. (Hammersley) S.; m. Rosemary Lippie, Aug. 31, 1957 (dec.); children: Joshua E., Rachel Marie. BA, Ind. U., 1958, MA, 1960, PhD (Univ. fellow), 1968. Grad. asst. divsn. libr. sci. Ind. U., 1959-60, reference asst., 1960-61; spl. intern Libr. of Congress, 1961-62, reference libr., sr. bibliographer, 1962-65; dir. regional campus librs. Ind. U., Bloomington, 1968-73, assoc. dean univ. librs., 1973-77; dir. librs. Ohio State U., Columbus, 1977-2000, prof. emeritus libr. sci., 2000—, coord. univ. oral history program, 2001—. Mem. Libr. Svcs. and Constrn. Act Adv. Com. of Ind., 1971-76; mem. Adv. Coun. on Fed. Libr. Programs in Ohio, 1977-85, chmn., 1980-81; adv. coun. Libr. Svcs. and Tech. Act, 1997-99; mem. ARL Office Mgmt. Studies Adv. Com., 1977-81, ARL Task Force on Nat. Libr. Network Devel., 1978-83, bd. dirs., 1981-84, chmn., 1981-83, com. on preservation, 1985-88, vice-chmn., 1989-90, chmn., 1991-92, task force on scholarly comm., 1983-87, com. stats. and measurement, 1993-99, chmn., 1997-98; network adv. com. Libr. Congress, 1981-88; libr. study com. Ohio Bd. Regents, 1986-87; mem. steering com. Ohio Libr. and Info. Network (OhioLINK), 1987-90; vice-chmn. Ctr. Rsch. Librs., 1993-94, chmn., 1994-95, sec., chmn. membership com., 1990-93; adv. coun. OhioLink Libr., 1992-2000, chmn., 1991-92, policy adv. coun., governing bd., 1991-92. Contbr. articles to profl. jours. Trustee Online Computer Libr. Ctr. Inc., 1977-78; del. Online Computer Libr. Ctr. Users Coun., 1983-91; rsch. librs. adv. com. Online Computer Libr. Ctr., 1989-95, vice-chmn., chmn.-elect, 1993-94, chmn., 1994-95; bd. dirs. Ohio Network of Librs. Ohionet, 1977-87, chmn., 1980-82, 86-87, treas., 1983-86; mem. Columbia U. Sch. Libr. Svc. Conservation Programs, vis. com., 1987-90; nat. adv. coun. to commn. on preservation and access, 1989-92; treas. Monroe County (Ind.) Mental Health Assn., 1968-76; budget rev. com. United Way, 1975-77; bd. dirs. Mental Health Assn. Recipient citation for participation MARC Insts., 1968-69, Disting. Alumni award Ind. U., 1978, OhioLINK Founders award, 2002. Mem. ALA, Ohio Libr. Assn. (bd. dirs. 1980-83), Assn. Coll. and Rsch. Librs. (bd. dirs. 1977-81, com. on activities model for 1990, 1981-82, chmn. libr. sch. curriculum task force 1988-89), Ohio State U. Retirees Assn. (pres.-elect 2004-05, pres., 2005-06), Acad. Libr. Assn. Ohio, Torch Club (pres. 1993-94), Phi Kappa Phi (pub. rels. officer 1982-83, sec. 1983-85), Phi Eta Sigma, Alpha Epsilon Delta, Beta Phi Mu. Home: 724 Olde Settler Pl Columbus OH 43214-2924 Office: Ohio State U William Oxley Thompson Meml Libr 1858 Neil Ave Columbus OH 43210-1286 Office Phone: 614-688-0204. Business E-Mail: studer.2@osu.edu.

STUDIN, JAN, publishing executive; Grad., Ithaca Coll., NY, 1978. From acct. mgr. to v.p. Woman's Day mag. Hachette Filipacchi Media Inc., 1982—95, v.p., advt. dir., 1995—96, v.p., pub. NYC, 1996—2002; v.p., pub. Parents mag. Meredith Corp., 2002—06, v.p., pub. Better Homes & Gardens mag., 2006—08, v.p. corp. sales, 2008—. Office: 125 Park Ave New York NY 10017 also: Meredith Corp 325 Lexington Ave New York NY 10017 Office Phone: 212-557-6600, 212-499-2000.

STUDWELL, WILLIAM EMMETT, librarian, writer; b. Stamford, Conn., Mar. 18, 1936; s. Alfred Theodore and Mary Alice (Baker) S.; m. Ann Marie Stroia, Aug. 28, 1965 (dec. 2003); 1 child, Laura Ann. BA, U. Conn., 1958, MA, 1959; MLS, Cath. U. Am., 1967. Tech. abstracter Libr. Congress, Washington, 1963-66, asst. editor decimal classification office, 1966-68; head libr. Kirtland C.C., Roscommon, Mich., 1968-70; head/prin. cataloger No. Ill. U., DeKalb, 1970-2000; freelance writer, editor, 2001—. Mem. US Adv. Com. to Chemistry Sects., Universal Decimal Classification, 1968-72; chmn. adv. group Libr. Rsch. Ctr., Urbana, Ill., 1982-84. Author: Chaikovskii, Delibes, Stravinskii, 1977, Christmas Carols, 1985, Adolphe Adam and Leo Delibes, 1987, Ballet Plot Index, 1987 (named one of Outstanding Academic Books, Choice Mag., 1989), Cataloging Books, 1989, Library of Congress Subject Headings, 1990, Opera Plot Index, 1990, Christmas Card Songbook, 1991, Subject Access to Films and Videos, 1992, Popular Song Reader, 1994, Christmas Carol Reader, 1995 (named one of the Best Christmas Books, Pub.'s Weekly Mag., 1995), National and Religious Song Reader, 1996, Americana Song Reader, 1997, Minor Ballet Composers, 1997, State Songs of the United States, 1997 (academic best seller), Publishing Glad Tidings, 1998, College Fight Songs, 1998, Barbershops, Bullets, and Ballads, 1999, Circus Songs, 1999, The End of the Year, 1999, The Classic Rock and Roll Reader, 1999, They Also Wrote, 2000, The Big Band Reader, 2000, The Clandestine Classical Music Reader, 2000, Forward! Forward! Is the Word, 2000, College Fight Songs II, 2001, Lest We Forget, 2001, A Fable, A Fantasy, and a Farewell, 2002, The French Violin School, 2002, Suzannah's Redemption, or The Devil Gets His Due, 2003, The Man Who Invented God and Other Fantastic Tales, 2004, Ten Terrible Tales, 2005, College Fight Songs III, 2005, The Christmas Carol in the New Millennium, 2006, An Easy Guide to Christmas Carols, 2006, Seven Deadly Singles, 2007, Final Flights of Fancy, 2008, The Clandestine Classical Music Reader, 2008, Fabulous Fables and Fantastic Fantasies, 2009, Beautiful Winners Before Beautiful Dreamer, 2009; asst. editor Western Assn. of Map Librs. Info. Bull., 1989—94; editor: Music Reference Svcs. Quar., 1991—99, Resources in Music History Book Series, 1999—2008, The Millennia Collection, 2000—; contbg. editor Technicalities, 1996—2004; contbr. articles to profl. jours.; Cons. (films) A Christmas Carol. US expert on Christmas Carols; internat. recognized expert on Am. Coll. fight songs; internat. leader to devel. standardization code for libr. congress subject headings; leading internat. proponent multinat., multicultural and multilingual subject access sys. Named most productive author among librs. in US, Coll. and Rsch. Librs. Mag., 1983-87, 93-97, Outstanding Alumnus, Sch. Libr. and Info. Sci., Cath. U. America, 2003. Mem. Ill. Assn. Coll. and Rsch. Librs. (exec. bd. 1980-85, newsletter editor 1980-85, lifetime achievement award 1992), Ill. Libr. Assn., Librs. for Social Responsibility (editor newsletter 1986-87, bd. dirs. 1986-94). Home: 3332 S Forrester St Bloomington IN 47401-7115

STUEBER, NANCY, museum director; m. Dan Stueber. BS in Environ. Biology and Terrestrial Ecology, U. Pitts. Mgr. cmty. events and temporary exhibits Ore. Mus. Sci. and Industry, Portland, 1981, v.p. exhibits, COO, interim pres., pres. Bd. mem. Portland Streetcar, Inc., Ore. Natural Step Network. Mem.: AAM, Ore. Women's Forum, Assn. Sci.-Tech. Centers (bd. v.p.), Portland Ore. Visitors Assn. (bd. chair 2006—07). Office: Ore Mus Sci and Industry 1945 SE Water Ave Portland OR 97214-3354 Office Phone: 503-797-4514. Office Fax: 503-797-4500.

STUEBING, EDWARD WILLIS, research scientist; b. Cin., Sept. 9, 1942; s. Edward Norman and Ruth Marcella (Glass) S.; m. Mary Ann Brown (div. 1980); children: Barbara Jean, Jennifer Jane. BS with high honors, U. Cin., 1965; PhD, Johns Hopkins U., Balt., 1970. Rsch. scientist U.S. Army Frankford Arsenal, Phila., 1971—77, U.S. Army, Edgewood R&D Ctr., Aberdeen Proving Ground, Md., 1977—; joint svcs. bus. area mgr. CB Def. Supporting Sci. and Tech., 1994—2003, chief scientist for physical scis., 1999—2001, team leader, br. chief aerosol sci., 1992—. Adj. prof. Drexel U., Phila., 1973-1976; invited lectr. nat. and internat. scientific meetings. Contbr. articles to profl. jours., book chapters Dir. Civic Assn., Kingsville, Md., 1989-92; pres. Gunpowder Valley Conservancy, Md., 1990-94, treas., 1995—; elder Presbyn. Ch., Franklinville, Md., 1993—. Capt. U.S. Army, 1970-71. Recipient Army R&D Achievement award, 1974, 85, medal for Meritorious Civilian Svc., 1984, The Outstanding Fed. Profl. of 1984 award Fed. Exec. Bd., 1984, William H. Walker award, 1989. Mem. Am. Assn. for Aerosol Rsch. (chmn. nat. meeting 1983, dir. 1998—2001), Am. Chem. Soc., Am. Phys. Soc., Phi Beta Kappa, Sigma Xi. Avocations: trombone, sailing. Home: PO Box 233 Gunpowder MD 21010-0233 Office: 5183 Blackhawk Rd Bldg E5951 RDCB-DRT-A Aberdeen Proving Ground MD 21010-5424 Office Phone: 410-436-3089.

STUEBNER, JAMES CLOYD, real estate developer, contractor; b. Phila., Dec. 15, 1931; s. Erwin A. and Frances (Quinn) Stuebner; children: Kathleen, Stephen, James, Susan, Elizabeth. BA, Dartmouth Coll., 1953. Sales engr. Rohm & Haas Co., Phila., 1956-69; pres. Structural Plastics Corp., Mpls., 1961-69; pres., gen. ptnr. Stuebner Properties, Mpls., 1969—; pres. Northland Inn and Exec. Conf. Ctr., 1988—; CEO Five Star Realty and Devel. Co., Mpls., 1992—. Boone 94 Properties (Sleep Inn Hotel), 1998. Mem. Minn. Conv. Ctr. Commn., St. Paul, 1988; commr. Minn. Econ. Devel. Commn., St. Paul, 1985; bd. dirs. Bach Soc. of Minn., Mpls., 1986—, Minn. Orchestral Assn., Mpls., 1988-91. Sgt. U.S. Army, 1953-55. Mem. Nat. Assn. Office and Indsl. Parks (bd. dirs. Minn. chpt. 1976-85, 81-90, pres. 1978-80, 92-93, nat. pres. 1983-84, v.p. 1981-81, Developer of Yr. award 1987, Minn. Bus. Person of Yr. award 1990, vice chmn. indsl. devel. forum 1996, chmn. 1997). Avocations: sailing, running, singing.

STUEHRENBERG, PAUL FREDERICK, librarian; b. Breckenridge, Minn., Mar. 14, 1947; s. Henry Ernest Frederick and Marian Violet (Sandberg) S.; m. Suzanne Elaine Draper, June 14, 1969 (div. Apr. 1982); m. Carole Lee DeVore, Aug. 1, 1983. BA, Concordia Sr. Coll., 1968; MDiv, Concordia Sem., 1972; STM, Christ Sem., 1974; MA, U. Minn., 1978, PhD, 1988. Asst. libr. U. Minn., Mpls., 1974-82; monographs libr. Yale Divinity Libr., New Haven, 1982-91, div. libr., 1991—; adj. assoc. prof. in theol. lit. Yale Divinity Sch., New Haven, 1993—. Asst. pastor Christ Meml. Luth. Ch., Plymouth, Minn., 1974-82; adj. pastor Bethesda Luth. Ch., New Haven, 1984—; sec. Luth. Student Found., Mpls., 1978-81. Contbr. articles to profl. jours. Sec. North Haven (Conn.) Libr. Bd., 1989-2003. Mem. Am. Theol. Libr. Assn. (pres. 2004-05), Soc. Bibl. Lit., Am. Acad. Religion, North Haven Meml. Libr. Assn. Home: 280 Bayard Ave North Haven CT 06473-4307 Office: Yale U Div Sch Libr 409 Prospect St New Haven CT 06511-2167 E-mail: paul.stuehrenberg@yale.edu.

STUEWER, SHERRI K., oil industry executive; BS in Engring., Cornell U., 1973, MS in Engring., 1975. Mgr. Baytown refinery Exxon Mobil Corp., gen. mgr. Exxon Co. USA supply dept., strategic planning mgr., v.p. safety, health, and environ. Pres., bd. mem. Houston Regional Monitoring Corp.; mem. bd. trustees Engring. Coll. Coun. Cornell U.; chmn. industry adv. bd. Internat. Energy Agy.; bd. mem. Galveston Bay Found. Bd. mem. Baytown C. of C., YMCA Met. Dallas. Office: Exxon Mobil Corp Hdqs 5959 Las Colinas Blvd Irving TX 75039-2298*

STUFFT, DERRY L., education educator; EdD, Ind. U. Pa., Indiana. Cert. superintendent Pa. Asst. prof. edn. U. Scranton, Pa., 2005—. Office: Univ Scranton 137 McGurrin Hall Scranton PA 18510 Business E-Mail: stufftd2@scranton.edu.

STUFKEN, JOHN, statistician, educator; s. Maria Stufken; m. Lili Chen, Apr. 18, 1990; children: Sharon, Byron. PhD, U. Ill., Chgo., 1986. Prof. Iowa State U., Ames, 1997—2002; program dir. NSF, Arlington, Va., 2000—03; prof. & head U. Ga., Athens, 2003—. Editor, Am. statistician Am. Statis. Assn., Alexandria, Va., 2009—. Elected fellow, Inst. Math. Stats., 2000, Am. Statis. Assn., 2001. Avocation: racquetball. Office: Univ Ga Dept Stats Athens GA 30602 Office Phone: 706-542-5232.

STUHAN, RICHARD GEORGE, lawyer; b. Braddock, Pa., July 1, 1951; s. George and Pauline Madeline (Pavlocik) S.; m. Mary Ann Cipriano, Aug. 23, 1975; children: Brendan George, Sara Katherine, Brian Christopher, Caitlin Emily. BA summa cum laude, Duquesne U., 1973; JD, U. Va., 1976. Bar: Va. 1976, D.C. 1977, U.S. Ct. Appeals (D.C. cir.) 1977, U.S. Ct. Appeals (4th cir.) 1977, U.S. Claims Ct. 1979, U.S. Supreme Ct. 1980, U.S. Ct. Appeals (3d cir.) 1981, U.S. Ct. Appeals (11th cir.) 1982, U.S. Dist. Ct. (no. dist.) Ohio 1985, Ohio 1986. Assoc. Arnold & Porter, Washington, 1976-84; of counsel Jones Day, Cleve., 1984-86, ptnr., 1987—. Pres. Womankind Maternal and Prenatal Care; chmn. devel. com. Doan Brook Watershed Partnership. Mem. Va. Law Review, 1974-76. Recipient Gold Medal for Gen. Excellence, Duquesne U., 1973; named Ohio Super Lawyer, Law and Politics Media, Inc. Mem. Cleve. Bar Assn. (chmn. jury svc. com.), Internat. Assn. Def. Counsel, Order of Coif. Democrat. Roman Catholic. Avocations: tennis, swimming, basketball, home repair. Home: 2865 Falmouth Rd Shaker Heights OH 44122-2838 Office: Jones Day 901 Lakeside Ave Cleveland OH 44114-1190 Home Phone: 216-561-3595; Office Phone: 216-586-7148. Business E-Mail: rgstuhan@jonesday.com.

STUHR, ELAINE RUTH, former state legislator; b. Polk County, Nebr., June 19, 1936; m. Boyd E. Stuhr, 1956; children: Cynthia (Stuhr) Zluticky, Teresa (Stuhr) Robbins, Boyd E., Jr. BS, U. Nebr. Tchr. jr. and sr. vocat. h.s. Nebr. schs.; senator Nebr. Unicameral, Lincoln, 1995—2006; chmn. Nebr. retirement sys. com.; vice chair natural resources com.; commr. edn. com. of states; farmer Bradshaw, Nebr. Former asst. instr. U. Nebr., Lincoln; participant farmer to farmer assignment to Russia with Winrock, Internat., 1993, to Lithuania with Vol. Overseas Coop. Asistance, 1993; former pres. Agrl. Womens Leadership Network; former mem. bd. dirs. Feed Grains Coun., Nebr. Corn Bd. Past pres., bd. dirs. Found. for Agrl. Edn. and Devel.; former mem. exec. com. and bd. dirs. Agrl. Coun. Am.; nat. pres. Women Involved in Farm Econs., state pres.; mem. adv. com. Nebr. Extension Sv.; bd. dirs. Heartland Ctr. for Leadership Devel.; past chmn. Nebr. Agrl. Leadership Coun. Republican. Business E-Mail: elainestubr@mainataycomm.net. E-mail: estuhr@unicam.state.ne.us.

STUIVENGA, DOUGLAS R., engineering educator; s. William Glenn and Joy Stuivenga; m. Brenda S. Cardwell, July 29, 1979; 1 child, Drexler Cameron Scott. BS, Oreg. State U., Corvallis, 1982, MEd, 1985. Cert. in engring., Project Lead Way, 2007. Engring. tchr. McNary HS, Keizer, Oreg., 1982—. Recipient Unsung Heroes award, ING, 2006. Office: McNary HS 595 Chemawa Rd N Keizer OR 97303

STUKENBERG, MICHAEL WESLEY, lawyer; b. Freeport, Ill., Feb. 22, 1951; s. Wesley W. and Nancy Jack (Baker) S.; m. Amanda Reed Eggert, July 21, 1973; children: Sarah Reed, William Robinson. BA, Princeton U., 1973; JD, Vanderbilt U., 1976. Bar: Tex. 1977, U.S. Tax Ct. 1977, U.S. Dist. Ct. (so. dist.) Tex. 1982. Assoc. firm Branscomb P.C., Corpus Christi, Tex., 1976-81, shareholder, 1981—. Gov. Art Mus. South Tex., Copus Christi, 1990-96; dir., pres. Corpus Christi Estate Planning Coun., 1989-98; trustee, chair bd. trustees YMCA Corpus Christi, 1997-. Fellow Am. Coll. Trust and Estate Counsel; mem. ABA, Tex. Bar Assn. (tax sect.), Tex. Acad. of Probate and Trust Lawyers, Coll. of State Bar of Tex., Corpus Christi Yacht Club. Episcopalian. Home: 3502 Aransas St Corpus Christi TX 78411-1302 Office Phone: 361-888-9261. E-mail: mstukenberg@branscombpc.com.

STULBERG, BERNARD NATHAN, orthopaedic surgeon, research scientist; b. Kalamazoo, Aug. 2, 1948; s. Julius and Esther (Lieberman) S.; m. Carolyn Sue McComish, Oct. 16, 1976; children: Jonah James, Benjamin L., Micah Adam, John Samuel. BA, U. Mich., 1970, MD, 1974. Diplomate Am. Bd. Orthopaedic Surgery. Intern U. Chgo., 1974-75, resident in surgery, 1974-76; resident in orthop. surgery Hosp. for Spl. Surgery, NYC, 1979, fellow in orthop. rsch., 1980; staff surgeon in orthop. surgery Cleve. Clinic Found., 1980-90, staff scientist dept. musculoskeletal rsch., 1985-90; head divsn. arthritis surgery Case Western Res. U., Cleve., 1990-92; dir. Cleve. Ctr. Joint Reconstrn., 1992—2008, Cleve. Clinic, 2008—. Cons. Johnson & Johnson Orthopaedic Divsn., Inc., New Brunswick, N.J., 1983-89, Techmedia Corp., 1986-94, Implex Corp., 1994-2004, Wright Med., 1994-99, Collaborative Clin. Rsch. Sci. Adv. Bd., 1995-97. Contbr. orthopaedic articles to profl. jours.; patentee in field. ABC Exch. fellow Am. Orthopaedic Assn., 1987. Mem. AMA, Am. Acad. Orthop. Surgeons (chmn. FDA device adv. bd. 1996-2007), Orthop. Rsch. Soc. (bd. dirs. 1988-89), Am. Orthop. Assn., Mid-Am. Orthop. Assn., The Hip Soc., The Knee Soc., Ohio Orthop. Soc., Cleve. Orthop. Club, Internat. Soc. Tech. in Arthroplasty (pres. 1994-95), Phi Beta Kappa, Phi Kappa Phi, Pi Sigma Alpha. Jewish. Avocations: music, violin, tennis, golf, long distance running. Home: 7470 Water Fall Trl Chagrin Falls OH 44022-3967 Office: Cleve Clinic Orthop & Rheumatology Inst 1730 W 25th St Ste 4E Cleveland OH 44113 Office Phone: 216-363-3300. Business E-Mail: stulbeb@ccf.org.

STULL, DONALD LEROY, architect; b. Springfield, Ohio, May 16, 1937; s. Robert Stull and Ruth Branson; m. Patricia Ann Ryder, Dec. 29, 1959 (div. Dec. 1985); children: Cydney Lynn, Robert Branson, Gia Virginia. BArch, Ohio State U., 1961; MArch, Harvard U., 1962. Registered arch. Calif., Conn., Fla., Ky., Maine, Md., Mass., Mo., N.H., N.J., N.Y., Pa., R.I., Tenn., Va., D.C., Wash. Pres. Stull Assocs., Inc., Boston, 1966-83, Stull and Lee, Inc., Boston, 1983—. Mem. Loeb fellowship com. Harvard Grad. Sch. Design, Cambridge, 1969-80; mem. adv. bd. Boston Archtl. Ctr., 1972-80, Mus. Nat. Ctr. of Afro-Am. Artists, Boston, 1978—90, Ohio State U. Sch. Architecture, 1980—95; design prof. Harvard Grad. Sch. Design, 1974-81; mem. vis. design studio, Rice U., Houston, spring 1993; mem. vis. com. Yale Sch. Art and Architecture, New Haven, 1972-76, William Henry Bishop chair Yale Sch. Architecture, 1975; mem. nat. presdl. design award jury Nat. Endowment for Arts, 1984, 88; bd. overseers The Inst. of Contemporary Art, Boston, 1996-98. Trustee Shaw U., 1973-75, Boston Found. for Architecture, 1992—97; mem. design adv. panel, Balt., 1976-80; chmn. Mass Art Commn., Boston, 1978-80; commr. Boston Art Commn., 1980-92; mem. Design Adv. Group, Cambridge, 1980-90, 94—; commr. Boston Civic Design Commn., 1987—1998; adv. com. Suffolk Sch. Bus. Mgmt., 1989-95; bd. dirs Hist. Boston, 1990-98, Mus. of Afro-Am. History, Boston, 1979—1995; trustee Mass. Coll. Art, 1995-2000, 03-05. Recipient Presdl. Design award Nat. Endowment for Arts, 1988; named one of Outstanding Young Men of Boston, 1969, Outstanding Young Men in Am., 1970, Centennial Yr. Outstanding Alumnus Ohio State U., 1970. Fellow AIA (nat. design com. 1972-84); mem. Boston Soc. Archs. (bd. dirs. 1969, 1999-2001, AIA Regional Design award 1975, 80-89, Honor award 1997), Nat. Coun. Archtl. Registration Bds., Mass. Soc. Archs. (bd. trustees 1995). Office: Stull and Lee Inc 38 Chauncy St Ste 1100 Boston MA 02111-2301 Office Phone: 617-426-0406. E-mail: dstull@stullandlee.com.

STULL, EVALYN MARIE, artist; b. Hays, Kans., June 7, 1949; d. Harold Kenneth Gossett and Helen Marie Loreg; m. Dennis Eugene Kincaid, Dec. 4, 1967 (div. 1968); children: Pamela Sue Kincaid, Mark Allen Kincaid; m. Kenneth Eugene Stull, Dec. 4, 1973 (dec. July 27, 2006); children: Daniel Eugene, Carl Andrew. A in Gen. Studies, Morgan CC, Ft. Morgan, Colo., 1994. Owner Stull's Kinder Day Care, Fort Morgan, Colo., 1994, Paintings by Evalyn Stull, Chase, Kans., 2001—07; with Sunflower Diversified, Greatbend, Kans., 1998—99. Bd. dirs. Rice County Arts Coun., Sterling Coll., Kans., 2003—06. Exhibitions include Kans. State Fair, Hutchinson, 1996—98. Achievements include regconition for painting a mural on a carport. Home and Office: 201 Cedar/PO Box 134 Chase KS 67524

STULL, FRANK WALTER, elementary school educator; b. Easton, Pa., June 4, 1935; s. George Washington and Minnie Elizabeth S.; m. Darlene Joy Hunsicker, Aug. 2, 1958; children: James, Ronald, Wendy. BS, East Stroudsburg State Coll., 1956; MEd, Lehigh U., 1966. Cert. tchr., N.J. Tchr. Korea Heung-Up Bank, Seoul, Korea, 1957-58, Howell Twp. Elem. Sch., Freehold, NJ, 1958-59, Holland Twp. Elem. Sch., Milford, NJ, 1959-91. Bd. dirs., sec., treas., mgr. Hunterdon County Sch. Employees Fed. Credit Union, Phillipsburg, N.J., 1969-87, mem. adv. com., 1995; merit badge counselor Boy Scouts Am., 1970-84, cubmaster, 1971-72; treas., mem. Hist. Preservation Commn. Holland Twp., 1993—; bd. govs. Riegel Ridge Cmty. Ctr., 1997-2000; trustee, scholarship coord. C&E Found., 1997—. Recipient Meritorious Svc. award N.J. Credit Union League, 1988, Tchr. Recognition award State N.J. Gov., 1987, Disting. Achievement award for rsch. and preservation of history of Holland Twp. and surrounding areas; named Outstanding Elem. Tchr. Am., 1972; Experienced Tchr. in Geography fellow Pa. State U., 1967. Mem. NEA, Holland Twp. Edn. Assn., Hunterdon County Edn. Assn., N.J. Edn. Assn., Phi Delta Kappa (chartered mem. Zeta Gamma chpt.). Avocations: photography, travel. Home and Office: 2040 Lehigh St Apt 606 Easton PA 18042-3852

STULMAKER, RICHARD M., retired social studies educator; b. Bklyn., Sept. 23, 1940; s. Arthur M. and Sophe Stulmaker; children: Alissa A. Hughes, Kenneth L. BA, SUNY Albany, MA, 1964. Cert. secondary sch. tchr. NYS, 1964. Soc. sci. tchr. Herkimer Ctrl. Sch., NY, 1964—2001; sociology tchr. Mohawk Valley CC, Utica, 1970—85; adj. prof. sociology Utica Coll., NY, 1988—. Solicit mcht., sponsors, walkers CROP, Herkimer, 1995. Capt. USAR, 1964—69, Utica. Avocations: carpentry, travel, reading. Home: Oak Ridge Terrace Herkimer NY 13350 Office: Utica Coll 1600 Burrstone Rd Utica NY 13502 Personal E-mail: thirdplatoon@bluefrognet.net. Business E-Mail: rstulma@utica.edu.

STULTING, ANDRIES ANDRIESSEN, ophthalmologist; b. Cape Town, South Africa, Aug. 29, 1948; s. Andries Andriessen and Magdalena (Van Huyssteen) Stulting; m. Lemainé Fouché, Dec. 15, 1973; children: Lizette, Liesl. MB ChB, U. Pretoria, 1973, MMed in Ophthalmology, 1981. Intern S.A. Def. Force, Pretoria, 1974; sr. houseman H.F. Verwoerd and Kalafong Hosps., Pretoria, 1975-76, med. officer, 1976, sr. med. officer, 1976-77, sr. med. officer, registrar dept. ophthalmology, 1977-81, sr. specialist, 1982; head dept. ophthalmology U. of the Free State, 1982—. V.p. Colls. of Medicine of South Africa, 1998—2007. Chmn. Bloemfontein Children's choir, 1992-97; chmn. Free State Govern Sch. Bodies, 1993-97; vice chmn. South African Schs. Governing Bodies, 1993-97; chmn. Ctrl. H.S., 1992-97. Recipient Bloemfonteiner of Yr., Publicity Com. of Bloemfontein, 1996. Fellow ACS, Am. Acad. of Ophthalmology; mem. Ophthalmol. Soc. of South Africa (pres. 1989-91, 97-99), Health Professions Coun. of South Africa, South African Med. Assn. (past vice chmn., past pres. free state br.). Dutch Reformed Ch. Avocations: reading, writing, light classical music, sport photography. Home: 50 Gascony Crescent Bloemfontein 9301 South Africa Office: Dept Ophthalmology PO Box 339 Bloemfontein South Africa Home Phone: 27514362163; Office Phone: 27514052151. Personal E-mail: aaseyedoc@lantic.net. Business E-Mail: stulinga@fshealth.gov.za.

STULTS, WALTER BLACK, management consultant, trade association administrator; b. Hightstown, NJ, Oct. 25, 1921; s. C. Stanley and Nettie M. (Black) S.; m. Ann D. Haynes, June 28, 1947 (dec. 2002); children: Andrew Haynes, Thomas Stanley; m. Jean Morris Curtin, 2003. BA, Williams Coll., 1943; MA (Woodrow Wilson fellow), Princeton U., 1949. Teaching asst. Princeton (N.J.) U., 1946-49; legis. asst. to U.S. Senator Robert Hendrickson, Washington, 1949-50; staff dir. U.S. Senate Small Bus. Com., Washington, 1950-61; pres. Nat. Assn. Small Bus. Investment Cos., Washington, 1961-86; prin. W.B. Stults, Cons., Chapel Hill, NC, 1979-99. Dir. Pardee & Curtin Lumber Co., Pardee Resources Co., Phila.; chmn. Coun. Small and Ind. Bus. Assns., 1976-81. Pres. Carol Woods Residents Assn.; dir. Carol Woods Retirement Comty., 1995-97, 2001-06. With USAAF, 1943-46. Mem. Am. Soc. Assn. Execs., The Exchequer Club, Masons. Congregationalist.

STULTZ, CILLA HOLMES, psychologist; d. Jeffrey Lynn and Cynthia Anne Holmes; m. Jay Allen Stultz, July 12, 1998. BA in Psychology, U. Tex.-San Antonio, 1994, MS in Psychology, 1997; MA in Sch. Psychology, Trinity U., 1999. Nat. cert. sch. psychologist Md., cert. tchr. Tex., 1999, lic. specialist in sch. psychology, pscyhol. assoc. Lic. specialist sch. psychology Judson Ind. Sch. Dist., San Antonio, 1999—2003, Northside Ind. Sch. Dist., San Antonio, 2003—. Examiner Tex. RioGrande Legal Aid, San Antonio, 2005—. Contbr. articles to profl. jours.; presenter posters. Mem. Deerfield Homeowners' Assn., San Antonio, 2002—. Grantee Grad. Student Small Grant Program, U. Tex.-San Antonio, 1996; Pauline W. and Samuel W. Cochran fellow, 1996—97. Mem.: Tex. Coun. Adminstrs. of Spl. Edn. (assoc.). Episcopalian. Avocations: travel, scuba diving.

STULTZ, NEWELL MAYNARD, retired political science professor; b. Boston, June 13, 1933; s. Irving Washburn and Marjorie May (MacEachern) S.; m. Elizabeth Petronella Olckers, Apr. 6, 1958; children: Elliot Andries, Amy Elizabeth. AB, Dartmouth Coll., 1955; MA, Boston U., 1960, PhD, 1965; MA hon., Brown U., 1968. Fulbright exchange scholar U. Pretoria, South Africa, 1955-56; asst. prof. polit. sci. Northwestern U., Evanston, Ill., 1964-65; asst. prof. to prof. polit. sci. Brown U., Providence, 1965—2003, assoc. grad. dean, 1970-74, assoc. dean of faculty, 1993-98, assoc. provost, 1998-2000; ret., 2003. Vis. fellow Yale U.-South African Research Program, 1977; vis. prof. U. South Africa, Pretoria, 1980; James Gathings lectr. Bucknell U., Lewisburg, Pa., 1980 Author: Afrikaner Politics in South Africa, 1974, Who Goes to Parliament?, 1975, Transkei's Half Loaf, 1979, (bibliography) South Africa, 1989, 2d edit., 1993; co-author: South Africa's Transkei, 1967; co-editor: Governing in Black Africa, 1970, 2d edit., 1986 V.p. World Affairs Council R.I., 1983. Served as lt. (j.g.) USN, 1956-59. Fulbright fellow, 1955-56; NDEA grantee, 1959-62; Ford Found. fellow, 1962-64; Rockefeller Found. fellow, 1976-77 Unitarian Universalist. Home: 371 New Meadow Rd Barrington RI 02806-3729 Office: Brown U Dept Polit Sci PO Box 1844 Providence RI 02912-1844 Business E-Mail: newell_stultz@brown.edu.

STUMBO, GREGORY D., state legislator, former state attorney general; b. Huntington, W.Va., Aug. 14, 1951; s. Harold James and Pluma Jean (Martin) Stumbo; m. Mary Karen Henderson, Aug. 18, 1973; children: Brooks, Elizabeth Morgan, Kassidy Ream. BA in Gen. Sci., U. Ky., Lexington, 1973; JD, U. Louisville, 1975. Asst. county atty. Floyd County, Prestonsburg, Ky., 1977; trial commr. to dist. ct. Adminstrv. Office of Cts., State Ky., Prestonsburg, 1978; mem. Ky. House of Reps., Frankfort, 1980—2004, majority fl. leader, 1985—2003; atty. gen. State of Ky., 2004—07; house spkr. Ky. House of Reps., Frankfort, mem. Dist. 95, 2008—. Bd. dirs. First Guaranty Nat. Bank, Martin, Ky. Mem. Gov.'s Task Force on Coal Transp., Frankfort, 1983, Ky. Lottery Commn., Frankfort, 1988, Ky. Task Force on Edn. Reform, 1989—. Recipient Disting. Svc. award Ky. Cir. Judges Assn., 1980, Cert. of Appreciation, Western Ky. U., Bowling Green, 1982, Disting. Alumni award, U. Louisville, 1985. Mem. ABA, Ky. Bar Assn. Democrat. Baptist. Avocations: hunting, fishing, golf. Home: Box 1473 108 Kassidy Dr Prestonsburg KY 41653 Office: 700 Capitol Ave Capitol Rm 309 Frankfort KY 40601 also: 702 Capitol Ave Annex Rm 303 Frankfort KY 40601 Home Phone: 606-886-9953; Office Phone: 502-696-5300, 502-564-2363.*

STUMP, DAVID JAMES, philosopher, educator; b. Santa Monica, Calif., Mar. 21, 1955; s. John and Sarah Stump. BA, U. Calif., Berkeley, 1977; MA, Northwestern U., Ill., 1984, PhD, 1988. Prof., philosophy U. San Francisco, 1992—. Editor: Disunity of Science. Postdoctoral fellowship, NSF, 1989-1990. Mem.: The Internat. Soc. History of Philosophy of Sci. (steering com. 2003—06). Office: U San Francisco 2130 Fulton St San Francisco CA 94118

STUMP, JOHN SUTTON, retired lawyer; b. Clarksburg, W.Va., Aug. 7, 1929; s. John Sutton and Helen (Mannix) S.; m. Elaine Claire Scammahorn, Sept. 14, 1968; children— John Sutton IV, James Felix. Student, Washington and Lee U., 1946-47, LL.B., 1957; BS in Commerce, U. N.C., 1951. Bar: W.Va. 1957, Va. 1957, D.C. 1983. Assoc. Jackson, Kelly, Holt & O'Farrell, Charleston, W.Va., 1957-58, Boothe, Dudley, Koontz & Boothe, Alexandria, Va., 1958-61, Boothe, Dudley, Koontz & Blankingship, Fairfax and Alexandria, Va., 1962-63; ptnr. Boothe, Dudley, Koontz, Blankingship & Stump, Fairfax and Alexandria, 1963-71, Boothe, Prichard & Dudley, 1971-87, McGuire, Woods, Battle & Boothe LLP, 1987-99. Served to lt. comdr. USNR, 1951-54, 61-62. Fellow Am. Coll. Trial Lawyers; mem. Am. Law Inst. Office: 1750 Tysons Blvd Mc Lean VA 22102-4208 Home: 21145 Cardinal Pond Ter Apt 130 Ashburn VA 20147 Office Phone: 703-712-5457. Business E-Mail: jstump@mcguirewoodsemeritus.com.

STUMPE, WARREN ROBERT, county official, retired engineering executive; b. Bronx, NY, July 15, 1925; s. William A. and Emma J. (Mann) S.; children: Jeffrey, Kathy, William. BS, U.S. Mil. Acad., 1945; MS, Cornell U., 1949; MS in Indsl. Engring, N.Y. U., 1965; grad., Command and Gen. Staff Coll., 1972, Army War Coll., 1976; PhD (hon.), Milw. Sch. Engring., 1982. Registered profl. engr., N.Y., Fla., Wis. Commd. 2d lt., C.E. U.S. Army, 1945, advanced through grades to capt., 1954; with (65th Engr. Bn.), 1945-48; asst. prof. mechanics U.S. Mil. Acad., 1951-54; resigned, 1954; from capt. to col. Res., 1958-79; dep. gen. mgr., gen. engring. div. AMF, Stamford, Conn., 1954-63; exec. v.p. Dortech, Inc., Stamford, 1963-69; dir. systems mgmt. group Mathews Conveyor div. REX, Darien, Conn., 1969-71; dir. research and devel. Rexnord, Inc., Milw., 1971-73, v.p. corp. research and tech., from 1973, v.p. bus. devel. sector, 1981-83, v.p., chief tech. officer, 1983-86; pres. Rexnord Techs., Milw., 1986-87; v.p. Radian Corp., Milw., 1987—90; civilian aide to sec. army for State of Wis., 1981-85; alderman City of Mequon, 1994—97, pres. coun., 1996—97, county supr., 1998—. Mem. adv. bd. technology transfer program U. Wis.-Whitewater. Contbr. articles to profl. jours. Founder, pres. No. Little League, Stamford, 1965-69; pres. Turn of River Jr. High Sh. PTA, 1967-68; vice chmn. for Wis. Dept. Def., Nat. Com. Employer Support Guard and Res.; bd. regents Milw. Sch. Engring.; mem. liaison coun. Coll. Engring., U. Wis., also mem. indsl. adv. coun.; mem. adv. coun. Marquette U.; mem. Wis. Gov.'s Task Force on Energy, Coun. Great Lakes Govs.' Regional Econ. Devel. Commn., 1987-88; bd. dirs. MRA-Inst. Mgmt., Inc. Mem. Am. Water Pollution Control Fedn., Indsl. Rsch. Inst. (pres., dir.), Wis. Assn. Rsch. Mgrs. (founder), West Point Soc. Wis., Tau Beta Pi, Phi Kappa Phi. Clubs: Wis., Ozaukee Country. Office Phone: 262-241-9560. Personal E-mail: warrenstumpe@aol.com, wrs1945@hotmail.com.

STUMPF, BERNHARD JOSEF, physicist, educator; b. Neustadt der Weinstrasse, Rhineland, Germany, Sept. 21, 1948; arrived in U.S., 1981; s. Josef and Katharina (Cervinka) Stumpf. Diploma in physics, Saarland U., Saarbrucken, Germany, 1975, Dr.rer.nat., 1981. Rsch. asst. physics dept. Saarland U., Saarbrucken, 1976-81; rsch. assoc. Joint Inst. Lab. Astrophysics, U. Colo., Boulder, 1981-84; instr. physics NYU, NYC, 1984-86, asst. rsch. scientist Atomic Beams Lab., 1984-85, assoc. rsch. scientist, 1985-86; vis. assoc. prof. physics dept. U. Windsor, Ont., Canada, 1986-88; assoc. prof. physics dept. U. Idaho, Moscow, 1988—. Chmn. Conf. Atomic and Molecular Collisions Excited States, Moscow, 1990. Contbr. articles to profl. jours. German Sci. Found. postdoctoral fellow, U. Colo., 1981—83. Mem.: AAAS, AAUP, Nat. Assn. Acads. Scis. (sec. 2004—06), Optical Soc. Am., Am. Chem. Soc., Am. Phys. Soc. (chmn. N.W. conf. Moscow 2004), German Phys. Soc. Home: 825 W C St Moscow ID 83843-2108 Office: U Idaho Dept Physics Moscow ID 83844-0903 Business E-Mail: stumpf@uidaho.edu.

STUMPF, DAVID ALLEN, pediatric neurologist; b. LA, May 8, 1945; s. Herman A. and Dorothy F. (Davis) S.; children: Jennifer F., Kaitrin E.; m. Elizabeth Dusenbery, Feb. 2, 1989; children: Todd Coleman, Shilo Walker. BA, Lewis and Clark Coll., 1966; MD cum laude, U. Colo., 1972, PhD, 1972. Diplomate Am. Bd. Pediat., Am. Bd. Psychiatry and Neurology, lic. MD State of Ill. Pediatric intern Strong Meml. Hosp., Rochester, NY, 1972-73, resident, 1973-74; resident in neurology Harvard Med. Sch., Boston, 1974-77; dir. pediatric neurology U. Colo. Health Sci. Ctr., Denver, 1977-85; chief neurology Children's Meml. Hosp., Chgo., 1985-89; chmn. neurology, Benjamin and Virginia T. Boshes prof. Northwestern U., 1989-98, prof. neurology and pediatrics, 1999—2001; pres. and CEO Oyxis, LLC, 1999—2001; med. dir. United Healthcare, Chgo., 2005—. Mem. sci. adv. com. Muscular Dystrophy Assn., 1981-87; bd. dirs. Northwestern Meml. Corp., Chgo. Mem. editl. bd. Neurology, 1982-87; contbr. articles to sci. jours. Recipient Lewis and Clark Coll. Disting. Alumni award, 1991; NIH grantee, 1979-84; Muscular Dystrophy Assn. grantee, 1977-89; March of Dimes grantee, 1983-85. Fellow Am. Acad. Neurology (treas. 2005-07); mem. Child Neurology Soc. (counsellor 1982-84, pres. 1985-87), Am. Neurol. Assn., Am. Pediatric Soc., Soc. Pediatric Rsch., Internat. Child Neurology Assn. (sec. 2002-04). Presbyterian. Home: 540 Judson Ave Evanston IL 60202-3084 Office Phone: 312-424-6905. E-mail: david@stumpf.org.

STUMPF, JOHN GERARD, bank executive; b. Pierz, Minn., 1953; BS in Acctg., St. Cloud State U., 1976; MBA in Fin., U. Minn. V.p. loan adminstrn. Norwest Nat. Bank, 1982—83, sr. v.p., chief credit officer, 1982—89; chmn., CEO Norwest Bank Ariz., 1989—91; regional pres. Greater Colo./Ariz Norwest Bank, Colo., 1991—94, head Tex., 1994—98; head southwestern banking group Wells Fargo & Co., San Francisco, 1998—2000, exec. v.p. we. banking group, 2000—02, group exec. v.p. cmty. banking, 2002—05, pres., COO, 2005—07, pres., CEO, 2007—. Bd. dirs. Visa U.S.A. Inc., 2005—, Wells Fargo & Co., 2006—. Bd. dir. San Francisco Zool. Soc., Bay Area chpt. Jr. Achievement, San Francisco Com. on Jobs; trustee San Francisco Mus. Modern Art. Mem.: Fin. Services Roundtable, Calif Bus. Roundtable. Office: Wells Fargo & Co 420 Montgomery St San Francisco CA 94163*

STUMPF, PAUL GEORGE, obstetrician-gynecologist; b. Bklyn., June 26, 1948; s. George Valentine and Rita Josephine (Kunz) S. BA in Biology, Fordham U., 1969; MD cum laude, SUNY, Downstate, 1973. Intern L.A. County-U. So. Calif. Med. Ctr., 1973-74, resident in ob.-gyn., 1974-77; fellow in reproductive endocrinology U. So. Calif., LA, 1977-79; program dir., dir. reproductive endocrinology Jersey Shore Med. Ctr., Neptune, N.J., 1985—. Chief reproductive endocrinology Pa. State Coll. Medicine, Hershey, 1983-85; clin. prof. U. Medicine and Dentistry N.J., 1993—. Co-author: Prolog: Reproductive Endocrinology, 1995; contbr. chpts. to books. Fellow Am. Coll. Ob.-Gyn. (vice chmn. N.J. sect. 1994-97, sec., 1991-94); mem. Am. Soc. Reproductive Medicine, Resolve (adv. bd. 1991—), Soc. Reproductive Endocrinologists, Soc. Reproductive Surgeons. Office: Jersey Shore Med Ctr 1945 Corlies Ave Neptune NJ 07753-4896

STUMPF, WALTER ERICH, cell biology and pharmacology professor, researcher; b. Oelsnitz, Sachsen, Germany, Jan. 10, 1927; arrived in U.S., 1963; m. Ursula Emily Schwinge, May 20, 1961; children: Andrea, Martin, Carolin, Silva. MD summa cum laude, Humboldt U., Berlin, 1952; PhD in Pharmacology, U. Chgo., 1967; D of Human Biology (hon.), U. Ulm, Germany, 1987. Resident in neurology and psychiatry Humboldt U., Berlin, 1954-57, U. Marburg, Germany, 1957-61, resident in radiobiology, 1961-62; rsch. assoc. U. Chgo., 1963-67, asst. prof., 1967-70; assoc. prof. U. N.C., Chapel Hill, 1970-73, prof., 1973-95, mem. labs. for reproductive biology and neurobiology program, mem. Cancer Rsch. Ctr., Carolina Population Ctr., mem. curriculum in toxicology. Vis. psychiatrist Maudsley Hosp., London, 1959; vis. prof. Max-Planck Inst. for Cell Biology, Wilhelmshaven, Germany, 1975, U. Ulm, 1981, U. Sao Paulo, Brazil, 2000-02; rsch. advisor Chugai Pharm. Co., Ltd., Tokyo, 1992-95; lectr. U. São Paulo, 1997, 2000, Ain Shams U., Cairo, 1998; cons. Harris Mfg. Co., North Billerica, Mass., Rsch. Triangle Inst., Chemistry and Life Scis. Divsn., Rsch. Triangle Park, N.C., Merck Sharp and Dome, Westpoint, Pa., Glaxo Wellcome, Rsch. Triangle Park; exec. com. NRC, Inst. of Lab. Animal Resources, NAS, 1979-81, com. Inst. of Lab. Animal Res., 1978-81, com. Soc. for Exptl. Biology and Medicine, 1987-92, founder Internat. Inst. Drug Distbn. Cytopharmacology and Cytotoxicology, Chapel Hill, 1995—. Editor: Autoradiography of Diffusible Substances, 1969, Anatomical Neuroendocrinology, 1975, Autoradiography and Correlative Imaging, 1995; author: Drug Localization in Tissues and Cells, 2003; mem. editl. bd. Neuroendocrinology Letters, 1979-87, Exptl. Aging Rsch., 1975-85, Jour. Histochemistry and Cytochemistry, 1982-90, Cell and Tissue Rsch., 1982-88, Molecular and Cellular Neurosci., 1989-94, Biomed. Rsch., 1991-94, Histochemistry, 1992-96; contbr. articles to profl. jours. Recipient Humboldt Found. award, 1989. Mem. AAAS, Am. Assn. Anatomists, N.Y. Acad. Scis., Soc. for Exptl. Biology and Medicine, Soc. for Neurosci., Endocrine Soc., Internat. Brain Rsch. Orgn., Am. Soc. Zoologists, Histochem. Soc. (coun. 1977-81), Histochem. Gesellschaft (Feulgen lectureship 1982), Internat. Soc. Study Xenobiotics (charter), Internat. Inst. Drug Distbn. Cytopharmacology and Cytotoxicology (founder). Home: U NC Sch Medicine 2612 Damascus Church Rd Chapel Hill NC 27516-8043 Office: Internat Inst Drug Distribution Cytopharmacology & Cytotoxicology Chapel Hill NC 27516 Office Phone: 919-942-8646. Business E-Mail: stumpfwe@email.unc.edu.

STUNKARD, ALBERT JAMES, psychiatrist, educator; b. NYC, Feb. 7, 1922; s. Horace Wesley and Frances (Klank) Stunkard. BS, Yale U., 1943; MD, Columbia U., 1945; MD (hon.), U. Edinburgh, 1992, La. State U., 2006. Intern in medicine Mass. Gen. Hosp., Boston, 1945—46; resident physician psychiatry Johns Hopkins Hosp., 1948—51, rsch. fellow psychiatry, 1951—52; 1rsch. fellow medicine Columbia U. Svc., Goldwater Meml. Hosp., NYC, 1952—53; Commonwealth rsch. fellow, then asst. prof. medicine Cornell U. Med. Coll., 1953—57; mem. faculty U. Pa., 1957—73, 1976—, prof. psychiatry, 1962—73, 1976—, Kenneth Appel prof. psychiatry, 1968—73, chmn. dept., 1962—73; prof. psychiatry Med. Sch., Stanford U., 1973—76. Contbr. 500 articles on psychol., physiol., sociol., therapeutic and genetic aspects of obesity to profl. jours. Capt. M.C. AUS, 1946—48. Recipient Disting. Svc. award, Am. Psychiat. Assn., 1994, Goldberger award, AMA, 1990, Willendorf award, Internat. Assn. Study of Obesity, 1998, Sarnat award mental health, NAS Inst. Medicine, 2004, Disting. Achievement medal medicine, Columbia U. Coll. Physicians and Surgeons, 2005; fellow, Ctr. Advanced Study in Behavioral Scis., 1971—72. Mem.: Soc. Behavioral Medicine (past pres.), Assn. Rsch. Nervous and Mental Diseases (past pres.), Am. Psychosomatic Soc. (past pres.), Acad. Behavioral Medicine Rsch. (past pres.), Am. Assn. Chmn. Depts. Psychiatry (past pres.), Inst. Medicine of NAS. Achievements include contributions to the behavioral, pharmacological, community and surgical treatment of obesity and to understanding of sociological, physiological, psychological and genetic aspects of the disorder; contributions also to nosology and treatment of the eating disorders. Office: U Pa Sch Medicine Dept Psychiatry 3535 Market St 3rd Flr Philadelphia PA 19104-2641

STUNTZ, LINDA GILLESPIE, lawyer, former federal agency administrator; b. Bellefontaine, Ohio, Sept. 11, 1954; d. J. Bradshaw Gillespie and Freda Taylor; m. Reid P.F. Stuntz, May 23, 1981; children: Joseph Gillespie, Grace Reid. AB, Wittenberg U., 1976; JD, Harvard U., 1979. Bar: D.C. 1979, U.S. Dist. Ct. D.C. 1980, U.S. Temp. Emergency Ct. Appeals 1980, U.S. Ct. Appeals (D.C. cir.) 1980, U.S. Supreme Ct. 1983. Assoc. Jones, Day, Reavis & Pogue, Washington, 1979-81, 87-89; assoc. minority counsel Energy and Commerce Com., U.S. Ho. of Reps., Washington, 1981-86, minority counsel, staff dir., 1986-87; dep. under sec. for policy, planning and analysis US Dept. Energy, Washington, 1989-92, acting asst. sec. for fossil energy, 1991, acting asst. sec. for domestic & internat. energy policy, 1992, acting dep. sec., 1992, dep. sec., 1992—93; ptnr. Van Ness Feldman, Washington, 1993—95; prin., founding ptnr. Stuntz Davis & Staffier P.C., Washington, 1995—. Bd. dirs. Schlumberger Ltd., 1993—, Raytheon Co., 2004—. Mem. Fed. Energy Bar Assn. Republican. Office: Stuntz Davis & Staffier PC 555 Twelfth St NW Ste 630 Washington DC 20004 Office Phone: 781-522-3000.

STUNTZ, WILLIAM JOHN, law educator; b. Hyattsville, Md., July 3, 1958; s. John Walter and Marian Johnson Stuntz; m. Ruth Anne Councill, Aug. 2, 1980; children: Sarah Ruth, Samuel David, Andrew William. AB in History and English, Coll. of William and Mary, 1980; JD, U. Va., 1984. Law clk. to Hon. Louis H. Pollak, Phila., 1984-85; law clk. to Assoc. Justice Lewis H. Powell Jr. US Supreme Ct., Washington, 1985-86; asst. prof. law U. Va., Charlottesville, 1986-90, prof., 1990-96, E. James Kelly rsch. prof., 1991—94, Horace W. Goldsmith rsch. prof., 1995—2000, class of 1962 prof. law, 1996—2000; prof. law Harvard Law Sch., Cambridge, Mass., 2000—06, Henry J. Friendly prof. law, 2006—. Vis. prof. law Yale U., New Haven, Conn., 1996-97, Harvard U., 1998. Co-author: Constitutional Criminal Procedure, 1995, Supplement to Comprehensive Criminal Procedure, 2000, Comprehensive Criminal Procedure, 2001, Supplement to Comprehensive Criminal Procedure, 2004; contbr. articles to profl. journals. Bd. dirs. Ctr. for Christian Study, Charlottesville, 1993-97. Fellow: Am. Acad. Arts & Scis. Presbyterian. Office: Harvard Law Sch Areeda 327 1563 Massachusetts Ave Cambridge MA 02138 Office Phone: 617-496-0555. Office Fax: 617-496-4865. Business E-Mail: stuntz@law.harvard.edu.

STUPAK, BART (BARTHOLOMEW THOMAS STUPAK), United States Representative from Michigan, lawyer; b. Milw., Feb. 29, 1952; m. Laurie Ann Olsen; children: Ken, Bart Jr.(dec.). AA in Criminal Justice, Northwestern Mich. C.C., Traverse City, 1972; BS in Criminal Justice, Saginaw Valley State Coll., Mich., 1977; JD, Thomas M. Cooley Law Sch., Lansing, Mich., 1981. Patrolman Escanaba City Police Dept., 1972-73; state trooper Mich. Dept. State Police, 1973-84; instr. State Police Tng. Acad., 1980-82; atty., 1981-84, Hansley, Neiman, Peterson, Beauchamp, Stupak, Bergman P.C., 1984-85; ptnr. Stupak, Bergman, Stupak P.C., 1985-88; mem. Mich. Ho. of Reps., 1989-90; prin. Bart T. Stupak P.C., 1991—; mem. US Congress from 1st Mich. dist., 1993—, mem. commerce subcom., ranking dem. oversights/investigation, telecom./Internet, environment/hazardous materials, commerce trade, consumer protection. Active vol. Wildlife Unltd., Menominee County Hist. Soc., Menominee Woods & Streams Assn.; coach Menominee Youth Baseball Assn.; nat. committeeman Boy Scouts America; fin. com. Holy Spirit Cath. Ch.; adv. com. Bay Pines Juvenile Detection Ctr.; bd. dirs. Cmty. Action Agy. Named Fed. Legislator of Yr., Mich. Credit Union League, Legislator of Yr., Great Lakes Maritime Task Force, 2003. Mem.: State Employees Retirees Assn., Knights of Columbus, Sons of Am. Legion, Nat. Rifle Assn., Elks Club. Democrat. Roman Catholic. Office: US Congress 2352 Rayburn House Office Bldg Washington DC 20515-2201 also: Iron County Courthouse Ste 3 2 S Sixth St Crystal Falls MI 49920-1438 Office Phone: 202-225-4735, 906-875-3751. Office Fax: 202-225-4744, 906-875-3889. E-mail: stupak@mail.house.gov.*

STUPAK, RONALD JOSEPH, dean, management educator, researcher, author, consultant; b. Allentown, Pa., Nov. 28, 1934; s. Frank and Rose (Sisko) S.; m. Dolores Barbara Stupak, June 14, 1958 (dec. Nov. 1994); 1 child, Valeska Celina; m. Katherine Newman, Jan. 1, 1997. BA summa cum laude, Moravian Coll., 1961, LLD, 1998; MA, Ohio State U., 1964, PhD, 1967; Exec. Cert., Fed. Exec. Inst., Charlottesville, Va., 1973. Sales planner Pa. Power and Light Co., Allentown, 1961-63; instr. to prof. Miami U., Oxford, Ohio, 1966-74; prof. to assoc. dir. Fed. Exec. Inst., Charlottesville, 1974-84; prof. and dir. U. So. Calif., L.A./Washington, 1984-95; disting. scholar-in-residence Nat. Ctr. for State Cts., Williamsburg, Va., 1994-95; exec. v.p. Sydron Corp., Bethesda, Md., 1993-97; dean Ctr. Effective Orgnl. Leadership, disting. faculty rsch. scholar of mgmt. Mt. Vernon Coll., Washington, 1995-97; prin., exec. v.p., sr. cons. EMCO, LLC, Earlysville, Va., 1997—2001; prin. Fording Brook Assocs., Bethesda, 2002—. Author: The Shaping of Foreign Policy, 1968, American Foreign Policy, 1979, The Assistant Secretaries, 1979, War as an Instrument of Policy, 1999, Handbook of Public Quality Management, 2001, Handbook of Technology Management, 2006. Chmn. Students for Kennedy, Bethlehem, Pa., 1960-61; coord. Ethnics for Johnson, Columbus, Ohio, 1963-64; bd. visitors U. N.C., Asheville, 1988-91; mem. Va. Strategic Coun., Richmond, 1990-94; advisor Lt. Gov.'s Office, Richmond, 1990-94; trustee Moravian Coll., 1998-2001. With U.S. Army, 1955-57. Recipient Commenius award Moravian Coll., 1974, Outstanding Tchg. award U. So. Calif. Sch. Pub. Adminstrn., 1992, Warren E. Burger award, 1996; named Outstanding Young Man of Am., 1961, Disting. Scholar, Nat. Ctr. for State Cts., 1994, Warren Burger award, 1996; Mershon fellow, 1963-67. Mem. Am. Soc. for Pub. Adminstrn. (life, Nat. Capital chpt. dir. 1985-88), Travelers Protective Assn., Fed. Exec. Inst. Alumni Assn. Democrat. Avocations: sports, film, food, poetry, aerobics. Home: 3241 Golden Rain Rd 7 Walnut Creek CA 94595 Office Phone: 925-934-5645. Personal E-mail: ronstupak@mac.com.

STURCKOW, FREDERICK W. (RICK), astronaut; b. La Mesa, Calif., Aug. 11, 1961; s. Karl H. and Janette R. Sturckow; m. Michele A. Street. BS in Mech. Engring., Calif. Poly. State U., 1984. Commd. 2d lt. USMC, 1984, advanced through grades to lt. col.; with MCAS, Beaufort, SC, Sheik Isa Air Base, Bahrain, 1990; mission comdr. Operation Desert Storm; F/A-18 E/F project pilot Naval Air Warfare Ctr.-Aircraft Divsn., Patuxent River, Md., 1993; astronaut NASA, Houston, 1994—, with Vehicle Systems and Ops. Br., also served as dep. shuttle ops. br., astronaut office, lead for Kennedy Space Ctr. Ops. support, chief astronaut office, Capcom Br. Pilot STS-88 Endeavor Mission (first Internat. Space Station assembly mission), 1998, STS-105 Discovery Mission, 2001; crew comdr. STS-117 Atlantis Mission, 2007. Decorated Single Mission Air medal with combat "V", 4 Strike/Flight Air medals, Def. Superior Svc. medal, Navy and Marine Corps Commendation medal, Navy and Marine Corps Achievement medal, NASA Space Flight medals (2). Mem.: Soc. Exptl. Test Pilots, Marine Corps Assn. Achievements include logged 4,000 flight hours in over 50 different aircraft; logged 568 hours in space; pilot STS-88 Endeavour (1998) and STS-105 Discovery (2001). Avocations: flying, physical training. Office: Astronaut Office/CB NASA Johnson Space Ctr Houston TX 77058

STURGELL, ROBERT ALLAN (BOBBY STURGELL), former federal agency administrator; b. 1959; m. Lynn A. Sturgell; 1 child. BS, US Naval Acad.; JD, U. Va., 1994. Bar: 1994. Flight op. super. and line pilot flying the B-757 and B-767 United Airlines; atty. Shaw Pittman, Washington; naval aviator instr. on F-14, F-18, F-16 and A-4 aircraft Navy Fighter Weapons Sch. (Topgun); chmn. primary adv. & coord. Nat. Trans. Safety Bd. (NTSB); sr. counsel FAA, Washington, dep. adminstr., 2003—09, acting adminstr., 2007—09. Recipient Va Trial Lawyers award.*

STURGES, DIANA, medical educator; d. Tudor and Veronica Botnaru; m. George Sturges, Sept. 19, 1998; 1 child, Lucia Veronica Josephine. MD, State Med. & Pharmacy U., Chisinau, Moldova, 1997; MA in Pub. Policy and Mgmt., U. Southern Maine, Portland, 1999. Asst. project officer, youth program UNICEF, Moldova, Chisinau, 2002—03; asst. prof. Ga. Southern U., Statesboro, 2004—. Fellow SCOUT fellowship, Civic Edn. Project, 2003; Muskie fellowship, US Dept. Edn., 1997. Mem.: APHA, Human Anatomy & Physiology Soc. Office: Ga Southern Univ Dept Health & Kinesiology PO Box 8076 Statesboro GA 30460 Business E-Mail: dsturges@georgiasouthern.edu.

STURGES, JOHN SIEBRAND, management consultant; b. Greenwich, Conn., Feb. 12, 1939; s. Harry Wilton and Elizabeth Helen Sturges; m. Anastasia Daphne Sturges, May 6, 1967; children: Christina Aurora, Elizabeth Athena. AB, Harvard U., 1960; MBA, U. So. Calif., 1965; postgrad., NYU, 1972, U. Mich., 1982; PhD, Columbia U., 1997; ThD, Am. Coll., 1997, PhD, 2000. Cert. profl. mgmt. cons., sr. profl. in human resources; cert. mgmt. cons. V.p. pers. and adminstrv. svcs. Equitable Life Assurance Soc. US, NYC, 1965—79; sr. v.p. pers. Nat. Westminster Bank USA, NYC, 1979-82; corp. sr. v.p. adminstrn. and human resources Willis-Corroon Corp., NYC, 1982-84; mng. dir. human resources Marine Midland Bank, NYC, 1984-87; mng. dir. Siebrand-Wilton Assocs., NYC, 1986-87, pres., 1987—2006, mng. dir., 2007—. Bd. dir. Spencer Savings Bank, Elmwood Park, NJ, 2007-; lay reader, Stephen minister St. Peters Episcopal Ch., Freehold, NJ, 1972—. Lt. USNR, 1960-65. Fellow Am. Coll.; mem. Commerce Assocs., Soc. Human Resource Mgmt. (dir. 1979—), Inst. Mgmt. Cons. (bd. dirs. 1992-), Harvard Club (Princeton; dir. 1991-97), Nassau Club, Monmouth Boat Club, Beta Gamma Sigma (dir. N.Y. 1978—), Phi Kappa Phi. Republican.

STURGES, MOLLY, performing company executive, composer; MA in composition, Wesleyan U. Dir. edn. Ctr. Contemporary Arts, Santa Fe; co-founder, artistic dir. Littleglobe Inc., Santa Fe, 2005—; co-founder, mem. BING pop musical ensemble, 2001—; founder, primary vocalist mJane ensemble, N.Mex., 2003—. Guest artistic dir. The Creative Ctr.: Arts for People with Cancer, NYC; creator, dir. Moment intergenerational project, Cork, Ireland, 2005; artist in residence Santa Fe Opera; creator, dir. Memorylines: Voces de Nuestras Jornadas, Santa Fe. Composer, performer: live music for silent films, 2001—, sub)merge, 2001, In Situ, 2005, La Reina Roja, 2004, Night, 2005; singer: (albums) (with mJane) Prayers from the Underbelly; dir.: (Operas) Cuentos del Valle, 2006. Fellow US Artists, 2008. Office: Littleglobe Inc 223 N Guadalupe #427 Santa Fe NM 87501 Office Phone: 505-989-1437. E-mail: molly@littleglobe.org.*

STURGES, SHERRY LYNN, recording industry executive; b. Long Beach, Calif., Dec. 11, 1946; d. Howard George and Alice Myrtle Fairbairn; m. Jeffery Alan Sturges, Dec. 30, 1969; children: Allisun Malinda, Jay. Grad. high sch., Las Vegas, Nev. V.p. Soultime, Inc., Las Vegas, 1968-69, Universe, Inc., Las Vegas, 1971-76; co-developer, owner Fun Trax Music Video and Audio Recording Studios, Westwood, Calif., 1986—. Creative cons. John Debella Show, 1990, M.T.V., L.A., 1990, KCET-TV, L.A., 1990,KTLA-TV, L.A., 1991. Co-writer song The Sharing of Love for TV series Murder, She Wrote, 1996, feature film The Ride, 1997; song writer (film) The Ride, 1997. Officer PTA, Woodland Hills, Calif., 1977-86, pres., 1984-86; vol. Connie Stevens Charity

Orgn., Beverly Hills, Calif., 1980-84; vol. Crossroads Sch. for Arts and Sci., Westwood Meth. presch., West L.A. Bapt. Sch., Northridge United Meth. Ch., St. Vincent's Parents Coun., St. Joseph the Worker Sch., Chatsworth H.S., Sepulveda Nursery Sch., Nat. Neurofibromatosis Found., Life Steps Found., Westwood Village Assn., San Joaquin Valley Actors Repertory Co., 1997—. Recipient Outstanding Contribution award L.A. Unified Sch. Dist., Oxnard Unified Sch. Dist., 1998, 99. Mem. Am. Soc. Composers, Authors and Pubs. Republican. Avocations: collecting dolls, plates and figurines. Home: 29468 Sequoia Rd Santa Clarita CA 91387-6246

STURGES, SIDNEY JAMES, pharmacist, educator, investment and development company executive; b. Kansas City, Mo., Sept. 29, 1936; s. Sidney Alexander and Lenore Caroline (Lemley) S.; m. Martha Grace Leonard, Nov. 29, 1957 (div. 1979); 1 child, Grace Caroline; m. Gloria June Kitch, Sept. 17, 1983. BS in Pharmacy, U. Mo., 1957, post grad.; MBA in Pharmacy Adminstrn., U. Kans., 1980; PhD in Bus. Adminstrn., Pacific Western U., 1980; cert. in Gerentology, Avila Coll., 1986. Registered pharmacist, Mo., Kans.; registered nursing home adminstr., Mo.; cert. vocat. tchr., Mo. Pharmacist, mgr. Crown Drugs, Kansas City, Mo., 1957-60; pharmacist, owner Sav-On-Drugs and Pharmacy, Kansas City, 1960-62; ptnr. Sam's Bargain Town Drugs, Raytown, Mo., 1961-62; pharmacist, owner Sturges Drugs DBA Barnard Pharmacy, Independence, Mo., 1962—; pres., owner Sturges Med. Corp., Independence, Mo., 1967-1977, Sturgess Investment Corp., Independence, 1967-1978, Sturwood Investment Corp., Independence, 1968—, Sturges Agri-Bus. Co., Independence, 1977—, Sturges Devel. Co., 1984—; bd. dirs. Comprehensive Mental Health Corp., Truman Med. Ctr., 1992; instr. pharmacology Penn Valley C.C., 1976-92; instr., lectr. various clubs and groups. Contbr. articles to profl. jours. Bd. dirs. Independence House, 1981-83; mem. Criminal Justice Adv. Commn., Independence, 1982—. Recipient Outstanding award Kans. City Alcohol and Drug Abuse Council, 1982. Mem. Mo. Sheriffs Assn., Mo. Pharm. Assn. (pharmacy dr. 1981, Pharmacists Against Drug Abuse award 1989), Mo. Found. Pharm. Care, U. Mo. Alumni Assn. Home and Office: Sturges Co 16805 E Cogan Rd Ste B Independence MO 64055-2815 Office Phone: 816-478-0764.

STURGILL, BRAD, finance educator; b. Winston-Salem, NC, May 31, 1981; s. Tony and Karon Sturgill. PhD, NC State U., Raleigh, 2003—. Economics instr. NC State U., 2005—08; vis. instr. economics Appalachian State U., Boone, NC, 2008—. Recipient Brashear prize, Appalachian State U., 2003. Independent. Christian. Achievements include research in empirical and theoretical analysis of Factor Augmenting Technical Progress. Avocations: running, hiking, reading. Home: 169 China Creek Rd Blowing Rock NC 28605 Office: Appalachian State Univ 3102 Raley Hall Boone NC 28608

STURGIS, KATHY ANN, lawyer; b. NYC, Aug. 28, 1952; d. Irv DeKoff and Belle DeKoff Shouse; m. Radford Russell Sturgis, May 30, 1976. BA, Mt. Holyoke Coll., 1977; JD cum laude, Stetson U., 1986. Bar: Fla. 1986. Family services aide Dept. Health and Rehab. Services, Ft. Myers, Fla., 1974-77; legis. aide Fla. Ho. of Reps., Ft. Myers and Tallahassee, 1977-79; exec. dir. Voluntary Action Ctr., Lee County, Fla., 1979-80; owner Dance Fitness Unltd., Cape Coral, Fla., 1980-83; law clk. to circuit judges Fla. 20th Jud. Cir., Ft. Myers, 1985; assoc. Peper, Martin, Jensen, Maichel & Hetlage, Ft. Myers, 1986—92; gen. master Division of Adminstrv. Hearing, Fort Myers, 1996—2006; judge compensation claims Ft. Myers Dist., 2006—. Admissions rep. Mt. Holyoke Coll., SW Fla., 1982—86; secretariat mem. Gulf Coast Cursillo, Lee County, 1983; campaign coordinator Com. to Retain Judge Sturgis, Lee County, 1982; bd. dirs. Edison Women's Ctr., Lee County, 1978, Imaginarium Group Inc., 1990-95, sch. bd. chmn. SW Fla. Christian Acad., mem. SW Fla. Cmty. Found. Women's Legacy Fund, 2007-, co chair, 2009-. Charles A. Dana scholar Stetson U., 1985-86. Mem. Lee County Bar Assn. (pres. 1992), Fla. Bar Assn. (law related edn. com. 1987—). Clubs: Rotary, Calusa Inns of Ct., P.E.O. Presbyterian. Avocations: ballroom dancing, watching football, hockey, reading. Office: Division of Adminstrv Hearing 2080 McGregor Blvd Fl 3 Fort Myers FL 33901 Office Phone: 239-338-2459. Office Fax: 239-338-2928. Business E-Mail: kathy_sturgis@doah.state.fl.us.

STURGULEWSKI, ARLISS, state legislator; b. Blaine, Wash., Sept. 27, 1927; BA, U. Wash., Seattle, 1949; LLD (hon.), U. Alaska, Anchorage, 1993. Mem. Assembly Municipality of Anchorage; interim exec. dir. Alaska Sci. and Tech. Found., 1995. Vice chmn. New Capital Site Planning Commn., mem. Capital Site Selection Com.; chmn. Greater Anchorage Area Planning and Zoning Commn.; mem. Alaska State Senate, 1978-93; Rep. nominee Office Gov. Alaska, 1986, 90. Home: 2957 Sheldon Jackson St Anchorage AK 99508-4469 Office: 3201 C St Ste 405 Anchorage AK 99503-3967 Office Phone: 907-561-5286. Business E-Mail: a.sturgulewski@swallingcpas.com.

STURKEN, CRAIG C., retail executive; Sr. v.p. Big Star Food Stores, 1989—90; chmn. Can. ops. Spartan Stores Inc., 1990—93, group v.p. Mich. ops., then pres. A&P Mich., 1993—97, chmn., CEO midwest region, 1997—2000, pres., CEO atlantic region, 2000—03, chmn., pres., CEO, 2003—07, chmn., CEO, 2007—08, exec. chmn., 2008—. Office: Spartan Stores 850 76th St SW Grand Rapids MI 49518

STURM, WILLIAM CHARLES, lawyer; b. Milw., Aug. 4, 1941; s. Charles William and Helen Ann (Niesen) S.; m. Kay F. Sturm, June 10, 1967; children: Patricia, Elizabeth, Katherine, William, Susan. BS in Bus. Adminstrn., Marquette U., 1963; JD, 1966. Bar: Wis. 1966, U.S. Dist. Ct. (ea. dist.) Wis. 1966, U.S. Supreme Ct. 1980. Sole practice, Milw., 1966—77; ptnr. Rausch, Hamell, Ehrle & Sturm, S.C., Milw., 1977—81, Rausch, Hamell, Ehrle, Sturm & Blom, Milw., 1981-83, Rausch, Hamell, Ehrle & Sturm, 1983-95, Rausch, Hamell, Sturm & Israel S.C., 1995-98, Rausch, Sturm, Israel & Hornik, S.C., 1999—2009, Rausch, Sturm, Israel Enerson & Hornik, LIC, 2009—. Asst. prof. Marquette U., 1982-91; lectr. U. Wis., Milw., 1991-97, sr. lectr. 1997-2002. Contbr. articles to profl. jours. Mem. adv. bd. Pallotine Order, 1985—; bd. dirs. Pius XI H.S., 2002-2004. Recipient Editors award Wis. Med. Credit Assn., 1980, Recipient Outstanding Alumni Pius XI H.S., 2002. Mem. ABA, Wis. Bar Assn., Comml. Law League Am. (exec. coun. midwestern dist. 1981-83, 86-88, chmn. state membership com. 1981-88, nat. nominating coun. 1984-86, 1988-89, 2004-05, sec., 2d v.p. midwestern dist. 1989-90, 1st v.p. midwestern dist. 1990-91, chmn. 1991-92, nat. bd. govs. 1997-2000, pres. elect 2000-01, pres. 2001-02, mem. nat. fin. com. 2008-), Acad. Legal Studies in Bus., Midwest Bus. Law Assn. (sec. 1988-89, v.p. 1989-90, pres. 1990-91), Healthcare Fin. Mgmt. Assn., Beta Alpha Psi (faculty v.p. Psi chpt. 1985-88, Eta Theta chpt. 1992-99), Midwest Bus. and Health Assn. (v.p. procs. 1987-88, v.p. program 1988-89, pres. 1989-90), Westmoor Country Club (Milw.); Kiwanis (pres. 1979, lt. gov. div. 5, 1980). Office: 2448 South 102nd St Milwaukee WI 53227 Office Phone: 414-328-1400. E-mail: wsturm@wiscollect.com.

STURMAN, DEBORAH MUSCHA, attorney; d. Herman Getzie and Gladys Freiman Sturman; 1 child, Rachel Zipporah. Prix D'Excellence, Royal Brussels Conservatory Music, Belgium, 1992; JD, UCLA, 1995. Bar: Calif. 1995, D.C. 2000, NY 2001. Of counsel Milberg Weiss Bershad Hynes Lerach LLP, NYC, 1995—2001, Milberg, Weiss, Bershad, Schulman, 2001—06, Sturman LLC, 2006—; legal columnist Mgr. Mag., Hamburg, Germany, 2003—. Musician (French horn soloist): Telemann Concerti Mozart Chamber Music for winds, 1982; musician: (French horn sect. leader) Royal Philharmonic Belgium; musician: West German Broadcasting Orch.; dir.(prodr.): (radio and TV) Singing and Swinging in the Cloister Tavern, 1984, The Woodwind Quintet in Old and New Clothes, 1985; contbr. articles to numerous profl. jours. Mem.: Calif. Holocaust Era Ins. Oversight Com., Hadassah (life). Democrat. Jewish. Achievements include research in holocaust slave Labour Litigation against German industry resulting in compensation of approximately $6 billion for victim of the Holocaust. Avocations: music, writing. Office: Sturman LLC 7 Dey St New York NY 10007 Business E-Mail: sturman@sturman.ch.

STURMAN, SUSAN, music educator; b. Fairview Park, Ohio, Nov. 17, 1962; children: Nathaniel Spayd, Jordan Spayd, Joshua Spayd. MusM, Northwestern U., Evanston, Ill., 1986. Prof. cello Del Mar Coll., Corpus Christi, Tex., 1989—; prin. cello Corpus Christi Symphony Orch., Tex., 2004—. String chair Corpus Christi Internat. Competition, 2007—. Editor: (music) Bach Chorale for Two Cellos. Mem.: Suzuki Assn. Americas, Tex. Music Educators Assn., Coll. Music Soc. Office: Del Mar Coll 101 Baldwin Corpus Christi TX 78404 Office Fax: 361-698-1620; Home Fax: 361-698-1612. Business E-Mail: ssturman@delmar.edu.

STURNER, LYNDA, performing company executive; b. Buffalo, July 1, 1941; d. Samuel and Rachel Louise Sturner; m. Jerome S. Traum, Sept. 23, 2001 (dec.); children: Daniel Matthew Traum, Edward Hart Traum stepchildren: David A. Traum, Norman Traum. BFA, Boston U., 1963. Instr. Boston U., 1983. Actor: (Broadway plays) Oliver, 1964—66, Bingo the Musical, 2007; prodr.: Triangle Prodns., 1981—87; co-prodr.: The Juniper Tree, 1982; artistic dir.: Playwrights Forum Inc., 1982—88; Provincetown Repertory Theatre, 2004—05; playwright: Woman's Project Lab., 1989—97; contbg. author: TheaterMania.com, 1999—2007; author: (plays) Look What You Made Me Do, 2000 (Audience Choice award, 2001), Art Brute, 2001, The Death of Huey Newton; co-author Sextet, 2001. Bd. dir. Castle Hill Truro Ctr. for the Arts, 1980—99, Music Theatre Group, NYC, v.p., 1981—2001; bd. dir. Provincetown Theatre Co., 1999—2003; co-pres. League of Profl. Theatre Women, NYC. Mem.: League of Profl. Theatre Women, Screen Actors Guild, Actors Equity Assn. Democrat. Jewish. Personal E-mail: lynda_sturner@yahoo.com.

STURROCK, PETER ANDREW, space science and astrophysics educator; b. South Stifford, Essex, Eng., Mar. 20, 1924; came to U.S., 1955; s. Albert Edward and Mabel Minnie Sturrock; m. Marilyn Fern Stenson, June 29, 1963; children: Deirdre, Colin; 1 child from previous marriage, Myra. BA, Cambridge U., Eng., 1945, MA, 1948, PhD, 1951. Scientist Telecomms. Rsch. Establishment, Malvern, England, 1943-46, Nat. Bur. Standards, Washington, 1949-50, Ecole Normale Superieure, Paris, 1950-51, Atomic Energy Rsch. Establishment, Harwell, 1951-53; fellow St. John's Coll., Cambridge U., 1952-55; rsch. assoc. Stanford (Calif.) U., 1955-61, prof. dept. applied physics, 1961-98, dir. Inst. for Plasma Rsch., 1964—74, 1980—83; dep. dir. Ctr. for Space Sci. and Astrophysics, 1983-92, dir., 1992-98. Author: Static and Dynamic Electron Optics, 1955, Plasma Physics, 1993, The UFO Enigma, 1999, A Tale of Two Sciences, 2009; editor: Plasma Astrophysics, 1967, Solar Flares, 1980, Physics of the Sun, vols. I, II, III, 1986. Recipient Gravity prize Gravity Found., 1967, Hale prize Am. Astron. Soc., 1986, Henryk Arctowski medal NAS, 1990, Space Sci. award AIAA, 1992; European Ctr. for Nuclear Rsch. fellow, 1957-58. Fellow AAAS, Royal Astron. Soc., Am. Phys. Soc.; mem. Internat. Astron. Union, Internat. Acad. Astronautics, Soc. Sci. Exploration (pres. 1982-2001, Dinsdsale prize 2006). Office: Stanford U Dept Physics Varian Bldg Rm 302 Stanford CA 94305

STURTEVANT, BRERETON, retired lawyer, federal official; b. Washington, Nov. 24, 1921; d. Charles Lyon and Grace (Brereton) S. BA, Wellesley Coll., 1942; JD, Temple U., 1949; postgrad., U. Del., 1969-71. Bar: D.C. 1949, Del. 1950. Research chemist E.I. duPont DeNemours & Co., 1942-50; law clk. Del. Supreme Ct., 1950; gen. practice law Wilmington, Del., 1950-57; partner Connolly, Bove & Lodge, Wilmington, 1957-71; Examiner-in-Chief U.S. Patent and Trademark Office Bd. Appeals, Washington, 1971-88. Adj. prof. law Georgetown U., 1974-79. Trustee Holton-Arms Sch., Bethesda, Md., 1977-96, chmn. or mem. all coms., trustee emerita, 1997—. Mem. ABA, Exec. Women in Govt. (charter mem., chmn. 1978-79) Clubs: Wellesley College, Washington-Wellesley (pres. 1982-84). Episcopalian. Achievements include first woman law clerk for the Delaware Supreme Court; first woman US Patent Office examiner-in-chief. Home: 5209 Pimlico Ct Fairfax VA 22032-2623

STURTEVANT, PETER MANN, JR., television news executive; b. Northampton, Mass., Feb. 27, 1943; s. Peter Mann and Katharine Bryan (Hobson) S.; m. Anne Elizabeth Fitzpatrick, July 12, 1969 (div. Dec. 1984); 1 child, Amanda Hadden; m. Toni E. Siegel, Apr. 14, 1985; 1 child, Gillian Lee. BA in Polit. Sci., Wilmington Coll., 1965; MA in Journalism, U. Iowa, 1967. Assoc. prodr. CBS News, Washington, 1967-71, bur. chief Viet Nam Saigon, 1971-73, nat. news editor NYC, 1974-80, asst. v.p. spl. events, 1981-83, producer 60 Minutes, 1984-85; exec. bus. news editor CNN, NYC, 1985-86; prodr. Today's Bus. Buena Vista TV, NYC, 1987; dir. news coverage CNBC, Fort Lee, NJ, 1988-90, v.p., mng. editor Ft. Lee, NJ, 1991-94; sr. v.p. Internat. Bus. News NBC, 1994-98; disaster relief, instr. Am. Red Cross, 1999—. Trustee Wilmington Coll., 2000—. Named Disting. Alumnus, Wilmington Coll., 1975, 97; named to Journalism Hall of Fame, U. Iowa Grad. Sch. Journalism, 1988; named to Wilmington Coll. Sports Hall of Fame, 1997. Mem. Nat. Acad. Cable Programming (nominated ACE award 1992, 93, 94), Soc. Profl. Journalists, Deadline Club N.Y., The Asia Soc., Overseas Press Club (bd. dirs.). Episcopalian. Avocations: racquet sports, landscaping, travel, stamp collecting/philately, parenting. Home: 90 Riverside Dr # 8D New York NY 10024-5306

STURTZ, DONALD LEE, surgeon, military officer, educator; b. Coshocton, Ohio, Apr. 18, 1933; s. Walter Raymond and Helene Josephine (Kubic) S.; m. Alice Marie McGuire, June 11, 1955; children: Jimalee, Janel. BS, US Naval Acad., Annapolis, Md., 1955; MD, U. Pa., Phila., 1965; diploma med. care catastrophe, Soc. Apothecaries London, 1996. Diplomate Am. Bd. Surgery. Surg. resident USN, Phila., 1965-70, ship's surgeon, 1970-71; staff surgeon Bethesda Naval Hosp., USN, 1971-80; chief of surgery San Diego Naval Hosp., USN, 1980-84; exec. officer Oakland Naval Hosp., USN, Calif., 1984-85; prof. clin. surgery USN, Bethesda, Md., 1985-87, commd. Naval Med. Command, 1987-88, Atlantic fleet surgeon, Supreme Allied Command surgeon Norfolk, Va., 1989-91; prof. surgery USUHS, Bethesda, Md., 1991—. Contbr. articles to profl. jours. Mem. nat. adv. cabinet Guideposts, 1980—. Recipient B.D. Larrey award for Surgical Excellence, Surgical Dept. USUHS, Bethesda, 1988, Exceptional Svc. medal, Uniformed Svcs. U., 1998. Fellow ACS (gov. 1985-88); mem. Am. Assn. for Surgery of Trauma, Assn. Mil. Surgeons, USN Inst. Republican. Presbyterian. Avocations: travel, gardening, antiques, music, reading. Office: USUHS Dept Surgery 4301 Jones Bridge Rd Bethesda MD 20814-4799 Home Phone: 302-644-4541; Office Phone: 301-295-9825. Personal E-mail: sturtz@aol.com.

STUTTS, JAMES F., lawyer, energy executive; b. Dec. 1944; BA in English, U. Va., 1967; MBA, U. Pa., 1970; JD, U. Richmond, 1977. Bar: Va. 1977, Pa. 1992. V.p. corp. fin. Wheat, First Securities; ptnr. McSweeney, Stutts & Burtch, Richmond, Va.; assoc. McGuire, Woods, Battle & Boothe, LLP, Richmond, Va., 1985—87, ptnr., 1987—97; v.p., gen. counsel Dominion Resources Inc., Richmond, Va., 1997—2007, sr. v.p., gen counsel, 2007—. Office: Dominion PO Box 26532 Richmond VA 23261-6532*

STUTZ, CATHLEEN KINSELLA, education educator; m. Guy Stutz. BA in English, U. Pa., 1983, MS in Ed., 1983; EdD, Boston U., 1995. Asst. prof. edn. Assumption Coll., Worcester, Mass., 1995—, chair dept. edn., 2003—. Recipient US Prof. of Yr. award, Carnegie Found. for Advancement of Tchg. and Coun. for Advancement and Support of Edn., 2006. Office: Dept Edn Assumption Coll 500 Salisbury St Worcester MA 01609 Office Phone: 508-767-7553.

STUTZMAN, DONNA J., minister; b. Lemoyne, Ohio, Apr. 29, 1936; d. David O. Kaser and Opal M. Stockwell; m. Darrell A. Stutzman, June 7, 1958 (dec. Sept. 1993); children: Denzel, Devon, Dawn, Dara, Desmond. BS in Child and Family Cmty. Svc., Bowling Green State U., Ohio, 1987; MA in Christian Psychology, Cornerstone U., Lake Charles, La., 1992. Ordained minister Nat. Conservative Christian Ch., 1999; lic. social worker Ohio. Pvt. piano tchr., Wauseon, Ohio, 1958—; case mgr. Fulton County Maumee Valley Guidance Ctr., Defiance, Ohio, 1987—89; assoc. pastor First Ch. of God, Wauseon, 1989—91; mental health profl. Fulton County Health Ctr., Wauseon, 1991—99; social worker, music coord. Fulton Manor Nursing Home, Wauseon, 1998—; hospice chaplain Cmty. Health Profls., Archbold, Ohio, 1999—; pastor Hope Christian Fellowship, Wauseon, 1991—; in-patient hospice chaplain Defiance, Ohio, 2007—. Spirituality group facilitator Fulton County Health Ctr. Psychiat. Unit, 2003—. Vol. coord. Habitat for Humanity, 2003. Mem.: AAUW, Am. Acad. Bereavement, Am. Assn. Christian Counselors, Nat. Christian Counselors Assn., Phi Upsilon Omicron. Avocations: reading, music. Home: 701 Burr Rd Unit 5 Wauseon OH 43567 E-mail: donna.01@embargmail.com.

STUTZMAN, THOMAS CHASE, SR., lawyer; b. Portland, Oreg., Aug. 1, 1950; s. Leon H. and Mary L. (Chase) S.; m. Wendy Jeanne Craig, June 5, 1976; children: Sarah Anne, Thomas Chase Jr. BA with high honors, U. Calif. Santa Barbara, 1972; JD cum laude, Santa Clara U., 1975. Bar: Calif. 1976; family law specialist. Pvt. practice, San Jose, Calif., 1976—79; pres., sec., CFO Thomas Chase Stutzman, PC, San Jose, 1979—. Instr. San Jose State U., 1977—78. Bd. dirs. Santa Cruz Campfire, 1978-80, Happy Hollow Park, 1978-80, 83-86, Pacific Neighbors, pres., 1991-92. Mem. Calif. Bar Assn., Santa Clara County Bar Assn. (chmn. environ. law com. 1976-78, exec. com. family law), San Jose Jaycees (Dir. of Yr. 1976-77), Lions (dir. 1979-81, 2d v.p. 1982-83, 1st v.p. 1983-84, pres. 1984-85), Scottish Rite, Masons, Phi Beta Kappa. Congregationalist. Office: 1625 The Alameda Ste 626 San Jose CA 95126-2207 Home Phone: 408-997-7454; Office Phone: 408-294-4600. Business E-Mail: stutzman@tomstutzman.com.

STUZIN, JAMES M., plastic surgeon; b. Miami, Fla., June 1, 1952; BA, U. Fla., Gainesville, 1974, MD, 1978. Cert. in gen. surgery 1985, in plastic surgery 1989. Intern, gen. surgery U. Wash. Hosps., Seattle, 1978—79, resident, gen. surgery, 1979—83; fellow, plastic surgery NYU Hosps., NYC, 1984—86; craniofacial fellow U. Miami Hosps., Fla., 1986, UCLA Sch. Medicine, 1987, asst. clin. prof., plastic surgery, 1987; clin. instr., dept. plastic surgery U. Miami Sch. Medicine, Fla., 1989—95, clin. asst. prof., plastic surgery, 1995—. Chmn. Am. Bd. Plastic Surgery, 2008—. Mem. editl. bd. Annals of Plastic Surgery, 1993—; co-editor: Jour. of Plastic and Reconstructive Surgery; co-author: Facial Skin Resurfacing, 1998. Mem.: Am. Soc. for Aesthetic Plastic Surgery (pres. 2006), Alpha Omega Alpha, Phi Beta Kappa. Office: 3225 Aviation Ave Ste 100 Coconut Grove FL 33133 Office Phone: 305-854-8828.

STWALLEY, WILLIAM CALVIN, physics and chemistry professor; BS, Calif. Inst. Tech., 1964; PhD, Harvard U., 1968. Asst. prof. U. Iowa, Iowa City, 1968-72, assoc. prof., 1972-75, prof. dept. chemistry, 1975-93, prof. dept. physics and astronomy, 1977-93, dir. Iowa Laser Facility, 1979-93, dir. Ctr. for Laser Sci. and Engring., 1987-89, George Glockler prof. physical scis., 1988-93; program dir. NSF, Washington, 1975-76 (leave of absence); prof. and head dept. physics, prof. chemistry U. Conn., Storrs, 1993—, bd. trustees disting., prof., 2002—. Program chmn. Internat. Laser Sci. Conf., 1985, co-chmn., 1986, chmn., 1987; lectr. Chinese Acad. Scis., 1986. Editor books in field; contbr. numerous articles to profl. publs. Recipient Conn. medal of sci., 2005—; Japan Soc. for Promotion of Sci. fellow, 1982; Sloan fellow, 1970-72; numerous grants in field, 1970—. Fellow AAAS, Am. Phys. Soc. (sec.-treas. divsn. chem. physics 1984-90, vice chair/chair Topical Group on Laser Sci. 1989-92, vice chair/chair divsn. atomic, molecular and optical physics 2005-08), Optical Soc. Am. (William F. Meggers award 1998), Conn. Acad. Sci. and Engring., Conn. Acad. Arts and Scis.; mem. Am. Chem. Soc. Office: U Conn Unit 3046 Dept Physics Storrs Mansfield CT 06269-3046 Office Phone: 860-486-4924. Business E-Mail: w.stwalley@uconn.edu.

STYCOS, MARIA NOWAKOWSKA, retired adult education educator; b. Lwow, Poland, June 4, 1937; arrived in U.S., 1964; d. Marian Zygmunt Nowakowski and Julia Demska Nowakowska; m. Joseph Mayone Stycos; 1 child, Marek. BA, U. London, 1958; MA, Cornell U., 1967, PhD, 1977. Part time asst. prof. Ithaca Coll., NY, 1975—81; dir. Handwerker Art Gallery, Ithaca, NY, 1981—82; asst. prof. SUNY, Cortland, 1982—86; sr. lectr. Cornell U., 1986—2006; ret., 2006. Cons. Cornell U. project in San Jose, Costa Rica, 1986; faculty adv. com. Johnson Mus. Art, Cornell U. Co-author (with E. Sanchez-Blake): Voces Hispanas Siglo XXI Entrevistas con autores en DVD, 2005; contbr. chapters to books, articles to profl. jours. Planning bd. mem. Village of Lansing, NY, 2002—. Mem.: MLA, AILCFH. Avocations: music, art, gardening, travel, poetry. Business E-Mail: mns2@cornell.edu.

STYER, DENISE MARIE, psychologist; d. Kenneth James and Mary Ellen Styer; 1 child, James Kenneth Marketti. BA, U. Wis., Milw., 1990; MA, Alfred Adler Inst. Minn., 1995; PsyD, Adler Sch. Profl. Psychology, 2001. Lic. Profl. Counselor Ill., 2001. Therapist, intake coord. SAFE Alternatives, Naperville, Ill., 2000—01; clin. coord. Self Injury Recovery Svcs. Alexian Bros. Behavioral Hosp., Hoffman Estates, Ill., 2001—. Mem.: APA (prevention rschr. adv. bd. 2005). Home: 537 E Constitution Dr Apt 2 Palatine IL 60074-1911 Personal E-mail: drdenisestyer@comcast.net.

STYER, JOANNE LOUISE, retired dietician; b. Melin, Oreg., Nov. 23, 1931; d. Raymond Louis Hosford and Gladys Lorraine Loomis; m. Lawrence Henry Styer, Aug. 20, 1955. BS in Foods and Nutrition and Instnl. Mgmt., U. Wis., Stout, 1954; postgrad., George Washington U., U. Md., U.S. Internat. U. Lic. reg. dietitian. Intern St. Mary's Hosp., Rochester, Minn., 1955; chief therapeutic dietitian Glen Dale Hosp., Washington, 1956; chief dietitian George Washington U. Med. Ctr., Washington, 1956—68; asst. dir. food svc. Montgomery County (Md.) Pub. Schs., 1968—69, dir. food svc., 1969—92; dietetic cons. Carriage Hill Nursing Home; ret. Cons. N.Y.C. Homeless Food Svc., Montgomery County Pub. Schs., USDA Commodity Processing, N.Y.C. Prison Food Svc. Evaluation; mem. adv. bd. D.C. Dairy Coun.; mem. industry adv. bd. Nat. Frozen Food Assn. Mem. editl. review panel Sch. Food Svc. Rsch. Review. Past chmn. nutrition com. D.C. Heart Assn.; nutrition com. Am. Heart Assn.; food chmn. Montgomery County Disaster Com.; nutrition com. Montgomery County Heart Assn.; expert task force USDA, Am. Cancer Soc. Named Disting. Alumni, U. Wis., Stout, 1989. Mem.: Md. Sch. Bus. Ofcls. (sect. chmn. food svc.), Md. Sch. Food Svc. Assn. (past pres.), D.C. Dietetic Assn. (past pres.), Md. Dietetic Assn., Am. Dietetic Assn. (chmn. dietetic practice group for sch. food svc.). Home: 11342 Kings Valley Dr Damascus MD 20872 Personal E-mail: lcapthook1@aol.com.

STYLES, ANGELA BARBEE, lawyer, former federal official; b. Dallas, 1967; BA with Distinction, U. Va., 1990; JD with Honors, U. Tex., 1994. Legis. aide Congressman Joe Barton, Washington; assoc. Miller & Chevalier, Washington, 1996—2001, ptnr., 2003—06; with Budget Oversight Office Gen. Services Adminstrn., Washington, 2001; counselor to the dir. Office Mgmt. & Budget, Exec. Office of the Pres., Washington, adminstr. Office Procurement Policy (OFPP), 2001—03; ptnr. Crowell & Moring LLP, Washington, 2007—. Articles editor: Am. Jour. Criminal Law. Recipient Leadership award, Small Bus. Adminstrn. (SBA), 2003, Women Impacting Pub. Policy Leadership award, 2003. Mem.: ABA (chair legis. coordinating com. sect. pub. contract law, vice chair acctg., cost and pricing com.), Order of the Coif. Republican. Office: Crowell & Moring 1001 Pennsylvania Ave NW Washington DC 20004 Office Phone: 202-624-2500. Office Fax: 202-628-5116. E-mail: astyles@crowell.com.*

STYLES, BONNIE W., museum director, archaeologist; b. Mesa, Ariz., Nov. 11, 1950; d. Lois M. and James E. Whatley; m. Thomas R. Styles, May 15, 1976; children: Megan A., Todd E. BA in Anthropology, Ariz. State U., 1972; MA in Anthropology, Northwestern U., 1973, PhD in Anthropology, 1978. Chair, assoc. curator anthropology Ill. State Mus., 1977—83, chair, curator anthropology, 1983—88, dir. scis. Springfield, 1988—99, assoc. dir., 1999—2006, dir., 2006—. Mem. nat. accreditation commn. for mus. Am. Assn. Mus., 2007—; presenter in field. Project dir. (natural history exhbn.) Changes (IAM Superior Achievement, 2004); contbr. articles to profl. jours. Sci. adv. com. Ill. River Coordinating Coun.; bd. dirs. Natural Sci. Collections Alliance, 1999—2002, Soc. for Am. Archaeology, 1997—2000; pres. Ill. Archaeol. Survey, Champaign-Urbana, Ill., 1983—85. Named Prin. Investigator Emeritus, NSF, 2007; grantee, Inst. Mus. and Libr. Svcs., 2001—03; Miss. RiverWeb Mus. Consortium grant, NSF, 1998—2001, Mus. Tech. Acad. grant, 2004, Learning Opportunities grant, Inst. Mus. and Libr. Svcs., 2003—05, MuseumLink grant, US Dept. Commerce, 1997—2000. Fellow: Ill. State Acad. Sci. (bd. of directors 1998—2001), AAAS; mem.: Soc. Am. Archaeology, Ill. State Mus. Soc. (exec. sec. 2005—), Am. Assn. Mus. (mem. accreditation com. 2007—), Assn. Sci. Mus. Dirs. (sec.-treas. 2006—), Midwest Archaeol. Conf. (pres. 2006—), Am. Quaternary Assn. (bd. dirs. 1997—2000, sec. 1998—2004), Sigma Xi. Achievements include research in prehistoric subsistence practices. Avocations: travel, hiking. Office: Ill State Mus Sys 502 S Spring St Springfield IL 62706 Office Fax: 217-785-2857. Business E-Mail: director@museum.state.il.us.

STYLES, NAOMI, biology professor; b. Tocoma Pk., Md., Oct. 9, 1956; d. Delbert Alexander Patton and Frances Blackley; m. Roger Styles, Nov. 29, 1996. BS, North Carolina State U., Raleigh, 1982, MS, 1988. Biology, anatomy, physiology instr. Western Piedmont CC, Morganton, NC, 1992—. Mem.: Assn. Southeastern Biologist, NCSU Xi, Sigma Xi. Office: Western Piedmont CC 1001 Burkemont Ave Morganton NC 28655 Personal E-mail: styles1@bellsouth.net. Business E-Mail: nstyles@wpcc.edu.

STYLIANOPOULOS, ARETI LEONIDAS, music educator; b. York, Pa., Mar. 17, 1968; d. Leonidas Konstantinos Stylianopoulos and Leonidas Stylianopoulos Sophia; children: Robert Bruce Thompson, Tristan James Thompson. BALA, Purchase Coll., SUNY, 1996; MA in Classics, U. London, Egham, Surrey, Eng., 2000; MA in Drama, U. Toronto, Ont., Can., 2000. Paralegal sec. Karafotias Law Offices, Athens, Attica, Greece, 1987—88; ESL tchr. Trinity Found., Athens, 1997—98; tech. events coord. U. Pitts., 2000—, tchg. asst., 2000—01; adj. instr. U. Mary Wash., Fredericksburg, Va., 2005—. Asst. choir dir. Christ the Savior Orthodox Ch., Aquia, Va., 2004—08. Grant, Greek Orthodox Episcopate NY, 1995—96. Mem.: Rappahanock Music Soc. (active mem. 2005—08, occasional spkr.). Avocations: exercise, dance, travel, swimming, piano. Home: 3 Sunkist Ct Fredericksburg VA 22407 Office: Univ Mary Washington 1301 College Ave Fredericksburg VA 22401 Office Phone: 540-903-4215. Personal E-mail: aretileonidas@yahoo.com. Business E-Mail: astylian@umw.edu.

STYMIEST, BARBARA, bank executive; 1 child. MBA, Richard Ivey Sch. Bus. Audit ptnr., Fin. Svcs. Group Ernst & Young, 1978—87; exec. v.p., CFO Nesbitt Burns Corp., Ltd., Canada, 1992—99; chair, bd. govs. Toronto Stock Exch. (now TSX Group Inc.), 1997—99, CEO, bd. dirs., 1999—2004; COO, fin. group Royal Bank Can., 2004—09, group head, strategy, treasury & corp. services, 2009—. Mem. ICAO Task Force, 1996; gov. Can. Investor Protection Fund, 1996; chair Joint Industry Coord. Com., 1995—97; alt. gov. Can. Securities Inst., 1995, gov., 1997—; mem. task force on std. setting CICA, 1996—98; mem. Royal Bank Can. Group Exec. Mem. ofcl. Bd. Forest Hills United Ch., 1984; bd. mem. Rehab. Inst. Toronto, 1996, Hincks Dellcrest Children's Ctr., 1990—97, chair, bd. dirs., 1993—96. Named one of 50 Most Powerful Women, Fortune Mag., 2005, 50 Most Powerful Internat. Women in Bus., 2008, 25 Most Powerful Women in Banking, US Banker, 2007, 2008; named to Internat. Power 50, Forbes mag., 2008. Fellow: Inst. Chartered Accts. Ont. (grantee). Office: Royal Bank Canada 200 Bay St M5J 2J5 Toronto ON Canada*

STYSLINGER, LEE JOSEPH, JR., manufacturing executive; b. Birmingham, Ala., June 28, 1933; s. Lee Joseph and Margaret Mary (McFarl) S.; m. Catherine Patricia Smith, Apr. 30, 1960; children: Lee Joseph III, Jon Cecil, Mark Joseph. Student, U. Ala., 1952. Pres., chief exec. officer Altec, Inc. and predecessors, truck equipment mfrs., Birmingham, 1956-89, chief exec. officer, chmn. bd., 1989-92, chmn., 1992—. Bd. dirs. Jemison Investment Co., Birmingham, Ala., Electronic Healthcare Systems. Mem. Country Club Birmingham, Mountain Brook Club, Shoal Creek Club, Willow Point Golf and Country Club, Jupiter Island Club (Hobe Sound, Fla.), Seminole Golf Club (Juno Beach, Fla.), Lyford Cay Country Club (Bahamas), Rotary, NY Yacht Club (N.Y.C.). Roman Catholic. Home: 3260 E Briarcliff Rd Birmingham AL 35223-1305 Office: 210 Inverness Center Dr Birmingham AL 35242-4834

SU, BIN, architecture educator; b. Nanjing, Jiangsu, China, June 3, 1961; s. Jinkui Su and Xiuzhen Pan; m. Hua Zhang, Sept. 28, 1992; 1 child, Ranny. B of Engring. in Naval Architecture, Harbin Engring. U., China, 1983; MPhil in Architecture, U. Auckland, New Zealand, 1994, PhD (hon.) in Architecture, 1999. Engr. China State Shipbuilding Corp., Beijing, 1983—90; assoc. prof. architecture Unitec New Zealand, Auckland, 2000—. Mem.: ASHRAE (2006), ASCE. Home: 13c Haughey Ave Hillsborough Auckland New Zealand Office: Unitec New Zealand Carrington Rd Mt Albert Auckland New Zealand Office Fax: 0064 9 8154343. Business E-Mail: bsu@unitec.ac.nz.

SU, CHING-HUA, materials scientist; b. Taipei, Taiwan, Oct. 10, 1954; s. Draw-Ming Su and Kuo-In Ho; m. Yuk Yin Ma Su, May 19, 1995; children: Jeanne, Wynne, Charmain, Grace. BS in Materials Science, National Tsing-Hua U., Taiwan, 1976; PhD in Materials Science, Marquette U., Milw., 1985. Rsch. asst. Marquette U., 1979-84; sr. scientist U. Space Rsch. Assn., Huintsville, Ala., 1985-93, dir., 1993-94; rsch. scientist NASA/Marshall Space Flight Ctr., Huintsville, Ala., 1994—. Cons. in field. Author: (books) Semiconductor & Semimetals, 1983, Current Research Topics in C. Growth, 1995. Avocations: travel, bridge, basketball. Office: EM30 NASA Marshall Space Flight Ctr Huntsville AL 35812 Business E-Mail: ching.h.su@nasa.gov.

SU, EDWIN, orthopedist; s. Philip and Wen-Huey Su; m. Karen Lin, Nov. 7, 1998; children: Justin, Steven. MD, Cornell U. Med. Coll., NYC, 1997. Lic. NY, 1997. Attending orthopedic surgeon Hosp. Spl. Surgery, NYC, 2003—. Active contbr. Hosp. Spl. Surgery Charitable found., NYC, 2003—07. Fellow: Am. Acad. Orthopedic Surgeons. Achievements include research in hip and knee surgery. Office: Hosp Spl Surgery 535 E 70th St New York NY 10021

SU, GEORGE SHENGHUI (SHENG-HUI SU), chemist, medical researcher, educator; b. Shanghai, Mar. 9, 1941; came to U.S., 1992; s. Cheng-Ye and Zao-Fu (Hwang) S.; m. Qi Qi Zhang, Mar. 8, 1967; 1 child, Junjie. BS in Pharmacy, Shanghai Med. U., 1962, PhD in Med. Chemistry, 1966. Vis. rsch. fellow Inst. Microbial Chemistry, Tokyo, 1981—83; v.p., rsch. and dev. dir. Shanghai Inst. Pharm. Industry, 1983—89, rsch. prof., 1989—92; rsch. scientist BioGenex Labs., San Ramon, Calif., 1992-95, sr. rsch. scientist, mgr. R & D, 1995-99, dir. R & D, 2000—09; v.p. & CTO Biomics Biotech., Nantong, China, 2009—. Guest prof. Shanghai Inst. Pharm. Industry, 1993—. Contbr. articles to profl. jours. Mem. AAAS, Am. Chem. Soc., Chinese Am. Chem. Soc., Sino-Am. Pharm. Assn. Achievements include patents in field; development of novel synthetic process for antibiotics Amikacin, Tobramycin, cephalosporins and penicillins; invention of novel technology for DNA synthesis applied in oligonucleotide labeling and signal amplification. Home: 2 Craydon Ct San Ramon CA 94583-3906 Personal E-mail: geoshsu@yahoo.com.

SU, HUA, medical educator; d. Zuyou Su and Rongzhen Cao; m. Jianqin Ye, Mar. 2, 1957; 1 child, Julia Ye. MD, Nanjing Med. U., China, 1982. Cert. ednl. commn. for fgn. med. grads. Ednl. Commn. US, 1997. Asst. prof. Xian Med. U., 1986—87, lectr., 1987—89, assoc. prof., 1994—; postgrad. rschr. U. Calif., San Francisco, 1992—96, asst. rsch. physician, 1996—2003, asst. prof., 2003—. Contbr. articles to profl. jours. Recipient Distinctive Rsch. Paper award, Conf. Electron Microscopy in North-West China, 1987, Xian Br. Chinese Med. Assn., 1988; grantee, Nat. Family Planning Assn. China, 1986, Xian Med. U., 1986; Cheng scholar, Chinese Adminstrn. Health, 1989. Mem.: Am. Heart Assn. (Scientist Devel. grantee 2005), Am. Soc. Gene Therapy. Office: Univ California San Francisco 513 Parnassus Ave HSW 901B San Francisco CA 94143-0793 Office Fax: 415-476-2956. Business E-Mail: hua.su@ucsf.edu.

SU, KENNETH C. H., gynecologist; b. Taipei, Taiwan, Apr. 6, 1966; s. Hsin-chi and Wen-shu Su; m. Roxanne Chung-li Ku; 1 child, Erin H. MD, St. Louis U., 1993. Diplomate Am. Bd. ob-gyn., 1999. Resident physician SCHI, Sagina, Mich., 1993—97; physician Valley ob-gyn., Saginaw, 1997—2003; urogynecology fellow Ind. U., Indpls., 2003—06; staff urogynecologist Kaiser Permanente, San Diego, 2006—07, Riverside, Calif., 2008—. Office: Kaiser Permanente 10800 Magnolia Ave Riverside CA 92505 Office Fax: 951-353-5740.

SU, MENG, science educator; m. Hong Wang, Oct. 1, 1992; children: Madeline, Matthew. PhD, Southern Ill. U., Carbondale, 2000. Assoc. prof. Pa. State U., Behrend Coll., Erie, 1999—. Contbr. scientific papers to profl. jour. Mem.: Assn. Computing Machinery. Office: Pa State Erie Behrend Coll 4205 College Dr Erie PA 16563

SU, ZHENG, statistician; b. Harbin, Heilongjiang, China, May 2, 1978; s. Wendi Su and Shufang Yin. PhD, Stanford U., Calif., 2005. Asst. prof. SUNY, Stony Brook, NY, 2006—07; sr. biostatistician Genentech Inc., South San Francisco, 2007—. Vis. asst. prof. Stanford U., Calif., 2007. Contbr. articles to profl. jours. Recipient Outstanding Tchr. award, SUNY Stony Brook, 2006—07. Mem.: Am. Assn. Cancer Rsch. Achievements include research in identified prognostic factors for cancer. Office: Genentech Inc 1 DNA Way South San Francisco CA 94080 Office Fax: 650-742-8619. Business E-Mail: su.zheng@gene.com.

SUAREZ, LUIS EDGARDO, civil engineering educator; b. Jujuy, Argentina, May 14, 1957; came to U.S., 1983; s. Luciano and Maria Mercedes (Colche) S.; m. Rosana Martinez-Cruzado, Dec. 30, 1994. MS in Engring. Mechanics, Va. Poly Inst., 1984, PhD in Engring. Mechanics, 1986. Jr. engr. Atomic Energy Commn. Argentina, Cordoba, 1981; instr. part-time dept. of structures U. Cordoba, 1981-82, asst. prof. grad. programs, 1987-89; rsch. asst. engring. sci. and mechanics Va. Poly. Inst., Blacksburg, 1983-86, asst. prof. engr. sci. and mechanics dept., 1986-87; asst. prof. gen. engring. dept. U. P.R., Mayaguez, 1989-91, assoc. prof. gen. engring. dept., 1991-96, prof. civil engring., 1996—. Proposal reviewer U.S. Army Rsch. Office, Mayaguez, 1991, NSF, Washington, 1994-95, 2007-08; paper reviewer Jour. Vibration and Acoustics, Jour. Engring. for Industry, Jour. Engring. Structures, Jour. Engring. Mechanics, Jour. Vibration and Control, AIAA Jour., Jour. of Sound and Vibration, Jour. Nonlinear Dynamics; panelist to select scholarships Battelle, Raleigh, 1991-92; chmn. 5th Pan Am. Congress of Applied Math., 1997, tech. chmn. South Eastern Conf. Theoretical and Applied Mechanics Congress, 2001, 06. Co-author: Multinational Seismic Design Codes, Handbook, 1992, A Visual Introduction to SAP 2000, 2002; mem. editl. bds. Jour. Engineering Structures, Jour. Vibration and Control, Mechanics Bulletin; co-editor Jour. Revista Internacional de Desastres Naturales, Accidentes e Infraestructura Civil; contbr. articles to profl. jours. Cunningham fellow Va. Poly. Inst., 1986, Disting. prof., dept. gen. engring., 1994, Disting. prof. civil engring., 1996, 99, 2005; grantee U.S. Army Rsch. Office, 1990, Nat. Ctr. for Earthquake Engring. Rsch., 1992-96, Langley Rsch. Ctr. NASA, 1999, FEMA, 2001-03, U.S. Army Corps. Engrs., 2003-05, U.S. Geol. Survey, 2003-04. Mem. ASCE, ASME, AIAA, Soc. Exptl. Mechanics, Earthquake Engring. Rsch. Inst., Am. Soc. Engring. Edn., Am. Acad. Mechanics, Sigma Xi (Rsch. award Va. Tech. chpt. 1987). Roman Catholic. Achievements include development of methods for seismic analysis of mechanical equipment that are used in industry, several methods for dynamic analysis of large structural systems. Home: PO Box 3914 Marina Sta Mayaguez PR 00681-3914 Office: Univ Puerto Rico Civil Engring Dept PO Box 9000 Mayaguez PR 00681-9000 Home Phone: 787-832-5217; Office Phone: 787-832-4040 ext. 3669. Business E-Mail: luis.suarez3@upr.edu.

SUAREZ, MILDRED, speech pathology/audiology services professional, educator; children: Gabriel Andres, Victor Manuel, Daniel Armando, Alejandro Javier. MS, Eastern Ill. U., Charleston, 1981. Cert. speech lang. pathologist Fla., 1981. Dir. Speech Pathology & Ednl. Ctr. Inc., Miami, 1981—, pres., 1981—; prof. Fla. Internat. U., Miami, 2007—. Named Outstanding Alumni of Yr., Eastern Ill. U., 1997. Mem.: Fla. Speech and Hearing Assn., Am. Speech and Hearing Assn. Office: Speech Pathology and Ednl Ctr 8510 SW 8 St Miami FL 33144 E-mail: speechatspec@aol.com.

SUAREZ, RAY (REGNER SUAREZ), alderman; b. Yauco, PR, Oct. 26, 1946; m. Marta Suarez. Adminstrv. asst. Office of Mayor, Chgo.; asst. commr. Dept. Streets & Sanitation, Chgo., 1974-91, coord. Comprehensive Employment & Training Act (CETA) program; alderman, 31st ward Chgo. City Coun., 1991—, chmn. housing & real estate com., 1994—. Apptd. mem. Ill. Job Training Coordinating Coun., 1989. Served with USMC, Vietnam. Mem.: Caballeros de San Juan, Puerto Rican Lion's Club. Office: 4502 W Fullerton Ave Chicago IL 60639-1934 also: City Hall 121 N La Salle St Rm 203 Office 19 Chicago IL 60602 Office Phone: 312-744-6102. Business E-Mail: rsuarez@cityofchicago.org.*

SUAREZ, SALLY ANN TEVIS, health facility administrator, nurse, consultant; b. Jersey City, Jan. 23, 1944; d. Paul John and Gertrude Marie (Clancey) Tevis; 1 child, Maria E. Diploma, St. Mary Hosp. Sch. Nursing, 1965; BA in Health Edn. and Nursing, Jersey City State Coll., 1966, MA in Health Sci., 1977. Staff nurse St. Mary Hosp., Hoboken, N.J., 1965, Bayonne (N.J.) Hosp., 1966, Jersey City Med. Ctr., 1965-66; adminstr. Hoboken Med. Arts Family Health Ctr., 1969-75; adj. faculty Jersey City State Coll., 1976-77; adminstrv. supr. St. Mary Hosp., Hoboken, 1977-80; dir. North Hudson Commn. Action Corp. Clinic, West New York, N.J., 1979-88; nursing clin. dir. St. Mary Hosp., Hoboken, 1988-89; corp. dir. nursing Francisan Health System N.J., 1989-92; dir. maternal child health svcs. St. James Hosp., Newark, 1992-93, dir. Family Care Ctr., Cathedral Healthcare Sys., 1993-97, dir. nursing, 1992—97; ind. cons., 1995—; v.p. Med. Resource Network, 1997—2003; med. case mgr. MCR, 2000—03, Corvel Corp., 2003—04; coord. family health ctr. North Hudson Cmty. Action Corp., 2004—06; coord. case mgmt. U. Medicine and Dentistry N.J. Univ. Hosp., 2006—. Instr. nursing St. Mary Hosp. Sch. Nursing; cons. Creative Concepts in Counseling, Rutherford, N.J., 1979-82, Com. for Cytogenetics, Newark, 1986-88; cons. in health svcs., 1996—; v.p. Med. Resource Network, 1998-2003; case mgr. workers' compensation, critical care MCR, 2000-2003; case mgr. workers' compensation CorVel Corp., 2003-2004; health ctr. coord. North Hudson Cmty. Action Corp. Health Ctr., 2004-2006; case mgr. and coord UMDNJ, 2006—. Active Hudson County ARC, 1984-88, United Way, 1984-94; mem. Hudson County Perinatal Consortium Bd., 1987-92, Gateway Consortium, 1993-96; mem. adv. bd. Health Start, 1995-97, N.J. Assn. Women Bus. Owners, 1996-98; bd. dirs. Passaic Head Start; mem. adv. bd. Harrison Care Inst., 2005—. Mem. U.S. Assn. Women Bus. Owners, Am. Cancer Soc., N.J. Family Planning Forum (exec. com. 1980-86), Family Planning Assn. N.J. (exec. com. 1986-88). Roman Catholic. Avocation: alternative healing. Home: 113 Wilson Ave Rutherford NJ 07070-2726 Home Phone: 201-935-4989; Office Phone: 973-972-4655. Personal E-mail: narsesrch@aol.com. Business E-Mail: suarezst@umdnj.edu.

SUAREZ-ALMAZOR, MARIA E., rheumatologist, educator; PhD in Med. Scis., U. Alberta, 1993. Cert. MD U. Alberta, 1979. Rsch. assoc. U. Alberta, Edmonton, Canada, 1993, asst. prof., 1993—97, assoc prof., 1997—2000, Baylor Coll. Medicine, Houston, 2003—06; Barnts family Disting. prof., dept gen. intenal medicine U. Tex., MD Anderson Cancer ctr., Houston, 2006—. Contbr. articles to numerous profl. jours. Dir. Houston Ctr. Edn. & Rsch. Therapeutics, 2007—. Recipient K24 mentor award, NIH, 2008—09. Mem.: Clin. & Translational Scis., Am. Coll. Rheumatology. Office: Univ Tex MD Anderson Cancer Ctr1515 Holcombe Blvd Unit 1465 Rm FCT13 5034 Houston TX 77030 Fax: 713-563-4491. Business E-Mail: msalmazor@mdanderson.org.

SUAREZ-IÑIGUEZ, ENRIQUE, education educator; b. Mex. City, July 22, 1948; s. Enrique Suarez Alvarez and Paz Iñiguez de Suarez. BA in Polit. Sci., Nat. Autonomous U. Mex., Mexico City, 1973, PhD, 1978; postgrad., U. Paris I Sorbonne, 1973—74, Cornell U., Ithaca, NY, 1986—87. From assoc. prof. level A to prof. level B Nat. Autonomous U. Mex., Mexico City, 1975—83, chmn. ctr. ednl. rsch., 1983—85, dir. jour. perfiles educativos, 1983—85, prof. level C, 1996, pres., Polit. Philosophy Acad., Dept. Polit. Sci., 2008; vis. prof. govt. Cornell U., Ithaca, 1986—87; from nat. rschr., level i to nat. rschr. iii Nat. Rsch. Sys., Mexico City, 1985—2000; chmn., grad. dept. Dept. of Polit. and Social Sciences, Mexico City, 1992—95, dir., jour. revista mexicana de ciencias politicas y sociales, 1992—95. Cons. in field; mem. editl. bd. Philosophy of Social Scis. Recipient Nat. Rschr. award, Nat. Rsch. Sys., 1985, Prof. Recognition award, Nat. Autonomous U. Mex., 1997, Univ. Tchg. award, 2004, Raúl Cardiel Reyes medal, Dept. Polit. and Social Sci., 2006, Silver medal to acad. merit, 2007; named IBC Forenist Educators of World, Cambridge, 2008. Fellow: Mexican Sociology Assn., Mexican Acad. Sci. Roman Catholic. Avocations: reading, movies, music, travel, football. Office: Nat Autonomous Univ Mexico Dept Political Sci Ciudad Universitaria Mexico City 04510 Mexico Office Phone: 52-55-5665-1233. Office Fax: 52-55-5622-9419. Personal E-mail: esiiguez2002@yahoo.com.mx.

SUBAIR, SAAD OSMAN ABDALLA, science educator; s. Osman Abdalla and UmSalamah AbdulBagi Subair; m. Nusaiba Ahmed Jaafar; children: Raiya Saad, Hiba Saad, Mohammed Saad. BSc with honors, U. Khartoum, Sudan, 1991; MSc in Genetics, U. Putra Malaysia, Serdang, 1994; postgrad. diploma in computer sci., U. Tech. Malaysia, Kuala Lumpur, 1996; MSc in Computer Sci., U. Tech. Malaysia, Skudai, 1998, PhD in Computer Sci., 2005. Rschr. U. Tech. Malaysia, Kuala Lumpur and Skudai, 1996—98; leading Internet programmer Ministry Islamic Affairs, Doha, Qatar, 1998—2000; lectr. Ajman U., Abu Dhabi, United Arab Emirates, 2000—02; asst. prof. Alghurair U., Dubai, United Arab Emirates, 2005—. Dep. dean Ajman U., Fujairah, United Arab Emirates, 2000—01; dir. info. tech. ctr. Alghurair U., 2005—; head bioinformatics and co-founder Computational Modeling Rsch. Lab., Abu Dhabi, 2006—. Contbr. articles to profl. jours. Head Poultry Com., Shambat, Sudan, 1987—89; founder, chief editor Green Color Paper (English/Arabic), U. Khartoum; founder Internat. Student Assn., U. Putra Malaysia, 1993—94. Recipient award and prize, Ministry Islamic

Affairs, Doha, 1999; named Best PhD Student, U. Tech. Malaysia, 2005. Achievements include research in a new method for predicting protein secondary structure using artificial neural networks and information theory. Office: Al-Ghurair U Sheikh Zayed Rd 37374 Dubai United Arab Emirates Office Fax: 97143393055. Personal E-mail: saad_subair@hotmail.com. Business E-Mail: saad@agu.ac.ae.

SUBEDI, BIDYA RAJ, school system administrator, statistician, consultant; arrived in US, 2000; s. Tirtha Raj and Subhadra Subedi; m. Bijaya Baral Subedi, Mar. 9, 1987; children: Bibidh, Bibek. BS, Tribhuvan U., Kathmandu, Nepal, 1991; MA, Mich. State U., East Lansing, 1996; PhD, Fla. State U., Tallahassee, 2005. Lectr. Tribhuvan U., Kathmandu, 1991—2000; tchg. asst. Fla. State U., Tallahassee, 2000—04; evaluation specialist Sch. Dist. Palm Beach County, West Palm Beach, Fla., 2004—. Evaluator Trungram Internat. Acad., Kathmandu, 1998—99; rsch. asst. Fla. Dept. Edn., Tallahassee, 2003—04; stats. cons. U. Ctrl. Fla., Orlando, Fla., 2004—05. Chief editor: Sagar - A Nepali Lit. Jour., 2006. Mem.: Internat. Napali Literary Soc. (pres. INLS FL chpt. 2007—09), Am. Edn. Rsch. Assn. Home Phone: 561-967-4165. Business E-Mail: subedib@palmbeach.k12.fl.us.

SUBLER, EDWARD PIERRE, advertising executive; b. Shelby, Ohio, Mar. 24, 1927; s. Leo John and Dorotha (Armstrong) S.; m. Alice Ellen Carpenter, Sept. 8, 1956; children: Leo, Scott, Dorotha. BA, Denison U., Granville, Ohio, 1950; grad. advanced mgmt. course, Emory U., Atlanta. Mgr. product advt. Westinghouse Electric Co., Mansfield, Ohio, 1950—65; mgr. advt. and sales promotion Bell & Howell Co., Chgo., 1965-69; v.p. mdsg. Westinghouse Consumer Products Co., 1969-76; sr. v.p. Ketchum Advt., Pitts., 1976-92, ret., 1992; v.p. Pacific Garden Co., Millheim, Pa., 1998—2005, pres., bd. dir. Trustee BCB Anglers, Baie Jeanne Assn., Tanglewood Assn. Served with USN, 1945-46. Mem. Am. Mktg. Assn., Am. Assn. Advt. Agencies (regional chmn.), Catawba Island Club, Bus./Profl. Adv. Assn. (Pitts. Advt. Exec. of Yr. 1988), US Power Squadron, Baie Jeanne Assn. (bd. dir.). Home: 2465 Circleville Rd Unit 122 State College PA 16803-3390 Personal E-mail: esubler@yahoo.com.

SUBLETT, SHERRY LAKE, junior high school educator; b. Wahiawah, Hawaii, July 21, 1957; d. Charles Edward Lake, Jr. and Jean Powell Lake; m. Bill Roy Sublett, Sept. 17, 1977. BS, Auburn U., Ala., 1978; Master's degree, U. Ala., Tuscaloosa, 1982. Tchr. Huffman Elem., Birmingham, 1979—80, John S. Jones Elem., Rainbow City, Ala., 1980—93, Moody Mid. Sch., Ala., 1993—2002, Moody Jr. HS, 2002—. Mem. Leeds Comty. Chorus, 1994—, Leeding Ladies, Leeds, 1997—. Named John S. Jones Tchr. of Yr., John S. Jones Elem., 1987, Ala. Spl. Educator of Yr., CEC, 1999, St. Clair County Secondary Tchr. of YR., St. Clair Bd. Edn., 2005. Mem.: NEA, Ala. Edn. Assn., Alpha Delta Kappa (officer internat. chpt. 1986—). United Methodist. Avocations: reading, hiking, singing, travel. Office: Moody Jr HS 600 High School Dr Moody AL 35004

SUBOLESKI, STANLEY C., federal agency administrator, mining engineer; b. 1941; BS, Pa. State U., 1963, PhD in Mining Engring., 1978; MS, Va. Tech. U., 1968. Mining engr. North American Coal Corp., 1963—65; gen. supt. Underground Mines, Ctrl. Div. Consolidation Coal Co., 1969—74; v.p. mining divsn. Continental Ill. Nat. Bank, 1977—81; v.p. mining devel, treas. A.T. Massey Coal Co., 1981—88, v.p. ops. strategy, pres. United Coal Co., v.p. Norfolk Southern Ops., 1993—97; cons. mining engr., 2000—01; exec. v.p., interim COO Massey Energy Co., 2001—03; commr. Fed. Mine Safety and Health Review Commn., Washington, 2003—. Instr. Va. Tech. U., 1965—69, prof., head Dept. Mining Engring., 1998—2000; instr. Pa. State U., 1974—77, Centennial prof. mining engring., chmn. Mining Engring. Sect., 1988—93. Mem.: NAE, Soc. Mining, Metallurgy and Exploration (mem. exec. com. Coal and Energy Div.). Office: Fed Mine Safety and Health Review Commn 601 New Jersey Ave NW, Ste 9500 Washington DC 20001 Office Phone: 202-434-9921.

SUBRAHMANYAM, SOMASHEKAR RAMACHANDRAN, mechanical engineer; s. Vasanthamma Sarasamma; m. Anuradha Narasimhaswamy Melkote, Dec. 30, 1993; children: Prianka Melkote, Neha Melkote. Doctorate, Rensselaer Poly. Inst., Troy NY, 1997. Cert. in exec. mgmt. leadership MIT, 2008. Sr. software engr. Computervision, San Diego, 1995—97; modeling expert Autodesk Inc, Novi, Mich., 1997—. Author: Autodesk LT, 2008. Mem.: ASME. Achievements include patents for CAD and solid modeling. Home: 29250 Fieldstone Farmington MI 48334

SUBRAMANI, VELU, chemist, researcher; arrived in US, 2002; s. Subramani Kuppan and Meenakshi Subramani; m. Amutha Velu Rathinam, Mar. 27, 1996; 1 child, Niraimathy-Nyorai Velu. PhD, Indian Inst. Tech., 1996. Rsch. scholar Indian Inst. Tech., Madras, Tamil Nadu, India, 1992—96; rsch. assoc. Nat. Chem. Lab., Pune, Maharastra, India, 1996—97; fcs fellow Swiss Fed. Inst. Tech., Lausanne, Switzerland, 1997—98; fellow Nat. Indsl. Rsch. Inst. Nagoya, Japan, 1998—2000; rsch. assoc. Agy. Indsl. Sci. and Tech., Nagoya, 2000—02, Pa. State U., Univ. Park, Pa., 2002—. Contbr. articles to profl. jours. Recipient Inventor Incentive award, 2003; fellow, Indian Inst. Tech., Madras, India, 1992, 1994, Switzerland Fed. Govt., 1997, Sci. and Tech. Agy. of Japan, 1998. Mem.: ACS (corr.; subscription mgr. 2004). Achievements include patents in field; development of new Catalytic process for hydrogen production; new technology for removing sulfur from transportation fuels for fuel cell applications. Office: Rsch Triangle Inst Ctr for Energy Tech 3040 Cornwallis Rd Research Triangle Park NC 27709 Home: 1576 Tara Belle Pkwy Naperville IL 60564-8197 Personal E-mail: subravelu@hotmail.com. Business E-Mail: velu@rti.org.

SUBRAMANIAM, SHIVAN SIVASWAMY, insurance company executive; b. Madras, India, Feb. 15, 1949; came to U.S., 1970; s. Kodaganullor Sivaswamy and Seethalakshmi S. B.E. in Mech. Engring. with honors, Birla Inst. Tech., Pilani. India, 1970; MS in Ops. Research, Poly. Inst. Bklyn., 1972; S.M. in Mgmt., MIT, 1978. Indsl. engr. Midland Container Corp., Ridgewood, N.J., 1971-74; mgmt. sci. analyst Allendale Ins. Co., Johnston, RI, 1974-76, sr. mgmt. sci. analyst, 1976-77, sr. fin. staff officer, 1978-80, v.p., treas., 1980-83, sr. v.p. fin., chief fin. officer, 1983-91, exec. v.p., 1991-92, pres., 1992-93, pres., CEO, 1993-95, chmn., pres., CEO, 1995—99; pres., CEO FM Global, Johnston, RI, 1999—2002, chmn., pres., CEO, 2002—. Mem. Fin. Execs. Inst. (membership chmn. 1982-84, Providence chpt. pres. 1985-86), Nat. Assn. Corp. Treas. Office: FM Global 1301 Atwood Ave Johnston RI 02919

SUBRAMANIAN, SHYAM, sleep physician director; b. Mumbai, India, Jan. 17, 1971; s. M. Subrmaanian and A. Subramanian; m. Uma Subramanian. MD, Case Western Res. U., Cleve., 2001. Diplomate in sleep medicine Am. Bd. Med. Specialties, 2000, in pulmonary medicine Am. Bd. Med. Specialties, 2000, in critical care Am. Bd. Med. Specialties, 2000. Cons. Pitts. Pulmonary Assoc., 2004—05; dir. BCM Sleep Ctr., Houston, 2005—, Harris County Sleep Ctr., 2005—. Contbr. articles to profl. jours. Fellow: ACCP. Office: Baylor Coll Medicine 100019 S Main Houston TX 77025 Office Fax: 713-798-3303. Business E-Mail: ssubrama@bcm.edu.

SUBRAMANIAN, VIJAY, mechanical engineer; Rschr. U. Fla., Gainesville, 2002—08. Achievements include research in autonomous vehicle guidance systems.

SUBUDHI, PRASANTA KUMAR, agricultural studies educator; PhD in Genetics, Indian Agrl. Rsch. Inst., New Delhi, 1992. Asst. prof. Orissa U. Agr. & Tech., Bhubaneswar, India, 1992—94; project scientist Internat. Rice Rsch. Inst., LosBanos, Luzon, Philippines, 1994—96; postdoc. rsch. assoc. Tex. Tech U., Lubbock, 1996—2000; asst. prof. La. State U. Agrl. Ctr., Baton Rouge, 2001—07, assoc. prof., 2007—. Recipient Tifton Team Rsch. award, La. State U. Agrl. Ctr., 2007; Rice Biotechnology fellowship, Rockefeller Found., 1994—96. Mem.: Agronomy Soc. America, Crop Sci. Soc. America (assoc. editor 2007—), Gamma Sigma Delta Soc., Sigma Xi. Office: La State Univ Sch Plant Environ & Soil Sci Baton Rouge LA 70803 Office Fax: 225-578-1403. Business E-Mail: psubudhi@agctr.lsu.edu.

SUCATO, DANIEL J., orthopaedic surgeon; s. Justin and Ilde Sucato; m. Lisa Sucato; children: Daniel, Emma, Matthew. BA magna cum laude, Canisius Coll., Buffalo, 1987; MD, U. Buffalo, 1991, MS in Biophysics, 1997. Orthopaedic resident U. Buffalo, 1991—97, basic sci. rsch. fellow, 1992—93; pediatric orthopaedic surgery fellow Tex. Scottish Rite Hosp., Dallas, 1997—98, assoc. prof. orthopaedic surgery, U. Tex. at Southwestern Med. Ctr., Dallas, 1998—. Active staff mem. Children's Med. Ctr. Dallas. Contbr. articles to profl. jours., including Jour. Bone and Joint Surgery; cons. reviewer Spine, Jour. of Spinal Cord Medicine, Jour. of Bone and Joint Surgery, Jour. Pediat. Orthop., mem. editl. bd. Spine Universe. Active smem. Recipient Dr. William Beaumont award, AMA, 2005; Hip Preserving fellowship, Bern, Switzerland, 1998, SRS Internat. Traveling Fellow, 2003. Mem.: N.Am. Spine Soc., Tex. Med. Assn., Pediatric Orthopaedic Soc. N.Am., Am. Acad. Orthopaedic Surgeons, Scoliosis Rsch. Soc. Office: Texas Scottish Rite Hosp 2222 Welborn St Dallas TX 75219 Office Fax: 214-559-7570. Business E-Mail: dan.sucato@tsrh.org.

SUCEAVA, BOGDAN DRAGOS, mathematics professor, writer; b. Curtea de Arges, Romania, Sept. 27, 1969; s. Ion and Elisabeta Suceava; m. Linica Pirvu, July 30, 1994; 1 child, Albert Christian. PhD, Mich. State U., East Lansing, 2002. Assoc. prof. math. Calif. State U., Fullerton. Author: (novel) Miruna, A Tale (Assn. Bucharest Writers Fiction award, 2008), Coming from an Off Key Time, Vincent the Immortal. Mem.: Am. Math. Soc., Union of Romanian Writers, Pen Club West. Office: Calif State Univ Fullerton Dept Math Fullerton CA 92834-6850 Personal E-mail: bsuceava@yahoo.com. Business E-Mail: bsuceava@fullerton.edu.

SUCHA, GEORGE R., education educator; b. McKeesport, Pa., Feb. 12, 1947; s. George J. and Elizabeth Sucha; m. Nancy J. Sucha, Oct. 9, 1977; children: Gregory Nichols, Joseph, Keith Nichols, Carolyn Ellsworth. MA in Edn., Edinboro U., Pa., 1990. Cert. tchr. Pa. Dept. Edn., 1969. Secondary sch. adminstr. NE Sch. Dist., Pa., 1969—99; asst. prof. Gannon Univ., Erie, Pa., 1999—. Sch. dir. NE Sch. Dist., Pa., 2000—. Mem.: P.A.S.S.P. Liberal. Office: Gannon Univ 109 Univ Sq Erie PA 16541 Office Phone: 814-871-5762. Business E-Mail: sucha001@gannon.edu.

SUCHANEK, WOJCIECH LUKASZ, materials scientist, researcher; b. Oswiecim, Poland, 1969; arrived in US, 1999, permanent resident, 2004; s. Franciszek and Lucyna Suchanek; m. Figen Suchanek, 1996; 1 child, Melissa Ann. BS, U. Mining and Metallurgy, Cracow, Poland, 1991, MS, 1992; DSc, Tokyo Inst. Tech., 1996. Rsch. assoc. Tokyo Inst. Tech., Materials and Structures Lab., 1996—98; postdoctoral fellow U. Pierre Marie Curie, Lab. Chimie Matière Condensée, Paris, 1998—99; rsch. assoc. dept. ceramic and materials engring. Rutgers U., Piscataway, NJ, 1999—2001; rsch. scientist Sawyer Tech. Materials LLC (formerly Sawyer Rsch. Products), Eastlake, Ohio, 2001—04, sr. rsch. scientist, 2004—07, R & D Direct Ceramics, 2007—. Contbr. chapters to books, highly cited review papers and articles to profl. jours. Recipient Young Rschr. award, IUMRS Internat. Conf., 1997; fellow, Centre Internat. Etiudants Stagiaires, 1998—99; scholar, Ministry Edn., Sci. and Culture of Japan (Monbusho), 1993—96; Rsch. grantee, Rsch. Inst. Solvothermal Tech, Japan, 1998—2001. Achievements include patents in field; patents pending in field. Avocations: travel, photography, classical music, movies, sports. Office: Sawyer Tech Materials LLC 35400 Lakeland Blvd Eastlake OH 44095 Office Fax: 440-951-1480. Personal E-mail: w_suchanek@yahoo.com. Business E-Mail: wls@sawyerllc.com.

SUCHENEK, MAREK ANDRZEJ, computer science educator; b. Warsaw, May 2, 1949; arrived in US, 1986, naturalized, 1999; s. Tadeusz Aleksander and Barbara Krystyna (Zych) Suchenek; m. Ewa Aleksandra Czerny, July 30, 1974 (div. 1991); m. Cynthia M. Vincent, July 6, 2001. MSc in Math. Engring., Warsaw Tech. U., 1973, PhD in Tech. Scis. with distinction, 1979. Instr. Warsaw Tech. U., 1973-79, asst. prof., 1979-88; assoc. Nat. Inst. for Aviation Rsch., Wichita, 1987-90; vis. asst. prof. Wichita (Kans.) State U., 1986-88, assoc. prof., 1988-89, assoc. prof., chair, 1989-90; prof. Calif. State U.-Dominguez Hills, Carson, 1990—, co-chair, 1996—97, chair, 1997-98, 2001—02. Adj. prof. Pepperdine U., Malibu, Calif., 1999; mem. organizing com. Internat. Symposium on Methodologies for Intelligent Sys., 1989-90; program com. Ann. Ulam Math. Conf., 1990-91, Internat. Conf. on Computing and Info., 1992-94; referee NSF, 1990-92, Annals of Math. and Artificial Intelligence, 1992-93, Jour. Logic Programming, 1992-94; presenter in field. Author: (with Jan Bielecki) ANS FORTRAN, 1980, (with Jan Bielecki) FORTRAN for Advanced Programmers, 1981, 2nd edit., 1983, 3rd edit., 1988 (Minister of Sci. Higher Edn. and Techs. prize 1982); reviewer Zentralblatt fur Mathematik, 1980-89, Math. Revs., 1989-91, Jour. Symbolic Logic, 1998-2000; contbr. articles to profl. jours. Rsch. grantee Polish Govt., 1974-76, 85-86, FAA, 1988-90, NASA, 1997. Avocations: swimming, target shooting. Office: Calif State U Dominguez Hills 1000 E Victoria St Carson CA 90747-0001 Home: 5605 Van Gogh Way Yorba Linda CA 92887-5604 Business E-Mail: suchenek@csudh.edu.

SUCHMAN, ANTHONY LEE, physician, consultant; BA, Cornell U., Ithaca, NY, 1975; MD, 1979; MA, U. Hertfordshire, England, 2002. Cert. Am. Bd. Internal Medicine, 1982. Exec. dir. Highland PO, Rochester, NY, 1995—96; ceo and chief med. officer Strong Health Managed Care Orgn., Rochester, 1997—99; sr. cons. founder Relationship Centered Health Care, Rochester, 2000; clin. prof. medicine U. Rochester, 2000. Chair, bd. dirs. Am. Acad. Comm. Healthcare, 2000—07. Contbr. articles to 100 profl. jours. Office: 990 S Ave Ste 207 Rochester NY 14620

SUCIU, JAMES N., sales executive; BS in Mech. Engring., Purdue U. Regional sales mgr., mktg. & bus. devel. GE Co., Singapore, regional sales mgr. China; mgmt. positions in comml. ops. GE Energy Products; v.p. energy services sales GE Power Systems; pres. global sales GE Energy (formerly GE Power Systems), Atlanta, 2004—. Office: GE Energy 4200 Wildwood Pkwy Atlanta GA 30339 Office Phone: 678-844-6000. Office Fax: 678-844-6690.*

SUDA, KATIE JOY, pharmacist, educator; d. George E. and Helen K. Suda. PharmD, Drake U., Des Moines, 1999. Assoc. prof., dir. U. Tenn., Memphis, 2005—. Office: Univ Tenn 930 Madison Ave Ste 890 Memphis TN 38163 Office Phone: 901-448-3744. Business E-Mail: ksuda@utmem.edu.

SUDAN, RAVINDRA NATH, electrical engineer, physicist, educator; b. Chineni, Kashmir, India, June 8, 1931; came to U.S., 1958, naturalized, 1971; s. Brahm Nath and Shanti Devi (Mehta) S.; m. Dipali Ray, July 3, 1959; children: Rajani, Ranjeet. BA with first class honors, U. Punjab, 1948; diploma, Indian Inst. Sci., 1952, Imperial Coll., London, 1953; PhD, U. London, 1955. Engr., Brit. Thomson-Houston Co., Rugby, Eng, 1955-57; Engr. Imperial Chem. Industries, Calcutta, India, 1957-58; research assoc. Cornell U., Ithaca, N.Y., 1958-59, asst. prof. elec. engring., 1959-63, assoc. prof., 1963-68, prof., 1968-75, IBM prof. engring., 1975—2001, IBM prof. engring. emeritus, 2001—, dir. Lab. Plasma Studies, 1975-85, dep. dir. Cornell Theory Ctr., 1985-87, prof., 1987—. Cons. Lawrence Livermore Lab., Los Alamos Sci. Lab., Sci. Applications Inc., Physics Internat. Co.; vis. research asso. Stanford U., summer 1963; cons. U.K. Atomic Energy Authority, Culham Lab., summer 1965; vis. scientist Internat. Center Theoretical Physics, Trieste, Italy, 1965-66, summers 1970, 73, Plasma Physics Lab. Princeton U., 1966-67, spring 1989, Inst. for Advanced Study, Princeton, N.J., spring 1975; head theoretical plasma physics group U.S. Naval Research Lab., 1970-71, sci. adviser to dir., 1974-75; chmn. Ann. Conf. on Theoretical Aspects of Controlled Fusion, 1975, 2d Internat. Conf. on High Power Electron and Ion Beam Research and Tech., 1977 Mem. editl. bd. Physics of Fluids, 1973-76, Comments on Plasma Physics, 1973, Nuclear Fusion, 1976-84, Physics Reports, 1990—; co-editor Handbook of Plasma Physics; contbr. over 220 articles to sci. jours. Recipient Gold medal Acad. Scis. of the Czech Republic, 1993. Fellow IEEE, AAAS, Am. Phys. Soc. (Maxwell prize 1989), Nat. Rsch. Coun. (chmn. Plasma Sci. com. 1993—). Achievements include patents (with S. Humphries, Jr) intense ion beam generator.

SUDARSKY, JERRY M., industrialist; b. Russia, June 12, 1918; s. Selig and Sara (Ars) S.; m. Mildred Axelrod, Aug. 31, 1947; children: Deborah, Donna (dec.). Student, U. Iowa, 1936—39; BS in Chem. Engring., Poly. U. Bklyn., 1942; DSc (hon.), Poly. U. NY, 1976; PhD Hebrew U. Jerusalem (hon.), 2002. Founder, CEO Bioferm Corp., Wasco, Calif., 1946-66; cons. to Govt. of Israel, 1966—72; founder, chmn. Israel Chems., Ltd., Tel Aviv, 1967-72; chmn. I.C. Internat. Cons., Tel Aviv, 1971-73; vice chmn., bd. dirs. Daylin, Inc., LA, 1972-76; pres., chmn. J.M.S. Assocs., LA, from 1976; vice chmn. bd. dirs. Jacobs Engring. Group Inc., Pasadena, Calif., 1982-94; chmn., CEO Health Sci. Prop. Holding Corp., 1994-97; chmn. Alexandria Real Estate Equities, Pasadena, 1997—2007, chmn. emeritus, from 2007. Patentee in field of indsl. microbiology. Bd. govs. Hebrew U., Jerusalem; trustee Polytechnic U. NY, 1976—; bd. dirs. Mgmt. Edn. Assn., UCLA, 1990-99. Served with USNR, 1943-46. Recipient Richard J. Bolt award for supporting industries, Chem. Heritage Found., 2008. Mem. AAAS, Am. Chem. Soc., Brentwood Country Club, Sigma Xi. Died Apr. 4, 2009.

SUDBRINK, JANE MARIE, sales and marketing executive; b. Sandusky, Ohio, Jan. 14, 1942; niece of Arthur and Lydia Sudbrink. BS, Bowling Green State U., 1964; postgrad., Kinderspital-Zurich, Switzerland, 1965. Field rep. Random House and Alfred A. Knopf Inc., Mpls., 1969-72, Ann Arbor, Mich., 1973, regional mgr. Midwest and Can., 1974-79, Can. rep., mgr., 1980-81; psychology and ednl. psychology adminstrv. editor Charles E. Merrill Pub. Co. div. Bell & Howell Corp., Columbus, Ohio, 1982-84; sales and mktg. mgr. trade products Wilson Learning Corp., Eden Prairie, Minn., 1984-85; fin. cons. Merrill Lynch Pierce Fenner & Smith, Edina, Minn., 1986-88; sr. editor Gorsuch Scarisbrick Pubs., Scottsdale, Ariz., 1988-89; regional mgr. Worth Publs., Inc. - von Holtzbrinck Pub. Grp., NYC, 1988-97; mktg. assoc. Harcourt Brace Coll. Pubs., Northbrook, Ill., 1997-98, cons. Mid-Atlantic Region, Midwest, Manitoba, Can., 1998—; mktg. assoc. W.W. Norton & Co., Northbrook, Ill., 1998—. Lutheran. Home and Office: 3801 Mission Hills Rd Northbrook IL 60062-5729 Business E-Mail: jsudbrink@wwnorton.com.

SUDBURY, DAVID MARSHALL, lawyer; b. Blytheville, Ark., Oct. 31, 1945; s. John Graham and Avis Wheatley (Miller) S.; m. Holly Jane Ritger, Dec. 27, 1967; children: Erin Elizabeth, Gregory Marshall. BA, So. Meth. U., 1967, JD, 1970. Bar: Tex. 1970, Okla. 1971, US Dist. Ct. (we. dist. Okla.) 1971, US Dist. Ct. (so. dist. Tex.) 1974, US Dist. Ct. (no. dist. Tex.) 1976, US Ct. Appeals (5th cir.) 1979, US Supreme Ct. 1981. Asst. sec., atty. Wilson & Co. Inc., Oklahoma City, 1970-74; ptnr. Nelson and Harding, Houston, 1974-76; v.p., gen. counsel, sec. Comml. Metals Co., Irving, 1976—2007, sr. v.p., sec., gen. counsel, 2007—. Bd. dirs. Dallas Repertory Theatre, 1982-85; bd. dirs. The 500 Inc., Dallas, 1978-82, pres., 1980-81. Mem. ABA, Tex. Bar Assn., Dallas Bar Assn. (bd. dirs. corp. counsel sect. 1987-93, chmn. 1992-93), Houston Bar Assn., Okla. Bar Assn., Am. Soc. Corp. Secs. (dir. 1984-86, pres., officer Dallas regional group 1978-81). Office: Comml Metals Co 6565 N MacArthur Blvd #800 Irving TX 75039-2461 Office Phone: 214-689-4300.

SUDDABY, GLENN T., federal judge, former prosecutor; b. 1956; BA, SUNY, 1980; JD, Syracuse U., 1985. Bar: NY 1986, Mass. 1986, Fed. Dist. Ct. 1986. Asst. dist. atty. Onondaga County Dist. Atty.'s Office, 1986—89; assoc. Menter, Rudin & Trivelpiece, Syracuse, NY, 1989—92; chief asst. dist. atty. Onondaga County Dist. Atty.'s Office, 1992; 1st chief asst. dist. atty. Onandaga County Dist. Atty.'s Office, 1998—2002; US atty. (no. dist.) NY US Dept. Justice, 2002—08; judge US Dist. Ct. (no. dist.) NY, 2008—. Office: US Dist Ct PO Box 7198 100 S Clinton St Syracuse NY 13261 Office Phone: 315-448-0672.

SUDDENDORF, MATTHEW L., band director; b. Cin., Nov. 25, 1979; s. Lawrence R. and Joan M. Suddendorf; m. Kathryn E. Collins, June 27, 2003; 1 child, Meredith E. MusB cum laude, Miami U., 2002; MusM in Edn., U. Cin., 2005. Cert. tchr. music K-12 Ohio. Asst. band dir. Norwood City Schs., Ohio, 2002—05, U. Cin. Bearcat Bands, 2005—07; dir. bands Little Miomi HS, Morrow, Ohio, 2007—. Author: (reference handbook) Music Instruction for Hearing Impaired Students Following the UDL Model, 2007. Mem.: Ohio Music Educators Assn., Music Educators Nat. Conf., Phi Mu Alpha (warden 2000—02). Roman Catholic. Avocations: travel, scuba diving, car restoration, volunteer work. Office: 3001 East US Morrow OH 45152 Personal E-mail: mattsuddendorf@yahoo.com.

SUDHAKAR, NORI, materials scientist, researcher; s. Siva Prasad Venkata and Parameswari Nori. PhD in Physics, Indian Inst. Tech., Kanpur, 2004. Rschr. low temperature lab. physics dept. Indian Inst. Tech., Kanpur, 1990—2005; postdoctoral rsch. assoc. materials sci. and engring. NC State U., Raleigh, 2006—. Contbr. articles to profl. jours. Mem.: Metals, Minerals and Materials Soc. Achievements include research in synthesis of novel transitiona metal oxides, nanomagnetic materials, study of electro-transport and magnetic properies of exotic materials showing giant magnetoresitance at low temperatures. Home: Apt # 205 2516 Avent Ferry Rd Raleigh NC 27606 Office: NC State U Materials Sci and Engring Raleigh NC 27695-7907 Office Fax: 919-515-7724. Personal E-mail: norisud@gmail.com. E-mail: nsudhak@ncsu.edu.

SUDHIVORASETH, NIPHON, pediatrician, immunologist, allergist; b. Bangkok, 1940; MD, Chulalongkorn Hosp. U., Bangkok, 1966. Diplomate Am. Bd. Pediatrics, Am. Bd. Allergy and Immunology. Intern Ch. Home Hosp., Balt., 1967-68; resident in pediatrics St. Lukes Hosp., NYC, 1968-69, Beth Israel Hosp., NYC, 1969-70; fellow in allergy Metro Hosp., N.Y. Med. Coll., NYC, 1970-72; staff Marshall Meml. Hosp., Tex., 1978—; pvt. practice. Mem. AMA, Am. Acad. Allergy, Asthma, and Immunology, Am. Acad. Pediats., Am. Coll. Allergy and Immunology. Office: PO Box 2087 705 S Grove St Marshall TX 75670-5220 Personal E-mail: drniphonsudhi@yahoo.com.

SUDHOF, THOMAS CHRISTIAN, molecular genetics educator; b. Göttingen, Germany, Dec. 22, 1955; Degree in medicine, RWTH, Aachen, Germany, 1977; MD, Georgia Augusta U., Göttingen, Germany, 1982. Postdoctoral fellow Max-Planck-Inst. Biophysikallsche Chemie, Göttingen, 1982-83; postdoctoral fellow dept. molecular genetics U. Tex. Southwestern Med. Ctr., Dallas, 1983-85, asst. prof. dept. molecular genetics, 1987-89; asst. investigator U. Tex. Southwestern Med. Ctr., Howard Hughes Med. Inst., Dallas, 1986-89, investigator, 1991—, assoc. prof. dept. molecular genetics, 1989-91, prof. dept. molecular genetics, 1991—2008, Gill disting. chair neurosci. rsch., 1995—2008, dir. center for neurosci., 1997—2006, adj. prof. neurosci., 2008—; Avram Goldstein prof. molecular and cellular physiology Stanford U. Sch. Medicine, 2008—. Loyd B. Sands disting. chair in neurosci.; mem. molecular, cellular and devel. neurobiology rev. com. NIMH, 1995—. Mem. editl. bd. Jour. Biol. Chemistry and of Neuron; contbr. numerous articles to profl. publs. Recipient W. Alden Spencer award Columbia U., 1993, Wilhelm Feldberg award, 1994, Molecular Biology award NAS, 1997, MetLife award for Alzheimers Rsch. MetLife Found., 2004, Freedom to Discover Achievement award for Neuro-Science, Bristol-Myers Squibb, 2004, Bernhard Katz awward, Biophysical Soc., 2008, Passano Found. award, 2008. Mem.: NAS, Inst. Medicine. Office: Howard Hughes Med Inst Stanford Sch Medicine 1050 Arastradero Rd B249F Palo Alto CA 94304-5543 Office Phone: 650-721-1418, 650-721-1421. Office Fax: 650-498-4585. E-mail: tcs1@stanford.edu.*

SUDKAMP, THOMAS, science educator; b. Elkhorn, Wis., Sept. 8, 1953; s. Donald J. and Mary Sudkamp; m. Janice Edwards Sudkamp, Jan. 8, 1993; 1 child, Elizabeth Regina. BS, U. Wis., 1974; MS, U. Notre Dame, 1978, Wright State U., 1981; PhD, U. Notre Dame, 1978. Prof. info. sci. Wright State U., Dayton, 1982—. Assoc. editor IEEE Trans. on Fuzzy Systems, IEEE Trans. on Systems, Man, and Cybernetics; area editor Internat. Jour. Approximate Reasoning, Fuzzy Sets & Sys. Author: Languages and Machines: An Introduction to the Theory of Computer Science; mem. editl. bd.: Internat. Jour. Computational Intelligence Rsch., Fuzzy Sets and Sys. Mem.: Internat. Fuzzy Systems Assn. (v.p. 2003—05), North Am. Fuzzy Info. Processing Soc. (pres. 2000—02). Office: Wright State U 3640 Colonel Glenn Hwy Dayton OH 45435 E-mail: tsudkamp@cs.wright.edu.

SUDMEYER, ALICE JEAN, art gallery owner; b. Goldbeach, Oreg., Feb. 17, 1946; d. Harold Leo Enz Sr. and Zoa Jane (Mercer) Enz; m. Larry Gene Orrell, Jan. 11, 1970 (div. July 1974); children: Aaron Jay, Zoa Jean Easterling; m. Larry Everett Sudmeyer, Apr. 28, 1978. A Fine Arts and Letters, Mt. Hood C.C., 1977. Adminstr. dir. Art's OK!, San Diego, 1987—93; with Margaret Harwell Art Mus., Poplar Bluff, Mo., 1999—; owner, operator, artist Alice Jean Sudmeyer Artworks Gallery and Studio, Fredericktown, 2000—. With USAR, 1970—2006, ret. USAR, 2006. Decorated Liberation of Kuwait medal, Army Commendation medal, Southwest Asia medal. Mem.: DAV (life), VFW (life), Am. Legion (life). Avocations: gardening, yoga, music. Home and Office: 715 South Wood Ave Fredericktown MO 63645 Personal E-mail: jean4me@charter.net.

SUDWEEKS, STERLING N., medical educator; s. Richard R. and Jo Sudweeks; m. Claudia Gibb, June 2, 1990; children: Reeve, Devin, Sarah, Adalyn, Emma. PhD, U. UT, Salt Lake City, 1997. Postdoc. fellow Nat. Inst. Environ. Health Scis., Rsch. Triangle Pk., NC, 1997—2001; faculty Brigham Young U., Provo, Utah, 2001—. Office: Brigham Young Univ 574 Widb Provo UT 84602

SUE, MICHAEL ALVIN, allergist; b. LA, Apr. 15, 1956; MD, U. Chgo., 1980. Diplomate Am. Bd. Internal Medicine, Am. Bd. Allergy and Immunology. Intern, resident and fellow West Los Angeles VA Med. Ctr., LA, 1980-86; allergist Kaiser Permanente, Panorama City, Calif., 1986—. Fellow Am. Coll. Allergy, Asthma, and Immunology; mem. Am. Acad. Allergy, Asthma, and Immunology. Office: Kaiser Permanente 13652 Cantara St Panorama City CA 91402-5497 Office Phone: 818-375-1720.

SUEDFELD, PETER, psychologist, educator; b. Budapest, Hungary, Aug. 30, 1935; emigrated to US, 1948, naturalized, 1952; s. Leslie John and Jolan (Eichenbaum) Field; m. Gabrielle Debra Guterman, June 11, 1961 (div. 1980); children: Michael Thomas, Joanne Ruth, David Lee; m. Phyllis Jean Johnson, Oct. 19, 1991. Student, U. Philippines, 1956-57; BA, Queens Coll., 1960; MA, Princeton U., 1962, PhD, 1963. Rsch. assoc. Princeton U.; lectr. Trenton State Coll., 1963-64; vis. asst. prof. psychology U. Ill., 1964-65; asst. prof. psychology Univ. Coll. Rutgers U., 1965-67, assoc. prof., 1967-71, prof., 1971-72, chmn. dept., 1967-72; prof. psychology U. B.C., Vancouver, 1972-2001, head dept., 1972-84, dean faculty grad. studies, 1984-90, disting. scholar-in-residence, P. Wall Inst. Adv. Studies, 2000, dean and prof. emeritus, 2001—. Chmn. Can. Antarctic Rsch. Program, 1994—98; Disting. vis. scholar Ohio State U., 2000—03; affiliated prof. U. Haifa, 2005—; cons., lectr. in field. Author: Restricted Environmental Stimulation: Research and Clinical Applications, 1980; editor: Attitude Change: The Competing Views, 1971, Personality Theory and Information Processing, 1971, The Behavioral Basis of Design, 1976, Psychology and Torture, 1990, Restricted Environmental Stimulation: Theoretical and Empirical Developments in Flotation REST, 1990, Psychology and Social Policy, 1991, Light from the Ashes, 2001, Understanding the Bush Doctrine, 2007; editor Jour. Applied Social Psychology, 1975-82; assoc. editor Environment and Behavior, 1992—; contbr. articles to profl. jours. Served with US Army, 1955-58. Recipient Antarctica svc. medal, NSF, US Navy, 1994, Zachor award, Parliament of Can., 2000; grantee, NIMH, 1970—72, Can. Coun., 1973—2006, Nat. Rsch. Coun. Can., 1973—90, NIH, 1980—84, Can. Space Agy., 2003—, Def. Rsch. and Dev. Can., 2007—. Fellow Royal Soc. Can., Can. Psychol. Assn. (pres. 1998-99, Donald O. Hebb award 2001), APA, Am. Psychol. Soc., Acad. Behavioral Medicine Resch., Soc. Behavioral Medicine, NY Acad. Sci., Royal Can. Geog. Soc.(hon.); mem. Internat. Soc. Polit. Psychol. (v.p. 1999-2001, Harold D. Lasswell award 2001, Roberta Sigel award 2005), Internat. Acad. Astronautics (corr.), Soc. Exptl. Social Psychology, Phi Beta Kappa, Sigma Xi. Office: U BC Dept Psychology Vancouver BC Canada V6T 1Z4 Home Phone: 604-687-8886; Office Phone: 604-822-5713. Business E-Mail: psuedfeld@psych.ubc.ca.

SUELTZ, PATRICIA C., information technology executive; BA in Polit. Sci., Occidental Coll. With Installation and Repair Divsn. Pacific Telephone and Telegraph Co.; from various tech. positions to gen. mgr. Java Software IBM Corp., 1979—98, gen. mgr. Java Software, 1998—99; exec. v.p., gen. mgr. Software Sys. Group Sun Microsystems Inc., 1999—2002, exec. v.p. Enterprise Svcs. Group, 2002—04; pres. mktg., tech. and sys. Salesforce.com Inc., San Francisco, 2004, pres. global ops., 2004—05, exec. v.p., 2004—05; CEO SurfControl Plc, Scotts Valley, Calif., 2005—07, LogLogic, Inc., San Jose, Calif., 2007—. Bd. dirs. Delphi Automotive Sys., Amgen Inc., Cyber Security Industry Alliance, 2007—. Trustee Am. Found. for the Blind, 2005—. Named one of 50 Most Powerful Women in Bus., Fortune Mag., 2000; fellow, Rockefeller Found. Office: LogLogic Inc 110 Rose Orchard Way Ste 200 San Jose CA 95134

SUEN, CHING YEE, computer scientist, educator, researcher; b. Chung Shan, Kwang Tung, China, Oct. 14, 1942; s. Stephen and Sin (Kan) S; m. Sheung Ling Chan, May 12, 1970; children: Karwa, Karnon. BSc in Engring., U. Hong Kong, 1966, MSc in Engring., 1968; MASc., U. B.C., 1970, PhD, 1972. Asst. prof. computer sci. Concordia U., Montreal, Can., 1972-76, assoc. prof., 1976-79, prof., 1979—, chmn., 1980-84, dir. Centre for Pattern Recognition and Machine Intelligence, 1988—, assoc. dean faculty engring. and computer sci., 1993-97, disting. chair artificial intelligence and pattern recognition, 2001—. Vis. scientist Rsch. Lab. of Electronics, MIT, Cambridge, 1975, 76, 78-79; invited prof. Ecole Polytechnique Fédérale de Lausanne, Switzerland, 1979, Institut de Recherche d'Informatique et d'Automatique, Rocquencourt, France, 1976, 78, 79, founder, Vision Interface, 1986; founder, co-chmn. Internat. Conf. on Document Analysis and Recognition, St.-Malo, France, 1991, Tsukuba Sci. City, Japan, 1993, chmn., Montreal, Can., 1995; founder, chmn. Internat. Workshop on Frontiers in Handwriting Recognition (hon. chair, 2002), gen. chair Internat. Conf. on Pattern Recognition, Quebec City, Canada, 2002; organizer numerous confs. Author: Computational Analysis of Mandarin, 1979, Computational Studies of the Most Frequent Chinese Words and Sounds, 1986, (with Z.C. Li, T.D. Bui, Y.Y. Tang) Computer Transformation of Digital Images and Patterns, 1989; editor: (with R. De Mori) Computer Analysis and Perception Vol. 1, Visual Signals, 1982, Computer Analysis and Perception Vol. 2, Auditory Signals, 1982, (with R. De Mori) New Systems and Architectures for Automatic Speech Recognition and Synthesis, 1985, (with R. Plamondon and M.L. Simner) Computer Recognition and Human Production of Handwriting, 1989, Frontiers in Handwriting Recognition, 1990, Operating Expert System Applications in Canada, 1992, (with P.S.P. Wang) Thinning Methodologies for Pattern Recognition, 1994, (with M. Cheriet et al.) Character Recognition Systems, 2007; assoc. editor: Signal Processing, 1979-2006, Pattern Recognition Letters, 1982—, Pattern Recognition, 1983-2005, dep. editor, 2005-06, editor-in-chief, 2007-; assoc. editor: IEEE Transactions on Pattern Analysis and Machine Intelligence, 1986-89, Internat. Jour. Pattern Recognition and Artificial Intelligence, 1986—, Pattern Analysis and Applications, 1998—2006, Internat. Jour. on Document Analysis and Recognisation, 1998-2006; founder, editor-in-chief: Computer Processing of Chinese and Oriental Langs., 1982-93; adviser: IEEE Transactions on Pattern Analysis and Machine Intelligence, 1989-92; author more than 450 publs.; patentee in field. Recipient award Fedn. Chinese Can. Profls., 1988; Rsch. fellow Concordia U., 1998; Swire scholar U. Hong Kong, 1967, ITAC/NSERC award Info. Tech. Assn. Can. and Natural Scis. and Engring. Rsch. Coun. Can., 1992, Internat. Assn. Pattern Recognition and Internat. Conf. Document Analysis and Recognition award, 2005, Concordia ENCS Lifetime Rsch. Achievement award, Lifetime Citation award, 2008. Fellow IEEE (advisor Computer Soc.), Royal Soc. Can., Internat. Assn. for Pattern Recognition; mem. (life) Chinese Lang. Computer Soc. (v.p. 1987-90, pres. 1990-93, award 1988), Can. Image Processing and Pattern Recognition Soc. (pres. 1984-90, award 1997). Office: Concordia Univ Dept Computer Sci 1455 Maisonneuve W Ste VE-3-189 Montreal PQ Canada H3G 1M8 Office Phone: 514-848-2424 7950.

SUEN, HON CHI, thoracic surgeon; MB BS, U. Hong Kong, Hong Kong. Diplomate Am. Bd. Surgery, 1998, Am. Bd. Thoracic Surgery, 2000. Pres. Ctr. Cardiothoracic Surgery, Inc, St. Louis, 2006—. Contbr. scientific papers to profl. publs. Recipient Prize, Brit. Assn. Pediatric Surgeons, 1983, Outstanding Excellence award, DePaul Health Ctr., 2005, Resident Rsch. award, Assn. Academic Surgeons, 1992; nominee Outstanding Compassion award, DePaul Health Ctr., 2005; scholar Scholarship, Singapore Govt., 1975—76. Fellow: RCS, RCPS, ACS, Coll. Surgeons Hong Kong; mem.: St. Louis Met. Med. Soc., St. Louis Thoracic Surg. Soc., Soc. Thoracic Surgeons. Office: Ctr Cardiothoracic Surgery 10004 Kennerly Rd 110A Saint Louis MO 63128 Office Fax: 314-543-5202.

SUEN, STEPHEN, investment company executive; b. Hong Kong, Oct. 2, 1954; s. Kam Hing Suen and Shiu Kwan Li; m. Anna Chim Suen, May 28, 1984; 1 child, Eliott Hancock. B in Social Sci., U. Hong Kong, 1978; M in Commerce, U. NSW, Sydney, Australia, 1987; MA in Buddhist Studies, U. Hong Kong, 2004. Assoc. dir. Macquarie Bank Ltd., Sydney, 1984—89; mng. dir. Treasure Land Property Consultants Ltd., Hong Kong, 1990—2000; pres. China-Way Corp. Ltd., Hong Kong, 2001—03; CEO Global Call Ltd., Hong Kong, 2001—06, chief advisor, 2006—. Dir. Macquarie Topest Mgmt. Ltd., 2005—, Macquarie Goodman Hong Kong Logistics Fund, 2006—. Mem.: Real Estate Assn. Guangzhou (vice-chair 1994—2003), Hong Kong Chamber Profl. Property Cons. (v.p. 1996—), Estate Agts. Authority, Hong Kong Soc. Accts., Australian Soc. Accts., Chartered Inst. Bankers U.K. (assoc.). Avocations: golf, skiing, music. Office: Rm 2402 24/F Harcourt House 39 Gloucester Rd Wanchai Hong Kong Personal E-mail: stephensuen@china-way.com.hk.

SUER, MARVIN DAVID, architectural consultant; b. Phila., Apr. 4, 1923; m. Gertrude Litvin, 1947; children: Marsha Suer Clark, Sharon, Deborah Suer Berman. BArch, U. Pa., 1950. Registered architect, Pa. Ptnr. Suer & Livingston, 1961-62, Suer, Livingston & Demas, 1962-69; dir. tech. prodn. Eshbach, Pullinger, Stevens & Bruder, Phila., 1969-74; assoc. Ballinger, Phila., 1974-79, Bartley Long Mirenda, Phila., 1979-85, S.T. Hudson Internat., Phila., 1986-95; archtl. cons., 1996—. Archtl. works include State Hosp. for Crippled Children addition, 1964, Huey Elem. Sch., Phila., 1964, Dist. No. 4 Health Ctr., Phila., 1967, Stephen Smith Towers, 1969, Foxchase Br. Libr., 1969. Chmn. bd. trustees Phila. Found. for Architecture, 1980-81. With C.E., AUS, 1943-46. Fellow AIA (pres. Phila. chpt. 1968, 125th Yr. citation 1982); mem. Tau Sigma Delta. Home: 305 Overlook Ave Willow Grove PA 19090-2806

SUESS, JAMES FRANCIS, retired clinical psychologist; b. Evanston, Ill., Aug. 8, 1950; s. James Francis and Rae Love (Miller) S.; m. Linda Grace Powell, July 31, 1976; 1 child, Misty Lynne. BS, U. So. Miss., 1974, MS, 1978, PhD, 1982. Lic. psychologist, NY, Ala.; diplomate Am. Bd. Profl. Psychology, Am. Bd. Med. Psychotherapists, Profl. Assn. Custody Evaluators, Am. Coll. Forensic Examiners, Am. Bd. Forensic Medicine. Assoc. psychologist State of Miss., Ellisville, 1978-80; clin. psychologist SUNY Med. Sch./Erie County Med. Ctr., Buffalo, 1982-84, supervising clin. psychologist, 1984-87, assoc. dir., 1987—2005; prof. dept. psychology Clinic South Ala., 2001—05; prof. emeritus SUNY, 2005—. Dir. practica SUNY Med. Sch., 1982-90, faculty counsel, 1988—; cons. Buffalo Dept. Social Svcs., 1985—; mem. spkrs. bur. Erie Alliance for Mentally Ill, 1986—; vis. prof. U. Guadalajara Sch. Medicine, 1985—; clin. dir. Stickney Adolescent Ctr. Mobile MHC, 1993-97; clin. dir. Physicans' Psychiat. Clinic, 1997—; CEO Stillwood Clin. Group, 1998—; adj. prof. dept. psychology U. South Ala., 2000—; clin. dir. Adm. Mc Collough Inst. of Rejuvenology. Author: Annotated Bibliography of Sex Roles, 1972, Personality Disorder and Self Psychology, 1991, (textbook) Enduring My Journey Throug Life: The Borderline Personality Disorders, 2005; contbr. chpts. to books, numerous articles to refereed jours. including Perceptual and Motor Skills, Jour. Clin. and Consulting Psychology, Am. Annals of Deaf, Assessment of Children. Mem. small bus. adv. coun. Nat. Congl. Com., 2005—. With USAR, 1969-76. Fellow Am. Orthopsychiat. Assn. (life, diplomate), Soc. Personality Assessment; mem. APA, Am. Bd. Forensic Exam (life), Ala. Lic. Psychol. (pres.), Mobile Assn. Psychol. (pres.). Home: 507 Evergreen Rd Mobile AL 36608-3845 Office: The Stillwood Clin Grp 717 Executive Park Dr Ste B Mobile AL 36606-2843 Office Fax: 251-342-8599. Personal E-mail: drjfsuess@comcast.net, andfsuess@ymail.com.

SUFFOLK, RANDALL, museum director, curator; BA, Conn. Coll.; MA in higher edn. adminstrn., Columbia U.; MA in art hist., Bryn Mawr Coll. Assoc. W. Graham Arader III Galleries, Phila., NYC; cons. Arts Corp., Ltd., Phila.; curator The Hyde Collection, Glen Falls, NY, 1995—98, dep. dir., 1998—99, acting dir., 1999—2000, dir., 2000—07; exec. dir., CEO Philbrook Mus. Art, Tulsa, Okla., 2007—. Mem. strategic planning com. Univ. Art Mus., SUNY, Albany; review panel mem. for Spl. Opportunity Stipend Grants NY State Coun. on Arts. Bd. dirs. Adirondack/Lake George Regional Tourism Bd., The Feeder Canal Alliance. Office: Philbrook Mus Art PO Box 52510 Tulsa OK 74152 Office Phone: 918-749-7941.

SUGAHARA, BYRON MASAHIKO, transportation executive; b. Jan. 22, 1940; s. Kay and Yone (Kuwahara) Sugahara; m. Nancy Shaw Hall, June 5, 1977; children: Christopher, Abigail, Alexandra. BA, Harvard Coll., 1962. From v.p. to pres. Gt. Am. Lines, Roseland, NJ, 1985—. Bd. dirs. Peck Sch., Morristown, NJ, 1993—95. 1st lt. US Army, 1963—65. Mem.: Am. Bur. Shipping, Tokyo Club, Henryville Conservation Club. Avocations: fly fishing, golf. Office: Great American Lines 5 Becker Farm Rd Ste 4 Roseland NJ 07068-1779 Home: 533 Indian Harbor Rd Vero Beach FL 32963

SUGAR, JOEL, ophthalmologist; m. Anita Sue Gerber; children: Nicole, Daniel. BA, U. Mich., Ann Arbor, MD, 1969. Cert. Am. Bd. Ophthalmology, 1975. Capt. US Army Reserves, 1970—79; prof. ophthalmology U. Ill. Coll. Medicine, Chgo., 1975—; vice head, ophthalmology U. Ill., prof., 1975—. Med. dir. Ill. Eye Bank, Chgo., 1985—. Contbr. articles to profl. jours. Office: Univ Il Eye and Ear Infir 1855 W Taylor Chicago IL 60612 Business E-Mail: joelsuga@uic.edu.

SUGAR, JOSEPH ROBERT, musician, conductor, educator; b. Worcester, Mass., Dec. 14, 1928; s. Elias George and Emily Angeline (David) Sugar; m. Clara Anne Steele, Dec. 26, 1955; children: Thomas Elias, Robert Albert. AA, Bergen Jr. Coll., Teaneck, NJ, 1948; BA, LI U., 1950; MA, Columbia U., 1955; profl. diploma, 1956. Brass instr. LI U., NY, 1949, prof., advisor to music chmn. for courses music edn. C. W. Post Coll. Greenvale, NY, 1990—, dir. music edn., 1990-2001; asst. bands. Ind. U., Bloomington, Ind., 1950; dir. Instrumental Music, Matawan, NJ, 1954-56; band dir. Upsala Coll., East Orange, NJ, 1956-57; band. dir., instr. music Bethpage Elem. Sch., NY, 1957-66; instr. baton twirling Bethpage HS, 1957-67; band. dir. Hewlett-Woodmere Jr. HS, NY, 1966-78; asst. band dir., instr. baton twirling Hewlett HS, 1967-69, band dir., 1983-84, dir. jazz ensemble, 1983-89; band dir. Dowling Coll., Oakdale, NY, 1977-79; dist. dir. music Hewlett-Woodmere Pub. Schs., 1978-89. Summer band sch. co-dir., Manasquan, NJ, 1955—64; creative music cultural workshop, Bethpage, 1959—62; dir. NY Jazz Ensemble, Hempstead, 1976, Kismet Shrine Temple Band, 1997—2008; clinician numerous music festivals, 1970—; choral dir., instrumentalist Air Force Band of Rockies, 504th Air Force Band, Colorado Springs; band master emeritus Kismet Shrine, 2009—. Performer: Indpls. Symphony Orch., 1950, MATS Hdg. Band Westover AFB, 1950—51, Joe Sugar and the Big Band, 1980—2006; musician (numerous entertainers including): Vic Damone, Diahann Carroll, Al Martino, Jerry Vale, Georgia Gibbs, Toni Arden, Johnny Ray, Eddie Fisher, Cab Calloway, Marilyn Michaels, Frankie Lane, Henny Youngman, Anna Maria Alberghetti, Patti Page, Bobby Rydell, Buddy Greco, Billy Eckstine, Julius La Rosa, The Four Aces, Don Cornell, Connie Francis; musician: (with Audio-Fidelity) (albums) 20th Century Fox, Paramount, MGM, 1958—61; author: Where Are We Headed in Music Education?, 1960, Twirling Tips in 3 Volumes, 1963, Presidents March, 1982; composer, condr.: albums Ten Nights in a Harem, 1963. Mem. Boy Scouts Am.; youth choir dir. Levittown Presbyn. Ch., NY, 1966. With USAF, 1950—52. Recipient Merit award, Music Belongs, 1972, 1st Pl. award, E. Nat. Music Festival, 1977, Apprecation of Outstanding Leadership award, Black Music Caucus, 1982, cert. of Merit award, NY State Senate, 1982, citation, Town of Hempstead, 1982, Oustanding Ret. Band Dirs. award, NY State Band Dirs. Assn., 2007, Disting. Svc. award, Hewlett-Woodmere Pub. Schs., 1989, Ricky Pub. Svc. award, Usdan Music Camp, 2008, Lifetime Achievement award, 2008, Usdan Art Ctr., Adjunct Faculty Recognition award, C.W. Post, 2008, Masonic-Daniel Scouting Bd. award, 2009, Rickie award, Assemblyman Harvey Weisenberg; named Man of the Yr., Wantagh C. of C., 1979; named to Tchr. Hall of Fame, Hewlett-Woodmere Pub. Schs., 1990; grantee, Ford Found., 1962. Mem.: DAV (life), NY State Coun. Music Adminstrs. (Disting. Svc. award 1990), Internat. Trumpet Guild, Nat. Assn. Jazz Educators, Nassau Music Educators Assn. (pres. 1970, mem. adv. bd. 1980—81, Pres. award 1970, Svc. award 1973, 1987), NY State Sch. Music Assn. (pres. 1980—82, Disting. Svc. award 1989), NY State Adminstrs. Music Edn. (pres. 1987—90), Music Educators Nat. Conf. (life; pres. ea. divsn. 1985—87), Wantagh Friends Libr., Jones Beach Power Squadron (sr.), Masonic 60Yr. Pin Damascus Lodge, Kiwanis (past pres., award 1979), Am. Legion (past cmdr., award 1978), Masons (50 Yr. award, 50 Yr. BSA award, Outstanding Adj. award), Wantagh Spiked Shoe (past pres., award 1979), Wantagh Dads and Booster (past pres.), Tri M, Kappa Kappa Psi, Phi Delta Kappa, Phi Mu Alpha (life). Republican. Home: 1594 Milburn Ct Wantagh NY 11793-3330 Office: LI U CW Post Coll Music Dept 720 Northern Blvd Greenvale NY 11548-1319 Home Phone: 516-781-9346; Office Phone: 516-299-3014. Business E-Mail: jsugar@liu.edu.

SUGAR, RONALD D., aerospace transportation company executive; b. Toronto, July 1948; m. Valerie Sugar; 2 children. BSEE summa cum laude, UCLA, 1968, MS, 1969, PhD, 1971. Dir. advanced R & D programs TRW Inc., Cleve., 1981-83, chief engr., dep. program mgr. Milstar Satellite payload program, 1983-87, v.p., gen. mgr. space comms. divsn., 1987-92, v.p. strategic bus. devel. space and def. sector, 1992-94, exec. v.p., CFO, 1994-96, exec. v.p., gen. mgr. automotive electronics group, 1996-98, exec. v.p. spl. projects, 1998-99, pres., COO space and info. sys. sector, 1999-2000; pres., COO Litton Industries, Inc., Woodland Hills, Calif., 2000—01, Northrop Grumman Corp., LA, 2001—03, pres., CEO, chmn., 2003—06, chmn., CEO, 2006—. Mem. adv. com. Nat. Security Telecom. Adv. Com.; bd. dirs. Chevron Corp., 2005—. Nat. trustee Boys & Girls Clubs of Am.; mem. bd. vis. UCLA Anderson Sch. Mgmt., 2008—; dir. LA Philharmonic Assn.; trustee U. So. Calif.; nat. fundraising chmn. Pearl Harbor Meml. Fund. Recipient Engring. Alumnus of the Yr., UCLA, 1996, Daniel Epstein Engring. Mgmt. award, U. So. Calif., 2003, Semper Fidelis award, USMC Found., 2003, John R. Alison Leadership to Nat. Def. award, Air Force Assn., 2003, Eisenhower Disting. Citizen award, Army Distaff Found. Fellow: Royal Aeronautical Soc., Am. Inst. of Aeronautics and Astronautics; mem.: NAE, Aerospace Industries Assn. (vice chmn., former chmn.), Assn. US Army. Office: Northrop Grumman Corp 1840 Century Park E Los Angeles CA 90067-2199*

SUGARMAN, ALAN WILLIAM, educational consultant; b. Boston, Sept. 26, 1924; s. Henry and Dorothy (Adams) S.; m. Alice Mulhall, 1974; children: Michael, Susan, Ellen, William, Jane, James. BS, Boston U., 1948; MA, Columbia U., 1949, EdD, 1967; postgrad., SUNY, Albany, 1954-56. Entrance examiner Boston U., 1947-48; tchr. Public Schs. Hudson, NY, 1950-54, prin. jr. high sch., 1954-56, prin. sr. high sch., 1956-61; prin. Spring Valley (N.Y.) Sr. High Sch., 1961-67; dir. secondary edn. Ramapo Central Sch. Dist. No. 2, Spring Valley, 1967-69, asst. supt. instrn., 1969-73; prin. Ramapo Sr. High Sch., Spring Valley, 1969; supt. schs. Connetquot Central Sch. Dist. Islip, Bohemia, NY, 1973-80, Ft. Lee (N.J.) Sch. Dist., 1980—2000; nat. spkr., cons., 2000—. Adj. prof. NY U., NYC, U. PR, Rio Piedras, Hofstra U., 1967—; prof. Fordham U., NYC, 1969. Athletic dir. East River Day Camp, N.Y.C., summer 1949; group worker St. John's Guild, summer 1950; asst. dir. Tenn. Work Camp, Unitarian Service Com., summer 1951; dir. spl. activities Hudson Youth Bur., Hudson, N.Y., summer 1952; exec. dir. Jewish Community Center, Hudson, 1953-56; chmn. vis. coms. Middle States Commn. Colls. and Secondary Schs., 1958-76; chmn. county leadership tng. com., mem. Rockland County exec. council Boy Scouts Am., 1956; bd. dirs. Bergen County Red Cross; corr. sec. Rockland County Negro Scholarship Fund, Inc.; pres. Spring Valley Youth Activities Com., 1956-58; bd. dirs., past campaign co-chmn. Greater Hudson Community Chest; bd. dirs., 2d v.p. Hudson Youth Recreation Center, 1958-61; bd. dirs. Rockland County br. Am. Cancer Soc., 1958-61, Columbia Meml. Hosp., 1959-61; chmn. Town of Islip Health Usage Com., 1973; bd. dirs. Am. Heart Assn. N.J. affiliate, 1993—. Served with AUS, 1944-46, ETO. Recipient Disting. Svc. award Hudson Jr. C. of C., 1960, Ft. Lee Citizen of Yr. award VFW, Bergen County Citizen of Yr. award VFW, 1989, N.J. State Elks Alcohol and Drug Prevention award, 1989, St. Michael's award, 1992, PBA Silver Life Card award, 1993, EIA award Greek Orthodox Archdiocese, 1993; named Adminstr. of Yr., Fordham U., 1990, B'nai Brith Man of Yr., 1995; Fort Lee Sports Complex renamed Dr. Alan W. Sugarman Sports Complex in his honor. Mem. Nat. Honor Soc. Secondary Schs. (hon.), Nat. PTA (hon. life), Am. Assn. Sch. Adminstrs., Assn. Supervision and Curriculum Devel., Nat. Sch. Public Relations Assn., Assn. Sch. Bus. Ofcls., Nat. Soc. Study Edn., DAV, VFW, Jewish War Vets., Rotary (bd. dirs.), Phi Delta Kappa (Adminstr. of Yr. award 1990), Kappa Delta Pi, Pi Gamma Mu. Office: 400 Fairview Ave Fort Lee NJ 07024 Home: 494 Country Club Dr Egg Harbor City NJ 08215-5132 Personal E-mail: amwsintac@msn.com.

SUGARMAN, MICHAEL, physician, rheumatologist; b. Galveston, Tex., May 26, 1945; s. Harold and Amelia Sugarman; m. Hilda Roberta Krug, Aug. 26, 1967; children: Jason, Steven. BS, U. Calif., Berkeley, 1966; MD, U. Calif., San Francisco, 1970. Diplomate Am. Coll. Physicians, Am. Coll. Rheumatology. Rheumatologist Fullerton (Calif.) Internal Medicine Ctr., Fullerton, Calif., 1976-94. Pres. St. Jude Heritage Med. Group, 1996—. Bd. trustees St. Jude Hosp. Fellow Am. Coll. Rheumatology, Orange County Rheumatism Soc.; mem. AMA, Orange County Med. Assn. Office: St Jude Heritage Med Group 433 W Bastanchury Rd Fullerton CA 92835-3404 Home Phone: 714-525-4422.

SUGARMAN, MYRON GEORGE, lawyer; b. San Francisco, Nov. 7, 1942; s. Irving Carden and Jane Hortense (Weingarten) S.; m. Cheryl Ann Struble, June 8, 1968 (div. 1993); children: Andrew, Amy, Adam; m. Cynthia Wilson Woods, Apr. 16, 1994. BS, U. Calif., Berkeley, 1964, JD, 1967. Bar: Calif. 1967, US Tax Ct. 1994. Assoc. Cooley Godward Kronish LLP, San Francisco, 1972-77, ptnr., 1977—. Served to capt. US Army, 1968-71. Fellow Am. Coll. Trust and Estate Counsel, Am. Coll. Tax Counsel, Am. Bar Found.; mem. U. Calif. Alumni Assn. (bd. dirs. 1985-88), U. Calf. Berkeley Found. (bd. trustees), San Francisco Tax Club (pres. 1990), San Francisco Grid Club, Order of Coif, Phi Beta Kappa, Beta Gamma Sigma. Avocations: skiing, tennis. Office: Cooley Godward Kronish LLP 101 California St 5th Fl San Francisco CA 94111-5800 Office Phone: 415-693-2040. Office Fax: 415-693-2222. Business E-Mail: msugarman@cooley.com.

SUGARMAN, PAUL RONALD, lawyer, educator, academic administrator; b. Boston, Dec. 14, 1931; m. Susan J. Sugarman; children: Amy J., Ellen L. AA, Boston U., 1951, JD cum laude (Law Week award 1954, asso. editor law rev. 1952-54), 1954; LLD (hon.), Suffolk U., 1989. Bar: Mass. 1954, U.S. Supreme Ct. 1965. Ptnr. Sugarman & Sugarman, Boston, 1967-90, 94—; prof. law, dean Suffolk U. Law Sch., Boston, 1990-94. Mem. Atty. Gen. Mass. Hwy. Law Study Commn., 1965, Mass. Gov.'s Select Com. on Jud. Needs, 1976; bd. bar overseers Supreme Jud. Ct., 1984-88, chmn., 1985-88; advocate Am. Bd. Trial Advocates; spl. master, commr. Boston Mcpl. Ct. Report Supreme Jud. Ct. of Mass., 1990. Trustee Mass. Bar Found., 1980-81; bd. visitors Boston U. Sch. Law, 2005—. Served as officer AUS, 1955-58. Recipient Courageous Adv. award, Mass. Acad. Trial Attys., 1984, William O. Douglas First Amendment Freedom award, Anti-Defamation League, 1986, Silver Shingle award for svc. to legal profession Boston U. Sch. Law, 1989, Jurisprudence award Am. Orgn. for Rehab. through Tng. Fedn., 1991, Civil Justice award Am. Bd. trial Adv., 1993, Lifetime Achievement award, Mass. Acad. Trial Attys., 2007, Charles P. Kindregan, Jr. award, Suffolk U. Law Sch., 2008. Fellow: Internat. Soc. Barristers, Mass. Bar Found., Am. Coll. Trial Lawyers, Am. Bar Found.; mem.: ATLA (gov. 1966—68, pres. Mass. chpt. 1968—70), ABA, Boston U. Sch. Law Alumni Assn. (pres. 1979—80), Boston Bar Assn., Mass. Bar Assn. (pres. 1976—77, chmn. com. on recall of ret. judges 1982—86, chmn. Jud. Adminstrn. Sect. Coun., chmn. 2000—01, Task Force on Jud. Conduct Commn., Gold Medal award 1991). Office: Sugarman and Sugarman PC One Beacon St Boston MA 02108 Business E-Mail: psugarman@sugarman.com.

SUGARMAN, PAUL WILLIAM, lawyer; b. Cambridge, Mass., July 31, 1947; s. Louis Edward and Natalie (Waldman) S.; m. Susan Lee Richard, July 16, 1978; children: Sarah, Emily, Hannah. BA magna cum laude (hon.), Harvard U., 1969; JD, Yale U., 1975. Bar: Calif. 1976, US Dist. Ct. (no. dist.) Calif. 1976, US Ct. Appeals (9th cir.) 1976. Law clk. to judge U.S. Dist. Ct. (no. dist.) Calif., San Francisco, 1975-76; assoc. Heller, Ehrman, White & McAuliffe, San Francisco, 1976-81, ptnr., 1982; shareholder Heller, Ehrman LLP, San Francisco. Spkr. in field. Contbr. articles to profl. jour. Vol. U.S. Peace Corps, Ethiopia, 1969-72. Mem. ABA (litig., tort & ins. practice sect.), Calif. Bar Assn., San Francisco Bar Assn., Phi Beta Kappa. Home: 1200 Sunnyhills Rd Oakland CA 94610-1818 Office: Heller Ehrman LLP 333 Bush St San Francisco CA 94104-2806 Office Phone: 415-772-6000, 415-772-6217. Office Fax: 415-772-6268. Business E-Mail: paul.sugarman@hellerehrman.com.

SUGG, BARNEY ALAN, academic administrator; b. Helena, Ark., 1938; married; 1 child, Jenifer. BS, U. Ark., 1960, MEd, 1970, PhD. Pres. Corpus Christi State U., Tex.; pres U. Ark. System, Little Rock, 1989—. Office: U Ark Sys Office of Pres 2404 North University Ave Little Rock AR 72207 Office Phone: 501-686-2505.*

SUGG, JEANNE D., library director; m. John Sugg; 1 child, James; 1 child, Jeff. BA, Trevecca Nazarene U., Nashville; MLS, Vanderbilt U. Peabody Coll. Libr. coord. Arabian-Am. Oil Co., Saudi Arabia, 1981—89; dir. pub. svcs. Tenn. State Libr. & Archives, Nashville, 1989, dir., 1991, asst state libr., archivist for admin., 1992—2005, state libr. & archivist, 2005—. Mem.: ALA, Tenn. Historical Soc., Tenn. Libr. Assn., Chief Officers State Libr. Agencies. Office: Tenn State Libr & Archives 403 7th Ave N Nashville TN 37243 Office Phone: 615-741-7996. Office Fax: 615-532-9293. Business E-Mail: jeanne.sugg@state.tn.us.

SUGG, ROBERT PERKINS, retired judge; b. Eupora, Miss., Feb. 21, 1916; s. Amos Watson and Virgie Christian (Cooper) S.; m. Elizabeth Lorraine Carroll, June 23, 1940; children: Robert Perkins, Charles William, John David. Student, Wood Jr. Coll., 1933—34, Miss. State U., 1935—37, Jackson Sch. Law, 1939—40; LLM (hon.), Miss. Coll. Sch. Law, 2007. Bar: Miss. Practice law, 1940; chancery judge, 1951—71; assoc. justice Miss. Supreme Ct., 1971—83; county pros. atty. Webster County, Miss., 1949—50; spl. chancery judge Hinds, Scott and Jasper counties, Miss., 1989; sr. judge, 1990—2000. Mem. adv. coun. Nat. Ctr. for State Cts., 1973-79. Bd. govs. Miss. Jud. Coll., 1973-80; literacy missions assoc. Home Mission Bd. of So. Bapt. Conv., 1983—; tchr. internat. class First Bapt. Ch., Jackson, Miss., 1980-2004, 08-, tchr. adult Bible class, 1973-2002, mem. fin. com. 1995-98, vision com. 1996-97, legal com. 1998-2001, missions com., 1997-2001. Named Outstanding Citizen, Eupora Jr. C. of C., 1970, Alumnus of Year, Wood Jr. Coll., 1973; recipient Svc. to Humanity award Miss. Coll., 1976, Literacy Missions Svc. award Home Mission Bd. of So. Bapt. Conv., 1995. Mem. Miss. State Bar, CAP (Miss. Wing, squadron comdr. 1974-76), Am. Legion (post comdr. 1950) Democrat. Baptist (chmn. bd. deacons 1964). Home: 1067 Meadow Heights Dr Jackson MS 39206-6021 Personal E-mail: justicesugg@comcast.net.

SUGGS, TERRELL (TERRELL RAYNONN SUGGS), professional football player; b. Mpls., Oct. 11, 1982; Student in secondary edn./history, Ariz. State U., Tempe. Defensive end Balt. Ravens, 2003—. Recipient Hendricks award, 2002, Bronko Nagurski award, 2002, Lombardi Trophy, 2002, Morris Trophy, 2002; named Freshman of Yr., Pac-10 Conf., 2000, Defensive Player of Yr., 2002, Defensive Rookie of Yr., AP, 2003; named to Am. Football Conf. Pro Bowl Team, NFL, 2004, 2006, 2008. Office: Balt Ravens M&T Bank Stadium 1101 Russell St Baltimore MD 21230*

SUGIHARA, KENZI, publishing executive; b. Kearny, NJ, Oct. 4, 1940; s. Kyuichi and Shinobuko (Yamaguchi) S.; m. Roslyn Forbes, Dec. 1966; children: Kenichi, Takeo, Akira, Fumio; m. Nancy Elizabeth Kirsh, June 8, 1981; 1 child, Toshiro. BA, NYU, 1963. Supr. McGraw Hill, Inc., NYC, 1965-67; assoc. dir. coll. product dept. Harcourt Brace Jovanovich Inc., NYC, 1978-82, dir. electronic pub., 1982-83; v.p., pub. Bantam Electronic Pub. div., pub. Bantam Reference Books, Bantam Profl. Books, Bantam Doubleday Dell, NYC, 1983-93; v.p., pub. Random House Reference & Electronic Pub. (Random House Inc.), NYC, 1993-95; pres. Sugihara and Rose, NYC, 1995—; pres., pub. ToExcel divsn. Kaleidoscope Software Corp., NYC, 1998—2001; pub. Iuniverse; CEO, pres. SelectBooks, Inc., NYC, 2001—. Democrat. Presbyterian. Home: 585 West End Ave Apt 15D New York NY 10024-1715 Office: SelectBooks Inc One Union Sq West Ste 909 New York NY 10003 Office Phone: 212-206-1997. Business E-Mail: kenzi@selectbooks.ccom.

SUGIKI, SHIGEMI, ophthalmologist, educator; b. Wailuku, Hawaii, May 12, 1936; s. Sentaro and Kameno (Matoba) Sugiki; m. Bernice T. Murakami, Dec. 29, 1958; children: Kevin S., Boyd R. AB, Washington U., St. Louis, 1957, MD, 1961. Intern St. Luke's Hosp., St. Louis, 1961-62; resident in ophthalmology Washington U., 1962-65; chmn. dept. ophthalmology Straub Clinic, Honolulu, 1965-70, Queens Med. Ctr., Honolulu, 1970-73, 80-83, 88-90, 93-2000; clin. prof. ophthalmology Sch. Medicine U. Hawaii, 1997. Maj. M.C., AUS, 1968-70. Decorated Hawaiian N.G. Commendation medal, 1968. Fellow ACS; mem. AMA, Hawaii Med. Assn., Honolulu County Med. Soc., Am. Acad. Ophthalmology, Contact Lens Assn. Ophthalmologists, Pacific Coast Oto-Ophthal. Soc., Pan-Pacific Surg. Assn., Am. Soc. Cataract and Refractive Surgery, Am. Glaucoma Soc., Internat. Assn. Ocular Surgeons, Am. Soc. Contemporary Ophthalmology, Washington U. Eye Alumni Assn., Hawaii Ophthal. Soc., Rsch. To Prevent Blindness. Home: 2398 Aina Lani Pl Honolulu HI 96822-2024 Office: 1380 Lusitana St Ste 714 Honolulu HI 96813-2443 Personal E-mail: vision2damax@yahoo.com.

SUGIMOTO, MITSUSHIGE, medical association administrator, researcher; b. Numazu, Shizuoka, Japan, Aug. 21, 1970; s. Hiroshi and Tomie Sugimoto; m. Yoko Yanagino; children: Masataka, Tatsuya. MD, Hamamatsu U. Sch. Medicine, Japan, PhD, 2006. Diplomate Japanese Govt., 1998. Resident internal medicine Hamamatsu U. Sch. Medicine, Shizuoka, 1996—, med. staff and asst. prof., 2001—08; med. staff gastroenterology Seirei Hamamatsu Gen. Hosp., 1997—2001; fellow Michael E. DeBakey Veterans Affairs Med. Ctr. and Baylor Coll. Medicine, Houston, 2008—. Councilor Japanese Soc. Gastroenterology, Tokyo, 2006—, Japan Gastroent. Endoscopy Soc., Tokyo, 2006—, Japanese Gastroent. Assn., Tokyo, 2008—; editl. bd. gastrointestinal cancer rev. letters Gastrointestinal Cancer Rev. Letters, Beijing, 2009—. Contbr. articles to profl. jours. (award Japanese Soc. Clin. Pharmacology and Therapeutics, 2006). Grant, Japanese Govt., 2007. Mem.: Japanese Soc. Gastrointestinal Endoscopy, Japanese Soc. Clin. Pharmacology, Japanese Soc. Gastroenterology, Japanese Soc. Internal Medicine, Japanese Gastroent. Assn., Japanese Soc. Clin. Oncology, Japanese Soc. Helicobacter. Office: Michael E DeBakey Veterans Affairs 2002 Holcombe Blvd Houston TX 77030 Office Fax: 713-794-7280. Business E-Mail: sugimoto@bcm.edu.

SUGISHITA, JONEA GENE, marketing executive, copywriter; d. Robert Dee and Linda Susan Boysen. BS in Mktg., Mgmt. and Psychology, Calif. Luth. U., 2004, MBA in Mktg. and Fin., 2005; grad. Global Bus. Program in Internat. Mgmt., FH-Joanneum, Graz, Austria, 2003. Profl. cert. marketer Am. Mktg. Assn., 2005, cert. bus. communicator Bus. Mktg. Assn., 2005. Mktg. comm. specialist and copywriter UBS Fin. Svcs. Inc., Ventura, Calif., 2003—04; pub. rels. copywriter NBC, Universal and Calif. Luth. U., Burbank, Calif., 2004—04; mgmt. cons., copywriter Jonea Gene Mktg. PR, Myrtle Beach, SC, 1999—; mng. editor The Breeze, Myrtle Beach, 2006—07; writer The Weekly Surge, 2006—08. Author (copywriter): (mktg. plan) DECA Learn & Earn Project (11th Pl. in Nation, 2000). Recipient Pub. Rels. Firm of Yr., Conway C. of C., 2007. Mem.: Am. Advt. Fedn., Am. Mktg. Assn., Myrtle Beach C. of C. (small bus. coun.), Conway Area C. of C. (bd. dirs.), Sigma Beta Delta, Psi Chi. Avocations: feng shui, time with family, husband and friends, exercise. Office: 4214 Mayfair St Ste F Myrtle Beach SC 29577 Office Phone: 843-839-4607. Business E-Mail: jonea@joneagene.com.

SUGIYAMA, MASANO, chemical engineer, researcher; BS in Chem. Engring., U. Ariz., Tucson, 2004. Undergrad. rsch. asst., NSF/SRC engring. rsch. ctr. environmentally benign semiconductor mfg. U. Ariz., 2002—04; rsch. asst., dept. chem. engring. and material cci. U. Minn., Mpls., 2004—. Recipient Best Poster prize, 12th Internat. Conf. Crystallization Biol. Macromolecules, 2008; Young Scientist fellow, 11th Internat. Conf. Crystallization Biol. Macromolecules, 2006.

SUGIYAMA, TAKEHARU, physical chemist; b. Fukuoka, Japan, May 1, 1973; s. Yoshikuni and Chikako Sugiyama; m. Hiromi Sugioka, Mar. 3, 2004. BS in Chemistry, Kyushu U., Fukuoka, Japan, 1997, MS in Applied Physics and Chemistry, 1999, PhD in Phys. Chemistry, 2002. Spl. postdoctoral rschr. inst. phys. and chem. rsch. Rikagaku Kenkyujo, Wako, Saitama, Japan, 2002—06; postdoctoral rschr. Kanto Gakuin U., Yokohama, Japan, 2006—09; rschr. Japan Synchrotron Radiation Rsch. Inst., Hyogo, Japan, 2009—. Contbr. articles to profl. jours. Mem.: Surface Sci. Soc. Japan, Phys. Soc. Japan, Japan Soc. Analytical Chemistry, Chem. Soc. Japan. Achievements include development of laser-based microspot photoemission spectroscopy and its application to organic molecular films on surfaces. Office: Japan Synchrotron Radiation Rsch Inst 1-1-1 Kouto Sayo-gun Hyogo 679-5198 Japan Office Fax: +81-791-58-0802. Business E-Mail: sugiyama@spring8.or.jp.

SUGRA, CYNTHIA MARIEL, marketing executive; d. Michael A. and Silvia A. Sugra. Degree music, UCLA. Cert. Music Bus./Audio Engring. UCLA. CEO/owner Studio 7 Media, LLC, LA, 2001—, Tripp Factor Music, LA, Hotllama Media LLC, LA. Cons. in field. Office: Studio 7 Media PO Box 963 Torrance CA 90508-0963 Business E-Mail: cyndee@studio7media.com.

SUGRUE, THOMAS J., history and social sciences professor; b. Detroit, July 24, 1962; s. Thomas J. and Sharon R. Sugrue; m. Dana L. Barron, May 30, 1993; children: Anna Linn Barron, John Michael Barron. BA in History summa cum laude, Columbia U., 1984; BA in History with honors, Cambridge Univ., 1986; AM in History, Harvard U., 1987; MA in History, Cambridge U., 1989; PhD in History, Harvard U., 1992. Lectr. history U. Pa., Phila., 1991—92, asst. prof. history, 1992—97, assoc. prof. history, 1997—98, assoc. prof. history and sociology, 1998—2000, Bicentennial Class of 1940 prof. history and sociology, 2000—04, Kahn prof. history and sociology, 2004—; Lawrence Stone prof. Princestone U., 2009. Rsch. fellow Brookings Instn., Washington, 1990—91; vis. assoc. prof. NYU, NYC, 1998; trustee and vice chair of bd. Hist. Soc. Pa., Phila., 2000—; dir. Urban History Assn., Cin., 2000—02, Social Sci. History Assn., 2008—; vis. prof. Ecole des Hautes Etudes en Sciences Sociales, Paris, 2002, Harvard U., 2008. Author: The Origins of the Urban Crisis (Bancroft Prize in History 1998, Taft Prize in Labor History 1997, President's Book Award SSHA, 1996, Urban History Assn. Best Book Award 1997); editor: (book series) Politics and Culture in Modern America, 2003—; editor, author (collection of essays) W.E.B. DuBois, Race, and the City, 1998, The New Suburban History, 2006; author: (book) Sweet Land of liberty: The Forgotten Struggle For Civil Rights in the North, 2008 (finalist LA Times Book prize, 2008). Founding mem. Scholars, Artists, and Writers for Social Justice, NYC, 1996—98; vice chair and commr. Phila. Hist. Commn., Phila., 2001—08; bd. chair Bread and Roses Cmty. Fund, 2004—. Recipient Phi Beta Kappa, Columbia U., 1983, Sidney Hillman Found. award. for Nat. Teach-In with the Labor Movement., 1997, Disting. Lectr., Orgn. of Am. Historians, 2002—, John Simon Guggenheim fellowship, 2005; grantee program in non-profits, univs., cmtys., schs., Kellogg Found. through U. Pa.Ctr. Cmty. Partnerships, 1998—2001, grant for Conf. (co-PI), Nat. Endowment Humanities, 1994-96; fellow, Alphonse Fletcher Sr. Found., 2005; scholar, Harry S. Truman Found., 1982-84, 1986-88, Josephine De Kármán Found. fellow, 1989-90, Com. for Rsch. on the Urban Underclass, Dissertation grant and fellow, Social Sci. Rsch. Coun., 1990-91, Am. Coun. of Learned Societies fellow, ACLS, 1995-96. Mem.: Inst. for Advanced Study, Social Sci. History Assn. (program com. chair 1997—98), Am. Studies Assn. (exec. com. mem. 2008—), Am. Sociol. Assn., Urban History Assn. (bd. mem., prize com. mem., program com. mem. 2000—04), Orgn. of Am. Historians (program com. 2001—03). Avocations: architecture, travel, gardening. Home: 129 Carpenter Ln Philadelphia PA 19119 Office: U Pa 208 College Hall Philadelphia PA 19104 Personal E-mail: thomas.sugrue@gmail.com. Business E-Mail: tsugrue@sas.upenn.edu.

SUGUMARAN, MANICKAM, biology professor; s. Manickam Chettiar and Sakunthala Manickam; m. Geetha Rani Sugumaran, Apr. 11, 1980; children: Keerthi, Karthik. BSc, St. Joseph's Coll., Trichy, India, 1969; MSc, Loyola Coll., Chennai, India, 1971; PhD, Indian Inst. Sci., Bangalore, 1979. Assoc. dean grad. studies U. Mass., Boston, 2001—03, chmn. biology, 2004—07, biology prof., 1991—. Contbr. articles to sci. publs. D-Liberal. Hindu. Office: Univ Mass Boston 100 Morrissey Blvd Boston MA 02125 Office Phone: 617-287-6650. Business E-Mail: manickam.sugumaran@umb.edu.

SUH, BYUNGSE, medical educator; b. Ansung, Republic of Korea, Mar. 6, 1941; came to U.S., 1964; s. Sang Keun and Chong Sang (Lee) S.; m. Youngjoo Lee, Dec. 21, 1974; children: Jason, Jessica, Janice. BS, Chungang U., Seoul, Korea, 1962; MA, U. Kans., 1967, PhD, 1969; MD, U. Miami, 1973. Diplomate Am. Bd. Internal Medicine; diplomate Am. Bd. Infectious Diseases. Asst. prof. medicine Temple U. Sch. Medicine, Phila., 1978-83, assoc. prof. medicine, 1983-90, prof. medicine, 1990—. Contbr. articles to profl. jours. Pres. Korea Ilsan Handicapped Children Support Assn., 1983—. Recipient Presdl. award, Republic of Korea, 1994. Fellow Infectious Diseases Soc. Am., Am. Coll. Physicians, Coll. Physicians Phila.; mem. Am. Soc. Microbiology, Alpha Omega Alpha. Republican. Roman Catholic. Office: Temple U Sch Medicine Sect Infectious Diseases 3401 N Broad St Philadelphia PA 19140 Office Phone: 215-707-1982. Business E-Mail: bingsuh@temple.edu.

SUH, CHANG HO, polymer engineer; b. Daegu, Republic of Korea, May 26, 1963; s. Jinmoo and Giok Hwang Suh; m. Younghee Kim Suh, Dec. 22, 1990; children: Hyukjoon Michael, Wonik John. BS in Textile Engring., Kyunghee U., Seoul, Republic of Korea, 1986; MS in Textile Engring., Yeungnam U., Gyungsan, Republic of Korea, 1988; PhD in Polymer Engring., U. Akron, Ohio, 1995. Group leader, Rsch. & Devel. Ctr. Toray Saehan Inc., Seoul, Republic of Korea, 1995—2004, bus. team leader, Adminstrn. Planning & Mgmt. Divsn., 2004—05, team leader, Rsch. & Devel. Ctr., 2004—05, project leader, Advanced Materials Rsch. Ctr., 2005—06, new bus. team leader and project leader, 2006—, gen. mgr., 2006—. Contbr. scientific papers to profl. pubs. Recipient Tech. Devel. prize, 1997, 1998, 2001, 2002. Mem.: Korean Carbon Soc., Membrane Soc. Korea, Soc. Plastic Engrs., Korean Inst. Chem. Engrs., Polymer Soc. Polymer, Korean Soc. Rheology. Roman Catholic. Achievements include patents for biaxially stretched polyester film; voided polyester film; flame retarded polyethylene micro porous film; polyethylene micro porous film for a rechargeable battery separator; manufacturing process of coextruded polyethylene micro porous film for a rechargeable battery separator; patents pending in field. Avocation: golf. Office: Toray Saehan Inc 16F LG Mapo Bldg 275 Gongduk Dong Mapo Gu Seoul 121 721 Republic of Korea Office Phone: 82 23279 1471, 02-3279-1479. Office Fax: 82232791015. Business E-Mail: chsuh@toraysaehan.com.

SUH, DAE-SOOK, political science professor; b. Hoeryong, Korea, Nov. 22, 1931; came to U.S., 1952; s. Chang-Hee and Chong-Hee (Paek) S.; m. Yun-Ok Park, Oct. 29, 1960; children: Maurice, Kevin. BA, Tex. Christian U., 1956; MA, Ind. U., 1958; PhD, Columbia U., 1964. Asst. prof. U. Houston, 1965-67, assoc. prof., 1968-71; prof. polit. sci., dir. Ctr. for Korean Studies, U. Hawaii, Honolulu, 1972-95, Korea Found. prof. policy studies, 1994-99; George L. Paik prof. Yonsei U., 1999; prof. polit. sci. U. Hawaii, Manoa, Hawaii, 1972—. Vis. prof. polit. sci. UCLA, 2005. Author: The Korean Communist Movement, 1967, Documents of Korean Communism, 1970, Korean Communism, 1980, Kim Il Sung, 1988, Kim Il Sung and Kim Jong Il, 1996. Mem. Conv. Ctr. Authority, Honolulu, 1989-94. Grantee Social Sci. Rsch. Coun.-Am. Coun. Learned Socs., 1963, East-/West Ctr., Columbia U., 1971, The Woodraw Wilson Internat. Ctr. for Scholars, 1985, Fulbright, 1988. Mem. Am. Polit. Sci. Assn. (life), Assn. for Asian Studies. Avocations: tennis, golf. Office: U Hawaii Manoa Dept Political Sci 2424 Maile Way Honolulu HI 96822-2223 Home: 5150 Via EL Molino Thousand Oaks CA 91320-6996 Personal E-mail: daesook@roadrunner.com.

SUH, KEUN TAE, management consultant, educator; b. Ulsan, Kyong Nam, Republic of Korea, May 5, 1939; s. Won Ki Suh and Bok Chool Choi; m. Kyong Nam Park, Apr. 6, 1969; children: Dong Whan, Sung Jin. BA, Pusan Nat. U., Korea, 1963, MA, 1966; PhD, Pusan Nat. Fisheries U., Korea, 1982. Prof. Pusan Nat. U., 1969—2004, chmn. dept. fgn. trade, 1985—88, dean Coll. Bus., 1990—92, dir. Asian Rsch. Inst., 1993—95, hon. prof., 2004—. Sr. bus. advisor Hwaseung Group, Pusan, 1980—85; vis. prof. Seoul Nat. U., 1978—79, U. Calif., Berkeley, 1983—84, Waseda U., 1995—96; pres. Korea Trade Rsch. Inst., Seoul, 1991—92, Ulsan Devel. Inst., Republic of Korea, 2001—; mem. adv. bd. Presdl. Com. on Balanced Nat. Devel., Seoul, 2003—; spkr. in field. Author: Principle of International Trade, 1989, International Economics, 1995, Theory of International Commerce, 1999. Chmn. Ulsan IT Forum, 2003—06; mem. adminstr. com. Fund-Raising Campaign for Social Welfare, Ulsan, 2006—. 2d lt., 1963—65, Republic of Korea. Recipient Nat. Svc. Merit of Green Strips, Korean Govt., 2004; grantee, 1986; fellow, Inst. Developing Econ., Japan, 1988—89, Korea-Japan Found., 1995—96. Mem.: Assn. Rsch. Inst. Korea-Japan Straits (chmn. 2006—), Korea Trade Rsch. Assn. (sr.), Korean Econ. Assn. (sr.; v.p. 2000—01). Home: 967-3 Ilsan-Dong Dong-Gu Ulsan 682-050 Republic of Korea Office: Ulsan Devel Inst 758-2 Yeonam-Dong Buk-Gu Ulsan 683-804 Republic of Korea

SUH, KYOUNGWON, science educator, researcher; b. Republic Of Korea; BS in Computer Engring., Seoul Nat. U., Republic of Korea, 1991; MS in Computer Sci., Rutgers, State U. NJ, New Brunswick, 2000; PhD in Computer Sci., U. Mass., Amherst, 2007. Rsch. engr. LG Electronics Inc., Seoul, 1993—98; rsch. intern Telcordia Techs., Morristown, NJ, 1999, Thomson Paris Rsch. Lab., 2006; asst. prof. Ill. State U., Normal, 2007—. Contbr. articles to profl. jours. (Best Paper award, 2008). Office: Ill State Univ Sch Info Tech Campus Box #5150 Old Union Bldg Normal IL 61790-5150

SUH, NAM PYO, mechanical engineering educator; b. Seoul, Apr. 22, 1936; arrived in U.S., 1954, naturalized, 1963; s. Doo Soo and Joon Joo (Lee) S.; m. Young Ja Surh; children: Mary M., Helen H., Grace J., Caroline Y. SB, MIT, 1959, SM, 1961; PhD, Carnegie-Mellon U., 1964; D of Engring. (hon.), Worcester Poly. Inst., 1986; LHD (hon.), U. Mass., Lowell, 1988; D of Tech. (hon.), Royal Inst. Tech., Sweden, 2000. Devel. engr. Guild Plastics Inc., Cambridge, Mass., 1958-60; sr. rsch. engr., project mgr. USM Corp., Beverly, Mass., 1961-65; asst. prof. U. SC, Columbia, 1965-68, assoc. prof., 1968-69; assoc. prof. mech. engring. MIT, Cambridge, 1970-75, prof., 1975—, Ralph E. and Eloise F. Cross prof., 1989—, dir. Lab. Mfg. and Productivity, 1977-84, dir. industry polymer processing program, 1973-84, dir. Mfg. Inst. (now Park Ctr. for Complex Sys.), 1989—2006, Cross prof., dept. head mech. engring., 1991-2001; presdl. appointee asst. dir. for engring. NSF, Washington, 1984-88; pres. Korea Advanced Inst. Sci. and Tech., 2006—. Bd. dirs. Axiomatic Design Software, Inc., Boston, Tribotek, Inc., Burlington, Mass., Parker Vision, Inc., Jacksonville, Fla., Therma Wave, Inc., Fremont, Calif., Integrated Device Tech., Inc., San Jose, Calif.; former cons. Lawrence Livermore Nat. Lab.; advisor Korea Elec. Power Rsch. Inst.; former mem. sci. and tech. rev. bd. Nat. Engring. Lab., mem. NRC rev. panel, 1986—90; mem. vis. com. (statutory) Nat. Inst. Stds. and Tech., 1990—94; mem. tech. adv. com. Alcan Aluminum Corp., 1989—90; editor advanced mfg. series Oxford U. Press; hon. prof. Univ. Hong Kong, 2003—; disting. vis. prof. Korea Advanced Inst. of Sci. and Tech., 2002—; cons. prof. Shangai Jiatong U., 2005. Author (with A.P.L. Turner): Mechanical Behavior of Solids, 1975; author: The Principles of Design, 1990; author: (with others) Manufacturing Engineering, 1990; author: Axiomatic Design: Advances and Applications, 2001, Complexity: Theory and Applications, 2005; co-author: Axiomatic Design and Fabrication of Composite Structures, 2006; editor (with N. Saka): Fundamentals of Tribology, 1980; editor: (with N. Sung) Science and Technology of Polymer Procs., 1979; editor: The Delamination Theory of Wear, 1977; editor: (with B.M. Kramer) University/Industry Cooperation, 1982; former co-editor-in-chief Robotics and Computer Aided Manufacturing, contbr. over 280 articles to profl. jours. Former chmn. bd. Korean-Am. Soc. New Eng., 1979. Recipient Best Paper award, Soc. Plastics Engrs., 1981, Citation Classic, Inst. for Sci. Info., 1981, Disting. Svcs. award, NSF, 1988, Mainstream Am. award, 1991, scholarly award, Korea Broadcasting Svc., 1994, The Mensforth Internat. Gold Medal, U.K. Instn. Elec. Engrs., 2000, The Hills Millennium Internat. award, U.K. Instn. Engr. Designers, 2001, Gold medal of Honor, Acad. Transdisciplinary Learning and Advanced Studies, 2006, Gen. Nicolau award, CIRP, 2006; named Fed. Engr. of Yr., NSF/NSPE, 1987; USM Corp. fellow, 1962—63. Fellow: ASME (Gustus L. Larson Meml. award 1976, Blackall award 1982, W.T. Ennor Mfg. Tech. award 1993, Best Tribology Paper award 1993, Ho.-Am. prize for Engring. Ho.-Am. com. 1997), Soc. Mfg. Engrs. (F.W. Taylor Rsch. award 1986); mem.: AAAS, Korean Acad. Sci. and Engring., Royal Swedish Acad. Engring. Sci. (fgn.), Internat. Acad. Prodn. Engring., Am. Soc. Engring. Edn. (Centennial medal 1993, Gen. Nicolau award 2006), Phi Kappa Phi, Pi Tau Sigma, Sigma Xi. Achievements include holder 50 U.S. patents. Office: MIT Rm 35-237 Dept Mech Engring Cambridge MA 02139 Office Phone: 617-253-2225.

SUH, RHEA S., federal agency administrator; b. 1970; d. Chung-Ha and Young-Ja Suh. BA in Environ. Sci., magna cum laude, Columbia U., NYC, 1992; MEd in Adminstrn., Planning & Social Policy, Harvard U., Cambridge, Mass., 1998. Former HS tchr., NYC; sr. legis. asst. to Senator Ben Nighthorse Campbell US Senate, Colo., 1993—96; environment prog. officer William & Flora Hewlett Found., Menlo Park, Calif., 1998—2007; conservation & sci. prog. officer David & Lucile Packard Found., Los Altos, Calif., 2007—09; asst. sec. for policy, mgmt. & budget US Dept. Interior, Washington, 2009—. Cons. US Nat. Park Svc.; bd. dirs. Environ. Grantmakers Assn. Recipient Fulbright Fellowship, Marshall Fellowship. Mem.: Asian-Am./Pacific Islanders Philanthropy Assoc. Office: US Dept Interior 1849 C St222 NW Washington DC 20240*

SUH, SANG WON, medical educator; s. Myung Suk Suh and Tae Suk Jang; m. Min Sohn; 1 child, Dyne. MD, Hallym U., Chun Cheon, Kang Won Do, Republic Of Korea, 1988; PhD, U. Tex., Galveston, 2001. Asst. adj. prof. U. Calif., San Francisco, 2001—; rsch. assoc. prof. Hallym U. Med. Sch., 2008—. Lt. Navy, 1991—94, Jin Hae, Korea. Recipient Best Presentation award, Am. Diabetes Assn., 2001, Career Devel. award, Juvenile Diabetes Rsch. Found., 2006; fellowship, Danish Med. Acad., 1997, Postdoc. fellowship, Juvenile Diabetes Rsch. Found., 2003, Rsch. grant, Dept. Def., 2008. Mem.: Soc. Zinc Biology. Achievements include research in zinc translocation into neuron after brain ischemia. Home: 80 Middlefield Dr San Francisco CA 94132 Office: Univ Calif San Francisco Neurology 4150 Clement St San Francisco CA 94121 Business E-Mail: sang.suh@ucsf.edu.

SUH, SANGWON, environmental scientist, educator; b. Seoul, Republic of Korea, June 9, 1973; s. Jae-Young Suh and Kyong-Ja Ahn; m. Yunki Lee, Dec. 25, 1999; children: Jungho Stefan, Youngju Marina, Minju Sophie. BS in Environ. Engring., Ajou U., Suwon, 1998, MS in Environ. Engring., 2000; PhD in Environ. Scis. cum laude, Leiden U., Netherlands, 2004. Rsch. scientist Inst. Environ. Scis., Leiden U., Netherlands, 2002—04, assoc. fellow, 2004—. Chair indsl. ecology input-output analysis group Soc. Environ. Toxicology and Chemistry Europe, 2003—06; rsch. assoc. Carnegie Mellon U., Pitts., 2004—05; asst. prof. U. Minn., Twin Cities, 2005—; advisor Eco-Indsl. Devel. Coun., 2006—. Subject editor: Internat. Jour. Life Cycle Assessment, 2003—, mem. editl. bd.: Econ. Sys. Rsch., 2006—. Sgt. Korean Army, 1993—96. Recipient Article award, POSCO, Ltd., 1998, Best Paper award, Soc. Environ. Toxicology and Chemistry Europe, 2003; fellow, AT&T, 2004—05, Inst. Environ. Scis., Leiden U., 2004—. Achievements include research in mathematical basis for environmental and economic systems analysis; patents for system and method for optimizing industrial processes to minimize environmental interventions. Office: U Minn 1390 Eckles Ave Saint Paul MN 55108 Office Fax: 612-624-3005.

SUH, TAEWON, marketing and business educator; s. KyungSuk Suh and YongSung Lee; m. Soyoung Lee; children: Don Dongchan, Jeremy Dongjoo. PhD, Sogang U., Seoul, 1998, St. Louis U., 2004. Asst. prof. Tex. State U., San Marcos, 2003—. Contbr. articles to profl. jours. Recipient Best Paper award, Jour. Am. Acad. Bus., 2005, Gary V. Wood Rsch. award, Tex. State U., 2007, Best Paper award, AMA, 2008. Baptist. Office: Tex State Univ 601 University Dr San Marcos TX 78666

SUH, WONSUK WARREN, radiation oncologist; s. Chai-Pill and Myung-Hi Suh; m. Jeewon Park, Nov. 22, 2000; children: Ryan Joonwon, Sidney Chaewon. BA, Cornell U., 1991; MD, U. Chgo., 1996; MPH, Harvard U., 1996. Diplomate internal medicine and radiation oncology. Resident internal medicine Mayo Clinic, Rochester, Minn., 1996—99; from radiation oncology resident to chief resident U. Mich., Ann Arbor, 2000—04; faculty radiation oncologist Dana-Farber/Brigham & Women's Cancer Ctr., Boston, 2004—. Contbr. articles to profl. jours. Recipient H. Hughes award, 1990; named Eminent Scientist Yr. in Radiation Oncology, Internat. Rsch. Prom Coun., 2006—07. Mem.: Am. Coll. Radiology (mem. appropriateness criteria expert panel, rectal and anal cancers 2006—), Am. Soc. Therapeutic Radiation and Oncology (health svcs. outcome rsch. leadership com. 2004—, adj. prostate radiation panel chair 2007—), Am. Soc. Clin. Oncology (mem. new tech. com., PET evaluation 2002—, Merit award 2003). Office: Cancer Ctr Santa Barbara 300 W Pueblo St Santa Barbara CA 93105 Home: 2275 Feather Hill Rd Santa Barbara CA 93108 Office Phone: 617-732-7936, 805-682-7300.

SUHR, KARL FRIEDRICH, school librarian; b. Seward, Nebr., Jan. 30, 1969; s. John David and Norma Jean Suhr; m. Michelle Kathryn Brosz, Dec. 27, 1993; children: Anwyn Noelle, Greta Shenandoah. BA in Music, Concordia U., Seward, Nebr., 1992; MS in Info. Sci., U. North Tex., Denton, 1993. Libr. asst. III U. Nebr. Music Libr., Lincoln, 1994—96; reference libr. Nova Southeastern U., Davie, Fla., 1996—99; electronic resources reference libr. Kent Libr., SouthEast Mo. State U., Cape Girardeau, Mo., 1999—. Contbr. articles to profl. jours. Office: Kent Libr South East Mo State Univ 1 University Plz Cape Girardeau MO 63703 Office Fax: 573-651-2666. Business E-Mail: ksuhr@semo.edu.

SUHR, MOON JA MINN, dance educator; b. Seoul, Korea, Nov. 20, 1940; came to U.S., 1967; d. Jang-shik and Yang-keun (Kang) Minn; m. Paul T. Suhr, Sept. 5, 1970; children: Grace E.S. Van Doren, Abraham Wonduk. BS, Ewha Women's U., Seoul, 1963; MA, U. No. Colo., 1969; PhD, Tex. Woman's U., 1988. Cert. community coll. instr. and elem. and intermediate labanotation cert., Calif. Instr. dance Kongju (Korea) Tchrs. Coll. and Kongju Mid. and High Sch., 1963-64, Sookmyung Girl's Mid. and High Sch., Seoul, 1964-67; lectr. Calif. Poly. State U., San Luis Obispo, 1969-71, from asst. prof. to prof. dance, 1972—2008, prof. emeritus. Founder, dir., choreographer, performer Orchesis Dance Co., dir. 30th ann. dance prodn. Author: Korean Folk and Ethnic Dance, 1985, 6 textbooks; contbr. articles to The New Life mag., The Korean Dance mag. Vol. tchr. EDNH, 2005—. PEO Internat. Peace scholar, 1968, Aileen S. Lockhart scholar, 1983-85; Creative Activity and Research Effort grantee, 1982. Mem. Nat. Dance Assn., AAHPERD, PEN, Congress on Rsch. and Dance, Calif. Dance Educators Assn., Dance Notation Bur., Pilates Physicalmind Inst., Phi Beta Delta. Clubs: Eleven Book (Seoul) (pres. 1960-63). Methodist. Avocations: reading, writing, sewing, tai chi, classical music. Home: 175 San Jose Ct San Luis Obispo CA 93405-1532 Office: Calif Poly State U Dance Dept San Luis Obispo CA 93407

SUHR, PAUL AUGUSTINE, lawyer; b. Sonwunri, Chonbuk, Korea, Jan. 20, 1940; arrived in US, 1966; s. Chong-ju and Oksuk (Pang) So; m. Angeline M. Kang Suhr; 1 child, Christopher. BA, Campbell Coll., Buies Creek, NC, 1968; MA, U. N.C., Greensboro, 1970; MS, U. N.C., Chapel Hill, 1975; JD, N.C. Cen. U., 1988. Bar: NC 1989, US Dist. Ct. (ea. and mid. dist.) NC 1989, US Ct. Appeals DC 1990, US Ct. Appeals (4th cir.) 1992. Bibliographer NC Divsn. of State Libr., Raleigh, 1975-78; dir. Pender County Pub. Libr., Burgaw, NC, 1978-80; libr. Tob. Lit. Svc., NC State U., Raleigh, 1980-85; pvt. practice law Law Offices of Paul A. Suhr, PLLC, Raleigh and Fayetteville, NC, 1989—. Author short stories and novelettes various lit. mags., jours. and revs. Mem. Human Resources and Human Rels. Adv. Commn., City of Raleigh, 1990-95, chmn., 1994-95. NC Humanities Com. grantee, 1979-80; recipient Presdl. award President of Korea, 1992. Mem. ABA, ATLA, Am. Immigration Lawyers Assn., NC Bar Assn., NC Trial Lawyers Assn., Wake County Bar Assn. (bd. dirs. 1996-97, 2003—), DC Bar Assn. Democrat. Roman Catholic. Avocations: gardening, fishing, writing. Office: 1110 Navaho Dr Ste 502 Raleigh NC 27609-7322 Office Phone: 919-876-4707. Personal E-mail: paulsuhr@aol.com.

SUHRHEINRICH, RICHARD FRED, federal judge; b. Lincoln City, Ind., 1936; BS, Wayne State U., 1960; JD cum laude, Detroit Coll. Law, 1963; LLM (hon.), U. Va., 1990, Detroit Coll. Law, 1992. Bar: Mich. Law clerk Stringari, Fritz & Fiott, 1963; assoc. Moll, Desenberg, Purdy, Glover & Bayer, 1963—67; asst. prosecutor Macomb County, 1967; ptnr. Rogensues, Richard & Suhrheinrich, 1967; assoc. Moll, Desenberg, Purdy, Glover & Bayer, 1967—68; ptnr. Kitch, Suhrheinrich, Saurbier & Drutchas, 1968—84; assoc. prof. law Detroit Coll. Law, 1975—85; judge US Dist. Ct. (ea. dist.) Mich., Detroit, 1984—90, US Ct. Appeals (6th cir.), Lansing, 1990—2001, sr. judge, 2001—. Law prof. Thomas M Cooley Law Sch., 2003—; mem. State of Mich. Atty. Discipline Bd., Atty. Grievance Commn. Bd. trustees Brighton Hosp. Mem.: Ingham County Bar Assn., State Bar Mich., Mich. State Univ.-Detroit (bd. trustees 1985—2003, pres. 1999—2001). Office: US Ct Appeals 6th Cir USPO & Fed Bldg 315 W Allegan St Rm 241 Lansing MI 48933-1514*

SUI, ANNA, fashion designer; b. Dearborn Heights, Mich., 1955; d. Paul and Grace S. Grad., Parsons Sch. Design. Founder, designer Anna Sui, 1988—. Opened outlet SoHo dist., 1992, NYC, Anna Sui Boutiques, Osaka, Tokyo, 1997; designer Sui Anna Sui, 1995-, Anna Sui cosmetic line, fragrance line, 1999, skincare line, 2000. First runway show, 1991. Recipient Perry Ellis award new fashion talent Coun. Fashion Designers Am., 1992. Achievements include launching an Anna Sui Boho Barbie with Mattel, 2006. Office: c/o Rachna Shah KCD 450 W 15th St Ste 604 New York NY 10011

SUI, LEI, technical leader; b. Haiyang, Shandong, China, Nov. 10, 1977; s. Aimin Sui and Juxiang Liu; m. Li Liu, Sept. 22, 2001; children: David Liu, Peter Fukai. BS in Elec. Engring., Naning U., China; MS in Mech. Engring., Boston U., Mass.; PhD, 2005. Ultrasound rschr. Saoirse Corp., Cambridge, Mass., 2006; tech. leader -ultrasonics and transducers Gen. Electric Enterprise Solutions—Sensing, Billerica, Mass., 2006—. Achievements include patents pending for two.

SUITER, JANE, science educator; b. Waterloo, Iowa, June 21, 1948; d. Alfred and Luella Schneider; children: Jeremy, Jon. BS, Briar Cliff U., Sioux City, Iowa, 1970; MS in Tchg., Coe Coll., Cedar Rapids, Iowa, 1998. Tchr. Don Bosco HS, Gilbertville, Iowa, 1970—74; substitute tchr. Cedar Rapids Schs., 1977—91, tchr., 1991—; online course facilitator Am. Meteorol. Soc., Washington, 2003—; adj. instr. Kirkwood CC, Cedar Rapids, 2004—. Mem.: NEA, Iowa State Edn. Assn., Nat. Sci. Tchr. Assn. Home: 3415 26th Ave Marion IA 52302 Office: Kennedy HS 4545 Wenig Rd Ne Cedar Rapids IA 52402 Personal E-mail: volleys621@msn.com. Business E-Mail: jsuiter@cr.k12.ia.us.

SUITOR, DORCAS P., elementary school educator; b. Albany, Vt., Aug. 5, 1944; d. Abner Joseph and Eulalee Dorothy Poutry; m. David Douglas Suitor, Dec. 24, 1966; children: Daphne Joan Morris, Dorothea Joy Alter. BS in Edn., Johnson State Coll., 1966. Cert. tchr. Vt. Tchr. 2d grade C.P. Smith Sch., Burlington, Vt., 1966—67, Swanton Elem. Sch., 1967—71; tchr. title I Sheldon Elem. Sch., 1973—75, St. Anne's Elem. Sch., Swanton, 1974—75; tchr. 1st grade Swanton Elem. Sch., 1975—94, tchr. k-1, 1994—99, tchr. 1st grade, 1999—. Mem. adv. bd. Project Scope, Swanton, 2002—06; mem. local stds. bd. Franklin Northwest Dist., 1999—; mem. tech. task force Swanton Elem. Sch., 1999—2006, grade 1 math leader, 2005—; presenter in field. Mentor new tchr. FNW Supervisory Union, Swanton, 2003—; supr. student tchrs. U. Vt. and Johnson State Coll. Swanton Elem. Sch., 2001—04; trustee Meml. United Meth. Ch., Swanton, 2005—, Swanton Town Libr., 2005—. Recipient Outstanding Vt. Tchr. award, 2006. Mem.: ASCD, Nat. Coun. Tchrs. Math., Franklin Northwest NEA (30 Yrs. Svc. to Children award 1999), Vt. Coun. Reading. Democrat. United Methodist. Avocations: reading, cooking, making educational games, gardening. Home: 17 Dunning St Swanton VT 05488 Office: Swanton Elem Sch 113 Grand Ave Swanton VT 05488 Personal E-mail: davdor1@aol.com.

SUKAPDJO, WILMA IRENE, language educator; b. Indpls., Nov. 8, 1936; d. Wilson Homer and Della Irene Warren; m. Humam Sukapdjo, Apr. 12, 1960; children: Tina, Stephen, Amye. AB, Butler U., Indpls., 1958, MS, 1967; postgrad., Trinity Coll. of the Bible and Sem., Newburgh, Ind. Tchr. French U. Wis., Madison, Gadjah Mada U., Jogjarkarta, Indonesia, Plainfield H.S., Ind., Columbus Jr. H.S., Ben Davis H.S., Indpls.; tchr. langs. Iupui Continuing Edn., Wilhum Acad., Carmel, 1999—2007, Oasis, Indpls. Vol. guide Eiteljorg Indian Mus., Indpls. Recipient Di Vinci Diamond award, Cambridge, England, 2006. Fellow: Am. Biog. Assn. (life), Internat. Biographic Assn. Eng. (life); mem.: Smithsonian Instn., Colonial Williamsburg Found., Japan Am. Soc. Ind., Tomodachi Japan-Am. Club (pres.), Omicron Psi, Phi Kappa Phi. Republican. Presbyterian. Avocation: travel. Office: Wilhum Acad Foreign Lang 622 S Range Line Rd Ste Q Carmel IN 46032-2152 Office Phone: 317-843-2874.

SUKAR, ABDULHAMID I., economics professor; s. Ibrahim A. Sukar and Kedija Y. Khalifa; m. Jewahir M. Abubeker, Aug. 20, 1990; children: Ibrahim A., Nabil A., Ida A. PhD, Tex. Tech U., Lubbock, 1989. Prof. Cameron U., Lawton, Okla., 1987—. Recipient Disting. Rsch. award, SW Okla. Advanced Tech., Fulbright Lectureship and Rsch. award, State Dept., 1999—2000, Sch. Bus. Lifetime Rsch. award, Cameron U., 2003; named to Faculty Hall of Fame, 2007. Home: 2404 Ne 35 Lawton OK 73507 Office: Cameron Univ 2800 WGore Lawton OK 73507 Business E-Mail: abduls@cameron.edu.

SUKAWATY, ANDREW J., telecommunications industry executive; b. 1955; m. Laura Sukawaty; children: Jennifer, David. BBA, U. Wis., 1977; MBA, U. Minn., 1982. With US WEST, Inc., AT&T, Northwestern Bell; CEO Mercury One-2-One, London, COO, 1989—94; CEO NTL Ltd., 1994—96, Sprint PCS, 1996—98, pres., COO, 1998—2000; pres. Cable Ptnrs. Europe LLC, London, 2000—; chmn. Inmarsat Holdings Ltd., London, 2003—, CEO, 2004—. Chmn. Xyratex Group Ltd., 1996—2000; bd. dirs. Powerwave Technologies, Inc., 1998—, Inmarsat

Holdings Ltd.; non-exec. dir. mmO2, PLC (formerly BT Wireless), 2001—; chmn. Telenet; advisor Gen. Atlantic Ptnrs. Adv. com. Kan. Cancer Inst., Kan. City Equity Ptnrs. Mem.: Cellular Telephone and Internet Assn. (CTIA) (former chmn.). Office: Inmarsat plc 99 City Rd London EC1Y 1AX England also: Cable Ptnrs Europe LLC 2th Fl, Foxglove House 166-168 Piccadilly London W1J 9EF England Office Phone: +44 (0)20 7728 1777. Office Fax: +44 (0)20 7728 1142.

SUKI, DIMA, epidemiologist; d. Chafic Salim Abi-Said and Hiam Sami Nasrallah; m. Rabih Suki, Aug. 8, 1988; children: Yara, Tina. BS, Am. U. Beirut, Lebanon, 1986; MS, Am. U. Beirut, 1988, diploma in Tchg., 1987; PhD, U. Tex., Houston, 1993. Asst. epidemiologist, dept. med. specialties U. Tex. M.D. Anderson Cancer Ctr., Houston, 1992—93, rsch. assoc., dept. med. specialties, 1993—97, asst. epidemiologist, dept. neurosurgery, 1997—2004, asst. prof., dept. neurosurgery, 1997—2004, 2004—, assoc. epidemiologist, dept. neurosurgery, 2004; adj. assoc. prof. Baylor Coll. Medicine Dept. neurosurgery, Houston, 2007. Cons. U. Texas, Houston Sch. Pub. Health, 1993. Mem.: Assn. Clin. Rsch. Profl., Soc. Clin. Rsch. Assocs., Soc. Neuro-Oncology, Soc. Epidemiologic Rschrs. Avocations: art, reading, gardening. Office: MD Anderson Cancer Ctr 1515 Holcombe Blvd Unit 442 Houston TX 77030 Office Phone: 713-792-2400. Office Fax: 713-794-4950. Business E-Mail: dsuki@mdanderson.org.

SUKLE, ROBERT J., language educator; b. Paonia, Colo., Aug. 5, 1943; s. John and Helen M Sukle. MA, Cornell U., Ithaca, NY, ABD, 1974. Dir., Japanese FALCON program Cornell U., 1988—, dir., Japanese tchr. tng. workshop, 1989—2006. Pres. Nat. Assn. Self Instructional Lang. Programs, 2004—06. Office: Cornell Univ Dept Asian Studies 388 Rockefeller Hall Ithaca NY 14853

SUKO, LONNY RAY, judge; b. Spokane, Wash., Oct. 12, 1943; s. Ray R. and Leila B. (Snyder) Suko; m. Marcia A. Michaelson, Aug. 26, 1967; children: Jolynn R., David M. BA, Wash. State U., 1965; JD, U. Idaho, 1968. Bar: Wash. 1968, U.S. Dist. Ct. (ea. dist.), Wash. 1969, U.S. Dist. Ct. (we. dist.), Wash. 1978, U.S. Ct. Appeals (9th cir.) 1978. Law clk. U.S. Dist. Ct. Ea. Dist., Wash., 1968—69; assoc. Lyon, Beaulaurier & Aaron, Yakima, Wash., 1969—72; ptnr. Lyon, Beaulaurier, Weigand, Suko & Gustafson, Yakima, Wash., 1972—91; ptnr., shareholder Lyon, Weigand, Suko & Gustafson, Yakima, Wash., 1991—95; U.S. magistrate judge Yakima, Wash., 1971—91, 1995—2003; judge U.S. Dist. Ct., 2003—. Mem.: Phi Kappa Phi, Phi Beta Kappa. Office: PO Box 2726 Yakima WA 98907-2726

SUKOFF RIZZO, STACEY J., research scientist; married. BS, Rutgers U. Cook Coll., NB, NJ, 1995; attending, U. Coll. London, 2008. Rsch. technician Wistar Inst., Phila., 1995—96; assoc. scientist Merck Rsch. Labs. Sibia Neurosci., San Diego, 1999—2001, Wyeth Rsch., Princeton, NJ, 1996—99, sr. rsch. scientist, 2003—; rsch. scientist Aventis Pharms., 2001—03. Named Rsch. Scientist of Yr., Wyeth Rsch. Neurosci. Discovery, 2006. Mem.: NY Acad. Scis., Soc. Neurosci. Achievements include patents for serotonergic agents for treating sexual dysfunction. Business E-Mail: rizzos@wyeth.com.

SUKUMAR, NARAYANASAMI, research scientist; s. Duraisami and Navaneetham Narayanasami; m. Lakshmipriya Padaveti, Sept. 15, 1999; 1 child, Sahana Lakshmi. PhD, U. Madras, India, 1995. Staff scientist NE-CAT, Argonne Nat. Lab, Argonne, Ill., 2003—. Contbr. articles to various internat. jours. Merit scholar, India U. Grants Commn. Mem.: AAAS, Am. Crystallographic Assn. Avocation: photography. Home: 1123 Selma Ln Naperville IL 60540

ŠULC, VLADIMÍR, mechanical engineer; m. Mercy Das. M, Czech Tech. U., Prague, 1986. Compressor engr. Refrigeration & Food Rsch. Inst., Prague, 1986—93, Thermo King Corp., Bloomington, Minn., 1993—2002; sr. compressor engr. Ingersoll Rand, Bloomington, 2002—04, sr. R & D engr., 2004—. Office Phone: 952-887-2570. Business E-Mail: vsulc@thermoking.com.

SULEIMAN, ORHAN HUSSEIN, radiological physicist; b. NYC, Apr. 19, 1948; s. Hussein and Faize (Emin) S.; m. Perihan Hussein; children: Yildiz, Feray, Murat. BS, U. Fla., 1970, MS, 1972; PhD, Johns Hopkins U., 1989. Health physicist State of Fla. Broward County, Ft. Lauderdale, 1972-75, Dept. Army Aberdeen (Md.) Proving Ground, 1975-77, Ctr. Devices and Radiol. Health FDA, Rockville, Md., 1977—. Author of 21 papers and profl. articles. Pres. Md. Am. Turkish Assn., Columbia, 1986-87. Recipient Long-term Tng. award USPHS, Washington, 1986. Mem. Health Physics Soc., Phi Kappa Psi (pres., treas. 1970-72, Solon E. Summerfield scholar 1971). Muslim. Avocations: gardening, astronomy. Office: FDA HFZ-240 5600 Fishers Ln Rockville MD 20852-1750

SULENTIC, ROBERT E., real estate company executive; BA, U. Iowa; MBA, Harvard U. Various positions Trammell Crow Co., Dallas, 1984—94, pres. Trammell Crow NE, Inc., 1995—98, exec. v.p., nat. dir. devel. and investment, 1997—98, exec. v.p., CFO, 1998—2000, pres., CEO, 2000—06, chmn., 2002—06; group pres. EMEA, Asia Pacific, develop. & investment CB Richard Ellis, LA, 2006—09; group pres., devel. svcs., Asia Pacific and Europe, Middle East and Africa CB Richard Ellis Group Inc., CFO, pres., devel. svcs., 2009—. Bd. dirs. Staples, Inc.; bd dirs. Trammell Crow Co., 1997—2006; bd. dirs. CB Richard Ellis Group Inc., 2006—09. Office: CB Richard Ellis 11150 Santa Monica Blvd Los Angeles CA 90025 Office Phone: 310-405-8900. Business E-Mail: bsulentic@cbre.com.*

SULG, MADIS, manufacturing executive, entrepreneur; b. Tallinn, Estonia, May 25, 1943; came to U.S., 1950; s. Hand Eduard and Erika (Turk) S.; m. Mary Diane Detellis, Dec. 30, 1967; children: Danielle Marie, Michaella Erika. SB in Engring. Mgmt., MIT, 1965, SM in Mgmt., 1967. Cons. Barss, Reitzel & Assocs., Cambridge, Mass., 1970—71; mgr. planning and research Converse Rubber Co., Wilmington, Mass., 1971—75; dir. bus. planning and devel. AMF, Inc., Stamford, Conn., 1975—79; sr. v.p. planning and devel. Bandag, Inc., Muscatine, Iowa, 1978—88; pres. Prime Investments, 1988—, Muscatine Natural Resources Corp., 1981—88; chmn., CEO Sieg Auto Parts, Davenport, Iowa, 1989—93; COO Hammer's Plastic Recycling, Iowa Falls, Iowa, 1994, PURethane, Inc., West Branch, Iowa, 1994—98; COO, Bytec, Inc., Clinton Township, Mich., 1999—2001; prin. M&D Mgmt. Assocs., 1989—; mng. mem. Maddi's Gallery, LLC, 2001—, Maddi's Southern Bistro, LLC, 2007—. With U.S. Army, 1968-70. Presbyterian. Avocations: bridge, jogging, swimming. Home: 11238 Home Place Lane Charlotte NC 28227 Personal E-mail: madissulg@aol.com.

SULICK, MICHAEL J., federal agency administrator; b. NYC, 1948; BA in Russian Studies, MA in Russian Studies, Fordham U., Bronx, NY; PhD in Comparative Lit., CUNY. Joined CIA, Washington, 1980, chief intelligence ops., Russia and Poland, chief, Ctrl. Eurasia divsn., chief counterintelligence, assoc. dep. dir. ops., 2004; ret., 2004—07; dir., nat. clandestine svc. CIA, 2007—. Mem. editl. bd.: Studies in Intelligence. Served with USMC, Vietnam. Recipient Clandestine Svc. Medallion, CIA, Dir. Ctrl. Intelligence medal, Disting. Career Intelligence medal, Presdl. Order of Merit, Govt. of Poland. Office: Ctrl Intelligence Agency Office of Dir Nat Clandestine Svc c/o Office Pub Affairs Washington DC 20250*

SULKIN, HOWARD ALLEN, academic administrator; b. Detroit, Aug. 19, 1941; s. Lewis and Vivian P. (Mandel) S.; m. Constance Annette Adler, Aug. 4, 1963; children— Seth R., Randall K. PhB, Wayne State U., 1963; MBA, U. Chgo., 1965, PhD, 1969; LHD (hon.), De Paul U., 1990. Dir. program rsch., indsl. rels. ctr. U. Chgo., 1964-72; dean Sch. for New Learning, De Paul U., Chgo., 1972-77; v.p. De Paul U., Chgo., 1977-84; pres. Spertus Inst. Jewish Studies, Chgo., 1984—2009, chancelor, 2009—, CEO. St. Paul's vis. prof. Rikkyo U., Tokyo, 1970—; cons., evaluator North Ctrl. Assn., Chgo., 1975—. Contbr. articles to profl. jours. Sec.-treas. Grant Park Cultural and Ednl. Cmty., Chgo., 1984—; bd. dirs. Chgo. Sinai Congregation, 1972—, pres., 1980-83; bd. dirs. Grant Park Conservancy, Legacy Charter Sch., Parliament of World's Religions, 1989—, chmn., 1989-; mem. exec. com. Loop Alliance, bd. dirs. Hegeler Carus Found., 2001-. Mem.: Aldert Pick Found., The Standard. Office: Spertus Inst of Jewish Studies 610 S Michigan Ave Chicago IL 60605-1901

SULKOWSKI, HUBERTUS VICTOR, lawyer; b. Csikszereda, Hungary, Apr. 1, 1943; arrived in U.S., 1957; s. Alfred Viktor and Ingeborg (Brumowski) S.; m. Christine Barbara Joosten, July 26, 1969 (div. Jan. 6, 1994); m. Evelyne Marie-France Sylvie Meunier, Dec. 9, 2000; children: Nikolas Alexander, Erica Elizabeth, Christopher Victor. BA, Trinity Coll., Hartford, Conn., 1966; JD, Boston Coll., 1969. Bar: N.Y., U.S. Supreme Ct.; avocat Paris Bar. Assoc. Jackson Nash, NYC, 1969-71, Mendes & Mount, NYC, 1971-72; ptnr. Donovan Leisure, NYC, 1984-87; assoc. Shearman & Sterling, NYC, 1972-84, ptnr., 1987—, founder, mng. ptnr. Budapest office, 1991-97, mng. ptnr. Paris office, 1992—97. Bd. dirs. Rhodia, 1999—. Mem. The Univ. Club of N.Y.C., Cercle d l'Union Interaliée (Paris), Hungarian Knights of Malta. Roman Catholic. Office: Shearman & Sterling 114 Avenue des Champs-Elysees 75008 Paris France Office Phone: 011 33 1 53 89 70 00. Business E-Mail: hsulkowski@shearman.com.

SULL, WONHEE, telecommunications industry executive; BS, Seoul Nat. U.; MS in Computer Sci. and Engring., U. Mich.; PhD in Elec. and Computer Engring., Purdue U. Sr. mem. tech. staff Microelectronics and Computer Tech. Corp.; sr. engr. GE Med. Sys.; asst. rsch. prof. U. Miami, Fla.; dir. Platform R&D Ctr., SK Telecom, Republic of Korea, v.p.; pres., COO HELIO LLC (formerly SK-EarthLink), Westwood, Calif., 2005—08, bd. dirs., CEO, 2008—. Office: HELIO LLC 10960 Wilshire Blvd Ste 600 Westwood CA 90024

SULLAM, JOANNE D., environmental artist; d. T and Jo Helfert; life ptnr. A Martinez; children: Melissa J, Julianne S. Student, Sch. Visual Arts, NYC, 1981—85. Artist, NY. Wildlife-nature art, (Excellence Visual Art Alliance award, Muttontown, NY, 1999). Project grant, The LI Arts Coun., 2002—03. Mem.: Woodstock Artists Assn. & Mus. Woodstock, NY. Personal E-mail: daydreams58@hotmail.com.

SULLEBARGER, JOHN THOMPSON, internist, cardiologist, educator; b. Plainfield, NJ, May 2, 1957; s. Franklyn Jackson and Joanne Abbott (Aspinall) S.; m. Lorrie Jeanne Miller, June 14, 1980; children: Jeffrey Franklyn, Melissa Jeanne. Student, U. Mainz, 1977; AB, Dartmouth Coll., 1979; MD, Johns Hopkins U., 1983. Intern U. Rochester, NY, 1983-84, resident in medicine, 1984-86, fellow in cardiology, 1986-89, from sr. instr. to asst. prof., 1989-92; asst. prof. U. South Fla., Tampa, 1992-96, assoc. prof., 1997-99; dir. CCU Tampa Gen. Hosp., 1997—; clin. assoc. prof. U. South Fla., Tampa, 2004—. Dir. Cardiac Catheterization Lab. James Haley VA Hosp., Tampa, 1992—99; dir. interventional cardiology U. South Fla., 1994—99; attending physician Strong Meml. Hosp., Rochester, 1989—92; pres. Fla. Cardiovascular Inst., 2004—; chief cardiology Tampa Gen. Hosp., 2008—. Author: (with others) book chapters; contrb. articles to profl. jours. Chmn. Bd. Christian Svc., 1st Bapt. Ch., Rochester, 1991-92. Fellow ACP, 1992, Am. Coll. of Cardiology, 1991, Counc. on Clin. Cardiology of Am. Heart Assn., 1991, N.Y. Cardiological Soc., 1992. Fellow ACP, Soc. Cardiac Angiography and Interventions, Am. Coll. Cardiology, N.Y. Cardiol. Soc.; mem. Am. Heart Assn. (fellow coun. on clin. cardiology), Tampa Internat. Heart Found. (founder 2004-). Avocation: music. Office: 509 S Armenia Ste 200 Tampa FL 33609 Office Phone: 813-353-1515.

SULLENBARGER, DANIEL JAMES, oil industry executive, lawyer; b. Greenville, Ohio, Apr. 25, 1951; s. James Lee and Doris Evelyn (Roark) S.; m. Lauren Jean Drehs, Aug. 10, 1974; children: Jennifer Ann, Erin Michelle, Kylie Marie. BA, Bowling Green State U., 1973; JD, Ohio No. U., 1976. Bar: Ohio 1976, U.S. Dist. Ct. (no. dist.) Ohio 1977, U.S. Ct. Appeals (7th cir.) 1978, U.S. Ct. Appeals (5th cir.) 1985, Tex. 1985. Atty. pipeline div. Marathon Oil Corp., Findlay, Ohio, 1976-78, atty. mktg. div., 1978-80, legal adviser prodn. div. London, 1980-84, atty. prodn. div. Houston, 1984-86, sr. counsel refining, mktg., supply, transp. and adminstrn., 1986-88, sr. counsel offshore and Gulf Coast prodn., 1988-90, sr. counsel adminstrn. and spl. projects, 1990-91, gen. atty. refining, mktg. supply and transp. Findlay, Ohio, 1991—94, group counsel-Worldwide Exploration & Production Houston, 1994—98, v.p. Human Resources and Environment, 1998—2000, v.p. Health, Environment, Safety, 2000—05, v.p. corp. responsibility, 2005—08, v.p. corp. compliance & ethics, 2008—. Mem. gen. com. Am. Petroleum Inst.; chmn. exec. com. Internat. Petroleum Ind. Environ. Conservation Assn. Bd. dirs. Hancock County Mental Health Assn., Findlay, 1976-80; chmn. City of Findlay Bd. of Zoning Appeals, 1978-80; mem. exec. com. Houston Clean City Commn. Recipient awards for Excellence Lawyer's Coop. Pub. Co., 1975,76. Mem. ABA, Ohio State Bar Assn., Tex. State Bar Assn., Houston Bar Assn. Avocation: recreational and competitive running. Office: Marathon Oil Corp 5555 San Felipe Rd Houston TX 77056*

SULLENBERGER, CHESLEY BURNETT, III, (SULLY SULLENBERGER), pilot, airline safety consulting company executive; b. Denison, Tex., Jan. 23, 1951; s. Chesley Burnett and Barbara Sullenberger; m. Lorrie Sullenberger; 2 children. BS in Psychology, USAF Acad., Colo., 1973; MS in Indsl. Psychology, Purdue U., West Lafayette, Ind., 1973; MPA, U. No. Colo., Greenley, 1979. Cert. Flight Instr. (Airplane Single and Multi-Engine, Glider, Instrument Airplane), Flight Engr. (Turbojet Powered), Ground Instr. (Advanced and Instrument). Fighter F-4 pilot, capt. USAF, 1973—80; pilot, capt. on Airbus A319/320/321 US Airways, 1980—; founder, pres., CEO Safety Reliability Methods, Inc. (SRM), 2007—. Panel mem. High Reliability Orgn. Internat. Conf., Deauville, France, 2007; participated in several USAF and Nat. Transportation Safety Bd. accident investigations; safety and reliability cons. and spkr. Co-author (with Jeffrey Zaslow): Highest Duty: My Search for What Really Matters, 2009. Recipient Outstanding Cadet in Airmanship award, 1973; co-recipient (with crew of 1549) Key to NYC, 2009; named one of The World's Most Influential People, TIME mag., 2009; vis. scholar, Ctr. for Catastrophic Risk Mgmt., U. Calif. Berkeley. Mem.: Air Line Pilots Assn. (served as local air safety chmn., mem. noise abatement com., rep. during negotiations leading to adoptions of adv. circular 91-53). Key achievements and contributions with US Airways: served as Check Airman, supervising and instructing other airline pilots upgrading from First Officer to Captain and to different aircraft. Recognized as one of best Check Airman/Line Instructors; Spearheaded efforts to improve maintenance efforts of MD-80 fleet, focusing on reliability of air conditioning systems. Helped identify and reduce number of faulty air conditioning systems from 24 to zero on fleet. Received formal commendation from MD-80 Fleet Manager for work on this project; Instrumental in delivering better, more competitive passenger service by presenting and receiving approval for suggestion to apply for and receive lower-than-standard takeoff minima in Canada; Realized operational safety and efficiency improvements by providing numerous suggestions that improved company gate charts that pilots use taxiing to/from airport gates; Enhancing situational awareness and safety by incorporating entry/exit taxiways on airport charts used by pilots to transition from gate areas to runways, working closely with airline vendor that provides pilot charts; Improving efficiency and reliability of air service in National Airspace System. Identified hundreds of FAA Instrument Landing System procedures used by all operators to land at airports that utilized incorrect visibility minima and collaborated with chart vendor to correct them; Selected as airline pilot representative to work with vendor that provides Flight Management System (FMS) for several of airline's aircraft to improve software and hardware that positively impacted operational safety and efficiency of airline operations. FMS improvements led to savings in both time and money (1% savings in fuel costs); Driving force behind development of airline's first CRM course and presenting course to hundreds of USAirways pilots. Significantly reduced number of operational incidents and realized reduction in number of altitude deviations. Course focuses on multidisciplinary approach involving leadership, communication, decision-making and error management-airline went from 5 major accidents to zero; Served as NASA Aviation Safety Research Consultant evaluating cockpit systems for reducing runway incursions. Co-authored published technical paper on crew decision-making errors in aviation working with NASA Ames researchers which provided blueprint for safer pilot training, procedures and standardization; Instrumental in guiding all aviation groups to adopt safer, more uniform standard with respect to departure procedures that ultimately was incorporated into new FAA standard for all operators; Teamed with SFO to adopt new airport taxiway signage that met latest FAA standards while improving safety and operational efficiency; Played integral role working with ATA, FAA, NATCA and NTSB to improve operations and investigate several major airline accidents. As member of ALPA National Noise Abatement Committee, directly involved in development of FAA Advisory Circular 91-53 which set new standard for aircraft noise abatement departure procedures industry-wide and improved safety and standardization; Key contributor/member of National Transportation Safety Board Survival Factors Group during investigation of major airline accident at LAX, leading to improved airline procedures and training for emergency evacuations of aircraft; Participated in joint FAA/ALPA All-Weather Flying Committee simulator study of Head-Up-Display (HUD) symbology effectiveness during low visibility landings; Widely recognized as pilot advocate and champion of high professional standards that consistently result in safer, smoother and more efficient flights. Employ leadership-by-example approach in the facilitation of CRM courses, teaching captains to be more effective leaders and make better decisions; Pilot from US Airways Flight 1549 that safely landed in the Hudson River in NYC on January 15th, 2009 saving all 155 passengers. Office Phone: 925-997-9332. Office Fax: 925-648-1166. E-mail: sully@safetyreliability.com.*

SULLENDER, JOY SHARON, retired elementary school educator; b. Bloomington, Ind., Apr. 9, 1932; d. Fred Laymond and Edith (Parrish) Medaris; m. Sullender Charles E. (dec.) BS, Ind. U., 1959, MS, 1965; postgrad., Ind. U./Purdue U., Indpls., 1991. Cert. tchr. elem. edn. 1-8. Tchr. Monroe Sch., Salem, Ind., 1952-55, Pekin (Ind.) Sch., 1955-61, Highland Park (Ill.) Sch., 1961-62, George Julian Sch. #57, Indpls., 1962—2000; ret., 2000. Mem. prin.'s adv. coun. Indpls. Pub. Schs., 1985-95, supts. adv. coun., 1982-90; state mentor student tchrs., 1969—. Author col.: Let's Be Informed, 1993-95. Class sponsor Best Friends, Indpls., 1990—; vol. Toys for Foster Children, Indpls., 1991—; workshop presenter Alpha Epsilon State, Anderson, South Bend, 1994, 95. NSF grantee, 1971. Mem. PTA (tchr. rep. 1993-95), Ind. Sch. Women's Club (v.p. 1989-91, pres. 1992-94), Woman's Dept. Club (v.p. 2002—, corr. sec. 2007-), Omega Chpt. Alpha Upsilon State (pres. 1978-80, state com. 1989—, state corr. sec. 1997-99, historian 2008-). Home: 1310 N Bazil Ave Indianapolis IN 46219-4244

SULLIVAN, ALFRED DEWITT, academic administrator; b. New Orleans, Feb. 2, 1942; s. Dewitt Walter and Natalie (Alford) Sullivan; m. Marilyn Janie Hewitt, Sept. 1, 1962 (div. May 1989); children: Alan, Sean; m. Dorothy Madeleine Hess, Apr. 1993. BS, La. State U., 1964, MS, 1966; PhD, U. Ga., 1969. Asst. prof. Va. Poly. Inst. and State U., Blacksburg, 1969—73; assoc. prof., then prof. Miss. State U., Starkville, 1973—88; dir. Sch. Forest Resources Pa. State U., University Park, 1988—93; dean coll. natural resources U. Minn., St. Paul, 1993—2002, vice provost academic programs & facilities Mpls., 2002—06, spl. asst. to pres., 2006—. Assoc. Danforth Found., 1981. Contbr. articles to profl. jours. Fellow, Am. Coun. Edn., 1987—88, NDEA fellow, U. Ga., 1966—69. Mem.: Soc. Am. Foresters. Office: U Minn 234 MorH 0262 100 Church St SE Minneapolis MN 55455 Office Phone: 612-626-3838. E-mail: sulli031@umn.edu.

SULLIVAN, AMANDA, science educator; d. Harold and Debra Davis; m. Rashard Sullivan, Aug. 6, 2005. PhD in Kinesiology, U. Ark., Fayetteville, 2006. Grad. tchg. asst. U. Ark., 2004—06; asst. prof. U. Evansville, Ind., 2007—. Mem.: Ind. AHPERD (adaptive phys. edn. com. mem. 2007—).

SULLIVAN, ANDREW MICHAEL, online journalist, editor, news blogger; b. South Godstone, Surrey, Eng., Aug. 10, 1963; m. Aaron Tone, Aug. 27, 2007. BA, Magdalen Coll., Oxford; MPA, Harvard U. John F. Kennedy Sch. Govt., 1986, PhD, 1990. Editl. writer, intern The Daily Telegraph, London; intern The New Republic, 1986, assoc. editor, then dep. editor, 1990, acting editor, 1991, editor, 1991—96; faculty mem. govt. dept. Harvard John F. Kennedy Sch. Govt., 1987; blogger, editor andrewsullivan.com, 2000—, The Daily Dish, 2001; columnist TIME Mag., 2000—07; blog writer time.blogs.com, 2006—07; sr. editor and blogger Atlantic Monthly (TheAtlantic.com), 2007—. Testimony before Congress on Defense of Marriage Act, 1996; freelance writer Wall St. Jour., Washington Post, Daily Telegraph, Esquire, NY Mag. Author: Virtually Normal: An Argument About Homosexuality, 1995, Love Undetectable: Notes on Friendship, Sex, and Survival, 1998, Same-Sex Marriage: Pro and Con, 2004, The Conservative Soul: How We Lost It, How to Get It Back (Hardcover), 2006, Intimations Pursued: The Voice of Practice in the Conversation of Michael Oakeshott, 2007, (essays) The Politics of Homosexuality, 1993, What's So Bad About Hate, 1999; contbg. writer, columnist NY Times Mag., regular contbr. NY Times Book Review, weekly columnist London Sunday Times, contbg. columnist The Advocate, LA, Calif., contbg. editor NY Sun, regular guest Real Time with Bill Maher, Chris Matthews Show, guest appearances Nightline, Face the Nation, Meet the Press, Crossfire, Hardball, The O'Reilly Factor, Larry King Show, Reliable Sources, Hannity and Colmes, and many others. Named Editor of Yr., Adweek Mag., 1996; named one of The 50 Most Powerful People in DC, GQ mag., 2007, The 25 Most Influential Liberals in US Media, Forbes mag., 2009; Harkness Fellowship, Harvard John F. Kennedy Sch. Govt., 1984. Office: 180 W 20th St #12 T New York NY 10011 also: Atlantic Monthly Group The Watergate 600 NH Ave NW Washington DC 20037 Office Phone: 202-508-4444, 212-406-2000, 212-522-1212. Office Fax: 202-628-9383, 212-522-0003. E-mail: andrewmsullivan@aol.com, andrew@andrewsullivan.com.*

SULLIVAN, AUSTIN PADRAIC, JR., retired diversified food company executive; b. Washington, June 26, 1940; s. Austin P. and Janet Lay (Patterson) Sullivan; m. Judith Ann Raab, June 1, 1968 (dec. Oct. 1995); children: Austin P. III, Amanda, Alexander; m. Marie Elise de Golian, Aug. 1, 1997 (dec. Nov. 2007); stepchildren: Lauren Gibbons, Georgia Gibbons, Samuel Gibbons. BA cum laude, Princeton U., 1964. Spl. asst. to dep. dir. N.J. Office Econ. Opportunity, Trenton, NJ, 1956—66; prof. staff mem. Com. on Edn. and Labor, U.S. Ho. of Rep., Washington, 1967—71, legis. dir., 1971—76; dir. govt. relations Gen. Mills, Inc., Mpls., 1976—78, v.p., corp. dir. govt. rels., 1978—79, v.p. pub. affairs, 1979—93, v.p. corp. comm. and pub. affairs, 1993—94, sr. v.p. corp. rels., 1994—2005; ret., 2005. Lectr. fed. labor market policies Harvard U., Mass., 1972—76, Boston U., 1972—76. Mem. Nat. Commn. on Employment and Tng., 1979—81, U.S. Sec. Agr. Adv. Com. on Agrl. Biotech., 2000—03; chmn. Governor's Coun. on Employment and Tng., 1976—82; bd. dir., exec. com. Urban Coalition Mpls., 1978—80, Guthrie Theatre, Mpls., 1978—84, Minn. Citizens for the Arts, 1980—83; co chmn. Governor's Commn. on Dislocated Workers, Minn., 1988—89; chmn. Pub. Affairs Coun., 1993—94; bd. dir. Minn. C. of C., 1993—99; trustee Minn. Pub. Radio, 1999—; bd. advisors Dem. Leadership Coun., 1986—. Served in USMC, 1957—59. Recipient Eleanor Roosevelt Fellow in Interracial Rels., 1964—65. Mem.: Grocery Mfr. Assn. (govt. affairs coun. 1991—2004, chmn. biotech. task force 1999—2004), Coun. of Pub. Affairs Exec. (chmn. 1989—90), Medica (bd. dir. 2001—), Greater Mpls. C. of C. (exec. com. 1980—86, 1990—93, bd. dir.), Mpls. Club (bd. governor's 2001—). Home: 17830 County Rd 6 Minneapolis MN 55447-2905 Office: Ste 252 700 Twelve Oaks Center Dr Wayzata MN 55391 Personal E-mail: austinsullivan@gmail.com.

SULLIVAN, BARRY, lawyer, educator; b. Newburyport, Mass., Jan. 11, 1949; s. George Arnold and Dorothy Bennett (Furbush) S.; m. Winnifred Mary Fallers, June 14, 1975; children: George Arnold, Lloyd Ashton. AB cum laude, Middlebury Coll., 1970; JD, U. Chgo., 1974. Bar: Mass. 1975, Ill. 1975, Va. 1995, US Dist. Ct. (no. dist.) Ill. 1976, US Ct. Appeals (7th cir.) 1976, US Ct. Appeals (10th cir.) 1977, US Supreme Ct. 1978, US Ct. Appeals (11th cir.) 1986, US Ct. Appeals (5th and 9th cirs.) 1987, US Ct. Appeals (fed. cir.) 1993, US Ct. Appeals (DC cir.) 1994, US Ct. Appeals (4th cir.) 1997, US Ct. Appeals (2d and 3d cirs.) 2002, US Ct. Appeals (6th and 8th cirs.) 2004, US Dist. Ct. (ctrl. dist.) Ill. 2006. Law clk. to judge John Minor Wisdom U.S. Ct. Appeals (5th cir.), New Orleans, 1974-75; assoc. Jenner & Block, Chgo., 1975-80; asst. to solicitor gen. of U.S. U.S. Dept. of Justice, Washington, 1980-81; ptnr. Jenner & Block, Chgo., 1981—94, 2001—09; prof. law Washington and Lee U., Lexington, Va., 1994-2001, dean, 1994-99, v.p., 1998-99; Fulbright prof. U. Warsaw, Poland, 2000—01; lectr. in law U. Chgo., 2001—02; spl. asst. state's atty. Cook County, Ill., 2002—03. Vis. fellow Queen Mary and Westfield Coll., U. London, 2001; spl. asst. atty. gen. State of Ill., 1989—90; lectr. in law Loyola U., Chgo., 1978—79, Cooney & Conway chair and prof. law, 2009—; adj. prof. law Northwestern U., Chgo., 1990—92, 1993—94, vis. prof., 1992—93; vis. prof. Ctr. for Am. law studies U. Warsaw, 2002—03, 2005; sr. lectr. Irving B. Harris Grad. Sch. Pub. Policy, U. Chgo., 2005—; Jessica Swift Meml. lectr. constl. law Middlebury Coll., 1991; Rufus Monroe and Sophie Payne lectr. U. Mo., Columbia, 2003; Charles L. Ihlenfeld lectr. pub. policy and ethics W.Va. U., 2005. Assoc. editor U. Chgo. Law Rev., 1973-74; mem. editl. bd. Dublin U. Law Jour., 2004-; contbr. articles to profl. jours. Mem. nat. adv. bd. Ctr. for Religion, The Professions, and The Pub., U. Mo., Columbia, 2003—; trustee Cath. Theol. Union at Chgo., 1993—2003, trustee emeritus, 2003—; mem. vis. com. Irving B. Harris Grad. Sch. Public Policy Studies U. Chgo., 2001—, U. Chgo. Divinity Sch., 1987—2001; mem. adv. panel Fulbright Sr. Specialist Program, 2001—04; mem. adv. bd. Internat. Human Rights Law Inst. DePaul U., 2003—; trustee U. Chgo. Court Theatre, 2003—05; mem. bd. visitors Southern Ill. U. Sch. Law, 2006—09; mem. adv. bd. Project DV-Leap, George Washington U. Law. Sch., 2006—, Cmty. Renewal Soc. Chgo., 2006—. Fellow, Woodrow Wilson Found., 1970; scholar, Yeats Soc., 1968; Nat. Honor scholar, Univ. Chgo., 1970—74. Fellow Am. Bar Found., Phi Beta Kappa; mem. ABA (chmn. coord. com. on AIDS 1988—94, standing com. on amicus curiae briefs 1990—97, coun. sect. individual rights and responsibilities 1993—98, sect. legal edn. com. on law sch. adminstrn. 1994—98, chair sect. legal edn. com. on professionalism 1999—2000, co-chair sect. individual rights/responsibilities com. amicus briefs 2002—04, mem. sect. legal edn. stds. rev. com. 2002—05, co-chair sect. individual rights/responsibilities com. bill rights 2002—07, mem. standing com. amicus curiae briefs 2004-07, mem. coun. sect. legal edn. 2006-09, mem. standing com. profl. discipline, 2007—), Lawyers Club Chgo., Supreme Ct. Hist Soc. (Ill. membership chair 2002—03), Ill. State Bar Assn., Appellate Lawyers Assn., Am. Law Inst., Bar Assn. 7th Fed. Cir. (vice chmn. adminstrn. justice com. 1985—86), Va. State Bar (chair sec. on edn. lawyers 1998—99) Democrat. Roman Catholic. Home: 5555 S Everett Apt A1-2 Chicago IL 60637 Office: Loyola Univ Chgo Sch Law 25 E Pearson St Chicago IL 60611

SULLIVAN, BRENDAN PAUL, state official, consultant, communications educator; b. Boston, Apr. 20, 1949; s. Francis Joseph and Margaret Rita (McDonough) S.; m. Debra Marie Fitzgerald, Feb. 11, 1988; children: Erin, Patrick. BS, Boston State Coll., 1970; MA in Comms., Fairfield U., 1976; MBA, Boston Coll., 1995. Tchr. Boston Pub. Schs., 1970-81; mgr. adminstrn. Mass. State Lottery, Braintree, 1981-91; asst. clk.-magistrate Commonwealth of Mass. Superior Ct., Brockton, 1993—. Adj. prof. Massasoit C.C., Brockton, 1996—, mem. mediation adv. bd., 1999—; sr. lectr. Northeastern U., Boston, 2009-. Mem. Plymouth County Dem. League, Abington, Mass., 2000—. Mem.: Furnace Brook Golf Club (gov. 1976—). Democrat. Roman Catholic. Avocations: golf, fishing, coaching baseball. Home: 220 Plymouth Ave Quincy MA 02169 Office: 72 Belmont St Brockton MA 02301-5248 Office Phone: 508-583-8250 377. E-mail: brensullivan@comcast.net.

SULLIVAN, BRENDAN V., JR., lawyer; b. Providence, Mar. 11, 1942; AB, Georgetown U., 1964, JD, 1967. Bar: RI 1967, DC 1970, US Dist. Ct. DC 1970, US Ct. Appeals (DC cir.) 1970, US Supreme Ct. 1972, US Dist. Ct. Md. 1974, US Ct. Appeals (3d cir.) 1979, US Ct. Appeals (4th cir.) 1981, US Ct. Appeals (6th cir.) 1991, US Ct. Appeals (9th cir.) 1996, US Ct. Fed. Claims 1998, US Ct. Appeals (fed. cir.) 2003, US Ct. Appeals (2d cir.) 2007. Mem. Williams & Connolly LLP, Washington. Lectr. Practicing Law Inst., 1981—, Md. Inst. for Continuing Profl. Edn. of Lawyers, Inc., 1979—, D.C. Criminal Practice Inst., 1975-81. Author: Grand Jury Proceedings, 1981, Techniques for Dealing with Pending Criminal Charges or Criminal Investigations, 1983, White Collar Criminal Practice Grand Jury, 1985. Capt. US Army, 1968—69. Named one of 75 Best Lawyers In Washington, Washingtonian mag., 2002, 100 Most Influential Lawyers, Nat. Law Jour., 2006. Fellow Am. Coll. Trial Lawyers; mem. ABA, R.I. Bar Assn., D.C. Bar. Office: Williams & Connolly LLP 725 12th St NW Washington DC 20005-5901 Office Phone: 202-434-5800.

SULLIVAN, CHARLES, dean, educator, author; b. Boston, May 27, 1933; s. Charles Thomas and Marion Veronica (Donahue) S.; divorced; children: Charles Fulford, John Driscoll, Catherine Page; m. Gail McNealy Greene, Feb. 19, 2008. BA in English, Swarthmore Coll., 1955; MA, NYU, 1968, PhD in Social Psychology, 1973; MPA, Pa. State U., 1978. Predoctoral fellow NYU, 1964-68; postdoctoral fellow Ednl. Testing Svc., Princeton, NJ, 1973-74; asst. prof. psychology Ursinus Coll., Collegeville, Pa., 1973-78; mgmt. cons., 1978-86; adj. prof. Pa. State U., Radnor, Pa., 1978-80; prof., head dept. pub. adminstrn., dir. student svcs. Southeastern U., Washington, 1986-89; asst. dean Grad. Sch. Arts and Scis. Georgetown U., Washington, 1989-92, assoc. dean Grad. Sch. Arts and Scis., 1992-97, professorial lectr., dept. psychology, 1994-95; exec. dir. Doylestown Found., Doylestown, Pa., 1958-73; assoc. dean, prof. Coll. Profl. Studies U. San Francisco, 1997-98. Adj. prof. social and behavioral scis. U. Md., 1984-96; lectr., spkr. on lit. and art Cooper-Hewitt Mus., N.Y.C., Nat. Soc. Arts and Letters, Washington, Martin Luther King Jr. Libr., Washington, Met. Mus. Art, N.Y.C., Smithsonian Instn., Washington, Children's Book Fair, N.Y.C., Nat. Mus. Women in Arts, Lombardi Cancer Rsch. Ctr., Georgetown U., Arts Club of Washington, Phillips Collection, Corcoran Gallery of Art, U. San Francisco Multicultural Lit. Program, Nat. Mus. Am. History, New Coll. of Calif., others, various apptd. & elected positions in local govt., Bucks County, Pa., 1967-1978. Author: Alphabet Animals, 1991, The Lover in Winter, 1991, Numbers at Play, 1992, Circus, 1992, Cowboys, 1993, A Woman of A Certain Age, 1994, Out of Love, 1996, American Folk, 1998, In a Certain Place, 1999, The Lovers' Companion, 2002; editor: America in Poetry, 1988, 2d edit., 1992, 3d edit., 1996, Imaginary Gardens, 1989, Ireland in Poetry, 1990, Children of Promise, 1991, 2d edit., 2001, Loving, 1992, American Beauties, 1993, Here Is My Kingdom, 1994, Fathers and Children, 1995, Imaginary Animals, 1996, Dancing in the Wind, 2002; contbr. poems in various periodicals. Trustee Folger Poetry Bd., 1988-92; Nat. Soc. Arts and Letters, 1992-94, 2002-04, Am. Acad. Liberal Edn., 1995—, San Francisco Art Inst., 2000-05, Pacific Ctr. for Photog. Arts, 2003—05; pres. Am. Found. Arts, 1995—; collectors com. Nat. Gallery Art, Washington, 1998-2006; mem. Dir.'s Cir., San Francisco Mus. Modern Art, 1998-2006. Recipient Best Books for Young Adults award, Young Adult Libr. Svcs. Assn., 1992, 1998, Best Books for Teens award, N.Y. Pub. Libr., 1992, 1993. Mem.: Inverness Yacht Club, The Family Club, Cosmos Club. Personal E-mail: artsfound@earthlink.net. Business E-Mail: kezaco@earthlink.net.

SULLIVAN, CHRISTOPHER DAVID, real estate broker, attorney; b. NYC, Oct. 6, 1966; m. Anne Marie Houlihan, Sept. 3, 1966. JD, U. of the Pacific, 1997. Bar: Nev. 2002, Utah 1998. Mng. ptnr. Sullivan/Brown The Law Firm, Las Vegas, Nev., 2004—; broker, owner Chris Sullivan Realty, Las Vegas, 2005—. Mem. Urban Land Inst., Las Vegas, 2004—. Bd. dirs. Project Sunshine, Las Vegas, 2003—06. Mem.: Clark County Bar Assn., State Bar of Utah (assoc.), State Bar of Nev. (assoc.). Office: Sullivan-Brown 332 S Jones Blvd Las Vegas NV 89107 Office Fax: 702-567-0116. E-mail: thisisyourleader@yahoo.com.

SULLIVAN, COLLEEN ANNE, anesthesiologist, educator; b. Lucknow, India, Feb. 11, 1937; arrived in U.S., 1961; d. Douglas George and Nancy Irene (MacLeod) Sullivan; m. Alexander Walter Gotta, July 17, 1965; 1 child, Nancy Colleen Gotta. MB, ChB, U. St. Andrews, Scotland, 1961. Diplomate Am. Bd. Anesthesiology, Am. Coll. Anesthesiologists. Rotating intern Nassau Hosp. (now Winthrop U. Hosp.), Mineola, N.Y., 1961-62; clin. instr. Cornell U., NYC, 1962-64; resident in anesthesiology N.Y. Hosp./Cornell U., 1962-64; fellow in anesthesiology Meml. Sloan-Kettering Cancer Ctr., NYC, 1964-67, asst. prof. Cornell U. Med. Coll., 1978-79; assoc. dir. anesthesia St. Mary's Hosp.-Cath. Med. Ctr., Bklyn., 1968-78; clin. assoc. prof. SUNY, Bklyn., 1979-90, clin. dir. anesthesia, 1990-93, clin. prof. anesthesiology, 1990-97. Clin. dir. anesthesia Kings County Hosp., Bklyn., 1983—90, med. dir. ambulatory surg. unit, 1993—97. Contbr. chapters to books, articles to profl. jours. Mem.: N.Y. State Soc. Anesthesiologists (mem. ho. of dels. 1983—97, asst. editor Sphere 1990—95, mem. com. sci. program 1990—97), Woman's Club Great Neck (bd. dirs. 2005). Republican. Roman Catholic. Avocations: reading, cooking. Personal E-mail: colleenag@optonline.net.

SULLIVAN, CONNIE CASTLEBERRY, artist; b. Cin., Jan. 8, 1934; d. John Porter and Constance (Alf) Castleberry; m. John J. Sullivan, June 6, 1959; children: Deirdre Kelly, Margaret Graham. BA, Manhattanville Coll., 1957. Spl. lectr. Cin. Contemporary Art Ctr., 1984, Toledo Friends of Photography, 1991, U. Ky. Art Mus., 1993, Dennison U. Sch. Art, 1993, El Instituto de Estudios Norte Americanos, Barcelona, 1994, Ctr. for Photography, Bombay, India, 1997, Miami U. Art Mus., Oxford, Ohio, 1998, Alice and Harris K. Weston Gallery, Aronoff Ctr. for the Arts, Cin., 2000, Columbus Mus. Art, Ohio, 2001, Mus. Fine Arts St. Petersburg, Fla., 2002. One-woman shows include Contemporary Art Ctr. Cleve., 1982, Cin. Contemporary Arts Ctr., 1983, Fogg Art Mus., Cambridge, Mass., 1983, 90, Neikrug Gallery, N.Y.C., 1984, Camden Arts Ctr., London, 1987, Evanston Art Ctr., Chgo., 1987, Silver Image Gallery Ohio State U., Columbus, 1988, Jean-Pierre Lambert Galerie, Paris, 1988, 96, David Winton Bell Gallery, Brown U., Providence, 1989, Toni Burckhead Gallery, Cin., 1989, Rochester Inst. Tech., 1991, Fotomus. im Münchner Stadtmus., Munich, 1992, U. Ky. Art Mus., Lexington, 1993, Internat. Photography Hall, Kirkpatrick Mus. complex, Oklahoma City, 1993, Institut d'Estudios Fotografics de Catalunya, Barcelona, Spain, 1994, Cheekwood Art Mus., Nashville, 1994, Museo Damy di Fotografia Contemporanea, Brescia, Italy, 1995, Photography Gallery U. Notre Dame, Ind., 1995, Louisville Visual Art Assoc., Watertower, Louisville, KY, 1995, Jean-Pierre Lambert Galarie, 1996, Museo Damy, Milan, 1997, Ctr. for Photography, Bombay, India, 1997, Miami U. Art Mus., Oxford, Ohio, 1998, Aronoff Ctr. for the Arts, Cin., 2000, Foto Fest, Houston, 2000, Visual Studies Workshop Gall. Rochester, NY, 2000, NuNatte Duo Centre Photography, OP Photo Gall., Hong Kong, 2000, Columbus Mus. Art, 2001, Mus. Fine Art, St. Petersburg, Fla., 2002; exhibited in numerous group shows including Robert Klein Gallery, Boston, 1981, Cin. Art Mus., 1981, 84, 85, 93, Witkin Gallery, N.Y.C., 1984, Milw. Art Mus., 1986, Dayton (Ohio) Art Inst., 1987, J.B. Speed Art Mus., Louisville, 1988, Trisolini Gallery Ohio U., 1989, Ohio U., Athens, 1989, Centre Nat. Photographie, Paris, 1989, Cleve. Ctr. for Contemporary Art, 1991, Tampa Mus. Art, 1991, 93, Images Gallery, 1991, Dayton Art Inst./Mus. Contemporary Art Wright State U., Dayton, 1992, Bowling Green State U. Sch Art, 1992, Carnegie Arts Ctr., Covington, Ky., 1993, POLK Mus. Art, Lakeland, Fla., 1993, Tampa (Fla.) Mus. Art, 1993, Adams Landing Fine Art Ctr., Cin., 1995, Checkwood Mus. Art, Nashville, 1995, Photo Forum Gallery, 1995, 96, Jean-Pierre Galerie, 1996, Soros Ctr. Contemporary Art, Kiev, Ukraine, 1996, Dom Khudozhnikiv, Kharkiv, Ukraine, 1996, Wolf Photographic Galleries, Cin., 1996, Columbus Mus. Art, 1996, Mus. fine Arts, St. Petersburg, Fla., 1997, Louisville Visual Art Assn., Water Tower, 1997, Mus. Damy di Fotografia Contemporanea, Brescia, Italy, 1998, Kharkiv Mcpl. Art Gallery, Kharkiv, Ukraine, 1999, Jean-Pierre Lambert Gallery, Paris, 1999, Huntington (W.Va.) Mus. Art, 2000, Centre Socio-Cultural Galerie Pierre Tal Coat, Hunnebont, France, 2000, Weston Gallery, Aranoff Ctr. Arts, Cin., 2005, Carl Solway Gallery, Cin., 2006, Dorothy and Lawson Reed Gallery, U. Cin., 2007, Light Factory, Charlotte, NC, 2008, New Orleans Mus. Art, 2008; represented in numerous permanent collections Tampa Mus. of Art, Mûnchner Stadt Mus., Munich, Germany, Museo Damy, Brescia, Italy, Ctr. Creative Photography, Tucson, Detroit Inst. Arts, Biblioteque National, Paris, Internat. Photography Hall of Fame and Mus., Kirkpatrick Ctr. Mus. Complex, Okla. City, Nelson Gallery-Atkins Mus., Kansas City, Ctr. for Photography, Bombay, Milw. Art Mus., Mus. Photography Arts, San Diego, Musee Nat. D'Art Modern, Cin. Art Mus., High Mus., Atlanta, Mus. Fine Arts, St. Petersburg, Fla., Centre Georges Pompidou, Paris, Denver Art Mus., Boston Mus. Fine Arts, Stanford U. Mus. Art, Palo Alto, Indpls. Art Mus., New Orleans Mus. Art, Fogg Mus., Cambridge, Mass., numerous others; also pvt. collections; author: Petroglyphs of the Heart, Photographs by Connie Sullivan, 1983; work represented in numerous publs. Trustee Images Ctr. for Fine Photography, Cin., 1986-94. Recipient Juried Show, Toledo Friends Photography, 1986, Best of show, 1988, Images Gallery, 1986, Pres.'s Coun. for Arts award, Manhattanville Coll., 1991, Treasure of the Month award, Mus. Fine Arts St. Petersburg, Fla., 1995; named Hyde Park Living Person of Yr., 1996; grantee Aid to Individual Artists grantee, Summerfair, 1987, travel grantee, Ohio Arts Coun., 1995, 1997, 2000, Artist Projects, 1999; fellow Arts Midwest fellow, NEA, 1989—90; Individual Artist fellowship, Ohio Arts Coun., 2002. Mem. McDowell Soc. Avocations: travel, reading, gardening, music. Home: 1950 Mount Vernon Dr Fort Wright KY 41011 Office Phone: 859-344-6446. Fax: 859-344-8008. E-mail: 1csullivan@fuse.net.

SULLIVAN, DANIEL EDMOND, fundraising executive; b. Alexandria, La., Jan. 22, 1946; s. Edmond James and Ruth (Morris) S.; m. Camille Lafleur Broussand, June 13, 1970; children: Daniel Edmond Jr., Parish Coughlin. Student, La. State U., 1964-67; BS, Northwestern State U., Natchitoches, La., 1968. Field underwriter N.Y. Life Ins. Co., New Orleans, 1968-70; asst. dir. Tulane U. Alumni Fund, New Orleans, 1970-71; assoc. dir. La. Civil Svc. League, New Orleans, 1971-73, exec. v.p., 1973—, also bd. govs., 1973—; bd. of gov. La. Orgn. for Jud. Excellence, 1992—2008, v.p., 1995—2008. Mem. com. La. Joint Legis. Com., 1982-2008, La. Atty. Disciplinary Bd., 2009-; mem. pub. adminstrn. tng. adv. com. U. New Orleans, 1983-90; trustee LA Jud. Excellence Found., 2002-. Bd. dirs. Young Audiences New Orleans, 1974-78. Named Hon. Alumnus Tulane U., 1977. Mem. Nat. Soc. Fund Raising Execs. (cert.), Am. Arbitration Assn. (panel of arbitrators), Royal Soc. St. George, Northwestern State U. Alumni Assn. (bd. dirs. 1974-84), New Orleans Lawn Tennis Club (bd. govs. 1978-80), Stratford Club, Pickwick Club. Republican. Roman Catholic. Home: 919 Short St New Orleans LA 70118-2730 Office: La Civil Svc League 810 Union St Ste 305 New Orleans LA 70112-1426

SULLIVAN, DANIEL F., retired academic administrator, sociologist, educator; b. Jan. 19, 1944; m. Ann H. Sullivan; 3 children. BS in Math., St. Lawrence U., 1965; PhD in Sociology, Columbia U., 1971; DSc (hon.), Clarkson U., 2009. Ctrl. office supr. NY Tel. Co., Syracuse, 1966—67; rsch. assoc. Barnard Coll., 1969—73, instr. sociology, 1970—71; asst. prof. sociology, sr. rsch. assoc. Cornell U., 1974—76; asst. prof. sociology Carleton Coll., 1971—79, assoc. prof. sociology, 1979—86, dean acad. devel. and planning, 1979—81, v.p. for planning and devel., 1981—86, sec. of the coll., 1981—86; pres. Allegheny Coll., Meadville, Pa., 1986—96, prof. sociology, 1986—96; pres., prof. sociology St. Lawrence U., Canton, NY, 1996—2009, pres. emeritus, 2009—. Mem. adv. com. NSF Divsn. Undergrad. Edn., 1991—; chair bd. trustees St. Lawrence Aquarium and Ecol. Ctr., 1998—; bd. dirs. N.Y. Commn. for Ind. Colls. and Univs., mem. exec. com., 2003; trustee Commn. on Ind. Colls. and Univs., 2002—. Co-author: Research on Human Subjects: Problems and Processes of Social Control in Bio-Medical Experimentation, 1973, Applying Market Research in College Admissions, 1983, What Works: Building Natural Science Communities, 1991. Mem.: Western Pa. Hist. Soc. (trustee 1994—), Am. Assn. Colls. and Univs. (bd. dirs. 2003—). Office: St Lawrence Univ 23 Romoda Dr Canton NY 13617 Office Phone: 315-229-5892. Business E-Mail: dsullivan@stlawu.edu.*

SULLIVAN, DANIEL JOSEPH, theater critic; b. Worcester, Mass., Oct. 22, 1935; s. John Daniel and Irene Ann (Flagg) S.; m. Helen Faith Scheid, 1965; children: Margaret Ann, Benjamin, Kathleen. AB, Holy Cross Coll., 1957; postgrad., U. Minn., 1957-59, U. So. Calif., 1964-65, Stanford U., 1978-79. Reporter Worcester Telegram, Mass., 1957, Red Wing Republican Eagle, Minn., 1959, St. Paul Pioneer Press, 1959-61; music and theater critic Mpls. Tribune, 1961—64; comedy writer Dudley Riggs' Brave New Workshop, 1961-64; music, theater reviewer NY Times, 1965—68; theater critic L.A. Times, 1969-90. Dramaturg Eugene O'Neill Theatre Ctr., Waterford, Conn., 1972-73, 93-98; instr. O'Neill Nat. Critics Inst., Waterford, 1977-92, assoc. dir., 1993-98, dir., 1999—; adj. prof. U. Minn., Mpls., 1990—; juror theater panel Nat. Endowment for Arts, 1983; juror Pulitzer Prize for Drama, 1985, 89, 92; pres. LA Drama Critics Circle, 1970-71, Ctr. for Arts Criticism, St. Paul, 1992-95. Mem. Am. Theater Critics Assn. (founding). Office Phone: 612-522-9053. Personal E-mail: sulli008@yahoo.com.

SULLIVAN, DANIEL S., state attorney general; married; 3 children. B in Economics magna cum laude, Harvard U.; JD, MS in Fgn. Svc. cum laude, Georgetown U. Law clk. to Hon. Andrew Kleinfeld US Ct. Appeals (9th cir.); law clk. to Chief Justice Warren Matthews Alaska Supreme Ct.; atty. Perkins Coie, LLP; dir., acting sr. dir. Internat. Econ. Directorate The White House, Washington; asst. sec. for econ. energy and bus. affairs US Dept. State, Washington, 2006—09; atty. gen. State of Alaska, Juneau, 2009—. With USMC, strategic advisor, spl. asst. to comdr. U.S. Ctrl. Command (CENTCOM) USMC, 2005—06. Decorated Def. Meritorious Svc. Medal; recipient Outstanding Svc. award, Nat. Security Coun.; named one of 10 Outstanding Young Americans, U.S. Jr. C. of C. Republican. Office: Office of the Atty Gen PO Box 110300 Diamond Courthouse Juneau AK 99811-0300 Office Phone: 907-465-2133. Office Fax: 907-465-2075. Business E-Mail: attorney.general@alaska.gov.*

SULLIVAN, DENNIS JOSEPH, bishop; b. NYC, Mar. 17, 1945; s. John and Hanorah (Hayes) Sullivan. BA, St. Joseph's Seminary, Dunwoodie, NY, 1967; MDiv, St. Joseph's Seminary, Dunwoodie, 1970. Ordained priest Archdiocese of New York, NY, 1971; pastor St. Elizabeth's Parish, NYC, Saints Philip & James, Bronx, NY, 1976—82, St. Teresa's Parish, NYC, 1982—2003, Saints John & Paul Parish, Larchmont, NY, 2003—04; ordained bishop, 2004; aux. bishop Archdiocese of New York, NY, 2004—, vicar gen. Roman Catholic. Office: Office of the Vicars Gen 19th Fl 1011 1st Ave New York NY 10022 Office Phone: 212-371-1011 ext. 2956. E-mail: chancery@archny.org.

SULLIVAN, DIANE P., lawyer; b. Elizabeth, NJ; BA cum laude, Fairfield U., 1984; JD, U. Pa., 1987. Bar: NJ 1987, U.S. Dist. Ct. (NJ Dist.) 1987, U.S. Dist. Ct. (So. and ea. dist. NY) 2003. Ptnr. mass torts and product liability group Dechert LLP, Princeton, NJ, 2001—. Bd. trustees Trial Attys. NJ, 2000—04; mem. policy com. Dechert LLP; lectr. in field. Named one of Top 40 Litigators Under 40, Nat. Law Jour., 2002, The Nation's Top Litigators, The Nat. Law Jour., 2007, Top 10 Lawyers in the Country, Lawyers Weekly USA, 2005. Mem.: ABA, Internat. Assn. Def. Counsel (mem. trial acad. faculty 2002), Def. Rsch. Inst., NJ State Bar Assn. Office: Dechert LLP 902 Carnegie Ctr Ste 500 Princeton NJ 08540-6531 Office Phone: 609-955-3200. Office Fax: 609-955-3259.

SULLIVAN, DONAL D., federal judge; b. 1931; Attended, Loyola U., Chgo., 1949-50, Ill. Inst. Tech., 1952-54; LLB, De Paul U., 1957. Bar: Oreg. 1957, Ill. 1958. 1st asst. U.S. atty. for Oreg., Portland, 1962-65; clk. U.S. Dist. Ct. Oreg., Portland, 1966-69, bankruptcy judge, 1969—98; ret., 1998; recalled, 1998—. Office: US Bankruptcy Ct 1001 SW 5th Ave 7th Fl Portland OR 97204-1147

SULLIVAN, EARL LE ROY, political science professor, former academic administrator; b. Anaconda, Mont., Aug. 11, 1942; s. Earl Richard Sullivan and Margaret Jones; m. Jean Ann Wendell, Aug. 10, 1963; children: Mark, Erin, Colin. BA in Polit. Sci., Seattle U., 1964; PhD in Internat. Rels., Claremont U., 1970. Asst. prof. U. Portland, Oreg., 1967-73, chair social sci., 1970-73; from asst. to full prof. Am. U., Cairo, 1973—, chair polit. sci., 1994-97, provost, chief academic officer, 1998—2008. Vis. scholar Von Grunebaum Ctr., UCLA, 1984-85, U. Utah, Salt Lake City, 1991-92. Author: Women in Egyptian Public Life, 1986, Social Background and Bureaucratic Behavior in Egypt, 1990; editor: Contemporary Study of the Arab World, 1991, Multilateral Diplomacy and the United Nations Today, 1999, 2d edit., 2005; chair editl. bd. Cairo Papers in Social Sci., 1982-84, 87-88. Mem. bd. trustees Cairo Am. Coll., 1974-84, chair bd. trustees, 1974-79. Mem. Am. Soc. Internat. Law, Middle East Studies Assn. Avocations: reading, hiking, camping, fishing, music. Office: Am U Cairo 113 Kasr el Aini St PO Box 2511 Cairo 11511 Egypt also: 420 Fifth Ave, 3rd Fl New York NY 10018-2729 Office Phone: 202-797-5190. E-mail: tims@aucegypt.edu.

SULLIVAN, EDWARD DELANO, lawyer, investor; s. Joseph Daniel and Eugenia Rose Sullivan; m. Elizabeth Wilhelmina Frank, June 26, 1954; children: Elizabeth Sullivan Rolfe, Kathleen Sullivan Fleming, Maureen Sullivan Fengler, Caroline Sullivan Piper, Alice Sullivan Tucker, April Sullivan Fitzgerald, Virginia Elaine. BS in Bus. Adminstrn., U. Conn., Storrs, 1954; JD, U. Okla. Coll. Law, Norman, 1958; grad. Judge Advocate Course Res., U. Va., Charlottesville, 1965; grad. Nat. Sec. Seminar, Indsl. Coll. of Armed Forces, 1974; grad. Sr. Staff Judge Advocate course, Air U., 1976; grad., U.S. Air Force War Coll., 1978. Bar: Okla. 1958, Conn. 1960, U.S. Supreme Ct. 1967, Fla. 1979; cert. in mgmt. devel. Fla. Atlantic U., 1977, pub. purchasing officer Nat. Inst. Govtl. Purchasing, lic. comml. pilot with seaplane rating FAA. Pvt. practice, Bridgeport, Conn., 1960—, Fort Lauderdale, Fla., 1979—. Dir. Nat. Inst. Govtl. Purchasing, 1965—68. Col. JAG USAF, 1954—84. Decorated Commendation medal with Oak Leaf Cluster USAF, Humanitarian medal, Meritorious Svc. medal, Legion of Merit medal; recipient Committment to Corporate Spirit plaque, Warren Robins AFB, GA, 1984, Boston Bar Assn. award, 1971; named Hon. Lt. Col. Aide-de-Camp, Ala. State Militia, 1976, Hon. Mayor, City of San Antonio, 1996, Most Experienced Mem., Am. Bar. Assn., 2008. Mem.: SAR (chpt. pres. 1990—91, Fla. state pres. 1998—99, nat. trustee 1999—2000, pres. coun. of state pres.'s 1999—2000), ABA (sr.), Overseer Plymouth Plantation Mus. (Commd. a Ky. Col.), Pilgrim Hall Mus. (trustee), Ga. Govtl. Purchasing Assn. (hon.), Freedon Found. (life), Air Force Assn., Delano Kindred (com. mem.), Gen. Soc. of Mayflower Descendants (asst. gen. 1996—99, dep. gov. gen. 1999—2002, counsellor gen. 2003—05, gov. gen 2005—08), Mil. Officers Assn. Am. (life), Nat. Gavel Soc. (life), Res. Officers Assn. U.S. (life), Hugenot Soc. Fla. (pres. (Louis Du Bois chpt.)), Alden Kindred, Pilgrim John Howland Soc., Phi Alpha Delta. Address: 2837 NE 27th St Fort Lauderdale FL 33306-1912

SULLIVAN, EDWARD JOSEPH, lawyer; b. Bklyn., Apr. 24, 1945; s. Edward Joseph and Bridget (Duffy) S.; m. Patte Hancock, Aug. 7, 1982; children: Amy Brase, Molly Elsasser, Mary Christine. BA, St. John's U., 1966; JD, Willamette U., 1969; MA, cert. Urban Studies, Portland State U., 1973; LLM, Univ. Coll., London, 1978; diploma in law, Univ. Coll., Oxford, 1984; MA, U. Durham, 1999. Bar: Oreg. 1969, D.C. 1978, Wash. 2001, U.S. Dist. Ct. Oreg. 1970, U.S. Ct. Appeals (9th cir.) 1970, U.S. Supreme Ct. 1972. Counsel Washington County, Hillsboro, Oreg., 1969-75; legal counsel Gov. of Oreg., Salem, 1975-77; ptnr. O'Donnell, Sullivan & Ramis, Portland, Oreg., 1978-84, Sullivan, Josselson, Roberts, Johnson & Kloos, Portland, Salem and Eugene, Oreg., 1984-86, Mitchell, Lang & Smith, Portland, 1986-90, Preston Gates & Ellis, Portland, 1990—2003; owner Garvey Schubert Barer, Portland, Oreg., 2003—. Bd. dirs., pres. Oreg. Law Inst. Contbr. numerous articles to profl. jours. Chmn. Capitol Planning Commn., Salem, 1975-77, 78-81. Mem. ABA (local govt. sect., com. on planning and zoning, adminstrv. law sect.) Oreg. State Bar Assn., D.C. Bar Assn., Wash. State Bar Assn., Am. Judicature Soc., Am. Polit. Sci. Assn. Democrat. Roman Catholic. Office: Garvey Schubert Barer 121 SW Morrison Ste 1100 Portland OR 97204-3141 Office Phone: 503-228-3939. Business E-Mail: esullivan@gsblaw.com.

SULLIVAN, EUGENE JOHN JOSEPH, manufacturing executive, director; b. NYC, Nov. 28, 1920; s. Cornelius and Margaret (Smith) S.; m. Gloria Roesch, Aug. 25, 1943; children: Eugene John Joseph, Edward J., Robert C., Elizabeth Ann Hansler. BS, St. John's U., 1942, D in Commerce, 1973; MBA, NYU, 1948. With chem. divsn. Borden, Inc., NYC, 1946—, beginning as salesman, successively asst. sales, 1957-58, exec. v.p., 1958-64; pres. Borden Chem. Co. divsn. Borden, Inc.; v.p. Borden, Inc., 1964-67, exec. v.p., 1967-73, pres., COO, 1973-79, chmn., pres., CEO, 1979-86; prof. St. John's U., 1987—2003. Bd. dirs. W.R. Grace & Co.; chmn. bd. dirs. Hamilton Fund; trustee Atlantic Mut. Ins. Co. Trustee, vice chmn., past sec. St. John's U., chmn. bd. dirs., 1999—; trustee N.Y. Med. Coll., Cath. Health Assn., Cath. Charities U.S.A., 1999—; chmn. Commn. on Cath. Health Care. Served as lt. USNR, 1942-46; lt. Res. Mem. Coun. Fgn. Rels., Knights of Malta, Knights of Holy Sepulchre, Knights of St. Gregory, Univ. Club, Plandome Country Club.

SULLIVAN, EUGENE RAYMOND, federal judge; b. St. Louis, Aug. 2, 1941; s. Raymond Vincent and Rosemary (Kiely) S.; m. Lis Urup Johansen, June 18, 1966; children: Kim, Eugene II. BS, U.S. Mil. Acad., 1964; JD, Georgetown U., 1971; HDL (hon.), New Eng. Sch. Law, 2001. Bar: Mo. 1972, D.C. 1972. Law clk. to Hon. M.C. Matthes US Ct. Appeals (8th Cir.), St. Louis, 1971—72; assoc. Patton Boggs & Blow LLP, Washington, 1972—74; asst. spl. counsel to Pres. The White House, Washington, 1974; trial counsel US Dept. Justice, Washington, 1974—82; dep. gen. counsel Dept. Air Force, US Dept. Def., Washington, 1982—84; gen. counsel USAF, Washington, 1982—86; gov. of Wake Island, 1984—86; judge US Ct. Appeals for the Armed Forces, Washington, 1986—2002, chief judge, 1990—95, sr. judge, 2002—; co-founder, prin. Gavel Consulting Group, 2003—; sr. partner Freeh Group Internat. Mem. Fed. Commn. To Study Honor Code at West Point, 1989-90. Author: (book) The Majority Rules, 2005, The Report to the Judiciary, 2008. Trustee U.S. Mil. Acad., 1989—; bd. Duke Law, Ethics, and Nat. Security Ctr., 2001-. Airborne ranger US Army, 1964—69, Vietnam, ranger instr. Decorated Bronze Star, Air medal, airborne badge, ranger badge, others; Castle award, West Point Soc., 2001, Medal of Justice, Romania, Medal of Defense, 1st Class, Hungary, Defense Minister Citation, ROC; installed as Disting. Mem. Army Ranger Training Brigade, 2006. Republican. Roman Catholic. Avocation: writing. Business E-Mail: esullivan@gavelconsultinggroup.com, judgesullivan@west-point.org, judgesullivan@freegroup.com.*

SULLIVAN, FRANK, JR., state supreme court justice; b. Mar. 21, 1950; s. Frank E. and Colette (Cleary) S.; m. Cheryl Gibson, June 14, 1972; children: Denis M., Douglas S., Thomas R. AB cum laude, Dartmouth Coll., 1972; JD magna cum laude, Ind. U., 1982; LLM, U. Va., 2001. Bar: Ind. 1982. Mem. staff Office of U.S. Rep. John Brademas, 1974-79, dir. staff, 1975-78; with Barnes & Thornburg, Indpls., 1982-89; budget dir. State of Ind., 1989-92; exec. asst. Office of Gov. Evan Bayh, 1993; assoc. justice Ind. Supreme Ct., 1993—. Chair Ind. Supreme Ct. Judicial Technology & Automation Com. Mem. ABA (chair appellate judges conf. 2008-09), Ind. State Bar Assn., Indpls. Bar Assn. Home: 5854 Lawton Loop West Dr Indianapolis IN 46216-2009 Office: Ind Supreme Ct State House Rm 321 Indianapolis IN 46204-2728 Home Phone: 317-549-3926; Office Phone: 317-232-2548.*

SULLIVAN, FRANK C., manufacturing executive; BA, U. N.C., 1983. Various comml. lending corp. fin. 1st Union Nat. Bank and Harris Bank, 1983-87; regional sales mgr. AGR Co. RPM Internat. Inc., 1987-89, dir. corp. devel., 1989-91, v.p., 1991-93, CFO, 1993-98, exec. v.p., 1998-99, pres., 1999—2002, pres., CEO, 2002—08, chmn., CEO, 2008—. Bd. dir. Timken Co. Bd. mem. Greater Cleveland Chpt., Am. Red Cross, Cleveland Rock & Roll Hall of Fame & Mus. Morehead scholar, 1983. Mem.: Cuyahoga County Bluecoats. Office: RPM International PO Box 777 2628 Pearl Rd Medina OH 44256 Office Phone: 330-273-5090.

SULLIVAN, GEORGE EDWARD, writer; b. Lowell, Mass., Aug. 11, 1927; s. Timothy Joseph and Cecilia Mary (Shea) S.; m. Muriel Agnes Moran, May 24, 1952; 1 son, Timothy. BS, Fordham U., Bronx, NY, 1952. Pub. relations mgr. Popular Library, NYC, 1952-55; pub. relations dir. AMF, NYC, 1955-63. Adj. prof. Fordham U. Author: Mathew Brady, His Life and Photographs, 1994 (named a Notable Children's Trade Book in Field of Social Studies, Nat. Coun. Social Studies and Children's Book Coun., Teenage Book of Yr. NY Pub. Libr., Recommended Children's Book for Reading and Sharing, 1994, Recommended as a Book of Gt. Interest, Gt. Books for Boys, 1998), Slave Ship, The Story of the Henrietta Marie, 1994 (named Best Book of 1994 Selection, Parents Mag., Best Children's Book of Yr. Selection, Children's Book Com., Bank St. Coll. Edn.), The Day Women Got the Vote, 1994, Pitchers: Twenty Seven of Baseball's Greatest, 1994(named Teenage Book of Yr., NY Pub. Libr., A Recommended Book for Reluctant Young Adult Reader, ALA), Black Artists in Photography, 1995, Women War Spies, 1996, Alamo, 1996, Black Artists as Photographers, 1840-1940, 1996(named Teenage Book of Yr., NY Pub. Libr., A Best Children's Book of Yr. Selection, Children's Book Com., Bank St. Coll. Edn.), Glovemen: Twenty-Seven of Baseball's Greatest, 1996 (named a Teenage Book of Yr., NY Pub. Libr., A Recommended Book for Reluctant Young Adult Reader, ALA), Not Guilty: Six Times When Justice Failed, 1996, To the Bottom of the Sea, 1998, Burnin' Rubber: Behind the Scenes in Stock Car Racing, 1998, One Hundred Years in Photographs, 1999, Picturing Lincoln: Famous Photographs that Popularized the President, 1999(Selected as a Notable Social Studies Trade Book, Children's Book Coun., named a Best Children's Book of Yr. Selection, Children's Book Com., Bank St. Coll. Edn.), Portraits of War, Civil War Photographers and Their Work, 2000, One Hundred Years in Photographs, 2000, The Civil War at Sea, 2001 (Selected as a Notable Social Studies Trade Book, Children's Book Coun., named a Teenage Book of Yr., NY Pub. Libr.), In Their Own Words: Lewis & Clark, 2001, In Their Own Words: Harriet Tubman, 2001, In Their Own Words: Helen Keller, 2001 (named a Best Children's Book of Yr. Selection, Children's Book Com., Bank St. Coll. Edn.), Power Football, 2001, In Their Own Words: The Wright Brothers, 2002 (Selected by US Agy. for Internat. Devel. to Promote Reading in North Africa, reprinted in Arabic), In Their Own Words: Abraham Lincoln, 2002 (Named a Best Children's Book of Yr. Selection, Children's Book Com., Bank St. Coll. Edn.), The Civil War Photographs of Mathew Brady, 2004, Journalists at Risk: Reporting America's Wars, 2005, Built to Last, 2005, Berenice Abbott, Photographer: An Independent Vision, 2006, Helen Keller: Her Life in Pictures, 2007, Knockout: The Photobiography of Boxer Joe Louis, 2008, Mr. President, A Book of US Presidents, 2009 Served with USN, 1945-48. Mem. PEN, Authors Guild, Soc. Children's Book Writers & Illustrators. Roman Catholic. Personal E-mail: gjsbooks@rcn.com.

SULLIVAN, GEORGE MURRAY, transportation executive, consultant, retired mayor; b. Portland, Oreg., Mar. 31, 1922; s. Harvey Patrick and Viola (Murray) S.; m. Margaret Eagan, Dec. 30, 1947; children: Timothy M., Harvey P. (dec. July 1996), Daniel A., Kevin Shane, Colleen Marie, George Murray, Michael J., Shannon Margaret, Casey Eagan. D.P.A. (hon.), U. Alaska, 1981. Line driver Alaska Freight Lines, Inc., Valdez-Fairbanks, 1942-44; US dep. marshal Alaska Dist., Nenana, 1946-52; mgr. Alaska Freight Lines, 1952-56; Alaska gen. mgr. Consol. Freightways Corp. of Del., Anchorage, 1956-67; mayor of Anchorage, 1967-82; exec. mgr. Alaska Bus. Council, 1968; sr. cons. to pres. Western Air Lines Inc., 1982-87; former legis. liaison for Gov. of Alaska; now cons. Past mem. Nat. Adv. Com. on Oceans and Atmosphere, Joint Fed.-State Land Use Planning Commn.; past chmn. 4-state region 10 adv. com. OEO; mem. Fairbanks City Council, 1955-59, Anchorage City Council, 1965-67, Greater Anchorage Borough Assembly, 1965-67, Alaska Ho. of Reps., 1964-65. Trustee U. Alaska Found.; chmn. Anchorage Conv. and Visitors Bur.; bd. dirs. Western council Boy Scouts Am., 1958-59. Served with U.S. Army, 1944-46. Mem. Nat. Def. Transp. Assn. (life mem., pres. 1962-63), Nat. League Cities (dir.), Pioneers of Alaska, Alaska Mcpl. League (past pres.), Anchorage C. of C. (exec. com. 1963-65, treas. 1965-66, dir.), Alaska Carriers Assn. (exec. com.), Alaska Transp. Conf. (chmn.), U.S. Conf. Mayors (exec. com.), VFW (comdr. Alaska 1952) Clubs: Elks. Home and Office: George M Sullivan Co 1345 W 12th Ave Anchorage AK 99501-4252 Office Phone: 907-272-2918. *America is truly the land of opportunity, and I feel that the success with which God has blessed my life attests to this fact. I have been blessed four times. Not only was I born in America, but I have lived my life in Alaska. My other two blessings are my wonderful and supportive wife and our eight healthy children.*

SULLIVAN, GORDON R., military association executive, retired military officer; b. Boston, Sept. 25, 1937; s. Russsell Edgar and Penuel Edith (Gordon) S.; m. Miriam Gay Loftus, June 20, 1965; children: John, Mark, Elizabeth. BA in History, Norwich U., 1959, D Mil. Sci. (hon.), 1991; MA in Polit. Sci., U. N.H., 1974. Commd. 2d lt. U.S. Army, 1959, advanced through grades to gen., 1990, ret., 1995; student Armor Officer Basic Course U.S. Army Armor Sch., Ft. Knox, Ky., 1959-60; platoon leader Co. B, 1st Medium Tank Bn., 66th Armor, 2d Armored Div., Ft. Hood, Tex., 1960; student Armor Communication Class U.S. Army Armor Sch., Ft. Knox, 1960; communications officer 1st Medium Tank Bn., 66th Armor, 2d Armored Div., Ft. Hood, 1960-61; comdr. Co. A, 1st Medium tank Bn., 66th Armor,. 2d Armored Div., Ft. Hood, 1961; bn. communications officer 3d Medium Tank Bn. (Patton), 40th Armor, U.S. Army Pacific, Republic of Korea, 1961-62; platoon leader Co. A 3d Medium Tank Bn., 40th Armor, U.S. Army Pacific, Korea, 1962; asst. civil guard/self def. corps advisor 21st Inf. Div., Mil. Assistance Adv. Group, Vietnam, 1962-63; adminstrv. officer, later exec. asst. Office of Asst. Chief of Staff, J2 Div., Mil. Assistance Command, Vietnam, 1963-64; student Armor Officer Advanced Course U.S. Army Armor Sch., Ft. Knox, 1964-65; S-4 (Logistics) 3d Bn., 32d Armor, 3d Armored Div., U.S. Army Europe, 1965-66; comdr. Co.A, 3d Bn., 32d Armor, 3d Armored Div., U.S. Army Europe, 1966; assignment officer, later staff officer Combat Arms Sect., Mil. Pers. Div., Office of Dep. Chief of Staff for Pers., U.S. Army Europe, 1966-68; student U.S. Army Command Gen. Staff Coll., Ft. Leavenworth, Kans., 1968-69; pers. svcs. officer Plans and Ops. Div., G-1, Hdqrs., I Field Force, Vietnam, 1969-70; pers. mgmt. officer Pers. Actions Sect., Armor Br., Office of Pers. Ops., Washington, 1970-73; student Internat. Rels. U. N.H., Durham, 1973-74; comdr. 4th Bn., 73d Armor, 1st Inf. Div. (Forward), U.S. Army Europe, 1975-76; chief of staff 1st Inf. Div. (Forward), U.S. Army Europe, 1976-77; student U.S. Army War Coll., Carlisle Barracks, Pa., 1977-78; asst. chief of staff G-3 (Ops.)/Dir. Plans and Tng., 1st Inf. Div. and Fort Riley, Kans., 1978-79, G-3 (Ops.), VII Corps, U.S. Army Europe, 1980-81; comdr. 1st Brigade, 3d Armored Div., U.S. Army Europe, 1981-83; chief of staff 3d Armored Div., U.S. Army Europe, 1983; asst. comdt. U.S. Army Armor Sch., Ft. Knox, 1983-85; dep. chief of staff for support Cen. Army Group, Europe, 1985-87; dep. comdt. U.S. Army Command and Gen. Staff Coll., Ft. Leavenworth, 1987-88; comdg. gen. 1st Inf. Div. (Mechanized), Ft. Riley, 1988-89; dep. chief of staff for ops. and plans US Army, Washington, 1989-90, vice chief of staff, 1990-91, chief of staff, 1991-95; pres. Coleman Federal, 1995—97; pres., COO Assn of the US Army, Arlington, Va., 1998—. Bd. dirs Newell Rubbermaid, 1999-, Electronic Warfare Associates, Inc., Inst. Def. Analysis Co-author (with Michael V. Harper) Hope Is Not a Method, 1996; editor: Portrait of an Army, 1991. Chmn. bd. trustees, Norwich U., chmn. emeritus Marshall Legacy Inst. Decorated D.S.M., Def. Superior Svc. medal, Legion of Merit, Bronze Star, Purple Heart, Meritorius Svc. medal with oak leaf cluster, Joint Svc. Commendation medal, Army Commendation medal with oak leaf cluster, Army Achievement medal, Combat Infantryman badge. Mem. Assn. of U.S. Army, Armor Assn. Office: Assn of the US Army 2425 Wilson Blvd Arlington VA 22201

SULLIVAN, GREGORY PATRICK, principal engineer; b. Boston, Aug. 10, 1963; s. Paul David and Thomasina Sullivan; m. Alisa Dean Sullivan, Aug. 19, 1989; children: Benjamin Patrick, Margaret Marie, Aidan Thomas. BS in Physics, U. Oreg., 1987; BSME, Oreg. State U., 1991; MS in Bldg. Engring., MIT, 1995. Registered profl. engr., Oreg. & Wash. Market analyst Applied Strategies, Inc., Natick, Mass., 1985-91; found. prin. engr. Efficiency Solutions, Richland, Wash., 1991—. Contbr. articles to profl. jours. V.p., bd. dirs. Benton Affordable Housing Assn., Richland, Wash., 1999—; soccer coach Tri-City Youth Soccer Assn., Richland, 1998—. Mem. ASME, Am. Soc. Heating, Ventilation and Air Conditioning Engrs., Assn. Energy Engrs. Avocations: ice hockey, skiing, ultimate frisbee.

SULLIVAN, GREGORY PAUL, secondary school educator; b. Buffalo, June 13, 1957; s. Jerome Patrick and Gloria Mae (Struble) S.; m. Sarah Davis Houston, May 17, 1986; children: Patrick Benjamin, Ryan Christopher. BS in Indsl. Edn., State U. Coll., Oswego, NY, 1979; MA in Indsl. Edn., Ball State U., 1983. postgrad. collegiate profl. teaching cert. Grad. asst. mfg. lab. Ball State U., Muncie, Ind., 1982-83; tchr. tech. edn. John Rolfe Mid. Sch., Richmond, Va., 1979-86, Horton Mid. Sch., Pittsboro, N.C., 1986-88, Dunbar Mid. Sch., Lynchburg, Va., 1988-93; supr. career-tech. programs Lynchburg City Schs., 1993—. Coord./judge regional and nat. mfg. contest Tech. Edn. and Collegiate Assn., 1988—; coord. Eisenhower Grant, 1991-92. Asst. dir. Camp Minnehaha, Minnehaha Springs, W.Va., 1979-88. Named Va. Tchr. of Yr., Va. Dept. Edn., 1993. Mem. Soc. Mfg. Engrs. (internat. edn. com. career guidance 1984, 91), Internat. Tech. Edn. Assn. (mem. editl. rev. bd. The Tech. Tchr., delphi com. critical issues and concerns tech. edn. 1992), Coun. Tech. Tchr. Edn. (student svcs. com. 1991), Va. Tech. Edn. Assn. (v.p. 1997, 98), Va. Coun. Tech. Edn. Suprs. (pres. 1997), Phi Delta Kappa, Epsilon Pi Tau, Kappa Delta Pi. Avocations: intramural sports, golf, tennis, running. Office: Lynchburg City Schools PO Box 2497 Lynchburg VA 24505-2497 Home: 311 Rowland Dr Lynchburg VA 24503-2619

SULLIVAN, HARRY TRUMAN, research scientist; b. Camden, Ala., Mar. 21, 1952; s. Ernest Curley and Luticia Ann (Aaron) B.; m. Sandra Carol Jackson, Nov. 13, 1976; 1 child, Asha Nicole. AA, So. Tech. Inst., Marietta, Ga., 1976; BS in Computer Sci., Ga. State U., 1989. Instrumentation technician Ga. Power Co., Baxley, 1976-78; electronic technician Micromeritics Instrument Corp., Atlanta, 1978-80, GEC Avionics, Inc., Atlanta, 1980-82; electronic technician II Ga. Inst. of Tech., Atlanta, 1982—. Mem. IEEE, Assn. for Computing Machinery. Avocation: tang soo do. Office Phone: 404-894-2947. Personal E-mail: harrysul@bellsouth.net.

SULLIVAN, HUGH DAVID, investment company executive; b. Detroit, Oct. 18, 1958; s. Brian and Ann (Carswell) S.; m. Julie Heisel, May 17, 1986. BS in Engring., U. Mich., 1980; MPPM, Yale U., 1982. Prodn. supr. GM, Flint, Mich., 1982, strategic planner, 1983, product mgr., 1983-84; assoc. mergers and acquisitions dept. 1st Boston Corp., NYC, 1984-87, v.p. Chgo., 1988, dir. mcht. banking, 1989-91; mng. ptnr. Carrus Ptnrs., Chgo.; owner, pres. Kalfact Plastics Co.; various positions including co-head Americas origination, head tech., head global prin. investment origination Merrill Lynch & Co., Inc., NYC, 1997—2006, vice chmn., mem. exec. client coverage group, 2006—, head investment banking, Germany, Austria and Switzerland, 2008—. Bd. dirs. Briggs Industries Inc., Tampa, Fla., Blodgett Oven Co., Interstate Brands Corp. Office: Merrill Lynch & Co Inc 4 World Fin Ctr 250 Vesey St New York NY 10080 Office Phone: 212-449-1000.

SULLIVAN, JAMES F., physicist, researcher; b. Cin., Mar. 7, 1943; s. James E. and Alma L. (Lienesch) S.; m. Sylvia J. Kasselmann, Aug. 16, 1969; 1 child, Robert L. BS, Xavier U., Cin., 1965, MS, 1969. Instr. physics Brebeuf Prep. Sch., Indpls., 1965-67, OMI Coll. Applied Sci., U. Cin., 1968-71, asst. prof. physics, 1971-77, assoc. prof. physics, 1977-88, prof. physics, 1988—; dept. head math., physics, computing tech. U. Cin. OMI Coll. of Applied Sci., 2002—. Summer faculty rschr. Solar Energy Rsch. Inst., Golden, Colo., 1980; mem. high sch. evaluation team N. Ctrl. Assn., Cin., 1983-85; vis. prof. Arcada Polytechnic Inst., Finland, 2001; rep. U. Cin. Grad. Ceremony, Delta Acad. Mansoura, Egypt, 2004. Author: Technical Physics, 1988; Co-author: Laboratory Manual for General Physics, 1973, 83, 90, 92, Physics for Technology Laboratory Manual, 1995, 97. Organizer of events St. Xavier H.S. Alumni, Cin., 1983—; vol. examiner Am. Radio Relay League for U.S.

Fed. Comm. Commn., Newington, Conn., 1984—; judge physics category Ohio State Sci. Fair, Columbus, Ohio, 1986—; chief negotiator faculty and librs. U. Cin., 1995. Received John B. Hart award (disting. svc. to Southern Ohio sect. of Am. Assn. of Physics Tchrs.), 2001; named Faculty Mem. of Yr., Gamma Alpha chpt. Tau Alpha Phi, 1983. Fellow Ohio Acad. Sci.; mem. AAUP (v.p. U. Cin. chpt. 1994-96, bd. dirs. 2004—), Am. Assn. Physics Tchrs. (founder, past pres., assoc. sec. So. Ohio sect. 1993—, com. on instrnl. media 1994-98, chief organizer and presenter Fundamentals of Radio workshop Toronto 1985, Columbus, Ohio 1986, Bozeman, Mont. 1987, Orono, Maine 1992, Boise, Idaho 1993, South Bend, Ind. 1994, College Park, Md. 1996, Denver, 1997, com. on metric measurements, 2000-03), Ohio Valley Amateur Radio Assn. (pres. 1997—), Am. Soc. Engring. Edn. Achievements include supervising successful attempt of OMI Coll. Applied Sci. contact of shuttle Challenger during STS-51F mission, 1985. Office: Univ Cin 2220 Victory Pkwy Cincinnati OH 45206-2822

SULLIVAN, JAMES FRANCIS, university administrator; b. Pitts., Sept. 15, 1930; s. Francis P. and Leona C. (Patterson) S.; m. Carol Rea, Sept. 10, 1955; children— Leslie Ann, Daniel Paul. BA, Dartmouth Coll., 1953; MS, U. Colo., 1956; PhD, U. Pitts., 1965. Asst. city mgr., Monterey, Calif., 1957-60; city mgr. Ojai, Calif., 1960-62; asst. prof. U. Pitts., 1965-66; vice-chancellor U. Calif. at Riverside, 1969-74; assoc. prof. Grad. Sch. Adminstrn., 1974-78; assoc. dir. Dry Lands Rsch. Inst., 1974-78; vice chancellor U. Calif., Davis, 1978-91, dean univ. extention, 1980-91, vice chancellor Santa Cruz, 1995-96, asst. v.p. systemwide Office of Pres., 1996-97; v.p. Calif. State U., Northridge, 1998—2000, 2006—07. Served with USAF, 1954-55. Home: 1005 Rodeo Rd Pebble Beach CA 93953-2720 Personal E-mail: jfs53@ao.com.

SULLIVAN, JAMES GERALD, small business owner; b. Bad Axe, Mich., Sept. 13, 1935; s. John Thomas and Frances Eugena (O'Henley) Sullivan; m. Florence Marie Tack, Sept. 12, 1959; children: Kevin Michael, Kathleen Marie. Student, U. Detroit, 1957—58, Highland Park Coll., 1959—60. Owner Jerry's Barber Shop, Kinde, Bad Axe, Mich., 1963-66, 79—; purchasing agt. Thumb Elec. Coop., Ubly, Mich., 1966-79, Walbro Corp., Cass City, Mich., 1979-80; sales rep. Thumb Blanket, Bad Axe, Mich., 1980-81, Sta. WLEW, Bad Axe, 1981-82; regional mgr. Pri Am. Fin. Svcs., Bad Axe, 1985—2008; treas. Colfax Twp., Bad Axe, 1979-90; rural letter carrier U.S. Postal Svc., Bad Axe, 1982-98, ret., 1998; distbr. Enagic USA Inc., Kangen Water, 2009. Loss clk., Toplis & Harding Wagner & Gliddon, Detroit, 1959-61; inventory control clk., Carrick Products Co., Royal Oak, Mich., 1957-59. Pres. Huron County Twp. Assn., Mich., 1988—90; leader Boy Scouts Am., Bad Axe, 1975—77; lector Ushers Club, Sacred Heart Ch., Eucharistic min. With US Army, 1954—56. Mem. Huron County Rural Letter Carriers Assn. (pres. 1988-2003), Armed Forces Vets. Club of the Nat. Rural Letter Carriers Assn. (Mich. divsn., state sec. 1999—), Am. Legion, 4-H Club (pres. 1948-50), Lions (pres. 1979-80, 2006-07), Cmty. Club (pres. 1976-77), KC (mem. coun. #1546), Tip of the Thumb Dance Club (pres. 2005). Republican. Roman Catholic. Avocations: gardening, golf, swimming, fishing. Home: 122 W Richardson Rd Bad Axe MI 48413-9108

SULLIVAN, JAMES LEO, organization executive; b. Somerville, Mass., Dec. 11, 1925; s. James Christopher and Anna Agnes (Kilmartin) S.; m. Anne Dorothy Hevner, Jan. 20, 1951; children: Maura, Mark, Lianne, Christopher. BS in History and Govt. cum laude, Boston Coll., 1950, MEd in Adminstrn. and Fin., 1958; DCS (hon.), Suffolk U., 1990. Asst. town mgr., Arlington, Mass., 1957-62; town mgr. Watertown, Conn., 1962-65; chief adminstrv. officer Town of Milton, Mass., 1965-68; city mgr. Cambridge, Mass., 1968-70, 74-81, Lowell, Mass., 1970-74; sr. rsch. asst. MIT, Cambridge, 1970-71; pres. Greater Boston C. of C., 1981-91, H.M.S. Mktg., Boston, 1991—. Chmn. Mass. Gov.'s Local Govt. Adv. Com., 1978; del. to Orgn. Econ. and Coop. Devel., Paris, 1979; chmn. New Eng.-Can. Bus. Coun., 1983; pres. Careers for Later Years, 1983; bd. dirs. Input-Output Computer Svcs., Imugen Inc., Mass. Bus. Devel. Corp., New Eng. Cert. Devel. Corp. Trustee Emerson Coll., 1984-88, mem. fin. and investment com., 1985-88; bd. dirs. Bunker Hill C.C. Coll. Found., 1988—; mem. Adv. Com. on Reorgn. of Mass. Ct. Sys., 1991—, chmn. budget subcom. 1991—; bd. overseers Univ. Hosp. Boston. With USN, 1943-46. Mem. Mass. League of Cities and Towns (pres. 1978), Mass. Mayors Assn., Internat. City Mgmt. Assn., Nat. League Cities, Am. C. of C. Execs. (bd. dirs. 1988—), World Trade Club (bd. govs. 1986—). Home Phone: 978-453-4350. Personal E-mail: jls1225@aol.com.

SULLIVAN, JAMES M., hotel executive; BS, Boston Coll.; MBA, Univ. Conn. Sr. auditor Arthur Andersen & Co.; mgmt. positions Harrah's Entertainment, Holiday Inns Inc., Kentucky Fried Chicken, Heublein Inc., Marriott Corp., Washington, 1980—83; chmn., pres., CEO Tenly Enterprises Inc., 1983—86; v.p. M&A Marriott Internat. Inc., Washington, 1986—89, sr. v.p. fin. lodging, 1989—90, sr. v.p. lodging devel., 1990—95, exec. v.p. lodging devel., 1995—. Bd. dir. Integra Life Sciences, 1992—. Office: Marriott Internat Inc 1 Marriott Dr Washington DC 20058-0001

SULLIVAN, JANE, theater educator, director; d. O. Charles and Eileen Mary Brouk; m. Michael David Sullivan, June 7, 1986; children: Mark Patrick, Zoe Elizabeth. MA, Essex U., Cohchester, Eng., 1980. Adminstrv. asst. Rep. Bill Emerson, Wash., 1981—82; prof. Jefferson Coll., Hillsboro, Mo., 1982—, dir., theatre, 1983—; costumer Act Inc., St. Louis, 2008—, Mustard Seed Theatre, St. Louis, 2008—. Recipient Governor's award, State Mo., 1995, Assessment award, Jefferson Coll., 2000, Faculty Innovation award, Mo. CC Assn., 2001, Innovative Faculty award, 2001, Assessment Award, Jefferson Coll. Mem.: Mo. C.C. Assn., Phi Theta Kappa Xi Zeta Chpt. (Tchr. of Yr. award 2007—08).

SULLIVAN, JANET NELSON, dermatologist, department chairman, health facility administrator; b. Salt Lake City, Feb. 3, 1950; d. Richard Knowlton Nelson, Marian Foote Nelson; m. David J. Schiller; children: Naomi Schiller, Erika children: Rachel Schiller, Molly Nestor. BA, Antioch Coll., 1972; MD, Ohio State U., 1987. Diplomate Am. Bd. Dermatology. Resident internal medicine Mich. State U. Associated Hosp., Lansing, 1987—89; resident dermatology U. Hosp. Cleve., 1989—92; asst. clin. prof. dermatology Case Western Res. U., Coll. Medicine, Cleve., 1992—97; staff physician Ohio Permanente Med. Group, Cleve., 1992—97; asst. med. dir. Hudson Health Plan, Tarrytown, NY, 1997—98, chief med. officer, 1998—. Chair NY Diabetes Coalition, Tarrytown, NY, 2004—06, Westchester Diabetes Coalition, NY, 2001—03; adv. bd. Taking On Diabetes, 2002; Ctr. for Medicaid and Medicare Svcs./AMA adv. group Electronic Performance Measurement Specifications Project, 2003; mem. doctor's office quality info. tech. task force IPRO Quality Improvement Orgn., 2005—07; mem. Pay For Performance Task Force, Nat. Com. Quality Health Care, Washington, 2005; mem. quality and clin. com Taconic Health Info. Cmty. Regional Health Info. Org., 2005—. With patient safety & quality com. performance workgroup Am. Acad. Dermatology, 2009, quality assurance quality improvement task force mem.; child health project adv. com. mem. CHCS-NCQA, 2009; child health measurement adv. panel for NCQA CHMAP, 2009; bd. dirs. Nat. Quality Forum, Washington, 2003—07; mem. validation group Pub. Health Data Standards Consortium Rev. of HL7-EHR Functional Model, 2004; mem. N.Y. State Dept. Health SSI Task Force, 1999—2000, Westchester County Bioterrorism Med. Adv. Com., NY, 2001. Mem.: AMA, NY Quality Alliance (cert. value exchange 2007—), NY Acad. Medicine, Assn. Clinicians for the Underserved, Women's Dermatology Soc., Westchester County Med. Soc., Med. Soc. State N.Y., Am. Acad. Dermatology, Alpha Omega Alpha. Office: Hudson Health Plan 303 S Broadway Ste 321 Tarrytown NY 10591-5410 Office Fax: 914-631-1615.

SULLIVAN, JEFFREY C., prosecutor; BA, JD, Gonzaga U. Prosecutor Yakima County, Wash., 1975—2002; chief criminal divsn. (we. dist.) Wash. US Dept. Justice, Seattle, 2002—, interim US atty. (we. dist.) Wash., 2007—. Office: US Attys Office 700 Stewart St Ste 5220 Seattle WA 98101-1271 Office Phone: 206-553-7970. Office Fax: 206-553-0882.*

SULLIVAN, JERRY STEPHEN, electronics executive; b. Havre, Mont., July 17, 1945; s. Patrick Joseph and Evangeline (O'Neil) S.; m. Sharon Lee Horton, June 17, 1967; children: Garrett, Mindy, Darren. BS, U. Colo., 1967, MS, 1969, PhD, 1970; advanced mgmt. program, Harvard U. Bus. Sch., 1986. Tech. mgr. N.V. Philips Co., Eindhoven, Netherlands, 1971-75; group dir. N.Am. Philips Corp., Briarcliff Manor, NY, 1975-80; dir. Tektronix, Beaverton, Oreg., 1981-83, div. gen. mgr., 1983-85, corp. dir., 1985-88; v.p. Microelectronics & Computer Tech. Corp., Austin, Tex., 1988-92; pres., CEO, Design Techs. Inc., Austin, 1992—. Chmn. bd. MBA Techs., Inc., Phoenix; bd. dirs. Sherpa Corp., San Jose, Calif., Ontos, Inc. Boston, MBA Tech. Inc., Phoenix; mem. adv. bd. Ctr. Integrated Sys., Stanford U., Palo Alto, Calif., 1982—. Mem. adv. com. Coll. Engring., U. Tex., Austin, 1989—, bd. dirs. Edn. Found., 1990—. Mem. IEEE, Am. Phys. Soc., Assn. Computing Machinery, Am. Mgmt. Assn., Nat. Assn. Corp. Dirs. Avocations: scuba diving, golf, chess, sailing. Office: Design Techs Inc 107 Ranch Rd 620 S Austin TX 78734-3942

SULLIVAN, JIM, artist; b. Providence, Apr. 1, 1939; s. James Henry, Jr. and Frances Winifred (Welch) S.; m. Marie-Louise Paulson. BFA, R.I. Sch. Design, 1961; postgrad., Stanford U., 1962-63. Prof. art Bard Coll., Annandale-on-Hudson, NY, 1966—95, prof. emeritus, 1995—. Oneman shows Paley and Lowe Gallery, N.Y.C., 1971, 73, Henri Gallery, Washington, 1974, Fischback Gallery, N.Y.C., 1974, Willard Gallery, N.Y.C., 1978, Nancy Hoffman Gallery, N.Y.C., 1980, 82, 84, 86, 88, 2004, Dart Gallery, Chgo., 1984, Foker Skulima Gallery, Berlin, Germany, Anne Jaffe Gallery Bay Harbor Islands, Fla. 1990; exhibited in group shows including, Whitney Mus., Mus. Modern Art, Columbus Gallery Fine Arts, Worcester Art Mus., Queens Mus., McNay Art Mus., San Antonio, De Cordova Mus., Lincoln, Mass., Carie Secrist Gallery, 2006, Corcoran Gallery Art, Washington; pub. collections including Met. Mus., Whitney Mus., Albany State Mus., Wadsworth Atheneum, Philip Morris Inc., Owens Corning Coll., Amerada Hess. Juror Fulbright Fellowship Program, 1996, 1999; bd. dirs. Schoharie Land Trust. Recipient Hinda and Richard Rosenthal award, Am. Acad. Arts and Letters, 1973; grantee Stanford U., 1962—63, R.I. Sch. Design European Honors program, Rome, 1960—61, Nat. Endowment for Arts, 1982; Fulbright fellow, 1961—62, Guggenheim fellow, 1972—73. Address: Box 219 Rum Hill Rd Jefferson NY 12093 also: 59 Wooster St New York NY 10012

SULLIVAN, JOHN A., United States Representative from Oklahoma; b. Tulsa, Okla., Jan. 1, 1965; s. Daniel and Mag Sullivan; m. Judith Marie Beck; children: Tommy, Meredith, Sydney, Daniel. BBA, Northeastern State U., Tahlequah, Okla., 1992. Real estate broker; mem. Okla. State House Reps., 1995—2002, US Congress from 1st Okla. dist., 2002—, mem. energy and commerce com., co-chair Congl. Fatherhood Caucus, vice chair Congl. Native Am. Caucus. Republican. Office: US House Reps 434 Cannon House Office Bldg Washington DC 20515-3601 Office Phone: 202-225-2211. Office Fax: 202-225-9187.*

SULLIVAN, JOHN CORNELIUS, JR., lawyer; b. Erie, Pa., Oct. 23, 1927; s. John Cornelius and Catherine J. S.; m. Helen E. Kennedy, Feb. 3, 1951; children: John III, Timi Ann, Michael, Elizabeth. BA in Econs., Allegheny Coll., 1953; LLB, Dickinson Sch. Law, 1959. Bar: Pa. 1960, U.S. Supreme Ct. 1976. Sales rep. IBM Corp., 1953-56; mem. firm Nissley, Clecker & Fearen, Harrisburg, Pa., 1959-63, Nauman, Smith, Shissler & Hall, Harrisburg, 1964—97, of counsel, 1997—. Asst. city solicitor City of Harrisburg, 1964-68, city solicitor, 1968-70; gen. counsel Harrisburg Redevel. Authority, 1964-68, Harrisburg Mcpl. Authority, 1964-87; solicitor Silver-Spring Twp., 1970-81; dir. accounts and fin. City of Harrisburg, 1963; mem. Pa. House of Reps., 1963-64. Assoc. editor Dickinson Law Rev., 1958-59; editor Dauphin County Reporter, 1961-63. Chmn. bd. dirs. Harrisburg Pub. Library, 1965-73; bd. dirs., sec. Harrisburg Hosp.; bd. dirs. Harrisburg Hosp. Found., 1975-89. Mem. Pa. Bar Assn., Dauphin County Bar Assn. (past. dir.), The Pa. Soc. (N.Y.C.), Phi Gamma Delta. Home: 107 Sample Bridge Rd Mechanicsburg PA 17050-1940 Office: 200 N 3rd St Fl D18 Harrisburg PA 17101-1518

SULLIVAN, JOHN DOMINIC, theater producer, writer; b. La Crosse, Wis., Oct. 6, 1963; s. Arthur John and Eleanor Elizabeth (Skemp) Sullivan. BFA, U. Wis., Superior, 1986. Asst. dir. Duluth Playhouse, Minn., 1985; freelance arts cons. La Crosse, Wis., 1993—; play prodr. Great River Steamboat Co., La Crosse, Wis., 1996—97; stage mgr. La Crosse Cmty. Theatre, Wis., 1997; mng. dir. Fairbanks Shakespeare Theatre, Alaska, 1997. Author: (plays) Murder on the Mississippi, 1996, The Cabaret Killer, 1997. Democrat. Roman Catholic.

SULLIVAN, JOHN F., III, lawyer; BBA with highest honors, U. Okla., 1984; JD with honors, U. Houston, 1987. Bar: Tex. 1987, US Dist. Ct. (so., ea., no., and we. dists.) Tex., US Ct. Appeals (5th cir.), bar: US Supreme Ct. Joined Fulbright & Jaworski LLP, Houston, 1987—, ptnr. and chair, hiring com. Assoc. editor Houston Law Rev. Trustee Oncology Svcs. Found. Fellow: Tex. Bar Found., Houston Bar Found.; mem.: ABA, Tex. Assn. Civil Trial and Appellate Specialists, State Bar of Tex., Houston Bar Assn., Tex. Assn. Def. Counsel, Order of Coif, Beta Gamma Sigma. Office: Fulbright & Jaworski LLP Ste 5100 1301 McKinney Houston TX 77010-3095 Office Phone: 713-651-5637. Office Fax: 713-651-5246. Business E-Mail: jsullivan@fulbright.com.

SULLIVAN, JOHN J., lawyer, former federal agency administrator; b. Boston, 1959; m. Grace Rodriguez; 3 children. BA in History & Polit. Sci., Brown U., 1981; JD, Columbia U., 1985. Law clk. to Hon. John Minor Wisdom US Ct. Appeals (5th Cir.); law clk. to Justice David H. Souter US Supreme Ct.; counselor to asst. atty. gen. Office Legal Counsel US Dept. Justice, 1991; dep. gen. counsel George H.W. Bush Re-Election Campaign, 1992; ptnr. Mayer, Brown, Rowe & Maw, LLP, 1993—2004; legal counsel, dep. gen. counsel US Dept. Def., Washington, 2004—05; gen. counsel US Dept. Commerce, Washington, 2005—08, dep. sec., 2008—09; ptnr. Gibson, Dunn & Crutcher LLP, Washington, 2009—. Office: Gibson Dunn & Crutcher LLP 1050 Connecticut Ave NW Washington DC 20036 Office Phone: 202-955-8565. Office Fax: 202-530-9681. E-mail: jsullivan@gibsondunn.com.*

SULLIVAN, JOHN L., political science professor; BA summa cum laude, Univ. Minn., 1967; PhD, Univ. NC, 1970; Postdoctoral Rsch. Fellow, Yale Univ., 1970—71. Faculty, dept. statistcs, polit. sci. Iowa State Univ., 1971—72; faculty, polit. sci. Ind. Univ., 1972—75; faculty, dept. polit. sci. Univ. Minn., 1975—, prof., 1983—99, regents' prof., 1999—, Arleen C. Carlson chair in Am. politics, 2001—04. Vis. prof. Victoria Univ. of Wellington, New Zealand, 1984; adj. assoc. prof., Hubert H. Humphrey Inst. Pub. Affairs Univ. Minn., 1975—83, co-dir. Ctr. for Study of Polit. Psychology, 1995—2004; Benedict disting. vis. prof. Carleton Coll., 1991, 98, 2000, 01. Co-editor (founder): Political Methodology, 1972—85; co-editor: Quantitative Applications to the Social Sciences, 1979—86, American Journal of Political Science, 1985—88, Political Psychology, 1997—2004; editl. bd. American Political Science Review, 1996—2001. Recipient Harold Lasswell award for Disting. Scientific Contributions, Internat. Soc. Polit. Psychology, 2002. Fellow: Am. Acad. Arts & Scis. Office: Coll Liberal Arts Twin Cities Campus Univ Minn 101 Pleasant St SE Minneapolis MN 55455 Office Phone: 612-624-4305. Business E-Mail: jsull@umn.edu.

SULLIVAN, JOHN LOUIS, JR., retired search company executive; b. Macon, Ga., Aug. 27, 1928; s. John Louis and Elizabeth (Macken) S.; m. Barbara Boyle, Aug. 17, 1974; children: John, Katherine, Betsy, Ted. AB in Econs., Duke U., 1950; MBA, U. Pa., 1957; postgrad. Advance Mgmt. Program, Harvard U., 1975. Br. mgr. IBM, Phila., 1962-63, mgr. edn. Endicott, N.Y., 1963-64; asst. to pres. Data Procesing Div. IBM, White Plains, N.Y., 1965-67; dist. mgr. Data Processing Div. IBM, Washington, 1967-69; mgr. eastern and fed. regions Memorex Corp., 1969-71; v.p. mktg. Infonet div. Computer Sci. Corp., El Segundo, Calif., 1971-75; exec. v.p. Fin. Service Group-ADP Inc., Clifton, N.J., 1975-77; sr. v.p. Heidrick & Struggles Inc., San Francisco and Los Angeles, 1977-82, dir., 1977-82, office mgr., 1979-82; v.p., mng. dir. Korn-Ferry Internat., Los Angeles, 1982-87, v.p., mng. ptnr. Boston, 1987-94; ret., 1994. Bd. dirs., mem. exec. com. March of Dimes, Los Angeles County; bd. regents Mount St. Mary's Coll., L.A.; chmn. bd. Latin Am. Resource Ctr.; bd. dirs. Coalition St. Simons and Sea Island. Served to lt. (j.g.) USN, 1950-53. Mem. Harvard U. Bus. Sch. Alumni Assn. (dir.). Clubs: Regency (Los Angeles), Bankers (San Francisco), Atheneum (Pasadena), Mission Hills (Rancho Mirage), Calif. Yacht (Los Angeles), Harvard (Boston), Newcomers (pres.), Rotary (bd. dirs.). Democrat. Home Phone: 912-634-8747.

SULLIVAN, JOSEPH MARTIN, bishop emeritus; b. Bklyn., Mar. 23, 1930; s. Thomas and Margaret Sullivan. Attended, Manhattan Coll.; grad., Immaculate Conception Sem., Huntington, NY, 1956; MA, Fordham U. Sch. Social Work, 1961; MPA, NYU. Ordained priest Diocese of Bklyn., NY, 1956; priest Our Lady of Lourdes, Queens Village, NY, 1956—59; asst. dir. child care divsn. Cath. Charities, Bklyn., 1961—65, dir. child care divsn., 1965—68, exec. dir., 1969—79, exec. v.p. bd. trustees, 1979; ordained bishop, 1980; aux. bishop Diocese of Bklyn., NY, 1980—2005, aux. bishop emeritus, 2005—. Chmn. Cath. Med. Ctr. of Bklyn. & Queens; bd. dirs. Cath. Charities USA. Mem.: US Cath. Conf. (chmn. Social Devel. & World Peace dept.). Roman Catholic. Office: 75 Greene Ave PO Box C Brooklyn NY 11202

SULLIVAN, KATHLEEN, elementary school educator; b. Vt. Grad., Pa. State Univ. Tchr. Quaker Sch., Phila., Ripton Sch., 1991—92, Warren (Vt.) Sch., 1992—. Leader Vt. Math. Network, 1994—. Named Vt. Tchr. of Yr., 2007. Office: Warren Elem Sch 293 School Rd Warren VT 05674 Home Phone: 802-496-5867; Office Phone: 802-496-2487. Business E-Mail: katie@warrenschool.org.

SULLIVAN, KATHLEEN MARIE, lawyer, educator; b. Sault Sainte Marie, Mich., Aug. 20, 1955; BA, Cornell U., 1976, Oxford U., Eng., 1978; JD, Harvard U., 1981. Bar: NY 1982, US Supreme Ct. 1985, Mass. 1988, Calif. 2006. Law clk. to Hon. James L. Oakes US Ct. Appeals (2nd cir.), 1981-82; pvt. law practice, 1982-84; asst. prof. law Harvard U., Cambridge, Mass., 1984-89, prof., 1989-93, Stanford U. Law Sch., Calif., 1993—, Robert E. Paradise fellow, 1995-96, Stanley Morrison prof., 1996—, dean, Richard E. Lang prof. law, 1999—2004; of counsel Quinn Emanuel Urquhart Oliver & Hedges LLP, Redwood Shores, Calif., 2005—. Vis. prov. U. So. Calif. Law Ctr., 1991, Stanford U., 1992; lectr., commentator on constnl. law. Co-editor: (with Gerald Gunther) Constitutional Law, 15th edit., 2004. Named one of The 100 Most Influential Lawyers in America Nat. Law Jour., 2000, 2006, 50 Most Influential Women Lawyers in America, 2007, 100 Most Influential Lawyers in Calif., Daily Jour.; recipient Albert M. Sacks-Paul A. Freund award for Tchg. Excellence, Harvard U., 1992, John Bingham Hurlbut award for Excellence in Tchg. Stanford U., 1996. Fellow Am. Acad. Arts and Scis, Am. Philosophical Soc.; bd. trustees, The Century Found. Office: Quinn Emanuel Urquhart Oliver & Hedges LLP 51 Madison Ave 22nd Fl New York NY 10010 also: Stanford U Law Sch Crown Quadrangle 559 Nathan Abbott Way Stanford CA 94305-8610 Office Phone: 650-801-5000. Business E-Mail: sullivan@law.stanford.edu.*

SULLIVAN, KATHRYN D., geologist, former astronaut, science association executive; b. Paterson, NJ, Oct. 3, 1951; d. Donald P. and Barbara K. Sullivan (dec.). BS in Earth Scis., U. Calif., Santa Cruz, 1973; PhD in Geology, Dalhousie U., Halifax, NS, Can., 1978; Dr. (hon.), Halhousie, Halifax, NS, Can., 1985, SUNY, Utica, 1990, Stevens Inst., 1992, Ohio Dominican U., 1998, Kent State U., 2002; Doctorate (hon.), St. Bonaventure U., 2005. Astronaut NASA, 1979—93, mission specialist flight STS-41G, 1984, mission specialist flight STS-31, 1990, payload comdr. flight STS-45, 1992; chief scientist NOAA, Washington, 1993—96; pres., CEO Ctr. Sci. and Industry, Columbus, Ohio, 1996—2005, sci. advisor; dir. Battelle Ctr. for Math. and Sci. Edn. Policy John Glenn Sch. Pub. Affairs, Ohio State U., Columbus, Ohio, 2006—. Adj. prof. Rice U., Houston, 1985-92, geology, Ohio State U., Columbus, Ohio; mem. Nat. Commn. on Space, 1985-86; mem. exec. panel Chief of Naval Ops., 1988-96; chair, Ohio Aerospace and Defense Adv. Coun., 2003; mem. Nat. Sci. Bd., 2004—, vice chmn., 2006—; served on Pews Oceans Commn.; advisor, Nat. Geographic, Smithsonian Inst., Pub. TV; bd. dirs. Am. Electric Power. Oceanography officer, Capt. USNR; private pilot. Recipient Space Flight medal NASA, 1984, 90, 92, Exceptional Svc. medal, 1988, 91, Nat. Air and Space Mus. trophy Smithsonian Instn., 1985, Outstanding Leadership medal, 1992, AAS Space Flight Achievement award, 1991, AAS Prather Eva award, 1992, Lone Sailor award, US Navy Meml. Found., 1997, Juliette award for Nat. Women of Distinction, Girl Scouts U.S.A., 2002, Aviation Week & Space Tech. Aerospace Legend award, 2005; named one of Ten Outstanding Young People of the World award, Jaycees Internat., 1987, Ten Outstanding Young Americans award, US Jaycees, 1987; inductee Ohio Veteran's Hall of Fame, 2001, Ohio Women's Hall of Fame, 2002, Astronaut Hall of Fame, 2004. Fellow AAAS; mem. AIAA (Haley Space Flight award, 1991, Legends Aerospace Laureate 2005), Geol. Soc. Am.,

Am. Geophys. Union, Soc. Women Geographers, Nat. Sci. Bd. (Public Svc. award, 2003), Explorers Club, Woods Hole Oceanographic Institution, Assn. Space Explorers. First Am. woman to walk in space.

SULLIVAN, KENNETH WAYNE, engineer; b. NYC, Apr. 15, 1957; s. William A. and Helen J. Sullivan; m. Christina A. Eastwood, Sept. 10, 1983 (div. Apr. 1997); children: Daniel, Sarah; m. Lucina Ibarra, Aug. 26, 2006. AAS, SUNY, Farmingdale, 1978, BS, 2003; MBA, Dowling Coll., Oakdale, NY, 2007. Draftsman, jr. designer Cosentini Assoc., NYC, 1981—84; sr. designer Syska & Hennessy Engrs., NYC, 1984—88; project engr. Sikorski Engring. Assn., Jericho, NY, 1990—93, Lehr Assocs., NYC, 1993—99, Sear Brown, Melville, NY, 1999—2003; project mgr. Estee Lauder Co., 2003—05, AKF Engrs., NYC, 2005—06, Parsons Brinckerhoff, NYC, 2006—. Evening instr. Inst. Design & Constrn., Bklyn. Contbr. articles to profl. publs. Recipient award, Am. Sch. and U. Archtl. Portfolio, 2000. Mem.: ASHRAE, Project Mgmt. Inst., Nat. Trust Hist. Preservation, Delta Mu Delta. Roman Catholic. Avocations: reading, history, music, running. Office: Parsons Brinckerhoff One Penn Plz New York NY 10001 Home: 70 Lincoln Ave Apt B21 Rockville Centre NY 11570 Office Phone: 212-631-3716. Personal E-mail: sullk11801@yahoo.com.

SULLIVAN, KEVIN B., museum administrator, former lieutenant governor, state legislator; b. Hartford, Conn., Aug. 20, 1949; s. John (dec.) and Gwendolyn Price (Bancroft) S.; m. Carolyn Thornberry, 1985. AB with honors, Trinity Coll., 1971; JD, U. Conn., 1982. Polit. cons. in pvt. practice, West Hartford, Conn., 1973-74; adminstrv. clk. edn. com. Conn. House of Reps., Hartford, 1974-76; legis. asst. State Commr. Edn., 1976-81; atty. Byrn Slater Sandler Shulman & Rouse, Hartford, 1981—; councilman Town of West Hartford, 1981-86, mayor, 1983-85, dep. mayor, 1985-86; mem. from Dist. 5 Conn. Senate, Hartford, 1986—2004, Pro Tempore, 1997—2004; lt. gov. State of Conn., 2004—07; pres., CEO The Children's Mus., Conn., 2007—. Chmn. edn. com., mem. internship and transp. coms., dep. minority leader Conn. State Senate. Active Nat. Legis. Found.; participant U. Va.'s Program for Emerging Polit. Leaders; v.p., cmty. and instl. rels. Trinity Coll., West Harford. Mem. ABA, Hartford Bar Assn., League of Women Voters, State Capitol Vietnam Veterens Meml. (founder), Greater Hartford Jaycees (Man of Yr. 1983), Rotary Club, Pi Gamma Mu. Democrat. Office: Children's Mus 950 Trout Brook Dr West Hartford CT 06119 Office Phone: 860-231-2824. Office Fax: 860-232-0705. Business E-Mail: ksullivan@thechildrensmuseumct.org.

SULLIVAN, LAWRENCE MATTHEW, lawyer; b. Wilmington, Del., Sept. 5, 1937; BA Philosophy, Kings's Coll., 1959; JD, Cath. U. Am., 1964. Bar: DE Supreme Ct. 1965, US Dist. Ct./DE 1966, US Supreme Ct. 1985. Pvt. practice, 1965—2000; asst. county atty. New Castle County, 1966—67, register of wills, 1966—70; pub. defender State of Del., 1970; instr. bus. and real estate law Wilmington Coll., 1969—78; assoc. prof. Real Estate Law Wilmington Coll., 1969—78; adj. prof. Real Estate Law DE: Tech. and Cmty. Coll., 1978—80, DE State Coll., 1980—82; instr. bus. and real estate law Del Tech. and Cmty. Coll., 1978—80, Del. State Coll., 1980—82, Brandywine Coll.; vice chmn. and mem. various com., Criminal Justice Coun., Del. Co-author: Del. Fundamentals of Real Estate, 1980. Recipient Reginald Heber Smith award, Nat. Legal Aid and Defender Assn., 2006, Highest award, Am. Bar Assn., Charles H. Dorsey, Jr. award, Reginald Heber Smith award; named Del. Outstanding Young Rep. of Yr., Del., 1965, Wilmington's Young Man of Yr., Wilmington Del., 1966, one of Outstanding Young Men of Am., 1968. Mem.: ABA (Charles H. Dorsey, Jr. award 2006), DE Supreme Ct. Planning Com. (vice chair), Crime Reduction Task Force, New Castle County Officials Assn. (pres. 1968—70), Del Trial Lawyers Assn., Del. Bar Assn., Trial Lawyers Am., Am. Arbitration Assn., Sentencing Accountability Commn., Gov. Crime Reduction Task Force, Del. Agy. to Reduce Crime, Del Supreme Ct. Commn. on Del. Ct. 2000, Del Supreme Ct. Planning and Long Range Ct. Planning Com., Phi Alpha Delta. Office: Lawrence M Sullivan Pub Defender Del 1010 Concord Ave # 201 Wilmington DE 19802-3367

SULLIVAN, LOUIS WADE, medical educator, former United States Secretary of Health & Human Services; b. Atlanta, Nov. 3, 1933; s. Walter Wade and Lubirda Elizabeth (Priester) S.; m. Eve Williamson, Sept. 30, 1955; children: Paul, Shanta, Halsted. BS magna cum laude, Morehouse Coll., Atlanta, 1954; MD cum laude, Boston U., 1958. Diplomate: Am. Bd. Internal Medicine. Intern N.Y. Hosp.-Cornell Med. Ctr., NYC, 1958-59, resident in internal medicine, 1959-60; fellow in pathology Mass. Gen. Hosp., Boston, 1960-61; rsch. fellow Thorndike Meml. Lab. Harvard Med. Sch., Boston, 1961-63; instr. medicine Harvard Med. Sch., 1963-64; asst. prof. medicine N.J. Coll. Medicine, 1964-66; co-dir. hematology Boston U. Med. Ctr., 1966; assoc. prof. medicine Boston U., 1968—73; dir. hematology Boston City Hosp., 1973-75; prof. medicine & physiology Boston U., 1973—75; dean Sch. Medicine, Morehouse Coll., Atlanta, 1975—83; pres. Morehouse Sch. Medicine, Morehouse Coll., Atlanta, 1981—89, 1993—2002, pres. emeritus, 2002—; sec. US Dept. Health & Human Services, Washington, 1989-93. Non-exec. dir. GM, 1993-2002; bd. dirs. 3M Co., 1993-, Henry Schein Inc., 2003-, Bristol-Myers Squibb Co., CIGNA Corp., Equifax Inc., Georgia-Pacific Corp., United Therapeutics Corp.; mem. sickle cell anemia adv. com. NIH, 1974-75; ad hoc panel on blood diseases Nat. Heart, Lung Blood Disease Bur., 1973, Nat. Adv. Rsch. Coun., 1977; mem. med. adv. bd. Nat. Leukemia Assn., 1968-70, chmn., 1970; researcher suppression of hematopoiesis by ethanol, pernicious anemia in childhood, folates in human nutrition. Mem. Sec. of Edn.'s Commn. on Future of Edn., 2005. John Hay Whitney Found. Opportunity fellow, 1960-61; recipient Honor medal Am. Cancer Soc., 1991. Mem. Assn. Am. Physicians, Am. Soc. Hematology, Am. Soc. Clin. Investigation, Clin. and Climatological Soc., Inst. Medicine, Phi Beta Kappa, Alpha Omega Alpha. Episcopalian. Office: Morehouse Sch Medicine Office of the Pres Emeritus 133 Peachtree St Ste 4040 Atlanta GA 30303 Office Phone: 404-752-1933.*

SULLIVAN, MARCIA WAITE, lawyer; b. Chgo, Nov. 30, 1950; d. Robert Macke and Jacqueline (Northrop) S.; m. Steven Donald Jansen, Dec. 20, 1975; children: Eric Spurlock, Laura Macke, Brian Northrop. BA, DePauw U., 1972; JD, Ind. U., 1975. Assoc. Arnstein, Gluck, Weitzenfeld & Minow, Chgo., 1975-76; ptnr. Greenberger and Kaufmann, Chgo., 1976-86, Katten Muchin Rosenman LLP, Chgo., 1986—. Adj. prof. Kent Coll. Law, Ill. Inst. Tech., Chgo., 1991—94; pres. Chgo. Real Estate Exec. Women, 2000—01. Mem. editl. adv. bd.: Real Estate Chgo., 2001—02. Mem. NNCREW Found. Grant Making Com, 2003—04. Mem.: ABA, Chgo. Bar Assn. Avocations: bicycling, cross country skiing, gardening, camping. Office: Katten Muchin Rosenman LLP 525 W Monroe St Chicago IL 60661-3693 Home Phone: 847-256-2496; Office Phone: 312-902-5535. Business E-Mail: marcia.sullivan@kattenlaw.com.

SULLIVAN, MARGARET M., editor-in-chief; d. John and Elaine (Saab) Sullivan; children: Alex, Grace. BA in English, Georgetown U., 1979; MS with distinction, Medill Sch. Journalism, Northwestern U., 1980. Clk. Washington bur. Gannett News Svc., 1977—80; Buffalo-area stringer NY Times, 1984—89; reporter, news-feature reporter, columnist Buffalo News, 1980—87, asst. city editor, 1987—89, asst. mng. editor, 1989—98, mng. editor, 1998—99, editor, v.p., 1999—. Instr. journalism SUNY, Buffalo, 1991—93. Recipient Award for Internat. Understanding, Rotary Found., 1987, Young Leadership award, YMCA, 1987; named One of Buffalo's Outstanding Young Bus. Leaders, Bus. 1st newspaper, 1992; named to Medill Sch. Journalism Hall of Achievement, 2003. Mem.: Kappa Tau Alpha. Office: Buffalo News 1 News Plaza PO Box 100 Buffalo NY 14240 Office Phone: 716-849-4480. E-mail: mmsullivan@buffnews.com.*

SULLIVAN, MARGARET M., biologist, educator; d. Charles Watson and Ann McGee McKay; m. Jacob Edwin Sullivan, May 17, 1974 (dec. June 14, 2003); children: Margaret-Ann, Mary-Katherine, Jacob Edwin III. BS, MS, U. Ala., 1973; MEd, Ala. State U., 1991. Cert. tchr. Ala., 1991. Adj. prof. Huntingdon Coll., Montgomery, Ala., 1975—84; tchr. Montgomery Pub. Sch., 1993—2003; adj. prof. Troy U. Montgomery, 1999—; tchr. Elmore County Sch., Millbrook, Ala., 2003—05; environ. scientist Ala. Dept. Environ. Mgmt., Montgomery, 2005—. Dist. trainer Montgomery County Sch., 1997—2002; cons. Ala. Wildlife Fedn., Montgomery, Ala., 2001, Dallas County Sch., Selma, Ala., 2002. Leader Girl Scouts Am., Montgomery, Ala., 1987—97; co-chair Ala. Dance Theatre Com., Montgomery, 1990—2000; v.p. Montgomery Zoo, Ala., 1990—92. Recipient Outstanding Environ. Program award, Legacy, Ptnrs. in Environ. Edn., 1998, NSTA/FDA Profl. Devel. Program participant, Nat. Sci. Tchr. Assn., 2003, edn. grant, Ala. Electric Coop., 2004, 2005; named Toyota Internat. Tchr., Toyota, USA, 2002, Outstanding Svc. Team leader, Girl Scouts Am., 1992, Outstanding Svc. Team Vol., 1995; finalist Outstanding Tchr., State Farm, 1999; grantee, Cmty. Found. of Montgomery, 1998—2000, Legacy, Ptnrs. in Environ. Edn., 1999, 2002, America's Unsung Heroes, Star Ins., 2000, Alagasco, 2000, Ala. Power Co., 2001; fellow Operation Pathfinder, Ala., Miss. Sea Grant, 1995; Eleanor Roosevelt fellow, AAUW, 2002. Mem.: Ala. Sci. Tchr. Assn., Nat. Marine Edn. Assn., Nat. Sci. Tchr. Assn., Delta Kappa Gamma. Office: Ala Dept Environ Mgmt 1350 Coliseum Blvd Montgomery AL 36109

SULLIVAN, MARIAN TOTH, epidemiologist, researcher; b. Pitts., July 4, 1955; d. William E. and Mildred C. Toth; m. Joseph Hearst Sullivan, June 5, 1982; children: David, Linda, William Hearst. BS in Microbiology, U. Notre Dame, Ind., 1977; MS in Biochemistry, Clemson U., SC, 1980; MPH, Johns Hopkins U., Md, 1991. Asst. prof. Erskine Coll., Due West, SC, 1980—83; chemist Clemson U., 1983—85; project leader ARC, Rockville, Md., 1986—97; exec. dir. Nat. Blood Data Resource Ctr., Bethesda, 1997—2003; rsch. epidemiologist RTI Internat., Rockville, 2003—. Recipient Congl. Testimony, Commerse Com.-Oversight and Investigations Subcommittee, 1999, ARC Tiffany award, ARC, 1996, Career Author award, RTI Internat., 2005. Mem.: Assn. Prevention, Tchg. and Rsch. (Rsch. Grant 2004). Roman Catholic. Office: RTI Internat 6110 Executive Blvd Ste 902 Rockville MD 20852 Business E-Mail: msullivan@rti.org.

SULLIVAN, MARK J., federal agency administrator; b. Arlington, Mass. m. Laurie Bell; 3 children. BA, St. Anselm Coll. Spl. agent office inspector gen. HUD, 1978—83; spl. agent U.S. Secret Svc., U.S. Dept. Homeland Security, Detroit, 1983—90, spl. agent fraud divsn. Washington, 1990—91, spl. agent presdl. protection divsn., 1991—96, asst. spl. agent in charge office protective ops., 1996—97, resident agent in charge Columbus, Ohio, 1997—98, spl. agent in charge conterfeit divsn., 1998—99, asst. spl. agent in charge presdl. protective divsn., 1999—2000, dep. asst. dir. office protective ops. fed. sr. exec. svc., 2000—02, dep. spl. agent in charge vice presdl. protective divsn., 2002—03, dep. asst. dir. office human resources and training, asst. dir. office protective ops., 2003—06, dep. dir., 2006, dir., 2006—. Recipient Disting. Presdl. Rank award, 2005. Office: US Secret Svc Personnel Divisn 245 Murray Dr Bldg 410 Washington DC 20223*

SULLIVAN, MARTIN EDWARD, museum director; b. Troy, NY, Feb. 9, 1944; s. John Francis and Helen Edna (Lynch) S.; m. Katherine Mary Hostetter, May 9, 1981; children: Abigail, Bethany. BA in History, Siena Coll., 1965; MA in History, U. Notre Dame, 1970, PhD in History, 1974. Exec. dir. Ind. Commn. for Humanities, Indpls., 1972-75; dir. pub. programs NEH, Washington, 1976-81; pres. Inst. on Man and Sci., Rensselaerville, NY, 1981-83; dir. NY State Mus., State Edn. Dept., Albany, 1983-90, Heard Mus., Phoenix, 1990-99, Historic St. Mary City, Md., 1999—2008, Smithsonian Nat. Portrait Gallery, Washington, 2008—. Trustee Am. Indian Ritual Object Repatriation Found., N.Y.C., 1992-98; chmn. U.S. Govt. Cultural Property Adv. Com., 1995-2003. Author: Museums, Adults and the Humanities, 1981, Inventing the Southwest: The Fred Harvey Company and Native American Art, 1996; contbr. articles to profl. jours. Trustee Am. Fedn. Arts, 1994-98; mem. Native Am. Repatriation Act Adv. Com., 1992-2005. With U.S. Army, 1966-68. Mem. Am. Assn. Mus. (v.p. 1990-93, mem. accreditation commn. 1997—; named to Centennial Honor Roll, 2006). Democrat. Office: Nat Portrait Gallery Smithsonian Inst PO Box 37012 Washington DC 20013-7012 Office Phone: 212-633-8300.

SULLIVAN, MARTIN J., former insurance company executive; b. Essex, Eng., 1955; married; 3 children. With fin. dept. Am. Internat. Underwriters Ltd., 1971—83, property mgr., 1983—88, London office mgr., regional mktg. mgr. for U.K. and Ireland, 1988—89, asst. mng. dir., 1989—91, CEO, 1991—93, pres., UK/Ireland div., 1993—95, pres., 1997—98; sr. v.p. Am. Internat. Group, Inc. (AIG), 1995—98, exec. v.p. NYC, 1998—2002, co-COO, 2002—05, vice chmn., 2002—05, pres., CEO, 2005—08; chmn. Transatlantic Holdings, Inc., 2006—. Bd. dirs. Am. Internat. Group, Inc. (AIG), 2002—08, Transatlantic Holdings, Inc., 2005—. Recipient Leadership award, The Am. Ireland Fun, 2007, Order of the British Empire, Queen Elizabeth II, 2007. Office: Transatlantic Holdings Inc 80 Pine St New York NY 10005

SULLIVAN, MARY ANN, artist; b. Columbus, Ohio, June 17, 1952; d. Thomas Joseph and Mary Jane (neeHouck) Sullivan; 1 child, Benjamin James. BFA in Illustration, Columbus Coll. Art and Design, 1974. Designer, illustrator Gibson Greeting Cards, Cin., 1974—78; freelance comml. artist Artwear, Albuquerque, 1984—90; exhibiting fine artist Fine Arts Ctr. En Taos, Taos, N.Mex., 1984—86, Spangler Cummings Gallery, Columbus, 1984—88, El Taller Gallery, Taos, N.Mex., 1984—94, Roberta Kuhn Gallery, Columbus, 1988—92, various galleries, 1992—. Songs of the Earth, 1976, one-woman shows include El Taller Gallery, N. Mex., 1988, 1990, Wilmington Coll., 2001, exhibited in group shows at Ohio State Fair, 1974—2001, Spangler Cummings Gallery, Ohio, Roberta Kuhn Gallery, Grand Ctrl. Galleries, N.Y.C., 1985, Society of Illustrators, NYC, others. Mem.: Ohio Art League. Achievements include evolving 2 dimensional art work into 3 dimensional assemblages in 2001-2009. Avocations: books, interior decorating.

SULLIVAN, MARY E., retired secondary educator, former state legislator; b. June 29, 1932; m. Charles M. Sullivan; children: Charles M. Jr., Ethel M., Mary E., Kathleen M., Mark C., Ursula M. AB, Regis Coll., 1954; MA, Boston Coll., 1955. Asst. prof. stats. Bentley Coll., Waltham, Mass., 1966-72; asst. prof., registrar Husson Coll., 1973-79; mem. staff Maine Dept. Manpower Affairs Rsch., 1980-81; math. tchr. John Bapst Meml. H.S., 1981-97; also mem. Maine Ho. of Reps., 1992-94. City councilor City of Bangor, Maine, 1985—, mayor, 1988-89. Mem. Maine Munic Assn. (past pres.). Democrat. Home: 143 Bright St Waltham MA 02453-6584

SULLIVAN, MARY ROSE, retired English language educator; b. Boston, May 13, 1931; d. John Joseph and Elinor Mary (Crotty) Sullivan BA, Emmanuel Coll., Boston, 1952; MA, Cath. U. Am., 1957; PhD, Boston U., 1964. Tchr. Woburn Pub. Schs., Mass., 1957-60; faculty Emmanuel Coll., Boston, 1960-66; prof. English U. Colo., Denver, 1966-96; ret., 1996. Book reviewing staff San Diego Mag., 1980—90. Author: Browning's Voices in the Ring and the Book, 1969; co-editor: (3 vols.) letters of E.B. Browning to M.R. Mitford, 1836-54, 1983, Women of Letters: Selected Letters of E.B. Browning to M.R. Mitford, 1987, Crime Classics, 1990, Elizabeth Barrett Browning: Selected Poetry and Prose, 1993; editl. bd. English Lang. Notes, 1970-96. Served to capt. USNR, 1952—83. Am. Coun. Learned Socs. fellow, 1973. Mem. MLA, Boston Browning Soc., Mystery Writers of Am.

SULLIVAN, MICHAEL EVAN, investment company executive; b. Phila., Dec. 30, 1940; s. Albert and Ruth (Liebert) S. BS, N.Mex. State U., 1966, MA, 1967; BS, U. Tex., 1969; MBA, U. Houston, 1974; MS, U. So. Calif., 1976, MPA, 1977; BS in Acctg., U. La Verne, Calif., 1981; PhD in Adminstrn., U. So. Calif., 1983. Sr. adminstrv. and tech. analyst Houston Lighting & Power Co., 1969—74; electronics engr. US Govt., Point Mugu, Calif., 1974—77; mem. tech. staff Hughes Aircraft Co., El Segundo, Calif., 1977—78; staff program adminstr. Ventura divsn. Northrop Corp., Newbury Park, Calif., 1978—79; divsn. head engring. Navastrogru, Point Mugu, 1978—82; br. head, divsn. head spl. programs head operational sys. Pacific Missile Test Ctr., Calif., 1983—90, head tech. devel. office, head capability devel., 1993—98; regional coord. far west, exec. com., exec. bd. Fed. Lab. Consortium, 1999—. CNO, dir. rsch., devel. and acquisiiton The Pentagon, Washington, 1987-88, dir. rsch. devel. test and evaluation and tech., 1990-93; pres., chmn. bd. Diversified Mgmt. Sys., Inc., Camarillo, Calif., 1978—. Author: The Management of Research, Development, Test and Evaluation Organizations; Organization Behavior Characteristics of Supervisors-Public versus Private Sectors; Self-Actualization in RDT & E Organizations: Self-Actualization in a Health Care Agency; others. V.p., bd. dirs. Ventura County Master Chorale and Opera Assn.; bd. dirs. So. Calif. Assn. of Pub. Adminstrn. (also mem. fin. com., programs com., student aid com., exec. bd., exec. com. fed. lab. consortium). Served with U.S. Army, 1958-62. Ednl. Rsch. Info. Clearing House fellow, 1965-67, Ednl. Rsch. Tng. Program fellow N.Mex. State U., 1967. Mem. IEEE, Am. Math. Soc., Math. Assn. Am., Am. Statis. Assn., IEEE Engring. Mgmt. Soc., Am. Soc. Pub. Adminstrn., So. Calif. Assn. Pub. Adminstrn. (bd. dirs., various coms.), Assn. Fedn. Tech. Transfer Execs., Fed. Mgrs. Assn., Am. Assn. Individual Investors, Mcpl. Mgmt. Assts. So. Calif., Acad. Polit. Sci., Internat. Soc. for the Sys. Scis., Assn. MBA Execs., Tech. Transfer Soc., Internat. Fedn. for Sys. Rsch., Phi Kappa Phi, Pi Gama Mu. Home: PO Box 273 Port Hueneme CA 93044-0273 Office: PO Box 447 Camarillo CA 93011-0447

SULLIVAN, MICHAEL J., lobbyist, former prosecutor; b. Oct. 3, 1954; m. Terry Sullivan, 1975; children: Joseph, Kelly, Allyson, James. BA, Boston Coll., 1979; JD, Suffolk U., 1983. Assoc. Bolles & Pritchard, 1983—90; ptnr. McGovern & Sullivan, 1990—95; mem. Mass. Ho. Reps. from Dist. 7, 1991—95; dist. atty. Plymouth County, Mass., 1995—2001; US atty. Dist. Mass. US Dept. Justice, Boston, 2001—09, acting dir. Bur. Alcohol, Tobacco, Firearms & Explosives (ATF) Washington, 2006—09; ptnr. The Ashcroft Group, LLC, Washington, 2009—. Office: The Ashcroft Group LLC 1399 New York Ave NW Ste 950 Washington DC 20005 Office Phone: 202-942-0202. Office Fax: 202-942-0216.*

SULLIVAN, MICHAEL J., labor union administrator; b. Indpls., 1945; Former sheet metal worker Brad Snodgrass Sheet Metal Inc., R.M. Cotton Inc., Nyland Sheet Metal Inc.; apptd. bus. rep. Sheet Metal Workers' Internat. Assn. (SMWIA), 1973, bus. mgr., fin. sec.-treas., Local 20, 1979—94, mem. gen. exec. coun., 1983—94, gen. sec.-treas., 1994—99, gen. pres., 1999—. Pres. SMWIA's Mich.-Ind. Coun., Ind. Bldg. & Constrn. Trades Coun.; apptd. mem. Ind. Workers Compensation Commn., Hoosier Alliance Against Drugs. Office: SMWIA 1750 New York Ave NW 6th Fl Washington DC 20006*

SULLIVAN, MICHAEL PATRICK, food service executive; b. Dec. 5, 1934; s. Michael Francis and Susan Ellen (Doran) S.; m. Marilyn Emmer, June 27, 1964; children: Katherine, Michael, Maureen, Bridget, Daniel, Thomas. BS, Marquette U., 1956; JD, U. Minn., 1962. Bar: Minn. 1962, U.S. Dist. Ct. Minn. 1962, U.S. Supreme Ct. 1975, U.S. Ct. Appeals (8th cir.) 1978. Assoc. Gray, Plant, Mooty, Mooty & Bennett, Mpls., 1962-67, ptnr., 1968-87, mng. ptnr., 1976-87; pres., CEO Internat. Dairy Queen, Inc., Mpls., 1987-2001, chmn. bd., 2001—. Bd. dirs. The Valspar Corp., Allianz Life Ins. Co. N.Am., Opus Corp.; instr. U. Minn. Law Sch., 1962-67; lectr. continuing legal edn.; spl. counsel to atty. gen. Minn., 1971-79, 82-84; bd. dirs. Met. Mpls.YMCA, chmn. bd. dirs., 1997-99; pres. Uniform Law Commn., 1987-89. Contbr. articles to profl. jours. Bd. regents St. John's U., 2000; bd. dirs. YMCA Met. Mpls.; bd. trustees St. Paul Sem. Served with USN, 1956-59. Mem. ABA (ho. of dels., 1984-89), Minn. Bar Assn. (gov. 1974-86), Hennepin County Bar Assn. (pres. 1978-89), Am. Bar Found., Am. Law Inst., Am. Arbitration Assn. (bd. dirs.), Order of Coif. Roman Catholic. Office: Internat Dairy Queen 7505 Metro Blvd Minneapolis MN 55439-3020

SULLIVAN, MIKE, city councilman, small business owner; m. Kim Sullivan; 1 child. Lic. real estate broker. Owner, pres. Mar-Max Supply, Inc., Channelview, Tex.; mgr. First World Realty, Houston; councilman, Dist. E Houston City Coun., 2008—. Bd. trustees Humble Ind. Sch. Dist., 2004—; ex-officio dir. Bay Area Houston Econ. Partnership. Active Good Shepherd Episcopal Ch., Kingwood, Tex.; bd. dirs. Hosp. Corp. America, Kingwood Med. Ctr. Office: City Hall Annex 900 Bagby 1st Fl Houston TX 77002 Office Phone: 832-393-3008. Office Fax: 832-393-3279. Business E-Mail: districte@cityofhouston.net.*

SULLIVAN, MORTIMER ALLEN, JR., lawyer; b. Buffalo, Sept. 19, 1930; s. Mortimer Allen Sr. and Gertrude (Hinkley) S.; m. Maryanne Calella, Nov. 20, 1965; children: Mark Allen, Michael John. BA, U. Buffalo, 1954. Bar: N.Y. 1964, U.S. Dist. Ct. (we. dist.) N.Y. 1966, U.S. Dist. Ct. (no. dist.) N.Y. 1967, U.S. Supreme Ct. 1970. Counsel liability claims Interstate Motor Freight System, Grand Rapids, Mich., 1964-82. V.p. J.P.M. Sullivan, Inc., Elmira, N.Y., 1959-67; govt. appeal agt. U.S. Selective Service System, 1967-71; dep. sci. staff Erie County (N.Y.) Sheriff's Office, 1971—, lt., 1986—. Inventor (with others) in field; creator, dir. video depiction JudiVision, 1969; composer High Flight, 1983. Chmn. com. on Constn. and Canons Episcopal Diocese of Western N.Y., 1975-96; bd. dirs. Erie County Law Enforcement Found., Inc., 1987—, vice chair, 2008-; bd. dirs. Orchard Park (N.Y.) Symphony Orch., 1975-97, v.p., 1977-79, 91-94. With USAF, 1954-57; spl. agt. Air Force Office of Spl. Investigations, 1972-87, col. res. ret. Decorated Legion of Merit. Mem. Erie County Bar Assn. (chmn. law and tech.

com., 1970-81), Transp. Lawyers Assn., Kappa Alpha Soc., Wanakah (N.Y.) Country Club. Republican. Avocation: aviation. Home: 19 Knob Hill Rd Orchard Park NY 14127-3917 Office: PO Box 1003 Orchard Park NY 14127-8003 Home Phone: 716-662-3270; Office Phone: 716-667-7800. Personal E-mail: masulaw@aol.com.

SULLIVAN, OWEN, employment services executive; Grad., Marquette U., Milw. Various sales, sales mgmt. and product mgmt. positions IBM; pres. Fin. Svcs. Group Metavante, pres. Enterprise Solutions Group; owner Sullivan Advisors, LLC; exec. v.p., CEO Jefferson Wells subs. Manpower, Inc., 2003—, CEO Right Mgmt. subs., 2004—. Bd. dirs. Ministry HealthCare, Circuit Check Inc. Bd. dirs. Children's Hosp. and Health Sys., Inc.

SULLIVAN, PATRICIA A., academic administrator; b. SI, NY; m. Charles Sullivan. AB cum laude, St. John's U., 1961; MS in Biology, NYU, 1964, PhD in Biology, 1967. Tchg. fellow, NIH pre-doctoral fellow NYU; post-doctoral fellow in cell biology Upstate Med. Ctr., Syracuse, NY; vis. fellow Cornell U., 1976; tchr. Wells Coll., NY; dir. biology honors program Tex. Woman's U., 1979-81; dean Salem Coll., Winston-Salem, 1981-87; v.p. acad. affairs Tex. Woman's U., 1987-94, interim pres., 1993-94; chancellor U. N.C., Greensboro, 1995—. Pres. Assn. Tex. Colls. and Univs. Acad. Affairs Officers, Assn. So. Colls. for Women, N.C. Assn. Chief Acad. Officers; active numerous coms. Tex. Higher Edn. Coordinating Bd.; lectr. in field. Contbr. articles to profl. jours. Office: U NC at Greensboro Office of Chancellor PO Box 26170 Greensboro NC 27402-6170

SULLIVAN, PATRICIA LYNNE, political science professor; d. Paul Joseph and Lynne Morgan Sullivan. PhD in Polit. Sci., U. Calif. Davis, 2004. Asst. prof. U. Ga., Athens, 2005—; assoc. dir. cmty. involvement ctr. Rice U., Houston, 1996—98. Dir., internat. conflict resolution GLOBIS, U. Ga., 2007—. Recipient Lilly Tchg. Fellow, U. Ga., 2008—; Jr. Faculty Rsch. grant, Smith Richardson Found., 2008—. Achievements include research in statistical model predicting war outcomes. Office: Univ Ga Dept Internat Affairs Athens GA 30602-1492

SULLIVAN, PATRICIA MARIE, elementary school educator; b. Evergreen Park, Il., Jan. 12, 1953; d. Roger James and Marion Helen (Sabo) Sullivan; m. Gerald Michael Karl, June 23, 1977; children: Andrew Michael Karl, Regan James Karl. BA in History, U. Ill., Chgo., 1974; MA in Reading, St. Xavier U., Chgo., 2002. Cert. reading specialist Ill. Tchr. asst. Sch. Dist. 163, Park Forest, Ill., 1989—93, tchr. 1st grade, 1993—2002, reading coach, 2002—05, reading specialist, 2005—. Vol. women's aux. Am. Legion, Park Forest, 2000—. Mem.: LWV, Alpha Upsilon Alpha, Kappa Delta Phi. Office: Sch Dist 163 Forest Trail Sch 215 Wilson Park Forest IL 60466

SULLIVAN, PATRICIA W. (TERRY SULLIVAN), real estate trainer; b. Hempstead, NY, July 25, 1936; d. Gilbert Hudson and Vera (Morgan) Wehmann; m. Richard J. Sullivan, June 8, 1957 (div. Apr. 1982); children: Katherine, Gillian Stewart, Adam W. BS, Skidmore Coll., 1958; MS, Syracuse U., 1965. Mgr. Purtell & Wigdale, Inc., Cedarburg, Wis., Merrill Lynch Real Estate, Cedarburg; office mgr. Coldwell Banker Real Estate, Cedarburg; sales mgr. Coldwell Banker Residential Brokerage, Mequon, WI; owner, trainer, cons. Terry Sullivan Tng. and Seminars, Belgium, Wis., 1991—2007; sales exec. Coldwell Banker, Mequon, Wis. Contbr. articles to profl. jours. Named Wis. Cert. Real Estate Brokerage Mgr. of Yr., 1990. Mem.: Wis. Cert. Residential Brokers (cert., pres. 1988), Wis. Cert. Residential Specialists (cert., pres. 1982, Cert. Residential Specialist of Yr. 1983), Wis. Realtors Assn. (v.p. 1982—83, bd. dirs. 1983—86, GRI 1975, Instr. of Yr. 1988, Disting. Svc. award 1992), Realtors Nat. Mktg. Inst. (dir. RS coun. 1983—86, CRS 1978, CRB 1981), Ozaukee Bd. Realtors (pres. 1979, bd. dirs. 1977—79, Realtor of Yr. 1979), Women's Coun. Realtors (pres. Milw. chpt. 1982, bd. dirs. 1983—90, PMN 2005, WCR of Yr. 1983), Nat. Women's Coun. Realtors (pres. 1990), Nat. Assn. Realtors (bd. dirs. 1989—90, Omega Tau Rho award 1983, Outstanding Educator of Yr. award for medium states 1989). Office: 1339 W Mequon Rd Mequon WI 53092

SULLIVAN, PATRICK ALLEN, strategic management educator; b. Peoria, Ill., Oct. 31, 1932; s. Francis Richard and Carmela Marie (Smith) S.; m. Gwendolyn Jo Herndon, Aug. 25, 1958; children: Richard John, Sharon Louise Little, Patrick Michael, Cecelia Anne, Catherine Marie Markee. BCE, Marquette U., 1955; MBA, San Diego State U., 1975; DBA, U.S. Internat. U., San Diego, 1988. Engr. USMC, 29 Palms, Calif., 1958-63, USN, San Diego, 1963—87, mgmt. analyst, 1987—88; asst. prof. strategic mgmt. U.S. Internat. U., San Diego, 1988-89, assoc. prof. strategic mgmt., 1989-94, prof. strategic mgmr., 1994—2000, prof. emeritus, 2000—. Ptnr. Sullivan and Assocs. Mgmt. Cons., San Diego, 1988-2005; pres. Ansoft Inst., 2001-2006. Pres. St. Pius Ch. Parish Coun., Chula Vista, Calif., 1984. 1st lt. USMC, 1955-58. Mem. ASCE (life), Japan Strategic Mgmt. Soc. (dir.), K.C., Chi Epsilon, Tau Beta Pi, Sigma Iota Epsilon, Beta Gamma Sigma. Republican. Roman Catholic. Home: 98 E Emerson St Chula Vista CA 91911-3545 Personal E-mail: patsullivan2@cox.net.

SULLIVAN, PATRICK JAMES, lawyer; b. Orange, Calif., Sept. 17, 1943; s. Leo Charles Sullivan and Virginia (Wohosky) Souza; m. Pamela Pressler, Aug. 17, 1974; children: Shannon, Erin. BA, U. So. Calif., 1965; JD, Loyola U., Los Angeles, 1974. Bar: (Calif.) 1974, (U.S. Ct. Appeals (9th cir.)) 1978, (U.S. Supreme Ct) 1979, U.S. Ct. Appeals (3d cir.) 1983, U.S. Tax Ct. 1986, U.S. Ct. Appeals (2d and 8th cirs.) 1989. Trial atty. U.S. Dept. Justice, Washington, 1974—75; ptnr. Sullivan, Jones & Archer, San Diego and San Francisco, 1975—83, Hewitt, Sullivan & Marshall, San Diego, 1983—87, King & Ballow, 1987—90, The Sullivan Law Firm, San Diego, 1990—. Arbitrator San Diego Superior Ct., 1979—83; lectr. U. Calif. Securities Regulations Inst., 1985; chmn. Am. Law Inst. Anti-Trust Conf., 1988, 91; mem. faculty Hastings Ctr. for Trial and Appellate Advocacy, 1989—92, Calif. Continuing Edn. of Bar, 1989—. Served to 1st lt. US Army, Vietnam. Decorated Bronze Star. Fellow: Am. Bar Found. (life); mem.: ABA (litigation and anti-trust sects., ho. dels.), Am. Bd. of Trial Advocates, Nat. Inst. Trial Adv. (faculty 1986—), Am. Judiciary Soc., Am. Law Inst., Am. Inn Ct. (master 1992—2002), Rotary (Newhall, Calif.). Republican. Roman Catholic. Home: 335 Whitewood Pl Encinitas CA 92024-3137 Office: 810 Mission Ave Ste 300 Oceanside CA 92054

SULLIVAN, PEGGY, librarian, consultant; b. Kansas City, Mo., Aug. 12, 1929; d. Michael C. and Ella (O'Donnell) Sullivan. AB, Clarke Coll., Dubuque, Iowa, 1950; MS in Libr. Sci., Cath. U. Am., 1953; PhD, U. Chgo., 1972. Children's pub. libr., Mo., Md., Va., 1952-61; sch. libr. specialist Montgomery County Pub. Schs., Md., 1961-63; dir. Knapp Sch. Librs. Project, 1963—68, Jr. Coll. Libr. Info. Ctr., 1968-69; asst. prof. U. Pitts., 1971-73; dir. Office Libr. Pers. Resources, ALA, Chgo., 1973-74; dean of students, assoc. prof. U. Chgo. Grad. Libr. Sch., 1974-77; asst. commr. ext. svcs. Chgo. Pub. Libr., 1977-81; dean No. Ill. U. Coll. Profl. Studies, DeKalb, 1981-90; dir. univ. librs. No. Ill. U., 1990-92; exec. dir. ALA, 1992-94; dean Rosary Coll. Grad. Sch. Libr. and Info. Sci., 1995-97; rep. Tuft & Assocs., 1995—98. Instr. grad. libr. edn. programs, 1958—73; sr. ptnr. Able Cons., 1987—92; assoc. Tuft & Assocs., 1995—98. Author: The O'Donnells, 1956, Many Names for Eileen, 1969, Problems in School Media Management, 1971, Carl H. Milam and the American Library Association, 1976, Opportunities in Library and Information Science, 1977; co-author: Public Libraries: Smart Practices in Personnel, 1982; editor: Realization: The Final Report of the Knapp School Libraries Project, 1968. Mem.: ALA (hon.), Ill. Libr. Assn., Cath. Libr. Assn., Caxton Club, Chgo. Lit. Club. Roman Catholic. Home and Office: 2800 N Lake Shore Dr Apt 816 Chicago IL 60657-6266 Office Phone: 773-549-5361. Business E-Mail: pslibcon@alumni.uchicago.edu. *Opportunities to use my abilities in a variety of public services have enriched my life, as I hope the results have enriched and empowered others.*

SULLIVAN, PENNY MCIVER, theater and speech educator; b. Hope, Ark., Sept. 25, 1964; d. Arthur William and Willie Mae McIver; m. Michael Lee Sullivan, May 29, 1987; 1 child, Mandy Sullivan Touchstone. BS, So. Ark. U., Magnolia, 1986, BE. Cert. educator State Bd. Edn., Tex., 1998. Speech tchr., English Stephens Pub. Schs., Ark., 1988—96, Karnack ISD, Tex., 1996—98; speech tchr., drama Waskom HS, Tex., 1998—, theatre dir., 1998—. Dir.: (play) Dance Real Show in Jackson (Bronze medal, 2005). Sponsor Internat. Thespian Soc., Waskom, 2005. Mem.: Tau Beta Sigma. Liberal. Methodist. Office: Waskom HS 255 School Ave Waskom TX 75692 Office Fax: 903-687-2897.

SULLIVAN, RICHARD JOSEPH, federal judge; b. Manhasset, NY, 1964; BA, Coll. William and Mary, 1986; JD, Yale U., 1990. Bar: NY 1993. Law clk. to Hon. David M. Ebel US Ct. Appeals (10th Cir.), 1990—91; assoc. Wachtell Lipton Rosen & Katz, 1991—94; asst. US atty. (so. dist.) NY US Dept. Justice, NYC, 1994—2005; dep. gen. counsel Marsh & McLennan Companies, Inc., 2005—07; gen. counsel Marsh Inc., 2006—07; judge US Dist. Ct. (so. dist.) NY, 2007—. Recipient Henry L. Stimson Medal, City Bar Assn., 2003. Office: Daniel Patrick Moynihan US Courthouse 500 Pearl St, Rm 615 New York NY 10007 Office Phone: 212-805-0264.

SULLIVAN, ROBERT EDWARD, lawyer; b. San Francisco, May 18, 1936; s. Edward C. S. and Mary Jane (Sullivan); m. Maureen Lois Miles, June 14, 1958 (dec. 1972); children: Teresa Ann, Andrew Edward, Edward Braddock; m. Lynn Bryant, Aug. 28, 2002. BS, U. San Francisco, 1958; LLB, U. Calif-Berkeley, 1961. Bar: Calif. 1962. Assoc. Pillsbury, Madison & Sutro, San Francisco, 1963-70, ptnr., 1971—2000, Pillsbury Winthrop LLP, San Francisco, 2001—05, Pillsbury Winthrop Shaw Pittman LLP, San Francisco, 2005—. Lectr. bus. law Calif. Continuing Edn. Bar and Practicing Law Inst.; v.p., treas., dir. MPC Ins., Ltd., 1986-93. Contbr. articles to profl. jours. Bd. dirs., exec. com. mem., sec. San Francisco Opera Assn., 1993-2007. 1st lt. U.S. Army, 1961-63. Mem. ABA, State Bar Calif. (com. corps. 1979-82, chmn. 1981-82, mem. exec. com. bus. law sect. 1982-85, vice chmn. 1983-84, chmn. 1984-85, advisor 1985-86, mem. partnership com. 1990-92, chmn. ltd. liability co. drafting com. 1992-93), San Francisco Bar Assn., Bankers Club San Francisco (bd. dirs., sec.). Democrat. Roman Catholic. Office: Pillsbury Winthrop Shaw Pittman LLP 50 Fremont St San Francisco CA 94105-2228

SULLIVAN, ROBERT EMMETT, pediatric dentist, educator; b. Sioux City, Iowa, May 28, 1932; s. Joseph A. and Daisy B. (Stanieforth) S.; m. Mary Ann Haerer, Sept. 22, 1961. BA, Morningside Coll., 1954; DDS, U. Nebr., 1961, MSD, 1963. Diplomate Am. Bd. Pediat. Dentistry. Prof., chair pediat. dentistry U. Nebr. Coll. Dentistry, Lincoln, 1963—; prof. pediats. U. Nebr. Coll. Medicine, Omaha, 1969—. Contbr. articles to profl. jours. With U.S. Army. Fellow Am. Acad. Pediat. Dentistry, Am. Coll. Dentists, Internat. Coll. Dentistry; mem. ADA, VFW, Am. Soc. Dentistry for Children, N.E. Nebr. Dental Assn., Lincoln Dist. Dental Assn. Democrat. Avocation: music. Home: 2530 Ridge Rd Lincoln NE 68512-2418

SULLIVAN, ROBERT S., college dean; BA in Math., Boston Coll., 1966; PhD in Ops. Mgmt., Pa. State U., 1968; MBA in Prodn. Mgmt., Cornell U., 2003. Various U. Tex., Austin, 1968—91; dean graduate sch. Indsl. Adminstrn. Carnegie Mellon U., Pitts., 1991-95; dir. IC2 inst. U. Tex., Austin, 1995-97; dean Kenan-Flagler U. N.C., Chapel Hill, 1998—2003; dean Rady Sch. Mgmt. U. Calif., San Diego, 2003—. Peace Corps. vol. Addis Ababa U., 1968-70. Office: U Calif Rady Sch Mgmt 9500 Gilman Dr La Jolla CA 92093-0093 Office Phone: 858-822-0830. Business E-Mail: rss@ucsd.edu.

SULLIVAN, ROY MICHAEL, aerospace engineer, researcher; b. Pitts., Pa., July 30, 1960; s. Jeremiah Bonaventure and Majorie Lorain Sullivan; m. Traci Ann Fabian, Dec. 31, 1988; children: Bonny Skye Palsa, Kyle Michael, Clare Eyles, Conor Fallon, Emma Doran. BS, The Pa. State U., U. Park, Pa., 1982; MS, The U. Va., Charlottesville, Va., 1984; PhD, The Pa. State U., U. Park, Pa., 1990. Registered profl. engr., Va., 1983. Aerospace engr. Marshall Space Flight Ctr. NASA, Huntsville, Ala., 1985—98, sr. rsch. engr. Glenn Rsch. Ctr. Cleve., 1998—. Adj. faculty The U. Ala., Huntsville, Ala., 1991—98. Achievements include development of analytical methods for the thermo-mechanical behavior of high temparature composite materials.

SULLIVAN, SHAUN STUART, lawyer; b. Albany, NY, Dec. 25, 1940; s. Charles Patrick and Dorothy Beatrice (Stuart) S.; m. Bonnie Sullivan; children: Sara Stuart, Jennifer Landon. AB with honors, Fairfield U., 1962; LLB, Fordham U., 1966. Bar: N.Y., Conn., U.S. Dist. Ct. (so. dist.) N.Y., U.S. Dist. Ct. Conn., U.S. Ct. Appeals (2d cir.), U.S. Supreme Ct. Assoc. Cahill, Gordon, NYC, 1966-69, Wiggin & Dana, New Haven, 1969—. Fellow Am. Coll. Trial Lawyers (chair ADR comm., chair state of Conn. 1997-99, Best Lawyers 1987-2005), Internat. Acad. Trial Lawyers (chmn. state of Conn. 2004—); mem. Internat. Bar Assn. (chair litig. sect. bus. law 1999-2001), Am. Bar Found., Conn. Bar Found, Federal Bar Coun. Home: 40 Cliff St New Haven CT 06511-1344 Office Phone: 203-498-4400. Business E-Mail: ssullivan@wiggin.com.

SULLIVAN, SHEILA C., critical care nurse, educator; b. Berea, Ky., May 13, 1960; d. Curtis Warren and Lorretta Ann (Cunningham) Cox; m. William Barry Sullivan, June 26, 1982; children: Curtis, Bryan, Caitlin. BSN, Harding U., 1982. Cert. ACLS instr., BCLS instr., CCRN. Preceptor coord. Richland Meml. Hosp., Columbia, S.C., 1983-85, head nurse; staff RN Bapt. Med. Ctr., Little Rock, Ark., 1987-90; case mgr. Bristol Regional Med. Ctr., 1990-94; nursing faculty S.W. Va. C.C., Richland, 1994—. Recipient Going the Extra Mile award. Mem. AACN. Office: S W Va C C P O Box SVCC Richlands VA 24641

SULLIVAN, STEVE, professional hockey player; b. Timmins, Ont., Can., July 6, 1974; m. Kristen Sullivan; children: Aidyn, Garner, Drake, Karlisle. Left wing Albany River Rats (AHL), 1994—96, NJ Devils, 1996—97, Toronto Maple Leafs, 1997—99, Chgo. Blackhawks, 1999—2004, Nashville Predators, 2004—. Recipient Bill Masterton Meml. Trophy, 2009. Office: Nashville Predators 501 Broadway Nashville TN 37203*

SULLIVAN, STEVEN R., lawyer; b. St. Louis, Aug. 1960; BBA summa cum laude, U. Mo., St. Louis, 1981; JD with distinction, U. Mo., Kans. City, 1994. CPA 1982. Atty. Arthur Andersen & Co., Kohn, Shands, Elbert, Gianoulakis & Giljum, 1985—87, Union Electric Co. (now Ameren EU), 1987—95; assoc. gen. counsel Anheuser-Busch Co., 1995—98; v.p. regulatory policy, gen. counsel, sec. Ameren EU, 1998—2003; sr. v.p. govtl./regulatory policy, gen. counsel, sec. Ameren Corp., St. Louis, 2003—. Mem.: Mo. Bar Assn., Bar Assn. Met. St. Louis, Mo. Soc. CPA., Am. Soc. Corp. Sec., Edison Electric Inst. Office: Ameren Corp 1 Ameren Plz 1901 Chouteau Ave Saint Louis MO 63103 Office Phone: 314-621-3222. Office Fax: 314-554-3801.*

SULLIVAN, STUART FRANCIS, anesthesiologist, educator; b. Buffalo, July 15, 1928; s. Charles S. and Kathryn (Duggan) S.; m. Dorothy Elizabeth Faytol, Apr. 18, 1959; children: John, Irene, Paul, Kathryn. BS, Canisius Coll., 1950; MD, SUNY, Syracuse, 1955. Diplomate Am. Bd. Anesthesiology. Intern Ohio State U. Hosp., Columbus, 1955—56; resident Columbia Presbyn. Med. Ctr., 1958—60; fellow Columbia-Bellevue Hosp. Ctr., NYC, 1960—61; instr. anesthesiology Columbia U. Coll. Physicians and Surgeons, NYC, 1961—62, assoc., 1962—64, asst. prof., 1964—69, assoc. prof., 1969—73; prof. dept. anesthesiology UCLA, 1973—91, vice chair anesthesiology, 1974—77, exec. vice chair, 1977—90, acting chmn., 1983—84, 1987—88, 1990—91, prof. emeritus, 1991—. Capt. M.C., USAR, 1956-58. Fellow NIH, 1960-61; recipient research career devel. award NIH, 1966-69. Mem. Assn. Univ. Anesthetists, Am. Physiol. Soc., Am. Soc. Anesthesiologists. Home: 101 Foxtail Dr Santa Monica CA 90402-2047 Office: UCLA Sch Medicine Dept Anesthesiology Los Angeles CA 90095-0001

SULLIVAN, TERESA ANN, law and sociology educator, academic administrator; d. Gordon Hager and Mary Elizabeth S.; m. H. Douglas Laycock, June 14, 1971; children: Joseph Peter, John Patrick. BA, Mich. State U., 1970; MA, U. Chgo., 1972, PhD, 1975. Asst. prof. sociology U. Tex., Austin, 1975-76, assoc. prof. sociology, 1981-87, dir. women's studies, 1985-87, prof. sociology, 1987—, prof. law, 1988—, assoc. dean grad. sch., 1989-90, 1992-95, chair dept. sociology, 1990-92, vice provost, 1994-95, v.p., grad. dean, 1995—2002; asst. prof. sociology U. Chgo., 1977-81; exec. vice-chancellor acad. affairs U. Tex. Sys., 2002—06; provost, exec. v.p. academic affairs U. Mich., Ann Arbor, 2006—. Pres. Southwestern Sociol. Assn., 1988-89; mem. faculty adv. bd. Hogg Found. Mental Health, 1989-92; mem. sociology panel NSF, 1983-85. Author: Marginal Workers Marginal Jobs, 1978; co-author: As We Forgive Our Debtors, 1989 (Silver Gavel 1990), Social Organization of Work, 1990, 4th edit., 2007; co-author: The Fragile Middle Class, 2000; contbr. articles and chpts. to profl. jours. Bd. dirs. Calvert Found., Chgo., 1978, CARA, Inc., Washington, 1985; mem. U.S. Census Bur. Adv. Com., 1989-95, chmn., 1991-92; mem. sociology panel NSF, 1983-85; trustee St. Michael's Acad., 1996-2001. Leadership Tex. 1994. Fellow AAAS (liaison to Population Assn. Am. 1989-91, chair sect. K 1996), Sociol. Rsch. Assn., Am. Sociol. Assn. (sec. 1995—, editor Rose Monograph Series 1988-92), Philos. Soc. Tex., Soc. Study of Social Problems (chair fin. com. 1986-87), Population Assn. Am. (bd. dirs. 1989-91, chair fin. com. 1990-91), Assn. Grad. Schs. (pres. 2001-2002). Roman Catholic. Avocation: reading. Office: 503 Thompson St Ann Arbor MI 48109-1340 Home: 2197 Gray Fox Ct Ann Arbor MI 48103 Office Phone: 734-764-9292. Business E-Mail: tsull@umich.edu.

SULLIVAN, THOMAS CHRISTOPHER, coatings company executive; b. Cleve., July 8, 1937; s. Frank Charles and Margaret Mary (Wilhelmy) S.; m. Sandra Simmons, Mar. 12, 1960; children: Frank, Sean, Tommy, Danny, Kathleen, Julie. BS, Miami U., Oxford, Ohio, 1959. Div. sales mgr. Republic Powdered Metals, Cleve., 1961-65, exec. v.p., 1965-70; chmn. bd., CEO RPM, Internat., Medina, Ohio, 1971—2002, chmn. bd., 2003—08. Bd. dirs. Cleve. Clinic Found., Kaydon Corp., Ann Arbor, Mich. Trustee emeritus Culver (Ind.) Ednl. Found.; former trustee Cleve. Tomorrow; bd. advisors Urban Cmty. Sch., Cleve., Malachi House, Cleve.; trustee City Year Cleve.; trustee Cath. Diocese of Cleve. Found. Lt. (j.g.) USNR, 1959-60. Mem.: Nat. Assn. Securities Dealers (bd. govs. 1986—88, long-range strategic planning com.), Nat. Paint and Coatings Assn. (past chmn. bd., CEO, mem. exec. com.). Roman Catholic. Office: RPM Internat 2628 Pearl Rd Medina OH 44256-7623

SULLIVAN, THOMAS JAMES, retired manufacturing company executive; b. Franklin, NH, Mar. 26, 1923; s. James J. and Helen (Mullin) S.; m. Anne Clark, Aug. 31, 1963. AB, Holy Cross Coll., 1947; JD, Harvard U., 1949. With Gen. Dynamics Corp., 1949-61, asst. div. mgr., 1959-61; sr. assoc. Harbridge House, Cambridge, Mass., 1961-63; with Hydraulic Research & Mfg. Co., Valencia, Calif., 1963-71, v.p., 1964-68, exec. v.p., 1968-69, pres., 1969-71; v.p. Textron, Inc., Providence, 1971-73; pres. Walker/Parkersburg (W. Va.) Co., 1973-81, Sprague Meter, Bridgeport, Conn., 1981-84, Dimetrics Inc., Diamond Springs, Calif., 1984-86. Served with USAAF, 1943-46. Fellow Nat. Contract Mgmt. Assn. Home: 2186 Augusta Ct San Luis Obispo CA 93401-4500 E-mail: tsullivan0323@aol.com.

SULLIVAN, THOMAS PATRICK, lawyer; b. Evanston, Ill., Mar. 23, 1930; s. Clarence M. and Pauline (DeHaye) Sullivan; m. Anne Landau; children from previous marriage: Margaret Mary, Timothy Joseph, Elizabeth Ann. Student, Loras Coll., 1947—49; LLB cum laude, Loyola U., Chgo., 1952; LLD (hon.), U. Notre Dame, 2006. Bar: Ill. 1952, N.Mex 1997. Assoc. Jenner & Block, Chgo., 1954—62, ptnr., 1963—77, 1981—; US atty. (no. dist.) Ill. US Dept. Justice, Chgo., 1977—81. Co-chair Ill. Gov.'s Commn. Capital Punishment, 2000—02; chair Capital Punishment Reform Study Com., 2005—. Contbr. articles to profl. jours. With US Army, 1952—54. Decorated Bronze Star; recipient Medal of Excellence, Loyola U. Law Sch., 1965, Ill. Pub. Defender Assn. award, 1972, Justice John Paul Stevens award, 2000, Ctr. on Wrongful Convictions award, Northwestern U., 2003, Albert E. Jenner, Jr. Pro Bono award, 2003, Damen award, Loyola U. Law Sch., 2004, Lifetime Achievement award, Legal Assistance Found. Chgo., 2005, The Am. Lawyer Mag., 2007; named Laureate, Acad. Ill. Lawyers, Person of Yr., Chgo. Lawyer Mag., 2004. Fellow: Ill. Bar Assn. (Legal Legends award Am. Const. Soc., Chgo. Lawyer Chpt. 2008), Am. Coll. Trial Lawyers; mem.: ABA (John Minor Wisdom Pub. Svc. and Professionalism award 2003), Am. Coast Soc., Chgo. Coun. Lawyers (Commitment to Justice award 2007), Am. Judicature Soc. (Justice award 2004), Am. Law Inst., Fed. Bar Assn., Chgo. Bar Assn., Fed. 7th Cir. Bar Assn. Office: Jenner & Block 330 N Wabash Ave Ste 4700 Chicago IL 60611-5697 Office Phone: 312-923-2928. Business E-Mail: tsullivan@jenner.com.

SULLIVAN, TIMOTHY, lawyer; b. Detroit, May 16, 1948; s. Paul Gilmary and Virginia (Rosier) S.; m. Marsha Rosenberg Sullivan, June 19, 1971; children: Eileen A., Hugh V. BA Journalism, U. Mich., 1970; JD, Georgetown U., 1975. Bar: Va. 1975, D.C. 1976. Contract negotiator

CIA, Washington, 1973-75; assoc. Fried, Frank, Harris, Shriver & Kampelman, Washington, 1975-78; ptnr. Capell, Howard, Knabe & Cobbs P.A., Washington, 1978-83, Dykema Gossett, Washington, 1983-95, Adduci, Mastriani & Schaumberg, LLP, 1995—2001. Lectr. in field. Narrator (audio cassette) How to Negotiate Government Contracts, 1986. Citizen mem. Alexandria Commn. Persons with Disabilities, Va., 1992-99, vice-chmn. 1997-98, 98-99. Sgt. U.S. Army, 1970-73. Mem. ABA, Nat. Contract Mgmt. Assn., U. Club Washington (bd. govs. 2003-2004, sec. 2003-05, v.p. 2005-06, pres. 2006-07), Congl. Country Club (v.p. 1998-99, bd. govs. 1995-2000, pres. 1999-2000). Roman Catholic. Avocations: reading, sports. Office: Thompson Coburn LLP 1909 K St NW 6th Fl Washington DC 20006-1167

SULLIVAN, TIMOTHY E., bank executive; B, U. Ill.; MBA, U. Calif., Berkeley. Various tech. and ops. mgmt. positions including chief info. officer First Interstate Bank, Ariz.; chief info. officer Kaiser Found. Health Plan; exec. v.p., group tech. exec. Wells Fargo, San Francisco; corp. exec. v.p., chief info. officer SunTrust Banks, Inc., Atlanta, 2003—. Office: SunTrust Banks Inc PO Box 4418 Atlanta GA 30302-4418 Office Phone: 404-588-7711. Office Fax: 505-827-6173.

SULLIVAN, TIMOTHY JACKSON, museum administrator, retired academic administrator, educator; b. Ravenna, Ohio, Apr. 15, 1944; s. Ernest Tulio and Margaret Elizabeth (Caris) Sullivan; m. Anne Doubet Klare, Jan. 21, 1973. AB, Coll. William and Mary, Williamsburg, Va., 1966; JD, Harvard U., Cambridge, Mass., 1969; LLD (hon.), U. Aberdeen, Scotland, 1993, Old Dominion U., Norfolk, Va., 2005, Centre Coll., Danville, Ky., 2007. Asst. prof. law Coll. William and Mary, Williamsburg, Va., 1972—75, assoc. prof., 1975—78, prof., 1978—85, Bryan prof. law, dean, 1985—92, pres., 1992—2005, pres. emeritus, 2005—; exec. asst. for policy to Gov. Charles S. Robb State of Va., Richmond, Va., 1982—85; atty. Freeman, Drapers' Co., London, 1992; pres., CEO The Mariners Mus., Newport News, Va., 2006—. Vis. prof. law U. Va., Charlottesville, 1981; exec. dir. Gov.'s Commn. on Va.'s Future, Richmond, 1982—84; vice-chmn. Gov.'s Commn. on Fed. Spending, Richmond, 1986; mem. Gov.'s Fellows Selection Com., 1985—90, Gov.'s Commn. on Sexual Assault and Substance Abuse on the Coll. Campus (chmn. enforcement subcom.), 1991—92; counsel Commn. on Future of Va.'s Jud. Sys., 1987—89; chair VA Rhodes Scholarship Commn., 1998—2003; mem. Livery Drapers Co., 2003; chair appeals panel Internat. Commn. Holocaust Era Ins. Claims, 2002—06. Mem. Va. State Bd. Edn., Richmond, 1987—92; chair Gov.'s Task Force on Intercollegiate Athletics, 1992—93; pres. The Mariner's Mus., Newport News, Va., 2006—. Decorated Bronze Star; named Outstanding Virginian, Va. 4-H Found., 1999. Fellow: Va. Bar Fedn., Am. Bar Fedn.; mem.: ABA, Va. Bar Assn., Va. State Bar, Am. Arbitration Assn. (bd. dirs. 2000—03), Cosmos Club, Univ. Club (Washington), Bull and Bear Club, Omicron Delta Kappa, Phi Beta Kappa. Democrat. Avocations: wine, swimming, reading, golf. Office: Coll William and Mary Office of Pres Emeritus PO Box 8795 Williamsburg VA 23187-8795 also: The Mariners Museum 100 Museum Dr Newport News VA 23606 Home Phone: 757-220-0423; Office Phone: 757-591-7707. Business E-Mail: tjsull@wm.edu, tsullivan@marinersmuseum.org.

SULLIVAN, TRUDY (GERTRUDE FULHAM SULLIVAN), apparel company executive; b. 1949; m. Michael Sullivan; children: Catherine, Anne. BA, Manhattanville Coll.; grad. studies, Simmons Coll. Buyer Jordan Marsh; mgmt. positions with The Avenue, Decelle, T. Deane, Filene's; pres. J. Crew Group, Inc., 1997—2001; group pres. Liz Claiborne casual & Liz Claiborne woman Liz Claiborne, Inc., NYC, 2001—02, exec. v.p., 2002—06, pres., 2006—07; pres., CEO The Talbots, Inc., Hingham, Mass., 2007—. Bd. dirs. The Talbots, Inc., 2007—. Office: The Talbots 1 Talbots Dr Hingham MA 02043*

SULLIVAN, WALTER FRANCIS, bishop emeritus; b. Washington, June 10, 1928; s. Walter Francis and Catherine Jeanette (Vanderloo) Sullivan. BA, St. Mary's Sem. U., Balt., 1947; STL, St. Mary's Sem. U., 1953; JCL, Catholic U. Am., 1960. Ordained priest Diocese of Richmond, Va., 1953; assoc. pastor St. Andrew's Parish, Roanoke, Va., St. Mary's Parish, Fort Monroe, Va.; sec. diocesan tribunal Diocese of Richmond, Va., 1960-65, chancellor Va., from 1965; rector Sacred Heart Cathedral, Richmond, 1967—70; ordained bishop, 1970; aux. bishop Diocese of Richmond, Va., 1970-74, bishop Va., 1974—2003, bishop emeritus Va., 2003—. Bd. dirs. Christian Children's Fund, Richmond, Va., Churches' Ctr. Theology & Pub. Policy, Washington, Va. Interfaith Ctr. Pub. Policy, Cath. Com. Appalachia; bishop-pres. Pax Christi USA, 1991—. Roman Catholic. Office: Catholic Diocese Of Richmond 7800 Carousel LN Richmond VA 23294-4201

SULLIVAN, WILLIAM E., wholesale distribution executive; b. 1955; BSBA in Acctg. and Mktg., Georgetown U.; MBA in Mgmt. and Fin., Northwestern U. Mem. comm. lending group First Nat. Bank, Chgo.; mem. tax divsn. Ernst & Ernst; various positions including CFO Jones Lang LaSalle, 1984—2001; chmn., CEO SiteStuff, Inc., Austin, Tex., 2001—05; founder, pres. Greenwood Advisors, Inc., Greenwood Village, Colo., 2005—07; CFO ProLogis, Denver, 2007—. Mem.: AICPA. Office: ProLogis 4545 Airport Way Denver CO 80239 Office Phone: 303-567-5000, 800-566-2706.*

SULLIVAN, WILLIAM FRANCIS, lawyer; b. San Francisco, May 6, 1952; s. Francis Michael and Jane Frances (Walsh) S.; children: Matthew, Meghan, Kathleen; m. Kait Sullivan. AB, U. Calif., Berkeley, 1974; JD, UCLA, 1977. Bar: Calif. 1977, U.S. Dist. Ct. (no. dist.) Calif. 1977, U.S. Ct. Appeals (9th cir.) 1977, U.S. Dist. Ct. (ea. dist.) Calif. 1978, U.S. Ct. Appeals (D.C. cir.) 1979, U.S. Ct. Appeals (fed. cir.) 1985, U.S. Dist. Ct. (so. dist.) Calif. 1986, U.S. Dist. Ct. (cen. dist.) Calif. 1990, U.S. Supreme Ct. 1986. Assoc. Chickering & Gregory, San Francisco and Washington, 1977-81, Brobeck, Phleger & Harrison, San Diego and San Francisco, 1981-84, ptnr., 1984—2002, mng. ptnr. San Diego, 1992-96, 2001—03, securities litig. group leader, 2002—03, firmwide mng. ptnr., 1996-98; ptnr. Paul Hastings Janofsky & Walker LLP, San Diego and LA, 2003—, chair nat. securities litig. practice group, mem. litig. steering com., 2003—. Named Calif. Lawyer of Yr. in Securities, Chambers USA, 2006—09; named an Best Lawyers in Am. Mem. ABA, Assn. Bus. Trial Lawyers (bd. govs. San Diego chpt. 1993-95, bd. govs. LA chpt., 2009-), Calif. Bar Assn. (litig. sect.), LA County Bar Assn., San Diego Bar Assn., Barristers Club San Francisco (bd. dirs. 1984-86, pres. 1985), Calif. Young Lawyers Assn. (bd. dirs. 1986-89, sec. 1987-99, 1st v.p. 1988-89), Am. Arbitration Assn. Democrat. Roman Catholic. Home: 1089 Prospect Blvd Pasadena CA 91103 Home Phone: 626-584-1909; Office Phone: 213-683-6000. Business E-Mail: williamsullivan@paulhastings.com.

SULLIVAN, WILLIAM J., state supreme court justice; b. Waterbury, Conn., Mar. 12, 1939; Student, St. Thomas Sem., 1958-59; BA in Polit. Sci., Providence Coll., 1962; B in Civil Law, Coll. William and Mary, 1965, JD, 1970. Priv. practice, Waterbury, 1967—78; civil service commr. State of Conn., 1974—75; corp. counsel City of Waterbury, 1976—78; judge Conn. Superior Ct., 1978-97, Conn. Appellate Ct., 1997-99; assoc. justice Conn. Supreme Ct., 1999-2001, chief justice, 2001—06, sr. justice, 2006—09; judge trial referee, 2009—. Captain US Army, 1965—66. Decorated 2 Bronze Stars for meritorious svc. US Army, Air Medal. Office: Superior Ct House 400 Grand St Waterbury CT 06702 Office Phone: 860-757-2116, 203-236-8200.

SULLIVAN, WILLIAM MICHAEL, JR., lawyer; b. Norwalk, Conn., May 18, 1958; s. William Michael and Teresa Barbara Sullivan; m. Jennifer Lynn Miller, June 20, 1992; children: Conor Royal, Alexis Bailey, Jack Nicholas, William Michael III. BA in English magna cum laude, Tufts U., Medford, Mass., 1980, MA in English, 1981; JD, Cornell U, Ithaca, NY, 1985. Bar: Conn. 1985, US Dist. Ct. Conn. 1985, NY 1986, US Dist. Ct. (so. and ea. dists.) NY 1986, US Ct. Appeals (DC cir.) 1992, US Dist. Ct. DC 2000, US Ct. Appeals (4th cir.) 2004, US Dist. Ct. (ea. dist.) Mich. 2006, US Ct. Appeals (2nd cir.) 2006. Atty. Manhattan Dist. Atty.'s Office; asst. US atty. US Attys. Office, Washington, 1991—2002; ptnr. Winston & Strawn, Washington, 2004—. Faculty Trial Advocacy Inst., U. Va. Law Sch.; TV expert legal commentator, spkr. in field. Contbr. articles to profl. jours. Recipient awards and commendations, FBI/Dept. of Justice; named one of Washington DC Superlawyers, 2007. Mem.: ABA, Asst. US Attys. Assn., Am. Inn of Ct. Roman Catholic. Avocations: golf, reading, running, travel. Office: Winston & Strawn LLP 1700 K St NW Washington DC 20006-3817 Office Fax: 202-282-5100. Business E-Mail: wsullivan@winston.com.

SULLIVAN, WILLIAM P., electronics executive; b. Yakima, Wash., 1949; BS, U. Calif.-Davis. With Hewlett-Packard Co., 1976—99, various positions, 1976—95, gen. mgr. Optical Comm. Divsn., 1995—97, gen. mgr. Comm. Semiconductor Solutions Divsn., 1997—98, gen. mgr., v.p. Components Group (now Semiconductor Products Group), 1998—99; senior v.p., gen. mgr. SPG Agilent Technologies Inc. (spin-off from HP Co.), 1999—2002; exec. v.p., COO Agilent Technologies Inc., 2002—05, pres., CEO, 2005—. Bd. dir. Children's Discovery Mus., San Jose, Calif., Lumileds, URS Corp., 2006—, Avnet Inc. Office: Agilent Technologies Inc 5301 Stevens Creek Blvd Santa Clara CA 95051-7201

SULLIVAN STEMBERG, MAUREEN, interior designer; b. Brookline, Mass., July 8, 1951; d. Loretta McDermott and Herbert Michael Sullivan; m. Thomas George Stemberg, Mar. 11, 1975 (div. Sept. 0, 1989). AA in polit. sci., Newton Jr. Coll., 1969—71; degree in art history, Boston Coll., 1972—73; Fine Arts Program, Mus. of Fine Arts Sch., 1973—75; Architecture and Design, Boston Ctr. of Architecture, 1982—85. ASID, MA, 1987. CEO, interior designer Interiors of Wellesley, Inc., Wellesley, Mass., 1977—80; CEO, head designer Maureen Sullivan Stemberg Interiors, Boston-Palm Beach, 1980—98; design and fashion editor Palm Beach Illus., Palm Beach, Fla., 1990—95; CEO BabySuites.Com, Boston, 2003—04; chief creative officer Connoisseur Pub., Inc., Boston, 2004—. Chmn. and co-chairman, ann. flower show Mass. Hort. Soc., Boston, 1990—94. Designer Mahaney Baseball Club House, U. Maine (Top 5 Design winner for Baseball Complex Devel., 1994), Various Hotel Interiors (Top 20 Hotel Designers for Holiday Inns Inc., 1991), Trump Plaza, other Club Colette, Palm Beach, Fla.; contbr. articles to mag. Fund raiser Barcelona Summer Olympics, Mass., Spain, 1990—92, Am. Cup, Boston, 1993—95; trustee Boston Opera Co., 1977—81. Mem.: United Way of Mass. Bay, Nat. Trust for Hist. Preservation, Dana Farber Cancer Inst. Pediat. (hon.; dir. 1996—97), Nat. Musuem of Women in the Arts (hon.; coun. mem. 1991—93), Am. Soc. of Interior Designers (assoc.).

SULLIVAN-SZUTS, BETTY ANNE, academic administrator, educator; b. Phila., Dec. 23, 1939; d. Rowland Thomas and Elizabeth Catherine Moriarty; m. Robert Lloyd Sullivan, Sept. 21, 1957 (div.); children: Lisa Anne Sullivan, Brent Rowland Sullivan, Jamie Alexandra Sullivan; m. Ivan Ramon Szuts, May 6, 1995. BS in Home Econs. Edn., Douglass Coll., New Brunswick, NJ, 1975; EdM in Supervision and Adminstrn., Rutgers U., New Brunswick, N.J., 1978, EdD in Adult and Continuing Ednl. Adminstrn., 1989. Cert. sch. adminstr. NJ, prin./supr. NJ, tchr. home econs. NJ. Tchr. home econs. Freehold Regional HS Dist., NJ, 1975—80; state supr. home econs. edn. NJ State Dept. Edn., Trenton, 1980—81; dir. and tchr. in-svc. Rutgers U., New Brunswick, NJ, 1981—89; vice prin. Monmouth County Vo-Tech H.S. Dist., Middletown, NJ, 1990—91; dir. Suffolk County Respite Care Program, Patchogue, NY, 1991—94; dir. gerontology program and instr. aging courses Union County Coll., Cranford, NJ, 1994—96; supr. student tchrs. Georgian Ct. Coll., Lakewood, NJ, 1994—96; vis. prof. dept. sociology Wheaton Coll., Norton, Mass., 1996—97; dir. model Tex. safe home program N.W. Assistance Ministries, Houston, 2000—02; grant coord. N. Harris Coll., 2002—03; seminar leader Spirited Elder and Assocs. Adj. prof. profl. studies grad. program LI U., Southampton, NY, 1991—94; rschr. Aging Tex. Well Coalition, 2002—; seminar leader Spirited Elder and Assocs., 2004—; presenter in field. Author: Spiritual Elders: Women of Worth in the Third Millennium, 1999. Chair edn. Harris County Area Agy. Aging, tng. com.; chair adv. bd. Acad. Lifelong Learning, North Harris Coll.; mem. Acts 16:5 task force Presbytery New Covenant, Houston; ruling elder Northwoods Presbyn. Ch., 2006—. Recipient Cmty. Svc. award, North Harris Coll., 2003; The Aging Tex. Well grantee, 2002—03. Mem.: Phi Delta Kappa, Kappa Delta Pi, Omicron Nu. Avocations: tennis, ballroom dancing, writing, playing the organ. Home: Spirited Elder and Assocs 314A Sharon Way Monroe Township NJ 08831-1743 Personal E-mail: bettyanne.ivan@sbcglobal.net.

SULLOWAY, FRANK JONES, social sciences educator, historian; b. Concord, NH, Feb. 2, 1947; s. Alvah Woodbury and Alison (Green) Sulloway; 1 child, Ryan. AB summa cum laude, Harvard U., Cambridge, Mass., 1969, AM in History Sci., 1971, PhD in History Sci., 1978. Jr. fellow Harvard U. Soc. Fellows, 1974-77; mem. Sch. Social Sci. Inst. Advanced Study, Princeton, NJ, 1977-78; rsch. fellow Miller Inst. Basic Rsch. Sci. U. Calif., Berkeley, 1978-80, vis. Miller rsch. prof., 1999—2000, vis. prof., 2000—; rsch. fellow MIT, Cambridge, 1980-81, vis. scholar, 1989-98; postdoctoral fellow Harvard U., Cambridge, 1981-82, vis. scholar, 1984-89; rsch. fellow U. Coll., London, 1982-84; Vernon prof. biography Dartmouth Coll., Hanover, NH, 1986. Author: (book) Freud, Biologist of the Mind, 1979 (Pfizer award History Sci. Soc., 1980), Born to Rebel, 1996; contbr. articles to profl. jours. Recipient Randi award, Skeptics Soc., 1997, Golden Plate award, Am. Acad. Achievement, 1997; fellow, NEH, 1980—81, NSF, 1981—82, John Simon Guggenheim Meml. Found., 1982—83, MacArthur Found., 1984—89, Dibner Inst., MIT, 1993—94, Ctr. Advanced Study Behavioral Scis., Stanford, Calif., 1998—99. Fellow: AAAS (mem. electorate nominating com. sect. L 1988—91, 1994—97), Assn. Psychol. Sci., Linnean Soc. London; mem.: History Sci. Soc. (mem. fin. com. 1987—92, mem. com. devel. 1988—92), Human Behavior and Evolution Soc., Am. Psychol. Soc. Home: 1709 Shattuck Ave Apt 205 Berkeley CA 94709-1753 Office: U Calif Dept Psychology IPSR 4125 Tolman Hall Berkeley CA 94720-1603 Home Phone: 510-540-9336; Office Phone: 510-642-7139. Business E-Mail: sulloway@berkeley.edu.

SULLY, IRA BENNETT, lawyer; b. Columbus, Ohio, June 3, 1947; s. Bernie and Helen Mildred (Koen) S.; m. Nancy Lee Pryor, Oct. 2, 1983. BA cum laude, Ohio State U., 1969, JD summa cum laude, 1974. Bar: Ohio 1974, U.S. Dist. Ct. (so. dist.) Ohio 1974. Assoc. Schottenstein, Garel, Swedlow & Zox, Columbus, 1974-78; atty. Borden, Inc., Columbus, 1978-80; sole practice Columbus, 1980—. Instr. Real Estate Law Columbus Tech. Inst., 1983-88; title ins. agt. Sycamore Title Agy., Columbus, 1983—. Bd. dirs. Rsch. Franklin County Celeste for Gov., Columbus, 1978; asst. treas. Pamela Conrad for City Coun., Columbus, 1979; treas. Leland for State Rep., Columbus, 1982, 84, Leland for City Atty., Columbus, 1985; active Ohio Dem. Bldg. Com., 1995-98; commentator Sta. WOSU, Columbus, 1980; trustee Ohio State U. Undergrad. Student Govt. Alumni Soc., 1997—, pres., 2000—. Mem. ABA, Ohio Bar Assn., Columbus Bar Assn., Agonis Club (Columbus). Democrat. Jewish. Avocations: running, coin collecting/numismatics. Home: 200 Reinhard Ave Columbus OH 43206-2616 Office: 844 S Front St Columbus OH 43206-2543

SULTAN, MARK R., plastic surgeon; b. NJ; BS, Brandeis U.; MD, Columbia U. Coll. Physicians and Surgeons, 1982. Diplomate rgery, Am. Bd. Plastic Surgery. Resident in gen. surgery Columbia-Presbyn. Med. Ctr., NYC, 1983—87, resident in plastic surgery, 1987—88, 1989—90; fellow in head and neck surgery/microvascular reconstrn. Emory U. Affiliated Hosps., Atlanta, 1988—89; attending physician dept. plastic surgery St. Luke's Roosevelt Hosp., NYC, 1998—, chief divsn. plastic and reconstructive surgery, Beth Israel Hosp., NYC; pvt. practice plastic surgery NYC. Assoc. prof. clin. surgery Columbia U. Coll. Physicians and Surgeons, NYC. Recipient Allen O. Whipple award for Outstanding Performance in Surgery; named one of NY's Top Doctors, NY mag. Mem.: Am. Assn. Plastic Surgery, Soc. Reconstructive Microsurgery, NY Head and Neck Soc., Northeast Regional Soc. Plastic and Reconstructive Surgeons, Am. Soc. Reconstructive Microsurgery, Am. Soc. Plastic and Reconstructive Surgeons, Am. Soc. Aesthetic Plastic Surgery, Alpha Omega Alpha Soc., Phi Beta Kappa. Office: 1100 Park Ave New York NY 10128 Business E-Mail: samson@slrsurgery.com, msultan@chpnet.org.

SULTAN, TERRIE FRANCES, museum director; b. Asheville, NC, Oct. 28, 1952; d. Norman and Phyllis Ellen (Galumbeck) Sultan; m. Christopher French, June, 1988. BFA, Syracuse U., 1973; MA, John F. Kennedy U., 1985. Exhbn. dir. Source Gallery, San Francisco, 1982-83; adj. curator Oakland (Calif.) Mus., 1984-85; dir. pub. affairs and pub. programs New Mus. Contemporary Art, NYC, 1986-88; curator contemporary art Corcoran Gallery of Art, Washington, 1988—99, interim chief cur., 1999; dir. Blaffer Gallery, U. Houston, 2000—08, The Parrish Art Museum, LI, 2008—. Founding bd. mem. Etant donné, French-Am. Endowment for Contemporary Art. Author: Representation and Text in the Work of Robert Morris, 1990, Redefining The Terms of Engagement: The Art of Louise Bourgeois, 1994, Neik Kemps: Behind the Facade of Analytical Order (a Series of Propositions), 1995, Painting Outside Painting, 1995, Petah Coyne: black/white/black, 1996, Ida Applebroog: Nothing Personal Paintings 1987-1997, 1998; also exhbn. catalogues. Recipient Chevalier, Ordre des Arts et Lettres, 2003. Mem. Am. Assn. Museums, Coll. Art Assn., ArTable. Democrat. Office: Parrish Art Mus 25 Job's Ln Southampton NY 11968 Office Phone: 631-283-2118 ext. 12.

SULTAN BIN MUHAMMAD AL-QASIMI, SHEIKH **See SHEIKH SULTAN AL-QASIMI, BIN MUHAMMAD**

SULTANIK, EVAN ANDREW, computer scientist; m. Nadezhda Belov, June 1, 2008. MS in Computer Sci., Drexel U., Phila., 2006. Rsch. asst. Drexel U., 2001—. Contbr. articles to profl. publs.

SULTANOV, MARAT, bank executive; b. Bishkek, Kyrgyz, Dec. 5, 1960; married; 2 children. Cand. math. scis., Moscow Inst. Steel and Fusions, postgrad. Tutor Kyrgyz Nat. Inst., 1987-92, head dept., 1992; dep. chmn. Nat. Bank Kyrgyzstan, Bishkek, 1993, chmn., then former chmn.; chmn. parliamentary budget and fin. com. Kyrgyzstan Govt., Bishkek. Office: Ministry Fin 720874 Bishkek 58 Bul Erkinduk Kyrgyzstan

SULTZBAUGH, JOHN STEPHAN, retired historian, educator, researcher; b. Harrisburg, Pa., July 25, 1950; s. John Leroy Sultzbaugh and Kathryn Mikhailovna Sass; m. Gayle Rene Reitenbach, May 3, 1980; children: Elisabeth Yvonne, Andrew John. B.Humanities summa cum laude, Pa. State U.-Harrisburg, 1972, MA, 1975; PhD, Greenwich U., Norfolk Island, Australia, 1999. Cert. tchr. Pa. Hydrologist USGS, Harrisburg, Pa., 1973—74; hydrologic technologist Susquehana River Basin Commn., Mechanicsburg, Pa., 1974—75; tchr. history, govt. Upper Dauphin Area Sch. Dist., Lykens, Pa., 1975—2005. Adj. journalist and photographer Upper Dauphin Sentinel, Millersburg, Pa., 1978—88, Daily News, Lebanon, Pa., 1981—83, Sunday Pa., Lebanon, 1982, Pa. Mag., Harrisburg, 1990; mem. Nat. Jr. Honor Soc. Bd./Upper Dauphin Area Sch. Dist., 2002—03; coord. student assistance program Upper Dauphin Sch. Dist., 1991—98; cons. reader Pa. History Textbook Commn., Harrisburg, 2003. Contbr. poetry in jours. Recipient Editors award, Poetry.com, 2004. Mem.: Tech. Inst. Music Educators, Nat. Edn. Assn., Am. Soc. Authors, Composers and Pubs., Intersoc. Color Coun., Mensa. Democrat. Eastern Orthodox. Achievements include patents for variable pitch fluid impeller; research in blending colored music for instructional and therauputic applications; entry in Guniness Book of World Records. Avocations: aquatics, classical music, photography, philosophy. Home: 261 Romberger Rd Elizabethville PA 17023 Office: Upper Dauphin Area Sch Dist 2668 State Rt 209 Lykens PA 17048

SULYK, STEPHEN, archbishop emeritus; b. Balnycia, Western Ukraine, Oct. 2, 1924; s. Michael and Mary (Denys) Sulyk. Student, Ukrainian Cath. Sem. of Holy Spirit, Fed. Republic Germany, 1945—48, St. Josaphat's Sem., 1948—52; Licentia in Sacred Theology, Cath. U. Am., 1952. Ordained priest Archeparchy of Phila. (Ukrainian), 1952, archbishop, 1981—2000, archbishop emeritus, 2000—; assoc. pastor Omaha, 1952, Bklyn., 1953, Minersville, Pa., 1954, Youngstown, Ohio, 1955; pastor Ch. Sts. Peter and Paul, Phoenixville, Pa., 1955, St. Michael's Ch., Frackville, Pa., 1957—61, Assumption of Blessed Virgin Mary Ch., Perth Amboy, NJ, 1962—81; sec. Archeparchy Chancery, 1956—57; adminstr. St. Nicholas, Phila., 1961. Vice-chmn. Priests Senate, 1977—78, chmn.; pres. Ascension Manor, Inc.; archbishop Ukrainian Rite Caths. Archeparchy Phila., Met. Ukrainian-Rite Caths. USA; chmn. ad-hoc inter-rite com. Nat. Cath. Conf. Bishops/US Cath. Conf., 1991. Mem.: Presidium of Synod of Ukrainian Cath. Bishops (treas.), Coll. Bishops of Roman Cath. Ch., Providence Assn. Am. (Supreme Protector). Roman Catholic. Office: Archdiocese of Phila 827 N Franklin St Philadelphia PA 19123-2004

SULZBERGER, ARTHUR OCHS, JR., newspaper publisher; b. Mt. Kisco, NY, Sept. 22, 1951; s. Arthur Ochs Sulzberger and Barbara Winslow Grant; m. Gail Gregg, May 24, 1975 (separated); children: Arthur Gregg, Ann Alden. BA, Tufts U., 1974; grad. Prog. for Mgmt. Dev., Harvard U. Bus. Sch., 1985. Reporter The Raleigh Times, Raleigh,

1974—76; corr. AP, London, 1976—78; Washington corr. NY Times, 1978—81, city hall reporter, 1981, asst. metro editor, 1981—82, group mgr. advt. dept., 1983—84, sr. analyst corp. planning, 1985, prodn. coordinator, 1985—87, asst. pub., 1987—88, dep. pub., 1988—92, pub., 1992—; chmn. NY Times Co., 1997—. Author: (book) The Page One: Major Events, 1920-1995 as Presented in The New York Times, 1995. Chmn. NY Outward Bound Ctr., 2002—. Office: The NY Times 620 8th Ave New York NY 10018-1618*

SUMANASEKERA, GAMINI UDAYA, physics professor; b. Liyanwala, Sri Lanka, Apr. 4, 1956; s. Piyasena and Somawathie Sumanasekera; m. Wasana Kumarihamy Ratnayake, Aug. 20, 1990; children: Thimira Udana, Ruchira Udara. PhD, Ind. U., Bloomington, 1995. Sr. rsch. assoc. Pa. State U., State Coll., 1999—2002. Home: 4625 Shenandoah Dr Louisville KY 40241 Office: Univ Louisville Louisville KY 40292 Office Fax: 502-852-0742. Business E-Mail: gusuma01@gwise.louisville.edu.

SUMANASEKERA, WASANA KUMARIHAMY, medical educator; d. Karunarathna and Swarna Jayasilie Ratnayake; m. Gamini Udaya Sumanasekera, Aug. 23, 1990; children: Thimira Udana, Ruchira Udara, Mihira Dylan. BS, U. Colombo, Sri-Lanka, 1990; MS, U. Ky., Lexington, 1999, Eastern Ky. U., Richmond, 1997; PhD, Pa. State U., State Coll., 2003. Tchg. asst. Eastern Ky. U., 1995—97; Grad. Ctr. Toxicology fellow U. Ky., 1997—98, toxicology rsch. asst., 1998—99; life scis. consortium fellow Pa. State U., 1999—2001, rsch. asst., 2001—03; Am. Heart Assn. fellow U. Louisville, 2004—06, vol. instr. teach rsch. projects for HS students, 2004—07, adj. prof., 2005—08; rsch. assoc. Inst. Molecular Cardiology, Louisville, 2007—08; asst. prof. Coll. Pharmacy, Sullivan U., Louisville, 2008—. Regional sci. fair judge, biochemistry sect. Jefferson County Pub. Schs., Louisville, 2006—08; vis. prof. Bellarmine U., 2007. Author: (poetry) Daddys Little Girl (Editor's Choice award, 2007). Sunday sch. tchr. Ohio Vihara, Cin., 2004—05, various religious activities. Recipient Honor scholar, U. Colombo, 1991. Mem.: Soc. Toxicology, Am. Assn. Colls. Pharmacy, Am. Heart Assn. Achievements include patents pending for carbon nanotube membranes for microfluidic-based separations. Avocations: swimming, travel, music. Home: 4625 Shenandoah Dr Louisville KY 40241 Office: Coll Pharmacy Sullivan Univ 2100 Gardiner ln Louisville KY 40205

SUMANT, ANIRUDHA, materials scientist, researcher; arrived in US, 1998; children: Alkesh, Suchir. PhD, U. Pune, India, 1998. Postdoctoral fellow Argonne Nat. Lab., Ill., 1998—2001, materials scientist, 2006—; scientist Light Matrix Techs., Inc., 2001—02, MER Corp., Tucson, 2001—02; staff scientist U. Wis., Madison, 2002—06. Mem.: Am. Vacuum Soc. (chmn. group 2007—). Achievements include patents pending in field. Office: Argonne Nat Lab 9700 S Cass Ave Argonne IL 60439 Business E-Mail: sumant@anl.gov.

SUMBRY, JO ANN, academic administrator, educator; b. Columbus, Ga., Apr. 29, 1958; 1 child, Gerald Dion Griffin. BS, Ala. State U., Montgomery, 1979; MS, Troy State U., Phenix City Campus, 1980; EdD, Nova Southeastern U., Fort Lauderdale, Fla., 2005. Cert. tchr. Dept. Edn., Ala., 1989, tchr. & prin. Dept. Edn., 1991. Tchr. Mother Mary Mission, Phenix City, Ala., 1979—80, Russell County Sch. Sys., Seale, Ala., 1980—90, Phenix City Sch. Sys., 1990—92; asst. prin. Opelika City Sch. Sys., Ala., 1992—95, prin., 1995—2001; sys. wide curriculum dir. Macon County Sch. Sys., Tuskegee, Ala., 2001—02; chief academic officer, prin. Cornerstone Schs. Ala., 2006—07; coord. field-based experiences Tuskegee U., Ala., 2002—06, asst. dean, NCATE coord., 2007—. Ednl. cons. LightSpan, Inc., 2002—03. Chairperson Ninth Episcopal Dist. Conf. AME Ch., Birmingham, 2008—09; assoc. min. Lee's Chapel AME Ch., Auburn, Ala., 2007—09; co-pastor Woodlawn United Meth. Ch., Birmingham, 2006—07; assoc. pastor St. Luke AME Ch., Opelika, 2001—07. Named Tchr. of Yr., Phenix City Sch. Sys., 1991—92. Home: 287 Pecan Ct Auburn AL 36830 Office: Tuskegee Univ 70-400 Bioethics Bldg Tuskegee Institute AL 36088 Home Fax: 334-887-0097. Personal E-mail: sumbryj@bellsouth.net.

SUMICHRAST, ROBERT T., dean, business educator; BS in Physics, Purdue U., 1979; PhD in Mgmt. Sci., Clemson U., 1984. Asst. prof. mgmt. sci. Va. Tech, 1984—90, assoc. prof., 1990—96, prof. mgmt. sci. and info. tech., 1996—98; assoc. dean grad. and internat. programs Pamplin Coll. Bus., 1998; dean, Ourso disting. prof. of bus. E. J. Ourso Coll. Bus., La. State U., 2003—07; dean, Simon S. Selig, Jr. chair for econ. growth Terry Coll. Bus., U. Ga., 2007—. Mem. Decision Scis. Inst. (DSI), Inst. Ops. Rsch. and the Mgmt. Scis. (InfORMS). Office: Terry Coll of Bus, U Ga Office of Dean 335 Brooks Hall Athens GA 30602-6254 Office Phone: 706-542-8100. Office Fax: 706-542-3835. E-mail: busdean@terry.uga.edu.*

SUMIDA, GERALD AQUINAS, lawyer; b. Hilo, Hawaii, June 19, 1944; s. Sadamy and Kimiyo (Miyahara) S. AB summa cum laude, Princeton U., 1966; JD, Yale U., 1969. Bar: Hawaii 1970, U.S. Dist. Ct. Hawaii 1970, U.S. Ct. Appeals (9th cir.) 1970, U.S. Supreme Ct. 1981. Rsch. assoc. Ctr. Internat. Studies, Princeton U., 1969; assoc. Carlsmith, Ball, Honolulu, 1970-76, ptnr., 1976-99; gen. counsel Asian Devel. Bank, 1999—2008; ptnr. Carlsmith Ball LLP, Honolulu, 2008—. Mem. cameras in courtroom evaluation com. Hawaii Supreme Ct., 1984-86. Co-author: (with others) Legal, Instutional and Financial Aspects of An Inter-Island Electrical Transmission Cable, 1984, Alternative Approaches to the Legal, Instutional and Financial Aspects of Developing an Inter-Island, Electrical Transmission Cable System, 1986; editor Hawaii Bar News, 1972-73; contbr. chpts. to books. Mem. sci. and statis. com. Western Pacific Fishery Mgmt. Coun., 1979-99; mem. study group on law of armed conflict and the law of the sea Comdr. in Chief Pacific, USN, 1979-82; chmn. Pacific and Asian Affairs Coun. Hawaii, 1991, pres., 1982-91, bd. govs., 1976-96; bd. govs. ARC, 1994-2000, mem. exec. com., 1996-2000, chmn. human resources com., 1996-2000, chmn. Hawaii chpt., 1983-99, bd. dirs., 1983-99, vice chmn., 1990; chmn. Hawaii C. of C., 1997-98, bd. dirs., 1990-99; vice chmn. Honolulu Com. Fgn. Rels., 1983—; pres., dir., founding mem. Hawaii Ocean Law Assn., 1978—; mem. Hawaii Adv. Group for Law of Sea Inst., 1977-85; pres. Hawaii Inst. Continuing Legal Edn., 1979-83, dir., 1976-87; pres., founding mem. Hawaii Coun. Legal Edn. Youth, 1980-83, dir., 1983-88; chmn. Hawaii Commn. Yr. 2000, 1976-79; mem. Honolulu Cmty. Media Coun., 1976-99, exec. com., 1976-84, legal coun., 1979-83; bd. dirs. Hawaii Imin Centennial Corp., 1983-90, Hawaii Pub. Radio, 1983-88, Legal Aid Soc. Hawaii, 1984; founding gov., exec. v.p., chmn. rules and procedures Ctr. Internat. Comml. Dispute Resolution, 1987—; exec. com. Pacific Aerospace Mus., 1991—; exec. com. Pacific Islands Assn., 1988—; exec. com. Asia-Pacific Ctr. Res. Internat. Bus. Disputes, 1991-95; mem. Coun. Asia-Pacific Dispute Rsch. Ctrs., 1991-95; bd. dirs. U.S. C. of C., 1998—; mem. Pacific Basin Econ. Coun., 1993—; mem. mgmt. com. PBEC-U.S. Nat. Com., 1994-99. Recipient cert. of appreciation Gov. of Hawaii, 1979, resolutions of appreciation Hawaii Senate and Ho. of Reps., 1979; grantee Japan Found., 1979. Mem. ABA, Hawaii Bar Assn. (pres. young lawyers sect. 1974, v.p. 1984), Japan-Hawaii Lawyers Assn., Am. Soc. Internat. Law, Internat. Bar Assn., Am. Judicature Soc., Inter-Pacific Bar Assn., Internat. Law Assn., Plaza Club (Honolulu), Colonial Club (Princeton). Democrat. Office: Carlsmith Ball LLP ASB Tower Ste 2200 1001 Bishop St Honolulu HI 96813 Business E-Mail: gsumida@carlsmith.com.

SUMLIN, MARGARET BROWN (MARGIE SUMLIN), retired special education educator; b. Ann Arbor, Mich., Nov. 2, 1950; d. Willis Radcliff and Eulalie (Draughon) Brown. BS, U. Ala., 1972; MA, U. South Ala., 1976. Cert. spl. edn. tchr., Ala. Spl. edn. tchr. Morningside Elem. Sch., Tuscaloosa, Ala., 1972-73; spl. edn. tchr., community coord. A.P. Brewer Developmental Ctr., Mobile, Ala., 1973-75; spl. edn. tchr. Crichton Elem. Sch., Mobile, 1975-77, Scarborough Mid. Sch., Mobile, 1977-82, Cornerstone Group Home, Mobile, 1982; spl. edn. tchr., edn. coord. Brookwood Recovery Ctr., Mobile, 1984-90, Wilmer Hall Children's Home, Mobile, 1991, art therapy tchr., 1991—92; spl. edn. coord., tchr. The Murray Sch. at Wilmer Hall, Mobile, 1992—2002, prin., spl. edn. coord., 2003—08. Ednl. cons. Parkside Recovery Ctr., Mobile, 1989-90; art therapy coord. Wilmer Hall Children's Home, 1991—; founder, organizer Friends of Wilmer Hall, 1992—. Author: (program model) Classroom Structure for Emotionally Disturbed Students, 1984. Bd. dirs. Women of Ch., St. Paul Ch., Mobile, 1991—, Mobile Pub. Libr., 1992—; vol. fundraiser Am. Cancer Soc., 1992; vol. tutor Project Hope Group Home, 1974, Rotary Rehab. Ctr., 1976; vol. coord. Vol. Mobile, 1982, Mobile County Sch. System, 1984; bd. dirs. Cornerstone Group Home (pres. 1985-86); vol. Mobile Pre-Sch. for the Deaf, 1979, Rotary Rehab. Ctr. In-Patient Svcs., 1977. Named a Point of Light by Pres. George Bush, 1991. Mem. Jr. League of Mobile (vol. fundraiser 1990-91), Nat. Soc. of Colonial Dames of Am. Episcopalian. Avocations: reading, hand sewing, beach activities.

SUMMA, PHILIP, lawyer; b. Phila., Oct. 1, 1951; s. Felix and Carlotta Rose Summa; m. Mary Louise Potter, Sept. 9, 1989; children: Philip Daniel, Mary Catherine, Sarah Elizabeth, Rachel Louise, Rebekah McLean. BA, Gettysburg Coll., Pa., 1973; MS, NC State U., Raleigh, 1975; JD, Campbell U., Buies Creek, NC, 1983. Bar: NC 1983. Pres. Summa, Additon & Ashe P.A., Charlotte, NC, 1997—. Mem.: ABA, Fourth Circuit Jud. Conf., Licensing Exec. Soc., Am. Chem. Soc., NC Bar Assn. (bd. govs. 2005—). Office: Summa Additon & Ashe P A 11610 N Community House Rd Charlotte NC 28277 Office Fax: 704-945-6701. Business E-Mail: psumma@summalaw.com.

SUMMER, DONNA (LA DONNA ADRIAN GAINES), singer, songwriter, actress; b. Boston, Dec. 31, 1948; d. Andrew and Mary Gaines; m. Helmut Sommer (div.); 1 child, Mimi; m. Bruce Sudano; children: Brooklyn, Amanda. Has sold over 20 million records. Singer, 1967—; actress: (German stage prodn.) Hair, 1967-75, (Vienna Folk Opera prodns.) Porgy and Bess, (German prodns.) The Me Nobody Knows, (cable TV spl.) Donna Summer Special, 1980; recorded albums including The Wanderer, Star Collection, Love To Love You Baby, Love Trilogy, Four Seasons of Love, I Remember Yesterday, The Deep, Shut Out, Once Upon A Time, Bad Girls, On The Radio, Walk Away, She Works Hard For The Money, Cats Without Claws, All Systems Go, 1988, Another Place and Time, 1989, Mistaken Identity, 1991, Endless Summer, 1994, Christmas Spirit, 1994, I'm a Rainbow, 1996, Live & More Encore, 1999, Crayons, 2008; subject My Life VH1 Concert, 1999; recorded theme song for Hunchback of Notre Dame, Disney; forerunner of disco style. Named Best Rhythm and Blues Female Vocalist, Nat. Acad. Rec. Arts and Scis., 1978, Best Female Rock Vocalist, 1979, Favorite Female Pop Vocalist, Am. Music Awards, 1979, Favorite Female Vocalist of Soul Music, 1979, Soul Artist of Yr., Rolling Stone mag., 1979; recipient Best Favorite Pop Single award, 1979, Best-selling Black Music Album for Female Artist award Nat. Assn. Record Merchandizers, 1979, Ampex Golden Reel award for album On the Radio, 1979, Best-selling Album for Female Artist, 1980, Ampex Golden Reel award for single On the Radio, 1980, Ampex Golden Reel award for album Bad Girls, Best of Las Vegas Jimmy award for best rock performance, 1980, Grammy award for best inspirational performance, 1984. Office: 2401 Main St Santa Monica CA 90405-3515

SUMMER, EMILY EUGENIA, artist, educator; d. Charles Edgar and Emily Eugenia Summer. BS, Miss. U. for Women, 1945; LHD (hon.), MIss. U. for Women, 2005; MA, Columbia U., 1948. Supr. art Clarksdale (Miss.) City Schs., 1948—49; adj. prof. art Miss. U. for Women, Columbus, 1949—58, assoc. prof. art, 1958—78, prof. art, 1978—80, asst. dean Sch. Arts and Scis., 1980—82, head divsn. fine and performing arts, 1982—85, prof. emerita art, 1985—. One-woman shows include Ricks Meml. CArnegie Libr., Yazoo City, Miss., 1962, First Nat. Bank, Jackson, Miss., 1974, Mcpl. Libr., Amory, Miss., 1975, Miss. State U., Starkville, 1978, Rosenzweig Arts Ctr., Columbus, 2001, Fine Arts Gallery, Miss. U. for Women, 02, exhibitions include Hunter Gallery, 1963, Birmingham Mus. Art, 1968, Nat. Arts Club, 1980, numerous others, exhibited in group shows at Itawamba Jr. Coll. Gallery, Fulton, Miss., 1986, Hinds C.C. Gallery, Raymond, Miss., 1987, Shelton State C.C. Gallery, Tuscalloosa, Ala., 1988, Miss. U. for Women, 1970—86, Miss. Mus. Art, Jackson, 2002, 2007, Miss. Gov.'s Mansion, 2001, Walter Anderson Mus. Art, Ocean Springs, Miss., 2007, Represented in permanent collections Miss. Mus. Art, exhibitions include Eugenia Summer: Legacy of Creativity, Miss. U. for Women, 2009, also numerous pvt. and corp. collections. Bd. govs. artist registry Brooks Meml. Art Mus., Memphis, 1971—72; Miss. rep. bd. dirs. Southeastern Coll. Art Assn., 1964—71; rschr., trainer Nat. Mus. Am. Art, Washington, 1992—93; mem. Columbus/Lowndes County United Way, 1997—. Recipient Alumni Achievement award, Miss. U. for Women, 1986, Honored Artist, Nat. Mus. Women Artists, 2001, Lowndes County Alumni Svc. award, Plymouth Bluff Ctr., Columbus, 2003, Medal of Excellence, Miss. U. for Women, 2003, numerous others; Eugenia Summer Art Gallery named in her honor, Miss. U. for Women, 2002, Danforth assoc., 1977—83, rsch. grantee, Miss. U. for Women, 1976, 1978, 1979. Mem.: Miss. Mus. Art Rembrandt Soc., Nat. Audubon Soc., Lauren Rogers Mus. Art, Nat. Mus. Women in Arts (honored artist 2002), Coll. Art Assn. Am. (life), Nature Conservancy, John Muir Soc., Sierra Club, Garden Clubs Miss. (life), Kappa Pi, Phi Kappa Phi. Democrat. Roman Catholic. Home: 915 5th Ave S Columbus MS 39701

SUMMER, WARREN R., pulmonologist, director; b. Bayonne, NJ, Apr. 22, 1940; m. Lillian R. Horlick, Aug. 19, 1962; children: Lori Machiorlette, Renee Melchiode, Ross. MD, Georgetown Med., Wash., 1965. Sect. chief pulmonary medicine LSUMC, New Orleans, 1983—2005, dir. morial asthma & respiratory disease ctr., 1995—, dir. clin. pulmonary rsch., 2005—. Lt. USN, 1968—70. Recipient award, LSUMC, 1987—. Office: LSUHSC 1901 Perdido St New Orleans LA 70112 Office Fax: 504-564-4295. Personal E-mail: redoak1@cox.net. Business E-Mail: wsumme@lsumc.edu.

SUMMERFIELD, GALE, director, educator; children: Tai Hsiao, Thomas Hsiao. PhD, U. Mich., 1987. Assoc. prof. Monterey (Calif.) Inst. Internat. Studies, 1987—98, U. Ill., Champaign, Ill., 1998—, dir. WGGP, 1998—. Author: Women and Gender Equity in Development Theory and Practice, Women's Rights to House and Land: China, Laos, Vietnam; contbr. articles to profl. jours. Bd. dirs. Nat. Coun. Rsch. on Women, NYC, 2004—05; trustee Assn. Social Econs., 2002—05. Office: University of Illinois at Urbana 910 South Fifth St Champaign IL 61820 Office Fax: 217-333-6270. Business E-Mail: summrfld@uiuc.edu.

SUMMERFIELD, JOHN ROBERT, textile curator; b. St. Paul, Feb. 21, 1917; s. Isaac and Irene (Longini) S.; m. Anne Benson, July 14, 1945. SB in Mech. Engring., MIT, 1938; MBA, U. Calif., Berkeley, 1947, PhD in Econs., 1954. Asst. prof. Sloan Sch. Mgmt., MIT, 1952-54; br. chief CIA, Washington, 1954-56; project leader The Rand Corp., Santa Monica, Calif., 1956—62; corp. economist Douglas Aircraft Co., Santa Monica, Calif., 1962—66; v.p. econ. planning Western Airlines, LA, 1966-70; staff v.p. econ. planning Pan Am. Airways, NYC, 1970-71; pres. Summerfield Assocs., Pacific Palisades, Calif., 1972-92; vis. curator Fowler Mus. Cultural History, UCLA, 1993—. Co-curator exhbns. of antique Minangkabau ceremonial textiles from West Sumatra, Textile Mus., Washington, 1990-91, Santa Barbara (Calif.) Mus. Art, 1991, Bellevue (Wash.) Art Mus., 1992, Utah Mus. Fine Art, 1992, Fowler Mus. of Cultural History, UCLA, 1999, Iris and B. Gerald Cantor Gallery, Coll. Holy Cross, 2003, 05, 07. Served to lt. USNR, 1942-45. E-mail: summrfld@arts.ucla.edu.

SUMMERS, CAROL, artist; b. Kingston, NY, Dec. 26, 1925; s. Ivan Franklin and Theresa (Jones) S.; m. Elaine Smithers, Oct. 2, 1954 (div. Aug. 1967); 1 child, Kyle; m. Joan Ward Toth, May 6, 1974 (dec. 1998); 1 child, Ethan. BA, Bard Coll., 1951, DFA (hon.), 1974. Tchr. Hunter Coll., Sch. Visual Arts, Haystack Mountain Sch. Crafts, Bklyn. Mus. Art Sch., Pratt Graphic Art Ctr., Chelterham Twp. Art Ctr., Valley Stream Community Art Ctr., U. Pa., Columbia Coll., U. Calif., Santa Cruz, San Francisco Art Inst., U. Utah, Logan, Art Study Abroad, Paris, Casa de Espiritus Alegres Marfil, Mex., USIS workshop tour, India, 1974, 79; folk art and textiles tour leader to Rajasthan & Gujarat, India, 1995-2009. Represented in permanent collections at, Mus. Modern Art, Bklyn. Mus., N.Y. Pub. Libr., Libr. of Congress, Nat. Gallery, Victoria and Albert Mus., London, Bibliotheque Nationale, Paris, Kunstmuseum, Basil, Lugano (Switzerland) Art Mus. Grenchen (Switzerland) Art Mus., Malmo (Sweden) Mus., Los Angeles County Mus., Phila. Mus., Balt. Mus., Seattle Mus., Boston Mus., Art Inst. Chgo., Am. embassies in Russia, Can., India, Thailand, Fed. Republic Germany and Eng.; traveling exhibit, Mus. Modern Art, 1964-66; retrospective exhbn. Brooklyn Mus., 1977, Nassau County Mus. Art, 1990, Belles Artes, San Miquel de Allende, Mex., 1992, Miami U. Art Mus., Oxford, Ohio, 1995, Egon Schiele Centrum Česky Krumlov, Czech Republic, 1997-98; 50-yr. retrospective at Mus. Art and History, Santa Cruz, 1999, Woodstock (N.Y.) Artists Assn., 1999, Museo del Peublo de Guanajuato, Mex., 2007; author: A Treasury of Indian Folk Textiles, 2002, Another Treasury of Indian Folk Textiles, 2006. Served with USMCR, 1944-48, PTO. Recipient Outstanding Printmaker award, Mid Am. Print Coun., 2004; named Artist of Yr., Santa Cruz County Arts Commn., 2001; fellow, Louis Comfort Tiffany Found., 1955, 1960, John Simon Guggenheim Found., 1959, Fulbright, Italy, 1961; study grantee, Italian govt., 1954—55, rsch. grantee, Coun. Internat. Exch. Scholars, India, 1993—94. Mem. NAD (academician, 1994-), Calif. Soc. Printmakers. Office Phone: 831-423-0181. Personal E-mail: carol@casaspirit.com.

SUMMERS, CATHLEEN, film producer; b. Chgo. d. Paul and Elizabeth Summers; m. Patrick Crowley. BA, U. So. Calif., 1973. Film editor, comml. producer, dir.'s asst. Roman Polanski, Rome, 1972; story editor Albert S. Ruddy Prodns. Paramount Pictures, LA, 1973-74; exec. asst. Columbia Pictures, Burbank, Calif., 1974, story editor, 1974-76; devel. exec., v.p., producer Martin Ransohoff Prodns. Columbia Pictures, 1976; sr. v.p. Tri-Star Pictures, Century City, Calif., 1984-87; motion picture producer Cathleen Summers Prodns., LA, 1989—; ptnr. ESN, Film Prodn. Resource Co.; cons., ptnr. Estudio Network. Motion picture producer, ptnr. Summers-Kouf Prodns., Burbank, 1986-87; motion picture producer Cathleen Summers Prodns., L.A., 1987, Summers-Quaid Prodns., Century City, Culver City, Calif., 1988—. Producer: (motion picture) Stakeout, 1987, DOA, 1991, Vital Signs, 1990, Mystery Date, 1991, Dogfight, 1991, The Sandlot, 1993, Stakeout II, 1993; exec. prodr. Derivations, Who New/The Real Deal, 2003. Co-founder Diane Thomas Scholarship, UCLA, 1988—; bd. dirs. L.A. chpt. Nat. Parkinsons Found.; founding bd. dirs. U.S. Comedy Arts Festival, Aspen, Colo. Mem. Am. Film Inst. (pres. 3d Decade Coun. 1995, 96, 97). Personal E-mail: july4bu@charter.net.

SUMMERS, CHARLES E., JR., military officer, former state senator; b. Danville, Ill., Dec. 26, 1959; m. Ruth Summers; children: Tricia, Chas. AA, Blackhawk Coll.-East; BS, U. Ill., Urbana-Champaign, 1984. Mem. Maine State Senate from Dist. 31, 1991—95, mem. Taxation com.; pub. affairs officer US Navy, 1995—; state dir. for US Senator Olympia Snowe, 1995—2004; New England regional adminstr. US Small Business Adminstrn., 2005—07. Owner Charlie's Beverage Warehouse, 1992—95. Lt. comdr. USNR, 2001—. Mem.: Free and Accepted Masons, Am. Legion, Vets. of Foreign Wars. Republican. Methodist. Office: 107 Exchange St Portland ME 04101 Office Phone: 207-883-5105. E-mail: charlie@summersforcongress.org.*

SUMMERS, DAVID STEWART, neurologist, consultant; b. Canton, Ohio, Feb. 16, 1932; s. William Edward and Stewart (Jordan) Summers; m. Ada Ernestine Cumber, Nov. 30, 1957; children: David Stewart II, Timothy C. BS, Va. State U., Petersburg, 1954; MD, U. Va., Charlottesville, 1959. Diplomate Am. Acad. Pain Mgmt. Resident in neurology SUNY, Syracuse, 1960—63; asst. prof. neurology U. Rochester, NY, 1968—72; asst. prof. U. Utah Coll. Medicine, Salt Lake City, 1972—76; staff neurologist St. Vincent Health Ctr., Erie, Pa., 1976—91, Meadville Med. Ctr., Pa., 1991—93; neurologist Warren State Hosp., Pa., 1993—2000; investor, 2000—. Cons. Reflex Sympathetic Dystrophy Assn., Erie, 1988—97; mem. adv. coun. HHS, Washington, 1974—77. Contbg. author The Black Humanist Experience, 2003; contbr. articles to profl. jours. Supporter City Mission, Erie, 1991—; Planetary Soc., 2005—, Am. United Separation Ch. and State, NOW, ACLU, Am. Humanist Assn., People for the Am. Way, Ctr. Reproductive Law and Policy, Planned Parenthood, The Freedom from Religion Found., others; advisor to gov. Coun. Black Affairs, Salt Lake City, 1975; mem. Human Rights Campaign, Population Connection. Capt. M.C. USAR, 1964—67, Landstuhl, Germany. Grantee, Nat. Med. Fellowships, 1956—59; A. A. Rockefeller scholar, Williamsburg, Va., 1951—54. Mem.: AAAS, NAACP, African Sci. Fellows, Nat. Ctr. for Sci. Edn., The Planetary Soc., Nat. Soc. Scabbard & Blade, NY Acad. Scis., Menninger Soc., Am. Epilepsy Soc., Nat. Med. Assn., Am. Acad. Neurology, U. Va. Alumni Assn., Am. Legion (life). Democrat. Avocations: reading, hiking, walking. Office Phone: 814-392-3273. Personal E-mail: dssmd1@gmail.com.

SUMMERS, HORACE KENNETH, biology professor; b. Mandeville, Jamaica, July 11, 1945; s. Lorel Osbourne and Edna Mae Summers; m. Linda Sue James, July 27, 1968; children: Chad Kenneth, Saraya Dawn Lopez-Cepero. BS, Howard U., Washington, 1968, DDS, 1973; MA in Adult Edn., U. South Fla., Tampa, 1997. Pvt. practice, Mandeville, 1973—74, St. Albans, NY, 1979—87; dentistry educator, gen. dentist Wascana Inst. Applied Arts & Scis., Regina, Saskatchewan, Canada,

1975—78; clin. instr. NY U. Coll. Dentistry, Manhattan, 1986—87; gen. dentist Children's Aid Soc., Manhattan, NY, 1985—87; dental educator Pasco Hernando CC, New Port Richey, Fla., 1988—2001, prof. biology, 2001—. With Jehovah's Witnesses, Spring Hill, Fla., 1991. Recipient Excellence award, NISOD- Nat. Inst. Staff & Orgnl. Devel., 2009. Home: 8199 Nightingale Rd Brooksville FL 34613 Office: Pasco Hernando CC 10230 Ridge Rd New Port Richey FL 34654

SUMMERS, LARRY (LAWRENCE HENRY SUMMERS), federal official, economist, former United States Secretary of the Treasury; b. New Haven, Nov. 30, 1954; s. Robert Summers and Anita A. (Summers); m. Victoria Joanne Perry, 1984 (div.); children: Pam, Ruth, Harry; m. Elisa New, Dec. 11, 2005. BS, MIT, 1975; PhD, Harvard U., 1982. Mem. faculty MIT, 1979-82; domestic policy economist Coun. Econ. Advisors, Exec. Office of the Pres., 1982-83; v.p. devel. economics, chief economist The World Bank, 1991-93; prof. economics Harvard U., Cambridge, Mass., 1983-93, Nathaniel Ropes prof. polit. economy, 1987—91, pres., 2001—06, Charles W. Eliot U. prof., 2006—08; under sec. for internat. affairs US Dept. Treasury, Washington, 1993-95, dep. sec., 1995-99, sec., 1999-2001; Arthur Okun Disting. Fellow in Econ., Globalization, and Governance Brookings Instn., Washington, 2001; mng. dir. D.E. Shaw & Co. LP, NYC, 2006—09; asst. to Pres. for econ. policy The White House, Washington, 2008—; dir. The Nat. Econ. Coun., Washington, 2008—. Author: Understanding Unemployment, 1990; co-author Reform in Eastern Europe, 1991; editor series Tax Policy and the Economy; contbr. numerous articles to profl. jours. Recipient Alan Waterman Award NSF, 1987, John Bates Clark Medal, Am. Econ. Assn., 1993, Disting. Achievement Award Boys' & Girls' Club Greater Washington, 2000, Disting. Svc. Award Golden Slipper Club & Charities 2000, Econ. Patriot Award Concord Coalition, 2000, Stephen P. Guggan Award Inst. Internat. Edn., 2000; named one of The 100 Most Influential People, TIME mag., 2005, The Top 25 Market Movers, US News & World Report, 2009 Fellow NAS, Econometric Soc., Am. Acad. Arts and Scis., Brookhaven Sci. Assocs. (bd. dirs.), Nat. Acad. Sci. Democrat. Office: The National Economic Council 1600 Pennsylvania Ave Washington DC 20500*

SUMMERS, LORRAINE DEY SCHAEFFER, retired librarian; b. Phila., Dec. 14, 1946; d. Joseph William and Hilda Lorraine (Ritchey) Dey; m. F. William Summers, Jan. 28, 1984. BA, Fla. State U., 1968, MS, 1969. Ext. dir. Santa Fe Regional Libr., Gainesville, 1969-71; pub. libr. cons. State Libr. of Fla., Tallahassee, 1971-78, asst. state libr., 1978-84; dir. adminstrv. svcs. Nat. Assn. for Campus Activities, Columbia, SC, 1984-85; asst. state libr. State Libr. of Fla., Tallahassee, 1985—2001, ret., 2001—. Bd. dirs., sec. Southeastern Libr. Network, Inc.; cons. in field. Contbr. articles to profl. jours. Del. Pres.'s Com. on Mental Retardation Regional Forum, Atlanta, 1975; del. Fla. Gov.'s Conf. on Libr. and Info. Svcs., 1978, 90. Mem. ALA (orgn. com. 1979-83, coun. 1982-84, 93-97, resolutions com. 1983-85, mem. legislation com. 1993-95, nominating com. 1996, awards com. 1998-99, Spectrum awards jury 1999-2000), Assn. Specialized and Coop. Libr. Agys. (dir. 1976-82, chmn. planning and orgn. com. 1976-80, chmn. nominating com. 1980-81, chmn. by laws com. 1985-86, exec. bd. state libr. agy. sect. 1983-86, pres. 1987-88, chmn. stds. rev. com. 1990-92), Southeastern Libr. Assn. (exec. bd. 1976-80, v.p., pres.-elect 1994-96, pres. 1996-98, past pres. 1998-2000, nominating com. 2000-02), Fla. Libr. Assn. (sec. 1978-79, dir. 1976-80, nominating com. 1995-96), Zonta (dir. 1992-95, sec. 1999-2001, mem. svc. com. 2007-), United Nat. Comm.(chmn. 2009-). Democrat. Methodist. Personal E-mail: lorrainesummers@comcast.net.

SUMMERS, PAUL G., lawyer, former state attorney general; b. Somerville, Tenn., Mar. 28, 1950; 1 child, Isaac. BS, Miss. State U., 1972; JD, U. Tenn., 1974. Bar: US Ct. Mil. Appeals 1975, Tenn. Supreme Ct. 1975, US Supreme Ct. 1979. Dist. atty. gen. 25th Jud. Dist., Somerville, Tenn., 1982—90; judge Tenn. Ct. Criminal Appeals, Nashville, 1990—99; atty. gen. State of Tenn., Nashville, 1999—2006; ptnr. Waller, Lansden, Dortch & Davis LLP, Nashville, 2006—. Adj. prof. law U. Memphis; former adj. faculty Cumberland U.; pres. elect Tenn. Dist. Atty.'s Gen. Conf.; mem. Ct. Criminal Appeals, 1990—99; lectr. in field. Former mem. Tenn. Sentencing Commn.; col. Tenn. Army N.G. With USAF. Decorated Legion of Merit, Meritorious Svc. medal with Oak Leaf Cluster. Mem.: Tenn. Dist. Attys. Gen. Conf. (pres.), Tenn. Bar Assn. (former gov.). Democrat. Avocations: racquetball, rollerblading, Karate (black belt), martial arts. Office: Waller Lansden Dortch & Davis LLP Ste 2700 511 Union St Nashville TN 37219 E-mail: paul.summers@wallerlaw.com.

SUMMERS, ROBERT, economics professor; b. Gary, Ind., June 20, 1922; s. Frank and Ella (Lipton) Samuelson; m. Anita Arrow, Mar. 29, 1953; children: Lawrence Henry, Richard Fredric, John Steven. BS, U. Chgo., 1943; PhD, Stanford, 1956; postgrad. (Social Sci. Research Council fellow), King's Coll., U. Cambridge, Eng., 1951-52. Instr. Stanford, 1949-50; mem. faculty Yale, 1952-59, asst. prof., 1956-59; staff mem. Cowles Found., 1955-59; economist RAND Corp., Santa Monica, Calif., 1959-60, cons., 1960-80. Mem. faculty U. Pa. Wharton Sch., 1959—, prof., 1967—, chmn. grad. group in econs., 1967-70, 73-76 Author: (with Lawrence R. Klein) The Wharton Index of Capacity Utilization, 1966, (with others) Strategies for Research and Development, 1967, (with others) A System of International Comparisons of Gross Product and Purchasing Power, 1975, (with others) International Comparisons of Real Product and Purchasing Power, 1978, (with others) World Product and Income, 1982; contbr. articles to profl. jours. Served with AUS, 1944-46. Ford Found. faculty rsch. fellow London Sch. Econs., 1966-67; NSF grantee 1957-59, 63-66, 80-82, 86-90, 92-94, 95-97, 97-2000, 00—03; resident scholar Rockefeller Found. Study Ctr., 1986. Fellow: AAAS, Am. Econ. Soc. (disting.), Econometric Soc. Home: 1400 Waverly Rd V-11 Gladwyne PA 19035-1271 Office: U Pa Dept Econ Philadelphia PA 19104-6297 Home Phone: 610-645-8660. E-mail: rsummers@econ.upenn.edu.

SUMMERS, SANDRA LINDEMANN, language educator; b. Karlsruhe, Germany, June 19, 1963; m. T. Stran Summers, Dec. 28, 1985; children: Berta Jane, Erik Stran. PhD, Duke U., Durham, NC, 2004. Cert. in bus. Duesseldorf, Germany, 2002, in medieval studies Duke U., 2004. Lectr., Germanic langs. U. NC, Chapel Hill, 2004—. Home: 3618 Stoneybrook Dr Durham NC 27705 Office: Univ NC Chapel Hill 438 Dey Hall Chapel Hill NC 27599 Business E-Mail: slsummer@email.unc.edu.

SUMMERS, SUZANNE FRANCES HEMENWAY, elementary school educator; b. Charleston Twp., Mich., June 23, 1950; d. Robert Walter and Irene (Hodges) Hemenway; m. Jacob George Summers, June 23, 1973; children: Braxton, Jennifer, Dondra. BS in Home Econs., E. Carolina U., 1972; MEd, Campbell U., 1997. Lic. elem. tchr., NC; cert. ESL instr., cert. tchr. Nat. Bd. Profl. Tchg. Standards, Va., 2005. Substitute tchr. Wake County Pub. Schs., Raleigh, N.C., 1973-74; presch. tchr. Greenwood Forest Bapt. Kindergarten, Cary, N.C., 1978-80; substitute tchr. Wake County Pub. Schs., Raleigh, 1980-96, tchr. elem., 1996—; tchr. Cary Elem. Sch. 2d team chair Cary Elem. Sch., rep. sch. improvement 2d and 3d grades; chmn. Wake County Pub. Schs., mem. sci. leadership com., mem. elem. sci. dept. steering com., K5 rep. elem. leadership com. Mem. NEA, NC Assn. Educators, Kappa Delta Pi, Phi Kappa Phi, Phi Upsilon Omicron. Republican. Baptist. Avocations: cooking, decorating homes. Home: 239 E Cornwall Rd Cary NC 27511-3907 Office Phone: 919-460-3455. Business E-Mail: ssummers@wcpss.net.

SUMMERS, WILLIAM COFIELD, science educator; b. Janesville, Wis., Apr. 17, 1939; s. Crosby Hungerford and Rebecca Delores (Cofield) S.; m. Wilma Jean Poos, July 24, 1965; 1 child, Emily Alexandra. BS, U. Wis., 1961, MS, 1963, Phd, MD, 1967; MAH, Yale U., 1977. Post-doctoral fellow MIT, Cambridge, Mass., 1967-68; asst. prof. Yale U., New Haven, 1968-70, assoc. prof., 1970-77, prof., 1977—. Cons. NIH, Bethesda, Md., 1976—. Editor Nucleic Acids Research Jour., 1977-79, Gene jour., 1984-91; contbr. articles to profl. jours. Cons. Anna Fuller Fund, New Haven, 1973-88, Searle Scholars Program, Chgo., 1980-84; trustee Leukemia Soc. Am., N.Y.C., 1981-85, Yale-China Assn., New Haven, 1982-88, 94-98. Mem. Am. Soc. for Microbiology, History Sci. Soc., Am. Assn. History of Medicine. Office: Yale U Box 208114 New Haven CT 06520-8114 E-mail: william.summers@yale.edu.

SUMMERS, WILLIAM LAWRENCE, lawyer; b. Ravenna, Ohio, Mar. 6, 1942; s. Samuel Long and Harriet Cordellia (Jones) S.; m. Barbara A. Herbert; children: Melinda Ann, Shannon Lea, Heather Colleen, Kelly Lynn, Michael Patrick, Kevin James. BA in Polit. Sci. and Sociology, Kent State U., 1965; postgrad., U. Miami, 1966; JD, Cleve. State U., 1969. Bar: Ohio 1969, Ky. 1988, U.S. Dist. Ct. (no. dist.) Okla. 1971, U.S. Ct. Appeals (6th cir.) 1973, U.S. Ct. Appeals (3d and 5th cirs.) 1979, U.S. Ct. Appeals (8th and 5th cirs.) 1981, U.S. Ct. Appeals (7th cir.) 1982, U.S. Ct. Appeals (9th and 10th cirs.) 1983, U.S. Ct. Appeals (11th cir.), 1984, U.S. Supreme Ct., 1973, U.S. Tax Ct. 1973, U.S. Dist. Ct. (so. dist.) Ala. 1984, U.S. Dist. Ct. (so. dist.) Ohio 1985, U.S. Dist. Ct. (ea. and we. dists.) Ky. 1988. Ptnr. Summers & Vargas Co. LPA, Cleve. and Lexington, Ky., 1969—. Cons. on death penalty State Pub. Defender, Santa Fe, 1980-83; lectr. in field. Named one of Ten Outstanding Young Men of Cleve., Cleve. Jaycees, 1972, Five Outstanding Young Men of Ohio, Ohio Jaycees, 1972. Fellow Am. Acad. Trial Lawyers (Roscoe Pound award 1971); mem. ABA (criminal justice sect.), Ohio State Bar Assn. (ho. of dels. 1973-75, 2002-2004), Cuyahoga County Bar Assn. (trustee 1972-76, treas. 1976-79, pres. 1982-83, other coms.), Cuyahoga County Bar Assn., Cuyahoga County Criminal Ct. Bar Assn. (pres. 1977-79), Fed. Bar Assn., Portage County Bar Assn., Ohio Assn. Criminal Def. Lawyers (bd. dirs. 1988—), Ky. Assn. Criminal Def. Lawyer (bd. dirs. 1987-2000), Bar Assn. Greater Cleve., Nat. Assn. Criminal Def. Lawyers (trustee 1977-88, chmn. various coms. Pres.'s award 1981, 1986, 90, Robert C. Heeney award 1982), Am. Judicature Soc., Thoroughbred Club Am., Delta Theta Phi, Canterbury Golf Club, Elks. Roman Catholic. Avocation: thoroughbred horse breeding. Home: 17549 Merry Oaks Trl Chagrin Falls OH 44023-5643 Office: 55 Public Square Ste 2000 Cleveland OH 44113 Home Phone: 440-543-5500; Office Phone: 216-591-0727. Personal E-mail: wlslawyer@aol.com.

SUMMERTREE, KATONAH See WINDSOR, PATRICIA

SUMMITT, PAT (PATRICIA SUE SUMMITT), women's college basketball coach; b. Henrietta, Tenn., June 14, 1952; d. Richard and Hazel Head; m. R.B. Summitt (div.); 1 child, Ross Tyler. BS in Phys. Edn., U. Tenn., Martin, 1974; MS in Phys. Edn., U. Tenn., Knoxville, 1975. Head coach U. Tenn., Knoxville, 1974—. Head coach 1st US Jr. Nat. team, 1977 (2 gold medals in internat. play), US Nat. team William R. Jones Cup Games, 1979, World Championships, 1979, Pan Am. Games, 1979 (2 gold medals, 1 silver medal); asst. coach US Women's Olympic Basketball team, 1980-84, head coach, 1984 (gold medal); assoc. athletics dir., U. Tenn.; past v.p. USA BASKETBALL; past Olympic rep. adv. com. to USA BASKETBALL; bd. trustees Basketball Hall of Fame; bd. dirs. Women's Basketball Hall of Fame. Author: (books) Reach For The Summit, 1998, Raise the Roof, 1998. Active Big Bros./Big Sisters; active spokesperson United Way, Race for the Cure, Juvenile Diabetes; hon. chair Tenn. Easter Seal Soc., 1985, 87, 88, 89; Tenn. chair Am. Heart Assn., 1994. Recipient Silver medal, US World U. Games, 1973, Gold medal, Pan Am. Games, 1975, Silver medal, Olympic Games, 1976, Wooden award, 1997, ARETE Award for Courage in Sports, 1999, Dick Enberg award, Coll. Sports Info. Dirs. Am., 2007, John R. Wooden Award's Legends of Coaching award, 2008, ESPY award, Best Coach-Mgr., ESPN, 2008, Joe Lapchick Character award, 2008; named Women's Basketball Coaches Assn./Converse Coach of Yr., 1983—95, Naismith Coach of Yr., 1987, 1989, 1994, 1997, Naismith Coach of Century, 2000; named one of Women of Yr., Women in Sports and Events, 1999, 10 Most Powerful People in Coll. Sports, 2007, America's Best Leaders, US News & World Report, 2007; named to Women's Sports Found. Hall of Fame, 1990, Nat. Assn. Sport and Phys. Edn. Hall of Fame, 1996, Women's Basketball Hall of Fame, 1999, Basketball Hall of Fame, 2000. Mem. Chi Omega. Achievements include leading the Lady Vols to the NCAA Championship, 1987, 89, 91, 96, 97, 98, 2007, 2008; led the Lady Vols to the Southeastern Conf. Championship, 1980, 85, 90, 93, 94, 95, 98, 99, 2000, 01, 02, 03, 04; became the all-time winningest coach in NCAA basketball history, March 21, 2005; first Division 1 coach to record 1,000 career victories, Feb. 5, 2009. Avocations: cooking, golf, running, water-skiing, boating. Office: U Tenn 207 Thompson-Boling Ctr and Arena 1600 Phillip Fulmer Way Knoxville TN 37996-4610 Office Phone: 865-974-0600.*

SUMNER, GORDON, JR., retired military officer; b. Albuquerque, July 23, 1924; s. Gordon and Esstella (Berry) S.; m. Frances Fernandes, May, 1991; children: Ward T., Holly Rose. AS, N.Mex. Mil. Inst., Roswell, 1943; BA, La. State U., 1955; MA, U. Md., 1963. Commd. 2d. lt. US Army, 1944, advanced through grades to lt. gen., 1975, ret., 1978; founder, chmn. Cypress Internat., 1978-96; chmn. La Mancha Co., Inc., 1981-89, Sumner Assoc. Cons. US Depts. State and Def; amabassador at large for Latin Am.; spl. advisor US Dept. State; nat. security advisor Pres.' Bi-Partisan Commn. Ctrl. Am.; cons. Los Alamos Nat. Lab. Contbr. articles to profl. jours. Decorated D.S.M., Silver Star, Legion of Merit with three oak leaf clusters, D.F.C., Air medal with 13 oak leaf clusters, Bronze Star, Army Commendation medal with oak leaf cluster, Purple Heart. Mem. Phi Kappa Phi, Pi Sigma Alpha. Office: La Mancha Co 100 Cienega St Ste D Santa Fe NM 87501-2003 Office Phone: 505-984-8041.

SUMNER, GORDON MATTHEW See STING

SUMNER, KELLY, computer game company executive; With Commodore Computers, 1979—92, mng. dir. UK, 1992—93; pres., CEO GameTek Inc., 1993—97; pres. Take Two Interactive Software Europe Ltd., 1997—2000; CEO, pres. pub. unit Take Two Interactive Software, 2000—06; CEO RedOctane Inc., Sunnyvale, Calif., 2006—. Office: Redoctane Inc 444 Castro St Ste 140 Mountain View CA 94041-2073

SUMRULD, BILL, history professor; PhD, Southwestern Bapt. Theol. Sem., Ft. Worth, 1985. Latin instr. Southwestern Bapt. Theol. Sem., 1981—85; instr., eccles. Latin St. Thomas More Inst., Ft. Worth, 1986—87; prof., history and religion U. SW, Hobbs, N.Mex., 1988—. Contbr. articles to jours. Deacon Northside Bapt. Ch., Hobbs, 2003—08. Office: Univ SW 6610 Lovington Hwy Hobbs NM 88240

SUMUKADAS, NARENDAR, finance educator; BS in Tech., Kakatiya U., Warangal, India, 1983; MBA, U. Man., Winnipeg, Canada, 1991; PhD, U. Western Ont., London, Ontario, Canada, 1997. Asst. prof. U. Hartford, West Hartford, Conn., 1999—2005, assoc. prof., 2005—. Office: Univ of Hartford 200 Bloomfield Ave West Hartford CT 06117

SUMWALT, ROBERT LLEWELLYN, III, federal agency administrator, pilot; b. Columbia, SC, June 30, 1956; s. Robert Llewellyn Jr. and Joyce (Mills) S.; m. Anne Macdonald, Dec. 22, 1978; 1 child, Kaylyn Mackenzie. BS, U. S.C., 1979. Flight engr., first officer Piedmont Airlines, Winston-Salem, N.C., 1981-83, chief flight engr., 1983, capt., airline instr. Charlotte, NC, 1984-89; capt. U.S. Airways, Charlotte, 1989—2005; mgr. aviation SCANA Corp., 2005—06; mem. Nat. Transp. Safety Bd. (NTSB), Washington, 2006—, vice chmn., 2006—08. Chmn. Richland County Airport Commn., Columbia, S.C., 1987-89; pres. Aviatrends, Inc., Columbia, 1992—; aviation safety rsch. cons. NASA Aviation Safety Reporting Sys.; mem., Air Line Pilots Assn. Accident Investigation Bd., 2002-04, US Airways Flight Ops. Quality Assurance, 2002-04; instr. Aviation Safety & Security Program, U. So. Calif., 2003- Author: Terminal Checklist, 1991; editl. adv. bd. Profl. Pilot Mag., Alexandria, Va., 1986—; contbr. articles to profl. jours. Recipient Laura Taber Barbour award, Flight Safety Found., 2003, Air Safety award, Air Line Pilots Assn., 2004. Mem. Airline Pilots Assn. (chmn. human hactors and ergonomics com.). Presbyterian. Achievements include research on aviation safety and aircraft accident investigation. Office: Nat Transp Safety Bd (NTSB) 490 L Enfant Plz SW Washington DC 20594*

SUN, ANDY, dentist; b. Ping-Dong, Taiwan, Nov. 23, 1953; s. Shi-Kia Sun and Su-Ju Chen; m. Shu-Yun Hsiung, Mar. 11, 1978; children: Han-Wei, Wan-Lin. DDS, Nat. Taiwan U., Taipei, 1978, PhD in Immunology, 1992. Attending physician Nat. Taiwan U., 1989—; assoc. prof. Fu-jen Cath. U., Taipei, 1993-94, Shih Hsin U., Taipei, 1996—2003, prof., 2003—. Vis. prof. Tianjin Med. U., China, 1999—, Hu-Bei Traditional Chinese Med. Coll., China, 1999—; vis. assoc. prof. Shanghai Traditional Chinese Med. U., China, 1999-2003, prof., 2003—. Contbr. articles to profl. jours. Mem. ctrl. com. KMT, Taipei, 1995-98. Lt. Taiwan armed forces, 1978-80. Recipient Outstanding in Immunology Rsch. award Found. Immunology Rsch., 1987. Mem.: Formosan Med. Assn., NY Sci. Coun., Chinese Soc. Immunology, Straits Acad. and Cultural Exch. Assn. (v.p. 1997—2001, pres. 2001—), Univ. and Coll. Lectrs. Assn. (pres. 1998—). Roman Catholic. Avocations: speech, singing, meditation, qigong. Office: Nat Taiwan U Hosp No 1 Chang-te St Taipei 100 Taiwan Office Phone: 886-2-23123456 ext. 67702. Personal E-mail: andysun.sun@msa.hinet.net. Business E-Mail: andysun7702@yahoo.com.tw.

SUN, BRIAN A., lawyer; BA magna cum laude, U. Southern Calif., LA, 1976, JD, 1979. Bar: Calif. Law clk. Hon. A Andrew Hauk US Dist. Ct. (ctrl. Calif.), 1979—80; asst. US atty., criminal divsn. US Attorney's Office, LA, 1982—86; chief, fin. investigations unit US Dept. Justice, 1984—86; ptnr. Jones Day, LA. Dep. gen. counsel Ind. Commn. on the LA Police Dept., 1992; lawyer rep. Ninth Cir. Jud. Conf.; adj. prof. Southwestern U. Law Sch.; trial advocacy lectr. US Dept. Justice. Contbr. articles to profl. jours. Bd. mem. Constl. Rights Found., Southwestern U. Law Sch., bd. trustees; bd. dirs. Bet Tzedek. Recipient Am. Jewish Congress award, 2001; named Best of Bar in LA, LA Bus. Jour., 2007; named one of 100 Most Influential Lawyers in Calif., LA Daily Jour., America's 500 Leading Lawyers, Lawdragon, 2005, 50 Most Influential Minority Lawyers in America, Nat. Law Jour., 2008. Fellow: Am. Coll. Trial Lawyers; mem.: LA County Bar Assn. (chmn. litig. sect. 2000, Def. Atty. of Yr. 2003), Nat. Asian Pacific Am. Bar Assn. (past pres.), Southern Calif. Chinese Lawyers Assn. (past pres., Disting. Svc. award 2003), Com. of 100. Avocation: Tae Kwon Do. Office: Jones Day 555 S Flower St 50th Fl Los Angeles CA 90071 Office Phone: 213-243-2858. Office Fax: 213-243-2539. Business E-Mail: basun@jonesday.co.*

SUN, CHANGQUAN CALVIN, medical researcher, educator; b. China; married. PhD, U. Minn., Mpls., 2000. Prin. scientist Pfizer, Kalamazoo; sr. scientist Amgen Inc., Thousand Oaks, 2005—08; asst. prof. U. Minn., 2008—. Mem.: AAAS, ACS, Am. Assn. Pharm. Scientists (New Investigator award 2008). Business E-Mail: sunx0053@umn.edu.

SUN, DAZHI, engineering educator; s. Jianmin Sun and Shirong Chen; m. Miao Zhuang; 1 child, Matthew. PhD, U. Ill., Urbana-Champaign, 2005. Rsch. scientist Tex. Transp. Inst., San Antonio, 2005—06; asst. prof. Tex. A&M U., Kingsville, 2006—. Recipient 1st Pl. Sci. and Tech. awards, China Hwy. and Transp. Soc., 2006. Mem.: Inst. Transp. Engrs. (student chpt. advisor, Best Paper award, Ill. sect. 2004, Best Paper award, Dist. 4 2005). Office: Tex A&M Univ Kingsville 700 University Blvd MSC 194 Kingsville TX 78363

SUN, DONGLIAN, meteorologist; d. Detian Sun and XianZhi Shiao; m. XiaoBiao Fan, May 1, 1990; 1 child, Jean Fan. BS in Synoptic Dynamics, Nanjing Inst. Meteorology, China, 1986; MS in Numerical Model and Simulation, Chinese Acad. Meteorol. Scis., Beijing, 1989, U. Md., College Park, 1998, PhD in Satellite Remote Sensing, 2003. Sr. scientist Raytheon ITSS Inc, Lanham, Md., 1998—2000; sr. software engr. Titan/AverStar, Vienna, Va., 2000—01; rsch. scientist, severe weather ctr. lead George Mason U., Fairfax, Va., 2001—. Achievements include development of new algorithms for improving atmospheric water vapor, surface temperature and emissivity retrieval from current and future satellite measurements; the study of coastal upwelling, hurricanes, and earthquakes by combining numerical model simulations with satellite remote sensing. Home: 21700 Seneca Ayr Dr Boyds MD 22030 Office: George Mason Univ Rsch Bldg 1 Room #252 MS:5C3 4400 University Dr Fairfax VA 22030 Office Fax: 703-943-1980; Home Fax: 703-993-1980. Personal E-mail: dsun@gmu.edu. Business E-Mail: sun@atmos.umd.edu.

SUN, HONGWEI, mechanical engineer; b. Liaoyang, China, Sept. 17, 1962; d. Dingxian Sun and Suzhi Zheng; m. Shaofu Wu, Dec. 30, 1985; children: Jenny Wu, Kevin Wu. BS, Beijing U. Aeronautics, 1982, MS, 1984; PhD, U. Ill., Chgo., 1991. Profl. engr., Tex. Rsch. engr. Aurora Pump, Ill., 1991-94; lead design engr., sr. engr. Suzer Pumps, Brookshire, Tex., 1994—; sr. cons. engr. Mustang Engring., 2002—. Patentee in field; contbr. articles to profl. jours. Mem. ASME (assoc.), Tau Beta Pi. Avocations: singalong, swimming. Office Phone: 281-206-6309. Fax: 281-206-1309. E-mail: vicki.sun@mustangeng.com.

SUN, HUI, industrial engineer, operations research analyst; b. Luoyang, Henan, China, May 21, 1973; arrived in US, 2001; s. Yubao Sun and Jun Xu. BEng, Hefei U. Tech., China, 1993; PhD, U. Tenn., Knoxville, 2005. Cert. SAS Inst. Inc., NC, 2006. Rsch. asst. U. Tenn., 2001—05; design engr. Millennium Transit Svcs., LLC., Roswell, N.Mex., 2006—. Indsl. engr. Inst. Project Planning and Rsch. Ministry Machinery Industry, Zhengzhou, Henan, China, 1993—2001. Contbr. articles to profl. jours. Mem.: Inst. Ops. Rsch. and Mgmt. Scis., Inst. Indsl. Engrs. Achievements include research in improving the performance of manufacturing systems and supply chain using advanced optimization techniques. Personal E-mail: hui.sun@utalum.org.

SUN, JIAMING, social sciences educator; m. Fang Liu; 1 child, Jeffery. PhD, U. Ill., Chgo., 2005. Assoc. prof. sociology Fudan U., Shanghai, 1985—97; assoc. prof., sociology and criminal justice Tex. A&M U. Commerce, 2005—. Office Phone: 903-886-5322. Personal E-mail: jmsunsh@yahoo.com.

SUN, JIANXIN, medical educator, researcher; s. Guiying Shen; m. Yong Sun, Jan. 1, 1990; children: Peter Y., Chris H. PhD, Chinese Acad. Scis., Shanghia Inst. Biochemistry, 1998. Instr. Harvard Med. Sch., Boston, 2002—05; asst. prof. NJ. Med. Sch., Newark, 2005—. Scientist Devel. Grant, Am. Heart Assn., 2006—09. Mem.: Am. Heart Assn. Home: 3 Short Hills Cir1A Millburn NJ 07041 Office: Bristol-Myers Squibb Company 311 Pennington-Rocky Hills Rd Pennington NJ 08534 Office Fax: 609-818-7877.

SUN, JIE, R & D engineer; s. Xiexiu Wang and Rongxin Sun. PhD, Pa. State U., State Coll., 2008. Sr. process engr. Vishay Gen. Semiconductor, Tian Jin, 1996—2000; R & D engr. Intel Corp., Santa Clara, Calif., 2008—. Fellow: Kodak; mem.: IEEE (sr. George Smith award 2005), Sigma Xi. Personal E-mail: jasonusa800@hotmail.com.

SUN, LI, chemist, researcher; d. Demin Sun and Chunlan Lu; m. Jiangyan Shi, Nov. 26, 2003. BS, U. Sci. and Tech. China, Hefei, 1998; MS, Rensselaer Poly. Inst., Troy, NY, 2002, PhD, 2007. Staff chemist Merck & Co., Inc., West Point, Pa., 2003—05, rsch. chemist, 2006—07, sr. rsch. chemist, 2008—. Office: Merck & Co Inc WP75A-303 Sumneytown Pike West Point PA 19486 Business E-Mail: li_sun@merck.com.

SUN, LIPENG, chemist; Postdoc. fellow Northwestern U., Evanston, Ill., 2003—06; rsch. assoc. NC State U., Raleigh, 2006—. Mem.: AAAS, Am. Chem. Soc., Sigma Xi.

SUN, LUZHE, pharmacology educator, researcher; b. Guongzou, China, Sept. 12, 1958; came to U.S., 1984; m. Junhua Yang, July 13, 1985; children: Lisa Y., Ryan Y. BS, Shanghai Fisheries Coll., China, 1982; PhD, Rutgers U., 1990. Rsch. assoc. Baylor Coll. Medicine, Houston, 1990-92; rsch. asst. prof. Med. Coll. Ohio, Toledo, 1992-95; asst. prof. U. Ky., Lexington, 1995—. Mem. Am. Assn. Cancer Rsch., Am. Soc. Biochemistry & Molecular Biology. Achievements include discovery of autocrine transforming growth factor beta in cancer cells that can act to suppress malignant progression. Office: U Ky 800 Rose St # Ms-311 Lexington KY 40536-0001

SUN, QIANG, scientist, educator; arrived in US, 2002, permanent resident, 2006; s. Li Xian Sun and Si Ying Hou; m. Qian Wang, July 4, 1987; 1 child, Tony. BS in Physics Edn., Southwest U., Chongging, China, 1984, MS in Theoretical Physics, 1987; PhD in Condensed Matter Physics, Nanjing U., China, 1996. Asst. prof. Tohoku U., Sendai, Japan, 1997—2003; rsch. asst. prof. Va. Commonwealth U., Richmond, 2003—. Contbr. articles to profl. jours. Recipient Outstanding Rsch. award, Japan Inst. of Metals Rsch., 2000. Mem.: Japan Soc. Nano Sci. and Tech., Am. Materials Rsch. Soc., Am. Chem. Soc., Am. Physical Soc. Achievements include research in nanostructures applied to spin electronics, catalysis, biomedicine, enviornmental science, and hydrogen storage. Office: Va Commonwealth Univ W Main St 1020 Richmond VA 23284-2000 Office Fax: 804-828-7073. Business E-Mail: qsun@vcu.edu.

SUN, QUNHUI, research scientist; s. Maiqiu Sun and Xuyun Yang; m. Bairao Zhou; 1 child, Xueyang. PhD, Zhongshan U., China, 1991. Asst. scientist IPST Inc., Atlanta, 2001—03; rsch. scientist Ga. Inst. Tech., Atlanta, 2003—. Vis. scientist CSIRO, Melbourne, Victoria, Australia, 2000—01. Recipient 1st Guanghua award, Zhongshan U., 1991. Office: Ga Inst Tech 500 10th St NW Atlanta GA 30332 Office Fax: 404-894-4778. Business E-Mail: qunhui.sun@ipst.gatech.edu.

SUN, ROBERT ZU JEI, manufacturing company executive, inventor, educator; b. Shanghai, July 5, 1948; s. David C.H. and Evelyn (Lee) S.; m. Nan Jennifer Ronis, Sept. 20, 1986; children: Matthew Nyland, Michael Elias. BS in Elec. Engring., U. Pa., 1970. Sr. project engr. Drexelbrook Engring. Co., Horsham, Pa., 1970—78; pres., chmn. bd. Suntex Internat., Inc., Easton, 1981—. Inventor 24 Math Game, Mhing Card Game; author First In Math. online program; 5 patents in field. Pres. Coalition of Religious and Civic Orgns., Easton, 1979-81; mem. transition team Pa. Gov.-elect Tom Ridge, 1994; apptd. by Gov. Ridge to Pa. State Bd. Edn., 1995, Team Pa. Amb. Coun., 1999; mem. fin. comm. Moravian Acad., 2001, trustee, 2004-08, chair audit com., 2006; planning commr. City of Easton, 2005; mem. Eisenhower Commn., 2006; bd. dir. State Theatre, Ctr. For Arts, 2008. Recipient 2 Excellence awards for Mhing pkg. Nat. Paperbox and Pkg. Assn., 1984-85, Gop Congl. Medal Distinction, 2008; named Asian Entrepreneur of Yr., 2008. Office: 3311 Fox Hill Rd Easton PA 18045 Office Phone: 610-253-5255. E-mail: bob@24game.com.

SUN, SHU-WEI (RICHARD SUN), science educator; s. Hui-Ci Sun and Fu-Mei Shih; m. Hsiao-Fang Liang; children: Angelina, Rachel. PhD, Nat. Yang-Ming U., Taipei, 2002. Rsch. instr. Wash. U., St. Louis, 2002—08; asst. prof. Loma Linda U., Calif., 2008—. Contbr. articles to profl. publs. Rsch. grant, Nat. Multiple Sclerosis, 2006—. Mem.: Internat. Soc. Magnetic Resonance Medicine. Office: Loma Linda Univ 11175 Campus St CSPA1010 Loma Linda CA 92354 Personal E-mail: sun.mri@gmail.com.

SUN, WANXIAO, remote sensing educator; m. Gang Xu. BS, Nanjing U., China, 1986; MS, Chinese Acad. Scis., 1989; PhD, Johannes Gutenberg U. Mainz, Germany, 1999. Postdoctoral fellow U. Calif., Berkeley, 2001—02; asst. prof. So. Ill. U., Carbondale, 2002—06, Grand Valley State U., Allendale, Mich., 2006—. Contbr. articles to profl. jours. Grantee Rsch. grant, NASA, U. Md., 2004—07. Mem.: Am. Soc. Photogrammetry and Remote Sensing, Assn. Am. Geographers. Achievements include development of data fusion techniques; research in land-use and land cover classification; mapping plant function types. Avocations: travel, sports. Office: Grand Valley State Univ 1 Campus Dr Allendale MI 49401 Office Fax: 616-331-2328. Business E-Mail: sunwa@gvsu.edu.

SUN, WEI, electrical engineer; b. Jilin, China, Sept. 15, 1969; arrived in US, 1997; m. Xeqin Wu, July 15, 1997; 1 child, Olivia Qing. BEE, Xidian U., China, 1992; MS, Chinese Acad. Telecom. Tech., 1995; PhD, Stevens Inst. Tech., 2001. Mem. tech. staff Bell Labs Lucent Technologies, Holmdel, NJ, 2001—02; post-doctoral rsch. fellow Villanova U., Pa., 2002—04; asst. prof. Temple U., Phila., 2004—05; sr. comm. engr. Magnolia Broadband Inc., Bedminster, NJ, 2005—. Author: Signal Processing for Mobile Communications Handbook, 2004; contbr. scientific papers to profl. jours. Mem.: IEEE, Eta Kappa Nu. Home: 104 Bluebird Dr Hillsborough NJ 08844 Personal E-mail: wsun@ieee.org.

SUN, WEI, pharmaceutical executive, researcher; PhD, U. Southern Calif., LA. Sr. biostatistician Catalyst Pharm. Rsch., Pasadena, Calif., 2005—07; sr. rsch. biostatistician Bristol-Myers Squibb, Plainsboro, NJ, 2007—. Contbr. scientific papers.

SUN, XIANKAI, research scientist; Attending, Calif. Inst. Tech., Pasadena, 2004—. Rsch. asst. Calif. Inst. Tech., 2004—. Contbr. scientific papers. Recipient award, Ministry Edn., Chinese Govt., 2008; fellowship, IEEE, 2008, Li Ming fellowship, Caltech, 2008. Mem.: SPIE, IEEE, OSA. Achievements include patents pending for hybrid waveguide systems and related methods. Office: Calif Inst Tech 1200 E Calif Blvd MC128-95 Pasadena CA 91125

SUN, YANG, computer engineer; PhD, Rice U., Houston, 2005—. Student intern Tex. Instruments, Dallas, 2007, 2008—; hardware engr. S3 Graphics, Co. Ltd., Shanghai, 2003—04, Conexant Sys., 2004—05. Contbr. scientific papers (Best paper award, 2008). Scholar Excellent student, Zhejiang U., 1997—2000; Motorola scholarship, Motorola China, 1999, Rice Fellowship, Rice U., 2005. Mem.: IEEE. Achievements include research in high throughput LDPC decoder design for wireless system and parallel turbo decoder and high speed MIMO detector design for 4G wireless systems. Office: Rice Univ 6100 Main St Electrical & Computer Engr Houston TX 77005 Business E-Mail: ysun@rice.edu.

SUN, YING-HSUAN, research scientist; b. Taipei, Taiwan, May 22, 1964; s. Tien-Shou Chou and Mei-Shieh Sun; m. Chiu-Yueh Hung, Nov. 21, 1964; children: Katherine Hung, Isabella Hung. BS, Nat. Taiwan U., 1987; MS, N.C. State U., 1994, PhD, 2001. Rsch. scientist Bio-Informatics Group, Inc., Cary, NC, 2001—03; rsch. assoc. N.C. State U., Raleigh, 2003—06. Contbr. articles to profl. jours. Biotechnology fellow, N.C. State U., 1998. Mem.: AAAS, Taiwanese Am. Assn. (pres. N.C. chpt. 2003—04), Am. Soc. Plant Biologists, N.Y. Acad. Sci. Achievements include patents pending for micro RNA in trees. Office: Forest Biotech Group NCSU 2500 Partners II 840 Main Campus Dr Raleigh NC 27695 E-mail: yhsun@unity.ncsu.edu.

SUN, YONGSHENG VICTOR, educator; PhD, Wash. State U., Pullman. Tenured faculty Inner Mongolia Tchrs. U., Hohhot, China, 1987—93, Columbia Basin Coll., Pasco, Wash., 1994—, divsn. trainer, 2008. Pres. Tri-Cities Chinese Am. Assn., Richland, Wash., 2003—05; bd. mem. Tri-Cities Chinese Lang. Sch., Richland, 2003—08. Recipient 2nd prize, Inner Mongolia Tchrs. U., 1987, Outstanding Adviser award, 1988, Tchg. and Leadership Excellence award, Nat. Inst. Staff and Orgnl. Devel., 1996, Outstanding Svc. award, Asian Am. Assn., CBC, 1997, George Brain Adminstrv. Leadership award, Wash. State U., 2005, Dorothy Cook award, 2005, Outstanding Instr. award, Columbia Basin Coll., 1995, Outstanding Faculty award, 2001, 2008, 2009, Exceptional Faculty award, 2005; Faculty Devel. grant, 2000, 2004, 2005, Doctoral fellow, Wash. State U., 2006.

SUN, YUEFENG, research scientist, educator; b. Liangshan, Shandong, China, Apr. 5, 1962; s. Xueqian Sun and Shuyuan She; m. Lilai Yan; 1 child, Yusha Yan Sun. BS, Petroleum U. China, Donying, Shandong, 1981; MS, Columbia U., NYC, 1988, PhD, 1994. Geophysicist China Nat. Petroleum Corp., Urumqi, Xinjiang, 1982—87; grad. tchg. fellow Columbia U., NYC, 1988—94; postdoctoral fellow Lamont Doherty Earth Obs., Columbia U., Palisades, 1995—97, Doherty rsch. scientist, 1998—2005; assoc. prof. The Petroleum Inst., Abu Dhabi, 2005—06, Tex. A&M U., College Station, 2007—. Mem.: Am. Assn. Petroleum Geologists, Soc. Exploration Geophysicists (assoc.), Am. Geophys. Union (assoc.). Achievements include invention of work on relating permeability to wave velocity implemented and referred to as the Sun model by Shell Oil Co., which improves world hydrocarbon reserves and production; research in theory invention; patents for method of estimation of gas hydrates; systems and methods of detecting living organisms in rocks. Office: TAMU 3115 College Station TX 77843 Home: 721 Aster Dr College Station TX 77845 Personal E-mail: yfsun3@yahoo.com. Business E-Mail: sun@geo.tamu.edu.

SUN, YUZHI, mechanical engineer, researcher; m. Dongsheng Wu; children: Huijia Emily Wu, Erik Huicheng Wu. PhD, Mich. State U., East Lansing, 2004. Rsch. assoc. Iowa State U., Ames, 2005—07, U. Ala., Huntsville, 2008—. Office: Dept Mech & Aerospace Engring 301 Sparkman Dr Huntsville AL 35899

SUN, ZUO, aerospace engineer, researcher; b. Shenyang, Liaoning, China, July 3, 1970; arrived in U.S., 1996; s. Dianfu Sun and Shuxiang Liu; m. Xinxin Zhou. PhD in Theoretical and Applied Mechanics, Northwestern U., 2001; MS, BS, Tsinghua U. Sr. mech. engr. Corning (N.Y.) Inc., 2001—02; rsch. scientist Va. Tech, Blacksburg, 2002—03; mech. engr. GE Global Rsch. Ctr., Schenectady, NY, 2003—06; sr. aerospace engr. Boeing Co., 2006—. Cons. Hewlett-Packard Corp., Portland, Oreg., 2001—02, State Nuc. Safety Bur. in China, Beijing, 1993—95. Contbr. articles to profl. jours. Recipient First Class award, Tsinghua U., Beijing, 1989; Grad. fellow, 1994, Grad. scholar, Northwestern U., 1997—2003. Mem.: ASME, AIAA (corr.), Sigma Xi (hon.). Achievements include development of new models to predict long term behavior and life of composite materials; tools to characterize micro/nano scale systems; physics-based modeling of commercial aircraft engines; design of Micro-electro-mechanical Systems; investigation of adhesion science. Personal E-mail: zuosun@yahoo.com.

SUND, RICK (RICHARD W. SUND), professional sports team executive; b. Elgin, Ill., 1951; s. Bob Sund; m. Lea E. Sund; children: Hali, Patrick. Student, Northwestern U.; M in Athletic Adminstrn., Ohio U., 1974. With Milw. Bucks, 1974—78; player pers. dir. to v.p. ops. Dallas Mavericks, 1979—93; player pers. cons. Seattle SuperSonics, 1994—95, gen. mgr., 2001—07, cons., 2007—08; v.p. player pers. to exec. v.p. basketball ops. Detroit Pistons, 1995—2001; exec. v.p., gen. mgr. Atlanta Hawks, 2008—. Named to Ill. HS Basketball Coaches' Hall of Fame. Avocation: golf. Office: Atlanta Hawks Centennial Tower 101 Marietta St NW Ste 1900 Atlanta GA 30303*

SUNDARAM, NARAYAN, electrical engineer; PhD, Va. Tech, Blacksburg, 2007. Asst. mgr. Brit. Phys. Labs Ltd., Bangalore, 2000—02; grad. rsch. asst. Va. Tech, Blaksburg, 2002—07; vis. rsch. engr. Alstom Power, Baden, Switzerland, 2004; postdoc. rsch. assoc. Pa. State U., State Coll., Pa., 2007—08; lead engr. Creative Power Solutions, Inc., Fountain Hills, Ariz., 2008—. Contbr. articles to profl. jours. Mem.: ASME.

SUNDARAM, SENTHIL K., pediatrician, educator; s. Gurumoorthy Sundaram and Mathurambal Sitharam; m. Sarala Somasi; 1 child, Avaneeth Kumar. MD, All India Inst. Med. Sci., New Delhi, 2000. Asst. prof. pediat. and neurology Wayne State U., Detroit, 2005—. Fogarty Internat. Vis. fellow, Nat. Inst. Health, Bethesda, Md., 2000—03. Mem.: Soc. Nucelar Medicine. Business E-Mail: ssundaram@pet.wayne.edu.

SUNDARAM, SRINIVASAN, finance educator; b. Bangalore, India, Aug. 18, 1951; m. Kavery Nanaiah; children: Vani, Varun. PhD, U. Cin., 1991. Asst. prof, fin. U. Wis., Eau Claire, 1988—91; prof. fin. & ins. Ball State U., Muncie, Ind., 1991—. Editor: Am. Jour. Bus. HS soccer coach Burris Ind. Acad., Muncie. Mem.: MidWest Fin. Assn. Office: Ball State Univ Miller Coll Muncie IN 47306-0345

SUNDARAM, V. RAMANAN, hematologist, educator; b. Calicut, Tamil Nadu, India, June 21, 1933; s. Tarakad Appadoraier and Seetha Sundaram; m. Chitraleka Rajagopalan; children: Srikumar Ramanan, Radhika Anusha Ramanan. MD, Vellore: CMC, Tamil Nadu, 1959; MS in Pharmacology, W.Va. U., Morgantown, 1976; MRCP, Royal Coll. Physicians, Edinburgh. Cert. State Conn., 1976. Prof. medicine U. Conn. Sch. Medicine, Farmington, 1976—; sr. attending physician St Francis Hosp., Hartford, 1993—. Chief hematology Mt. Sinai Hosp., Hartford, Afghanistan, 1976—86. Contbr. scientific papers. Founder trustee Conn. Valley Hindu Temple Soc., Middletown, Conn. Recipient Tchg. awards, U. Conn. Sch. Medicine. Fellow: Royal Coll. Physicians. Office: St Francis Hosp 1000 Asylum Ave # 2004 Hartford CT 06105

SUNDARARAJAN, VIJAY, systems engineer; s. Trivandrum Padmanabhan and Chellammal Sundararajan; m. Anuradha Ganesh Joshi, Nov. 3, 2006; 1 child, Sruti Chellam Vijay. PhD, U. Minn., Mpls., 2000. Sys. engr. Tex. Instruments, Dallas, 2000—06, sys. engring. mgr., 2006—. Mem. tech. program com. IEEE Signal Processing Soc., Dallas, 2009. Contbr. articles to profl. jours. Charitable contbr. United Way, Smile Train, Asha Edn., Dallas, 2000—09. Mem.: IEEE. Achievements include patents for algorithm, architecture & design of wireless communication systems. Office: Tex Instruments Inc 12500 TI Blvd Dallas TX 75243

SUNDARESAN, THARUN, science educator; PhD in Cellular and Molecular Biology, U. Hyderabad, India, 1994. Rsch. assoc. HHMI Howard Hughes Med. Inst., U. Ariz., Tucson, 1995—2003; asst. prof., dept. biochemistry Uniformed Svcs. U., Bethesda, Md., 2003—. RO1, Nat. Insts. Health, 2006—. Mem.: RNA Soc. Office: Uniformed Svcs Univ 4301 Jones Bridge Rd Bethesda MD 20876

SUNDBERG, CARL-ERIK WILHELM, telecommunications executive, researcher; b. Karlskrona, Sweden, July 7, 1943; arrived in US, 1984; s. Erik Wilhelm and Martha Maria (Snaar) S. MEE, U. Lund, Sweden, 1966, PhD, 1975. Tchr., rsch. asst., lectr. U. Lund, 1966-75, rsch. prof. (docent), 1977-84; rsch. fellow European Space Agy., Nordwijk, The Netherlands, 1975-76; disting. mem. tech. staff AT&T Bell Labs., Murray Hill, NJ, 1984-96, Lucent Technologies, Bell Labs., 1997-2000; with media signal processing rsch. dept. Agere Sys., 2000—01, iBiquity Digital, Warren, NJ, 2002—03; prin., owner SundComm, Sunnyvale, Calif., 2003—. Cons. L.M. Ericsson, Gothenburg, Sweden, 1976-77, Bell Labs., Crawford Hill, NJ, 1981-82; instr. Carl Cranz Gesellschaft, Oberpfaffenhofen, Fed. Republic Germany, 1990-93; vis. prof Korea U., Seoul, 2003-05 Co-author: Digital Phase Modulation, 1986, Source-Matched Mobile Communications, 1995; contbr. articles to profl. jours.; patentee in field. Served in Swedish Navy, 1968. Fellow IEEE (Best Paper award 1986, guest editor Jour. on Selected Areas in Comm. 1988-89, 2005-06, 2 papers named among 50 most influential 2002), IEE Marconi Premium (Best Paper award 1989); mem. Swedish Union Radio-Scientifique Internat Lutheran. Avocations: travel, history, photography. Home and Office: SundComm 395 Ano Nuevo Ave Apt 1107 Sunnyvale CA 94085 Office Phone: 973-906-0109. Business E-Mail: cews@ieee.org.

SUNDBERG, MARSHALL DAVID, biology professor; b. Apr. 18, 1949; m. Sara Jane Brooks, Aug. 1, 1977; children: Marshall Isaac, Adam, Emma. BA in Biology, Carleton Coll., 1971; MA in Botany, U. Minn., 1973, PhD in Botany, 1978. Lab. technician Carleton Coll., Minn., 1973-74; teaching asst. U. Minn., Mpls., 1974-76, rsch. asst., 1976-77; adj. asst. prof. Biology U. Wis., Eau Claire, 1978-85, mem. faculty summer sci. inst., 1982-85; instr. La. State U., Baton Rouge, 1985-88, asst. prof. Biology, 1988-91, coord. dept. Biology, 1988-93, assoc. prof. Biology, 1991-97; prof., chair dept. biol. scis. Emporia State U., 1997—. Author: General Botany Laboratory Workbook, 5th revision, 1984, General Botany 1001 Laboratory Manual, 1986, General Botany 1002 Laboratory Manual, 1987, Biology 1002 Correspondence Study Guide, 1987, Boty 1202: General Botany Laboratory Manual, 1988, Biol 1208: Biology for Science Majors Laboratory Manual, 1988, 2d edit., 1989, Instructor's Manual for J. Mauseth, Introductory Botany, 1991; contbr. articles to profl. jours. Brand fellow U. Minn., 1976-77, Faculty Grants scholar U. Wis., 1984-85. Fellow Linnaean Soc. London; mem. NSTA, AAAS, Am. Inst. Biol. Scis. (coun. mem. at large 1992-95, edn. com. 1994-95, 98-2002), Nat. Sci. Tchrs. Assn., Assn. Biology Lab. Edn., Bot. Soc. Am. (chmn. tchg. sect. 1985-86, workshop com. tchg. sect. 1983-84, slide exch./lab. exch. tchg. sect. 1980-89, edn. com. 1991, 92, editor Plant Sci. Bull. 2000—, Charles H. Bessey award 1992, Centennial award 2006), Internat. Soc. Plant Morphologists, Nat. Assn. Biology Tchrs. (Outstanding 4-Yr. Coll. Tchr. award 1997, 2003), Soc. Econ. Botany, The Nature Conservancy, Sigma Xi (chpt. sec. 1982-84, 93-95, 2000-02, v.p. 1984-85, 96-97, pres. 1996, 99, 2005). Home: 1912 Briarcliff Ln Emporia KS 66801-5404 Office: Emporia State U Dept Biol Scis 1200 Commercial St Emporia KS 66801-5087

SUNDBERG, RICHARD JAY, chemistry professor; b. Sioux Rapids, Iowa, Jan. 6, 1938; BS, U. Iowa, 1959; PhD, U. Minn., 1962. Faculty dept. chemistry U. Va., Charlottesville, 1964-74, prof., 1974—. Author (with F. A. Carey) Advanced Organic Chemistry, 5th edit., 2007. Served to 1st lt. U.S. Army, 1962-64 Mem. Am. Chem. Soc. Lutheran. Office: U Va Dept Chemistry Box 400319 Charlottesville VA 22904-4319 Office Phone: 434-924-3233. Personal E-mail: rjs1d@virginia.net.

SUNDBERG, RUTH DOROTHY, hematologist, educator; b. Chgo., July 29, 1915; d. Carl William and Ruth (Chalbeck) S.; m. Robert H. Reiff, Dec. 24, 1941 (div. 1945). Student, U. Chgo., 1932-34; BS, U. Minn., 1937, MA, 1939, PhD, 1943, MD, 1953. Diplomate: Am. Bd. Pathology. Instr., asst. prof. anatomy U. Minn., 1939-53, assoc. prof., 1953-60, prof., 1960-63, prof. of lab. medicine and anatomy, 1963-73, prof. lab. medicine, pathology and anatomy, 1973-84, emeritus prof., 1984—; hematologist, dir. Hematology Labs., 1945-74, hematologist, co. dir., 1974-84. Editorial bd.: Soc. Exptl. Biology and Medicine, until 1975; mem. editorial bd.: Blood, 1960-67; assoc. editor, 1967-69.

Recipient Lucretia Wilder award for research in anatomy, 1939 Mem.: Sigma Xi. Home (Winter): 12558 Shanandoah Ct Marco Island FL 34145-5023 Home: 6690 Morgans Run Rd Loveland OH 45140-7205

SUNDE, DOUGLAS, plastic surgeon; b. Evanston, Ill., May 18, 1960; s. Edward Albert and Marilyn S.; m. Linda Neff, 1989. AB, Stanford U., 1982; MD, U. Calif., San Francisco, 1986. Diplomate Am. Bd. Plastic Surgery. Resident in plastic surgery Stanford (Calif.) U., 1986-92, clin. instr., 1992; fellow in aesthetic surgery Manhattan Eye Ear and Throat Hosp., NYC, 1990; fellow in hand, microsurgery Davies Med. Ctr., San Francisco, 1993; pvt. practice Monterey, Calif., 1994—. Clin. asst. prof. Stanford Med. Ctr., 1998—. Contbr. articles to profl. jours. Named Nat. Merit scholar 1977. Fellow ACS; mem. Am. Bd. Plastic Surgery, Am. Soc. Plastic Reconstructive Surgery, Calif. Soc. Plastic Surgery, Alpha Omega Alpha. Office Phone: 831-372-0200.

SUNDEL, MARTIN, management consultant, psychologist, educator; b. Bronx, NY, Sept. 22, 1940; s. Louis and Pauline (Brotman) S.; m. Sandra Stone, Aug. 22, 1971; children: Adam Daniel, Jenny Rebecca, Ariel Pauline. BA cum laude, St. Mary's U., 1961; MSW., Our Lady of the Lake Univ., 1963; MA, PhD, U. Mich., 1968. Social group work supr. Valley Cities Jewish Cmty. Ctr., Van Nuys, Calif., 1963-65; asst. prof. U. Mich. Sch. Social Work, Ann Arbor, 1968-71; dir. rsch. and evaluation River Region Mental Health-Mental Retardation Bd., Louisville, 1972-77; assoc. clin. prof. dept. psychiatry and behavioral sci., adj. prof. Kent. Sch. Social Work, U. Louisville, 1974—77; sr. research assoc. The Urban Inst., Washington, 1977-80; pvt. practice psychology Dallas, 1980-95; Dulak Disting. prof. U. Tex., Arlington, 1980-89, prof., 1980-95, Fla. Internat. U., Miami, Fla., 1995-2000; faculty assoc. S.E. Fla. Ctr. on Aging, 1996-2000; pres. Sundel Cons. Group, 2000—. Mental health cons. UN High Commn. for Refugees in Cyprus, 1993-95; profl. adv. coun. Dallas Geriatric Rsch. Inst., 1980-89; long-range planning com. Dallas Jewish Coalition for the Homeless, 1986-95; coordinating com. Arlington Human Svcs. Project, 1981-90, Mayor's Forum on Human Svc. Needs Assessment, Ft. Worth, 1983-86; vis. prof. U. So. Calif. Sch. Social Work, spring 1985; sr. consortium rsch. fellow, Dept. Def., 1996-99. Author: (with Sandra Stone Sundel) Behavior Change in the Human Services, 1975, 5th edit., 2005; Be Assertive, 1980; co-author: Women at Midlife, 2002; co-editor: Assessing Health and Human Service Needs, 1983, Individual Change Through Small Groups, 2d edit., 1985, Midlife Myths, 1989; mem. editl. bds. and cons. to profl. jours. Named Nat. Table Tennis Champion, U1600 Round Robin Age Group of 40 Yrs. and Older, 2005; fellow, Harvard U. Lab. Cmty. Psychiatry, Boston, 1971—72. Fellow Prescribing Psychologists Register (diplomate), Internat. Coun. Prescribing Psychology (diplomate in psychopharmacology); mem. Behavior Therapy and Rsch. Soc. (charter clin. fellow). Home: 3804 Barbados Ave Hollywood FL 33026-4659 Personal E-mail: sundelm@bellsouth.net.

SUNDERMAN, DUANE NEUMAN, chemist, research and development company executive; b. Wadsworth, Ohio, July 14, 1928; s. Richard Benjamin and Carolyn (Neuman) S.; m. Joan Catherine Hoffman, Jan. 31, 1953; children: David, Christine, Richard. BA, U. Mich., 1949, MS, 1954, PhD in Chemistry, 1956. Researcher Battelle Meml. Inst., Columbus, Ohio, 1956-59, mgr., 1959-69, assoc. dir., 1969-79, dir. internat. programs, 1979-84; sr. v.p. Midwest Rsch. Inst., Kansas City, Mo., 1984-90, exec. v.p., 1990-94, Golden, Colo., 1990-94. Dir. Nat. Renewable Energy Lab., Golden, Colo., 1990-94, dir. emeritus, 1994—. Contbr. numerous articles to profl. jours. Bd. dirs. Mid-Ohio chpt. ARC, 1982-83, U. Kansas City, 1985-90, Mo. Corp. for Sci. and Tech., Jefferson City, 1986-90, Colo. Energy Sci. Ctr., 2000-04. With USNR, 1949—59. Mem. Am. Chem. Soc. Presbyterian. Avocation: paleontology.

SUNDERMAN, MARK A., finance educator; s. Glenn E. and Mary C. Sunderman; m. Judy K. Green, Aug. 18, 1974; children: Mark A. Jr., Gabrielle S. BS in Fin., U. Ill., Urbana, 1974, MS in Fin., 1976, PhD in Fin., 1986. Grad. rsch. asst. U. Ill., Urbana; instr. bus. Spring Arbor Coll., Mich., 1976—77; instr. fin. NorthWest Mo. State U., Maryville, 1977—78, Ill. State U., Normal, 1978—83; prof. fin. U. Wyo., Laramie, 1986—2008, chair faculty senate, 2006—07; prof. and morris fogelman real estate chair excellence U. Memphis, 2008—. Bd. dirs. Am. Real Estate Soc., 2004—. Recipient eOT Excellence in Online Tchg. award, eCollege, 2002, Disting. R & D award, Internat. Assn. Assessing Officers, 1991—92. Mem.: Tenn. Assn. Assessing Officers, Acad. Fin. Svc., Internat. Assn. Assessing Officers, Am. Real Estate Soc., Fin. Mgmt. Assn., Am. Real Estate and Urban Economics Assn. Office: Univ Memphis Fogelman Coll Bus and Econ Memphis TN 38152-3120 Office Fax: 901-678-2685. Business E-Mail: msndrman@memphis.edu.

SUNDERMEYER, MICHAEL S., lawyer; b. Kansas City, Mo., Feb. 8, 1951; s. Edgar W. and Ruth (Shobe) S.; m. Susan Talarico; children: Kim Marie, Mark Shobe. BA, U. Kans., 1973; JD, U. Va., 1976. Bar: D.C., Md., Va., U.S. Dist. Ct. D.C., U.S. Dist. Ct. Md., U.S. Dist. Ct. (ea. dist.) Va., U.S. Dist. Ct. (no. dist.) Okla., U.S. Ct. Appeals (D.C. cir.), U.S. Ct. Appeals (2d, 3d, 4th, 5th, 6th, 9th and 11th cirs.). Law clk. to Hon. John Minor Wisdom U.S. Ct. Appeals (5th cir.), New Orleans, 1976-77; law clk. to Hon. Harry A. Blackmun U.S. Supreme Ct., Washington, 1977-78; assoc. Williams & Connolly, Washington, 1978-84, ptnr., 1985—. Editor-in-chief Va. Law Rev., 1975-76. Mem. ABA. Office: Williams & Connolly LLP 725 12th St NW Washington DC 20005-5901 Office Phone: 202-434-5000. E-mail: msundermeyer@wc.com.

SUNDHEIM, NANCY STRAUS, lawyer, computer company executive; b. Phila., June 25, 1951; B in Hist., U. Pa., 1973; JD, Harvard U., 1978. With Arnold & Porter, Washington, Ropes & Gray, Boston, Dechert, Price & Rhoads, Phila.; chief acquisitions counsel Unisys Corp., Blue Bell, Pa., 1987, dep. counsel, head corp. law group, 1990, corp. v.p., corp. sec., 1999, mem. exec. com., 1999—, sr. v.p., sec., gen. counsel, 2001—. Office: Unisys Corp Unisys Way Blue Bell PA 19424 Office Phone: 215-986-4011. Office Fax: 215-986-2312.

SUNDICK, SHERRY SMALL, author, journalist, poet; b. Washington, July 17, 1946; d. Charles Haskell and Ruth (Behrend) Small; B.A., Am. U., 1970; m. Gary Norman Sundick, Aug. 3, 1969; children— Amy Beth, Suzanne Faye. Columnist, Today Newspapers, Rockville, Md., 1973-75; journalist The Jour. Newspapers, Chevy Chase, Md., 1975—, The Potomac Almanac, 1976-80. Recipient N.Am. Mentor Mag. Ann. Mentor Poetry award, 1973. Mem. Nat. League Am. Pen Women, Writers Center, World Poetry Soc. Jewish. Author: Celebration, 1977; (with Ruth Small) Potpourri, 1978; contbr. articles to various mags. and jours. including Md. Mag., No. Va. Mag. Design, Maine Life, Feelings, Smile, The Pen Women, Haiku Headlines, others. Address: 11809 Hunting Ridge Ct Potomac MD 20854-2152

SUNDIN, MATS JOHAN, professional hockey player; b. Sollentuna, Sweden, Feb. 13, 1971; Center Que. Nordiques, 1990—94, Toronto Maple Leafs, 1994—2008, capt., 1997—2008; center Vancouver Canucks, 2008—. Mem. Team Sweden, Canada Cup, 1991, Team Sweden, World Cup of Hockey, 1996, 2004, Team Sweden, Olympic Games, Nagano, Japan, 1998, Salt Lake City, 2002, Torino, Italy, 06. Recipient Mark Messier Leadership Award, 2008; named to Swedish League All-Star Team, 1990—91, 1991—92, NHL All-Star Game, 1996—2004, Second All-Star Team, NHL, 2002, 2004. Achievements include being the first overall draft pick in NHL entry draft, 1989; being a member of gold medal winning Swedish Hockey Team, Torino Olympics, Italy, 2006. Office: Vancouver Canucks 800 Griffiths Way Vancouver BC V6B 6G1 Canada*

SUNDLOF, STEPHEN FREDERICK, federal agency administrator, veterinarian; b. Peoria, Ill., May 4, 1951; m. Sandra Linden Sundlof; children: Christofer Linden, Thomas Michael. BS in Zoology/Chemistry with honors, So. Ill. Univ., Carbondale, Ill., 1973; MS in Veterinary Toxicology, U. Ill., Coll. Veterinary Med. Sciences, Urbana, Ill., 1976, BS in Veterinary Medicine with honors, 1977, DVM in Veterinary Medicine with honors, 1980, PhD in Veterinary Toxicology, 1980. Diplomate Am. Bd. Vet. Toxicology. Rsch. asst., dept. physiology and pharmacology U. Ill., Coll. Vet. Medicine, Urbana, Ill., 1973—76, rsch. asst., dept. veterinary biosciences, 1976—80; asst. prof., dept. preventative medicine Coll. Vet. Medicine, U. Fla., Gainesville, Fla., 1980—86, prof., dept. physiological sciences, 1995, assoc. prof., dept. physiological sciences, 1986—95; dir. Ctr. for Vet. Medicine FDA, Rockville, 1994—2008, Ctr. for Food Safety & Applied Nutrition College Park, Md., 2008—. Chmn., drug abuse com., Fla. Vet. Med. Assn., 1982-85; divsn. leader, divsn. toxicology and pathophysiology, dept. preventative medicine, 1982-83; animal drug coordinator, So. Region IR-4 Project, 1982-94; vice-chair, Ineragency Coordinating Com. for Animal Production Food Safety, 1995-; rep., Fla. Prescription Abuse Data Synthesis Com, Coll. Vet. Medicine and Fla. Vet. Med. Assn., 1984-86; courtesy prof., dept. physiological sciences, Coll. Vet. Medicine, U. Fla., Gainesville, Fla., 1996; mem. US Pub. Health Svc. spl. oversight com. to review allegations of mismanagement and abuse of authority by the US FDA, Ctr. for Vet. Medicine, 1986-87; Am. Vet. Med. Assn. delegate to the WHO/FAO Codes Alimentarius Com. on Residues of Vet. Drugs in Foods, 1986-94; Inst. Food Technologists delegate to the Food Safety Workshop, 1989; mem., vet. medicine adv. com., US FDA, 1991-94, chmn. 1993-94; chmn., WHO/FAO Codes Alimentarius Com. on Residue of Vet. Drugs in Foods, 1994-; temporary advisor, WHO/FAO Joint Expert Com. on Food Additives, 1995-; mem. steering com. on Internat. Cooperation on Harminization of Tech. Requirements for Registration of Vet. Medicinal Products, Office of Internat. Epizootics, 1995-; mem. external adv. bd., Inst. Food Sci. and Engrng, Tex. A7M U., 1996-97; mem., USDA Food Safety and Inspection Svc., Food Rsch. Working Group, 1996-97; US Delegate to the Codex Alimentarius Internat. Ad Hoc Task Force on Animal Feeding, 1999-2004; mem., WHO/FAO, Office of Internat. Epizootics expert consultation on non-human antimicrobial usage and antimicrobial resistence, 2004; US delegation to Japan to discuss trade implications following finding of BSE-positive cow in US, 2004-; presenter in field. Editoral reviewer, Journal Veterinary Pharmacology and Therapeutics, 1988-; contbr. articles to profl. jours. Recipient Presidential Exec. Rank award Meritorious Exec. Rank, 1999; named Hon. Diplomate, Am. Vet. Epidemiology Soc., 1996, Disting. Practitioner in the Nat. Acad. Practice in Vet. Medicine, Nat. Acad. Practices, 1997. Mem. Am. Acad. Vet. Pharmacology and Therapeutics (pres.-elect 1993-95, pres. 1995-97), Am. Acad. Vet. and Comparative Toxicologists, Am. Vet. Med. Assn. (President's award, 1997), Am. Bd. Veterinary Toxicology. Office: Ctr Food Safety & Applied Nutrition FDA 5100 Pain Branch Pkwy College Park MD 20740

SUNDLUN, BRUCE, former governor; b. Providence, Jan. 19, 1920; s. Walter I. and Jan Z. (Colitz) Sundlun; m. Susan Garvin Dittelman, Jan. 1, 2000; children: Tracy, Stuart, Peter, Kara; stepchildren: Heather Conover, Max Dittelman. BA, Williams Coll., 1942; LLB, Harvard U. & Sch., 1949; grad., Air Command and Staff Sch., 1948; DSBA (hon.), Bryant Coll., 1980; DBA (hon.), Roger Williams Coll., 1980; LLD (hon.), Johnson and Wales U., 1993, Williams Coll., 1993, U. RI, 1998; DHL (hon.), New Eng. Inst. Tech., 2005; DPS (hon.), RI Coll., 2008. Bar: RI 1949, DC 1949. Asst. US atty., Washington, 1949-51; spl. asst. to US atty. gen., Washington, 1951-54; ptnr. Amram, Hahn & Sundlun, Sundlun, Tirana & Scher, Washington, 1958—76; v.p., gen. counsel, dir. Outlet Co., Providence, 1960-76, Outlet Comms. Inc.; pres., CEO Outlet Co., Providence, 1976-84, chmn. bd., CEO, 1984-88. Pres. Exec. Jet Aviation, Inc., Columbus, Ohio, 1970—76; apptd. by Pres. Kennedy incorporator, bd. dirs. Comm. Satellite Corp., 1962—92; bd. dirs. Worthington Industries, Nat. Bank of Washington, Miriam Hosp. Mem. adv. group Nat. Aviation Goals, 1961; chmn. Inaugural Medal Com., Washington, 1961, 65; vice chmn. Inaugural Parade Com., 1961; appointed by Pres. Carter, bd. visitors USAF Acad., 1978-80; mem. RI Capital Center Commn., 1980, RI Legis. Pay Commn., 1980; vice chmn. Providence Rev. Com., 1981, chmn., 1982-85; mem. Providence Sch. Bd., 1985-90; mem. Providence Housing Authority, 1987, chmn. 1987-90; elected del. Dem. Nat. Conv. 1964, 68, 80, 88, 92, RI Constl. Conv., 1985; Dem. candidate for gov. RI, 1986, 88, 90, 92; gov. RI, 1990-92, 1992-95; mem. exec. com. Dem. Gov. Assn., 1990-94; vice chmn. CONEG, 1992-94, chmn., vice chmn. Com. on Economy Nat. Gov. Assn., 1992-94, chmn., 1994, chmn. NE Gov. Assn., 1994; pres. Washington Internat. Horse Show, 1970-75, trustee, 1975-90; pres. Providence Performing Arts Ctr., 1978-90; bd. dirs. Touro Synagogue, Newport, RI, 1979—2008, Miriam Hosp., 1985-90; bd. dirs. Temple Beth El, Providence, 1979-84, v.p., 1984-88, pres.,1989-1991; bd. dirs. Trinity Repertory Theater, 1980-90, chmn., 1984-90; trustee RI Philharm. Orch., 1981-90; trustee Providence Preservation Soc., 1981-90, v.p., 1987-90; trustee Newport Art Mus., 1985, pres., 1987-91; founding chmn., pres. Providence Found., 1985-86; pres. RI C. of C. Fedn., 1981-84, bd. dirs., 1977-81; pres. Greater Providence C. of C., 1978-81, bd. dirs. 1976-85; bd. dirs. New Eng. Coun., 1978, vice chmn., 1980-81, chmn., 1981-83; trustee Bryant Coll., 1989-98; gov.-in-residence U. RI, 1995—; dir. Providence Facilities Mgmt. Corp., 1998—; appointed by Pres. Clinton dir. Nat. Security Edn. Bd., 2000-05; dir. Sargent Rehab. Ctr., 1995-08, Ft. Adams Found., 2000-08. Lt. USAAF, 1941—45, capt. USAF, 1945—, ret. col., 1980. Decorated D.F.C., Air medal with oak leaf cluster, Purple Heart; chevalier Legion d'Honneur (France); Prime Minister's medal (Israel). Mem.: Aurora Assn., Providence, RI, Spouting Rock Beach Assn., Newport, RI, Dunes Club (Narragansett, RI), Hope Club(Providence), Clambake Club (Middletown, RI), Delta Upsilon. Democrat. Office: Univ RI Carlotti Bldg #213 Kingston RI 02881 Home Phone: 401-423-3663; Office Phone: 401-874-4000. Business E-Mail: sundlun@uri.edu.

SUNDQUIST, DON, lobbyist, former governor; b. Moline, Ill., Mar. 15, 1936; s. Kenneth M. and Louise (Rohren) S.; m. Martha Swanson, Oct. 3, 1959; children: Tania, Andrea, Donald Kenneth. BA, Augustana Coll., 1957. Div. mgr. Josten's, Inc., 1961-72; exec. v.p. Graphic Sales of Am., Memphis, 1972, pres., 1973-82; mem. 98th-103rd Congresses from 7th Tenn. dist., Washington, 1983-94; gov. State of Tenn., Nashville, 1995—2003; co-founder, prin. Sundquist Anthony LLC, Washington. Vice chmn. bd. Bank of Germantown, Tenn. Past mem. White House Commn. Presdl. Scholars; past chmn. Jobs for High Sch. Grads. of Memphis; chmn. Congl. Steering Com. George Bush for Pres., 1988, 92; nat. campaign mgr. Howard Baker for Pres., 1979; dir. com. ops., alt. del. Republican Nat. Conv., 1980; chmn. Shelby County Rep. Party, 1975-77; alt. del. Rep. Nat. Conv., 1976; exec. com. Rep. Nat. Com., 1971-73; nat. chmn. Young Rep. Nat. Fedn., 1971-73; sec. Bedford County Election Commn., 1968-70; chmn. Tenn. Young Rep. Fedn., 1969-70; dir. Mid-South Coliseum, Am. Council Young Polit. Leaders, 1972-74, U.S. Youth Council, 1972-75; bd. govs. Charles Edison Meml. Youth Fund; nat. adv. bd. Distributive Edn. Clubs Am.; mem. U.S. del. study tour, People's Republic of China, 1978, study tour, USSR, 1975. Served with USN, 1957-59. Mem. Kiwanis. Republican. Lutheran. Office: Sundquist Anthony LLC 51 Louisiana Ave NW Washington DC 20001 Office Phone: 202-347-3900. Office Fax: 202-347-4448.

SUNDQUIST, JAMES LLOYD, retired political scientist; b. West Point, Utah, Oct. 16, 1915; s. Frank Victor and Freda (Carlson) S.; m. Beth Ritchie, Dec. 25, 1937 (dec. 1982); children: Erik L., Mark L., James K.; m. Geraldine Coote, Dec. 3, 1983. Student, Weber Coll., 1932-34, HHD (hon.), 1990; student, Northwestern U., 1934-35; BS, U. Utah, 1939; MS in Pub. Adminstrn, Syracuse U., 1941; DDS (hon.), Carthage Coll., 1987. Reporter Salt Lake Tribune, 1935-39; adminstrv. analyst U.S. Bur. Budget, 1941-47, 49-51; reports and statistics officer Office Def. Moblzn., 1951-53; dir. mgmt. control European Command, U.S. Army, Berlin, 1947-49; asst. to chmn. Democratic Nat. Com., 1953-54; asst. sec. to gov. NY, 1955-56; asst. to U.S. Senator Clark, 1957-62; dep. under sec. agr., 1963-65; sr. fellow Brookings Instn., 1965-85, emeritus, 1985—, dir. govtl. studies, 1976-78; adj. prof. Smith Coll., 1975-78. Sec. platform com. Dem. Nat. Conv., 1960, 68 Author: Politics and Policy: The Eisenhower, Kennedy and Johnson Years, 1968, Making Federalism Work, 1969 (Louis Brownlow award for best pub. adminstrn. book), Dynamics of the Party System, 1973, 2d edit., 1983, Dispersing Population: What America Can Learn form Europe, 1975, The Decline and Resurgence of Congress, 1981 (Hardeman prize for best book on Congress), Constitutional Reform and Effective Government, 1986, 2d edit., 1992, Deseret Boy: Memories of a Utah Childhood, 2003; editor: Internat. Rev. Adminstrv. Scis., 1980—89, Beyond Gridlock?, 1993, Back to Gridlock?, 1995. Mem. Gov.'s Commn. on Va.'s Future, 1983-84 Recipient Exceptional Civilian Svc. award War Dept., 1945, Lifetime Achievement award Maxwell Sch. (Syracuse U.) Alumni Assn., 1994; sr. Rsch. fellow U. Glasgow, Scotland, 1972-73. Mem. Nat. Acad. Pub. Adminstrn., Am. Soc. Pub. Adminstrn., Am. Polit. Sci. Assn. (treas. 1980, Charles E. Merriam award 1985, Eldersveld award 1994), Am. Acad. Arts and Scis. Home: 900 N Taylor St Unit 2117 Arlington VA 22203 Office Phone: 703-294-4226. E-mail: jlsundquist@aol.com.

SUNDQUIST, LEAH RENATA, military officer; b. El Paso, Tex., July 22, 1963; d. Dominic Joseph and Patricia Ann (Manley) Bernardi; m. David Curtis Sundquist, June 23, 1990. AA, N.Mex. Mil. Inst., 1983; BS, U. Tex., El Paso, 1986; MEd in Curriculum and Instrn., City U., Bellevue, Wash., 1996. Field exec. Rio Grande Girl Scout Coun., El Paso, 1983-84; customer teller M-Bank, El Paso, 1984-85; soccer coach St. Clements Sch., El Paso, 1985; substitute tchr. El Paso Sch. Dist., 1986; commd. 2nd lt. U.S. Army, 1983, advanced through grades to maj., 1997, plans/exercise officer Ft. Lewis, Wash., 1990, ops. officer, 1990-1991; comdr. hdqs. Hdqs. Co. 141st Support Bn. U.S. Army N.G., 1996-97; dir. Childrens World Learning Ctr., Federal Way, Wash., 1992-94; phys. edn. specialist, tchr. K-6 Kent (Wash.) Elem. Sch., 1994-2001; health fitness tchr. Camas (Wash.) Mid. Sch., 2001—02; ops. and tng. officer bn. U.S. Army N.G., 1997-99, exec. officer, 1999—2002, bn. comdr., 2002—; recruiting Oreg. N.G., 2004—. Coord. NCCJ, El Paso, 1979-81; v.p. Jr. Achievement, El Paso, 1980-81; adult tng. vol. Girl Scout Coun., El Paso, 1981-83; bd. dirs. Pacific Peaks coun., 1993-99, chair nominating com., 1996, jr. troop leader Totem coun. Girl Scouts U.S., 1996, chair program policies rev. com., 1997, trainer instrn. of adults, tng. coord. team mem., 1997—; bd. dirs. Jr. League Tacoma, 1993, 94, staff devel. coun. mem., 1997-2000, design com., 1998—. 3rd Res. Officer Tng. Corps scholar, 1981-83, H.P. Saunder scholar, 1982; recipient Humanitarian Svc. medal Great Fires of Yellowstone, U.S. Army, 1988, Gold award Girl Scouts U.S.A., 1981; decorated Nat. Def. Svc. medal Desert Storm; meritorius Svc. medal, 1991. Mem. NEA, Wash. Edn. Assn., Assn. U.S. Army, Oreg. Army Nat. Guard Assn., Assn. U.S. Army, Air Def. Artillery Assn., Zeta Tau Alpha (sec. 1983-85, house mgr. 1984-86). Republican. Roman Catholic. Avocations: soccer, fishing, hunting, skydiving, rafting. Home: 1315 SE 16th Ave Canby OR 97013 Office Phone: 503-280-8160. Business E-Mail: leah.sundquist@us.army.mil.

SUNDQUIST, M. ALEXANDRA (ALIX SUNDQUIST), diplomat, consultant; arrived in US, 1962; m. Erik Lindon Sundquist, Mar. 1, 1975; 1 child, Karin Alexandra. BA in Govt. cum laude, Smith Coll.; MA in Econ., N.Y. U. Entered fgn. svc. U.S. Dept. State, 1979; with Chase Manhattan Bank, NYC, Chemical Bank, NYC, 1970—75; comml. attache U.S. Embassy, Jeddah, Saudi Arabia, 1980—82, 1st sec. (energy attache) Paris, 1982—86, consul gen. Bordeaux, 1991—94, counselor econ. affairs Rabat, Morocco, 1995—98; economist Bur. Econ. and Bus. Affairs Dept. State, Washington, 1986—90, chief spl. trade activities divsn., 1998—99; ret., 1999; ind. fgn. affairs advisor, 1999—. Cons. U.S. Dept. State, Washington, 2000; chargé d'Affaires, Valletta, Malta; trade policy advisor Bill Bradley Pres. Campaign. Mem.: Am. Fgn. Svc. Assn., Middle East Inst., Diplomatic and Consular Officers, Retired, Inc. (gov., trustee DACOR Bacon Ho. Found.). Address: 3016 N Florida St Arlington VA 22207-1808 Personal E-mail: masundq@aol.com.

SUNDSTROM, HAROLD WALTER, public relations executive; b. Chgo., Jan. 26, 1929; s. Elmer A. and Rosalind Lillian (Busse) S.; m. Mary Olin, Oct. 1, 1955; children: Geoffrey Lee, Lori Lynn, Deborah. AA, Wright Jr. Coll., 1949; BA, Mich. State U., 1952, MA, 1954. Fgn. svc. info. officer USIA, Tokyo, Jakarta, Seoul, 1955-61; sr. pub. rels. assoc. Eli Lilly and Co., Indpls., 1962-66; v.p., dir. pub. rels. Eisenhower People to People Program, Kansas City, Mo., and Copenhagen, 1966-68; govt. and pub. affairs rep. North Ctrl. States Automobile Mfrs. Assn., Kansas City, 1968-69; speechwriter, pub. rels. cons. Commdr.-in-Chief U.S. Pacific Forces, Aiea, 1969-75; pres. No. Ariz. Comm., Inc., Flagstaff, 1975-79; asst. sec., dir. pub. affairs U.S. Internat. Trade Commn., Washington, 1977-87; v.p. pub. affairs and publs. Export-Import Bank U.S., Washington, 1987-89; pres. Halamar, Inc., Manassas, Va. and Easley, SC, 1983—, Silver Springs, Fla., 1983-98. Mem. Pres.'s Consumer Affairs Couns., 1977-89; freelance writer and poet. Author: The American West, 1956, Indonesia: Its People and Politics, 1957, Garuda, Introducing Indonesia, 1962, Faces of Asia: Korea, 1965, The Northern Arizona Scene, 1976, American Collie Champions, Vol. I, 1979, Vol. II, 1980, Vol. III, 1987, Collies - A Complete Pet Owners Manual, 1994, 2d edit., 2005; editor, pub. Hawaiian Dog Rev., The Alaska Cir., The Arizona Cir., Internat. Lhasa Apso Rev., Sandwich Isles Dog Gazette, 1972-76, Collie Cues, 1983-86, Travel Writer, Honolulu Sun Press, 1972-76. Active Civil War Preservation Trust, Colonial Williamsburg, Hist. Mount Vernon, Va. With U.S. Army, 1947-48, 52-53. Recipient People to People Disting. Svc. award, 1967, George Washington Honor medal Freedom Found., 1968, Silver Beaver award Boy Scouts Am., 1975. Fellow Japan Soc. N.Y., Pub. Rels. Soc. Am. (past pres. Hawaii chpt., Silver Anvil award 1973); mem. Dog Writers Assn. Am. (pres. 1984-92, Disting. Svc. award 1993), Dog Writers Ednl.

Trust (vice chmn., chmn. 1999-2005), Collie Club Am. (pres. 1984-86), Collie Club Am. Found. (life, pres. 1990-92), Am. Kennel Club (del. 1986—), Pi Sigma Alpha, Phi Kappa Sigma. Republican. Avocations: pure-bred dog breeding and showing, travel, photography, conservation, preservation of historic properties. Home and Office: 1 Wadsworth Ct Greer SC 29651

SUNDSTROM, MARY CHARY, psychologist; d. Harry and Julie Brenner; m. Robert Sundstrom, July 1, 1977; children: Julianne, Carl, Eric. EdS, U. Mich., Ann Arbor, 1974. Cert. in special and regular edn., sch. psychologist NC, 1974. Sch. psychologist Wake County Pub. Schs., Raleigh, NC, 1992—. Bd. mem. Nat. Alliance Mentally Ill, Raleigh, 2003—07. Mem.: Nat. Assoc. Sch. Psychologists. Office: East Cary Mid Sch 1111 SE Maynard Rd Cary NC 27511

SUNDWALL, DAVID N., state agency administrator, public health service officer; b. Murray, Utah; m. Catherine Sundwall; 3 children. MD, Univ. Utah. Adminstr. Health Resources & Svcs. Adminstrn.; v.p., med. dir. Am. Healthcare Sys., 1988—94; pres. Am. Clinical Laboratory Assn., 1994—2003, sr. med. & sci. officer; asst. surgeon gen. USPHS, Washington, 2003—05; exec. dir. Utah Dept. Health, Salt Lake City, 2005—. Vol. physician HealthCare for the Homeless Project, Washington; clinical assoc. prof. family med. Georgetown Univ.; assoc. prof. Univ. Utah Sch. Med. Contbr. articles to profl. jours. Trustee Spelman Coll., Atlanta. Mem.: AMA, Am. Acad. Family Physicians. Office: Utah Dept Health 4th Fl CHB Box 141000 Salt Lake City UT 84114-1000 Office Phone: 801-538-6111. Office Fax: 801-538-6306.*

SUNEJA, MANISH, physician; s. Subhash Chander and Shashi Suneja; married. MD, Armed Forces Med. Coll., Iowa, 2002. Asst. prof. U. Iowa Hosp. and Clinics, Iowa City, 2006—. Multiple sci. grants. Fellow: Am. Assn. Medicine. Personal E-mail: manish_suneja@hotmail.com.

SUNG, GYUNG TAK, urologist, department chairman; b. Daegu, Republic of Korea, Aug. 15, 1958; s. Ui Joon Sung and Won Ok Rho; m. Sung Jong Kyung, Feb. 7, 1989; children: Seh-Rin, Catherine, Christine. Degree, State U. NJ, 1981, Busan Coll. Medicine, Republic of Korea, 1987, Busan Nat. Grad. Sch., 1990. Resident neurology Pusan Nat. U. Hosp., Busan, 1988—92; asst. prof. Coll. Medicine Dong-N U., Busan, 1995—98, chmn. dept. urology Coll. Medicine, 2002—; rsch. fellow dept. urology Cleve. Clinic Found., 1999, co-dir. laparoscopic rsch., 1999—2001, mem. staff Urol. Inst., 2001—02. Cons. in field. Co-editor: Robotic Surgery In Urology, 2003; co-author: Laparoscopic Prestatertomy, 2003, Retropa-Floneoscope Adrenarectomy: Lateral Approach, 2003. Recipient Video award, World Congress Endourology and Shockwave, 2001. Mem.: The Korean Urol. Assn., World Endourology and Shockwave Soc. (Academic Paper 2d prize 2002), Am. Urol. Assn. (Best Video 1st prize 1999, Best Video hon. mention 2001, Best Video 2d prize 2002). Avocations: jazz, golf. Office: Dept Urology Dong A Univ Hosp 3Ga1 Dongdaesin dong Seo gu Busan Republic of Korea 602 715 Home: 7430 W Cross Creek TRL Brecksville OH 44141-3185 Office Phone: 82 51-240-5446. Personal E-mail: sunggt@daunet.donga.ac.kr.

SUNG, KYONGJE, medical researcher; married. PhD, Purdue U., West Lafayette, 2005. Rsch. assoc. Ctr. Cognitive Neurosci., Duke U., Durham, NC, 2005—08, Johns Hopkins U. Sch. Medicine, Balt., 2008—. Mem.: APA, Soc. Math. Psychology, Assn. Psychol. Sci.

SUNG, KYU-TAIK, social worker, gerontologist, educator, researcher; b. South Kyungsang, Republic of Korea, Sept. 9, 1930; arrived in U.S., 1967; s. Jang Hwan Sung and Kyu Soon Nam; children: Choon-ho, Jin-ho, Yoon-ho, Vera. BA, Seoul Nat. U., 1956, MA, 1961; MSW, U. Mich., 1972, PhD, 1974. Prof. U. Wis. Sch. Social Work, Madison, 1975—78; prof. dept. social work Yonsei U., Seoul, Republic of Korea, 1978—96; prof. Mich. State U. Sch. Social Work, East Lansing, Mich., 1996—98; Frances Wu endowed chair prof. U. So. Calif. Sch. Social Work, 1999—2004; vis. prof. U. Mich. Sch. Social Work, Ann Arbor, 2004—. Dir., founder Ctr. for Social Welfare Rsch. Yonsei U., 1982—96; exec. dir., founder Elder Respect, Inc., 2002—; sr. rschr. Korean Inst. Gerontology; presenter/spkr. in field. Author: Social Welfare Administration, 1993, Filial Piety in Modern Times: A New Look at Intergenerational Relationship, 1995, Filial Piety in Modern Times: Changing Expressions in Modern Times, 1996, Filial Piety in Modern Times: Timely Adaptation and Practicing Patterns, 2000, Filial Piety in Modern Times: Care and Respect for the Elderly, 2005, Care and Respect for the Elderly: Filial Piety in Modern Times in East Asia, 2005; contbr. articles to profl. jours. With US Army, 1950—53. Mem.: Korean Acad. Social Welfare (past pres.), Korean Gerontol. Soc. (past pres.). Democrat. Achievements include identified components of filial piety (East Asian value of care and respect for the elderly) based on empirical data and introduced them in US profl. jours. Avocations: collecting Buddhist paintings, visiting museums. Office Phone: 734-936-8645.

SUNGOLOWSKY, JOSEPH, literature educator; s. Aaron Gerson and Esther (Berger) Sungolowsky; m. Honey Himelstein, Aug. 20, 1967; children: Robert Yves, Elissa Jeanine Garrel. Baccalauréat-ès-Lettres, Lycée Masséna, Nice, France, 1950; BA, Yeshiva U., 1955; Oridination, Rabbi Isaac Elchanan Theol. Sem., Yeshiva U., NYC, 1957; MA, NYU, NYC, 1957; PhD, Yale U., New Haven, 1962. Instr. french Yale U., 1957—62; asst. prof. french Vassar Coll., Poughkeepsie, 1962—65; asst. prof. to prof. Queens Coll., CUNY, Flushing, 1965—2000, adj. prof. french, 2000—; vis. prof. Bar-Ilan U., Ramat-Gan, Israel, 1980—80; adj. prof. french Yeshiva U., Stern Coll. Women, 2005—. Author: (book) Beaumarchais, Reflections of the Holocaust in Art & Literature, Alfred de Vigny & le dix-huitième siècle; contbr. chapters to books, articles to profl. jours. Recipient Chevalier award, Ordre Palmes Académiques, 1994. Home: 136-14 76th Rd Flushing NY 11367-2822 Office: Queens Coll City Univ NY 65-30 Kissena Blvd Flushing NY 11367-1597 Office Fax: 718-997-5072. Business E-Mail: joseph.sungolowsky@qc.cuny.edu.

SUNI, ELLEN Y., dean, law educator; BA magna cum laude, CCNY; JD magna cum laude, Boston U. Law clerk to chief justice Mass. Supreme Jud. Ct., dep. legal asst. to justices; dir. legal writing prog. Boston U. Sch. Law, asst. dean, lectr.; faculty mem. U. Mo.-Kansas City Sch. Law, 1980—, assoc. dean, 1993—96, 2003—04, interim dean, prof. law, 2004—05, Marvin Lewis Rich faculty scholar, dean, prof. law, 2005—. Fed. prosecutor U.S. Atty. Office, 1987—88; mem. Eighth Cir. Criminal Jury Instrns. Sub-com.; bd. mem. Pub. Interest Litigation Clinic, Police Law Inst. Contbr. articles to law jours. Legal dir. Kansas City Youth Ct.; pres. Midwestern Innocence Project. Recipient Legal Leader of Yr. Award, 2004. Office: Univ Mo-Kansas City Sch Law 5100 Rockhill Rd Kansas City MO 64110 Office Phone: 816-235-2372. E-mail: sunie@umkc.edu.*

SUNIA, IPULASI AITOFELE TOESE F., Lieutenant Governor of American Samoa; b. Mar. 26, 1943; JD, U. San Francisco. Various gov. positions including asst. atty. gen., temp. dist. ct. judge Ter. of Am. Samoa, territorial treas., 1997—2003, lt. gov., 2003—. Democrat. Office: Office Lt Governor Territory American Samoa Pago Pago AS 96799 Office Phone: 684-633-4116. Office Fax: 684-633-2269.

SUNOSKY, JAMES T., lawyer; m. Laura E. Danielson; children: Zachary J., Zoey E. BS, Tex. Tech U., Lubbock, 1995; MS, U. North Tex., Denton, 1998; JD, South Tex. Coll. Law, Houston, 2001. Bar: Tex. 2001, US Dist. Ct., Tex. (so. dist.) 2002, US Dist. Ct., Tex. (ea. dist.) 2003. Assoc. atty. Boston & Hughes, PC, Houston, 2001—06; sr. assoc. atty. Ireson & Weizel, PC, Houston, 2006—. Office: Ireson & Weizel PC 700 Louisiana Ste 1200 Houston TX 77002 Office Fax: 713-228-1160. Business E-Mail: jsunosky@iwlegal.com.

SUNSHINE, LOUISE MINTZ, real estate marketing executive; b. Dec. 2, 1940; d. Nelson E. Mintz and Elizabeth (Pressman); m. Abraham Sunshine, 1962 (div. 1980); children: Suzanne Sunshine Mendel, Paul, Samuel; m. Martin S. Begun, Feb. 1997. BA, Brandeis U, 1962; attended and studied real estate and bus. postgraduate courses, NYU. Exec. v.p., ptnr. Trump Organization, 1975—85; founder, chmn.,CEO The Sunshine Group, Ltd., 1986—2005; chmn. emeritus Corcoran Sunshine Mktg. Group, 2005—06; develop. dir. Alexico Group, LLC, 2006—; co-chair woman, founder Sundezio, 2006—; founder, co-chair women Domineum.com, 2008—. Former state treas. Democratic Party; former fin. chairwoman NY State Democratic Party; bd. dirs. Cathedral of St. John Divine; mem. real estate develop. adv. bd. Columbia U.; commr. NYC Commn. on Women's Issues; with NYC Job Develop. Authority; vice chmn. State Thruway Authority; pres. NYU Hosp. Ladies' Auxillary; mem. Urban Land Inst.; bd. trustee Dalton. Mem.: Internat. Real Estate Fedn., Real Estate Bd. NY, Econ. Club NY. Democrat. Avocation: spending time with grandchildren. Office: Alexico Group LLC 150 E 58th St 33rd Fl New York NY 10155*

SUNSHINE, ROBERT A., federal official; Sr. assoc. Simat, Helliesen and Eichner, Inc.; prin. analyst Budget Analysis Divsn. Congl. Budget Office, Washington, chief natural and physical resources cost estimates unit, 1978—94, dep. asst. dir., 1995—99, dep. dir., 2007—, acting dir., 2008—. Recipient James L. Blum Award, Am. Assn. Budget and Program Analysis, 2003. Office: Congl Budget Office Ford House Office Bldg, 4th Fl Second and D Streets, SW Washington DC 20515 Office Phone: 202-226-2700. Office Fax: 202-225-7509.*

SUNSHINE, STEVEN H., lawyer; AB, UCLA, 1973, JD, 1976. Bar: Calif. 1976. Ptnr., mem. exec. com. Bryan Cave LLP, Irvine, Calif. Office: Bryan Cave Llp 3161 Michelson Dr Ste 1500 Irvine CA 92612-4414 Office Phone: 949-223-7200. E-mail: shsunshine@bryancave.com.

SUNSTEIN, BRUCE DAVID, lawyer; b. Phila., May 27, 1944; s. David E. and Phylis (Eisenberg) S.; 1 child, Aaron E. BS, MIT, 1965; MA, Ind. U., 1969; JD, U. Calif., Berkeley, 1973. Bar: Calif. 1973, U.S. Dist. Ct. (no. dist.) Calif. 1973, U.S. Ct. Appeals (9th cir.) 1973, U.S. Patent and Trademark Office 1974, Mass. 1977, U.S. Tax Ct. 1977, U.S. Supreme Ct. 1977, U.S. Ct. Appeals (1st cir.) 1978, U.S. Ct. Appeals (fed. cir.) 1982. Assoc. Cooper, White & Cooper, San Francisco, 1973-77; ptnr. Bromberg & Sunstein LLP, predecessor firms, Boston, 1977—. Contbr. articles to profl. jours.; author: Investor Relations Meets Intellectual Property, 2003. Named one of top Boston lawyers, Boston Mag., 2002. Mem.: Boston Patent Law Assn., Boston Bar Assn., Mass. Bar Assn., Licensing Execs. Soc., Am. Intellectual Property Lawyers Assn., IEEE, ABA. Office: Bromberg & Sunstein LLP 125 Summer St Ste 1100 Boston MA 02110-1618 Office Phone: 617-443-9292. Office Fax: 617-443-0004. Business E-Mail: bsunstein@bromsun.com.

SUNSTEIN, CASS ROBERT, law educator; b. Salem, Mass., Sept. 21, 1954; m. Samantha Power. AB, Harvard U., 1975, JD, 1978. Law clk. to Hon. Benjamin Kaplan Supreme Jud. Ct. of Mass., 1978—79; law clk. to Hon. Thurgood Marshall US Supreme Ct., Washington, 1979-80; atty.-advisor, Office of Legal Counsel US Dept. Justice, Washington, 1980-81; asst. prof. U. Chgo. Law Sch., 1981—83, U. Chgo. Law Sch. & U. Chgo. dept. polit. sci., 1983—85, prof. law, 1985—88, Karl N. Llewellyn Prof. Jurisprudence, 1988—93, Karl N. Llewellyn Disting. Svc. Prof. Jurisprudence, 1993—2008; Felix Frankfurer prof. law, dir. Program on Risk Regulation Harvard Law Sch., 2008—. Assoc. editor Ethics, 1986—88; bd. editors Studies Am. Polit. Devel., 1989—, Constitutional Polit. Econ., 1991, Jour. Polit. Philosophy, 1991—; contbg. editor The Am. Prospect, 1989, The New Republic, 1999—; vis. prof. Columbia Law Sch., NYC, 1986, Harvard Law Sch., Cambridge, Mass., 1987, 2005; co-dir. Ctr. Constitutionalism Ea. Europe U. Chgo., 1990—97; mem. Presdl. Adv. Com. Pub. Svc. Obligations of Digital TV, 1997—98; cons. project on social norms IRS, 1999—. Author: (book) After the Rights Revolution: Reconceiving the Regulatory State, 1990, Democracy and the Problem of Free Speech, 1993 (Goldsmith Book Award, 1994), The Partial Constitution, 1993, Legal Reasoning and Political Conflict, 1996, Free Markets and Social Justice, 1997, One Case At A Time: Judicial Minimalism on the Supreme Court, 1999, Designing Democracy: What Constitutions Do, 2001, Republic.com, 2001, Free Markets and Social Justice, 2002, Risk and Reason, 2002, The Cost-Benefit State, 2002, Why Societies Need Dissent, 2003, The Second Bill of Rights: Franklin Delano Roosevelt's Constitutional Vision and Why We Need It More Than Ever, 2004, The Laws of Fear: Beyond the Precautionary Principle, 2005, Radicals in Robes: Why Extreme Right-Wing Courts Are Wrong for America, 2005, Republic.com 2.0, 2006, Infotopia: How Many Minds Produce Knowledge, 2006, A Constitution of Many Minds: Why the Founding Document Doesn't Mean What It Meant Before, 2009; co-author: Administrative Law and Regulatory Policy, 1999, The Cost of Rights, 1999, Constitutional Law, 2001, Punitive Damages: How Juries Decide, 2002; co-author: (with David Schkade, Lisa Ellman, & Andres Sawicki) Are Judges Political? An Empirical Investigation of the Federal Judiciary, 2006; co-author: (with Richard H. Thaler) Nudge: Improving Decisions about Health, Wealth, and Happiness, 2008; editor: Feminism and Political Theory, 1990, Behavioral Law and Economics, 2000; co-editor: The Bill of Rights and the Modern State, 1992, Clones and Clones: Facts and Fantasies About Human Cloning, 1998, The Vote: Bush, Gore & the Supreme Court, 2001, Animal Rights: Current Controversies and New Directions, 2004. Mem.: ABA (vice chmn. Sect. Govtl. Orgn. & Separation Powers 1986—87, coun. Sect. Adminstr. Law 1987—88, vice-chmn. Jud. Rev. Com. 1991—, co-chair Com. Regulatory Policy 2001—, Cert. Merit Award 1991), Am. Acad. Arts and Sci., Am. Law Inst., Inst. Medicine Com., World Wildlife Fund. Office: Harvard Law Sch Areeda 225 1563 Massachusetts Ave Cambridge MA 02138 Office Phone: 617-496-2291. E-mail: csunstei@law.harvard.edu.*

SUNTZEFF, NICHOLAS BORIS, research astronomer; b. Berkeley, Calif., Nov. 22, 1952; s. Nicholas Matveevich and Jeanette Lydia (Argo) S.; m. Jeruška Vladislavic Brtetevic, Mar. 21, 1987; 1 child, Lara Thais. BS in Math. with distinction, Stanford U., 1974; MS, PhD in Astronomy and Astrophysics, U. Calif., Santa Cruz, 1981. NSF postdoctoral fellow U. Wash., Seattle, 1981-82; Las Campanas fellow Mt. Wilson and Las Campanas Obs., Pasadena, Calif., 1982-85; asst. astronomer Cerro Tololo Inter-Am. Obs., La Serena, Chile, 1986-90, assoc. astronomer, 1991—. Mem. CTIO adv. com. NOAO, Tucson, 1984-86. Contbr. articles to Astron. Jour., Astron. Soc. Pacifi, Nature, Monthly Notices Royal Astron. Soc., Astrophysical Jour., Astronomy and Astrophysics. Carnegie fellow Mt. Wilson and Las Campanas Obs., 1983. Mem. Am. Astron. Soc., Astron. Soc. Pacific (R. Trumpler award 1987), Internat. Astron. Union, Phi Beta Kappa. Eastern Orthodox. Achievements include research in stellar populations, galactic structure, stellar astrophysics, origin and evolution of galaxies, and supernovae. Office: Texas A&M Univ Dept Physics 4242 TAMU College Station TX 77843

SUNUNU, JOHN EDWARD, former United States Senator from New Hampshire; b. Boston, Sept. 10, 1964; s. John H. Sununu; m. Kitty (Halloran) Sununu; 3 children BS in Mech. Engring., Mass. Inst. Tech., 1986, MS in Mech. Engring., 1987; MBA with honors, Harvard Grad. Sch. Bus., 1991. Design engr. Remec, Inc., 1987-90; mgr., ops. specialist Pittiglio, Rabin, Todd & McGrath, 1990-92; CFO, dir. ops. Teletrol Sys. Inc., Manchester, NH, 1992—96; cons. JHS Assocs., Ltd.; mem. US Congress from 1st NH Dist., 1997—2003; US Senator from NH, 2003—09. Bd. dirs. Time Warner Cable Inc., 2009—. Active NH C. of C., NH Bus. and Industry Assn., NH High Tech Coun. Recipient Friend of the Taxpayer award, Americans for Tax Reform, Guardian of Small Bus. award, Nat. Fedn. Independent Bus., Spirit Enterprise award, US C. of C. Mem.: NH Bus. and Industry Assn. Republican. Roman Catholic.*

SUNUNU, JOHN HENRY, political organization administrator, former White House chief of staff, former governor of New Hampshire; b. Havana, Cuba, July 2, 1939; s. John Sununu Sr. and Victoria Dada; m. Nancy Hayes, 1958; children: Catherine, Elizabeth, Christina, John, Michael, James, Christopher, Peter. BS, MIT, 1961, MS, 1962, PhD, 1966; DSc (hon.), Nathaniel Hawthorne Coll., 1983; LLD (hon.), U. NH, 1983, New Eng. Coll., 1984, Washington & Jefferson Coll., 1985, Colby-Sawyer Coll., 1989, St. John's Coll., 1989, Manhattan Coll., 1989, Dowling Coll., 1989, Wake Forest U., 1990, Marquette U., 1990, Suffolk U., 1990, Iona Coll., 1990; LHD (hon.), New Eng. Coll. Optometry, 1986; Doctorate in Pub. Adminstrn. (hon.), Nowich U., 1987, Rivier Coll., 1989; Doctorate in Pub. Svc. (hon.), U. SC, 1991. Founder, chief engr. Astro Dynamics, 1960-65; pres. JHS Engring. Co. & Thermal Rsch. Inc., Salem, NH, 1965-82; assoc. prof. mech. engring. Tufts U., 1966-82, assoc. dean Coll. Engring., 1968-73; mem. NH Ho. of Reps., 1973-74, Gov.'s Energy Coun., 1973-78; chmn. Gov.'s Com. on NH Future, 1977-78; mem. Gov.'s Adv. Com. on Sci. and Tech., 1977-78; gov. State of NH, Concord, 1983-89; chief of staff to Pres. The White House, Washington, 1989-91, counsellor to Pres., 1991-92; pres. JHS Associates, Ltd., 1992—; ptnr. Trinity Internat. Ptnrs.; chmn. NH Republican Party, 2009—. Co-host Crossfire, CNN, 1992-98; cons., spkr. in field. Adv. bd. tech. and policy program MIT, 1984-89; chmn. Coalition Northeastern Govs., 1985-86; vice chmn. Alliance Acid Rain Control; trustee George Bush Presdl. Libr., mem. Nat. Acad. Engring. Mem. ASME (hon.), NAE, Nat. Govs. Assn. (vice chmn. 1986-87, chmn. task force on tech., task force on acid rain, chmn. 1987-88), Rep. Govs. Assn. (chmn. 1985-86), New England Govs.' Assn. (chmn. 1984-85, vice chmn. adv. commn. on intergovtl. rels.). Republican. Roman Catholic. Office: JHS Associates Ltd 49 Linden Rd Hampton Falls NH 03844 Office Phone: 603-890-1630. Office Fax: 603-890-1634. E-mail: chairman@nhgop.org.*

SUNY, RONALD GRIGOR, political science professor, history professor; b. Phila., Sept. 25, 1940; s. Goorken George and Arax Kesdekian Suny; m. Armena Pearl Marderosian, Aug. 14, 1971; children: Grikor Suni, Sevan Siranoush Suni, Anoush Tamar Suni. PhD, Columbia U., NYC, 1968. Charles Tilly collegiate prof. social and polit. history U. Mich., Ann Arbor, 2005—, dir. Eisenberg Inst. Hist. Studies, 2009—; emeritus prof. polit. sci. and history U. Chgo., 2005—. Author: (book) The Soviet Experiment, Revenge of the Past, The Making of the Georgian Nation; editor: The Cambridge History of Russia: The Twentieth Century. Guggenheim fellowship. Office: Dept History 435 S State St Ann Arbor MI 48109 Business E-Mail: rgsuny@umich.edu.

SUPAK, CATHY POERNER, athletic trainer, educator; b. San Antonio, Tex. d. John and Jo Ann Poerner; m. Ray Supak; children: Amanda, Cameron. BS in Edn., Tex. State U., San Marcos, 1984. Cert. athletic trainer Bd. Certification-Nat. Athletic Trainer Assn., 1987, lic. Tex. State Bd. Athletic Trainers, 1984; cert. tchr. State Bd. Edn., Tex., 1984. Athletic trainer/tchr. La Porte H.S., Tex., 1984—87; staff athletic trainer Christus St John Sports Medicine, Nassau Bay, Tex., 1992—2004, supr. athletic tng. svcs., 2004—. Vol. Boy Scouts, Houston, 1996; chair Tex. State Bd. Athletic Trainers, 2007—. Recipient Cert. of Merit, ARC, 1999, Disting. Alumnus award, Dept. Phys. Edn. and Sports Sci., 1999. Mem.: Greater Houston Athletic Trainers Assn. (pres. 1998—2001, Bobby Gunn Svc. award 1999), SW Athletic Trainers Assn. (com. chair 2004—06), Nat. Athletic Trainers Assn. (Athletic Trainer Svc. award 2004). Home: 14714 Graywood Grove Lane Houston TX 77062

SUPANICH, BARBARA ANN, physician; b. Detroit, Sept. 24, 1952; d. Donald George and Mildred Mary (Stanovich) Supanich. BS in Chemistry, Mercy Coll. Detroit, 1974; MD, Mich. State U., 1980. Diplomate Am. Bd. Family Practice, Am. Bd. Hospice and Palliative Medicine, 2006, lic. physician Mich., Fla., Md.; joined Sisters of Mercy, 1973. Resident in family practice Creighton U. Affiliated Hosps., Omaha, 1980—83; pvt. practice Eaton Rapids, Mich., 1983—86, Houghton Lake, Mich., 1986—92; fellow in clin. ethics Ctr. Ethics Mich. State U., East Lansing, 1992—93, asst. prof. family practice, 1993—97, assoc. prof., 1998, assoc. chair clin. svcs., dept. family practice, 1995—99, assoc. residency dir. family practice residency Munson, 1999—2005; fellow palliative medicine and hospice care Mayo Clinic, Jacksonville, Fla., 2005—06; med. dir. palliative medicine, sr. svcs. Holy Cross Hosp., Silver Spring, Md., 2006—. Cons. Mich. Dept. Cmty. Health, Lansing, 1996—99. Contbr. chapters to books, articles to profl. jours. Recipient Teacher-Scholar award, Mich. State U., Coll. Human Medicine, 1998, Two Thousand Notable American Women award, 2003, Palliative Care Program award, Greater Wash. Partnership, 2009; named Am.'s Top Family Dr., Palliative Medicine Dr., 2007. Fellow: Am. Acad. Hospice and Palliative Medicine (Outstanding award 2009), Am. Acad. Family Physicians (bd. dirs., regional dir. 2000—04, 2d v.p. 2004—05); mem.: Md. Acad. Family Physicians, Am. Med. Women's Assn. Democrat. Roman Catholic. Avocations: swimming, bicycling, walking, mystery and science fiction novels, movies. Home: 4013 Postgate Terr Apt 201 Silver Spring MD 20906 Office: Holy Cross Hosp 1500 Forest Glen Rd Silver Spring MD 20910 Home Phone: 301-828-0748; Office Phone: 301-754-7910. Personal E-mail: barbsupanich@comcast.net.

SUPANVANIJ, JANIKAN, finance educator; b. Bangkok, Aug. 6, 1971; d. Vitaya and Sopha Supanvanij. BBA, Thammasat U., Bangkok, 1993; MFN in Fin., St. Louis U., 1995, MBA in Fin. and Econs., 1997, PhD in Fin., 2003. Cert. tchg. skills. Internat. banking facility fgn. exch. dealer The Thai Mil. Bank, Ltd., Bangkok, 1993; instr. St. Louis U., 1997—2003; asst. prof. St. Cloud State U., Minn., 2003—06, assoc. prof., 2006—09, prof., 2009—. Contbr. articles to profl. jours. Recipient Rsch. Collaboration award, St. Cloud State U., 2000—05, Disting. Rsch. award, 2000—05, Tchg. Excellence award, 2004—05, Best Paper award, Assn. Global Bus., 2004, 2005; finalist Tchg. Excellence award,

Acad. Fin., 2007. Mem.: St. Louis U. Grad. Student Assn. (webmaster 1997—2002, GSA rsch. symposium program co-chair 2001—02, pres. 2002—03), Beta Gamma Sigma, Alpha Epsilon Lambda. Office: St Cloud State U 720 4th Ave S Saint Cloud MN 56301

SUPATTO, WILLY, research scientist; b. Clamart, France, July 25, 1978; s. Jean-Claude and Francoise Supatto; m. Aurelie Bertin. Degree in Engring., ESPCI, Paris, 2002; PhD, U. Paris, 2005. Postdoc. fellow Calif. Inst. Tech., Pasadena, 2006—. Office: Calif Inst Tech 1200 E California Blvd MC 139-74 Pasadena CA 91125 Office Fax: 1 626 449 5163. Business E-Mail: supatto@caltech.edu.

SUPERNEAU, DUANE WILLIAM, geneticist, physician; b. Ogden, Utah, Dec. 31, 1950; s. Richard Edwin and Mary Ellen Superneau; children: Adam, Ashley, Allison. BA, Carroll Coll., 1973; MD, U. Wash., 1977. Diplomate Am. Bd. Pediat., Am. Bd. Med. Genetics. Asst. prof. dept. med. genetics U. So. Ala., Mobile, 1982-87, assoc. prof. dept. med. genetics, 1987-91; chief sect. med. genetics Ochsner Clinic, New Orleans, 1991—2005; dir. Genetic Svcs. La., Baton Rouge, 2005—. Clin. asst. prof. La. State U., New Orleans, 1992—. Bd. dirs. The ARC Greater New Orleans, 1991—, pres. 1994-96; bd. dirs. ARC of La., 1994—, pres., 1999-2001; bd. dirs. Jefferson Parish Human Svcs. Authority, Jefferson Parish, La., 1992-99. Roman Catholic. Office: Genetic Svcs of La 5339 O'Donovan Dr Baton Rouge LA 70808 Office Phone: 225-231-5381. Business E-Mail: duane.superneau@womans.org.

SUPINO, PHYLLIS GAIL, medical researcher, educator; m. Rene Patrick Supino, June 7, 1980; children: Lisa Michelle, Christopher Davies. BS in Biol. Scis., CCNY, 1964; EdD in Sci. Edn., Rutgers U., New Brunswick, NJ, 1976. Instr. psychology, rsch. assoc. in cognitive psychology Princeton U., 1975—77; dir. rsch. and evaluation The Ednl. Improvement Ctr. divsn. NJ. State Dept. Edn., West Orange, 1977—79; adj. instr. environ. and cmty. medicine, adj. instr. family medicine Robert Wood Johnson Med. Sch./U. Medicine and Dentistry NJ, Piscataway, 1979—90; asst. prof. pub. health in medicine, dir. data mgmt. Cornell U. Med. Coll., NYC, 1990—95; rsch. assoc. prof. emergency medicine, rsch. assoc. prof. med. edn., dir. rsch. in emergency medicine Mt. Sinai Sch. Medicine, NYC, 1996—99; assoc. rsch. prof. pub. health in medicine, dir. data mgmt., epidemiology and ednl. programs Weill Cornell Med. Coll., NYC, 1999—. Mem. editl. bd.: Cardiology, reviewer: Med. Edn.; contbr. chapters to books, articles to profl. jours. Vol. Morocco VI US Peace Corps, Washington. Recipient Phi Delta Kappa award, Rutgers U., 1976, The Howard Gilman award, The Howard Gilman Found., 1995, Best Mentor of the Yr. award, Mt. Sinai Sch. Medicine, 1998, Best Nat. Sci. Abstract award, Am. Soc. Nuc. Cardiology and Internat. Affiliates, 2001; grantee Pilot Rsch. award, Weill Med. Coll. of Cornell U. Fellow: NY Acad. Medicine; mem.: Heart Valve Soc. Am., Am. Soc. Nuc. Cardiology, Am. Heart Assn., Am. Statis. Assn., Cardiology (editl. bd. Cardiology), Am. Fedn. for Med. Rsch., Kappa Delta Pi (life). Achievements include development of first comprehensive approved course on clinical research methodology for physicians at Weill Medical College and Mount Sinai School of Medicine; first course on hypothesis and protocol design for physicians at WMC; Research mentor to more than 50 residents, fellows and junior faculty in medicine. Avocations: theater, vocal music.

SUPP, DOROTHY M., medical educator, researcher; b. NYC, 1965; m. P. Supp Andrew. BS, Cornell U., Ithaca, NY, 1986; PhD, U. Cin., 1994. Rsch. investigator Shriners Burns Hosp., Cin., 1997—; assoc. prof. U. Cin., 2004—. Editl. bd. mem. Burns Jour., 2000—. Mem.: AAAS, Assn. Advancement Wound Care, Internat. Soc. Burn Injuries, Wound Healing Soc., Soc. Investigative Dermatology. Office: Shriners Burns Hosp Cin 3229 Burnet Ave Cincinnati OH 45249

SUPPA-FRIEDMAN, JANICE DESTEFANO, secondary school educator, consultant; b. Morristown, NJ, Apr. 27, 1943; d. Eugene Arthur and Isabella Vienna (Bottiglia) DeS.; m. Dennis Suppa, June 28, 1964 (div. May 1994); children: Julie Ann, Chad Dennis; m. Michael Jac Friedman, Oct. 7, 1995. BS in Edn., Bowling Green State U., 1964; MA in Edn., Va. Poly. Inst. & State U., 1977, cert. advanced grad. study, 1990. Cert. secondary tchr., Va. Tchr. English and reading Northwood (Ohio) Jr. High Sch., 1964—66; tchr. English and history Canaseraga (N.Y.) Ctrl. Schs., 1966—67; tchr. English and reading Marstellar Jr. High Sch., Manassas, Va., 1967—72; tchr. English Taylor Jr. High sch., Warrenton, Va., 1973—74; tchr. English and reading, lang. arts specialist, dept. head, lead tchr. Brentsville Dist. Mid.-Sr. High Sch., Nokesville, Va., 1975—99; reading specialist Graham Park Middle Sch., Dumfries, Va., 1999—2000; ednl. cons., 2000—; co-tchr./mentor Fredericksburg City Pub. Sch., 2004. Ednl. cons. So. Region Coll. Bd., 2001—, Nat. Coll. Bd., 2007—; reader for advanced placement lit. and composition exam, 1996, 1998—2003; adj. prof. Old Dominion U., 1999, No. Va. C.C., 1992—94, George Mason U., 2003—04; advanced placement English tchr. mentor Coll. Bd., 2004—05. Editor newsletter Spinning Wheel, 1991-94; contbr. articles to profl. jours. Va. English Bull. Tour guide George Washington Fredericksburg Found. at Kenmore Mansion and Plantation and George Washington's Ferry Farms, Va., 2001—04; officer of election Stafford County, 2001—04; vol. Visitor Use Asst. and Survey Adminstrn. Shenandoah Nat. Pk., 2005—. Grantee Va. Comm. of the Arts, 1994-95, 2000, Prince William Edn. Found., 1996, 2000, Greater Washington Reading Coun., 1999, 2000, Va. Opera Assn., 2000, So. States Southland Corp., 2000. Mem. NATE (pres. 1992-94), Nat. Coun. Tchrs. English (coord. Va. state Achievement in Writing awards 1995-01, SCOA Region 2 rep. 2009-, judge Va. state forensics finals 2000-03, judge Va. state excellence in lit. mags. 1998-02), Va. Assn. Tchrs. English (exec. bd. 1992—, v.p. 2001-02, pres.-elect 2002-03, pres. 2004, 05, Nat. Coun. Tchrs. English liaison 2007-, Svc. award 1993, Frances Weimer award 2007), Phi Delta Kappa; Fellow Ctrl. Va. Writing Project UVA, 2008. Avocations: reading, music, hiking, swimming, yoga, snorkeling. Personal E-mail: suppaf@aol.com, jdsfriedman@aol.com.

SUPPE, FREDERICK, historian, educator; b. Schenectady, NY, 1947; s. Charles and Eleanor Suppe; m. Ann Blakey. AB, Princeton U., NJ, 1969; MA, U. Minn., Mpls., 1973, PhD, 1981. Assoc. prof. Ball State U., Muncie, Ind., 1989—. Treas. Charles Homer Haskins Soc., 1995—; vis. fellow Harris-Manchester Coll., Oxford U., 1997; pres. Celtic Studies Assn. N.Am., 2008—; vis. asst. prof. Clemson U., SC. Author: (book) Military Institutions on the Welsh Marches. Fulbright fellowship, Fulbright Commn., 1974—76. Office: Ball State Univ History Dept Muncie IN 47306 Office Fax: 765-285-5612. Business E-Mail: fsuppe@bsu.edu.

SUPPES, CHRISTINE JOHNSON, publishing executive; b. LA, Mar. 3, 1953; d. Robert and Jane Johnson; m. Patrick Suppes; children: Alexandra Christine, Michael Patrick. Copygirl/editl. asst. San Francisco Examiner, 1972—73; pres. Gravure At Home, Stanford, Calif., 1997—2001; pub., editor-in-chief www.Fashionlines.com, Stanford, Calif., 1999—2007; chief designer Jewels by Christine, 2002—; freelance fashion designer, 2007—. Advt. cons. Clarum Corp., Palo Alto, Calif., 1997—, Gravure Corp., Dallas, 1997—2000; chief designer www.jewelsbyChristine.com, Stanford, Calif., 2003—; freelance fashion writer; Am. rep. Of Silk, of Gold and Silver Assn., France. Author: Amanda Prescott, 1984, Clinic, 1985; contbr. revs. to San Francisco Chronicle, articles to SF Moda. Organizer, Teacher's Fund Bing School, Stanford, 1995—; mem. Peninsula chpt. NARAL, Palo Alto, 1997—2000; supporter ARC, Palo Alto, 2001, St. Vincent de Paul Soc., Couture Coun. Mus. FIT. Recipient Angel of Fashion com. award, N.Y.C., 1999—. Mem.: Fine Art Mus. San Francisco, Couture Circle, Fashion Group Internat., Camera Nazionale della Moda Italiana, Federation Francaise de la Couture. Office: Fashionlines 678 Mirada Ave Stanford CA 94305 Office Phone: 650-380-1825. Business E-Mail: suppes@fashionlines.com.

SUPPES, PATRICK, statistician, philosopher, psychologist, educator; b. Tulsa, Mar. 17, 1922; s. George Biddle and Ann (Costello) Suppes; m. Joan Farmer, Apr. 16, 1946 (div. 1970); children: Patricia, Deborah, John Biddle; m. Joan Sieber, Mar. 29, 1970 (div. 1973); m. Christine Johnson, May 26, 1979; children: Alexandra Christine, Michael Patrick. BS, U. Chgo., 1943; PhD (Wendell T. Bush fellow), Columbia U., 1950; LLD, U. Nijmegen, Netherlands, 1979; Dr. honoris causa (hon.), U. Rene Descartes, Paris, 1982, U. Regensburg, Germany, 1999, U. Bologna, Italy, 1999. Instr., Stanford U., 1950—52, asst. prof., 1952—55, assoc. prof., 1955—59, prof. philosophy, statistics, psychology and edn., 1959—92, prof. emeritus. Founder, CEO Computer Curriculum Corp., 1967—90. Author: Introduction to Logic, 1957, Axiomatic Set Theory, 1960, Sets and Numbers, books 1-6, 1966, Studies in the Methodology and Foundations of Science, 1969, A Probabilistic Theory of Causality, 1970, Logique du Probable, 1981, Probabilistic Metaphysics, 1984, Estudios de Filosofia y Metodologí de la Ciencia, 1988, Language for Humans and Robots, 1991, Models and Methods in the Philosophy of Science, 1993, Representation and Invariance of Scientific Structures, 2002; author: (with Davidson and Siegel) Decision Making, 1957; author: (with Richard C. Atkinson) Markov Learning Models for Multiperson Interactions, 1960; author: (with Shirley Hill) First Course in Mathematical Logic, 1964; author: (with Edward J. Crothers) Experiments on Second-Language Learning, 1967; author: (with Max Jerman and Dow Brian) Computer-assisted Instruction, 1965—66, Stanford Arithmetic Program, 1968; author: (with D. Krantz, R.D. Luce and A. Tversky) Foundations of Measurement, Vol. 1, 1971, Vol. 2, 1989, Vol. 3, 1990; author: (with M. Morningstar) Computer-Assisted Instruction at Stanford, 1966-68, 1972; author: (with B. Searle and J. Friend) The Radio Mathematics Project: Nicaragua, 1974-75, 1976; author: (with Colleen Crangle) Language and Learning for Robots, 1994; author: (with Mario Zanotti) Foundations of Probability with Applications, 1996. Served to capt. USAAF, 1942-46. Recipient Nicholas Murray Butler Silver medal, Columbia U., 1965, Disting. Sci. Contbr. award, APA, 1972, Tchrs. Coll. medal for disting. svc., 1978, Nat. medal Sci., NSF, 1990, Henry Chauncey award for disting. svc., Ednl. Testing Svc., 2003, Lakatos Book Award prize, London Sch. Econs., 2003, Lauener Prize in Philosophy, Lauener Found., 2004; fellow, Ctr. for Advanced Study Behavioral Scis., 1955—56, NSF, 1957—58. Fellow: APA, AAAS, Assn. Computing Machinery, Am. Acad. Arts and Scis.; mem.: NAS, Chilean Acad. Scis., European Acad. Scis. and Arts, Norwegian Acad. Sci. and Letters (fgn.), Russian Acad. Edn. (fgn.), Am. Ednl. Rsch. Assn. (pres. 1973—74), Internat. Union History and Philosophy of Sci. (pres. divsn. logic, methodology and philosophy of sci. 1975—79), Finnish Acad. Sci. and Letters, Internat. Inst. Philosophy, Croatian Acad. Scis. (corr.), Brazilian Acad. Philosophy (corr.), Nat. Acad. Edn. (pres. 1973—77), Acad. Internat. de Philosophie des Scis. (titular), Am. Math. Soc., Assn. Symbolic Logic, Am. Philos. Soc., Am. Philos. Assn., Math. Assn. Am., Sigma Xi. Office Phone: 650-725-6030. E-mail: psuppes@stanford.edu.

SUPUT, RAY RADOSLAV, librarian; b. Columbus, Ohio, May 13, 1922; s. Elias and Darinka (Balac) S.; m. Mary Grace Hansen, May 23, 1953 (dec. Nov. 1980); children: David Ray, Dorothy Mary; m. Milana Preradov, July 12, 1986. BA, Ohio State U., 1950; MSL.S., Case Western Res. U., 1951, PhD, 1972; MA, U. Chgo., 1955. Librarian Northwestern U., Evanston, Ill., 1951-52; reference and circulation librarian Law Library, U. Chgo., 1952-54, cataloger, 1954-57; asso. librarian Garrett-Evang. Theol. Sem., Evanston, 1957-58, head librarian, 1958-64; asst. dir. libraries and adj. lectr. dept. Slavic and E. European langs. Sch. Library Sci. Case Western Res. U., Cleve., 1964-67, acting dir. libraries, 1967-68; adj. instr. Case Western Res. U. (Sch. Library Sci.), 1965-69; librarian Case Western Res. U. (Freiberger Library), 1968-69; dir. univ. library, head dept. and prof. library sci. Ball State U., Muncie, Ind., 1969-78, univ. librarian, head dept. and prof. library service, 1978-81, prof. library service, also adj. prof. library sci., 1981-82, chmn. dept. library and info. sci., prof. library sci., 1982-87, prof. library sci., info. sci. emeritus, 1987—. Contbr. articles to profl. jours. Nat. Endowment for Humanities and Council on Library Resources Inc. grantee. Mem.: ALA, Serb Nat. Fedn., African Violet Soc. Am., Am. Theol. Libr. Assn. (life). Eastern Orthodox.

SURACI, CHARLES XAVIER, JR., retired federal agency administrator, air transportation executive, consultant; b. Washington, Feb. 10, 1933; s. Charles Xavier and June Celcia (Hunter) Suraci; m. Florence Patricia De Mino, May 23, 1970. Cadet, Widener U., 1951—55; grad., Nat. Acad. Broadcasting Sch., Washington, 1959; student, Columbia Union Coll., 1962-63, 72, Catholic U., 1969; grad. extension course, CAP Staff Coll., 1974; BA, Calif. Christian Coll., 1977, HHD (hon.), 1977; grad., USAF Inspectors Gen. Sch., Eglin AFB, Fla., 1982; also grad. numerous other govt. schs. and courses. Served with USAF, 1953-57; enlisted CAP, 1957, commd. 1st lt., 1961; advanced through ranks to Col. CAP USAF Aux, 1974; co-founder Wheaton-Silver Spring Cadet Squadron; comdr. Nat. Capital Wing, 1973-76; dep. chief of staff cadet activities Middle East region, 1977-79, dir. cadet tng., 1979-82, insp. gen., 1982—. With Henry Diamond Lab. U.S. Army, Adelphi, Md., 1963—, materials publs. asst. Harry Diamond Lab., 1963—68, later asst. to motor transp. officer, now supply specialist, logistics sect.; bd. dirs. Centro Tepeyac Crisis Pregnancy Ctr., Silver Springs, Md. Mem. youth com. YMCA, Silver Spring, 1962—69, mem. bd. mgmt., 1967—; bd. dirs. Am. Youth Com.; mem. Commn. on Children and Youth Bd., Montgomery County, Md., Montgomery County Juvenile Ct. Com., 1978—86; co-chmn. Right to Life com. KC-Rosensteel Coun.; bd. dirs. Pregnancy Aid Ctr., College Park, Md.; choir mem. Blessed Sacrament Cath. Ch., Washington. Recipient Leader and Svc. award, YMCA Silver Spring, 1968, 1969, CAP Meritorious Svc. award, Dept. Def., 1969, 1977, Cert. of Commendation, Pres. Richard Nixon, 1970, CAP Exceptional Svc. award, Congressman Lester Wolff of N.Y., 1972, award, Montgomery County C. of C., 1973, Commendation, Gov. of Tenn., 1975, Letter of Commendation, Washington Mayor Walter Washington, 1977, Outstanding Patriotic Civilian Svc. award, Dept. Def., 1977, Md. Vol. Cmty. honor award, Montgomery County, 1981, Vol. Activist award, 1984, George Washington honor medal, Valley Forge Freedom Found., 1995, Patrick Henry medal for Patriotic Achievement, Mil. Order of World Wars, 1995, Honor, Md. Ho. Dels., 1974, D.C. Govt., 1977, numerous AF and CAP ribbons and medals, Dept. of Army Spl. Act or Svc. award, Dept. of Army Superior Performance award, 1987, Cmty. Svc. award, Wheaton-Kensington News, Bethesda Chevy Chase Current, Montgomery County Press Assn., 1990, Outstanding Support Aviation Career Day Tuskegee Airmen and Commdg. Gen. of D.C., Air Nat. Guard, 1992, Spl. award for tng. over 1000 youth cadets in CAP in 31 yrs., State of Md., 1986, Plaque Name Displayed at U.S. Army-Harry Diamond Lab., Pro-Life award, KC-Rosensteel Coun., 1992, 1999—2002, Frank G. Brewer Meml. Aerospace award-CAP Mid. East Region HQ, 1984, 1991, 1992, CAP-USAF Aux. Meritorious Svc. award, Mid. East Region HQ, 1993, Cert. Appreciation Aerospace Edn. of Md., Air Force Assn., 1993—95, Exceptional Svc. award, USAF Aux., 1994—95, Sr. Officer of Yr. Mid East Region, USAF Aux.-CAP, 1998, Colonel Robinson Lifetime Leadership award, Nat. Capital Wing, 2001, Leadership award, Cen. East Region Air Force Assn., 2001, numerous others, 50th Yr. award, Blessed Sacrament Ch., 2007; named Air Man of Month, USAF, 1956, Grand Marshall Meml. Day Parade, Rockville, Md., 1971, Man of Yr. State of Md., Air Force Assn., 1993; nominee Pres.'s Vol. Action award, Pres. of U.S., 1988, 1991. Mem.: Md. Pvt. Industry Coun. (bd. dirs. Opportunity Skyway program), Md. Press. Assn. Montgomery County, Nat. Officers Assn., Mil. Order of World Wars (jr. vice comdr. Bethesda chpt. 1996—, Outstanding staff officer of the yr. 2005), Tuskegee Airmen Inc., Fed. Ret. Employees Assn., Army Aviation Assn., Navy League, Nat. Aerospace Assn., Air Force Assn. (v.p. aerospace edn. Thomas W. Anthony chpt. 1996—, pres. Thomas W. Anthony chpt. 1998—, bd. dirs., nat. liaison officer to Civil Air Patrol-Aux. USAF 2004, Medal of Merit 1990, Exceptional Svc. award 1991, Disting. Svc. as Inspector Gen. 1991, Exceptional Svc. award 1994, Commd. Officer of Yr. 1995, Spl. Cert. Appreciation 1996, Mem. Distinction award Thomas W. Anthony chpt. 2000—02, Cen. East Region Chpt. Pres. of Yr. for State of Md. 2002, named Outstanding Mem. 2004, Outstanding Pres. of the Thomas W. Anthony chpt. 2004, Thomas W. Anthony Chptr. pres. of the Yr. 2005, Pres. of Yr. Thomas Anthony chpt. 2006, pres. of Yr. Thomas W. Anthony Chpt., Ctrl. East Recon 2008), Alumni Assn. Widener U., Andrews AFB Officers Club, KC (chmn. Pro-Life Father Rosensteel coun., Outstanding Leadership Pro-Life activities 1990—91, Outstanding Svc. award 1993—94, Honored Guest of Yr. 1996—97, Outstanding Cmty. award 2003, 2004, Achievement award of the Yr. 2005), Chester Lodge. Democrat. Achievements include 2 plaques in his name displayed at Columbia Union Coll., Takoma Park, Md., Widener U. (formerly Pa. Mil. Coll.), Chester. Home: Rock Creek Hills 9817 La Duke Dr Kensington MD 20895-3156 Office: USAF Aux CAP Mid East Region Hdqrs Office of Insp Gen 9817 La Duke Dr Kensington MD 20895-3156 Office Phone: 301-585-0081.

SURACI, PATRICK JOSEPH, clinical psychologist; b. Rochester, NY, May 31, 1936; s. Frank and Josephine Rosalie (Marino) S. PhD in Psychology, New. Sch. for Social Rsch., NYC, 1981. Cert. clin. psychologist, N.Y. Intern in clin. psychology Morrisania Neighborhood Family Care Ctr., Montefiore Hosp., NYC, 1979-80; staff psychologist N.Y. Police Dept., 1981-83; pvt. practice NYC, 1982—. Adj. lectr. N.Y. Inst. Tech., N.Y.C., 1975-78, John Jay Coll. Criminal Justice, CUNY, 1973-81; adj. asst. prof. dept. psychology Baruch Coll., CUNY, 1983-92; vol. Manhattan Ctr. for Living, 1994-96, Police Orgn. Providing Peer Assistance, 2001—. Author: Male Sexual Armor. Erotic Fantasies and Sexual Realities of the Cop on the Beat and the Man in the Street, 1992. Mem. The Nat. Arts Club. With U.S. Army, 1959-62. Mem. Actors Equity. Office Phone: 212-473-5966. Personal E-mail: drsuraci@aol.com.

SURANOVIC, STEVEN M., science educator; b. Chgo., Feb. 22, 1960; s. Richard L. and Bette Suranovic; m. Debra Fortman, May 1, 1982 (div.); children: Ben, Katelyn. BS in Math., U. Ill., Champaign, 1981; PhD in Economics, Cornell U., Ithaca, NY, 1988. Asst. prof. George Washington U., Washington, 1988—94, assoc. prof., 1994—. Fulbright fellow, Inst. Internat. Edn. China, 2002.

SURAWICZ, BORYS, physician, educator; b. Moscow, Feb. 11, 1917; came to U.S., 1951, naturalized, 1956; s. Josef and Mathilda (Solowieczyk) S.; m. Frida G. Van Klaveren, July 19, 1946; children: Christina M., Nina M., Tanya S., Serge J. MD, Stefan Batory U., Wilno, Poland, 1939. Mem. staffs hosps., Germany, Norway, 1945-49; staff De Goesbriand Meml. Hosp., Burlington, Vt., 1951-53, Phila. Gen. Hosp., 1953-55; instr. cardiology U. Pa., Phila., 1954-55; instr. U. Vt., Burlington, 1955-57, asst. prof. clin. and expt. medicine, 1957-62; chief div. cardiology U. Ky. Coll. Medicine, Lexington, 1962-81, assoc. prof. medicine, 1962-66, prof., 1966-81; prof. medicine Ind. U. Sch. Medicine, Indpls., 1981—. Cons. VA Hosp., Indpls. Editor: (with E.D. Pellegrino) Sudden Cardiac Death, 1964, (with C. Fisch) Digitalis, 1969; (with E. Prystowsky, C.P. Reddy) Tachycardias, 1985, Electrophysiologic Basis of ECG and Cardiac Arrhythmics, 1995, Chou's Electrocardiography in Clinical Practice, 2001, 2008, Doctors in Fiction Lessons from Literature, 2009; mem. editl. bds. profl. jours. Mem. AMA, ACP, Am. Heart Assn., Assn. Univ. Cardiologists (pres. 1978), Am. Coll. Cardiology (master; pres. 1979), Am. Physiol. Soc., Sigma Xi. Office Phone: 317-338-6227. Personal E-mail: bsurawic@yahoo.com.

SURBONE, ANTONELLA, medical oncologist, bioethics researcher; b. Turin, Italy, Aug. 11, 1957; d. Walter and Anita (Pugno) S.; 1 child, Francesco Akira. MD, U. Turin, 1982; postgrad., U. Milan, Italy, 1987-92. Fellow Nat. Cancer Inst., Milan, 1983-84, asst., 1988-91, vis. assoc. Bethesda, Md., 1985-87; attending Meml. Sloan-Kettering Cancer Ctr., NYC, 1990-91; vice chmn. dept. oncology Santa Chiara Hosp., Pisa, Italy, 1991-94; attending, mem. Meml. Sloan-Kettering Cancer Ctr., 1994—. Prof. Oncology and Ethics Italy, U.S., 1992—; investigator Nat. Cancer Inst., Bethesda, 1987—. Editor, author: Annals of the New York Acad. Scis., 1993, 97; editor: Critical Review in Oncology-Hematology; contbr. articles to profl. jours. Mem. UNICEF, Italy and U.S., 1985—. Fellow ACP; mem. AAAS, AMA, Italian Assn. for Med. Oncology (coord. 1993—), Am. Soc. Clin. Oncology, N.Y. Acad. Scis., Am. Assn. for Cancer Rsch., Multinat. Assn. for Supportive Care in Cancer, Internat. Soc. for Psycho-oncology, European Soc. for Med. Oncology, Amnesty Internat. Avocations: ballet dancing, philosophy.

SURENDRA, BASTI, ophthalmologist, educator; s. Gopal and Shantha Basti; m. Shobha Basti; children: Vinay Basti, Neha Basti. MBBS, Kasturba Med. Coll., Mangalore, 1987. Cert. in medicine II., 2004. Cons. L V Prasad Eye Inst., Hyderabad, Andhra Pradesh, India, 1992—97; assoc. prof. ophthalmology Northwestern U. Feinberg Sch. Medicine, Chicago, 2004—. Contbr. to numerous profl.jours. Recipient Achievement award, Am. Acad. of Ophthalmology, 2008, Beem Fisher award, Chgo. Ophthalmological Soc., 2003, C S Reshmi award, All India Ophthalmological Society, 1996, Best Paper of Session, Am. Soc of Cataract Refractive Surgery, 2004; grant, Nat. Eye Inst., 1996. Mem.: Am. Soc. Cataract and Refractive Surgery, Am. Acad. of Opthalmology (head, cornea splty. info. team, o.n.e.network 2005—). Avocations: tennis, music. Office: Northwestern Memorial Faculty Foundation 675 N St Clair Galter Suite 15-150 Chicago IL 60611 Business E-Mail: sbasti@northwestern.edu.

SURENDRAN, SANKAR, research scientist; s. Ponniah and Perumal (Valliammal) S.; m. Indira Surendran, Dec. 4, 1997, 1 child: Subrajit. BS, Madurai Kamaraj U., Tamil Nadu, 1984; MS, Mohanlal Sukhadia U., Udiapur, India, 1987, PhD, 1992. Postdoc. fellow U. Tex. Med. Br.,

1999—2004, instr., 2005—06. Vis. scientist Nat. Inst. Neurosci., Japan, 1998. Contbr. articles to profl. jours. Sci. and Tech. rsch. fellow, India, 1993; Indian Coun. Agrl. Rsch. sr. rsch. fellow, 1995. Fellow Assn. of Zoologists; mem. AAAS, Indian Assn. Biomed. Scientists, Indian Soc. for Vet. Immunology and Biotech., Internat. Brain Rsch. Orgn., Soc. for Devel. Biologists, Soc. Exptl. Biology and Medicine, Am. Soc. Naturalists, Molecular Biology Soc. Japan. Avocations: reading articles, chess, computer games. Office: Lsuhsc 1901 Perdido St New Orleans LA 70112-1393 Personal E-mail: sankar_surendran@yahoo.com.

SURESH, SUBRA, materials engineer, educator; B in Tech., Indian Inst. Tech., 1977; MS, Iowa State U., 1979; ScD, MIT, 1981. Asst. prof. engring. Brown U., 1983; R. P. Simmons Endowed Professorship MIT, 1993, head Dept. Materials Sci. and Engring., 2000—06, Ford Prof. of Engring., 2002—, dean Sch. Engring., 2007—. Clark B. Millikan Endowed Chair for visiting professorship Calif. Inst. Tech., Pasadena, 1999—2000. Author: Fatigue of Materials, 2nd ed., 1998; co-author (with A. Mortenson): Fundamentals of Functionally Graded Materials, Institute of Materials, 1998; co-author: (with L.B. Freund) Thin Film Materials: Stress, Surface Evolution and Failure, 2003; contbr. articles to profl. jours. Recipient Outstanding Scientific Accomplishment award, U.S. Dept. of Energy, 1982, Robert Lansing Hardy Gold medal, The Metallurgical Society of AIME, 1983, Champion H. Matthewson Gold medal, 1985, Presidential Young Investigator award, NSF, 1985—90, Ford Found. Rsch. award, 1985—87, Allied Signal Found. Rsch. award, 1989, Allied Signal Found. Merit award, 1990, Disting. Alumnus award, Indian Inst. of Technol., 1997, Acta Materialia Gold medal, 2006, European Materials medal, Fedn. European Materials Societies, 2007; named one of The Most "Highly Cited Researchers" in the World in the broad area of Materials Science, Inst. for Scientific Info., 2002. Fellow: TMS (Disting. Scientist/Engineer award 2001), ASME, ASM Internat., Am. Acad. Arts and Sciences, Am. Ceramic Society (Ross Coffin Purdy award 1992); mem.: US Nat. Acad. Engring., NAE, Materials Rsch. Society of India (hon.). Achievements include patents in field. Office: MIT Room 8-303 77 Massachusetts Ave Cambridge MA 02139

SURGUCHOV, ANDREI P., biochemist, ophthalmologist, researcher; m. Irina G. Surgucheva; 1 child, Alexei A. Surguchev. DS, PhD, Moscow State U. Head lab. molecular biology Cardiology Rsch. Ctr., Moscow, 1986—91; asst. prof. Baylor Coll. Medicine, Houston, 1992—95; sr. rschr. U. Utah, Salt Lake City, 1995—98; prof. Washington U., St. Louis, 1998—2001; prof., rsch. biologist VA Med. Ctr. and Kans. U. Med. Ctr., Kansas City, Mo., 2001—. Grantee, Alzheimer's Disease Rsch. Ctr., 1999, Reevs Found., 1999, NIH, 2001—04, VA, 2005. Mem.: Am. Acad. Neurology, Soc. Neurosci., Assn. Rsch. Vision and Ophthalmology. Office: VA Med Ctr 4801 Linwood Blvd Kansas City MO 64128 Business E-Mail: asurguchov@kumc.edu.

SURI, JASJIT S., research scientist; BS in Computer Engring., Regional Engring. Coll., Bhopal, India, 1988; MS, U. Ill., Chgo., 1991; PhD in Elec. Engring., U. Wash., 1997. Lectr. dept. electronic and computer engring. Regional Engring. Coll., Bhopal, 1988-89; rsch. asst. biomed. visualization dept. U. Ill., Chgo., 1989-90; rsch. programmer image sci. group IBM Palo Alto (Calif.) Sci. Ctr., summer 1990-91; rsch. assoc. U. Wash., Seattle, 1992-97; rsch. software engr. radiation treatment planning group Siemens Med. Sys., Calif., 1991-92; rsch. scientist Gammex Inc., Middleton, Wis., 1997, Sch. Medicine, U. Wis., Madison, 1997; rsch. scientist software devel. TSI, N.Y., 1997; rsch. staff scientist image guided surgery dept. Image Processing & Computer Graphics Picker Internat., Cleve., 1999—, Eigen, Robotic surgery, 2005—09. With Bharat Heavy Elec. Ltd., Bhopal, 1986, Larson & Tubro Ltd., Bombay, India, 1987, Nat. Info. Tech. Ltd., Bhopal, 1987; presenter in field; mem. Mayo Clinic Procs., Rochester, Minn.; rev. com. Internat. Conf. in Pattern Analysis and Applications, Plymouth, Eng., 1998. Author: (with others) Model Based Segmentation, 2d. rev. edit., 2000; mem. editl. bd. Radiology, Jour. Computer Assisted Tomography, Internat. Jour. Pattern Analysis and Applications, Internat. Conf. Pattern Analysis and Applications; contbr. over 300 articles. to profl. jours.; patentee in field. Scholar Regional Engring. Coll., 1985-88; fellow AIMBE. Mem. IEEE, Assn. Computing Machinery, Artificial Intelligence, Optical Engring. Soc. Am., Engring. in Medicine and Biology Soc. (mem. editl. bd.), Am. Assn. Artificial Int., USENIX-Tcl/Tk. Office: Eigen LLC 13366 Grass Valley Ave Grass Valley CA 95945 Home Phone: 916-797-4942; Office Phone: 916-749-5628. Personal E-mail: jsuri@comcast.net.

SURKIN, ELLIOT MARK, lawyer; b. Phila., Apr. 22, 1942; s. Hersh M. and Minnie (Shore) S.; m. Carol E. Foley, May 26, 1973; 1 child, Jennifer Dykema. AB, Princeton U., 1964; LLB, Harvard U., 1967. Bar: Mass. 1967. Assoc. Hill & Barlow, P.C., Boston, 1967-73, mem., 1973—2003, chmn. mgmt. com., 1988-92, chmn. real estate dept., 1996-2001; mng. ptnr. Boston DLA Piper, 2003—. Lectr. law Harvard U., 1975-96, MIT, Ctr. for Real Estate, 1996—. Chmn. bd. Boston Ctr. Arts, 1972-81, dir., mem. exec. com., 1981-83; trustee, mem. exec. com. Citi Performing Arts Ctr. (formerly Wang Ctr. for Performing Arts), Boston, 1980-2007, mem. fin. com., 1995-2005, vice chmn. bd., 1997-2005, dir. clk., mem. exec. com., 2007—; mem. New Eng. com. Legal Def. Fund NAACP, 1976-93; chmn. bd. Trustees of Reservations, 1997-2003, bd. dir., 2003-06, chmn. Chappaquiddick local com. 1986-97, trustee 1985—, mem. standing com. 1994-2003, mem. exec. com. 1996-2003; dir. Sheriff's Meadow Found., 1994-97. Mem. ABA, Am. Law Inst., Am. Coll. Real Estate Lawyers, Mass. Bar Assn., Boston Bar Assn., St. Botolph Club, Harvard Club of Boston, Edgartown Yacht Club, Country Club of Brookline, Mass., Kiawah Island Club. Office: DLA Piper 33 Arch St 26th Fl Boston MA 02110-1447 Office Phone: 617-406-6030. Office Fax: 617-406-6130. Business E-Mail: elliot.surkin@dlapiper.com.

SURLES, CAROL D., academic administrator; b. Pensacola, Fla., Oct. 7, 1946; d. Elza Allen and Versy Lee Smith; divorced; children: Lisa Surles, Philip Surles. BA, Fisk U., 1968; MA, Chapman Coll., 1971; PhD, U. Mich., 1978. Personnel rep. U. Mich., Ann Arbor, 1973-78, vice-chancellor-adminstrn. Flint, 1987-89; exec. asst. to pres., assoc. v.p. for human resources U. Ctrl. Fla., Orlando, 1978-87; v.p. acad. affairs Jackson State U., Miss., 1989-92; v.p. adminstrn. and bus. Calif. State U., Hayward, 1992-94; pres. Tex. Woman's U., Denton, 1994-99, Ea. Ill. U., Charleston, 1999—2001. Trustee Pub. Broadcasting Ch. 24, Orlando, 1985-87; bd. dirs. First State Bank, Denton, Tex., Tex.-N.Mex. Power Co., TNP-Enterprise. Recipient Outstanding Scholar's award Delta Tau Kappa, 1983. Mem. AAUW, Am. Assn. Colls. and Univs., Golden Key Honor Soc., Mortar Bd. Soc., Dallas Citizens' Coun., Dallas Women's Found., Coun. of Pres. (Austin, Tex.), Phi Kappa Phi, Alpha Kappa Alpha. Episcopal. Avocation: piano. Home: 1227 Parasol Pl Pensacola FL 32507

SURLES, RICHARD HURLBUT, JR., retired law librarian; b. Norfolk, Va., Mar. 28, 1943; s. Richard H. and Elda Florine (Belvin) S.; m. Judith Louise Coffin, May 29, 1964; children— Stephanie Anne, Richard H. BA, Tex. A&M U., 1963; JD, U.Houston, 1967; M.L.L., U.Wash., 1969. Bar: Colo. 1971. Asst. to law librarian U. Houston, 1966-68; asst. to law librarian King county Law Library, Seattle, 1968-69; dir. of law library, prof. law U. Denver, 1969-71, U. Tenn., Knoxville, 1971-76, U. Oreg., Eugene, 1976-81, U. Ill., Champaign, 1981—98; ret., 1998. Author: Legal Periodical Management Data, 1977 Mem. Am. Assn. Law Libraries Republican. Personal E-mail: Beretta@KTC.com.

SURMA, JOHN P., JR., metal products executive; b. Pitts., 1954; BS in Acctg., Pa. State U., 1976. CPA. Acct. Price Waterhouse, 1976—81, mgr., 1981—85, sr. mgr., 1985—87, ptnr., 1987—97; sr. v.p. fin. and acctg. Marathon Oil Co., 1997—98; pres. Speedway SuperAmerica LLC, 1998—2000; sr. v.p. supply and transp. Marathon Ashland Petroleum LLC, 2000, pres., 2001; asst to chmn. USX Corp., 2001; vice chmn., CFO US Steel Corp., 2002—03, pres., COO, 2003—04, pres., CEO, 2004—06, chmn., pres., CEO, 2006—. Exec. staff asst. to vice chmn. Fed Res. Bd. Pres. Exec. Exch. Program, 1983; bd. dirs. Mellon Fin. Corp., 2004—, Calgon Carbon Corp., 2000—, NAM; dir. & mem. exec. com. Internat. Iron & Steel Inst.; mem. Pa. Bus. Roundtable. Dir., mem. exec. com. Allegheny Conf. Cmty. Devel.; mem. bd. visitors U. Pitts. Katz Grad. Sch. Bus., Pa. State U. Smeal Coll. Bus. Mem.: AICPA, Pitts. Celebrity Hockey Team. Office: US Steel Corp 600 Grant St Pittsburgh PA 15219-2800 Office Phone: 412-433-1121.*

SURMAN, OWEN STANLEY, psychiatrist; b. Boston, Apr. 21, 1943; s. Aaron Harry and Edith Anne (Silver) S.; m. Lezlie Anne Humber, July 19, 1969 (dec. Nov. 5, 1994); children: Craig Bruce Hackett, Kathleen Bridget Lezlie; m. Amy Johnson, Oct. 1, 2000. BSc with honors, McGill U., 1964, MD, CM, 1968. Diplomate Am. Bd. Psychiatry and Neurology. Intern Balt. City Hosp., 1968—69; clin. fellow in medicine Johns Hopkins U., Balt., 1968—69; resident in psychiatry Mass. Gen. Hosp., Boston, 1969—72; clin. fellow in psychiatry Harvard Med. Sch., Boston, 1969—72; clin. asst. in psychiatry Mass. Gen. Hosp., Boston, 1975—76, asst. in psychiatry, 1977—80, asst. psychiatrist, 1980—86, assoc. psychiatrist, 1986—89, psychiatrist, 1990—; instr. psychiatry Harvard U. Med. Sch., Boston, 1975—80, asst. prof., 1980—90, assoc. prof., 1990—. Psychiat. cons. Boston Ctr. Heart Transplant, 1988-94; mem. ethics com. Mass. Ctr. Organ Transplantation, 1988—; mem. subcom. Human Studies, Mass. Gen. Hosp., 1982—, acting chmn., 1996-97, co-vice-chmn., 1999-2001, cons. transplant unit, 1975—, vice-chmn. xenotransplant adv. com., 1997-98, living related partial liver donor oversight com., 2000—; mem. Inst. for Study of Smoking Behavior and Policy, John F. Kennedy Sch. Govt., 1982-89; vis. prof. Tokyo U., 2001; mem. N.Y. State Com. on Quality Improvement in Living Liver Donation, 2002—. Contbr. articles and letters to profl. jours., chpts. to books, The Wrong Side of an Illness: A Dr.'s Love Story, 2008. Bd. dirs. Unitarian-Universalist Area Ch., Sherborn, Mass., 1983-86, 93-96; advancement officer troop 1 Boy Scouts Am., Sherborn, 1983-91. Lt. comdr. M.C., USNR, 1972-75. Grantee Milton Fund, 1969-70, Upjohn Corp., 1982-84, Burroughs Wellcome Co., 1984-85, Eli Lily Corp., 1989, 90-92. Fellow Am. Psychiat. Assn. (Disting.), Am. Acad. Psychosomatic Medicine (ethics com., awards com. 1994-97); mem. AAAS, Mass. Med. Soc., N.Y. Acad. Scis., Mass. ACLU, Libr. of Boston Athenaeum, Ford Hall Forum, New Eng. Poetry Club, Boston Authors Club. Avocation: creative writing. Office: Mass Gen Hosp Wang ACC 815 15 Parkman St Boston MA 02114 Office Phone: 617-724-0846. Business E-Mail: osurman@partners.org. E-mail: ossurman@yahoo.com.

SUROVELL, EDWARD DAVID, real estate company executive; b. Washington, Mar. 20, 1940; s. Samuel and Florence Deborah (Starfield) S.; m. Barbara Ann Bartelmes, Apr. 26, 1958 (div. Jan. 1974); children: David Alexander, Claire Katherine; m. Natalie A. Sallade, June 3, 1999. BA, Columbia U., 1962; postgrad., U. Mich., 1968-71. Lic. real estate broker, Mich. Copy editor Harcourt, Brace & World, Inc., NYC, 1963-65; editor Princeton (N.J.) U. Press, 1965-67, Scott, Foresman Co., Glenview, Ill., 1967-68, U. Mich., Ann Arbor, 1968-72; real estate agt. Fletcher & Klein, Inc., Ann Arbor, 1973-75; sales mgr. Charles Reinhart Co., Ann Arbor, 1975-82; pres. Edward Surovell Realtors, Ann Arbor, 1982—. Mem. Ann Arbor City Planning Commn., 1988-91, 95-98, Downtown Devel. Authority, Ann Arbor, 1991-95; trustee Ann Arbor Dist. Libr., 1996—, pres., 2004—06; trustee Libr. Mich. Found., 2005-; bd. dirs. Mich. Shakespeare Festival, 1999—, Chamber Music Am., 2004—; mem. Mich. Bd. Profl. Cmty. Planners, 1988-92. Mem. Nat. Assn. Realtors, Ann Arbor Area Bd. Realtors (pres. 1985, Realtor of Yr. 1990), Univ. Mus. Soc. (bd. dirs. 1992-98, trustee Mich. Ctr. for the Book 1998-2002), Mich. Hist. Commn. (bd. mem. 2005—, pres. 2007—), Mich. Hist. Found. (bd. dirs. 2007—), Hist. Soc. Mich. (trustee 1992—), Eastern Mich. U. Found. Bd. (bd. dirs. 2008-). Avocations: book collecting, arts philanthropy. Home: 1000 Forest Rd Ann Arbor MI 48105-1047 Office: Edward Surovell Realtors 1884 W Stadium Blvd Ann Arbor MI 48103-4504 Office Phone: 734-741-5599. Business E-Mail: esurovell@surovell.com.

SUROWIEC, ANDREW JULIUS, biophysicist, researcher; b. Lwów, Poland, Apr. 13, 1940; arrived in US, 1986; s. Jan Jakub and Maria (Knobloch) S.; m. Irene Regina Baranowski, Apr. 27, 1977; 1 child, Caroline Maria. Engr., Tech. U., Gliwice, Poland, 1962, MS, 1964; PhD, Silesian U., Katowice, Poland, 1972. Cert. elec. engring. Asst. prof. Silesien Sch. Medicine, Katowice, 1964-82; postdoctoral fellow Ctr. d'Etude L'Energie Nucleaire, Mol, Belgium, 1973-74; disting. vis. scientist U. Ottawa, Ont., Canada, 1983-87; asst. prof. Bowman U. Sch. Medicine, Winston-Salem, NC, 1987-88, U. So. Calif., LA, 1988-93; sr. physicist Centennial Med. Ctr., Nashville, 1993—2005. Peer reviewer: Cancer, Internat. Jour. Am. Cancer Soc., 1993; contbr. articles to Physics in Medicine and Biology, Bioelectromagnetics, IEEE Transactions Biomed., Internat. Jour. Hyperthermia, Biopolymers, Jour. Chem. Soc. Faraday Transactions. Grantee Nat. Sci. and Engring. Rsch. Coun., 1985. Fellow Radiation Rsch. Soc.; mem. Internat. Clin. Hyperthermia Soc., N.Y. Acad. Scis. Achievements include patent for recording system for rotating viscometer; finding of simulated materials for electromagnetic studies and cancer treatment; findings of dielectric spectroscopy of normal and cancer tissues; finding of dielectric and hydrodynamic properties of DNA. Home: 8209 Londonberry Rd Nashville TN 37221-4640 Home Phone: 615-673-0205. Personal E-mail: andsur@aol.com.

SURPRISE, JUANEE, chiropractor, nutrition consultant; b. Gary, Ind., Apr. 28, 1944; d. Glenn Mark and Willia Ross (Vasser) Surprise; m. Peter E. Coakley, Feb. 12, 1966 (div. Jan. 1976); children: Thaddeus, Mariah, Darius; m. Robert T.Howell, Feb. 24, 1984. RN, Phila. Gen. Hosp. Sch. Nursing, 1965; D of Chiropractic summa cum laude, Life Chiropractic Coll., Marietta, Ga., 1981. Diplomate Am. Acad. Pain Mgmt., Coll. Clin. Nutrition, Chiropractic Bd. Clin. Nutrition, Thompson tech., Nimmo receptor tonus tech.; cert. acupuncturist. Staff nurse Children's Hosp., Balt., 1966-67; charge nurse Melrose-Wakefield Hosp., Mass., 1967-68; hosp. adminstr. Animal Hosp. of Wakefield, Mass., 1967-79; chiropractor Chiropractic Clinic of Greenville, NC, 1982-84, Family Chiropractic Clinic, Denton, Tex., 1984—; dean Sch. Nutrition Quantum-Veritis Internat. Univ. Sys., 2003—09; dir. Ctr. Clin. Sci., Parker Coll. Chiropractic, Dallas, 1996-97, dir. diplomate and certification programs, 1997-2000. Postgrad. faculty Northwestern U. Health Scis., 2000—. Mem., chmn. Cmty. Planning Commn., North Reading, Mass., 1976-79; chmn. bldg. com. Immaculate Conception Ch., Denton, 1987-90, parish coun., 1990-92; v.p. Property Owners Assn., 2000-02. Fellow Am. Acad. Integrated Medicine; mem. Am. Assn. Pain Mgmt., Am. Chiropractic Assn., Am. Chiropractic Bd. on Nutrition (past pres.), Tex. Chiropractic Assn. (past chair), Chiropractic Bd. Nutrition (sec.), Pi Tau Delta. Republican. Roman Catholic. Avocation: health education. Office: Family Chiropactic Clinic 400 N Loop 288 Ste 120 Denton TX 76209 Office Phone: 940-566-0000.

SURRIDGE, STEPHEN ZEHRING, lawyer, writer; b. NYC, Dec. 12, 1940; s. Robert George and Florence Elizabeth (Zehring) S.; m. Helen Frances McKenna, Mar. 15, 1969; children: Christopher S., Jonathan R., Matthew W., Martha H. BA magna cum laude, Yale U., 1962; MBA (with distinction), JD, U. Mich., 1969. Bar: Wis. 1969, Mich. 1969. Assoc. Quarles & Brady, Milw., 1969-76, ptnr., 1977-89; freelance writer, tchr., 1990—. Author: (monograph) Seven Thunders of Revelation, 1985, Revelation Revisited, 1995, Fatima's 'Third Secret' is Future Warning, 2004. 1st lt. US Army, 1963—65. Mem. Phi Beta Kappa. Mem. Christian Ch. Home: 4480 N Ardmore Ave Milwaukee WI 53211-1418

SURRY, MELINDA OWEN, reading coach; d. Marvin Edward and Joyce Carole Owen; m. Daniel Wayne Surry. BS, Jacksonville State U., Ala., 1988; Ednl. Specialist, U. Ala., Tuscaloosa, 1996, MA, 1993. Nat. bd. cert. tchr. Nat. Bd. for Profl. Tchg. Stds., 2005, cert. adminstr. U. Ala., Tuscaloosa, 2000. Elem. sch. tchr. W. E. Striplin Elem., Gadsden, Ala., 1988—2001; asst. prin. Eichold-Mertz Elem., Mobile, Ala., 2001—03; coach Ala. Reading Initiative McDavid-Jones Elem., Citronelle, Ala., 2003—. Master coach Ala. Reading Initiative Ala. State Dept. Edn., Foley, 2006. Vol. Habitat for Humanity, Gadsden, Ala., 1999—2000; vol. Food for the Bereaved St. Dominic Cath. Ch., Mobile, 2002—06. Named Tchr. of Yr., Striplin Elem., 1991—92; grantee, Ala. Power, 1997—98. Mem.: ASCD, Ala. Network Nat. Bd. Cert. Tchrs., Nat. Coun. Tchrs. English, Internat. Reading Assn., Kappa Delta Pi, Pi Lambda Theta, Kappa Delta Epsilon. Roman Catholic. Avocations: travel, sporting events, concerts, gardening. Office: McDavid-Jones Elementary 16520 Highway 45 Citronelle AL 36522

SURWIT, RICHARD SAMUEL, psychology professor; b. Bklyn., Oct. 7, 1946; s. David and Ethel S.; m. Sandra E. Cummings, May 23, 1982; children: Daniel Alan, Sarah Jeanne. AB, Earlham Coll., 1968; PhD, McGill U., Montreal, Que., Can., 1972; postgrad., Harvard U., Boston. Postdoctoral fellow Harvard Med. Sch., 1972-74, instr., 1974-76, asst. prof., 1976-77; assoc. prof. psychiatry Duke U. Med. Ctr., Durham, NC, 1977-83, prof., 1980, 83—, vice chmn., 1993—; chief divsn. med. psychology Duke U., 1997, prof. psychology, 1991—; chmn. bd. dir. ZyCare Inc. (formerly Healthware Corp.), Chapel Hill, 1983—. Author: Fear: Learning to Cope, 1978, Behavioral Approaches to Cardiovascular Diseases, 1982, The Mind-Body Diabetes Revolution, 2004. Recipient rsch. devel. award NIMH, 1980, rsch. scientist award NIMH, 1993. Fellow APA, Soc. Behavioral Medicine (pres. 1994), Acad. Behavioral Medicine Rsch. Achievements include co-discovery in 1997, of UCP2, a novel gene related and diabetes and immunity; co-developer of the Diacare diabetes disease management system, Coag-Care anticoagulation management system; patents in field. Home: 3804 Sweeten Creek Rd Chapel Hill NC 27514-9706 Office: Duke U Med Ctr PO Box 3842 Durham NC 27702-3842 Business E-Mail: richard.surwit@duke.edu.

SURYANARAYANAN, SIDDHARTH, electrical engineer, educator; s. Trichur Subramanian Suryanarayanan and Geetha Viswanathan; m. Sujatha Kalyanam, Dec. 15, 2006. PhD, Ariz. State U., Tempe, 2004. Faculty rsch. assoc. Ariz. State U., 2004—05; asst. scholar scientist Fla. State U., Tallahassee, 2005—08; asst. prof. Colo. Sch. Mines, Golden, 2008—. Contbr. articles to profl. jours. Collaborative Rsch. grant, US Nat. Sci. Found., 2007—. Mem.: IEEE. Achievements include patents pending for system and methods for determining masking signals for empirical mode decomposition (EMD) and for demodulating intrinsic mode functions obtained from application fo EMD. Office: Colo Sch Mines 1610 Ill St Brown Hall 326 Golden CO 80401 Office Fax: 303-273-3602. Business E-Mail: ssuryana@mines.edu.

SUSANIN, TIMOTHY SCOTT, lawyer, health products executive; b. 1963; m. Barbara Susanin. BA in History with honors, Franklin & Marshall Coll., 1985; JD, Villanova U., 1988. Asst. US atty. (ea. dist.) Pa. US Dept. Justice, asst. US atty. DC; ptnr. Gibbons PC, 2001—08; v.p., chief counsel, dispute mgmt. WellCare Health Plans Inc., 2008, sr. v.p., gen. counsel, sec., 2009—. Assoc. ind. counsel US Senate Whitewater Investigation, 1998—2000. Worked US Navy Judge Adv. General's Corps, 1988—92. Office: WellCare Health Plans Inc 8735 Henderson Rd Tampa FL 33634 Office Phone: 813-290-6200. Office Fax: 813-262-2802.*

SUSIC, DINKO, physiologist; b. Ogulin, Croatia, Mar. 9, 1945; s. Dinka Vajs, Emanuel Vajs (Stepfather); m. Jovana Djokic, Nov. 19, 1977; 1 child, Ana. MD, Med. Sch., U. Belgrade, Serbia, 1969, PhD, 1976. Prof. physiology U. Belgrade, 1988—93; dir. Inst. Med. Rsch., 1990—93; staff scientist Ochsner Med. Found., New Orleans, 1993—. Contbr. chapters to books. Achievements include research in pathophysiology of hypertension. Office: Ochsner Clinic Found 1520 Jefferson Hwy New Orleans LA 70121 Office Fax: 504-842-5947. Personal E-mail: dinkosusic@yahoo.com. Business E-Mail: dsusic@ochsner.org.

SUSKIND, RONALD STEVEN, journalist, writer; b. Kingston, NY, Nov. 20, 1959; s. Walter Burton and Shirley Lila (Berman) Suskind; m. Cornelia Kennedy, May 4, 1986; children: Walter Kennedy, Harry Owen. BA in Govt. and Fgn. Affairs, U. Va., 1981; MS in Journalism, Columbia U., 1983. No. Va. field coord. Charles Robb for Gov., Alexandria, Va., 1981; campaign mgr. John Downey for U.S. Senate, New Haven, 1982; news asst., interim reporter The New York Times, 1983—85; city/state reporter The St. Petersburg Times, Fla., 1985—86; sr. editor Boston Bus. Mag., 1987—88, editor, 1988—90; staff reporter The Wall St. Jour., Boston, 1990—93, sr. nat. affairs writer Washington, 1993—2000, project reporter; contr. NY Times Mag., Esquire Mag. Instr. advanced journalism Harvard U., Cambridge, Mass., 1987—93; commentator Sta. WBUR, Boston, 1989—93. Author: (non-fiction) A Hope in the Unseen: An American Odyssey from the Inner City to the Ivy League, 1998, The Price of Loyalty: George W. Bush, the White House, and the Education of Paul O'Neill, 2004 (Investigative Reporter's and Editor's Book of Yr. award, 2004), The One Percent Doctrine: Deep Inside America's Pursuit of Its Enemies Since 9/11, 2006, The Way of the World: A Story of Truth and Hope in an Age of Extremism, 2008 (Publishers Weekly bestseller). Recipient Pulitzer Prize for feature writing, 1995, Benjamin Fine award, Nat. Assn. Secondary Sch. Prins., 1995, Nat. Writing award, Ball State U., 1995, Bus. Book of Yr. award, Forbes Mag., 2004. Office: c/o The Harry Walker Agency Inc 21st Fl 355 Lexington Ave New York NY 10017 Business E-Mail: ronsuskind@ronsuskind.com.

SUSLICK, KENNETH SANDERS, chemistry professor; b. Chgo., Sept. 16, 1952; s. Alvin and Edith Suslick. BS with honors, Calif. Inst. Tech., 1974; PhD, Stanford U., 1978. Rsch. and tchg. asst. Stanford (Calif.) U., 1974-78; chemist Lawrence Livermore (Calif.) Lab., 1974-75; asst. prof. U. Ill., Urbana, 1978-84, assoc. prof., 1984-88, prof. chemistry, 1988—; prof. Beckman Inst. for Advanced Sci. and Tech., Urbana, 1989-92; prof. materials sci. and engring. U. Ill., Urbana, 1993—, William H. and Janet Lycan prof. chemistry, 1997—2004, Marvin T. Schmidt prof. chemistry, 2004—; founder ChemSensing, Inc., 2001—. Dir. Sch. Chem. Scis., U. Ill., 2009, vis. fellow Balliol Coll., Inorganic Chemistry Lab., Oxford (Eng.) U., 1986; cons. in field. Editor: High Energy Processes in Organometallic Chemistry, 1987, Ultrasound: Its Chemical, Physical and Biological Effects, 1988, Comprehensive Supramolecular Chemistry, vol. 5, 1996; co-editor: Sonochemistry and Sonoluminescence, 1999; editl. bd. Ultrasonics, 1992-96, Ultrasonic Sonochemistry, 1996—, Accounts of Chemical Research, 2005—, Jour. Am. Chem. Soc., 2006-; patentee isotope separation by photochromatography, sonochemistry, protein microspheres, drug delivery, blood substitutes, sensors, smell-seeing, artificial olfaction; contbr. articles to profl. jours. Recipient Rsch. Career Devel. award NIH, 1985-90, NSF Spl. Creativity award 1992-94, Material Rsch. Soc. medal, 1994, R.S.C. Sir George Stokes medal 2007-08; fellow DuPont Found., 1979-80, Sloan Found., 1985-87; A.C.S. Sr. Cope scholar, 2004. Fellow AAAS, Am. Acoustical Soc. Royal Soc. Arts, Mfrs. and Commerce (Silver medal 1974), Materials Rsch. Soc. (medal 1994); mem. Am. Chem. Soc. (chmn. sect. 1987-89, Nobel Laureate Signature award 1994, Sr. Cope Scholar award 2004). Avocations: sculpting, music. Office: U Ill Dept Chemistry 600 S Mathews Ave Urbana IL 61801-3602 Business E-Mail: ksuslick@uiuc.edu.

SUSLOV, VLADIMIR MIKHAYLOVICH, physics professor, researcher; b. St. Petersburg, Russia, Mar. 14, 1947; m. Nina Vyacheslavovna Sorochinskaya. MS, Leningrad State U., St. Petersburg, 1976; PhD, St. Petersburg State U., 1987. Cert. theoretist Leningrad State U., 1976. Sr. rsch. assoc., math. & computational physics St. Petersburg State U., 1993—; rsch. prof. NC Ctrl. U., Durham, 1997—, tchr., 2002—. Recipient award, NCCU, 2007; Rsch. grant, Faddeev Equations Configuration Space, 2002—03. Mem.: Am. Phys. Soc. Office: NC Ctrl Univ 1891 Fayetteville St Durham NC 27707 Business E-Mail: vsuslov@nccu.edu.

SUSMAN, LOUIS B., United States Ambassador to the United Kingdom, retired investment banker; b. St. Louis, Nov. 19, 1937; m. Marjorie Susman; 2 children. AB, U. Mich., 1959; JD, Washington U., 1962. Sr. ptnr. Thompson & Mitchell Law Firm, St. Louis, 1981—89; with Salomon Bros., 1989—98; chmn. N.Am. customer com. Citibank's global relationship bank and Solomon Smith Barney's investment bank Citigroup Inc. (formerly Salomon Bros.), 1998—2000, vice chmn. global corp. and investment bank, 2000—09; US amb. to the United Kingdom US Dept. State, London, 2009—. Mem. adv. dir. D&K Healthcare Resources, Inc., 1998—. Mem. Dem. Nat. Com., 1972—82; nat. fin. chmn. John Kerry for Pres., 2003—04; co-chmn. fin. com. Bill Bradley for Pres., 1999—2000; Mo. fin. chmn. Richard Gephardt for Pres., 1998; bd. dirs. St. Louis Cardinals Baseball Team, 1975—89. Democrat. Office: US Embassy 8400 London Pl Washington DC 20521*

SUSMAN, MILLARD, geneticist, educator; b. St. Louis, Sept. 1, 1934; s. Albert and Patsy Ruth S.; m. Barbara Beth Fretwell, Aug. 18, 1957; children: Michael K., David L. AB, Washington U., St. Louis, 1956; PhD, Calif. Inst. Tech., 1962. With microbial genetics research unit Hammersmith Hosp., London, 1961-62; asst. prof. genetics U. Wis., Madison, 1962-66, assoc. prof., 1966-72, prof., 1972—2002, prof. emeritus, 2002—, chmn. lab. genetics, 1971-75, 77-86, assoc. dean med. sch., 1986-95, acting dean Sch. Allied Health Professions, 1988-90, vice dean med. sch., 1994-95, spl. advisor to the dean med. sch., 1995; dir. Ctr. for Biology Edn., Madison, 1996—2002. Phage course instr., Cold Spring Harbor, N.Y., 1965; v.p. scis., Wis. Acad. Scis., Arts and Letters, 2000—. Co-author: Life on Earth, 2d edit., 1978, Human Chromosomes: Structure, Behavior, Effects, 3d edit., 1992; contbr. articles to sci. jours. Mem Genetics Soc. Am., AAAS, Sigma Xi, Phi Beta Kappa, Phi Eta Sigma, Omicron Delta Kapp. Home: 2707 Colgate Rd Madison WI 53705-2234 Office: 2432 Genetics/Biotech Ctr Bldg Madison WI 53706 Office Phone: 608-263-5075. Business E-Mail: msusman@wisc.edu.

SUSMAN, MORTON LEE, lawyer; b. Aug. 6, 1934; m. Nina Meyers, May 1, 1958; 1 child, Mark Lee. BBA, So. Meth. U., 1956, JD, 1958. Bar: Tex. 1958, U.S. Dist. Ct. (so. dist.) Tex. 1961, U.S. Ct. Appeals (5th cir.) 1961, U.S. Supreme Ct. 1961, U.S. Ct. Appeals (11th cir.) 1981, DC 1988, U.S. Ct. Appeals (DC cir.) 1988, N.Y. 1990, Colo. 1996. Asst. U.S. atty., Houston, 1961-64; 1st asst. U.S. atty., 1965-66; U.S. atty., 1966-69; ptnr. Weil, Gotshal & Manges and predecessor firm Susman & Kessler, Houston, 1969-97; ret., 1998. Lt. USNR, 1958—61. Fellow: Am. Coll. Trial Lawyers, Tex. Bar Found.; mem.: FBA (dir., Younger Fed. Lawyer award 1968), ABA, Tex. Bar Assn. Democrat.

SUSMAN, SALLY S., pharmaceutical executive, former cosmetics executive; b. 1961; Student, London Sch. Econs.; BA, Conn. Coll., 1984. Legis. asst. US Senate Com. Commerce, Sci. & Transp., 1987—93; dep. asst. sec. for legis. & intergovernmental affairs US Dept. Commerce, 1993—95; with pub. rels. Am. Express Co., 1990—93, v.p. corp. affairs Europe London, 1995—97, v.p. worldwide corp. affairs & comm., 1997—2000; sr. v.p. global comm. The Estée Lauder Cos. Inc., NYC, 2000—05, exec. v.p. global comm., 2005—08; sr. v.p. worldwide comm., chief comm. officer Pfizer Inc., NYC, 2008—. Commr. NYC Commn. Women's Issues; bd. dirs. Nat. Partnership Women and Families, Parsons Sch. Design, Gina Gibney Dance; trustee Conn. Coll., New Sch. U. Mem.: Arthur W. Page Soc. Office: Pfizer Inc 235 E 42nd St New York NY 10017*

SUSMAN, STEPHEN DAILY, lawyer; b. Houston, Jan. 20, 1941; m. Ellen Spencer, 1999; children: Stacy Kuhn, Harry. BA magna cum laude, Yale U., 1962; JD with highest honors, U. Tex., 1965. Bar: Tex. 1965, US Supreme Ct. 1970, DC 1999, NY 2000, Colo. 2002. Law clk. to Hon. John R. Brown US Ct. Appeals (5th cir.), New Orleans, 1965-66; law clk. to Justice Hugo L. Black US Supreme Ct., Washington, 1966-67; ptnr. Fulbright & Jaworski LLP, Houston, 1966-75; spl. counsel to atty. gen. Mandell & Wright, P.C., Houston, 1975-80; founding ptnr. Susman Godfrey LLP, Houston, 1980—. Vis. prof. law U. Tex., Austin, 1975; chmn. adv. com. on discovery Tex. Supreme Ct. Contbr. articles to profl. jours. Mem. Nat. Coun. of Human Rights First; mem. bd. visitors Anderson U. Cancer Found.; mem. devel. bd. U. Tex. Health Sci. Ctr.; mem. Yale Art Gallery, Yale Devel. Found. Recipient ADL Jurisprudence award, 1995, Disting. Counselor award, State Bar Tex., 2005; named one of The Nation's Top Litigators, The Nat. Law Jour., 1989, 2006 Mem. ABA (antitrust sect., mem. coun. litig. sect., chmn. task force on fast track litig.), Houston Bar Assn., Dallas Bar Assn., DC Bar Assn., NY Bar Assn., Colo. Bar, State Bar Tex., Am. Law Inst., Assn. Trial Lawyers Am., Am. Bar Trial Advs., Houston Bar Assn., Southwestern Legal Found. Rsch. Fellows, Yale Club (Houston, NYC), Houston Trial Lawyers Assn. (dir.), Tex. Assn. Civil Trial and Appellate Specialists (former pres., dir.), Order of the Coif, Friars, Phi Delta Phi. Avocations: skiing, hiking. Office: Susman Godfrey LLP Ste 5100 1000 Louisiana St Houston TX 77002-5096 Home Phone: 713-522-1856; Office Phone: 713-653-7801. Office Fax: 713-654-6670. Business E-Mail: ssusman@susmangodfrey.com.

SUSSBERG, MILTON JOEL, marketing professional; b. New Rochelle, NY, Oct. 5, 1949; s. Darwin Ralph and Carol G Sussberg; m. Linda Aland, June 27, 1971; children: Matthew H, Jordan A. BBA with distinction, U. Wis., Madison, 1971; MBA, Columbia U., 1973. Car. mktg. & sales Pearl-Wick Corp., Long Island City, N.Y., 1973-76; v.p. M. Ware Assocs., NYC, 1976-79, Meteor/SKelly, Inc., Stamford, Conn., 1979-84; pres. Robot-Coupe Internat., Norwalk, Conn., 1984-86; CEO, founder Sussberg & Co., Inc., Chappaqua, NY, 1986—; owner Savannah (Ga.) Sand Gnats Baseball Club, 1991—2005. Adj. prof. mktg. Fordham U., Bronx, NY, 1996—99. Mem.: Phi Kappa Phi. Avocations: golf, skiing.

SUSSER, SAM L., oil industry and consumer products company executive; married; 3 children. BBA in Fin., U. Tex., Austin. With corp. fin. divsn. and mergers and acquisitions group Salomon Bros. Inc., NYC and Dallas, 1985—87; founder Susser Holdings Corp. (formerly Southguard Corp.), 1988, pres., CEO. Mem. adv. coun. Tex. A&M U. Coll. Bus., Corpus Christi; trustee Driscoll Found.; dir. Tex. State Aquarium, USS Lexington Mus. Office: Susser Holdings 4525 Ayers St Corpus Christi TX 78415-1401 Office Phone: 361-884-2463. Office Fax: 361-884-2494.

SUSSKIND, LAWRENCE ELLIOTT, urban planner, mediator, educator; b. NYC, Jan. 12, 1947; s. David J. and Marjorie H. (Friedman) S.; m. Miriam Mason, June 8, 1968 (div. Dec. 1982); m. Leslie Webster Tuttle, Dec. 12, 1982; children: Noah Gates, Lily Webster. AB in Sociology, Columbia U., 1968; M.C.P., MIT, 1970, PhD in Urban Planning, 1973. Asst. prof. urban and environ. planning MIT, Cambridge, 1971-74, assoc. prof., 1974-82, prof., 1982-95, Ford prof., 1995—, head dept., 1978-82, dir. MIT-Harvard Pub. Disputes Program, 1980—; exec. dir. program on negotiation Harvard Law Sch., 1984-87, visiting prof. law, 2001—. Founder Consensus Bldg. Inst., 1993—. Author: Paternalism, Conflict and Co-Production, 1983, Proposition 1 1/2; Its Impact on Massachusetts, 1983, Resolving Environmental Regulatory Disputes, 1983, Breaking the Impasse, 1987, Environmental Diplomacy, 1994, Reinventing Congress for the 21st Century, 1995, Dealing With an Angry Public, 1996, Consensus Building Handbook, 1999, Negotiating on Behalf of Others, 1999, Negotiating Environmental Agreements, 1999, Better Environmental Policy Studies, 2001, Transboundary Environmental Negotiation, 2002, Breaking Robert's Rules, 2006, Multiparty Negotiation, 2008, The Cure for Our Broken Political Process, 2008, Built-to-Win, 2009; sr. editor, founder Environ. Impact Assessment Rev., 1980-96; mem. editl. bd. Negotiation Jour., 1984—. Recipient Disting. Planning Educator award, Assn. Collegiate Sch. Planning, 2005, Global Environment award, Internat. Assn. Impact Assessment, 2007. Mem. Am. Inst. Cert. Planners, Assn. for Conflict Resolution. Jewish. Office: MIT 9-332 Cambridge MA 02139 Office Phone: 617-492-1414. Business E-Mail: susskind@mit.edu.

SUSSKIND, LEONARD, physicist, educator; BS, CCNY, 1962; PhD, Cornell U., 1965. NSF postdoc. fellow Cornell U., Ithaca, NY, 1965-66; asst. prof. physics Belfer Grad. Sch. Sci. Yeshiva U., NYC, 1966—68, assoc. prof., 1968—70, prof., 1970—79; prof. physics Stanford U., Stanford, Calif., 1979—, Felix Bloch prof. physics, 2000—. Visiting prof. Physics U. Tel Aviv 1971-72. Co-author (with James Lindesay): An Introduction To Black Holes, Information And The String Theory Revolution: The Holographic Universe, 2004; author: The Cosmic Landscape: String Theory and the Illusion of Intelligent Design, 2005, The Black Hole War: My Battle with Stephen Hawking to Make the World Safe for Quantum Mechanics, 2008. Recipient Pregel award 1975, J.J. Sakurai prize 1997; Loeb lectr. Harvard U. 1976. Mem. AAAS, Nat. Acad. Sci. Achievements include being credited as the father of String Theory; co-inventor, Holographic Principle. Office: Stanford Univ Dept Physics Varian Bldg 382 Via Pueblo Mall Rm 332 Stanford CA 94305-4060 Business E-Mail: susskind@stanford.edu.

SUSSKIND, TERESA GABRIEL, publishing executive; came to U.S., 1945; d. Aaron and Betty (Fox) Gabriel; m. Charles Susskind, May 1, 1945; children: Pamela Pettler, Peter Gabriel, Amanda. Student, U. London, 1938-40. Profl. libr. Calif. Inst. Tech., Pasadena, 1946-48, Yale U., New Haven, 1948-51, Stanford (Calif.) U., 1951-52, SRI Internat., Menlo Park, Calif., 1953; founder, pres. San Francisco Press, Inc., 1959—. Active in cultural affairs; bd. govs. San Francisco Symphony, 1986-89. With Women's Royal Naval Svc., 1943—45. Mem. Town and Gown Club (Berkeley, Calif.; pres. 1984-85). Office: 660 Spruce St Berkeley CA 94707-1730

SUSSMAN, BARRY, writer, demographer, editor; b. NYC, July 10, 1934; s. Samuel and Esther (Rosen) S.; m. Peggy Earhart, Jan. 20, 1962; children: Seena, Shari. BA, Bklyn. Coll., 1956. Reporter Herald Courier, Bristol, Va., 1960-62, mng. editor, 1962-65; editor Washington Post, 1965-69, city editor, 1970-73, spl. Watergate editor, 1972-74, pollster, pub. opinion analyst, 1975-87; co-founder, co-dir. Washington Post-ABC News poll, 1981-87; columnist Washington Post Nat. Weekly, 1983-87; mng. editor nat. affairs UPI, Washington, 1987; ind. pub. opinion analyst and pollster, 1988—. Adv. bd. Innovation news media cons. group, 1994—; editor Watchdog Project of the Nieman Found. for Journalism at Harvard U., 2003—. Author: The Great Coverup: Nixon and the Scandal of Watergate, 1974, What Americans Really Think, 1988, (with Lowell P. Weicker, Jr.) Maverick, 1995; editor: (with J.A. Giner) Innovations in Newspapers: The 1999 Global Report, 1999, The 2000 Global Report, 2000, The 2001 Global Report, 2001, 02, 03, 04. Recipient Drew Pearson award for Nat. Reporting, 1972, 1st Prize award Washington Newspaper Guild, 1973, Editor of Yr. award Washington Newspaper Guild, 1973. Mem. Am. Assn. for Pub. Opinion Rsch. (exec. coun. 1985-87), Am. Soc. Newspaper Editors. Jewish. Avocation: chess. Office Phone: 301-983-1287. Personal E-mail: bsussman@his.com. Business E-Mail: bsussman@niemanwatchdog.org.

SUSSMAN, BONNIE KAUFMAN, art dealer, interior designer, consultant; b. Mpls., Apr. 2, 1932; d. Samuel S. and Marie A. (Green) Kaufman; m. Ross A. Sussman, Dec. 19, 1954 (div. May 1985); children: David, Peter, Marianne. BS in Home Econs., U. Minn., 1954. Designer Sch. Design, Mpls., 1954-57; owner, designer Contemporary Interiors, Mpls., 1957-70; owner, dir. Peter M. David Gallery, Mpls., 1970—; food specialist Simek's, Inc., 1997—2003; realtor Ecklund Swedlund Homes, 2004—05. Mem. mem. Minn. Coun. Chs. Com. on Christian/Jewish Rels., 1991—, co-chair, 1994—; bd. dirs. Goldstein Gallery, U. Minn., 1994-95. Mem. Met. Art Dealers Assn. (pres. Mpls.-St. Paul chpt. 1976-85), Phi Upsilon Omicron, Omicron Nu. Home and Office: 3412 Oak Ridge Rd 109 Minnetonka MN 55305 Office Phone: 952-938-5192. Personal E-mail: bksussman@yahoo.com.

SUSSMAN, GERALD, publishing company executive; b. Balt., Feb. 21, 1934; s. Hyman Jacob and Sylvia (Applebaum) S.; m. Arla Ilene Ellison, Aug. 25, 1963; children: Daniel Leonard, Andrew Louis. BA, U. Md., 1956. Co-founder, prin. Investors Service of Md., Balt., 1956-60; coll. traveller Oxford U. Press, Inc., NYC, 1961-62, coll. sales mgr., 1962-69, gen. advt. mgr., 1970-73, v.p., dir. mktg., 1974-79, sr. v.p., dir. mktg., 1979-83, sr. v.p., dir. adminstrn. and planning, 1983—97; project mgr. Guide to the Sandia Mountains. V.p. Friends of Sandia Mountains. Mem. Assn. Am. Pubs. (chmn. mktg. com.), Assn. Am. Univ. Presses (chmn. mktg. com. 1980-81), Pubs. Advt. Club, Phi Alpha Theta. Home: 10424 City Lights Dr NE Albuquerque NM 87111-7536 Office: Oxford U Press Inc 198 Madison Ave Fl 9 New York NY 10016-4341 Personal E-mail: agsuss@comcast.net.

SUSSMAN, GERALD, social sciences educator; PhD, U. Hawaii, Honolulu, 1983. Asst. prof. Ohio U., Athens, 1984—87; assoc. prof. Emerson Coll., Boston, 1987—94; prof. Portland State U., Oreg., 1994—. Cons. UN, NYC, 1983—84. Author: (books) Global Electioneering: Campaign Consulting, Communications, and Corporate Financing, Communication, Technology and Politics in the Information Age; author: (editor) Global Productions: Labor in the Making of the Information Society, Transnational Communications: Wiring the Third World; author: Branding Democracy: The US Propaganda Regine and Post-Soviet Europe. KOPB cmty. adv. bd. mem. Oreg. Pub. Broadcasting, Portland. Recipient Henry Luce Rsch. Travel award, U. Mich., 1990, 1993. Business E-Mail: sussmang@pdx.edu.

SUSSMAN, HENRY STEPHEN, literature and language professor; b. Phila., Feb. 10, 1947; s. Albert and Rosalie Sussman; m. Carol Frances Jacobs; children: Tamara Jacobs, Nadia Rebecca Jacobs. BA, Brandeis U., Waltham, Mass., 1968; PhD, Johns Hopkins U., Balt., 1975. Julian Pk. prof., comparative lit. U. Buffalo, 2002—; vis. prof., germanic langs. & lits. Yale U., New Haven, 2003—. Author: (literary criticism) Idylls of the Wanderer, High Resolution: Critical Theory & the Problem of Literacy. Mem.: MLA, Kafka Soc. America (pres. 2004—08), Am. Comparative Lit. Assn., Inst. Critical Climate Change (program dir. 2006). Jewish. Avocations: writing, travel, photography, films, art. Office: Yale Univ Dept German Wlh 309 New Haven CT 06520 Office Fax: 203-432-8164.

SUSSMAN, JANET I., social sciences educator; b. NYC, Sept. 24, 1952; d. Joseph I. and Selma H. Sussman. BA, Douglas Coll., 1974. Pub. Harcourt Brace, NYC, 1974—76, Van Nostrand Reinhold, NYC, 1975—77, Sky & Telescope Mag., Cambridge, Mass., 1977—80, Wholistic Edn. & Svcs., Inc., Charlotte, NC, 1984—90, No. Star Dimensions, Charlotte, 1986—; pub., cons. Time Portal Pubs., Fairfield, Iowa, 1993—. Author: Timeshift: The Experience of Dimensional Change, 1996, The Reality of Time, 2005; musician: (CD) Bridges, 2002, Subtle Bodies, 2007. E-mail: timeport@lisco.com.

SUSSMAN, JOSEPH, engineering educator, researcher; BCE, City Coll. NY; MSCE, U. NH; PhD, MIT. Dir. ctr. transp. & logistics MIT, Cambridge, Mass., 1986—91, JR East prof. civil & environ. engring. & engring. systems. Author: (book) Introduction to Transportation Systems, 2000, Perspectives on Intelligent Transportation Systems, 2005. Recipient Effective Teaching award, MIT Dept. Civil & Environ. Engring., 1997, Tech. Leadership award, Move Mass. 2000, 1998, Disting. Contbn. award, Coun. Univ. Transp. Ctrs., 2003. Mem.: ASCE, Intelligent Transp. Systems Mass. (bd. dirs. 1996—2001, ann. Joseph M. Sussman Leadership award instituted 2002), Intelligent Transp. Systems Am. (bd. dirs. 1995—2001), Transp. Rsch. Bd. (exec. com. mem. 1991—98, exec. com. chmn. 1994, Roy W. Crum award for Disting. Rsch. 2002), Transp. Rsch. Forum, Am. Soc. Engring. Edn., Boston Soc. Civil Engrs. (life). Achievements include development of new methodology for regional strategic transportation planning, ReS/SITE (Regional Strategies for the Sustainable Intermodal Transportation Enterprise); Complex, Large-Scale, Integrated, Open Systems (CLIOS) process; worked extensively on intelligent transportation systems in the U.S., Bangkok, Western Europe and Japan. Office: Mass Inst Tech Bldg 1-163 77 Massachusetts Ave Cambridge MA 02139-4307 Office Phone: 317-253-4430. Business E-Mail: sussman@mit.edu.

SUSSMAN, LAUREEN GLICKLIN, retired elementary school educator; b. NYC, Mar. 21, 1953; d. Harry and Ruth (Goldstein) G.; m. Alan Neil Sussman, May 30, 1977; children: David Efrem, Adam Jacob, Daniel Joshua. BA, Bklyn. Coll., 1974; MS, MSc, Hofstra U., 1998. Cert. tchr. nursery-6, spl. edn. tchr. all grades. Sec. McCann-Erickson, Inc., NYC, 1974-75; adminstrv. asst., tour operator EasTours divsn. Fgn. Tours, NYC, 1975-78; adminstrv. asst. Alan N. Sussman, CPA, Woodmere, NY, 1978-96; kindergarten tchr. Hebrew Acad. Long Beach (N.Y.), 1996-97; jr. HS tchr. Torah Acad. Girls, Far Rockaway, NY, 1997—2007; ret., 2007. Participant Instrumental Enrichment/IRI Skylight, N.Y., 1995, 98, Dynamic Assessment project Touro Coll., N.Y.C., 1996; CSE parent rep., adv. Lawrence (N.Y.) Pub. Schs., 1992-97; trainer Life Tech., Cedarhurst, N.Y., 2004—05. Contbr. articles to profl. jours. Mem. Spl. Edn. PTA Lawrence Schs., 1986-2003, Sisterhood Congregation Bais Tefilah, 1990-2003; mem. Sisterhood Young Meadow Jewish Ctr., chair social action, Israel affairs, 1979-81; mem. adv. bd. Kulanu of the South Shore of Nassau County, 2000—; mem. Sisterhood Kehillah Aish Kodesh, Emunah of Am. Mem.: AMIT Women (Masada chpt.), OTSAR (founder Nassau County chpt. 1987—, nat. bd. dirs., pres. Nassau chpt. 1987—2002). Democrat. Avocations: Israeli and simcha dancing, walking, reading, needlepoint. Personal E-mail: lauglick@aol.com.

SUSSMAN, LEONARD RICHARD, foundation executive; b. NYC, Nov. 26, 1920; s. Jacob and Carrie (Marks) S.; m. Frances Rukeyser, May 9, 1942 (div. 1958); m. Marianne Rita Gutmann, May 28, 1958; children: Lynne, David William, Mark Jacob. AB, NYU, 1940; MS in Journalism, Columbia U., 1941. Copy editor N.Y. Morning Telegraph, news editor radio sta. WQXR, 1941; cable editor San Juan (P.R.) World Jour., also corr. Business Week mag., 1941-42; editor fgn. broadcast intelligence svc. FCC, 1942; press sec. to Gov. of P.R., 1942-43; dir. info. in N.Y. for Govt. of P.R., 1946-49; regional dir., then nat. exec. dir. Am. Coun. Judaism, 1949-66; cons. pub. affairs cons. Nationwide Ins. Cos. (and indsl. subs.), 1955-57; mem. editorial com. Coun. Liberal Chs., 1956-59; exec. dir. Freedom House, 1967-88, 96, sr. scholar in internat. communications, 1988—; evaluator Fulbright Program Bd. Fgn. Scholarships, 1990-92; exec. dir. Willkie Meml., 1970-88. Adj. prof. journalsim and mass comm. NYU, N.Y.C., 1990-99; adj. prof. Sch. for Internat. and Pub. Affairs, Columbia U., 2000-01; organizer, dir. Freedom House/Books USA, 1968-85; editor Freedom at Issue, bimonthly, 1970-81; mem. U.S. Dels. to Conf. World Communicaiton Yr./83, 1982-83; organizer acad. confs.; participant Internat. Conf. on Press Freedom, Venice, Italy, 1976, 77, Cairo, 1978, Talloires, 1981, 83, San Jose, Costa Rica, Johannnesburg, and Santiago Chile, 1987, others; panel competition in space Congl. Office Tech. Assessment, 1982-83. Author: American Press-Under Siege?, 1973, Mass News Media and The Third World Challenge, 1977, Glossary for International Communications: Warning of a Bloodless Dialect, 1983, Spanish version, 1987, Power, The Press and the Technology of Freedom: The Coming of Age of ISDN, 1990, The Culture of Freedom: The Small World of Fulbright Scholars, 1992, Good News Bad News, 1994, Can A Free Press Be Responsible? To Whom?, 1995, The Press: Pressed and Oppressed, 1995, The Journalist as Pariah: Press Freedom, 1996, The Global Airscape, 1996, Democracy, Yes; Press Freedom, Maybe, 1997, Press Law Epidemic: Press Freedom, 1997, Global Warning: Press Controls Fuel the Asian Debacle, 1998, The News of the Century, 1999, Censor Dot Gov: The Internet and Press Freedom, 2000, Press Freedom in Our Genes, A Human Need, 2001, How Free? The Web and the Press, 2001, Democracy's Advocate: The Story of Freedom House, 2002, The Press at War: Marksman and Target, 2002, repub. in Freedom and Responsibility Yearbook, 2001-2002, A Global Survey of Media Independence, 2003, A Passion for Freedom: My Encounters with Extraordinary People, 2004, Historic Aspects of Freedom of the Press and New World Information and Communication in the Encyclopedia of International Media and Communications, 2003, The Unesco Withdrawral Syndrome: Shoot The UN in Americans for UNESCO, 2005, Footnotes to Freedom: 8 Decades of Striving, 2007, Freedom House in Encyclopedia of Human Resource, 2009; editor: Three Years at the East-West Divide, 1983, Today's American: How Free?, 1986; contbr. chpts. to books, articles to profl. jours. and newspapers; project dir.: Big Story-How the American Press and Television Reported and Interpreted the Crisis of Tet-1968 in Vietnam and Washington, 1977; editor: textbook series, also quar. mag. Issues, 1953-66; mem. editl. bd. Polit. Comm. and Persuasion. Trustee Internat. Coun. on Future of Univ., 1973-84; bd. dirs. World Press Freedom Com., 1977—; chmn. Friends of Survey Mag. Charitable Trust, London, 1978-92; mem. U.S. Nat. Commn. for UNESCO, 1979-85, vice chmn., 1983-85; mem. U.S. dels. to internat. conf. on space, African Aid, UNESCO, London Info. Forum; mem. Internat. Freedom of Expression Exch., 1995-2003, mem. coun., 1997-99. 2001-2002. Decorated Legion of Merit; recipient Ann. First Amendment award N.Y. br. Soc. Profl. Journalists, 1988. 1st Bullen award World Press Freedom Com., 2008. Mem. Internat. Inst. Comm., Internat. Press Inst., Internat. Assn. Mass Comm. Rsch., Century Club. Home: 215 E 73d St New York NY 10021-3653 Office: 120 Wall St Fl 26 New York NY 10005-3904 Business E-Mail: sussman@freedomhouse.org.

SUSSMAN, MICHAEL DAVID, orthopedic surgeon; b. Balt., Feb. 20, 1943; s. Sidney and Leonora H. (Applebaum) S.; m. Nancy Evans Whiteley, Aug. 13, 1971; children: Evans (dec.), Tovah. AB, Washington and Lee U., 1963; MD, U. Md., Balt., 1967. Diplomate Am. Bd. Orthopaedic Surgery. Intern, jr. resident surgery Med. Coll. Va., Richmond, 1967-69; rsch. assoc. NIH, Bethesda, Md., 1969-71; resident orthopaedic surgery Johns Hopkins Hosp., Balt., 1971-75; fellow pediatric orthopaedic surgery Childrens Hosp. Med. Ctr., Boston, 1975-76; from asst. prof. to prof. dept. orthopaedic surgery and dept. pediat. U. Va., Charlottesville, 1976—92, head div. pediatric orthopaedics, 1985—92; chief med. staff Shriners Hosps. for Children, Portland, Oreg., 1992—99, staff surgeon, 1999—. Mem. rsch. adv. bd. Shrine Hosp., 1984—92; mem. grant rev. bd. Orthopaedic Rsch. Edn. Found., 1985—86. Mem. editl. bd.: Jour. Pediatric Orthopedics, Jour. Pediatric Orthopedics B, Childrens Orthopedics; contbr. articles to profl. jours., chapters to books. Bd. dirs. Bloomfield Inc., Ivy, Va., 1979-83, Dyslexia Ctr., Charlottesville, 1987-92. Served to lt. commdr. USPHS, 1969-71. Frank Ober fellow, 1976, Gianestras-Schmerge Traveling fellow, 1978. Fellow Am. Acad. Orthopaedic Surgery (com. on pediatric orthopaedics 1986—89), Am. Acad. Cerebral Palsy and Devel. Medicine (sci. program com. 1986—, membership com. 1986—, pres. 2001-03), Am. Acad. Pediat., Scoliosis Rsch. Soc.; mem. Pediatric Orthopaedic Soc. (Arthur H. Huene award, 2000). Democrat. Jewish. Office: Shriners Hospitals Children 3101 SW Sam Jackson Park Rd Portland OR 97239-5090 Office Phone: 503-221-3424. Office Fax: 503-221-3490. Business E-Mail: msussiman@shrinenet.org.

SUSSMAN, PAUL I., dentist; BA, Boston U.; DMD, Wash. U. Pvt. practice, Rochester, NY. Mem.: Dental Orgn. Conscious Sedation, Am. Dental Assn., NY State Dental Soc., Seventh Dist. Dental Soc., Monroe County Dental Soc., Am. Acad. Cosmetic Dentistry (founder, former pres. Upstate NY Chap., treas., com. mem. Give Back a Smile Program), Acad. Gen. Dentistry, Internat. Assn. Dental Rsch., Alpha Omega Dental Fraternity. Office: 324 Greece Ridge Center Dr Rochester NY 14626 Office Phone: 585-227-4390, 585-227-5215.

SUSSMAN, STEVEN YALE, preventive medicine and psychology educator; b. Chgo., Mar. 16, 1955; s. Max and Rosamond (Vishny) S.; m.; 3 children. BS, U. Ill., Champaign-Urbana, 1976; PhD, U. Ill., Chgo., 1984. Rsch. assoc. U. So. Calif., LA, 1984-86, asst. prof. rsch. Pasadena, 1986-88, asst. prof., 1988-92, assoc. prof. Inst. Health Promotion-Disease Prevention Rsch. LA, 1992—98, prof., 1999—. Mem. expert adv. group on spitting tobacco prevention and cessation Nat. Cancer Inst., Rockville, Md., 1992; editor, chpt. 4, 2010 Surgeon Gen.'s Report on Tobacco Use in Young People. Contbr. over 330 articles on health behavior research to profl. publs. Grantee Nat. Cancer Inst., 1987-92, Nat. Inst. Drug Abuse, 1992—, Tobacco Related Disease Rsch. Program, 1992-. Mem. Am. Acad. Health Behavior, Am. Psychol. Assn. Office: 1000 S Fremont Ave Ste 5108 Alhambra CA 91803 Office Phone: 626-457-6635. Business E-Mail: ssussma@usc.edu.

SUSSNA, EDWARD, economist, educator; b. Phila., Nov. 26, 1926; s. Louis and Manya (Prytzycka) Sussna; m. Sylvia Fishman, Mar. 8, 1953; children: Audrey Francine, Ellen Sondra. BA, Bklyn. Coll., 1950; MA, U. Ill., 1952, PhD, 1954. Instr. U. Ill., 1952-54; asst. prof. Lehigh U., 1956-57; prof. bus. adminstrn. and econs. U. Pitts., 1957—; dir. ctr. for exec. edn. Grad. Sch. Bus. U. Pitts., 1983-89; dir. mgmt. program for execs. Center for Econ. Edn., Grad. Sch. Bus., acad. dir. study program in Hong Kong and Peoples Republic China, spring 1989, 95; inaugural prof. MBA program Bratislava Sch. Econs., Slovakia, 1996. Vis. Fulbright prof. U. Tehran, Iran, adviser, 1972—73; cons. Bur. Budget, HEW, Dept. Transp., UN Indsl. Devel. Orgn., Bell Tel. Co., Alcoa, Westinghouse Corp., NSF, Pitts. Nat. Bank, Japanese Regional Bankers Assn., others; vis. prof. UCLA, 1970, Ecole Superieure des Scis. Economiques et Commerciales, Paris, 1976—77, U. E. Asia, Hong Kong, Macau, 1986; vis. scholar Internat. Inst. Mgmt., Berlin, 1982. Contbr. articles to profl. jours. With U.S. Mcht. Marine, 1944—47, with US Army, 1954—56. Ford Found. Fellowship Vis. prof., Harvard, 1960—61, Ford Found. Fellowship Guest scholar, Brookings Instn., 1962—63. Mem.: Strategic Mgmt. Inst., Am. Fin. Assn., Am. Econ. Assn., Omicron Delta, Beta Gamma Sigma. Home: 1538 S Negley Ave Pittsburgh PA 15217-1420 Personal E-mail: sussna@katz.pitt.edu.

SUSTER, SAUL, medical educator, director; s. Juan and Raquel Suster; m. Jenny Iturralde, Mar. 22, 1980; children: David, Dana. MD, Cath. U. Sch. Medicine, Guayaquil, Ecuador, 1976. Diplomate Am. Bd. Pathology, 1998. Prof. Ohio State Med. Ctr., Columbus, 1998—2007, vice-chairman, 1998—2007, dir. anatomic pathology, 1998—2007; prof. Med. Coll. Wis., Milw., 2007—, chmn., dept. pathology, 2007—. Editor-in-chief, annals diagnostic pathology Elsevier Pub. Co., Phila., 1997—. Editor (author): (textbook) Modern Surgical Pathology. Mem., bd. dir. and contbr. Found. Thymic Cancer Rsch., NYC, 2003—08. Recipient Joanne Vandenberge Hill award, U. Tex. Md. Anderson Cancer Ctr., 2003. Fellow: Coll. Am. Pathologists (surg. pathology com. 2006—08). Jewish. Achievements include research in study of cancer involving the chest cavity, including tumors of the lung, pleura and mediastinum. Avocations: travel, reading, music. Office: Med Coll Wis 9200 W WI Ave Milwaukee WI 53226 Business E-Mail: ssuster@mcw.edu.

SUTARIYA, VIJAYKUMAR BHADABHAI, medical educator; b. Saravaniya, Gujarat, India, May 1, 1979; s. Bhadabhai Chakubhai and Kantaben Mepabhai Sutariya; m. Minaxi Vijaykumar Pambhar. PhD, M.S. U. Baroda, Vadodara, Gujarat, 2007. Cert. pharmascist Pharmacy Coun. India, 2000. Postdoc. fellow Butler U., Indpls., 2007—08; asst. prof. Northeastern U. Coll. Pharmacy, Rootstown, Ohio, 2008—. Lectr. Indukaka Ipcowala Coll. Pharmacy, Vallabh Vidyanagar, Gujarat, 2006. Contbr. articles to rsch. papers (3rd Best prize, 2004). Mem.: Am. Assn. Pharm. Scientist. Home: 1925 Chippewa Pl Kent OH 44240 Office: Neoucom 4209 St Rt 44 Rootstown OH 44272-0095 Office Phone: 330-325-6485. Personal E-mail: vsutariya@yahoo.co.in. Business E-Mail: vsutariya@neoucom.edu.

SUTER, ROBERT EDUARD, emergency physician, educator; b. Decatur, Ill., Aug. 29, 1961; s. Robert Koester and Erika Ilse Suter; children: Robert E. Jr., Joseph E., Jennifer E. B, Washington U., 1982; M in Healthcare Adminstrn., Des Moines U., 1989, D of Osteopathy, 1989. Diplomate Am. Bd. Emergency Medicine. Chmn. Emergency Svcs. Eisenhower Army Med. Ctr., Ft. Stewart, Ga., 1993—95; chmn. emergency svcs. Providence Hosp. and Med. Ctrs., Detroit, 1995—97; regional med. dir. Questcare Med. Svcs., Dallas, 1997—2001; chmn. emergency dept. Spring Br. Med. Ctr., Houston, 2001—06; dir. emergency med. practice mgmt. and health policy U. Tex. Southwestern. Pres. Tex. Emergency Physicians; prof. Med. Coll. Ga., U. Tex. S.W. Bd. dirs. alumni assn. Des Moines U. Col. US Army, 1978—. Recipient Founders award, Continuing Edn. Coord. Bd. for EMS, 2004, Wackerle Founders award, Emergency Medicine Residents Assn., 1998, Alumnus of the Yr., Des Moines U., 2005, Order of IFEM, 2008. Fellow: Am. Coll. Osteopathic Emergency Physicians, Am. Coll. Emergency Physicians (pres. bd. dirs. 2001—06); mem.: Emergency Medicine Found. (chair 2006), Internat. Fed. Emergency Medicine (pres. 2006), Soc. for Academic Emergency Medicine. Cath. Mailing: P O Box 670785 Dallas TX 75367 Home: 5926 St Marks Cir Dallas TX 75230

SUTER, SCOTT HAMILTON, literature and language educator; b. Harrisonburg, Va., Oct. 30, 1962; s. Stanley Heatwole and Norma Hamilton Suter; m. Geraldine Poppke, June 10, 2007; children: Anna Elizabeth, Ian Hamilton. MA, U. NC, Chapel Hill; PhD, George Wash. U. Assoc. prof. english & Am. studies Bridgewater Coll., Va., 2002—. Author: (book) Shenandoah Valley Folklife; exhibitions include A Great Deal of Stone and Earthen Ware: The Rockingham County, Virginia, School of Folk Pottery. Sr. Fulbright scholarship, USIS, 1996—97.

SUTER, STEVEN E., veterinarian, educator; MS in Biochemistry, NY Med. Coll.; PhD in Molecular Biology, U. Pa., VMD. Diplomate oncology Am. Coll. Veterinary Internal Medicine. Intern U. Pa. Mathew J. Ryan Veterinary Teaching Hosp., 2000—01; resident U. Calif. Veterinary Med. Training Hosp., 2001—03, lectr in med. oncology, 2003—05; med. oncologist Sacramento Animal Med. Group, 2005; asst. prof. oncology NC State U. Coll. Veterinary Medicine, 2006—, med. dir. Canine Bone Marrow Transplant Unit. Office: 4700 Hillsborough St Raleigh NC 27606 Office Phone: 919-513-0813. Office Fax: 919-513-7301. E-mail: steven_suter@ncsu.edu.*

SUTERA, SALVATORE PHILIP, mechanical engineer, educator; b. Balt., Jan. 12, 1933; s. Philip and Ann (D'Amico) S.; m. Celia Ann Fielden, June 21, 1958; children: Marie-Anne, Annette Nicole, Michelle Cecile. BS in Mech. Engring, Johns Hopkins, 1954; postgrad., U. Paris, 1955-56; MS, Calif. Inst. Tech., 1955; PhD, Cal. Inst. Tech., 1960; MA (hon.), Brown U., 1965. Asst. prof. mech. engring. Brown U., Providence, 1960-65, asso. prof., 1965-68, exec. officer div. engring., 1966-68; prof. dept. mech. engring. Washington U., St. Louis, 1968-97, chmn. dept., 1968-82, 86-97, Spencer T. Olin prof. engring. and applied sci., 1997—2003, prof. biomed. engring., 1997—2003, sr. prof., 2003—07; interim dean Sch. Engring. Washington U., St. Louis, 2008—. Vis. prof. U. Paris VI, 1973. Assoc. editor: Jour. Biomech. Engring., 1993-97; mem. editorial bd. Circulation Rsch., 1975-82. Pres. St. Louis-Lyon Sister Cities, Inc., 2000—. Fulbright fellow Paris, 1955; recipient Nat. Marconi Sci. award UNICO, 1999. Fellow ASME, Am. Inst. of Med and Biol. Engring. (founding); mem. Biomed. Engring. Soc. (bd. dirs. 1997-2000), Internat. Soc. Biorheology, N.Am. Soc. Biorheology (pres.-elect 1986-89, pres. 1989-90), Am. Soc. Artificial Internal Organs, Am. Soc. Engring. Edn., AAAS (Lindbergh award St. Louis sect. 1988), AIAA, European Acad. Sci., Tau Beta Pi, Pi Tau Sigma. Republican. Roman Catholic. Achievements include research in fluid mechanics, heat transfer, blood flow, rheology of suspensions. Home: 830 S Meramec Ave Saint Louis MO 63105-2539 Office Phone: 314-935-6540. Business E-Mail: sps@wustl.edu.

SUTHERLAND, ALAN ROY, business educator; b. NYC, Jan. 15, 1944; s. Arthur Abbott and Margaret Louise S. BFA, Pratt Inst., Bklyn., 1964; MPA, NYU, 1969, PhD, 1984. Personnel dir. Manhattan Psychiat. Ctr., NYC, 1966-72; dep. dir. Rockland Children's Psychiat. Ctr., Orangeburg, NY, 1972-74, L.I. Devel. Ctr., Melville, NY, 1974-78, dir., 1978-80; program dir. Vols. Am., NYC, 1983-86; sr. staff officer Nat. Acad. Scis., Washington, 1986-88; dep. dir. U.S. Interagy. Coun. on Homeless, Washington, 1988-89; exec. dir. Travelers Aid Internat., Washington, 1989-91, AIDS Ctr. of Queens County, Rego Park, NY, 1992-96; chair dept. mgmt. studies Southeastern U., Washington, 1998-99. Prof. U. Md., College Park, 1998—, program dir. U. Md. U. Coll., Adelphi, Md., 1998-. Editor: Homlessness, Health and Human Service Needs. Recipient citation N.Y.C. Coun., 1986, Stanley J. Drazak Excellence in Tchg. award U. Md., 2004. Mem. ASPA, World Futurist Soc. Lutheran. Avocation: weightlifting. Office: Univ of Maryland 3501 University Blvd E Adelphi MD 20783-7998

SUTHERLAND, ALLAN C., engineering executive; BS in Accountancy, U. Ill., Urbana-Champaign, 1985; MS in Taxation, DePaul U., Chgo. Sr. mgr. tax dept. Ernst & Young; mgr. fed. tax Ill. Tool Works Inc. (ITW), Glenview, Ill., 1993, dir. worldwide tax planning, v.p. leasing and investments, 1996—98, sr. v.p. taxes and investments, 1998—. Mem. commerce coun. U. Ill. Coll. Bus. and Adminstrn.; mem. fin. adv. coun. DePaul U. Mem.: AICPA, Ill. CPA Soc., Execs.' Club Chgo. Office: Ill Tool Works 3600 W Lake Ave Glenview IL 60026-1215 Office Phone: 847-724-7500. Office Fax: 847-657-4572.*

SUTHERLAND, DAVID E.R., surgeon; married. BA, Augustana Coll., Rock Island, Ill., 1962; MD, U. Minn., Mpls., 1966, PhD, 1977. Dir. Diabetes Inst. Immunology and Transplantation, Mpls.; chair Golf Classic, Mpls., 2003—08; head, divsn. transplantation U. Minn., prof., dept. surgery, instr., dept. surgery, 1976—77, asst. prof., dept. surgery, 1977—80, assoc. prof., dept. surgery, 1980—86, John S. Najarian, physician, 2008—, surg. chair clin. transplantation, 2008—. Cons. Qualifying Exam. Com., 1987—90. With med. corps. US Army, 1968—70, 3rd Surg. Hosp., Vietnam. Recipient Resident Rsch. award, Assn. Academic Surgery, 1973, John J. Richard Macleod award, Childrens Diabetes Found. Denver, 1980, Outstanding Achievement award, Augustana Coll. Alumni Assn., 1981, Outstanding Achievement medal, City Lyon, 1984, Silver Needle award, Am. Diabetes Assn., 1984, David Rumbough award, Juvinille Diabetes Internat., 1990, Student Rsch. Forum First prize, U. Tex., Galveston, 1966, Allan T. H. Bluhm Meml. award, U. Minn., 1965, Rsch. award, 2008, Dorfman Jour. Paper award, Acad. Psychosomatic Medicine, 1993, Physician's Recognition award, AMA, 1974, 1977, 1980, 1980, 1983, 1986, 1989, 1992, 1993, 1995, Pioneer award, ASTS-Roche, 2007; named Internat. Lectr., Can. Diabetes Assn., 1992; fellow, All India Inst. Diabetes. Mem.: Greek Surg. Soc. (hon. mem. 1991), Soc. Med. Chirurgica Bononiensis, Med. and Surg. Soc. (Bologna). Office: Univ Minn Med Sch 420 Delaware St 11-200PWB MMC280 Minneapolis MN 55455 Office Fax: 612-624-7168. Business E-Mail: dsuther@umn.edu.

SUTHERLAND, DONALD, actor; b. St. John, NB, Can., July 17, 1935; m. Lois Hardwick, 1959 (div. 1966); m. Shirley Douglas, 1966. (div. 1970); children: Kiefer, Rachel; m. Francine Racette, 1972; children: Roeg, Rossif, Angus. Grad., U. Toronto, 1958. Actor: London Acad. Music and Dramatic Art, Perth Repertory Theatre, Scotland, also Nottingham, Chesterfield, Bronley, Sheffield, (plays) The Spoon River Anthology, The Male Animal, The Tempest, August for People (London debut), On a Clear Day You Can See Canterbury, The Shewing Up a Blanco Posnet, Enigma Variations, 2000, Ten Unknowns, 2001 (films) The World Ten Times Over, 1963, The Castle of the Living Dead, 1964, Dr. Terror's House of Horrors, 1965, Fanatic, 1965, The Bedford Incident, 1965, Promise Her Anything, 1966, The Dirty Dozen, 1967, Billion Dollar Brain, 1967, Oedipus the King, 1967, Sebastian, 1968, Interlude, 1968, Joanna, 1968, The Split, 1968, Start the Revolution Without Me, 1970, The Act of the Heart, 1970, M*A*S*H, 1970, Kelly's Heroes, 1970, Alex in Wonderland, 1970, Little Murders, 1971, Klute, 1971, Johnny Got His Gun, 1971, Lady Ice, 1973, Steelyard Blues, 1973, Don't Look Now, 1973, Alien Thunder, 1974, S*P*Y*S, 1974, The Day of the Locust, 1975, End of the Game, 1975, Fellini's Casanova, 1976, 1900, 1976, The Eagle Has Landed, 1976, The Kentucky Fried Chicken Movie, 1977, The Disappearance, 1977, Blood Relatives, 1978, Animal House, 1978, Invasion of the Body Snatchers, 1978, The Great Train Robbery, 1979, Murder by Decree, 1979, Bear Island, 1979, A Man, A Woman and a Bank, 1979, North China Commune (voice), 1980, Nothing Personal, 1980, Ordinary People, 1980, Eye of the Needle, 1981, Gas, 1981, The Disappearance, Blood Relative, Threshold, 1981, Max Dugan Returns, 1983, Crackers, 1984, Heaven Help Us, 1985, Revolution, 1985, The Wolf at the Door, 1986, The Trouble with Spies, 1987, The Rosary Murders, 1987, Apprentice to Murder, 1988, Lock Up, 1989, Lost Angels, 1989, A Dry White Season, 1989, Bethune: The Making of a Hero, 1990, Buster's Bedroom, 1991, Backdraft, 1991, JFK, 1991, Eminent Domain, 1991, Cerro Torre: Schrei aus Stein, 1991, Buffy the Vampire Slayer, 1992, The Setting Sun, 1992, Shadow of the Wolf, 1992, The Railway Station Man, 1992, Younger and Younger, 1993, Six Degrees of Separation, 1993, The Shadow Catcher (voice), 1993, Red Hot, 1993, Benefit of the Doubt, 1993, Punch, 1994, The Puppet Masters, 1994, Disclosure, 1994, Outbreak, 1995, Bethune: The Making of a Hero, 1990, FTA, A Time to Kill, 1996, Hollow Point, 1996, The Shadow Conspiracy, 1997, The Assignment, 1997, Fallen, 1997, Without Limits, 1998, Free Money, 1998, Toscano, 1999, CSS Hunley, 1999, Virus, 1999, Instinct, 1999, Panic, 2000, Space Cowboys, 2000, The Art of War, 2000, Threads of Hope (voice), 2000, Final Fantasy: The Spirit Within(voice), 2001, Da wan, 2001, Five Moons Plaza, 2003, The Italian Job, 2003, Baltic Storm, 2003, Cold Mountain, 2003, Aurora Borealis, 2005, Fierce People, 2005, Pride & Prejudice, 2005, Lord of War, 2005, An American Haunting, 2005, Land of the Blind, 2006, Ask the Dust, 2006, Beerfest, 2006, Sleepwalkers, 2007, Reign Over Me, 2007, Fool's Gold, 2008; (TV films) Terry-Thomas, 1963, Marching to the Sea, Hamlet at Elsinore, 1964, The Death of Bessie Smith, 1965, The American Civil War, 1965, The Sunshine Patriot, 1968, Bethune, 1977, The Saint, The Avengers, Gideon's Way, The Champions, The Winter of Our Discontent, 1984, Ordeal By Innocence, 1984, Quicksand: No Escape, 1992, The Lifeforce Experiment, 1994, Oldest Living Confederate Widow Tells All, 1994, Citizen X, 1995 (Emmy award), Natural Enemy, 1997, Behind the Mask, 1999, The Hunley, 1999, The Big Heist, 2001, Uprising, 2001, Path to War, 2002, Salem's Lot, 2004, Frankenstein, 2004; (TV mini series) A Farewell to Arms, 1966; (TV series) Commander in Chief, 2005-06, Dirty Sexy Money, 2007-09; guest appearance Suspense, 1963, Gideon's Way, 1965, The Saint, 1965, 1966, Man in a Suitcase, 1967, 1968, The Name of the Game, 1969, (voice) The Simpsons, 1996 and others; narrator The Poky Little Puppy's First Christmas, 1992; exec. prodr. Steelyard Blues, 1973. Decorated officier dans l'Ordre des Artes et des Lettres (France); officer Order of Can.

SUTHERLAND, DONALD SINCLAIR, musician, educator; b. Kearny, NJ, May 27, 1939; s. Sinclair Ross Watt and Helen Angus Sutherland; m. Phyllis May Brynjulson, June 7, 1968; children: David Alan, Kaaren Sutherland Lally. MusB, Syracuse U., NY, 1961, MusM, 1963. Faculty Sch. of Music Syracuse (N.Y.) U., 1963—71; coord. Organ Dept. Peabody Conservatory Johns Hopkins U., Balt., 1975—. Adj. faculty Hamilton Coll., Clinton, NY, 1970—71. Musician: Nat. Symphony Orch., Balt. (Md.) Symphony, City London (Eng.) Symphonia, Athenee Theatre, Queen Elizabeth Hall, Notre Dame, Stephandsdom, Westminster Abbey. Fund raiser Bethesda (Md.) Cares, 1984—99; dir. music ministries Bradley Hills Presbyn. Ch., Bethesda, Md., 1969—71; organist, choir master First Universalist Ch., Syracuse, 1962—71. Recipient Disting. Alumni award, Syracuse U., 1988, Excellance in Tchg. award, Johns Hopkins U., 1997, Recognition and Appreciation award, The County Exec. of Montgomery County, Md., 1999. Mem.: Am. Guild Organists (sec. 2002—, dean Syracuse (N.Y.) chpt. 1968—70, dean D.C. chpt. 1978—80), Pi Kappa Lambda. Home: 721 Tobacco Run Drive Bel Air MD 21015-1331 Office: Peabody Institute of the Johns Hopkins U 1 East Mount Vernon Place Baltimore MD 21202

SUTHERLAND, DONALD WOOD, retired cardiologist; b. Kansas City, Mo., July 29, 1932; s. Donald Redeker and Mary Frances (Wood) S.; m. Margaret Sutherland, Sept. 11, 1954 (div. 1994); children: Kathleen Sutherland, Ellen Baltus, Richard, Ann, Julia McMurchie; m. Roslyn Ruggiero Elms, Mar. 31, 1995. BA, Amherst Coll., 1953; MD, Harvard U., 1957. Intern, resident Mass. Gen. Hosp., Boston, 1957-60; fellow in cardiology U. Oreg., Portland, 1961-63; pvt. practice Portland, 1963—2006; ret. Assoc. clin. prof. medicine Oreg. Health Sci. U., Portland, 1967—; chief of staff St. Vincent Hosp. and Med. Ctr., Portland, 1971-72. Contbr. articles to profl. jours. Fellow Am. Heart Assn., Am. Coll. Cardiology (pres. Oreg. chpt. 1972); mem. Multnomah Athletic Club, North Pacific Soc. Internal Medicine (pres. 1985), Pacific Interurban Clin. Club (pres. 2000). Avocations: flying, scuba diving. Home: 4405 SW Council Crest Dr Portland OR 97239 Home Phone: 503-243-2535. Personal E-mail: dwscardio@comcast.net.

SUTHERLAND, KIEFER, actor; b. London, Eng., Dec. 21, 1966; s. Donald and Shirley Douglas S.; m. Camelia Kath, Sept. 12, 1987 (div. 1990); 1 child, Sarah Jude; m. Kelly Winn, June 29, 1996 (div. May 16, 2008)) Stage appearances include (theater) Throne of Straw, 1977; actor: (films) Max Dugan Returns, 1983, The Bay Boy, 1984 (Genie award nominee 1984), At Close Range, 1986, Crazy Moon, 1986, Stand By Me, 1986, The Lost Boys, 1987, The Killing Time, 1987, Promised Land, 1987, 1969, 1988, Bright Lights, Big City, 1988, Young Guns, 1988, Renegades, 1989, Chicago Joe and the Showgirl, 1990, Flashback, 1990, Flatliners, 1990, (voice only) The Nutcracker Prince, 1990, Young Guns II, 1990, Article 99, 1991, Twin Peaks: Fire Walk With Me, 1992, A Few Good Men, 1992, The Vanishing, 1993, The Three Musketeers, 1993, The Cowboy Way, 1994, Eye for an Eye, 1995, A Time to Kill, 1996, The Last Days of Frankie the Fly, 1996, Freeway, 1996, Truth or Consequences N.M, 1997, Dark City, 1997, Sweetheart of the Song Tra Bong, 1998, Ground Control, 1998, (voice) Dinosaur, 1998, The Breakup, 1998, Dark City, 1998, Woman Wanted, 1999, The Red Dove, 1999, Hearts and Bones, 1999, Beat, 2000, Picking Up the Pieces, 2000, Ring of Fire, 2000, The Royal Way, 2000, The Right Temptation, 2000, To End All Wars, 2001, Paradise Found, 2001, Desert Saints, 2002, Dead Heat, 2002, Behind the Red Door, 2002, Phone Booth, 2002, Taking Lives, 2004, Jiminy Glick in La La Wood, 2004, (voice) The Wild, 2006, The Sentinel, 2006, Mirrors, 2008, (voice) Monsters vs. Aliens, 2009; (TV movies) Trapped in Silence, 1986, Brotherhood of Justice, 1986, Last Light, 1993; (TV series) 24, 2001-(Best Performance by Actor in TV Series Drama Golden Globe award 2002, Best Performance by Actor in a Drama Series Golden Satellite award 2002, nominee Outstanding Lead Actor in Drama Series Emmy award 2002, Screen Actors Guild Award for best actor in a drama series, 2004, Screen Actors Guild Award for Outstanding Performance by a Male Actor in a Drama Series, 2006, Emmy Award for Outstanding Lead Actor in a Drama Series, 2006). Office: William Morris Agency attn: Steve Dontanville 151 El Camino Dr Beverly Hills CA 90212

SUTHERLAND, L(EWIS) FREDERICK, food products executive; b. Charleston, W.Va., Jan. 1, 1952; s. Lewis Frederick and Dorothy Louise (Droddy) S.; m. Barbara Hall Hoover, Aug. 24, 1974; children— Matthew, Mark BS, Duke U.; MBA, U. Pitts. V.p. Chase Mahattan Bank, NYC; asst. treas. Aramark Corp., Phila., 1980-83, treas., 1983-85, v.p., treas., 1985-87, v.p. corp. fin. and devel., 1987-91, sr. v.p., 1991-93, exec. v.p. and pres. Uniform Svcs. sector, 1993-96, exec. v.p., CFO, 1997—. Trustee WHYY, Phila.; bd. dirs. Consol. Edison. Trustee People's Light and Theatre Co. Named Treas. of Yr., Cash Flow mag., 1987. Office: Aramark Corp 1101 Market St Ste 45 Philadelphia PA 19107

SUTHERLAND, MARION IDA, music educator; b. Merrill, Wisc. d. Edwin August and Erna Martha Hackbarth; m. Robert D. Sutherland, Sept. 22, 1962. B in Music Edn., St. Louis Inst. of Music, 1954; M in Music, Eastman, 1956. Cert. music educator 1974. Music tchr. St. Louis Inst. Music, Clayton, Mo., 1956—58; acting vocal music dir. Carleton Coll., Northfield, Minn., 1959—60; choral music dir. Concordia Coll., River Forest, Ill., 1960—61, Chippewa Falls Mid. Sch., Wis., 1975—81; music educator St. Therese Sch., Schofield, Wis., 1981—85, St. Paul's Sch., Bloomer, Wis., 1988—93; piano and voice educator Wausau Conservatory Music, Wis., 1982—2003; ret., 2003. Mem. libr. bd. St. Louis Inst. Music, Clayton, 1956—58; cert. music adj. Wis. Music Festivals, 1982—2000, master music adj., 2000—. Author: (booklet) Life of P. Tschaikovsky, 1963. Full Yr. scholarship, Eastman, 1955—56. Mem.: Nat. Assn. of Tchrs. of Singing, Kiwanis Club (pianist 1948—50), Rotary Club (pianist 1945—50, Internat. Found. fellowship for European study 1958—59), Sigma Alpha Iota (life). Lutheran. Avocations: reading, walking, swimming, needlecrafts. Home: 2815 County Highway 1 Chippewa Falls WI 54729-2656 Home Phone: 715-627-7945; Office Phone: 715-627-7945.

SUTHERLAND, MARY (MARCUS), pianist, composer, conductor; d. T. Frederick Sholtis and Veronica Kuharik; m. Howard Lawrence Sutherland, Apr. 6, 1997; children: Jennifer, Nancy. MusB, DePaul U., 1967; MusM, U. Ky., 1978; postgrad., U. Memphis, 1978—80. Tchr., vocal coach, Memphis, 1978—94, St. Louis, 1994—; pianist Opera Memphis, Memphis Symphony Chorus, Regional Met. Opera, 1980—94; pianist, narrator, mgr. Sutherland Duo, St. Louis, 1992—; condr., art dir., mgr. devel. Midwest Chorale, St. Louis, 1994—2002; pianist Clayton H.S., St. Louis, 1997—; dir. music Overdue Theater Co., 2004—. Composer: (CD) Exaltation: Songs of Women-Sacred Solos, 2005, Premier: The Winter's Tale, A Musical Romance, 2005. Mentor, St. Louis, 1996—2002; Oasis tutor, 2002—06. Recipient Best Achievement in Musical Direction award, Arts for Life, 2004, 2008; grantee Pres.'s fellow, U. Memphis, 1978—80. Mem.: Am. Composers Forum, Pi Kappa Lambda. Democrat. Avocations: reading, travel, theater. Home: 3104 Longfellow Blvd Saint Louis MO 63104 Office: The Sutherland Duo 3104 Longfellow Blvd Saint Louis MO 63104 Personal E-mail: msongmaker@yahoo.com.

SUTHERLAND, ROXANE Y., communications educator; m. Dean A. Sutherland; children: Jason D., Jaret A. AA, Clark Coll., Vancouver, 1987; BA, Evergreen State Coll., Olympia, Wash., 1989; MS, Portland State U., Oreg., 1992. Comm. & humanities divsn. chair Clark Coll., 2000—, faculty pres., AHE, 2001—03. Bd. mem. Leadership Clark County, Vancouver, 2000—06, Clark County Sheriff's Adv. Com., Vancouver, 2003—. Bd. mem. Clark Coll. Alumni Assn., 2000—08; endowment Clark Coll. Found., 1998—2008. Mem.: Nat. Comm. Assn. Avocations: bicycling, boating. Office: Clark Coll 1933 Fort Vancouver Way Vancouver WA 98663 Business E-Mail: rsutherland@clark.edu.

SUTHERLAND, VANNA RAE, psychiatrist; BS in Biology, Tulane U., New Orleans, 1992, MD, 1996. Cert. Am. Bd. Psychiatry Neurology, 2001. Resident in psychiatry U. Calif., San Francisco, 1996—2000; adult psychiatrist City and County of San Francisco, 2000—03; adult psychiatrist student health ctr. Hastings Coll. Law, San Francisco, 2000—06; pvt. practice San Francisco, 2000—05, San Mateo, Calif., 2005—. Mem.: No. Calif. Psychiat. Soc., Am. Psychiat. Assn. Office: 205 E Third Ave Ste 207 San Mateo CA 94401 Office Phone: 650-375-8077.

SUTHERLIN, MICHAEL W., paper company executive; BSIE/BBA, Tex. Tech. Univ.; MBA, Univ. Tex., Austin. Mgmt. positions through pres. & COO Varco Internat. Inc., 1976—2003; pres., COO Joy Global Inc., Milw., 2003—06, pres., CEO, 2007—. Office: Joy Global Inc 100 E Wisconsin Ave Milwaukee WI 53202

SUTHERS, JOHN WILLIAM, state attorney general; b. Denver, Oct. 18, 1951; s. William Dupont and Marguerite A. (Ryan) S.; m. Janet Gill, May 21, 1976; children: Alison, Catherine. BA in Govt. magna cum laude, U. Notre Dame, 1974; JD, U. Colo., 1977. Bar: Colo. 1977, U.S. Dist. Ct. Colo. 1977, U.S. Ct. Appeals (10th cir.) 1979, U.S. Supreme Ct. 2003. Dep. dist. atty. 4th jud. dist. State of Colo., Colorado Springs, 1977-79, chief dep. dist. atty. 4th jud. dist., 1979-81, dist. atty. 4th jud. dist., 1989—97; assoc. Sparks, Dix, Enoch, Colorado Springs, 1981-82; ptnr. Sparks, Dix, Enoch, Suthers & Winslow, Colorado Springs, 1982-89; sr. counsel Sparks, Dix, Colorado Springs, 1997—99; exec. dir. Colo. Dept. Corrections, 1999—2001; US atty. dist. Colo. US Dept. Justice, 2001—05; atty. gen. State of Colo., Denver, 2005—. Mem. adv. bd. Sec. of State, Denver, 1983—89; Colo. commr. Uniform State Laws, 1993—97. Author: Fraud and Deceit, 1982, No Higher Calling, 2008. Pres., chmn. bd. dirs. Cmty. Corrections of Pikes Peak Region, Inc., 1984—87; bd. dirs. Crimestoppers, Inc., Colorado Springs, 1985—88; mem. exec. com. Colo. Dist. Atty.'s Coun., 1992—97, pres., 1994—95, treas., 1993; El Paso County Rep. Ctrl. com. Colorado Springs, 1985—2001; Colo. State Rep. Ctrl. com., 1989—2001. Zimmerman Found. scholar, 1970-74. Mem. Colo. Bar Assn. (com. chmn.), El Paso County Bar Assn. (pres. 1990-91), Notre Dame Colorado Springs (pres. 1983-84). Republican. Roman Catholic. Avocations: baseball cards, golf. Office: Colo Dept Law 1525 Sherman St 5th Fl Denver CO 80203 Office Phone: 303-866-3557. Business E-Mail: john.suthers@state.co.us.*

SUTIN, NORMAN, senior chemist emeritus, researcher; b. Ceres, Sept. 16, 1928; arrived in US, 1956, naturalized; s. Louis and Clara (Goldberg) S.; m. Bonita Sakowski, June 29, 1958; children: Lewis Anthony, Cara Ruth. B.Sc., U. Cape Town, S. Africa, 1948, M.Sc., 1950; PhD, Cambridge U., Eng., 1953. Research fellow Durham U. (Eng.), 1954-55; research assoc. Brookhaven Nat. Lab., Upton, NY, 1956-57, assoc. chemist, 1958-61, chemist, 1961-66, sr. chemist, 1966—2001, dept. chmn., 1988-95; ret., 2001; sr. chemist emeritus, 2007; affiliate Rockefeller U., NYC, 1958-62; vis. fellow Weizmann Inst., Rehovoth, Israel, 1965; vis. prof. SUNY-Stony Brook, 1968, Columbia U., NYC, 1968-69, Tel Aviv U., Israel, 1973-74, U. Calif.-Irvine, 1977, U. Tex. Austin, 1979; disting. prof. Rutgers U., 1999—2001. Editor: Comments on Inorganic Chemistry Jour., 1980-87; mem. editorial bd. Jour. Am. Chem. Soc., 1985-89, Inorganic Chem., 1986-89, Jour. Phys. Chem., 1987-92; contbr. articles to profl. jours. Mem. NAS, Am. Acad. Arts and Scis., Am. Chem. Soc. (recipient award for disting. svc. in advancement of inorganic chemistry 1983).

SUTLEY, NANCY HELEN, federal official; b. NYC, Apr. 20, 1962; BA in Govt., Cornell U., Ithaca, NY, 1984; MA in Pub. Policy, Harvard U. John F. Kennedy Sch. Govt., Cambridge, Mass. Spl. asst. to the adminstr. EPA, Washington, sr. policy advisor to the regional adminstr., region 9 San Francisco; dep. sec. for policy & intergovernmental rels. Calif. Environ. Protection Agy., 1999—2003; energy advisor to Gov. Gray Davis State of Calif., Sacramento, 1999—2003; dep. mayor, energy & environment City of L.A., 2005—09; chair, Council on Environmental Quality The White House, Washington, 2009—. Mem. Calif. State Water Resources Control Bd., 2003—05; bd. dirs. Met. Water Dist. So. Calif., 2005—09, chair, water planning and stewardship com., mem. exec. com., spl. com. on Bay-Delta, mem. comm. and legis. com., IRP steering com., 2005—09. Mem. lesbian, gay, bisexual and transgender steering com. Senator Hillary Clinton's Presdl. Campaign, 2008. Democrat. Office: The White House 1600 Pennsylvania Ave NW Washington DC 20500*

SUTMAN, FRANK XAVIER, retired academic administrator, chemist, writer, educator; b. Newark, Dec. 20, 1927; s. Joseph L. and Ella (Joyce) S.; m. Mabel Ranagan, Apr. 1, 1956; children: Frank J., Catherine J., Elizabeth A. AB, Montclair State U., 1949, MA, 1952; EdD, Columbia U., 1956. Tchr. pub. secondary schs., NJ, 1949-55; instr. chemistry Upsala Coll., 1953-55; asst. prof. Wm. Paterson Coll., 1955-57; chmn., assoc. prof. natural scis. Inter-Am. U. P.R., 1957-58; prof. gen. edn., chmn. SUNY, Buffalo, 1958-62; prof. sci. edn., chmn. dept. secondary edn., dir. Merit Bilingual Ctr., Sci. Lab. Stds. Temple U., Phila., 1962—82; dean edn. Fairleigh Dickinson U., 1982—89; vis. scientist Nat. Sci. Found., 1989—93; sr. scholar U. Miami, 1995—2000, Morgan State U., 1999—2002, Temple U., Phila, 1998—2004; sr. scholar, tchg. intern supr. Richard Stockton Coll., NJ, 2004—. Tech. rsch. staff Exxon Engring. & Rsch. Lab., Linden, N.J., 1955; vis. lectr. Rutgers U.; cons. India AID Project; vis. prof., scientist Hebrew U., Israel; exec. dir. curriculum devel. coun., Rowan U., N.J., 1993-2003; del. OAS Coun. Sci. Edn. and Culture, 1971; dir. Environ. Edn. Conf. Environ. Protection Svc., Jerusalem, 1975; cons. fed., state, local sch. dists.; dir. sci. tech. project Huazhong U., China, 1980-87; co-dir. chem. edn. conf. Tianjin Normal U., 1984. Author: Concepts in Chemistry, 1962, 2d edit., 1968, What Kind of Environment Will Our Children Have?, 1971, Chemistry in Today's Environment (U.S. and Israel), 1977, Educating Personnel for Bilingual Settings: Today and Beyond, 1979, Learning English Through Science, 1986, Improving Learning in Science and Basic Skills Among Diverse Student Populations, 1995, We Need a Better Understanding of Inquiry in Instruction, Harvard Edn. Letter, 2000, The Science Quest: Using Inquiry/Discovery to Enhance Student Learning, 2008, World Perspective on HIV & AIDS Epidemic, Haryana, India, 2008. Active Haddonfield (N.J.) Bd. Edn., 1976-79; v.p. alumni bd. Montclair State U., 1982-89; mem. chem. and tech. bd. Burlington County Coll., 1994—. Recipient Air Force Assn. award, 1968, N.J. Gov.'s Albert Einstein Edn. award, 1987, award Hispanic Congress of Pa., 1980, Alumni Citation Montclair State U., 1988. Fellow AAAS; mem. NSTA, Am. Chem. Soc., Am. Assn. Colls. Tchr. Edn. (chief instnl. rep. 1968-87), Nat. Assn. Rsch. Sci. Tchg. (pres.), N.J. Gov.'s Acad., Coun. Sci. Soc. Presidents, Sigma Xi, Phi Delta Kappa (pres. Temple U. chpt. 2000-02). Home: 311 W Royal Ave Linwood NJ 08221-1458 Personal E-mail: fmsutman@msn.com. *Personal success is achieved when one accepts the paradoxes of human activity and conflict, criticism and praise, and gives of one's self for worthy causes.*

SUTNICK, ALTON IVAN, internist, dean, educator, researcher, consultant; b. Trenton, NJ, July 6, 1928; s. Michael and Rose (Horwitz) S.; m. Mona Reidenberg, Aug. 17, 1958; children: Amy Sutnick Plotch, Gary Benjamin Sutnick. AB, U. Pa., 1950, MD, 1954; student in Biomed. Math., Drexel U., 1961—62; student in Biometrics, Temple U., 1969—70. Diplomate Am. Bd. Internal Medicine. Rotating intern Hosp. U. Pa., 1954—55, resident in anesthesiology, 1955—56, resident in medicine, 1956, USPHS postdoctoral research fellow, 1956—57; asst. instr. anesthesiology, then asst. instr. medicine U. Pa. Sch. Medicine, 1955—57; resident in medicine Wishard Meml. Hosp., Indpls., 1957—58, chief resident in medicine, 1960—61; resident instr. medicine Ind. U. Sch. Medicine, Indpls., 1957—58; USPHS postdoctoral research fellow Temple U. Hosp., 1961—63; instr., then assoc. in medicine Temple U. Sch. Medicine, 1962—65; mem. faculty U. Pa. Sch. Medicine, 1965—75, assoc. prof. medicine, 1971—75; clin. asst. physician Pa. Hosp., 1966—71; research physician, then assoc. dir. Inst. Cancer Research (now Fox Chase Cancer Ctr.), Phila., 1965—75; vis. prof. medicine Med. Coll. Pa., Phila., 1971—74; prof. medicine Drexel U. Coll. Medicine (formerly Med. Coll. Pa.), 1975—; dean Med. Coll. Pa., 1975—89, sr. v.p., 1976—89; v.p. Ednl. Commn. Fgn. Med. Grads, 1989—95; dir. internat. med. edn. Carelift Internat., 1997—2005. Dir. clin. devel. Am. Oncologic Hosp., Phila., 1973-75; attending physician Phila. VA Hosp., 1967-89, Allegheny U. Hosps., 1971-95; cons. in field; mem. U.S. nat. com. Internat. Union Against Cancer, 1969-72; mem. Nat. Conf. Cancer Prevention and Detection, 1973, Nat. Cancer Control Planning Conf., 1973; vice chmn. Gov. Pa. Task Force Cancer Control, 1974-76, chmn. com. cancer detection, 1974-76; mem. health rsch. adv. bd. Commonwealth of Pa., 1976-78; mem. diagnostic rsch. adv. group Nat. Cancer Inst., 1974-78; chmn. coord. com., comprehensive cancer ctr. program Fox Chase Cancer Ctr., U. Pa. Cancer Ctr., 1975; cons. WHO, Govt. of India, 1979, Govt. of Indonesia, 1980, entire S.E. Asia region, 1981, U. Zimbabwe, 1989, Minister of Health of Poland, 1992, Israel Sci. Coun., 1992, U. Autonoma de Guadalajara, Mex., 1993, Generalitat de Catalunya, Spain, 1993, Ministry of Health Russian Fedn., 1993, Inst. de Pos-Graduacae Medica Carlos Chagas, Brazil, 1993, Fondazione Smith Kline, Italy, 1995, Assn. Med. Schs. Europe, 1995-99, U. Jordan, 1995, U.S.-China Ednl. Inst., 1996, Georgian Postgrad. Med. Found., 1996, Instituto Universitario de Ciencias Biomedicas, Argentina, 1996, faculty of medicine U. Saarland, Germany, 1996, Ctr. for Med. Edn., Ben Gurion U., Israel, 1996-, Hungarian Nat. Health Ins. Fund, 1996, Carelift Internat., 1997, Intercoll., Cyprus, 1997, Open Soc. Inst., 1997-99, Aieti Med. Sch., Republic of Georgia, 1997-2001, Tartu U., Estonia, 1998-99, WHO European Office, 1998, Vilnius U. and Kaunas Med. U., Lithuania, 1998-99, U. Zagreb, Croatia, 1998-99, Larnaca Hosp., Cyprus, 1998, Netherlands and Russian med. schs., Temple U., Govt. of Republic of Georgia, others; faculty of medicine Moldova State Med. and Pharm. U., 1997-, vis. prof., 2002, prof. assoc., 2003-; rep. for internat. med. and health scis. edn. MCP Hahnemann U. of the Health Scis., 1996-99; adv. com. Open Soc. Inst. Muskie Fellowship Program, 1997, working group on implementation of presdl. policy on internat. edn., 2000, selection comm. Internat. Consortium for the Advancement of Med. Edn., 2001-05; mem. adv. com. internat. health program Temple U., 2005—. Author numerous articles in field.; asst. editor: Annals Internal Medicine, 1972-75; mem. editl. bd. other med. jours. Bd. dirs. Israel Cancer Rsch. Fund, 1975—95, Am. Assocs. for Democracy in Georgia, 2000—; nat. bd. dirs. Am. Assocs. Ben Gurion U., 1991—; bd. Internat. Med. Scholar Program, 1988—89, Sight Savers Internat., 1988—91; adv. commn. Internat. Participation Phila. '76, 1973—76; bd. dirs. Phila. Coun. Internat. Visitors, 1972—77; nat. bd. dirs. Phila. divsn. Am. Assocs. Ben Gurion U., 1986—, assoc. chair, 1993—95, 2000—. Capt. M.C. US Army, 1958—60. Recipient Torch of Learning award Am. Friends of Hebrew U., 1981, medal Ben Gurion U. of Negev, Israel, 1985, medal U. Cath. de Lille, France, 1987, medal U. Belgrade, Yugoslavia, 1988, Founder's award and medal Med. Coll. Pa., 1989, St. Thomas Aquinas award Santo Tomas U. Med. Alumni Assn., The Philippines, 1989, medal Kiev Med. Inst., Ukraine, 1991, Benjamin Albagli medal Inst. de Pos-Graduacao Medica Carlos Chagas, Brazil, 1993, shield Coll. Physicians and Surgeons, Pakistan, 1993, medal Ukrainian State Med. U., 1994, medal Universidad de Cantabria, Spain, 1999, medal Hadassah-Hebrew U. Dental Sch., 1999, Negev award Am. Assocs., Ben Gurion U., 2000. Fellow ACP (internat. adv. network), Coll. Physicians Phila. (censor 1977-86, councillor 1977-86); mem. AMA (Arnold and Marie Schwartz award in medicine, 1976, Dr. William Beaumont award), AAAS, Am. Fedn. Clin. Rsch. (pres. Temple U. chpt. 1964-65), Am. Assn. Cancer Rsch., Am. Soc. Clin. Oncology, Am. Dermatoglyphics Assn., Assn. Am. Cancer Insts., Assn. Am. Med. Colls., Northeast Consortium on Med. Edn. (treas. 1983-89, chmn. 1986-87), Coun. of Deans of Pvt. Free-Standing Med. Schs. (co-founder, nat. chmn. 1983-85), Pa. Coun. Deans (chmn. 1987-89), Am. Cancer Soc. (vice chmn. service com. Phila. div. 1974-76, bd. dirs. 1974-80, chmn. awards com. 1976), Am. Lung Assn., Am. Heart Assn., NAFSA-Assn. Internat. Educators, Pan Am. Med. Assn., Phila. Coop. Cancer Assn., N.Y. Acad. Scis., Pa. Heart Assn., Heart Assn. Southeastern Pa., Pa. Med. Soc., Phila. County Med. Soc. (chmn. com. internat. med. affairs 1964-72, Strittmatter award 2006), Pa. Lung Assn., Phila. Assn. for Clin. Trials (bd. dirs. 1980-81), Health Systems Agy. Southeastern Pa. (gov. bd., exec. com. 1983-87, sec. 1985-87), Am. Assn. Ben Gurion U. (bd. dirs. 1986—), Soc. des Medecins Militaires Français, Assn. Med. Edn. in Europe, Soc. Española de Educacion Medica, Internat. Med. Sch. Affiliates Consortium (co-founder, vice chmn. 1985-87), Phi Beta Kappa, Sigma Xi, Alpha Omega Alpha (councillor 1963-65). Achievements include discovery of association of hepatitis B surface antigen with hepatitis; performed 1st studies of pulmonary surfactant in adult human lung disease; developed cancer screening system based on risk status; pioneer in describing non-A non-B hepatitis C, pioneer in showing relationship of body iron stores to cancer susceptibility and life expectancy; organized first symposium on problems of foreign medical graduates; coined word "ergasteric" for lab.-contracted disease; responsible for advances in assessment of clinical competence; demonstrated validity of clinical competence assessment using standardized patients; demonstrated reliability of clinical competence assessment across six different languages and cultures; medical education advisor to over 50 countries, with a measurable impact on health care delivery system. Personal E-mail: altonsutnick@msn.com.

SUTOO, DEN'ETSU, neuroscientist, researcher; b. Tendo, Yamagata, Japan, May 29, 1952; s. Den'ichiro and Kikue (Shinohara) S.; m. Sumi Inoue, Mar. 20, 1976; children: Lemi, Ken'etsu. B of Hygienic Sci., Kitasato U., Tokyo, 1975, PhD, 1989. Rschr. U. Tsukuba, Japan, 1975—, expert officer, 1990—92, head officer, 1992—. Cons. Tosoh Corp., Tokyo, 1977-90, Jeol Ltd., Tokyo, 1978-97, Nikon Corp., Tokyo, 1983—, Taisho Pharm. Co. Ltd., Tokyo, 1996—, Yamato Sci. Co., Ltd., Tokyo, 1999—. Author: The Vulnerable Brain and Environmental Risks, 1994, Trends in Exercise and Health Research, 2005; contbr. articles to profl. jours. Fellow Japanese Sci. Jamboree, Tokyo, 1970—; exec. mem. Tsukuba Children's Art Contest, Tokyo, 1984—; adviser preservation of stickleback, Yamagata, Japan, 1998—; spl. judge Intel Internat. Sci. and Engring. Fair, Phoenix, 2005. Recipient Spl. award U.S. Patent Office, 1969, Prime Min. award Japanese Govt., 1969; Grant award Toyota Found., Tokyo, 1987, Yamaha Music Found., Tokyo, 2005. Fellow Japanese Pharmacological Soc., Japanese Finalist Club; mem. NY Acad. Scis. Buddhist. Avocations: classical music, bicycling, photography, gardening, fishing. Home: 3-22-13 Namiki Tsukuba 305-0044 Japan Office: U Tsukuba Inst Med Sci Tsukuba 305-8575 Japan Home Phone: 81-29-851-0125; Office Phone: 81-29-853-3113. Office Fax: 81-29-854-9817. Personal E-mail: den@sutoo.jp.

SUTPHEN, JAMES L., pediatrician; b. Aug. 9, 1946; MD, Columbia U., NYC, 1972. Cert. in pediat., in pediatric gastroenterology 2005. Residency in pediat. Johns Hopkins U., Balt.; fellowship in clin. nutrition, pediatric gastroenterology Harvard Med. Sch. Boston Children's Hosp.; prof., dept. pediat. U. Va. Health Sys., Charlottesville, head, divsn. pediatric gastroenterology, nutrition. Contbr. articles to profl. jours. Named to Best Doctors in America, Best Doctors, Inc. Office: Univ Va Health Sys Divsn Pediat Gastroenterology Nutrition PO Box 800386 Charlottesville VA 22908-0386 Office Phone: 434-924-2457. Office Fax: 434-924-8798. Business E-Mail: jls5z@virginia.edu.

SUTPHEN, MONA K., federal official; b. 1967; m. Clyde Williams, 2001; 2 children. BA in Internat. Rels., Mount Holyoke Coll., South Hadley, Mass., 1989; MSc in Internat. Polit. Economy, London Sch. Econs. Various positions as fgn. svc. officer US Dept. State, 1991—2000, including office of High Rep. Sarajevo, then Human Rights Bur., consular, polit. officer US Embassy Bangkok, spl. asst. to nat. security adv. Samuel R. Berger, adv., dep. chief of staff to amb. Bill Richardson NYC; dir. strategic planning/policy Currenex, Inc., NYC; v.p., mng. dir. Stonebridge Internat. LLC, Washington, 2001—09; dep. chief of staff for policy to Pres. The White House, Washington, 2009—.

Mng. dir. Civitas Group llc, Washington; bd. dirs. Internat. Human Rights Law Grp., Washington. Co-author: The Next American Century: How the US Can Thrive as Other Powers Rise, 2008. Mem. steering com. Ron Brown Scholar Prog., Charlottesville, Va. Mem.: Women's Fgn. Policy Grp., Coun. Fgn. Rels. Democrat. Office: The White House Dep Chief of Staff 1600 Pennsylvania Ave NW Washington DC 20500*

SUTPHIN, BRIAN, information technology executive; Grad. in Econs., U. Wis., Madison; law degree, Stanford U., Calif. Pvt. practice atty.; various sr. mgmt. positions in mktg., bus. devel. and engring. Sun Microsystems, Inc., Santa Clara, Calif., v.p. bus. devel., exec. v.p. corp. devel. & alliances, mem. exec. mgmt. group. Office: Sun Microsystems Inc 4150 Network Cir Santa Clara CA 95054 Office Phone: 650-960-1300.

SUTTELL, PAUL ALLYN, state supreme court justice; b. Providence, Jan. 10, 1949; s. Allyn Kingsley and Pauline Louise (Stickney) S.; m. Mary Wood Cissel, May 24, 1980; children: William Theodore Stickney, Grace Wood. BA, Northwestern U., Evanston, Ill., 1971; JD, Suffolk U. Sch. Law, Boston, 1976. Assoc. Beals & DiFiore, Providence, 1977-90; legal counsel RI Home Minority Leader, 1979-82; mem. RI Ho. of Reps., Providence, 1983—90; assoc. justice RI Family Ct., Providence, 1990—2003; justice RI Supreme Ct., 2003—, chief justice, 2009—. Mem. Little Compton (RI) Rep. Town Commn., 1981-90; del. RI Rep. State Com., 1981-90, Rep. Nat. Conv., 1988; bd. dirs. Friends of Sakonnet Lighthouse; bd. dirs. Little Compton Hist. Soc., chmn., 1999—; mem. bd. deacons Little Compton Congregational Ch., 1995-99, chair, 1997-99. Mem. Sakonnet Preservation Assn., R.I. Agrl. Lands Preservation Com. Office: RI Supreme Ct Frank Licht Judicial Complex 250 Benefit St Providence RI 02903 E-mail: psuttell@counts.state.ri.us.*

SUTTER, BRENT COLIN, professional hockey coach, retired professional hockey player; b. Viking, Alta., Can., June 10, 1962; m. Connie Sutter; children: Merrick, Brandon, Brooke. Center NY Islanders, 1981—91, capt., 1987—92; center Chgo. Blackhawks, 1991—98; owner, pres. Red Deer Rebels (Western Hockey League), 1999—, gov., gen. mgr., head coach, 1999—2007; head coach NJ Devils, 2007—09, Calgary Flames, 2009—. Head coach Can. Nat. Jr. Team, 2005—07. Named to NHL All-Star Game, 1985. Achievements include being a member of Stanley Cup Champion New York Islanders, 1982, 1983. Office: Calgary Flames PO Box 1540 Stn M Calgary AB T2P 3B9 Canada also: Red Deer Rebels 4847C - 19th St Red Deer AB T4R 2N7 Canada E-mail: bsutter@reddeerrebels.com.

SUTTER, DARRYL JOHN, professional sports team executive, former professional hockey coach; b. Viking, Alta., Can., Aug. 19, 1958; m. Wanda Sutter; children: Brett, Christopher, Jessie. Player Chgo. Blackhawks, 1980-86, asst. coach, 1987-88, assoc. coach, 1991-92, head coach, 1992-95, cons., 1995-97; head coach San Jose Sharks, 1997—2002, Calgary Flames, 2002—06, gen. mgr., 2003—. Recipient Dudley Red Garrett Meml. Trophy, 1980, Commrs. Trophy, 1990; named to Alberta Sports Hall of Fame, 2000. Office: Calgary Flames PO Box 1540 Stn M Calgary AB Canada T2P 3B9

SUTTER, DIANE, television executive; b. Dec. 9, 1950; d. George Edward and Dorothy Ann (Deckard) S.; m. James M. Stuart, Sept. 21, 1974 (div. Nov. 1984). BA in Polit. Sci., Allegheny Coll., 1972; MS in Pub. Rels., Am. U., 1974. Pub. rels. Congressman William S. Conover, 27th Dist. Pa., Washington, 1972; press sec. Congressman Robert P. Hanrahan, 3d Dist. Ill., Washington, 1973; dir. comm. D.C. Bicentennial, Washington, 1975; acct. exec. Sta. WPEZ, Pitts., 1975-78, sales mgr., 1978-79; v.p., mgr. Sta. WTKN/WWSW, Pitts., 1979-83; corp. v.p., gen. mgr. Sta. WTVQ-TV (ABC affiliate), Lexington, Ky., 1989-91; exec. v.p. ops. Shamrock Broadcasting, Inc., Burbank, Calif., 1991-93; pres. Shamrock TV, Burbank, Calif., 1994-95; pres., CEO Shooting Star Broadcasting, Sherman Oaks, Calif., 1996—. Chmn. ABC Talk Radio Affiliate Bd., 1983-87. Contbr. articles to newspapers. Mem. adv. bd. Women's Polit. Caucus, Allegheny County, Pitts., 1979-89; bd. dirs. Support Ctr. Cancer, 1988-90, United Way Bluegrass, 1990-91, Jr. Achievement Bluegrass, 1990-91; mem. devel. com. Holygrove Children's Home. Recipient Leadership award, Nat. Assn. Broadcasters, 2009. Mem. Am. Women Radio and TV (nat. sec., treas. 1982-84, nat. pres.-elect 1987-88, nat. pres. 1988-89, Nat. Achievement award 1994), Nat. Assn. Broadcasters (legis. com. 1983—), Hollywood Radio and TV Soc., Hollywood Women's Polit. Com., Pitts. Radio Orgn. (pres. 1982-83), Pitts. Radio/TV Club (dir. 1979-84), TV Assn. Bluegrass (pres. 1988-90). Republican. Home: 50 Boatswains Way Apt 406 Chelsea MA 02150-4062*

SUTTER, ELAINE JOYCE, elementary school educator; b. Chetek, Wis., Sept. 2, 1932; d. William J. and Alba Odela (Thompson) Owen; m. Lester E. Sutter, Jr., Nov. 25, 1955; children: Virginia Leigh Sutter Bartlett, Victoria Lynn Sutter Smith. Student, Moody Bible Inst., 1954; BS, Ill. State U., 1966, MEd, 1973. Tchr. 2d grade Lincon Sch. Dist. 709, Morton, Ill., 1966-73; tchr. 2d and 3d grades Grundy Sch. Dist. 709, Morton, 1973-93; substitute tchr. Sch. Dist. 709, 1993—. Mem. AAUW. Republican. Mennonite. Avocation: travel. Office: Grundy Sch 400 S 4th Morton IL 61550-2617

SUTTER, ELEANOR BLY, retired diplomat; b. NYC, Oct. 21, 1945; d. Samuel M. and Sylvia Gertrude Bly; children: Deborah Nelson, Willis. BA, Swarthmore Coll., 1966; MA, Am. U., 1978; diploma in strategic studies, U.S. Army War Coll., 1997. Instr. English Thammasat U., Bangkok and Udornthani Tchr. Tng. Coll., 1967-71, Lomonosov State U., Moscow, 1973-74; rschr. Kennan Inst. for Advanced Russian Studies, 1977-79; fgn. svc. officer Office Soviet Internal Affairs Dept. of State, 1979-80, fgn. svc. officer Office of Strategic Nuc. Policy, 1986-88, fgn. svc. officer Office of Soviet Union Affairs, 1988-90, office dir. Washington, 1997-99, sr. inspector Office Inspector Gen., 1999-2001, dir. Office of Proliferation Threat Reduction, 2001—02; fgn. svc. officer U.S. Embassy, Kinshasa, 1980-82, London, 1982-85, Moscow, 1990-92, charge d'affaires ad interim Bratislava, 1993, dep. prin. officer, 1993-95, dep. chief of mission, 1995-96. Exec. dir., exec. sec., advisor U.S. Del. to Nuclear and Space Talks, Geneva, 1987-91; teaching fellow Russian lit. The Am. U., 1976-77; escort interpreter and translator Dept. of State, 1976. Co-author: Final Report of the Kennan Institute's Soviet Research Institutes Project, 1981. Founder Camp Wocsom, Moscow, 1974. Mem. Am. Fgn. Svc. Assn. Avocations: music, folk dance. Office: care of Fgn Svc Lounge Dept State Washington DC 20520

SUTTER, ELOUISE C., retired art educator; b. Jersey City, Feb. 10, 1925; d. Alfredo G. Conte and Asunta Maddalena; m. John H. Sutter, Sept. 2, 1956; children: Susan, Maria, Sally. BS, Columbia U., 1947; MA, Stanford U., 1953; PhD, Wright Inst., Berkeley, Calif., 1984. Art tchr., supr. Milford Sch., Milford, Del., 1947—51, Newark Sch., Del., 1951—52. Mem. World Affairs Coun., San Francisco, 1956—; pres. bd. Oakland YWCA, Calif.; bd. dirs. Ctr. for Human Devel., Pleasant Hill, 1983—97. Mem.: Am. Humanistic Soc. Democrat. Presbyn. Avocations: archaeology, travel, reading, art. Home: 3627 Klamath St Oakland CA 94602

SUTTER, JANE ELIZABETH, conservationist, science educator; b. St. Louis, Nov. 27, 1939; d. Richard A. and Elizabeth Henby Sutter. AB in Sociology and English, Vassar Coll. for Women, Poughkeepsie, NY, 1961; MA in Health Facilities Mgmt., Webster Coll., St. Louis, 1979. Healthcare analyst, Chgo. and St. Louis, 1966-83; asst. dir. radio, TV and motion picture dept. AMA, Chgo., 1966-67; staff coord., rsch. assoc. Chgo. water quality study and environ. health study Inst. of Medicine of Chgo., 1967-69; dir. environ. health planning Comprehensive Health Planning, Inc., Chgo., 1969-73; spl. asst. to Mary Hastings Bradley early African explorer, 1973—75; planning assoc., spl. asst. to med. dir. Sutter Clinic, St. Louis, 1975-84; vol. activist, educator; founder, dir. Wild Birds for the 21st Century, 1994—; ednl. writer www.wildbirds.org. Author: City Approved Medical Emergency Plan of Operation O'Hare International and Midway Airports, 1971. Chmn. Opera Theatre of St. Louis Newsletter, Recitative, Vol. 1, No. 1, 1980, Vol. 1, No. 2, 1980; co-founder, com. mem. 1st Internat. Alewife Festival of Chgo., Chgo. Yacht Club, summer 1968; appointee Gov.'s Com. for Pure Air and Water, Chgo., 1968; spl. advocate N.Am. Migratory Birds particularly hummingbirds. Mem. Ladue Chapel, Mo. Bot. Garden, St. Louis Artists' Guild (mem. artists' sect. 1992-95, portraitist), Mo. Bird Conservation Initiative, Neotropical Bird Club (UK), Bradenton C. of C, River des Peres Yacht Club. Avocations: gardening, writing, poetry, physical therapy.

SUTTER, LAURENCE BRENER, lawyer; b. NYC, Feb. 5, 1944; s. Meyer and Beatrice Sutter; m. Betty A. Satterwhite, June 9, 1979. AB, Columbia Coll., 1965; JD, N.Y.U., 1976. Bar: N.Y. 1977, U.S. Dist. Ct. (so. and ea. dists.) N.Y. 1977. Assoc. Shea & Gould, NYC, 1976-80, Meyer, Suozzi, English & Klein P.C., Mineola, NY, 1980-82; assoc. counsel publs. Gen. Media Comm., Inc., NYC, 1982-96, sr. v.p., gen. counsel, sec., 1997—2004; sr. counsel Friend Finder Networks Inc., 2004—. With N.Y. Army N.G., 1966-72. Mem. Assn. of Bar of City of N.Y. (mem. com. on civil rights 1986-89, mem. com. on comm. and media law 1989-92, mem. com. on copyright and lit. property 1994-97), First Amendment Lawyers Assn., Nat. Arts Club, Orient (N.Y.) Yacht Club (dir. 1997-2000, sec. 2000-2001), Early Music America(dir., 2007-) Democrat. Jewish. Avocations: music, sailing. Office Phone: 212-702-6105.

SUTTER, RICHARD C., anthropologist, educator; b. NY; married. PhD, U. Mo., Colombia, 1997. Prof. anthropology, Fort Wayne, Ind., 1998—. Fulbright scholarship, J. William Fulbright Fgn. Scholarship Bd., 1994, Rsch. grant, NSF, 1999—2001. Mem.: Am. Assn. Phys. Anthropologists, Soc. Am. Archaeology, Soc. Am. Archaeology, Lambda Alpha Theta. Office: Ind U-Purdue U Ft Wayne Dept Anthropology Fort Wayne IN 46805

SUTTER, WILLIAM PAUL, lawyer; b. Chgo., Jan. 15, 1924; s. Harry Blair and Elsie (Paul) S.; m. Helen Yvonne Stebbins, Nov. 13, 1954; children: William Paul, Helen Blair Sutter. AB, Yale U., 1947; JD, U. Mich., 1950. Bar: Ill. 1950, Fla. 1977, U.S. Supreme Ct. 1981. Assoc. Hopkins & Sutter (and predecessors), Chgo., 1950-57, ptnr., 1957-89, of counsel, 1989—2001. Mem. Ill. Supreme Ct. Atty. Registration Commn., 1975-81 Contbr. articles on estate planning and taxation to profl. jours. Chmn. Winnetka Caucus Com., 1966-67; pres., trustee Lucille P. Markey Charitable Trust, 1983-98; precinct capt. New Trier Twp. (Ill.) Rep. party, 1960-68; asst. area chmn. New Trier Rep. Orgn., 1968-72; trustee Gads Hill Center, pres., 1962-70, chmn., 1971-80; trustee Northwestern Meml. Hosp., 1983-98, life trustee, 1998—; bd. dirs. Chgo. Hort. Soc., 1982-2005, life dir., 2005—; mem. dean's coun. Sch. Medicine, Yale U., 1991-97; bd. visitors Waisman Ctr., U. Wis., 1996-2002; corr. sec. Yale U. Class of 1945, 1990—. Served to 1st lt. AUS, 1943-46 Fellow Am. Bar Found., Am. Coll. Trust and Estate Counsel (bd. regents 1977-83, exec. com. 1981-83); mem. ABA (ho. dels. 1972-81, chmn. com. on income estates and trusts, taxation sect. 1973-75), Ill. Bar Assn. (bd. govs. 1964-75, pres. 1973-74), Chgo. Bar Assn. (chmn. probate practice com. 1963-64), Am. Law Inst., Internat. Acad. Estate and Trust Law, Am. Judicature Soc., Ill. LAWPAC (pres. 1977-83), Order of Coif, Phi Beta Kappa, Phi Delta Phi, Chi Psi, Indian Hill Club, Gulf Stream Golf Club, Country Club Fla., Ocean Club (Fla.) (bd. govs. 1993-99, sec. 1993-97, pres. 1997-99), Lawyers Club Chgo. Episcopalian. Home: 2 Par Club Cir Village Of Golf FL 33436 Personal E-mail: WPSutter@aol.com.

SUTTERFIELD, J. S., engineering educator; b. St. Louis, Dec. 17, 1939; s. Marvin and Beulah G. (Morgan) Sutterfield; m. Janice R. Pipkin, June 4, 1960; children: Kimberly Ann Gasbarra, Kelly Lynn Meyer. BSME and Applied Math., U. Mo., Rolla, 1962, MSME and Applied Math., 1970, PhD in Engring. Mgmt., 1994. Registered profl. engr., Mo. Aerospace engr. McDonnell Astronautics, St. Louis, 1962—67; sr. acquisitions mgr., dep. program mgr., chief engr. Aviation and Troop Command, St. Louis, 1967—97; instr. physics Duchesne H.S., St. Charles, Mo., 1999—2001; assoc. prof. oper. mgmt. Fla. A&M U., 2001—. Adj. prof. S.E. Mo. State U., Cape Girardeau, 2000—01; pres. Tng. for Svc., St. Louis, 1975—92; v.p. ops. Reach Comms., Bridgetor, Mo., 1985—90. Contbr. articles to profl. publs. Officer Piney-Z Homeowners, Tallahassee, 2004—05; amb. Bond Grade Sch., Tallahassee, 2003—05. Named Disting. Prof., Alpha Kappa Alpha, 2004. Mem.: Engring. Mgmt. Soc. Avocations: history, philosophy, classical music, mathematics. Home: 1171 Landings Loop Tallahassee FL 32311 Office: Fla A&M U 1 SBI Plz Tallahassee FL 32307 Office Phone: 850-412-7723.

SUTTERLIN, JAMES SMYRL, political science professor, researcher; b. Frankfort, Ky., Mar. 15, 1922; s. Frederick J. and Agnes (Douglas) S.; m. Betty C. Berven, June 24, 1950 (dec. Jan. 1989); children: Rose E., Sabrina, Jamie Ann, James E.; m. Renate Craine, Dec. 27, 1997. BA, Haverford Coll., 1943; postgrad., Harvard U., 1949-67; degree in jurisprudence (hon.), Kyung Hee U., Seoul, Korea, 1973. Vice-consul U.S. Fgn. Svc., Berlin, 1946-48; polit. officer U.S. Mission, Berlin, 1951-54; 1st sec. U.S. Embassy, Tel Aviv, 1954-56; desk officer U.S. State Dept., Washington, 1956-60; 1st sec. U.S. Embassy, Tokyo, 1960-63, counselor Bonn, 1963-68; dir. U.S. Dept. State, Washington, 1969-72, insp.-gen., 1972-74; dir. UN, NYC, 1974-87; dir. rsch. L.I. U., Bklyn., 1985-87, adj. prof., 1985—; fellow/lectr. Yale U., New Haven, 1988—2006; visiting fellow, 2006—. Author: Berlin—Symbol of Confrontation, 1989, UN and the Maintenance of Security, 1995, The United Nations in Iraq: Defanging the Viper, 2003. Elder Presbyn. Ch., Port Chester, N.Y., 1976-96; chmn. Samaritan House, White Plains, N.Y., 1990-95; pres. Wainwright House, Rye, 1995-96; chmn. acad. coun. on the UN Brown U., 1995-97. 1st lt. U.S. Army, 1945-46. Recipient Grosse Verdienstkreuz award, Fed. Republic of Germany, 1974. Mem. UN Assn. of U.S.A., Am. Coun. on Germany, Coun. Fgn. Rels., Phi Beta Kappa. Avocation: gardening. Home: 17 N Chatsworth Ave Apt 6k-l Larchmont NY 10538-2126 Office: Yale U 34 Hillhouse Ave New Haven CT 06511-3704 Office Phone: 914-834-3902. Personal E-mail: jsutter728@aol.com.

SUTTIE, JOHN WESTON, biochemist; b. La Crosse, Wis., Aug. 25, 1934; married; 2 children. BS, U. Wis., 1957, MS, 1958, PhD, 1960. Fellow biochemist Nat. Inst. Med. Rsch, England, 1960-61; asst. prof. to assoc. prof. biochemistry U. Wis., Madison, 1961-69, prof., 1969—2001, chair nutrition sci., 1988-97, Katherine Berns Van Donk Steenbock prof. nutrition, 2000, prof. emeritus, 2002—. Mem. Bd. on Agriculture & Natural Resources, 1996—2001, Food and Nutrition Bd., 2004—07. Assoc. editor Jour Nutrition, 1991-97; editor Jour. Nutrition, 1997-2003; asst. editor Ann. Rev. Nutrition, 2005—. Recipient Disting. Achievement in Nutrition Rsch., Bristol-Myers Squibb/Mead Johnson, 2002. Fellow Am. Heart Assn. Coun. Nutrition, Physical Activity and Metabolism, Am. Soc. for Nutrition (Osborne and Mendel award 1980, Mead Johns award 1974, Conrad Elvehjem award, 2004); mem. NAS, Am. Soc. Expl. Biology and Medicine, Am. Soc. Biochemistry and Molecular Biology, Internat. Soc. Thrombosis and Hemostasis (Hemostasis Career award 1989). Business E-Mail: suttie@biochem.wisc.edu.

SUTTLE, HELEN JAYSON, retired elementary school educator; b. Plattsburgh, NY, Dec. 13, 1925; d. Harold Lincoln Jayson and Blanche Rabideau Jayson Woods; widowed, 1993; 1 child, Adolphia Helen Suttle Blanton. BA in Edn., Limestone Coll., 1961; MA in Edn., Winthrop U., 1973. Cert. tchr., S.C. Tchr. Madden Elem. Sch., Spartanburg, S.C., 1961-71, West Jr. High Sch., Gaffney, S.C., 1971-81, L.L. Vaughn Elem. Sch., Gaffney, S.C., 1981-88; substitute tchr. Gaffney Dis. 1, 1988—; ret. Vol. SC Budget Control Bd., Upstate Carolina Med. Ctr., Meals on Wheels, Literacy Assn., local soup kitchen; chmn. Cherokee County Rep. Com.; v.p. Ch. Women's Guild, pres., 1998—; dir. religious edn. Sacred Heart Ch., 2001—; pres. Sacred Heart Sr. Citizens Club; treas. ch. com. Greenville Deanery; pres.-elect Piedmont Deanery, 2002—; Eucharistic min., lector; mem. exec. bd. SC Coun. Cath. Ch. Women, 1998—, chair family commn., 1998—; pres. Piedmont Deanery, 2002—03; trustee Limestone Coll. Named Woman of Yr., S.C. Coun. Cath. Women Greenville Deanery, 1996, Alumna of Yr., Limestone Coll., 2004. Fellow Internat. Biog. Assn. (life, dep. gov. Am. chpt.), Limestone Coll. Alumni Assn. (pres., chpt. pres.), Fountain Club (charter mem.), Kalosophia Honor Soc. Roman Catholic. Avocations: writing, art, gardening, crafts.

SUTTON, BETTY, United States Representative from Ohio, lawyer; b. Barberton, Ohio, July 31, 1963; m. Doug Sutton; 2 children. BA in Polit. Sci., Kent State U., Ohio, 1985; JD, U. Akron, Ohio, 1990. Coun.-at-large Barberton City Coun., 1990-91; v.p. Summit County Coun., 1991-92; mem. Ohio Ho. Reps. from dist. 47, 1993—2000; atty. Faulkner, Muskovitz & Phillips LLP, 2001—06; mem. US Congress from 13th Ohio dist., 2007—, mem. rules com., judiciary com., 2007—. Recipient Friend of Edn. award, Barberton Edn. Assn., Am. Jurisprudence award, Fed. Bar Assn., 1989, Outstanding Performance in Const. Law award, 1989. Mem.: ABA, Fed. Dem. Women, Summit County Trial Lawyers, Ohio Acad. Trial Lawyers (Legislator of Yr.), Assn. Trial Lawyers America, Akron Child Guidance Adv. Coun. Democrat. Office: 1721 Longworth House Office Bldg Washington DC 20515 also: 1655 W Market St Rm 435 Akron OH 44313 Office Phone: 330-865-8450. Office Fax: 330-865-8470.*

SUTTON, BEVERLY JEWELL, psychiatrist; b. Rockford, Mich., May 27, 1932; d. Beryl Dewey and Cora Belle (Potes) Jewell; m. Harry Eldon Sutton, July 7, 1962; children: Susan, Caroline. MD, U. Mich., 1957. Diplomate Am. Bd. Pediat., Am. Bd. Psychiatry and Neurology. Rotating intern St. Joseph Mercy Hosp., Ann Arbor, Mich., 1958; resident in child psychiatry Hawthorne Ctr., Northville, Mich., 1958-62; resident in pediat. U. Hosp./U. Mich. Med. Ctr., Ann Arbor, 1959-61; resident in psychiatry Austin (Tex.) State Hosp., 1962-64, dir. children's svc., 1964-89, dir. psychiat. residency program, 1989—, dir. tng. and rsch., 1993-98. Cons. in field. Contbr. articles to profl. jours. Active numerous civic orgns. Recipient Outstanding Achievement award, YWCA, 1989, Jackson Day award, Tex. Soc. Child and Adolescent Psychiatry, 1989, Showcase award, Tex. Dept. Mental Health/Mental Retardation, 1990. Fellow Am. Acad. Child and Adolescent Psychiatry (life), Am. Psychiat. Assn. (Disting. fellow), Am. Pediatric Assn.; mem. Group for Advancement Psychiatry, Tex. Soc. Child and Adolescent Psychiatry (pres. 1979-80, Jackson Day award), Tex. Soc. Psychiat. Physicians (Disting. Svc. award 1990), AMA, Tex. Med. Soc., Am. Genetics Soc. Office: Seton Shoal Creek Hosp 3501 Mills Ave Austin TX 78731 Business E-Mail: bsutton@seton.org.

SUTTON, BRIAN K., construction executive; b. Bardstown, Ky., Aug. 25, 1970; s. Myron Keith Sutton and Laura Elizabeth Sutton Cozine. BA, Transylvania U., Lexington, KY, 1993. Southeast regional methods & procedures field mgr. BellSouth Corp./Cingular Wireless, Ashland, Ky., 1996—2004; dir. mktg. Hagan Enterprises, Bardstown, 2004—08; bus. mgr. J.L. Hutchins Builders, 2007—; dir. Optimist Internat., 2009—. Exec. vice-president Nelson County Edn. Endowment Fund, Bardstown, Ky., 2007—; program co-chair Leadership Nelson County, Bardstown, Ky., 2007—; amb. Bardstown-Nelson County Chamber of Commerce, Bardstown, Ky., 2007—; mem. Kiwanis Internat., Bardstown, Ky., 2007—; chmn. of fin. Optimist Internat., Bardstown, Ky., 2007—, dir., 2009—; exec. dir. Optimist Club Bardstown, 2009—. Author: (poem) Valdez (Nat. Poet's Antholgy Award, 1989). Recipient BellSouth Corp. Shining Star of the Yr., BellSouth Corp., 1998, 1999, Pres.'s Vol. Svc. award, 2003—07, Vol. Svc. award, Pres.'s Call to Svc., 2008; named Amb. of Yr., C. of C., 2009, Bardstown Nelson Co., 2008. Democrat. Office: JL Hutchins Builders 106 Manor Ave Ste 101 Bardstown KY 40004-2270 Home Phone: 502-349-9242. Office Fax: 502-349-1370. Personal E-mail: briankstton@msn.com. Business E-Mail: briank@bardstowncable.net.

SUTTON, CECE (CECILIA STEWART SUTTON), bank executive; b. Charlotte, NC, 1956; 2 children. BA in Psychology, U. SC, 1978; MBA, Winthrop U., 1993. Branch mgr. First Union Corp., Raleigh and Cary, NC, consumer credit sales mgr. Charlotte, NC, 1984—86, consumer banking mgr. Greenville, SC, 1986—89, consumer bank training dir. Charlotte, NC, 1988—89, area exec. Rock Hill, SC, 1989—92, head SC Gen. Banking Group Greenville, SC, 1992—93, area exec. Rock Hill, SC, 1993—95, consumer banking exec. SC, exec. v.p. SC, 2001; exec. v.p., head retail & small bus. banking Wachovia Corp. (merged with First Union Corp), Charlotte, 2001—08; pres. retail banking group Morgan Stanley, NYC, 2008—. Chmn. Consumers Bankers Assn., 2006—. Active United Way. Named one of 25 Most Powerful Women in Banking, US Banker, 2007, 25 Women to Watch, 2008, 50 Most Powerful Women in Bus., Fortune mag., 2007, 2008. Office: Morgan Stanley 1585 Broadway New York NY 10036*

SUTTON, DAVID E., anthropologist, educator; b. NYC, Apr. 1, 1963; s. Samuel and Constance R. Sutton; m. Bethany A. Rowe, Aug. 24, 1988; children: Samuel Evan Herman Rowe-Sutton, Maxwell Ivan Rowe-Sutton. BA, U. Chgo., Ill., 1985, MA, 1987, PhD, 1995. Rsch.

fellow St. Peter's Coll., Oxford U., England, 1996—98; asst. prof. anthropology U. NH., Durham, 1998—99; assoc. prof. anthropology Southern Ill. U., Carbondale, 1999—. Editor: (anthropological collection) The Restaurants Book; contbr. scientific papers to profl. jours. Assoc. editor Global Studies Culture & Power, Carbondale, 2000—. Recipient Outstanding Tchr. award, Souther Ill. U. Carbondale, 2008. Mem.: Am. Anthrop. Assn. (exec. program com. mem. 2008—). Office: Southern Ill Univ Mailcode 4502 Carbondale IL 62901 Office Fax: 618-453-5037. Business E-Mail: dsutton@siu.edu.

SUTTON, FERRON, engineering educator; married. BS in Applied Sci. Indsl. Tech., MS in Edn. Instrnl. Tech. and Design. Instr. engring. & design tech. ENMU, Roswell, N.Mex., 1998—. Office: ENMU-Roswell 52 University Blvd Roswell NM 88203 Office Fax: 575-624-7188. Business E-Mail: ferron.sutton@roswell.enmu.edu.

SUTTON, FRANCIS XAVIER, social services administrator, consultant; b. Oneida, Pa., July 7, 1917; s. Frank James and Rose Marie (Burns) S.; m. Ruth Jacqueline Young, Aug. 24, 1948 (dec. July 2002); children: Peter, Sean, Philip, Elizabeth. BS, Temple U., 1938; MA, Princeton U., 1940, Harvard U., 1941, PhD, 1950; DLitt (hon.), Aga Khan U., Karachi, 2003. Jr. fellow, Soc. Fellows Harvard U., Cambridge, Mass., 1946-49, asst. prof., lectr., 1949-54; program officer, overseas rep. Ford Found., NYC, 1954-67, dep. v.p., acting v.p., 1968-83; cons. Ford Found. and Harvard U., 1983-85; acting pres. Social Sci. Rsch. Coun., NYC, 1985-86, also bd. dirs., chmn., 1985-92; cons. Rockefeller Found, U.S. Agy. for Internat. Devel. and World Bank, NYC and Washington, 1987-92; acting dir. Rockefeller Study and Conf. Ctr., Bellagio, Italy, 1990-92; cons. Aga Khan U., 1992—. Author: The American Business Creed, 1956; editor: A World to Make/Development in Perspective, 1989; contbr. articles to profl. jours. and chpts. to books. Pres. Am. Found. for Intellectual Coop. with Europe, N.Y.C., 1987-93; mem. bd. fgn. scholarships Dept. State, Washington, 1961-63; bd. dirs. Nat. Ctr. on Adult Literacy, U. Pa., Phila., 1990-97; mem. adv. bd. Ctr. on Philanthropy, City Univ., N.Y.C., 1988—. Capt. U.S. Army Air Corps, 1941-45. Fellow AAAS; mem. Council on Fgn. Relations, Assn. for Asian Studies (Disting. Service award 1984). Clubs: Century Assn. (N.Y.C.). Democrat. Avocation: piano playing. Home: 80 Bellair Dr Dobbs Ferry NY 10522-3504 E-mail: fxsutton@aol.com.

SUTTON, G. KATHERINE HALLETT, nurse; b. Denver, Mar. 9, 1920; d. Lucius Felt Hallett and Genevieve Folsom (Pfeiffer) Taylor; m. John B. Sutton, Feb. 26, 1949 (dec. Mar. 1957); children: John, Lawrence, Stephen, Katherine Anne, Minou. BA, La. State U. Nurse ob-gyn. Glen Cove (N.Y.) Hosp.; head nurse N.Y. Neurol. Inst., NYC; floor nurse Jefferson-Hillman Hosp., Birmingham, Ala.; nurse ICU Highland Hosp., Shreveport, La.; supr. Schumpert Hosp., Shreveport, La. Mem. Order of Daus. of the King. Episcopalian. Avocation: church. Home: 5910 Roma Sr Apt 24 Shreveport LA 71105-4572

SUTTON, GEORGE PAUL, rocket propulsion engineer, writer, educator; b. Sept. 5, 1920; s. Fred Charles and Augusta Amalie (Landegger) S.; m. Kathleen M. Sutton, July 1944 (dec. July 1952); m. Yvonne B. Sutton, Apr. 1954 (dec. Dec. 1992); children: Christine, Marilyn. BS in Mech. Engring., Calif. Inst. Tech., 1942, MS, 1943, postgrad., 1943-46. Registered profl. engr., Calif. Devel. engr. Aerojet Corp., Pasadena/Asuza, Calif., 1943-46; asst. to pres., exec. dir. engring. Rocketdyne (now Pratt & Whitney Rocketdyne), Canoga Park, Calif., 1946-69; chief scientist Advanced Rsch. Project Agy., Dept. Def., Pentagon, Washington, 1959-60; v.p. Envirotech Corp., Menlo Park, Calif., 1969-74, Johnston Pump Co., Glendora, Calif., 1975-77; lab. assoc., program leader, asst. divsn. leader Lawrence Livermore Nat. Lab., Livermore, Calif., 1977-88, part time, 1988-00. Pres., v.p. Am. Rocket Soc., 1945-59; instr. mech. engring. Calif. Inst. Tech., Pasadena, 1943-46; Hunsaker prof. aero. engring. MIT, Cambridge, 1958-59; exec. v.p. Sumitomo Jukikai Envirotech, Tokyo, 1971-74. Author: Rocket Propulsion Elements, 1949, 8th edit., 2009, A History of Liquid Propellant Rocket Engines, 2006; contbr. articles to profl. jours. Mem. Sci. Adv. Bd. USAF, 1960-71. Fellow: AIAA (past pres., Pendray award 1951, 2002); mem.: ASME, Soc. Mfg. Engrs.

SUTTON, GREGORY PAUL, obstetrician, gynecologist; b. Tokyo, Dec. 12, 1948; (parents Am. citizens); s. Vernon S. And Vonna Lou (Streeter) S.; m. Judith Craigie Holt, June 26, 1977; children: Anne Craigie, James Streeter. BS in Chemistry with honors, Ind. U., 1970; MD, U. Mich., 1976. Diplomate Am. Bd. of Ob/Gyn. Prof. gynecol. oncology Ind. U. Sch. Medicine, Indpls., 1986-97; Mary Fendrich Hulman prof. Gynecologic Oncology Ind. U. Sch. Med., Indpls., 1997-2000; dir., gynecologic oncology St. Vincent Hosp. and Health Svcs., 2000—01. Cancer Clin. fellow Am. Cancer Soc., Phila., 1981-83; recipient Career Devel. award Am. Cancer Soc., 1986-89. Fellow: Am. Coll. Obstetrics and Gynecology (chair Ind. sect. 2000—03); mem.: ACS (com. on cancer, Ind. state liaison), Nat. Cancer Inst. (grampian cancer steering com. mem. 2008—), Hoosier Oncology Group, Soc. of Gynecologic Oncologists, Bayard Carter Soc., Ind. State Med. Soc., Marion County Med. Soc., Gynecologic Oncology Group (cert. Spl. Competence in Gynecologic Oncology 1985). Avocations: swimming, bicycling, woodworking, sailing, crossword puzzles. Office: 8301 Harcourt Rd Ste 202 Indianapolis IN 46260-1453 Office Phone: 317-415-6740. E-mail: gsutton@stvincent.org.

SUTTON, HARRY ELDON, geneticist, educator; b. Cameron, Tex., Mar. 5, 1927; s. Grant Edwin and Myrtle Dovie (Fowler) S.; m. Beverly Earlene Jewell, July 7, 1962; children: Susan Elaine, Caroline Virginia. BS in Chemistry, U. Tex., Austin, 1948, MA, 1949; PhD in Biochemistry, U. Tex., 1953. Biologist U. Mich., 1952-56, instr., 1956-57, asst. prof. human genetics, 1957-60; assoc. prof. zoology U. Tex., Austin, 1960-64, prof., 1964-99, chmn. dept. zoology, 1970-73, asso. dean Grad. Sch., 1967-70, 73-75, v.p. for research, 1975-79, Ashbel Smith prof. emeritus molecular genetics and microbiology, 2000—. Mem. adv. council Nat. Inst. Environ. Health Scis., 1968-72, council sci. advs., 1972-76; mem. various coms. Nat. Acad. Scis.-NRC; cons. in field; bd. dirs. Associated Univs. for Research in Astronomy, 1975-79, Argonne Univs. Assn., 1975-79, Univ. Corp. for Atmospheric Research, 1975-79, Associated Western Univs., 1978-79 Author: Genes, Enzymes, and Inherited Disease, 1961, An Introduction to Human Genetics, 1988, Genetics: A Human Concern, 1985; editor: First Macy Conference on Genetics, 1960, Mutagenic Effects of Environmental Contaminants, 1972, Am. Jour. Human Genetics, 1964-69. Trustee S.W. Tex. Corp. Public Broadcasting, 1977-80, sec., 1979-80; bd. dirs. Ballet Austin, 1978-84, 98-2004; mem. Austin Arts Commn., 1991-95. Served with U.S. Army, 1945-46. Mem. AAAS, Am. Soc. Human Genetics (dir. 1961-69, pres. 1979), Genetics Soc. Am., Am. Soc. Biochem. and Molecular Biology, Am. Chem. Soc., Tex. Genetics Soc. (pres. 1979), Am. Genetic Assn., Headliners Club (Austin), Town and Gown Club. Achievements include research and publications in human genetics. Home: 1103 Gaston Ave Austin TX 78703-2507 Office: Univ Tex Sect Molecular Genetics & Microbiology Austin TX 78712 Business E-Mail: eldon.sutton@mail.utexas.edu.

SUTTON, JEFFREY PAUL, physician, scientist, administrator; b. NYC, July 6, 1958; MD, U. Toronto, Ontario, Can., 1982, MSc in Med. Sci., 1985, PhD in Physics, 1988. Resident Harvard Med. Sch., Boston, 1988-91; vis. scientist brain & cognitive scis. MIT, Cambridge, 1988-95; facaulty Harvard Med. Sch., Boston, 1991—2002; founder. dir. neural sys. grp. Mass. Gen. Hosp., 1995—2002; pres., inst. dir. Nat. Space Biomed. Rsch. Inst., Houston, 2001—. Recipient Career Rsch. Scientist award, NIH, Presidents Citation, Soc. NASA Flight Surgeons. Office: Nat Space Biomed Rsch Inst One Baylor Plaza NA 425 Houston TX 77030 Office Phone: 743-798-7412. Office Fax: 743-798-7413.*

SUTTON, JEFFREY S., federal judge; b. Dhahran, Saudi Arabia, 1960; BA, Williams Coll., 1983; LLB, Ohio State Univ., 1990. Clk. Second Circuit Ct. for Judge Thomas Meskill, 1990—91, Supreme Ct. for Justice Scalia and ret. Justice Powell, 1991—92; assoc. Jones, Day, Reavis & Pogue, Columbus, Ohio, 1992—95; adj. law prof. Ohio State Univ., Ohio, 1994—; Solicitor Ohio State, Ohio, 1995—98; ptnr. Jones, Day, Reavis & Pogue, Columbus, Ohio, 1998—2003; judge US Ct. Appeals, (6th cir.), Cin., 2003—. Office: Office Clerk US Ct Appeals 6th Cir 532 Potter Stewart US Cthse 100 E 5th St Cincinnati OH 45202-3988*

SUTTON, JOE, playwright, educator; s. Frank and Toby Sutton; m. Anne Travers, Sept. 19, 1986; children: James, Nick. BA, Dartmouth Coll., Hanover, NH, 1976; MFA, U. Calif., Davis, 1990. Vis. assoc. prof. Dartmouth Coll., 1999—. Author: (plays) Complicit, Voir Dire (nominated Pulitzer Prize, Best Play Am. Theater Critics Assn., 1995), As It Is In Heaven, The Third Army; co-author (with C. Filloux and T. Mccraneyl) The Breach; author Restoring the Sun; composer (with Lewis Flinn): (musical) The Winner. Recipient fellowship, NEA, 1999, 2007, NYFA, 1989, 1999, 2007, NJ. Arts Coun., 1989, 1999, 2007;, NEA, 1989. Mem.: Dramatists Guild. Personal E-mail: jsut@juno.com. Business E-Mail: joseph.d.sutton@dartmouth.edu.

SUTTON, JOHN F., JR., lawyer, dean, educator; b. Alpine, Tex., Jan. 26, 1918; s. John F. and Pauline Irene (Elam) S.; m. Nancy Ewing, June 1, 1940; children: Joan Sutton Parr, John Ewing. JD, U. Tex., 1941. Bar: Tex. 1941, U.S. Dist. Ct. (we. dist.) Tex. 1947, U.S. Ct. Appeals (5th cir.) 1951, U.S. Supreme Ct. 1960. Assoc. Brooks, Napier, Brown & Matthews, San Antonio, 1941; spl. agt. FBI, Washington, 1942—45; assoc. Matthews, Nowlin, Macfarlane & Barrett, San Antonio, 1945—48; ptnr. Kerr, Gayer & Sutton, San Angelo, Tex., 1948—50, Sutton, Steib & Barr, San Angelo, 1951—57; prof. U. Tex.-Austin, 1957—65, William Stamps Farish prof., 1965—84, A.W. Walker centennial chair, 1984—88, emeritus, 1988—, dean Sch. Law, 1979—84. Editor: (with Wellborn) Materials on Evidence, 8th edit., 1996, (with Dzienkowski) Cases and Materials on Professional Responsibility of Lawyers, 1989, (with Schuwerk) Guideline to the Texas Disciplinary Rules of Professional Conduct, 1990, (with Dzienkowski) Cases and Materials on Professional Conduct, 2d edit., 2002; contbr. articles to profl. jours. Served to 1st lt. JAGC USAR, 1948—53. Fellow Am. Bar Found. (life), Tex. Bar Found. (life); mem. ABA (com. on ethics 1970-76), State Bar Tex. (com. on rules of profl. conduct), Philos. Soc. Tex., Order of Coif, U. Tex. Club, Phi Delta Phi, North Austin Rotary (pres. 1969). Presbyterian. Home: 3830 Sunset Dr San Angelo TX 76904-5956 Office: U Tex Sch Law 727 E Dean Keeton St Austin TX 78705-3224 Business E-Mail: jsutton@mail.law.utexas.edu.

SUTTON, JOHN PAUL, lawyer; b. Youngstown, Ohio, July 24, 1934; m. Jane Williamson, Aug. 20, 1958; children: Julia, Susan, Elizabeth. BA, U. Va., 1956; JD, George Washington U., 1963. Bar: Calif. 1965. Patent examiner U.S. Patent Office, Washington, 1956, 59-62; law clk. U.S. Ct. Customs and Patent Appeals, Washington, 1962-64; assoc. Flehr, Hohbach, Test, Albritton & Herbert, San Francisco, 1964-68; ptnr. Limbach, Limbach & Sutton, San Francisco, 1969-91; spl. counsel Heller, Ehrman, White & McAuliffe, San Francisco, 1992-95; of counsel Medlin & Carroll, San Francisco, 1995, Bryan, Hinshaw & Barnet, San Francisco, 1996-99; sole practice San Francisco, 2000—. Adj. instr. Practicing Law Inst., 1968-69; continuing edn. program Calif. State Bar, 1972, 75, U. Calif. Law Sch., Berkeley, 1975, 84. Contbr. articles to legal jours. Served with USNR, 1956-59. Mem.: Am. Chem. Soc., Fedn. Internat. des Conseils en Propriete Indsl. (pres. U.S. sect. 2003—06), State Bar Calif. (exec. com. patent sect. 1975—77), San Francisco Patent Law Assn. (pres. 1976), Calif. Patent Law Assn. (pres. 1975). Democrat. Episcopalian. Home and Office: 123 Race St Grass Valley CA 95945 Home Phone: 530-477-8538; Office Phone: 530-477-8535. Personal E-mail: JohnPSutton@earthlink.net.

SUTTON, JOHNNY KEANE, lobbyist, former prosecutor; b. June 1960; B in Internat. Bus., U. Tex., 1983, JD, 1987. Criminal trial prosecutor Harris County Dist. Atty. Office; asst. dist. atty. Harris County Dist. Atty.'s Office, 1987—95; criminal justice policy dir. to Gov. State of Tex., 1995—2000; assoc. dep. atty. gen. US Dept. Justice, Washington, 2001; policy coord. Bush-Cheney Transition Team, US Dept. Justice; US atty. (we. dist.) Tex. US Dept. Justice, 2001—09: ptnr. The Ashcroft Group, LLC, Washington, 2009—. Avocation: baseball (played for the Longhorns, starting lef-fielder on 1983 Nat. Championship team).*

SUTTON, JULIA, musicologist, dance historian; b. Toronto, July 20, 1928; d. Samuel L. and Anne R. (Rubin) Sumberg. AB summa cum laude, Cornell U., 1949; MA, Colo. Coll., 1952; PhD, U. Rochester, 1962. Instr. music history New Sch. for Social Rsch., 1962-63; instr. music Queens Coll., CUNY, 1963-66; instr. music history and musicology New Eng. Conservatory Music, 1967—90, instr. and prof. musicology, 1967—90, chmn. dept. music history and musicology, 1971-90, chmn. faculty senate, 1971-73, prof. emerita, 1992. Vis. asst. prof. George Peabody Coll. for Tchrs., 1966-67; instr. NYU, summers 1963, 64; pvt. tchr. piano, 1949-65; lectr., rsch. dir. in musicology, music as related to the dance; presenter numerous workshops and summer insts. on Renaissance dance. Dance dir. N.Y. Pro Musica prodn. An Entertainment for Elizabeth, Caramoor, N.Y., Saratoga, N.Y., U. Ariz., Stanford U., UCLA, 1969, ann. nationwide tours, 1970-1973; dance dir. Descent of Rhythm and Harmony, Colorado Springs, Colo., 1970, Renaissance Revisited, Phila., 1972, An Evening of Renaissance Music and Dance, York U., Toronto, 1974; author: Jean Baptiste Besard's Novus Partus 1617, 1962; editor: Thoinot Arbeau: Orchesography 1588, 1967; translator, editor: Fabritio Caroso: Nobiltà di dame 1600, 1986, reprinted 1995; producer, co-dir. (tng. video) Il Ballarino, 1991; contbr. numerous articles to profl. jours. and Internat. Ency. of Dance, The New Grove Dictionary of Music and Musicians 1st and 2d edit., Die Musik in Geschichte und Gegenwart, 1st edit.; editor-in-chief Dances for the King, 2008. Mem. Am. Musicological Soc., Soc. of Dance History Scholars, Phi Beta Kappa. Office Phone: 617-879-0032. Personal E-mail: jsutton@rcn.com.

SUTTON, KAREN E., museum director; b. New Brunswick, NJ, Aug. 26, 1952; d. Alfred Michael and Carmen (Collado) Sutton; children: Sloane, Brooke, Devon, Megan, Christopher. BA, Hofstra U., 1974; postgrad., NYU, 1987—89. Asst. to dir. Mus. Am. Folk Art, NYC, 1975-76, acting dir., 1976-77, bd. dirs., exec. com. officer, 1980-88, gallery dir., 1989-92, dir. ops., 1992-94, dep. dir. planning and adminstrn., 1994-95; v.p. Sotheby's, NYC, 1995-96, sr. v.p. adminstrn., 1996-2001, sr. v.p. worldwide mktg., 2001—08, sr. v.p., Global Client Devel., pvt client gr., 2008. Bd. dirs. Family Dynamics, N.Y.C., 1976-80. Mem.: NY Women in Real Estate, Cosmopolitan Club (younger members chmn.). Democrat. Episcopalian. Office: Sotheby's 1334 York Ave New York NY 10021-4806 Home: 132 E 72 St New York NY 10021 Home Phone: 212-535-5935; Office Phone: 212-606-7410. E-mail: karen.sutton@sothebys.com.

SUTTON, LEE, biology professor; s. Leonard F. and Jerri Sutton; m. Brooks Sykes, May 31, 2003; 1 child, Charlie. PhD, NC State U., Raleigh, 2002. Lic. 100 ton capt. USCG, 1997. Biology prof. East Carolina U., Greenville, NC, 2002—. Participant Jeanie B Tall Ships, Pepsi Am.'s Sail, 2006; sailing capt., instr. Outer Banks Sail and Kayak.

SUTTON, LYNN SORENSEN, librarian; b. Detroit, July 31, 1953; d. Leonard Arthur Edward and Dorothy Ann (Steele) Sorensen. AB, U. Mich., 1975, MLS, 1976. Dir. Med. Libr. South Chgo. Cmty. Hosp., 1976-77; corp. dirs. librs. Detroit-Macomb Hosp. Corp., Detroit, 1977-86; dir. librs. Harper Hosp., Detroit, 1987-88; dir. Sci. and Engring. Libr. Wayne State U., Detroit, 1989-95, dir. undergrad. libr., 1996—2004; dir. Z. Smith Reynolds Libr. Wake Forest U., Winston-Salem, NC, 2004—. Cons. Catherine McAuley Health Sys., Ann Arbor, Mich., 1993. Contbr. articles to profl. jours. Mem. ALA, Assn. Coll. and Rsch. Librs. (budget and fin. com. 1995—), Mich. Health Scis. Librs. Assn. (pres. 1987-88), Met. Detroit Med. Libr. Group (pres. 1983-84), Phi Beta Kappa, Beta Phi Mu. Office: Z Smith Reynolds Libr Wake Forest U Box 7777 Reynolda Station Winston Salem NC 27109 Office Phone: 336-758-5090. Business E-Mail: suttonls@wfu.edu.

SUTTON, NEAL S., lawyer; b. Grand Forks, ND, Sept. 9, 1945; BA, U. Houston, 1969, JD, 1972. Bar: Tex. 1972, US Ct. Appeals (5th cir.) 1972. Atty. pvt. practice; gen. counsel, sec. Cameron Iron Works (acquired by Cooper Industries Inc. in 1989), Houston, 1977—89; assoc. gen. counsel Cooper Industries Inc., Houston, 1989—91; v.p., sec., gen. counsel Smith Internat. Inc., Houston, 1991—92, v.p. adminstrn., gen. counsel, sec., 1992—94, sr. v.p. adminstrn., gen. counsel, sec., 1994—2006, sr. v.p. law, 2006—. Adj. assoc. prof. adminstrv. sci. Rice U. Jones Grad. Sch. Adminstrn., 1989—93; gulf coast dist. dir. Petroleum Equipment Suppliers Assn. Bd. dirs. Harris County Edn. Found., 1997—. Mem.: Am. Corp. Counsel Assn. (dir. Houston chpt. 1984—87, pres. Houston chpt. 1985—86, mem. nat. bd. dirs. 1988—96), State Bar Tex., Houston Bar Assn. (dir. corp. counsel sect. 1991—93), ABA. Office: Smith Internat Inc PO Box 60068 Houston TX 77205-0068

SUTTON, PETER CAMPBELL, museum director; b. Boston, Mar. 30, 1949; s. Francis Xavier and Jacqueline (Young) S.; m. Mary Lynn Riesmeyer, Mar. 7, 1981; children: Page Alicia, Spencer Burns. AB magna cum laude, Harvard U., 1972; MA, Yale U., 1975, PhD, 1978. Finley fellow Nat. Gallery Art, Washington, 1978-79; asst. curator European paintings Phila. Mus. Art, 1979-83, assoc. curator, 1983-85; Mrs. Russell W. Baker curator European paintings Mus. Fin. Arts, Boston, 1985; exec. dir., CEO Bruce Mus., Greenwich, Conn. Author: Pieter de Hooch, 1980, Dutch Art in America, 1986, Northern European Paintings in the Philadelphia Museum of Art, 1990, Dutch and Flemish Paintings, The Harold Samuel Collection, 1992; (exhbn. catalogues) Masters of Seventeenth Century/Dutch Genre Painting, 1984, Masters of 17th Century Dutch Landscape Painting, 1987-88, Prized Possessions, 1992, The Age of Rubens, 1993-94, numerous others; contbr. articles, revs. to profl. jours. Shaw travelling fellow, 1972-73, Yale U. fellow, 1973-76, David E. Finley fellow Nat. Gallery Art, 1976-79; Kress travel grantee, 1975. Mem. Coll. Art Assn. (Alfred Barr award 1986), Union Boat Club.

SUTTON, PHILIP D(IETRICH), psychologist, educator; b. June 20, 1952; s. Clifton C. and Ida-Lois (Dietrich) S.; m. Kathleen E. Duffy, June 17, 1973; children: Heather, Shivonne. BA, So. Ill. U., 1974; MA, U. Chgo., 1975; PhD, U. Utah, 1979. Lic. psychologist, Colo. Psychologist VA Hosp., Salt Lake City, 1975-76; psychology intern Salt Lake Cmty. Mental Health Ctr., 1976-77; counselor, instr. Counseling Ctr. U. Utah, 1976-78; counselor, acting dir. spl. svcs. program Met. State Coll., Denver, 1978-80; staff psychologist Kaiser-Permanente Health Plan, 1980—83; pvt. practice Boulder, 1983—. Adj. prof. U. Colo., 1979-83; cons. spl. program for disacvantaged students in higher edn. HEW, 1980. Mem. APA, Biofeedback Soc., Am. Soc. Behavioral Medicine. Office: Box 1781 Nederland CO 80466 Office Phone: 720-406-0400. Personal E-mail: pdsphd@aol.com.

SUTTON, ROBERT EDWARD, investment company executive; b. Burlington, Vt., July 3, 1943; s. Rollin Robert and Blanche Margaret (Deforge) S.; m. Julie Robin Levine, Feb. 1, 1975; children: Katherine Vanessa, David Robert. BA in Econs., St. Michaels Coll., 1962-66. V.p. Compretic, Inc., Beverly Hills, Calif., 1967-70; brokerage cons. Conn. Gen. Life Ins. Co., Denver, 1970-74; pres. The Core Corp., Denver, 1975-80; mng. dir. Willshire Investments & Holding Co., Denver, 1981-91; pres., chmn. Gen. Capital, Inc., Denver, 1991-93; pres, CEO WK Capital Advisors, Inc., Denver, 1994—; prin., owner Sutton Motorsports, 2002—; co-owner MBZ Motorsports, 2005—06. Dir. Nat. Assn. Indep. Contr., Denver. 1991—, Nat. Endowment Trust, Denver, 1990—, Tri Corp, Denver, 1980-89, Nat. Acceptance Corp., LA, 1991—, Nat. Investment Holdings, LA, 1990—99; chmn. Centrix Findmiol, LLC, 1998—06, EIF, Inc., 1998—06, Centrix Fin., LLC. Mem. Nat. Rep. Eagles, Washington, 1986-90, Inner Circle, Washington, 1985-90, Denver Ctr. Performing Arts, 1976-86; bd. trustees St. Michaels Coll., Burlington, Vt.; bd. dirs. St. John's Hospice, Make-a-Wish Found. Mem. Am. Cancer League, Glenmoor Country Club. Home: 4949 South Fairfax St Littleton CO 80121 Office Phone: 303-773-4210.

SUTTON, RONNIE NEAL, state legislator, lawyer; b. Pembroke, NC, June 17, 1941; s. Willie French and Vergie Mae (Oxendine) S.; m. Genny Chavis, June 19, 1967; children: Ronette, Fonda Lynn. BA, U. West Fla., 1970; MS, Naval War Coll., 1977; MA, Ctrl. Mich. U., 1979; JD, U. N.C., 1985. Commd. ensign USN, 1958, advanced through grades to comdr., ret., 1982; atty. Sutton Law Office, Pembroke, 1985—; mem. Dist. 47 N.C. House of Reps., 1993—. Bd. dirs. Lumber River Legal Svcs., Pembroke, N.C. Cancer Inst., Lumberton. Chmn. Robeson County Dem. Party, Lumberton, 1991-92. Mem. Pembroke Kiwanis Club (pres. 1991-92, Kiwanian of Yr. 1992). Democrat. Methodist. Home: 2940 Philadelphus Rd Pembroke NC 28372-8308 Office: NC House of Representatives 16 W Jones St Rm 1321 Raleigh NC 27601-1096 Home Phone: 910-775-9090; Office Phone: 919-715-0875. Business E-Mail: Ron.Sutton@ncleg.net.

SUTTON, WILLIAM G., JR., (WOODY SUTTON), federal agency administrator, retired military officer; b. Brunswick, Ga., 1948; m. Claudia A. Mansfield. BS, U.S. Naval Acad., 1970; MS Naval Architecture, Marine Engring., MIT. Commd. ensign USN, 1970, advanced through grades to rear admiral, ASW officer USS Jonas Ingram, weapons officer USS Suribachi, ops. officer, navigator, exec. officer USS Kidd, comdr. USS Callaghan Straits of Hormuz, comdr. Destroy Squadron Twenty-Four, naval aide to Pres. Reagan, dir. programs, Navy Office of Legis. Affairs; instr. naval sys. engring. US Naval Acad.; chief of staff Comdr. Second Fleet, Comdr. Striking Fleet USN, dir. jt. staff comdr. jt. task force Haitian Ops., comdr. Naval Surface Group, Mid. Pacific, 1996-99, comdr. Pearl Harbor Naval Base, 1996-99; dir. programs, Office Legis Affairs Dept. of Navy, US Dept. Def.; pres. Air-Conditioning & Refrigeration Inst., 2002—07; asst. sec. for mfrs. & services, Internat. Trade Adminstrn. US Dept. Commerce, Washington, 2007—. Office: US Dept Commerce 1401 Constitution Ave NW Washington DC 20230*

SUTTON-CREECH, DONNA LYNN, gifted and talented educator; b. Arcadia, La., Dec. 14, 1963; d. Jerry Lamar and Betty Muse Sutton; m. Stephen Orel Creech, July 9, 2005; 1 child, Spencer Kyle Sutton Creech. BA, La. Tech. U., 1984, MA, 1985, EdD in curriculum and instruction, 2002. Compensatory edn. tchr. Bienville Parish Sch. Sys., Arcadia, La., 1985—90; parttime computer instr. Northwest La. Tech. Coll., Minden, La., 2002—04; gifted program tchr. Bienville Parish, Sch. Sys., Arcadia, 1990—. Computer workshop presenter Bienville Parish La. Libr., Arcadia, La., 2003. Publr. genealogy column, Bienville Democrat. Participant Tech Rome 1987, La. Tech. U. Recipient Daughters of Am. Revolution Outstanding Jr. Mem. award, Dorcheat-Bistineau, 1997; named Tchr. of Yr., Ringgold Elem. Sch., 1995; La. Heritage Edn. grant, La. Divsn. Archaeology and Hist., 2003. Mem.: DAR (Dorcheat-Bistineau chpt. officer, vice regent, historian, chpt. chair, Dorcheat-Bistineau chpt. scholarship com., Good Citizens award), Phi Delta Kappa, Krewe of Gemini, Colonial Dames Seventeenth Century (state jr. mem. chair 2001—04, Martha Randolph chpt. v.p. 2002—04, state pages chair), Nat. Soc. Magna Carta Dames and Barons, USA Order of Crown of Charlemagne. Republican. Baptist. Avocations: genealogy, reading, travel, painting.

SUTTON-STRAUS, JOAN M., journalist; b. Mimico, Ont., Can., Nov. 30, 1932; d. Frederick Edward and Anna May (Taylor) Treble; m. Walter J. Sutton, Feb. 1955 (div. 1979); children: Walter John, Deborah Anne.; m. Oscar S. Straus, Mar. 1982. Fashion editor Toronto Telegram, 1972; lifestyle editor, daily columnist Sutton's Place, Toronto Sun, 1972-79; daily commentator Sta. CFRB, Toronto, 1974-77; columnist Toronto Star, 1979; agt. gen. to U.S. Ont., 1990-91; columnist Toronto, Calgary, Edmonton and Ottawa Sun. Fin. Post, 1992-94. Author: Lovers and Others, 1974, Once More with Love, 1975, Clothing and Culture, 1975, Lovelines, 1979, All Men are not Alike, 1980, A Legacy of Caring, 1996. Former mem. adv. bd. Peggy Guggenheim Mus.; former trustee Am. Acad. Dramatic Arts; nat. gov. The Shaw Festival; trustee Am. Friends of Can., The Banff Ctr.; dir. Citizens Com. for N.Y.C., dir. emeritus, trustee The Fred Lavanburg Found. Decorated Canada medal; recipient Judy award Garment Salesmen Ont., 1964; named Can. Woman of Yr., N.Y.C., 1990; honored with Freedom of City of London, Theodore Roosevelt award, 2007.

SUUBERG, ERIC MICHAEL, chemical engineering educator; b. NYC, Nov. 23, 1951; s. Michael and Aino (Berg) S.; m. Ina Inara Vatvars, Apr. 26, 1987; 1 child, Alessandra Anna. BSChemE, MSChemE, MIT, 1974, BS in Bus. Mgmt., 1974, MS in Bus. Mgmt., 1976, ScD in Chem. Engring., 1978. Asst. prof. chem. engring. Carnegie-Mellon U., Pitts., 1977-81; asst. prof. engring. Brown U., Providence, 1981-84, assoc. prof. engring., 1984-90, prof. engring., 1990—, rep. exec. com. fluids, thermal and chem. processes group, 1991—97, 2006—, assoc. dean faculty, 2003—05; co-dir. Brown, Superfund Basic Rsch. Program, 2005—. Vis. scientist Centre National de la Recherche Scientifique, Mulhouse, France, 1988; invited lectr. Ministry Edn., Monbusho, Japan, 1991, 93, 2003; vis. prof. Tallinn Tech. U., 2001. Mem. internat. editl. bd. Fuel, 1988—, mem. editl. adv. bd. Energy and Fuels, 1990—93, 1998—2000, Americas editor Fuel, 2000—, contbr. over 100 articles to books and profl. jours. Elected mem. Estonian Am. Nat. Coun., N.Y.C., 1984-99, v.p. 1996-99, bd. dirs. 2002—. Vice Chancellor's Rsch. Best Practice fellow U. Newcastle, Australia, 1995; Fulbright scholar, 2000-01. Mem. AIChE, Combustion Inst., Am. Chem. Soc. (chmn. divsn. fuel chemistry 1991, bd. dirs.-at-large 1995-97, trustee 2002—, H.H. Storch award in fuel chemistry Am. Chem. Soc. 1999). Office: Brown Univ Divsn Engring Box D Providence RI 02912 E-mail: eric_suuberg@brown.edu.

SUVA, LARRY JOHN, orthopedic researcher; arrived in US, 1989, permanent resident, 1991; s. Ladislav John and Maureen Suva; m. Dana Gaddy, Aug. 10, 2002; children: Megan Kurten children: Megan Kate Suva-Urwin, Jack William Suva-Urwin. BS in Chemistry and Biochemistry, Swinburne U., Melbourne, 1981; PhD in Medicine, U. Melbourne, Australia, 1989. Post-doctoral fellow Merck Rsch. Labs., West Point, Pa., 1989—92; asst. prof. med. sch. Harvard U., Boston, 1992—97; assoc. dir. GlaxoSmithKline, Phila., 1997—2000; prof. U. Ark., Little Rock, 2000—. Mem.: Endocrine Soc., Am. Soc. Bone and Mineral Rsch. (mem. coun. 2000—03). Achievements include patents for diagnosis of breast cancer; calcium receptor antagonists for osteoporosis; tumor derived PTHrP antibodies. Avocations: skiing, bicycling. Office: UAMS 4301 West Markham Little Rock AR 72205 Office Fax: 501-686-8987. Business E-Mail: suvalarryj@uams.edu.

SUWAT, LIPTAPANLOP, Thailand government official; b. Ratchaburi Province, Thailand, Feb. 9, 1955; married. BS in Civil Engring., Kasetsart U.; MS in Transport Engring., Purdue U. Dep. min. Ministry of Transport and Comm., 1990-92, min., 1996, Ministry of Sci., Tech. and Environ., 1995, Ministry of Industry, Bangkok, 1998—2001; dep. prime min., 2004—; min. Justice, 2005. Sec. gen. Chart Pattana Party. Recipient 1996 Knight Grand Cordon (Special Class) of the Most Exalted Order Of the White Elephant, Thailand. Buddhist. Office: Ministry of Industry Rama VI Rd Ratchathewi Bangkok 10400 Thailand

SUWYN, MARK A., paper company executive; b. Denver, Aug. 12, 1942; BS in Chemistry, Hope Coll., Holland, Mich., 1964; PhD in Inorganic Chemistry, Wash. State U., Pullman, 1967. R & D to gen. mgmt. positions DuPont Co., 1967-91, sr. v.p. imaging and med. products, 1989-92; exec. v.p. distbn., dir. Internat. Paper, Purchase, NY, 1992-95; chmn., CEO La.-Pacific Corp., Portland, Oreg., 1996—2004, NewPage Corp., 2006—. Chmn. & CEO NewPage Corp. Office: NewPage Corp 8540 Gander Creek Dr Miamisburg OH 45342

SUYDAM, JOHN J., lawyer; b. NYC, 1960; BA, SUNY, Albany, 1982; JD, NYU, 1985. Bar: NY 1986. Chmn. O'Sullivan, LLP, NY; head O'Melveny & Myers, LLP, NY, mem. policy com., co-chair merger and acquisitions/private equity practice group, 2002—06; chief legal officer, v.p. Apollo Investment Corp., NYC, 2006—. Mem.: ABA. Office: Apollo Investment Corp 9 W 57th St New York NY 10019

SUYENAGA, ELSIE SAKAE, retired elementary school educator; b. Honolulu, Dec. 19; d. Shigeharu Shimizu-Jinbo and Misao Jinbo; m. James Saburo Suyenaga; 1 child, Matthew Masao. BA, Pasadena Coll., 1963; postgrad., U. Hawaii, 1963—81. Sec. Nuuanu Bapt. Ch., 1954—62; tchr. Ewa Beach (Hawaii) Elem. Sch., 1964—89. Exch. tchr. Laurel Elem. Sch. LA Sch. Dist., 1968—69; advisor student coun. Laurel Elem. Sch. Sec. Palisades Cmty. Assn., 1977; treas. Neighborhood Bd., Pearl City, 1982; legis. chmn., treas. Pearl City Cmty. Assn., 1984—85; treas. local chpt. PTA; active polit. campaigns. Recipient Student Coun. Advisor award, Ewa Beach Elem. Sch., 1978, Dist. award, PTA, 1976, Merit Cert., Pearl City Cmty. Assn., 1977, Recognition award, Ewa Beach Kiwanis, 1986; Fed. grant, 1963. Mem.: DAV, Am. Mus. Natural History, Hawaii Edn. Assn. (bd. trustees 1986—), Leeward Tchrs. Assn. (treas., polit. sect. chmn. 1986), Hawaii State Tchrs. Assn. (dir. 1981—83, sec. fin. com. 1981, vice-chmn. 1982, Merit Cert. 1969), Alpha Delta Kappa (treas. Lambda chpt. 1980—81). Democrat. Baptist. Home: 6354 San Diego Ave Riverside CA 92506 E-mail: suyenaga@charter.net.

SUZIEDELIS, VYTAUTAS A., retired engineering corporation executive; b. Kaunas, Lithuania, June 22, 1930; s. Simas and Antanina S. BS, Northeastern U., 1954; MS, NYU, 1955. With Stone & Webster Engring. Corp., Boston, 1956-90, chief power engr., 1972-74, v.p., 1974-76, sr. v.p., 1976-79, exec. v.p., 1979-87, dir., 1975-87, cons., 1987-90; pres. Vasair Corp., Brockton, Mass., 1977-91; ret., 1991. Mem. ASME, Aircraft Owners and Pilots Assn., Pi Tau Sigma (hon.). Republican. Roman Catholic. Home: 6849 Grenadier Blvd Ph 5 Naples FL 34108-7223 Personal E-mail: vasuziedelis@cs.com.

SUZUKI, AKANE, metallurgist; BS, Tokyo Inst. Tech., 1999, MS, 2001, PhD, 2003. Postdoc. rsch. fellow U. Mich., Ann Arbor, 2003—07; metallurgist GE Global Rsch., Niskayuna, NY, 2007—. Rsch. fellowship, Japan Soc. Promotion of Sci., 2001—03. Mem.: Minerals, Metals & Materials Soc. (Magnesium Tech. award 2005), Iron and Steel Inst. Japan, Japan Inst. Metals, Sigma Xi, Materials Rsch. Soc. Office: GE Global Rsch 1 Research Cir Niskayuna NY 12309

SUZUKI, AKIRA, physics professor; b. Tokyo, Apr. 14, 1949; s. Masatsugu and Takako (Tanbo) S.; m. Keiko Sawamura, Sept. 13, 1992. BSc, Sci. U. Tokyo, 1973; PhD, U. Reading, Eng., 1982. Rsch. assoc. Purdue U., West Lafayette, Ind., 1982-85; chief scientist Canon Inc. Rsch. Ctr., Atsugi, Japan, 1986-93; assoc. prof. Sci. U. Tokyo, 1993-98, prof. physics, 1998—, chmn., 2002—08; prof. Inst. Pure and Applied Physics Tokyo U. Sci., 1998—. Author: Foundation of Statistical Thermodynamics; contbr. articles to profl. jours. Mem. IEEE, Am. Phys. Soc., NY Acad. Scis. Avocations: tennis, golf, music. Office: Sci U Tokyo Ctr Solid State Physics 1-3 Kagurazaka Tokyo 162 Japan

SUZUKI, BOB H., retired academic administrator; b. Jan. 1936; BS in Aeronautics, PhD in Aeronautics, Calif. Inst. Tech., Pasadena; MS in Mech. Engring., U. Calif., Berkeley. Formerly v.p. acad. affairs Calif. State Univ., Northridge; pres. Calif. State Poly. Univ., Pomona, 1991—2003; ret., 2003. Recipient Human Rights award Leadership Asian and Pacific Island Affairs, NEA, 1976, Order of Rising Sun, Japanese Govt., 2003. Home: 3012 W Ross Ave Alhambra CA 91803 Personal E-mail: bsuzuki1@charter.net.

SUZUKI, EDWARD M., chemist; b. Seattle, June 16, 1947; m. Joanne F. Tanabe, Aug. 17, 1975. BS, U. Wash., Seattle, 1970; PhD, Oreg. State U., Corvallis, 1975. Rsch. chemist Nat. Marine Fisheries Svc., NOAA, Seattle, 1975—79; forensic scientist Wash. State Crime Lab., Seattle, 1979—2001, supervising forensic scientist, 2001—08. V.p. Lake Wash. Chpt. Japanese Am. Citizens League, Bellevue, 2005—07. Recipient Wash. State Patrol Chief's award, Wash. State Crime Lab., 1991; fellow, Am. Bd. Criminalistics, 1998. Fellow: Am. Acad. Forensic Scis. (Gen. Sect. award 1988); mem.: Coblenz Soc., Soc. Applied Spectroscopy, Northwest Assn. Forensic Scientists, Am. Chem. Soc., Phi Beta Kappa (puget sound chpt., Inspirational and Scholarship award 1968). Achievements include research in forensic chemistry. Office: Wash State Crime Lab 2203 Airport Way South Bld A Suite 250 Seattle WA 98134 Office Fax: 206-262-6033. Business E-Mail: edward.suzuki@wsp.wa.gov.

SUZUKI, HIDETARO, violinist; b. Tokyo, June 1, 1937; arrived in U.S., 1956; s. Hidezo and Humi (Sakai) S.; m. Zeyda Ruga, May 16, 1962; children: Kenneth Hideo, Nantel Hiroshi, Elina Humi. Diploma, Toho Sch. Music, Tokyo, 1956, Curtis Inst. Music, 1963. Prof. violin Conservatory Province Que., Canada, 1963-79, Laval U., Quebec, Canada, 1971-77, Butler U., Indpls., 1979—. Concertmaster Que. Symphony Orch., 1963-78, Indpls. Symphony Orch., 1978-2005; performed as concert violinist Can., U.S., Ea. and Western Europe, Cuba, Japan, S.E. Asia, India, USSR 1951-; guest condr. orchs. in numerous concerts, broadcasts, 1968—; mem. jury Mont. Internat. Competition, 1979, Internat. Violin Competition, 1979, jury for Internat. Violin Competition of Indpls., 1982, 86, 90, 94; artistic dir. Suzuki and Friends chamber music series, 1980-, founder Pro Musica Washington, 2007-; rec. artist (CDs, violin and piano) Dialogue, Dialogue II, Pas de deux.

SUZUKI, HOWARD KAZURO, retired anatomist, educator; b. Ketchikan, Alaska, Apr. 3, 1927; s. Goerge K. and Tsuya S.; m. Tetsuko Fujita, Sept. 12, 1952; children: Georganne, Joan, James, Stanley. BS, Marquette U., 1949, MS, 1951; PhD, Tulane U., 1955. Instr. anatomy Yale U. Sch. Medicine, 1955-58; asst. prof. anatomy U. Ark. Med. Center, Little Rock, 1958-62, asso. prof., 1962-67, prof., 1967-70; prof. anatomy, asso. dean health related professions U. Fla., Gainesville, 1970-71; prof. anatomy U. Fla. (Coll. Medicine), 1970-71; dean U. Fla. (Coll. Health Related Professions), 1971-79; prof. anatomy U. Fla. (Coll. Medicine and Health Related Professions), 1979-90, ret., 1990. Cons. NIH, VA, NASA; vis. research prof. U. Utah Sch. Medicine, 1962 Contbr. articles to profl. jours. Bd. dirs. Civitan Regional Blood Bank, 1977—; regional v.p. Fla. Retarded Citizens Assn., 1974-76; mem. Fla. Adv. Council on Vocat. Edn., 1978-86, chmn., 1981; active United Way. Fellow AAAS; mem. Soc. Exptl. Biol. Medicine, Am Assn. Anatomists, Am. Soc. Allied Health Professions, Am. Soc. Marine Artists, Sigma Xi. Episcopalian. Home: 4331 NW 20th Pl Gainesville FL 32605-3436 E-mail: hksuzuki@aol.com.

SUZUKI, ICHIRO, professional baseball player; b. Kasugai, Japan, Oct. 22, 1973; m. Yumiko Suzuki. Player Orix Blue Waves, Japan, 1992—2001; right fielder Seattle Mariners, 2001—. Mem. Japanese nat. team World Baseball Classic, 2006, 09. Recipient 8 Gold Glove awards, Nippon Profl. Baseball League, Matsutaro Shoriki prize, 1994—95, Silver Slugger award, 2001, 2007, Gold Glove award, 2001—08; named Pacific League MVP, 1994—96, Am. League Rookie of Yr., 2001, Am. League MVP, 2001, Maj. League All-Star Game MVP, 2007; named to Am. League All-Star Team, 2001—09, All-Tourney Team, World Baseball Classic, 2006. Achievements include becoming the second player in Major League Baseball history named Rookie of the Year and MVP in the same season, 2001; leading the American League in: at bats, 2001, 2004-08; hits, 2001, 2004, 2006-08; singles, 2001-08; batting average, 2001, 2004; stolen bases, 2001; setting MLB records for hits (262) and singles (225) in a season, 2004; member of the World Baseball Classic winning Japanese national team, 2006, 2009; recording his 3,000 career hit (Japanese League and MLB), 2008; tying the MLB record for consecutive 200 hit seasons (8), 2001-08; becoming the Japanese all-time hits leader, 2009. Office: Seattle Mariners PO Box 4100 Seattle WA 98104*

SUZUKI, JON BYRON, medical educator, periodontist, microbiologist; s. George K. and Ruby Suzuki. BA in Biology, Ill. Wesleyan U., 1968; PhD in Microbiology magna cum laude, Ill. Inst. Tech., 1971; DDS magna cum laude, Loyola U., 1978. Lic. lab. dir. Hawaii Dept. Health. Med. technologist Ill. Masonic Hosp. and Med. Ctr., Chgo., 1966—67; instr. lab. in histology and parasitology Ill. Wesleyan U., Bloomington, 1967—68; med. technologist Augustana Hosp., Chgo., 1968—69; rsch. assoc., instr. microbiology Ill. Inst. Tech., Chgo., 1968—71; clin. rsch. assoc. U. Chgo. Hosps., 1970—71; clin. microbiologist St. Luke's Hosp., Columbia Coll., Physicians and Surgeons, NYC, 1971—73; assoc. med. dir. Paramed Tng. and Registry, Vancouver, BC, Canada, 1973—74; dir. clin. labs. Registry of Hawaii, 1973—74; chmn. clin. labs. edn. Kapiolany C.C., U. Hawaii, Honolulu, 1974; lectr. periodontics, oral pathology Loyola U. Med. Ctr., Maywood, Ill., 1974—90; lectr. stomatology Northwestern U. Dental Sch., Chgo., 1982—90; NIH rsch. fellow depts. pathology and periodontics Ctr. for Rsch. in Oral Biology, U. Wash., Seattle, 1978—80; prof. dept. periodontics and microbiology U. Md. Coll. Dental Surgery, Balt., 1980—90; attending faculty divsn. dentistry and oral and maxillofacial surgery Johns Hopkins Med. Inst., Balt., 1985—96; practice specializing in periodontics Balt. and Pitts.; prof., dean Sch. Dental Medicine U. Pitts., 1989—2000, prof., dir. periodontics residency program, 2002—04. Cons. Dentsply Internat., York, Pa., U.S. Army, Walter Reed Med. Ctr., Washington, U.S. Army, Ft. Gordon, Ga., USN, Nat. Naval Med. Command, Bethesda, The NutraSweet Col, Chgo., FDA, Rockville, Md., 1995—, Phillips Oral Health Care, Snoqualmie, Wash.; oral biology/medicine study sect. NIH, Bethesda, 1985-90; nat. adv. dental rsch. coun. NIH/NIDCR, Bethesda, 1994-98; vis. scientist Moscow State U., USSR, 1972, NASA, Houston, 1976-92; lectr. Internat. Congress allergology, Tokyo, 1973. Author: Clinical Laboratory Methods for the Medical Assistant, 1974; mem. editl. bd. Jour. Clinical Dentistry, Jour. Practical Hygiene, Jour. Acad. Gen. Dentistry; contbr. articles on rsch. in microbiology, immunology and dentistry to profl. jours. Instr. water safety ARC, Honolulu, 1973—90. Recipient Pres.'s medallion Loyola U., Chgo., 1977; named Alumnus of Yr., Ill. Wesleyan U., 1977, Loyola U., Chgo., 1997. Fellow Acad. Dentistry Internat., Am. Coll. Dentists, Internat. Coll. Dentists, Am. Coll. Stomatognathic Surgeons; mem. ADA (chair coun. sci. affairs 1998), AAUP, Am. Acad. Periodontology (diplomate), Am. Dental Edn. Assn., Am. Inst. Biol. Scis., Internat. Soc. Biophysics, Internat. Soc. Endocrinologists, Ill. Acad. Sci., Am. Internat. Assn. Dental Rsch. (pres. Md. chpt.), Am. Coll. Microbiology (diplomate, examiner), Am. Soc. Clin. Pathology (specialist microbiology), N.Y. Acad. Scis., Sigma Xi, Omicron Kappa Upsilon (past nat. pres., exec. sec. 1989—, treas. 2006—), Beta Beta Beta. Office: Temple Univ Dentistry Office of the Dean 3223 N Broad St Philadelphia PA 19140 Office Phone: 215-707-7667. Business E-Mail: jon.suzuki@temple.edu. E-mail: jsuzuki@temple.edu.

SUZUKI, MAKOTO, thoracic surgeon; b. Aomori, Japan, May 28, 1962; s. Takashi and Chikako Suzuki; m. Orie Suzuki, May 5, 1967; children: Yu, Ai. MD, Chiba U., Japan, 1989, PhD. Thoracic surgeon Chiba U., Japan, 1989—. Postdoctoral fellow Southwestern Med. Ctr., Dallas, 2001—03. Office: Dept Thoracic Surgery Chiba Univ 1-8-1 Inohana Chuo-ku Chiba 260-8670 Japan Office Fax: 81-43-226-2172. E-mail: smakoto@faculty.chiba-u.jp.

SUZUKI, NORIYASU, physician, psychologist, journalist; b. Sanjo, Niigataken, Japan, Oct. 20, 1947; s. Souroku and Haru Suzuki. Degree in physics, Nihon U.; degree in journalism, Tokyo U. With USHHSC, San Chico, Japan; mathematician Army Coll. U. Home: 1-7-4 Cinema House Sanchiku Sanjo 955-0041 Japan Office: 1-7-2 USHHSC San Chico Santo Niigata Japan

SUZUKI, OSAMU, automotive executive; b. Gero, Gifu, Japan, Jan. 30, 1930; s. Shunzo and Toshiko S.; m. Shoko Suzuki, 1958; 3 children. Student, Chuo U., Japan, 1953. Joined Suzuki Motor Co. Ltd., 1958, various mgmt. positions, 1958-63, dir., 1963-66, jr. mng. dir., 1967-72, sr. mng. dir., 1973-77, pres., 1978-2000, chmn., 2000—. Recipient Sitara-i-Pakistan award Govt. of Pakistan, 1985, Honor with Blue Ribbon medal, 1987, Mid. Cross of Order of Rep. Hungary, 1993, Second Class Order of the Rising Sun, Gold and Silver Star, 2000. Avocation: golf. Office: Suzuki Motor Corp 300 Takatsuka-cho Hamamatsu 432-8611 Japan

SUZUKI, TADAO, retired corporate financial executive; b. Japan, Jan. 16, 1930; m. Takako Suzuki. Grad., Keio U., Japan, 1951; postgrad., Northwestern U., Evanston, Ill., 1952. With Ajinomoto Co, Inc., 1951—, vice chmn., 1987—; corporate auditor Ajinomoto Corp., 2002—; pres. Mercian Corp., Tokyo, 1987; ret. Mem.: Corporate Governance Forum of Japan (chmn.), Japan Winery Assn., Fedn. of Employers Associations, Fedn. of Economic Organizations. Office: Mercian Corp 5-8 Kyobas Hi 1-Chrome Chuo-ku Tokyo 104 Japan

SUZUKI, YASUHIKO, retired law educator; b. Mishima, Japan, Sept. 6, 1936; arrived in U.S., 68; s. Heiji and Hiro Suzuki; m. Kyoko Teraizumi Suzuki, May 14, 1961; children: Iori, Anri, Claude. LLB, Chuo U., Tokyo, 1960; LLM, Georgetown U., 1972. V.p. Nissan Motor Corp., Gardena, Calif., 1968—85; chmn. bd. dirs. Pacific Trade & Investment Corp., Washington, 1985—90; prof. U. Va., Charlottesville, 1991—93, Showa Joshi U., Tokyo, 1994—96, George Mason U., Fairfax, Va., 1996—2003. Vice chmn. Automobile Importers Am., Washington, 1975—85; lectr. in field. Author: Washington Lobby, 1990, The American Nation, 1999, The Constitution of the United States - The Evolving Constitution, 2000, Is the Second Amendment Anachronism? - The Right to Keep and Bear Arms, 2003. Bd. dirs. Japanese C. of C., NYC, 1978—85, Washington, 1979—85. Recipient cert. of recognition for outstanding contbns. and efforts, Humane Soc. of Washington, DC, 1980, Youth for Understanding, 1981; named to Automotive Hall of Fame, 1984. Mem.: Internat. Law Inst. Japan, Acad. Polit. Sci. Home: 31242 Avenida Terramar San Juan Capistrano CA 92675

SUZUKI, YOICHIRO, retired asset management company executive; b. Tokyo, Sept. 20, 1932; s. Hideo and Matsuko (Nagata) S.; m. Kimiko Fujita, Mar. 29, 1963; 1 child, Tetsu. BA, Tokyo U., 1956. Exec. v.p. Nissei BOT Asset Mgmt. Corp., NYC, 1984-87; CEO BOT Touche Remnant Ltd., London, 1987-89, Bank of Tokyo Asset Mgmt. Ltd., 1989-92; mng. dir. Nat. Mut. Funds Mgmt. (Japan) Ltd., Tokyo, 1992-99; sr. advisor AXA Investment Mgrs. Tokyo Ltd., 1999; ret., 1999. Avocation: golf. Home: 4-6-11-1511 Yushima Bunkyo-ku Tokyo 113-0034 Japan Fax: 813-3811-5898. E-mail: yosuzuk@nifty.com.

SUZUKI, YUKIKO, language educator; b. Tokyo, June 21, 1962; d. Morio and Masako Shiratori; m. Akira Suzuki, Mar. 27, 1988; children: Nobiru, Koso. English tchr. Jr. HS, Yokyo Met. Govt., 1984—2006; prof. Japanese lang. Niagara U., 2007. Tchr. Buffalo Nihongo Club, 2006. Personal E-mail: yukikos155@hotmail.com.

SUZUKI-LAITILA, JUNKO KIANNA, biology professor; d. Yutaka and Toshie Suzuki. MS in Biology, Toho U., Chiba, Japan, 1992. Bacteriologist Japan Food Rsch. Labs., Shibuya-ku, Tokyo, 1992—95; instr. Antelope Valley Coll. CC, Lancaster, Calif., 2007—. Environment protection specialist NAF Atsugi USN, 2001—02, Ayase, Japan. Decorated Letter Commendation. Office: Antelope Valley Coll 3041 West Ave K Lancaster CA 93536 Business E-Mail: jlaitila@avc.edu.

SVAHN, JOHN ALFRED, federal agency administrator; b. New London, Conn., May 13, 1943; s. Albert Russell and Esther Marilu (Caffero) S.; m. Jill Weber, July 12, 1977; children: Kirsten Marie, John Alfred III. BA in Polit. Sci, U. Wash., 1966; postgrad., U. Pacific, 1970-73, Georgetown U., 1973-74. Spl. asst. to dir. Calif. Dept. Public Works, 1968-70; chief dep. dir. Calif. Dept. Social Welfare, 1971-73, dir., 1973; acting commr. Community Services Adminstrn., HEW, Washington, 1973-74; commr. Assistance Payments Adminstrn., 1973-76; dep. adminstr. Social and Rehab. Service, 1974-75; adminstr. Social and Rehab. Svcs., 1975-76; mgr. Haskins and Sells, 1976-79; pres. John A. Svahn, Inc., Annapolis, Md., 1979-81; U.S. commr. social security Balt., 1981-83; undersec. HHS, Washington, 1983-84; assst. to Pres. for policy devel. Washington, 1984-86; chmn. Maximus Inc., Washington, 1988-94; U.S. commr. Commn. for Study of Alternatives for Panama Canal, 1987-92; exec. v.p. The Wexler Group, Washington, 1995—; chmn. Captial Assocs., Inc., 1994—; bd. dirs. Logisticare, Inc., 2000—, EpicEdge, Inc., 2001—. Mem. Nat. Devel. Disability Adv. Council, 1975-76, Pres.'s Transition Team, 1980-81, Calif. Health Care Commn., 1972, pub. affairs com. United Way Am., 1987—; chmn. Govs. Commn. on Corrections Health Care, Md., 1990—; assoc. mem. Calif. Republican State Cen. Com., 1970-72; bd. dirs. Nat. Aquarium, Balt.; bd. dirs. Health Care Svcs. NAS Inst. Medicine, 1987-92; bd. dirs. Logisticare, Inc., 2001-; bd. dirs. Epic Edge, Inc., 2001-04; mem. Gov.'s Privatization Coun., 1992—. Served to lt. USAF, 1966-68. Named Outstanding Young Man in HEW, 1974; recipient Sec.'s citation, 1975, Adminstr.'s spl. citation, 1975 Mem. Annapolis Yacht Club, Sailing Club of the Chesapeake, Kent Island Yacht Club, Phi Delta Phi, Zeta Psi. Republican. Office: 4790 Caughlin Pkwy 317 Reno NV 89509 Personal E-mail: jacksvahn@aol.com.

SVALYA, PHILLIP GORDON, lawyer; b. Mich., June 28, 1943; s. John Michael and Ann Marie Svalya; children: Daniel Gordon, Karina Renee. BS, U.S. Naval Acad., Annapolis, Md., 1966; JD, U. Santa Clara, Calif., 1973. Bar: Calif. 1974, U.S. Dist. Ct. (no. dist.) Calif. 1974. Pvt. practice, Sunnyvale, Mountain View, Calif., 1974-81, Cupertino, Calif., 1981—. Officer, bd. dir. Albanian Health Fund, Phillis Found., Johnston Hope Found., Lt. USN, 1966-70, capt. USN SEAL ret., 1970-91. Mem. Calif. Bar Assn., Santa Clara County Bar Assn., Santa Clara County Trial Lawyers Assn., Sunnyvale/Cupertino Bar Assn., Underwater Demolition Team-SEAL Assn., Million Dollar Advocates Forum. Republican. Avocation: hiking. Office: Phillip G Svalya Inc 10455 Torre Ave Cupertino CA 95014-3203 Office Phone: 408-252-5211.

SVARLIEN, JOHN E., classicist, educator; b. Gainesville, Fla., Jan. 20, 1954; s. Jarle Oscar and Mattie Eugenia Svarlien; m. Diane Arnson Svarlien, Nov. 27, 1987; children: Aaron Atticus, Corinna Miriam. PhD, U. Tex., Austin, 1987. Vis. asst. prof. classics Ctr. Coll., Danville, Ky., 1987—93; prof. classics Transylvania U., Lexington, Ky., 1993—. Co-dir. Greece program Ky. Inst. Internat. Studies, 2004—06. Contbr. articles to profl. jours. Recipient Bingham award, Transylvania U., 2002. Mem.: Classical Assn. Mid. West and South (regional v.p. 1998—2003), Am. Philol Assn. Avocation: travel. Home: 619 Baldwin Ave Lexington KY 40502 Office: Transylvania Univ 300 North Broadway Lexington KY 40508 Office Fax: 859-281-3655. Business E-Mail: jsvarlien@transy.edu.

SVAROVSKY, SERGEI A., engineering educator; b. Tomsk, Russia, Apr. 20, 1967; s. Aleksandr P. Svarovsky and Yulia A. Svarovskaia; children: Katherine S. Swarovski, Michelle S. Swarovski. PhD, W.Va. U., Morgantown, 2000. Assoc. rsch. prof. Biodesign Inst., Tempe, Ariz., 2006—; CEO IBPT Corp., Scottsdale, Ariz., 2007—. Contbr. scientific papers (NIH Fellow award, 2002). Rsch. grant, Wallace Rsch. Initiative, 2008. Mem.: Internat. Union Against Cancer. Achievements include patents for artificial lectin mimics; invention of carbohydrate encapsulated quantum dots; charged hard core microparticles; long term hypothermic preservation of biological tissues and cells; heterobifunctional pseudo-oligosaccharides as pan-selectin inhibitors and anti-inflammatory agents. Avocations: photography, travel, running. Personal E-mail: ssvarovs2002@yahoo.com. Business E-Mail: sergei.svarovsky@asu.edu.

SVEHLAK, STEVEN ANDREW, plastic surgeon; b. Derby, Conn., Oct. 14, 1966; BS in Biology, U. Conn., Storrs, Conn.; MD, NY Med. Coll., Valhalla NY, 1994. Cert. Am. Bd. Surgery, 2001, Am. Bd. Plastic Surgery, 2003, lic. Calif. Bd. Medicine, DC Bd. Medicine. Surg. intern, gen. surgery Stamford Hosp., Columbia U. Coll. Physicians and Surgeons, Stamford, Conn., 1994—99; resident, gen. surgery Columbia Presbyn. Med. Ctr. Program in Surgery, Stamford, Conn.; resident, plastic surgery George Wash. U. Med. Ctr., Washington, 1999—2001, fellow, plastic surgery, 2001, Children's Nat. Med. Ctr., Washington; hosp. appt. plastic surgery Midway Hosp., West LA, Calif., Cedars Sinai Hosp., LA; advanced cosmetic surgery tng. fellowship Dr. Richard Ellenbogen, Beverly Hills, Calif., 2002; plastic surgeon Sunset Cosmetic Surgery, LA. Lectr. and presenter in field. Contbr. articles to profl. jours.; featured on Dr. 90210. Fellow: Am. Coll. Surgeons; mem.: AMA, Calif. Med. Assn., Am. Soc. Plastic Surgeons (candidate assoc.), Northeastern Soc. Plastic Surgery. Office: Sunset Cosmetic Surgery 9201 Sunset Blvd Ste 805 Los Angeles CA 90069 Office Phone: 310-858-9100. E-mail: drssvehlak@yahoo.com.*

SVEINSSON, LINDA RODGERS, engineering company executive; b. Tuscaloosa, Ala., July 1, 1938; d. Eric and Sarah Ella (Haughton) Rodgers; m. Hjalmar Sveinsson, May 29, 1971; children: Martha M. Moreno, Stephen R.M. Moreno, III. BA in Math., Birmingham-So. Coll., 1960; MS in Indsl. Engring., U. Ala., 1972. Sys. analyst U. Ala. Med. Ctr., Birmingham, 1967-69; sys. mgr. Internat. Data Sys., New Orleans, 1969-70; computer scientist Computer Scis. Corp., Silver Spring, Md., 1973-76; computer sys. specialist Sys. Devel. Corp., McLean, Va., 1976-78; mem. tech. staff Bell Labs., Holmdel, NJ, 1978—80, tech. supr. Columbus, Ohio, 1980—85; mgr. bus. devel. No. Telecom., Inc., Research Triangle Park, N.C., 1985-88; dept. mgr. network ops. and mgmt. systems GTE Fed. Systems, Ctr., 1988-94; cons. Bell Atlantic, 1994-95, AT&T Solutions, 1996-97, Noblis, 1998—. Mem. IEEE, Phi Beta Kappa, Alpha Pi Mu. Republican. Methodist. Office: 3150 Fairview Park Dr S Falls Church VA 22042 Office Phone: 703-610-2911. Business E-Mail: linda.sveinsson@noblis.org.

SVENDSBYE, LLOYD AUGUST, retired academic administrator, theologian, educator; b. Hamlet, ND, May 26, 1930; s. Anders A. and Gudrun J. (Birkelo) S.; m. Annelotte Frieda Erika Moertelmeyer, Dec. 20, 1958. BA, Concordia Coll., Moorhead, Minn., 1951, DD (hon.), 1983; BTh, Luther Theol.Sem., 1954; postgrad, U. Erlangen, Germany, 1954-55, Columbia U., 1959-60; ThD, Union Theol. Sem., 1966; LLD (hon.), Gettysburg Coll., 1977; LHD (hon.), Kilian C.C., 1992. Ordained to ministry, 1955; asst. pastor Our Saviours Luth. Ch., Mpls., 1955-56; adminstrv. asst. to dir. 3d Assembly Luth. World Fedn., 1956-57; asst. prof. religion Concordia Coll., 1957-59; asst. pastor Trinity Luth. Ch., Bklyn., 1959-61; chmn. dept. religion Concordia Coll., 1962-66; editor in chief Augsburg Publ. House, Mpls., 1966-71; v.p., dean St. Olaf Coll., 1971-74; pres., prof. ch. history Luther Theol. Sem., St. Paul, 1974-82; pres. Northwestern Luth. Theol. Sem., 1976-82; pres., prof. ch. history Luther Northwestern Theol. Sem., 1982—87; pres. Augustana Coll., Sioux Falls, SD, 1987-92; ret., 1992. V.p. Am. Luth. Ch., 1981-87; Mem. Am. Luth. Ch.-Luth. Ch. Am. coop. com., 1974-78; Luth. World Fedn. Com. on Info. Services, 1971-76; mem. Com. on Luth. Unity, 1978-82, Commn. To Form a New Luth. Ch., 1982-86; mem. ch. coun. Normandale Luth. Ch., 2003—, pres., 2005-07; mem. steering com. Tuesday Open House Mindekirken, 2004—; bd. dirs. Norway House, 2005—. Chmn. senate dist. 49A, Dem. Farm Labor Com., 1970-71; bd. dirs. Luth. Brotherhood, 1970-95, Luth. Gen. and Health Care Sys., Park Ridge, Ill., 1981-87; trustee Luth. Deaconess Hosp., Mpls., 1970-71, Fairview-Southdale Hosp., 1975-87, Fairview Cmty. Hosps., 1979-87. Recipient Alumni Achievement award Concordia Coll., 1974, Christus Lux Mundi award Luther Seminary, St. Paul, 2009. Mem. Phi Beta Kappa. Home: 2500 Quentin Ct Minneapolis MN 55416-1900 Home Phone: 952-927-0987. Personal E-mail: annelloy@aol.com.

SVENGALIS, KENDALL FRAYNE, law librarian, publishing executive, educator, writer; b. Gary, Ind., May 16, 1947; s. Frank Anthony and Alvida Linnea (Matheus) S.; children: Hillary Linnea, Andrew Kendall; m. Ellen Christine Haffling, June 16, 2001. BA, Purdue U., 1970, MA, 1973; MLS, U. R.I., 1975. Reference librarian Roger Williams Coll., Bristol, RI, 1975, Providence (R.I.) Coll., 1975-77; asst. law librarian R.I. State Law Library, Providence, 1976-82, state law librarian, 1982—2002. Adj. prof. libr. and info. studies U. R.I., 1987-2006; pres. RI Law Press, 1996—. Author: The Legal Information Buyer's Guide and Reference Manual, 1996 (Best Legal Reference Book of 1996), 13th edit., 2009, Gary, Indiana: A Centennial Celebration, 2006; editor: The Criv Sheet, 1988—94; contbr. articles to profl. jours. Chmn. jud. branch United Way Com. R.I., 1980; pres. Verdandi Male Chorus, 2000—. Recipient AALL Joseph L. Andrews Bibliographical awd. Mem. Am. Assn Law Librs. (state, ct. and county libr. spl. interest sect., Connie E. Bolden Significant Publ. award 1993, 99, bd. dirs. 1986-88, 96-99), Law Librs. New Eng. (treas. 1983-85, v.p. 1985-86, pres. 1986-87), Com. on Rels. with Info. Vendors (editor 1988-94), New Eng. Law Libr. Consortium (v.p. 1990-92, pres. 1992-94), Jussi Bjorling Soc. (v.p.), R.I. Swedish Heritage Assn. (pres.), Verdandi Swedish Male Chorus (pres.). Republican. Lutheran. Home: 204 Wyassup Rd North Stonington CT 06359 Office Phone: 860-535-0378. Personal E-mail: ksven@comcast.net, rilawpress@comcast.net.

SVENSON, CHARLES OSCAR, investment banker; b. Worcester, Mass., June 28, 1939; s. Sven Oscar and Edahjane (Castner) S.; m. Sara Ellen Simpson, Nov. 15, 1968; children: Alicia Lindall, Tait Oscar. AB, Hamilton Coll., 1961; LL.B., Harvard U., 1964; LL.M., Bklyn. Law Sch., 1965. Bar: N.Y. 1965, U.S. Dist. Ct. (so. dist.) N.Y. 1965, U.S. Ct. Appeals (2d. cir.) 1965. Atty. Dewey, Ballantine, Bushby, Palmer & Wood, NYC, 1964-68; v.p. Goldman Sachs & Co., NYC, 1968-75; sr. v.p. Donaldson, Lufkin & Jenrette, NYC, 1975-89, mng. dir., 1989-2000; sr. mng. dir. Brock Capital Group LLC, NYC, 2002—. Trustee Kirkland Coll., Clinton, N.Y., 1976-78, Hamilton Coll., Clinton, 1979-83, 90- Adirondack Mus. Nat. History, 2002-; pres. Harvard Law Sch. Assn. NYC, 2007-. Mem. ABA, N.Y. State Bar Assn., Assn. of Bar of City of N.Y. Clubs: Tuxedo (Tuxedo Park, N.Y.); Harvard (N.Y.C.). Home: 1185 Park Ave New York NY 10128-1308 Office: 622 Third Ave 12th Fl New York NY 10017 Office Phone: 212-209-3000. Business E-Mail: csvenson@brockcapital.com.

SVENSSON, CRAIG KARL, pharmaceutical sciences educator, dean; b. Balt., Feb. 6, 1957; s. Emil Leonard and Teresa Jane (Nugent) Svensson; m. Susan Jane Morey, July 7, 1984; children: Kate Marie, Eric David. BS, U. Md. Sch. Pharmacy, 1979, PharmD, 1981; PhD, SUNY, Buffalo, 1984. Poison info. specialist Md. Poison Ctr., U. Md., 1979—81; cons. clin. pharmacokinetics lab. Buffalo Gen. Hosp., 1981—82; postdoc. fellow dept. pharmaceutics SUNY, Buffalo, 1984-85; asst. prof. dept. pharm. scis. Wayne State U. Coll. Pharmacy, Detroit, 1985-91, assoc. prof., 1991—98, prof., 1998—2003, assoc. chmn. dept. pharm. scis., 1999—2003; Lynn & Sharon Bighley prof. pharm. scis. U. Iowa Coll. Pharmacy, Coralville, 2003—06, head divsn. pharmaceutics, 2003—06; prof. medicinal chemistry/molecular pharmacology Purdue U. Coll. Pharmacy, Nursing & Health Scis., West Lafayette, Ind., 2006—, dean, 2006—. Mem. Barbara Ann Karmanos Cancer Inst., Wayne State U., 1992—2003; mem. exec. coun., adv. coun. U. Iowa Coll. Pharmacy, 2003—06; cons. Warner Lambert/Parke-Davis, Ann Arbor, Mich., Pyro Pharm., Inc., Costa Mesa, Calif., 2001, Oxford Biomed. Rsch., Mich., 2002, Pfizer Global Rsch. & Devel., 2004. Rep. US Pharmacopeial Conv., 1996—2003. Recipient Meritorious Rsch. award, Am. Fedn. Clin. Rsch., 1982, James A. Shannon Dir.'s award, NIH, 1992; named Tchr. of Yr., Wayne State U. Coll. Pharmacy, 2003, U. Iowa Coll. Pharmacy, 2005. Mem.: AAAS, Soc. Toxicology, Soc. Investigative Dermatology, Internat. Soc. Study of Xenobiotics, Am. Soc. Pharmacology & Experimental Therapeutics (sec.-treas. drug metabolism divsn. 2003—06), Am. Assn. Colleges of Pharmacy, Am. Assn. Pharmaceutical Scientists, Rho Chi. Office: Purdue U Heine Pharmacy Bldg Rm RHPH 108 575 Stadium Mall Dr West Lafayette IN 47907 Office Phone: 765-494-1368. Office Fax: 765-494-7880. Business E-Mail: svensson@purdue.edu.*

SVENSSON, ROBERT CHARLES WILHELM, physicist, researcher; b. Göteborg, Sweden, Sept. 11, 1947; s. Carl-Eric George and Lilly Maria S. BS in Physics, Göteborgs U., 1983, MS in Physics, 1991, PhD in Environ. Scis. with specialization in Phys. Chemistry, 1994. Lectr. Merchant Marine Acad., Göteborg, 1983—; physicist Applied Scis., Inc., Cedarville, Ohio, 1991-92; electronic design engr. Göteborg, 1982—; instr. Merchant Marine Acad., Göteborg, 1982-93; asst. prof. Chalmers U. Tech., Göteborg, 1994-96, assoc. prof., 1996—. Organizer Conf. TEC '93, Chalmers U. of Tech., 1993; guest speaker workshop, U. Eindhoven, Holland, 1993; cons. physicist Applied Scis., Cedarville, 1991-92, Space Exploration Assoc., 1993; specialist Thermionic Energy Conversion Conf.; presenter MIT, 1999; invited TEC specialist US Nat. Rsch. Coun. 2000; invited spkr., Russia, 2003; vis. rsch. prof. W.Va. U., Morgantown, 2004-06, 07. Contbr. articles to profl. jours; patentee in field. Mem. ASME, Soc. Automotive Engrs. Liberal. Lutheran. Achievements include patents for TEC field; method for heat-to-electricity conversion in cars. Avocations: artistic photography, electronics design, power sports. Home: Dörravägen 1 Landvetter S-43893 Sweden Office: Chalmers U Tech S-40272 Gothenburg Sweden Office Phone: 46 31 772 5728, 46 31 772 1000. Personal E-mail: drlomo@yahoo.com. Business E-Mail: term@chalmers.se, rcsvensson@mail.wvu.edu.

SVETKEY, LAURA PAT, nephrologist; b. Carlisle, Pa., Sept. 19, 1951; d. Edward Robert and Marcia Tuchman (Wallace) S.; m. Charles Michael van der Horst, May 17, 1980; children: Anna Svetkey. Student, Barnard Coll., 1969-70; BA, Sarah Lawrence Coll., 1974; MD, Harvard U., 1979; postgrad., Duke U., 1988—. Diplomate Nat. Bd. Internal Medicine, Am. Bd. Internal Medicine; lic. physician, N.C., N.Y. Intern internal medicine Montefiore Hosp. and Med. Ctr., Bronx, NY, 1979-80, resident, 1980-82; fellow divsn. gen. internal medicine Duke U. Med. Ctr., Durham, NC, 1982-83, assoc. medicine divsns. nephrology & gen. internal medicine, 1983-86, co-dir., dir. Duke Hypertension Ctr., 1985—, asst. prof. medicine divsn. nephrology, 1986-93, sr. fellow Ctr. for Study Aging and Human Devel., 1990—, assoc. prof., 1994—, mem. Stedman Nutriton Ctr., 1992—; staff physician dept. medicine Lincoln Community Health Ctr., Durham, NC, 1983-84. Cons. NC Commr. Agr.; ad hoc rev. com. NIDDK, NIH, 1990; adv. com. on status of women dept. medicine Duke U. Med. Ctr., 1987—; mem. spl. emphasis panel NHLBI, NIH, 1993; instr., moderator, speaker, presenter various organizations, 1984-93. Contbr. articles to profl. jours., chpts. to books. Mem. Am. Soc. Hypertension, Am. Soc. Nephrology, Internat. Soc. Hypertension in Blacks, Am. Heart Assn. (Kidney Coun.). Office: Duke U Med Ctr PO Box 3075 Durham NC 27715-3075 Office Phone: 919-419-5840, 919-668-7630. Office Fax: 919-419-5841. E-mail: svetk001@mc.duke.edu.*

SVEUM, DALE CURTIS, professional baseball coach; b. Richmond, Calif., Nov. 23, 1963; m. Darlene Sveum; children: Brittane, Rustin. Infielder Milw. Brewers, 1986—91, Phila. Phillies, 1992, Chgo. White Sox, 1992, Oakland Athletics, 1993, Seattle Mariners, 1994, Pitts. Pirates, 1996—97, 1999, NY Yankees, 1998; third base coach Boston Red Sox, 2004—05, Milw. Brewers, 2005, bench coach, 2006—08, interim mgr., 2008, hitting coach, 2008—. Achievements include being a member of the World Series Championship winning Boston Red Sox, 2004. Office: Milw Brewers Miller Pk One Brewers Way Milwaukee WI 53214*

SVIGGUM, INGVAR, automotive executive; b. Hafslo, Norway, 1945; married; 2 children. Trainee Ford Norway, 1963, mng. dir., 1985—87; mng. dir., v.p. Ford Spain, 1987—89; dir. mktg. plans and programs Ford Europe, 1989—98, exec. dir. European sales ops., 1998—99, v.p. European sales ops., 1999—2008, v.p. mktg., sales and svc., 2008—; vice chmn. Ford-Werke AG, 1996—97; v.p. Ford Motor Co. Office: Ford Motor Co PO Box 685 Dearborn MI 48126-0685*

SVIKIS, DACE SUSAN, medical educator; b. Milw., Sept. 5, 1959; d. Gunars Karlis and Biruta Svikis; m. Roy Wilson Pickens, Sept. 12, 1987; children: Marks Alexander Pickens, Kristopher Janis Pickens. PhD, U. Minn., Mpls., 1989. Lic. MD Bd. Examiners, Psychology. Asst. prof. Johns Hopkins Sch. Medicine, Balt., 1990—96, assoc. prof., 1997—99, Va. Commonwealth U., Richmond, 1999—2004, prof., 2004—. Program dir. Ctr. Addiction and Pregnancy, Balt., 1992—99; dep. dir. VCU Inst. Women's Health, Richmond, 2001—. Contbr. articles to profl. jours. (Dan Anderson award, Hazelden, 1998). R01 award, NIH (NIDA/NIAAA), 1997—. Fellow: Coll. Problems Drug Dependence (bd. mem., comm. chairperson 2007—). Achievements include research in study interventions pregnant drug abusing women. Home: 12204 Loxton Way Glen Allen VA 23059 Office: Va Commonwealth Univ 1001 E Broad St Old City Hall 350A Richmond VA 23298 Office Fax: 804-827-1502. Business E-Mail: dssvikis@vcu.edu, dssvikis@hsc.vcu.edu.

SVINICKI, KRISTINE L., commissioner; b. 1966; BS in Nuc. Engring., U. Mich., 1988. Energy engr. Wis. Pub. Svc. Commn.; nuc. engr. Office. Nuc. Energy, Sci., Tech., Office Civilian Radioactive Waste Mgmt., Idaho Ops. Office, 1990—97; sr. policy adv. to Senator Larry Craig US Senate, Washington, 1997—2004, profl. staff mem. Armed Svcs. Com., 2005—08; commr. US Nuclear Regulatory Commn. (NRC), Washington, 2008—. Task force mem., global nuc. materials mgmt. Ctr. Strategic Internat. Studies; expert adv. panel mem. US Nuc. Regulatory Commn. Stennis Congl. fellow, 108th Congress, 2003—04. Mem.: Am. Nuc. Soc. (former mem. spl. com. nuc. non-proliferation). Office: US Nuclear Regulatory Commn 11555 Rockville Pike Rm 18G1 Rockville MD 20852 Office Phone: 301-415-1850. Business E-Mail: CMRSVINICKI@nrc.gov.*

SVIOKLA, JOHN JULIUS, technology consultant; b. Brockton, Mass., July 3, 1957; s. Sylvester Charles and Katherine Bravendar (McCaig) S.; m. Eileen Marie Harvey, Aug. 12, 1987; children: John, Michael, Patrick. BA, Harvard U., 1979, MBA, 1983, D of Bus. Adminstrn., 1986. Banker Mark Twain Bank Inc., St. Louis, 1986; asst. prof. to assoc. prof. Harvard Bus. Sch., Boston, 1986—98; v.p. DiamondCluster Internat., Chgo., 1998—2001, vice chmn., 2000—. Dir. Cosmo, Inc., Braintree, Mass., Ctr. Expert Systems, Cambridge, Mass. Dir. Found. Faces of Children-At-Children's Hosp., Boston, 1987. Recipient Detur prize Harvard U., 1979; IBM fellow Harvard, 1982. Mem. Am. Assn. Artificial Intelligence, Inst. Mgmt. Sci. Clubs: Harvard Faculty (Cambridge); Harvard (Boston). Avocations: drawing, bicycling, yoga. Office: Diamond Mgmt & Tech Cons 875 North Michigan Ave Ste 3000 Chicago IL 60611

SVOBODA, JANICE JUNE, nurse; d. Alfred A. and Jessie (Boor) Hinke; m. Glenn R. Svoboda, July 20, 1957; children: Melora, Kevin, Craig. Diploma, Luther Hosp., Eau Claire, Wis., 1954; student, U. Wis., Madison, 1955—57; BS in Health Edn. cum laude, U. Wis., Milw., 1980; student, Alverno Coll., Milw., 1991-92. Cert. U. Wis., 1955. Pub. health nurse Ozaukee County, Wis., 1979, 86; asst. instr. nursing Milw. Area Tech. Coll., 1979-83; instr. seminar Cardinal Stritch Coll., Milw., 1985-87; nutritional counselor Nutri-Sys., Grafton, Wis., 1987-90. Instr. seminar Milw. Area Tech. Coll., 1983, 90, coping with stress course, 1985-86, assertiveness training course, 1985, health seminars Alverno Coll., Milw., 1991-95, designed and implemented alternative health and healing seminar, Alverno Coll., 1994-97; pvt. practice holistic nurse cons., nutrition and herbal therapy, 1997—; lectr. pub. on nutrition and anti aging. Mem. Am. Holistic Nurses Assn. (cert. and recert.), Ctr. for Sci. in the Pub. Interest. Office Phone: 262-377-1242.

SVOBODA, JOANNE DZITKO, artist, educator; b. Dec. 24, 1948; d. John Richard and Joanna Frances (Rygiel) Dzitko; m. Peter W. Svoboda, Sept. 3, 1972; children: Kimberly Anne, Lauren Anne. Student, Parsons Sch. Design, 1966, Kean Coll., 1970; BA, Jersey City State Coll., 1970, MA, 1975; postgrad., Tchrs. Coll., Columbia U., 1972, Chubb Inst., 1983-84. Art tchr., Jersey City, 1966-70, Henry Snyder H.S., Jersey City, 1970-80; tng. specialist Johnson & Johnson Baby Products, Skillman, N.J., 1984-89; cons., 1989—; pres. Mgmt. Strategies Internat., 1991—. Computer instr. Raritan Valley C.C., 1999—. Exhibited Courtney Gallery, Jersey City State Coll., 1970, 74, Long Valley, 1979-80; contbr. articles in field to various publs. Trustee Jersey City Mus. Assn.,

1973-79, chmn. fine arts dept., 1972-79; mem. curriculum revision com. Jersey City Bd. Edn., 1976; mem. Washington Twp. Shade Tree Commn., 1979-81, chmn., 1981; mem. Washington Twp. Hist. Heritage Commn., 1981-85; active encouraging establishment of hist. zone Long Valley, landmarks, Jersey City and Washington Twp. Grantee N.J. State Dept. Edn., 1973; recipient awards N.J. Fedn. Jr. Woman's Clubs: black and white photography, 1979, crafts, 1979, 1st pl. color photography, 1980, free form, 1981. Mem. Am. H.S. Assn. (asst. exec. dir. 1997-99, 2000-), Inst. Raritan Valley CC. (2000-). Office: PO Box 1216 Marshalls Creek PA 18335 Office Phone: 570-223-9600. E-mail: joan@joansvoboda.com.

SVOBODA, PATRICIA HELEN, art historian; d. Ladislav Maurice and Marie Martina (Vojta) S. BFA in Graphic Design, U. Wash., Seattle, 1974, BA in Art History, 1974, MA in Art History, 1980. Graphic artist freelance, Seattle, Washington, 1971—86; art history rschr. for exhbns. Collaboration of Seattle Art Mus. & U. Wash., Seattle, 1977—78; graphic artist U. Rsch. Tech. Edn. Ctr., Rockville, Md., 1984; graphic artist, adminstrv. asst. US Dept. Commerce Office Publs. Svc., Washington, 1984—88; lectr. art history Phillips Collection, Washington, 1987—; coord. rsch. Smithsonian Instn. Nat. Portrait Gallery, Washington, 1988—; lectr. art history Georgetown U., Washington, 1989—97. Rep. Art Svcs. Internat., Alexandria, Va., 1990-92; contbr. Inst. for Classical Studies, Prague, Czech Republic, 1993-94, Inst. for the Classical Tradition, Boston U., 1995, Mus. of Decorative Arts, Prague, Czech Republic, 1996. Author: Zoe Dusanne, 1980; interviewer for Northwest Traditions, 1978; prin. work includes Seattle YMCA mural Olympic Race, 1982; contbr. articles to profl. jours. Keyworker Combined Fed. Campaign, Washington, 1985-88; participant Internat. Partnerships among Mus. Programs Am. Assn. Mus., 2003-05. Recipient Nat. Pks. Svc. Purchase Prize award Soc. Illustrators, 1974, Performance award Smithsonian Instn., 1989-2008 Mem. Am. Assn. Mus., Internat. Coun. Mus., Coll. Art Assn., Czechoslovak Soc. Arts & Scis., Internat. Soc. for Classical Tradition, U. Wash. Alumni Assn. Avocations: literature, history, langs., music, photography. Office: Smithsonian Instn Nat Portrait Gallery Victor Bldg-Ste 410 PO Box 37012 Washington DC 20013-7012 Business E-Mail: svobodap@si.edu.

SWAD, STEPHEN MARK, former mortgage company executive; b. Aug. 10, 1961; married; 2 children. BBA, U. Mich. CPA. Dep. chief acct. SEC, 1995; ptnr. KPMG LLP, 1998; v.p., dep. contr. Time Warner, 1998, v.p. financial planning and analysis, exec. v.p. finance & admin. Turner Entertainment Group, 2002—03; exec. v.p., CFO America Online, Inc., 2003—07; CFO Fannie Mae (Fed. Nat. Mortgage Assn.), 2007—08.*

SWADENER, JOHN GREGORY, mechanical engineering lecturer; s. Nina and John Richard Swadener; m. Kay Swadener, June 23, 1984; 1 child, Michael John. PhD, U. Tex., 1998. Rsch. asst. prof. U. Tenn., Knoxville, Tenn., 1998—2001; tech. staff mem. Los Alamos Nat. Lab., Los Alamos, N.Mex., 2001—. Adj. faculty mem. U. Memphis, 2002—05. Fellow Texas Space Grant Consortium, NASA, Ripperger Engineering Mechanics. Mem.: Materials Rsch. Soc. D-Liberal. Protestant. Avocations: hiking, travel. Office: Aston Univ Sch Engring Aston Triangle Birmingham B4 7ET England Office Phone: 44 121 204 3536. Business E-Mail: j.g.swadener@aston.ac.uk.

SWAFFAR, GLENDA JEAN, director; d. Glen Edward and Imagean Perkins; m. J.D. Swaffar, Aug. 27, 1992; children: Leeann Glynette Pratt, Mark Tillman Pratt. BA, U. Mo., Columbia, 1969; MS summa cum laude, U. Mo.-Kans. City, 1988, Edn. Specialist, 1990. Cert. tchr./media specialist Mo. Dept. Elem. and Secondary Edn., 1983. Media specialist Hickman Mills HS, Kans. City, 1985—99, instrnl. facilitator, A+ coord., 1999—. Adv. com. Tchr. Edn. U. Mo., Kans. City; elector for bishop Episcopal Ch., Kans. City, 1984—85. Mem.: Mo. Assn. Sch. Librs. (assoc.), Am. Assn. Sch. Librs. (assoc.), ASCD (assoc.), Internat. Reading Assn. (assoc.), Phi Kappa Phi. Achievements include successfully writing grant to secure funding and then led staff of 100 teachers through a three-year improvement process to prepare our school for designation by the state as an A+ high school. Avocations: reading, travel, swimming, scrapbooks, fabric arts. Office: Hickman Mills HS 9010 Old Santa Fe Rd Kansas City MO 64138 Office Phone: 816-316-7259. Office Fax: 816-316-7248. Personal E-mail: gswaffar@hotmail.com. Business E-Mail: glendas@hickmanmills.org.

SWAFFORD, LESLIE EUGENE, physician assistant, consultant; b. Long Beach, Calif., Aug. 31, 1950; s. Leslie Eugene Swafford, Sr. and Kathryn Shirley (Gros) Jarvis; children: Jayson Patrick, Jonathan Allyn, Jude Christopher, Joshua Douglas; m. Cheryl Kaleen Killman, Apr. 10, 1993; 1 child, Lesli Tayte. BS in Allied Health, physician asst. degree of completion, George Washington U., 1978; postgrad. in Occupl. Medicine, U. Cin., 1994-95; M. in Physician Asst. Studies, U. Nebr., 2001. Cert. physician's asst. NCCPA, ACLS, PALS, ATLS, CDC AIDS Counselor, EBT (Alco-Sensor IV), EBT (EC/IR) QAP, TTT, lic. JBORPA. Chief EEG technologist Group Health Assn., Washington, 1974-76; physician asst. Pediat. Assocs., Frederick, Md., 1978-81, Heart Inst. for Care, Amarillo, Tex., 1981-84, Maricopa County Medicine Assocs., Avondale-Goodyear, Ariz., 1984-89; mgr. Samarital Occupl. Health Svcs. Samaritan Health System, Phoenix, 1989-98; dir. employee health/occupl. medicine, worker's comp program Maryvale Hosp. Med. Ctr., Phoenix, 1998, MRO asst., dir. adminstr. respiratory protection program, 1998-2001; with Emergency Assocs. Ariz. St. Joseph's Emergency Rm. and Trauma Ctr., Phoenix, 2001—05. Med. edn. and policy cons. Occupl. Health and Med. Edn. Consultants; adminstr. drug test program Samaritan Health Svcs., Phoenix, 1991—95; mem. com. Ariz. Rural Health Conf., 1992—96; adj. asst. prof. physician asst. tng. program Kirksville Coll. of Osteo. Medicine, Phoenix, 1995—; instr. Calif. Tech. Contbr. articles to profl. jours. Chmn. sex edn. com. North Ctrl. Accreditation-Aqua Fria H.S., Avondale, Ariz., 1991; physician asst. Camp Geronimo (Boy Scouts of Am.), Phoenix, 1989-94; team mem. Young People's Beginning Experience Grief Recovery Program for Children, Phoenix, 1989-93; mem. com. Ariz. Dept. Health Svcs.-Robert Wood Johnson Application, Phoenix, 1992-93. With USN, 1969-74. Recipient scholarship NIH, 1976, Squibb Pharm. Rural Physician Asst. of Yr. award honorable mention Am. Acad. Physician Assts., 1987, Dr. Paul L. Singer award for disting. cmty. svc. Samaritan Found., 1991. Fellow Ariz. State Assn. Physician Assts. (pres.-elect 1990-91, pres. 1991-92, chmn. Ariz. physician asst. tng. program task force 1990-94). Republican. Christian. Avocations: fishing, hiking, softball, basketball, golf. Home: 17723 Cactus Flower Dr Goodyear AZ 85338-5232 Office: Banner Estrella Med Ctr ER 9201 Ww Thomas Rd Phoenix AZ 85037 Office Phone: 623-910-1204.

SWAGEL, PHILLIP L., economics professor, former federal agency administrator; b. 1966; married; 3 children. AB in Economics, Princeton U., 1987; MS, Harvard U., 1990, PhD, 1993. Economist Fed. Reserve Bd., 1992—94, Internat. Monetary Fund, 1996—2002; sr. economist Coun. Econ. Advisors, Exec. Office of the Pres., 2000—01, chief of staff, 2002—05; resident scholar Am. Enterprise Inst., 2005—06; asst. sec. for econ. policy US Dept. Treasury, Washington, 2006—09. Vis. asst. prof. Northwestern U., 1994—96; adj. prof. economics U. Chgo. Booth Sch. Bus., 2009—. Office: U Chgo Booth Sch Bus 5807 South Woodlawn Avenue Chicago IL 60637 Office Phone: 773-702-8453. E-mail: phillip.swagel@chicagobooth.edu.*

SWAIL, WATSON SCOTT, educational association administrator; b. Winnipeg, Manitoba, Canada, July 29, 1962; s. Gordon Emerson and Florence Eva Swail; m. Pamela P. Pearsall, June 13, 1991; children: Watson Tyler, Pearse Tyson, Luke Alexander. B of Edn., U. Man., Winnipeg, Can., 1985; MS, Old Dominion U., Norfolk, Va., 1991; EdD, George Wash. U., Washington, 1995. Tchr. St. Vital Sch. Divsn., Winnipeg, Manitoba, Canada, 1986—90, Hampton City Schs., Va., 1991—93; assoc. dir. policy analysis Coll. Bd., Washington, 1996—2000; sr. policy analyst SRI Internat., Rosslyn, Va., 2000—01; exec. dir. The Pell Inst., Washington, 2001—02; pres., CEO Ednl. Policy Inst., Virginia Beach, Va., 2002—. Author: Retaining Minority Students in Higher Education. Achievements include research in framework for student retention in higher education; development of crriculum for middle school technology. Office: Educational Policy Institute 2400 Princess Anne Rd Virginia Beach VA 23456-3409 E-mail: wswail@educationalpolicy.org.

SWAILES, HEIDI ROBIN, counselor; b. Germany, May 31, 1948; d. Walter and Elfriede Raudleht; m. William E. Swailes, May 19, 1968. BA, U. Wash., Seattle, 1981; M in Counseling, Seattle U., 1984. Cert. Chem. Dependency Profl. Wash. State, 1988, Lic. Mental Health Counselor Wash. State, 1989, Master Addiction Counselor Nat. Assn. Alcohol and Drug Abuse Counselors, 1996. Asst. dir. First Step CD Treatment Prgram, Bellevue, Wash., 1989—90; dir. clin. svcs. Care Unit Hosp., Kirkland, Wash., 1990—91; dir. spl. programs CPC Fairfax Hosp., Kirkland, Wash., 1991—93; supr. Value Behavioral Health, Bellevue, Wash., 1993—96; dir. NW Alternatives, Lynnwood, Wash., 1996—98; exec. dir. Family Counseling Svc., Lynnwood, Wash., 1998—2002; clin. supr. United Treatment Therapy, Bellevue, Wash., 2002—. Pres. Puget Sound Dual Disorder Coalition, Kirkland, Wash., 1992—93; bd. dirs. Alcohol Studies Program Bellevue Cmty. Coll., Wash., 1993; treas. Employee Assistance Profl. Assn. Pacific NW, Seattle, 1995; pres EWR, Inc., Bellevue, Wash., 2002—, dir., 2002—. Co-author: (book) Money In Your Life, 1986. Mem.: Am. Mental Health Counselors Assn., Nat. Assn. Alcohol Drug Abuse Counselors. Office: EWR, Inc PO Box 1525 Bellevue WA 98009

SWAILES, WILLIAM E., counseling administrator; b. Balt., July 28, 1945; m. Heidi Robin Raudleht, May 19, 1968. Registered counselor State Wash., 1988. Stockbroker Foster & Marshall, Bellevue, Wash., 1978—81; investment mgr. Advanced Personal Finances, Medina, Wash., 1982—; chmn. EWR, Inc., Bellevue, 2002—. Author: (book) Money in your Life, 1986. Chgo. area chmn. Ill. Coll. Rep. Fedn., 1968—69; hon. chmn. for Wash. state NRCC Bus. Adv. Coun., 2004; founder, min. Leyden Tolerants Ch., 1973—. With US Army, 1964—67, Germany and Vietnam. Recipient Ronald Reagan Rep. Gold medal, Nat. Rep. Congl. Com., 2004, Wash. State Businessman of Yr., 2005, Congl. medal of distinction, 2006; Monmouth Honor scholar, Monmouth Coll., 1963. Mem.: Am. Assn. Retired Persons (past pres. Bellevue chpt.).

SWAILS, JOHN WASHINGTON, III, history professor, director; b. Hamlet, NC, Sept. 16, 1948; s. John Washington and Glenda Baldwin Swails; m. Joy Williams Swails, Dec. 7, 1969; children: John Washington IV, Jana Lynette Pitts, Jaffa Marie Szymanski, Jessica Joy Smith, Joel Matthew. AB, U. Ga., Athens, 1969; MA, U. Ga., 1972, PhD, 1983; MA, Brandeis U., Waltham, Mass., 1975. Dir. condr. Israel and middle east studies Oral Roberts U., Tullsa, Okla., 1998—2007, dir.,mid. east studies and prof. history, 2008—. Mem.: ASMEA. Office: Oral Roberts Univ 7777 S Lewis Ave Tulsa OK 74171

SWAIM, MARK WENDELL, physician, molecular biologist, hepatologist, essayist, gastroenterologist, photographer; b. Winston-Salem, NC, Dec. 4, 1960; s. Donnie Lee and Bernice Earline (Brown) S. BA summa cum laude, U. N.C., 1983; MD, Duke U., 1990, PhD with honors, 1990. Diplomate Am. Bd. Internal Medicine, Am. Bd. Gastroenterology and Hepatology. Resident dept. medicine Duke U. Med. Ctr., Durham, NC, 1990-93; postdoc. fellow, dept. pharmacology Nat. Taiwan U., Taipei, 1992; fellow gastroenterology Duke U. Med. Ctr., Durham, NC, 1993-97, clin. med. instr., 1994-2000, fellow in advanced hepatology and transplant hepatology, 1997-98, attending physician, 1998-2000, Durham VA Med. Ctr., 1998-2000; asst. prof. medicine Gastrointestinal Ctr., U. Tex.-M.D. Anderson Cancer Ctr., Houston, 2000—02; dir., prin. investigator, med. dir. Regional Rsch. Inst., Jackson, Tenn., 2002—; founder Southeastern Liver Inst., Jackson, 2002—; hepatologist, gastroenterologist Ctr. Liver Diseases, Laurea McKennan U. Med. Ctr., Sioux Falls, SD, 2009. Assoc. dept. medicine Duke U., 1998-2000; instr. clin. medicine Duke U. Sch. Medicine, 1994-2000, mem. admissions com.; instr. U. Tenn. Sch. Medicine, 2004—; asst. prof. medicine Gastrointestinal Ctr., U. Tex. M.D. Anderson Cancer Ctr., Houston; vis. med. resident Nat. Taiwan U., Taipei, 1991, 92; vis. physician Saratov (Russia) Med. U., 1995; faculty senator U. Tex. M.D. Anderson Cancer Ctr., 2000-02; book rev. panelist The Pharos of Alpha Omega Alpha; cons. physician Al-Jazeira Hosp., Abu Dhabi, United Arab Emirates; mem. med. adv. bd. Axium Pharms., Inc.; cons. Intermune Pharms, Forest Pharms., Three River Pharms., Coley Pharms. Axcan Pharms. Contbr. articles to profl. jours., Ency. Brit. Great Ideas Today, 1996; photography pub. in Am. Photo. Recipient Brody award for history of medicine, 1998, Davison award for tchg. excellence, 2000; NIH Med. Sci. Tng. Program fellow, 1983-90, numerous acad. scholarships and grants. Fellow: ACP (winner assocs. competition 1994), Am. Coll. Forensic Examiners; mem.: Internat. Liver Cancer Assn., European Assn. for Study of Liver, Houston Acad. Medicine, Tex. Med. Assn., Am. Liver Found. (bd. dirs. Tex. chpt.), Engel Soc., Reticuloendothelial Soc., Am. Assn. for Study Liver Diseases, Am. Soc. for Gastrointestinal Endoscopy, Am. Coll. Gastroenterology, Sigma Pi Sigma, Phi Lambda Upsilon, Sigma Xi, Phi Beta Kappa, Alpha Omega Alpha (pres. Duke chpt. 1989). Avocations: photography, chamber music, writing, travel. Home: 61 Valley Oak Loop Jackson TN 38305 Office: 45 Physicians Dr Jackson TN 38305 Personal E-mail: markswaim@msn.com.

SWAIMAN, KENNETH FRED, pediatric neurologist, educator; b. St. Paul, Nov. 19, 1931; s. Lester J. and Shirley (Ryan) S.; m. Phyllis Kammerman Sher, Oct. 1985; children: Lisa, Jerrold, Barbara, Dana. BA magna cum laude, U. Minn., 1952, BS, 1953, MD, 1955; postgrad., 1956-58. Diplomate Am. Bd. Psychiatry and Neurology, Am. Bd. Pediatrics, Am. Bd. Psychiatry and Neurology with Spl. Competence in Child Neurology. Intern Mpls. Gen. Hosp., 1955-56; resident in pediatrics, fellow in pediatrics to chief resident U. Minn. Hosp., 1956-58, spl. fellow in pediatric neurology, 1960-63, dir. pediatric neurology tng. program, 1968-94, various to interim head dept. neurology, 1994-96; chief pediatrics U.S. Army Hosp., Ft. McPherson, Ga., 1958-60; asst. prof. pediatrics, neurology U. Minn. Med. Sch., Mpls., 1963-66, prof., dir. pediatric neurology, 1969-96, mem. internship adv. coun. exec. faculty, 1966-70, interim head dept. neurology, 1994-96; postgrad. fellow pediatric neurology Nat. Inst. Neurologic Diseases and Blindness, 1960-63, assoc. prof., 1966-69. Cons. pediatric neurology Hennepin County Gen. Hosp., 1963—, Mpls., St. Paul-Ramsey Hosp., St. Paul Children's Hosp., Mpls. Children's Hosp.; vis. prof. numerous univs. including Loyola U., 1982, U. N.Mex., 1982, U. Ind. Med. Sch., 1983, U. Kyushu, Shiga, Nagoya, Tokyo, 1985, Driscoll Children's Hosp., Corpus Christi, Tex., 1986, Inst. Nacional de Pediatria, Mexico City, 1986, U. de Concepion, Chile, 1989, Beijing U. Med. Sch., 1989, Xian Med. U., China, 1989, Children's Hosp. of Mich., Detroit, 1990, Hong Kong Child Neurology Soc., 1995, Tartu, Estonia, 1997, Krem, Austria, 1997, Santiago, Chile, 1997, Kaunas, Lithuania, 1998, ICNA Ednl. Seminar, Tartu, 1998, Montevideo, Uruguay, 1999, others; lectr. in field; guest worker NIH, NICHD, Bethesda, Md., 1978-79, 79-81. Author: (with Francis S. Wright) Neuromuscular Diseases in Infancy and Childhood, 1969, Pediatric Neuromuscular Diseases, 1979, (with Stephen Ashwal) Pediatric Neurology Case Studies, 1978, 2d edit., 1984, Pediatric Neurology: Principles and Practice, 1989, 4th edit., 2006; editor: (with John A. Anderson) Phenylketonuria and Allied Metabolic Diseases, 1966, (with Francis S. Wright) Practice Pediatric Neurology, 1975, 2d edit., 1982, Pediatric Neurology: Principles and Practice, 4th edit., 2006; mem. editl. bd. Annals of Neurology, 1977-83, Neurology Update, 1977-82, Pediatric Update, 1977-85, Brain and Devel. (Jour. Japanese Soc. Child Neurology), 1980—, Neuropediatrics (Stuttgart), 1982-92, Chinese Jour. Pediat., 2009; editor-in-chief: Pediatric Neurology, 1984—; contbr. articles to sci. jours. Chmn. Minn. Gov.'s Bd. for Handicapped, Exceptional and Gifted Children, 1972-76; mem. human devel. study sect. NIH, 1976-79, guest worker, 1978-81. Served to capt. M.C. U.S. Army, 1958-60. Fellow Am. Acad. Pediatrics, Am. Acad. Neurology (rep. to nat. coun. Nat. Soc. Med. Rsch., A.B. Baker Neurol. Edn. Lifetime Achievement award 2005); mem. Soc. Pediatric Rsch., Ctrl. Soc. Clin. Rsch., Ctrl. Soc. Neurol. Rsch., Internat. Soc. Neurochemistry, Am. Neurol. Assn., Minn. Neurol. Soc., AAAS, Midwest Pediatric Soc., Am. Soc. Neurochemistry, Child Neurology Soc. (1st pres. 1972-73, Hower award 1981, Founder's award 1996, chmn. internat. affairs com., 1991-96, mem. long range planning com. 1991-97, chmn. fin. com. 1995—), Internat. Assn. Child Neurologists (exec. com. 1975-79, chmn. global edn. com. 1996-99), Profs. of Child Neurology (1st pres. 1978-80, mem. nominating com. 1986-92), Japanese Child Neurology Soc. (Segawa award 1986, mem. nominating com. 1986-92, chair internat. affairs com. 1991—, mem. long range planning com. 1991-98), Soc. de Psiquiatria y Neurologia de la Infancia y Adolescencia, Internat. Child Neurology Assn. (chair internat. edn. com. 1996-99), Lithuanian Child Neurology Soc. (hon., mem. 2000—), Child Neurology Found. (pres. 2000-03), Phi Beta Kappa, Sigma Xi. Office: Pediatric Neurology 1821 University Ave W Saint Paul MN 55104-2801 E-mail: pncomm@qwestoffice.net.

SWAIN, DAVID O., manufacturing executive; b. Lizton, Ind., July 30, 1942; B of Aeronautical Engring., Purdue U., D (hon.), Rose-Hulman Inst. Tech. Engr. Gemini project McDonnell Douglas, 1954—72, engr. tactical missile programs,, tomahawk and harpoon/standoff land attack missile, 1972—87; v.p., gen. mgr. strategic bus. devel. McDonnell Douglas Astronautics Co., 1987—91; sr. v.p., c-17 program mgr. McDonnell Douglas Aerospace, 1981—94; v.p., gen. mgr. advances sys. and tech. Phantom Works McDonnell Douglas, 1994—97; v.p. engring. The Boeing Co., 1997—99; pres. Boeing Phamtom Works, 1999—2001; exec. v.p. The Boeing Co., 2002—, chief operating officer integrated defense systems, 2003—. Chmn. NASA Aerospace Tech. Adv. Com. Bd. dirs. Nat. Action Coun. Minorities in Engring., Chgo.'s Mus. Sci. and Industry. Recipient Disting. Engring. ALumnus award, Purdue U., 1993, Outstanding Aerospace Engr. award, 1999, Indsl. Rsch. Inst. medal, 2006. Fellow: AIAA, Royal Aeronautical Soc.; mem.: Soc. Automotive Engrs. Office: The Boeing Co PO Box 516 Saint Louis MO 63166

SWAIN, DONALD CHRISTIE, retired academic administrator, historian, educator; b. Des Moines, Oct. 14, 1931; s. G. Christie and Irene L. (Alsop) S.; m. Lavinia Kathryn Lesh, Mar. 5, 1955; children: Alan Christie, Cynthia Catherine. BA, U. Dubuque, 1953; MA in History, U. Calif., Berkeley, 1958, PhD, 1961; D (hon.), U. Louisville, 1995, Bellarmine Coll., 1995. Asst. rsch. historian U. Calif., Berkeley, 1961-63, mem. faculty Davis, 1963-81, prof. history, 1970-81, acad. asst. to chancellor, 1967-68, asst. vice chancellor acad. affairs, 1971, vice chancellor acad. affairs, 1972-75; acad. v.p. U. Calif. System, Berkeley, 1975-81; pres. U. Louisville, 1981-95, pres. emeritus, 1995—, prof. history, 1981-95; ret., 1995. Author: Federal Conservation Policy, 1921-33, 1963, Wilderness Defender: Horace M. Albright and Conservation, 1970; co-editor: The Politics of American Science 1939 to the Present, 1965. Recipient William B. Hellestine award Wis. State Hist. Soc., 1967, Disting. Tchg. award U. Calif., Davis, 1972, Wilson Wyatt award U. Louisville Alumni Assn., 1995; named Louisvillian of Yr., 1995. Democrat. Presbyterian. Personal E-mail: dcsandlls@aol.com.

SWAIN, JUDITH LEA, cardiologist, educator; b. Long Beach, Calif., Sept. 24, 1948; m. Edward W. Holmes. BS in Chemistry with deptl. honors, UCLA, 1970; MD, U. Calif., San Diego, 1974. Diplomate Am. Bd. Internal Medicine, cardiovasc. disease; lic. physician Calif., Pa., N.C. Intern in medicine Duke U. Med. Ctr., 1974-75, resident in medicine, 1975-76, fellow in cardiology, 1976-80, assoc. in medicine, 1979-81, from asst. prof. medicine to assoc. prof. medicine, 1981-91, asst. prof. physiology, 1981-88, assoc. prof. microbiology & immunology, 1988-91, Herbert C. Rorer prof. med. scis., prof. genetics, 1991-92, mem. molecular biology grad. group, 1991-92, chief cardiovasc. divsn., 1991-92; chair dept. medicine Stanford (Calif.) U., 1996—2006; dir. Coll. Integrated Life Scis. U. Calif., San Diego, 2004—06; exec. dir. Singapore Inst. Clinical Sciences Agy. for Sci. Tech., & Rsch. (A*STAR), 2006—; Lie Ying Chow prof. medicine Nat. U. Singapore, 2006—. Vis. asst. prof. dept. genetics Harvard Med. Sch., Boston, 1985-86; mem. search com. for dir. Ctr. for Aging, Duke U. Med. Ctr., 1991—, mem. exec. com. deptl. awards selection, 1992—, chmn. combined degree dir. search com., 1993, mem. clin. rsch. ctr. adv. com., 1993-94, mem. grad. student admissions com., 1993, mem. search com. for chief cardiovasc. surgery, 1992, dept. medicine intern selection com., 1992—; mem. instnl. rev. com. Pa. Muscle Inst., 1993; cardiology adv. com. Nat. Heart, Lung, & Blood Inst., 1989-93; dir. USA-Russia Cardiovasc. Rsch. Program, 1992—; mem. NIH Task Force on Heart Failure, 1992-93, dirs. standing com. on clin. rsch. NIH, 1995—; cons. Netherlands Rsch. Initiative in Molecular Cardiology, 1993; external adv. com. Ctr. for Prevention of Cardiovasc. Disease, Harvard Sch. Pub. Health, 1993—; adv. coun. NHLBI, 1995—, Friends of NHLBI com., 1996—, lectr. in field.; bd. dirs, Lexico Pharmaceuticals Inc., 2007-. Exec. editor: Trends in Cardiovascular Medicine, 1990-93; mem. editl. bd. Circulation Rsch., 1991—, Circulation, 1991—, Jour. Clin. Investigation, 1992—; cons. editor: Circulation, 1993—; contbr. articles to med. jours. Mem. exec. com. Coun. on Basic Sci., Am. Heart Assn., 1986-93, chmn. Katz Prize Award Com., 1989-92, rsch. rev. com., 1990-93, fellowship rsch. com., 1992—, program com., 1992—, mem. Levine Young Investigator Awards Com., Coun. on Clin. Cardiology, 1994—, mem. Basic Sci. Coun.; bd. dirs. Southeastern Pa. Heart Assn., 1992—. Recipient Bristol-Myers Squibb Cardiovasc. Achievement award, 1992, also numerous rsch. grants. Fellow Am. Coll. Cardiology (internat. edn. com. 1994—, chair cardiovasc. rsch. com. 1996—), Coll. Physicians of Phila.; mem. Assn. Univ. Cardiologists, Assn. Am.

Physicians, Assn. Prof. of Cardiology, Am. Soc. Cell Biology, Am. Fedn. Clin. Rsch., Am. Soc. Clin. Investigation (pres.-elect 1994—, councilor 1991—), Internat. Soc. Heart Rsch. (councilor 1988—), Interurban Clin. Club, Clin. and Climitol. Soc., John Morgan Soc, Inst. Medicine (coun. mem.). Office: Singapore Inst Clinical Sciences 30 Medical Dr 117609 Singapore Singapore also: Nat U Hosp Main Bldg Level 3 5 Lower Kent Ridge Rd 119074 Singapore Singapore E-mail: judith_swain@sics.a-star.edu.sg.*

SWAIN, KRISTIN A., museum director; d. Grace Amylon Waterman. Degree in Art History, Sweet Briar Coll., 1974. Various adminstrv. positions Rockwell Mus. of Western Art (formerly Rockwell Mus.), Corning, NY, 1976—83, collections supr., 1983—84, interim dir., 2002, exec. dir., 2002—; program mgr. Corning Inc. Found., 1984—86, exec. dir., 1986—90, pres., 1990—. Bd. trustees Rockwell Mus. of Western Art (formerly Rockwell Mus.), 1984—, pres. bd. trustees; bd. dirs. Alliance of NY State Arts Coun., Clemens Ctr., Market St. Restoration Agy., 171 Cedar Arts Ctr. Mem. contbns. coun., Conf. Bd. and Corp. Assocs. United Way of Am.; dir. Elmira Savings Bank; bd. dirs. United Way of Southern Tier, Glove House, Southeast Steuben County Pub. Libr. Office: Rockwell Mus of Western Art 111 Cedar St Corning NY 14830 Office Phone: 607-937-5386. Business E-Mail: swaink@rockwellmuseum.org.

SWAIN, LAURA TAYLOR, federal judge; b. Bklyn., 1958; d. Justus E. and Madeline V. (Allgood) Taylor; m. Andrew J. Swain, 1991. AB, Harvard U., 1979, JD, 1982. Bar: Mass. 1982, N.Y. 1983, U.S. Dist. Ct. (so. and ea. dists.) N.Y. 1983. Law clk to chief judge U.S. Dist. Ct. (so. dist.) N.Y., 1982-83; assoc. Debevoise & Plimpton, NYC, 1983-95, counsel, 1995-96; U.S. bankruptcy judge U.S. Bankruptcy Ct., Bklyn., 1996-2000; judge U.S. Dist. Ct. (So. Dist.), NY, 2000—. Mem. N.Y. State Bd. Law Examiners, Albany, 1986-96; mem. multistate bar exam. com. Nat. Conf. Bar Examiners, 1987-99, mem. testing, R&D devel. com., 1990-94, mem. long range planning com., 1994-96; cons. N.Y. Profl. Edn. Project, 1995-96; adv. com. for fules of bankruptcy procedure Judicial Conf. U.S., 2002-; chair, 2007-. Co-contbr. articles on employee benefits, employee stock ownership plans, acctg. and bankruptcy to profl. publs.; contbg. author: New York Insurance Law, 1991. Trustee Diocese of N.Y. (Episcopal), 1991-92; mem. Dessoff Choirs, N.Y.C., 1984-92; bd. dirs. Episcopal Charities, Inc., 1996-2003, Coalition Consumer Bankruptcy Debtor Edn., 1998—2006; bd. mgrs. Haven Relief Fund Soc., 2005-. Mem. ABA, Assn. of Bar of City of N.Y., Met. Black Bar Assn., N.Y. State Bar Assn., Nat. Conf. Bankruptcy Judges, Nat. Assn. Women Judges, Fed. Judges Assn. (bd. dirs. 2005-). Episcopalian. Avocation: music. Office: US Courthouse 500 Pearl St Rm 755 New York NY 10007

SWAIN, MARY ANN PRICE, university official; b. Chardon, Ohio, Apr. 20, 1941; d. A. David and Mary A. Price; m. Donald B. Swain, June 27, 1964; children: Judy, Brenda. BA in Psychology, DePauw U., 1963; MA in Psychology, U. Mich., 1964, PhD in Psychology, 1969. Dir. Sch. Nursing Doctoral Program U. Mich., Ann Arbor, 1975—76, chmn. dept. nursing rsch., 1977—82, assoc. v.p. acad. affairs, 1983—93, interim co-dir. pers., 1986—88, interim dir. affirmative action, 1988—89, interim v.p. student svcs., 1990—92; provost and v.p. acad. affairs SUNY, Binghamton, 1993—. Evaluation site visotor U. Balt. Sch. Law, 1996—97, Tes. Wesleyan U., 1998—99, U. Va. Sch. Nursing, Charlottesville, 1994—95; chmn. coun. acad. affairs Nat. Assn. State Univs. and Land Grant Colls., 1998—99. Co-author (with H. Erickson and E. Tomlim): Modeling and Role-modeling: A Theory and Paradigm for Nursing, 1983. Chmn. campaign United Way Broome COunty, Binghamton, 1998—99; pres. bd. dirs. Vis. Nurses Assn. Huron Valley, Ann Arbor, 1989—92. Named Woman of Distinction, Girl Scouts, 2007; fellow Woodrow Wilson fellow, 1963. Mem.: Am. Psychol. Soc., Am. Assn. Higher Edn., Am. Soc. Quality Control, Sigma Theta Tau, Phi Beta Kappa, Golden Key Hon. Soc. Office: SUNY at Binghamton Provost Office PO Box 6000 Binghamton NY 13902-6000 Office Phone: 607-777-2141. E-mail: mswain@binghamton.edu.

SWAIN, PAUL JOSEPH, bishop; b. Newark, NY, Sept. 12, 1943; s. William and Gertrude (Mohr) Swain. BA, Ohio Northern U., 1965; MA in Polit. Sci., U. Wis., 1967, JD, 1974; MDiv, Blessed John XXIII Nat. Sem., Weston, Mass., 1988. Ordained priest Diocese of Madison, Wis., 1988; ordained bishop, 2006; bishop Diocese of Sioux Falls, SD, 2006—. Pvt. practice, Madison, Wis., 1974—79; legal counsel, dir. policy Gov. Lee Sherman Dreyfus, Wis., 1979—83. Intelligence officer USAF, 1967—72, Vietnam. Decorated Bronze star. Mem.: Knights of Columbus (chaplain U. Wis. coun.), Equestrian Order of the Holy Sepulchre of Jerusalem. Roman Catholic. Office: Cath Diocese of Sioux Falls 523 N Duluth Ave Sioux Falls SD 57104 Office Phone: 605-334-9861. Office Fax: 605-334-2092.

SWAIN, ROBERT, artist; b. Austin, Tex., Dec. 7, 1940; s. Robert O. and Beth (Brower) S.; m. Annette Carol Leibel, Oct. 4, 1969. BA, Am.U., 1964. Prof. fine arts Hunter Coll.; vis. artist to various schs., univs., including Bklyn. Mus. Art Sch., 1975, 77, 78; dept. architecture Harvard U. Grad. Sch. Design, 1977 One-man shows, Thenan Gallery, N.Y.C., 1965, Fischbach Gallery, N.Y.C., 1968-69, Everson Art Museum, N.Y.C., 1974, Susan Galdwell Gallery, N.Y.C., 1974, 75, 78, Tex. Gallery, Houston, 1975, Columbus (Ohio) Gallery Fine Arts, 1976, Nina Freundenhein Gallery, Buffalo, 1978, group shows include, Mus. Modern Art, N.Y.C., 1968, Grand Palais, Paris, 1968, Kunsthaus, Zurich, Switzerland, 1969, Tate Gallery, London, 1969, Corcoran Gallery Art, Washington, 1969, Whitney Mus. Am. Art, N.Y.C., 1971, Albright-Knox Gallery, Buffalo, 1971, Mus. Modern Art Internat. Circulating Exhbn.-Latin Am., 1974-75; represented in permanent collections, Corcoran Gallery Art, Walker Art Center, Mpls., Va. Mus. Fine Arts, Richmond, Everson Art Mus., Columbus Gallery Fine Arts, Detroit Inst. Art, Albright-Knox Mus., works include archtl. installations, Am. Republic Ins. Co., Des Moines, 1969, N.K. Winston Corp., N.Y.C., 1969, Schering Labs., Bloomfield, N.J., 1970, Skidmore, Owings and Merrill, N.Y.C., 1970, Kahn & Mallis Assos., N.Y.C., 1972, Harris Bank, Chgo., 1977, Powell/Kleinschmidt Chgo., 1977, Travenol Labs., Deerfield, Ill., 1977, Skidmore, Owings and Merrill, Chgo., 1977. John Simon Guggenheim Meml. Found. fellow, 1969; Nat Endowment for Arts grantee, 1976 Home and Office: 57 Leonard St Fl 4 New York NY 10013-2919

SWAINE, LUCAS, social sciences educator; b. Ottawa, Ontario, Canada, Nov. 13, 1969; s. Frederick Ronald and Catherine Isabel Swaine; m. Meghan Elizabeth Liegel, Sept. 14, 2007. BA, U. Man., Winnipeg, 1991, MA, 1992; PhD, U. Sussex, England, 1995; MA, PhD, Brown U., Providence, 1999. Head tutor Brown U., 1997—98; gifford rsch. fellow U. St. Andrews, Fife, Scotland, 1999—2001; postdoc. rsch. fellow Boston Coll., Chestnut Hill, 2001; Govt. asst. prof. Dartmouth Coll., Hanover, NH, 2001—07, Govt. assoc. prof., 2007—. Author: (book) The Liberal Conscience: Politics and Principle in a World of Religious Pluralism (Best Book award, 2007). Recipient Excellence Tchg. award, Dartmouth Coll. Student Assembly, 2003, John M. Manley Huntington award, Dartmouth Coll., 2007, Pres. award, Brown U., 1995; Jack E. Thomas 1974 Family fellowship, Dartmouth Coll., 2007—08. Mem.: Nat. Assn. Scholars, Soc. Philosophy & Pub. Affairs, New Eng. Polit. Sci. Assn. (sect. chair 2002—03, exec. coun. 2004—06, ann. conf. program chair 2006), Am. Soc. Polit. & Legal Philosophy, APA, Am. Polit. Sci. Assn. Office: Dartmouth Coll Silsby Hall Hanover NH 03755 Office Fax: 603-646-2152. Business E-Mail: lucas.swaine@dartmouth.edu.

SWAINSON, JOHN A., software company executive; b. Can. 3 children. BS in Engring., U. British Columbia. Joined as systems engr. IBM, Vancouver, Canada, 1978, various mgmt. positions in mktg. and services and mfg. and devel., mgr. market devel. and support, IBM Canada Software Solutions Lab. Toronto, Canada, 1991—93, dir. application devel. mktg., software solutions div., 1993—94, v.p., application devel. solutions and dir., IBM Canada Software Solutions Lab. Toronto, Canada, 1994, gen. mgr. applications and integration middleware, 1997—2004, v.p. sales software div., 2004; pres. Computer Associates Internat. Inc., Islandia, NY, 2004—05, CEO-elect, 2004—05; pres., CEO Computer Associates Internat. Inc. (now named CA, Inc.), Islandia, NY, 2005—08, CEO, 2008—. Mem. IBM Worldwide Mgmt. Coun., IBM Strategy Team, IBM Sr. Leadership Team; bd. gov. IBM Acad. Technology. Office: Computer Assocs Internat Inc (CA Inc) One Computer Assocs Plz Islandia NY 11749

SWAISGOOD, HAROLD EVERETT, biochemist, educator; b. Ashland, Ohio, Jan. 19, 1936; s. Ray Weaver and Jennie (Morr) S.; m. Janet Cromwell, Sept. 15, 1956; children: Mark Harold, Ronald Ray. BS, Ohio State U., 1958; PhD in Chemistry (NIH fellow), Mich. State U., 1963. Rsch. asst. Mich. State U., 1958-63; rsch. assoc. NIH, 1963—64; asst. prof. food sci. and biochemistry N.C. State U., 1964-67, assoc. prof., 1967-72, prof., 1972-84, William Neal Reynolds prof., 1984—2001, prof. emeritus William Neal Reynolds, 2001—, Alumni Disting. Grad. Rsch. prof., 1997. Vis. prof. U. Lund, Sweden, 1974, chmn. biotech. program, 1986-92; bd. mem. Coun. Agrl. Sci. and Tech., 2004—07. Editor for Ams., Comments on Agr. and Food Chemistry; assoc. editor Jour. Food Biochemistry, 1983-2000; mem. editl. bd. Jour. Dairy Sci, 1975-85, Jour. Food Sci. 1978-83; regional editor Nahrung-Food, 1995-2002; contbr. articles, chpts. to profl. publs. USPHS fellow, 1963-64. Fellow Am. Chem. Soc. (agriculture food chem. divsn., award advancement of application of agrl. and food chemistry sponsored by IFF 1994), Am. Dairy Sci. Assn. (pres. 1999-2000, dairy rsch. found. award, 1985, Borden award 1987); mem. AAAS, Am. Inst. Nutrition, Am. Soc. Biochemists and Molecular Biologists, Inst. Food Technologists, Coun. Agrl. Sci. and Tech. (bd. dir.), Sigma Xi, Phi Kappa Phi, Gamma Sigma Delta. Democrat. Methodist. Achievements include research in protein structure, interactions, and functionality; characteristics and applications of immobilized enzymes; patents in field. Office: NC State U Dept Food Sci Raleigh NC 27695-7624 Business E-Mail: harold_swaisgood@ncsu.edu.

SWALES, LARRY D., oil industry executive; b. Clearfield, Pa., Aug. 24, 1949; m. Ya-Hui Laurie Pan, June 26, 2004. BS in Chem. Engring., Okla. State U., Stillwater, 1971, MS in Chem. Engring., 1972. R&d engr. Celanese Fibers Co., Pearisburg, Va., 1972—73; engr., mgr. Exxon Co, USA, Baton Rouge, 1975—84, advisor mktg. Houston, 1984—89, advisor, supply, 1989—91, advisor, planning, 1991—94, advisor, pub. affairs, 1994—95; issues advisor Exxon Mobil Corp., Irving, Tex., 1995—2003, advisor, emergency preparedness & response, 2003—. Bd. dir. Baton Rouge Arts Com., Baton Rouge, 1983—84, Helios Ensemble, Dallas, 2006—09. First lt. US Army, 1973—75, Fort Bragg, NC. Recipient Internat. Web Page award, 1998. Mem.: Pub. Affairs Coun. Avocations: singing, running. Home: 2026 Cottonwood Valley Cir S Irving TX 75038 Personal E-mail: ldswale@verizon.net.

SWALIN, RICHARD ARTHUR, scientist, company executive; b. Mpls., Mar. 18, 1929; s. Arthur and Mae (Hurley) S.; m. Helen Marguerite Van Wagenen, June 28, 1952; children: Karen, Kent, Kristin. BS with distinction, U. Minn., 1951, PhD, 1954. Rsch. assoc. GE, 1954-56; mem. faculty U. Minn., Mpls., 1956-77, prof., head Sch. Mineral and Metall Engring., 1962-68, assoc. dean Inst. Tech., 1968-71, dean Inst. Tech., 1971-77; acting dir. Space Sci. Center, 1965; v.p. tech. Eltra Corp., NYC, 1977-80; v.p. R & D Allied-Signal Corp., Morristown, NJ, 1980-84; dean Coll. Engring. and Mines U. Ariz., Tucson, 1984-87, prof., 1984-94; pres. Ariz. Tech. Devel. Corp., Tucson, 1987; prof. emeritus U. Ariz., Tucson, 1995—. Guest scientist Max Planck Inst. für Phys. Chemie, Göttingen, Fed. Republic Germany, 1963, Lawrence Radiation Lab., Livermore, Calif., 1967; cons. to govt. and industry; bd. dirs. emeritus Medtronic Corp., BMC Industries; corp. adv. bd. AMP Inc., 1990-93. Author: Thermodynamics of Solids, 2d edit, 1972; Contbr. articles to profl. jours. Dir. div. indsl. coop. U. Ariz. Found., 1985-86; trustee Midwest Research Inst., 1975-78, Sci. Mus. Minn., 1973-77, Nat. Tech. U., 1983-90. Recipient Disting. Teaching award Inst. Tech., U. Minn., 1967, Leadership award U. Minn. Alumni, 1993; NATO sr. fellow in sci., 1971. Mem. Sigma Xi, Tau Beta Pi, Phi Delta Theta, Gamma Alpha. Home: 3975 E Clock Tower Ln 323 Meridian ID 83642 Personal E-mail: rswalin@gmail.com.

SWALLOW, KATHLEEN CLINEDINST, chemistry professor; b. Balt., Jan. 21, 1948; d. Clinton Richard and Virginia Catherine (Martin) Clinedinst; m. Stephen Thaxter Swallow, June 20, 1970; children: Lindsey Ellen, Clinton Peloubet. BS, U. Richmond, 1970; PhD, MIT, 1978; Dr. Honoris Causa, U. West, Timisoara, Romania, 2006. Asst. prof. Wellesley Coll., Mass., 1977—82, 1989—90; pres. Interstate Labs., Newburyport, Mass., 1980—82; mgr. Analytical Labs MODAR, Inc., Natick, Mass., 1982—85; sr. assoc. Gradient Corp., Cambridge, Mass., 1986—89; from assoc. prof. to prof. Merrimack Coll., North Andover, Mass., 1990—97, prof., 1997—, dean sci. and engring. dept., 1998—2003. Chair dept. chemistry Merrimack Coll., North Andover, 1995—97, 2005—; vis. scientist, prof. MIT, 1996—; Fulbright sr. specialist in environ. sci., 2004—; cons. MODAR, Inc., 1985—92. Contbg. author: Ground Water Quality and Analysis at Hazardous Waste Sites, 1992; patentee supercritical water oxidation. Moderator, Town of West Newbury, 1985—; chmn. governing bd. First Religious Soc. of Newburyport, 1984, 2002. Disting. Alumna Westhampton Coll. Class of 1970, Richmond, Va., 1995 Mem. Am. Chem. Soc. (chmn. Norris com. northea. sect. 1996), Sigma Xi, Gamma Sigma Epsilon, Phi Beta Kappa Unitarian Universalist. Home: 131 River Rd West Newbury MA 01985-1103 Office: Merrimack Coll 315 Turnpike St North Andover MA 01845-5806 Business E-Mail: kathleen.swallow@merrimack.edu.

SWALM, THOMAS STERLING, aviations systems and weapons consultant, retired military officer; b. San Diego, Sept. 28, 1931; s. Calvin D. and Margaret A. (Rynning) S.; m. Charlene La Vern Garner, June 26, 1954; children: Edward Steven, Lori Ann. BS, U. Oreg., Eugene, 1954; MS in Pub. Adminstrn., George Washington U., Washington, 1964; grad., Air Command and Staff Coll., Montgomery, Ala., 1964; MA, Nat. War Coll., Washington, 1974. Commd. USAF, 1954, advanced through grades to maj. gen., 1982, instr. fighter-interceptor weapons sch. Tyndall AFB, Fla., 1956, pilot 434th Fighter-Day Squadron George AFB, Calif., 1957-58, engring. test pilot and flight examiner 50th Tactical Fighter Wing, 10th Tactical Fighter Squadron Toul-Rosieres AFB, France, and Hahn AFB, Fed. Republic Germany, 1958-61, hdqrs. 12th Waco, Tex., 1961-64, instr. pilot, flight examiner 4453d Combat Crew Tng. Wing Davis-Monthan AFB, Ariz., 1965-66, flight comdr. 12th Tactical Fighter Wing Cam Ranh Bay AFB, Republic Vietnam, 1966-67; comdr. air-to-air flight, instr. and chief R&D/OT&E sect. Fighter Weapons Sch., Nellis AFB, Nev., 1967-70; comdr., leader Thunderbirds USAF, 1970-73, chief fighter attack directorate Kirtland AFB, N.Mex., 1974-75, dep. dir. test and evaluation, 1975-76, from vice comdr. to comdr. 8th Tactical Fighter Wing Kunsan AFB, Republic of Korea, 1976-78, comdr. 3d Tactical Fighter Wing Clark AFB, Philippines, 1978-79, comdt. 57th Fighter Weapons Wing, comdt. fighter weapons sch. Nellis AFB, Nev., 1979-80, comdr. 833d air div. Holloman AFB, N.Mex., 1980-81, comdr. tactical air warfare ctr. Eglin AFB, Fla., 1981-86, ret., 1986; pres. T. Swalm and Assocs., Ft. Walton Beach, Fla., 1986-91; v.p. Melbourne Systems Div. Grumman Corp., 1991-95; pres. T. Swalm and Assocs., Melbourne, Fla., 1995—; cons. weapons and aviation sys. V.p. Applications Group Internat., Inc., Atlanta, 1986—89; bd. dirs. Nat. Correlation Working Group. Mem. editorial bd. Jour. Electronic Def., 1983-86; contbr. articles to profl. jours. Hon. chmn. Heart Assn., Las Vegas, Nev., 1972; exec. dir. Boy Scouts Am., Las Vegas and Alamagordo, N.Mex., 1970-81; chmn. AFA Scholarship Found., 1989-91; active Fla. Govs. Coun. for TQM, 1992-94; bd. dirs. Jr. Achievement, Ctrl. Fla., 1992-94; mem. USAF scientific adv. bd., 1994-98. Decorated D.S.M., Legion of Merit with two oak leaf clusters, DFC, Air medal with 14 oak leaf clusters, Vietnam Service medal with three service stars, Republic Vietnam Campaign medal; recipient R.V. Jones Trophy Electronic Security Command, 1984, Exceptional Civilian Svc. award USAF, 1999. Mem. Air Force Assn. (exec. advisor), Jerome Waterman award 1985, Jimmy Doolittle fellow 1986), Thunderbirds Pilots Assn., Old Mission Beach Athletic Club (founder), Assn. Old Crows (editl. bd. R.V. Jones trophy 1984), Order of Daedalians (flight capt.), Melbourne C of C. (trustee 1993-95), Sigma Nu. Republican. Presbyterian. Avocations: golf, tennis, sailing.

SWAMIKANNU, XAVIER, environmental engineer, state official; b. Penang, Malaysia, Aug. 1, 1958; s. Swamikannu Savarimuthu and Rosary Swamikannu; m. Laveeza Bhatti, Apr. 21, 1959; 1 child, Romin Swamikannu Savri. PhD in Environ. Sci. & Engring., U. Calif., LA, 1994. Environ. engr. Calif. EPA - Water Quality Control Bd., LA, 1989—99, chief, coastal storm water program, 1999—2003, spl. asst., storm water pollution control, 2003—04, chief storm water permitting, 2005—. Tech. adv. on storm water pollution USEPA Office of Water, Washington, 1989—; expert panelist Nat. Water Rsch. Inst., Pomona, Calif., 1997—97; mem. com. NAS/NRC, 2006—. Lector St. Anastasia Cath. Ch., LA, 1999—2004. Named Disting. scholar, U. Calif., 1993. Mem.: ASCE, Water Environment Fedn., Internat. Water Assn., Am. Water Works Assn. Roman Catholic. Achievements include development of water quality design stds. for Calif; So. Calif. storm water monitoring; Santa Monica Bay restoration policy; storm water pollution control. Avocation: travel. Home: 7732 Stewart Ave Los Angeles CA 90045 Office: Calif EPA - Water Quality Control Bd 320 W 4th St Los Angeles CA 90013 Office Fax: 213-576-6625; Home Fax: 310-242-9222. Business E-Mail: xswamikannu@waterboards.ca.gov.

SWAMINATHAN, SETHURAMAN, pediatrician, cardiologist; b. Chennai, India, 1967; MBBS, U. Madras, India, 1990; MD in Pediat., U. Calicut, India, 1993. Diplomate Am. Bd. Pediat. (sub-bd. cardiology), Indian Bd. Pediat. Asst. prof. clin. pediat. Miller Sch. Medicine, U. Miami, 2001—. Mem.: Am. Soc. Echocardiography. Achievements include research in tissue Doppler echocardiography in children. Office: U Miami Miller Sch Medicine 1611 NW 12 Ave Rm 5043 Miami FL 33156 Office Fax: 305-324-6012.

SWAMINATHAN, SRIVIDHYA, literature and language professor; d. Subramania and Nalini Swaminathan. PhD, Pa. State U., Univ Pk., 2002. Asst. prof. LI U., Bklyn., 2003—. Office: Long Island Univ One University Plaza Brooklyn NY 11201 Business E-Mail: srividhya.swaminathan@liu.edu.

SWAMY, GEETA K., obstetrician, gynecologist; MD, U NC Sch. Medicine, Chapel Hill, 1997. Resident ob-gyn U. Pitts., 2001; fellow in maternal-fetal medicine Duke U. Med. Ctr., 2004; ob-gyn Duke Perinatal Durham-Fetal Diagnostic Ctr. Office: 2608 Erwin Rd Ste 200 Durham NC 27705 Office Phone: 919-681-5220. Office Fax: 919-681-7861.*

SWAN, BARBARA J., lawyer, utilities executive; BA in History, Macalester Coll., St. Paul, 1973; JD, William Mitchell Coll. of Law, St. Paul, 1979. Atty. Axley Brynelson Law Firm, 1981—87; assoc. gen. counsel Wis. Power and Light (subs. Alliant Energy), 1987—93, gen. counsel, 1993—94, v.p., gen. counsel, 1994—98, pres., 2004—; exec. v.p., gen. counsel Alliant Energy, 1998—. Mem. Edison Electric Inst. Gen. Counsel Com. Bd. mem. Nat. Assn. Mfrs., 2001—07; pres. Alliant Energy Found., 2004—; bd. mem. Forward Wisconsin, Madison Symphony Orch., 2004—, Greater Madison C. of C., 2005—, Am. Players Theater, 2007—, Arcadian networks Advisory Bd., 2008—. Office: Alliant Energy PO Box 77007 4902 N Biltmore Ln Madison WI 53707-1007 Office Phone: 608-458-3431. E-mail: barbaraswan@alliantenergy.com.

SWAN, GEORGE STEVEN, law educator; b. St. Louis; s. Raymond Albert and Lorene Catherine (Kennedy) Swan. BA, Ohio State U., 1970; JD, U. Notre Dame, 1974; LLM, U. Toronto, 1976, SJD, 1983. Bar: Ohio 1974, U.S. Dist. Ct. (so. dist.) Ohio 1975, U.S. Supreme Ct. 1987, U.S. Ct. Appeals (6th and 11th cirs.) 1993, U.S. Ct. Appeals (10th cir.) 1994, DC 1997, Ga. 1997, Fla. 1997, U.S. Dist. Ct. (no. dist.) Ga. 1997, Minn. 1998, La. 1999, Mass. 1999; cert. NE 1998, CLU, ChFC, CFP. Asst. atty. gen. State of Ohio, Columbus, 1974-75; jud. clk. Supreme Ct. Ohio, Columbus, 1976-78; asst. prof. Del. Law Sch., Wilmington, 1980-83, assoc. prof., 1983-84; prof. law St. Thomas U. Law Sch., Miami, Fla., 1984-88; jud. clk. U.S. Ct. Appeals (7th cir.), Chgo., 1988-89; assoc. prof. N.C. Agrl. & Tech. State U., Greensboro, 1989—. Vis. prof. John Marshall Law Sch., Atlanta, 1996—97, Atlanta, 2000—01. Contbr. articles to profl. jours. Mem.: Minn. Bar, Am. Polit. Sci. Assn., Fin. Planning Assn., Soc. Fin. Svc. Profls., La. State Bar Assn., Nebr. State Bar Assn., Mass. Bar Assn., Fla. Bar, State Bar Ga., DC Bar, Ohio State Bar Assn., Phi Kappa Phi. Office: Merrick Hall 1601 E Market St Greensboro NC 27411 Office Phone: 336-334-7656 ext 7022. Business E-Mail: swan@ncat.edu.

SWAN, IVE ARLINGTON, territorial supreme court justice; b. St. Thomas, VI; m. Gertrude Niles Drue. BA, Morgan State U., Balt., 1967; JD, Howard U. Sch. Law, 1970; course completion, U. Nev. Nat. Jud. Coll., Reno, Am. Acad. Jud. Edn. Bar: US Supreme Ct., US Ct. Appeals (DC), US Ct. Appeals (3rd cir.), US Dist. Ct. (DC), VI. Legal intern VI Dept. Justice, dep. asst. atty. gen., asst. atty. gen., criminal and family law divsns. civil and adminstrv. law divsns., atty. gen., 1978—81; pvt. practice atty., 1981—87; judge Territorial Ct. the VI, 1987—2006, Superior Ct. the VI, 2006; assoc. justice Supreme Ct. the VI, 2006—. Mem.: Soc. Atty. Generals Emeritus, Am. Judges Assn., Nat. Bar Assn., VI Bar Assn., Washington, DC Bar Assn. Office: Supreme Ct the VI PO Box 590 St Thomas VI 00804*

SWAN, JAMES C., United States Ambassador to Djibouti; BS in Fgn. Svc., Georgetown U., Washington; MA in Internat. Rels., Johns Hopkins Sch. Advanced Internat. Studies; M in Security Studies, Nat. War Coll., 2005. Fgn. svc. assignments US Dept. State, Port-au-Prince, Haiti, Managua, Nicaragua, chief polit. sect. Yaounde, Cameroon, 1992—94, Somalia watcher Nairobi, Kenya, 1994—96, desk officer Democratic Republic of Congo, 1996—98, dep. chief of mission Brazzaville, Republic of the Congo, Kinsasha, Democratic Republic of Congo, 2001—04, dir. analysis Africa, Bur. Intelligence and Rsch., 2005—06, dep. asst. sec. state African Affairs, 2006—08, US amb. to Djibouti, 2008—. Office: DOS Amb 2150 Djibouti Pl Washington DC 20521-2150*

SWAN, MARA E., employment services executive; BBA, U. Buffalo; M in Indsl. Rels., U. Minn. Human resources mgr. Miller Brewing Co.; chief people officer global ops. Molson Coors Brewing Co.; sr. v.p. global human resources Manpower, Inc., Milw., 2005—.

SWAN, MICHAEL K., lawyer; b. Kilgore, Tex. BBA, Tex. A&M, 1964; LLB, Univ. Tex., 1967. Bar: Tex. 1967, US Supreme Ct. 1971, US Dist. Ct. (so., no., we., ea. districts) Tex., cert.: Civil Trial Law, Tex. Bd. Legal Specialization. Assoc. Reynolds White Allen & Cook, 1971—75, mng. ptnr., 1981—88; ptnr., gen. litig. Andrews Kurth, 1988—92, ptnr. in charge, 2000—07; head ptnr. litig. practice Akin Gump Strauss Hauer & Feld LLP, Houston, 1992—. Mem. JAGC US Army, 1967—71. Fellow: Houston Bar Found., Tex. Bar Found.; mem.: ABA, Am. Bd. Trial Advocates, State Bar of Tex. (dir. 1982—85), Houston Bar Assn., Phi Alpha Delta. Office: Akin Gump Strauss Hauer & Feld LLP 44th fl 1111 Louisiana St Houston TX 77002-5200 Office Phone: 713-220-5862. Office Fax: 713-236-0822. Business E-Mail: mswan@akingump.com.

SWAN, PATRICIA BRINTNALL, academic administrator, researcher; b. Hickory, NC, Oct. 21, 1937; d. Philip Earle and Mary Lucille (Farmer) Brintnall; m. James Byron Swan, Apr. 23, 1962; children: Kathryn Ann, Deborah Lee. BS, U. N.C., 1959; MS, U. Wis., 1961, PhD, 1964. Rsch. assoc. U. Wis., Madison, 1963—64, U. Minn., St. Paul, 1964—65, asst. prof., 1965—68, assoc. prof., 1968—73, prof., 1973—89; assoc. dean U. Minn. Grad. Sch., Mpls., 1987—89; prof. Iowa State U., Ames, 1989—2001, prof. emeritus, 2002—, vice provost, dean, 1989—91, 1992—99, interim provost, 1991—92. Program coord. SEA-USDA, Washington, 1979-80; bd. dirs. Fedn. of Am. Socs. for Exptl. Biology, Bethesda, Md., 1988-91; mem. Bd. Agr., NRC, Washington, 1992-94; mem. Grad. Rsch. Examination Bd., 1996-2002. Contbr. over 80 tech. articles to profl. jours. Pres. U. Minn. Faculty Polit. Action Com., Mpls., 1984-87; bd. dirs. Ames Econ. Devel. Commn., 1991-99. Recipient Disting. Alumni award U. Wis., 1994. Fellow Am. Soc. Nutrition Sci., Am. Inst. Nutrition (sec. 1981-84, historical and biographical editor Jour. Nutrition); mem. Nat. Agrl. Biotech. Coun. (chair 1996-97), Rsch. Coun. of Iowa (pres. 1994-96). Home: 1301 Crest Ridge Ct Nashville TN 37221-4336 E-mail: pswan@iastate.edu.

SWAN, PEER ALDEN, public utility executive; b. Beverly, Mass., 1944; s. E.M. and Stella Swan; m. Nancy Carol Mosier, Jan. 24, 1969; children: Michael, Ashley. AA, Orange Coast Coll., Costa Mesa, Calif., 1966; BA, Calif. State U., Fullerton, 1973. Fin. analyst Brunswich, Costa Mesa, 1974-76; asst. treas. Pacific Sci. Co., Newport Beach, Calif., 1977-84, treas., 1984-98. Dir. SC Bancorp, Downey, Calif., 1992-97, Met. Water Dist. of So. Calif., 1999-2002, Assn. Calif. Water Agys, 2008-. Dir. Irvine (Calif.) Ranch Water Dist., 1979—, Orange County Sanitation Dist., Fountain Valley, Calif., 1985—2001, So. Calif. Water Com., Irvine, 1984—92, Nat. Water Rsch. Inst., Fountain Valley, 1991—2001. Capt. US Army, 1966—71, Vietnam. Avocations: sailing, hiking. Home: 7 Terraza Dr Newport Coast CA 92657-1510 Business E-Mail: pswan@ix.netcom.com.

SWAN, PHILIP GEORGE, librarian, educator, director, artist; b. Camp Springs, Md., Feb. 7, 1969; s. Philip George and Diana Morse Swan; m. Jennifer Marguerite Hubert, Sept. 27, 2001. BA, U. Mich., 1991; MA, Coll. William and Mary, 1994; MS in Info., U. Mich., 1996. Libra, asst. mgr. Queensborough Pub. Libr., Jamaica, NY, 1997—99; head libr., assoc. prof. Hunter Coll., NYC, 2000—. Chesebrough Pond's Nat. Arts Competition, 1987, juried exhibition, The Haven (Second Pl. Nationally, 1987), Dansforth Gallery, 2000, Longbeach Island Found. Arts, 2002, exhibited in group shows at Santorelli Gallery, 2007, Hun Gallery, NY, 2008, Korous House, Washington, 2008; author: (peer reviewed article) Collection Building (Emerald Publishing's 2003 Highly Commended Award, 2002); contbr. articles to profl. jours. Scholar, Coll. William and Mary and Colonial Williamsburg Found., 1993—94. Mem.: ALA, Libr. Assn. CUNY (co-chair 2002—04, co-chair electronic info. svcs. com. 2002—04), Assn. Coll. and Rsch. Libr. (coll. libr. sect. comm. com. 2001—04). Office: Hunter Coll 129 E 79th St 2nd Flr New York NY 10075

SWAN, ROBERT H., Internet company executive; BS in Mgmt., SUNY, Buffalo; MBA, SUNY, Binghamton. Fin. positions Gen. Electric, 1985—99; CFO GE Transportation Systems, 1994—97; v.p. fin. GE Med. Systems, 1997—98; v.p. fin., CFO GE Lighting, 1998—99, Webvan Group, 1999—2001, COO, 2000—01, CEO, 2001; CFO, exec. v.p. TRW Inc., 2001—02; exec. v.p., CFO EDS, Plano, Tex., 2003—06; sr. v.p. fin., CFO eBay Inc., San Jose, Calif., 2006—. Office: eBay Inc 2145 Hamilton Ave San Jose CA 95125 Office Phone: 972-604-6000. Office Fax: 972-605-6033.

SWANER, LYNN E., education educator; d. Norris S and Susan L Gaynor; m. Damon K Swaner, Aug. 10, 1996; 1 child, Ashley E. EdD, Columbia U., 2003. Nat. cert. counselor, lic. mental health counselor, approved clin. supr. Asst. prof. C.W. Post Campus of L.I. U., Brookville, NY, 2005—. Cross-site evaluator, mem. planning bd. Bringing Theory to Practice Project, Am. Assn. Colls. and Univs., Washington, 2004—. Contbr. articles to profl. jours. Sec. South Yaphank Cmty. Assn., Yaphank, NY, 2004—05. Recipient Binghamton U. award for the Humanities, 1996; grantee Cost Study Coll. Expenditures, 2007—. Mem.: Phi Beta Kappa. Achievements include commissioned literature review on mental health, engaged learning, and civic development published by Am. Assn. Colls. and Univs. Office: CW Post Campus of LI U Dept of Counseling 720 Northern Blvd Brookville NY 11548

SWANK, ANNETTE MARIE, software designer; b. Lynn, Mass., Nov. 9, 1953; d. Roland Paterson and Rita Mary (Edwards) S. BSEE and Computer Sci., Vanderbilt U., 1975; M of Engring. Sci., Pa. State U., 2003. Lead programmer GE, Phila., 1975-80; system analyst SEI Corp., Wayne, Pa., 1980-82; mgr., designer Premier Systems, Inc., Wayne, Pa., 1982-85, dir., 1985-88, tech. advisor, 1988-90, tech. architect, 1990-92, Funds Assocs. Ltd., Wayne, 1992-99; sr. bus. analyst First Data Investor Svcs. Group, Berwyn, Pa., 1999; prin. bus. analyst PFPC Inc., King of Prussia, 1999—2000, v.p., mng. dir. SURPAS bus. unit Berwyn, Pa., 2000—. Mem. exec. coun. internat. bus. critical sys. Hewlett Packard, 2002—. Designer: (programming lang. and data dictionary) Vision, 1985. Treas. Master Singers, Plymouth Meeting, Pa., 1987-88. Mem. Assn. Computing Machinery, Gamma Phi Beta (com. chmn. alumna Phila. 1986-87). Avocations: singing, dance, bowling, bridge, wine tasting. Office: PNC GIS Inc 760 Moore Rd King Of Prussia PA 19406 Home: 948 Marshall DR Pottstown PA 19465

SWANK, HILARY, actress; b. Lincoln, Nebr., July 30, 1974; d. Stephen and Judy Swank; m. Chad Lowe, Sept. 28, 1997 (div. Nov. 1, 2007). Attended, Santa Monica Coll. Co-founder 2S Films, 2008—. Actress (films) Buffy the Vampire Slayer, 1992, The Next Karate Kid, 1994, Sometimes They Come Back...Again, 1996, Kounterfeit, 1996, The Way We Are, 1997, Heartwood, 1998, Boys Don't Cry, 1999 (Golden Globe award for Best Actress, 2000, Acad. award for Best Actress, 2000), Affair of the Necklace, 2000, The Gift, 2000, Insomnia, 2002, The Core, 2003, Million Dollar Baby, 2004 (Boston Film Critics best actress award, 2004, SAG award for outstanding performance by female actor in leading role, 2005, Golden Globe award for Best Actress, 2005, Acad. award for Best Actress, 2005), The Black Dahlia, 2006, The Reaping, 2007, P.S. I Love You, 2007, Birds of America, 2008, (TV films) Cries Unheard: The Donna Yaklich Story, 1994, Terror in the Family, 1996, Dying to Belong, 1997, The Sleepwalker Killing, 1997, Iron Jawed Angels, 2004, (TV series) Evening Shade, 1991—92, Camp Wilder, 1992, Leaving LA, 1997, Beverly Hills, 90210, 1997—98, actress, exec. prodr. (films) 11:14, 2003, Freedom Writers, 2007, TV appearances Growing Pains, 1985, Harry and the Hendersons, 1991. Recipient Little Screen/Big Star award, TV Land, 2006, Emery award, Hetrick-Martin Inst., 2006, star on the Hollywood Walk of Fame, 2007; named one of 100 Most Influential People, TIME mag., 2005. Avocations: sky diving, river rafting, skiing, swimming. Office: c/o Jason Weinberg Untitled Entertainment (LA) 331 N Maple Dr 3rd Fl Beverly Hills CA 90210*

SWANK, MICHAEL LAWSON, orthopedist; MD, NW U., Chgo., 1992. Pres. Cin. Orthop. Rsch. Inst., 2003—. Office: Cin Orthop Rsch Inst 8250 Kenwood Crossing Way Ste 101 Cincinnati OH 45236 Office Fax: 513-221-1962.

SWANKIN, DAVID ARNOLD, lawyer, consumer products company executive; b. Boston, Jan. 18, 1934; s. Max and Anne (Rotefsky) S.; m. Jeanne Phyllis Herrick; 1 dau., Sheryl. AB, Brandeis U., 1954; MS, U. Wis., 1957; JD, George Washington U., 1962. Mgmt. intern U.S. Dept. Labor, Washington, 1957-60, spl. asst. to asst. sec. labor, 1961-63, dep. asst. sec. labor, 1967; dir. Bur. Labor Standards, 1967-68; exec. sec. Pres.'s Consumer Adv. Council, Washington, 1964; exec, dir. Pres's Com. on Consumer Interests, Washington, 1965-66; Washington rep. Consumer's Union, 1969-71; exec. dir. Consumer Interests Found., 1971-73; sr. partner Swankin & Turner, 1973—. Pres. Citizen Advocacy Ctr. 1994—; cons. U.S. Dept. Labor; pres. Citizen Advocacy Ctr., 1994—. Mem. president's coun. Brandeis U., 1968-69; mem. PEW Health Profls. Commn., 1997-98. Served with AUS., 1954-56. Recipient Jump award U.S. Govt., 1969 Office: 1400 16th St NW Washington DC 20036-2217 Home: 102 Gresham Pl Falls Church VA 22046 Business E-Mail: davidswankin@cacenter.org.

SWANN, CHARENA RAI, psychotherapist, social worker; b. Chambersburg, Pa., June 18, 1962; d. Nathaniel McNabb and Brenda Keepler; m. Lynn Swann, June 23, 1991; children: Shafer, Braxton. BA Social Work, Calif. U. Pa., Calif., Pa., 1984; MA Social Work, U. Pitts., 1985, PhD, 2002. Psychiatric soc. worker Western Psychiatric Inst. & Clinic, Pitts., 1984—; psychotherapist Sewickley Valley Hosp., Pitts., 1995—. Adv. bd. Summerbridge Pitts., 1999—2002; bd. mem. Children's Mus., 1998—. Fundraiser, mentor Girls Hope Pitts., 1998—2002. Mem.: Am. Psychol. Soc., Link, Jack and Jill of Am. Baptist. Avocations: reading, exercise.

SWANN, LYNN CURTIS, management consultant, retired professional football player; b. Alcoa, Tenn., Mar. 7, 1952; s. Willie and Mildred (McGarity) Swann; m. Bernadette Robi, June 10, 1979 (div. 1983); m. Charena Shaffer; children: Shaffer, Braxton. BA in Pub. Rels., U. So. Calif., 1974. Wide receiver Pitts. Steelers, 1974—83; football and sports broadcaster ABC Sports, 1976—2006; pres. Swann, Inc., 1976; mng. dir. Diamond Edge Capital Ptnrs., LLC, 2008—. Chmn. President's Coun. Phys. Fitness and Sports, 2002—05; bd. dirs. Transdel Pharmaceuticals, Inc., H. J. Heinz Co., 2003—, Harrah's Entertainment, Inc., 2008—. (film appearances) The Last Boy Scout, 1991, The Program, 1993, The Waterboy, 1998; (TV appearances)Omnibus, 1980, Mister Rogers Neighborhood, 1981, '83, Paper Chase, 1984, Hotel, 1984, Love American Style, 1985, Family Matters, 1991, Drew Carey Show, 1991; host, narrator: Britten's Young Person's Guide to Orchestra, Wheeling Symphony Orch., 1982; host: Arts Alive, PBS, 1984; talk show host: Pittsburgh 2Day, 1985; panelist, host To Tell the Truth, 1990-91. Mem., Big Bros./Big Sisters Assn., 1980-, pres., 1993-95; trustee Pitts. Ballet Theatre, creator youth scholarship program; bd. dirs. Scott Newman Juvenile Drug and Alcohol Prevention Found., U. So. Calif. Sch. Journalism Alumni Assn.; Republican candidate Gov. of Pa., 2005. Named NFL All-Pro, 1975, 77, 78; Super Bowl X MVP, 1976, Pitts. Multiple Sclerosis Athlete of Yr., 1980, NFL Man of Yr., 1981; named to NFL Pro Bowl 1975, 77, 78, NFL Hall of Fame Team of Decade/1970's, AP, UPI, Kodak All Am. Teams, Pop Warner Hall of Fame, Coll. Football Hall of Fame, 1993, NFl Pro Football Hall of Fame, 2001, Bay Area Hall of Fame, 2002; recipient Image award NAACP, 1979, Ebonics Soc. award, Outstanding Alumni award U. So. Calif., 1984, Oleg Cassini Competitors Fashion award, 1985. Mem. Screen Actors Guild, AFTRA. Republican. Baptist. Achievements include being selected a member of the Pittsburgh Steelers All-Time Team and the Super Bowl Silver Anniversary Team. Office: Swann Inc 506 Hegner Way Sewickley PA 15143-1552 Office Phone: 412-749-4988.*

SWANN, RICHARD ROCKWELL, lawyer, banker; b. Orlando, Fla., May 7, 1940; s. Pervie P. and Maesther (Mears) Swann; m. Doris Orr (dec. Oct. 1983); children: Dorothy Orr, Christian Mears, Campbell Thornal, Doris Reed. AB, Duke U., 1961, JD, 1963. Bar: Fla. 1963. Mem. Swann & Haddock, Orlando, 1963—90, Swann & Hadley, 1990—. Jr. achievement bd., Orlando, 1964—68, Downtown Orlando Coun., 1969—71; appointee of Gov. Askew Orange County Budge Commn., Orlando, 1971, Orange County Expy. Authority, Orlando, 1973—75; dir. Overseas Pvt. Investment Corp., Washington, 1977—82; bd. govs. Overseas Investment Reins, 1978—82; dir., appointed by Gov. Graham Fla. High Speed Rail Commn., Orlando, 1984—88; bd. visitors Terry Sanford Sch. Inst. Pub. Policy, Duke U., 1989—92; gen. counsel, dir. Am. Heritage Homes USA, Inc., 1995—2000, Jefferson Nat. Title Ins. Co., 1997—2003; dir. Property Gen., Inc., Orlando, 2003—, Comml. Vehicle Ins. Co. SC, 2004—, Surrey Homes, LL, Orlando, 2008—; chmn. bd. 1st Fidelity Savs. & Loan, Orlando, Am. Pioneer Savs. Bank, Orlando, Am. Pioneer, Inc., Orlando. Mem.: ABA, Fla. Bar Assn., Orange County Bar Assn. Democrat. Office: 1031 W Morse Blvd Ste 350 Winter Park FL 32789 Office Phone: 497-647-2777. Business E-Mail: rswann@swannhadley.com.

SWANSEN, SAMUEL THEODORE, lawyer; b. Milw., June 6, 1937; s. Theodore Lawrence and Clarinda Dingwall (Crittenden) S.; m. Donna Rae Elizabeth Maloney, June 27, 1959; children: Jessica Swansen Bonelli, Theodor Arthur, Christopher Currie. AB, Dartmouth Coll., 1959; JD, U. Wis., 1962. Bar: Wis. 1962, Pa. 1964, U.S. Supreme Ct. 1969, accredited estate planner: Nat. Assn. Estate Planners & Couns. 1995. Law clk. to presiding justice Wis. Supreme Ct., Madison, 1962-63; assoc. Dechert, Price & Rhoads, Phila., 1963-68, 70-73, ptnr., 1973-93; asst. dist. atty. City of Phila. Dist. Atty.'s Office, 1968-70, chief frauds div., 1969; pvt. practice Phila., 1963—93, Blue Bell, Pa., 1994—. Adj. prof. law Temple U., Phila., 1970-80; lectr. Pa. Bar Inst., Nat. Bus. Inst., Ctr. Profl. Edn., 1985—. Editor, author U. Wis. Law Rev., 1960-62. Corp. mem. Anna T. Jeanes Found., Fox Chase, Phila, 1985—93, Associated Svcs. for the Blind, Phila, 1974—91, Bach Festival of Phila., 1989—2009, pres., 1993—97, 2003—06; founding dir. Global Bach Cmty., 2000—, pres., 2001—, 2003—06; violinist Southeastern Pa. Symphony Orch. (formerly North Penn Symphony Orch.), 1973—; trombonist North Penn Symphony Orch., 1973—; mem. Nat. Network of Estate Planning Attys., 1993—2008, Nat. Acad. Elder Law Attys., 1993—, Wealth Counsel, 2005—; bd. dirs. Friends Rehab. Program, Inc., Phila., 1966—73, 1985—94, Franklin Found., Phila., 1969—; v.p., sec., bd. dirs. Foulkeways at Gwynedd, 1979—97, pres., 1986—97, emeritus dir., 1997—; chmn. bd. dirs. Friends Life Care at Home, Inc., 1990—2007, bd. dirs., 1990—, Friends Retirement Concepts, Inc., Gwynedd, sec. bd. dirs., 1985—96; hon. bd. dirs. Friends Neighborhood Guild; pres. Greater Phila. Fedn. Settlements, 1970—72; dir., sec. Energy Islands Internat., Inc., 1963—; pres. emeritus Foulkeways at Gwynedd, 1997; mem. Gwynedd Monthly Meeting of Friends, 1974—. Fellow Esperti Peterson Inst. Wealth Strategies Planning, 1996—. Mem. ABA, Pa. Bar Assn., Phila. Bar Assn., Montgomery County Bar Assn., Dartmouth Club Phila., Delta Upsilon, Phi Delta Phi. Republican. Mem. Soc. Of Friends. Home: 221 Morris Rd Ambler PA 19002-5202 Office: 660 Sentry Pky Ste 200 Blue Bell PA 19422-2317 Office Phone: 610-834-9810. Personal E-mail: sts@samswansen.com.

SWANSON, AL, oil industry executive; With Santa Fe Snyder Corp.; sr. v.p. fin., treas. Plains All Am. Pipeline, LP, Houston, 2007—08, sr. v.p. fin., CFO, 2008—. Office: Plains All Am Pipeline LP 333 Clay St Ste 1600 Houston TX 77002 Office Phone: 713-646-4100. Business E-Mail: apswanson@paalp.com.*

SWANSON, DAVID C., publishing executive; Account exec. R.H. Donnelley, 1985, exec. v.p. sales, 1995—97, exec. v.p., gen. mgr. proprietary ops., 1997—98, exec. v.p. corp. strategy, 1998—99, pres. Donnelley Directory Svcs., 1999—2000, pres., COO, 2000—02, bd. dirs., 2001—, CEO, 2002—, chmn., 2002—06. Bd. dirs. Yellow Pages Assn., 2003—, v.p. bd. dirs. Office: RH Donnelley 1001 Winstead Dr Cary NC 27513 Office Phone: 919-297-1600.

SWANSON, DAVID HENRY, retired economist, educator, consultant; b. Anoka, Minn., Nov. 1, 1930; s. Henry Otto and Louise Isabell (Holiday) S.; m. Suzanne Nash, Jan. 19, 1952 (dec. Sept. 1990); children: Matthew David, Christopher James; m. Joanne Perkins, Feb. 1, 1991. BA, St. Cloud State U., 1953; MA, U. Minn., 1955; PhD, Iowa State U., 1987. CPCU. Econ. area devel. dept. No. State Power Co., Mpls., 1955-56, staff asst., v.p. sales, 1956-57, economist indsl. devel. dept., 1957-63; dir. area devel. dept. Iowa So. Utilities Co., Centerville, 1963-67, dir. econ. R&D, 1967-70; dir. New Orleans Econ. Devel. Coun., 1970-72; divsn. mgr. Kaiser Aetna Tex., New Orleans, 1972-73; dir. corp. rsch. United Svcs. Automobile Assn., San Antonio, 1973-76; pres. Lantern Corp., San Antonio, 1974-79; adminstr. bus. devel. State of Wis., Madison, 1976-78; dir. Ctr. Indsl. Rsch. and Svc. Iowa State U., Ames, 1978-89, mem. mktg. faculty Coll. Bus. Adminstrn., 1979-85; dir. econ. devel. lab Ga. Inst. Tech., 1989—93; adv. to mfg. extension program Nat. Inst. Stds. U.S Dept. Commerce, 1993—96; prin. rshch assoc., econ. devel. Insts. Ga. Insts. Tech., Atlanta, 1996-99, ret., 1999. Cons. Indsl. Modernization and Univ. Ext., Mexico, 1997—2000, Tech. Tng. and Indsl. Ext., Poland, 1998—2000, Mendes England & Assocs. Polish Project, 1998—2000; dir. Iowa Devel. Commn., 1982—83; mem. adv. bd. Iowa Venture Capital Fund, 1985—88; dir. Applied Strategies Internat. Ltd., 1983—88; dir. econ. devel. lab. Ga. Inst. Tech., Atlanta, 1989—93; mem. adv. bd. Nat. Tech. Transfer Ctr, 1992—96; exec. on loan Nat. Inst. Stds. and Tech., 1993—96; chmn. Iowa Curriculum Assistance Sys., 1984—85; cons. Ctr. for Indsl. Rsch., Iowa State U., 1998—2001; award evaluator Fed. Lab. Consortium, 1999—2008. Mem. Iowa Airport Planning Coun., 1968-70; mem. adv. coun. Office Comprehensive Health Planning, 1967-70; mem. adv. coun. Ctr. Indsl. Rsch. and Svc., 1967-70, New Orleans Met. Area Com., 1972-73; mem. Iowa Dist. Export Coun., 1977-88; mem. Atlanta Dist. Export Coun., 1989-96; mem. region 7 adv. coun. SBA, 1978-88; dir. Mid-Continent R&D Coun., 1980-84; chmn. Iowa del. White House Conf. on Small Bus., 1980; chmn. Gov.'s Task Force on High Tech., 1982-83; chmn. Iowa High Tech. Coun., 1983-86; mem. adv. com. U. New Orleans, 1971-73; county fin. chmn. Rep. Party, 1966-67; bd. dirs. Greater New Orleans Urban League, 1970-73, Indsl. Policy Coun., 1984-88, Suwanee Crossroads Inc., 2001-04; mem. Iowa Gov.'s Export Coun., 1984-89; v.p. Iowa Sister State Friendship Com., 1985-87, pres., 1988; chmn. nat. adv. coun. Fed. Lab. Consortium, 1985-98, chmn., 1993-96, mem., 1985, award reviewer, 1998—; mem. Ga. Tech. Faculty Assembly, 1990-92; pres. Chattahoochee Run Homeowners Assn., 1997-99; mem. planning com. Internat. Tech. Transfer Conf., 1997; mem. adv. com. Ga. Oglethorpe Quality Award, 1997-99, quality examiner, 1998-99, Georgians Mfg., 1997-99; mem. Suwanee Planning and Zoning Bd. Appeals, 1999, chair, 2000-03; vice chmn. econ. devel. com. Suwanee Cmty. Betterment Program, 1999-2000; chmn. transition com. Chattahoochee Run Neighborhood Assn., 2000; chair Suwanee Day Festival, 2001-02. With USAF, 1951-52. Mem. Am. Indsl. Ext. Alliance (pres. 1992-96, editor 1998-2000), Nat. Assn. Mgmt. Tech. Assistance Ctrs. (pres. 1985, bd. dirs. 1982-86), Tech. Transfer Soc. (bd. dirs. 1984-94, v.p. 1987-90, pres.-elect 1991-92, pres. 1992-93), Oak Ridge Assoc. Univs. (tech. transfer adv. coun. 1992-95), Ga. Fin. Developers Assn., Ga. 2000, Profl. Developers Assn., Nat. Univ. Continuing Edn. Assn., Internat. Coun. Small Bus., Rotary (bd. dirs. 1986-88), Toastmasters (past pres.), Marston Club (Iowa State U. Coll. Engring.), Alumni Admissions Coun. (Iowa State U.), Kiwanis (sec. 2004—), Spruce Creek Country Club Vets. Assn. Episcopalian. Home: 13320 SE 97th Terrace Rd Summerfield FL 34491 Personal E-mail: swansondh@mindspring.com.

SWANSON, DAVID P., lawyer; b. 1955; BA, St. Cloud State U., 1978; JD, Vanderbilt U., 1981. Bar: Ill. 1981, Minn. 1983. Ptnr., co-chair, project devel., fin. group Dorsey & Whitney LLP, Mpls., and chair, agribus., coop. law. Dir. North Country Devel. Fund, Ralph K. Morris Found. Recipient Honored Cooperator award, Nat. Coop. Bus. Assn. Mem.: Nat. Soc. of Accountants for Cooperatives, Nat. Coop. Bus. Assn. Office: Dorsey & Whitney LLP Ste 1500 50 S Sixth St Minneapolis MN 55402-1498 Office Phone: 612-343-8275. Office Fax: 612-340-7800. Business E-Mail: swanson.dave@dorsey.com.

SWANSON, DIANE LORAINE, business management and economics educator, researcher; b. Manhattan, Kans., Oct. 6, 1950; d. Harold Albin Swanson and Betty Jo Lusby; m. Michael Dale Scott, Aug. 5, 1970 (dec. July 19, 1975); 1 child, Christopher William Scott. BS Mgmt. and Fin., Avila U., Kansas City, Mo., 1980; MA Econs., U. Mo., Kansas City, 1982; PhD Bus. Adminstrn., U. Pitts., 1996. Instr. econs., interim dir. Inst. Mgmt. Old Dominion U., Norfolk, Va., 1984—86; asst. prof. fin.

Hampton U., Va., 1987—88; asst. prof. bus. econs. U. Pitts., 1988—89; assoc. prof. mgmt. Robert Morris U., Pitts., 1989—97; prof. Kans. State U., Manhattan, 1997, prof. mgmt., 2008—, prof. Von Waaden, 2003—; instr. corp. continuing ethics edn. acctg. Lindburg & Vogel, 2005. Mem. Pres.'s Commn. on Women Kans. State U., Manhattan, 2000—01, mentor Developing Scholars Program for Minority Students, 2000—01; instr. exec. edn. program Nat. Assn. Credit Mgmt., 2005—; founder, chair Bus. Ethics Edn. Initiative Kans. State U., 2002—; instr. continuing edn. tax profls., Kans., 2005; presenter in field; spkr. in field. Co-editor: Advancing Business Ethics Education Book, 2008; book rev. editor, consulting editor: Internat. Jour. Orgnl. Analysis, 1994—2005, mem. editl. bd.: Ethics in Film, 2005—07, Organizational Analysis, Research in Management, Education and Development Books Series, 2005, mem. editl. team spl. issues: Acad. Mgmt. Rev., 2005, mem. editl. bd.:, 2007—, Business Ethics Quarterly, 2008—, Ethics in Practice Book Series, 2006—, Media Reference, 2002—; mem. editl. bd. Bus. & Soc., 2008—; contbg. editor: Managing Ego Energy, 1994; spl. issue editor: Jour. Individual Employment Rights, 2002—03, assoc. editor: Business Ethics and Society Encyclopedia, 2004—08 (award); assoc. editor website Acad. Mgmt. Profl. Devel., 2005; assoc. editor: Acad. Mgmt. Profl. Devel. in Ethics, 2005, reviewer: Acad. Textbooks, 1998—2009; contbr. chapters to books, articles to profl. jours.; co-author: (book) Integrative Corporate Citizenship, 2008. Co-founder Nat. Campaign to Improve Bus. Ethics Edn., 2002—; bd. dirs. Women's Intercultural Network, San Francisco, 1994—2002, People's Coop., Manhattan, 1998—2000, All Acad. Task Force on Mentoring, 2002—07. Recipient nat. award for tchg. excellence, Bell and Howell, 1982, award for entrepreneurial leadership, Advances in Mgmt. Conf., 1996, Best Article on Bus. and Soc. award, Internat. Assn. for Bus. and Soc. and Calif. Mgmt. Rev., 1999, Internat. Outstanding Bus. Ethics Educator award, 2004, Japha Hon. for rsch. on exec. compensation, U. Colo., 2004; grantee, Beard Ctr. for Ethics, Duquesne U., 2000, Australian Grad. Sch. Mgmt., 2000—01;, David Berg Family Found. in Bus. Ethics fellow, 1994, Weatherford fellow, Oreg. State U., 2004. Mem.: Bus. Ethics Quarterly, Acad. Mgmt. Review (editl. bd. mem. 2008—), Nat. Acad. Mgmt. (governing bd. Social Issues in Mgmt. 1998—2005, sponsors internat. tchg. ethics website 2001—, chair nat. ethics curriculum devel. com. 2003—05, editl. bd. Ethics in Practice Book Series 2006—), Beta Gamma Sigma. Democrat. Avocations: yoga, meditation, travel, gardening. Office: Kans State U 101 Calvin Hall Manhattan KS 66506 Office Phone: 785-532-4352. Business E-Mail: swanson@ksu.edu.

SWANSON, DON RICHARD, university dean; b. LA, Oct. 10, 1924; s. Harry Windfield and Grace Clara (Sandstrom) S.; m. Patricia Elizabeth Klick, Aug. 22, 1976; children— Douglas Alan, Richard Brian, Judith Ann. BS, Calif. Inst. Tech., 1945; MA, Rice U., 1947; PhD, U. Calif., Berkeley, 1952. Physicist U. Calif. Radiation Lab., Berkeley, 1947-52, Hughes Research and devel. Labs., Culver City, Calif., 1952-55; research scientist TRW, Inc., Canoga Park, Calif., 1955-63; prof. Grad. Library Sch., U. Chgo., 1963-92, dean, 1963-72, 77-79, 86-90, prof. bio-sci. coll. divsn. and divsn. humanities, 1992-96, prof. emeritus, 1996—. Mem. Sci. Info. Council, NSF, 1960-65; mem. toxicology info. panel Pres.'s Sci. Advisory Com., 1964-66; mem. library vis. com. Mass. Inst. Tech., 1966-71; mem. com. on sci. and tech. communication Nat. Acad. Scis., 1966-69 Editor: The Intellectual Founds. of Library Education, 1965, The Role of Libraries in the Growth of Knowledge, 1980; co-editor: Operations Research: Implications for Libraries, 1972, Management Education: Implications for Libraries and Library Schools, 1974; mem. editorial bd.: Library Quarterly, 1963-93; contbr.: chpt. to Ency. Brit, 1968—; sci. articles to profl. jours. Trustee Nat. Opinion Research Center, 1964-73; Research fellow Chgo. Inst. for Psychoanalysis, 1972-76. Served with USNR, 1943-46. Recipient Award of Merit Am. Soc. for Info. Sci. and Tech., 2000. Mem.: Am. Soc. for Info. Sci. Home: 5468 S Ingleside Ave Chicago IL 60615-5062 Business E-Mail: d-swanson@uchicago.edu.

SWANSON, DONALD ALAN, geologist; b. Tacoma, July 25, 1938; s. Leonard Walter and Edith Christine (Bowers) S.; m. Barbara Joan White, May 25, 1974. BS in Geology, Wash. State U., 1960; PhD in Geology, Johns Hopkins U., 1964. Geologist U.S. Geol. Survey, Menlo Park, Calif., 1965—68, 1971—80, Hawaii National Park, 1968—71, sr. geologist Cascades Volcano Obs. Vancouver, Wash., 1980—90, rsch. scientist-in-charge, 1986—89, sr. geologist Seattle, 1990—96; assoc. dir. Volcano Systems Ctr. U. Wash., 1993—96; scientist-in-charge Hawaiian Volcano Obs., 1997—2004. Affiliate prof. U. Wash., 1992—; adj. prof. U. Hawaii, 2002--; cons. U.S. Dept. Energy, Richland, Wash., 1979-83; volcanologist New Zealand Geol. Survey, Taupo, 1984; advisor Colombian Volcano Obs., Manizales, 1986. Assoc. editor Jour. Volcanology and Geothermal Rsch., 1976—, Jour. Geophys. Rsch., 1992-94; editor Bull. of Volcanology, 1985-90, exec. editor, 1995-99; contbr. numerous articles to profl. jours. Recipient Superior Svc. award U.S. Geol. Survey, 1980, Meritorious Svc. award U.S. Dept. Interior, 1985, Disting. Svc. award, U.S. Dept. Interior, 2005; postdoctoral fellow NATO, 1964-65. Fellow Geol. Soc. Am., Am. Geophys. Union, AAAS; mem. Sigma Xi. Avocation: hiking. Home: 417 Linaka St Hilo HI 96720-5927 Office: US Geol Survey Hawaiian Volcano Obs PO Box 51 Hawaii National Park HI 96718-0051 Office Phone: 808-967-8863. Business E-Mail: donswan@usgs.gov.

SWANSON, DONALD FREDERICK, retired food company executive; b. Mpls., Aug. 6, 1927; s. Clayton A. and Irma (Baiocchi) S.; m. Virginia Clare Hannah, Dec. 17, 1948; children— Donald Frederick, Cynthia Hannah, Janet Clare Webster. BA, U. Minn., 1948. With Gen. Mills, Inc., 1949-85, div. v.p., dir. marketing flour, dessert and baking mixes, 1964-65, v.p., gen. mgr. grocery products div., 1965-68, v.p., corporate adminstrn. officer consumer foods group, fashion div., transp. and purchasing depts., advt. and marketing services, 1969, exec. v.p. craft, game and toy group, fashion group, direct marketing group, travel group, dir., 1968-76, sr. exec. v.p. consumer non-foods, 1976-85, chief financial officer, 1977-79, sr. exec. v.p. restaurants and consumer non-foods, 1981-85, vice chmn. restaurants and consumer non-foods, 1981-85. Ret. chmn. bd. Soo Line Corp. Served with AUS, 1946-47. Mem. Mpls. Club, Wayzata Country Club, Royal Poinciana Golf Club, Phi Kappa Psi. Home: 2171 Gulf Shore Blvd N Apt 504 Naples FL 34102-4685

SWANSON, DONALD ROLAND, retired English literature and language educator; b. Pitts., Nov. 20, 1927; s. Roland E. and Ruth Amelia (Uddstrom) S.; m. Willa Gray, Sept. 3, 1955. BA, Washington and Jefferson Coll., Washington, Pa., 1953; MA, U. Conn., 1955; PhD, Rutgers U., 1965. Instr. U. Conn., Storrs, 1953-55; editor Prentice-Hall, Inc., NYC, 1955; instr. Upsala Coll., East Orange, NJ, 1955-58, asst. prof., 1958-66, assoc. prof., 1966-71; prof. English Wright State U., Dayton, Ohio, 1971—98, editor univ. monographs, 1975-87, dir. Press, 1987-89, dir. grad. studies in English, 1992—98; prof. emeritus, 1998—. Treas. N.W. Priority Bd., Dayton, 1980-81; mem. Citywide Crime Com., Dayton, 1980-81. With USN, 1945-46. Mem. Modern Lang. Assn. Am., Coll. English Assn. (dir. 1974-77), Northeast Modern Lang Assn., Midwest Modern Lang. Assn. Home: 1550 Benson Dr Dayton OH 45406-4514 Personal E-mail: donald.swanson@wright.edu.

SWANSON, JEFFREY, sociologist, researcher, educator; b. St. Paul, Mar. 24, 1957; s. Wallace Leroy and Charlotte Dillon Swanson; m. Pamela Ruth Mydske, Aug. 23, 1983; children: Angela Nicole, Alexandra Jane, Matthew Thomas. BA, Westmont Coll., Santa Barbara, Calif., 1979; PhD, Yale U., New Haven, 1985. Asst. prof. psychiatry and behavioral scis. U. Tex. Med. Br., Galveston, 1985—91; postdoctoral fellow U NC, Chapel Hill, NC, 1991—93, Duke U. Med. Ctr., NC, 1991—93; prof. psychiatry and behavioral scis. Duke U. Sch. Medicine, Durham, 1993—; mem. John D. and Catherine T. MacArthur Found. Rsch. Network on Mandated Cmty. Treatment, 2002—. Author: Echoes of the Call: Identity and Ideology among American Missionaries in Ecuador, 1995; contbr. over 130 articles to profl. and acad. jours. Grantee Ind. Rsch. Scientist Career Award, NIMH, 2004—. Progressive. Achievements include seminal research studies on links between violent behavior and severe mental illnesses, effectiveness of involuntary outpatient mental health treatment, and psychiatric advance directives. Office: Duke Univ Sch Medicine Dumc 3071 Durham NC 27701

SWANSON, LORI A., state attorney general, lawyer; b. Dec. 16, 1966; m. Gary Swanson. BA in Journalism and Polit. Sci. with distinction, U. Wis., Madison, 1989; JD magna cum laude, William Mitchell Coll. Law, St. Paul, 1995. Atty. Hatch, Eiden & Pihlstrom, Mpls., 1995—99; dep. atty. gen. State of Minn., St. Paul, 1999—2002, solicitor gen., 2003—06, atty. gen., 2007—. Chair consumer adv. coun. Fed. Res. Bd. Govs., Washington, 2004—. Democrat. Office: Office of Atty Gen 1400 Bremer Tower 445 Minnesota St Saint Paul MN 55101 Office Phone: 651-296-3353.*

SWANSON, LYNNETTE SUE, special olympics coordinator, special education educator; d. Carl Robert and Betty Jane Krambier; m. David John Swanson, June 2, 1984. BS cum laude, Brenau U., Gainesville, Ga., 2004. Cert. spl. edn. Ga., 2005. Spl. edn. paraprofl. Gwinnett County Pub. Schs., Lawrenceville, Ga., 1994—2000, coord. spl. olympics, 2000—; asst. coach athletics Spl. Olympics World Games, Shanghai, 2007. Coach Ga. women's volleyball team Spl. Olympics USA, Dublin, 2003. Mem.: Nat. Rlwy. Hist. Soc., Kappa Delta Pi, Phi Theta Kappa. Avocations: volunteer coaching, travel, crafts. Home: 4875 Five Forks Trickum Rd Lilburn GA 30047 Office: 590 Old Snellville Hwy Lawrenceville GA 30045 E-mail: lynnette_swanson@gwinnett.k12.ga.us.

SWANSON, PEGGY EUBANKS, finance educator; b. Ivanhoe, Tex., Dec. 29, 1936; d. Leslie Samuel and Mary Lee (Reid) Eubanks; m. B. Marc Sommers, Nov. 10, 1993. BBA, U. North Tex., 1957, M. Bus. Edn., 1965; MA in Econs., So. Meth. U., 1967, PhD in Econs., 1978. Instr. El Centro Coll., Dallas, 1967-69, 71-78, bus. div. chmn., 1969-71; asst. prof. econs. U. Tex., Arlington, 1978-79, asst. prof. fin., 1979-84, assoc. prof., 1984-86, chmn. dept. fin. and real estate, 1986-88, prof. fin., 1987—, interim dean Coll. Bus. Adminstrn., 1999—2000, John and Judy Goolsby disting. prof., 2004—. Expert witness various law firms, primarily Tex. and Calif., 1978—; cons. Internat. Edn. Program, 1992-99; curriculum cons. U. Monterrey, Mexico, 1995, New Saudi Arabia U., 1999. Contbr. articles to acad. profl. jours. Vol. Am. Cancer Soc., Dallas, Arlington, 1981—, Meals on Wheels, Arlington, 1989—; mem. adv. bd. Ryan/Reilly Ctr. for Urban Land Utilization, Arlington, 1986-88. Mem. Fin. Exec. Inst. (chmn. acad. rels. 1987-88), Internat. Bus. Steering Com. (chmn. 1989-91), Am. Fin. Assn., Am. Econ. Assn., Fin. Mgmt. Assn. (hon. faculty mem. Nat. Honor Soc. 1985-86, program com. 1998-99), Southwestern Fin. Assn. (program com. 1987-88, 96), Midwest Fin. Assn. (program com. 1997-98, 98-99), Acad. of Internat. Bus. (program com. 1992-95), Acad. Disting. Tchrs., Phi Beta Delta (membership com. 1987-89). Republican. Episcopalian. Avocations: tennis, gardening. Home: 4921 Bridgewater Dr Arlington TX 76017-2729 Office: U Tex at Arlington PO Box 19449 Arlington TX 76019-0001 Office Phone: 817-272-3841. Business E-Mail: swanson@uta.edu.

SWANSON, RICHARD SPRAGUE, oncologist, surgeon; b. Winchester, Mass., 1954; MD, Harvard Med. Sch., 1980. Intern Mass. Gen. Hosp., Boston, 1980-81, resident in gen. surgery, 1981-87, fellow, 1983; fellow surg. oncology M.D. Anderson Cancer Ctr., Houston, 1987-89; mem. staff U. Mass. Med. Ctr., Worcester; chief surg. oncology; assoc. prof. surgery U. Mass. Mem. AMA, Mass. Med. Soc., Am. Soc. Clin. Oncology, New Eng. Surg. Soc., Boston Surgical Soc., Soc. Surg. Oncology, Soc. for Surgery of Allimentary Tract. Office: U Mass Med Ctr 55 Lake Ave N Worcester MA 01655-0002

SWANSON, RICHARD WILLIAM, retired statistician; b. July 26, 1934; s. Richard and Erma Marie (Herman) Swanson; m. Laura Yoko Arai, Dec. 30, 1970. BS, Iowa State U., Ames, 1958, MS, 1964. Ops. analyst Stanford Rsch. Inst., Monterey, Calif., 1958—62; statistician ARINC Rsch. Corp., Washington, 1964—65; sr. scientist Booz-Allen Applied Rsch., Vietnam, 1965—67, LA, 1967—68; sr. ops. analyst Control Data Corp., Honolulu, 1968—70; mgmt. cons. Honolulu, 1970—73; exec. v.p. SEQUEL Corp., Honolulu, 1973—75; bus. cons. Hawaii Dept. Planning and Econ. Devel., Honlulu, 1975—77; tax rsch. and planning officer Dept. Taxation, 1977—82; ops. rsch. analyst U.S. Govt., 1982—89, shipyard statistician, 1989—97; ret., 1997. Mem.: Hawaiian Acad. Sci., Sigma Xi. Home: 583 Kamoku St Apt 3505 Honolulu HI 96826-5241 Home Phone: 808-949-4868. Personal E-mail: hnlrichardswanson@msn.com.

SWANSON, ROBERT LAWRENCE, oceanographer, academic program administrator; b. Balt., Oct. 11, 1938; s. Lawrence Wilbur and Hazel Ruth Swanson; m. Dana Lamont, Sept. 12, 1963; children: Lawrence Daniel, Michael Nathan BSCE, Lehigh U., 1960; MS Oceanography, Oreg. State U., 1965, PhD Oceanography, 1971. Cert. hydrographer. Commd. ensign U.S. Coast and Geodetic Survey (now NOAA), 1960, advanced through grades to capt., 1978; ops. officer U.S. Pathfinder, 1965; comdg. officer U.S. Marmer, 1966; chief oceanog. divsn. Nat. Ocean Survey, NOAA, Rockville, Md., 1969—72; mgr. Marine Ecosys. Analysis, N.Y. Bight project, Stony Brook, 1973—78; dir. Office Marine Pollution Assessment NOAA, Rockville, 1978—83, rsch. assoc. Sea Grant Stony Brook, 1983—84; comdg. officer U.S. Rschr., Miami, Fla., 1984—86; chief internat. activities group NOAA, Rockville, 1986, exec. dir. Office Oceanic and Atmospheric Rsch., 1986—87; dir. Waste Reduction and Mgmt. Inst. SUNY, Stony Brook, 1987—, assoc. dean Sch. Marine and Atmospheric Scis., 2003—. Adj. prof. Marine Scis. Rsch. Ctr., SUNY, Stony Brook, 1976—; mem. Suffolk County Coun. Environ. Quality, 1988—, vice chair, 1996—2006, chair, 2006—; mem. N.Y. State Oversight Com. Brookhaven Nat. Lab., 1996—2006; mem. Coastal Mgmt. Commn. Villages Head-of-the-Harbor and Nissequogue, 1994—2002; chmn. Coastal Mgmt. Commn. Villages Head Harbor and Nissequogue, 1995—97, 1999—2001; trustee Three Village Hist. Soc., 1994—2002; co-chair L.I. Environ. Econ. Roundtable, 1995—2000; adv. bd. Evan Liblit Meml. Fund, 1998—; trustee Village of Head of the Harbor, 2002—, deputy mayor, 2006—; cons. in field. Co-author, co-editor: Oxygen Depletion and Associated Benthic Mortalities in N.Y. Bight, 1979; co-editor: Floatable Wastes and the Region's Beaches; mem. editl. bd. N.Y. Bight Monograph Series, 1973-81, Chemistry and Ecology, 1995-2003; co-author Images of America, Stony Brook, 2003; co-pub. Waste Mgmt. Rsch. Report, 1988-95; mem. adv. bd. L.I. Hist. Jour., 1995-2003, mem. editl. bd., 2004- Recipient Karo award Am. Soc. Mil. Engrs., 1972; Silver medal Dept. Commerce, 1973; Program and Adminstrn. Mgmt. award NOAA, 1975, Unit citation, 1981; sr. exec. fellow John F. Kennedy Sch. Govt., Harvard U., 1983, Spl. Achievement award, 1987, NOAA Corps. Commendations, 1987; named Man of Yr. for environment Three Village Times, 1998 Mem. N.Y. Acad. Scis., ASCE (chmn. hydrography and oceanography com. 1972-74), AAAS, Am. Geophys. Union, Marine Tech. Soc. (chmn. marine pollution com. 1982-92), Cosmos Club, Sigma Xi (pres. SUNY Stony Brook chpt. 1998—) Presbyterian. Home: 46 Harbor Hill Rd Saint James NY 11780-1217 Office: SUNY Waste Reduction And Mgmt Ins Stony Brook NY 11794-5000 Office Phone: 631-632-8704. Business E-Mail: lswanson@notes.cc.sunysb.edu.

SWANSON, ROY ARTHUR, classicist, educator; b. St. Paul, Apr. 7, 1925; s. Roy Benjamin and Gertrude (Larson) S.; m. Vivian May Vitous, Mar. 30, 1946; children: Lynn Marie (Mrs. Gerald A. Snider), Robin Lillian (dec.), Robert Roy (dec.), Dyack Tyler, Dana Miriam (Mrs. Jon Butts). BA, U. Minn., 1948, BS, 1949, MA, 1951; PhD, U. Ill., 1954. Prin. Maplewood Elementary Sch., St. Paul, 1949-51; instr. U. Ill., 1952-53, Ind. U., 1954-57; asst. prof. U. Minn., Mpls., 1957-61, assoc. prof., 1961-64, acting chmn. classics, 1963-64, prof. classics, chmn. comparative lit., 1964-65; prof. English Macalester Coll., St. Paul, 1965-67, coord. humanities program, 1966-67; prof. comparative lit. and classics U. Wis.-Milw., 1967—, prof. English, 1990-96, prof. emeritus, 2003—, chmn. classics dept., 1967-70, 86-89, chmn. comparative lit., 1970-73, 76-83, coord. Scandinavian studies program, 1982-96. Cons. St. Paul Tchrs. Sr. High Sch. English, 1964 Author: Odi et Amo: The Complete Poetry of Catullus, 1959, Heart of Reason: Introductory Essays in Modern-World Humanities, 1963, Pindar's Odes, 1974, Greek and Latin Word Elements, 1981, The Love Songs of the Carmina Burana, 1987, Pär Lagerkvist: Five Early Works, 1989, Blue Margin, 2008; editor Minn. Rev., 1963-67; Classical Jour., 1966-72; contbr. articles to profl. jours. With AUS, 1944-46. Decorated Bronze Star; recipient Disting. Teaching award U. Minn., 1962, Disting. Teaching award U. Wis.-Milw., 1974, 91, 99, Pub. Hong. Profl. Career Educator, 2005. Home: 11618 N Bobolink Ln Mequon WI 53092-2804 Office: U Wis French/Italian/Comp Lit PO Box 413 Milwaukee WI 53201-0413 Business E-Mail: rexcy@uwm.edu.

SWANSON, STEVEN R., astronaut; b. Syracuse, NY, Dec. 3, 1960; s. Stanley and June Swanson; m. Mary Drake Young; 3 children. BS in Engring. Physics, U. Colo., 1983; MAS in Computer Sys., Fla. Atlantic U., 1986; PhD in Computer Sci., Tex. A&M U., 1998. Software engr. GTE, Phoenix; sys. engr. aircraft ops. divsn. NASA, Johnson Space Ctr., Houston, 1987—89, flight simulation engr. for shuttle tng. aircraft, 1989—98, astronaut, mission specialist candidate, 1998—. Crew mem., spacewalker STS-117 Atlantis Mission, 2007; mission specialist STS-119 Discovery Mission, 2009. Recipient NASA Exceptional Achievement medal, Johnson Space Ctr. Cert. Accomodation, Flight Simulation Engrng. award. Mem.: Phi Kappa Phi. Avocations: mountain biking, basketball, skiing, weightlifting, running, woodworking. Office: Astronaut Office/CB NASA Johnson Space Ctr Houston TX 77058*

SWANSON, SUSAN MARIE, children's book author, educator; b. Chgo., May 19; married; 2 children. MFA in English, U. Mass., Amherst. Tchr. COMPAS Writers & Artists in Schools prog., St. Paul. Tchr. summer arts prog. St. Paul Acad., Friends Sch. of Minn. Author: (children's books/poetry) Getting Used to the Dark: 26 Night Poems, 1997, Letter to the Lake, 1998, The First Thing My Mama Told Me, 2002 (Charlotte Zolotow Honor book, 2003, NY Times Best Illustrated Book, 2003), To Be Like the Sun, 2008, The House in the Night, 2008 (Randolph Caldecott Medal, ALA, 2009); editor: Northern Lights: Selected Works from the COMPAS Writers & Artists in the Schools Program, 2001; contbr. poetry to anthologies. Grantee poetry fellowships, Bush Found., McKnight Found., Minn. State Arts Bd. Office: COMPAS 75 Fifth St W Ste 304 Saint Paul MN 55102 Office Phone: 651-292-3249. Personal E-mail: susanmarieswanson@mac.com.*

SWANSON, VICTORIA CLARE HELDMAN, lawyer; b. Aug. 28, 1949; d. Paul F. and Anne F. (Thomas) Schmitz; m. Louis M. Heldman, Sept. 21, 1971 (div. 1973); m. John Askins, Feb. 28, 1975 (div. 1977); m. Thomas C. Swanson, Feb. 13, 1988 (div. 2004); m. Spellman T. Richard, Oct. 11, 2008. BA in journalism with distinction, Ohio State U., 1972; JD, U. Detroit, 1975. Bar: Mich. 1975, Colo. 1984, U.S. Dist. Ct. (ea. and we. dists.) Mich. 1975, U.S. Ct. Appeals (6th cir.) 1977, U.S. Ct. Appeals (3d cir.) 1980, U.S. Supreme Ct. 1983, U.S. Ct. Appeals (10th cir.) 1984, U.S. Ct. Appeals (5th cir.) 1989, cert.: NBTA (civil trial advocate) 1994. Assoc. Lopatin, Miller, Bindes & Freedman, Detroit, 1973—76; ptnr. Schaden, Swanson & Lampert, Detroit, 1977—90, Sears, Anderson & Swanson, P.C., Colorado Springs, Colo., 1991—96, Sears & Swanson, Colorado Springs, 1997—. Adj. prof. U. Detroit Sch. Law, 1982. Author (chpt.): (non-fiction) Anatomy of a Personal Injury Lawsuit, 1992; author, editor: handbook Colorado Auto Litigators Handbook, 1995, Colorado Courtroom Handbook, 1998, author, editor: 2nd edit., 2006, Colorado Evidence Handbook, 2005; co-author (with Richard F. Schaden): (non-fiction) Product Design Liability, 1982; co-author: (with others) Women Trial Lawyers: How They Succeed in Practice and in the Courtroom, 1986. Mem.: Mich. Trial Lawyers Assn., Colo. Trial Lawyers Assn. (past pres., Kripke Lifetime Achievement award 2005), Am. Assn. Justice, Colo. Bar Assn., Mich. Bar Assn. Home Phone: 719-481-4210; Office Phone: 719-471-1984. Business E-Mail: victoria@searsandswanson.com.

SWANSON, WALLACE MARTIN, lawyer; b. Fergus Falls, Minn., Aug. 22, 1941; s. Marvin Walter and Mary Louise (Lindsey) S.; children: Kristen Lindsey, Eric Munger. BA with honors, U. Minn., 1962; LL.B. with honors, So. Methodist U., 1965. Bar: Tex. 1965. Assoc. Coke & Coke, Dallas, 1965-70; ptnr. firm Johnson & Swanson, Dallas, 1970-88; prin. Wallace M. Swanson, P.C., Ennis, Tex., 1988—; chmn., CEO Ace Cash Express Inc., Irving, Tex., 1987-88, State St. Capital Corp., 1990—. Served with USNR, 1960-65. Mem. Tex. Bar Found., State Bar Tex. (securities com. 1972-86, chmn. 1978-80, coun. bus. law sect. 1980-86), Crescent Club. Methodist. Address: 6234 FM 879 Ennis TX 75119 Office Phone: 214-520-7000. Personal E-mail: wallaceswanson@yahoo.com.

SWANSON, WILLIAM FREDIN, III, manufacturing executive; b. Pitts., Mar. 6, 1960; s. William Fredin Jr. and Marjorie Beatrice (Davis) S.; m. Jane Anne Crosby, June 30, 1990; children: Elisabeth Anne, William Fredin IV. BSME, U. Va., 1982; M in Mgmt., Northwestern U., 1985. Asst. to v.p. mfg. Bridgestone/Firestone, Inc., Akron, Ohio, 1985-87, project mgr. Decatur, Ill., 1987-89, operating mgr., 1989-92; plant mgr. Am. Roller Co., Walkerton, Ind., 1992-95, mfg. mgr. Union Grove, Wis., 1995—2002; pres. Diamond Holding Corp., Marietta, Ga., 2002—07; CEO Signs and More, Inc., Cartersville, Ga., 2007—. Mem. alumni admissions orgn. Kellogg Grad. Sch. Mgmt., Northwestern U., Evanston, Ill., 1986-97, CEO roundtable Cobb County, 2002—; chmn. long range planning com. Antioch (Ill.) United Meth. Ch., 1997-98, adminstrv. coun., 2000-02, lay leader, 2001-02; coach youth soccer YMCA, 2003-2004, t-ball, 2004, basketball, 2004-2005; bd.dir. & v.p.

Bartow County Bus. Assn. Mem.: Bartow Bus. Assn. (v.p. 2008—). Avocations: golf, spectator sports, reading. Home: 1701 Kenbrook Ct Acworth GA 30101 Office: Signs and More Inc 481 E Main St Cartersville GA 30121 Personal E-mail: wfswansoniii@bellsouth.net. Business E-Mail: bills@signsmoreinc.com.

SWANSON, WILLIAM HENRY, defense equipment manufacturing company executive; b. Bakersfield, Calif., Feb. 9, 1949; s. William H. and Rosemary O. (Pavicich) Swanson; m. Cheryl K. Allen, Dec. 21, 1968. BSIE, Calif. Poly. State U., 1972; MBA, Golden Gate U., 1977; JD (hon.), Pepperdine U., 2002. Assoc. engr. Raytheon Co., 1972—74, project engr., 1974—75, mfg. program mgr., 1975—77, test engring. mgr., 1977—80, mgr. mfg. group, 1980—81; mfg. mgr. Equipment div. Waltham, Mass., 1981—83; plant mgr., Missile Systems div. Andover, Mass., 1984—90; asst. gen. mgr., Missile Systems div., 1989—90; sr. v.p., gen. mgr., Missile Systems div., 1990—95; exec. v.p. Raytheon Co., 1995—2002; gen. mgr. Electronic Systems div., 1995—97; chmn., CEO Raytheon Systems Co., 1997—99; pres., Electronic Systems div., 1999—2002; pres. Raytheon Co., 2002—03, pres., CEO, 2003—04, chmn., CEO, 2004—. Mem. President's Nat. Security Telecommunications Adv. Com.; bd. dirs. Raytheon Co., 2003—, Sprint Corp., 2004—05, Sprint Nextel Corp., 2005—08. Exec. com. Bus.-Higher Edn. Forum; mem. Sec. Air Force Adv. Bd.; bd. adv. CIA Officers Meml. Found.; bd. dir. Medal Honor Found., Rose Fitzgerald Kennedy Greenway Conservancy; mem. Calif. Poly. State U. President's Cabinet, Pepperdine U. Bd. Regents. Recipient Captains Industry Award, Inst. Indsl. Engr., Semper Fidelis Award, USMC Scholarship Found., 2002, Laurel Award, Aviation Week & Space Tech., 2003; named Outstanding Indsl. Engring. Grad., Calif. Poly. State U., 1972, Outstanding Indsl. Engring. Alumni, 1981. Fellow: Royal Aero. Soc. (UK), Am. Inst. Aeronautics & Astronautics, Tau Beta Pi; mem.: Aerospace Industries Assn., Nat. Def. Indsl. Assn., Air Force Assn., Navy League (Rear Adm. John J. Bergen Leadership Medal for Industry), Assn. US Army, Blue Key, Alpha Pi Mu. Republican. Roman Catholic. Office: Raytheon Co 870 Winter St Waltham MA 02451

SWANSON, ZONA LUCIEL, retired elementary school educator; b. Orr, ND, Nov. 14, 1923; d. Fred L. and Hilda Dora (Rose) Neumann; m. Lyle R. Swanson, June 23, 1943; children: Barbara Jean Swanson Serr, Daniel Raymond. AA, Mayville State Tchrs., ND, 1941—43; BA, Mayvill State Tchrs., ND, 1959; MEd, U. ND, Grand Forks, 1966. Elem. tchr., rural schools, Larimore, ND, 1950—52; tchr., grades 1-8, small town sch. Kempton, 1954—59; tchr., grades 5-8, small town sch. Arvilla, 1952—54; tchr., grades 5 & 7, AFB Grand Forks, 1959—69; tchr., grade 6 Viking Grade Sch., Grand Forks, 1969—89; ret., 1989. Sec. Grand Forks Edn. Assn., 1960—61; pres. ND Classroom Tchr.'s Assn., Bismarck. Active Girl Scouts, US, Civil Air Patrol, Farmer's Union, Larimore United Luth. Ch. Mem.: VFW, NEA (life), ND Edn. Assn. (life), Am. Legion. Democrat. Lutheran. Avocations: stamp collecting/philately, reading, doll collecting, teddy bear collecting. Home: 2429 W Fallcreek Ct Grand Forks ND 58201

SWANSTROM, LEE LERAY, surgeon; b. Douglas, Wyo., Apr. 3, 1957; married. Grad., U. Colo., U. Paris, France; MD, Creighton U., 1983. Cert. Am. Bd. Surgery. Resident, gen. surgery Emanuel Hosp., Portland, Oreg., 1983—88; fellow, surgical endoscopy U. Western Ont., Canada; clin. prof. Oreg. Health Scis. Univ., Portland, Oreg.; dir., Gastrointestinal and Minimally Invasive Surgery Clinic (GMIS) Oreg. Clinic, Portland, Oreg., program dir., minimally invasive surgery; chmn., sect. gen. and vascular surgery Legacy Emanuel and Good Samaritan Hosp. Mem. Natural Orifice Surgery Consortium for Assessment and Rsch.; dir. Legacy Minimally Invasive Surgery Program. Co-editor-in-chief Surgical Innovation; contbr. articles to prof. jours. Recipient Golden Scalpel award for Excellence in Tchg., Maricopa Med. Ctr., Phoenix, Ariz., 2005—06; named one of Portland Monthly Top Docs, 2006—07. Fellow: Am. Coll. Surgeons; mem.: Soc. for Surgery of the Alimentary Tract (mem. exec. com.), Soc. Am. Gastrointestinal and Endoscopic Surgeons (past pres.). With a team of surgeons, performed the first transgastric endoscopic cholecystectomy, NOTES (Natural Orifice Translumenal Endoscopic Surgery-removing the gall bladder without making incisions on the surface of the skin, also less pain, less risk of infection and reduced recovery time) in the US in 2007. Office: Oreg Clinic GMIS Good Samaritan Med Bldg 1040 NW 22nd Ste 560 Portland OR 97210 Address: 2055 Exchange St Ste 270 Astoria OR 97103 Office Phone: 503-325-9597. Office Fax: 503-281-0561, 503-281-0575.

SWANSTROM, THOMAS EVAN, economist; b. Green Bay, Wis., May 17, 1939; s. Alfred Enoch and Elizabeth Nan (Thomas) S.; m. Nancy Anne Roche; children: Amy, Scott. Student, U. Notre Dame, 1957-59; BA, U. Wis., 1962, MA, 1963; postgrad., Am. U., 1963-66. Economist, U.S. Bur. Labor Statistics, Washington, 1963-66. Dir. rsch/Population Ref. Bur., Washington, 1966-68; economist Sears, Roebuck & Co., Chgo., 1968-70, market analyst, 1970-72, mgr. catalog rsch., 1972-75, asst. mgr. econ. rsch., 1974-80, chief economist, 1980-90; pres. Consumer Econs., Chgo., 1991-. Contbr. articles to industry publs. Mem. Conf. Bus. Economists, The Caxton Club, The Literary Club. Home Phone: 312-315-7829. Personal E-mail: tevanswan@aol.com.

SWARAY, STEVEN MUSTAPHA, banker, economist; b. Pujehun, Sierra Leone, May 20, 1954; m. Miata; children: Siata, Sonia. BSc economics with honors, U. Sierra Leone; MA economics. Gov. Ctrl. Bank Sierra Leone, 1993-96, deputy gov., 1992-93; budget and finance controller Mono River Union, 1988-92; industrial development officer UNIDO, Vienna, Austria, 1990; lecturer, acting chrm. Dept. Economics U. Sierra Leone, 1983-88, lecturer, Dept. Economics, 1980-83. Office: care Ctrl Bank Sierra Leone Siaka Stevens St PO Box 30 Freetown Sierra Leone

SWARBRICK, JOHN BRIAN, JR., athletics director, lawyer; b. Yonkers, NY, Mar. 19, 1954; s. John Brian and Mary Catherine (Comey) S.; m. Kimberly Ann Hudgens, Oct. 15, 1983; children: Kathleen Marie, Connor John, William Calvin, Christopher Robert. BA magna cum laude, U. Notre Dame, Ind., 1976; JD, Stanford U., Calif., 1980. Bar: Ind. 1980, U.S. Dist. Ct. (so. dist.) Ind. 1980, U.S. Ct. Appeals (7th cir.) 1982, U.S. Supreme Ct. 1984. Assoc. Baker & Daniels, Indpls., 1980-86, ptnr., 1987—; pres., CEO LMiV, LLC, Indpls.; athletic dir. U. Notre Dame, 2008—. Pres. Sports Mktg. Ind., Indpls., 1988-91. Assoc. editor: US Diving Safety Manual, USGF Gymnastics Safety Manual. Sports commr. US Olympic Festival, 1982; competition dir. 10th Pan Am. Games, Indpls., 1984-87; mem. Penrod Soc., Indpls., 1987—; chmn. World Gymnastics Championship, 1991, Ind. Sports Corp., 1992-2001; adv. com. World Rowing Championships, 1994; v.p. Indpls. 2012 Super Bowl Com. Mem. Phi Beta Kappa. Democrat. Roman Catholic. Office: U Notre Dame C113 Joyce Ctr Notre Dame IN 46556 Office Phone: 574-631-6107, 317-237-1402. Business E-Mail: jack.swarbrick@bakerd.com.

SWARD, ANDREA JEANNE, information and computer scientist, musician; b. Hackensack, NJ, June 25, 1951; d. George Frederick and Carol Jeanne (Snoad) Lankow; m. Jeffrey Edwin Sward, June 7, 1975. Student, U. Minn., Duluth, 1969-72; BA in Psychology, Calif. State U., Fullerton, 1973, MS in Info. Sci., 1974, MS in Edn., 1976; cert. Bus. Intelligence and Data Warehousing, U. Calif. Irvine, 2003. Librarian, prof. Calif. State U., Fullerton, 1972—97; violist Anaheim Cultural Arts Ctr. Orch., Calif., 1978-80, Anaheim Civic Light Opera, 1978-80, Calif. European Tour Orch., Fullerton, 1978-79, Fullerton Cmty. Orch., Fullerton, 1978—86; computer programmer, analyst Hughes Aircraft, Fullerton, 1980-81, Smith-Kline/Beckman, Fullerton, 1981-83, ConAgra/Hunt-Wesson, Irvine, 1983—2004; librarian Downey City Library, Calif., 1985, Orange Pub. Library, Calif., 1985—90, Huntington Beach Library, Calif., 1985—; sys. analyst New Century Mortgage, Irvine, Calif., 2004—07; IT analyst Lehman Brothers, Irvine, Calif., 2007; sys. data analyst Kelley Blue Book, 2007—. Adj. faculty CC Dist., Calif., 1993—2002. Editor: Vis À Vis: An Interdisciplinary Journal, 1972—74; contbr. articles to profl. jours. Mem., contbr. Newport Harbor Art Mus., Newport Beach, Calif., 1975—, Los Angeles County Mus. of Art, 1975—, ACLU, 1976—, Cousteau Soc., 1978—, Audubon Soc., 1985—, Amigos de Bolsa Chica, 1985—, Spl. Olympics, 1987—; wildlife rehabilitator Wetlands and Wildlife Care Ctr., Orange County, 1999—. Fridley (Minn.) Edn. Assn. scholar, 1969, Spl. Edn. Assn. scholar, 1972; Edwin Carr fellow, 1976; Ptnrs. in Excellence grantee, 1979. Mem. ALA, Assn. for Computing Machinery, Calif. Library Assn., Calif. Reading Assn., Reading Educators Guild, Penguini Poets and Philosophers Guild of Placentia (co-founder). Democrat. Avocations: sports, reading, dance, theater, art. Home: PO Box 7019 Huntington Beach CA 92615-7019 Office Phone: 949-260-7427. E-mail: ajsward@yahoo.com.

SWARLIS, LINDA, library and information scientist; d. Clarence Leroy and Helen Louise Jacobs; m. Gary W. Piggram; children: Amber, Andrew. BS in Edn., Clarion U., Pa., 1979; MLS, U. Pitts., Pa., 1984; PhD. Libr. dir. Winchester Thurston Sch., Pittsburgh, Pa., 1984—88, Sewickley Acad., Sewickley, Pa., 1988—95; head libr. Lincoln H.S., Gahanna, Ohio, 1995—97; dir. of info. services and libr. Columbus Sch. for Girls, Columbus, Ohio, 1997—. Pres. Pitts. Area Ind. Schools Assn., Pa., 1989—95. Recipient Outstanding Svc. award, Gahanna Kiwanis Club for Key Club Leadership, 1995—97; Distance Ind. scholarship, U. North Tex., 2004—. Office: Columbus Sch for Girls 56 S Columbia Ave Columbus OH 43209 Office Fax: 614-252-0571. E-mail: lswarlis@columbusschoolforgirls.org.

SWAROVSKI, NADJA, apparel designer; b. Wattens, Austria, May 5, 1970; d. Helmut and Danna Swarovski; m. Rupert Adams, May 25, 2002. BA in Art History and Fgn. Lang, So. Methodist U., Dallas. With Sotheby's, NYC; sales commn. and distribution position D. Swarovski & Co., Hong Kong, 1995, v.p. internat. communications. Creator Crystal Palace Project, 2002. Office: Swarovski 14-15 Conduit St 2nd Fl London W1S 2XJ England

SWART, SUSAN, federal official; B, Va. Commonwealth Univ.; grad., Nat. War Coll. Various Fgn. Svc. positions US State Dept., 1989—2006, spl. asst Bureau of Adminstrn. Washington, info mgmt. positions Caracas, Venezuela, office dir. customer svc. Bureau Info. Mgmt. Washington, info. mgmt. officer Cairo, dep. dir. Ea. Asia & Pacific affairs Washington, dean Sch. Applied Info. Tech., dep. CIO bus. planning & customer svc. & chief knowledge officer, 2006—08, CIO Info. Resource Mgmt., 2008—. Office: US State Dept 2201 C St NW Washington DC 20520*

SWARTOUT, WILLIAM R., mathematician, educator, director; s. Charles W. and June Swartout; m. Janet P. Swartout, 2008 (dec.); children: Robin, David. BS in Math. Scis. with distinction, Stanford U., Palo Alto, Calif., 1974; MS in Elec. Engring. & Computer Sci., MIT, Cambridge, Mass., 1977, PhD in Computer Sci., 1981. Dir., intelligent sys. divsn. U. So. Calif. Info. Scis. Inst., Marina del Rey, 1989—99; dir. of tech. U. So. Calif. Inst. for Creative Technologies, Marina del Rey, 1999—. Rsch. assoc. prof. computer sci. U. So. Calif., 1985—2006, rsch. prof. computer sci., 2006—. Mem. Air Force Sci. Adv. Bd., Washington, 2003—07, Bd. Army Sci. and Tech., Washington, 2004—, Joint Forces Command Transformation Adv. Group, 2004. Fellow: Am. Assn. Artificial Intelligence (mem. bd. councilors 1989—92); mem.: Assn. Computing Machinery (chair Spl. Interest Group on Artificial Intelligence 1985—87). Presbyterian. Achievements include pioneering research in automatic program explanation, and development of virtual humans. Avocations: photography, bicycling. Office: Univ So Calif Inst Creative Technologies 13274 Fiji Way Marina Del Rey CA 90292

SWARTZ, B. K., JR., (BENJAMIN KINSELL SWARTZ JR.), archaeologist, educator; b. LA, June 23, 1931; s. Benjamin Kinsell and Maxine Marietta (Pearce) S.; m. Cyrilla Casillas, Oct. 23, 1966; children: Benjamin Kinsell III, Frank Casillas. AA summa cum laude, L.A. City Coll., 1952; BA, UCLA, 1954, MA, 1958; PhD, U. Ariz., Tucson, 1964. Curator Klamath County Mus., Oreg., 1959-61, rsch. assoc., 1961-62; asst. prof. anthropology Ball State U., Muncie, Ind., 1964-68, assoc. prof., 1968-72, prof., 1972-2001, prof. emeritus, 2001—. Vis. sr. lectr. U. Ghana, 1970-71; exch. prof. U. Yaoundé, Cameroon, 1984-85, summer vis. prof. UNLV, 2009-; field rschr. N.Am. and West Africa; mem. exec. bd., pres. Am. Com. to Advance the Study of Petroglyphs and Pictographs and its rep. to Internat. Fedn. Rock Art Orgns.; mem. overseas ed. bd. Rock Art Rsch.; mem. adv. bd. Am. Com. for Preservation of Archaeol. Collections. Contbr. revs. and articles to profl. jours.; author books, monographs in field, including: West African Culture Dynamics, 1980, Indiana's Prehistoric Past, 1981, Rock Art and Posterity, 1991, Procs. of Ist Internat. South African Rock Art Assn. Conf., 1991. Klamath County chmn. Oreg. Statehood Centennial, 1959. With USN, 1954-56. Fellow AAAS, Ind. Acad. Sci.; mem. Current Anthropology (assoc.), Soc. Am. Archaeology, Internat. Com. Rock Art, Sigma Xi, Lambda Alpha (nat. coun., exec. sec.). Home: 805 W Charles St Muncie IN 47305-2235 Personal E-mail: 01bkswartz@bsu.edu.

SWARTZ, JON DAVID, psychologist, educator; b. Houston, Dec. 28, 1934; s. Orville Elmo and Nina June (Baker) S.; m. Carol Joseph Hampton, Oct. 20, 1966; children: Eric Jason McFarland, Sally Katherine Baker, Edward Joseph Bryson. BA, U. Tex., Austin, 1956, MA, 1961, PhD, 1969, postgrad., 1973-74. Rsch. and tng. asst. dept. psychology U. Tex., 1956-62, asst. prof. dept. ednl. psychology, 1969-72; assoc. prof. psychology, chmn. U. Tex.-Permian Basin, 1974-78, chmn. anthropology and sociology, 1975-78, field dir., 1962-65; asst. dir. Austin Longitudinal Rsch. project, 1965-69, co-dir., 1969-74; research scientist Hogg Found. for Mental Health, 1972-74; prof. edn. and psychology Southwestern U., Georgetown, Tex., 1978-90, vis. prof. psychology, 1991, dir. testing and guidance, 1978-81, holder Brown vis. chair, 1978-82, assoc. dean for librs. and learning resources, 1981-90; coord., adminstrv. head Killeen office Cen. Counties Ctr. for MHMR Svcs., Temple, Tex., 1990-91; chief psychol. svcs. Temple, Tex., 1991-99; pvt. practice Tex., 2000—. Lectr. Nat. U., Mexico, 1962, U. Ctrl. Tex., 1994, Temple Coll., 1994. Author: (with W.H. Holtzman) Inkblot Perception and Personality, 1961, (with C.C. Cleland) Mental Retardation: Approaches to Institutional Change, 1969, Administrative Issues in Institutions for the Mentally Retarded, 1972, Exceptionalities Through the Lifespan: An Introduction, 1982, Multihandicapped Mentally Retarded, 1973, (with W.H. Holtzman, R. Diaz-Guerrero) Personality Development in Two Cultures, 1975; editor: (with C.C. Cleland, L.W. Talkington) Profoundly Mentally Retarded, 1976, (with R.K. Eyman, C.C. Cleland) Research with the Profoundly Retarded, 1978, Holtzman Inkblot Technique: An Annotated Bibliography (supplement), 1988, (with R.C. Reinehr, W.H. Holtzman) Holtzman Inkblot Technique: An Annotated Bibliography 1956-1982, 1983, (with R.C. Reinehr) Handbook of Old-Time Radio, 1993, Holtzman Inkblot Technique: Research Guide and Bibliography, 1999, Southwestern University Bibliographic Series, 1986-1990, Historical Dictionary of Old-Time Radio, 2008; contbr.: Handbook of Texas, 1996; editl. assoc. Current Anthropology, 1971-77; assoc. editor: Am. Corrective Therapy Jour., 1971-81, Exceptional Children, 1982-84; mem. editl. bd. Tex. Psychologist, 1979-83, Phi Kappa Phi Jour./Nat. Forum, 1976-80; editl. cons. Mental Retardation, 1972-77; rev. editor Jour. Biol. Psychology, 1972-80, Revista Interamericana de Psicologia, 1983-89; reviewer Sci. Books, Films, 1978—; cons. editor Jour. Personality Assessment, 1981-90; spl. features editor: Scientifiction: The First Fandom Report, 2002—; rev. editor The National Fantasy Fan, 2003—; frequent contbr. Paperback Parade, 2004—;contbr. Big Little Times, 2008-; contbr. over 500 articles to profl. jours. Mem. Mayor's Drug Abuse Panel, Odessa, Tex., 1975-78; chmn. adv. bd. Human Potentials Ctr., Permian Basin Cmty. Ctrs. for Mental Health and Mental Retardation, Odessa and Midland, Tex., 1975-78; bd. govs. Mood-Heritage Mus., 1984-90. US Office Edn. fellow, 1964-66, U. Tex. fellow, 1973-74; recipient Franklin Gilliam prize Humanities Rsch. Ctr. U. Tex., 1965, Spencer Rsch. award Nat. Acad. Edn., 1972, Faculty Fellowship award Southwestern U., 1981. Fellow AAAS, Am. Psychol. Soc., Soc. Personality Assessment (life); mem. Western Rsch. Conf. on Mental Retardation, Am. Acad. Mental Retardation, Southwestern Psychol. Assn., Bell County Psychol. Assn., Sigma Xi, Psi Chi, Mu Alpha Nu, Delta Tau Kappa, Phi Kappa Phi, Phi Delta Kappa, Nat. Fantasy Fan Fedn. (Franson award 2005, 07), First Fandom. Personal E-mail: jon_swartz@hotmail.com. *All my life I have had teachers, in school and out, who challenged me to do more than I thought I was capable of doing. Any success I have achieved, I owe to them and their efforts in my behalf.*

SWARTZ, KATHERINE (B. KATHERINE SWARTZ), economist, educator; m. Frank Levy; 2 children. BS, MIT, 1972; MS, U. Wis., Madison, 1974, PhD, 1976. Lectr. Goldman Sch. Pub. Policy, U. Calif., Berkeley, 1976—77; asst. prof. economics U. Md., College Park, 1977—82; rsch. assoc. health policy Urban Inst., 1982—85, sr. rsch. assoc. health policy Washington, 1986—92; assoc. prof. pub. policy Brown U., 1989—90; assoc. prof. health policy and mgmt. Harvard Sch. Pub. Health, Boston, 1992—2000, prof. health economics and policy, 2001; dir. Robert Wood Johnson Scholars in Health Policy Rsch. Prog. Harvard U., 2005—. Editor Inquiry, 1995—2007; vis. scholar Russell Sage Found., NYC, 2000—01. Author: Reinsuring Health: Why More Middle-Class People are Uninsured and What Government Can Do, 2006. Mem.: Inst. Medicine, Nat. Acad. Social Ins., Assn. Pub. Policy Analysis and Mgmt. (sec. 1991—93, v.p. 2002—04, pres. 2007—, David Kershaw award 1991). Office: Harvard Sch Pub Health Kresge Bldg 404 677 Huntington Ave Boston MA 02115 Office Phone: 617-423-4325. Office Fax: 617-432-4494. E-mail: kswartz@hsph.harvard.edu.*

SWARTZ, MICHAEL D., statistical geneticist; b. Boston, Jan. 24, 1974; s. Robert J. and Adele M. Swartz. BA, BS, Trinity U., San Antonio, 1997; MA, Rice U., Houston, 2002, PhD, 2004. Instr. dept. epidemiology M.D. Anderson Cancer Ctr., U. Tex., Houston, 1999—2004, post-doctoral fellow, 2004—; rsch. asst. prof. stats. dept. Tex. A&M U., College Station, 2004—06. Contbr. articles to profl. jours. Vol. Kairos Found., Houston, 1989. Recipient Chairman's award for svc. to dept. stats., Rice U. Dept. Chair, 2002; fellow Tng. fellowship in cancer prevention, Nat. Cancer Inst., M.D. Anderson. Cancer Ctr., 2006—, Nat. Cancer Inst. & Dept. Stats., Tex. A&M U., 2004—06; Keck fellowship in computational biology, Keck Ctr., Rice U., 1998—2000, Tng. fellowship in cancer prevention, Nat. Cancer Inst., M.D. Anderson Cancer Ctr., 2000—04. Mem.: Am. Stats. Assn., Internat. Genetic Epidemiology Soc., Phi Beta Kappa. Achievements include development of a new method for gene mapping. Avocation: swing dancing. Office: U Tex MD Anderson Cancer Ctr Dept Epidemiology Unit PO Box 301439 Houston TX 77230 Business E-Mail: mdswartz@mdanderson.org.

SWARTZ, MORTON NORMAN, medical educator; b. Boston, Nov. 11, 1923; s. Jacob H. and Janet (Heller) Swartz; m. Cesia Rosenberg, Sept. 18, 1956; children: Mark David, Caroline Joan. BA, Harvard Coll., 1945; MD, Harvard U., 1947; MD (hon.), U. Geneva, Switzerland, 1988. Diplomate Am. Bd. Internal Medicine. Med. intern and resident Mass. Gen. Hosp., Boston, 1947—50, chief resident in medicine, 1953—54, chief infectious disease unit, 1956—90, chief James Jackson Firm, med. svcs., 1990—; USPHS postdoctoral rsch. fellow Johns Hopkins U., McCollum-Pratt Inst. Enzymology, Balt., 1954—56; assoc. prof. medicine Harvard Med. Sch., Boston, 1967—73, prof., 1973—, prof. medicine, 2007. Vis. assoc. prof. biochemistry Stanford Med. Sch., Palo Alto, Calif., 1969—70; chmn. Nat. Inst. Child Health and Devel., 1995—97, bd. sci. counselors. Co-author: Osteomyelitis, 1971; editor: Current Clinical Topics in Infectious Diseases, 1980—2002; assoc. editor: New Eng. Jour. Medicine, 1981—2002; contbr. articles to profl. jours. 1st lt. US Army, 1950—52. Mem.: ACP (Disting. Tchr. award 1989), Inst. Medicine, Infectious Diseases Soc. Am. (Bristol award 1984, Feldman award 1989, Soc. Citation award 2003), Assn. Am. Physicians, Am. Soc. for Clin. Investigation, Am. Soc. Biochemistry and Molecular Biology. Jewish. Avocations: biology, birdwatching, cosmology. Office: Mass Gen Hosp Dept Medicine Bulfinch Bldg #127 Boston MA 02114-2696 Home: 101 Monmouth St Apt 917 Brookline MA 02446-5637 Business E-Mail: mswartz@partners.org.

SWARTZBAUGH, DOROTHY STOEPPELWERTH, middle school educator; b. Lawrence, Kans., Oct. 19, 1939; d. Walter William and Leona Stoltenberg Stoeppelwerth; m. Richard Grey Swartzbaugh, Oct. 27, 1962; children: Alfred Walter, Richard Andrew, Anne Elizabeth, Frederick Allen. BA in History and German, Valparaiso U., 1961; MA in German Lit., Ohio State U., 1966; PhD in German Lit. and Comparative Lit., U. Ill., 1982. Cert. tchr. Ill. Tchr. Hamilton Twp. Schs., Columbus, Ohio, 1962—64; German instr. Ea. Ky. U., Richmond, 1966—68, U. Miss., Oxford, 1968—72; tchr. Mattoon Mid. Sch., Ill., 1979—2008; adj. asst. prof. Ea. Ill. U., Charleston, 1997—2001; faculty Ea. Ill. U., Sch. Continuing Edn. Presenter in field. Recipient Key award, Phi Delta Kappa, 1988, Excellence award, Ill. Math. and Sci. Academy, 1988. Home: 880 7th St Charleston IL 61938

SWARTZBAUGH, MARC L., lawyer; b. Urbana, Ohio, Jan. 3, 1937; s. Merrill L. and Lillian K. (Hill) S.; m. Marjory Anne Emhardt, Aug. 16, 1958 (deceased May 20, 2000); children: Marc Charles, Kathleen Marie, Laura Kay. BA magna cum laude, Wittenberg Coll., 1958; LLB magna cum laude, U. Pa., 1961. Bar: Ohio 1961, U.S. Dist. Ct. (no. dist.) Ohio 1962, U.S. Claims Ct. 1991, U.S. Ct. Appeals (6th cir.) 1970, U.S. Ct. Appeals (3d cir.) 1985, U.S. Ct. Appeals (Fed. cir.) 1995, U.S. Supreme Ct. 1973. Law clk. to judge U.S. Ct. Appeals (3d cir.), Phila., 1961-62;

assoc. Jones, Day, Reavis & Pogue, Cleve., 1962-69, ptnr., 1970-98; ret., 1998; cons., 1998—. Note editor U. Pa. Law Rev., 1960-61; co-author: Ohio Legal Ethics, 2001, Ohio Legal Ethics Law under the New Rules, 2006; contbr. articles to profl. jours. Co-chmn. Suburban Citizens for Open Housing, Shaker Heights, Ohio, 1966; v.p. Lomond Assn., Shaker Heights, 1965-68; trustee The Dance Ctr., Cleve., 1980-83; amb. People to People Internat., 1986; chmn. legal divsn. Cleve. campaign United Negro Coll. Fund, 1989-96; tutor Cleve. Reads, 2003; endower of keyboard instruments chair, Cleve. Orch., 2004, mem. exec. com. Assn. Continuing Edn, CWR U., 2009-. Mem. ABA (mem. ctr. profl. responsibility, sr. lawyers divsn.), Fed. Bar Assn., Ohio Bar Assn., Cleve. Bar Assn., Rowfant Club, Order of Coif, Beta Theta Pi. Democrat. Avocations: poetry, painting, music, photography, book collecting. Office: Jones Day N Point 901 Lakeside Ave E Cleveland OH 44114-1190

SWARTZLANDER, EARL EUGENE, JR., engineering educator, former electronics company executive; b. San Antonio, Feb. 1, 1945; s. Earl Eugene and Jane (Nicholas) S.; m. Joan Vickery, June 9, 1968. BSEE, Purdue U., 1967; MSEE, U. Colo., 1969; PhD, U. So. Calif., 1972. Registered profl. engr., Calif., Colo., Tex. Devel. engr. Ball Bros. Rsch. Corp., Boulder, Colo., 1967-69; Hughes fellow, mem. tech. staff Hughes Aircraft Co., Culver City, Calif., 1969-73; mem. rsch. staff Tech. Svc. Co., Santa Monica, Calif., 1973-74; chief engr. Geophys. Systems Corp., Pasadena, Calif., 1974-75, staff engr. to sr. staff engr., 1975-79, project mgr., 1979-84, lab. mgr., 1985-87; dir. ind. R&D TRW Inc., Redondo Beach, Calif., 1987-90; Schlumberger Centennial prof. engring. dept. elec. and computer engring. U. Tex., Austin, 1990—2006, prof., 2006—. Gen. chmn. Internat. Conf. Wafer Scale Integration, 1989, Internat. Conf. Application Specific Array Processors, 1990, 94, 11th Internat. Symposium on Computer Arithmetic, 1992, 31st Ann. Asilomar Conf. on Signals, Sys., and Computers, 1997, others; chmn. 3d Internat. Conf. Parallel and Distributed Sys., Taiwan, 1993, 12th Internat. Conf. on Application-Specific Systems, Architectures and Processors, 2000; mem. tech. adv. bd. ECIT, Queen's U., Belfast, 2005—, Arithmatica. Author: VLSI Signal Processing Systems, 1986; editor: Computer Design Development, 1976, Systolic Signal Processing Systems, 1987, Wafer Scale Integration, 1989, Computer Arithmetic Vol. 1 and 2, 1990, Application Specific Processors, 1996; editor-in-chief Jour. of VLSI Signal Processing, 1989-95, IEEE Transactions on Computers, 1991-94, IEEE Transactions on Signal Processing, 1995; editor: IEEE Transactions on Computers, 1982-86, IEEE Transactions on Parallel and Distributed Systems, 1989-90; hardware area editor ACM Computing Revs., 1985—; assoc. editor: IEEE Jour. Solid-State Circuits, 1984-88; contbr. more than 300 articles to profl. jours. and tech. conf. procs. Bd. dirs. Casiano Estates Homeowners Assn., Bel Air, Calif., 1976-80, pres., 1978-80; bd. dirs. Benedict Hills Estates Homeowners Assn., Beverly Hills, Calif., 1984-2006, pres., 1990-95. Recipient Disting. Engring. Alumnus award Purdue U., 1989, U. Colo., 1997, Outstanding Elec. Engr. award Purdue U., 1992, knight Imperial Russian Order St. John of Jerusalem (Knights of Malta), 1993. Fellow: IEEE (hist. com. 1996—2004, fellows com. 2000—03, 3d Millennium medal 2000); mem.: Assn. for Computing Machinery, IEEE Solid-State Cirs. Coun. (bd. govs. 1986—91, sec. 1992—93, treas. 1994—97), IEEE Signal Proc. Soc. (bd. govs. 1992—94), IEEE Computer Soc. (bd. govs. 1987—91, Golden Core award 1996), Omicron Delta Kappa, Sigma Tau, Eta Kappa Nu. Office: U Tex Austin Dept Elec Computer Engring Austin TX 78712 Office Phone: 310-702-5756, 512-471-3923. Business E-Mail: e.swartzlander@ieee.com.

SWARTZMAN, DANIEL, lawyer, educator; m. Arlene L. Swartzman, Aug. 22, 1981; children: Alexandra D., Samantha G., Simon G. BA in Sociology, U. Wash., Seattle, 1972; JD cum laude, Northwestern U. Sch. Law, Chgo., 1975; MPH, U. Ill., Chgo., 1978. Cert.: Ill. (law practitioner) 1975. Dir. legal svcs. Chgo. Lung Assn., 1975—81; dir. Midwest Environ. & Indsl. Health Tng. Ctr., 1991—95; ptnr. Schoenfield, Swartzman & Massin, 1992—2004; asst. prof. UIC Sch. Pub. Health, Chgo., 1978—85, assoc. dean, 1998—2005, assoc. prof., 1985—, assoc. divsn. dir., 2005—; ptnr. DiVincenzo Schoenfield Swartzman, 2004—. Author: (book) Cost-Benefit Analysis in Environmental Regulations: Politics, Ethics, Methods, Principles of Public Health Management. Mem. Nat. Air Conservation Commn., Washington, 1978—80, Nat. Clean Air Coalition, Washington, 1978—81; mem., pres. Ill. Environ. Coun., Springfield, 1976—83; mem. Health & Medicine Policy Rsch. Group, 1987—89; mem., pres. Temple Sholom, 1998—. Recipient Golden Apple award, Student Body, 1985, 1993, 2002, Tchr. Recognition award, UIC Coun., 1997, 2003, Disting. Tchrs. award, Assn. Schs. Pub. Health, 2008; fellow Clin. fellowship, Northwestern U. Sch. Law, 1973;, 1974, Pub. Health fellowship, Chgo. Lung Assn., 1977. Mem.: Alpha Kappa Delta, Delta Omega. Jewish. Office: UIC Sch Pub Health 1603 W Taylor M/C 923 Chicago IL 60612

SWARTZ NEUHARDT, SHAREN, lawyer; b. Dayton, Ohio, Oct. 16, 1951; d. Robert Earl and Naomi Ruth (Price) Swartz; children: Ann, Robert; m. David A Neuhardt. BA, Northwestern U., Evanston, Ill., 1973; JD, Georgetown U., Washington, 1976. Bar: Ohio 1976, U.S. Dist. Ct. (so. dist.) Ohio 1977. Assoc. Morgan, Lewis & Bockius, Washington, 1976; assoc., shareholder Smith & Schnacke, Dayton, 1977-89; v.p., gen. counsel Mead Data Ctrl., Inc., Dayton, 1987-90; ptnr. Thompson Hine LLP, Dayton, 1990—. Mem. Fed. Bar Admissions Com., Dayton; adv. bd. U. Dayton Ctr. for Law and Tech. Bd. trustees Planned Parenthood Miami Valley, 1995—2002, Tecumseh Land Trust, Premier Cmty. Health Partners, Miami Township and Yellow Springs Cmty. Improvement Corp. Mem. ABA, Ohio State Bar Assn., Dayton Bar Assn., Phi Beta Kappa. Democrat. Office: Thompson Hine LLP 2000 Courthouse Plz NE Dayton OH 45402

SWATOS, WILLIAM HENRY, JR., priest, sociologist; b. Paterson, NJ, Sept. 25, 1946; s. William H. Sr. and Lucille (MacNab) S.; children (by previous marriage): Giles S., Eric B.; m. Joanne Longstreet, Oct. 29, 2002. AB with honors, Transylvania U., 1966; MDiv summa cum laude, Episc. Theol. Sem., Lexington, Ky., 1969; MA, U. Ky., 1969, PhD in SOcial Theory with honors, 1973. Ordained to ministry Episcopal Ch., 1969. Mem. sociology faculty King Coll., Bristol, Tenn., 1973-80; vicar St. Mark's Episc. Ch., Silvis, Ill., 1980-94; mem. sociology faculty No. Ill. U., 1984-88; chair dept. edn. Diocese of Quincy, 1988-90, 93-96. Mem. faculty Black Hawk and Scott CC, Moline, Ill., Bettendorf, Iowa, 1988-96; adj. prof. Augustana Coll., Rock Island, Ill., 2005—; priest-in-charge Christ Ch. Limestone Twp., Ill., 2006—. Editor: Sociol. Analysis/Sociology of Religion, 1989-94, The Power of Religious Publics, 1999, The Protestant Ethic Turns 100, 2005, On the Road to Being There, 2006; editor-in-chief Encyclopedia of Religion and Society, 1998; mng. editor Interdisciplinary Jour. Rsch. on Religion, 2004—; co-author Sociology of Religion, 2nd edit., 2008; contbr. articles to profl. jours. Recipient Templeton prize in humility theology, 1996; full grantee World Soc. Found., Zurich, Switzerland, 1987, grantee NEH, 1974, 79, 85, 89, rsch. grantee Soc. for the Sci. Study of Religion, 1984-85, 91-92; Inst. Studies Religion sr. fellow Baylor U, 2004—; named Disting. Alumnus Dept. Sociology, U. Ky., Lexington, 1990. Fellow Soc. Sci. Study of Religion (program chair 2004); mem. Assn. for the Sociology of Religion (editor 1989-94, book rev. editor 1986-88, exec. coun. 1984-86, exec. officer 1996—, gen. editor Religion and the Social Order Series 2004—), Religious Rsch. Assn. (sec. 1990-91, bd. dirs. 1986-89, exec. officer 1994—). Home and Office: 618 SW 2nd Ave Galva IL 61434-1912 E-mail: bill4329@hotmail.com.

SWATT, STEPHEN BENTON, communications executive, consultant; b. LA, June 26, 1944; s. Maurice I. and Lucille E. (Sternberger) S.; m. Susan Ruth Edelstein, Sept. 7, 1968; 1 child, Jeffrey Michael. BSBA, U. Calif., 1966, M in Journalism, 1967. Writer San Francisco Examiner, 1967; reporter United Press Internat., LA, 1968-69; producer news Sta. KCRA-TV, Sacramento, 1969-70, reporter news, 1970-79, chief polit. and capitol corres., 1979-92; mng. ptnr. NCG Porter Novelli, Sacramento, 1992—2003, sr. counselor, 2003—. Adj. prof., guest lectr. Calif. State U., Sacramento. Contbr. articles to profl. jours. With USCG, 1966. Recipient No. Calif. Emmy NATAS, 1976-77, Pub. Svc. award Calif. State Bar, 1977, Exceptional Achievement Coun. advancement and Support of Edn., 1976, Nat. Health Journalism award Am. Chiropractic Assn., 1978. Mem. Soc. Profl. Journalists (8 awards), Capitol Corres. Assn., U. Calif. Alumni Assn., Sacramento Press Club. Avocations: hiking, jogging, fishing. Office: Porter Novelli 1215 K St # 2100 Sacramento CA 95814 Office Phone: 916-443-3354. Business E-Mail: steve.swatt@porternovelli.com.

SWAYNE, KENNETH E., engineering educator; BSEE, U. Tenn., Knoxville, 1988; AS in Math., Cleve. State Comm. Coll., 1984; MS in Engring., U. Tenn., Knoxville, 1992; MA in Theol. Studies, Southern Bapt. Theol. Sem., Louisville, 2005. Lic. profl. engr., Tenn., 1993, La., 1993. Project engr. J.M. Huber Corp., 1989—92; instrument engr. Am. Cyanamid, 1992—94; IC&E sect. leader Thermatrix Inc., 1995—98, sr. instrument engr., 1995—98; owner Swayne & Assocs., 1998—2001; asst. prof. Pellissippi State Tech. Comm. Coll., Knoxville, 2001—05, EET program coord., 2001—05, seat com. mem., 2004—05, faculty senate mem., 2004—08, EET program coord., 2006—, assoc. prof., 2006—, student success coord., 2007—08, faculty senate comm. officer, 2007—. Cons., 2001—08; adv. com. mem. Farragut HS, Knoxville, 2006—07; textbook reviewer Delmar Pubs., 2004. Project bus. cons. JTPA, Athens, Tenn., 1989—92; mem. Rotary Internat., Etowah, Tenn., 1989—92, sec., 1990—92, treas., 1990—92; mem. IEEE, 1987—2008, faculty advisor, 2001—04; sunday sch. tchr. Local Ch., 1994—2005, scholarship com. mem., 1997—98, long range planning com. mem., 1998—99, trainer, 2003—05, bylaws com. mem., 2008—09, deacon; chmn. Christian life com. McMinn-Meigs Bapt. Assn., Athens, 2003—05; bd. mem. Athens Youth Baseball Assn., 2006—08; mem. Am. Assn. Engring. Educators, 2004—08; baseball coach Athens Youth Baseball Assn., 2004—08. Recipient Math. award, Cleve. State Comm. Coll., 1984. Mem.: Instrument Soc. America, Tau Beta Pi, Eta Kappa Nu, Phi Kappa Phi. Avocations: skiing, racquetball, tennis, weightlifting.

SWAYZE, CHARLES J., JR., lawyer; b. Greenwood, Miss., May 14, 1944; BBA, Univ. Miss., 1966, JD, 1969; LLM, George Washington Univ., 1973. Bar: Miss. 1969, US Ct. Mil. Appeals 1969, US Supreme Ct. 1973. Prosecuting atty. City of Greenwood, Miss., 1974—75, Leflore County, 1976—2000; mem. Whittington, Brock & Swayze PA, Greenwood, Miss. Pres. So. Conf. of Bar Pres. Capt. JAGC US Army, 1969—73. Fellow: Miss. Bar Found., Am. Bar Found.; mem.: ABA, Miss. Bar Assn. (pres. 2004), Phi Delta Phi. Office: Whittington Brock & Swayze PA 308 Fulton St PO Box 941 Greenwood MS 38930

SWAYZE, PATRICK, actor, dancer; b. Houston, Aug. 18, 1952; s. Jesse Wayne & Patsy Swayze; n. Lisa Niemi, June 12, 1975 Student, Harkness Sch., Joffrey Ballet Sch. Actor: (films) Skatetown, USA, 1979, The Outsiders, 1983, Staying Alive, 1983, Uncommon Valor, 1983, Red Dawn, 1984, Grandview, USA, 1984, Youngblood, 1986, Dirty Dancing, 1987, Steel Dawn, 1987, Tiger Warsaw, 1988, Road House, 1989, Next of Kin, 1989, Ghost, 1989, Point Break, 1991, City of Joy, 1992, Father Hood, 1993, Tall Tale, 1994, To Wong Foo, Thanks for Everything, Julie Newmar, 1995, Three Wishes, 1995, Letters From a Killer, 1997, Vanished, 1998, Black Dog, 1998, Without a Word, 1999, The Winddrinker, 2000, Wakin' Up In Reno, 2000, Forever Lulu, 2000, Green Dragon, 2001, Donnie Darko, 2001, One Last Dance, 2003, 11:14, 2003, George and the Dragon, 2004, Dirty Dancing: Havana Nights, 2004, Keeping Mum, 2005, Jump!, 2007, Christmas in Wonderland, 2007; (TV movies) The Comeback Kid, 1980, Return of the Rebels, 1981, The Renegades, 1982, King Solomon's Mines, 2004, Icon, 2005; (TV mini-series) North and South, 1985, North and South: Book II, 1986; (TV series) Renegades, 1983, The Beast, 2009; (TV appearances) M*A*S*H, 1981, Amazing Stories, 1986, Whoopi, 2004; (Broadway plays) Goodtime Charley, Grease; (off-Broadway) Guys and Dolls, 2006. Recipient Aftonbladet TV prize for Best Fgn. TV Personality, 1988, Golden Apple award, Male Star of Yr., ShoWest award, 1992 Office: William Morris 151 S El Camino Dr Beverly Hills CA 90212-2775

SWAZEY, JUDITH POUND, academic administrator, science educator; b. Bronxville, NY, Apr. 21, 1939; d. Robert Earl and Louise Titus (Hanson) Pound; m. Peter Woodman Swazey, Nov. 28, 1964; children: Elizabeth, Peter. AB, Wellesley Coll., 1961; PhD, Harvard U., 1966. Rsch. assoc. Harvard U., 1966-71, lectr., 1969-71, rsch. fellow, 1971-72; cons. com. brain scis. NRC, 1971-73; staff scientist neuroscis. rsch. program MIT, Cambridge, 1973-74; assoc. prof. dept. socio-med. scis. and cmty. medicine Boston U., 1974-77, prof., 1977-80, adj. prof. Schs. Medicine and Pub. Health, 1980—; exec. dir. Medicine in the Pub. Interest, Inc., Boston and Washington, 1979-82, 89-93; pres. Coll. of the Atlantic, Bar Harbor, Maine, 1982-84, Acadia Inst., Bar Harbor, 1984-2001, founding pres., sr. scholar, 2001—07. Mem. Army Sci. Bd., 1987-92. Author: Reflexes and Motor Integration, the Development of Sherrington's Integrative Action Concept, 1969, (with others) Human Aspects of Biomedical Innovation, 1971, (with R.C. Fox) The Courage to Fail, a Social View of Organ Transplants and Hemodialysis, 1975, rev. edit., 1978, 02 (hon. mention Am. Med. Writers Assn., C. Wright Mills award Am. Sociol. Assn.), Chlorpromazine in Psychiatry, a Study of Therapeutic Innovation, 1974, (with K. Reeds) Today's Medicine, Tomorrow's Science, Essays on Paths of Discovery in the Biomedical Sciences, 1978; editor: (with C. Wong) Dilemmas of Dying, Policies and Procedures for Decisions Not to Treat, 1981, (with F. Worden and G. Adelman) The Neurosciences: Paths of Discovery, 1975, (with R.C. Fox) Spare Parts, Organ Replacement in American Society, 1992, Japanese transl., 1999, (with C. Messikomer and A. Glicksman) Society and Medicine. Essays in Honor of Renée Fox, 2002, (with R.C.Fox) Observing Bioethics, 2008; assoc. editor IRB: A Jour. of Human Subjects Rsch., 1979-00; mem. editl. bd. Sci. and Engring. Ethics, 1994—; contbr. articles to profl. jours. Mem. Maine Dept. Human Svcs. Bioethics Adv. Com. (chair 1991-94); mem. Commn. on Rsch. Integrity, 1994-95; bd. dirs. Maine Bioethics Network, 1994-99. Wellesley Coll. scholar, 1961; Wellesley Coll. Alumnae fellow Harvard U., 1966, NIH predoctoral fellow, 1966, Radcliffe Coll. Coll. grad. fellow, 1966. Fellow AAAS (sci. freedom and responsibility com. 1986-89, nominations com. 2003-2004), Inst. Medicine of NAS (mem. health scis. policy bd. 1986-89), Grad. Record Exam. (bd. dirs. 1987-91), Phi Beta Kappa, Sigma Xi (mem. ethics com. 2004-). Office: PO Box 243 Bar Harbor ME 04609-0243 Office Phone: 207-288-3295. Personal E-mail: swazey.jp@gmail.com.

SWEARENGIN, ASHLEY, Mayor, Fresno, California; b. Tex. m. Paul Swearengin; children: Sydney, Samuel. BS in bus. adminstrn., MS in bus. adminstrn., Calif. State U., Fresno. Dir. cmty. and econ. devel. Calif. State U., Fresno, 2000—08; co-founder, COO Regional Jobs Initiative, Fresno, 2002—05; lead exec. Calif. Partnership for the San Joaquin Valley, 2005—08; mayor City of Fresno, Calif., 2009—. Mem. Fresno Utility Commn., Calif. Commn. Econ. Devel., 2007. Named Alumnus of the Yr., Leadership Fresno, 2007; named one of Fresno's Top Bus. and Profl. Women of the Yr., Marjaree Mason Ctr., 2006. Office: Office of the Mayor 2600 Fresno St Fresno CA 93721 Office Phone: 559-621-8000. Office Fax: 559-621-7990. E-mail: mayor@fresno.gov.*

SWEARER, WILLIAM BROOKS, lawyer; b. Hays, Kans. Grad., Princeton U., 1951; law degree, U. Kans., 1955. Bar: Kans. 1955. Pvt. practice, Hutchinson, Kans., 1955—; ptnr., now counsel Martindell, Swearer & Shaffer, LLP, Hutchinson, 1955—. Mem. Kans. Bd. Discipline for Attys., 1979-92, chmn., 1987-92; mem. Kans. Commn. on Jud. Qualifications, 2003-. With U.S. Army, 1952-53, Korea. Mem. ABA (ho. of dels. 1995-2000), Am. Bar Found. (state chair 1998-2002), Kans. Bar Assn. (pres. 1992-93, various offices, mem. coms.), Kans. Assn. Sch. Attys. (pres. 1989-90), Reno County Bar Assn. Office: PO Box 1907 Hutchinson KS 67504-1907 Office Phone: 620-662-3331. Business E-Mail: wbs@martindell-law.com.

SWEARINGEN, LAURA COLLEEN, music educator, director; b. St. Louis, Apr. 10, 1973; d. Paul Andrew and Karen Marie Hogan; m. Gary William Swearingen, Aug. 16, 1997; children: Sawyer Hogan children: Shane Michael, Zoe Nichole. MusB, So. Ill. U., Edwardsville, 1995; MusM, Webster U., St. Louis, 1999. Choir dir. Brentwood Sch. Dist., Mo., 1993—2003; music tchr. Hillsboro Sch. Dist., Mo., 1996—98; choir dir. Festus Sch. Dist., Mo., 1998—99, Lindbergh Sch. Dist., St. Louis, 2003—. All-state choir coord. St. Louis Suburban Music Educators Assn., 2006—. Singer: (voice recital) Art Song by French Composers, (mezzo-soprano soloist) Brahm's Requiem; prodr.: (show choir competition show) Money, Gangsters; singer: St. Louis Chamber Chorus. Mem.: NEA, Mo. Music Educators Assn., Mo. State Tchrs. Assn., Mo. Choral Dirs. Assn., Am. Choral Dirs. Assn., St. Louis Irish Arts, Sigma Alpha Iota (pres. 1994—95). Conservative. Roman Catholic. Avocations: exercise, reading, geocaching, sports. Office: Lindbergh HS 4900 S Lindbergh Blvd Saint Louis MO 63126 Office Fax: 314-729-2443. Business E-Mail: lswearingen@lindberghschools.ws.

SWEATMAN, KELLY, information technology executive; Student, Loyola Coll., Balt., 1983; BA in Bus. Mgmt., Washington Coll., Chestertown, Md., 1985; MBA, U. Md., College Park, 1987. Asst. to contr. Balt. Window Factory, 1983—85; ops. rsch. analyst MIE MSS (Shock Trauma), Balt., 1986—87; officer MNC Info. Svcs., Balt., 1987—96; v.p. MBNA Tech., Newark, Del., 1996—. Recipient MBNA Hallmark award, MBNA Tech., 1998. Mem.: AAUW, Balt. Choral Arts Soc. Home: 826 Contry Club Rd Havre De Grace MD 21078-2105

SWEATT, ERMELINDA ESPINOLA, retired mathematics educator; d. Edmund Joseph and Mary Sylvia Espinola; m. Ronald Burnett Sweatt, Feb. 13, 1971; children: Tanya Sylvia, Jason Safford Edmund. BA in Math., Nasson Coll., Springvale, Maine, 1969; MA in Secondary Math. Edn., U. Conn., Storrs, 1974. Math. educator cert. Conn., dept. chairperson cert. Conn. Tchr. Ayer Jr.-Sr. HS, Mass., 1969—71, Plainfield HS, Conn., 1971—2005, dept. chairperson, 1987—2008; acct. Bustins Builders LLC, Bustins Island, Maine, 1980—. Cooperating & mentor tchr. Conn. Dept. Edn., Hartford, 1978—2005; advisor Plainfield Nat. Honor Soc., 1987—2005. Chairperson numerous dist. coms. Plainfield Pub. Schs., 1971—2005; coach girls field hockey Plainfield HS, 1971—73, coach girls cross country, 1974—80; officer Cottagers Assn. Bustins Island, 1979—88; exec. bd. Conn. Assn. Nat. Honor Socs. Recipient Outstanding Conn. Tchr. of Math., Conn. Dept. Edn., 1992, 2000. Mem.: NEA, Busting Island Village Corp. (sec. 2008—), Plainfield Edn. Assn., Nat. Coun. Tchrs. Math., Conn. Edn. Assn., VFW Aux. Avocations: reading, writing, drawing, swimming, golf. Home: 37 Cooney Rd Pomfret Center CT 06259

SWEDISH, JOSEPH, insurance company executive; b. Richmond, Va. BS, U. NC, Charlotte, 1973; M in health adminstrn., Duke U., 1979. Pres., CEO Ea. Fla. Divsn. Columbia/HCA Healthcare Corp., 1994—99, Centura Health, Colo., 1999—2005, Trinity Health, Mich., 2005—. Past chmn. Colo. Hosp. Assn.; mem. bd. Am. Hosp. Assn. Regional Policy Bd.; dir. Cross Country Healthcare, Fla., 2001—. Mem. econ. devel. coun. Metro Denver C. of C.; mem. bd. Metro Denver Boy Scouts, Colo. Forum, Colo. Concern. Recipient Univ. Medal, Bd. Regents U. Colo.; named E & Y Entrepreneur of Yr., Ernst & Young, 2003. Fellow: Am. Coll. Healthcare Exec. Office: Trinity Health 27870 Cabot Dr Novi MI 48377*

SWEED, PHYLLIS, publishing executive; b. NYC, Dec. 6, 1931; d. Paul and Frances (Spitzer) S.; m. Leonard Bogdanoff (dec. Oct. 1975); children: Patricia Romano (dec. June 1994), James Alan (dec. Feb 29, 2008) BA, NYU, 1950. Asst. buyer Nat. Bellas Hess, NYC, 1950; assoc. editor Fox-Shulman Pub., NYC, 1951-57; significant products and components editor Product Engring. mag. McGraw-Hill Pub., NYC, 1957—61; mng. editor Haire Pub., NYC, 1962-66; editor Gifts & Decorative Accessories Mag., 1966-78; sr. v.p. Geyer-McAllister Pub., NYC, 1978-98, editor-in-chief, co-pub., 1978—98; dir. editl. devel. Gifts & Decorative Accessories, NYC, 1998-99; prin. P.S. Comms. & Mktg., 1999—2008; editor-in-chief, pub. Gift Executive, 1999. Bd. dirs. Frances Hook Scholarship Fund, 1989-96. Recipient Editl. Excellence award Indsl. Mktg., 1964, Nat. Assn. Ltd. Edit. Dealers award, 1993, 96, MagWeek Excellence award, 1992, Dallas Mktg. Ctr. award, 1969, 80, 82. Mem. Nat. Assn. Ltd. Edit. Dealers (assoc.), Internat. Furnishings and Design Assn. Avocations: gardening, collecting antique Belleeck. Office: 505 LaGuardia Pl Ste 17D New York NY 10012-2004 Personal E-mail: psweed505@aol.com.

SWEELY, GAY CARYLL, art historian, educator; b. Chgo., May 30, 1946; d. Irvin Ray Malewicki and Carol Mae Schultz; m. Stephen Wallis Sweely, Oct. 21, 1978; children: Eric, Chad. BA in Art History, Ill. Wesleyan U., 1968; MA in Art History, U. Utah, 1973; PhD Ad Eundem, Canterbury U., New Zealand, 1988; PhD in Art and Archtl. History, U. Melbourne, 1998; PhD (hon.), Nat. Cath. U., Australia, 1998; MA (hon.), U. Ballarat, 1999, Flinders U., 1999. Art history, slide libr. U. Utah, Salt Lake City, 1969—71; dir. of pub. rels. Air Force Sgts. Assn., Washington, 1973—75; sr. tech. editor U.S. Bur. Census, 1975—79; mgr. IBM Corp., Manassas, Va., 1979—83; instr. No. Va. C.C., 1980—85; instr. art history U. Canterbury, Christchurch, New Zealand, 1988; lectr. and rschr. U. Ballarat, Australia, 1991—2000; lectr., vis. asst. prof. Ea. Ky. U., Richmond, 2000—. Co-author: Becoming Australians, 2001; contbr. articles to profl. publs. and jours. in field. Elected ofcl. Cen. Com. St. of Md., 1974—75; with outreach svcs. First United Meth. Ch., Richmond, Ky., 2000—. Named Internat. Educator of Yr., Cambridge, 2004, Art Educator Yr., Art Educators Assn., 2005; named to William Howard Taft Hall of Fame, 2004. Mem.: Ky. Art Edn. Assn., Kappa Pi, Alpha Omicron Pi, Phi Kappa Phi (sec. chpt. 122

2003—). Methodist. Avocations: writing, editing. Home: 745 Caleast Rd Richmond KY 40475 Office: Ea Kentucky Univ Dept of Art and Design 309 Campbell Richmond KY 40475 E-mail: gc.sweely@eku.edu.

SWEEM, BILLY DON, bishop, religious organization administrator; b. Bartlesville, Okla., Aug. 7, 1942; s. Verl D. and Viola J. (Benner) Sweem; m. Roberta Marie Hawthorn, Dec. 26, 1990; children: Mark A., Kevin L., Chad D. Diploma, Internat. Bible Inst. & Sem., Portsmount, Fla.; DD magna cum laude, Bethel Full Gospel Sem., Okla., 1980; M in Christian Counseling, 1984; PhD, Internat. Bible Inst. & Sem., Portsmount, Fla., 1988. Ordained to ministry Gospel Mins. and Chs. Internat., 1991, Ind. Assemblies Fellowship, 1991. Evangelist Lighthouse Temple, Colorado Springs, 1977—80, Tulsa, 1980—85; youth pastor Echoes of Faith, Las Vegas, Nev., 1985-89; exec. dir. Billy Sweem Gospel Ministries, Tulsa, 1990—. Evangelist United Meth. Coop. Ministries, Tulsa, 1990—. Missionary India, Pakistan and Philippines. Special interest in church planting and mission works with orphans and troubled teens world-wide. Home: Internat Independent Assemblies Inc St Luke Ind Assemblies Ministries PO Box 2171 Bartlesville OK 74005-2171 Home Phone: 918-213-4791; Office Phone: 918-214-7506, 918-338-0927. Personal E-mail: revdrbsweem@yahoo.com.

SWEENEY, ANNE M., cable television company executive; b. Nov. 4, 1957; m. Philip Miller; children: Rosemary, Christopher. BA, Coll. of New Rochelle, NYC, 1979; EdM, Harvard U., 1980. With Nickelodeon/Nick at Nite, 1981-93, sr. v.p. program enterprises; chmn., CEO FX Networks, Inc., NYC, 1993—96; exec. v.p. Disney/ABC Cable Networks, pres. Disney Channel Walt Disney Co., 1996—98, pres. Disney/ABC Cable Networks, Disney Channel, 1998—2000, pres. ABC Cable Networks Group, Disney Channel Worldwide, 2000—04, co-chair Media Networks divsn., pres. Disney/ ABC TV Group, 2004—. Bd. dirs. Hulu, 2009—, Mus. Radio & TV, Lifetime TV, Paley Ctr. for Media (formerly Mus. TV and Radio), Am. Film Inst.; hon. chair Cable Positive. Bd. trustees Coll. of New Rochelle, Harvard U. Ptnrs. Coun.; hon. chair Cable Positive; bd. dirs. Walter Kaitz Found, Spl. Olympics Internat. Recipient Lucy award, Women in Film, 2002, Chair Award, Caucus for TV Prodrs., Writers, and Dirs., 2003, President's award, Cable TV Pub. Affairs Assn., 2004, Muse award, NY Women in Film and TV, 2004, Disting. Vanguard award for Leadership, Nat. Cable and TV Telecomm. Assn., 2009, Matrix award, NY Women in Comm., Inc., 2009, Golden Mike award for Outstanding Contributions to Broadcasting, Broadcasters Found. America, 2009; named one of 100 Most Powerful Women in Entertainment, Hollywood Reporter, 2004—07, 50 Women to Watch, Wall St. Jour., 2005, 2006, 100 Most Powerful Women, Forbes mag., 2005—09, Next 20 Female CEOs, Pink Mag. & Forté Found., 2006, 50 Most Powerful Women in Bus., Fortune mag., 2006, 2007, 2008; named to Hall of Achievement, Am. Advt. Fedn., 1996; inductee, Cable Ctr. Hall of Fame, 2007. Mem. Nat. Acad. Cable Programming (bd. dirs.), Women in Cable NY (founding mem.), Women in Cable (Exec. of Yr. 1994, Woman of Yr. 1997, Advocate Leader award So. Calif. Chpt. 1998). Office: The Walt Disney Co 500 S Buena Vista St Burbank CA 91521*

SWEENEY, CLAYTON ANTHONY, lawyer, business executive; b. Pitts., Oct. 20, 1931; s. Denis Regis and Grace Frances (Roche) S.; m. Sally Dimond, Oct. 4, 1958; children: Sharon, Lorrie, Maureen, Clayton Anthony, Tara, Megan. BS, Duquesne U., 1957, LLB, 1962. Bar: Pa. 1962, U.S. Supreme Ct. 1968. Supr. transp. claims H.J. Heinz Co., Pitts., 1955-57; mgr. market research Murray Corp. Am., Pitts., 1957-62; ptnr. Buchanan, Ingersoll, Rodewald, Kyle and Buerger, Pitts., 1962-78; sr. v.p. Allegheny Ludlum Industries, Inc., Pitts., 1978-81; exec. v.p., chief adminstrv. officer Allegheny Internat., Inc., Pitts., 1981-84, vice chmn., 1984-85; ptnr., mng. dir. Dickie, McCamey & Chilcote, Pitts., 1986-98, also bd. dirs.; pres. Sweeney Metz Fox McGrann & Schermer, 1998-2000; with Schnader Harrison Segal & Lewis, LLP, Pitts., 2000—. Bd. dirs. Wilkinson Sword Group Ltd., U.K., Landmark Savs. and Loan Assn., Liquid Air N.Am., Halbouty Energy Co., Koppers Holding Corp., Koppers Industries, Inc., Schaefer Mfg., Inc., Schaefer Marine, Inc., Schaefer Equipment, Inc.; adj. prof. Duquesne U. Sch. Law; lectr. Pa. Bar Inst.; mem. procedural rules com. Supreme Ct. Pa. Named Disting. Alumnus Sch. Law Duquesne U., 1997. Bd. dirs. Met. Pitts. Pub. Broadcasting, Inc., Diocesan Sch. Bd., Roman Cath. Diocese Pitts., Toner Inst., Christian Assocs. of Southwestern Pa., Wesley Inst., Inc., Jr. Achievement S.W. Pa., YMCA Western Pa.; chmn. Seton Hill Coll.; mem. St. Thomas More Sch. Bd., Bethel Park, Pa.; chmn. St. Francis Med. Ctr., St. Francis Health System; chmn. bd. DePaul Inst. With U.S. Army, 1953-55. Named one of 100 Most Disting. Living Alumni, Duquesne U. Century Club, 1978. Mem. Acad. Trial Lawyers Allegheny County, ABA, Pa. Bar Assn., St. Thomas More Soc. Home: 232 Thornberry Cir Pittsburgh PA 15234-1025 Office: Schnader Harrison Segal & Lewis LLP Ste 2700 Fifth Ave Pl 120 Fifth Ave Pittsburgh PA 15222-3010 Home Phone: 412-835-8548, 716-386-6143; Office Phone: 412-577-5225. Business E-Mail: csweeney@schnader.com.

SWEENEY, DAVID BRIAN, lawyer; b. Seattle, June 23, 1941; s. Hubert Lee and Ann Louise (Harmon) S.; m. Janice Kay Goins, June 18, 1983; children: Stuart, Jennifer, Ann, Katharine. BA Magna cum laude, Yale U., 1963; LLB, Harvard U., 1967. Bar: Wash. 1968, U.S. Dist. Ct. (we. dist.) Wash. 1968, U.S. Ct. Appeals (9th cir.) 1968. Assoc. Roberts, Shefelman, Lawrence, Gay and Moch, Seattle, 1968-75; ptnr. Roberts, Shefelman, Lawrence, Gay & Moch (then Robert & Shefelman, then Foster, Pepper & Shefelman), 1976—2002; of counsel Smith & Zuccarini, P.S., Bellevue, Wash., 2002—. Mem. Seattle-King County Bar Assn., Wash. State Bar Assn., ABA, Estate Planning Coun. Seattle, College Club, Harbor Club. Home: 17506 SE 46th St Bellevue WA 98006-6527 Office: Smith & Zuccarini PS 2155 112th Ave NE Bellevue WA 98004 Home Phone: 425-641-8323; Office Phone: 425-990-1586. Business E-Mail: d.sweeney@smithzuccarini.com.

SWEENEY, DEIDRE ANN, lawyer; b. Hackensack, NJ, Mar. 17, 1953; AB cum laude, Mt. Holyoke Coll., 1975; JD, Fordham U., 1978. Assoc. Curtis, Mallet-Prevost, Colt & Mosle, NYC, 1978—84, Eaton & Van Winkle, NYC, 1984—86; ptnr. Jacobs, Persinger & Parker, NYC, 1986—2002; of counsel McCanliss and Early, LLP, NYC, 2002—. Trustee Sidney & Judith kranes Charitable Trust, 2009—, Lighthouse Internat., Planned Giving Adv. Com., 2009—. Mem. Assn. of Bar of City of N.Y.

SWEENEY, JACK, publishing executive; b. Jersey City; m. Ellie Sweeney; children: Jake, Jessica. BA in English, King's Coll., Wilkes-Barre, Pa. With adv. dept. Washington Post, 1968—74; adv. dir. Trenton Times, 1974—78, Boston Herald, 1978—80, Houston Chronicle, 1980—83, dir. sales and mktg., 1983—86, v.p. sales and mktg., 1986—91, v.p., gen. mgr., 1991, assoc. pub., 1998—2000, pres., 1998—, pub., 2000—. Exec. com., bd. trustees United Way Tex. Gulf Coast; exec. com., bd. dirs. Greater Houston Partnership; chmn. Be A Super Host Com. Super Bowl 2004, Houston. Mem.: Tex. Daily Newspaper Assn. (Pat Taggart Meml. Award 2000), Newspaper Assn. Am. Office: Houston Chronicle 801 Texas Ave Houston TX 77002*

SWEENEY, JAMES, application developer; s. Mary Blakeney; m. Jennifer Sweeney. BS, Davis and Elkins Coll., West Va., 1994; MS, U. North Fla., Jacksonville, 2007. Software engr. Mayo Clinic, Jacksonville, 2003—. Contbr. articles to profl. jours. Mem.: Assn. Computing Machinery.

SWEENEY, JAMES LEE, engineering educator; b. Waterbury, Conn., Mar. 22, 1944; s. James Wallace and Aletha B. S.; m. Susan L. Van Every, Aug. 21, 1971; children: Erin, Ryan, Regan, Wesley. BSEE, MIT, 1966; PhD in Engring.-Econ. Sys., Stanford U., 1971. With Stanford U., 1967—, prof. engring.-econ. sys., 1971—, chmn. dept. engring.-econ. sys., 1991—, prof. and chmn. dept. ops. rsch., engring.-econ. sys., 1996—99, prof. mgmt. sci. and engring., 2000—; sr. fellow Hoover Inst., 2001—; dir. office energy sys., modeling and forecasting U.S. Fed. Energy Adminstrn., Washington, 1974-76. Dir. Energy Modeling Forum, 1978-85, chmn. Inst. Energy Studies, 1981-84, cons. faculty Sch. of Law, 1980-82, mem. steering com. Ctr. Econ. policy Rsch., 1982—, dir., 1984-86; sr. fellow Ctr. for Econ. Policy Rsch., 1997—; dir. Precourt Energy Efficiency Ctr.; cons. Cornerstone Rsch., NRC, Exxon Mobil. Author: The California Electricity Crisis, 2001; co-author: Macroeconomics Impacts of Energy Shocks, 1987, Fuels to Drive Our Future, 1990; editor: Handbook of Natural Resources and Energy Economics, 1985, 93; contbr. numerous publs., in field to profl. jours. Bd. pres. Stanford Campus Residential Leaseholders, 1998—. Recipient Disting. Svc. award Fed. Energy Adminstrn., 1975, Adelman-Frankel award US Assoc. Energy Econs., 2007. Mem. Am. Econ. Assn., Internat. Assn. Energy Econs. (Past v.p. for publs.), Rotary (past pres.), Menlo Circus Club, Eta Kappa Nu, Tau Beta Pi. Home: 445 El Escarpado Stanford CA 94305-8430 Office: Stanford University 473 Via Ortega Stanford CA 94305-4121 Office Phone: 650-723-2847. Business E-Mail: jim.sweeney@stanford.edu.

SWEENEY, JILLIAN C., marketing professor; PhD, Curtin U. Bus. Sch., Perth, Western Australia, 1994. Assoc. prof. U. Western Australia, 2001—07, prof. Crawley, 2007—08; fellow and exec. Anzmac, 2001—07. Chair Market Rsch. Soc. Western Australia, 2002—04. Office: M261 UWA Bus Sch UWA 35 Stirling Highway Wa Crawley 6009 Australia Office Fax: 08 6488 1004. Business E-Mail: jsweeney@biz.uwa.edu.au.

SWEENEY, JOHN E., former United States Representative from New York; b. Troy, NY, Aug. 9, 1955; m. Gayle Ford; 3 children. AA in Liberal Arts, Hudson Valley CC, 1978; BA in Polit. Sci. and Criminal Justice, Russell Sage Coll., 1981; JD, Western New Eng. Sch. Law, 1991. Bar: NY 1991. Dir. Rensselaer County Stop-DWI prog., Troy; ptnr. Cholakis, Sweeney and Wollowitz, Troy, 1991—95; exec. dir., chief counsel NY State Rep. Party, 1992—94; commr. labor State of NY, Albany, 1995-97, dep. chief of staff to Gov. George Pataki, 1997—98; mem. US Congress from 20th NY dist., 1999—2007, mem. Rep. steering com., mem. appropriations com., vice chmn. transp., treasury and housing and urban devel. appropriations subcommittee. Recipient President's award, Mental Health Assn. NY State, Inc., 2002, Friend of Farm Bur. award, NY Farm Bur., 2004, Guardian award, Partnership for Drug-Free Am., 2004. Republican. Roman Catholic.

SWEENEY, JOHN JOSEPH, labor union administrator; b. Bronx, NY, May 5, 1934; m. Maureen Power; children: John, Patricia. Degree in Econs., Iona Coll., New Rochelle, NY, 1956; degree (hon.), Oberlin Coll., U. Mass., Amherst, U. Balt., Cath. U. Law Sch., U. Toledo Coll. Law. Clk. IBM; rschr. Internat. Ladies' Garment Workers, 1956; contract dir., NYC Local 32B Svc. Employees Internat. Union (SEIU), 1960, asst. to pres. Local 32B, 1972, v.p. Local 32B, 1973—76, pres. Local 32B, 1976—81, pres. SEIU, 1980—95; v.p. AFL-CIO, 1980—95, pres., 1995—. Pres. Trade Union Adv. Com., 2000—. Author: America Needs A Raise: Fighting for Economic Security and Social Justice, 1996; co-author: Solutions for the New Work Force, 1989; co-editor: Family & Work: Bridging the Gap, 1987. Mem.: Dem. Socialists of America. Office: AFL-CIO 815 16th St NW Washington DC 20006-4104 Office Phone: 202-637-5000.*

SWEENEY, JOSEPH DUDLEY, law educator, political organization worker; b. Omaha, Aug. 5, 1944; s. William Dudley Sweeney and Catherine Teresa Malone. BS in Agrl. Sci. and Animal Sci., U. Ariz., 1972; JD, Alexander Hamilton Evening Law Sch., 1995. Prof., adminstr. Alexander Hamilton Evening Law Sch., Tucson, 1978—, Union Western Sem., Tucson, 1985—. Founder, dir. Nat. Svc. Lobby, 1988—. Mem.: KC. Republican. Avocations: sports, exercise, reading, video production. Home: 1411 N 3rd Ave Tucson AZ 85705 Office: Alexander Hamilton Law Coll 1411 N 3rd Ave Tucson AZ 85705 Office Phone: 520-617-0656.

SWEENEY, JOSEPH J., lawyer, manufacturing executive; AB, Harvard Coll., 1970; JD, Boston U., 1973. Sr. atty. Data Gen. Corp.; v.p., gen. counsel MIPS Computer Systems, Inc.; v.p. adminstrn. MIPS Technologies, Inc.; with Applied Materials Inc., Santa Clara, Calif., 1993—, group v.p. legal affairs & intellectual property, corp. sec., 2002—05, sr. v.p., gen. counsel, corp. sec., 2005—. Office: Applied Materials 3050 Bowers Ave PO Box 58039 Santa Clara CA 95054-3299

SWEENEY, MARGARET MARY, federal judge; b. 1955; BA in History, Coll. Notre Dame, Md., 1977; JD, Delaware Law Sch., 1981. Bar: Supreme Ct. Pa., DC Ct. Appeals. Master Delaware Family Ct., 1981—83; atty. Fedorko, Gilbert, & Lanctot, 1983—85; law clk. to Honorable Loren A. Smith US Ct. Fed. Claims, 1985—87; trial atty. gen. litig. sect., environ. and nat. resources divsn. US Dept. Justice, 1987—99, atty. advisor office intelligence policy and review; spl. master US Ct. Fed. Claims, 2003—05, judge, 2005—. Mem.: US Ct. Fed. Claims Bar Assn. (mem. bd. 1990—, pres. 1999). Office: US Ct Fed Claims 717 Madison Pl NW Washington DC 20005 Office Phone: 202-219-9657.*

SWEENEY, MARK, dentist; m. Julie Sweeney; children: Julian, Marcus, Clark;children from previous marriage: Mason, Danielle. Grad., U. Tex., Austin, 1975; DDS, U. Tex., San Antonio, 1979. Pvt. practice, Austin, Tex., 1975—; cosmetic dentist Veneers USA, Austin Dental Spa. Mem.: ADA, Am. Endodontic Soc., Acad. Gen. Dentistry, Capital Area Dental Soc., Am. Acad. Cosmetic Dentistry, Tex. Dental Assn., Ken Olsen Study Group. Avocation: tennis. Office: Veneers USA 3305 Northland, Ste 515 Austin TX 78731 Office Phone: 512-380-1300.

SWEENEY, NEAL JAMES, lawyer; b. Paterson, NJ, Nov. 1, 1957; s. Bernard Thomas and Mary Agnes (Keneally) S.; m. Mary Elizabeth Finocchiaro, Oct. 27, 1984; children: Daniel Fulton, Clare Kenneally, Moira Ann. BA in History and Polit Sci., Rutgers U., 1979; JD, George Washington U., 1982. Bar: Ga. 1982, US Dist. Ct. (no. dist.) Ga. 1982, US Dist. Ct. (no. dist.) Tex. 1982, US Claims Ct. 1984, US Ct. Appeals (5th cir.) 1987. Assoc. Smith, Currie & Hancock, Atlanta, 1982-87, ptnr., 1988-98; ptnr. Construction and Pub. Contracts Practice Kilpatrick Stockton LLP, Atlanta, 1998—. Co-author: Construction Business Handbook, 1985, Holding Subcontractors to Their Bids, 1986, Subcontractor Default, 1987, The New AIA Design and Construction Documents, 1988, Proving and Pricing Claims, 1995, Fifty State Construction Lien and Bond Law, 2000, Who Pays For Defective Design?, 1997, Design-Build Contracting Claims, 1999, Design-Build Contracting Handbook, 2001; editor: Construction Subcontracting, 1991, Common Sense Construction Law, 1997, Aspen Construction Law Update, 1992—; notes editor G.W.U.J. Internat. Law and Econs., 1981-82. Mem. ABA (pub. contract law sect., forum com. on constrn. industry), Atlanta Bar Assn. (bd. mem. construct law sect.), Am. Arbitration Assn. (panel of arbitrators), Water Environment Fedn. (editl. adv. bd. 1994-97), Design Build Inst. of Am. (pres. SE chpt. 2006-07). Roman Catholic. Home: 120 Forrest Lake Dr NW Atlanta GA 30327 Office: Kilpatrick Stockton LLP 1100 Peachtree St NE Ste 2800 Atlanta GA 30309-4530 Office Phone: 404-815-6616. Office Fax: 404-541-3408. Business E-Mail: nsweeney@kilstock.com.

SWEENEY, PATRICK J., medical educator; m. Eve McGrath, July 12, 1969; children: Erin Christine Brousseau, Andrew P. BS, Loyola U., Chgo., 1967; MD, St. Louis U., 1971; MPH, U. Calif., Berkeley, 1978; PhD, U. Miss., Oxford, 1987. Cert. Am. Bd. Ob-Gyn., 1977. Assoc. prof. ob-gyn. U. Tenn., Memphis, 1978—87; prof. ob-gyn. Brown U., Providence, 1987—, assoc. dean, medicine, 1991—. Bd. mem. Alliance CME, Birmingham, Ala., 1997—2003. Maj. USAR, 1975—77, Fort Bragg, NC. Avocations: travel, photography. Office: Women & Infants Hosp 101 Dudley St Providence RI 02905 Office Fax: 401-453-7684. Business E-Mail: psweeney@wihri.org.

SWEENEY, PAUL W., JR., lawyer; BA cum laude, U. So. Calif., 1972; JD, Columbia U., 1975. Bar: D.C. 1975, Calif. 1984. White House Fellow Chief of Staff Asst. to Pres. for Intergovernmental Affairs, Washington, 1979—81; adminstrv. ptnr. & mem. mgmt. com Kirkpatrick & Lockhart Nicholson Graham LLP, LA. Contbr. articles to profl. jours. Bd. dir. Prevent Child Abuse Am., Hollywood Wilshire YMCA, Public Counsel. Mem.: Am. Law Inst. Office: Kirkpatrick & Lockhart Nicholson Graham LLP 7th Fl 10100 Santa Monica Blvd Los Angeles CA 90067-4003 Office Phone: 310-552-5055. Office Fax: 310-552-5001. Business E-Mail: psweeney@klng.com.

SWEENEY, RICHARD EDWARD, biomedical engineer, consultant; BS in Engring., Widener U., Chester, Pa., 1975; PhD in Biomed. Engring., U. Va., Charlottesville, 1980. Vis. lectr. physics Salisbury State Coll., Md., 1983; v.p. sci. and engring. DAKKRO Corp., Denver, 1985—98; adj. asst. prof. Widener U., 1992; pres. RESECO Rsch. Engring. Consultants, Nottingham, Pa., 1998—. Contbr. articles to profl. jours. Mem.: Sigma Xi, Nat. Rsch. Achievements include patents for automated method of identifying and archiving nucleic acid sequences. Avocation: photography. Home: PO Box 554 Nottingham PA 19362 Personal E-mail: reseco@rcn.com.

SWEENEY, SARINA MARIE, psychologist, consultant; b. Chester, Pa., Nov. 20, 1978; d. William T. and Catherine M. Sweeney. BS, St. Joseph's U., Phila., 1997—2001; MA in Counseling Psychology, Immaculata U., 2004. Cert. sch. psychologist Pa., 2004. Therapeutic support staff Pvt., West Chester, Pa., 1999—2003; behavior specialist cons. Chester County Intermediate Unit, Downingtown, Pa., sch. psychologist, 2004—. Mem.: APA, Nat. Assn. Sch. Psychologists, Chi Sigma Iota. Office: Chester County Intermediate Unit 455 East Boot Rd Downingtown PA 19335

SWEENEY, SHAWNA ELIZABETH, political science professor, researcher; b. New Bedford, Mass., Aug. 9, 1967; d. John Brennan and Elizabeth Theresa Sweeney. BA magna cum laude, U. Mass., Dartmouth, 1992; MA, SUNY, Binghamton, 1997, PhD, 2006. Sr. rsch. assoc. Ctr. Policy Analysis, U. Mass. Dartmouth, 1998—; asst. prof. policy studies dept. U. Mass., Dartmouth, 2005—. Guest editl. asst. spl. issue Spill Sci. and Tech. Bull., 2001—02; human rights cons. World Bank, 2003—06; rsch. asst. SUNY Human Rights Data Set funded by NSF and World Bank, Binghamton, NY, 2006—06; ofcl. coord. ann. policy studies lecture series U. Mass., Dartmouth; inaugural affiliate econ. rights working group Human Rights Inst. U. Conn. Grantee, NSF, 2003—06; scholar, SUNY Binghamton, 1993—98. Mem.: Internat. Studies Assn., So. Polit. Sci. Assn., Am. Polit. Sci. Assn. Avocations: travel, animal welfare, photography, kayaking, hiking. Office: U Mass Dartmouth 285 Old Westport Rd Dartmouth MA 02719 Business E-Mail: ssweeney@umassd.edu.

SWEENEY, TIM, computer game developer, programmer; Founder, CEO, chief architect Epic Games (founder originally under name Potamac Computer Games, formally called Epic MegaGames, Inc.), 1991—. Credited to game ZZT, 1991, Onesimus: A Quest for Freedom, 1992, Kiloblaster, 1992, Jill of the Jungle: Jill Saves the Prince, 1992, Jill of the Jungle: Jill Goes Underground, 1992, Jill of the Jungle, 1992, Brix, 1992, Zone 66, 1993, Xargon, 1993, Solar Winds: The Escape, 1993, Traffic Department 2192, 1994, Jazz Jackrabbit, 1994, Unreal Engine, 1995—98, Tyrian, 1995, Extreme Pinball, 1995, Tyrian 2000, 1999, The Wheel of Time, 1999, Unreal Tournament, 1999, Deus Ex, 2000, Deus Ex (Game of Year Edit.), 2001, Unreal Tournament 2003, 2002, Unreal Championship, 2002, Tactical Ops: Assault on Terro, 2002, Unreal II: The Awakening, 2003, Devastation, 2003, Unreal Tournament 2004, 2004, Thief: Deadly Shadows, 2004, Shadow Ops: Red Mercury, 2004, Star Wars: Republic Commando, 2005, Grand Theft Auto: Liberty City Stores, 2005, Brothers in Arms: Road to Hill 30, 2005, Gears of War (Limited Collector's Edit.), 2006. Co-recipient Rave Award-Games, WIRED Mag., 2007. Avocation: exotic sports cars. Office: Epic Games Inc 620 Crossraods Blvd Cary NC 27518-6965

SWEENY, PETER MICHAEL, lawyer, director; b. Boston, Aug. 17, 1947; s. John Sweeny and Marguerite Veronica (Caulfield) Shine; m. Sousan Fakhry Omana Sweeny, Dec. 18, 1981; children: Kaitlin Anne, Lauren Elizabeth, Hannah Sousan, Mora Katherine. BA, Georgetown U., 1971; JD, Seton Hall U., 1974. Bar: Va. 1976, US Dist. Ct. (ea. dist.) Va. 1977, US Ct. Appeals (4th cir.) 1977, DC 1978, US Dist. Ct. DC 1978, US Ct. Appeals (D.C. cir.) 1978, US Supreme Ct. 1979; diplomate Ct. Practice Inst. Staff atty. Occpl. Safety & Health Rev. Commn., Washington, 1974—76; assoc. Ashcraft & Gerel, Alexandria, Va., Washington, 1977—84, ptnr., 1985—86, Thacher, Swiger, Sweeny & Day, Fairfax, Va., 1986—89; pvt. practice, 1989—. Mem.: AAJ, ABA, Loudoun County Bar Assn., Va. State Bar. Democrat. Home: 36552 Innisbrook Cir Purcellville VA 20132-9010 Office Phone: 571-258-0900. Personal E-mail: pmsweeny@mac.com.

SWEERE KOMSTADIUS, LORI, insurance company executive; BA in Orgnl. Behavior and Comm., Concordia Coll.; grad. human resources exec. program, U. Mich. Assoc. A.T. Kearney, Inc., Heidrick & Struggles, Inc.; human resources assoc. The St. Paul Companies, Nat. Computer Systems, Eden Prairie, Minn.; various leadership positions CNA Fin. Corp., Chgo., 2001—04, exec. v.p. human resources, 2004—07; exec. v.p. human capital UnitedHealth Group, Inc., Minnetonka, Minn., 2007—. Chair, pers. com. USO of Ill. Office: United-Health Group Inc 9900 Bren Rd E Minnetonka MN 55343 Office Phone: 952-936-1300. Office Fax: 952-936-1949.*

SWEET, CHAD CREIGHTON, consulting firm executive, former federal official; b. 1969; m. Julie Terese Spellman, Oct. 3, 2004. BA in Polit. Sci., Internat. Rels., East Asian Studies, Columbia U., 1991. Directorate ops. CIA, 1991—93; v.p. Morgan Stanley, 1994—96, Goldman Sachs & Co., 1996—2006; spl. asst. to sec., dep. chief of staff US Dept. Homeland Security, 2006—07, chief of staff, 2006—09; co-founder, mng. prin. The Chertoff Group, Washington, 2009—. Avocations: fishing, hunting, politics.*

SWEET, HARVEY, set and lighting designer; b. Detroit, Oct. 27, 1943; s. Sam and Rose Sweet; m. Susan Perrett, Mar. 16, 1964 (div. Mar. 1975); children: Deborah Anne, Rebecca Lynn, Jason Aaron; m. Patricia Ravn, Sept. 9, 1978 (div. July 1987); m. Peggy Lynn Krueger, May 12, 2007; 1 stepchild, Caitlin M. Dugan. BS, Ea. Mich. U., 1965; MS, U. Wis., 1967, PhD, 1974. Instr. U. ND, Grand Forks, 1967-69; asst. prof. Boise State Coll., Idaho, 1972-73; instr. U. Wis., Madison, 1973-74; prof. of theater arts U. No. Iowa, Cedar Falls, 1974-89; dir. lighting Landmark Entertainment Group, LA and Tokyo, 1989-91; cons. Advanced Tech., Tokyo, 1991; tech. writer Walt Disney Imagineering, Glendale, Calif., 1992; project mgr., sr. designer, sr. estimator, tech. writer Tru Roll, Inc., Glendale, Calif., 1993-99; project mgr. estimator tech. sales LVH Entertainment Sys., Oxnard, Calif., 1999—2002, mgr. theatrical rigging divsn., 2002—03, v.p. rigging systems, 2003—04, v.p. installation sys. and sales, 2004—05; v.p. sales LA Propoint, 2005—09; sr. tech. product mgr. Electronic Theatre Controls, 2009—. Owner, operator Sweet Studios Theatrical Equipment, Cedar Falls, 1981-89; dir. theater tech. and design U. No. Iowa, 1974-89; mem. tech. stds. working group Entertainment Svcs and Tech. Assn., 2002-2004, mem. rigging cert. working group, 2002-2004, mem. fire safety curtain stds. task group, 2003—04, chair, 2004-08, E1.22 Fire Safety Curtain Stds., chair E1.6-1Powered Rigging Stds. Task Group, 2005-. Author: Graphics for the Performing Arts, 1982, Handbook of Scenery, Properties and Lighting I and II, 1988, 2nd edit., 1995, The Complete Book of Drawing for the Theatre, 1995; scenic designer Summer Repretory Theatre, 1988, Timberlake Playhouse, 1988-89; lighting designer, scenic designer, tech. dir. various coll. theatrical prodns., 1964-89; themed lighting designer Sanrio Puroland, Tokyo, 1989, exec. dir. lighting, 1990. Mem. US Inst. for Theatre Tech. (vice commr. 1979-81, commr. 1981-87, mem. graphic stds. bd. 1979-86, chair edn. commn. 1983-88, mem. publs. com. 1986-89, bd. dirs. 1989). Avocations: travel, cooking. Office: Electronic Theatre Controls 3031 Pleasant View Rd Middleton WI 53562 Office Phone: 608-824-5458.

SWEET, MERRILL HENRY, II, retired biology professor; b. Chgo. Heights, Ill., Sept. 5, 1935; m. Sonia E. Stevens, May 15, 2008; children: Lisa Sweet Smith, Merrul H. II, Earl David, Wendy Hardin. BS, U. Conn., Storrs, 1958, PhD, 1963. Prof. emeritus Tex. A&M U., Coll. Station, Conn., 1963—. Rsch. assoc. Nat. Mus. Natural History, Washington, 2009. Contbr. articles to profl. jours. Mem.: NSF (grant 1958—63, 1967—69). Achievements include discovery of seed feeding habits of the rhyparochromidae. Home: 2900 Chaparral Cir Bryan TX 77802 Office: Tex A&M Univ Dept Biology College Station TX 77843 Office Phone: 979-774-5607. Business E-Mail: msweet@bio.tamu.edu.

SWEET, ROBERT MARTEN, urologic surgeon, medical simulation scientist/administrator; b. San Antonio, Tex., Oct. 24, 1969; s. Roger Charles and Gail Juliet Sweet; m. Ania Sweet; 1 child, Cody Benjamin. BS, U. of Wis., Madison, 1996; MD, U. of Minn., Minneapolis, 1997. Diplomate Am. Bd. of Urology, 2005. Urology resident U. of Wash., Seattle, 1997—2003, acting asst. prof., 2003—05; co-founder and med. dir. Red Llama Inc., Seattle, 2003—; asst. prof. urologic surgery U. of Minn., Minneapolis, Minn., 2005—, dir. of med. sch. simulation programs, 2005—. Urology clerkship dir. U. of Minn. Med. Sch., Minneapolis, Minn.; cons. Med. Edn. Technologies Inc., Sarasota, Fla., 2005—, Gyrus/ACMI Corp., Maple Grove, Minn., 2005—; asst. prof. of urology U. of Wash., Seattle, 2005—; co-dir. endourology fellowship U. of Minn. Dept. of Urologic Surgery, Minneapolis, Minn., 2006—, assoc. dir. urology residency program, 2008—. Musician: (blues keyboardist) Late Night Trash; contbr. articles to profl. jours. Founder U. of Minn. SimPORTAL Simulation PeriOperative Resource for Tng. and Learning, Minneapolis, Minn., 2007—09; co-founder Inst. for Surg. and Interventional Simulation, U. of Wash. Recipient, Phi Kappa Phi, 1989, Alpha Omega Alpha, 1997, Warren H. Chapman Resident Rsch. award, U. of Wash. Dept. of Urology, 2000—01, Endourological Soc. Internat. Ann. Essay Contest (3rd Pl.), Endourological Soc., 2001, J. Tate Mason award, NW Urol. Soc., 2001, Pfizer Scholar award for Outstanding Contbn. to Urology, 2002, U. of Wash. Innovators award, U. of Wash., 2004—05, Inventors award, U. of Minn., 2008; grantee Funding for rsch., ACMI, 2000—02, NIH, 2003—05, Transfer Gap Initiative Fund, 2005, DHHS-AHRQ x 2, 2005—09, Inst. for Engring. in Medicine, 2007—09, Minn. Med. Found., 2007—08, Med. Edn. Technologies Inc., 2008—09, Olympus/Gyrus ACMI Corp., 2008—09, Vincent Johnson Breakthrough Fund, U. of Minn., 2009; scholar, Am. Cancer Soc., 1995—96. Fellow: ACS (assoc.; accreditation surveyor); mem.: Minn. Urol. Soc., Soc. for Simulation in Healthcare, Inst. for Engring. and Medicine, Assn. for Surg. Educators, Soc. for U. Urologists, Soc. for Laparoendoscopic Surgeons (chair of urology and simulation coms. 2007—09), Am. Urol. Assn. (laparoscopic and robotic com. mem. 2008—09), Endourological Soc., Soc. of Industry Leaders. Achievements include invention of 3D virtual reality models of the human body and of the genitourinary tract; virtual reality TURP simulator; ultrasound simulator; Co-Founder of the Institute for Surgical and Interventional Simulation, University of Washington; patents pending for Virtual reality modeling; SimPraxis cognitive simulation engine; novel virtual reality collision detection/response. Avocations: swimming, racquet sports, keyboards. Office: Univ of Minnesota Medical Sch 420 Delaware St SE MMB A580 Minneapolis MN 55455 Office Phone: 612-626-3386.

SWEET, WILLIAM, educator, author, administrator; b. Edmonton, Alberta, Can., Apr. 22, 1955; s. William Donald and Joyce Leila (Taylor) S. DEA, U. Sorbonne, Paris, 1987; PhD, U. Ottawa, Can., 1994; DPh, St. Paul U., Can., 1996. Lectr. U. Saskatchewan, Saskatoon, Can., 1980-83, Coll. de l'Outaouais, Hull, Que., Can., 1983-85, U. Ottawa, 1983-85, 87-88, Carleton U., Ottawa, 1989-90; asst. prof. to prof. St. Francis Xavier U., Antigonish, Nova Scotia, Canada, 1990—2007; prof. philosophy. v.p. acad. St. Thomas U., New Brunswick, Canada, 2007—. Sec.-gen. World Union of Cath. Philos. Socs., Washington, 1998—. Author: Idealism and Rights, 1997, Religious Belief: The Contemporary Debate, 2003, Religion, Science and Nonscience, 2003, Responses to the Enlightenment, 2008; editor: Collected Works of Bernard Bosanquet, 1999, God and Argument, 1999, The Bases of Ethics, 2000, Idealism, Metaphysics, and Community, 2001, Philosophy, Culture and Pluralism, 2002, Philosophical Theory and the Universal Declaration of Human Rights, 2003, Bernard Bosanquet: Essays in Philosophy and Social Policy, 1883-1922, 2003, Husserl and Stein, 2003, Approaches to Metaphysics, 2004, The Philosphy of History, 2004, Politics, Ethics and Challenges to Democracy, 2005, Collected Works of A.R. Lord, 2006, Freedom of Religions, 2006, Philosophy of Religion, 2006, Bernard Bosanquet and the Legacy of British Idealism, 2007, Religion and The Challenges of Science, 2007. Chair of senate. St. Francis Xavier U., Antigonish, 1995-96, chair of faculty of arts, 1998-2000, chair univ. faculty, 2001-02, pres. faculty assn. 2002-04; mem. St. Martha's Regional Hosp. Mission Assurance Adv. Coun., 1999-2005; mem. ethics com. Ea. Regional Health Bd., Nova Scotia, 1999-2000; pres. St. Xavier Faculty Assn., 2002-04; mem. Guysborough Antigonish Strait Health Authority, 2002-03. Rsch. grantee Social Scis. and Humanities Rsch. Coun. of Can., 2000—; Dr. S. Radhakrishnan Endowment Lectr., Madras, 2002; Nimishakkavi K. Subbaiah Naidu Endowment lectr. U. Madras, India, 1999, Royal Inst. of Philosophy lectr. U. Wales, Cardiff, 1999; Dharma Endowment lectr., Bangalore, India, 2001; Dr. S. Radhakrishnan Endowment lectr, 2002, Prin. William Miller Meml. Lectr., Madras, India, 2004, Lo Kuang chair philosophy and culture, Taipei, Taiwan, 2004, aquinas Lectr., New Brunswick, 2008. Mem. Can. Jacques Maritain Assn. (pres. 1999-2006), Can. Soc. for Study of Religion (mem. exec. and mem. sec. 1999-2001), Can. Philos. Assn. (bd. dirs. 1997-99, v.p. 2006-07, pres. 2007), Can. Soc. Christian Philosophers (v.p. 1996-99, pres. 2000-02), Istituto Internazionale Jacques Maritain (v.p. 2002—), Internat. Fedn. Philosophy Socs. (steering com. 2003—). Avocations: travel, rock climbing, literature. Office: St Francis Xavier Univ PO Box 5000 Antigonish NS Canada B2G 2W5 Business E-Mail: wsweet@stu.ca.

SWEETBAUM, MARSHALL DAVID, lawyer; b. NYC, May 17, 1925; s. Samuel and Esther Sweetbaum; 1 child, Joel. BA, Queens Coll., NYC, 1948; LLB, Fordham U., NYC, 1951. Bar: N.Y. Assoc. McCarthy McGrath, NYC, 1951—63; pvt. practice law New Hyde Park, NY, 1964—. Editor: Fordham Law Rev., 1949—51. Cpl. US Army, 1943—45. Mem.: ABA, N.Y. County Lawyers Assn., Nassau County Bar Assn., Lions. Home: 121 Terrace Ct Woodbury NY 11797 Office: 3000 Marcus Ave New Hyde Park NY 11042

SWEETENHAM, PAUL, retail executive; With Allders Internat., 1984; area mgr. Burton Group; retail ops. dir. Champion Sports; head retail ops. T.K. Maxx TJX Cos., Inc., 1993—94, planning and distbn. dir. T.K. Maxx, 1994—95, divisional mdse. mgr. T.K. Maxx, 1995—97, sr. mdse. mgr. T.K. Maxx, 1997, asst. v.p. T.K. Maxx, gen. mdse. mgr., v.p. T.K. Maxx, 1998—99, sr. v.p., gen. mdse. mgr. T.K. Maxx, 1999—2000, pres. T.K. Maxx, 2001—06, pres. T.K. Maxx Europe, 2006—07, sr. exec. v.p., group pres. Europe, 2007—. Office: TJX Cos Inc 770 Cochituate Rd Framingham MA 01701 Office Phone: 508-390-1000. Office Fax: 508-390-2091.

SWEETLAND, DALE A., former county official, former dairy farmer; b. Oneida, NY, 1949; m. Susan Sweetland; 2 children. Attended, SUNY, Cobleskill, 1968—69. Lic. property and casualty ins. agent NY. Owner operator Sweetland Farms Dairy Farm, 1967—97; supr. Town of Fabius, 1988—93; legislator, dist. 12 Onondaga County Legislature, NY, 1994—2008, chmn., 2002—08, dir., legis. budget rev., 2008; northeast crop ins. mgr. Fireman's Fund Agribusiness; sr. northeast mktg. agent Crop Growers' Ins. Services. Chair, pub. works and social services com. Onondaga County Legislature, vice-chmn. county facilities, transportation and ways & means coms. Mem. Onondaga County Drug and Alcohol Abuse Commn.; bd. dirs. Leadership Greater Syracuse, Elmcrest Children's Ctr., Syracuse Symphony. Mem.: Pompey Lions Club. Republican. Mailing: 8305 Route 80 Fabius NY 13063

SWEETNAM, JAMES E., automotive executive; BS in Applied Sci. and Engring., US Mil. Acad., West Point, NY; MBA, Harvard U. Various engring. positions Air Products and Chems.; various mgmt. positions Can. Liquid Air; exec. dir. Drivetrains Cummins Engine Co., 1988—89; pres. Cummins Electronics, 1989—93; group mng. dir. Holset Engring. Co. Ltd. subs., v.p. Cummins Engine Co., 1993—97; v.p., gen. mgr. Heavy-Duty Transmission Divsn. of Truck bus. Eaton Corp., Cleve., 1997—2000, ops. v.p. Heavy-Duty Transmission Clutch and Aftermarket Ops. for Truck bus., 2000—01, sr. v.p., pres. Truck Group, 2001—08; pres., CEO Dana Holding Corp., Toledo, 2009—. Bd. dir. Dana Holding Corp., Lubrizol Corp.; trustee Ideastream. Bd. trustees ideastream, Cleve. Office: Dana Holding PO Box 1000 Toledo OH 43697 Office Phone: 419-535-4500. Office Fax: 419-535-4643.*

SWEETSER, MARIE-ODILE GAUNY, retired language educator; b. Verdun, Meuse, France, Dec. 28, 1925; arrived in US, 1949; d. Eugene Auguste and Madeleine (Schwab) Gauny; m. Franklin Pratt, Dec. 17, 1955; 1 child, Caroline Gauny Sweetser. Grad., U. Nancy, France, 1945; MA, Bryn Mawr Coll., Pa., 1950; PhD, U. Pa., Phila., 1956. Instr. Mills Coll., Oakland, Calif., 1957-60; from asst. prof. to assoc. prof. French CUNY, 1960-69; from assoc. prof. to prof. French U. Ill., Chgo., 1969-97, ret., 1997. Adv. bd. Papers on French Seventeenth Century Lit., Paris. Seattle, Tübingen, Germany. Author: Les Conceptions dramatiques de Corneille d'après ses écrits théoriques, 1962, La Dramaturgie de Corneille, 1977, La Fontaine, 1987, Parcours Lafontainien D'Adonis Au Livre XII des Fables, 2004; contbr. articles to profl. jours. Marcelle Pardé scholar, 1949-50, Newberry Libr. Found. fellow, 1980. Mem. Mouvement Corneille (bd. dirs. 1980-1990), Soc. des Amis de la Fontaine (v.p. 1996-2008), Ctr. Internat. Rencontres sur le 17th Siecle (bd. dirs. 1991—). Avocations: music, theater. Home: 311 Hirst Ct Lake Bluff IL 60044-2754

SWENDIMAN, ALAN ROBERT, lawyer; b. Arlington, Va., Apr. 5, 1947; s. Robert Charles and Jessie (Birse) S.; m. Kathleen Shea, Oct. 8, 1977; children: Shelley Christine, Robert Alan. AB in Polit. Sci., U. N.C., 1969; JD, Georgetown U., 1973. Bar: Md. 1973, D.C. 1974, U.S. Dist. Ct. D.C. 1974, U.S. Dist. Ct. Md. 1974, U.S. Ct. Appeals (D.C. cir.) 1974, U.S. Ct. Appeals (4th cir.) 1974, U.S. Supreme Ct. 1980. Law clk. to chief judge US Dist. Ct. Md., 1973-74; ptnr. Jackson & Campbell, P.C., Washington, 1974—92, 1993—2005, 2009—, mng. ptnr., 1989-90; gen. counsel Fed. Labor Rels. Authority, Washington, 1992-93, Gen. Services Adminstrn., Washington, 2005—06; spl. asst. to Pres., dir. adminstrn. office The White House, Washington, 2006—08; gen. counsel US Agy. for Internat. Develop. (USAID), Washington, 2008—09. Edn. appeal bd. US Dept. Edn., 1982—90; gen. counsel Legal Svcs. Corp., Washington, 1983—84; adj. prof. George Mason Law Sch., 1988—91; mem. White House Presdl. Personnel, 1989. Gen. counsel Nat. Capital Cmty. Found.; past chmn. bd. Columbia Lighthouse for the Blind; bd. dirs. Jr. Achievement, Leadership Greater Washington, Providence Hosp. Found.; trustee Goodwill of Greater Washington; bd. dirs. Greater Wash. Bd. Trade. Mem. DC Bar Assn., Md. Bar Assn., Montgomery County Bar Assn., Jud. Conf. DC Cir., U. NC Alumni Assn., Barristers Club, Counsellors Club, DC, Rotary, Phi Beta Kappa, Phi Eta Sigma. Office: Jackson & Campbell PC 1120 20th St NW Ste 300 S Washington DC 20036-3437 Office Phone: 202-457-1600. Business E-Mail: aswendiman@jackscamp.com.*

SWENSEN, CLIFFORD HENRIK, JR., psychologist, educator; b. Welch, W.Va., Nov. 25, 1926; s. Clifford Henrik and Cora Edith (Clovis) S.; m. Doris Ann Gaines, June 6, 1948; children: Betsy, Susan, Lisa, Timothy, Barbara BS, U. Pitts., 1949, MS, 1950, PhD, 1952. Diplomate Am. Bd. Profl. Psychology. Instr. U. Pitts., 1951-52; clin. psychologist VA, 1952-54; from asst. prof. to assoc. prof. U. Tenn., Knoxville, 1954-62; assoc. prof. psychology Purdue U., West Lafayette, Ind., 1962-65, prof., 1965—99, prof. emeritus, 1999—, dir. clin. tng., 1975-85; vice chair U. Senate, 1994-95. Vis. prof. U. Fla., 1968-69, U. Bergen, Norway, 1976-77, 83-84; cons. VA, 1981 White House Conf. on Aging, others; Am. Psychol. Assn.-NSF Disting. Sci. lectr., 1968-69; Fulbright-Hays lectr., Norway, 1976-77 Author: An Approach to Case Conceptualization, 1968; Introduction to Interpersonal Relations, 1973; contbr. chpts. to books, articles to profl. jours. Mem. Ind. Gov.'s Task Force Alzheimer's Disease and Related Senile Dementia, 1998—; bd. dirs. Ind. Assn. Homes and Svcs. Aging, 2007-. Served with USN, 1944-46 Recipient Gordon A. Barrows Meml. award for disting. contributions to psychology, 1990; named to Hall of Fame, Brentwood Pa. H.S., 2001. Fellow APA (pres divsn. cons. psychology 1976-77, Presdl. citation 1999, Cert. achievement 2000), Assn. for Psychol. Sci., Soc. Personality Assessment, Am. Assn. Applied and Preventive Psychology, Acad. Clin. Psychology; mem. Midwestern Psychol. Assn., Southeastern Psychol. Assn., Ind. Psychol. Assn., Gerontol. Soc., Sigma Xi, Psi Chi. Republican. Mem. Ch. of Christ Home: 1700 Lindberg Rd 229 West Lafayette IN 47906 Office: Purdue U Dept Psychol Scis West Lafayette IN 47907 Office Phone: 765-494-6977. Business E-Mail: cswensen@psych.purdue.edu.

SWENSEN, DAVID FREDERICK, investment advisor; b. River Falls, Wis., Jan. 26, 1954; s. Richard David and Grace Marie (Hartman) Swensen; m. Susan Candler Foster, June 26, 1982 (div.); children: Tory, Alex, Tim. BA, BS, U. Wis., River Falls, 1975; MA, Yale U., 1976, M in Philos., 1978, PhD in Econs., 1980. Assoc. Salomon Bros., NYC, 1979-82; sr. v.p. Lehman Bros., NYC, 1982-85; chief investment officer Yale U., New Haven, 1985—; adj. prof. investment strategy, lectr. econs. Yale Coll., Yale Sch. Mgmt., 1985—. Bd. dirs. Endowment Advs. Inc., Endowment Realty Investors Inc.; trustee Carnegie Inst. Wash., 1991—; bd. mem., treas. Hopkins Sch. Com. Trustees Inc., 1998—; mem. investment com. Yale New Haven Hosp., 2000—, Courtauld Inst. Art, 2002—; trustee Brookings Inst., Washington, 2004; fellow Berkeley Coll., Yale U. Internat. Ctr. Fin.; mem. President's Econ. Recovery Advisory Bd., 2009—. Author: Pioneering Portfolio Management: An Unconventional Approach to Institutional Investment, 2000, Unconventional Success: A Fundamental Approach to Personal Investment, 2005. Fellow: Am. Acad. Arts & Scis.; mem.: Tchrs. Ins. & Annuity Assn. of America (trustee 2003—), Am. Fin. Assn., Am. Econ. Assn., Yale U. Elizabethan Club. Avocations: squash, tennis, skiing, bicycling. Office: Yale Sch Mgmt Box 208200 135 Prospect St New Haven CT 06520-8200 E-mail: swen@invsmtp.invest.yale.edu.*

SWENSON, ADA PEREZ, artist; m. Roy Swenson, Oct. 30, 1994; children: Miguel Weissman, Wendy Robin Weissman. Student, Stony Brook U., 1965—66, Indian River C.C., 2002—05, Art Student League, 1951—54; studied with, Richard Cardoff, 1965—68, John Seerey Lester, 2004. Coord. art exhibits Indian River County Main Libr., Vero Beach, 2004—. Art coord. Cultural Coun. Indian River, 2007; artist-in-residence Everglade Nat. Park, 2005—07. One-woman shows include Bahia Redonda Resort and Marina, Venezuela, 1999, Port de Plaisance, St. Maarten, Netherlands, 1999, Harbor Village, Bonaire, Netherlands, 1999, Vero Beach Main Libr., Fla., 2002—06, Count Down Studio, N.Y.C., 2000—06, 2006, Everglades Nat. Park Mus., Homestead, Fla., 2005, exhibitions include Vero Beach Mus., Vero Beach Main Libr., 2001—04, 2005, 2006, Meghan Candler Gallery, Vero Beach, 2004, 2005, 2006, Arte Direct Galley, Naples, Fla., 2004—06, Everglades Nat. Park Visitors Ctr. Mus., 2005—06, Represented in permanent collections U. Fla. Rsch. Ctr., Ft. Pierce, S.C. State Park, Dillon, Littman Jewelers, Bonaire, Count Down Studio, Everglades Nat. Park; art coord. for cultural coun. Indian River Main Libr., Vero Beach, 2006, Jr. League Indian River. Recipient Scholastic Art award, Pratt U., 1948, awards, AE Backus Mus., Ft. Pierce, 2002, Ctr. for the Arts, Vero Beach, 2002, Everglades Nat. Park, 2004. Mem.: Vero Beach Art Club, Nat. Acad. Profl. Plein Air Painters, Am. Impressionist Soc., Plein Air Painters of East Coast, Fla. Watercolor Soc. Home: 256 Marina Dr Fort Pierce FL 34949 Office Phone: 772-595-3158. Personal E-mail: adaswenson@comcast.net.

SWENSON, CONSTANCE RAE, lawyer; d. Albin Linus Peterson and Lillian; m. Keith Howard Swenson, June 20, 1970; children: Jeffrey, Melissa, Stacy, Justin. BA in Zoology, Rockford Coll., Ill., 1968; BA in French with honors, Portland State U., 1996; diploma in Law Studies, East China Sch. Law and Politics, Shanghai, 1988; diploma in Spanish, El Centro Idiomas y Estudios, Mex., 1993; cert. in Environ. and Natural Resources Law, Northwestern Sch. Law, Portland, 1990. Bar: Oreg. 1991, Esquire Dist.: Oreg. 1991, atty., counselor: US Ct. Appeals (4th cir.) 2001. Librarian asst. Rockford Pub. Libr., Ill., 1968—69; law internship internat. banking Crédit de Nord, Paris, 1989; atty. Connie Swenson, Atty., Portland, Oreg., 1991—93, 2000—; art dept. asst. Portland State U. Bookstore, 1993—96, 1997; realtor Century 21, Gresham, Oreg., 1997; student asst. to adminstr. Portland State U., Oreg., 1997—98, Client Security Fund Com. Oregon State Bar. Hearings officer Multnomah Animal Ctrl., 2003—. Adv. council U. Oreg., Eugene, 2003—; arbitrator Better Bus. Bur., Portland, 2006—. Recipient Advocate award, 2005. Mem.: Multnomah Bar Assn. Mem. Evangelical Covenant Ch. Avocations: ice skating, hiking, travel. Office: Connie Swenson Atty 465 NE 181 Ave #149 Portland OR 97230 Office Phone: 503-997-9477. Business E-Mail: swenson997@mail.com.

SWENSON, CYNTHIA CUPIT, psychologist, educator; d. Joseph E. and Bobbie D. Cupit. PhD, Fla. State U., Tallahassee, 1991. Psychologist Dozier Sch. Boys, Marianna, Fla., 1988—90; assoc. prof. Med. U. SC, Charleston, 1993—. Assoc. dir. Family Services Rsch. Ctr., Charleston, 2005—. Dir.: (djole) Children's West African Dance Company. Founding bd. mem. Gethsemani Cir. Friends, North Charleston, SC, 2004—09; co-dir. Project OKURASE, Okurase, Ghana, 2006—09. Grant, Nat. Inst. Mental Health, 2000—06. Mem.: Internat. Soc. Prevention Child Abuse and Neglect. Achievements include development of a treatment model for families where child abuse and neglect have occurred. Office: Med Univ SC 67 President St Ste MC406 Charleston SC 29425 Business E-Mail: swensocc@musc.edu.

SWENSON, GABRIEL J., biology professor; b. Augusta, Ga., Apr. 22, 1978; m. Summer Seklecki Swenson. MS in Applied & Environ. Microbiology, Ga. State U., Atlanta, 2006; attending, U. SC., 2009—. Biology prof. Paine Coll., Augusta, 2006—. Office: Paine Coll 1235 15th St Augusta GA 30901

SWENSON, GEORGE WARNER, JR., engineering educator; b. Mpls., Sept. 22, 1922; s. George Warner and Vernie (Larson) Swenson; m. Virginia Laura Savard, June 26, 1943 (div. 1970); children: George Warner III, Vernie Laura, Julie Loretta, Donna Joan; m. Joy Janice Locke, July 2, 1971. BS, Mich. Coll. Mining and Tech., Houghton, 1944, E.E., 1950; MS, MIT, Cambridge, 1948; PhD, U. Wis., Madison, 1951. Asso. prof. elec. engring. Washington U., St. Louis, 1952-53; prof. U. Alaska, 1953-54; asso. prof. Mich. State U., 1954-56; faculty U. Ill., Urbana, 1956—, prof. elec. engring. and astronomy, 1958-88, prof. emeritus, 1988—, acting head dept. astronomy, 1970-72, head dept. elec.

and computer engring., 1979-85. Dir. Vermilion River Obs., 1968-81; vis. scientist Nat. Radio Astronomy Obs., 1964-68; cons. to govt. agys. and other sci. bodies; resident cons. US Army Constrn. Engring. Rsch. Lab., 1988--; adj. prof. elec. engring. Mich. Technol. U., 1996—. Author: Principles of Modern Acoustics, 1953, An Amateur Radio Telescope, 1980; co-author: Interferometry and Synthesis in Radio Astronomy, 1986, 2d edit., 2001, also Russian edits.; contbr. articles to profl. jours. 1st lt. signal corps US Army, WWII. Recipient citation for disting. service to engring. U. Wis., 1984; Guggenheim fellow, 1984-85 Fellow IEEE, AAAS; mem. NAE, Am. Astron. Soc., Internat. Sci. Radio Union (U.S. nat. com. 1965-67, 80-82), Internat. Astron. Union, Inst. Noise Control Engring. (cert.), Sigma Xi, Eta Kappa Nu, Tau Beta Pi, Phi Kappa Phi. Achievements include chairing conceptual design group which produced the concept/proposal for the Very Large Array of National Radio Astronomy Observatory; designed and built two large innovative radio telescopes for the University of Illinois. Home: 1107 Kenwood Rd Champaign IL 61821-4718 Office: U Ill 328 CSL 1308 W Main St Urbana IL 61801-2307 Office Phone: 217-333-4498.

SWENSON, PATRICIA J., literature and language professor; d. Oscar C. and Marie F. Swenson; m. Steven P. Brilliant, June 22, 1991. BA, Loyola Marymount U., LA, 1984; MA, Calif. State U., Northridge, 1993; MFA, Goddard Coll., Plainfield, Vt., 1996. Coord. Calif. State U., 1991—2001, prof., 1991—, webmaster, 2000—, amb., Ctr. Excellence Learning & Tchg., 2000—02, lectr. rep., dept. English ednl. tech. com., 2008—. Editl. bd. mem. New Voices. Contbr. articles to profl. jours. U. Online Instrnl. Design grant, Calif. State U., 1997—2008, Judge Julian Beck Instrnl. Devel. grant, 1997, 1999, 2002, GTE Online Composition grant, 1999—2001, Office Online Instrn. Course Re-Design grant, 2007. Office: Calif State Univ Northridge 18111 Nordhoff St Northridge CA 91330 Business E-Mail: pat.swenson@csun.edu.

SWENSON, SARA, librarian, educator; d. Jon and Julene Swenson; m. Claude Sigmund. BA, St. Olaf Coll., Northfield, Minn., 1993; MLIS, St. Catherine U., St. Paul, 1994. Cert. tchr. Nat. Bd. Profl. Tchg. Standards, 2003. Libr. Edina Pub. Schs., Edina, Minn., 1998—; reference libr. Minn. Hist. Soc., St. Paul, 1998—; adj. faculty Cardinal Stritch U., Milw., 2003—, Hamline U., St. Paul, 2006.

SWENSSON, EARL SIMCOX, architect; b. Nashville, July 28, 1930; s. Earl Ebenezer and Viola Lazelle (Simcox) Swensson; m. Suzanne Dickenson, June 6, 1953; children: Krista, Lin, Kurt. BS in Bldg. Design, Va. Poly. Inst. and State U., 1952, MSArch, 1953, U. Ill., 1955. Registered 28 states. Founder, prin. Earl Swensson Assocs., Inc., Nashville, 1961—. Adj. prof. Va. Poly. Inst. and State U., Blacksburg, 1971—72, Auburn U., 1976—83; lectr. in field; apptd. chairholder Jennings and Rebecca Jones Chair of Excellence in Urban and Regional Planning, Mid. Tenn. State U., 1999—2008. Contbr. articles to profl. jours.; author (with Richard L. Miller): (books) New Directions in Hospital and Healthcare Facility Design, 1995; author: Hospital and Healthcare Facility Design 2d edit., 2002, A Passion for Design: Human-Centered Architecture and Synergenial Practice, 2008. Mem. arch. program adv. coun. Auburn U., 1990—94; bd. dirs. Metro Arts Commn., 1979—86; Middle Tenn. Health Systems (pres. 1972) AIA, 1984—; bd. advisors U. Tenn. Sch. Arch., 1982, chmn., 1985—88. Recipient Jefferson award, Am. Inst. Pub. Svc. (Nashville chpt.), 1985, Hall Fame, Nashville Alliance Pub. Edn., 2008; named Outstanding Nashvillian of Yr., Downtown Kiwanis Club, 1992, One of Top 100 Alumni of Greatest Distinction Throughout 128-yr. History, Va. Poly. Inst. and State U., 2001. Presbyterian. Achievements include patents for systamodule for pharmacies. Office: Earl Swensson Assocs 2100 W End Ave Ste 1200 Nashville TN 37203-5239 Office Phone: 615-329-9445.

SWERDLOFF, RONALD S., physician, educator, researcher; b. Pomona, Calif., Feb. 18, 1938; s. Julius Lewis and Eva (Kelman) S.; m. Christina Wang; children: Jonathan Nicolai, Peter Loren, Paul Im, Michael Im. BS, U. Calif., 1959, MD, 1962. Diplomate Am. Bd. Internal Medicine, Am. Bd. Endocrinology. Intern U. Wash., Seattle, 1962-63, resident, 1963-64; rsch. assoc. NIH, Bethesda, Md., 1964-66; resident UCLA Sch. Medicine, 1966-67; rsch. fellow Harbor-UCLA Med. Ctr., Torrance, Calif., 1967-69, asst. prof., 1969-72, assoc. prof. divsn. Endocrinology, 1972-78, chief divsn. Endocrinology, 1973—, prof., 1978—, assoc. chair dept. medicine, 1997—; dir. UCLA Population Rsch. Ctr., Torrance, 1986-92, Mellon Found. Ctr. in Reproductive Medicine, 1997—. Dir. WHO Collaborating Ctr. Reproduction, Torrance, NIH Contraceptive Clin. Trials Ctr., 2005—, Torrance; cons. WHO Geneva, 1982-90, NIH, Bethesda, 1982—, UN Fertility Planning Assn., Geneva, 1983—, Am. Bd. Internal Medicine, Phila., 1989—; inaugural lectr. Australian Soc. Reproductive Biology, Perth, 1990; mem. tech. adv. com. Contraceptive R & D Agy. (CONRAD, AID), 1992—. Editor: 3 books; contbr. chapters to books 100, articles 250 to profl. jours. Bd. dirs., vice chair Harbor-UCLA Rsch. and Edn. Inst; bd. dirs. Scaplanes Corp. Recipient Sherman Mellinkoff award, UCLA, 1998. Fellow: ACP; mem.: We. Soc. Clin. Rsch. (pres. 1983—84, Sherman Mellinkoff award UCLA, Mayo Soley award 2000), Endocrinology Soc., Pacific Coast Fertility (pres. 1984, Outstanding Rsch. award 1976, 1984, Wyeth award 1984, Squibb award), Am. Soc. Clin. Rsch. (pres. we. sect. 1972—73), Am. Assn. Physicians, Am. Soc. Andrology (pres. 1992—93, Serono award 1986, Disting. Andrologist award 2004). Office: Harbor UCLA Med Ctr Divsn Endocrinology 1000 W Carson St Torrance CA 90502-2004 Office Phone: 310-222-1867. Business E-Mail: swerdloff@labiomed.org.

SWERDLOW, MARTIN ABRAHAM, retired pathologist, educator; b. Chgo., July 7, 1923; s. Sol Hyman and Rose (Lasky) Swerdlow; m. Marion Levin, May 19, 1945; children: Steven Howard, Gary Bruce. Student, Herzl Jr. Coll., 1941—42; BS, U. Ill., 1945; MD, U. Ill., Chgo., 1947. Diplomate Am Bd Pathology. Intern Michael Reese Hosp. and Med. Center, Chgo., 1947-48, resident, 1948-50, 51-52, mem. staff, 1974—2008, chmn. dept. pathology, v.p. acad. affairs, 1974-90; pathologist Menorah Med Ctr, Kansas City, Mo., 1954—57. Asst prof, pathologist Univ Ill Col Med, Chicago, 1957—59, assoc prof, 1959—60, clin prof, 1960—64, prof, pathologist, 1966—72, assoc dean, prof pathology, 1970—72; prof pathology, chmn Univ Mo, Kansas City, 1972—74; prof pathology Univ Chicago, 1975—89, Geever prof, head pathology emeritus, 1993—; mem comt standards Chicago Health Sys Agency, 1976—. With MC US Army, 1944—45. Recipient Alumnus of the Yr Award, Univ Ill Col Med, 1973, Instructorship Award, Univ Ill, 1960, 1965, 1968, 1971, 1972. Mem.: Inst. of Medicine, Am. Soc. Dermatopathology, Internat. Acad. Pathology, Coll. Am. Pathologists, Am. Soc. Clin. Pathologists, Chgo. Pathology Soc. (pres 1980—). Jewish. Business E-Mail: maswerdl@uic.edu. *My credo these years has been to care about patients, students, colleagues, employees, my institution and the many publics I serve. Honesty and thoroughness has been a basic life style, irrespective of the cost. With all, competence is a necessity and ongoing. Continuous responsibility for my education and learning is my way of living.*

SWETMAN, GLENN ROBERT, literature and language professor, poet; b. May 20, 1936; s. Glenn Lyle and June (Read) S.; m. Margarita Ortiz, Feb. 8, 1964 (div. 1979); children: Margarita June, Glenn Lyle Maximilian, Glenda Louise. BS, U. So. Miss., 1957, MA, 1959; PhD, Tulane U., 1966. Instr. U. So. Miss., 1957-58, asst. prof., 1964-66; instr. Ark. State U., 1958-59, McNeese U., 1959-61; instr. English Univ. Coll. Tulane U., 1961-64, spl. asst. dept. elec. engring., 1961-64; assoc. prof. La. Inst. Tech., 1966-67; prof., head dept. langs. Nicholls State Coll., Thibodaux, La., 1967-69, head dept. English, 1969-71, prof., 1971-91; prof. emeritus William Carey Coll., Gulfport, Miss., 1991—. Writer in residence, prof. English William Carey Coll., Gulfport, 1991—; ptnr. Breeland Pl., Biloxi, 1960—; stringer, corr. Shreveport Times, La., 1966—; ptnr. Ormuba, Inc., 1975—; cons. tech. writing Union Carbide Corp., Am. Fedn. Tchrs. State v.p. Nat. Com. to Resist Attacks on Tenure, 1974—. Book reviewer Jackson State Times, Miss., 1961; contbr. poetry to various publs. including Poet, Prairie Schooner, Trace, Ball State U. Forum, Film Quar., Poetry Australia, numerous others worldwide; author: (books of poems) Tunel de Amor, 1973, Deka #1, 1973, Deka #2, 1979, Shards, 1979, Concerning Carpenters, 1980, Son of Igor, 1982, Poems of the Fantastic, 1990, Oh What Tangled Web, 2007, Deka 3, 2008, Naked Chains of Haiku Sentyu, 2009, Aaron of the Night High Island, 2009, Biloxi:A Bankers Pay Book, 2nd edit., 2009, History of the People's Bark of Biloxi, 2009; contbr. numerous articles to encys.; cons. editor (poetry) Paon Press, 1974—, Scott-Foresman, 1975; mem. editl. bd. Scholar and Educator, 1980—. Subdivsn. coord. Rep. Party, Hattiesburg, Miss., 1964. With AUS, 1957. Recipient Poetry awards KQUE Haiku contest, 1964, Coll. Arts contest, LA, 1966, Black Ship Festival, Yoqosuka, Japan, 1967, Green World Brief Forms award Green World Poetry Editors, 1965. Mem. MLA, S. Cen. MLA, So. Literary Festival Assn. (v.p. 1975-76, 82-83, pres. 1984-85), Coll. Writers Soc. La. (pres. 1971-72, exec. dir. 1983—), IEEE, Am. Assn. Engring. Edn., La. Poetry Soc. (pres. 1971-74, 86—), Internat. Boswellian Inst., Nat. Fedn. State Poetry Socs. (2d v.p., nat. membership chmn. 1972-74, pres. 1976-77), Nat. Soc. Scholars and Educators (bd. dirs. 1982—, sec. exec. bd. 1986—, sec. bd. dirs. 1968—, sec. soc. 1989—, exec. edn. 2001-), Am. Fedn. Tchrs. (chpt. pres. 1973-78), Nat. Fedn. State Poetry Socs. (1st v.p. 1975-76, exec. bd. 1972—), Phi Eta Sigma, Omicron Delta Kappa. Home: PO Box 146 Biloxi MS 39533-0146 Office: William Carey Coll 1856 Beach Dr Gulfport MS 39507-1508

SWETNAM, MICHAEL S., think-tank executive; b. Espanola, N.Mex., Aug. 18, 1952; s. Fred R. and Grace M. (Thompson) S.; m. Karen T. Swetnam, June 15, 1971; children: Kelly M., Kevin M.; 1 foster child, Gerry Wild. BSEE, U. Okla., 1979. Program mgr. Nat. Security Agy., Ft. Meade, Md., 1980-83; R&D mgr. RAF Edzell, Scotland, 1983-86; dir. ctrl. intelligence staff CIA, Washington, 1986-90; mgr. strategic investments GTE Corp., Rockville, Md., 1990-92, dir. info. sys., 1992-94; co-founder Potomac Inst. for Policy Studies, Washington, 1994, chmn., 1994—; v.p. Pacific-Sierra Rsch. Corp. Spl. cons. Pres.' Fgn. Intelligence Adv. Bd., Washington, 1990—92; mem. Tech. Adv. Group to US Senate Spl. Select Com. on Intelligence, Washington; bd. dirs. Space and Defense Sys. Inc., Gov. Bd. of Potomac Inst. of New Zealand, Dragon Hawk Entertainment Inc. Co-editor: Cyber Terrorism and Information Warfare: Threats and Responses, 1999; co-author: ETA: Profile of a Terrorist Group, 2001, Usama bin Laden's al-Qaida: Profile of a Terrorist Network, 2001; contbr. articles to profl. jours. Bd. dirs. Boy Scouts UK, Scotland, 1982-83; No. UK Scout Master, 1984-85; mem. Canyon (N.Mex.) Sch. Bd., 1970; pres. Pershinghill PTA, Ft. Meade, 1982-83, Cockroaches, Washington, 1992-95, Corp. Vol. Coun., Montgomery, Md., 1992-94; candidate from 5th dist. Md. for U.S. Ho. of Reps., Bowie, 1992; chmn. P.G. County Tax Referendun, Bowie, 1992. Comdr. USN, 1972-90. Recipient Presdl. Unit citation Naval Rsch. Lab., 1991. Mem.: Term Limits Referendum Com. (chmn. 1992—93), Armed Forces Comms. and Electronics Assn., Security Affair Svc. Assn., Md. Bus. Roundtable (pres. 1993), Montgomery County Corp. Vol. Coun. (pres. 1993), Montgomery County Corp. Partnership for Managerial Excellence (pres. 1993), Old Crows. Republican. Roman Catholic. Achievements include invention of of glucose tape tester. Office: Potomac Inst for Policy Studies 901 N Stuart St, Ste 200 Arlington VA 22203 Office Phone: 703-525-0770. Office Fax: 703-525-0299.

SWETS, JOHN ARTHUR, psychologist, researcher; b. Grand Rapids, Mich., June 19, 1928; s. John A. and Sara Henrietta (Heyns) Swets; m. Maxine Ruth Crawford, July 16, 1949; children: Stephen Arthur, Joel Brian. BA, U. Mich., 1950, MA, 1953, PhD, 1954. Instr. psychology U. Mich., Ann Arbor, 1954—56; asst. prof. psychology MIT, Cambridge, 1956—60, assoc. prof. psychology, 1960—63; v.p. Bolt Beranek & Newman Inc., 1964—69, sr. v.p., 1969—74, gen. mgr. rsch., devel. and cons., dir., 1971—74; chief scientist BBN Labs., 1975—98, chief scientist emeritus, 1998—; sr. rsch. assoc. dept. radiology Brigham and Women's Hosp., 1997—. Lectr. dept. clin. epidemiology Harvard Med. Sch., 1985—88, dept. health care policy, 1988—; mem. corp. Edn. Devel. Ctr., Newton, Mass., 1971—75; Regent's prof. U. Calif., 1969; advisor vision com., com. on hearing and bioacoustics NAS-NRC, 1960—96; mem. Commn. on Behavioral Social Scis. and Edn., NRC, 1988—92, vice chair, 1992—93, chmn., 1993—96; ex-officio mem. governing bd. NRC, 1994—96, mem. various coms., 1960—. Author: Signal Detection Theory and ROC Analysis in Psychology and Diagnostics, 1996; co-author (with D.M. Green): Signal Detection Theory and Psychophysics, 1966; co-author: (with R.M. Pickett) Evaluation of Diagnostic Systems: Methods From Signal Detection Theory, 1982; editor: Signal Detection and Recognition by Human Observers, 1964; editor: (with L.L. Elliott) Psychology and the Handicapped Child, 1974; editor: (with D. Druckman) Enhancing Human Performance, 1988; mem. editl. bd. Med. Decision Making, 1980—85, Psychol. Sci., 1989—94, 1999—2002, Psychol. Rev., 1995—97, Jour. Exptl. Psychology: Applied, 1995—97, Human Factors, 1997—2001; contbr. articles to profl. jours. Mem. bd. dirs. German-Am. Rsch. Coun. Found., 1999—2001; mem. corp. Winchester Hosp., Mass., 1981—84. Fellow vis. rsch. fellow, Philips Labs., The Netherlands, 1958. Fellow: APA (Disting. Sci. Contbn. award 1990), AAAS (coun. 1986—89), Am. Psychol. Soc., Soc. Exptl. Psychologists (chmn. 1986, exec. com. 1986—89, Howard Crosby Warren medal 1985), Am. Acad. Arts and Scis., Acoustical Soc. Am. (exec. coun. 1968—71); mem.: NAS (chmn., Troland award com. 1991, chair psychology sect. 1998—2001, nominating com. 2001), Soc. Math. Psychology, Psychometric Soc., Psychonomic Soc., Tequesta Country Club, Sigma Alpha Epsilon, Sigma Xi. Congregationalist (Moderator). Home: 10411 SE Terrapin Pl 103-C Tequesta FL 33469-1827 E-mail: swets@bbn.com.

SWETT, RICHARD NELSON (DICK), former ambassador, former congressman; b. Bryn Mawr, Pa., May 1, 1957; s. Philip Eugene Sr. and Ann (Parkhurst) S.; m. Yvonne Katrina Lantos, Aug. 29, 1980; children: Chelsea, Sebastian, Keaton, Chanteclaire, Kismet, Atticus, Sunday. BA in Architecture, Yale U., 1979. Lic. contractor, Calif.; lic. architect, Calif., N.H. Arch. Skidmore Owings & Merrill, San Francisco, 1979-82; pres. Bastion Group, Inc., San Mateo, Calif., 1982-87; project mgr. Grosvenor Properties, San Francisco, 1986-87; pres. Veritas Group Inc., Gilford, NH, 1987-90; mem. US Congress from 2nd N.H. Dist., Washington, 1991—95, mem. pub. works and transp. com., 1991-95, mem. sci., space, and tech. com., 1991-95, mem. select com. on aging, 1991-95; US amb. to Denmark US Dept. State, Copenhagen, 1998-2001; pres. Swett Assocs., Bow, NH, 2001—; sr. counselor APCO Worldwide, 2001—. State chmn. U.S. Olympic Com., 1992—98; founding mem. adv. bd. European Ctr. of Calif., 2001—06; mem. U.S. Govt. Gen. Svcs. Adminstrn. Archtl. Peer Rev. Bd., 2000—; bd. dirs. AeroSat Corp., Amherst, NH, 2001—. Author: Leadership by Design: Creating an Architecture of Trust; contbg. author: A Nation Reconstructed. Bd. advisors Hans Christian Andersen Found., Denmark, 2001—, Architects for Humanity, NYC, 2001—, Abildsø Found., Oslo, 2002—, Project for Pub. Spaces, NYC, 2003—. Presented 1st Comdr. Order of Danabrog, Queen Margrethe II of Denmark, 2001; named as one of Top Ten Outstanding Young Ams., U.S. Jr. C. of C., 1993. Fellow AIA, Design Futures Coun. (sr.); mem. Nat. Hist. Preeservation Soc., Ind. Power Producers N.H. Assn., Yale Club N.H., Sierra Club, Winnipesaukee Yacht Club. Democrat. Avocations: athletics, piano, art, sailing. Home Phone: 603-774-0314; Office Phone: 603-774-1072. Business E-Mail: rnswett@swettassociates.com. E-mail: info@swettassociates.com.

SWETT, STEPHEN FREDERICK, JR., artist, educator; b. Englewood, NJ, Sept. 14, 1935; s. Stephen Frederick and Frances (Gulotta) S.; m. Annette Palazzolo, Nov. 18, 1961; children: Susan, Kimberly Ann, Stephen Laurence. BA, Montclair State Coll., 1959, MA, 1965; EdD in Ednl. Adminstrn., Rutgers U., 1976; grad., North Light Art Sch., 1995. Tchr. Long Branch (N.J.) H.S., 1961-62, Roselle Park (N.J.) H.S., 1962-73; rsch. asst. Rutgers U., New Brunswick, NJ, 1973-74; instrnl. supr. Elmwood Park (N.J.) Schs., 1974-76, Morris Hills Regional Schs., Denville, NJ, 1976-77; asst. prin. Lawrence H.S., Lawrenceville, NJ, 1977-79; prin. Stafford Intermediate Sch., Manahawkin, NJ, 1979-94; recreation and art cons., 1994—. Participant NSF Inst. in physics, chemistry and math. Seton Hall U., 1964, Newark Coll. Engring., 1965, Stevens Inst. Tech., summers 1966-68; rschr. sch. fin. Exhibited in group shows at Sheldon Meml. Art Gallery, 1998, Period Gallery, Omaha, 1998, 99, Montserrat Gallery, N.Y.C., 2000, The Looking Glass Art Gallery, Hawley, Pa., 2000, Annette Howell Turner Ctr. for the Arts, Valdosta, Ga., 2004, Schacknow Mus. Fine Arts, Plantation, Fla., 2005, 06. With US Army, 1959—61. Mem. Roselle Park Edn. Assn. (pres. 1971-73), Nat. Soc. Study Edn., Am. Assn. Physics Tchrs., Am. Inst. Physics, Am. Assn. Sch. Adminstrs., N.J. Assn. Sch. Adminstrs., Nat. Assn. Elem. and Mid. Sch. Adminstrs., Phi Delta Kappa (sec. Rutgers chpt. 1977-80, v.p. 1980-82, pres. 1983-84). Home: 306 Tenth Ave Belmar NJ 07719-2313

SWHIER, CLAUDIA VERSFELT, lawyer; b. Mineola, NY, Jan. 15, 1950; d. William Holly and Ruth (Gerland) Versfelt; children: James Robert, Jeffrey William. BA in Philosophy magna cum laude, Yale U., 1972; JD cum laude, Harvard U., 1975. Bar: Ind. 1975. Assoc. Barnes & Thornburg, Indpls., 1975-82, ptnr., 1982—. Mem. ABA, Ind. Bar Assn., Indpls. Bar Assn. Republican. Presbyterian. Avocations: skiing, swimming, aerobics. Office: Barnes & Thornburg 11 S Meridian St Indianapolis IN 46204 Office Fax: 317-231-7433. Business E-Mail: cswhier@btlaw.com.

SWIATEK, KAZIMIERZ CARDINAL, cardinal, archbishop emeritus; b. Walga, Oct. 21, 1914; Attended, Diocesan Seminary of Pinsk, Belarus. Ordained priest Diocese of Pinsk, Belarus, 1939, parochial vicar, 1939—44, parish priest, 1954—89, vicar gen., 1989—91, apostolic adminstr., 1991—2006; imprisoned by KGB, 1941, 1944—54; ordained bishop, 1991; archbishop Archdiocese of Minsk-Mohilev, Belarus, 1991—2006, archbishop emeritus, 2006—; elevated to cardinal, 1994; cardinal-priest S. Gerardo Maiella, 1994—. Pres. Cath. Bishops Conf. of Belarus, 1999—2006. Recipient Fidei Testis award, Pope John Paul II, 2004. Roman Catholic. also: Pl Swobody 9 220030 Minsk Belarus

SWIATYCKI, GERSHON See BARNETT, GARY

SWIBEL, STEVEN WARREN, lawyer; b. Chgo., July 18, 1946; s. Morris Howard and Gloria Swibel; m. Leslie Swibel; children: Deborah, Laura. BS, MIT, 1968; JD, Harvard U., 1971. Bar: Ill. 1971, U.S. Dist. Ct. (no. dist.) Ill. 1971, U.S. Tax Ct. 1973, U.S. Ct. Appeals (7th cir.) 1981. Assoc. Sonnenschein Carlin Nath & Rosenthal, Chgo., 1971-78, ptnr., 1978-84, Rudnick & Wolfe, 1984-93, Schwartz, Cooper, Chartered, Chgo., 1993—2008, Dykema Gossett PLLC, Chgo., 2008—. Adj. prof. taxation Ill. Inst. Tech. Kent Coll. Law, Chgo., 1989—2001; lectr. in field. Contbr. articles to profl. jours. Ednl. counselor MIT, 1979—; bd. dirs. MIT Alumni Fund, 1992—95, MIT Enterprise Forum, Chgo., 2002—08, Kids in Danger, 1998—, Ragdale Found., 1987—2000, treas., 1987—92. Recipient Lobdell Disting. Svc. award, MIT Alumni Assn., 1989. Mem.: ABA (com. partnerships sect. taxation), Chgo. Bar Assn. (mem. exec. subcom. 1984—2004, chmn. subcom. real estate and partnerships 1986—87, vice-chmn. 1988—89, chmn. 1990, mem. fed. taxation com.), Ill. Bar Assn., MIT Club (sec. 1980—87, dir. Chgo. chpt. 1980—91, pres. 1987—89, dir. Chgo. chpt. 1996—), Met. Club, Sigma Xi, Eta Kappa Nu, Tau Beta Pi. Office: Dykema Gossett PLLC 10 S Wacker Dr Ste 2300 Chicago IL 60606 Office Phone: 312-627-5676. Business E-Mail: sswibel@dykema.com.

SWIBINSKI, EDWARD THOMAS, internist, endocrinologist, educator; b. Jersey City, Jan. 26, 1950; s. Stanley Adolph and Celina Frances (Szymanski) S. BA, Rutgers U., 1972; MD, N.Y. Med. Coll., 1975. Diplomate Am. Bd. Internal Medicine, Am. Bd. Endocrinology and Metabolism. Resident in medicine N.Y. Med. Coll., NYC, 1975-78; gen. internist Nat. Health Svcs. Corp., Camden, NJ, 1978-79; fellow in endocrinology Hosp. of U. Pa., Phila., 1979-80; fellow in endocrinology -R.W. Johnson Med. Sch. U. Medicine and Dentistry N.J., Piscataway, NJ, 1980-81, clin. prof. medicine R.W. Johnson Med. Sch. Mem. ACP, Phila. Endocrinology Soc. (v.p. 1993-94, bd. dirs. 1991-96, pres. 1994-95), Camden County Med. Soc., Phi Beta Kappa, Alpha Omega Alpha, Am. Diabetes Assn., Endocrine Soc., Am. Assn. Clin. Endocrinologists. Roman Catholic. Office: 1210 Brace Rd Cherry Hill NJ 08034-3213 Home Phone: 856-424-2052; Office Phone: 856-795-3597. Personal E-mail: marvoor@aol.com.

SWICK, TODD J., medical association administrator; b. NYC, Feb. 8, 1950; s. Adele Hantman; m. Marilyn L. Farkas, June 22, 2002; m. Lisa C. Bleiweiss, Apr. 14, 1973; children: Jennifer P., Blair J., Chad M. Ruoff. B. and MD, SUNY, Stony Brook, NY, 1974. Med. dir. Houston Sleep Ctr., 1999—; sect. chief divsn. sleep medicine Meth. Neurol. Inst., Houston, 2006—. Fellow: Am. Acad. of Sleep Medicine, Am. Acad. of Neurology (life). Office: Houston Sleep Ctr Ste 525 7500 San Felipe Houston TX 77063 Office Fax: 713-465-9248. E-mail: tswick@houstonsleepcenter.com.

SWICKRATH, MICHAEL JACOB, research scientist; b. Lima, Ohio, Nov. 10, 1980; s. Mary Pamela and William Keith Swickrath; m. Amber Nicole Wanner, May 12, 2007. BS in Chem. Engring., Ohio State U., Columbus, 2004; PhD in Chem. Engring., Case Western Res. U., Cleve., 2008. Grad. student rschr. Case Western Res. U., Cleve., 2004—08; postdoc. assoc. U. Minn., Twin Cities, Mpls., 2008—. Tech. cons. Infoscitex Corp., Boston, 2008—. Contbr. articles to profl. sci. jours. Advt. com. chair Polymeric Innovations NE Ohio, Cleve., 2007—08; exec. com. mem. Case Western Res. U. Grad. Student Senate, Cleve.,

2007—08; com. mem. Case Western Res. U. Diekhoff Award Selection Com., Cleve., 2007—08. Mem.: Assn. Rsch. Vision and Ophthalmology, AIChE, Phi Eta Sigma, Alpha Lambda Delta. Office: Univ Minn Twin Cities 100 Union St SouthEast Minneapolis MN 55455

SWID, STEPHEN CLAAR, communications executive, director; b. NYC, Oct. 26, 1940; s. David and Selma (Claar) S.; m. Nan Goldman, Mar. 1, 1963; children: Robin, Scott, Jill. BS, Ohio State U., 1962. Mgmt. trainee Alside Aluminum Co., Akron, Ohio, 1962-63; securities analyst Dreyfus Fund, NYC, 1963-66; sr. investment officer Oppenheimer Fund, NYC, 1966-67; gen. ptnr. City Associates, 1967-69, Swid Investors, NYC, 1970-78; co-chmn. bd. Gen. Felt Industries Inc., Saddle Brook, NJ, 1974-86, Knoll Internat., 1977-86; chmn. bd., CEO SBK Entertainment World, Inc., NYC, 1986-89; chmn., CEO SCS Comm., NYC, 1989—2007, SESAC, 1992—. Trustee Solomon R. Guggenheim Mus., New Sch. U.; mem. vis. com. 20th century art Met. Mus. Art; past trustee Horace Mann Sch., NYC.; former exec. vp. bd. dirs. Lenox Sch. NY; dir. Mcpl. Art Soc. Mem.: Coun. Fgn. Rels. Office: SESAC Inc 152 W 57th St New York NY 10019-3310 Office Phone: 212-752-4050.

SWIDARSKI, THOMAS W., manufacturing executive; B in Mktg., U. Dayton, Ohio; M in Bus. Mgmt., Cleve. State U. With various financial firms; mgr. PNC Bank; joined Diebold, Inc., Canton, Ohio, 1996—, sr. v.p., financial self-svc. group, pres., COO, 2005, pres., CEO, 2005—. Bd. dir. Diebold, Inc., Canton, Ohio, 2003—. Office: Diebold Inc 5995 Mayfair Rd PO Box 3077 Canton OH 44720-8077*

SWIECA, HENRY ALEXANDER, hedge fund manager; b. NYC, 1957; s. Marion and Julia Swieca; m. Estee Swieca; 4 children. BA, SUNY, Stony Brook, 1978; MBA in Fin., Columbia Bus. Sch., NYC, 1982. With Merrill Lynch & Co., 1979; fl. trader NY Futures Exch., 1982; investment adv. Dillon Read & Co.; co-founder Dubin & Swieca, 1984; co-founder, mng. ptnr., co-CEO Highbridge Capital Mgmt. LLC, 1992—. Mem. exec. com. Am. Israel Pub. Affairs Com. Named one of 50 Best Paid Hedge Fund Managers, Alpha Mag., 2007, Forbes Richest Americans; named to 'The World's Billionaires' list, Forbes mag. Republican. Office: Highbridge Capital Mgmt LLC 9 W 57th St New York NY 10019 Office Phone: 212-287-4977. Business E-Mail: henrys@hcmny.com, henrys@highbridge.com.*

SWIECH, ALAN M., human relations executive; BSBA, SUNY, Buffalo; MS, Rensselaer Polytechnic Inst., Troy, NY. V.p., adminstrn., N.Am. Akebono Corp.; v.p., human resources Cambridge Industries Inc.; sr. leadership position (indsl., employee rels.) United Technologies Corp.; v.p., human resources, supply chain ops. Chemtura Corp., sr. v.p., human resources, 2009—. Office: Chemtura Corp 199 Benson Rd Waterbury CT 06749 Office Phone: 203-573-2000. Office Fax: 203-353-5424.*

SWIENTON, GREGORY T., transportation company executive; BBA in Mktg., Loyola U., Chgo., 1971; MBS in Bus. Admin., U. Chgo. Various sales and mktg. positions Ill. Bell and AT&T, Chgo., Mpls., 1971-82; former v.p., gen. mgr. DHL Airways, Inc., Chgo. and Houston; mng. dir. We. & Ea. Europe DHL Worldwide Express, Brussels, 1988—90, exec. dir. Europe and Africa, 1991—94; exec. v.p. Intermodal Bus.Unit Burlington No. Railroad, 1994—95; sr. v.p. Industrial Bus. Unit Burlington No. Santa Fe Corp., 1995—99; pres., COO Ryder System, Inc., Miami, 1999—2000, chmn., CEO, 2000—. Mem. bd. dir. St. Thomas Univ. Bd. Trustees. Office: Ryder System Inc PO Box 20816 Miami FL 33102-0816

SWIER, CAROL ANN, English educator; b. Brookings, SD, Aug. 10, 1951; d. William Joseph and DeLores Jean Fleissner; m. Ronald Duane Swier; children: Scott Ronald, Brooke DeLores. BS, Dakota State U., Madison, SD, 1982. Acad. skills instr. Dakota State U., 1981—86; english tchr. Madison Jr. High, 1986—88, Summit Sch., SD, 1988—90, Bridgewater Sch., SD, 1990—2005, Rosholt Sch., SD, 2005—07; english instr. Oldham Ramona Sch., SD, 2007—. Club leader Go Getters 4-H Club, Emery, SD, 1995—2000; officer Emery Cmty. Booster Club, 1998—2000; pres. Hanson County 4-H Leaders, Alexandria, SD, 2000—01, active, 2002—05; tchr. Bible and Sunday Sch., Madison and Emery, 1986—94; active Ch. Bd. Edn. Edn., Madison, 2008. Recipient Who's Who Among Am. Tchrs., 1984. Conservative. Lutheran. Avocations: reading, gardening, walking. Home: 45097 Jackson Rd Madison SD 57042 Office: Rosholt Sch PO Box 106 Rosholt SD 57260 Business E-Mail: carol.swier@k12.sd.us.

SWIERENGA, ROBERT, humanities educator, researcher; b. Chgo., June 10, 1935; s. John R. and Marie Ann Swierenga; m. Joan Boomker Swierenga, June 16, 1956. BA in Edn., Calvin Coll., 1953—57; MA in History, Northwestern U., 1957—58; PhD in History, U. of Iowa, 1962—65. Cert. secondary tchr. Mich. State Bd. Edn., 1965. Social studies tchr. Pella Christian H.S., Iowa, 1958—61; history instr. Calvin Coll., Grand Rapids, Mich., 1961—62, asst. prof., 1965—68; prof. Kent State U., Ohio, 1968—96; rsch. prof. Hope Coll., Holland, Mich., 1996—. Bd. trustees Calvin Coll., 1976—82. Author: The Forerunners, 1994, Faith and Family, 2000, Dutch Chicago, 2002, Elim, 2005, Old Wing Mission, 2008. Elder Akron Christian Ref. Ch., Ohio, 1970—89; elder, clk. Pillar Christian Ref. Ch., Holland, Mich., 2002—05. Decorated knight-Order of Netherlands Lion, Queen Beatrix of Netherlands at Holland, Mich.; named Disting. Alumnus, Calvin Coll., 2003. Mem.: Agrl. History Soc. (pres. 1996—97), Conf. Faith and History, Assn. for Advancement of Dutch Am. Studies (pres. 2000—02). Republican. Mem. Christian Reformed Ch. Achievements include research in Dutch immigration databases, CD #269 Family Tree Maker. Avocations: walking, choral singing. Office: A C Van Raalte Inst Hope Coll Nine E 10th Street Holland MI 49422 Office Phone: 616-395-7172. Business E-Mail: swierenga@hope.edu.

SWIERINGA, ROBERT JAY, accounting educator, former dean; BA in Econs., Augustana Coll., 1964; MBA in Acctg. and Econs., U. Denver, 1965; PhD in Acctg. and Complex Orgns., U. Ill., 1969. Asst. prof. acctg. Grad. Sch. Bus., Stanford U., Calif., 1968-74; assoc. prof. acctg. Johnson Grad. Sch. Mgmt., Cornell U., Ithaca, NY, 1974-81, prof. acctg., 1981-85, 1997—, Anne and Elmer Lindseth dean, 1997—2007; mem. Fin. Acctg. Standards Bd., Norwalk, Conn., 1986—96; prof. in practice acctg. Yale Sch. Mgmt., 1996—97. Bd. dirs. GE, 2002—; adv. bd. mem. Columbia Bus. Sch. Ctr. for Excellence in Fin. Reporting and Security Analysis, 2003—; mem. editl. bd. Jour. Acctg. Rsch., 1975—97, Acctg. Horizons, 1996—. Co-author: (with R.T. Sprouse) Essentials of Financial Statement Analysis, 1972, (with R.H. Moncur) Some Effects of Participative Budgeting on Managerial Behavior, 1975; (with T.R. Dyckman) Cases in Financial Accounting, 1980, rev. 1981, 3rd edit. 1989; (with H. Bierman Jr.) Financial Accounting: An Introduction, 1987. Grantee Nat. Assn. Accts., 1970, Peat, Marwick, Mitchell & Co. Found., 1976; Recipient Justice Found. Award for Outstanding Teaching, Cornell U., 1976, PhD Alumni of Yr. Award, Accountancy Dept. U. Ill., 1988, Alumni Outstanding Achievement Award, Augustana Coll., 1989, Alumnus of Yr. Award, Sch. Accountancy U. Denver, 1994. Mem. Am. Acctg. Assn. (inducted into Northeast Regional Hall of Fame, 1996), Beta Gamma Sigma, Beta Alpha Psi, Assn. to Advance Collegiate Schs. of Bus. (peer review teams mem., 2001-), Grad. Mgmt. Admissions Coun. (bd. dirs., 2001-05, vice chair, 2002-03, chair, 2003-04). Office: Johnson Grad Sch of Mgmt Cornell U 337 Sage Hall Ithaca NY 14853-6201 Office Phone: 607-255-0422. Office Fax: 607-255-6889. E-mail: rjs22@cornell.edu.

SWIFT, CALVIN THOMAS, electrical and computer engineering educator; b. Quantico, Va., Feb. 6, 1937; s. Thomas and Elsie (Hill) S.; m. Joanne Taylor, Sept. 5, 1959; children: Pamela, Janet. BS, MIT, 1959; MS, Va. Poly. Inst., 1965; PhD, William and Mary Coll., 1969. Research engr. N. Am. Aviation Co., Downey, Calif., 1959-62; aerospace technologist NASA, Hampton, Va., 1962-81; prof. elec. and computer engring. U. Mass., Amherst, 1981—2001, prof. emeritus, 2001—. Cons. engring. Amherst, 1981—; co-founder ProSensing (formerly Quadrant Engring., Inc.), Amherst, 1982; v.p. spl. projects team Limited Liability Corp., 2006. Editor: Transactions on Geoscience and Remote Sensing, 1980-84; assoc. editor: Jour. Oceanic Engring., 1980-84. F.L. Thompson fellow NASA, 1977; faculty fellow U. Mass., 1997. Fellow IEEE (life); mem. Internat. Union Radio Sci. (chmn. Commn. F 1988-91), Antennas and Propagation Soc. (adminstrv. com. 1974-77, 80-85), Geosci. and Remote Sensing Soc. (adminstrv. com. 1978-86, pres. 1985, Disting. Achievement award 1994). Office: U Mass Dept Elec & Computer Engring Amherst MA 01003 Personal E-mail: calswift@comcast.net.

SWIFT, CONSTANCE REDMOND, special education educator; b. Cleve., Aug. 31, 1950; d. Charles Clovis and Sally McMahon Redmond; m. Robert Jeffrey Swift, Sept. 17, 1977 (div. Aug. 1, 1990); children: Robert J., Michael F., J. Patrick, Sally M., Terrence M. BS in Psychology, Loyola U., Chgo., 1972; postgrad., Sam Houston State U., Houston, 1991—93; MA in Counseling Psychology, Sam Houston State U., Huntsville, Tex., 1997. Cert. tchr., spl. edn., tchr., master reading and ESL Tex. Pre-trial coun. Harris County Criminal Ct., Houston, 1990—91; spl. edn. tchr. Houston Ind. Sch. Dist., 1991. Psychology prof. Kingwood Coll., Houston, 1998—; guided studies prof. Houston CC, 2001—03; mem. attendance com. Houston Ind. Sch. Dist., 2004—06, mem., shared decision making com., 2005—; v.p. Swift Entertainment, 2004—06. Social dir. United Way, Houston, 1990—91; active Centre Stage Theatre, Kingwood, 1995—2006. Mem.: Houston Fedn. Tchrs. Democrat. Roman Catholic. Avocations: tennis, reading, working out. Home: 4545 Kingwood Dr Kingwood TX 77345-2617 Office Phone: 713-805-5966. E-mail: constance_swift@hotmail.com.

SWIFT, DAVID A., lawyer; b. Piqua, Ohio, Nov. 4, 1952; s. Charles Joseph and Margaret Clara Swift; m. Karen Ann Zelenka, June 23, 1979; children: Matthew, Nicole, Daniel. BA, Miami U., Oxford, Ohio, 1975; JD, Ohio State U., Columbus, 1978. Bar: Ohio 1978. Assoc. ptnr. Porter, Wright, Morris and Arthur, Columbus, 1978—90; counsel, ptnr. Vorys, Sater, Seymour, Pease LLP, Columbus, 1990—. Bd. dirs. Boys & Girls Club Columbus, Columbus, 1998—2005; pres. Worthington Youth Boosters, Ohio, 2000—01. Fellow: Am. Coll. Trust and Estate Coun. (Best Lawyers in Am.); mem.: Am. Bar Assn., Ohio Bar Assn., Columbus Bar Assn. Roman Catholic. Avocations: golf, sports. Office: Vorys Sater Seymour Pease LLP 52 E Gay St Columbus OH 43215 Office Phone: 614-464-8370. Personal E-mail: daswift@vorys.com.

SWIFT, DAVID L., manufacturing executive; b. Wilbraham, Mass. married. BA in Math. & Physics, Amherst Coll., Mass., 1980; M in Electronics Engring., Dartmouth Coll., Hanover, NH; MBA, Harvard Bus. Sch., 1999. Chmn., pres. Greater Asia Region Eastman Kodak Co., Shanghai, pres. Kodak Profl. Group; exec. v.p. N.Am. region Whirlpool Corp., Benton Harbor, Mich., 2001—05, pres. Whirlpool N.Am., 2006—07; pres., CEO Goodman Global, Inc., Houston, 2008—. Bd. dirs. Whirlpool Corp., 2006—07, Goodman Global, Inc., 2008—. Office: Goodman Global Inc 5151 San Felipe Blvd Ste 500 Houston TX 77056

SWIFT, EDWARD FOSTER, III, investment banker; b. Chgo., Nov. 1, 1923; s. Theodore Philip I and Elizabeth (Hoyt) S.; m. Joan McKelvy, July 2, 1947; children: Theodore Philip II, Edward McKelvy, Lockhart McKelvy, Elizabeth Hoyt; m. Carol Coffey Whipple, June 21, 1968. Grad., Hotchkiss Sch., 1941; BA, Yale U., 1945. With Esmark, Inc. (formerly Swift & Co.), 1947-75, asst. to v.p. charge meat packing plants, 1958, asst. v.p., 1958-59, v.p. for provisions, fgn., casings and storage, 1959-64, exec. v.p., 1964-75; vice-chmn. Chgo. Corp., 1975-79; vice chmn. Bacon, Whipple & Co., Chgo., 1980-84; mng. dir. A.G. Becker Paribas Inc., Chgo., 1984-85; with E.F. Hutton and Co., Chgo., 1985-87; mng. dir. Shearson Lehman Hutton Inc, Chgo., 1987-92. Bd. dirs. Santa Fe Pacific Pipelines, Inc. Chmn. So. Ind. chpt. United Negro Coll. Fund, 1956; trustee Northwestern U., Evanston, Ill.; bd. dirs. Northwestern Meml. Hosp., Chgo. Served to capt. U.S. Army, 1942-46. Mem. Chgo. Assn. Commerce and Industry (bd. dirs.), Scroll and Key, Chgo. Club, Racquet Club, Econ. Club, Valley Club, Comml. Club, Onwentsia Club, Old Elm ClubBirnam Wood Golf Club, Aurelian Honor Soc. Home: 1100 Pembridge Dr Apt 129 Lake Forest IL 60045

SWIFT, FRANK MEADOR, lawyer; b. NYC, Dec. 27, 1911; s. Frank Meador and Alberta (Rankin) S.; m. Harriet Elizabeth Simpson, May 30, 1944 (dec. Jan. 2003); children: Frank Meador (dec.), Thomas Lamar. Student, Emory U., 1930-32; LL.B., U. Ga., 1935. Bar: Ga. 1935. Partner Swift, Currie, McGhee & Hiers, Atlanta, 1965-82, of counsel, 1982—. Served to comdr. USNR, 1942-46. Mem. Am., Ga. bar assns., Lawyers Club Atlanta, Clubs: Piedmont Driving. Republican. Presbyterian. Office: Swift Currie McGhee & Hiers 1355 Peachtree St NE Ste 300 Atlanta GA 30309-3238 Home: 12 Renegar Way Apt 220 Saint Simons Island GA 31522

SWIFT, JANE MARIA, educational consultant, former governor; b. North Adams, Mass., Feb. 24, 1965; d. John Maynard and Jean Mary (Kent) Swift; m. Charles T. Hunt, Feb. 19, 1994; 3 children. BA in Am. Studies, Trinity Coll., Hartford, Conn., 1987; LLD, Mass. Coll. Liberal Arts, 1999; LLD (hon.), Pine Manor Coll., 1999; DBA (hon.), Asumption Coll., 1999. Exec. mgmt. trainee G. Fox. & Co., Hartford, 1987-88; adminstrv. aide Sen. Peter C. Webber, Boston, 1988-90; mem. Mass. State Senate, Boston, 1991-96, 3d asst. minority leader, 1993-96; coord. strategic devel. of regional airports Mass. Port Authority, Boston, 1997; dir. consumer affairs and bus. regulation Commonwealth of Mass., lt. gov., 1999-2001, gov., 2001—03; ptnr. Arcadia Ptnrs., Boston; founder, prin. WNP Consulting LLC. Fellow Kennedy Sch. Govt. Inst. Politics; bd. dirs. Animated Speech Corp., Sally Ride Sci., Suburban Propane. Republican. Roman Catholic. Home and Office: 580 Henderson Rd Williamstown MA 01267-2214 Office Phone: 413-458-3900. E-mail: jane@wnpconsulting.com.

SWIFT, JOHN FRANCIS, retired health care advertising company executive; b. NYC, June 15, 1935; s. John F. and Mary Veronica (Kehoe) S.; m. Eleanor H. Cunniff, Oct. 10, 1964; children— John Francis, Sharon Ann. BS in Bus. Adminstrn, Seton Hall U., 1960, postgrad., 1960-61. Mktg. research mgr. Lederle Labs. div. Cyanamid Internat., 1960-63; account exec. Robert A. Becker Advt. Agy., NYC, 1963-66; mgr. new products Chesebrough Ponds Co., NYC, 1966-68; v.p. Frohlich Intercon Co., NYC, 1968-72; pres., CEO, Lavey/Wolff/Swift, Inc., NYC, 1972-91, chmn., CEO, 1991-94; pres., CEO, BBDO Health & Med. Comms. Inc., 1977-91; chmn., CEO Health & Med. Comm. Inc., 1991-95, chmn. emeritus, 1995—, ret., 1995; vice-chmn. Lyons Lavey Nickel Swift, Inc., 1995—. Bd. govs. Cathedral Healthcare Systems, 1991-2004; chmn. emeritus Cathedral Healthcare Found., 1994-2004. Served with USN, 1955-57. Named to, Med. Advt. Hall of Fame, 2004. Mem. Pharm. Advt. Coun. (pres. 1979), Bio-Med. Mktg. Assn., Baltusrol Golf Club (Springfield, NY), Canoe Brook CC (Summit, N.J.), Manasquan River Golf Club, Skytop Club (Pa.), Royal Palm Yacht and Country Club, Boca Raton Resort and Club, N.Y. Athletic Club. Home: 12 Melrose Ln Green Village NJ 07935 also: 600 S Ocean Blvd Boca Raton FL 33432-6265 also: 76 Bay Point Harbour Point Pleasant NJ 08742-5509

SWIFT, JONATHAN, television personality, educator; b. Glasgow, Scotland, Apr. 26, 1932; arrived in U.S., 1948, naturalized, 1954; s. John Francis and Catherine Little (McGowan) S. MA, Wayne State U., 1957; postgrad., Ecole Normale Superieure, Paris, 1954-55; studied with Georges Jouatte, 1954-56; cert., Conservatoire Nat. de Musique, France, 1955; postgrad., U. Mich., 1959, Cambridge U., 1981; PhD, Mich. State U., 1983. On-camera tchr. French Sta. WTVS, Detroit, 1955-56, tchr. Am. lit., 1960-62; instr. French Wayne State U., Detroit, 1955-60; tchr. English, French and social studies Detroit Pub. Schs., 1957-64; tchr. English and history Glasgow Corp. Schs., 1967; tchr. English and French Livonia (Mich.) Pub. Schs., 1967; chmn. English dept. Stevenson H.S., Livonia, 1970-78, dir. Sch. Global Edn., 1978-98; dir. Ctr. Internat. Studies Madonna U., Mich., 1998—. Sr. lectr. Mich. State U. Debut in opera as Alfredo in La Traviata, 1961; host PBS TV and cmty. TV series Global Connections, Time Out for Opera, Dining Out With Jonathan Swift; leading tenor with Detroit Piccolo Opera Co., 1981-96, Detroit Grand Opera Assn., 1965, Mich. Opera Co., 1961-64; concert soloist with major symphonies in U.S., Can., Europe, Australia, 1961-81; appeared as tenor soloist in various radio and TV programs, 1961-81; rec. artist with Scotia and Andis, U.K.; contbr. articles and poems to profl. and lit. jours. Mem. adv. bd. Am. Mid.-East Christian Congress, 2003—; bd. trustees Mich. Opera. Recipient French Govt. medal, 1954, tribute, Mich. State Legislature, 1984, NEA Applegate-Dorros award, 1987, MEA Siddall Internat. award, 1987, Philo Farnsworth award, Alliance Cmty. Media, 1990, 1994, 1995, 1998, 1998, 1999, 2000, Hometown award, Nat. Fedn. Local Cable Programmers, 1994, 1999, 2001, Nat. TV award, Nat. Assn. Telecomm. Officers and Advs., 1995, Human Rels. award, Livonia, 1999, Multi-Cultural award, Birmingham, Mich., 2000, 2004; named Fulbright scholar, 1954—55; named to Hall of Fame, Mich. Model UN, 1999. Mem.: Confrerie de la Chaine des Rotisseurs, Descs. Knights of Garter, Soc. Friends of St. George. Roman Catholic. also: 4200 Telegraph Rd # 489 Bloomfield Hills MI 48302-2038 Office Phone: 734-432-5669. Personal E-mail: jonathanswift32@yahoo.com. E-mail: jswift@madonna.edu.

SWIFT, MARY LOU, art dealer, financial consultant; b. Syracuse, NY, July 25, 1942; d. Andrew G. Swift and E.R. Ensle. BA, Sarah Lawrence Coll., Bronxville, NY, 1964; postgrad, U. Pa., 1964-66, NYU Bus. Sch., 1967-69, N.Y. Inst. Finance, 1967-69. Registered stockbroker N.Y. Stock Exch. and Nat. Assn. Securities Dealers. Adminstrv. head of syndicate dept. Drexel Harriman Ripley, NYC, 1966-71; product mgr. Fieldcrest Mills, NYC, 1971-74; acct. supr. advtg. Rosenfeld Sirowitz Lawson, NYC, 1974-76, BBDO, NYC, 1976-78, Cavalieri, Kleier, Pearlman, NYC, 1978-79; bus., mktg. cons. Mary Lou Swift & Co., NYC, 1979-81; instnl. stockbroker Mabon Securities, NYC, 1981-91; Gerard Klauer Mattison, NYC, 1992-93; pvt. art dealer internat. modern and contemporary art Mary Lou Swift Fine Arts, NYC, 1994—. Cons. Miller Tabak & Co., Inc., 1994—2006. Recipient Undergraduate Fellowship (2) Am. Mus. Nat. History, 1962, 63. Avocations: golf, travel, languages. Office: Mary Lou Swift Fine Arts 161 Breese Ln PO Box 1496 Southampton NY 11969-1496 Personal E-mail: mlswifty@yahoo.com.

SWIFT, MICHAEL RONALD, internist, educator; b. NYC, Feb. 5, 1935; s. Herbert Allen and Estelle (Clafter) S.; m. Ronnie Elaine Gorman, Nov. 27, 1971; children— Melissa, Amy, Laura. BA, Swarthmore Coll., 1955; MA in Math., U. Calif.-Berkeley, 1958; MD, NYU Sch. Med., 1962. bd. cert. Am. Bd. Internal Medicine, 1969, Am. Bd. Med. Genetics, 1987. Intern med. Coll. Physicians and Surgeons, NY, 1962—63; asst. resident med. NYU Bellevue Hosp., 1963—64; Instr., then asst. prof. NYU Sch. Medicine, NYC, 1966-70; asst. prof. med., 1970; assoc. prof., then prof. U. N.C., Chapel Hill, 1972-92, also chief genetics div.; prof. pediatrics, dir. Inst. for Genetic Analysis Diseases N.Y. Med. Coll., NYC, 1992—2001, prof. med., pathology, 1998. Dir. Inst. Genetic Analysis Common Diseases, 1994—2001, Disease Insight Rsch. Found., 2004—; CEO Sci. dir. Life Testing LLC (now GenDex LLC), 2001—. Author: Malignant Neoplasms in the Families of Patients with Ataxia Telangiectasia, 1976, Breast Cancer and other Cancers in Ataxia-Telangiectasia Families, 1987, Incidence of Cancer in 161 Families affected by Ataxia-Telangiectasia, 1991, Molecular Genotyping shows that Ataxia Telangiectasia Heterozygotes are Predisposed to Breas Cancer, 1996. Mem. AAAS, Am. Soc. Human Genetics, Alpha Omega Alpha. Achievements include discovery of Mutations in the A-T gene predispose carriers in the general population to cancer, particularly female breast cancer. Avocations: hiking, fishing, travel, theater. Personal E-mail: msuriftmd@gmail.com.

SWIFT, PEGGY LYNETTE, elementary school educator; b. Forrest City, Ark., Aug. 6, 1969; d. Paul Edward Tabron and Willean Hicks; m. Leonard Terrell Swift, July 3, 1993; 1 child, Symone Sydnee. BS, U. Ark., Pine Bluff, 1992; MS in Edn., Ark. State U., Jonesboro, 2003. Cert. reading specialist Ark. 6th grade classroom tchr. Ector County Ind. Sch. Dist., Odessa, Tex., 1992—93; 4th grade classroom tchr. Marion Sch. Dist., Ark., 1993—2001; literacy coach Earle Sch. Dist., Ark., 2003—. Named Master Edcuator, Reading Renaissance /Accelerated Reading. Mem.: Memphis RAW Readers and Writers Sistaz, Alpha Kappa Alpha (life). Democrat. Baptist. Home: 601 Charles Wood Dr Marion AR 72364 Office: Earle Sch Dist PO Box 637 Earle AR 72331 Office Fax: 870-735-1704. Business E-Mail: leonardswift@aol.com.

SWIFT, RONNIE GORMAN, psychiatrist, educator; b. NYC, Sept. 13, 1948; d. Joseph Harry Gorman and Mollie Samuels; m. Michael Ronald Swift, Nov. 27, 1971; children: Melissa, Laura, Amy. BS, CCNY, 1969; MD, U. N.C., Chapel Hill, 1975. Lic. physician N.Y., N.C. Resident U. N.C., Chapel Hill, 1978; pvt. practice psychiatry Chapel Hill, 1979—92; psychiatrist, dir. divsn. psychiatry genetics N.Y. Med. Ctr., Valhalla, 1992—97; chief psychiatry Met. Hosp. Ctr., NYC, 1998—, assoc. med. dirs., 1999—. Clin. assoc. prof. dept. psychiatry U. N.C., Chapel Hill, 1982—83, 1990—92, rsch. scientist Biol. Sci. Rsch. Ctr., 1988—92; assoc. prof. dept. psychology NY Med. Coll., Valhalla, 1992—2005, assoc. chmn. dept. psychiatry, 2004—, First Sidney E. Frank vis. prof., 2005; dir. outpatient svcs., dept. psychiatry Westchester County Med. Ctr., NY, 1995—98; network chief psychiatry and behavioral health svcs. Generations+/No. Manhattan Health Network, Health and Hosps. Corp. Orgn., NYC, 2001—; med. dir. Open Gate Residential

Ctr., Somer, NY, 1992—; chief psychiatry Westchester Inst. Human Devel., N.Y. Med. Coll. Orgn., Valhalla, 1999—2001; cons., spkr. in field; mem., chairperson CME adv. bd. Neurosci. Edn. Inst., Carlsbad, Calif., 2006—; v.p. med. bd. Met. Hosp. Ctr., 2006—; psychiat. commentator various programs Fox 5 News. Contbr. articles to profl. jours. Fellow Falk fellow, Am. Psychiat. Assn., 1979. Mem.: Am. Psychiat. Assn., World Psychiat. Assn. (hon.), Alpha Omega Alpha. Avocations: cooking, reading, travel. Office: Metropolitan Hospital Center 1901 First Ave New York NY 10029

SWIFT, STEPHEN JENSEN, federal judge; b. Salt Lake City, Sept. 7, 1943; s. Edward A. and Maurine (Jensen) S.; m. Lorraine Burnell Facer, Aug. 4, 1972; children: Carter, Stephanie, Spencer, Meredith, Hunter. BS, Brigham Young U., 1967; JD, George Washington U., 1970. Trial atty. US Dept. Justice, Washington, 1970-74, asst. US atty. tax divsn. San Francisco, 1974-77; v.p., sr. tax counsel Bank America N.T. & S.A., San Francisco, 1977-83; judge US Tax Ct., Washington, 1983—98, 2000—08, sr. judge, 2008—. Adj. prof. Golden Gate U., San Francisco, 1976-83, 2005-08, U. Balt., 1987-2008. Mem. ABA, Calif. Bar Assn., DC Bar Assn. Office: US Tax Ct 400 2nd St NW Washington DC 20217-0002 Office Phone: 202-521-0760.*

SWIFT, TAYLOR, country singer; b. Wyomissing, Pa., Dec. 13, 1989; d. Scott and Andrea Swift. Singer: (albums) Taylor Swift, 2006, Songs of the Season, 2007, Fearless, 2008 (Album of Yr., Acad. Country Music Awards, 2009, Choice Music Album: Female Artist, Teen Choice Awards, 2009), (songs) Tim McGraw, 2006 (Breakthrough Video of Yr., Country Music TV, 2007), Teardrops On My Guitar, 2006, Our Song, 2006 (Video of Yr., Female Video of Yr., Country Music TV, 2008); actor: (films) Hannah Montana: The Movie, 2009. Recipient Songwriter of Yr. award, Nashville Songwriters Assn., 2007, Horizon award, Country Music Assn., 2007, Top New Female Vocalist award, Acad. Country Music, 2008, Crystal Milestone award, 2009, Favorite Female Country Artist award, Am. Music Awards, 2008, Choice Music: Female Artist, Teen Choice Awards, 2009. Office: c/o Troy Tomlinson Sony/ATV Tree Publishing 8 Music Sq W Nashville TN 37203*

SWIG, KENT M., real estate company executive; b. San Francisco, Jan. 20, 1961; m. Elizabeth Swig; children: Simon, Oliver. BA in Chinese History, Brown U.; JD, U. Calif., Berkeley. V.p. The Swig Co. (formerly Swig, Weiler & Dinner Devel. Co.), San Francisco, prin., bd. dirs.; exec. v.p. The Macklowe Orgn., pres. Manhattan Pacific Mgmt. Co., Inc.; co-founder, pres. Swig Equities, LLC (formerly Swig Burris Equities), 2001—, co-chair Brown Harris Stevens; owner, co-chair Terra Holdings, LLC; owner, pres. Helmsley Spear, LLC; owner Falcon Pacific Construction, LLC. Chmn. real estate and construction industries State of Israel Bonds, nat. bd. dirs., 2004. Bd. mem. Downtown Alliance, Wall Street Rising, Assn. Builders and Owners of NY, Bus. Execs. for Nat. Security; v.p. Realty Found. of NY; pres. Am. Friends of the Jaffa Inst. Recipient Man of Yr. Award, Big Brothers/Big Sisters of NY, 2000; named Man of Yr., Realty Found. of NY, 2005. Office: Swig Equities, LLC 770 Lexington Ave New York NY 10065 also: 450 Sansome St San Francisco CA 94111 Office Phone: 212-508-7373. Office Fax: 212-508-7488.*

SWIGER, ANDREW P., oil industry executive; m. Sherry Swiger. BSc in Petroleum Engring., Colo. Sch. Mines, Golden, 1978. Ops. engr. to various staff and managerial upstream assignments Mobile Oil, 1978—96, gen. mgr. mfg. Singapore, 1996—99, pres., gen. mgr., Mobil Oil Can., 1999—2001; corp. prodn. advisor ExxonMobil Corp., Irving, Tex., v.p. Africa London, 2001—03, chmn., prodn. dir., ExxonMobil Internat. Ltd., lead country mgr., UK and Ireland, 2003—04, exec. v.p., ExxonMobil Prodn. Co., pres., ExxonMobil Gas & Power Mktg. Co., sr. v.p., 2009—. Chmn. Esso Exploration and Prodn., Mobil North Sea. Bd. dirs. US-Kazakhstan Bus. Assn.; mem. Greater Houston Partnership Bus. Issues Adv. Com. Mem.: Internat. Assn. Oil and Gas Prodrs. (vice chmn. bd. dirs.). Office: ExxonMobil Corp 5959 Las Colinas Blvd Irving TX 75039-2298

SWIGER, ELINOR PORTER, lawyer; b. Cleve., Aug. 1, 1927; d. Louie Charles and Mary Isabelle (Shank) Porter; m. Quentin Gilbert Swiger, Feb. 5, 1955; children: Andrew Porter, Calvin Gilbert, Charles Robinson. BA, Ohio State U., 1949, JD, 1951. Bar: Ohio 1951, Ill. 1979. Sr. assoc., now of counsel Robbins, Schwartz, Nicholas, Lifton & Taylor, Ltd., Chgo., 1979—. Author: (book) Mexico for Kids, 1971, Europe for Young Travelers, 1972, The Law and You, 1973 (Literary Guild award), Law in Everyday Life, 1977, Careers in the Legal Professions, 1978, Women Lawyers at Work, 1978. Mem. Glenview (Ill.) Fire and Police Commn., 1976—86; chmn. Glenview Zoning Bd. Appeals, 1987—97. Mem.: Chgo. Bar Assn. (chmn. legis. exec. com. 1990—92), Women Bar Assn. Ill., Ill. Coun. Sch. Attys. (past chmn.), Ohio State U. Coll. Law Alumni Coun., Soc. Midland Authors. Republican. Home: 1933 Burr Oak Dr Glenview IL 60025 Office: Robbins Schwartz Nicholas Lifton & Taylor 20 N Clark St Ste 900 Chicago IL 60602-4115

SWIGER, ELIZABETH DAVIS, chemist, educator; b. Morgantown, W.Va., June 27, 1926; d. Hannibal Albert and Tyreeca Elizabeth (Stemple) Davis; m. William Eugene Swiger, June 2, 1948 (dec.); children: Susan Elizabeth Swiger Knotts-Case, Wayne William; m. James E. Coleman, Dec. 11, 2004. BS in Chemistry, W.Va. U., 1948, MS in Chemistry, 1952, PhD in Chemistry, 1964. Instr. math. Fairmont State Coll., 1948-49, instr. math. and phys. sci., 1956-57, instr. chemistry, 1957-60, from asst. prof. to assoc. prof., 1960—66, prof., 1966-92, chmn., divsn. sci., math, and health careers, 1991-92; NSF fellow rsch. W.Va. U., Morgantown, 1963-64, prof. emerita, 1992. Advisor Am. Chem. Soc. student affiliates, 1965-88. Author: Morton Family History, 1984-2004, Davis-Winters Family History, 1994—, Civil War Letters and Diary of Joshua Winters, 1991, 2d edit., 1996; contbr. articles to profl. jour. Chmn. Blacks Chapel Meml. Found., 1993—; rep. adv. coun. to Bd. Regents Fairmont State Coll., Charleston, W.Va., 1977—78, rep. instl. bd. advisors, 1990—92. NSF grantee, 1963; named Outstanding Prof. W.Va. Legislature, Charleston, 1990. Mem.: Am. Chem. Soc. (advisor student affiliates 1965—88, sec. chmn. North W.Va. 1975—83), W.Va. Acad. Sci. (life; pres. 1978—79, exec. com. edn. chmn. 1990—93), Nature Conservancy (bd. dir. W.Va. chpt. 1970—86, chmn. 1980—82), Prickett's Fort Meml. Found. (life; bd. dir. 1988—2000, chmn. elect 1990—92, chmn. 1992—96, bd. dir 2002—), Marion County Hist. Soc. (life), Fairmont Lions Club, Morning Gardeners Garden Club (pres. 1999—2003). Republican. Methodist. Avocations: local history, genealogy, gardening, quilting. Home: 1599 Hillcrest Rd Fairmont WV 26554-4807 Home (Winter): 242 Laird Dr Freeport FL 32439

SWIGERT, JAMES MACK, lawyer; b. Carthage, Ill., Sept. 25, 1907; s. James Ross and Pearl (Mack) S.; m. Alice Francis Titcomb Harrower, July 7, 1931 (dec. 1990); children: Oliver, David Ladd, Sally Harper (Mrs. Hamilton). Student, Grinnell Coll., 1925-27; SB, Harvard U., 1930, LLB, 1935. Bar: Ill. 1935, Ohio 1937. With Campbell, Clithero & Fischer, Chgo., 1935-36, Taft, Stettinius & Hollister, Cin., 1936—, ptnr., 1948-79, sr. ptnr. and chmn. exec. com., 1979-85, of counsel, 1985—. Dir., mem. exec. com. Union Cen. Life Ins. Co., 1963-79; dir., chmn. audit com. Philips Industries, 1975-82. Author articles on labor rels. and labor law. Bd. dirs. Cin. Symphony Orch., 1976-78; trustee, chmn. exec. com. Am. Music Scholarship Assn., 1987-92. Recipient Lifetime Achievement in Law award, Cin. Bar Fund, 2002, Great Living Cincinnatian award, 2004. Mem.: Harvard Law Club (past pres.), Recess Club (past pres.), Tennis Club (past pres.), Queen City Club, Queen City Optimists Club (past pres., psat bd. dirs.), Cin. Country Club (past v.p., dir.). Republican. Presbyterian. Home: 2121 Alpine Pl Cincinnati OH 45206-2690 Office: 425 Walnut St Ste 1800 Cincinnati OH 45202 Home Phone: 513-221-4983; Office Phone: 513-357-9360. Business E-Mail: swigert@taftlaw.com.

SWIGGER, KEITH, library and information scientist, educator; b. Hutchinson, Kans., Feb. 3, 1943; s. Paul Clarke and Loneta (Miller) S.; children: Jessica, Nathaniel; m. Cindy Johnson Potter, Nov. 29, 1997. BA, U. Chgo., 1965, MA, 1975, Ind. U., 1967; PhD, U. Iowa, 1973. Sketchwriter Marquis Who's Who, Chgo., 1963-67; teaching asst. Ind. U., Bloomington, 1967, U. Iowa, Iowa City, 1968-73, lectr., 1973-74, libr., 1976-77; asst. prof. East Tex. State U., Commerce, 1977-81; asst. prof. libr. scis. Tex. Woman's U., Denton, 1981-85, assoc. prof., 1985-89, prof., 1989—, interim dean Sch. Libr. Sci., 1991-92, dean Sch. Libr. and Info. Studies, 1992-2000, dir. Sch. Libr. and Info. Studies, 2001—02, dir. Ctr. for Consulting and Planning, 1997—, dean Coll. Profl. Edn., 2000—03, dir. Gear Up fed. grant program, 2002—03. Mem. adv. com. continuum libr. edn. We. Coun. State Librs., 2003—07; cons. in field. Co-editor Jour. of Youth Svcs., 1997-2000; contbr. numerous articles to profl. jours. Bd. dirs. ACLU, Denton, 1990-92, Emily Fowler Pub. Libr., Denton, 1995-97, vice chair, 1997; mem. Tex. Edn. Tech. Coord. Coun., 2000-03; delegate Tex. Dem. Party state convention, 2004. Rsch. grantee OCLC, Inc., 1990-91, Career Tng. grantee U.S. Office Edn., 1990-98; postdoctoral fellow Coun. on Libr. Resources U. Chgo., 1974-75; recipient Svc. award Nat. Storytelling Assn., 1998. Mem. ALA, Assn. Coll. and Rsch. Librs., Nat. Wildlife Fedn., Sierra Club, World Wildlife Fund, Audubon Soc., Ft. Worth Botanical Soc, Nat. Coun. Pub. History. Democrat. Office: Tex Womans U Sch Libr Info Studies PO Box 425438 Denton TX 76204-5438 Personal E-mail: keithswigger@charter.net.

SWIMMER, ROSS OWEN, federal official; b. Oklahoma City, Oct. 26, 1943; s. Robert Otis and Virginia Marie (Pounder) S.; m. Margaret Ann McConnell, June 30, 1965; children— Joseph Ross, Michael David. BA, U. Okla., 1965, JD, 1967. Bar: Okla. 1967. Partner firm Hanson, Peterson, Thompkins, Oklahoma City, 1967-72; counsel Cherokee Nation, Tahlequah, Okla., 1972-74, prin. chief, 1975-85; exec. v.p. 1st Nat. Bank, Tahlequah, 1974, pres., 1974-84; asst. sec. Indian Affairs Dept. Interior, 1985-89; of counsel Hall, Estill, Hardwick, Gable, Golden & Nelson, Tulsa, 1989—92; spl. trustee Am. Indians US Dept. Interior, Washington, 2003—. Mem. ABA, Okla. Bar Assn., Cherokee Nat. Hist. Soc. (pres. 1979-80), Okla. Hist. Soc. Republican. Office: US Dept Interior 1849 C St NW Rm 5140 Washington DC 20240 Personal E-mail: rswimmer@sbcglobal.net.*

SWIMM-MCMAHON, KATHERINE LYNN, educator; d. Ray Leeroy Swimm and Linda Lee Hardy-Swimm; m. Brian McMahon, Apr. 1, 2002. PhD, U. Miss., Oxford, 2002. Adj. prof. Liberty U., Lynchburg, Va., 2006—. Personal E-mail: bkmcmahon41@yahoo.com.

SWINAND, ANDREW, advertising executive; b. 1968; m. Laura Swinand; children: Tanner, Georgia. BS in Economics, U. Pa. Wharton Sch. Bus., 1990. Account supr. BBDO, LA, 1994—96; brand mgr. beauty care divsn. The Procter & Gamble Co., Cin., 1997—99; mktg. dir. Reflect.com, San Francisco, 1999—2000; gen. mgr. Starcom USA, San Francisco, 2000—02, Chgo., 2002—05, exec. v.p., 2005—06; pres., chief client officer Starcom Worldwide, 2006—08; pres., COO Denou (subs. Publicis Grp.), 2008; pres. global ops. Starcom MediaVest Grp., 2008—. Served in 3rd Infantry Divsn. USAR, 1990—94. Named one of 40 under 40, Crain's Chgo. Bus. mag., 2005; named to Advt. Hall of Achievement, Am. Advt. Fedn., 2008; scholar Reserve Officers' Training Corps, US Army. Office: Starcom MediaVest Grp Global Hdqs 35 W Wacker Dr Chicago IL 60601 Office Phone: 312-220-3535. Office Fax: 312-220-6530.*

SWINBURN, CAROL DITZLER, retired state and municipal agency administrator; b. Washington, July 9, 1945; d. John Nevin and Mildred Peterman Ditzler; m. Charles Swinburn, Dec. 16, 1972; children: Ann Elizabeth, Catherine Knowles. BA, Ursinus Coll., Collegeville, Pa., 1967. Founder, dir. The Healthy Gourmet, West Chester, Pa., 1990—95; campaign exec. United Way, Alexandria, 1994—95; acting dir., counselor Women's Empowerment Program, Alexandria, 1995—97; dir., co-ord. Alexandria Criminal Justice Svcs., Va., 1997—2004; sr. staff Alexandria Cmty. Criminal Justice Bd., 1997—2004. Author: (cookbook) Recipes from the Healthy Gourmet Cooking Classes. Shelter staff vol. Domestic Violence Program, Alexandria, 1995—97; shelter staff vol. teen runaway shelter This Way House, Alexandria, 1994—95; parent edn. chair PTO, Alexandria, 1994—96, mem., fundraising chair Chadds Ford, Pa., 1986—90; bd. dirs. Delray Beach Club Apts. Condo Assn., 2006—08. Named Woman of Yr., Alexandria Commn. on Women, 1997. Mem.: NOW, Planned Parenthood, Emily's List, Hammock Dunes Club. Democrat. Avocations: travel, yoga. Home: 23 Montilla Pl Palm Coast FL 32137 also: 4 San Gaboriel Ln Palm Coast FL 32137

SWINBURN, CHARLES, retired rail transportation executive; b. Bowness on Windermere, Cumbria, Eng., Apr. 11, 1942; came to U.S., 1949; s. Joseph and Myra (Sullivan) S.; m. Carol Ann Ditzler, Dec. 16, 1972; children: Ann Elizabeth, Catherine Knowles. BA in Psychology, Princeton U., NJ, 1963; MBA, Harvard U., Cambridge, Mass., 1971; JD, U. Pa., Phila., 1993. Industry analyst US Dept. Transp., Washington, 1971-73, chief Industry Analysis Div., 1973-76, dep. asst. sec., 1979-83; assoc. adminstr. fed. assistance Fed. R.R. Adminstrn., Washington, 1976-79; v.p. FS Rollins Environ. Svcs. Inc., Wilmington, Del., 1983-90; atty. Morgan, Lewis & Bockius, Washington, 1993—2004; CEO RailAmerica, Inc., Boca Raton, Fla., 2004—07. Capt. USMC, 1963-69; major USMCR, 1970-75. Decorated DFC (2), Air medal (35); recipient Presdl. Disting. Exec. award, 1980, Dept. Transp. Meritorious Achievement award, 1976, 78, 81 Personal E-mail: chaarles@aol.com.

SWINBURN, PETER, brewery company executive; married; 2 children. BSc in Econs. with honors, U. Wales. Joined Coors Brewing Co., 1974; sales dir. Bass Brewers, 1994—2002; dir. Grolsch UK; COO Coors Brewers Ltd., 2002—03, pres., CEO, 2005—07; pres. Coors Brewing Worldwide, 2003—05; pres., CEO Coors Brewing Co., 2007—08, Molson Coors Brewing Co., 2008—. Chmn. Tradeteam; bd. dirs. Molson Coors Brewing Co., 2008—. Office: Molson Coors Brewing Co 1225 17th St Ste 1875 Denver CO 80202 E-mail: peter.swinburn@molsoncoors.com.

SWINDELL, ARCHIE CALHOUN, JR., statistician, consultant; b. Sept. 26, 1936; s. Archie Calhoun and Louise Evelyn (Ellis) S.; m. Dolores Dyer Holland, Dec. 28, 1962 (dec.); children: Randy Zidick, Matthew Earle. BS in Chemistry, So. Meth. U., 1958; M in Nutritional Sci., Cornell U., 1965, PhD in Biochemistry, 1968. NIH postdoctoral fellow Duke U. Med. Ctr., Durham, NC, 1968-70; rsch. sci. positions in biochemistry, pharmacology, stats. Pfizer, Inc., Groton, Conn., 1970-95; statis. cons., 1995—. Contbr. articles on cholesterol metabolism, hormone action, cell culture, actions of drugs, data analysis, stats. to profl. jours., 1968-2008; patentee several anti-atherosclerosis agts. Active Town Coun., Groton, 1991-95, Bd. of Edn., 1997—2008; bd. dirs. LEARN, 2001-07. With US Army, 1958—61. Mem. AAAS, Am. Statis. Assn., Am. Heart Assn., Am. Assn. Artificial Intelligence, Sigma Xi, Conn. Botanical Soc., Math. Assn. Am. Avocations: nature photography, hiking, botany. Home and Office: 192 Monument St Groton CT 06340-3915 Home Phone: 860-449-8658; Office Phone: 860-449-8658. Personal E-mail: swindellac@tvcconnect.net.

SWINDELL, RUSSELL A., II, legislative staff member; Dist. dir., Rep. Bob Etheridge US House of Reps., NC, acting chief of staff to Rep. Bob Etheridge Washington, 2009—. Democrat. Office: 1533 Longworth House Office Bldg Washington DC 20515 Office Phone: 202-225-4531. Office Fax: 202-225-5662.*

SWINDLE, RALPH WILSON, JR., research psychologist; b. Palo Alto, Calif., Nov. 17, 1951; s. Ralph Wilson and Jewel Marie Swindle; m. Renee Marie Pobuda, May 8, 1983; children: David Michael, Jeremy Christopher, Natalie Diane. BA Magna Cum Laude in social ecology, U. Calif., Irvine, 1973; PhD in clin. cmty psychology, Ind. U., 1983. Cert. Psychologist, Health Svcs. Provider Ind. Health Svcs. Profl. Bur., 1984. Psychol. intern Quinco Cons. Ctr., Columbus, Ind., 1977—78; program evaluator So. Ctrl. Cmty. Mental Health Ctr., Bloomington, Ind., 1978—87; rsch. psychologist VA Health Svcs. R&D, Stanford U., Palo Alto, Calif., 1987—94, VA Health Svcs. R&D, Ind. U., Indpls., 1994—99; mgr., US rsch., global health outcomes Eli Lilly & Co., Indpls., 1999—2005, sr. rsch. scientist, 2005—07, rsch. advisor, 2007—08, rsch. fellow, 2008—. Contbr. chapters to books, more than 65 articles to profl. jours. Recipient Nicolas Aeberhardt award, Outstanding Freshman, U. Calif., Irvine, 1969; grantee NIMH Rsch. Grant (Heller & Swindle), NIMH, 1995-1998; fellow Clin. Traineeship in Alcoholism Rsch., NIAAA, 1975-1977; Summer fellow in Evaluation Rsch., NIMH, 1975, Pre-Doctoral Clin. Tng. fellowship, 1973-1975. Office: Outcomes Rsch Global Health Outcomes DC 5024 Lilly Corp Ctr Indianapolis IN 46285 Office Fax: 317-276-8268. Personal E-mail: pobudaswindle@earthlink.net. Business E-Mail: swindle@lilly.com.

SWING, ELIZABETH SHERMAN, education educator; b. Boston, June 29, 1927; d. James Beatty and Hilda (Ford) Sherman; m. Peter Gram Swing, May 27, 1948; children: Pamela, Timothy (dec.), Bradford. AB cum laude, Harvard U., 1949, MA, 1952; PhD, U. Pa., 1979. Tchr. English Marple Newtown HS, Pa., 1966-73; rsch. asst. U. Pa., Phila., 1973-75; asst. prof. West Chester State U., 1975-77, St. Joseph's U., Phila., 1978-84, assoc. prof., 1984-89, prof. edn., 1989—99, prof. emeritus, 1999—. Co-coord. commn. V, World Congress of Comparative Edn. Socs., Prague, 1992, co-coord. European commn., 1996. Author: Bilingualism and Linguistic Segregation in the Schools of Brussels, 1980; Editor: Inside Dunwoody, 2005; co-editor: Problems and Prospects in European Education, 2000; mem. editl. bd. European Edn., 1983—; contbr. articles to profl. jours. Collaborative com. Phila. Schs. and Colls., 1983-90; bd. dirs. Orchestra 2001, 1997-2003. Decorated knight Order of Crown (Belgium), 1989; recipient Legion of Honor award Chapel of Four Chaplains, 1984; grantee NEH Summer Seminar, 1981, U.S. Dept. Edn., 1984-87, Fulbright Found., 1989-90; vis. fellow U. London Inst. Edn., 1989-90. Mem. AAUP, Comparative Edn. Soc. Europe, Comparative and Internat. Edn. Soc. (bd. dirs. 1988-91, historian 1999-2008, hon. fellow 2000). Home: 3500 West Chester Pike Newtown Square PA 19073-4101 Personal E-mail: eswing1@verizon.net.

SWINNEY, DABO, college football coach; b. Ala., Nov. 20, 1969; m. Kathleen Bassett, 1994; children: Will, Drew, Clay. B in Commerce & Bus. Adminstrn., U. Ala., 1993, MBA, 1995. Grad. asst. coach U. Ala. Crimson Tide, 1993—95, wide receivers, tight ends coach, 1996—97, tight ends coach, 1997—98, wide receivers coach, 1998—2001; pvt. bus. Ala., 2001—03; wide receivers coach Clemson U. Tigers, 2003—08, interim head coach, 2008, head coach, 2008—. Office: Clemson Univ Athletic Dept PO Box 31 Clemson SC 29633*

SWINSON, SARA HOPE, writer, artist; b. Denver, Sept. 10, 1964; d. Honey Constance Harriet Shulman and Thomas Stanley Swinson. BA in Bible and Religion, Montreat, NC, 1993; MA in Exegetical Theology, Covenant Theol. Sem., Mo., 1996. Social worker MERS, Goodwill Industries, St. Louis, 1998—2005; media coord. Zip for Senate, Jefferson County, Mo., 2005; with hosp. chaplaincy, clin. pastoral edn. St. Louis U. Hosp., 2005—06; vocat. evaluator, social worker Lakes Country Resource Ctrs., St. Louis, 2005—06; hosp. chaplain, resident in clin. pastoral edn. St. Luke's Hosp., St. Louis, 2006—08. Columnist St. Louis Suburban Jours., 2004—05; staff writer, music journalist Nighttimes.com, St. Louis, 2005—; freelance writer St. Louis Post-Dispatch. Writer (humor columns, social critiques, revs.) Opinion Shaper's Columnist, archaeological (byzantine mosaic floor) Abila of the Decapolis; exhibit, Prophetic Self-Portrait, Bird Series. Staff writer New City Fellowship's Mainliner, St. Louis, 2001—. Mem.: Focus 11 Artists Collective, St. Louis Writer's Guild, St. Mary's Hosp. Bioethics Com. (com. mem. representing patient's rights 2001—03), Ctr. for Culture and Bioethics. Independent. Avocations: travel, painting, acting, collecting globes and pens. Home: 10331 Oxford Hill Dr Apt 3 Saint Louis MO 63146 Personal E-mail: shswinson@yahoo.com.

SWINTON, TILDA (KATHERINE MATILDA SWINTON), actress; b. London, Nov. 5, 1960; m. John Byrne; children: Xavier, Honor. Degree in Eng. Lit., Cambridge U., Eng., 1983. Actress (films) Caravaggio, 1986, Egomania - Insel ohne Hoffnung, 1986, Friendship's Death, 1987, Aria, 1987, L' Ispirazione, 1988, Degrees of Blindness, 1988, Das Andere Ende der Welt, 1988, The Last of England, 1988, War Requiem, 1989, Play Me Something, 1989, The Garden, 1990, Edward II, 1991 (Volpi Cup for Best Actess, Venice Film Festival, 1991), The Party: Nature Morte, 1991, Man to Man, 1992, Orlando, 1992 (Best Actress, Thessaloniki Film Festival, 1992, Golden Space Needle award for Best Actress, Seattle Internat. Film Festival, 1993), Wittgenstein, 1993, Blue, 1993, Remembrance of Things Fast: True Stories Visual Lies, 1994, Female Perversions, 1996, Conceiving Ada, 1997, Love Is the Devil: Study for a Portrait of Francis Bacon, 1998, The War Zone, 1999, The Beach, 2000, Possible Worlds, 2000, The Deep End, 2001 (Best Actress, Boston Soc. Film Critics, 2001, Sierra award for Best Actess, Las Vegas Film Critics Soc. Awards, 2002), Vanilla Sky, 2001, Teknolust, 2002, Adaptation, 2002, Young Adam, 2003 (Best Actress in Scottish Film, BAFTA awards, 2004), The Statement, 2003, Absent Presence, 2005, Constantine, 2005, Broken Flowers, 2005, The Chronicles of Narnia: The Lion, the Witch and the Wardrobe, 2005, Sleepwalkers, 2007, The Man from London, 2007, Michael Clayton, 2007 (Best Supporting

Actress, Brit. Acad. Film and TV Arts, 2008, Acad. award for Best Actress in a Supporting Role, 2008), Burn After Reading, 2008, The Curious Case of Benjamin Button, 2008, The Limits of Control, 2009, actress, prodr. Thumbsucker, 2005, Stephanie Daley, 2006, actress (TV series) Zastrozzi: A Romance, 1986, Your Cheatin' Heart, 1990, Shakespeare: The Animated Tales, 1992, (TV films) Offene Universum, 1993, The Somme, 2005. Recipient Bemen Film award, 2001. Office: Hamilton Hodell Ltd 5th Fl 66-68 Margaret St London W1W 8SR England Office Phone: 020 7636 1221. Office Fax: 020 7636 1226.*

SWIONTKOWSKI, MARC FRANCIS, orthopedist; b. Elizabeth, NJ, Sept. 15, 1951; s. William Robert and Agnes Eileen (Baker) S.; m. Beth Ellen, Sept. 2, 1972. BA, Calif. State U., 1973; MD, U. So. Calif., 1979. Gen. surgeon U. Wash., Seattle, 1979-80, resident orthop., 1980-84, assoc. prof., 1988-91, prof., 1991-97; orthopedic cons. KIlimanjoro Christian Med. Ctr., Moshi, Tanzania, 1984; rsch. assoc. Lab. for Experiment, Davos, Switzerland; asst. prof. surgery Vanderbilt U., Nashville, 1985-86, assoc prof., 1986-88; prof., chair dept. orthop. surgery U. Minn., Mpls., 1997—2007, prof. dept. orthop. surgery, 2007—. Fellow Am. Acad. Orthopaedic Surgery, Soc. Internat. Chgo., Chirurgie Orthopaedic Traumatology, Am. Coll. Surgery, Am. Bd. Orthopaedic Surgery (bd. dirs. 1999-2007), Am. Bd. Med. Specialties (bd. dirs. 2007-08). Democrat. Avocations: bicycle riding, carpentry. Office: U Minn Dept Ortho Surgery 2450 Riverside Ave Minneapolis MN 55454

SWIRE, EDITH WYPLER, music educator, violist, violinist; b. Boston, Feb. 16, 1943; d. Alfred R. Wypler Jr. and Frances (Glenn) Emery Wypler; m. James Bennett Swire, June 11, 1965; 1 child, Elizabeth Swire Falker. BA, Wellesley Coll., Mass., 1965; MFA, Sarah Lawrence Coll., Bronxville, NY, 1983; postgrad., Coll. of New Rochelle, 1984-85, Sarah Lawrence Coll., 2000—. Tchr. instrumental music, viola, violin The Windsor Sch., Boston, 1965-66; tchr., dir. The Lenox Sch., NYC, 1967-76; music curriculum devel. The Nightingale-Bamford Sch., NYC, 1968-69; head of fine arts dept. The Lenox Sch., NYC, 1976-78, head of instrumental music, 1978-80; founder, dir., tchr. string sch. Serpentine String Sch., Larchmont, 1981—96. Mem. founding com. Inter Sch. Orch., N.Y.C., 1972, trustee, 1976-85; panelist Nat. Assn. Ind. Sch. Conf., N.Y.C., 1977. Mem. music and worship com., Larchmont Ave. Ch., 1978-82, 88. Mem. Westchester Musicians Guild, N.Y. State Music Tchrs. Assn., Music Tchrs. Nat. Assn., Music Tchrs. Coun. Westchester (program com.), Violin Soc. Am., Wellesley in Westchester, Am. String Tchrs. Assn., The Viola Soc. of N.Y. Avocations: chamber music, mind/body healing, palliative care. Home and Office: 4 Mill Pond Ln New Rochelle NY 10805 Personal E-mail: edieswire@lrsoft.com.

SWIRNOFF, LOIS, artist, educator; b. Bklyn., May 9, 1931; d. Harold and Fannie (Goldstein) Swirnoff; m. Richard Boyce (dec.); 1 child, Dr. Joshua Avram Boyce; m. J. G. Charney (dec.). Cert. of graduation, Cooper Union Art Sch., NYC, 1951; BFA, Yale U., 1953, MFA summa cum laude, 1956; studied with Josef Albers. Instr. art Wellesley (Mass.) Coll., 1954-58; from asst. prof. to prof. emerita UCLA, 1965—90, prof. emerita, 1990—; lectr. Harvard U., Cambridge, Mass., 1968-75; assoc. prof., chmn. art dept. Skidmore Coll., Saratoga Springs, N.Y., 1977-81; guest artist Cooper Union Art Sch., 1990-91, adj. prof., 1991—; Feltman chair Cooper Union, NYC, 2000—02. Author: Dimensional Color, 1989, WW Norton, Van Nostrand Reinhold, 1992, 2nd edit., 2003, The Color of Cities, 2000 (Honorable Mention Best Book on Arch. and Urban Studies, Assn. Am. Pubs., Version in Mandarin Pub. in Beijing Van, China, 2008); one-woman shows include Farnsworth Mus., 1958, Swetzoff Gallery, Boston, 1962, Inst. Internat. Edn., N.Y.C., 1978—79, NAS, Washington, 1982—83, The Woman's Bldg., L.A., Bradford Coll. Laura Knott Gallery, 1988, Wellesley Coll., Gallery BAI, N.Y.C., 1996, N.Y. Sch. of Interior Design, 2000—01, Parson's Sch. Design, 2005, exhibited in group shows at City Art Mus., St. Louis, 1951, Bklyn. Mus., 1951, Munson-Williams Proctor Inst., Unica, N.Y., 1956, Swetzoff Gallery, 1963—65, Inst. Contemporary Art, Boston, 1961, LaJolla (Calif.) Mus., 1968, L.A. County Mus., 1968, Represented in permanent collections Addison Gallery Am. Art at Andover, Wellesley Coll., Mary I. Bunting Inst., Radcliffe Coll, UCLA, Parsons Sch. Design, also pvt.collections, exhibitions include The Light of Manhattan, NYSID, 2008;: 2d edit., 2003. Fulbright fellow, Florence, Italy, 1951-52, Yale-Norfolk summer fellow, 1953, fellow Mary I. Bunting Inst., Radcliffe Coll., 1961-63, Yaddo fellow, 1985, 1987; Mellon faculty grantee Skidmore Coll., 1981, grantee Graham Found., 1988, 98, Internat. Interior Design Assn., 2004-05. Studio: 80 Monmouth St Brookline MA 02446-5607 Office Phone: 617-731-5071. Personal E-mail: lswirnoff@earthlink.net.

SWISHER, NICK (NICOLAS THOMPSON SWISHER), professional baseball player; b. Columbus, Ohio, Nov. 25, 1980; s. Steve and Lillian Swisher. Attended, Ohio State U., Columbus, 1999—2002. First baseman Oakland Athletics, 2004—08, Chgo. White Sox, 2008; outfielder, first baseman NY Yankees, 2008—. Host Swisher Unscripted (Emmy award). Founder Swish's Wishes; amb. Entertainment Industry Found., Women's Cancer Rsch. Fund. Named Freshman of Yr., Big Ten Conf., 1999. Office: NY Yankees Yankee Stadium One E 161st St Bronx NY 10451*

SWISHER, STEPHEN G., thoracic surgeon; BA in Hist., Stanford U., 1982, BS in Biology, 1982; MD, U. Calif., 1986. Diplomate Nat. Bd. Med. Examiners, AM. Bd. Surgery, Am. Bd. Thoracic Surgery, lic. Tex. State Bd. Med. Examiners, Calif. State Bd. Med. Examiners. Intern U. Calif., Los Angeles Med. Ctr., 1986—87, resident, 1987—88, fellow surgical oncology, 1988—90, resident gen. surgery, 1990—93; clin. instr. gen. surgery U. Calif. Los Angeles Med. Ctr., 1993—94; registrar gen. surgery Nottingham, England, 1991; prof. surgery U. Tex., M.D. Anderson Cancer Ctr., fellow cardiothoracic surgery, 1994—96, jr. faculty assoc. to asst. prof. to assoc. prof. to prof., dept. throacic and cardiovascular surgery, 1995—; chmn., prof. surgery, dept. thoracic and cardiovasc. surgery St. Luke's Episc. Hosp., Tex. Heart Assn., 1994—96. Dir. esophageal cancer program, dept. thoracic and cardiovascular surgery U. Tex., M.D. Anderson Cancer Ctr., 2002—05, APN/PA dept. liaison, dept. thoracic and cardiovascular surgery, 2003—, dep. chair academic affairs, dept. thoracic and cardiovascular surgery, 2004—; reviewer various profl. jours.; speaker various nat. and internat. confs. Contbr. articles various profl. jours. and abstracts, chapters to books. Mem. ACS, 1982—86, 1996—98, assoc. fellow to fellow, 1998—2000; mem. Am. Med. Student Assn., 1982—86, Western Student Rsch. Med. Com., 1983—86, AMA, 1986—98. Recipient Yale Book award, Menlo Sch., 1977, Fairclough award, Stanford U., 1982, Lange Publ. award, UCSD Med. Sch., 1986, Pres. award, Soc. Leukocyte Biology, 1989, Golden Scalpel Chief award, UCLA Med. Ctr. Resident, 1993; named one of Best Doctors in Am., 2005; nominee Clin. Scientist award in translational rsch., Burroughs Wellcome, 2000; numerous rsch. grants. Mem.: Denton A. Cooley Cardiovascular Soc., Harris County Med. Soc., Tex. Med. Assn., Longmire Surgical Soc., Am. Assn. Thoracic Surgery, Am. Coll. Surgeons Oncology Group, Soc. U. Surgeons, Internat. Soc. Gastointestinal Cancer, Am. Soc. Gastrointestinal Oncology, Am. Radium Soc., Am. Assn. Cancer Rsch., So. Thoracic Surgical Assn., Soc. Thoracic Surgeons, Am. Bd. Thoracic Surgery, Internat. Soc. Diseases Esophagus, Am. Soc. Clin. Oncology, Internat. Assn. Study Lung Cancer, Soc. Surgical Oncology, Soc. Thoracic Radiology (hon.), Peruvian Soc. Med. Oncology (hon.), Gen. Thoracic Surgical Club, Phi Beta Kappa. Achievements include patents for induction of apoptotic or cytotoxic gene expression by adenoviral mediated gene codelivery; patents pending for methods of enhancing immune induction involving MDA7; proapoptotic adenoviral vectors and methods of use thereof; multigene vectors; compositions and methods involving MDA7 for the treatment of cancer. Office: Thoracic Cardiovascular Surgery 1515 Holcombe Blvd Unit 445 FC9 2044 Houston TX 77030

SWISTEK, RONALD JAMES, special education educator; b. Chgo., Aug. 24, 1969; s. Walter V. and Joyce E. Swistek; m. Carolyn L. Swistek, Dec. 8, 2001; children: Sean J., Catherine A. BS in Edn., Jacksonville State U., Ala., 1991; Med, Armstrong Atlantic State U., Savannah, Ga., 2007. Cert. in behavioral Sci.Edn. GAPSC, Ga., 1999, in economics edn. GAPSC, Ga., 1999, in geography Edn. GAPSC, Ga., 1999, in history Edn. GAPSC, Ga., 1999, polit. Sci. Edn. GAPSC, Ga., 1999, special edun. Gen. Curriculum GAPSC, Ga., 2004, in special Edn. social sci. cognitive level GAPSC, Ga., 2005, Reading Edn. GAPSC, Ga., 2007. Adjuct instr. Lanier Tech. Coll., Gainesville, Ga., 2007—08; tchr. Lumpkin County Sch. Sys., Dahlonega, Ga., 2008—. Ednl. tchr. U.S. Space Acad., Huntsville, Ala., 1991—94, counselor, 1991—94; edn. programs coord. Big Bros., Big Sisters, Huntsville, 1995—98; edn. coord. Eckerd Youth Alternatives, Suches, Ga., 1998—2008; com. chmn. dept accreditation SACS/CASI, peer rev. team dept accreditation. Alumnus Sigma Phi Epsilon Frat., Richmond, Va. Recipient Disting. Tchr. Yr., Ga. Dept. Juvenile Justice, 2001—02. Mem.: P.A.G.E. R-Conservative. Roman Catholic. Achievements include development of curriculum Eckerd Academy, Blue Ridge. Avocations: fishing, hiking, canoeing, climbing, baseball. Personal E-mail: swistek@windstream.net.

SWISTEL, DANIEL GEORGE, surgeon; b. Mar. 4, 1953; AB, Harvard Coll., 1975; MD, Rutgers U., 1979. Intern/resident gen. surgery St. Lukes/Roosevelt, 1979—84; resident in cardiovasc. surgery Albert Einstein/Montefiore Hosp. Med. Ctr., 1984—86; chief divsn. cardiothoracic surgery St. Luke/Roosevelt Hosp. Ctr., NYC, 1998—, co-dir. hypertropthic cardiomyopathy program; sr. attending Lenox Hill Hosp. Assoc. prof. surgery Columbia U. Coll. Physicians and Surgeons, 1996—; co-dir. Hypertrophic Cardiopathy Program, 1998—2008; pres. bd. dirs. Ukrainian Inst. Am., NYC; pres. NY Thoracic Soc., 2009—. Home: 25 E 86th St Apt 13D New York NY 10028-0553 Office Phone: 212-523-4088, 212-434-3000. E-mail: dwistel@chpnet.org.

SWITZ, ROBERT E., telecommunications executive; BS in Mktg. and Econs., Quinnipiac Coll., 1969; MBA in Fin., U. Bridgeport, 1973. Sr. fin. mgmt. staff PepsiCo., AMF, Olin Corp.; v.p. European ops., ventures and fin. Burr-Brown Corp., Tucson, 1988-94; CFO ADC Telecom., 1994—2003, sr. v.p. to exec. v.p., 1997—2003, pres. broadband access & transport group, 2000—01, pres., CEO, 2003—. Bd. dirs. Hickory Tech. Corp., Mpls. Youth Trust. Office: ADC Telecommunications 13625 Technology Dr Eden Prairie MN 55344 E-mail: bob_switz@adc.com.

SWITZER, BARRY, sportscaster, retired professional football coach; b. Crossett, Ark., Oct. 5, 1937; s. Frank and Louise Switzer; m. Kay Switzer, 1963 (div. 1983); children: Greg, Kathy, Dove. BA, U. Ark., 1960. Asst. football coach U. Ark. Razorbacks, 1960-65, U. Okla. Sooners, 1966-72, head coach, 1973-89, Dallas Cowboys, 1994—97; studio analyst FOX NFL Sunday, 2008—. Author: Bootleggers's Boy, 1990. Served with US Army. Recipient Jim Thorpe Lifetime Achievement award, 2004; named Walter Camp Coach of Year, 1973; named to College Football Hall of Fame, 2002. Achievements include head coach of the AP/UPI NCAA National Champions University of Oklahoma Sooners, 1974, 75, 85; head coach of Super Bowl XXX Championship winning Dallas Cowboys, 1996. Office: c/o FOX Sports PO Box 900 Beverly Hills CA 90213-0900

SWITZER, CAROLYN JOAN, artist, educator; b. Petoskey, Mich., Apr. 20, 1931; d. Eugene Constant and Burnis Hazel (Lower) S. Student, Wayne State U., 1954-55, St. John's Coll., Santa Fe, N.Mex., 1993; BA, Mich. State U., 1953, MA, 1964. Cert. tchr., Mich. Art tchr. Ferndale Bd. of Edn., 1953-56, Birmingham Bd. of Edn., Mich., 1956-96; pvt. tchr. drawing and painting. Cons. Girl Scouts U.S., Birmingham, Petoskey, Mich.; mem. Crooked Tree Arts Coun., Petoskey; deacon, mem. choir First Presbyn. Ch. of Petoskey. Recipient Recognition award Birmingham Edn. Assn. Coun., 1967, Outstanding Sr. Woman, Lantern Night MSU, 1953. Mem. AAUW (scholar, Mich. State U., 1962), PEO, Nat. Art Edn. Assn., Mich. Art Edn. Assn., Mich. Edn. Assn., Detroit Inst. Art, Nat. Mus. for Women in Arts, Mich. Coun. for Arts, Art Study Club of Petoskey, Zonta Internat., Crooked Tree Arts Ctr. Petoskey, Little Traverse Hist. Soc. Avocations: music/singing, reading, exercise class, walking, photography. Home: 805 Lindell Ave Petoskey MI 49770-3159

SWITZER, JANET, psychologist administrator; b. Dodge City, Kans., June 17, 1932; d. Thomas Marion and Rozella (White) S. BA, Antioch Coll., 1955; MA, Clark U., 1957, PhD, 1961. Lic. psychologist. Various ednl. and rsch. positions, 1952-57; clin. intern Judge Baker Guidance Clinic, Boston, 1957-58; teaching asst. Clark U., Worcester, Mass., 1961-63, lectr., 1963; supervising psychologist Worcester Youth Guidance Ctr., 1958-63; sr. supervising psychologist Reiss-Davis Child Study Ctr., LA, 1963-65; dir. tng. Marianne Frostig Ctr. for Ednl. Therapy, LA, 1965-67; lectr. ednl. psychology dept. U. Hawaii, Honolulu, 1966; lectr. extension faculty UCLA, 1967-80; exec. dir. Switzer Ctr., Torrance, Calif., 1966-94; exec. dir. emeritus, 1994—. Author: Norris Educational Achievement Test, 1992; contbr. articles to profl. jours. Pres. Calif. Assn. Pvt. Spl. Edn. Schs., Sacramento, 1977-78, legis. chair, 1978-82. Fellow Am. Orthopsychiat. Assn., Am. Ednl. Therapy Assn. (adv. bd. 1979—); mem. Am. Psychol. Assn., Calif. Psychol. Assn., La. County Psychol. Assn., Coun. on Exceptional Children, Orton Dyslexia Soc. Democrat. Avocations: gardening, stained glass, fishing, antique collecting. Office Phone: 310-328-3611.

SWITZER, JAY A(LAN), chemistry educator; b. Cin., May 14, 1950; s. William K. and Virginia H. (Gray) S.; m. Barbara A. Smith, Aug. 18, 1972; 1 child, Eric R. BS in Chemistry, U. Cin., 1973; MA in Inorganic Chemistry, Wayne State U., 1975, PhD in Inorganic Chemistry, 1979. Rsch. chemist Union Oil Co. Calif. (UNOCAL), Brea, 1979-84, sr. rsch. chemist, 1984-86; assoc. prof. materials sci. and engring. U. Pitts., 1987-90; prof. chemistry, sr. investogator Ctr. for Materials Rsch. U. Mo., Rolla, 1990—. Mem. Electrochem. Soc. (vice chmn. So. Calif. sect. 1985-86), Am. Chem. Soc., Materials Research Soc., Am. Ceramic Soc. Office: Univ Mo 103 Materials Rsch Ctr Rolla MO 65409-0001

SWITZER, JO YOUNG, college president; b. Huntington, Ind., Mar. 4, 1948; d. John Frederick and Miriam Lucile (Kindy) Young; children: Sarah Kate Keller, John Christian Keller. BA, Manchester Coll., 1969; MA, U. Kans., 1977, PhD, 1980; postdoctoral, Ind. U., 1983, Harvard U., 1995. Asst. instr. U. Kans., Lawrence, 1977-79; asst. prof. Ind. U.-Purdue, Ft. Wayne, Ind., 1979-82; assoc. prof. Manchester Coll., North Manchester, Ind., 1982-87, Ind. U.-Purdue, Ft. Wayne, Ind., 1987-93; v.p., dean for acad. affairs and prof. comm. studies Manchester (Ind.) Coll., 1993—2004, pres., 2004—. Bd. dirs. BCA Study Abroad Consortium, Indpls. Peace Inst. Recipient E. C. Buehler award U. Kans., 1978; grantee NEH, 1983. Mem. Central States Comm. Assn. (Outstanding Young Educator award 1982), Coun. Ind. Colls. (bd. dirs.), Ind. Coll. Ind. (exec. bd. mem.), Am. Coun. on Edn., Am. Assn. Colls. and Univs. Office: Manchester Coll Office of Pres 604 E College Ave North Manchester IN 46962-1276 Office Phone: 260-982-5050. Office Fax: 260-982-5042. Business E-Mail: jyswitzer@manchester.edu.

SWITZER, JON REX, architect; b. Shelbyville, Ill., Aug. 22, 1937; s. John Woodrow and Ida Marie (Vadalabene) S.; m. Judith Ann Heinlein, July 7, 1962; 1 child, Jeffrey Eric. Student, U. Ill., 1955-58; BS, Millikin U., 1972; MA, U. Ill., Springfield, 1981. Registered architect Ill., Mo., Ohio, Colo.; registered interior designer, Ill. Arch. Warren & Van Praag, Inc., Decatur, Ill., 1970-72; prin. Decatur, 1972-81, Bloomington, Ill., 1981-83; arch. Hilfinger, Asbury, Cufaude, Abels, Bloomington, 1983-84; ptnr. Riddle/Switzer, Ltd., Bloomington, 1984-86; with bldg., design and constrn. divsn. State Farm Ins. Cos., Bloomington, 1986-89; arch. The Riddle Group, Bloomington, 1989-91; prin. J. Rex Switzer, Arch., Bloomington, 1991—. Elder Presbyn. Ch., 1996. With U.S. Army, 1958-61. Mem. AIA (emeritus, pres. Bloomington chpt. 1983, Decatur chpt. 1976, v.p. Ill. chpt. 1986-87, sec. 1985, treas. 1984), Am. Archtl. Found., Chgo. Architecture Found., Nat. Trust Hist. Preservation, Frank Lloyd Found., Decatur C. of C. (merit citation 1974, merit award 1979), Am. Legion, Masons (32d degree). Republican. Presbyterian. Avocations: swimming, hunting, fishing, reading, drawing. Home: 9 Mary Ellen Way Bloomington IL 61701-2014 Office: 2412 E Washington St Ste 6A Bloomington IL 61704-1613

SWITZER, KATHLEEN HENDERSON, administrative law judge, clinical nurse specialist; d. Carroll Vincent and Vera Elaine (Morey) Henderson; m. Ronald L. Switzer, Nov. 27; children: Kendall Scott, Douglas Kent, Sherry Lynn Rowe. BS with distinction, Mont. State U., Bozeman, 1969; MS, U. Ariz., Tucson, 1976; JD, U. Utah Coll. Law, Salt Lake City, 1987. Bar: Utah; RN Mont. Judicial clerk US Dist. Ct., 10th Cir. Ct. Appeals, Salt Lake City, 1987—89; legal counsel GTE Health Sys. Inc., Salt Lake City, 1993—96; atty. Fabian & Clendenin, Salt Lake City, 1993—96; adminstrv. law judge Utah Labor Commn., Salt Lake City, 1996—2000; US Indian probate judge Dept. Interior, Salt Lake City, 2000—01; US adminstrv. law judge Social Security Adminstrn., Salt Lake City, 2001—. Judge protempore 3rd Dist. Ct., Salt Lake City, 2000—01; bd. dirs. Ft. Douglas Mus. Assn, Salt Lake City, 2007, Women Lawyers Utah, Salt Lake City; ex officio bar commr. Utah State Bar, Salt Lake City. Contbr. articles to law jours.; author: (book chpt.) Disaster Nursing: Planning, Assessment and Intervention, 1985 (Am. Jour. Nursing Book Yr. award, 1986). Vet. Persian Gulf War, Nuremburg, Germany, 1990—91; trustee First Meth. Ch., Salt Lake City. Col. USAR, Ft. Douglas, Utah, comdr. 5th Brigade 104th Divsn. USAR, 2000—02, Salt Lake City. Decorated Legion of Merit US Army, Meritorious Svc. medal (First Oak Leak Cluster), Commendation medal (Fourth Oak Leaf Cluster), Achievement medal (Second Oak Leaf Cluster); recipient Outstanding Student award, Army Command and Gen. Staff Coll.; named Utah Woman Lawyer of Yr., 2008. Fellow: Am. Assn. Nurse Attys. (Outstanding Advocate award 1994); mem.: Sigma Thela Tau (hon.). Achievements include female US administrative law judge in Salt Lake City; first Army nurse selected for brigade command; first Army nurse selected as Army Detailed Inspector General. Office: Disability Adjucation and Rev Bennett Fed Bldg Ste 3102 Salt Lake City UT 84138 Office Phone: 801-524-4449. Office Fax: 801-294-7686. Business E-Mail: switzer@xmission.com.

SWITZER, MAURICE HAROLD, journalist; b. Toronto, Ont., Can., Mar. 28, 1945; s. Harold Switzer and Ruby (Marsden) Hicks; m. Mary Helene Pavlik (dec.); children: Andrea Zimperi, Adin, Lisa Doracka. Student, Trent U., Peterborough, Ont., 1964-65. Journalist Belleville (Ont.) Intelligencer, Canada, 1965-67, sports editor, 1967-72, mng. editor, 1972-79, Oshawa (Ont.) Times, 1979-81; pub. Timmins (Ont.) Daily Press, 1981-86, Sudbury (Ont.) Star, 1986-92, Winnipeg (Man.) Free Press, 1992-94; owner Media Help Svcs., 1994—. Mem. faculty Aboriginal Media First Nations Tech. Inst., 1996—97; dir. comm. Assembly of First Nations, Ottawa, 1997—2000, Union Ont. Indians, North Bay, 2000—; mem. faculty Aboriginal Leadership and Mgmt. program Banff Ctr., 1998—2005; prof. comms. Huntington U., Sudbury, Ont., Canada, 2001—08. Author: Bruno Cavallo a Conversation, 1991. Mem. elders coun. Mississaugas of Alderville First Nation. Office Phone: 705-497-4127. Personal E-mail: swimau@anishinabek.ca.

SWITZER, ROBERT LEE, biochemistry professor; b. Clinton, Iowa, Aug. 26, 1940; s. Stephen and Elva Delila (Allison) S.; m. Bonnie George, June 13, 1965; children: Brian, Stephanie. BS, U. Ill., 1961; PhD, U. Calif., Berkeley, 1966. Research fellow Lab. Biochemistry, Nat. Heart Inst., Bethesda, Md., 1966-68; asst. prof. biochemistry U. Ill., Urbana, 1968—73, assoc. prof., 1973—78, prof. biochemistry and basic med. scis., 1978—2002, prof. emeritus, 2002—, dept. head, 1988—93. Mem. biochemistry study sect. NIH, 1985-89, chmn., 1987-89; guest prof. U. Copenhagen, 1995; mem. microbial physiology and genetics study sect., NIH, 1998-2000. Author: (with Liam F. Garrity) Experimental Biochemistry, 3rd rev. edit., 1999; mem. bd. editors Jour. Bacteriology, 1977-82, 1985—2002, Archives Biochemistry and Biophysics, 1977-98, Jour. Biol. Chemistry, 1980-85; contbr. articles to profl. jours. NSF predoctoral fellow, 1961-66; NIH postdoctoral fellow, 1966-68; Guggenheim fellow, 1975. Fellow Am. Acad. Microbiology; mem. Am. Soc. for Biochemistry and Molecular Biology, Am. Soc. Microbiology, Am. Chem. Soc., AAAS, Sigma Xi. Home: 404 W Michigan Ave Urbana IL 61801-4948 Office: U Ill Dept Biochemistry 600 S Mathews Ave Urbana IL 61801-3602 Office Phone: 217-333-3940. Business E-Mail: rswitzer@illinois.edu.

SWITZER, SHARON CECILE, language educator, researcher; PhD, Lesley U., Cambridge, Mass., 2003. Dir. of ESL Martha's Vineyard Sch. Dist., Martha's Vineyard, Mass., 2000—04; asst. prof. East Stroudsburg U., Pa., 2004—. Bd. dirs. Pa. TESOL E., Phila., 2004—. Bd. dirs. Pocono Svcs.s for Family and Children, East Stroudsburg, 2005—06. Grantee Head Start Rsch. scholar, Adminstrn. Children Youth and Families, 1999—2001. Mem.: TESOL. Avocations: painting, travel, yoga. Office: East Stroudsburg University 200 Prospect St East Stroudsburg PA 18301

SWOAP, DAVID BRUCE, government and state agency administrator, consultant, art director; b. Kalamazoo, Aug. 12, 1937; s. Orlo Frederick and Aileen Esther (Hempy) S. BA in Govt. with honors, Denison U., 1959; MA in Govt., Claremont Grad. Sch., 1961; DSc (hon.), U. Osteo. Medicine and Health Scis., Des Moines, 1981. Asst. sec. Calif. State Pers. Bd., Sacramento, 1972-73; chief dep. dir., acting dir. Calif. State Dept. Social Welfare, 1973, dir., 1973-74, Calif. State Dept. Benefit Payments, 1974-75; sr. rsch. asso. Rep. Study Com., U.S. Ho. of Reps., Washington, 1975-76; profl. staff mem. U.S. Senate Com. on Fin.,

1976-79; legis. dir. U.S. Senator William L. Armstrong, 1979-81; dep. sec. HHS, 1981-83; sec. health and welfare State of Calif., Sacramento, 1983-85; ptnr. Franchetti & Swoap, San Francisco, 1985-90; owner Mana Olana Farms, Hakalau, Hawaii, 1989—97; vice chmn. Sacramento Advs., 1991-98; owner The David Bruce Gallery, Carlsbad, Calif., 1995-97. Chmn. bd. Hope Unltd. for Children, Los Alamitos, Calif., 1991—96, bd. mem., 2007—, mem. adv. bd., 1996—2007, chmn. adv. bd., 1996—2003. Elder Presbyn. Ch.; bd. dirs. Friends of SOS Children's Villages, 1989-91; bd. regents John F. Kennedy U., 1990-93; mem. Healthy Families Dorchester adv. bd., 2002-05, Md. State Bd. of Physicians, 2003-05. Rotary Club Found. fellow, 1961-62 Mem. Wycliffe Assocs., Phi Beta Kappa, Delta Upsilon. Republican.

SWOFFORD, BETH, agent; Motion picture agent Creative Artists Agency (CAA), Beverly Hills. Trustee Mus. of Contemporary Art, LA; media com. mem. Gold Mus. Modern Art, 2007—09. Named one of Top 200 Collectors, ARTnews Mag., 2004—08, The 100 Most Powerful Women in Entertainment, Hollywood Reporter, 2004, 2005, 2006, 2007, The 50 Smartest People in Hollywood, Entertainment Weekly, 2007. Avocation: Collector of Contemporary Art. Office: Creative Artists Agy 2000 Ave of the Stars Los Angeles CA 90067 also: PO Box 240002 Los Angeles CA 90024

SWONGER, CHRIS, lobbyist, beverage company executive; With Nat. Rep. Senatorial Com.; sr. lobbyist UST, Inc.; sr. v.p. corp. affairs Allied Domecq Spirits & Wine N.Am., v.p. govt. affairs; sr. v.p. corp. affairs Jim Beam Brands Worldwide, 2005—, Beam Global Spirits & Wine, Inc. Office: Beam Global Spirits & Wine, Inc 1301 K St NW, #250W Washington DC 20005 Office Phone: 202-962-0551.*

SWONGER, THOMAS K. H., JR., insurance company executive; s. Thomas K. H. and Mary Helen Swonger; m. Claudia Maria Arteaga, Feb. 6, 2004; children: Richard Thomas, Karli Elizabeth, Thomas K. H. III. BS in Bus. Mgmt., U. Phoenix, Orlando, Fla., 2001—04, MBA, 2004—05. Cert. in workers compensation WCCP, Fla., 1996. Mil. police US Army, Karlsruhe, Germany, 1987—92; police officier Daytona Beach Police Dept., Fla., 1992—93; claims examiner Exec. Risk Cons., Longwood, Fla., 1993—97; sr. claims examiner, claims supr. Gallagher Bassett Svcs., Orlando, Fla., 1997—2004; claims mgr. Sedgwick Claims Mgmt. Svcs., Lake Mary, Fla., 2004—. Youth instr. St. Issac Joques, Orlando, 2003—05. Specialist US Army, 1987—92, Germany, paratrooper US Army, 1988. Decorated Good Conduct medal US Army, Drivers medal, Forgien Svc. medal, Combat citation. Mem.: WCCP (assoc.). Office: Sedgwick CMS 255 Primera Blvd Ste 400 Lake Mary FL 32746 Office Fax: 407-833-4111. Business E-Mail: tswonger@sedgwickcms.com.

SWONK, DIANE CATHERINE, economist; b. Kalamazoo, Apr. 8, 1962; AB in Economics, U. Mich., 1984, MA in Applied Economics, 1985; MBA in Fin., U. Chgo., 1989. From assoc. economist to dep. chief economist Bank One Corp. (formerly First Chgo. Corp.), 1985-96; chief economist, sr. v.p. Bank One Corp., 1998—2004; sr. mng. dir., chief economist Mesirow Financial Holdings, Inc., Chgo., 2004—. Clinical prof. fin. DePaul U. Kellstadt Grad. Sch. Bus., 2001—; mem. Congressional Budget Office Panel of Econ. Advisors. Author: The Passionate Economist: Finding the Power and Humanity Behind the Numbers, 2003 Bd. dirs. Workforce City of Chgo., 1995—; mem. advisory bd., The Chgo. Conservation Ctr.; bd. mem., U. Mich. Alumni Assn. Named one of 40 Under 40, Crains Chgo. Bus., 1993; named Fin. Voice of Midwest, Chgo. Tribune, 1994, Woman of Achievement, Girl Scouts Am., Ill., 1997, Bus. Leader of the Yr., YWCA Metropolitan Chgo., The Top Woman in Fin. in Chgo., Today's Chgo. Woman, 1999 Mem. Nat. Assn. Bus. Econs. (bd. dirs. 1996—, regional chair 1990-97, v.p. 1998-99, pres. 1999-00), Soc. Automotive Analysts (bd. dirs.), Chgo. Assn. Bus. Economists, Internat. Conf. for Comml. Bank Economists, Conf. of Bus. Economics, Econ. Club of Chgo. Office: Mesirow Financial Holdings Inc 350 N Clark Chicago IL 60654 Office Phone: 312-595-7122. E-mail: dswonk@mesirowfinancial.com.*

SWOPE, DONALD DOWNEY, retired banker; b. Martinsville, Ill., Feb. 26, 1926; s. Roy V. and Dorothy Irene (Downey) S.; m. Earla Long Markert, Aug. 16, 1960. BS, Ind. State U., 1950. With Ill. Savs. and Loan Commn., Springfield, Ill., 1950-77, chief dept. commr., 1971-77; exec. v.p. Bank for Savs. & Loan Assn., Chgo., 1977-81, pres., 1981-90. Bd. dirs. Country Fair White Elephant, Green Valley, Ariz., 1981-2008, treas., 1981-84. With USNR, 1944-63. Mem. VFW (life), Nat. Assn. State Savs. and Loan Suprs. (pres. 1972-73), Am. Legion (life), Kiwanis (pres. Crete, Ill. 1977-78, treas. Green Valley, Ariz. 1994, 95), Elks (life, treas.). Home Phone: 520-625-9732. Personal E-mail: dds777@msn.com.

SWOPE, JEFFREY PEYTON, lawyer; b. Evanston, Ill., June 11, 1945; s. Oliver P. and Elspeth E. (Cahill) S.; m. Linda Lee, Aug. 26, 1967; children: Matthew, Gregory, Timothy. AB, Harvard U., 1967, JD, 1970. Bar: Mass. 1970, U.S. Dist. Ct. Mass. 1971, U.S. Ct. Appeals (1st cir.) 1973, U.S. Ct. Appeals (Fed. Cir.) 1974, U.S. Supreme Ct. 1979. Assoc. Edwards Angell Palmer & Dodge, Boston, 1970-76, ptnr., 1977—. Treas. Social Law Libr., Boston, 1984-2003, pres., 2003-. Treas. Ella Lyman Cabot Trust, Holliston, Mass., 1979-. Home: 54 Hyde St Newton MA 02461-1206 Office: Edwards Angell Palmer & Dodge LLP 111 Huntington Ave Boston MA 02199-7613

SWYGERT, HAYWOOD PATRICK, law educator, retired academic administrator; b. Phila., Mar. 17, 1943; s. LeRoy and Gustina (Rogers) Huzzy; children: Haywood Patrick Jr., Michael Branson. AB in History, Howard U., 1965, JD cum laude, 1968. Bar: D.C. 1968, Pa. 1970, N.Y. 1970. Law clk. to chief judge U.S. Ct. Appeals (3d cir.), Phila., 1968—69; assoc. Debevoise, Plimpton, Lyons & Gates, NYC, 1969—70; adminstrv. asst. to Congressman Charles B. Rangel NY, 1971—72; spl. asst. dist. atty. Phila., 1973; from asst. prof. to prof. law Temple U., 1972—90, v.p. adminstrn., 1982—88, exec. v.p., 1988—90; pres. SUNY, Albany, 1990—95, Howard U., Washington, 1995—2008, prof. law, 2008—. Bd. dirs. United Tech. Corp., Hartford Fin. Svcs. Group; adv. bd. Ctrl. Intelligence Agy., 2002; chmn. HBCU Capital Fin., 2002—. Gov.'s rep. Southeastern Pa. Transp. Authority, 1987—90; bd. trustees Inst. Pub. Adminstrn., 1992—99; exec. com. Pub. Law Ctr., Phila., 1980—88; bd. dirs. NY State Coun. on Humanities, 1991—95; chmn. ednl. structure, policies and practices NY State Spl. Commn., 1993—95; co-chmn. joint task force grad. edn. Nat. Assn. State Univs. and Land Grant Colls./Am. Assn. State Coll. and Univs., 1993—95; chmn. capital financing program adv. bd. Historically Black Colls. and Univs., 2002—06; mem. founding coun. Smithsonian Instn.'s Nat. Mus. of African Am. History and Culture, 2004; mem. DC Emancipation Commemoration Commn., 2004, Brown vs. Board Edn. Commemoration Commn., 2002, US Nat. Commn. UNESCO, 2004; bd. dirs. New Cmty. Devel. Corp., HUD, 1980—82, Nat. Pub. Radio, 1995—96; mem. Commn. Presdl. Debates. Recipient Bldg. Industry Assn. Achievement award, DC, Spl. Friend award, Am. Friends of Lubavitch, 2003, Edn. award, Nat. Conf. Cmty. & Justice, 2003, Chmn. award, Congl. Black Caucus 34th Ann. Legis. Conf., 2004, Legend award for outstanding leadership in edn., Nat. Urban League, 2005. Mem.: ABA, Victory Funds (trustee 1994—2002), Middle States Assn. Colls. and Schs. (commn. on higher edn. 1992—95). Office: Howard U 2400 6th St NW Washington DC 20059-0002 Office Phone: 202-806-2500. E-mail: hswygert@howard.edu.

SYDOW, MICHAEL DAVID, SR., executive lawyer; b. Dec. 12, 1950; children: Kristen, David, Wyatt. BA, Southwestern U., 1973; JD with honors, U. Tex., 1976. Bar: Tex. 1976, U.S. Ct. Claims 1977, U.S. Ct. Appeals (5th cir.) 1977, U.S. Dist. Ct. (so. dist.) Tex. 1977, U.S. Dist. Ct. (ea. dist.) Tex. 1979, U.S. Supreme Ct. 1980, U.S. Dist. Ct. (no. dist.) Tex. 1985, U.S. Dist. Ct. (we. dist.) Tex. 1986; cert. in civil trial law Tex. Bd. Legal Specialization. Trial atty. Office Gen. Counsel USN, Arlington, Va., 1976-77; mem. firm Eastham, Watson, Dale & Forney, Houston, 1977-84, Hagans & Sydow, LLP, Houston, 1985-90, Reynolds & Sydow, LLP, Houston, 1993-94; pvt. practice, 1990-93; with Sydow & McDonald, LLP, 1995-97, shareholder, 2002—, Verner, Liipfert, Bernhard, McPherson & Hand, Houston, 1997—2002; CEO Tex. Syngas, 2004—. Fellow Tex. Bar Found., Houston Bar Found.; mem. Houston Bar Assn. (chmn. jud. liaison com. 1988-90, Pres.'s award 1990), Maritime Law Assn. U.S. (mem. com. on gen. average 1977-88, practice and procedures com. 1988—), State Bar Tex., Phi Delta Phi. Office: Sydow & McDonald 4900 Woodway Ste 900 Houston TX 77056 Home: 4400 Post Dak Pkwy Ste 2360 Houston TX 77027 Office Phone: 713-622-9700. Office Fax: 713-552-1949. Business E-Mail: msydow@sydowmcdonald.com.

SYED, ELIZABETH CHANCE, health facility administrator, critical care nurse; b. Clermont, Fla., Oct. 18, 1958; d. Brooker Lawson and Beulah Catharine (Lord) Chance; m. Mohsin M. Syed, Dec. 30, 1993; children: Adam, Jibran. B in Gen. Studies, Howard Payne U., 1981; MA in Comm. without thesis, SW Bapt. Theol. Sem., 1985; ADN, Ea. N.Mex. U., 1988. Cert. CCRN, program nurse sr. options, med. office mgr. Critical care nurse Meml. Hosp. & Med. Ctr., Midland, Tex., 1990—94, Angelo Cmty. Med. Ctr., San Angelo, Tex., 1992; staff nurse ICU Med. Ctr. Hosp., Odessa, Tex., 1998; mental health nurse Glenwood Hosp., Midland, Tex., 1998—99; practice adminstr. Family Care Clinic and Med. Spa of Midland, 1998—, Cypur Clinic, Housten, Tex. Instr. ACLS. Mem. Cmty. Chorale, Farmington, N.Mex., 1981, Roswell, N.Mex., 1989-90. Mem. AACN (rsch. assoc. Thunder Project 1991-92). Avocation: music. Office: Family Care Clinic 4506 Briarwood Ave Midland TX 79707-2642 Office Phone: 432-689-6818. Business E-Mail: elizabeth@medicalspaofmidland.com.

SYED, IBRAHIM BIJLI, medical educator, physicist; b. Bellary, India, Mar. 16, 1939; came to US, 1969, naturalized, 1975; s. Syed Ahmed Bijli and Mumtaz Begum (Maniyar) S.; m. Sajida Shariff, Nov. 29, 1964; children: Mubin, Zafrin. BS with honors, Veerasaiva Coll., Bellary U., Mysore, 1960; MS with honors and distinction, Bangalore U., Mysore, 1962; diploma, U. Bombay, 1964; DSc, Johns Hopkins U., Balt., 1972; PhD (hon.), Malta, 1985. Cert. hazard control officer, 1980, internat. health care safety profl., 1980; diplomate Am. Bd. Radiology, Am. Bd. Health Physics. Lectr. physics Veerasaiva Coll., Bellary U., Mysore, 1962-63; med. physicist, radiation safety officer Victoria Hosp., India, 1964-67, Bowring and Lady Curz on Hosp. & Postgrad. Med. Rsch. Inst., Bangalore, India, 1964-67; cons. med. physicist, radiation safety officer Ministry of Health, Govt. of Karnataka, India, 1964-67, Bangalore Nursing Home, India, 1964-67; med. physicist, radiation safety officer Baystate Med. Ctr., Springfield, Mass., 1973-79; assoc. prof. Springfield Tech. C.C.; also adj. prof. radiology Holyoke C.C., Mass., 1973-79; asst. clin. prof. nuclear medicine U. Conn. Sch. Medicine, Farmington, 1975-79; cons. med. physicist Mercy Hosp., Springfield, 1973-79, Wing Meml. Hosp., Palmer, Mass., 1973-79; med. physicist, radiation safety officer VAMC, Louisville, 1979—, exec. officer radiation safety com., 1979—; prof. medicine U. Louisville Sch. Medicine, 1979—, dir. nuclear med. scis., 1980—; mem. Instl. Review Bd. Veterans Admin. Medical Ctr., Louisville, 2000—. Guest lectr. religious studies program U. Louisville, 1979—; vis. prof. Bangalore U., 1987—88, Gulbarga U., India, 1987—88; vis. scientist Bhabha Atomic Rsch. Ctr., Bombay; invited spkr. Veerasaiva Coll., Bellary, India, 1996, Vijayanagar Coll., Hospet, 1996, Vajayanagar Inst. Med. Scis., Bellary, 1996, Deccan Coll. Med. Scis., Hyderabad, India, Bhabha Atomic Rsch. Ctr., Bombay, 1997, 15th Ann. Islamic Conf. New Eng., Islamic Coun. New Eng., 1999, Coun. for a Parliament of the World's Religions, Cape Town, South Africa, 1999, Garden City Coll. Bangalore, 2000, Veerasaiva Coll., Bellary, 2000, Islamic Rsch. Found., Mumbai, India, 2001, Islamic Assn. of Essex, England, 2001, Assn. Muslim Social Scientists, Detroit, 2001, Darus Salam, Bangalore, India, 2005; invited faculty Assn. Muslim Social Scientists, Dallas, 2005; invited spkr. Islamic Orgn. Med. Scis., Cairo, 2002; PhD thesis examiner Allahabad U., 1996—; course dir. licensing for nuclear cardiologists U. Louisville, 1980—, mem. admissions com. nuclear medicine program, 1980—; guest relief examiner Am. Bd. Radiology, 1991, 2005; examiner in radiol physics, 1995, 97, 98, 2000; examiner in radiol. physics, 03, 05, 06; mem. panel of examiners Am. Bd. Health Physics; PhD thesis examiner U. Delhi, Internat. Inst. for Advanced Study, Clayton, Mo., 1985—. Allahabad (India) U., 1996—2005; faculty mem. Med. Physicists of India Ann. Meeting, 1987; IAEA tchr. expert in nuclear medicine on mission to People's Republic of Bangladesh, 86; to Guatemala, 94; founder, pres. Islamic Rsch. Found. Internat., Louisville, 1988—; convener Internat. Conf. on Islamic Renaissance: Action Plan for the 21st Century, Chgo., 1995; cons. Coun. Sci. and Indsl. Rsch., Govt. India, 0809—, Am. Coun. Sci. and Health, 1980—; cons. gastroenterology and urology divsn. FDA, HHS, 1988—, cons. radiopharm. divsn., 1989—; cons. Govt. India in nuclear medicine, diagnostic radiol. physics, therapeutic radiol. physics and radiation safety, 1992; cons. radiol. and med. nuc. physics Govt. India, Un Devel. Program, 1992; convenor Internat. Conf. on Islamic Renaissance, Chgo., 1995; guest spkr. Muslim Cmty. Ctr., Chgo., 1988; invited spkr. objective studies and Islamic voice, Bangalore, 96, Parliament of World Religions, Chgo., 1993, Cape Town, South Africa, 99, Cooper Mosque, Mississauga, Ont., Canada, 2002; invited faculty Assn. of Muslim Social Scientists, Dallas, 2005; invited spkr. Darus Salam, Bangalore, India, 2005. Author: Radiation Safety for Allied Health Professionals, Radiation Safety Manual, 1979, Intellectual Achievements of Muslims, 2002, Qur'anic Inspirations, 2007; contbg. editor Jour. of Islamic Food and Nutrition Coun. of Am., 1986—, health and sci. column Muslim Jour., 1989—; freelance writer Minaret Bi-weekly, NYC, 1975—, Islamic Voice, India, 1988—, Al-Balaagh, Lenasia, South Africa, 1989—, AL'FURQAN Internat., Norcross, Ga., 1990, Message Internat., Jamaica, NY, 1990, Minaret Monthly Mag., LA, 1995—, The Message, London, 1998—, The Minaret, Botswana, 1998—; editor: Science and Technology for the Developing World, 1988; mem. editl. bd. Jour. Islamic Med. Assn., 1981—; regular contbr. Pres.'s Page; manuscript reviewer for sci. and med. jours., 1973; assoc. editor AAlim, 1998—; contbr. more than 100 articles to sci. jours.; pub. internat. more than 300 articles on various topics of Islam in jours. and mags. Moderator fgn. policy workshop U.S. Dept. State, Louisville, 2000; spkr. Dayton Islamic Ctr., Dayton, 2000, Muslim Student Assn. U. Cin., 2000, Muslim Cmty. Ctr., Chgo., 2001; invited spkr. Muslim Assn. of Cleve. East, 2002, Biotech. Conf., Kuala Lumpur, Malaysia, 2007; adv. bd. Partnership to Prevent Child Abuse, Louisville, 2007—; bd. dir. Nur Islamic Sch., Louisville, 2003, Am. Muslim Assn. Louisville, 2003—; bd. dirs. Islamic Ctr. of Louisville, 1992—; founder, mgr., trustee Bijli Found. Charitable Trust, Bellary, India, 2005—. Recipient Disting. Cmty. Svc. award India Cmty. Found., 1982, Hind Rattan Jewel of India Title award Govt. India, 1994, Disting. Svc. award, Am. Bd. radiology, 2008; WHO fellow, Govt. India scholar Bhabha Atomic Rsch. Ctr., Bombay, 1963-64; USPHS fellow Johns Hopkins U., 1969-72. Fellow Inst. Physics (UK), Am. Inst. Chemists, Royal Soc. Health, Am. Coll. Radiology, Internat. Acad. Med. Physics; mem. Am. Assn. Physicists in Medicine, Am. Coll. Nuclear Medicine, Health Physics Soc., Am. Acad. Health Physics, Soc. Nuclear Medicine (faculty mem. ann. meeting 1987, convenor internat. conf. 1995), Nat. Assn. Ams. of Asian Indian Descent (chmn. state pub. rels. com. 1982—), Islamic Med. Assn. N.Am. (life, faculty 1994, 96, 98), Internat. Inst. Islamic Medicine (faculty Orlando, Fla. 1996, 97, Birmingham, UK 1998), Islamic Soc. N.Am. (faculty Chgo. 1998), Islamic Soc. Balt. (founding mem.), Islamic Cultural Ctr.(sec. 1999-), Louisville, Islamic Assn. Maritime Provinces Can., Halifax, N.S. (asst. sec. 1967-69), Health Physics Soc. (chmn. med. health physics com. 1989—, affirmative action com. 1984—), Am. Assn. Physicists in Medicine (biol. effects com.), Assn. Muslim Scientists and Engrs. N.Am. (program chmn. ann. conf. 1987, treas. 1987-88, sec. 1988—), AAUP, Soc. Nuc. Medicine India (life, faculty mem. ann. meeting 1987, invited spkr. and faculty ann. meeting 1996), Assn. Med. Physicists India (life, invited spkr. and faculty ann. meeting Madras 1996), Med. and Biol. Physics (divsn. Can.) Assn. Physicists, Hosp. Physicists Assn., NY Acad. Scis., Islamic Assn. Maritime Provinces of Can., Ky. Med. Assn., Jefferson County Med. Soc. (assoc.), Am. Muslim Assn. Louisville (bd. dirs. 2003—), Assn. Muslim Social Scientists, Sigma Xi Islamic. Home: 7102 W Shefford Ln Louisville KY 40242-4642 Office: 800 Zorn Ave Louisville KY 40206-1499 Office Phone: 502-287-6262. Business E-Mail: irfi@iname.com.

SYED, IMRAN SHAFI, cardiologist, consultant; s. Sabir Ali and Nosheen Syed; m. Meher Khalid Rahman, Jan. 2, 2004; 1 child, Sulayman Aaryan. MD, Aga Khan U., Karachi, Pakistan, 1999. Diplomate Am. Bd. Internal Medicine, 2004, Nat. Bd. Echocardiography, 2008, Certification Bd. Cardiac Computed Tomography, 2008, Certification Bd. Nuc. Cardiology, 2008, Am. Coll. Cardiology, 2009. Sr. assoc. cons. Mayo Clinic, Rochester, Minn., 2008—. Contbr. articles to profl. jours. Fellow: Am. Coll. Cardiology; mem.: Soc. Cardiac Magnetic Resonance, Soc. Cardiovasc. Computed Tomography, Am. Soc. Nuc. Cardiology, Am. Soc. Echocardiography, Am. Heart Assn. Office: Mayo Clinic 200 1st St SW Rochester MN 55905

SYED, MUBIN ISAAC, interventional radiologist, neuroradiologist; s. Ibrahim Bijli and Sajida Syed; m. 3 children. BA summa cum laude, Boston U.; MD, Boston U. Sch. Medicine, 1989. Bd. cert. in diagnostic radiology Am. Bd. Radiology, 1994, cert. of added qualifications in vascular and interventional radiology Am. Bd. Radiology, 1998, 2008, of added qualifications in neuroradiology Am. Bd. Radiology, 1999. Resident in medicine U. Louisville Affiliated Hosps., 1989—90, Ind. U. Med. Ctr., Indpls., 1990, resident in radiology, 1990—94, fellow in neuroradiology, 1994—95, fellow in vascular and interventional radiology, 1995—96; vis. fellow Miami Vascular Inst., 1996; ptnr. Diagnostic Imaging Assocs. Ohio, Springfield, 1996—2001, Radiology Physicians Springfield, 2001—06; pres. Dayton Interventional Radiology, 2005—; clin. assoc. prof. radiol. scis. Wright State U. Sch. Medicine, Dayton, Ohio, 2006—; summer rsch. fellow NIH, Bethesda, Md., 2007. Faculty, spkr. Otsuka Pharms., 1999—2004; spkr., moderator Genentech, 2000—01; faculty, keynote spkr., cons. Stryker Interventional Pain, 2002—09; faculty, spkr. Arthrocare Inc., 2004—08; med. dir. MedScan Middletown Open MRI, 2004—08; spkr. Possis Inc., 2006—08; faculty, spkr. Bacchus Vascular, 2006—08, Am. Soc. Internat. Pain Physicians, 2007—. Author: (book) Radiology for Non Spinal Pain Interventions, 2009; Contbr. articles to profl. jours., chapters to books, presenter in field,. Chmn. movie com. Coll. of Liberal Arts Forum, Boston U., 1984-85, del., 1983-84. NIH Summer Rsch. fellow, 1987; Nat. Merit scholar, 1983, William Marshall Warren scholar Boston U., 1985; recipient Silver medal U.S. Acad. Decathlon, 1983, named Practice Leader CME Tchg. Vertebroplasty to Physicians; Nominee Physician of Yr., Cmty. Mercy Health Ptnrs., 2006. Fellow: Soc. Interventional Radiology (faculty, instr. 2003-08, Cert. Recognition for Disting. Faculty 2005), Am. Coll. Radiology, AMA; Mem. Montgomery County Med. Soc., Ohio State Med. Assn., Ohio State Radiol. Soc., Am. Soc. Spine Radiology, Radiol. Soc. N.Am., Am. Roentgen Ray Soc., Internat. Soc. Clin. Densitometry, Vascular Access Soc. America, Am. Soc. Interventional Pain Physicians, Am. Soc. Neuroradiology (sr.), Islamic Med. Assn. N.Am., Assn. Physicians Indian Origin, Assn. Physicians Pakistani Decent N. Am., Mercy Med. Ctr. (Credentials Com., Continuing Med. Edn. Com., Cancer Com.), Nat. Geographic Soc. (life), Islamic Rsch. Found. (bd. trustees), Phi Beta Kappa. Muslim. Avocations: music composition, chess, tennis, table tennis, running. Home: 3108 Henderson Ct Springfield OH 45503-1307 Office: Dayton Interventional Radiology 3075 Governors Pl Blvd Ste 120 Dayton OH 45409 Office Phone: 937-424-2580. Office Fax: 937-424-2581. Business E-Mail: mubinsyed@aol.com.

SYED, RIZVI SAJJAD HAIDER, engineering educator, researcher; s. Syed Riasat Hussain Rizvi and Riasat Najma; m. Syeda Qurat-ul-Ain Zaidi. Diploma in Computer Sci., AT&T Edn. Ctr., Pakistan, 1996; BS in Computer Engring., Sir Syed U. Engring. & Tech., Karachi, Pakistan, 2000; MS in Computer Engring., Old Dominion U., Norfolk, Va., 2005; PhD Student, U. Bridgeport, Conn., 2006—08. Cert. UNIX sys. adminstr. DEC Tng. Ctr. Pakistan, 1999, in windows network adminstrn. 1997. Tester and analyst Tech. Application Ctr., Norfolk, 2003; sr. rsch. asst. Old Dominion U., Norfolk, 2003—05, rsch. asst. Va. Modeling, Analysis, and Simulation Ctr., 2005—06; adj. faculty Computer Sci. & Engring. Dept., U. Bridgeport, 2006—, sr. rsch. asst. wireless and mobile comm. lab., 2007—. Contbr. scientific papers (Best Paper award, 13th IEEE Symposium on Computers and Comm., 2008). Program com. mem. Spring Simulation Multiconf., San Diego, 2008—; reviewer Instn. Engring. and Tech., Jour. IET Signal Processing, Stevenage, Hertfordshire, 2008, Jour. Supercomputing, Springer, NYC, 2008, Elsevier Editl. Sys.; chair World Congress in Computer Sci. Computer Engring. and Applied Computing, Las Vegas, 2008. Office: Univ Bridgeport 121 University Ave Tech Bldg 162D Bridgeport CT 06601 Business E-Mail: srizvi@bridgeport.edu.

SYED, YASSER FOUAD KHADERI, electrical engineer; b. Halifax, Nova Scotia, Can., Sept. 9, 1968; s. Asif Syed, Amtul Syed; m. Romana Yasser Shahdad; 1 child, Arva Hanan. BS cum laude, Rensselaer Polytechnic Inst., 1990; MS Elec. Engring., U. So. Calif., LA, 1992; DPhil Elec. Engring., U. Tex., 1999. Sr. systems engri. SpectraPoint Wireless, Richardson, Colo., 1996—2000; project dir. emerging digital video tech. CableLabs, Louisville, 2000—. Assoc. mem. INCITS, Washington, 2000—; del. MPEG USA; chmn, adv. codes Drafting Group SCTE, 2005—. Named Dean's List, Rensselaer Polytechnic Inst., 1986—90; grantee, Tex. Instruments, 1998; scholar, Hewlett-Packard, 1990. Mem.: IEEE (sr.), Greater Dallas Indo- Am. C. of C. (bd. dirs. 1999—2000), Alpha Phi Omega, Eta Kappa Nu, Tau Beta Pi. Office:

Cable Television Laboratories Inc 400 Centennial Pkwy Louisville CO 80027 Home Phone: 720-565-9189; Office Phone: 303-661-3319. Personal E-mail: yasser_syed@ieee.org.

SYGULA, ANDRZEJ, chemist, researcher; b. Suloszowa, Krakow, Poland, Aug. 31, 1952; came to U.S. 1990; s. Wladyslaw Sygula and Krystyna Sygula-Morawiec; m. Renata Solska, Jan. 19, 1976; 1 child, Peter. MS in Chemistry, Jagiellonian U., Krakow, 1976, PhD in Chemistry, 1982. Asst. prof. Jagiellonian U., 1983-90; sr. rsch. assoc. La. State U., Baton Rouge, 1990-93, asst. prof., researcher, 1993—. Contbr. articles to profl. jours., books. Avocations: books, chess, tennis. Office: La State U Dept Chemistry Choppin Hall Baton Rouge LA 70803

SYKES, ALAN O'NEIL, lawyer, educator; b. Bethesda, Md., Oct. 10, 1954; s. Alan O'Neil and Emily (Adams) S.; m. Maureen J. Gorman, June 29, 1980; children: Madeleine, Sophie. BA, Coll. William and Mary, 1976; JD, Yale U., 1982, PhD in Econs., 1987. Bar: Mass., D.C. Atty. Office of Arnold & Porter, Washington, 1982-86; asst. prof. law U. Chgo., 1986-90, prof. law, 1990—, Frank and Bernice Greenberg prof., 1996—. Vis. prof. law Harvard U., Cambridge, Mass., 1991, NYU, 1996. Author: (book) Product Standards for Internationally Integrated Goods Markets, 1995; co-author: Legal Problems of International Economic Relations, 2002; co-editor: Implementing the Uruguay Round, 1997. NSF fellow, 1976-79. Mem. ABA, Am. Econ. Assn., Am. Law and Econs. Assn. (bd. dirs. 1999—). Office: U Chgo Sch of Law 1111 E 60th St Chicago IL 60637 Home: 534 Chimalus Dr Palo Alto CA 94306-2707 Business E-Mail: alan_sykes@law.uchicago.edu.

SYKES, CHARLES E., dean; s. Delmar and Thelma Sykes; m. Katherine L. Sykes; children: Nicole Mitchel-Sykes, Amber Mitchell-Sykes. PhD in Mgmt., Union Inst. and U., Cin., 2003. Asst. prof. Harris-Stowe State U., St. Louis, 2003—05, exec. dir. bus. sch., 2005—06, asst. dean, bus., 2006—. Mem.: Am. Assn. Mgmt. Democrat. Avocations: walking, boxing, travel. Office: Harris-Stowe State Univ 5707 Wilson Ave Saint Louis MO 63104 Office Fax: 314-877-0379. Personal E-mail: csykes@msn.com. Business E-Mail: sykesc@hssu.edu.

SYKES, DAVID TERRENCE, lawyer; b. Phila., Oct. 24, 1937; s. David Malcolm and Hester Lydia (Kliphouse) Sykes; m. Mary Carlisle Ferguson, Nov. 5, 1966; children: David Graham, Matthew Carlisle. BA, Hamilton Coll., 1959; LLB, Temple U. Sch. Law, Phila., 1965. Bar: Pa. 1965, US Dist. Ct. (ea. dist.) Pa. 1965, US Ct. Appeals (3rd cir.) 1965, Supreme Ct. Pa., US Supreme Ct. 1975, cert.: Am. Bd. Certification (bus. bankruptcy specialist). Assoc. Duane Morris LLP, Phila., 1965—71, ptnr., 1972—2004, of counsel, 2004—, chmn. reorganization & fin. sect., 1972—93, mem. ptnrs. bd., 1981—2004, mng. ptnr., 1994—97, vice chmn., 1998—2004. Law lectr. Temple U. Sch. Law, 1983—88; co-founder, past chair Ea. Dist. Pa. Bankruptcy Conf.; co-founder, pres. bd. dirs. Consumer Bankruptcy Assistance Project. Contbr. articles to profl. jours. Bd. vis. Temple U. Sch. Law; pres. PTA, mem. bd. trustees Chestnut Hill Acad., 1985—87. Active duty USN, 1959—62, U.S.S. Springfield. Recipient Equal Justice award, Cmty. Legal Svcs., 1996; named a SuperLawyer, Phila Mag., 2006; named one of America's Leading Bus. Lawyers, Chambers USA, 2003—, Corp. Counsel mag.'s Best Lawyers, 2005. Fellow: Am. Coll. Investment Counsel; mem.: ABA (Nat. Pub. Svc. award 1999), Am. Bankruptcy Inst., Assn. Comml. Fin. Attorneys, Internat. Bar Assn., Comml. Law League of America, Am. Coll. Bankruptcy (v.p. 1997—2001, dir. 2001—05, pres. 2005—07, charter fellow, Disting. Svc. award 2008), Phila. Bar Assn. (chmn. bus. law sect. 1983, chmn. banking & fin. institutions com. 1989, First Union Fidelity award 2000), Pa. Bar Assn. Democrat. Episcopalian. Avocations: skiing, golf. Office: Duane Morris LLP 30 S 17th St Philadelphia PA 19103-7396 Office Phone: 215-979-1500. Office Fax: 215-689-4429. Business E-Mail: Sykes@duanemorris.com.*

SYKES, DIANE S., federal judge, former state supreme court justice; b. Milw., Dec. 23, 1957; 2 children. BA, Northwestern U., 1980; JD, Marquette U., 1984. Reporter Milw. Jour.; law clk. to Hon. Terence T. Evans US Dist. Ct. (ea. dist.) WI, 1984—85; assoc. Whyte & Hirschboeck S.C., 1985—92; judge Milw. County Ct., 1992—99, Wis. Supreme Ct., Madison, 1999—2004, US Ct. Appeals (7th cir.), 2004—. Mem.: Am. Law Inst., St. Thomas More Soc., Milw. Lawyers Chpt., Federalist Soc., Seventh Cir. Bar Assn., Wis. Bar Assn. Office: US Ct Appeals 7th Cir 716 US Court House 517 E Wisconsin Ave Milwaukee WI 53202 also: Dirksen Fed Bldg Rm 2742 219 S Dearborn St Chicago IL 60604 Office Phone: 414-727-6988.*

SYKES, GRESHAM M'CREADY, sociologist, educator, artist; b. Plainfield, NJ, May 26, 1922; s. M'Cready and Beatrice (Evans) S.; m. Carla Adelt, July 13, 1946. AB summa cum laude, Princeton U., 1950; PhD (Woodrow Wilson fellow 1950-51, Univ. fellow 1951-52), Northwestern U., 1953; MA (hon.), Dartmouth Coll., 1961. Instr. sociology Princeton U., 1952-54, asst. prof., bicentennial preceptor, 1954-58; assoc. prof. Northwestern U., Evanston, Ill., 1958-60; prof. sociology Dartmouth Coll., Hanover, NH, 1960-63, chmn. dept., 1961-63; exec. officer Am. Sociol. Assn., 1963-65; research prof. law and sociology, dir. adminstrn. of justice program U. Denver, 1965-72; chmn. dept. sociology U. Houston, 1973; prof. sociology U. Va., Charlottesville, 1974-88, chmn. dept., 1978-81, emeritus prof., 1988—. Chmn. Salzburg (Austria) Seminar in Am. Studies, summer 1965; working as artist, with frequent group and one-man exhbn., 1988—. Author: Crime and Society, rev. edit., 1967, The Society of Captives, 1958, 2nd edit. 2007, Law and the Lawless, 1969, Social Problems in Am., 1971, Criminology, 1978, rev. edit., 1992, The Future of Crime, 1980; criminology editor Jour. Criminal Law, Criminology and Police Sci., 1959-64; assoc. editor Rev. Am. Sociol. Assn., 1960-62, Contemporary Sociology, 1977-80, Criminology, 1980-84; contbr. articles and revs. to Ency. Britannica, profl. jour. Served to capt., C.E. AUS, 1942-46, ETO. Recipient Edwin H. Sutherland award Am. Soc. Criminology, 1980. Home: 2197 Shepherds Ridge Road Charlottesville VA 22901 Business E-Mail: gms6m@virginia.edu.

SYKES, LINDA DIANE, retired elementary school educator; b. Indpls., Aug. 23, 1950; d. Theodore Ross and Mary Elizabeth Willits; m. Gregory Allen Sykes, Nov. 29, 1946; children: Amanda Ruth, Bryan Paul. MusB in Edn., U. Evansville, Indi., 1972; MusM, Butler U., Indpls., 1976. Tchr. elem. music Jac-Cen-Del Schs., Osgood, Ind., 1972—73; tchr. music grades k-12 NHJ United Sch. Corp., Trafalgar, 1974—86; tchr. elem. music MSD Warren Twp., Indpls., 1986—2008. Indpls. Alumnae chpt. pres. Sigma Alpha Iota, 1984—88, 1999—2000; vestry mem. St. Matthews Episcopal Ch., Indpls., 2006—09; pres., bd. mem. Sounds Hope Alumni Assn., North Webster, Ind. Mem.: Ind. Kodaly Educators (founding pres. 1993—99), Orgn. Am. Kodaly Educators (midwest divsn. pres. 2003—05). Episcopalian. Avocations: travel, reading, needlecrafts, scrapbooks. Home: 5619 Allan Ct Indianapolis IN 46239 Personal E-mail: lsykes4188@aol.com.

SYKES, MEGAN, immunologist; b. Toronto, Can., 1958; MD, Univ. Toronto, 1982. Cert. Am. Bd. Internal Medicine. Resident, medicine Montreal Gen. Hosp., Univ. Toronto, 1982—85; joined Mass. Gen. Hosp., Boston, 1990—, chief, bone marrow transplantation sect., Transplantation Biology Rsch. Ctr., and head, Cellular Immunology Lab; also prof., surgery and medicine Harvard Med. Sch., Boston. Served on Immunobiology Study Sect. NIH, 1996—2000; sci. adv. bd. Biotransplant, Inc., Immerge; trustee Roche Biomedical Rsch. Found. Author: 216 sci. jour. articles, book chapters. Recipient Jr. Faculty Rsch. award, Am. Cancer Soc., 1991, Wyeth-Ayerst Young Investigator award, Am. Soc. Transplantation, 1998, Astellas Basic Sci. Established Investigator award (Prof. Level), 2007. Office: Transplantation Biology Rsch Ctr MGH-East, Bldg 149-9019- 13th St Boston MA 02119 Office Phone: 617-726-4065. Office Fax: 617-726-4067. Business E-Mail: Megan.Sykes@tbrc.mgh.harvard.edu.

SYKES, MELVIN JULIUS, lawyer; b. Balt., Jan. 9, 1924; s. Philip Louis and Sara (Klein) S.; m. Judith Janet Konowitz, Sept. 24, 1950; children: David K., Rachel A. (dec.), Daniel E., Israel J. Grad., Balt. City Coll., 1940, Balt. Hebrew Coll., 1941; AB with honors, Johns Hopkins U., 1943; LLB magna cum laude, Harvard U., 1948. Bar: Md. 1949, U.S. Ct. Appeals (4th cir.) 1949, U.S. Dist. Ct. Md. 1950, U.S. Supreme Ct. 1955. Law clk. to Judge Morris A. Soper U.S. Ct. Appeals (4th cir.), 1948-49; pvt. practice Balt., 1949—. Draftsman Md. Dept. Legislative Reference, 1949—50; rsch. cons. Md. Commn. Adminstrv. Orgn., 1951—52; reporter Md. Commns. to Study Judiciary, 1953, Md. commns. to revise law relating to pub. svc. commn., 1953—55; mem. standing com. on rules of practice, procedure Md. Ct. Appeals, 1954—72, 1978—; mem. legis. coun. Commsn. on Revision Condemnation Laws, 1961—63; mem. Balt. Charter Revision Com., 1962—63; pres. Bar Libr. Balt., 1962—63; mem. Md. Constl. Conv. Commn., 1966—67; cons. Gov. Md. Commn. to Revise Testamentary Laws, 1967—69; mem. Gov. Md. Commns. to study state aid to nonpub. edn., 1969—71, Md. Code Revision Commn., 1970—78. Co-author: West's Maryland Procedural Forms, 1964, Jewish Law (Mishpat Ivri), Cases and Materials, 1999; co-translator Elon, Jewish Law--History, Principles, Sources, 1994. Mem. governing coun. Am. Assn. Jewish Edn., 1968—81; hon. bd. dirs. Balt. Jewish Coun., 1970—72, Inst. for Christian and Jewish Studies; bd. dirs. Balt. chpt. Am. Jewish Com.; former mem. and chmn. bd. trustees Balt. Hebrew U.; hon. bd. dirs. Balt. Neighborhoods. With USAF, 1943—45. Fellow Am. Coll. Trial Lawyers, (Md. Fellows Lifetime Achievement award, 2006), Am. Acad. of Appellate Lawyers, Am. Coll. Trust and Estate Counsel, Am. Bar Found., Md. Bar Found. (chmn. 1981-83), Balt. City Bar Found.; mem. ABA, Am. Law Inst., Md. Bar Assn., Balt. City Bar Assn., Am. Jewish Congress, Balt. Zionist Dist., B'nai B'rith, Phi Beta Kappa Democrat. Home: 3811 Fords Ln Baltimore MD 21215-2804 Office: Brown Goldstein & Levy LLP Ste 1700 120 E Baltimore St Baltimore MD 21202-6701 Home Phone: 410-358-6765; Office Phone: 410-962-1030. Business E-Mail: msykes@mjsykes.com.

SYKES, RICHARD NESBIT, retired history professor, department chairman; b. Charlotte, NC, Jan. 11, 1942; s. Richard Nesbitt and Sarah Elizabeth (Hovis) Sykes. BA in History and English summa cum laude, So. Wesleyan U., 1964; MA in Social Sci. and Reading Spec., Appalachian State U., 1965; PhD in History, Greenwich U., 2001. Cert. educator S.C., N.C. Instr. history and polit. sci. Gordon Coll., Barnesville, Ga., 1965—67; asst. prof. history and reading Gardner-Webb Coll., Boiling Springs, NC, 1967—69; instr. history and reading Ctrl. Piedmont C.C., Charlotte, 1969—70; coord. secondary reading Chester County Schs., 1971—73; reading specialist Williamsburg County Schs., 1973—74; reading diagnostician Chesterfield County Schs., 1974—79; tchr., reading specialist Lancaster County Schs., SC, 1979—90; prof. history Aiken Tech. Coll., SC, 1990—2005, dept. chair, 2001—05, ret., 2006. Recipient medal, Nat. Inst. Staff and Orgnl. Devel., 2000, Gov.'s Disting. Prof. award, S.C. Commn. on Higher Edn., 2000; named Faculty Mem. of Yr., Aiken Tech. Coll., 1999. Mem.: SC State Employees Assn., SC Tech. Edn. Assn. (Educator of Yr. Aiken Tech. Coll. 1991—92), Nat. Geog. Soc., Smithsonian Instn. Avocations: reading, walking, fishing. Home: 838 Osbon Dr Aiken SC 29801-4154 Home Phone: 803-641-9930.

SYKES, WANDA, comedienne, actress; b. Portsmouth, Va., Mar. 7, 1964; m. Alex Sykes, Oct. 25, 2008; children: Olivia Lou, Lucas Claude. BS, Hampton U. Actor: (TV series) Best of Chris Rock, 1999, Larry David: Curb Your Enthusiasm, 1999, Crank Yankers, 2003—, Wanda Does It, 2004, The New Adventures of Old Christine, 2006—09, Back at the Barnyard, 2007—08; (films) Tomorrow Night, 1998, Nutty Professor II: The Klumps, 2000, Down to Earth, 2001, Pootie Tang, 2001, Monster-in-Law, 2005 (Outstanding Supporting Actress in a Theatrical Film, BET Comedy award, 2005), Clerks II, 2006, My Super Ex-Girlfriend, 2006, (voice) Over the Hedge, 2006, Barnyard: The Original Party Animals, 2006, CondomNation, 2006, Evan Almighty, 2007, License to Wed, 2007; actor, writer (TV series) The Chris Rock Show, 1997—2000 (Emmy award for outstanding writing, 1999), The Downer Channel, 2001, writer, creator, actor, prodr. Wanda at Large, 2003, writer The Keenen Ivory Wayans Show, 1997, guest appearances include The Drew Carey Show, Chappelle's Show, appears on Inside the NFL, 2002—; author: Yeah I Said It, 2004. Recipient Am. Comedy award for Funniest Female Stand-Up Comic, 2001. Office: c/o William Morris Agy One William Morris Pl Beverly Hills CA 90212*

SYKIOTIS, GERASIMOS, biomedical researcher, geneticist; US, 2003; MD, U. Patras, 1997, PhD, 2003. Resident internal medicine Patras U. Hosp., 1998—2000; postdoctoral rsch. assoc. U. Rochester Med. Ctr., NY, 2003—07; investigator Novartis Insts. for Biomed. Rsch., Cambridge, Mass., 2007—09; clin. rsch. fellow Reproductive Endocrinology Mass. Gen. Hosp., Harvard Med. Sch., 2009—. Contbr. articles to 20 scholarly rsch. jours., med. textbooks. Mem.: AAAS, Endocrine Soc., Hellenic Bioscientific Assn. USA, Hellenic Med. Assn., Nat. Postdoctoral Assn., Soc. Free Radical Biology and Medicine, Genetics Soc. Am., Am. Assn. Cancer Rsch. Home: 177 Gerry RD Chestnut Hill MA 02467-3185

SYKORA, PETR, professional hockey player; b. Plzen, Czechoslovakia, Nov. 19, 1976; m. Reynata Sykora. Center Cleve. Lumberjacks, 1993—94, Detroit Vipers, 1994—95, Albany River Rats; right wing NJ Devils, 1995—2002, Anaheim Mighty Ducks, 2002—06, NY Rangers, 2006, Edmonton Oilers, 2006—07, Pitts. Penquins, 2007—09. Mem. Czech Republic Nat. Hockey Team, World Cup of Hockey, 1996, 2004, Czech Republic Nat. Hockey Team, Olympic Games, Salt Lake City, 2002. Named to All-Rookie Team, NHL, 1996. Achievements include being a member of Stanley Cup Champion New Jersey Devils, 2000, Pittsburgh Penguins, 2009.*

SYLK, LEONARD ALLEN, manufacturing executive, real estate developer; b. Phila., Feb. 25, 1941; s. Harry S. and Gertrude (Bardy) S.; m. Barbara Ann Lovenduski, Dec. 1, 1975; children: Tristan, Tyler, Galen. BS in Econs., U. Pa., 1963; MBA, Columbia U., 1965. Cert. comml. property builder. Founder, chmn. bd., CEO Shelter Systems Corp., Hainesport, NJ, 1965-99; ret.; prin. and CEO Property Mgmt. Svcs., Hainesport, 1996—. Vice chmn. USA Bancshares, Inc., 1998-2000; chmn., bd. govs. Mid. East Forum; trustee Nat. Bldg. Sys. Coun., 1986—; presdl. advisor on housing trade with Soviet Union, 1990; bldg. industry advisor US Dept. Commerce, 1997-99; mem. adv. bd. Franklin and Marshall Coll., 2006-09; mem. adv. bd. Hosp. U. Pa., 2006, guest lectr., Columbia U. Grad. Sch. Bus., 2007-. Contbr. articles to industry publs. Chmn. ann. awards dinner Jewish Nat. Fund, Phila., 1987, v.p., bd. dir.; bd. dirs. Phila. Orch. Assn., 1990-98, emeritus, 1999—; trustee Roman Cath. HS, Phila., 2003—; bd. dir. Pa. Ballet, 1994-99, exec. com., 1996-99, vice-chmn., pres., 1998; bd. dir. Resources for Childrens' Health, 1993-96, Acad. Music, Phila., 1990-96, Rock Sch. of Pa. Ballet, 1995-98, Young Scholars Charter Sch., 2000—; bd. dir. Jewish Nat. Fund, 1987—, v.p., 2000—; trustee Hahnemann U. and Hosp., 1991-96; vice chmn., trustee St. Christopher's Hosp. Children, Phila., 1994-2002, chmn. St. Christophers Found. Children, 1999, v.p., bd. dirs., 1999-2002; chmn. 1999, bd. dirs., vice chmn. St. Peter's Sch, Phila., 1995-03; trustee Allegheny U. Hosps., 1999—; bd. dirs. Hosp U. Pa. Cancer Ctr., 2004-; NJ chmn. Builders Bush, 1988; mem. Phila. Coun. for Excellence in Edn., 2006; mem. adv. bd. Columbia U. Grad. Sch. Bus., 2006-, lectr., instr., 2008-. Recipient Tree of Life award presented by R. Hon. Margaret Thatcher, 1995, Leadership award, Roman Cath. Sch. Sys., 2006; named Man. of Yr., 1988, Man of Yr., NJ C. of C., 2002, 2001. Mem. Nat. Assn. Homebuilders (com. chmn., nat. bd. dir. 1984—, mem. exec. com. 1990, 97, fundraising chmn. 1991, Man of Yr. in Industrialized Housing 1990), Wood Truss Coun. Am. (bd. dir. 1983—, pres. 1987, named to Hall of Fame 1990), Builders League South Jersey (v.p., bd. dir. 1984-94), NJ Builders Assn. (bd. dir., com. chmn., exec. com. 1990-96), Merion Civic Assn. (bd. dir. 1999-2001), Le Club (NYC), Atlantic City Country Club, Vesper Club, Union League, Capitol Club (Washington), Masons, United Way Million Dollar Roundtable. Republican. Home: 350 N Highland Ave Merion Station PA 19066-1708 Office: Property Mgmt Svcs PO Box 9 Hainesport NJ 08036-0009 Office Phone: 609-261-4300. Business E-Mail: info@hainesport.us.

SYLLA, RICHARD EUGENE, economics professor; b. Harvey, Ill., Jan. 16, 1940; s. Benedict Andrew and Mary Gladys (Curran) S.; m. Edith Anne Dudley, June 22, 1963; children: Anne Curran, Margaret Dudley. BA, Harvard U., 1962, MA, 1965, PhD, 1969. Prof. econs. and bus. N.C. State U., Raleigh, 1968-90; Henry Kaufman prof. history fin. insts. and markets NYU, NYC, 1990—, prof. econs., 1990—, acting chmn. dept. econs., 2002—03. Cons. Citibank NA, N.Y.C., 1979-82, Chase Manhattan Bank, N.Y.C., 1983-85; vis. prof. U. Pa., Phila., 1983, U. N.C., Chapel Hill, 1988; rsch. assoc. Nat. Bur. of Econ. Rsch., 1983—; trustee Mus. Am. Fin., 2002—, vice chmn., 2007—. Author: The American Capital Market, 1975; co-author: Evolution of the American Economy, 1980, 2d edit., 1993, A History of Interest Rates, 1991, 4th edit., 2005; co-editor: Patterns of European Industrialization, 1991, Anglo-American Financial Systems, 1995, The State, The Financial System, and Economic Modernization, 1999; editor Jour. Econ. History, 1978-84. Study fellow NEH, 1975-76; Rsch. grantee NSF, 1985-94, 98-02, 2008-, Sloan Found., 1995-97. Mem. Am. Econs. Assn., Econ. History Assn. (v.p. 1987-88, trustee 1977-88, Arthur H. Cole prize 1970, pres. 2000-01), Bus. History Conf. (trustee 1991-94, 2002-04, pres. 2005-06), So. Econ. Assn. (v.p. 1981-82), Cliometrics Soc. (trustee 1997-2000, trustee chair 1998-2000). Avocations: golf, hiking, stamp collecting/philately, arts. Office: NYU 44 W 4th St New York NY 10012-1106 Home: 425 Main St PH2B New York NY 10044 Home Phone: 212-673-2131; Office Phone: 212-998-0869. Business E-Mail: rsylla@stern.nyu.edu.

SYLVESTRE, JEAN GUY, former national librarian; b. Sorel, Que., Can., May 17, 1918; s. Maxime Arthur and Yvonne Marie (Lapierre) S.; m. Francoise Poitevin, Feb. 27, 1943; children: Marie, Jean, Paul. BA, U. Ottawa, 1939, B.Ph., 1940, MA, 1942, D.L.S. (hon.), 1969, D.Litt. (hon.), 1970, LL.D. (hon.), 1974, 75, 82. Translator Dept. Can. Sec. of State, 1942-44; editor Wartime Info. Bd., 1944-45; asst. pvt. sec. to minister of justice, 1945-47; pvt. sec. to sec. of state for external affairs, 1947-48; pvt. sec. to prime minister, 1948-50; adminstrv. officer Dept. Resources and Devel., 1950-53; asst. librarian Library of Parliament, Ottawa, Ont., 1953-56, asso. parliamentary librarian, 1956-68, nat. librarian, 1968-83; pres., chmn. bd. Can. Inst. for Hist. Microprodns., 1983-86; chmn. Ottawa Valley Book Festival, 1988-92; hon. chmn., 1993—. Author: Louis Francoeur, journaliste, 1941, Situation de la poésie canadienne, 1941, Anthologie de la poésie canadienne-française, 1943, 58, 64, 66, 68, 74, Poétes catholiques de la France contemporaine, 1944, Sondages, 1945, Impressions de théâtre, 1950, Amours, délices et orgues, 1953, Panorama des lettres canadiennes-francaises, 1964, Canadian Writers, 1964, Literature in French Canada, 1967, A Century of Canadian Literature, 1967, The Future of the National Library of Canada, 1980, Guidelines for National Libraries, 1987 French, Spanish and Arabic edits., 1988; also articles in profl. jours., encys.; editor: A Canadian Errant (J.P. Manion), 1960; editor: Canadian Universities Today, 1961, Structures sociales du Canada francais, 1967. Chmn. Gov. Gen.'s Lit. Awards, 1960-62; organizer, chmn. World Poetry Conf., Expo 1967; chmn. Can. Council Com. on Aid-to-Publs., 1960-68; lectr. U. Ottawa Library Sch., 1954-71; v.p. Can. Library Week Council, 1965-67; Bd. dirs. Can. Writers Found., pres., 1960-61. Decorated comdr. Ordre International du Bien Public, officer Order of Can.; comdr. Order of Merit of Poland; recipient Centennial medal., Outstanding Pub. Service award, Internat. Fedn. Libr. Assn. medal. Fellow Royal Soc. Can. (hon. sec. 1959-62, pres. sect. I 1963-64, hon. libr. 1969-91, pres. 1973-74); mem. Can. Libr. Assn. (life), Ont. Libr. Assn. (hon. life), Can. Assn. Info. Sci. (pres. 1971-72), Assn. Scis. et Techniques de la Documentation (life). Home: 2286 Bowman Rd Ottawa ON Canada K1H 6V6

SYMANZIK, JUERGEN, statistician, educator; m. Natascha Vukasinovic; 1 child, Alexandar. MS in Stats., U. Dortmund, Germany, 1991, MS in Computer Sci., 1992; PhD, Iowa State U., Ames, Iowa, 1996. Postdoctoral fellow Iowa State U., Ames, 1997, George Mason U., Fairfax, Va., 1997—99; asst. prof. Utah State U., Logan, 1999—2005, assoc. prof. dept. math. and stats., 1999—, 2005—. Assoc. editor Computational Statistics, 1998—2005, regional editor, 2005—. Cochmn. Interface Found. N.Am., Fairfax, Va., 2002—; mem. PTO. Mem.: Statis. Computing and Statis. Graphics (coun. sects. rep., sect. statis. graphics 2002—04, program chair-elect sect. statis. graphics 2005, 2006), Internat. Assn. Statis. Computing, Am. Statis. Assn. (mem. Utah chpt. 1999—, chpt. rep. Utah chpt. 2001—03, conf. co-chair ann. meeting 2003, v.p. Utah chpt. 2004, pres. Utah chpt. 2005, past pres. Utah chpt. 2006), Interface Found. of N.Am. (bd. dirs. 2002—07). Office: Utah State U Dept Math and Stats Logan UT 84322-3900 Business E-Mail: symanzik@math.usu.edu.

SYMBORSKA, WISLAWA See SZYMBORSKA, WISLAWA

SYME, DANIEL BAILEY, rabbi, institution executive; b. Sharon, Pa., Feb. 6, 1946; s. Monte Robert and Sonia (Hendin) S.; m. Jill Susan Young; 1 child, Joshua. BA, U. Mich., Ann Arbor, 1967; BHL, MAHL, Hebrew Union Coll.-Jewish Inst. Religion, Cin., 1972; MEd, Columbia U., 1977, EdD, 1980. Ordained rabbi, 1972. Asst. dir. Nat. Fedn. Temple Youth, 1972-73; rabbi Stamford (Conn.) Fellowship for Jewish Learning, 1973-77; asst. nat. dir. edn. Union of Am. Hebrew Congregations, NYC, 1973-77, dir., 1977—; asst. dir. Commn. Jewish Edn. for Reform Movement, NYC, 1973-77, dir., 1977—, Union of Am. Hebrew Congregations TV Inst., NYC, 1982-83, exec. asst. to pres., 1983-85, v.p., 1985-91, sr. v.p., 1991-96; sr. rabbi Temble Beth El, Bloomfield Hills, Mich., 1996—. Chmn. coalition for Alternatives in Jewish Edn., N.Y.C., 1978-80; mem. Nat. Assn. Temple Educators, 1972-91, Commn. on Teaching of Israel and Zionism, World Zionist Orgn., 1980-84; dir.-at-large Jewish Nat. Fund, Jewish Fedn. Met. Detroit, 2000—, internat. bd. Meml. Found. for Jewish Culture; nat. cabinet mem. Am. Zionist Movement, v.p. Am. Zionist Youth Movement; bd. dirs. United Israel Appeal, Ecumenical Inst., Jewish Nat. Fund. Author: 100 Essential Books for Jewish Readers, Finding God, My Body is Something Special, Prayer Is Reaching, I'm Growing, I Learn About God, Books Are Treasures, Jewish Home, What Happens After I Die?, Why I Am a Reform Jew, Drugs, Sex and Integrity, The Jewish Wedding Book, The Book of the Jewish Life; exec. prodr. T.V. programs A Conversation with Menachem Begin, 1981, Choosing Judaism, 1981, To See the World Through Jewish Eyes, 1983, A Conversation with Yitzchak Navon, 1983, You Can Go Home Again, Jewish Youth and Cults, 1984; contbr. articles to religious publs. Mem. Rabbinic Adv. Coun., United Jewish Appeal, Nat. Religious Edn. Assn. (exec. bd.), Nat Coun. Jewish Edn. (exec. bd.), Econ. Club Detroit (bd. dirs.), Jewish Nat. Fund (bd. dir.). Office: 7400 Telegraph Rd Bloomfield Hills MI 48301-3876

SYMENS, MAXINE BRINKERT TANNER, retired marketing professional; b. Primghar, Iowa, June 12, 1930; d. George Herman and Irene Marie (Dahnke) Brinkert; m. Jack Frederiksen Tanner, Dec. 28, 1950 (dec. Oct. 1976); m. Delbert Glenn Symens, Sept. 26, 1981. BS magna cum laude, Westmar Coll., 1970. Cert. tchr., Iowa. Elem. tchr. Rural Sch. O'Brien Co., Primghar, 1949-54, Gaza (Iowa) Com. Sch., 1954-60; secondary tchr. Primghar Com. Sch., 1960-81; fitness salon owner Slim 'N' Trim, George, Rock Rapids, Iowa, 1982-87; restaurant owner George Cafe, 1985-90, Pizza Ranch, 1988-96; with network mktg. divsn. Espial, 1997-99; dir. Coastal Vacations, 2000—03, Delmax Liquidations, 2004, Delmax Debt Arbitration, 2004—05. Advt. sales cons. Antique & Gift Shop, 1998-2000. Pres. Primghar Edn. Assn., 1970-71. Mem. George C. of C., George Kiwanis Club (sec. 1991-2005), Delta Kappa Gamma. Lutheran. Home: 307 Dell St NE George IA 51237-1030 E-mail: delmax@mtcnet.net.

SYMES, STEVEN JAMES KENNETH, chemistry professor; b. Okla. City, June 25, 1969; s. Ronald W. and Peggy L. Symes, Joan E. Symes (Stepmother). BA in Physics, Wash. U., St. Louis, 1992; PhD in Analytical Chemistry, U. Ark., Fayetteville, 1996. Postdoc. rsch. assoc. NASA Johnson Space Ctr., Houston, 1996—98; assoc. prof. chemistry U. Tenn., Chattanooga, 1999—. Mem.: Meteoritical Soc., Am. Chem. Soc. Avocations: travel, scuba diving, backpacking, skiing, guitar. Office: Univ Tenn Chattanooga 615 McCallie Ave Dept 2252 Chattanooga TN 37403 Business E-Mail: steven-symes@utc.edu.

SYMINGTON, W. STUART, IV, (WILLIAM STUART SYMINGTON IV), United States Ambassador to Rwanda; b. 1952; m. Susan Symington; 2 children. BA, Brown U.; JD, Columbia U. Law clk. US Dist. Ct. (ea. dist.) Mo.; atty. NYC, London, Paris, St. Joseph, Mo.; fgn. svc. officer US Dept. State, 1986—, amb. aide, worked with under sec. for polit. affairs on Latin Am. and African issues, served in Sudan and North Korea, aide to US permanent rep. to UN, dep. chief mission Niger, 2001—03, dep. dir. West African Affairs, Agrican Bur., worked with amb. to Iraq, 2004—05, US amb. to Djibouti, 2006—08, US amb. to Rwanda Kigali, 2008—. Pearson fellowship Staff of Congressman Ike Skelton; tchr. Joint Forces Staff Coll., Nat. Defense U., Norfolk. Office: Am Embassy 2210 Kigali Pl Washington DC 20521*

SYMONE, RAVEN (RAVEN-SYMONÉ CHRISTINA PEARMAN), actress, singer; b. Atlanta, Dec. 10, 1985; d. Christopher B. Pearman and Lydia Gaulden. Actor: (TV series) The Cosby Show, 1989—92, A Different World, 1989, The Fresh Prince of Bel-Air, 1992, Hangin' with Mr. Cooper, 1994—97, Happily Ever After: Fairy Tales for Every Child, 1998, My Wife and Kids, 2001, (voice) Kim Possible, 2002—07, That's So Raven, 2003—07 (Blimp Award for Favorite TV Actress, Kids' Choice Awards, 2004, 2005, Outstanding Performance, Children's Program, NAACP Image award, 2005, 2006, 2007, 2008), Fillmore!, 2004, Higglytown Heroes, 2005; (films) The Little Rascals, 1994, Doctor Dolittle, 1998, Dr. Dolittle 2, 2001, The Princess Diaries 2: Royal Engagement, 2004, (voice) Fat Albert, 2004, Everyone's Hero, 2006, College Road Trip, 2008, (voice): (video) Kim Possible: The Secret Files, 2003, That's So Raven: Supernaturally Stylish, 2004, That's So Raven: Raven's Makeover Madness, 2006, Raven Symone: Raven's Postcards from Spain, 2006; (TV films) The Cheetah Girls, 2003, (voice) Kim Possible: A Sitch in Time, 2003, Kim Possible: So the Drama, 2005, Zenon: Z3, 2004, For One Night, 2006; prodr.: (TV series) That's So Raven, 2006; actor, co-prodr.: (TV films) The Cheetah Girls 2, 2006; singer: (soundtrack) Ella Enchanted, 2004, That's So Raven, 2004, The Princess Diaries 2: Royal Engagement, 2004. Former amb. Children First program; spkr. for Nat. Safe Kids Campaign. Home: c/o Internat Creative Mgmt 8942 Wilshire Blvd Beverly Hills CA 90211-1934

SYMONS, EDWARD LEONARD, JR., lawyer, educator, investment advisor; b. Pitts., Dec. 21, 1941; s. Edward Leonard and Lillian Mae (Daniel) S.; m. Louise Quinn, July 18, 1970; children: Amy, Colin. BA, Cornell U., 1963; JD summa cum laude, U. Pitts., 1969. Assoc., ptnr. Reding, Blackstone, Rea & Sell, Pitts., 1969-72; asst. atty. gen., chief counsel Pa. Dept. Banking, Harrisburg, 1972-74; prof. law U. Pitts. Sch. Law, 1974-98; chmn. Symons Capital Mgmt., Inc., 1983—. Tax cons., Wash., 1987, Del., 95; exec. v.p. investments Smithfield Trust Co., 1996—2000; mem. adv. coun. Conflict Resolution Ctr. Internat., 1994—2004; mem. bd. internat. scholars Ctr. for Comml. Law Studies, Queen Mary and Westfield Coll., U. London, 1993—2004. Co-author: Pennsylvania Professional Corporations, 1974, Banking Law Teaching Materials, 1984, 3d edit., 1991, Regulation of Financial Institutions, 1998; contbr. articles to profl. jours. Commr., Mt. Lebanon, Pa., 1976—80; chmn. St. Clair Hosp. Found., Pitts., 1996—2006; bd. dirs. Performing Arts for Children, Pitts., 1980—84, Mt. Lebanon Hosp. Authority, 1993—2004, St. Clair Hosp., 1995—. 1st. lt. arty., AUS, 1964—66. Mem.: Order Coif. Home Phone: 412-854-1977; Office Phone: 412-344-7690.

SYMONS, JOSEPH KEITH, bishop emeritus; b. Champion, Mich., Oct. 14, 1932; Student, St. Thomas Sem., Bloomfield, Conn., St. Mary Sem., Balt. Ordained priest Diocese of St. Augustine, Fla., 1958; ordained bishop, 1981; aux. bishop Diocese of St. Petersburg, Fla., 1981—83; bishop Diocese of Pensacola-Tallahassee, Fla., 1983-90, Diocese of Palm Beach, Fla., 1990—98, bishop emeritus Fla., 1998—. Roman Catholic. Office: PO Box 109650 Palm Beach Gardens FL 33410-9650

SYMS, MARCY, retail executive; MS in Pub. Rels., Boston U.; postgrad., Harvard U.; D (hon.), Bryant Coll. Chief operating officer Syms Corp., Secaucus, N.J., 1992-97; pres. Syms Corp, 1983—; CEO Syms Corp., Secaucus, N.J., 1998—. Bd. sirs. Stanley Blacker, Inc., Am. Materials, Eau Claire, Wis.; bd. dirs. Syms Corp, 1983—; bd. sirs. Rite Aid Corp., 2005—. Author: Mind Your Own Business, Keep it in the Family; columnist Family Bus. Mag. Founding bd. dirs. Sy Syms Sch. Bus. Yeshiva U., 1985—; bd. dirs. NY Chapter Am. Hearth Assn., NJ Economic Growth Coun. Recipient Disting. Bus. Leader of Yr. award Monmouth U., Marvin Feldman award Fashion Inst. Tech., Disting. Alumni award boston U., Good Citizen award Coun. Sr. Ctrs. & Svcs. of N.Y.C., Inc., Lewis Rudin medal for Civic Leadership, New York Leadership Ctr., 2008. Mem. Young Pres.' Orgn., Com. of 200, Internat. Women's Forum, Econ. Club N.Y. Office: Syms Corp One Syms Way Secaucus NJ 07094 Office Phone: 201-902-9600. Office Fax: 201-902-9874.*

SYN, WING-KIN, gastroenterologist, hepatologist, researcher; b. Singapore, 1972; s. Y. and W. Syn. MBChB with honors, U. Sheffield, 1998. Intern Royal Hallamshire Hosp., Sheffield, England, 1998—99; sr. ho. officer in medicine U. Hosp. Birmingham, West Midlands, England, 1999—2001; sr. ho. officer in hepatology King's Coll. Liver Unit, London, 2001—02; gastroenterology and hepatology specialist registrar Liver and Hepatobiliary Unit, 2002—07, advanced hepatology specialist registrar, 2006—07, hepatologist, 2007; rschr. divsn. gastroenterology Duke U., Durham, NC, 2007—, U. Birmingham, England, 2008—. Clinician Nat. Health Svc., 1998—2007; rschr. Duke U., 2007. Recipient Bronze Medal, U. Sheffield, 1994, Travel Fellowship award, Midlands Gastroenterology Soc. Mem.: Med. Rsch. Soc., ACP, Brit. Soc. Gastroenterology, European Assn. Study of Liver, Royal Coll. Physicians. Office: Duke Univ GSRB-1 DUMC 3256 595 LaSalle Street Durham NC 27710 Business E-Mail: wing-kin.syn@duke.edu.

SYNEK, MIROSLAV, physicist, chemist, world affairs consultant; b. Prague, Czech Republic, Sept. 18, 1930; came to U.S., 1958, naturalized, 1963; s. Frantisek and Anna (Kokrment) S.; children: Mary Rose, Thomas Robert. Cert., Indsl. Chemistry Tech. Sch., Prague, 1946-50; cert. in liberal arts, Prague, 1951; MS in Physics with distinction, Charles U., Prague, 1956; PhD in Physics, U. Chgo., 1963. Analytical chemist Indsl. Medicine Inst., Prague, 1950-51; rsch. physicist Acad. Scis., Prague, 1956-58; from asst. to assoc. prof. De Paul U., Chgo., 1962-67; prof. Tex. Christian U., Ft. Worth, 1967-71; lectr., rschr. U. Tex., Austin, 1971-75; tenured faculty U. Tex., San Antonio, 1975-95. Sci. advisor Tex. Edn. Agy., Austin, 1971-73, U. Tex., 1971-73; advisor Student Physics Soc., active numerous univ. coms. Contbr. numerous articles to sci. jours., abstracts to presentations. Campaigner United Way, San Antonio, 1975-95; judge Alamo Sci. Fairs and Tex. Acad. of Sci. Fairs, annually; grand award judge Internat. Sci. and Engring. Fairs, 1998, 99. Rsch. grantee Robert A. Welch Found., 1968-71, 76-83, 93-95. Fellow AAAS, Am. Phys. Soc. (life), Tex. Acad. Sci., Am. Inst. Chemists; mem. NEA, Tex. State Tchrs. Assn., AAUP, DAV Comdrs. Club, Am. Assn. Physics Tchrs., Am. Acad. Polit. Sci., Am. Mus. Natural History, Libr. Congress, Smithsonian Instn., Nat. Trust Hist. Preservation, N.Y. Acad. Scis., Am. Chem. Soc. (San Antonio edn. com. chmn.), Czechoslovak Nat. Coun. Am. (dist. sec. Chgo. 1961-63, chmn. 1967), Czechoslovak Soc. Arts and Scis. Am., Internat. Soc. Poets (disting. mem.), Sheriffs' Assn. Tex. (assoc.), San Antonio Astron. Assn., World Affairs Coun. San Antonio (diplomat mem.), Bexar County Czech Heritage Soc. of Tex., Sigma Xi (life), Sigma Pi Sigma (sustaining). Roman Catholic. Achievements include research in atomic structure calculations of laser-active lanthanides, analytical relativistic self-consistent field theory, approximate estimate of the extra-terrestrial intelligence probability, nuclear age requiring free elections, main dangers of our times, suggested priorities for human society. Home and Office: Independent Consultant PO Box 5937 San Antonio TX 78201-0937 Personal E-mail: m.synek@juno.com.

SYNNOTT, AIDAN JOHN, lawyer; b. Cork, Ireland, July 1, 1964; arrived in U.S., 1987; s. Edward Christopher Synnott and Nora Mary Angela Walsh; m. Elizabeth Lauren Grayer, May 11, 2002; 1 child, Catherine Eve. B of Civil Law, Univ. Coll. Cork, 1985; LLM, U. Mich., 1989. Bar: Ireland 1987, NY 1989, US Dist. Ct. (so. and ea. dists.) NY 1989, US Ct. Appeals (2nd cir.) 1992, US Supreme Ct. 1993, US Dist. Ct. (no. dist.) Calif. 1993, US Dist. Ct. (no. dist.) NY 2001, US Ct. Appeals (9th cir.) 2003, US Ct. Appeals (3rd cir.) 2005, US Ct. Appeals (6th cir.) 2006, Barrister at Law: Hon. Soc. of King's Inns, Dublin 1987. With Paul, Weiss, Rifkind, Wharton & Garrison LLP, NYC, 1988—2000, ptnr., 2000—. Assoc. editor: Antitrust Law Jour., 2000—07. Named Alumnus of Yr. in Law, Univ. Coll. Cork, 2004. Fellow: Am. Bar Found.; mem.: ABA (mem. leadership antitrust sect. 2000—07), NY State Bar Assn. (chair com. on antitrust 1999—2002), Bar Assn. City NY (mem. pro bono com. 2002—05). Home: 124 Hudson St New York NY 10013 Office: Paul Weiss Rifkind Wharton & Garrison LLP 1285 Avenue of the Americas New York NY 10019-6064

SYNNOTT, MARCIA GRAHAM, history professor; b. Camden, NJ, July 4, 1939; d. Thomas Whitney and Beatrice Adelaide (Colby) S.; m. Willard Edwin Sharp, June 16, 1979; children: Willard Sharp, Laurel Beth Sharp. AB, Radcliffe Coll., 1961; MA, Brown U., 1964; PhD, U. Mass., 1974. History tchr. MacDuffie Sch., Springfield, Mass., 1963-68; instr. U. S.C., Columbia, 1972-74, asst. prof., 1974-79, assoc. prof. history, 1979-97, dir. grad. studies history dept., 1990-92, prof. history, 1997—2005, emeritus prof. history, 2005—. Author: The Half-Opened Door, 1979; contbr. essays to books, articles to profl. jours. Active university-wide cmty. svc. projects. Grantee, Am. Coun. Learned Socs., 1981; Fulbright scholar, 1988. Mem. Am. Hist. Assn., So. Hist. Assn., Orgn. Am. Historians (membership com. 1990-93), S.C. Hist. Assn. (pres. 1994-95), History of Edn. Soc. (mem. editl. bd. 1996, 97, 98, bd. dirs. 2000-02). Avocations: history, skiing, walking. Office: U SC Dept History Columbia SC 29208-0001 Office Phone: 803-777-2585. Business E-Mail: synnott@mailbox.sc.edu.

SYNNOTT, WILLIAM RAYMOND, retired management consultant; b. Fall River, Mass., Dec. 29, 1929; s. William Joseph and Marie Aurore (Labrie) S.; m. Suzanne Pauline Moseley, Oct. 21, 1967; children—Dianne, Mark, Amy Grad. cert., Rutgers U., 1958; BS summa cum laude, Boston U., 1973; grad. advanced mgmt. program, Harvard Bus. Sch., 1973. Sr. v.p. Bank of Boston, 1967-87; sr. dir. The Yankee Group, Boston, 1987-88; dir. Nolan Norton & Co., Lexington, Mass., 1988-91; pres. W.R. Synnott Assocs., Wellesley Hills, Mass., 1990-94; ret., 1994. Lectr., seminar leader on info. technology worldwide. Author: The Information Weapon, 1987; co-author: Information Resource Management, 1981. Served as sgt. U.S. Army, 1951-53, Korea. Avocations: skiing, tennis, golf. Home: 1924 Springberry Cir Naples FL 34109 Personal E-mail: wilsyn@aol.com.

SYPHER, FRANCIS J., writer, editor, educator; s. Francis J. and Mildred A. Sypher; m. Marie-Claire Cournand, 1966 (div. 1969); m. Eleanor C. Kramer, 1970 (div. 1983); 1 child, Eleanor H. AB, Columbia U., NYC, 1963, AM, 1964, PhD, 1968. Prof. Columbia U., 1965—68, U. NY, Albany, 1968—75. Author: (books) Saint Agnes Chapel of the Parish of Trinity Church, 2002, Frederick L. Hoffman, His Life and Works, 2002, Letitia Elizabeth Landon, 2004, New York Society of the Cincinnati: Biographies of Original Members and Other Continental Officers, 2004, Landon Bibliography, 2005, The Donald M. Liddell Collection, 2007, Histories of New York Regiments of the Continental Army, 2008; editor: Landon's Works, 1990, 15th vol., 2007, Minutes of Coroners Proceedings, 2004, St. Nicholas Soc. Geneaiogical Record, 2007; contbr. articles to profl. jours.;, editor (writer). Rsch. grant, NY State Regents Fellowship, 1963—65, SUNY Rsch. Found., 1974, Mellon Found. Pub., 1974, Fulbright Sr. Lectureship Am. Lit., 1981—83, 1986—88. Mem.: Soc. Colonial Wars State NY, Grolier Club, Huguenot Soc. Am., NY State Soc. Cin., St. Nicholas Soc. City NY (editor), Cosmos Club. Office: FDR Station PO Box 1125 New York NY 10150-1125 Personal E-mail: fjsypher@usa.net.

SYPOLT, DIANE GILBERT, retired judge; b. Rochester, NY, June 14, 1947; d. Myron Birne and Doris Isabell (Robie) Gilbert; m. Dwight Douglas Sypolt; children: Andrew, David Weinstein. BA, Smith Coll., Northampton, Mass., 1969; postgrad., Stanford U., 1977-78, Georgetown U., 1978; JD, Boston U., 1979. Bar: D.C. 1979, Mass. 1979. Law clk. to judge D.C. Ct. Appeals, Washington, 1979-80; assoc. Peabody, Lambert & Meyers, Washington, 1980-83; asst. gen. counsel Office of Mgmt. and Budget, Washington, 1983-86; dep. gen. counsel U.S. Dept. Edn., Washington, 1986-88, acting gen. counsel, 1988-89; legal counselor to V.P. of U.S., White House; counsel Pres.'s Competitiveness Coun., Washington, 1989-90; judge U.S. Ct. Fed. Claims, Washington, 1990—2005; ret., 2005. Recipient Young Lawyer's award Boston U. Law Sch., 1989. Mem. Fed. Am. Inn of Ct. (Master), Federalist Soc., Pets on Wheels. Personal E-mail: dgsypolt@yahoo.com.

SYPOLT, JENNIFER LYNN, legislative staff member; Exec. asst., scheduler, Rep. William Lipinski US House of Reps., Washington, adminstrv. asst., chief of staff to Rep. Daniel Lipinski, 2005—. Democrat. Office: 1717 Longworth House Office Bldg Washington DC 20515 Office Phone: 202-225-5701. Office Fax: 202-225-1012.*

SYPOLT, SHIRLEY RAE, elementary school educator; b. Farmville, Va., Sept. 9, 1953; d. Benifield and Ruth Bethel Burnett; m. Russell Eugene Sypolt, Jr., Sept. 1, 1974; children: Russell Eugene III, Jason Michael, Ryan Alexander. AS, Southside Va. CC, Keysville, 1973; BS in Edn., U. Nebr., Omaha, 1991; MSc in Tchg. Environ. Edn., Christopher Newport U., Newport News, Va., 2001. Lic. early childhood k-4, mid. grades 4-8 Va. Bd. Edn., cert. mid. childhood generalist Nat. Bd. Profl. Tchg. Stds., 2005. Pre-sch. tchr. Greenfield Childhood Devel. Ctr., Bossier City, La., 1986—88; sub. tchr. Bossier Parish Sch. Dist., 1988—89, Omaha Pub. Schs., Nebr., 1992; 5th grade tchr. Hampton City Schs., Va., 1992—; k-5 sci. instrnl. leader Cooper Elem. Schs., 1999—. State facilitator, project learning tree Va. Dept. Forestry, Richmond, 1999—; state facilitator, project WET Va. Dept. Environ. Quality, Richmond, 1999—; state facilitator, project WILD Va. Dept. Game, Richmond, 2000—; adj. prof. Christopher Newport U., 2002—05; edn. adv. panel Nat. Wildlife Fedn., 2002—; exec. adv. com. Gov.'s Environ. Edn., 2001; adv. com. Project Learning Tree, 2000—. Author: (poem) Earth's Rock Cycle, 2002, project WILD k-12 curriculum & activity guide. Chair Sch. Pride in Action Com., Hampton, 1998—, Hampton Clean City Commn., 2004—. Recipient Pres.' Coun. Environ. Quality Tchr. Tng. award, NEETF, 2001, Outstanding Educator award, Nat. Project Learning Tree, 2001, Presdl. award for Excellence in Math. & Sci. Tchg., Nat. Sci. Found., 2003. Mem.: NSTA (Disting. Tchg. award 2003), Nat. Wildlife Fedn. Leaders Club, Soc. Elem. Presdl. Awardees, Assn. Presdl. Awardees in Sci. Tchg. Republican. Protestant/Methodist. Avocations: gardening, reading. Home: 6 Encore Ct Hampton VA 23666 Office: Cooper Elem Magnet Sch 200 Marcella Rd Hampton VA 23666 Office Phone: 757-825-4645. Personal E-mail: shirleysyp@aol.com.

SYRON, RICHARD FRANCIS, former mortgage company executive, economist; b. Boston, Oct. 25, 1943; s. Dominick Richard and Elizabeth (McQuire) S.; m. Margaret Mary Garatoni, Oct. 21, 1972; children: Erin Elizabeth, Brendan Paul. BS in Econs.-Acctg. with high honors, Boston Coll., 1966; MA in Econs., Tufts U., 1969, PhD in Econs., 1971. Dep. dir. budget Commonwealth of Mass., 1973-74; v.p., economist Fed. Res. Bank of Boston, 1974-82, sr. v.p., econ. advisor, 1982-85; exec. asst. to sec. U.S. Dept. Treasury, Washington, 1979-80, dep. sec. for econ. policy, 1980-81; asst. to Chmn. Paul Volcker Fed. Res. Sys., Washington, 1981-82; pres., CEO Fed. Home Loan Bank of Boston, 1986-88, Fed. Res. Bank of Boston, 1989-94; chmn. Am. Stock Exch., NYC, 1994-99; chmn., CEO Thermo Electron, Waltham, Mass., 1999—2002, exec. chmn., 2002—03; chmn., CEO Fed. Home Loan Mortgage Corp. (Freddie Mac), McLean, Va., 2003—08. Bd. trustees Boston Coll.; past chmn. Boston Pvt. Industry Coun.; bd. dirs. McKesson Corp., Nabors Industries. Author: Urban Fire Insurance, 1972; contbr. articles to profl. jours. Mem. Fed. Open Market Com., 1989—94. Teaching fellow Tufts U., 1966-69. Mem.: Comml. Club Boston, Boston Econ. Club, Clover Club Boston.

SYTSMA, DAVID ALLEN, history professor, department chairman; b. Chgo., Nov. 3, 1949; s. Bernard and Phyllis Jean Sytsma; m. Sharon Elizabeth Coleman, May 4, 1974; children: Janine Anne, Sarah Marie Halstead, Katharine Marie. PhD, North Ill. U., DeKalb, 1985. Assoc. prof. Rockford Coll., Ill., 1986—89, history prof., 1995—, dept. chmn., 1998—. Recipient Photography award, US Local Bus. Assn., 2008. Mem.: Phi Alpha Theta. Liberal. Avocation: photography. Office: Rockford Coll 5050 E State St Rockford IL 60601 Business E-Mail: dsytsma@rockford.edu.

SYTSMA, FREDRIC A., lawyer; b. Grand Rapids, Mich., Jan. 12, 1944; BA, Mich. State U., 1964; JD, U. Mich., 1968. Bar: Mich. 1968. Mem. Varnum, Riddering, Schmidt & Howlett, Grand Rapids. Fellow Am. Coll. Trust and Estate Counsel; mem. ABA, State Bar Mich. (mem. coun. probate and estate planning sect. 1977—, chmn. 1986-87), Grand Rapids Bar Assn. Office: Varnum Riddering Schmidt & Howlett PO Box 352 333 Bridge St NW Grand Rapids MI 49501-0352 Office Phone: 616-336-6000. Business E-Mail: fasytsma@varnumlaw.com.

SYVERTSON, CLARENCE ALFRED, management consultant, engineer; b. Mpls., Jan. 12, 1926; s. Alfred and Esther Louise (Goertemiller) S.; m. Helen Hammond Gonnella, May 4, 1953 (dec. May 1981); 1 child, Marguerite Louise.; m. JoAnn Mary Caruso, May 8, 1982; 1 stepchild, Lynn S. Sechrest. B. Aero. Engring., U. Minn., 1946, MS, 1948, DSc (hon.), 2004; postgrad., Stanford U., 1950—57; grad., Advanced Mgmt. Program, Harvard U., 1977. Research scientist Ames Aero. Lab., NACA, Moffett Field, Calif., 1948-58; exec. dir. Joint Dept. Transp./NASA Civil Aviation Research and Devel. Policy Study, 1970-71; with Ames Research Center, NASA, Moffett Field, 1958-84, dep. dir., 1969-78, dir., 1978-84. Adv. bd. Coll. Engring., U. Calif., Berkeley, 1980-85; cons. prof. Stanford U., 1985-88; hon. prof. Northwestern Poly. U., Xian, China, 1998. Served with U.S. Army, 1946-47. Recipient invention and contbn. award NASA, 1964, Exceptional Svc. medal, 1971, Disting. Svc. medal, 1984, Outstanding Achievement award U. Minn., 1982, Comdrs. award for civilian service U.S. Army, 1984 Fellow AIAA (Lawrence Sperry award 1957), Am. Astronautical Soc., Calif. Coun. Sci. and Tech.; mem. Nat. Acad. Engring. Home: 14666 Springer Ave Saratoga CA 95070-5748

SYVERUD, KENT DOUGLAS, dean, law educator; b. Rochester, NY, Oct. 23, 1956; s. Warren Lukken and Janet (Thatcher) S.l; m. Ruth Chi-Fen Chen, May 22, 1982; children: Steven, Brian, David. BSFS, Georgetown U., 1977; JD, U. Mich., 1981, MA, 1983. Bar: D.C. 1982, Mich. 1993. Law clk. to Judge Oberdorfer US Dist. Ct. DC, Washington, 1983-84; law clk. Justice O'Connor US Supreme Ct., Washington, 1984-85; assoc. Wilmer, Cutler & Pickering, Washington, 1985-97; exec. sec. Mich. Law Revision Commn., Lansing, 1993-95; prof. U. Mich. Law Sch., Ann Arbor, 1987-97; dean, Garner Anthony prof. Vanderbilt U. Law Sch., Nashville, 1997—2005; dean, Ethan A. H. Shepley univ. prof. Wash. U. Law Sch., St. Louis, 2005—. Visiting prof. U. Tokyo, 1993, U. Pa., 1997; chair exec. com. Inst. CLE, Ann Arbor, 1995-97; chair, bd. trustees Law Sch. Admissions Coun., 2005-. Editor: Journal of Legal Education, 1998—2004. Mem. Am. Law Inst., Law and Soc. Assn. Office Phone: 314-935-6420. Business E-Mail: syverud@wulaw.wustl.edu.

SZABLYA, HELEN MARY, writer, language educator; b. Budapest, Hungary, Sept. 6, 1934; came to U.S., 1963; d. Louis and Helen (Bartha) Kovacs; m. John Francis Szablya, June 12, 1951; children: Helen, Janos, Louis, Stephen, Alexandra, Rita, Dominique-Mary. Diploma in Sales, Mktg., U.B.C., 1962; BA in Fgn. Lang., Lit., Wash. State U., 1976. Freelance writer, translator, 1967—; columnist Cath. News, Trinidad, West Indies, 1980-91; adult educator TELOS Bellevue (Wash.) C.C., 1987-89; adult educator Pullman-Spokane (Wash.) C.C., 1976-80; faculty Christian Writers' Conf., Seattle, 1983-88, Pacific N.W. Writers' Conf., Seattle and Tacoma, 1987—92; hon. consul for Wash., Oreg., Idaho Republic of Hungary, 1993—; pres. Consular Assn. WA, 2009—. Lectr. Washington Commn. for Humanities, 1987-89. Author (with others): Hungary Remembered, 1986 (Guardian of Liberty award, 1986, George Washington Honor medal, Freedoms Found. award, 1988); author: 56-os Cserkèszcsapat, 1986; author: (with others) The Fall of the Red Star, 1996, Hungarian transl., 1999 (1st prize Wash. Press Assn., 1st prize Nat. Fedn. Press Women); pub., editor Hungary Internat. newsletter, 1990—93, columnist Hungarian Bus. Weekly, 1994—95; translator: Emlèkezünk, 1986, Mind Twisters, 1987, A vörös csillag lehull, 1999. Recipient Nat. 1st place editl. Nat. Fedn. Press Women, 1987, Senator Tom Martin Meml. award Pacific N.W. Writers Conf., 1979, Pro Auxilio Civium Hungarorum, Min. Fgn. Affairs, Republic of Hungary, 2003, Order of Merit, Republic of Hungary, 2005, Pro Communitate, City of Pecs, Hungary, 2006; grantee Hungarian Am. Assn. Wash., 1986, Wash. Com. for Humanities, 1986; named Cmty. Woman of Yr. Am. Bus. Women Assn., 1990. Mem. AAUW, Wash. Press Assn. (pres. 1987-88, 1st and 2nd place awards, several editl. and profile awards 1983, 87, 89, 90, 91, 92, 96, Communicator of Achievement award 1987), Nat. Fedn. Press Women (Affiliate Pres.' award 1988, bd. dirs. edn. fund N.W. quadrant, mem. 21st century planning com.), Authors Guild, Am. Translators Assn., Arpad Acad. (Gold medal 1987), Nat. Writers Club, Internat. PEN Club, Sigma Delta Chi (editl. award 1989), Hungarian-Am. Coalition (bd mem. 1992—, chair bd. 2007), Am.-Hungarian Fedn. Avocations: children, reading, dance, swimming, travel. Home and Office: PO Box 578 Kirkland WA 98083-0578 Office Phone: 425-739-0631. Personal E-mail: szablyahj@aol.com.

SZABO, BARNA ALADAR, engineering educator; b. Martonvasar, Hungary, Sept. 21, 1935; arrived in US, 1967, naturalized, 1974; s. Jozsef and Gizella (Ivanyi) S.; m. Magdalin Gerstmayer, July 23, 1960; children: Mark, Nicholas. BASc., U. Toronto, Ont., Can., 1962; MS, SUNY, Buffalo, 1966, PhD, 1968; D honoris causa, U. of Miskolc, Hungary, 1998. Registered profl. engr., Mo. Mining engr. Internat. Nickel Co. Can., 1960-62; engr. Acres Cons. Services Ltd., Niagara Falls, Can., 1962-66; instr. SUNY, Buffalo, 1966-68; prof. Washington U., St. Louis, 1968—2006, sr. prof. mech. engring., 2006—; chmn. Engring. Software R&D, Inc., St. Louis, 1989—. Author: (with Ivo Babuska) Finite Element Analysis, 1991; contbr. articles to profl. jours. Fellow, St. Louis Acad. Sci. Fellow: US Assn. Computational Mechanics (founding mem.); mem.: Hungarian Acad. Sci. Office Phone: 314-935-6352. Business E-Mail: szabo@wustl.edu.

SZABO, DANIEL, federal official; b. Budapest, Hungary, Mar. 23, 1933; came to U.S., 1950, naturalized, 1954; s. Alexander and Maria (Berger) S.; m. Corinne Holiber, July 3, 1955; children— Nancy Beth, Peter Stuart. BA, CCNY, 1957; MA, Johns Hopkins U., 1959. Internat. economist U.S. Tariff Commn., 1959-60; desk officer for Vietnam, Cambodia and Laos U.S. Dept. Commerce, 1960-63; spl. asst. to U.S. Senator Jacob K. Javits, 1963-69; dep. asst. sec. state for Inter-Am. Affairs, Washington, 1969-74; sr. adviser Inter-Am. Devel. Bank, Washington, 1974—2008. Bd. dirs. Washington chpt., chmn. Md. legis. task force Am. Jewish Com.; Am. Jewish Com. advocate Md. Interfaith Legis. Com., 1999—. With US Army, 1954—56. Home: 11600 Danville Dr North Bethesda MD 20852-3716 Personal E-mail: ds3693@verizon.net. *In approaching life I want my work to represent a service to our society. I am attracted to new ideas and new ways of solving old problems.*

SZABO, DENIS, criminologist, educator; b. Budapest, Hungary, June 4, 1929; arrived in Can., 1958; s. Jenö and Catherine (Zsiga) Szabo; m. Sylvie Grotard; children: Catherine, Marianne. D in Social and Polit. Sci., U. Louvain, Belgium, 1956; diploma in Criminology, Sorbonne U., Paris, 1958; Doctorate (hon.), U. Sienna, Italy, 1983, U. Budapest, Hungary, 1985, U. Aix Marseille, 1992, Panteios U., 1996, U. Bucarest, 2004. Asst. in sociology U. Louvain, 1951—56; lectr. sociology Cath. Univ., Paris, Lyon, 1956—58; mem. rsch. group Ctr. Nat. de la Recherche Scientifique, Paris, 1954—58; asst. prof. to assoc. prof. U. Montreal, Canada, 1958—66, founder, dir. dept. criminology, 1960—70, prof., 1966—95; founder, dir. Internat. Ctr. Comparative Criminology, Canada, 1969—84; prof. emeritus U. Montreal, Canada, 1995—. Emeritus prof. law U. Ecuador, Quito, 1984. Author, editor: book Can. Criminal Justice Sys., 1977, Criminologie et Politique Criminelle, 1978, La Criminologie Empirique au PQ, 1985, Sci. et Crime, 1986, De L' Anthropologie a la Criminologie Comparee, 1993, La Criminologie: Ses Fondements et sa Fondation, 1998; author (with Marc LeBlanc): Le Traité de Criminologie Empirique, 1993, The Criminal Justice Sys., 2001. Decorated officer Order Can.; recipient Beccaria Award, German Soc. Criminology, 1970, Chevalier Des Arts et des Lettres, France, 1996; named Comdr., Nat. Order Merite Hungarian Republic, 1996. Fellow: Am. Soc. Criminology (exec. coun., Sutherland award 1968), Am. Sociol. Soc., Royal Soc. Can.; mem.: Acad. Sci. Morales et Politiques, Quebec Soc. Criminology (founder, 45 Yrs. Svc. award 2005), Can. Soc. Criminology (v.p. 1962—64), Hungarian Acad. Sci., Inst. France (corr.; corres. mem.), Basque Inst. of Criminology San Sebastian (hon.), Romanian Soc. Criminology (hon.; elected hon. mem. 2003), Medaille de l' Institut Basque de Criminology (hon.), Nat. Order Merit (comdr. Ivory Coast 1987), Internat. Assn. Sociology, Order Nat. du Que. (officer 1998—), Soc. de Criminology du Que. (sec.-gen. 1960—70), Soc. Criminology (v.p. 1962—64), Internat. Soc. Criminology (pres. 1978—85, hon. pres.). Roman Catholic. Avocations: swimming, gardening, travel. Home: 66 Carré Copp Georgeville PQ Canada J0B 1T0 Office: U Montreal Internat Ctr Com Criminology CP 6128 succursale Centre-ville Montreal PQ Canada H3C 3J7 Home Phone: 819-843-4343. Business E-Mail: denis.szabo@umontreal.ca.

SZABO, ISTVAN, film director; b. Feb. 18, 1938; s. Istvan and Maria (Vita) S.; m. Vera Gyurey, Dec. 29, 1961. Dir. Budapest Acad. Theatre and Film Arts, 1961; mem. Balaz B. Studio, Budapest; leading man Hungarian Film Studios, Budapest, 1961—; dep. head Objektiv studio, 1980—92; prof. Hungarian Film Sch., Budapest, 1970—; prof., docent Deutsche Film Fernsehakademie, Berlin, 1982—84. Dir.: (short films) Concert, 1961, Variations Upon a Theme, 1961, Te (You), 1963 (Grand prix de Tours), (short film) Budapest, amiert szeretem (Budapest, Why I Love It), (series segment) Alom a hazrol (Dream About the House), 1971, (documentary) Kegyelet (Piety), 1967, Varosterkep (City Map) (Grand prix of Oberhausen, 1977), (TV plays) Osbemutato (Premier), 1974, Katzenspiel (Cat Play), 1982; (films) Almodozasok kora (The Age of Day-Dreaming), 1964, Apa (Father), 1966 (Grand prix of Moscow, 1966), Szerelmes film (love film), 1970, Tuzolto utca 25 (25 Fireman's Street), 1973 (Grand prix of Locarno, 1974), Budapesti mesék (Budapes Tales), 1976, Bizalom (Confidence), 1979 (Silver Bear of Berlin, 1980, Acad. aaward nomination, 1981), Der Grüne Vogel (The Green Bird), 1979, Mephisto, 1981 (Acad. award for best fng. lang. film, 1982, David di Donatello prize, 1982, prize of Italian Critics, prize of Critics U.K., 1982), Redl ezredes (Col. Redl), 1985 (Brit. Acad. award, 1986, Acad. award nomination, 1986, Cannes Internat. Film Festival Jury prize), Hanussen, 1989 (Acad. award nomination, 1989), Meeting Venus, 1991, Sweet Emma Dear Böbe, 1992 (Silver Bear of Berlin, 1992, prize Italian Critics, 1992), (TV play) Offenbach, 1995, Steadying the Boat (BBC-TV), 1996, Sunshine, 1998—99 (Euro. Film Acad. award, 1999, Gemie award (Can.), Taking Sides, 2001, Being Julia, 2004, Relatives/Rokonok, 2006. Recipient Bela Balázs prize, 1967, Kossuth prize, 1975. Mem.: Assn. Hungarian Film Dirs. and Artists, Acad. Motion Picture Arts and Scis. Office Phone: 3612519369. E-mail: islfilm@t-online.hu.

SZABO, JOSEPH CLARK, federal agency administrator; b. Evergreen Park, Ill., Dec. 26, 1957; s. Joseph Frank and Shirley Jean (Clark) S. AAS, South Suburban Coll., 1984; BA, Governors State U., 1990. Train condr. Metra/ICG, Chgo., 1976-96; state dir. Ill. legis. bd. United Transp. Union, 1996—2009; adminstr. Fed. R.R. Adminstrn. (FRA), Washington, 2009—. Mem. labor/mgmt. com. Metra, Chgo. Chmn. Riverdale (Ill.) Zoning Bd./Plan Commn., 1981-86; commr. Ivanhoe Park Bd., Riverdale, 1982-87; trustee Village of Riverdale, 1987-97, mayor 1997-2000. Mem. United Transp. Union (sec.-treas. local 1290 1984-90, legis. rep. 1987-96, vice chmn. state legis. bd. 1992-96), Calumet Region Enterprise Zone (bd. dirs.), Calumet Region Indsl. Assn. (bd. dirs.), Dolton Riverdale Jaycees (treas. 1979-80, v.p. 1980-81, pres. 1981-82, Jaycee of Yr. 1980, 81, Disting. Svc. award 1981, Outstanding Local Pres. 1982, Outstanding Jaycee 1990), Elks. Methodist. Office: Federal Railroad Administration US Dept Transp 1200 New Jersey Ave Washington DC 20590*

SZABO, PETER JOHN, investment company executive, mining engineer, financial planner, lawyer; b. Bklyn., Nov. 22, 1946; s. Paul Simon and Marita Ellen (Coughlin) S.; m. Dorothy Anne Steward, Nov. 14, 1970; children: Peter, David, John Paul Steward. BS in Mining Engring., Columbia U., 1968; LLB, LaSalle Law Sch., 1975; MS in Fin. Planning, Coll. Fin. PLanning, 1994. registered profl. engr., CFP. Mining engr. Halecrest Co., Mt. Hope, NJ, 1973-74; mgr. solid fuels & minerals Ford, Bacon & Davis, NYC, 1974-75; asst. v.p. Mfrs. Hanover Trust Co., NYC, 1975-77, Irving Trust Co., NYC, 1977; v.p. Republic Nat. Bank of Dallas, 1977-80; mgr. bus. devel. AMOCO Minerals, Denver, 1980-84; investment broker B.J. Leonard, Denver, 1984-85; investment exec. Wedbush Nobel Cook, Denver, 1985; regional sr. v.p. Alliance Fund Distbrs., NYC, 1985-92, sr. v.p., 1992—. Mining engr. U.S. Bur. Mines, Dallas, 1971-72, IRS, Washington, 1972-73. Treas. Columbia Sch. Engring., 1968—. Lt. USMC, 1969-71, Vietnam, capt. Res. Mem. VFW (post sr. vice comdr. 1993-94, post comdr. 1994-95, all state team post comdrs. 1995, 16th dist. jr. vice comdr. 1995—, 16th dist. sr. vice comdr. 1996—, nat. aide-de-camp 1995-96), Mil. Order of the Cootie (sr. vice comdr. 1994-95). Republican. Roman Catholic. Avocations: sailing, golf, tennis, jogging. Home and Office: Alliance Fund Distbrs 810 Oxford Way Benicia CA 94510-3646

SZAKAL, ANDRAS KALMAN, immunologist, anatomist, educator; s. Andor Viktor and Maria Szakal; m. Norma Elisabeth Skinner; children: Andras Robert, Tamas Kalman. BA in Zoology, U. Colo., 1961, MA in Biology, 1963; PhD, U. Tenn., 1972. Rsch. biologist for immunology of carcinogenesis group divsn. biology Oak Ridge (Tenn.) Nat. Labs., 1972—74; prin. scientist Meloy Labs., Springfield, Va., 1974—79; assoc. prof. dept. anatomy, divsn. immunobiology Va. Commonwealth Univ./Med Sch., Richmond, 1979—91, prof. dept. anatomy and neurobiology and The Immunology Group, 1991—. Cons. electron microscopist in exptl. biology Oak Ridge Nat. Lab., 1969—70; cons. electron microscopist Lunar Receiving Lab., NASA Manned Spacecraft Ctr., Houston, 1969; cons. on electron micros. autoradiography Nat. Cancer Inst., NIH, Bethesda, Md., 1974. Contbr. articles to profl. jours. Grantee, NIH, Nat. Inst. on Aging, 1985—88, 1991—94, 1999—2004. Mem.: AAAS, Va. Acad. Sci., Am. Assn. Immunologists, Am. Assn. Anatomists. Achievements include discovery of Antigen Transport Cell; ICCOSOMEs and the role of follicular dendritic cells (FDCs) in aging. E-mail: aszakal@hsc.vcu.edu.

SZALDA, DAVID JOSEPH, chemistry educator; b. Buffalo, May 25, 1950; s. Aloysius and Florence Szalda; m. Victoria Anne Galgano, June 2, 1974; children: Dava, David. PhD, Johns Hopkins U., Balt., 1976. Prof. Baruch Coll., NYC, 1978—. Rsch. collaborator Brookhaven Nat. Lab., Upton, NY, 1981—. Office: Baruch Coll 1 Bernard Baruch Way New York NY 10010 Business E-Mail: dszalda@baruch.cuny.edu.

SZALKOWSKI, CHARLES C., lawyer; b. Amarillo, Tex., Apr. 14, 1948; s. Chester Casimer and Virginia Lee Szalkowski; m. Jane Howe, Dec. 28, 1971; children: Jennifer Lee, Stephen Claude. BA, BS in Acctg., Rice U., 1971; MBA, JD, Harvard U., 1975. Bar: Tex. 1975. Assoc. Baker Botts L.L.P., Houston, 1975-82, ptnr., 1983—, gen. coun., 2006—. Speaker in field. Chmn. ann. fund campaign Rice U., Houston, 1991-93, chmn. Fund Coun., 1995-96; chmn. adminstrv. bd. St. Luke's United Meth. Ch., Houston, 1994, chmn. bd. trustees, 1997, 2003; chmn. DePelchin Children's Ctr., Houston, 2002-04; bd. dirs. Meth. Children's Home, Waco, 1998-2001, 03—. Mem.: ABA (fed. regulation of securities com.), BJohnston (chmn. assoc. adv. bd. 2007—), Tex. Bus. Law Found. (mem. exec. com. 1988—, chmn. 1998—2000, bd. dirs.), Harvard Law Sch. Assn. Tex. (pres. 1983—84), Houston Bar Assn. (corp. counsel sect. 1989—90, chmn.), State Bar Tex. (chmn. bus. law sect. 1991—92), Am. Law Inst., Assn. Rice U. Alumni (bd. dirs. 1999—2002, pres. 2007—08), Harvard Bus. Sch. Club (Houston) (bd. dirs. 2000—04, 2006—09). Office: Baker Botts LLP 1 Shell Plz 910 Louisiana St Ste 3000 Houston TX 77002-4991 Office Phone: 713-229-1480.

SZAREK, STANISLAW JERZY, mathematics professor; b. Ladek Zdroj, Poland, Nov. 13, 1953; arrived in US, 1980, naturalized, 1994; s. Mieczyslaw and Bronislawa (Brzezinska) S.; m. Malgorzata Chwascinska, June 22, 1980 (separated 1996, div. 2002); children: Martina, Natalia; 1 stepchild, Olga; m. Margaretmary Daley, May 15, 2004; 1 child, Emily; stepchildren: Blake, Devin. M in Math., Warsaw U., Poland, 1976; PhD in Math. Scis., Polish Acad. Scis., Warsaw, 1979. Rsch. asst. Math. Inst. Polish Acad. Scis., Warsaw, 1976-79, rsch. fellow, 1979-83; asst. prof. Case Western Res. U., Cleve., 1983-87, prof., 1987—, chair math. dept., 1994-96, Levi Kerr prof., 2009; prof. U. Paris, 1996—. Vis. positions U. Ill., Urbana, 1980, Ohio State U., Columbus, 1981, U. Tex., Austin, 1981-83, Inst. des Hautes Etudes Scientifiques, Bures-Sur-Yvette, France, 1986-89, U. Paris, 1990, 92, 95, Math. Scis. Rsch. Inst., Berkeley, Calif., 1996; invited spkr. Internat. Congress Math., Madrid, 2006 Contbr. articles to profl. jours. Recipient Prize of Sci. Sec., Polish Acad. Scis., 1979, Langevin prize Acad. Scis., France, 2007; Rsch. grantee NSF, 1983—, U.S.-Israel Binat. Sci. Found., 1993-97, 2003—; Sloan fellow Alfred P. Sloan Found., 1986-88. Mem.: Am. Math. Soc. Avocations: skiing, sailing, diving, bridge, travel. Office: Case Western Res U Dept of Math Cleveland OH 44106 Home Phone: 216-283-0303; Office Phone: 216-368-2880. Business E-Mail: szarek@cwru.edu.

SZAREK, WALTER ANTHONY, chemist, educator; b. St. Catharines, Ont., Can., Apr. 19, 1938; s. Anthony and Sophia (Kania) S. BSc, McMaster U., 1960, MSc, 1962; PhD, Queen's U., 1964. Postdoctoral fellow in chemistry Ohio State U., Columbus, 1964-65; asst. prof. biochemistry Rutgers U., New Brunswick, N.J., 1965-67; asst. prof. chemistry Queen's U., Kingston, Ont., 1967-71, assoc. prof., 1971-76, prof., 1976—2003, emeritus prof., 2003—, dir. Carbohydrate Research Inst., 1976-85; founding mem., prin. investigator Neurochem, Inc., 1993—. Cons. to govt. and industry; mem. Premier's Coun. Tech. Fund., Queen's Chemistry Innovation Coun., 2006-. Mem. editl. adv. bd. Carbohydrate Rsch. jour., 1973-97, Jour. of Carbohydrate Chemistry, 1994-2001; contbr. articles to profl. jours. Recipient Tchg. Excellence award Queen's U. Arts and Sci. Undergrad. Soc., 1988-89, Tchg. Excellence in Chemistry award, 1993, 2000, 2002. Fellow Chem. Inst. Can.; mem. AAAS, Am. Chem. Soc. (chmn. divsn. carbohydrate chemistry 1982-83, councilor 2002—05, alternate councilor, 2005-, Claude S. Hudson award in carbohydrate chemistry 1989, Melville L. Wolfrom award 1992), Inst. Theol. Encounter with Sci. and Tech., Royal Soc. Chemistry, N.Y. Acad. Scis., Soc. Glycobiology. Roman Catholic. Office: Dept Chemistry Queens Univ Kingston ON Canada K7L 3N6 Home Phone: 613-544-4358; Office Phone: 613-533-2643. Fax: 613-533-6532. Business E-Mail: szarekw@chem.queensu.ca.

SZASZ, FERENC M., historian, educator; b. Davenport, Iowa, Feb. 14, 1940; s. Ferenc Paul Szasz and Mary Ineta Plummer; m. Margaret Connell, Aug. 1, 1969; children: Eric, Chris, Maria. BA, Ohio Wesley U., 1962; PhD, U. Rochester, 1969. Vis. instr. to prof. history U. N.Mex., Albuquerque, 1967—2003. Author: The Day The Sun Rose Twice, 1986, Scots in the North American West, 2000, Religion in the Modern American West, 2000; contbr. articles to profl. jours. Democrat. Mem. United Ch. Of Christ. Avocation: travel. Office: Univ N Mex Dept History MSC 06 3760 1 Univ of N Mex Albuquerque NM 87131 Home Phone: 505-266-7406; Office Phone: 505-277-2451. E-mail: fszasz@unm.edu.

SZASZ, THOMAS STEPHEN, psychiatrist, educator, writer; b. Budapest, Hungary, Apr. 15, 1920; came to U.S., 1938, naturalized, 1944; s. Julius and Lily (Wellisch) S.; m. Rosine Loshkajian, Oct. 19, 1951 (div. 1970); children: Margot Szasz Peters, Susan Marie Szasz Palmer. AB, U. Cin., 1941, MD, 1944; DSc (hon.), Allegheny Coll., 1975, U. Francisco Marroquin, Guatemala, 1979; LHD (hon.), Towson U., 1999; D Sc(hon.), SUNY, 2001. Diplomate: Nat. Bd. Med. Examiners, Am. Bd. Psychiatry and Neurology. Intern 4th Med. Service Harvard, Boston City Hosp., 1944-45; asst. resident medicine Cin. Gen. Hosp., 1945-46, asst. clinician internal medicine div. out-patient dispensary, 1946; asst. resident psychiatry U. Chgo. Clinics, 1946-47; tng. research fellow Inst. Psychoanalysis, Chgo., 1947-48, rsch. asst., 1949-50, staff mem., 1951-56; practice medicine, specializing in psychiatry, psychoanalysis Chgo., 1949-54, Bethesda, Md., 1954-56, Syracuse, NY, 1956—; prof. psychiatry SUNY Health Sci. Ctr., Syracuse, 1956-90, prof. psychiatry emeritus, 1990—. Vis. prof. dept. psychiatry U. Wis., Madison, 1962, Marquette U. Sch. Medicine, Milw., 1968, U. N.Mex., 1981; holder numerous lectureships, including C.P. Snow lectr. Ithaca Coll., 1970; E.S. Meyer Meml. lectr. U. Queensland Med. Sch.; Lambie-Dew orator Sydney U., 1977; Mem. nat. adv. com. bd. Tort and Med. Yearbook; cons. com. mental hygiene N.Y. State Bar Assn.; mem. research adv. panel Inst. Study Drug Addiction; adv. bd. Corp. Econ. Edn., 1977— Author: Pain and Pleasure, 1957, The Myth of Mental Illness, 1961, Law, Liberty and Psychiatry, 1963, Psychiatric Justice, 1965, The Ethics of Psychoanalysis, 1965, Ideology and Insanity, 1970, The Manufacture of Madness, 1970, The Second Sin, 1973, Ceremonial Chemistry, 1974, Heresies, 1976, Karl Kraus and the Soul-Doctors, 1976, Schizophrenia: The Sacred Symbol of Psychiatry, 1976, Psychiatric Slavery, 1977, The Theology of Medicine, 1977, The Myth of Psychotherapy, 1978, Sex by Prescription, 1980, The Therapeutic State, 1984, Insanity: The Idea and its Consequences, 1987, The Untamed Tongue: A Dissenting Dictionary, 1990, Our Right to Drugs: The Case for a Free Market, 1992, A Lexicon of Lunacy, 1993, Cruel Compassion, 1994, The Meaning of Mind, 1996, Fatal Freedom, 1999, Pharmacracy: Medicine and Politics in America, 2001, Liberation By Oppression: A Comparative Study of Slavery and Psychiatry, 2002, Words to the Wise: A Medical-Philosophical Dictionary, 2004, Faith in Freedom: Libertarian Principles and Psychiatric Practices, 2004, Szasz Under Fire: The Psychiatric Abolitionist Answers His Critics, 2004, My Madness Saved Me: The Madness and Mariage of Virginia Woolf, 2006, Coercion as Cure: A Critical History of Psychiatry, 2007, The Medicalization of Everyday Life, 2007, Psychiatry: The Science of Lies, 2008; Antipsychiatry: Quackery Squarch, 2009, editor: The Age of Madness, 1973; cons. editor of Psychiatry and Psychology: Stedman's Medical Dictionary, 22d edit, 1973; contbg. editor: Reason, 1974—, Libertarian Rev., 1986—; mem. editl. bd. Psychoanalytic Rev, 1965—, Jour. Contemporary Psychotherapy, 1968—, Law and Human Behavior, 1977—, Jour. Libertarian Studies, 1977—, Children and Youth Services Rev, 1978—, Am. Jour. Forensic Psychiatry, 1980—; Free Inquiry, 1980—. Comdr. M.C., USNR, 1954-56. Recipient Stella Feiss Hofheimer award U. Cin., 1944, Holmes-Munsterberg award Internat. Acad. Forensic Psychology, 1969; Wisdom award honor, 1970; Acad. prize Institutum atque Academia Auctorum Internationalis, Andorra, 1972; Distinguished Service award Am. Inst. Pub. Service, 1974; Martin Buber award Midway Counseling Center, 1974, Thomas S. Szasz award Ctr. Ind. Thought, 1990, Alfred R. Lindesmith award for achievement in field of scholarship and writing Drug Policy Found., 1991, Rollo May award APA, 1998; others; named Humanist of Year Am. Humanist Assn., 1973; Hon. fellow Postgrad. Center for Mental Health, 1961, Mencken award, 1981, Humanist Laureate, 1984, Statue of Liberty-Ellis Island Found. Archives Roster, 1986, George Washington award Am. Hungarian Found., 2003. Fellow Am. Psychiat. Assn. (life), Am. Psychoanalytic Assn., Internat. Psychoanalytic Soc., Western N.Y. Psychoanalytic Soc. Home: 4739 Limberlost Ln Manlius NY 13104-1405 Office: 750 E Adams St Syracuse NY 13210-2306 Personal E-mail: tszasz@aol.com.

SZCZUBLEWSKI, WENDY SUE, small business owner, musician, freelance/self-employed writer; b. Dunkirk, NY; d. Bernard and Rosemary Dougherty; m. Michael Szczublewski, June 26, 1999; 1 child, Preston Thomas. BA in polit. sci. cum laude, SUNY Coll. at Fredonia, 1987—91. Project mgr. Vanstar Corp., Vienna, Va., 1996—97; proposal mgr. RS Info. Systems, Inc., McLean, Va., 1997—98; writer/editor Computer Assoc. Internat., Inc., Herndon, Va., 1999—2002; pres. and ceo WoBop Music, Columbia, Md., 2002—; owner Szczublewski Music, Fairfax Station, Va., 2005—. Mem.: Nat. Guild of Piano Teachers, Am. Coll. of Musicians, MENSA. Avocations: baking, gardening, reading, bicycling, hiking. Mailing: PO Box 131 Fairfax Station VA 22039 Business E-Mail: wszczub@szczublewski.com.

SZCZYRBA, IGOR NICHOLAS, mathematical physicist, consultant; b. Prague, Czech Republic, May 20, 1946; s. Mikolaj and Rozalia Szczyrba; m. Halina Agnieszka Kocewiak; children: Rafal W, Anna P. MS, Warsaw U., 1969, PhD, 1973, Dr. Habilitatis, 1983. Tchg. and rsch. asst. Warsaw U., 1969—73, tenured prof., 1973—84; vis. prof. Warsaw Sch. Econs., 1973—77; rsch. fellow Inst. Theoretical Physics, Trieste, Italy, 1975; vis. prof. U. Heidelberg, Germany, 1977—81; asst. prof. U. No. Colo., Greeley, 1986—88, assoc. prof., 1988—90, full prof., 1990—. Linguistic cons. Internat. Lang. Engring., Boulder, Colo., 1988—99, LionBridge, Boulder, Colo., 2000—, Bowne Global Solutions, Montreal, Canada, 2003—; polit. scis. cons. U. No. Colo., Greeley, 1986—. Contbr. articles to profl. jours. Recipient Scholar of Yr. award, U. No. Colo., Coll. Arts and Scis., 1989, 2002—03. Mem.: Math. Assn. Am. Office: U No Colo Ross Hall Greeley CO 80639 Office Fax: 970-351-1225. E-mail: igor.szczyrba@unco.edu.

SZE, SARAH, sculptor; b. Boston, 1969; BA magna cum laude, Yale U., 1991; MFA, Sch. of Visual Arts, NYC, 1997. One-woman shows include, Mus. of Fine Arts, Boston, Inst. of Contemporary Art, London, The Found. Cartier, Paris, Walker Art Ctr., Mpls., 2002, The Whitney Mus. Am. Art, N.Y.C., 2003, Mus. of Contemporary Art, Chgo, Victoria Miro Gallery, London, 2006, exhibited in group shows, The Whitney Mus. of Am. Art, N.Y.C., The Carnegie Mus. of Art, Pitts., Mus. Modern Art, San Francisco, 48th Venice Biennial, The L.A. (Calif.) Mus. Contemporary Art, 1999, Bionale of Lyon, 2009. Recipient Paula Rhodes Meml. award, 1997, award, Louis Comfort Tiffany Found., 1999, Lotus Club Found. Prize, 2003; fellow John D. and Catherine T. MacArthur Found, 2003.

SZEFLER, STANLEY JAMES, pediatrics and pharmacology educator; b. Buffalo, Aug. 24, 1948; s. Stanley and Bernice Laura (Platt) Szefler; m. Christine M. Drezek, Dec. 26, 1970; children: David, Paul. BS, SUNY, Buffalo, 1971, MD, 1975. Resident pediat. Children's Hosp. Buffalo, 1975—77; postdoctoral fellow in clin. pharmacology and allergy immunology SUNY, Buffalo, 1977—79, asst. prof. pediat. and pharmacology, 1979—82; assoc. prof. pediat. and pharmacology U. Colo., Denver, 1982—90, prof. pediat., pharmacology, 1990—. Dir. clin. pharmacology Children's Hosp., Buffalo, 1979—82, Nat. Jewish Ctr. for Immunology and Respiratory Medicine, Denver, 1982—. Contbr. articles to profl. jours. Mem. steering com., Asthma Camp for Children Am. Lung Assn., Denver, 1987—96. Maj. USAR, 1979—88. Grantee NIH, 1980—84, 1990—, FDA, Denver, 1988—91. Fellow: Am. Acad. Pediat. (liaison mem. com. drugs), Am. Acad. Allergy, Asthma and Immunology (chmn. asthma, rhinitis and respiratory disease interest sect. 1995—97). Avocations: literature, history, reading. Office: Nat Jewish Med & Rsch Ctr Dept Pediat 1400 Jackson St Denver CO 80206-2761 Business E-Mail: szeflers@njc.org.

SZEGO, CLARA MARIAN, cell biologist, educator; b. Budapest, Hungary, Mar. 23, 1916; arrived in U.S., 1921, naturalized, 1927; d. Paul S. and Helen (Elek) S.; m. Sidney Roberts, Sept. 14, 1943. AB, Hunter Coll., 1937; MS, U. Minn., 1939, PhD, 1942; DSc (hon.), CUNY, 2007. Instr. physiology U. Minn., 1942-43; Minn. Cancer Rsch. Found. fellow, 1943—44; rsch. assoc. OSRD, Nat. Bur. Stds., 1944-45, Worcester Found. Exptl. Biology, 1945-47; rsch. instr. physiol. chemistry Yale U. Sch. Medicine, 1947-48; mem. faculty UCLA, 1948—, prof. biology, 1960—. Contbr. articles to profl. jours., book chapters and revs. Garvan fellow U. Minn., 1939; Guggenheim fellow, 1956; named Woman of Year in Sci. Los Angeles Times, 1957-58; named to Hunter Coll. Hall of Fame, 1987. Fellow AAAS; mem. Am. Physiol. Soc., Am. Soc. Cell Biology, Endocrine Soc. (CIBA award 1953), Soc. for Endocrinology (Gt. Britain), Biochem. Soc. (Gt. Britain), Internat. Soc. Rsch. Reproduction, Phi Beta Kappa (pres. UCLA chpt. 1973-74), Sigma Xi (pres. UCLA chpt. 1976-77). Home: 1371 Marinette Rd Pacific Palisades CA 90272-2627 Office: U Calif Dept Molecular Cell & Devel Biology Los Angeles CA 90095-1606 Business E-Mail: cmszego@ucla.edu.

SZELENYI, IVAN, adult education educator; b. Budapest, Apr. 17, 1938; came to the U.S., 1981; s. Gusztav and Julianna (Csapo) S.; m. Valeria Vanilia Majoros; children: Szonja, Lilla, Balazs. PhD, Hungarian Acad. Scis., Budapest, 1973, DSc, 1990; doctorate (hon.), Budapest U. Econs., 1992; DLitt (hon.), Flinders U., 1997; dr. rer.pol. h.c. (hon.), Friedrich-Alexander U., 2003. Rsch. fellow Hungarian Acad. Scis., Budapest, 1963-75; found. prof. Flinders U., Adelaide, Australia, 1975-80; prof. U. Wis., Madison, 1981-86; disting. prof. CUNY Grad. Ctr., 1986-88; prof. UCLA, 1988-99; William Graham Sumner prof. sociology Yale U., New Haven, 1999—. Author: Urban Inequalities under State Socialism, 1983, Socialist Entrepreneurs, 1988 (C. Wright Mills award 1989); co-author: Intellectuals on the Road to Class Power, 1979, Making Capitalism without Capitalists, 1998, Theories of New Class, 2004, Patterns of Exclusion, 2006. Mem. Hungarian Acad. Scis; fellow Am. Acad. Arts and Sci. Business E-Mail: ivan.szelenyi@yale.edu.

SZELIGA, VICTORIA L, retired social studies educator; b. Williamsport, Pa., Nov. 29, 1950; d. George E. Mayer and Dorothy M. Thomas; m. Martin Szeliga, Jan. 15, 1972; children: Christopher M., Bryan J. MA, U. No. Colo., Greeley, 1975. Tchr. Dist. #11, Colorado Springs, Colo., 1973—83, Acad. Dist. #20, 1983—2006. Author: (ednl. materials) Book Bridges #1. Blood donor Penrose Hosp., Colorado Springs, Colo., 1976—; pres. Home Owners Assn., Canon City, Colo., 2007—. Named Tchr. of Yr., Rockrimmon Elem., 1986; grantee, Pikes Peak Coalition Ctr., 1985, 1987, Colo. Endowment Humanities, 1991, Colo. Geog. Alliance, 1992, Acad. Dist. #20, 2001; scholar, Nat. Geog. Soc., 1997, Econ. Tchr. award, Found. Tchg. Econ., 2001. Achievements include development of science, social studies and technology curricula. Avocations: reading, hunting, fishing, hiking. Home: 433 Aspen Grove Guffey CO 80820

SZENBERG, MICHAEL, economics professor, editor, consultant; b. Sosnowiec, Poland, Apr. 8, 1934; came to US, 1961, naturalized, 1966; s. Henry and Sara (Rosensaft) S.; m. Miriam Silverstein, Sept. 2, 1962; children: Naomi, Avi. Student, Bar Ilan U., 1959—61; BA summa cum laude, L.I. U., 1963; PhD, CUNY, 1970. Faculty Bklyn. Ctr. L.I. U., 1965—, prof. econ. Bklyn. Ctr., 1974—83; disting. prof. econs. Lubin Grad. Sch. Bus. Pace U., 1983—; chmn. fin. and econ., 2000—; dir. Ctr. Applied Rsch., 1994—2007. Adj. prof. Hunter Coll., 1970-76, Pace U., 1975-83; founder, dir. Lecture Bur. Econ., 1973; chmn. 1st Met. Grad. Conf. Econ., 1973; assoc. Ctr. Tech. Assessment, Newark Coll. Engring., 1973; vis. prof. econ. NYU, 1977-79; cons. in field. Author: Econ. of the Israeli Diamond Industry, 1973, The Welfare Effects of Trade Restrictions: A Case Study of the United States Footwear Industry, 1977, The Economics of the American Footwear Industry, 2d edit., 1984, Paul Samuelson On Being an Economist, 2005, Distressed Industries in the Era of Globalization 2007Franco Modigliani, A Mind that Never Rests 2008, Encyclopedia Entries, Samuelsonian Economics and the Twenty-First Century 2006; editor: Essays in Economics, The John Commons Meml. Lectures, 1986, Eminent Economists: Their Life Philosophies, 1992, Passion and Craft, Economists at Work, 1999, New Frontiers in Economics, 2004, Reflections of Eminent Economists, 2004; co-editor: Oxford U., Press Handbooks in Economics; assoc. editor: Am. Economist, 1973-75, editor-in-chief, 1975—; contbr. articles to profl. jours., chpt. to books. Served with Israeli Air Force, 1956-59. Recipient Dean Hudson award L.I. U., 1962, Am. Coll. Abroad award, 1962, Dean Abelson award CUNY, 1963; fellow econs. CUNY, 1963; grantee Israel Diamond Inst., 1970; recipient Irving Fisher Monograph award, 1971; fellow Internat. Honor Soc. in Econ., 1972; grantee Dept. Labor, 1975; recipient Kenan award Pace U., 1983, Schalkenbach Found. Rsch. award, 1987, First Prize Recognition award, 1989, Tchr. of Yr. Pace U., 1992, Tchg. Excellence award Acad. Bus. Admin., 1993, Achievement award CUNY, 1993, Outstanding Publ. award Pace U., 1993-95, scholarly rsch. award Pace U., 1996, Lubin Tchr. of Yr. award Pace U., 1999; Eugene Lang Regional fellow, Pace U. Nat. Bus. and Econ. Assn. Mem. Internat. Trade and Fin. Assn., Internat. Fedn. Sci. Editors, Ea. Econ. Assn., Am. Econ. Assn., Assn. Cultural Econs., Internat. Honor Soc. Econs. (exec. bd. 1975—, regional dir. 1971-74), Optimates Soc. (pres. 1972-80). Home: 1442 E 9th St Brooklyn NY 11230-6405 Office Phone: 212-618-6529. Business E-Mail: mszenberg@pace.edu.

SZERI, ANDRAS Z., engineering educator; b. Nagyvarad, Hungary, June 6, 1934; came to U.S., 1967; s. Andras F. and Julie (Farkas) S.; m. Mary J. Parkinson, Apr. 25, 1962; children: Andrew J., Elizabeth C., Maria J. BS with honors, U. Leeds, 1959, PhD, 1962. Rsch. engr. English Electric Co., Stafford, 1962—64; prof. Universidad Santa Maria, Valparaiso, Chile, 1964—66; asst. prof. U. Pitts., 1967—70, assoc. prof., 1970—76, prof. math., 1977—93, prof. mech. engring., 1977—94, chmn. dept. mech. engring., 1984—87, William Kepler Whiteford prof. engring., 1990—94; Robert Lyle Spencer prof. mech. engring., chmn. U. Del., Newark, 1994, acting dean Coll. Engring., 1998—2000. Cons. Westinghouse Electric Co., Pitts., 1967-82; external examiner U. W.I., 1989-95. Author: Tribology: Friction, Lubrication, and Wear, 1980, Fluid Film Bearings, Theory, and Design, 1998, 2d edit., 2005. Fellow ASME (assoc. editor Jour. Tribology 1978-87, tech. editor 1987-93); mem. Am. Acad. Mechanics, The Soc. Rheology, Soc. Engring. Sci., Soc. Natural Philosophy. Office: U Del Dept Mech Engring Newark DE 19716 Office Phone: 302-831-2008. Business E-Mail: szeri@udel.edu.

SZERLAG, CHESTER THEODORE, health care executive; MBA, U. Chgo., 1984. Exec. dir. U. Chgo., 1980—. Contbr. articles to profl. jours.; mem. editl. bd.: Enterprise Imaging and Radiation Oncology Management Jour. Pres. elect Chgo. Health Exec. Forum, 2009; bd. trustee Village of Woodridge, Ill., 1997—2005; vice chmn. U. Chgo. Credit Union, Ill., 2001—. Recipient Gold medal, Soc. Radiation Oncology Adminstrs., 1991. Fellow: Am. Coll. Healthcare Execs.; mem.: Healthcare Fin. Mgmt. Assn., Radiol. Soc. N.Am. (chair assoc. sci. consortium), Am. Coll. Med. Practice Execs. (cert. med. practice exec. 2004), Soc. Radiation Oncology Adminstrs. (pub. chair, past treas., past. pres., past chmn.), Woodrige Club (pres. 2005—06), Rotary Internat. (asst. dist. gov. 2008—). Office: Univ Chgo 5758 S Maryland Ave MC 9006 Chicago IL 60637 Business E-Mail: cszerlag@radonc.uchicago.edu.

SZETELA, CHERYL WAHL, educator; m. Andrew Wahl, June 8, 1996; children: Christopher Jacob Martins, Jessica Marie. BA, So. CT State U., Hamden, 2002; MPhil, Grad. Sch. and U. Ctr., CUNY, 2005, PhD in ABD, 2008. Part time prof. Quinnipiac U., Hamden, 2006—; adj. prof. Norwalk CC, Conn., 2006—08. Early mem. Moveon. Org., Conn., 2000—08; founding mem. Color Change Org., Conn., 2005—08. Recipient Sophomore Scholastic award, St. Cloud State U., 2000, Outstanding Graduating Sr. award, 2002; U. fellowship, Grad. Sch. and U. Ctr., 2003—06. Mem.: Phi Alpha Theta (Admittance award 2000).

SZEWS, CHARLES, transportation executive; BBA, U. Wis., Eau Claire. CPA. With Ernst & Young; v.p., contr. Fort Howard Corp., Green Bay, Wis.; v.p., CFO Oshkosh (Wis.) Truck Corp., 1996-97, exec. v.p., CFO, 1997—2007, pres., COO, 2007—. Office: Oshkosh Truck Corp 2307 Oregon St Oshkosh WI 54902

SZIGETI, JÁNOS, physicist; b. Budapest, Hungary, Oct. 11, 1936; s. György and Zsuzsanna (Ziffer) S.; m. Boglárka Gulyás, Aug. 7, 1967; children: Andrea, Zsófia. Diploma, Roland Eötvös U., 1960; PhD, U. Leningrad, 1972. With Ctrl. Rsch. Inst. for Physics, 1960—91; sr. scientist Rsch. Inst. for Particle and Nuc. Physics, 1991—96, sci. advisor, 1996—, head dept. laser spectroscopy, 1991—. Asst. scientific co-worker, 1960-66; scientific co-worker Acad. of Sci., 1966-72, sr. scientist, 1972-96, head dept. laser spectroscopy, 1993—, sci. advisor, 1996—; head of dept. Rsch. Inst. of Particles and Nuclear Physics, 1991—. Contbr. numerous articles to profl. jours. Mem. Roland Eötvös Phys. Soc., European Phys. Soc. Avocation: rowing on the danube. Home: Erzsebet u 27 app 40 1043 Budapest Hungary Office: Rsch Inst Particle & Nuc Physics PO Box 49 H-1525 Budapest Hungary Office Phone: 36-1-392-27-52. Business E-Mail: szigeti@rmki.kfki.hu.

SZKUTAK, TOM, corporate financial executive; married; 2 children. BS in Fin. magna cum laude, Boston U. Fin. mgmt. positions through exec. v.p. fin. GE Investments, CFO GE Lighting GE, 1982—2002; sr. v.p., CFO Amazon.com, Seattle, 2002—. Office: Amazon.com 1200 12th Ave S Seattle WA 98144

SZOKA, EDMUND CASIMIR CARDINAL, cardinal, archbishop; b. Grand Rapids, Mich., Sept. 14, 1927; s. Casimir and Mary (Wolgat) Szoka. BA, Sacred Heart Sem., 1950; JCB, Pontifical Lateran U., 1958, JCL, 1959. Ordained priest Diocese of Marquette, Mich., 1954; asst. pastor St. Francis Parish, Manistique, Mich., 1954—55; sec. to bishop Marquette, 1955—57, 1959—62; chaplain St. Mary's Hosp., Marquette, 1955—57; tribunal, defender of bond Marquette, 1960—71; asst. chancellor Diocese of Marquette, 1962—69, chancellor, 1970—71; pastor St. Pius X Ch., Ishpeming, Mich., 1962—63, St. Christopher Ch., Marquette, 1963—71; ordained bishop, 1971; bishop Diocese of Gaylord, Mich., 1971—81; archbishop Archdiocese of Detroit, 1981—90; elevated to cardinal, 1988; cardinal-priest Ss. Andrea e Gregorio al Monte Celio, 1988—; pres. prefecture of econ. affairs of Holy See Rome, 1990—97; pres. Pontifical Commn. for Vatican City State, 1997—2001; pres. Governatorate of Vatican City State, 2001—06; pres. emeritus, 2006—. Sec.-treas. Mich. Cath. Conf., Lansing, 1972—77; chmn. region VI Nat. Conf. Cath. Bishops, 1972—77; treas., adminstrv. bd. and adminstrv. com., budget and fin. com. Nat. Conf. Cath. Bishops/U.S. Cath. Conf., 1981—84; mem. Secretariat of State 2d sect. Coun. for Rels. with States. Trustee Nat. Shrine of the Immaculate Conception, Washington, 1981—90; chmn. bd. trustees Cath. Telecomm. Network Am., 1984—90; trustee, exec. com., chmn. com. for univ. rels. Cath. U. Am, 1981—90. Mem.: Congregation for Clergy, Congregation for Evangelization of Peoples, Congregation for Bishops, Congregation for Causes of Saints, Congregation for Insts. Consecrated Life and Socs. Apostolic Life. Roman Catholic. Mailing: Via Rusticucci 13 00193 Rome Italy

SZOKODY, ANIKO, pianist, educator; b. Szeged, Hungary, Apr. 24, 1973; arrived in U.S., 1997; d. Fedor Sandor Szokody and Zsuzsanna Szlovak; m. Willis Dee Ottery III, Mar. 1, 2002; 1 child, Willis David. MusB, Zoltan Kodaly Spl. Musical Secondary Sch., Kecskemet, Hungary, 1991; Piano Performer Artist Degree, tchrs. diploma, Franz Liszt Acad. Music, Budapest, Hungary, 1997; MusM in Piano Performance, Ind. U., 2000; artist diploma (hon.), Conservatorio Beethoven, Buenos Aires, 1997. Assoc. instr. piano Ind. U., Bloomington, 1998—2000; instrumental accompanist, chamber music coach Chautauqua Instn., 1999—2002, head instrumental accompanist, chamber music coach, 2002—06. Guest instr. piano Conservatorio Beethoven, Buenos Aires, 1996—97; studio pianist for cellist Janos Starker Ind. U., Bloomington, 1998—2000; pvt. piano instr., Albany, NY, 2000—; mem. piano faculty Luzerne Music Ctr., NY, 2007; piano faculty Union Coll., Schenectady, NY, 2007; organist Hist. St. George's Ch., Schenectady, NY, 2007—. Musician (pianist): (solo performances) Europe, North and South America. Grantee, Hungarian Nat. Cultural Found., 1996, Conservatorio Beethoven, 1996—97, for profl. career documentary, Hungarian Pub. TV, 2002; scholar, studio of Prof. Gyorgy Sebok, Ind. U., 1998—2000. Mem.: Luzerne Chamber Players, Am. Fed. Musicians, Capitol Chamber Artists, Adirondack Ensemble, N.Y. State Music Tchrs. Assn., Coll. Music Soc., Music Tchrs. Nat. Assn., Upper Hudson Musical Arts, Schenectady Musical Union, Albany Symphony Orch. Home: 819 Woodland Ave Schenectady NY 12309

SZOLNOKI, JOHN FRANK, special education educator, administrator; b. NYC, Apr. 16, 1956; s. Jacob and Anna (Reinwald) S.; m. Kathleen Bascetta, Dec. 28, 2004; children: Melissa Beth, David Jacob, Elizabeth, Eric. BS, Manhattan Coll., 1978; MS, Coll New Rochelle, 1981; MEd, Columbia U., 1983, EdD, 1988. Cert. tchr. spl. edn., sch. adminstr., supr., dist. adminstr., N.Y. Therapy aide Office Mental Health, N.Y. State Bronx Psychiat. Ctr., 1978; tchr. sci. 6th-8th grades Sts. Philip and James Sch., Archdiocese of N.Y., 1978-79; program supr. occpl. edn. classes St. Mary's Habilitation Inst. Inst. Applied Human Dynamics, Bronx, 1979-83; sch. supr. Assn. for Help of Retarded Children Bronx Habilitation Ctr., NYC, 1983-87; spl. educator Mt. Pleasant-Blythedale Union Free Sch. Dist., Valhalla, NY, 1987-88; spl. edn. educator Bd. Coop. Ednl. Svcs. So. Westchester, White Plains, NY, 1988—, Dobbs Ferry (N.Y.) H.S., 1995-96, Harrison (N.Y.) H.S., 1996-97, Hommocks Mid. Sch., Larchmont, NY, 2002—05, West Lake H.S., Valhalla, 2005—. Adj. prof. Western Conn. State U., Danbury, 1988-89, St. Thomas Aquinas Coll., Sparkill, N.Y., 1990, 91, Coll. New Rochelle, N.Y., 2001-, CUNY Hunter, 1994-99; team leader Bd. Coop. Ednl. Svcs., So. Westchester, 1989-93, site coord. extended sch. yr. program Rye Lake campus, 1991-95; presenter in field; Ctr. Spl. Edn. and Tng. Resource Ctr., workshop presenter supts. day, 1995; mem. So. Westchester Bd. coop. Ednl. Svcs. Vol. firefighter, sec. hook & ladder Harrison (N.Y.) Fire Dept., 1993-95, lt., 1996-97 capt., 1998-99 (Firefighter of Yr. 1990); mem. com. Very Spl. Arts,White Plains, N.Y., 1990; parent rep. exec. bd. Harrison Children's Ctr., 1991-93, 95—; lector, tchr. catechism St. Gregory the Gt. Roman Cath. Ch., 1994-95, Secular Franciscan Order, Roman Cath. Ch., 2002—; sec. St. Francis Fraternity, N.Y., 2003—; EMT vol. Harrison Ambulance Corps, 1993-94; aux. police officer N.Y.C. Police Dept., 1975-77; mem. Ctrl. Westchester Vicariate Coun., Archdiocese of N.Y., 1998—99; mem. parish coun. St. Gregory the Great, 1998—99; panel mem. surrogate decision making com. N.Y. State Commn. on Quality Care for the Mentally Disabled, 1999—. Grantee: Readers Digest Found., Westchester Edn. Coalition, 1990, Innovation Network, Westchester, Rockland Impact II, Adaptor award, 1991, 92, 93, 94, 95, 97, 98, 2000 Mem. Am. Assn. on Mental Retardation (rsch. project norming examiner adaptive behavior scale 1991), Coun. for Exceptional Children (pres. Hunter Coll. chpt. 1997-2000, regional rep. to bd. dirs. N.Y. State Fedn. 1990-93, treas. 1993-96, exec. bd. dirs. 1993-96, del. Nat. conv. 1998, co-chair N.Y. state conv. 1997, sec. 2002—, co-chmn. promotion/publicity subcom. local arrangements com. nat. annual conv. 2002, v.p. NY State Fedn. Chpts. Coun. Exceptional Children, 2003-04, pres.-elect, 2004-05, NY State CEC pres. 2005-), Kappa Delta Pi, Phi Delta Kappa. Avocation: marathon running. Office: Bd Coop Ednl Svcs So Westchester 1606 Old Orchard St White Plains NY 10604-1049 Home: 51 Holmes Ave Hartsdale NY 10530-1339 Office Phone: 914-948-7271. Personal E-mail: johnszolnoki@aol.com.

SZONNTAGH, EUGENE L., chemical engineer, educator, chemist, historian, archaeometrist, organologist; b. Budapest, Hungary, July 31, 1924; arrived in US, 1957; s. Jenö Szonntag and Anna Vaisz; m. Nora Jenser, July 27, 1950; children: Desi, Thomas. Diploma in Chem. Engring., Tech. U. Budapest, 1948, DTech, 1975, PhD, 1999; postgrad, Tech. U., Austria, 1957, Bryn Mawr Coll., 1970. Registered profl. engr., Pa.; profl. indsl. hygienist. Chem. engr. Hungarian R.R., Budapest, 1948—50; asst. to assoc. prof. Veszprem U., Hungary, 1950—56; from scientist to sr. scientist Leeds and Northrup Co., North Wales, Pa., 1957—72; prin. engr. Honeywell, Inc., Ft. Washington, Pa.; dir. ops. Continuing Edn., Inc., 1972—73; prin. engr. Honeywell, Inc., Clearwater, Fla., 1973—86; assoc. prof. U. South Fla., Tampa, 1987—91, prof., 1991—2007. Author: (book) Atmospheric Sampling and Analysis of Chemical Agents, 2009; Contbr. over 100 articles to profl. jours., 8 chpts. to books; 38 patents in field. Dir. music, organist emeritus St. Alfred's Ch., Palm Harbor, Fla., 1983—93; dir. music, organist Faith Luth. Ch., 1994—95, Holy Spirit Episcopal Ch., Safety Harbor, Fla., 1996—2008. Recipient Indsl. Rsch. 100 award Chromatography, 1964, Star Inventor award Honeywell, 1982. Mem. Am. Chem. Soc., Am. Inst. Archaeology, Am. Musical Instrument Soc., Organ Hist. Soc., Instrument Soc. Am. (historian 1978-82), Am. Guild Organists (acad.; cert. choir master, chpt. dean 1970-72, 84-86). Avocations: collecting musical instruments, travel, archaeology, photography. Home: 1161 Cane Mill Ln Bradenton FL 34212 Office: U South Fla MDC-56 13201 Bruce B Downs Blvd Tampa FL 33612 Home Phone: 941-708-6699. Personal E-mail: e.szonntagh@verizon.net.

SZOSTAK, (M.) ANNE, consulting firm executive, former bank executive; b. London, June 23, 1950; BA in sociology, Colby Coll., Waterville, Maine, 1972; student, Husson Coll., 1992. Pres. Fleet Nat. Bank, Providence, 1980—82; sr. VP Fleet Nat. Bank, 1982—85, exec. VP, 1985—88, corp. VP, head human resources, 1988—91; pres., COO Fleet Bank Maine, 1991—94; sr. v.p. human resources FleetBoston Fin. Corp., 1994—98, exec. v.p., dir. human resources & diversity, 1998—2004; chmn., CEO Fleet RI, RI, 2001—03; pres., CEO Szostak Partners LLC, 2004—. Bd. dirs. Tupperware Corp., 2000-, Belo Corp., 2004-, Spherion Corp., 2005-, Choicepoint, Inc., 2005-, Cadbury Schweppes plc, 2008- Chmn. Boys & Girls Clubs of Am., 2003—; bd. mem. United Way Women's Leadership Com. Recipient Disting. Alumni Award, Colby Coll., Leadership Award, New England Coun.,

1993, Athena Award, YWCA Outstanding Women's Gala, 2002; named to Human Resources Honor Roll, Human Resources Exec. Mag., 2001. Office: 17 Virginia Ave Providence RI 02906 Office Phone: 401-383-9363.

SZOSTAK, JACK WILLIAM, molecular biologist, educator; b. London, Nov. 9, 1952; s. William J. and Viola (Munford) S.; m. Terri-Lynn McCormick, May 29, 1993. BS in Cell Biology, McGill U., Montreal, Can., 1972; PhD in Biochemistry, Cornell U., Ithaca, NY, 1977. Rsch. assoc. in biochemistry Cornell U., Ithaca, NY, 1977-79; asst. prof. dept. biol. chemistry Harvard Med. Sch./Sidney Farber Cancer Inst., Boston, 1979-83; assoc. prof. dept. biol. chemistry Harvard Med. Sch./Dana Farber Cancer Inst., Boston, 1983-84; assoc. prof. dept. genetics Harvard Med. Sch., Boston, 1984-87, prof., 1988—; assoc. molecular biologist, dept. molecular biology Mass. Gen. Hosp., Boston, 1984-87, molecular biologist, dept. molecular biology, 1988—, Alex Rich Disting. Investigator, dept. molecular biology, 2000—; investigator Howard Hughes Med. Inst., 1998—. Cons. Genetics Inst., 1980-87; mem. site visit team, NIH, 1982; mem. Presdl. Young Investigator Review Panel, 1984; mem. Nat. Sci. Found. Review Panel, 1985, NASA Exobiology Study Sect., 1997; NATO Advanced Study Course on RNA, Spetses, Greece, 1994; program dir., Genetics Cancer and Inherited Disease Tng. Grant, Harvard Med. Sch., 1986-92; mem. sci. adv. bd. Gilead Scis., Inc., 1990-98, Trans-Karyotic Therapies, Inc., 1990—, Cubist, Inc., 1993-97; ad hoc mem., NIH Molecular Biology Study Sect., 1992; mem. Subcommittee of Professors, Harvard Med. Sch., 1992-94, preliminary qualifying exam com., 1996-97, com. on postdoctoral fellow, 1997-98; mem. com. on sr. appointments, Mass. Gen. Hosp., 1992-97; co-chair, Nucleic Acids Gordon Conf., 1993, Keystone Symposium on RNA, 1996; Can. reallocation exercise external reviewer, NRC, 1998, mem. workshop on size limits of microorganisms, 1998, co-chair com. on the origin and evolution of life, 2003-; mem. partners com. on sr. appointments, 1997-; mem. bd. tutors, biochemical sciences, Harvard U., 2000-; mem. NIH Intramural Review Panel, 2001; invited lectr., Agouron Inst. Sponsored Geobiology Course, Catalina Island, 2002; vis. fellow, Brasenose Coll. and Astor Lectr., Oxford U., 2005; tchr. Introductory Lecture, RNA World Quarter Course, 2005. Contbr. articles to sci. jours. Recipient Louis Vuitton-Moet Hennesey 'Vinci of Excellence' award, 1996, Hans Sigrist prize U. Bern, Switzerland, 1997, Genetics Soc. Am. medal, 2000, Harrison Howe award, Am. Chemical Soc., Rochester sect., 2003; co-recipient Albert Lasker award for Basic Med. Rsch., Lasker Found., 2006 Fellow NY Acad. Scis.; mem. NAS (award in molecular biology, 1994), Am. Acad. Arts & Sciences. Achievements include patents in field. Office: Howard Hughes Med Inst Mass Gen Hosp Dept Molecular Biology Boston MA 02114 also: CCIB 7215 Simches Research Ctr 185 Cambridge St Boston MA 02114 Address: Mass Gen Hosp 32 Fruit St Boston MA 02114 Business E-Mail: szostak@molbio.mgh.harvard.edu.*

SZOT, PAULO, baritone, singer, actor; b. Sao Paulo, Brazil, 1969; Attended, U. Jagiellonski, Cracow, Poland. Profl. opera debut, São Paulo, Brazil, 1997; debut NYC Opera, 2003, Met. Opera, NYC, 2004, Téatre Municipal, Marseille, 2005, Nat. Opera, Bordeaux, France, 2006, Teatro Liceu, Barcelona, 2007; Broadway debut, 2008. Singer: (Operas) Carmen, Elixir of Love, Nozze di Figaro, La Boheme, Il Guarany, Eugene Onegin, Barber of Seville, Don Giovanni, Cavaleria Rusticana, I Pagliacci, Die Fledermaus, Manon, Tannhauser, Don Pasquale, Hansel und Gretel, Romeo e Juliette, The Merry Widow, Orfeu, Joanna de Flandres, The Fall of the House of Usher, Dido and Aeneas, Cosi fan Tutte, Maria Golovin, Portrait of Manon, Rita, (Broadway plays) South Pacific, 2008 (Outstanding Actor in a Musical, Outstanding Musical, Drama Desk awards, 2008, Tony award for leading actor in a musical, 2008). Recipient Premio Carlos Gomes award for Best Vocal Performance, 2000, Tony award for Best Actor in Musical, 2008, Brama Desu award for Outstanding Actor in Musical, 2008, Outer Critics Circle award for Outstanding Actor in Musical, 2008, Theatre World award for Best Actor in Musical; finalist Pavarotti Internat. Voice Competition, 1994—95. Office: care Philip Rinaldi Publicity 150 W 65th St New York NY 10023 Office Phone: 212-579-6700. Business E-Mail: pauloszot@uol.com.br.

SZUCHET, SARA, biochemist, educator; d. Szuchetin and Hendler. DPhil., Girton Coll., Cambridge U., 1963. Cert. physical biochemist Cambridge U., 1963. Postdoc. fellow Princeton U., NJ, 1963—66; rsch. assoc., asst. prof. SUNY, Buffalo, 1966—76. Prof. U. Chgo., 1976—. Contbr. articles to profl. jours. Grantee, Am. Cancer Soc., 1993—94; fellow, Consejo Nacional de Investigaciones Technicas, 1959—60, Oliver Gatty, Cambridge U., 1962—63, Nat. Rsch. Svc. award, NINDS, Nat. Inst. Health, 2001—02, Danna Haughton, NIH, NSF, NMSS, ACS, BRF; Sr. Fellowship, Nat. Multiple Sclerosis Soc., 1976—78, Fellowship, 1993—94, fellowship, Tacker-Price. Achievements include discovery of novel proteins. Office: Univ Chgo 5841 S Md Ave Chicago IL 60637

SZULIK, MATTHEW J., information technology executive; With Sapiens Internat., MapInfo Corp.; pres. Relativity Technologies, 1997—98; COO Red Hat, Inc., Raleigh, NC, 1998—99, CEO, 1999—2007, pres., 1999—2007, dir., 1999—, chmn., 2002—. Chmn. sci. and tech. bd. State NC Econ. Develop. Bd. Recipient 20/20 Vision award, CIO mag. Mem.: NC Electronics and Information Technologies Assn. (past chmn. and exec. dir.). Office: Red Hat Inc 1801 Varsity Dr Raleigh NC 27606-2072 Office Phone: 919-754-3700. Office Fax: 919-754-3701.

SZWARC, WLODZIMIERZ, operations research professor; b. Kowel, Poland, Apr. 9, 1924; s. Maksym and Raja (Frenkel) S.; m. Maria Bass, Aug. 17, 1954 (div. Mar. 3, 1976); children: Michal, Ryszard; m. Rae Briker Lagen, Nov. 5, 1990. MS, U. Wroclaw, Poland, 1952, PhD in Math., 1960. Asst. prof. Tech. U., Wroclaw, 1952-60, adj. prof., 1960-67, assoc. prof., 1967-69; vis. prof. Carnegie-Mellon U., Pitts., 1970-71, U. Wis., Milw., 1971-72, prof. ops. rsch., 1972—97, prof. emeritus, 1997—. Cons. Inst. Inner Trade, Warsaw, 1959-68, Budapest, 1963-64, Elec. Inst., Wroclaw, 1961-62, Transp. Inst., Warsaw, and Wroclaw, 1967-69. Assoc. editor Naval Rsch. Logistics, 1977; contbr. over 94 rsch. papers to sci. jours. Mem. Ops. Rsch. Soc. Am., Inst. Mgmt. Sci. Achievements include research on transportation and linear programming problems, optimization techniques, production scheduling, discrete optimization techniques, application of mathematics to managerial problems and combinatorial methods. Office: U Wis-Milw PO Box 742 Milwaukee WI 53201-0742 Home: 670 San Antonio Rd unit 33 Palo Alto CA 94306 Home Phone: 650-494-1665. Personal E-mail: wlodek.1@comcast.net.

SZYDLOWSKI, RALPH, retired metal products engineer; b. Alpena, Mich., Nov. 14, 1942; s. Chester and Bridget (Romel) Sedloske; m. Geraldine Bryson, Oct. 8, 1971; children: Denise E., George S., Ruth A., Regina M. Assoc. in Indsl. Tech. summa cum laude, Baker Coll., Flint, Mich., 1991, B of Indsl. Mgmt. summa cum laude, 1994. With Flint Metal Ctr., Draw Die Tryout, 1972-96; die maker Flint Metal Ctr., 1996—2001, formability cons., 1995—2001; die engr. tech. staffing divsn. Trialon Corp., GM Metal Fabricating divsn., 2003—05. Served with U.S. Army, 1962-69. Decorated Silver Star, Purple Heart. Mem. VFW, DAV, Am. Legion, Mil. Order of the Purple Heart, 26th Inf. Regt. Assn., Soc. 1st Inf. Divsn. Roman Catholic. Avocations: woodworking, travel, books. Personal E-mail: rsgs42@aol.com.

SZYGENDA, RALPH J., automotive executive; b. McKeesport, Pa., Sept. 6, 1948; BS in Computer Sci., U. Mo., 1970; MEE, U. Tex., 1975; ED (hon.), U. Mo. With Tex. Instruments Inc., 1972—93, v.p. info. sys. and svcs., chief info. officer, 1989, v.p., gen. mgr. Enterprise Sys. Bus. Unit, 1991; v.p., chief info. officer Bell Atlantic Corp., Arlington, Va., 1993—96, GM Corp., 1996—2000, group v.p., chief info. officer, 2000—. Bd. dir. Handleman Co.; mem. The Rsch. Bd. Editl. bd. mem. InformationWeek. Mem.: GM Automotive Stratey Bd., U. Mo. Sch. Mgmt. Info. Sys. (chmn. advisory bd.), InformationWeek Mag. (editl. bd.), Rsch. Bd. Home: GM Corp PO Box 33170 Detroit MI 48232-5170*

SZYGENDA, STEPHEN A., electrical and computer engineering educator, researcher; b. McKeesport, Pa., Oct. 5, 1938; s. Stephen A. Sr. and Elizabeth B. (Zolczer) S.; m. Marie A. Deli, Apr. 2, 1960; children: Stepahnie Burden, Diana Easton, Mark. BS, Fairleigh Dickinson U., 1965; MS, Northwestern U., 1967, PhD, 1968. Registered profl. engr., Tex. Engr. Comprehensive Design, NJ, 1959-62; mem. tech. staff Bell Tel. Labs., NJ, Ill., 1962-68; assoc. prof. elec. engring. and computer engring. U. Mo., Rolla, 1968-70; prof. elec. engring. and computer engring. So. Meth. U., Dallas, 1970-73, U. Tex., Austin, 1973-86, dir. Ctr. for Tech. Tng., 1986-89, Clint Murchison Sr. Chair of Free Enterprise prof., 1986-96, chmn. elec. and computer engring. dept., 1993-96; dean Sch. Engring. U. Ala., Birmingham, 1996-2000, So. Meth. U., Dallas, 2000—04, Cecil H. Green chair, 2004—. Pres. CCSS, Austin, 1972-81, Comsat Gen. Internat. Sys., Austin, 1981-83, SBI, Inc., Austin, 1985—; pres., CEO Rubicon Group, Austin, 1983-85; active Tex. Gov. Coun. for Sci. and Tech., 1984-87. Contbr. articles to profl. jours. Dir. Laguna Gloria Mus., Austin, 1981-83; pres. bd. Austin Ballet, 1983. With USN, 1956-59. Fellow IEEE (bd. dirs. 1973-75 Svc. awards 1977, 79, 83, 87, 96), IC2, Soc. for Design and Process Sci.; mem. Assn. Computing Machinery (Svc. award 1975, 79, 87, 88, Disting. lectr. 1991-95). Roman Catholic. Achievements include pioneering in CAD, simulation, fault tolerant computing, telecommunications, entrepreneurship, and software engineering. Home: 5227 Beckington Ln Dallas TX 75287 Office: Southern Methodist Univ Sch of Engring Dallas TX 75275 Office Phone: 214-768-3959. Personal E-mail: szygenda@msn.com.

SZYMANCZYK, MICHAEL E., tobacco products executive; BS in Finance, Indiana U., 1972. Various sales and gen. mgmt. positions Procter & Gamble, 1971-87; v.p. sales Kraft Inc., Glenview, Ill., 1987-88, v.p retail ops., 1988; sr. v.p. Swift-Eckrich Inc., 1989; sr. v.p. sales Philip Morris USA (now divsn. of Altria Grp., Inc.), NYC, 1990-97, pres., CEO, 1997—, chmn., 2002—; chmn., CEO Altria Group, Inc., 2008—. Mem.: Indiana U. Kelley Sch. of Bus. Dean's Adv. Council (chmn.), bd. trustees Va. Found. for Independent Coll. Office: Philip Morris USA Inc 120 Park Ave New York NY 10017-5592

SZYMANSKI, EDNA MORA, academic administrator; b. Caracas, Venezuela, Mar. 19, 1952; came to U.S., 1952; d. José Angel and Helen Adele (McHugh) Mora; m. Michael Bernard, Mar. 30, 1973. BS, Rensselaer Poly. Inst., Troy, NY, 1972; MS, U. Scranton, Pa., 1974; PhD, U. Tex., 1988. Vocat. evaluator Mohawk Valley Workshop, Utica, NY, 1974-75; vocat. rehab. counselor NY State Office Vocat. Rehab., Utica, 1975-80, sr. vocat. rehab. counselor, 1980-87; rsch. assoc. U. Tex., Austin, 1988-89; asst. prof. U. Wis., Madison, 1989-91, assoc. prof., 1991-93, assoc. dean sch. edn., 1993—97, dir. rehab. rsch. and tng. ctr., 1993-96, prof. rehab. psychology and spl. edn., 1993—99, chair dept. rehab. psychology and spl. edn., 1997-99, fellow tchg. acad., 1997; dean Coll. Edn. U. Md., College Park, 1999—2006; sr. v.p. acad. affairs, provost U. Maine, Orono, 2006—08; pres. Minn. State U. Moorhead, 2008—. Cons. Rsch. Assocs. Syracuse, NY, 1988-90. Author/co-author various book chpts.; co-editor: Rehabilitation Counseling Basics and Beyond, 1992, 98, 2005; co-editor Work and Disability, 1996, 2003, Rehabilitation Counseling Bull., 1994-2000; contbr. articles to profl. jours. Recipient Rsch. award Am. Assn. Counselor Edn. and Supr., 1991. Mem. ACA (chair rsch. com. 1992-94, Rsch. awards 1990, 93, 95), Am. Rehab. Counseling Assn. (pres. 1985-86, rsch. award 1989, 94, Disting. Profl. award 1997, James F. Garrett award for disting. career in rehab. rsch. 1999), Coun. Rehab. Edn. (chair rsch. com. 1990-95, v.p. 1993-95, 97), Nat. Coun. Rehab. Edn. (chair rsch. com. 1992-99, Rehab. Edn. Rschr. of Yr. 1993, New Career in Rehab. Edn. award 1990). Office Phone: 218-477-2243. Personal E-mail: emszy@aol.com.

SZYMANSKI, PATRICK JOSEPH, lawyer; b. Detroit, Jan. 18, 1949; s. Frank S. and Lillian F. (Mikula) S. Student, MIT, 1966-69; BA, Wayne State U., Detroit, 1973, JD, 1976. Bar: Mich. 1976, US Ct. Appeals (DC, 1st, 2nd and 4th cirs.) 1977, US Ct. Appeals (9th cir.) 1978, Calif. 1979, DC 1979, US Dist. Ct. (no. dist.) Calif. 1979, US Ct. Appeals (10th cir.) 1984, US Supreme Ct. 1985, US Dist. Ct. DC 1988, US Dist. Ct. Md. 1988, US Dist. Ct. Mich. (ea. dist.) 1991, US Ct. Appeals (3rd cir.) 1991. Appellate ct. br. NLRB, Washington, 1976-78, 83-88; assoc. Beeson, Tayer & Bodine, San Francisco, 1978-83, Baptiste & Wilder, P.C., Washington, 1988—2003. Mem. editl. bd. Wayne State U. Law Rev., 1975-76. Gen. counsel Internat. Brotherhood Teamsters, 1999—2006, Change to Win, 2006—. Democrat. Roman Catholic. Office: Change to Win 1900 L St NW Ste 900 Washington DC 20036 Office Phone: 202-721-6035. Business E-Mail: patrick.szymanski@changetowin.org.

SZYMBORSKA, WISLAWA (WISLAWA SYMBORSKA), poet; b. Bnin, Poland, July 2, 1923; m. Adam Wlodek (div.); m. Kornel Flipowicz (dec.). Student, Jagiellonian U., Cracow, 1945—48; LittD (hon.), Poznan U., 1995. Mem. editl. staff Zycie Literackie, 1953-81. Author: (poetry) That's Why We Are Alive, 1952, Questions Put to Myself, 1954, Calling Out to Yeti, 1957, Salt, 1962, Wiersze Wybrane, 1964, A Hundred Joys, 1967, Selected Poems, 1967, No End of Fun, 1967, Poems, 1970, There But for the Grace, 1972, Wybor wierszy, 1973, Tarsius and Other Poems, 1976, A Large Number, 1976, Sounds, Feelings, Thoughts: Seventy Poems, 1981, Selected Poems II, 1983, The People in the Bridge, 1986, The End and the Beginning, 1993, View with a Grain of Sand: Selected Poems, 1995, Poems: New and Collected 1957-1997, 1998, Miracle Fair: Selected Poems of Wislawa Szymborska, 2001, Nonrequired Reading: Prose Pieces, 2002, CHWILA, 2002. Decorated Knight's Cross, Order of Polonia Restituta, 1974; recipient Gold Cross of Merit, 1955, Goethe award, 1991, Herder prize, 1995, Polish PEN Poetry award, 1996, Nobel Lit. prize, 1996. Office: Zwigzel Literalow Polskich ul Krolewska 82m 18 30-079 Cracow Poland

TAAFFE, JAMES GRIFFITH, retired academic administrator, educator; b. Cin., Sept. 15, 1932; s. Griffith C. and Mary (Ropp) T.; m. Donna Click, June 8, 1955 (dec. 1986); children: Lauren Kathleen, Patrick Michael; m. Allison S. Blair, Nov. 7, 1987; 1 child, Michael Sean (dec. 2008). AB, Columbia U., 1954; MA, Ind. U., 1956, PhD, 1960. Instr. English Williams Coll., Williamstown, Mass., 1959-62; asst. prof. English Vassar Coll., 1962-64; from asst. prof. to prof. English Case Western Res. U., Cleve., 1964—, chmn. advanced placement in English, 1968-73, chmn. dept., 1969-72, asst. to pres., 1971-72, dean grad. studies, 1972-74, v.p. undergrad. and grad. studies, 1974-81, univ. v.p. acad. affairs, 1981-86, 2005, acting chair dept. theatre arts, 1989-90, prof. English emeritus, univ. v.p. acad. affairs emeritus, 2005; v.p. acad. affairs U. Ala., Tuscaloosa, 1990-91, prof. English, 1990—2005, provost, v.p. acad. affairs, 1991-96. Mem. Joint Coun., East Cleve. Sch. Dist., 1970. Co-author: A Milton Handbook, 1970; editor: Abraham Cowley, 1970; co-editor: Poems on Poetry, 1965, Reading English Poetry, 1971. Newberry Libr. fellow, 1964; Am. Philos. Soc. fellow, 1967, 69; NEH fellow, 1971. Home: 9201 Enterprise Ave NE Tuscaloosa AL 35406-1005 Personal E-mail: ajtaaffe@bellsouth.net.

TAALMAN, LAURA ANNE, mathematics professor; b. Norwich, Conn., Feb. 14, 1973; d. Juri Eino and Tania Jane Taalman; m. Philip Benjamin Riley, May 31, 1998; 1 child, Calvin Grey Riley. BS in Math., U. Chgo., 1994; MA in Math., Duke U., Durham, 1996, PhD in Math., 2000. Assoc. prof. math. James Madison U., Harrisonburg, Va., 2000—. Author: (textbook) Integrated Calculus (Texty award, 2006), (puzzle book) Color Sudoku; contbr. scientific papers. Recipient Trevor Evans award, Math. Assn. Am., 2003, Alder award, 2005, Disting. Tchr. award, James Madison U., 2008; Project Next fellowship, Math. Assn. Am., 2000—01, RUMC grant, NSF and Math. Assn. Am., 2005—08. Mem.: Text and Academic Authors Assn., Math. Assn. Am. (program chair 2006—08). Office: James Madison Univ Dept Math Roop Hall MSC 1911 Harrisonburg VA 22807 Business E-Mail: taal@math.jmu.edu.

TAAR, MIREILLE, language educator, interpreter; d. Elijah and Ilda (Nemni) Taar; m. Michel Chapelle; children: Corinne Chapelle, Philippe Chapelle, Eric Chapelle, Godefroy Chapelle. BA, UCLA, 1970, PhD, 1989; MA in Spanish and French, U. Tex., Austin, 1974. Cert. reiki level I 2005. Fgn. lang. educator Chapman U., Orange, Calif., 1982—86; prof. romance langs. Fullerton CC, Calif., 1986—. Technol. translations cons. DataWorks Corp., Irvine, Calif., 1991—92. Vol. Nat. Dem. Party, Ft. Meyers, Fla., 2008; mem. Jr. Scouts of America, 1982—84. Achievements include research and publishing in French literature. Avocations: literature, swimming, travel.

TAATI, POOPAK, media director; d. Abdol Ali Taati and Mahin Dokht Farzan. PhD in Sociology, U. Tex., Austin, 1988. Asst. prof. of sociology Minn. State U., Moorhead, 1988—92; prof. sociology Georgetown U., Washington, 1995—96; prof. social scis. Montgomery Coll., Germantown, Md., 1999—2003; freelance journalist BBC, 2003—05; dir. Media for Thought, 2004—06. Vis. prof. anthropology & sociology Wittenberg U., Springfield, Ohio, 1987—88. Prodr.: (documentary film/video) When Authorities Turn Violent, (educational film/video) When Different is Beautiful. Treas. Ctr. Iranian Rsch. and Analysis, 1988—89; mem. tchg. com. Am. Sociol. Assn., 1997—98; mem. Iranian Professionals Assn., Washington, 1993—94, Iranian-American Cultural Assn., 1996—97. Recipient Tchg. and Svc. award, Montgomery Coll., 2002; grantee, MIT, Cambridge, 1990, U.S. Inst. Peace, 1996; fellow, NEH, 1991, 1997. Mem.: Gulf 2000. Independent. Spiritual Moslem. Avocations: participation in cultural activities, movies, travel, exercise, sauna. Home: PO Box 25413 Los Angeles CA 90025-0413

TAAVILA, PIA SEIJA, literature and language professor; PhD, Mich. State U., East Lansing, 1985. Prof. English Gallaudet U., Washington, 1992—. Author: (poetry book) Moon on the Meadow. Mem. Temple Beth Sholom, Fredericksburg, Va., 2006—08. Office: Gallaudet University 800 Florida Avenue NE Washington DC 20002 Business E-Mail: pia.taavila@gallaudet.edu.

TABACHNICK, NORMAN DONALD, psychiatrist, educator; b. Toronto, Ont., Can., Feb. 21, 1927; BS, U. Ill., 1947, MD, 1949; PhD in Psychoanalysis, So. Calif. Psychoanalytic Inst., 1977. Diplomate Am. Bd. Med. Examiners, Am. Bd. Psychiatry and Neurology. Intern Michael Reese Hosp., 1949-50; resident in psychiatry U.S. VA Hosp., Bedford, Mass., 1950-51, U.S. AFB, Biloxi, Miss., 1951-52, L.A. County Gen. Hosp., 1953-54; staff psychiatrist Sepulveda VA Hosp., 1976-78; pvt. practice LA; mem. staff Resthaven Sanitarium, U. So. Calif. Med. Ctr., L.A. County, Westwood Hosp., Edgemont Hosp., Cedars-Sinai Med. Ctr.; mem. staff Neuropsychiatric Inst. UCLA; clin. prof. psychiatry U. So. Calif., LA, 1970-75, UCLA, 1975—2008, disting. clin. prof. psychiatry, 2008—. Hon. mem. med. staf. Resthaven Cmty. Med. Health Ctr., 1973; guest lectr. Cedars-Sinai Med. Ctr., 1985; mem. adv. bd. divsn. psychoanalysis Nassau County Med. Ctr.; mem. faculty Calif. Sch. Profl. Psychology, L.A. Ctr. Group Psychotherapy, Grad. Ctr. Child Devel. and Psychotherapy; cons. L.A. County Coroner's Office, 1963-70, Bur. Vocat. Rehab., Jewish Family Svc., profl. adv. bd. Resthaven Sanitarium, Marianne Frostig Sch. Ednl. Therapy, W. Valley Ctr. Edl. Therapy. Author: Accident or Suicide?, 1973; mem. edtl. bd. Jour. Acad. Psychoanalysis, book rev. editor, 1978; mem. edtl. bd. Internat. Jour. Psycho-analytic Psychotherapy, 1979-83; reviewer Am. Jour. Psychiatry, 1983—, Jour. Neuropsychiatry and Clin. Neuro Scis., 1988-90; contbr. articles to profl. jours.; cons. (film) Suicide Prevention: The Physician's Role, 1967, Highlights of the 1964 American Psychiatric Association; cons., participant The Thin Edge--Guilt., 1975; author book revs. Assoc. chief psychiatrist L.A. Suicide Prevention Ctr., 1968-76, prin. investigator; adv. com. Walter Briehl Human Rights Found., 1984; v.p., bd. dirs. Suicide Prevention Ctr., Inc.; bd. dirs. Inst. Suicide Prevention, L.A., 1996, chmn. funding a crisis line com., 1997; bd. dirs. We. divsn. Am. Found. Suicide Prevention, 1998, chair program com., 1999-2002. Recipient award for disting. creativity and leadership, Am. Found. for Suicide Prevention, 2003; rsch. grantee, Founds. Fund Rsch. Psychiatry, 1963, NIMH, 1970. Fellow Am. Psychiatric Assn. (life), Am. Acad. Psychoanalysis (pres. 1974, chmn. nominating com. 1975, trustee, chmn. com. on rsch., mem. editl. bd. The Acad., presdl. citation 1975); mem. Internat. Psychoanalytic Assn., Internat. Assn. Suicide Prevention, Am. Psychoanalytic Assn. (cert., mem. com. liason with AAAS 1977-80), Am. Assn. Suicidology, (founder, mem. editl. bd. Life-Threatening Behavior, cert. recognition 1996) Inst. Contemporary Psychoanalysis (founding mem., trustee 1990-93), So. Calif. Psychoanalytic Inst. (pres., tng. and supervising analyst, selection rsch. clin. assocs. com., dir. rsch. divsn. 1970-81, chief investigator 1976-88, chmn. com. rsch. award stds. 1979, pres.-elect 1980, 86, pres. 1981, 87-90, mem. tng. and supr. analyst, new ctr. for psychoanalysis), Am. Coll. Psychiatrists, Med. Rsch. Assn. So. Calif., So. Calif. Psychiat. Soc. (consultation and violence panel), L.A. County Med. Assn. Office: 505 N Bonhill Rd Los Angeles CA 90049-2325 Office Phone: 310-472-5044. Personal E-mail: ndtmd@aol.com.

TABACHNICK, STEPHEN ELY, English literature educator; b. NYC, Apr. 1, 1944; s. Nathaniel Ralph and Ruth (Fesman) T.; m. Sharon Eve Lazar, Mar. 20, 1975; children: Daphne, Orrin, Laurie. BA, U. Calif., Berkeley, 1966; MA, U. Chgo., 1967; PhD, U. Conn., 1971. Lectr. to assoc. prof. Ben Gurion U., Beersheva, Israel, 1971-84; vis. assoc. prof. UCLA, 1984-85; prof., chmn. dept. English Tenn. Tech. U., Cookeville, 1985-90; prof., chmn. Dept. English U. Okla., Norman, 1990-93, prof. English, 1994—2000; prof., chmn. dept. English U. Memphis, 2000—08, prof. English, 2009—. Author: Harold Pinter, 1973, T.E. Lawrence, 1978, Charles Doughty, 1981, Images of Lawrence, 1988,

Fiercer than Tigers: The Life and Works of Rex Warner, 2002, Lawrence of Arabia: An Encyclopedia, 2004; editor: The T.E. Lawrence Puzzle, 1984, Explorations in Doughty's Arabia Deserta, 1987, (novels) Teaching the Graphic, 2009. Office: Univ of Memphis Dept English Patterson Hall 467 Memphis TN 38152-3510 Home: PO Box 770126 Memphis TN 38177-0126 Office Phone: 901-678-2651.

TABAK, LAWRENCE A., federal agency administrator, dentist; b. Bklyn., Dec. 15, 1951; BS in Biology and Chemistry, CUNY City Coll., 1972; DDS, Columbia U., NYC, 1977; PhD in Oral Biology, SUNY, Buffalo, 1981. Cert. in Endodontics SUNY, Buffalo, 1985. Asst. prof. oral biology SUNY, Buffalo, 1980—81, asst. prof. endodontics and oral biology, 1981—85, assoc. prof., 1985—86; assoc. prof. dental rsch. & biochemistry U. Rochester Sch. Medicine & Dentistry, NY, 1986—92, prof., 1992—96, prof. dental rsch., biochemistry & biophysics, 1996—97, prof. dentistry, biochemistry & biophysics, 1998—2000; chair dept. dental rsch. Sch. Medicine and Dentistry, U. Rochester, 1995—97, sr. assoc. dean for rsch., 1998—2000; sr. investigator Nat. Inst. Diabetes, Digestive & Kidney Diseases NIH, 2000, dir. Nat. Inst. Dental & Craniofacial Rsch. (NIDCR), 2000—. Vis. scientist Nat. Inst. Dental Rsch., NIH, 1982—83. Contbr. articles to profl. jours. Named Alumnus of Yr., Columbia U. Sch. Dental & Oral Surgery, 1997. Fellow: AAAS; mem.: Inst. Medicine, Soc. Glycobiology, Am. Assn. Dental Rsch., Internat. Assn. Dental Rsch. (Disting. Scientist award 1996). Office: Nat Inst Dental and Craniofacial Rsch Bldg 31 Rm 2C39 31 Center Dr MSC 2290 Bethesda MD 20892 Office Phone: 301-496-3571. Office Fax: 301-402-2185. E-mail: lawrence.tabak@nih.gov.*

TABAK, STEVEN WILLIAM, cardiologist; b. LA, May 7, 1952; MD, Johns Hopkins U., 1977. Intern Cedars-Sinai Med. Ctr., LA, 1977-78, resident in internal medicine, 1978-81, fellow in cardiovascular disease, 1981-83; assoc. clin. prof. medicine UCLA; clin. chief of cardiology, chmn. cardiac catheterization com. Cedars-Sinai Med. Ctr., 1996-98. Pvt. practice., interventional cardiologist, Cardiovascular Med. Group So. Calif. Fellow Am. Coll. Cardiology; mem. AMA, ACP Office: 414 N Camden Dr Ste 1100 Beverly Hills CA 90210-4532 Office Phone: 310-278-3400. E-mail: tabak@evang.com.

TABAKA, SANDRA LEE, retired medical/surgical nurse; d. Elmer William and Elaine Verba Viehmann; m. John Lawrence Tabaka, Oct. 8, 1960 (div. Nov. 1985); children: James Lawrence, Anthony Michael, Theresa Lynn. ADN, St. Mary's Coll., O'Fallon, Mo., 1978; BSN, Webster U., 1993. RN Mo. Staff nurse St. Luke's Hosp., Chesterfield, Mo., 1978—82, assoc. head nurse, 1982—94, staff nurse, 1994—2004, ret., 2004. Founding mem. St. Charles Countians Against Hazardous Waste, 1982—84; bd. mem. Cedar Groves Townhomes Assn., St. Charles, 1999—2002. Mem.: Oncology Nursing Soc. (oncology cert. nurse). Home: 244 Cedar Grove Dr Saint Charles MO 63304

TABATABAEI, SHAHIN, urologist, educator; s. Alireza and Shahnaz Tabatabaei; m. Rozita Hashemi Nejad; children: Mateen, Kimia. MD, Nat. U. Iran, Tehran, 1990. Surg. rsch. fellow Harvard Med. Sch., Boston, 1994—97, surg. resident, 1997—2003, asst. prof. surgery, 2008—; asst. urology surgery Mass. Gen. Hosp., Boston, 2003—. Dir. prostate health program Mass. Gen. Hosp., Boston, 2008—. Recipient Pfizer Clin. Excellence award, Pfizer Pharm., 2001. Mem.: AMA, Am. Endourology Soc., Am. Urol. Assn. Achievements include patents for bladder clot evacuation catheter. Office: Mass Gen Hosp 55 Fruit St Boston MA 02114 Office Phone: 617-726-3574. Office Fax: 617-726-6131. Personal E-mail: shahintaba@gmail.com.

TABATZNIK, BERNARD, retired cardiologist; b. Mir, Poland, Jan. 8, 1927; arrived in US, 1959, naturalized, 1966; s. Max and Fay (Ginsberg) T.; m. Marjorie Turner, Jan. 8, 1956; children: Darron Mark, Keith Donald, Ilana Wendy; m. Charline Edwards Harmon, Aug. 7, 1992. BSc, U. Witwatersrand, South Africa, 1945, MB, BChir, U. Witwatersrand, South Africa, 1949. Intern Baragwanath Hosp., Johannesburg, 1950-51, Hillingdon Hosp., Ashford Hosp., also rsch. unit Can. Red Cross Meml. Hosp., Taplow, England, 1951-54; med. registrar Ashford Hosp., 1954-56, Johannesburg Gen. Hosp., 1956-58; physician Baragwanath Hosp., 1958-59; fellow in medicine Sch. Medicine Johns Hopkins U., Balt., 1959-60, fellow in cardiology, 1960-61, asst. prof. medicine, 1966-97, ret., 1997; head cardiopulmonary divsn. Sinai Hosp., Balt., 1961-72, assoc. chief medicine, 1964-72; chief cardiology dept. North Charles Gen. Hosp., Balt., 1972; also dir. med. edn., dir. Postgrad. Inst., coord. ambulatory svcs.; med. dir. Nurse Practitioner-Physician Asst. Program Ch. Hosp., Balt., 1987-90. Contbr. articles to profl. jours. Recipient Save-A-Heart Humanitarian award, 1977, Maimonides award, 1983, Shaarei Zion Humanitarian award, 1987. Fellow Royal Coll. Physicians (London); mem. South African Cardiac Soc., Am. Heart Assn., Md. Heart Assn. (chmn. health careers 1964-66), Am. Coll. Cardiology. Home: 63 Oakridge Dr Monterey VA 24465-2350 Personal E-mail: btabatznik@aol.com.

TABB, VANDOSTER LANGFORD, SR., retired military officer; b. Williamsburg, Va., June 4, 1935; s. George Edward and Mary Alice (Parker) Tabb; m. Evangelyn Maria Darby, May 26, 1965; m. Julia Spain (div. Oct. 2, 1961); children: Yolanda Agnes West Jenkins, Vandoster Langford Jr., Jacinda Lynn, Larticia Ann, Myrtinia Alores. BS in Acctg., Va. State U., Petersburg, 1959; MA in Mgmt. and Pub. Adminstrn., Webster U., St. Louis, 1978. Commd. 2d lt. US Army, 1959, detachment comdr. adv. group, 1968—69, post comptr. Ft. Holabird Balt., 1969—72, with adv. group, 1973—76, civic action officer 18th Airborne Corps, 1976—80; fin. mgmt. officer US Dept. of State, Washington, 1981—2000; ret., 2000. Career counselor, cons. US Dept. of State, 2000—. Budget officer Assoc. Md. Africa Societies, Inc, Ft. Washington, Md., 2004—07. Decorated Vietnam Campaign medal US Army, Combat Inf. Badge, Bronze Star medal, Bronze Medal for Meritorious Svc., Army Commendation Medal, Legion of Merit, Joint Svc. Commendation medal, Meritorious Svc. medal US Dept. of State, Washington, Superior Honor award. Mem.: NAACP, Rock, Inc, Am. Fgn. Svc. Assn., Mil. Officers Assoc. Am. (life). Democrat. Baptish. Avocations: bowling, travel, golf, movies, reading. Home: 1806 Williamsburg Ct Fort Washington MD 20744-4259 Office: US Dept State C St NW Washington DC 20522-4201 Home Phone: 301-292-2810; Office Phone: 703-302-7407. Office Fax: 703-302-7416. Personal E-mail: lank69@verizon.net. Business E-Mail: tabbvl@state.gov.

TABB, WALLER CROCKETT, retired allergist, immunologist; b. Richmond, Va., 1935; MD, U. Va., 1959. Diplomate Am. Bd. Internal Medicine, Am. Bd. Allergy and Immunology. Intern U. Va. Hosp., Charlottesville, 1959-60, resident in internal medicine, 1964-66, fellow in allergy/immunology and pulmonary medicine, 1966-67; mem. staff Lakeland (Fla.) Regional Med. Ctr., 1967—; pvt. practice Watson Clinic, Lakeland, ret., 1997. Fellow ACP, Am. Acad. Allergy and Immunology, Am. Coll. Chest Physicians; mem. Alpha Omega Alpha. Address: PO Box 178 Ware Neck VA 23178-0178 Home: 6102 WAre Neck Rd Ware Neck VA 23178 Personal E-mail: aroca2@earthlink.net.

TABB, WINSTON, library director; b. Tulsa, Okla. BA magna cum laude, Okla. Baptist U., 1963; MA in Am. Lit., Harvard U., 1964; MLS, Simmons Coll., Boston, 1972. Various positions with Libr. of Congress, Washington, 1972—2002, asst. chief Gen. Reading Room, 1978—84, chief Copyright Info. & Reference Dvsn., 1984—88, dir. Rsch. Svc., 1988—89, acting dep. libr., 1989—92, assoc. libr., 1992—2002; Sheridan Dean of Univ. Libr. Johns Hopkins U., Baltimore, 2002—, dir. Sheridan Libraries, 2002—, vice provost for arts, 2006—, dir. historic houses. Mem. Nat. Digital Libr. Fedn. Policy Com., Coun. Libr. & Info. Resources; mem. vis. com. Harvard Libr.; rsch. libr. adv. com. Online Computer Libr. Ctr. Past bd. mem. Soros Found. Served with US Army, in Thailand. Recipient Ainsworth Rand Spofford President's award, District of Columbia Libr. Assn., 2002. Mem.: ALA (Melvil Dewey medal 1998, Joseph W. Lippincott award 2007), Internat. Fedn. of Libr. Assns. & Insts. (chmn. profl. com. 2001—, vice chmn. profl. bd., chmn. nat. librs. sect., chmn. coordinating bd. for divsn. gen. rsch. librs., chmn. copyright and other legal matters com.). Office: Milton S Eisenhower Libr Johns Hopkins Univ 3400 N Charles St Baltimore MD 21218 Office Phone: 410-516-8328. Office Fax: 410-516-5080. E-mail: wtabb@jhu.edu.

TABBAL, NICOLAS G., plastic surgeon; b. Beirut, July 14, 1946; MD, Am. U., Beirut, 1972. Diplomate Am. Bd. Plastic Surgery, Am. Bd. Surgery. Intern Am. U. Med. Ctr., Beirut, 1971—72, resident in surgery, 1972—76; resident in plastic surgery Akron City Hosp., Ohio, 1977—79; fellow in gen. surgery Upstate Med. Ctr., Syracuse, NY, 1976—77; fellow in anesthetic surgery Manhattan Eye, Ear & Throat Hosp., 1979—80; fellow in plastic reconstructive surgery NYU Med. Ctr., 1980; pvt. practice plastic surgery NYC, 1980—; attending plastic surgeon Manhattan Eye, Ear, and Throat Hosp. Clin. instr. plastic surgery NYU Med. Ctr. Office: 521 Park Ave New York NY 10021-1840 Office Phone: 212-644-5800. Office Fax: 212-644-5828. Business E-Mail: mail@tabbal.us.

TABBARA, HADI, director, researcher; PhD, Iowa State U., Ames, 2000. Rsch. assoc. USDA-ARS, Phoenix, 2001—02; lab. mgr. Ariz. State U., Tempe, 2005—. Recipient, USAID, 1973—76. Mem.: Am. Chem. Soc., Phi Lambda Upsilon. Office: BioDesign Institute- Arizona State U 1001 S McAllister Tempe AZ 85281 Office Fax: 480-727-0889; Home Fax: 480-727-0889. Business E-Mail: hadi.tabbara@asu.edu.

TABEA, EMILE VICTOR, health facility administrator; b. Abidjan, Ivory Coast, June 6, 1959; arrived in US, 1982; s. Leon Kobe and Jeannette Saoua Tabea; m. Melanie Ayere Gbangninan, Dec. 20, 1990; children: Joel Victor, Eunice Victoire. MS, U. Mass., 1992. Cert. human svcs. profl. Mass. Instr. French and ESL U. Mass., Lowell, 1984—97; coord. Tewksbury Hosp., Mass., 1989, discharge planner dept. pub. health, 1989. Deacon Bethel Internat. Ch., Everett, Mass., 2003—05. Recipient Performance Recognition award, Commonwealth of Mass., 2000. Mem.: Internat. Reading Assn., Mass. Tchr. Assn. (assoc.). Mem. Independent Thinkers. Avocations: soccer, reading, travel. Home: 46 Barclay St Lowell MA 01851 Office: Tewksbury Hosp Dept Pub Health 365 East St Tewksbury MA 01876 Office Fax: 978-851-6743; Home Fax: 978-851-6743. Personal E-mail: emile_tabea@uml.edu. Business E-Mail: emile.tabea@state.ma.us.

TABER, CHRISTOPHER ROBERT, finance educator; b. New Haven, Dec. 9, 1966; s. Richard Hallock and Joanne Townsend Taber; m. Judith Anne Sontheimer, Sept. 15, 1990; children: Kathryn Lois, Rachel Helen, Andrew James. BS, MA, U. Chgo., PhD, 1995. Prof. Northwestern U., Evanston, Ill., 1995—, U. Wis., Madison, 2007—. Editor-in-Chief, jour. labor economics U. Chgo. Press, 2007. Home: 7522 Red Fox Tr Madison WI 53717 Office: Univ Wis Madison 1108 Observatory Dr Madison WI 53706 Business E-Mail: ctaber@ssc.wisc.edu.

TABER, DAVID O., urological surgeon; b. Panama City, Panama, June 30, 1938; s. Alden Pugh and Virginia (Kresler) Taber; m. Rebecca M.; children: Sharon Taber Silverman, Jeffrey, Andrew, Richard; m. Rebecca M. Taber, Dec. 20, 1987. BA, Syracuse U., 1959; MD, George Washington U., 1963. Diplomate Am. Bd. Urology. Urologic surgeon in pvt. practice, El Paso, Tex., 1973—; pres. El Paso County Med. Soc., 2008—. Chief med. staff Columbia West Hosp., El Paso, 1975-76, chief of urology, 1998-99; chief of surgery Sierra Med. Ctr., El Paso, 1977-78, chief of urology, 1995-97; prof. urology Tex. Tech Sch. Medicine, El Paso, 1998—. Mem. state com. on prostate cancer Am. Cancer Soc., Austin, 1998-99, bd. dirs. El Paso unit, 1999; mem. Tex. Rangers Found., Waco, 1998-2005; judge Santa Fe Indian Market; med. exec. com. El Paso County; founder Am. Mus. Served to lt. U.S. Army, 1963-72. Lt. col. US Army. Fellow ACS; mem. AMA, Urol. Soc. Internat., Urostomy Assn. (adv.), Tex. Urol. Soc., Am. Urol. Assn., Tex. Med. Assn. (del. 2009), Am. Fertility Soc., Am. Lithotripsy Soc., El Paso Med. Soc. (exec. com. 2004- sec. 2006-, pres. elect, 2007, pres., 2008-, named in Best Doctors in Am., Best Doctors in Tex.), Mason (32 degree), Elmaida Shrine, Rotary, Alpha Epsilon Delta, Pi Sigma. Episcopalian. Avocations: photography, diving instructor. Office: 2201 N Stanton St El Paso TX 79902 Office Phone: 915-533-0800. Personal E-mail: dotabermd@yahoo.com.

TABER, KENNETH W., lawyer; b. Nov. 28, 1956; BS summa cum laude, Univ. Pa., 1977; JD, Yale Univ., 1980. Bar: NY 1981, US Dist. Ct. (so., ea. dist. NY) 1981. Ptnr. Pillsbury Winthrop Shaw Pittman, NYC, litigator employment, co-chmn. nat. litig. practice. Founder Interfaith Legal Outreach, Westchester County, NY. Office: Pillsbury Winthrop Shaw Pittman 1540 Broadway New York NY 10036 Office Phone: 212-858-1813. Office Fax: 212-858-8405. Business E-Mail: kenneth.taber@pillsburylaw.com.

TABER, MARGARET RUTH, retired engineering technology educator; b. St. Louis, Apr. 29, 1935; d. Wynn Orr and Margaret Ruth (Feldman) Gould Stevens; m. William James Taber, Sept. 6, 1958 B of Engring. Sci., Cleve. State U., 1958, BEE, 1958; MS in Engring., U. Akron, 1967; EdD, Nova Southeastern U., 1976; postgrad., Western Res. U., 1959-64. Registered profl. engr., Ohio; cert. engring. technologist. From engring. trainee to tng. dir. TOCCO divsn. Ohio Crankshaft Co., Cleve., 1954-64; from instr. elec.-electronic engring. tech. to prof. Cuyahoga C.C., Cleve., 1964-79, chmn. engring. tech., 1977-79; assoc. prof. elec. engring. tech. Purdue U., West Lafayette, Ind., 1979-83, prof., 1983-2000, prof. emeritus, 2000—. Lectr. Cleve. State U., 1963-64; mem. acad. adv. bd. Cleve. Inst. Electronics, 1981—; cons. in field. Author: (with Frank P. Tedeschi) Solid State Electronics, 1976; (with Eugene M. Silgalis) Electric Circuit Analysis, 1980; (with Jerry L. Casebeer) Registers, 1980; (with Kenneth Rosenow) Arithmetic Logic Units, 1980, Timing and Control, 1980, Memory Units, 1980; 6809 Architecture and Operation, 1984, Programming I: Straight Line, 1984; contbr. articles to profl. jours. Bd. dirs. West Blvd. Christian Ch., deaconess, 1974-77, elder, 1977-79; deacon Federated Ch., 1981-84, 86-89, Stephen Leader, 1988—2002; mem. Cancer Support Group; vol. Lafayette Adult Resource Acad., 1992—; vol. ednl. resource, vol. tchr. Sunburst Farm/Rainbow Acres, Ariz., 1988—. Recipient Helen B. Schleman Gold Medallion award Purdue U., 1991, The Greater Lafayette Cmty. Survivorship award, 1994, Outstanding Alumni award U. Akron Coll. Engring., 1994, Disting. Alumni award, Cleve. State U., 2002; Margaret R. Taber Microcomputer Lab. named in her honor Purdue U., 1991; NSF grant, 1970-73, 78; Rainbow Acres Computer Lab named The Marge Taber Computer Lab., 2002, Golden Gift Time award, Greater Lafayette Vol. Bur. & United Way, 2008. Fellow Soc. Women Engrs. (counselor Purdue chpt. 1983-94, Disting. Engring. Educator award 1987); mem. IEEE (life sr.), Am. Cancer Soc. (co-chair svc. and rehab com. 1992-94, vol. coord. CanSurmount 1993-98, chair Cmty. Connections, mem. Resource, Info. and Guidance CoreTeam, 1994-98, v.p. Tippecanoe bd. dirs. 1996-98, relay for life hon. chair 1999), Am. Bus. Women's Assn. (ednl. chmn. 1964-66), Am. Soc. Engring. Edn., Am. Tech. Edn. Assn., Tau Beta Pi (hon.), Phi Kappa Phi. Avocations: robotics, computers. Home: 3036 State Rd 26 W West Lafayette IN 47906-4743 Office: Purdue U Elec Engring Tech Dept Knoy Hall Tech West Lafayette IN 47907

TABIN, JULIUS, lawyer, physicist; b. Chgo., Nov. 8, 1919; s. Sol and Lillian (Klingman) T.; m. Johanna Krout, Sept. 7, 1952; children: Clifford James, Geoffrey Craig. BS, U. Chgo., 1940, PhD in Physics, 1946; LLB, Harvard U., 1949. Bar: Calif., D.C. 1949, Ill. 1950. Jr. physicist metall. lab. U. Chgo., 1943-44; physicist Los Alamos Sci. Lab. (U. Calif.), N.Mex., 1944-45, Argonne Nat. Lab., AEC, Chgo., 1946; staff mem., group supr. Inst. Nuc. Studies, MIT, 1946-49; patent examiner U.S. Patent Office, Washington, 1949-50; assoc. firm Fitch, Even, Tabin & Flannery, Chgo., 1950-52; mem. firm Fich, Even, Tabin & Flannery, Chgo., 1952—. Lectr. U. Chgo., 1959. Mem. Am., D.C., Calif., Ill., Chgo. bar assns., Sigma Xi. Home: 162 Park Ave Glencoe IL 60022-1352 Office: 120 S La Salle St Chicago IL 60603-3403 Office Phone: 312-577-7000. Personal E-mail: cgtabin@aol.com. E-mail: jtabin@fitcheven.com.

TABLER, NORMAN GARDNER, JR., lawyer; b. Louisville, Oct. 15, 1944; s. Norman Gardner and Marie (Grant) T.; m. Dawn Carla Martin, May 6, 1989; 1 child, Rachel Ann Tabler. BA, Princeton U., 1966; MA, Yale U., 1968; JD, Columbia U., 1971. Bar: Ind. 1971, U.S. Dist. Ct. (so. dist.) Ind. 1971. Assoc. Baker & Daniels, Indpls., 1971-77, ptnr., 1978-96; sr. v.p. corp. affairs, gen. counsel, chief compliance officer, sec. Clarian Health Ptnrs., Inc., Indpls., 1996—. Adj. prof. Ind. U. Law Sch., Indpls., 1984-88; mem. adv. com. Ctr. for Law and Health, Ind. U., Indpls., 1987-91; mem. antitrust task force Ind. Dept. Health, 1993-94; lectr. Ind. U. Law Sch., 1992-96; chmn. bd. dirs. CH Assurance Ltd., 2002-, Clarian Health Risk Retention Group, Inc., 2004—. Bd. dirs. Ind. Repertory Theatre, Inc., Indpls., 1984-97, 2005-06, Indpls. Art Ctr., 1988-93, 2006-07, chmn., 1989-92, Indpls. 500 Festival, 1992-98, Brickyard 400 Festival, 1993-98; bd. dirs. Indpls. Pub. Broadcasting, 1992—, chmn., 1997-2001, 05-07; mem. Ind. Sec. of State's Com. on Revision of Ind. Nonprofit Corp. Act, 1989-92, Ind. Ednl. Fin. Authority, 1989-93; mem. Ind. Recreational Devel. Commn., 1993-2004, vice chmn., 2002-04; mem. Medicaid Task Force Ind. Commn. Health Policy, 1990-92, Ind. Commn. on CLE, 1999-2005; mem. nat. bd. lay reps. PBS, 1997-2003. Mem. ABA (health care com. sect. antitrust law, health law sect.), Ind. Bar Assn. (health law sect.), Indpls. Bar Assn. (health law sect.), Am. Health Lawyers Assn., Ind. Health and Hosp. Assn. (com. on hosp. governance 1999-2007), Ind. U. Parents Assn., Ind. U. Parents Ann. Fund (nat. chmn. 1995-98), Princeton Alumni Assn. Ind. (pres. 1988-97), Indpls. Athletic Club (bd. dirs. 1994-2000), Skyline Club (bd. govs. 1992—), Princeton Club N.Y., Lawyers Club (Indpls., pres. 2007—), Highland Golf & Country Club (Indpls.), Carmel Racquet Club (Ind.). Methodist. Avocations: reading biographies, squash, kayaking. Office: General Counsel & Sr VP Legal Dept Clarian Health Ptnrs Inc PO Box 1367 Indianapolis IN 46206-1367

TABOR, CURTIS HAROLD, JR., retired librarian, minister; b. Atlanta, July 3, 1936; s. Curtis Harold and Gerturde Olive (Casey) Tabor; m. Dorothy May Corbin, June 30, 1957 (dec. June 1996); m. Paulene C Pennington, July 12, 1997; children: Timothy M, John M. AA, Fla. Coll., Temple Ter., 1957; BA, Harding Coll., Ark., 1960; MA, Butler U., Indpls., 1969; MDiv, Bapt. Missionary Assn. Theol. Sem., Jacksonville, Tex., 1974; MLS, Tex. Woman's U., Denton, Tex., 1977. Min. Ch. of Christ, Bowling Green, Ky., 1960-61, Hamilton, Ont., Canada, 1961-64, Indpls., 1964-67, Nacogdoches, Tex., 1967-75, Dallas, 1976-77, Columbus, Miss., 1977-79, Tampa, Fla., 1993-97, Maryville, Tenn., 1997—; reference libr. Blount County Pub. Libr., 1998—2006; ret., 2006. Tchr. Great Lakes Christian Coll., Beamville, Ont, Canada, 1961—64; Bible chair dir Stephen F Austin State U., Nacogdoches, Tex., 1967—75; participant archeological excavations, Tell Gezer, Israel, 1969, Tell Lachish, Israel, 80; profl. libr. sci. Fla. Coll., Temple Terrace, 1979—85, libr. dir., 1985—97; prin., owner Tabor Properties, Inc., 2005—08. Author (with others): (book) Resurrection, 1973, Biblical Authority, 1974, The Lord of Glory, 1980, Making A Difference: Florida College, the First Fifty Years, 1996. Cub master Boy Scouts Am, Nacogdoches, Tex., 1970—75; pres Nacogdoches Baseball Asn, 1974—75; vol driving instr 55 Alive AARP, 1998—2001. Recipient Scouters Key, Cub Scouts Ams, 1975. Mem.: SAR, Tampa Bay Libr. Consortium (treas 1986—89), Beta Phi Mu, Eta Beta Rho. Republican. Mem. Ch. Of Christ. Avocations: amateur radio (KC4XS), locksmithing. Home: 2359 Six Mile Rd Maryville TN 37803-2739 Personal E-mail: haltabor@yahoo.com.

TABOR, EDWARD, medical researcher; BA, Harvard U., Cambridge, Mass., 1969; MD, Columbia U., NYC, 1973. Intern and resident Columbia-Presbyn. Med. Ctr., NYC, 1973-75; rsch. investigator Bur. Biologics, Bethesda, Md., 1975-83; dir. divsn. anti-infective drug products FDA, Rockville, Md., 1983-88; assoc. dir. for biol. carcinogenesis Nat. Cancer Inst./NIH, Bethesda, 1988-95; dir. divsn. transfusion transmitted diseases FDA, Bethesda and Rockville, Md., 1995-99; assoc. dir. med. affairs Office Blood Rsch. and Rev., FDA, Rockville, 1999—2005; exec. dir. Regulatory Consulting, Quintiles, Inc., Rockville, 2005—06; head regulatory affairs Am. Quintiles, Inc., Rockville, 2006—08; v.p. Quintiles, Inc., 2008—, head global regulatory strategy, 2008—. Author: Infectious Complications of Blood Transfusion, 1982; editor: Viruses and Liver Cancer, 2002, Emerging Viruses in Human Populations, 2007,(with others) Etiology, Pathology, and Treatment of Hepatocellular Carcinoma in North America, 1991, Hepatitis C Virus and its Involvement in the Development of Hepatocellular Carcinoma, 1995, Liver Cancer, 1997; contbr. more than 300 articles to profl. jours. Capt. USPHS, 1975-05. Achievements include formulation of US regulatory policy on antibiotics, anti-viral drugs, and blood transfusion safety, research in hepatitis viruses, hepatocellular carcinoma. Office: Quintiles Inc 1801 Rockville Pike Ste 300 Rockville MD 20852 Business E-Mail: edward.tabor@quintiles.com.

TABOR, PAMELA DALTON, elementary school educator, career planning administrator; b. Roanoke, Va., June 7, 1965; d. Thomas Eugene and Mary Ann DeLong Dalton; m. Ronald Lynn Tabor, June 6, 1987; children: Jeremy Lynn, Zachary Aaron. BS, Ky. Christian U., Grayson, 1987; MA, E. Tenn. State U., Johnson City, 1992; PhD, So. Cross U., Lismore, Australia, 2008. Cert. advanced profl. tchr. Md., math. recovery leader/trainer US Math. Recovery Coun. GED instr. Cherry Hill Adult Learning Ctr., Balt., 1993—96; tchr. Harford County Pub. Schs., Havre de Grace, Md., 1996—97, elem. math. specialist,

1997—. Profl. devel. cons., Havre de Grace, 2003—; bd. dirs. US Math Recovery Coun. Co-developer (professional development program) SNAP (Student Numeracy Assessment Progressions), Add+VantageMR; co-author: Teaching Number in the Classroom with 4-8 Year Olds; contbr. articles to profl. jours. Vol. parent tng. Aberdeen Proving Ground Youth Ctr., Apg, Md., 2006; vol. children's min. First Christian Ch., Havre de Grace, 1994—. Named Outstanding Young Women of Am., 1987. Mem.: ASCD, Nat. Coun. Tchrs. Math., Christian Women's Fellowship (v.p. 2006), Kappa Delta Pi. Independent. Avocations: reading, gardening, travel, puzzles. Home: 801 S Stokes St Havre De Grace MD 21078 Office: Harford County Pub Schs Roye-Wms 201 Oakington Rd Havre De Grace MD 21078 Business E-Mail: pamela.tabor@hcps.org.

TABUENCA-CORDOBA, MARIA-SOCORRO, education educator, researcher; b. El Paso, Tex., Dec. 9, 1955; d. Manuel Tabuenca-Gutierrez and Socorro Cordoba De Tabuenca. BA, U Tex., El Paso, 1976; MA, U. Tex., El Paso, 1979; PhD, SUNY, Stony Brook, 1997. Instr. El Paso CC, 1992—98; lectr. U. Tex., El Paso, 1993—, tchr. asst., 1996—98; regional dir. El Colegio de la Frontera Norte, Ciudad Juarez, Chihuahua, Mexico, 1995—99, dean NW region, 1999—2007. Vis. prof. N.Mex. State U., Las Cruces, 1998, U. Tex., El Paso, 2007—. Regional dir. Hunger Project Mex., Ciudad Juarez, 1984—85; adv. bd. Techo Comunitario Found., Ciudad Juarez, 1993—2006; mem. Immigration Mus., U. Tex., El Paso, 2002—04; bd. advisors folklife festival Rio Bravo/Rio Grande exhibit Smithsonian Instn., Washington/Ciudad Juarez, 1999—2003; student rep. Turner Fellows, SUNY, Stony Brook, 1990—92. Recipient Pres. Selection Com. for Nat. Poetry award, Instituto Sonorense De Cultura, 1995; W.B Turner fellow, Suny, Stony Brook, 1990—94, Transl. Of Chicana Authors grantee, Fideicomiso Para La Cultura Mexico-estados Unidos, 1996—97, Nat. Rsch. scholar, Consejo Nacional De Ciencia Y Tecnologia, 1998—, Cooperation US/Spain Latinos in Spain fellow, Instituto De Cooperacion Iberoamericana, Paso Del Norte Region Bldg. Project grantee, William and Flora Hewlett, 2001—03, Student Mobility Project grantee, Secretaria De Educacion Publica, 2004—. Mem.: MLA (assoc.), Latin Am. Studies Assn. (assoc.), Raza Assn. (assoc.). Roman Catholic. Achievements include research in methodology for study of borders' literatures between the US and Mexico. Avocations: reading, swimming, walking, travel, movies. Office: El Colegio de la Frontera Norte Ave Insurgentes # 3708 Chihuahua Ciudad Juarez Mexico Business E-Mail: tabuenca@colef.mx.

TABUENCA-MOYER, ROSAMARIA, language educator; d. Manuel and Maria Socorro Tabuenca. BA, Autonomous U. Chihuahua, Mex., 1973; MA, U. Tex., El Paso, 1983. Cert. in translation U. Tex., 1995. Lectr. Autonomous U., Ciudad Juarez, Chihuahua, 1973—78; Spanish instr. & translator BI Lang. Svcs., El Paso, 1979—83; instr. El Paso CC, 1984—2001; Spanish & u. studies lectr. U. Tex., 1984—, coord., 1999—2001, undergrad. Spanish advisor, 2006—. Translator Tabuenca Lang. Svcs., El Paso, 1983—99. Vol. Cancer & Chronic Disease Consortium, 1992—2005. Recipient Excellence award, The Breast & Cervical Cancer Control Program. Tex. Dept. Health, 2002. Mem.: Nat. Academic Advising Assn. Home: 2718 Aurora El Paso TX 79930 Office: Univ TX El Paso 500 W Univ El Paso TX 79968 Office Fax: 915-747-5292. Business E-Mail: tabuenca@utep.edu.

TACAL, JOSE VEGA, JR., retired public health official, veterinarian; b. Ilocos Sur, Philippines, Sept. 5, 1933; arrived in US, 1969; s. Jose Sr. and Cristina (Vega) T.; m. Lilia Caccam, 1959; children: Joyce, Jasmin, Jose III. DVM, U. Philippines, Quezon City, 1956; diploma, U. Toronto, 1964. Diplomate Am. Coll. Vet. Preventive Medicine; lic. vet., Calif. Provincial veterinarian Philippine Bur. Animal Industry, Manila, 1956-57; instr. vet. medicine U. Philippines, Quezon City, 1957-64, asst. prof., chmn. dept. vet. microbiology, pathology and pub. health, 1965-69; pub. health veterinarian San Bernardino (Calif.) County Dept. Pub. Health, 1970-83, sr. pub. health veterinarian, program mgr., sect. chief, 1984-2000. Zoonotic diseases lectr. Calif. State U., San Bernardino, 1984; lectr. U. Calif. Ext., Riverside, 1985; vis. prof. vet. pub. health U. Philippines at Los Banos, Laguna, 1988; participant 1st Internat. Conf. on Emerging Zoonoses, Jerusalem, 1996; presenter 4th Internat. Symposium on Ectoparasites of Pets, U. Calif., Riverside, 1997; presenter 8th Ann. Rabies in the Ams. Conf., Kingston, Ont., Can., 1997; rabies and ferret adv. group Calif. Dept. Health Svcs., 1998; presenter 48th Western Poultry Disease Conf., Vancouver, B.C., Can., 1999, 10th Rabies in Ams. Meeting, San Diego, 1999. Columnist LA Free Press, 1991, Pilipinas Times, 1993, Mabuhay Times, 1994-95; panelist Filipino-Ams. TV series The Many Faces of San Bernardino, California; contbr. more than 50 articles to profl. jours. Pres. Filipino Assn. of San Bernardino County, Highland, Calif., 1979; charter mem. Greater Inland Empire Filipino Assn., Highland, 1986—; del. First Filipino Media Conf. N.Am., LA, 1993; active San Bernardino County Africanized Honey Bee Task Force, 1993-2000, City of Highland Historic and Cultural Preservation Bd., 2006-08; v.p. Friends of the Highland Libr., 2006-09. Recipient Donald T. Fraser Meml. medal, U. Toronto, 1964, cert. of merit, Philippine Vet. Med. Assn., 1965, cert. of appreciation, Calif. State Bd. Examiners in Vet. Medicine, 1979, 1984, cert. of recognition, Congressman George E. Brown Jr., 42d Congl. Dist. Calif., 1994, Assemblyman Joe Baca, 62d Assembly Dist., Calif. State Legis., 1994, Vet. Medicine/Journalism award, Greater Inland Empire Filipino Assn., 1999, Cert. of Appreciation award, San Bernardino County Libr., Highland Br., 2005—06, Cert. of Recognition award, City of Highand, Calif., 2007—08, Proclamation, City Highland, Calif., 2008; named Vol. of Yr., Friends of Highland Libr., 2007; Colombo Plan Study fellow, Can./Philippine Govts., 1963—64, hon. fellow, Philippine Coll. Vet. Pub. Health, 2002. Mem.: ACLU, Highland Area Hist. Soc. (bd. mem. 2009), Calif. Rare Fruit Growers (Inland Empire chpt.), Soc. for Advancement of Rsch., Western Poultry Disease Conf., Am. Vet. Med. History Soc., U. Philippines Alumni Assn. (life), Phi Sigma, Phi Kappa Phi. Office: PO Box 1023 Highland CA 92346-1023

TACCHERI, UMBERTO, language educator; b. Rome, Apr. 29, 1958; s. Remo Taccheri and Ave Stefoni; m. Susan Meyer Taccheri, Jan. 20, 1990; children: Giulia Victoria, Isabel Rose, Claudia Raffaella. PhD in Roman Languages, U. Pa., Phila., 2000. Vis. instr. Duke U., Durham, NC, 1996—2000, vis. asst. prof., 2000; assoc. prof. italian language St. Mary's Coll., Notre Dame, Ind., 2001—08. Mem. Suzuki Music Sch., Granger, Ind., 2007—08. Lt. Inf., 1984—85, Pesaro, Italy. Recipient Salvatori Rsch. award, U. Pa., 1995. Home: 17343 Pencross Dr Granger IN 46530 Office: Saint Mary's Coll State 933 Notre Dame IN 46556 Business E-Mail: taccheri@saintmarys.edu.

TACHA, ATHENA, sculptor, artist, educator; b. Larissa, Greece, Apr. 23, 1936; arrived in U.S., 1963; MA, Nat. Acad. Fine Arts, Athens, Greece, 1959; MA in Art History, Oberlin Coll., 1961; PhD, U. Paris, 1963. Curator modern art Allen Art Mus., Oberlin, Ohio, 1963-73; prof. art Oberlin Coll., 1973-2000; adj. prof. art U. Md., College Park, 1999—. One-woman shows include Zabriskie Gallery, NY, 1979, 81, Max Hutchinson Gallery, NY, 1984, High Mus. Art, Atlanta, 1989, Cleve. Ctr. Contemporary Art, 1989, Franklin Furnace, NY, 1994, Found. for Hellenic Culture, NY, 2001, Marsha Mateyka Gallery, Washington, 2004, 08, Am. Univ. Mus., Washington, 2006, Kouros Gallery, NYC, 2007, others; prin. pub. commns. include sculptures at Am. Airlines Ctr., Dallas., City of Phila., Dept. Environ. Protection, Trenton, NJ, Case-Western Res. U., Cleve., Low Water Dam Riverfront Pk., Tulsa, Dept. of Transp., Hartford, Conn., Metrorail, Miami, Fla., Ecology Dept. U. Minn., St. Paul, Metro Morgan Blvd. Sta., Washington, DC, Light Rail Stas., Newark, NJ, Strathmore Music Ctr., Bethesda, Md., Bus. Sch., U. Wis., Madison, Muhammad Ali Plaza, Louisville, KY; collections include Hirshhorn Mus., Washington, Albright-Knox Art Gallery, Buffalo, Mus. Fine Arts, Houston, Nat. Coll. Fine Arts, Washington, Cleve. Mus. Art, Munson-Williams-Proctor Inst., Uttica, Nelson-Atkins Mus. Art, Kansas City, Allen Art Mus., Oberlin, Speed Art Mus., Louisville; author: (as A. T. Spear) Rodin Sculpture in the Cleveland Museum of Art, 1967, Brancusi's Birds, 1969; contbr. articles to profl. jours.; subject of books Cosmic Rhythms: Athena Tacha's Public Sculpture (E. McClelland), 1998, Dancing in the Landscape: The Sculpture of Athena Tacha, 2000. Recipient 1st prize May Show, Cleve. Mus. Art, 1968, 71, 79; NEA grantee, 1975; Bogliasco Found./Liguria Study Ctr. fellow, 2003, Bellagio Study Ctr. fellow, 2007. Home: 3721 Huntington St NW Washington DC 20015-1817 E-mail: atacha@umd.edu.

TACHA, DEANELL REECE, federal judge; b. Goodland, Kans., Jan. 26, 1946; m. John Allen Tacha; children: John Reece, David Andrew, Sarah Nell, Leah Beth. BA, U. Kans., 1968; JD, U. Mich., 1971. Spl. asst. to US Sec. of Labor, Washington, 1971—72; assoc. Hogan & Hartson, Washington, 1973, Thomas J. Pitner, Concordia, Kans., 1973—74; dir. Douglas County Legal Aid Clinic, Lawrence, Kans., 1974—77; assoc. prof. law U. Kans., Lawrence, 1974—77, prof., 1977—85, assoc. dean, 1977—79, assoc. vice chancellor, 1979—81, vice chancellor, 1981—85; judge US Ct. Appeals (10th cir.), Denver, 1985—, chief judge, 2001—07; mem. US Sentencing Commn., 1994—98; nat. pres. Am. Inns. Ct., 2004—08; pres. Nat.'l Inst. Trial Advocacy, Editl. Bd., 2007—. Office: US Ct Appeals 643 Massachusetts St Ste 301 Lawrence KS 66044*

TACHADO, SOUVENIR D., medical educator; s. Alfredo and Magdalena Tachado; m. Mona D. Domines; children: Alfred, Gerard, Souvenir Jr. MD, Cebu Doctors U., Philippines, 1983. Instr. medicine Harvard Med. Sch., Boston, 2002—. Deacon FBCS, Sudbury, Mass., 2007—09. Mem.: Am. Thoracic Soc. Achievements include discovery of malaria toxin. Home: 319 E Main St Marlborough MA 01752 Office: Beth Israel Deaconess Med Ctr 330 Brookline Ave Boston MA 02215 E-mail: stachado@bidmc.harvard.edu.

TACHDJIAN, RAFFI, pediatrician; b. July 8, 1969; BS, UCLA, 1992; MPH, Univ. Ala., Birmingham, 1994; MD, Morehouse Sch. Med., Atlanta, 2001. Cert. Am. Bd. Pediatrics, 2007. Epidemiologist in diphtheria surveillance Centers for Disease Control & Prevention, 1995—97; intern & resident in pediatrics Harvard Med. Sch., Mass. Gen. Hosp., 2001—04; fellow in pediatric immunology & rheumatology Mattel Children;s Hosp., UCLA, 2004—07. Vis. prof. Berklee Coll., Boston, 2004—; Chrysalis Mentor Am. Acad. of Allergy, Asthhma & Immunology, 2006. Contbr. articles to profl. jours. Mem.: Am. Acad. of Allergy, Asthma & Immunology, Am. Coll. of Allergy, Asthma & Immunology, Am. Acad. Pediatrics. Office: Mattel Children's Hosp MDCC 22-464 10833 LeConte Ave Los Angeles CA 90095-1752 Office Phone: 310-825-0731. Business E-Mail: rtachdjian@mednet.ucla.edu.

TACHI, SUSUMU, robotics educator; b. Tokyo, Jan. 1, 1946; m. Mayumi Yamamura, Mar. 20, 1973; 3 children. B in Math. Engring. and Info. Physics, U. Tokyo, 1968, MS in Math. Engring. and Info. Physics, 1970, PhD in Math. Engring. and Info. Physics, 1973. Mem. faculty engring. U. Tokyo, 1973-75, mem. faculty to prof. dept. info. physics and computing, 1989—; staff rschr. Ministry Internat. Trade and Industry Mech. Engring. Lab., Japan, 1975-78, sr. rsch. scientist, 1978-85, dir., 1985-90. Japanese Govt. award vis. scientist MIT, Cambridge, 1979—80; sr. adv. Nat. Inst. Advanced Indsl. Sci. and Tech./Ministry Internat. Trade and Industry, Japan, 1983—84, Ministry Internat. Trade and Industry, Japan, 1987. Contbr. articles to sci. jours., chapters to books; author: Tele-Existence and Virtual Reality, 1992, Virtual Tech. Lab., 1992, Telecommunication, Teleimmersion and Telexistence, 2003. Recipient IEEE Paper award, 1983, Ministry Internat. Trade and Industry award, Japan, 1988. Fellow: Japan Soc. Mech. Engring., Robotics Soc. Japan (founding dir., Tech. award 1991), Soc. Instrumentation and Control Engrs.; mem.: Virtual Reality Soc. Japan (founding pres.), Internat. Measurements Confederation (chmn. 1987, pres. 1996, IMEKO Disting. Svc. award 1997). Achievements include invention of a guide dog robot and tele-existence; patents in field. Office: Dept Info Physics and Computing U Tokyo 7-3-1 Hongo Bunkyo-ku Tokyo 113-8656 Japan E-mail: tachi@star.t.u-tokyo.ac.jp.

TACHNA, RUTH C., retired lawyer; b. NYC; d. Max and Rose (Rosenblatt) T.; m. Paul Bauman (dec.); children: Leslie Levy, Lionel Bauman. BA, Cornell U., 1935; LLB cum laude, Bklyn. Law Sch., 1937. Bar: N.Y. 1938, Calif. 1978, U.S. Dist. Ct. (so. dist.) N.Y. 1966, U.S. Ct. Appeals (2d cir.) 1966, U.S. Supreme Ct. 1956. Founding atty. Legal Aid, Westchester, N.Y., 1960-64; sr. ptnr., of counsel Tachna & Krassner, White Plains, NY, 1964—2001; ret. Prof. law Northrop U. Sch. Law, L.A., 1977-85; speechwriter for many office holders including Franklin D. Roosevelt. Group mng. editor Matthew Bender, N.Y.C., 1968-77; editor law rev. Bklyn. Law Sch., 1936-37. Staff atty., founder Legal Aid for Srs., Santa Monica, Calif., 1980-83, lectr. Writing Your Memoirs, 2007-09. Mem. Calif. Bar Assn., L.A. County Bar Assn. Home: 1951 N Honore Sarasota FL 34235 Home Phone: 941-342-1815.

TACHNER, LEONARD, lawyer; b. Bklyn., Jan. 18, 1944; BEE, CCNY, 1965; MSEE, Calif. State U., Long Beach, 1969; JD, Western State U., Fullerton, Calif., 1973. Bar: Calif. 1973, US Patent Office 1972. Supr. electronic counter measures sect. Ford Aerospace Corp., Newport Beach, Calif., 1969—73; patent atty. Reed C. Lawlor, LA, 1973—76, Rockwell Internat. Corp., Anaheim, Calif., 1976—78; ptnr. Fischer, Tachner & Strauss, Newport Beach, 1978—84; pvt. practice Irvine, Calif., 1984—. Instr. intellectual property Calif. State U., Long Beach, 1979—82; com. maintenance profl. competence Calif. State Bar, 1978—81. Mem. editl. bd. Western State U. Law Rev., 1972—73, columnist Interface Age mag., 1979—82, Bus.-to-Bus. mag., 1983—85. Mem.: Orange County Patent Law Assn., Calif. Bar Assn., Greater Irvine Indsl. League, Phi Kappa Phi. Office: 17961 Sky Park Cir Ste 38-E Irvine CA 92614 Home Phone: 949-786-7767; Office Phone: 949-752-8525. Personal E-mail: ltachner@aol.com.

TACK, LOIS CATHERINE, biochemist, researcher; d. James Christian and Joan Christine Otto; 1 child, Jesse Brian. PhD, Johns Hopkins U., Balt., 1979. Prin. investigator Salk Inst., La Jolla, Calif., 1983—89; automation human genome Gen. Atomics Corp., San Diego, 1991—94; biochemist Sequana Therapeutics, La Jolla, 1995—97; rsch. prof. U. Nev., Reno, 1999—2000; sr. scientist Packard Life Sci., Downers Grove, Ill., 2000—02; sr. applications scientist Perkin Elmer Inc., Waltham, Mass., 2002—. Contbr. articles to profl. jours. Mem.: Lab. Robotics Interest Group. Achievements include development of automated typing for tissue transplantation. Home: 201 N Adams St Westmont IL 60559 Office: Perkin Elmer Inc 2200 Warrenville Rd Downers Grove IL 60515 Business E-Mail: lois.tack@perkinelmer.com.

TACKETT, BILLY JOHN, electronics engineer, educator; b. Levelland, Tex., Jan. 22, 1969; s. Laura LaRae and Johnny Lewis Tackett; m. Melisa Ann Hough, Oct. 29, 1987; children: Matthew James, Christopher John, Autumn Elizabeth. AAS in Electronics Tech., South Plains Coll., Levelland, 1998. Cert. in aircraft maintenance FAA, 1991. Multiprobe pm and calibration group supr. Tex. Instruments, Houston, 1996—2006, equipment modification and devel., 1999—2006, HS student engring. mentor, 2003—06, safety team, 2003—06; equipment engring. technician X-Fab Tex., Lubbock, Tex., 2006—; instr. South Plains Coll., 2007—. Conservative. Baptist. Avocations: woodworking, fishing, camping. Office: South Plains Coll 1401 S College Ave Box 79 Levelland TX 79336 Business E-Mail: btackett@southplainscollege.edu.

TACKETT, KIMBERLY LYNN, pharmacist, educator; d. Alna Lee and Patricia Ellen Tackett; life ptnr. Mark Kevin Florence. BS in Biology, U. Ky., Lexington, 1991, BS in Pharmacy, 1997, PhD, 1998. Cert. Am. Assn. Diabetes Educators, 2002, Bd. Pham. spltys., 2004. Lab. technician U. Ky., Lexington, 1991—94; pharmacy practice resident Richland Meml. Hosp., Columbia, SC, 1998—99; retail pharmacist CVS Pharmacy, Aiken, SC, 1999—2001; clin. pharmacist Drs Hosp., Augusta, Ga., 2001—02, Beaufort Meml. Hosp., SC, 2002—04, clin. coord., 2004—07, interim dir., 2005—06; asst. prof. South U., Savannah, Ga., 2007—. Contbr. articles to profl. jours. Mem.: Ga. Soc. Health System Pharmacist (bd. mem. 2007—08), Am. Assn. Colls. Pharmacy (del. 2008—), Soc. Infectious Disease Pharmacist, Am. Coll. of Clin. Pharmacist. Office: S Univ Sch Pharmacy 709 Mall Blvd Savannah GA 31406 Office Fax: 912-201-8153. Business E-Mail: ktackett@southuniversity.edu.

TACKETT, NATALIE JANE, state administrator; b. Wausau, Wis. d. Roland Elsworth and Natalie (Zanon) Kannenberg; m. William Marshall Tackett, July 1975 (dec.); children: Roland, Scott, Renee, William. BA in English with highest honors, N.W. Mo. State U., 1966, MA in English, 1968. Instr. English Tarkio (Mo.) Coll., 1968-70, N.W. Mo. State U., Maryville, 1970-78; rsch. dir. Mo. Dept. Revenue, Jefferson City, Mo., 1978-81; rsch. analyst Mo. Ho. of Reps., Jefferson City, 1981-84; dir. oversight div. Mo. Gen. Assembly, Jefferson City, 1984—. Contbr. articles to profl. jours. Councilman N.W. Mo. Subarea Coun. Area II Health Sys. Agy., 1976-77; bd. dirs. Nodaway County Nursing Svcs. and Health Ctr., pres., 1974-76; gov.'s adv. coun. Comprehensive Health Planning, 1976; chmn. Nodaway County Citizen's Com. for a County Health Ctr., 1972-74; pres. Cole County Hist. Soc., 1996-1998, 2004—06. Recipient Outstanding Woman award Maryville chpt. Soroptimist Internat. 1975, Joy of Achievement award 1975. Mem. AAUW (legis. com. 1985-87, pres. Mo. div. 1983-85, Woman of Distinction award 1984, Outstanding Contbn. in the Area of Legis., Mo. div. 1987), Legis. Program Evaluation Soc. Office: Mo Gen Assembly Oversight divsn State Capitol Rm 132 Jefferson City MO 65101 Personal E-mail: natalie_tackett@yahoo.com, njtackett@gmail.com.

TACKETT, STEPHEN DOUGLAS, retired education services specialist; b. Waverly, Ohio, Apr. 27, 1939; s. James Elbert and Zelma Iola (Manahan) T.; m. Magdalena Schneider, Jan. 4, 1958; children: Doris, Janice, Jerry, Suzanne. AA, El Paso C.C., 1974; BS, SUNY, Albany, 1976; MA, Ball State U., 1979. Nat. cert. counselor. Enlisted US Army, 1955, advanced through grades to Command Sgt. Maj., 1973, ret., 1982; instr. Mt. Wachusett CC, Gardner, Mass., 1979-81; asst. dir. Evaluation US Army Sgts. Maj. Acad., Ft. Bliss, Tex., 1981-82; dir. substance abuse treatment Sun Valley Hosp., El Paso, Tex., 1982-84; from guidance counselor to ednl. svcs. officer US Army, Germany, 1984-86, 88-90; edn. advisor US Army Sgts. Maj. Acad., Fort Bliss, 1986—88, 1990—92; edn. svcs. specialist Mil. Entrance Processing Sta., El Paso, 1992—2002; ret., 2002. Mem. adv. bd. for Counselor Edn. U. Tex., El Paso, 1983. Cubmaster Boy Scouts Am., Ft. Leonard Wood, Mo., 1970-71, com. mem., Frankfurt, Germany, 1972-73, asst. scoutmaster, Kaiserslautern, Germany, 1976-79.

TACKETT, VITI LEE, writer; d. Clarence James and America Jane (Mason) Hunt; m. Floyd Vernon Tackett, July 2, 1953; children: Floyd Randall, Terry Lynn, Lucinda Gail Tackett/Hines. Diploma, Inst. Children's Lit., West Redding, Conn. Author: (novel series) Roseanna, Belle's Restless Heart, Beyond the Tempest, Rainbow's End, Girl on the Run, Two Roads, Summer's Dream, Betrayal, (novel) The Bargain, 2009; contbr. poems to anthology. Home: 85 Pond St Cabot AR 72023 Office Phone: 870-995-5406. Personal E-mail: goviti@hotmail.com, vititackett6@yahoo.com.

TACOPINA, JOSEPH, lawyer; b. Bklyn., Apr. 14, 1966; m. Patricia Ann MacDonald. BA, BS, Skidmore Coll., 1988; JD, U. Bridgeport, 1991. Bar: NY 1992, US Dist. Ct. (so. and ea. dists.) NY 1994. Assoc. Law Office of Bruce Cutler, NYC, 1980-92; asst. dist. atty. Kings County Dist. Atty.'s Office, Bklyn., 1992-95; ptnr. Altchiler & Tacopina, NYC, 1995-97; founder Law Offices of Tacopina Seigel & Turano, P.C. (formerly Law Offices of Joseph Tacopina, P.C.), NYC, 1994—. TV commentator Fox News, NYC, 1996—, Court TV, NYC, 1995—, also MSNBC, CNBC, NBC, ABC. Mem. Fed. Bar Coun., NY Counsel Def. Lawyers, NY State Assn. Criminal Def. Lawyers, (dir., chair legis. com. 1995—), Nat. Assn. Criminal Def. Lawyers (coord. legis. com. 1995—), Assn. of the Bar City of NY (mem. legis. com.). Office: Law Offices Tacopina Seigel & Turano PC 275 Madison Ave 35th Fl New York NY 10016 Office Phone: 212-227-8877. Office Fax: 212-619-1028. E-mail: jtacopina@tacopinalaw.com.*

TADDEO, ANNETTE, language services professional; b. Barrancabermeja, Columbia, Apr. 7, 1967; m. Eric Goldstein; 3 children. BA, U. North Ala., 1992; grad. exec. edn. prog., Dartmouth Tuck Sch. Bus., Hanover, NH. Founder, CEO comprehensive lang. svcs. co. LanguageSpeak, Miami, 1993—. Mem. exec. bd. Women Impacting Pub. Policy. Recipient Entrepreneurial Diversity award, Women Impacting Pub. Policy, Latina Excellence award, Hispanic Mag.; named Businesswoman of Yr., South Fla. Bus. Jour., Women in Internat. Trade; named one of Top 50 Latina Entrepreneurs in US, Hispanic Mag. Mem.: Miami-Dade County Women's C. of C., Dade-County C. of C. Democrat. Office: LanguageSpeak Hdqs 5975 Sunset Dr Ste 803 Miami FL 33143 Office Phone: 305-668-9797. Office Fax: 305-668-0435.*

TADEPALLI, RAGHU, dean; B in Commerce, M in Commerce, Andhra U., India; MBA, Ariz. State U.; PhD in Mktg., Va. Tech. Faculty mem. ND State U., U. Ill. at Chgo.; joined Xavier U., Cin., 1997, dean Grad. Sch. Bus., assoc. dean Williams Coll. Bus.; Murata dean F.W. Olin Grad. Sch. Bus., Babson Coll., Mass., 2009—. Contbr. articles to profl. jours. Office: FW Olin Grad Sch Bus Babson Coll 231 Forest St Babson Park MA 02457-0310 E-mail: rtadepalli@babson.edu.*

TADESSE, BEDASSA, economics professor, researcher; s. Tadesse Ayele and Jiituu Eeyii; m. Iftu G. Iftu Dorose, Oct. 22, 2004; 1 child, Solan B. PhD in Economics, Western Mich. U., Kalamazoo, 2003. Asst. prof. Jimma U., Ethiopia, 1993—98, U. Minn.-Duluth, 2003—. Contbr. rsch. papers. Recipient Grad. Creative Rsch. award, Western Mich. U., 2001. Mem.: Am. Economics Assn., Omicron-Delta and Epsilon (coord. 2006—08). Office: Univ Minn-Duluth 1318 Kirby Plaza 330G LSBE Duluth MN 55812 Office Fax: 218-726-6059.

TADESSE, MESFIN, botanist, biology professor, consultant, researcher; s. Tadesse Woldemeskel and Askale Ayetaged; m. Hirut Girma, Oct. 18, 1986; children: Sofonias Mesfin, Brook Mesfin. BSc, Haile Selassie 1st U., Addis Ababa, 1973; MSc, U. Minn., Mpls., 1976; PhD, Uppsala U., Sweden, 1984. Grad. asst. Haile Sellasie 1st U., Addis Ababa, 1973—74; asst. lectr. Addis Ababa U., 1976—77, dir., nat. herbarium, 1976—92, lectr., 1977—80, asst. prof., 1984—89, assoc. prof., 1989—93; adj. prof. Columbus State CC, 2001—; vis. prof., lectr. Ohio State U., Columbus, 1993—2002, curator vascular plants, 2003—. Cons. Ethiopian Toursim Orgn., Addis Ababa, 1989—92; external examiner botany Moi U., Eldoret, Kenya, 1990—92; external examiner in botany Dar-Es-Saalam U., Tanzania, 1991. Author: (booklet) Some Endemic Plants of Ethiopia, 1991, (book) Asteraceae of Ethiopia, 2004; contbr. articles to profl. jours. Chmn. Ethiopian Cmty. Orgn., Inc., Columbus, 2003—06. Recipient Leadership award, Ethiopian Cmty. Orgn., Inc., 2006; grantee, SAREC, Sweden, 1981—92, Young Scientist Rsch. award, UNESCO, 1989, Ministry Coffee & Tea Devel., Ethiopia, 1990; scholar, USAID, 1974—76. Mem.: Assn. pour l'etude de la Flore Taxonomique d'Afrique Tropicaux (assoc.). Achievements include research in scientific names of plants. Avocations: reading, writing, exercise. Office: Ohio State Univ 1315 Kinnear Rd Columbus OH 43212

TADROS, FAWZI M., educator; b. Mar. 12, 1934; came to U.S. 1967; BA in Library & Info. Scis., Cairo U., 1960; MA, U. Utah, 1972, Ind. U., 1973; MLS, U. Mich., Ann Arbor, 1974; PhD in Library & Info. Scis., Cairo U., 1979. Expert in libr. sci. Inspector Egyptian Nat. Libr., 1960-67; mem. faculty U. Utah, 1967-69, Ind. U., 1969-76; Arab area specialist Library of Congress, 1976—2007, dir., 2008—; mem., expert libr. sci. UNESCO, 1981-83. Cons. U. Libr. Saudi Arabia, Oman, Qatar, Bahrain, Kuwait, United Arab Emirates, Alexandria Libr. Com.; cons. for edn. and info. scis. UNESCO; vis. prof. Cairo U., U. Qatar, U. Bahrain, U. Oman; supr. World Global Gate Way between Libr. of Congress and Nat. Libr. Egyp; acting field dir. Cairo Office Libr. of Congress, 2007—. Pub. bibliography on the Holy Koran (among the best 60 Am. pub., 1994), others; contbr. articles to profl. jours. Mem. Congl. Del. State Qatar. Recipient Fulbright Sr. Awd., Univ. Qatar, 1990. Mem. AAUP, Middle East Studies Assn., Middle East Libr. Assn., Fulbright Assn., World Digital Libr. Achievements include first to exhibit in Qatar on the Holy Koran Manuscripts. Office Phone: 202-707-7311. Business E-Mail: ftad@loc.gov.

TADROS, MOHSEN SHOKRY, agriculturist; b. Cairo, Jan. 1, 1930; s. Shokry Tadros Boulos; m. Etedal Lala Tadros; children: Ramez, Karam. MSc, Cairo U., 1960; PhD, Ain Shams U., Cairo, 1965; degree (hon.), Ohio U., Athens, 1978. Cert. sr. ecologist Ecological Soc. Am. Bd. Profl. Certification, 1999. Biology tchr. High Agrl. Inst., Menia, Egypt, 1958-66, lectr. Kafr El Sheikh, Egypt, 1966-67, Tanta U., Kafr El-Sheikh, Egypt, 1968-77, assoc. prof., 1978-81, prof. agrl. zoology, 1982-89, prof. emeritus, 1990—. Cons., New Valley Govt. Kharga, Egypt 1952-55; rsch. supr., Tanta U., 1966—; vis. prof., State U. NJ, 1979-82; prin. investigator Link Project, NJ and Egypt, 1987-91. Author gen. zoology textbooks, 1976, 77. Recipient award, Tanta U., 1999. Mem. Ecol. Soc. Am., Entomol. Soc. US, Zool. Soc. Egypt, Entomology Soc. Egypt, Internat. Assn. Ecology, Acarological Soc. Am. Avocations: swimming, reading, tennis, gardening. Home Phone: 0020-4831250. Personal E-mail: mohsentadros@yahoo.com.

TADROS, NADER K., political organization worker, director; s. Kadry H Tadros and Soraya Labib; m. Amy Mariam Ekdawi; children: Youssef N., Nadine A. BA in English Lang., Ain Shams U., Cairo, 1981; Diploma in Social Devel., St. Francis Xavier U., Nova Scotia, Can., 1988; MA in Orgnl. Psychology, Columbia U., NYC, 1996. Mid. east and Egypt country dir. America's Devel. Found., Cairo, 1998—2001, mem. Alexandria, Va., 2008, dir., internat. tng., 2001—02; fellow GEM, 2000—01; program dir. Advocacy Inst., Washington, 2002—04; adj. prof. SAIS, Johns Hopkins U., Washington, 2002—05, Coady Internat. Inst., St. Francis Xavier U., 2003—05, Sch. Internat. Tng., Brattleboro, Vt., 2005—; founding dir., advocacy cons. facilitator People's Advocacy, Fairfax, Va., 2004—. Contbr. articles to profl. jours. Founding mem. Romanian Assn. Cmty. Devel., Bucharest, Romania, 1999. Mem.: Rotary. Democrat. Office: People's Advocacy 4031 University Dr Fairfax VA 22030 Office Fax: 1 (703) 652-5150. Personal E-mail: nktadros@msn.com. Business E-Mail: ntadros@peoplesadvocacy.org.

TAEKMAN, JEFFREY MARC, anesthesiologist; s. Michael Seymour and Ilene Roberta Taekman; m. Jeanne Marie Beckley, June 2, 1991; children: Joshua Beckley, Sarah Anne, Lauren Marie. BS, U. Calif., Davis, 1986; MD, Wake Forest U. Med. Ctr., Winston-Salem, NC, 1991. Asst. dean ednl. tech. Duke U. Sch. Medicine, Durham, NC, 2001—07; dir. human simulation patient safety ctr. Duke U., 2001—07. Office: Duke Univ Med Ctr 100 Trent Dr Durham NC 27710 Business E-Mail: jeffrey.taekman@duke.edu.

TAEKMAN, MICHAEL SEYMOUR, neurological surgeon; b. Chgo., June 30, 1937; s. Harry Joseph and Rose Anne (Sturner) T.; m. Ilene Roberta Erlich, Dec. 18, 1960; children: Jeffrey Marc, Jennifer Lynn, Jessica Beth. MD, U. Ill., Chgo., 1962. Diplomate Am. Bd. Neurol. Surgery. Intern U. Ill., Chgo., 1962—63, resident in gen. surgery, 1963—64, 1971; resident in neurosurgery U. Ill. Neuropsychiat. Hosp., Chgo., 1964—67; fellow U. Edinburgh, Scotland, 1967; attending neurosurgeon Chgo. Mcpl. Contagious Disease Hosp., 1967; pres. East Bay Med. Group, Berkeley, Calif., 1969—99. Asst. clin. prof. U. Calif., San Francisco, 1990-99, assoc. clin. prof., 1999—; instr. U. Ill., Chgo., 1963-67; lectr. U. Calif., Berkeley, 1975—1992; chmn. dept. surgery Childrens Hosp. Med. Ctr., Oakland, Calif., 1980-90; assoc. clin. prof., Stanford U., 1999—; assoc. prof. pediatric neurosurgery Leland Packard Childrens Hosp. Contbr. articles to profl. jours. Adv. mem. San Rafael Sch. Bd., 1976-77; med. examiner State Calif., Berkeley, 1976—, docent, chmn. acad. sci. Served to capt. USAF, 1964-71. Scholar Internat. Coll. Surgeons, 1967, Med. Rsch. Coun. Great Britain, 1967. Fellow ACS, Am. Assn. Neurol. Surgeons, Am. Assn. Pediatric Neurol. Surgeons; mem. Calif. Acad. Medicine, Alameda Contra Costa Med. Assn., Rafael Racket Club, Phi Eta Sigma. Republican. Jewish. Office: 4350 Clement St San Francisco CA 94121 Office Phone: 415-459-3616. Personal E-mail: michaeltaekman@sbcglobal.net.

TAESCH, RICHARD EDMUND, music educator; b. San Diego, Calif., Dec. 17, 1942; s. Edmond Thomas Taesch and Ann Marcella Simeone; m. Sandra Aiken, June 15, 1968 (div. Jan. 0, 1980). Attending, LA Valley Coll., 1960, Calif. State Lonj Beach, 1970, Adlor Music Acad., 1949—53, attending, 1959—63. Cert. lit. Braille Libr. of Congress, 1988, music Braille Libr. of Congress, 1992; proofreader 2003. Tchr. Adler Music Acad., Van Nuys, Calif., 1961—71; tchr. pvt. studio Van Nuys Music, 1971—94; tchr., chair dept. guitar So. Calif. Conservatory of Music, Sun Valley, 1976—, tchr., founder Braille music divsn., 1992—; tchr. L.A.City Coll., 1983—90, Chas Lewis Piano Studio, 1961—68; lab. Congress Transcribe Tng., 1984—92, 2006. Br. pres. Music Tchrs. Assn. Calif, San Fernando East Valley, 1971—79; music specialist Calif. Transcribers and Educators of Visually Handicapped, LA, 1996—. Author: An Introduction to Music for the Blind Student Parts I & II; contbr. articles to profl. jours.; author: Introduction to the Piano for the Blind Student. Founder Music Edn. Network for The Visually Impaired, 1996. Recipient Ptnr. Sch. Award, Blend School-LAUSD, 1999. Mem.: ASCAP, Nat. Assn. of Schools of Music, Nat. Braille Assn. Roman Catholic. Achievements include development of Cal Transcribers and Educators of the Visually Handicapped music committee; developed curriculum for teaching of braille music. Avocations: hiking, amateur radio. Office: SCCM Braille Music Divsn 8230 Fallbrook Ave W. Canoga Park CA 91304

TAEYMANS, OLIVIER N., veterinarian, educator; b. Antwerp, Belgium, Sept. 26, 1975; m. Inge Keppens; 1 child, Matthieu M. BA, U. Antwerp, 1997; DVM, Ghent U., Merelbeke, Belgium, 2000, PhD, 2008. Diplomate in vet. radiology ECVDI, 2005. Resident Ghent U., 2001—05, asst. prof., 2005—08, Tufts U., Norht Grafton, Mass., 2008—. Contbr. articles to profl. jours. Named Resident of Yr., 2003; Rsch. grant, Tufts U. Mem.: ACVR US Conn. MRI Socs., ECVDI (credential com. mem. 2006—). Achievements include research in cross sectional imaging of the canine thyroid gland. Office: Tufts Univ 200 Westboro Rd North Grafton MA 01536

TAFLOVE, ALLEN, electrical engineer, educator, researcher, consultant; s. Harry and Leah T.; m. Sylvia Hinda Friedman, Nov. 6, 1977; children: Michael Lee, Nathan Brent. BS with highest distinction, Northwestern U., 1971, MS, 1972, PhD Cabell Fellow, 1975. Assoc. engr. IIT Rsch. Inst., Chgo., 1975-78, rsch. engr., 1978-81, sr. engr., 1981-84; assoc. prof. Northwestern U., Evanston, Ill., 1984-88, prof., 1988—. Charles Deering McCormick prof., 2000—03; master Lindgren/Slivka Residential Coll. Sci. & Engring., 2000—05. Author: Computational Electrodynamics: The Finite-Difference Time-Domain Method, 1995, 3rd edit., 2005; co-author: Computational Electromagnetics: Integral Equation Approach, 1993; editor: Advances in Computational Electrodynamics: The Finite-Difference Time-Domain Method, 1998. Fellow: IEEE. Achievements include pioneer of finite-difference time-domain method in computational electrodynamics. Office: Northwestern U Dept Elec Engring and Computer Sci 2145 Sheridan Rd Evanston IL 60208-0834 Home Phone: 847-674-0597; Office Phone: 847-491-4127. Business E-Mail: taflove@ece.northwestern.edu.

TAFOYA, ARTHUR NICHOLAS, bishop; b. Alameda, N.Mex., Mar. 2, 1933; s. Nicholas and Rosita Tafoya. Student, St. Thomas Sem., Denver, Conception Sem., Mo. Ordained priest Archdiocese of Santa Fe, 1962; asst. pastor Holy Rosary Parish, Albuquerque, 1962-65; pastor Northern N.Mex., from 1965, San Jose Parish, Albuquerque; rector Immaculate Heart of Mary Sem., Santa Fe; ordained bishop, 1980; bishop Diocese of Pueblo, Colo., 1980—. Roman Catholic. Office: Diocese of Pueblo 1001 N Grand Ave Pueblo CO 81003-2915

TAFT, BOB (ROBERT ALPHONSO TAFT II), former governor, educator; b. Conn., Jan. 8, 1942; great grandson of William Howard Taft, 27th President of US; m. Hope Taft; 1 child, Anna. BA in Govt., Yale U., 1963; MA, Princeton U., 1967; JD, U. Cin., 1976. Budget officer, asst. dir. Ill. Bur. Budget, 1967—73; mem. Ohio Ho. of Reps., Columbus, 1976-80; commr. Hamilton County, Ohio, 1981-90; sec. of state State of Ohio, Columbus, 1991-99, gov., 1999—2007; disting. rsch. assoc. U. Dayton, Ohio, 2007—. Vol. Peace Corps., Tanzania, 1963—65. Republican. Protestant. Office: U Dayton 300 College Park Dayton OH 45469

TAFT, DAVID DAKIN, chemicals executive; b. Cleve., Mar. 27, 1938; s. Kingsley A. and Louise D. T.; m. Sararose Leonard, July 8, 1961; children: Amy Rose, Kingsley Leonard, Elisabeth. AB, Kenyon Coll., 1960; PhD in Chemistry, Mich. State U., 1963. Sr. rsch. chemist Archer-Daniels Midland, 1964-67; mgr. polymer rsch. Ashland Chem., 1967-72; dir. comml. devel. Gen. Mills Chems., 1972-74; v.p., dir. R&D, Henkel Corp., 1973-78, group v.p. consumer and splty. products, 1978-81, exec. v.p. chem. products div., dir., 1981-82; gen. mgr. materials div. Raychem Corp., Menlo Park, Calif., 1983-84; gen. mgr. Telecom group, 1983-86; v.p. Raychem Corp., 1984-93, v.p. manufacturing, 1986-93; COO Landec Corp., Menlo Park, Calif., 1993—2001, 2005—; pres., COO Dock Resins Corp., 2001—02; COO Apio, Inc., 2002—05. Author: Fundamentals of Powder Coatings; bd. editors: Rsch. Mgmt. Jour.; patentee in field. Trustee Mpls. Soc. Fine Arts, 1981-83, Kenyon Coll., 1990—2002; vice chmn. Mem. Comml. Devel. Assn., Indsl. Research Inst., Am. Chem. Soc., Kenyon Alumni Assn. (pres. 1978), Circus Club. Republican. Office: Landec Corp 3603 Haven Ave Menlo Park CA 94025-1010 Office Phone: 650-261-3695. E-mail: dtaft@landec.com.

TAFT, SHELDON ASHLEY, retired lawyer; b. Cleve., Mar. 2, 1937; s. Kingsley Arter and Louise Parsons (Dakin) T.; m. Rebecca Sue Rinehart, Dec. 26, 1962; children: Mariner R., Ashley A., Curtis N. BA, Amherst Coll., 1959; LLB, Harvard U., 1962. Bar: Ohio 1962. Assoc. Vorys, Sater, Seymour & Pease, Columbus, Ohio, 1965-69, 71-73; chief legal counsel Pub. Utilities Commn. Ohio, 1969-71; ptnr. Vorys, Sater, Seymour & Pease, Columbus, Ohio, 1974—2001, of counsel, 2002—04, ret., 2005. Ohio bd. advisors Chgo. Title Ins. Co., 1967-98. Rep. candidate for justice Ohio Supreme Ct., 1974; trustee Opera Columbus, 1989—, pres., 1991-93, life trustee, 1995—; trustee Columbus Bach Ensemble 2002—, pres. 2002-06; trustee Chamber Music Columbus, 2006—;trustee Columbus Symphony orchestra, 2007—; 1st lt. USAF, 1963-65. Mem. Ohio State Bar Assn. (pres. pub. utilities com. 1984-87), Columbus Bar Assn., Ohio Camera Collectors Soc. (pres. 1985-87), Rocky Fork Hunt and Country Club, Hillsboro Club (dir. 2008-, sec. 2009-), 41 Club, Review Club. Congregationalist. Avocation: camera collecting. E-mail: staft@columbus.rr.com.

TAFT, TIMOTHY NED, orthopedist, surgeon, sports medicine physician; s. Samuel Milton and Helen Taft; m. Judith Ann Huffman, Sept. 13, 1971; children: Todd Daniel, Rebecca Lynn Fecher. AB, Princeton U., NJ, 1964; MD, U. Mo., Columbia, Mo., 1969. Diplomate Am. Bd. Orthopaedic Surgery, 1978, lic. physician N.C., 1978. Intern, resident in orthopedics U. N.C., NC, 1969—74, prof., 1974—, dir. sports medicine, 1991—. Mem.: Spl. Olympics N.C. (chmn., bd. dirs.). Office: University of North Carolina 3154 Bioinformatics CB 7055 Chapel Hill NC 27599 Office Fax: 919-966-6750; Home Fax: 919-967-6750. Business E-Mail: ttaft@med.unc.edu.

TAFT, WILLIAM HOWARD, retired journalism educator; b. Mexico, Mo., Oct. 24, 1915; s. Raymond E. and Ferrie (Dains) T.; m. Myrtle Marie Adams, Jan. 18, 1941; children: Marie, William Howard, Alice. AB, Westminster Coll., 1937; B in Journalism, U. Mo., 1938, MA, 1939; PhD, Western Res. U., 1951. Dir. pub. rels. Hiram (Ohio) Coll., 1939-40, 47-48; asst. prof. journalism Youngstown (Ohio) Coll., 1946-48; prof. Defiance (Ohio) Coll., 1948-50; assoc. prof. Memphis State Coll., 1950-56; prof. U. Mo., Columbia, 1956-81, assoc. dean grad. programs, 1980-81, ret., 1981. Yearbook cons., 1957—. Author: Let's Publish That Top-Rated Yearbook, 1961, (with others) Modern Journalism, 1962, Missouri Newspapers, 1964, Missouri Newspapers, When and Where, 1808-1962, 1964, American Journalism History, 1968, rev. edit., 1977, Newspapers as Tools for Historians, 1970, (with others) Mass Media and the National Experience, 1971, Donrey Media; A Low Profile Group, 1976, Magazines for the Eighties, 1981, Encyclopedia of 20th Century Journalists, 1986, Missouri Newspapers and the Missouri Press Association, 125 Years of Service, 1867-1992, 1992, Wit and Wisdom of Country Editors, 1996, Show-Me Journalists: The First 200 Years, 2003, The Missouri Honor Medal, 2005, Missouri United Methodist Church, History to 2006, 2006, Created in Heaven A Love Story, 2008; contbr. articles to profl. jours. and encys. With USAAF, 1941-45. Recipient Faculty-Alumni citation U. Mo., 1979, Alumni Achievement award Westminster Coll., 1987, Dist. Svc. in Journalism medal U. Mo. Sch. Journalism, 2004; rsch. fellow Washington Journalism Ctr., 1967; inducted into Mo. Newspaper Hall of Fame, 2001 Mem. Assn. Edn. Journalism and Mass. Comm. (Presdl. award 1991), Boone County Hist. Soc. (past pres.), Kiwanis (life; past pres., Churchman of Yr. 1987, Kiwanian of Yr. 1993, Tablet of Honor 1997, George F. Hixson award), Delta Tau Delta (life), Pi Delta Epsilon, Kappa Tau Alpha (nat. treas., exec. dir. 1962-91). Methodist. Home: 107 Sondra Ave Columbia MO 65202-1416

TAFT, WILLIAM HOWARD, IV, lawyer; b. Washington, Sept. 13, 1945; s. William Howard and Barbara Hoult (Bradfield) T.; m. Julia Vadala, May 4, 1974; Maria Consetta, William Howard V, Julia Harris. BA, Yale U., 1966; JD, Harvard U., 1969. Bar: D.C. 1969. Assoc. Winthrop, Stimson, Putnam & Roberts, NYC, 1969-70; atty.-advisor to chmn. FTC, Washington, 1970; prin. asst. to dep. dir. Office Mgmt. & Budget, Exec. Office of the Pres., Washington, 1970-72, exec. asst. to dir., 1972-73; exec. asst. to sec. US Dept. Health Edn. & Welfare, Washington, 1973-76, gen. counsel, 1976-77; ptnr. Leva, Hawes, Symington, Martin & Oppenheimer, Washington, 1977-81; gen. counsel US Dept. Def., Washington, 1981-84, dep. sec., 1984—89, acting sec., 1989; perm. rep. U.S. Mission to NATO, Brussels, 1989—92; legal adv. US Dept. State, Washington, 2001—05; ptnr. Fried Frank Harris Shriver & Jacobson LLP, Washington, 1992—2001; of counsel Fried Frank Harris Shriver & Jacobson, 2005—; Warren Christopher prof. practice of internat. law and diplomacy Stanford Law Sch., 2007—. Vis. scholar Freeman Spogli Inst. for Internat. Studies, 2007—. Recipient Disting. Service award HEW, 1975 Mem. D.C. Bar Assn., Lit. Soc. (Washington) Clubs: Cosmos (Washington), Leo (Washington). Republican. Office: Fried Frank Harris Shriver & Jacobson LLP 1001 Pennsylvania Ave NW Washington DC 20004 Office Phone: 202-639-7164. Business E-Mail: taftwi@friedfrank.com.

TAGATZ, GEORGE ELMO, retired obstetrician, gynecologist, educator; b. Milw., Sept. 21, 1935; s. George Herman and Beth Elinore (Blain) T.; m. Susan Trunnell, Oct. 28, 1967; children: Jennifer Lynn, Kirsten Susan, Kathryn Elizabeth. AB, Oberlin Coll., 1957; MD, U. Chgo., 1961. Diplomate Am. Bd. Obstetricians and Gynecologists, Am. Bd. Reproductive Endocrinology (examiner, bd. reproductive endocrinology 1976-79). Rotating intern Univ. Hosps. of Cleve., 1961-62, resident in internal medicine, 1962-63; resident in ob-gyn U. Iowa, 1965-68; sr. research fellow in endocrinology U. Wash. dept. obstetrics and gynecology, 1968-70; prof. emeritus Med. Sch. U. Minn., 1970—96, 1996—. Fertility and maternal health adv. com. FDA, USPHS, HHS, 1982-86; cons. in field. Ad hoc editor: Am. Jour. Ob-Gyn, Fertility and Sterility; contbr. articles to profl. publs. Served with M.C. U.S. Army, 1963-65. Mem. AMA, Minn., West Metro med. socs., Minn. Obstet. and Gynecol. Soc., Am. Coll. Ob-Gyn (subcom. on reproductive endocrinology 1979-82), Endocrine Soc., Am. Fertility Soc., Central Assn. Obstetricians and Gynecologists, U. Iowa Ob-Gyn Alumni Soc. Home: 5828 Long Brake Trl Edina MN 55439-2622 Home Phone: 952-941-7930. Personal E-mail: george.tagatz@comcast.net.

TAGEN, JULIE, legislative staff member; Grad., U. Md., College Pk. Events mgr., corp. & founds. rels. Human Rights Campaign, 1997—99; devel. dir. Gay and Lesbian Victory Fund, 1999—2002; fin. cons. Senator John Kerry's Presdl. Campaign, 2004; cons. America Coming Together, 2004; dep. nat. fin. dir. Dem. Nat. Com., 2005—08; chief of staff to Rep. Alan Grayson US House of Reps., Washington, 2009—. Democrat. Office: 1605 Longworth House Office Bldg Washington DC 20515 Office Phone: 202-225-2176. Office Fax: 202-225-0999.*

TAGGART, BRUCE M., library administrator; BS in Pub. Adminstrn., Nichols Coll., Mass.; M in Pub. Adminstrn., U. Conn., PhD in Edn., 1993. Past assoc. dir. Computing Ctr. U. Conn.; exec. dir. Info. Tech. Portland State U., Oreg.; vice provost Libr. and Tech. Svc. Lehigh U., Pa., 2000—. Mem. Educause, Gov.'s Telecom. Adv. Com., Oreg., N.W. Academic Computing Consortia, Lehigh Valley Econ. Devel. Corp. Office: Libr and Tech Svc Lehigh U 8A E Packer Ave Bethlehem PA 18015 Office Phone: 610-758-3025. E-mail: bmt2@lehigh.edu.

TAGGART, CHRISTOPHER SCOTT, systems engineer; s. Donald John and Marlene Faulkner Taggart; m. Elizabeth Young Chu Pedro, Sept. 17, 1983; children: Ross Kenneth, Amy Elisabeth. BS, U. Rochester, NY, 1982; MS, U. Wash., Seattle, 1992; PhD, NC State U., Raleigh, 2008. Cert. profl. engr., Md., 1996. Navy officer Nuc. Power Tng. Unit, Ballston Spa, NY, 1982—83; officer US Navy Nuc. Power Sch., Orlando, Fla., 1982, US Navy Submarine Sch., Groton, Conn., 1983; submarine officer USS Atlanta SSN 712, Norfolk, Va., 1983—86, Comsubron 17, Silverdale, Wash., 1986—88; sys. engr. Alliant Techsys. Inc., Poulsbo, Wash., 1989—92, prin. sys. engr. Sykesville, Md., 1994—96; lead sys. engr. Gen. Dynamics Advanced Info. Sys., Greensboro, NC, 1996—2007, sys. & software engring. mgr., 2007—08, sr. bus. mgr., 2008—. Navy res. officer, comdr. Submarine Squadron Seventeen, Silverdale, 1989—93; commdg. officer Trident Refit Facility Res. Unit, Silverdale, 1993—94; navy res. officer, comdr. Submarine Force US Atlantic Fleet Res. Unit, Washington, 1994—98; commdg. officer Navy Computer & Telecom. Command Res. Unit, Norfolk, 1998—2000; navy res. officer Space & Naval Warfare Command Res. Unit, Charlotte, NC, 2000—02; commdg. officer Overseas Repair Facility RSV Unit, Greensboro, 2002—04, PEO Integrated Warfare Sys. Res. Unit, Washington, 2002—04, Office Naval Rsch. Global Res. Unit, Arlington, Va., 2004—06, navy res. officer, 2007—; insp. gen. category leader Naval Sea Sys. Command, Washington, 2006—07. Coach MathCounts, Greensboro, 2003—06; sch. tchr. St. Francis Episcopal Ch., Greensboro, 1997—2007, Holy Trinity Episcopal Ch., Greensboro, 2008—09; asst. scout master Boy Scouts Am., Greensboro, 2001—07; swimming referee NC HS Athletics Assn., Greensboro, 2003—. Mem.: SAR, Eta Kappa Nu, Tau Beta Pil, Phi Beta Kappa. Episcopalian. Avocations: exercise, history, movies. Office: Gen Dynamics AIS 5440 Millstream Rd Mc Leansville NC 27301 Business E-Mail: christopher.taggart@gd-ais.com.

TAGGART, JAMES JEFFREY, engineering educator; s. James Jeffrey and Anne Marie Taggart; m. Sonia Carias-Reyes, Dec. 27, 2002; children: Diego Miguel, Eduardo James. BSEd, Wesley Coll., Dover, Del., 1997; MA, Richard Stockton Coll. NJ., Pomona, 2000. Asst. prof., computer info. sys. Atlantic Cape CC, Mays Landing, NJ, 2000—. Office: Atlantic Cape CC 5100 Black Horse Pike Mays Landing NJ 08330 Business E-Mail: jtaggart@atlantic.edu.

TAGGART, THOMAS MICHAEL, lawyer; b. Sioux City, Iowa, Feb. 22, 1937; s. Palmer Robert and Lois Allette (Sedgwick) T.; m. Dolores Cecilia Baroway Renfro, Jan. 4, 1963; children: Thomas Michael Jr., Theodore Christopher; m. Mary Ann Gribben, Feb. 7, 1976. BA, Dartmouth Coll., 1959; JD, Harvard U., 1965. Bar: Ohio 1965, U.S. Dist. Ct. (so. dist.) Ohio 1967, U.S. Dist. Ct. (no. dist.) Ohio 1981, U.S. Supreme Ct. 1997. Ptnr. Vorys, Sater, Seymour & Pease, Columbus, Ohio, 1965—, now of counsel. Lectr. Ohio Legal Ctr. Inst., Ohio Mfrs. Assn., Capital U. Ctr. for Spl. and Continuing Legal Edn. Capt. USMC, 1959-63. Mem. ABA, Ohio Bar Assn. (bd. govs. 1991-99, liability ins. com. 1996-, pres. 1997-98, trustee Found. 1996-98, 2000—, pres 2005—, chair commn. on jud. evaluations 2000, Ohio Bar medal 1999), Columbus Bar Assn. (bd. govs., pres. 1989-90), Am. Bd. Trial Advocates, Columbus Area C. of C. Methodist. Home: 145 Stanbery Ave Columbus OH 43209-1465 Office: Vorys Sater Seymour & Pease 52 E Gay St Columbus OH 43215-3161 Business E-Mail: tmtaggart@vssp.com.

TAGIURI, CONSUELO KELLER, child psychiatrist, educator; b. San Francisco; d. Cornelius H. and Adela (Rios) Keller; m. Renato Tagiuri; children: Robert, Peter, John. BA, U. Calif.-Berkeley; MD, U. Calif.-San Francisco. Diplomate Am. Bd. Psychiatry and Neurology. Resident psychiatry Mass. Gen. Hosp., Boston; staff psychiatrist Children's Hosp., Boston, 1951-59; med. dir. Gifford Sch., Weston, Mass., 1965-85; chief psychiatrist Cambridge (Mass.) Guidance Ctr., 1961-84; mem. faculty dept. psychiatry Harvard Med. Sch., 1965—2002; cons. early childhood program Children's Hosp., 1985—. Contbr. articles in field to books. Fellow Am. Orth. Psychiat. Assn., Mass. Med. Soc., New Eng. Coun. Child Psychiatry.

TAGLIABUE, PAUL JOHN, lawyer, retired national football league commissioner; b. Jersey City, Nov. 24, 1940; s. Charles and Mary Tagliabue; m. Chandler M. Minter, Aug. 28, 1965; children: Drew, Emily. BA, Georgetown U., 1962; JD, NYU, 1965; LHD (hon.), Northeastern U., 1990; LLD (hon.), Colgate U., 2001. Bar: N.J. 1965, D.C. 1969. Policy analyst US Dept. Def., Washington, 1966—69; assoc. Covington & Burling LLP, Washington, 1969—74, ptnr., 1969—89, sr. of counsel, 2007—; commr. NFL, NYC, 1989—2006. Bd. dirs. Pro Football Hall of Fame, Nat. Urban League. Contbr. articles to profl. jours. Co-founder NFL Teacher of the Yr. Program, 1990; bd. governors United Way of America, 1998—99; bd. dirs. Georgetown U., 2006—, chmn. bd. dirs., 2009—. Recipient Meritorious Civilian medal, US Dept. Def., 1969, Humanitarians of the Yr. award, Cmty. Anti-Drug Coalitions of Am., 2004, Ellis Island Family Heritage award, 2004, Theodore Roosevelt award, NCAA, 2007; co-recipient Stay Close Individual Leadership award, PFLAG, 2005; named Sports Industrialist of the Yr., Sports Business Daily, 2000, Sports Executive of the Yr., Sports Business Journal, 2001, Most Powerful Person in Sports, The Sporting News, 2001; Gordon Grand Fellow, Yale U., 2001. Mem.: ABA (chmn. sports and entertainment industry com. antitrust sect. 1986), D.C. Bar Assn. Office: Covington & Burling LLP 1201 Pennsylvania Ave Washington DC 20004 E-mail: ptagliabue@cov.com.*

TAGLIAFERRI, LEE GENE, investment banker; b. Mahanoy City, Pa., Aug. 14, 1931; s. Charles and Adele (Cirilli) Tagliaferri; m. Maryellen Stanton, Apr. 29, 1962; children: Mark, John, Maryann. BS, U. Pa., 1957; MBA, U. Chgo., 1958. Div. comptroller Campbell Soup Co., Camden, NJ, 1958—60; securities analyst Merrill, Lynch, Pierce, Fenner & Smith, Inc., NYC, 1960—62; asst. v.p. US Trust Co. of NY, 1962—71; v.p. corp. fin. div. Laidlaw & Co., Inc., NYC, 1972—73; pres. Everest Corp., NYC, 1973—. Dir. Fairfield Communities Inc., UEC, Inc., LRA, Inc., Industrialized Bldg. Systems, Inc. Past pres. West Windsor Cmty. Assn.; trustee Schuyler Hall, Columbia, Madison Sq. Boys Club. With AUS, 1953—55. Mem.: Princeton Club (NYC), U. Pa. Club, K.C. Home: 77 Lillie St Princeton Junction NJ 08550-1307 Office: 1 Penn Plz New York NY 10119-0002

TAGLIAPIETRA, LINO, glass artist; b. Murano, Italy, 1934; Apprentice to, Archimede Seguso glass-making maestro, 1942. Instr. Pilchuck Glass Sch., Washington, 1979; master glassblower, designer Galliano Ferro Studio, Venini Studio, La Murrina Studio, Effetre Internat. Studio. Recipient Urban Glass award for Preservation of Glassworking Techniques, 1996, Lifetime Achievement award, Glass Art Soc., 1997, Urkunde Goldmedaille, Germany, 1997, Libensky award, Chateau Ste Michelle Vineyard and Winery and Pilchuck Glass Sch., 1998. Mem.: Am. Acad. Arts & Scis. (fgn. hon.). Mailing: care of Galleria Marina Barovier San Marco 3216 30124 Venice Italy Business E-Mail: info@linotagliapietra.com.

TAGUE, CHARLES FRANCIS, retired engineering, real estate and construction company executive; b. NYC, Aug. 16, 1924; s. Charles and Isabelle (Carey) T.; m. Alicia Patricia Murtha, Aug. 6, 1949; children: Patrick, Charles, Thomas, Mary Alicia Haberman, James, Beth Anne Giuliano BS, Fordham U., 1952. Auditor Scovell, Wellington & Co., NYC, 1951-57; comptroller Chem. Constrn. Corp., NYC, 1957-75; contr. Burns and Roe, Inc., Oradell, NJ, 1975-81; fin. dir. Alfred Sanzari Enterprises, Hasbrouck Heights, NJ, 1981-84; v.p. fin. Alexander Summer Co., 1984-93; ret., 1993. Fin. advisor Cath. Cmty. at Seabrook Village. Mem. Colts Neck (N.J.) Sports Found.; active Boy scouts Am.; mem. Lacawac Sanctuary Steering Com.; pres. parish coun. Ch. of Presentation; mem. pastoral coun. St. Thomas More Cath. Ch. With USNR, 1943-46, PTO, ETO, NATOUSA. Mem. Controllers Inst., Nat. Contract Mgmt. Assn., Assn. Govt. Accts., Scranton Club, Eagle Oaks Country Club. Democrat. Roman Catholic. Address: 4 Appleby Ct Jackson NJ 08527

TAGUE, FANELLA, language educator; d. Gene and Suzanne Bell; m. Matthew Tague; children: Gabriela, Micah. BA in Spanish, Meredith Coll., Raleigh, NC, 1998; MA in Hispanic Linguistics, Ohio State U., Columbus, 2000. Spanish tchr. Wakefield HS, Raleigh, 2001—05; adj. prof. Meredith Coll., 2002—. Mem.: FLANC. Office: Meredith Coll 3800 Hillsborough St Raleigh NC 27606 Business E-Mail: taguef@meredith.edu.

TAGUE, GREGORY FRANK, literature and language professor; b. Bklyn., Feb. 1, 1957; s. Joseph E. and Frances Tague; BA, Bklyn Coll., 1978; MA, Hunter Coll., NY, 1990; PhD, NY U., 1997. Prof. English St. Francis Coll., Bklyn., 1998—. Bd. mem. D.H. Lawrence Soc. North America, 2007—09. Mem.: MLA. Office: St Francis Coll 180 Remsen St Brooklyn NY 11201

TAGUE, JOHN PATRICK, air transportation executive; b. 1962; married; 2 children. Dir., then sr. v.p. Midway Airlines, 1985—91; exec. v.p. mktg. & planning ATA Airlines Inc., 1991—95; co-chmn., CEO The Pointe Group, 1995—97; pres., CEO ATA Holdings Corp., 1993—2002; exec. v.p., customer UAL Corp., 2003—04, exec. v.p. mktg., sales & revenue, 2004—06, exec. v.p., chief revenue officer, 2006—08, exec. v.p., COO, 2008—. Bd. dirs. Pacer Internat. Inc., 2002—05, United Airlines Inc., 2003—. Bd. trustees John G. Shedd Aquarium. Office: UAL Corp PO Box 66100 Chicago IL 60666

TAHA, ASSAD M., surgeon; b. Nabatieh, Lebanon, Dec. 12, 1955; came to U.S. 1980; s. Muhyddin S. and Hind (Jaber) T. BS, Am. U. Beirut, 1976, MD, 1980; PhD, Med. Coll. Ohio, Toledo, 1992. Diplomate Am. Bd. Surgery, Am. Bd. Surg. Critical Care. Surgery resident Good Samaritan Hosp., Cin., 1980-82, Med. Coll. Ohio, Toledo, 1982-85, attending surgeon, 1985-94, Am. U. of Beirut, 1994—, assoc. prof. surgery and physiology, 1994—. Dir. hyperbaric medicine Med. Coll. Hosp., Toledo, 1987—94, dir. surg. intensive care, 1988—94, assoc. prof. surgery; vis. surgeon surg. critical care Brigham & Women's Hosp., Harvard Med. Sch., Boston, 2000—01; vis. assoc. prof. Harvard U., 2000—01; vis. scholar trauma Ryder Trauma Ctr., U. Miami Sch. Medicine, Fla., 2003—04. Mem. editl. bd. European Jour. Emergency Surgery and Intensive Care; contbr. articles to profl. jours. Recipient AMA Physician Recognition award, 1987, 1991, 1997, 2000; grantee, Ohio Lions, 1987—92, Am. U.- Beirut U. Rsch. Bd., 1993—2000. Fellow ACS, AMA, Am. Heart Assn., Am. Physiologic Soc., Am. Soc. Gastrointestinal Endoscopy, European Assn. Trauma and Emergency Surgery, Royal Coll. Surgeons Can., Soc. Critical Care Medicine, Undersea and Hyperbaric Med. Soc., Am. Soc. Laser Medicine and Surgery, Am. Coll. Nutrition, Internat. Coll. Surgeons, Assn. Acad. Surgery, Shock Soc., European Soc. Intensive Care Medicine, World Assn. Disaster and Emergency Medicine, Soc. Am. GI Endoscopic Surgeons, World Med. Assn., Laser Inst. Am., Royal Soc. Medicine, Am. U. Beirut Alumni Assn., Am. Trauma Soc., Crit. Care Club, Disaster Med. Asst. Team; mem. AMA, AAUP. Avocations: chess, bridge. Office: Am U Beirut 3 Dag Hammarskjold Plz 8th Fl New York NY 10017-2303 Home Phone: 305-490-3682; Office Phone: 0119613628627, 305-468-2810. Office Fax: 212-583-7650, 0119611363291. Business E-Mail: at03@aub.edu.lb.

TAHANEY, MICHAEL HAMILTON, theatre professor, actor and director; s. Patrick Edward Tahaney and Patricia Tahaney (Dale) Hamilton; 1 child, Adam Michael. MFA in Theatre Arts, San Diego State U., Calif., 2000. Asst. prof. U. Ctrl. Fla., Orlando, 2001—02; BFA musical theatre program coord. East Carolina U., Greenville, NC, 2002—. Actor: (world premier cast) Thoroughly Modern Millie. Mem.: Va. Theatre Conf., NC Theatre Conf., Actors' Equity Assn., Phi Kappa Phi. Avocations: travel, art. Office: East Carolina Univ Messick Theatre 1001 E 5th St Greenville NC 27858 Personal E-mail: mhtahaney@aol.com. Business E-Mail: tahaneym@ecu.edu.

TAHAR, MOHAMMED ZRENDINI, physics professor; s. Smain and Selma Tahar. PhD in Physics, Boston U., 1991. Asst. prof., physics Coll. Brockport SUNY, 1997—2003, assoc. prof., physics, 2003—. Mem.: Soc. Physics Students, Inst. Physics, NY State Sect. Am. Assn. Physics Tchrs. (exec. bd. mem. to pres. 2005—), Am. Phys. Soc., Sigma Pi Sigma (councilor zone 2004—). Achievements include research in condensed matter and low temperature physics. Avocations: soccer, travel. Office: Coll Brockport State Univ NY 350 New Campus Dr Brockport NY 14420

TAHARI, ELIE, fashion designer; b. Israel; arrived in US, 1971; m. Rory Green, 2000; children: Jeremy, Zoe. Electrician Garment Dist., NYC, 1971; founder, designer Elie Tahari Co., NYC, 1973—; co-founder Theory LLC, NYC, 1997. Vol. New Yorkers for Children. Office: 11 W 42nd St New York NY 10036 Office Phone: 212-763-2000.*

TAHBAZ, CHRISTOPHER K., lawyer; BA cum laude, Columbia U., 1986, JD, 1990. Bar: NY 1991. Assoc. Donovan Leisure Newton & Irvine; mem. Debevoise & Plimpton LLP, NYC, 1994—, ptnr. litig. dept., mem. Mem.: ABA (mem. Litig. & Antitrust Sects.), NY Lawyers Pub. Interest, Inc. (chair, bd. dirs.), Internat. Bar Assn., Assn. Bar City NY. Office: Debevoise & Plimpton LLP 919 Third Ave New York NY 10022 Office Phone: 212-909-6543. E-mail: cktahbaz@debevoise.com.

TAHER, CECILIA, music educator; d. Hugo Alberto Taher and Maria Delia Giavedoni. MusB in Flute, U. Nat. del Litoral, Santa Fe, Argentina, 2001; MM in Flute Performance, U. Ark., Fayetteville, 2005; DMA in Flute Performance and Pedagogy, U. Iowa, Iowa City, 2006. Cert. in elem. music tchr. Santa Fe, 1998, in suzuki flute book 1 SAGWA Flute Inst., Alexandria, Va., 2008. Flute tchg. asst. U. Ark., Fayetteville, 2003—05, U. Iowa, 2006—. Flute instr. Liceo Mcpl. Jose Pedroni, Esperanza, Santa Fe, 2006, Liceo Mcpl. Santo Tome, Santo Tome, Santa Fe, 2006; pvt. flute lessons. Contbr. scientific papers. Recipient Artistic Merit award, Mozarteum Santa Fe, Argentina, 2000, 2002, Hon. Recital award, U. Ark. Sch. Music, 2004. Personal E-mail: ctaher@yahoo.es.

TAHERI, SAIED, engineering educator; b. Tehran, Iran, June 18, 1959; s. Mohammad and Nosrat Taheri; m. Homa Vanavi; children: Sina, Kasra, Sara. PhD, Clemson U., SC, 1990. Prin. engr. Goodyear Tire and Rubber Co., Akron, Ohio, 1998—2007; assoc. prof., dir. intelligent transp. Va. Poly. Inst. and State U., Blacksburg, 2007—. Grant, Dept. Def., 2007—. Mem.: Soc. Automotive Engrs. Achievements include research in bio inspired technology. Personal E-mail: saiedtaheri@gmail.com.

TAHIR, RABIA, pharmacist, educator; PharmD, St. John's U., Queens, 2005. Cert. practice resident Am. Soc. Health Sys. Pharmacists, 2006, NY State immunizer Am. Pharmacist Assn., 2005. Adj. prof. LI U., Bklyn., 2005—06; pharmacy practice resident Dept. Vets. Affairs, NYC, 2005—06; asst. clin. prof. St. John's U., 2006—08; adj. prof. Coll. Mt. St. Vincent, Bronx, NY, 2007; asst. prof. Touro Coll. Pharmacy, NYC, 2008—. Pharamcist Steinway Pharmacy, Queens, 2007—. Contbr. articles to profl. jours. Mem.: Pharmacy Leadership Soc., Am. Soc. Health Sys. Pharmacist, Am. Assn. Colls. Pharmacy, Am. Coll. Clin. Pharmacy, Phi Lambda Sigma Xi Chpt., Rho Chi Pharmacy Honor Soc. Office: Touro Coll Pharmacy 2090 Adam Clayton Powell Blvd 6th Fl New York NY 10027 Business E-Mail: rabia.tahir@touro.edu.

TAHIR-KHELI, RAZA A., physics professor; b. North West Frontier Province, Pakistan; m. Shirin R. Tahir-Kheli; children: Shehra J. Boldt, Kazim R. MA, U. Oxford, England, DPhil, 1962. Chmn. dept. physics, prof. Temple U., Phila., 1970—. Fellow: APS. Office: Temple Univ Dept Physics Philadelphia PA 19122 Office Phone: 215-204-7624. Personal E-mail: rtahirk@gmail.com. Business E-Mail: rtahirk@temple.edu.

TAHIR-KHELI, SHIRIN, federal official; BA, Ohio Wesleyan Univ.; MA, Univ. Pa., PhD in Internat. Rels. Mem. policy planning staff US State Dept., Washington, 1982—84; dir. political mil. affairs & dir. Near East & So. Asian affairs Nat. Security Council Staff, Washington, 1984—89; alt. US rep. for spl. political affairs UN, 1990—93; sr. fellow Ctr. Internat. Studies Princeton Univ., 1993—95; rsch. prof. & founding dir. So. Asia prog. Fgn. Policy Inst. Johns Hopkins Univ. Sch. Advanced Internat. Studies, Washington, 1995—2003; spl. asst. to the Pres. & sr. dir. for Democracy, Human Rights & Internat. Ops. Nat. Security Council, Washington, 2003—05; sr. adv. for UN reform, Office of the Sec. US State Dept., Washington, 2005—06, sr. adv. for women's empowerment, Office of the Sec., 2006—. Head US delegation UN Commn. on Human Rights, 2001; mem. US Commn. on Internat. Religious Freedom, Presdl. Commn. on Pub. Svc., 1992—93. Mem.: Council on Fgn. Rels. Office: US State Dept 2201 C St NW Washington DC 20520*

TAHMASSEBI, DARYOUSH, chemistry professor; b. Tehran, Iran, Mar. 21, 1965; PhD, Tarbiat Modarres U., Iran, 2007. Asst. prof. chemistry St. Francis Xavier U., Antigonish, Nova Scotia, Canada, 2000—01, Brandon U., Manitoba, 2001—05, Ind.-Purdue U. Ft. Wayne, 2005—. Postdoc. fellow U. Toronto, Ontario, Canada, 2008—09. Office: Ind-Purdue Univ Ft Wayne 2101 E Coliseum Blvd Fort Wayne IN 46805 Office Fax: 260-481-6070. Business E-Mail: tahmassd@ipfw.edu.

TAI, ELIZABETH SHI-JUE LEE, library director; b. Si-Ann, China, Aug. 12, 1942; arrived in U.S., 1965; d. Jun-Yee Lee and Fang-Yee Liu; m. Hsiang Tai, Dec. 29, 1969; children: Alan C., Victoria C., Brian C. BA in English Lang. and Lit., Nat. Cheng Kung U., Taiwan, 1965; M in Libr. and Info. Sci., Tex. Woman's U., 1967. Sr. libr. Queens (N.Y.) Borough Pub. Libr., 1967-73; asst. regional libr. Cin. Pub. Libr., Libr. for Blind and Physically Handicapped, 1973-75; libr. Ga. State Libr., Atlanta, 1975-78; dir. Poquoson (Va.) Pub. Libr., 1979—. Vol. ARC York County chpt., Va., 1980—; mem. York County Sch. Sys. Extend Program Coun., 1997; mem. Va. social svcs. bd. York County/City of Poquoson, 2002—; vice chmn. Peninsula Ret. Sr. Vol. Program Coun., Newport News, Va., 1994—99, chmn., 2000; bd. dirs. Peninsula Ret. Sr. Vol. Program, 2001—08, sec., 2002—05. Named City Employee of Yr., City of Poquoson, Va., 1989; recipient Letter of Commendation, Va. Gov. James Gilmore III, 2001, Unsung Hero/Heroine award Nat. Cheng Kung U. N.Am. Alumni and Found., 2003. Mem. ALA, Va. Libr. Assn., Va. Pub. Libr. Dirs. Assn. (region 3 rep. 2003-05, treas., 2004-08, Outstanding Pub. Rels. award 1998, 2001, 02, 04, 06, 07, Outstanding Facility award 1998, Outstanding Young Adult Program award 1999, Outstanding Children's Program award 1999, Outstanding Libr. Staff award 2003, Outstanding Va. Pub. Libr. Dir. award 2004), Va. Peninsula Chinese Am. Assn. (bd. mem. 2004—, pres. 2006-08), Tidewater Area Libr. Dirs. Coun.,Kiwanis Club (charter mem. Tabb chpt., chmn. youth program 2005—). Avocations: reading, gardening, swimming, tennis. Home: 129 Loblolly Dr Yorktown VA 23692-4254 Office: 500 City Hall Ave Poquoson VA 23662-1996 Office Phone: 757-868-3066. Business E-Mail: etai@poquoson-va.gov.

TAI, ROBERT H., science educator, researcher; s. Peter Yai-Po and Rosie P. Tai; m. Amy S. Lee, Jan. 15, 1967; children: Liana Grace, Miya Joy. BA in Math., 1986; BS in Physics, U. Fla., Gainesville, 1986; MS, U. Ill., Champaign, 1987; MEd, 1994; EdD, Harvard U. Grad. Sch. Edn., Cambridge, Mass., 1998. Physics tchr. Lyons Twp. H.S., Lagrange, Ill., 1990—92; physics tchr., curriculum specialist Wichita Falls Ind. Sch. Dist., Tex., 1992—93; asst. prof. Coll. Staten Island, CUNY, 1998—2001, U. Va., Charlottesville, 2001—07, assoc. prof., 2007—. Contbr. articles to profl. jours. Mem.: Am. Ednl. Rsch. Assn. Office: Univ Va 405 Emmet St S Charlottesville VA 22904

TAI, TSZE CHENG, aerodynamicist, researcher; b. Shaoxing, Chekiang, China, Apr. 29, 1933; arrived in U.S., 1963, naturalized, 1972; m. Shih Lin Sun, Aug. 27, 1965; children: Kuangheng, Kuangkai, Kuangshin. Diploma, Air Tech. Inst., Taiwan, Republic of China, 1957; MS, Clemson U., 1965; PhD, Va. Poly. Inst. and State U., 1968. Cert. in sr. civil svc. exam. 1960. Aircraft insp. Taoyuan Air Base, Taiwan, 1958—63; rsch. asst. Clemson U., 1963—65; grad. asst. Va. Poly. Inst. and State U., 1965—67, instr., 1967—68; sr. rsch. scientist Carderock divsn. Naval Surface Warfare Ctr., Bethesda, Md., 1968—2005. Chmn. panel US Navy Aero Ballistics Com., Washington, 1978—81; Lectr. von Karman Inst. Fluid Dynamics, Belgium, 1980. Prin. Potomac Chinese Sch., Md., 1981—82; sci. officer fluid mechanics Office Naval Resch., 1985—86. Recipient Eugene Brooks award, Naval Ship R&D CTR., 1979. Fellow: AIAA (assoc.); mem.: Sigma Xi (pres. David Taylor chpt. 1989—90). Achievements include obtained the world's first numerical solution to full inviscid transonic flow equations that detects the effect of entropy on the shock wave in 1970; research in aeodynamic development of US Navy's V-22 tilt-rotor aircraft in tail buffet alleviation, aerodynamic drag reduction, and fuel dumping. Personal E-mail: tszetai@yahoo.com.

TAI, WEON-PIL, materials scientist, researcher; b. Heongsung, Republic of Korea, Dec. 12, 1961; m. Kyong-Hee Heo, Jan. 12, 1991; children: Myung-Sik, Yi-Sik. BS, Kangwon Nat. U., 1985, PhD (hon.), 1993. Rschr. Nat. inst. Advanced Indsl. Sci. and Tech., Tosu, Japan, 1995—2000; prof. Inst. Advanced Materials, Inha U., Inchon, Republic of Korea, 2000—05; prin. rschr. Fine Chem. Industry Ctr., Ulsan Industry Promotion Techno Pk., Republic of Korea, 2005—. Referee Sensors & Actuators B, Jour., 2002—. With, 1995—97, Mil. Fellow, KOSEF, 1994. Achievements include research in dye-sensitized solar cell, chemical sensor, electronic ceramics, transparent conducting materials, nano paint, nano particles and materials organic/ inorganic composites. Home: 602 Hansung-Billa 1627-26 Shinjung-2 dong Nam-ku Ulsan 680-012 Republic of Korea Office: Fine Chem Industry Ctr Ulsan Industry Promotion Techno Pk 411 Daun-dong jung-gu Ulsan 681-340 Republic of Korea Home Phone: 82-52-274-3128; Office Phone: 82-52-219-8751. Personal E-mail: wptai1132@gmail.com. Business E-Mail: wptai@utp.or.kr.

TAIFI, MOHAMED, language educator, researcher; s. Moha Taifi and Hadda Oulamine; m. Khadija Bentouhami, June 1, 1974; children: Tarik, Adnane, Mehdi. PhD, U. Aix En Provence, France, 1986. Cert. tchr. Ecole Normale Superieure Rab, Maroc, 1972. Tchr. French Lycee Omar Ibn El Khattab, Meknes, Morocco, 1974—76; prof. Ctr. Pedagogique Regional, Meknes, 1976—77; rsch. dir. Sidi Mohammed U., Fes, 1986—93; faculty dean U. Mohammed Premier, Oujda, 1986—93; prof. Sidi Mohammed Ben Abdallah U., Fes, 1993—2002, Va. Mil. Inst., Lexington, 2002—. Mem. du conseil d'administration Biennale De La Langue Francaise, Paris, 1987—2008; pres., assn. des facultes et etablissements de lettres et scis. humaines Agence U. De La Francophonie, Paris, 1998—2005; pres. Assn. Mobilite Pour Tous, Fes, 2002—04; v.p. Assn. Cedre De Latlas, Azrou, 2004—08. Author: (novel) La Source Enragee, L' Appel de la Colline Chauve. Pres. Assn. Mobilite Pour Tous, Fes, 2002—04. Recipient Palmes Academiques de Paris, Republique Francaise, 2002, Disting. Tchr. award, Va. Mil. Inst., 2008; Rsch. grant, 2005, 2008. Mem.: Phi Kappa Phi (academic excellence award 2008). Avocations: reading, travel, soccer. Business E-Mail: taifim@vmi.edu.

TAI-SEALE, MING, science educator, consultant; d. Jianzhong Tai and Xiouhua Zhao; m. Thomas Scott Seale, July 23, 1988; children: Sahar Marguerite, Arin Minghua. MPH, Emory U., Atlanta, Ga., 1988; PhD, UCLA, 1995. Asst. prof. Tex. A&M Health Sci. Ctr., College Station, 2001—02, assoc. prof., 2002—09, prof., 2009—. Cons. to grant reviewers NIH, Bethesda, Md., 2001—, AHRQ. Recipient Mentored Scientist Career award, NIH, 2002—. Mem.: Health Economics Interest Group Acad. Health. (chair), Acad. Health Orgn. (Article Yr. award 2008), Am. Soc. Health Economists, Internat. Health Econs. Assn., Acad. Health (mem. adv. bd. health econs. interest group 2005—). Office: Taxes A&M Health Sci Ctr TAMU 1266 College Station TX 77843

TAIT, JOHN REID, lawyer; b. Toledo, Apr. 7, 1946; s. Paul Reid and Lucy Richardson (Rudderow) T.; m. Christina Ruth Bjornstad, Mar. 12, 1972; children: Gretchen, Mary. BA, Columbia U., 1968; JD, Vanderbilt U., 1974. Bar: Idaho 1974, US Dist. Ct. Idaho 1974, US Ct. Appeals (9th cir.) US Supreme Ct., Nez Perce Tribal Ct., Coeur d'Alene Tribal Ct. Assoc. Keeton & Tait, Lewiston, Idaho, 1974-76, ptnr., 1976-86, 89—, Keeton, Tait & Petrie, Lewiston, 1986-88. Chmn. bd. No. Rockies Action Group, Helena, Mont., 1985-86, bd. dirs., 1981-88; active Lewiston Hist. Preservation Commn., 1975-94, chmn., 1988-94; bd. dirs. Idaho Legal Aid Svcs., Boise, 1975-99, Idaho Housing Agy., Boise, 1984-91, St. Joseph Regional Med. Ctr. Found., Inc., 1989-94, Lewiston Ind. Found. for Edn., Inc., 1996—; Dem. precinct committeeman, 1976-86, state committeeman, 1977-94, 2000-08; del. Dem. Nat. Conv., 1980, 84; regional coord. Idaho State Dem. Party, 1996-99; treas. Larry LaRocco for Congress, 1990, 92. With U.S. Army, 1968-71. Counter-intelligence spl. agent US Army, 1968—71. Recipient Pro Bono Svc. award Idaho State Bar, 1988, Cmty. Recognition award Lewiston Intergovtl. Coun., 1992, Spl. Recognition award Idaho Legal Aid Svcs., 1993. Mem. ABA, Am. Assn. Justice, Idaho Trial Lawyers Assn. (regional dir. 1976-77, 86-88, 97-03), Idaho State Bar (worker's compensation sect. 2002—, chmn. 2004-06), Clearwater Bar Assn. (sec. 1974-76, pres. 1984-86), Consumer Attys. Calif., Workers Injury Law and Litig. Group (bd. dirs. 2002-), Idaho Pre Bench Commn. Office: Keeton & Tait PO Drawer E 312 Miller St Lewiston ID 83501-1944 Office Phone: 208-743-6231. Office Fax: 208-746-0962. Business E-Mail: lewlawus@lewiston.com.

TAIT, PATRICIA ANN, secondary school educator; b. Sacramento, Calif., Nov. 26, 1942; d. Frank Scott and Anna Mae (Chubbey) Smith; m. Arthur Fitzwilliam Tait, Jr., Dec. 27, 1968; children: Arthur Fitzwilliam III, Lauryn Kristine. BS in Edn., Tex. Western Coll., 1965; BA in English, U. Tex., El Paso, 1966, MA in English, 1974. Cert. secondary educator, English, ESOL, Fla., Tex. Tchr. English Cheyenne Mountain High Sch., Colorado Springs, 1966-69; tchr. English, dept. chairperson Christ the King Internat. Sch., Okinawa, Japan, 1970-71; pres. Accurate Secretarial and Typing Svc., 1971—; tchr. English Forest High Sch., Ocala, Fla., 1979—, co-chair Eng. dept., 1990—2000. Cons. Fla. Writing Project, Gainesville, 1984—; presenter Marion County Tchrs. English, Ocala, 1985—. Author: Joseph Conrad: The Development of Character in the Jungle, 1974. Named Master Tchr., State of Fla., 1983-84, 84-85. Mem. NEA, AFT, Nat. Coun. Tchrs. English, Fla. Coun. Tchrs. English, Marion County Tchrs. English, Marion County Edn. Assn., Fla. Tchrs. Profl. Edn. Assn. Democrat. Episcopalian. Avocation: equine activities. Home: 5109 SE 4th St Ocala FL 34471-3304 Address: 5000 SE Maricamp Rd Ocala FL 34480 Office: Forest High School 5000 SE Maricamp Rd Ocala FL 34480-7422 Home Phone: 352-694-7651; Office Phone: 352-671-4700. E-mail: pattait1@aol.com.

TAIT, ROBERT E., lawyer; b. Lima, Ohio, Sept. 3, 1946; s. Robert and Helen (Smith) T.; m. Donna G. Dome, June 22, 1968; children: Heather, Jennifer, Robert. BA, Kenyon Coll., Gambier, Ohio, 1968; JD, U. Mich., Ann Arbor, 1973. Bar: Ohio 1973, US Dist. Ct. (so. dist.) Ohio. 1976, US Dist. Ct. (no. dist.) Ohio 1976, US Dist. Ct. Md. 1980, US Ct. Appeals (6th cir.) 1981, US Supreme Ct. 1982. Ptnr. Vorys, Sater, Seymour & Pease, LLP, Columbus, Ohio, 1973—. Staff counsel Govs. Select Com. on Prevention Indsl. Accidents, Columbus, 1977-78. Served with US Army, 1969-70. Fellow Ohio Bar Found., Columbus Bar Found.; mem. ABA (litigation sect., products liability com.), Ohio Bar Assn. (worker's compensation com.), Columbus Bar Assn. (workers compensation and professionalism coms.), Def. Rsch. Inst. (bd. dirs., 2008-), Am. Bd. Trial Advocates, Assn. Def. Trial Attys. (exec. com. 1991-94, treas., 2002-07, v.p. 2007-08, pres. elect, 2008-09, pres., 2009), Dept. Energy and Contractors Attys. Assn., Fedn. Def. and Corp. Counsel (toxic torts com). Home: 2045 Wickford Rd Columbus OH 43221-4223 Office: Vorys Sater Seymour & Pease PO Box 1008 52 E Gay St Columbus OH 43215-3161 Home Phone: 614-488-4003; Office Phone: 614-464-6341. Business E-Mail: retait@vssp.com.

TAITT, EARL PAUL, psychiatrist, military officer; b. LA, Nov. 6, 1956; s. Earl and Mary (Freitas) T.; m. Puruca Estepa, May 11, 1985; children: Anamaria, Earl. AA, East L.A. Coll., 1976; BS, U. Calif., Irvine, 1978; MD, Northwestern U., Chgo., 1984. Commd. capt. U.S. Army, 1984, advanced through grades to maj., 1991; intern in psychiatry Tripler Army Med. Ctr., Honolulu, 1984-85; resident in psychiatry Eisenhower Army Med. Ctr., Ft. Gordon, Ga., 1985-88; staff psychiatrist Community Mental Health Ctr., Ft. Gordon, Ga., 1988; div. psychiatrist, chief mental health 10th Mountain Div., Ft. Drum, N.Y., 1988-90; staff psychiatrist Community Mental Health Ctr., Ft. Meade, Md., 1990—; chief resident in psychiatry U.S. Army Hosp., Ft. Gordon, Ga., 1988. Cons. Army Drug and Alcohol Program, Ft. Drum, 1988-90, Installation Detention Facility, Ft. Meade, 1990—. Mem. San Gabriel (Calif.) Mission Parish Coun., 1975-76; pres. Medicai Soc., L.A., 1976. Mem. Assn. U.S. Army, Order of Green Key. Republican. Roman Catholic. Home: 14403 Altamaha Ct Orlando FL 32837-5425 Office Phone: 407-856-8830.

TAKABE, KAZUAKI, surgeon, research scientist; b. Nishinomiya City, Hyogo, Japan, Aug. 12, 1966; s. Tokuji and Ayako T. MD, Niigata U., 1992; PhD, Yokohama City U., 1999. Rsch. trainee dept. legal medicine Niigata (Japan) U. Sch. of Medicine, 1992-93; surg. resident Niigata U. Hosp., 1993-94, Akita (Japan) Red Cross Hosp., 1994-95; surg. fellow Yokohama (Japan) U. Hosp., 1995-97; rsch. assoc. The Salk Inst., PBL, La Jolla, Calif., 1997—, Prof., chmn. gene diagnosis and therapy Internet Med. Coll., 2000—; com. mem. Soc. of Rsch. Fellows The Salk Inst., 1999—. Contbr. articles to profl. jours. Yoshida scholarship found. fellowship, 1997-2000. Mem. The Endocrine Soc., Internat. Liver Transplantation Soc., Internat. Assn. of Surgeons and Gastroenterologists, Japan Surg. Soc., Japanese Soc. of Gastroenterology, Japan Hepatology Soc. Office: Surg Onc Virginia Commonwealth Univ 1200 E Broad St WH7-402 PO Box 980011 Richmond VA 23298-0011

TAKAHASHI, TOKU, education educator, researcher; b. Godo, Gifu prefecture, Japan, June 20, 1950; s. Ikuyo Takahashi; m. Junko Narisada, Apr. 8, 1978; children: Ryota, Kota, Tomoko. PhD, Kobe U., Japan, 1985, MD, 1997. Cert. Physician Japanese Govt., 1977. Asst. rsch. scientist U. of Mich., Ann Arbor, 1996—2000; assoc. prof. Duke U., Durham, NC, 2000—. Grantee RO1, NIH NIDDK sect., 1999—. Office: Duke Univ Box 3479 Durham NC 27710 E-mail: ttakahas@duke.edu.

TAKAHASHI, YORIKO, psychology professor; m. Masaharu Takahashi; 1 child, Mariko. BA, Kyoto U., 1969, MA, 1971; PhD, Kyoto U., Japan, 1974. Assoc. prof., prof. Saga Art Coll., Kyoto, 1974—97; dean Koshien U., Takarazuka, Hyogo, Japan, 1997—. Author: (book) Rorschach Diagnosis, Tree Drawing Test, Introduction to Clinical Psychology. Mem.: Japanese Soc. Rorschach and Projective Methods, Japanese Assn. Clin. Drawings (pres.), Assn. Japanese Clin. Psychology. Home: 3-12-604 Maruhashi-cho Nishinomiya 662-0831 Japan Office: Koshien University 10-1 Momijigaoka Takarazuka 665-0006 Japan Office Phone: 81-797-87-8360. Office Fax: 81-797-87-8444.

TAKANIKOS-QUIÑONES, JOHN NICHOLAS, history professor; b. Sacramento, May 10, 1945; m. Barbara Ingersoll Takanikos; children: Alexandra Sophia Greenlee, Sonia Nicole Takanikos-Erickson, John Christopher Takanikos. PhD, U. Calif., Davis, 1971. Prof. history Sacramento City Coll., 1969—. Contbr. articles to profl. jour. Mem.: Phi Beta Kappa. Democrat. Avocations: music, travel. Office: Sacramento City Coll 3835 Freeport Blvd Sacramento CA 95822

TAKASU, YUKIO, ambassador; Grad. in law, U. Tokyo; grad., Oxford U. Merton Coll., Eng. Joined diplomatic svc. Ministry Fgn. Affairs, Japan, 1969, overseas posts London, Kuala Lumpur, Malaysia, NYC, Jakarta, Indonesia, Vienna, Washington, first sec. and counsellor, Japanese Mission to the UN NYC, 1981—88, dir., We. Europe divsn. Tokyo, 1989—92, dep. chief of mission Indonesia, 1992—93, amb. to the UN NYC, 1997—2000, dir. gen. multilateral cooperation dept. Tokyo, 2000—01, amb. to internat. orgns. Vienna, 2001—05, amb. human security, sci. and tech. cooperation and spl. envoy for UN reform, 2005—07, amb., perm. rep. to the UN NYC, 2007—; asst. sec. gen., contr. UN, NYC, 1993—97. Past pres. IAEA Gen. Conf.; vis. fellow Harvard U., Cambridge, Mass., 2006—07. Office: Perm Mission Japan to the UN 866 United Nations Plz 2d Fl New York NY 10017 Office Phone: 212-223-4300. Business E-Mail: mission@un-japan.org.*

TAKEI, HIDEKI, business educator; b. Yoriimachi, Saitama, Japan, Mar. 24, 1973; s. Tsuneo and Yuriko Takei; m. Helena Pavelkova, June 2, 2007. BA in Economics, Josai U., Saitama, 1995; MBA, Southern NH U., Manchester, 1998, MS in Internat. Bus., 2001, PhD in Bus. Adminstrn., 2004. Cert. retail sales specialist Japan C. of C. and Industry, 1994. Rschr. Tokyo Survey Rsch. Inc., 1998—99; adj. lectr. internat. bus. Southern NH U., 2000—04; dir., Ctr. Advanced Bus. Studies City U. Seattle, Vysoka Skola Manazmentu, Trencin, Slovakia, 2004—07, lectr. bus., 2004—05, sr. lectr. bus., 2005—07, dept. chair mktg. and communication, 2006—07; asst. prof. internat. bus. Juniata Coll., Huntingdon, Pa., 2007—09, Ctrl. Washington U., Ellenburg, Wash., 2009—. Localization advisor PUMATECH, Nashua, NH, 1999—2000; cons. SECTRA Inc., Lebanon, NH, 2003—04. Mem.: Mktg. Educators' Assn. Home: 833 Sakurazawa Yoriimachi Oosatogun Saitama 369-1202 Japan Office: Ctrl Washington Univ ITAM Dept 400 E University Way Ellensburg WA 98926 Personal E-mail: hidekitakei@hotmail.com. Business E-Mail: takei@juniata.edu.

TAKEMOTO, STEVEN KAN, medical educator; b. Pasadena, Calif., Mar. 2, 1956; m. Juna Beck. BS, UCLA, 1979; PhD, Toho U., Tokyo, 1995. Program analyst, tissue typing lab. UCLA, 1984—95, assoc. prof. dept. pathology, 2001—04; assoc. prof. dept. medicine St. Louis U.; assoc. prof. dept. orthop. surgery U. Calif., San Francisco, 2008—. Contbr. articles to profl. publs. Mem.: Am. Soc. Histocompatibility and Immunogenetics (com. mem. 1999—2004), Am. Soc. Transplantation (com. chmn. 1999—2001). Office: Univ Calif San Francisco 500 Parnassus Ave MU320W San Francisco CA 94143-0728 Office Fax: 415-476-1304. Business E-Mail: takemotos@orthosurg.ucsf.edu.

TAKENAKA, TOICHI, pharmaceutical executive; PhD. Former pres., CEO Yamanouchi Pharmaceutical Co.; pres., CEO Astellas Pharma Inc. (merger of Yamanouchi Pharmaceutical and Fujisawa Pharmaceutical), 2005, rep. dirs., chmn. Office: Astellas Pharma Inc 3-11 Nihonbashi-Honcho 2-chome Tokyo 103-8411 Japan*

TAKESHITA, OSCAR YASSUO, engineering educator; b. Sao Paulo, Oct. 28, 1966; PhD in Elec. Engring., U. Tokyo, 1997. Postdoctoral rsch. assoc. U. Notre Dame, Ind., 1997-99; asst. prof. Ohio State U., Columbus, 1999—. Mombusho scholar Ministry of Edn. of Japan, 1991-97; grantee Ind. Space Grant Consortium, 1998, Ohio State U., 1999. Mem. IEEE Info. Theory Soc., IEEE Comms. Soc. Office: Ohio State U 2015 Neil Ave Columbus OH 43210-1210 Fax: (614) 292-7596.

TAKEYAMA, AKIKO, anthropologist, educator; m. William Bond Steele. PhD, U. Ill., Urbana-Champaign, 2007. Grad. tchg. fellow U. Ill., 2006; asst. prof. U. Kans., Lawrence, 2007—. Contbr. articles to profl. jour. Student fellowship, Freeman Found., 2002, Doc. fellowship, Japan Found., 2004—05, Spl. Rsch. fellowship, Sch. Humanities and Sociologies, U. Tokyo, 2004—05, Ethnographic Rsch. Tng. grant, NSF, 2004, George L. Beslow Grad. fellowship, U. Ill., 2007, Dissertation Workshop fellowship, Asian Inst., U. Toronto, 2007. Mem.: Soc. East Asian Anthropology, Soc. Cultural Anthropology, Assn. Feminist Anthropology, Assn. Asian Studies, Am. Ethnol. Soc., Am. Anthrop. Assn. Office: Univ Kans 1415 Jayhawk Blvd 614 Fraser Hall Lawrence KS 66045 Business E-Mail: takeyama@ku.edu.

TAKHAR, PAWAN S., food and biological engineer; PhD, Purdue U., West Lafayette, Ind., 2001. Asst. prof. U. Idaho, Lubbock, Tex., 2002—05, Tex. Tech U., Lubbock, 2005—. Design engr. Patkol Pub. Co., Bangkok, 1996—97. Business E-Mail: pawan.takhar@ttu.edu.

TAKIZAWA, HIDEAKI, gastroenterologist; b. Saitama, Japan, July 17, 1960; s. Eiichi and Youko Takizawa; m. Kyoko Kimura, Nov. 10, 1991; children: Hiroki, Naoki. MD, Niigata U., Japan, 1985, DPhil, 1992. Resident Niigata U. Hosp., 1985, physician, 1988-90; rsch. fellow gastroenterology Niigata U., 1986-87; physician Kouseiren Murakami Hosp., Murakami, Japan, 1991; asst. chief gastroenterology Nagaoka Red Cross Hosp., Japan, 1992-96; chief gastroenterology Kido Hosp., Niigata, 1997-2000; dir. Endo Clinic, Niigata, 2001—. Author: Digestion, 1995; contbr. articles to profl. jours. Mem. Japanese Soc. Gastroenterology, Japanese Soc. Internal Medicine, Japan Gastroenterol. Endoscopy Soc. Office: Endo Clinic 1-4-11 Minami-Sasaguchi Niigata 950-0912 Japan

TAKIZAWA, YUKIO, medical ecologist; b. Shiojiri, Nagano, Japan, Dec. 8, 1932; s. Masaru and Tamae Takizawa; m. Tomiko Ogata, May 5, 1958; children: Eri, Hirotsugu. BA, Shinshu U., 1953; BM, Niigata U., Japan, 1957; MD, Niigata U., 1962. Diplomate Japan, 1958, Specialist in Occupational Health Supr. Occupational Health, 1993. Intern Niigata U. Hosp., 1958; assoc. prof. Niigata U. Sch. Medicine, Japan, 1964—73; prof. Akita U. Sch. Medicine, Japan, 1973—95, emeritus prof., 1995. Vis. prof. Kamazawa (Japan) U. Low-level Radioactivity Lab, 1958—62; dir. Environ. Rsch. Ctr. Akita U., 1977—95, Nat. Inst. Minimata Disease, Japan, 1995—2001; expert advisor Nuclear Safety Commn. Prime Minister's Office, Tokyo, 1979—2001; mem. food sanitation investigation coun. Ministry Health and Welfare, Tokyo, 1982—88; bd. dirs. Environ. Rev. Adv. Coun. Ministry Internat. Trade & Industry, Tokyo, 1983—; mem. UN Environ. Programme Environ. Effect Panel, Nairobi, Kenya, 1987—; mem. steering com. Kyoto U. Rsch. Reactor Inst., Kumatori, Osaka, Japan, 1992—94; trustee Akita U., 1993—95; advisor Nat. Inst. Minamata Disease, Minamata, Japan, 2001—, Nat. Inst. Radiological Scis., Chiba, Japan, 2001—06. Author: (Book) Mercury and the Environment, 1974, Environmental Effects of Ozone Depletion: UNEP 1998 Assessment, 1998; editor: Metylmercury Poisoning in Minamata and Niigata, Japan, 2001. Dir.-gen. Nat. Inst. for Minimata Disease, Minimata, Japan, 1995—2001; adv. Nat. Inst. for Minamata Disease, 2001—; dep. mayor Minamata City, Japan, 2003—06. Recipient Niigata Civic honor, Niigata City Prefecture, 1968, Mutsu Mcpl. honor, Mutsu City, Aomori Prefecture, 1985, 1994, Dir.-gen. prize, Sci. and Tech. Agy. Japanese Govt., 1986, Appreciation award, UN Environ. Protection Agy., 1988, Air Pollution prize, Japan Soc. Atmospheric Environ., 1991, Disting. Svc. award, Brewers' and Distillers' Assn. Japan, 1998; grantee, Asahi Press (Shinbun), Tokyo, 1970. Avocations: collecting paintings, calligraphy. Home: 34-9 Nakadai 2 Chome Itabashi Tokyo 174-0064 Japan Office Fax: 0966-63-6958. Business E-Mail: takizawa-y@sky.plala.or.jp.

TAKKE, KARYN COPPOCK, social worker, educator; b. Sacramento, June 13, 1961; d. Arthur Clifton Coppock and June Marie Betz; m. Vince Takke, Sept. 15, 1991; children: Jake Taylor, Kyle Hunter, Chad Brigham, Joshua Spencer. BS in Social Work, Brigham Young U., 1982; MSW, U. Tex., Austin, 1989. LCSW Utah. Dir. The Adoption Ctr., Orem, Utah, 2001—; med. social worker Intermountain Health Care-Home Care, Orem, 2002—05; pediat. continuum care mgr. Primary Children's Med. Ctr., Salt Lake City, 2005—. Adj. faculty Brigham Young U., Provo, Utah, 2003—, Utah Valley State Coll., Orem, 2003—. Mem., tchr. The Relief Soc., 1979—; vol. Sun Porch Group Home, Palo Alto, Calif., 1983—86; Sunday sch. tchr. LDS Ch., Utah, Calif., 1990—; bd. dirs. LDS Family Svcs., Fresno, Calif., 1999. Republican. Avocations: reading, gardening, needlework, baking. Office: Utah Valley State Coll Behavioral Sci Dept 800W University Pky #MC Orem UT 84058 Office Phone: 801-718-4375. Fax: 801-302-7301. E-mail: karyn.takke@intermountainmail.org.

TAKOOSHIAN, HAROLD, social psychology educator; b. NYC, Nov. 21, 1949; s. Alfred C. and Dorothy H. T. BA, CCNY, 1971; PhD in Social Psychology, CUNY, 1979. Lic. psychologist, N.Y. Prof. div. social scis. Fordham U., NYC, 1975—, dir., orgnl. leadership program, 2003—. Vis. prof. U. Talca, Chile, 1983, U. Atacama, Copiapo, Chile, 1984, 85; U.S. Fulbright scholar USSR, 1987-88; cons. projects for indsl. and govtl. orgn., 1979—. Editor: Bull. and Directory of Armenian Behavioral Scientists, 1988—, Feminism Survey, 1990—; (with W.M. Verdi) Short-Form Scale of Attitudes toward Terrorism, 1989, (with T.D. Guzewicz) Public Attitudes toward Homeless, 1991. Nat. bd. dirs. Alliance Guardian Angels, 1982-. Recipient Apple Polisher award WOR-TV, N.Y.C., 1981, Denmark Faculty Adv. award Psi Chi, 1988, Kurt Lewin award N.Y. State Psychol. Assn., 1990. Fellow APA, Soc. Psychol. Study Social Issues (chmn. N.Y.C. regional group 1991—), Soc. Tchg. Psychology; Am. Psychol. Assn. (pres., divsn. 52, internat. psychology 2003, pres., divsn. 1, gen. psychology 2006-07), Psi Chi (v.p. ea. region 1993-97, pres. 1998-99), Psi Beta (hon.) (Wolman award, 2006). Developer standardized scales, use of field experiment to study social issues. Office: Fordham Univ Div Social Sci New York NY 10023 Office Phone: 212-636-6393. Business E-Mail: takoosh@aol.com.

TAKUMI, ROY MITSUO, state legislator; b. Honolulu, Oct. 13, 1952; m. Wanda A. Kutaka; children: Aisha, Jaron. BA, Friends World Coll., 1991; MPA, U. Hawaii, 1993. Laborer Pearl Harbor Naval Shipyard; cmty. organizer Osaka, Japan, 1977-83; tchr. ESL; program dir. Am. Friends Svc. Com., Honolulu, 1984-90; polit. dir. Hawaii State AFL-CIO, Honolulu, 1990-92, comms. dir., 1992—; mem. Dist. 36 Hawaii House of Reps., Honolulu, 1992—. Precinct pres. Dem. Party; del. Dem. Party State Conv. Democrat. Office: Hawaii State Capitol 415 South Beretania St Rm 444 Honolulu HI 96813 Office Phone: 808-586-6170. Business E-Mail: reptakumi@capitol.hawaii.gov.

TALAG, TRINIDAD SANTOS, retired educator; b. Manila, Philippines, June 12, 1932; came to the U.S., 1954; d. Telesforo and Felisa A. Santos Talag. BS in Edn., U. Philippines, Quezon City, 1953; BS in Physical Edn., U. Oreg., 1955, MS in Physical Edn., 1956; PhD, U. Md., 1972. Instr. Centro Escolar U., Manila, Philippines, 1957-60; asst. prof. Northeastern U., Boston, 1962-66, Slippery Rock State Coll., Pa., 1966—73; assoc. prof. Elizabeth City State U., NC, 1989—90, prof., 1990—97; ret. NIH rsch. fellow, 1976-78. Mem. Bus. Profl. Women's Club, Am. Coll. Sports Medicine, Am. Alliance for Health, Phys. Edn., Recreation and Dance. Avocations: reading, theater. Home: 4632 Broad St Virginia Beach VA 23462

TALAGA, STEPHEN C., pianist, composer, music educator; b. Bay City, Mich., Apr. 30, 1962; s. Stephen E. and JoAnne E. Talaga; m. Jean A. St.Laurent, June 29, 1985; children: Lauren M., Stephen L. MusM, Western Mich. U., Kalamazoo, 1993. Radio prodr. CMU Pub. Radio, Mt. Pleasant, Mich., 1989; adj. prof. music Aquinas Coll., Grand Rapids, Mich., 1992—, Hope Coll., Holland, Mich., 1998—. Composer songs. Recipient DB award, Downbeat Mag., 1992. Mem.: Am. Fedn. Musicians, Phi Kappa Phi.

TALALAY, PAUL, pharmacologist, educator; b. Berlin, Mar. 31, 1923; arrived in U.S., 1940, naturalized, 1946; s. Joseph Anton and Sophie (Brosterman) Talalay; m. Pamela Judith Samuels, Jan. 11, 1953; children: Antony, Susan, Rachel, Sarah. SB, MIT, 1944; student, U. Chgo. Sch. Medicine, 1944—46; MD, Yale U., 1948; DSc (hon.), Acadia U., 1974. House officer, asst. resident surg. services Mass. Gen. Hosp., Boston, 1948—50; asst. prof. surgery U. Chgo., 1950—51, asst. prof. biochemistry, 1955—57, assoc. prof., then prof., 1957—63; asst. prof. Ben May Lab. Cancer Research, 1951—57, assoc. prof., then prof., 1957—63; John Jacob Abel prof., dir. dept., pharmacology and exptl. therapeutics Johns Hopkins Sch. Medicine, 1963—75, John Jacob Abel Distinguished Service prof., 1975—, Am. Cancer Soc. prof., 1958—63, 1977—. Sr. asst. surgeon USPHS, 1951—53; vis. prof. Guy's Hosp. Med. Sch., London, 1970, London, 1974—76; nat. adv. cancer coun. USPHS, 1967—71; vis. com. dept. biology MIT, 1964—67; bd. sci. advisers Jane Coffin Childs Meml. Fund for Cancer Rsch., 1971—80; bd. sci. consultants Sloan-Kettering Inst. Cancer Rsch., 1971—81. Hon. editl. adv. bd. Biochem. Pharmacology, 1963—68, editl. bd. Jour. Biol. Chemistry, 1961—66, Molecular Pharmacology, 1965—68, 1971—80, editor-in-chief, 1968—71. Recipient Premio Internationale la Madonnina Milan, 1978, Med. Alumni Disting. Svc. award, U. Chgo., 1978; fellow Guggenheim Meml., 1973—74; scholar Am. Cancer Soc., 1954—58. Fellow: Am. Acad. Arts and Scis.; mem.: NAS, AAAS (Theobald Smith award med. scis. 1957), Am. Soc. Pharm. and Exptl. Therpeutics, Am. Chem. Soc., Biochem. Soc., Am. Soc. Clin. Investigation, Am. Soc. Biochem. Molecular Biology, Am. Philos. Soc., Alpha Omega Alpha, Sigma Xi, Phi Beta Kappa. Home: 5512 Boxhill Ln Baltimore MD 21210-2039 Office: Johns Hopkins U Sch Medicine 725 N Wolfe St Baltimore MD 21205 Office Phone: 410-955-3499. Fax: 410-502-6818. Business E-Mail: ptalalay@jhmi.edu.

TALAMINI, MARK A., surgeon, department chairman; BA in Natural Sciences, Johns Hopkins U., 1978; MD, Johns Hopkins U. Sch. Medicine, 1981. Lic. Md., 1987, Calif., 2005, cert. Am. Bd. Surgery, 1988, Critical Care Bd., 1990. Intern Johns Hopkins Hosp., 1981—82, jr. asst. resident, 1982—83, sr. asst. resident, 1983—86, chief resident, 1986—87, asst. chief svc., 1987—88, dir. minimally invasive surgery, 1992—2004, dir. nutrition support svc., 1995—2005; fellow in surgical nutrition U. Cin. Sch. Medicine, 1984—85; instr. dept. surgery Johns Hopkins U. Sch. Medicine, 1987—88, asst. prof. dept. surgery, 1988—95, assoc. prof. dept. surgery, 1995—2001, prof. dept. surgery, 2001—05; prof. & chmn. dept. surgery U. Calif. Sch. Medicine, San Diego, 2005—; surgeon-in-chief U. Calif. Med. Ctr., 2005—. Editorial bd. mem. Surgical Laparoscopy & Endoscopy, 1990—, INSIGHTS, 1991—94, Jour. Gastrointestinal Surgery, 2003—; co-editor Jour. Laparoscopy, 1991—93; editor-in-chief Jour. Laparoendoscopic & Advanced Surgical Techniques, 2002—. Fellow: Am. Surgical Assn., Am. Coll. Surgeons; mem.: Western Surgical Assn., San Diego County Med. Soc., Baltimore Acad. Surgery, Southern Surgical Assn., Soc. U. Surgeons, Soc. Am. Gastrointestinal Endoscopic Surgeons, Soc. for Surgery of Alimentary Tract, Soc. for Laparoendoscopic Surgeons, Am. Soc. Clinical Nutrition, Assn. for Academic Surgery, Am. Soc. Parenteral & Enteral Nutrition, Halsted Soc., Crohn's & Colitis Found. Office: UCSD Medical Center Dept of Surgery 200 W Arbor Dr #8400 San Diego CA 92103-8400 Office Phone: 619-543-6453. Office Fax: 619-543-3763. E-mail: talamini@ucsd.edu.*

TALAMO, JONATHAN HASKELL, ophthalmologist, educator; b. Boston, Sept. 25, 1960; Student, Cornell U., Ithaca, NY, 1978-80; AB, Johns Hopkins U., Balt., Md., 1982, MD, 1986. Diplomate Am. Bd. Ophthalmology. Intern in medicine Children's Hosp. San Francisco-U. Calif., 1986—87; resident in ophthalmology Wilmer Ophthal. Inst., Johns Hopkins Hosp., Balt., 1987—90; clin. fellow ophthalmology, cornea and external disease Mass. Eye and Ear Infirmary-Harvard U. Med. Sch., Boston, 1990—91, asst. surgeon, 1992—95, sr. surgeon, 1995—, dir. gen. eye and cataract consultation svc., 1992—94, dir. keratorefractive surgery unit, 1992—95, acting dir. cornea svc., 1994—95, dir. cornea and external disease fellowship program, 1994—95; pvt. practice Providence, 1991—92, Boston, 1995—. Rsch. fellow in ophthalmology Harvard U. Med. Sch., 1984-85, clin. fellow in ophthalmology, 1990-91, instr. ophthalmology, 1992-94, asst. prof., 1994-95, asst. clin. prof., 1995-2005, assoc. clin. prof., 2005—; clin. fellow in ophthalmology Johns Hopkins U. Med. Sch., 1987-90; asst. clin. prof. dept. surgery Brown U. Sch. Medicine, Providence, 1991-93; attending surgeon Miriam Hosp., Providence, 1991-93, R.I. Hosp., Providence, 1991-93; med. adv. bd. Intralase Corp., 2003—. Author: The Excimer Manual: A Clincians Guide to Excimer Laser Surgery,1996; asst. editor jour. Refractive Surgery, 1994-99; mem. editl. bd. Ophthalmology Times, 1995—; contbr. 70 articles to profl. jours., chpts. to books. Tng. grantee USPHS, 1984, travel grantee Assn. for Rsch. in Vision and Ophthalmology, 1985, N.E. Corneal Transplant Rsch. Fund, 1993-94, Coherent Med., Inc., 1994-95; fellow Fight for Sight, 1985, Heed Ophthalmic Found., 1990. Mem. Am. Acad. Ophthalmology (Honor award 1998), Internat. Soc. Refractive Surgery (bd. dirs. 1995-2001), Am. Soc. Cataract and Refractive Surgery, Soc. Heed Fellows, New Eng. Ophthal. Soc., Mass. Soc. Eye Physiciand and Surgeons. Home Phone: 617-899-7233; Office Phone: 781-890-1023.

TALANO, JULIE M., medical educator; d. James and Joan Talano; m. Mattthew Regan, June 10, 1995; children: Natalie Regan, Elizabeth Regan, William Regan. BS, Georgetown U., Washington, 1991; MD, Ill., 1995. Asst. prof. pediat. Med. Coll. Wis., Milw., 2004—. Bd. mem. Children's Oncology Group, Chgo., 2006—07. Mem.: Am. Soc. Hematology. Achievements include research in pediatric bone marrow transplantation. Office: Med Coll Wis 8701 Watertown Plank Rd Milwaukee WI 53226

TALANOW, ROLAND, radiologist; s. Wilhelm Talanow and Irena Lozynska; m. Martina Paetzel. MD, Martin-Luther U. Halle Wittenberg, Germany, 2001, PhD, 2002; MD, USMLE, 2003. Lic. ECFMG, 2003. Editor-in-chief Jour. Radiology Case Reports. Author: (book) USMLE Help Step 2 CK, USMLE Help Step 2 CS, USMLE Help Step 3 CCS, 2007, USMLE Help Step 1 Q & A Biochemistry; contbr. articles to profl. jours. (RSNA and ECR award, 2006). Mem. bd. EduRad, Cleveland Heights, Ohio, 2006—; bd. mem. Assn. U. Radiologists, Oak Brook, Ill., 2008—. With German Army, 1990—91. Recipient Best Presentation award, Internat. Soc. Radiology, 2008. Mem.: AMA, SIIM, AUR, ACR, Am. Roentgen Ray Soc. (Ednl. grant 2008, Sci. Exhibit award 2006—08), ESR, Radiol. Soc. N.Am. (Merit award 2005, 2008). Achievements include invention of staging program for common female pelvic cancers; development of virtual anatomy; discovery of regulation of endothelin shearstress system; research in acute pulmonary embolism. Office: Cleve Clinic 9500 Euclid Ave Cleveland OH 44195

TALAPATRA, INDRAJIT, endocrinologist; b. Calcutta, West Bengal, India, Sept. 13, 1963; s. Debabrata and Shibani Talapatra; m. Sharmila Talapatra; 1 child, Avraneel. MBBS, U. Calcutta, India, 1988, diploma in Tropical Medicine and Hygiene, 1991, MD, 1995; postgraduate in Medicine, Royal Coll., UK, 2001. Med. practitioner various hosp., Calcutta, 1988—98; physician St. Mary's Hosp., Newport, Isle of Wight, England, 1999—2001; physician elderly medicine Countess Chester Hosp., Merseyside, England, 2001—02; physician endocrinology and diabetes Royal Albert Edward Infirmary, Wigan, Lancashire, England, 2002—. Contbr. articles to profl. jours. Mem.: RCP, European Congress Endocrinology, Glasgow Royal Coll. Physicians and Surgeons. Hindu. Avocations: chess, stamp collecting/philately, reading. Office: Royal Albert Edward Infirmary Wigan Lane Lancashire Wigan WN1 2NN England

TALAR, ANITA LOUISE, university librarian; b. Trenton, NJ, June 21, 1942; d. Leon Frank and Helen Johanna Talar. BA, Georgian Ct. U., Lakewood, NJ, 1965, MA, 1982; MLS, Rutgers U., New Brunswick, NJ, 1971; EdD candidate, Seton Hall U., South Orange, NJ, 2008. Cert. ednl. media specialist NJ, 1971, ednl. supt. 1982, 6th yr. specialist Rutgers U., 1981. Reference libr. Seton Hall U., 1982—, acting dean, 1996—97. Dir. libr. Georgian Ct. U., 1976—82; dir. sch. libr. Phillipsburg Cath. HS, NJ, 1970—76, St. Mary's HS, South Amboy, NJ, 1968—70, tchr. English, Perth Amboy, NJ, 1965—68, AV coord., 1965—68. Contbr. articles to profl. jours., chapters to books. Mem. McAuley Hall Health Care Ctr., Watchung, NJ, 1995—2000; pub. mem., com. instl. rev. and rsch. UMDNJ, Sch. Health Related Professions, Newark, 1990—2000; cmty. mem., IRB U. Medicine and Dentistry, Newark, 2000—03. Recipient Disting. Svc. award, ACRL, NJ, 1991, Rsch. award, 1992, Tech. Innovation award, 2002, Ray Murray Svc. award, NJ Assn. Libr. Assts., 1997—98, Outstanding Svc. award, Seton Hall U., 2004; named Woman of Yr., 2006. Fellow: Assn. Coll. and Rsch. Librs. (com. chair 1997—); mem.: ALA, NJ Libr. Assn. (bd. mem., coll. & u. sect. chair 1988—91), Religious Sister Mercy, Kappa Delta Pi (Recognition award 1991). Roman Catholic. Avocations: travel, reading. Home: 105 New England Ave P8 Summit NJ 07901-1839 Office: Seton Hall Univ 400 South Orange Ave South Orange NJ 07079-2671 Office Phone: 973-761-9795. Office Fax: 973-275-2119. Business E-Mail: talarani@shu.edu.

TALAREK, NICOLAS, geneticist, researcher; b. Marmande, France, Apr. 25, 1978; s. George Stanislas and Anne-Marie Elisabeth Talarek. BS in Molecular Cell Biology, U. Bordeaux, France, 1998, MS in Genetic Molecular Biology, 2001, PhD, 2004. Postdoctoral rschr. Dana Farber Cancer Inst., Boston, 2005—. Fellowship, French Ministry Rsch., 2001—04. Achievements include discovery of of Antiprion drugs; research in conservation of the Prion Mecanisms through evolution. Avocations: squash, movies, cooking, hiking. Office: Dana Farber Cancer Institue 44 Binney St Boston MA 02115

TALASKA, GLENN, medical educator; PhD, U. Tex. Med. Br., Galveston, 1986. Diplomate cih Am. Bd. Indsl. Hygiene, 1992. Prof. dept. environ. Health U. Cin. Coll. Medicine, 1987—. Vice chair, bei com. ACGIH, Cin. Edn. dir. Cin. Cycle Club, Cin., 2004—. Green Party. Achievements include research in identified specific DNA in human bladders related to smoking tobacco and occupational exposures. Office: Dept Environ Health Univ Cin 3223 Eden Ave Cincinnati OH 45267-0056 Business E-Mail: glenn.talaska@uc.edu.

TALBERT, ARTHUR THOMAS, music educator; b. Jackson, Miss., Aug. 29, 1925; s. Arthur William Talbert and Lucy Esther McIntosh. BA, Miss. Coll., 1948; MusM, La. State U., 1950; M of Sacred Music, Southwestern Bapt. Sem., 1954. Organist, choirmaster Cen. Bapt. Ch., NYC, 1954—55, 1st Bapt. Ch., Selma, Ala., 1955—56, 1st Meth. Ch., Booneville, 1956—59; instr. piano and organ N.E. Miss. Jr. Coll., Booneville, 1956—59; assoc. prof. Calif. Bapt. Coll., Riverside, 1960—69; organist, choirmaster Arlington Meth. Ch., Riverside, Calif., 1960—61, 1st Congl. Ch., San Bernardino, Calif., 1961—63, Lutheran Ch. of the Cross, Riverside, Calif., 1963—69; tchr. piano, organ Sul Ross State U., Alpine, Tex., 1969—70; organist 1st Congrl. Ch., Corona, 1975—80, March Air Force Base, Riverside, 1980—82, St. Albans Episcopal Ch., Houston, 1992—94, Salem Luth. Ch., 1994—2000, 1st Ch. Christ Scientist, Bellaire, 2000—02, Spring, 2002—. Organist 9th Ch. of Christ Scientists, 2002—. Mem.: Am. Guild of Organists (assoc.). Achievements include establishing the Talbert Scholarship Fund at Tokyo Conservatory of Music. Home: 791 Bateswood Dr #121 Houston TX 77079 Office Phone: 281-589-8073.

TALBERT, CHARLES HAROLD, theologian, educator; b. Jackson, Miss., Mar. 19, 1934; s. Carl E. and Audrey (Hale) T.; m. Betty O'Neal Weaver, June 30, 1961; children: Caroline O'Neil, Charles Richard. BA, Samford U., 1956, LittD (hon.), 1990; BD, So. Bapt. Theol. Sem., Louisville, 1959; PhD, Vanderbilt U., 1963. Asst. prof. Wake Forest U., Winston-Salem, NC, 1963-68, assoc. prof., 1968-74, prof., 1974-89, Wake Forest prof., 1989-96; disting. prof. religion Baylor U., Waco, Tex., 1996—. Author: Reading Luke, 1982, Reading Corinthians, 1987, Learning Through Suffering, 1991, Reading John, 1992, The Apocalypse, 1994, Reading Acts, 1997, Romans, 2002, Reading Luke-Acts in its Mediterranean Milieu, 2003, Reading the Sermon on the Mount, 2004, Literary Patterns, Theological Themes and the Genre of Luke-Acts, 2005, Paideia: Ephesians and Colossians, 2007. Postdoctoral fellow U. N.C., 1968-69, Soc. for Values in Higher Edn., 1971-72. Mem. Soc. Bibl. Lit. (editor SBL Dissertation Series, N.T. 1984-86, 87-89, editorial bd. jour. 1984-89), Cath. Bibl. Assn. (assoc. editor Cath. Bibl. Quar. 1991-98, pres. 1999-00), Nat. Assn. Bapt. Profs. Religion (pres. 1985), Studiorum Novi Testamenti Societas. Independent. Baptist. Home: 9602 Old Farm Rd Waco TX 76712-6402 Office: Baylor Univ Dept Religion PO Box 97284 Waco TX 76798-7284 Office Phone: 254-710-8622. Business E-Mail: charles_talbert@baylor.edu.

TALBERT, DEBRA KAISER, elementary school educator, artist; b. Louisville, May 14, 1970; d. John Richard and Gwen Richter Kaiser, Rochelle Weaver Kaiser (Stepmother); m. John Matthew Talbert, June 20, 1992; children: Alyssa Rose, Braden Richard. BFA, Murray State U., Ky., 1994, MA in Edn., 2001. Cert. tchr. Ky. Itinerant art tchr. Massac County Schs. Unit #1, Metropolis, Ill., 1994—97; art tchr. Reidland Elem. Sch., Paducah, Ky., 1997—. Webmaster, tech. leader Reidland Elem. Sch., 2001—03, coord. sch. tech., 2006—; mem. Sch. Based Decision Making Coun., Paducah, 2000—03; mem. dist. decision making coun. McCracken County Schs., Paducah, 2002, Dist. Tech. Leadership, 2008—; coach Dist. Assessment Acad., 2009—. Mem. Kentuckiana Girl Scouts, Louisville, 1976—87, unit mgr. Paducah, 1994—96; youth leader First Presbyn. Ch., Paducah, 2001—04. Named Outstanding Young Am., 1997. Mem.: McCracken County Edn. Assn., Ky. Edn. Assn. Office: Reidland Elem Sch 5741 Benton Rd Paducah KY 42003 Personal E-mail: jtalbert0001@comcast.net, johntalbert@att.net. E-mail: debra.talbert@mccracken.kyschools.us.

TALBOT, DONALD ROY, management consultant; b. Bridgeport, Conn., Jan. 23, 1931; s. Grant Edward and Elvera (Gilbert) T.; m. Beverly Rinebold, Aug. 15, 1953; children: Donna, Randall, Theodore, Timothy, Thomas. B in Marine Engring., N.Y. State Maritime Coll. Project engr. atomic power equipment div. GE, San Jose, Calif., 1952-58; mgr. nuclear labs., nuclear div. Martin Marietta Corp., Balt., 1958-62, project dir. nuclear div., 1962-67, dir. spl. studies Friendship, Md., 1967-71, project dir. environ. programs Balt., 1971-74, dir. environ. tech. ctr. Relay, Md., 1974-83, gen. mgr. environ. systems div. Columbia, Md., 1984-87; corp. v.p. Versar, Inc., Springfield, Va., 1987-89; pres. R.E. Mgmt. Svc., Inc., Towson, Md., 1989—. Recipient Antarctica Svc. medal Civil Engrs. Corps USN, 1965, Cert. of Appreciation Sec. Dept. Commerce, 1975 Avocation: outdoor activities. Home: 712 Hickory Lot Rd Baltimore MD 21286-1427 Office: R E Mgmt Svcs Inc PO Box 10614 Baltimore MD 21285-0614 Office Phone: 410-583-1334. Personal E-mail: remsdrt@varizon.net.

TALBOT, EMILE JOSEPH, French language educator; b. Brunswick, Maine, Apr. 12, 1941; s. Joseph Emile and Flora Talbot; m. Elizabeth Mullen, Aug. 6, 1966; children: Marc, Paul. BA, St. Francis Coll., Biddeford, Maine, 1963; MA, Brown U., 1965, PhD, 1968. From instr. French to prof. U. Ill., Urbana, 1967—86, prof., 1986—2004, prof. emeritus, 2004—, head dept. French, 1988-94. Editor: (book) La Critique Stendhalienne, 1979; author: Stendhal and Romantic Esthetics, 1985, Stendhal Revisited, 1993, Reading Nelligan, 2002; rev. editor: The French Rev., 1979—82, Quebec Studies, 1988—93, mem. editl. bd.:, 1993—96; mem. editl. bd. Quebec Studies, 2003—05; mem. editl. bd.: Nineteenth-Century French Studies, 1986—2003, La Revue Francophone, 1990—96, Etudes Francophones, 1996—2004, Nouvelles Etudes Francophones, 2004—; editor: Quebec Studies, 2004—09. Decorated chevalier Ordre des Palmes Académiques (France); recipient prize, Quebec, 2006; fellow, Ctr. Advanced Study U. Ill., 1973, Assoc., 1988, NEH, 1973—74, Camargo Found., France, 1976. Mem.: MLA, Am. Coun. Que. Studies (v.p. 1995—97, pres. 1997—99), Assn. Can. Studies in U.S., Am. Assn. Tchrs. French. Roman Catholic. Office: U Ill Dept French 707 S Mathews Ave Urbana IL 61801-3625 Home Phone: 217-351-6039; Office Phone: 217-244-2728.

TALBOT, LEE MERRIAM, ecologist, educator, administrator; b. New Bedford, Mass., Aug. 2, 1930; s. Murrell Williams and Zenaida (Merriam) T.; m. Martha Walcott Hayne, May 16, 1959; children: Lawrence Hayne, Russell Merriam. BA, U. Calif., Berkeley, 1953, MA, PhD, U. Calif., Berkeley, 1963. Biologist Arctic Research Lab., Point Barrow, Alaska, 1951; staff ecologist Internat. Union for Conservation, Brussels, 1954-56; ecologist, dir. East African ecol. research project Nat. Acad. Scis., Govts. of Kenya and Tanzania, 1959-63; wildlife advisor UN Spl. Fund, Africa, 1963-64; dir. S.E. Asia project Internat. Union for Conservation, 1964-65; resident ecologist, field rep. for internat. affairs Smithsonian Instn., Washington, 1966-70; sr. scientist, dir. internat. activities Pres.'s Council on Environ. Quality, Washington, 1970-78; sr. sci. advisor Internat. Council Sci. Unions, Paris, 1978-83; dir. conservation, spl. sci. advisor World Wildlife Fund Internat., Switzerland, 1978-80; dir. gen. Internat. Union for Conservation of Nature and Natural Resources, Gland, Switzerland, 1980-83; research fellow Environ. and Policy Inst., East West Ctr., 1983-87; vis. fellow World Resources Inst., Washington, 1984-89; sr. environ. advisor World Bank, 1984—; pres. Lee Talbot Assocs. Internat., 1991—; sr. prof. environ. scis., internat. affairs and pub. policy George Mason U., Va., 1994—, affiliate prof. geography, 2007—. Cons. UNESCO, World Bank, Asian Devel. Bank, Nat. Geog. Soc., Inter-Am. Devel. Bank, The Nature Conservancy, U.S. Govt., U. Calif., UN Spl. Fund, WHO, UN Environment Program, UN Univ., UN Devel. Programme, African and Asian Govts.; conservation coord. Internat. Biol. Program, 1965-70; bd. dirs. Defenders of Wildlife; mem. corp. NY Bot. Gardens; mem. sci. adv. coun. Nat. Pks. Conservation Assn., Bailey Wildlife Compensation Trust; founding trustee Inst. Ecosys. Studies, NY, 2006; mem. pres.'s coun. Population Reference Bur., 2007—. Author 17 books and monographs; contbr. more than 280 articles to profl. jours. Active Boy Scouts Am., Geneva, 1980-82, Washington, 1987-95. With USMC, 1953-54. Decorated officer Order of Lion (Senegal); recipient Regents Lectureship award U. Calif., Santa Barbara, 1986, Pierre Chaleur prize French Acad. Scis., 1993, Festschrift Career Accomplishments award George Mason U., 2003, World Commn. Protected Areas East Asia award, 2005; named Disting. Alumnus, 1953 Officer Candidate Sch., USMC, 2003; Centenary Symposium named in his honor Bombay Natural History Soc., 2003; Excellence in Achievment award U. Calif., 2008, Explorers medal Explorers Club, 2009. Fellow Royal Geog. Soc., Royal Soc. Arts, AAAS, N.Y. Zool. Soc.; mem. Am. Inst. Biol. Scis. (Disting. Scientist award 1979), Acad. Medicine, World Conservation Union (hon.), Am. Assn. for Club of Rome, Am. Soc. Mammalogists, Ecol. Soc., Wildlife Soc. (Outstanding Publ. award 1963), Soc. for Conservation Biology, Internat. Soc. for Ecol. Econs., Boone and Crockett Club (N.Y.C.), Explorers Club (N.Y.C., medal, 2009), Cosmos Club (Washington), Sigma Xi, Phi Kappa Sigma. Achievements include incorporation of ecological principles in international development; development of new principles for management of wild resources; biodiversity conservation; definition of ecosystem dynamics of tropical savannahs including role of fire, feeding habits and migrations of wild herbivores; development and negotiation of national legislation and international agreements for environmental protection. Home: 6656 Chilton Ct Mc Lean VA 22101-4422

TALBOT, LYNN K., language educator; d. Gerald Byron and Elizabeth Ferguson Talbot; m. Michael Squires, June 27, 1987; 1 child, Andrew Squires. BA, U. Calif., Davis, 1973; MA, Middlebury Coll., Vt., 1974; PhD, U. Wis., Madison, 1982. Asst. prof. Spanish Va. Tech., Blacksburg, 1982—87, Roanoke Coll., Salem, Va., 1987—91, assoc. prof. Spanish, 1991—98, prof. Spanish, 1998—. Contbr. articles to profl. publs. Mem.: MLA, D. H. Lawrence Soc. N.Am., Am. Assn. Tchrs. Spanish and Portuguese, Am. Pilgrims on Camino. Office: Roanoke Coll 221 College Ln Salem VA 24153 Business E-Mail: talbot@roanoke.edu.

TALBOT, MARK ROSS, philosophy educator; b. Warren, Ohio, Jan. 3, 1950; s. Thomas Wagar and Jeanette Lind Talbot; m. Cynthia Sue Jefferies, Feb. 24, 1978; 1 child, Kimberly Lyn Lumkes. PhD in Philosophy, U. Pa., Phila., 1993. Asst. prof. philosophy Calvin Coll., Grand Rapids, Mich., 1987—92, Wheaton Coll., Ill., 1992—94, assoc. prof. philosophy, 1994—. Vice chair coun. Alliance of Confessing Evangelicals, 2000—04. Author: Signs of True Conversion, 2000; exec. editor: Modern Reformation Mag., 2002—04, mem. adv. coun.: English version of Bible Good News Pubs./Crossway Books, 1999—, consulting editor: Edification: Jour. for Soc. Christian Psychology; co-editor (with Robert C. Roberts): Limning the Psyche, 1997; co-editor: (with R. Lints and M.S. Horton) Personal Identity in Theological Perspective, 2006; contbr. articles to profl. pubs. Recipient Leland Ryken Tchg. Excellence Humanities award, 2008—09. Home: 1410 Mayo Ave Wheaton IL 60187-9055 Office: Wheaton Coll 501 College Ave Wheaton IL 60187 Business E-Mail: mark.talbot@wheaton.edu.

TALBOT, MARTHA HAYNE, conservationist, biologist; b. San Francisco, Aug. 3, 1932; d. Francis Bourn and Anna (Walcott) Hayne; m. Lee Merriam Talbot, May 16, 1959; children: Lawrence Hayne, Russell Merriam. BA, Vassar Coll., 1954. Co-founder, asst. dir. student conservation program U.S. Nat. Parks, 1955-59; co-dir. East African Ecol. Rsch. Project, Kenya and Tanzania, 1959-63; asst. dir. S.E. Asia Project, Internat. Union for Conservation of Nature/Natural Resources, 1964-65; asst. coord. Internat. Biol. Programme, London, 1966; rsch. assoc. Smithsonian Instn., Washington, 1966-75; mem., treas. Fairfax County Park Authority, Fairfax, Va., 1973-77; sec.-treas. Talbot Racing Assocs., McLean, Va., 1983—; owner, dir. Talbot Hayne Vineyard, St. Helena, Calif., 1988—; sec.-treas. Lee Talbot Assocs. Internat., McLean, 1991—. Bd. dir. Student Conservation Assn., 1966-78, 83-87, hon. dir., 1987— (Svc. Honor award), Defenders of Wildlife, 1974-77, Audubon Naturalist Soc., 1975-78, Rachel Carson Coun., 1975-94, treas., 1994-98, v.p., 1998—. Co-author: Introduction to the Landscape, East Africa, 1961; co-editor: Conservation in Tropical South East Asia, 1968; contbr. articles to profl. jours. Leader Boy Scouts Am., Geneva, 1978-83, transp. coord., McLean, 1989-95 Recipient Outstanding Pub. award The Wildlife Soc., 1963, Cinema Golden Eagle award Documentary Film, 1968, Disting. Alumna award Katharine Branson Sch., 1981, Conservation Svc. award U.S. Dept. Interior, 1986, Bd. Tribute to co-founder, Student Conservation Assn., 1984, Resolution of Honor, 1999; N.Y. Zool. Soc. grantee, 1961; co-recipient World Comm. on Protected Areas East Asia award, 2005. Mem. Soc. Woman Geographers (bd. dir. 1972-75, treas. 1984-89, treas. Washington group 1990-96, pres. 2008-, Outstanding Achievement award, 2008), Napa Valley Grape Growers Assn., Rachels Network, Explorers Club, Woman's Nat. Dem. Club. Avocations: backpacking, hiking, bicycling, travel, swimming. Home: 6656 Chilton Ct Mc Lean VA 22101-4422

TALBOT, MARY LEE, minister; b. Cleve., Apr. 18, 1953; d. Richard William and Mary Helen (Jacobs) T. BA, Coll. Wooster, 1975; MDiv, Andover-Newton Theol. Sch., 1979; MPhil, Tchrs. Coll. Columbia U., 1990; PhD, Columbia U., 1997. Ordained to ministry Presbyterian Ch. (U.S.A.), 1981. Asst. in ministry Grace Congl. Ch., Framingham, Mass., 1975-78; resources coord. Women's Theol. Coalition, Boston, 1977-79; assoc. editor Youth Mag., Phila., 1979-80; co-dir. youth and young adult program Presbyn. Ch. U.S.A., NYC, 1981-88; cons. in religious edn. NYC, 1988-90; dir. continuing edn. Pitts. Theol. Sem., Pitts., 1990—2001; interim pastor Hebron U.P. Ch., Clinton, 2002—03, supply pastor, 2004—07; dir. Discipleship and Spiritual Formation, Presbytery Western NY, 2008. Bd. dirs. Christian Assn., U. Pa., 1979-81; mem. religion com. Chautauqua Inst., 1988-91. Author, editor Suicide and Youth, 1981, (newsletter) Trackings, 1986—88; editor: Racism and

Anti-Racism, 1982, One Fantastic Book, 1982, My Identity: A Gift from God, 1987, A Guidebook for Presbyterian Youth Ministry, 1988, God's Gift of Sexuality, 1989, Celebrate Bible Study, 1990, The C.L.S.C. Banner Book, 2004; contbr. articles to popular mags., profl. jours. Bd. dirs. Christian Assn., U. Pa., 1979-81. Recipient English award Bus. and Profl. Women, 1971. Mem. Assn. Presbyn. Ch. Educators, Assn. Presbyn. Clergywomen, Religious Edn. Assn. (bd. dirs. 1986-91), History of Edn. Soc., Kappa Delta Pi, AAUW, Internat. Assn. Women Ministers Democrat. Office Phone: 716-668-1995. Personal E-mail: mltalbot@aol.com.

TALBOT, MAXIME, professional hockey player; b. Lemoyne, Que., Can., Feb. 11, 1984; Center Gatineau Olympiques (QMJHL), 2000—04, Wilkes-Barre/Scranton Penguins (AHL), 2004—06, Pitts. Penguins, 2005—. Recipient Guy Lafleur Trophy, QMJHL, 2003, 2004. Achievements include being a member of Stanely Cup Champion Pittsburgh Penguins, 2009. Office: Pittsburgh Penguins 66 Mario Lemieux Pl Pittsburgh PA 15219*

TALBOT, NYNA LUCILLE, psychologist, writer; b. Warrington, Eng., May 24, 1954; d. John Robert Talbot and Lois June Snow. MA, Calif. Inst. Integral Studies, 1997, PhD, 2000; BA, Elmhurst Coll., 1976. Sr. tech. writer Hitachi Data Sys., Santa Clara, Calif., 1986—2006; clinical psychologist Royal Cornhill Hosp., Aberdeen, Scotland, 2007—08; pvt. practice Scotland, 2009—. Clin. psychology intern San Mateo County Emergency Response Team, 1990—91, San Mateo County Mental Health Svcs., Half Moon Bay, 2000—01. Clin. psychology intern mem. Red Cross, San Mateo, 1990—91. Mem.: Internat. Coun. Psychologists, Assn. Transpersonal Psychology, APA. Achievements include research in the relationship of companionship coupling in two significant populations. Avocations: painting, poetry. Home: Dogshillock Aberchirder by Huntly Aberdeenshire AB54 7PS Scotland Personal E-mail: drnyna@yahoo.com.

TALBOT, PAMELA, public relations executive; b. Chgo., Aug. 10, 1946; BA in English, Vassar Coll., 1968. Reporter Worcester, Mass. Telegram and Gazette, 1970—72; account exec. Daniel J. Edelman, Inc., Chgo., 1972—74, account supr., 1974—76, v.p., 1976—78, sr. v.p., 1978—84, exec. v.p., gen. mgr., 1984—90; pres. Edelman West, Chgo., 1990—95; pres., CEO Edelman U.S., 1995—. Recipient Silver Anvil award, Publicity Club Chgo., 1985, Golden Trumpet award, 1982, 1985; named a Pub. Rels. All Star, PR Mag. Mem.: Pub. Rels. Soc. Am., Chgo. Network, Execs. Club Chgo. Office: Edelman Pub Rels 200 E Randolph Dr Ste 6300 Chicago IL 60601-6436 Business E-Mail: pam.talbot@edelman.com.

TALBOT, PHILLIPS, retired Asian affairs specialist; b. Pitts., June 7, 1915; s. Kenneth Hammet and Gertrude (Phillips) T.; m. Mildred Aleen Fisher, Aug. 18, 1943 (dec. June 20, 2004); children: Susan Talbot Jacox, Nancy, Bruce Kenneth (dec.). BA, U. Ill., 1936, BS in Journalism, 1936; student, London Sch. Oriental Studies, 1938—39, Aligarh Muslim U., India, 1939—40; PhD, U. Chgo., 1954; LLD (hon.), Mills Coll., 1963, Elmhurst Coll., Ill., 2007. Reporter Chgo. Daily News, 1936-38, corr. India and Pakistan, 1946-48, 49-50; assoc. Inst. Current World Affairs, 1938-41, 46-51; instr. U. Chgo., 1948-50, Columbia U., NYC, 1951; exec. dir. Am. Univs. Field Staff, 1951-61; asst. sec. Near Eastern and S. Asian affairs Dept. State, 1961-65; U.S. amb. to Greece, 1965-69; pres. Asia Soc., NYC, 1970-81, pres. emeritus, 1981—. Phi Beta Kappa vis. scholar, 1973-74. Author: (with S.L. Poplai) India and America, 1958, India in the 1980s, 1983, An American Witness to India's Partition, 2007.; editor: South Asia in the World Today, 1950. Life trustee Aspen Inst., US-Japan Found.; counselor United Bd. for Christian Higher Edn. in Asia; elder Presbyn. Ch. 2d lt. cav. Officers Res. Corps, 1936; 1st lt. NG, 1937-38; lt. comdr. USNR, 1941-46. Recipient Padma Shri honors, India, 2002, Bharatiya Shiromani Purskar award, 2006. Mem. Am. Acad. Diplomacy, Coun. Am. Ambs., Coun. Fgn. Rels., Century Assn., Cosmos Club. Address: 200 E 66th St New York NY 10065-9178 Personal E-mail: talbotp@pipeline.com.

TALBOT, PIERRE JOSEPH, microbiologist, researcher; b. Quebec City, Que., Can., July 11, 1956; s. Arthur and Suzanne (Hudon) T.; children: Natalie, Benoit, Dominic. BSc in Biochemistry, Laval U., Ste-Foy, Que., 1977; PhD in Biochemistry, U. B.C., Vancouver, 1981. Rsch. assoc. Scripps Clinic and Rsch. Found., La Jolla, Calif., 1981-84; asst. prof. Inst. Armand-Frappier U. Que., Laval, 1984-89; assoc. prof. Inst. Armand-Frappier, Laval, Que., 1989-92, prof., 1992—, dir. Human Health Rsch. Ctr., 1998—2001; dir. INRS Inst. Armand-Frappier, 2002—07. Com. reviewer Med. Rsch. Coun., Ottawa, Ont., Can., 1989-96, 98-2000, Multiple Sclerosis Soc., Toronto, Ont., 1993-96, Nat. Sci. Engring. Res. Coun., Ottawa, 1999-2002, Can. Inst. Health Rsch., 1998—. Mem. editl. bd. Viral Immunology, San Antonio, 1990-99; contbr. articles to Virology, Jour. Virology, Annals Neurology, Jour. Immunology. Fonds de la Recherche en Santé du Que. scholar of exceptional merit, 1992-97. Mem. AAAS, Am. Soc. Virology, Am. Soc. Microbiology, Can. Soc. Microbiologists (Fisher Sci. award 1987, Roche Diagnostics award 2002), Can. Soc. Immunology, Assn. Can.-Francaise Pour L'Avancement des Scis., Internat. Soc. Neuroimmunology, Internat. Soc. Neurovirology. Achievements include research in immuno- and molecular biology of neurotropic coronaviruses and possible involvement in neurologic disease. Office: INRS Inst Armand-Frappier 531 Boul Des Prairies Laval PQ Canada H7V 1B7 Home: 92 ch du Grand Moulin Deux Montagnes PQ Canada J7R 3C7 Home Phone: 450-623-3268; Office Phone: 450-687-5010. Business E-Mail: pierre.talbot@iaf.inrs.ca.

TALBOT, SUZANNE DAVIDSON, psychologist; b. Hartford, Conn., Sept. 13, 1968; d. Robert Stuart and Kathleen Davidson; m. David Peter Talbot, Aug. 14, 1993; children: Hannah Louise, Meghan Margaret. BS in Psychology, Trinity Coll., Hartford, 1990; MA in Sch. Psychology, U. Conn., Storrs, 1992, degree in Sch. Psychology, 1993. Cert. NASP, 1993. Sch. psychologist North Stonington Pub. Schs., Conn., 1994—98, Groton Pub. Schs., Mystic, Conn., 1998—. Com. mem. Mystic Congl. Ch., 2008; sec. Regional Multicultural Magnet Sch. Mgmt. Team, New London, Conn., 2004—08. Named Young Careerist, Bus. and Profl. Women's Group, 1998. Mem.: NASP, Conn. Assn. Sch. Psychologists. Democrat. Congregationalist. Avocations: swimming, camping, travel. Home: 98 Castle Hill Rd Pawcatuck CT 06379-1987 Office: Cutler Mid Sch 160 Fishtown Rd Mystic CT 06355 Office Fax: 860-572-5834. Personal E-mail: sdtalbot@sbcglobal.net. Business E-Mail: stalbot@groton.k12.ct.us.

TALBOTT, BEN JOHNSON, JR., lawyer; b. Louisville, May 2, 1940; s. Ben Johnson and Elizabeth (Farnsley) Talbott; m. Sandra Riehl, Oct. 19, 1963; children: Elizabeth, Betty, John, Ben, Sandra. AB magna cum laude, Xavier U., Cin., 1961; LLB, Harvard U., 1964. Bar: Ky. 1965, U.S. Ct. Appeals (6th cir.) 1967. Law clk. to presiding justice U.S. Dist. Ct. Ky., Louisville, 1964-65; assoc. Middleton, Reutlinger & Baird, Louisville, 1965-68, ptnr., 1968-80, Westfall, Talbott & Woods, Louisville, 1980-2000, Talbott & Talbott, PLLC, Louisville, 2000—04, Bardenwerper, Talbott & Roberts, PLLC, Louisville, 2004—. Atty. Stitzel-Weller Distillery, 1970—72, Louisville Gen. Hosp., 1974—83, Louisville and Jefferson County Bd. Health, 1974—80, U. Louisville, 1980—95. Mem. adv. bd. Louisville 15, Sta. WKPC-TV, bd. dirs., 1972—74, pres., 1974; past bd. dirs. U. Louisville Found., U. Louisville Med. Sch. Fund Orgn.; bd. dirs. Louisville Theatrical Assn., 1971—, pres., 1975—76, chmn., 1977—78; bd. dirs. Def. Enterprise Fund, 1994—2006, Macauley Theatre, 1975, TARC Adv. Com., 1971, Jefferson County Capital Constrn. Com., 1971, Louisville Orch., 1976—86, pres., 1979—81; bd. dirs. Ky. Ctr. Arts, 1983—2006, Louisville Lung Assn., 1974—75, treas., 1975; bd. dirs. Hist. Homes Found., 1972—78, 1995—97, 2000—01, 2002—06, v.p., 1978, 2002—06, advisor, atty., 1978—98; bd. regents Whitehall, 1993—2001; bd. dirs. asst. treas. Gen. Soc. May Flower, 2004; bd. dirs. Ky. Soc. Mayflower Desenlants, 2009; trustee U. Louisville, 1970—79, sec., 1974, vice chmn., 1975, chmn. fin. com., 1976. Named an Outstanding Young Man of Louisville, Louisville Jaycees, 1976. Mem.: SAR, ABA, Ky. Soc. Mayflower Descs. (bd. dirs. 2009—), Gen. Soc. Mayflower Descs. (asst. treas. 2009—), Louisville Bar Assn. (past mem. exec. com.), Def. Rsch. and Trial Lawyers Assn., Ky. Bar Assn. (chmn. 1989, Gen. Practice Session of CLE), Alden Kindred Am., Inc., Soc. Colonial Wars, Mayflower Soc., St. Andrews Club, Louisville Boat Club, Pendennis Club, Harvard Law Sch. Assn. Ky. (sec. 1965, pres. 1989—), Filson Hist. Soc., Louisville Country Club, U. Louisville Club, Country Club Fla., Gulf Stream Bath and Tennis Club, Big Sand Lake Club, Phi Kappa Phi (treas. Louisville chpt. 1990—, bd. dirs.). Avocations: golf, tennis, skiing, fishing. Home: 566 Blankenbaker Ln Louisville KY 40207-1167 Office: Bardenwerper Talbott & Roberts PLLC 8311 Shelbyville Rd Louisville KY 40222 Home Phone: 502-895-8251; Office Phone: 502-426-6688. Business E-Mail: lynn@bardlaw.net.

TALBOTT, CHARLES W., JR., agricultural studies educator; b. Syracuse, NY, July 26, 1949; life ptnr. Nadine Annette Perry; children: Heather Kaley Berinyuy, Thomas Joseph George, Jesse Valentine Robert. PhD in Animal Sci., NC State U., Raleigh, 1994. Rschr. NC A&T SU, Greensboro, 1994—2005; agrl. edn. educator W. Va. U., Putnam, 2009—. Rep. Heifer Internat., Bamenda, Cameroon, 1983—89. Contbr. articles to profl. jours. (honor, 2003). Dir. Sustainable Integrated Sys. Transforming Agr., Fraziers Bottom, W.Va., 2005—. Grant, Golden Leaf Found., USDA, 1998—. Mem.: Am. Livestock Breeds Conservancy. Achievements include research in promotion of small scale farming systems and genetic biodiversity. Home: 6909 Black Oak Rd Fraziers Bottom WV 25082 Business E-Mail: chucktalbott293@aol.com.

TALBOTT, EVELYN ELEANOR, epidemiologist, educator; d. Frank Peter OShinsky and Josephine Mary Oshinsky; m. John Bartlett Talbott, July 11, 1971; children: Jacqueline Elizabeth, John Bradley. MPH, U. Pitts., 1971, DrPH, 1976. Cert. epidemiologist Grad. Sch. Pub. Health, 1975. Prof. U. Pitts., 1976—. Epidemioloigist Nat. Rsch. Coun., Washington, 2006—. Fellow: Am. Heart Assn., Am. Health Assn. Coun. on Epidemiology and Prevention. Achievements include research in environmental epidemiology. Avocations: hiking, running. Office: Univ Pitts 130 DeSoto St Pittsburgh PA 15261 Home Fax: 412-624-7397. Business E-Mail: eot1@pitt.edu.

TALBOTT, FRANK, III, lawyer; b. Danville, Va., Mar. 26, 1929; s. Frank and Margaret (Jordan) Talbott; m. Mary Beverley Chewning, July 11, 1952; children: Beverley, Frank IV. BA, U. Va., 1951, LLB, 1953. Bar: Va. 1952. With firm Meade, Talbott & Tate, Danville, 1956—59, Talbott, Wheatley & Talbott, Danville, 1959—66; with Dan River Inc., 1966-76, v.p., gen. counsel, 1968-76; ptnr. firm Clement, Wheatley, Winston, Talbott & Majors, Danville, 1977-78; individual practice law Danville, 1979-92; gen. counsel Va. Mfrs. Assn. Inc., 1983-92; of counsel Woods, Rogers PLC, Danville, Va., 1992—. Chmn. adv. bd. NationsBank, Danville, 1984-94. Vice-chmn. Danville Sch. Bd., 1964-70; trustee Va. Student Aid Found., 1963-68; bd. dirs. United Fund Danville, 1959-63, Meml. Hosp., Danville, 1977-90. Served with AUS, 1953-56. Decorated Commendation medal. Fellow Am. Bar Found. (life); mem. Va. Bar Assn. (v.p. 1965-66, exec. com. 1967-70), Danville Bar Assn. (pres. 1965-66), Am. Judicature Soc., Newcomen Soc., U. Va. Alumni Assn. (bd. mgrs.), Danville Golf Club, Farmington Country Club, Country Club Va., Country Club of North Carolina, Delta Psi, Phi Alpha Delta. Methodist. Home: 221 Salisbury Cir Danville VA 24541-5571 Office: 341 Main St Danville VA 24541 Office Phone: 434-797-8206.

TALBOTT, STROBE, think-tank executive; b. Dayton, Ohio, Apr. 25, 1946; s. Nelson S. and Josephine (Large) T.; m. Brooke Lloyd Shearer, Nov. 14, 1971; children: Devin Lloyd, Adrian Nelson. BA, Yale U., 1968, MA (hon.), 1976; MLitt, Oxford U., Eng., 1971. East European corr. TIME mag., 1971-73, US Dept. State corr., 1973-75, White House corr., 1975-77, diplomatic corr., 1977-84, chief Washington bur. & fgn. affairs columnist, 1984-89, editor at large, 1989-94; amb. at large & spl. advisor to the sec. on the new independent states US Dept. State, Washington, 1993—94, dep. sec., 1994—2001; pres. Brookings Instn., Washington, 2002—. Editor, translator: Khrushchev Remembers, 1970, (with Edward Crankshaw) Khrushchev Remembers: The Last Testament, 1974, The Age of Terror: America & The World After September 11, 2001; author: Endgame: Inside Story of SALT II, 1979, Deadly Gambits: Reagan Administration & Arms Controls, 1984, The Russians and Reagan, 1984, Reagan and Gorbachev, 1987, The Master of the Game: Paul Nitze and the Nuclear Peace, 1988, (with Michael Beschloss) At the Highest Levels: The Inside Story of the End of the Cold War, 1993, The Russia Hand: A Memoir of Presidential Diplomacy, 2002, (with Robert L. Suettinger) Beyond Tiananmen: The Politics of U.S.-China Relations 1989-2000, 2003, Engaging India: Diplomacy, Democracy, and the Bomb, 2004. Trustee Yale U. 1976-82, Hotchkiss Sch., 1982-87; bd. dirs. Carnegie Endowment Internat. Peace; Council on Fgn. Relations. Recipient Edward Weintal Prize for Disting. Diplomatic Reporting Georgetown U., Overseas Press Club award, Stanley Hillman award. Office: Brookings Instn 1775 Massachusetts Ave NW Washington DC 20036 Office Phone: 202-797-6000.*

TALBOTT, SUSAN LUBOWSKY, museum director, curator, arts administrator; b. Bklyn., Jan. 16, 1949; children: MacKay, Maggie. BFA, Pratt Inst., 1970, MFA, 1975. Asst. coord. exhbns. Pratt Inst., Bklyn., 1972—75; gallery dir. SUNY, Brockport, 1975—77; asst. curator McCrory Corp., NYC, 1977—80; asst. dir. Queens Mus., Flushing, NY, 1980—82; br. dir. Whitney Mus. Am. Art at Philip Morris, NYC, 1982—87, Whitney Mus. Am. Art at Equitable Ctr., NYC, 1987—89; dir. visual arts program Nat. Endowment for Arts, Washington, 1989—92; dir. Southeastern Ctr. for Contemporary Art, Winston-Salem, NC, 1992—98; dir., chief exec. Des Moines Art Ctr., 1998—2005; dir. Smithsonian Arts Smithsonian Instn., 2005—08; dir. Wadsworth Atheneum Mus. Art, Hartford, Conn., 2008—. Author: (exhbn. catalog) George Ault, 1988; co-author: (exhbn. catalogs) Spaces '88, 1988, Yasuo Kuniyoshi, 1990. Bd. dirs. 42d Street Edn., Theater and Culture, NYC, 1982-87; mem. Art Table, Inc., N.Y.C., 1988-89. Avocation: tennis. Office: Wadsworth Atheneum 660 Main St Hartford CT 06103 Office Phone: 860-278-2670.

TALENT, JAMES MATTHES, former United States Senator from Missouri; b. Des Peres, Mo., Oct. 18, 1956; m. Brenda Lyons, 1984; children: Michael, Kathleen Marie, Christine. BA in Polit. Sci., Washington U., 1978; JD, U. Chgo. Law Sch., 1981. Law clk. to Hon. Richard A. Posner US Ct. Appeals (7th Cir.), 1982—83; adj. prof. law Washington U. Sch. Law, 1984—86; mem. Mo. State Ho. Reps., 1985—93, minority leader, 1989-93; mem. US Congress from 2nd Mo. Dist., 1993—2001, mem. edn. and the workforce com., armed svcs. com., chmn. small bus. com., 1993—2001; US Senator from Mo., 2002—07. Legislative Achievement award Mo. Hosp. Assn., 1989, Legis. of Yr. award Dept. Mo. Veterans Fgn. Wars, Spirit Enterprise award, Mo. C. of C., 1990, Nat. Public Policy award Nat. Assn. Women Bus. Owners, Lifetime Achievement award Vietnam Veterans of Am. 2000, Lawmaker of Yr. award Independent Electrical Contractors, Inc., 2004 Mem. Mo. Bar Assn. (Award for significant contbns. to adminstrv. justice 1989), Mo. C. of C. (Spirit of Enterprise award 1990), Order of the Coif. Republican. Presbyterian.

TALERMAN, ALEKSANDER, pathologist, educator; b. Warsaw, Jan. 8, 1932; came to U.S., 1979; s. Nattali and Stanislawa (Naiman) T.; m. Karin Margaretha Barkland, Feb. 28, 1962; children: Robert Alexander, Edward Mark Olof. MB, BChir, U. Sheffield, Eng., 1957, MD, 1968. Lectr. pathology U. London, 1965-70; sr. lectr. pathology, head dept. pathology Rotterdam Cancer Inst., Netherlands, 1970-79; prof. pathology and ob-gyn. U. Chgo., 1979—90; Peter A. Herbut prof. pathology and cell biology Thomas Jefferson U., Phila., 1990—. U. and rsch. inst. cons. Co-author: Atlas of Germ Cell Tumors, 1989; editor: Pathology of the Testis and its Adnexa, 1985; contbr. articles to profl. jours. With Royal Air Force, 1960-63. Recipient Silver medal German Cancer Soc., 1979. Fellow Royal Coll. Pathologists; mem. Internat. Soc. Gynecol. Pathologists (exec. coun. 1976-82, sec. 1982-86, pres. 1990-92), Internat. Acad. Pathology, European Soc. Pathology, Path. Soc. Great Britain and Ireland, French Gynecopathology Soc. (hon.) Home: 243 S 4th St Philadelphia PA 19106-3803 Office: Thomas Jefferson Univ Dept Pathology Main Bldg 11th & Walnut Sts Rm 285Q Philadelphia PA 19107-5244 Home Phone: 215-592-4689; Office Phone: 215-955-2433. Office Fax: 215-923-1969. Personal E-mail: mtaleman@aol.com.

TALESE, GAY, writer, former journalist; b. Ocean City, NJ, Feb. 7, 1932; s. Joseph Francis and Catherine (DiPaola) Talese; m. Nan Ahearn, June 10, 1959; children: Pamela, Catherine. BA in Journalism, U. Ala., 1953. Copyboy NY Times, NYC, 1953—54, staff writer, 1956—65. Vis. writer U. So. Calif. Profl. Writing Program. Author: New York - A Serendipiter's Journey, 1961, The Bridge: The Building of the Verrazano-Narrows Bridge, 1964, The Overreachers, 1965, The Kingdom and the Power, 1969, Fame and Obscurity, 1970, Honor Thy Father, 1971, Thy Neighbor's Wife, 1981, Unto the Sons, 1992, Origins of a Nonfiction Writer, 1996, A Writer's Life, 2006; co-author (with Barbara Lounsberry): The Literature of Reality, 1995; editor: Italians in America: A Celebration, 2001, The Gay Talese Reader, 2003; regular contbr. Esquire mag., Sunday Times. Served with US Army, 1954—56. Recipient George Polk Career award, 2008. Mem.: PEN (v.p. 1984—87, bd. dirs.), Phi Sigma Kappa. Achievements include recognition as helping define literary journalism or "new nonfiction reportage", also known as New Journalism. Office: c/o Knopf Publicity Dept 1745 Broadway 21st Fl New York NY 10019-4511 Office Fax: 212-753-3820.

TALIAFERRO, PHILIP, III, lawyer; b. Cin., July 10, 1937; s. Philip II and Shirley (Denny) T.; children from previous marriage: Greg, Gina, Laura Elizabeth, Morgan; m. Diana Perryman, Nov. 12, 1989; 1 child, Philip IV. BA in Bus., Centre Coll., Danville, Ky., 1959; JD, U. Ky., 1962. Bar: Ky. 1962, US Dist. Ct. (ea. dist.) Ky. 1966, US Dist. Ct. (so. dist.) Ohio 1966, US Ct. Appeals (6th cir.) 1968, US Supreme Ct. 1970, Ohio 1991. Sr. ptnr. Taliaferro, Shirooni, Carran & Keys, PLLC, Covington, 2007—. Bd. editors U. Ky. Law Jour., 1960-62; asst. prosecutor Kenton County, Ky., 1967-72; personnel bd. Commonwealth Ky., 1972-87; chmn. emeritus 1988; adj. prof. Salmon P. Chase Coll. Law No. Ky. U., 1984-2001; spl. justice Ky. So. Ct., 1994; faculty mem. NITA, 1992-96, 99; lectr. in field. Mem. Greater Cin. Tall Stacks Commn., Inc., 1989-92, sec., 1990-92, trustee, 1990-92; mem. pres.'s coun. Dan Beard Coun. Boy Scouts Am., 1990—2007; chmn. Kenton County, Ky. Bicentennial Commn., 1990-92; trustee Covington Ladies Home, Inc., 1991-93; bd. dirs. Common Cause Ky., 1991-2001, No. Ky. Bd. Regents, 1987-90, 92-98; vice chmn. bd. regents No. Ky. U., 1992-93; founding trustee No. Ky. Leadership Found.; Master of Bench Salmon P. Chase Inn of Ct., 1993-. Lt. (JAG) USNR, 1962-66, Vietnam, with USNR, 1966-69. Recipient Outstanding Dedication and Svc. to State Employees award Ky. Assn. State Employees, 1983, Outstanding Leadership, Accomplishments and Kinship to Career Employees, Ky. State Tenure Club, 1984, Award of Merit, Transitions, 1985, Silver Beaver award Boy Scouts Am., 1996; named Boss of Yr., No. Ky. Legal Secs. Assn., 1991. Fellow: Internat. Acad. Trial Attys.; mem. ABA, Am. Arbitration Assn. (arbitrator), Am. Assn. Justice, Am. Inns Ct., Cin. Bar Assn., Ky. Bar Assn., No. Ky. Bar Assn. (Disting. Svc. award 1995), Ky. Justice Assn. (regional v.p. 1981, 82, treas. 1983, sec. 1984, v.p. 1986, bd. govs. 1987-2005, Outstanding Trial Lawyer of Yr. award 1996), Louisville Bar Assn., Centre Coll. Alumni Assn. (dir., Disting. Alumnus award 2002), Am. Legion, Navy League US (no. Ky. chpt.), Mil. Order Fgn. Wars, VFW, Omicon Delta Kappa, Phi Delta Phi. Office Phone: 859-291-9900. Business E-Mail: ptaliaferro@tmsck.com.

TALIAFERRO, ROBERT See BROOKE, TAL

TALIAFERRO, SUMAYAH JAMILA, dermatologist; d. Debra Taliaferro. MD, Brown Med. Sch., Providence, 2002. Cert. Ga., 2007. Co-author: (textbook) Fitzpatrick's Dermatology in General Medicine, Titzpatrick's Dermatology in General Medicine; contbr. articles to profl. jour. Mem.: Am. Acad. Dermatology, Nat. Med. Assn., Women's Dermatol. Soc., Atlanta Dermatol. Assn., Atlanta Med. Assn. Office: Metro Atlanta Dermatology 285 Blvd NE Ste #430/410 Atlanta GA 30312 Office Fax: 404-681-5444.

TALL, ALAN R., molecular biologist, educator; MB, BS, U. Sydney, 1970. Intern Royal Prince Alfred Hosp., 1971, resident, 1972; sr. resident Boston City Hosp., 1973—74, chief resident, 1975—76, asst. visiting physician, 1976—77; fellow in gastroenterology Boston U. Hosp, 1974—75; asst. prof. medicine Boston U., 1977, Columbia U. College Physicians & Surgeons, 1978—81, assoc. prof. medicine, 1982—89, prof. medicine, 1989, dir. Specialized Ctr. Rsch in Atherosclerosis, 1990—96, dir. Specialized Ctr. Rsch. in Molecular Medicine & Atherosclerosis, 1997—; attending physician Presbyterian Hosp., 1989. Scientific adv. bd. Gladstone Rsch. Found., 1992—; bd. scientific counselors NHLBI. Mem.: Assn. Am. Physicians, Am. Heart Assn. (program com. 1985—86, Arteriosclerosis coun. 1987—89, rsch. com. 1999—2000), Am. Soc. Clinical Investigation. Office: Columbia University Division of Molecular Medicine 630 W 168th St P&S 8-401 New York NY 10032 Office Phone: 212-305-9418. Office Fax: 212-305-5052.*

TALL, SUSAN PORTER, music educator; b. NYC, Apr. 16, 1942; m. Alan R. Tall, July 27, 1979; 1 child, Alexander A.; m. Burton F. Porter (div.); 1 child from previous marriage, Anastasia Porter. BA, Montclair State U., 1965; MA in Musicology, NYU, 1973; postgrad., U. Ill., 1978—80. Instr. music Am. Sch. London, 1966—68; instr. music, dir. inst. music Russell Sage Coll., Troy, NY, 1971—74; grad. asst. in conducting U. Ill., Champagne-Urbana, 1978—79; mem. faculty music Tenafly Sch. Sys., NJ, 1980—; facilitator Music K-12, 1995—. Dir. music, condr. Presbyn. Ch., Tenafly, 1980—90, 1995—2005, North Jersey Symphony Orch., Tenafly, 1984—89, Concerto Orch. N.J., Tenafly, 1986—88; guest condr. in field. Organizer, dir. Fanfare for Humanity, Tenafly, 2001, 2005, THS Chorus and Orch. Benefit, Tenafly, 2005. Recipient Disting. Tchg. award, Tenafly H.S., 2002, Tchr. Recognition award, Gov., N.J., 2002, Disting. Leadership in Arts Edn. award, Gov. of N.J., 1997; named Tchr. of Yr., Tenafly Sch. Dist., 2002; nominee Disting. Secondary Sch. Tchg. award, Princeton U., 1990. Mem.: N.J. Music Educators Assn. (Master Tchr. award 1997). Avocation: classical guitar. Home: PO Box 104 Cresskill NJ 07626 Office: Tenafly Sch Dist Dept Music 19 Columbus Dr Tenafly NJ 07626 Office Phone: 201-816-6621. Business E-Mail: stall@tenafly.k12.nj.us.

TALLACKSON, JEFFREY STEPHEN, lawyer; b. Washington, May 10, 1943; s. John Robert and Betty Marcelle (Crockett) T.; m. Christine Ann Johnson, Aug. 10, 1974. BA, Yale U., 1965; LLB, Columbia U., 1968. Bar: N.Y. 1968. Law clk. to judge US Dist. Ct. (so. dist.) NY, 1968-70; assoc. Milbank, Tweed, Hadley & McCloy, NYC, 1970-78, ptnr., 1979-87; exec. v.p., gen. counsel, sec. Am. Savs. Bank, White Plains, NY, 1987-92; ptnr. Lowy & Tallackson, NYC, 1993-96; pvt. practice, 1996-2000, 2007—; counsel Brauner, Baron, Rosenzweig & Klein, LLP, NYC, 2000—06. Mem. exec. com. N.Y. Law Inst., N.Y.C., 1980-87; bd. dirs., exec. v.p., gen. counsel, sec. Riverhead Savs. Bank., 1988-92; chmn. com. on banking law and regulation Community Banking Assn. N.Y. State, 1990-92; sec. banking law com. of the Assn. of Bar of City of N.Y., 1997-2000. Mem. ABA, N.Y. State Bar Assn., Assn. Bar City N.Y. Democrat. Home: 1060 New Forge Rd II Ancram NY 12502-5005 Office: 2 Penn Plaza Ste 1910 New York NY 10121 Home Phone: 518-851-7212; Office Phone: 212-292-4978. Business E-Mail: tallacksonlaw@hughes.net, jtallackson@hughes.net.

TALLANT, STEVEN HALL, academic administrator, social worker; b. Winston-Salem, NC, Dec. 29, 1948; s. Daniel Hoge and Wanda Jean (Nance) T.; m. Karen Marie Snider, June 29, 1974; children: Matthew Hoge, Sean Edward. AA, Paris Jr. Coll., 1969; BA, U. Fla., 1975; MSW, U. Utah, 1977; PhD in Social Welfare, U. Wis., 1985. Lic. social worker. Unit social worker Sacred Heart Home, Pueblo, Colo., 1977-78; chief social work svcs. USAF Hosp., Ellsworth AFB, S.D., 1978-82, dir. alcoholism rehab. ctr. Scott AFB, Ill., 1985-87; dir. family support ctr. 1605 Air Base Group, Lajes Field, Portugal, 1987-89, 3380 Air Base Group, Keesler AFB, Miss., 1989; chief Air Force Family Rsch. The Pentagon, Washington, 1991—94; prof. social work U. Wis., Eau Clair, 1994—2000, assoc. vice chancellor, dir. grad. programs, 2000—04, assoc. vice chancellor academic affairs, 2004, interim provost, vice chancellor academic affairs, 2004, 2005—07, provost, vice chancellor academic affairs, 2007—08; pres. Tex. A&M U., Kingsville, 2008—. Contbr. articles to profl. jours. Lt. col. USAF, 1978-94. Named to Alpha Kappa Delta, 1975, Phi Kappa Phi, 1975, Phi Kappa Phi, 1977; recipient Charles I. Schottland award U. Utah, 1977. Mem. NASW. Democrat. Avocations: camping, hiking, golf, fishing. Office: Tex A&M U - Kingsville Office of Pres 700 University Blvd Kingsville TX 78363*

TALLCHIEF, MARIA, former ballerina; b. Fairfax, Okla., Jan. 24, 1925; d. Alexander Joseph and Ruth Mary (Porter) Tallchief; m. Henry Paschen, Jr., June 3, 1956; 1 child, Elise Paschen. DFA (hon.), Lake Forest Coll., Ill., Colby Coll., Waterville, Maine, 1968, Ripon Coll., 1973, Boston Coll., Smith Coll., 1981, Northwestern U., Evanston, Ill., 1982, Yale U., 1984, St. Mary of the Woods Coll., 1984, Dartmouth Coll., 1985, St. Xavier Coll., 1989, U. Ill., 1997. Ballerina Ballet Russe de Monte Carlo, 1942-47; with NYC Ballet Co., 1947-65, prima ballerina, 1947-60; founder Chgo. City Ballet, 1981, artistic dir., 1981—87; now ballet dir. Lyric Opera Chgo., 1979—. Ballerina Ballet Russe de Monte Carlo, 1942—47, N.Y.C. Ballet Co., 1947—65, prima ballerina, 1947—60; founder Chgo. City Ballet, 1979; dir. ballet Lyric Opera Chgo., 1979—. Prima ballerina Am. Ballet Theatre, 1960, founder Sch. Chgo. Ballet, guest star Paris Opera, 1947, Royal Danish Ballet, 1961, created role Danses Concertantes, 1944, Night Shadow, 1946, Four Temperaments, 1946, 1946, Orpheus, 1948, The Firebird, 1949, Bourée Fantastique, 1949, Capriccio Brillante, 1951, A la Françaix, 1951, Swan Lake, 1951, Caracole, 1952, Scotch Symphony, 1952, The Nutcracker, 1954, Allegro Brillante, 1956, The Gounod Symphony, 1958; performer: (films) Presenting Lily Mais, 1943, Million Dollar Mermaid, 1953. Recipient Disting. Svc. award, U. Okla., 1972, Dance Mag. award, 1960, Jane Addams Humanitarian award, Rockford Coll., 1973, Order of Lincoln award, 1974, Bravo award, Rosary Coll., 1983, award, Dance Educators Am., 1956, Achievement award, Women's Nat. Press Club, 1953, Capezio award, 1965, Nat. Medal of Arts, Pres. Clinton, 1999; named Hon. Princess, Osage Indian Tribe, 1953; named to Nat. Women's Hall of Fame, 1996, Internat. Women's Forum Hall of Fame, 1997. Mem.: Nat. Soc. Arts and Letters. Office: Lyric Opera Ballet 20 N Wacker Dr Ste 860 Chicago IL 60606-2874

TALLEDO, OSCAR EDUARDO, medical educator; b. Sullana, Piura, Peru, Aug. 1, 1929; s. Jorge Antonio and Flora Natividad (Cordova) T.; m. Jeanette McCarley, June 8, 1959; children: Roy Anthony, Paul Frederick, Linda Jeanette. BS, San Marcos U., 1948, MD, 1955. Diplomate Am. Bd. Ob-Gyn., Am. Bd. Laser Surgery. Intern Crawford W. Long Hosp., Atlanta, 1956-57, resident, 1957-58, Med. Coll. Ga., Augusta, 1958-60, fellow in gynecology, 1960-61, chief gynecologic oncology, 1961—, prof. ob-gyn, 1970—, instr., 1961-63, asst. prof., 1963-68, assoc. prof., 1968-71, prof., 1971—, acting chmn., 1981-82. Nat. Heart Inst. grantee, 1965 Fellow Am. Coll. Ob-Gyn, ACS, Gynecologic Oncology Soc.; mem. Soc. Gynecologic Investigation, AMA, Am. Fertility Soc., Richmond County Med. Soc., Ga. Ob-Gyn Soc., So. Med. Assn., S. Atlantic Assn. Ob-Gyn, Gyn-Urology Soc., Ga. Med. Assn. Clubs: Augusta Country. Lodges: Rotary (chmn. world community service com., Augusta 1983). Presbyterian. Home: 817 Aumond Pl W Augusta GA 30909-3106 Office: Med Coll Ga Dept Gyn Oncology Dept Ob Gyn Augusta GA 30912 Personal E-mail: cordoba@comcast.net. Business E-Mail: ctalledo@mail.mcg.edu.

TALLENT, STEPHEN EDISON, lawyer; b. Columbus, Nebr., Aug. 10, 1937; s. William E. and Helen Tallent; m. Martha Sutcliffe, Apr. 6, 1971; 1 child, Jennifer Diane. BA, Stanford U.; JD, U. Chgo.; LLD (hon.), Lincoln U. Bar: Calif. 1963, U.S. Dist. Ct. (so. and cen. dists.) Calif. 1965, U.S. Dist. Ct. (so. and ea. dists.) N.Y. 1989, U.S. Ct. Appeals (D.C. cir. 1981), U.S. Ct. Appeals (2d cir.) 1987, U.S. Ct. Appeals (3d. cir.) 1980, U.S. Ct. Appeals (4th cir.) 1982, U.S. Ct. Appeals (9th cir.) 1968, U.S. Ct. Mil. Appeals 1965, U.S. Supreme Ct. 1973. Ptnr. Gibson, Dunn & Crutcher, LA, 1962-96; pvt. practice Washington, 1997—. Former adj. prof. Loyola Law Sch., L.A.; mem. vis. com. U. Chgo. Law Sch.; former mem. Calif. Atty. Gen.'s adv. com. for Evaluation of Anti-Organized Crime Programs; mem. L.A. Town Hall, L.A. World Affairs Council; mem. bd. visitors Stanford Law Sch.; founding dir. Am. Employment Law Coun., 1993—. Fellow Coll. Labor and Employment Lawyers (founding, pres. and gov. 1995—); mem. ABA (chair labor and employment law sect. 1998-99), Indsl. Rels. Rsch. Assn. Home: PO Box 512 Reedville VA 22539-0512 Office: 1050 Connecticut Ave NW Ste 900 Washington DC 20036-5320 Home Phone: 804-453-6832; Office Phone: 202-955-8552.

TALLENT-RUNNELS, MARY K., psychology professor, researcher; b. Houston, July 13, 1948; d. Thomas A. and Arleen E. Tallent. BS, U. Houston, 1971; MS, Southern Ill. U., Carbondale, 1974; PhD, Tex. A&M U., Coll. Sta., 1985. Tex. tchr.'s cert. 1971. Prof. Tex. Tech U.-Coll. Edn., Lubbock, 1985—, assoc. dean adminstrn., 1995—2001. Contbr. articles to profl. jour. Recipient Pres.'s Outstanding Tchg. award, Tex. Tech U., 1992. Mem.: SW Ednl. Rsch. Assn. (pres. 1993—94, Outstanding Rsch. Paper award 1986—87), Nat. Assn. Gifted Children, Am. Ednl. Rsch. Assn. (bd. mem. divsn. C 2001—05, Award of Svc.). Avocations: travel, reading. Home: 3706 61St Lubbock TX 79413 Office: Tex Tech Univ PO Box 41071 Lubbock TX 79409 Office Fax: 806-742-2179. Business E-Mail: mary.runnels@ttu.edu.

TALLETT, ELIZABETH EDITH, biopharmaceutical company executive; b. London, Apr. 2, 1949; d. Edward and Edith May (Vickers) Symons; m. James Edward Wavle Jr.; children: James Edward Tallett, Alexander Martin Tallett, Christopher Andrew Wavle. BS with honors, Nottingham U., Eng., 1970. Ops. rsch. analyst So. Gas Bd., 1970-73; mgmt. svcs. mgr. Warner-Lamber (UK), Eastleigh, England, 1973-77, strategic planning mgr., 1977-81; internat. dir. strategic planning Warner-Lambert, Morris Plains, NJ, 1981-82, corp. dir. strategic planning, 1982-84; head mktg., ops./exec. com. mem. Parke-Davis, Morris Plains, 1984-87; exec. v.p. therapeutic products Centocor, Malvern, Pa., 1987-89, pres. pharms. div., 1989-92; pres., CEO Transcell Techs., Inc., Monmouth Junction, NJ, 1992-96, Dioscor, Inc., Stockton, 1996—2003; prin. Hunter Ptnrs. LLC, 2002—. Bd. dirs. Prin. Fin. Group, Inc., Varian, Inc., Coventry Health Care, Inc., IntegraMed Am. Inc., Meredith Corp. Inc. Contbr. articles to profl. jours. Chmn. NJ Mus. Contemporary Sci. Avocations: acting, badminton, travel, skiing.

TALLEY, ANDRÉ LEON, editor-at-large; b. Washington, 1949; BA in French Lit., NC Ctrl. U.; M in French Lit., Brown U. Worked for Andy Warhol, 1975; reporter Women's Wear Daily, 1977; apprentice to Diana Vreeland, Costume Inst. NY's Met. Mus.; fashion editor Ebony mag., 1982; fashion news dir. Vogue mag., NYC, 1983—88, creative dir., 1988—95, editor-at-large, 1998—; Paris fashion editor W mag., 1995, Paris bur. chief, 1995—98. Amb. Vogue mag., Moscow, 2004; trustee Savannah Coll. Arts and Design, SC; curator Ann. Oscar fashion show, 2007. Columnist Life with André, Vogue mag.; author: (books) A.L.T.: A Memoir, 2003, A.L.T. 365+, 2005. Recipient Eugenia Sheppard award, Coun. Fashion Designers of Am., 2003; named to Power 150, Ebony mag., 2008. Office: Vogue Conde Nast Publications 4 Times Sq Ste 17 New York NY 10036-6518

TALLEY, BRENDA S., performing arts center director, theatrical light designer; b. Las Vegas, Nev., Jan. 17, 1955; d. Wanda Marie and Milton Rex Linn; m. Donald P. Kennedy, June 7, 1975 (div. Nov. 19, 2001); m. Douglas L. Talley, Nov. 29, 2003; children: Ryan Rex Kennedy, Krista Marie Kennedy, Dawnie Rose Kennedy, Breanna (Annie) Linn Kennedy. AA in Gen. Studies, C.C. So. Nev., 1989; BA in Bus. Mgmt., St. Regis U., 2002. Ho. mgr. C.C. So. Nev. Performing Arts Ctr., 1996—2000; performing arts ctr. asst. dir. C.C. So. Nev., 2000—02, performing arts ctr. dir., 2002—. Mem. C.C. So. Nev. Lecture Com., 2000—; chmn. C.C. So. Nev. Honors Com., 2000—02, Campus Environment Coun., North Las Vegas, 2000—02; mem. Nev. C.C. Conf., 2001—02. V.p. Tule Springs Preservation Com., Las Vegas, 1998—2003; vice chair Congress of States Nat. Parent Tchr. Assn., Chgo., 1999—2001; pres. Nev. Parent Teachers Assn., Las Vegas, 1999—2001. Recipient Hon. Life Membership, Nat. PTA, 1994, Nev. PTA, 1996, Parent Hall of Fame, Clark County Sch. Dist., 1996, High Honors, Phi Theta Kappa, 1989. Mem.: AAUP (assoc.), Nev. Faculty Alliance (assoc.). Democrat. Lds Ch. Avocations: theater, rapelling, hiking, camping, music. Office: Community College Southern Nevada 3200 East Cheyenne Ave North Las Vegas NV 89030

TALLEY, CHARLES RICHMOND, retired bank executive; b. Richmond, Va., Dec. 23, 1925; s. Charles Edward and Marie (Thorckmorton) Talley; m. Anne Marie Smith, June 4, 1948 (dec. Feb. 16, 2007); children: Laurie Anne, Charles Richmond Jr. BA in Econs, U. Richmond, 1949; postgrad., Rutgers U., 1959-61, Northwestern U., 1954-55; grad. exec. program, U. Va., 1974. Asst. cashier 1st & Mchts. Nat. Bank, Richmond, 1955-57, asst. v.p., 1957-63, v.p., 1963-69, sr. v.p., 1969-73, exec. v.p., 1973-84; corp. exec. officer Sovran Bank N.A., 1984-86, ret., 1986. Bd. dirs. Security Atlantic Life Ins. Co.; v.p., bd. dirs. Security Atlantic Ins. Agency; bd. dirs. Sovran Properties Inc.; vice-chmn., bd. dirs. Va Edn. Loan Authority, 1983—87, chmn., 1988—91; v.p., mem exec. com. Richmond Eye and Ear Hosp., pres., 1988—91. Pres Richmond Jr Cof C, 1960—61; treas Richmond chpt Nat Found, 1956—; pres Baptist Extension Bd Va, 1973—75; bd dirs Commonwealth Eye and Ear, 1986—89, Richmond Symphony Orchestra, Richmond Better Bus Bur. With USNR, 1944—46. Mem.: Richmond Clearing House Asn (pres 1977), Richmond Metropolitan CofC (bd dirs 1979—89), The Tartan Golf Course (Irvington, Va), Bull and Bear Club, Willow Oaks Country Club Richmond (pres 1971), Rotary (bd dirs Richmond 1981—83). Home: 4301 Stratford Rd Richmond VA 23225-1060 also: Bldg 2 Unit 2 The Green At Tides Lodge Irvington VA 22480

TALLEY, HAYWARD LEROY, communications executive; b. Nov. 3, 1923; s. Roy and Reta (Hayward) T.; m. Emma Mae Chandler, Sept. 2, 1950; children: Brian, Kevin. BS, U. Ill., 1948. Chief engr. Sta. WOKZ-AM-FM, Alton, Ill., 1948-50; pres., gen. mgr. Talley Broadcasting Corp. (sta. WSMI AM and FM), Litchfield, Ill., 1950—; pres. Talley Broadcasting Co. (sta. KBKB AM and FM), Ft. Madison, Iowa, 1960-99, North Cen. Iowa Broadcasting Co. (stas. KLSS, KSMN), Mason City, 1963-83, Talley Broadcasting Corp. (sta. WAOX), Staunton, Ill., 1999—. Chmn. ofcl. bd. Meth. Ch., 1961-63, 65-66, chmn. ch. coun., 2003-05; adv. bd. Lewis & Clark Coll., 1978—; adv. coun. St. Francis Hosp., 1992—. With Signal Corps, U.S. Army. Recipient Vincent T. Wasilewski Broadcaster of Yr. award, Ill. Broadcasters Assn., 2002. Mem.: Ill. Broadcasters Assn., Nat. Assn. Broadcasters, Am. Legion, Masons, Rotary (pres. Litchfield Club 1989—90). Home: 1414 N Harrison St Litchfield IL 62056-1209 Office: Sta WSMI PO Box 10 Litchfield IL 62056-0010

TALLEY, JOSEPH EUGENE, psychologist; b. Springfield, Mass., May 27, 1949; s. Joseph Addison and Miriam Louise (Ayers) T.; m. Vibeke Absalon, Jan. 3, 1981; children: Kirsten, David, Jonathan. BA, U. Richmond, 1971; MA, Radford Coll., 1973; PhD, U. Va., 1978. Diplomate Am. Bd. Profl. Psychology; lic. psychologist, NC; cert. health svc. provider, NC. Faculty Duke U. Med. Ctr., Durham, NC, 1977—2005, prof. med. psychology, 2005—, with counseling and psychol. svcs., 1977—, asst. dir., 2006—; gen. practice psychotherapy Durham, 1980—. Author: Study Skills, 1981, Performance Prediciton of Law Enforcement Personnel, 1990, The Predictors of Successful Very Brief Psychotherapy, 1992, Seeking Something Sacred: Managing Our Frustrations, Losses and Fears, 2001; author, editor: Counseling and Psychotherapy Services, 1985, Counseling and Psychotherapy with College Students: A Guide to Treatment, 1986, Multicultural Needs Assessment with College and University Populations, 1995; contbr. articles to profl. jours. Bd. deacons Hillsborough Presbyn. Ch., NC, 1983-85, chmn., 1985, bd. elders, 1987-94, 2002-07, v.p. bd. trustees, 1992-94; bd. dirs. Orange County Mental Health Assn., Chapel Hill, NC, 1982-83, mem. legis. com., 1983, site visitor for accreditation. Named Disting. Practitioner, Nat. Acads. Practice, 2009. Fellow APA (awards com. divsn. 17, 2002-05, chair awards com. 2006-07, chair Leona Tyler lifetime achievement award com., 2007-08), Am. Acad. Clin. Psychology, Am. Acad. Counseling Psychology, Am. Acad. Counseling Psychology (pres. 1995-97, pres. emeritus 2008, Disting. Svc. award 2002); mem. Am. Bd. Profl. Psychology (sec., treas. coun. of pres.'s psychology splty. acads. 1997-98, chmn., CEO 2000-03, spl. liaison to related groups 2003—, past chmn., CEO 2003-05, exec. bd. and spl. liaison to congress and related profl. groups, 2005—, Disting. Contbns. award 2002, chair and CEO emeritus, 2008-), NC Psychol. Assn., Nat. Soc. Clin. Hypnosis (cert. and approved cons., supr. and practitioner, ethics com. 1995-97), Phi Kappa Phi, Omicron Delta Kappa, Psi Chi, Phi Kappa Sigma. Democrat. Presbyterian. Home: 134 E Tryon St Hillsborough NC 27278-2550 Office: Duke U Counseling & Psychol Svcs PO Box 90955 214 Page Bldg Durham NC 27708-0955 Office Phone: 919-660-1000. Business E-Mail: jtalley@duke.edu.

TALLEY, MICHAEL FRANK, lawyer; b. Chesterfield, SC, Aug. 14, 1945; s. Frank and Rosena A. Talley; m. Dianne Wright, May 24, 1980; children: Michanna, Michael. BA, S.C. State U., 1966; MA, Howard U., 1971, JD, 1976. Bar: S.C. 1976, U.S. Dist. Ct. S.C. 1976, U.S. Ct. Appeals (4th cir.) 1976, U.S. Ct. Appeals (11th cir.) 1994. French instr. S.C. State U., Orangeburg, 1970-71, Tenn. State U., Nashville, 1971-73; staff atty. Presdl. Clemency Bd., White House, Washington, 1975; atty. Bishop Law Firm, Greenville, S.C., 1976-77, Talley, Green & Lewis, Greenville, 1977-87, Talley Law Firm, Greenville, 1987—. French lab. instr. Howard U., Washington, 1973-76. Bd. dirs. Legal Svcs. for Western S.C., Greenville, 1978-82. Earl Warren Legal fellowship NAACP Legal Def. Fund, 1973-76; recipient Cert. of Appreciation S.C. Bar Pro Bono Program, 1991. Mem. S.C. Bar Assn., Nat. Bar Assn., Greenville C. of C., Kappa Alpha Psi. Avocations: fishing, travel, swimming, reading. Home: 208 Boling Rd Greenville SC 29611-7604 Office: Talley Law Firm 206 Green Ave Greenville SC 29601-3436 Office Phone: 864-233-6229. Personal E-mail: talleylaw@aol.com.

TALLEY, NICHOLAS JOSEPH, medical educator, research scientist, physician; b. Perth, Australia, Jan. 9, 1956; arrived in U.S., 2002; s. Nicholas Alexander and Irene Mary Talley; m. Catherine Elizabeth Davies, Dec. 30, 2004; children: Nicholas Stephen, Matthew Jonathon, Nicole Sarah, Luke James. MB, BS, U. NSW, 1979; PhD, U. Sydney, 1987; MD, U. NSW, 1993, M in Med. Sci., 2003. Resident med. officer/registrar Prince of Wales Hosp., Sydney, 1979—83; rsch. fellow, prof. registrar Royal North Shore Hosp., Sydney, 1983—87; rsch. fellow Mayo Clinic, Rochester, Minn., 1987—88, asst. prof. medicine, 1988—91, assoc. prof., 1991—93; head divsn. medicine, prof. medicine Nepean Hosp., Sydney, 1993—2001; area dir. medicine Westworth Area Health Svc., Nepean Hosp., Sydney, 2001—02; prof. medicine, cons. Mayo Clinic Coll. Medicine, Rochester, 2003—, prof. epidemiology, 2007—; chair dept. internal medicine Mayo Clinic, Jacksonville, 2007—. Author: Examination Medicine, 1985, 5th edit., 2006, Clinical Examination, 1988, 5th edit., 2006, Internal Medicine, 1990, 2d edit., 2000, Clinical Gastroenterology, 1996, 2d edit., 2006, Multiple Choice Questions in Clinical Examination, 1996, Pocket Clinical Examination, 1998, 3d edit., 2009, Conquering Irritable Bowel Syndrome, 2006, GI Epidemiology, 2007, Handbook of Gastroenterology, 2007; asst. editor Am. Jour. Gastroenterology, 1992-97; co-editor-in-chief, Am. Jour. Gastroenterology, 2004-09; mem. editl. bd. Gastroenterology, 1993-98, Jour. Clin. Gstroenterology, 1994-2008, Alimentary Pharmacology and Therapeutics, 1995-03, editor-in-chief, 2009-, Jour. Gastroenterology and Hepatology, 1994-98, editor, 1998-03; contbr. articles and revs. to profl. jours., chpts. to books. Pres. Miranda br. Young Liberals, Sydney, 1976; wing comdr. Royal Australia Air Force, 2000. Postgrad. rsch. scholar Nat. Health and Med. Rsch. Coun., Australia, 1984-85. Fellow ACP, Royal Australasian Coll. Physicians, Am. Coll. Gastroent., Australian Faculty Pub. Health Medicine (founding mem.), Royal Coll. Physicians (London and Edinburgh); fellow Am. Gastroent. Assn., Gastroent. Soc. Australia, Brit. Soc. Gastroenterology, Functional Brain Gut Rsch. Group (pres.). Avocations: tennis, writing, travel, jogging, martial arts. Office: Mayo Clinic 4500 San Pablo Rd Jacksonville FL 32224 Business E-Mail: talley.nicholas@mayo.edu.

TALLEY, PATRICK A., JR., lawyer; b. July 3, 1955; m. Sharon P. Talley, Aug. 11, 1985; children: Sarah Ilene, Patrick A. III, Peyton J. BA, Armstrong Coll., Savannah, Ga., 1976; MA, La. State U., Baton Rouge, 1979, JD, 1982; LLM in Energy & Environ. Law, Tulane U., New Orleans, 1993. Bar: La. 1982, Tex. 1982, US Dist. Ct. (ea. dist.) La. 1982, US Ct. Appeals (5th cir.) 1983, US Dist. Ct. (mid. and no. dists.) La. 1983. With Milling, Benson, Woodward Law Firm, New Orleans, 1982—87, ptnr., 1987—96, Frilot LLC Law Firm, New Orleans, 1996—, mem. mgmt. cosmetic, 2005—. Bd. trustees Acad. Sacred Heart, chmn., 2003—05, mem. legal com., mem. exec. com., chmn. com. trustees; bd. trustees St. George's Episcopal Sch., chmn. com. trustees; mem. environ. task force La. Recovery Authority; v.p. New Orleans Charter Schs. Found.; mem. parish coun. Holy Name Jesus Ch., mem. sch. bd.; mem. cmty. appeal Archdiocese New Orleans; bd. dirs. New Orleans Charter Schs. Found.; mem. exec. com. Southeastern La. Coun., Boy Scouts Am.; bd. dir. La. Children's Mus. Mem.: ABA, La. Bar Found. (mem. grants com. 2000—), Baton Rouge Bar Assn., La. Assn. Def. Counsel, Nat. Assn. Railroad Trial Counsel (mem. exec. com. 2000—, v.p. southwestern region 2006—07), Southeastern Admiralty Law Inst., Maritime Law Assn. US (mem. transp. hazardous substances com., mem. stevdoring and terminal ops. com.), La. State Bar Assn. (ho. dels. 1994—, chair fed bench bar liaison com., mem. 5th cir. jud. conf., mem. bar admissions com.), Kappa Alpha Internat. Fraternity (pres. 2008—). Office: STE 3700 1100 Poydras St New Orleans LA 70163-1138 Business E-Mail: ptalley@frilot.com.

TALLEY, RICHARD WOODROW, accountant; b. Birmingham, Ala., Sept. 10, 1941; s. Alton Woodrow and Alta O. (Tittle) T.; m. Anita Marcell Moses, Jan. 14, 1966; children: Richard Woodrow Jr., Leah Michelle. BS in Commerce and Bus. Adminstrn., U. Ala., 1964. CPA Ala. Pres. Talley, Maulding & Peete, PC, Decatur, Ala., 1964—. Officer Boy Scouts Am., Decatur, Austin Band Boosters, Decatur, PTA, Decatur; mgr. coach Dixie Youth Baseball, Decatur; deacon Ch. of Christ. Served as sgt. USAR, 1964-70. Named Boss of Yr. Decatur Jaycees, 1980. Mem. AICPA, Tenn. Soc. CPAs, Ala. Soc. CPAs, Commerce Execs. Soc. U. Ala., Lions (sec. 1982-83, treas. 1985-86, sec.-treas. 1994-95). Avocations: genealogy, photography. Home: 1266 Brandywine Ln SE Decatur AL 35601-4582 Office: Talley Mauldin & Peete PC PO Box 2067 Decatur AL 35602-2067 Home Phone: 256-355-1264; Office Phone: 256-353-1421. Business E-Mail: richard@tmpcpa.com.

TALLEY, ROBERT COCHRAN, academic administrator, cardiologist; b. May 26, 1936; m. Katherine Ann Plocar; children: Andrew, Katherine, David. BS, U. Mich., 1958; MD, U. Chgo., 1962. Diplomate Nat. Bd. Med. Examiners (mem. medicine com. 1984-88, com. chair 1988-93). Asst. prof., dept. physiology and medicine U. Tex. Med. Sch., San Antonio, 1969—71; head, sect. cardiovascular diseases, 1971—75, assoc. prof., dept. medicine, 1971—75; acting chief medicine VA Hosp., San Antonio, 1974, chief cardiology svc., 1973—75; chmn. dept. internal medicine U. SD Sch. Medicine, Sioux Falls, 1975—87, Freeman prof. medicine, 1984—87, interim v.p., dean, 1986—87, v.p., dean, 1987—2004, dir. residency program, 2004—. Mem. liaison com. med. edn., 1998—. Contbr. articles to med. jours. Surgeon USPHS, 1966—68. Tchg. scholar, Am. Heart Assn. U. Chgo., 1972—75. Fellow: ACP, Am. Coll. Cardiology; mem.: AMA, Liaison Com. on Med. Edn., Assn. Am. Med. Coll. (mem. coun. deans new dean mentoring program, mem. adminstrn. bd. coun. deans 1999—2004), Am. Fedn. Clin. Rsch., Am. Heart Assn. (bd. dirs. Dakota affiliate). Home: 1305 Cedar Ln Sioux Falls SD 57103-4512 Office: U SD Sch Medicine 1400 W 22nd St Sioux Falls SD 57105-1505

TALLEY, ROBERT MORRELL, aerospace company executive; b. Erwin, Tenn., Mar. 13, 1924; s. Robert Taylor and Anna Laura (Morrell) T.; m. Mary Sue Williams, June 5, 1948; children: David, Carol. Student, East Tenn. State Coll., 1942-43, U. Va., 1943-44; BS U. S.C., 1945; MS, U. Tenn., 1948, PhD, 1950. Chief infrared br., chief solid state div. U.S. Naval Ordnance Lab., White Oak, Md., 1951-58; mgr. lab. Santa Barbara Rsch. Ctr. subs. Hughes Aircraft, Calif., 1958-69, v.p. Calif., 1969-76, pres. Calif., 1976-89, ret. Contbr. articles to profl. jours.; patentee in field. Trustee, hon. alumnus U. Calif.-Santa Barbara Found.; bd. dirs. Ptnrs. in Edn., Santa Barbara. With USN, 1943-46. Fellow Am. Phys. Soc.; mem. Optical Soc. Am., LaCumbre Club, Sigma Xi

TALLEY, TRUMAN MACDONALD, retired publisher, editor; b. NYC, Feb. 3, 1925; s. Truman Hughes and Helen Nicholson (Macdonald) Talley; m. Madelon DeVoe, Oct. 17, 1953 (dec. 1997); children: Melanie, Macdonald, Marina; m. Susannah H. Chapman, Feb. 6, 2008. Grad. cum laude, Princeton U., NJ, 1949. Assoc. editor New Am. Libr. of World Lit., NYC, 1949-59, editl. v.p., 1959-64; pres., editl. dir. Weybright & Talley, NYC, 1966-78; pub. Truman Talley Books/Times Books, NYC, 1978-82; with E.P. Dutton, 1983-98, St. Martin's Press, NYC, 1998—2008; ret., 2008. Mem.: PEN. Personal E-mail: trumantalley@aol.com.*

TALLEY, VERNON ANDREW, museum administrator; b. Balt., Feb. 13, 1968; s. Kenneth Franklyn Talley; m. Nancy Rae Gerhart, Dec. 30, 1988; 1 child, Rhiannon Victoria. BA in Art History, Calif. State U., LA, 1996; MA in Mus. Studies, U. Okla., Norman, 2007. Exhibit tech. Calif. African Am. Mus., LA, 1995—98, registrar interpretive collections, 1998—2009; registrar Nat. Mus. African Am. History & Culture, 2009—. Presenter ann. meeting Associated Hist. Socs. LA County, 2003—03; presenter ann. conf. Packing, Art Handling & Crating Info. Network, Portland, 2003—03, Calif. Hist. Soc., 2008. Mem. NAACP, Balt., 2004—06. Sgt. US Army, 1989—91. Decorated Army Achievement medal US Army, Army Commendation medal; Joseph Uribe Meml. scholar, Calif. State U., LA, 1994, MA Alumni scholar, U. Okla., 2007. Mem.: Packing, Art Handling & Crating Info. Network, Am. Assn. Museums (registrar's com.), Am. Legion, Phi Kappa Phi, Golden Key Nat. Honor Soc. Independent. Office: Smithsonian Nat Mus African Am History & Culture 600 Maryland Ave SW Ste 7001 Washington DC 20024 Office Phone: 202-633-7358. Office Fax: 202-633-7364. Business E-Mail: talleyv@si.edu.

TALLIA, ALFRED F., physician, educator; married, 1982. MPH, MD, Robert Wood Johnson Med. sch., New Brunswick, NJ, 1978. Diplomate Am. Bd. Family Medicine, 1982. Prof. and chmn. dept. family medicine Robert Wood Johnson Med. Sch., New Brunswick, 2007—. Mem. bd. Nat. Bd. Med. Examiners, Phila., 1992—2007. Contbr. articles to profl. jours. Fellow: Am. Acad. Family Physicians. Office: Robert Wood Johnson Med Sch 1 RW Johnson Pl New Brunswick NJ 08903

TALLMADGE, MARK MYRON, lawyer; b. Neptune, NJ, Sept. 21, 1957; m. Therese Noonan. BBA, U. Notre Dame, Ind., 1979, JD, 1982. Bar: NJ 1982, Ill. 1986, US Dist. Ct. NJ 1982, US Dist. Ct. (so. dist.) NY 1986, US Dist. Ct. (ea. dist.) NY 1986, US Ct. Appeals (3d cir.) 1998, US Ct. Appeals (2nd cir.) 2007. Law clk. US Dist. Ct. NJ, Newark, 1983; lawyer Stryker, Tams & Dill, Newark, 1984—86, Bressler, Amery & Ross, P.C., Florham Pk., NJ, 1986—. Scoutmaster Troop 28 Boy Scouts Am., Chatham, NJ, 1997—2009. Mem.: ABA, Nat. Conf. Insurance Guaranty Funds, NJ Def. Assn., Def. Rsch. Inst., NJ State Bar Assn. (mem. ins. law com.), Profl. Liability Underwriting Soc. Office: Bressler Amery & Ross PC 325 Columbia Turnpike Florham Park NJ 07932 Office Fax: 973-514-1660. Business E-Mail: mtallmadge@bressler.com.

TALLMAN, ANN MARIE, lawyer; b. Iowa; BS in Psychology and Polit. Sci., with distinction and spl. honors, U. Iowa; JD, U. Calif. Berkeley, Boalt Hall Sch. Law. Atty. Kutak Rock, Denver; dep. dir. & head Planning and Community Develop. Agy. City and County of Denver; with Fannie Mae, Pasadena, Calif., 1994—2004; pres., CEO Fannie Mae Found., Washington, 1998—99; pres., gen. counsel MALDEF (Mexican Am. Legal Def. and Edn. Fund), LA, 2004—06. Bd. mem. MALDEF (Mexican Am. Legal Def. and Edn. Fund), 1998—2006; bd. dirs. J. C. Penney Company, Inc., 2006—. Founding bd. mem. Hispanic PAC USA; exec. dir. Colo. Hispanic League, 1990.

TALLMAN, DENNIS EARL, professor, research scientist; b. Bellefontaine, Ohio, Apr. 23, 1942; s. Maurice Earl and Mary Elizabeth Tallman. PhD, Ohio State U., Columbus, 1968. Postdoctoral rsch. assoc. Cornell U., Ithaca, NY, 1968—70; asst. prof. chemistry N.D. State U., Fargo, 1970—73, assoc. prof. chemistry, 1973—78, prof. chemistry, 1978—2006, rsch. prof. dept. coatings and polymeric materials, 2007—. Co-dir. Corrosion/Coatings Rsch. Ctr. N.D. State U., Fargo, 2000—. Contbr. articles to profl. jours. (Fred Waldren Award for Outstanding Rsch., 2000); N.Am. editor: Jour. Solid State Electrochemistry, 1997—2007. Recipient postdoctoral fellowship, NIH, 1968—70, numerous rsch. grants, NSF, Dept. of Def., NIH, and EPA, 1970—. Mem.: Nat. Assn. of Corrosion Engrs., Electrochem. Soc., Am. Chem. Soc. (lobbied Congress for increases in fed. rsch. funding 2000—03), Soc. for Electroanalytical Chemistry (life; bd. dirs. 1998—2002), Phi Kappa Phi, Sigma Xi, Phi Lambda Upsilon. Avocations: four-wall handball, skiing, canoeing, biking, backpacking. Office: ND State Univ Dept Coatings & Polymeric Materials Fargo ND 58108-6050 Business E-Mail: dennis.tallman@ndsu.edu.

TALLMAN, EVE, library director; Dir. Grand County Pub. Libr., Moab, Utah. Recipient Merit award, Utah Humanities Coun., 2005, Best Small Libr. in Am., Libr. Jour., 2007. Mem.: Utah Libr. Assn. (vice-chair pub. com.). Office: Grand County Pub Libr 257 E Ctr St Moab UT 84532 Office Phone: 435-259-1111. Office Fax: 435-259-1380. E-mail: eve@moablibrary.org.

TALLMAN, RICHARD C., federal judge, lawyer; b. Oakland, Calif., 1953; s. Kenneth A. and Jean M. Tallman; m. Cynthia Ostolaza, Nov. 14, 1981. BSc, U. Santa Clara, 1975; JD, Northwestern U., 1978. Bar: Calif. 1978, Wash. 1979, US Dist. Ct. (no. dist.) Calif. 1979, US Dist. Ct. (we. dist.) Wash. 1979, US Dist. Ct. Hawaii 1986, US Ct. Fed. Cl. 1999, US Ct. Appeals (9th cir.) 1979, US Dist. Ct. (ea. dist.) Wash. 1998, US Supreme Ct. 1997. Law clk. to Hon. Morrell E. Sharp US Dist. Ct. (we. dist.) Wash., Seattle, 1978—79; trial atty. US Dept. Justice, Washington, 1979—80; asst. US atty. (we. dist.) Wash., Seattle, 1980—83; assoc., then ptnr. Schweppe, Krug & Tausend, PS, Seattle, 1983—89; mem. Bogle & Gates, PLLC, Seattle, 1990—99; ptnr. Tallman & Severin, LLP, Seattle, 1999—2000; apptd. US cir. judge US Ct. Appeals (9th cir.), 2000—. Chmn. western dist. Wash. Lawyer Reps. to Ninth Cir. Jud. Conf., 1996—97. Instr. Nat. Pk. Svc. Seasonal Ranger Acad., Everett, Mt. Vernon, Wash., 1983—93; chmn. Edmonds C.C. Found., Lynnwood, Wash., 1990—92; gen. counsel Seattle-King County Crime Stoppers, 1987—99; mem. exec. bd. Chief Seattle coun. Boy Scouts Am., 1997—; chmn. US Jud. Conf. Adv. Com. Criminal Rules, 2007—. Mem.: Fed. Judges Assn. (bd. dirs. 2002—06), King County Bar Assn., Fed. Bar Assn. (we. dist. trustee 1992—93, v.p. 1994, pres. 1995), Wash. Athletic Club, Rainier Club. Office: Park Place Bldg 1200 Sixth Avenue 21st FL Seattle WA 98101-3123

TALLMER, MARGOT SALLOP, psychologist, gerontologist, psychoanalyst; b. NYC, Sept. 8, 1925; d. Harry and Mildred (Schifrin) Sallop; m. Jonathan Tallmer, Apr. 12, 1949 (dec.); children: Mary, Megan, Jill, Andrew. MS, NYU, 1948; MA, Yeshiva U., 1962, PhD, 1967; cert. in psychotherapy and psychoanalysis, NYU, 1976. Faculty dept. psychol. founds. Hunter Coll., NYC, 1969-76, assoc. prof., 1976-79, prof., 1979—94, prof. emeritus; staff psychologist Mt. Sinai Hosp., NY, 1967-68; pvt. practice NYC, 1979—; faculty NY Ctr. for Psychoanalytic Tng., NY. Lectr. N.Y. Ctr. Psychoanalytic Tng. Author: Sex in Later Life, 1996; editor: Sex and Life Threatening Illness, HIV Testing Positive, The Child and Death, Sexuality and the Older Adult; co-author: Suicide in the Elderly; mem. editl. bd. in Psychoanalysis, Psychoanalytic Rev.; contbr. chpts. to textbooks, articles to profl jours. Mem. APA, N.Y. State Psychol. Assn. (past pres. divsn. adult devel. and aging), Nat. Psychol. Assn. for Psychoanalysis (trustee 1972-2005, bd. dir. 1972—). Address: 515 E 85th St New York NY 10028-0246 Personal E-mail: mamadoc4@n.y.c.rr.om. E-mail: mamadoc4@gmail.com.

TALLON, DALE, professional sports team executive; b. Rouyn-Noranda, Can., Oct. 19, 1950; m. Meg Tallon; 2 children. Defenseman Vancouver Canucks, 1970—73, Chgo. Blackhawks, 1973—78, Pitts. Penguins, 1978—80; color analyst Chgo. Blackhawks, 1981—97, dir. player personnel, 1998—2002, color analyst, 2002—03, asst. gen. mgr., 2003—05, gen. mgr., 2005—09, sr. advisor hockey ops., 2009—. Named to NHL All-Star Team, 1971, 1972. Office: c/o Chicago Blackhawks 1901 W Madison St Chicago IL 60612*

TALMADGE, MARY CHRISTINE, nursing educator administrator; b. Monticello, Ga., Nov. 6, 1940; d. Herbert Pope and Margaret (Allen) T.; m. Larry Benson, Aug. 10, 1962 (div. 1975). Diploma, Crawford W. Long Hosp. Sch. of Nursing, Atlanta, 1961; BSN, U. Dayton, 1966; MPH, U. Hawaii, 1971, PhD, 1989. RN; cert. Family Life Edn. Staff charge nurse Crawford W. Long Hosp., Atlanta, 1961-62; instr. LPN program Dayton (Ohio) Bd. Edn., 1963-66; instr. Miami Valley Hosp. Sch. of Nursing, Dayton, 1967-69; clin. nurse specialist Hawaii State Hosp., Kaneohe, 1970-77, dir. nursing, 1978-80; adminstrv. asst. to dir. health Hawaii State Dept. of Health, Honolulu, 1977-78; clin. nurse specialist Windward Community Counseling Ctr., Kaneohe, 1980-83; asst. prof. U. Hawaii, 1983-85; assoc. prof. Hawaii Loa Coll., Kaneohe, 1987-89; assoc. prof., acting dept. head Ga. So. U., Statesboro, 1990-93; prof., chair dept. nursing Calif. State U., Long Beach, 1993—2001. Cons. Tokyo Women's Med. Coll. Sch. of Nursing, 1988-90; local and internat. healthcare orgns, charter mem., Nat. Womens History Mus., pres. Altrusa Internat. Statesbores Ga., 2008-09, 2009-, mem., Nature Conservatory, Restored Family Farm, Nat. Registry Historic Homes. Sec., mem. Gov.'s Commn. on Mental Health and Criminal Justice, Honolulu, 1978-80; mem., chmn. Windward Oahu Svc. Area Bd. on Mental Health and Substance Abuse, Honolulu, 1985-86; candidate Neighborhood Bd. Kaneohe, 1988; bd. dirs. New Beginnings for Children; chair nursing task force, health com. Statesboro C. of C. Recipient Cmty. Svc. award African-Am. Caucus, Ga. So. U., 1993. Mem. Nat. League Nursing, Sigma Theta Tau, Phi Kappa Phi (faculty 1995) Ga. Trust Hist. Preservation, Nat. Trust Hist. Preservation, Nat. Wildlife Fedn., Sierra Club, Smithsonian Instn. contbg. mem., Humane Soc., Nat. Parks Conservation Assn., Nat. Audubon Soc., Democrat. Methodist. Avocation: breeder and handler of miniature schnauzers. Personal E-mail: mct@frontiernet.net.

TALMADGE, PHILIP ALBERT, retired judge, state senator; b. Seattle, Apr. 23, 1952; s. Judson H., Jr. and Jeanne C. Talmadge; m. Darlene L. Nelson, Sept. 6, 1970; children: Adam, Matthew, Jessica, Jonathan, Annemarie. BA magna cum laude, Yale U., 1973; JD, U. Wash., 1976. Bar: Wash. 1976. Atty. Karr Tuttle Campbell, 1976—89; pres. Talmadge & Cutler, P.S., 1989—95; senator State of Wash., 1979—94; justice Supreme Ct. Wash., 1995—2001; ptnr. Talmadge Law Group PLLC, 2001—07, Talmadge-Fitzpatrick, 2008—. Author: The Nixon Doctrine and the Reaction of Three Asian Nations, 1973; editor: Law Rev., 1975—76; contbr. articles to profl. jours. Chair Senate Judiciary Com., 1981, 1983—87, Senate Health and Human Svcs. Com., 1992—95, Wash. Senate, 1978—94, ways and means com. Fellow: Am. Assn. Appellate Lawyers; mem.: Wash. Appellate Lawyers Assn., King County Bar Assn., Wash. State Bar Assn. Office: Talmadge-Fitzpatrick 18010 Southcenter Pkwy Tukwila WA 98188 Business E-Mail: phil@talfitzlaw.com.

TALMAGE, DAVID WILSON, retired microbiologist, educator, dean; b. Kwangju, Korea, Sept. 15, 1919; s. John Van Talmage and Eliza (Emerson) Talmage; m. LaVeryn Marie Hunicke, June 23, 1944; children: Janet, Marilyn, David, Mark, Carol. Student, Maryville Coll., Tenn., 1937—38; BS, Davidson Coll., NC, 1941; MD, Washington U., St. Louis, 1944. Intern Ga. Baptist Hosp., 1944—45; resident medicine Barnes Hosp., St. Louis, 1948—50, fellow medicine, 1950—51; asst. prof. pathology U. Pitts., 1951—52; asst. prof., then assoc. prof. medicine U. Chgo., 1952—59; prof. medicine U. Colo., 1959—; prof. microbiology, 1960—86, disting. prof., 1986—, chmn. dept., 1963—65, assoc. dean, 1966—68, dean, 1969—71; dir. Webb-Waring Lung Inst., 1973—83, assoc. dean for rsch., 1983—86. Mem. nat. council Nat. Inst. Allergy and Infectious Diseases, NIH, 1963—66, 1973—77. Author (with John Cann): Chemistry of Immunity in Health and Disease; editor: Jour. Allergy, 1963—67; editor: (with M. Samter) Immunological Diseases. With M.C. AUS, 1945—48. Scholar Markle, 1955—60. Mem.: Am. Assn. Immunologists, Am. Acad. Allergy, Inst. Medicine, NAS, Alpha Omega Alpha, Phi Beta Kappa. Home Phone: 303-388-1898.

TALMAGE, KENNETH KELLOGG, consumer products company executive; b. Morristown, NJ, Jan. 16, 1946; s. Edward Taylor Hunt Jr. and Dorothy Rogers Talmage. BA, Claremont Men's Coll., 1968; MBA, Boston U., Brussels, 1976. Aide to U.S. ambassador to Austria, Vienna, 1969-72; asst. to chmn. Fin. Com. to Re-elect Pres. Nixon, 1972-73; assoc. Hon. Leonard K. Firestone, LA, 1973-74; attaché Am. Embassy, Brussels, 1974-77; mgmt. cons. strategic planning and fin. Arthur D. Little, Inc., Cambridge, Mass., 1977-80; pres. Boston Co. of New Orleans, 1980—81; sr. v.p. Boston Safe Deposit & Trust Co., 1980-87; pres. Lloyd's, Inc., Denver, 1987-92. Pres. Sprague Corp., Cape Elizabeth, Maine, 1978-79; bd. dirs. Monterey Water Co., pres., 1995-97, chmn., CEO, 1997—; bd. dirs. Pure West Industries, Inc., vice-chmn., 1993-95. Mem. exec. com. Outward Bound, U.S.A., 1980—85; dir. Vols. for Outdoor Colo., 1988—94, Breckenridge Outdoor Edn. Ctr., 1989—92; advisor Hurricane Island Outward Bound Sch., Maine, 1987—2005, bd. trustee, 1979—87, chmn. bd. trustees, 1980—83; bd. trustee Colo. Outward Bound Sch., 1990—96, vice chmn., 1995—96, bd. govs., 1996—2005; bd. trustees Outward Bound Profl., 2005—. With USNR, 1968—69. Home: PO Box 1526 Carmel CA 93921-1526 Office: Monterey Water Co 1158 S Main St Manteca CA 95337-9505 Personal E-mail: kktalm@aol.com.

TALMAGE, LANCE ALLEN, obstetrician, gynecologist, military officer; b. Vandergrift, Pa., Feb. 23, 1938; s. Guy Wesley and Martha Lois (Bradstock) T.; m. Diana Elizabeth Heywood, June 23, 1962; children: Tamara, Lance Jr., Tenley. BS in Chem. Engring., U. Toledo, Ohio, 1960; MD, U. Mich., 1964. Flight surgeon 24th Infantry Divsn. US Army, 1966-69; resident U. Mich. Med. Ctr., Ann Arbor, 1969-73; clin. prof. U. Toledo Coll. Medicine, 1987—; med. dir. Ctr. for Women's Health, Toledo, 1987—2003. Brigadier gen. 112th Med. Brigade Ohio Army Nat. Guard, Columbus, 1995-97; pres. med. staff Toledo Hosp., 1989-91, chair dept. Ob-gyn., 1979-86; pres. Toledo Lucas County Acad. Medicine, 1994-95; mem. Toledo Hosp. Found. Bd., 2000-05, Ohio State Med. Bd., 1999—, supervising sec., 2003-. Cabinet mem. United Way, Toledo, 1994-96; hon. chmn. March of Dimes Mothers-March, Toledo, 1989; pres. Ottawa Hills Athletic Boosters, Ohio, 1986-88, team physician, 1981-2003; trustee U. Toledo Found., 1999—. Decorated Legion of Merit; recipient Disting. Alumni award, Waite H.S., 1996, Garde Nationale Trophy, N.G. Assn. U.S., 1998, Outstanding Team Physician, Ohio H.S. Athletic Assn., 2002, Gold T award, U. Toledo, 2009, Blue T award, 2002, Outstanding Chem. Engr. Grad. award, 2002—03; named to, Ohio Vets. Hall Fame, 2001. Fellow ACS, ACOG (dist. chair 1996-99, v.p. 2000-01, Disting. Dist. Svc. award, 2004), Fedn. State Med. Bds. (editl. com. 2007-08, bd. dirs. 2008); mem. AMA (mem. ho. of dels.), Am. Soc. Reproductive Medicine, Ohio State Med. Assn. (pres. 1998-99), Pi Kappa Phi Alumni Assn. (Beta Iota chpt. Hall of Fame), U. Toledo Alumni Assn. (trustee 1996-2002, pres. 2000-01, athletic com., 2005—09), Res. Officers Assn., Soc. Med. Cons. to Armed Forces, Am. Legion Post 335, Mil. Officers Assn. Am. (life), Assn. Mil. Surgeons US (life), Nat. Guard Assn. US (life). Republican. Lutheran. Office: The Toledo Hosp 2150 W Ctrl Ave Toledo OH 43606 Home Phone: 419-535-1605; Office Phone: 419-291-2193. Personal E-mail: latalmage@bex.net.

TALMI, YOAV, conductor, composer; b. Kibbutz Merhavia, Israel, Apr. 28, 1943; m. Erella Gottesmann; 2 children. Diploma, Rubin Acad. Music, Tel Aviv; postgrad., Julliard Sch. Music; D (hon.), Laval U., 2001. Artistic dir., condr. Gelders Symphony Orch., Arnhem, 1974-80; prin. guest condr. Munich Philham. Orch., 1979-80; artistic dir. Israel Chamber Orch., 1984-88; music dir. New Israeli Opera, 1985-89, San Diego Symphony Orch., 1990-96, Waterloo Festival, NJ, 1994-95, Que. Symphony, Can., 1999—, Hamburg (Germany) Symphony, 2000—04. Guest condr. Berlin Philharm., Munich Philharm., London Philharm., Philharmonia, Royal Philharm., Concertgebouw, Paris Orch. Nat., Israel Philharm., NHK Symphony, Tokyo, New Japan Philharm., Vienna Symphony, St. Petersburg Philharm., Pitts. Symphony, Detroit Symphony, St. Louis Symphony, Houston Symphony, Dallas Symphony, Montreal Symphony, N.Y. Chamber Symphony, LA Chamber Orch., Oslo Philharm., Tonhalle Orch., Zurich, others; head conducting dept. Buchmann-Mehta Sch. Music U., Tel Aviv, 2009. Composer: Dreams for choir a capella, Music for Flute and Strings; Overture on Mexican Themes (recorded), 3 Monologues for Flute Solo (pub.), Inauguration Fanfare, Elegy for Strings, Timpani, and Accordion, 1997, Suite on Israeli Songs, The Double Marriage of Figaro; recs. include: Bruckner 9th Symphony (Oslo Philharm.), Tchaikovsky 1st Symphony (Quebec Symphony), Gliere 3d Symphony, Brahms Sextet/4 Serious Songs, Rachmaninov's Isle of the Dead, Berlioz: Symphonie Fantastique, Overtures, Harold in Italy, Romeo and Juliette (San Diego Symphony), Tchaikowsky/Schoenberg, Bloch/Barber/Grieg/Puccini (Israel Chamber Orch.), DeBussyis and Beach Orchestrations, Tchaikovsky's Symphony No. 1 (Quebec Symphony); (with Erella Talmi) works for flute and piano. Recipient Boskovitch prize for composition, Israel, 1965, Koussevitzky Meml. Conducting prize, Tanglewood, 1969, Ruppert Found. Condr. competition award, London, 1973, Frank Peleg prize, Israeli Govt.'s Ministry Culture, 2008, named Officer Nat. Que., Que. Govt., 2009. Home: PO Box 1384 Kefar Sava 44113 Israel Office: Michal Schmidt Artists Internat 59 E 54th St Ste 83 New York NY 10022 Office Phone: 212-421-8500. Home Fax: 972-9-765-6553. E-mail: talmi@netvision.net.il.

TALMOR, MIA, plastic surgeon; d. Shlomo and Dolly Talmor; m. Seth Plancher, May 30, 1993. BS with Honors, U. Mich., Ann Arbor, 1990; MD with Honors, Cornell U., NYC, 1993. Diplomate Am. Bd. Plastic Surgery, 2002, Am. Bd. Surgery, 2000. Asst. prof. surgery Weill Cornell Med. Coll., NYC, 2001—08, assoc. prof. surgery, 2008—; pres. NY Regional Soc. Plastic and Reconstructive Surgeons, NYC, 2008—. Office: New York Presbyn Hosp 425 E 61 st St New York NY 10065

TALOR, ZVI, nephrologist; b. Haifa, Israel, Aug. 4, 1944; came to U.S., 1979; s. Moshe and Sarah (Thaler) T. BSc, Hebrew U., Jerusalem, 1967, MSc, 1970, MD, 1972. Bd. cert. in internal medicine. Intern Rambam Hosp., Haifa, Israel, 1973, resident internal medicine, 1975-77, fellow nephrology, 1978-79; rsch. assoc. dept. medicine U. Chgo., 1980-81; acting chief of nephrology Little Rock VA Med. Ctr., 1983-85; chief of nephrology West-Side VA Med. Ctr., Chgo., 1986-91, Asheville (N.C.) VA Med. Ctr., 1991-92; assoc. prof. of med. U. Ill., 1988-91; chief of nephrology Cath. Med. Ctr. of Bklyn. and Queens, Brooklyn, 1992—; clin. assoc. prof. Cornell U. Med. Coll., Elmhurst, N.Y., 1992-94; assoc. prof. medicine Yeshiva U., Bronx, 1994—.

TALUKDER, ASHIT, research scientist; b. Hyderabad, Andhra Pradesh, India; m. Shampa Talukder. BS, Osmania U., India, 1992; MS, Iowa State U., Ames, 1994; PhD, Carnegie Mellon U., Pitts., 1999. Sr. rsch. scientist Jet Propulsion Lab., NASA, Caltech, Pasadena, Calif., 1999—; rsch. asst. prof. U. Southern Calif., LA, 2003—; sr. rschr. Childrens Hosp. LA, 2003—. Tech. organizing com. mem. SPIE Def. and Security Symposium, Optical Pattern Recognition, Orlando, Fla. Mem.: SPIE. Achievements include patents for remote, non-contacting personnel bio-identification using microwave radiation; computer implemented plaque analysis system. Office: NASA Jet Propulsion Lab 4800 Oak Grove Dr MS 300-123 Pasadena CA 91109 Business E-Mail: ashit.talukder@jpl.nasa.gov.

TALWALKAR, ABHI Y. (ABHIJIT Y. TALWALKAR), computer company executive; b. Pune, India, 1965; BEE, Oreg. State Univ., 1985. Sr. engring., mktg. mgmt. Sequent Computer Sys. (now part of IBM), Bipolar Integrated Tech. Inc., Lattice Semiconductor Inc.; with Intel Corp., Santa Clara, Calif., 1993—2005, various positions including v.p., gen. mgr., enterprise platform group, v.p., co-gen. mgr., digital enterprise group; pres., CEO, dir. LSI Logic Corp., Milpitas, Calif., 2005—. Office: LSI Logic Corp 1621 Barber Ln Milpitas CA 95035 Office Phone: 408-433-8000.

TALWALKAR, SAMEER S., pathologist, researcher; s. Sadanand C. and Ranjana S. Talwalkar; m. Shruti Pai, Jan. 22, 2005. MD, U. of Mumbai, 2000. Med. intern K.J. Somaiya Med. Coll., U. of Mumbai, Maharashtra, India, 2000—01; rsch. fellow - hematology Bhavans SPARC Rsch. Ctr., U. of Mumbai, 2001—02; rsch. fellow gynecologic pathology U. of So. Calif., LA, 2002—03; resident anatomic and clin. pathology U. of Louisville Sch. of Medicine, Louisville, 2003—07; clin. fellow hematopathology U. of Tex., M.D. Anderson Cancer Ctr., Houston, 2007—08; clin. fellow molecular pathology U. Pitts., Pa., 2001; hematopathology & molecular genetic pathology fellow CPA Lab., Louisville, 2009—. Contbr. articles to profl. jours. Recipient Chairman's Recognition award - Outstanding Resident of the Yr., U. of Louisville, Dept. of Pathology, 2004, Distinction in Physiology, U. of Mumbai, 1997, Best Painting award, All India Drawing Contest, 1985; scholar Sir Dorabji Tata Trust scholar, Tata Trust, 2002. Mem.: AMA, Am. Soc. of Clin. Pathology, U.S. and Can. Acad. of Pathology, Coll. of Am. Pathologists (resident forum del. 2005—). Achievements include research in microarray-based charecterization of patients with Chronic Lymphocytic Leukemia. Office: CPA Lab 2307 Greene Way Louisville KY 40220 Personal E-mail: drsameerst@gmail.com.

TAM, SEE-YING SEBASTIAN, biomedical researcher, consultant, entrepreneur; arrived in USA, 1973, naturalized, 1988; s. Chung-Kwai Tam and Wai-Fong Yan; m. Mindy Ming-Chin Tsai, July 13, 1991; children: Jessica, Andrew. BS, Columbia U., NYC, 1977, MS, 1980; PhD, Yale U., New Haven, Conn., 1986. Postdoctoral fellow MIT, Cambridge, Mass., 1986—91; instr. Beth Israel Deaconess Hosp., Harvard Med. Sch., Boston, 1991—99; sr. rsch. scientist Stanford U., Calif., 1999—; founder, pres. Apollonian Biosystems Ltd., Hong Kong, 2008—. Cons. DiagCor Biosci. Ltd., 2007—. Contbr. articles to profl. jours. including Nature Immunology, Molecular and Cellular Biology, European Jour. Immunology, Blood, others. Recipient Nat. Rsch. Svc. award, NIH, 1986—89. Mem.: Internat. Soc. Stem Cell Rsch., Am. Assn. Immunologists, Soc. Neuroscience, Yale Club (Silicon Valley, Hong Kong), Phi Beta Kappa. Achievements include patents for molecular cloning and characterization of RabGEF1; generation of RabGEF1 knock-out mouse. Avocations: swimming, classical music, Chinese philosophy. Office: Stanford Univ Sch Medicine 269 Campus Dr CCSR#3255 Stanford CA 94305 Office Fax: 650-736-0073. Business E-Mail: stam@stanford.edu.

TAM, SUNNY WING YEE, physicist; s. Yin-Tso Tam and Yuk-Ying Sham Tam; m. Miho Ujimoto, Jan. 14, 1998; 1 child, Laurence Yoshina Ka-Ming. BA, U. of Calif., 1985—89; PhD, MIT, 1989—96. Rsch. asst. MIT, Cambridge, Mass., 1989—96, postdoctoral assoc., 1996—2000, rsch. scientist, 2000—06, rsch. affiliate, 2006—; assoc. rsch. prof. Plasma and Space Sci. Ctr., Nat. Cheng Kung U., Tainan, 2006—08; assoc. prof. Inst. Space Astrophysical and Plasma Scis., Nat. Cheng Kung U., Taiwan, 2008—. Team on polar wind rsch. Internat. Space Sci. Inst., Bern, Switzerland, 2000; chief guest editor Jour. Atmospheric and Solar-Terrestrial Physics, 2007; prin. investigator Nat. Ctr. for High-Performance Computing, Taiwan, 2006—07, Nat. Sci. Coun., 2007—, Nat. Space Orgn., Taiwan, 2007—; reviewer, lectr., spkr. in field; co-chmn. 2007 NCTS Plasma Sci. Workshop, Taiwan. Contbr. scientific papers. Co-convenor Asia Ocenia GeoSciences Soc. Meeting. Grantee, Nat. Ctr. for High-Performance Computing, Taiwan, 2006—07, Nat. Sci. Coun., Taiwan, 2007—; Edward Frank Kraft scholar, U. Calif., Berkeley, 1986, James Monroe McDonald scholar, Physics Dept., U. Calif., Berkeley, 1988, Rsch. grantee, NSF, 1996—2005, NASA, 2000—06. Mem.: Am. Geophys. Union (co-convener spl. session Fall mtg. 2005), Golden Key, Phi Beta Kappa Soc., Sigma Pi Sigma. Avocations: soccer, Scrabble, backgammon, fencing.

TAMADDON, SINA, information technology executive; b. Aug. 27, 1957; V.p. Advanced Tech. Software Alliance Inc.; v.p. profl. svcs. NeXT, 1994—96, v.p. Europe, 1996—97; sr. v.p. worldwide svc. and support Apple Computer Inc., v.p. and gen. mgr. Newton Group, sr. v.p. applications Cupertino, Calif., 1997—. Office: Apple Computer Inc 1 Infinite Loop Cupertino CA 95014 Office Phone: 408-996-1010.

TAMARELLI, ALAN WAYNE, venture capitalist; b. Wilkinsburg, Pa., Aug. 13, 1941; s. John Adam Tamarelli and Florence Eleanor (Heacock) T.; m. Carol Ann Crawford, Aug. 3, 1963; children: Robin Carol, Alan Wayne. BS, Carnegie Mellon U., 1963, MS, 1965, PhD, 1966; MBA, NYU, 1972. Engr. Exxon Corp., Linden, NJ, 1966, project leader, 1968-70; corp. planner Engelhard Minerals & Chem. Corp., Newark, 1970-71, asst. to exec. v.p., 1971-74, gen. mgr., 1974-77, v.p., 1977-79, group v.p., 1979-81; sr. v.p. Engelhard Corp., Iselin, NJ, 1981-83; chmn., chief exec. officer Dock Resins Corp, Linden, NJ, 1983—2000; pres. AWT Private Investments, 2000—. Mem. exec. com. nat. adv. coun. for environ. policy and tech. U.S. Dept. Environment Protection, Gov's. Econ. Task Force, N.J.; mem. exec. com. Alliance for Union County; chmn. Jumpstart N.J., Joseph Priestley Soc. Capt. U.S. Army, 1966-68. NSF fellow, 1963-66 Mem. Synthetic Organic Chems. Mfrs. Assn. (chmn., vice chmn., bd. govs.), Am. Chem. Soc., N.Y. Paint and Coatings Assn. (chmn., pres., v.p., sec., treas., bd. dirs.), Chem. Industry Coun. (chmn., bd. dirs., exec. com.), N.J. Energy Rsch. Inst. (founding trustee), Am. Mgmt. Assn., N.Y. Acad. Scis., Scabbard and Blade, Rotary (pres., v.p., sec. Linden Club), Linden Indsl. Assn. (pres.), Joseph Priestley Soc. (chmn.), Shakespeare Theater of N.J. (bd. dirs.), Sigma Xi, Tau Beta Pi, Phi Kappa Phi, Omicron Delta Kappa. Home: 49 Wexford Way Basking Ridge NJ 07920-2432 Office Phone: 908-581-4308.

TAMARGO, RAFAEL J., neurological surgeon, educator; b. Havana, Cuba, Mar. 22, 1958; AB magna cum laude, Princeton U., NJ, 1980; MD, Columbia U., NYC, 1984. Diplomate Am. Bd. Neurol. Surgery. Intern Columbia Coll. Physicians and Surgeons, NYC, 1984—85; resident in neurosurgery Johns Hopkins Hosp., Balt., 1985—92, active staff, 1992—, from assoc. prof. neurosurgery to Walter E. Dandy prof., 1998—2004, Walter E. Dandy prof., 2004—, assoc. prof. of otolaryngology, 2002—04, prof. otolaryngology, 2004—. Fellow ACS; mem. Am. Assn. Neurol. Surgeons. Office: Johns Hopkins Hosp 600 N Wolfe St Meyer 8-181 Baltimore MD 21287-0001 Office Phone: 410-614-1533. Business E-Mail: rtamarg@jhmi.edu.

TAMARO, GEORGE JOHN, retired consulting engineer; b. Weehawken, NJ, Mar. 16, 1937; s. Giorgio Angelo and Giacomina T.; m. Rosemary Ann Volta, June 24, 1961; children: Peter Louis, Jean Marie, Paul Anthony, Mark Joseph. BCE, Manhattan Coll., 1959; MCE, Lehigh U., 1961; M of Archtl. Tech., Columbia U., 1969. Profl. engr., N.Y., N.J., D.C., Md., Pa., Calif., Ill., La., Wis., Wash., R.I.; structural engr., Ill., Mass.; geotech. engr., Calif.; chartered engr., U.K.; registered European engr. Staff engr. Port Authority NY & NJ, NYC, 1961—71; v.p., chief engr. ICOS Corp. Am., NYC, 1971—80; sr. ptnr. Mueser Rutledge Cons. Engrs., NYC, 1980—2006; ret., 2007. Patentee in field; author tech. papers. Chmn. Bergen County Planning Bd., N.J., 1978-82; vice-chair Leonia (N.J.) Planning Bd., 1971-89; mem. Bd. Adjustment, Leonia, 1974-76; councilman Borough Governing Body, Leonia, 1972. Mem. ASCE (hon., Martin S. Kapp Found. Engr. award 1987, Homer Gage Balcom award 2002, Ralph B. Peck medal 2003, Friedman Profl. Recognition award 2003, OPAL award for engring. design 2004, Ernest E. Howard award 2006), NSPE (Annual award 2006), Am. Assn. Engring. Socs. (John Fritz medal 2005), Lehigh U.(Lynn Beedle award), Nat. Acad. Engring., Internat. Soc. Soil Mechs. and Found. Engrs., Deep Found. Inst. (Disting. Svc. award), The Moles (past pres., Outstanding Achievement in Constrn. award 2003, Beavers' award for outstanding achievement in heavy engring. constrn. 2004), Chi Epsilon (hon. mem. award 1990), Tau Beta Pi. Avocations: sailing, photography.

TAMAYO, JAMES ANTHONY, bishop; b. Brownsville, Tex., Oct. 23, 1949; BA magna cum laude, U. St. Thomas, Houston, MA; grad., St. Mary's Sem., Houston. Ordained priest Diocese of Corpus Christi, Tex., 1976; assoc. pastor St. Patrick Parish, 1976—81, adminstr., 1981; asst. pastor Corpus Christi Cathedral, 1981—82; assoc. pastor St. Pius X Parish, 1982—85; pastor St. Andrew by the Sea Parish, 1986—90, Blessed Sacrament Parish, Laredo, Tex., 1990—93; vicar, adminstr. Western vicariate Diocese of Corpus Christi, Tex., 1993; aux. bishop Archdiocese of Galveston-Houston, Tex., 1993—2000; ordained bishop, 1993; bishop Diocese of Laredo, Tex., 2000—. Staff mem. Cath. Charities, 1975—81; v.p., bd. dirs. Cath. Legal Immigration Network. State chaplain Cath. Daughters Am.; state coun. chaplain Knights of Columbus, Tex.; nat. episcopal advisor Cursillo Movement, Tex.; regional exec. bd. mem., mem. Hispanic com. on scouting Boy Scouts Am.; mem. Leadership Houston; bd. dirs. United Way of Tex. Gulf Coast, Houston; mem. fin. com. Inst. Hispanic Culture, Houston. Chaplain with the rank of major USAFR. Mem.: US Conf. Cath. Bishops (subcom. on Youth of the Secretariat 1996—99, Internat. Policy com. 1996—99, com. on Hispanic Affairs 1999—, subcom. on Hispanic Liturgy 1999—, com. on Pastoral Practices 1999—), US Cath. Conf., Nat. Conf. Cath. Bishops (Nat. Adv. coun. 1996—99, Adminstrv. bd. 1996—99), US Res. Officers Assn. (life), USAF Assn. (life). Roman Catholic. Address: Diocese of Laredo 1901 Corpus Christi St PO Box 2247 Laredo TX 78043-2247 Office Phone: 957-727-2140. Office Fax: 956-727-2777.

TAMBELLINI, STEVE, professional sports team executive, former professional hockey player; b. Trail, BC, Can., May 14, 1958; m. Denise Tambellini; children: Trisha, Jeff, Adam. Center NY Islanders, 1979—81, Colorado Rockies, 1981—82, NJ Devils, 1982—83, Calgary Flames, 1983—85, Vancouver Canucks, 1985—88, v.p. bus. ops., sr. v.p. hockey ops., 1997—98, v.p. player personnel, 1998—2004, v.p., asst. gen. mgr., 2004—08; gen. mgr. Edmonton Oilers, 2008—. Mem. Team Can., Olympic Games, Calgary, 1988, dir. player personal, Salt Lake City, 2002; gen. mgr. Team Can., World Hockey Championships, 2003, 05; dir. hockey ops. Team Can., World Cup of Hockey, 2004. Former pres. Canucks For Kids Fund. Recipient Jake Milford Plaque, 2004, BC Humanitarian of Yr. Award, BC Hockey Hall of Fame, 2006; named to BC Hockey Hall of Fame, 2004. Achievements include being a member of Stanley Cup Champion New York Islanders, 1980. Office: Edmonton Oilers Hockey Club 11230 - 110 St Edmonton AB T5G 3H7 Canada

TAMBLYN, AMBER ROSE, actress; b. Santa Monica, Calif., May 14, 1983; d. Russ and Bonnie Tamblyn. Actor: (TV series) General Hospital, 1995—2001, Joan of Arcadia, 2003—05, The Unusuals, 2009; (films) Live Nude Girls, 1995, Rebellious, 1995, Johnny Mysto: Boy Wizard, 1996, The Ring, 2002, The Sisterhood of the Traveling Pants, 2005, Stephanie Daley, 2006, The Grudge 2, 2006, Blackout, 2007, Spiral, 2007, Normal Adolescent Behavior, 2007, The Sisterhood of the Traveling Pants 2, 2008; (TV films) Prep, 2002, Babylon Fields, 2007, The Russell Girl, 2008, (guest appearances): Buffy the Vampire Slayer, 2001, Boston Public, 2002, Twilight Zone, 2002, CSI: Miami, 2002, Without a Trace, 2003, Punk'd, 2003. Office: c/o Hyler Mgmt 20 Ocean Park Blvd Ste 25 Santa Monica CA 90405

TAMBOR, JEFFREY, actor, theater director, educator; b. San Francisco, July 8, 1944; m. Kasia Ostlun, Oct. 6, 2001; children: Gabriel Kasper, Eve Julia. BA, San Francisco State; MFA, Wayne State U. Acting tchr. Milton Katselas' Acting Workshops, Beverly Hills, Calif. Actor (theatre) Sly Fox, 1976 (Broadway and L.A.), Measure for Measure, The Hands of the Enemy, Flea in Her Ear, American Mosaic; (films) ...And Justice For All, 1979, Saturday the 14th, 1981, Dreamchasers, 1982, The Man Who Wasn't There, 1983, Mr. Mom, 1983, No Small Affair, 1984, Desert Hearts, 1985, Three O'Clock High, 1987, Brenda Starr, 1989, Lisa, 1990, City Slickers, 1991, Life Stinks, 1991, Pastime, 1991, Article 99, 1992, Crossing the Bridge, 1992, The Webbers, 1993, A House in the Hills, 1993, Radioland Murders, 1994, Heavyweights, 1995, My Teacher's Wife, 1995, Big Bully, 1996, Dr. Dolittle, 1998, There's Something About Mary, 1998, Meet Joe Black, 1998, Muppets From Space, 1999, Teaching Mrs. Tingle, 1999, Girl Interrupted, 1999, Pollock, 2000, How the Grinch Stole Christmas, 2000, Never Again, 2001, Get Well Soon, 2001, Scorched, 2002, The Freshman, 2002, Malibu's Most Wanted, 2003, My Boss's Daughter, 2003, Nobody's Perfect, 2004, Hellboy, 2004, Funky Monkey, 2004, (voice) The SpongeBob SquarePants Movie, 2004, The King of Central Park, 2006, Slipstream, 2007, The Chubbchubbs Save Xmas, 2007, Superhero Movie, 2008, Hellboy II: The Golden Army, 2008, (voice) Monsters vs. Aliens, 2009, The Hangover, 2009; (TV series) The Ropers, 1979-80, Hill Street Blues, 1981-87, 9 to 5, 1982, Mr. Sunshine, 1986, (voice) Jonny Quest, 1986, Max Headroom, 1987-88, Studio 5-B, 1989, American Dreamer, 1990, The Larry Sanders Show, 1992-98 (Emmy award nominee 1993), Me & George, 1998, (voice) The Lionhearts, 1998, Everything's Relative, 1999, The Lot, 1999, (voice) Sammy, 2000, That Was Then, 2002, 3-South, 2002, Hollywood Squares (announcer), 2002-03, Arrested Development, 2003-06, Welcome to the Captain, 2008; (TV episodes) M*A*S*H, Barney Miller, L.A. Law, The Golden Girls, Empty Nest, Who's The Boss, Doogie Houser, M.D., Equal Justice, Murder She Wrote, Tales From The Crypt (Dead Right) (TV movies) Eddie and Herbert, 1977, Alcatraz: The Whole Shocking Story, 1980, A Gun in the House, 1981, The Star Maker, 1981, Pals, 1981, The Awakening of Candra, 1981, Take Your Best Shot, 1982, The Zertigo Diamond Caper, 1982, Cocaine: One Man's Seduction, 1983, Sadat, 1983, The Three Wishes of Billy Grier, 1984, Wildfire, 1986, A Quiet Little Neighborhood, a Perfect Little Murder, 1990, The Burden of Proof, 1992, 1775, 1992, (voice) Jonny's Golden Quest, 1993, Another Midnight Run, 1994, (voice) Jonny Quest vs. the Cyber Insects, 1995, The Man Who Captured Eichmann, 1996, Weapons of Mass Distraction, 1997, Eloise at the Plaza, 2003, Eloise at the Plaza, 2003, Eloise at Christmastime, 2003, The Muppets' Wonderful Wizard of Oz, 2005; (TV spls.) Living and Working in Space: The Countdown Has Begun; (TV miniseries) Robert Kennedy and His Times, 1985; dir. for numerous theatre companies including Seattle Repertory Theatre, Actors Theatre of Louisville, Milw. Repertory Theatre, Acad. Festival Theatre, Chgo., San Diego Shakespeare Festival, South Coast Repertory Theatre, Loeb Drama Ctr., Cambridge, Mass., Sky Light Theatre, L.A. Office: Care The Gersh Agency c/o Leslie Siebert 232 N Canon Dr Beverly Hills CA 90210-5302

TAMBOUR, SOPHIE, research scientist; b. Liège, Belgium, Sept. 26, 1979; Attending, U. Liège, Belgium, 2009. Rschr. FNRS, Liège, 1998—.

TAMBS, LEWIS ARTHUR, diplomat, historian, educator; b. San Diego, July 7, 1927; s. Fred B. and Marguerite Johanna (Tambs) Jones; m. Phyllis Ann Greer, 1982. BS, U. Calif., Berkeley, 1953; MA, U. Calif., Santa Barbara, 1962, PhD, 1967. Plant engr. Std. Brands, San Francisco, 1953—54; pipeline engr. Creole Petroleum Co., Caracas, Maracaibo, Venezuela, 1954—57; gen. mgr. Cacyp, Maracaibo, 1957—59; instr. Creighton U., 1965—67, asst. prof., 1967—69; prof. history Ariz. State U., Tempe, 1969—82, 1987—2002, dir. Ctr. L.Am. Studies, 1972—76; cons. NSC, 1982—83; U.S. amb. to Colombia, 1983—85; U.S. amb. to Costa Rica, 1985—87; ret., 2002. Author: East European and Soviet Economic Affairs, 1975, Historiography, Method and History Teaching, 1975, Hitler's Spanish Legion, 1979; editor: United States Policy Toward Latin America, 1976, Inter-American Policy for the 80's; co-editor: Santa Fe IV, 2000, English translation of Karl Haushofer's Geopolitics of the Pacific, 2002; co-author periodical guides; contbr. articles to profl. jours. Bd. dirs. Ariz.-Mex. Commn., 1974-82, Coun. Inter-Am. Security, 1979-90. With U.S. Army, 1945-47, 50-51. Faculty grantee, Ariz. State U., 1970, 1971, 1974, 1978, 1979. Roman Catholic. E-mail: lewtambs@aol.com.

TAMBURINE, JEAN HELEN, sculptor, painter, illustrator; b. Meriden, Conn., Feb. 20, 1930; m. Eugene E. Bertolli. Student, Art Students League, NYC, 1948-50; student of Jon Corbino, John Groth, Carlo Ciampaglia, Elisabeth Gordon Chandler. Exhibited group shows Rockport Art Assn., Mass., North Shore Arts Assn., Gloucester, Mass., George Walter Vincent Mus., Springfield, Mass., Hudson Valley Art Assn., NY, Pearl S. Buck Found., Phila., Am. Artists Profl. League, NY, Acad. Artists Assn., Springfield, Pen and Brush, NY; heritage bronze commd. by Wallingford Pub. Library, 1986, Conn.; represented in permanent collections Conn. State Library, Middletown, Nashville Pub. Library, Strong Sch., Hartford, Conn., L'Heure Joyeux, Paris; also pvt. collections; author, designer, illustrator: Almost Big Enough, 1963, I Think I Will Go to the Hospital, 1965, How Now, Brown Cow, 1967. Recipient Assoc. Members prize Acad. Artists, Founders prize Pen and Brush, 1981, 1st prize for sculpture Arts and Crafts Assn. of Meriden, Conn.; named to Meriden Hall of Fame. Mem. Rockport Art Assn. (Martha Moore Meml. award 1983), North Shore Arts Assn., Acad. Artists Assn., Salmagundi Club, Am. Artists Profl. League, Am. Medallic Sculpture Assn., FIDEM, Authors Guild. Home and Office: The Bertolli Studio 73 Reynolds Dr Meriden CT 06450-2532

TAMBURRO, PETER JAMES, JR., secondary school educator; b. Hoboken, NJ, Jan. 20, 1947; s. Peter James and Rose Catherine (Verta) Tamburro; m. Andrea Everitt Huber, Aug. 21, 1976 (div. 1998); children: Peter James III, Christopher Harding, Matthew Everitt. BA in Polit. Sci, Dickinson Coll., 1969; MAT in Social Studies, Trenton State Coll., 1973. Cert. secondary sch. tchr., social studies N.J. Tchr. Morris Sch. Dist., NJ, 1973-76, Hanover Park Regional HS Dist., East Hanover, NJ, 1976—2005, Frisch HS, 2005—. Cross country coach Hanover Park HS, 1983—2003, volleyball coach, 1990—98, asst. basketball coach, 1994—2001; judge Bicentennial Com., NJ; asst. basketball coach Caldwell Coll., 1989—93; cons. Hist. Commn., East Hanover, 1989—92; cons. for developing Advanced Placement history programs, reader Advanced Placement exams ETS; mem. hist. com. Washington Twp., 1994—97, curriculum adv. com., 1996—97; adj. prof. William Paterson U., NJ, 1999—; chess coach Frisch HS, 2005—, table tennis coach, 2006—; spkr. in field. Author: (book) Gateway to Morris, 1993, Learn Chess from the Greats, 2000; editor (with Dale Brandreth): The Chess Diary of Rudolph Spielmann; editor: Atlantic Chess News, 1973—76, 2000—02, Teaching Chess Step by Step, 2006; contbr. articles to chess mags.; nationally syndicated columnist: U.S. Chess Fedn., 1994—2001, columnist: Chessmates, Newark Star Ledger, 1997—, feature writer: Chess Life for Kids; host internet radio show Openings for Amateurs, www.chess.fm. Mem. Hist. Commn., Washington Twp., NJ, 1994—96; scoutmaster Boy Scouts Am., 1994—97; team capt. Rep. Nat. Conv., 2000; Rep. County Committeeman Hanover Twp., NJ, 1984—88; legis. aide Assemblyman Robert Martin, Trenton, 1985—89; Rep. County Committeeman Morristown, NJ, 2002—03. Named N.J.'s Outstanding Tchr. History, DAR, 1990, Cross Country State Section Champions, 1987, 2000, 2001, 2002, Morris County Coach of the Yr., Cross Country, 2000; grantee, NSF, 1978, Dodge Found., Madison, N.J., 1987; fellow Taft Inst. Two Party Govt., Fairleigh Dickinson U., 1984, Woodrow Wilson Found., 1991, Nat. Coun. Basic Edn., Washington, 1993. Mem.: Chess Journalists Am. (v.p. 1990—99, pres. 1999—2003, awards 1995, 1996, 1997, 2002, 2003, Journalist of Yr. 2006, awards 2006), US Chess Fedn. (nat. chmn. hist. com. 1994—99), NJ Edn. Assn., Hanover Park Regional Ednl. Assn. (v.p. 1994—95, pres. 1995—2001, chief negotiator 2003—05), Morris County Hist. Soc., Nat. Coun. Social Studies. Avocations: rare books, chess. Home: 22 Budd St Morristown NJ 07960-5304 Office: Frisch Sch Paramus NJ 07652

TAMERON, ALEXIS C., legislative staff member; Former polit. dir. Ariz. Dem. Party; dist. dir. to congressman Harry Mitchell US House of Reps., Washington, 2007—08, chief of staff, 2009—. V.p. Young Dems. of America Nat. Conv., San Francisco, 2005. Mem.: Latino Leaders Network. Democrat. Office: US House Reps 2434 Rayburn House Office Bldg Washington DC 20515 Office Phone: 202-225-2190. Office Fax: 202-225-3446.*

TAMEZ, LORRAINE DIANE, writer, nurse; b. Pueblo, Colo., Nov. 26, 1950; d. Daniel and Mary Ann (Abeyta) Tamez; children: David, Christopher, Lauren. AA in Creative Writing, Trinidad State Jr. Coll.; BA in Lit., U. Md. Cert. LPN nurse, Trinidad State Jr. Coll., Colo. Poetry editor Purgatoire Mag., 1997-98; editor, Trinidad Plus News, Chronicle News. Author: December Snow, 1996, Prairie Woman, 2000, Legends of Peoples of the Earth, Indian Folklore, 2003; contbr. poetry (as L.D. Tames), short stories various mags. With U.S. Army, 1969-71. Mem. PEN New Eng., Western Writers Am., Phi Betta Kappa. Democrat. Roman Catholic. Avocations: photography, photojournalism, poetry. Home and Office: PO Box 181 Trinidad CO 81082-0181

TAMIKO, WASHINGTON SUZETTE, theater educator; b. Houston, Aug. 1, 1967; d. Roosevelth Washington. MFA, U. Calif., 1992. Assoc. prof. theatre Chapman U., Orange, Calif., 1997—. Dir.: (play) Waiting for Godot (Spl. Award, 2002). Respondent KC-ACTF, Orange, Los Angeles, 1997—2008. Named one of Educator of Yr., KC-ACTF, 2005.

Mem.: SAG (actor 1998—2008), Actors Equity (actor 1994—2008). Achievements include development of American Noh Theatre. Home: 611 S Palm Street E La Habra CA 90631 Office: Chapman Univ One University Dr Orange CA 92866 Personal E-mail: atsumuri1998@yahoo.com. Business E-Mail: washingt@chapman.edu.

TAMKE, GEORGE WILLIAM, venture capitalist; b. Beacon, NY, May 16, 1947; s. George William and Josephine Edna (Carbone) Tamke; m. Christine Barbara MacLeod, June 28, 1969; children: Kara Lee, Shannon. BSChemE, Vanderbilt U., 1969; MS in Mgmt. Sci., Stanford U., 1979. With IBM, NY, Fla., Calif., Ga., Minn., 1969—86, dir. orgn. planning and sec. to corp. mgmt. com. White Plains, NY, 1981—82, v.p. mfg. Communication Products div., 1982—83, v.p. display products Communication Products div., 1983—84, asst. group exec. Info Systems, Products Group, 1984—86; pres. Cullinet Software, Inc., Westwood, Mass., 1986—87, COO, 1987—88; exec. v.p. Emerson Electric Co., St. Louis, 1989—; principal Clayton, Dubilier & Rice, 2000—; CEO Kinkos, 2001, chmn., 2001—04, Culligan Internat., 2004, Hertz Corp., 2005—06, Servicemaster Co., 2007—. CEO Astec (BSR) Plc, Hong Kong, 1989—; bd. dir. Target Corp. Contbr. articles to profl. jours. Avocations: tennis, golf. Office: Clayton Dubilier & Rice 375 Park Ave 18th Fl New York NY 10152-1899

TAMKIN, CURTIS SLOANE, real estate development company executive; b. Boston, Sept. 21, 1936; s. Hayward and Etta (Goldfarb) T.; m. Priscilla Martin, Oct. 18, 1975; 1 child, Curtis Sloane. BA in Econs., Stanford U., Calif., 1958. V.p., treas., dir. Hayward Tamkin & Co., Inc., mortgage bankers, LA, 1963-70; mng. ptnr. Property Devel. Co., LA, 1970-82; pres. The Tamkin Co., 1982—2000; chmn. Tamkin Capital Group L.L.C., 1999—. Mem. bd. govs. Music Ctr. LA, 1974—98; pres. LA Master Chorale Assn., 1974—78; mem. vis. com. Stanford U. Librs., 1982—86; vice-chmn. bd. dirs., mem. exec. com. LA Philharm. Assn., 1985—2006, vice chmn. bd., 2004—06, chmn. bd. overseers, 2001—07. Lt. (j.g.) USNR, 1960—63. Mem.: Hoover Instn. on War, Revolution and Peace, Stanford U., Nat. Coun. World Wildlife Fund, Pacific Council Internat. Policy, L.A. Jr. C. of C. (dir. 1968—69), Founders League L.A. Music Ctr. (pres. 1988—98, chmn. emeritus 1998—, cheualiers du Tastevin 2008—), Hillcrest Country Club, Burlingame Country Club. Home: 1230 Stone Canyon Rd Los Angeles CA 90077-2920 Office: 9460 Wilshire Blvd Beverly Hills CA 90212-2732

TAMM, JAYANTI, writer; b. Norwalk, Conn., Sept. 2, 1970; d. Rudra and Samarpana Tamm; m. Duane Patrick Dietz, June 2, 2005; 1 child, Nadira Juliet Dietz. MFA, Am. U., Washington, 2000. Prof. Ocean County Coll., Toms River, NJ, 2005—. Author: (book) Cartwheels in a Sari: A Memoir of Growing Up Cult, (plays) The Suicide Bomber. Vol. Big Bros. Big Sisters, Newton, NJ, 2005—. Office: Ocean County Coll College Dr Toms River NJ 08754

TAMMARO, KELLY ANN, pharmacist, researcher; b. Methuen, Mass., Mar. 9, 1978; s. Joseph Peter and Sheila Ann DiBurro; m. Daniel Pasquale Tammaro, Aug. 10, 2003. PharmD, Mass. Coll. Pharmacy and Allied Health Scis., Boston, 2002. Cert. pharmacist NH, 2002, Mass., 02. Pharmacy practice resident Boston VA Healthcare Sys., 2002—03, clin. oncology pharmacist, 2003—, clin. trials heme/oncology rsch. coord., mgr., 2005—. Mem.: Am. Soc. Hosp. Pharmacist. Achievements include research in effects of oxaliplatin induced neurotoxicity. Office: Boston VA Healthcare Sys 150 South Huntington Avenue Boston MA 02130 Business E-Mail: kelly_tammaro_va@yahoo.com.

TAMMEUS, WILLIAM DAVID, journalist, columnist; b. Woodstock, Ill., Jan. 18, 1945; s. W. H. and Bertha H. (Helander) T.; m. Marcia Bibens, Nov. 29, 1996; children: Lisen Tammeus Mann, Kate Tammeus Willaredt; stepchildren: Christopher L. Johnston, Daniel Bednarczyk, Kathryn W. Bednarczyk, David Bednarczyk. BJ, U. Mo., Columbia, 1967; postgrad., U. Rochester, 1967-69. Reporter Rochester (N.Y.) Times-Union, 1967-70; reporter Kansas City (Mo.) Star, 1970-77, columnist, 1977—2008; blogger Faith Matters, 2004—; syndicated columnist N.Y. Times News Svc., 1989-99, Knight Ridder/Tribune Info. Svcs., 2000—06; ret., 2006. Author: A Gift of Meaning, 2001, They were Just People: Stories of Rescue in Poland During the Holocaust, 2009; editor-at-large Presbyn. Outlook, 1993; contbg. editor Mo. Life mag., 1980-81; commentator Sta. KCPT-TV, 1979-90, colunist, 2009-. Co-recipient Pulitzer prize for gen. local reporting of Hyatt Regency Hotel disaster, 1982; recipient 1st pl. opinion-editl. divsn. Heart of Am. award Kansas City Press Club, 1991, 93, 1st pl. column divsn., 1994, 1st pl. award best column/humor divsn. Mo. Press Assn., 1997, 2002, Best In-Depth Reporting on Religion award Am. Acad. Religion, 2001, David Steele Disting. Writer award Presbyn. Writers Guild, 2003, 1st pl. religion coverage Kans. Press Assn., 2004, Wilbur Column Writing award, Religion Communicators Coun., 2005, 1st pl. best feature column divsn. Mo. Press Assn., 2006. Mem. Nat. Soc. Newspaper Columnists (v.p. 1990-92, pres. 1992-94, 1st pl. items divsn. Writing award 1992, 3d place humor writing, 1999, 2000), Soc. Profl. Journalists. Presbyterian. Personal E-mail: wtammeus@kc.rr.com.

TAMMINGA, CAROL ANN, neuroscientist; b. Grand Rapids, Mich., Jan. 26, 1946; d. Samuel William and Freda (Hekman) T.; children: Cristan Fredericka, Bonnie Michael. BS, Calvin Coll., 1966; student, U. Tubingen, Fed. Republic of Germany, 1966-67; MD, Vanderbilt U., 1971. Lic. physician, Ill., Md. Vivian Allen fellow Vanderbilt Med. Sch., 1968-71; intern in medicine Blodgett Meml. Hosp., Grand Rapids, Mich., 1971-72; resident in psychiatry U. Chgo., 1972-74, chief resident in psychiatry, 1974-75, instr. dept. psychiatry, 1975-77, asst. prof. psychiatry, 1978-79; assoc. prof. psychiatry U. Md., Balt., 1979-85, chief inpatient rsch. program, 1979—, prof. psychiatry, 1985—. Chief clin. investigator Manteno (Ill.) State Hosp., 1975-79; chief clin. biochemistry unit Nat. Inst. Neurologic & Communicative Diseases & Stroke NIH, Bethesda, Md., 1979-85; mem. treatment devel. and assessment rsch. rev. com. NIMH, 1981-85, 90-94, 96-99; mem. FDA Psychopharm Adv. Com., 1990-92, 97—, chair, 1991-92, 98—; mem. Inst. Medicine, NAS, 1998—; cons. in field. Author: Schizophrenia: Scientific Progress, 1988, Schizophrenia Research, 1989; editorial bd. Am. Jour. Psychiatry, Biol. Psychiatry, Jour. Nervous and Mental Diseases, Schizophrenia Bull., Schizophrenia Rsch., Functional Neurology, Progress in Neuroendocrinimmunology, Progress in Neuro-Psychopharmacology and Biol. Psychiatry; contbr. articles to Archive Gen. Psychiatry Sci., Am. Jour. Psychiatry, Jour. Neural Transmission, Lancet, Physiol. Behavior, and other. Recipient McAlpin award Nat. Assn. Mental Health, 1979, Dean award, 1995; Beauchamp scholar, 1971; Found. for Rsch. in Psychiatry fellow, 1975-76, NIMH fellow, 1978-79. Mem. AAAS, Am. Psychiatric Assn., Am. Coll. Neuropharmacology, Internat. Psychoneuroendocrine Soc., Soc. Neurosci., Biol. Psychiatry. Achievements include research in schizophrenia. Office: U Md PO Box 21247 Baltimore MD 21228-0747 E-mail: ctamming@MPRC.umaryland.edu.

TAMPAS, JOHN P., radiologist; married; children: Jessica, Peter, Andrea, Christiana. BS, U. Vt., 1951, MD, 1954. Diplomate Am. Bd. Radiology. Radiology resident U. Vt., Burlington, 1957—60; teaching fellow pediat. radiology L.A. Children's Hosp., 1960—61; NIH Nat. Heart Inst. resident fellow cardiovascular radiology U. Ind., Indpls., 1961—62; attending radiology Med. Ctr. Hosp. Vt., Burlington, 1962—; asst. prof. radiology Coll. Medicine U. Vt., 1962—70; prof. & chmn. dept. radiology Med. Ctr. Hosp. Vt., Burlington, 1970—96. Contbr. articles to profl. jours. Recipient Karl Jefferson Thompson Meml. Excellence in Tchg. award, 1969, 1975; scholar, James Picker Found./NRC, 1962—65. Fellow: Am. Coll. Radiology (pres. 1987—88, bd. chancellors, emergency radiology com., accreditation com., chmn. mem. ins. com., adminstrv. affairs commn., radiologic practice commn., Gold medal 1996); mem.: AMA, Vt. Med. Soc., Vt. Radiol. Soc., Assn. Univ. Radiologists, Soc. Chmn. Acad. Radiology Depts., New Eng. Roentgen Ray Soc., Radiol. Soc. N.Am., Am. Roentgen-Ray Soc. (pres. 1982—83, Gold medal 1992), Soc. Pediat. Radiology, Alpha Omega Alpha. Office: Fletcher Allen Health Ctr 111 Colchester Ave Burlington VT 05401-1416 also: Hosp Vt Med Ctr Dept Radiology Burlington VT 05401

TAMURA, SHIGEMI, electric power industry executive; b. 1938; Chmn. Tokyo Elec. Power Co., Inc., 2002—08. Co-dir. Rsch. Inst. Urban & Environ. Devel.; dir. bd. dirs. e7 Fund, 2003; dir. AOC Holdings Inc.; rep. pres. Inst. Rsch. and Innovation; mem. exec. com. Japan-U.S. Bus. Council. Mem.: Assn. Radio Industries and Businesses (dir. 2005—), Engring. Acad. Japan.

TAN, ALFREDO CHENG, engineering educator, director; s. Chua Tan and Boc Lee Cheng; m. Rose Mary Ang; children: Christopher Michael, Alfred Vincent. BS in Mech. Engring., Adamson U., Manila, Philippines, 1979, BS in Elec. Engring., 1980; MS in Elec. Engring., Stevens Inst. Tech., Hoboken, NJ, 1984, PhD in Elec. Engring., 1988. Cert. mech. engr., Philippine Bd. Mech. Engring., 1981, asst. elec. engr., Philippine Bd. Elec. Engring., 1981. Dir., sch. engring. and engring. tech. Fairleigh Dickinson U., Teaneck, NJ, 1996—2003, prof. elec. engring., 1988—, dir., gildart haase sch. computer sci. and engring., 2003—. Contbr. scientific papers. Recipient 2nd Pl., Philippine Asst. Elec. Engr. Licensure Exam., 1981, Disting. Faculty award, Fairleigh Dickinson U., 2003, Profl. Achievement award, Philippine Chinese Assn. Am., 2008; grantee grant, John Victor Machuga Found., grants, Paterson Sch. Dist., 2007;, Mech. Contractors Assn. NJ, 2003, Greg Olsen Found., 2005, Toyota USA Found., 2005—, John Victor Machuga Found., 2005—, Exxon Mobil Found., 2005—, Paterson Sch. Dist., 2005—, PSE&G, BAE Sys., 2005—. Mem.: IEEE (vice chairman signal processing chpt. 2001, award 2003), Eta Kappa Nu. Office: Fairleigh Dickinson Univ 1000 River Rd Teaneck NJ 07666 Business E-Mail: tan@fdu.edu.

TAN, AMY RUTH, writer; b. Oakland, Calif., Feb. 19, 1952; d. John Yueh-han and Daisy Ching (Tu) Tan; m. Louis M. DeMattei, Apr. 6, 1974. Student, Linfield Coll., McMinnville, Oreg.; BA in Linguistics/English, with honors, San Jose State U., Calif., 1973, MA in Linguistics, 1974; LHD (hon.), Dominican Coll., San Rafael, 1991. Specialist lang. devel. Alameda County Assn. for Mentally Retarded, Oakland, 1976-80; project dir. M.O.R.E., San Francisco, 1980-81; mng. editor Emergency Medicine Reports newsletter, San Francisco; freelance writer, 1981-88. Lit. editor West mag. LA Times. Author: (novels) The Joy Luck Club, 1989 (Gold award for fiction, Commonwealth Club, 1990, Bay Area Book Reviewers award, 1990), The Kitchen God's Wife, 1991, The Hundred Secret Senses, 1995, The Bonesetter's Daughter, 2001, The Opposite of Fate: A Book of Musing, 2003, Saving Fish from Drowning, 2005, (children's books) The Moon Lady, 1992, The Chinese Siamese Cat, 1994, (Operas) The Bonesetter's Daughter, 2008; prodr.; (films) The Joy Luck Club, 1993. Recipient Best Am. Essays award, 1991. Office: c/o Putnam Publicity 375 Hudson Street New York NY 10014

TAN, CHADE-MENG, application developer, educator; b. Singapore; Jolly Good fellow Google Inc., Mountain View, Calif., 2000—. Pres. Tan Teo Charitable Found. Recipient Outstanding Young Alumni award, Nanyang Technol. U., 2008. Office: Google Inc 1600 Amphitheatre Pky Mountain View CA 94043 Business E-Mail: meng@google.com.

TAN, CHIN-TUAN, medical educator, engineering educator, consultant; s. Yan-Heng Tan and Bok-Lian Ang; m. Junko Matsumoto; 1 child, Xiu-Jun Hidetoshi. PhD, Nanyang Technol. U. Sch. Elec. and Electronic Engring., Singapore, 2000. Adj. assoc. prof., dept. elec. & computer engring. NY U., Bklyn., 2007—, rsch. asst. prof., dept. otolaryngology NYC, 2008—. Cons. Samsung Electronics Co. Ltd. Telecom. R&D Ctr. Codec Lab., Suwon-City, Gyeonggi-do, 2008—. Grantee, Nokia, Finland, 2001—03, Deafness Rsch. Found., 2008—. Mem.: Audio Engring. Soc., Acoustical Soc. America. Achievements include patents for quality of sounds subjected to spectral distortion. Office: NY Univ Otolaryngology 550 1st Ave NBV 5E5 New York NY 10016 Office Fax: 212-263-8257. Business E-Mail: chin-tuan.tan@nyumc.org.

TAN, DONGFENG, pathologist, educator; s. Tan Jiaqi and Tang Shubao; m. Helen Zhou. Degree in Medicine, Tongji Med. Coll., Wuhan, 1987. Diplomate Am. Bd. Pathology, 1998. Rsch. scientist Columbia U., NYC, 1990—94; resident pathology Yale Sch. Medicine, New Haven, 1994—98; fellow tumor pathology Meml. Sloan-Kettering Cancer Ctr., NYC, 1998—99; asst. prof. Roswell Pk. Cancer Ctr. & SUNY, Buffalo, 1999—2004; assoc. prof. MD Anderson Cancer Ctr. & U. Tex. Health Sci. Ctr., Houston, 2004—. Vis. scholar Essen U., Germany, 1987—90. Recipient award, Am. Profl. Registry.

TAN, ENG MENG, immunologist, biomedical researcher; b. Seremban, Malaysia, Aug. 26, 1926; arrived in US, 1950; s. Ming Kee and Chooi Eng (Ang) T.; m. Liselotte Filippi, June 30, 1962; children: Philip, Peter. BA, Johns Hopkins U., 1952, MD, 1956. Intern Duke U., Durham, NC, 1956-57; resident, fellow Case-We. Res. U., Cleve., 1957-62; rsch. assoc. Rockefeller U., NYC, 1962—65; asst. prof. Washington U. Sch. Medicine, St. Louis, 1965—67; assoc. mem. and mem. Scipps Rsch. Inst., LaJolla, Calif., 1967—77; prof. Scripps Rsch. Inst., LaJolla, Calif., 1982—2006, prof. emeritus, 2006—; prof. U. Colo. Sch. Medicine, Denver, 1977-82. Chmn. allergy & immunology rsch. com. NIH, Bethesda, Md., 1982-84; mem. nat. arthritis adv. bd. HHS, Washington, 1981-85; hon. prof. Shanghai Jiao Dong U., Zhengzhou U., China. Contbr. chapters to books, articles to profl. jours. Recipient US Sr. Scientist award, Humboldt Found., Germany, 1986, Ciba-Giegy-Internat. League against Rheumatism award, 1989, Carol Nachman award, Wiesbaden, Germany, 1989, Lee Howley Sr. award, Arthritis Found., 1989, Paul Klemperer award and medal, NY Acad. Medicine, 1993, City Medicine award, Durham, NC, 1996, Disting. Med. Alumnus award, Duke U., 2000, Mayo Soley award, Western Soc. Clin. Investigation, 2002, Japan Rheumatism Found. Internat. prize, 2003, Meritorious Svc. award, European League Against Rheumatism, 2005, Lifetime Achievement award, 8th Internat. Lupus Congress, China, 2007; named to Nat. Lupus Hall Fame, 1984. Fellow AAAS; mem. Am. Coll. Rheumatology (pres. 1984-85, chmn. Blue Ribbon com. Future Acad. Rheumatology 1997-98, Disting. Investigator award 1991, Gold medal award 1998), Assn. Am. Physicians, Am. Soc. Clin. Investigation, Western Assn. Physicians (v.p. 1980-81), Am. Assn. Immunologists, Brazilian Soc. Rheumatology (hon.), Australian Rheumatism Assn. (hon.), Brit. Soc. Rheumatology (hon.), Mex. Nat. Acad. Medicine (hon.). Achievements include research on antibodies and antigens in cancer and in autoimmune diseases, systemic lupus erythematosus, scleroderma, Sjogren's syndrome, myositis and mixed connective tissue disease; relationship of autoantibodies to pathogenesis. Home: 8303 Sugarman Dr La Jolla CA 92037-2224 Office: Scripps Rsch Inst 10550 N Torrey Pines Rd La Jolla CA 92037-1000 Office Phone: 858-784-8686. Business E-Mail: emtan@scripps.edu.

TAN, GANG, engineering educator; married. B in Engring., Tsinghua U., Beijing, China, 1999; MA, Princeton U., NJ, 2001, PhD, 2005. Rsch. summer intern NEC Labs Am., Princeton, 2004, Microsoft Rsch., Redmond, Wash., 2002, cons. rschr., 2007—08; asst. prof. computer sci. Boston Coll., 2005—08; asst. prof. computer sci. and engring. Lehigh U., Bethlehem, Pa., 2008—. Contbr. articles to profl. sci. jours. Faculty fellowship, Boston Coll., 2008, Collaborative Rsch. grant, NSF, 2008—. Mem.: IEEE, USENIX, ACM. Achievements include patents pending for tamper response mechanism. Office: Lehigh Univ 19 Memorial Dr W Bethlehem PA 18034

TAN, JUN, psychology professor, researcher; s. Tan and Zhang; m. Jin Zeng, July 4, 1999; 1 child, Justin. MD, 3rd Mil. Med. U., Chongqing, China, 1992; PhD, Fudan U., Shanghai, 1992. Assoc. prof. dept. psychiatry U. South Fla. Silver Child Devel. Ctr., 2004—07, Robert A. Silver chair, prof., 2007—, dir. Devel. Neurobiology Lab., 2007—. Recipient Investigator-Initiated award, Alzheimer Assn., 2003, Investigator award, Inst. Study of Aging, 2006. Achievements include patents for evaluating the therapeutic effectiveness of agents in reducing Alzheimer's disease pathology. Office: Univ S Fla 3515 E Fletcher Ave Tampa FL 33613 Office Fax: 813-974-1130. Business E-Mail: jtan@hsc.usf.edu.

TAN, LIQIN, artist, educator; arrived in US, 2000, permanent resident, 2003; s. Hong Jun Tan and Bing Xi Xian; m. Kuan Dong; children: Ju, Shelly. Diploma in Fine Arts, Hengyang Tchrs. Coll., Hengyang, China, 1981; cert. in Art History, Ctrl. Acad. Fine Arts, Beijing, 1984; BA, Hunan Normal U., ChangSha, China, 1987; MA, Concordia U., Montreal, Can., 1993; cert. in Animation, Sharidan Coll., Ont., Can., 1995, cert., 1996; cert. in Softimage/XSI, Nat. Animation and Design Ctr., Can., 2000; cert. in Softimage/XSI Character Animation, Mesmer Animation Lab., Seattle, 2003. Cert. in advanced Softimage instrn. AVID Tech. Inc., Can., 1999. Instr. art Hengyang Tchrs. Coll., China, 1981—85; exec. art editor Hunan Art Pub. Ho., ChangSha, China, 1985—87; dir. art 12 Sources Arts Inc., Mississauga, Ont., Canada, 1991—96; lectr. Ngee Ann Poly., Singapore, 1997—2000; prof. Rutgers U., Camden, NJ, 2000—. Adj. prof. digital media ctr. Seneca Coll., Toronto, Canada, 2000; visiting prof. China Comm. U., 2007—; adj. prof. Perking U., 2008—. Exhibitions include Hopkins Ho. Gallery, Hadden, 2002 (Best of Show award, 2002), Int'l Digital Media & Arts Assn., 2004 (Best of Show award iDEAa Exhbn., 2004), Da Vinci Art Alliance, Phila., 2004 (Gold medal, 2004), Ctr. Digital Art, LA, 2004 (Second Pl. award, 2004), Gallery Internat., Balt., 2004 (Excellence award, 2004), Period Gallery, Omaha, 2004 (Excellence award, 2004), Shanghai Duolun Museum of Modern Art, 2005, The Noyes Museum of Arts, NJ, 2006, Butler Inst. Am. Art, Ohio, 2006 (First Pl. 5th Ann. Digital Art and Computer Animation Juried Competition award, 2006), Modern Art Mus. Forth Worth, 2006, Prix Ars Electronic, 2007—08 (Excecllent & 1st. prize, 3rd China Academic award), Beijing World Art Mus., 2008, LaSalle U. Art Mus., 2009. Final judging pres. 3rd China Internat. Student Animation Festival, 2008. Grantee, Rutgers U., 2001—08, Lindback Found., 2002, Bildner Family Found., 2003—05; John W. O'Brien Grad. fellowship, Concordia U., 1987. Mem.: AAUP, SIGGRAPH (juror art gallery 2006—07, assoc. art panel organizer 2007, curator students' print/animation competition 2007—), CGIV Penang, Malaysia (juror 2008), Internat. Conf. on IV London, UK (joror art gallery 2008), Internat. Media and Arts Assn. Office: Rutgers Univ 314 Linden St Camden NJ 08102 Office Phone: 856-225-6247. Office Fax: 856-225-6330. Personal E-mail: liqintan@gmail.com. Business E-Mail: ltan@camden.rutgers.edu.

TAN, LI-SU LIN, accountant, insurance company executive, consultant, registered investment advisor representative; b. Keelung, Taiwan, Republic of China, Mar. 7, 1956; arrived in US, 1985; d. I-Chang and Sung-Mei (Chen) Lin; m. Bert T. Tan, Aug. 19, 1985; children: Patricia Tan, Peter Puwen Tan, Lotus Tan. BBA, Nat. Taiwan U., 1978; MBA, Ill. Inst. Tech., Chgo., 1991. CPA, Ill., Taiwan; lic. ins. agt., Ill. Asst. mgr. T.N. Soong & Co. (mem. firm Arthur Anderson & Co., SC), Taipei, 1978—85; practitioner Li-Su Lin, CPA, Taipei, 1981—85, Li-Su Lin Tan, CPA, Naperville, Ill., 1988—90; pres. Lisu L. Tan & Co., Ltd., CPAs, Naperville, 1990—; agt. Mut. Omaha Co., Lombard, Ill., 1991—94, Met. Life and Affiliated Cos., Bloomingdale, Ill., 1993—98, GE Fin. Assurance, Schaumburg, Ill., 1999—. Chair family Naperville Chinese Assn., 1990. Mem.: AICPA (tax divsn., quality control program), Ill. Soc. CPA, Chinese Women's League Chgo. Assn. (bd. dir. 2006—), Amitabha Buddhist Libr. Chgo. (pres. 2003—, bd. dir.), Buddha's Light Internat. Assn. (pres. Chgo. chpt. 2002—04, bd. dir.), Chinese Am. Culture Found. (pres. 2001—, bd. dir.), Nat. Taiwan U. Alumni Assn. Greater Chgo. (bd. dir. 1999—2003), World Taiwanese C. of C. (dep. treas. 1998—99), Taiwanese C. of C. N.Am. (treas. 1998—99, bd. dir.), Greater Chgo. Area Taiwanese Am. C. of C. (bd. dir. 1995—2006), Taipei First Girls High Alumni Assn. (treas. 1990—94). Buddhist. Avocations: travel, art, photography. Office: Lisu L Tan & Co Ltd CPAs 24W500 Maple Ave #107 Naperville IL 60540 Office Phone: 630-416-9422. Business E-Mail: lisu@lisutancpas.com.

TAN, MASAKI, surgeon, director; b. Akita, Japan, Feb. 13, 1946; s. Chiyoshi and Masae (Akahira) T.; m. Keiko Takahashi, Jan. 28, 1975; children: Hiroki, Chihiro. MB, Tohoku U., Sendai, Japan, 1971, MD, 1978; LLB, Kinki U., Osaka, Japan, 1985. Asst. prof. dept. surgery Tohoku U., Sendai, 1973-85; head dept. surgery Ohfunato Prefectural Hosp., Japan, 1985-88, Kitakami Prefectural Hosp., Japan, 1988-94, Isawa Prefectural Hosp., Mizusawa, Japan, 1994-98; vice dir. Wakayanagi Hosp., Kurihara, Japan, 1998—. Author: Recent Advances in Chemotherapy, 1985, New Applications of OK-432, 1986. Mem. AAAS, Am. Chem. Soc., NY Acad. Sci. Avocations: reading, movies, music, travel. Office: Wakayanagi Hosp 23-4 Kawakitaharahata Wakayanagi Kurihara Miyagi Japan Home Phone: 0228324122; Office Phone: 0228322335. Personal E-mail: mtan@mve.biglobe.ne.jp. Business E-Mail: mtan09-28-04ocn.com@eos.ocn.ne.jp.

TAN, SONGXIN, science educator; m. Zixing Shen; 1 child, Kyle Tan. PhD, U. Nebr., Lincoln, 2004. Asst. prof. SD State U., Brookings, 2004—. Mem.: IEEE, SPIE. Achievements include research in lidar remote sensing, machine vision, and image processing. Business E-Mail: songxin.tan@sdstate.edu.

TAN, TJIAUW-LING, psychiatrist, educator; b. Pemalang, Java, Indonesia, June 2, 1935; came to U.S., 1967; naturalized, 1972; s. Ping-Hoey and Liep-Nio (Liem) T.; m. Esther Joyce Kho, June 2, 1961; children: Paul Budiman, Robert Yuling, Alice Ayling. BS, U. Indonesia Faculty Medicine, 1957, MD, 1961; postgrad., U. Indonesia, Jakarta, 1961-65,

UCLA, 1967-71, Pa. State U., 1971-72. Diplomate Am. Bd. Psychiatry and Neurology, Gen. Psychiatry, Bd.Psychiatry & Neurology, Geriat. Psychiatry. Lectr. psychiatry U. Indonesia, Jakarta, 1965-67; psychiat. cons. Ctrl. Gen. Hosp., Jakarta, 1965-67; postdoctoral fellow UCLA Brain Rsch. Inst., 1967-69; asst. rsch. psychiatrist, dept. psychiatry Neuropsychiat. Inst., UCLA, 1969-70; asst. prof. psychiatry Pa. State U., 1972-87, assoc. prof. psychiatry, 1987-99, prof. psychiatry, 1999—. Chief inpatient psychiatry Univ. Hosp. Milton S. Hershey Med. Ctr., 1972-2005, dir. Behavioral Medicine Clinic, co-dir. Biofeedback Lab., 1975—2005; cons. psychiatry Family and Children's Svc. Lebanon County, Lebanon, Pa., 1971-79. Contbr. articles to profl. jours. Bd. dir. Retarded Children's Assn. Dauphin County, Inc., 1971—73. Fellow Am. Psychiat. Assn. (disting. life), Pa. Psychiat. Soc.; mem. Ctrl. Pa. Psychiat. Soc., Assn. Advancement Behavior Therapy, Assn. Applied Psychophysiology and Biofeedback, Soc. Behavioral Medicine, Assn. Psychophysiol. Study of Sleep, Am. Assn. for Geriat. Psychiatry, Am. Geriat. Soc. Democrat. Presbyterian. Home: 1478 Bradley Ave Hummelstown PA 17036-9143 Office: Pa State U Coll Medicine Dept Psychiatry 500 University Dr Hershey PA 17033-2390 Home Phone: 717-566-3009; Office Phone: 717-782-6430. Business E-Mail: lingtan@psu.edu.

TAN, WANPENG, physicist; b. China; married. PhD, Mich. State U., East Lansing, 2002. Rsch. faculty mem. U. Notre Dame, Ind., 2007—, Joint Inst. Nuc. Astrophysics, 2007—. Contbr. articles to sci. jours. (Overseas Young Returning Scientist award, CCAST, 2003). Mem.: Am. Phys. Soc. Achievements include research in nuclear astrophysics including the understanding of the ignition conditions of X-ray bursts; nuclear reaction physics including original work on nuclear isospin fractionation, isoscaling, and particle correlations. Office: Univ Notre Dame 225 Nieuwland Sci Hall Notre Dame IN 46556

TAN, XIANGLIN, epidemiologist, researcher; married. MB, Tongji Med. Coll., HuaZhong U. Sci. and Tech., Wuhan, China, 1999, MS, 2002; D in Medicine, German Cancer Rsch. Ctr., U. Heidelberg, 2006. Postdoc. fellow, dept. health Wadsworth Ctr., NYS, Albany, 2006—08; rsch. assoc. Albert Einstein Coll. Medicine, Bronx, NY, 2008—. Fellowship, Prevent Cancer Found., Chemoprevention, 2007. Office: Albert Einstein Coll Medicine 1301 Morris Pk Ave Bronx NY 10461 Business E-Mail: xtan@aecom.yu.edu.

TAN, YONG, electronics engineer; m. Ye Lu, Oct. 31, 2006. BS in Engring., Tongji U., Shanghai, 1999, MS in Engring., 2002; DEng, U. Mass., Lowell, 2005. EIT SC, 2006. Project engr. WPC, Inc., Savannah, Ga., 2005—; rsch. asst. U. Mass., Lowell, tchg. asst. Contbr. scientific papers to profl. jours. Office: WPC Inc 2201 Rowland Ave Savannah GA 31404 Business E-Mail: tanyong21th@hotmail.com.

TANABE, CHARLES Y., lawyer; b. Denver, Nov. 27, 1951; BA cum laude, U. Colo., 1973; JD, U. Calif., Berkeley, 1976. Bar: Colo. 1976. Atty. Sherman & Howard LLC, Denver; gen. counsel Liberty Media Corp., Englewood, Colo., 1999—2001, sr. v.p., sec., gen. counsel, 2001—07, exec. v.p., sec., gen. counsel, 2007—. Bd. dir. FUN Technologies Inc. Mem. ABA, Phi Beta Kappa. Office: Liberty Media Corp 12300 Liberty Blvd Englewood CO 80112

TANACHAIWIWAT, SAPON, information technology manager; b. Bangkok; married. PhD in Elec. Engring., U. Southern Calif., LA, 2007. Rsch. asst. U. Southern Calif., 2001—07; project mgr. Innovative Scheduling Inc., Gainesville, 2007—.

TANAGHO, EMIL ABDELSAYED, urologist, eductor; b. Tahte, Egypt, Aug. 12, 1929; came to U.S., 1963; m. Mona Fawzy Armanious; children: Radgia, Nancy, Rafik. MB, ChB, Alexandria U., Egypt, 1952, MSurg in Urology, 1957. Resident in surgery Alexandria U., 1953-54, resident in urology, 1955-57, clin. demonstrator urology, 1957-59; lectr. urology Alexandria u., 1959-62; rsch. urologist Inst. Urology, London, 1962-63, U. Calif., San Francisco, 1963-64; asst. prof. urology Alexandria U., 1964-66, U. Calif., San Francisco, 1967-70, assoc. prof., 1970-72, prof., 1972, 76—, chmn. dept., 1976-96. Recipient Declaration of Merit, Govt. of Egypt, 1978, Jacob K. Javits Neurosci. award, 1985, Valentine medal N.Y. Acad. Medicine, 1997. Mem. Am. Urology Assn. (Disting. mem. 1995, cons. internat. rels. 1985, postgrad. instrn. com. western sect. 1977-87), Urodynamic Soc. (chair common neurophysiology 1978). Home: 408 Biscayne Dr San Rafael CA 94901-8319 Office: 400 Parnassus A-610 PO Box 330 Box 0330 San Francisco CA 94104-0330

TANAKA, HIROSHI L., atmospheric scientist; b. Shibata, Niigata, Japan, Dec. 22, 1957; came to U.S. 1981; s. Wazoh and Chieko T.; m. Masayo Takagi, Oct. 18, 1981; children: Daiki, Lisa. BSc in Geoscience, U. Tsukuba, Japan, 1980; PhD in Atmospheric Sci., U. Mo., Columbia, 1988. Sr. rsch. specialist atmospheric scis. U. Mo., Columbia, 1981-88; asst. prof. Geophys. Inst. U. Alaska, Fairbanks, 1988-91; asst. prof. Inst. Geoscience U. Tsukuba, Japan, 1991-2001, assoc. prof. life and environ. sci., 2001—05, prof. Ctr. Computational Scis., 2005—. Contbr. articles to sci. jours. Mem. Am. Meteor Soc. (Fathest North pres. 1990-91), Japan Meteor Soc. (Yamamoto Shono award 1992), Sigma Xi (Grad. Student award 1988). Home: 2511-1 Saiki Tsukuba 305-0028 Japan Office: U Tsukuba Ctr Computational Scis Tsukuba 305-8577 Japan Business E-Mail: tanaka@sakura.cc.tsukuba.ac.jp.

TANAKA, ICHIRO, fluid mechanics scientist, educator; b. Kobe, Japan, Sept. 12, 1931; s. Hisao and Kimie Tanaka. B in Engring., Osaka U., Japan, 1953; M in Engring., Osaka U., 1955, D in Engring., 1963. Asst. Osaka U., 1959—67, assoc. prof. to prof., 1967—95; vis. scientist Stevens Inst. Tech., NJ, 1963—65; dir. Osaka U. Libr., 1993—95, prof. emeritus, 1995. Pres. Kansai Soc. Naval Archietects Japan, 1992—96. Contbr. articles various profl. jours.; co-author: Fluid Dynamics of Resistance and Propulsion, 1997; contbr. chapters to books Ship Design Handbook, 1976. Recipient Man of Merit award, Soc. Naval Arch. Japan, 1986, Naval Architecture Tech. award, 1996. Mem.: Soc. Naval Arch. and Marine Engrs., Japan Soc. Naval Arch. and Ocean Engrs. (hon.). Avocation: classical music. Home: 4 20 16 Soyama Cho Kita Ku Kobe 651 1145 Japan

TANAKA, ICHIROU, science educator; b. Takada, Japan, Aug. 9, 1961; s. Kei-ichiro and Iku Tanaka. BS, U. Tokyo, 1984, MS, 1987, DSc, 1990. Postdoctoral fellow Japan Soc. Promotion of Sci., Tokyo, 1990—92, Primate Rsch. Inst., Inuyama, Japan, 1996—2001; assoc. prof. Yokkaichi (Japan) U., 2001—. Mem. adv. bd. Primates, Inuyama, 2003—. Mem.: Primate Soc. Japan, Anthrop. Soc. Nippon. Achievements include discovery of three phases of lactation, weaning age, milk secretion in pregnancy, delousing (hygienic function of grooming) and social transmission of grooming techniques in Japanese macaques (snow monkeys). Avocations: oil painting, contemporary art, model railroads. Office: Yokkaichi U 1200 Kayo-cho Yokkaichi 512-8512 Japan Office Fax: 81-593-365-6630. Business E-Mail: itanaka@yokkaichi-u.ac.jp.

TANAKA, J(EANNIE) E., lawyer; b. LA, Jan. 21, 1942; d. Togo William and Jean M. Tanaka. BA, Internat. Christian U., Tokyo, 1966; MSW, UCLA, 1968; JD, Washington Coll., 1984. Bar: Calif. 1984, U.S. Dist. Ct. (cen., no. dists.) Calif. 1985, U.S. Ct. Appeals (9th cir.) 1985, D.C. 1987. Instr. Aoyama Gakuin, Meiji Gakuin, Sophia U., Tokyo, 1968-75; with program devel. Encyclopedia Britannica Inst., Tokyo, 1976-78; instr. Honda, Mitsubishi, Ricoh Corps., Tokyo, 1975-80; with editorial dept. Simul Internat., Tokyo; assoc. Seki and Jarvis, LA, 1984-86, Jones, Day, Reavis & Pogue, LA, 1986-87, Fulbright, Jaworsky and Reavis, McGrath, LA, 1987-89; asst. counsel Unocal, LA, 1989-91; pvt. practice LA, 1991—; counsel Calif. Dept. Corps., LA, 1993—. Active Japan-Am. Soc., L.A., 1984-95, Japanese-Am. Citizens League, L.A., 1981, 92—, Japanese Am. Cultural and Cmty. Ctr., 1986-89; vol. Asian Pacific Am. Legal Ctr. So. Calif., 1985-86. Mem. Japanese-Am. Bar Assn., Mensa. Democrat. Mem. Foursquare Meth. Ch. Avocations: languages, martial arts. Office Phone: 310-712-1947.

TANAKA, JUNJI, educational administrator; b. Osaka, Japan, Nov. 22, 1929; s. Waichiro and Hide T.; m. Chieko, Mar. 5, 1957; children: Keiji, Eiko. BA in Econs., Kinki U., Japan, 1956; cert. in librarianship, Doshisha U. Local employee USIA, 1957; sr. advisor Am. Ctr., Osaka, 1970; exec. dir. Japan Inst. for Internat. Study, Osaka, 1973—; pres. JIIS Corp. Ltd., 1988—. Ednl. counseling svcs. internat. student and personnel exchange programs; pres. Japan Youth Devel. Assn., 1996-2005, internat. youth exchange program dir., 2005-; bd. dirs. Brain Dynamics Co., Ltd.; chmn. Japan Nat. Com. for Operation of Chinese Proficiency Test, 2005-. Recipient Meritorious Honor award USIA, 1968. Mem. Nat. Assn. Fgn. Student Advisors, Osaka C. of C. and Industry, Japan-Am. Soc., Tokonaka City Japan-China Friendship Assn. (pres. 2004-), Rotary. Buddhist. Home: 17-20 4 chome Kumano-cho Toyonaka City Osaka 560 0014 Japan Office: Kyoiku Ctr Bldg 5-1-1 Honmachi Toyonaka-shi Osaka 560-0021 Japan Office Phone: 06-6857-3395 ext. 3399. E-mail: j-tanaka@md.neweb.ne.jp.

TANAKA, KOUICHI ROBERT, hematologist, educator; b. Fresno, Calif., Dec. 15, 1926; s. Kenjiro and Teru (Arai) T.; m. Grace Mutsuko Sakaguchi, Oct. 23, 1965; children: Anne M., Nancy K., David K. BS, Wayne State U., 1949, MD, 1952. Cert. in internal medicine Am. Bd. Internal Medicine, 1961, recertified in internal medicine Am. Bd. Internal Medicine, 1974, cert. in hematology Am. Bd. Internal Medicine, 1972. Intern Los Angeles County Gen. Hosp., 1952—53; resident, fellow Detroit Receiving Hosp., 1953—57; instr. Sch. Medicine UCLA, 1957—59, asst. prof. medicine, 1959—61, assoc. prof. medicine, 1961—68, prof. Sch. Medicine, 1968—97, prof. emeritus, 1998—. Chief hematology divsn. Harbor-UCLA, Torrance, Calif., 1961—97, chief hematology, 1998—2000. Author 137 rsch. publs. Served US Army, 1946—48. Recipient Disting. Alumni Svc. award, Wayne St. U. Sch. Med. Alumni Assn., Med. Alumni Assn. Disting. Svc. award, UCLA. Master ACP (gov. So. Calif. region I 1993-97); mem. Am. Fedn. Med. Rsch., We. Soc. Clin. Investigation, Am. Soc. Hematology, Internat. Soc. Hematology, We. Assn. Physicians, Am. Soc. Clin. Investigation, Assn. Am. Physicians, Sigma Xi, Alpha Omega Alpha. Achievements include research on red cell metabolism. Home: 4 Cayuse Ln Rancho Palos Verdes CA 90275-5172 Office: Dept Med Box 400 Harbor-UCLA Med Ctr Torrance CA 90509 Home Phone: 310-377-7687; Office Phone: 310-222-3695.

TANAKA, RICHARD I., computer company executive; b. Sacramento, Dec. 17, 1928; s. G. and Kei Tanaka; m. Edith M. Arita, Aug. 18, 1951; children: Steven Richard, Jean Elizabeth, John Richard, Anne Mariko. BS with highest honors, U. Calif., Berkeley, 1950, MS, 1951; PhD, Calif. Inst. Tech., 1958. Sr. rsch. engr. N.Am. Aviation, Inc., 1951-54; mem. tech. staff Hughes Aircraft Co., 1954-57; dept. mgr., sr. mem. computer rsch. Lockheed Missiles & Space Co., Palo Alto, Calif., 1957-65; sr. v.p. Cal Comp (Calif. Computer Products, Inc.), Anaheim, 1966-77; pres. Internat. Tech. Resources Co., Tustin, Calif., 1977-80; pres., CEO Systonetics, Inc., Fullerton, Calif., 1980-86; pres. Lundy Electronics & Sys., Inc., Glen Head, NY, 1986-89; chmn., CEO, pres. Scan-Optics, Inc., Manchester, Conn., 1989-97; chmn., CEO V-Sys., Inc., San Juan Capistrano, Calif., 1999-2000; pres. ITR Co., Santa Ana, Calif., 2000—. Vis. prof. U. Calif., Berkeley, 1962 Author: Residue Arithmetic and Its Applications to Computer Technology, 1967. Hughes fellow Calif. Inst. Tech., 1955-57 Fellow IEEE (pres. computer soc. 1965-66, centennial medal, Golden Core award 1996); mem. Internat. Fedn. Info. Processing (pres. 1974-77, hon. life mem., U.S. del.), Am. Fedn. Info. Processing Socs. (pres. 1969-71, disting. service award 1983), Phi Beta Kappa, Tau Beta Pi, Eta Kappa Nu. Home: 10321 Shadyridge Dr Santa Ana CA 92705-1568 Personal E-mail: ritanaka@cox.net.

TANAKA, RICHARD KOICHI, JR., architect, planner; b. San Jose, Calif., Oct. 16, 1931; s. Richard Inoru and Mae Yoshiko (Koga) T.; m. Barbara Hisako Kumagai, Oct. 7, 1961; children: Craig, Todd, Sandra, Trent. BArch, U. Mich., Ann Arbor, 1954; M in Urban Planning, Calif. State U., San Jose, 1978. Arch., planner Steinberg Group, San Jose, L.A., 1954. Chair, bd. dirs. Happi House Restaurants, Inc., 1972—. Author: American on Trial, 1988. Dir. Human Rels. Com., San Jose, 1969-73; past pres., trustee East Side HS Dist., San Jose, 1971-92, Japanese Am. Citizens League, San Jose; dir., pres. Bicentennial Com., San Jose, 1974-77; past pres. Tapestry and Talent, 1976-80; mem. bd. govs. NCCJ, San Jose, 1976—, Boy Scouts Am., San Jose, 1978—; bd. dirs. Santa Clara County Sch. Bd. Assn., 1980—, Calif. CC Trustees, 1993-2002, pres., 1997-98; pres. Internment of Local Japanese Ams., San Jose, 1984—; trustee San Jose/Evergreen CC, 1992—, pres., 1993-94, 97-98, 2001-02, 07-08. Mem. AIA, Am. Planning Inst., Constrn. Specification Inst., Rotary. Avocations: golf, painting. Home: 14811 Whipple Ct San Jose CA 95127-2570 Office: 60 Pierce Ave San Jose CA 95110-2819 Personal E-mail: rktanaka@sbcglobal.net.

TANANBAUM, STEVEN ANDREW, investment consultant; b. NYC, June 26, 1965; s. David Jay and Elizabeth (Belfer) Tananbaum. BA in Econs., Vassar Coll., 1987. Analyst Kidder, Peabody & Co., NYC, 1987-89; investment specialist MacKay Shields, NYC, 1989—91, head high yield grp., 1991—97, lead portfolio mgr. hedge fund area, 1997; sr. mng. mem., founding ptnr. GoldenTree Asset Mgmt., LP, NYC, 2000—, CEO, chief investment officer. Cons. Nat. Retirement Progs., 1987—89. Bd. dirs. Citymeals-on-Wheels, NYC; mem. corp. fund bd. John F. Kennedy Ctr. Performing Arts. Named one of Top 200 Collectors, ARTnews mag., 2006—08. Republican. Office: GoldenTree Asset Mgmt LP 300 Park Ave 21st Fl New York NY 10022

TANAY, EMANUEL, psychiatry professor, writer; s. Bunim Tenenwurzel and Betty Kowarski-Tenenwurzel; m. Sandra Jean Eddy, Aug. 13, 1970; children: Elaine Nina Meleski, Anita Hirsch-Tanay, David Emanuel. MD, U. Munich, 1951. Cert. in emanuel tanay State Mich., 1957, diplomate Am. Bd. Psychiatry and Neurology, 1959, cert. in commendation chmn. task force Occupl. Psychiatry Am. Psychiat. Assn., 1970, in emanuel tanay Am. Bd. Forensic Psychiatry, 1979. Assoc. dir. dept. psychiatry Detroit Receiving Hosp., 1958—63; clin. prof. psychiatry Wayne State U. Sch. Medicine, Detroit, 1971—; assoc. prof. Wayne State U. Law Sch. Pres. Mich. Psychiat. Soc., Lansing, 1981—82; mem. exec. com. World Psychiat. Assn., Vienna. Author: (books) Murderers: Study of Homicide, Passport to Life: Reflections of a Holocaust Survivor; co-author: Massive Psychic Trauma in Survivors of Nazi Persecution, Vietnam Veteran - Victim of War. Pres. Jewish Cmty. Coun. Grosse Pointe, Mich.; v.p. Mich. Assn. Marriage, Family and Divorce, Detroit; mem. Internat. Assn. Genocide Scholars. Recipient Flag award, Mich. State Med. Soc., 1969, Exemplary Psychiatrist award, Nat. Alliance Mentally Ill, 1992, Fellowship award, Am. Coll. Psychiatrists, 1992, Golden Apple award, Am. Acad. Psychiatry, 1998; Disting. fellow, Am. Acad. Forensic Sciences, 2008—, Disting. Life fellow, Am. Psychiatrics Assn., 2008—. Mem.: Am. Psychiat. Assn. Democrat. Achievements include research in psychology of homicide and post traumatic stress disorder. Avocations: sailing, skiing. Office: 2980 Provincial Dr Ann Arbor MI 48104 Business E-Mail: drtanay@umich.edu.

TANCER, EDWARD F., lawyer, utilities executive; b. 1961; BA in Polit. Sci., U. Fla., Gainesville, JD. Bar: Fla. 1985. Atty. FPL Energy, Juno Beach, Fla., 1988, v.p., gen. counsel, 2001—05; asst. sec. FPL Group Inc., Juno Beach, Fla., 1997—, assoc. gen. counsel, 2003—05, v.p., gen. counsel, 2005—08; asst. sec. Fla. Power & Light Co., 1997—, sr. v.p., gen. counsel, 2005—08, vice chmn., sr. v.p. state govt. affairs, 2008—. Office: FPL Group Inc 700 Universe Blvd PO Box 14000 Juno Beach FL 33408 Office Phone: 561-694-4644. Office Fax: 561-694-4640.*

TANCER, MANUEL E., psychiatrist; married. MD, U. Ariz. Coll. Medicine, Tucson, 1984. Diplomate Am. Bd. Psychiatry & Neurology, 1990. Assoc. chair Wayne State U. Sch. Medicine, Detroit, 1999—2003, prof. & chair, 2003—. Office: Wayne State Univ Sch Medicine 4201 St Antoine UHC 9B Detroit MI 48201

TANCREDI, JAMES J., lawyer; b. Hartford, Conn., Apr. 1, 1954; s. Joseph I. and Angelina C. (Lanza) T.; children: Lauren, Jamie, Brian. BA in Urban Studies and Polit. Sci., Coll. Holy Cross, Worcester, Mass., 1976; JD, U. Conn., Storrs, 1979. Bar: Conn. 1979, US Dist. Ct. Conn. 1979, US Ct. Appeals (2d cir.) 1982, US Dist. (so. dist.) NY 1988, US Supreme Ct., 1991; cert. comm. bankruptcy specialist, ABI. From assoc. to ptnr. Day Pitney LLP, Hartford, Conn., 1979, chmn. bankruptcy and distressed assets groups. Editor: CT Bankruptcy Desk Book. Bd. dirs. Conn. Mental Health Assn., Hartford, 1986-89, 2001-04. Mem. ABA (bus. sect.), Am. Bankruptcy Inst., Conn. Bar Assn. (exec. com. mem. bankruptcy section), Hartford County Bar Assn. (dir., comml. law 1997-2004, sec. 2009), Conn. Turnaround Mgmt. Assn. (dir. 2004—, pres. 2008, chmn. 2009). Office: Day Pitney LLP 242 Trumbull St Hartford CT 06103 also: 875 Third Ave New York NY 10001 Office Phone: 212-829-3600, 860-992-2464, 860-275-0331. Business E-Mail: jjtancredi@daypitney.com.

TANCREDI, LAURENCE RICHARD, medical educator, psychiatrist; b. Hershey, Pa., Oct. 15, 1940; s. Samuel N. and Alvesta (Pera) T. AB in English, Franklin and Marshall Coll., 1962; MD, U. Pa., 1966; JD, Yale U., 1972. Diplomate Am. Bd. Neurology and Psychiatry; Bar: N.Y. 1982. Sr. profl. assoc. Inst. Medicine, NAS, Washington, 1972-74; fellow in psychiatry Columbia U. Coll. Physicians and Surgeons, NYC, 1974-75; postdoctoral fellow in psychiatry Yale U. Med. Sch., New Haven, 1975-77; assoc. prof. psychiatry Med. Sch. NYU, NYC, 1977-84; Kraft Eidman prof. medicine and law U. Tex. Health Sci. Ctr., Houston, 1984-92, dir. health law program, 1983-92; clin. prof. psychiatry NYU, 1992—; clin. prof. health care scis. U. Calif., San Diego, 1993—2003; mem. staff Brookhaven Nat. Labs. Clin. Ctr., 1994-96; pvt. practice NYC, 1994—. V.p. bd. dirs. Internat. Acad. Law and Mental Health, 1987—95, bd. dirs., 2002—07, v.p., 2003—07; mem. adv. com. on transplantations Health Care Fin. Adminstrn., Dept. Health and Human Svcs., 1981—84; mem. nat. adv. bd. NIMH Ctr. Study of Pub. Mental Health N.Y. State Office Mental Health, 1994—99; cmty. svcs. bd. Dept. Mental Health, Mental Retardation and Alcohol Svcs., City of N.Y., 1995—2001; mem. sci. adv. com. Am. Suicide Found., 1995—; cons. Commn. on Med. Profl. Liability; co-prin., investigator study ABA, 1978—80; cons. in field. Fellow: Am. Coll. Psychiatry, N.Y. Acad. Med. Office: 129B E 71st St New York NY 10021-4201 Office Phone: 212-288-5197. Personal E-mail: lrtancredi@yahoo.com.

TANCREDO, TOM (THOMAS GERARD TANCREDO), retired United States Representative from Colorado; b. North Denver, Dec. 20, 1945; s. Gerald and Adeline (Lombardi) Tancredo; m. Jackie Tancredo; 2 children. BA in Polit. Sci., U. North Colo., 1968. Tchr. Drake Jr. H.S.; mem. Colo. State Ho. Reps., 1977-81; regional rep. US Dept. Edn., 1981-93; mem. US Congress from 6th Colo. Dist., 1999—2009; mem. edn. and workforce, budget, internat. rels., and resources committees. Author: In Mortal Danger: The Battle for America's Border and Security, 2006. Republican. Evangelical Presbyterian Church.*

TANDBERG, GERILYN GAY, theater educator, retired costume designer; b. Rugby, ND, Aug. 23, 1942; d. Otto and Edna Tandberg; m. Maurice Berger, Aug. 2, 1980. BS in English, Minot State U., ND, 1963, BS in French, 1963, MA, BS in Edn., 1963; PhD, U. Minn., Mpls., 1973; postgrad., U. London, Courtauld Inst., Ctrl. Sch. Design, St, Martin's Sch. Arts & Ctrl. London Inst., U. Tex., U. Calif., Long Beach. Cert. in tchg. State ND. Asst. prof. Minot State U., ND, 1966—73; costume designer and historian, dept. theatre La. State U., Baton Rouge, 1973—2009. Critic Am. Coll. Theatre Festival, 1975—79, state chair, 1976—80; costume designer Ctrl. State U., Okla., 1981—82; costume cons. 5 films, 1975—2000; mem., theatre advisory bd. La. State Arts Coun., 1981, 82; costume designer U. Tulsa, Okla., 1986—87; reviewer Dress Jour. Am. Costume Soc., 1991—2003; co-chair, region 6 conf. Costume Soc. Am., New Orleans, 1996, bd. dir., region 6 conf., 96; v.p. Theatres La.; lectr. in field. Author: General Learning Press; Theatre Crafts, 1987; contbr. articles to profl. jours.; designed costumes for over 100 plays, musicals, operas at La. State U. Officer pub. rels. flotilla 4-10 and regional divsn. iv Coast Guard Aux., Baton Rouge, New Orleans, 1980—2006. Recipient Outstanding Svc. citation, S.W. Theatre Assn., Gold Medallion, Am. Coll. Theatre Festival, 1984; grantee, Women's and Gender Studies Program, La. State U., 1995, Manship Found., 1996, The Student Tech. Fee Grant, 2000—02. Mem.: Costume Soc. Am. (mem. bd. 1988—91, v.p. 1988—91). Democrat. Unitarian Universalist. Avocations: boating, reading, vintage clothing, jewelry, scrimshaw and buttons. Mailing: PO Box 2083 Baton Rouge LA 70821 Home Phone: 225-753-9808. Personal E-mail: gtandberg1@cox.net.

TANDEL, SUJIT KASHINATH, physicist, researcher; b. Mumbai, India, Feb. 9, 1971; s. Kashinath Hari and Vijaya Kashinath T. BSc in Physics, U. Bombay, 1991, MSc in Physics, 1994, PhD in Nuclear Physics, 1998. Rsch. fellow U. Bombay, 1994-97, lectr. in physics, 1997—. Contbr. articles to profl. jours. Coun. Scientific Indsl. Rsch. fellow, 1995. Avocations: hiking, reading. Office: Univ of Massachusetts Lowel 1 University Ave Lowell MA 01854

TANDLER, BERNARD, cell biology educator; b. Bklyn., Feb. 18, 1933; s. Arthur and Pauline (Solomon) T.; m. Helen Weisman, Dec. 25, 1955 (dec. Aug. 14, 1986); children: Janice Dena, Evan Charles. BS, Bklyn. Coll., 1955; AM, Columbia U., 1957; PhD, Cornell U., 1961; DMD (hon.), U. Cagliari, 1997. Instr. anatomy NYU, NYC, 1962-63; assoc. Sloan Kettering Inst., 1963-67; asst. prof. cell biology Cornell U., NYC, 1965-67; assoc. prof. Case Western Res. U., Cleve., 1967-72, prof. oral biology, 1972-91, acting chmn. dept. oral biology, 1987-89. Affiliate prof. oral biology U. Wash., Seattle, 1993—; vis. prof. U. Copenhagen, 1973, U. Cagliari, 1983, Kyushu Dental Coll., 1994-98, bio. sci. Case We. Res. U., 2003—; sr. rsch. scientist Tex. Tech U., Lubbock, 1999-01; cons. NIH, NSF, VA. Author: (with C.L. Hoppel) Mitochondria, 1972; assoc. editor: Anatomical Record, 1974-98; guest editor: Microscopy Rsch. and Technique, 1993-94, European Jour. Morphology, 1995-2000, 02—; contbr. chpts. to books, articles to profl. jours. Recipient Disting. Alumnus award Bklyn. Coll., 1981, Robert E. Kennedy award for Acad. Freedom, Ohio chpt. AAUP, 1992, Disting. Scientist award Am. Assn. Dental Rsch., 1999; USPHS fellow, 1957-62. Mem. Am. Assn. Anatomists, Am. Soc. Cell Biology, Electron Microscopy Soc. Am., Japanese Soc. Oral Biology, Japanese Assn. Anatomists, Internat. Assn. Dental Rsch. (Disting. Scientist award 1999) Am. Soc. Mammalogists, Italian Soc. Anatomy (hon.), Sigma Xi. Office Phone: 216-368-0563. Business E-Mail: bernard.tandler@case.edu.

TANDON, RAJIV, psychiatrist, educator; b. Kanpur, India, Aug. 3, 1956; arrived in US, 1984, naturalized, 1988; s. Bhagwan Sarup and Usha (Mehrotra) T.; m. Chanchal Nammi Vohra; children: Neeraj, Anisha, Gitanjali. Student, St. Xavier's Coll., Bombay, India, 1974; BS, All India Inst., New Delhi, 1980; MD, Nat. Inst. of MH, India, 1983. Sr. resident Mental Health and Neuro-Scis., India, 1983-84; resident U. Mich. Hosps., Ann Arbor, 1984-87, attending psychiatrist, 1987-2000. Dir. schizophrenia program, dir. hosp. svcs. divsn. U. Mich., Ann Arbor, 1987—2000, assoc. prof., 1993—99, prof., 1999—2004; cons. Lenawee County Cmty. Mental Health, Adrian, Mich., 1985—99. Author: Biochemical Parameters of Mixed Affective States; Negative Schizophrenic Symptoms: Pathophysiology and Clinical Implications; contbr. over 250 articles to profl. jours. Recipient Young Scientist's award Biennial Winter workshop on Schizophrenia, 1990, 92, Travel award Am. Coll. Neuropsychopharmacology/Mead, 1990, Rsch. Excellence award Am. Assn. Psychiatrists from India, 1993, Sci. award, Best Drs. in Am. award, 1994-98, Gerald Klerman award for outstanding rsch. by a Nat. Alliance for Rsch. in Schizophrenia and Depression young investigator, 1995, FuturPsych award CINP, 1997. Mem. Am. Psychiat. Assn. (Wisniewski Young Psychiatrist Rschr. award 1993), World Fedn. Mental Health, Soc. for Neurosci., N.Y. Acad. Scis., Soc. Biol. Psychiatry, Mich. Psychiat. Soc. Independent. Hindu. Office Phone: 850-488-9998, 352-294-0400. Business E-Mail: tandon@ufl.edu.

TANDY, CARLA M., dancer, educator; b. Redlands, Calif., July 21, 1923; d. Charles Raymond and Alice Vilora Lane Weaver; m. Henry Cecil Taylor (div.); children: Kim Michael Taylor, Craig Alan Taylor, Kelye Anette Taylor Allen; m. Robert Tandy (dec.). BA, U. Redlands, 1945; MA, Mills Coll., Oakland, Calif., 1978. Dancer Christopher Beck's Theater Co., San Francisco, 1975—89, Am. Dance Therapy Assn., 1977—2007. Pvt. tchr.; dance therapist Calif. Sch. Blind and Deaf, Palo Alto, 1976—78, Stanford U., Palo Alto, 1978, Altenheim, Oakland, 1976—78, Ctr. of Elders Independence, Oakland, 1991—2006; instr. Religious Soc. Friends, Palo Alto, Calif. Author: Rhythm, A Guide for Creative Movement, 1974, 1975. Mem.: NAACP. Democrat.

TANDY, KAREN POMERANTZ, communications executive, former federal agency administrator; b. Ft. Worth, 1954; married; 2 children. Grad., Tex. Tech. U., Tex. Tech. Law Sch., 1977. Law clk. No. Dist. Tex.; asst. U.S. atty. (ea. dist.) Va. US Dept. Justice, 1979—90, asst. U.S. atty. (we. dist.) Wash., 1979—90, supr. dept. drug and forfeiture litig. criminal divsn., 1990—99; assoc. dep. atty. gen., dir. Organized Crime Drug Enforcement Task Forces, US Dept. Justice, 1999—2003, mgr., 2001—03; adminstr. Drug Enforcement Adminstrn. (DEA), Alexandria, Va., 2003—07; sr. v.p. global govt. rels. & pub. policy divsn. Motorola, Inc., Schaumburg, Ill., 2007—. Chief asset forfeiture unit U.S. Attys. Office Western Dist., Wash., 1988—90; clk. Chief Judge of No. Dist., Tex.; dep. chief Narcotics and Dangerous Drug Sect.; lectr. in field. Recipient Atty. Gens. award for disting. svc., Award for Extraordinary Achievement, US Dept. Justice, Award for Superior Svc., U.S. Atty. Dir., Disting. Alumni award, Tex. Tech U., 2006.*

TANE, SUSAN JAFFE, retired manufacturing company executive; b. NYC; d. Irving and Beatrice (Albert) J.; m. Irwin R. Tane; children by previous marriage: Robert Wayne, Stephen Mark. BS, Boston U., 1964; postgrad., Hofstra U., C.W. Post U. Elem. sch. tchr., Long Beach, NY, 1964-67; pres. Fashions by Appointment, Glen Cove, NY, 1967-71; adminstrv. asst. Peerless Sales Corp., Elmont, NY, 1967-71; from sales mgr. to mktg. dir. United Utensils Co., Inc., Port Washington, NY, 1973-78; v.p. ops. and control United Molded Products divsn. United Utensils Co., Inc., Port Washington, 1978-80; v.p. mktg. Utensco, Port Washington, 1980-88. Bd. dirs. Peerless Aerospace Corp. Co-inventor plastic container and handling assembly, publ. Nevermore, The Edgar Allan Poe collection of Susan Jaffe Tane, 2006. Life mem. Ronald McDonald House; friend N.Y. Pub. Libr.; pres. Susan Jaffe Tane Found., Am. Jewish Congress, mem. bd. adv.; life mem. Hadassah; chair Commn. for Women's Equality/Am. Jewish Congress; bd. dirs. Poe Found. Mem. Boston U. Alumni Assn., Cornell Weil Med. Coll., Ptnrs. in Leadership, Shareholder ASsn. Rsch. and Edn. Leadership Coun., Poe Studies Assn. (sponsor), Boston U. (sponsor poetry workshop), Lotos Club, Grolier Club. Personal E-mail: suetane@optonline.net.

TANEJA, INDU, medical educator, researcher; b. Bhilai, Madhya Pradesh, India, July 4, 1962; d. Bhagwan Das and Gyan Devi Manocha; m. Indu Manocha, Oct. 1, 1987; children: Aanchal, Anjali. MBBS, Pt. JNM Med. Coll., Raipur, MP, India, 1982, MD, 1986; PhD, All India Inst. Med. Scis., New Delhi, 2004. Postdoc. fellow dept. pharmacology Vanderbilt U., Nashville, 2003—06; asst. prof. dept. pediat. NY Med. Coll., Hawthorne, 2006—. Contbr. scientific papers. Recipient Intramural award, NY Med. Coll., 2006. Mem.: Assn. Physiologists and Pharmacologists India, Soc. Neurosci., Am. Autonomic Soc., Am. Physiol. Soc., Am. Heart Assn. (SDS award 2007, Postdoc. fellowship 2005). Home: 200 Diplomat Dr #4K Mount Kisco NY 10549 Office: NY Med Coll 19 Bradhurst Ste 1600 S Hawthorne NY 10532 Personal E-mail: indu_taneja@hotmail.com. Business E-Mail: indu_taneja@nymc.edu.

TANEJA, RAJAT, computer software company executive; BSEE, Jadavpur U., India; MBA, Wash. State U., Pullman. Various technical positions Wipro Technologies; desktop & open systems products and tech. solutions profl. Digital Equipment Corp.; joined Microsoft Corp., Redmond, Wash., 1996, licensing ops. profl., the Americas & Europe, gen. mgr. bus. divsn., corp. v.p. worldwide comml. search, 2008—. Office: Microsoft Corp One Microsoft Way Redmond WA 98052-6399*

TANENBAUM, EDWARD, lawyer; b. NYC, May 12, 1949; BA magna cum laude, Queens Coll., 1971; JD, Fordham Univ., 1974; LLM in Taxation, NYU, 1980. Bar: NY 1975. Ptnr., chmn., internat. tax group, mem., fed. income tax group Alston & Bird LLP, NYC. Mem.: ABA, Bar Assn. City NY, NY Bar Assn., Internat. Tax Inst. (past pres.), Nat. Coun., Internat. Fiscal Assn. Office: Alston & Bird LLP 90 Park Ave New York NY 10016-1387 Office Phone: 212-210-9425. Office Fax: 212-210-9444. Business E-Mail: edward.tanenbaum@alston.com.

TANENBAUM, JAY HARVEY, lawyer; b. NYC, Nov. 17, 1933; s. Leo Aaron and Regina (Stein) T.; m. Linda Goldman, May 28, 1961; children: Susan Hillary, Steven Eric. BA, Hobart and William Smith Colls., 1954; LLB, Union U., 1957, JD, 1961. Bar: N.Y. 1957, U.S. Dist. Ct. (so. dist.) N.Y. 1961, U.S. Supreme Ct. 1967. Internat. trader Associated Metals and Minerals Corp., NYC, 1960-64; pvt. practice, NYC, 1964—. Corp. counsel Internat. Gate Corp., Gen. Gate Corp. Named to Knighthood, His Royal Highness The Prince of Cittanova and His Royal Highness The Prince of Trabzon, 2001. Mem. N.Y. State Bar Assn., N.Y. Trial Lawyers Assn., Bronx County Bar Assn. Clubs: St. James (London), Le Club (N.Y.).

TANENBAUM, JOEY, real estate developer; m. Toby Tanenbaum. PhD (hon.), Ryerson U., 2003. Chmn., CEO Jay-M Enterprises Ltd., Jay-M Holdings Ltd. Trustee Royal Ontario Mus., Art Gallery of Ontario; hon. chmn. Can. Psychiat. Rsch. Found. Recipient Order of Can.; named one of Top 200 Collectors, ARTnews mag., 2003—08. Avocation: Collector of 19-century European art; Cycladic and Neolithic art. Address: 317 Dundas St W Toronto ON M5T 1G4 Canada

TANENBAUM, LARRY (LAWRENCE TANENBAUM), construction executive, professional sports team executive; married; 2 children. BS in Econs., Cornell U., 1968. Pres., CEO Kilmer Van Nostrand Co. Ltd. (KVN), 1968—2000, 2000—; chmn. Kilmer Capital Ptnrs.; owner Kilmer Sports Inc.; chmn. bd. Maple Leaf Sports & Entertainment, 2003—; gov. Toronto Maple Leafs, Toronto Raptors, Toronto FC. Exec. com. bd. mem. CUC Broadcasting Ltd., 1977—94; former chmn. Warren Paving & Materials Group Ltd.; bd. dirs., chair fin. com. Lafarge N.Am.; mem. planning com. NBA Bd. Govs. Vice-chmn. bd. dirs. Mt. Sinai Hosp.; co-chmn. rsch. com. Samuel Lunenfeld Rsch. Inst.; bd. dirs. Baycrest Centre for Geriatric Care; mem. dean's adv. coun. Schulich Sch. Bus., York U.; mem. nat. bd. Can. Coun. Christians & Jews; mem. bd. dirs. Miller Thomson Found.; founding mem. Can. Coun. Israel and Jewish Advocacy. Office: Kilmer Capital Ptnrs Scotia Plaza, Ste 2700 40 King St W, Box 127 Toronto ON M5H 3Y2 Canada also: Maple Leaf Sports & Entertainment 40 Bay St, Ste 400 Toronto ON M5J 2X2 Canada Office Phone: 416-635-6100. Office Fax: 416-635-7697.

TANENBAUM, WILLIAM ALAN, lawyer; b. Rochester, NY, Feb. 16, 1954; s. Burton David and Millicent (Kroll) T.; m. Judy Ellen Hertz, June 15, 1986. BA with highest honors, Brown U., 1976; JD, Cornell U., 1979. Ptnr. Kenyon & Kenyon, NYC, Rogers & Wells, NYC. Lectr. in field. Co-author A Guide to European Data Protection and Privacy Laws for U.S. Companies, contbr. articles to profl. jours. Mem. ABA, NY State Bar Assn. (litigation com., intellectual property litigation com.), Intellectual Property Law Assn., Computer Law Assn. (founding co-chmn. ann. outsourcing conf., pres. 1995-96), NY Intellectual Property Law, Copyright Soc. USA, Am. Arbitration Assn. (panel arbitrators), Phi Beta Kappa. Avocation: sailing. Office: Kaye Scholer LLP 425 Park Ave New York NY 10022 Home Phone: 212-570-0871; Office Phone: 212-836-7661. Business E-Mail: wtanenbaum@kayescholer.com.

TANENHAUS, DAVID SPINOZA, historian, educator; b. Iowa City, Iowa, Jan. 8, 1968; s. Joseph and Gussie Tanenhaus; m. Virginia Louise Pitts, Oct. 25, 2001; m. Jenifer Lee Stenfors, July 27, 1997 (dec. Sept. 9, 1999). BA, Grinnell Coll., Iowa, 1990; MA, U. of Chgo., 1991, PhD, 1997. Asst. prof. history U. of Nev., 1997—; asst. prof. law William S. Boyd Sch. of Law, Las Vegas, 2002—03, assoc. prof., 2003—. Author: Juvenile Justice in the Making, 2004; editor: A Century of Juvenile Justice; contbr. chpt. to book. Adv. Juvenile Ct. Centennial Com., Washington, 1999, Children and Family Justice Ctr., Northwestern U. Sch. of Law, Chgo., 2001. Mellon Postdoctoral Long Term Fellowship, The Newberry Libr., 2000—01. Mem.: Am. Soc. for Legal History, Orgn. of Am. Historians, Am. Hist. Assn. Office: U of Nevada 4505 Maryland Pkwy Las Vegas NV 89123

TANENHAUS, SAM, editor; m. Kathryn Bonomi; 1 child. BA in English, Grinnell Coll., 1977; MA in English Lit., Yale U., 1978. With publicity Farrar, Straus and Giroux; with trade, acad., and crossover books Oxford Univ. Press, Chelsea House; contbg. editor Vanity Fair, 1999—2004; asst. editor op-ed page N.Y. Times, 1997—99, editor book rev., 2004—, editor week in review, 2008—. Juror on biography Pulitzer Prize Com., 2000; affiliated writer Sch. Journalism NYU, 2002—03. Author: Literature Unbound: A Guide for the Common Reader, 1984, Louis Armstrong: Biography of a Musician, 1989, Whittaker Chambers: A Biography, 1997 (L.A. Times Book prize for biography, 1997, finalist Nat. Book award for nonfiction, 1997, finalist Pulitzer prize for biography, 1998); contbg. author: Wall St. Jour., Washington Post; contbg. author Boston Globe, LA Times, N.Y. Times Mag., Nat. Rev., New Criterion, N.Y. Rev. Books, New Republic, Am. Scholar, Commentary. Recipient award, John M. Olin Found., Bradley Found.; grantee, NEH, 1997; Media fellow Hoover Instn., Stanford U., 2000, 2002. Mem.: Soc. Am. Historians (mem. exec. bd.). Office: The NY Times 620 Eighth Ave New York NY 10018 Business E-Mail: tanenhaus@nytimes.com.

TANEY, FRANCIS XAVIER, JR., lawyer; b. Camden, NJ, Aug. 31, 1970; s. Francis Xavier Sr. and Clara Mary Taney; m. Sheila Ann FitzPatrick, Oct. 26, 1996; children: Patrick Francis, Bridget Ann. BA in Econs. summa cum laude, Drew U., 1992; JD, U. Pa., 1995. Bar: Pa. 1995, NJ 1995, US Dist. Ct. (ea. dist.) Pa. 1995, US Dist. Ct. (NJ) 1995, US Ct. Appeals (3d cir.) 1996. Assoc. Klehr, Harrison, Harvey, Branzburg & Ellers, Cherry Hill, NJ, 1995—96, Piper & Marbuy LLP, Phila., 1996—97, Saul, Ewing, Remick & Saul LLP, Phila., 1997—2001, Buchanan Ingersoll and Rooney, P.C., Phila., 2001—03, shareholder, 2004—. Guest lectr. Pa. State U. Gt. Valley Campus, Malvern, 2004—; spkr. in field. Contbr. articles to profl. jours., chpt. to book.; editor: U. Pa. Law Sch. Law Rev., 1994—95. Pres. steering com. Drew U. Phila. Area Alumni Club, 1999—2002. Recipient Pa. Rising Star (atty.) award, Law and Politics Mag. and Phila. Mag., 2005—07, Lawyer on First Track award, Pa., 2008. Mem.: ABA, Am. Soc. Inventors (bd. advisors 2009—), Open Metaverse Found. (bd. dirs. 2008—), Entrepreneurs' Forum (bd. dirs. 2008—, pres.-elect 2009—), Phila. New Media Assn. (bd. dirs. 2007—), Friendly Sons of St. Patrick, Phi Beta Kappa, Omicron Delta Epsilon. Avocations: tennis, music. Office: Buchanan Ingersoll and Rooney PC Two Liberty Pl Ste 3200 Philadelphia PA 19102 Office Fax: 215-665-8760. Business E-Mail: francis.taney@bipc.com.

TANG, CHINPEI, mechanical engineer, researcher; b. Ipoh, Perak, Malaysia, Dec. 21, 1980; Diploma in Engring. and Applied Scis., Inti Coll. Malaysia, Nilai, Negeri Sembilan, 2000; BS in Mech. Engring. with honors, U. Buffalo, 2002, MS in Mech. Engring., 2004, PhD in Mech. Engring., 2009. Cert. in computational sci. U. Buffalo Ctr. Computational Rsch., 2006. Tchg. asst. dept. mech. and aerospace engring. U. Buffalo, 2002—07, rsch. asst. dept mech. and aerospace engring., 2003—09, mem. faculty dept. mech. and aerospace engring., 2006, 2008; post-doctoral rsch. assoc. Erik Jonsson Sch. Engring. and Computer Sci., U. Tex., Dallas, 2008—. Quality assurance engr. Winfield Industries, Inc., Buffalo, 2007. Contbr., reviewer (to profl. jours. articles). Recipient Profl. Devel. award, NY State Grad. Student Employees Union, 2003; scholar, U. Buffalo, 2002—08. Mem.: IEEE, ASME, ASEE, Nat. Geographic Soc., Sigma Xi, Tau Beta Pi, Golden Key. Achievements include development of complete theoretical and software/hardware implementation infrastructure to design, analyze, and control a cooperative collective system of multiple robotic mobile manipulators; research in cooperative and distributed robotics, parallel mechanisms, screw theory, geometric methods in kinematics and dynamics, diferentially flat control systems, nonholonomic systems, mechatronics. Avocations: photography, travel, computer hardware and software. Office: Univ Texas Erik Jonsson Sch of Engrg & CS 800 W Campbell Rd EC33 Richardson TX 75080 Business E-Mail: chinpei@utdallas.edu.

TANG, ESTHER DON, real estate developer, consultant, social worker; b. Tucson, Mar. 5, 1917; d. Don Wah and Yut (Gnan) Fok; m. David W. Tang, June 14, 1942; children: Patricia Karen Tang Crowley, Diana Cheryl Tang Simoes, David. Jr., Elizabeth Carol. Student, Draughn's Bus. Sch., San Antonio, 1936, U. Ariz., 1938-41, DHL, LHD, U. Ariz., 1992. Owner, operator supermarket, Tucson, 1940-66; exec. dir. Pio Decimo Ctr., Cath. Diocese, Tucson, 1966-85; cons., ptnr., vice chmn. bd. Netwest Devel. Corp., Tucson, 1985—. Prodr.: (video) Tapestry of Tucson (award winning). Mem. Tucson Airport Authority, 1975—, Pima County Crime and Pub. Safety Coun., 1999; chmn. Tucson-Taichung Sister Cities, 1979-91; chmn. Tucson Sister Cities Steering Com., 1984—, Sister Cities Assn. Tucson, 1990, Ariz. Pers. Bd.; chmn. bd. dirs. Pima Community Coll., 1975-85; pres. bd. dirs. Pima Coun. on Aging, 1986-90; coord. US Bicentennial, Tucson; mem. adv. bd. Ariz. Dept. Econ. Security; master of ceremonies to welcome Pres. Clinton, City of Tuscon, 1999. Named Woman of Yr., City of Tucson, 1955, Woman of Yr. in Adminstrn., 1968, Lady Comdr. the Holy Sepluchre Jerusalem; recipient Disting. Friend of the Humanities award Nat. Adv. Bd., 1989, Jefferson award Ariz. Daily Star, 1987, Svc. award Pima Coun. on Aging, 1987-89, Disting. Svc. award U. Pima CC Found., 1988, Roots and Wings Cmty. award, 1988, Rosie award So. Ariz. Ctr. Against Sexual Assault, 1990, Lifetime Achievement award YWCA, 1992, 93, La Doña de los Descendientes del Precido de Tucson, 1997-98, centennial alumni award U. Ariz., 1998, Pan-Asian Cmty. Leadership award, 1999, Arthritis Humanitarian award, 1999, Altrusa Women in Svc. award, 2000, Asia Am. Times Devel. Mgmt. Excellence award, 2000, Voices into the Millennium award Ariz. Border Patrol, Dynamic Duo—Pointing Lives in New Directions award Compass Health Care, Congl. Recognition, 2002, Lulac Nat. Presdl. citation, 2002, award Agave Ariz. Hist. Tape TV, 2002, Lifetime award U. Ariz. Coll. Agr. and Life Sci., 2002; Learning Svc. Bldg. and Gallery named in her honor, U. Ariz., 2001; named Ariz. History Maker State of Ariz. Hist. League, 2003, 15th annual Cath. Found. Honoring Esther Don Tang, 2004; featured as an active activist Foothills Publ., 2005; named to Hall of Fame Tucson H.S. Badger Found., 2006. Mem. Soroptimist (hon., Women Who Helped Build Tucson award), Rotary Club Tucson (4 way test award 1998) Cath. Found. Diocese of Tucson (honorable mention, honoree Corner Stone Gala, 2004). Roman Catholic. Avocations: travel, cooking, golf. Home: 701 E Camino De Los Padres Tucson AZ 85718-1921

TANG, IRVING CHE-HONG, mathematician, educator; b. Macau, China, Dec. 29, 1931; came to U.S., 1948; s. Man-yan and Susie Wei-chun (Chung) T. BS, U. Calif., Berkeley, 1952; MS, U. Ill., 1953; DS, Washington U., St. Louis, 1965. Chartered engr., Brit. Engring. Coun. Design engr. Friden Calculators, San Leandro, Calif., 1955-56; staff engr. IBM Corp., San Jose, Calif., 1956-66; postdoctoral fellow U. Oslo, 1966-68; head math. dept. NSW Inst. Tech., Sydney, 1969-76, Hong Kong Poly., 1977-89; prof. math. Phillips U., Enid, Okla., 1989-91, Oklahoma City C.C., Rose State Coll., 1991-94, Okla. State U., Oklahoma City, 1994—97, 1999—2009, Ednl. Testing Svc., Princeton, N.J., 1997-99, Kalpan U., 2009—. Contbr. articles to profl. jours. Mem. Hong Kong Math. Soc. (pres. 1977-81), Sigma Xi, Tau Beta Pi, Eta Kappa Nu. Home Phone: 405-692-2771. Personal E-mail: tangic31@gmail.com.

TANG, JAY X., physics professor; m. Luning Han; children: Irene, Albert. PhD, Brandeis U., Mass., 1995. Asst. prof. physics Ind. U., Bloomington, 1999—2002, Brown U., Providence, 2003—, assoc. prof., 2008—. Contbr. articles to profl. sci. jours. Grants, NSF, 2000, 2004, 2008. Mem.: Am. Phys. Soc. Office: Brown Univ 184 Hope St Providence RI 02912 Office Phone: 401-863-2292. Office Fax: 401-863-2024. Personal E-mail: jxtang2001@yahoo.com. Business E-Mail: jay_tang@brown.edu.

TANG, JENNY CC, music educator; d. Sing Cheng Tang and Lai Hah Chow; m. David Birkin. MusM in Piano Performance, New Eng. Conservatory Music, Boston, 1991; PhD in Piano Performance, New Eng. Conservatory Music, 1997; Artist Diploma in Piano Performance, Longy Sch. Music, Cambridge, MA, 1994. Piano instr. Wellesley Coll., Mass., 2003—, vis. lectr., 2007—. Musician (Piano). Home: 261 Linden St Waltham MA 02452 Office: Wellesley Coll Dept of Music 106 Central St Wellesley Hills MA 02481 Business E-Mail: jtang@wellesley.edu.

TANG, JIANWU, geochemist, researcher; b. Shaoyang, Hunan, China, Dec. 2, 1970; s. Kelai Tang and Yuanzhen Yang; m. Xiaomei Jing; children: Zhiyao, Guo. PhD, Old Dominion U., Norfolk, Va., 2005. Postdoc. rschr. Graz U. Tech., Styria, Austria, 2005—08, Tulane U., New Orleans, 2008—. Contbr. articles to profl. jours. Recipient Best paper award, Chinese Soc. Mineralogy, Petrology and Geochemistry, 1995, Sci. and Tech. Progress award, Sichuan Provincial Govt., 1997. Mem.: Sigma Xi. Achievements include first to rare earth element, complexation with organic matter for the whole REE series; research in paradoxical observation of temperature-dependence of strontium incorporation into calcite; strontium incorporation and calcium isotope fractionation during calcite formation and gave a new mechanism to interpret calcium isotope fractionation; mineral surface not only as free ions but also as aqueous dicarbonato complexes at relatively high pH. Home: 6451 Center St New Orleans LA 70124 Office: Tulane Univ 6823 Saint Charles Ave New Orleans LA 70118

TANG, JOHN, network technician, information scientist, educator; b. Hong Kong, Oct. 21, 1959; s. Chew Sang and Miu King Tang; m. Juana Teresita Enriquez, Mar. 15, 1990; 1 child, Jonathan Alexander. BA, San Francisco State U., 1981; MA, San Francisco State Univeristy, 1983; PhD, U. of Va., 1991. MIS mgr. Oakland Pvt. Industry Coun., Oakland,

Calif., 1991—95; IT mgr. Western Human Nutrition Rsch. Ctr., San Francisco, 1995—98; network analyst Shaman Pharms., South San Francisco, Calif., 1995—98; instr. The Computer Learning Ctr., San Francisco, 1997—2001; adj. prof. City Coll. of San Francisco, 2000—; prof. DeVry U., Fremont, Calif., 2002—. Founder/pres. easyRE.net, Fremont, Calif., 2003—; founder, CEO Home Opportunities Inc., Oakland, Calif., 2003—. Contbr. articles to profl. jours., chpts. to books. Pres. Dance for Power, Oakland, 1993—98; mem. of bd. of advisors American-Viet League, Oakland, 1991—2003. Recipient Dupont fellow, U. of Va., 1984—88, Grad. Achievement award, San Francisco State U., 1983. Roman Catholic. Avocations: creative writing, travel. Office: DeVry Univ 6600 Dumbarton Cir Fremont CA Home: 5948 Balboa Dr Oakland CA 94611-2319 Personal E-mail: jltang@sbcglobal.net. Business E-Mail: jtang@fre.devry.edu.

TANG, KWONG-TIN, physics professor, researcher; m. Pauline Tang; children: Scott, Stephen. BS, U. Wash., Seattle, 1960; PhD, Columbia U., NYC, 1965. Prof. physics Pacific Luth. U., Tacoma, 1967—; vis. scientist Max-Planck Inst., Gottingen, Germany, 1975—2002. Bd. mem. Atomic and Molecular Scis., Taipei, Taiwan, 1980—98. Author book; contbr. articles to sci. jours. Recipient Disting. Sr. US Scientist award, Alexander von Humboltd Found., 1992; fellow, APS, 2006. Office: Pacific Luth Univ Dept Physics Tacoma WA 98447 Business E-Mail: tangka@plu.edu.

TANG, LIANG, optics scientist; s. Xinhua Tang and Bin Lu; m. Yang Lu, Aug. 8, 2008. PhD, Stanford U., Calif., 2008. Cert. in entrepreneurship Stanford Grad. Sch. Bus., 2006. Dir. Hua Yuan Sci. & Tech. Assn., San Jose, Calif., 2006—08; sr. scientist Sharp Labs. Am., Camas, Wash., 2008—; editor Fiber & Integrated Optics, Phila., 2008—. Contbr. articles to profl. jours. Mem.: IEEE, IEEE Communication Soc., IEEE Laser & Electro-Optics Soc. (Best Paper award 2008), Optical Soc. Am., Adv. Bd. Open Optics Jour., Adv. Bd. Jour. Optoelectronics & Advanced Materials, Adv. Bd. Fiber & Integrated Optics, Sigma Xi. Achievements include design of first plasmonic photodetector at near-infrared wavelengths; research in method to dramatically improve the efficiency of nanoscale photodetectors, interaction of optical antennas with semiconductor; development of plasmonic effect in silicon CMOS. Avocations: tennis, piano, travel, swimming. Home: 905 SE 136th Ave H2 Vancouver WA 98683

TANG, LIE, agricultural engineer, educator; b. Zigong, Sichuan, China, Sept. 19, 1967; s. Mingkuan Tang and Nengliang Yin; m. Xiaoli Hong, Dec. 17, 1990; children: Anthony, Justin. BS, Jiangsu U., China, 1989; MS, Zhejiang U., China, 1994; PhD, U. Ill. Urbana-Champaign, 2002. Vis. scholar Cath. U. Leuven, Belgium, 1995—97; asst. prof. Royal Vet. and Agrl. U., Copenhagen, 2002—03, Wageningen U., Netherlands, 2003—04, Iowa State U., Ames, 2004—. Mem.: Am. Soc. Agrl. and Biol. Engrs. Achievements include research in corn plant spacing sensing system using real-time machine vision; optimal field coverage path planning for agricultural field equipment, agricultural robotics for weed control and other autonomous operations. Office: Iowa State Univ 203 Davidson Hall Ames IA 50011 Office Phone: 515-294-9778. Office Fax: 515-294-2255. Business E-Mail: lietang@iastate.edu.

TANG, PAUL C., lawyer; b. Hong Kong, Oct. 4, 1952; arrived in US, 1958, naturalized, 1964; m. Shirley Tang; children: Elizabeth, Margaret. BA, Harvard U., 1974; JD, Columbia U., 1977, MBA, 1978. Bar: NY 1981, NJ 1994. Tax acct. Deloitte & Touche, 1978—80; mem. Phillips Nizer, 1980—85, ptnr., 1985—87; co-founder law firm, 1987—89; ptnr. Reid & Priest, 1989—93; exec. v.p., gen. counsel, sec. Burlington Coat Factory Warehouse Corp., NJ, 1993—. Mem.: ABA, Arbitrator for Fin. Industry Regulatory Authority, NJ State Bar Assn., NY State Bar Assn. Office: Burlington Coat Factory 1830 Rt 130 Burlington NJ 08016-3020 Business E-Mail: paul.tang@coat.com.

TANG, PAUL C., medical administrator, educator; b. May 20, 1953; BS, Stanford U., Calif., 1975, MS, 1976; MD, U. Calif., San Francisco, 1981. Cert. in internal medicine Am. Bd. Internal Medicine, Pa., 1984. Program mgr. Hewlett-Packard Laboratories, Palo Alto, Calif., 1984—94; assoc. prof. medicine Northwestern U. Med. Sch., Chgo., 1994—98; med. dir., info. systems Northwestern Meml. Hosp., Chgo., 1994—98; v.p. Epic Rsch. Inst., Mountain View, Calif., 1998—2000; v.p., chief med. info. officer Palo Alto Med. Found., Mountain View, 1998—; consulting assoc. prof. medicine Stanford U. Sch. Medicine, 2007—. Chmn. Am. Med. Informatics Assn., Bethesda, Md., 2006—07. Fellow: ACP, Healthcare Info. Mgmt. Systems Soc., Coll. Healthcare Info. Mgmt. Execs., Am. Coll. Med. Informatics; mem.: Inst. Medicine. Achievements include research in electronic health records and decision support; personal health records and disease management; patents for clinical decision support. Avocation: photography. Office: Palo Alto Medical Found 2350 W El Camino Real Mountain View CA 94040 Business E-Mail: paultang@stanford.edu.

TANG, QIUHONG, research scientist; PhD, U. Tokyo, Japan, 2006. Rsch. assoc. U. Wash., Seattle, 2006—. Contbr. articles to profl. jours. Mem.: Am. Geophys. Union. Office: Univ WA Civil & Envir Engring Box 352700 Seattle WA 98195-2700

TANG, SHAO-JUN, biologist, educator; PhD, U. Toronto, Can., 1998. Postdoctoral assoc., Howard Hughes med. inst. Calif. Inst. Tech., Pasadena, 1998—2001; asst. prof. U. Calif., Irvine, 2001—. Contbr. articles to profl. jours. Recipient Developing Scientist award, Am. Heart Assn., 2003, New Investigator award, US Dept. Def., 2004; grantee, Whitehall Found., 2002-2005, Tuberous Sclerosis Complex Alliance, 2007—; scholar, EJLB Found., 2003; Counaught Grad. fellowship, U. Toronto, 1991-1992, Doctoral Open fellowship, 1995-1997, Restracom Doctoral fellowship, Hosp. Sick Children, Toronto, 1995-1997. Mem.: Soc. Neurosci. Achievements include research in the molecular mechanisms critical for memory formation. Office: Univ Calif 303 Qureshey Rsch Lab Irvine CA 92697 E-mail: shaojun2002@yahoo.com.

TANG, SHENSHENG, research scientist; m. Guangpu Shi Tang; children: Grace, Michael. BSEE, Tianjin U., China, 1990; MSEE, China Acad. Telecom. Tech., Beijing, 1997; PhD in Elec. Enging., U. Toledo, 2006. Hardware engr. East China Electronic Measurement Inst., Benbu, Anhui, China, 1990—94; project mgr., sys. engr. China Acad. Telecom. Tech., Beijing, 1997—2001; rsch. fellow George Mason U., Fairfax, Va., 2006—. Reviewer profl. jours. and confs.; tech. program com. mem. several internat. confs. Contbr. articles profl. jours. and confs. Mem.: IEEE (sr.), Sigma Xi.

TANG, TERRY, editor, lawyer; BA, Yale Univ., 1980; JD, NYU, 1983. Atty. Preston Thorgrimson Ellis & Holman, Seattle, 1983; staff writer Seattle Weekly, 1984—89; editl. writer Seattle Times, 1989—97; mem. editl bd. New York Times, 1997—2000, Op-Ed page editor, 2000—03, dep. tech. editor, 2003—. Editor (mng.): Rev. of Law & Social Change, 1982—83. Nieman fellow, Harvard Univ., 1992—93. Office: New York Times 620 8th Ave New York NY 10018 Office Phone: 212-556-7745. Office Fax: 212-556-1448. Business E-Mail: tang@nytimes.com.

TANG, WEI, software engineer; s. Shenhua Tang and Lanfen Zhang. BA, Tsing Hua U., Beijing, 1987, MS, 1990; PhD, U. Pa., Phila., 2001. Rschr. Tsinghua U., 1987—90; engr. Siemens, Beijing, 1990—92; software engr. and rschr. Lucent Tech., Homdel, NJ, 1994—99; rschr. U. Pa., Phila., 1994—2001; sr. software engr. Motorola Inc, South Plainfield, NJ, 1999—. Achievements include research in wireless channel modeling. Avocations: piano, volleyball, guitar, vocal singing. Personal E-mail: wtang0327@yahoo.com.

TANG, WILLIAM C., electrical engineer; b. Hong Kong, Mar. 9, 1958; m. Pauline Yuen, Jan. 26, 1963. PhD, U. Calif., Berkeley, 1990. Mem. tech. staff TRW, Inc., Redondo Beach, Calif., 1981-82; assoc. engr., scientist IBM Corp., San Jose, Calif., 1982-84; rschr. U. Calif., Berkeley, 1986-90; sr. rsch. engr. Ford Motor Co., Dearborn, Mich., 1990-93; sr. rsch. mgr. Ford Microelectronics, Inc., Colorado Springs, Colo., 1993-96; tech. group supr. Jet Propulsion Lab., Pasadena, Calif., 1996-99; program mgr. Def. Advanced Rsch. Projects Agy., Arlington, Va., 1999—. Fellow Inst. Physics (editl. bd. 1994). Office: Def Advanced Rsch Project Agy 3701 N Fairfax Dr Arlington VA 22203 Fax: 703-696-2206. E-mail: wtang@darpa.mil.

TANG, XIAOLEI, immunologist; s. Hui Tang and Jiafen Yu; m. Yan Xie; m. Dongqin Zhang (div.); children: Wade X., Liyan. MD, Wannan Med. Coll., Wu Hu, An Hui Province, China, 1988; MS, Fudan Med. Sch. (formerly Shanghai Med. U.), China, 1993; PhD, U. Ariz., Tucson, 2001. Cert. in immunology Chinese Acad. Scis., 1996, methods in cell and molecular biology Adademia Sinica Max-Planck Guest Lab., 1996. Physician Huang-Shan City Hosp., An Hui Province, China, 1988—90; ms candidate in microbiology and immunology Fudan Med. Sch., Shanghai, 1990—93, lectr. and scientist, 1993—97; postdoc. fellow Torrey Pines Inst. for Molecular Studies, San Diego, 2002—06; rsch. fellow Harvard Med. Sch., Dana-Farber Cancer Inst., Boston, 2006—. Recipient Outstanding Student, Shanghai Bur. Edn., 1991, Outstanding Student Shanghai Med. U., Fudan Med. Sch., 1992. Mem.: Reuters Insight. Achievements include research in Definition of pathogenic role of newly discovered soluble survival factors from accessory cells in autoimmune diseases; discovery and cloning of a new subset of regulatory CD8 T cells bearing CD8alphaalpha homodimer and cloning technology for studying Qa-1 restricted CD8 T cells; development of Qa-1 tetramer strategy for the study of Qa-1 restricted CD8+ T cells; definition of mechanisms leading to preferential killing of T helper 1 cells by Qa-1 restricted Cd8+ T cells. Avocations: soccer, basketball, tennis. Office: Dana-Farber Cancer Inst Harvard Med Sch 44 Binney St SM 722 Boston MA 02115 Office Fax: 617-632-4630. Personal E-mail: charles.x.l.tang@cheerful.com. Business E-Mail: xiaolei_tang@dfci.harvard.edu.

TANG, XIAOLI, medical educator; d. Xudong Tang and Boxian Wu; m. Philip H. Russell, Oct. 23, 2008; 1 child, Sheng P. Russell-Tang. PhD, Rensselaer Poly. Inst., Troy, NY, 2005. Software engr. EasyPax Inc., Toronto, Ont., Canada, 2000; vis. asst. prof. U. Miami, Coral Gables, Fla., 2005; postdoc. fellow Mass. Gen. Hosp., Havard Med. Sch., Boston, 2006—07, U. Calif. San Diego, La Jolla, 2007—08; asst. prof. U. NC, Chapel Hill, 2008—. Contbr. articles to rsch. papers. Grant, Ctr. Image Processing Rsch., 2001—04. Mem.: IEEE, The Am. Assn. Physicists Medicine. Achievements include research in fluoroscopic tracking of multiple implanted fiducial markers using multiple object tracking. Personal E-mail: xiaoli.tang@gmail.com. Business E-Mail: xiaoli_tang@med.unc.edu.

TANG, YAO LIANG, medical educator, researcher, surgeon; b. Shanghai, July 14, 1970; s. HaiChuan Tang and MeiJuan Liang; m. Yan Shen, Oct. 27, 2000; 1 child, SongTing. MD, Shanghai 2nd Med. U., 1993; PhD, Fudan U., Shanghai, 2002. Diplomate physician Ministry of Health P.R. China, 2000. Cardiac surgeon Shanghai Inst. of Cardiovasc. Diseases, Shanghai, Shanghai, 1997—2002; postdoctoral fellow University of South Fla., St. Petersburg, 2003—04; asst. prof. U. of South Fla., Tampa, 2004—; postdoctoral fellow U. of Fla., Gainesville. Ad hoc reviewer Can. Inst. of Health Rsch. (CIHR), Ottawa, Ont., 2005—, Nat. Med. Rsch. Coun. (NMRC), Singapore, 2005—. Contbr. articles to profl. jours. Recipient Outstanding Postdoctoral Fellow Rsch. award, Am. Heart Assn. (Fla./Puerto Rico Affiliate), 2003, Young Investigator award, Am. Coll. of Cardiology Found., 2004, Dr. Jeff Isner Young Investigator award, Mass. Gen. Hosp., 2004, Melvin L. Marcus award, Am. Heart Assn., 2004. Mem.: Am. Heart Assn., Sigma Xi (Outstanding Postdoctoral Fellow award 2004). Buddhism. Achievements include patents pending for vigilant cell system for enhancing grafted cell survial in ischemic myocardium; stem cell beacon system for targeting stem cells to ischemic myocardium for repair; vigilant vector for cardioprotection; invention of adult cardiac stem cells for heart repair. Avocations: swimming, travel. Home: 2870 N Towne Apt 13 Pomona CA 91767 Office: Keck Grad Inst Applied Life Scis 535 Watson Dr Claremont CA 91711 E-mail: tangyl888@hotmail.com.

TANG, YUE, financial analyst; s. Xiangrong Tang and Jiayin Zhang. BS in Genetics, Fudan U., Shanghai, 1998; M.S. in Molecular Pharmacology and Toxicology, U. So. Calif., 2001; MBA, U. Notre Dame, 2003. Cert. NASD. Founder BioRoad Gene Devel. Ltd. (now United Gene Ltd.), Shanghai, 1997—99; equity analyst Needham & Co., NYC, 2003—05; equity analyst, portfolio mgr. BB Biotech, Boston, 2005—. Provost scholar, U. Notre Dame, 2001—02. Mem.: NY Acad. of Scis., Oxygen Club Calif. Achievements include research in metabolic pathways to dopamine mediated by nitric oxide in dopaminergic neurons.

TANGALOS, ERIC G., internist, geriatrician, educator; MD, Stritch Sch. Medicine. Cert. geriatric medicine Am. Bd. Internal Medicine. Fellow Mayo Grad. Sch. Medicine; med. dir. Bethany Samaritan Heights, 1981—; prof. medicine Mayo Clinic, chmn. dept. primary care internal medicine, 1997—2006. Fellow: Am. Coll. Physicians (former gov.); mem.: Alzheimer's Assn., Am. Med. Dirs. Assn. (former pres.). Office: 200 First St SW Rochester MN 55905*

TANGHERLINI, DANIEL MARK, federal agency administrator; b. 1967; m. Theresa Tangherlini; children: Cassandra, Francesca. BA in Pub. Policy Studies, U. Chgo., 1990, MA in Pub. Policy Studies, 1991; MBA, U. Pa., Phila., 2001. Various positions including budget preparation specialist and spl. asst. to assoc. dir. for gen. govt. & fin. Office Mgmt. & Budget, Exec. Office of Pres., 1991—97; sr. program analyst policy office US Dept. Transp., 1998; CFO Met. Police Dept., Washington, 1998—2000; acting dir. Divsn. Transp. DC Dept. Pub. Works, 2000—02; dir. DC Dept. Transp., 2002—06; interim gen. mgr. Washington Met. Area Transit Authority, 2006—07; city adminstr., dep. mayor Washington, 2007—09; asst. sec. for mgmt., CFO, chief performance officer US Dept. Treasury, Washington, 2009—. Office: US Dept Treasury 1500 Pennsylvania Ave NW Washington DC 20220*

TANGHERLINI, FRANK ROBERT, physics educator; b. Boston, Mar. 14, 1924; s. Emiliano Francesco Tangherlini and Rosa (Robinson) Leclaire; m. Jane Kjaergaard Kjems, Jan. 2, 1960 (div. 1979); children: Arne E.(dec.), Timothy R., Daniel M., Niels L. SB in Physics cum laude, Harvard U., Cambridge, Mass., 1948; MS in Physics, U. Chgo., 1952; PhD in Physics, Stanford U., Calif., 1959. Rsch. engr. Convair-Gen. Dynamics, San Diego, 1952—55; postdoctoral fellow NSF, Copenhagen, Naples, 1958—60; rsch. assoc. U. NC, Chapel Hill, 1960-61; asst. prof. Duke U., Durham, 1961-64; assoc. prof. George Washington U., Wash. DC, 1964-66; sci. assoc. Danish Space Rsch. Inst., Lyngby, Denmark, 1966-67; assoc. prof. Coll. of the Holy Cross, Worcester, Mass., 1967-94. Vis. scientist Internat. Ctr. Theoretical Physics, Trieste, Italy, 1973—74. Author: Introduction to the General Theory of Relativity, 1961, (novels) Catholic Girl and Atheist 194, (book of poetry) Love is not Always Commutative, 2004; contbr. articles to profl. jours. Chmn. Cub Scouts Am., Auburn, Mass., 1975—77. With US Army, 1943—46, with US Army, 1944—45, ETO. Vis. scholar, Harvard U., 1988—89; Travel grantee, NSF, 1980, 1984. Mem.: AAUP, Am. Phys. Soc., Balboa Tennis Club, Stanford Club San Diego, Harvard Club San Diego, U. Chgo. Club San Diego, Sigma Xi. Achievements include research in velocity of light, dimensionality of space, the classical electron, Snell's law, relativity and quantum mechanics, gravitation and cosmology. Avocations: poetry, history, philosophy. Office Phone: 858-638-7362. Personal E-mail: frtan96@sbcglobal.net.

TANGIRALA, VENKAT E., aerospace engineer, researcher; s. Sarma S. Tangirala; married. Cert. aerospace engr., U. Mich., 1986. Combustion specialist ACRi, Combustion Ctr. Excellence, Cin.; sr. rsch. scientist GE Global Rsch., Niskayuna, NY, 1997—. Contbr. articles to profl. jours. Fellow: AIAA. Office: GE Global Rsch Ctr 1 Rsch Cir Niskayuna NY 12309

TANGLAO AGUAS, FRANCIS, performing arts association administrator, educator; s. Pedro Aguas and Aida Tanglao; m. Gin P. Pangilinan. AA cum laude, De Anza Coll., Cupertino, Calif., 1993; BA magna cum laude, U. Calif., LA, 1995, MFA in Dramatic Writing, Theatre & Film, 2000. Irwin endowed asst. prof. theatre and film Ateneo Manila U., Philippines, 2001—03; vis. asst. prof. drama and film Kenyon Coll., Gambier, Ohio, 2004—05; asst. prof. theatre Coll. William and Mary, Williamsburg, Va., 2005, founding dir. pan Asian studies, 2008—; founding artistic dir. Internat. Performance Arts Exch., IPAX, Williamsburgv, 2006—08; vis. asst. prof. theater Georgetown U., Washington, Va. Playwright, dramaturg, artistic liason, dir. Asian Am. Theatre Co., San Francisco, 2005—. Author (director, actor): (stage play) When the Purple Settles (Palanca award for Lit., 2002, Philippine Lit. prize), (one man play) The Sarimanok Travels (James Pendleton Found. prize, 1995); author: (dance theatre epic) Ramayana La'ar (NAACP Image Award, Best Play, Best Dir. (Va. Gazette), 2007); dir.: (stageplay) Topdog Underdog by Suzan Lori Parks (Kennedy Ctr. Am. Coll. Theatre Festival Regional Nominee, 2008). Hon. artistic dir. Lahi Arts Philippine Nat. Day Assn., Sacramento, 2004—08. Recipient Outstanding Prof. award, NAACP William and Mary Chpt., 2007. Mem.: Dramatists Guild. Liberal. Office: Coll William and Mary PO Box 8795 Williamsburg VA 23187 Office Fax: 757-221-2636. Business E-Mail: fjtang@wm.edu.

TANGNEY, MICHAEL J., consumer products company executive; With Colgate, 1971, various US and internat. mgmt. positions in L.Am. and Europe; pres. Colgate-Mex. Colgate-Palmolive Co., pres. Colgate-L.Am., exec. v.p., pres. Colgate-L.Am., 2000—07, COO Colgate Europe, Greater Asia, Africa, 2007—. Office: Colgate Palmolive Co 300 Park Ave New York NY 10022-7499 Office Phone: 212-310-2000. Office Fax: 212-310-3284.

TANGUAY, ALEX, professional hockey player; b. Sainte-Justine, Que., Can., Nov. 21, 1979; Left wing Colo. Avalanche, 1999—2006, Calgary Flames, 2006—08, Montreal Canadiens, 2008—09, Tampa Bay Lightning, 2009—. Player NHL YoungStars Game, 2002, NHL All-Star Game, 2004. Achievements include being a member of Stanley Cup Champion Colo. Avalanche, 2001. Office: Tampa Bay Lightning St Pete Times Forum 401 Channelside Dr Tampa FL 33602

TANGUY-TRACEY, SHEILA ANNE, artist, poet; b. Morristown, NJ, Dec. 19, 1955; d. Eugene Joseph and Francoise Marie-Thérèse Tracey; m. Abdul Aziz Hanif, Nov. 13, 1978 (div. Sept. 12, 1984); children: Aisha M. Hanif, Dianne Al Hady; m. Zafar Iqbal Kabli, Aug. 4, 1986 (div. 1992); children: John A. Tracey Kabli, Sammy F. Tracey Kabli. AA, Monterey Peninsula Coll., 1997; BA with distinction, Calif. State U., Monterey Bay, 2000. Gen. class lic. Grove Comm. Costume model Sunset Ctr., Carmel by the Sea, Calif., 1995—2005; art docent Monte Vista Sch., Monterey. Exhibitions include Maritime Mus., 2000, Borders' Books Inc., Sandy City, Calif., 2000—04, Interim, Monterey, 2004—08, Dickman Ctr., New Monterey, Calif., 2004—05, Nat. League Am. Pen Women, 2004—06. Recipient Editor's Choice award, Internat. Soc. Poetry, 2000, Cert. of Achievement, Resource Coun. Intrim, 2004—05; grantee Monterey Maritime Mus., 2000. Fellow: Internat. Soc. Poetry; mem.: Art Nat. League Pen Women (sec. 2004—08), Interim Cmty. Coun. (coun. mem. 2004—08). Avocation: sculpting. Home and Studio: Apt 3 6 Arkwright Ct Pacific Grove CA 93950 Office Phone: 831-372-7059. Personal E-mail: sheilah2597@sbcglobal.net.

TANI, DANIEL M., astronaut; b. Ridley Park, Pa., Feb. 1, 1961; m. Jane Egan. BS in Mech. Enging., MIT, 1984, MS in Mech. Enging., 1988; DSc (hon.), Elmhurst Coll., Ill., 2003. Design engr. Hughes Aircraft Corp., El Segundo, Calif.; dept. exptl. psychology dept. Bolt Beranek and Newman, Cambridge, Mass., 1988; sr. structures engr. Orbital Scis. Corp., Dulles, Va., 1988, mission ops. mgr., Transfer Orbit Stage, launch ops. mgr.; astronaut NASA, 1996—, mission specialist, 1998—, with Astronaut Office Computer Support Br. Crew support astronaut Expedition-4; mission specialist-2 STS-108 Endeavor Mission to Internat. Space Station, 2001; crew mem. on the Aquarium Undersea Rsch. Habitat for 9 days as part of NEEMO-2 Mission (NASA Extreme Environ. Mission Ops.), 02; trained and qualified as back-up flight engr. Expedition-11, launched from Soyuz TMA-6, 2005; flight engr. Expedition 15 and 16; astronaut, will perform 3 spacewalks and numerous robotic ops. support of the installation and checkout of Node-2 STS-120 Discovery Mission to the Internat. Space Station, will return aboard STS-122, 2007. Recipient Outstanding Tech. Achievement award, Orbital Scis. Corp., 1993, NASA Spaceflight medal, 2001, Japanese-Am. Citizen League's Nikkei of the Biennium for Sci. and Tech., 2002, Excellence award in Sci. and Tech., US Pan Asian Am. C. of C., 2003. Mem.: Aircraft Owners and Pilots Assn., Japanese Am. Citizens League, Alpha Delta Phi. Achievements include logged over 11 days in space; mission specialist STS-108 Endeavour, 2001; with Peggy Whitson made history, marked the 100th spacewalk at the space station, December, 2007. Avocations: golf, flying, running, tennis, music. Office: Astronaut Office/CB NASA Johnson Space Ctr Houston TX 77058

TANI, LLOYD YASUO, pediatrician, educator; b. LA, Aug. 6, 1956; s. Lorraine Hiroko Tani; m. Yvette Friede Tani, May 30, 1990; children: Ryan Yasuo, Jaclyn Christine. BA in Biology, UCLA, 1978; MD, U. Calif., LA, 1982. Diplomate Nat. Bd. Med. Examiners, 1986, Am. Bd. Pediatrics, 1987, pediatric cardiology Am. Bd. Pediatrics, 1991, lic. Utah, 1989. Internship and residency pediat. Baylor Coll. Medicine, 1982—86, fellowship pediat. cardiology, 1986—89; pediat. cardiologist

Sch. Medicine U. Utah, 1989—, prof. pediat. Sch. Medicine, 1989—, assoc. dir. divsn. pediat. cardiology, 2002—07, dir. divsn. pediat. cardiology, 2007—. Mem.: Utah Med. Assn., Am. Acad. Pediatrics, Am. Soc. Echocardiography, Am. Heart Assn. Office: University of Utah School of Medicine 100 N Medical Drive Salt Lake City UT 84113 Office Fax: 801-662-5404.

TANICK, MARSHALL HOWARD, lawyer, educator; b. Mpls., May 9, 1947; s. Jack and Esther (Kohn) T.; m. Cathy E. Gorlin, Feb. 20, 1982; children: Lauren, Ross. BA, U. Minn., 1969; JD, Stanford U., 1973. Bar: Calif. 1973, Minn. 1974. Law clk. to presiding justice U.S. Dist. Ct., Mpls., 1973-74; assoc. Robins, Davis & Lyons, Mpls., 1974-76; ptnr. Tanick & Heins, P.A., Mpls., 1976-89, Mansfield & Tanick, Mpls., 1989—. Prof. constrn., real estate and media law U. Minn., Mpls., 1983—, Hamline U., St. Paul, 1982—; prof. constl. law William Mitchell Coll. Law, 1994. Editor: Hennepin Lawyer, Bench, Bar and Litigation mag.; contbr. articles to mags. Avocation: writing. Home: 1230 Angelo Dr Minneapolis MN 55422-4710 Office: Mansfield Tanick Cohen Pa 220 S 6th St Ste 1700 Minneapolis MN 55402-4511 Office Phone: 612-339-4295. Business E-Mail: mtanick@mansfieldtanick.com.

TANIELIAN, MATT, lobbyist; Staff atty. Fed. Election Commn.; counsel to Senator Robert Toricelli US Senate, chief counsel Judiciary Subcommittee on Adminstrv. Oversight and the Courts; v.p. Info. Tech. Coun.; dir. govt. affairs and pub. policy Cisco Sys., 2003—07; co-founder, ptnr. Franklin Sq. Group LLC, Washington, 2008—. Office: Franklin Sq Group LLC 900 7th St NW, Ste 750 Washington DC 20001*

TANIGUCHI, KEIJI, engineering educator; b. Tuyama, Okayama, Japan, Nov. 20, 1934; s. Teijyu and Kazue (Ebara) T.; m. Jyunko Ariki, Mar. 25, 1962; children: Yosikazu, Teruaki, Haruko. B in Engring., Kinki U., Japan, 1964; DEng, Osaka U., Japan, 1972. Designer Osaka Gear Works Japan, 1953—56; enlisted Japanese Air Force, 1956, advanced through grades to 1st lt., 1962, resigned, 1964; rsch. assoc. Osaka U., 1964-73; assoc. prof. engring. Fukui U., 1973—76, prof., 1976—2000; cons. Noda Elec. Corp., 2000—04, ING Corp., 2004. Prof. (hon.) Xi'an U. Tech., China, 1996, Fukui U., 2000. Author: Introduction to Signal Processing, 2001, Micro Wave Circuit Design, 2004, Image Processing for Practical Application, 2005, Antennas and Radio-Wave Propagation, 2006, Discharge Phenomena and Their Applications, 2007, Practical Sensing Technologies, 2008, Fundamentals and Practices of Sensing Technologies, 2009, 10 others; contbr. 150 tech. papers to profl. jours.; patentee in field. Achievements include 24 patents. Avocations: coaching swimming, skiing instruction. Office: Bunkyo 1-13-17 Fukui-shi Fukui 910-0017 Japan

TANIGUCHI, SHOICHI, library and information scientist, educator; b. Japan, Sept. 19, 1958; BS, U. Libr. and Info. Sci., Tsukuba, Japan, 1985; PhD in Libr. and Info. Sci., Keio U., Tokyo, 2005. Rsch. assoc. U. Libr. and Info. Sci., 1988—95, assoc. prof., 1995—2002; assoc. prof. U. Tsukuba, 2002—06, prof., 2006—. Mem.: Am. Soc. Info. Sci. and Tech. Office: U Tsukuba 1-2 Kasuga Tsukuba Ibaraki 305-8550 Japan Home: 4-417-103 Matsushiro Tsukuba 305-0035 Japan E-mail: taniguch@slis.tsukuba.ac.jp.

TANIGUCHI, TADATSUGU, biology professor, researcher; b. Wakayama-ken, Japan, Jan. 1, 1948; s. Takashi and Tomiko Taniguchi; m. Yoko Tsuchihashi, Apr. 30, 1977; 1 child, Masanori. BS, Tokyo U., 1971; PhD, U. Zurich, 1978. Chief Japanese Found. for Cancer Rsch., 1983—84; prof. Inst. Molecular and Cellular Biology Osaka U., Japan; prof. Dept. Immunology, Grad. Sch. Medicine U. Tokyo. Recipient Hammer prize, 1985, Hideyo Nguchi Meml. award, 1985. Mem.: Am. Assn. Cancer Rsch. (co-chmn. internat. affairs com. 2003—07), NAS. Mailing: Am Assn for Cancer Rsch Internat Affairs Committee 615 Chestnut St 17Th Fl Philadelphia PA 19106

TANKS, ASHLEY, legislative staff member; Dep. press sec. constituent services, Rep. David Scott US House of Reps., Washington, 2007—. Democrat. Office: Dist Office 173 N Main St Jonesboro GA 30236 Office Phone: 770-210-5073. Office Fax: 770-210-5673. Business E-Mail: Ashley.Tanks@mail.house.gov.*

TANNA, ANGELO PETER, ophthalmologist, educator, researcher; m. Carola Ann Tanna. BA, Johns Hopkins U., 1989; MD, Columbia U. Coll. of Physicians and Surgeons, 1994. Glaucoma Fellowship Johns Hopkins Hosp. / Md., 1999. Internship Grad. Hosp., Md., 1995; ophthalmology residency Wilmer Eye Inst., Md., 1998; attending ophthalmologist Johns Hopkins Bayview Med. Ctr., Baltimore, Md., 1998—99; dir., glaucoma svc. Northwestern Med. Faculty Found., Chicago, Ill., 1999—; asst. prof. of ophthalmology Northwestern U. Feinberg Sch. of Medicine, Chicago, Ill., 1999—. Dir., glaucoma svc. Northwestern Med. Faculty Found., Chicago, Ill., 1999—; editl. bd. mem. Survey of Ophthalmology, Brookline, Mass., 2000—. Contbr. articles various profl. jours. Recipient Frey prize in engring., Northwestern U., 2003; named to Best Drs. in Am., Best Drs., Inc., 2005—. Fellow: Am. Acad. of Ophthalmology; mem.: Ophthalmology Mgmt. (editl. bd. mem. 2007—), Am. Glaucoma Soc., Alpha Omega Alpha. Office: NW Med Faculty Found 675 N Saint Clair Ste 15-150 Chicago IL 60611 Office Phone: 312-908-8152.

TANNEN, RICHARD LAURENCE, nephrology educator; b. NYC, Aug. 31, 1937; s. Harold and Fannie (Rosenberg) T.; m. Elizabeth Whitney Harriman, Aug. 8, 1964 (div. Apr. 1990); m. Vivien Baraban, Nov. 17, 1990; children: Bradford, Whitney, Jennifer, Alison, Julie. Student, Vanderbilt U., 1957; MD, U. Tenn., Memphis, 1960. Rsch. internist Walter Reed Inst. Rsch., Washington, 1966-69; assoc. prof., co-dir. nephrology unit U. Vt., Burlington, 1969-78; prof., chief nephrology divsn. U. Mich., Ann Arbor, 1978-88; prof., chmn. dept. medicine U. So. Calif., LA, 1988-95; vice dean for rsch. U. Pa., Phila., 1995-97, prof. medicine, 1995—, sr. vice-dean, 1997—2002. Established investigator Am. Heart Assn., 1971-76. Co-editor: Fluids and Electrolytes, 1986, 3d edit., 1996; contbr. more than 130 sci. articles to profl. jours. Maj. U.S. Army, 1966-69. Recipient Merit award NIH, 1986-94, Disting. Alumnus award U. Tenn., 1991. Fellow ACP; mem. Am. Soc. Nephrology (pres. 1991-92), Am. Soc. Clin. Investigation, Assn. Am. Physicians, Nat. Kidney Found. (regional v.p. 1984-87, Pres.'s award 1986). Jewish. Avocations: tennis, travel. Office: U Pa Sch of Med 295 John Morgan Bldg Philadelphia PA 19104 Office Phone: 215-898-2270. Business E-Mail: tannen@mail.med.upenn.edu.

TANNENBAUM, BERNICE SALPETER, national religious organization executive; b. NYC; d. Isidore and May Franklin; 1 child, Richard Salpeter. BA, Bklyn. coll. Chmn. Commn. on the Status of Women of the World Jewish Congress; mem. exec. bd. Am. sect. World Jewish Congress; chmn. internat. affairs com.; mem. Zionist Gen. Coun.; active Exec. World Zionist Orgn. Bd. dirs., mem. gen. assembly Jewish Agy.; bd. dirs., v.p. United Israel Appeal; mem. exec. com. Am. Zionist Movement; former chair Hadassah mag.; nat. pres. Hadassah, 1976-80; nat. chmn. Hadassah Internat., 1984-95; liaison Hadassah Found.; sec. Jewish Telegraphic Agy.; bd. govs. Hebrew U. Office: Hadassah 50 W 58th St New York NY 10019-2590

TANNENBAUM, MICHAEL J(AY), physicist; b. NYC, Mar. 10, 1939; s. Morris and Ann Tannenbaum; m. Barbara C. Moshinsky, July 15, 1973; children: Nina Fay, Lisa Marie. AB in Physics magna cum laude, Columbia Coll., NYC, 1959; MA in Physics, Columbia U., NYC, 1960, PhD, 1965. Vis. scientist CERN, Geneva, 1965-66, 91, attache scientifique, 1973-84; from asst. prof. to assoc. prof. Harvard U., Cambridge, Mass., 1966-71; assoc. prof. Rockefeller U., NYC, 1971-80; physicist Brookhaven Nat. Lab., Upton, NY, 1980-87, sr. physicist, 1987—, group leader, 2001—08. Program adv. com. Fermilab, Batavia, Ill., 1972—75; exec. coun. PHENIX Experiment at the Relativistic Heavy Ion Collider, 1994—2003, Sci. Coun. Lab. Leprince-Ringuet, Ecole Polytechnique, France, 2002—05, Coun. Brookhaven Nat. Lab., 2002—05. Contbr. articles to profl. jours. Ernest Kempton Adams fellow, 1965, NSF fellow, 1959-63, 66, Alfred P. Sloan Found. fellow, 1967-69. Fellow: AAAS, Am. Phys. Soc.; mem.: NY Acad. Scis., Sigma Xi, Phi Beta Kappa. Achievements include measurement of the statistics of the muon; discoveries in hard-scattering of quarks and gluons; jet-quenching in collisions of nuclei at the Relativistic Heavy Ion Collider. Office: Physics Dept Brookhaven Nat Lab Bldg # 510C Upton NY 11973-5000 Home: 5 Arabian Ct East Moriches NY 11940 Office Phone: 631-344-3722. Business E-Mail: mjt@bnl.gov.

TANNENBAUM, MIKE (MICHAEL B. TANNENBAUM), professional sports team executive; b. NYC, 1969; m. Michelle Tannenbaum; children: Ella Morgan, Jacob Harry. BA in Acctg. & Sports Mgmt., U. Mass., 1991; JD cum laude, Tulane Law Sch. Bar:, Sports Law. Player personnel asst. New Orleans Saints, 1994, Cleve. Browns, 1995; with NY Jets, 1997—, team dir., pro. player devel., 2000, asst. gen. mgr., dir. pro. personnel, 2001—03, sr. v.p., football ops., asst. gen. mgr., 2003—06, gen. mgr., 2006—08, exec. v.p., gen. mgr., 2008—. Office: NY Jets 1000 Fulton Ave Hempstead NY 11550*

TANNENBERG, DIETER E.A., retired manufacturing executive; b. Chevy Chase, Md., Nov. 24, 1932; s. E.A. Wilhelm and Margarete Elizabeth (Mundhenk) T.; m. Ruth Hansen, Feb. 6, 1956; 1 child, Diana Sylvia Tannenberg BSME, Northwestern U., 1959. Ret. registered profl. engr., Ohio, Ill., Ind., Wis., N.J. Supervising engr. Flexonics div. Calumet & Hecla, Inc., Chgo., 1959-61, chief engr., 1961-63, program mgr. advanced space systems, 1963-65, dir. mfg. services, 1965-67; dir. mfg. engring. SCM Corp., Cortland, NY, 1967-69; tech. dir. internat. Singer Co., NYC, 1969-71; v.p. ops. internat. div. Addressograph-Multigraph Corp., Cleve., 1971-74; mng. dir. Addressograph Multigraph GmbH, Frankfurt/Main, W. Ger., 1974-78; v.p., gen. mgr. Europe, Middle East, Africa AM Internat. Inc., Chgo., 1978-79; pres. AM Bruning div., 1979-82, AM Multigraphics Div., Mt. Prospect, Ill., 1982-86; corp. v.p. AM Internat., Inc., 1981-83, corp. sr. v.p., 1983-86; chmn. bd. dirs., pres., chief exec. officer Sargent-Welch Sci. Co., Skokie, Ill., 1986-89; pres., CEO ExhibitGroup, Inc., Elk Grove Village, Ill., 1990-91, Bell & Howell Document Mgmt. Products Co., Chgo., 1991-94, Bell & Howell Postal Sys. Inc., Chgo., 1994-97; corp. v.p. Bell & Howell Co., Skokie, Ill., 1991-97. Chmn. AM Internat. GmbH, Frankfurt, 1977-86 Contbr. chpts. to handbooks, articles to tech., trade mags.; patentee in machinery field Served with M.I., U.S. Army, 1953-56 Named Man of Yr. Quick Print Mag., 1985 Mem. NSPE (life), ASME (life), Assn. Reprodn. Materials Mfrs. (bd. dirs. 1979-82, v.p. 1980-82), Nat. Assn. Quick Printers (bd. dirs. 1982-84), Nat. Printing Equipment and Supplies Mfg. Assn. (bd. dirs. 1983-86, chmn. govt. affairs com. 1985-86), Computer and Bus. Equipment Mfg. Assn. (bd. dirs. 1983-86, 91-93), Soc. Am. Value Engrs. (hon. v.p. 1985—), Value Found. (trustee 1985—), Pi Tau Sigma.

TANNENWALD, PETER, lawyer; b. Washington, Apr. 8, 1943; s. Judge Theodore and Selma (Peterfreund) T.; m. Carol B. Baum, May 25, 1969; 1 child, Jonathan Mark. AB, Brown U., 1964; LLB, Harvard U., 1967. Bar: U.S. Dist. Ct. D.C. 1968, U.S. Ct. Appeals (D.C. cir.) 1968, U.S. Supreme Ct. 1972. Assoc. Arent, Fox, Kintner, Plotkin & Kahn, Washington, 1967-74, ptnr., 1975-94; v.p. Irwin, Campbell & Tannenwald, P.C., Washington, 1995—2007; mem. Fletcher, Heald & Hildreth, 2008—. Columnist The LPTV Report, 1988-92. Mem. cmty. coun. Sta. WAMU-FM, Washington, 1986-93, 94-97, 2003—; dir. Brown Broadcasting Svc., Inc., Providence, 1970—; chmn. maj. law firms divsn. Nat. Capital Area affiliate United Way, 1977-79. Mem. Harvard Law Sch. Assn. D.C. (pres. 1979-80), Harvard Law Sch. Assn. (sec. 1982-84). Avocations: electronics, photography. Office: Fletcher Heald & Hildreth PLC 1300 N 17th St 11th Fl Arlington VA 22209-3801 Office Phone: 703-812-0400. Business E-Mail: tannenwald@fhhlaw.com.

TANNER, BARBARA ANN, pediatrics nurse; b. Paia, Maui, Hawaii, Apr. 26, 1938; d. Samuel S.F. and Aileen L.Y. (Mau) Hew; m. Edwin Paul Tanner, Jan. 22, 1960; children: Rhonda, Bonnie, Eugene. BSN, U. Colo., 1960; cert. PNP, U. Hawaii, 1982; MS, U. Hawaii at Manoa, 1990. Cert. pediatric nurse practitioner, cmty. health nurse, advanced practice nurse. Evening charge nurse Maui Meml. Hosp., Wailuku; pub. health nursing supr. Hale Makua Home Health Svc., Wailuku; pub. health nurse State. Dept. Health, Wailuku, pediatric nurse practitioner, project mgr. perinatal support svcs., 1990-95; clin. asst. prof. U. Hawaii, Manoa, 1997—2006; pediat. nurse specialist Maui Family Support Svc. Early Head Start, 2002—. Commr. Maui County Commn. on Children and Youth, 1998-2000; mem. Hawaii Bd. Nursing, 2002-08. Chair Keiki Booster Coalition, 1997. Recipient Educenter for Nursing Leadership award, 1990, Innovation in Improving Health Care Quality Mgmt. award Am. Coll. Physician Execs., 1992, March of Dimes Maui Divsn. Leadership award, 1992, State award for excellence Am. Acad. of Nurse Practitioners, Healthy Mothers, Healthy Babies Nat. Achievement award, 1993, Sustained Superior Performance award Hawaii Dept. Health, 1994, March of Dimes chpt. of the Pacific, Maui County Excellence in Maternal and Child Health Care award, 1996; Ann L. Clark Nursing Rsch. Fund grantee, 1990. Mem. Nat. Assn. Pediatric Nurse Assocs. and Nurse Practitioners, Hawaii Nurses Assn. (bd. dirs., Excellence in Nursing Practice award 1991), Maui Nurses Assn. (pres., sec., bd. dirs.), Sigma Theta Tau (Gamma Psi chpt. 1991). Home: 175 Ehilani St Makawao HI 96768-8315 Personal E-mail: bmauigirl2000@yahoo.com.

TANNER, BRUCE L., aerospace transportation executive; b. 1959; m. Vicki Tanner; 1 child. BBA, U. Mich., 1981; MBA, U. Tex., Arlington, 1990. Fin. mgmt. positions Lockheed Martin, Bethesda, Md., 1982—97, v.p. bus. mgmt. aeronautics bus. area, 1997—2002, CFO elec. systems bus. area, 2002—06, v.p. fin. & bus ops. aeronautics bus. area, 2006—07, exec. v.p., CFO, 2007—. Office: Lockheed Martin 6801 ROckledge Dr Bethesda MD 20817-1836*

TANNER, DANIEL, education educator; b. NYC, Sept. 22, 1926; s. Jack and Lillian (Jupiter) T.; m. Laurel Nan Jacobson, July 11, 1948 (div. 1988). BS with honors, Mich. State U., 1949, MS, 1952; PhD, Ohio State U., 1955. Asst. prof. edn. San Francisco State Coll., 1955-60; assoc. prof. edn., coord. Midwest program on airborne TV instrn. Purdue U., 1960-62; assoc. prof. edn., assoc. dir. internat. program for edn. leaders Northwestern U., 1962-64; assoc. prof. rsch. divsn. tchr. edn. CUNY, 1964-66; prof. edn., dir. Ctr. for Urban Edn., U. Wis.-Milw. Sch. Edn., 1966-67; prof. edn., dir. grad. programs in curriculum theory and devel. Grad. Sch. Edn., Rutgers U., New Brunswick, NJ, 1967—, chmn. dept. curriculum and instrn., 1969-72, faculty rsch. fellow, 1974-75, 88-89. Vis. faculty U. Kansas City, 1956, Tchrs. Coll. Columbia, 1966, Emory U., 1968, SUNY, Binghamton, 1968, U. London, 1975, King Abdulaziz U., Saudi Arabia, 1992, U. Iowa, 1996; disting. lectr. ASCD, 1985, 86, Dewey Meml. lectr., 1984, Raths Meml. lectr., SUNY, 1984; Leadership Inst. lectr. U. Del., 1990; disting. lectr. Rider U., 1996; vis. scholar U. London Inst. Edn., 1974-75; rev. bd. coll. work-study program US Office Edn., 1965; mem. symposium on comparative curriculum history Inst. Sci. Edn. Kiel U., Fed. Republic Germany, 1989; del. leader Citizen Amb. Program, People-to-People Internat., Republic of South Africa, 1996, China, 1997, Dem. Citizenship Project Czech Republic, USIA, 1996-98; cons. U. Tex. Med. Ctr., 1961-62, Chgo. Sch. Survey, 1964-65, ctr. Urban Edn., NYC, 1964-65, West Chgo. Sch. Survey, 1963-64, Nat. Ednl. TV Ctr., NYC, 1963, Campbell County Sch. Survey, Va., 1970, Memphis Schs., 1977-78, Perth Amboy Schs., NJ, 1996-97; ASCD Commn. on Gen. Edn., 1980-81, West Orange, NJ, Curriculum Study, 1984, ASCD Commn. on Secondary Sch. Practices, 1985, ASCD Ednl. Policy Task Force, 1985, NASSP Curriculum Coun., 1985-95; SUNY Buffalo External Evaluation, 1988; dir. Nat. Curriculum Inst., Washington, 1987; delivered Founder's Day address Delaware Valley Coll., 1985, keynote address Nat. Conf. Citizen Edn., Palacky U., Czech Rep., 1998, raywid lectr. Soc. Profs. Ed., 2008-. Author: Schools for Youth: Change and Challenge in Secondary Education, 1965, Secondary Curriculum: Theory and Development, 1971, Secondary Education: Perspectives and Prospects, 1972, Using Behavioral Objectives in the Classroom, 1979, Supervision in Education, 1987, History of the School Curriculum, 1991, Crusade for Democracy: Progressive Education at the Crossroads, 1991, 2d edit., 2002; co-author: Teen Talk: Curriculum Materials in Communications, 1971, Curriculum Development Theory Into Practice, 4th edit., 2007, History of the School Curriculum, Chinese rev. edit., 2006; co-editor: Improving the School Curriculum, 1988, Restructuring for an Interdisciplinary Curriculum, 1992, Curriculum Issues and the New Century, 1995; founding editor, contbg. author: Rsch. Rev. for Sch. Leaders, 1996, 98, 2000, Philosophy Edn. Ency., 1996, Ency. Edn., 2d edit., 2003, Curriculum Issues, 87th Yearbook NSSE, 1988, 98th Yearbook, 1999, Ency. Ednl. Rsch., 5th edit., 1982, Readings in Edn. Psychology, 1965, Yearbook of the Assn. for Student Tchg., 1962, Great Debate, Our Schools in Crisis, 1959, Educational Issues in a Changing Society, 1964, Programs, Teachers and Machines, 1964, Views on American Schooling, 1964, Tng. America's Tchrs., 1975, Curriculum and Instruction, 1981, Experiencing Dewey, 2005, Intricate Palette, 2005, Chicago Comparision to the Child, 2009; contbg. editor: Ednl. Leadership, 1969-74; mem. editl. bd. Tex. Tech. Jour. Edn., 1984-89, Tchg. Edn., 1986-90, Jour. Curriculum Supervision, Edn. and Culture, 2007-; editl. cons.: Ency. of Ednl. Rsch., 5th edit., 1982, Ency. of Edn., 2d edit., 2003, Jour. Ednl. Psychology. Trustee Delaware Valley Coll., Doylestown, Pa., 1981-95; bd. dirs. Ohio State Alumni Assn. N.J., 1990-96. Recipient Excellence award, Edn. Press Am., 1989, Disting. Educator award, Rider U., 1996, Disting. Scholarship award, Soc. Profs. Ed., 2008; grantee, Rutgers Rsch. Coun., 1988—89, 2000—01; Univ. scholar, Ohio State U., 1955, Disting scholarship, Soc. Profs. Edn., 2008. Fellow AAAS, AERA, John Dewey Soc. (bd. dirs. 1985-88, archivist 1989-, chmn. lectrs. commn. 1999-2004, pres. 2001-03), Am. Ednl. Rsch. Assn. (Lifetime Achievement award 2006); mem. AAUP, N.Y. Acad. Scis., Am. Polit. Sci. Assn., Am. Ednl. Studies Assn., Nat. Soc. Study Edn., Phi Kappa Phi, Phi Delta Kappa (Svc. award 1957). Home: 23 Highwood Rd Somerset NJ 08873 Office: Grad Sch Edn Rutgers U New Brunswick NJ 08901-1183 Office Phone: 732-846-8855. Office Fax: 732-932-6803. Personal E-mail: dantan@rci.rutgers.edu. *The essential quality of education and life is growth. Hence problems must be seen as opportunities and not as limitations if solutions are to be found and progress is to be made.*

TANNER, DAVID ARDEN, biologist, researcher; b. Provo, Utah, Oct. 24, 1975; s. David Earl and Susan Elizabeth Tanner; married. PhD, U. Calif., Riverside, 2007. Postdoc. fellow Utah State U., Logan, 2007—; adj. biology faculty Mt. San Jacinto Coll., Calif., 2007. Mem. missionary LDS Ch., Japan, 1994—96. Grant, Nat. Wildlife Svc., 2007, Army Corp Engrs., 2009. Mem.: Entomol. Soc. Am. Independent. Office: Utah State Univ Biology Dept 5305 Old Main Hill Logan UT 84322 Business E-Mail: dtanner@biology.usu.edu.

TANNER, DOUGLAS ALAN, lawyer; b. Palo Alto, Calif., Aug. 30, 1953; s. Bernard R. and Caroline (Orris) Tanner; m. Carol Scilacci, May 28, 1977; children: Lauren Elizabeth, Wynn Ann, Leigh Caroline. AB in History, Stanford U., 1974, MBA, JD, Stanford U., 1978. Bar: Calif. 1978, U.S. Dist. ct. (no. dist.) Calif. 1978, U.S. Ct. Appeals (9th cir.) 1979, N.Y. 1987. Law clk. to judge U.S. Ct. Appeals (9th cir.), San Francisco, 1978-79; assoc. Orrick, Herrington & Sutcliffe, San Francisco, 1979-83, ptnr. San Jose, Calif., 1984-86, NYC, 1986-89, Milbank, Tweed, Hadley & McCloy, LA, 1989-92, Hong Kong, 1992-2001, Palo Alto, Calif., 2001—04, NYC, 2004—, ptnr., head global securities group. Mem.: San Francisco Barristers (chmn. corps. com. 1981—82), Order of Coif, Phi Beta Kappa. Episcopalian. Office: Milbank Tweed Hadley & McCloy LLP 1 Chase Manhattan Plaza New York NY 10021 Home Phone: 212-734-3841. Office Fax: 212-530-5219. Business E-Mail: dtanner@milbank.com.

TANNER, HAROLD, investment banker; b. NYC, May 7, 1932; s. Irving and Pauline (Steinlauf) T.; m. Estelle Newman, July 6, 1957; children: David, James, Karen. BS, Cornell U., 1952; MBA, Harvard U., 1956. V.p., dir. Blyth & Co. Inc., NYC, 1956-69; exec. v.p. New Court Securities Corp., NYC, 1969-76, Blyth Eastman Dillon & Co., Inc., NYC, 1977-80; ptnr. Salomon Bros. Inc., 1980-81, mng. dir., 1981-87; pres. Tanner & Co., Inc., NYC, 1987—. Co-founder Vol. Urban Cons. Group. Pres. emeritus Am. Jewish Com.; former chmn. Transatlantic Inst.; chmn. Conf. Pres. Major Jewish Orgns.; chmn. bd. trustees emeritus Cornell U.; trustee Russell Sage Found., Revson Found., Classroom Inc. Lt. (j.g.) USNR, 1952—54. Mem. Coun. on Fgn. Rels., Century Country Club, Harmonie Club. Home: 2 Morris Ln Scarsdale NY 10583-6053 Office: Tanner & Co 950 Third Ave New York NY 10022-1029

TANNER, HELEN HORNBECK, historian, consultant; b. Northfield, Minn., July 5, 1916; d. John Wesley and Frances Cornelia (Wolfe) Hornbeck; m. Wilson P. Tanner, Jr., Nov. 22, 1940 (dec. 1977); children: Frances, Margaret Tanner Tewson, Wilson P., Robert (dec. 1983) AB with honors, Swarthmore Coll., 1937; MA, U. Fla., 1949; PhD, U. Mich., 1961. Asst. to dir. pub. rels. Kalamazoo Pub. Schs., 1937-39; with sales dept. Am. Airlines Inc., NYC, 1940-43; tchg. fellow, then tchg. asst. U. Mich., Ann Arbor, 1949-53, 57-60, lectr. ext. svc., 1961-74, asst. dir. Ctr. Continuing Edn. for Women, 1964-68; project dir. Newberry Libr., Chgo., 1976-81, rsch. assoc., 1981-95, sr. rsch. fellow, 1995—. Expert witness in Indian treaty litig., 1963—; dir. D'Arcy McNickle Ctr. for Indian History, 1984-85; mem. Mich. Commn. Indian Affairs, 1966-70; cons. in field Author: Zespedes in East Florida 1784-1790, 1963, 89, General Green Visits St. Augustine, 1964, The Greeneville Treaty, 1974, The Territory of the Caddo Tribe of Oklahoma, 1974, The Ojibwas, 1992; editor: Atlas of Great Lakes Indian History, 1987, The Settling of North America: An Atlas, 1995, Powhatan's Mantle, 2006,

Beyond Red Power, 2007. Named to Mich. Women's Hall of Fame, 2006; NEH grantee, 1976, fellow, 1989; ACLS grantee, 1990. Mem. Am. Soc. Ethnohistory (pres. 1982-83), St. Augustine Hist. Soc., Conf. L.Am. History, Soc. History Discoveries, Chgo. Map Soc., Hist. Soc. Mich., Ctr. French Colonial Studies. Home: 5178 Crystal Dr Beulah MI 49617-9618 Personal E-mail: hhtanner@charter.net.

TANNER, JIMMIE EUGENE, retired dean; b. Hartford, Ark., Sept. 27, 1933; s. Alford C. and Hazel Ame (Anthony) Tanner; m. Carole Joy Yant, Aug. 28, 1958; children: Leslie Allison, Kevin Don. BA, Okla. Baptist U., 1955; MA, U. Okla., 1957, PhD, 1964. Prof. English Okla. Bapt. U., Shawnee, 1958—64, 1965—72; assoc. prof. Franklin Coll., Ind., 1964—65; v.p. acad. affairs Hardin-Simmons U., Abilene, Tex., 1972—78, La. Coll., Pineville, 1978—80; dean William Jewell Coll., Liberty, Mo., 1980—97, prof., 1997—2003, interm pres., 1993—94; ret., 2003. Contbg. author: The Annotated Bibliography of D. H. Lawrence, Vol. 1, 1982, Vol. 2, 1985. Mem. Shawnee Sch. Bd., 1966—72; edn. commn. So. Bapt. Conv., 1967—72; bd. dirs. Mo. Coun. for Humanities, 2003—. So. Fellowships Fund fellow, 1960—61, Danforth fellow, 1962—63. Mem.: SAR. Democrat. Baptist. Avocations: tennis, photography. Home: 609 Lancelot Dr Liberty MO 64068-1023 *As I reflect on my life, the thought that presses on me is my incredible luck at having been born in America in the 20th century, my good fortune in having the opportunity for education, for a satisfying career, for supportive family, friends, mentors at every stage of my life. I must recognize any accomplishment as communal as well as individual.*

TANNER, JOHN S., United States Representative from Tennessee, lawyer; b. Halls, Tenn., Sept. 22, 1944; s. E.B. and Edith (Sumners) Tanner; m. Betty Ann Portis, Sept. 2, 1967; children: Elizabeth Tanner Atkins, John Portis. BBA, U. Tenn., Knoxville, 1966; JD, U. Tenn. Sch. Law, 1968. Bar: Tenn. 1968. Mem. Tenn. State Ho. Reps., 1976-88, US Congress from 8th Tenn. dist., 1989—, mem. nat. security com., 1989—97, mem. sci. com., 1989—97, mem. ways and means com., 1997—, mem. Sportsmen's Caucus. V.p. NATO Parliamentary Assembly. Former mem. bd. visitors US Mil. Acad., USAF Acad.; bd. visitors US Naval Acad.; active vol. Obion County Cancer Soc. Lt. USN, 1968—72, col. Tenn. Army N.G., 1974—2000. Recipient Outdoor Life Conservation award, Pub. Svc., Silver Bayonet award, AMVETS. Mem.: Obion County Bar Assn., Obion County C. of C., Rotary Club. Democrat. Avocations: golf, hunting. Office: US Ho Reps 1226 Longworth Ho Office Bldg Washington DC 20515-4208 Office Phone: 202-225-4714.*

TANNER, JONATHAN D., educational association administrator; b. Cedar Rapids, Iowa, Apr. 18, 1964; s. Richard Elmer and Jean Ellen Tanner. MusB, Coe Coll., Cedar Rapids, 1982—86; MS in Libr. & Info. Sci., Pratt Inst., New York, 2001—05. Sr. account rep. Weill Cornell Med. Coll., NYC, 1994—97, account adminstr., 1998—2006. Freelance libr. cons. Mem. Archivists Roundtable Met. NY, NYC, 2006, Mid Atlantic Regional Archivists Conf., Vienna, Va. Mem.: Spl. Librs. Assn., Soc. Am. Archivists. Avocations: swimming, tennis, exercise, mountain biking, mountain hiking. Home: 135 W 225th St #6L New York NY 10463 Office: Weill Med Coll Cornell Univ 575 Lexington Ave #640 New York NY 10463 Personal E-mail: tannerjonathan@hotmail.com.

TANNER, LAUREL NAN, education educator; b. Detroit, Feb. 16, 1929; d. Howard Nicholas and Celia (Solovich) Jacobson; m. Daniel Tanner, July 11, 1948; m. Kenneth J. Rehage, Nov. 25, 1989. BS in Social Sci, Mich. State U., 1949, MA in Edn., 1953; EdD, Columbia U., 1967. Pub. sch. tchr., 1950-64; instr. tchr. edn. Hunter Coll., 1964-66, asst. prof., 1967-69; supr. Milw. Pub. Schs., 1966-67; mem. faculty Temple U., Phila., 1969—, prof. edn., 1974-89, prof. emerita, 1993—; prof. edn. U. Houston, 1989-96; affiliate prof. U. Washington, 2009—. Vis. professorial scholar U. London Inst. Edn., 1974—75; vis. scholar Stanford U., 1984—85, U. Chgo., 1988—89; curriculum cons., 1969—; disting. vis. prof. San Francisco State U., 1987. Author: Classroom Discipline for Effective Teaching and Learning, 1978, La Disciplina en la enseñanza y el Aprendizaje, 1980, Dewey's Laboratory School: Lessons for Today, 1997; co-author: Classroom Teaching and Learning, 1971, Curriculum Development: Theory into Practice, 1975, 4th edit., 2007, Supervision in Education: Problems and Practices, 1987, (with Daniel Tanner) History of the School Curriculum, 1990; editor Nat. Soc. Study Edn. Critical Issues in Curriculum, 87th yearbook, part 1, 1988. Faculty rsch. fellow Temple U., 1970, 80, 81; recipient John Dewey Rsch. award, 1981-82, Rsch. Excellence award U. Houston, 1992, Outstanding Writing award Am. Assn. Colls. Tchr. Edn., 1998; Spencer Found. rsch. grantee, 1992. Mem. ASCD (dir. 1982-84), Soc. Study Curriculum History (founder, 1st pres. 1978-79), Am. Edn. Rsch. Assn. (com. on role and status of women in ednl. R & D 1994-97, Lifetime Achievement award 2007), Profs. Curriculum Assn. (Factotum 1983-84, chair membership com. 1994-95), Am. Ednl. Studies Assn., John Dewey Soc. (bd. dirs. 1989-91, pres. 2000-01), Alumni Coun. Tchrs. Coll. Columbia U. Office Phone: 206-441-4602. *In my view, America has progressed over the years, and the best days are still to come. We have the single necessary resource to solve our most urgent problems and achieve our deepest moral values — human intelligence.*

TANNER, MARTIN ABBA, statistician, educator; b. Highland Park, Ill., Oct. 19, 1957; s. Meir and Esther Rose (Bauer) T.; m. Anat Talitman, Aug. 14, 1984; 1 child, Noam Ben. BA, U. Chgo., 1978, PhD, 1982. Asst. prof. stats. and human oncology U. Wis., Madison, 1982-87, assoc. prof., 1987-90; dir. lab., prof. and dept. chair biostatistics U. Rochester, 1990-94; prof. dept. statistics Northwestern U., 1994—. Cons. Kirkland & Ellis, 1980-82; mem. Nat. Inst. Allergy and Infectious diseases study sect., 1994-98; reviewer NIH, NSF, VA. Assoc. editor Jour. Am. Stat. Assn., 1987-99; editor Jour. Am. Statis. Assn., 1999-03, Chapman & Hall, 2002-; contbr. articles to profl. jours. Recipient New Investigator Rsch. award NIH, 1984, Mortimer Spiegelman award Am. Pub. Health Assn., 1993; NSF grantee, 1983, 95, NIH grantee, 1986—. Fellow Royal Statis. Soc., Am. Statis. Assn. (Continuing Edn. Excellence award); mem. AAAS, Mensa, Sigma Xi. Avocations: classical guitar, medieval poetry. Office: Northwestern U 2006 Sheridan Rd Evanston IL 60208-0852 Home Phone: 847-491-2700; Office Phone: 847-491-2700. Business E-Mail: mat132@northwestern.edu.

TANNER, STEPHEN LOWELL, retired literature educator; b. Ogden, Utah, Apr. 18, 1938; s. Nathan Russell Tanner and Dorothy Berenice Woods; m. Madlyn Gillespie, Aug. 18, 1961; 1 child, Elizabeth. PhD, U. Wis., Madison, 1969. Prof. U. Idaho, Moscow, Utah, 1969—78, Brigham Young U., Provo, 1978—2006. Contbr. literary criticism. Recipient The Lionel Trilling award, The Levy Found., 1999, Karl G. Maeser Disting. Faculty Lecture, Brigham Young U., 2004. Mem. Lds Ch. Avocation: fly fishing. Home: 1108 E 2620 N Provo UT 84604 Personal E-mail: sltanner@gmail.com.

TANNER, W(ALTER) RHETT, lawyer; b. Athens, Ga., May 16, 1938; s. Johnnie Bryson and Walterette (Arwood) T.; m. Carolyn Laverne Watson, Nov. 11, 1967; 1 child, Walter Rhett (dec. 1989). AB cum laude, U. Ga., 1960, JD cum laude, 1962. Bar: Ga. 1961. With Hansell & Post, Atlanta, 1964—89, Jones, Day, Atlanta, 1989—99. Panelist Am. Arbitration Assn., 1995—. Bd. dirs. Atlanta Symphony Orch., 1975—95, mem. exec. com., 1977—86, v.p., 1978, chmn. maj. gifts campaign, 1980, bd. counsellors, 1996—; mem. Leadership Atlanta, 1980, Leadership Ga., 1982; mem. bd. visitors Grady Meml. Hosp., 1983—92; trustee Ga. Legal History Found., 1986—, pres., 1996—2008; hon. chmn. Atlanta Decorators Show House, 2002; mem. Rotary Club, 2003—08; bd. dirs., vice chmn. Sr. Citizens Svc. Met. Atlanta, Inc., 2000—, chmn.; chmn., bd. dirs. Highlands-Cashiers Chamber Music Festival, 2006—08; chmn. Sr. Citizens Found., 2005—. Lt. comdr. USNR, ret. Mem. Atlanta Bar Assn. (bd. dirs. 1982-87, exec. com. 1983-87), State Bar Ga. (vice chmn. bar and media com. 1979-82), Atlanta Bar Found. (trustee 1985-91), U. Ga. Alumni (pres. chpt. 1973-74, chmn. Atlanta/Met. coun. 1975, mem. state bd. mgrs., v.p. 1976-78), Gridiron, Capital City Club, Phi Beta Kappa, Omicron Delta Kappa, Phi Kappa Phi, Phi Delta Phi, Delta Tau Delta.

TANNO, JOHN W., university librarian; b. Bklyn., Sept. 28, 1939; s. John C. and Hildegarde (Whitaker) T.; children: Maria Elena, Luisa. AA, Phoenix Jr. Coll., 1959; MusB, Ariz. State U., 1963; MusM, U. So. Calif., 1965, MLS, 1970. Music librarian SUNY, Binghamton, 1965-68; order librarian Claremont Colls., Calif., 1970; music librarian U. Calif., Riverside, 1970-72, head monographs sect., 1972-78, asst. univ. librarian, 1978-83, assoc. univ. librarian, 1983—2002, assoc. univ. libr. Davis, 2002—. Mem. ops. com. So. Regional Library Facility, 1984—, task group Intercampus Transp., 1984, negotiating team CLSI, 1981-84, bldg. com. So. Regional Compact Shelving Facility, 1979-82, steering com. Univ. Bibliographic Access System, 1978-82; chair Systemwide Ops. and Planning Adv. Group, 2001-04. Editor Soundboard, 1976-80; contbr. articles to profl. jours. Mem. ALA, The Music Library Assn., Coll. Music Soc., Assn. Recorded Sound Collections, Guitar Found. Am. (exec. com. 1976-80), Beta Phi Mu. Home: 130 Eastbrook Cir Sacramento CA 95835 Office: Gen Libr U Calif Davis 100 NorthWest Quad Davis CA 95616-5292 Office Phone: 530-752-2110. Business E-Mail: jwtanno@ucdavis.edu.

TANNON, JAY MIDDLETON, lawyer; b. Augusta, Ga., Feb. 24, 1956; BA summa cum laude, Univ. N.C., 1978; JD, U. Va., 1982; MBA cum laude, U. Louisville, 1983. Bar: Ky. 1982, DC, 2004. Ptnr. Brown, Todd & Heyburn, Louisville, 1987—2000, exec. com., 1997—2000; exec. committee Frost, Brown, Todd LLC, 2000—04; chmn. Kentucky WorldTrade Ctr., 1999—2004; ptnr., co-chairs, Private Equity practice, head DC & No. Va. Corp. & Securities Group Pillsbury Winthrop Shaw Pittman LLp, 2004—06; ptnr., co-chair Pvt. Equity Group DLA Piper LLP, Washington, 2006—08; ptnr. Energy Practice Steering Com., 2008—; co-founder Novus Energy Ptnrs. LP, 2008—. Chmn., founder Comml. Dispute Resolution Inc., 1986—90; co-founder US-China Bus. Mediation Ctr., 2004; chmn. Ky. Export Coun., 2001—04; svcs. adv. com. US Trade Rep., 2002—06; global edn. ctr. adv. bd. U. NC, 2003—; exec. com. Evermore Investments LLC; mem. So. Tech. Coun., 2004—07; mem. steering com. Internat. Bus. Exchange Coun., 2004—06. Contbg. author Ky. Bus. Acquisitions; contbr. articles to profl. jours. Bd. dirs. U. Louisville Sch. Bus., 1985-88, Independent Industries, Inc. 1988-95. Hearst Found. scholar, 1974, Johnston scholar U. N.C., 1976, Phillips scholar U. N.C., 1977, du Pont scholar U. Va., 1979; named one of Best Lawyers in Am., Woodward-White, Am.'s Leading Bus. Lawyers Chambers & Ptnrs. Mem. ABA, Internat. Bar Assn., Ky. Bar Assn., D.C. Bar Assn. Office: DLA Piper 500 8th St NW Washington DC 20004 Office Phone: 202-799-4204. Business E-Mail: jay.tannon@dlapiper.com.

TANOUS, JAMES JOSEPH, lawyer, insurance company executive; b. Olean, NY, Sept. 11, 1947; s. Michael F. and Philomena M. (Eade) T.; m. Constance M. Griffin, Nov. 27, 1982; children: James M., Michele P. BA, St. Bonaventure U., 1969; JD, U. Va., 1972. Bar: N.Y. 1973, U.S. Dist. Ct. (we. dist.) 1973, U.S. Ct. Appeals (2d cir.) 1973. Ptnr., chmn. exec. com. Jaeckle Fleischmann & Mugel, LLP, Buffalo, 1973—2007; exec. v.p., sec., gen. counsel Erie Ins. Group, Erie, Pa., 2007—. Served to capt. USAR, 1971-79 Mem. ABA, N.Y. State Bar Assn. Office: Erie Ins Group 100 Erie Ins Pl Erie PA 16530

TANOUS, PETER JOSEPH, investment advisor; b. NYC, May 21, 1938; s. Joseph Carrington and Rose Marie (Mokarzel) T.; m. Barbara Ann MacConnell, Aug. 18, 1962; children: Christopher, Helene, William. BA in Econs., Georgetown U., 1960. With Smith Barney & Co., Inc., NYC, 1963-78, 2d v.p., mgr. Paris office, 1967, v.p., 1968-78, resident European sales mgr. in Paris, 1969-71, internat. sales mgr., 1971-78, 1st v.p., 1975-78; chmn. bd. Petra Capital Corp., NYC, 1978-81; pres. Lynx Investment Advisory Inc., Washington, 1992—; dir. The Atlantic Coun., Washington. Exec. v.p. Bank Audi (USA), NYC, 1984—92; del. U.S.-Saudi Arabian Joint Econ. Commn. Bus. Dialogue; bd. dirs. MPS Group, Inc. (formerly Modis Profl. Svcs., Inc.), Jacksonville, Fla., Christian Children's Fund, Worldcare Ltd., Cambridge, Mass. Author: Investment Gurus, 1997, The Wealth Equation, 1999, Investment Visionaries, 2003, (book) Kiplinger's Build a Winning Portfolio, 2008; co-author (with Arthur Laffer and Steven Moore): The End of Prosperty, 2008. Trustee Browning Sch., NYC, 1987—93. Recipient Nat. Order of Cedar, Govt. of Lebanon, 2002. Office: 1100 Connecticut Ave NW Washington DC 20036-4101

TANOV, ROMIL R., mechanical engineer, researcher; b. Rousse, Bulgaria, July 10, 1962; arrived in U.S.A., 96; s. Rayko I. Tanov and Ekaterina Y. Tanova; m. Nadya T. Georgieva, June 23, 1988; children: Radostin R., Srebrina R. Tanova. MSc, U. for Architecture, Civil Engring. and Geodesy, Sofia, Bulgaria, 1988; PhD, U. Cin., 2000. Asst. prof. U. Rousse, Bulgaria, 1989—96; rsch. asst. U. Cin., 1996—2000; applied mechanics engr. Ctr. Advanced Product Evaluation divsn. Ind. Mills & Mfg. Inc., Westfield, Ind., 2000—04; sr. engr. Abaqus Inc., Cin., 2004—. Reviewer Finite Elements in Analysis and Design, Internat. Jour. of Solids and Structures, AIAA Jour.; contbr. articles to sci. jours. R.T. Davis scholar, U. Cin., 2000. Mem.: ASME, Internat. Assn. for Computational Mechanics, U.S. Assn. for Computational Mechanics, Am. Soc. for Composites, Soc. Automative Engr. Office: Dassault Sys SIMULIA Corp Cin Office 9075 Centre Pt Dr Ste 410 West Chester OH 45069 Business E-Mail: romil.tanov@3ds.com.

TANPHAICHITR, KONGSAK, rheumatologist, allergist, immunologist, internist; b. Bangkok, Feb. 22, 1946; came to U.S., 1971; s. Boonchoo and Hong (Nayakovit) T.; m. Sirirat Tareesung, June 17, 1973; children: Saksiri Marc, Marisa. Student, Mahidol U., Bangkok, Thailand, 1964-66, MD cum laude, 1970. Diplomate Am. Bd. Internal Medicine, Am. Bd. Rheumatology, Am. Bd. Allergy and Immunology; cert. Rheumatologist Royal Coll. Physicians Can. Straight med. intern Detroit Gen. Hosp.-Wayne State U., 1971-72; resident Barnes Hosp.-Washington U., St. Louis, 1972-74, fellow in rheumatology and immunology, 1974-76; instr. in medicine Washington U., 1976-77, asst. prof. medicine, 1977-97, assoc. prof. clin. medicine, 1997—2004, prof. clin. medicine, 2005—; attending physician Barnes Hosp., 1976—, Jewish Hosp. of St. Louis, 1981—. Dir. Allergy, Rheumatology & Immunology Specialists, St. Louis; cons. rheumatology Washington U., St. Louis, 1976—. Author: Amyloid Fibrils in Joint Fluid, 1976, Studies of Tolerance in NZB/NZW Mice, 1977, Vasculitis and Multiple Sclerosis, 1980, Buddhism and Science, 1987, Buddhism: Answers to Common Questions, 1990, Buddhism Answers Life, 1995, 2006, Mindfulness: The Key to Perfect One's Life, 1997, Mind and Universe, Mindfulness and Stress Management, 1998, Awakened Life for the New Millennium, 2000, Ethics and Morality, 2000, Parenting, 2000, Buddhism Beyond Non-Violence, 2001, Mom, 2001, The Best, the Worst and the Horrible of 9/11, 2001, Miracle of the Buddha's Wisdom, 2002, Mindfulness Amidst the Evolving World, 2003, Self-Awareness: The Neglected Essence of Life, 2003, Universal Language, Laws, and Community, 2004, Dharma In Action, 2006; editor: Vipassana 101, 2004, World Peace, 2004, Dependent Arising: Center of all Truths, 2004, Essence of Life: Mindfulness and Self-Awareness, 2005, Buddhism: The Ultimate Self-Improvement System, 2005, Science on Mind & Mindfulness, 2005, Buddhism and Qualia, 2006, Buddhism & Medicine, 2006, How Brain, Mind and Consciousness Work, 2007, PDR on Theravada Buddhism, 2007, The Buddha and Healthcare, 2008; author: Buddhist Genesis, 2009. Dharma tchr., bd. dirs., sec. Wat Phrasriratanaram Buddhist Temple, St. Louis, 1983—; co-dir. Buddhist Coun., St. Louis, 1985-90; chmn. Buddhist Coun. Greater St. Louis, 1999—. Recipient Dharma Wheel Pillar award, Royal Thai Crown Princess Sirindhorn, 2008; named Am.'s Top Physician, Consumers' Rsch. Coun. Am., 2003—. Fellow: ACP, Royal Coll. Physicians Can., Am. Coll. Rheumatology, Am. Acad. Allergy, Asthma, and Immunology; mem.: Thai-Am. Physicians Found. (treas., bd. dirs. 2000—), Thai Physicians Assn. Am. (treas. Midwest chpt. 1994, sec. Midwest chpt. 1997, nat. treas. 1998, nat. bd. dirs. 1999—2001, nat. treas. 2000), UN Assn. Greater St. Louis (bd. dirs. 2004—07), UN Assn. U.S.A., Thai Assn. Greater St. Louis (pres.), Thai Temple Karate Shorinryu Club (Black Belt). Avocations: Karate, karaoke, insight meditation. Home: 12413 Ladue Rd Saint Louis MO 63141-8100 Office: Allergy Rheum & Immun Specs 11115 New Halls Ferry Rd Florissant MO 63033-7613 Home Phone: 314-878-1014; Office Phone: 314-839-4339. Personal E-mail: kongsakt@sbcglobal.net.

TANSELLE, GEORGE THOMAS, language educator, foundation administrator; b. Lebanon, Ind., Jan. 29, 1934; s. K. Edwin and Madge R. (Miller) T. BA magna cum laude, Yale U., 1955; MA, Northwestern U., 1956, PhD, 1959. Instr. Chgo. City Jr. Coll., 1958-60, U. Wis., Madison, 1960-61, asst. prof., 1961-63, assoc. prof., 1963-68, prof. English, 1968—78; v.p. John Simon Guggenheim Meml. Found., 1978—2006; adj. prof. English and comparative lit. Columbia U., 1980—. Mem. Planning Inst. Commn. on English, 1961; exec. com. Ctr. for Edits. Am. Authors, 1970-73; adv. com. for drama for bicentennial Kennedy Ctr., 1974-76; mem. Soviet-Am. symposium on editing Ind. U., 1976; adv. com. Howells Meml., Kittery Point, 1976-78; exec. com. Ctr. for Scholarly Edits., 1976-81; mem. nat. adv. bd. Ctr. for Book, Libr. of Congress, 1978—; adv. bd. Burton's Anatomy of Melancholy, 1978—, Pub. and Printing History, A Guide to Manuscript Resources in the U.S., 1980—; bd. dirs. Lit. Classics of U.S., Inc., 1979—, chmn. editl. standards com., 1979—, corp. sec., 1989—; adv. com. N.Am. imprints program, 1980-92; Hanes lectr. U. NC, 1981; adv. coun. Rosenbach Mus. and Libr., 1980-83, Ind. U. Inst. Adv. Study, 1983-90; faculty Summer Rare Book Sch., Columbia U., 1984-87; adv. bd. Ctr. for Am. Culture Studies, Columbia U., 1985-94, Blake Archive, 1998—, Ctr. for Renaissance and Baroque Studies, U. Md., 1990—; adv. coun. Am. Trust for the Brit. Libr., 1987-92, Am. Literary Manuscripts project, 1988—; Rosenbach lectr. U. Pa., 1987; bd. dirs. 18th Century Short-Title Catalogue/N.Am., Inc., 1988—, chmn., 1994—, Mark Twain Edition Project, 1991—; vis. com. Lilly Libr., 1988-92; adv. com. Writings of J.F. Cooper, 1990—; Sandars lectr. Cambridge U., 1997; bd. dirs. Am. Newspaper Repository, 1999—; faculty Beineke Libr. Master Classes, 1999-; adv. bd. Cambridge edit. of Jonathan Swift, 2002-. Author: Royall Tyler, 1967, Guide to the Study of United States Imprints, 1971, A Checklist of Editions of Moby-Dick, 1976, Selected Studies in Bibliography, 1979, The History of Books as a Field of Study, 1981, Textual Criticism since Greg, 1987, expanded edit., 2005, A Rationale of Textual Criticism, 1989, Parkman Dexter Howe Library, Hawthorne and Melville, 1989, Textual Criticism and Scholarly Editing, 1990, Libraries, Museums, and Reading, 1991, A Description of Descriptive Bibliography, 1992, The Life and Work of Fredson Bowers, 1993, Literature and Artifacts, 1998, Italian transl., 2004, The Pleasures of Being a Scholar-Collector, 2006, Bibliographical Analysis: A Historical Introduction, 2009; co-editor: The Writings of Herman Melville, 1968—, Samuel Johnson's Translation of Sallust, 1993; editor: Library of Am. Melville, 1982-83, Books as a Way of Life: Essays by Gordon N. Ray, 1988, The Art Deco Book in France by Gordon N. Ray, 2005; mem. editorial bd. Contemporary Literature, 1962-91, Abstracts of English Studies, 1964-78, Papers of Bibliog. Soc. Am, 1968-80, Resources for American Literary Study, 1971—, Analytical and Enumerative Bibliography, 1977—, Review, 1978—, Am. Literature, 1979-82, Literary Research, 1986-90, Common Knowledge, 1991—, Book History, 1996-2005, Leviathan, 1998-, Textual Cultures, 2006-; contbr. articles to books and profl. jours. Mem. coun. Friends of Columbia U. Librs., 1990-94; bd. dirs. Friends of Lilly Libr., 1990-92. Recipient Kiekhofer Teaching award U. Wis., 1963, Jenkins award for bibliography, 1973; Guggenheim fellow, 1969-70; Am. Council Learned Socs. fellow, 1973-74; Nat. Endowment for the Humanities fellow, 1977-78, Laureate award Am. Printing History Assn., 1987. Mem. MLA (mem. exec. com. bibliog. evidence group 1974-75, methods of lit. rsch. div. 1979-83, chmn. 1982, mem. Hubbell award Com. Am. lit. sect. 1978-82, chmn. 1982, mem. com. on prize for ind. scholars 1983-87, chmn. 1985-87, chmn. ad hoc com. on future of print record 1993-95), Modern Humanities Rsch. Assn., Bibliog. Soc. London (pres. Am. Friends 1992—), Bibliog. Soc. Australia, Bibliog. Soc. Am. (mem. council 1970-94, vice chmn. publs. com. 1974-76, chmn. 1981-84, sec. 1976-78, chmn. com. on regional groups, 1978-80, 2d v.p. 1978-80, 1st v.p. 1980-82, pres. 1984-88, hon. mem., 2004), Bibliog. Soc. U. Va. (pres. 1992—), Oxford, Cambridge, Edinburgh, Birmingham, No. Ill., Can. bibliog. socs. (mem. coun. 1996—), Soc. for Bibliography of Natural History, Printing Hist. Soc. (Am. corr. 1970-84), Am. Printing Hist. Assn. (trustee N.Y. chpt. 1979-85), Pvt. Librs. Assn., Ind. Rsch. Librs. Assn. (com. on standards for rare book cataloging in machine-readable form 1978-79), Fellows Morgan Libr., Manuscript Soc. (bd. dirs. 1974-79), Am. Pub. Libr. Film Project (bd. advisors 1993—), Am. Antiquarian Soc. (mem. publs. com. 1972-81, chmn. com. 1978-81, mem. coun. 1974-92, hon. councillor, 1992—, del. to Am. Coun. Learned Socs. 1978-93, exec. com. dels., 1987-89, chmn. exec. com. program on book in Am. culture 1983-89, com. on edn., 1982-85, chmn., 1983-85, chmn. com. on libr. 1988-91), Soc. Textual Scholarship (adv. bd. 1979—, pres. 1981-83), The Johnsonians (chmn. 1993), Melville Soc. (pres. 1982, Electronic Melville Com. 1997—), Book Club Calif., Typophiles, Guild Book Workers, Wis. Acad. Scis., Arts and Letters, Renaissance Soc. Am., Am. Soc. 18th-Century Studies, Renaissance English Text Soc., Assn. Documentary Editing (chmn. Julian Boyd award com. 1986, Boydston award com. 1995), Soc. Scholarly Pub., Assn. internationale de bibliophilie (NY corr., Bulletin de bibliophilie, 1996-), Soc. History of Authorship, Reading and Pub. (bd. dirs. 1993—), Century Club, Yale Club, Caxton Club, Grolier Club (publs. com. 1979-82, 83-87, 97—, coun. 1980—, small exhbns. com. 1979-87, chmn. 1980-82, sec. 1982-86, chmn. libr. com. 1985-86, 90-2002, pres. 1986-90, hon. mem., 2007), Odd Volumes, Phi Beta Kappa. Home: 420 E 51st St # 10D New York NY 10022

TANSEY, RICHARD J., research scientist; b. Winchester, Mass., Sept. 26, 1944; s. Joseph and Ruth Tansey; m. Julie Tansey; children: Kara, Joseph, Kevin. BS in Physics, U. NH., Durham, 1966; MS in Physics, Lowell Tech Inst., Mass., 1970, PhD in Physics, 1975. Assoc. fellow Avco Everett Rsch. Ctr., Mass., 1980—86, Boeing, LEOS, West Hills, Calif., 1998, fellow, 1987, 1999, Lockheed Martin, Advanced Tech. Ctr., Palo Alto, 2004—. Contbr. scientific papers. Group leader Youth Basketball League, Thousand Oaks, Calif., 1992—97. Recipient pres. award, Rockwell, 1982; fellowship, NASA, 1967—72. Mem.: SPIE. Avocations: water-skiing, skiing, baseball. Office: Lockheed Martin 3251 Hanover Palo Alto CA 94304 Business E-Mail: richard.j.tansey@lmco.com.

TANSILL, FREDERICK JOSEPH, lawyer; b. Washington, Feb. 27, 1948; s. Frederick Riker and Mary Eileen (Loftus) T.; m. Joan Louise Trefsgar, July 10, 1971; children: Brendan Frederick, Brooke Charlotte, Charlotte Trefsgar. BA with honors, Brown U., 1970; JD, Georgetown U., 1974, LLM in Taxation, 1982. Bar: D.C. 1974, U.S. Tax Ct. 1976, Va. 1983. Assoc. Cross, Murphy & Smith, Washington, 1974-77; ptnr. Bird & Tansill, Washington, 1977-79; assoc. Ober, Grimes & Shriver, Washington, 1979-81; ptnr. Lewis, Mitchell & Moore, Vienna, Va., 1981-86; counsel Boothe, Prichard & Dudley, McLean, Va., 1986-87; ptnr. McGuire, Woods, Battle & Boothe, McLean, 1987-90; shareholder Verner, Liipfert, Bernhard, McPherson & Hand, Chartered, McLean, 1990-97; owner-mgr. Frederick J. Tansill & Assocs., LLC, McLean, 1997—. Gen. counsel No. Va. Cmty. Found., 1995-98, 1st v.p., 1998-99, pres., 1999-2000; mem. Estate Planning Coun. Washington, 2007—. Fellow Am. Coll. Trust and Estate Counsel; mem. ABA, Internat. Bus. Bar, Va. Bar Assn. (exec. coun. taxation sect. 1989-92, coun. and legis. com. wills sect. 1993-99—, trusts and estate sect. 1983-99, bd. govs. 1988-96, chmn. bd. govs. 1991-92, co-chmn. spl. task force lawyers as fiduciaries 1993-95), D.C. Bar Assn. (steering com. estates, trusts and probate law sects. 1995-97, co-chair 1997-99), Fairfax County Bar Assn. (will sect. 1986, chmn. tax sect. 1987-88, CLE com. 1988-89), No. Va. Estate Planning Coun. (exec. com. 1987-92, pres. 1990-91), Tower Club (bd. dirs. 1988—). Office: Frederick J Tansill & Assocs 1355 Beverly Rd Ste 215 Mc Lean VA 22101-3654 Office Phone: 703-847-1359. Office Fax: 703-847-1357. Business E-Mail: fred@fredtansill.com.

TANSKY, BURTON M., department store executive; b. 1938; married BA, U. Pitts., 1960. With Kaufmann's, 1961-67; from asst. store mgr. to mgr. Filenes, Boston, 1967-71; mdse. mgr. Rikes, Dayton, Ohio, 1971-74; v.p. Forbes and Wallace, Springfield, Ohio, 1974, I. Magnin, San Francisco, 1974-77; from sr. v.p. to exec. v.p. Saks and Co., NYC, 1977-80, pres., 1980—94; chmn., CEO Saks & Co., NYC, 1990—94, Neiman Marcus Stores, Dallas, 1994—98; exec. v.p. Neiman Marcus Group, Dallas, 1998, pres., COO, 1998—2001, pres., CEO, 2001—; interim CEO Bergdorf Goodman, 2004. Bd. dir. Internat. Flavors & Fragrances, 2003—. Named a Chevalier de la Legion d'Honneur, Govt. France, 2002. Office: Neiman Marcus Group One Marcus Sq 1618 Main St Dallas TX 75201-2581

TANSMAN, ALAN, language educator; b. Havana, Cuba, Feb. 10, 1960; s. Aaron Bernard Tansman and Carlotta Stokamer; m. Paula Varsano, June 2006. MSJ, Columbia, NYC, 1982; PhD, Yale, New Haven, 1989. Prof. Georgetown U., Washington, 1995—2001, East Asian Lang. and Cultures, Berkeley, Calif., 2001—. Office: UC Berkeley 3431 Dwinelle Berkeley CA 94720-2230

TANT, MARTIN RAY, chemical and biomedical engineer; b. Seneca, SC, Apr. 10, 1953; s. Larry Ray and Doris Jo Anne (Alexander) T. BS, Old Dominion U., 1975; MS, Va. Tech., 1979, PhD, 1986; postgrad. in Biomed. Sci., East Tenn. State U., 2003—. Chemist Naval Mine Engrng. Facility, Yorktown, Va., 1975-76; chem. engr. Naval Surface Warfare Ctr., Dahlgren, Va., 1979—82; sr. rsch. engr. Dow Chem. USA, Freeport, Tex., 1986-88; rsch. assoc. Eastman Chem. Co., Kingsport, Tenn., 1988—. Co-editor Ionomers: Synthesis, Structure, Properties and Applications, 1997, High-Temperature Properties and Applications of Polymeric Materials, 1995, Structure and Properties of Glassy Polymers, 1998; contbr. over 50 publs. to books and profl. jours. Cunningham Dissertation fellow, 1985. Mem.: AIChE, Am. Assn. Pharm. Scientists, Am. Chem. Soc., Sigma Xi. Office: Eastman Chem Co PO Box 1972 Kingsport TN 37662-1972 Office Phone: 423-229-2147. Business E-Mail: tant@eastman.com.

TANTEH, VICTOR NKANGAMI, information technology educator; b. Ekona, Buea, South West Province, Cameroon, July 28, 1972; s. Dominic Tarry and Mary Tanteh, Beatrice Akenji Tanteh (Stepmother). BS in Computer Engring., Ga. Inst. Tech., 2000; BS in Gen. Sci., Morehouse Coll., 2000. Assoc. applications specialist Schlumberger, San Jose, Calif., 2000—01; tech. coord. Humphries Elemenatry Sch., Atlanta, 2001—, DigitalBash, 2005—; CEO, pres. Tanvicktech Cons., Inc., Austell, Ga., 2005—. Tech. cons. Forchuteck Consulting, Douglasville, Ga., 2000—02. Tech. coord. Solid Found. Home Sch., Stone Mountain, Ga.; sec. gen. Social Dem. Front, Atlanta, 1998—99; capt. Atlanta (Ga.) Lions Soccer Team, 2003—04. Recipient Leadership and Outstanding Svcs. award, Am. U. in Cairo, 1994, Math. award, Morehouse Coll., 1997, Outstanding Performance award, Morehouse Soccer Team, 1997, 1998. Mem.: IEEE (assoc.). Roman Catholic. Avocations: travel, soccer, swimming, horseback riding, sports. Office: Humphries Elementary School 3029 Humphries Dr SE Atlanta GA 30354 Home: 3401 Cook Rd Powder Springs GA 30127-1171 Office Fax: 404-362-2408. Personal E-mail: tanvic14@yahoo.com. Business E-Mail: vtanteh@atlanta.k12.ga.us, vtanteh@tanvicktech.com.

TANTILLO, ANDREW M., legislative staff member; BA in Polit. Sci., Marquette U., Milw., 1997; JD, Georgetown U. Law Ctr., Washington, 2005. Asst. to chief of staff for congressman David Obey US House of Reps., Washington, 1997, legis. corr., 1997—97, legis. asst., 1998—2001, legis. counsel to congressman Brian Higgins, 2005—07, dep. chief of staff, then chief of staff, 2007—; sr. fed. rels. specialist Lockridge Grindal Nauen P.L.L.P., Washington, 2001—05. Democrat. Mailing: US House Reps 431 Cannon House Office Bldg Washington DC 20515 Office Fax: 202-225-0347, 202-225-3306. Business E-Mail: andy.tantillo@mail.house.gov.*

TANTILLO, MARY DARLENE, nurse; b. Rochester, NY, July 28, 1960; d. Salvatore Augustus and Constance Tantillo; m. Odysseus Adamides, Oct. 2, 1993; 1 child, Odysseus Alexander Adamides. AAS in Nursing, Monroe C.C., Rochester, NY, 1980; BS in Nursing, Nazareth Coll. Rochester, NY, 1982; MS in Psychiat. Mental Health Nursing, U. Rochester Sch. Nursing, NY, 1986; PhD, Adelphi U., Garden City, NY, 1992. Profl. RN, N.Y., 1980. Nurse mgr. behavioral medicine unit U. Rochester/Strong Meml. Hosp., 1985—86, clinician II clin. nurse specialist cons., 1986—90, assoc. dir. adult ambulatory svcs.-psychiatry, 1990—94, adminstrv. dir. ambulatory svcs.-psychiatry, 1994—98, dir. eating disorder treatment svc., 1997—2000; dir. eating disorders program Unity Health Sys. Dept. Psychiatry and Behavioral Health, Rochester, 2000—, dir. We. N.Y. Comprehensive Care Ctr. for Eating Disorders, 2005—. Chair legis. com. Rochester Area Psychiat. Mental Health Nurse Clin. Specialist Group, 1986—94; chairperson Rochester Consortium on Eating Disorders, 1990—93; coord. Jean Baker Miller Tng. Inst. Rsch. Network, Wellesley, Mass., 1996—; pres., bd. dirs. Mental Health Assn., Rochester, 2002—05, bd. dirs. Acad. Eating Disorders, Northbrook, Ill., 2002—05, chairperson credentialing task force, 2004—; clin. assoc. prof. psychiatry U. Rochester Med. Ctr., 2004—; co-chair Rochester Eating Disorders Cmty. Adv. Bd., 2004—. Mem. mental health outreach Spiritus Christi Ch., Rochester, 2000—. Recipient Ann. Outstanding Nurse award for Excellence in Patient and Family Nursing, U. Rochester Dept. Psychiat. Nursing, 1984, Rsch. award, Sigma Theta Tau Internat. Inc. Epsilon xi Chpt., 1996, Gottschalk Mental Heatlh Rsch. award, Mental Health Assn., 1996, Excellence in the Treatment of Eating Disorders, Excellus, Blue Cross/Blue Shield of Rochester, 2002—, Woman of Influence in Health Care, Girl Scouts Genesee Valley, Inc., 2005; fellow, Acad. Eating Disorders, 2003. Fellow: Acad. Eating Disorders; mem.: Nat. Ctr. Addictions and Substance Abuse, Nat. Alliance for the Mentally Ill, Nat. Eating Disorders Assn., AAUW, Sigma Theta Tau Internat., Wellesley Centers for Women, Nat. Registry Cert. Group Psychotherapists, Jean Baker Miller Tng. Inst., Am. Group Psychotherapy Assn., Rochester Area Group Psychotherapy Soc., Genesee Valley Nurses Assn. Democrat-Npl. Catholic. Avocations: bicycling, hiking, dance, swimming, crafts. Office: Unity Health System Dept of Psychiatry 835 W Main St Rochester NY 14611 Office Fax: 585-368-6540. Business E-Mail: mtantillo@unityhealth.org.

TANTUM, JAMES KENT, artist, publisher; b. Miami, Fla., Dec. 7, 1964; s. James Kent Tantum and Penelope Elaine Davis. BA, Temple U., 1990; MFA, San Francisco Art Inst., 2005. Facilitator, presenter World Game Inst., Phila., 1994—2001, asst. dir. mktg., 1996—2001; owner Tantum Mfg., San Francisco, 1998—; sr. fellow Cultural Studies and Analysis, Phila., 2002—06. Author: Teleological Expressionism, 1998, Time, Ontology, Reality, and Me, 2002, Wreeder's Notes, 2009; co-author: Sex Notes, 1998; author of short stories; photographer A Year in the Life of Rittenhouse Square Show, 1995; artist (calendar) Jim Calendar, 1997-2009; designer Pogany flatware, 1996, Childhood Fantasy Series, 2004-09, Wrax cd rack, 1995; creator, M.C., Jim's Ann. All-Invitational RoadRally, 1995—2005, Tomorrow, Boxed edit., 2009; featured Phila. Weekly, 2001; co-founder performance troupe Parsley, 2001; performer Phila. Fringe Festival 2001, 02, 03. Fellow Murphy fellow in the fine arts, San Francisco Found. Mem.: Golden Key. Avocations: travel, art. Home and Office: Tantum Mfg 1214 York St San Francisco CA 94110 Personal E-mail: jameskttantum@yahoo.com.

TANUR, JUDITH MARK, statistician, sociologist, educator; b. Jersey City, Aug. 12, 1935; d. Edward Mark and Libbie (Berman) Mark; m. Michael Isaac Tanur, June 2, 1957; children: Rachel Dorothy, Marcia Valerie. BS, Columbia U., 1957, MA, 1963; PhD, SUNY, Stony Brook, 1972. Analyst Biometrics Rsch., NYC, 1955-67; lectr. SUNY, Stony Brook, 1967-71, from asst. prof. to prof. sociology, 1971-94, Disting. tchg. prof., 1994—2006, Disting. tchg. prof. emerita, 2006—. Cons. NBC, NYC, 1976—89, Lang. of Data Project, Los Altos, Calif., 1980—89, Inst. for Rsch. on Learning, 1994—95; mem. com. on nat. stats. NAS, 1980—87, com. on applied and theoretical stats., 1997—2000; trustee NORC, U. Chgo., 1987—; bd. dirs. Social Sci. Rsch. Coun., 2000—06, mem. Vietnam Population Health Study Advisory Com., 2007—; mem. adv. com. SBE, NSF, 2000—06. Author: The Subjectivity of Scientists and the Bayesian Approach, 2001; editor: Internat. Ency. of Social Scis., 1963—67, Statistics: A Guide to the Unknown, 1972, Internat. Encyclopedia of Statistics, 1978, Cognitive Aspects of Survey Methodology, 1984, Questions About Questions, 1991, Cognition and Survey Research, 1999, Visualizing Social Science: Photographs of Rachel Tanur, 2008, Pleasures of Statistics Autobiography of Frederick Mosteller, 2009; contbr. articles to sci., stats., and social sci. jours. Bd. dirs. Vis. Nurse Svc., Great Neck, N.Y., 1970-2000; bd. govs. Gen. Soc. Survey, Chgo., 1989-92. Recipient Geoffrey Marshall Mentoring award, Northeastern Assn. Grad. Schs., 2005, Innovators award, Am. Assn. Pub. Opinion Rsch., 2005, Outstanding Achievement award, NY Chpt. Am. Assn. Pub. Opinion, 2007; Sr. rsch. fellow, Am. Statis. Assn./NSF/Bur. Labor Stats., 1988—89. Fellow AAAS, Am. Statis. Assn. (Founders award 1997), Assn. Psychol. Sci.; mem. Internat. Statis. Inst., Am. Sociol. Assn., Phi Beta Kappa. Home: PO Box 280 Montauk NY 11954 Office: SUNY Dept Sociology Stony Brook NY 11794-4356 Office Phone: 631-668-2965. Business E-Mail: jtanur@notes.cc.sunysb.edu.

TANYI, RUTH A., family practice nurse practitioner, lifestyle diseases consultant; b. Cameroon, West Africa; arrived in US, 1987, naturalized; d. Johnson and Mercy Tanyi. BS in Journalism, U. Wis. River Falls, 1993; BSN, Met. State U., St. Paul, 1999; MSN, U. Wis. Eau-Claire, 2002; DrPH in Lifestyle Diseases & Prevention, Loma Linda U., Calif. Cert. nurse practitioner, Am. Acad. Nurse Practitioner & Am. Nurses Credentialing Ctr., 2002, health fitness specialist, Am. Coll. Sports Medicine, 2005, nutrition specialist, Am. Coll. Nutrition, 2007. Family nurse practitioner Preventive Care & Wellness Svcs., Loma Linda, Calif., 2002—, lifestyle & disease prevention cons., 2004—; TV exec. prodr. Lifestyle & Preventive Care TV Show, Loma Linda, 2005—. Guest spkr. Radio & Television Programs Lifestyle Related Diseases & Prevention, 2004—; reviewer Jour. Advanced Nursing, 2003—, Jour. Am. Acad. Nurse Practitioner, 2008; med. journalist, host exec. prodr., creator Lifestyle & Preventive Care Television Show, 2005—; key note & plenary spkr., creator Lifestyle & Disease Annual Conf., 2007—; creator Preventive Care Today Television Show, 2007. Contbr. scientific papers, to numerous sci. poster presentations. Vol. health educator on lifestyle practices & diseases prevention Abundant Living Family Ch., Rancho Cucamonga, Calif., 2008. Recipient Student Rsch. award, U. Wis. Eau-Claire, 2002, Golden Lamp award for Bad Sugar, Television Series, Best Media Depictions Nurses Television, 2006, Glen Blix award Excellence Preventive Care, Loma Linda U., Sch. Public Health, 2009; Selma Andrews scholarship, 2008. Mem.: Am. Coll. Sports Medicine, Am. Coll. Nutrition, Sigma Theta Tau Internat. Honor Soc. of Nursing. Achievements include research in spirituality & health in various populations. Avocations: reading, dance. Home and Office: Preventive Care & Wellness Svcs Theta Taw Internat PO Box 1185 Loma Linda CA 92354 Office Phone: 909-557-7269. Personal E-mail: rtanyi@yahoo.com.

TANYUK, KATHRYN MARY, medical/surgical nurse, educator; b. Montague, Mass. d. Daniel John and Helen Mary (Kopec) Tanyuk. Diploma, Mercy Hosp. Sch. Nursing, Springfield, Mass., 1970; BS in Nursing Edn., Cen. Conn. State U., 1980; MA in Counseling, St. Joseph Coll., West Hartford, Conn., 1994. RN, Conn.; cert. continuing edn. and staff devel., ANCC. Asst. head nurse recovery room Hartford Hosp., Conn., 1972-76, pediatric cardiology nurse clinician Conn., 1976-81, staff nurse coronary ICU Conn., 1981-82, instr. div. nursing edn. and rsch. Conn., 1982—2000; staff nurse Bristol Hosp., Bristol, Conn., 2001—05, clin. edn., 2005—. Appt. adv. bd. Wilcox Coll. Nursing, Middletown, Conn.; lectr. on cardiol to area instns.; condr. workshops on basic and advanced arrhythmia interpretation. Mem. ANA, Nat. Nursing Staff Devel. Orgn. Office Phone: 860-585-3360. Business E-Mail: ktanyuk@bristolhospital.org.

TANZI, RUDOLPH EMILE (RUDY TANZI), neuroscientist, researcher, educator; b. Providence, Sept. 18, 1958; s. Rudolph Anthony and Anne Marie (Macari) Tanzi; m. Dora Marta Kovacs, May 24, 2002. BS in Microbiology, U. Rochester, 1980, BA in History, 1980; PhD in Neurobiology, Harvard U., 1990. Rsch. asst. genetics unit to prof. Mass. Gen. Hosp., Boston, 1980—99, prof. neurology, 1999—, dir. Genetics and Aging Unit, 1999—. Instr. neurology Harvard U. Med. Sch., 1990—92, asst. prof. to prof., 1992—; bd. sci. counselors Nat. Inst. Aging; chmn. sci. adv. bd. Blanchette Rockefeller Neurosciences Inst. Editl. bd. Neuron, 1994—; co-editor: Molecular Mechanisms of Dementia, 1997, Presenilins and Alzheimer's Disease, 1998, Alzheimer's Disease: Advances in Genetics, Molecular and Cellular Biology, 2006; co-author: Decoding Darkness: The Search for the Genetic Causes of Alzheimer's Disease, 2001; contbr. articles to profl. jours. Adv. bd. Lifeboat Found. Recipient Nathan Shock New Investigator award, Gerontology Soc. Am., 1993, Met. Life award, 1995, Potamkin prize, 1995; fellow French Found., 1991, Pew scholar in biomed. scis., 1993. Fellow: AAAS; mem.: Am. Soc. Human Genetics, Am. Soc. for Neurosci. Avocations: skiing, tennis, scuba diving, piano. Office: Mass Gen Hosp - East Genetics and Aging Rsch Unit 114 16th St Charlestown MA 02129 Office Phone: 617-726-6845. Office Fax: 617-724-1949. E-mail: tanzi@helix.mgh.harvard.edu.*

TAO, JIANG, engineering educator; s. Yequan Jiang and Guohua Yao; m. Chunju Huang; 1 child, Haotian Jiang. PhD, Huazhong U. Sci. and Tech., Wuhan, China, 2004. Cert. engr., TI Co., Shanghai, 2001. Postdoc. rschr. U. Mich., Dearborn, 2006—07; prof. Huazhong U. Sci. and Tech., 2008—. Contbr. scientific papers. Mem.: IEEE. Office Fax: 0086-27-87795845. Personal E-mail: unique.tao.jiang@gmail.com.

TAO, JIANMIN, chemistry educator, researcher; b. Kunming, China, May 2, 1960; s. Hua Tao and Ruiying Li; m. Limei Liu, May 10, 1995; 1 child, Xing Tao. BS, Yunnan Normal U., Kunming, 1982; MS, U. Sci. and Tech. China, 1988; postgrad., Tulane U., 1999. Asst. prof. chemistry Yunnan Normal U., 1982-96, assoc. prof., 1997—. Contbr. articles to profl. jours. including Jour. Chem. Physics, Phys. Rev. A, others. Grantee Sci. Found. China, 1997, Basic Rsch. and Applied Rsch. Coun. of Yunnan, 1997, Yunnan Normal U., 1997. Mem. AAAS, N.Y. Acad. Scis. Avocations: playing bridge, ping pong/table tennis, dance. Office: Tulane U Dept Physics New Orleans LA 70118

TAO, JIANNING, research scientist; s. Changlai Tao and Meiying Zeng; m. Xiaofan Li, Dec. 10, 2004; 1 child, Arthur; m. Jianxiong Liu, May 1, 1993 (div. Mar. 5, 2001); 1 child, Junling. BS, Sichuan U., Chengdu, China, 1991; MS, West China U. Med. Sci., Chengdu, China, 1996; PhD, U. Tenn., Memphis, 2004. Rsch. assoc. Zhejiang Chinese Med. U., Zhejian, 1991—93; lectr. Sichuan U., China, 1996—98; postdoctoral rsch. fellow St. Jude Children's Rsch. Hosp., Memphis, 2004—05, Baylor Coll. Medicine, Houston, 2005—. Contbr. articles to profl. jours. Fellow, Baylor Coll. Medicine, 2005, 2006, 2007. Mem.: Soc. Investigative Dermatology (assoc.), Soc. Devel. Biology (assoc.). Achievements include discovery of finding three novel genes in vertebrate Xenopus frog, (Xenopus Grhl1, Grhl2, Grhl3). Business E-Mail: tao@bcm.edu.

TAO, LI, application developer; s. Linzhong Li and Zhengzai Peng; m. Jing Xiao. PhD, Ill. Inst. Tech., Chgo., 2006. Sr. rsch. assoc. Ill. Inst. Tech., 2006—07; software engr. Siemens Energy Inc., Minnetonka, Minn., 2007—. Contbr. articles to profl. publs. Office: Siemens Energy Inc 10900 Wayzata Blvd Minnetonka MN 55305 Personal E-mail: taoli_sjtu@yahoo.com.

TAO, RAN, economics professor, researcher; d. Zhixin Tao and Guihua Fan; m. Yun-Lung Hsiao, May 18, 2008. BA with 1st class, Shandong U., China, 2001; MS, Lancaster U., Eng., 2002; PhD, Claremont Grad. U., Calif., 2008. Clin. asst. prof. Claremont Grad. U., 2008—. Summer intern Inland Revenue, London, 2002; rsch. assoc. Nat. Water Rsch. Inst., Fountain Valley, Calif., 2003—06, U. La Verne, Calif., 2005, Nat. Devel. and Reform Com., Beijing, 2007—. Contbr. articles to profl. jours., chapters to books. Mem.: Asia-Pacific Econ. Assn., Western Econ. Assn., Am. Econ. Assn., Phi Beta Kappa. Office: Claremont Grad Univ 150 E 10th St Claremont CA 91711 Business E-Mail: nancy.tao@cgu.edu.

TAO, RAN, immunologist, researcher; s. Hongchao Tao and Haimin Xu. MD, Zhejiang U. Sch. Medicine, Hangzhou, 1997. Postdoc. fellow Children's Hosp. Phila. & U. Pa., 2003—07; sr. clin. fellow Starzl Transplantation Inst., UPMC, Pitts., 2007—. Contbr. scientific papers. Recipient Young Investigator award, Am. Transplantation Soc. Mem.: Am. Soc. Transplant Surgeons. Achievements include research in deacetylase inhibition promotes the generation and function of regulatory T cells. Office: Starzl Transplantation Inst UPMC 3459 Fifth Avenue Pittsburgh PA 15213 Home Phone: 412-334-6212. Office Fax: 412-647-5480. Business E-Mail: taor@upmc.edu.

TAO, SHIQUAN, chemistry professor; b. Machen, Hubei, China, Sept. 3, 1961; m. Junfang Zhang; 1 child, Keane Jian. DSc, Hiroshima U., 1996. Asst. rsch. prof. Miss. State U., Starkville, 2002—03, assoc. rsch. prof., 2004—07; asst. prof. West Tex. A&M U., Canyon, 2007—. Contbr. chapters to books. Mem.: Am. Chem. Soc. Office: West Tex A&M Univ WTAMU PO Box 60787 Canyon TX 79016 Business E-Mail: stas@wtamu.edu.

TAO, TERENCE CHI-SHEN, mathematics professor; b. Adelaide, South Australia, Australia, July 17, 1975; arrived in US, 1992; s. Billy and Grace Tao; married. BSc with honors in Math., Flinders U., 1991, MSc in Math., 1992; PhD in Math., Princeton U., 1996. Asst. rschr. Flinders Med. Ctr., 1992—94, Princeton U., 1993—94; Hedrick asst. prof. UCLA, 1996—98, acting asst. prof., 1999, asst. prof., 2000, prof., 2000—. Mem. Math. Scis. Rsch. Inst., 1997; vis. fellow U. NSW, Sydney, 1999—2000, vis. prof., 2000; long-term prize fellow Clay Math. Inst., Boston, 2001—03; hon. prof. Australian Nat. U., 2001—03; mem. sci. adv. bd. Australian Math. Scis. Inst., 2002—; mem. adv. bd. Internat. Math. Rsch. Surveys (IRMS), 2003—. Reviewer Zentralblatt Math., 1998—2005, assoc. editor J. Am. Math. Soc., 2002—04, full editor, 2004—06, assoc. editor Am. Jour. Math., 2002—, Dynamics of Partial Differential Equations, 2003—; author: Solving Mathematical Problems: A Personal Perspective, 1992, 2006, Analysis Vol. I, Analysis Vol. II, 2006. Recipient Bronze medal, Internat. Math. Olympiad, 1986, Silver medal, 1987, Gold medal, 1988, medal, Flinders U., 1992, Fulbright postgraduate award, Fulbright Assn., 1992—95, Salem prize, Salem Prize Com., 2000, medal, Australian Math. Soc., 2005, Bocher Meml. prize, Am. Math. Soc., 2000, Fields medal, Internat. Math. Union, 2006, SASTRA Ramanujan prize, 2006, Alan T. Waterman award, NSF, 2008; co-recipient Levi L. Conant prize, Am. Math. Soc., 2005; named one of Brilliant 10, Popular Sci. mag., 2006; Packard Found. fellow, David & Lucille Packard Found., 1999—, Rsch. fellow, Sloan Found., 1999—2001, MacArthur Fellow, John D. and Catherine T. MacArthur Found., 2006. Fellow: Royal Soc. UK; mem.: NAS, Australian Acad. Sci. (corr.). Achievements include research in partial differential equations), combinatorics, number theory and harmonic analysis which is an advanced form of calculus that uses equations from physics. Office: UCLA Dept Math Math Sciences 5622 MS 6364 405 Hilgard Ave Los Angeles CA 90095-1555 Office Phone: 310-206-4844. Business E-Mail: tao@math.ucla.edu.

TAO, ZHINING, environmental scientist; b. Nanjing, Jiangsu, China, 1970; m. Qin Wang. PhD, U. Ill., Urbana, 2003. Asst. profl. scientist Ill. State Water Survey, Champaign, 2004—08; atmospheric scientist U. Ill., Champaign, 2008—. Mem.: Am. Geophys. Union. Achievements include research in climate change impact on air quality; study of terrestrial carbon sequestration; biogeo-interaction. Office: Univ Ill 2204 Griffith Dr Champaign IL 61820 Business E-Mail: ztao@illinois.edu.

TAPAN, MUCIP, engineering educator, consultant; b. Van, Turkey, Jan. 23, 1977; s. Hikmetullah and Zuleyha Tapan; m. Emine Asli Gezen, Apr. 15, 2003; children: Abdullah Bera, Muhammed Yasir, Agah Server. PhD (hon.), Syracuse U. L.C. Smith Coll. Engring., NY, 2007. Asst. prof. YYU Muh. Mim. Fak. Ins. Muh., Van, 2007—; engr. Nat. Grid, Syracuse, 2005—07. Cons. Sistemyapi-Bateg Consortium, Istanbul, Turkey, 2007—. Scholar, TOBB, 1994—99, Turkish Govt., 2005—07. Mem.: Tmmob Imo, ACI, Phi Beta Delta (hon.). Avocations: table tennis, tennis, boating, swimming, travel. Home: 1824 Birgul Sk 1/12 Van 65100 Turkey Office: Yuzuncu Yil Univ MuhMimFak Zeve Kampusu Van 65080 Turkey Business E-Mail: mtapan@syr.edu.

TAPELLA, ROBERT CHARLES, federal official; b. Calif. BS in Graphic Comm., Calif. Polytechnic State U., San Luis Obispo, 1991. Dist. rep. for Congressman Bill Thomas US Congress, 1986—93; profl. staff mem. US Ho. of Reps., 1996—2000; strategic comm. cons., 2000—02; dep. chief of staff US Govt. Printing Office, 2002—04, chief of staff, 2004—07, pub. printer, CEO, 2007—. Recipient Honored Alumni award, Calif. Polytechnic State U., 2008. Office: US Govt Printing Office 732 N Capitol St NW Washington DC 20401 Office Phone: 202-512-0000.*

TAPKEN, MICHELLE G., prosecutor; BA in Edn., U. SD, 1967, MA in Ednl. Psychology, 1970, JD, 1989. Bar: South Dakota; lic. Psychologist. Fed. law clerk, Lincoln, Nebr., 1989—90; prosecutor US Atty. Office, Sioux Falls, SD, 1990—2001; interim US atty. Dist. SD US Dept. Justice, 2001, 2002, 1st asst. US atty. Dist. SD, 2005—. Recipient Director's award, US Dept. Justice, 1996, 2006. Office: 325 S 1st Ave Sioux Falls SD 57104

TAPLEY, EARL MAYS, retired college dean; b. Marietta, Ga., Nov. 8, 1913; s. Joel David and Emma Melissa (Quarles) T.; m. Ruby Jewell Franklin, June 5, 1935; children: Dwight Lowell, Sharon Roselle, Ruth Annette. AB, Vanderbilt U., 1945; MA, George Peabody Coll., Nashville, 1946; PhD, U. Chgo., 1955. Ordained to ministry, Meth. Ch. Pastor various chs., Ga., Tenn., Ill., 1935-46; dean, academic v.p., interim pres. Lee U., Cleveland, Tenn., 1946—53; assoc. prof., asst. to pres., dir. spl. svcs., head dept. psychology U. Chattanooga, 1953-57; prof., dir. research U. Evansville, Ind., 1957-59, prof., dept. head, 1959-65, dean, grad. sch., 1965-79, grad. dean emeritus, 1979—, dir. internat. studies and travel, 1970—86; assoc. minister First United Meth. Ch., Dunedin, Fla., 1986-90, The Meth. Temple, Evansville, 1980-86. Accreditation cons.; leader comparative edn. study groups USSR, 1969-79, China, 1978-84. Author: Teaching General Education in Junior Colleges, 1955, General Education in the College Curriculum, 1957, The Way It Was, 1994, 2d edit., 2000; contbr. articles to profl. jours. Named to Hall of Fame, Dunedin, 2003. Mem. AAUP (chpt. pres. 1962-64), Ind. Assn. Grad. Schs. (pres. 1972-74), Dunedin Com. Aging, Rotary, Phi Delta Kappa, Phi Kappa Phi. Avocations: writing, computers, boating, sport fishing, fishing. Home: 700 Beach Plz Apt 950 Dunedin FL 34698-6646 Personal E-mail: earltap@tampabay.rr.com.

TAPLIN, MARY-ELLEN, medical educator; AB, Mt. Holyoke Coll., South Hadley, Mass., 1982; MD, U. Mass., 1986. Diplomate Am. Bd. Internal Medicine, Am. Bd. Oncology. Assoc. prof. medicine Dana-Farber Cancer Inst., Harvard Med. Sch., Boston, 2003—. Mem. staff Sair Hosp.-Clinic. Office Fax: 617-632-2165.

TAPLIN, WINN LOWELL, historian, retired federal agency administrator; b. Saint Albans, Vt., Oct. 3, 1925; s. Winn Lowell and Elinor (Cunningham) T.; m. Ellajean Allard, July 16, 1949; children: Leslie Taplin Baumann, Mark Allard. BSCE, U. Mich., 1946, AB, 1948, AM, 1950, PhD, 1956. Oper. officer CIA, Washington, Saigon, Bucharest, Geneva, Bangkok, 1955-81; cons. Stowe, Vt., 1981-94, Sarasota, Fla., 1994—; tchr. Am. and intelligence history U. South Fla.-Sarasota Campus, 2007—. Author: Secret New England: Spies of the American Revolution, 1991, We Vermonters, 1992. Mem. U.S. del. to UN Commn. on Human Rights, 1969; pres. Vt. Hist. Soc., 1989-93, trustee, 1983-96; mem. Sarasota Geneal. Soc., v.p., 1999-2001, pres., 2001—03; pres. Mansfield View Water Corp., Stowe, 1989-92. 1st lt. USMC, 1943-46, 50-52, Korea. Decorated Bronze Star, Intelligence Medal of Merit, Korean War Purple Heart, 1951. Mem. DAV, Central Intelligence Retirees Assn., Assn. Former Intelligence Officers, First Day Cover Soc., Am. Philatelic Assn., Soc. Mayflower Descendants (Sarasota Tilley chpt., dir. 2005-), Am. Legion, U. Mich. Club Sarasota (dir. 1994-04, pres. 2009-), Sigma Chi. Avocations: historical research, genealogy, classical music, stamp collecting/philately. Home: 4468 Calle Serena Sarasota FL 34238-5641 Home Phone: 941-924-7719. Personal E-mail: winn.ej@juno.com.

TAPP, SHELLEY RAYE, marketing educator; b. Paducah, Ky., June 5, 1953; d. David Donald and Beatrice (Guill) T. BA, Agnes Scott Coll., 1975; MS, Ga. Inst. Tech., 1977; PhD, Ind. U., 1986. Lectr. Murray (Ky.) State U., 1978-79; assoc. instr. Ind. U., Bloomington, 1979-84; asst. prof. U. Nebr., Lincoln, 1984-89, St. Louis U., 1990—. Contbr. articles in consumer research field, 1982—. Cons. Goodwill Industries, Lincoln; pres. Lincoln Civic Chorus, 1986-89. George Holmes fellow U. Nebr., 1986, Ind. U. fellow, 1979-82, 83. Mem. Assn. Consumer Rsch., Am. Acad. Advt., Am. Mktg. Assn. (v.p. 1985-87), Jr. Women's League (cons.), Lincoln Needleworkers Guild (pres. 1987-89). Democrat. Avocations: classical voice performance, reading, needlecrafts. Office: St Louis Univ Sch Bus 3674 Lindell Blvd Saint Louis MO 63108-3302 Home: 5621 W 43rd Ave Amarillo TX 79109-5201

TAPPÉ, ALBERT ANTHONY, architect; b. Pitts., Aug. 12, 1928; s. Albert Anthony and Martha Ann (McKee) T.; m. Jean Bates, June 27, 1963; children: Eliza Bruce, Albert Anthony III. Student, William and Mary Coll., 1947-48, Fontainebleau Fine Art and Music Sch., 1951; BS, U. Va., 1952; M.Arch., MIT, 1958, M.City Planning. Designer McLeod & Ferrara (Architects), Washington, 1954-55; planner Boston City Planning Bd., 1957-58; architect, planner Architects Collaborative, Cambridge, Mass., 1958-61; ptnr. Huygens & Tappé, Inc. (architects and planners), Boston, 1962-80; pres. A. Anthony Tappé & Assocs., Inc., Boston, 1980—. Instr. dept. city planning MIT, 1959-60; instr. office exec. edn. Harvard U., 1989—; cons. architect Mass. Bur. Library Extension, 1965-76; chmn. bldg. commn., Brookline, Mass., 1977, mem. bd. examiners, Brookline; v.p. Guild Religious Architecture; mem. Back Bay Archtl. Commn.; bd. dirs. Boston Archtl. Ctr., 1980, bd. overseers, 2001-; vis. architect Am. Acad. Rome, 1997. Author: Guide to Planning a Library Building, 1967; important works include: Longy Concert Hall, Cambridge, Mass., Campus NH Coll., Franklin Park Zoo, Boston, Lynn Inst. for Savs., Interfaith Religious Ctr., Columbia, Md., student housing W.Va. Wesleyan Coll., Hotel, Costa Smeralda, Sardinia, Newton Pub. Libr., Beverly Pub. Libr., Am. Coll., Athens, Greece, Morse Inst. Library, Natick, Mass., Newton Public Library, Mass., Ctrl. Sch., Longmeadow, MA.; also residences in US, France, Switzerland, housing projects in New Eng. Served with AUS, 1946-47, 52-54. Recipient Prog. Architecture Design award, 1966, 1st place single family category Plywood Design Awards Program, 1973, award Merit, 1974 Fellow AIA (mem. nat. urban planning design com. 1975, citation, hon. mentions 1969, 1st honor award 1970, honor award New Eng. Regional Council 1976); mem. Mass. Assn. Architects (exec. com.), Boston Soc. Architects (dir., v.p. 1981-82, pres. 1982-83, award 1998), Am. Inst. Planners, Am. Planning Assn., Am. Inst. Cons. Planners, Ecoles D'Art Americanes Fontainebleau (trustee 2003-), Harvard Travelers Club. Clubs: Union Boat (Boston), Eastern Point Yacht (Gloucester, Mass.), Harvard Club (Boston), Bass Rocks Golf Club (Gloucester, Mass.). Office: Tappe Assocs Inc 6 Edgerly Pl Boston MA 02116-5327 Business E-Mail: aatappe@tappe.com.

TAPPEINER, II, JOHN C., forester, educator; b. LA, Dec. 15, 1934; s. John Cummings Tappeiner and Whilhelmina Behr; m. Susan Elisabeth Burtnett; children: Aileen A. Runde, Elisabeth Peter Tappeiner. MS in Forestry, UC Berkeley, PhD, 1966. Assoc. prof. Forestry U. Mex., 1968—73; regional silviculturist US Forest Svc., 1973—80; emeritus prof. Coll. Forestry Oreg. State U., Corvallis, 1980—. Contbr. articles to profl. jours. (award, 2001). With Com. Forests, Washington, 2008. Lt. USN, 1957—59. Recipient Rschr. of Yr. award, Oreg. Soc. Am. Forestry, 1997. Mem.: Soc. Am. Forestry. Roman Catholic. Avocations: bicycling, skiing, reading. Home: 2841 NW Monterey Pl Corvallis OR 97330 Office: Coll Forestry Oreg State Univ Corvallis OR 97331 Office Phone: 541-737-3055. Business E-Mail: john.tappeiner@orst.edu.

TAPPER, JAKE, television journalist, news correspondent; b. NYC, Mar. 12, 1969; m. Jennifer Tapper; 1 child, Alice. BA in Hist., magna cum laude, Dartmouth Coll., Hanover, NH, 1991; student, U. So. Calif. Sch. Cinema-TV. With pub. affairs firm Powell Tate, Washington; with Handgun Control Inc., 1997; sr. writer Washington City Paper, 1998—99; Washington corr. Salon.com, 1999—2002; joined ABC News, 2003, nat./sr. polit. corr. DC bur., then sr. White House corr., 2008—. Host TV news show Take Five, CNN, 2001; corr. series entertainment news specials VH1, 2002; host Sundance Channel, 2003; regular contbr. Good Morning America, Nightline, World News with Charles Gibson, This Week with George Stephanopoulos, ABCNews-.com, ABC NewsNOW. Author: Body Slam: The Jesse Ventura Story, 1999, Down and Dirty: The Plot to Steal the Presidency, 2001; contbr. (polit. comic strip featured in Roll Call) Capitol Hell, 1994—2003, contbr. cartoons Am. Spectator mag., LA Times, Phila. Inquirer, contbg. writer The New Yorker, NY Times Mag., Washington Post, LA Times, Weekly Standard. Office: ABC News 7 W 66th St New York NY 10023*

TAPSCOTT, ED, professional sports team executive; m. Janis Thomas; 1 child, Logan. B, M, Tufts U., Medford, Mass.; JD, Am. U. Coll. Law, 1980. Asst. coach Am. U. Eagles, 1978—82, head coach, 1982—90; player agent Advantage Internat., Washington, 1990—91; v.p. player pers., v.p. basketball ops. NY Knicks, interim pres., gen. mgr.; front office cons. Milw. Bucks, Phoenix Suns; on-air TV analyst Fox Sports, Comcast Sports Net; pres., COO Bobcats Basketball Holdings, LLC, Charlotte, 2003—06, pres., CEO, 2006; dir. player devel./programs Washington Wizards, 2007—, interim head coach, 2008—09. Bd. mem. United Way Ctrl. Carolinas, Urban League Ctrl. Carolinas, U. NC Charlotte Belk Coll. Bus., Charlotte Ctr. City Ptnrs., Charlotte Chamber, Johnson C. Smith U. Bd. Visitors, YMCA Greater Charlotte, Winston-Salem State U. Leadership Sch. Named one of Most Influential Minorities in Sports, Sports Illus., Power 50 in the City of Charlotte, Charlotte Mag., 2004; named to Stafford H. Cassell Hall of Fame, Am. U., 2006. Office: Washington Wizards 601 F St NW Washington DC 20004*

TAPSCOTT, STEPHEN, literature educator; life ptnr. Andrew Rosing. PhD, Cornell U., Ithaca. Prof. Lit MIT, Cambridge, 1975—. Author: (poems) Mesopotamia Another Body, Penobscot. Home: 66 Martin St Cambridge MA 02138 Office: MIT 77 Mass Ave Cambridge MA 02141 Personal E-mail: stephentapscott@hotmail.com.

TARAGIN, DAVIRA SPIRO, curator; d. Herman Frank and Edith Mae Spiro; m. Marvin Maynard Taragin, June 22, 1975; 1 child, Charles Steven. BA, Barnard Coll., NYC, 1973; MA, George Wash. U., Washington, 1975. Curator ednl. svcs. and grant rsch. Fayetteville Mus. Art, NC, 1976—77; curator, edn. coord. Mich. Artrain, Detroit, 1977—78; various positions ranging from rsch. assoc. to curator of 20th-century decorative arts and design Detroit Inst. Arts, Detroit, 1978—90; curator 19th and 20th-century glass Toledo Mus. Art, 1990—2002, dir. Ctr. for Glass, 2001—02; dir. exhbns. and programs Racine Art Mus., Wis., 2002—08; ind. writer Chihuly Inc., Portland Press, 2009. Adviser Assn. Israel's Decorative Arts, NYC, 2003—; contbr. to Web site Dale Chihuly Studio, Seattle, 2004—; mem. curatorial adv. panel New Art Forms Internat. Expn., Chgo., 1988—90. Exhbn. and publ., Design in America: The Cranbrook Vision 1925-1950 (Charles F. Montgomery prize, 1983), Contemporary Crafts and the Saxe Collection (Hon. Mention, AAM Publs. award, 1993), Furniture by Wendell Castle, The Alliance of Art and Industry: Toledo Designs for a Modern America (Hon. Mention, AAM Publs. award, 2002), Women's Tales: Four Leading Israeli Jewelers, 2006; curator, author (exhbn. and catalog) Bigger, Better, More: The Art of Viola Frey, 2009; exhbn. and brochure, Material Response: Michael James at RAM, 2006, exhbn. and catalog, Automobile and Culture-Detroit Style, 1985, Art to Art: Paley, Dine, Statom Respond to Toledo's Treasures, 1996, Contemporary Directions: The William and Maxine Block Collection, 2002—03, Introducing RAM: Its Building and Collections, 2003, The Artist Responds: Albert Paley and Art Nouveau, 2004, Drawing Out The Collection: John McQueen Responds to RAM, 2004, Diane Simpson: Window Dressing, 2007, Arline Fisch: Creatures from the Deep, 2008, Ornament as Expression: Jewelry of Arline Fisch, 2008. Bd. dirs. Toledo Modern Art Group, 1992—2000. Recipient Legal Issues in Mus. Adminstrn. scholarship, ALI-ABA, 2004, David Lloyd Kreeger award Hon. Mention, 1975, Internat. Partnership Among Museums grant, administered by Am. Assn. of Museums and funded by Dept. of State's Bur. of Ednl. and Cultural Affairs, 2003—05; grantee, Ctr. Craft, Creativity and Design, U. NC, 2005—09. Mem.: Friends of Fiber Art, Soc. of North Am. Goldsmiths, Glass Art Soc. Business E-Mail: taragindm@att.net.

TARAN, LEONARDO, classicist, educator; b. Galarza, Argentina, Feb. 22, 1933; came to U.S., 1958, naturalized, 1976; s. Miguel and Liuba Taran; m. Judit Sofia Lida, Dec. 10, 1971; 1 child, Gabriel Andrew. Legal degree, U. Buenos Aires, 1958; PhD in Classics, Princeton U., 1962. Jr. fellow Inst. Rsch. in Humanities, U. Wis., 1962-63, Ctr. Hellenic Studies, Washington, 1963-64; asst. prof. classics U. Calif., LA, 1964-67; mem. faculty Columbia U., NYC, 1967—, prof. Greek and Latin, 1971—, Jay prof. Greek and Latin, 1987—, chmn. dept., 1976-79; emeritus, 2004. Mem. Inst. Advanced Study, Princeton, N.J., 1966-67, 78-79; trustee Assn. Mems. Inst. Advanced Study, 1974-79; mem. mng. com. Am. Sch. Classical Studies, 1976-. Author: Parmenides, 1965, Asclepius of Tralles, Commentary to Nicomachus' Introduction to Arithmetic, 1969, Plato, Philip of Opus and the Pseudo-Platonic Epinomis, 1975, Anonymous Commentary on Aristotle's De Interpretatione, 1978, Speusippus of Athens, 1981, Collected Papers (1962-1999), 2001; co-author: Eraclito: Testimonianze e imitazioni, 1972; mem. editl. bd.: Columbia Studies in the Classical Tradition, 1976-80. Am. Coun. Learned Socs. fellow, 1966-67, 71-72, Guggenheim Found. fellow, 1975, NEH fellow, 1986-87; grantee Am. Philos. Soc., 1963, 71, 75, Am. Coun. Learned Socs., 1968, 72, NEH, 1985-87, 88-89. Mem. Am. Philol. Assn., Classical Assn. Atlantic States, Soc. Ancient Greek Philosophy, Assn. Guillaume Budé. Home: 39 Claremont Ave New York NY 10027-6802 Office: Columbia U 615 Hamilton Hall New York NY 10027 Business E-Mail: lt1@columbia.edu.

TARANIK, JAMES VLADIMIR, geologist, educator; b. LA, Apr. 23, 1940; s. Vladimir James and Jeanette Downing (Smith) T.; m. Colleen Sue Glessner, Dec. 4, 1971; children: Debra Lynn, Danny Lee. BSc in Geology, Stanford U., 1964; PhD, Colo. Sch. Mines, 1974. Chief remote sensing Iowa Geol. Survey, Iowa City, 1971-74; prin. remote sensing scientist Earth Resources Observation Systems Data Ctr., U.S. Geol. Survey, Sioux Falls, SD, 1975-79; chief non-renewable resources br., resource observation div. Office of Space and Terrestrial Applications, NASA Hdqrs., Washington, 1979-82; dean mines Mackay Sch. Mines U. Nev., Reno, 1982-87, prof. geology and geophysics, 1982—98, Arthur Brant chair of geophysics, 1998—; pres. Desert Rsch. Inst., Univ. and C.C. Sys. Nev., 1987-98, Regents's prof. and pres. emeritus, 1998—; adj. prof. geology U. Iowa, 1971-79; vis. prof. civil engring. Iowa State U., 1972-74; adj. prof. earth sci. U. S.D., 1976-79; HQ program scientist space shuttle OSTA-1 Payload on STS-2 NASA, 1981—82, large format camera expt. for heat capacity mapping mission and for magnetic field satellite mission; liaison, 1981—82; dir. NOAA Coop. Inst. Aerospace Sci. & Terrestrial Applications, 1986-94; program dir. NASA Space Grant consortium Univ. and C.C. Sys. Nev., Reno, 1991—2005, dir. NASA EPSCOR program, 1998—2005; bd. dirs. NASA Challenger Learning Ctr., Reno, 2006—; dir. Great Basin Ctr. Geothermal Energy, 2000—03; acting dean Mackay Sch. Mines, 2003; dir. Mackay Sch. Earth Sci. and Engring., U. Nev, 2004—. Team mem. Shuttle Imaging Radar-B Sci. Team NASA, 1983-88, NASA space applications adv. com., 1986-88; chmn. remote sensing subcom. SAAC, 1986-88; chmn. working group on civil space commercialization Dept. Commerce, 1982-84, mem. civil operational remote sensing satellite com., 1983-84; bd. dir. Newmont Mining Corp., 1986-; adv. com. NASA Space Sci. and Applications Com., 1988-90, Nat. Def. Exec. Res., 1986-94, AF studies bd., com. on strategic relocatable targets, 1989-91; pre-launch rev. bd., NASA, Space Radar Lab., 1993-94; fed. lab. rev. task force, NASA, 1994-96; prin. investigator Japanese Earth Resources Satellite, 1991-94; environ. task force MEDEA, Mitre Corp., McLean, Va., 1993-98; mapping scis. com. Nat. Rsch. Coun., 2001-04; cons. Jet Propulsion Lab., Calif., Hughes Aircraft Corp., Lockheed-Marietta Corp., Mitre Corp., TRW; developer remote sensing program and remote sensing lab. State of Iowa, ednl. program in remote sensing Iowa univs. and U. Nev., Reno; program scientist 2d space shuttle flight Office Space and Terrestrial Applications Program; mem. terrestrial geol. applications program NASA, 1981-82; co-investigator Can. Radarsat Program, 1995-97; mem. geol. scis. bd., NAS; dept. of energy prin. investigator nuclear non-proliferation sci. program, 2004-. Contbr. articles to profl. jours. Bd. dirs. Mountain States Legal Found., 2000—, sec., 2006-, Northwest Mining Assn., 2006-08. Served with C.E. U.S. Army, 1965-67; mil. intellegence officer Res. Decorated Bronze Star medal; recipient Spl. Achievement award U.S. Geol. Survey, 1978, Exceptional Sci. Achievement medal NASA, 1982, NASA Group Achievement award Shuttle imaging radar, 1990, NASA Johnson Space Ctr. Group Achievement award for large format camera, 1985; NASA prin. investigator, 1973, 83-88, prin. investigator French Spot-1 Program to Evaluate Spot 1986-88; NDEA fellow, 1968-71. Fellow: AAAS, AIAA (assoc.), Am. Soc. Photogrammetry Remote Sensing, Explorers Club, Geol. Soc. Am.; mem.: IEEE (sr.), N.W. Mining Assn. (trustee 2005—), Mining and Metall. Soc. Am., St. Mary's Hosp. Found., Soc. Econ. Geologists, Am. Geol. Inst. Found. (trustee 1999—), Am. Astron. Soc. (sr.), Am. Inst. Metall. Engrs., Soc. Mining Engrs. Am. (gen. chmn. ednl. sustainability task force 2005—), Am. Assn. Petroleum Geologists (chmn. rsch. com. 2000—), Am. Geophys. Union, Soc. Exploration Geophysicists, Internat. Acad. Astronautics. Home: PO Box 7175 Reno NV 89510-7175 Office Phone: 775-682-8735, 775-784-6987. Personal E-mail: jtaranik@uncedo.com. Business E-Mail: jtaranik@mines.unr.edu. *I have always been in awe of the universe in which we live and the little time we have on earth to perceive and understand it.*

TARANTINO, CHERYL, literature and language professor; Lectr. French & Italian U. Calif., Riverside, 2005—. Curriculum cons. Heritage Oak Pvt. Edn., Yorba Linda, Calif., 2007—08. Recipient Comparative Lit. Outstanding Tchg. Asst. award, U. Calif., 2003—04. Mem.: Am. Coun. Tchg. Fgn. Lang.

TARANTINO, DOMINIC A., retired professional services firm executive; b. San Francisco, Aug. 1, 1932; m. Leona Lazzareschi, July 24, 1954; children: John Robert, Stephen, Leanne. BS, U. San Francisco, 1954. With Price Waterhouse, 1957-98, mem. policy bd. and mgmt. com., 1979-93, vice chmn. tax svcs., 1982-88, co-chmn. bd., mng. ptnr., 1988-93; chmn. Price Waterhouse World Firm, 1995-98; ret., 1998. Mem. IRS Commr.'s Adv. Group, 1978. Trustee U. San Francisco, 1996—2005, chair bd. trustees, 1999—2003, chair Capital Campaign, 2001—07, chair bd. trustees emeritus, 2005—; treas., bd. dirs. Bus. Opportunities for Leadership Diversity, 1988—. Recipient Delta Sigma Pi Career Achievement award, 1997. Mem. AICPA (bd. dirs. 1988-95, vice chair 1992-3, chmn. 1993-94, Dixon Meml. award 1990, Gold medal for disting. svc. 2000). Address: 549 Indian Field Rd Mead Point Greenwich CT 06830

TARANTINO, LOUIS GERALD, lawyer, management consultant; b. Bridgeport, Conn., Sept. 7, 1934; s. Louis Gerald and Mary Louise (Boyle) T. BA, U. Pa., 1955, LLB, 1958. Bar: Conn. 1958, N.Y. 1960. Assoc. Beekman & Bogue, 1959—67, ptnr., 1968—76; pres., bd. dirs. Berkeley Mgmt. Assocs., Inc., Boston, 1994—2003. Mem. enterprise adv. bd. Photonics Ctr., Boston U., 1999-2004; bd. dirs. Midnight Trader, Inc., Bethesda, Md., Celsense., Inc., Pitts. Mem. Bar Assn. City N.Y., N.Y. Bar Assn., Conn. Bar Assn., Huguenot Soc. Pa., St. Anthony Hall, Knickerbocker Club, India House N.Y.C. Home: One Devonshire Pl Apt PH309 Boston MA 02109

TARANTINO, QUENTIN JEROME, film director, scriptwriter; b. Knoxville, Tenn., Mar. 27, 1963; s. Tony and Connie Tarantino. Co-founder (with Lawrence Baker) A Band Apart Records. Actor:

(films) My Best Friend's Birthday, 1987, Eddie Presley, 1993, (voice) The Coriolis Effect, 1994, Sleep With Me, 1994, Somebody to Love, 1994, Destiny Turns on the Radio, 1995, The Anatomy of Horror, 1995, Desperado, 1995, Girl 6, 1996, Steven Spielberg's Director's Chair, 1996, Full Tilt Boogie, 1997, Little Nicky, 2000, Planet of the Pits, 2004, Epreuves d'artistes, 2004, (voice) Diary of the Dead, 2008; actor, writer & prodr.: films From Dusk Till Dawn, 1996, writer (story): films Natural Born Killers, 1994, writer, dir. & prodr.: films Kill Bill: Vol. 1, 2003, Kill Bill: Vol. 2, 2004, actor, writer & dir.: films Reservoir Dogs, 1992, Pulp Fiction, 1994, actor (voice), writer & dir.: films Jackie Brown, 1997; exec. prodr. From Dusk Till Dawn 2: Tex. Blood Money, 1999, From Dusk Till Dawn 3: The Hangman's Daughter, 2000; exec. prodr.: (films) Hostel, 2005, Daltry Calhoun, 2005, Freedom's Fury, 2006; actor, writer, prodr. & dir.: films Grindhouse, 2007; prodr. Iron Monkey, 2001; writer, dir. (films) Inglourious Basterds, 2009; writer, prodr.: Curdled, 1996, actor, writer, prodr., dir.: (with Alexandre Rockwell, Robert Rodriguez & Allision Anders) Four Rooms, 1995; exec. prodr.: God Said, 'Ha!", 1998; TV appearances Golden Girls, 1998, 1990, All-American Girl, The Muppets' Wonderful Wizard of Oz, 2005; dir.: (TV series) ER, episode 'Motherhood', 1994, Jimmy Kimmel Live, episode 5/18/2004. Recipient Building Bridges award, Asian Excellence Awards, 2006, Kirk Douglas award for Excellence in Film, 2009; named one of Time Mag. 100 Most Influential People, 2005. Home: 8439 W Sunset Blvd West Hollywood CA 90069-1921

TARAS, PAUL, physicist, researcher; b. Tunis, Tunisia, May 12, 1941; emigrated to Can., 1957, naturalized, 1962; s. Wladimir and Benita (Koort) T.; m. Marja-Leena Malinen, Aug. 3, 1963; children: Lisa Helene, Michele Anne. BASc., U. Toronto, 1962, MA, 1963, PhD, 1965. Asst. prof. physics U. Montreal, Que., Canada, 1965-70, assoc. prof., 1970-76, prof., 1976—. Spokesman U. Montreal in rsch. projects. Helios, SDC, Babar. Rsch. on nuclear and particle physics; co-managed conception and constrn. of 8pi Spectrometer, Chalk River Nuclear Labs, 1984-86; contbr. articles to profl. jours.; presenter papers to profl. confs. U. Toronto, Province of Ont., U.K. Atomic Energy Authority fellowships; France-Que., NRC, Natural Scis. and Engring. Research Council Can. grantee. Mem. Am. Phys. Soc., Can. Assn. Physicists, Soc. Galilée (mem. exec. bd.), Babar Collaboration (bd. dirs.). Home: 1639 Norway Rd Montreal PQ Canada H4P 1Y3 Office: U Montreal Groupe Physique des Particules Montreal PQ Canada H3C 3J7 Home Phone: 514-735-8392. Business E-Mail: taras@lps.umontreal.ca.

TARASENKO, OLGA, biologist, educator; d. Elizaveta Grebenyuk; m. Pierre Alusta. MD, Kyrgyz State Med. Acad., Kyrgyzstan, 0190, PhD, 1998. Postoctoral rsch. assoc. Poly. U., NYC, 2001—05; asst. prof. U. Ark., Little Rock, 2005—. Mentor biology club U. Ark., 2005—06. Recipient Med. Student Conf. First prize, Kyrgyz State Med. Acad., 1990, Appreciation cert., Polytechnic U., 2002; named Exceptional Inventions award, Govt. of Kyrgyz Republic, State Agy. of Sci. and Intellectual Properties, 2004; grantee, European Sch. Transfusion Medicine, 1993; fellow, Union Hematological Ctr., Moscow, Russia, 1991, Rsch. Inst. Hematology and Blood Transfusion, St. Petersburg, Russia, 1991, 1992; scholar, Asian Devel. Bank, 1999—2001. Mem.: Am. Soc. Biology and Biochemistry, Kyrgyz Soc. Allergy and Immunology (assoc.), MidSouth Computational Biology and Bioinformatics Soc. (assoc. grantee 2006), Am. Soc. Microbiology (assoc.), Sigma Xi Sci. Rsch. Soc. (assoc.). Achievements include research in detection and inhibition of bacterial spores; patents for protective immunogenetics factors against tuberculosis; patents pending for glycoconjugate sensors; inhibitors of sporeforming pathogens; destruction of spores through glycoconjugate enhanced phagocytosis. Office: University of Arkansas at Little Rock 2801 South University Little Rock AR 72204

TARASI, LOUIS MICHAEL, JR., lawyer; b. Cheswick, Pa., Sept. 9, 1931; s. Louis Michael and Ruth Elizabeth (Records) T.; m. Patricia Ruth Finley, June 19, 1954; children: Susan, Louis Michael III, Elizabeth, Brian, Patricia, Matthew. BA, Miami U., Ohio, 1954; JD, U. Pa., 1959. Bar: Pa. 1960, U.S. Dist. Ct. (we. dist.) Pa. 1960, U.S. Ct. Appeals (3d cir.) 1964, U.S. Supreme Ct. 1969, U.S. Dist. Ct. (we. dist.) Tex. 1988, U.S. Ct. Appeals (5th cir.) 1989, U.S. Ct. Appeals (4th cir.) 1994, U.S. Ct. Fed. Claims 1987, U.S. Dist. Ct. Colo. 1998; cert. civil trial adv. Nat. Bd. Trial Advocacy. Assoc., owner Burgwin, Ruffin, Perry & Pohl, Pitts., 1960-68; ptnr. Conte, Courtney & Tarasi, Beaver County, Pa., 1968-78, Tarasi & Tighe, Pitts., 1978-82, Tarasi & Johnson, P.C., Pitts., 1982-95, Tarasi & Assocs., P.C., Pitts., 1995-99, The Tarasi Lawfirm, P.C., Pitts., 1997-2001, Tarasi & Tarasi, P.C., Pitts., 2001—. Mem. parish coun. St. James Ch., Sewickley, Pa.; active Sewickley Borough Allegheny Coun., 1978-1982. With U.S. Army, 1954-56. Fellow: Internat. Soc. Barristers; mem.: Am. Coll. Barristers (sr. counsel), Am. Bd. Trial Advs., Melvin Belli Soc., St. Thomas More Soc. (award 1991), West Pa. Trial Lawyers Assn. (pres. 1975), Pa. Bar Assn., Allegheny County Bar Assn., Acad. Trial Lawyers Allegheny County, Pa. Trial Lawyers Assn. (pres. 1979—80), Assn. Trial Lawyers Am. (gov., rep.). Democrat. Roman Catholic. Avocations: reading, golf, lecturing. Home: 1 Way Hollow Rd Sewickley PA 15143-1192 Office: Tarasi & Tarasi PC 510 3d Ave Pittsburgh PA 15219-2107 Home Phone: 412-741-8534; Office Phone: 412-391-7135. Business E-Mail: lmt@tarasilaw.com.

TARASIEWICZ, TAMARA, painter; b. Hajnowka, Poland, Feb. 23, 1950; arrived in US, 1996; d. Wlodzimierz and Anastazja Rygorowicz; m. Sergiusz Tarasiewicz, Aug. 28, 1976; children: Radek, Anna. ADN, Med. Sch., Poland, 1970; B, Tchrs. Med. Sch., Poland, 1976; M, Med. Academy, Poland, 1982. Nurse ZOZ, Hajnowka, Poland, 1982—88; painter Bialowieza, Poland, 1988—96; art gallery dir. Forest Mus. and Gallery, Bialowieza, 1994—96; painter Chgo., 1997—; art gallery dir. Tammy's Gallery, 1998—2001. New Art International, 2002—05, Trends, 2007, Masters of Today, 2008, one-woman shows include, Poland, Russia, France, Germany, US, Can., 1991—, Tamara Tarasiewicz Art, Byelorussian TV, 1992—; contbr. art to popular mags., chapters to books; author: (book) Russ, Petru. Trends London.:MOT., 2007, Russ, Petru. Masters Today. London.:MOT., 2008, International Contemporary Masters, 2009, Creative Genius, 2009—. Recipient Art of Hajnowka Region First prize, Poland, 1992—93, Bialowieza Mayor award, Dist. Bialowieza, Poland, 1993, Cert. Recognition, George H. Ryan Office Gov., Chgo., 2001—02, Cook County Treas. Maria Pappas, Chgo., 2005, Renee Denmark Meml. award, Northern Ind. Arts Assn., 2005, Distinction award, 2d Art Biennial Medial Mus., London, 2007, Excellence prize, 2007. Mem.: Broward Art Guild, Stamford Art Assn., Art Assn. Harrisburg, Am. Soc. Contemporary Artists (Samueal Rosen award 2007), Provincetown Art Assn. Mus., Nat. Assn. Women Artists, Chgo. Artists' Coalition, Oil Painters of America, No. Ind. Arts Assn., Tall Grass Arts Assn. Personal E-mail: info@tamaratarasiewicz.com.

TARAZAGA, PABLO ALBERTO, research scientist; b. San Luis, Argentina; m. Vanessa Tarazaga; 1 child, Pablo Lucas. BS in ME, U. PR, Mayaguez, 2002; PhD candidate, Va. Tech, Blascksburg, 2002—; MS, Va. Tech, Blacksburg, 2004. Grad. student asst. Va. Tech, 2002—. Contbr. articles to profl. jours. GSRP fellow, NASA, 2004—06. Mem.: AIAA.

TARBUTTON, LLOYD T., hotel executive, consultant; DCS in Mktg., Pacific Western U. Grad. Realtors Inst.; cert. franchise exec., La. State U., cert. hotel adminstr. Divsn. sales mgr. Reuben H. Donnelley Corp. (advt. agy.), Norfolk, Va., 1953-58; chmn. bd., dir. Tarbutton Assocs., Inc., Norfolk, 1962—; founder, dir., pres., chmn. bd. Econo Lodges of Am., Norfolk, 1967-83; chmn. bd. emeritus Econo Lodges of Am. (formerly Econ-Travel Motor Hotel Corp.), Norfolk, 1983—. Co-founder, chief judge Franchising Hall of Fame, Washington, 1979-82; co-founder, chmn. Coun. Franchise Suppliers, Washington, 1986-88. Author: Franchising--The How To Book, 1986. Trustee Edn. Found. Old Dominion U., 1979-86, chmn. bd. trustees Ctr. Econ. Edn., Old Dominion U., 1983-84. Recipient Hon. Tchr. award Maury High Sch., Norfolk, 1959. Mem. Internat. Franchise Assn. (hon. life, chmn. bd. dirs., chmn. 1st Asian Symposium on Franchising, Tokyo 1978, 1st European Symposium on Franchising, Amsterdam 1978, 1st So. Pacific Symposium on Franchising, Jakarta 1991), 1st Ea. Europe Franchise Symposiums (Varna, Bulgaria, 2000, inducted into Franchise Hall of Fame 2000), Internat. Coun. Hotel/Motel Mgmt., Realtor's Inst. Norfolk (chmn. 1965), Internat. Sales Execs. Club (Distinguished Sales award 1957), Internat. Platform Assn., Airplane Owners and Pilots Assn., Cavalier Golf and Yacht Club, Town Point Club, Naples Grande Resort Hotel & Tennis Club, The Club at Pelican Bay. Presbyterian. Office Phone: 239-877-3000. *I believe the greatest assist to my progress in business and personal life came when I became more aware of the "value of self" and thus others.*

TARDE, JERRY (GERARD TARDE), editor-in-chief; married; 2 children. Grad., Northwestern U. Sch. Journalism, 1978. Asst. editor Golf Digest Condé Nast Publs., assoc. editor, 1979—82, sr. editor, 1982—84, 1984—90, chmn., editor-in-chief, 1990—; v.p. NY Times Mag. Grp. (Golf Digest former umbrella co.), 1990—98, editl. dir., 1998—2001; chmn., editl. dir. Golf Digest Publs., 2001—. Office: Golf Digest 750 3rd Ave 3rd Fl New York NY 10017 Office Phone: 212-630-2700. Office Fax: 212-630-3296.*

TARDIF, DONNA LYNN, elementary school educator; BS in Elem. Edn., Univ. Maine, Farmington, 1990; MS in Curriculum, Va. Commonwealth Univ.; cert. of Adv. Study in Literacy, Univ. So. Maine. Tchr., 1992—, Montello Elem. Sch., Lewiston, Maine, 2001—. Named Maine Tchr. of Yr., 2006. Office: Montello Elem Sch 407 East Ave Lewiston ME 04240 E-mail: dtardif@lewnet.avcnet.org.

TARDIFF, JILL ALEXANDRIA, publishing executive, photographer; b. Morristown, NJ, Apr. 8, 1953; d. Howard James Tardiff and Jean Elizabeth Cook; m. Paul Edward Kozlowski, Feb. 11, 1984. BA in liberal arts, Coll. St. Elizabeth, 1975. Cert. teacher, K-12 NJ, 1975. Mgr. retail Hallmark Cards Inc./Flagship, NYC, 1976—81; mgr./gen. mgr. Doubleday Book Shops/Flagship, NYC, 1981—91; sales mgr./dir. of sales Tiffany & Co., NYC, 1991—93; entrepreneur, self-propr. Bamboo River Assocs., Hoboken, NJ, 1993—; mng. editor/sr. rschr. Lintel Press, NYC, 1993—94; assoc. editor BookWire Online, NYC, 1995—98; contbg. editor/project mgr. Pubs. Weekly, NYC, 1996—; mgr. advt. Persimmon, Asian Lit., Arts, and Culture Mag., NYC, 1999—2002. Profl. spkr./tour facilitator Bamboo River Associates, Hoboken, 1991—; sec./bd. dirs. Contemporary Asian Culture Inc., NYC, 1999—; adv. bd. mem. Women's Ink., NYC, 1999—2004. Contbr. book Bob Vila's Guide to Historic Homes Series; reporter Shinbunka Weekly, Tokyo, 1995—2000. Mem.: AAUW (assoc.), Internat. Women's Writing Guild (hon.), N.Y. Women in Comm. (assoc.), Women's Nat. Book Assn. (assoc.; main rep. UN DPI/NGO 2000—, nat. v.p., pres. elect 2002—04, nat. pres. 2004—06), Women's Nat. Book Assn. (assoc.; newsletter editor/v.p. N.Y.C. chpt. 1997—2000, pres. N.Y.C. chpt. 2000—, immediate past nat. pres. 2006—), Editl. Freelancers Assn. (assoc.), Diev Donné Papermill (assoc.), Japan Soc. (assoc.), Asia Soc. N.Y. (assoc.). Avocations: travel, photography, gardening, architecture, paper making. Office: Bamboo River Associates 625 Madison StSte 2 Hoboken NJ 07030-6305 Personal E-mail: jat-bambooriver@worldnet.att.net.

TARDIO, THOMAS A., public relations executive; V.p. strategic planning and other positions Columbia Pictures Industries, 1979-88; CFO, v.p. adminstrn. Rogers & Cowan, Inc., LA, 1988-89, exec. v.p. entertainment sect., 1989-91, pres., 1991-95; CEO Rogers & Cowan, LA, 1995—. Mem. Pub. Rels. Soc. Am., Nat. Acad. Recording Arts and Scis., Pub. Communicators L.A., Contry Music Assn. Office: Rogers & Cowan 8687 Melrose Ave 7th Fl Los Angeles CA 90069

TARGOVNIK, SELMA E. KAPLAN, dermatologist; b. NYC, Apr. 22, 1936; d. Harry A. and Helen (Goodstein) Kaplan; m. Jerome H. Targovnik, Dec. 2, 1961; children: Nina Rebecca, Labe Eric (dec.), Diane Michelle. BA, NYU, 1957; MD, Albert Einstein Col. Medicine, 1961. Diplomate Am. Bd. Dermatology. Intern Kaiser Found. Hosp., San Francisco, 1961-62; resident in internal medicine Bellevue Hosp., NYU Med. Ctr., 1962-63, U. Colo. Med. Ctr., Denver, 1963-64; rsch. fellow, resident in dermatology Boston U. Med. Ctr., 1964-66, mem. staff, 1968-69, NYU Med. Ctr., 1966-68, St. Joseph's Hosp., Phoenix, 1969—98, Good Samaritan Hosp., Phoenix, 1969—, Carl Hayden VA Hosp., Phoenix, 1998—. Mem. staff St. Joseph's Hosp., Phoenix, St. Luke's Hosp., Phoenix; chief divsn. dermatology Good Samaritan Hosp., Phoenix, 1985-90; adj. assoc. prof. Midwestern U. Coll. Medicine, Glendale, Ariz., 1998—; clin. assoc. prof. dermatology Kirksville Coll. Osteopathic Medicine, 2000—, clin. assoc. prof. dermatology, 1998; supr. physicians assts., med. students, residents Carl Hayden VA Hosp., Phoenix, 1998-. Bd. dirs. ACLU, Ariz., 1973-78, 83-94, Congregation Beth El, Phoenix, 1971-75, Flagstaff Festival of the Arts, 1984-86; active Jewish Nat. Fund; adv. bd., Lowell Obs. Flagstaff, Ariz., 2007-. Fellow Am. Acad. Dermatology, Assocs. for the Weizmann Inst. Sci., Assocs. for the Technion Inst.; mem. Am. Technion Soc. (bd. dirs. 1988-92, pres. Ariz. divsn. 1990-92), Dermatology Found., Sonoran Dermatologic Soc., Southwestern Dermatologic Soc., Pacific Dermatological Soc., Noah Worcester Dermatol. Soc., Phi Beta Kappa, Mu Chi Sigma, Pi Delta Phi, Beta Lambda Sigma. Democrat. Jewish. Home: 3706 E Rancho Dr Paradise Valley AZ 85253 Office Phone: 602-628-8117. Fax: 602-667-6813. Personal E-mail: selmaderm@cox.net.

TARLETON, EARL RUSSELL, JR., lawyer; b. Hollywood, Calif., 1954; s. Earl Russell Tarleton and Dolores Jean Huss; m. Ann Marie Dewey, 2000; children from previous marriage: Russell Bradford, Charlotte Vanessa, Jonathan Elias, Joshua Thomas. BS in Indsl. Tech.-Aeronautics, Utah State U., Logan, 1982; JD, U. Utah, Salt Lake City, 1986; MS in Elec. Engring., U. Wash., Seattle, 1998. Bar: US Patent and Trademark Office 1985, US Ct. Appeals (9th Cir.) 1987, Wash. Bar 1987, US Dist. Ct. (Wash. dist.) 1987, Utah 1992, US Dist. Ct. (UT dist.) 1992, US Ct. Appeals 1992, US Ct. Appeals (10th Cir.) 1994, US Ct. Appeals (5th Cir.) 2008. Ct. reporter LA mcpl. cts., 1975—76; founder, pres. Intermountain Coll. Ct. Reporting, Salt Lake City, 1978—81; assoc. atty. Christenson, O'Connor, Johnson & Kindness, Seattle, 1986—89, Tresk, Britt & Rossa, Salt Lake City, 1991—94; ptnr. Cassidy, Vance & Tarleton, Kirkland, Wash., 1989—91; of coun. Graham & James, Seattle, 1994—97; with Seed I.P. Law Group PLLC, Seattle, 1997—. Mem. SAR, Calif., 1975—; unit commr. Boy Scouts Am., Maltby, Wash., 2005—07, scoutmaster, 2007—. Mem.: Washington. State/Patent Law Assoc., American Intellectual Property Law Assoc. Mem. Lds Ch. Achievements include patents for Rotary Vane Nozzle. Avocation: flying. Office: Seed Intellectual Property Law Group 701 Fifth Ave Ste 5400 Seattle WA 98104 Office Phone: 206-622-4900. Office Fax: 206-682-6031. Business E-Mail: russt@seedip.com.

TARLETON, JESSE S., retired business educator; b. Upper Darby, Pa., Nov. 1, 1928; s. Leslie Sauren and Jessie Dorothy (Sommers) T.; m. Lavonne Catherine Olson, June 25, 1955; children: Lesley Omary., David T. BS in Chem. Engring., Pa. State U., 1952; PhD in Chem. Engring., Cornell U., 1958; MBA, Coll. William and Mary, 1970; postgrad., Am. Grad. Sch. Internat. Mgmt., (Thunderbird), 1974. Cert. planning commr., Va.; cert. US Track and Field ofcl. Tchg. asst. Sch. Chem. Engring. Cornell U., Ithaca, NY, 1952-53, 55-57; rsch. engr. E.I. duPont de Nemours, Wilmington, Del., 1957-59; various positions in prodn. and engring. to sr. engr. Dow Badische Co. formerly Dow Chem. Co., Williamsburg, Va., 1959-70; from asst. prof. to prof. bus. adminstrn. Coll. William and Mary, Williamsburg, Va., 1970—97, prof. emeritus, 1997—. Spkr. in field. Contbr. chpts. to books, articles to profl. jours. Rep. Richmond Rd. transp. study group City of Williamsburg, 1992-94, regional issues com., 1991-95, mem. beautification adv. com., 1987-91, mem. planning commn., 1987-95, vice chmn., 1994-95, mem. econ. devel. authority, 1996-2007, chmn. 2003-05; mem. investment bd. Greater Peninsula Workforce, 2004—08. With US Army, 1946—48. Standard Oil of Ind. fellow, 1953-55. Mem. AIChE, Acad. of Mgmt., Acad. Internat. Bus., Decision Scis. Inst., Am. Prodn. and Inventory Control Soc., James River Assn., Nat. Ry. Hist. Soc., Nat. Assn. Railroad Passengers, Kiwanis Club of Williamsburg (sec. 1965-74, dir., com. chmn.), Colonial Road Runners, Phi Kappa Phi, Tau Beta Pi, Sigma Tau, Phi Lambda Upsilon, Alpha Chi Sigma. Avocations: travel, railroading, reading, walking. Home Phone: 757-229-2791. Personal E-mail: thetarletons@gmail.com.

TARLOV, ALVIN RICHARD, foundation administrator, physician, educator; b. Norwalk, Conn., July 11, 1929; s. Charles and Mae (Shelinsky) T.; m. Joan Hylton, June 12, 1956 (div. 1976); children: Richard, Elizabeth, Jane, Suzanne, David. BA, Dartmouth Coll., 1951; MD, U. Chgo., 1956. Intern Phila. Gen. Hosp., 1956-57; resident in medicine U. Chgo. Hosps., 1957-58, 62-63, research assoc., 1958-61; asst. prof. medicine U. Chgo., 1963-68, assoc. prof., 1968-70, prof., 1970-84, prof. medicine, 2006—, chmn. dept. medicine, 1969-81; chmn. grad. med. edn. nat. adv. com. HHS, Washington, 1980; pres. Henry J. Kaiser Family Found., Menlo Park, Calif., 1984-90; sr. scientist New Eng. Med. Ctr., Boston, 1990-99, exec. dir. The Health Inst., 1995-99; prof. pub. health Harvard U., Boston, 1990-99; prof. of medicine Tufts U., 1990-99. Dir. Tex. Program for Soc. and Health, James Baker III Inst. for Pub. Policy, Rice U., 1999-2005. Pres. Med. Outcomes Trust, Inc., 1993-2000; chmn. bd., pres. Mass. Health Data Consortium, 1994-98. Served to capt. U.S. Army, 1958-61. Recipient Research Career Devel. award NIH, 1962-67; John and Mary Markle Found. scholar, 1966-71. Mem. ACP (master), Inst. Medicine of Nat. Acad. Scis. Home: 25 Oakcrest Ln Hastings On Hudson NY 10706 Home Phone: 914-478-1868. Personal E-mail: atarlov@gmail.com.

TARNOFF, JEROME, lawyer; b. June 22, 1931; s. Meyer and Anne (Soshnick) T.; children: Marcy Jane, Margery Lynne; m. Nancy Radin, 1990. AB, Syracuse U., 1952; JD, Columbia U., 1957. Bar: NY 1957, U.S. Dist. Ct. (so. and ea. dists.) NY 1960, U.S. Ct. Appeals (2d cir.) 1961. Ptnr. Sheldon and Tarnoff, NYC, 1957-78, Feldesman, D'Atri, Tarnoff & Lubitz, NYC, 1978, Baskin and Sears, P.C., NYC, 1979-84, Baskin & Steingut P.C., 1984-85, Berger & Steingut, 1986-92, Morrison, Cohen LLP, NYC, 1993—. Contbr. articles to legal jours. Chmn. policy com. NY Dem. Party, 1975-78, vice chmn. NY County, 1978—, mem. nat. com., 1980-88; mem. Cmty. Planning Bd. #8, 1966-75; bd. dirs. Grand St. Settlement, 1973—1981, Assoc. Y's of NY, 1972-88. With U.S. Army, 1952-54. Recipient Disting. Svc. award NAACP, 1975, Cert. Achievement, El Diario-La Prensa, 1977. Mem. ABA, NY State Bar Assn., Assn. Bar City of NY, N.T. County Lawyers, Am. Arbitration Assn. (nat. panel arbitrators), Phi Alpha Delta, Sunningdale Country Club (Scarsdale, NY), Harmonie Club (NYC), Audubon, Masons. Jewish. Office: Morrison Cohen LLP 909 Third Ave New York NY 10022 Home Phone: 212-988-5842; Office Phone: 212-735-8632. Business E-Mail: jtarnoff@morrisoncohen.com.

TARNOFF, PETER, federal agency administrator, consultant; b. NYC, Apr. 19, 1937; s. Norman Tarnoff and Henrietta (Goldfarb) Laing; m. Daniele Oudinot, Jan. 13, 1962 (div. Oct. 1981); children: Nicholas, Alexander; m. Mathea Falco, Dec. 24, 1981; 1 child, Benjamin. Student, U. Paris, 1956-57, postgrad., 60-61; BA, Colgate U., 1958; postgrad., U. Chgo., 1958-60. Joined Fgn. Svc., Dept. State, 1961; spl. asst. to amb. Am. Embassy, Bonn, Fed. Republic Germany, 1969; trainee Nat. Sch. Adminstrn., Paris, 1970; prin. officer Am. Consulate Gen., Lyon, France, 1971-73; dep. chief of mission Am. Embassy, Luxembourg, 1973-75; dir. Office Rsch. and Analysis for Western Europe Dept. State, Washington, 1975-76, exec. sec. Dept. State, 1977-81, fgn. affairs fellow San Francisco, 1981-82; exec. dir. World Affairs Coun. No. Calif., San Francisco, 1983-86; pres., dir. Coun. on Fgn. Rels., NYC, 1986-93; under sec. state for polit. affairs Dept. State, Washington, 1993-97; pres. Internat. Adv. Corp., San Francisco, 1997—. Office: Internat Adv Corp 2028 Green St San Francisco CA 94123-4813 Home Phone: 415-567-4241; Office Phone: 415-235-2547. Personal E-mail: iacmail@aol.com.

TARNOVE, LORRAINE, medical association executive; b. Atlantic City, July 26, 1947; d. Leonard Robert Tarnove and Jeanne Tarnove Yudkin; m. Steven B. Friedman, July 1, 1969; 2 children. BA, U. Md., 1969. Pres. Lorraine Tarnove Consulting, Columbia, Md., 1985-93; exec. dir. Am. Med. Dirs. Assn., Columbia. Contbr. chapters to books. Office: AMDA 10840 Little Patuxent #760 Columbia MO 21044 Office Phone: 301-596-5774. E-mail: ltarnove@amda.com.*

TARONJI, JAIME, JR., lawyer; b. NYC, Nov. 20, 1944; s. Jaime and Ruth T.; m. Mary Taronji, May 16, 1970; children: Ian A., Mark N., Nicole V. BA, George Washington U., 1972; JD, Georgetown U., 1976. Bar: Va. 1977, DC 1978. Asst. to dep. staff dir. U.S. Commn. on Civil Rights, Washington, 1972-76; antitrust atty. FTC, Washington, 1976-79; antitrust counsel Westinghouse Electric Corp., Pitts., 1979-81; group legal counsel Dana Corp., Toledo, 1982-88; v.p., gen. counsel Packaging Corp. Am. subs. Tenneco, Evanston, Ill., 1988-95; law v.p. NCR Corp., Dayton, 1996-99; v.p., gen. counsel, sec. Dayton Superior Corp., Dayton, 1999—2003; of counsel antitrust practice group Howrey LLP, Washington, 2004—; atty., gen. counsel FTC, Washington, 2006—. Mem. adv. bd. Corp. Counsel Inst., Georgetown U. Law Ctr. Author: The 1970 Census Undercount of Spanish Speaking Persons, 1974; editor: Puerto Ricans in the U.S., 1976. Capt. M.I., U.S. Army, 1965-70, Vietnam. Mem. ABA (antitrust sect.), Hispanic Nat. Bar Assn., Hispanic Bar Assn. DC. Democrat. Roman Catholic. Office: FTC 600 Penn Ave NW Washington DC 20580 Office Phone: 202-383-7406, 202-326-2420.

TAROY-VALDEZ, LOLITA B., nursing educator; b. Cogon, Mindanao, Philippines, Sept. 3, 1951; d. Horonio Taroy and Florentina Lucagbo Bequiso; married, May 28, 1990. BSN, Mountain View Coll.,

Philippines; MN, U. Philippines, Diliman, Quezon City, 1981. Cert. AACN, 1994. Dir. Hongkong Adventist Sch. Nursing, 1985—88; asst. prof. Southwestern Adventist U., Keene, Tex., 1991—. Dean Mountain View Coll. Sch. Nursing, Valencia, Bukidnon, Philippines, 1982—85. Coord. mission trips to Philippines Healing Outreach Profl. Endeavor, Keene, 2004—05, sec., 2000—06. Recipient President's award for svc., Mountain View Coll. Sch. Nursing Alumni Assn., 1997, Leadership award, 1997; named one of Gt. 100 Nurses, Dallas /Ft. Worth Hosp. Council-Nurse Exec. Forum and Tex. Nurses Assn., 2002. Home: 2725 Hill Ln Cleburne TX 76031 Office: Southwestern Adventist U Hillcrest Keene TX 07659 Home Fax: 817-641-9988. Personal E-mail: valdezl@swau.edu.

TARPEH-DOE, LINDA DIANE, retired controller; b. Laramie, Wyo., Mar. 19, 1957; d. Leland Dean and Marilyn Lee (McClurg) Wheeler; m. Nyenpan Tarpeh-Doe, Jan. 16, 1982 (div. Nov. 1985); 1 child, Nyenpan Tarpeh-Doe II. BS in Acctg., U. Colo., 1979. CPA, Cert. Govt. Fin. Mgr. Asst. auditor First Bank Holding Co., Lakewood, Colo., 1979-80; internat. devel. intern USAID, Monrovia, Liberia, 1981-82, sys. acct. Washington, 1982-84, fin. analyst Kingston, Jamaica, 1984-88, macs coord. Washington, 1988-93, contr. Colombo, Sri Lanka, 1993-97, REDSO, Nairobi, Kenya, 1997-2000, USAID/Ethiopia, Addis Ababa, 2000—02, USAID, Jakarta, Indonesia, 2002—07. Democrat. Methodist. Avocations: music, reading. Home: 3851 Paseo Del Prado Boulder CO 80301-1527

TARPGAARD, PETER THORVALD, naval architect; b. Knoxville, Tenn., Sept. 25, 1937; s. Peter Thorvald and Edith Margurite (Mees) T.; m. Judith Ann Burgess; 1 child, Andrew Christian. BS, U.S. Naval Acad., 1959; MSME, MIT, 1968, naval engr., 1968, PhD, 1970. Spl. project asst. Office Chief of Naval Devel., Washington, 1970—73; profl. staff U.S. Arms Control & Disarmament Agy., Washington, 1973—76; design supr. Portsmouth Naval Shipyard, Portsmouth, NH, 1976—79; prin. analyst Congressional Budget Office, Washington, 1979—85; mgr. submarine programs Draper Lab., Cambridge, Mass., 1985—92; prof. U.S. Naval War Coll., Newport, RI, 1992—97; mgr. Noesis Inc., Arlington, Va., 1997—. Cons. Congressional Office of Tech. Assessment, Washington, 1991-92. Contbr. articles to profl. jours. With U.S. Navy, 1959-79. Mem. Soc. Naval Architects & Marine Engrs., Assn. for Public Policy Analysis & Mgmts., U.S. Naval Inst. Episcopalian. Home: 5 Longmeadow Ave Middletown RI 02842-5225 Office: Noesis Inc 4100 N Fairfax Dr Ste 800 Arlington VA 22203-1663 Home Phone: 401-848-5142; Office Phone: 703-741-0300. E-mail: ptarpgaard@alum.mit.edu.

TARPLIN, LINDA E., lobbyist; m. Richard J. Tarplin. Head health care legis. for Rep. Bill Frenzel; dep. asst. sec. legis. Office of Legis. Affairs, Washington; legis. and policy positions US Dept. Health and Human Svcs.; spl. asst. legis. affairs to pres. George H.W. Bush The White House; founding prin. OB-C Group (formerly O'Brien & Calio), 1993; ptnr. Tarplin, Downs & Young, LLC, 2006—. Office: Tarplin, Downs & Young, LLC 1212 New York Ave, NW, Ste 1050 Washington DC 20005 Office Phone: 202-898-4733. Office Fax: 202-898-4769.*

TARPLIN, RICHARD J., lobbyist, former federal agency administrator; b. Tarrytown, NY, Dec. 23, 1959; m. Linda Eisheid, Oct. 6, 1990; 2 children. BA with honors, Skidmore Coll., 1981. Legis. asst. to Rep. Leon E. Panetta State of Calif., 1982-85, mem. profl. staff senate labor and resources com., 1985-88; staff dir. subcom. children, family, drugs alcoholism US Senate, 1988-93; prin. dep. asst. sec. legis. HHS, Washington, 1993-96, asst. sec. legis., 1997—2001; chmn. bd., mng. dir. Timmons and Co., Washington, 2001—08; prin. Tarplin Strategies, LLC, 2008—. Vol. Dem. Nat. Convention, liaison to Dem. mem. of congress, 2000, 04. Named one of 50 Top Lobbyists, Washingtonian mag., 2007. Democrat. Office: Tarplin Strategies, LLC 975 F St NW Washington DC 20004 Office Phone: 202-885-9405.*

TARPY, THOMAS MICHAEL, lawyer; b. Columbus, Ohio, Jan. 4, 1945; s. Thomas Michael and Catherine G. (Sharshal) T.; m. Mary Patricia Canna, Sept. 9, 1967; children: Joshua Michael, Megan Patricia, Thomas Canna, John Patrick. AB, John Carroll U., 1966; JD, Ohio State U., 1969. Bar: Ohio 1969, U.S. Dist. Ct. (so. dist.) Ohio 1972, U.S. Dist. Ct. (no. dist.) Ohio 1974, U.S. Ct. Appeals (6th cir.) 1982, U.S. Supreme Ct. 1997. Assoc. Vorys, Sater, Seymour & Pease LLP, Columbus, 1969-76, ptnr., 1977—85, 1985—87, 1987—2005; v.p. Liebert Corp., Columbus, 1985-87. Chmn. Columbus Graphics Commn., 1980; mem. Columbus Area Leadership Program, 1975. With U.S. Army, 1969-75. Fellow Coll. Labor and Employment Lawyers, Ohio Mgmt. Lawyers Assn. (founding mem.); mem. ABA, Ohio Bar Assn., Columbus Bar Assn. Office: Vorys Sater Seymour & Pease LLP PO Box 1008 52 E Gay St Columbus OH 43215-3161 E-mail: tmtarpy@vssp.com.

TARR, CURTIS W., management consultant, educator; b. Stockton, Calif., Sept. 18, 1924; s. F.W. and Esther (Reed) T.; m. Elizabeth May Myers, 1955 (div. 1978); children: Pamela Elizabeth, Cynthia Leigh; m. Marilyn Van Stralen, 1979 (div. 1991); m. Mary Katherine Stegmiller, 1992. BA, Stanford U., 1948, PhD, 1962; MBA, Harvard U., 1950; L.H.D., Ripon Coll., 1965, Grinnell Coll., 1969, Lincoln Coll., 1980; LL.D., Lawrence U., 1974, Ill. Wesleyan U., 1980. Rsch. asst., instr. Harvard U., 1950-52; v.p. Sierra Tractor & Equipment Co., Chico, Calif., 1952-58; staff mem. 2d Hoover Commn., 1954-55; asst. dir. summer session Stanford U., 1961-62, dir., 1962-63, asst. dean humanities and scis., 1962-63, lectr. bus. sch., 1962-63; pres. Lawrence U., Appleton, Wis., 1963-69; asst. sec. for manpower and res. affairs Air Force, 1969-70; dir. SSS, Washington, 1970-72; under sec. state for security assistance, 1972-73; acting dep. under sec. state for mgmt., 1973; from v.p. parts distbn. and matrials mgmt. to v.p. mgmt. devel. Deere & Co., Moline, Ill., 1973—83; dean, prof. Johnson Sch. Mgmt., Cornell U., 1984—89, prof. mgmt., 1989-90, dean emeritus, 1990—; vice chmn. Intermet Corp., 1992-95. Bd. dirs. Phyton Corp., Ithaca, N.Y., 1985-2002, State Farm Ins. Companies, 1985-98, Banta Corp, 1976-95, Intermet Corp., 1984-98; mem. Internat. Rsch. Coun. Ctr. for Strategic and Internat. Studies, Washington, 1989-92; dir. Ulysses S. Grant Assn., 1985-09; adj. prof. mgmt. Emory U., 1991-93. Author: Private Soldier, 1976, By the Numbers, 1981, Youth, 1994. Trustee Inst. Paper Chemistry, 1963-69, Morehouse Sch. Medicine, Atlanta, 1994—2004; chmn. Task Force on Govt. Orgn., Fin. and Tax Distbn. for State Wis., 1967-69; chmn. Def. Manpower Commn., 1974-76, Ill. State Scholarship Commn., 1978-79, Quad Cities Grad. Study Ctr., 1982-84, Rep. candidate for Congress 2d Dist., Calif., 1958; trustee Am. Coll., Bryn Mawr, Pa., 1989-92; dir. Bethesda Home, Savannah, Ga., 1989-2003, The Mighty 8th Air Force Mus., Savannah, 1999-2004. With AUS, 1943-46, ETO. Recipient Exceptional Civilian Service medal Air Force Dept., 1970; Distinguished Service award SSS, 1975 Mem. Univ. Club (Chgo.), Cosmos Club (Washington). Methodist. Personal E-mail: curtis.tarr@sbcglobal.net.

TARR, JOEL ARTHUR, historian, educator; b. Jersey City, May 8, 1934; s. Max Alfred and Florence (Levin) Tartalsky; m. Arlene Green, Sept. 2, 1956 (dec. June 1969); children: Michael Jay, Joanna Sue; m. Tova Brafman, Aug. 11, 1978; children: Maya Leah, Ilana Ariel. BS, Rutgers U., 1956, MA, 1957; PhD, Northwestern U., Evanston, Ill., 1963. Asst. prof. Calif. State U., Long Beach, 1961-66; vis. prof. U. Calif., Santa Barbara, 1966-67; asst. prof. Carnegie Mellon U., Pitts., 1967-70, assoc. prof., 1969-72, prof. history and pub. policy, 1973-90, Richard S. Caliguiri prof. urban and environ. history and policy, 1990—2004, Richard S. Caliguiri univ. prof. history and pub. policy, 2004—, dir. program in tech. and soc., 1975-87, co-dir. program in applied history and social sci., 1978-86, acting dean Sch. Urban and Pub. Affairs, 1986, assoc. dean Coll. Humanities and Social Sci., 1988-91, acting dean Coll. Humanities and Social Sci., 1991-92, acting head dept. history, 1992-93, Univ. prof., 2004—. Author: A Study in Boss Politics, 1971; editor: Patterns of City Growth, 1974, Retrospective Technology Assessment, 1977, Transportation Innovation and Spatial Change in Pittsburgh, 1850-1934, 1978, Pittsburgh-Sheffield: Sister Cities, 1986, Technology and the Rise of the Networked City in Europe and America, 1988, The Search for the Ultimate Sink: Urban Pollution in Historic Perspective, 1996, Devastation and Renewal: An Environmental History of Pittsburgh and Its Region, 2003; Co-Author: Horses in Cities: Living Machines in the 19th Century, 2007. Bd. dirs. Action Housing, Pitts., 1983; trustee Hist. Soc. Western Pa., 1993-2000. NEH fellow, 1969-70; grantee NSF, 1975-80, 83-85, 95-98, NOAA, 1982-84; recipient Robert Doherty prize for contbns. to excellence in edn., 1992, Choice Outstanding Acad. Book award, 1997, cert. Commendation Am. Soc. State and Local History, 2005, Hon. Lewis Mum Ford prize, Society City & Regional Planners, Leonardo da Vinci medal, Soc. History Tech. Mem. AAAS, Pub. Works Hist. Soc. (pres. 1982-83, Abel Wolman prize 1989), Orgn. Am. Historians, Pub. History Assn., Am. Soc. Environ. History, Soc. for the History of Tech.(Leonardo da Vinci medal, 2008), Urban History Assn. (pres. 1999). Democrat. Jewish. Home: 5418 Normlee Pl Pittsburgh PA 15217-1116 Office: Carnegie-Mellon U Schenley Pk Pittsburgh PA 15213 Office Phone: 412-268-2609. Business E-Mail: jt03@andrew.cmu.edu.

TARR, KENNETH J., retired investment company executive; b. 1945; BA, U. Pa., 1967; MBA, Columbia U., 1971. With Chem. Bank, NYC, 1971-72; asst. v.p. Standard and Poors/Inter Capital, NYC, 1972-74; founder, mgr. S&P/Market Insights, NYC, 1974-75; v.p. Kuhn Loeb and Co., NYC, 1975-77; asst. v.p. Bessemer Trust Co., NYC, 1977-80, v.p., 1980-82, sr. v.p., 1982-91, dir. rsch., 1984; pres., dir. Suisse Asset Mgmt., Inc., NYC, 1991-93; mng. prin. Weiss, Peck & Greer, LLC, NYC, 1994-97; exec. v.p., regional head pvt. banking Am.'s Deutsche Bank AG, NYC, 1997-99; ret., 2000. Mem.: NY Yacht Club.

TARR, RALPH WILLIAM, lawyer, former federal government official; b. Bakersfield, Calif., Sept. 29, 1948; BA, Dartmouth Coll., 1970; MPA, Calif. State U., Sacramento, 1973; JD, U. Calif., Hastings, 1976. Staff asst. Calif. Gov. Ronald Reagan, 1971—73; extern to assoc. justice Calif. Supreme Ct., 1976; rsch. atty. to presiding justice Ct. Appeal (5th dist.) Calif., 1976-77; assoc. Baker, Manock & Jensen, Fresno, Calif., 1977-81, dir., mem. exec. com., 1981-82; mem. adminstrv. com. Fed. Register, Washington, 1982-85; dep. asst. atty. gen. US Dept. Justice, Washington, 1982-84, acting asst. atty. gen., 1984-85; solicitor US Dept. Interior, Washington, 1985-89, counselor, 1989-90; pvt. practice LA, 1990—. Home: 24011 Alder Pl Calabasas CA 91302-2394 Office: Atty At Law 24011 Alder Pl Calabasas CA 91302-2394 Office Phone: 818-591-7846. Personal E-mail: ralphwtarr@gmail.com.

TARR, ROBERT JOSEPH, JR., publishing and retail executive; b. Freeport, NY, Dec. 7, 1943; s. Robert Joseph and Janet Christman (Laughton) T.; m. Molly Worthington Upton, Feb. 28, 1970; children: William Upton, Robert Joseph, III, David Worthington. BS, U.S. Naval Acad., 1966; MBA, Harvard U., 1973; MA, Fletcher Sch. Law & Diplomacy, 1976. Asst. v.p. corp. fin. Paine Webber Jackson Curtis, Boston, 1973-75; dir. corp. planning, then v.p., treas. Gen. Cinema Corp., Chestnut Hill, Mass., 1976-78, sr. v.p., 1978-83, exec. v.p., COO, 1983-85, pres., COO, 1985—92; pres., CEO, COO Harcourt Gen., Inc. (Gen. Cinema Corp., 1993), Chestnut Hill, Mass., 1991-97. CEO, COO The Neiman Marcus Grp., Inc., 1987—92, pres., bd. dirs., CEO, COO, 1991—97, pres., 2007; bd. dirs. WESCO Internat., Inc.; chmn., pres., CEO HomeRuns.com, Inc., 1999—2001; spl. ptnr. Chartwell Investments, NYC, 2002—07. Lt. USN, 1966-71. Mem.: Nanea Golf Club, Old Sandwich Golf Club, Briar's Creek Club, The Oyster Harbors Club, Wianno Yacht Club, Kiawah Island Club. Home: 58 River Marsh Ln Johns Island SC 29455-5202 Personal E-mail: rjtjr12@aol.com.

TARRANCE, VERNON LANCE, JR., research and development company executive; b. Harlingen, Tex., Dec. 4, 1940; s. Vernon Lance Sr. and Mary Gilmore (Rea) T.; m. Eugenia Aline McCuistion, July 2, 1966 (dec.), Debora, July 14, 2007; children: Vernon Lance III, Haloway McCuistion (dec.), Kyle Rea. BA, Washington & Lee U., 1962; postgrad., U. Mich., 1971; MA with distinction, Am. U., 1973; postgrad., Harvard U., 1973-74. Dir. rsch. Tex. Rep. Com., Austin, 1964-67, Rep. Nat. Com., Washington, 1969-70; spl. asst. to dir. U.S. Census Bur., Washington, 1970-73; v.p. Decision Making Info. Inc., Santa Ana, Calif., 1974-77; pres., founder Tarrance, Hill, Newport & Ryan, Houston, 1977-92; pres., mng. dir. Gallup China Ltd., Beijing, 1993-95; vis. prof. polit. sci. Tex. A&M U., College Station, 1995-96; scholar in residence Washington and Lee U., Va., 1996; mng. dir. Burson-Marsteller, Washington, 1997-99. Bd. dirs. Gallup Orgn., 1987-92; cons. Gallup Internat. Rsch. Ctr., Lincoln, Nebr.; co-chmn. adv. adjustment panel U.S. Census, 1990. Co-author: The Ticket Splitter, 1972, Checked and Balanced, 1998; editor: Texas Precinct Votes '66, '68, '70. Sr. strategist, sr. advisor Senator John McCain for Pres. 2008. Fellow John F. Kennedy Inst. Politics Harvard U., 1973-74; named one of 150 People Who Influence Fed. Govt. Nat. Jour. Mag., 1986. Mem.: Raleigh Tavern Philos. Soc. (founder), Am. Polit. Sci. Assn., Kappa Sigma. Avocations: mountain trekking, golf, aviculture, travel. E-mail: lanceterrancejr@aol.com.

TARRANT, ALISON, broadcast executive, marketing professional; b. 1970; Assoc. to v.p., grp. dir. nat. broadcast divsn. Universal McCann, 1993—2000; dir. promotions Kids' WB! to v.p. integrated sales and mktg. Warner Bros. TV Network, 2000—06; sr. v.p. integrated sales and mktg. CW TV Network, 2006—. Mem. media coun. Paley Ctr. for Media. Named a Woman to Watch, Advt. Age, 2008. Office: CW TV Network 4000 Warner Blvd Burbank CA 91522 Office Phone: 818-977-2500. Office Fax: 818-954-7667. Business E-Mail: alison.tarrant@cwtv.com.*

TARRANT, CHRISTINE GLORIA, music educator; d. Nick and Bessie Boulos; m. Timothy Michael Tarrant, May 1, 2004; children: John Nicholas, Victoria Kathleen 1 stepchild, Joseph John. BS, U. Ill., 1992, MS, 1997. Tchr. choral, music Marquardt Mid. Sch., Glendale Heights, Ill., 1992—98, Timber Ridge Mid. Sch., Plainfield, Ill., 1998—99, Heritage Grove Mid. Sch., Plainfield, Ill., 1999—2002, Drauden Point Mid. Sch., Plainfield, 2002—05. Children's choral dir. Hinsdale (Ill.) Children's Choir, 1997—97, United Meth. Ch., Downers Grove, Ill., 1997—99; youth choral dir. All Saints Greek Orthodox Ch., Joliet, Ill., 2000—03. Recipient Fine Arts award, Bloom Sch. Dist., 1988. Mem.: Am. Choral Dirs. Am., Alpha Delta Pi. Greek Orthodox. Avocations: reading, exercise.

TARRANT, RICHARD J(OHN), classicist, educator; b. Bklyn., Apr. 4, 1945; s. John Joseph and Bertha (Slaney) T.; m. Jacqueline Brown, Sept. 14, 1968. BA, Fordham U., 1966; DPhil, Oxford U., 1972; AM (hon.), Harvard U., 1982. P.S. Allen jr. research fellow Corpus Christi Coll., Oxford, England, 1968-70; lectr. Univ. Coll., Toronto, Ont., Canada, 1970-71, asst. prof., 1971-74, assoc. prof., 1974-79; prof. U. Toronto, 1979-82; prof. Greek and Latin Harvard U., Cambridge, Mass., 1982-87, Carl A. Pescosolido prof. Roman civilization, 1987-93, Pope prof. Latin language and Literature, 1993—, Harvard Coll. prof., 1999—2004, chmn. dept., 1988-94, acting dean Grad. Sch. Arts and Scis., 1995-96. Vis. Mellon prof. Inst. for Advanced Study, Princeton, 1991-92; vis. fellow Corpus Christi Coll. U. Oxford, 1992. Author: Greek and Latin Lyric Poetry in Translation: A Bibliographical Survey, 1972, Seneca, Agamemnon, 1976, (with others) Texts and Transmission: A Survey of the Latin Classics, 1983, Seneca's Thyestes, 1985, Ovid's Metamorphoses, 2004; editor Phoenix: Jour. Classical Assn. Can., 1978-82, Harvard Studies in Classical Philology, 1985-88, 93-94; editorial bd. Toronto Medieval Latin Texts, 1977—, Cambridge Classical Texts and Commentaries, 1992—; advisory bd. Text: Transactions of the Soc. for Textual Scholarship, 1994—, Materiali e discussioni comitato scientifico, 2002—; contbr. articles to profl. jours. Cabot fellow, 1993—94, 2004—05, Marshall scholar, 1966—69. Mem. Am. Philol. Assn. (bd. dirs. 1987-89, v.p. publs. 1992-95), Cambridge Philol. Assn., Classical Assn. Can., Classical Assn. New Eng., Phi Beta Kappa. Office: Harvard U Dept Classics Boylston Hall 204 Cambridge MA 02138 Home Phone: 617-864-7919; Office Phone: 617-496-3611. Business E-Mail: tarrant@fas.harvard.edu.

TARRANT, SASHA RANAE ADAMS, history professor; b. Torrington, Wyo., July 20, 1967; d. Bryan Robert Adams and Donna Joy Grimes; m. Glenn Durwood Tarrant, July 2, 1985; children: Sheila Ranae, Margo Elizabeth. BA in History, U. Houston, Clear Lake, 1994, MA in History, 1996; AA, Brazosport Coll., Lake Jackson, Tex. Rschr., tchg. asst. U. Houston, Clear Lake, 1995—96; tchg. asst. Tex. A&M U., Coll. Sta., 1997—98; intern U. Space Rsch. Assn., NASA Johnson Space Ctr., Houston, 1998—99; honors program dir., asst. prof. history Brazosport Coll., 1999—. Steering com. Viewing the Past Through Different Lenses: The African Am. Legacy in the Lower Brazos Valley Symposium, Lake Jackson, Tex., 2001; pres. Gulf Coast Intercollegiate Honors Coun., Houston, 2004—05; co-chair com. Nat. Collegiate Honors Coun., Lincoln, Nebr., 2005—07. Editor: Antifeminism in America; author: (handbook) Texas Community College Student Day Handbook. Troop leader Girl Scouts of Am., Lake Jackson, 2000—04. Recipient Tchr. of Excellence award, Nat. Inst. Staff and Orgnl. Devel., 2002—03, 2006—07, Martha Wash. award, SAR, 2006; named Orgn. Leader of Yr., U. Houston, Clear Lake, 1995—96. Mem.: AAUW (expanding your horizons coord. com. 1996), Tex. State Hist. Assn. Home: 1611 McFadden Lake Jackson TX 77566 Office: Brazosport Coll 500 College Dr Lake Jackson TX 77566 Office Fax: 979-230-3592.

TARRIO, CHARLES, physicist; b. Middletown, Conn., Dec. 20, 1960; s. Frank R. and Frances Tarrio; m. Danielle Partello, Feb. 17, 1995; 1 child, Alyssa Partello Tarrio. BS, Bates Coll., Lewiston, Maine, 1982; PhD, U. of Va., Charlottesville, 1991. Physicist Nat. Inst. of Stds. and Tech., Gaithersburg, Md., 1991—. Recipient Dept. of Commerce Silver medal, U.S. Dept. of Commerce, 2004, Arthur S. Flemming award for applied sci., George Wash. U., 2003, Dept. of Commerce Bronze medal, U.S. Dept. of Commerce, 1994. Mem.: SPIE, Optical Soc. of Am. Office: Nat Inst Stds and Tech Stop 8410 100 Bureau Dr Gaithersburg MD 20899

TARRO, GIULIO, virologist; b. Messina, Italy, July 9, 1938; s. Emanuele and Emanuela (Iannello) Tarro; 1 adopted child, Giuseppe. MD, U. Naples, 1962, postgrad. in nervous diseases, 1968, PhD in Virology, 1971; postgrad. in med. and biol. scis., Roman Acad., 1979; degree in medicine (hon.), U. Pro Deo, Albany, NY, 1989; degree in immunology (hon.), St. Theodora Acad., NY, 1991; degree in bioethics (hon.), Constantinian U., Cranston, RI, 1996. Asst. in med. pathology Naples U., Italy, 1964-66; rsch. assoc. divsn. virology and cancer rsch. Children's Hosp., Cin., 1965-68; asst. prof. rsch. pediat. U. Cin. Coll. Medicine, 1968-69; rsch. fellow Nat. Rsch. Coun., Naples, 1966-74, rsch. chief, 1974; prof. oncologic virology Coll. Medicine U. Naples, 1971-85, prof. microbiology and immunology Sch. Specialization, 1972—2006; chief divsn. virology D. Cotugno Hosp. Infectious Diseases, Naples, 1973—2006, pres. ethic com., 1998—2007, head dept. diagnostic labs., 2003—06, emeritus, 2006—. Sr. scientist Nat. Cancer Inst. Frederick Ctr., Md., 1973; project dir. Nat. Cancer Inst., Bethesda, Md., 1971-75; edn. min. rep. Zool. Sta., Naples, 1975-79; cons. Italian Pharmacotherapic Inst., Rome, 1980-98, med. dir., 2006-07; nat. com. on bioethics, 1995-98; ethics com. Basilicata Oncologic Hosp., 2005-; pres. De Beaumont Bonelli Found. Cancer Rsch., Naples, 1978—, European Group Econ. Interest, Rsch. and Devel., Naples, 2003-07, Campania Tech. and Ecology Ctr., 2004-09; dean faculty natural and phys. scis. Nobile Accademia di Santa Teodora Imperatrice, 1993-2003; dept. head medicine Naples People U., 2000-05; sci. coord. extracorporeal hyperthermia in HCV patients First Circle Med., Mpls., 2000-03; vice chmn., gen. sec. sci. adv. bd. Unihart Biotech Pharm., London, 2005-07; chmn. com. on biotechs. and virusphere World Acad. Biomed. Techs., UNESCO, Paris, 2007-; adj. prof. dept. biology Temple U. Coll. Sci. and Tech., Phila., 2007—, pres. sci. com. Moravia U. Gonzaga Inst. Naples, 2008-, hon. pres. Norman Acad. Rome, 2009- Author: Virologia Oncologica, 1979, Patologia dell'AIDS, 1991, Con il Cancro si Puó Vivere, 1992, AIDS Cosa Possiamo Fare Cosa Dobbiamo Sapere, 1994, Pocket File Research Collection, 1997, 6th edit., 2003, To Prevent Is To Win, 1998, Bioethics and Culture of Prevention, 2001, Health Without Borders, 2004, 2d edit., 2007, Safety No Limits, 2008; editor-in-chief: Internat. Jour. Clin. Investigation, 2000—, Cotugno News, 2003—, Fratres, 2004—; contbr. more than 375 articles to profl. jours. Pres. Sci. Cultural Com., Torre Annunziata, Italy, 1984, Tumor Prevention Assn., Rome, 1984; mem. acad. senate Constantinian U., Providence, 1990, U. Pro Deo, NY, 1994; hon. acad. U. Sancti Cyrilli, Valletta, Malta, 2001; mem. UNESCO-Hebrew U. Jerusalem Internat. Sch. Molecular Biology and Microbiology, UNESCO-World Acad. Biomed. Techs.; hon. rector Ruggero II U., Fla., 2003. Maj. Italian Navy, 1982-84, lt. col., 1993-95. Decorated comdr. Nat. Order of Merit, Star of Europe, knight grand cross Sovereign Constantinian Order St. George, gt. officer Italian Republic; recipient Internat. Lenghi award Lincei Acad., 1969, Gold Microscope award Italian Health Min., 1973, Knights of Humanity award Internat. Register of Chivalry, Malta, 1978, Gold medal of culture award Pres. Italian Republic, 1975, Culture award, 1985, 1st prize in biomed. rsch., Italian Acad. Arts and Scis., 1987, Castello di Pietrarossa award, Italy, 1991, Gold Cesare award Padova, 1991, 20th Century award in Medicine, 1994, Gold Little Horse, Transnat. European Fedn., Rome 1996, King Manfredi award Manfredonia, 1999, Equestris Ordinis S. Sepulcri of Jerusalem, Rome, 1999, Gold medal of health Pres. Italian Republic, 1999, Saint Catherin award, Siena, 2003, Sorrento in the World award, 2004, Medal of Culture Ministry, 2005, Knight of Solidarity Internat. award Norman Acad., Rome, 2006, hon. pres. 2009-, St. Pio for Peace award City of Fiuggi, 2006, Tables of Law award Internat. Assn. Cath. Apostleship, Naples, 2006, 32nd Casentino International. award in medicine Poppi-Arezzo, 2007, Grand Cross Internat. Acad.

State Wyo., 2008, award Pres. Italian Rep, Silver medal, 2008, others. Fellow: AAAS; mem.: Norman Acad. (hon. pres. 2009—), Am. Chem. Soc., European Soc. Clin. Virology, NY Acad. Scis., Nat. Order Journalists, AIDS Soc. Asia and the Pacific, Assn. Res. Prevention of Cancer (sci. com. 1995), Italian Assn. Viral Study and Rsch. (pres. 1995—), Italian Soc. Immuno-Oncology (v.p. 1975—, pres. 1990—2008), Internat. League Drs. for Abolition of Vivisection (pres. 1992—), Internat. Assn. Leukemias, Am. Assn. Cancer Rsch., Am. Soc. Microbiology, Rotary, Lions (pres. Pompei chpt. 1987—89, pres. com. fight cancer 1989—90, vice gov. dist. 1991—92, pres. com. fight cancer 1992—94, pres. com. sci. and life 1994—95, pres. com. fight drug addiction and AIDS 1995—97, pres. com. transplant and donations 1998—99, pres. com. oncology 2000—02, pres. com. on stem cells 2002—03, dist. dir. operative area ethics and social solidarity 2003—04, pres. Pompei chpt. 2004—06, dist. dir. operative area health and rsch. 2006—, Melvin Jones fellow 1993, 2004, 2008). Roman Catholic. Achievements include patents in field; discovery of RSV virus in infant deaths in Naples and of tumor liberated protein as a tumor associated antigen, 100 kilodalton protein overexpressed in lung tumors and other epithelial adenocarcinomas. Office Phone: 39-081-5463222. E-mail: gitarro@tin.it.

TARR-WHELAN, LINDA, political organization worker, consultant; b. Springfield, Mass., May 24, 1940; d. Albert and Jane Zack; m. Keith Tarr-Whelan; children: Scott, Melinda. BSN, Johns Hopkins U., 1963; MS, U. Md., 1967; PhD in Public Svc. (hon.), Chatham Coll.; PhD in Humane Letters (hon.), Plymouth State U., 2007. Program dir. AFSCME AFL-CIO, Washington, 1968-74, union area dir., 1974-76; adminstrn. dir. N.Y. State Labor Dept., Albany, N.Y., 1976-79; dep. asst. to pres. Carter White House, Washington, 1979-80; dir. govt. rels. NEA, Washington, 1980-86; CEO, pres. Ctr. for Policy Alternatives, Washington, 1986—2000, bd. dirs., 1985—2002; mng. dir. Tarr-Whelan Assoc. Inc., St. Helena Island, SC, 2000—07. Apptd. Ambassador U.S. rep. UN Commn. on Status of Women, 1996-2001, apptd. mem. pres. adv. bd. trade 2001-2003. Bd. dir., Corp. Voices for Working Families. Recipient Disting. Grad. award Johns Hopkins U. Alumini Assn., 1981, Woodrow Wilson award, Johns Hopkins U., 2003, Breaking the Glass Ceiling award, 1996; leadership fellow Japan Soc., 1987-88; named one of 50 Most Powerful Women in Washington, Ladies Home Jour. Democrat. Avocations: walking, travel. Home: Tarr-Whelan Assoc Inc PO Box 1012 Saint Helena Island SC 29920 Business E-Mail: ltw@tarr-whelan.com.

TARTAKOVSKY, DANIEL M., applied mathematician; b. Kazan, Russia, Sept. 9, 1969; PhD, U. of Ariz., 1996. Tech. staff mem. Los Alamos Nat. Lab., N.Mex., 1998—. Contbr. articles to profl. jours.

TARTAR ESCH, STACY, literature and language professor; b. Phila., Mar. 11, 1963; d. Jerry Tartar and Eleanor Hammill; m. James Esch, Mar. 17, 1995; 1 child, Devin Casey Esch. MA in Lit., West Chester U. Pa., 1987. Instr. Del. County CC, Media, Pa., 1987—93, Drexel U., Phila., 1988—91, CC Phila., 1991—93, St. Louis CC, Florissant Valley, 1993—97, West Chester U. Pa., 1998—, Immaculata U., 2004—. Donator Mil. Order Purple Heart, West Chester, 2001. Home: 330 West Barnard St West Chester PA 19382 Office: West Chester Univ Pa 720 S High St West Chester PA 19383 Personal E-mail: stacyesch@gmail.com. Business E-Mail: startar@wcupa.edu.

TARTER, CURTIS BRUCE, physicist, science administrator; b. Louisville, Sept. 26, 1939; s. Curtis B. and Marian Turner (Cundiff) T.; divorced; 1 child, Shana Lee; m. Gabriela Odell, 2003. BS, MIT, 1961; PhD, Cornell U., 1967. Tchg. asst. Cornell U., Ithaca, NY, 1961—63, rsch. asst., 1964—67; physicist, summers Lawrence Radiation Lab., Livermore, Calif., 1962—63; staff mem. theoretical physics divsn. U. Calif., Lawrence Livermore Nat. Lab., 1967—69, group leader macroscopic properties of matter, 1969—71, assoc. divsn. leader, 1971—74, group leader opacities, 1972—78, divsn. leader, 1974—84; dep. assoc. dir. for physics Lawrence Livermore Nat. Lab., 1984—88, assoc. dir. for physics, 1988—94, dep. dir., 1994, dir., 1994—2002, assoc. dir. at large, 2002—04, dir. emeritus, 2004—. Sr. scientist Applied Rsch. Labs. Aeronutronic divsn. Philco-Ford Corp.; cons. Hertz Found., field com. study on astronomy in the 80's, NRC, 1980; mem. Army Sci. Bd., Washington, 1989-96; adj. prof. dept. applied sci., U. Calif., Davis, 1999-2002; mem. Calif. Coun. on Sci. and Tech., 1996-2002, Pacific Coun. on Internat. Policy, 1998—, lab. opers. bd. DOE, 1998-2002, Nuc. Energy Rsch. Adv. Bd., 1999-2002, Coun. Fgn. Rels., 1999—; bd. dirs. Draper Lab; chair nuc. weapons assessment com. AAAS. Contbr. numerous articles to profl. jours. Recipient Roosevelts Gold Medal award for sci., NNSA Gold medal for disting. svc., U.S. Dept. Energy Exceptional Pub. Svc. award, Sec. of Energy's Gold award. Fellow AAAS (cons. commn. US Strategic Posture 2008-09), Calif. Coun. Sci. and Tech., Am. Phys. Soc. (phys. policy com. 2002-05); mem. Am. Astron. Soc., Internat. Astron. Union. Avocations: golf, running, music. Office: Lawrence Livermore Nat Lab PO Box 808 Livermore CA 94551-0808 Office Phone: 925-422-4169. Business E-Mail: tarter1@llnl.gov. E-mail: cbtarter@yahoo.com.

TARTER, FRED BARRY, advertising executive; b. Bklyn., Aug. 16, 1943; s. Irving and Edna (Kupferberg) T.; m. Lois; children: Scott Andrew, Heather Michelle, Megan Elizabeth. Attended, CCNY, 1962—68. Pres. Jamie Publ. Hootenanny Enterprises, Inc., 1962-65; mdse. dir. Longines Symphonette Soc., 1965-67; with Universal Comm., Inc., NYC, 1967—, pres., CEO, 1969-74; exec. v.p. Deerfield Comm., Inc., NYC, 1974-87, pres., CEO, 1977-88; pres. Deerfield Books, Inc., NYC, 1988-89; pub. S.E.W. mag., NYC, 1977-88; pres. The Rainbow Group Ltd., NYC, 1988—; chmn. Stagebill Mag., 1997-2001; pres., CEO The Lakeside Group of Co., 2001—. Exec. prodr. Joanne Carson's VIP's Miss Am. Teenager Pageant, 1972—73; prodr. Marriage Counselor, 1994, Spenser: Pale Kings & Princes, 1995, Spenser: A Savage Place, 1995, Spenser Judas Goat, 1995, Hearts Adrift, 1995, Ceremony, 1996, Wounded Heart, 1996, Reasons of the Heart, 1996, Lover's Leap, 1996; chmn. Stagebill Enterprises, LLC, 1997—2001; vice-chmn. Affinity Comm., Inc., 1997—2001, Inscap, LLC; pres., CEO The Telephone Co. LLC, 1999—2003; pres. The Programme Exch., U.K. Ltd.; bd. dir. Boardwalk Entertainment, Ltd., Lakeside Group, Inc., Cinema Events, LLC, Money Mailer LLC. Office: Lakeside Group Ltd 210 E 39th St New York NY 10016-2754 Personal E-mail: ftarter@lakesideglobal.com. *An integral part of success is the capacity for failure. Persistence, combined with responsibility, has proven to be the winning combination time and again.*

TARTIR, SAMIR, science educator; s. Yacoub and Intesar Tartir; m. Nadyin Aarag, Nov. 20, 1980; 1 child, Leen. Attending, U. Ga., Athens, 2004—. Instr. Phila. U., Amman, Jordan, 2003; sr. database developer & analyst Intergrant Inc., San Diego, 2000—03. Personal E-mail: s_tartir@hotmail.com.

TARTT, BLAKE, lawyer; b. Houston, Mar. 16, 1929; s. Herbert Blake and Bernice (Schwalm) T.; m. Barbara Jean Moore, Jan. 30, 1960; children: Blake III, Courtnay Elias. BBA, So. Meth. U., Dallas, 1949, JD cum laude, 1959. Bar: Tex. 1959. Assoc. Fulbright & Jaworski, Houston, 1959-70, ptnr., 1970-2000, Beirne, Maynard & Parsons, LLP, Houston, 2000—. Mem. Tex. Commn. on Jud. Conduct, 1996-2001; bd. dirs. Nat. Judicial Coll. Bd. dirs. Mus. Fine Arts, Houston; mem. bd. visitors Nat. Jud. Coll. Served to 1st lt. USAF, 1951-55, Korea. Decorated Air medal. Fellow Am. Bar Found. (chmn. fellows 1987, life), Tex. Bar Found. (chmn. bd. 1974-75, chmn. fellows 1978-79, life), Am. Coll. Trial Lawyers; mem. ABA (ho. of dels. 1976-99, state del. 1990-99, standing com. fed. jud. 1996-99, chair 1997, bd. govs. 2001-04), Am. Bd. Trial Advocates (advocate), Houston Bar Found. (life., chmn., bd. dirs. 1992), Fed. Bar Assn., Internat. Assn. Def. Counsel, Am. Judicature Soc. (bd. dirs. 1984-88), So. Conf. Bar Pres. (pres. 1984), State Bar Tex. (dir. 1972-75, exec. com. 1975-76, pres. elect 1982-83, pres. 1983-84), Houston Bar Assn., Am. Law Inst., Tex. Jud. Commn., Citizens Commn. on the Tex. Judiciary, Tex. Commn. Jud. Conduct, Houston Philos. Soc., Coronado Club, Forest Club, Argyle Club (San Antonio), Reform Club (London), Delta Theta Phi, Alpha Tau Omega. Episcopalian. Office: Beirne Maynard & Parsons 1300 Post Oak Blvd Houston TX 77056-3028 Office Phone: 713-960-7331. Business E-Mail: btartt@bmpllp.com.

TARULLO, DANIEL K., federal official, law educator; b. Boston, Nov. 3, 1952; AB summa cum laude, Georgetown U., 1973; MA, Duke U., 1974; JD summa cum laude, U. Mich., 1977. Bar: D.C. 1978. Assoc. Arnold & Porter LLP, 1977-78; atty. antitrust divsn. US Dept. Justice, 1978-79; spl. asst. to under sec. US Dept. Commerce, 1980-81; asst. prof. law Harvard U., Cambridge, Mass., 1981-87; chief employment counsel US Senate Com. on Labor & Human Resources, 1987-89; internat. counsel Shearman & Sterling, Washington, 1989-93; asst. sec. econ. & bus. affairs US Dept. State, Washington, 1993—96; dep. asst. to Pres. for econ. policy The White House, 1996—97, asst. to Pres. for internat. econ. policy, 1997—98; prof. law Georgetown U. Law Ctr., 1999—; sr. econ. adv. Barack Obama Presdl. Campaign, 2008; mem. bd. govs. Fed. Res. Sys., Washington, 2009—. Econ. advisor Clinton-Gore Transition Team, 1992; personal rep. to G7/G8 Groups, The White House, 1995-98; non-resident sr. fellow, Ctr. for Am. Progress; Frederick H. Schultz prof. internat. economics policy, Princeton U., 2004, vis. prof. law, Harvard Law Sch., 2005 Articles editor Law Rev.; contbr. articles to profl. jours. Mem. Order of Coif, Phi Beta Kappa. Office: Federal Reserve System 20th St & Constitution Ave NW Rm 2010 Washington DC 20551 also: Georgetown University Law Center Hotung 6017 600 New Jersey Ave NW Washington DC 20001 E-mail: dtarullo@americanprogress.org.*

TARVER, ANTONIO DEON, professional boxer; b. Orlando, Fla., Nov. 21, 1968; Boxer Pan-Am. Games, 1996; profl. boxer, 1997—. Winner vacant world title vs. Montell Griffin, light heavyweight divsn. World Boxing Coun., 2003, Internat. Boxing Fedn., 2003; winner world title vs. Roy Jones Jr. by knockout, light heavyweight divsn. World Boxing Coun., 2004, World Boxing Assn., 2004, Internat. Boxing Orgn., 2004, winner world title vs. Glen Johnson, light heavyweight divsn., 05, winner world title def. vs. Roy Jones Jr. by unanimous decision, light heavyweight divsn., 05, winner vacant world title vs. Elvir Muriqi, light heavyweight divsn., 07, winner world title def. vs. Danny Santiago by tech. knockout, light heavyweight divsn., 07. Actor: (films) Rocky Balboa, 2006. Recipient Bronze medal, US Olympics, Atlanta, 1996. Office: Star Boxing 991 Morris Pk Ave Bronx NY 10462 Office Phone: 718-823-2000. Office Fax: 718-823-6330.

TARVER, BETTY GAIL, music educator; d. Garland E. and Evelyn J. Schiller; m. Robert D. Tarver, July 20, 1991. AA, Temple Jr. Coll., 1978; B of Music Edn., Sam Houston State U., Huntsville, Tex., 1980. Cert. Kodaly Sam Houston State U. Music tchr. Magnolia Elem. Sch., Tex., 1980—83, Bear Br. Elem. Sch., Magnolia, 1983—. Dir. Bear Branch Elem. Choir. Named Tchr. of Yr., Bear Branch Elem. Sch., 2008. Mem.: Assn. Tex. Profl. Educators (assoc.), Tex. Music Educators Assn. (assoc.). Avocations: travel, piano. Office: Bear Branch Elem Sch 8909 FM 1488 Magnolia TX 77354

TASCO, MARIAN B., councilwoman; b. Greensboro, NC, Nov. 26, 1937; d. Thomas and Alice Bratcher Benton; m. Thomas Earle Williams, Nov. 28, 1981 (dec.); 1 child, Charles III. Student, Bennett Coll., 1956-58; BS, Temple U., 1965. Coord. task force Phila. Urban Coalition, 1970-76; dir. constituent svc. Congressman William Gray III, Phila., 1978-83; commr. Voter Registration Phila., 1983-87; councilwomen, dist. 9 Phila. City Coun., 1987—. Chmn. fin. com., pub. health and human services com. Phila. City coun.; vice chmn. ethics com., whole coun. com. Phila. City Coun. Cons., trainer YWCA, Inst. Pub. Leadership; trustee Bennett Coll.; chmn. Phila. Gas Commn.; bd. dirs. Bd. of City Trusts, Bd. City Towns. Named Outstanding Alumnae, Bennett Coll. Nat. Alumni Assn., 1975, Woman of Yr. Pa Fedn. Dem. Women, 1998; recipient Winners award Women's Alliance for Job Equity, 1986, Civil Rights award Phila. Affirmative Action Coalition, 1986, Achievement award United Negro Coll. Fund Phila. Chpt., 1986, Woman Achievement award March of Dimes, 1999. Mem. Nat. League Cities (mem. adv. bd.), Women in Mcpl. Govt. (past pres. govt. bd.), Nat. Polit. Congress Black Women, Nat. Coalition 100 Black Women, Pa. Women's Campaign Fund, Women's Way, Family Planning Coun. Pa., Women's Way, Health Watch, Delta Sigma Theta. Democrat. Baptist. Office: Phila City Coun City Hall Rm 577 Philadelphia PA 19107 Office Phone: 215-686-3455. Office Fax: 215-686-1938. Business E-Mail: marian.tasco@phila.gov.

TASH, PAUL CLIFFORD, editor, publishing executive; b. South Bend, Ind., July 17, 1954; s. Robert N. and Barbara R. (Eller) T.; m. Karyn E. Krayer, Aug. 19, 1983; children: Kaley Marie, Kendyl Barbara. BA summa cum laude, Ind. U., 1976; LLB, Edinburgh U., Scotland, 1978. Reporter St. Petersburg Times, 1978-83, city editor, 1983-86, metro editor, 1986-89, editor, pub. Fla. Trend Mag., 1990-91, Washington bur. chief, 1991-92, exec. editor, 1992-2000, dep. chmn., 1997—2004, editor & pres., 2000—04, editor, 2004—; chmn. & CEO Times Pub. Co., 2004—. Bd. dirs. Times Pub. Co., Newspaper Assn. Am., Com. to Protect Journalists, Pulitzer Prize Bd., Western Commn. Fla. Coun. 100, Fla. Trend Mag., Congressional Quar., Poynter Inst. Media Studies. Chmn. Fla. First Amendment Found.; mem. adv. bd. Ind. U. Sch. Journalism. Marshall Aid Commemoration Commn. scholar, 1976-78; recipient Kappa Tau Alpha Hall of Fame award U. So. Fla. Sch. Mass Comm., 2009. Mem.: Fla. First Amendment Found., Tampa Bay Area Com. on Fgn. Rels., Am. Soc. Newspaper Editors, Fla. C. of C. Office: St Petersburg Times 490 1st Ave S Saint Petersburg FL 33701-4204 Mailing: PO Box 1121 Saint Petersburg FL 33731-1121 Office Phone: 727-893-8887. Office Fax: 727-892-2328. E-mail: ptash@sptimes.com.*

TASHIMA, ATSUSHI WALLACE, federal judge; b. Santa Maria, Calif., June 24, 1934; s. Yasutaro and Aya (Sasaki) Tashima; m. Nora Kiyo Inadomi, Jan. 27, 1957; children: Catherine Y., Christopher I., Jonathan I. AB in Polit. Sci., UCLA, 1958; LLB, Harvard U., 1961. Bar: Calif. 1962. Dep. atty. gen. State of Calif., 1961—67; atty. Spreckels Sugar divsn. Amstar Corp., 1968—72, v.p., gen. atty. Spreckels Sugar divsn., 1972—77; ptnr. Morrison & Foerster, LA, 1977—80; judge US Dist. Ct. (ctrl. dist.), LA, 1980—96, US Ct. Appeals (9th cir.), Pasadena, Calif., 1996—2003, sr. judge, 2003—. Mem. Calif. Com. Bar Examiners, 1978—80. With USMC, 1953—56. Mem.: ABA, LA County Bar Assn. Democrat. Office: Richard A Chambers US Ct Appeals PO Box 91510 125 S Grand Ave Pasadena CA 91109-1510*

TASHMAN, LAITH, civil engineer, educator; b. Zarka, Jordan, Nov. 28, 1976; s. Suleiman and Ebtisaam. BSCE (hon.), U. Jordan, 1999; MSCE, Wash. State U., 2000; PhD in Civil Engring., Tex. A&M U., 2003. Engr. trainee Byrom Clark Roberts, Manchester, England, 1998—98; site engr. and quality control mgr. TAC Group, Amman, Jordan, 1999—99; grad. rsch. asst. Wash. State U., 1999—2002, instr., 2001; grad. rsch. asst. Tex. A&M U., College Station, 2003; asst. prof. Wash. State U., 2004—. Assoc. dir. Wash. ctr. for x-ray tomography and imaging tec. Wash. State U., 2004—. Contbr. articles to profl. jours. Recipient John Orsborn Outstanding Grad. Student award, Washington State U., 2001, Morris K. Snyder award; named Winner of the Graduate Oral Engring. (I) Presentation, Tex. A&M U., 2003; grantee, Wash. State U., 2000, 2002, Tex. A&M U., 2003; scholar, The Assn. Asphalt Paving Technologists, 2003; Rsch. Edn. Found. scholar, NAPA. Mem.: ASCE (assoc.), Internat. Grad. Student Assn., Grad. and Profl. Student Assn. (senator 2000—02, Senator of Yr. 2002), KC. Avocations: reading, travel, chess, jogging, soccer. Office: Washington State University Department of Civil & Environmental Eng Pullman WA 99164-2910 Office Fax: 509-335-7632. Business E-Mail: ltashman@wsu.edu.

TASKONAK, BURAK, medical educator, dentist; s. Erim Hakki and Leyla Taskonak. DDS, Ind. U., Indpls.; PhD, U. Fla., Gainesville, 2000—04. Cert. dentistry Ind., 2008, Fla., 2008. Rsch. assoc. Tex. A&M U., Dallas, 2004—05; asst. prof. Ind. U., Indpls., 2005—. Bd. mem. Acad. Dental Materials, Portland, Oreg., 2007—. Contbr. articles to profl. jours. Recipient Oral Health Rsch. award, Ind. U., 2006—07; Rsch. grant, Matsumoto U., 2007—08, ESPE. Mem.: Am. Assn. Dental Rsch., Internat. Assn. Dental Rsch. Achievements include patents pending for multilayer tape-cast and reaction-bonded dental ceramics. Office: Indiana Univ Sch Dentistry 1121 West Michigan St Indianapolis IN 46202 E-mail: btaskona@iupui.edu.

TASLIDERE, EZGI, science educator; d. Kadir and Nihal Taslidere. BS, Mid. East Tech. U., Ankara, Turkey, 2000, MS, 2002; attending, Drexel U., Phila., 2002—. Registered yoga tchrs. Yoga Alliance, 2009. Internship Info. Technologies & Electronics Rsch. Inst., Ankara, Turkey, 1998, ASELSAN Electronic Industries Inc., Ankara, 1999, electronic design engr., 1999—2002; rsch. asst. Drexel U., Phila., 2002—, tchg. asst., 2004—. Contbr. articles to profl. jours. Mem.: IEEE Women Engring., IEEE. Office: Drexel Univ 3120-40 Market St Ste 312 ECE Dep Philadelphia PA 19104 Business E-Mail: et43@drexel.edu.

TASMAN, ALLAN, psychiatry educator; b. Louisville, Feb. 8, 1947; s. Goodman and Zelda Tasman; m. Cathy Faye Goldstein, May 24, 1970. BA in Chemistry, Franklin and Marshall Coll., 1969; MD, U. Ky., 1973. Diplomate Am. Bd. Psychiatry and Neurology. Resident in psychiatry U. Ky. Med. Sch., Lexington, 1973—74, U. Cin. Med. Ctr., 1974—76; asst. prof. psychiatry U. Conn. Med. Sch., Farmington, 1976—82, assoc. prof. psychiatry and tenure, 1982—88, prof. psychiatry, 1988—91; prof. psychiatry and behavioral scis., tenure and chmn. U. Louisville Sch. Medicine, 1991—. Editor: Annual Review of Psychiatry, 1989-92, Clinical Challenges in Psychiatry, 1993, Less Time to Do More, 1993; sr. editor: Textbook of Psychiatry, 1997, 2d edit., 2003, 3rd edit., 2008, assoc. editor Am. Jour. Psychotherapy, 1999—; founding dep. editor Jour. Psychotherapy Practice and Rsch., 1992-99; founding editor Jour. Psychiatry Practice Rsch., 2008-. Recipient Alpha Omega Alpha Faculty award, 2002, Nat. Alliance Mental Illness Exemplary Psychiatrist award, 2002, Pres.'s Disting. Faculty award for svc. to the profession, U. Louisville, 2003, St. Clair award, Ky. Psychiat. Assn., 2007, Disting. Alumnus award, U. Ky. Coll. Medicine, 2008. Fellow Am. Psychiat. Assn. (disting., v.p. 1996-98, pres.-elect 1998-99, pres. 1999-2000, Nancy Roeske award for excellence in med. student edn. 1991, Irma Bland award for excellence in resident tchg. 2005), Royal Coll. Psychiatrists, Am. Assn. Dirs. Psychiat. Residency Tng. (pres. 1993-94); mem. Assn. Acad. Psychiatry (pres. 1993-94, Educator of Yr. award 2000), Am. Assn. Chmn. Depts. Psychiatry (pres. 1996-97, 97-98), World Psychiat. Assn. (bd. dirs. 2002—, sec. for edn. 2005—), Pacific Rim Coll. Psychiatrists (pres. 2006—). Office: Univ Louisville Dept Psychiatry 401 E Chestnut St Louisville KY 40202

TASOOJI, MICHAEL B., retail executive; m. Linda Tasooji; 3 children. BS in Internat. Trade and Quantitative Bus. Analysis, U. So. Calif., MBA in Internat. Fin. and Bus. Econs. With Getty Oil Co., Columbia Pictures Studio; v.p. application systems Bergen Brunswig Corp.; v.p. info. svcs. Disneyland, 1995—2000; sr. v.p., chief info. officer Walt Disney Attractions, 2000, Walt Disney Co., 2000—03; exec. v.p., chief info. officer Gap, Inc., 2003—. Office: Gap Inc 2 Folsom St San Francisco CA 94105 Office Phone: 650-952-4400.

TASSE, MARIE JEANNE, retired art educator; b. Worcester, Mass., Mar. 25, 1925; d. Paul Charles and Marie Antoinette (DesRosiers) T. AB, Anna Maria Coll., 1955; MA, U. Notre Dame, 1962; PhD, Boston U., 1972. Tchr. music., dir. choir St. John's Sch., Newton, Mass., 1945-50, Notre Dame High Sch., Central Falls, R.I., 1950-53; instr. to prof. Anna Maria Coll., Paxton, Mass., 1953—75; from assoc. prof. to prof. Marietta (Ohio) Coll., 1975-92, chmn. art dept., 1977-82, cons. to faculty, 1981-85, dir., instr. Inst. for Learning in Retirement, 1992—; advisor Anna Maria Coll. Bd., 1977—81. Founder Marietta Calligraphy Soc., 1981—; dir. Letters at an Exhbn., Marietta, 1984, 86, 88, 92, 99, 2003, 2005, By Women's Hands Exhbn., Marietta, 1989-91. Calligrapher wall hangings, handmade books, broadsides (Merit award 1991). Pres., v.p. bd. The Marietta Chorale, 1978-88; dir. St. Mary's Ch. Choir, Marietta, 1978-88; bd. dirs. Artsbridge, Marietta/Parkersburg, 1981-94, Blennerhasset Hist. Found., 2000—. Recipient Art Educator award Artsbridge, 1991, Alumni award for profl. achievement, 2001; named Zonta Woman of Yr., 2006. Mem. Nat. Soc. Arts and Letters (local pres., v.p. bd. 1982—, nat. resolutions chair 1988-90, nat. career liaison 1992-94, organizer A Showcase of the Arts 1992—, editor Career Award Winner 1994, nat. editor membership directory 1994-2000, nat. historian 1996-98, nat. pres., 2000-02), Sr. Arts Com. (chair 2008-). Roman Catholic. Avocations: music, needlecrafts, reading, travel.

TASSÉ, ROGER, lawyer, former Canadian government official; b. Montreal, Que., Can., 1931; BA, Coll. St. Marie, Montreal, 1952; Lic. in Law, U. Montreal, 1955; diploma d'Etudes Superieures, U. Ottawa, Ont., Can., 1957. Bar: Que. 1956, Ont. 1986; called to Queens Counsel 1971. Joined Dept. Justice, 1956, civil law counsel for Can. govt., from 1957, supt. bankruptcy, 1965-68, asst. dep. min. consumer and corp. affairs, 1968-72; dep. min. Dept. of Solicitor Gen., 1972-77; dep. min. of justice, atty. gen. of Can., 1977-85; ptnr. Land Michener Lash Johnston, Toronto and Ottawa, Noel Décary Aubry & Assocs., Hull, Que., 1985-88; exec. v.p. legal and environ. affairs Bell Can., 1988-91; of counsel Fraser & Beatty, Toronto, 1992-95, Gowling, Lafleur & Henderson, Ottawa, 1995—. Prin. constl. advisor to Spl. Joint Com. of the Senate and the House of Commons on a Renewed Can., 1991-92. Mem. Citizens' Forum on Canada's Future, 1990; co-chair task force Can.

Mags., 1993; mem. DTH Panel, 1995. Decorated officer Order of Can. Avocations: skiing, tennis. Office: Gowling Lafleur Henderson LLP 160 Elgin St Ste 2600 Ottawa ON Canada K1P 1C3 Office Phone: 813-786-0208. Fax: (613) 563-9869. E-mail: roger.tasse@gowlings.com.

TASSINARI, MELISSA SHERMAN, teratologist, developmental toxicologist; b. Lawrence, Mass., Sept. 26, 1953; m. R. Peter Tassinari; children: Michael, Emily, Sara. AB, Mt. Holyoke Coll., 1975; postgrad., U. St. Andrews, Scotland, 1973-74; PhD, Med. Coll. Wis., 1979. Diplomate Am. Bd. Toxicology. Rsch. asst. in orthopedic surgery., Lab. Human Biochemistry Children's Hosp. Med. Ctr., Boston, 1981-83; rsch. affiliate in toxicology Forsyth Dental Ctr., Boston, 1983-86, staff assoc. dept. toxicology, 1986-89; asst. prof. cell biology U. Mass. Med. Ctr., Worcester, 1989-91; head reproductive and developmental toxicology Pfizer Inc., Groton/New London, Conn., 1991—99; group dir. worldwide safety scis. Pfizer Global R&D, Groton/New London, Conn., 2001—04, sr. dir. worldwide regulatory policy and intelligence, 2004—. Rsch. fellow oral biology Harvard Sch. Dental Medicine, Boston, 1978-81, instr. oral biology and pathophysiology, 1981-83; asst. prof. biol. scis. Wellesley Coll., Mass., 1985-91, biology Simmons Coll., Boston, 1986-87. Contbr. abstracts, articles to profl. jours. Mem. Teratology Soc. (coun. mem. 2000-07, v.p. 2004, pres. 2005-06), Neurobehavioral Teratology Soc., Mid. Atlantic Reprodn. and Teratology Assn. (steering com. 1994), Midwest Teratology Assn., Soc. Toxicology, Orgn. Teratogen Info. Svcs., Drug Info. Assn. Office: Pfizer Inc 6025 B5220 50 Pequot Ave New London CT 06320

TASSIOPOULOS, APOSTOLOS K., vascular surgeon; b. Trikala, Greece, Oct. 8, 1965; arrived in US, 1992; s. Konstantinos A. Tassiopoulos and Vasiliki D. Tassiopoulou; m. Yianna Darsinos Tassiopoulos, Aug. 23, 2003; 1 child, Vasia. MD, Aristotle U., Thessaloniki, Greece, 1989. Resident gen. surgery Upstate Med. U., Syracuse, 1993—99; fellow vascular surgery Loyola U. Med. Ctr., Haywood, Ill., 1999—2001; sr. attending Cook County Hosp., Chgo., 2001—06; asst. prof. surgery Rush U. Med. Ctr., Chgo., 2002—06, SUNY, 2006—. Contbr. chapters to books. Fellow: Am. Coll. Surgeons; mem.: Am. Assn. Vascular Surgery, European Soc. Vascular Surgeon (assoc.). Home: 5 Bayberry Ct Miller Place NY 11764 Office: SUNY Med Ctr HSC Level T-19 Rm 090 Stony Brook NY 11794

TASSLER, NINA, broadcast executive; married; 2 children. BFA, Boston U. With Roundabout Theatre Co., NYC; dir. TV Triad Artists, Inc.; dir. movies & miniseries, pres. drama devel. Warner Bros. TV, 1990—97; with CBS Corp., 1997—; v.p. drama CBS Prodns., 1997—98; sr. v.p. drama devel. CBS Entertainment, 1998—2003, exec. v.p. drama series devel., 2003—04, pres. Los Angeles, 2004—. Recipient Imagen award, 2005; named one of The 100 Most Powerful Women in Entertainment, Hollywood Reporter, 2006, 2007, America 's Top Women in Bus.-Game Changers, Pink mag. & Forté Found., 2007.

TASSONE, GELSOMINA (GESSIE), metal products executive; b. NYC, July 8, 1944; d. Enrico and A. Cira (Petriccione) Gargiulo; children: Ann Marie, Margaret, Theresa, Christine; m. Armando Tassone, Mar. 20, 1978. Student, Orange County Community Coll., 1975-79, Iona Coll., 1980—. Head bookkeeper Gargiulo Bros. Builders, NYC, 1968-72; pres., owner A&T Iron Works, Inc., New Rochelle, NY, 1973—. Recipient Profl. Image award Contractors Coun. Greater NYC, 1986; named Businesswoman of Yr., Contractors Coun. Greater NYC, 1985, NY State Small Bus. Person of Yr., 1988, Entrepreneur of Yr., Inc. mag., 1990; company named a Successful Small Bus. Co. Westchester County C. of C./BSBA, 1986-88. Mem. Nat. Ornamental and Miscellaneous Metal Assn., Builders Inst. Westchester and Putnam County, Westchester Assn. Women Bus. Owners, Profl. Women in Constrn., New Rochelle C. of C. Office: A&T Iron Works Inc 25 Cliff St New Rochelle NY 10801-6803 Office Phone: 914-632-8992. Personal E-mail: gesjames@aol.com. Business E-Mail: info@atironworks.com, info@atironworks.inc.

TASTO, JAMES P., orthopedist, educator; b. Chgo., Dec. 9, 1938; s. Nicholas Tasto and Monica Flynn; m. Noreen Tasto; children: James Jr., Brian, Patrick, Tricia Tasto-Levien. MD, Loyola U., Chgo., 1965. Physician Alvarado Orthopedics, San Diego, 1970—88, San Diego Sports & Orthopedic Medicine, 1988—, owner, 1988—. Pres. Alvarado Knee Rsch. Inst., San Diego, 1989—; program dir. SD Arthroscopy & Sports Medicine Fellowship Program, 1992—; clin. prof., dept orthopedics U. Calif., San Diego, 2002—, chmn. bd., 2002—. Contbr. articles to 50 profl. jour. publs. and 500 sci. presentations. (Lloyd W. Taylor award, 2004). Recipient Francis West award; named one of Top Drs., San Diego.

TATA, GIOVANNI, publishing executive; b. Taranto, Italy, Apr. 26, 1954; came to U.S., 1974, naturalized, 1982; s. Vito and Angela (Colucci) T.; m. Brenda Susan Smith, Feb. 14, 1978; children: Elizabeth Ariana, Katherine Allison, Margaret Anne, Michael Anthony, Hanna Amelia. BS cum laude, Brigham Young U., 1977, MA, 1980; grad. cert. area studies, U. Utah, 1980, PhD, 1986; postgrad., U. Turin, Italy, 1980-81. Archaeologist Utah State Hist. Soc., Salt Lake City, 1979; instr. dept. langs. U. Utah, Salt Lake City, 1983-85; Mediterranean specialist Soc. Early Hist. Archaeology, Provo, Utah, 1978-91; rsch. fellow Direzione Gen. Cooperazione Sci. Culturale e Technica, Rome, 1980-81; mus. curator Pioneer Trail State Park, Salt Lake City, 1982-83; instr. dept. art Brigham Young U., Provo, 1982-84, dir. creative works, 1996—; rsch. curator Utah Mus. Fine Arts, Salt Lake City, 1985-87; pres. Mus. Info. Sys., 1987-93, Transoft Internat., Inc., 1988—. Chmn. 35th Ann. Symposium on the Archaeology of the Scriptures, 1986, Taras Devel. Corp., 1994—97, MuseMedia, Inc., 1995—2000. Patentee method and system for computerized learning, response, and evaluation. Brigham Young U. scholar. Mem.: Intellectual Property Owners Assn., Assn. Univ. Tech. Mgrs., Nat. Coun. Museums, Am. Assn. Museums. Republican. Mem. Ch. Jesus Christ of Latter-day Saints. Home Phone: 801-224-4973; Office Phone: 801-422-3724. Business E-Mail: giovanni_tata@byu.edu. E-mail: tata@lexinet.com.

TATAR, ARNOLD MARSHALL, internist, educator; b. Chgo., June 26, 1933; s. Louis and Rose Goldberg Tatar; m. Marina Deull-Wirszup, Aug. 30, 1959; children: Carolyn Beth, Audrey Michelle, Lauren D. W. BA in Chemistry, U. Ill., 1954; BS in Medicine, U. Ill., Chgo., 1955, MD cum laude, 1957. Lic. physician, Ill.; cert., recert. Am. Bd. Internal Medicine. Resident in internal medicine Michael Reese Hosp. and Med. Ctr., Chgo., 1957-60, chief med. resident, 1960-61, attending physician, 1961—2001; pres. Drs. Tatar Tatar Buchanan Hunt Suh and Lavery, Chgo., 1961—; attending physician Northwestern Meml. Hosp., Chgo., 1991—. Assoc. prof. internal medicine U. Chgo., 1973-91; asst. prof. internal medicine Northwestern U., Evanston/Chgo., 1991—; dir. med. intensive care Michael Reese Hosp., Chgo., 1969-76, dir. investigative hypertension clinic, 1964-76, pres. med. staff, 1988-90, hosp. trustee, 1982-91. Contbr. rsch. articles to profl. jours. Pres. Parent-Tchr. Orgn., John F. Kennedy Sch., Highland Park, Ill., 1970-72. Lt. col. U.S. Army, 1967-69. Decorated Commendation medal US Army; named one of Chgo.'s Top Drs., Chgo. Mag., 1997, 2001, 2004, Outstanding Primary Care Physicians in U.S., Town and Country Mag., 1999. Fellow Am. Coll. Chest Physicians, Am. Coll. Angiology, Am. Heart Assn. (coun. on hypertension, coun. on clin. cardiology), Am. Soc. Internal Medicine. Avocations: music, theater, dance, bicycling, photography. Home: Apt 5-East 189 E Lake Shore Dr Chicago IL 60611 Office: Drs Tatar Tatar Buchanan Hunt Suh and Lavery Ste 1801 111 W Washington Chicago IL 60602

TATARINOV, KIRILL, computer software industry expert; b. Moscow, Sept. 17, 1964; came to US, 1994; s. Lev Gorinshteyn and Inna Tatarinova; m. Oksana Grekina Tatarinov, Jan. 18m 1986; children: Katherine, Konstantin. MS in Elec. Engring., Moscow U. Railroad Engring., 1986; MBA, Houston Bapt. U., 1997. Tech. lead Fibronics Ltd., Haifa, Israel, 1990-91; dir. R&D Patrol Software Pty. Ltd., Sydney, 1991-94; v.p. R&D BMC Software, Inc., Houston, 1994-98, v.p. strategic planning, 1998-2000, sr. v.p., chief tech. officer, 2000—02; corp. v.p. mgmt. & solutions divsn. Microsoft Corp., 2002—07; corp. v.p. Microsoft Bus. Solutions. Inventor: System for monitoring and managing computer resources, 1997, 99. Office: Microsoft Corp Microsoft Bus Solutions 1 Microsoft Way Redmond WA 98052-6399 Office Phone: 425-707-8978. E-mail: kirill@tatarinov.com.

TATARSKII, VALERIAN IL'ICH, physics researcher; b. Kharkov, USSR, Oct. 13, 1929; s. Il'ya A. and Elizabeth A. (Lapis) T.; m. Maia S. Granovskaia, Dec. 22, 1955; 1 child, Viatcheslav V. MS, Moscow State U., 1952; PhD, Acoustical Inst. Acad. Scis., 1957; DSc, Gorky State U., 1962. Scientific rschr. Geophys. Inst. Acad. Sci. USSR, Moscow, 1953-56, Inst. Atmospheric Physics, Acad. Sci. USSR, Moscow, 1956-59, sr. scientific rschr., 1959-78, head lab., 1978-90; head dept. Lebedev Phys. Inst. Acad. Sci., Moscow, 1990-91; sr. rsch. assoc. U. Colo. Coop. Inst. for Rsch. in Environ. Sci., Boulder, 1991—2001; sr. rsch. scientist Zel Techs. and NOAA/Phys. Sci. Dept., Boulder, 2001—06, Radio Hydro Physics LLC, Boulder, 2006—. Author: Wave Propagation in a Turbulent Medium, 1961, 67, The Effect of the Turbulent Atmosphere on Wave Propagation, 1971, Principles of Statistical Radiophysics, 1989; contbr. articles to profl. jours. Recipient USSR State prize, 1990. Fellow Optical Soc. Am. (Max Born award 1994), Inst. Physics; mem. Russian Acad. Sci., USA Nat. Acad. Engring., NY Acad. Sci., MIT Electromagnetic Soc. Avocations: classical music, fine art, photography. Office: Radio Hydro Physics NOAA Phys Sci Dept Mail Stop ZelTech 325 Broadway St Boulder CO 80305-3328 Personal E-mail: vtatarskii@hotmail.com.

TATE, CURTIS E., JR., management educator; b. Trezvant, Tenn., July 5, 1920; s. Curtis E. and Mary Kathryn (Haskins) T.; m. Evelyn Ruth Mann, Apr. 12, 1945 (div. May, 1969); m. Mary Jim Combs, Aug. 28, 1977; children: Curtis Emory, Milton Oglesby. Student, N. Ga. Coll., 1943-44, U. Ga., 1945-46; AB, Bethel Coll., 1946; MS, U. Tenn., 1952. Clk. Family Gen. Grocery, Trezevant, Tenn., 1938-42; clk. purchasing dept. P&G Defense Corp., Milan, Twnn., 1942; plant mgr. Keathley Pie Co., Memphis, 1946-50; instr. Furman U., Greenville, S.C., 1952-53; bus. mgr. Lander Coll., Greenwood, S.C., 1953-56; from asst. to assoc. prof. Coll. of Bus. Adminstrn. U. Ga., Athens, 1956—91; prof. emeritus Terry Coll. of Bus. U. Ga., Athens, 1991—. Bd. dirs. Flexible Products, Inc., Marietta, Ga., 1968-76; asst. to dean fund raising Terry Coll. Bus., 1991-98. Co-author: Successful Small Business Management, 1975, latest rev. edit., 1985, Complete Guide to Your Own Business, 1977, Dow-Jones-Irwin Business Papers, 1977, Bus. Policy: Administrative, Strategic and Constituency Issues, 1983, 92, Managing for Profits, 1984, Small Business Management and Entrepreneurship, 1992. With U.S. Army, 1942-45, ETO. Fellow N. Am. Case Rsch. Assn. (sec., v.p., bd. dirs., pres. so. casewriters, Outstandinc Case Contbr. 1992), Acad. Mgmt., NACRA (past pres. adv. coun. 1998), Kiwanis, Sigma Iota Epsilon, Beta Gamma Sigma. Home and Office: 1640 Broadlands Dr Watkinsville GA 30677-2288

TATE, DANIEL CLYDE, JR., lobbyist, former legislative aide; b. Athens, Ga., Dec. 14, 1966; s. Danny Clyde and Ruth (McGaughey) T. BA, Amherst Coll., 1988. With spl. events CNN, Washington, 1989; legis. dir. Congressman W.J. Tanzin, Washington, 1989-93; dep. asst. sec. for House liaison US Dept. Energy, Washington, 1993-95; spl. asst. to Pres. for legis. affairs The White House, Washington, 1995—97; lobbyist Cassidy & Assoc., Washington, 1998—2000, Lemunyon Group, Washington, 2001—03, Capitol Solutions, Washington, 2003—. Field worker Mondale for Pres., Maine, 1984; issues aide Robb for Senate, Fairfax, Va., 1988; vol. Clinton-Gore Campaign, Washington and Pa., 1992. Avocations: lacrosse, golf, skiing. Office: Capitol Solutions 659 C St SE Washington DC 20003 Office Fax: 202-544-3350.*

TATE, DEBORAH TAYLOR, former commissioner; b. Murfreesboro, Tenn., 1956; d. Louis Carlton Taylor; m. William H. Tate; children: Will, Taylor, Carlton. BA, U. Tenn., 1977, JD, 1980. Cert.: Tenn. Supreme Ct. (Rule 31 Mediator). Atty., sr. policy advisor to Gov. Lamar Alexander and Gov. Don Sundquist, Tenn.; dir. Tenn. Regulatory Authority, 2000—06, chmn., 2003—04; commr. FCC, Washington, 2006—09. Former dir. state and local policy ctr. Vanderbilt Inst. for Pub. Policy Studies; guest lectr. Vanderbilt U.; chair bd. dirs. Centerstone; bd. mem. Vanderbilt Children's Hosp., Martha O'Bryan Center Found., Ct. Appointed Spl. Advocates. Elder Westminster Presbyn. Ch.; bd. mem. League of Women Voters, Tenn. Voices for Children, Tenn. Tomorrow, Inc. Recipient award for Outstanding Pub. Svc., Common Sense Media, Good Scout award, Boy Scouts of America, Carol Reilly award, NY State Broadcasters Assn., Touchstones of Leadership award for Pub. Svc., Women in Cable TV, YW award, Acad. Women of Achievement, Jerry Duvall Pub. Svc. award, Phoenix Ctr. for Advanced Pub. Policy Studies. Fellow: Nashville Bar Found.; mem.: Lawyer's Assn. for Women, Nashville Bar Assn. Republican.*

TATE, ELEANOR ANN, educational association administrator; d. Fred and Rachel Beckman; m. Robert Dennis Tate, Aug. 9, 1959; children: Michael, Susan. BA, U. Wyo., Laramie, 1958; MEd, U. Nev. Las Vegas, LA, 1983. Dir., profl. devel. ctr. U. Nev. Las Vegas, 1996—2004, coord., profl. devel. ctr., 2004—. Bd. mem. South Nev. Human Resource Assn., Las Vegas, ASTD, Nev. Adult Edn. Assn. Program developer (microcomputer programs devel.) (ASTD Chpt. Contbn. award, 1996, ASTD Disting. Svc. award, 1995). Leader Boy Scouts Am., Las Vegas, 1973—76; active & chmn. Jr. Mesquite, Las Vegas; sunday sch. dir. and tchr. Trinity Meth. Ch., Las Vegas, 1972—76. Mem.: PEO, Delta Delta Delta Alumni Assn. (pres. 1964—2008). Avocations: travel, sewing, reading, gardening. Home: 2408 Plaza Del Grande Las Vegas NV 89102 Office: Univ Nevada Las Vegas 4505 S Md Pky Las Vegas NV 89154-1019 Business E-Mail: ann.tate@unlv.edu.

TATE, HAROLD SIMMONS, JR., lawyer; b. Taylors, SC, Sept. 19, 1930; s. Harold Simmons and Cleone (Clayton) T.; m. Elizabeth Anne Coker, Dec. 22, 1952; children— Mary Elizabeth Anne, Martha Coker, Virginia Clayton. Degree in internat. law and rels. cum laude, Harvard U., 1951, postgrad., 1954, JD, 1956; MA, U. SC, 2005; PhD, U. SC., 2008. Bar: S.C. 1956. Ptnr. Haynsworth Sinkler Boyd, PA, Columbia, SC, 1962—. Chmn. adv. com. US Dist. Ct. (SC), 1984-2006; lectr. Am. Law Inst.-ABA seminars; adv. com. on rules and procedures US Ct. Appeals (4th cir.), 1990-95. Co-author: South Carolina Appellate Practice, 1985; bd. editors Federal Litigation Guide Reporter, 1985—; co-draftsman S.C. Rules of Evidence, 1995; contbr. articles and book revs. to profl. jours. Chmn. Richland County Mental Health Ctr., 1965-66; co-chmn. Columbia Hearing and Speech Ctr., 1962-64; mem. admission and scholarship com. Harvard U., 1961—; chmn. subcom. on legislation, legislation and fin. study commn. Gov.'s Adv. Group on Mental Health Planning, 1963-65; chmn. Columbia Bd. Supervisors of Registration, 1961-70; pres. Columbia Philharm. Orch., 1966-67, Town Theatre, 1967-70; bd. trustee Richland County Pub. Libr., 1973-78, Hist. Columbia Found., 1971-75, Caroliniana Soc., 1978—, Bostick Charitable Trust, 1968—, Archaeol. Rsch. Trust, 2000-2003; bd. mgrs. SC Hist. Soc., 1993-99, 2002-2008; commr. SC Commn. of Archives and History, 1995—; bd. dirs. Charleston Libr. Soc., 2009-. Capt. US Army, 1951—53. Recipient DuRant award Disting Pub. Svc., 2001. Fellow Am. Coll. Trial Lawyers; mem. ABA, Am. Law Inst., Am. Judicature Soc., SC Bar Assn., Assn. Bar City NY, Richland County Bar Assn., Harvard Law Sch. Assn. SC (sec.-treas. 1968-70, pres. 1988—), Columbia Drama Club (pres. 1963-64), Palmetto Club (sec. 1963-70, pres. 1973-76), Forum Club, Harvard Club NYC, Harvard Club SC, Carolina Yacht Club. Episcopalian. Office: Haynsworth Sinkler Boyd PA Fl 22 1201 Main St Ste 2200 Columbia SC 29201-3232 Home: 41 King St Charleston SC 29401 Office Phone: 803-779-3080. Business E-Mail: state@hsblawfirm.com.

TATE, JITENDRA S., engineering educator; s. Sarjerao B. and Kamal S. Tate; m. Sanyogita Deshpande; 1 child, Yash. PhD in Mech. Engring., NC A & T State U., Greensboro, 2004. Mfg. engr. Tata Motors, Pune, Maharashtra, India, 1986—87, Thermax Ltd., Pune, Maharashtra, 1990—91; lectr. mech. engring. Bharati Vidyapeeth's Coll. Engring., Pune, 1991—2000; grad. rsch. asst. NC A&T State U., 2000—04, rsch. assoc., 2004—05; asst. prof. mfg. engring. Ingram Sch. Engineeirng, Tex. State U., San Marcos, 2005—. Contbr. articles to profl. jours. Mem.: ASME, Soc. Advancement Material and Process Engring., Am. Soc. Engring. Edn. Liberal. Hindu. Achievements include research in mechanical and thermal performance of soy based polyurethane glass composites; automation of vacuum assisted resin transfer molding; development of fire retardant nano modified phenolic glass composites. Avocations: travel, reading, cricket. Office: Tex State Univ Ingram School Engineering San Marcos TX 78666 Office Fax: 512-245-7771. Personal E-mail: jittate@yahoo.com. Business E-Mail: jt31@txstate.edu.

TATE, JOHN TORRENCE, mathematics professor, researcher; b. Mpls., Mar. 13, 1925; BA, Harvard U., 1946; PhD, Princeton U., 1950. With Harvard U., 1954—90; Sid W. Richardson chair math. U. Tex., Austin, 1990—. Co-recipient Leroy P. Steele prize Am. Math. Soc., 1995, Cole prize in number theory, 1956, Wolf prize in math. Wolf Found., Israel, 2003. Mem. Nat. Acad. Scis., Academie des Scis. (Paris), mem. London Mathematical Society. Office: Univ Texas at Austin Dept Math 1 University Station C1200 Austin TX 78712-0257 Office Phone: 512-471-7127, 512-471-7711. Office Fax: 512-471-9038. E-mail: tate@math.utexas.edu.

TATE, JOHN WILLIAM, consumer products company executive, former food products executive; BA in Econs., U. Tex., 1972. Various fin. and gen. mgmt. positions Dole Food Co. Inc., Westlake Village, Calif.; CFO fresh vegetables divsn. Dole Food Co., 1993-96, CFO Dole Europe Paris, CFO Westlake Village, Calif., 1998—2000, Krispy Kreme Doughnuts, Inc., Winston-Salem, NC, 2000—02; COO Krispy Kreme Doughnuts Inc., Winston-Salem, NC, 2002—04; exec. v.p., COO Restoration Hardware, Inc., Corte Madera, Calif., 2004—. With USAF, 1973-79. Office: Restoration Hardware Inc 15 Koch Rd Ste J Corte Madera CA 94925

TATE, KRISTOPHER, Internet company executive; Lead web arch. Meetroduction LLC; founder, chief tech. officer BlueBridge Technologies Group, Japan, 2002—, Zooomr Inc., 2006—; co-founder, chief technologist AM6.jp, Japan, 2009—.

TATE, ROSEMARY, special education educator; b. Sept. 7, 1956; BS in Spl. Edn., U. DC, Washington, 1980, M in Reading, 1988. Non-categorical cert. spl. edn. K-12 DC, 1981. Spl. edn. tchr. DC Pub. Schs., Washington, 1985—. Mentor tchr. Trinity Coll., Washington, 2003. Leader Girl Scout Troop #3819; mem. Girl Scout Coun. Nation Capitol; supr. Jr. Usher Bd.; Sunday sch. tchr. Metropolitan AME Ch., Washington, asst. advisor, Young People's Dept., Sarah Allen Missionary Sch. Recipient cert. of appreciation, Howard U. Sch. Edn., Washington, 2006; Adopt-a-Classroom grantee, Washington, 2001—06, Opera for Students grantee, Washington Post, 2003—05. Mem.: Coun. Exceptional Children. Home: 761 Quebec Pl NW Washington DC 20010

TATE, SHEILA BURKE, public relations executive; b. Washington, Mar. 3, 1942; d. Eugene L. and Mary J. (Doherty) Burke; m. William J. Tate, May 2, 1981 (dec. Aug. 1998); children: Hager Burke Patton, Courtney Paige Patton Manzel; m. John K. Youel, Nov. 26, 2005. BA in Journalism, Duquesne U., 1964; postgrad. in mass comm., U. Denver, 1975—76. Rsch. asst. Westinghouse Air Brake Co.; asst. account exec. Falhgren and Assocs.; copywriter Ketchum, MacLeod and Grove, 1964—66; account exec. Burson-Marsteller Assocs., Pitts., 1967, sr. v.p. Washington, 1985—87; pub. rels. mgr. Colo. Nat. Bank, Denver, 1967—70; account exec. Hill and Knowlton, Inc., Houston, 1977—78, v.p. Washington, 1978—81; dep. to the chmn. Hill and Knowlton Inc., Washington, 1987—88; press sec. to First Lady White House, Washington, 1981—85; press sec. George Bush for Pres. Campaign, 1988; press sec. to Pres.-elect George Bush, 1988—89; vice chmn. Cassidy and Assocs. Pub. Affairs, Washington, 1989—91; pres. Powell Tate, Washington, 1991—99, vice-chmn., 1999—. Bd. dirs., former mem. Corp. for Pub. Broadcasting, vice chmn., 1990—92, chmn., 1992—94. Mem. nat. adv. bd. The Salvation Army; adv. bd. Am. Acad. Family Physicians, Kansas City, Kans. Mem.: Nat. Press Club, Belfair Club, Farmington Country Club, Washington Golf and Country Club, Duquesne U. Century Club. Office: Powell Tate 700 13th St NW Ste 1000 Washington DC 20005-5926 Home Phone: 703-536-0477. Business E-Mail: state@webershandwick.com.

TATE, STONEWALL SHEPHERD, lawyer; b. Memphis, Dec. 19, 1917; m. Janet Graf; children: Adele Shepherd, Shepherd Davis, Janet Reid Walker. BA, U. Southwestern (now Rhodes Coll.), Memphis, 1939; JD, U. Va., 1942; LLD (hon.), Samford U., 1979, Suffolk U., 1982, Capital U., 1989, Rhodes Coll., 1993. Bar: Va. 1941, Tenn. 1942. Chmn. emeritus Martin, Tate, Morrow & Marston, P.C. (and predecessor firms), Memphis, 1947—. Chmn. pres.'s coun. Rhodes Coll., 1995-96, sec. bd. trustees, 1967-77, 80-84. Pres. Episcopal Churchmen of Tenn., 1961-62; sec. standing com. Episcopal Diocese of Tenn., 1969-71; pres. Chickasaw Coun. Boy Scouts Am., 1967-78. With USNR, 1942-46; comdr. USNR; ret. Decorated Order of Cloud Banner (China); recipient Silver Beaver award Boy Scouts Am., 1963, Disting. Eagle Scout award, 1980, Disting. Svc. medal Rhodes Coll., 1978, Disting. Alumni award, 1991, Lawyers' Lawyer award Memphis Bar Assn., 1990; Memphis Rotary Club Civic Recognition award, 1983, Paul Harris fellow, 1985. Fellow Am. Bar Found., Am. Coll. Trust and Estate Counsel, Internat. Acad.

Estate and Trust Law, Coll. Law Practice Mgmt. (hon.), Tenn. Bar Found., Memphis Bar Found. (Benjamin L. Hooks award 2003), Shelby County Bar Found.; mem. ABA (chmn. standing com. on profl. discipline 1973-76, chmn. standing com. on scope and correlation of work 1977, chmn. task force on lawyer advt. 1977, pres. ABA 1978-79, chmn. standing com. on lawyer competence 1986-92, mem. coun. sr. lawyers divsn. 1997-2001, 2004-), Am. Judicature Soc. (past bd. dirs.), Am. Law Inst., Lawyer-Pilots Bar Assn., Tenn. Bar Assn. (pres. 1963-64, recipient of William M. Leech, Jr., Public Svc. award, 2005), Memphis and Shelby County Bar Assn. (pres. 1959-60), Nat. Conf. Bar Pres. (pres. 1972-73, Alumnus of Yr. 1996), U.S. 6th Cir. Jud. Conf. (life), U. Va. Law Sch. Alumni Assn. (mem. exec. coun. 1974-77), Rhodes Coll. Alumni Assn. (pres. 1951-53), Rotary (pres. 1982-83, bd. dirs. 1974, 80-84, 89-90, 2007-), Raven Soc., Order of Coif, Phi Beta Kappa, Omicron Delta Kappa, Phi Delta Phi, Sigma Alpha Epsilon (highest effort award N.Y.C. Alumni Assn. 1979). Office: Martin Tate Morrow & Marston PC 6410 Poplar Ave Ste 1000 Memphis TN 38119-4843 Business E-Mail: sstate@martintate.com.

TATEISHI, PETER, legislative staff member; married. Field rep., Rep. Daniel Lungren US House of Reps., Washington, 2005, intergovtl. affairs staff, Rep. Daniel Lungren, 2006—07, dep. chief of staff to Rep. Daniel Lungren, 2009—. Cons. Ione Band of Miwok Indians, Calif., 2008. Republican. Office: 2262 Rayburn House Office Bldg Washington DC 20515 Office Phone: 202-225-5716. Office Fax: 202-225-1298.*

TATEL, DAVID STEPHEN, federal judge; b. Washington, Mar. 16, 1942; s. Howard Edwin and Molly (Abramowitz) Tatel; m. Edith Sara Bassichis, Aug. 29, 1965; children: Rebecca, Stephanie, Joshua, Emily. BA, U. Mich., 1963; JD, U. Chgo., 1966. Bar: Ill. 1966. Instr. U. Mich., Ann Arbor, 1966—67; assoc. Sidley & Austin, Chgo. and Washington, 1967—69, 1970—72; dir. Chgo. Lawyer's Com., 1969—70, Nat. Lawyers Commn. for Civil Rights Under Law, Washington, 1972—74; assoc. Hogan & Hartson, Washington, 1974—77, ptnr., 1979—94; dir. Office for Civil Rights US Dept. Health Edn. & Welfare, Washington, 1977—79; judge US Ct. Appeals (DC cir.), Washington, 1994—. Lectr. Stanford U. Law Sch., 1991—92; co-chmn. Nat. Lawyers Com. for Civil Rights Under Law, Washington, 1989—91; chmn., bd. dirs. Spencer Found., Chgo., 1990—97. Bd. dirs. Carnegie Found. for Advancement in Tchg., Stanford, Calif., 1997—. Office: US Ct Appeals 333 Constitution Ave NW US Courthouse Washington DC 20001-2866*

TATLOCK, ANN, writer; married. Author: (novels) A Room of My Own, 1998 (Silver Angel award, Excellence in Media, 1999), A Place Called Morning, 1998, All the Way Home, 2002 (First Place Adult Fiction, Midwest Ind. Publ. Assn., 2002, Christy award Contemporary Fiction, 2003), I'll Watch the Moon, 2003 (First Place Gen. Fiction, Midwest Ind. Publ. Assn., 2003, Best of Genre Christian Fiction, Libr. Jour., 2003), Things We Once Held Dear, 2006. Mailing: Bethany House Publ 11400 Hampshire Ave Minneapolis MN 55438 E-mail: anntatlock@yahoo.com.

TATLOCK, ANNE M., retired trust company executive; b. White Plains, NY, July 1, 1939; d. John and Kathleen (McGrath) McNiff; m. William Tatlock, Apr. 29, 1967; children: Julina, Kerry, Christopher. BA, Vassar Coll., 1961; MA in Econs., NYU, 1968. 1st v.p. Smith Barney Harris Upham, NYC, 1962-84; exec. v.p. Fiduciary Trust Internat., NYC, 1984-94, pres., 1994—99, pres., CEO, 1999—2000, chmn., CEO, 2000—06, ret., 2006. Bd. dirs. Fortune Brands, Deerfield, Ill., Franklin Resources, San Mateo, Calif., Merck, NJ, Fiduciary Trust Internat. Trustee Am. Ballet Theatre, N.Y.C., 1994-, pres., 1998-2001; trustee Vassar Coll., 1994-2006, The Teagle Found., N.Y.C., 1995-2006; trustee Andrew W. Mellon Found., NYC, 1995—, chmn., 2003—; trustee Cultural Instns. Retirement Sys., NYC, 1989-2005, chmn., 1996-2001; trustee Howard Hughes Med. Inst., Md., 2000—, vice chmn. The Conf. Bd., NYC, 2001-08, Mayo Found., Minn., 2002—, Nat. Sept. 11 Meml. & Mus., 2005—. Fellow: Am. Acad. Arts and Scis. (elected 2004); mem.: Coun. on Fgn. Rels.

TATMAN, DAVID C., state banking agency administrator; Grad., U. Oreg. Sch. Law, 1981. Bar: Oreg. 1981. With Oreg. Divsn. Fin. & Corp. Securities, 1988—, chief enforcement securities sect., dep. adminstr., 2004—05, acting adminstr., 2005—06, adminstr., 2006—; spl. asst. atty. gen. Oreg. Dept. Justice. Office: Dept Consumer & Bus Svcs Divsn Fin and Corp Securities PO Box 14480 Salem OR 97309-0405 Office Phone: 503-378-4140. Office Fax: 503-947-7862. E-mail: david.c.tatman@state.or.us.*

TATOM, JOHN ANTHONY, economist; b. Little Rock, Dec. 8, 1945; s. Vaughn L. and Dorothy L. (Huggins) T.; m. Cecelia A. Chamberlain, Aug. 20, 1966 (div. 1982); children: Shawn, Sharon, Sydney; m. Kathleen I. Rudd, July 3, 1986; 1 stepchild, Todd K. Hentschel. BA, U. Dallas, 1967; MA, U. Chgo., 1968; PhD, Tex. A&M U., 1971. Asst. prof. econs. Albion (Mich.) Coll., 1971-73, U. Redlands (Calif.), 1973-75, U. Ga., Athens, 1975-76; sr. economist Fed. Res. Bank of St. Louis, 1976-82, rsch. officer, 1982-84, asst. v.p., 1984-95; v.p. Union Bank of Switzerland, 1995—98, exec. dir., 1998—2000; exec.-in-residence De-Paul U., Chgo., 2000—03; vis. prof., 2003—05; dir. rsch. Networks Fin. Inst., 2005—. Adj. assoc. prof. Washington U., St. Louis, 1985-87; sr. fellow Tax Found., 2003-04; assoc. prof. Ind. State U., 2005—. Editorial adv. bd. Jour. Econs. and Bus., 1985-95; contbr. articles to profl. jours. Mem. Am. Econ. Assn., Nat. Assn. Bus. Economists (chpt. v.p. 1990-91, pres. 1991-92), Missouri Valley Econs. Assn. (bd. dirs. 1983-85, pres. 1993-94), Western Econs. Assn. Home: 8633 Gordonshire Dr Indianapolis IN 46278 Office: Networks Fin Inst 2902 N MeridianSt Indianapolis IN 46208 Office Phone: 317-536-0281 ext 712. Business E-Mail: john.tatom@isunetworks.org.

TATREAU, (DOLORES) MAXINE, artist; b. Minden, Iowa, Sept. 6, 1929; d. Charles Ross Teninty and Hester Evaline Peterson Teninty Hadfield; m. Donald Max Tatreau, Aug. 18, 1949; children: Douglas M., Dean M., Kevin L. Student, U. No. Iowa, 1947, Iowa State Tchrs. Coll, U. Nebr., Omaha. Receptionist, typesetter Neola (Iowa) Gazette Newspaper, 1946—47; rural sch. tchr. Neola, 1947—48; office worker Orchard and Wilhelm Furniture Co., Omaha, 1948—50; comptometer operator Western Elec., Omaha, 1950—53; office worker Western Elec. (AT&T Tech.), Omaha, 1969—86; artist Tatreau Studio, 1972—; represented by Wickwire Gallery, Hendersonville, NC, Carolina Gallery Art, Spartenburg, SC, Twigs & Leave, Waynesville, NC. Pres. Art League Henderson County, 2004. Exhibitions include Kans. Watercolor Soc. Competition (Purchase award, 1988), Rocky Mountain Nat. Watercolor Soc., Phi Theta Kappa Six State Regional Competition, Brand Libr. and Art Gallery, Glendale, Calif., Passageway Gallery, Omaha, Asheville Gallery of Art, 2000—04, Aberdale, Wales, 2004, many others, invitational exhibitions, Edina Art Ctr., Mpls., Conn Gallery, Landrum, SC, Wichita Art Gallery, Kans., Statehouse Gallery, Lincoln, Nebr., many others, numerous corp. and pvt. collections in US and Europe. Den mother Boys Scouts Am., Omaha; wedding coord. 1st Luth. Ch., Omaha, Sunday sch. tchr., children's summer bible sch. leader, circle leader. Mem.: Kans. Watercolor Soc. (signature) (Purchase award), So. Watercolor Soc., Upstate Visual Arts Greenville, SC, Watercolor Soc. NC, Tryon Painters and Sculptors, Nat. Watercolor Soc., Art League Henderson County, Internat. Soc. Exptl. Artists (signature), Nat. Mus. Women (charter). Lutheran. Avocations: golf, bridge, jewelry making, quilting, church choir. Home and Studio: 2701 Kalmia Ln Hendersonville NC 28791-1838

TATSURO, BABA, health products executive, medical educator; b. Shimonoseki, Yamaguchi, Japan, Feb. 6, 1958; s. Shigeo and Asako Baba; m. Masako Baba, Nov. 29, 1990; 1 child, Yusuke Baba. BS in Precision Engring., Osaka U., Japan, 1981, MS in Precision Engring., 1983; DEng (hon.), Kobe U., Japan, 2006. Dep. mgr. ultrasound sys. devel. dept. Toshiba Med. Sys. Corp., Otawara, Japan, 1983—. Contbr. articles to profl. jours. Fellow: Japan Soc. Ultrasonics Medicine; mem.: IEEE, Acoustical Soc. Japan, Profl. Engrs. Assn. Japan. Avocations: movies, music, baseball, computers. Home: 1920-2 Usuba Otawara 324-0035 Japan Office: 1385 Shimoishigami Otawara 324-8550 Japan Business E-Mail: baba@us.nasu.toshiba.co.jp, ezdo03014@nifty.ne.jp.

TATSUTA, KUNIAKI, organic chemistry educator; b. Osaka, Japan, Dec. 1, 1940; s. Naraji and Sadame (Ohnishi) T.; m. Yoko Nakamura, Apr. 28, 1965; children: Yoshiyuki, Hiroyuki, Miwa. B., Keio U., Yokohama, Japan, 1963, M., 1965, PhD, 1968. Researcher Takeda Chems., Osaka, 1968-69; asst. dept. applied chemistry Keio U., Yokohama, 1969-73, asst. prof. dept. applied chemistry, 1973-77; postdoctoral fellow dept. chemistry Harvard U., Cambridge, Mass., 1973-75; assoc. prof. dept. applied chemistry Keio U., Yokohama, 1977-86, prof. dept. applied chemistry, 1986-92, Waseda U., Tokyo, 1993—. Vis. prof. dept. chemistry Cambridge (Eng.) U., 1988-89, Oxford U., Eng., 2006; chmn. dept. applied chemistry Keio U., Yokohama, 1991-92; chmn. dept. applied chemistry Waseda U., Tokyo, 2000-02, dean Grad. Sch. Sci. and Engring., 2004—. Recipient Imperial medal with Purple Ribbon (Emperor), 2002, Fujihara award, 2008, prize, Japan Acad., 2009. Mem. Japan Antibiotics Rsch. Assn. (councilor 1980—, Sumiki-Umezawa award 1988), Soc. Organic Synthetic Chemistry (v.p. 1989-91, pres., 2004—, award 1998), Chem. Soc. Japan (v.p. 1990—, award 1985, 2001), Fujihara award, 2008, Japan Acad. prize, 2009. Home: 2-26-7 Matsunoki Suginami 166-0014 Japan Office: Waseda U Grad Sch Sci Engr 3-4-1 Ohkubo Shinjuku 169-8555 Japan

TATTA, JOSEPH, language educator; b. Toro, Molise, Italy, Dec. 24, 1933; arrived in US, 1947; s. Andrea and Louise Jean Tatta; m. Carol Tatta; children: Jo, Andrew, Sue, Ben. BA, Eastern U., St. Davids, 1955; MA, U. Penn., Phila., 1957. History tchr. Thehaverford Sch., Pa., 1958—95; Italian instr. Am. Coll., Pa., 1975, Villanova U., 1995—97, Mainline Sch. Adults, Pa., 1964—, Eastern U., St. Davids, 2004—. Exec. dir. Am. Film Ctr., St. Davids, Pa., 1962—98; pres. Circolo Italiano, Strafford, Pa., 2009—; exec. sec. Phila Area Soccer Coach Assn., Pa., 1977—. Vice pres. Valley Book Civic Assn., Wayne, Pa., 1960—65; mem. Radnor Sch. Bd. Ad Hoc Com., 1970; coach Wayne Little League, 1970—80. Recipient Knight award, Govt. Italy, 2007; named one of Outstanding Men of America. Mem.: Circolo Mainline (pres. 1999—). Independent. Roman Catholic. Avocations: reading, walking, cooking. Home: 341 Rock Land Rd Wayne PA 19087

TATTER, STEPHEN BRADLEY, neurosurgeon, educator; b. St. Joseph, Mich., July 20, 1960; s. Jordan Bradley and Mary Ellen Tatter; m. Kathleen Marie Ghiorsi, May 19, 1990; children: Grace Susanna, Abigail Elizabeth, James Bradley, John Stephen. BS, U. Mich., Ann Arbor, 1982; PhD, Rockefeller U., NY, 1989; MD, Cornell U. Med. Coll., NY, 1990. Diplomate neurol. surgeon Am. Bd. Neurol. Surgery, 2004. Fellow Harvard U., Cambridge, Mass., 1991—97; Dixie & Liang Yee Soo prof. dept. neurosurgery Wake Forest U. Sch. Medicine, Winston-Salem, NC, 1997—. Contbr. articles to profl. jours. Pres. Forsyth, Stokes, Davie County Med. Soc., Winston-Salem, NC, 2008. Mem.: Am. Assn. Neurol. Surgeons. Achievements include research in delivery of therapeutic agents into the brain. Office: Wake Forest Univ Sch Medicine Med Ctr Boulevard Winston Salem NC 27157-1029

TATUM, ARTHUR, III, lexicographer, educator, pianist; b. Sumpter, SC, July 7, 1935; s. Art Tatum and Lillie Bell. Cert. tchr. Prin. Youth in Action, NYC, 1964-67; prin., tutor Cmty. Action, NYC, 1968-72; performer Jazz Hall of Fame, LA, 1975-79; music tutor Morgan Coll., Balt., 1980-83, Coppin State Coll., Balt., 1985-90, lang. tutor, 1995-96. Author: (Ebonese dictionary) Afro American Language, 1994, (gospel in ebonese) Gospel According to St. Matthew, 1996, Solar-Harmonic Systems (original method for reading and writing music). Lang. tutor Neighborhood Youth Corp., Charles Villa Balt., 1995-97. Avocations: sand-lot baseball, golf, table-tennis.

TATUM, BEVERLY DANIEL, academic administrator, writer, psychology and education educator; b. Tallahaassee, Sept. 27, 1954; d. Robert Alphonse and Catherine Faith (Maxwell) Daniel; m. Travis James Tatum, July 28, 1979; children: Travis Jonathan Daniel, David Alexander Daniel. BA, Wesleyan U., 1975; MA in Psychology, U. Mich., 1976, PhD, 1984; MA in Religious Studies, Hartford Seminary. Lic. clin. psychologist. Asst. prof. Dept. Psychology Westfield State Coll., Mass., 1983—86, assoc. prof. Mass., 1986—89; assoc. prof. Dept. Psychology and Edn. Mt. Holyoke Coll., South Hadley, Mass., 1989—96, prof., 1996—, dept. chair, 1997—98, dean, v.p. student affairs, 1998—2002, acting pres., 2002; pres. Spelman Coll., Atlanta, 2002—. Lectr. dept. black studies U. Calif., Santa Barbara, 1980-83, counseling psychologist, 1979-83; vis. scholar Stone Ctr., Wellesley Coll., 1991-92; chair, bd. dirs. Equity Inst., Emeryville, Calif., 1987-89; bd. dirs. Ga. Power, 2008- Author: Assimilation Blues: Black Families in a White Community, 1987, Why Are All the Black Kids Sitting Together in the Cafeteria?: And Other Conversations About Race, 1997, Can We Talk About Race?: And Other Conversations in an Era of School Resegregation, 2007; contbr. articles to profl. jours. Recipient Brock Internat. Prize in Edn., 2005; named one of The 100 Most Influential Georgians, Ga. Trend mag., 2008; fellow APA Minority Program, 1976—79, U. Calif., 1980—81, Ford Found., 1991. Mem. APA, Am. Psychol. Soc., Ea. Psychol. Assn., Mass. Psychol. Assn., Assn. Women in Psychology, Assn. Black Psychologists, Atlanta Rotary Club, Metro Atlanta C. of C. Office: Spelman Coll Office of Pres 350 Spelman Lane SW Atlanta GA 30314-4399

TATUM, CHANNING, actor; b. Cullman, Ala., Apr. 26, 1980; m. Jenna Dewan, July 11, 2009. Actor: (films) Coach Carter, 2005, Supercross, 2005, Havoc, 2005, She's the Man, 2006 (Choice Breakout Make, Teen Choice Awards, 2006), Step Up, 2006, A Guide to Recognizing Your Saints, 2006 (co-recipient Best Actor, Gijón Internat. Film Festival, Special Jury Prize, Sundance Film Festival, 2006), Battle in Seattle, 2007, The Trap, 2007, Step Up 2: The Streets, 2008, Stop-Loss, 2008 (Choice Movie Actor: Drama, Teen Choice Awards, 2008), Fighting, 2009, Public Enemies, 2009, (guest appearance): (TV series) CSI: Miami, 2004. Avocation: Kung Fu. Office: c/o Management 360 9111 Wilshire Blvd Beverly Hills CA 90210*

TATUM, MARK A., sports association executive; b. 1969; m. Lisa Skeete Tatum; children: Tai Aidan, Kylan Ming. BS in Bus. Mgmt. & Mktg., Cornell U., 1991; MBA, Harvard Bus. Sch., 1998. Sales mgr. Proctor and Gamble Co., 1991—95; with sports mktg. dept. Pepsi-Cola Co., 1997; regional sales mgr. Clorox Co., 1995—97; with corp. sponsorship and mktg. dept. Maj. League Baseball, 1999—2000; v.p. bus. devel. NBA, 1999, sr. dir., grp. mgr. mktg. properties, dir. mktg. partnerships, 2001—04, sr. v.p. mktg. partnerships, 2004—09, exec. v.p. mktg. partnerships, 2009—. Cornell Black Alumni Assn.; Cornell Alumni Mentor Prog. Named one of 40 Under 40, Sports Bus. Jour., 2006—08. Office: NBA Olympic Tower 645 5th Ave Fl 10 New York NY 10022*

TATUPU, LOFA, professional football player; b. San Diego, Nov. 15, 1982; s. Mosi Tatupu. Attended, U. Maine, U. So. Calif., LA. Linebacker Seattle Seahawks, 2005—. Named 1st Team All-Pro, AP, 2007; named to All-Rookie Team, PWF/PFWA, 2005, Nat. Football Conf. Pro Bowl Team, NFL, 2005—07. Achievements include being a member of the Bowl Championship Series, National Championship winning University of Southern California Trojans, 2003, 2004. Office: Seattle Seahawks 800 Occidental Ave S Ste 200 Seattle WA 98134*

TATUSOVA, TATIANA A., research scientist; d. Akop Gasparovich Mamikonov and Larisa Konstantinovna Mamikonova; children: Alexey Tatusov, Michael Tatusov. PhD, Moscow State U., 1988. Sci. fellow Inst. Molecular Biology, Moscow, 1988—93; sr. data analyst MSD Inc., Bethesda, Md., 1993—98; staff scientist NIH, Bethesda, 1998—. Author: (sci. book) BioInformatics. Russian folk music KAP US, Bethesda, 1998—2008. Recipient Performance award, NIH, 2005. Mem.: ASM. Achievements include research in web design and develpoment. Office: NIH 9000 Rockville Pike Bethesda MD 20892

TATYREK, ALFRED FRANK, retired chemist, environmental engineer; b. Hillside, NJ, Jan. 23, 1930; s. Frank Peter and Frances (Luxa) T. BS, Seton Hall U., 1954; postgrad., Rutgers U., 1956—57. Rsch. chemist Bakelite divsn. Union Carbide, Bloomfield, NJ, 1953—58, U.S. Radium Corp., Morristown, NJ, 1958—62; analytical chemist insp. Chem. Procurement Dist. U.S. Army, NYC, 1962—64, rsch. chemist Picatinny Arsenal Dover, NJ, 1964—73; chem. materials engr. U.S. Army Armament Rsch., Devel. and Engring. Ctr., NJ, 1973—95; ret. Cons. pyrotechnics, polymer materials and environ. chemistry. Patentee pyrotechnic compositions, chemiluminescent compounds and processes, crank case oil vacuum purification sys. for internal combustion engines, method for the removal of thermoset potting compound from the electronics package of a munitions item; lectr., contbr. publ. on mountaineering expdns. and adventures in the great mountain ranges of N.Am., S.Am., Europe and Africa to mags.; contbr. more than 50 sci. and tech. publs. 1st aid instr. ARC, Essex County, NJ, 1969-82; chief 1st aid Maplewood CD, NJ, 1971-91; patrol dir. Nat. Ski Patrol, Phoenicia, NY, 1978-84, sr. status, 1979-, lifetime Nat. Ski patroller So. NY and NJ region, 1993-; life mem. Blood Ctr. NJ. Staff sgt. NJ Air N.G., 1948-57. Decorated Comdr.'s Pub. Svc. award US Army, 1996; recipient 35 Yr. Svc. award Nat. Ski Patrol, 2006, 35 Yr. Svc. awrd, 2006. Mem. Nat. Soc. Inventors, Sigma Xi Sci. Rsch. Soc. (pres. Picatinny chpt. 1974-75, 79-80, 85-86), Nat. Assn. Underwater Instrs. (cert. basic and advanced diver and underwater photographer 1971-, cert. Nitrox diving 1999), Magician's Roundtable, Internat. Magicians Soc. (life), Alpine Club Can. (life), N.J. Animal Rights Alliance, Appalachian Mountain Club (life; hiking leader), Sierra Club. Roman Catholic. Climbed 15,771 feet Mt. Blanc, highest mountain peak in Europe; climbed to highest summit on Point Uruhu on 19,730 feet on Mt. Kilimanjaro, highest mountain peak in Africa, 1972; leader of climb on Matterhorn and Monte Rosa, Switzerland's highest peak; mountain expdns. in U.S. and Can. including 3 first ascents in No. Cascades of Wash. (S.E. ridge of Mt. Goode, Aug. 1963, Peak 7732 via the Snow Chute, Aug. 1964, East ridge of Bear Mountain Aug. 1964); undersea photography expeditions to Caribbean and South Pacific coral reefs. Home: 27 Orchard Rd Maplewood NJ 07040-1919 Personal E-mail: atatyrek@verizon.net. *"God has given us a world rich in physical and intellectual beauty as well as intriguing scientific discovery. To earn these rewards we must seek out and meet the challanges of life, not as distasteful burdens, but as true opportunities upon which to build where others have failed or left off, using all the infinite resources that God has given to all of us".*

TAUB, EDWARD, psychology researcher; b. Bklyn., Oct. 22, 1931; s. Samuel Hart and Ida Pearl (Kimmel) T.; m. Mildred Allen Taub, Aug. 13, 1959. BA, Bklyn. Coll., 1953; MA, Columbia U., 1959; PhD, NYU, 1969. Rsch. asst. Columbia U., NYC, 1956; rsch. asst. dept. exptl. neurology Jewish Chronic Disease Hosp., NYC, 1957-60, rsch. assoc., 1960-68; dir. Behavioral Biology Ctr., Inst. for Behavioral Rsch., 1968-83; assoc. dir. Inst. for Behavioral Rsch., 1978-83; univ. prof. psychology U. Ala., Birmingham, 1986—2000, 2000—; standing guest prof. U. Konstanz, Germany, 1995—2002; guest prof. U. Jena, Germany, 1996—2002. Asst. prof. dept. psychiatry Johns Hopkins U., Balt., 1972-82; vis. prof. grad. program dept. psychology CUNY, 1984-85; vis. prof. U. Tuebingen, U. Muenster, Humboldt U., Germany, 1993—2001. Contbr. articles to profl. jours. Recipient Pioneering Rsch. Contbn. award, 1989, Disting. Scientist of 1998 award, Assn. of Applied Psychophysiology and Biofeedback, Ireland prize for scholarly distinction, U. Ala., Birmingham, 1997, Humboldt Rsch. award, 2000; fellow Guggenheim Found., 1983—84. Fellow AAAS (pres. psychol. sect. 2009), APA (exec. com. divsn. 6, Disting. Sci. award for the applications of psychology 2004), Soc. for Behavioral Medicine, Am. Psychol. Soc. (charter, William James Fellow award 1997); mem. Soc. for Neurosci. (named one of 10 leading translational rsch. projects in neurosci. in the 20th Century 2003), Biofeedback Soc. Am. (pres. 1978-79, Outstanding Rsch. Contbn. award 1988), Am. Physiol. Soc. (exec. com. neurosci. sect. 1988-91). Achievements include invention of technique of thermal biofeedback; Constraint-Induced Movement therapy for rehabilitation for stroke, traumatic brain injury, spinal cord injury, cerebral palsy and other motor disorders due to neurological injury. Office: U Ala at Birmingham 712 CPM 1530 3d Ave S Birmingham AL 35294-0018 Office Phone: 205-934-2471. Business E-Mail: etaub@uab.edu.

TAUB, JESSE J., electrical engineering researcher; b. NYC, Apr. 27, 1927; s. Julius and Ida (Orlansky) T.; m. Eva Pollack, Dec. 24, 1955 (dec. Nov. 1973); children: Richard Lawrence, Jocelyn Cara, Suzanne Mara; m. Naomi Etta Trachtenberg, June 30, 1974. BEE, CCNY, 1948; MEE, Poly. U., 1949. Group leader microwave electronics, Material Lab. USN, Bklyn., 1949-55; engr. Airborne Instruments Lab., Mineola, NY, 1955-58, sect. leader, 1958-61, engring. cons., 1961-75; chief scientist AIL Systems Inc., Melville, NY, 1975-93; cons., 1993—. Mem. engring. adv. bd. N.Y. Tech., Hofstra U. Author: (with others) Microwave Measurements, 1963; contbr. numerous papers to profl. publs.; patentee microwave techniques With USN, 1945-46. Fellow IEEE (Centennial medal 1984, 3rd Millenium medal 2000, C.A. Fowler award 1993, Region 1 awards 2001, 06, adminstrv. com. 1972-74, program chmn. microwave symposium, steering com., chmn. L.I. sect. awards, USAB Divsn. award 2002); mem. Archaeology Inst. Am., LI Soc. (v.p.).

Democrat. Jewish. Avocations: classical musician, contract bridge, archaeology. Home and Office: 115 Northgate Cir Melville NY 11747-3045 Personal E-mail: jjtaub@aol.com.

TAUB, MARY LOUISE, biochemist; b. Chgo., Sept. 26, 1948; d. Theodore William and Judith (Marcus) T. BA, U. Calif., San Diego, 1971; PhD, U. Calif., Santa Barbara, 1976. Postdoctoral fellow U. Calif., San Diego, 1976-79; asst. prof. biochemistry SUNY, Buffalo, 1979-85, assoc. prof. biochemistry, 1985—. Office: SUNY 140 Farber Hall Dept Of Biochemistry Buffalo NY 14214

TAUB, RICHARD PAUL, social sciences educator; b. Bklyn., Apr. 16, 1937; s. Martin Glynn and Frances (Israel) T.; m. Doris Susan Leventhal, Aug. 14, 1961 (dec. Feb. 1996); children: Neela Robin, Zachariah Jacob; m. Betty G. Farrell, June 21, 2000. BA, U. Mich., 1959; MA, Harvard U., Cambridge, Mass., 1962, PhD in Social Relations, 1966. Asst. prof. sociology Brown U., Providence, 1965-69; from asst. prof. to Paul Klapper prof. of social scis. U. Chgo., 1969—, assoc. dean Coll. of Univ., 1982-86, chmn. dept. comparative human devel., 2000—09. Adv. bd. Neighborhood Preservation Initiative, 1993-2000; chair adv. bd. Nat. Comty. Devel. Initiative, 1991-95; dir. South Ark. Rural Devel. Study, 1988-96; Disting. visitor Mac Arthur Found., 1998. Author: Bureaucrats Under Stress, 1969; (with D. Garth Taylor and Jan Dunham) Paths of Neighborhood Change, 1984, Community Capitalism, 1988; (with Doris L. Taub) Entrepreneurship in India's Small Scale Industries, 1989, Doing Development in Arkansas, 2004; (with William Julius Wilson) There Goes the Neighborhood, 2006; editor: (with Doris L. Taub) American Society in Tocqueville's Time and Today, 1974; contbr. articles to profl. jours. Chmn. bd. St. Thomas the Apostle Sch., Chgo., 1983-86; bd. dirs. Hyde Park Kenwood Cmty. Conf., Chgo., 1972-75; bd. seminary Coop Bookstore, Chgo., 1994—. Angell scholar U. Mich., 1956; Woodrow Wilson fellow Harvard U., 1959-60, W.E.B. DuBois Inst. fellow, 1997-98; grantee Am. Inst. Indian Studies, Ford Found., MacArthur Found., NSF, Wieboldt Found., Nat. Inst. Justice; recipient Quanctrell award U. Chgo., 1976, Outstanding Grad. Tchg. award U. Chgo., 2004. Mem. Am. Sociol. Assn., Midwest Sociol. Soc. Avocations: hiking, music. Office: Univ Chgo 5730 S Woodlawn Ave Chicago IL 60637 Office Phone: 773-702-3971. Business E-Mail: rpt2@uchicago.edu.

TAUB, ROBERT G., legislative staff member; b. Gloversville, NY, Oct. 12, 1964; m. Cynthia L. Jorgenson, Aug. 12, 1964; 2 children. BS in Polit. Sci. cum laude, Am. U., Washington, 1986, MA in Polit. Sci., 1987. Dist. staff asst. for Glenn Harris NY State Assembly, 1979—81; administr. Convention II, Inc., 1983—84; staff asst. for Rep. Sherwood L. Boehlen US House of Reps., staff asst. for Rep. Peter W. Rodino Jr., 1984—86, staff dir. Subcom. Postal Svc. House Com. on Gov. Reform, 1998—2001; chief of staff for Rep. John McHugh US House Rep., Washington, 2000—; staff assoc. Fulton County Planning Dept., 1985; rsch. asst. for Austin Mitchell Mem. of Parliament British House of Commons; staff asst. Mark A. Siegel & Assoc. Inc., 1987; evaluator Gen. Acctg. Office, 1987—89, eveluator to sr. evaluator San Francisco, 1990—95, profl. staff mem. chief investigator to sr. profl. staff mem., 1995—97; rsch. dir. Lee L. Verstandig & Assoc. Inc., 1990. Recipient Special Commendation award, Gen. Acctg. Office, 1988, 1989, 1993, Outstanding Performance award, 1993, 1994. Mem.: Pi Sigma Alpha, Pi Alpha Alpha. Jewish. Office: Office of Congressman John McHugh 438 Cannon House Office Bldg Washington DC 20515*

TAUB, THEODORE CALVIN, lawyer; b. Springfield, Mass., Jan. 1, 1935; s. Samuel and Sara Lee (Daum) T.; m. Roberta Mae Ginsburg, Aug. 23, 1959; children: Tracy, Andrew, Adam. AB, Duke U., 1956; JD, U. Fla., 1960. Bar: Fla., 1960, U.S. Supreme Ct. Atty. Shumaker, Loop & Kendrick, LLP, Tampa. Asst. city atty. City of Tampa, 1963-67; city atty. City of Temple Terrace, Fla., 1974-2007; panelist in field. Contbr. articles to profl. jours. Chmn. Tampa-Hillsborough (Fla.) County Expy. Authority, 1974-84; mem. Hillsborough County Charter Commn., 1966-69, Local Govt. Mgmt. Efficiency Com., 1979, State of Fla. Environ. Efficiency Study Commn., 1986-88; founder Tampa Bay Performing Arts Ctr. Fellow: Am. Bar Found; mem. ABA (chmn. real property litigation com. 1981-86, chmn. com. on housing and urban environ. 1989-91), Am. Coll. Real Estate Lawyers (bd. govs.), Am. Land Title Assn. (lenders' counsel group), Fla. Bar Assn. (bd. cert. real estate lawyer), Fla. Jaycees (pres.), Tau Epsilon Phi. Democrat. Jewish. Home: 4937 Lyford Cay Rd Tampa FL 33629-4828 Office: Bank of Am 101 E Kennedy Blvd Ste 2800 Tampa FL 33602-5869 Office Phone: 813-227-2351. Business E-Mail: ttaub@slk-law.com.

TAUBENFELD, HARRY S., lawyer; b. Bklyn., June 27, 1929; s. Marcus Isaac and Anna (Engelhard) T.; m. Florence Spatz, June 17, 1956; children: Anne Gail Weisbrod, Stephen Marshall. BA, Bklyn. Coll., 1951; JD, Columbia U., 1954. Bar: NY 1955, U.S. Supreme Ct. 1965, U.S. Dist. Ct. (so. and ea. dists.) NY 1976. Assoc. Benjamin H. Schor, Bklyn., 1955-58; ptnr. Zuckerbrod & Taubenfeld, Cedarhurst, NY, 1958—. Village atty. Village of Cedarhurst, 1977-88, trustee, 1989-2001; mem. bd. Downtown Cedarhurst Bus. Improvement Dist., 1993; legis. chmn., counsel Nassau County Village Ofcls., 1979-86, v.p., 1991-93, pres., 1993-94, mem. exec. com., 1989-99, chmn. intergovtl. liaison com., 1991-93; mem. legis. com. NY State Conf. Mayors, 1979-87, 92-93; mem. exec. bd. Tri-County Village Ofcls., 1991-95, pres., 1993-94; arbitrator Am. Arbitration Assn. Dist. Ct. Nassau County, 1980—, Assessment Rev. Panel, Supreme Ct., Nassau County, 1981—; mem. Constl. Bicentennial Com., 1987-89; adv. bd. First Am. Title Ins. Co. of N.Y., 2004-. Del. World Zionist Congress, 1977, 82, 87; mem. Zionist Gen. Coun., 1977-83; assoc. chmn. Am. Zionist Fedn., 1985-87; pres. Herut Zionists Am., 1977-79; v.p. Hartman YMHA, 1983-87; hon. trustee Cong. Beth Shalom, Lawrence, N.Y., 1990-2001; nat. bd. dir. Zionist Orgn. Am.; bd. govs. Jewish Agy., 1983-92; mem. exec. com. World Zionist Orgn., 1983-92; trustee United Jewish Appeal, 1986-91; bd. dir. United Israel Appeal, 1986-91; hon. vice chmn., bd. dir. Jewish Nat. Fund, 1987-89; nat. bd. dir. Am. for a Safe Israel; hon. pres. World Coun. Herut Hatzoa, Jerusalem, Internat. Bd. Youthtown of Israel. Recipient Centenial award Jabotinsky Found. 1981, Betar Youth award World Betar 1982, award Internat. League for Repatriation of Russian Jews 1977, Youth Towns of Israel Leadership award 1973, Israel Bonds Leadership award 1976, Life Time Achievement award Israel Bonds 1991, Defender of Jerusalem award 1991, Israel Bonds Menachem Begin Leadership award, 1999. Mem.: Internat. Assn. Jewish Lawyers and Jurists, Beth El Synagogue Ctr. New Rochelle, NY, Zionist Orgn. Am. (nat. bd. 1996—), B'nai B'rith, Jewish War Vets. Home: 21 N Chatsworth Ave Larchmont NY 10538 Office: 575 Chestnut St Cedarhurst NY 11516-2223 Personal E-mail: handf21n@verizon.net.

TAUBER, MARK J., retired lawyer; b. Detroit, Mar. 25, 1949; s. Max M. and Beatrice R. (Roth) T.; m. Anita L. Tilben, June 23, 1970; children: Melissa A., Benjamin M., Allison B. BA with honors, U. Mich., 1970; JD with honors, George Washington U., 1973. Bar: D.C. 1973, Md. 1974, US Dist. Ct. (DC, MD. dist.), US Ct. Appeals (1st, 3d, 4th, 7th, 11th, DC cir.), US Supreme Ct. 1980. From assoc. to ptnr. Pierson, Ball & Dowd, Washington, 1973—82; ptnr., chair comm. practice group Piper & Marbury, Washington, 1982—99; ptnr. Piper, Marbury, Rudnick & Wolfe, Washington, 1999—2002; ptnr., chair comm. practice group Piper Rudnick LLP, Washington, 2002—04; ptnr., chair comm., e-commerce and privacy practice group DLA Piper, Washington, 2005—06; ret., 2007. Assoc. editor: George Washington Law Rev., 1972—73. Home: 110 St Martin Dr Palm Beach Gardens FL 33418 Office Phone: 561-626-4632. Office Fax: 561-626-0174.

TAUBES, CLIFFORD HENRY, mathematician, educator; b. Rochester, NY, 1954; AB, Cornell U., 1975; PhD in Physics, Harvard U., Cambridge, Mass., 1980. Postgraduate fellowship Harvard U., Cambridge, 1980—83; prof. math U. Calif., Berkeley, 1983—85, Harvard U., 1985—, William Petschek prof. math., chair math. dept., 2005—. Recipient Oswald Veblen Geometry prize Am. Math. Soc., 1991, Elie Cartan prize French Math. Soc., 1993, Clay Rsch. award, 2008; co-recipient Shaw prize for Mathematical Sciences, The Shaw Prize Found., 2009 Fellow: Am. Assn. Advancement Sci.; mem.: NAS (Award in Mathematics 2008), Am. Acad. Sci. Office: Math Dept 504 Science Ctr Harvard U 1 Oxford St Cambridge MA 02138-2901 Office Phone: 617-495-5579. Office Fax: 617-495-5132. Business E-Mail: chtaubes@math.harvard.edu.*

TAUBIN, ALEXANDER, computer scientist, educator; b. Leningrad, May 16, 1953; arrived in Japan, 1993; s. Rafail and Leonora (Rivlina) T.; m. Tatiana Magnitskaia, July 6, 1996. MSc, Elec. Engring. Inst., Leningrad, 1976; PhD, Elec. Engring. Inst., 1981. Engr. Krasnaya Zaria Co., Leningrad, 1976-78; researcher Inst. for Socio-Econ. Problems, Leningrad, 1978-89; sr. researcher TRASSA Rsch. & Devel. Co., St. Petersburg, Russia, 1989-93; prof. U. Aizu, Aizu-Wakamutsu, Japan, 1993—. Co-author: Self-Timed Control of Concurrent Processes, 1990, Concurrent Hardware, 1994. Mem. IEEE (sr.), Assn. Computing Machinery. Office Phone: 617-353-1235. Business E-Mail: taubin@bu.edu.

TAUBMAN, A. ALFRED, real estate developer; b. Pontiac, Mich., Jan. 31, 1924; s. Philip and Fannie Ester (Blustin) T.; m. Reva Kolodney, Dec. 1, 1949 (div. July 1977); children: Gayle Kalisman, Robert S., William S.; m. Judith Mazor, June 17, 1982. Student, U. Mich., 1945-48, LLD (hon.), 1991; student, Lawrence Inst. Tech., 1948-49, DArch (hon.), 1985; D in Bus. (hon.), Eastern Mich. U., 1984; D in Edn. (hon.), Mich. State U., 1993; HHD (hon.), No. Mich. U., 1995. Chmn. The Taubman Co., Bloomfield Hills, Mich., 1950—, Taubman Ctrs., Inc., Bloomfield Hills, Mich., 1992—. Prin. shareholder Sotheby's Holdings, Inc., N.Y.C., 1983-2001. Author: Threshold Resistance: The Extraordinary Career of a Luxury Retailing Pioneer, 2007. Trustee Ctr. for Creative Studies, Detroit, Harper-Grace Hosps., Detroit; chmn. emeritus Archives Am. Art Smithsonian Inst., Washington, U. Pa. Wharton Real Estate Ctr., Phila.; pres. Arts Commn. of Detroit; mem. nat. bd. Smithsonian Assocs.; established Taubman Ctr. for State and Local Govt. Harvard U., Cambridge, Mass., chmn. Mich. Partnership for New Edn., Program in Am. Instns., U. Mich., Brown U.'s Pub. Policy and Am. Instns. Program; prin. benefactor A. Alfred Taubman Health Care Ctr. and A. Alfred Taubman Med. Libr., U. Mich.; bd. dirs. Detroit Renaissance, Inc., Friends of Art and Preservation in Embassies, Washington; active State of Mich. Gaming Commn. Recipient Bus. Statesman award Harvard Bus. Sch. Club of Detroit, 1983, Sportsman of Yr. award United Found. Detroit, SE Mich. Chpt. March of Dimes Birth Defects, 1983; named Michiganian of Yr. The Detroit News, 1983; named one of Forbes' Richest Americans, 2006 Mem. Urban Land Inst. (trustee), Nat. Realty Com. (bd. dirs.).

TAUBMAN, JANE ANDELMAN, literature and language professor; b. Boston, Oct. 23, 1942; d. Hyman M. and Esther (Rosenthal) Andelman; m. William Chase Taubman; children: Alexander, Phoebe. BA, Radcliffe Coll., 1964; MA, Yale U., 1968, PhD, 1972. Instr. Russian Smith Coll., Northampton, Mass., 1968-72; asst. prof. Russian Amherst (Mass.) Coll., 1973-83, assoc. prof. Russian, 1983-89, prof. Russian, 1989—. Author: A Life Through Poetry: Marina Tsvetaeva's Lyric Diary, 1989, Russian transl., 2000, Cinetek: Asthenic Syndrome, 2000, Kira Muratova, 2004; co-author: Moscow Spring, 1989; co-editor: Marina Tsvetaeva: One Hundred Years, 1994. Woodrow Wilson Found. fellow, 1964—, Am. Coun. Learned Socs.-SSRC, 1974, trustee-faculty fellow Amherst Coll., 1978, fellow Nat. Def. Title VI, 1965-68; grantee Am. Philos. Soc., 1975, Amherst Coll., 1991, 94, IREX grantee USSR, 1988. Mem. AAUP, Am. Assn. Tchrs. Slavic and East European Langs., Am. Assn. Slavic Studies, Am. Coun. Tchrs. of Russian. Office: Amherst Coll Dept Russian Amherst MA 01002 Office Phone: 413-542-2047. Business E-Mail: jataubman@amherst.edu.

TAUBMAN, NICHOLAS FRANK, United States Ambassador to Romania; b. Roanoke, Va., 1935; s. Arthur and Grace Taubman; m. Eugenia L. Taubman. BS in Economics, The Wharton Sch., U. Pa.; Degree (hon.), Hollins U., 1992. Dir. Shenandoah Life Ins. Co.; pres., CEO Advance Auto Parts, Inc., 1969—2005; pres. Mozart Investments, Roanoke, Va.; US amb. to Romania US Dept. State, Bucharest, 2005—. Mem. Roanoke City Coun., 1976-78; served in US Army, 1957-58, 1960-61 Recipient Disting. Svc. award, Roanoke Jaycees, 1978, Brotherhood Citation, Nat. Conf. of Christians and Jews, 1981. Jewish. Office: US Embassy 5260 Bucharest Pl Washington DC 20521*

TAUBMAN, PAUL J., diversified financial services company executive; b. 1961; BS, U. Pa., 1982; MBA, Stanford U. Grad. Sch. Bus., 1986. Joined Morgan Stanley, NYC, 1982, with mergers and acquisitions dept., 1986—2007, v.p., 1991—93, prin., 1993—95, mng. dir., co-head global mergers and acquisitions, 2003—07, global co-head investment banking, 2007—. Recipient Rainmaker award, Dealmaker mag., 2006; named a Top Rainmaker for uber-bankers, Dealmaker nag., 2007. Office: Morgan Stanley 1585 Broadway New York NY 10036 Office Phone: 212-761-7929.*

TAUBMAN, PHILIP M., editor; b. 1948; s. Howard Taubman; m. Felicity Barringer. BA, Stanford U., 1971. Reporter NY Times, 1979, Moscow bur. chief, 1986—88, Washington (DC) editor, 1989—92, dep. nat. editor, 1993—94, asst. editorial page editor, 1994—2002, dep. editorial page editor, 2002—03, Washington (DC) bur. chief, 2003—07, assoc. editor, nat. security investigative reporter, 2007—. Author: Secret Empire: Eisenhower, the CIA & the Hidden Story of America's Space Espionage, 2003. Recipient George Polk award, 1981, 1983. Office: NY Times Washington Bur 7th Fl 1627 I St Washington DC 20006 Office Phone: 202-862-0300. Office Fax: 202-862-0340. E-mail: taubman@nytimes.com.

TAUBMAN, WILLIAM CHASE, political science professor, writer; b. NYC, Nov. 13, 1941; s. Howard and Nora (Stern) T.; m. Jane Dea Andelman, May 18, 1969; children: Alexander, Phoebe. AB, Harvard U., 1962; MA, Columbia U., 1965, cert. of Russian Inst., 1965, PhD, 1969; MA (hon.), Amherst Coll., Mass., 1978. Instr. Amherst Coll., 1967-69, asst. prof., 1969-73, assoc. prof., 1973-78, prof. dept. polit. sci., 1978-83, Bertrand Snell prof., 1983—. Mem. planning staff U.S. Dept. State, Washington, 1970-71; mem. bd. Internat. Rsch. and Exch. Bd., N.Y.C., 1971-74, mem. selection com., 1984-85; vis. assoc. prof. Yale U., New Haven, spring 1975; chmn. adv. com. Cold War Internat. History Project, Woodrow Wilson Ctr., Washington, 1993—; mem. Internat. Acad. Adv. Group, Russian Fgn. Ministry Archives, 1992-97; assoc. Davis Ctr. for Russian Studies, Harvard U., pres. Am. Assn. Advancement Slavic Studies, 2008-. Author: The View from Lenin Hills, 1967; Governing Soviet Cities, 1973; Stalin's American Policy, 1982, Khrushchev: The Man and His Era, 2003 (Nat. Book Critics Circle award, 2004, Pulitzer Prize for biography, 2004, Wayne S. Vucinich Book prize Am. Assn. for Advancement of Slavic Studies 2004, Robert H. Ferrell Book prize 2004); co-author: (with Jane Taubman) Moscow Spring, 1989; editor, translator: Khrushchev on Khrushchev (Sergei N. Khrushchev), 1990; editor: Globalism and Its Critics, 1973; co-editor: Nikita Khrushchev, 2000. Named Alumnus of Yr., Harriman Inst., Columbia U., 2003; fellow Woodrow Wilson Nat. Found., 1962, Ford Found., 1963-67, Coun. Fgn. Rels., 1970-71, Rockefeller Found., 1983, Columbia U. Harriman Inst., 1987, Fulbright-Hays Found., 1988, NEH, 1992, 2008, Woodrow Wilson Internat. Ctr. for Scholars, 2000, Guggenheim Found., 2006; grantee Nat. Coun. Soviet and East European Rsch., 1984 Mem. Coun. Fgn. Rels., Authors Guild. Home: 43 Hitchcock Rd Amherst MA 01002 Office: Amherst Coll Dept Polit Sci Amherst MA 01002 Home Phone: 413-256-8858; Office Phone: 413-542-2420. E-mail: wctaubman@amherst.edu.

TAUC, JAN, retired physics professor; b. Pardubice, Czechoslovakia, Apr. 15, 1922; arrived in US, 1969, naturalized, 1978; s. Jan and Josefa (Semonska) T.; m. Vera Koubelova, Oct. 18, 1947; children: Elena (Mrs. Milan Kokta), Jan. Ing.Dr. in Elec. Engring., Tech. U. Prague, 1949; RNDr., Charles U., Prague, 1956; Dr.Sc. in Physics, Czechoslovak Acad. Scis., 1956. Scientist microwave research Sci. and Tech. Research Inst., Tanvald and Prague, 1949-52; head semiconductor dept. Inst. Solid State Physics, Czechoslovak Acad. Scis., 1953-69; prof. exptl. physics Charles U., 1964-69, dir. Inst. Physics, 1968-69; mem. tech. staff Bell Telephone Labs., Murray Hill, NJ, 1969-70; prof. engring. and physics Brown U., 1970-83, L. Herbert Ballou prof. engring. and physics, 1983-92, L. Herbert Ballou prof. emeritus, 1992—, dir. material research lab., 1983-88. Dir. E. Fermi Summer Sch., Varenna, Italy, 1965; vis. prof. U. Paris, 1969, Stanford U., 1977, Max Planck Inst. Solid State Research, Stuttgart, Germany, 1982; UNESCO fellow, Harvard, 1961-62 Author: Photo and Thermoelectric Effects in Semiconductors, 1962, also numerous articles; editor: The Optical Properties of Solids, 1966, Amorphous and Liquid Semiconductors, 1974; co-editor: Solid State Communications, 1963-92. Recipient Nat. prize Czechoslovak Govt., 1955, 69; Sr. U.S. Scientist award Humboldt Found., 1981, Silver medal Union of Czechoslovak Mathematicians and Physicists, 1992; Jan Tauc Grad. Fellowship in Engring. at Brown U. in his honor, 2003. Fellow AAAS, Am. Phys. Soc. (Frank Isakson prize 1982, David Adler award 1988); mem. NAS, European Phys. Soc. (founding), Czechoslovak Acad. Scis. (corr. 1963-71, 90-91, fgn. 1991-92, Hlavka medal 1992, de Scientia et Humanitate Optime Meritis medal 2003), Czech Learned Soc. (hon.), Wash. State Acad. Scis. (founding mem. 2008). Business E-Mail: jan.tauc@brown.edu.

TAUER, ED, Mayor, Aurora, Colorado; m. Betsy Tauer; 1 child. MBA, U. Colo; BME, Colo. State U. Mem. Aurora City Coun., 1997—; mayor City of Aurora, Colo., 2003—. Bd. dirs. Aurora Econ. Develop. Coun. Mem. Denver Regional Coun. Govts., Regional Air Quality Coun., Linkages for Older Adults, Fitzsimons Redevelopment Authority; chmn. Commn. & Youth Programs. Mem.: Nat. League of Cities, US Conf. Mayors, Village East Neighborhood Assn., Aurora C. of C. Republican. Avocations: Sports, family activities, making wood furniture. Office: Office of Mayor 15151 E Alameda Pkwy 5th Floor Aurora CO 80012 Office Phone: 303-739-7015. E-mail: etauer@auroragov.org.*

TAUFIK, TAUFIK, electrical engineer, educator; s. Oton and Sumarlik Sanusi; m. Made A. Hartanti, Nov. 28, 1997; children: Fawwaz Huzayfa, Wafiqa R. Farhana. BSEE, No. Ariz. U., 1993; MSEE, U. Ill., Chgo., 1995; DEng, Cleve. State U., 1999. Rsch. asst. U. Ill., Chgo., 1995—96, Cleve. State U., 1996—99; power electronics engr. Capstone Microturbine, Tarzana, Calif., 1996; hardware engr. Rockwell Automation, Mayfield Heights, Ohio, 1997—98; power electronics engr. Picker Internat., Cleve., 1998—99; asst. prof. elec. engring. Cal Poly State U., San Luis Obispo, 1999—2004, assoc. prof. elec. engring., 2004—. Cons. San Diego Gas and Electric, 2001; power supply engring. cons. Rantec Power Systems, Los Osos, 2002—04. Named Best Lab Instr., Cal Poly, 2003, 2005, Prof. of Yr., 2005, Best Lecture Instr., 2002, 2005, Most Supportive Prof., Soc. Women Engrs., 2005; grantee, Rantec Power Systems, 2001, 2003, Calif. Energy Commn., 2001, Cal Poly, 2002, 2004;, State Faculty Support Grant. Mem.: IEEE Indsl. Electronics Soc., IEEE Industry Applications Soc., IEEE Power Engring. Soc., IEEE Power Electronics Soc., IEEE Ctrl. Coast Sect. (chair 2004—05). Achievements include building a photovoltaic facility; research in efficiency improvement in high-density DC-DC converters; providing power in digital society; transmission circuit breaker replacement criteria. Office: Cal Poly State U Elec Engring Dept 1 Grand Ave San Luis Obispo CA 93407 Office Fax: 805-756-1458. Business E-Mail: taufik@calpoly.edu.

TAUGER, MARK BERNARD, historian; s. Herbert and Marilyn June Tauger; m. Eva Segert, Jan. 9, 1987; children: Naomi Segert, Nathan Vaclav, Eliana Pamela. BA in Music, UCLA, 1976, MA in Music, 1980, PhD in History, 1991. Asst. prof. History Dept., W.Va. U., Morgantown, 1992—2000, assoc. prof., 2000—. Recipient Eric Wolf prize, Jour. Peasant Studies, 2003—04; grantee, Internat. Rsch. Exchs. Bd., 1987, 1993, 1997. Mem.: Am. Assn. Advancement Slavic Studies. Achievements include discovery of series of famines in the history of the USSR and India, documented environmental causes. Office: W Va Univ History Dept 202 Woodburn Hall Morgantown WV 26506-6303 Office Fax: 304-293-3616. Business E-Mail: mark.tauger@mail.wvu.edu.

TAUKE, THOMAS JOSEPH, telecommunications company executive, former United States Representative from Iowa; b. Dubuque, Iowa, Oct. 11, 1950; s. Joseph A. and Esther M. (Reicher) Tauke; m. Beverly Tauke, 2 children. BA magna cum laude, Loras Coll., 1972; JD, U. Iowa, 1974. Bar: Iowa 1974. Mem. Curnan, Fitzsimmons, Schilling and Tauke, Dubuque, 1976-79, Iowa Gen. Assembly, 1975-79, US Congress from 2nd Iowa dist., 1979—91; v.p. govt. affairs NYNEX, Washington, 1991—97, exec. v.p. govt. affairs, 1991—97; sr. v.p. govt. rels. Bell Atlantic Corp., 1997—2000; sr. v.p. pub. policy & external affairs Verizon Comm. Inc., 2000, exec. v.p. pub. affairs, policy and comm., 2004—. Del. Rep. Nat. Conv., 1976; chmn. 2nd Congl. Dist. of Iowa Rep. Party, 1974-77; mem. Iowa Rep. Ctrl. Com., 1974-77; chmn. Dubuque County Rep. Party, 1972-74 Mem. pastoral coun. Roman Catholic Archdiocese of Dubuque, 1971-73; trustee Mt. Mercy Coll., Cedar Rapids, Iowa. Mem. ABA, Iowa Bar Assn., Dubuque County Bar Assn., Dubuque C. of C., Cedar Rapids Area C. of C. Clubs: Rotary, Junipera Serra. Office: Verizon Comm Inc 1095 Ave Americas New York NY 10036*

TAULBEE, THOMAS LESTER, psychotherapist, educator; b. Normal, Ill., June 12, 1947; s. Marion L. and Marjorie S. T. BS, Ill. State U., 1970; MS, Tex. A&M U., 1971, EdD, 1973. Cert. marriage and family therapist; cert. sports counselor; ordained min. Psychotherapist Human

Resource Devel. Ctr., Dallas, 1974-76; prof. psychology Richland Coll., Dallas, 1976—, prof. history, 1994—. North Tex. regl. dir. Nat. Inst. Sports, 2000-2003, nat. coord. of divsn. chmn., 2002-03; bd. advisors Revival Fires Ministries, Branson West, Mo., 1997-99, bd. dirs. Sports Sys. Internat., 2001-2003, mem. sports chaplaincy adv. com. U.S. Coun. for Sports Chaplaincy, 2002-2003, exec. dir., exec. v.p., chief orgnl. officer, 2003; pres., founder Internat. Escorted Tour Svc., 2004—; internat. tour guide, with nat. and internat. cos., 1980—. Co-author: Psychology from a Personal Perspective, 1992, rev. edit., 1997; editor, co -author: Personal Applications of Psychology, 1997. Dir. Superior Student Roundtable, Parker, Tex., 1993, 1996—; bd. dirs. U.S. Coun. for Sports Chaplaincy, 2003—. Recipient Nat. Inst. for Staff and Orgnl. Devel. excellence award U. Tex., 2004; Ctr. for Behavioral Studies U. North Tex., Denton, 1973-74; named Basketball All-Am., Ill. State U., 1969; named to Ill. State U. Athletic Hall of Fame. Mem. Tex. Jr. Coll. Teachers Assn., Nat. Assn. Scholars, Assn. Behavior Analysis. Avocations: world travel, scuba diving, cooking. Office: Richland Coll 12800 Abrams Rd Dallas TX 75243-2173 E-mail: taulbee@verizon.net.

TAUR, YUAN, physicist, researcher; b. Nanchang, Jiangxi, China, Sept. 27, 1946; arrived in U.S., 1968; s. Tang and Ping-Chung Seh Taur; m. Betty Chu, Apr. 20, 1974; children: Ying, Hsuan. BS in Physics, Nat. Taiwan U., 1967; PhD in Physics, U. Calif., Berkeley, 1974. Postdoctoral fellow U. Calif., Berkeley, 1974—75; rsch. assoc. Goddard Inst. Space Studies NASA, NYC, 1975—79; mem. tech. staff Rockwell Internat. Sci. Ctr., Thousand Oaks, Calif., 1979—81; rsch. staff mem., mgr. T. J. Watson Rsch. Ctr. IBM, Yorktown Heights, NY, 1981—2001; prof. U. Calif., San Diego, 2001—. Co-author: Fundamentals of Modern VLSI Devices, 1998; contbr. articles to profl. jours. Fellow IEEE (subject editor Electron Device Letters 1996-99, editor-in-chief 1999—). Achievements include 14 patents. Office: U Calif San Diego Dept Elec and Computer Engring La Jolla CA 92093 Office Phone: 858-534-3816. Business E-Mail: taur@ece.ucsd.edu.

TAURASI, DIANA LURENA, professional basketball player; b. Glendale, Calif., June 11, 1982; d. Mario Taurasi and Lili. Grad. in Sociology, U. Conn., 2004. Player Phoenix Mercury, Ariz., 2004—. Mem. USA Basketball Women's Sr. Nat. Team, Athens, Greece, 2004, Beijing, 08. Recipient Honda award for Women's Basketball Finalist, 2001—02, Honda Trophy Award, 2003, Wade Trophy, 2003, ESPY award, Best Female Coll. Athlete, ESPN, 2003, 2004, ESPY award, Best Female Athlete, 2004, Gold medal, women's basketball, Athens Olympic Games, 2004, Beijing Olympic Games, 2008; named Big East Preseason Rookie of Yr., 2000—01, Most Outstanding Player of NCAA East Region, 2000—01, Big East Championship Most Outstanding Player, 2000—01, Kodak All-Am. and AP Second Team All Am., 2001—02, Naismith Player of Yr., 2001—02, 2003, Big East First Team Performer, 2002—03, NCAA Final Four and East Regional Most Outstanding Player, 2003, Nat. Player of Yr., US Basketball Writers Assn., 2003, Preseason All-Am., 2003, WNBA Rookie of Yr., 2004, WNBA Peak Performer, 2006, Female Athlete of Yr., USA Basketball, 2006; named to Big East All-Rookie Team, 2000—01, NCAA Mideast Region All-Tournament Team, 2001—02, All Big-East First Team, 2002, Big East All-Tournament Team, 2002, 2003, All-WNBA First Team, 2004, 2006, WNBA Western Conf. All-Star Team, 2005—07. Achievements include winning a WNBA Championship as a member of the Mercury, 2007. Office: Phoenix Mercury 201 E Jefferson St Phoenix AZ 85004

TAURO, JOSEPH LOUIS, federal judge; b. Winchester, Mass., Sept. 26, 1931; s. G. Joseph and Helen Maria (Petrossi) T.; m. Elizabeth Mary Quinlan, Feb. 7, 1959 (dec. 1978); children— Joseph L., Elizabeth H., Christopher M.; m. Ann Lefavour Jones, July 12, 1980. AB, Brown U., 1953; LLB, Cornell U., 1956; JD (hon.), U. Mass., 1985, Suffolk U., 1986, Northeastern U., 1990, New Eng. Sch. Law, 1992, Boston U., 1997, Brown U., 1998. Bar: Mass. 1956, D.C. 1960. Assoc. Tauro & Tauro, Lynn, Mass., 1958-59; asst. U.S. atty. Dept. Justice, Boston, 1959-60; ptnr. Jaffee & Tauro, Boston and Lynn, Mass., 1960-71; chief legal counsel Gov. of Mass., Boston, 1965-68; U.S. atty. Dept. Justice, Boston, 1972; judge U.S. Dist. Ct., Boston, 1972—; chief judge U.S. Dist. Ct., Mass., 1992-99. Mem. exec. com. Cornell Law Assn., Ithaca, N.Y., 1968-71; mem. adv. coun. Cornell Law Sch., Ithaca, 1975-80; vis. prof. law Boston U. Law Sch., 1977—; mem. Jud. Conf. U.S., 1994-97, mem. com. on operation of jury sys., 1979-86, mem. adv. com. on codes of conduct, 1988-94. Trustee Brown U., 1978—, Mass. Gen. Hosp., Boston, 1968-72, Children's Hosp. Med. Ctr., Boston, 1979-94. 1st lt. U.S. Army, 1956-58. Recipient Disting. Alumnus award Cornell U. Law Sch., 1992, Brown Bear award Brown U., 1993; named one of 10 Outstanding Young Men, Greater Boston Jaycees, 1966. Fellow Am. Bar Found.; mem. Mass. Bar Assn., Boston Bar Assn. (coun. 1968-71), D.C. Bar Assn., Boston Yacht Club (Marblehead, Mass.). Republican. Roman Catholic. Avocations: sports, reading, music, films, theater. Office: 1 Courthouse Way Ste 7110 Boston MA 02210-3009 Office Phone: 617-748-9288.

TAUSAN, CAROL A., music educator; b. Holyoke, Mass., Mar. 14, 1958; d. Eugene A. and Margaret M. Miller; m. Jon Criss Tausan, June 20, 1994. MA, Chapman U., Colorado Springs, Colo., 1994; MusB, Nebr. Wesleyan U., 1980. Cert. tchr. Fla., 1996, Nat. Bd. Profl. Tchg. Stds., 2005. Music tchr. Mary Our Queen Sch., Omaha, 1980—86, Panorama Mid. Sch., Colorado Springs, 1987—94, Turman Elem. Sch., Colorado Springs, 1994—96, Garden Elem. Sch., Venice, Fla., 1996—. Choir dir. Panorama Mid. Sch., Colorado Springs, Colo., 1987—94, gifted and talented coord., 1988—92; mem. authentic assessment com. Harrison Sch. Dist. #2, Colorado Springs, Colo., 1989—90; mem. coun. Curriculum, Instrn. and Assessment Coun., Colorado Springs, Colo., 1990—92; choir dir. Turman Elem. Sch., Colorado Springs, Colo., 1994—96, Garden Elem. Sch., Venice, Fla., 1996—, mem. faculty leadership com., 1996—; team leader Garden Elem., Venice, Fla., 1999—; mem. lang. arts com. Garden Elem. Sch., Venice, Fla., 1999—2002, bldg. rep. Sarasota Classified/Tchrs. Assn., 2001—02, sr. bldg. rep., 2002—; mem. com. Cmty./Schs. Partnership for Arts, Sarasota, Fla., 1997—, Renaissance Com., Venice, Fla., 2001—03; mem.music textbook adoption com. Sch. Bd. of Sarasota County, Fla., 2002—03. Choir dir. (performance) St. Mary's Cath. Ch., Bellevue, Nebr., 1982—84, All-City Eighth Grade Chorus, Sun Fiesta Parade (Best Edn. Entry, 1997), Venetian Holiday Festival. Grantee Sing out for Am., The Edn. Found. of Sarasota, 1997—98, The Magnificent 7, Edn. Found. of Sarasota, 1998—99, Hooray for the Red, White and Blue, 1998—99, All Am. Celebration, 1999—2000, Rockin' and Readin', 2000—01, Young Americans and Proud of It, 2000—01, True to the Red, White, and Blue, 2002—03, Rockin' and Readin', Cmty. Found. of Sarasota County, 2000-2001, The Merry Minstrel, 2002-2003, Recorders - An instrumental Opportunity, 2002-2003, Create and Communicate with Recorders, 2003-2004, You Can BEAT This!, 2003-2004, Got Recorders?, 2004—05; African Artist-in-Residence, Arts for a Complete Edn./Fla. Alliance for Arts Edn., 1998—99, grant, Musical Expression Through Recorders, 2007—08. Mem.: Colo. Music Educators Assn., Fla. Music Educators Assn., Music Educators Nat. Conf. Home: 427 Pebble Creek Ct Venice FL 34285 Office: Garden Elem Sch 700 Center Rd Venice FL 34285 Personal E-mail: candcofppcc@comcast.net.

TAUSCHER, ELLEN O'KANE, federal agency administrator, former United States Representative from California; b. Newark, Nov. 15, 1951; 1 child, Katherine. BS in Early Childhood Edn., Seton Hall U., 1974. With Bache Securities, NYC, 1974—79; officer NY Stock Exch., 1980—83; with Bear Stearns Companies Inc., 1983—85, Drexel Burnham Lambert, NYC, 1985—89; founder, CEO Child Care Registry Inc., 1991—96; mem. US Congress from 10th Calif. dist., 1997—2009, regional whip, 2008—09; mem. US House Armed Services Com., US House Transp. & Infrastructure Com.; under sec. for arms control & internat. security US Dept. State, Washington, 2009—. Co-chair US Senate Campaign Dianne Feinstein, 1992, 1994; mem. Blue Dog Coalition; co-chair Troop Capitol Hill: Hon. Girl Scout Caucus, Intelligent Transp. Sys. Caucus, Dept. Energy Facilities Caucus, Iraqi Women's Caucus, 2004—; chair New Dem. Coalition, 2005—, co-chair Entitlement Reform Task Force; com. mem. N. Am. Treaty Orgn. Parliamentary Assembly; nat. vice chair Dem. Leadership Coun. Author: The ChildCare Sourcebook, 1996. Bd. vis. US Mil. Acad.; bd. mem. Alumnae Resources, Battered Women's Alternative, Breast Cancer Fund, Bus. Execs. for Nat. Security, Calif. Symphony; bd. regents Seton Hall U. Democrat. Roman Catholic. Office: US Dept State 2201 C St NW Washington DC 20520*

TAUSSIG, ANDREW RICHARD, investment banker; b. Abington, Pa., Aug. 27, 1951; s. Ralph J. and Sally G. Taussig; m. Susan Fierman, June 25, 1978. BA, Trinity Coll., Hartford, Conn., 1973; JD, Georgetown Law Sch., Washington, DC, 1976; MBA, U. Pa. Wharton Grad. Sch., Phila., 1978. Bar: Pa. 1976, NY 1978. Corp. atty. Willkie, Farr & Gallagher, NYC, 1978-82; investment banker, mng. dir. CS First Boston, NYC, 1983—2005; head retail investment banking First Boston Corp., NYC, 1988—2005; vice chmn., global head, investment banking Lehman Brothers, NYC, 2005—. Bd. dirs. Big V. Supermarkets, Fla., NY, Pueblo Internat., Pompano, Fla. Named a Top Rainmaker for consumer/retail, Dealmaker mag., 2006, 2007. Office: Lehman Brothers 745 Seventh Ave New York NY 10019 Office Phone: 212-526-7000. Office Fax: 212-526-0739.

TAVAKKOLIZADEH, ALI, surgeon; s. Abdulhossein Tavakkolizadeh and Mehranghiz Saidi. MB, Royal London Hosp. Med. Coll., Eng., 1993. Anatomy demonstrator United Med. and Dental Schools of Guy's and St Thomas's Hospitals, London, 1995—96; basic surg. tng. Wessex Deanary, England, 1996—98; rsch. fellow Brigham and Women's Hosp., Harvard Med. Sch., Boston, 1998—2000; surg. specialist registrar East Anglian Deanary, Cambridge, England, 2000—01; surg. resident Brigham and Women's Hosp., Harvard Med. Sch., Boston, 2001—05, adv. minimally invasive fellowship, 2005—06, assoc. surgeon, 2006—. Instr. surgery Harvard Med. Sch., 2005—. Author: (original paper) American Journal of Physiology, Journal of Surgical Research, Journal for Parentral and Enteral Nutrition, (review article) Transplantation Reviews, (letter) Lancet, (review article) Journal for Parentral and Enteral Nutrition. Recipient Japan Surg. Soc. Travel Grant, Japan Surg. Soc., 2000, AGA Travel Award to World Congress of Gastroenterology, Am. Gastroenterology Assn., 2002, GRG/AGA Fellow Travel Award, Gastroenterology Rsch. Group, 2000. Fellow: Royal coll. of Surgeons of Eng.; mem.: Am. Gastroenterology Assn., Soc. for Surgery of Alimentary Tract. Office: Brigham and Women's Hospital 75 Francis Street Boston MA 02115 E-mail: atavakkolizadeh@partners.org.

TAVANA, MADJID, science educator; b. Tehran, Iran, Aug. 28, 1957; Postdoc. diploma, Wharton Sch. U. Pa., Phila., 1987. Prof. info. sys. and decision scis. La Salle U., Phila., 1984—, lindback disting. chair, MIS, 2005—. Dir. Ctr. Tech. and Mgmt.; exec. dir. E-Commerce Inst. Recipient Space Act award, NASA. Achievements include invention of data flow petri nets, NASA. Office: La Salle Univ 1900 W Olney Ave Philadelphia PA 19141 Office Fax: 267-295-2854. Business E-Mail: tavana@lasalle.edu.

TAVARES, CHARLETA B., city councilwoman; Student, Spelman Coll., Atlanta, Ohio State U. Assoc. dir. Pub. Children Svcs. Assn. of Ohio; chief children's protection sect. Office Ohio Atty. Gen.; mem. from 22nd dist. Ohio House of Reps., 1993—99; councilwoman Columbus City Coun., 1999—, chair health, housing & human svcs. com., com. on workforce devel., mem. transp. com., recreation com., parks & zoning com., fin. com., pub. svc. com., devel. com. Exec. dir. Multiethnic Advocates for Cultural Competence, Columbus, 2006—; pres. Ohio Suicide Prevention Found.; vice-chair Columbus/Franklin County Housing Adv. Bd.; mem. Franklin County Family & Children First Coun.; founding mem. Ohio chpt., former v.p. Nat. Coalition of 100 Black Women. Del Dem. Nat. Convention, 1988, 1992, 1996, 2000. Recipient YWCA Woman of Achievement award, 2001, Legis. Leadership award, Nat. Alliance for Mentally Ill, Ohio Hispanic Coalition award, Friends of Homeless Leadership award, Living Faith award, Met. Area Ch. Coun., Martin Luther King, Jr. Humanitarian award, Columbus Edn. Assn.; named Pub. Ofcl. of Yr., SE Mental Health, Legislator of Yr., Ohio chpt. NASW. Mem.: Ohio Mcpl. League, Ohio Bus. & Profl. Women's Orgn., Women in Mcpl. Govt. Democrat. Mailing: 1237 Medford Rd Columbus OH 43209 also: Columbus City Coun 90 W Broad St 2nd Fl Columbus OH 43215-9015 Office Phone: 614-645-2537. E-mail: aide_rechilton@columbus.gov.*

TAVARES, SAMANTHA, psychologist, educator; b. Bahia, Brazil, Oct. 23, 1968; arrived in U.S., 1984; d. Jose and Clarice Maria Tavares; 1 adopted child, Satyana Lua 1 child, Titus Sol. BA in Chinese Lang. Studies, Taipei, 1988; BA in Asian Studies, UCLA, 1990; M in Psychology, Forest Inst. Profl. Psychology, 1993; MA in Ea. Religion, U. Hawaii, 2000; PhD in Clin. Psychology, Am. Schs. Profl. Psychology, 1995. Lic. psychologist Hawaii, 1996, cert. hypnotherapist 1994, level II cert. Eye Movement Desensitization and Reprocessing. 1998, cert. holistic therapist 2000. Sch. counselor Han Guan Inst., China, 1986—88; pvt. practice clin. psychology Honolulu, Kailua, Hawaii, 1995—; clin. psychologist Dept. Health, Honolulu, 1996—98; clin. supr. Alaka'I Na Keiki, Inc., 1996—; clin. psychologist evaluator Dept. Edn. Dist. Hawaii, 1997—2000; assoc. prof. Holos U. Grad. Seminary, 2000—; faculty staff Inst. for Sci. Med. Intuition, 2000—04. Co-founder Samba Axe Hawaii, 1993—; dance instr., performer, 1993—; project dir. Support Adoption Hawaii, 2005—; exec. dir. Hawaii Hearts Helping Adoptions, 2005. Author: (compact disk, cassette tape) Transformative Liberation, 2005. Avocations: dance, yoga, meditation, running, surfing. Office: 43 Oneawa St Kailua HI Office Phone: 808-261-3731. E-mail: dr.tavaressam@yahoo.com.

TAVÁREZ, DAVID EDUARDO, anthropologist, educator; b. Ciudad Juárez, Chihuahua, Mex. s. David Tavárez-Soltero and Estela Bermúdez-Ávila; m. Elisabeth Tavárez. BA, Harvard Coll., 1992; PhD, U. Chgo., 2000. Asst. prof. Latin Am. & Iberian studies Bard Coll., Annandale, NY, 2000—03; asst. prof. anthropology Vassar Coll., Poughkeepsie, NY, 2003—. Co-author: (book) Chimalpahin's Conquista: An Indigenous Historian's Reading of López de Gómara's Conquest of Mexico; author: Invisible Wars: Evangelization Projects and Indigenous Clandestine Devotions in Colonial Mexico. Fellowship, Mellon Found., 1998—99, grants, Found. Advancement Mesoam. Studies, 1997, 2003, Rsch. fellowship, Nat. Endowment Humanities, 2004, Collaborative grant, 2005—07. D-Liberal. Avocations: travel, dance, jazz, cooking. Office: Vassar Coll 126 Raymond Ave Poughkeepsie NY 12604

TAVEGGIA, THOMAS CHARLES, retired management consultant, educator; b. Oak Lawn, Ill., June 15, 1943; s. Thomas Angelo and Eunice Louise (Harris) Taveggia; m. Brigitte I. Adams, Jan. 23, 1965; children: Michaela, Francesca. BS, Ill. Inst. Tech., 1965; MA, U. Oreg., 1968, PhD, 1971. Prof. U. Oreg., Eugene, 1970, U. B.C., Vancouver, Can., 1970-73, U. Calif., Irvine, 1973-74, Ill. Inst. Technology, Chgo., 1974-77; mgmt. cons. Towers, Perrin, Forster, & Crosby, Chgo., 1977-80; ptnr. Manplan Cons., Chgo., 1980-81, Coopers & Lybrand, San Francisco, 1981-86, Touche Ross, San Francisco, 1986-88; prof. Calif. Sch. Profl. Psychology, Berkeley, 1988-98, U. Ariz., Tucson, 2000—05. Author: (with Dubin and Arends) From Family and School to Work, 1967; (with Dubin) The Teaching-Learning Paradox: A Comparative Analysis of College Teaching Methods, 1968; (with Dubin and Hedley) The Medium May Be Related to the Message: College Instruction by TV, 1969; contbr. articles to profl. jours. Grantee, Calif. Sch. Profl. Psychology, 1993—98; NDEA Title IV fellow, 1967—71, U. B.C. faculty rsch. grantee, 1970, 1971, 1973. Home: 3622 Edgewater Dr Enid OK 73703 Personal E-mail: taveg@aol.com.

TAVERNA, RODNEY ELWARD, financial services company executive; b. Springfield, Ill., Aug. 8, 1947; s. Jerome Thomas and Virginia (Holcomb) T.; m. Cheryl Ann Walters, Sept. 4, 1968 (div. 1983); children: Lara Lyn, Melinda Marie, Ryan Thomas; m. Caroline Whiffen, Apr. 1985. BA, U. Mo., 1969; MBA in Fin., Nat. U., 1988. Commd. 2d lt., supply officer USMC, 1969, advanced through grades to maj., 1979; supply officer Central Svcs. Agy., Danang, Vietnam, 1970-71, Marine Air Control Squadron, Futenma, Okinawa, 1977-78; logistics officer Hdqrs. Marine Corps Recruit Depot, Paris Island, S.C., 1972-75; support officer Marine Barracks, Treasure Island, San Francisco, 1975-77; regimental supply officer 1st Marine Divsn., Camp Pendleton, Calif., 1978-79, asst divsn. supply officer, 1985-88; brigade supply officer 1st Marine Brigade, Kaneohe Bay, Hawaii, 1980-82; exec. officer 1st Maintenance Bn., Camp Pendleton, 1982-85; asst div. supply officer 1st Marine Div., 1985-88; pres. Freedom Fin. Group, 1991—2000; br. mgr. WMA Securities, Inc., 1994-97; sr. field dir. Premier Fin. Am., 1997-2000; CEO Freedom Fin. Solutions, Inc., 2000—; pres. Best Discount Benefits, 2003—; founder Smart Consumer Group, 2003—. Owner, mgr. Opportunities Unltd., Oceanside, Calif., 1985-91; cons. Incentive Leasing Corp., San Diego, 1985-86, The Profit Ctr., Santa Ana, Calif., 1991; founding mgr. Meditrend Internat., San Diego, 1987-88; founding dir. Am. 3-D Corp., Henderson, Nev., 1990-91. Mem.: Fed. C. of C. (bd. advisors 2002—03). Republican. Avocations: computers, skiing, racquetball, scuba diving. Office: PO Box 4022 Oceanside CA 92052 Home Phone: 760-631-4300; Office Phone: 760-631-4300. Business E-Mail: ceo@freedomfinancialsolutionsinc.com.

TAVERNER, PAMELA JOHNSON, secondary school educator; b. Benton, Ill., July 3, 1948; d. Elmer Ellsworth and Ruth Elizabeth (Claybourn) Johnson; m. Clyde K. Taverner, June 29, 1990. AB, Friends U., 1971; M in Comm., Wichita State U., 1981. Cert. tchr. Kans., Mo. Tchr. Elk Valley H.S., Longton, Kans., 1971—72, Summersville H.S., Mo., 1972—75, Clearwater H.S., Kans., 1975—2007. Comm. cons. Fourth fin. Corp., Wichita, 1989—93; mem. bd. examiners Nat. Coun. Accreditation Tchr. Edn., 2002—. Named Outstanding Tchr./Dir., Assn. Kans. Theatre, 1993. Mem.: NEA (dir. 2001—07), Heartland Ret. Educators (tres. 2009—), South Ctrl. Kansas NEA (tres., pres. elect., pres.), Kansas NEA (dirs. 1989—95, exec. com. 1991—92, dirs. 2001—07, exec. com. 2001—07), Kans. Exemplary Educators Network (pres. 1977—78, outstanding mem. 1990, pres. 2001), Clearwater Tchrs. Assn. (pres. 1977—78, 2001, Oustanding Mem. 1990), Nat. Coun. Tchrs. English, Parents-FLAG (bd. dirs. Wichita chpt. 1993—95). Democrat. Mem. Soc. Of Friends. Avocations: victorian restoration, needlecrafts, gourmet cooking. Home: 1551 Fairview Ave Wichita KS 67203-2635 Office: Clearwater High Sch PO Box 248 Clearwater KS 67026-9176 Home Phone: 316-264-7880.

TAVISS, PATRICIA ANN, management consultant, library association executive; b. Toronto, Ont., Can., Jan. 11, 1955; came to US, 1984; d. Norman Elward and Catherine (Johnson) Larter; m. Michael L. Taviss, Apr. 28, 1984. BA in English and Psychology, York U., Toronto, 1978; MLS, U. Western Ont., 1980; M in Arts and Orgnl. Mgmt., U. Phoenix Online, 2004. Children's libr. Grande Praire (Can.) Pub. Libr., 1980-84; reference libr. Memphis-Shelby County Pub. Libr., 1984-86; systems mgr. Lane Pub. Libr., Hamilton, Ont., 1986-89; installation cons. CLSI, Boston, 1989-91; pres. TurboTraining, Carmel, Ind., 1991—2001; pres., chief change catalyst Pat Taviss Consulting, Saddlebrooke, Ariz., 2001—. Mem. C. of C., Rewood City, Calif.; vol. lit. tutor Project READ, Redwood City Pub. Libr., 2000—02. Recipient Pres's. award for outstanding contract instr., LMB Microcomputer, 1992. Mem.: Pub. Libr. Assn., Orgnl. Devel. Network, Continuing Libr. Edn. Network and Exchange Round Table (pres.-elect 2006—07, pres. 2007—), Calif. Libr. Assn., Calif. Assn. Libr. Trustees and Commissioners (prog. co-chair 2003—), Bay Area Orgn. Devel. Network, Am. Mgmt. Assn., ALA. Avocations: travel, reading, gardening.

TAVLIN, MICHAEL JOHN, real estate company and manufacturing executive; b. Lincoln, Nebr., Dec. 16, 1946; BEd, Okla. City U., 1970; JD, U. Nebr., 1973; LLM in Taxation, Washington U., St. Louis, 1977. Bar: Nebr. 1973, Mo. 1974. Ptnr. Nelson & Harding, Lincoln, 1973-77; sr. tax. mgr. Deloitte & Touche, Lincoln and Tulsa, 1979-84, PriceWaterhouseCoopers, Tulsa, 1984-86; v.p., treas., sec. Aliant Comm. Inc. and subs., Lincoln, 1986-99; sr. v.p., CFO, treas., sec. Interactive Intelligence, Inc. and subs., Indpls., 1999—2001; CFO, gen. counsel Speedway Motors, Inc. and Speedway Properties, Lincoln, 2001—. Bd. dirs., treas. Cmty. Health Endowment, Lincoln, 1998-2004; bd. dirs. Woods Charitable Fund, Lincoln, 2000-06, pres., 2005-06. Named Disting. Alumnus Oklahoma City U., 1995. Office: Speedway Motors Inc PO Box 81906 Lincoln NE 68501 Office Phone: 402-323-3122.

TAVOULARIS, MARJORIE OSTERWISE, psychiatrist; b. Mt. Pleasant, Pa., May 28, 1938; d. Robert Russell and Violet Jane (Watson) Osterwise; m. James Harry Tavoularis, May 23, 1962 (div. 1987); children: Laura, Suzanne, Diana, Patricia. BS, U. Pitts., 1961, MD, 1966; postgrad., Pitts. Psychoanalytic Inst., 1976-85; PhD, Calif. Psychoanalytic Inst., 1996. Rotating intern St. Francis Gen. Hosp., 1966-67; resident in psychiatry U. Pitts. Western Psychiat. Inst., 1967-70; staff psychiatrist St. Frances Med. Ctr., Pitts., 1972-85, Kern Med. Ctr., Bakersfield, Calif., 1986-89; sr. psychiatrist Calif. Correctional Inst., Teachapi, 1989-91, Calif. Parole OP Clinic, Bakersfield, 1991-96; psychiatrist pvt. practice, Pitts. & Bakersfield, 1972—2006; chief psychiatrist CPS-Corcoran, 1995-96, Pelican Bay State Prison, 1996. Chief mental health svcs. Calif. Dept Correction, 1996-97, Kern County MH 1997-2008; Vet.'s Adminstr. Outpatient Clinic, 2001-05, Chestnut Ridge Counselling, 2007-2009, Family Svc. West Pa., 2005-. Mem. Am. Psychiat. Assn., Ctrl. Calif. Psychiat. Soc., Kern County Med. Soc., Pa.

Psychiat. Soc. (pres. 1984-85), Pitts. Psychiat. Soc. (pres. 1981-82), Pa. Med. Soc. Avocation: duplicate bridge (life master). Home: 1340 W Pittsburgh St Scottdale PA 15683 Home Phone: 724-220-2422. Personal E-mail: moojiet2@aol.com.

TAW, DUDLEY JOSEPH, sales executive, director; b. Cleve., Mar. 11, 1916; s. William C. and Ella (Gedeon) T.; m. Louise E. Forshey, Sept. 10, 1938; children: Judith (Mrs. William W. Beck, Jr.), Dudley Joseph. Student, Hiram Coll., 1938. With McKesson & Robbins, Inc. (pharm. co.), after 1937, sales mgr. Boston, 1947, v.p. sales NYC, 1953-60; v.p. Revlon, Inc., NYC, 1960-64; v.p. mktg. East Ohio Gas Co., Cleve., 1964-74, pres., 1975-81, chmn., 1981-82, Middtaw, Ltd., Inc., 1982. Bd. dirs. No. New England Gas Corp., First Union Mgmt. Co., Biskind Devel. Co., Vt. Gas Systems Inc. Mem. Better Bus. Bur., Cleve., chmn., 1973; trustee Lakewood Hosp.; treas. Salvation Army, Cleve. With USNR, 1946-47. Named Sales Exec. of Year Sales and Mktg. Execs. Cleve., 1966, Man of Year, 1977 Mem. Sales and Mktg. Execs. Cleve. (pres. 1969-70), Westwood Country Club, Union Club, Pepper Pike Club, Rotary (pres. Cleve. 1972-73). Methodist. Home: Apt 302 22500 Lake Rd Cleveland OH 44116-1025

TAWEEL, JANICE M., artist, educator; b. Ennis, Tex., Nov. 24, 1950; d. Josh H. and Evelyn M. Rivers; m. George M. Taweel, Nov. 24, 1973 (dec. Aug. 21, 1996); 1 child, Lorie M. BS, Lamar U., Beaumont, Tex., 1976. Cert. in all level art Tex. Edn. Agency, 1976, tchr. Tex. Edn. Agency., 1976, in elem. edn. Tex. Edn. Agency., 1990. Florist Designs by Delle Florist, Houston, 1968—69; credit/ billing lead Rogers Enterprises, Beaumont, Tex., 1976—90; owner Jan's Art, Beaumont, Tex., 1980—90; co-owner George's Boot and Shoe Repair, Beaumont, Tex., 1980—90; art educator Dallas Ind. Sch. Dist., Dallas, 1991—; owner The Artist Paper Trail, Dallas, 2004—. Sch. site coord. ArtsPartners, Dallas, 1999—, Crayola Dream-Makers, Dallas, 1999—2007; academic art sponsor Adamson H.S. Academic Fair, Dallas, 1999—; sch. site coord. Dallas Mus. of Art/ Go Van Gogh, Dallas, 1999—. Prin. works include pop art and tool series Mushrooms, Iris, The Villiage, Nature on the Lake, The Hummingbird, Our Texas Past, Pink Azalea, Mosaics. Sponsor Future Educators, Dallas, 2005. Grantee, Hispanic Salute North Tex. Ford Dealers, 2001, Jr. League of Dallas, 2002, 2003. Mem.: Dallas Art Educator Assn. (assoc.). Independent. Bapt. Avocations: painting, travel, photography, art, crafts. Office: The Artist Paper Trail 8229 Cr 3823 Murchison TX 75778

TAY, SAVAS, physicist, researcher; m. Ayse Tay. BS, Marmara U., Istanbul, 2000; PhD, U. Ariz., Tucson, 2007. Rsch. assoc. Howard Hughes Med. Inst., Stanford, Calif., 2007—; rsch. assoc. bioengring. dept. Stanford U., 2007—. Contbr. articles to profl. jour. Founder Found. Intercultural Dialogue, Tucson, 2005—07. Mem.: Optical Com. Turkey, Optical Soc. Am., SPIE. Muslim. Achievements include development of photorefractive polymer composite that operates at the optical communication wavelength; infra-red emitter based on a diamond-like material for use in sensors and thermal cameras; discovery of mammalian cell responses to external stimuli such as bacterial products. Avocation: martial arts.

TAYLER, IRENE, retired English literature educator; b. Abilene, Tex., July 13, 1934; d. B. Brown Smith and Madeline (Bowron); m. Edward W. Tayler, June 3, 1961 (div. 1971); children: Edward Jr., Jesse; m. Saul Touster, Jan. 14, 1978. BA in Philosophy, Stanford U., 1956, MA in Am. Lit., 1961, PhD in English Lit., 1968. Tchr. Breadloaf Sch. of Eng., Middlebury, Vt., 1970, 71, 75, 76; teaching asst. Stanford U., Calif., 1958-60; lectr. Columbia U., NYC, 1961-71; asst. prof. CUNY, 1971-73, assoc. prof., 1973-76, MIT, Cambridge, 1976-82, prof., 1982-96, sec. of the faculty, 1993-95, retired, 1996. Chair gov. com. The English Inst., 1981. Author: Blake's Illustrations to the Poems of Gray, 1971, Holy Ghosts: The Male Muses of Emily and Charlotte Bronte, 1990; editor; Samuel Bak: Between Worlds, Paintings and Drawings from 1946 to 2001, 2002; contbr. articles to profl. jours.; chpts. to books. Internat. Inst. Edn. fellow U. Munich, 1957-58; Wilson fellow Stanford U., 1961-62; NEH sr. scholar fellow, 1980; Mac Vicar faculty fellow MIT, 1993-2003; ACLS study grantee, 1968-69; Faculty Rsch. Found. grantee CUNY, 1972-73; first occupant Thomas Meloy chair rhetoric MIT, 1979-83. Mem.: St. Botolph Club (Boston) (pres. 2000—03). Personal E-mail: itayler@mit.edu.

TAYLOE, DAVID T., JR., pediatrician; b. Phila., Mar. 24, 1949; MD, U. NC Sch. Medicine, 1974. Intern pediat. St. Christopher's Hosp. Children, Phila., 1974—75, resident pediat., 1975—76; resident NC Meml. Hosp., Chapel Hill, 1976—77; pvt. practice pediatrician Goldsboro, NC, 1977—. Contbr. articles to profl. jours. Fellow: Am. Acad. Pediat. (NC chpt. pres. 1993—95, nat. pres. 2008—). Address: Goldsboro Pediat 2706 Medical Office Pl Goldsboro NC 27530 Office: AAP Nat Hdqs 141 Northwest Point Blvd Alden IL 60001*

TAYLOR, ALICE P., medical researcher; PhD, Cornell U., NYC, 1996. Postdoc. fellow dept. internat. medicine Cornell U. Med. Sch., NYC, 1996—98; rschr. Ctr. Molecular Medicine & Immunology-Garden State Cancer Ctr., Belleville, NJ, 1998—. Vol. Meml. Sloan Kettering Hosp., NYC, 1993—2008. Mem.: Sigma Xi. Achievements include discovery of tumor-inhibiting peptides.

TAYLOR, ALLAN BERT, lawyer; b. Cin., June 28, 1948; s. H Ralph and Henrietta Taylor; m. Sally Ann Silverstein, June 6, 1971; children: Rachel Elizabeth, Karen Ruth. AB magna cum laude, Harvard U., 1970, M in Pub. Policy, 1975, JD magna cum laude, 1975. Bar: Conn 1975, US Ct Appeals (DC cir) 1977, US Dist Ct (so dist) NY 1979, US Ct Appeals (2d cir) 1979, US Supreme Ct 1979, US Ct Appeals (1st and 10th cirs) 1991. Law clk. to J. Skelly Wright D.C. Cir., Washington, 1975-76; law clk. to Thurgood Marshall U.S. Supreme Ct., Washington, 1976-77; assoc. Day, Berry & Howard, Hartford, Conn., 1977-83, ptnr., 1983—. Overseer Bushnell Meml Hall Corp, Hartford, 1992—. Bd. dirs. Hartford Infant Action Project, 1990—2006, pres., 1999—2005; elected mem Hartford City Coun, 1981—87; mem. Hartford Bd. Edn., 1989—93, v.p., 1991—93; mem. Conn. State Bd. Edn., Hartford, 1994—2005, chair, 2005—; chmn. charter revision comns. City of Hartford, 1999—2002; bd dirs Conn Asn Bds Educ, Hartford, 1989—93, Hartford Stage Co, 1993—2001. Mem.: ABA, Hartford Bar Asn, Conn Bar Asn, Phi Beta Kappa. Democrat. Jewish. Avocation: reading. Home: 238 Whitney St Hartford CT 06105-2270 Office: Day Pitney LLP 242 Trumbull St Hartford CT 06103-1212 Home Phone: 860-233-8087; Office Phone: 860-275-0225. Business E-Mail: abtaylor@daypitney.com.

TAYLOR, ALLAN RICHARD, retired banker; b. Prince Albert, Sask., Can., Sept. 14, 1932; s. Norman and Anna Lydia (Norbeck) T.; m. Shirley Irene Ruston, Oct. 5, 1957; children: Rodney Allan, Leslie Ann. LLD (hon.), U. Regina, Sask., 1987, Concordia U., Montreal, Can., 1988; DBA (hon.), Laval U., Quebec City, Can., 1990; LLD (hon.), Queen's U., Kingston, Ont., 1991; Doctorate of Univ. (hon.), U. Ottawa, 1992. With Royal Bank of Can., Toronto, Ont., 1949-95, pres., COO, dir., 1983-86, chmn., CEO, dir., 1986-94, chmn., 1994-95, ret., 1995. Bd. dirs. NeuroSci. Can. Found., Montreal; mem. adv. coun. Can. Exec. Svc. Overseas; former chmn. Can. Bankers Assn.; past pres. Internat. Monetary Conf. Former chmn. corp. program IMAGINE; mem. adv. bd. Can. Found. AIDS Rsch.; chmn. hon. adv. bd. Can. Assn. for Cmty. Living. Decorated officer Order of Can. Address: 200 Bay St 29th Fl South Tower Toronto ON Canada M5J 2J5 E-mail: allan.taylor@rbc.com.

TAYLOR, ALLEN, nutritionist, educator; PhD in Organic Chemistry, Rutgers U. Dir. & sr. scientist Lab. Nutrition & Vision, Jean Mayer USDA Human Nutrition Rsch. Ctr. on Aging; prof. dept. biochemistry Sackler Sch. Grad. Biomedical Sciences; assoc. prof. dept. ophthalmology Tufts U. Sch. Medicine; prof. Friedman Sch. Nutrition Sci. & Policy Tufts. U. Office: Tufts University Jean Mayer USDA HNRCA 711 Washington St Boston MA 02111-1524 Office Phone: 617-556-3156. Office Fax: 617-556-3132. E-mail: allen.taylor@tufts.edu.*

TAYLOR, ANDREW C., rental and leasing company executive; b. 1947; BSBA, Denver U., 1970. With RLM Leasing Co., San Francisco, 1970—73, Enterprise Rent-A-Car, St. Louis, 1973—, pres., COO, 1980—91, CEO, 1991—, chmn., 2001—. Dir. Anheuser Busch Co., Commerce Bancshares; pres., CEO Crawford Group. Trustee, conference co-chair National Urban League; trustee Washington U., St. Louis Symphony Orch.; bd. dirs. United Way Greater St. Louis; life trustee Mo. Bot. Garden. Office: Enterprise Rent-A-Car 600 Corporate Park Dr Saint Louis MO 63105-4204

TAYLOR, ANDREW T., JR., radiologist, educator; b. Jackson, Tenn., Jan. 14, 1942; MD, Duke U., 1968. Cert. nuclear medicine Splty. Bd. 1, internal medicine Splty. Bd. 2. Resident U. Hosp.-U.C.S.D., San Diego, 1970, 1972—74, intern, 1969; co-dir. nuc. medicine Emory U. Sch. Med., prof. radiology, 2002—. Mem.: Am. Bd. of Nuclear Medicine (past chair). Office: Emory U Sch of Medicine Radiology 1440 Clifton Rd Atlanta GA 30322

TAYLOR, ANN, writer, educator; d. Gideon S. and Elizabeth L. Stoltzfus; m. James R. Taylor III, Feb. 18, 1983 (dec. Sept. 1995). BA, Ea. Mennonite U., Harrisonburg, Va., 1966; MEd, Millersville U., Pa., 1979; EdD, Temple U., Phila., 1995. Caseworker Lancaster Welfare Dept., Pa., 1969-72, Rockingham County Welfare Dept., 1966—67, Lancaster County Probation Parole Dept., 1967-69; parole agent Pa. Bd. Probation and Parole, Harrisburg, 1972-85; human resource cons., trainer Taylor Assocs., Lancaster, 1985—2004; psychotherapist, career counslor Greystone Psychol. Ctr., 1990—97; founder Kid Brilliance Program, 2005—. Adj. prof. bus. mgmt. Pa. State U., Lancaster, 1979-2000, continuing edn. dept. Franklin and Marshall Coll., Lancaster, 1979-90; free lance trainer Hamilton Bank, Lancaster, 1985-91, Armstrong World Industries, Lancaster, 1987, 91; adv. com. staff trainer Vantage Drug and Alcohol Facility, Lancaster, 1983-85; trainer, public spkr., 1979-92; instr., field rschr., Kid Brilliance Program, Reynold Mid. Sch., Lancaster, Pa. Co-author: Fire Up Your Brilliance. Vol. Lancaster County Mental Health Ctr., 1983-94; seminar leader Fulton County (Pa.) C. of C., 1985-86, York County C. of C., Pa., 1985-86, Lancaster County C. of C., 1985-88. Mem.: ACA. Democrat. Episcopalian. Avocations: travel, reading, gardening, hiking, walking. Office: 214 E King St Lancaster PA 17602 Office Phone: 717-394-6859. Personal E-mail: brilliance@comcast.net.

TAYLOR, ANNA DIGGS, federal judge; b. Washington, Dec. 9, 1932; d. Virginius Douglass and Hazel (Bramlette) Johnston; m. S. Martin Taylor, May 22, 1976; children: Douglass Johnston Diggs, Carla Cecile Diggs. BA, Barnard Coll., 1954; LLB, Yale U., 1957. Bar: D.C. 1957, Mich. 1961. Atty. Office Solicitor Gen. US Dept. Labor, 1957-60; asst. prosecutor Wayne County, Mich., 1961-62; asst. US atty. (ea. dist.) Mich. US Dept. Justice, 1966; ptnr. Zwerdling, Maurer, Diggs & Papp, Detroit, 1970-75; asst. corp. counsel City of Detroit, 1975-79; judge US Dist. Ct. (ea. dist.) Mich., Detroit, 1979—. Hon. chair United Way, Cmty. Found., S.E. Mich.; trustee emeritus Detroit Inst. Arts; co-chair, vol. Leadership Coun.; vice-chair Henry Ford Health Sys. Mem. Fed. Bar Assn., State Bar Mich., Wolverine Bar Assn. (v.p.), Yale Law Assn. Episcopalian. Office: US Dist Ct 740 US Courthouse 231 W Lafayette Blvd Detroit MI 48226-2700

TAYLOR, ANTHONY BALDWIN, civil engineer; b. Nassau, Bahamas, Nov. 25, 1971; came to U.S., 1990; s. Anthony Baldwin Sr. and Ruth Inez (McKenzie) T.; m. Kaaryn Wilaine Rogers, July 2, 1994; children: Anthony Baldwin III, Andrew Benjamin, Antonia Beth. BSCE, NC State U., 1994; PhD, Columbia State U., 1997. Owner, engr. TNT Constn., Nassau, 1992-94; constrn. engr. Greenman Pedersen Inc., Durham, NC, 1994-96; resident engr. Parsons, Butner, 1996—2000, dir. engring. Newport, 2000—03, v.p., program mgr. Atlanta, 2003—. Mem. ASCE, Assn. for Advancement of Cost Engring. Avocations: reading, writing, basketball, sport shooting, fishing. Business E-Mail: tony.taylor@parsons.com.

TAYLOR, ANTHONY BASIL, bishop; b. Ft. Worth, Apr. 24, 1954; s. Basil and Rachel (Roth) Taylor. Attended, Univ. Okla.; BA, St. Meinrad Sem., Ind.; attended, No. Am. Coll., Rome, 1976—80; D in Biblical Theol., Fordham Univ., 1989. Ordained priest Archdiocese of Oklahoma City, 1980; assoc. pastor Sacred Heart parish, Okla. City, 1980—82, Queen of All Saints Mission, Sayre, Okla., 1982—86, Holy Rosary parish, Bronx, NY, 1986—88; vicar for ministries Archdiocese of Oklahoma City, 1988—2008; founding pastor St. Monica parish, Edmond, Okla., 1993—2003; pastor Sacred Heart parish, Okla. City, 2003—08; ordained bishop, 2008; bishop Diocese of Little Rock, Ark., 2008—. Roman Catholic. Office: Diocese of Little Rock PO Box 7565 2500 N Tyler St Little Rock AR 72217 Office Phone: 501-664-0340. Office Fax: 501-664-9075.

TAYLOR, ASHLEY L., JR., lawyer; BA, Va. Mil. Inst., Lexington, 1990; JD, Wash. & Lee U., Lexington, Va., 1993. Bar: Va., US Supreme Ct., US Ct. Appeals (4th cir.), US Dist. Ct. (ea. Va. dist.). Law clk. US Dist. Ct., 1993—95; assoc. Kaufman & Canoles, Norfolk, Va., 1995—98; dep. atty. gen. State of Va., 1998—2001; assoc. Troutman Sanders LLP, 2001—02, ptnr., 2003—. Former dir. Va. Mil. Inst. Athletic Assn.; commr. US Commn. on Civil Rights, 2004—. Contbr. articles to profl. jours. Mem. Commn. on Va. Courts in the 21st Century. Named one of Top 40 Under 40, Style Weekly, 2007, 50 Most Influential Minority Lawyers in America, Nat. Law Jour., 2008; named to Va. Super Lawyers, civil litig. def., 2006—09. Mem.: ABA (chmn. state atty. gen. subcom., former mem. exec. coun., young lawyers divsn., State and Local Govt. Sect. Up and Comer of Yr. 1999), Va. Bar Assn. (former mem. exec. com., young lawyers divsn., mem. com. on fed. judgeships, ea. dist.). Office: Troutman Sanders LLP 1001 Haxall Point PO Box 1122 Richmond VA 23218-1122 Office Phone: 804-697-1286. Office Fax: 804-698-6018. Business E-Mail: ashley.taylor@troutmansanders.com.*

TAYLOR, BARBARA ANN OLIN, writer, educational consultant; b. St. Louis, Feb. 8, 1933; d. Spencer Truman and Ann Amelia (Whitney) Olin; m. F. Morgan Taylor Jr., Apr. 5, 1954; children: Spencer O., James W., John F., Frederick Morgan. AB, Smith Coll., 1954; MBA, Northwestern U., 1978, PhD, 1984; LHD, U. New Haven, 1995. Mem. faculty Hamden (Conn.) Hall Country Day Sch., 1972-74; cons. Booz, Allen & Hamilton, Inc., Chgo., 1979; program assoc. Northwestern U., Evanston, Ill., 1982; co-founder, exec. dir. Nat. Ctr. Effective Schs. R&D, Okemos, Mich., 1986-89, rsch. assoc., 1987; chmn. Nat. Ctr. for Effective Schs. Resource and Devel. Found., 2002—03; cons. on effective schs. rsch. and reform Nat. Ctr. Effective Schs. R&D U. Wis., Madison, 1990-96; pres. Excelsior! Found., Chgo., 1994—. Mem. exec. com. Hudson Inst. New Am. Schs. Devel. Corp. Design Team, 1990—94; Danforth Disting. lectr. U. Nebr., Omaha, 1993. Co-author: (book) Making School Reform Happen, 1993, Keepers of the Dream, 1994, The Revolution Revisited: Effective Schools and Systemic Reform, 1995; editor: Case Studies in Effective Schools Research, 1990; contbr. articles to profl. jours. Co-chair Coalition Housing and Human Resources, Hartford-New Haven, 1970—73; co-chair steering com. Day Care Conn., Hartford, 1971—73; trustee U. New Haven, 1961—71, Smith Coll., Northampton, Mass., 1984—90, Choate Rosemary Hall Sch., 1973—78, Lake Forest Coll., 1996—, Hudson Inst., 1989—97, Northwestern U., 1998—2002; pres. Jr. League New Haven, 1967—69, NCCJ, New Haven, 1971—73. Recipient Humanitarian award, Mt. Calvary Bapt. Ch., 1988, Outstanding Alumna award, John Burroughs Sch., 1994, Pres.'s award, U. New Haven, 1998, Alumni Merit award, Northwestern U., 2004. Mem.: ASCD, Nat. Staff Devel. Coun., Nat. Commn. Citizens Edn. (bd. dirs. 1980—86), Phi Delta Kappa (Internat. award Outstanding Svc. 2000). Episcopalian.

TAYLOR, BARBARA MAE HELM, artist, educator; b. Salina, Kans., Aug. 4, 1940; d. Wilber John and Mildred Mae (Walters) Helm; m. Walter Luther Taylor, II, Feb. 11, 1957; children: Walter Luther III, Natalie Sue Taylor Estes, Laura Marie, Toby Clark. AA, East Ark. C.C., Forrest City, 1990; BFA, Ark. State U., Jonesboro, 1992, MA, 1994. Portrait painter Barbara Taylor Art Studio, Palestine, Ark., 1992—. Adj. prof. Mid South C.C., West Memphis, Ark., 1996—98, East Ark. C.C., Forrest City, Ark., 1998—2006. Author: Every One and Me; numerous art shows, (award). Country fiddle player Ark. Gospel Assn., Forrest City, 1994—; violin player Bethel Bapt. Ch., Forrest City, 2008—. Mem.: Art Exchange, Smithsonian Soc., Audubon Soc., Little Rock Art Links, Am. Soc. Portrait Artists (assoc.), Ark. Artist Registry (life), Delta Art Soc. (v.p. 1999—2000), Memphis Art Links, St. Francis Art Club (life; founder, pres. 2000—), Gamma Beta Phi (life). Avocation: birdwatching. Home: 523 Saint Francis 867 Palestine AR 72372 Office: Barbara Taylor Art Studio 493 St Francis Co 867 Palestine AR 72372-8936 Business E-Mail: barbhelmtaylor@arkansas.net.

TAYLOR, BARRY LLEWELLYN, microbiologist, educator; b. Sydney, May 7, 1937; arrived in US, 1967; s. Fredrick Llewelyn and Vera Lavina (Clarke) T.; m. Desmyrna Ruth Tolhurst, Jan. 4, 1961; children: Lyndon, Nerida, Darrin. BA, Avondale Coll., Cooranbong, New South Wales, 1959; BSc with honors, U. New South Wales, Sydney, 1966; PhD, Case Western Res. U., 1973; postgrad., U. Calif., Berkeley, 1973-75. Vis. postdoctoral fellow Australian Nat. U., Canberra, 1975-76; asst. prof. biochemistry Loma Linda (Calif.) U., 1976-78, assoc. prof. biochemistry, 1978-83, prof. biochemistry, 1983—, prof., chmn. dept. microbiology and molecular genetics, 1988-2000, interim dir. Ctr. for Molecular Biology, 1989-94, 96-98, v.p. for rsch. affairs, 2000—06, prof. microbiology and molecular genetics, 2006—. Contbr. articles to profl. publs. Rsch. grantee Am. Heart Assn., 1978-85, NIH, 1981—. Mem. Am. Soc. Microbiology, Am. Soc. Biochemistry and Molecular Biology. Office: Divsn Microbiology and Molecular Genetics Loma Linda U Loma Linda CA 92350-0001 Office Phone: 909-558-4881. Business E-Mail: bltaylor@llu.edu.

TAYLOR, BENJAMIN CRAIG, orthopedist; b. Mich. s. Julie Taylor; m. Jennifer Taylor; children: Avery, Allison. Med. Degree, Ohio State U., Columbus, 2005. Orthopaedic surgeon Mt. Carmel Med. Ctr., Columbus, 2005—. Orthopaedic Traumatology fellowship, Grant Med. Ctr. Mem.: Am. Acad. Orthopaedic Surgeons, Orthopaedic Trauma Assn., Alpha Omega Alpha. Achievements include research in differences in techniques of lower extremity amputations. Avocations: travel, golf, cooking. Office: Mt Carmel Med Ctr 793 West State St Columbus OH 43222

TAYLOR, BONNITA KAY, biology professor; b. Columbus, Ohio, Dec. 22, 1953; d. Walter Eugene Taylor and Erma Eleanor Mauger; m. Julius Manning Glinter, Nov. 8, 1986. MS, Ea. Mich. U., Ypsilanti, 1991. Adult edn. tchr. Plymouth-Canton Sch., Mich., 1986—92; quality assurance technician Kroger Co., Livonia, 1977—86; prof. biology Schoolcraft Coll., Livonia, Mich., 1991—. Recipient Presdl. Recognition award, Schoolcraft Coll., 2007. Mem.: Mich. CC Biologists. Office: Schoolcraft Coll 18600 Haggerty Rd Livonia MI 48152

TAYLOR, BYRON KEITH, industrial engineer; b. Portsmouth, Va., July 9, 1955; s. Robert Lee and Joyce Sue (Cox) T.; m. Barbara Sue Keene, Aug. 27, 1977; 1 child, Joshua Lee. BS in Indsl. Engring., Va. Poly. Inst. and State U., 1980; MBA, Ariz. State U., 2002. Indsl. engr. Deere & Co. (Harvester), East Moline, Ill., 1980-81, 83-84, product engr., 1981-83, prodn. engr., 1984-90, module owner, 1990-93; sr. engr. new product devel., 1993-95; supr. engring. John Deere, Davenport (Iowa) Works, 1995-97; mgr. loader fabrications John Deere, Davenport Works, 1995-97; mgr. header and sheet metal mfg. John Deere Harvester Works, East Moline, Ill., 1998-99, mgr. supply mgmt., 1999—2001, mgr. mfg., 2001—04; dir. quality worldwide agrl. divsn. Deere and Co. World Hdqs., Moline, Ill., 2005—09, dir. global strategic quality Agr. & T Divsn., 2009—. Mem. engring. curriculum devel. panel Black Hawk Coll., Moline, Ill., 1989; tech. del. conf. Citizen's Amb. program Soviet Union, 1990. Program chmn. Meth. Mens Club, Colona, Ill., 1985; advisor Jr. Achievement, East Moline, 1986-87, cons., 1988; bd. dirs. Handicapped Devel. Ctr., Davenport, 2000—; dir. Deere Harvester Credit Union, East Moline, 2000—. Named Young Engr. of Yr. Quad-Cities Engring. and Sci. Coun., 1989-90. Mem. Inst. Indsl. Engrs. (sr., dir. pub. rels. chpt. 46, 1986-87, pres.-elect 1988-89, pres. 1989-90). Republican. Avocation: golf. Office: Deere & Co World Hdqs One John Deere Pl Moline IL 61265

TAYLOR, CELIANNA ISLEY, information systems specialist; b. Youngstown, Ohio; d. Paul Thornton and Florence (Jacobs) Isley; divorced; children: Polly, Jerry, Jim. BA in Philosophy, Denison U., 1939; MLS, Western Res. U., 1942. Worked in several pub. libs. and univ. librs., 1939-50; head Libr. Cataloging Dept. Battelle Mem. Inst., Columbus, Ohio, 1951-53; head pers. office, assoc. prof. libr. adminstrn. Ohio State U. Librs., Columbus, 1954-65; coord. info. svcs., assoc. prof. libr. adminstrn. Nat. Ctr. for Rsch. in Vocat. Edn., Ohio State U., Columbus, 1966-70; sr. rsch. assoc., adminstrv. assoc., assoc. prof. libr. adminstrn. dept. computer and info. sci. Ohio State U., Columbus, 1970-86, assoc. prof. emeritus Univ. Librs., 1986—. Mem. Task Force on a Spl. Collections Database, Ohio State U. Librs., Columbus, 1988-89, comm. systems and recs. coord. Ohio State U. Retirees Assn.,

Columbus, 1992-93, info. specialist, MacForum, Ohio State U., Columbus, 2001-2004; cons. profl. orgns. including Ernst & Ernst CPA's and Oreg. State Sys. of Higher Edn., 1961-82. Author: (with J. Magisos) Guide for State Voc-Tech Edn. Dissemination Systems 1971; editor: (with A.E. Petrarca, and R.S. Kohn) Info. Interaction 1982; Highlights-Coun. for Ethics in Econs., 1997—; contbr. several articles to profl. jours.; designer info. sys.: CALL Sys., 1977-82, Channel 2000 Proj. Home Info. Svc., 1980-81, Continuing Education Info. Ctr., 1989-90, Human Resources (HUR) Sys., 1976-77,1979-82, DECOS, 1975-86, Computer-asst. libr. Sys., Optical Scan Sys., 1972-73, ERIC Clearinghouse for vocat. edn., 1966-70. Chmn. subcom. on design, info. and ref. com. Columbus United Cmty. Coun., 1972-73; bd. dirs. Columbus Reg. Info. Svc., 1974-78, Cmty. Info. Referral Svc., Inc. 1975-81; dir. Computer Utility for Pub. Info. Columbus, 1975-81; acct. coord. Greater Columbus Free-net, 1994-98; info. specialist, coord. LWV Met. Columbus Website Com., 2001-02; judge Laws of Life Ohio Statewide H.S. Essay Contest, 2005—; interprofessional pub. policy panel on tech. and ethics, Interprofessional Commn. Ohio, 2006-07. Mem. ALA, Assn. Computing Machinery (Ctrl. Ohio chpt.), Am. Soc. Info. Sci. and Tech., Assn. Faculty and Profl. Women Ohio State U., Columbus Metro Club, Coun. for Ethics in Econs., World Future Soc., Coun. for Ethical Leadership, Olympic Indoor Tennis Club. Avocations: birdwatching, gourmet cooking, tennis, exercise. Home and Office: 3471 Greenbank Ct Columbus OH 43221-4724 Office Phone: 614-876-0069.

TAYLOR, CHARLES A. (CHUCK TAYLOR), oil industry executive; b. Ind., 1957; BS in Engring., Purdue U., Ind., 1980; MBA, Tulane U., New Orleans, 1992. Drilling engr. to domestic and internat. engring. and mgmt. positions in upstream operations in the US, Indonesia, the UK and Nigeria Chevron Corp.; mgr. asset devel., area ops. mgr., Bekasap Strategic Bus. Unit Caltex Pacific, Duri, Sumatra, Indonesia, 1996—99; gen. mgr. Chevron UK, Aberdeen, Scotland, 1999—2003; gen. mgr., joint venture Chevron Nigeria Ltd. and Nigerian Nat. Petroleum Co., Nigeria, 2003—07; v.p. health, environment and safety Chevron Corp., 2007—. Chevron rep., bd. dirs. Offshore Prodrs. Trade Sect., UK Offshore Operators Assn.; Chevron rep., oil and gas sector Step Change Initiative. Recipient Allen R. Vorholt award, Tulane U., 1992. Mem.: Beta Gamma Sigma. Office: Chevron Corp Hdqs 6001 Bollinger Canyon Rd San Ramon CA 94583*

TAYLOR, CHARLES ELLETT, biologist, educator; b. Chgo., Sept. 9, 1945; s. Stewart Ferguson and Barbara (Ellett) Taylor; m. Minna Glushien, June 22, 1969. AB, U. Calif., 1968; PhD, SUNY, Stony Brook, 1973. Prof. U. Calif., Riverside, 1974-80, UCLA, 1980—. Cons. artificial life and population genetics; dir. UCLA Cognitive Sci. Rsch. Program, 1990—99; mem. adv. bd. Computer Mus. Fishtank. Co-author: Artifical Life II, 1992, Artifical Life VI, 1998; editor: Artificial Life, 1997—2001; assoc. editor: IEEE Transactions on Evolutionary Computing, 1997—99; assoc. editor Artifical Life and Robotics, 1999—, Artificial Life, 2002—; mem. editl. bd.: Internat. Jour. Distributed Sensor Networks, 2004—; contbr. articles to profl. publs. Office: Dept Ecology and Evolutionary Biology UCLA Box 951606 Los Angeles CA 90095-1606 E-mail: ctaylor@ucla.edu.

TAYLOR, CHARLES HART, former United States Representative from North Carolina; b. Brevard, NC, Jan. 3, 1941; m. Elizabeth Owen; 3 children. BA, Wake Forest U., 1963, JD, 1966. Owner-operator Transylvania Tree Farms, Brevard, NC; founder, chmn. bd. Blue Ridge Savings Bank, Asheville, NC; dir. Fin. Guaranty Corp.; mem. NC State Ho. Reps., Raleigh, 1967—73, minority leader, 1969—73; mem. NC State Senate, Raleigh, 1973—75, minority leader, 1973—75; mem. US Congress from 11th NC dist., 1991—2007, mem. appropriations com., chmn. interior, environment and related agencies subcommittee. Bd. visitors US Mil. Acad. West Point. Recipient Golden Bulldog award, Watchdogs of the Treasury, 1997—98, Guardian of Small Bus. award, Nat. Fedn. Ind. Bus., 1997—98, Voting Achievement award, Nat. Farmers Union, 1997—98, Friend of the Taxpayer award, Ams. for Tax Reform, Nat. Environ. Edn Leadership award, Nat. Environ. Edn. and Tng. Found., 2005; named to Congl. Honor Roll, Seniors' Coalition. Mem.: Western NC Environ. Coun. (vice chair), NC Pks. and Recreation Coun. (chair), NC Energy Policy Coun., NC Bd. Transp. Republican. Baptist.

TAYLOR, CHAROLETTE OLIVIA, primary school educator; b. Chgo., Aug. 2, 1979; d. Jerome Alvin and Velma Louise Taylor. BA in Elem. Edn., Tougaloo Coll., Miss., 2002, AA in Early Childhood Edn., 2002. Tchr. pre-K Walton Elem., Jackson, Miss., 2002—. Tutor, mentor upward bound Tougaloo Coll., 1998. Active Ameri Corps Campus Link, Jackson, 2000—01. Grantee, Edn. Found. Trust, Jackson, 2003. Mem.: Assn. for Childhood Edn. Internat., So. Early Childhood Assn., Miss. Early Childhood Assn.

TAYLOR, CHERYL MEAGAN, pre-school administrator; b. Syracuse, NY, Apr. 28, 1977; d. Michael Charles and Terry Lynn Birmingham; m. James Allen Taylor, June 15, 1995; children: Joshua Alan, Samantha Lynn, Makayla Louise, Alyssa Meagan. Degree in presch. edn., Polk C.C., Lakeland, Fla., 2004. Office mgr., owner Choice Comm. Inc., Lakeland, Fla., 1993—2003; preschool owner Taylor Learning Ctr. Inc., Lakeland, 2003—. Recipient Vol. of Yr., Polk County Sch. Bd., 2003. Home: 4319 Creek Ct Lakeland FL 33811 Office: Taylor Learning Center Inc 827 Oak Ln Lakeland FL 33813 Home Fax: 863-709-9493. Personal E-mail: james4tlc@tampabay.rr.com.

TAYLOR, CHRISTINE, actress; b. Allentown, Pa., July 30, 1971; d. Skip and Joan Taylor; m. Ben Stiller, May 13, 2000; children: Ella Olivia, Quinlin Dempsey. Actor: (films) Calendar Girl, 1993, Showdown, 1993, The Brady Bunch Movie, 1995, Breaking Free, 1995, The Craft, 1996, A Very Brady Sequel, 1996, Cat Swallows Parakeet and Speaks, 1996, Campfire Tales, 1997, The Wedding Singer, 1998, Overnight Delivery, 1998, Denial, 1998, Kiss Toledo Goodbye, 1999, Desperate But Not Serious, 1999, Zoolander, 2001, Dodgeball: A True Underdog Story, 2004, The First Year's A Bitch, 2004, Room 6, 2006, Kabluey, 2007, Dedication, 2007, License to Wed, 2007; (TV films) Here Come the Munsters, 1995, To the Ends of Time, 1996, Heat Vision and Jack, 1999. Office: United Talent Agy 9560 Wilshire Blvd Ste 500 Beverly Hills CA 90212

TAYLOR, CINDY B., oil industry executive; BBA, Tex. A&M Univ. CPA. Acctg. mgmt. positions Ernst & Young, 1984—92; v.p., contr. Cliffs Drilling Co., 1992—99; CFO L.E. Simmons & Associates, 1999—2000; sr. v.p., CFO Oil States Internat., Inc., Houston, 2000—06, pres., COO, 2006—07; pres., CEO Oil States Internat., inc., Houston, 2007—. Bd. dirs. Boots & Coots Internat. Well Control Inc., Global Industries Ltd., Tidewater Inc., 2008—. Office: Oil States Internat 333 Clay St Houston TX 77002

TAYLOR, CORA HODGE, social worker; b. Fayetteville, NC, Nov. 25, 1942; d. John Marlin and Cora Louise (Mitchell) Hodge; m. Charles L. Taylor, June 26, 1965; children: Charles L., John M. BS, N.C. Coll., Durham, 1963; MSW, U. N.C., Chapel Hill, 1965. Clin. social worker VA Hosp., Bedford, Mass., 1965-68, 73-79; chief social worker Regional Health Center, Wilmington, Mass., 1978-79; clin. social worker VA Hosp., Bedford, Mass., 1979-91, supervisory social worker geriatrics and long term care, 1991—2000, coord. contract programs, 1993—. Field instr. Boston U. Sch. Social Work, 1979-87, Smith Coll. Sch. of Social Work, 1986-89; instr., cons. primary care residents Tufts U. Med. Sch., Regional Health Center, Wilmington, Mass., 1978-79. Mem. Town Meeting, Billerica, Mass., 1981-2000; precinct clk., 1981, 82, 89, precinct chmn., 1984, 85, 86; deacon first Congl. Ch., 1986—; women vets. coord. VA Bedford; Social Work Leadership Tng. program, 1998; mem. bd. commrs. Housing Authority Atlantic Beach, SC, 2003-04. Mem. LWC (dir. 1970-73), Acad. Cert. Social Workers, Nat. Assn. Social Workers, Afro-Am. Club The Villages, Hope Luth. Ch. (The Villages), Jozz Lovers Club.

TAYLOR, DANIEL RUSSELL, JR., lawyer; b. Clarksville, Tenn., July 6, 1946; s. Daniel Russell Taylor and Effie Mae Winslow; m. Gwynne Stephens Taylor, May 24, 1975; children: Edward Winslow, William Brinson. Grad., U.S. Mil. Acad., West Point, NY, 1968; JD, Wake Forest U., Winston-Salem, NC, 1976. Sr. ptnr. Kilpatrick Stockton, LLP, Winston-Salem, 1978—. With US Army, 1968—73. Home: 700 Arbor Road Winston Salem NC 27104 Office: Kilpatrick Stockton LLP 1001 W Fourth Street Winston Salem NC 27101 Business E-Mail: dantaylor@kilpatrickstockton.com.

TAYLOR, DARRELL RICHARD, art gallery director, artist; b. Nashville, Jan. 10, 1961; s. Melvin Richard Taylor and Nancy Ledbetter (Taylor) Briggs; m. Christina Moose Taylor (div.); 1 child, Matthew Harrison; life ptnr. Mark Stephen McCusker. BFA, U. Iowa, 1996, MA, 1998, MFA, 1999. Co-artistic dir. Habeas Corpus, Iowa City, 1997—2007; prodn. asst. dance dept. U. Iowa, Iowa City, 1998—2001; acting dir. UNI Gallery of Art, U. No. Iowa, Cedar Falls, 2001—02, art gallery dir., 2003—. Standing mem. art and architecture com. U. No. Iowa, 2001—, chair, 2008—. Author: (exhbn. catalog) Transformations in the Nervepool: The Rituals and Zoacodes of Ebon Fisher, 2005. Sec. Cedar Valley Cultural Alliance, Cedar Falls, 2005; chair UNI Mus. Adv. Bd., 2008, Cedar Falls Pub. Art Com.; tenor sect. leader Nashville Symphony Chorus, 1990. Recipient Charles Massey award, Mid. Tenn. State U., 1992; grantee, Iowa Arts Coun., 2002, 2004, Humanities, Iowa Veridian Credit Union, 2007, Elizabeth Firestone Graham Found.; Mendieta Meml. scholar, U. Iowa, 1997, grant, IMLS, 2005, 2008. Mem.: Coll. Art Assn., Cedar Falls Pub Art Com. Democrat. Avocation: dance. Office: UNI Gallery of Art U No Iowa 104 KAB Cedar Falls IA 50614 Home: 421 Adams St Waterloo IA 50703 Home Phone: 319-331-2464; Office Phone: 319-273-6134. Office Fax: 319-273-7333. Business E-Mail: galleryofart@uni.edu.

TAYLOR, DAVE, professional sports team executive, retired professional hockey player; b. Levack, Ont., Can., Dec. 4, 1955; m. Beth Duken, July 11, 1981; children: Jamie, Katie Ann. Attended, Clarkson U. Right wing LA Kings, 1977—94, capt., 1985—89, mem. front office, 1993—97, gen. mgr., 1997—2006, dir. amateur devel., 2006—07; dir. player personnel Dallas Stars, 2007—. Player NHL All-Star Game, 1981, 82, 86, 94. Recipient Bill Masterton Meml. Trophy, 1991, King Clancy Meml. Trophy, 1991; named NHL Exec. of Yr., Hockey News, 2001; named to Second All-Star Team, 1981. Achievements include having his number, 19, retired by LA Kings, 1995. Office: Dallas Stars 2601 Avenue of the Stars Frisco TX 75034

TAYLOR, DAVID J., photographer; b. 1968; BFA in studio art/photography, Tufts U., 1989; MFA in visual design/photography, U. Oreg., 1994. Grad. tchg. fellow U. Oreg., 1993—94; adj. prof. Oreg. Coll. Art and Craft, 1995—97, Linfield Coll., McMinnville, Oreg., 1995—99, dir. Renshaw Gallery, 1997—99; asst. prof. N.Mex. State U., Las Cruces, 1999—2003, assoc. prof., 2003—. Represented in permanent collections Mus. Contemporary Photography, Columbia Coll., Chgo., Wash. State Arts Commn., Olympia, one-man shows include Obscura Gallery, Portland, Oreg., 1994, U. Oreg. Mus. Art, Eugene, 1995, Quartersaw Gallery, Portland, 1998, Soc. Contemporary Photography, Kansas City, 2001, Ironton Studios and Gallery, Denver, 2001, SPAS Gallery, Rochester Inst. Tech., NY, 2008, exhibited in group shows at Human Relationships with Place and Time, CUNY: Lehman Coll., 1995, Nature and History, Renshaw Gallery, Linfield Coll., McMinnville, Oreg., 1995, Constructs, Benton County Hist. Mus., Philomath, Oreg., 1996, Harvesting the Land, Ball State U. Mus. Art, Muncie, Ind., 1997, From Tractors to Tornadoes, Whatcom Mus., Bellingham, Wash., 1999, Re-Imagining the West, SF Camerawork, San Francisco, 2001, Regarding Water in the West, Landmark Arts, Tex. Tech. U., 2004, Water, Northlight Gallery, Ariz. State U., 2004, Passing Through/Settling In, Stanlee & Gerald Rubin Ctr. Visual Arts, U. Tex. El Paso, 2006. Recipient Purchase award, Biennial Photography Exhbn., 1994, Merit award, 1998; fellow John Simon Guggenheim Found., 2008; David McCosh meml. scholarship, U. Oreg., 1993, Faculty Devel. grant, Linfield Coll., 1997, Faculty minigrant, N.Mex. State U., 2000, 2002, 2004, Nexus Press project grant, Atlanta Contemporary Art Ctr., 2001, pvt. commn., Ryan & Sanders, LLP, 2003, pub. commn., US Gen. Services Adminstrn., 2004, Horak Devel./US Border Patrol, 2006. Office: Bonni Benrubi Gallery 52 E 76th St New York NY 10021 Studio: 428 W Griggs Ave Las Cruces NM 88005 Office Phone: 505-646-2547.*

TAYLOR, DAVID WYATT AIKEN, retired clergyman; b. Tsingkiangpu, Kiangsu, China, Dec. 13, 1925; s. Hugh Kerr and Fanny Bland (Graham) T.; m. Lillian Ross McCulloch, Aug. 25, 1951; children: Frances Bland, David Wyatt. BA, Vanderbilt U., 1949; B.D. cum laude, Union Theol. Sem. Va., 1952; Th.M., Princeton Theol. Sem., 1953; D.D. (hon.), King Coll., Bristol, Tenn., 1959. Ordained to ministry Presbyn. Ch. U.S., 1952. Pastor chs., Elkton, Va., 1953-55, Bristol, Va., 1955-62; ednl. sec. bd. world missions Presbyn. Ch. U.S., 1962-68, program div. dir., 1968-73, ecumenical officer gen. assembly mission bd. Atlanta, 1973-82; pastor Orange Park Presbyn. Ch., Orange Park, Fla., 1982-86; gen. sec. for strategy and interpretation Consultation on Ch. Union, Princeton, NJ, 1986-88, gen. sec., 1988-93; ret., 1993. Instr. Bible Presbyn. Jr. Coll., Maxton, N.C., 1951; mem. program bd., div. Christian edn. Nat. Council Chs., 1965-69, bd. mgrs., dept. edn. for mission, 1962-68, mem. program bd., div. overseas ministries, 1968-78, mem. governing bd., 1976-80, chmn. governing bd. credentials com., 1978; chmn. Church World Service, Inc., 1973-75; mem. adminstrn. and fin. com. Nat. Council Chs., 1973-75, mem. commn. on faith and order, 1978-93; mem. commn. on interchurch aid World Council Chs., 1973-75; mem. 5th Assembly, 1975; rep. Presbyn. Ch. U.S. to World Alliance Ref. Chs., 1976-82; bd. dirs. Presbyn. Survey mag., 1963-68; mem. Consultation on Ch. Union, 1974-93; chmn. Nat. Ecumenical Officers Assn., 1978-81; exec. coun. NC Coun. Chs., 2003—. Bd. dirs. Abingdon Presbytery's Children's Home, Wytheville, Va., 1958-62. Served with AUS, 1944-46, PTO. Mem. Sigma Chi. Presbyterian. Home: 3113 Glenhope Ct Cary NC 27511 Personal E-mail: taylor3@mindspring.com.

TAYLOR, DAWN M., biomedical engineer, educator; BFA with Highest Honors, U. Ariz., 1983; MS in Bioengineering, Ariz. State U., 2001, PhD in Bioengineering, 2002. Rsch. scientist, biomedical engring. Cleve. FES Ctr. Excellence, Cleve. VA Med. Ctr., 2002—; rsch. assoc., dept. biomedical engring. Case Western Reserve U., 2003—04, asst. prof., dept. biomedical engring., 2004—. Develop. and ran an in-house med. graphic svc. Mayo Clinic Scottsdale, 1988—94; adj. investigator, dept. orthop. MetroHealth Med. Ctr., 2004—; adj. investigator, dept. neuroscience Lerner Rsch. Inst., Cleve. Clinic Found., 2006—; adj. investigator, dept. neurosurgery Case Western Reserve U., 2007—; invited spkr. in field. Contbr. several articles to profl. peer-reviewed jours., chapters to books. Recipient Vodovnik award for Excellence in Student Rsch. on Functional Elec. Stimulation, Internat. Functional Elec. Stimulation Soc., 2001, NIH Neural Prosthesis Workshop Student Travel award, 2001; Whitaker Found. Grad. Student Fellowship, 1996—2001, Philanthrophic Ednl. Orgn. Scholarship, 2000—01, several grants awarded as principal investigator and collaborative efforts. Office: Case Western Reserve U Dept Biomedical Engring Wickenden 101 10900 Euclid Ave Cleveland OH 44106-7207 Office Phone: 216-368-2476. Office Fax: 216-778-4259. Business E-Mail: dxt42@case.edu.*

TAYLOR, DIANA LANCASTER, investment company executive, former state official; b. Summit, NJ, Feb. 6, 1955; d. Edwin Douglas and Lois Johnston (O'Neill) Taylor. AB, Dartmouth Coll., 1977; MBA, Columbia U., 1979-81. Analyst N.Y. State Dept. Soc. Service, NYC, 1977-79; assoc. Smith, Barney, Harris, Upham, NYC, 1981-82, Lehman Brothers Kuhn Loeb, NYC, 1982-83, v.p., 1983-84, Donaldson, Lufkin & Jenrette, NYC, 1984-86, sr. v.p., mgr. short-term banking, 1987-88, sr. v.p., mgr. edn. fin. group, 1987-88; founding ptnr. M.R. Beal & Co., 1988—90, pres., 1990—93; exec. v.p., head capital markets Muriel Siebert & Co., 1993—95; sr. v.p. pub. fin. Smith Mitchell Investment Group Inc., 1996—99; asst. sec. for pub. authorities State of NY, 1999; v.p. govtl. & regulatory affairs KeySpan Energy, NYC, 2000—02; CFO LI Power Authority, NY, 2001—02; dep. sec. for state authorities State of NY, 2002—03, dep. sec. for fin. & housing, 2003, supt. banks, 2003—07; mng. dir. Wolfensohn & Co. LLC, NYC, 2007—. Bd. dirs. Fannie Mae (Fed. Nat. Mortgage Assn.), 2008—, Citigroup Inc., 2009—, Allianz Global Investors Fund Mgmt, LLC, Brookfield Properties, LLC, Sotheby's Holdings, Inc. Bd. dirs. YMCA Greater NYC, Hudson River Park Trust, The After Sch. Corp., NYC Transit Mus., Bklyn. Acad. Music; bd. trustees Dartmouth U., 2008—. Named one of The 50 Most Powerful Women In NYC, 2007. Office: Wolfensohn & Co LLC 1350 Ave of the Americas 29th Fl New York NY 10019*

TAYLOR, DONALD, retired manufacturing executive; b. Worcester, Mass., June 2, 1927; s. John A. B. and Alice M. (Weaver) T.; m. Ruth L. Partridge, June 24, 1950; children: Linda Taylor Robertson, Donald, Mark, John. BSME, Worcester Poly. Inst., 1949; grad., Northeastern U. Mgmt. Devel. Program, 1962, Harvard Bus. Sch. Advanced Mgmt. Program, 1979. Registered profl. engr., Mass. With George J. Meyer Mfg. Co., Milw., 1954-69; pres. mfg. div. A-T-O, Inc., 1969; exec. v.p. Nordberg div. Rex Chainbelt, Inc., Milw., 1969-73; v.p. ops. Rexnord Inc., Brookfield, Wis., pres., chief operating officer, 1978-85, chief exec. officer, from 1985, chmn., 1985-88; pres. Nordberg Machinery Group, Milw., 1973-78. With USNR, 1951—54. Mem. ASME, Milw. Country Club, Milw. Town Club, Univ. Club, Masons. Office: 1 Runnymede Dr North Hampton NH 03862-2328

TAYLOR, DUNCAN PAUL, pharmacologist, researcher; b. Bremerton, Wash., Feb. 4, 1949; s. Alan Earl and Barbara Eleanor (Thiel) T.; m. Jeanne Louise Damgaard, Apr. 8, 1972; 1 child, Jack Xander. BS in Chemistry, Calif. Inst. Tech., 1971; PhD in Biochemistry, Oreg. State U., 1978. Technician analytical svcs. Carnation Co. Rsch. Labs., Van Nuys, Calif., 1967-70; Peace Corps vol. Princess Margaret Secondary Sch., St. Johns, Antigua and Barbuda, 1971-73; grad. tchg. and rsch. asst. biochemistry and biophysics Oreg. State U., Corvallis, 1973-77; rsch. assoc. sect. biochemistry and pharmacology NIMH, Bethesda, Md., 1977-79; scientist, neuropharmacologist, rsch. assoc. Pharm. divsn. Mead Johnson & Co., Evansville, Ind., 1979-80; sr. scientist, group leader Pharm. div. Mead Johnson & Co., Evansville, Ind., 1980-82; sr. scientist, group leader, neuropharmacologist Pharm. R & D divsn. Bristol-Myers Co., Evansville, 1982-83, sr. rsch. scientist, mgr., 1983-85, rsch. fellow preclin. ctrl. nervous sys. rsch., 1985-89; sr. rsch. fellow preclin. ctrl. nervous sys. rsch. Pharm. Rsch. Inst. Bristol-Myers Squibb Co., Wallingford, Conn., 1989-94; dir. pharmacology Symphony Pharms., Malvern, Pa., 1994-95; cons., 1995-96; analyst bus. devel. Pharmacia & Upjohn, Kalamazoo, 1996-98, dir. strategic rsch. assessment, 1998—2003, Biovail Techs., Ltd., Bridgewater, NJ, 2004—05; sr. dir. strategic intelligence Biovail Pharms., Inc., Bridgewater, 2005—07; prin. MT Enterprises, Kalamazoo, 2007—08; sr. dir. bus. devel. SK Life Sci., Fair Lawn, NJ, 2008—. Mem. external adv. bd. dept. chemistry U. So. Miss.; grant reviewer NSF, 1981, 82, Med. Rsch. Coun. Can., 1987, 88; frequent presenter to profl. confs.; cons. in field. Contbr. numerous articles and abstracts to profl. jours. Bd. dirs. Posey County chpt. Am. Cancer Soc., 1983—85; mem. Tri-State Cursillo Cmty.; mentor Horizons Leadership Acad., Evansville-Vanderburgh Sch. Corp., 1985; cons. Project Bus. Jr. Achievement, 1988; mem. chancel choir 1st United Meth. Ch., Mt. Vernon, Ind., 1979—86; mem. adult choir South Congl. Ch., Middletown, Conn., 1986—96, deacon, 1987—90, 1995—96, co-chmn., 1989—90, 1996, mem. coun., 1989—90, mem. task force on long-range planning, 1989—90; mem. adult choir 2d Reformed Ch., Kalamazoo, 1997—2004, mem. handbell choir, 1997—2004, mem. worship coun., 1997—99, elder, 1998—2001, consistory mem., 1998—2001, ch. outreach coun., 2000—01; mem. Grace United Ch. of Christ, Flemington, NJ, 2005—, trustee, 2006—, coun. moderator, 2006—. Scholar Carnation Co., 1967-70, Calif. State scholar, 1967-68, 70; rsch. fellow NSF, 1970, Cold Spring Harbor Labs., 1974. Fellow: Am. Inst. Chemists; mem.: Lic. Exec. Soc., Am. Acad. Neurology, Internat. Brain Rsch. Orgn.-World Fedn. Neuroscientists, Fedn. Am. Socs. for Exptl. Biology, European Brain and Behavior Soc., Brit. Brain Rsch. Assn, Soc. for Neurosci. (v.p. Conn. chpt. 1989—93), Am. Soc. for Pharmacology and Exptl. Therapeutics, Am. Chem. Soc., Phi Lambda Upsilon, Sigma Xi. Democrat. Achievements include patent for method and treatment of ischemia in the brain; made significant efforts in identification and development of new antipsychotics and antidepressants; identification of potential mechanism of action of the antipsychotic BMY14802; research in receptors, in etiology, expression and pharmacotherapy of psychiatric disorders. Home: 11 Jockey Ln Flemington NJ 08822-1599 Business E-Mail: dtaylor@sklsi.com.

TAYLOR, E. DENNIS, English language educator, editor; b. Balt., Feb. 26, 1940; s. Frank Edmund and Mary Chester Taylor; m. Mary Barber Brown, Aug. 28, 1966; children: John Edmund, Frank Matthew, Kathryn Elizabeth Wall, MaryRebecca Hayden. PhD, Yale U., 1965. Emeritus editor Religion and the Arts, Boston Coll., Chestnut Hill, 1996—; emeritus prof. English dept. Boston Coll., Chestnut Hill, Mass., 1971—. Author: (scholarly work) Hardy's Metres and Victorian Prosody, 1988, Hardy's Literary Language and Victorian Philology, 1998, Hardy's Poetry 1860-1928, 1998 (Macmillan/Hardy Soc. prize, 1990), Jude the Obscure, 1998, Shakespeare and the Culture of Christianity in Early Modern England, 2003. Democrat. Home: 24 Riverdale Rd Concord MA 01742 Office: Boston Coll Carney 447 Chestnut Hill MA 02467 Home Phone: 978-369-3336; Office Phone: 978-844-4929. E-mail: taylor@bc.edu.

TAYLOR, E. JANE, lawyer; b. Niagra Falls, NY, Dec. 16, 1954; BA cum laude, Kent State U., 1977; JD, U. Akron, 1980. Bar: Ohio 1981, U.S. Dist. Ct. No. Dist. Ohio 1981, U.S. Ct. Appeals (6th cir.) 1985, U.S. Dist. Ct. So. Dist. Ohio 2002. Assoc. atty. Guy Lammert & Towne, Akron, Ohio, 1981—90, ptnr., 1990—. Mem. Akron Law Rev., 1979—80. Mem. bd. trustees United Way Summit County, 1995—2002, past chair svc. rev. team, mem. cmty. investment coun., chair portfolio coun. improving health and wellness, past mem. planning and allocations com., co-chair task force multi-yr. funding. Named one of 100 Women of Distinction, Akron Area YWCA, 2001. Mem.: ABA, Comml. Law League Am., Ohio Women's Bar Assn., Nat. Conf. Bar Presidents, Ohio State Bar Assn. (mem. coun. delegates 1996—2003, mem. bd. govs. 2000—03, pres.-elect 2004—, pres. 2005), Akron Bar Assn. (chair bar applicants and students com. 1988—90, mem. bankruptcy and comml. law sect. 1989—, bd. trustees 1990—93, v.p. 1993—94, pres. 1994—95, outstanding com. chairperson 1997—98). Office: Guy Lammert & Towne 2210 First National Tower Akron OH 44308 Office Phone: 330-535-2151. Office Fax: 330-535-9048. E-mail: guylaw2210@aol.com.

TAYLOR, EDNA JANE, retired employment program counselor; b. Flint, Mich., May 16, 1934; d. Leonard Lee and Wynona Ruth (Davis) Harvey; children: Wynona Jane MacDonald, Cynthia Lee Zellmer. BS, No. Ariz. U., 1963; MEd, U. Ariz., 1967. Tchr. h.s. Sunnyside Sch. Dist., Tucson, 1963—68; employment program counselor employment devel. State of Calif., Canoga Park, 1968—98; ret., 1998. Mem. adv. coun. Van Nuys Cmty. Adult Sch., Calif., 1983-96, steering com., 1989-91, leadership coun., 1991-92; mem. adv. coun. Pierce CC, Woodland Hills, Calif., 1979-81; first aid instr., recreational leader ARC. Mem. AARP, NAFE, Internat. Assn. of Pers. in Employment Security, Calif. Employment Counselors Assn. (state treas. 1978-79, state sec. 1980), Delta Psi Kappa (life). Avocations: writing, tennis, health and fitness, gardening.

TAYLOR, EDWARD CURTIS, chemistry professor; b. Springfield, Mass., Aug. 3, 1923; s. Edward Curtis and Margaret Louise (Anderson) T.; m. Virginia Dion Crouse, June 29, 1946; children: Edward Newton, Susan Raines. Student, Hamilton Coll., 1942-44, DSc (hon.), 1969; AB, Cornell U., 1946, PhD, 1949. Postdoctoral fellow Nat. Acad. Scis., Zurich, Switzerland, 1949-50; DuPont postdoctoral fellow chemistry U. Ill., 1950-51, faculty, 1951-54, asst. prof. organic chemistry, 1952-54; faculty Princeton U., 1954—, prof. chemistry, 1964—, A. Barton Hepburn prof. organic chemistry, 1966—, A. Barton Hepburn prof. organic chemistry emeritus, 1997—, chmn. dept. chemistry, 1974-79, sr. rsch. scientist, 1997—, sr. scholar, 2007—. Vis. prof. Technische Hochschule, Stuttgart, Fed. Republic Germany, 1960, U. East Anglia, 1969, 71; Disting. vis. prof. U. Buffalo, 1968, U. Wyo., 1977; Backer lectr. U. Groningen, Holland, 1969; mem. chemistry adv. com. Office Sci. Research, USAF, 1962-73, Cancer Chemotherapy Nat. Service Ctr., 1958-62; mem. internat. adv. bd. Ctr. Medicinal Chemistry, Bar-Ilan U., Israel, 1994—; cons. rsch. divs. Parke-Davis Co., 1951-56, Procter & Gamble, 1953-80, Smith Kline & French, 1956-62, Eastman Kodak Co., 1965-83, Tenn. Eastman Co., 1968-83, Eli Lilly & Co., 1962-2002, Burroughs Wellcome Co., 1983-95, E.I. duPont de Nemours & Co., 1986-90, Polaroid Corp., 1986-2001, Dow Elanco Co., 1989-96, DuPont Merck Pharm. Co., 1990-97, Dow AgroScis., 1997-2003, DuPont Pharms. Co., 1997-2001. Author: (with McKillop) Chemistry of Cyclic Enaminonitriles and o-Aminonitriles, 1970, Principles of Heterocyclic Chemistry: film and audio courses, 1974; editor (with Raphael and Wynberg) Advances in Organic Chemistry, vols I-V, 1960-65, (with Wynberg) Vol VI, 1969, vols. VII-IX, 1970-79 (with W. Pfleiderer) Pteridine Chemistry, 1964, The Chemistry of Heterocyclic Compounds, 1968—, General Heterocyclic Chemistry, 1968—; organic chemistry editl. advisor John Wiley & Sons, Inc., 1968—; mem. editl. adv. bd. Jour. Medicinal Chemistry, 1962-66, Jour. Organic Chemistry, 1971-75, Synthetic Communications, 1971—, Heterocycles, 1973—, Chm. Substructure Index, 1971—, Advances in Heterocyclic Chemistry, 1983—, Pteridines, 1989—. Recipient rsch. awards, SmithKline and French Found., 1955, Hoffmann-LaRoche Foun., 1964—65, Ciba Found., 1971, Disting. Hamilton award, 1977, U.S. Sr. Scientist prize, Alexander von Humboldt Found., 1983, Disting. Alumni medal, Hamilton Coll., 1990, F. Gowland Hopkins medal, 1993, Thomas Alva Edison award, R&D Coun. NJ, 2004; sr. faculty fellow, Harvard U., 1959, Guggenheim fellow, 1979—80. Fellow N.Y. Acad. Scis., Am. Inst. Chemists; mem. Am. Chem. Soc. (award for creative work in synthetic organic chemistry, 1974, chmn. organic chemistry div. 1976-77, Arthur C. Cope scholar award 1994, Heroes of Chemistry award 2006), German Chem. Soc., Royal Soc. London, Internat. Soc. Heterocyclic Chemistry (5th Internat. award 1989), Phi Beta Kappa, Sigma Xi, Phi Kappa Phi. Achievements include patents for Alimta. Home: 288 Western Way Princeton NJ 08540-5337 Office Phone: 609-258-3914. Business E-Mail: etaylor@princeton.edu.

TAYLOR, EDWARD STEWART, obstetrician, educator; b. Hecla, SD, Aug. 20, 1911; s. Robert Stewart and Sylvia Frances (Dewey) T.; m. Ruth Fatherson, June 15, 1940; children: Edward Stewart, Elizabeth Dewey Taylor Bryant, Catherine Wells Taylor. BA, U. Iowa, 1933, MD, 1936. Diplomate Am. Bd. Ob-Gyn (dir. 1962-69). Intern, Hurley Hosp., Flint, Mich., 1936-37; splty. tng. ob-gyn L.I. Coll. Hosp., 1937-41; prof. ob-gyn, chmn. dept. Sch. Medicine, U. Colo., 1947-76, clin. prof., 1976-81, prof., chmn. emeritus, 1981—. Nat. cons. ob-gyn to surg. gen. USAF, 1958-62. Author: Manual of Gynecology, 1952, Essentials of Gynecology, 4th edit.; editor: Beck's Obstetrical Practice, 10th edit.; editor-in-chief for obstetrics: Obstetrical and Gynecol. Survey, 1967-92. Trustee Denver Symphony Orch., 1979-85. Served to lt. col. AUS, 1942-45. Endowed ob-gyn. chair U. Colo., 1999. Fellow ACS, Am. Coll. Obstetricians and Gynecologists (Disting. Svc. award 1984); mem. AMA, Am. Gynecol. Soc. (v.p. 1974-75), Am. Assn. Obstetricians and Gynecologists (pres. 1970-71), Ctrl. Assn. Obstetricians and Gynecologists, S.W. Obstet. and Gynecol. Soc. (hon.), Am. Gynecol. and Obstet. Soc., Assn. Profs. Ob-Gyn (pres. 1974-75), Western Surg. Soc., Finnish Gynecol. Soc. (hon.), University Club, Alpha Omega Alpha. Congregationalist. Home: 80 S Dexter St Denver CO 80246-1051

TAYLOR, EDWIN R., music director; b. Port Huron, Mich., Sept. 4, 1952; s. Leroy E. and Virgene M. Taylor; m. Faith A. Ferry, Sept. 28, 1996; children: Jenelle F. Ferry, Jordan W. Ferry, Colton W. Ferry. MusB, Westminster Choir Coll., Princeton, NJ, 1975, MusM, 1979; postgrad., UCLA, 1996. Music dir. Covenant Presbyn. Ch., Fort Myers, Fla., 1984—98; co-dir. Gulf Coast Opera Co., Fort Myers, Fla., 1996—2001; chorus master SW Fla. Symphony Chorus, Fort Myers, 1997—98; music dir. Venice United Ch. Of Christ, Fla., 1998—2001; min. music, music dir. The First Congl. Ch., Ridgefield, Conn., 2001—. Adj. prof. Fla. Gulf Coast Univ., Fort Myers, 1999—2001; concert series dir. The First Congl. Ch., Ridgefield, 2001—; guest condr. Wapping Cmty. Ch., South Windsor, Conn., 2004—08; singer Yale Camerata, New Haven, 2005—06. Composer: (anthem for choir, organ, brass, percussion) Sing Praise To God Who Reigns Above, (anthem for male chorus) In The Bleak Midwinter, (hymntunes) Farmer, Crown Chase, Simpson, Duncan, Faithsong, Sluyter, King's Crown, Harding, Emory, Spring Hill Lane, St. Patrick's, Liberation, Presbyterian Hymnal, 1990, Christian Sci. Hymnal Supplement, 2009, Duncan, (for brass quintet) Lo, How A Rose E'er Blooming, Angels We Have Heard On High, (for piano) Songs Of Home, (for choir and congregation) Missa Memoria, 2009; arranger: for choir, organ, brass, percussion O Praise Ye The Lord, for brass, organ, percussion Feierlicher Einzug, for handbells, organ, brass, percussion, chair The Great Gate of Kiev, Processional March, Rigaudon, Trumpet Tune, Prelude, Jesus Walked This Lonesome Valley. Mem.: Westminster Choir Coll. Alumni Assn. (class agt. 1984—90, alumni coun. mem. 1994—96), Choristers Guild (v.p. 2006), Fairfield-West Chpt. Am. Guild Organists (mem. exec. bd. 2002—05, dean 2006—08), Aircraft Owners and Pilots Assn. Achievements include first to Conduct the modern-day premiere of Sousa's The Last Crusade. Avocations: flying, writing, cooking, travel. Home: 34 Spring Hill Ln Bethel CT 06801-2724 Office: The First Congregational Church 103 Main St Ridgefield CT 06877 Business E-Mail: music@firstcongregational.com.

TAYLOR, ELIZABETH (DAME ELIZABETH ROSEMOND TAYLOR), actress; b. London, Feb. 27, 1932; d. Francis Lenn and Sara Viola (Warmbrodt) Taylor; m. Conrad Nicholas Hilton Jr., May 6, 1950 (div. Feb. 1, 1951); m. Michael Wilding, Feb. 21, 1952 (div. Jan. 30, 1957); children: Christopher Edward, Michael Howard; m. Michael Todd, Feb. 2, 1957 (dec. Mar. 22, 1958); 1 child, Elizabeth Frances; m. Eddie Fisher, May 12, 1959 (div. Mar. 6, 1964); m. Richard Burton, Mar. 15, 1964 (div. June 26, 1974); 1 adopted child, Maria; m. Richard Burton, Oct. 10, 1975 (div. Aug. 1, 1976); m. John W. Warner, Dec. 4, 1976 (div. Nov. 7, 1982); m. Larry Fortensky, Oct. 6, 1991 (div. Oct. 31, 1996). Student, Byron House, Hawthorne Sch., Metro-Goldwyn-Mayer Sch. Ptnr., cons. House of Taylor Jewelry, Inc, 2005—. Actress: (films) There's One Born Every Minute, 1942; Lassie Come Home, 1943; The White Cliffs of Dover, 1944; Jane Eyre, 1944; National Velvet, 1944; Courage of Lassie, 1946; Cynthia, 1947; Life with Father, 1947; A Date with Judy, 1948; Julia Misbehaves, 1948; Little Women, 1950; Conspirator, 1950; The Big Hangover, 1950; Father of the Bride, 1950; Quo Vadis, 1951; Father's Little Dividend, 1951; A Place in the Sun, 1951; Callaway Went Thataway, 1951; Lover is Better Than Ever, 1952; Ivanhoe, 1952; The Girl Who Had Everything, 1953; Elephant Walk, 1954; Rhapsody, 1954; Beau Brummel, 1954; The Last Time I Saw Paris, 1954; Giant, 1956; Raintree County, 1957; Cat on a Hot Tin Roof, 1958; Suddenly, Last Summer, 1959; Scent of Mystery, 1960; Butterfield 8, 1960 (Acad. award for Best Actress, 1960); Cleopatra, 1963; The V.I.P.'s, 1963; The Sandpiper, 1965; Who's Afraid of Virginia Woolf?, 1966 (Acad. award for Best Actress, 1966); The Comedians, 1967; Reflections in a Golden Eye, 1967; Dr. Faustus, 1967; Boom!, 1968; Secret Ceremony, 1968; Anne of the Thousand Days, 1969; The Only Game in Town, 1970; Under Milkwood, 1971; X, Y and Zee, 1972; Hammersmith is Out, 1972; Night Watch, 1973; Ash Wednesday, 1973; That's Entertainment, 1974; The Driver's Seat, 1974; Blue Bird, 1975; Winter Kills, 1977; A Little Night Music, 1977; The Mirror Crack'd, 1980; Young Toscanini, 1988; The Flintstones, 1994; Actress, prodr. The Taming of the Shrew, 1967; Actress: (TV films) Divorce His-Divorce Hers, 1973; Victory at Entebbe, 1977; Return Engagement, 1979; Between Friends, 1982; Malice in Wonderland, 1986; There Must Be a Pony, 1986; Poker Alice, 1987; Sweet Bird of Youth, 1989; These Old Broads, 2001; (TV miniseries) North and South, 1985; (TV series) General Hospital, 1981; All My Children, 1984; Hotel, 1984; The Simpsons, 1993; The Nanny, 1996; Murphy Brown, 1996; High Society, 1996; theatre appearances include: (Broadway plays) The Little Foxes, 1981; Private Lives, 1983; narrator: (documentaries) Genocide, 1981; exec. prodr.: (films) Number 13, 1962; exec. prodr.: (films) Oz, 1967; assoc. prodr.: (films) The Caretaker, 1963; author: (autobiography) Elizabeth Taylor, 1965, Elizabeth Taylor Takes Off: On Weight Gain, Weight Loss, Self Esteem and Self Image, 1988, Elizabeth Taylor: My Love Affair with Jewelry, 2002; co-author (with Richard Burton): (novels) World Enough and Time, 1964; lic. (fragrances) Elizabeth Taylor's Passion, Passion for Men, White Diamonds/Elizabeth Taylor, Elizabeth Taylor's Diamonds & Emeralds, Diamonds and Rubies, Diamonds & Sapphires, Elizabeth Taylor Black Pearls. Active philanthropic, relief, charitable causes internationally, including Israeli War Victims Fund for the Chaim Sheba Hosp., 1976, UNICEF, various children's hosps., med. clinics, Botswana; initiated Ben Gurion U. - Elizabeth Taylor Fund for Children of the Negev, 1982; supporter AIDS Project, LA, 1985; founder, nat. chmn. Am. Found. for AIDS Rsch. (AmFAR), 1985—, internat. fund, 1985—; founder Elizabeth Taylor AIDS Found., 1991—. Recipient Legion of Honor (for work with AmFAR), France, 1987, Aristotle S. Onassis Found., 1988, Jean Hersholt Humanitarian Acad. award (for work as AIDS advocate), 1993, Life Achievement award, Am. Film Inst., 1993, BAFTA Fellowship Award, British Acad. Film and Television Arts, 1999, Presdl. Citizen's Medal, 2001, Humanitarian award for AIDS Activism, Macy's Passport event, 2007; named Comdr. Arts Letters, France, 1985, an honoree with dedication of Elizabeth Taylor Med. Ctr. Whitman - Walker Clinic, Washington, 1993, Dame Comdr. of Order of British Empire (DBE), Her Majesty Queen Elizabeth II, 1999; named a Kennedy Ctr. Honoree, John F. Kennedy Ctr. for the Performing Arts, 2002; named to The Calif. Hall of Fame, 2007. Address: Elizabeth Taylor AIDS Found PO Box 55995 Sherman Oaks CA 91413*

TAYLOR, ELIZABETH JANE, investment advisor, real estate company and marketing executive; b. Tiffin, Ohio, Oct. 27, 1941; d. Albert Joseph Lucas and Mary Jane Siebenaller-Swander; m. Gaylen Lloyd Taylor, July 11, 1977. Student, Heidelberg Coll., 1961, Austin CC, Tex., 1983-84; grad., Real Estate Edn. Ctr., 1984, Inst. Real Estate, 1988, Real Estate Inst., 1989; Tex. Realtors Inst., 1989; student, Rockhurst Coll., 1991-92. Dir. regional mktg. Sibrow, Inc., Ottawa, Can., 1981-83; realtor assoc. Alliance Sales, Austin, 1985-88; assoc. Broadway Comml. Investments, 1988-91; prin. Taylor & Assocs. Internat. Mktg. & Bus. Devel., 1980-98. Cons. Hypnosis Conn., Ohio, Tex. and Ariz., 1967—; tchr. mktg. and bus. devel., 1980-96. Author: Letters from Home, 1986, Unfinished Business, 2001, Reflections and Dreams, 2002, Unfinished Business, 2002, Southwest Celebration, 2003, A Dark and Stormy Night, 2003, Soul's Music, 2003, A Christmas Collection, 2003, Sourdough & More, 2003, 2007, Joy of Poetry, 2004, A Treasury of Poetry, 2005, Marketing Yourself As a Freelance Writer, 2005; contbr. Best New Poets of 1986, American Poetry Anthology, vol. VI., #3, 1986; columnist Austin Women Mag., 1984-86, (poetry) Desert Spirts, 2007. V.p. Am. Congress on Real Estate, 1982-83; arbitrator Better Bus. Bur., 1984-89, sr. arbitrator, Austin, 1989-95; spkrs. bur. Austin Womans Ctr., 1985-88; v.p. Austin World Affairs Coun., 1984-94; adv. panel Austin Woman Mag., 1984-86. Nominee to Tex. Womens Hall of Fame, 1984. Mem. NAFE (network dir. 1980-88), Am. Biog. Inst. Rsch. (hon., bd. advisors 1988). Avocations: writing, behavior research. Home: 3926 E Cherokee St Phoenix AZ 85044-3827 Personal E-mail: elizabethlucastaylor@yahoo.com.

TAYLOR, ERROL BANCROFT, lawyer; b. Kingston, Jamaica, Nov. 24, 1955; s. Samuel George and Etta Maud (Champagnie) T.; m. Paula Whitfield, July 8, 1989; children: Bradford Russell, Kyle Bancroft. BA in Biology, SUNY, Oswego, 1977; JD, NY Law Sch., 1987. Bar: NY 1988, US Dist. Ct. (So. and Ea. Dists.) NY 1988, US Ct. Appeals (fed. cir.) 1991, US Supreme Ct. 2006. Sr. rsch. assoc. Squibb Corp., New Brunswick, NJ, 1977-81, asst. rsch investigator, 1981-87; assoc. atty. Fitzpatrick, Cella, Harper & Scinto, NYC, 1987-93, ptnr., 1994—2003, Milbank, Tweed, Hadley & McCloy, LLP, NYC, 2003—. Lectr. in field. Bd. dirs. Oswego Coll. Found., 1997—. Named one of Top 10 Litigators, Nat. law Jour., 2003. Mem. ABA, Am. Intellectual Property Law Assn., Fed. Cir. Bar. Assn., Nat. Bar. Assn., N.Y. Intellectual Property Law Assn., Assn. Bar for the City N.Y. (patent com. 1994-97). Office: Milbank, Tweed, Hadley & McCloy LLP 1 Chase Manhattan Plz New York NY 10005-1413 Office Phone: 212-530-5545. Office Fax: 212-822-5545. Business E-Mail: etaylor@milbank.com.

TAYLOR, FRANCES O'CONNELL, lawyer; b. Atlanta, Oct. 24, 1951; d. James Joseph and Julia (Chesser) O'Connell; m. Simon R.H. Taylor, Apr. 25, 1987; children: Katherine, Emma. BA honors, U. Fla., 1973; JD honors, U. Ga., 1978; LLM, London Sch. Econs., 1986. Bar: Md. 1988, U.S. Ct. Appeals (D.C. cir.) 1983, U.S. Ct. Appeals (4th cir.) 1983, U.S. Ct. Appeals (6th cir.) 1984, U.S. Ct. Appeals (2d cir.) 1987, U.S. Ct. Appeals (5th cir.) 1987. Sr. counsel, trial counsel Nat. Labor Rels. Bd., Washington, 1979—88; assoc. Shawe and Rosenthal, Balt., 1988—95, Gordon Feinblatt Rothman Hoffberger and Hollander LLC, Balt., 1995—98, mem., 1998—2005, Taylor & Ryan, LLC, Balt., 2005—. Contbr. The Employment Law Deskbook, 1990; co-author, editor The Maryland Handbook on Labor and Employment Law. Bd. dirs. Pumpkin Theatre, Balt., 1995—, chair, 1998—2003; chair, bd. dir. Goodwill Industries Chesapeake, Balt., 2009—, officer, bd. dirs., 1996—. Recipient Top 100 Women in Md. award, Daily Record, 2002, 2004, 2009, 2009, Cir. of Excellence award, 2009; named one of Best Lawyers in America, 2006—09. Mem.: ABA, Am. Immigration Lawyers Assn. Office: Taylor & Ryan LLC CommerCtr E Ste 265 1777 Reisterstown Rd Baltimore MD 21208 Office Phone: 410-412-3462. Office Fax: 800-254-4971. Business E-Mail: ftaylor@taylor-ryan.com.

TAYLOR, FRANCIS MICHAEL, auditor, municipal official; b. Munich, 1960; came to the U.S., 1961; BS, Va. Tech., 1982. CPA Va., cert. internal auditor. Pub. acct. Brown, Edwards, Co., Roanoke, Va., 1982-84; controller ARC Roanoke, Inc., Roanoke, 1984-87; audit supr. City of Roanoke, 1987-94; city auditor City of Stockton (Calif.), 1994—. Nat. coord. com. Key Nat. Indicators Initiative. Mem. AICPA, Nat. Assn. Local Govt. Auditors (chair peer review com., past pres.), Calif. Soc. CPAs, Inst. Internal Auditors, Bay Area Local Govt. Auditors, Brookside Country Club (mem. fin. club). Office: 22 E Weber Ave Ste 325 Stockton CA 95202-1951

TAYLOR, FRED, professional football player; b. Belle Glade, Fla., June 27, 1976; m. Andrea Taylor; children: Nataajah, Inari. BS in Sociology, U. Fla., Gainesville. Running back Jacksonville Jaguars, Fla., 1998—2009, New Eng. Patriots, 2009—. Spokesman Leukemia Soc. Am., Lymphoma Soc. Am., Glades Asthma Project. Named FedEx Air & Ground NFL Player of Yr., 2007; named to Am. Football Conf. Pro Bowl Team, NFL, 2007. Office: New Eng Patriots One Patriots Pl Foxboro MA 02035*

TAYLOR, GARY, literature and language professor; life ptnr. Celia R. Daileader; children: Isaac, Joshua Daniel, Michael. BA in English and Classics, U. Kans., Lawrence, 1975; PhD in English lit., U. Cambridge, Eng., 1978. Editor: William Shakespeare, Complete Works, Collected Works of Thomas Middleton; author: (book) Castration: An Abbreviated History of Western Manhood, Reinventing Shakespeare: A Cultural History, Buying Whiteness: Race, Cultural, and Identity from Columbus to Hip Hop, Cultural Selection. Fellowship, John Simon Guggenheim Found., 2002—03. Office: English Dept Fla State Univ Tallahassee FL 32306-1580 Business E-Mail: gtaylor@fsu.edu.

TAYLOR, GARY KENNETH, accountant, educator; b. Lancaster, Ohio, Feb. 18, 1965; s. Gary Keith and Lola Carol Taylor; m. Jennifer Lynn Drumm; children: Mackenzie Rae, Gregory Kyle. PhD, Ohio State U., Columbus, 1996. CPA Ohio, 1988. Acct. Ernst & Whinney, Columbus, 1987—91; assoc. prof. U. Ala., Tuscaloosa, 1996—. Contbr. articles to profl. jours. on acctg. Mem. and pres. bd. Holy Spirit Regional Sch., Tuscaloosa, 1991—98; baseball coach Holy Spirit Mid. Sch. Recipient U. Wide Alumni Tchg. award. Home: 4634 Brook Highland Ln Tuscaloosa AL 35406 Office: Culverhouse Sch Accountancy 326 Alston Hall Box 870220 Tuscaloosa AL 35487-0220 Business E-Mail: gtaylor@cba.ua.edu.

TAYLOR, GENE (GARY EUGENE TAYLOR), United States Representative from Mississippi; b. New Orleans, Sept. 17, 1953; m. Margaret Gordon; children: Sarah, Emily, Gary. BA, Tulane U., New Orleans, 1976; student, U. So. Miss., Hattiesburg. Sales rep. Stone Container Corp.; city councilman Bay St. Louis, Miss., 1981—83; mem. Miss. State Senate, 1984-89, US Congress from 4th Miss. dist., 1989—, mem. house armed svcs. com., mem. transp. and infrastructure com., chmn. subcommittee on seapower and expeditionary forces, co-chair Shipbuilding Caucus, Nat. Guard and Res. Caucus, Coast Guard Caucus and Expeditionary Warfare Caucus; mem. Conservative Dems.' Blue Dog Coalition. With USCGR, 1971—84. Mem.: Rotary Club, Lions Club, Kappa Sigma. Democrat. Roman Catholic. Office: US House Reps 2269 Rayburn House Office Bldg Washington DC 20515-2405 Office Phone: 202-225-5772. Office Fax: 202-225-7074.*

TAYLOR, GEORGE KIMBROUGH, JR., lawyer; b. Atlanta, Aug. 28, 1939; s. George Kimbrough and Helen Whiteside (Shepard) T.; m. Carol Ann McKinney, July 1, 1961 (div. 1976); children: George Kimbrough III, Thomas Haynes; m. Triska Ashley Drake, Oct. 2, 1981. BA, Emory U., 1961; LLB, U. Va., 1964. Bar: Ga. 1964, U.S. Dist. Ct. (no. dist.) Ga. 1964, U.S. Ct. Appeals (11th cir.) 1964. Assoc. Kilpatrick & Cody, Atlanta, 1964-70, ptnr., 1970-96, Kilpatrick Stockton LLP (formerly Kilpatrick & Cody), 1997—. Bd. dirs. Ont. Reins. Co. Ltd., Atlanta; chmn., bd. dirs. MFI Am., Inc., Atlanta, 2003—06. Chmn. bd. dirs. Spl. Audiences, Inc., Atlanta, 1985-87; bd. dirs. Atlanta Symphony Orch., 1986—; trustee Woodruff Arts Ctr., Atlanta, 1997—; bd. dirs. Atlanta Opera, 1995—, Ga. Humanities Coun., Atlanta, 1986-93, Ga. Conservancy, 1979-85; bd. dirs. Ga. Trust for Hist. Preservation, 2002—, vice chair, 2004-2008;chair 2008-; bd. dirs. Ga. Coun. Internat. Visitors, Atlanta, 1987-94, pres., 1993; bd. dirs. Brit.-Am. Bus. Group, 1989-95, pres., 1994; bd. visitors Emory U., Atlanta, 1993-96, Brit.-Am. Bus. Coun., 1997—, chmn. 1997-98; mem. alumni coun. U. Va. Law Sch., 1995-98; active Leadership Atlanta. Woodrow Wilson fellow, 1961. Mem. ABA, Internat. Bar Assn., Atlanta Bar Assn., Order of Coif, Soc. Internat. Bus. Fellows, Capital City Club, Phi Beta Kappa, Omicron Delta Kappa. Democrat. Avocations: sailing, skiing. Office: Kilpatrick Stockton LLP 1100 Peachtree St NE Ste 2800 Atlanta GA 30309-4530 Office Phone: 404-815-6500. Business E-Mail: ktaylor@kilpatrickstockton.com.

TAYLOR, GEORGE PEACH, JR., aerospace transportation executive, retired military officer; b. Birmingham, Ala. BA in Physics and Russian Language, Rice U., Houston, Tex., 1975; MD, Baylor Coll. Medicine, 1978; MPH, Harvard Sch. Pub. Health, Boston, Mass., 1984; attended, Nat. War Coll., Fort Lesley J. McNair, Washington, DC, 1992—93. Lic. Tex. Advanced through grades to gen. USAF, 2002;

resident USAF Sch. of Aerospace Medicine, Brooks AFB, Tex., 1984—85; chief flight medicine, squadron flight surgeon USAF Clinic, Kadena AFB, Japan, 1979—81; chief aerospace medicine Detachment 3 Air Force Flight Test Ctr., Henderson, Nev., 1981—83; chief aerospace medicine, comdr. air transportable hosp. USAF Hosp., Torrejon AFB, Spain, 1985—88; med. inspector active duty forces Air Force Inspection and Safety Ctr., Norton AFB, Calif., 1988—90; chief aerospace medicine USAF Hosp., Air Force Flight Test Ctr., Edwards AFB, Calif., 1990—92; comdr. and dir. base med. svcs. 75th med. group Ogden Air Logistics Ctr., Hill AFB, Utah, 1993—95; chief aerospace med. divsn., later dep. dir. Air Force Med. Ops. Agy., Bolling AFB, Washington, 1995—96; assoc. dir. to dir. med. programs and resources USAF, 1996—97, command surgeon Ramstein AFB, Germany, 1997—2000, Air Combat Command, Langley AFB, Va., 2000—02; asst. surgeon gen. expeditionary ops., sci. & tech. USAF, Washington, 2002, spl. asst. to surgeon gen. Air Force, 2002, surgeon gen., 2002—06; sr. mng. dir. fed. practice PriceWaterhouseCoopers, LLP, Washington, 2006—09; v.p. health & human services info. tech. divsn. Northrop Grumman Corp., McLean, Va., 2009—. Chmn., base realignment and closure Joint Med. Cross Svc. Group, 2002—05; disting. prof. mil./emergency medicine Uniformed Svcs. U. Health Svcs. Decorated DSM, Def. Superior Svc. medal, Legion of Merit with oak leaf cluster, Bronze Star medal, Meritorious Svc. medal with four oak leaf clusters, Air Force Commendation medal, Air Force Achievement medal, Air Force Recognition Ribbon, Gold Cross of Honor of the Bundeswehr Germany; recipient Malcom C. Grow award for Air Force Flight Surgeon of Yr. Fellow: Aerospace Med. Assn. (former coun. mem.), Am. Coll. Preventive Medicine; mem.: AMA (Air Force delegate), Soc. US Air Force Flight Surgeons (former pres.), Assn. Military Surgeons of U.S. (life Founders Medal), Am. Soc. Aerospace Medicine Specialists (former pres.). Office: Northrop Grumann Information Technology 7575 Colshire Dr Mc Lean VA 22102 Office Phone: 703-713-4000.*

TAYLOR, GLEN A., printing, direct mail and technology executive, professional sports team owner; b. Apr. 20, 1941; m. Becky Taylor; children: Terri, Jean, Taylor Moor, Jeff, Kendahl. BS in Math., Physics and Social Sci., Mankato State U., 1962; student, Harvard Grad. Sch. Bus.; D (hon.), Mankato State U., 1997. Chmn., CEO Taylor Corp., North Mankato, Minn., 1975—2001, chmn., 2001—; mem. Minn. State Senate, 1980—90; owner NBA Minn. Timberwolves and Minn. Lynx, Mpls., 1995—. Recipient Sales Exec. of Yr. award, Sales and Mktg. Execs. Mpls./St. Paul, 1999; named Exec. of Yr., Corp. Report mag., 1987; named one of Forbes' Richest Ams., 2006; named to Minn. Hall of Fame, Twin Cities Monthly mag., 2002. Office: Taylor Corp 1725 Roe Crest Dr North Mankato MN 56003-1807 also: Minn Timberwolves Target Ctr 600 1st Ave N Minneapolis MN 55403-1416*

TAYLOR, GRANT DAVID, urologist; b. Arlington, Tex., Feb. 14, 1974; s. Michael Albert and Lynda Lavelle Taylor; m. Carla Ranee Nedderman, July 5, 1995; children: Benjamin Grant, Sarah Ranee. BS, John Brown U., Siloam Springs, Ariz., 1996; MD, U. Tex. Houston Med. Sch., 2000. Lic. Tex. State Bd. Med. Examiners, 2002, Tenn. State Bd. Med. Examiners, 2005, diplomate Am. Bd. Urology, 2007. Intern MD Anderson Rsch., Houston, 1997; intern gen. surgery U. Tex. Southwestern, Dallas, 2000—01, resident urology, 2001—05; urologist Johnson City Urol. Clinic, Tenn., 2005—. Faculty adv. bd. Quest Diagnostics. Contbr. articles to profl. jours., chapters to books. Scholar, John Brown U., 1992—96. Mem.: AMA, Christian Med. and Dental Soc. (internat. med. missionary 2006—), Americal Urol. Assn., Endourological Soc., Tenn. Med. Assn., Alpha Omega Alpha, Alpha Chi (pres. 1994—95). Office: Johnson City Urol Clinic 300 W Watauga Ave Johnson City TN 37604

TAYLOR, HAROLD ALLEN, JR., industrial minerals consultant; b. San Jose, Calif., June 27, 1936; s. Harold Allen and Marie Anna (Briody) T.; m. Theresa Josephine Kustritz, Aug. 29, 1963; children: Harold Allen III, Ruth F., Jonathan L.E. BA, Brown U., 1958; MA, U. Minn., 1968. Project leader Office Mineral Supply, U.S. Bur. Mines, Mpls., 1968-70, commodity specialist divsn. ferrous metals Washington, 1970-74; commodity analyst U.S. internat. Trade Commn., Washington, 1974-80; sr. commodity specialist br. indsl. minerals U.S. Bur. Mines, Washington, 1980-95; pres. Basics Mines, Summit Point, W.Va., 1995—. Pub., editor Dimension Stone Advocate News, Graphite Advocate News, Bismuth Advocate News, Indium Advocate News, 2000—; contbr. articles to profl. jours. & to stone-related wikis on Wikipedia. Pres. Arlington (Va.) Interfaith Coun., 1994, 95. Mem. AIME (sec 1983-84, 1st vice chmn. 1984-85, chmn. 1985-86, exec. adv. bd. mineral econs. subsect. 1981-83, 87-91), ASTM (chmn. subcom. nomenclature of com. on dimension stone 1987-2004, sec. of com. 1990-95), Soc. Govt. Economists (chmn. materials policy panels, 1979-84), Capitol Metals Forum (steering com. 1979-85), Toastmasters (pres. 1978, 81, 87, 91, asst. area gov. 1978-79, area gov. 1979-80, dep. divsn. lt. gov. 1989-90), Sigma Gamma Epsilon Address: PO Box 185 Summit Point WV 25446-0185 Office Phone: 304-725-6619. E-mail: bmhtayl@earthlink.net.

TAYLOR, HARRIS C., endocrinologist, consultant; b. Bklyn., Apr. 30, 1940; s. William and Florence Ruth T.; m. Diana Kahn, Sept. 3, 1962; children: Brian David, Rebecca Lynn. BS, Queens Coll., 1961; MD, U. Chgo., 1965. Diplomate Am. Bd. Internal Medicine, Am. Bd. Endocrinology and Metabolism. Cons. endocrinologist Kaiser Found., Cleve., 1972-86; chief divsn. endocrinology Luth. Med. Ctr., Cleve., 1977-96, dir. endocrinology & radioimmunoassay lab., 1978-96, dir. internal medicine residency, 1985-94, dir. rsch., internal medicine residency program Fairview Health Sys., 1996—. Sr. clin. instr. Case Western Res. U. Sch. Medicine, Cleve., 1977-81, clin. asst. prof., 1981-88, clin. assoc. prof. medicine in endocrinology, 1988-2003, clin. prof., 2003—; prin. investigator NIH, 2006-08, co-prin. investigator, 2008-. Contbr. articles to profl. jours. Chmn. program com. Diabetes Assn. Cleve., 1976-81, exec. com., 1978-85, pres.-elect, 1981-82, pres., 1982-84. Sr. asst. surgeon USPHS, 1966-68. Named One of Best Drs. in Cleve., Cleve. Mag., 1998, 2002, 2004. Fellow: ACP (reviewer Annals of Internal Medicine 1986—2008, Master Tchr. award 2001), Am. Coll. Endocrinology (editl. bd. Endocrine Practice 1997—2004); mem.: Endocrine Soc., Am. Assn. Clin. Endocrinologists, Phi Beta Kappa. Jewish. Avocations: stamp collecting/philately, classical music. Office: Fairview Gen Hosp Dept Medicine 18101 Lorain Ave Cleveland OH 44111 Home Phone: 216-921-7393; Office Phone: 216-476-7369. Personal E-mail: dkthct62@sbcglobal.net.

TAYLOR, HARRY, real estate broker; b. NJ; 1 child, Christopher. BA, Colgate U., Hamilton, NY. Comml. real estate broker Whiteside Properties, 1993—96, Taylor Real Estate Group, LLC, 1996—. Cmty. vol. NC Outward Bound Sch.; leader Habitat for Humanity, 1995—96; bd. mem. Big Brothers, Denver, Boulder, Colo., 1985—87; bd. mem., bd. pres., adv. com. Youth Homes Inc., 1987—; bd. mem., pres. Charlotte Folk Soc., 2002—. Served with USAF. Mem.: Sierra Club. Democrat. Avocations: banjo, mandolin, fiddle. Office: Taylor Real Estate Group Ltd 611 Templeton Ave Ste 106 Charlotte NC 28203-4557

TAYLOR, HENRY SPLAWN, retired literature educator, poet; b. Loudoun County, Va., June 21, 1942; s. Thomas Edward and Mary Marshall (Splawn) Taylor; m. Mooshe Taylor, 2002. BA, U. Va., Charlottesville, 1965; MA, Hollins Coll., Va., 1966. Instr. English Roanoke Coll., Va., 1966—68; asst. prof. U. Utah, 1968—71; faculty Am. U., Washington, 1971—2003, prof. lit., 1976—2003, co-dir. MFA program in creative writing, 1982—2003, dir. Am. studies program, 1983—84. Dir. writer's conf. U. Utah, 1970—72; writer-in-residence Hollins Coll., 1978; poet-in-residence Wichita State U., 1994, Randolph-Macon Woman's Coll., 1997; prof. poetry U. Cin., 2002. Author: (poetry) The Horse Show at Midnight, 1966, Breakings, 1971, An Afternoon of Pocket Billiards, 1975, Desperado, 1979, The Flying Change, 1985 (Pulitzer prize, 86), Understanding Fiction: Poems 1986-96, 1996, Brief Candles: 101 Clerihews, 2000, Crooked Run, 2006, Poetry: Points of Departure, 1974; editor: The Water of Light: A Miscellany in Honor of Brewster Ghiselin, 1976; author: Compulsory Figures: Essays on Recent American Poets, 1992, (cassette) Landscape with Tractor, 1985; contbg. editor: Hollins Critic, 1971—78, 1997—; editl. cons.: Magill's Literary Annual, 1972—90, cons. editor: Poet Lore, 1977—84; translator (with others): The Children of Herakles, 1981; translator: Plautus' The Weevil, 1995, Sophocles' Electra, 1998. Recipient Pulitzer Prize, Poetry, 1986, Michael Braude award for light verse, Am. Acad. Arts and Letters, 2002, Aiken Taylor award in Modern Am. Poetry, 2004; grantee, NEH, 1980—81; fellow, Nat. Endowment Arts, 1978, 1986. Mem.: PEN, Fellowship of So. Writers, Am. Lit. Translators Assn. Democrat. Mem.Soc.Of Friends.

TAYLOR, HOLLY ANN, music educator; b. Midland, Tex., Oct. 11, 1978; d. Thomas Woods and Donna Louise Hughston; m. Mark Alan Taylor, July 22, 2006. MusB in Music Edn., George Mason U., Fairfax, Va., 2003, M in Music Performance, 2006. Cert. tchr. Va., 2003. Music/strings tchr. Fairfax County Pub. Schs., 2003—. Freelance performer Haase Quartet, Fairfax, 1999—. Mem.: Music Educators Nat. Conf. Personal E-mail: holly.taylor@fcps.edu.

TAYLOR, IAN LOGAN, dean; b. Eng. MD, PhD, Liverpool Med. Sch. Fellow in gastrointestinal rsch. UCLA, mem. Wadsworth V.A. Tng. Program, various positions, prof. medicine; chief of gastroenterology Duke U., 1986—89, dir. Sarah W. Stedman Ctr. for Nutritional Studies, 1989—90, prof. physiology, dept. cell biology, 1990—93; prof. and chmn. dept. medicine Med. U. S.C., 1993—2001, pres. U. Med. Assocs., 1999—2001; dean Sch. Medicine Tulane U., 2001—05; dean Coll. Medicine SUNY Health Sci. Ctr., Bklyn., 2006—. Office: Coll Medicine SUNY Health Sci Ctr 470 Clarkson Ave Brooklyn NY 11203

TAYLOR, JACK CRAWFORD, rental and leasing company executive; b. 1922; With Lindburg Cadillac, St. Louis, 1944-50, Forrest Cadillac, St. Louis, 1951-56; chmn. bd. Enterprise Rent-A-Car, St. Louis, 1980—2001, chmn. emeritus, 2001—. Served with USN. Named one of Forbes Richest Americans, 2006, World's Richest People (with family), Forbes Mag., 2007, 2008. Office: Enterprise Rent-A-Car 600 Corporate Park Dr Saint Louis MO 63105-4204

TAYLOR, JAMES C., writer; b. Nashville, Oct. 17, 1924; s. James Custer Taylor and Winnie Olive Duncan. AB in Journalism and Psychology, U. Ky., 1941; postgrad., Vanderbilt U., 1941, Notre Dame U., Ind., 1942, Kans. U., 1942. Sports writer Topeka State Jour., Kans., 1950—52; reporter, editor Kansas City Star, Mo., 1953—57; sr. editor TV Guide Mag., 1957—82; fgn. corr. Internat. Am., various locations, 1982—2000; ret., 2000. Guest columnist CDL Report, World Intelligence Rev.; lectr. in field. Author: (book) Dubious Duty, 1976, Pearl Harbor II, 1978, Khadafy, Man or Myth, 1984. Referee H.S. football games, Ariz., 1980—2000. With French Foriegn Legion, Algeria, lt. comdr. USNR, 1941—61. Recipient Outstanding Book award, Mark Twain Soc., St. Louis, 1958, Del Oro award, Fria Ord, Stockholm, 1982; nominee Nobel Peace prize, 2008. Republican. Roman Catholic. Home: 5519 N 77th Pl Scottsdale AZ 85250

TAYLOR, JAMES C., language educator; s. Clarence S. and Shirley S. Taylor; m. Diana L. Correa, Dec. 16, 1999; 1 child, Emily B. BA in Spanish, Va. Commonwealth U., Richmond, 1994, BA Magna Cum Laude, 2000, MA in Tchg. Spanish, 2000. Spanish tchr. Hanover County Pub. Schs., Ashland, Va., 2000—01; claims coord., translator Mondial Assistance, Richmond, 2001—; adj. instr., spanish Va. Commonwealth U., 2002—. Translator: Spanish BCBS Claim Forms. Missionary Ch. Jesus Christ Latter-day Sts., Mendoza, Argentina, San Juan, St. Louis, 1994—96. Mem.: Golden Key Nat. Honor Soc.

TAYLOR, JAMES STACEY, philosopher, educator; s. Thomas Begg and Betty Jean Taylor; m. Margaret Ellen Ulizio, July 21, 2001; 1 child, Octavia MargaretBegg. MLitt, MA, PhD, Bowling Green State U., Ohio, 2000. Asst. prof. Coll. NJ, Ewing, 2005—. Dir. Ethics Initiatives, Baton Rouge, 2001—05; editl. bd. Jour. Medicine and Philosophy, Houston, 2006—; mng. editor Jour. Value Inquiry, Dordrecht, Netherlands, 2007—. Contbr. monograph, articles to profl. jours. Advisor IHEU-Appignani Ctr. for Bioethics at the UN, New York, NY, 2005—08. Recipient Grieve prize, St Andrews U., 1991—92; Hume fellowship, Inst. Humane Studies, 1996, grant, Cecile and Philip Berbier Fund, 2001—04, Vis. scholar, Social Philosophy & Policy Ctr., 2007. Mem.: Soc. Value Inquiry (pres. 2006—07). Achievements include research in advocates posthumous organ conscription. Office: Coll NJ 2000 Pennington Rd Ewing NJ 08628 Business E-Mail: jtaylor@tcnj.edu.

TAYLOR, JAMES VERNON, musician; b. Boston, Mar. 12, 1948; s. Isaac M. and Gertrude (Woodard) T.; children: Sarah Maria, Benjamin Simon. Student, Milton Acad., Mass., 1962-66, Arlington Sch., Belmont, Mass., 1966-67. Recorded for Apple Records, 1968, Warner Bros. Records, 1970—77. Musician: (albums) James Taylor, 1968, Sweet Baby James, 1970, Mud Slide Slim & the Blue Horizon, 1971, One Man Dog, 1972, Walking Man, 1974, Gorilla, 1975, In the Pocket, 1976, JT, 1977, Flag, 1979, Dad Loves His Work, 1981, That's Why I'm Here, 1985, Never Die Young, 1988, New Moon Shine, 1991, Live in Rio, 1991, Live, 1993, Hourglass, 1997 (Grammy award, Best Pop Vocal Album), Live at the Beacon Theatre, 1998, October Road, 2002, A Christmas Album, 2004, James Taylor at Christmas, 2006, One Man Band, 2007, Covers, 2008, (songs) Fire & Rain, 1970, You've Got a Friend, 1971 (Grammy award, Best Male Pop Vocal Performance, 1972), Handy Man, 1977 (Grammy award, Best Male Pop Vocal Performance, 1978), Don't Let Me Be Lonely Tonight, 2001 (Grammy award, Best Male Pop Vocal Performance), (with Alison Krauss) How's the World Treating You, 2003 (Grammy award, Best Country Collaboration with Vocals). Recipient Billboard Century award, 1998; named one of 100 Greatest Artists of Rock & Roll, VH1, 1998, 100 Greatest Artists of All Time, Rolling Stone, 2004; named to Rock & Roll Hall of Fame, 2000. Office: Borman Entertainment Ste 401 1250 6th St Santa Monica CA 90401-1638 Office Phone: 310-656-3150.

TAYLOR, JANET R., Mayor, Salem, Oregon; b. 1942; m. Duane Taylor; 5 children. Student, Chemeketa C.C. Lic. pvt. pilot 1981. Co-founder, exec. Taylor Metal Products, Salem, Oreg.; mayor City of Salem, Oreg., 2003—. Past chairwoman Salem Econ. Devel. Corp., S.E. Mill Creek Neighborhood Assn.; mem. Willamette River Bridge Task Force; sponsor A.C. Gilbert Discovery Village. Mem.: Salem Area C. of C. (v.p.), Salem Futures, Salem City Club, Salem Downtown Rotary. Office: 555 Liberty St SE Rm 220 Salem OR 97301 Office Phone: 503-588-6159. Business E-Mail: jtaylor@cityofsalem.net.*

TAYLOR, JASON PAUL, professional football player; b. Pitts., Sept. 1, 1974; m. Katina Taylor; 2 children. BA in Polit. Sci. & Criminal Justice, U. Akron, 1997. Defensive end Miami Dolphins, 1997—2008, 2009—, Washington Redskins, 2008—09. Contestant (dance competition) Dancing with the Stars, 2008 (2nd Pl. finish, 2008). Founder Jason Taylor Found., 2004—. Named NFL Defensive Player of Yr., AP, 2006, NFL All-Pro, 2006, Walter Payton Man of Yr. award, 2007; named to Am. Football Conf. Pro Bowl Team, 2000, 2002, 2004—06. Office: c/o Miami Dolphins 7500 SW 30th St Davie FL 33314*

TAYLOR, JEAN ELLEN, mathematics professor, researcher; d. Richard and Donna Taylor; m. John Mark Guckenheimer, Apr. 18, 1969 (div.); m. Frederick J. Almgren, Oct. 6, 1973 (dec. 1997); 1 child, Karen Taylor Almgren stepchildren: Ann Almgren, Robert Almgren; m. William T. Golden, July 8, 2001 (div.). AB summa cum laude, Mt. Holyoke Coll., 1966, DSc (hon.), 2001; MS in Chemistry, U. Calif., Berkeley, 1968; MS in Math., U. Warwick, Coventry, Eng., 1971; PhD, Princeton U., 1973. Instr. MIT, Cambridge, Mass., 1972-73; asst. prof. Rutgers U., New Brunswick, N.J., 1973-77, assoc. prof., 1977-82, prof., 1982-87, prof. II, 1987—2002, prof. emeritus, 2002—; vis. scholar Courant Inst., NYU, 2002—. Mem. Inst. for Advanced Study, Princeton, N.J., 1974-75, 77-78, 85, 95-96; Miller vis. prof. U. Calif., Berkeley, 1999; vis. scholar Stanford (Calif.) U., 1989; visitor Princeton U., 1980-81; mem. Geometry Computing Group (permanent faculty of the Nat. Sci. and Tech. Ctr. for Computational and Visualization of Geometric Structures); cons. Nat. Bur. Standards, Gaithersburg, Md.; guest expert 3-2-1 Contact program Children's TV Workshop, 1978; mem. exec. com. Conf. Bd. of the Math. Scis., 2000-2002; lectr. in field. Contbr. articles in math., physics and materials sci. to profl. jours. Mem. at large of bd. dir. Black Rock Forest Consortium, 2000—07. Recipient Presdl. Pub. Svc. award Rutgers Coll. Class of 1962, 1999; Sloan Found. fellow, 1976-78; NSF grad. fellow, 1966-72, hon. fellow Woodrow Wilson Found.; rsch. grantee NSF, 1973—97, Air Force Office Sci. Rsch., 1987-94. Fellow: AAAS (bd. dir. 1995—99, chair sect. 2004—05), Assn. for Women in Sci., Am. Acad. Arts and Scis.; mem.: Soc. for Indsl. and Applied Math., Assn. for Women in Math. (pres. 1999—2001, nominating com. chair 2003—04), Math Assn. Am., Materials Rsch. Soc., Am. Math. Soc. (nominating com. 1977—78, coun. 1984—89, exec. com. 1985—88, v.p. 1994—97, trustee 2003—08, chair bd. trustees 2006—07), Assn. Princeton Grad. Alumni (governing bd. 1999—2003), Phi Beta Kappa (vis. scholar 2006—07). Democrat. Achievements include proof, in the context of Geometric Measure Theory, that the singular set in a mathematical model for soap bubble clusters and soap films on wire frames is what is physcally observed, thereby solving a 100 year old problem; development of mathematical models for treating shapes of surfaces and interfaces for crystalline materials and use of them to model crystal growth. Office: Courant Inst 251 Mercer St New York NY 10012 Business E-Mail: jtaylor@cims.nyu.edu.

TAYLOR, JEFFREY A., lawyer, former prosecutor; m. Marcia Taylor. BA in History, Stanford U., 1987; JD, Harvard Law Sch., 1991. Law clk. to Hon. John C. Mowbray Supreme Ct. Nev., 1991—92; asst. US atty. (so. dist.) Calif. US Dept. Justice, 1995—99, counselor to atty. gen. John Ashcroft and Alberto Gonzales, 2002—06, US atty. Dist. DC, 2006—09; counsel US Senate Judiciary Com., 1999—2002; head Americas Fraud Investigation & Dispute Services (FIDS) Ernst & Young LLP, 2009—. Recipient Edmund J. Randolph award, US Dept. Justice, 2006. Office: Ernst & Young LLP 5 Times Sq New York NY 10036*

TAYLOR, JEFFREY LEE, political science educator, writer; b. Spencer, Iowa, Jan. 30, 1961; s. James Lee and Judith Lane (Crowder) Taylor; m. Shirley Jean Bentz, Dec. 29, 1990; children: William Taylor (dec.), Jane Taylor, David taylor. BA magna cum laude, Northwestern Coll., 1983; MA, U. Iowa, 1985; PhD, U. Mo., 1997. Libr., instr. No. State U., Aberdeen, S.D., 1985-90; libr. Lincoln U., Jefferson City, Mo., 1994-95, Univ. Ctr. Rochester, Minn., 1997—2008; instr. polit. sci. Rochester Cmty. and Tech. Coll., 1999—2008; asst. prof. polit. sci. Western Ill. U., Macomb, 2007—08, Jacksonville State U., Ala., 2008—. Instr. S.D. Pub. Library Tng. Inst., Pierre, 1987, Southea. Libraries Coop., Rochester, 1997-98. Author: From Radical to Respectable, 1997, Where Did the Party Go?, 2006; musician (guitarist), vocalist: Cornboy, 1997—2006. Chair Boone County Green Party, Columbia, Mo., 1994-96, Mo. Green Party, 1996; chair Olmsted County Green Party, Rochester, 2001-02; co-mgr. McGaa for Senate, 2002. State of Iowa scholar, 1979. Mem. Am. Polit. Sci. Assn., Acad. Polit. Sci. Mem. Soc. Of Friends. Office Phone: 507-285-7233, 256-782-5651.

TAYLOR, JEFFREY SCOTT, lawyer; b. Chgo., May 24, 1967; s. Robert David and Betty Jane Taylor; m. Wendy Dawn Moore, Aug. 7, 1993; children: Addison Louise, Kallista Antoinette. BA, Colo. State U., 1991; JD cum laude, John Marshall Law Sch., Chgo., 1995. Bar: Ill. 1995. Assoc. Williams, Montgomery & John, Chgo., 1995—2002; ptnr. Spesia, Ayers & Ardaugh, Joliet, Ill., 2002—. Mem.: Ill. Trial Lawyers Assn., Ill. State Bar Assn. (assoc.). Home: 15912 Hometown Dr Plainfield IL 60586 Office: Spesia Ayers & Ardaugh 1415 Black Rd Joliet IL 60435 Office Fax: 815-846-2410. Business E-Mail: jtaylor@spesia-ayers.com.

TAYLOR, JILL BOLTE, neuroanatomist; b. 1959; BA in Biology and Physiol. Psychology, Ind. U., Bloomington, 1982; PhD in Neuroanatomy, Ind. U., 1991. Rsch. asst. Ind. U., Terre Haute Ctr. Med. Edn., Med. Gross Anatomy Lab., Neurosci. Lab., Med. Histology Lab., 1983—91; postdoctoral fellow, Dept. Neurobiology, Lab. Visual Physiology Harvard Med. Sch., Boston, 1991—93; rsch. assoc., asst. neuroanatomist, Lab. Structural Neurosci. McLean Hosp., Dept. Psychiatry, Harvard Med. Sch., 1993—97; cons. neuroanatomist, brain cancer Midwest Proton Radiotherapy Inst. Tchg. asst., instr. Ind. U., 1985—89; tchg. asst., vis. lectr. Terre Haute Ctr. Med. Edn., 1985—91; vis. lectr. DePauw Coll., 1990—91; brain bank assoc., spokesperson McLean Brain Tissue Resource Ctr., 1993—95; instr. Harvard Sch. Dental Med., 1993—96; course dir. Rose Hulman Inst. Tech., Dept. Applied Biology, Biomedical Engring., 1999, Ind. U., Dept. Kinesiology, 2004—06; vol. lab. instr. Ind. U. Sch. Medicine, 2004—06, adjunct instr., Bloomington Med. Sci. Prog., 2005—; mem. planning com. Crisis Intervention Trainingprog., 2006—; founder Bloomington Brain Tumor Support Grp., 2007—; nat. spokesperson, psychiat. disorders Harvard Brain Tissue Resource Ctr. Author: My Stroke of Insight: A Brain Scientist's Personal Journey, 2006 (Publishers Weekly bestseller); contbr. articles to profl. jours. Vol. Am. Heart Assn., Am. Stroke Assn., 2000—02; singer for inmates Monroe County Jail, 2006, instr. drug awareness prog., 2006—; mentor to Eagle Scouts Bloomington, Terre Haute, Columbus, 2006—; mentor women's basketball team Ind. U., 2007—. Recipient Excellence award for contribution in advocacy, Mass. Alliance Mental Illness, 1995, Indpls. Mini-Marathon Celebration of Life award, Nat.

Alliance Mental Illness, 2007, Distinguished Alumni award, Ind. U., 2007; named Mem. of Yr., Nat. Alliance Mental Illness, 2003; named one of The 100 Most Influential People in the World, TIME mag., 2008. Mem.: Nat. Alliance Mental Illness (bd. dirs. 1996—97, pres. greater Bloomington area 2005—). Achievements include design of anatomically correct stained glass brains. Office: Jill Bolte Taylor PhD PO Box 1181 Bloomington IN 47402 Personal E-mail: drjill@drjilltaylor.com.*

TAYLOR, JIMMY LYNN, retired family practice physician, administrator; b. Franklin County, NC, May 11, 1936; s. Herman Benjamin and Ruby Lynn (Perry) T.; m. Dorothy Keenum, Sept. 4, 1960; children: Gregory Scott, Sonya Lynn Taylor Loper. AA, Mars Hill Coll., 1956; BS, Wake Forest U., 1958; MD, Wake Forest U. Sch. Medicine, 1962. Postdoctoral fellow Greenville (S.C.) Gen. Hosp., 1962-63; staff physician USPHS Indian Hosp., Pine Ridge, SD, 1963-65, chief of obstetrics, 1964-65; family physician, co-founder Monroe (N.C.) Family Med. Ctr., 1965, family physician, ptnr., 1965-95; student physician Wingate (N.C.) U., 1987-94; med. dir. Brian Ctr. Nursing Facility, Monroe, 1992-95. H.S. team physician, 1965—75. Lt. comdr. USPHS, 1963-65. Recipient Head Start Child Care Achievement award N.C. Head Start Assn., 1990. Fellow Am. Acad. Family Physicians; mem. Am. Bd. Family Practice (diplomate), N.C. Acad. Family Physicians, N.C. Med. Soc., Union County Med. Soc. (pres. 1976-77). Republican. Baptist. Avocations: golf, fishing, gardening, bridge, collecting autographed first edition books. Home: 1657 Pageland Hwy Monroe NC 28112-8737 Office: Monroe Family Med Ctr 1420 E Franklin St Monroe NC 28112 Personal E-mail: jtaylor28112@yahoo.com, jtaylor6@carolina.rr.com.

TAYLOR, JOB, III, lawyer; b. NYC, Feb. 18, 1942; s. Job II and Anne Harrison (Flinchbaugh) T.; m. Mary C. August, Oct. 24, 1964 (div. 1978); children: Whitney August, Job IV; m. Sally Lawson, May 31, 1980; 1 child, Alexandra Anne. BA, Washington & Jefferson Coll., 1964; JD, Coll. William and Mary, 1971. Bar: N.Y. 1972, Mass. 2003, U.S. Dist. Ct. (no., so. ea. and we. dists.) N.Y. 1973, U.S. Ct. Appeals (2d cir.) 1973, U.S. Ct. Claims 1974, U.S. Tax Ct. 1974, U.S. Supreme Ct. 1975, U.S. Ct. Appeals (9th cir.) 1976, U.S. Ct. Mil. Appeals 1977, U.S. Ct. Appeals (D.C. and 10th cirs.) 1977, D.C. 1981, U.S. Ct. Internat. Trade 1981, U.S. Ct. Appeals (fed. cir.) 1982, U.S. Dist. Ct. (no. dist.) Calif. 1983, U.S. Ct. Appeals (6th cir.) U.S. Dist. Ct., 1987, U.S. Ct. Appeals (3d cir.) 1990, U.S. Dist. Ct. Conn. 1996. Ptnr. Olwine, Connelly, Chase, O'Donnell & Weyher, NYC, 1971-85, Latham & Watkins, NYC, 1985—. Served to lt. USN, 1964-68. Mem. ABA, Assn. Bar City N.Y., La Confrerie des Chevaliers du Tastevin, Racquet and Tennis Club, Wee Burn Country Club (Darien, Conn.). Republican. Episcopalian. Avocations: squash, tennis, golf, reading. Office Phone: 508-240-3069. Personal E-mail: job.taylor@retiredpartner.lw.com.

TAYLOR, J(OCELYN) MARY, museum director, educator, zoologist; b. Portland, Oreg., May 30, 1931; d. Arnold Llewellyn and Kathleen Mary (Yorke) T.; m. Joseph William Kamp, Mar. 18, 1972 (dec.); m. Wesley Kingston Whitten, Mar. 20, 2001. BA, Smith Coll., 1952; MA, U. Calif., Berkeley, 1953, PhD, 1959. Instr. zoology Wellesley Coll., 1959-61, asst. prof. zoology, 1961-65; assoc. prof. zoology U. B.C., 1965-74; dir. Cowan Vertebrate Mus., 1965-82, prof. dept. zoology, 1974-82; collaborative scientist Oreg. Regional Primate Research Ctr., 1983-87; prof. (courtesy) dept. fisheries and wildlife Oreg. State U., 1984-95; dir. Cleve. Mus. Nat. History, 1987-96, dir. emerita, 1996—. Adj. prof. dept. biology Case Western Res. U., 1987-96. Assoc. editor Jour. Mammalogy, 1981-82. Contbr. numerous articles to sci. jours. Trustee Benjamin Rose Inst., 1988-93, Western Res. Acad., 1989-94, U. Circle, Inc., 1987-96, The Cleve. Aquarium, 1990-93, Cleve. Access to the Arts, 1992-96; corp. bd. Holden Arboretum, 1988-98, The Cleve. Mus. Natural History, 1996—, The Catlin Gabel Sch., 1998-2000, The Inst. for the Northwest, 1999—2001. Recipient Lake County Environ. award, Lake county metro parks.; Fulbright scholar, 1954-55; Lalor Found. grantee, 1962-63; NSF grantee, 1963-71; NRC Can. grantee, 1966-84; Killam Sr. Rsch. fellow, 1978-79 Mem.: Rodent Specialist Group of Species Survival Commn. (chmn. 1989—93), Assn. Sci. Mus. Dirs. (v.p. 1990—93), Cooper Ornithol., Australian Mammal Soc. (hon. life), Am. Soc. Mammalogists (1st v.p. 1978—82, pres. 1982—84, hon. life, Hartley T. Jackson award 1993), Soc. Women Geographers, Sigma Xi. Home: 2718 SW Old Orchard Rd Portland OR 97201-1637 E-mail: taylorwhitten@comcast.net.

TAYLOR, JOEL SANFORD, retired government agency administrator, retired lawyer; b. Hazleton, Pa., Oct. 8, 1942; s. Robert Joseph and Alice Josephine (Sanford) T.; m. Donna Rae Caron, Mar. 26, 1967; children: Jason, Adam, Jeremy. BA in Polit. Sci. and Internat. Rels., Swarthmore Coll., 1965; LLB, Columbia U., 1968. Bar: NY 1969, US Ct. Appeals (2d cir.) 1970, US Dist. Ct. (no. dist.) Ohio 1974, US Supreme Ct. 1974, US Dist. Ct. (so. dist.) Ohio 1975, US Ct. Appeals (6th cir.) 1975, US Dist. Ct. (ea. dist.) Ky. 1979. Law clk. hon. Constance B. Motley US Dist. Ct., NYC, 1968-69; assoc. Paul, Weiss, Rifkind, Wharton & Garrison, NYC, 1969-72; exec. asst. Ohio Office Budget and Mgmt., Columbus, 1972-74; asst. atty. gen. Ohio Atty. Gen., Columbus, 1974-83, chief counsel, 1983-91; ptnr. Dinsmore & Shohl, Columbus, 1991-2000; dir. fin. and mgmt. City of Columbus, 2000—09. Pres. Ohio Sundry Claims Bd., Columbus, 1972-74, Ohio State Controlling Bd., Columbus, 1973-74; mem., bd. trustees Ohio State Tchrs. Retirement Sys., Columbus, 1986-91, Solid Waste Authority Ctrl. Ohio, 2001—09. Mem.: Nature Conservancy, Nat. Wildlife Fedn., Columbia Law Alumni Assn. Home Phone: 614-237-5854; Office Phone: 614-645-7036. Business E-Mail: joeitaylar@alum.swathmore.edu.

TAYLOR, JOHN BRIAN, economist, educator; b. Yonkers, NY, Dec. 8, 1946; s. John Joseph and Lorraine (Crowley) T.; m. Raye Allyn Price, Dec. 30, 1972; children: Jennifer Lynn, John Andrew. AB in Econs. summa cum laude, Princeton U., 1968; PhD, Stanford U., 1973. Asst. prof. econs. Columbia U., NYC, 1973-77, assoc. prof., 1977-79, prof., 1979-80; prof. econs. and pub. affairs Princeton U., 1980-84; prof. economics Stanford U., 1984—93, Mary & Robert Raymond prof. economics, 1993—, dir. Ctr. for Econ. Policy Rsch., 1994-97, dir. Introductory Econs. Ctr., 1997-2001; under sec. for internat. affairs US Dept. Treasury, Washington, 2001—05. Vis. prof. econs. Yale U., 1980; sr. staff economist Pres.'s Coun. Econ. Advisers, 1976—77, mem., 1989—91; econometric cons. Townsend-Greenspan and Co., NY, 1978—81; rsch. advisor Fed. Res. Bank, Phila., 1981—84; rsch. assoc. Nat. Bur. Econ. Rsch., 1980—; rsch. economist Bank of Japan, Tokyo, 1987, hon. adviser, 1994—2001; panel of econ. advisers Congl. Budget Office, 1995—2001; sr. fellow Hoover Instn., 1996—. Author: (non-fiction) Macroeconomics, 1986, Macroeconomic Policy in the World Economy, 1993, Economics, 1995, Unemployment, Inflation, and Monetary Policy, 1998, Monetary Policy Rules, 1999, Handbook of Macroeconomics, 2000, Global Financial Warriors: The Untold Story of International Finance in the Post 9/11 World, 2007, Getting Off Track: How Government Actions and Interventions Caused, Prolonged and Worsened the Financial Crisis, 2009; co-editor: Am. Econ. Rev., 1985—89; assoc. editor: Econometrica, 1981—85, Jour. Econ. Dynamics and Control, 1978—85, Jour. Monetary Econs., 1978—83, Jour. Econ. Perspectives, 1997—2001, mng. editor: Internat. Jour. Ctrl. Banking, 2005—; contbr. articles to profl. jours. NSF grantee, 1979-81, 81-83, 83-86, 86-89, 92-95; Guggenheim Found. fellow, 1983-84. Fellow Econometric Soc., Am. Acad. of Arts and Sci.; mem. Am. Econ. Assn. (exec. com. 1991-94, v.p. 2000-01). Office: Stanford University 579 Serra Mall Stanford CA 94305 Office Phone: 650-723-9677. Business E-Mail: johnbtaylor@stanford.edu.*

TAYLOR, JOHN CALVIN, dentist; b. Cin., July 22, 1914; s. John Calvin Taylor V and Magdala Elizabeth Siehl; m. Adah Packard Boggs, Mar. 7, 1941; children: Sarah, Margaret, Virginia, John, Frederick, Alison, Carla. BSc, Muskingum Coll., 1937; BD, Cedarville Sem., 1939; DDS, U. Pitts., 1949; cert. excellence in Hindi and Urdu, Lang. Sch., Landour, India, 1940-41. Diploma Acad. Gen. Dentistry, Am. Biog. Inst., 2005; cert. in med. missions, wildlife and theology, Internat. Biog. Ctr., 2009. Missionary Reformed Presbyn. Synod, Roorkee, India, 1939-46; moderator Reformed Presbyn., Pitts., 1946—47; nat. missions missionary Presbyn. Bd. Home Missions, Pitts., Tyre, Pa., 1947-52; missionary dentist United Presbyn., Pitts., Seattle, 1953-59; dir. Meth. Mission Hosp. Dental Clinic, Bariely, India, 1954—55; founder Dental Clinic Landour Cmty. Hosp., Mussoorie, India, 1955-59; pres. Rotary Club Internat., Mount Union, Pa., 1964-65; pastor 3 chs. Mt. Union, Johnsonburg and St. Mary areas, 1964-68; founder Shanta Bhawan Hosp. Dental Clinic, Katmandu, Nepal, 1968, Missionary Dentist, Inc., 1977; dental missionary svc. E.L.W.A. Hosp., Liberia, 1977, Tank Hosp., Pakistan, 1980—81, Sahiwal Hosp., Pakistan, 1981, Shell Clinics, Ecuador, 1983; provider free dental care India, 1978—2001; founder Oral Clinic Ctr., Dera Dun, India, 1981—. Tchr. emergency dentistry Vellore (India) Med. Coll., 1958; dentist Youth With a Mission, Mercy Ship, Hawaii, 1985. Author: Wildlife in India's Tiger Kingdom, 1980, Face the Devil's Roar, 1995, God's Kingdom helps Animal Kingdoms, 2005, The Creator God Saves Lives- Some Eternally, 2009 Co-founder, life mem. Wildlife Preservation Soc., Dehra-Dun, India, 1954—, organizer, founder Rajpur Wildlife Cheetal Pk., 1954—. Recipient Cert. of Honor for 50 Yrs. of Dedicated Svc. to Dentistry, ADA, 1999. Mem. Herminie Lions Club (fgn. chmn., Lions Hat award), N.Am. Hunting Club, NRA. Republican. Presbyterian. Avocations: zoology, hunting, taxidermy, photography, music. Home Phone: 724-446-7732; Office Phone: 724-446-7732. Personal E-mail: tgrtlr@juno.com.

TAYLOR, JOHN JACKSON (JAY), writer, retired diplomat; b. Little Rock, Dec. 4, 1931; s. Alfred Wesley and Annie Laurie (Cain) T.; m. Elizabeth Rose, July 9, 1954; children: John Jr., Laurie, Amy, Cynthia. BA, Vanderbilt U., 1952; MA, U. Mich., 1968. 3d sec. U.S. Fgn. Svc., Accra, Ghana, 1957-59, 2d sec. Taichung and Taipei, China, 1960-65; Chinese affairs analyst Dept. State, Washington, 1966-67; staff assoc. Ctr. for Chinese Studies, U. Mich., Ann Arbor, 1967-68; U.S. consul Sarawak, Sabah and Brunei, Kuching, Malaysia, 1968-70; chief external affairs reporting U.S. Consulate Gen., Hong Kong, 1970-74; officer-in-charge Chinese affairs Dept. State, Washington, 1974-75; staff mem. E. Asian affairs Nat. Security Coun., Washington, 1975-77; polit. counselor U.S. Embassy, Pretoria/Capetown, 1977-80, polit. cons. Peking, 1980-82; rsch. fellow Fairbank Ctr. for East Asian Studies Harvard U., Cambridge, Mass., 1982-83; dir. East Asian analysis Dept. State, Washington, 1983-85; dep. asst. sec. state Bur. Intelligence and Rsch., Dept. State, Washington, 1986-87; chief of mission U.S. Interests Sect., Havana, Cuba, 1987-90; diplomat in residence Carter Presdl. Ctr., Emory U., 1990-92; sr. mem. State Task Force 2000, 1992-93; sr. assoc. Global Bus. Access; assoc. in rsch. Fairbank Ctr. for East Asian Studies, Harvard U.; prodr., writer, dir. ?Why Prodns. Guest faculty Emory U. and Spelman Coll. Author: China and Southeast Asia, 1974, 1976, The Dragon and the Wild Goose, 1987, 1990, The Rise and Fall of Totalitarianism, 1993, The Generalissimo's Son, 2000, (PBS documentary) Ubuntu, African and Afrikaner, 2000, Chiang Kai-shek and the Struggle for Modern China, 2009; contbr. China and National Security, 1985, columns in newspapers Washington Post, L.A. Times, NY Times, Interviwee: PBS, VOA, BBC, CBS, FOX. Served as Naval Aviator with USMC, 1953-57. Mem.: Wash. Inst. Fgn. Affairs, Fgn. Svc. Assn. E-mail: jaytaylor888@sprintmail.com.

TAYLOR, JOHN JOSEPH, nuclear engineer, researcher; b. Hackensack, NJ, Feb. 27, 1922; s. John J.D. and Johanna F. (Thibideau) T.; m. Lorraine Crowley, Feb. 5, 1943; children: John B., Nancy M., Susan M. BA, St. John's U., Jamaica, NY, 1942, DSc (hon.), 1975; MS, U. Notre Dame, Ind., 1947. Mathematician Bendix Aviation Corp., Teterboro, NJ, 1946-47; engr. Kellex Corp., NYC, 1947-50; v.p. water reactor divsn. Westinghouse Electric Corp., Pitts., 1950-81; v.p. nuc. power Electric Power Rsch. Inst., Palo Alto, Calif., 1981-95; energy cons., 1995—. Adv. com. Oak Ridge Nat. Lab., Tenn., 1973-83, Brookhaven Nat. Lab., Upton, NY, 1986-92, Inst. for Nuc. Power Ops., 1988-95; adv. com. Argonne Nat. Lab., Ill., 1980-86, bd. dirs.; cons. Office Tech. Assessment, Washington, 1975-93; internat. adv. group IAEA, Vienna, Austria, 1992-95; nuc. rsch. rev. com. NRC, 1995-97; mem. US-Russian Commn. on Weapons Plutonium Disposition, 1996-2001, Nat. Acad. Bd. Radioactive Waste Mgmt., 1998-2001, DOE Nuc. Energy Rsch. Adv. Bd., 1998-2002; co-chair Atoms for Peace Study, Livermore Lab., 2003-04; com. on rev. of Dept. Energy Nuc. Energy R&D, Nat. Acad., 2006-07. Co-author: Reactor Shielding Manual, 1953, Naval Reactor Physics Manual, 1956, Nuclear Power, Policy and Prospects, 1987, Management and Disposition of Excess Weapons Plutonium, 1995; contbr. articles to profl. jours. Bd. regents emeritus St. Mary's Coll., Moraga, Calif., Bd of Regents, St. Patrick's U. Calif. Lt. (j.g.) USN, 1942—45. Recipient Order of Merit Westinghouse Electric Corp., 1957, George Westinghouse Gold medal ASME, 1990. Fellow AAAS, Am. Phys. Soc., Am. Nuc. Soc. (bd. dirs., Walter Zinn award 1993, Nuclear Builders award, 2007); mem. NAE (chair), Elec. Power/Energy Sys. Engrs. Republican. Roman Catholic. Office: Electric Power Rsch Inst PO Box 10412 3412 Hillview Ave Palo Alto CA 94304-1344 Home: 620 Sand Hill Rd Apt 303b Palo Alto CA 94304-2069

TAYLOR, JOHN LOCKHART, retired municipal official; b. NYC, Nov. 4, 1927; s. Floyd and Marian (Lockhart) T.; m. Barbara Becker, July 19, 1952; children: Catherine Fair, Robert, William, Susan. AB, Middlebury Coll., 1952; M.Govtl. Adminstrn., U. Pa., 1956. Reporter Providence Jour.-Bull., 1952-54; adminstrv. intern City of Xenia, Ohio, 1955-56; mcpl. mgr. Borough of Narberth, Pa., 1956-60, Twp. of Lakewood, N.J., 1960-64; asst. city mgr. Fresno, Calif., 1964-65; city mgr., 1965-68, Kansas City, Mo., 1968-74, Berkeley, Calif., 1974-76; lectr. U. Pa., 1957-58, Golden Gate U., 1977; sr. urban mgmt. specialist Stanford Research Inst., 1977-80; dir. Internat. Devel. Center, 1980-82; clk. of bd. suprs. City of San Francisco, 1982-98, spl. asst., 1998—2000. Pres. Calif. Clks. Bd. Suprs. Assn., 1988-89. Served with USN, 1945-48. Mem. Internat. City Mgrs. Assn., Mcpl. Execs. Assn. (pres. 1991-93, 98). Address: 1005 Creston Rd Berkeley CA 94708-1503 E-mail: misterclerk@sbcglobal.net.

TAYLOR, JOHN MCKOWEN, lawyer; b. Baton Rouge, Jan. 20, 1924; s. Benjamin Brown and May (McKowen) T.; 1 child, John McKowen. BA, La. State U., 1948, JD, 1950. Bar: La. 1950, U.S. Ct. Appeals (5th cir.) 1959, U.S. Supreme Ct. 1960. Assoc. Taylor, Porter, Brooks, Fuller & Phillips, Baton Rouge, 1950-55, Huckaby, Seale, Kelton & Hayes, Baton Rouge, 1955-58; ptnr. Kelton & Taylor, Baton Rouge, 1958-61; pvt. practice, Baton Rouge, 1961—. With AUS, 1943—46, maj. USAR, 1946—, ATO, ETO, PTO. Mem. ABA, AAAS, La. State Bar Assn., Baton Rouge Bar Assn., Mil. Order of World Wars, Am. Radio Relay League, Baton Rouge Country Club, City Club of Baton Rouge, Baton Rouge Amateur Radio Club, Camelot Club, SAR, Sigma Chi, Pi Gamma Mu, Phi Delta Phi. Republican. Presbyterian. Home and Office: 2150 Kleinert Ave Baton Rouge LA 70806-6712 Office Phone: 225-343-1928. E-mail: jmcktaylor@cox.net.

TAYLOR, JOHN READ, JR., hedge fund manager; b. NYC, July 16, 1943; s. John Read and Patricia (Green) Taylor; m. Sandra Shackelford Brown, June 28, 1969 (div. 1988); 1 child, Louise Tiffany; m. Joyce Manis, Jan. 28, 1989; 1 child, John Read III. AB in Romance Langs., Princeton U., 1965. Asst. mgr. Chem. Bank, NYC, 1969-73, founder Fgn. Exch. Adv. Svc., 1972; asst. v.p. First Nat. Bank Chgo., 1973-74; v.p. Citibank, NYC, 1974-78, Gessellschaft fur Trendanalysen, NYC, 1978-79; pres. EMCOR Mgmt., NYC, 1979-81; chmn., CEO, chief investment officer FX Concepts, Inc., NYC, 1981—. Chmn. J3 Biologics, Inc., NYC, 1992—98, US Transgenics, Inc., 1999—2002, Am. Integrated Biologics, Inc., 2002—07, Am. Detection Techs., Inc., 2002—, Inspiration Biopharms., Inc., 2005—. Contbr. articles to profl. jours. Bd. dirs. Hemophilia Assn. NY, 1990—96; chmn. bd. dirs. Coalition for Hemophilia B, NY, 1990—97. Office: FX Concepts Inc 225 W 34th St Ste 710 New York NY 10122-0710*

TAYLOR, JOSEPH EVANS, law educator; Student, Calif. State U., Sacramento; JD, Loyola U., LA, 1961; MBA, Pepperdine U., Malibu, Calif., 1986. Bar: Calif. 1962. Asst. chief dep. Sacramento Dist. Atty.'s Office, 1964-79; sr. atty. Ventura Dist. Atty.'s Office, 1979-86; counsel Lagerlof, Senecal, Drescher & Swift, Ventura, L.A., Calif., 1987; pub. defender County of Riverside, Calif., 1987-92; prof. law McGeorge Sch. Law, 1992—; judge pro tem Sacramento County Superior Ct., 1993—. Co-author trial practice cases. Named Prof. of Yr., U. Pacific McGeorge Sch. Law, 2004. Mem. Sacramento County Mgmt. Assn. (co-founder, v.p., past pres.), Calif. Dist. Attys. Assn. Office: McGeorge Sch Law 3200 5th Ave Sacramento CA 95817-2799

TAYLOR, JOSEPH HOOTON, JR., radio astronomer, physicist; b. Phila., Mar. 29, 1941; s. Joseph Hooton and Sylvia Hathaway (Evans) T.; m. Marietta Bisson, Jan. 3, 1976. BA in Physics, Haverford Coll., 1963; PhD in Astronomy, Harvard U., 1968; DSc (hon., U. Chgo., 1985, U. Mass., 1994. Research fellow, lectr. Harvard U., 1968-69; asst. prof. astronomy U. Mass., Amherst, 1969-72, assoc. prof., 1973-77, prof., 1977-81; prof. physics Princeton U., 1980—, James McDonnell Disting. prof. physics (now emeritus), 1986—, dean of faculty, 1997—2003. Author: Pulsars, 1977. Recipient Dannie Heineman prize in astrophysics, Am. Inst. Physics/Am. Astron. Soc., 1980, prize in gravitation and cosmology, Tomalla Found., 1985, Magellanic Premium award, Am. Philos. Soc., 1990, Einstein prize laureate, Albert Einstein Found., 1993, Wolf prize in physics, Wolf Found., Israel, 1992, Nobel Prize in Physics, Nobel Found., 1993, Carty Award for Advancement of Scis., Schwartz-child Medal; fellow MacArthur fellow, 1981. Fellow: Am. Phys. Soc., Am. Acad. Arts and Scis.; mem.: Internat. Astron. Union, Internat. Sci. Radio Union, Am. Astron. Soc., Am. Philos. Soc., NAS (Draper Medal). Mem. Soc. Of Friends. Achievements include discovery of first binary pulsar - a twin star system that provides a rare natural laboratory in which to test Albert Einstein's prediction that moving objects emit gravitational waves. Office: Princeton U Dept Physics 215 Jadwin Hall PO Box 708 Princeton NJ 08544-0001 Business E-Mail: joe@pulsar.princeton.edu.*

TAYLOR, JOSHUA AARON, computer scientist; BS, Rensselaer Poly. Inst., Troy, NY, 2005, MS, 2007. Rschr. Rensselaer AI & Reasoning Lab, 2003—. Christian edn. Korean Presbyn. Ch. Albany, Schenectady, NY, 2007—08. Business E-Mail: tayloj@cs.rpi.edu.

TAYLOR, JUNE RUTH, retired minister; b. Annapolis, Md., June 27, 1932; d. Benjamin and Naomi Medora (Dill) Michaelson; m. Thomas Wayne Taylor, Mar. 20, 1954; children: Rebecca Susan Taylor DeLameter, Michael Steven. AB, Goucher Coll., 1952; MRE, Presbyn. Sch. of Christian Edn., Richmond, Va., 1954; MDiv., McCormick Theol. Sem., 1978. Ordained to ministry Presbyn. Ch. (U.S.A.), 1976. Min. Christian Edn. Congl. United Ch. of Christ, Arlington Heights, Ill., 1974-79; dir. pastoral svcs. Presbyn. U. Hosp., Pitts., 1979-89; dir. chaplaincy svcs. Ephrata (Pa.) Community Hosp., 1991-96; ret., 1996; interim pastor Kreutz Creek Presbyn. Ch., Hellam, Pa., 2001; interim parish vis. Highland Presbyn. Ch., Lancaster, Pa., 2004. Chaplain Rush-Presbyn. St. Luke's Med. Ctr., Chgo., 1976-78; chair exec. com. Presbyn. Assn. Specialized Pastoral Ministries, Louisville, 1987-89; bd. dirs. Cocalico Place; parish assoc. Krentz Creek Presbyn. Ch., 2007-. Book reviewer in field. Fellow Assn. Profl. Chaplains (sec. exec. com. 1985-87); mem. Soc. Chaplains, Hosp. Assn. Pa. (pres. 1983), Assn. Profl. Chaplains (cert.), Assn. for Clin. Pastoral Edn. (clin.), Rotary (liaison to Boys and Girls Club S.W. Pitts. chpt. 1990-91, v.p., program chair Denver-Adamstown club 1996-97, pres.-elect 1997-98), York North Rotary Club (chmn. vocation svc. 2003-2005), Mental Health Assn. York County (bd. dirs. 1999—2005), Gamma Phi Beta Alumnae Club (pres. 1990-91).

TAYLOR, KATHLEEN P., hotel executive; married; 3 children. BA, U. Toronto, 1980; MBA, York U., 1984; JD, Osgoode Law Sch. Atty. Goodmans law firm; with Four Seasons Hotels and Resorts, Toronto, 1989—, v.p., gen. counsel, 1992—93, sec., bd. dirs., 1993, sr. v.p., 1993—95, sr. v.p. corp. planning and devel., 1995—97, exec. v.p., 1997—98, exec. v.p., chief corp. officer, 1998—99, pres. worldwide bus. ops., 1999—2007, pres., COO, 2007—. Dir. Royal Bank Canada, mem. audit com., human resources com. Cabinet mem. United Way of Greater Toronto; chair Endowment Giving portfolio; bd. dirs. The Hosp. for Sick Children Found. Mem.: Schulich Sch. Bus. (mem. internat. adv. coun.), Am. Hotel and Motel Assn. (mem. industry real estate financing adv. coun.), World Travel and Tourism Coun. Office: Four Seasons Hotels and Resorts 1165 Leslie St Toronto ON M3C 2K8 Canada Office Phone: 416-449-1750. Office Fax: 416-441-4374.

TAYLOR, KATHRYN L., Mayor, Tulsa; b. 1955; d. Jim and Lola Taylor; m. Bill Lobeck; 1 child. BA in Journalism, Okla. U., JD, 1981. Atty. pvt. practice; v.p., gen. counsel Thrifty Car Rental, 1988—2003; sec. Dept. Commerce State of Okla., 2003—05; mayor city of Tulsa, 2006—. Bd. mem. Tulsa Energy Authority; mem. Tulsa Parks and Recreation Bd.; bd. mem. Tulsa Energy Authority. Recipient Pinnacle award for community svc., Mayor's Commn. on Status of Women, 2003, Mona Lambird Spotlight award, Okla. Bar Assn., 2003, Headliners award, Tulsa Press Club, 2004. Office: Office of Mayor City Hall 200 Civic Ctr 11th Fl Tulsa OK 74103 Office Phone: 918-596-7411. Office Fax: 918-596-9010.*

TAYLOR, KELLEY M., music educator; b. Alexandria, Va., Aug. 20, 1974; d. Carol L. Shelby. BSE in Music Edn., U. Ark., Fayetteville, 1996; MusM, Southern Meth. U., Dallas, 2006. Cert. secondary edn. music tchr. Tex., 1996. Asst. band dir. Austin Acad., Garland, Tex., 1999—2000; head band dir. Classical Ctr. Brandenburg, Garland,

2000—. Home: 5601 Naaman Forest Blvd 1736 Garland TX 75044 Office: Classical Ctr Brandenburg MS 626 Nickens Rd Garland TX 75043 Home Fax: 972-926-2633. Business E-Mail: kmvanhoo@garlandisd.net.

TAYLOR, KENNETH BROOKS, retired marketing executive; b. Pensaola, Fla., Jan. 1, 1938; s. Brooks and Helen (McFaden) Taylor; m. Claire Marie Kennedy, Oct. 8, 1977; children: Cynthia, Randy, Tracey. AA, Pensacola Jr. Coll., 1958; BS, Fla. State U., Tallahassee, 1960; grad. student, U. Md., College Pk., 1965—69. Intelligence analyst Westinghouse Corp., 1968—70; mktg. rep. Computer Scis. Corp., Falls Church, Va., 1970—73; mktg. mgr. Interdata Corp., Arlington, Va., 1973—76; sr. sales exec. Digital Equip. Corp, Lanham, Md., 1976—80; sales mgr. Harris Computer, Washington, 1980—83; br. mgr. Sys. Engring. Labs., Lanham, Md., 1983—86; v.p. mktg. Altos Computers, Falls Church, Va., 1986—89; dir. mktg. Computer Data Sys., Rockville, Md., 1990—93; mktg. dir. CACI, Arlington, Va., 1993—96; cons. in field, 1994—96; ret., 1996. Tchr. Montgomery County Schs., Md., 1997—2002. V.p. Jaycees, Md., 1964—74; HS baseball, basketball umpire, 1984—2006; official, 1986—. Comdr. USN, 1961—67. Mem.: Nat. Assn. Sports Officials, US Naval Res. Assn., Lexington Veterans Assn. (comdr. 2006—), Internat. Basketball Official Org., Barbershop Harmony Soc., Kiwanas. Democrat. Methodist. Avocations: sports officiating, tennis, golf, politics, singing. Home: 16180 Edgemont Dr Fort Myers FL 33908 Personal E-mail: kbtaylor38@aol.com.

TAYLOR, KENNETH DOUGLAS, stockbroker, finance and computer consultant, educator; b. Topeka, Nov. 21, 1942; s. Olin Orlando and Lola Louise (Conley) T.; AB, George Washington U., 1964, MS in Stats., 1966; MS in Computer Sci. SUNY, 1990, PhD in Math. Eurotech, 1992, (univ. fellow); student of Peter Hilton; postgrad., McGill U., 1974, Bowdoin Coll., U. Montreal; m. Joy Ellen Rice, May 25, 1973 (div. Nov. 1981); m. Elizabeth Flanagan Brunner, May 6, 1995. Registered rep./stockbroker, options principal. Sr. programmer C-E-I-R, Inc., 1963, 69; instr. Army Map Svc., 1964-65; student instr. McGill U., 1966-71; rsch. assoc. U. Va. Med. Sch., 1972; fin. and computer cons., Plymouth, N.Y., 1973-87; computer scientist USAF, 1989-90; broker Russell Hawkes Assoc./Linsco/Pvt. Ledger, 1993-94, LESKO Fin Svcs, 1994—; sec. Richmond (Va.) Computer Club, 1977. Contbr. articles to profl. jours. Summer grantee NSF, Can. Research Council. Mem. ASTM, Am. Math. Soc. Home: PO Box 288 Montrose PA 18801-0288 Office: LESKO Fin Svcs Centre Plz 53 Chenango St Binghamton NY 13901-2820 Home Phone: 570-278-2899.

TAYLOR, KRISTÍN JÓNÍNA, musician, educator; b. Kans. City, Jan. 15, 1976; d. Ronald Lee and Vigdís A. Taylor. MusB, U. Mo., Kans. City, 1997, MusM, 1999; MusD, U. Cin., 2006. Pvt. practice, Forest City, Iowa, 1990—; asst. prof. piano Waldorf Coll., Forest City, 2005—. Musician: (conference presentation) The complete solo piano works of Thorkell Sigurbjörnsson, (guest soloist) Concert with UMKC Conservatory Orchestra, Concert with Independence Symphony Orchestra, (radio appearances) Performances on National Icelandic Radio Service, (solo performance - salurinn concert hall) The complete solo piano works of Thorkell Sigurbjörnsson, (recital) Mpls. Inst. Art, Piano works of Nordic Composers, (recital at reykjavík arts festival) Sunday Matinée with Schumann, (solo recital) Salurinn Concert Hall, (guest soloist) Recital with CCM Philharmonia Orchestra, Concert with CCM Philharmonia Orchestra, Concert with UMKC Conservatory Orchestra, Concert with Jefferson City Symphony Orchestra. Recipient Grand prize Winner, Naftzger Young Artist Competition, 1997; finalist, Music Teachers Nat. Assn. Coll. Competition, 1999; grant, Fulbright Assn., 2004—05. Mem.: Coll. Music Soc., Music Tchrs. North Iowa (v.p. 2007—09), Iowa Music Tchr. Assn., Music Tchrs. Nat. Assn., Mu Phi Epsilon Profl. Music Frat. (scholarship chmn. 2008—09, Bernstein-Crosman Piano award 1998, 1998, Presl. award 2002, grant 2004). Office: Waldorf Coll 106 S Sixth St Forest City IA 50436

TAYLOR, LANCE JEROME, economics professor; b. Montpelier, Idaho, May 25, 1940; s. Walter Jerome and Ruth (Robinson) T.; m. Yvonne S.M. Johnsson, May 31, 1963; children: Ian Lance, Signe Marguerite. BS with honors, Calif. Inst. Tech., 1962; PhD, Harvard U., 1968. Instr. econs. Harvard U., Cambridge, Mass., 1967-68, asst. prof., assoc. prof., 1970-74; research assoc. MIT, Cambridge, 1968-70, prof. econs., 1974-93, New Sch. for Social Rsch., NYC, 1993—. Vis. prof. U. Brasilia, 1974, Pontifical Cath. U. Rio de Janeiro, 1981, U. Delhi, 1987-88, Stockholm Sch. Econs., 1990; Marshall lectr. Cambridge U., 1986-87; cons. World Bank, UN, various fgn. govts. Author: Macro Models for Developing Countries, 1979, Models of Growth and Distribution for Brazil, 1980, Structuralist Macroeconomics, 1983, Varieties of Stabilization Experience, 1988, Income Distribution, Inflation, and Growth, 1991, The Market Meets its Match: Restructuring the Economies of Eastern Europe, 1994, Global Finance at Risk, 2000, Restructuring Macroeconomics: Structuralist Proposals and Critiques of the Mainstream, 2004. Fulbright fellow, 1962-63 Mem. Am. Econ. Assn., Royal Econ. Soc. Home: PO Box 378 Washington ME 04574-0378 Office: New School for Social Rsch Grad Faculty 65 5th Ave New York NY 10003-3089 E-mail: lance@blacklocust.com.

TAYLOR, LAVONNE TROY, editor; b. Riverside, Calif., May 20, 1941; d. Troy Virgil Bradstreet and R. Victoria (Freeman) Chambers; m. Robert Martin Taylor, May 15, 1958 (div. 1975); children: Dana Freeman, Timothy Rene; m. Herman Pickell, Feb. 14, 1985; children: Marianne, Barry, David. Cert. personal trainer Am. Coun. on Exercise, 2003. Reporter Thousand Oaks (Calif.) Chronicle; with prodn. News Chronicle, Thousand Oaks, prodn. supr., 1979-81; with prodn. Ind. Jour., Thousand Oaks, Herald Examiner, LA, L.A. Times; asst. mgr. Publ. Typography, Agoura, Calif., 1981-85; owner Excellence Enterprises, LA, 1982—; sr. editor arts Glencoe/McGraw-Hill Sch. Pub., Mission Hills, Calif., 1987-96; actress, 1997—2006; copy chief Shape mag., 1997—2005. Spkr. various writers clubs. Editor, pub. L.A. My Way, 1991, On the Wings of Song, 1994; mng. editor The BookWoman, 1991-93, The Taylor Trust. Mem. pub. rels. com. Conejo Players Theatre, Thousand Oaks, 1970-75, Betty Mann for 38th Assembly Dist., Agoura, 1975-76. Mem. NAFE, Am. Coll. Sports Medicine, Nat. Writers Club (pres. 1990-91, Merit Svc. award 1991), Women's Nat. Book Assn. (L.A. chpt. pres. 1992-93, newsletter editor, bd. dirs.). Avocations: reading, writing, gardening, music, art. Home Phone: 661-267-2220. Home Fax: 1-908-673-1179. Personal E-mail: lavonne.taylor@sbcglobal.net.

TAYLOR, LAWRENCE DOW, geologist, educator; b. Boston, Oct. 6, 1932; s. Theodore and Dorothea Mae (Dow) T.; m. Jean Ann Ryland, Sept. 24, 1955; children: Charles, Keith. AB, Dartmouth Coll., 1954, MA, 1958; PhD, Ohio State U., 1962. Geologist geophysics br. U.S. Geol. Survey, Boston, and Greenland, 1954-55, geologist fuels br. Denver, 1958; rsch. assoc. Dartmouth Coll., Hanover, N.H., and Greenland, 1957-58, Ohio State U. Inst. Polar Studies, Columbus, Ohio, and Antarctica, 1962-63, Glacier Bay, Alaska, 1959-60; asst. prof. Coll. of Wooster, Ohio, 1963-64, Albion (Mich.) Coll., 1964-68, assoc. prof., 1968-77, prof., 1977-98, prof. emeritus, 1998—, chair dept. geol. scis., 1968-85. Chief glaciologist Trans-Antarctic Traverse, NSF, U.S. Antarctic Rsch. Program, 1962-63. Contbr. articles to profl. jours. With US Army, 1955—57. Grantee NSF, 1960, 62-63, 65, 69, Hewlett Melon Found., 1981, Pew Sci. Program, 1991, Albion Coll., 1992-97; recipient Exemplary Tchr. award United Meth. Ch., 1997, Mich. Campus Compact Cmty. Svc. award, 1998, Antarctic Svc. Congl. medal; Taylor Hills, Antarctica, named in his honor. Fellow Geol. Soc. Am., Am. Quaternary Assn., Am. Geophys. Union, Nat. Assn. Geology Tchrs. (pres. East Ctrl. sect. 1984-85), Explorers Club, Rotary, Sigma Xi. Avocations: mountain climbing, backpacking, cross country skiing, tennis. Office: Albion Coll Dept Geol Scis Albion MI 49224 Business E-Mail: ltaylor@albion.edu.

TAYLOR, LELAND BARIDON, lawyer; b. Poughkeepsie, NY, July 5, 1920; s. Alexander J. and Elsie Jane (Van Wyck) T.; m. Rosemary Olcott Coon, June 24, 1945; children: Barry Eugene, Craig Cameron, Mark Alexander, Meg Olcott Taylor Casey. BS, Syracuse U., 1942, JD, 1948. Bar: N.Y. 1948, U.S. Dist. Ct. (no. dist.) N.Y. 1954, U.S. Supreme Ct. 1958. Ptnr. Fitzgerald, Taylor, Pomeroy & Armstrong and predecessor, Cortland, NY, 1948-2000; of counsel Pomeroy, Armstrong & Casullo, Cortland, NY, 2000—. Judge City of Cortland, 1952-57; bd. dirs. First Nat. Bank of Dryden. Former trustee Cortland Free Libr., 1950-2007. With Supply Corps, USNR, 1942-45. Named Cortland County Jr. C. of C. Young Man of Yr., 1952, N.Y. State Young Man of Yr., N.Y. State Jaycees, 1953, Syracuse U. Letterman of Distinction, 1977. Fellow N.Y. Bar Found., Am. Bar Found.; mem. ABA, N.Y. State Bar Assn. (v.p. 1974-76, sec. 1976-79, chmn. fin. com. 1979-84), Cortland County Bar Assn., Rotary (Paul Harris fellow), Masons. Presbyterian. Address: 16 Tompkins St Cortland NY 13045-2541 Office Phone: 607-756-7501.

TAYLOR, LEONARD STUART, engineering educator, consultant; b. NYC, Dec. 28, 1928; m. Lillian Rachel Schlang, Apr. 11, 1954; children: Robin Jolie, Allyn Lise. AB, Harvard Coll., 1951; MSc, N.Mex. State U., 1955, PhD, 1960. Microwave engr. Raytheon Mfg. Co., Bedford, Mass., 1950-55; research physicist Gen. Electric Co., Phila., 1960-63; assoc. prof. Case Western Res. U., Cleve., 1964-67; prof. U. Md., College Park, Md., 1967-96, prof. emeritus, 1996—. Cons. USN, Silver Spring, Md., 1967-96. Contbr. articles to profl. jours; inventor Microwave Scalpel, Implantable Microwave Hyperthermia Applicator and numerous others. With US Army, 1955—57. Recipient Disting. Alumni award, N.Mex. State U., 1975, Outstanding Contbn. award, U. Md. Coll. Engring., 2002. Fellow IEEE (life), Am. Soc. for Laser Medicine and Surgery; mem. Am. Phys. Soc. (life), Optical Soc. of Am., Bioelectromagnetics Soc. Avocations: tennis, music. Office: U Md ECEE Dept College Park MD 20742-0001 Office Phone: 301-405-3741. Business E-Mail: taylor@umd.edu.

TAYLOR, LESLIE M., theater educator; MFA, NY U., 1981. Chair, theater studies Emory U., Atlanta, 2000—; exec. dir., ctr. creativity and arts Emory Univ., 2008—. Pres. Out Hand Theater, Atlanta, 2006—08. Office: Emory Univ Clifton Rd Atlanta GA 30312 Business E-Mail: ltayl04@emory.edu.

TAYLOR, LESLIE RONALD, psychologist; b. Jeffersonville, Ind., May 25, 1934; s. Leslie Christopher and Nora Cordelia (O'Neal) T.; children: Deborah Susan, Michael Brooks. BA, DePauw U., 1956; MA, Ohio U., 1958; PhD, Purdue U., 1961; MS, Fla. State U., 1973. Lic. psychologist, Ohio. Psychology intern VA, Ind., 1958-61; psychologist Divsn. Corrections, Waukesha, Wis., 1961-63; prof. Muskingum Coll., New Concord, Ohio, 1963-85; dir. outpatient and partial hospitalization programs Marymount Hosp. Mental Health Ctr., Garfield Heights, Ohio, 1985-97; asst. prof. Ala. A&M, 1999—2003; counselor Ala. State Cert. Addition, 2004—. Cons. in field, 1965-85. Contbr. articles to profl. jours. Named Outstanding prof. Phi Theta Beta, 1979-80. Mem. APA, Sigma Xi. Avocations: aviation, music, cooking, woodworking, recipe collecting. Personal E-mail: ltaylor209@aol.com.

TAYLOR, LINDSAY DAVID, JR., health care executive, bank executive, federal agency administrator; b. Balt., Dec. 15, 1945; s. Lindsay David Sr. and Lillian Helen (Wagner) T.; children: Sarah Ruth, John David, Margaret Katherine. B in Mech. Engring., Rensselaer Poly. Inst., 1967; MBA, Dartmouth Coll., 1969. Bus. assoc. U.S. Steel Corp., Pitts., 1968-70; spl. asst. to asst. sec. for health HEW, Washington, 1970-71, mgr. operational planning, 1971-74, dep. asst. sec. mgmt., 1977-79; programming officer World Bank, Washington, 1974-76; dir. exams. and supervision Fed. Home Loan Bank Bd., Washington, 1979-81; exec. v.p. Perpetual Bank, Alexandria, Va., 1981-89; pres., CEO Columbia (Md.)-FreeState Health Sys., 1989-91, Preferred Health Network, 1992-96; CEO Alpha Health Plan, 1997-99; COO NPD, LLC, Bethesda, Md., 1999—, Nat. Assn. Cmty. Health Ctrs., Washington, 2001—. Cons. Nat. Acad. Pub. Adminstrn., Washington, 1985—86, Ctr. for Advancement of Health, Washington, 1988—89, Diabetex Corp., Balt., 1996—2003, Latin Am. Youth Ctr., 2003—04; trustee Md. Sci. Ctr., 1996—2000; co-chair Greater Balt. Health Care Coun., 1996—2001, Leadership Md., 1996; mem. bd. advisors Found. for Island Health, 2001—06; mem. adv. bd. WAMU Pub. Radio, 1985—88; bd. dirs. Hospice No. Va., 1984—88; chmn. Washington Employers Coalition on Day Care, 1983—90; chair CHC Funding, LLP, 2002—06; bd. dirs. Capital Link, 2003—08. Recipient Mgmt. Improvement award Pres. U.S., 1973, 77; Edward Tuck scholar, South Dakota Comm. Health Leadership award, 2008 Mem. Ctr. for Excellence in Govt. (prin. 1986-07), Washington Coun. Govts. (devel. policy com. 1986-89, mem. editl. adv. bd. Managed Care 1989-95), Tau Beta Pi, Pi Tau Sigma. Avocations: photography, folk music instruments, travel, wilderness, coaching youth baseball and basketball. Office: 4800 Montgomery Ln Ste 1000 Bethesda MD 20814-3472 also: Ste 210 7200 Wisconsin Ave Bethesda MD 20814 E-mail: LDavidTaylor@yahoo.com.

TAYLOR, LISA DEITSCH, lawyer, arbitrator, mediator; b. East Orange, NJ, Oct. 27, 1961; d. Thomas Alan Sr. and Marian (Rubin) Deitsch; m. Lindsey Handley Taylor, Dec. 29, 1984. BA cum laude, Columbia U., 1983; MA, JD, Duke U., 1986. Bar: NJ 1986, NY 1987, DC 1989, Tenn. 1996, Pa. 2003, Fla. 2004, US Dist. Ct. NJ 1986, US Dist. Ct. (so. and ea. dists.) NY 2005, US Ct. Appeals (3d cir.) 1991, US Supreme Ct. 1991; cert. arbitrator US Dist. Ct., 2002—; qualified mediator NJ Adminstrv. Office of the Cts., 2005-. Law clk. Duke U. Counsel and Med. Ctr. Legal Counsel, Durham, 1984—86, Coastal Healthcare Group, Inc., Durham, NC, 1985—86, Supreme Ct. NJ, Morristown, 1986—87; assoc. LeBoeuf, Lamb, Leiby & MacRae, NYC, 1987-89, Shanley & Fisher, P.C., Somerville, NJ, 1989-90, Morristown, NJ, 1990-96; dir., atty., co-chair health care practice group Hannoch Weisman, Roseland, NJ, 1996—99; atty., mem. firm St. John & Wayne, LLC, Newark, 1999—2006, Stern & Kilcullen LLC, Roseland, 2006—; counsel to fed. monitor U. Medicine & Dentistry of NJ, 2006—07. Lectr. practice mgmt. seminars AMA, 1989, 90, 91, 92, 93, 94, 95; program faculty Am. and Nat. Health Lawyers Assn. Physician, 1992, 99, 2000-02, 2005; cert. mem. Million Dollar Adv.'s Forum. Author: The Biggest Legal Mistakes Physicians Make and How to Avoid Them., 2005, Representing Physicians Handbook, 2006; contbr. chpt. to Hospital Law in North Carolina, 1987, Health Law Practice Guide, 2005, updated 2006, 2008, Physician's Comprehensive Guide to Negotiating, 2007; contbr. articles to profl. jours. Trustee Barnard Coll., Columbia U., NYC, 1981-83; mem. Town of Livingston Adv. Health Com., 1989-97, vice chmn., 1991, 94, 95; bd. dirs. Advanced Cmty. Health Systems, Inc. and subsidiaries, 1994-98, chmn., 1997-98; mem. dist. ethics com. Supreme Ct. NJ, 1998-2002, chair 2001-02; contr. editor Healthcare Fraud & Abuse Newsletter 1999-2002; editl. adv. bd. Med. Staff Briefing Dispute Resolver, Am. Health Lawyers Assn. Alternative Dispute Resolution Svc., 1997—; bd. dirs. Alzheimer's Assn., 2000-02; mem. Nat. Arbitration Forum Panel of Arbitrators, 2004-. Named one of 10 Outstanding Physicians Practice Attys., Nightingale's Healthcare News, 2004, NJ's Leading Women and Minority Attys., NJ Law Jour., 2005, Top 100 NJ Super Lawyers, NJ Monthly Mag., 2005, 2006, 2007, 2008, 2009, NY Area's Top Lawyers, 2008; named to Best Lawyers in America, 2009. Mem. ABA (planning com. health law sect. 2009), Am. Arbitration Assn. (arbitrator 1998-, mediator 2006-), Am. Health Lawyers Assn. (bd. appt. ADR Task Force, 2001-04, 2008-, vice chair Physician Orgn. Practice Group 2002-08), NJ State Bar Assn. (immediate past chair, bd. dirs., health and hosp. law and banking law sects., Disting. Svc. award, 2007). Office: Stern and Kilcullen LLC 75 Livingston Ave Roseland NJ 07068 Office Phone: 973-535-2624.

TAYLOR, LYNDON CLINT, lawyer, energy executive; b. Lawton, Okla., June 9, 1958; s. Clinton Harold and Doris Lee (Nance) T. BS of Indsl. Engring., Okla. State U., 1981; JD, U. Okla., 1984. Bar: Okla. 1984, U.S. Dist. Ct. (we. dist.) Okla. 1985, D.C. 1986. Assoc. Watson & McKenzie, Okla. City, 1984-86; assoc. through mng. ptnr. energy practice Skadden, Arps, Slate, Meagher & Flom LLP, Houston, 1986—2005; stet. gen. counsel Devon Energy Corp., Okla. City, 2005—07, exec. v.p., gen. counsel, 2007—. Republican. Avocation: golf. Office: Devon Energy Corp 20 N Broadway Oklahoma City OK 73102-8260*

TAYLOR, MARILYN JORDAN, architectural firm executive; m. Brainerd O. Taylor; children: Brainerd I., Alexis. Degree in govt. and urban affairs, Harvard Coll., 1969; MArch, U. Calif., Berkeley; postgrad., MIT. Joined Skidmore, Owings & Merrill LLP, Washington, 1971, urban designer, dir. design stations program of N.E. Corridor Improvement Project, 1978—85, chmn. NYC, 2001—04, chief urban design and planning practice, 1985—, ptnr., 1987—. Past pres. N.Y.C. chpt. AIA; chmn. Nat. AIA Regional and Urban Design Com.; vis. prof. Harvard Grad. Sch. Design; David Rockefeller fellow N.Y.C. Partnership, fellows adv. com. Key projects include N.J. Performing Arts Ctr., Newark, Riverside South, Manhattan, NYNEX Hdqs., Battery Park City, Penn Sta. Redevelopment Project, various airports, many others. Chmn. Urban Land Inst., 2005—; bd. dirs. NYC Bldg. Congress (chmn. 2002-04), Comml. Real Estate Women N.Y., Inst. for Urban Design. Recipient Profl. Leadership award, Profl. Women in Constrn., 2001; named Woman of Yr., Comml. Real Estate Women N.Y., 1998; named one of Most Influential Women in Am. Real Estate, GRID mag., 2001, The 100 Most Influential Women in NYC Bus., Crain's NY Bus., 2007; named to List of Most Influential Women, Crain's N.Y., 1996, 2000. Office: Skidmore Owings and Merrill LLP 14 Wall St New York NY 10005

TAYLOR, MARISA, literature and language professor; MFA in Creative Writing, U. Mont., Missoula, 1998. English instr. South Tex. Coll., McAllen, 1999—. Vol. Get Out the Vote, McAllen, 2008—08.

TAYLOR, MARK, former lieutenant governor; b. Atlanta, May 7, 1957; m. Sacha Taylor; 1 child. Degree in polit. sci., Emory U.; degree in law, U. Ga. Exec. Fred Taylor Co., Albany; mem. Ga. Senate, Atlanta, 1987—99; asst. adminstrn. floor leader then adminstrn. floor leader Gov. Zell Miller; sec. transp. com.; mem. appropriations, ethics, ins. and labor, rules coms.; lt. gov. State of Ga., Atlanta, 1999—2007. Mem. bd. dirs. March of Dimes, Albany/Dougherty 2000 Partnership, Throneateeska Heritage Found. Mem. Ga. Bar Assn., Dougherty County Bar Assn., Leadership Albany (charter), Artesian City Sertoma Club (past pres.), Rotary. Democrat. Methodist. Office: Taylor One Georgia Inc PO Box 250241 Atlanta GA 30325 Office Phone: 404-816-5724. Office Fax: 404-846-8579.

TAYLOR, MARY, state official; M in Taxation, U. Akron. CPA. Sr. mgr. Bober, Markey, Fedorovich & Co.; state rep. dist. 43 Ohio Ho. of Reps., Columbus, 2002—06, mem. edn., econ. devel. & environ. ways and means; state auditor State of Ohio, 2007—. Councilwoman, fin. com. chair, mem. rules & pers. and intergovtl. and utilities coms. Green (Ohio) City Coun., 2001—. Republican. Mailing: 3431 Parfoure Blvd Uniontown OH 44685 Home Phone: 330-699-3031; Office Phone: 614-466-1790.

TAYLOR, MARY LEE, retired academic administrator; b. Amarillo, Tex., Nov. 13, 1931; d. David Kelly and Bessie F. (Peck) McGehee; m. Lindsey Taylor, Sept. 13, 1950 (dec. Aug. 1985); children: Gary, Kent, Ronald. BS, W. Tex. State U., 1959; MEd, Tex. Tech U., 1975. Tchr. Mesquite (Tex.) Pub. Schs., 1961-63; resource tchr. Amarillo Pub. Schs., 1971-79, supr., 1979-80; reading instr. Amarillo Coll., 1981-88, asst. prof. reading, 1988-93, assoc. prof., 1994-95; ret., 1995. Project dir. Tex. Edn. Agy., Austin, 1984-85, 85-86, Amarillo Coll., 1988-89. Instr. GED Ctr. for Neighborhood Ministries, Phoenix, 2001—02. Mem. Tex. Assn. for Children with Learning Disabilities (meritorious svc. award 1985), Coll. Reading and Learning Assn. (spl. interest group leader 1987-89, cert. 1988, editor newsletter 1987-89), Am. Assn. Cmty. and Jr. Colls., North Plains Assn. for Learning Disabilities (pres. 1987-88, coord. accessibility svcs. 1993—), Tex. Assn. Developmental Educators (membership chmn. 1992-93), Assn. of Higher Edn. and Disabled Students.

TAYLOR, MATTHEW A., lawyer; b. Bryn Mawr, Pa., May 11, 1964; BA in English, Boston Coll., 1986; JD, Georgetown U. Law Ctr., 1989. Assoc. Emmet, Marvin & Martin, 1989—91; trial lawyer Taylor & Taylor, 1991—97; assoc. Duane Morris LLP, Phila., 1997—99, ptnr., 1999—, chmn. trial practice group, 2008—. Bd. mem. Covenant House Pa., M-Able, Inc.; bd. governors Malvern Prepatory Sch. Named one of America's Leading Lawyers in Business, Chambers USA, 2008, 2009. Mem.; Def. Rsch. Inst., Internat. Assn. Def. Counsel (vie chmn. technology com.), Phila. Bar Assn., Pa. Bar Assn. Office: Duane Morris LLP 30 S 17th St Philadelphia PA 19103 Office Phone: 215-979-1140. Office Fax: 215-689-4437. E-mail: MATaylor@duanemorris.com.*

TAYLOR, MICHAEL E., mathematics professor; AB, Princeton Univ., 1967; PhD, Univ. Calif., Berkeley, 1970. William R. Kenan, Jr. prof. math. Univ. NC, Chapel Hill. Fellow: Am. Acad. Arts & Scis.; mem.: Soc. Industrial and Applied Math., Math. Assn. Am., Am. Math. Soc. Office: Math Dept Univ NC Chapel Hill NC 27599-3250 Business E-Mail: met@math.unc.edu.

TAYLOR, MICHAEL LESLIE, lawyer; b. Boonville, Mo., Nov. 2, 1954; s. Paul Howard and Nora Lee T.; m. Janet S. Finke, June 23, 1990. AA, Kans. City Cmty. Coll., 1977; BGS, U. Kans., 1979, JD, 1982. Bar: Mo. 1982, US Dist. Ct. Mo. 1982, US Ct. Appeals (10th cir.) 1986, US Ct. Appeals (8th cir.) 1987, US Supreme Ct. 1999. Assoc. atty. Watkins, Boulware, Lucas & Miner, St. Joseph, Mo., 1982-85, ptnr., 1986-87, Watkins, Boulware, Lucas, Miner, Murphy & Taylor, St. Joseph, Mo.,

1987—2002, Murphey, Taylor, Siemens & Elliott, St Joseph, 2002—. Instr. Mo. Western State Coll., St. Joseph, 1985-94. Bd. mem. Midland Empire Diabetes Assoc., St. Joseph, 1984; mem. United Way Allocations Com., St. Joseph, 1985-86; pres. East Hills Homes Assn., St. Joseph, 1987-89, Ctr. Court Homes Assn., 2001-02; co-chair Leadership Tomorrow, St. Joseph, 1985-88; pres. Center Court Homes Assoc., St. Joseph, 2002-2003. Recipient Outstanding Vol. Svc. to the City award City St. Joseph, 1985, Lon O. Hocker Meml. Trial Lawyer award Mo. Bar Found., 1989. Fellow Am. Acad. Matrimonial Lawyers; mem. ABA, Mo. Bar Assn., St. Joseph Bar Assn., Million Dollar Advocates Forum. Avocations: reading, tennis, weightlifting. Office: Murphy Taylor Siemens & Elliott 3007 Frederick Ave Saint Joseph MO 64506 Office Phone: 816-364-6677. Business E-Mail: miketaylor@mtselaw.com.

TAYLOR, MILDRED D., author; b. Jackson, Miss., Sept. 13, 1943; d. Wilbert Lee and Deletha Marie (Davis) Taylor. BA in Edn., U Toledo, 1965; MA, U Colo., 1969. Vol., tchr. English and history Peace Corps, Ethiopia, 1965-67, then recruiter U.S., 1967-68; study skills coord. black edn. program U. Colo., 1969-71. Author: (children's fiction) Song of the Trees, 1975 (Coun. on Interracial Books for Children award 1975), Roll of Thunder, Hear My Cry, 1976 (Newbery medal, 1977), Let the Circle Be Unbroken, 1981, The Gold Cadillac, 1987 (Christopher award), The Friendship and Other Stories, 1987, Mississippi Bridge, 1990 (Christopher award), The Road to Memphis, 1990, The Well, 1995 (winner Jane Addams book award, 1996), The Land, 2001 (Coretta Scott King award, L.A. Times Book award, Scott O'Dell award, Pen USA award). Address: care Dial Books For Young Readers 375 Hudson St New York NY 10014-3658

TAYLOR, NANCY ELIZABETH, lobbyist, lawyer; b. Salt Lake City, Apr. 6, 1956; d. Calvin Walker and Dorothy (Cope) Taylor; m. Christopher Robbins Bowen, Jan. 22, 1978; children: Elizabeth Grant Bowen, Alexandra Taylor Bowen. BS, U. Utah, 1979; JD, Cath. U., 1988. Bar: DC. Health policy dir. Senate Com. on Labor and Human Resources, Washington, 1981-91; ptnr. Law Offices of Deborah Steelman, Washington, 1991-93; prin. shareholder, nat. co-chair health law dept. Greenberg Traurig LLP, Washington, 1993—. Spkr. in field. Testimony presentor Rep. Nat. Conf., 1992. Recipient Commr. award, FDA, 1989; named one of 50 Top Lobbyists, Washingtonian mag., 2007. Mem. Nat. Health Lawyers, Women & Gov. Rels., Food and Drug Law Inst. Republican. Mem. Lds Ch. Office: Greenberg Traurig LLP 2101 L St, NW, Ste 1000 Washington DC 20037 Office Phone: 202-331-3133. Office Fax: 202-331-0133. Business E-Mail: taylorn@gtlaw.com.*

TAYLOR, NATHALEE BRITTON, retired nutritionist, freelance/self-employed writer; b. Lubbock, Tex., June 8, 1941; d. Nathaniel E. and Dessie Pauline (Moss) Britton; children by previous marriage: Clay H., Bret N. Courtney. BS in Home Econs., Tex. Tech U., 1963. Home economist Pioneer Gas, Lubbock, Tex., 1963-65; dietitian Tex. Tech U., Lubbock, 1966-71; home economist South Plains Electric Co-op., Lubbock, 1986; mgr. quality control Rip Griffins Enterprises, Lubbock, Tex., 1987; sales rep. Time Chem., Lubbock, 1987—2003; with Sentry, Lubbock; mktg. rep. Dodson Group Ins., Lubbock, Farmers Ins., Lubbock, Southwestern Bell Wireless; ret., 2003. Ranch Historian. Co-author: (cookbook) From Our House to Yours, 1975; columnist: Lubbock Lights (mag.) Ranch Record, Nat. Ranching; presenter: (TV show) Southwestern Cooking Sta. KTXT; contbr. articles to profl. publs. Bd. dirs. Am. Heart Assn., Lubbock, 1985-87; mem. Home Economist in Bus., pres. Lubbock chpt., 1985; culinary co-chmn. Lubbock C. of C. Arts Festival, 1982, 83, 84; mem. Write for Nat. Ranching Heritage Ctr., Lubbock., Womens Studies Cmty. Connection. Named Lincoln County Fair Queen. Mem. Tech. Home Econs. Alums (sec./treas.), Am. Home Econs. Assn. (v.p., sec./treas.), Bd.-Cove, Soroptimist (v.p. Lubbock club). Democrat. Achievements include competing in reining horse competition. Avocations: gardening, writing, cooking, horseback riding. Personal E-mail: nathaleet@ranch-horses.com.

TAYLOR, NELLIE RUBY, artist, author, dramatist, director, producer, host, poet, singer, filmmaker; b. Lundale, W.Va., Apr. 18, 1946; d. John Otis and Blanche L. (Wright) Taylor; m. Ivan Lee Hurt, July 31, 1965 (div. Nov. 1982); children: Ivan Lee Hurt Jr., Bradley Allen Hurt. Student, Gallipolis Bus. Coll, Buckeye Hills Career Ctr., Hocking Tech. Sch., Nelsonville, Ohio; AA, Kans.; MA, Pa., 1995. Cert. pathologist, scientist William K. Sterin. Agent A.L. Williams Ins., Athens, Ohio, 1984—87; adminstr. Cleve. Sch., 1987—; nursing Mary Farmers Nurses, Cleve. Heights, Ohio, 1987—2002; tchr. Manor-Care, Mayfield Heights, Ohio, 2002—. Involved with Career Ladder Program Cleve. Mcpl. Sch. Adminstrn.; tchr. Head Start Gallia-Meigs Head Start Sch., Cheshire, Ohio, mem. bd. of mental retardation and devel. disabilities; founder, pres. Mean Corp. Author: Mean: You the Creative One, Mental Education; inventor Hopter-Copter Acar-Airplane; prodr., dir., host: (television) In Time Like These, Time Warner Cleve.; Represented in permanent collections Portrait of Bill Clinton, Presdl. Libr., Little Rock, Ark., painting, The Tree of Love, Apples of Gold, Black Gold, Libraries and Books, Bob Hope, portraits, William Shakespeare, Queen Elizabeth II, Prince Phillip, Pres. Nelson Mandella, Pres. John Zemin, Prince Charles, Princess Diana, Bob Evans, others. Recipient Award of Excellence, Ohio Sch. Bd. Assn, 1985—87, Award of Excellence in speaking, PhD Harris, Black Story Teller's Assn., Lifetime Congl. award, US Congress 11th Dist., 1998, Plaque of Excellence in Edn., Ohio Sch. Bds. Assn., USA Lifetime Congl. award Humanities, Black Story award of Excellence. Mem.: Am. Fedn. Tchrs. Achievements include represented as permanent leader, justice, tolerance new civil rights mem. ctr. with Rosa Parks, Montgomery, Ala; The Path of King, The Path of America, The Freedom Journey Continues, a speeches telling the history of freedom in the USA until present time (MLK day 2004 in Gallipolis and 2007 in Shaker Heights); history of genealogy and education Washington DC. Avocations: writing, travel, poetry, drama. Home Phone: 216-253-3616; Office Phone: 216-225-8645. Personal E-mail: taylor7715@roadrunner.com, taylor7715@adelphia.net.

TAYLOR, NICHOLAS C., lawyer, state agency administrator, energy executive; b. Washington, Sept. 18, 1937; s. James Spear Taylor and Helen Livingston MacGregor Strauss; m. Catherine Blaffer, d. Jan. 1, 1999; m. Elizabeth Carol Burke, July 25, 2004; children: Nicholas Van Campen, Katherine C., Christie. AB, Harvard U., 1959; JD, Georgetown U., 1963. Bar: DC 64, NY 66, Tex. 71. Assoc. Wilson, Woods & Villalon, Washington, 1964-65, Shearman & Sterling, NYC, 1965-70, Locke, Liddell, Sapp, Dallas, 1970-74; shareholder Stubbeman, McRae, Sealy, Laughlin & Browder, Inc., Midland, Tex., 1974-93; atty. Midland, 1993—; pres. Mexco Energy Corp., Midland, 1983—; chmn., mem. State Securities Bd. of Tex., 1995—2003. Pres. Mexco Energy Corp., 1983—; mem. Tex. Ethics Commn., 2006—. Mem. Tex. Jud. Coun., 1990-95. Recipient Am. Jurisprudence prizes for constnl. law, oil, and gas taxation So. Meth. U. Law Sch. Mem. Natural Gas Prodrs. Assn., Permian Basin Petroleum Assn. (bds. dirs. 2002-03). Episcopalian. Office: 214 W Texas Ave Ste 1101 Midland TX 79701-4616 E-mail: mexco@sbcglobal.net.

TAYLOR, NICOLE RENÉE (NIKI TAYLOR), model, shop owner; b. Miami, Fla., Mar. 5, 1975; d. Ken and Barbara Taylor; m. Matt Martinez (div. 1996); children: Jake Martinez, Hunter Martinez; m. Burney Lamar, Dec. 27, 2006; 1 child, Ciel Taylor Lamar. With Tri Star Sports and Entertainment Group, Brentwood, 2006—; owner Abbie and Jesse's, Cool Springs, Tenn., 2006—, Franklin, Tenn., 2006—. Contracts with L'Oreal, 1990-92, Cover Girl Makeup; appeared in Seventeen (cover girl) 1989, Vogue, Elle, Mademoiselle, Harper's Bazaar; modeled for Yves Saint Laurent, Karl Lagerfeld; modeled swimsuit Sports Illus., 1997, cover Sports Illus. Calendar, 1998. Founder Begin Found. Achievements include appearing on over 320 magazine covers worldwide; youngest model to appear on the cover of Vogue; holds the world record for being the youngest model to receive a six figure deal. Office: TriStar Entertainment Group Suite 200 215 Ward Circle Brentwood TN 37027 Office Phone: 615-309-0969. Business E-Mail: tristar@tristarse.com.*

TAYLOR, PATRICIA NAIL, mathematics and science educator; b. Birmingham, Ala., Apr. 13, 1973; d. Cecil Thomas Nail and Mickie Kelley Sullivan; m. John Lynwood Taylor, May 4, 1996; 1 child, Levi Thomas. B in Elem. Edn. cum laude, U. Ala., 1996, M, 2000. Fourth grade tchr. Jefferson County Bd. Edn. Fultondale Elem., 1996—. Grade level chair Fultondale Elem., Ala., 2004—06, discipline com. chair, 2004—06, mem. textbook com., 2005—07, mem. scheduling com., 2003—06; mem. Red Ribbon Week Com., Ala. Reading Initiative, Math Team Grade Level; SIP team - 4th grade tchr. Math Steering Com. Mem.: Ala. Edn. Assn. Avocations: horseback riding, softball. Office: Fultondale Elem 950 Central Rd Fultondale AL 35068

TAYLOR, PAUL B., choreographer; b. Allegheny County, Pa., July 29, 1930; s. Paul B. and Elizabeth (Pendleton) Taylor. Student, Syracuse U., 1949—52, Juilliard Sch. Music, 1952—53; PhD (hon.), Duke U., 1983, Conn. Coll., 1983, Syracuse U., 1986, Juilliard, 1988, SUNY, Purchase, 1988, Calif. Inst. Arts, 1989, Skidmore Coll., 1995. Artistic dir. Paul Taylor Dance Co., 1954. Dancer Mercé Cunningham Co., 1954, Martha Graham, 1955—62, Paul Taylor Dance Co., 1954—74. Dancer Paul Taylor Dance Co. has performed in over 450 U.S. cities and 60 countries, PBS TV Dance in Am., Live From the Am. Dance Festival, Two Landmark Dances, Three Modern Classics, The Wrecker's Ball, The Taylor Co.: Recent Dances, Am. Masters, Paul Taylor, Dancemaker, Acts of Ardour, choreographer (partial list) Aureole, 1962, Private Domain, 1969, Esplanade, 1975, Cloven Kingdom, 1976, Airs, 1978, Le Sacre du Printemps (the Rehearsal), 1980, Arden Court, 1981, Mercuric Tidings, 1982, Sunset, 1983, Roses, 1985, Last Look, 1985, Musical Offering, 1986, Ab Ovo Usque ad Mala, 1986, Syzygy, 1987, Speaking in Tongues, 1988, Company B, 1991, Funny Papers, 1994, Offenbach Overtures, 1995, Eventide, 1996, Piazzolla Caldera, 1997, The Word, 1998, Cascade, 1999, Arabesque, 1999, Black Tuesday, 2001, Promethian Fire, 2002, Dante Variations, 2004, Klezmerbluegrass, 2004, Spring Rounds, 2005, Banquet of Vultures, 2005; author (autobiography): Private Domain, 1987 (Nat. Book Critics Cir. award for biography, 1987). Decorated Chevalier des Arts et Lettres, elevated to Officier France, Comdr. Legion of Honor; recipient Internat. Cir. of Criticism for Artistic Rsch. and Cultural Exch. award, Festival Nations, Paris, 1962, Best Fgn. Attraction prize, Critics of Chile, 1966, Capezio Dance award, 1967, Creative Arts award, Brandeis U., 1978, Dance Mag. award, 1980, Samuel H. Scripps Am. Dance Festival award, 1983, Arts award, State N.Y., 1987, Lions of Performing Arts award, N.Y. Pub. Libr., 1989, Emmy award, Speaking in Tongues, 1992, Kennedy Ctr. Honors award, 1992; named Dancer of Yr., London's Dance and Dancers, 1965; named to Nat. Mus. Dance Hall of Fame, 1995; Guggenheim fellow, 1961, 1966, 1983, MacArthur Found. fellow, 1985. Office: Paul Taylor Dance Co 551 Grand St Lbby A New York NY 10002-4282 Office Phone: 212-431-5562.

TAYLOR, PAULETTE ANN, special education educator, consultant; b. Plainfield, NJ, June 8, 1948; d. Arthur John and Bess Ealy Taylor. AA, Centenary Coll. for Women, Hackettstown, NJ, 1968; BS in Edn., U. Tenn., Knoxville, 1970; MEd, Memphis State U., Tenn., 1973. Cert. English tchr. (7-12) N.J. Bd. Edn., 1970, English/Psychology tchr. (7-12) Tenn. Bd. Edn., 1970, Spl Edn. tchr. (with endorsements) Tenn. Bd. Edn., 1970, English tchr. (9-12) Minn. Bd. Edn., 1976, Spl. Edn. tchr. (k-12) Minn. Bd. Edn., 1976, Secondary tchr. (with approvals in English, Mental Disabilities Resouce) Iowa Bd. Edn., 1977, Spl. Edn. tchr. (k-12) Iowa Bd. Edn., 1977, Ednl. Cons. Iowa Bd. Edn., 1977. Para-educator Willis Sch. of Ednl. Therapy, Bound Brook, NJ, 1971; English tchr. Marshall County Sr. HS, Lewisburg, Tenn., 1971—72; spl. edn. tchr. Coro Lake Elem. Sch., Memphis, 1973—76, Inver Grove Heights Jr. High, Minn., 1976—77, Black Hawk Jr. HS, Pleasant Valley, Iowa, 1977—88; spl edn./ednl. cons. Miss. Bend Area Edn. Agy., Bettendorf, 1988—2007. Mem. negotiations team Pleasant Valley Edn. Assn., 1979—85, pres. elect, 1981—82, pres., 1982—84, past pres., 1984—85; pres. elect Miss. Bend UniServ Unit, 1985—86, pres., 1986—87, past pres., 1987—88; exec. bd. mem., profl. staff orgn. Miss. Bend Area Edn. Agy., 1989—, membership co-chair, profl. staff orgn., 1993—, mentor for new cons., 1995; vol. practicum supr. St. Ambrose U., Bettendorf/Davenport. Vol. Homework Hotline, Betttendorf, 1986—96; exec. bd. mem./grant reader Riverboat Devel. Authority, Davenport, 1989—99; bd. dirs. Scott. Co. Hist. Preservation Soc., Davenport, 1980—85, 1991—96, awards com., 1980—85, 1992, 1994, 1996, hist. homes tour organ. com. mem., 1984—95; bd. dirs. Neighborhood Housing Svc., Davenport, 1987—89; mem. organizing/steering com. East Bluff Neighborhood Dist., Davenport, 2004—06. Mem.: NEA (del. to 3 conventions 1982—86), Coun. for Exceptional Children, Iowa State Edn. Assn. (del. to 7 conventions 1981—87), Cornbelt Running Club (vol.), Delta Kappa Gamma (mem. program com., mem. membership com.). Democrat. Meth. Avocations: reading, gardening, exercise, computers.

TAYLOR, PEYTON TROY, JR., oncologist, educator; b. Tuscaloosa, Ala., July 21, 1941; s. Peyton Troy, Sr. and Frances (Sutter) Taylor; m. Helena Ström, Sept. 23, 1967; children: Annika, Karin, Sarah. BS, U. Ala., 1963, MS, 1968; MD, Med. Coll. Ala., 1968. Intern U. Va. Hosp., Charlottesville, 1968-69, resident, 1969-70, 72-75; asst. prof. ob-gyn. U. Va., Charlottesville, 1976-79, assoc. prof., dir. divsn. ob-gyn. Health Scis. Ctr., 1981-87, Richard N. and Louise R. Crockett prof., 1987—, med. dir. Cancer Ctr., 1996—2008, dep. med. dir. Cancer Ctr., 2008—; clin. assoc. surgery Nat. Cancer Inst., Bethesda, Md., 1970-72. Assoc. prof. U. Ala., Birmingham, 1979—81. Contbr. articles to profl. jours. With USPHS, 1970—72. Recipient Disting. Alumnus, U. Ala. Med. Alumni Assn., 2000. Fellow: ACS, Am. Coll. Obstetricians and Gynecologists; mem.: So. Surg. Assn., Internat. Gynecol. Cancer Soc., Am. Assn. Cancer Rsch., Am. Soc. Clin. Oncology, Soc. Surg. Oncology, Soc. Gynecol. Oncologists, Assn. Acad. Surgeons. Episcopalian. Avocations: sports, travel. Office Phone: 434-924-9933. Personal E-mail: peyton.taylor@virginia.edu. Business E-Mail: ptt9y@virginia.edu.

TAYLOR, PHILIP CRAIG, physics professor; b. Paterson, NJ, Mar. 17, 1942; s. Philip D. and Elizabeth E. Taylor; m. Muriel A. Allison, Dec. 20, 1969; children: Allison T. Severson, Heather M. Porreca. BA, Carleton Coll., 1964; PhD, Brown U., 1969. Postdoctoral rsch. assoc. NAS, Washington, 1969—71; rsch. physicist Naval Rsch. Lab., Washington, 1971—80, supervisory rsch. physicist, 1980—82; prof. physics U. Utah, Salt Lake City, 1982—2001, chmn. Dept. Physics, 1989—98, disting. prof. physics, 2001—05; prof. physics Colo. Sch. Mines, Golden, Colo., 2005—. Dir. Dixon Laser Inst., Salt Lake City, 1998—2005; assoc. dir. Colo. Energy Rsch. Inst., Golden, 2005; dir. Renewable Energy Materials Rsch. Sci. & Engring. Ctr. Recipient Rsch. Publ. award, Naval Rsch. Lab., 1975, Oustanding Profl. Contributions medal, Brown U., 1992, Disting. Rsch. award, U. Utah, 2002. Fellow: Am. Phys. Soc. (chmn. four-corners sect. 2000—02); mem.: AAAS, Materials Rsch. Soc., Am. Assn. Physics Tchrs. Office: Colorado School of Mines 1523 Illinois Street Golden CO 80401-1887 Office Fax: 303-273-3919. Business E-Mail: pctaylor@mines.edu.

TAYLOR, PHILIP RAYMOND, lawyer; b. Dublin, Ga., Nov. 1, 1933; s. Evan Augustus and Eula Bush Taylor; m. Elizabeth Lester Taylor (div.); children: Emily Taylor Fendig, Lester Taylor Odachowski. AB, Mercer U., Macon, Ga., 1955, JD, 1957. Bar: Ga. Ptnr. Harris, Watkins, Taylor & Davis, Macon, Ga., 1958—80, Fendig, McLemore, Taylor, Whitworth & Durham, Brunswick, Ga., 1980—2001; sr. ptnr. Taylor, Odachowski, Sperry & Crossland, St. Simons, Ga., 2001—05. Bd. visitors Mercer U. Law Sch., Macon, Ga., 1998—2004, chmn. bd. visitors, 2002—04. Mem. editl. bd Mercer Law Rev., 1956—57. Mem. Ga. State Ho. of Reps., Atlanta, 1961—62; chmn. Macon-Bibb County Dem. Exec. Com., Macon, Ga., 1964—68, Macon-Bibb County Bd. of Elections, Macon, Ga., 1969—80. Capt. USAR, 1962—78. Fellow: Am. Coll. Trial Lawyers, Am. Bd. Trial Lawyers; mem.: ABA, Am. Acad. Healthcare Attys., Def. Rsch. Inst., Ga. Soc. Hosp. Attys., Brunswick-Glynn County Bar Assn., Ga. Def. Lawyers Assn. (bd. dirs. 1967), Delta Theta Phi. Avocations: travel, fishing, hunting. Office: Taylor Odachowski Sperry & Crossland 300 Oak St Ste 200 Saint Simons Island GA 31522 Office Phone: 912-634-0955. Business E-Mail: ptaylor@toslaw.com.

TAYLOR, RALPH ARTHUR, JR., lawyer; b. Washington, Jan. 19, 1948; s. Ralph Arthur Sr. and Mary Florence Taylor; m. Joanna Lamb Moorhead, Jan. 30, 1988; children: Alison M., John Duncan. BS in Engring. with honors, Princeton, 1970; JD, U. Va., 1975. Bar: Va. 1975, D.C. 1976, Md. 1989, U.S. Dist. Ct. D.C. 1977, U.S. Dist. Cts. (ea. and we. dists.) Va. 1986, U.S. Dist. Ct. Md. 1988, U.S. Dist. Ct. Colo. 1998, U.S. Ct. Appeals (4th cir.) 1991, U.S. Ct. Appeals (D.C. cir.) 1977, U.S. Ct. Appeals (6th cir.) 1991, U.S. Ct. Claims 1985, U.S. Supreme Ct. 1980. Program advisor US EPA, Boston, 1970-72; assoc. Steptoe & Johnson, Washington, 1975-84, Shaw, Pittman, Potts, & Trowbridge, Washington, 1984-86, ptnr., 1986—2000, leader tech. and intellectual property litigation group, co-leader Yr. 2000 practice group; ptnr. Dorsey & Whitney, LLP, Washington, 2000—05, co-chair intellectual property litig. group, 2000—03, chair intellectual property litig. group, 2003—05; ptnr., litig., intellectual property groups Arent Fox LLP, Washington, 2005—. Assoc. editor Litigation News, 1985-99, exec. editor, 1999-2004; notes editor Va. Law Rev., 1974-75; contbg. author: International Technology Transfers, 1995; co-chair com. newsletters com. ABA Litigation Sect., 2004-07, coun. mem., 2007-. Pres. Cloisters West Homeowners Assn., Washington, 1989, 1990, 1625 Q St. Condo. Assn., Washington, 1982—86; bd. dirs. Am. Liver Found., nat. capital chpt., pres., 2004—09; mem. grad. bd. trustees Princeton Quadrangle Club. Lt. USPHS, 1970—72. Mem. Order of the Coif, Met. Club (Washington), Barristers, Princeton Club (Washington), Chevy Chase Club, Lawyers Club, Internat. Assn. Defense Counsel. Protestant. Avocations: sailing, skiing, tennis, golf. Office: Arent Fox LLP 1050 Connecticut Ave NW Washington DC 20036-5339

TAYLOR, RAYMOND MASON, lawyer, educator, former government official; b. Washington, NC, Jan. 1, 1933; s. Thaddeus Raymond and Mary Ada (Mason) T.; m. Rachel High; 1 dau., Elizabeth Lee Taylor Garber (Mrs. Kenneth Richard Garber). AB, U. N.C.-Chapel Hill, 1955, JD, 1960. Cert. law librarian Am. Assn. Law Libraries, 1968. Bar: N.C. 1960, U.S. Dist. Ct. (ea. dist.) N.C. 1960, U.S. Supreme Ct. 1970, U.S. Ct. Appeals (4th, 5th, 6th, 7th, 8th and 9th cirs.) 1977, U.S. Ct. Internat. Trade 1978, U.S. Ct. Appeals (11th cir.) 1981, U.S. Ct. Appeals (D.C. cir.) 1983, U.S. Ct. Mil. Appeals 1983. Staff reporter Washington (N.C.) Daily News, 1952, 54; adminstrv. asst. CD, Winston-Salem and Forsyth County, NC, 1955; adminstrv. intern City of Winston-Salem, 1958; research asst. Assoc. Justice N.C. Supreme Ct., Raleigh, 1960-61; assoc. Gardner, Connor & Lee, Wilson, NC, 1961-64; adj. instr. bus. law Atlantic Christian Coll. (now Barton Coll.), Wilson, 1962-63, adj. prof., 1963-64; marshal, librarian N.C. Supreme Ct., 1964-77; sole practice Raleigh, NC, 1977—81, 1983—84, 1988—. Asst. U.S. atty., chief of appellate sect. Eastern Dist. N.C., 1981-82; supt. documents of U.S., asst. pub. printer of U.S., assoc. gen. counsel U.S. GPO, Washington, 1982-83; ptnr. Hall, Hill, O'Donnell, Taylor, Manning & Shearon, 1985-87; vis. lectr. econs. and bus. law N.C. State U., Raleigh, 1967-85; project dir. Fed. Jud. Ctr. Study of Fed. Ct. Libraries, 1976-77; dir. N.C. Law Research Facilities Study, 1970; chmn. State and Ct. Law Libraries of the U.S. and Can., 1973-74; mem. Info. Industry Coun. to Pub. Printer of U.S., 1981-83. Author: Federal Court Libraries, 1981. Mem., sec. southeastern area coun. Am. Jr. Red Cross, 1949-50, internat. study visitor, Europe, 1950; chmn. Parents' Day Campbell U., 1979, chmn. Parents Fund, 1981-82; mem. Wake County Libr. Commn., 1979-81. Served with CIC, U.S. Army, 1955-57. Recipient NC Soc. County and Local Historians award, 1955, Tar Heel of Week award, 1971, Excellence award Soc. Tech. Communication, 1976. Mem. ABA, NC Bar Assn. (chmn. legis. com. elder law sect. 2002-03), Nat. Acad. Elder Law Attys. (state coord. 1991-95), SCV, Order Golden Fleece (pres. 1958-59), West Raleigh Rotary (pres. 1992-93, Paul Harris fellow 1992, Holoman Disting. Svc. award 1997), Pi Sigma Alpha, Phi Delta Phi, Omicron Delta Kappa, NC Supreme Ct. Hist. Soc. (trustee 1999-). Home: 3073 Granville Dr Raleigh NC 27609-6917 Office: 503 Oberlin Rd Ste 203 Raleigh NC 27605-1327 Office Phone: 919-832-8440.

TAYLOR, REGINA, actress; b. Dallas, Aug. 22, 1960; d. Nell Taylor. Student, So. Meth. U. TV appearances include (movies) Crisis at Central High, 1981, Howard Beach: Making the Case for Murder, 1989, Children of the Dust, 1995, Hostile Waters, 1997, The Third Twin, 1997, Strange Justice, 1999, Cora Unashamed, 2000, In from the Night, 2006, (TV series) I'll Fly Away, 1991-93 (Emmy award nominee best actress in a drama 1993, Golden Globe award), Feds, 1997, The Education of Max Bickford, 2001-02, The Unit, 2006- (Outstanding Actress in a Drama Series, NAACP Image award, 2008); films include Lean on Me, 1989, Losing Isaiah, 1995, Clockers, 1995, The Keeper, 1995, Spirit Lost, 1996, A Family Thing, 1996, Courage Under Fire, 1996, The Negotiator, 1998; stage appearances include Romeo and Juliet, 1986, King Lear, 1987, The Tempest, 1988, one-woman show Escape From Paradise, 1994. Office: c/o Anonymous Content 3532 Hayden Ave Culver City CA 90232

TAYLOR, REGINALD L., lawyer, consultant; s. Marvin E. Goode and Debra D. Randolph, Martin D. Randolph (Stepfather); life ptnr. Chris Aaron Porter, Oct. 30, 2004. MBA, JD, U. Mo., Kansas City, PhD, 2003. Bar: Mo. 2002, Kans. 2004. Asst. prof. U. Mo., Kansas City, Mo., 2002—04; in-house counsel Total Sodding & Seeding, Inc, Belton, Mo.,

2006—. Youth min. Spruce St. Matthew BC, Kansas City, 1992—95. Capt. USMC. Mem.: ABA (assoc.). Office: Total Sodding & Seeding Inc PO Box 746 Belton MO 64012 Office Fax: 816-331-8706. Business E-Mail: rtaylor.totalsod@sbcglobal.net.

TAYLOR, RICHARD EDWARD, physicist, researcher; b. Medicine Hat, Alta., Can., 1929; arrived in U.S., 1952; s. Clarence Richard and Delia Alena Taylor; m. Rita Jean Bonneau, 1951; 1 child, Norman Edward. BS, U. Alta., 1950, MS, 1952; PhD, Stanford U., 1962; DHC (hon.), U. Paris-Sud, 1980; DSc, U. Alta., 1991; LLD (hon.), U. Calgary, Alta., 1993; DSc (hon.), U. Lethbridge, Alta., 1993, U. Victoria, B.C., Can., 1995; DHC (hon.), U. Blaise Pascal, 1997; DSc (hon.), Carleton U., Ottawa, Ont., 1999, U. Liverpool, UK, 1999, Queen's U., Kingston, Ont., 2000. Boursier Lab. de l'Accelerateur Lineaire, Orsay, France, 1958—61; physicist Lawrence Berkeley Lab., Berkeley, Calif., 1961—62; staff mem. Stanford Linear Accelerator Ctr., 1962—68, assoc. prof., 1968—70, prof., 1970—2003, assoc. dir., 1982—86, Lewis M. Terman Prof., 1993—99, emeritus prof., 2003—. Recipient Nobel prize in Physics, 1990; named Companion, Order of Can., 2005, Can. Hall of Fame, Ottawa; fellow Guggenheim Found., 1971—72, von Humboldt Found., 1982. Fellow: AAAS, Royal Soc. London, Royal Soc. Can., Am. Acad. Arts and Scis.; mem.: NAS (fgn. assoc.), Can. Assn. Physicists, Am. Phys. Soc. (W.K.H. Panofsky prize divsn. particles and fields 1989). Achievements include first to conduct investigations concerning deep inelastic scattering of electrons on protons and bound neutrons, which have been of essential importance for the development of quark model in particle physics. Office: Stanford Linear Accelerator Ctr M/S 43 2575 Sand Hill Rd Menlo Park CA 94025-7015 E-mail: retaylor@slac.stanford.edu.

TAYLOR, RICHARD WILLIAM, investment banker, portfolio manager; b. Toledo, Sept. 16, 1926; s. Everett Ellsworth and Hazel (Broer) T.; m. Lyn Westerlund, Sept. 11, 1954; children: Julie Everett, Richard William, Alison Nichols, Jennifer Broer, Liane Westerlund. BS, U.S. Naval Acad., 1949; postgrad., U. Calif., 1952. Mem. Ohio Ho. of Reps. (100th gen. assembly from 9th Dist.); asst. mgr. Navy sales Martin Aircraft, Balt., 1953-56; with McKinsey & Co. (mgmt. cons.), NYC, 1956-60; asst. to v.p. Cerro Corp., NYC, 1960-62, spl. asst. to pres., 1965; pres. Cerro Aluminum Co., NYC, 1962-65; successively v.p., exec. v.p., pres. and CEO Carter, Walker & Co., Inc., 1967-69; pres., CEO Burton, Dana, Westerlund, Inc., NYC, 1969—; v.p. Sterling, Grace & Co., Inc., 1971-74, sr. v.p. corp. fin., 1980-81; v.p. corp. fin. Moseley, Hallgarten, Estabrook & Weeden Inc., 1975-80; v.p. Kidder, Peabody & Co. Inc., 1981-93; dir. investments, pvt. client divsn. Oppenheimer & Co., 1993—. Bd. dirs., pres., chmn. fin. com. YWCA Retirement Fund, Inc. With USN, 1944-52. Decorated Air medal, Navy Commendation medal. Mem. U.S. Naval Acad. Alumni Assn., U.S. Naval Inst. Home: Apt D 132 Heritage Hill Rd New Canaan CT 06840-4631 Office: Oppenheimer & Co Inc 200 Park Ave New York NY 10166 Home Phone: 203-801-9604; Office Phone: 212-667-4022.

TAYLOR, RICHARD WIRTH, retired political science professor; b. Cleve., Jan. 15, 1923; s. Robert and Irmgard (Wirth) T.; m. Sadie White, Sept. 19, 1946; children: Peter, Karla, Mark, Stephen. BA, U. Ill., 1947, MA, 1948, PhD, 1950. Instr. polit. sci. U. Minn., Mpls., 1950-52; asst. prof. polit. sci. Lehigh U., Bethlehem, Pa., 1952-55, Wis. State U., Stevens Point, 1955-56; vis. asst. prof. Northwestern U., Evanston, Ill., 1956-57; assoc. prof. Coe Coll., Cedar Rapids, Iowa, 1957-60, chmn., prof., 1960-67; prof. polit. sci. Kent State U., Ohio, 1967-92, prof. emeritus Ohio, 1992—, chmn. Ohio, 1974-82. Vis. prof. Karl-Marx-Universität, Leipzig, Fed. Republic Germany, 1990. Co-exec. editor Peace and Change, 1986-87. Policy com. Friends Com. Nat. Legis., Washington, 1964-85, exec. com., 1986-87; acad. adv. com., ombudsman com. Internat. Bar Assn., Edmonton Alta., Can., 1980—; active Friends World Com. on Consultation, 1991-98, Am. Friends Svc. Com., 2000-07, clk. Lake Erie Yearly Meeting, 1977-79. Home: 115 Kendal Dr Oberlin OH 44074-1905

TAYLOR, ROBERT BROWN, physician, educator, writer; b. Elmira, NY, May 31, 1936; s. Olaf C. Taylor and Elizabeth (Place) Brown; m. Anita Dopico; children: Diana Taylor Root, Sharon Taylor Oliverio. Student, Bucknell U., 1954-57; MD, Temple U., 1961. Diplomate Am. Bd. Family Medicine. Gen. practice medicine, New Paltz, NY, 1964-78; faculty physician Sch. Medicine Wake Forest U., Winston-Salem, NC, 1978-84; prof. dept. family medicine Oreg. Health Scis. U. Sch. Medicine, Portland, 1984—, chmn., 1984-98, prof. emeritus family medicine, 1998—. Mem. comprehensive part II com. Nat. Bd. Med. Examiners, Phila., 1986-91. Author: Common Problems in Office Practice, 1972, A Primer of Clinical Symptoms, 1973, The Practical Art of Medicine, 1974; editor: Family Medicine: Principles and Practice, 1978, 6th edit., 2003, Health Promotion: Principles and Clinical Applications, 1982, Difficult Diagnosis, 1985, Difficult Medical Management, 1991, Difficult Diagnosis II, 1992, Fundamentals of Family Medicine, 1996, 3rd edit, 2003, Manual of Family Practice, 1997, 2d edit., 2002, Taylor's Review of Family Medicine, 1998, Manual of Ten-Minute Diagnosis, 2000, The Clinician's Guide to Medical Writing, 2004, Taylor's Diagnostic and Therapeutic Challenges, 2005, Taylor's Cardiovascular Diseases, 2006, Academic Medicine: A Guide for Clinicians, 2006, Taylor's Musculoskeletal Problems and Injuries, 2006, White Coat Tales: Medicine's Heroes, Heritage and Misadventures, 2008; contbg. editor Physicians Mgmt. Mag., 1972-99; editl. bd. Family Practice Rsch. Jour., 1980-90, Female Patient, 1984-2006, Am. Family Physician, 1990-98, Jour. Family Practice, 1990-93, Med. Tribune, 1993-99. Served as surgeon USPHS, 1961-64. Recipient J. David Bristow MD award, Oreg. Health Scis. U., 1993, F. Marian Bishop Leadership award, Soc. Tchrs. Family Medicine Found., 2007. Fellow Am. Acad. Family Physicians (sci. program com., Thomas W. Johnson award 1998, bd. curators found. archives, John G. Walsh Lifetime Achievement award 2003, Outstanding Sci. Paper award 1982); mem. Soc. Tchrs. Family Medicine (bd. dirs., Excellence cert. 1989), Assn. Am. Med. Colls., Am. Assn. for Study Headache, World Orgn. Family Doctors (chmn. sci. program com.), Portland City Club, Multnomah Athletic Club, Phi Beta Kappa (award 1957), Alpha Omega Alpha (award 1961). Home: 1414 SW 3rd Ave Apt 2904 Portland OR 97201-6629 Office: Oreg Health Sci U Sch Medicine Mail Code FM 3181 SW Sam Jackson Park Rd Portland OR 97239-3098 Home Phone: 503-241-1826; Office Phone: 503-494-6611.

TAYLOR, ROBERT LAWRENCE, JR., medical educator; s. Robert Lawrence and Mary S Taylor; m. Jane Rachel Young, June 9, 1990; children: Rachel M., Rebecca J. BA, Carson-Newman Coll., Jefferson, Tenn., 1975; MS, Auburn U., Ala., 1978; PhD, Miss. State U., Starkville, 1981. Postdoc. fellow Med. Coll. Va., Richmond, 1982—84; prof. U. NH., Durham, 1984—. Recipient Nat. Leadership Devel. Program award, ESCOP-ACOP, 2004—05, award, Nat. Animal Germplasm Program, 2004—08, Assoc. Jour. Editor award, Poultry Sci. Assn., 2005—, Centennial Symposium Invited Spkr. award, 2008. Mem.: World's Poultry Sci. Assn., Soc. Exptl. Biology & Medicine, Poultry Sci. Assn., Am. Assn. Immunologists. Independent. Office: Univ NH Kendall Hall 129 Main St Durham NH 03824 Office Fax: 603-862-3758. Business E-Mail: bob.taylor@unh.edu.

TAYLOR, ROBERT LEWIS, management educator; b. Pitts., Dec. 10, 1939; s. Robert William and Elinor (Miller) T.; m. Linda Taylor Shapiro, Oct. 28, 1988; 1 step child, Kara; children by previous marriage: Rob, Mike. AB in Am. Studies, cum laude, Allegheny Coll., 1961; MBA, Ohio State U., 1966; D in Bus. Adminstrn., Mgmt., Ind. U., 1972. Asst. prof., dir. rsch. USAF Acad., Colorado Springs, Colo., 1971-77, assoc. prof., dir. instrn. dept. econ., geography, mgmt., 1977-79, prof. mgmt., head dept. econs., geography, mgmt., 1980-81; assoc. dean Coll. Letters and Sci., head div. Bus. and Econs., Carl N. Jacobs Prof. of Bus. U. Wis., Stevens Point, 1981-84; dean Coll. Bus. Pub. Adminstrn. U. Louisville, 1984—2003, dean emeritus and prof. of mgmt., 2003—. Chmn. bd. dirs. Ky. Wood Floors, Louisville, 1988-98, AACSB: Internat., Tampa, Fla., 1999-2000; bd. advisors Rawlings Co., Louisville; bd. dirs. Stock Yards Bancorp,; cons., advisor Kellogg Nat. Fellowship program Kellogg Found., bd. dirs. Innovative Production Inc., 2007-, Battle Creek, Mich., 1985-89. Co-editor: Contemporary Issues in Leadership, 1984, 6th edit., 2006, Leadership Challenges for Today's Manager, 1988, Military Leadership: In Pursuit of Excellence, 6th edit., 2009; contbr. articles to profl. jours Chmn. Mayor's Strategic Planning Group, Louisville, 1986—; mem. Gov.'s Econ. Devel. Com., Frankfort, Ky., 1987-89, exec. com. Bus. Advs., 1988-92, task force on econ. devel. Ky. Legis. Rsch. Coun., 1991, Leadership Louisville, 1986, Leadership Ky., 1987; bd. dirs. Metro United Way, 1999—, Ctr. Nonprofit Excellence, 2005—, Louisville Public Media, 2006—; bd. trustees Jewish Hosp. Healthcare Svcs., Louisville, 2000—07; active St. Michael Orthodox Ch. Mem. Acad. Mgmt. (proceedings editor 1976-77, newsletter editor 1983-86), Louisville C. of C. (bd. dirs., exec. com 1990-94), Sigma Xi, Beta Gamma Sigma, Pi Gamma Mu. Avocations: travel, walking, stamp collecting/philately, reading. Home: 1516 Sylvan Way Louisville KY 40205-2408 Office: U Louisville 375 College of Bus Louisville KY 40292-0001 Office Phone: 502-852-4786. Business E-Mail: rltayl01@gwise.louisville.edu.

TAYLOR, ROBERT MORGAN, electronics executive; b. Orange, NJ, May 13, 1941; s. Morgan H. M. Taylor and Grace Anna (Bonynge) Loding; m. Sandra Ruth Cox, Sept. 11, 1965; children; Scott Joseph, Karen Lynne. BA in Chemistry, Williams Coll., 1963; PhD in Chemistry, Pa. State U., 1968; MBA, Drexel U., 1973. Scientist Leeds & Northrup Co., North Wales, Pa., 1968-70, sr. scientist, 1970-72, prin. scientist, 1972-84, corp. scientist, 1984-85, dir. R&D, 1985-92, dir. analytical mktg., 1990-93; v.p. The Capital Controls Group, Colmar, Pa., 1993-99; pres. RMT Cons., Lansdale, Pa., 1999—. Contbr. articles to profl. jours. Chmn. indsl. com. Montgomery County (Pa.) Sci. Rsch. Competition, 1987-99. Mem. IEEE, Electrochem. Soc. (fin. com. 1971-73, controlling mems. com. 1977), Am. Chem. Soc., Instrument Soc. Am. (sr.), Indsl. Rsch. Inst. (rep.). Achievements include patents for for water analysis (5). Personal E-mail: rmtconsulting@comcast.net.

TAYLOR, ROGER DALE, lawyer; b. Booneville, Ark., Apr. 6, 1950; s. Carl Edward and Amanda (Wilkins) T.; m. Elizabeth Payne, Feb. 20, 1988; children: Zachary, Grace, Greta, Wilkins. BSEE, U. Ark., 1972; JD with honors, George Washington U., 1980. Bar: DC 1980, Tex. 1981, Ga. 1996. Assoc. Vinson & Elkins, Houston, 1981-83, Busby, Rehm & Leonard, Washington, 1983-85, Finnegan, Henderson, Farabow, Garrett & Dunner LPP, Washington, 1985-90, ptnr. Tokyo, 1990-92, Washington, 1992-96, Atlanta, 1997—; mng. ptnr. Atlanta Office Finnegan, Henderson, mem. exec. com.; ptnr. Alston & Bird, Atlanta, 1996-97. Adj. prof. Catholic U. Law Sch., Washington, 1992—95. Mem. Am. Intellectual Property Assn., Atlanta Soc. Clubs, Licensing Execs. Soc. (chmn. Japan com. 1994—), World Trade Ctr. Atlanta, Order of the Coif, Tau Beta Phi, Etta Kappa Nu. Office: Finnegan Henderson 3500 Suntrust Plz 303 Peachtree St NE Atlanta GA 30308-3201 Home: 552 Wood Valley Dr SW Marietta GA 30064-3359

TAYLOR, ROGER LEE, academic administrator, lawyer; b. Canton, Ill., Apr. 6, 1941; s. Ivan and Pauline Helen (Mahr) T.; m. E. Anne Zweifel, June 13, 1964. BA, Knox Coll., 1963; JD cum laude, Northwestern U., 1971. Bar: Ill. 1971, U.S. Dist. Ct. (no. dist.) Ill. 1971, U.S. Dist. Ct. (no. dist.) Tex. 1975, U.S. Ct. Appeals (7th cir.) 1972, U.S. Ct. Appeals (5th and 11th cirs.) 1981, U.S. Supreme Ct. 1975. Assoc. Kirkland & Ellis, Chgo., 1971-78, ptnr., 1978—; pres. Knox Coll., Galesburg, Ill., 2002—. Trustee Knox Coll., pres. 2002; trustee Ill. Hist. Preservation Agy., dir. Assoc. Coll. of Midwest, dir. Assoc. Coll. of Ill. Mem. Order of Coif, Univ. Club, Soangetaha Country Club (Galesburg, Ill.). Office: Knox College Galesburg IL 61401

TAYLOR, RONALD D., mathematics professor; s. Ronald D. and Martha S. Taylor; m. Kirsten Lee Rafferty, Dec. 15, 2007. BS, Concord Coll., Athens, 1991, BA, 1994; MMth, Winthrop U., Rock Hill, 1993; PhD, Bowling Green State U., 2000. Assoc. prof. math. Berry Coll., Mount Berry, Ga., 2000—; ofcl. scorer Rome Braves Baseball Club, Ga., 2003—. Recipient Tchg. Excellence Award, Berry Coll., 2008, Project NEXT Fellow, Math. Assn. Am., 2003. Mem.: Math. Assn. Am. (co-dir. project NEXT-SE). Methodist. Avocations: reading, Tae Kwon Do. Office: Berry Coll 2277 Martha Berry Highway Mount Berry GA 30149

TAYLOR, RONALD LEE, academic administrator; b. Urbana, Ill., Nov. 11, 1943; s. Lee R. and Katherine L. (Becker) Taylor; m. Patricia D. Fitzimmons, Mar. 10, 1973; children: Jamie, Lara, Meredith, Dana. AB, Harvard U., 1966; MBA, Stanford U., 1971. Asst. contr. Bell & Howell, Chgo., 1971-73; pres., CEO DeVry Inc., Chgo., 1973—2004, CEO, 2004—06, co-founder, sr. advisor, 2006—. Cons. evaluator Higher Learning Commn., North Ctrl. Assn. Colls. and Schs., 1985—2006; bd. dirs. Am. Edn. Group, Inc., 2007—. Trustee Rehabilitation Inst. Chgo.; mem. mgmt. bd. Stanford U. Sch. Bus., 2003—06. 1st lt. US Army, 1966—69. Decorated Commendation medal US Army, Oak Leaf Cluster; recipient Outstanding Pub. Svc. medal, Sec. Def., 1998. Achievements include feature in Crain's Mag. Chgo., 2006. Office: DeVry Inc 1 Tower Ln Ste 2350 Oakbrook Terrace IL 60181-4663 Business E-Mail: rtaylor@devry.com.

TAYLOR, RONALD LEWIS, sociology educator; b. St. Petersburg, Fla., Feb. 27, 1941; s. David T. and Lillian (Bell) Miller; m. Bernice E. Chavis, Dec. 24, 1967; children: Kevin, Darryl. BA, Bethune-Cookman Coll., 1962; MA, Howard U., 1964; PhD, Boston U., 1973. Dean of men Bethune-Cookman Coll., Daytona Beach, Fla., 1964-65, dir. fin. aid, 1965-67; instr., lectr. Boston U., 1967-70; rsch. assoc., cons. Army Bur. Rsch., Ft. Devens, Mass., 1971-73; asst. prof. U. Conn., Storrs, 1972-78, assoc. prof., 1978-90, chair dept. sociology, 1981-86, prof. sociology, 1990—, dir. Inst. African-Am. Studies, 1993-99, vice provost multicultural and internat. affairs, 1999—2009. Nat. adv. bd. Ctr. Nat. Policy, Washington, 1991—; grant review panel Ctrs. for Disease Control, Atlanta, 1991-93. Editor: Black Youth in America, 1990, Minority Families in the U.S., 1994, African-American Youth, 1995; co-editor: The Black Male in America, 1977; mem. editl. bd. Jour. African-Am. Male Studies, 1991-93; editor Race and Soc. Assn. Black Sociologists, 1995-2003 Mem. AAUP (U. Conn. chpt. pres. 1993-94), Am. Sociol. Assn. (com. on coms. 1991-93, nominations com. 1994-96), Eastern Sociol. Soc. (chair elections 1991-93, v.p. 2003-04) Home Phone: 860-872-0596. Business E-Mail: ronald.taylor@uconn.edu.

TAYLOR, S. BROOKE, lawyer; b. Port Angeles, Wash. BA in Polit. Sci., Stanford U., 1965; JD, U. Va., 1968. Bar: Wash. 1968. Dep. prosecuting atty. Clallam County, 1969—70, prosecuting atty., 1970—75; co-owner, ptnr. Taylor & Taylor P.S., Port Angeles, 1975—90, Platt Irwin Taylor, Port Angeles, 1991—. Spkr. in field. Dir., pres. Clallam County Family YMCA; dir. G.M. Lauridsen Found.; dir., pres. Clallam County Cmty. Mental Health Ctr.; mem., dir. Port Angeles C. of C.; mem. Penninsula Coll. Found. Named Citizen of Yr., Clallam County, 1999. Mem.: ABA, Assn. Trial Lawyers Am., Wash. State Trial Lawyers Assn., Clallam County Bar Assn. (pres. 1981), Wash. State Bar Assn. (mem. bd. govs. 2000—02, treas. 2001—02, chmn. facilities com. 2001—, liaison dist. and mcpl. ct. judges assn. 2003—04, pres.-elect 2004, pres. 2005), Kiwanis Club (dir.). Achievements include contributions to the Washington State Bar Association's "Diversity Amendment" (later called the "Taylor Draft") which expanded the Association's definition of diversity and led to the creation of three governor-at-large positions. Office: Platt Irwin Taylor 403 S Peabody Port Angeles WA 98362 Office Phone: 360-457-3327. Office Fax: 360-452-5010.

TAYLOR, SARAH ANN, oncologist, educator; b. Wichita, Kans., July 2, 1950; Grad., Cornell Coll., Iowa; MD, U. Kansas Sch. Medicine, 1975. Cert. Internal Medicine, Med. Oncology. Intern, internal medicine U. Kansas Med. Ctr., 1975—76, resident, oncology, 1976—78, fellow, 1978—80, hosp. appointment, 1980—, med. dir., Palliative Care Svcs., 1987—; prof. internal medicine, divsn. hematology/oncology U. Kansas, med. dir., hematology, oncology fellowship program. Named one of Kansas City Super Doctor, Kansas City Mag. Mem.: FDA, CIRB. Office Phone: 913-588-6029. Office Fax: 913-588-4085.

TAYLOR, STEPHAN F., psychiatrist, educator; s. David E. Taylor and Deborah Hogan; m. Elizabeth Stumbo; children: Rachel, Sarah. BA, Northwester U., Evanston, 1980; MD, Wash. U., St. Louis, 1988. Cert. psychiatry ABPN, 1993, diplomate Nat. Bd. Med. Examiners, 1989. Asst. prof. psychiatry U. Mich., Ann Arbor, 1998—2003, assoc. prof. psychiatry, 2003—, adj. assoc. prof. psychology, 2005—, vice chair, instl. rev. bd. med., 2008—. Co-director Psychiat. Neuromodulation Program; ad hoc reviewer, dept. vet. affairs NIMH, 1998—, NIDA, 1998—, NIAAA, 1998—, Wellcome Trust, 1998—; co-dir. Psychiatry Affective Neuroimaging Lab., Ann Arbor, 2000—; editl. bd. mem. Biol. Psychiatry, 2008—. Contbr. articles to profl. publ. Recipient Young Investigator award, NARSAD, 1996, Young Scientist award, Biennial Winter Workshop Schizophrenia, 1993, Mentor Neuroimaging award, Dana Found., 2008; named one of Am.'s Top Psychiatrists, Consumers Rsch. Coun., 2006; Laughlin fellow, Am. Coll. Psychiatrists, 1991, R01s grant, NIMH, 1997—, K08 grant, 1997—. Mentor Young Investigators grant, NARSAD, 2007—08. Mem.: AAAS, Internat. Congress Schizophrenia Rsch. (program com. mem. 2007), Soc. Biol. Psychiatry (program com. mem. 2007—, Dista Travel award 1992), Soc. Neurosci., Psychiat. Rsch. Soc. (pres. 2007—08), Am. Coll. Neuropsychopharmacology, Phi Beta Kappa. Office: Univ Mich 4250 Plymouth Rd Ann Arbor MI 48109-2700 Office Fax: 734-936-7868. Business E-Mail: sftaylor@umich.edu.

TAYLOR, STEPHEN LLOYD, toxicologist, food scientist, educator; b. Portland, Oreg., July 19, 1946; s. Lloyd Emerson and Frances Hattie (Hanson); m. Susan Annette Kerns, June 23, 1973; children: Amanda, Andrew. BS in Food Sci. Tech., Oreg. State U., 1968, MS in Food Sci. Tech., 1969; PhD in Biochemistry, U. Calif., Davis, 1973. Research assoc. U. Calif., Davis, 1973-74, research fellow, 1974-75; chief food toxicology Letterman Army Inst., San Francisco, 1975-78; asst. prof. food toxicology U. Wis., Madison, 1978-83, assoc. prof., 1983-87; head dept. food sci. technology, dir. Food Processing Ctr. U. Nebr., Lincoln, 1987—2004, prof. dept. food sci. tech., 2004—. Cons. in field. Contbr. articles to profl. jours. Fellow: Inst. Food Technologists (divsn. chmn. 1981—82, sect. chmn. 1984—85, exec. com. 1988—91); mem.: Soc. Toxicology, Am. Chem. Soc., Am. Acad. Allergy, Asthma and Immunology. Democrat. Presbyterian. Home: 941 Evergreen Dr Lincoln NE 68510-4131 Office: U Nebr Dept Food Sci Tech Lincoln NE 68583-0919 Home Phone: 402-488-6477; Office Phone: 402-472-2833. Business E-Mail: staylor2@unl.edu.

TAYLOR, STEVE HENRY, zoologist; b. Inglewood, Calif., Mar. 18, 1947; s. Raymond Marten and Ardath (Metz) T.; 1 child, Michael Travis; m. Sarah Margaret Young, May 14, 1993. BA in Biology, U. Calif.-Irvine, 1969. Animal keeper Los Angeles Zoo, 1972-75, assoc. curator, 1975-76; children's zoo mgr. San Francisco Zoo, 1976-81; zoo dir. Sacramento Zoo, 1981-88; dir. Cleve. Met. Zoo, 1989—. Bd. dirs. Sacramento Soc. Prevention Cruelty to Animals, 1983-87, Sacramento Red Cross, 1988-89, Conv. and Visitor Bur. of Greater Cleve., 1995-03, 06-, Leadership Cleve. Class 1997; mem. admissions com. United Way, 1999. Recipient Robert P. Bergman Impact award Convention & Visitors Bur. Greater Cleve., 2000. Fellow Am. Assn. Zool. Parks and Aquariums (infant care diet advisor 1979, 85, bd. dirs. 1987-93, pres. 1991-92, chmn. pub. edn. com. 1987-89, bd. regents, mgmt. sch., chmn. accreditation com. 1998, 99, Outstanding Svc. award 1979, 85, 88, 89, 91, 95, 98, 99, 2001); mem. Conservation Breeding Specialist Group, World Assn. Zoos and Aquariums, Sierra Club, Audubon Soc. Democrat. Home: 1265 Elmwood Rd Rocky River OH 44116-2236 Office: Cleveland Metroparks Zoo 3900 Wildlife Way Cleveland OH 44109-3132 Home Phone: 440-333-7564; Office Phone: 216-635-3331. Business E-Mail: sht@clevelandmetroparks.com.

TAYLOR, STEVEN W., state supreme court justice; b. Henryetta, Okla., June 7, 1949; m. Mary Taylor; 1 child. BA in Polit. sci., Okla. State U., 1971; JD, U. Okla. Coll. Law, 1974. Atty. Gotcher, Gotcher & Taylor, Okla., 1978—84; councilman McAlester City, 1980—82, mayor, 1982—84; judge Okla. Dist. Ct., 1984—94; dist. judge, chief judge 18th Jud. Dist., 1994—2004; presiding judge E. Ctrl. Jud. Adminstrv. dist., 1997—2003; justice Okla. Supreme Ct., Oklahoma City, 2004—, vice chief justice, 2009—. Pres. Okla. Jud. Conf., 1990. Mem. bd. dirs. Okla. Heritage Assn., Okla. Med. Rsch. Found. Served atty. & judge USMC, 1970—78. Mem.: Pittsburg County Bar Assn., Okla. Bar Assn. (Jud. Excellence award 2003, Outstanding Okla. Judge of Yr. 2003). Office: Okla Supreme Ct Rm 200 State Capital Bldg Oklahoma City OK 73105 Office Phone: 405-521-3844. Business E-Mail: steven.taylor@oscn.net.*

TAYLOR, STUART ROSS, geochemist, writer; b. Ashburton, New Zealand, Nov. 26, 1925; s. Thomas Stuart and Anne Grace (Lloyd) T.; m. Noel Elvie White, May 21, 1958; children: Susanna, Judith, Helen. BSc, U. New Zealand, 1948, MSc, 1951; PhD, Ind. U., 1954; DSc, Oxford U., 1978. Lectr. U. Oxford, Eng., 1954-58; sr. lectr. U. Cape Town, South Africa, 1958-60; professorial fellow Australian Nat. U., Canberra, 1961-90, vis. fellow, 1990-99, prof. emeritus, 1997; prof. U. Vienna, 1992, 96. Vis. scientist Lunar and Planetary Inst., Houston, 1969-90. Author: Lunar Science: Post-Apollo View, 1975, Planetary Science, 1982, Solar System Evolution, 1992, (with others) Continental Crust, 1985, Destiny or Chance: Our Solar System and Its Place in the Cosmos, 1998, Solar System Evolution, 2d edit., 2001; contbr. more than 220 articles to profl. jours. Recipient Goldschmidt medal Geochem. Soc., 1993, Gilbert award Geol. Soc. Am., 1994, Bucher medal Am. Geophys.

Union, 2002; co recipient Planetary Crusts Cup, 2009; Asteroid 5670 named Rosstaylor, 1997. Fellow Royal Soc. New Zealand (hon.), Australian Acad. Sci., Geol. Soc. London (hon.), Geol. Soc. India (hon.); mem. NAS (fgn. assoc.), Meteoritical Soc. (pres. 1989-90, Leonard medal 1998), Companion (AC) Order of Australia (hon.). Office: Australian Nat U Dept Geology Canberra 0200 Australia E-mail: ross.taylor@anu.edu.au.

TAYLOR, SUE KAY, science educator; b. Cherokee, Iowa, Feb. 9, 1958; d. Virgil Harry Schlinz; m. Stephen Lee Jarvis (div.); children: Stephanie Cady, Jason Lindsay; m. Brooks R. Taylor. BA in Edn., Wayne State Coll., Nebr., 1986; post grad., Marycrest Coll., Davenport, Iowa, 1986—89, U. No. Iowa, Cedar Falls, 1990—96, post grad., 2003, post grad., 2002, Morningside Coll., Sioux City, 1996—98, Iowa State U., Ames, 1997, Iowa Ctrl. Cmty. Coll., Fort Dodge, 1999. Cert. tchr. Iowa, endorsements in biology, anatomy, physiology, gen. sci., chemistry, physics, phys. edn. and coaching Iowa. Tchr. jr. high biology St. John's Cath. Sch., Bancroft, Iowa, 1987—89, Holy Family Schs., Sioux City, 1989—95; tchr. phys. sci., biology, chemistry and physics Albert City-Truesdale Combined Sch. Dist., 1995—99; substitute tchr. Pocahontas Area Combined Sch. Dist., 2000; tchr. biology, chemistry and TAG Schaller- Crestland Combined Sch. Dist., Early, 2000—03; tchr. biology, anatomy and physiology, health Pocahontas Area Combined Sch. Dist., 2003—. Advisor Nat. Honor Soc.; asst. H.S. softball and basketball; head softball and volleyball; jr. high softball and volleyball; jr. high athletic dir.; advisor dist. and state sci. fairs; faculty sponsor Iowa State Bar Assn. Mock Trial State Tournament; volleyball official. Named AEA 12 Demonstration Sci. Classroom. Mem.: NEA, Character Edn. Com., Ia. State Edn. Assn., Nat. Sci. Tchrs. Assn., Iowa Girls HS Athletic Union (volleyball official), Optimist Club Pocahontas, Delta Kappa Gammaa Upsilon. Republican. Roman Catholic. Avocations: kayaking, gardening, house remodeling, motorcycling. Office: Pocahontas Area CDS Pocahontas IA 50574 Office Phone: 712-335-4848.

TAYLOR, SUSAN L., former magazine editor, philanthropist; b. NYC, Jan. 23, 1946; d. Lawrence and Violet (Weekes) Taylor; m. William Bowles (div.); 1 child, Shana Nequai; m. Khephra Burns, 1989. BA in Sociology, Fordham U., 1991; doctorate (hon.), Spelman Coll., Bennett Coll., U. Del., Fisk U., Lincoln U., Dillard U. Founder, rschr., developer, pres. Nequai Cosmetics, 1970—72; freelance writer, beauty editor Essence Mag., NYC, 1970—71, fashion, beauty editor, 1971—80, editor-in-chief, 1980—2000, editl. dir., 2000—08; founder, dir. Nat. Cares Mentoring Movement (formerly Essence Cares Initiative), 2006—. Exec. prodr. and host to exec. coord., v.p. TV prog. Essence Essence Comm. Inc. Author: In the Spirit: The Inspirational Writings of Susan L. Taylor, 1993, Lessons in Living, 1995; co-author (with husband Khephra Burns): Confirmation: The Spiritual Wisdom That Has Shaped Our Lives, 1997; contbr. articles to mags.; exec. prodr.: Essence Awards and Essence Music Festival; spkr. in field. Mem. rsch. com. in black edn. Assn. Ednl. Rsch.; co-chair Danny Glover for Shared Interest (to raise money to build housing in rural areas of S. Africa); bd. dir. Joint Ctr. for Polit. and Econ. Studies, Washington; mem. adv. bd. Black Adminstr. in Child Welfare; mem. La. Recovery Authority. Recipient Henry Johnson Fisher award, 1998, President's award, NAACP Image award, 2006; named to Power 150, Ebony mag., 2008. Mem.: Women in Comm. (Matrix award), Am. Soc. Mag. Editors (inducted into Hall of Fame 2002), Nat. Assn. Black Journalists. Office: Nat Cares Mentoring Movement 230 Peachtree St Ste 530 Atlanta GA 30303 Office Phone: 404-584-2744. Office Fax: 404-525-6222.

TAYLOR, SUZONNE BERRY STEWART, real estate broker; b. Memphis, Sept. 27, 1926; d. Andrew Cleveland and Sue Hodge (Berry) Stewart; m. Robert Allen Taylor, Sr., June 15, 1946; children: Robert A. Jr., Suzonne Stewart Taylor Davids. Student, Rhodes Coll., Memphis, 1948, U. S.C., Columbia, 1969. Cert. residential specialist CRS Coun., 1996; grad. Realtors Inst.; cert. real estate broker; accredited buyer's rep. Am. Bd. Realtors. Sales agt. E. Roy Stone Realtors, Greenville, SC, 1967—69; real estate broker Aven Assoc. Realtors, Dover, Del., 1970—80, Emerson & Co. Realtors, Dover, 1980—2000; assoc. broker ERA Harrington Realty, Dover, 1998—. Active Cresent Music Club, Greenville, 1955, Wildwood Garden Club, Greenville, 1960; mem., costume chmn. Greenville Little Theater, Jr. League Greenville, 1956-66, sustaining mem., 1966—, emeritus sustaining mem. Jr. League Wilmington, Del., 1999—, dir., 1999. Recipient Beyond Excellence award, ERA, 2004, 2005. Mem. Nat. Bd. Realtors, Del. Bd. Realtors, Kent County Bd. Realtors, Del. Hist. Soc., Biggs Mus., Alpha Omicron Pi, Friends of Old Dover, Dover Rotary Club, Dover Rotary Club (bd. dirs.). Republican. Episcopalian. Home: 517 Greenhill Rd Dover DE 19901-3766 Office: ERA Harrington Realty 516 Jefferic Blvd Dover DE 19901 Home Phone: 302-678-0153; Office Phone: 302-736-0800. Business E-Mail: staylor@harringtonera.com.

TAYLOR, TERESA A., telecommunications industry executive; b. 1963; BS, U. Wis., LaCrosse. With US West (now Qwest), 1988—2000; exec. v.p. products and pricing group Qwest Comm. Internat., Inc., Denver, 2000—03, exec. v.p. wholesale markets group, 2003—04, exec. v.p., chief human resources officer, 2004—07, exec. v.p., chief adminstrv. officer, 2007—08, exec. v.p. Bus. Markets Group (BMG), 2008—09, pres., COO, 2009—. Co-head State Job's Cabinet State of Colo., 2008—09; bd. dirs. Colo. Inst. Tech., Colo. Children's Campaign, Colo. Symphony Orch. Office: Qwest Comm Internat Inc 1801 California St Denver CO 80202 Office Phone: 303-992-1400. Office Fax: 303-896-8515.*

TAYLOR, TERRY R., editor, educator; b. Valley Forge, Pa., Oct. 4, 1952; d. Thomas R. and Anna P. (Bystrek) T. BA in Journalism, Temple U., 1974. Reporter gen. assignments, sch. news Charlotte (N.C.) News, 1974-77; supr., writer AP, Phila., 1977-81, supr., writer sports desk NYC, 1981-85, asst. editor sports, 1985-87, dep. editor sports, 1987-91, asst. chief bur., 1991-92, editor sports, 1992—; asst. editor sports N.Y. Times, 1991. Assoc. in journalism Columbia U., N.Y.C., 1991-95; adv. bd. Honda Awards, 1996—06. Mem. Internat. Olympic Com. Press Commn., 2005—. Recipient John A. Domino Meml. award St. Bonaventure U., 1996, Founder's award Temple U., 1999; inductee Delaware County Sports Hall of Fame, 1998. Roman Catholic. Achievements include first woman sports editor at the AP. Office: AP Sports 450 W 33rd St New York NY 10001

TAYLOR, THOMAS TEMPLETON, history professor; s. Ralph Samuel and Ruth Templeton Taylor; m. Mechelle Bostick Bostick, Aug. 15, 1975; children: Erin Ruth, Sarah Elisabeth, Samuel James. BA, UNC, Greensboro, MA, 1978; PhD, U. Ill., Urbana-Champaign, 1983. Prof. Wittenberg U., Springfield, Ohio, 1988—. Dept. chair Wittenberg U., 1997—2002, faculty devel. adminstr., 1999—2001, dir., 2008—. Bd. mem. Clark County Hist. Soc., Springfield, Ohio, 1995—2000, pres., 2006—08; v.p. Westcott House Found., Springfield, Ohio, 2000—03, Southern Ohio Synod Evang. Luth. Ch. Am., Columbus; pres. Ohio Acad. History, 2004—05. Recipient Outstanding Tchg. award, Omicron Delta Kappa, Wittenberg U., 1991, Ohio Acad. History, 2001. Mem.: Federalist Soc., Orgn. Am. Historians, Hist. Soc., Am. Polit. Sci. Assn., Am. Hist. Soc. Independent. Lutheran. Home: 2716 Rebecca Dr Springfield OH 45503 Office: Wittenberg Univ PO Box 720 Springfield OH 45501 Office Fax: 937-327-6340. Business E-Mail: ttaylor@wittenberg.edu.

TAYLOR, THOMAS WILLIAM, lawyer; b. Columbus, Ind., Feb. 11, 1943; s. Virgil W. and Margaret Emma (Voiles) T.; m. Linda Kay Followell, Jan. 1, 1964; children: Pamela Kay, William Lansing. AB with honors, Ind. U., 1965; LLB cum laude, Harvard U., 1968. Bar: Mass. 1968, U.S. Dist. Ct. Mass. 1969. Assoc. Ropes & Gray, Boston, 1968-78, ptnr., 1978-98, of counsel, 1999—. Lectr. Pres.'s urban policy program seminars U.S. Coun. of Mayors, 1982; chmn. tax panel nat. workshop Coun. of Infrastructure Financing Authorities, 1993; vol. astronomer Chaco Obs., Chaco Culture Nat. Hist. Park, 2000, 2006, prin. astronomer, 2001, 2005. Vol. Wilderness First Responder, 2002—; snowboard instr. Nashoba Valley Ski Area, 1999—2005, staff trainer, 2003—05. Mem. Nat. Assn. Bond Lawyers (opinions com., chmn. securities law panel Washington workshop 1992, lectr. atty.'s workshop Chgo. 1983-97), Am. Coll. Bond Counsel (founding fellow), Appalachian Mountain Club Stewardship Soc. Avocations: rock climbing, orienteering, trumpet playing, canoeing. Office: Ropes & Gray 1 International Pl Fl 4 Boston MA 02110-2624

TAYLOR, VOLNEY, retired information company executive; b. Portsmouth, Ohio, Dec. 6, 1939; s. Lafayette and Martha Louise (Frederick) T.; m. Kathleen Ann MacMahon, May 17, 1969; children: Lafayette, Lloyd MacMahon, Kerry Erin, Frederick Daly. BS in Indsl. Engring. Ohio State U., 1962; MBA, Harvard U., 1966. Assoc. mem. McKinsey & Co., Inc. (mgmt. cons.), NYC, 1966-72; exec. v.p., dir. Funk & Wagnalls, Inc., NYC, 1972-74; v.p. fin. Reuben H. Donnelley Co., NYC, 1974-76; dir. corp. planning Dun & Bradstreet Corp., NYC, 1976-77, v.p. corp. planning, 1977-78, corp. v.p., 1979-80, sr. v.p., 1980-82, exec. v.p., 1982-96; gen. mgr. Official Airline Guides, Oak Brook, Ill., 1978-79; chmn. bd. dirs. Dun & Bradstreet Info. Svcs., Murray Hill, N.J., 1991-2000; chmn. bd., CEO Dun & Bradstreet Corp., Murray Hill, 1996-2000; ret., 2000. Bd. dirs. Dun & Bradstreet, Inc., Dun & Bradstreet Europe, Dun & Bradstreet Internat., Dun's Mktg. Svcs., Inc., Moody's Investors Svc.; bd. dirs. Reuben H. Donnelley Corp., pres., 1988-90. Served to lt. (j.g.) USNR, 1962-64. Mem. Harvard Bus. Sch. (N.Y.C.) Club, Beta Theta Pi.

TAYLOR, WALTER WALLACE, retired lawyer; b. Newton, Iowa, Sept. 18, 1925; s. Carrol W. and Eva (Greenly) T.; m. Mavis A. Harvey, Oct. 9, 1948; children: Joshua Michael (dec. 1980), Kevin Eileen, Kristin Lisa, Jeremy Walter, Margaret Jane, Melissa E., Amy M. AA, Yuba Coll., 1948, AB, 1950; MA, U. Calif., 1955; JD, McGeorge Coll. Law, 1962. Adminstrv. analyst USAF, Sacramento, 1951-53; personnel, rsch. analyst Calif. Personnel Bd., Sacramento, 1954-56; civil svc., personnel analyst, chief counsel, gen. mgr. Calif. Employees Assn., Sacramento, 1956-75; staff counsel, chief profl. stds. Calif. Commn. Tchr. Credentialing, 1975-88, ret., 1988. Staff counsel State Office Real Estate Appraiser Licensing and Certification, 1992-94, ret.; tchr. discipline civil service, personnel cons. Author: Know Your Rights, 1963-64. Served USCGR, 1943-46. Mem. Calif. State Bar, Am., Sacramento County Bar Assns. Democrat. Home: 4572 Fair Oaks Blvd Sacramento CA 95864-5336 Business E-Mail: walttaylor@surewest.net.

TAYLOR, WILLIAM B., JR., United States Ambassador to Ukraine; married; 2 children. Grad., US Mil. Acad., 1969; MA in Pub. Policy, Harvard U., 1977. Dir. Office Emergency Preparedness Dept. Energy; mem. staff Senator Bill Bradley; dir. Def. Dept., Washington; spl. dep. def. adv. US Amb. to NATO, Brussels, 1987—92; coord. US Assistance to Europe and Eurasia US Dept. State, Washington, 1992—2002, spl. rep. Donor Assistance to Afghanistan Kabul, 2002—03, Afghanistan coord., 2003, dir. Iraq Reconstruction Mgmt. Office Baghdad, Iraq, 2004—05, mem. Quartet Spl. Envoy Jerusalem, 2005—06, US amb. to Ukraine Kiev, 2006—. Infantry officer US Army, 1969—75, Vietnam and Germany. Office: DOS Amb 5850 Kiev Pl Washington DC 20521-5850*

TAYLOR, WILLIAM COLTON, physician, educator; b. Boston, Jan. 25, 1948; s. Manuel and Marjorie Taylor; m. Julia Katherine Landau, Dec. 4, 1983; children: Rachel, Hannah, Daniel, Benjamin, Jessica. BA, Yale U., New Haven, Conn., 1970; MD, U. Pa., Phila., 1974. Cert. bd. Am. Bd. of Internal Medicine, 1977. Sr. physician Beth Israel Deaconess Med. Ctr., Boston, 1996—; assoc. prof. medicine Harvard Med. Sch., Boston, 1994—; assoc. physician Brigham and Women's Hosp., Boston, 2006—.

TAYLOR, WILLIAM JAMES (ZAK), lawyer; b. Milw., Jan. 26, 1948; s. William Elmer and Elizabeth Emily (Lupinski) T.; m. Marlou Belyea, Sept. 20, 1975; children: Danielle Belyea, James Zachary Belyea. BA in Econs., Yale U., 1970; JD, Harvard U., 1976. Bar: Calif. 1976, US Dist. Ct. (cen. dist.) Calif. 1976, US Dist. Ct. (no. dist.) Calif. 1977, US Ct. Appeals (9th cir.) 1977, US Dist. Ct. (ea. dist.) Calif. 1980, US Supreme Ct. 1980, US Tax Ct. 1988. Law clk. to hon. Shirley M. Hufstedler U.S. Ct. Appeals (9th cir.), LA, 1976-77; assoc. Broebeck, Phleger & Harrison, San Francisco, 1977-83; ptnr. Broebeck, Phleger and Harrison, San Francisco, 1983-95; shareholder Taylor & Jenkins, P.C., Oakland, Calif., 1995-96, Chilvers & Taylor, P.C., Oakland, 1996-99; of counsel Brobeck, Phleger & Harrison, LLP, San Francisco, 2000—03, Morgan Lewis & Bockius, LLP, San Francisco, 2003—04, ptnr., 2004—. Bd. dirs. Berkeley (Calif.) Law Found., 1988-91, Legal Svcs. for Children (recipient Jean Waldman Child Advocacy award, San Francisco 1988), 1983-89; co-chmn. Attys. Task Force for Children, San Francisco, 1983-89. Editor-in-chief Harvard Civil Rights, Civil Liberties Law Rev., 1976; bd. editors No. Dist. Calif. Digest, 1978-83; co-author: California Antitrust Law, 1991; contbg. editor: Calif. Bus. Law Reporter, 1995—, Antitrust Law Developments, 1997, 4th edit., 2002. With US Army, 1970—73. Mem. ABA, Bar Assn. San Francisco (bd. dirs. 1986-87, chair antitrust sect. 1987, chair fed. cts. sect. 1995-97; award of merit 1987), Am. Bus. Trial Lawyers Assn., Am. Health Lawyers Assn., Calif. Soc. Healthcare Attys., Barristers of San Francisco (bd. dirs. 1980-82, v.p. 1982-83). Democrat. Office: Morgan Lewis & Bockius LLP 1 Market Spear Tower San Francisco CA 94105-1420 Office Phone: 415-442-1315. Business E-Mail: wtaylor@morganlewis.com.

TAYLOR-BROCHET, ANDREA, language educator; b. Providence, June 1, 1959; d. Paul Beekman and Alexandra Fatio Taylor; m. Stéphane Jean Brochet, Dec. 11, 1993; children: Adrien Manuel Cirou, Charles Lancelot Brochet, Nia Florence Brochet. BA in French, Duke U., Durham, NC, 1982, BA in Psychology, 1982, MA in Tchg. English. Human resources cons. Eurotec & Synergie, Chartres, France, 2002—05; lang. cons. C. of C. d'Industrie, Chartres, 2005—07; adj. prof. French Seattle Pacific U., 2008—. Cons. MEDEF, ANPE, GRETA, Chartres, 2001—07; cert. corp. coach, Chartres, 2005—08. Home: 8603 8th Ave NE Seattle WA 98115 Personal E-mail: ataylorbrochet@gmail.com.

TAYLOR-CLARK, KALAHN ALEXANDRA, medical researcher; d. Katherine Marion Clark. MPH, Tufts U. Sch. Medicine, Boston, 2001; PhD, Harvard U., Cambridge, Mass., 2006. Rschr. Harvard U. Sch. Pub. Health, 2001—04; lectr. Tufts U., Medford, Mass.; lead rsch. cons. Opportunity Agenda, NYC, 2005—08; sr. rsch. assoc. Brookings Instn., Washington, 2008—. Contbr. articles to profl. sci. jours.

TAYLOR-DUNN, CORLISS LESLIE, marriage and family therapist; d. Hilary Oliver and Sally Wilkins Taylor; m. David Charles Dunn, Aug. 2, 1975 (dec. Apr. 6, 2001). BA in Performing Arts, classically trained dramatic soprano, Ctrl. State U., 1971; MA in Marriage & Family Therapy, Azusa Pacific U., Calif., 1995; student in Counseling for the Ministry, Biola U., 1991—93; DS in Psychology, Calif. Coast Coll., 2006. Lic. marriage & family therapist Bd. of Behavioral Scis., Calif., 2000. Psychotherapist Helicon Youth Ctr., Riverside, Calif., 1998—2001, Genesis Counseling Svcs., San Bernardino, Calif., 2002—02; pvt. practice Fort Garland, Colo., 2003—; pres., CEO, tchr. The Dunn Ctr. of Ft. Garland, Fort Garland, 2002—. Pres., CEO, nationwide safe house planter, tchr. www.freudsfunstuff.com, Fort Garland, 2002—; tchr. music, drama and dance Cmty. Ctr.; presenter in field. Author: (plays) (with Sandra Reaves-Phillips) Musical, Opening Night, 1981—82 (nominated for 3 off-Broadway Audelco awards, 1983); composer: Musical, Performer in Fall, 2008; dir.: Musical, Opening Night; author: (plays) Sojourner; The Story of an Ex-Slave (The Brody Art award Calif.Commn. Nat. Edn. Arts Assn., 1987); actor: (plays, Broadway) Ella, Bubbling Brown Sugar, 1977, Rockette Spectacular, Pin 'N Needles, Don't Bother Me I Can't Cope, (Broadway tour) Ruth in Raisin, 1976, 1988—89; prodr.: (TV films) Safehouse; creator (world view game) Logical Conclusion. Mem. Friends of the Fort support com. Fort Garland Mus., Colo.; founder Buffalo Soldiers Essay Contest Colo. Schs.; established David Charles Dunn scholarship Bilola U., 2002; mem. steering com. Rural Philanthropy Days; bd. dirs. Cmty. Revitalization Com. Mem.: Va. Assn. Marriage & Family Therapist, Am. Assn. Marriage and Family Therapists (licentiate), Calif. Assn. Marriage and Family Therapists (licentiate), Internat. Fellowship Christians and Jews, Costilla County C. of C. (mktg. com. 2003). Republican. Avocations: gardening, travel, acting, interior decorating, performing. Personal E-mail: ctaylordunn@aol.com.

TAYLOR-FISHWICK, DAVID, immunologist, educator; m. Judith Taylor-Fishwick. BS; PhD, London U., 1993. Dir., cell & molecular islet biology East Va. Med. Sch., Norfolk, 2000—08, assoc. prof., medicine, 2006—. Contbr. chapters to books to profl. jours. Rsch. grant, Commonwealth Health Rsch. Bd. Achievements include patents for anti-INGAP assay aystem; INGAP displacement assays; patents pending for composition & method for treating diabetes. Office: Eastern VA Med Sch 700 W Olney Rd Norfolk VA 23507 Office Fax: 757-446-5803. Business E-Mail: taylord@evms.edu.

TAYLOR-WHITE-GRIGSBY, QUEEN DELORIS, minister, consultant; b. Oklahoma City, Aug. 21, 1948; d. Barnett C., Sr. and M. Bedell Boles Dewitt Taylor; m. Walter Thomas White II, Nov. 26, 1966 (div. June 1976); children: Walter Thomas III, Robin Orlando; m. James O. Grigsby, Sept. 19, 1976 (dec. Dec. 1976); 1 child, James Jumaané. BS, Howard U., 1970; M in Counseling, Liberty U., 1988. RN Va., 1983; ordained to ministry Ray Deliverance Found., 1989; cert. housing specialist Housing Specialist Inst., 1972. Housing cons. Montgomery County, Rockville, Md., 1971—73; founder, cons., pres. Taylor & Co., Richmond, Va., 1973—; assoc. cons. Trust Inc., Richmond, Va., 1973—80, Orgnl. Devel. Cons., Richmond, 1979—81; founder, pastor Tangible Substance God Is Love Ch., 1985—; founder, min. Man Child Ministries, Phoenix, 1988—. RN tng. J. Sargent Reynolds CC, Richmond, 1982—83; practitioner Richmond Meml. Hosp., 1982—83; adv. nursing rights & charges, 1983—; cons. in field, 1972—2007. Author: numerous poems. Advocate child and adult welfare Dept. Corrections, Commonwealth Va., 1974-75, vol. Ariz. Dept. Corrections, Phoenix, 1990, Ark. Dept. Corrections, 1994—, Okla. City Dept. Corrections, 1995—, advocate tchr. rights, 1991; active tchr. rights Phoenix Pub. Sch. Sys., 1992; supr. elections County Election Bd., Maricopa County, Ariz., 1987-88; trainer, developer Internat. Transactional Analysis counseling model for abused women and their families in YWCA residential housing programs, 1992; coord. Y-Splash program Maricopa County YWCA, 1992-93, grant writer, 1992, Mich. County YWCA, Better Living Ctr. 1995-; active food programs and ministry Internat. Healing Cathedral/Hall of Deliverance Found. and Desert Moon Mission, 1985-93; active children and youth program Phoenix Women's League, 1991-92; active Las Guias Heard Mus. Guild, 1990-93; docent Okla. Zoo., 2004-07; vol. VA, 2004-07, Column Writers, 2005; planning commn., Montgomery County, Md., 1972-73, Regional Coun. Govts., Washington, 1972-73; dir. children's program United Meth. Ch., Richmond, 1977, Childrens Programme Cirst Child Settlement Home, 1972-, SE Washington DC Yeachin 1965-. Lucille McMahn scholar, 1965, Nellie Green scholar, 1965, Philip Morris scholar, 1983; recipient Danforth Leadership award, 1965, Golden Poet award, World of Poetry, 1991-92; named Internat. Woman of Yr., 2000-06. Mem. Soc. Tng. and Devel., Friends Libr. Republican. Avocations: reading, swimming, hunting, fishing, camping. Office: Taylor & Co 1138 N Bath Ave Oklahoma City OK 73117-2602 Office Phone: 405-834-8695.

TAYMAN, JEFF, retired economics professor; b. Balt., Dec. 4, 1951; s. Bernard and Sheila Tayman; m. Melinda Davis, Sept. 27, 1988. PhD, Fla. State U., Tallahassee, 1979. Sr. demographer San Diego Assn. Govts., 1982—99, dir. tech. svcs., 1999—2006; lectr., econ. dept. U. Calif., 2003—, La Jolla. Author: (book) State and Local Population Projections, Methodology and Analysis (Walt Terrie award Best Paper Applied Demography, 1999). Pecas com. mem. UC Davis, Calif., 2007; transp. modeling com. mem. San Diego Assn. Govts., 2007. Home: 2142 Diamond St San Diego CA 92109 Personal E-mail: jtayman@san.rr.com.

TAYMOR, JULIE, theater, film and opera director, designer; b. Newton, Mass., Dec. 15, 1952; d. Melvin L. and Betty Taymor. BA in folklore and mythology, Oberlin Coll., 1974; attended, L'Ecole Mimet Theatre in Paris, France, Herbert Berghof Studio, NYC. Founder Teatr Loh. Dir. Way of Snow, The Transposed Heads, 1984, The Tempest, 1986, Liberty's Taken, 1985, Juan Darién, 1988, Fool's Fire, 1992, Titus Andronicus, 1994, Oedipus Rex, 1992, The Magic Flute, Salomé, The Flying Dutchman, The Lion King, 1997, (Tony awards for best director and costume design 1998), The Green Bird, 2000, (films) Titus, 1999 (Acad. award nominee), Frida, 2002 (two Acad. awards), Across the Universe, 2007, operas, classical plays and exptl. theater projects; prodr. Shakespeare plays and operas; designer puppets, masks, imaginative costumes and other visual elements. MacArthur grantee, Watson fellow, 1974-79, Obie awards, 1988, Golden Plate award, Acad. Achievement, 2006, Women in Hollywood Tribute award Elle Mag., 2008. Mailing: CAA 162 Fifth Ave New York NY 10010

TAYPE, CARMEN AMELIA, physician; d. Mauro Benigno Taype and Francisca Perez; m. Roberts Jonathan David, Feb. 3, 2007. MD, U. Peruana Cayetano Heredia, Peru, 2001, MSc, 2003; PhD, U. Leeds, Eng., 2008. Rschr Lab. Rsch. & Devel., U. Peruana Cayetano Heredia,

Lima, 1998—2004; rsch. trainee Pulmonary & Critical Care Divsn., Feinberg Sch. Medicine, Northwestern U., Chgo., 2003—03, Sch. Medicine, U. Libre de Bruxelles, Brussels, 2004, IRD Montpellier, France, 2005, 2007; internal medicine resident St. Barnabas Hosp. Albert Einstein Coll. Medicine, Bronx, NY, 2008—. Medic San Martin de Porres, Lima, 2001—02. Recipient Travel award, Internat. Conf. Am. Thoracic Soc., San Diego, 2005, Internat. Conf. Am. Thoracic Soc., Orlando, 2004, Minority Trainee Travel awards, Internat. Conf. Am. Thoracic Soc., San Diego, 2009; grantee Grant, Concytec, Fundación Inst. Hipólito Unanue & U. Peruana Cayetano Heredia, 1998—99; Marie Curie fellowship, European Union, U. Leeds, 2004—08, Grant, U. Peruana Cayetano Heredia, 2004, Proyecto VIGIA, Peru, 2002, Travel grant, European Respiratory Soc., Ann. Congress, 2002. Fellow: Am. Thoracic Soc.; mem.: ACP, Peruvian Coll. Physicians. Home Phone: 516-532-9075. Personal E-mail: carmentaype@yahoo.com.

TCHAKO, ABRAHAM, engineering educator; s. Peter and Eliza Njipe; m. Kontchie Tiako, Dec. 22, 1996; children: Stevie, Joey, Lizzy, Marina. PhD, CUNY Grad Ctr., NYC, 2005. Cert. European welding engr., DVS, Berlin, 1992. Writing fellow CUNY Grad Ctr., 1999—2001, tchg. fellow, 2002—04; vis. asst. prof. Union Coll., Schenectady, NY, 2005—. Actor: (play) Ancient Combattant. Founder Laakam, e.V, Berlin, 1989—94. Mem.: ASME, ASEE, Engrs. Without Borders, Sigma Xi, SWE. Achievements include research in partial discectomy of fusion of C-Spine. Office: Union Coll 807 Union St Schenectady NY 12308 Personal E-mail: somtchako@yahoo.com. Business E-Mail: tchakoa@union.edu.

TCHANTCHOU, FLAUBERT, medical researcher; arrived in US, 2001; s. Gabriel Tchana and Touwoud Monique; m. Wyllie Christiane Njinou Noupet, Apr. 12, 2003; 1 child, Francesca Gabrielle Tchatch. BSc, Yaounde U., Cameroon, 1992; diploma in tropical med. biology, Inst. Tropical Medicine, Antwerp, Belgium, 1999; MSc, Free U. Brussels, 2001; PhD, U. Mass., Lowell, 2005. Tchr. and rsch. asst. U. Douala, Cameroon, 1996—98; rsch. asst. U. Mass., 2002—05; postdoctoral rsch. fellow So. Miss. U., Hattiesburg, 2005, U. Md., Balt., 2005—. Assoc. rev. editor Jour. Alzheimer's Disease, 2006—. Mem.: AAAS, Am. Physiol. Soc., Am. Assn. Pharm. Sci. Office: U Md Sch Pharmacy 20 N Pine St Baltimore MD 21244

TCHEGUS, ROBERT PAUL, lawyer; b. Simcoe, Ont., Can., June 13, 1962; s. Bohdan and Nellie Elsie Tchegus; m. Deborah Anne Berry, Aug. 10, 1996. LLB, Queen's U. at Kingston, Ont., Can., 1986. Lic.: Law Soc. Upper Can. (barrister and solicitor) 1988, cert.: Law Soc. Upper Can. (real estate law specialist) 2004, lic.: Province of Ont. (notary pub.) 1988. Student-at-law The Corp. of the City of Kingston, 1984—87; assoc. Cunningham, Swan, Carty, Little & Bonham, Kingston, 1987—95, ptnr., 1995—. Spl. lectr. Law Soc. of Upper Can., Kingston, 1996—98; dir. Greater Kingston Homebuilders Assn., 2000—01; mem. adv. bd. The Salvation Army, Kingston, 2003—; former tchr. St. Lawrence Coll. Applied Arts and Tech., Kingston, 2003—05; part-time mem. Assessment Rev. Bd., Toronto, Canada, 2006—; coun. Queen's U., Kingston, 2008—; govt. coun. Ontario Bar Assn., 2008—; governing coun. mem. Canadian Bar Assn., 2008—. Contbr. articles to profl. jours. Pres., treas. The Kingston Family Y.M.C.A., 1995—99; v.p., dir. Grenville Pk. Co-operative Housing Assn. Ltd., Kingston, 2003. Mem.: Can. Bar Assn. (assoc.), Soc. Ont. Adjudicators and Regulators (assoc.), Ont. Bar Assn. (assoc.), Frontenac Law Assn. (assoc.; pres. real property sect. 1988—94), The Rideau Trail Assn. (life). Avocations: squash, cross country skiing. Office: Cunningham Swan Carty Little & Bonham 201-1473 John Counter Blvd Kingston ON Canada K7M 8Z6 Office Fax: 613-542-9814. Business E-Mail: rtchegus@cswan.com.

TCHEN, CHRISTINA M. (TINA TCHEN), federal official, lawyer; b. Columbus, Ohio, 1956; BA cum laude, Radcliffe Coll., Harvard U., Cambridge, Mass., 1978; JD cum laude, Northwestern U. Sch. Law, Chgo., 1984. Bar: Ill. 1984. Assoc. Skadden, Arps, Slate, Meagher & Flom LLP, Chgo., 1984—92, ptnr., 1992—2009; dep. asst. to Pres., dir. pub. liaison The White House, Washington, 2009—. Appt. mem. Rules Adv. Com., Civil Justice Reform Act Com., and Magistrate Judge Merit Selection Com. Fed. Dist. Ct. Chgo.; exec. dir. White House Coun. on Women & Girls, 2009—. Contbr. articles to profl. jours. Bd. trustees U. Chgo. Med. Ctr.; bd. dirs. Chgo. Pub. Libr., 2003—, Harvard Alumni Assn., Chgo. Bar. Found., Chgo. Area Found. Legal Svcs.; chair bd. dirs. Field Found. Ill., 2004—. Recipient Women of Achievement award, Anti-Defamation League, 1996; named Person of Yr., Chgo. Lawyer mag., 1994; named one of Top Three Women Bus. Lawyers in Ill., Leading Lawyers Network, 2007; named to Chambers USA: America's Leading Lawyers for Bus., 2008, Best Lawyers in America 2009. Mem.: ABA (appt. mem. pres. adv. coun. on diversity in profession 2004, co-chair Minority Trial Lawyer Task Force, co-chair, Comml. & Banking Litigation Com.), Women's Bar Assn. Ill. (Leadership award 1999). Democrat. Office: The White House 1600 Pennsylvania Ave NW Washington DC 20500*

TCHENG, JAMES ENLOU, physician; b. Covington, Ky., Sept. 15, 1956; s. John T.L. and Marlena Y.N. (Wang) T.; m. Mary Ann Powers, Aug. 13, 1983. BS, U. Cin., Ohio, 1978; MD, Johns Hopkins U., Balt., 1982. Diplomate Am. Bd. Internal Medicine, Am. Bd. Cardiovascular, Am. Bd. Interventional Cardiology. Intern Wash. U., St. Louis, 1982-83, resident, 1983-85; critical care physician DePaul Health Ctr., Bridgeton, Mo., 1985-86; fellow in cardiology Duke U. Med. Ctr., Durham, N.C., 1986-88, assoc. medicine, 1988-89, asst. prof. medicine, 1990-96, assoc. prof. medicine, 1997—, assoc. prof. cmty. and family medicine, 2004—. Fellow, Soc. of Cardiac Angrography and Interventions, European Soc. of Cardiology. Fellow Am. Coll. Cardiology; mem. ACP. Avocations: computers, classical music. Office: Duke U Med Ctr 403 Hock Plaza 2424 Erwin Rd Durham NC 27705 Office Phone: 919-668-8796. Business E-Mail: tchen001@mc.duke.edu.

TCHESLAVSKI, GLEB, engineering educator; b. Noginsk, Moscow region, Russia, Sept. 26, 1972; s. Valery Cheslavsky and Galina Guseva; m. Albina Karimova, Oct. 26, 2007. Engr., Bauman Moscow State Tech U., 1997; PhD, Va. Tech, Blacksburg, 2005. Tchg. asst. Va. Tech, 2001—05; postdoctoral fellow U. Houston, 2006—07; vis. asst. prof. Lamar U., 2007—08, asst. prof., 2008—. Office: Lamar Univ EE Dept 211 Redbird ln Box 10029 Beaumont TX 77710-0029

TCHOBANOGLOUS, GEORGE, civil engineering educator; b. Patterson, Calif., May 24, 1935; s. Christo and Penelope (Megdani) T.; m. Rosemary Ash, June 16, 1957; children: Kathryn, Lynn, Julianne. BCE, U. Pacific, 1958; MCE, U. Calif., Berkley, 1960; PhD, Stanford U., 1969; D in Engring. (hon.), Colo. Sch. Mines, 2005. Registered profl. engr., Calif. Research engr. U. Calif.-Berkeley, 1960-62; cons. Metcalf & Eddy Engrs., Palo Alto, Calif., 1963-81, Nolte & Assocs., Sacramento, 1981—, Calif. Water Resources Control Bd., 1972-80; assoc. prof. U. Calif.-Davis, 1970-76, prof. engring., 1976—2004, prof. emeritus, 2004—. Prin. author: Wastewater Engineering: Collection, Treatment, Disposal, 1972; author: (with R. Smith and R. Crites) Wastewater Management: A Guide to Information Sources, 1976, (with H. Theisen and R. Eliassen) Solid Wastes: Engineering Principles and Management Issues, 1977, (with Schroeder) Water Quality: Characteristics, Modeling, Modification, 1985, (with Peavy and Rowe) Environmental Engineering, 1985, (with H. Theisen, S.A. Vigil) Integrated Solid Waste Management: Engineering Principles and Management Issues, 1993, (with R. Crites) Small and Decentralized Wastewater Management Systems, 1998; co-author: Wastewater Engineering: Treatment, Disposal, Reuse, 1991, 4th edit., 2002; author, editor: Wastewater Engineering: Collection and Pumping of Wastewater, 1981; co-editor: Pumping Station Design, 1989 (with F. Burton and D. Stensel) Wastewater Engineering: Treatment and Reuse, 4th ed., 2002, co-editor: (with F Kreith) Solid Waste Handbook, 2d edit., 2002; contbr. numerous articles to profl. jours. Mem. bd. Calif. Integrated Waste Mgmt.; lectr. T.R. Camp, 1990. Recipient Waste to Energy Rsch. and Tech. Coun. Disting. award, 2004. Mem. AAAS, ASCE, NAE (Wiert Svc. award, 2004, Rsch. Edn. award, 2004), Assn. Environ. Engring. Profs. (bd. dirs., past pres.), Am. Acad. Environ. Engrs., Water Environ. Fedn. (Gordon Maskew Fair medal 1985, Jack Edward McKee medal 1999), Am. Water Works Assn. (Thomas R. Camp lectr. 1991), Nat. Water Rsch. Inst. (Athalie Richardson Irvine Clarke prize, 2003), Nat. Acad. Engring., Colorado Sch. Mines (hon. dr. engring. degree, 2006), AAEE and AEESP (Frederick Pohland Medal 2007) Home: 662 Diego Pl Davis CA 95616-0123 Office Phone: 530-756-5747.

TCHOU, JULIA, surgeon, educator; married. BS, Coll. Mt. St. Vincent, Riverdale, NY, 1982; MD, SUNY, Stony Brook, PhD, 1993. Cert. Am. Bd. Surgery, 2002. Asst. prof. surgery U. Pa., Phila., 2003—, asst. program dir., breast fellowship, sch. medicine, 2007—. Office: Univ Pa 3400 Spruce St Philadelphia PA 19104 Office Fax: 215-662-3354.

TCHOUMAK, ADELINA, corporate financial executive; b. Chishinau, Moldova, Feb. 16, 1974; arrived in U.S., 1990; d. Mercuriu and Olga Ciumac. BBA in Econs. cum laude, U. Anchorage, 1995. Performance analyst Clay Finlay Inc., NYC, 1996—2000, Oppenheimer Capital, 2000—02; asst. v.p., sr. performance analyst Citibank, 2002—04; ret., 2004. Sponsor Children Internat., Honduras, 2002—. Atheist. Avocations: reading, yoga. Home: 5108 Marcadas Rd NW Albuquerque NM 87114 Personal E-mail: tadelina@hotmail.com.

TCHOUNWOU, PAUL BERNARD, environmental health specialist, toxicologist, educator; b. Bangou, Cameroon, Aug. 14, 1960; came to U.S., 1985; s. Maurice and Christine (Kouanang) Seumo; m. Martha Namondo Mondoa, Aug. 3, 1990; children: Christine K., Hervey M., Solange S. BSc, U. Yaounde, Cameroon, 1983, MSc, 1984; MS in Pub. Health, Tulane U., 1986, ScD, 1990. Cert. toxicologist Nat. Environ. Health Assn.; registered sanitarian La. State Bd. Examiners for Sanitarians. Tchg. asst. Tulane Sch. Pub. Health, New Orleans, 1988—90; med. rschr. Inst. Med. Rsch., Yaounde, 1991—94; asst. prof. Faculty Medicine, Yaounde, 1992—94; rsch. assoc. Xavier and Tulane Univs., New Orleans, 1994—96; assoc. prof., dir. environ. sci. PhD program Jackson State U., 1996—; adj. assoc. prof. sch. pub. health Tulane U., 1999—2005; prof., dir. environ. sci. doctoral program Jackson State U., 2001—, dep. dir. Ctr. for Environ. Health, 2003—06, chair dept. biology, 2004—, interim assoc. dean coll. sci., engring. and tech., 2006—07; assoc. dean Coll. Sci. Engring. and Tech., 2007—. Adj. prof. Tulane U. Sch. Pub. Health, 2005—; environ. health cons. Orstom & UNICEF, Yaounde, 1992-93, U.S. AID, Kaele, 1991-93; rsch. supr. Tulane Sch. Pub. Health, New Orleans, 1994—; tng. and rsch. fellow U.S. AID, Washington, 1985-90; adj. assoc. prof. environ. health scis. Tulane U. Sch. Pub. Health and Tropical Medicine, 1999—. Editor-in-chief: Internat. Jour. of Environ. Rsch. and Pub. Health, 2003—, mem. editl. bd.: Internat. Jour. Environ. Toxicology and Water Quality, 1994—2005, guest editor: Internat. Jour. Molecular Scis., 2002—, regional editor: USA-Environ. Toxicology, 2002—, mem. overseas editl. bd.: Jour. Environ. Biology, 2002—; contbr. articles to profl. jours.; editor-in-chief: Environmental Toxicology, 2006—, mem. editl. bd.: Revs. on Environ. Health, 2003—. Grantee, Internat. Devel. Rsch. Ctr., 1992—93, Nat. Aeronautics and Space Adminstrn., 1977—99, NIH, 1998—, Nat. Oceanic and Atmospheric Adminstrn., 2001—, Dept. Army, 2002—03. Mem. APHA, AAUP, AAAS, Am. Assn. Cancer Rsch., Water Environ. Fedn., Cameroon Bioscis. Soc., Cameroon Assn. Epidemiology, Nat. Environ. Health Assn., N.Y. Acad. Scis., Miss. Acad. Sci., Soc. Environ. Toxicology and Chemistry, Soc. Toxicology, Delta Omega. Roman Catholic. Avocations: travel, playing tennis, watching tv sport programs. Home: 230 Clark Farms Rd Madison MS 39110-8112 Office: Jackson State U Coll Sci Engring and Tech PO Box 18540 Jackson MS 39217

TEAFORD, JON CHRISTIAN, retired history professor; b. Columbus, Ohio, Sept. 5, 1946; s. Robert Eugene and Virginia Hamilton Teaford. PhD, U. Wis., Madison, 1973. Prof. Purdue U., West Lafayette, Ind., 1975—2007. Author: (history book) The Municipal Revolution in America, 1975, City and Suburb: The Political Fragmentation of Metropolitan America, 1979, The Unheralded Triumph: City Government in America 1870-1900, 1984, The Twentieth-century American City, 1986, The Rough Road to Renaissance: Urban Revitalization in America, 1990, Cities of the Heartland: The Rise and Fall of the Industrial Midwest, 1993, Post-Suburbia: Government and Politics in Edge Cities, 1997, The Rise of the States, 2002, The Metropolitan Revolution: The Rise of Post-Urban America, 2006, (book) The American Suburb: The Basics, 2008. Business E-Mail: teaford@purdue.edu.

TEAGLE, RACHEL, museum director; PhD in Art History, Stanford U. Cur. San Francisco Mus. Modern Art; cur., co-dept. head Mus. Contemporary Art San Diego; exec. dir. Children's Mus. San Diego, 2007—. Office: Childrens Museum San Diego 200 W Island Ave San Diego CA 92101-6850 Office Phone: 619-233-8792.

TEAGUE, CRAIG M., chemistry professor; m. Mary Anne Armstrong, Sept. 2, 2001; children: Megan, Allison. BS, Mo. State U., Springfield, 1998; PhD, U. Ill., Urbana, 2003. Asst. prof. Cornell Coll., Mt. Vernon, Iowa, 2003—. Contbr. scientific papers. Bd. dirs. Vineyard Ch., Cedar Rapids, Iowa, 2006—08; bd. advisors mem. Mo. State U. Dept. Chemistry, 2005—08. Recipient Outstanding Grad. award, Mo. State U., 1998, Gaarde-Morton Jr. Faculty award, Cornell Coll., 2006. Mem.: Midwestern Assn. Chemistry Tchrs. Liberal Arts Colls, Am. Phys. Soc., Am. Chem. Soc., Sigma Pi Sigma, Phi Lambda Upsilon. Avocations: music, travel. Office: Cornell Coll 600 1st St SW Mount Vernon IA 52314 Business E-Mail: cteague@cornellcollege.edu.

TEAGUE, HARRY, United States Representative from New Mexico; b. Gracemont, Okla., June 29, 1949; m. Nancy Teague; 2 children. Founder, owner, pres. Teaco Energy Services, N.Mex.; mem. Lea County Bd. Commissioners, N.Mex., 1999—2006, chmn. N.Mex., 2003—06; mem. US Congress from 2nd N.Mex. Dist., 2009—. Bd. mem. Black Gold Race Track and Casino, LES Enrichment Facility; mem. N.Mex. State Transportation Com. Bd. mem. Lea County Big Brothers Big Sisters, Lea County Fair, Boys and Girls Club of Hobbs. Mem.: N.Mex. Oil and Gas Assn., Assn. Commerce and Industry. Democrat. Office: US Congress 1007 Longworth House Office Bldg Washington DC 20515-3102 also: Dist Office 200 E Broadway Ste 200 Hobbs NM 88240 Office Phone: 202-225-2365, 575-393-0510. Office Fax: 202-225-9599.*

TEAGUE, LAVETTE COX, JR., systems educator, consultant; b. Birmingham, Ala., Oct. 8, 1934; s. Lavette Cox and Caroline Green (Stokes) T. Student, Auburn U., 1951-54; BArch, MIT, 1957, MSCE, 1965, PhD, 1968; MDiv with distinction, Ch. Div. Sch. Pacific, 1979. Cert. computer profl. Inst. Cert. Computer Profls. Archtl. designer Carroll C. Harmon, Birmingham, 1957, Fred Renneker, Jr., Birmingham, 1958-59; architect Rust Engring. Co., Birmingham, 1959-62, Synergetics, Inc., Raleigh, NC, 1962-64, Rust Engring. Co., Birmingham, 1964-68; rsch. asst., instr., rsch. assoc. MIT, Cambridge, 1964-68; dir. computer svcs. Skidmore Owings & Merrill, San Francisco, Chgo., 1968-74; postdoctoral fellow UCLA, 1972; adj. assoc. prof. arch. and civil engring. Carnegie-Mellon U., Pitts., 1973-74; archtl. systems cons. Chgo., 1974-75, Berkeley, Calif., 1975-80, Pasadena, 1980-82, Altadena, Calif., 1982—. Lectr. info. systems Calif. State Poly. U., Pomona, 1980-81, prof., 1981-98, prof. emeritus, 1998—, asst. chair, 1990-91, chair, 1991-93, 96-98; Fulbright lectr., Uruguay, 1985; lectr. Peking U., 2004. Author: Event-Based Analysis and Design: An Introduction to Structured Methods, 2000; co-author: Structured Analysis Methods for Computer Information Systems, 1985, Object-Oriented Systems Analysis and Design with UML, 2005, Chinese edit., 2005. Mem. adv. bd. Ch. Div. Sch. of the Pacific. Recipient Tucker-Voss award MIT, 1967. Mem. AIA (Arnold W. Brunner scholar 1966), Assn. Computing Machinery, Sigma Xi, Phi Eta Sigma, Scarab, Scabbard and Blade, Tau Beta Pi, Chi Epsilon, Beta Gamma Sigma. Episcopalian. Home: 1696 N Altadena Dr Altadena CA 91001-3623 Office: 3801 W Temple Ave Pomona CA 91768-2557 Business E-Mail: lcteague@csupomona.edu.

TEAGUE, LETTIE, editor; b. Ind. d. H. Edward and Patricia Teague; m. Alan Richman, Oct. 2, 1994 (div. 2006). Grad., Kenyon Coll., Gambier, Ohio, 1983. Pub. rels. cons.; food, wine, and books editor Diversion mag., 1995—97; wine editor Food & Wine mag., 1997—2005, exec. wine editor, 2005—. Awards judge City and Regional Mag. Assn., 2007. Co-author, illustrator (books) Fear of Wine: An Introductory Guide to the Grape, 1995; author: (books) Educating Peter, 2007, (monthly column) Wine Matters (MFK Fisher Disting. Writing award James Beard Found., 2003, Mag. Columns award James Beard Found., 2005); guest appearances include (TV series) CNN, CNN Headline News, CNBC. Avocations: running, horseback riding, Cuban music. Office: Food & Wine mag 1120 Ave of Americas 19th Fl New York NY 10036*

TEAGUE, RANDAL CORNELL, SR., lawyer; b. Durham, NC, May 19, 1944; s. Roy M. Sr. and Lottie (Rhew) T.; children: R. Cornell, R. Townsend, Mary Robb Durham, James K.B. BA, Am. U., 1967; JD, George Washington U., 1971, LLM with highest honors, 1972; LLD (hon.), Allen U., 1973. Bar: Fla. 1972, D.C. 1972, U.S. Dist. Ct. D.C. 1972, U.S. Tax Ct. 1972, U.S. Ct. Mil. Appeals 1972, U.S. Ct. Appeals (D.C. and fed. cirs.) 1972, U.S. Ct. Appeals (5th cir.) 1973, U.S. Supreme Ct. 1975, Mass. 1979, U.S. Ct. Appeals (1st cir.) 1979, U.S. Dist. Ct. Mass. 1979, U.S. Ct. Internat. Trade. Coord. policy devel. Exec. Office of Pre. of U.S., Washington, 1971-73; chief of staff, legis. counsel to Rep. Jack F. Kemp Ho. of Reps., Washington, 1973-79; div. counsel Cabot Corp., 1979-81; counsel Vorys, Sater, Seymour & Pease LLP, Washington, 1981-83, ptnr., 1984—. Pres. Internat. Exch. Coun., 1984—; trustee Fund Am. Studies, Washington, 1976—, chmn., 1998—; trustee, dir. Air Force Acad. Found., Colorado Springs, Colo., 1983—; chmn. adv. com. voluntary aid U.S. AID, 1987-91; trustee Earth U., Costa Rica, 1987—, chmn., 2006-; councillor Atlantic Coun. of U.S., 1990—; co-founder Am. Inst. on Polit. and Econ. Sys., Charles U., Prague, 1993—; founder Internat. Inst. Polit. and Econ. Studies, Athens, Greece, 1996—; dir. Salzburg Seminar, 1997—. Named one of Outstanding Young Men Am., 1973; recipient George Washington medal Freedoms Found., 1978. Mem. Fla. Bar Assn., Mass. Bar Assn., D.C. Bar Assn., Univ. Club (Washington). Republican. Episcopalian. Office: Vorys Sater Seymour & Pease LLP 1828 L St NW Fl 11 Washington DC 20036-5109 Office Phone: 202-467-8817. Business E-Mail: rcteague@vorys.com.

TEAGUE, ROBERT COLE, physician; b. Waxahachie, Tex., June 13, 1930; s. Isaac Lawson and Frances (Cole) Teague; m. Virginia M. Teague, Nov. 11, 1960 (dec. May 1, 2005); children: Patrick, Michael. BA in Chemistry, Baylor U., Waco, Tex., 1951; MD, U. Tex., Galveston, 1955. Lic. physician Ariz.; cert. ABFB, 2005. Intern McLaren Hosp., Flint, Mich., 1955—56; med. officer, active duty USNR, 1956—58; physician family practice LaJolla, Calif., 1958—63, Phoenix, 1963—. Med. dir., pres. Vis. Nurse Svc., Phoenix; chmn. Family Practice Humana Hosp., 1984—86, past chmn.; chmn. Family Practice Good Samaritan Hosp., 1990—91. Fellow Am. Acad. Family Physicians (charter); mem. Ariz. Acad. Family Physicians (pres. 1988). Republican. Episcopalian. Avocation: travel. Office: 7200 W Bell Rd G-103 Glendale AZ 85308

TEAL, GILBERT EARLE, II, lawyer, coast guard officer; b. Lafayette, Ind., May 1, 1959; s. Gilbert Earle and Evangeline Maxine (Pipcr) T.; m. Mary Anne Liwoch, Oct. 3, 1987. AS, Western Conn. State U., 1979; BS, USCG Acad., 1983; MPA, George Mason U., 1988; JD, Coll. William and Mary, 1991. Bar: Va. 1991, U.S. Mil. Ct. Appeals 1991, U.S. Ct. Appeals (4th cir.) 1991, D.C. 1992, U.S. Ct. Claims 1992, U.S. Ct. Appeals (fed. cir.) 1992, U.S. Tax Ct. 1998, Alaska 1998, U.S. Dist. Ct. Alaska 1998, U.S. Ct. Appeals (9th cir.) 1998, U.S. Supreme Ct. 1998; designated mil. judge, 2001; appellate judge Coast Guard Ct. Criminal Appeals, 2004. Commd. ensign USCG, 1983, advanced through grades to capt., 2004; assigned to USCG Cutter Vigorous (WMEC 627), New London, Conn., 1983-85; intelligence officer COMDT (G-OIS-3) Hdqs. USCG, Washington, 1985-88; law clk. to chief trial judge Capt. Thomas Snook, USCG, NYC, 1989; law clk. USCG RTC Yorktown, 1990; staff atty. Maintenance and Logistics Command Atlantic, Governors Island, N.Y., 1991-94; legal officer USCG Support Ctr., Kodiak, Alaska, 1994-97; br. legal officer 17th Coast Guard Dist., spl. asst. U.S. Atty., Dist. of Alaska, Anchorage, 1997—2001; dep. staff judge adv. Maintenance and Logistics Command Atlantic, Norfolk, Va., 2001—04; chief legal policy and program devel., spl. asst. to the judge adv. gen. USCG Hdqrs., Washington, 2004—06; asst. counsel U.S. Navy Fleet and Indsl. Supply Ctr., Norfolk, 2006—. Adj. prof. law Coll. William & Mary Sch. Law, 2008—. Recipient Dirs. award for outstanding performance as spl. asst. U.S. atty. Dept. Justice, Exec. Office for U.S. Attys., 1998, Lawrence R. Schneider award U.S. Dept. Transp., 1999, Cert. of Commendation, Dept. of Justice Environ. Natural Resources Divsn., 2000. Mem. ABA, FBA, Va. State Bar, Va. Bar Assn., D.C. Bar, AK Bar Assn., Jud. Advs. Assn. (life), U.S. Naval Inst. (life), Nat. Eagle Scout Assn. (life), Army and Navy Club (Washington), Army-Navy Country Club (Arlington, Va.), Trout Unltd. (life), Coastal Conservation Assn. (life), Fedn. Fly Fishers (life), Masons, Shriners, Phi Delta Phi (life), Phi Delta Kappa. Avocation:

fishing. Office: Office of Counsel Fleet Indsl and Supply Ctr Norfolk VA 23511-1088 Home: 4769 Bristol Cir Williamsburg VA 23185 Office Phone: 757-443-1088. Business E-Mail: gilbert.teal@navy.mil.

TEAL, JOHN M., environmental scientist; b. Omaha, Nov. 9, 1929; s. Clarence William and Valentine Moline Teal; m. Susan B. Peterson, Dec. 30, 1979; children: Eric, Tanya Sanders; m. Mildred Mann, Dec. 30, 1950 (div. June 1978). AB, Harvard Coll., Cambridge, Mass., 1951; PhD, Harvard U., Cambridge, 1955. Cert. profl. wetland scientist Soc. Wetland Scientists, 1999. Asst. scientist U. Ga., Sapelo Island, 1955—59; asst. prof. Dalhousie U., Halifax, Nova Scotia, Canada, 1959—61; scientist Woods Hole Oceanog. Instn., Mass., 1961—94, scientist emeritus, 1994—. Ptnr. Teal Partners, Rochester, Mass., 1985—. Contbr. chapters to books (Phi Beta Kappa Sci. Book award, 1970). Recipient Lifetime Achievement award, Soc. Wetland Scientists, 2007. Independent. Avocations: farming, birdwatching. Home: 567 New Bedford Rd Rochester MA 02770

TEAL, TERESA, mathematics professor; b. Blakely, Ga., June 27, 1967; d. Calvin Holmes Sr. and Carolyn Holmes; 1 child, LaDarius. BS in Applied Math., Valdosta State U., Ga., 1989; MBA, U. Phoenix, 2001. Cert. tchr. Ga. Dept. Edn., 1995. Tchr. Early County Dept. Edn., Blakely, 1993—99; math. instr. Albany Tech. Coll., Ga., 1999—2006, Bainbridge Coll., Ga., 2006—. Owner 1st Beginnings Tutorial and Homework Svcs., Blakely, 2007. Home: 4211 Rockmine Rd Blakely GA 39823 Office: Bainbridge Coll 40 Harold Ragan Dr Blakely GA 39823 Personal E-mail: tteal@windstream.net.

TEARE, RICHARD WALLACE, retired foreign service officer; b. Cleve., Feb. 21, 1937; m. Jeanie Walter; 3 children. BA, Harvard U., 1958; diploma, Nat. War Coll., 1978. Joined Fgn. Svc., 1959; vice consul U.S. Consulate, Bridgetown, Barbados, 1960-62; consular officer U.S. Embassy, Manila, 1962-64, polit. officer Saigon, Vietnam, 1965-67, Mexico City, 1971-74, counselor for polit. affairs Vientiane, Laos, 1974-76, dep. chief mission Wellington, New Zealand, 1983-86, Canberra, Australia, 1986-89; dep. and acting prin. officer U.S. Consulate Gen., Nha Trang, Vietnam, 1973; intelligence and rsch. specialist Dept. State, 1967-69, desk officer Vietnam Working Group, 1969-71, spl. asst. to asst. sec. for East Asian and Pacific Affairs, 1976-77, dep. dir. Office Philippine Affairs, 1978-80, dep. and acting U.S. rep. for Micronesian Status Negotiations, 1980-83, dir. Office of Indonesia, Malaysia, Brunei and Singapore Affairs, 1989-92, spl. projects officer Office of Dir. Gen., 1992-93, U.S. amb. to Papua New Guinea, Solomon Islands and Vanuatu, 1993-96; fgn. policy advisor to the Commander in Chief U.S. Pacific Command, Camp Smith, Hawaii, 1996-98; dir. Ctr. Australian and New Zealand studies Sch. Fgn. Svc., Georgetown U., 1998—2004, sr. fellow, 2004—07; ret., 2007. Mem.: Australian and New Zealand Studies Assn. N.Am. (past pres.), U.S.-New Zealand Coun. (bd. dirs.), Am. Fgn. Svc. Assn., Historic Chevy Chase DC. Home: 3111 Oliver St NW Washington DC 20015-1654

TEAS, ROY KENNETH, marketing educator; b. Manhattan, Kans., Apr. 17, 1945; s. Chester Kenneth and Ruthella Teas; m. Susan Paula Teas; children: Sarah Calaway, David, Rachel, James. BS, Augustana Coll., Sioux Falls, SD, 1969; MBA, U. Okla., Norman, 1970, PhD, 1975. Operational auditor Std. Oil, Chgo., 1970; asst. prof. U. Wis., Oshkosh, 1975—79; assoc. prof. Iowa State U., Ames, 1979—85, prof., 1985—95, disting. prof., 1995—. Editl. rev. bd. Jour. Mktg., Chgo., contbg. reviewer; editl. rev. bd. Jour. Personal Selling Sales Mgmt., Chgo. Contbr. articles to profl. jours. Grantee Heggen Faculty fellow, Iowa State U., 2007; Hawkeye Bancorp. fellowship, 1984—86, Dean's Faculty fellow, 2005—. Home: 2003 Polk Dr Ames IA 50010 Office: Iowa State Univ Gerdin 3311 Ames IA 50010 Business E-Mail: rteas@iastate.edu.

TEASDALE, KENNETH FULBRIGHT, lawyer; b. St. Louis, Nov. 8, 1934; s. Kenneth and Ann (Fulbright) T.; m. Elizabeth Driscol Langdon, June 13, 1964; children: Caroline, Doug, Cindy. AB, Amherst Coll., 1956; LLB, Washington U., St. Louis, 1961. Bar: Mo. 1961. Atty. antitrust div. U.S. Dept. Justice, Washington, 1961-62; asst. counsel Dem. Policy Com. U.S. Senate, Washington, 1962—64, gen. counsel Dem. Policy Com., asst. to majority leader, 1963-64; assoc. Armstrong, Teasdale, Kramer & Vaughan, St. Louis, 1964-67, ptnr., 1967-86; mng. ptnr. Armstrong, Teasdale, Schlafly & Davis, St. Louis, 1986-93, chmn. of firm, 1993—. Trustee Sci. Ctr. St. Louis, St. Louis Art Mus.; trustee, St. Louis U.; mem. nat. coun. Washington U. Law Sch., 1988—. Mem. ABA, Bar Assn. Mo., Bar Assn. St. Louis, St. Louis Coalition for Plant and Life Scis., Old Warson Country Club. Episcopalian. Office: Armstrong Teasdale LLP Ste 2600 One Metropolitan Sq Saint Louis MO 63102-2733 Office Phone: 314-621-5070. Business E-Mail: kteasdale@armsteasdale.com.

TEBALDI, EDINALDO, economics professor; m. Analia M Tebaldi, May 16, 1992; children: Heloisa, Erik. PhD in Economics, U. NH, Durham, 2005, M, 2003, Fereral U. Ceara, Brazil, 2000. Vis. asst. prof. U. NH, 2006—07; asst. prof. Bryant U., Smithfield, RI, 2007—. Contbr. scientific papers publ. in profl. jours. Advisor Bryant Economics Student Assn., Smithfield, 2007. Recipient Elizabeth Bogan prize in Economics, U. NH, 2003, Outstanding Tchg. award, 2005; named Economics Prof. of Yr., 2006—07. Mem.: Am. Econ. Assn. Office: Bryant Univ 1150 Douglas Pike Smithfield RI 02917 Office Fax: 401-232-6068. Business E-Mail: etebaldi@bryant.edu.

TEBBETTS, JOHN BERYL, plastic surgeon; b. Ruston, La., Nov. 9, 1946; BS, Tulane Univ., 1968; MD, Univ. Tex. Med. Branch, Galveston, 1972. Cert. Am. Bd. Gen. Surgery, 1978, Am. Bd. Plastic Surgery, 1980, lic. Tex., 1972, Wyo., 1987. Intern LDS Hosp., Salt Lake City, 1972—73; resident in surgery Univ. Utah Affiliated Hospitals, 1973—77; resident in plastic surgery Southwestern Med. Sch., Dallas, 1977—79; asst. clin. prof. in plastic surgery Southwestern Univ.; attending staff plastic surgery Mary Shiels Hosp., Baylor Univ. Med. Ctr., Longview Regional Hosp.; plastic surgeon Board Certified Surgery-Dallas. Contbr. articles to profl. jours.; co-author (with Terrye B. Tebbetts): The Best Breast. Recipient Ralph Millard award, Canadian Soc. for Aesthetic Plastic Surgery, 1994. Mem.: AMA, Am. Assn. Plastic Surgeons, Am. Coll. Surgeons, Am. Coll. Emergency Physicians, Am. Soc. Plastic & Reconstructive Surgery, Am. Cleft Palate Assn., Am. Soc. Aesthetic Plastic Surgery (Walter Scott Brown award 1984, 1990, Simon Fredericks award 1990), Tex. Soc. Plastic Surgeons, Tex. Med. Assn., Dallas Soc. Plastic Surgeons, Dallas County Med. Soc. Office: Board Certified Surgery-Dallas Ste W-300 2801 Lemmon Ave Dallas TX 75204 Office Phone: 972-220-2712, 888-888-8769. Office Fax: 214-969-0933.

TEBBI, CAMERON K, hematologist, oncologist; b. Hamadan, Iran, Oct. 9, 1943; s. Mehdi and Iran A. Tebbi; m. Judith H Dautch, Apr. 24, 1982; children: Michael Lewis, David Nathan, Natalie Sarah. MD, U. Tehran, Iran, 1968. Lic. MD 1974. Med. dir., adolescent unit Roswell Pk. Meml. Inst., Buffalo, 1979—90; med. dir., pediatric hematology/oncology Tampa Children's Hosp., Fla., 1990—. Sci. rev. bd. Nat. Cancer Inst., Washington, 1998—. Contbr. over 230 articles & 2 books. Founder Children's Cancer Rsch. Group, Tampa, 2004. Recipient Medal Of Honor In Medicine, U. Tehran, 1968. Mem.: Histiocyte Soc., Internat. Soc. Pediat. Oncology, Am. Assn. Cancer Rsch., Am. Soc. of Clin. Oncology. Jewish. Office: Tampa Children's Hosp 3001 W ML King Blvd Tampa FL 33607 Office Fax: 813-554-8167. E-mail: cameron.tebbi@baycare.org.

TEBOH-EWUNGKEM, MIRANDA IJANG, education educator; d. Aaron Bagen and Christiana Enih Teboh; m. Julius Ewungwo Ewungkem, July 31, 1998; children: Jeswill Bagen Ewungkem, Julius Ewungwo Ewungkem Jr. BS in Math., U. Buea, 1996, MS in Math., 1998; PhD in Math., Lehigh U., 2003, MS in Stats, 2003. Tchg. asst. U. Of Buea, Cameroon, 1997—98; dean's fellow Lehigh U., Bethlehem, Pa., 1998—99, tchg. asst., 1999—2003, hsiung vis. asst. prof., 2003—04; vis. post doc U. Mich., 2004—04; vis. asst. prof. Lafayette Coll., Easton, Pa., 2004—, asst. prof., 2004—. Author: (conference book of abstracts) International Conference for Mathematics in Biology and Medicine, International Conference on Applied Math, International Conference on Mathematical Biology; contbr. articles to profl. jours. Landahl student travel grant, Soc. of Math. Biology, 2002, Travel grant, AWM, 2004, Reidler grant, Lehigh U., 2003, SMB Travel grant, SMB, 2004, Commonwealth scholarship, Commonwealth group, 1998. Mem.: Soc. of Indsl. and Applied Mathematicians, Soc. for Math. Biology, Am. Math. Soc., Assn. for Women in Math. Christian. Avocations: reading, tennis. Office: Lafayette Coll Pardee Hall 225A Easton PA 18042 Office Fax: 610 330 5721. Business E-Mail: tebohewm@lafayette.edu.

TEBOW, TIM (TIMOTHY RICHARD TEBOW), student athlete; b. Philippines, Aug. 14, 1987; s. Bob and Pam Tebow. Student, U. Fla., 2006—. Quarterback U. Fla. Gators, 2006—. Active Goodwill Gators. Recipient Heisman Meml. trophy, Heisman Trophy Trust, 2007, Maxwell award, 2007, 2008, Davey O'Brien award, 2007, James E. Sullivan award, US Amateur Athletic Union, 2007, ESPY award, Best Male Coll. Athlete, ESPN, 2008, Sports Spirit award, Disney, 2008; named SEC Offensive Player of Yr., AP, 2007, First Team All-SEC, 2007, First Team All-Am., 2007, SEC Offensive MVP, Sporting News, 2008; named to SEC All-Freshman Team, 2006, All-Am. Team, Walter Camp Found., 2007. Christian. Achievements include member of the BCS National Championship winning University of Florida Gators, 2006, 2008; becoming the fist NCAA Division I player with at least 20 rushing and 20 passing touchdowns; becoming the first underclassman to ever win the Heisman Trophy. Mailing: U Fla Gators Ben Hill Griffin Stadium Univ Ave & North South Dr Gainesville FL 32611*

TECCE, ANITA MERCEDES, literature, language and theatre professor; b. NYC, Dec. 30, 1949; d. Manuel John and Mercedes Maria Basoa; children: Justin Scott, Erica Michele, Marc Curtis. BA, St. John's U., Jamaica, NY, 1971; MA, Montclair State U., Upper Montclair, NJ, 1974, U. Tex., Tyler, 2000. Prof. English Laredo CC, Tex., 1991—94, Tyler Jr. Coll., 1994—2002; asst. prof. theatre & comm. Chesapeake Coll., Wye Mills, Md., 2003—. Theatrical dir. Peake Players, Wye Mills, Md., 2003—. Actor: (numerous theatrical prodns.). Bd. mem. Laredo Little Theatre, 1991—94, Somerset Valley Players, Somerville, NJ, 1987—91. Avocation: theater. Office: Chesapeake Coll PO Box 8 Wye Mills MD 21679 Business E-Mail: atecce@chesapeake.edu.

TECCO, ROMUALD GILBERT LOUIS JOSEPH, violinist, concertmaster; b. Toulon, Var, France, May 1, 1941; came to U.S., 1960; s. Raymond Charles and Angele (Cornille) T. Student, Paris Conservatoire, 1954-60; diploma, postgrad. diploma, Juilliard Sch. Music, 1967-68. Mem. N.Y. String Quartet, 1969-72; concertmaster Juilliard Ensemble, NYC, 1969-72, St. Paul Chamber Orch., 1972-98; soloist Chgo. Symphony, Bavarian Radio Orch., Orch. of Mex., Orchestre Colonne, Paris, Rotterdam Philharm.; performer numerous festivals, Sweden, Finland, France, Italy, U.S. Recs. with Aaron Copland and Lou Harrison Chamber Music. Served with French Navy, 1964-65, NATO hdqrs. Recipient first prize in violin Conservatoire Paris; recipient first prize chamber music Conservatoire Paris Mem. St. Paul Univ. Club.

TEDD, MONIQUE MICHELINE, artist; b. Sotteville-les-Rouen, France, Jan. 25, 1943; came to U.S., 1968; d. Maurice Joseph and Dolly Jeanne (Carpentier) T.; m. Asiat A. Ali, Dec. 23, 1967; 1 child, Asiat Allum Ali. MFA in Painting, Beaux-Arts Sch. of Rouen, Seine Rouen Maritime, France, 1967. Art tchr. Vernon, France, 1967-68; advt. Hahn J. Shoes, Washington, 1968-69, Magrams, Burlington, Vt., 1974—. Set decorator Lyric Theater, Burlington, Vt., 1975. One-woman shows include St. Michael's Coll., Winooski, Vt., 1972, 91, Peel's Gallery, Danby, Vt., 1978-79, Gov.'s Corridor, State Capital, Montpelier, Vt., 1980, The Living and Learning Ctr., U. Vt., Burlington, 1982, Passepartout Gallery, Winooski, 1983, Gallery Two, Woodstock, 1984; exhibited in group shows at The Gallery, Washington, 1969, N.Y. First Internat. Art Show, 1970, Galerie des Trois Arts, Burlington, Vt., 1970-71, Fleming Mus., Burlington, 1972, Frog Hollow, Middlebury, 1973, The Four Winds Gallery, North Ferrisburg, Vt., 1975, Norwich U. Armory Show, Hanover, N.H., 1976, Old Bergen Art Guild Touring Exhibit, 1978-80, Stratton Art Festival, Stratton, Vt., 1979, Women's Ednl. Ctr., Essex Junction, Vt., 1981-82, Pocketbook Wood Gallery, Montpelier, 1981-82, Window, a Women's View, Burlington, 1981-82, Passepartout Gallery, 1985, Smith Coll., 1985, Wood Art Gallery, Montpelier, 1985, 86, 87, Helen Day Ctr., Stowe, Vt., 1986-87, Gallery Two, 1991, Shelburne Mus., 1996, Beaux Arts Studio, Essex Junction, Vt., 1998—; selected for exhibit and calendars Paysage de France, a 12-city exhibit, 1965. Recipient 1st prize Rouen C. of C., 1964, 3rd prize Grand Prix Internat. of Deauville, 1987, open studio 7th Vt. Craft Coun., 2000. Home: 9 Seneca Ave Essex Junction VT 05452-3521 E-mail: teddali@verizon.net.

TEDDER, THOMAS FLETCHER, immunology educator, researcher; b. Chateauroux, France, May 14, 1956; came to U.S. 1959; s. Raymond Percy and Barbara (Hagemann) T. AA, Okaloosa-Walton C.C., Niceville, Fla., 1976; BS with honors, U. Fla., 1978, MS, 1980; PhD, U. Ala., Birmingham, 1984. Rsch. fellow in pathology Harvard Med. Sch., Boston, 1984-85, instr. pathology, 1986-88, asst. prof. pathology, 1988-93; assoc. prof. pathology Harvard U. Med. Sch., Boston, 1993; prof. immunology Duke U. Med. Ctr., Durham, NC, 1993—, chmn. dept. immunology, 1993—. Alter Geller prof. rsch. in immunology Duke U. Med. Ctr., 1997—; co-founder Angelica Therapeutics, Inc.; cons. in field. Assoc. editor Jour. Immunology, 1989-93, sect. editor, 1993-98, dep. editor, 2004-; contbr. numerous articles to med. jours., including Jour. Immunology, Nature, Lancet, Immunity. Recipient LeRoy Collins Disting. Alumnus award Fla. Assn. C.C.'s; named 25th Anniversary Disting. Alumnus, Okaloosa-Walton C.C., 1989; Damon Runyon-Walter Winchell rsch. fellow, 1985-87; scholar Leukemia Soc. Am., 1991-96, Stohlman scholar, 1995-96. Mem. Am. Soc. for Microbiology (Pres. fellow 1982), Am. Assn. Immunologists, Sigma Xi, Phi Kappa Phi. Achievements include identification and determination of structure and function of many human B lymphocyte cell-surface molecules. Office: Duke U Med Ctr Dept Immunology PO Box 3010 Durham NC 27710-0001 Office Phone: 919-684-3578. E-mail: thomas.tedder@duke.edu.

TEDESCHI, GEORGE, labor union administrator; Journeyman newspaper pressman Newsday, LI; mem. Graphic Comm. Internat. Union (GCIU), 1959—, v.p. & sec.-treas., Local 406C, pres., Nassau County 406C, 1972—2000, pres. GCIU (now Graphic Comm. Internat./Internat. Brotherhood Teamsters), 2000—. Pres. N.Am. Newspaper Conf. GCU, 1979—2000; mem. gen. bd. from Atlantic region GCIU, 1983—2000; mem. exec. bd. LI Fedn. Labor, AFL-CIO. Bd. dirs. Union Labor Life Ins. Co. (ULLICO); bd. dirs., sec. United Way LI. Office: GCIU 1900 L St NW Washington DC 20036 Office Phone: 202-462-1400 ext. 504. Office Fax: 202-721-0600. Business E-Mail: gtedeschi@gciu.org.*

TEDESCHI, JOHN ALFRED, historian, librarian, educator; b. Modena, Italy, July 17, 1931; came to U.S., 1939, naturalized, 1944; s. Caesar George and Piera (Forti) T.; m. Anne Wood Christian, Sept. 8, 1956; children: Martha, Philip, Sara. BA, Harvard U., 1954, MA, 1960, PhD, 1966. Bibliographer European history and lit. Newberry Library, Chgo., 1965-84, curator rare books and manuscripts, head dept. spl. collections, 1970-82, dir. Ctr. Renaissance Studies, 1979-84; curator rare books and spl. collections Meml. Library U. Wis.-Madison, 1984-96; ret., 1996. Lectr. history U. Chgo., 1969—71; vis. prof. U. Ill., Chgo., 1972—73, adj. prof., 1979—84. Co-editor: (series) Corpus Reformatorum Italicorum, 1968-96; editor-in-chief: Bibliographie Internat. de L'Humanisme et de la Renaissance, 1977-82; editor: Italian Reformation Studies in Honor of Laelius Socinus, 1965, (with Anthony Molho) Renaissance Studies in Honor of Hans Baron, 1971, (with Gustav Henningsen) The Inquisition in Early Modern Europe: Studies on Sources and Methods, 1986, The Prosecution of Heresy: Collected Studies on the Inquisition in Early Modern Italy, 1991 (transl. into Italian 1997), Tomasso Sassetti, Il Massacro di San Bartolomeo, 1995, The Italian Reformation of the Sixteenth Century and the Diffusion of Renaissance Culture: A Bibliography of the Secondary Literature (c. 1750-1997), 2000, The correspondence of Roland H. Bainton and Delio Cantimori, 1932-66, 2002; translator: (with Anne Tedeschi) The Cheese and the Worms. The Cosmos of a Sixteenth-Century Miller (Carlo Ginzburg), 1980 (named an Outstanding Acad. Book by Choice mag.), The Night Battles. Witchcraft and Agrarian Cults in the Sixteenth and Seventeenth Centuries (Carlo Ginzburg), 1983, Clues, Myths, and the Historical Method (Carlo Ginzburg), 1989, Hans Urs von Balthasar: A Theological Style (Angelo Scola), 1995, Domenico Scandella Known as Menocchio: His Trials Before the Inquisition (1583-1599) (Andrea Del Col), 1996, The Protestant Reformation in Sixteenth-Century Italy (Salvatore Caponetto), 1999, Books of the Body: Anatomical Ritual and Renaissance Learning (Andrea Carlino), 1999, The Jews in Mussolini's Italy (Michele Sarfatti), 2006 (named an Outstanding Acad. Book by Choice mag.); mem. editl. com.: Index des Livres Interdits (Sherbrooke), Collected Works of Erasmus (Toronto); mem. editl. bd.: Studi e Testi per la Storia Religiosa Italiana del '500 (Florence), The Peter Martyr Libr. (Kirksville, Mo.), Inquisizione e Società (Trieste); contbr. articles to profl. jours. Served with U.S. Army, 1954-56. Grantee Am. Philos. Soc., 1961; grantee NEH, 1967; Old Dominion fellow Harvard U. Ctr. Renaissance Studies, Florence, Italy, 1967-68; fellow Inst. Research in Humanities, U. Wis.-Madison, 1976-77; Huntington Library fellow, 1984. Mem. Am. Soc. Reformation Research (pres. 1972), Renaissance Soc. Am. (exec. bd. 1971-96), 16th Century Studies Conf. (pres. 1987), Archive of Congregation for the Doctrine of the Faith (Vatican City; pres. 1999-2002, scholarly adv. com.), Univ. Trieste, Congregation for the Doctrine of the Faith (the Vatican), Gen. Adminstrn. for Archives (Rome; pres. scholarly adv. com. for collaborative project to catalogue electronically dispersed Inquisitorial sources, 2004-; Livorno, Italy scholarly adv. com. to plan for 4th centenary of elevation to status of a city, 2004—06), Acad. Ambrosiana (Milan)(elected mem. 2008), Am. Hist. Assn., Am. Cath. Hist. Assn., Renaissance Soc. Am. Home: 57211 Rush Creek Rd Ferryville WI 54628 E-mail: tede@mwt.net.

TEDESCO, BARBARA L., dean, educator; b. Newark, Aug. 15, 1946; d. Guy R. and Evelyn A. Curry; m. Gary L. Thomas; 1 child, Jennifer L. PhD, Seton Hall U., South Orange, NJ, 2000. Assoc. dean NJ. Inst. Tech., Newark, 1986—. Home: 7 Vosseler Ct West Orange NJ 07052 Office: NJ Inst Tech Sch Mgmt Newark NJ 07102 Business E-Mail: tedesco@adm.njit.edu.

TEDESCO, MARK J., career military officer, physician; BS, Tufts U., Medford, Mass., 1980, MD, 1986; MPH in in Health Care Mgmt., Harvard Sch. Pub. Health, 1994. Diplomate Am. Bd. Family Medicine, Am. Bd. Preventive Medicine. Family practice residency, Ft. Belvoir, Va., 1986—89; aerospace medicine residency Brooks Air Force Base, San Antonio, 1994—95; various assignments as Army physician including, treatment platoon leader 24th Inf. Divsn. Saudi Arabia & Iraq, flight surgeon 224th Army Mil. Intelligence Battalion, flight surgeon Air Station Savannah at Hunter Army Airfield Ga.; transfer to USCG, 1997, comd. as. rear adm., various positions including med. readiness br. chief, Coast Guard Hdqs. Washington, med. dir. ops. for disaster response teams World Trade Ctr. Disaster site, 2001, chief operational medicine & med. readiness divsn., Coast Guard Hdqs., then chief med. officer, dir. Health, Safety & Work- Life, 2007—. Decorated Army Expert Field Medic Badge, Meritorious Svc. medal (3); named US Army Aerospace Medicine Specialist of Yr., 1997, USPHS Physician Exec. of Yr., 2005. Office: Coast Guard Hdqs 2100 Second St SW Washington DC 20593 Business E-Mail: mark.tedesco@uscg.mil.*

TEDFORD, CHARLES FRANKLIN, biophysicist; b. Lawton, Okla., June 26, 1928; s. Charles E. and Loula B. (Waters) Tedford; m. Julie Reme Sauret, Sept. 15, 1951; children: Gary Franklin, Mark Charles, Philip John. BS with distinction in Chemistry, S.W. Tex. State U., 1950; MS, 1954; postgrad. in radiobiology, Reed Coll., 1957; postgrad. in biophysics, U. Calif., Berkeley, 1961—63. With USN, 1945—47; commd. ensign., 1950; advanced through grades to capt., 1968; biochemist US Naval Hosp., San Diego, 1953—54, US Naval Biol. Lab., Oakland, Calif., 1954—56; sr. instr., radiation safety officer Nuclear, Biol. and Chem. Warfare Def. Sch., Treasure Island, Calif., 1956—61; asst. chief nuclear medicine div. Navy Med. Sch., Bethesda, Md., 1963—66; adminstrv. program mgr. radiation safety br. Bur. Medicine and Surgery, Washington, 1966—72; dir. radiation safety and health physics program Navy Regional Med. Ctr., San Diego, 1972—74; mgr. Navy Regional Med. Clinic, Seattle, 1974—78; ret., 1978; dir. radiation health unit Ga. Dept. Human Resources, Atlanta, 1978—79; dir. Ariz. Radiation Regulatory Agy., Tempe, 1979—91; chief Radiological Health Prog., Juneau, Alaska, 1991—93; ret., 1993; cons., 1993—. Elected chmn. Conf. Radiation Program Dirs., 1987. Contbr. articles to profl. jours. Decorated Legion of Merit, Meritorious Svcs. medal; recipient Ariz. Southwestern Low Level Radioactive Waste Compact Commr., 1990; named Ariz. Adminstr. of Yr. award, Ariz. Adminstrs. Assn., 1988. Mem.: Am. Nuclear Soc., Health Physics Soc. Home Phone: 480-860-0608.

TEDFORD, JACK NOWLAN, III, construction executive, small business owner; b. Reno, Jan. 1, 1943; s. Jack Nowlan Jr. and Elizabeth (Kolhoss) T.; m. Nancy Joanne Stiles, Feb. 27, 1971; children: Jack Nowlan IV, James Nathan. BS, U. Nev., 1966, MBA, 1969. Bus. mgr. Los Angeles Bapt. Coll., Newhall, Calif., 1969-71; v.p. Jack N. Tedford, Inc., Fallon, Nev., 1971-98; owner/broker Tedford Realty, Fallon,

1974-94; owner/mgr. Tedford Bus. Systems, Fallon, 1978-94; pres. JNT, Inc., Incline Village, Nev., 1994—. Pres., Jack N. Tedford, Inc., 1998—. Author numerous computer programs. Mem. Selective Svc. Local Bd., Fallon, 1971-76; chmn. City of Fallon Bd. Adjustment, 1972-95, chmn. Churchill Co. Reps., Fallon, 1976-80; mem. ctrl. com. Nev. Reps., 1976-2002; del. Nat. Conv., Detroit, 1980, Dallas, 1984; former coun. ofcls. Western Nev. Devel. Dist.; former treas. Lahontan Valley Environ. Alliance. Mem. Assn. Gen. Contractors (past pres., former v.p., treas. Nev. chpt., dir.), Nat. Bd. Realtors, State Bd. Realtors, Incline Village Bd. Realtors, CEDA Bus. Coun. (bd. dirs. 1991-97), Rotary (bd. dirs. 1980-81), Master's Coll. (bd. dirs. 1971-95), Slavic Gospel Assn. (bd. dirs.), Nat. Assn. Gen. Contractors (past bd. dirs. open shop com., closely held bus. com.), Fellowship of Cos. for Christ Internat. Republican. Baptist. Avocations: computers, golf. Home and Office: 1995 Champion Hills Dr Reno NV 89523 Business E-Mail: jnt@jntinc.com.

TEDROW, JOHN CHARLES FREMONT, soils educator; b. Rockwood, Pa., Apr. 21, 1917; s. John Wesley and Emma Grace (Younkin) T.; m. Mary Jane Lough, Mar. 20, 1943 (dec. Mar. 1991); children: John Charles Fremont, Thomas Lough (dec.). BS, Pa. State U., 1939; MS, Mich. State U., 1940; PhD, Rutgers U., 1950. Jr. soil technologist Dept. Agr., 1941-42, soil scientist, 1946-47; instr. Rutgers U., New Brunswick, N.J., 1947-50, asst. prof., 1950-53, assoc. prof., 1953-57, prof. soils, 1957—73, prof. II, soils, 1973—84, prof. emeritus, 1984—. Cons. N.S. Research Found., 1949—; sr. pedologist Boston U., 1953—; prin. investigator Arctic Inst. N.Am., Washington, 1955-68, NSF, 1961-62, Atomic Energy Commn., Washington, 1961-63; cons. to govt. and industry. Author: (with R.C. Murray) Forensic Geology: Earth Sciences and Criminal Investigation, 1974, Soils of the Polar Landscapes, 1977, (with K.A. Linell) Soil and Permafrost Surveys in the Arctic, 1981, Soils of New Jersey, 1986, (with R.C. Murray) Forensic Geology, 1991; editor in chief Soil Science, 1968-79; editor: Antarctic Soils and Soil Forming Processes, 1966. Lt. USN, 1942—46. Recipient Lindback Research award Rutgers U., 1978, Antarctic Service medal. Fellow Am. Soc. Agronomy, Soil Sci. Soc. Am., Arctic Inst. N.Am.; mem. Internat. Soc. Soil Sci., Am. Geophys. Union, Sigma Xi, Alpha Zeta (hon.), Phi Mu Delta. Achievements include investigation of polar soils in Alaska, Can., Greenland, Scandinavia, Siberia and Antarctica. Home: 5 Bluebird Ct Edison NJ 08820-3677 Office: Rutgers U Ecology Evolution and Natural Resources PO Box 231 New Brunswick NJ 08903-0231 Home Phone: 732-549-0819; Office Phone: 732-932-1588.

TEE, REBEKAH C., art educator; b. Woodsville, NH, Mar. 6, 1972; d. Lawrence E. and Susan A. Tee. MusB, Stephen F. Austin State U., Nacogdoches, Tex., 1997. Secondary art cert. Tex. Phys. edn. aide Aldine Ind. Sch. Dist., Houston, 1994—96, art tchr., volleyball coach, 1997—99; art tchr., soccer coach Clear Creek Ind. Sch. Dist., League City, Tex., 1999—2006; founding art tchr. KIPP, Inc., Houston, 2006—. Sponsor, tchr. Art Club/Nat. Art, Houston, 1998—; creator art scholarship and comty. svc. art clubs various schs. Mem.: Houston Area Art Suprs., Tex. Art Edn. Assn., Nat. Art Edn. Assn., Parents of Prodigies Art Booster Club (founder 2002). Avocations: running, bicycling, rollerblading, attending art openings, creating films and art. Home: PO Box 132098 Houston TX 77219 Office: KIPP Inc 10711 Kipp Way Dr Houston TX 77009

TEECE, MARK A., chemistry professor; PhD, Bristol U., Eng. Asst. prof. SUNY-ESF, Syracuse, NY, 1999—2005, assoc. prof., 2005—. Office: SUNY-ESF 1 Forestry Dr Syracuse NY 13210

TEEGALA, BRAHMANANDA REDDY, electrical engineer, educator; b. Narpala, India, May 16, 1979; s. Aswartha Reddy and Nallamma Teegala. B in Elec. and Electronics Engring., G. Pulla Reddy Engring. Coll., Kurnool, India, 2001; ME, Osmania U., Hyderabad, India, 2003; PhD in Elec. Engring., Jawaharlal Nehru Tech. U., Anantapur, 2008. Asst. prof. G. Pulla Reddy Engring. Coll., 2003—07, assoc. prof., 2007—. Presenter in field; coord. elec. workshops; lectr. in field. Contbr. articles to profl. jours. Mem.: Indian Soc. For Tech. Edn. (life). Democrat. Hindu. Achievements include proposal and application of various advanced PWM methods for direct torque controlled induction motor drives for reduced steady state ripples in current, torque, and flux; research in direct torque control of induction motor. Avocations: reading, music. Home: Beside AG Bank Narpala Andhra Pradesh Anantapur 515425 India Office: G Pulla Reddy Engineering College Nandyal Road Andhra Pradesh Kurnool 518002 India Personal E-mail: tbnr@rediffmail.com. Business E-Mail: teegalabrahma@rediffmail.com.

TEEGEN, HILDY, dean, business educator; BA in Latin American Studies and Internat. Bus. and Fin., U. Tex., Austin, 1987, PhD in Internat. Bus., 1993. Instr. internat. bus. U. Tex., Austin, 1991—92; asst. prof. mktg. Coll. of William & Mary, Williamsburg, Va., 1996; asst. prof. George Washington U., Washington, 1996—2000, assoc. prof. internat. bus. and internat. affairs, 2000—05, prof., 2005—07, dir. Ctr. Internat. Bus. Edn. and Rsch. (CIBER), 2006—07; dean, USC Ednl. Found. chaired prof. internat. bus. Darla Moore Sch. Bus., U. SC, Columbia, 2007—. Bd. mem. Palmetto Inst. Co-author: US Economic Sanctions: Philosophy and Efficacy, 2001, Case Studies of Economic Sanctions: The Chinese, Cuban and Iranian Experiences, 2003; co-editor: Globalization and NGOs: Transforming Business, Governments and Society, 2003, NGOs and the Millennium Development Goals: Citizen Action to Reduce Poverty, 2007; contbr. articles to profl. jours. Bd. mem. United Way of the Midlands of SC, Ctr. Internat. Private Enterprise, Washington; mem. Midlands Bus. Leadership Group, SC. Liberty Fellow, 2008. Mem.: Assn. for Advancement of Collegiate Schs. of Bus. (mem. task force Globalization of Bus. Edn.), Bus. Assn. of Latin Am. Studies, Acad. Mgmt., Acad. Internat. Bus. Office: Moore Sch Bus U SC 1705 College Street Columbia SC 29208 Office Phone: 803-777-3176. Office Fax: 803-777-9123. E-mail: teegen@moore.sc.edu.*

TEEGUARDEN, DENNIS EARL, forest economist, educator; b. Gary, Ind., Aug. 21, 1931; s. Gary Leon and Mary Dessa (Purciful) T.; m. Sally Annette Gleason, Dec. 23, 1954; children: Jason Earl, Julie Annette, Justin Gary. BS in Forestry with honors, Mich. Tech. U., Houghton, 1953; M.Forestry, U. Calif., Berkeley, 1958, PhD in Agrl. Econs. (Bidwell research fellow 1962-63), 1964. Rsch. aid U.S. Forest Service, 1957; asst. rsch. specialist U. Calif., Berkeley, 1958-63, mem. faculty, 1963-91, prof. forestry econs. Sch. Forestry, 1963-91, S.J. Hall prof. forest econs., 1989-91, prof. emeritus, 1991—, chmn. dept. forestry and resource mgmt., 1978-86, acting dir. forest products lab., 1987-88, assoc. dean for acad. affairs, 1990-92, assoc. dean rsch. and extension, 1992-93. Mem. Calif. Commn. on Agr. and Higher Edn., 1993-95, com. scientists Dept. Agr., 1977-80; cons. in field; mem. adv. bd. U. Calif. Forest Products Lab., 1994-98; mem. adv. coun. Alberta Heritage Found. for Sci. and Engring. Rsch., 2001-03. Co-author: Forest Resource Management: Decision-Making Principles and Cases, 1979; contbr. articles to profl. jours. Trustee Mich. Tech. Fund, Mich. Tech. U., Houghton, 1994-2004, life trustee, 2004—. Lt. USNR, 1953-57, Korea. Recipient Outstanding Alumnus award Mich. Tech. U., 1993, Berkeley citation U. Calif., Berkeley, 1994, Outstanding Svc. award Mich. Tech. Alumni Assn., 2007; grantee U.S. Forest Svc., Bur. Land Mgmt.; named to Honor Acad. Sch. Forestry and Wood Products, Mich. Tech. U., 1995. Fellow Soc. Am. Foresters; mem. Western Forest Economists, Calif. Water Fowl Assn. Home: 4732 Westwood Ct Richmond CA 94803-2441 Office: U Calif Coll Natural Resources Berkeley CA 94720-0001

TEEHEE, KIMBERLY KAY, federal official; b. Chgo., 1968; BA in Polit. Sci., Northeastern State U., Tahlequah, Okla.; JD, U. Iowa Coll. Law, Iowa City. Law clk., divsn. law and justice Cherokee Nation Okla.; dep. dir. Native Am. outreach Dem. Nat. Com.; dir. Native Am. outreach Pres. Clinton's Presdl. Inauguration Com.; sr. advisor, Rep. Dale Kildee US House of Reps., Washington, 1998—2009; sr. policy advisor Native Am. affairs Domestic Policy Coun. The White House, Washington, 2009—. Tribal mem. Cherokee Nation Okla. Recipient Bur. Nat. Affairs award. Office: The White House Domestic Policy Coun 1600 Pennsylvania Ave NW Washington DC 20500*

TEEM, PAUL LLOYD, JR., bank executive; b. Gastonia, NC, Mar. 10, 1948; s. Paul Lloyd Sr. and Ruth Elaine (Bennett) T. BA, U. N.C., 1970; Cert., Inst. Fin. Edn., Chgo., 1984, Diploma, 1985, Degree of Distinction, 1989. Cert. tchr. N.C., cert. consumer credit exec.; lic. real estate broker; lic. lay Eucharistic minister. Exec. v.p., sec. Citizens South Bank, Gastonia, NC, 1983—; exec. v.p., sec., bd. dirs. Citizens South Fin. Svcs. Inc., Gastonia, 1988—; exec. v.p., sec. Citizens South Holdings, Mut. Holding Co., Gastonia, 1998—2002, Citizens South Banking Corp., Gastonia, 1998—. Bd. dirs. Gastonia Mchts. Assn., Inc., 1981-83; lay reader, lay eucharistic min. Episcopal Ch. Decorated Order Purple Cross, Legion of Honor. Fellow Soc. Cert. Credit Execs.; mem. Nat. Soc. Sons and Daus. of Pilgrims, SAR, Sons of Confederate Vets., Mil. Order of Stars and Bars, Masons (32d degree, bd. dirs., Disting. Svc. award 1987, Gold Honor award 1988, Active Legion of Honor 1989, Order of the Purple Cross of York 1990), Shriners, KT, Royal Order of Scotland, Hon. Order Ky. Cols., Phi Alpha Theta. Democrat. Avocation: genealogy. Home: 1208 Poston Cir Gastonia NC 28054-4634 Office: Citizens South Bank PO Box 2249 Gastonia NC 28053-2249 Office Phone: 704-884-2262. Business E-Mail: paul.teem@citizenssouth.com.

TEEMANT, MELANIE J., middle school educator; BS in Elem Edn., Univ. Nev., Las Vegas; MS student in Ednl. Leadership, Nova Southeastern Univ. Tchr. Clark County Sch. Dist., 1997—, Wengert Elem. Sch., Las Vegas, 1997—2001; reading tchr. Bob Miller Mid. Sch., Henderson, Nev., 2001—. Named Nev. Tchr. of Yr., 2007. Office: Bob Miller Middle Sch 2400 Cozy Hills Dr Henderson NV 89052 E-mail: mteemantx6@msn.com.

TEEPE, CHRISTOPHER JOHN, literature and language professor; b. Huntington, NY, July 23, 1976; s. Wilhelm and Patricia Teepe. PhD, U. Buffalo, 2006. Vis. prof. English U. Albany, NY, 2006—07; lectr. English Skidmore Coll., Saratoga Springs, 2007—08; vis. asst. prof. English Siena Coll., Loudonville, 2008—. Mem.: Phi Kappa Phi. Independent. Home: 395 State St Albany NY 12210 Office: Siena Coll 515 Loudonville Rd Loudonville NY 11211 Personal E-mail: christeepe@hotmail.com. Business E-Mail: cteepe@siena.edu.

TEER, DIANE, food products executive; B, Univ. Western Ontario; MBA, McMaster Univ. Mgmt. positions Procter & Gamble, Nabob Coffee Co., Kraft Canada; sr. mgmt. positions Campbell Soup Co., 1996—2005, v.p. gen. mgr. beverage div., v.p. No. Am. soup innovation, pres. new growth div. & mktg. services; pres. culinary products ConAgra Foods, Omaha, 2006—08, pres. consumer frozen foods, 2006—. Bd. dir. Am. Frozen Food Inst., 2006—. Office: ConAgra Foods 1 ConAgra Dr Omaha NE 68102-5001

TEERLINK, J(OSEPH) LELAND, real estate developer; b. Salt Lake City, July 16, 1935; s. Nicholas John and Mary Luella (Love) T.; m. Leslie Dowdle, Nov. 5, 1975; children: Steven, David, Andrew, Suzanne, Benjamin. Student, U. Utah, Salt Lake City, 1953-55. Sales rep. Eastman Kodak Co., Salt Lake City, 1960-69; founder Graphic Systems, Inc., Salt Lake City, 1969-82, pres., 1969-79, chmn. bd., 1979-82; founder Graphic Ink Co., Salt Lake City, 1973, pres., 1975-79, chmn. bd., 1979-82; founder G.S.I. Leasing Co., Salt Lake City, 1975, pres., 1975-82; chmn. bd. Graphic Sys. Holding Co., Inc., Salt Lake City, 1978-82; dir. leasing and acquisitions Terra Industries, Inc., real estate developers, 1982—2007, ptnr., 2007—; ptnr. to GM Life In Focus, 2007; ptnr. and Cons. Spotlight Home Tours. Bd. dirs. ARC, Salt Lake City, 1979-82; co-founder, dir. Hope Living Ctr. Found. for Mothers and Children, 1993-99; vice consulate of the Netherlands for Utah, 1977-92; mem. active corps of execs., SBA, 1979-83; adv. bd. House of Hope Mothers and Children Utah Alcoholism Found., 1992-94. Recipient Masters award Salt Lake Bd. Realtors, 1993; named Small Businessman of Yr. for Utah, SBA, 1978 Mem. Graphic Arts Equipment and Supply Dealers of Am. (dir. 1978-82), Printing Industry of Am., Nat. Assn. Indsl. and Office Parks (pres. Utah chpt. 1986-87), Nat. Fedn. Ind. Businessman, Million Dollar Club (life). Republican. Mem.Lds Ch. Home: 2984 Thackeray Pl Salt Lake City UT 84108-2517 Office: 6975 Union Park Ctr Midvale UT 84047-4135 Home Phone: 801-582-7528; Office Phone: 801-566-6653, 801-699-9928. Business E-Mail: leet@terrautah.com.

TEES, RICHARD CHISHOLM, psychology professor emeritus; b. Montreal, Que., Can., Oct. 31, 1940; s. Ralph Charles and Helen Winnifred (Chisholm) T.; m. Kathleen F. Coleman, Sept. 1, 1962; children: Susan M., Carolyn V. BA, McGill U., 1961; PhD, U. Chgo., 1965. Asst. prof. U. B.C., Vancouver, Canada, 1965-67, assoc. prof., 1969-75, prof. psychology, 1975—, head dept. psychology, 1984—94, 1999—2004, U. B.C. Okanogen transition mgmt. exec., 2004—07, acting dep. vice chancellor, acad. v.p., 2006. Rsch. prof. U. Sussex, Brighton, Eng., 1972-73, 77-78; chmn. grant selection panel Nat. Scis. and Engring. Rsch. Coun. Can., Ottawa, 1993-96, B.C. Health Care Rsch. Found., Vancouver, 1984-87; chmn. studentship com. Med. Rsch. Coun., Ottawa, 1985-92; chmn. Can. Coun. Dept. Psychology, 1987-93; mem. B.C. Degree Quality Assessment Bd., 2006—; chair bd. dirs. Cetacea Networks Corp., 2005—. Author: (with Kolb) Cerebral Cortex of the Rat, 1990; mem. editl. bd. Can. Jour. Exptl. Psychology, 1975-84, 87—; contbr. articles to profl. jours., chpts. to books. Rsch. fellow Killam Found., 1972-73, 77-78; Rsch. fellow Can. Coun., 1972-73. Fellow APA, Am. Psychol. Soc., Can. Psychol. Assn.; mem. Soc. for Neurosci., Psychonomic Soc., Can. Soc. Brain, Behaviour, and Cognitive Sci. (pres. 1997-98, Richard C. Tees Leadership award, 2004), U. B.C. Senate, Nat. Ctr. Excellence Can. Stroke Network. Office: U BC Dept Psychology Vancouver BC Canada V6T 1Z4 Home: 4506 W 14th Ave Vancouver BC V6R 2Y4 Canada Home Phone: 604-224-6030. Business E-Mail: rtees@psych.ubc.ca.

TEESON, DOUGLAS H., museum director; M in Ocean Engring., U. RI; M in Mgmt. Sci., Mass. Inst. Tech.; attended, Harvard U. Inst. Pres. Mystic Seaport; supt. USCG. Office: CT Mystic Seaport 75 Greenmanville Ave PO Box 6000 Mystic CT 06355-0990

TEETERS, NANCY HAYS, economist; b. Marion, Ind., July 29, 1930; d. S. Edgar and Mabel (Drake) Hays; m. Robert Duane Teeters, June 7, 1952; children: Ann, James, John. AB in Econs., Oberlin Coll., 1952, LLD, 1979; MA in Econs., U. Mich., 1954, postgrad., 1956—57, LLD (hon.), 1983, Bates Coll., 1981, Mt. Holyoke Coll., 1983. Tchg. fellow U. Mich., Ann Arbor, 1954—55, instr., 1956—57, U. Md. Overseas, Germany, 1955—56; staff economist govt. fin. sect. Bd. Govs. of FRS, Washington, 1957—66, mem. bd., 1979—84; economist Bur. Budget, 1966—70; economist (on loan) Coun. Econ. Advs., 1962—63; sr. fellow Brookings Instn., 1970—73; sr. specialist Congl. Rsch. Svc., Library Congress, Washington, 1973—74; asst. dir., chief economist Ho. of Reps. Com. on Budget, 1974—78; v.p., chief economist IBM, Armonk, NY, 1984—90. Author: (with others) Setting National Priorities: The 1972 Budget, 1971, Setting National Priorities: The 1973 Budget, 1972, Setting National Priorities: The 1974 Budget, 1973; contbr. articles to profl. publs. Recipient Comfort Starr award in econs. Oberlin Coll., 1952; Disting. Alumnus award U. Mich., 1980 Mem. Nat. Economists Club (v.p. 1973-74, pres. 1974-75, chmn. bd. 1975-76, gov. 1976-79), Am. Econ. Assn. (com. on status of women 1975-78), Am. Fin. Assn. (dir. 1969-71) Democrat.

TEETS, PETER B., former civilian military employee; b. Feb. 1942; BS, U. Colo., 1963, MS in Applied Math., 1965, DSc (hon.), 1990; MS in Mgmt., MIT, 1978. Engr. Martin Marietta Denver Aerospace, Colo., 1963—70, mgr., Titan IIIC inertial guidance system Colo., 1970—75, program mgr. Transtage Project & dir. Space Systems Colo., 1975—80, v.p. bus. devel. Colo., 1980—82, v.p., gen. mgr. aerospace strategic & launch systems divsn. Colo., 1982—85, pres. Colo., 1985—93, Martin Marietta Space Group, Bethesda, Md., 1993—95; pres., COO Lockheed Martin Info. & Services, Bethesda, Md., 1995—97, Lockheed Martin Corp., Bethesda, Md., 1997—99; under sec. Dept. Air Force, US Dept. Def., Washington, 2001—05, acting sec., 2005; dir. Nat. Reconnaissance Office, Washington, 2001—05. Bd. trustees The Aerospace Corp, El Segundo, Calif., 2005—. Recipient Sloan Fellow Award, W. Stuart Symington award, 2004. Fellow: Am. Astronautical Society, Am. Institute of Aeronautics and Astronautics; mem.: Nat. Acad. Engring.

TEETS, WALTER RALPH, accounting educator; b. Boulder, Colo., Oct. 1, 1950; s. Otis E. and Elsie (Purchase) T.; m. Mary Anne Clougherty; stepchildren: Katherine Kuder, Elizabeth Wierman B in Music Edn., U. Colo., Boulder, 1973; MMus, U. Wis., Madison, 1976; MS in Edn., U. Wis., Whitewater, 1981, MS in Acctg., 1985; PhD, U. Chgo., 1989. Asst. prof. Wash. U., St. Louis, 1986-89, U. Ill., Urbana-Champaign, Ill., 1989-94, Gonzaga U., Spokane, Wash., 1994-99, assoc. prof., 1999—; prof. resident Dept. Profl. Practice, KPMG LLP, 2007—08. Continuing profl. edn. spkr. Gonzaga U., 1996—2009, Wash. Soc. CPAs, numerous others; vis. assoc. prof. U. Notre Dame, 2000. Editor Fin. Reporting Jour., 1998—2002, spl. guest editor Issues in Acctg. Edn., 2001—03, assoc. editor Jour. Derivatives Acctg., 2003—; contbr. articles to profl. jours. Recipient Outstanding Acctg. Educator award Wash. Soc. CPAs, 1998-99; Acad. acctg. fellow Office of Chief Acct., U.S. SEC, 1997-98. Mem. Am. Acctg. Assn. (editor Fin. Reporting Jour. newsletter Fin. Acctg. and Reporting sect. 1998—02), Wash. Soc. CPAs (bd. dirs. Spokane chpt.), K.C. (fin. sec. 1990-93, 99-2003, treas. 2005-07), Govtl. Acctg. Standards Bd. (derivatives acctg. adv. com. mem. 2008-). Avocations: music, cross country skiing, fourwheeling. Office: Gonzaga Univ 502 E Boone Ave Spokane WA 99258-0001 Office Phone: 509-323-3416. Office Fax: 509-323-5811. Business E-Mail: teets@gem.gonzaga.edu.

TEEVAN, JAIME, application developer, researcher; b. Stanford, Calif., Sept. 5, 1976; d. James Ripley and Connie Monroe Teevan; m. Alexander Marliave Hehmeyer, June 15, 2002; 1 child, Griffin Alexander Teevan Hehmeyer. BS, Yale U., New Haven, Conn., 1998; M, MIT, Cambridge, Mass., 2001; student, MIT, 2001—. Financial Technology Option MIT Sloan Sch., 2003. Software engr. Infoseek Corp., Sunnyvale, Calif., 1998—99; rsch. asst. MIT, Cambridge, Mass., 1999—; rsch. intern Microsoft Rsch., Redmond, Wash., 2004. Editor: (book) Personal Information Management, (magazine) CACM Special Issue on Personal Information Management. Grad. student coun. rep. MIT, Cambridge, Mass., 2002—03, inst. rep., faculty com. on the libr. sys., 2003—05. Recipient J. Edward Meeker prize, Yale U., 1995, Bloch prize, 1995, Master's Cup, Timothy Dwight Coll., 1998; Grad. Rsch. fellowship, NSF, 1999—2003. Mem.: Spl. Interest Group on Computer-Human Interaction, Spl. Interest Group on Info. Retrieval, Assn. for Computing Machinery. Achievements include patents pending for systems, methods, and interfaces for providing personalized search and information access; research in personalized search and personal information management. Office: Mass Inst of Tech 32 Vassar St G472 Cambridge MA 02139 E-mail: teevan@mit.edu.

TEFF, JUSTIN SAMUEL, lawyer; b. Washington, Oct. 8, 1976; s. Stephanie K. Teff and Richard T. Dykes (Stepfather). BA, SUNY, Albany, 1998; JD, Albany Law Sch., NY, 2001. Bar: NY 2002. Assoc. atty. Stockton, Barker & Mead, Albany, 2002—06; with Spl. Funds Conservation Com., Albany, 2006—07. Chair, founder First Book - Albany, Albany; dem. ward leader, treas. Ward 11 Dem. Com., 2006—07. Master: Masons. Democrat. Office: Law Office of Ralph M Kirk 146-148 Barrett St Schenectady NY 12305 Home: 397 STATE ST APT N Albany NY 12210-1215 Personal E-mail: justinteff@hotmail.com.

TEFFT, JOHN F., United States Ambassador to Georgia; b. Madison, Wis. m. Mariella Cellitti; children: Christine, Cathleen. BA, Marquette Univ.; MA in History, Georgetown Univ. Various positions to rank of min./counselor US Sr. Fgn. Svc., 1972—; internat. affairs adv. Nat. War Coll., Washington, 2003—04; dep. chief, US Mission to Moscow US Dept. State, 1996—99, charge d'affaires Moscow, 1996—97, US amb. to Lithuania, 2000—03, dep. asst. sec. state European and Eurasian Affairs, 2004—05, US amb. to Georgia, 2005—. Recipient Disting. Honor award, US Dept. State. Office: US Dept State 7060 Tbilisi Pl Washington DC 20521-7060*

TEGNELIA, JAMES A., federal agency administrator; b. Monessen, Pa., 1942; BS in Physics, Georgetown U.; MS in Engring., George Washington U., 1975; PhD in Physics, Catholic U. Am. Supr. rsch. physicist to mgr. US Army Night Vision Lab., 1971—76; asst. under sec., acting. dep. under sec. Office Undersecretary Defense Rsch. Engring. US Dept Def., 1982—85; program mgr. and officer dir. Defense Advance Rsch. Projects Agy., 1976, dep. dir., 1985, acting dir.; v.p. engring. Martin Marietta Corp., v.p. bus. devel. Electronics Group; v.p. bus. devel., Energy and Environment Sector Lockheed Martin Corp., 1995, pres., Advanced Environ. Systems, Inc., 1996—98; exec. v.p., dep. dir. Sandia Nat. Lab., 1993, v.p. defense programs; dir. US Strategic Command Ctr. Combating Weapons Mass Destruction, 2004—, Defense Threat Reduction Agy., Ft. Belvoir, Va., 2004—. Mem. exec. coun., bd. dirs. Albuquerque C. of C., 1994—95; bd. dirs. Anderson Sch. U. N.Mex., Sandia Sci. and Tech. Pk., Tech. Ventures Corp., Laguna Industries, Inc.; bd. adv. George Washington U. Sch. Engring.; chmn. Greater Albuquerque US Saving Bond Campaign, 1995; chmn. State N.Mex. US Savings Bond Campaign, 1996; chmn. Army Sci. Bd.; co-chmn. Nat. Lab. Nat. Security Adv. Panel; campaign chmn. United Way Ctrl. N.Mex., 1996. Served with US Army, 1968—71, one yr. tour

Vietnam. Recipient Bronze Star Medal, Civilian Meritorious Svc. Medal, Sr. Exec. Svc. Meritorious Svc. award. Mem.: Soc. Sigma Xi. Office: Defense Threat Reduction Agy 8725 John J Kingman Rd Stop 6201 Fort Belvoir VA 22060-6201

TEGTMEIER, RONALD EUGENE, physician, surgeon; b. Omaha, Jan. 16, 1943; s. Harvey and Edna T.; children: Anne, Amy; m. Victoria Susan, June 28, 1985; children: Justina Becerra, Gregory Galvan, Mark Tegtmeier. AB, Dartmouth Coll., 1965; BMS, Dartmouth Med. Sch., 1966; MD, Harvard Med. Sch., 1968. Diplomate Am. Bd. Plastic Surgery. Internship in surgery U. Colo. Med. Ctr., Denver, 1968-69, residency in gen. surgery, 1969-70; plastic surgery preceptorship Kingston-upon-Hull, England, 1973; residency in plastic surgery U. Mexico, Albuquerque, 1974-76, fellowship, 1976; plastic surgeon pvt. practice Arvada, Colo., 1977—, Artistic Ctr. for Cosmetic Surgery, Golden, Colo., 1988—. Pres. Clear Creek Valley Med. Soc., Lakewood, Colo., 1983-84; speaker of ho. Colo. Med. Soc., denver, 1985-87. Author: Aesthetica Tapes, 1988—; contbr. numerous papers and publs. to profl. jours. Named Outstanding Bus. Person, Arvada Jaycees, 1978; recipient Arvada Image award, 1981, Denver Post Gallery of Fame award, 1979. Mem. Am. Soc. Plastic and Reconstructive Surgeons, Am. Soc. for Aesthetic Plastic Surgery, Am. Soc. Laser Medicine and Surgery, Am. Acad. of Anti-Aging Medicine. Avocations: scuba, music, skiing, tennis, model trains, flying, aquariums. Home: 103 Bee Creek Ct Georgetown TX 78633-5321

TEHLE, DAVID M., retail executive; b. 1956; BA in Econs., U. Wis., 1978; MBA in Fin. and Acctg., U. Mich., 1980. Fin. acctg. Tex. Instruments, Inc., 1980—86; fin. mgmt. Ryder Sytem, Inc., 1987—93; v.p., CFO Hat Brands, Inc., 1993—96; v.p. fin. divsn. The Stanley Works, 1996—97; exec. v.p., CFO Haggar Corp., 1997—2004, Dollar Gen. Corp., 2004—. Bd. dirs. Jack in the Box, Inc., 2004—. Mem.: Am. Apparel & Footwear Assn. Office: Dollar Gen Corp 100 Mission Ridge Dr Goodlettsville TN 37072 Office Phone: 615-855-4000. Office Fax: 615-855-5180.

TEHOVNIK, EDWARD JOSEPH, neuroscientist; s. John Mlinar and Antonia Tehovnik; m. Arlete Tehovnik, June 26, 2003. PhD, U. Toronto, 1988. Prin. rsch. scientist MIT, Cambridge, 2005—. Contbr. scientific papers. Mem.: Soc. Neurosci. Achievements include development of visual prosthesis for the blind. Office Fax: 617-324-3725.

TEHRANI, FLEUR TAHER, electrical engineer, educator, researcher; b. Tehran, Iran, Feb. 16, 1956; arrived in US, 1984; d. Hassan and Pourandokht (Monfared) Tehrani; m. Akbar E. Torbat, June 16, 1997. BSEE, Sharif U. Tech., Tehran, 1975; DIC in Comm. Engring., Imperial Coll. Sci. and Tech., London, 1977; MSc in Comm. Engring., U. London, 1977, PhD in Elec. Engring., 1981. Registered profl. engr., Calif. Comm. engr. Planning Orgn. Iran, Tehran, 1977—78; lectr. A elec. engring. Robert Gordon's Inst. Tech., Aberdeen, Scotland, 1982—83; lectr. II elec. engring. South Bank U., London, 1983—84; asst. prof. elec. engring. Calif. State U., Fullerton, 1985—91, assoc. prof. elec. engring., 1991—94, prof. elec. engring., 1994—. Vis. assoc. prof. elec. engring. Drexel U., Phila., 1987-88; sys. cons. Telebit Corp., Cupertino. Calif., 1985; engring. cons. PRD, Inc., Dresher, Pa., 1989-92; mem. NASA/Am. Soc. Engring. Edn. summer faculty Jet Propulsion Lab., Calif. Inst. Tech., Pasadena, 1995, 96; dir. pharm. engring. program Calif. State U., Fullerton, 1999-2001 Contbr. articles to profl. jours. Recipient Best Rsch. Manuscript award Assn. for Advancement Med. Instrumentation, 1993, NASA/Am. Soc. Engring. Edn. Recognition award for rsch. contbns., 1995, 96 Fellow: Instn. Engring. and Tech., Inst. Advancement of Engring.; mem.: IEEE (sr.), Assn. Profs. and Scholars Iranian Heritage (pres. 1991—92), Grad. Women in Sci. (life), Women in Sci. and Engring. (chair Calif. State U. chpt. 1990—91), Sigma Delta Epsilon (life). Achievements include patents for biomedical engineering that have been licensed and manufactured worldwide; invention of ventilatory assist devices and adaptive support ventilation-ASV. Avocations: music, literature, poetry, stamp collecting/philately. Office: Calif State U Coll Engring and Computer Sci 800 N State Coll Blvd Fullerton CA 92831-3547 Business E-Mail: ftehrani@fullerton.edu.

TEHRANY, ARMIN M., orthopedic surgeon, educator; b. Phila., Mar. 4, 1970; s. Jamshid M. and Shala R. Tehrany; m. Valerie Laury, Oct. 27, 2002; children: Jacqueline, Natalie. BA, CUNY, Bklyn., 1991; MD, NYU, 1994. Orthopedic resident Lenox Hill Hosp., NYC, 1994—99; shoulder arthroscopy fellow Baylor Coll. Medicine, San Antonio, 1999—2000; orthopedic attending Richmond Orthopedic Assocs., SI, NY, 2000—; asst. clin. prof. dept. orthop. surgery Mt. Sinai Sch. Medicine, NY; attending orthop. surgeon Richmond Orthop. Assocs., 2000—07, Staten Island Med. Group, NY, 2000—07. Master instr. Arthroscopy Assn. N.Am., Rosemont, Ill., 2001—. Contbr. chapters to books, articles to publs. Bd. dir. NYSSOS; with AANA Young Mems. Task Force, AANA Comm. Com.; adv. bd. NYCMS Young Physicians.; bd govs. Poly Prep Country Day Sch. Recipient 2d pl., Isakos, 2001. Mem.: NY U. Sch. Medicine Alumni Assn., Richmond County Med. Soc., NY County Med. Soc., Medical State Soc. NY, NY State Soc. Orthop. Surgeons, Am. Orthopedic Soc. Sports Medicine, Internat. Soc. Arthroscopy, Knee Surgery, and Orthopaedic Sprots Medicine, Arthroscopy Assn. N.Am., Am. Acad. Orthopedic Surgeons. Avocations: tennis, guitar. Office: 515 Madison Ave New York NY 10022 Business E-Mail: armin@tehrany.com.

TEICH, MALVIN CARL, electrical engineering educator; b. NYC, May 4, 1939; s. Sidney R. and Loretta K. Teich SB in Physics, MIT, 1961; MSEE, Stanford U., 1962; PhD in Quantum Electronics, Cornell U., 1966. Research scientist MIT Lincoln Lab., Lexington, Mass., 1966-67; prof. engring. sci. Columbia U., NYC, 1967-96, prof. emeritus, 1996—, chmn. dept. elec. engring., 1978-80, mem. Columbia Radiation Lab., faculty applied physics dept. NYC; prof. elec. computer engring., biomed. engring., physics Boston U., 1995—. Mem. Photonics Ctr., Boston U., also Ctr. Adaptive Sys., Hearing Rsch. Ctr.; mem. sci. bd. Inst. Physics, Czech Acad. Scis., Prague. Author: (with B.E.A. Saleh) Fundamentals of Photonics, 1991, (with S.B. Lowen) Fractal Based Point Processes; dep. editor Quantum Optics, 1988-92; bd. editors Jour. Visual Comm. and Image Representation, 1989-92, Jemná Mechanika a Optika, 1994—; contbr. articles to profl. jours.; patentee in field; expert in patent and trade secret litigation. Recipient Citation Classic award Inst. for Sci. Info., 1981; Meml. Gold medal of Palacky U., Czech Republic, 1992; Guggenheim Meml. Found. fellow, 1973. Fellow AAAS, IEEE (Browder J. Thompson Meml. prize 1969, Morris E. Leeds award 1997), Optical Soc. Am. (editl. adv. panel Optics Letters 1977-79), Am. Phys. Soc., Acoustical Soc. Am.; mem. Sigma Xi, Tau Beta Pi. Office: Boston U Dept Elec and Computer Engr 8 Saint Mary's St Boston MA 02215-2421 Office Phone: 617-353-1236. Business E-Mail: teich@bu.edu.

TEICHER, HENRY EARL, retired education educator; b. Jersey City, July 9, 1922; s. Leo and Anna Binn Teicher; m. Anne Severin, Aug. 14, 1962; 1 child, Rikke Jordahn. BA, State U. Iowa, 1946; MA, Columbia U., 1947, PhD, 1950. From asst. prof. to prof. Purdue U., West Lafayette, Ind., 1951—67; asst. prof. Stanford U., Palo Alto, Calif., 1955—56; assoc. prof. NYU, NYC, 1960—62; prof. Columbia U., NYC, 1967—68, Rutgers U., New Brunswick, NJ, 1968—93; ret., 1993. Cons. Radio Corp. Am., Indpls., 1967. Author: Probability Theory: Independence, 1977, Interchangeability, 1987, Martingales, 1997; contbr. articles to profl. jours. With US Army, 1943—46. Fellow: Inst. Math. Statis.; mem.: Phi Beta Kappa. Avocations: reading, music. Home: 6510 City Pl Edgewater NJ 07020

TEICHER, MORTON IRVING, social worker, anthropologist, educator; b. NYC, Mar. 10, 1920; s. Sam and Celia (Roth) T.; m. Mildred Adler, Oct. 4, 1941; children: Phyllis Margaret, Oren Jonathan. BS in Social Sci., CCNY, 1940; MSW, U. Pa., Phila., 1942; PhD, U. Toronto, 1956. Chief social worker in New Eng. VA, 1946-48; chief social worker Toronto Psychiat. Hosp., 1948—56; asst. prof., clin. tchr. U. Toronto, 1948-56; cons. Oppenheimer Coll., No. Rhodesia, Zambia, 1962-63; dean, prof. Yeshiva U. Sch. Social Work, 1956-72; prof. U. N.C. Sch. Social Work, Chapel Hill, 1972-81, 83-85, dean, 1972-81, adj. prof. dept. anthropology, 1972-85, dean emeritus, 1985—; prof. sociology and psychiatry, dir. U. Miami Ctr. on Aging, Coral Gables, 1981-83; instr. Fla. Internat. U. Elders Inst., 1987-88; faculty mentor Walden U., 1992—. Seminar assoc. creativity in sci. NYU, 1959-73; cons. Bar Ilan U., Israel, 1965-69, VA, 1965-69; cons., vis. prof. Henrietta Szold Inst., Jerusalem, 1975; preceptor Ctrl. Inst. Mgmt., Sr. Civil Svc., Israel, 1975; external examiner U. Zambia, 1968-69; cons. in field, 1950—; cons. U. W.I., 1982; chmn. U.S. com. Internat. Coun. Social Welfare, 1978-79; mem. adminstrv. bd. Sch. Pub. Health, U. N.C., 1974-79; mem. bioethics com. Mt. Sinai Hosp., Miami, 2007—. Author: Windigo Psychosis, 1960, Looking Homeward: A Thomas Wolfe Photo Album, 1993; co-author Distant Partners, 1990; sr. editor Inside Books, 1988-89; co-editor: Reaching the Aged, Data-Based Planning in the Field of Aging, 1982; book rev. editor: Jour. Jewish Communal Service, 1961-68, Jewish Floridian, 1982-86; mem. editorial bd. Human Orgn., 1963-66, Jour. Am. Soc. Cybernetics, 1970-72, Ednl. Gerontology, 1978-84; book reviewer South Fla. Jewish Jour., Nat. Jewish Post and Opinion, Jerusalem Post, Libr. Jour., Pubs. Weekly; also contbr. numerous articles to profl. jours., books. Rsch. chmn. Westchester Dem. Com., 1958-62; bd. dirs. Lake Success Capital Corp., 1967-71; trustee Wurzweiler Found., 1966-90, Coler Found., 1970-72; participant Fla. Gov.'s Challenge Program, 1981; exec. sec. Nat. Conf. Jewish Communal Svc., 1968-70; mem. exec. com. Miami chpt. Am. Jewish Com., 1981-83, mem.-at-large nat. exec. coun., 1980-82; bd. dirs. N.Y. Social Work Recruiting Ctr., 1960-70; mem. policy bd. Carolina Population Ctr., 1973-77; bd. dirs. Internat. Conf. Jewish Communal Svc., 1965-85, Hillel, U. Miami, 1981-83, Beth David Synagogue, Miami, 1991-2005; pres. Durham-Chapel Hill Jewish Fedn., 1980; mem. planning and budgeting com. Project Renewal Commn., Miami Jewish Fedn., 1981-2008; adv. coun. Sch. Social Work Barry U., 1986-2000; mem. ethics com. Miami Jewish Home and Hosp. for Aged, 1997—. grant application reviewer, Children's Trust, Miami, 1st lt. AUS, 1942-46, CBI. Recipient Disting. Alumnus cert. U. Pa., 1979, Rita Turner award Walden U., 1996; Louis Round Wilson Libr. fellow U. N.C., 1995—. Fellow Am. Anthropol. Assn.; mem. AAUP, Am. Assn. Ret. Persons (v.p. South Miami Beach chpt. 1992), Acad. Cert. Social Workers, Nat. Assn. Social Workers (chmn. Westchester chpt. 1960-62, mem. commn. ethics 1964-67, mem. exec. com. Ea. N.C. chpt. 1972-74, chmn. profl. advancement travel com. 1980-83), Thomas Wolfe Soc. (dir. 1981—, v.p. 1985-87, pres. 1987-91, Citation of Merit 1992). Anthrop. field work among the Eskimo and Iroquois; tour leader to internat. social welfare confs. in Athens, Helsinki, Nairobi, The Hague, San Juan, Jerusalem, Hong Kong, and Brighton, Eng. Home: Jockey Club III # 1851 11111 Biscayne Blvd Miami FL 33181-3404 Business E-Mail: morton.teicher@waldenu.edu.

TEICHER, OREN JONATHAN, trade association executive; b. Toronto, Can., Aug. 7, 1949; arrived in US, 1956; s. Morton Irving and Mildred (Adler) Teicher; m. Alison Eden Greene, June 20, 1976; children: Carrie Lee, Jessica Anne, Zachary Saul. BA in Pub. Affairs, George Washington U., 1972. Adminstrv. asst. US House of Reps., Washington, 1974-80; dir. corp. comm. March of Dimes Birth Defects Found., White Plains, NY, 1980-84; exec. dir. Americans for Constl. Freedom, NYC, 1987-90; assoc. exec. dir. Am. Booksellers Assn., Tarrytown, NY, 1990-95, dir. govt. affairs, 1995-97, pres., COO, 1997—2009, CEO, 2009—. Founding pres. Am. Booksellers Found. for Free Expression, 1990—98; chmn. Media Coalition, NYC, 1992—94. Trustee White Plains Libr., 1995—2000; del. Dem. Nat. Conv., 1992, 1996. Jewish. Office: ABA 828 S Broadway Tarrytown NY 10591-6602 Office Phone: 914-591-2665. Business E-Mail: oren@bookweb.org.*

TEICHLER, STEPHEN LIN, lawyer; b. Charleston, W.Va., Jan. 30, 1952; s. Alfred H. and Marjorie R. (Dunbar) Teichler; m. Dana Ruth Hegerle, Aug. 6, 1977; children: Adam Reed, Ryan Stephen. BA, U. Va., 1974, JD, 1977. Bar: Va. 1977, DC 1979, US Supreme Ct., Supreme Ct. Va., US Ct. Appeals 1st, 2nd, 4th, 5th, 6th, 11th & Fed. Circuits, US Dist. Ct. DC, US Dist. Ct. Ea. Dist. Va. Atty. Dept. Air Force Office of Gen. Counsel, Washington, 1977-80; assoc. Baker & Botts LLP, Washington, 1980—88, ptnr., 1988—95, Metzger, Hollis, Gordon & Alprin, Washington, 1995-97, Duane Morris LLP, Washington, 1997—, chair firm energy and resources practice group, 2003—. Capt. USAF, 1977-80. Mem.: Energy Bar Assn., Va. State Bar Assn., DC Bar. Lutheran. Office: Duane Morris LLP 505 9th St NW Ste 1006 Washington DC 20004 Office Phone: 202-776-7830. Office Fax: 202-776-7801. Business E-Mail: slteichler@duanemorris.com.

TEICHLER, ULRICH CHRISTIAN, higher education educator, researcher; b. July 23, 1942; s. Johannes and Erika (Petersen) T.; m. Yoko Urata; children: Nils-Erik Shinichiro, Matthias Tim Yoshio. Diplom-Soziologe, Free U. Berlin, 1968; PhD, U. Bremen, 1975; D (hon.), U. Turku, Finland, 2006. Rsch. fellow Max-Planck Inst. Ednl. Rsch., Berlin, 1968-78; guest rschr. Nat. Inst. Ednl. Rsch., Tokyo, 1970-72; prof. for rsch. on higher edn. and work U. Kassel, Hessen, Germany, 1978—, v.p., 1980-82, dir. internat. ctr. higher edn. rsch., 1978—. Fellow Netherlands Inst. for Advanced Study, Wassenaar, 1985-86; vis. prof. Sch. Edn. and Social Policy Northwestern U., Evanston, Ill., 1986-92; Japan SAP fellow Nagoya U., 1992; prof. Coll. Europe, Bruges, 1994-96, Hiroshima U., 2004; vis. rsch. prof. Open U., 2007—. Author: Bibliography on Japanese Education, 1974, Theologie und gesellschaftliche Praxis, 1974, Der Arbeitsmarkt für Akademiker in Japan, 1975, Geschichte und Struktur des japanischen Hochschulwesens, 1975, Das Dilemma der modernen Bildungsgesellschaft, 1976, Admission to Higher Ed. in the US, 1978, Die neuen Beamtenhochschulen, 1980, Higher Ed. and the Needs of Soc., 1981, Der Arbeitsmarkt für Hochschulabsolventen, 1981, Gesamthochschule-Erfahrungen, Hemnisse, Zielwandel, 1981, Bildung und Beschäftigung, 1981, Beispiele praxisorientierten Studiums, 1981, Implementation of Higher Education Reforms: The German Gesamthochschule, 1981, Higher Ed. and the Labour Market in the Fed. Republic of Germany, 1982, Hochschulzertifikate und betriebliche Einstellungspraxis, 1984, Convergence of Growing Variety: The Changing Organisation of Studies, 1988, Auslandsstudium im Vergleich, 1988, Changing Patterns of the Higher Education System, 1988, Europäische Hochschulsysteme, 1990, The Impact of Study Abroad Programmes on Students and Graduates, 1990, Experiences and Careers of Science and Engineering Fellows Supported by the European Community, 1990, Bestand und Perspektiven der Weiterbildung, 1991, Learning in Europe, 1991, Handbook of Higher Education Diplomas in Europe, 1992, Transition to Work, 1994, Berufsbild der Lehrenden und Forschenden an Hochschulen, 1995, Study Abroad and Early Career, 1996, Bestand und Entwicklungsrichtungen der Weiterbildung in Schleswig-Holstein, 1996, The ERASMUS Experience, 1997, Integrating Europe through Co-operation Among Universities, 1997, European Research Fellowships 1987-1993, 1997, Der Übergang von Bildungs- zum Beschäftigungssystem in Japan, 2000, Hochschule und Arbeitswelt, 2003, Graduados y Empleo, 2005, Hochschulstrukturen im Umbruch, 2005, Hochschulsysteme und Hochschulpolitik, 2005, Reformas de los Modelos de la Educación Superior, 2006, Yôroppa no Kyôiku Kaikaku, 2006, Higher Education and Graduate Employment in Europe, 2006, Wege zur Professur, 2007, Die Internationalisierung der Hochschulen, 2007, Higher Education Systems, 2007, Higher Education and the World of Work, 2009, The Professional Value of ERASMUS, 2009, Sistemas Compartidos de Essenza Superior en Europe; editor: Praxisorientierung des Studiums, 1979, Hochschule und Beruf, 1979, Praxisorientierung als institutionelles Problem der Hochschule, 1980, Hochschule und Beruf - Forschungsperspektiven, 1981, Gesamthochschule Kassel 1971-1981, 1981, Hochschule und Beruf in Polen und in der Bundesrepublik Deutschland, 1983, Berufstätigkeit von Hochschulabsolventen, 1983, The Compleat University: Break from Tradition in Germany, Sweden and the U.S.A., 1983, Hochschule und gesellschaftliche Entwicklung in Polen und der Bundersrepublik Deutschland, 1984, Forschungsgestand Hochschule, 1984, Hochschule - Beruf - Gesellschaft, 1988, Der Berufsstart von Hochschulsbsolventen, 1990, Das Hochschulwesen in der Bundesrepublik Deutschland, 1990, Hochschulabsolventen im Beruf, 1992, Higher Education and Work, 1995, Academic Mobility in a Changing World, 1996, Berufliche Kompetenzentwicklung im Bildungs- und Beschäftigungssystem in Japan und Deutschland, 1998, Higher Edn. Rsch., 2000, The Inst. Basis of Higher Ed. Rsch., 2000, Credits on deutschen Hochschulen, 2000;; Erfolgreich von der Uni in den Job, 2001, Challenges of the 21st Century in Japan and Germany, 2002, Erasmus in the Socrates Programme, 2002, Das Sokrates Programm: Erfahrungun der ersten fünf Jahre, 2003, Hochschule und Arbeitswelt, 2003, Universität auf dem Prüfstand, 2003, EURODATA, 2006, The Formative Years of Scholars, 2006, Careers of University Graduates, 2007, Universities as Centers of Research and Knowledge Creations: An Endangered Species, 2008, Hochschulsysteme in Neuer Verantwortung, 2008; contbr. articles to profl. jours. Recipient Coun. Internat. Ednl. Exch. prize, 1997, Comenicus prize UNESCO, 1998, DAAD Erasmus Spl. prize, 2008. Fellow: Soc. Rsch. Higher Edn.; mem.: European Assn. Instl. Rsch., Consortium Higher Edn. Rschrs., Acad. Europaea, Internat. Acad. Edn. Home: Haroldstr 11 D-34128 Kassel Hessen Germany Office: U Kassel Internationales Zentrum für Hochschuforschung Moenchebergstr 17 Hessen D-34109 Germany Office Phone: 49-561-8042415. Business E-Mail: teichler@incher.uni-kassel.de.

TEILLON, LOUIS PIERRE, JR., lawyer; b. NYC, Nov. 15, 1943; AB, Yale U., 1965; LLB, Columbia U., 1968. Bar: Pa. 1968. Mem. Heckscher, Teillon, Terrill & Sager, P.C., West Conshohocken, Pa. Mem. Am. Coll. Trust and Estate Counsel, Pa. Bar Assn. (real property, probate and trust sects.), Phila. Bar Assn. (past chmn. probate sect.). Office: Heckscher Teillon Terrill & Sager PC 100 Four Falls Corp Ctr Ste 300 West Conshohocken PA 19428 Office Phone: 610-940-4169. Fax: 610-940-6042. E-mail: perry@htts.com.

TEIMAN, RICHARD BARRY, lawyer; b. Bklyn., May 19, 1938; AB, Princeton U., 1959; LLB, Harvard U., 1962. Bar: N.Y. 1963. Ptnr. Winston & Strawn LLP and predecessor Cole & Deitz, NYC, 1968—2008. Trustee Citizens Budget Commn., 1993-2007. Mem. Assn. Bar City N.Y. (com. admiralty 1975-78, 87, chair 1988-91, 03-06), Maritime Law Assn. (com. maritime financing 1980—, chmn. subcom. Recodification U.S. Ship Mortgage Act 1986-91, chmn. subcom. USCG, citizenship and related matters 1988-94), Phi Beta Kappa. Home: 5 Pryer Ln Larchmont NY 10538-4012 Office: Winston & Strawn LLP 200 Park Ave Rm 4100 New York NY 10166-4193 Home Phone: 914-834-8827; Office Phone: 212-294-6730. Business E-Mail: rteiman@winston.com, rteiman@optonline.net.

TEIN, MICHAEL, lawyer; BA, Yale U., 1988; JD, U. Pa., 1992. Bar: Mass. 1992, Fla. 1993. Ptnr. Lewis Tein, P.L., Miami, Fla., 2005—. Office: Lewis Tein PL 3059 Grand Ave Coconut Grove FL 33133 Office Fax: 305-442-6744. E-mail: tein@lewistein.com.

TEIRSTEIN, ALVIN STANLEY, physician; b. NYC, Apr. 3, 1927; BA, Adelphi Coll., 1949; MD, SUNY, Bklyn., 1953. Intern Mt. Sinai Hosp., NYC, 1953-54; resident Bronx VA Hosp., 1954-55, Mt. Sinai Hosp., 1955-56, chief resident, 1957, asst. attennding physician, 1958-66; attending cardio-pulmonary lab. Bronx VA Hosp., 1958-64; assoc. attending physician Mt. Sinai Hosp., 1966-74, attending physician, 1974, acting chief pulmonary div., 1974-75, dir. pulmonary div., 1975—. Assoc. clin. prof. Mt. Sinai Sch. Medicine, 1968, clin. profl., 1974, prof. medicine, 1975, Florette and Ernst Rosenfeld and Joseph Solomon prof. medicine, 1977. Cardio-pulmonary lab. fellow Bronx VA Hosp., 1956, Mt. Sinai Hosp., 1958-59, Dazian fellow, 1959-61. Fellow Am. Coll. Chest Physicians, Am. Coll. Physicians; mem. Nat. Assn. Med. Dirs. of Respiratory Care, N.Y. State County Med. Socs., N.Y. Lung Assn., Assn. Pulmonary Program Dirs., Soc. Occupational Environ. Health. Office: Mt Sinai Pulmonary Assocs 5 E 98th St 10th fl Box 1232 New York NY 10029-6574 Business E-Mail: alvin.thirstein@mason.edu.

TEIRSTEIN, PAUL SHEPHERD, cardiologist, educator; b. NYC, July 5, 1955; s. Alvin Stanley and Alice Teirstein. BA in Biology, Vassar Coll., 1976; MD, CUNY, 1980. Diplomate Am. Bd. Internal Medicine and Cardiovascular Diseases. With Lab. of Vision Rsch. NIH, Bethesda, Md., 1977-79; intern and resident Brigham & Women's Hosp., Boston, 1980-83; fellow in cardiology Stanford U., Calif., 1983-86; fellow in advanced coronary angioplasty Mid-Am. Heart Inst., Kansas City, Mo., 1986-87; fellow in stents, artherectomy and lasers NIH, Bethesda, 1987; dir. interventional cardiology Scripps Clinic and Rsch. Found., La Jolla, Calif., 1987—, chief cardiology, 2006—; cardiologist Ctr. for Interventional Vascular Therapy, NY-Presbyn. Hosp.l/Columbia U. Med. Ctr. Prof. medicine Columbia Med. Ctr. NY Presbyn. Hosp., NYC, 2006—; presenter in field. Recipient Harold Lampert Rsch. Prize, 1980, Saul Horowitz, Jr. Meml. Award, Mt. Sinai Sch. Medicine, 1995, Spirit of Scripps Award, 1998, Erasmus Thoraxcenter Interventional Cardiology Award, 1998; named Skaggs Clin. Scholar, Scripps Rsch. Inst., 1998; named to Best Doctors in Am., 1994—97, Am.'s Top Doctors, Castle Connolly Medical LTD, 2001—05; grantee NSF, 1975. Fellow: Am. Coll. Cardiology; mem.: Assn. for Rsch. in Vision and Ophthalmology, Alpha Omega Alpha, Beta Beta Beta. Office: Scripps Clinic & Rsch Found 10666 N Torrey Pines Rd S1-056 La Jolla CA 92037-1092 also: Ctr Interventional Vascular Therapy 161 Fort Washington Ave 5th FL New York NY 10032 Office Phone: 858-554-9905, 212-305-7060. Office Fax: 212-342-3660. E-mail: pteirstein@crf.org.

TEITELBAUM, DONALD GENE, United States Ambassador to Ghana; BA in Fgn. Affairs, U. Va., 1985. Joined US Fgn. Svc., 1985; fgn. svc. assignments US Dept. State, Dominican Republic, Guyana, Kenya, Somalia, Sudan, Lebanon, Uganda, dep. chief of mission Pretoria, South Africa, chargé d'affairs, 2005—06, US amb. to Ghana Accra, 2008—; dir. African affairs Nat. Security Coun., Washington. Recipient Superior Honor award, US Dept. State, Meritorious Honor award, Award for Valor. Office: DOS Amb 2020 Accra Pl Washington DC 20521-2020*

TEITELBAUM, MICHAEL EDWARD, electrical engineer; b. Queens, NY, Oct. 19, 1976; s. Ira Teitelbaum and Sheila Jones. PhD in Elec. Engring., U. Del., Newark, 2003. Rsch. asst. U. Del., 2003—08. Contbr. articles to profl. jours. Achievements include patents in fields. Personal E-mail: mtstock2000@gmail.com.

TEITELBAUM, PHILIP, psychologist; b. Bklyn., Oct. 9, 1928; s. Bernard and Betty (Schechter) T.; m. Osnat Boné; children: Benjamin, Daniel, David, Jonathan, Gideon. BS, CCNY, 1950; MA, Johns Hopkins U., 1952, PhD, 1954. Instr., asst. prof. physiol. psychology Harvard U., 1954-59; assoc. prof. psychology U. Pa., Phila., 1959-63, prof., 1963-73; prof. psychology U. Ill.-Urbana-Champaign, 1973-85, emeritus prof., 1985—; Disting. prof. Ctr. Advanced Studies, 1980-85; grad. research prof. U. Fla., Gainesville, 1984—. Author: Fundamental Principles of Physiological Psychology, 1967; editor: (with E. Satinoff) Motivation: Handbook Behavioral Neurobiology, 1983, (with Osnat Teitelbaum) Does Your Baby Have Autism, 2008; contbr. chpts. to books; contbr. articles to profl. jours. Fellow Ctr. for Advanced Study in Behavorial Scis., Stanford U., 1975-76, Fulbright fellow Tel Aviv U., 1978-79, Guggenheim fellow, 1984-85, Carnegie Found. fellow Inst. Neurol. Scis., U. Pa. Med. Sch., 1958-59. Fellow APA (pres. div. physiol. psychology, disting. sci. contbn. award 1978), Am. Psychol. Soc. (William James fellow); mem. NAS, AAAS, Am. Physiol. Soc., Soc. for Neurosci., Soc. Exptl. Psychology. Home: 2239 NW 17th Ave Gainesville FL 32605-3909 Office Phone: 352-392-0615, 352-392-2180. Personal E-mail: teitelb@hotmail.com.

TEITELBAUM, STEVEN, plastic surgeon; b. LA, Aug. 22, 1962; AB, U. Calif. Berkeley; MD, UCLA, 1988. Lic. Mass., 1989, Calif., 1993, DEA, 1993, cert. Am. Bd. Plastic Surgery, 1997, Am. Bd. Plastic Surgery, 2006, Am. Bd. Surgery, 1995. Intern Harvard/Beth Israel Hosp., Boston, 1988—89, gen. surgery resident, chief resident, 1989—93; plastic & reconstructive surgery resident U. Southern Calif., 1993—95; at Santa Monica/ULCA Med. Ctr., 1995—2006, St. John's Hosp., Santa Monica, Calif., 1995—, UCLA Ctr. Health Sciences, 2006—; asst. clin. prof. plastic surgery UCLA David Geffen Sch. Medicine, 2006—; pvt. practice Santa Monica, Calif. Guest editor Aesthetic Surgery Jour., 2002—, Plastic & Reconstructive Surgery, 2006—. Chair new leadership div. Israel Bonds; state pres. Am. Jewish Congress; bd. mem. Maestro Found. U. Calif. Presdl. rsch. grant, 1982, Heart Assn. rsch. grant, 1985. Mem.: Internat. Soc. Aesthetic Plastic Surgeons, Internat. Ultrasonic Soc., Am. Coll. Surgeons, Calif. Soc. Plastic Surgeons, Bay Surg. Soc., LA Soc. Plastic Surgery (bd. dirs. 2005—, sec. 2005—), Calif. Soc. Plastic Surgery (ethics com. 2000—, co-chair exhibits com. 2001—04, co-chair legis. com. 2003—, exec. coun. 2006—), Calif. Med. Assn. (alt. del. 2004), Am. Soc. Plastic Surgeons (legis. com. 2002—04, exhibits com. 2004—06, performance metrics task force 2007—), Am. Soc. Aesthetic Plastic Surgery (govt. rels. com. 2001—03, electronic comms. com. 2003—, breast implant task force exhibits com. 2004, practice rels. com. 2004—, emerging trends task force & innovative procedures com. 2005—). Avocations: sailing, triathlon, photography, piano, scuba diving. Office: 1301 20th St Ste 350 Santa Monica CA 90404 Office Phone: 310-315-1121. Office Fax: 310-315-9921. Business E-Mail: steve@drteitelbaum.com.

TEITELL, CONRAD LAURENCE, lawyer, writer; b. NYC, Nov. 8, 1932; s. Benson and Belle (Altman) T.; m. Adele Mary Crummins, May 26, 1957; children: Beth Mary, Mark Lewis. AB, U. Mich., 1954; LL.B., Columbia U., 1957; LL.M., N.Y. U., 1968. Bar: N.Y. 1958, D.C., 1968. Mem. Prerau & Teitell, NYC and White Plains, NY, 1964-96, Cummings & Lockwood, Stamford, Conn., 1996—. Dir. Philanthropy Tax Inst., Old Greenwich, Conn., 1964—; adj. prof. U. Miami Law Sch., 1980—. Author: Philanthropy and Taxation, 5 vols., 1993-2009; editor, pub. Taxwise Giving, 1964—; contbr. articles to legal jours. Served with U.S. Army, 1957. Recipient Disting. Svc. to Higher Edn. award Am. Coll. Pub. Relations Assn., 1970, Disting. Svc. award Nat. Com. on Planned Giving, 1990, Harrison Tweed Spl. Merit award Am. Law Inst./ABA, 1992. Lifetime Achievement award Am. Coun. Gift Annuities, 2008. Fellow Am. Coll. Trust and Estate Counsel; mem. ABA (former co-chmn. com. charitable giving, trusts, founds.), Assn. of Bar of City of N.Y. Home: 16 Marlow Ct Riverside CT 06878-2614 Office: Cummings & Lockwood 6 Landmark Sq Stamford CT 06901 also: PO Box 299 Old Greenwich CT 06870-0299 Office Phone: 203-351-4164. Business E-Mail: cteitell@cl-law.com.

TEITELMAN, RICHARD B., state supreme court judge; BA in Math., U. Pa., 1969; JD, Washington U., 1973. Bar: Mo. 1974. Pvt. practice, St. Louis, 1974-75; staff atty. Legal Svcs. Ea. Mo., St. Louis, 1975-76, mng. atty., 1976-80, exec. dir., gen. counsel, 1980—; judge Mo. Ct. Appeals (ea. dist.), 1998—2002, Mo. Supreme Ct., 2002—. Bd. dirs. Citizens for Mo.'s Children, St. Louis, 1988—. Recipient Durward K. McDaniel award Am. Coun. of Blind, 1986. Mem. The Mo. Bar, Kansas City Met. Bar Assn., Mound City Bar Assn., Lawyers Assn., St. Louis, Women Lawyers' Assn. Greater St. Louis, St. Louis County Bar Assn., Am. Blind Lawyers Assn., Am. Judicature Soc. (bd. dirs. 1986-2005), St. Louis Bar Found., Leadership St. Louis. Office: Mo Supreme Court PO Box 150 Jefferson City MO 65102 Home Phone: 314-367-5541; Office Phone: 573-751-1004. Business E-Mail: rteitelm@courts.mo.gov.*

TEITGE, ROBERT A., medical association administrator; b. LA, Oct. 18, 1942; s. Allan Bernhard and Barbara Hodges (Means) T.; m. Louise Janet Hirschmann, Dec. 28, 1968; children: Erika, Stefan, Shera, Mieke. AB, Stanford U., 1964; MS, U. Puget Sound, 1965; MD, U. So. Calif., 1969. Diplomate Am. Bd. Orthopedic Surgery. Intern RI Hosp., Providence, 1969-70; resident in orthopedic surgery LA County-U. So. Calif. Med. Ctr., 1970-74; postgrad. fellow in sports medicine Kaplan Jobe Clinic, Inglewood, Calif., 1976-77; orthopedic surgeon Tacoma Orthopedic and Fracture Clinic, 1977-79, Palo Alto Med. Clinic, Calif., 1979-80; dir. Ctr. for Athletic Medicine Henry Ford Hosp., Detroit, 1980-84; prin. Teitge Orthopedic Assocs., P.C., Warren, Mich., 1984—. Team physician Stanford U., 1979-80, Detroit Lions Profl. Football Team, 1980-84, Detroit Red Wings Profl. Hockey Team, 1982-88, Detroit Drive Profl. Football Team, 1987-88; orthopedic cons. Detroit Tigers Profl. Baseball Team, 1980-84, Detroit Pistons Profl. Basketball Team, 1984-94, 96—; chief med. officer sports medicine U.S. Figure Skating Championship, 1994, World Cup U.S.A., 1994; prof. Wayne State U. Sch. Medicine. Contbr. articles to profl. jours. Trustee AO Found., Berne, Switzerland, 1985-90; Maj. USAF, 1974-76. Mem. AMA, Am. Acad. Orthopedic Surgeons, Am. Orthopedic Soc. for Sports Medicine, Mid-Am. Orthopedic Assn., Mich. State Med. Soc., Acad. Orthopedic Soc., Wayne County Med. Soc., Detroit Acad. Orthopedics, Organ Procurement Agy. Mich. Office: 4050 E 12 Mile Rd Warren MI 48092-2594

TEIXEIRA, ARTHUR ALVES, food engineer, educator, consultant; b. Fall River, Mass., Jan. 30, 1944; s. Arthur Araujo and Emelia (Alves) T.; m. Jean E. Lamb, Dec. 26, 1966 (dec. Dec. 1983); children: A. Allan, Scott C.; m. Marjorie St. John, June 28, 1986; 1 stepchild, Craig St. John. PhD, U. Mass., 1971. Registered profl. engr., Fla., Mass. Rsch. engr. Ross Labs., Columbus, Ohio, 1971-73, R&D group leader, 1973-77; sr. cons. Arthur D. Little, Inc., Cambridge, Mass., 1977-82; assoc. prof. U. Fla., Gainesville, 1982-89, prof., 1989—. Sci. advisor Escola Superior de Biotecnologia, Porto, Portugal, 1991-96, FMC Corp., Santa Clara, Calif., 1989-92; internat. cons., Albania, Australia, Belgium, Brazil, Bulgaria, Chile, Cuba, Eng., France, Germany, Hungary, Indonesia, Ireland, Israel, Kenya, Netherlands, Poland, Portugal, Peru, Romania, South Africa, Spain; reviewer USDA, Washington, 1991—. Author: Computerized Food Processing Operations, 1989, Food Physics, 2007; contbr. 14 chpts. to books, 70 articles to profl. jours. Judge Internat. Sci. Fair, Orlando, Fla., 1991. Recipient Fulbright scholar award, Portugal, 1990—91, Golden Retort award of Merit, IFTPS, 1994, Sr. Faculty award, U. Fla. chpt. Gamma Sigma Delta, 1996, Tchr. of Yr. award, U. Fla. Coll. Engring., 1996, Fulbright scholar award, Peru, 2000, Disting. Food Engr. award, IAFIS/FPEI/ASAE, 2001, Marvin Tung Achievement award, 2005, Disting. Alumni award, Durfee H.S., 2007. Fellow Am. Soc. Agrl. Engrs. (dir. 1988-90, Paper awards 1988-89, 2001, assoc. editor Transactions of ASAE 1985—); mem. AIChE, Am. Soc. Agr. and Biol. Engrs., Inst. Food Technologists (mem. editl. bd. 1980-83, 2003—), Am. Soc. Engring. Edn., Inst. Thermal Process Specialists, Coun. on Agrl. Sci. and Tech., R & D Assocs., Gamma Sigma Delta (chpt. pres. U. Fla. 1999-2000), Sigma Xi, Alpha Epsilon, Tau Beta Pi. Roman Catholic. Achievements include design of on-line process control system to assure safety of sterilized canned foods; tech. and economic feasiblity for radiation sterilization of disposable feeding devices; research in computer optimization and control of food sterilization processes, mathematical modelling of bacterial spore population dynamics in processed foods, and anaerobic composting for solid waste management on long-term NASA space missions. Office: U Fla Rogers Hall Gainesville FL 32611-0570 Home Phone: 352-335-3608; Office Phone: 352-392-1864. E-mail: atex@ufl.edu.

TEIXEIRA, EDUARDO V., mathematics professor; b. Sao Paulo, Brazil, Apr. 9, 1976; s. Arthur and Maria Clecia Teixeira; m. Katiuscia C. Teixeira, June 30, 2001; 1 child, Amanda. PhD in Math. (hon.), U. Tex., 2005. Hill asst. prof. Rutgers U., Piscataway, NJ, 2005—08; prof. math. U. Fed. Ceara, Forteleza, Brazil, 2006—. Grantee, NSF, 2006; Associated Rsch. fellowship, CNPQ, 2008. Mem.: Brazilian Acad. Sci. Office: Univ Fed Ceara Av Humberto Monte Fortaleza Ceara 60455-760 Brazil

TEIXEIRA, MARK CHARLES, professional baseball player; b. Severna Park, Md., Apr. 11, 1980; s. John and Margy Teixeira; m. Georgia Leigh Williams, Dec. 7, 2002. Attended, Ga. Inst. Tech., Atlanta. First baseman Tex. Rangers, 2003—07, Atlanta Braves, 2007—08, LA Angels, Anaheim, 2008, NY Yankees, 2009—. Mem. Team USA, World Baseball Classic, 2006. Founder Mark Teixeira Charitable Fund, 2006—. Recipient Silver Slugger award, 2004—05, Gold Glove award, 2005—06; named to Am. League All-Star Team, Maj. League Baseball, 2005, 2009. Achievements include becoming the fifth player in Major League history to hit 100 home runs in his first three seasons, 2005. Office: NY Yankees Yankee Stadium One E 161st St Bronx NY 10451*

TEJADA, MIGUEL ODALIS, professional baseball player; b. Bani, Dominican Republic, May 25, 1974; m. Alesandra Tejada; children: Alexa, Miguel. Shortstop Oakland Athletics, Calif., 1997—2003, Balt. Orioles, 2004—07, Houston Astros, 2008—. Mem. Dominican Republic nat. team World Baseball Classic, 2009. Recipient Silver Slugger award, 2004, 2005; named Am. League MVP, 2002, All-Star Game MVP, Maj. League Baseball, 2005; named to Am. League All-Star Team, 2002, 2004—06, Nat. League All-Star Team, 2008, 2009. Achievements include leading the American League in: runs batted in (149), 2004; doubles (50), 2005; winning the All-Star Home Run Derby, 2004. Avocations: dominoes, music. Mailing: c/o Houston Astros Minute Maid Pk 501 Crawford St Houston TX 77002*

TEJADA, RITA MARÍA, literature and language professor; children: Rita Marie Guzmán, Lara Adamilka Guzmán. BA in Edn., U. Católica Madre y Maestra, Santiago, Dominican Republic, 1986; MA, Emory U., Atlanta, 1993; PhD, Fla. State U., Tallahasse, 1995. Prof. Pontificia U. Católica Madre y Maestra, 1987—93; assoc. prof. Luther Coll., Decorah, Iowa, 1996—. Contbr. articles to profl. jours. (Dominican Republic Nat. Lit. award, 2007). Mem. Evang. Luth. Ch. America, Decorah, 2008—. Fulbright scholarship, Fulbright-Laspau Orgn., 1991—93. Lutheran. Avocations: travel, reading, hiking, movies. Office: Luther Coll 700 College Dr Decorah IA 52101 Business E-Mail: tejadari@luther.edu.

TEJNIL, EDITA, engineering company executive; BS, U. Calif., Berkeley, MS, 1994, PhD, 1997. Staff process engr. Intel Corp., Santa Clara, Calif., 1997—2005; sr. imaging scientist ASML MaskTools, Santa Clara, 2005—07; tech. mktg. engr. Mentor Graphics Corp., San Jose, Calif., 2007—. Fellowship, NSF, 1992—95, Intel Found., 1995—97. Mem.: SPIE. Achievements include patents for advanced lithography and photomask technology.

TEKUT, THOMAS FRANCIS, chemistry professor; b. Wiesbaden, Hesse, Germany, Aug. 20, 1962; s. Kenneth Francis and Susanna Elisabeth Tekut; m. Kim Hwaeun Song, Jan. 12, 2002; 1 child, Jennifer Elizabeth. BS, Hardin-Simmons U., Abilene, Tex., 1984; MS, Abilene Christian U., 1988; PhD, Tex. Tech U., Lubbock, 1992. Assoc. prof. chemistry N.Mex Mil. Inst., Roswell, 1998—. Contbr. articles to profl. jours. Mem.: Am. Chem. Soc. Libertarian. Avocations: reading, travel, video games, basketball, bicycling. Office: N Mex Mil Inst 101 W College Blvd Roswell NM 88201 Business E-Mail: tekut@nmmi.edu.

TELEKI, STEPHANIE, policy analyst; PhD, UCLA Sch. Pub. Health, 2002. Health policy analyst RAND, Santa Monica, Calif., 2002—; project mgr. and co-pi Kaiser Permanente, Calif. Office: Rand 1776 Main St Santa Monica CA 90407 Office Phone: 310-393-0411. Business E-Mail: teleki@rand.org.

TELEMAN, SILVIU, mathematician, educator; b. Corbeni, Romania, Aug. 21, 1931; arrived in U.S., 1986; m. Ecaterina Cioranescu, May 15, 1962; children: Calin Nicolae Stefan, Constantin. BS, M. Eminescu H.S., 1950; MS in Math., U. Bucharest, 1957, PhD of Math., 1968. Editor Inst. Romanian-Soviet Studies Romanian Acad. Sci., Bucharest, 1960—62; reader, chmn., lectr., dean Pedagogical Inst., Pitesti, Romania, 1962—68; rschr. Inst. Math. Romanian Acad. Scis., Bucharest, 1968—86; vis. prof. dept. math. Ind. U., Bloomington, 1986—87; Otto Szasz vis. prof. dept. math. U. Cin., 1987—88; vis. prof. dept. math. U. Mich., Ann Arbor, 1988—89; assoc. prof. Dept. Math. U. PR, San Juan, 1989—95, prof. Dept. Math., 1995—. Author: Theory of Harmonic Algebras, with Applications to Von Neumann Algebras and Cohomology of Locally Compact Spaces (de Rham's Theorem), 1971 (Gh. Tzitzeica award, 1971), An Introduction to Choquet Theory, with Applications to Reduction Theory, 1980; contbr. articles to profl. jours. Recipient Order of Work 3d Class, Pres. Romania, 1967, Rep. Presdl. Legion of Merit, Rep. Presdl. Legion Exec. Bd., 1997, Rep. Sen. Medal of Freedom, Rep. mems. of U.S. Senate, 1999. Mem.: AAAS, N.Y. Acad. Scis., Math. Assn. Am., Am. Math. Soc. Avocation: music. Home Phone: 518-813-4781. Personal E-mail: silviu.teleman@gmail.com.

TELES, FLAVIA R.F., clinical investigator, dental educator; d. Cesar Luiz and Ana Cristina Rocha Fonseca; m. Ricardo Palmier Teles, Feb. 22, 2003; 1 child, Isabella Rocha Fonseca. DDS, Fed. U. Rio de Janeiro Sch. Dentistry, 1996; DMSc, Harvard Sch. Dental Medicine. Cert. periodontist Dentistry Coun. Rio de Janeiro, 2000. Asst. prof. periodontology Pontificia Cath. U. Dental Inst., 2000—03; rsch. dentist Forsyth Inst., Boston, 2003—; adj. faculty Mt. Ida Coll., Newton, Mass., 2007—. Ad hoc reviewer Internat. Jour. Oral and Maxillofacial Implants, Hanover Pk., Ill., 2009, Jour. Periodontology, Chgo., 2009. Instl. NRSA Postdoc. grant, NIH NIDCR, 2006—, Loan Repayment Program fellowship, NIH, 2007—. Mem.: Am. Assn. Dental Rsch. Achievements include research in study of the microbiota of the oral cavity with emphasis on minute biofilm samples and uncultivated, unrecognized bacterial species. Office: Forsyth Inst 140 The Fenway Boston MA 02115 Office Fax: 617-262-4021. Business E-Mail: fteles@forsyth.org.

TELESETSKY, WALTER, federal agency administrator; b. Boston, Jan. 22, 1938; s. Keril and Nellie (Krelka) T.; m. Sharron-Dawn Lamp, July 15, 1961; children: Stephanie Ann, Anastasia Marie. BS in Mech. Engring., Northeastern U., 1960; MBA, U. Chgo., 1961; postgrad., Harvard U., 1977. Engr. trainee Chrysler Corp., Detroit, 1956-59; rsch. asst. Microtech Rsch. Co., Cambridge, Mass., 1959-60; engr. Allis Chalmers Mfg. Co., Milw., 1960-61; mem. tech. staff The Mitre Corp., Bedford, Mass., 1962-68; sr. mem. tech. staff Data Dynamics, Inc., Washington, 1969; phys. scientist NOAA, Rockville, Md., 1970-71, U.S. Gate Project coord., 1972-74, dir. U.S. Global Weather Experiment Project Office, 1974, dir. Program Integration Office, 1975-77, dir. Programs and Tech. Devel. Office, 1977-79, dir. Programs and Internat. Activities Office, 1979-81; dep. assoc. dir. for tech. svcs., chief AFOS ops. div. Nat. Weather Svc., Silver Spring, Md., 1981-86, dir. Office of Systems Ops., 1986-2000, dir. Office Operational Sys., 2000—02. Liaison to NAS coms. on atmospheric scis., geophysics studies and internat. environ. programs, 1975-81; U.S. coord. U.S./Japan Coop. Program in Natural Resources, 1980-88; chmn. U.S.-Japan Marine Resources and Engring. Coordination Com., 1980-88; U.S. del. governing coun. UN Environ. Program and World Meteorol. Orgn.; mem. commn. for Basic Systems World Meteorol. Orgn., 1988-2002; speaker in field. Contbr. articles to profl. publs. Recipient Silver medal Dept. Commerce, 1975, Gold medal Dept. Commerce, 1998. Mem. AAAS, Am. Geophys. Union, Am. Meteorol. Soc., Am. Soc. Mech. Engrs., Marine Tech. Soc. Home: 16 Eton Overlook Rockville MD 20850-3003

TELFER, MARGARET CLARE, internist, hematologist, oncologist; b. Manila, Apr. 9, 1939; came to U.S., 1941; d. James Gavin and Margaret Adele (Baldwin) T. BA, Stanford U., 1961; MD, Washington U., St. Louis, 1965. Diplomate Am. Bd. Internal Medicine, Am. Bd. Hematology, Am. Bd. Oncology; lic. Ill., Mo. Resident in medicine Michael Reese Hosp., Chgo., 1968, fellow in hematology and oncology, 1970, assoc. attending physician, 1970-72, dir. Hemophilia Ctr., 1971—, interim dir. div. hematology and oncology, 1971-74, 81-84, 89—, attending physician, 1972—, Rush-Presbyn. St. Luke's Hosp., 1999—, Olympia Fields (Ill.) Hosp., 1999—2006, Cook County Hosp., Chgo., 2000—, dir. hematology/oncology fellowship, 2004—; asst. prof. medicine U. Chgo., 1975-80, assoc. prof. medicine, 1980-85, assoc. prof. clin. medicine, 1985-89; assoc. prof. medicine U. Ill., Chgo., 1990-2001, Rush U., Chgo., 2001—. Mem. med. adv. bd. Hemophilia Found. Ill., 1971, chmn., 1972—83, lectr. annual symposium, 1978—84; mem. med. adv. bd. State of Ill. Hemophilia Program; dir. hematology-oncology fellowship program Michael Reese Hosp., 1971—75, 1981—84, 1989—2000, dir. Cook County Fellowship Program, 2004—, mem. numerous coms.; lectr. in field. Contbr. articles to profl. jours. Fellow ACP; mem. Am. Soc. Clin. Oncology, Am. Assn. Med. Colls., Am. Soc. Hematology, World Fedn. Hemophilia, Blood Club (Chgo.), Thrombosis Club (Chgo.). Office: Stroger Cook County Hosp Rm 750 Adminstrn Bldg 1900 W Polk Chicago IL 60612 Office Phone: 312-864-7250. Business E-Mail: mtelfer@ccbhs.org.

TELFORD, SAM ROUNTREE, JR., zoologist; b. Winter Haven, Fla., Aug. 25, 1932; s. Sam Rountree Telford and Ann Marion Frances Schiller; m. Michiko Miyazawa, Dec. 20, 1959; children: Sam Rountree III, Randolph Stuart, Robert Miyazawa. BA, U. Va., Charlottesville, 1955; MS, U. Fla., Gainesville, 1959; PhD, U. Calif., LA, 1964. NIH postdoc. fellow Inst. Infectious Diseases, U. Tokyo, 1965—67; vertebrate ecologist Gorgas Meml. Lab., Panama, 1967—70; asst. prof. U. Fla., 1970—73; med. zoologist WHO, Acarigua, Venezuela, 1973—74, Karachi, Pakistan, 1975—77, Geneva, 1977—78, Rangoon, Myanmar, 1978—80; project leader Danish Internat. Devel. Agy., Morogoro, Tanzania, 1981—85. Ecol. cons., Fla., 1985—98. Contbr. scientific papers. Sgt. US Army, 1956—59, Tokyo. Mem.: Am. Soc. Parasitologists. Democrat. Avocations: reading, gardening. Home Phone: 352-375-4214.

TELINGATOR, CYNTHIA J., psychiatrist, director; MD, Chgo. Med. Sch., 1989. Cert. in adult psychiatry, neurology Mass., 1994, in child, adolescent psychiatry, neurology 1995. Tng. dir., child, adolescent psychiatry Cambridge Health Alliance, Mass., 2000—. Mem.: APA, MPS (co-chmn. 2007—), NECCAP (pres. elect 2009—), AADPRT (henderson com. mem. 2003—), AACAP. Office: Cynthia J Telingator MD 6 Bigelow St Cambridge MA 02139

TELLEEN, JUDY, counselor; b. Chgo., Dec. 13, 1942; d. Kurt Theodore and Gertrude Lillian Lockwood Johnson; m. David Roger Telleen, June 15, 1964; children: Karin, Kirstin, Erik. BA, Lawrence U., 1964; MA, U. Mich., 1967, PhD, 1970. Program dir. counseling svcs. Asian Human Svcs., Chgo., 1994-95, coord. of counseling svcs., 1995-96, coord. of case mgmt., 1997-98; adj. prof. Gov.'s State Univ., University Park, Ill., 1995-99; counselor Arlington Heights, Ill., 1999—. Adv. com. mem. Bd. Suprs. and Sch. Bd., Va., 1993; mem. Pub. Policy and Legis. com. Ill. Counseling Assn., 1994, mem. governing coun., 2000—. Author: (book) A Predictive Model of the Cumulative Academic Achievement of Indian Students, 1970, (monograph) Guidance Factors Influencing Indian Students to Attend the University of Michigan, 1971; mem. editl. bd. (periodical) Ill. Counseling Assn. Quarterly, 1995—98. Youth adv. Bridge Youth & Family Svcs., Palatine, Ill., 1994—96; chairperson learning com. All Saints Luth. Ch., Palatine, 1993—2001. Mem. Am. Counselor's Assn., Ill. Counselor's Assn., Ill. Assn. of Couples & Family Couns. (pres.), Ill. Assn. for Multicultural Counseling, Ill. Assn. Mental Health Counselors, Assn. for Multicultural Counseling Develop., Internat. Assn. Marriage & Family Counselors, Internat. Assn. Addictions & Offender Counselors, Pi Lambda Theta, Phi Kappa Phi. Lutheran. Office: Ste 102 1040 S Arlington Heights Rd Arlington Heights IL 60005-3162

TELLEM, ARN, media company executive, agent; b. Phila. m. Nancy Reiss. BA, Haverford Coll., 1976; JD, U. Mich. Law Sch., 1979. Cert. player agent Maj. League Baseball Players Assn., Nat. Basketball Players Assn. Ptnr. Manatt, Phelps and Phillips; exec. v.p., gen. counsel LA Clippers, 1982—88; founder, CEO Tellem & Assocs. (acquired by SFX Entertainment), 1989—99; with SFX Entertainment, 1999—2004, CEO, SFX Sports, 2005—06; prin., mgmt. Wasserman Media Group, 2006—07, pres., mgmt., 2007—. Adj. prof. law U. Southern Calif.; spkr. in field. Bd. mgrs. Haverford Coll. Named Top Agent, Sports Bus. Jour., 2004; named one of The Most Powerful People in Sports, The Sporting News, 1998, 2001—04, The Most Influential People in the World of Sports, Bus. Week, 2007, 2008. Mem.: ABA, State Bar Calif. Office: Wasserman Media Group 12100 W Olympic Blvd Ste 400 Los Angeles CA 90064

TELLEM, NANCY REISS, broadcast executive; b. Danville, Calif., Dec. 13, 1953; m. Arn Tellem; children: Michael, Matthew, Eric. BA in Polit. Sci., U. Calif., Berkeley, 1975; JD, Hastings Coll. Law, 1979. Intern to Congressman Ron Dullums, Washington, 1974; with legal affairs dept. Lorimar TV; joined Warner Bros. TV, 1987, exec. v.p. bus. and fin. affairs; exec. v.p. bus. affairs CBS Entertainment, exec. v.p. CBS Prodns. CBS, 1997—98, pres. CBS Entertainment, 1998—2004; pres. CBS Paramount Network TV Entertainment Group, 2004—. Bd. dirs. ThirdAge Media. Named one of The 100 Most Powerful Women in Entertainment, Hollywood Reporter, 2005—07, The 100 Most Powerful Women, Forbes mag., 2007, 2008. Avocations: tennis, yoga, hiking, photography. Office: CBS Entertainment 7800 Beverly Blvd Los Angeles CA 90036

TELLER, PAULINE IVANCOVICH, artist; b. Ross, Calif., May 3, 1914; d. Baldo Aloysius and Marian Barron Ivancovich; m. Frederic de Peyster Teller II, Aug. 29, 1941; children: Joan Teller Coda, Peter Ivancovich, Anne Teller, Frederic de Peyster III. BFA, Dominican Coll., 1936. One-woman shows include San Francisco Mus. Modern Art, 1940, Dominican Coll. Libr., 1975, Ross Valley Clinic, 1976, Marin Civic Ctr. Adminstrn. Bldg Gallery, 1981, Mus. Mission San Juan Capistrano, 1987, Hobar Gallery, Santa Barbara, Calif., 1989, San Francisco City Coll. Gallery, 2008; exhibits include San Francisco Art Assn., 1939, Fine Arts Bldg GGIE, 1940, San Francisco Women Artists, 1945, Marin Soc. Artists, 1936-85, Terra Linda Art Assn., 1936-85, Soc. Western Artists, 1936-85, Marin Art Guild, 1970-85, Calif. State Fair, Sacramento, 1970-85, Gilbert Gallery, San Francisco, 1970-85, Shorebirds Gallery, Tiburon, 1970-85, L.A. Design Ctr., 1987, Village Artistry, Carmel, Calif., 1988-89, Linda Vida Gallery, Ruidoso, N.Mex., 1988-89, Hobar Gallery, Santa Barbara, Calif., 1989-90, Vigil Gallery, Sonoma, Calif., 1990, Nevada City, Calif., 1990, Linda Lundeen Gallery, Las Cruces, N.Mex., 1991, Projects Gallery, San Rafael, Calif., 1991, Arlene Siegel Gallery, N.Mex.; represented in permanent collections at Mrs. J.H. Dollar, Hr., Kentfield, Dr. Gary Boero, San Rafael, Domonican Coll., Leafy Mayhew, Sacramento, Stanford (Calif.) U., San Domenico Sch. San Anselmo, Calif., Stanford U. Hosp., Saiter Packard Children's Hosp., Stanford, Calif., others. Mem. Nat. Mus. Women in Arts (charter). Home: 1065 S Eliseo Dr Greenbrae CA 94904-2143

TELLES, CYNTHIA ANN, psychologist; b. El Paso, Tex., Aug. 10, 1952; d. Raymond Lawrence and Delfina Telles; m. David Jimenez (div. Aug. 1991); 1 child, Raymond Jimenez. BA, Smith Coll., Northampton, Mass., 1974; PhD in Clin. Psychology, Boston U., 1982. Cert. psychologist, Calif. Psychologist U. Hosp. Boston U. Med. Ctr., 1977-78; rsch. fellow psychology dept. Spanish Speaking Mental Health Rsch. Ctr. UCLA, 1978-79, co-investigator, rsch. diagnostician, ucla dept. psychiatry, 1982-84, investigator and mgr. Spanish instrument tng. Epidemiologic Catchment Area Program Dept. Psychiatry, 1981-87; clin. project dir., co-investigator NIMH Grant, 1984-86; investigator NIMH, 1986-90; project dir., co-prin. investigator Calif. State Dept. Mental Health Grant, 1986—; psychologist adult outpatient dept. UCLA Neuropsychiat. Inst., 1979-80; dir. UCLA Spanish Speaking Psychosocial Clinic, 1980—. Media psychologist for TV and radio; cons. Boston City Police, 1975, Boulder County Community Mental Health Ctr., 1978, Spl. Svc. for Groups, LA, 1982, Ministry of Health, Lima, Peru, 1982, NIMH, 1984—, LA County Dept. Mental Health, 1985—, Calif. Sch. Profl. Psychology, 1986—; presenter in field; teaching fellow Boston U. Sch. Medicine, 1975-78; lectr. dept. psychiatry UCLA, 1980-85, asst. clin. prof., 1986-96, assoc. clin. prof., 1996-, mem. faculty adv. com. Chicano Studies Rsch. Ctr., 1988—; bd. dirs. United Calif. Bank, 1994-2002, Kaiser Health Plan and Hosps., 2004-, Calif. Cmty. Found., 2005-. Author: (with others) Psychiatric Epidemiology and Prevention: The Possibilities, 1985, Violence and Homicide in Hispanic Communities, 1988; contbr. articles to profl. jours.; mem. editorial bd. Hispanic Jour. Behavioral Scis., 1978-79; ad hoc reviewer Psychology of Women Quar., 1986-87. Bd. dirs. Coalition Pro-Salud Hispana, Boston, 1977-78, Nat. Hispanic Psychol. Assn., 1984-86, Ctr. for Study of Youth in Groups/Teen Line, Dept. of Psychiatry, Cedars-Sinai Med. Ctr., 1986-88, NCCJ, Southern Calif., 1990—, El Centro Human Svcs. Corp., 1988-90, Calif. Commerce Found., Calif. Endowment, 2001-, bd. chair, 2004-; mem. Nat. Adv. Com. on Hispanic Women and AIDS, Ctrs. for Disease Control and Hispanic Designers Inc., 1989—; pres., founder Hispanic Health Found., 1988-98. Boston U. Grad. scholar, 1975-79, APA Minority fellow, 1975-79; recipient Humanitarian award East LA Coll., 1988, Civic and Cmty. Leadership award Nat. Network of Hispanic Women, 1989, First Annual Achievement award for mental health pub. svc. APA Minority Fellowship Program, 1989, Crystal Eagle award CORO Found., 2006, Pioneer for Justice award Mex. Am. Found., LA, 2006, others. Mem. Nat. Hispanic Psychol. Assn. (charter), APA. Roman Catholic. Office: UCLA Dept Psychiatry 300 Ucla Medical Plz Los Angeles CA 90095-8346 Office Phone: 310-825-4568.

TELLEZ, CLAUDIA, hematologist, oncologist, educator; MD, U. Ill., Chgo., 1990. Cert. Internal Medicine, 1997, Oncology, 1997, Hematology, 1998. Residency in internal medicine Northwestern Meml. Hosp., 1990—93, fellowship in hematology and oncology, 1993—96; instr. clin. medicine Northwestern Med. Sch.; ptnr. Hematology Oncology Assoc. Ill. Prin. investigator for two clin. trials. Office: Hematology Oncology Associates Ill 676 N St Clair Ste 2140 Chicago IL 60611*

TÉLLEZ KUENZLER, LUIS, former government official, investment banker; b. Mexico City, Mex., 1958; Grad., Inst. Tech.; PhD in Econs., MIT. Gen. dir. fin. & planning Sec. Fin. & Pub. Credit, 1988; undersec. planning Sec. Agrl. & Hydraulic Resources, chief staff of Pres. of Mex., 1996—97; sec. Energy, Mines & Parastatal Industry Govt. Mexico, Mexico, 1997—2000; exec. v.p., CEO Desc, S.A. de C.V., Mexico, 2001—03; mng. dir. The Carlyle Group, S. de R.L. de C.V., Mexico City. Dir. Fomento Economico Mexicano, S.A. de C.V., 2001—. Named Global Leader of Tomorrow, World Econ. Forum, Leader for the New Millennium, Time mag. Office: The Carlyle Group Montes Urales 720 Col Lomas de Chapultepec 11000 Mexico City Mexico Office Phone: 52 55 52498020. Office Fax: 52 55 52498030. Business E-Mail: mexico@carlyle.com.

TELLIER, RICHARD DAVIS, management educator; b. Darby, Pa., Feb. 18, 1942; s. Joseph Campbell and Jane Grace (Davis) T.; m. Susan Gammon, June 10, 1974; children: John-Jo and Tiekka (twins). BSEE, Drexel U., 1967; MBA, Fla. State U., 1971, DBA, 1973. Elec. engr. Philco-Ford Corp., Phila., 1960-67; aerospace sys. engr. GE, Cape Canaveral, Fla., 1967-70; lectr. Fla. State U., Tallahassee, 1970-73; prof. mgmt. Calif. State U., Fresno, 1973-2000, chmn. dept. mgmt. and mktg., 1979-84, assoc. dean Sch. Bus., 1984-85, asst. dean, 1990-92, assoc. provost acad. resources, 1995-99, prof. emeritus, 2000—. Cons. ops. mgmt., market rsch. orgnl. behavior. Author: Operations Management: Fundamental Concepts and Methods, 1978, Production and Operations Management Test Bank, 1990; contbr. articles to profl. jours. Grantee 1975; recipient Meritorious Performance award, 1987, 88, 90. Mem. Ops. Research Soc. Am., Phi Kappa Phi. Home: 8294 N Academy Ave Clovis CA 93619-9454 Office: Calif State U Shaw and Maple Ave Fresno CA 93740-0001 Business E-Mail: rickt@csufresno.edu.

TELLMAN, WILLIAM C., dentist; BS in Biology, Purdue U., 1980; DDS, Ind. U., 1985. Founder, dentist Castleton Cosmetic & Family Dentistry, Indpls.; dir. Blue Triangle Dental and Wellness Ctr. Vol. dentist Gennesaret Free Clinic, 1986—, bd. dirs., 1996—; former clin. instr. Dept. Restorative Dentistry Ind. University Sch. Dentistry. Mem.: ADA, Am. Acad. Cosmetic Dentistry, Acad. Computerized Dentistry, Am. Acad. Gen. Dentistry, Indpls. Dist. Dental Soc., Ind. Dental Assn. Office: 5750 E 91st St Indianapolis IN 46250 Office Phone: 866-406-5992, 317-849-3280. Office Fax: 317-849-3868.

TELLOCK, GLEN E., manufacturing executive; b. 1961; BBA, Univ. Wis., Madison, 1983. CPA. Audit mgr. Ernst & Whinney; fin. planning mgr. Denver Post Corp.; dir. acctg. The Manitowoc Co., Inc., Manitowoc, Wis., 1991—92, corp. contr., 1992—98, v.p. fin., treas., 1998—99, sr. v.p., CFO, 1999—2002, sr. v.p., pres. Crane segment, 2002—07, pres., CEO, 2007—09, chmn., pres., CEO, 2009—. Vice-chmn. Assn. Equip. Manufacturers. Office: The Manitowoc Co Inc 2400 S 44th St Manitowoc WI 54221-0066*

TELOWITZ, MARILYN MARIE, English and social studies educator; b. St. Louis, Oct. 31, 1952; d. Nicholas John and Audrey Mulhern Telowitz. BA, U. Mo., Columbia, 1972; cert. 7-12 in English and social studies, U. Mo., St. Louis, 1975. Tchr. English and social studies Rosary HS, St. Louis, 1977—2003, chairperson English dept., 1982—2003; tchr. English and social studies Trinity Cath. HS, St. Louis, 2003—, dean humanities, 2003—04, chairperson English dept., 2004—06, academic dean, 2006—. Mem. Spanish Lake Cmty. Assn., Mo., 2005—. Mem.: Nat. Coun. for Social Studies, Nat. Coun. Tchrs. English. Democrat. Roman Catholic. Avocation: travel. Home: 804 Vista Pointe Saint Louis MO 63138 Office: Trinity Cath H S 1720 Redman Rd Saint Louis MO 63138

TELZROW, MICHAEL E., museum director, historian; BA, U. Ctrl. Fla., 1993; MA in History, U. Wis., Milw., 1996. Curator asst. Wis. Veterans Mus., Madison, Wis., 1995—97; curator history Neville Pub. Mus., Green Bay, 1997—2002; dir. rsch. and interpretation Mighty Eighth Air Force Mus., Savannah, Ga., 2003—05; exec. dir. Nat. Railroad Mus., Green Bay, 2006—. Contbr. articles to profl. jours. Office: Nat Railroad Mus 2285 S Broadway Green Bay WI 54304 Office Phone: 920-437-7623. E-mail: metelzrow@nationalrrmuseum.org.

TEMAM, ROGER M., mathematician, educator; b. Tunis, Tunisia, May 19, 1940; s. Ange M. and Elise (Ganem) T.; m. Claudette Cukorja, Aug. 21, 1962; children: David, Olivier, Emmanuel. M in Math., U. Paris, 1962, DSc, 1967. Asst. prof. math. U. Paris, 1960-67, prof., 1967—2003, emeritus prof., 2003—; dir. Inst. Sci. Computing and Applied Math. Ind. U., Bloomington, 1986—. Prof. Ecole Polytechnique, Paris, 1968-85, 2007-; mem., French Acad. Scis. Author: Numerical Analysis, 1969, 2d edit., 2001, Navier-Stokes Equations, 1977, rev. edit., 2001, Mathematical Problems in Plasticity, 1983, Infinite Dimensional Dynamical Systems in Mechanics and Physics, 1988, 2nd edit., 1997; co-author: Convex Analysis and Variational Problems, 1976, rev. edit., 1999, Dynamic Multilevel Methods and the Numerical Simulation of Turbulence, 1999, Navier-Stokes Equations and Turbulence, 2001; assoc. editor: profl. jours.; contbr. articles to profl. jours. Recipient several prizes; named Most Prolific Advisor in Math., Math. Genealogy Project. Mem. AAAS, Am. Math. Soc., Am. Phys. NY Acad. Scis.; fellow Soc., Soc. Indsl. and Applied Math. (first pres. French chpt. 1983-87). Office: Ind U Dept Math Rawles Hall Bloomington IN 47405

TEMAN, ELLY, medical researcher; d. Nissan and Rhisa Teman; m. Abraham Solomon, Oct. 1, 2003; 1 child, Uriel Moshe Solomon. BA, Hebrew U., Jerusalem, 1998, MA, 2000, PhD, 2006. Contbr. articles to profl. jours. (Best Essay award, 2002, Raphael Patai prize, 2004, Herbert Blumer award, 2004).

TEMARES, STEVEN H., retail executive; BA, Rutgers U., 1980; JD, U. Pa., 1983. Assoc. Real Estate Group Schulte Roth & Zabel LLP, NYC, 1983—85; counsel Universal Maritime Svc. Corp., NYC, 1986—88; atty. Real Estate Group Riker Danzig Scheler Hyland & Perretti, Morristown, NJ, 1988—92; from dir. real estate, gen. counsel to exec. v.p. Bed, Bath & Beyond Inc., Union, NJ, 1992—97, exec. v.p., COO, 1997—99, pres., COO, 1999—2003, pres., CEO, 2003—06; CEO Bed, Bath & Beyond, Inc., Union, NJ, 2006—. Office: Bed Bath & Beyond Inc 650 Liberty Ave Union NJ 07083

TEMBREULL, MICHAEL A., automotive executive; Grad., Stanford U., Calif., 1985. Gen. mgr. PACCAR, Inc., 1985—90, sr. v.p., 1990-92, exec. v.p., 1992-95, bd dirs., 1994—, vice chmn., 1995—; prin. fin. officer, vice chmn. PACCAR Fin. Corp. Office: PACCAR PO Box 1518 Bellevue WA 98009 Office Phone: 425-468-7400. Office Fax: 425-468-8216.

TEMERLIN, LIENER, advertising executive; b. Ardmore, Okla., Mar. 27, 1928; s. Pincus and Julie (Kahn) T.; m. Karla Samuelsohn, July 23, 1950; children: Dana Temerlin, Ray, Lisa Temerlin Gottesman, Sandy Gottesman. BFA, U. Okla., 1950. Assoc. editor Sponsor Mag., NYC, 1950-51; from copywriter to COO Glenn Advt. Inc., Dallas, 1952—74; pres. Glenn, Bozell & Jacobs, Inc., 1974-79; chmn. bd. dirs. Bozell & Jacobs Inc., 1979-86, Bozell, Jacobs, Kenyon & Eckhardt, Dallas, 1986-89; chmn. Bozell, 1989-92, Temerlin McClain, Irving, Tex., 1992—2001; pres. Temerlin Cons., 2001—. Bd. dirs. East/West Inst. Chmn. Winston Churchill Found. award dinner, 1986; chmn. Dallas Symphony Assn., 1986-88, pres., 1984-86, bd. govs., 1982-84, pres. coun., 1989—; mem. Blair House Restoration Com., 1987-88; vice-chmn. Am. Film Inst., 1992-93, bd. dirs., 1992-2000, hon. trustee, 2000; bd. dirs. United Way of Met. Dallas Exec. Com., 1986-89, Dallas Bus. Com. for Arts, 1989, Dallas Citizen's Coun., 1984-86, 92; trustee Southwestern Med. Found., 1988—, mem. adv. com., 2003—; trustee com. univ. devel. So. Meth. U., mem. exec. bd., 1990-91, bd. dirs. Tate lectr. series, 2002—; trustee and chmn. of devel. com. Dallas Mus. Art, 1993-96; steering com. Susan G. Komen Found., 1989-91, art acquisition com. Meyerson Symphony Ctr., 1989-92, exec. coun. Daytop/Dallas, 1989—; chmn. grand opening fortnight Morton H. Meyerson Symphony Ctr., 1989; active Madison Coun. Libr. Congress, Washington, 1991-2002; hon. chair rsch. dinner Am. Lung Assn. Tex., 1996; corp. chmn. Sr. Citizens Greater Dallas for Spirit of Generations Award to Stanley Marcus, 1997; fundraising campaign chmn. Lieberman Rsch. Bldg., Baylor Med. Ctr., 1997; hon. chmn. ann. dinner Make A Wish Found., 1998; exec. bd. Meadows Sch. Arts, So. Meth. U., 2001; co-chair ann. fundraising event Vogel Alcove Child Care Ctr. for the Homeless, 2001; adv. cons. Dallas Ctr. Performing Arts, 2003-; chmn., founder & festival dir., Am. Film Inst. Dallas Internat. Film Festival, 2006-08. Lt. field arty. US Army, Korea. Decorated Bronze Star; recipient Bill D. Kerss award Dallas Advt. League, 1983, Brotherhood award NCCJ, 1984, Susan G. Komen Found. for Breast Cancer Rsch. Cmty. award, 1989, Neiman Marcus (formerly James K. Wilson) Silver Cup award, 1990, Linz award 1990, Silver Medal award Dallas Advt. League, 1991, Vol. Fundraiser of Yr. award Nat. Soc. Fundraising Execs., 1991, Inst. Human Rels. award Am. Jewish Commn., Dallas, 2003; named Dallas Father of Yr., 1991, Best Man in Advt. award McCall's Mag., 1992; named Temerlin Advt. Inst. for Edn. and Rsch. in his honor So. Meth. U. Sch. Advt., 2001; inducted into Am. Advt. Hall Fame, 2004. Mem.: Am. Film Inst. (hon. trustee), Dallas CC Dist. (bd. dir. 1982), Dallas Citizens Coun. (bd. dir. 1984—86, 1992—95), Dallas C. of C. (bd. dir. 1982), Dallas Ambassadors Forum (adv. coun. 1993), Am. Heart Fund (chmn. Cmty. Relation Com. and Keystone Gifts Com. 1977, Dallas chpt. bd. dir.). Business E-Mail: connie.beebe@temerlinconsulting.com.

TEMES, GABOR CHARLES, electrical engineering educator; s. Erno and Rozsa (Angyal) Wohl-Temes; m. Ibi Kutasi-Temes, Feb. 6, 1954; children: Roy Thomas, Carla Andrea. Dipl.Ing., Tech. U. Budapest, 1952, DSc (hon.), 1991; Dipl. Phys., Eotvos U., Budapest, 1954; PhD, U. Ottawa, Ont., Can., 1961. Asst. prof. Tech. U. Budapest, 1952-56; project engr. Measurement Engring. Ltd., 1956-59; dept. head No. Electric Co. Ltd., 1959-64; group leader Stanford Linear Accelerator Center, 1964-66; corp. cons. Ampex Corp., 1966-69; prof. elec. engring. UCLA, 1969-90, chmn. dept., 1975-80; dept. head Oreg. State U., Corvallis, 1990—. Cons. Xerox Corp., ANT GmbH Author: (with others) Introduction to Circuit Synthesis and Design, 1977, Analog MOS Integrated Circuits for Signal Processing, 1986; assoc. editor: (with others) Jour. Franklin Inst, 1971-82; co-editor, contbg. author: (with others) Modern Filter Theory and Design, 1973, Oversampling Delta-Sigma Data Converters, 1991. Recipient Western Electric Fund award Am. Soc. Engring. Edn., 1982, Humboldt Sr. Rsch. award, 1991; NSF grantee, 1970— Fellow IEEE (life, editor Transactions on Circuit Theory 1969-71 Best Paper award 1969, 81, 85, Centennial medal 1984, Edn. award 1987, Tech. Achievement award 1989, Grad. Tchg. award 1998, Millenium medal 2000, CAS Golden Jubilee medal 2000, Gustav Robert Kirchhoff award 2006, Mac Valkenburg award, 2009). Home: 7100 NW Grandview Dr Corvallis OR 97330-2708 Office: Oreg State U Dept Elec Engring Corvallis OR 97331 Personal E-mail: temes@ieee.org. Business E-Mail: temes@ece.orst.edu.

TEMESGEN, HAILEMARIAM, statistician, educator; m. Yodit Dagne, Dec. 23, 1965; children: Nebiy Temesgen, Adam Temesgen. PhD, U. BC, Vancouver, 1999. Cert. in forestry BC, 2000. Asst. prof. Oreg. State U., Corvallis, 2003—. Office: Oreg State Univ 280 Peavy Hall Corvallis OR 97333 Business E-Mail: hailemariam.temesgen@oregonstate.edu.

TEMIRKANOV, YURI KHATUEVICH, conductor, music director; b. Nal'chik, Russia, Dec. 10, 1938; s. Khatu Sagidovich and Polina (Petrovna) Temirkanov; m. Irina Guseva; 1 child. Grad., Leningrad Conservatory, Russia, 1966. Condr. Maly Opera and Ballet Theatre, Leningrad, 1966; chief condr. Leningrad Philharm. Orch., 1967—76, Kirov Opera and Ballet Theatre Orch., 1976—88; prof. Leningrad Conservatory, 1979; artistic dir. Leningrad Symphony Orch. (now St. Petersburg Philharm.), 1988; mus. dir., prin. condr. St. Petersburg Philharm.; condr. Baltimore Symphony Orch., Md., 1992, Md., 1995, Md., 1998—2000, dir. music Md., 2000—06, music dir. emeritus, 2006—. Chief guest condr. London Royal Philharm. Orch., 1992; guest condr. Berlin Philharm., Vienna Philharm., l'Orch. Paris, Dresden Staatskapelle, Amsterdam's Royal Concertgebouw, NY Philharm., Phila. Orch., Boston Symphony, Chgo. Symphony, San Francisco Symphony Orch., LA Philharm., Calif., Danish Nat. Radio Symphony; condr. laureate Royal Philharm., London; Rec. artists BMG/RCA, 1988. Musical dir. (Operas) Peter I (Petrov), 1975, War and Peace (Prokofiev), 1976, Dead Souls (Schedrin), 1978, Pushkin (Petrov), 1979, Queen of Spades (Tchaikovsky), 1979. Vice chmn. bd. All-Russian Theatrical Soc. Recipient 1st prize, USSR Contest for Condrs., 1967, USSR State Prize, 1976; named People's Artist of Kabardino-Balkarian Autonomous Republic, People's Artist of Russian Soviet Fed. Socialist Republic. Office: Balt Symphony Orch Meyerhoff Symphony Hall 1212 Cathedral St Baltimore MD 21201-5545*

TEMKIN, ANN, curator; b. 1960; AB magna cum laude, Harvard U.; PhD in art history, Yale U. Curatorial asst., painting and sculpture dept. Mus. Modern Art, NYC, 1984—87, curator, painting and sculpture dept., 2003—08, chief curator painting and sculpture, 2008—; asst. curator twentieth-century art Phila. Mus. Art, 1987—90, Muriel and Philip Berman curator modern and contemporary art, 1990—2003. Co-curator Thinking is Form: The Drawings of Joseph Beuys, Phila. Mus. Art, 1993, Constantin Brancusi, 1995, Raymond Pettibon, 1998—99, curator Alice Neel, 2000—01, Barnett Newman, 2002, Color Chart: Reinventing Color, 1950 to Today, Mus. Modern Art, NYC, 2004—08, Against the Grain: Contemporary Art from the Edward R. Broida Collection, 2006. Office: Mus Modern Art 11 W 53 St New York NY 10019-5497

TEMKIN, HARVEY L., lawyer; b. Madison, Wis., Jan. 1, 1952; s. Joe L. and Sylvia Temkin; m. Barbara, June 13, 1976; children: James, Daniel, Eli. BA, U. Wis., 1974; JD, U. Ill., 1978. Bar: Wis. 1978. Assoc. Foley & Lardner, Madison, 1978—83; prof. Tulane Law Sch., New Orleans, 1983-87; ptnr. Foley & Lardner, Madison, 1987—2002; shareholder Reinhart Boerner Van Deuren, s.c., Madison, 2002—. Lectr. U. Wis. Law Sch., 1990-93; mem. U.S. Senator Feingold's Bus. Adv. Group. First v.p. Hillel Found., Madison, 1982-83, bd. dirs., 1987-95; chmn. edn. com. Beth Israel Synagogue, Madison, 1980-82; chmn. Jewish edn. panel Madison Jewish Cmty. Coun., 1993-98, bd. dirs., 1998-03; bd. dirs. Hospice Care, Inc. Fellow Am. Coll. Real Estate Lawyers (chmn. title insurance coverage subcom.), Am. Coll. Mortgage Attys.; mem. ABA (real property probate and trust sect., reporter significant legis. panel 1983-85, significant lit. panel 1985-87), Downtown Madison, Inc. (chmn. 1989-91), Hospice Care Inc. (bd. dirs. and audit com.). Office: Reinhart Boerner Van Deuren 22 East Mifflin St PO Box 2018 Madison WI 53701-2018 Business E-Mail: htemkin@reinhartlaw.com.

TEMKIN, ROBERT HARVEY, accountant; b. Boston, Oct. 21, 1943; s. Max and Lillian (Giller) T.; m. Ellen Phyllis Band, Sept. 25, 1966; 1 child, Aron; m. Debra Gottlieb, Oct. 3, 1998; 1 child, Rachel; m. Douglas Moore, Feb. 28, 1999; 1 child, Joshua. BBA, U. Mass., 1964. CPA, Mass.; Cert. in fin. forensics. With Ernst & Young LLP, 1964—72, 1973—2002, ptnr., 1976—2002, nat. dir. auditing standards, 1980-88; prin. Robert H. Temkin, CPA, 2002—. Assoc. prof. NYU, 1982. Bd. dirs. Jewish Home for Elderly of Fairfield County, 1979—, pres., 1985-87; mem. Bd. Edn., Weston, Conn., 1983-87; dir. United Synagogue of Conservative Judaism, 1984-99, 2004-08; bd. dirs., chmn. bd. dirs. Jewish Cmty. Ctrs. Greater Boston, 2003-05; mem. exec. com. Combined Jewish Philanthropies of Greater Boston, 1995-99, 2000-06, bd. dir. 1993-2006; treas. Synagogue Coun., Mass., 1988-93; dir., v.p. Greater Boston C. of C., 1989-97; dir. Hillel Found., U. Mass., 1992-99; mem. Town of Barnstable Mass Comprehensive Fin. Adv. Com., 2007. Recipient Acctg. Alumni award U. Mass., 1978, Alumnus Award Sch. Mgmt. U. Mass., 1986; Cmtys. of Excellence award Combined Jewish Philanthropies, 2003. Mem. AICPA (staff dir. commn. on auditors responsibilities 1976-78, peer rev. com. 1982-84, auditing stds. bd. 1984-88, chmn. internat. auditing task force 1988-90), Mass. Soc. CPAs (Silver medal 1964), N.Y. State Soc. CPAs, Mass. Bd. Pub. Accountancy (sec. 1996, 2001, chmn. 1997, 2002, 2006-07),Hyannis (MA) Rotary, Hyannis Yacht Club (assoc.). Office: 275 Millway PO Box 255 Barnstable MA 02630 Home: 294 Millway PO Box 1209 Barnstable MA 02630 Office Phone: 508-362-5518.

TEMKO, STANLEY LEONARD, lawyer; b. NYC, Jan. 4, 1920; s. Emanuel and Betty (Alderman) T.; m. Francine Marie Salzman, Mar. 4, 1944 (dec. Dec. 1998); children: Richard J., Edward J., William D. AB, Columbia U., 1940, LLB, 1943. Bar: N.Y. 1943, D.C. 1951. Practice in, NYC, 1943, 46-47; law clk. Mr. Justice Wiley Rutledge, U.S. Supreme Ct., Washington, 1947-48; legal counsel Econ. Coop. Adminstrn., 1948-49; assoc. Covington & Burling, Washington, 1949-55, ptnr., 1955-90, sr. counsel, 1990—. Editor-in-chief: Columbia Law Rev, 1942-43. Trustee Beauvoir Sch., 1963-69; trustee Columbia U., 1980-91, trustee emeritus, 1991—, mem. bd. visitors Sch. Law, 1961-98, mem. emeritus, 1999—; mem. bd. govs. St. Albans Sch., 1967-73, chmn., 1971-73. 2nd lt. U.S. Army, 1943-46. Decorated Bronze Star; recipient medal for conspicuous alumni svc. Columbia U., 1979, Excellence medal Columbia U. Law Sch., 2004. Fellow Am. Bar Found. (chmn. rsch. com. 1970-72); mem. ABA, Am. Law Inst., D.C. Bar Assn., Columbia U. Sch. Law Alumni Assn. (pres. 1982-84), Met. Club, Nat. Press Club, Phi Beta Kappa. Home: Apt 618 700 New Hampshire AVe NW Washington DC 20037 Office: Covington & Burling 1201 Pennsylvania Ave NW Washington DC 20004-2401 Home Phone: 202-342-0811; Office Phone: 202-662-5514. Business E-Mail: stemko@cov.com.

TEMME, MARCIA E. See HARDCASTLE, MARCIA E.

TEMPELIS, CONSTANTINE HARRY, immunologist, educator; b. Superior, Wis., Aug. 27, 1927; s. Harry and Thelma Marie (Hoff) T.; m. Nancy Louise Foster, Aug. 27, 1955; children: William H., Daniel S. BS, U. Wis.-Superior, 1950; MS, U. Wis.-Madison, 1953, PhD, 1955. Project assoc. immunology U. Wis., Madison, 1955-57; instr. immunology U. W.Va., Morgantown, 1957-58; asst. rsch. immunologist U. Calif., Berkeley, 1958-66, assoc. prof. immunology, 1966-72, prof., 1972-95, prof. emeritus, 1995—, prof. grad. sch., 1996—. Vis. scientist Wellcome Rsch. Labs., Beckenham, Kent, Eng., 1977-78, U. Innsbruck, Austria, 1985, 90, 91; cons. in field. Contbr. articles to profl. jours. Served with USNR, 1945-46. Recipient Rsch. Career Devel. award, 1965-70; Fogarty sr. internat. fellow NIH, 1977-78 Mem. AAAS, Am. Assn. Immunologists, Fedn. Am. Soc. Exptl. Biology, Sigma Xi. Office: U Calif Sch Pub Health Berkeley CA 94720-0001 Home Phone: 510-524-7742; Office Phone: 510-642-3744. Business E-Mail: chtemp@berkeley.edu, champ@berkeley.edu.

TEMPLE, DONALD, retired allergist, dermatologist; b. Chgo., May 21, 1933; s. Samuel Leonard and Matilda Eve (Riff) T.; m. Sarah Rachel Katz, Sept. 29, 1957; children: Michael A., Matthew D., Madeline B. AB in Biology cum laude, Harvard U., 1954; MD, U. Chgo., 1958. Diplomate Am. Bd. Allergy and Immunology, Am. Bd. Dermatology, Nat. Bd. Med. Examiners; lic. Intern Michael Reese Hosp., Chgo., 1958-59; resident in dermatology U. Chgo. Hosps., 1959-62; clin. asst., dept. dermatology Boston U. Sch. Medicine, 1963-64; clin. instr. dermatology dept. Stanford U. Med. Sch., 1965; preceptee in allergy Offices of Leon Unger, M.D., and Donald Unger, M.D., Chgo., 1965-69; pvt. practice Des Plaines, Ill., 1969-76; with allergy dept. Glen Ellyn (Ill.) Clinic, 1972-97; ret., 1997. Dermatology and allergy staff Louis A. Weiss Hosp., Chgo., 1965-73, allergy sect. Loyola U. Med. Ctr., Maywood, Ill., 1977-80, exec. and contract medicine coms. Glen Ellyn; clin. asst. prof. dermatology Abraham Lincoln Sch. Medicine, U. Ill., 1972-75; clin. asst. prof. medicine sect. allergy and dermatology, Loyola U., 1977-85; mem. staff Cen. DuPage Hosp., Winfield, Ill., 1973-97, Glen Oaks Med. Ctr., Glendale Heights, Ill., Glendale Heights Cmty. Hosp., 1980-92. Contbr. articles to profl. jours. Bd. dirs. Am. Lung Assn., DuPage, McHenry counties, 1980-91; chmn. Contract Medicine, HMO Com., Glen Ellyn Clinic, 1985, mem. exec. com., 1988-92. Fellow Am. Coll. Chest Physicians, Am. Assn. Cert. Allergists, Am. Coll. Allergists, Am. Acad. Allergy, Ill. Soc. Allergy and Clin. Immunology, Chgo. Dermatol. Soc.; mem. AMA, Ill. State Med. Soc., DuPage County Med. Soc., Chgo. Med. Soc., Fla. Med. Assn. Collier County Med. Soc. Jewish. Avocations: sailing, investing. Home: 6585 Nicholas Blvd Ph 3 Naples FL 34108-7210 E-mail: don.temple@post.harvard.edu.

TEMPLE, DONALD EDWARD, medical association administrator; b. NYC, Nov. 28, 1946; s. James Edward and Helen Louise (Gannon) Temple; m. Lucy Chirinos de Lorentzen, Feb. 23, 1974 (div. 1989); 1 child, Gail Marie. BBA, St. Francis Coll., Bklyn., 1968. Vol. U.S. Peace Corps, Lima, Peru, 1968-72; asst. to pres., gen. mgr. Barrons Ednl. Series, Inc., Hauppauge, NY, 1973-78; dir. supply svc. Am. Lung Assn., NYC, 1978-84; bus. mgr. Am. Jour. Respiratory and Critical Care Medicine, NYC, 1985—2008, Am. Jour. Respiratory Cell and Molecular Biology, 1989—2008, Procs. Am. Thoracic Soc., NYC, 2004—08; dir. bus. affairs Am. Lung Assn., NYC, 1985-89, dep. mng. dir. bus. affairs, 1990-94; dir. bus. affairs Am. Thoracic Soc., NYC, 1994—2007, dep. exec. dir. bus. affairs, 2007—08. Mem. mailers tech. adv. com. U.S. Postal Svc., Washington, 1987—93. Vol. L.I. Assn. AIDS Care, 1994—98. Recipient Merit award, Soc. Tech. Communication, 1990. Mem.: South Shore Audubon Soc. (bd. dirs. 2009—), N.Y. Soc. Assn. Execs., Healthcare Mktg. Comm. Coun., Am. Soc. Assn. Execs., Alliance Non-Profit Mailers (bd. dirs., chmn. tech. com. 1986—94, v.p. 1990—94), Soc. Scholarly Pub. Home: 63 Vanderwater St Farmingdale NY 11735-5235

TEMPLE, LARRY EUGENE, lawyer; b. Plainview, Tex., Dec. 26, 1935; s. Herman Edward and Grace Eileen (Ivey) T.; m. Laura Louann Atkins, Feb. 23, 1963; children: Laura Allison, John Lawrence. BBA, U. Tex., 1957, LLB with honors, 1959; LLD (hon.), Lamar U., 1985. Bar: Tex., U.S. Dist. Ct. (we. dist.) Tex., U.S. Ct. Appeals (5th cir.), U.S. Supreme Ct. Law clk. to justice Tom Clark U.S. Supreme Ct., Washington, 1959-60; assoc. Powell, Rauhut, McGinnis, Reavley & Lochridge, Austin, Tex., 1960-63; legal adminstrn. asst., exec. asst. (chief of staff) Tex. Gov. John B. Connally, Austin, 1963-67; spl. counsel to pres. Lyndon Baines Johnson, Washington, 1967-69; pvt. practice Austin, 1969—. Bd. dirs. Temple-Inland, Inc., Guaranty Bank, 1991-2008. Mem. U. Tex. Cancer Found., Houston, 1978-84, U. Tex. Devel. Bd., Austin, 1980-85, 90—, chmn., 1993-95; pres. U. Tex. Ex-Students Assn., 1997-98; mem. Tex. Higher Edn. Coordinating Bd., Austin, 1983-89, chmn., 1983-87; chmn. Select Com. for Higher Edn., Austin, 1985-87; bd. dirs. Lyndon B. Johnson Found., 1986—, vice chmn., 1989-2000, pres., 2000—; trustee U. Tex. Law Sch. Found., 1989-2007. Recipient Faculty award U. Tex. Law Sch., 1987, Humanitarian award Austin region NCCJ, 1988, Santa Rita award U. Tex. System, 1989, Disting. Alumnus award U. Tex., Austin, 1990, Mirabeau B. Lamar medal Assn. Tex. Colls. and Univs., 1990, Pro Bene Meritis award U. Tex., 1991 Outstanding Alumnus award U. Tex. Law Sch., 1999, Presdl. Citation award U. Tex., 2001, Leon Green award Tex. Law Rev., 2003; named a Tex. Super Lawyer, 2003-09; Named one of Best Lawyers in Am., 1994—. Fellow: Tex. Bar Found.; mem.: ABA, Tex. Bar Assn. (chmn. legis. com. 1980, 1983—86), Tex. Jr. Bar Assn. (chmn. bd. dirs. 1967), Austin Bar Assn. (Disting. Lawyer award 2004). Democrat. Episcopalian. Home: 2606 Escondido Cv Austin TX 78703-1610 Office: 400 W 15th St Ste 1510 Austin TX 78701-1648 Home Phone: 512-453-7936; Office Phone: 512-477-4467. Business E-Mail: larry@larrytemple.com.

TEMPLE, SALLY, neuroscientist, educator; b. Eng. children: Rebecca, Sam, Josh. BA, U. Cambridge, Eng., 1982; PhD, Univ. Coll. London, 1986. Postdoctoral fellow Columbia U., U. Miami; prof. neuropharmacology/neurosci. Albany Med. Coll., 2001—; founder, sci. dir. NY Neural Stem Cell Inst. SUNY, Albany, 2007—. Adj. faculty mem. Rensselaer Polytechnic Inst., SUNY, Albany; mem. med. adv. bd. NY Stem Cell Found.; mem. Internat. Soc. Stem Cell Rsch., 2004—, bd. dirs., 2006—. Contbr. articles to profl. jours.; spkr. in field. Named a MacArthur Fellow, The John D. and Catherine T. MacArthur Found., 2008; fellow Alden March Bioethics Inst. Achievements include research in the mechanisms by which embryonic progenitor cells divide into highly specialized neurons and support cells; development of a culture system in which single CNS progenitor cells can divide and differentiate into clones of neurons and glial cells; advancement in developing effective clinical treatments for central nervous system damage due to trauma, neurodegenerative diseases, malignancy, or stroke. Office: SUNY Dept Biomed Sci Empire State Plz C236 Albany NY 12201 Office Phone: 518-473-7553.*

TEMPLE, WAYNE CALHOUN, historian, writer; b. Richwood, Ohio, Feb. 5, 1924; s. Howard M. and Ruby March (Calhoun) T.; m. Lois Marjorie Bridges, Sept. 22, 1956 (dec. Apr. 1978); m. Sunderine Wilson, Apr. 9, 1979; stepson, James C. Mohn. AB cum laude, U. Ill., 1949, AM, 1951, PhD, 1956. Rsch. asst. history U. Ill., 1949-53, tchg. asst., 1953-54; curator ethnohistory Ill. State Mus., 1954-58; editor-in-chief Lincoln Herald, Lincoln Meml. U., 1958-73, assoc. editor, 1973—, also dir. dept. Lincolniana, dir. univ. press, John Wingate Weeks prof. history, 1958-64; with Ill. State Archives, 1964—, now chief dep. dir. Lectr. U.S. Mil. Acad., 1975; sec.-treas. Nat. Lincoln-Civil War Council, 1958-64; mem. bibliography com. Lincoln Lore, 1958—; hon. mem. Lincoln Sesquicentennial Commn., 1959-60; advisory council U.S. Civil War Centennial Commn., 1960-66; maj. Civil War Press Corps, 1962—; pres. Midwest Conf. Masonic Edn., 1985; mem. adv. com. Abraham Lincoln Bicentennial Commn., 2000—. Author: Indian Villages of the Illinois Country: Historic Tribes, 1958, rev. edits., 1966, 77, 87, Lincoln the Railsplitter, 1961, Abraham Lincoln and Others at the St. Nicholas, 1968, Alexander Williamson-Tutor to the Lincoln Boys, 1971, (with others) First Steps to Victory: Grant's March to Naples, 1977, Lincoln and Grant: Illinois Militiamen, 1981, Stephen A. Douglas: Freemason, 1982, Lincoln as a Lecturer, 1982, By Square and Compasses: The Building of Lincoln's Home and Its Saga, 1984, Lincoln's Connections with the Illinois and Michigan Canal, 1986, Dr. Anson G. Henry: Personal Physician to the Lincolns, 1988, Abraham Lincoln: From Skeptic to Prophet, 1995, Thomas and Abraham Lincoln as Farmers, 1996, Alexander Williamson: Friend of the Lincolns, 1998, By Square and Compass: Saga of the Lincoln Home, 2002, The Taste Is In My Mouth a Little...Lincoln's Victuals and Potables, 2004, Abraham Lincoln and Illinois' Fifth Capitol, 2006, Abraham Lincoln's Travels on the River Queen, 2007; co-author: Illinois's Fifth Capitol: The House that Lincoln Built, 1988; contbg. author: Capitol Centennial Papers, 1988; editor: Campaigning with Grant, 1961, 72, The Civil War Letters of Henry C. Bear, 1961; 71 radio scripts A. Lincoln 1809-1959, Indian Villages of the Illinois Country: Atlas Supplement, 1975; mem. editl. bd. Am. Biog. Inst., 1971—, Ency. Indians of Ams., 1973—; contbr. articles to profl. jours., encys. Sponsor Abraham Lincoln Bay, Washington Nat. Cathedral; mem. Ill. State Flag Commn., 1969—; trustee, regent Lincoln Acad. Ill., 1970-82, Bicentennial Order Lincoln, 2009; bd. govs. St. Louis unit Shriners Hosps. for Crippled Children, 1975-81; commissioning com., hon. crew mem. and plank owner USS Springfield submarine, 1990—; hon. crew mem. USS Abraham Lincoln aircraft carrier, 1989—. With U.S. Army, 1943-46, gen. Res. (ret.). Decorated Bronze Star Medal, Silver Citizenship medal SAR, 1993, Literary Merit Gold medal Ill. Lodge of Rsch., 1993; recipient Order of Arrow Boy Scouts Am., 1957, Scouters award, 1960, Scouter's Key, also medallion, 1967, Lincoln medallion Lincoln Sesquicentennial Commn., 1960, award of Achievement U.S. Civil War Centennial Commn., 1965, Algernon Sydney Sullivan medallion, 1969, Distinguished Service award Ill. State Hist. Library, 1969, 77, I.H. Duval Distinguished Service award, 1971, legion of honor Internat. Supreme Council, Order of De Molay, 1972, Disting. Service award Civil War Round Table of Chgo., 1983, 91, George L. Cashman award Civil War Round Table Springfield, 2009, Cert. Excellence Ill. State Hist. Soc., 1985, Archbishop Richard Chenevix Trench award, 1999; Lincoln Diploma Honor, Lincoln Meml. U., Harrogate, Tenn., 1963, Lifetime Achievement award 2001; named Hon. Ky. Col., Marshal of Okla. Territory. Fellow Royal Soc. Arts (life); mem. NRA, KT (Red Cross Constantine), Lincoln Group D.C. (hon.), U. Ill. Alumni Assn., Ill. State Hist. Soc., Board of Advisors, The Lincoln Forum, Ill. Profl. Land Surveyors Assn., Ill. State Dental Soc. (citation plague 1966), Res. Officers Assn., Lincoln Fellowship of Wis., Iron Brigade Assn. (hon. life), Mil. Order Loyal Legion U.S. (hon. companion), Mil. Order Fgn. Wars U.S., Army and Navy Union, Masons (33 degree, Meritorious Svc. award, grand rep. from Grand Lodge of Colo.), Shriners, Kappa Delta Pi, Phi Alpha, Phi Alpha Theta (Scholarship Key award), Chi Gamma Iota, Phi Beta Kappa, Tau Kappa Alpha, Alpha Psi Omega, Sigma Pi Beta (Headmaster), Sigma Tau Delta (Gold Honor Key award for editorial writing), Zeta Psi. Presbyterian (elder). Home: 1121 S 4th Street Ct Springfield IL 62703-2200 Office: Ill State Archives Springfield IL 62756-0001 Office Phone: 217-782-3501. *Only in America could a poor farm boy from Ohio work his way through a great university, like the University of Illinois, and receive a doctor's degree. Life has been kind to me, and I have tried hard and worked hard. I am proud to be an American.*

TEMPLEMAN, LYDIA, retired assistant principal; b. Sydney, 1913; arrived in U.S., 1946; d. Giuseppe and Maria Concetta Lo Schiavo; m. Bruce Liscum Templeman, May 20, 1950; 1 child, Geoffrey. BA, Sydney U., 1934, diploma in Edn., 1935; grad., Royal Acad. London, 1935; MA, U. Mich., 0950, B of Econs., 1956. Tchr. NSW Dept. Edn., Sydney, Australia, 1936—46, Jackson, Mich. Edn. Dept., 1947—91; asst. prof. Fullerton, Calif. Dept. Edn., 1967—91; ret., 1991. Owner, operator Bren Travel Svcs., Calif., 1965—88. Author: Travel Agency Operation, 1988, Dollars and Sense, 2004; tour dir. Europe, 1956—80. Mem.: Calif. Ret. Tchrs. Assn. Democrat. Roman Catholic. Avocations: sailing, motor boats.

TEMPLETON, BRAD, information technology executive, software engineer, entrepreneur; b. Can., 1960; s. Charles Templeton and Sylvia Murphy. B in Math., U. Waterloo, 1982. First employee with Personal Software/Visicorp; founder ClariNet Communications Corp., Waterloo, Canada, 1989, pub., 1989—98; founder Looking Glass Software Ltd.; chmn. bd. dirs. Electronic Frontier Found.; CEO Caller App Inc., 2007—. Bd. dirs. Foresight Inst. for Nanotech, BitTorrent, Inc. Author: (CD-ROM) Hugo and Nebula Anthology 1993, 1993; contbr. articles to profl. jours. Named one of 50 Most Important People on the Web, PC World, 2007. Achievements include invention of the world's first ever ".com" company. Avocations: photography, writing, acting, singing. Office: Electronic Frontier Found 454 Shotwell St San Francisco CA 94110

TEMPLETON, CHELNECA (CHELLY TEMPLETON), education educator; b. Ashland, Ky., Jan. 2, 1952; d. Ray and Edna Kegley; m. Gary Templeton, Dec. 29, 1972; children: Gary Wayne Jr., Jonathan Ryan, Natalie Rae. BA in Elem. Edn., U. Ky.; MA in Early Childhood Edn., Marshall U.; EdD, Fla. Atlantic U. Gifted tchr. Mohawk Trads Smoky Row Elem., Carmel, Ind., 1993—97; assoc. prof. edn. Palm Beach Atlantic U., Fla., 2002—. Grantee tchg. fellowship, Eli Lilly, 1993. Mem.: ASCD, Am. Edn. Rsch. Assn., Nat. Assn. Edn. Young Children, Oxford Roundtable (del. 2004), Phi Kappa Phi. Home: 5154 Monterey Ln Delray Beach FL 33484 Office: Palm Beach Atlantic U 901 S Flagler Dr Delray Beach FL 33416 Business E-Mail: chelly_templeton@pba.edu.

TEMPLETON, JOHN MARKS, JR., retired pediatric surgeon, foundation administrator; b. NYC, Feb. 19, 1940; s. John Marks and Judith Dudley (Folk) T.; m. Josephine J. Gargiulo, Aug. 2, 1970; children: Heather Erin, Jennifer Ann. BA, Yale Coll., 1962; MD, Harvard U., 1968; degree (hon.), Beaver Coll., Buena Vista U., Va. Commonwealth U., Alvernia Coll. Intern Med. Coll. Va., Richmond, 1968-69, resident, 1969-73; dir. trauma program U. Pa. and Children's Hosp. Phila., 1989—95, prof. pediat. surgery, 1995. Chmn. bd. Templeton Growth Fund, Ltd. Assoc. editor: Textbook of Pediatric Emergencies, 1993; pub. 6000 Name Geneology, 1997, A Searcher's Life, 1999, Thrift and Generosity, 2004. Chmn. health and safety, exec. bd. Cradle of Liberty coun. Boy Scouts Am.; mem. exec. bd. Eastern U., Fgn. Policy Rsch. Inst., Nat. Recreation Found., Coll. Physicians Phila., Melmark Charitable Found.; nat. bd. dirs., pres. Pa. divsn. Am. Trauma Soc.; bd. dirs. Nat. Bible Assn.; elder Proclamation Presbyn. Ch.; pres. John Templeton Found. With M.C., USNR, 1975-77; bd. mem. Am. Trauma Soc., Foreign Policy Rsch. Inst., Nat. Bible Assn., EAST Found., John Templeton Found., Session and Proclamation Presbyterian Ch. Barclay fellow Green Templeton Coll., Oxford U., fellow George H. Gallup Internat. Inst. Mem. ACS, AMA, Am. Pediat. Surg. Assn., Am. Acad. Pediats., Am. Assn. Surgery Trauma, Ea. Assn. Surgery Trauma, Phila. Coll. Physicians, Union League, Order Charlemagne, Lyford Cay Club, Merion Cricket Club, Athenaeum Club London, Rotary Internat., White's London, United Oxford and Cambridge U. Club (London). Republican. Evangelical. Office: 300 Conshohocken State Rd Ste 500 West Conshohocken PA 19428 Personal E-mail: templeton.pembroke@comcast.net.

TEMPLETON, RICHARD K., electronics executive; BSEE, Union Coll., NY, 1980. Various positions Tex. Instruments, Inc., Dallas, 1980—91, v.p. semiconductor group, 1991—94, mgr. worldwide application specific products, 1993—96, sr. v.p. semiconductor group, 1994—96, exec. v.p., pres. semiconductor group, 1996—2004, COO, 2000—04, pres., CEO, 2004—08, chmn., pres., CEO, 2008—. Bd. dirs. Tex. Instruments, Inc., 2003—, Semiconductor Industry Assn. Mem. Bus. Roundtable, Dallas Chief Exec. Roundtable. Office: Tex Instruments Inc PO Box 660199 Dallas TX 75266-0199 Office Phone: 972-995-2011. Office Fax: 972-995-4360.

TEMPLIN, DONALD C., lawyer; b. Jacksonville, Fla., Nov. 10, 1945; BA, Yale U., 1967; JD, U. Okla., 1970. Bar: Okla. 1970, Tex. 1972, admitted to practice: US Supreme Ct., US Ct. Appeals (Fed. Cir.), US Ct. Appeals (5th Cir.), US Ct. Appeals (9th Cir.), US Ct. Appeals (10th Cir.). Ptnr., Intellectual Property Litig. Group Haynes and Boone LLP, Dallas, head, Litig. Sect. Lectr. in field. Contbr. articles to profl. jours. Chmn., exec. com. March of Dimes Birth Defect Found. of North Tex., 1998—99. Capt. USMC, 1971—73. Fellow: Am. Coll. Trial Lawyers; mem.: State Bar Tex., ABA (Intellectual Property Sect.), Okla. Bar Assn., Am. Bd. Trial Adv., Order of Coif. Office: Haynes and Boone LLP 3100 NationsBank Plz 2323 Victory Ave Dallas TX 75219-7657 Office Phone: 214-651-5590. Office Fax: 214-200-0593. Business E-Mail: don.templin@haynesboone.com.

TEMPLIN, NOREEN, finance educator; d. Orlando and Mabel Penner; m. Trey Templin, May 29, 1999; children: Andrew, Braeden. BBA in Internat. Bus., Wichita State U., Kans., 1998, MA in Economics, 2000. Investment rep. Edward Jones Investment, Wichita, 2000—03; adj. instr. Wichita State U., 2004—. Debt cons. Lain Empowering Solutions, Elbing, Kans., 2004—. Named Adj. Instr. of Yr., Wichita State U., 2007. Home: PO Box 22 Elbing KS 67114

TEMPLIN, ROY W., manufacturing executive; B in Acctg., Ind. U., Bloomington. CPA. With Price Waterhouse, Indpls., NCR Corp., Dayton, Ohio; various positions including dir. corp. acctg. and dir. corp. fin. Cummins Engine Co., Columbus, Ind.; v.p. fin., chief acctg. officer Kimball Internat. Inc.; corp. v.p., contr. Whirlpool Corp., Benton Harbor, Mich., 2003—04, exec. v.p., CFO, mem. exec. com., 2004—. Office: Whirlpool Corp 200 N M-63 Benton Harbor MI 49022-2692

TEMPORITI, JOHN J., lawyer, former political organization administrator; b. 1949; BA, Cardinal Glennon Coll., 1971; JD, St. Louis U., 1975. Chief of staff to mayor City of St. Louis, 1981—85; ptnr., mem. mgmt. com. Gallop, Johnson & Neuman, St. Louis, 1985—97, of counsel, 2007—; exec. v.p. UniGroup, 1997; pres., CEO Mayflower Van Lines, 1998—99, Vanliner Insurance Co., 1999—2004; chief govtl. affairs St. Louis County, 2004—07; chmn. Mo. Dem. Party, 2007—09. Mem. Democratic Nat. Com. (DNC), 2007—09. Mem.: ABA, Bar Assn. of Met. St. Louis, Mo. Bar Assn. Democrat. Office: Gallop Johnson & Neuman 101 S Hanley Ste 1700 Saint Louis MO 63105 Office Phone: 314-615-6007. Office Fax: 314-615-6001.*

TEMSCH, RICHARD, research and development company executive, consultant; b. Vienna, Dec. 21, 1950; s. Erna and Franz Temsch; m. Fatima Fernandez, Aug. 28, 2000. PhD in Chemistry, U. Vienna, 1978.

Cert. in Russian U. Vienna, 1978, in Polish U. Vienna, 1978, in Serbo-Croatian U. Vienna, 1978, in French U. Vienna, 1978, in Italian U. Vienna, 1978. Expert World Bank, Tbilisi, Georgia; export mgr. Biotronik, Maintal, Germany, 1979—92; pres. Missing Link Internat. Consulting Corp., San Francisco, 1992—; adviser selection strategic ptnrs. biotechnology Medipolis, Oulu, Finland, 1995—2000; chief tech. adviser biomedical engring. ctrs. UN Indsl. Devel. Orgn., Sarajevo, Bosnia-Herzegovina, 1999—2001; evaluator, support program leather sector Austrian Ministry Fgn. Affairs, Kampala, Uganda, 2002; internat. expert UN Indsl. Devel. Orgn., Vienna, 2003—. Lectr. economy post-crisis countries Naval Postgrad. Sch., Monterey, Calif., 2001—; faculty mem., cultural seminars Afghanistan Can. Forces, Ottawa, 2007—. Contbr. scholarly articles. Local, program coord. internat. rels. forum Commonwealth Club Calif., San Francisco, 1995—2008. Mem.: Austrian Internat. Cons. (Winner of Project of the Month 2008), Am. Chem. Soc. Business E-Mail: richard@themissinglinkconsulting.com.

TEN, CHEE-WOOI, electrical engineer, researcher; b. Alor Star, Kedah Darul Aman, Malaysia, May 30, 1978; s. Kin-Kok Ten and Sow-Geit Teh; m. Sheu-Sheu Tan. BSEE, Iowa State U Sci. and Tech., Ames, 1999, MSEE, 2001, PhD in Electric Power Engring., 2006—. Summer intern Mid Am. Energy, Des Moines, 2000; network application engr. Siemens Energy Mgmt. and Info. Sys., Singapore, 2002—05; rschr. Iowa State U Sci. and Tech., 2005—. Contbr. articles to profl. jours. Mem.: IEEE. Achievements include research in power system visualization; power infrastructure cybersecurity. Avocations: badminton, jogging, swimming, basketball, bicycling. Home: 2549 Jalan Sultanah Taman Lumba Kuda Alor Setar Kedah Darul Aman 05250 Malaysia Office: Iowa State Univ 2215 Coover Hall Ames IA 50011-3060 Personal E-mail: cheewooi@gmail.com. Business E-Mail: cheewooi@iastate.edu.

TENDER, GABRIEL CLAUDIU, neurosurgeon, consultant; s. Vasile and Maria Tender; m. Deborah Elizabeth Burch, Nov. 4, 2006; 1 child, Liliana Arres. MD, La. State U., New Orleans, 2008. Cert. neurosurgery La., 2005. Neurosurgery resident La. State U., New Orleans, 1999—2005, asst. prof. neurosurgery, 2005—. Cons. Trans1, Stryker, New Orleans, 2007—. Contbr. scientific papers (Resident award, 2004). Spine surgery devel. LSU, New Orleans, La., 2005—08. NASS grant, North Am. Spine Soc., 2006. Mem.: Congress Neurol. Surgeons. Achievements include research in pain, complex spine. Office: La State Univ 2020 Gravier St Ste 326 New Orleans LA 70112

TENDLER, DAVID, investment company executive; b. NYC, Jan. 15, 1938; s. Philip and Pearl (Berman) T.; m. Beatrice Weisberg, Oct. 11, 1958; children: Pearl, Karen. BBA in Internat. Econs., CCNY, 1959. With Philipp Bros. Co., 1960—, mgr. Far Eastern ops., 1968-75, pres. NYC, 1975—; dir. parent corp. Engelhard Minerals & Chems. Corp. (name changed to Phibro Corp. 1981), NYC, 1975-85, vice chmn. bd., 1979-81, chmn. bd., CEO, 1981—; co-chmn., co-CEO Phibro-Salomon Inc., NYC, 1983-84; ptnr. Tendler Beretz, L.L.C. Ltd., NYC, 1985—. Chmn. subcom. trade U.S.-German Dem. Rep. Trade and Econ. Coun., 1978—84; bd. dirs., mem. exec. com. U.S./USSR Trade and Econ. Coun., 1979—85, U.S.-China Bus. Coun., 1983—94, 1994—2005; bd. dirs. V.I. Techs., Inc., Watertown, Mass., 1994—2007, Savient Pharm., East Brunswick, NJ, 2004—07, Agrifos Fertilizer Inc., Pasadena, Tex., 2005—07. Mem. bd. overseers NYU Grad. Sch. Bus., 1981-85; trustee Lenox Hill Hosp., 1981-94; trustee, mem. exec. com. N.Y. Blood Ctr., 1987—; bd. dirs., mem. exec. com. Fgn. Policy Assn., 1983-96; bd. dirs. Ctr. for the Advancement of Women, N.Y.C., 1999-2007; mem. adv. coun. Weissman Ctr. for Internat. Bus., Baruch Coll., 2001. Recipient Torch of Liberty award metals and metal products divsn. Anti-Defamation League, 1976, Edith and Herbert Lehman award Henry St. Settlement, 1982; named Man of Yr., Fgn. Trade Soc., Baruch Coll., CUNY, 1985. Office: Tendler Beretz LLC 150 E 52nd St New York NY 10022-6017 Office Phone: 212-593-0550. Personal E-mail: tenchan@aol.com.

TENENBAUM, ANN G., art association administrator; b. Savannah, Ga., June 1961; m. Thomas H. Lee; children: Stephen Zachary, Robert Schiff. Grad., Sarah Lawrence Coll. Mem. vis. com. dept. photogs. Met. Mus. Art, 1996—2005, trustee, 2005—; vice chmn. bd. trustees Dia Art Found., NYC, 1994—2006. Co-pres. bd. trustees Film Soc. Lincoln Ctr. for Performing Arts; founding mem. bd. govs. Bard Coll. Ctr. Curatorial Studies; bd. dirs. Sarah Lawrence Coll., Channel 13/WNET, Studio Mus., Harlem, Second Stage Theatre, Guild Hall East Hampton; mem. chmn.'s coun. Mus. Modern Art. Recipient Leo award, Ind. Curators Internat., 2003, Child Advocacy award, NYU Child Study Ctr., 2003; named one of Top 200 Collectors, ARTnews mag., 2003—08. Avocation: Collector of Modern and contemporary art; Egyptian art. Office: c/o Met Mus Art 1000 5th Ave New York NY 10028

TENENBAUM, BERNARD HIRSH, entrepreneur, educator; b. Long Beach, NY, Dec. 23, 1954; s. Abraham Benjamin and Helen Pearl (Wahrhaft) T. BA, Columbia Coll., NYC, 1976; postgrad., Stanford U., Calif., 1976-77; MBA, U. Pa., Phila., 1981. Mgr. Lido Beach (N.Y.) Hotel, 1976-77; gen. mgr. Sound Spectrum, Huntington, N.Y., 1977-78; dir. Small Bus. Ctr., Phila., 1980-84; asst. dir. Entre Ctr., Phila., 1984-85, assoc. dir., 1986-88; prof. entrepreneurial studies, dir. Fairleigh Dickinson U., Madison, N.J., 1988-93; v.p. corp. devel. Russ Berrie & Co., Inc., 1993-97; founding dir. George Rothman Clin. Prof.of Entrepreneurial Studies, George Rothman Inst. of Entrepreneurial Studies; pres. Children's Leisure Products Group, NYC, 1997—; mng. ptnr. China Cat Capital, LLC, 2006—; advisor Bel Air Ptnrs., 2000—. Cons. Phila. Phillies, 1984-85; bd. dirs., Unger Global, Franklin Mint., Syms Corp., 2006-. Del. Securities Exchange Commn. on Small Bus. Capital Formation, 1984-86; vice chmn. Small Bus. Devel. Ctr. adv. bd., Phila., 1983—; bd. dirs. Pvt. Industry Council, Phila., 1983-88; chmn. Small Bus. Fair, Phila., 1983-88. Mem. Phila. C. of C. (vice chmn. small bus. coun. 1982-86, chmn. 1986-88), Venture Assn. N.J. (v.p.). Democrat. Jewish. Avocations: swimming, sports cars, music, literature, films. Office: Bel Air Ptnrs 71 Tamarack Cir Skillman NJ 08558 Office Phone: 609-252-1125. Office Fax: 609-252-1322. E-mail: bernie@btenenbaum.com.*

TENENBAUM, INEZ MOORE, federal agency administrator, former school system administrator; b. Hawkinsville, GA, Mar. 8, 1951; m. Samuel J. Tenenbaum. BS in Edn., U. Ga., Athens, 1972, MSE in Edn., 1974; JD, U. S.C. Law Sch., Columbia, 1986. Tchr. Elementary Sch.; dir. rsch. S.C. House of Reps., 1977-83; atty. Sinkler & Boye, P.A., Columbia, SC, 1986-92; supt. S.C. Dept. Edn., Columbia, SC, 1999—2007; chmn. US Consumer Product Safety Commn., Bethesda, Md., 2009—. Founder S.C. Ctr. Family Policy. Democrat. Methodist. Office: US Consumer Products Safety Commn 4330 E West Highway Bethesda MD 20814*

TENENBAUM, JEFFREY S., lawyer; b. Boston, Oct. 29, 1968; BA, Univ. Pa., 1990; JD, Catholic Univ. Am., 1996. Bar: DC. Legis. asst. U.S. Ho. Reps., 1990—93; legal sect. mgr., govt. affairs analyst Am. Soc. Assn. Exec., Washington, 1993—95; of counsel Venable LLP, Washington, 1999—2003, ptnr., Nonprofit Assns., Trade & Profl. Assns. practices, 2003—. Spkr. in field. Author: Association Tax Compliance Guide; contbr. articles to profl. jours., magazines, newspapers; mem. editl. adv. bd. Assn. Law & Policy, 2000—, Nonprofit Tax & Financial Strategies, 1996—2002. Recipient Chairman's award, Greater Washington Soc. Assn. Exec., 1997, Ctr. for Assn. Leadership, 2004; named Outstanding Nonprofit Lawyer of Yr., Bus. Law Sect., ABA, 2006; named a Top Washington Lawyer, Washington Bus. Jour., 2004. Mem.: Am. Soc. Assn. Exec. Office: Venable LLP 575 7th St NW Washington DC 20004 Office Phone: 202-344-8138. Office Fax: 202-344-8300. Business E-Mail: jstenenbaum@venable.com.

TENENBAUM, JOSEPH, cardiologist; b. Neptune, NJ, Feb. 11, 1946; s. Sol and Marilyn Tenenbaum; m. Marilou Faith Jones, May 19, 1978; 1 child, Mollie Rodriguez. BA, Brandeis U., 1968; MD, Harvard U., 1974. Diplomate Am. Bd. Internal Medicine, Am. Bd. Cardiology. Edgar Leifer clin. prof. medicine Columbia U., NYC, 1979—; attending physician, interim chair dept. medicine Presbyn. Hosp., NYC, 2001—03. Fellow Am. Coll. Cardiology; mem. Columbia Faculty Practice Orgn. (chmn. 2000-03) Office: 161 Fort Washington Ave New York NY 10032-3713 Office Phone: 212-305-5288.

TENER, CAROL JOAN, retired secondary school educator, consultant; b. Cleve., Feb. 10, 1935; d. Peter Paul and Mamie Christine (Dombrowski) Manusack; m. Dale Keith Tener, Feb. 13, 1958 (div. Aug. 1991); children: Dean Robert, Susan Dawn Tener Belair. Student, Cleve. Mus. Art, 1948-53, Cleve. Art Inst., 1953-54; BS in Edn. cum laude, Kent State U., 1957; MS in Supervision, Akron U., 1974; postgrad., Kent State U., 1964, 81, 88-90, Akron U., 1975, postgrad., 1979, John Carroll U., 1982, 83, 85-86, Ohio U., 1987, Baldwin Wallace Coll., 1989. Cert. permanent K-12 tchr., Ohio; cert. vol. counselor for Ohio sr. health ins. Ohio Dept. Ins. Stenographer Equitable Life Iowa, Cleve., 1953-54; tchr. elem. art Cuyahoga Falls (Ohio) Bd. Edn., 1957-58, 62-63, 65-68, tchr. jr. high sch., 1968-69; tchr. high sch. Brecksville (Ohio)-Broadview Heights Sch. Dist., 1969-94; chmn. dept. art Brecksville-Broadview Heights (Ohio) HS, 1979—94, chmn. curriculum devel., 1982, 1989, quality deployment team employee recognition district- wide bd. level, 1993—94; ret., 1994. Instr. for children Kent State U., 1956; advisor, prodr. cmty. svc. in art Brecksville Broadview Heights Bd. of Edn., 1969-94; former tchr. recreation and adult art edn. City of Cuyahoga Falls, 1967-68; com. mem. North Ctrl. evaluation com. Nordonia H.S., Nordonia City, Ohio, 1978, Solon H.S., Solon City, Ohio, 1989; chmn. north ctrl. evaluation com. Garfield Heights H.S., 1991; chair pilot program curriculum devel. com. in art/econs. Brecksville-Broadview Heights H.S., 1985-86, 86-87; spkr. in field. Contbr. articles to newspapers, brochures, mags.; commd. artist for mural Brecksville City's Kids Quarters, 1994, Christopher Columbus/John Glen portraits in relief commemorating Columbus Day, 1961, Wooster (Ohio) Products Co.; editor Greater Cleve. chpt. Ohio Ret. Tchrs. Assn., 1998-2002; contbr. to Resources for You, 2003, Ohio Sr. Health Ins. Info. Program, Ohio Dept. Ins., 2001—. Chmn. Artmart Invitational Exhibit PTA, 1982-94; active Meals on Wheels program in Brecksville and Broadview Hts., 1995-98, Heart Disease collection, 1995, Stow-Glen Assisted Living Visitations, 1994-95, NCR Assisted Living transp. provision to hosps. and dr. in neighboring county; trustee, sec. Gettysburg Devel. Block Group Parma, 1995-96, Kids Quarters, 1994; Med Save fraud vol. Cuyahoga County Dept. Sr. and Adult Svcs., 2000-2002, spkrs. bur.; sr. health ins. info. program, cert. vol. counselor OSHIIP County Dept. Ins., Ohio Dept. Ins., 2001-, vol. coord. spkr. and healthfair mktg., OSHIIP, 2004-05. Recipient Ohio Coun. on Econ. Edn. award, 1985-86, award for significant svc. to cmty. Ret. and Sr. Vol. Program of USA, 1996, Svc. award Greater Cleve. Chpt./Ohio Ret. Tchrs. Assn., 1998, Outstanding Svc. award Sr. Medicare Patrol Projects, Cert. of Appreciation, U.S. Dept. Health and Human Svcs. Adminstrn. on Aging, 2002; Pres.'s scholar Kent State U., 1954-57; Resolution to thank a Med-Save Project Vol. signed by Cuyahoga County Commrs. Tim McCormack, pres., Jimmy Dimora, v.p., and Peter Lawson Jones, commr. Mem.: NAFE, ASCD, NEA (life), AAUW, S.W. Area Ret. Educators (co-chair 1996—98, program chair 1996—98, program coord. 1999—2000), Nat. Mus. Women in Arts, Cleve. Mus. Art, Acad. Econ. Edn., Brecksville Edn. Assn., Internat. Platform Assn., Nat. Art Edn. Assn., Ohio Ret. Tchrs. Assn. (life; registration chair 1997—98, pres.-elect Cleve. chpt. 1998, program chair 1998, interim editor 1998, circulation mgr. 1998—2002, chpt. pres. 1999, editor 1999—2002, trustee 2000, guest spkr. on newsletter writing and pub. 2000, nominating chair 2000—01, by-law chair 2000—01, Pub. Rels. awards 1999—2002), Phi Delta Kappa Pi. Roman Catholic. Avocations: photography, collecting books on architecture, painting. Home: 7301 Sagamore Rd Parma OH 44134-5732 Office Phone: 440-885-2231.

TENET, GEORGE JOHN, investment company executive, former CIA director; b. Flushing, NY, Jan. 5, 1953; m. A. Stephanie Glakas; 1 child, John Michael BS in Fgn. Svc., Georgetown U., 1976; MIA, Columbia U., 1978. Legis. asst. to Sen. H. John Heinz III Senate Select Com. on Intelligence, Washington, 1985-86, designee to vice chair Sen. Patrick J. Leahy, 1986-89, dir. oversight of arms control negotiations Soviet Union/US, 1989-93, staff dir. to chmn. Senator David Boren, 1993; mem. presdl. transition team Nat. Security Coun., Washington, 1993-95, spl. asst. to pres., sr. dir. intelligence programs, 1995-97; dep. dir. CIA, Washington, 1995-96, acting dir., 1996-97, dir., 1997—2004; disting. prof. in practice of diplomacy Edmund Walsh Sch. Fgn. Svc. Georgetown U., Washington, 2004—07, sr. rsch. assoc. Inst. Study of Diplomacy, 2004—07; mng. dir. Allen & Co. LLC, NYC, 2008—. Sr. rsch. assoc. Inst. for the Study of Diplomacy, Washington, 2004—; bd. dirs. L-1 Identity Solutions, Inc. (formerly Viisage Tech. Inc.), 2005—, Guidance Software, Inc., 2005—08; ind. non-exec. dir. QinetiQ Group plc, 2006—08; bd. dirs. QinetiQ N. Am., 2008—. Author: At the Center of the Storm: My Years at the CIA, 2007 Recipient Presdl. Medal of Freedom, The White House, 2004. Office: Allen & Company LLC 711 5th Ave New York NY 10022

TEN EYCK, DOROTHEA FARISS, real estate agent; b. Pulaski County, Va., Dec. 2, 1923; d. Orel Cronk and Esther Mildred (Rexrode) Fariss; m. George Ten Eyck, Jan. 4, 1947 (dec.); m. John S. Kreeger, Aug. 27, 1965 (dec.); m. Robert L. Ten Eyck, Oct. 30, 1994; 6 children Student, Ind. U. Market rsch. Proctor & Gamble, Cin., 1944-47; ptnr. Santee Builders, 1960—63. Pres. women's com. Cin. Art Mus., mem. adv. com., docent emeritus; mem. Elder Indian Hill Ch. Independent. Presbyterian. Avocations: golf, gardening, travel, volunteerism. Home: 3032 Alpine Ter Cincinnati OH 45208-2925

TENG, CHRISTINA T., molecular biologist, researcher; b. Kuming, Yunan, China, July 23, 1942; d. Wellington Sj Tu and Sonia Sl O'Young; m. Ching Sung Teng, July 11, 1964; children: Janet In, Peggy Yn. PhD, U. Tex., Austin, 1966—69. Postdoc. resh. Rockefeller U., New Yori, 1969—71; rsch. fellow Nat. Brookhaven Nat. Lab., Stony Brook, NY, 1971—73; asst. prof. Baylor Coll. Medicine, Houston, 1973—81, NC State U., Raleigh, NC, 1981—83; expert NIEHS, NIH, Rsch. Triangle Pk., NC, 1981—83, prin. investigator, 2008—. Sect. head NIEHS, NIH. Mem.: Endocrine soc. Achievements include patents for screen for lactoferrin gene polymorphism. Office: Lrdt NIEHS NIH 111 TW Alexander Dr Durham NC 27709 Office Fax: 919-541-1978. Business E-Mail: teng1@niehs.nih.gov.

TENG, RENLI, pharmacologist, director; m. Lisa Zhang. PhD, Coll. Pharmacy, U. Ky., Lexington, 1992. Sr. dir. Astra Zeneca, Wilmington, Del., 1998—. Mem.: AAPS. Achievements include research in pharmacokinetics & clinical pharmacology. Office: AstraZeneca 1800 Concord Pike Wilmington DE 19850

TENG, WENYUAN WILLIAM, dean; 1 child, Jason. PhD. in Bus. Adminstrn., U. Memphis, 1998. Cert. fin.mgr. Dean bus. sch. King Coll., Bristol, Tenn., 2005—. Treas. and deacon Chinese Ch. Greater Tri-Cities. Mem.: Inst. Cert. Mgmt. Accts., CFA Inst., Am. Economics Assn. Office: Sch Bus King Coll 1350 King Coll Rd Bristol TN 37620 Business E-Mail: wyteng@king.edu.

TENGEL, JEFFREY J., bank executive; B in Acctg., Marquette U., Milw.; MBA, Case Western Res. U., Cleve. Corp. mgmt. trainee Nat. City Corp., 1986, various positions in corp. banking, mergers and acquisitions, credit, structured fin. divsn. mid. market corp. banking group, chief credit officer Wholesale Banking, chief credit officer, exec. v.p. comml. banking - nat. Mem. adv. com. Case Western Res. U. Office: Nat City Corp Nat City Ctr 1900 E Ninth St Cleveland OH 44114-3484 Office Phone: 216-222-2000.

TENGLUND, ANN M., librarian; d. Carl Arnold and Alice Taylor Tenglund. MS in Edn., St. Bonaventure U., NY; MLS, Syracuse U., NY, 1999; postgrad., Nova Southeastern U., Ft. Lauderdale, Fla., 2006—. Cert. K-12 reading tchr. NY, N-6 elem. tchr. NY, 7-12 bus. edn. tchr. NY. Libr. St. Bonaventure U., St. Bonaventure, NY, 1982—. Presenter in field. Treas. Immanuel Luth. Ch., Olean, NY, 1993—2006. Mem.: ALA, Am. Ednl. Rsch. Assn., Assn. Study Higher Edn., Assn. Instl. Rsch., Assn.Coll. and Rsch. Librs. (com. mem. 2003—04). Office: St Bonaventure U 3261 West State Rd Saint Bonaventure NY 14778 Office Fax: 716-375-2389. Business E-Mail: ateng@sbu.edu.

TENHAGEN, ALLISON MAE, psychologist; d. Bill and Mary Erickson; m. Steve Tenhagen, July 29, 2006. BS, U. Whitewater, MSE, 2005. Sch. psychologist Beloit Turner Sch. Dist., Wis., 2004—, varsity volleyball coach, 2007—. Named All-Am. Volleyball Divsn. III, Am. Volleyball Coaches Assn., 2000—01, Nat. Player of Yr., 2001, Wis. Sportswomen of Yr., 2001. Mem.: Wis. Sch. Psychologists Assn.

TENHOEVE, THOMAS, academic administrator; b. Bklyn., Oct. 1, 1935; s. Thomas and Adeline Ruth (Vander Hill) T.; m. Suzanne Underwood, June 7, 1957; children: Thomas III, Carol, Timothy. AB, Hope Coll., 1956; MA, U. Mich., 1957; PhD, U. Toledo, 1965; postgrad., U. Western Mich.; EdD (hon.), Northwestern Coll., 1995. Biology tchr. South Haven. Mich. Pub. Schs., 1957-58; biology instr. Northwestern Coll., Orange City, Iowa, 1958-63; supr. biology student tchrs. U. Toledo, Ohio, 1963-65; acad. dean, acting pres. Northwestern Coll., Orange City, 1965-70; pres. Butler (Pa.) County Community Coll., 1970-84, Oakton Community Coll., Des Plaines, Ill., 1984-95. Dir. CoVest Banc, 1987—99. Bd. dirs. Sister Cities Internat., 1986-95, 1998-2004, nat. v.p., treas., 2001-04; trustee Northwestern Coll., 1988-95; mem. Ill. C.C. State Found. Bd., 1993-95, Ill. Math. and Sci. Acad. Selection Bd., 1986, 87, Cook County Sheriff's Scholarship Panel; exec. com. Golden Corridor, 1986-92; vol. Good Samaritan Ministries, 2001-. Recipient Pacesetter award Nat. Coun. for Community Rels., 1986, Orchard Village award, Skyway Conf. Hall of Fame. Mem. Am. Coun. on Internat. Intercultural Edn. (chmn. 1992-95), Coun. North Ctrl. Two-Yr. Colls. (state rep. 1988-92, exec. bd. 1989-95, 2d v.p. 1990-91, 1st v.p. 1991-92, pres. 1992-93).

TENKE, CRAIG E., neuroscientist, consultant; b. Port Jefferson, NY, Oct. 19, 1950; s. Emery and Ruth Irene Tenke; m. Jo-Ann Bullock; children: Elizabeth Ann, Connie Jean. BA summa cum laude, SUNY, Stony Brook, 1972; MA in Neuropsychology, Queens Coll., Flushing, NY, 1976; PhD in Neuropsychology, CUNY, 1983. Postdoc. trainee in neurosci. Albert Einstein Coll. Medicine, Bronx, NY, 1987. Adj. lectr., dept. psychology Queens Coll., NYC, 1973—80, rsch. asst. dept. psychology; sci. computer programmmer NY, 1981—88; rsch. assoc. dept. neurosci. Albert Einstein Coll. Medicine, 1987—88; rsch. scientist NYS Psychiat. Inst., NYC, 1988—; rsch. assoc. dept. psychiatry Columbia U., NYC, 2003—. Mem. grant rev. Stanley Med. Rsch. Inst., 2006; assoc. editor. Clin. Neurophysiology. Contbr. scientific papers, articles to med. jours. Ruling elder Presbyn. Ch. Moriches, Ctr. Moriches, NY, 1998—2008; mem. coun. edn. Presbytery LI, NY, 2001—06. Recipient Schizophrenia Rsch. award, NYS Psychiat. Inst., 1991—93; grants, NIMH, 1988—. Mem.: AAAS, Am. Pain Soc., NY Acad. Scis., Soc. Neurosci. Independent. Presbyterian. Achievements include development of application quantify brain generators of scalp-recorded electrical activity; methods to identify. Office: NYS Psychiat Inst Columbia Univ 1051 Riverside Dr New York NY 10032-2695

TENKORANG, FRANK A., economist, educator; m. Comfort Duodu; children: Nana Ama, Kojo. PhD, Purdue U., West Lafayette, Ind., 2006. Asst. prof. U. Nebr., Kearney, 2006—. Mem.: Agrl. & Applied Economics Assn. Office: Univ Nebr Kearney WSTC 306C 905 W 25th St Kearney NE 68849 Business E-Mail: tenkorangf1@unk.edu.

TENNANT, JOHN RANDALL, management consultant; b. North Bend, Wash., Aug. 23, 1940; s. Maurice Andrew and Jane Downing (Vinnedge) T.; m. Nikki Mae Priem, July 17, 1965 (div.); children: Ann Elizabeth, Randall Warren; m. Deborah Ann Francis, Oct. 25, 1986 (div.); 1 child, Alyssa Jane; m. Carol A. McDonnell, Feb. 2, 2005. BS in Indsl. Engring., Stanford U., 1962; MBA, U. Wash., 1966. Registered profl. engr., Wash. Sr. rsch. engr. Boeing Co., Seattle, 1962-68; mgr. Price Waterhouse, Seattle, 1968-73, ptnr. Tokyo, 1973-79, Los Angeles, 1979-89; founder, CEO, Manex, Inc., Newport Beach, Calif., 1989—; dir. subs. Price Waterhouse Assocs., Pacific region, 1975-79. Mem. John Tracy Clinic Men's Com., Santa Catalina Island Conservancy, pres., 1985-87; capt. Long Beach Mounted Police. Mem. NSPE, Japan Computer Assn. (founder, pres. 1976-77), Japan Modapts Assn. (founder), Japan Am. Soc., Inst. Mgmt. Cons., Am. Inst. Indsl. Engrs. (pres. Seattle chpt. 1970-71), Data Processing Mgmt. Assn., Tokyo Lawn and Tennis Club, L.A. Country Club, Jonathan Club, Empty Saddle Club, Los Rancheros Visitadores Club, Los Caballeros Club. Home: 332 Sunset Ct Oak View CA 93022 Office Phone: 310-618-0299. Personal E-mail: tennantrjohn@aol.com.

TENNANT, NATALIE E., state official; b. 1967; m. Erik Wells, June 20, 1998; 1 child, Delaney. Grad., W. Va. U., 1991. TV anchor, reporter, W.Va.; co-owner Wells Media Group LLC; sec. state State of W. Va., Charleston, 2009—. Mem.: Am. Heart Assn. (bd. mem. Great Rivers Affiliate). Democrat. Office: Office Sec State Bldg 1 Suite 157 K 1900 Kanawha Blvd East Charleston WV 25303-0770 Business E-Mail: wvsos@wvsos.com.*

TENNEN, LESLIE IRWIN, lawyer, consultant; b. Toronto, Aug. 26, 1952; came to U.S., 1961; s. Edward and Elsie (Liberbaum) T.; m. Patricia MargaretSterns. BA with distinction, U. Ariz., Tucson, 1973, JD, 1976; Mount Scopus, Hebrew U., Jerusalem, 1975. Bar: Ariz. 1977, US Dist. Ct. Ariz. 1979, US Ct. Appeals (9th cir.) 2007. Sole practice, Tucson, 1977—79; ptnr. Sterns and Tennen, Phoenix, 1979—. Cons. internat. law and aerospace activities; lectr. univs., colls. and law schs., UN(Vienna); mem. Ariz. Space Commn., 1994-2000, inventor, profl. aviation and aerospace congresses and seminars in N.Am., Europe, Asia, S.Am., Australia; judge Jessup Internat. Moot Court Competition, 1982, 83, 85, 92; dir., treas. Assn. US Mems. Internat. Inst. Space Law; com. mem. U. Belarusian Culture Internat. Orgn. Mem. editl bd. Space Regulations Libr.; contbr. Ariz. Law Rev., 1975-76; contbr. articles to profl. jours. Precinct committeeman State Dem. Conv., 1972-73. Received highest score Ariz. Bar Exam., Feb. 1977. Mem. AIAA (sr.), Ariz. Bar Found., Internat. Eurasian Acad. Scis., Internat. Inst. Space Law (Appreciation award 1998, Disting. Svc. award 2006), Internat. Acad. Astronautics, Am. Soc. Internat. Law, Soc. Aerospace Communicators Inc., Internat. Law Assn., Planetary Soc., Fedn. Aerospace Socs. in Tucson (exec. bd.). Office: 2915 N 16th Ave Phoenix AZ 85015 Office Phone: 602-254-5197. Business E-Mail: LTennen@astrolaw.com.

TENNER, SCOTT, physician, researcher; b. Boston, June 26, 1963; s. Mark Joel and Brenda Pearl Tenner; m. Monica Tenner; 1 child, Samantha. BS, George Washington U., 1985, MS, 1987, MPH, MD, 1991. Resident George Washington U. Med. Ctr., Washington, 1988-94; fellow Brigham and Women's Hosp., Harvard Med. Sch., Boston, 1994—. Author: Pocket Guides to Disease, 1991. Mem. Alpha Omega Alpha. Avocations: european history, philosophy of science, painting, racquetball. Office: Brigham and Women's Hosp 75 Francis St Boston MA 02115-6106

TENNESON, MICHAEL GUNNAR, biology professor; s. Corinne Tenneson; m. Cheryl L. Combs, Sept. 3, 1977; children: Gabriel Michael, Joshua Elijah, Anna Mishael. PhD, U. Mo., Columbia, 2001. Prof. biology Evangel U., Springfield, Mo., 1987—. Office: Evangel Univ 1111 N Glenstone Ave Springfield MO 65802

TENNESSEN, KENNETH J., retired entomologist; b. Ladysmith, Wis., June 10, 1946; s. Joseph A. Tennessen and Lydia Perger; m. Sandra F. Erdman; children: Jeffrey J., Gregory A. PhD, U. Fla., Gainesville, 1975. Biologist TVA, Muscle Shoals, Ala., 1975—2002; cons. Wis. Dept. Natural Resources, Madison, Wis., 2004—. With US Army, 1970—71. Recipient Hammer award, TVA, 1995. Mem.: Dragonfly Soc. Americas (pres. 1996—97). Achievements include discovery of 12 new species of dragonflies. Home: 125 N Oxford St Wautoma WI 54982 Home Phone: 920-787-2171. Personal E-mail: ktennessen@centurytel.net.

TENNEY, JANE MORRIS, real estate developer; d. Mendel Morris and Floreine Welch; m. Mark William Tenney, June 1, 1974; m. Daniel Marston Shepherd, Mar. 16, 1957 (div.); children: Daniel Vincent Shepherd, David Morris Shepherd. BS, U. Ky., 1962. Sales rep. IBM, South Bend, 1975—80; pres. Technivest, Inc., South Bend, Ind., 1980—88; mgr. bus. incubator Control Data, South Bend, 1984—89; owner, pres. Tenney Assocs., Inc, Niles, Mich., 1992—. Land developer Longmeadow Residential and Comml. Cmty., Niles, Mich., 1997—. Elected del. White Ho. Conf. of Small Bus., Washington, 1984—84. Recipient Demonstration Project on Watershed Devel. Design, Conservation Fund, 1997, Women of Yr., Four Flags C. of C., 2003. Mem.: Nat. Assn. of Realtor, Nat. Home Builders Assn. Office: Tenney Assocs Inc 126 Churchill Ln Niles MI 49120

TENNEY, SARAH G., music educator; b. NYC, Apr. 30, 1948; d. John Wool Griswold and Margaret Brett Tenney. BA, Bennington Coll., 1971; MusM, New Eng. Conservatory, 1976. Founder Spectrum Young Audiences Trio, Boston, 1976-80; marimba, percussion tchr. Rivers Music Sch., Weston, Mass., 1976-80, 85—, St. Ann's Sch., Bklyn., 1980-85; founder, dir. Marimba Magic, Weston, 1987—; tchr. improvisation Northeastern U., Boston, 1991-95. Percussionist on 6 Revel records; percussionist/timpanist in Christmas Revels, 1980—; presenter in field. Composer: (composition/musical) Gamelon Dream, 1989, Mysterious Waltz, 1991, Whole Tone Dream, 1996, Adventures, 1999, Machines, 2000, Jaja Mani Dreams, 2001, Drum Circle, 2002, 3 Canons, 2003, Moving Music, 2004, More Moving Music, 2005, April Fool's Music, 2007; composer: (with Martha Rogers) Returning to Mt. Greylock, 2008; composer: Circles, 2009. Concert performer Concerts for Children, 1976-80, Cambridge World's Fair, 1997, 98, Clarimba Duo, 2002—03, WCRB Cartoonfest, Symphony Hall, 2005, World Premiers Marimba Mague With Boston Musica Viva, 2003, 05, 08. Recipient Am. Composers Forum grant. Mem. Music Tchrs. Nat. Assn. (conf. presenter 1991), Musicians Union, Music Educators Nat. Conf. (presenter ea. conf. 1992, 96), Percussive Arts Soc. (presenter internat. conv. 1989, 97), Orff Schulwerk Assn. (presenter nat. conf. 1996) presenter European Piano Tchrs. Assn., Internat. Conf., Budapest, 2000, Internat. Marimba Conf., Belgium, 1992, All State Mass. Conf., 2007 Office: The Rivers Sch Conservatory 337 Winter St Weston MA 02493-1072 Office Phone: 781-235-6840.

TENNIES, ROBERT HUNTER, headmaster; b. Bogotá, Colombia, Aug. 19, 1952; s. Leo C. and Ruth (Winston) T.; m. Ruth Ellen Fischer, June 14, 1975; children: Debbie, Julie. BS, Wheaton Coll., Ill., 1973; MA, U. South Fla., 1975; EdS, Fla. Atlantic U., 1978, EdD, 1982. Sci. tchr. Cypress Lake Middle Sch., Ft. Myers, Fla., 1973-77, Boca Raton (Fla.) Christian Sch., 1977-78, asst. adminstr., 1978-84, headmaster, 1984—, min. of children, 1984-90; interim. min. of edn., 1991-93. Spkr. Internat. Conf. Religious Edn., Petrozavodsk, Russia; mem. Nat. Rev. Panel Blue Ribbon Schs., 1999. Recipient Excellence in Edn. award Nat. Assn. Elem. Prins., 1990, 97, Presentation award, Internat. Children Educators Conf., Hong Kong, China, 2008. Mem. Assn. of Christian Schs. Internat. (chair Fla. accreditation commn., 2007), Nat. Assn. Elem. Sch. Prins. Avocation: camping. Home: 2415 NW 30th Rd Boca Raton FL 33431-6214 Office: Boca Raton Christian Sch 315 NW 4th St Boca Raton FL 33432-3739 Office Phone: 561-391-2727. Business E-Mail: bocachristian@bocachristian.org.

TENNIHILL, SALLY KAY, writer, music educator; b. Columbus, Feb. 14, 1941; d. Wayne Harris and Ruth Anne Downs; m. Jack Tennihill (dec.), Oct. 17, 1961; children: John, Ralph, Myrtle, Joe. Student, Ohio State U., 1959—61; BA in English, Northwest Mo. State U., 1985, MA in English, 1987. Tchr. piano, Maryville, Mo., 1970—; cert. nurse asst. Nodaway Nursing Home, Maryville, Mo., 1982-84; grad. asst. Northwest Mo. State U., Maryville, Mo., 1985-86, tchg. asst., 1986-87; substitute tchr. St. Joseph (Mo.) Sch. Bd., 1988-93; stringer St. Joseph News-Press, 1988-92. Mem. Univ. Players, 1982—85. Actor: Mid Summer Night's Dream, 1982, Texas Trilogy, 1983, Ten Little Indians, 1990, Do Not Disturb, 1994; dir.: Nodaway County Theatre Co., 1991—96, Everybody Loves Opal, 1996; author: (one act musical, romantic comedy) Steak, Potatoes and a Little Romance, 1995; editor: (creative mag.) Envy's Sting, 1985—86; contbr. poems and short stories to books/anthologies; Reenactment Julia Dent. Grant, S Grant Festival, Cincinatti Ohio, 1998; contbr. articles jour. Mem. Coalition Against Domestic Violence, Maryville, Mo., 1987-96, Prison Fellowship, Maryville, 1996, Willa Cather Found., Maryville, 1993-96; head Women's Resource Ctr. Northwest Mo. U., Maryville, 1984-87; pres. M.S. Support Group, Maryville, 1995-96; v.p. Nodaway County Civil War Roundtable, pres. 1996-2002. Recipient Mattie Dykes Creative Writer scholarship, Presdl. Scholar's scholarship. Mem. AAUW, Retired Tchrs. Maryville, Sons and Daus. of the Civil War, NW Mo. Multiple Sclerosis Support Group. Home: 123 Park Ave Maryville MO 64468-1347 Office Phone: 660-562-3339.

TENNIMON, DANNIE EARL, academic administrator, educator; b. Selma, Ala., Mar. 15, 1947; s. Earl and Mary Tennimon; m. Lori Dee Krehbiel, Feb. 7, 1991; m. Kathy Leann McCowan, Aug. 31, 1968 (div. Feb. 1, 1991); children: Tara Lee Faulkner, Shelby Danielle, Brandi Kay Miller, Shandon Earl. BA, Auburn U., Ala., 1970; MEd, Boston U., 1975; MA in Tchg., Troy State U., 1995. Commd. lt. U.S. Army, 1970, advanced through grades to lt. col., 1988, ret., 1994; asst. to pres. Troy State U., Montgomery, Ala., 1996—2004; coord. instl. rsch., effectiveness and planning Troy U., Montgomery, 2004—. Adj. instr. history Troy U., Montgomery, 1998—; presenter in field. Deacon Millbrook Presbyn. Ch., Ala., 1996—2001, ruling elder, 2001—. Decorated Bronze Star with oak leaf cluster U.S. Army, Meritorious Svc. award with 2 oak leaf clusters, Joint Svc. Meritorious Svc. award. Mem.: Soc. Coll. and U. Planning (assoc.), Assn. Instnl. Rsch. (assoc.), So. Assn. Instnl. Rsch. (assoc.), Ala. Assn. Instnl. Rsch. (assoc.; pres. 2003—04), Gamma Beta Phi (assoc.). Avocations: travel, backpacking, military history. Home: 46 Pine Mountain Court Millbrook AL 36054 Office: Troy University PO Drawer 4419 Montgomery AL 36103-4419 Office Fax: 334-241-8619; Home Fax: 334-285-1257. Personal E-mail: ltennimon@yahoo.com. Business E-Mail: dtennimon@troy.edu.

TENNISON, LYNDEN, rail transportation executive; m. Sue Tennison; 1 child. B, U. Tex., Arlington. Various mgmt. and tech. positions AT&T and Southwestern Bell Tel., 1979—87; with SABRE divsn. Am. Airlines; with Union Pacific Corp., Omaha, 1992—, pres., CEO Nexterna, 1998—2001, v.p. info. techs., chief tech. officer Union Pacific RR, 2001—05, sr. v.p., chief info. officer, 2005—. Bd. dirs. Applied Distbn. Group. Office: Union Pacific Corp 1400 Douglas St Omaha NE 68179 Office Phone: 402-544-5000.

TENORIO, PEDRO AGULTO, former Resident Representative from Northern Mariana Islands; b. Saipan, Aug. 8, 1941; BA in Geology, U. Hawaii, MS in Hydrology. Sen. No. Marianas Congress of Micronesia, 1972—74; mem. No. Marianas Polit. Status Commn., 1973—76; exec. dir. No. Marianas Office Transition Studies and Planning, 1975—77, Marianas Pub. Land Corp., 1977—81; legis. adv. 1st Commonwealth No. Mariana Islands (CNMI) Legislature, 1977—81; lt. gov. CNMI, 1981—89; resident rep. from the Northern Mariana Islands US Congress, Washington, 2001—09. Mem. Rep. Nat. Com., Presdl. Victory Team. Mem.: Nat. Rep. Club Capitol Hill, Lions Club East Manoa. Republican.*

TENPAS, RONALD JAY, lawyer, former federal agency administrator; b. 1963; m. Kathryn Dunn; children: Nathaniel, William. BA in Internat. Rels., Mich. State U., 1985; degree in Philosophy, Politics & Economics, Oxford U., Balliol Coll., Eng., 1987; JD, U. Va., 1990. Law clk. to Hon. Louis H. Pollak US Dist. Ct. (ea. dist.) Pa., 1990—91; law clk. to Chief Justice William H. Rehnquist US Supreme Ct., Washington, 1991—92; law clk. to Hon. Howard Holtzmann Iran-U.S. Claims Tribunal, The Hague, Netherlands, 1992—93; assoc. Carlton Fields, P.A., Tampa, Fla., 1993—97; asst. US atty. (mid. dist.) Fla. US Dept. Justice, 1997—99, asst. US atty. Md., 1999—2003, branch chief Dist. Md. So. Divsn., 2001—03, US atty. (so. dist.) Ill., 2003—05, assoc. dep. atty. gen., 2005—07, asst. atty. gen. for environment & nat. resources, 2007—09; ptnr. Morgan, Lewis & Bockius LLP, Washington, 2009—. Editor in chief Va. Law Rev. Recipient Edmund J. Randolph Award for Outstanding Svc., US Dept. Justice; Rhodes scholarship, 1985—87, Hardy Cross Dillard scholarship, 1987—90. Mem.: Md. Fed. Bar Assn. (bd. governors), Am. Assn. Rhodes Scholars. Office: Morgan, Lewis & Bockius LLP 1111 Pennsylvania Ave NW Washington DC 20004 Office Phone: 202-739-5435. Office Fax: 202-739-3001. E-mail: rtenpas@morganlewis.com.

TENSER, BETH HILLARY, graphics designer, art director; b. Balt., Nov. 4, 1966; d. David Elliott and Myrna Pruzon Tenser. BA, Adelphi U., 1991; MA, NY Inst. Tech., 1993. Dir. art Island Art & Restoration, Elmont, NY, 1991—96, Bond Distbg. Co., Balt., 1997—; co-founder Creative Cups A Breast Cancer Fundraiser on LI, 2009—. Singer (Nat. Anthem): Oriole Pk. at Camden Yards, 2003; Poster Competition, 1989, Liver Let Die, 1991, Outback Steakhouse's Annual Golf Tournament, 1997—, Howard County Hosp. Cancer Ctr. Fundraiser, 2006—. Pres. resident student assn. Adelphi U., Garden City, NY, 1989—91; co-founder Annual Celebrate Life Charity for Lou Gehrig's Disease, Md., 2007—. Recipient Academic Excellence in Leadership, Provosts, 1991. Mem.: The Babe Ruth Mus. Democrat. Avocations: singing, sports, travel, photography, volunteer work. Home: 2 High Stepper Ct #102 Baltimore MD 21208 Office Phone: 443-418-1060. Personal E-mail: btenser@verizon.net.

TENUTA, LUIGIA, lawyer; b. Madison, Wis., June 4, 1954; d. Eugene P. and Nancy (Gardner) T. AB in Internat. Studies with honors, Miami U., Oxford, Ohio, 1976; JD, Capital U., 1981; postgrad., Pontifical Coll. Josephinum, 1987-88. Bar: Ohio 1981. With internat. mktg. dept. Dresser Industries, Columbus, Ohio, 1976-80, analyst strategic planning, 1980, mgr. internat bus. planning Stratford, Conn., 1981; pvt. practice law Columbus, 1981—. Former mem. devel. com. Miami U. Mem. Ohio Bar Assn., Columbus Bar Assn. Roman Catholic. Office: 6400 Riverside Dr Dublin OH 43017-5197

TEODORESCU, VICTORIA JEAN, surgeon; b. Newark, June 1, 1952; MD, NYU Sch. Medicine, 1985. Diplomate Am. Bd. Surgery with subspecialty in gen. vascular surgery. Intern Mt. Sinai Med. Ctr., NYC, 1985-86, resident surgery, 1986-91, fellow vascular surgery, 1991-92; hosp. appt. Bronx VA Med. Ctr., NYC; asst. prof. surgery Mt. Sinai Sch. Medicine, NYC. Mem. AMA

TEPER, JEFFREY ALLEN, computer software company executive; b. 1964; s. Gary Teper; m. Sandy Rynczak, Sept. 14, 1991; 2 children. BS in Info. Systems and Finance, NYU; MBA, Harvard U. Sr. v.p. Colonial Consulting Corp., NYC; with Windows Corp., 1992—, dir. orgn. mktg. & info, gen. mgr. SharePoint Portal Server bus. group, 2001—07, corp. v.p. Office SharePoint Server group, Office bus. platform, 2007—. Office: Microsoft Corp SharePoint Server Group 1 Microsoft Way Redmond WA 98052-6399

TEPLÁN, ISTVÁN, SR., biochemist, researcher; b. Magyarkeszi, Hungary, Sept. 4, 1932; s. Katalin Kovacs; m. Tünde Soproni, 1957 (div. 1964); 1 child, István; m. Katalin Farkass-Jablanczy, 1965; 1 child, Attila. Master's degree, Eötvös Lorand U., Budapest, 1957, Univ. Dr., 1966; PhD, Lomonosov U., Moscow, 1966; DSc (hon.), Hungarian Acad. Sci. (HAS), Budapest, 1978. Rsch. asst. Pharm. Rsch. Inst., Budapest, 1957-59; rsch. assoc. Inst. Isotopes, Budapest, 1960-71; vis. scientist Rockefeller U., NYC, 1971-73; sr. scientist Semmelweis Med. U., Budapest, 1973—87, rsch. prof., 1987—2002; main adviser to the pres. HAS, 2002—. Gen. dir. Nat. Sci. Dept., 1973—2002. Contbr. sci. articles to internat. jours.; patents in field. Recipient Order of Labor, Pres. of the Republic (Silver medal 1970, Gold medal 1976), award of the Acad. Presidium of HAS, 1978, A Magyar Köztársaság Érdemrend Középkeresztje, 1996, Széchenyi-price, 2003. Mem. Hungarian Acad. Sci. (dep. gen. sec. 1995-96), European Peptide Soc., Am. Peptide Soc. Avocations: gardening, collecting old books, tennis. Home: Tövis u 35 H-1026 Budapest Hungary E-mail: teplani.tovis@citromail.hu.

TEPLEY, NORMAN, physics educator; b. Denver, Dec. 14, 1935; s. David Jack and Ida Elizabeth (Cohen) T.; m. Aviva Judith Rubin, June 24, 1959 (dec. June 1967); 1 child, Jamina Esther; m. Elaine Ruth Ash, Aug. 24, 1969; children: Philip Scott, Alan Joseph. BS, MIT, 1957, PhD, 1963; postgrad., Columbia U., 1957-59. Asst. prof. physics Wayne State U., Detroit, 1963-69; assoc. prof. physics Oakland U., Rochester, Mich., 1969-77, prof., 1977—, chmn. dept., 1983—. Vis. prof. physics U. Lancester, U.K., 1970; dir. neuromagnetism lab. Henry Ford Hosp., Detroit, 1988—; faculty research participant Argonne (Ill.) Nat. Lab., 1971. Mem. AAAS, Am. Phys. Soc., Sigma Xi. Precinct worker Detroit Dem. Com., 1972; bd. dirs. Hickory Grove Homeowners Assn., Bloomfield Hills, Mich., 1982, treas. 1982, pres. 1983. Research grantee Air Force Office Sci. Research, 1964-69, NSF, 1972, Office Naval Research, 1982, NIH, 1993—. Jewish. Office: Oakland U Dept Of Physics Rochester MI 48309

TEPLITZKY, JACKY, real estate broker; b. Chile; arrived in US, 1989; Mng. dir. Prudential Douglas Elliman, NYC. Mem. edn. com. Real Estate Bd. of NY; adj. prof. NYU; lectr. Real Estate Inst.; spkr. in field. Adv. bd. Pajama Program. Mem.: Women's Internat. Zionist Orgn., UJA Fedn. of NYC (mem. Lions of Judah, Real Estate Com., and Women Exec. Coun.). Office: Prudential Douglas Elliman Real Estate 575 Madison Ave New York NY 10022 Office Phone: 212-891-7263. Office Fax: 464-497-5136. E-mail: jteplitzky@elliman.com.*

TEPLOW, THEODORE HERZL, retired valve company executive; b. Brockton, Mass., Apr. 14, 1928; s. Edward Abraham and Evelyn (Stone) T.; m. Charlotte Leah Savitz, June 14, 1953; children: Rachel P., David I., Deborah R., Evan S., Jonathan P. BS, U.S. Mcht. Marine Acd., 1950; MBA, Harvard U., 1953; DHL honoris causa, Hebrew Coll., 1999; PhD honoris causa, Weizmann Inst. Sci., 2002. Mgmt. trainee to pres. Crosby Valve Inc. a Tyco Internat. Ltd. Co., Wrentham, Mass., 1953-82, cons., 1982—2001; dir. Emerson Investment Mgmt., Inc., Boston, 1985—2008. Cons. Firesafe Products Corp., N.Y.C., 1982-96; pres. Gateway Investment Corp., 2003—. Trustee Am. Mcht. Marine Mus. Found., Kings Point, NY, 1988—98, Rofeh Internat., Boston, 1990—, Hebrew Coll., Newton Center, Mass., 1971—2009, chmn., 1992—99, Hebrew Coll. Bd. Mgrs. of Trust Property, 1999—; trustee Kings Point Challenge, 1997—, US Mcht. Marine Acad., Kings Point, 2002—; v.p., bd. dirs. Internat. Catacomb Soc., Boston, 1982—99; asst. treas., dir. Am. Com. for Weizmann Inst. Sci., NY, 1987—2002, vice chair fin. and adminstrn., dir., 2002—; gov. Weizmann Inst. Sci., Rehovoth, Israel, 1991—; dir. Archives for Hist. Documentation, Boston, 1994—2009; bd. dirs. Nat. Ctr. Jewish Policy Studies, LA and Boston, 1993—2009, Cong. Beth El-Atereth Israel, Newton Center, 1975—85, Beth El Cmty. Hebrew Sch., Newton Center, 1965—86, US Mcht. Marine Acad. Alumni Found., Kings Point, 1957—, Stone Charitable Found., 1982—99. Comdr. USNR, ret. Recipient Outstanding Profl. Achievement award U.S. Mcht. Marine Acad. Alumni Assn., 1970, Meritorious Alumni Svc. award, 1990, Disting. Svc. award, 1995. Democrat.

TEPPER, CLIFFORD, allergist, immunologist, educator; b. Schenectady, NY, Oct. 26, 1922; s. Solomon B. and Annette (Lifset) T.; m. Cynthia S. Tepper; children: Stewart, Nancy, Henry, Audrey. Chief allergy dept. Ellis Hosp., Schenectady, 1990—; allergist allergy asthma immunology ctr. Albany (N.Y.) Med. Coll., 1992—, prof. pediats., 1973—. Co-dir. Schenectady Vol. Physicians Free Clinic; cons. in field. Trustee Schenectady Mus., 1987-99, Schenectady Pub. Libr., 1985—; pres. Antismoking Acad. Schenectady County; co-dir. Vol. Physician Clinic, Shcenectady County. Mem. Coll. Allergy and Immunology, Am. Acad. Pediatrics, Am. Acad. Allergy and Immunology, New Eng. Soc. Allergy (pres. 1990-92), N.Y. State Allergy Soc. (treas. 1993-95), Eastern Allergy Soc. (exec. com.), Physicians for Social Responsibility. Avocations: bird watching, art history. Home: 2216 Stoneridge Rd Niskayuna NY 12309-5524 Office: Allergy Asthma Immunology Ctr Albany Med Coll 1201 Washihngton Ave Ext Albany NY 12205 Fax: 518 452 2683. E-mail: tepperc@mail.amc.edu.

TEPPER, DAVID ALAN, hedge fund manager; b. Pitts., Sept. 11, 1957; m. Marlene Tepper, 1986; children: Brian, Randi, Casey. BA in Econs., with honors, U. Pitts., 1978; MS in Indsl. Adminstrn., Carnegie Mellon U., Pitts., 1982. Credit & securities analyst Equibank, Pitts., 1978—80; mem. treas. dept. Republic Steel, Ohio, 1982—84; with Keystone Mutual Funds, Boston, 1984—85; credit analyst Goldman Sachs, NYC, 1986, head trader high-yield desk, 1986—92; founder, pres. Appaloosa Mgmt., Chatham, NJ, 1993—. Mem. bus. bd. advisors Carnegie Mellon U. Tepper Sch. Bus. Named one of The World's 25 Highest-Paid Hedge Fund Managers, Institutional Investor/Alpha mag., 2003, 2004, Top 25 Hedge Fund Earners, 2006, 400 Richest Americans, Forbes mag., 2005, 2006, World's Richest People, 2006; named to Guru Hall of Fame, GuruFocus.com, 2007. Office: Appaloosa Mgmt 26 Main St Chatham NJ 07928 Office Phone: 973-701-7000.*

TEPPER, LLOYD BARTON, occupational and preventive medicine physician, educator; b. LA, Dec. 21, 1931; m. Lamonte Leverage; children: Jeffrey Hamilton, Evan Clothier. AB, Dartmouth Coll., 1954; MD, Harvard U., 1957, MIH, 1960, ScD in Hygiene, 1962. Diplomate Am. Bd. Preventive Medicine (trustee, vice chair, 1986-94), Am. Bd. Occupl. Medicine. Intern U. Calif., San Francisco, 1957—58; resident Harvard Sch. Pub. Health, 1959—62; rsch. fellow Harvard Med. Sch., Boston, 1958-59; clin. fellow Mass. Gen. Hosp., Boston, 1958-60; rsch. assoc. MIT, Cambridge, 1959-61; physician U.S. AEC, Washington, 1962-65; prof. environ. health U. Cin., 1965-72; assoc. dir. Kettering Lab., Cin., 1965-72; assoc. commr. U.S. FDA, Washington, 1972-76; corp. med. dir. Air Products and Chems., Inc., Allentown, Pa., 1976-97; adj. prof. medicine Jefferson Med. Coll., 1998—2001. Adj. prof. emergency medicine occupl. and environ. medicine U. Pa., 2000—. Editor: Jour. Occupl. Medicine, 1979—91. Fellow: Am. Acad. Occupl. Medicine (pres. 1980—81), Am. Coll. Occupl. and Environ. Medicine. Office Phone: 610-527-8918. E-mail: lbtepper@icdc.com.

TEPPER, LYNN MARSHA, gerontologist, educator; b. NYC, Mar. 16, 1946; m. William Chester Tepper, Aug. 27, 1967; children: Sharon Joy, Michelle Dawn. BS, SUNY, Buffalo, 1967; MA, Wayne State U., 1971; MS, Columbia U., 1977, EdM, 1978, EdD, 1980. Instr. John F. Kennedy Sch., Berlin, 1967-68, ednl. counselor, 1968-69; ednl. coordinator Army Edn. Ctr., Berlin, 1969-71; psychologist U.S. Dept. Def., Berlin,

1971-73; prof. gerontology L.I. U., 1979—2000, Mercy Coll., Dobbs Ferry, 1979—, Columbia U., NYC, 1982—. Cons. NATO, Naples, Italy, 1969-71, SHAPE, Brussels, 1969-71, Found. for Long Term Care, 1992—, others; dir. Gerontology Resource Ctr., Ctr. for Geriatrics and Gerontology, Columbia U., NYC, 1980-85, dir. Behavioral Sci. Program, 1982—; del. White House Conf. on Aging, 1980; clin. prof. Columbia U., 1982— Author: (textbooks) Long Term Care, 1993, Respite Care, 1993, Multidisciplinary Perspectives on Aging, 2004; contbr. articles to profl. jours., chpts. to books. Advisor Office on Aging, State of N.Y., Albany, 1980-90; dir. Mercy Coll., Inst. Gerontology, 1990—; trustee, St. Cabrini Nursing Home, 1988-98, Morningside Nursing Home, 1998—; bd. dirs. Found. Long Term Care. Brookdale Inst. on Aging fellow, 1983; rsch. grantee NIH, Nat. Inst. on Aging, Nat. Inst. Gen. Med. Sci., U.S. Dept. Edn., U.S. Bur. Health Professions, interdisciplinary geriat. tng. U.S. Dept. Health Resources Svcs. Adminstrn. Fellow Gerontol. Soc. Am.; mem. Am. Psychol. Assn. Avocations: hiking, bicycling. Office: Columbia U Med Campus Box 20 630 W 168th St New York NY 10032-3702

TEPVORACHAI, GORN, financial analyst; BS, MS, Case Western Res. U., Cleve., 2004, PhD, 2008. Lab. asst. Case Med. Sch., Cleve., 2002—05; rsch. asst. Case Western Res. U., 2003—08; analyst Bank Thailand, Pranakorn, Bangkok, 2008—. Recipient V-Fund award, Case Western Res. U., 2008, award, 2008; scholarship, Thai Govt., 1999—2004, Case Prime fellowship, Case Western Res. U., 2004—08. Mem.: IEEE, IEEE CIS (Conf. Traveling grant 2008), Golden Key Internat. Avocations: badminton, ballroom dancing, gardening. Home: 93 S Jackson St #6457 Seattle WA 98104 Office: Bank of Thailand IT Dept Bldg 1 5th Fl Zone 4 273 Samsen Rd Pranakorn Bangkok 10200 Thailand Office Phone: 66 85 7164667. Personal E-mail: gorn_mst@hotmail.com. Business E-Mail: gorn@case.edu.

TEQUILA, TILA See NGUYEN, TILA

TERADA, ALICE MASAE, retired elementary school educator; b. Hilo, Hawaii, Nov. 13, 1928; d. David Matsuo and Mitsuko (Sekido) Marutani; m. Harry T. Terada, Aug. 25, 1951; children: Suzanne T. Henderson, Keith Y., Lance S. Diploma, Queen's Hosp. Sch. Nursing, 1950; BS, We. Res. U., 1953; MEd, U. Hawaii, 1971. Cert. tchr., Hawaii. Registered nurse County Meml. Hosp., Hilo, Hawaii, 1950-51, U. Hosps., Cleve., 1952-53; lang. arts tchr. Dept. Edn., Honolulu, 1967-68; reading tchr. Reading Ctr., Honolulu, Hawaii, 1968-82; ret. Author: Under the Starfruit Tree, 1989, The Magic Crocodile, 1994. Mem. AAUW, Internat. Reading Assn., Zonta Club Internat., Zonta Club Honolulu (bd. dirs. 1996-97). Avocations: art, art history, porcelain antiques, yoga, swimming.

TERBORG-PENN, ROSALYN MARIAN, historian, educator; b. Bklyn., Oct. 22, 1941; d. Jacques Arnold Sr. and Jeanne (Van Horn) Terborg; 1 dau., Jeanna Carolyn Terborg Penn. BA in History, Queens Coll. CUNY, 1963; MA in History, George Washington U., 1967; PhD in Afro-Am. History, Howard U., 1978. Daycare tchr. Friendship House Assn., Washington, 1964-66; program dir. Southwest House Assn., Washington, 1966-69; adj. prof. U. Md.-Balt. County, Catonsville, 1977-78, Howard C.C., Columbia, Md., 1970-74; prof. history Morgan State U., Balt., 1969—, prof. emeritus, 2008, project dir. oral history project, 1978-79, coord. grad. programs in history, 1986—. Project dir. Assn. Black Women Hist. Rsch. Conf., Washington, 1982-83. Author: (with Thomas Holt and Cassandra Smith-Parker) A Special Mission: the Story of Freedman's Hospital, 1862-1962, 1975, African American Women in the Struggle for the Vote, 1850-1920, 1998; editor: (with Sharon Harley) The Afro-American Woman: Struggles and Images, 1978, 81, 97; (with Darlene Clark Hine and Elsa Barkley Brown) Black Women in America: An Historical Encyclopedia, 1993, 94; (with Sharon Harley and Andrea Benton Rushing) Women in Africa, 1987; (with Andrea Benton Rushing) Women in Africa and the African Diaspora: A Reader, 1996; (with Janice Sumler-Edmond) Black Women's History at the Intersection of Knowledge and Power, 2000; (with Robert L. Harris Jr.) The Columbia Guide to African American History, 2006; history editor Feminist Studies, 1984-89; mem. editl. bd. Md. Hist. Mag., 1988-94. Founding mem. Howard County Commn. for Women. Ford Found. fellow, 1980-81, Smithsonian Instn. fellow, 1982, 94-95, Howard U. grad. fellow in history, 1973-74; recipient Rayford W. Logan Grad. Essay award Howard U., 1973, Letitia Woods Brown Meml. prize for best article, 1988, Anna Julia Cooper award for disting. scholarship Sage Women's Ednl. Press, 1993, Letitia Woods Brown Meml. Book prize, 1998, Disting. Black Marylander in Edn. award, Towson Univ., 2003, Carter G. Woodson Scholars Medallion award Assn. Study African Am. Life and History, 2008, Outstanding Woman award Morgan State U., 2008. Mem. Assn. Black Women Historians (co-founder, 1st nat. dir. 1979-83, nat. treas. 1982-84, cert. outstanding achievement 1981, Lorraine A. Williams Leadership award 1998), Assn. Caribbean Historians(exec. com. mem., 1989-90, 2008-), Am. Hist. Assn. (mem. com. on women historians 1978-81, Joan Kelly Prize com. 1984-86, chair com. on women historians 1990-94), Assn. Study African Am. Life & History(mem. program com., 1979, 1985), Assn. for Study Worldwide African Diasporce(founding mem., mem-exec. bd., 2000-07),Orgn. Am. Historians (mem. black women's history project adv. com. 1980-81, nominations com. 2005-08), Alpha Kappa Alpha (mem. Internat. Archives and Heritage com. 1994-96). Office: Morgan State U 1700 E Cold Spring Ln Baltimore MD 21251-0002 Office Phone: 443-885-3190. Personal E-mail: rosalynterborgpenn@yahoo.com.

TERESI, JEANNE A., medical researcher, director; Sr. rsch. scientist Columbia U. Stroud Ctr., NYC, NY State Psychiat. Inst., NYC, 1974—. Adminstr. Rsch. Divsn., Hebrew Home Riverdale, NYC, 2009—, dir., 2009—.

TER HORST, JERALD FRANKLIN, public affairs counselor, former White House press secretary; b. Grand Rapids, Mich., July 11, 1922; s. John Henry and Maude (Van Strien) ter H.; m. Louise Jeffers Roth, Jan. 20, 1945(Dec. Mar. 21, 2009); children: Karen Bayens Morris, Margaret Fulton Robinson, Peter Roth, Martha Morgan Lubin. Student, Mich. State U., 1941-42; BA, U. Mich., 1947. Reporter Grand Rapids Press, 1946-51; mem. staff Detroit News, 1953-74, city and state polit. writer, 1953-57, fgn. assignments include Berlin crisis, Vietnam, Israel, Germany, USSR, Latin Am., 1959, Washington corr., 1958-60; chief Detroit News (Washington bur.), 1961-74; press sec. The White House, Washington, 1974; nat. affairs columnist Detroit News/Universal Press Syndicate, 1974-81; dir. nat. pub. affairs Ford Motor Co., 1981-91. Writer N.Am. Newspaper Alliance, 1958-74 Author: Gerald Ford and Future of the Presidency, 1974, The Flying White House: The Story of Air Force One, 1979; contbr. to mags. and TV documentaries. Bd. dirs. Nat. Press Found., 1982-98, WETA-TV (Channel 26), 1988-99, Brady Campaign to Prevent Gun Violence, 1992-2002; chmn. Gridiron Found., 1978-2005, Grad. Sch. Polit. Mgmt., George Washington U., 1985-96. Officer USMCR, 1943-46, 51-52. Recipient Conscience in Media award, Am. Soc. Journalists & Authors, 1975. Mem. Pub. Rels. Soc. Am., Soc. Profl. Journalists, Psi Upsilon. Presbyterian (elder). Clubs: Gridiron, Nat. Press. Overseas Writers. Home and Office: 100 Wesley Dr Apt 510 Asheville NC 28803-2091 Personal E-mail: terhorstjf@gmail.com.

TERHUNE, JERRY DAVID, biology professor, researcher; b. Louisville, Ky., Aug. 28, 1946; s. David Henry and Beatrice Mae Terhune; m. Bobbie Faye Tuggle; children: Rebecca Faye, Eric David. BS in Zoology, U. Louisville, 1975, MS in Limnology, 1975; ABD in Aquatic Ecology, U. L. & U. Minn. Cert. in wetlands evaluator Water Environment Inst., 2000, in soil and erosion prevention Louis. and Jefferson Co. MSD, 2001. With US Army, Fort Sam, Tex. & Louisville, 1969—78; environ. scientist Louisville & Jefferson Co. MSD, 1987—2002; prof. biology and environ. sci. Jefferson Comm. Coll., Louisville, 1976—. Sci. advisor werf Water Environment Rsch. Fedn., 1995—2001; sci. advisor USEPA, 1998—2000. Contbr. scientific papers. Sci. advisor Salt River Water Monitoring, Ky., 1995—2000, Beargrass Creek Assn., Louisville, 1992—2000; sci. advisor and trainer Water Monitoring Program Ky., Louisville, 1993—2000; sci. coop. US Geol. Svc., Louisville, 1990—2000. Conservative. Achievements include development of urban streams monitoing program. Avocations: target shooting, seashell collecting, reading. Home: 1822 Finchville Rd Shelbyville KY 40065 Office: Jefferson Cmty and Tech Coll 109 E Broadway Louisville KY 40202 Business E-Mail: jerry.terhune@kctcs.edu.

TERKELSEN, BRIAN J., entertainment marketing executive; BS in Bus Adminstrn., Bryant Coll., RI. Investment banker Barclay's Bank, Bankers Trust, Co., NY, 1985—92; co-founder, COO Eco-Challenge Lifestyles, Inc., 1993—98; v.p. programming/prodn., grp. gen. mgr. Quokka Sports, Inc., 1998—2001; v.p., gen. mgr. media entertainment Be Here Technologies, Inc., 2001—03; sr. v.p., dir. entertainment mktg. to exec. v.p., mng. dir. connectivetissue MediaVest USA, Inc., 2003—. Exec. prodr.: (TV series) Eco-Challenge (MTV), 1995, Extreme Games (ESPN), 1995; co-prodr.: Eco-Challenge (Discovery Channel), 1996—97. Office: MediaVest USA Inc 1675 Broadway New York NY 10019 Office Phone: 212-468-3602. Business E-Mail: brian.terkelsen@mediavestww.com.*

TERLAKY, TAMÁS, mathematics educator; b. Kaposvár, Somogy, Hungary, Jan. 10, 1955; arrived in The Netherlands, 1989; s. József and Edit (Kishonti) T.; m. Gabriella Török, Jan. 22, 1977; 1 child, Viktor. MSc in Math., Eövös U., Budapest, Hungary, 1979, PhD in Ops. Rsch., 1981; Habilitation, Hungarian Acad. Scis., Budapest, DSc, 1985. Ops. rsch. cons. Hungarian Oil and Gas Trust, Budapest, 1979-82; asst. prof. math. Eötvös U., 1982-89, assoc. prof., 1989—95, Delft U. Tech., Netherlands, 1990—99, rschr., 1989—90; assoc. prof. McMaster U., Hamelton, Ont., Canada, 1999—2008; prof. Can. Rsch. Chair Optimization, 2002—08; dir. Sch. Computational Engring. and Sci., 2005—08; chair, dept. indsl. and sys. engring., George N. and Stenia Kledanas endowed chair, prof. Lehigh U., Bethlehem, Pa. Lectr. various univs. and internat. confs., Bonn, London, Lisbon, 1985, Sofia, Tokyo, Jena, 1988, Paris, Calif., Cologne, 1990, Amsterdam, Grenoble, Marseille, 1991, Geneva, Zürich, Anaheim, New Brunswick, Ithaca, 1992, Lisbon, Kopenhagen, Budapest, Oviedo, 1993. Co-author: Theory and Algorithms for Linear Optimization: An Interior Point Approach, 1979, Self-Regularity: A New Paradigm for Interior Point Method; editor: Interior Point Methods in Mathematical Programming, 1996; founding editor-in-chief: Jour. Optimization and Engring.; editor procs.; contbr. chpts. to books, more than 150 articles to internat. math. jours., more than 200 other confs. Mem. SIAM, INFORMS, Math. Programming Soc., J. Bolyai Math. Soc. (G. Farkas award 1985), G. Farkas Ops. Rsch. Soc. Avocation: swimming. Office: Lehigh Univ 200 W Packer Ave Bethlehem PA 18015 Home: 4830 Brittany Hill Center Valley PA 18034 Personal E-mail: terlaky@hotmail.com. Business E-Mail: terlaky@lehigh.edu.

TERMAN, LEWIS MADISON, retired electrical engineer, researcher, director; b. San Francisco, Aug. 26, 1935; s. Frederick Emmons and Sibyl (Walcott) T.; m. Barbara Chertok, Aug. 28, 1958. BS in Physics, Stanford U., 1956, MSEE, 1958, PhD, 1961. Mem. rsch. staff T.J. Watson Rsch. Ctr., IBM, Yorktown Heights, NJ, 1961-89, sr. mgr., 1989-91, sr. mem. tech. planning staff, 1991-93; mgr. VLSI processor design IBM Rsch. Ctr., Yorktown Heights, NY, 1993-94, rsch. staff T.J. Watson Rsch. Ctr., 1994—2001, assoc. dir. Sys. Dept., 2003—06, rschr. emeritus, 2006—; pres. IBM Acad. Tech., Somers, 2001—03. Co-chmn. Symposium on Very Large Scale Integrated Technology, Systems and Application, Taiwan, 1989, 91, 93, 95, 97, 99, 01, 03, 05, 07 tech. program co-chmn., 1985, 87; tech. program chmn. Internat. Solid State Cirs. Conf., N.Y.C., 1983; chmn. Symposium on Very Large-Scale Integrated Tech., Kobe, Japan, 1985, San Diego, 1986, Symposium on Very Large-Scale Integrated Cirs., Karuizawa, Japan, 1988, Kyoto, Japan, 1989, Symposium on Low Power Electronics, San Diego, 1994; mem. tech. coun. IBM Acad. Tech., 1995-98. Contbr. articles to profl. jours. Pres. Twin Lakes Water Works Corp., S. Salem, N.Y., 1980—. Recipient IEEE Solid-State Cirs. Tech. Field award, 1995. Fellow: IEEE (chmn. tech. mtgs. coun. 1993—94, tech. activites bd. treas. 1995—98, chair strategic planning and rev. com. 1999—2000, v.p. elect tech. activities bd. 2000, v.p. tech. activities bd. 2001, treas. publs., svcs. and products bd. 2003, divsn. one dir., mem. bd. dirs. 2004—05, pres.-elect 2007, pres. 2008, past pres. 2009), AAAS; mem.: Nat. Acad. Enging., Circuits and Sys. Soc. of IEEE (adminstrv. com. 1981—83), IEEE Solid-State Circuits Soc. (editor jour. 1974—77, treas. 1988—89, v.p. 1996—97, pres. 1998—99), IEEE Electron Devices Soc. (v.p. 1988—89, pres. 1990—91, Disting. Svc. award 1995), IBM Acad. Tech. (co-chair tech. program com. 1996, chair components and processes com., tech. coun. 1996—98, pres. 2001—03, past pres. 2003—05). Achievements include patents in field. Avocations: music, theater, opera, hiking. Home: 61 Twin Lakes Rd South Salem NY 10590-1012 Office Phone: 914-763-5744.

TERMEER, HENRICUS ADRIANUS, pharmaceutical executive; b. Tilburg, Holland, Feb. 28, 1946; came to U.S., 1971, naturalized, 1999; s. Jacques and Mary (Van Gorp) T. Student, Econ. Coll. Erasmus U., Rotterdam, The Netherlands, 1969; MBA, Darden Sch., U. Va., 1973; DSc (hon.), U. Mass. Mgr. mgmt. svcs. Norvic Co., Norwich, England, 1969-71; mgr. internat. product planning Baxter Travenol, Inc., Deerfield, Ill., 1973-74, internat. mktg. mgr., 1975-76; gen. mgr. Travenol GMBH, Munich, 1976-79; v.p. Hyland Therapeutics divsn. Baxter Travenol, Glendale, Calif., 1979-81, exec. v.p., 1981-83; pres. Genzyme Corp., Inc., Boston, 1983—, COO, 1983-85, CEO, 1985—, chmn., 1988—. Bd. dir. Abiomed, Inc., Biotech. Industry Orgn., Pharma. Rsch. and Manufactures Am., Mass. High Tech. Coun., Mass. Gen. Hosp., Fed. Res. Bank Boston, MIT Corp; bd. assocs. Whitehead Inst. Biomedical Rsch.; mem. MIT Corp. vis. com. dept. biology; chmn. emeritus New England Healthcare Inst., 2002-06. Trustee Boston Mus. Sci., Harvard Med. Sch. Bd. Fellows, Biomedical Sci. Careers Project, 1994., dir. 1995; bd. dir. Project Hope; Served to 1st lt. Netherlands Royal Air Force, 1966-67. Recipient Torch of Liberty award, Anti-Defamation League, New England Region, 1995, The Governor's New Am. Appreciation award, 1997, Golden Door award, Internat. Inst. Boston, 1999, Genetic Disease Found. Humanitarian award, 1999, Franklin Delano Roosevelt Humanitarian award, March of Dimes, 2003, Cor Vitae award, Am. Heart Assn., 2003, Master Entrepreneur award, Ernst & Young, 2007; named Entrepreneur of Yr., Merrill Lynch and Ernst & Young, Inc., 1992, Renegade of Yr., Success Mag., 1995, Humanitarian of Yr., Cardinal Cushing Sch. for Exceptional Children, 1997. Fellow: Am. Acad. Arts & Sciences, Royal Coll. Physicians (hon.). Office: Genzyme Corp 500 Kendall St Cambridge MA 02142*

TERMINI, ROSEANN BRIDGET, law educator; BS magna cum laude, Drexel U., 1975; MEd, Temple U., 1979, JD, 1985, grad. in food and pharmacy law, 1998. Bar: Pa. 1985, U.S. Dist. Ct. (ea. dist.) Pa. 1985, DC 1986. Jud. clk. Superior Ct. Pa., Allentown, 1985-86; atty. Pa. Power & Light Co., Allentown, 1986-87; corp. counsel food and drug law Lemmon Co., Sellersville, Pa., 1987-88; sr. dep. atty. bur. consumer protection plain lang. law (Notable cases include: Waste Conversion case, 1990, violation of Pa. Solid Waste Mgmt. Act.) Office of Atty. Gen., Harrisburg, Pa., 1988-96; prof. Villanova U. Sch. Law, 1996-2000; prof. food and drug law Temple U. Sch. Pharmacy, Phila., 1998—, St. Joseph U., 2000—; prof. food and drug law Grad. Sch. John Hopkins U., 2005—; prof. grad. pharmacy/biotech master program U. Ga., 2005—. Adj. prof. law online life scis. on use food and drug law Widener U., 1993—; adj. prof. Dickinson Sch. Law; specialized food, drug, cosmetic and med. device law course dir. pres.'s coun. Immaculata Coll.; on-line distance learning legal issues pharmacy promotion and legal environ. bus. St. Joseph U., 2002—; instr. online exec. MBA program Drexel U., 2002—; mem. adv. bd. RXMD; spkr. Pa. Health Law Inst., 2007—. Author: Food, Drug and Medical Device Law: Topics and Cases, 2001, Health Law: Federal Regulation of Drugs, Biologics, Medical Devices, Foods and Dietary Supplements, 2003, Biologics, 2003, Medical Devices, 2004, Foods and Dietary Supplements, 2003, Statutory Supplement and Teacher's Manual, 2003;: 2d edit., 2004, Life Sciences Law Book and Statutory CD, 3rd edit., 2007, Federal Regulation of Drugs, Biologics, Medical Devices, Foods and Dietary Supplements; contbr. articles to profl. jours. Active Sr. Citizens Project Outreach, Hospice, 1986—; mem. St. Thomas More Law Bd. Mem.: ABA (mem. various coms.), Health Claim Found., Pa. Bar Assn. (ethics, exceptional children and environ. sects., profl. condr. 2008, Plain English award 1999), Bar Assn. DC, Drexel U. Alumni Assn., Temple U. Law Alumni Assn., Phi Alpha Delta, Omicron Nu. Avocations: tap dancing, hiking, cross country skiing. Personal E-mail: rtermini@lawyer.com. Business E-Mail: rtermini@fortipublications.com, info@fortipublications.com.

TERMUHLEN, PAULA, oncologist, surgeon; b. Dayton, Ohio, Dec. 30, 1962; d. Chester Paul and Loretta Jane Marcheski; m. David Forrest Termuhlen, Aug. 10, 1985; children: Christopher Valentin, Anka Marie, Sidharth Matthew, Christopher Valentin, Anka Marie, Sidharth Matthew. MD, Sch. Medicine, St. Louis U., 1989. Diplomate Am. Bd. Surgery, 1997. Gen. surgery residency program dir. Wright State U. Boonshoft Sch. Medicine, Dayton, Ohio, 2002—, chief, surg. oncology, 2005—. Treas. Assn. Program Dirs Surgery, Bethesda, Md., 2007—. Exec. Leadership fellowship, Am. Assn. Med. Colleges, Drexel U., 2008—. Fellow: ACS. Avocation: travel. Office: Wright State Surgical Oncology 1222 S Patterson Blvd Ste 220 Dayton OH 45409 Office Fax: 937-424-2479. Personal E-mail: dtermuhlen@woh.rr.com. Business E-Mail: paula.termuhlen@wright.edu.

TERNAR, MINE Y., artist, educator; b. Istanbul, Turkey, Apr. 18, 1961; d. Orhan Ternar and Gulbun Tok; 1 child, Dilara Ilayda Nur Ternar Kal. Student, State Acad. Fine Arts, Istanbul, 1979—80; BA in Liberal Arts, Bennington Coll., Vt., 1984; MA in Painting and Serigraphy, Mimar Sinan U., Istanbul, 1986; MFA in Art Practice, U. Calif., Berkeley, 1991. C.c. instr. credential fine and applied arts Bd. Govs. Calif. Cmty. Colls., tchg. credential adult edn. art Commn. Tchr. Credentialing. Papermaking and painting asst. to artist Sophie Healy Trout Paper, Eagle Bridge, NY, 1980—81; copywriter, illustrator Radar Advt. Agy., Istanbul, 1985—86; curatorial asst., intern Phoebe A. Hearst Mus. Anthropology, U. Calif., Berkeley, 1989—91, intern Berkeley Art Mus., 1990—91; vol. coord. Pro Arts Gallery, Oakland, Calif., 1991—92; mem. adj. faculty Calif. Coll. Arts, Oakland, 1992—93, San Francisco Art Inst., 1992—93; asst. dir. Cartoon Art Mus., San Francisco, 1993—94; cmty. outreach coord. Dean Lesher Regional Ctr. Arts, Walnut Creek, Calif., 1994—97; mem. adj. faculty dept. visual arts Cabrillo Coll., Aptos, Calif., 1994—98; mem. faculty dept. art City Coll. San Francisco, 1996—. Vol. outreach coord. Gilles Peres photo installation New Langton Arts, San Francisco, 1994; freelance designer, computer graphics Golden Touch Design, Berkeley, 1996—2000; intranet webmaster Coherent Laser Co., Santa Clara, Calif., 1997—98; faculty advisor Diego Rivera website City Coll. San Francisco, 1997—98, gallery dir., curator City Arts Gallery, 1998—2007, mem. works of art sub-com., acad. senate, 2002—. Author, co-prodr., collaborator (film/video) Conversations Across the Bosphorus, 1995; one-man shows include Osman Hamdi Hall, Mimar Sinan U., Istanbul, 1986, exhibitions include Lutfu Gunay Studio, Turkish-Am. Cultural Assn., Ankara, Turkey, 1978, Adnan Coker Studio, Istanbul State Gallery Fine Arts, 1985, Berkeley Art Mus., 1991, Worth Ryder Gallery, U. Calif., Berkeley, 1991, Walter/McBean Gallery, San Francisco Art Inst., 1992—93, KALA Artists Exhbn., 1997—98, Kala Artists' Ann., 1998—99, exhibited in group shows at Harcourts Modern and Contemporary Art Gallery, San Francisco, 1989, Berkeley Art Ctr., 1998, PRO ARTS Open Studios, 1996, Cabrillo College Gallery, 1997, exhibited in group shows, CCSF, 1998—. Recipient Winning design, Health Through Art: Signs of Recovery, Alameda County Cmty. Project, 1996—2000; grantee, City Coll. San Francisco, 1997—98, Vt. Studio Ctr., 2007; fellow, Calif. Student Aid Commn., 1990—91, KALA Art Inst., Berkeley, 1997; scholar, Univ. per Stranieri, Perugia, Italy, 1979, Bennington Coll., 1980—84. Mem.: Coll. Art Assn. Am., Turkish-Am. Assn. Calif. (assoc.; bd. dirs., dir. arts and culture 1994—97), U. Calif. Alumni Assn. (life), YMCA. Avocations: reading, swimming, films, music, travel. Office: City Coll San Francisco Art Dept 50 Phelan Ave San Francisco CA 94112 Office Fax: 415-239-3131. Business E-Mail: mternar@ccsf.edu.

TERNBERG, JESSIE LAMOIN, pediatric surgeon, educator; b. Corning, Calif., May 28, 1924; d. Eric G. and Alta M. (Jones) T. AB, Grinnell Coll., Iowa, 1946, ScD (hon.), 1970; PhD, U. Tex., Austin, 1950; MD, Washington U., St. Louis, 1953; ScD (hon.), U. Mo., St. Louis, 1981, ScD (hon.), 2008, Wash. U., 2008. Diplomate: Am. Bd. Surgery. Intern Boston City Hosp., 1953—54; asst. resident in surgery Barnes Hosp., St. Louis, 1954-57, resident in surgery, 1958-59; rsch. fellow Washington U. Sch. Medicine, 1957-58; practice medicine specializing in pediatric surgery St. Louis, 1966—; instr., DGMS trainee in surgery Washington U., 1959-62, asst. prof. surgery, 1962-65, assoc. prof. surgery, prof., 1965-71, prof. surgery, 1971-96, chief divsn. pediatric surgery, 1972-90, prof. emeritus, 1996—; mem. staff Barnes Hosp., 1959—90; gen. surgeon in chief Children's Hosp. of St. Louis, 1974-90. Mem. staff Children's Hosp., dir. pediatric surgery, 1972-90. Contbr. numerous articles on pediatric surgery to profl. jours. Trustee Grinnell Coll., 1984—. Recipient Alumni award Grinnell Coll., 1966, Faculty/Alumni award Washington U. Sch. Medicine, 1991, 2nd Century award 2006, 1st Aphrodite Jannopaulo Hofsommer award, 1993, Local Legend Changing the Face of Medicine award AMWA. Fellow AAAS; mem. SIOP, Am. Pediatric Surg. Assn., We. Surg. Assn. (2d v.p. 1984-85), St. Louis Med. Soc., Soc. Surgery of the Alimentary Tract, Am. Acad. Pediatrics, Soc. Pelvic Surgeons (v.p. 1991-92), Brit. Assn. Paediatric Surgeons, Assn. Women Surgeons (disting. mem. 1995), Mo. State Surg. Soc., St. Louis Surg. Soc. (pres. 1980-81), St. Louis Pediatric

Soc., Soc. Surg. Oncology, Pediatric Oncology Group (chmn. surg. discipline 1983-96), St. Louis Childrens Hosp. Soc. (pres. 1979-80), Acad. Sci. St. Louis (Trustees award 2002), St. Louis Met. Med. Soc. (hon., councilor, trustee), Barnes Hosp. Soc., Phi Beta Kappa, Sigma Xi, Iota Sigma Pi, Alpha Omega Alpha. Office: St Louis Childrens Hosp 1 Childrens Pl Saint Louis MO 63110-1002 Business E-Mail: ternbergj@wurna.edu.

TERNER, JAMES, chemistry educator; b. Reading, England, Mar. 27, 1951; came to U.S., 1955; s. Charles and Ruth Hilde (Cohn) T.; m. Ellen Cindy Shapiro, July 1, 1979; children: Steven, Jeremy, Benjamin, Zachary. BA, Brandeis U., Waltham, Mass., 1973; PhD, UCLA, 1979; post doctorate, Princeton U., NJ, 1979-81. Asst. prof. Va. Commonwealth U., Richmond, 1981-86, assoc. prof., 1986—. Fellow Alfred P. Sloan Found., 1985-87. Office: Va Commonwealth U Dept Chemistry 1001 W Main St Richmond VA 23284-9059

TERNING, JOHN, physics professor, researcher; PhD, U. Toronto, Ont., Can., 1990. Postdoc. fellow Yale U., New Haven, 1990—93; rsch. assoc. Boston U., 1993—96, U. Calif., Berkeley, 1996—99, prof. Davis, 2005—; rschr., lectr. Harvard U., Cambridge, Mass., 1999—2001; staff mem. Los Alamos Nat. Lab., N.Mex., 2001—04. Author: (book) Modern Super Symmetry. Super Conducting Supercollider fellowship, Tex. Nat. Rsch. Lab. Commn., 1992—93. Fellow: Am. Phys. Soc. (fellowship 2007). Achievements include research in electroweak symmetry breaking and cosmolgy in extra dimensions. Office: Univ Calif Davis One Shields Ave Davis CA 95616

TERNUS, MARSHA K., state supreme court chief justice; b. Vinton, Iowa, May 30, 1951; married; 3 children. BA, U. Iowa, 1972; JD, Drake U., 1977. Bar: Iowa 1977, Ariz. 1984. With Bradshaw, Fowler, Proctor & Fairgrave, Des Moines, 1977—93; justice Iowa Supreme Ct., Des Moines, 1993—, chief justice, 2006—. Former mem. Iowa Jury Instructions Com.; former bd. mem. Polk County Legal Aid Soc.; pres. bd. of counselors Drake U. Law Sch.; former mem. Iowa Supreme Ct. Commn. on Planning for the 21st Century, MultiState Perf. Test Policy Com., Nat. Conf. of Bar Examiners. Editor-in-chief: Drake Law Rev., 1976—77. Mem.: Iowa State Bar Assn. (bd. governors), Polk County Bar Assn. (pres. 1984—85), Order of Coif, Phi Beta Kappa. Office: Iowa Supreme Ct Jud Branch Bldg 1111 E Ct Ave Des Moines IA 50319-0001*

TERPSTRA, A. ELLEN, federal agency administrator; BS, Georgetown Univ. Sch. Fgn. Svc. Cons. Food & Agr. Org. UN; agr. policy analyst Congl. Rsch. Svc., Washington; trade negotiator & policy coord. Office of US Trade Rep., Washington; pres. U.S. Apple Assn., 1991—98; pres., CEO U.S. Rice Assn., 1998—2002; head Fgn. Agr. Svc. USDA, Washington, 2002—06, dep. undersecretary for farm & fgn. agr. services, 2006—. Office: USDA 1400 Independence Ave SW Washington DC 20250*

TERR, LENORE CAGEN, psychiatrist, writer; b. NYC, Mar. 27, 1936; d. Samuel Lawrence and Esther (Hirsch) Cagen; m. Abba I. Terr; children: David, Julia. AB magna cum laude, Case Western Res. U., 1957; MD with honors, U. Mich., 1961. Diplomate Am. Bd. Psychiatry and Neurology (subspecialty bd. child and adolescent psychiatry). Intern U. Mich. Med. Ctr., Ann Arbor, 1961-62; resident Neuropsychiat. Inst. U. Mich., Ann Arbor, 1962-64, fellow Children's Psychiat. Hosp., 1964-66; from instr. to asst. prof. Case Western Res. U. Med. Sch., Cleve., 1966-71; pvt. practice Terr Med. Corp., San Francisco, 1971—; from asst. clin. prof. to clin. prof. psychiatry Sch. Medicine U. Calif., San Francisco, 1971—. Lectr. law, psychiatry U. Calif., Berkeley, 1971—90, Davis, 1974—88; dir. Am. Bd. Psychiatry and Neurology, 1988—96, chair psychiatry coun., 1996. Author: Too Scared to Cry, 1990, Unchained Memories, 1994, Beyond Love and Work, 1999, Magical Moments of Change, 2008; contbr. articles to profl. jours.; exhibited works in art show at Canessa Gallery, San Francisco, 2002. Recipient Career Tchr. award, NIMH, 1967—69, Child Advocacy award, APA, 1994; named to Cleveland Heights H.S. Disting Alumni Hall of Fame, 2003; grantee project, Rosenberg Found., 1977, William T. Grant Found., 1986—87, Leon Lowenstein Found., 2002; scholar-in-residence, Rockefeller Found., Italy, 1981, 1988. Fellow: Am. Acad. Child and Adolescent Psychiatry (coun. 1984—87, Reiger award 2009), Am. Coll. Psychiatrists (program chair 1991—92, Bowis award 1993), Am. Psychiat. Assn. (Child Psychiatry Rsch. award 1984, Clin. Rsch. award 1987, Marmor Sci. award 2002); mem.: Phi Bet Kappa, Alpha Omega Alpha. Avocations: piano, walking, travel, gardening, needlepoint. Office: Terr Med Corp 450 Sutter St Rm 1336 San Francisco CA 94108-4204 Office Phone: 415-433-7800. Office Fax: 415-433-2130. E-mail: lenoreterrmd@sbcglobal.net.

TERRACCIANO, ANTHONY PATRICK, finance company executive; b. Bayonne, NJ, Oct. 27, 1938; s. Patrick and Grace Teracciano; m. Rity Cuddy, Apr. 20, 1963; children: Laura, Karen, Kenneth. BS in Econs., St. Peters Coll., 1960; MA in Philosophy, Fordham U., 1962. Exec. v.p. internat. Chase Manhattan Bank, NYC, 1974—76, exec. v.p., CFO, 1983—84, vice chmn. global banking, 1985—87; pres., COO Mellon Bank Corp., 1987—90; chmn., pres., CEO First Fidelity Bancorp, Newark, 1990—96; pres. First Union Nat. Bank, Summit, NJ, 1996—97; vice chmn. Am. Water Works Co. Inc., 1998—2003; non-exec. chmn. Dime Bancorp, Inc., NYC, 1999—2002, Riggs Nat. Corp., Washington, 2005; chmn. SLM Corp. (Sallie Mae), Reston, Va., 2008—. Bd. dirs. TradeCard, Inc., 1999—, Avaya, Inc., 2002—, Ikon Office Solutions, Inc., 2003—, Knoll, Inc., 2004—. Bd. dirs. N.Y. Philharm., Metro Newark C. of C.; mem. exec. coun. Better Bus. Bur., Newark; trustee Renaissance Newark, Inc., U. Medicine & Dentistry NJ, 2006-, Monmouth Med. Ctr.; mem. Coun. Fgn. Rels. 1st lt. U.S. Army, 1962-64. Mem. N.J. Bankers Assn. (exec. com.). Avocations: music, reading. Office: Sallie Mae 12061 Bluemont Way Reston VA 20190*

TERRACINA, ROY DAVID, entrepreneur; b. Chgo., Aug. 24, 1946; s. Angelo R. and Josephine T.; divorced; children: Joseph, Vincent, Angela, Peter, Paul. BS in Fin., Marquette U., 1968, MBA, 1972. Officer First Wis. Nat. Bank, Milw., 1968-71; account exec. Robert W. Baird Co., Milw., 1971-74; v.p. mktg. Midwest Retail Group, Milw., 1974-76; mgmt. cons. Anderson-Roethle, Milw., 1976-77; v.p., treas. Farm House Foods Corp., Milw., 1977-84; pres. Sterling Foods, Inc., San Antonio, 1984-93, pvt. investor, 1994—. Instr. personal fin. Marquette U.; instr. fin. Trinity U.; bd. dir. US Global Investors, JP Morgan Chase, San Antonio. Roman Catholic. Office: 7900 Callaghan Rd San Antonio TX 78229-2327

TERRAGNO, PAUL JAMES, information industry executive; b. Ogden, Utah, May 17, 1938; s. Charles L. and Florence E. (Gabardi) T.; m. Nancy Robinson, Aug. 26, 1961; children— Thomas C., Paul A., Teresa A. BA, U. Utah, 1960; MS, U. Wyo., 1962. Vice pres. Westat, Inc., Rockville, Md., 1962-70; vice pres. Remac Information, Gaithersburg, Md., 1970-76; dir. U.S. Patent Office, Washington, 1976-80; v.p. Pergamon Internat., McLean, Va., 1980-84; pres. Pergamon InfoLine, McLean, Va., 1984-87, Pergamon ORBIT InfoLine, McLean, 1987-89, Maxwell Online, Inc., 1989-92. Pres. Pergamon Orbit InfoLine, Ltd., London, 1984-89, Pergabase, Inc., Gainesville, Fla., 1985-92, pres. Topate Info. Svcs. Inc., 1992-97; dir. Eagle Design and Mgmt., Inc., Bethesda, Md. Contbr. articles to various publs. Mem. Am. Soc. Info. Sci. Roman Catholic. Office: 7830 Old Georgetown Rd Bethesda MD 20814-2432 Home: 1002 Elmcroft Blvd Apt 401 Rockville MD 20850-6657 E-mail: terragno@comcast.net.

TERRAS, AUDREY ANNE, mathematics professor; b. Washington, Sept. 10, 1942; d. Stephen Decatur and Maude Mae Bowdoin. BS with high honors in Math., U. Md., 1964; MA, Yale U., 1966, PhD, 1970. Instr. U. Ill., Urbana, 1968-70; asst. prof. U. P.R., Mayaguez, 1970-71, Bklyn. Coll., CUNY, 1971-72; asst. prof. math. U. Calif.-San Diego, La Jolla, 1972-76, assoc. prof., 1976-83, prof., 1983—. Prin. investigator NSF, 1974-88; vis. positions MIT, fall 1977, 83, U. Bonn West Germany, spring 1977, Inst. Mittag-Leffler, Stockholm, winter, 1978, Inst. Advanced Study, spring 1984, Math. Scis. Rsch. Inst., Berkeley, Calif., winter 1992, spring 1995, U. Aachen, Germany, 1998, Tsuda Coll., Tokyo, 1999, CRM, U. Montreal, 1999, U. Colo., Boulder, 2006, Newton Inst., Cambridge, Eng., 2007; dir. West Coast Number Theory Conf., U. Calif.-San Diego, 1976, AMS joint summer rsch. conf., 1984; Co-organizer, UCLA IPAM Workshops on Expanders, 2004, 2008; lectr. in field. Author: Harmonic Analysis on Symmetric Spaces and Applications, Vol. 1, 1985, Vol. II, 1988, Fourier Analysis on Finite Groups and Applications, 1999; editor: The Selberg Trace Formula and Related Topics, 1986; contbr. chapters to books, articles to profl. jours. Woodrow Wilson fellow, 1964, NSF fellow, 1964-68; NSF grantee Summer Inst. in Number Theory, Ann Arbor, Mich., 1973. Fellow: AAAS (nominating com. math. sect. project 2061); mem.: Assn. for Women in Sci., Assn. for Women in Math. (travel grants com. 1996, noether lectr. 2008), Soc. Indsl. and Applied Math., Math. Assn. Am. (program com. for nat. meeting 1988—90, chair joint program com. Am. Math. Soc. and Math. Assn. Am. 1991), Am. Math. Soc. (com. employment and ednl. policy com. on coms., coun., trans. editor, com. for the yr. 2000, western sect. program com., assoc. editor book revs. Bull., assoc. editor Notices). Achievements include research in harmonic analysis on symmetric spaces; number theory; graph theory. Office: U Calif San Diego Dept Math La Jolla CA 92093-0112

TERRASSE, ANTHONY P., plastic surgeon; b. Fla. BS magna cum laude, U. Notre Dame, 1979; MD, Vanderbilt U. Med. Sch., 1983. Cert. Am. Bd. Plastic Surgery, 1991. Residency in gen. surgery Northwestern Meml. Hosp., Chgo., 1983—86, residency in plastic surgery, 1986—89; staff mem. Lake Forest Hosp., Ill., 1983—, chmn. dept. of medicine Ill., 1999—; staff mem. Highland Park Hosp., Evanston Hosp., Glenbrook Hosp., Condell Med. Ctr., St. Joseph's Hosp.; plasic surgeon Terrasse Aesthetic Surgery & Skin Care, Lake Forest. Prof., plastic and reconstructive surgery Northwestern U., Evanston, Ill., 1990—. Mem. Lake Forest C. of C., 1990—; adv. bd. Lake Forest Health & Fitness Inst., 1994—. Named a Top Doctor, Castle Connelly; named one of Top Surgeons in Aesthetic Surgery, Consumers Rsch. Coun. America. Fellow: Am. Coll. Surgeons; mem.: Ill. State Med. Soc., Chgo. Soc. Plastic Surgery, Lipoplasty Soc. N.Am., Am. Soc. Aesthetic Plastic Surgery, Am. Soc. Plastic Surgeons. Office: 700D N Westmoreland Rd Lake Forest IL 60045*

TERRELL, CHARLES SHAUL, JR., educational administrator; b. Chgo., Oct. 1, 1930; s. Charles Shaul and Maxine (Kagley) Terrell; m. Roberta Lucille Fisher, Aug. 31, 1951; children: Gregory Allen, Kathleen Rae Smith. BA, LaVerne Coll., 1952; MA, San Diego State U., 1956; EdD, U. So. Calif., 1966. Tchr. Hudson Elem. Sch. Dist., La Puente, Calif., 1952—53, San Diego City Sch. Dist., 1955—56; tchr. social studies Azusa HS, Calif., 1956—58; counselor, 1957—60; dir. student activities, 1960—61; unit adminstr., 1961—63; prin., 1963—66; supt. Needles Unified Sch. Dist., Calif., 1966—69, Corona-Norco Unified Sch. Dist., Calif., 1969—77, San Bernardino City Unified Sch. Dist., Calif., 1977—82, San Bernardino County Sch. Dist., 1982—93; ret., 1993; pres. EDUCARE, Sch. Edn., U. So. Calif., LA, 1964; dir., past pres. Summer session instr. U. Calif.-Irvine, 1973—75; instr. Calif. State Coll., San Bernardino, 1977, U. So. Calif., L.A, 1990; cons. in field.; past pres. Nat. Soc. to Prevent Blindness, So. Calif.; bd. dirs. San Bernardino Cmty. Hosp.; chmn. San Bernardino County Drugs & Gangs Task Force. Cpl. USMC, 1953—55. Recipient award Merit, Corona C. of C., 1976. Mem.: Conf. State Ct. Adminstrs. Group (chmn. bd. 2003), San Bernardino CC Dist. (trustee 2001, clk. bd., pres.), San Bernardino Area C. of C. (bd. dirs., v.p. 1994—), Calif. Assn. County Supt. Schs. (pres. 1982—93), Small Sch. Dists. Assn. (exec. com.), Am. Assn. Sch. Adminstrs (supt. com. 1972—78), Coll. Bd. Western Regional Acad. Adv. Panel (chmn. Calif. del. 1979—90, mem. Nat. Ctr. for Improvement Learning 1980—84), Masons, Elks, Lions Rotary (past pres.). Republican. Presbyterian. Home: 3730 Osbun Rd San Bernardino CA 92404-2132 Office Phone: 909-475-8228. Personal E-mail: csterrell@eee.org.

TERRELL, ELISE I., humanities educator; b. Meridian, Miss., Aug. 29, 1980; d. Edgar Dalrymple Dale Ingels; m. Charles L. Terrell, May 28, 2005; 1 child, Catherine Grace. BA in Psychology & Sociology, Millsaps Coll., Jackson, Miss., 2002. Lic. tchr. Miss., 2009. Tchr. New Summit Sch., Jackson, 2002—04, Veritas Sch., Jackson, 2008—. Youth ministry intern Galloway United Meth. Ch., Jackson, 1998—2004. Mem.: Epsilon Sigma Alpha (life). Avocations: swimming, travel. Home and Office: Catherine Grace LLC 379 Kings Ridge Cir Brandon MS 39047 Business E-Mail: quayterrell@bellsouth.net.

TERRELL, G. IRVIN, lawyer; b. Houston, Sept. 28, 1946; s. George I. and Adella (Weichert) T.; m. Karen Steenberg, Jan. 8, 1984; 1 child, Katharine. BA, U. Tex., 1968, JD, 1972. Bar: Tex., US Supreme Ct., US Ct. Appeals (3d and 5th cirs.), US Dist. Ct. (so., no. and ea. dists.) Tex., US Dist. Ct. (we. dist.) Pa, US Dist. Ct. (so. dist.) NY. Assoc. Baker & Botts LLP, Houston, 1972-79, ptnr., 1980—. Mem. ABA, Houston Bar Assn., Internat. Soc. Barristers. Office Phone: 713-229-1231. Business E-Mail: irv.terrell@bakerbotts.com.

TERRELL, HELLENNA L., education educator; d. Ernestine Robinson and Herman L. Terrell. BS, Spelman Coll., Atlanta, 1986; MS, Jacksonville State U., Ala., 1995; EdD, U. Ala., Tuscaloosa, 1999. Dir. alumni affairs/pub. rels. Mary Holmes Coll., West Point, Miss., 1986—88; project dir. U.S. Dept. of Agr., Washington, 1988—91; asst. to exec. v.p. Talladega (Ala.) Coll., 1991—93; dean student life Tex. Coll., Tyler, 1993—95; dean multicultural initiatives U. Tenn., Chattanooga, 1997—2004; v.p. for student affairs St. Augustine's Coll., Raleigh, NC, 2004—07; dept. chair gen. studies U. Md. Ea. Shore, 2007—, dir. honors program, 2007—. Mem. Raleigh Rotary Club, 2006, Chattanooga Area Food Bank, 1997—2004, Chattanooga Theater Ctr., 1997—2004. Mem.: So. Assn. for Coll. Student Affairs, Nat. Asnn. of Student Pers. Administrs., Am. Assn. Univ. Pers., Am. Assn. Univ. Women. Office Fax: 410-621-3750. Business E-Mail: hlterrell@umes.edu.

TERRELL, HOPE PRICE, assistant principal; d. John Kenneth and Ruth Ward Price; m. Robert Steven Terrell, Oct. 10, 1970; children: Aaron Steven, Amber Lea. EdS, George Washington U., Washington, 1999. Cert. ednl. adminstr. Va. Instrnl. spl. Chesapeake Pub. Schs., Va., 1999—2002, asst. prin., 2002—. Com. chair Gt. Bridge Womans Club, Chesapeake, 2000—05; pres. Chesapeake Reading Assn., 1998—99, bd. dirs., 1996—2000. Named Tchr. of Yr., Pk. Elem., Chesapeake, 1993; fellow, Tidewater Writing Project, 1992. Mem.: Va. State Reading Assn. (corr.; found. chair 2004—06, governing coun. 2004—, bd. dirs. 2000—04, pres. 2002—03, Found. award). Home Fax: 757-546-8479. Personal E-mail: hopet123@gwu.edu. Business E-Mail: terrehpr@cps.k12.va.us.

TERRELL, J. ANTHONY, lawyer; b. NYC, Sept. 20, 1943; s. Claude M. and Kathleen L. (Prevost) Terrell; m. Karen E. Terrell; 1 child, Elizabeth S. BA, NYU, 1965, LLM (in Taxation), 1975; JD, Villanova U., 1968. Bar: NY. With Frueauff, Farrell, Sullivan & Bryan, NYC, 1970—74, ptnr., 1974; with Reid & Priest LLP, NYC, 1974—2003, ptnr., 1977; now ptnr. Dewey & LeBoeuf LLP, NYC. Named Best Lawyers in Am. (energy law), Best Lawyers, 1999—2009, America's Leading Lawyers for Bus. (transactional energy law), Chambers USA, 2005—08, NY Super Lawyers, Super Lawyers mag., 2006—08. Mem.: ABA, Nat. Assn. Bond Lawyers, Am. Bar Found., NYC Bar Assn., Internat. Bar Assn., Belle Haven Club, Coral Beach and Tennis Club, Met. Club. Office: Dewey & LeBoeuf LLP 1301 Avenue of the Americas New York NY 10019-6092 Office Phone: 212-259-7070. Office Fax: 212-259-6333. E-mail: jterrell@dl.com.

TERRENATO, NICOLA, archaeologist, researcher; b. Rome, Oct. 22, 1963; s. Luciano T. and Marina Frontali. Laurea, U. Rome I, 1988; PhD, Pisa U., Italy, 1994. Tchg. asst. U. Rome I, 1992-96; temp. lectr. U. Siena (Italy), 1996-98; rsch. fellow U. Durham (Eng.), 1996-98; asst. prof. U. N.C., Chapel Hill, 1998—. Area supr. N. Slope of Palatine Excavation, Rome, 1985-96; dir. Cecina Valley Survey, Pomarance, Italy, 1987—. Co-author: Introduzione All'Archeologia dei Paesaggi, 1994; contbr. articles to archeaol. jours. Project grantee Earthwatch, 1994-2000. Avocation: playing recorder. Office: U NC Dept Classics Chapel Hill NC 27599-0001

TERRILL, ROSS GLADWIN, writer, educator; b. Melbourne, Australia; arrived in U.S., 1965, naturalized, 1979; s. Frank and Miriel (Lloyd) Terrill. BA with honors, U. Melbourne; PhD, Harvard U., 1970. Tutor in polit. sci. U. Melbourne, 1962-63; staff sec. Australian Student Christian Movement, 1964-65; tchg. fellow Harvard U., 1968-70, lectr. govt., 1970-73, assoc. prof., 1974-78, rsch. assoc. E. Asian studies, 1970—, dir. student programs Ctr. Internat. Affairs, 1974-78; contbg. editor Atlantic Monthly, 1970-84; rsch. fellow Asia Soc., 1977—79. Vis. prof. Monash U., Melbourne, 1994—97, U. Tex., Austin, 1999—2003; pub. policy fellow Woodrow Wilson Ctr., 2008. Author: China Profile, 1969, China and Ourselves, 1971, 800,000,000: The Real China, 1972, R. H. Tawney and His Times, 1973, Flowers on an Iron Tree, 1975, The Future of China, 1978, The China Difference, 1979, Mao: A Biography, 1980, rev., 2000, White-Boned Demon, 1984, The Australians, 1987, Madam Mao, 1992, rev., 1999, China in Our Time, 1992, The Australians: How We Live Now, 2000, The New Chinese Empire, 2003; contbr. articles to Foreign Affairs, National Geographic, New Republic, Weekly Standard, New York Review of Books, Wilson Quarterly, others. Recipient Sumner prize, 1970, Nat. Mag. award, 1972, George Polk Meml. award outstanding mag. reporting, 1972, Book prize, L.A. Times, 2003. Mem.: PEN, Authors Guild, Harvard Club (N.Y.C.). Avocations: squash, music. Home: PO Box 230772 Astor Station Boston MA 02123-0772 Office Phone: 617-445-2542. Personal E-mail: rt5789@cs.com.

TERRIQUEZ-KASEY, LAURA MARIE, emergency nurse; b. Bronx, NY, May 12, 1950; d. Gilbert Manuel and Elizabeth (Arevena) Terriquez; m. William Kasey, July 23, 1988 (dec. May 1995). AAS, SUNY, Morrisville, 1971; BSN, Long Island U., 1980; MSN, CUNY, 1985. RN, N.Y., Tex. Commd. 2d lt. AUS, 1974, advanced through grades to maj., 1993; staff nurse emergency svc. Bellevue Hosp. Ctr., NYC, 1971-73, head nurse emergency svc., 1973-81, nursing supr., 1981-84; clin. nurse coord. South Nassau Cmty. Hosp., Oceanside, N.Y., 1984-85; staff nurse Brooke Army Med.Ctr., San Antonio, 1985-86; head nurse vascular surg. ward Brooke Army Med. Ctr., San Antonio, 1987-89, charge nurse, EMT, head nurse PACU, 1987-89; staff nurse med. ICU William Beaumont Army Med. Ctr., Ft. Bliss/El Paso, Tex., 1985-90, staff nurse trauma unit, 1990-91, head nurse trauma unit, 1991-92, asst. chief nurse, 1992-93; nurse mgr. emergency/trauma svcs. Bassett Health Care Sys., Cooperstown, N.Y., 1993-2000, adminstr. emergency and svc. tng. program, 1997-98, co-chair network adv. group, nurse advisor emergency svcs.; asst. clin. prof. SUNY Sch Nursing, Binghamton, 2000; asst. coun. prof. Sch. Nursing, Binghamton U. Instr. U. El Paso, Tex., 1991-92; mem. com. nursing adv. Southwest Organbank, El Paso, 1992—; adj. instr. U. Tex. Dept. Nursing, El Paso, 1992; Advanced Emergency Med. Technic Critical Care, N.Y. State Dept. Health sponsor for EMS programs, 2000-02; dir. Binghamton Program Abroad, Dominican Republic, 2004-08, lectr. in field. With disaster med. assistance team Team Houston, Tex., 2001; with disaster med. assistance team team response Anthrax Postal Response, NYC, 2001; mem. disaster med. assistance team NY Dept. Health and Human Svcs., NY, 2001; Ground Zero med. team World Trade Ctr., 2001; mem. hurricane disaster med. assistance team N.Y. Disaster Med. Assistance Team, FEMA, Fla., 2004—05. Decorated Army Commendation medal with 3 oak leaf clusters, Army Achievement award; recipient Meritorious Svc. award San Antonio Police Dept., 1988, Svc. award ARC, 1980, Cert. Appreciation N.Y. Emergency Med. Svcs., 1984, Chancellors award for internat. edn. program on cmty. health in Dominican Republic. Mem.: Red Cross So. Tier, Emergency Nurses Assn. (pres. rural nursing orgn. 2006), Am. Legion, Sigma Theta Tau. Achievements include development of disaster nursing courses. Avocations: swimming, biking. Home: 125 Park Dr Oneonta NY 13820 Office: Decker Sch Nursing Box 6000 SUNY Binghamton Binghamton NY 13902 Office Phone: 607-777-6033. Business E-Mail: kasey@binghamton.edu.

TERRIS, BRUCE JEROME, lawyer; b. Detroit, Aug. 3, 1933; s. Charles Z. and Ruth (Singer) T.; m. Shirley DuVal, Aug. 1958 (dec. 1976); m. Sally S. Gillespie, Sept. 10, 1977; children: Sally Phillips, Elizabeth, Jessica Kehimkar, Robert. AB summa cum laude, Harvard U., 1954, LLB magna cum laude, 1957; postgrad., Georgetown U., 1957-59. Bar: D.C. 1957, U.S. Supreme Ct. 1960. Atty. Internal Security Div. Dept. Justice, Washington, 1957-58; asst. to solicitor gen. Solicitor Gen.'s Office, Dept. Justice, Washington, 1958-65; co-chmn. Nat. Conf. Law and Poverty Office Econ. Opportunity, Washington, 1965; asst. dir. Nat. Crime Commn., Washington, 1965-67; cons. Community Relations Svc., Washington, 1967; asst. to v.p. Vice Pres.'s Office, Washington, 1967-68; vis. prof. law Cath. U. Am., Washington, 1967-68; sr. atty. Ctr. for Law and Social Policy, Washington, 1969-70; ptnr. Terris, Pravlik & Millian, Washington, 1970—. Author: Legal Services for the Elderly, 1972; contbr. articles to profl. jours.; article editor Harvard Law Review, 1956-57. Chmn. D.C. Dem. Cen. Com., Washington, 1968-72; bd. dirs. D.C. Home Rule Com., 1968-74; sec. D.C. Devel. Corp., 1974-77; bd. dirs. Coun. for Pub. Interest Law, 1976-81. Recipient Conservation Law award Nat. Wildlife Fedn., Washington, 1981; hon. fellow, commencement speaker U. Pa. Law Sch., 1977. Jewish. Office: Terris Pravlik & Millian 1121 12th St NW Washington DC 20005-4632 Office Phone: 202-204-8476. Business E-Mail: bterris@tpmlaw.com.

TERRIS, SUSAN, physician, cardiologist, researcher; b. Morristown, NJ, Sept. 5, 1944; d. Albert and Virginia Terris. BA in History, U. Chgo., 1967, PhD in Biochemistry, 1975, MD, 1976. Diplomate in internal medicine, endocrinology and metabolism, cardiovasc. disease Am. Bd. Internal Medicine. Resident in internal medicine Washington U., Barnes Hosp., St. Louis, 1976-78; fellow in endocrinology and metabolism U. Chgo., 1978-80, fellow cardiology, 1980-83, U. Mich., Ann Arbor, 1983-85, instr. cardiology, 1985-86; head cardiac catheterization lab., head cardiology Westland (Mich.) Med. Ctr., 1985. Contbr. articles to Jour. Biol. Chemistry, Am. Jour. Physiology, Am. Jour. Cardiology, Jour. Clin. Investigation, other profl. publs. Grantee Juvenile Diabetes Found., 1978-80, NIH, 1978-79. Mem. N.Y. Acad. Sci. Achievements include rsch. demonstrating dependence of intracellular degradation of insulin upon its prior adsorptive pinocytotic uptake by liver; studies on the electrophysiologie effect of cathecholamimes on sheep Parkinje fibers and on the hemodynamic effects of various drugs on the human circulatory system.

TERRITO, MARY C., health facility administrator, hematologist, educator; BS in Biology, Wayne State U., 1965, MD, 1968. Intern/resident in internal medicine Parkland Hosp., Dallas, 1971-73; fellow in hematology/oncology Harbor-U. Calif., LA, 1973-74, UCLA, 1974-75; rsch. assoc. Wadsworth VA Hosp., LA, 1975-81; asst. prof. dept. medicine UCLA, 1975-81, assoc. prof., 1981-96, prof., 1996—2007, dir. bone marrow transplant program Ctr. Health Scis., 1981—. Contbr. articles to profl. jours. Office: UCLA Bone Marrow Transplantation Program Ctr 42-121 CHS 10833 Le Conte Ave Los Angeles CA 90095-3075

TERRONES, GUILLERMO, research scientist; s. Eduardo Terrones-Langone and María Esther Maldonado-Zermeño; m. Kristine Marie Johnson, June 29, 1996; children: Taylor, Wesley, Arianne. BS, U. Iberoamericana, Mex. City, 1983; MS, U. Ariz., Tucson, 1987, PhD, 1991. Instr. U. Iberoamericana, 1983; grad. tchg. asst. U. Ariz., 1985—87, grad. rsch. asst., 1987—91; rsch. scientist Pacific NW Nat. Lab., Richland, Wash., 1991—96, sr. rsch. scientist, 1996—2002; scientist Los Alamos Nat. Lab., N.Mex., 2002—. Adj. lectr. Wash. State U., Tri Cities Campus, Richland, 1994—2002. Co-author: (textbook) Thermo-Fluids, Turbomachinery and Thermal Engines (in Spanish); contbr. articles to sci. jours., Dept. Energy tech. reports. Mem. Tri-Cities Hispanic Affairs Com., Wash., 1994—96. Recipient Outstanding Mentoring award, Pacific NW Nat. Lab., 1993, Outstanding Team Performance award, 1993, 2000, Outstanding Performance award, 2001; Grad. Coll. fellowship, U. Ariz., 1991. Achievements include design of liquid metal retrieval sampler. Office: Los Alamos Nat Lab PO Box 1663 MS T086 Los Alamos NM 87545 Business E-Mail: terrones@lanl.gov.

TERRUSO, LUIGI LEONARDO, artist, educator; b. Oct. 19, 1964; s. John James Terruso and (Ewashenko) Anne. BS in Studio Art with honors, CUNY, Staten Island, 1987; MFA, Yale U., 1994. Studio artist CUNY, 1987—, tchg. asst. to prof., 1987; instr. art lab. Snug Harbor Cultural Ctr., SI, NY, 1991—96; tchg. asst. Yale U. Sch. Art, New Haven, 1994; instr. Trumbull Coll., Yale Coll., New Haven, 1994; pvt. instr. Santa Fe, 2007—. Vis. artist Am. Acad. Rome, 2003—04, 2006—07; artist-in-residence Santa Fe Art Inst., 2005—06, Vt. Studio Ctr., Johnson, 1991, 97, 2005, Chautauqua Instn. Sch. Art, NY, 1991. One-man shows include Milton Gallery, Wash., Conn., 1998, Shneyer and Shen Ansonia Gallery, NYC, 1999, Smith and Thompson, 2000, 55 Mercer Gallery, 2005, exhibited in group shows at Gallery 313, 1990, Frank Bustemante Gallery, 1990, Foundry Gallery, DC, 1991, A.I.R. Gallery, NYC, 1991, Logan Gallery, Chautauqua, NY, 1991, Gale Gatesetal, Bklyn., 1999—2000, CJM Projects, NY, 2004, Lamia Ink!, Kyoto, Montpelier Cultural Arts Ctr., Laurel, Md., 1992, Yale U. Art and Architecture Gallery, New Haven, 1992—94, Snug Harbor Cultural Ctr., NYC, 1996, Bklyn. Waterfront Artists Coalition, 1992, 1992, 1998, Am. Acad. Arts and Letters, NYC, 2001, Nat. Acad. Mus., 2006, exhibitions include 183 Annual Survey Contemporary Am. Art, 2008, Nat. Acad. Mus., 2008, Century Assn., 2007—08, juried art, First Street Gallery, NY, 2008, Art Gotham, 2008. Mem. Century Assn., 2006—07, Art Gallery, NYC, 2007, James Cohan Gallery, NYC, 2007, Ober Gallery, Kent, Conn., 2009. Grantee, Santa Fe Art Inst., 2005—06; fellow, Vermont Studio Ctr., 1991, 1997, 2005; scholar, Joan Mitchell Found., 2006; Tenebaum scholar, CUNY, 1983—87. Mem.: Artists Fellowship, Inc., Century Assn., Harper Cons., Inc. (v.p. 1997—, bd. dirs. 1997—), Hanovarian Found. (bd. dirs. 2007—), Coll. Art Assn., Print Club NY. Avocation: travel. Studio: 526 W 26th St Studio 910 New York NY 10001

TERRY, ADAM, legislative staff member; m. Jenni Roberson. BA in Journalism, La. Tech U., 2003. Columnist The Ruston Daily Leader; spokesman for Rep. Rodney Alexander, US House of Reps., now chief of staff. Office: Office of Congressman Rodney Alexander 316 Cannon House Office Bldg Washington DC 20515 Office Phone: 202-225-8490. Office Fax: 202-225-5639. E-mail: adam.terry@mail.house.gov.*

TERRY, ANNE CURTIS, lawyer, writer; d. Charles and Florine Curtis; m. Edward H. Terry; children: Edward, Ellyn. BA, Fla. State U., Tallahassee, 1970; MA, U. Tex., Austin, 1972; JD, U. Fla., Gainesville, 1978. Bar: Fla. 1979. Tchg. asst./lectr. dept. geography U. Tex., Austin, 1972—74; appellate law clk. 1st Dist. Ct. of Appeals, Tallahassee, 1978—79; asst. atty. gen. Office of Fla. Atty. Gen., Tallahassee, 1980—86; staff counsel Fla. Legislature, Tallahassee, 1986—89; solo practitioner/firm owner Law Office of Anne Curtis Terry, Tallahassee, 1993—. Author: The Spirit in the South, 2006; contbr. legal opinions to ann. report of atty. gen. Fla. NDEA Title VI fellow, Inst. Latin Am. Studies, U. Tex., 1971-1972. Mem.: Phi Alpha Delta, Phi Kappa Phi. Democrat. Methodist. Achievements include represented Southern Christian Leadership Conference in First Amendment litigation; represented numerous plaintiffs in employment discrimination cases, based on disability, race and gender; represented clients in litigatic against home and plaintiff-relators in state and federal qui tam litigation; research in model ordinance for regulation of low frequency vibrations. Avocations: travel, photography, poetry, cooking, gardening. Office: Law Office of Anne Curtis Terry 6209 Verdura Way Tallahassee FL 32311

TERRY, CAROLE COSGROVE, retired small business owner, historian, researcher; b. San Francisco, Jan. 5, 1938; d. John Charles and Emile Dohrmann Cosgrove; m. Norman Berkley Terry, Feb. 14, 1970; children: Emilie Terry Meinadier, Brenda Jane. BA, Stanford U., Calif., 1959; MA, U. Nevada, Las Vegas, 2000, PhD candidate, 2001—. Cert. Merit Katherine Gibbs Sch., N.Y., 1960. Sec. asst. Hon. Herbert Hoover, NYC, 1959—60; exec. sec. E.F. Hutton & Co. Inc., LA, 1960—71; interim alumnae dir. Marlborough Sch., LA, 1991—92; owner, v.p., CFO Galleria Travel, Inc., Glendale, 1976—93; ret., 1994. Co-author (with Emilie D. Cosgrove): California Potpourri 1852-1936, 1966; contbg. editor: The Morelli House, 2008; contbr. articles to profl. jour., scientific papers. Treas. bd. mem. Sun City Quilters, 2002—05; stewardship team chair St. Andrew Luth. Ch., 2004—05, stewardship, counting chair, 1996—99; bd. mem., treas. Costume Coun., L.A. County Mus. Art, 1992—95; sec. bd. mem. Jr. League Las Vegas Endowment Bd., 2002—08; treas. bd. mem. Jr. League Las Vegas Sustainers, 2007; sec., pres. Jr. League Las Vegas Endowment Bd., 2008—; pres. Jr. League Las Vegas Sustainers, 2008—. E-mail: terrynandc@cox.net.

TERRY, CLIFFORD LEWIS, journalist; b. Highland Park, Ill., Jan. 19, 1937; s. Clifford Lewis and Isabelle (Marlow) T.; m. Patricia West Dickelman, Sept. 1, 1966; children: Christopher West, Scott Marlow. Student, Carleton Coll., Northfield, Minn., 1954-55; BA, Trinity Coll., Hartford, Conn., 1958; postgrad., Columbia U., 1962-63. Tchr., English and history Mt. Hermon (Mass.) Sch., 1958-59; police reporter City News Bur. Chgo., 1959-60; mem. staff Chgo. Tribune, 1960-94, movie critic, 1965-70; assoc. editor Chgo. Tribune (Sunday mag.), 1970-82, feature writer, 1982-85, TV critic, 1985-89, arts feature writer, 1989-94; ind. writer, 1994—. Author: Chicago: Off the Beaten Path, 2001, 3d edit., 2005. Served with AUS, 1960. Nieman fellow Harvard U., 1969-70 Mem. Phi Beta Kappa.

TERRY, EDWIN WELLINGTON, college librarian; b. Bklyn., Dec. 4, 1918; s. Edwin Wellington Roberts Terry and Ursaline Whittle McClane; m. Natalie Johnston (dec.); children: Brian Paul, Francesca Natalie. BA, Bklyn. Coll., 1941, MA, 1968; BSc with honors, Columbia U., 1946; MA, Columbia Tchrs. Coll., 1948; PhD, St. John's U., 1971. Cert. pub. libr. SUNY Dept. Edn., 1967. Cataloger Columbia U. Libr., NYC, 1946—47; acquisition asst. Queens Coll., Flushing, NY, 1948—59; dir. Dillard U. Libr., New Orleans, 1947—48, Nassau CC Libr., Garden City, 1960—67, Bronx CC Libr., 1967—78, staff mem., 1978—88; adj. libr. Bronx CC, 1988—93, Manhattan CC, NYC, 1993—2000. Chair two yr. coll. chief librs. SUNY, 1965; mem. ad hoc com. Nassau County Ctrl. Libr., 1965—66; pres. Nassau County Lib. Assn., 1965—66; chair profl. status com. Libr. Assn. of CUNY, 1978—80, chair publ. com., 1980—88; mem. adv. com. minority fellowship Queens Coll. Libr. Sch., 1966—90. Editor: Urban Academic Librarian, 1983—88; contbr. articles to profl. jours.; co-author: Core Collection in Nursing and Allied Health Sciences, 1990. Mem. Friends of U. Calif. San Diego Libr., 2004. Staff sgt. US Army, 1943. Recipient Cert. of Svc., Bronx CC Student Coun., 1968, Cert. of Merit, Bronx CC, 1988. Mem.: Archons of Colophon, Beta Phi Mu. Democrat.

TERRY, ELIZABETH HUDSON, personal care industry executive, realtor; d. Otis Hudson and (Russell) Evelena; m. Lester Terry; 1 child, Darric. Student, Clark Coll., Atlanta, 1966; BA business, Atlanta Sch. Bus., 1968; student, Dekalb Perimeter Coll., Decatur, Ga., 1978—83; cert. enterpreneurship program, U. Ga., 1993; cert., Speak Easy Sch., Atlanta, 1993. Lic. real estate salesperson Ga., 1996. Asst. dir. Count Jackson Studio, Atlanta, 1968—72; mgr. BellSouth Corp., Atlanta, 1970—97, Bank of Am., Atlanta, 1999—; wedding dir., cons. Weddings by Liz, Decatur, Ga., 1980—; realtor, sales assoc. Coldwell Banker Buckhead Brokers, Tucker, 1996—2000, Quest Realty Inc., Decatur, 2000—. Notary, Decatur; featured in numerous newspapers and mags.; guest appearances on several t.v. and radio shows. Author: Just Think About It, 1993. Mem. planning bd. sch. in Haiti; mem. Veracruz Homeowners Assn., Decatur, 2001—, Nat. Coalition of 100 Black Women's Assn., NAACP, United Negro Coll. Fund; pub. rels. advisor Uptown Social Club, Decatur; vol. Habitat for Humanity, Atlanta; asst. dir. The Colored People Prodn., Atlanta; program dir. Azusa St. Revival Prodn., 1995; asst. dir., program dir. Fix Me Jesus Prodn., Atlanta; mem. Jr. Achievement Mentoring Program, 1990—96; founding mem. Nat. Campaign Tolerance, 2005; mem. Beulah Bapt. Ch., Decatur; adv. bd., bd. dirs. Suncrest Resources, Inc., Stone Mountain, Ga., 1986. Recipient Pearl award, Diamond award, Ruby award, Emerald award, Gold award. Mem.: Midnight Expression Orgn., Chamber of Commerce, Rainbow Internat. chpt. (Am. Bus. Women's Assn.) (founder 1985—86, v.p. 1985—86, pres. 1986—87, chmn. Program Com., Woman of the Year 1985—86), Sphnix chpt. (Am. Bus. Women's Assn.) (exec. bd. secy. 1984, chmn. Extension Com., Woman of the Year 1984—85, Woman of Quarter 1985, Hand of Friendship award), St. Peter and Paul Parent-Teacher Assn., United Coun. for Negro Women Assn., Am. Bus. Women's Assn. (chpt. chmn. adminstrv. bd. 1986—88, chmn. mem. com., chmn. bus. assn. com., chmn. edn./scholarship com.), Starwood Vistana Vacation Assn., Toastmasters (v.p. edn. 2003—04, pres. Bank of Am. 2004—, A.T.M. Bronze award 2006, Competent Toastmaster award 2004, Competent Leadership award). Avocation: writing. Home: 3941 Veracruz Dr Decatur GA 30034 Office Phone: 770-374-4900.

TERRY, FRANCES JEFFERSON, retired psychiatric nurse practitioner; d. Walter Louis and Ruth Williams Jefferson; m. Robert Terry, Sept. 29, 1926; children: Deborah Ella Terry-Hays, Robert David, Michael Duane, William Brian, Walter Louis. BSN, Seattle U., 1951; MSN, U. Wash., Seattle, 1981. Lic. Advanced RN Practitioner, ANCC. Health enhancement-program nurse Ctrl. Area Sr. Ctr., Seattle; staff nurse Providence Hosp., Seattle; prescribing and consulting nurse Cmty. Ho. Mental Health Agy., Seattle; psychiat. mental health practitioner U. Wash.-Harborview Med. Ctr., Seattle; nursing instr. Shoreline CC, Seattle; nurse case mgr.-mental health U. Wash.; nursing instr. Seattle U.; dir. health svcs. NW Ctr. Developmentally Challenged, Seattle; sch. nurse Seattle Pub. Schs.; pub. health nurse Seattle King County Health Dept., Seattle. Diabetes support group vol. facilitator Joslin Diabetes Ctr., Seattle. Auditor, ch. coun. ImmaculateConception Ch., Seattle; mem. Seattle Ctrl. Cmty. Coll. Found. Recipient Cmty. Svc. award, Seattle U., 2004, honoree, Knights of Peter Claver Ladies, 2008, Black Heritage Soc. Wash. State, 2008, Wash. State Nurses Soc. Centennial Celebration, 2008; named Outstanding Nurse, U. Wash.-Harborview Med. Ctr., 1993; named to Hall of Fame, Wash. State Nurses Assn., 2000. Mem.: Cert. Ret. Nurse Amb. Cir., Am. Nurse Credentialing Ctr., Mary Mahoney Profl. Nurses Assn., Am. Nurses' Assn. (life), Alpha Kappa Alpha Sorority (life). Personal E-mail: bobfrater@comcast.net.

TERRY, FREDERICK ARTHUR, JR., lawyer; b. Buffalo, May 24, 1932; s. Frederick Arthur and Agnes Elizabeth (Tranter) T.; m. Barbara (Anderson). BA, Williams Coll., 1953; LLB, Columbia U., 1956. Bar: N.Y. 1957, U.S. Dist Ct. (so., no., and ea. dist.), N.Y., U.S. Tax Ct., U.S. Supreme Ct. Law clk. to Hon. Sterry R. Waterman U.S. Ct. Appeals (2d cir.), 1956—57; assoc. Sullivan & Cromwell LLP, NYC, 1957—64, ptnr., 1965—99, sr. counsel, 2000—. Trustee Harold K. Hochschild Found.; chmn. Flagler Found.; bd. dir. McIntosh Found., Weinman Found.; trustees coun. Nat. Gallery of Art; hon. trustee Natural Resources Def. Coun.; trustee emeritus Rockefeller U. Recipient David Rockefeller Extraordinary Svc. award, Rockefeller U., 2007. Mem. ABA, N.Y. State Bar Assn., Assn. Bar City of N.Y., River Club, Union Club, Maidstone Club, The Bathing Corp. Office: Sullivan & Cromwell LLP 125 Broad St Fl 25 New York NY 10004-2400 Office Phone: 212-558-3923.

TERRY, GARY A., lawyer, director, former trade association executive; b. Ogden, Utah, Apr. 2, 1935; s. Hyrum Aceal and Viola (Sorenson) T.; m. Carole Ann Eitel, June 23, 1962; children— Stephanie Ann, Brendan Gary BA in Polit. Sci., UCLA, 1964; JD, George Washington U., 1968. Bars: Va. 1969 D.C. 1969. Mem. staff U.S. Ho. of Reps., Washington, 1964-65; Washington staff Bethlehem Steel Corp., 1965-69; atty. HUD, Washington, 1969; exec. v.p. Am. Land Devel. Assn. (now Am. Resort Devel. Assn.), Washington, 1969-82, pres., 1982-91, also dir.; with Jones, Waldo, Holbrook & McDonough, Washington, 1991-95, St. George, 1995-97. Dir. Internat. Found. for Timesharing, Washington, 1981-91, mem. consultative council Nat. Inst. Bldg. Scis., Washington, 1982-85; U.S. rep. land use and town planning com. Internat. Real Estate Fedn., Brussels, 1984-91; mem. Found. for Internat. Meetings, Washington, 1984-92; del. Lincoln Inst. Land Policy, Harvard U., 1984, 85 Contbr. articles to profl. jours. Asst. to exec. dir. Presdl. Inaugural Com., 1969-70; mem. adv. bd. NOAA, Washington, 1972; bd. dirs. Zacchaeus Free Med. and Legal Clinics, Washington, 1991-95, co-chair lawyers com., 1992-95; bd. dirs. Celebrity Concert Series, St. George, 1999—2005, pres., 2004-05; chmn. Pioneer Ctr. for the Arts Found., St. George, 2000-02, bd. trustees, 1998-03. Seved with USN, 1953-56. Decorated Am. Spirit of Honor medal. Mem. Va. Bar Assn., D.C. Bar Assn. Mem. Lds Ch. Avocations: music, literature, flying, art, travel. Home: 952 Lizzie Ln Saint George UT 84790-2255 Personal E-mail: gaterry@earthlink.net.

TERRY, JAMES LAYTON, II, research scientist; b. Peoria, Ill., Apr. 8, 1951; s. James Layton and Mary Elizabeth Terry; m. Nixie G. Raymond, Sept. 12, 1998; children: Morgan Raymond, Jesse Raymond. BA, Denison U., Granville, Ohio, 1973; MS in Physics, Johns Hopkins U., Balt., 1975, PhD, 1978. Rsch. staff Mass. Inst. Tech., Cambridge, 1978—2006, prin. rsch. scientist, 2006—. Fellow: Am. Phys. Soc.; mem.: Phi Beta Kappa. Liberal. Achievements include research in magnetically confined high temperature plasmas. Avocation: running. Office: Mass Inst Tech NW 17-176 Cambridge MA 02139

TERRY, JAMES PHILIP, federal agency administrator; b. East Brookfield, Mass., 1946; m. Michelle Lambert; 2 children. BA in Geo-Chemistry, Va. U., 1968, MA; JD, Mercer U., 1973; LLM, George Washington U., 1980, LLD, 1982. Legal counsel to Chmn. Joint Chiefs of Staff US Dept. Def., Washington, 1992—95; adminstrv. judge bd. land appeals US Dept. Interior; dep. asst. sec. for global, regional & functional affairs US Dept. State, prin. dep. asst. sec. legis. affairs; chmn. bd. veterans appeals US Dept. Veterans Affairs, 2005—. Decorated Def. Superior Svc. medal, Legion of Merit, Bronze Star medal with Combat V, Purple Heart, Def. Meritorious Svc. medal, Navy Commendation medal (2), Def. Achievement medal, Combat Action Ribbon; recipient Superior Honor medal, US Dept. State, Navy Meritorious Svc. medal (3). Office: US Dept Veterans Affairs Lafayette Bldg 811 Vermont Ave NW Rm 845 Washington DC 20420 Office Phone: 202-565-5001. Office Fax: 202-565-5587.*

TERRY, JASON EUGENE, professional basketball player; b. Seattle, Sept. 15, 1977; s. Curtis Terry and Andrea Cheatham; m. Johnyika Terry; 4 children. BA in Gen. Studies, U. Ariz., Tucson, 1999. Guard Atlanta Hawks, 1999—2004, Dallas Mavericks, 2004—. Mem. US nat. team Goodwill Games, Brisbane, Australia, 2001. Founder Jason Terry Found. Recipient Cmty. Asst. award, NBA, 2002, Image Leader Award In Sports, Building Leaders for Tomorrow, 2007; named NCAA 1st Team All Am., AP, 1999, Nat. Player of Yr., Sports Illus., Basketball Times, 1999, Player of Yr., Pac-10 Conf., 1999, Sixth Man of Yr., NBA, 2009. Achievements include member of the NCAA Men's Basketball Championship winning University of Arizona Wildcats, 1997. Office: Dallas Mavericks The Pavilion 2909 Taylor St Dallas TX 75226 also: The Jason Terry Found PO Box 3095 Loganville GA 30052*

TERRY, JOHN ALFRED, Senior Judge, DC Court of Appeals; b. Utica, NY, May 6, 1933; s. Robert Samuel and Julia Berenice (Collins) T. BA magna cum laude, Yale U., 1954; JD, Georgetown U., 1960. Bar: D.C. 1960. Asst. U.S. atty. for D.C. US Dept. Justice, 1962-67; staff atty. Nat. Commn. Reform of Fed. Criminal Laws, Washington, 1967-68; pvt. practice law Washington, 1968-69; chief appellate divsn. U.S. Atty.'s Office for D.C. US Dept. Justice, 1969-82; judge DC Ct. Appeals, 1982—2006, sr. judge, 2006—. Mem. D.C. Bar (bd. govs. 1977-82), ABA, Phi Beta Kappa. Office: DC Ct Appeals 430 E St NW Washington DC 20001-2767*

TERRY, JOHN DAVID, telecommunications industry executive, educator; b. Norfolk, Va., Sept. 29, 1966; s. Deborah Kathleen Terry; 1 child, Amiel David. PhD, Ga. Inst. Tech., 1999. Prin. scientist Nokia Rsch. Ctr., Irving, Tex.; dir. baseband sys. engring. WiQuest Comm., Inc, Allen, Tex., 2004—05; pres., CEO, Terry Cons. Inc., Garland, Tex., 2001—. Spkr. in field. Author: OFDM Wireless LANs: A Theoretical Guide. Recipient Black Engr. award, U.S. Black Engrs., 2002, featured in, Ebony Mag., Oct., 2006, Black Enterprise Mag., Feb., 2007, NSBE Pioneer award, 2009; named Suggester of Yr., NASA Glen Rsch. Ctr., 1990; named one of Most Important Blacks in Rsch. Sci., Sci. Spectrum mag., 2004; Pres. fellow, Old Dominion U., 1993—97. Mem.: IEEE (sr.; former vice-chair), Tau Beta Pi. Achievements include patents for method and apparatus for higher dimensional modulation; hybrid dimensional, spherical space-time codes; an efficient realization of biorthogonal spherical space-time codes; patents pending for combined OTD and TCM for high data rate wireless LANs; decision feedback equalization for residual ISI cancellation for OFDM sys; adaptive modulation for OFDM sys. with CSI at the transmitter; adaptive coord. interleaving for improved diversity performance in WLAN sys; layered matrix modulation design criteria for high data rate wireless LAN application; hybrid ARQ for WLAN networks. Office Phone: 703-349-5641. Fax: 703-349-5131. Personal E-mail: terry.consult@comcast.net. Business E-Mail: john.terry@terryconsult.com.

TERRY, KEITH, performing company executive, dancer, body musician; Drummer Jazz Tap Ensemble; founder, artistic dir. Crosspulse non-profit arts orgs., Oakland, Calif., 1980—; founding mem. Slammin All-Body Band. Mem. faculty World Arts and Cultures UCLA, 1998—2004; dir., curator Body Tjak Project, 1980—, Internat. Body Percussion Performance Project, The Listening Project, UCLA, Internat. Body Music Festival, 2008. Fellow John Simon Guggenheim Meml. Found., 2008. Office: Crosspulse PO Box 3388 Oakland CA 94609 Office Phone: 510-601-9797. Office Fax: 510-601-9197. E-mail: info@crosspulse.com.*

TERRY, LAVERN, school system administrator; BS in Elem. and Spl. Edn., U. Del.; MEd in Spl. Edn., U. Md., College Park; EdD in Edn. Leadership, U. Del. From tchr. to chief academic officer Christina Sch. Dist., Del.; dep. supt. curriculum and instrn. Hartford Pub. Schs., Conn., 2005—08; commr. edn. VI Dept. Edn., St. Thomas, 2008—. Fellow Broad Urban Supts. Acad. Office: VI Dept Edn 44-46 Kongens Gade St Thomas VI 00802-6746 Office Phone: 340-774-2810. Office Fax: 340-779-7153.*

TERRY, LEE RAYMOND, United States Representative from Nebraska, lawyer; b. Omaha, Jan. 29, 1962; s. Leland R. Terry; m. Robyn L. Terry, Feb. 14, 1992; children: Nolan E., Ryan, Jack. BA in Polit. Sci., U. Nebr., Lincoln, 1984; JD, Creighton U. Sch. Law, Omaha, 1987. Bar:

Nebr. 1987, US Dist. Ct. Nebr. 1987. Staff atty. Schrempp & Salerno, Omaha, 1987-92; ptnr. Schrempp, Salerno & Terry, Omaha, 1992-93, Terry & Kratville, Omaha, 1993-98; mem. City Coun., Omaha, 1991—98, US Congress from 2nd Nebr. dist., 1999—, mem. energy & commerce com. Co-author: Trying the Soft Tissue Case in Nebraska, 1995. V.p. Omaha City Coun., 1993—94, pres., 1995—97; chair elect Am. Diabetes Assn., Great Plains, 1996—97, chair Nebr. area, 1997—97; co-chmn. Impact Aid Coalition. Recipient Spirit of Enterprise award, US C. of C., 2002; named an Outstanding Young Nebraskan, Nebr. Jaycees, 1997; named one of Ten Outstanding Young Omahans, Omaha Jaycees, 1994. Mem.: Nebr. Assn. Trial Attys. (dir. 1995), Suburban Rotary Club. Republican. Methodist. Avocations: travel, baseball. Office: US House Reps 1524 Longworth House Office Bldg Washington DC 20515-2702 Office Phone: 202-225-4155.*

TERRY, LEON CASS, neurologist, educator; b. Dec. 22, 1940; s. Leon Herbert and Zella Irene (Boyd) T.; m. Suzanne Martinson, June 27, 1964; children: Kristin, Sean. Pharm. D., U. Mich., 1964; MD, Marquette U., 1969; PhD, McGill U., 1982; MBA, U. So. Fla., 1994. Diplomate Am. Bd. Psychiatry and Neurology, Am. Bd. Med. Mgmt. Intern U. Rochester, NY, 1969-70; staff assoc. NIH, 1970-72; resident in neurology McGill U., Montreal, Que., Canada, 1972-75; MRC fellow, 1975-78; assoc. prof. U. Tenn., Memphis, 1978-81; prof. neurology U. Mich., Ann Arbor, 1981-89; assoc. prof. physiology, 1982-89; asst. chief neurology VA Med. Ctr., Ann Arbor, 1982-89; chmn. dept. neurology Med. Coll. of Wis., Milw., 1989—2000, prof. neurology and physiology, 1989—2003; chief med. officer Nexostherapeuticals, 2003—; pres., CEO Neurologic Cons., LLP, 2004—, Longevitech, 2004—. Dir. clin neurosci. ctr. and multiple sclerosis clinic, Med. Coll. Wis.; assoc. dean for amb. care, 1996-98; vice chief of staff Froedtert Hosp., 1994-97; chief of staff, 1997-98; chief med. officer cenegenics, 1997-98. Contbr. articles to profl. jours, chpts. to books. Served to lt. comdr. USPHS, 1970-72. NIH grantee, 1981-92; VA grantee, 1980-92; VA Clin. Investigator award, 1980-81. Mem. AMA, Am. Soc. Clin. Investigation, Cen. Soc. Clin. Investigation, Am. Neurol. Assn., Am. Coll. Physician Execs. (vice chmn. academic health ctr. soc. 1994-95, chair, 1995-98, leader forum health care delivery 1995-98), Am. Coll. Healthcare Execs., Endocrine Soc., Am. Acad. Neurology, Internat. Soc. Neuroendocrinilogy, Internat. Soc. Psychoeuroendocrinilogy, Soc. Neurosci., Soc. Rsch. Biol. Rhythms, Milw. Acad. Physicians, Wis. Neurol. Assn., Wis. State Med. Soc. (del.-elect 1995-96), Med. Soc. Milw. County, Milw. Neuropsychiatric Soc. (pres.-elect.). Avocations: pilot, skiing, scuba diving, computers. Office: Neurologic Consultnats LLC Ste 212 1009 W Glen Oaks Ln Mequon WI 53092 Home Phone: 414-234-9207; Office Phone: 262-241-8512. E-mail: cass@cass-terry.com.

TERRY, MICKEY THOMAS, music educator, director; b. Greenville, NC, Feb. 29, 1956; s. Thomas Lewis Terry and Beatrice Claudia Chapman. BA, East Carolina U., Greenville, NC, 1977, MA, 1980; PhD, Georgetown U., Washington, 1991. Adminstr. humanities program NEH, Washington, 1991; lectr. history Georgetown U., 1992—93; dir. music St. Rita's Cath. Ch., Alexandria, Va., 1996—2000; lectr. music Howard U., Washington, 1999—2000; dir. music St. Mary's Cath. Ch., Clinton, Md., 2001—; lectr. Howard U., Sch Div., Ch. Music, 2007—08. Vice chair African Heritage Cultural Inst., Mitchellville, Md., 2006. Mem.: Am. Guild Organists (mem. exec. bd. 1994—97, 1988—94). Democrat. Episcopalian. Avocations: reading, antiques. Personal E-mail: mickeythomasterry@verizon.net.

TERRY, ROBERT ARTHUR, literature and language professor, director; b. Texarkana, Ark., Feb. 10, 1938; m. Carolyn Rosalind Eason; children: Todd Eason McGowan, Thomas Watson McGowan, Natasha Elizabeth Chandler, David Matthews. BA, Hendrix Coll., Conway, Ark., 1960; MA, U. Ark., Fayetteville, 1963; PhD, U. Ariz., Tucson, 1969. Pastor Village, Ebenezer Meth. Charge, 1958—; grad. tchg. asst. U. Ark., 1961—63; asst. dir. freshman english U. Ariz., 1963—69; head, dept. english U. Alaska, Fairbanks, 1969—73; dir., divsn. gen. studies, prof. english So. Ark. U., Magnolia, 1973—. Reader, table leader Ednl. Testing Svc., Princeton, NJ, 1977—. Author: (textbook) How to Stay in College. Pres. South Ark. Symphony, Eldorado, Magnolia, Camden, 1998—. Mem.: Rotary Internat. Conservative. Methodist. Avocations: travel, fishing. Office: Southern Ark Univ 100 University St Magnolia AR 71754

TERRY, SARA, photographer, reporter; b. Detroit; BA in journalism, summa cum laude, Calif. State U., Long Beach, 1977. Reporter Anaheim Bulletin/Orange County Register, Calif., 1977—78; staff writer, founding reporter Monitor Radio Christian Sci. Monitor, 1978—89; freelance writer and photographer, 1990—; founder The Aftermath Project, 2000—. Author: Aftermath: Bosnia's Long Road to Peace, 2005. Recipient Overseas Press Club award, Corp. Pub. Broadcasting award, Clarion/Women in Communication award, Lucie Humanitarian award, Internat. Photography Awards, 2008; named one of Top Ten Female Reporters in the US, Iowa State U. Press, 1991; Alicia Patterson fellowship, 2005. Office: c/o Dominique Charlet Taïga Presse 19 rue Martel 75010 Paris France E-mail: saraterry@mindspring.com.*

TERRY, STEPHEN D., mechanical engineer, educator; s. David and Barbara Terry; m. Susan Anderson, June 14, 1997; 1 child, Andrew. PhD in Mech. Engring., NC State U., Raleigh, 2005. Ext. asst. prof. NC State U., 1995—. Mem.: ASHRAE. Office: NC State Univ Campus Box 7910 Raleigh NC 27695

TERRY, WAYNE GILBERT, healthcare educator, hospital administrator; b. Plymouth, Mass., Oct. 2, 1932; s. Lawrence Arthur and Betty Frances (Boutemain) Terry; m. Barbara Bromwell, Sept. 20, 1980; children: Karleton Wayne, Dale Duane, Kendrick Shane, Kristen Alayne, Tammye Van Clief, Wade Bromwell Delk. AA in Gen. Adminstrn., Allan Hancock Coll., Santa Maria Calif., 1960; BBA in Bus. Mgmt., U. Hawaii, Honolulu, 1966; MHA, Med. Coll. Va., Va. Commonwealth U., Richmond, 1973; PhD in Health Svcs. Mgmt., LaSalle U., 1999; PhD, Manderville, La., 1999. Commd. 2d lt. USAF Med. Svc. Corps, 1967, advanced through grades to maj., 1976; asst. adminstr. for registrar activities USAF Hosp., Orlando AFB, Fla., 1966-67; assoc. adminstr. aeromed. evacuation activities USAF, Hickam AFB, Hawaii, 1967-71; adminstrv. resident USAF Regional Hosp., Langley AFB, Va., 1972-73; CEO USAF Hosp., Columbus AFB, Miss., 1973-75; nat. health edn. and tng. program advisor Office of Surgeon Gen., Dept. of Air Force, Washington, 1975-78; dir. health professions pers. planning and policy divsn. Office of Asst. Sec. Def. for Health Affairs, The Pentagon, Washington, 1978-80; dep. project mgr./adminstrv. dir. King Faisal U. Teaching Hosp., Al-Khobar, Saudi Arabia, 1980-82; dep. project mgr., hosp. dir. North Yemen Healthcare Project, As-Salem Hosp., Sadah, Yemen Arab Republic, 1982-83; hosp. dir., CEO western area Armed Forces Hosps., Khamis Mushayt, Saudi Arabia, 1983-84; chief adminstr./commissioning team chief Orbit Summit Health, Ltd., Riyadh, Saudi Arabia, 1984-85; hosp. dir., adminstrv. dir. Truk State Dept. Health Svcs., Moen, Federated States of Micronesia, 1985-87; assoc. adminstr. support svcs. King Fahad Hosp., Saudi Arabian N.G., Riyadh, 1987-90; project mgr., CEO N.W. Armed Forces Hosps. Program, Tabuk, Saudi Arabia, 1990-98, cons. in health svcs. mgmt., 1998-99; cons., mediator in health svcs. mgmt. Crozet, Va., 1999-2000; exec. dir., CEO Southside Area Health Edn. Ctr. Longwood U., Farmville, Va., 2000—. Apptd. mil. cons. healthcare planning to the Air Force Surgeon Gen., 1979; apptd. preceptor program in healthcare adminstrn. U. Mich. for adminstrv. residents at N.W. Armed Forces Hosps. Programs, Tabuk, Saudi Arabia, 1993; supervisory bd. Royal Coll. Surgeons in Ireland, Dublin, 1990-98; cert. sr. grant specialist, reviewer, cons.; lectr., cons. in field. Contbr. articles to profl. jours. Warden to Am. Cmty. N.W. Region of Yemen Arab Republic to Am. Embassy in Sanaa, 1982-83, warden to Am. Cmty. N.W. Region of Saudi Arabia to Am. Embassy in Riyadh, 1990-99; mem. Internat. Sch. Sys. Coord. Com., Tabuk, 1990-99; bd. dirs. Taif Sch. Dist. Sys., Saudi Arabia, 1981-82; chmn., exec. com., bd. dirs. Ctrl. Va. Health Planning Agy., Richmond, Va., 2001-08; bd. dirs. Va. Tobacco Settlement Found., Regional Adv. Bd., Richmond, Va., 2001—, Southside Area Health Edn. Ctr., Longwood U., Farmville, 2001—; leadership and planning group Nat. Area Health Edn. Ctr. Assn., Balt., 2003-04, Va. Dept. Health Commr's. Healthcare Workforce Authority, 2008-, chmn., program adv. group. Va. Statewide AHEC, 2008-. Decorated Def. Meritorious Svc. medal, Air Force Meritorious Svc. medal with 3 Oak Leaf Clusters, Air medal with 3 Oak Leaf Clusters, Air Force Commendation medal with 3 oak leaf clusters, Republic of Vietnam Gallantry Cross with palm, Republic of Vietnam Svc. medal with 11 svc. stars, Korean Def. Svc. medal, Sec. of Def. Svc. medal/badge, Air Staff Svc. Badge Dept. Air Force, Air Force Chief Med. Svc. Corps badge; recipient Citation of Appreciation Nat. Coun. Social Welfare, Seoul, Republic of Korea, 1963, Citation of Appreciation award Suchan Province Gov., Choong Nam, Republic of Korea, 1963, award of merit Pacific Air Forces Command, Hickam AFB, Hawaii, 1965, Outstanding Jr. Officer in 22nd Air Force, USAF, 1970, Outstanding Rsch. award Med. Coll. Va., 1973, Personality of the South award, 1975, Men of Achievement award, Cambridge, Eng., 1982, Citation of Appreciation Gov. Truk State, Federated States of Micronesia, 1987, Citation of Merit Internat. Red Cross Commn., Bern, Switzerland, 1991, N.W. Armed Forces Hosps., Ministry Def. and Aviation, Tabuk, 1991, Citation of Appreciation Presidency of Gen. Staff Hdqs., Ministry of Def. and Aviation, Tabuk, 1992-93, 95-99, Disting. Alumni award Allan Hancock Coll., Santa Maria, 2000, Citation of Appreciation Longwood U., Va., 2006. Fellow Am. Coll. Healthcare Execs. (life), Royal Soc. Health; mem. Am. Hosp. Assn., Am. Mgmt. Assn. (life), Air Force Med. Svc. Corps Assn. (membership and awards com. 2003—, bd. dirs., newsletter editor 2005—), Assn. Mil. Surgeons of U.S., Air Force Assn; life mem., Vets. of Foreign Wars (2001-), The American Legion (2007-), Military Officer's Assn. of Am., Piedmont Region (2001-). Republican. Baptist. Avocations: tennis, coin collecting/numismatics, hiking. Office: Southside Area Health Edn Ctr Longwood Univ 201 High St Farmville VA 23909-1800 Home Phone: 434-392-3226; Office Phone: 434-395-2862. Business E-Mail: terrywg@longwood.edu.

TERRY, WILLIAM LEAKE, lawyer; b. Little Rock; s. David Dickson and Adolphine Fletcher Terry; m. Elizabeth Kilbury Terry, June 20, 1947; children: Elizabeth Terry Foti, Ellen Fletcher, Susan Terry Borne. Student, Princeton U., NJ, 1941—43; BS in Bus. Adminstrn., U. Ark., Fayetteville, 1948, LLB, 1950. Bar: Ark., US Ct. Mil. Appeals. Law clk. Ark. Supreme Ct. Justice, Little Rock, 1950; atty. Ark. State Hwy. Dept., Little Rock, 1951—53; ptnr. Friday, Eldredge and Clark, Little Rock, 1954—90, of counsel, 1991—. Bd. trustees Ark. Arts Ctr., Little Rock, 1968—72; ombudsman Ark. Com. Employer Support Guard and Reserve; bd. dirs. Ark. River Hist. Soc., Tulsa, MacArthur Mus. Ark., Little Rock, 2000—, Ctrl. Ark. Libr. Sys, Little Rock, 1991—2000, United Way Pulaski County, 1966—79, All Saints Episcopal. Sch., Vicksburg, Miss., 1968—70. Lt. col. USAF, 1943—45, with USAFR, with JAG. Decorated Disting. Flying Cross and Air medal with Oak Leaf Clusters. Mem.: Ark. Bar Found. (bd. dirs. 1969—72), Pulaski County Bar Assn. (pres. 1977—78), Kiwanis. Avocations: history, tennis, boating, hunting, travel. Home: 6323 Greenwood Rd Little Rock AR 72207 Office: Friday Eldredge & Clark 2000 Regions Ctr 400 w Capital Ave Little Rock AR 72201

TERSINE, BRENDA L., funeral director; b. Punxsutawney, Pa., June 2, 1948; d. G.J. and Mary V. tersine; m. Bill Goichberg, Feb. 20, 1993. BS in Edn., Indiana U. Pa., 1970; Diploma, Pitts. Inst. Mortuary Sci., 1971; MA, SUNY, Albany, 1985. Lic. funeral dir., N.Y., Pa. Embalmer, funeral dir., Punxsutawney, 1971-75; embalmer, funeral dir. Oliver H Bair, Phila., 1976-80; per diem substitute Phila. Bd. Edn., 1978-80; embalmer, anatomical gifts Albany Med. Coll., 1980-90; asst. prof. mortuary sci. Hudson Valley C.C., Troy, N.Y., 1980-90; funeral dir., embalmer Salisbury Mills, N.Y., 1990—. Contbg. author: Embalming History, Theory and Practice, 1990. Vice pres. adv. bd. Continental Chess, Salisbury Mills, 1991—; supportive counseling/crisis intervention YWCA, Troy, 1989-91. Mem. Acad. Profl. Funeral Svc. Practice (life), Funeral Svc. Ednl. Found., Nat. Funeral Dirs. Assn., Cath. daus. of Am. Democrat. Roman Catholic. Avocation: organizing chess tournaments.

TERWILLEGAR, JANE CUSACK, retired librarian, educator; b. Warsaw, NY, Nov. 7, 1935; d. James Scott and Estella B. (Ackerman) Cusack; m. Gordon H. Terwillegar, July 26, 1958 (div. Mar. 1989); children: Sarah Ann Terwillegar Smedley, Arne Matthew. BA, Elmira Coll., NY, 1957; MLS, SUNY, Geneseo, 1960; EdS, U. Ga., 1977. Cert. tchr., Fla. Instr. U. Ga., Athens, 1975-81; libr. Palm beach County Libr., West Palm Beach, Fla., 1981-83, Palm Beach County Schs., Royal Palm Beach, Fla., 1983-94, dist. libr. media svcs. mgr. West Palm Beach, 1994—2000; dir. Lake Park Public Libr., 2000—07. Lectr. Sch. Libr. and Info. Sci., U. South Fla., Tampa, 1987—, Nova U., Ft. Lauderdale, Fla., 1995—; task force mem. SUNLINK project Fla. Dept. Edn., 1995-2000; mem. adv. coun. Fla. Libr. Svcs. and Tech. Act., 1999-2003. Co-author: Commonsense Cataloging, 3d edit. 1983, 4th edit. 1990; contbr. articles to profl. jours. Pres. Staff Assn. Palm Beach Sch. Dist., 1997-99. Mem. ALA, AAUW (pres. No. Palm Beach br. 2001-05), Am. Assn. Sch. Librs. (exec. bd. 1990-94), Assn. for Libr. Svc. to Children (Newbery com. 1988-89), Fla. Assn. Media in Edn. (sec. 1988-89, bd. dirs. 1997—, pres. 1999-2001), Ednl. Media Assn. Fla. (pres. 1988), Kiwanis Club of Lake Park, Phi Beta Kappa, Phi Delta Kappa. Avocations: scuba diving, sports cars. Home: 911 Oak Harbour Dr Juno Beach FL 33408-2173

TERWILLIGER, GEORGE JAMES, III, lawyer, former federal agency administrator; b. New Brunswick, NJ, June 5, 1950; s. George James Jr. and Ruth Nancy (Mellilo) T.; m. Carol Anne Hitchings, Dec. 18, 1976; children: Sarah Katherine, George Zachary Grant, Virginia. BA in Communications, Seton Hall U., 1973; JD, Antioch Law Sch., 1978. Bar: D.C. 1978, U.S. Dist. Ct. D.C., 1979, U.S. Ct. Appeals (D.C. cir.) 1979, U.S. Dist. Ct. (so. dist.) Fla. 1980, U.S. Dist. Ct. Vt. 1981, U.S. Ct. Appeals (2d cir.) 1982, Vt. 1983, U.S. Supreme Ct. 1992, U.S. Ct. Appeals (4th cir.) 1993. Asst. US atty. DC dist. US Dept. Justice, Washington, 1978-81, asst. US atty. dist. Vt Burlington, 1981-86, US atty., 1986-91, dep. atty. gen. Washington, 1992-93; ptnr. McGuire, Woods, Battle & Boothe LLP, Washington, 1993—2000, White & Case LLP, Washington, 2000—. Co-founder Americans for a Better Country, 2003—. Named one of 100 Most Influential Lawyers, Nat. Law Jour., 2006. Mem. ABA, Vt. Bar Assn., D.C. Bar Assn., Rep. Nat. Lawyers Assn. (pres. 1994-95). Republican. Congregationalist. Avocations: skiing, tennis, fishing. Office: White & Case LLP 701 Thirteenth St NW Washington DC 20005 Business E-Mail: gterwilliger@whitecase.com.

TERWILLIGER, J. RONALD, real estate company executive; Grad., US Naval Acad.; MBA (hon.), Harvard U. Pres., COO Sea Pines Plantation Co., Hilton Head Plantation Co.; chmn., CEO Trammell Crow Residential, Atlanta, 1986—. Chmn. emeritus Wharton Real Estate Ctr.; mem. Fannie Mae Adv. Coun.; owner Atlanta WNBA team, 2007—. Mem. internat. bd. dirs. Habitat for Humanity; vice chmn. Atlanta Neighborhood Devel. Partnership; dir. Naval Acad. Found. Baker scholar, Harvard Grad. Sch. Bus. Mem.: Real Estate Roundtable, Urban Land Inst. (immediate past chmn.). Office: Trammell Crow Residential Two Buckhead Plz 3050 Peachtree Rd NW Ste 500 Atlanta GA 30305 Office Phone: 770-801-1600. Office Fax: 770-801-1256.

TERZIAN, GRACE PAINE, communications executive; b. Boston, Oct. 19, 1952; d. Thomas Fite and Grace Hillman (Benedict) Paine; m. Philip Henry Terzian, Oct. 20, 1979; children: William Thomas Hillman, Grace Benedict Paine. BA in Art History, Williams Coll., Williamstown, Mass., 1974. Art dir. The New Republic, Washington, 1976-78; asst. editor The Chronicle of Higher Edn., Washington, 1978-79; rsch. editor Archtl. Digest, LA, 1982-85; pub. The Women's Quar., Arlington, Va., 1994—2004; exec. dir. Allergy and Asthma Network Mothers of Asthmatics, 2004—06; v.p. comm. Hudson Inst., Washington, 2006—. Editor Ex Femina, 1996—2004; sr. v.p. Ind. Women's Forum, 1998-2004. Mem. Soc. Colonial Dames in Am., Phi Beta Kappa. Episcopalian. Home: 10505 Adel Rd Oakton VA 22124-1605 Office: The Hudson Inst 1015 15th St NW 6th Fl Washington DC 20005 Home Phone: 703-938-7321; Office Phone: 202-974-2400. Personal E-mail: gterzian@cox.net. Business E-Mail: gracet@hudson.org.

TERZIAN, PHILIP HENRY, journalist; b. Kensington, Md., July 5, 1950; s. L. A. and Louise (Anderson) Terzian; m. Grace Barrett Paine, Oct. 20, 1979; children: William Thomas Hillman, Grace Benedict Paine. BA in English, Villanova U., 1973; DTS, Episcopal Theol. Sem., Va., 1995; postgrad., Oxford U., Eng., 1976. Desk editor Reuters, Washington, 1973, U.S. News & World Report, Washington, 1973-74; asst. editor The New Republic, Washington, 1974-78; mem. policy planning staff Dept. State, Washington, 1978-79; asst. editor Anniston (Ala.) Star, 1979-80; assoc. editor Lexington (Ky.) Herald, 1980-82; asst. editor of editl. pages L.A. Times, 1982-86; editor of editl. pages Providence Jour., 1986-92, assoc. editor, syndicated columnist, 1992—2005; lit. editor The Weekly Standard, Washington, 2005—. Panelist Washington Wk. in Rev., C-SPAN, Fox News, Nat. Pub. Radio, Voice Am. Contbr. articles to newspapers and jours. Pres. Providence Com. Fgn. Rels., 1989—92. Recipient Edn. Writers award, Edn. Writers Am., 1981, Svc. to Preservation award, Ida Lee Willis Found., 1982, juror, Pulitzer Prize, 1994—95; named finalist Disting. Commentary, 1991; Travelling fellow, Am. Journalism Found. Mem.: The Lit. Soc. Washington DC, Nat. Book Critics Cir., Va. Hist. Soc., Am. Coun. on Germany, Va. Soc. Ornithology, Assn. Literary Scholars and Critics, Order Hosp. St. John of Jerusalem, St. Andrew's Soc. Washington, Wolver Beagles (hon. whip), Sons of Union Vets. of Civil War, Soc. King Charles the Martyr, Univ. Club, Nat. Beagle Club. Republican. Episcopalian. Home: 10505 Adel Rd Oakton VA 22124-1605 Office: The Weekly Standard 1150 17th St NW Washington DC 20036 Office Phone: 202-293-4900. E-mail: pterzian@weeklystandard.com.

TESCHER, ANN NOREEN, nurse; b. Milw., Mar. 23, 1955; d. John Thomas and Pauline Shillue Hotter; m. Ren James Tescher, Mar. 4, 2000; 1 child, Margaret MaLi. BSN, Vanderbilt U., Nashville, 1977; MSN, Duke U., Durham, NC, 1980; PhD, U. Wis., Milw., 2003—03. Cert. CCNS, AACN, 1979, AACN, 2000. Staff nurse St. Joseph's Hosp., Milw., 1977—79, VA Med. Ctr., Durham, 1980—84; instr. Duke U., 1981—84; clin. nurse specialist Rapides Gen. Hosp., Alexandria, La., 1984—86, Orlando Regional Med. Ctr., Fla., 1986—2001, Mayo Clinic, Rochester, Minn., 1991—. Contbr. articles to profl. jours. Recipient fellowship, Am. Acad. Critical Care Medicine, 2006, Bea Ratner award, Naval Res. Assn., 1996, Mary Hall award, Navy Nurse Corps, 1995, Navy and Marine Corps Commendation medal, Sec. Navy, 1996—97, 1999, 2003, 2005. Mem.: Assn. Mil. Surgeons, Cath. Med. Assn., Soc. Critical Care Medicine, AACN (nominating com. 1990—90). Office: Mayo Clinic 1216 2nd St SouthWest Rochester MN 55902 Home Fax: 507-255-4194. Business E-Mail: tescher.ann@mayo.edu.

TESELLE, EUGENE ARTHUR, JR., religion educator; b. Ames, Iowa, Aug. 8, 1931; s. Eugene Arthur and Hildegarde (Flynn) TeS.; m. Sallie McFague, Sept. 12, 1959 (div. Oct. 1976); children: Elizabeth, John; m. Penelope Saunders, Mar. 4, 1978; children: William, James, Thomas. BA, U. Colo., Boulder, 1952; BD, Princeton Theol. Sem., NJ, 1955; MA, Yale U., New Haven, Conn., 1960, PhD, 1963. Commr. to gen. assembly Presbyn. Ch. in U.S.A., 1993. Issues analyst Witherspoon Soc., 1987-93, 99-2005, pres., 1996-99; chmn. global missions com. Presbytery Mid. Tenn., 1989-93, mem. nominating com., 2002-05. Author: Augustine, the Theologian, 1970, Augustine's Strategy as an Apologist, 1974, Christ in Context, 1975, Thomas Aquinas: Faith and Reason, 1988, Living in Two Cities: Augustinian Trajectories in Political Thought, 1998, Augustine (Abingdon Pillars of Theology), 2006. Incorporator Belmont-Hillsboro Neighbors, Nashville, 1971, Consumer Coalition for Health, Nashville, 1980, Nashville Local, Dem. Socialists Am., 1983, Cen. Am. Solidarity Assn., Nashville, 1986. Presbyn. Grad. fellow, 1958, Rockefeller doctoral fellow, 1960, Kent fellow, 1961; recipient Thomas Jefferson award Vanderbilt U., 1996. Mem. Am. Acad. Religion, Am. Soc. Ch. History, Soc. for Values in Higher Edn., Workgroup on Constructive Christian Theology, Witherspoon Soc. (pres. 1995—99), Phi Beta Kappa. Home: 1925 19th Ave S Nashville TN 37212-3805 Home Phone: 615-297-2629. Personal E-mail: teselle@bellsouth.net.

TESIJA, KATHEE (KATHRYN A. TESIJA), retail executive; b. Feb. 1963; m. Mark Tesija. Merchandise analyst Target Corp., Mpls., 1986, sr. v.p. hardlines merchandising, 2001—08, exec. v.p. merchandising, 2008—. Office: Target Corp 1000 Nicollet Mall PO Box 1392 Minneapolis MN 55403*

TESLER, LAWRENCE GORDON, technology company executive; b. NYC, Apr. 24, 1945; s. Isidore and Muriel (Krechmer) T.; m. Shelagh Elisabeth Leuterio, Oct 4, 1964 (div. 1970); 1 child, Lisa Traci; m. Colleen Ann Barton, Feb. 17, 1987. BS in Math., Stanford U., 1965. Pres. Info. Processing Corp., Palo Alto, Calif., 1963—68; rsch. asst. Stanford U. Artificial Intelligence Lab., 1968—73; mem. rsch. staff Xerox Corp., Palo Alto, 1973—80; sect. mgr. Lisa divsn. Apple Computer, Inc., Cupertino, Calif., 1980—82, cons. engr., 1983—86, v.p. advanced tech., 1986—90, v.p. advanced products, 1990—92, v.p. engring., 1992—93, chief scientist, 1993—97, v.p. AppleNet divsn., 1996—97; pres. Stagecast Software, Inc., Redwood City, Calif., 1997—2001; v.p. engring. Amazon.com, Seattle, 2001—05; v.p. user experience and design Yahoo! Inc., Sunnyvale, Calif., 2005—08; product fellow 23 and Me Inc. Mt. View, Calif., 2008—. Mem. Computer

Sci. and Telecom. Bd., 1991-94. Contbr. articles to profl. jours., various computer software. Bd. dirs. Peninsula Sch., Menlo Park, Calif., 1974-78, Gorilla Found., Menlo Park, 2000—. Mem. IEEE, Assn. Computing Machinery (conf. co-chmn. 1987-88).

TESMER, NANCY ANN STUTLER, retired librarian; b. Aug. 25, 1934; d. Ernest Lynn and Sophrona Rebecca (Pepper) Stutler; m. John A. Tesmer, Sept. 10, 1980. Student, U. Akron, 1952—54; BA, Kent State U., 1956. Jr. asst. libr. E. Br. Libr., Akron, 1956—59; hosp. libr. VA Hosp., Northampton, Mass., 1959—61, med. libr. Brecksville, Ohio, 1961—65, chief libr., 1965—73, assoc. chief libr. Cleve., 1973—75, chief libr., 1975—. Chief Regional Libr. Svc., 1986—90. Mem.: N.E. Ohio Med. Libr. Assn., Med. Libr. Assn., Zeta Tau Alpha. Home: 8537 SW 90th Pl Unit G Ocala FL 34481-7516 E-mail: nst0825@aol.com.

TESREAU, CYNTHIA LYNN, elementary school educator; b. Jackson, Tenn., Apr. 29, 1960; d. Dewitt Talmadge and Brenda Lynn Coppedge; m. Kevin Paul Tesreau, Mar. 29, 1997; children: Kristen Lynn Burrage, Nick Lee Burrage. BS in Elem. Edn., U. of Houston, 1983; MA in Tchg., Cumberland U., Lebanon, Tenn., 2001. Cert. tchr., adminstr. Tenn., Administration Tenn., 2005. Tchr. Spring Br. Ind. Sch. Dist., Houston, 1984—87, Shelby County Schs., Memphis, 1987—. Women's ensemble leader Trinity Bapt. Ch., Memphis, 2003—06, women's mininstry team mem., 2003—06. Recipient, Patricia Ashcraft award for outstanding tchg., 2005; named Tchr. of Yr., Chimneyrock Elem. Sch., 2005, Bailey Station Elem. Sch., 2006, Shelby County Schs., 2006. Mem.: NEA (assoc.), Tenn. Ednl. Assn. (assoc.), Shelby County Ednl. Assn. (assoc.), Pi Delta Kappa (assoc.), Pi Lambda Theta (life). Baptist. Avocations: needlepoint, quilting, water sports, travel. Office: Bailey Station Elementary 3435 Bailey Station Elementary Collierville TN 38017 E-mail: ctesreau@scsk12.org.

TESSEMA, GEORGE, mathematician, educator; b. Addis Ababa, Ethiopia, May 20, 1942; arrived in U.S., 1985; s. Tessema Garedew and Woodnesh Tessema; m. Tafesech Mengistu; children: Thomas, Michael. BSc, Addis Ababa U., Ethiopia, 1966; MSc, Fla. State U., Tallahassee, Fla., 1970; PhD, SUNY, Albany, NY, 1991. Tchr. math. Ras Darghe H.S., Assela, Ethiopia, 1967—70; prof. math. Ketobe Coll. Tchr. Edn., Addis Ababa, 1971—85, Armstrong Atlantic State U., Savannah, Ga., 1993—94, Savannah State U., 1994—, with, 1994—. Mem.: Am. Math. Assn. Avocations: walking, ping pong/table tennis, soccer, reading. Office: Savannah State Univ Whiting Hall Rm 131 Savannah GA 31404

TESSIER, JACK T., biology professor; b. Oneida, NY, Feb. 13, 1971; s. Egwin J. Tessier and Frances M. Wright; m. Lisa M. Conner, July 31, 1999; children: Anna M., Abigail L. BA, SUNY Geneseo, 1994, MA, 1996; PhD, SUNY Coll. Environ. Sci. and Forestry, Syracuse, 2002. Asst. prof. Ctrl. Conn. State U., New Britain, 2002—07, SUNY, Delhi, 2007—. Contbr. articles to numerous publs. Finalist Excellence Tchg. award, Ctrl. Conn. State U., 2003—05. Mem.: NSTA, NY Flora Assn., Soc. Am. Foresters, Bot. Soc. Am., Ecol. Soc. Am. Office: SUNY Delhi 2 Main St 722 Evenden Tower Delhi NY 13753 Business E-Mail: tessiejt@delhi.edu.

TESTA, JAMES A., lawyer; b. Newark, Aug. 7, 1948; AB magna cum laude, Princeton U., 1970; JD, Harvard U., 1973. Bar: N.Y. 1974, U.S. Dist. Ct. (so. dist.) N.Y. 1975. Mem. Willkie Farr & Gallagher, NYC; shareholder Buchanan Ingersoll P.C., Princeton, NJ, Pitts.; ptnr. Testa & Monfried, Princeton, NJ; dep. gen. counsel Innophos Holdings, Inc., Cranbury, NJ. Mem. ABA (mem. bus. law sect.), N.Y. State Bar Assn., Phi Beta Kappa. Office: 259 Prospect Pleins Rd Cranbury NJ 08512 Personal E-mail: jatesta70@aol.com.

TESTA, JOSEPH R., geneticist, researcher, biologist; PhD in Biology, Fordham U., Bronx, NY, 1976. Diplomate Am. Bd. Med. Genetics. Cancer cytogeneticist U. Chgo., 1976-80; rsch. scientist Nat. Cancer Inst., Balt., 1980—82; prof. U. Md., Balt., 1980—89; sr. mem. rsch. staff, dir. Human Genetics Program, 1989—2008; Weg endowed chair human genetics Fox Chase Cancer Ctr., 1999—; co-leader Cancer Genetics & Signaling Program, Kidney Cancer Keystone Program, 2008—. Adj. lectr. Johns Hopkins U., Balt., 1983—87; vis. scientist Nat. Cancer Inst., Frederick, Md., 1987—89, mem. bd. sci. counselors, Bethesda, Md., 2005—. Assoc. editor: Cancer Rsch., mem. editl. bd.: Cancer Genetics & Cytogenetics, Leukemia Rsch., Genes Chromosomes & Cancer, Genes & Cancer; contbr. articles to profl. jours., chapters to books. Recipient Selikoff Cancer Rsch. award, Ramazzini Inst., 1999, Disting. Alumnus award, Southern Conn. State U., 2006, Stohlman Meml. Scholar award, 1987; scholar Leukemia Soc. Am., 1984—90; Spl. fellow, Leukemia Soc. Am., 1982—84. Mem. AAAS, ASHG, Am. Assn. Cancer Rsch., Am. Soc. Hematology, Am. Soc. Microbiology. Achievements include discovery of mutations associated with mesothelioma tumor formation; cloning of AKT2 gene; discovery of first alterations of AKT2 in human cancers. Office: Fox Chase Cancer Ctr 333 Cottman Ave Philadelphia PA 19111-2497 Office Fax: 215-214-1623. Business E-Mail: Joseph.Testa@fccc.edu.

TESTA, MICHAEL HAROLD, lawyer; b. NYC, 1939; m. Carol Waldenberg, 1962; 2 children. BS summa cum laude, NYU, 1958, LLB cum laude, 1961, LLM in Taxation, 1967. Bar: NY 1961. Assoc. White & Case, NYC, 1962-71, Skadden, Arps, Slate, Meagher & Flom, NYC, 1971-72, ptnr., 1972-91; conservation lawyer, sole practitioner Michael H. Testa, NYC, 1992—. Advisor U.S. del. to UN Conf. on Straddling Fish Stocks and Highly Migratory Fish Stocks, 1994-95, U.S. del. to Kyoto Internat. Conf. on Sustainable Contribution of Fisheries to Food Security, 1995, to N.W. Atlantic Fisheries Orgn., 1996, 98, to 22d Session of FAO Com. on Fisheries, 1997, to Western and Ctrl. Pacific Fisheries Conf., 1998-2001; adj. assoc. prof. law NYU Law Sch., 1986; mem. consultative com. to secs. state and commerce N.W. Atlantic Fisheries Conv., 1996-2002. Assoc. editor, contbr.: NYU Law Rev., 1960-61; contbr. articles to legal jours. Mem. planning bd. Town of Tuxedo (N.Y.), 1971-76. Served to capt. USAFR, 1961-72. Root-Tilden-Snow scholar, 1958-61. Mem. Order of Coif. Home: 860 UN Plz New York NY 10017 Office: Ste 28-424 4 Times Square New York NY 10036-6522

TESTER, JON(ATHAN), United States Senator from Montana, former state legislator, farmer; b. Havre, Mont., Aug. 21, 1956; m. Sharla Tester; children: Christine, Shon. BS in Music, U. Great Falls, 1978. Tchr. Big Sandy School District, 1978—80; farmer organic wheat, barley, lentils, peas, millet, buckwheat, alfalfa and hay; mem. Mont. Senate from Dist. 45, Helena, 1998—2005, 2005—06, minority whip, 2001—03, minority leader, 2003—05, pres., 2005—06; US Senator from Mont., 2007—. Mem. Big Sandy Sch. Bd., 1983—91, chmn., 1986—91. Named an Outstanding Agrl. Leader, Coll. Agrl., Mont. State U., 2005. Democrat. Office: US Senate B-40E Dirksen Senate Office Bldg Washington DC 20510 Office Phone: 202-224-3121. E-mail: jontester@yahoo.com.*

TESTERMAN, TRACI L., educator; m. David James McGee, June 17, 2001; children: Kyle McGee, Adriana McGee. PhD, U. Colo. Health Sci. Ctr., Denver, 1999. Postdoc. fellowship U. Md., Balt., 1999—2001; instr. U. South Ala., Mobile, 2001—05; asst. prof. La. State U. HSC, Shreveport, La., 2005—. Office: La State Univ HSC-Shreveport 1501 Kings Hwy Shreveport LA 71130-3932 Business E-Mail: tteste@lsuhsc.edu.

TETELMAN, ALICE FRAN, small business owner; b. NYC, Apr. 15, 1941; d. Harry and Leah (Markovitz) T.; m. Martin A. Wenick, Dec. 7, 1980. BA, Mt. Holyoke Coll., South Hadley, Mass., 1962. Rsch. and info. asst. Edn. and World Affairs, NYC, 1963-67; legis. asst. U.S. Sen. Charles Goodell, Washington, 1968-70; land use and energy specialist Citizens Adv. Com. on Environ. Quality, Washington, 1973-74; sr. assoc. prog. mgr. Linton & Co., Washington, 1971-73, 75-76; pub policy cons. Washington, 1977-78; adminstrv. asst. U.S. Congressman Bill Green (N.Y.), Washington, 1978-81; cons. The Precious Legacy Project, Prague, Czechoslovakia, 1982-83; Rep. staff dir. Select Com. on Hunger, U.S. Ho. of Reps., Washington, 1984-85; dir. State of N.J. Washington Office, 1986-90; exec. dir. Coun. of Gov.'s Policy Advisors, Washington, 1991-94; dir. Washington Office, The City of N.Y., 1994-98. Pres. Italian Vacation Villas, Washington. Bd. dirs. Republican Women's Task Force, Nat. Women's Polit. Caucus, 1976-80, Women in Senate and House (WISH) List, 1998-2001. European Community grantee, 1975. Mem. Ripon Soc. (nat. exec. com. 1971-73). Office: Italian Vacation Villas PO Box 9586 Washington DC 20016-9586

TETELMAN, EVAN DAVID, dentist, educator; b. Cleve., Sept. 1, 1953; s. Myron Phillip Tetelman and Hilda Epstein, Bernard Epstein (Stepfather); m. Terry Jean Rohfeld, June 15, 1975; children: Aaron Daniel, Michael Phillip, Jeremy Marc. AB in Zoology, Miami U., Oxford, Ohio, 1975; DDS, Ohio State U., Columbus. Restorative dentist Streem, Resnick, Tetelman & Young DDS Inc., Lyndhurst, Ohio, 1979—; attending dentist Mt. Sinai Med. Ctr., Cleve., 1980—98, Montefiore Home, Beachwood, Ohio, 1981—96; asst. prof. Case Western Res. U. Sch. Dental Medicine, Cleve., 1998—. Cons. lectr. Interpore Internat., Irvine, Calif., 1985—98, Nobel BioCare, Loma Linda, Calif., 1998—, Camlog Implants, Mellville, NY, 2005—06; del. rep. Ohio Dental Assn., Columbus, 2000—. Contbr. articles to profl. publs. (Daniel Verne Tchg. award, Cleve. Mt. Sinai Med. Ctr., 1998). Mem. Friends of Beachwood Libr., 1990, Beachwood 100, 1985; past pres. Congregation Bethaynu, Pepper Pike, Ohio, 1980; trustee Greater Cleve. Dental Soc., Cleve., 1995; v.p. Beachwood Boosters, 1985—2000. Mem.: Alpha Omega Dental Frat. (pres. treas. 1990), Acad. Gen. Dentistry, Am. Acad. Implant Dentistry, Acad. Osseointegration. Avocations: golf, skiing, scuba diving, softball, singing. Home: 2424 Allen Blvd Beachwood OH 44122 Office: Streem Resnick Tetelman & Young DDS In 29001 Cedar Rd Ste 660 Cleveland OH 44124 Personal E-mail: docet@hotmail.com. Business E-Mail: doct@wholelifedentistry.com.

TETER, ESTON JOE, musician, educator; b. Ft. Seybert, W.Va., Jan. 23, 1951; MusM, Peabody Conservatory, Balt., 1975. Music dir. Archdiocese Balt., Balt., 1987; vis. asst. prof. Loyola Coll., Balt., 2009—. Home: 501 W University Pky Baltimore MD 21210 Office: Loyola Coll Charles St Baltimore MD 21210 Personal E-mail: estonjoe@aol.com.

TETHER, ANTHONY JOHN, aerospace executive; b. Middletown, NY, Nov. 28, 1941; s. John Arthur and Antoinette Rose (Gesualdo) T.; m. Nancy Engle Pierson, Dec. 27, 1963 (div. July 1971); 1 child, Jennifer; m. Carol Suzanne Dunbar, Mar. 3, 1973; 1 child, Michael. AAS, Orange County C.C., NYC, 1961; BS, Rensselaer Poly Inst., 1963; MSEE, Stanford U., Calif., 1965, PhD, 1969. V.p., gen. mgr. Sys. Control Inc., Palo Alto, Calif., 1968-78; dir. nat. intelligence Office Sec. of Def., Washington, 1978-82; dir. strategic tech. DARPA, Washington, 1982-86; corp. v.p. Ford Aerospace, Newport Beach, Calif., 1986-90, LORAL, Newport Beach, 1990-92; corp. v.p., gen. mgr. Sci. Application Internat., Inc., San Diego, 1992-94; CEO Dynamics Tech. Inc., Torrance, Calif., 1994-96; CEO, pres. Sequoia Group, Newport Beach, Calif., 1996-2001; dir. def. advanced rsch. project agy. Office of Sec. of Def., Washington, 2001—. Bd. dirs. Condyne Tech., Inc., Orlando, Fla., 1990—92, chmn., 1990—92; dir. Orincon, La Jolla, Calif., 1996—99, Evans & Sutherland, Salt Lake City, 2001; mem. def. sci. bd. Army Sci. Bd. Task Forces, 1998—2002; cons. Army Sci. Bd., Def. Sci. Bd. Contbr. articles to profl. jours.; mem. editl. adv. bd. Scientific American. Recipient Nat. Intelligence medal DCI, 1986, Civilian Meritorious medal U.S. Sec. Def., 1986, Outstanding Pub. Svc. medal, Sect. Def., 2009. Mem. IEEE, Cosmos Club, Sigma Xi, Eta Kappa Nu, Tau Beta Pi. Avocations: amateur radio, skiing, golf. Home: 6400 Lyric Ln Falls Church VA 22044 Personal E-mail: ttether@aol.com.

TETI, LOUIS NICHOLAS, lawyer; b. Bryn Mawr, Pa., May 29, 1950; BA, Dickinson Coll., 1972; JD, Temple U., 1976, LLM in Taxation, 1981. Bar: Pa. 1976. Ptnr. MacElree Harvey, Ltd., West Chester and Kennett Square, Pa. With disciplinary bd. Supreme Ct. Pa., 2000-06, chair, 2004-05. Chair Paoli Hosp. Found, 2007—, Chester County Cmty. Found., 2008—; bd. dirs. Malvern Prep. Sch., 2006—. Fellow Am. Coll. Trust and Estate Counsel; mem. ABA (house dels. 1985-91, 99-2001, 04-07), Pa. Bar Assn. (chmn. young lawyers divsn. 1982-83, bd. govs. 1982-85, 91-94, 97-2001, pres. 1999-2000), Chester County Bar Assn. (sec. 1979-82, 86-88, v.p. 1989, pres.-elect 1990, pres. 1991, chair young lawyers sect. 1977, bd. dirs. 1977-92), Chester County Estate Planning Coun. (pres. 1988-89). Office: MacElree Harvey Ltd 17 W Miner St PO Box 660 West Chester PA 19381-0660 Home Phone: 610-873-5557; Office Phone: 610-840-0300. Fax: 610-429-4486. E-mail: lteti@macelree.com.

TETLIE, HAROLD, soldier, priest; b. Madison, Minn., Aug. 24, 1926; s. H. Ben and Anna (Mauland) T. BA cum laude, St. Olaf Coll., Northfield, Minn., 1951; MBA, U. Denver, 1956; postgrad., Cornell U., 1959—60; MDiv, Luther Sem., St. Paul, 1965. Ordained to ministry Am. Luth. Ch., 1965. Pastor Christ the King Chs. (True Caths.), Alice, Tex., 1965—, congregation supr., 1969—. Cir. parish priest, Nuevo Leon, Tamaulipas, Hidalgo, San Luis Potosi, Mex. Author numerous poems. Coord. Joint Action in Cmty. Svc., Inc., Alice, 1970—. Sgt. U.S. Army, 1945-46, PTO. Recipient Svc. to Mankind award Sertoma Club, Corpus Christi, Regional Vol. of Yr. award Joint Action in Cmty. Svc., 1991, Michael Madhusudan award for poem, Calcutta, 1996; Ky. Col., 1992. Mem. NEA (life), VFW (life), Am. Legion (life), 40 et 8 (life), Family Motor Coach Assn., Sons of Norway, Order of Ky. Col., Internat. Platform Assn., Thousand Trails, WWII Tank Destroyer Soc. (chaplain). Home and Office: Christ the King Chs PO Box 1607 Alice TX 78333-1607 *It is by the Power of Jesus Christ: He tells us in John 13:34: "Love one another, even as I loved you".*

TETREAULT, JAMES, automotive executive; b. Detroit, 1955; BS in environ. sci., U. Mich., 1978. Vehicle ops. dir. quality Ford Motor Co., Dearborn, Mich., 2000—02, dir. mfg., vehicle ops., 2002—05; v.p. mfg. Ford of Europe, 2005—08; v.p. N.Am. mfg. Ford Motor Co., Dearborn, Mich., 2008—. Office: Ford Motor Co PO Box 685 Dearborn MI 48126-0685*

TETREAULT, PAUL R., theater director, museum administrator; Grad., Emerson Coll., 1984. Sr. mgmt. Crossroads Theatre Co., NJ, Berkeley Repertory Theatre, Calif., Cir. Repertory Co., NYC; mng. dir. Alley Theatre, Houston, 1994—2004; producing dir. Ford's Theater, Washington, 2004—; dir. Ford's Theatre Soc., Washington, 2004—. Lectr. Bklyn. Coll., U. Houston, Rice U. Achievements include under his directorship, the Ford's Theater Society received the National Medal of Arts, 2008. Office: Fords Theatre 511 10th St NW Washington DC 20004 Office Phone: 202-638-2941. Office Fax: 202-347-6269.*

TETSURO, MOTOYAMA, electronics engineer; s. Yusuke and Junko Motoyama; m. Miriam Haydee Motoyama; children: Ken Motoyama, Marti Motoyama. PhD, Iowa State U., Ames, 1978. Engr. Ricoh Americas Corp., Cupertino, Calif., 1983—. Office: Ricoh Americas Corp 10460 Bubb Rd Cupertino CA 95014

TETTEGAH, SHARON YVONNE, university professor; b. Wichita Falls, Tex., Jan. 14, 1956; d. Lawrence Guice and Doris Jean (Leak) Oliver; 1 child, Tandra Ainsworth; m. Joseph Miller Zangai, Dec. 22, 1978 (div. 1983); 1 child, Tonia Monjay Zangai; m. George Tettegah, Apr. 28, 1989 (div. Sept. 2004); children: Nicole Jennifer, Michael Scott. AA, Coll. Alameda, 1985; BA, U. Calif., Davis, 1988, teaching cert., 1989, MA, 1991; PhD in Ednl. Psychology, U. Calif., Santa Barbara, 1997. Cert. elem. tchr., Calif., Online web-based tchg. and learning, Calif. State U., Hayward. Clk. II Alameda County Mcpl. Ct., Oakland, Calif., 1976-77; acct. clk. Alameda County Social Svcs., Oakland, 1977-78, eligibility technician, 1978-82; supervising clk. Alameda County Health Care Svcs., Oakland, 1982-84; tchr. Davis Joint Unified Sch. Dist., Calif., 1988-89, LA Unified Schs., 1990-92, Oakland Unified Sch. Dist., 1992—, tchr. sci. mentor, 1993—; tchg. asst. U. Calif., Santa Barbara, 1993-94; adminstrv. intern Oxnard Unified Sch. Dist., 1994, U. Calif. Cultural Awareness Program, Santa Barbara, 1994; rsch. cons. to vice chancellor students affairs, cons. tchr. edn. program, facilitor registrar's office U. Calif., Santa Barbara, 1995-96, rsch. asst. Grad. Sch. Edn., 1996—; asst. prof. tchr. edn. Calif. State U., Hayward, 1998—, cons. Cal Teach, Office of the Chancellor, 1999; asst. prof. U. Ill., Math, Sci. and Tech., Urbana Champaign, 2001—; faculty fellow Nt. Ctr. for Super Computing Applications, 2003—04, Bur. Ednl. Rsch, Coll. of Edn., U. Ill., Urbana Champaign, 2002—03, 2005—; mem. faculty ednl. psychology, divsn. cognitive sci. tchg. and learning and culture U. Ill., Urbana Champaign, 2005—, faculty affiliate Beckman Inst., 2005—, global campus faculty, 2008—; affirmative action officer U. Ill., Coll. Edn., 2008—; part time faculty Beckman Inst., Cognitive Neurosci. Biol. Intelligence, 2008—. Cons. U. Calif., Davis, 1988-89, Montessori Ctr. Sch., Santa Barbara, Calif., 1996, Oakland-Hayward Sch. Partnership, Oakland, 1998-99, Cal Teach, Office of the Chancellor, 1999; multicultural cons. Davis Unified Sch. Dist., 1988-89; edn. cons. Ednl. Testing Svc., Emeryville, Calif., 1994; cons., dir., 2000—; chair diversity com. of Santa Barbara Village Charter Sch.; mem. academic senate com. undergrad enrollment and admissions U. Calif. Santa Barbara, 1995, tchr. cross-cultural interactions course, summer, 1995; mem. academic affairs affirmative action com. U. Calif. Santa Barbara, 1995-96, grad. sch. of edn., grad. affairs and affirmative action comms. U. Calif. Santa Barbara, 1995-96; rsch. cons. Oakland Unified Sch. Dist., 1998-99, African Am. Literacy and Culture Project, Oakland Pub. Schs., Oakland, 1998—; gubernatorial appointee to State Interagy. Coord. Coun., 1999—; chmn. Com. on Rsch., Calif. State U., 2000-01, mem. Academic Senate, Hayward; faculty Univ. Ill., Urbana-Champaign, 2001, v.p. Distance Edn. Soc. of Info. Tech. and Tchr. Edn., 2003-2004, mem. chancellor's ad hoc cybersecurity com., 2003—; faculty fellow Nat. Ctr. Supercomputing Applications, 2005—, Buf. Ednl. Rsch., 2005—; panel reviewer NSF, 2005-06; mem. editl. bd. Urban Edn. Sage Press, 2005—. Contbr. articles to profl. jours. Mem. U. Calif. Santa Barbara Acad. Senate Bd. Undergraduate Admissions and Records; co-chair Diversity Com. Montecito-Santa Barbara Charter Sch.; pres. African-Am. Grad. and Profl. Students Orgn., Davis, 1988-89; gubernatorial appointee State Interagy. Coordinating Coun., Calif., 1999; commissioned Calif. Policy Makers Inst. Health & Poverty, Lt. Gov., 2001; bd. dirs. YMCA, 2004—. Recipient Charlene Richardson Acad. Honors award Coll. Alameda, 1985, Faculty Rsch. Bd. award U. Ill., 2004, Rsch. Bd. award, 2003-04, 2005-06; Calif. State Acad. fellow, 1989-91, Grad. Opportunity Acad. Excellence fellow, 1994-95, Vice Chancellors Acad. Achievement fellow U. Calif. Santa Barbara, 1995-96, Vice Chancellors Acad. fellow Grad. Divsn., 1995-96, 96-97, Critical Initiative in Rsch. fellow Vice Chancellors Office, 2005-06. Mem. APA, Am. Ednl. Researchers Assn., Calif. Sci. Tchrs. Assn., Calif. Advocacy for Math and Sci., Calif. Tchrs. Assn., Calif. Media Libr. Educators Assn., PTA, Multicultural Curriculum Assn., Supervision and Curriculum Leadership Assn., Bay Area Sci. and Tech. Educators Corsortium, Pan-African Students Assn., U. Ill. Urbana Champaign Acad. Senate, Media Psychology Am. Psychological Assn., Assn. of Computing Machinery, Am. Sociological Assn., Info. and Communications, Inernat. Soc. for Tech. in Edn., Spl. Interest Group, Kappa Delta Pi. Avocations: travel, reading, preparing gourmet foods, tennis. Office: Coll Edn Dept Curriculum & Instruction 1310 S Sixth St Champaign IL 61822 Office Phone: 217-265-6206. Business E-Mail: stettega@illinois.edu.

TETTLEBAUM, HARVEY M., lawyer; m. Ann Safier; children: Marianne, Benjamin. AB, Dartmouth Coll., 1964; JD, Washington U. Sch. Law, 1968, AM in History, 1968. Asst. dean Washington U. Sch. Law, 1969-77; asst. atty. gen., chief counsel Consumer Protection and Anti-Trust Div., 1970-77; pvt. practice Jefferson City, Mo., 1977-90; mem., chmn. health law practice group Husch & Eppenberger, LLC, Jefferson City, Mo., 1990—. Mem. selection com. US Magistrate, 1988; mem. Fed. Jud. Merit Selection Commn., 1991; bd. trustees James Madison Meml. Fellowship Found., 2008—. Contbr. articles to profl. jours. Treas. Mo. Rep. State Com., 1976—2004; v.p. Moniteau County R-1 Sch. Dist. Bd., 1991-95, pres., 1995-96; mem. Calif. R-1 Sch. Bd., 1990-96, v.p., 1993-95, pres., 1995-96. Recipient Legis. award, Legal Svcs. Ea. Mo., 1999; named one of Best Lawyers in Am., 2005—08. Mem. Am. Health Lawyers Assn. (bd. dirs. 1993-99, co-chair long-term care and the law program 1993-01, chair 2001—07, chair long-term care and law program 2001—07, former chair long term care practice group 1997-01), Am. Bar Assn. (mem. standing com. election law)Mo. Bar Assn. (health and hosp. law com., chmn. adminstrv. law com., vice chair delivery legal svc. com., Mo. statewide legal svc. com., President's award 2000, 03), Am. Health Care Assn. (legal com. 1994—, chair 2004-06), Rep. Nat. Lawyers Assn. (bd. dirs. 1988-, 1st v.p. 2002—, pres. 2003-06, Lawyer of Yr. 2006). Republican. Jewish. Home: 56295 Little Moniteau Rd California MO 65018-3069 Office: Husch & Eppenberger LLC Monroe House Ste 300 235 E High St PO Box 1251 Jefferson City MO 65102-1251 Office Phone: 573-761-1107. Business E-Mail: harvey.tettlebaum@husch.com.

TETZELI, RICK, magazine editor; m. Mari Blecher; 1 child, Jonah. BA in Comparative Lit., Middlebury Coll., Vt., 1983. Asst. editor Little, Brown; with FORTUNE Mag., 1990—93, assoc. editor, 1993—93, editor, 1996—97, sr. editor, 1997—99, asst. mng. editor, 1999, exec. dir.,

2000, dep. mng. editor, 2001—02; mng. editor Entertainment Weekly Time Inc., NYC, 2002—09, editor-at-large, 2009—. Office: Time Inc 1271 Ave Americas 34th Fl New York NY 10012 Office Fax: 212-522-6104, 212-522-8350.*

TEUBER, WILLIAM J., JR., corporate financial executive; B, Coll. of the Holy Cross; MS in Taxation, Bentley Coll.; MBA, Babson Coll. Ptnr. Audit and Fin. Adv. Svcs. Coopers & Lybrand LLP; v.p., contr. EMC Corp., Hopkinton, Mass., 1995—97, v.p., CFO, 1997—2000, sr. v.p., CFO, 2000—01, exec. v.p., CFO, 2001—06, vice-chmn., 2006—. Bd. dirs. Popular, Inc. Bd. trustees Babson Coll. Office: EMC Corp 176 South St Hopkinton MA 01748 Office Phone: 508-435-1000.

TEUBER MOORE, TERRI, legislative staff member; Comm. dir., Gov. Mike Johanns Office of Gov., Nebr.; pub. info. officer Nebr. State Patrol; comm. dir. USDA, Washington, 2005—07; dep. asst. to the Pres., dep. dir. comm. for policy and planning The White House, Washington, 2007—08; chief of staff to Senator Mike Johanns US Senate, Washington, 2008—. Republican. Office: Senate Russell Courtyard 1 Washington DC 20510 Office Phone: 202-224-4224. Business E-Mail: terri_moore@johanns.senate.gov.*

TEUFEL, HUGO, III, former lawyer, federal agency administrator; b. Albuquerque, July 25, 1961; s. Hugo Jr. and Carmen Margarite (Trujillo) T. BA in Econ., Met. State Coll., Denver, 1985; JD, Am. U., 1990; M in Nat. Security and Strategic Studies, Naval War Coll. Bar: Colo. 1990, US Ct. Fed. Claims 1991, US Ct. Appeals (DC cir.) 1991, US Ct. Appeals (10th cir.) Colo. 1992. Law clk. to chief judge Smith, US Ct. Fed. Claims, Washington, 1990-91; assoc. McKenna & Cuneo, Denver, 1991-96; dep. solicitor gen. Colo. Atty. Gen's. Office, Denver, 1997; with Hall and Evans, Denver; assoc. gen. counsel gen. law US Dept. Homeland Security, chief privacy officer, 2006—. Principal US/EU high level contact group US Dept. Homeland Security, chair cyber security subcommittee CIO Coun., officer Chief Freedom Info. Act. Sr. articles editor Adminstrv. Law Jour. Am. U., 1989-90. Mem. Federalist Soc. (chpt. chmn. 1996—). Republican. Lutheran. Office: US Dept Homeland Security Seventh & D Streets SW Washington DC 20528*

TEULÉ, FLORENCE, research scientist; d. Louis Francois and Marie Anne Andrée Teulé. PhD in Genetics, Clemson U., SC, 2003. Postdoc. fellow U. Wyo., Laramie, 2003—04, rsch. scientist, 2004—. Merit fellowship, French Ministry of Edn., 1995—96, Wade Stackhouse fellowship, Clemson U., 1999—2001. Roman Catholic. Avocation: martial arts/karate. Business E-Mail: fteule@uwyo.edu.

TEUTSCH, CLIFFORD L., editor-in-chief; b. NYC, 1950; m. Patrice Nelson. BA, Amherst Coll. With Daily Hampshire Gazette, Northampton, Mass., Hartford Courant, Conn., 1980—, local news reporter Conn., politics editor Conn., 1987—91, asst. mng. editor Conn., 1991—94, mng. editor Conn., 1994—2006, exec. editor & v.p. Conn., 2006—09. John S. Knight fellowship, Stanford. U., 1986—87.*

TEUTUL, PAUL JOHN, SR., television personality, mechanic; b. Yonkers, NY, May 1, 1949; m. Paula Teutul (div.); children: Paul Jr., Michael, Daniel, Kristin; m. Beth Dillon, July 29, 2007. Owner Orange County Iron Works, Inc., 1973—, Orange County Choppers, 1999—. Co-star: (TV series) Amercian Chopper: The Series, 2003—; actor(voice only): (TV appearances) King of the Hill, 2006, My Name Is Earl, 2008; (films) Wild Hogs, 2007; co-author (with Paul M. Teutul, Michael Teutul, Keith & Kent Zimmerman): Orange County Choppers: The Book, 2006; (with Paul M. Teutul, Michael Teutul) Orange County Choppers: The Tale of the Teutuls, 2006, (with Mark Yost) The Ride of a Lifetime: Doing Business the Orange County Choppers Way, 2009. Office: Orange County Choppers Inc 14 Crossroads Ct Newburgh NY 12550-5064 Office Phone: 845-457-1992. Office Fax: 845-457-4529.*

TEW, E. JAMES, JR., management services company executive; b. Dallas, July 7, 1933; s. Elmer James and Bessie Fay (Bennett) T.; children: Teresa Annette, Linda Diane, Brian James. Student, Arlington State Jr. Coll., 1955—57; BBA in Indsl. Mgmt., So. Meth. U., 1969; MS in Quality Systems, U. Dallas, 1972, MBA in Mgmt., 1975; EdD in Adult Edn., Nova U., 1986. Registered profl. engr., Calif. Mgr. quality assurance ops. Tex. Instruments Inc., Dallas, 1957-98; chmn. corp. metric implementation com. Texins Credit Union, co-chmn. credit com. Adj. faculty Richland Coll. Mountain View Coll., LeTourneau U.; precinct chmn., election judge, del. several county and state convs.; bus. computer info. systems adv. bd. U. North Tex., bd. dirs. ctr. for quality and productivity U. North Tex.; bd. examiners Malcolm Baldridge Nat. Quality award, U.S. Dept. Commerce, Nat. Inst. Standard and Tech., 1988, 89, 90, 91, 95, 96; chmn. panel judges, fellow Tex. Quality Award, 1993-2001; cons. nat. quality award Govt. Singapore, 1994; spkr. in field; bd. examiners Presdl. Quality Award, 1994-96, judge 1997-2000; quality examiner U.S. Army, 1996—; sr. quality examiner USAF, 1995-98, postdoctoral edn. in mediation and arbitration edn., 1998, 99; vol. mediator for dispute mediation svc., 1998—. Spkr. in field. Contbr. articles to profl jours. Decorated Army Commendation medal with oak leaf cluster, Meritorious Svc. medal, Legion of Merit. Fellow Am. Soc. Quality Control (cert. quality auditor, cert. quality mgr., cert. as quality and reliability engr., chmn. Dallas-Ft. Worth sect. 1974-75). Fellow U.S. Metric Assn. (cert., chmn. cert. bd. 1986-87); mem. U.S. Res. Officers Assn., Dallas C. of C. (chmn. world mfg. com. 1974-77, chmn. spl. tasl force career edn. adv. bd. 1973-74), Mensa (mem. air force blue ribbon commn. on assesments and evaluations 1996-98), Sigma Iota Epsilon, Phi Delta Kappa. Baptist. Clubs: Texins Rod and Gun (pres. 1969-70), Texins Flying, Masons (32 degree). Office Fax: 214-349-3686.

TEWARI, SHUBHA, physics professor; d. Krishna Kumar and Kamla Tewari; m. Narayanan Menon, Aug. 24, 1992; children: Achala Narayanan, Kabir Narayanan. PhD, U. Calif., 1993. Vis. asst. prof. Mt. Holyoke Coll., South Hadley, Mass., 2000—08, U. Mass., Amherst, 2008—. Mem.: Am. Phys. Soc.

TEWARSON, REGINALD PRABHAKAR, retired mathematics educator, consultant; b. Pauri, Garhwal, India, Nov. 17, 1939; came to U.S., 1957; s. Seth Narottam and Chand (Mani) Tewarson; m. Hedi Thomann, July 1, 1960 (div. Nov. 1990); children: Anita Jasmine, Monique Shanti; m. Ghenwah Albarazi, Apr. 16, 2003. MA, Agra U., 1952; PhD, Boston U., 1961. Lectr. Lucknow U., India, 1951—57; sr. mathematicisn Honeywell EDP, Wellesley Hills, Mass., 1960—64; leading prof. applied math. and stats. SUNY, Stony Brook, 1964—2000, leading prof. physiology and biophysics dept., 1964—2000, leading prof. emeritus, 2001—. Cons. NIH, Washington, 1971-74. Author: Sparse Matrices, 1973; mem. editorial bd. Applied Math. Letters, 1986-2004, Math. Computer Modeling, 1991-2004, Pan. Am. Math. Jour., 1991-2004; contbr. articles to profl. jours. Centenary scholar Govt. of India, 1946-50, Crusade scholar U.S. Coun. Chs., 1957-59; rsch. grantee NIH, 1973-97, Air Force Office Sch. Rsch. Math. and Info. Scis., 1983-85, NSF, 1993-95. Mem. Am. Math. Soc., Soc. Indsl. and Applied Math., Soc. for Math. Biology. Democrat. Achievements include pioneering research on sparse matrices based largely on own research; co-development of mathematical model of kidney concentrating mechanism, of computer model of neuronal function. Home: 22 Night Heron Dr Stony Brook NY 11790-1108 Office: SUNY Dept Applied Math And Stats Stony Brook NY 11794-0001 Office Phone: 631-632-8370. Personal E-mail: tewarson@optonline.net. E-mail: tewarson@ams.sunysb.edu.

TEWELL, JOSEPH ROBERT, JR., retired electrical engineer; b. Albany, NY, May 19, 1934; s. Joseph Robert and Florence Edna Tewell; m. Barbara Ann Johnson, Nov. 20, 1960; children— Patricia Ann, Donna Lynn, Joseph Robert, III. B.E.E., Rensselaer Poly. Inst., 1955, M.E.E., 1958. Rsch. engr. N.Am. Aviation, Inc., Downey, Calif., 1955; assoc. rsch. engr. Lockheed Aircraft Corp., Burbank, Calif., 1956; instr. Rensselaer Poly. Inst., 1957-64; sr. rsch. scientist Martin Marietta Corp., Denver, 1964-79, mgr. advanced programs Michoud, La., 1979-87, mgr. shuttle-C project, 1988-90, mgr. computer-aided productivity, 1991-93, mgr. sys. engring., 1994-96; ret., 1996. Cons. in field. Contbr. articles to profl. jours. Founding sponsor Challenger Ctr. Served with Army Security Agy., 1957. Recipient NASA Manned Awareness citation, 1970, NASA Skylab Achievement award, 1974, NASA New Tech. award, 1976, Tech. Achievement award Martin Marietta Corp., 1977, Sustained Performance award Martin Marietta Corp., 1981, NASA cert. of recognition, 1977, Author of Yr. award, 1986, also 38 publ. awards, 1965— Fellow Explorers Club; mem. AIAA, Smithsonian Assocs., Air and Space Mus., Unmanned Vehicle Sys., Nat. Audubon Soc., Sigma Xi, Eta Kappa Nu, Tau Beta Pi, Theta Chi. Achievements include invention of dual action single drive actuator; spacecraft docking and retrieval mechanism. Home and Office: 619 Legendre Dr Slidell LA 70460-3427

TEXTOR, ALICE MIDDLE, political science professor; b. Toledo, Ohio, Apr. 20, 1950; MS, U. Ariz., Tucson, 1977. Prof. and coach Northern Ill. U., Dekalb, 1977—81, Calif. State U., DH, Carson, 1981—88; tchr. Laytonville HS, Calif., 1989—2001; prof. student life coord. Folsom Lake Coll., Calif., 2001—. Office: Folsom Lake Coll 10 College Pky Folsom CA 95630 Office Fax: 916-608-6746. Business E-Mail: textora@flc.losrios.edu.

TEXTOR, ROBERT BAYARD, cultural anthropology educator, writer, consultant; b. Cloquet, Minn., Mar. 13, 1923; s. Clinton Kenney and Lillian (Nickles) T.; divorced; children: Alexander Robertson, Marisa Elizabeth. Student, Lafayette Coll., 1940—41, Antioch Coll., 1941—43; BA in Asian Studies, U. Mich., 1945; PhD in Cultural Anthropology, Cornell U., 1960. Civil info. and edn. officer Mil. Govt., Kyoto-Wakayama, Japan, 1946-48; rsch. fellow anthropology and S.E. Asia studies Yale U., 1959-60, assoc., 1960-61; rsch. fellow in stats. Harvard U., 1962-64; assoc. prof. edn. and anthropology Stanford U., 1964-68, prof. edn. and anthropology, 1968-86, prof. anthropology, 1986-90, prof. anthropology emeritus, 1990—; co founder EFR Source Inc., Spokane, Wash., 2008. Vis. prof. U. Saar, Saarbrücken, Germany, 1984-85; cons. Motorola, Inc., 1991-2001, Ministry of Planning, Kuwait, 1999; mem. S.E. Asia Coun., 1974-77; cons. cultural anthropology to govt. agys., 1957-58, 61-62. Author: (with Arthur S. Banks) A Crass-Polity Survey, 1963, A Cross-Cultural Summary, 1967, Roster of the Gods: An Ethnography of The Supernatural in a Thai Village, 6 vols., 1973, Austria 2005: Projected Sociocultural Effects of the Microelectronic Revolution, 1983,(with Sippanondha Ketudat) The Middle Path for the Future of Thailand, 1990; (with others) Uncompromising Integrity: Motorola's Global Challenge, 1998; editor, commentator: Margaret Mead and the World Ahead: An Anthropologist Anticipates the Future, 2005; editor, contbr. Cultural Frontions of The Peace Corps, 1966; editor, commentator; (with Ernst Eugen Veselsky and others) The Future of Austria: Opportunities and Dangers in the Age of Nanotechnology, 2006; assoc. editor Jour. Conflict Resolution, 1965-70; mem. editl. bd. Human Orgn., 1966-71, Jour. Cultural Futures, 1979-87; adv. editor Behavior Sci. Rsch., 1974-86. Bd. dirs. Vols. in Asia, Stanford, Calif., 1968-73; mem. Metro Portland Future Vision Commn., 1993-95; Served with U.S. Army, 1943-46. Fellow Rockefeller Found., 1951-52, fgn. area tng. fellow Ford Found., Thailand 1955-58, Carnegie fellow, 1958-59, Fulbright West Europe rsch. fellow, 1984-85, East-West Ctr. fellow, 1988-90; NSF grantee, Thailand, U.S., 1969-73, Volkswagen Found. grantee, Thailand and Germany, 1984. Fellow Am. Anthrop. Assn. (life, chair resource devel. com. 2003-04), Soc. Applied Anthropology; mem. Siam Soc. (life), Assn. Asian Studies (life), Council on Anthropology and Edn. (pres. 1974-75), AAUP (pres. Stanford chpt. 1975-76), Phi Kappa Phi. Home Phone: 503-223-6370. Personal E-mail: robertbtextor@comcast.net.

TEYAN, FREDERICK GENE, pediatrician; b. NYC, Sept. 16, 1938; s. Jack H. and Pearl A. (Chernesky) T.; m. Dec. 18, 1965; children: Frederick II, Julie, Jonathan. AB, St. Peter's Coll., 1960; MD, Seton Hall, 1964. Diplomate Am. Bd. Pediatrics. Intern Kings County Hosp., Bklyn., 1964-65, resident in pediat., 1969-70, L.I. Jewish Hosp., New Hyde Park, NY, 1970-71; pvt. practice, Rockville Centre, NY, 1971—. Major U.S. Army, 1966-69. Fellow Am. Acad. Pediatrics; mem. Nassau Pediatric Soc. Roman Catholic. Office: 36 Lincoln Ave Rockville Centre NY 11570-5768 Office Phone: 516-766-2602. Personal E-mail: fgjteyan@ix.netcom.com.

TEZAK, EDWARD GEORGE, mechanics educator; b. Steelton, Pa., Oct. 16, 1940; s. John Frank and Mary Cecilia (Shiprak) T.; m. Martha Katherine Leyko, Sept. 10, 1966; children: Christine Louise, Edward Scott. BS, U.S. Mil. Acad., 1963; MS in Astrodynamics, UCLA, 1967; PhD in Engring. Mechanics, Va. Poly. Inst. and State U., 1979. Commd. 2d lt. U.S. Army, 1963, advanced through grades to col., 1985; co. comdr., exec. officer B Co. 13th Engr. Bn., Camp Casey, Republic of Korea, 1964-65; engr. bn. advisor 6th ARVN Engr. Group, QuiNhon and DaNang, Vietnam, 1967-68; instr., then asst. prof. dept. mechanics U.S. Mil. Acad., West Point, NY, 1969-72, group dir. dept. mechanics, 1976-88, dep. head dept. mechanics, 1988, assoc. dean, 1989-93; plans officer U.S. Army Engr. Group, Saigon, Vietnam, 1972-73; USMA fellow Army War Coll., Carlisle, Pa., 1982-83; ret. U.S. Army, 1993; dean Sch. Info. Sys. and Engring. Tech. SUNY, Utica, 1993-97, dean Coll. Tech. Alfred State, 1998-99; assoc. prof. Alfred State Coll., 1999-2000, prof. mechanics, 2000—05, SUNY disting. svc. prof., 2005—; sec., treas. Coun. for Engring. Tech. NY State (CETNYS), 2000—. Mem. adv. bd. dept. math. U.S. Mil. Acad., 1993-97, mem. adv. bd. dept. civil and mech. engring., 2002-. Mem. Cmty. Counsel, Utica, 1994-97. Decorated Legion of Merit. Mem. ASME, Am. Soc. Engring. Edn. (bd. dirs., chair PIC III 1993-95, exec. com. mech. divsn., program chair, divsn. chair 1989-93, vice program chair engring. tech. divsn. 2001-02, program chair 2002-03, sec. engring. tech. divsn. 2004—, Outstanding Campus Liaison Rep. award Mid. Atlantic sect. 1991, Outstanding Tchr./Educator of Yr award St. Lawrence sect. 2001), NY State Engring. Tech. Assn. (exec. com. 2000—), Phi Kappa Phi, Am. Soc. Engring. Edn.(Fredrick J. Berger award, 2007) Roman Catholic. Avocations: bowling, golf, skiing. Home: 450 N Main St Wellsville NY 14895-1042 Business E-Mail: tezakeg@alfredstate.edu.

TEZANOS-PINTO, ROSA, Hispanic American literature educator; d. Alfredo Tezanos Pinto and Enriqueta Otiniano Tezanos Pinto; m. Jose L. Vargas Vila, Aug. 6, 1993; children: Sebastian Martin Valverde, Isabel Maria Valverde. BA, U. Miami, 1979, MA, 1994, PhD, 2002. Cons. and test evaluator U. Fla., Tampa, 1985—99; pres. Sigma Delta Pi, Miami, 1988—91; coord. symposia Michel de Certeau Ctr. for Critical Studies, Coral Gables, Fla., 1990—92; lectr. U. Miami, Coral Gables, 1992—99; dir. John Adams Pub. Co., Coral Gables, 1994—97; prof. of hispanic Am. lit. Lebanon Valley Coll., Annville, Pa., 1999—2006, coord. youth scholars program in Spanish, 2000—06, advisor Spanish club, 2001—06; dir. Alroquema Pub., Miami, 1999—; advisor Spanish majors and minors, open majors Lebanon Valley Coll., Annville, 2001—06, coord., meeting hispanic authors program, 2001—06; dir. Asociación de Poetas de América, Buenos Aires, 2000—; advisor Nat. Assn. of Fellowships Advisors, 2002—; prof. Ind. U. Purdue U., Indpls., 2006—. Rschr. Alroquema Pub. Co., Miami, 2003—. Editor: Redimiendo la Infancia en la estructura póetica, 2005, Nation and Narration in The LUSO - Hispanic World, 2008. Recipient Jayanca Disting. Visitor Diploma, Chiclayo, Peru, 2002, Comodoro Rivadavia Book Fair Plaque, Comodoro Rivadavia Book Fair (Argentina), 2001, Jaguar's Favorite Prof. award, Inst. Lit. Cultural Hispanic award; named Outstanding Woman Faculty Leader; Profl. grant, Lebanon Valley Coll., 2001—03, Boyer scholar. Mem.: Latin Am. Inst. Pa. (pres.), Assn. Cervantistas, Colloquium Com., Diversity Adv. Com., Círculo Panamericano, Instituto Literario y Cultural Hispánico, Casa del Poeta del Perú, Am. Assn. of Teachers of Spanish and Portuguese, Nat. Assn. of Fellowships Advisors, Grad. Fellowship Com., Sigma Delta Pi, Phi Sigma Iota. Achievements include research in the relationship in form and practice of poetic language and the Freudian psychoanalytic language; the hidden text of Infancy in the Poetic works of Ester de Izaguirre and Loreina Santos Silva and testimonial literature; publications in the USA, France, Spain, Argentina, Peru, Paraguay, Brazil, Puerto Rico, India, etc; presented papers at USA, Chile, Venezuela, Guatemala, Puerto Rico, Australia, Peru, Colombia, Paraguay, Argentina, Spain, France, India, Mexico and Brazil. Office: Ind Univ Purdue Univ Indpls 425 University Blvd CA545 Indianapolis IN 46202

TEZCUR, GUNES MURAT, political science professor; b. Ankara, Turkey, Oct. 31, 1979; s. Haldun Tezcur and Selma Kangal; m. Nazli Ozcan, July 14, 2005; 1 child, Babil. PhD, U. Mich., Ann Arbor, 2005. Asst. prof. Loyola U. Chgo., 2005—. Contbr. articles to profl. jours. Mem.: Am. Polit. Sci. Assn. Office: Loyola Univ Chgo 6525 N Sheridan Rd Chicago IL 60660 Office Fax: 773-508-3131. Business E-Mail: gtezcur@luc.edu.

THABAULT, PAULETTE J., state banking agency administrator; A in Nursing, U. Vt.; BSN, U. Wash.; MSN, Simmons Coll.; JD, New Eng. Sch. Law. Bar: Vt., Mass. Dep. commr. health care adminstrn. Vt. Dept. Banking, Ins., Securities and Health Care Adminstrn., Montpelier, 2003—05, commr., 2007—. Mem. devel. com. Alzheimer's Assn. Vt. and NH; bd. dirs. Cmty. Health Ctr. Burlington, Vt. Office: Vt Dept Banking Ins Securities and Health Care Adminstrn 89 Main St Drawer 20 Montpelier VT 05620-3101 Office Phone: 802-828-3307. Office Fax: 802-828-1477. E-mail: pthabault@bishca.state.vt.us.*

THACH, ROBERT EDWARDS, biology educator, former dean; b. Oklahoma City, Okla., Feb. 2, 1939; s. William Thomas and Mary Elizabeth (Edwards) T.; m. Carol Ann Schmidt, Sept. 23, 1959 (div. Aug. 1967); children: Catherine Anne, Robert Edwards Jr.; m. Sigrid Stumpp, Apr. 20, 1968; 1 child, Christopher Alexander. AB, Princeton U., NJ, 1961; PhD, Harvard U., 1964. Asst. prof. biochemistry and molecular biology Harvard U., Cambridge, Mass., 1966-69, assoc. prof. biochemistry and molecular biology, 1969-70; assoc. prof. biol. chemistry Wash. U., St. Louis, 1970-73, prof. biol. chemistry, 1973—, prof. biology, 1977—, chmn. biology, 1977-81, dean Grad. Sch. Arts and Scis., 1993—2008. Institutional biosafety com. Monsanto Co., St. Louis, 1980-83; mem. Grad. Record Exam. Bd., 1998-2003, chair 2001-2002;mem. North Ctr. Assn. Grad. Adv. Group, 1996-1998, Coun. Grad. Sch. Bd., 1997-2000, Emory U. Grad. Adv. Coun. 1996-2003, Assn. Grad. Sch. Exec. Com., 1998-2000, Mid. States Commn. Higher Edn. Team, 2004, Woodrow Wilson Found. Adv. Coun. 2000-05, co chair, 2001-05; organizer Internat. Grad. Scholarship Confs. China, 2005-. Mem. editorial bd. Jour. of Biol. Chemistry, 1984-89, Archives of Biochemistry and Biophysics, 1972-78; editor Enzyme, 1990-91; contbr. articles to profl. jours. including Sci., Nature, Cell, and Proc. Nat. Acad. Sci. Fellowship Woodrow Wilson Found., 1961-62, NSF, 1962-64, John Simon Guggenheim Meml. Found., 1969; grantee NSF, NIH, 1970-93. Fellow AAAS; mem. Am. Soc. of Biol. Chemists, Am. Soc. for Virology (Washington U. Arts & Sci. Dean's medal, 2008). Achievements include discovery of initiation codon "AUG" for mRNA translation, 5'-3' direction for mRNA translating, translational repressor for ferritin synthesis; devel. of methods for RNA synthesis. Office: Washington Univ 256 Busch Laboratory 1137 Saint Louis MO 63130 Office Fax: 314-935-4932. E-mail: thach@wustl.edu.

THACKER, PATRICIA ANN, nursing educator; b. Pikeville, Ky., Aug. 3, 1954; d. Jimmie and Arvie Coleman; m. Roger Dale Thacker, Aug. 13, 1973; 1 child, Tereshia Dalt-Hattie. Degree in Cosmetology, Pikeville Beauty Sch., 1977; BSN, Morehead State U., Ky., 1997. Cert. in advanced cardiac life support, Ky., 2008. Cosmetologist Ky Bd. Hairdressers, Pikeville, 1975—84; register nurse Ky. Bd. Nursing, Lousiville, 1984—90; assoc. prof. nursing faculty Bid Sandy Cmty. and Tech. Coll., Pikeville, 2001—. Clin. dir. pmh Pikeville Med. Ctr., 1990—2001. Mem. Pikeville Old Regular Bapt., 1990—2008.

THACKER, ROBERT GEORGE (BOB THACKER), marketing executive; b. Lincoln, Nebr., Dec. 17, 1947; s. George Leonard and Helen (Quimby) T.; m. Susan Deitemeyer, Mar. 20, 1970; children: Molly, Joshua, Gretchen. BA, U. Nebr., 1970. Writer Fahden Advt., Mpls., 1972-74, Ruhr, Paragon, Mpls., 1974-78, sr. writer, 1978-80, assoc. creative dir., 1980-84, v.p., creative dir., 1984-87, Campbell-Mithun, Mpls., 1987-89; v.p. mktg. Target Stores, Mpls., 1989—98; sr. v.p. mktg. Sears, Roebuck & Co., Hoffman Estates, Ill., 1998—99; pres., CEO BBDO Mpls., 1999—2004; sr. v.p. mktg. & advt. Office Max, 2005—. Instr. Coll. St. Thomas, St. Paul, 1982—. Recipient Clio award, 1976, 84, Emmy award, 1986, Communication Arts Ann. award 1975-87, Internat. Broadcasting award, 1978, Nat. Addy award, 1978, Show award NY Art Dirs., 1985, One Show award, 1985, Obie award, 1987; named a Media Maven Advt. Age, 2007. Mem. Minn. Art Dirs. and Copywriters Club (pres. 1978-79). Office: Office Max Royal St George Naperville IL 60563*

THACKER, STEPHEN BRADY, medical association administrator, epidemiologist; b. Independence, Mo., Dec. 30, 1947; m. 1976; 2 children. AB, Princeton U., 1969; MD, Mt. Sinai Sch. Medicine, 1973; MSc, London Sch. Hygiene and Tropical Medicine, 1984. Chief consolidated surveillance and commn. activity epidemiol. program office Ctrs. Disease Control and Prevention, Atlanta, 1978-83, dir. surveillance and epidemiol. studies, 1983-86, dir. epidemiol. program office, 1989—2004, acting dep. dir., 1998, acting dir. Nat. Ctr. Injury Prevention and Control, 1999-2000, acting dir. Nat. Ctr. Environ. Health, 1993-95, dir. Office of Workforce and Career Devel., 2004—; asst. dir. sci. Ctr. Environ. Health and Injury Control, Atlanta, 1986-89. Mem. steering com. Assn. Behavioral Sci. Med. Edn., 1971-74; assoc. Dept. Cmty. Medicine, Med. Ctr. Duke U., Durham, N.C., 1975-76; lectr.

Cmty. Ctr. Mt. Sinai Sch. Medicine, N.Y.C., 1978—, Sch. Medicine Emory U., Atlanta, 1985-86; cons. epidemiology Arab Republic Egypt, 1979-91; clin. asst. prof. cmty. health Sch. Medicine Emory U., 1986-91; adj. prof. Emory U. Sch. Pub. Health, 1992—. Editor: Epidemiologic Revs., 1990-2003. Clin. scholar Robert Wood Johnson Found., 1974-75; recipient Mosby Book award for excellence, 1973, Pub. Health Svc. Outstanding Svc. medal, 1987, Pub. Health Svc. Meritorious Svc. medal, 1988, 2002, Saul Horowitz Jr. Meml. award, 1990, Supervisory award for contbr. advantage of women, 1991, Pub. Health Svc. Commendation medal, 1991, Pub. Health Svc. Disting. Svc. medal, 1993, 2006, Pub. Health Svc. Surgeon Gen.'s Exemplary Svc. medal, 1993, Pub. Health Svc. Disting. Svc. medal, 1997, Medal of Excellence William C. Watson, Jr., 1996, Ray E. Brown award Assn. Mil. Surgeons of U.S., 2003. Achievements include rsch. public health surveillance, infectious disease, environ. health, injury prevention, alcohol abuse, health care delivery, meta-analysis, technology assessment. Office: Ctrs for Disease Control and Prevention MS E94 1600 Clifton Rd NE Atlanta GA 30333 Business E-Mail: sbt1@cdc.gov.

THACKER, WILLIAM D., physics professor; s. Herbert D. and Sarah Elizabeth Thacker; m. Doris Thacker; 1 child, William F. BS in Physics, MIT, Cambridge, 1978; MS in Physics, U. Ill., Urbana, 1980; PhD in Physics, U. Colo., Boulder, 1984. Lectr. U. Md., European Divsn., Nuremburg, Germany, 1984—85; postdoc. rsch. Max Planck Inst. Physics and Astrophysics, Munich, 1985—87; postdoc. rsch. and tchg. U. Kaiserslautern, Germany, 1987—89; asst. prof. Parks Coll. St. Louis U., Cahokia, Ill., 1989—93, assoc. prof., 1993—2001, prof., 2001—. Cons. NASA, Hampton, Va., 1997—2004. Fulbright scholarship, Fulbright Scholar Program, 1985—87. Mem.: Am. Phys. Soc. Avocations: swimming, hiking, reading. Office: St Louis Univ 3450 Lindell Blvd Saint Louis MO 63103 Business E-Mail: thackerwd@slu.edu.

THACKERAY, JONATHAN E., lawyer; b. Athens, Ohio, July 30, 1936; s. Joseph Eugene and Betty Rutherford (Boright) T.; m. Sandra Ann McMahon; children: Jennifer, Sara, Amy, Jonathan. AB cum laude, Harvard U., 1958, JD, 1961. Bar: Ohio 1961, U.S. Dist. Ct. (no. dist.) Ohio 1961, U.S. Supreme Ct. 1972, U.S. Ct. Appeals (6th cir.) 1973, U.S. Ct. Appeals (9th cir.) 1982, N.Y. 1993. Assoc. Vorys, Sater, Seymour & Pease, Columbus, Ohio, 1961, Baker & Hostetler, Cleve., 1965-72, ptnr., 1973-93; v.p., gen. counsel The Hearst Corp., NYC, 1993—2003; ret., 2003. Served to lt. USNR, 1961-65. Mem. ABA, Cleve. Bar Assn., Am. Law Inst. *Notable cases include: administrative proceedings leading to approval of joint newspaper operating agreements in Cincinnati, Seattle and Las Vegas; litigation of newspaper antitrust cases in Memphis, Trenton and Dallas.*

THACKSTON, EDWARD LEE, civil engineering educator; b. Nashville, Apr. 29, 1937; s. Guy Carleton and Sydney Virginia (Adams) T.; m. Betty Tucker, Mar. 19, 1961; children: Carol Elizabeth Thackston Nixon, Leah Virginia Thackston Hawkins. BE summa cum laude, Vanderbilt U., 1961; MS, U. Ill., 1963; PhD, Vanderbilt U., 1966. Registered profl. engr., Tenn. City engr. City of Lebanon, Tenn., 1959; design engr. City of Nashville, 1961-62; instr. Vanderbilt U., Nashville, 1965-66, asst. prof., 1966-69, assoc. prof., 1969-75, prof. engring., 1975-2000, chmn. dept. civil and environ. engring., 1980-99. Asst. to gov. for environ. affairs, State of Tenn., 1972-74; cons. in field. Author book, tech. reports; contbr. to profl. publs. Bd. dirs. Tenn. Environ. Coun., Nashville, 1971-76; bd. dirs. Tenn. Conservation League, Nashville, 1974-2003, v.p., 1977, pres., 1978-80; trustee Cumberland Mus., Nashville, 1986-92; trustee Cumberland U., Lebanon, 1996—, mem. exec. com., 1996-2002, 04—, sec.-treas., 2000-02, 04-07, chmn. 07—. Recipient Tenn. Lifetime Environ./Conservation Stewardship award State Tenn. 1996, Engr. of Yr. Mid. Tenn. Tenn. Soc. Prof. Engring., 2001, Landmark Paper award Assn. Environ. Engring. and Sci. Profs., 2001; named Tenn. Conservationist of Yr., 1974, Distinguished Alumnus Vanderbilt Univ. Sch. Engring., 2007. Fellow ASCE; mem. Am. Water Works Assn. (life), Water Environ. Fedn. (life), Assn. Environ. Engring. Profs. (emeritus, Landmark Paper award 2001), Tenn. Hist. Soc., Hillwood Country Club, Tau Beta Pi, Chi Epsilon. Republican. Episcopalian. Avocations: genealogy, history, photography, weightlifting. Business E-Mail: elt@vuse.vanderbilt.edu.

THADANI, UDHO, physician, cardiologist; b. Hyderabad, India, Apr. 1, 1941; came to U.S., 1980; s. Vensimal Mulchand and Gopi Thadani; m. Dorothy Ann Thadani, 1974; 1 child, Emma Sarala. MBBS, All India Inst. Med. Scis., New Delhi, 1964. Lic. physician, Okla., Ont., Can., Eng., India; cert. internal medicine, U.K., Can.; cert. cardiology, Can.; diplomate in internal medicine and cardiovasc. diseases Am. Bd. Internal Medicine. Intern All India Inst. Med. Scis., New Delhi, 1964-65, house physician, surgeon, 1965-66; house physician in medicine Joyce Green Hosp., Dartford, Kent, England, 1966-67; sr. house physician in medicine Kingston Gen. Hosp., Hull, England, 1967-69, registrar, rsch. fellow in medicine and cardiology, 1969-71, U. Leeds (Eng.), The Gen. Infirmary at Leeds, 1971-75; sr. rsch. fellow, clin. asst. medicine Queen's U., Kingston Gen. Hosp., Ont., Canada, 1975-78; asst. prof. medicine Queen's U., Kingston, 1978-80; staff physician Kingston Gen. Hosp., 1978-80; assoc. prof. medicine U. Okla. Health Scis. Ctr., Oklahoma City, 1980-83; prof. medicine Okla. U. Health Scis. Ctr., Oklahoma City, 1983—2001, prof. emeritus medicine, 2001, mem. cardiology fellowship com., 1980-82; dir. clin. cardiology Okla. U. Health Scis. Ctr. and VA Med. Ctr., Oklahoma City, 1980-87, cons. cardiologist, 1980—, vice chief cardiovasc. sect., 1981-99, dir. clin. rsch., 1987-99. Vice-chmn. rsch. and devel. com. VA Med. Ctr., Oklahoma City, 1989-92, chmn. physiology-pharmacology categorical rev. com., 1989-94, chmn. rsch. and devel. com., VA Med. Ctr. Oklahoma City, 1992-94, 2003-05; sr. rsch. fellow Ont. Heart Found., 1978-80, rsch. fellow, 1976-78; rsch. fellow dept. medicine Queen's U., Kingston, Ont., 1975-76; rsch. fellow U. Leeds, Pub. Health and Ciba Found., dept. medicine and cardiovasc. sect. Leeds Gen. Infirmary, 1971-75. Editor: Medical Therapy of Ischemic Heart Disease, 1992, Nitrates Updated, 1996; mem. editl. bd. panel Cardiology Drug Facts and Comparison, 1989; contbg. rev. panel Drug Facts and Comparisons, 1989—; mem. editl. bd. Internat. Jour. Cardiology, 1987-93, Cardiovascular Drugs and Therapy, 1987-2004, Heart Diseases, 1999-2004, Am. Jour. Pharmacology, 2000-04, Am. Jour. Cardiovasc. Drugs, 2003—, Cardiology, 2005—; reviewer Circulation, Jour. Am. Coll. Cardiology, Am. Jour. Cardiology, Brit. Heart Jour., Internat. Jour. Cardiology, Can. Jour. Cardiology, European Heart Jour., Annals of Internal Medicine, New Eng. Jour. Medicine, Archives of Internal Medicine, Cardiovasc. Drugs and Therapy, Drugs, European Jour. Pharmacology, Clin. Pharmacology and Therapeutics; contbr. over 200 articles to profl. jours., chpts. to books. Recipient Provost Rsch. award, OUHSC, 1995, James F. Hammarsten award for physicians of excellence award, VA Med. Ctr., Okla., 2003. Fellow: Coun. Clin. Cardiology Am. Heart Assn. (coun. rep. Okla. 1989—2000), Am. Coll. Cardiology (mem. cardiovasc. drug com. 1990—94), Royal Soc. Medicine London; mem.: Can. Cardiovasc. Soc., Royal Coll. Physicians U.K., Phi Kappa Phi (mem. FDA cardiovasc. and renal drugs adv. com. 1995—99). Avocations: gardening, tennis, travel. Office: Okla U Health Sci Ctr Cardiology Sect 920 SL Young WP 3120 Oklahoma City OK 73104 Office Phone: 405-271-4742. Business E-Mail: udho-thadani@ouhsc.edu.

THADDEUS, PATRICK, physicist, researcher; b. Wilmington, Del., June 6, 1932; s. Victor and Elizabeth (Ross) T.; m. Janice Petherbridge Farrar, Apr. 6, 1963 (dec. Dec. 2001); children: Eva, Michael; m. Valerie McCollom, Nov. 1, 2003. B.Sc., U. Del., 1953; MA, Oxford U., Eng., 1955; PhD, Columbia U., 1960; DSc (hon.), U. Chgo., 2003. Research assoc. Columbia Radiation Lab., 1960-61; research assoc. Goddard Inst. Space Studies, NYC, 1961-63, mem. sci. staff, 1963-86; mem. faculty Columbia U., 1965-86, adj. prof. physics, 1971-86; prof. astronomy and applied physics Harvard U., 1986-2000, Robert Wheeler Willson prof. applied astronomy, 2000—; mem. sci. staff Smithsonian Astrophys. Obs., 1986—. Vis. com. Nat. Radio Astronomy Obs., 1973-76, 91-94; mem. Astronomy Survey Com., 1978-80, 89-90; chair task group on Space Astronomy and Astrophysics, 1996-97; Fairchild Disting. Scholar Calif. Inst. Tech., 1994; Russell Marker lectr. Pa. State U., 1989; vis. fellow Inst. Astronomy, Cambridge, Eng., 1983. Author papers on microwave spectroscopy, optical and radio astronomy. Recipient Exceptional Sci. Achievement medal NASA, 1970, 85; John C. Lindsay Meml. award Goddard Space Flight Center, 1976; Alexander von Humboldt award, 1983; Herschel medal Royal Astron. Soc., 2001; Fulbright fellow, 1953-55. Fellow Am. Phys. Soc.; mem. Am. Astron. Soc., Am. Acad. Arts and Scis., Nat. Acad. Scis., Internat. Astronomical Union, Saturday Club, Sigma Xi. Address: 58 Garfield St Cambridge MA 02138-1802

THAGARD, NORMAN E., astronaut, physician, engineer, educator; b. Marianna, Fla., July 3, 1943; s. James E. Thagard and Mary F. Nicholson; m. Rex Kirby Johnson; children: Norman Gordon, James Robert, Daniel Cary. BS, Florida State U., 1965, MS, 1966; MD, U. Texas S.W. Med. Sch., 1977; LHD (hon.), Fla. Atlantic U. Intern, internal medicine Medical U. South Carolina, 1977-78; astronaut NASA, 1978-96, ret., 1996; mission specialist NASA Space Shuttle Challenger Flight STS-7, deployed satellites (ANIK C-2, PALAPA B-1), operated Remote Manipulator Sys., conducted experiments, 1983, NASA Spacelab-3 Mission STS-51 B, 1985, NASA Space Shuttle Atlantis Flight STS-30, deployed Magellan Venus exploration spacecraft, 1989; payload comdr. NASA Space Shuttle Discovery Flight STS-42, International Microgravity Lab.-1 module experiments, 1992; cosmonaut-rschr. Space Station MIR-18, 1995; prof. elec. engring., assoc. dean coll. rels. Coll. Engring. Fla. A&M U.-Fla. State U., Tallahassee, 1996—. Contbr. articles to profl. jours. With USMC, 1966-71, Capt. 1967-71, in Vietnam flew 163 combat missions. Decorated 11 Air medals, Navy Commendation medal with Combat V, Marine Corps E award, Vietnam Svc. medal, Vietnamese Cross of Gallantry with Palm. Fellow AIAA (assoc.); mem. IEEE, Assn. Space Explorers, Aerospace Med. Assn., Soc. for Human Performance in Extreme Environments, Phi Kappa Phi. Achievements include breaking U.S. space endurance record of 84 continuous days aboard the Russian space station Mir. Avocations: classical music, electronic design. Office: Fla A&M U-Fla State U Coll Engring 2525 Pottsdamer St Tallahassee FL 32310-6046 Fax: 850-487-6486. E-mail: nthagard@fsu.edu.

THAI, MY T., engineering educator; d. Minh B. Thai and Phuong T. Pham; m. Hoanh T. Ngo, July 24, 2005; 1 child, Bach Hy Ngo. PhD, U. Minn., 2005. Postdoc. U. Tex., Dallas, 2005—06; asst. prof. U. Fla., Gainesville, 2006—. Contbr. articles to profl. sci. jours. Grant, NSF, 2008—.

THAIN, JOHN ALEXANDER, former diversified financial services company executive; b. Antioch, Ill., May 26, 1955; m. Carmen M. Ribera; children: Zack, Nicole, Victoria, Alex. BS, MIT, 1977; MBA, Harvard U., 1979. CFO, head of ops., tech. & fin. The Goldman Sachs Group, L.P., 1994—99, co-CEO European ops., 1995—97, pres, co-COO, 1999; co-COO The Goldman Sachs Group, Inc., NYC, 1999—2003, pres., 1999—2004, COO, 2003—04; CEO NY Stock Exch., NYC, 2004—06, NYSE Group, Inc., NYC, 2006—07, NYSE Euronext, NYC, 2007; chmn., CEO Merrill Lynch & Co., Inc., NYC, 2007—08; pres. global banking, securities & wealth mgmt. Bank of America Corp., 2009. Bd. dirs. The Goldman Sachs Group, Inc., 1998—2004, NYSE Group, Inc., 2006—07, Merrill Lynch & Co., Inc., 2007—08, BlackRock Inc., 2008—; mem. MIT Corp., 2000—, MIT Sloan Sch. Mgmt. dean's adv. coun., INSEAD US Nat. Adv. Bd., Fed. Res. Bank NY Internat. Capital Markets Adv. Com., BritishAmerican Bus. Inc. Mem. James Madison Coun. Libr. Congress; gen. trustee Howard U.; trustee NY-Presbyn. Hosp.; gov. NY Presbyn. Found., Inc.; mem. adv. coun. MIT Sloan Sch. Mgmt. Mem.: Trilateral Commn., French Am. Found.*

THAKOR, ANJAN V., finance educator, consultant; m. Serry Thakor; children: Richard, Cullen. PhD in Finance, Northwestern U. Cert. in exceptional inspiration and guidance Doctoral Student Assn., Sch. Bus., Ind. U., 1980. Prof. fin. Ind. U., 1983—94; vis. assoc. prof. fin. Northwestern U., Evanston, Ill., 1983—85; vis. prof. fin. UCLA, 1987—88; Edward J. Frey prof. banking and fin. U. Mich., 2000—03; John E. Simon prof. fin. and sr. assoc. dean Wash. U. St. Louis, Olin Bus. Sch., 2003—. Dir. Western Fin. Assn., 1991—94; guest editor Spl. Issue Fin. Mgmt., 1993; mng. editor Jour. Fin. Intermediation, 1996—2005; v.p. Fin. Intermediation Rsch. Soc., 2003—05, pres., 2006—08; assoc. editor Jour. Banking and Fin. Author: (book) Credit, Intermediation and the Macro Economy: Models and Perspectives; co-author (with K. Cameron, R. Quinn, J. DeGraff): Competing Values Leadership: Creating Value in Organizations; co-author: (with J. Boquist and T. Milbourn) The Value Sphere: The Corporate Executive's Handbook for Creating and Retaining Shareholder Wealth; contbr. articles to profl. jours. Recipient J. Dwight Peterson Faculty fellowship, Ind. U., 1985, MBA Tchg. Excellence award, 1986, Outstanding Sr. Faculty Rsch. award, U. Mich. Bus. Sch., 1998, Outstanding Tchr. Doctoral Program award, 2003, Leadership award, 2003, Reid MBA Tchg. Excellence award, Wash. U. St. Louis, Olin Bus. Sch., 2005; grantee Grant, US Dept. Treasury, 1997—98; grant, Fed. Home Loan Bank Bd., 1983—84, Bank Adminstrn. Inst., 1983—85, Prochnow Ednl. Found., 1988—89, 1992, Gam Inst. Fin., 1990. Mem.: Am. Fin. Assn. (nominating com. mem. 1999), Nobel Prize Economics Nominating Com. (mem. 1993—2004), Third Biannual FIRS Conf., Anchorage, Alaska (organizer 2008), Second Biannual FIRS Conf., Shanghai (organizer 2006), Colo. Fin. Conf. (Estes Pk.) (organizer 2002), WDI and JFI Conf. (organizer 2002), Royal Econ. Soc., Estes Pk. Fin. Conf. (organizer 1999), Jour. Fin. Intermediation Symposium (organizer 1996—99), Ind. U. (organizer 1987, 1989, 1991), Western Fin. Assn. (program com. mem. 1985—98, 2006—07), Bd. Governors FRS (disting. vis. scholar 1993), Econometric Soc., Beta Gamma Sigma (disting. vis. scholar 1990). Avocations: painting, skiing, weightlifting. Office: Wash Univ Saint Louis One Brookings Dr Campus Box 1133 Saint Louis MO 63130-4899 Office Fax: 314-935-5218. Business E-Mail: thakor@wustl.edu.

THAKRE, TUSHAR P., physician, scientist; b. Saoner, Maharashtra, India, Nov. 10, 1977; s. Purushottam R. and Vaishali Thakre. MD, Govt. Med. Coll., Nagpur, India, 2001; PhD, U. North Tex. Health Sci. Ctr., Ft. Worth, 2007. Grad. tchg. asst. U. North Tex. Health Sci. Ctr., 2002—07; resident physician U. Mo., Kansas City, 2007—; pub. rels. officer Lata Med. Rsch. Found., Nagpur, Maharashtra, mem. bd. trustees, 2007—08. Contbr. articles to profl. jours. Recipient First prize, 1998, Fourth prize, 2004, Travel award, 2004. Office: Univ Mo Kansas City 1000 E 24th St Kansas City MO 64108

THAKUR, VINAY V., research scientist; b. Pune, Maharashtra, India, Apr. 7, 1974; s. Vijayraj K. and Champa V. Thakur; m. Reena V. Thakur, May 31, 1998; children: Sara V., Yash V. PhD, Nat. Chem. Lab., Pune, 2002. Diploma mgmt. Pune, 2000. Postdoc. assoc. Rutgers U., Piscataway, NJ, 2003—05; rsch. scientist Yale U., New Haven, 2005—. Contbr. to refree panel of internat. jours. Mem.: Nat. Chem. Lab., NY Acad. Sci., Am. Chem. Soc. Achievements include development of novel non-nucleoside reverse transcriptase inhibitors for HIV; discovery of new catalyst for aminobromination of olefins; new heterogeneous catalyst for asmmetric sulfoxidation and kinetic resolution of sulfoxides, new metal free catalytic system for aziridination of olefins. Home: 599 Prospect St Apt A New Haven CT 06511 Office: Yale Univ 225 Prospect St P O Box 108207 New Haven CT 06520 Office Phone: 203-432-8959. Office Fax: 203-432-6144. Business E-Mail: vinay.thakur@yale.edu.

THAL, SERGIO GUSTAVO, cardiologist, director, medical educator; b. Buenos Aires, Apr. 16, 1969; s. Samuel Nicolas Thal and Juana Abramovich; m. Ximena Pardo, Oct. 24, 1998; children: Lucila, Ivan Leon, Ilana. MD, U. Buenos Aires, Argentina, 1992. Cert. cardiologist Argentine Ministry of Pub. Health, 1998, Argentine Soc. Cardiology, 2003, Argentine Soc. Cardiology, 2008. Medicine resident Sanatorio Mcpl. Julio Mendez, Buenos Aires, 1993—95, cardiology fellow, 1995—98, chief cardiology, 1998—99, staff cardiologist, 1999—2004, Sanatorio Trinidad, Buenos Aires, 2001—04; fellow Cleve. Clinic, 2004—06; dir. cardiac electrophysiology So. Ariz. VA Health Care Sys., Tucson, 2007—; asst. prof. clin. medicine U. Ariz., 2007—. Consultor St Jude Med., 2008—; advisor Medtronic, 2009—. Recipient Tchg. award, Charles W Hall Jr Meml., 2008; Rsch. grant, Boston Sci., 2008. Mem.: Argentine Soc. Cardiology, Heart Rhythm Soc. Avocations: tennis, golf, travel. Office: Southern Ariz VA Health Care Sys 3601 S 6th Ave Mail Code 1-111C Tucson AZ 85723 Office Fax: 520-629-4636.

THAL, STEVEN HENRY, lawyer, consultant; b. NYC, Nov. 16, 1942; s. Michael and Mildred (Hirsch) T.; 1 child, Eric Alexander. BA, U. Mich., 1964, JD, 1967; postgrad., U. Tubingen, Fed. Republic Germany, 1967-68, New Sch. Social Rsch., NYC, 1971-72. Bar: N.Y., 1968, U.S. Ct. Appeals (2d cir.) 1969, U.S. Dist. Ct. (so. and ea. dists.) N.Y. 1969, U.S. Supreme Ct. 1973; cert. District Ct., Frankfurt, Germany. Ptnr. Thal & Youtt, NYC, 1972-84, Kaplan, Russin & Vecchi, NYC, 1984-88, Summit, Rovins & Feldesman, NYC, 1988-90, Oppenheimer Wolff & Donnelly, NYC, 1990-94, LeBoeuf Lamb Greene & MacRae, NYC, 1994—2003, Latham & Watkins, NYC, 2003—06, Internat. coun. to Phililp Nizer, NYC, 2007—. Pres. Export Assist Corp., Ft. Lee, N.J., 1988-94; trusted atty., Consulate Gen. of Fed. Repubic Germany, N.Y.C., 1986—, Austrian Trade Commn., N.Y.C., 1988—; Swiss Consulate, NYC, 2005-; fgn. legal cons., Frankfurt, Germany, 1991; vis. lectr. internat. legal matters, Law Faculty of Ludwig-Maximilians U., Munich, Germany, Ruprecht-Karls-U., Heidelberg, Germany; counsel German-Am. Partnership Program, 1998—. Fulbright scholar, 1967-68; grantee Ford Found., 1967-68, Deutsche Akademisches Austauchdienst, 1967-68. Mem. Internat. Bar Assn., N.Y. State Bar Assn. (internat. law com.), German Am. Lawyers Assn., Gesellschaft fuer Rechtsvergleichung, Deutscher Verein (NY) (pres. 2008-). Avocations: boating, fishing, camping. Office: Philip Nizer LLP 666 5th Ave New York NY 10103 Home Phone: 917-757-6200; Office Phone: 212-841-0742. Personal E-mail: stesq17@hotmail.com. Business E-Mail: sthal@phillipsnizer.com.

THALACKER, ARBIE ROBERT, lawyer, director; b. Marquette, Mich., Apr. 17, 1935; s. Arbie Otto and Jeanne (Emmett) T.; m. Rita Annette Skaaren, Sept. 11, 1956 (div. July 1992); children: Marc Emmett, Christopher Paul, Robert Skaaren; m. Deborah B. Garrett, Jan. 10, 1998. AB, Princeton U., 1957; JD, U. Mich., 1960. Bar: NY 1961, U.S. Ct. Appeals (2d cir.) 1962. Assoc. Shearman & Sterling, NYC, 1960—68, ptnr., 1968—2000, of counsel, 2001—. Dir. Detrex Corp., Detroit, 1981—, chmn. bd., 1993-96. Leader Rep. Dist. Com., 1966-68; pres. & trustee Greenwich Village Soc. for Hist. Preservation; trustee Naropa Univ.; bd. dirs. Meredith Monk House Found., Shambhala Internat. Mem. ABA, N.Y. Bar Assn., Assn. Bar City N.Y. (securities regulatory commn. 1975-78), Wine and Food Soc. (bd. dirs. 1976-78, 85-93, 94-2006), Chevaliers du Tastevin, Commanderie de Bordeaux, Siwanoy Country Club (bd. govs. 1976-79), Derby Club, Links Club, Verbank Hunting and Fishing Club. Office: Shearman & Sterling 599 Lexington Ave Fl C2 New York NY 10022-6069

THALER, DAVID SOLOMON, research scientist, educator; PhD, U. Oreg., Eugene, 1985. Postdoc. fellow U. Oreg., 1985—; vis. scientist U. Paris, 1987—88; rsch. assoc. U. Utah, Salt Lake City, 1988—90; sr. rsch. assoc. Rockefeller U., NYC, 1990—92, asst. prof., 1992—99, assoc. prof., 1999—. Contbr. scientific papers. Mem.: Genetics Soc. America. Achievements include research in molecular mechanisms of mutation and recombination. Office: Rockefeller Univ 1230 York Ave New York NY 10065-6307 Business E-Mail: thalerd@rockefeller.edu.

THALER, RICHARD WINSTON, JR., investment banker; b. Boston, Apr. 9, 1951; s. Richard Winston and Victoria Louise (Sears) T.; m. Mary Alice Gast, June 28, 1980; children: Julia Davis, Sarah Sears, Hannah Warren. BA in Am. Polit. History cum laude, Princeton U., 1973; MBA, Harvard U., 1978. Salesman Media Networks, NYC, 1973-74; banker Bank of Boston, Rio de Janeiro, 1975-77, Boston, 1978-80; mng. dir. investment banking Lehman Bros., NYC, 1980-96; vice chmn. Investment Banking Deutsche Bank Securities, NYC, 1996—2008; mng. ptnr. Lt. Island Ptnrs. LLC, 2008—. Adj. prof. fin. Morehouse Coll., Atlanta, 2007—; dir. Upper Manhattan Empowerment Zone, 2007—. Spl. gifts solicitor Princeton U. Ann. Giving, NYC, 1987—88, 1997—98, 2002—03, class agt., 1988—93; trustee Daily Princetonian, 1989—, pres. bd., 2004—; trustee Episc. Divinity Sch., Cambridge, Mass., 1995—2004, Plimoth Plantation, Plymouth, Mass., 1995—; del. Dem. Nat. Conv., 1996; active Dem. Leadership Coun.; mem. vestry Chapel of St. James the Fisherman, Wellfleet, Mass. Mem. Mass. Soc. Mayflower Descs., Harvard Club NY, Siwanoy Country Club, Univ. Cottage Club. Democrat. Episcopalian. Avocations: gardening, sailing, American political history, travel.

THALHAMMER, KRISTINA EMMA, political science professor; b. Sioux Falls, SD, Sept. 20, 1958; d. Korbinian and Katharina Rieger Thalhammer; m. David H. Anderson, Sept. 9, 1988; children: Daniel Anderson, Anna Anderson. PhD, U. Minn., Mpls., 1995. Prof. St. Olaf Coll., Norhtfield, Minn., 1994—, chair polit. sci., 2003—. Co-author: (nonfiction book) Courageous Resistance: The Power of Ordinary People. Vol. speaker's bur. Ctr. Victims Torture, Mpls., 2008—. Recipient Alumna award, Coll. St.Catherine, 2009. Roman Catholic. Office: Saint Olaf Coll 1520 Saint Olaf Ave Northfield MN 55057 Business E-Mail: thalhamm@stolaf.edu.

THALLER, MICHELLE LYNN, astronomer; b. Milwaukee, Nov. 28, 1969; d. Michael Lawrence Thaller and Hanna McDermott; m. Andrew John Booth. BA, Harvard U., Cambridge, Mass., 1992; PhD, Ga. State U., Atlanta, 1997. On-line sci. columnist C.S. Monitor, Boston, 1999—2004; outreach mgr., spitzer space telescope Calif. Inst. Tech., Pasadena, Calif., 2002—. Tv commentator History Channel, Pasadena, 2000—, Nat. Geog. Channel, Pasadena, 2002—; spaceship spitzer exec. prodr. Spitzer Sci. Ctr., Pasadena, 2003—; tv personality Discovery Channel, Pasadena, 2003—. Leader Spitzer Tchr. Rsch. Program, Pasadena, 2006—09; sci. spokesperson NASA, Pasadena, 1999—2009. Mem.: Am. Astron. Soc. Business E-Mail: thaller@ipac.caltech.edu.

THALLER, SETH RAY, plastic surgeon; b. NYC, June 22, 1949; m. Patricia Thaller; children: Cody, Lexi. BA, Lafayette Coll., 1971; MD, U. Louisville, 1975; DMD, Boston Sch. Dentistry, 1978; resident gen. surgery, St. Vincent's Hosp., 1978-80. Intern in internal medicine SUNY, Buffalo, 1975-76; resident in gen. surgery St. Vincent's Hosp., NYC, 1978-80; resident otalaryngology/head and neck surgery Mass. Eye and Ear Infirmary, 1980-83; resident in plastic surgery Albert Einstein Coll. Medicine Affiliated Hosps., 1983—85; craniofacial fellowship UCLA Sch. Medicine, 1986; clin. instr. NYU Sch. Dentistry, NYC, 1984-86; adj. asst. prof. plastic surgery U. Calif., LA, 1986, asst. prof. plastic surgery, 1987-93, acting chief divsn. plastic surgery, 1989, assoc. prof. plastic surgery Davis, 1993-95; prof. and chief divsn. plastic surgery U. Miami/Jackson Meml. Hosp. Mem.: ACS, Am. Assn Plastic Surgeons, Assn. Academic Chmn. Plastic Surgeons, Am. Soc. Maxillofacial Surgeons, Am Soc. Plastic & Reconstructive Surgeons, Am. Cleft Palate Craniofacial Assn., Am. Society for Aesthetic Plastic Surgery, AMA. Home: 11010 Paradela St Coral Gables FL 33156-4244 Office: Univ Miami Jackson Meml Hospital PO Box 16960 Miami FL 33101-6960 Office Phone: 305-585-5285.

THAMAN, MICHAEL H., building material systems executive; b. Mar. 5, 1964; BSEE, Princeton U., 1986, BS in Computer Sci., 1986. V.p. Mercer Mgmt. Cons., NYC, 1986—92; dir. corp. devel. Owens Corning, 1992-94, plant mgr. Toronto insulation facility, 1994-96, gen. mgr. OEM solutions group Louisville, 1996-97, v.p., pres. engineered pipe systems bus. Brussels, 1997-99, v.p., pres. exterior systems bus. Toledo, 1999-2000, sr. v.p., 2000—02, CFO, 2000—07, chmn., 2002—, pres., CEO, 2007—. Bd. dirs. Owens Corning, 2002—, FPL Group, Inc., 2003—. Office: Owens Corning One Owens Corning Pkwy Toledo OH 43659

THAMES, RICK, publishing executive, editor-in-chief; b. Laurinburg, NC; m. Debbie Thames; children: Nathan, Hunter, Lucy. AB in English, Pfeiffer U.; MS in Comm., U. Tenn., Knoxville. Reporter Fayetteville Observer, NC, 1978—80; various positions including mng. editor Miami News, 1980—88; various positions including govt. editor, city editor, assist. mng. editor, public editor Charlotte Observer, NC, 1988—96; editor Wichita Eagle, Kans., 1997—2004; v.p., editor Charlotte Observer, NC, 2004—. Chmn. adv. bd. Elliot Sch. of Comm., Wichita State U. Fellow: News Leadership 2009 Knight Digital Media Ctr.; mem.: NC Press Assn. (pres.), Am. Soc. of Newspaper Editors (mem. Freedom of Info. Com.), Kansas Press Assn. (bd. dirs.). Office: The Charlotte Observer PO Box 32188 600 S Tryon St Charlotte NC 28202 Office Phone: 704-358-5000. E-mail: rthames@charlotteobserver.com.

THAMHAIN, HANS JURGEN, management educator; b. Dresden, Saxony, Germany, Oct. 1, 1936; s. Hans Florenz Thamhain, Martha Thamhain; m. Ingrid Katharina Schwoch; children: Petra Lively, Thilo. BSEE, Ingenieurschule Koblenz, Germany, 1961; MSEE, U. Waterloo, Can., 1967; MBA, Syracuse U., 1972, PhD in Bus. Adminstrn., 1974. Elec. engr. Standard Electric Co.,ITT, Pforzheim, Baden-Wurttemberg, Germany, 1961—64, Westinghouse Corp., Hamilton, Ontario, Canada, 1964—67; project mgr. Gen. Electric Co., Syracuse, NY, 1967—75; bus. mgr. GTE/Verizon, Needham, Mass., 1975—81; assoc. prof. mgmt. Worcester Polytech. Inst., Worchester, Mass., 1981—87; prof. mgmt. Bentley U., Waltham, Mass., 1987—; dir. project mgmt. programs Bentley Coll., Waltham, Mass., 1987—. Vis. prof., guest lectr. numerous univs. and insts., 1981—; cons. in field. Author: Project Management for Small and Medium-Size Businesses, 1984, Engineering Program Management, 1985, Project Management Operating Guidelines, 1986 (Nat. Book award, AAP, 1993), Engineering Management, 1993, Management of Technology, 2005; contbr. articles to profl. jours. Scholar, Fulbright, 1998. Mem.: IEEE (life; publications adv. bd. 1985—, Engring. Mgr. of Year 2000), Project Mgmt. Inst. (publications adv. bd. 1990—93, cert., Dist. Contbn. award 1998, Rsch. Achievement award 2006), Am. Soc. Engring. Mgmt. (editl. bd. 1987—), Product Develop. Mgmt. Assn. (publications rev. bd. 1990—, cert.), Phi Beta Delta. Achievements include patents in field. Avocations: ironman triathlete, marathons. Home: 25 Lanewood Ave Framingham MA 01701-3660 Office: Bentley Univ Forest St Waltham MA Home Phone: 508-620-0370; Office Phone: 718-891-2189. Office Fax: 781-891-2896. Business E-Mail: hthamhain@bentley.edu.

THANKI, SANDIP G., educator; s. Gajendra M. and Asha G. Thanki; m. Tejal S. Rajyaguru, Dec. 25, 2001. PhD, U. Nev., Las Vegas, 2004. Asst. prof. Nev. State Coll., Henderson, Nev., 2005—. Musician: (live performances) Sitar Player. Office: Nev State Coll 1125 Nev State Dr Henderson NV 89002 Business E-Mail: sandip.thanki@nsc.nevada.edu.

THANNICKAL, THOMAS CHACKO, neurophysiologist, researcher; b. Alakode, Kerala, India, May 10, 1966; s. Chacko Varghese and Annaakutty Thannickal; m. Bincy Rose Pannikot, Sept. 2, 2000; children: Tobin Thomas, Ann Thomas. PhD, Mahatma Gandhi U., India, 1996. Rsch. officer All India Inst. Med. Sci., New Delhi, 1996—99; asst. rsch. neurophysiologist UCLA, Los Angeles, Calif., 1999—. Recipient Young Investigator Award, Am. Sleep Rsch. Soc., 2001, Finalist for Frank Brown Berry Prize, US Medicine, 2001, Post doctoral Rsch. Excellence, UCLA, 2001, Young Scientist Award, The Assn. Scientists Indian Origin in Am., 2002, Sleep Sci. Award, Am. Acad. Neurology, 2003. Roman Catholic. Achievements include discovery of Human Narcolepsy as a Neurodegenerative disease; Hypocretin (orexin) and Melanin, concentrating hormone (MCH), neuronal loss in Parkinson's disase. Office: UCLA Neurobiology Rsch 151A3 16111 Plummer St North Hills CA 91343 Office Fax: 818-895-9575. E-mail: thomastc@ucla.edu.

THAPAR, AMUL R., federal judge, former prosecutor; b. Troy, Mich., 1969; BS, Boston Coll., 1991; JD, U. Calif. Berkeley, 1994. Law clk. to Hon. S. Arthur Spiegel US Dist. Ct. (so. dist.) Ohio, 1994—96; law clk. to Hon. Nathaniel R. Jones US Ct. Appeals (6th Cir.), 1996—97; assoc. Williams & Connolly LLP, Washington, 1997—99, Squire, Sanders & Dempsey, Cin., 2001—02; asst. US atty. DC US Dept. Justice, Washington, 1999—2000; gen. counsel Equalfooting.com, 2000—01; asst. US atty. (so. dist.) Ohio US Dept. Justice, Cin., 2002—06, US atty. (ea. dist.) Ky. Lexington, 2006—07; judge US Dist. Ct. (ea. dist.) Ky., 2007—. Founder Street Law Inc., Cin., 1995; adj. prof. law U. Cin. Coll. Law, 1996—97, 2002—06; trial advocacy instr. George U. Law Ctr., 1999—2000. Office: US Dist Ct 101 Barr St Lexington KY 40507

THARAKAN, BINU, neuroscientist, researcher; b. Kottayam-Kerala, India, May 13, 1969; s. Varghese and Sosamma Tharakan; m. Mannisha Mary John, May 9, 2004. BSc, St. Berchman's Coll., Changanacherry, 1989; MSc, Agra U., India, 1991; PhD, Banaras Hindu U., Varanasi, India, 1998. Post doctoral fellow Nat. Ctr. Biol. Scis. Tata Inst. of Fundamental Rsch., Bangalore, Karnataka, India, 1998—2000, NIH, Bathesda, Md.; rsch. scientist Tex. A&M U. HSC, Scott and White Hosp., Temple, 2003—. Mem. Soc. for Neuroscience, Washington, 2004—. Asian fellow, Japan Neuroscience Soc. Mem.: Soc. Neuroscience, Am. Stroke Assn. (stroke coun., interdisciplinary working group on functional genomics, and translation biology), Internat. Soc. Stem Cell Rsch., Internat. Brain Rsch. Orgn. Office: Texas A&M U Scott and White Hosp 702 SW HK Dodgen Loop Temple TX 76504

THARNEY, LEONARD JOHN, education educator, consultant; b. New Haven, Nov. 6, 1929; s. Lillian A. Batey; m. Denise A. Gauvin, June 20, 1981; children: Karen L., Linda L. BS, Coll. of NJ, 1954; MEd, Rutgers U., 1959; postgrad., Lehigh U., Bethlehem, Pa., 1963-70, Columbia U.; grad., Command & Gen. Staff Coll., Ft. Leavenworth, Kans., 1972. Cert. secondary math. and sci. tchr., elem. tchr. Tchr. (elem. demonstration) Trenton State Coll., NJ, 1954-60; tchr. (jr. high demonstration) Ewing Twp. Sch., NJ, 1960-63; cons., evaluator Am. Coun. on Edn., Washington, 1975-95, field coord., 1995—2003; cons., evaluator Mid. States Assn., Phila., 1987—; prof. Trenton State Coll., 1963-92, dept. chmn., 1988-92, prof. emeritus, 1993—; cons., evaluator coll. and univ. programs Nat. Assn. Indsl. Tech., Ann Arbor, 2003—. Tchr. grad. courses curriculum and ednl. rsch. overseas sites, Spain, Cyprus, Saudi Arabia, Syria, 1981—; exch. prof. Worcester Coll. Higher Edn., England, 1984—85; presenter sci. edn. workshops AISA Internat. Conf., Nairobi, 1987; rep. Coll. to Prins. Tng. Ctr., London, 1994; mem. accrediting commn. Distance Edn. and Tng. Coun., Washington, 2000—; cons. in field. Co-author: 7 manuals for uniform constrn. codes. Col. US Army, 1947—81. Decorated Meritorious Svc. medal; recipient ACE award for Outstanding Svc. in Mil. Evaluations, 1987, cert. of appreciation, presdl. citation, 1989, spl. plaque award, Outstanding Svc. and Support award, 112th FA Assn., 1998, Internat. Outstanding Leadership award, People to People, Seoul, Republic of Korea, 2005, Internat. Pres. award, People to People, Berlin, 2007, Disting. Svc. award, Coll. NJ, 2005. Mem.: ASCD, Nat. Coun. Social Studies, Assn. for Edn. Tchrs. in Sci., Assn. Tchr. Educators, People to People Internat. (bd. dir. Trenton, NJ chpt. 1995—98, chpt. pres. 1998—, NJ del. various confs., internat. trustee 2000—), Am. Air Mus. in Britain (founding mem.), Torch Club Internat., the Trenton Club (bd. dir. 1998—2001, v.p. 2001—02, pres. 2002—03). Home: 20 Lawrenceville-Penning Rd Lawrenceville NJ 08648-1648 E-mail: ljmt.afa@att.net.

THAROOR, SHASHI, former international organization official, writer; b. London, Mar. 9, 1956; came to the US, 1975; s. Chandran and Lily (Menon) T.; m. Tilottama Mukherii, 1977 (div. 2000); children: (twins) Ishaan, Kanishk; m. Christa Giles, 2007. BA with honors, Delhi U., 1975; MA, Tufts U., 1976, MA in Law and Diplomacy, 1977, PhD, 1978. External affairs officer UN High Commn. for Refugees, Geneva, 1978-81, head sub-office and rep. Singapore, 1981-84, dep. chief of secretariat Geneva, 1984—87, exec. asst. to the dep. high commr., 1987-89; spl. asst. to under-sec. gen. for peace-keeping UN, NYC, 1989—96, prin. officer dept. peace-keeping ops., 1995-96, exec. asst. to the sec-gen., 1997-98, dir. comm. and spl. projects, Office of Sec.-Gen., 1998—2001, interim head of dept. of pub. info., 2001—02, under-sec. gen. for comm. & pub. info., 2002—07; writer Arcade Publishing, NYC. Author: Reasons of State, 1981, The Great Indian Novel, 1989 (Best Book of the Yr., Fedn. Indian Pubs. 1990, Best Book Eurasian region Commonwealth Writers prize 1990), Show Business, 1992, India: From Midnight to the Millennium, 1997, Riot, 2001, (with M.F. Husain) Kerala: God's Own Country, 2002, (short story collection) The Five-Dollar Smile, 1990, 2d edit., 93, Nehru: The Invention of India, 2003, Bookless in Baghdad, 2005, The Elephant, the Tiger and the Cellphone, 2007; columnist The Hindu, Times of India; contbg. editor, Newsweek Internat.; book reviewer Washington Post, The NY Times, others; contbr. articles to profl. jours. Mem. adv. bd. Vijay Amritraj Found.; bd. dirs. Fletcher Sch. Law and Diplomacy; advisor Internat. Com. of Red Cross, Geneva; with Coca-Cola Found., India. Named Global Leader of Tomorrow, World Econ. Forum, Davos, Switzerland, 1998. Fellow NY Inst. of the Humanities; mem. Internat. Inst. Strategic Studies (keynote spkr. 1995), Indian Internat. Ctr. Hindu. Avocations: reading, writing, cricket, theater.

THARP, MICHAEL D., medical educator; b. Columbus, Ohio, July 4, 1949; m. Robin Tharp, June 21, 1975; children: Kristin Jane Cornejo, Kelly Anne, Kathryn Pauline. BA, Ohio Wesleyan U., 1971; MD, Ohio State Med. Coll., 1974. Bd. cert. internal medicine Am. Bd. Internal Medicine, 1977, bd. cert. dermatology Am. Bd. Dermatology, 1980. Rsch. fellowship Duke Hosp., Durham, NC, 1979—80; resident Parkland Hosp., Dallas, 1974—77, Duke Hosp., Durham, NC, 1977—79; asst. prof. dermatology U. Tex. Southwestern Med. Sch., Dallas, 1980—85, assoc. prof. dermatology, 1985—87, U. Pitts. Sch. Medicine, Pitts., 1987—90, asst. prof. dermatology, 1990—95; prof., chair dept. dermatology Rush U. Med. Ctr., Chgo., 1995—. Editor: (book) Adult and Pediatric Dermatology, Dermatology Therapy. Mem.: Dermatology Found. (sec. 2005, v.p. 2009), Am. Profs. Dermatology (pres. 2008—), Soc. Investigative Dermatology (v.p. 2005—06), Am. Acad. Dermatology (bd. dirs. 2005—09), Chgo. Dermatol. Soc. (pres. 2002—03). Office: Rush U Med Ctr 707 S Wood St Annex 220 Chicago IL 60612 Office Fax: 312-942-7778.

THARP, ROLAND GEORGE, psychology professor; b. Galveston, Tex., June 6, 1930; s. Oswald Roland and Berma Lucille (Keefer) T.; m. Stephanie Dalton; children: Donald Martin, Thomas Roland, David Michael, Julie. Student, Middlebury Coll., 1956-60; BA cum laude, U. Houston, 1957; MA, U. Mich., 1958, PhD, 1961. Cert. Am. Bd. Examiners in Profl. Psychology. Reporter Tex. City Sun, 1946-47; mgr. Tharp Lumber Co., LaMarque, Tex., 1949-54; intern VA Hosp., Menlo Park, Calif., 1960; asst. prof. U. Ariz., Tucson, 1961-65, assoc. prof., 1965-68; prof., dir. clin. studies, dir. multicultural ctr. for higher edn. U. Hawaii, Honolulu, 1968-87; provost and v.p. for acad. affairs U.S. Internat. U., San Diego, 1987-89; prof. edn., psychology U. Calif., Santa Cruz, 1990—, rsch. prof. Berkeley; dir. Nat. Rsch. Ctr. for Diversity, 1995—; prof. U. Greenland, 2006—. Dir. Ctr. for Rsch. on Edn., Diversity and Excellence, 1996—; prin. investigator Kamehameha Early Edn. Program, Honolulu, 1969-89; field selection officer Peace Corps, Washington, 1965-67. Author: (poetry) Highland Station, 1978; co-author: Behavior Modification in the Natural Environment, 1969, Self-Directed Behavior, 1980, Rousing Minds to Life, 1988, Teaching Transformed, 2000; writer, producer, dir. film Scenes from the Life, 1981 (Purchase prize The Contemporary Mus. 1981). Mem. Bd. Psychologist Examiners, Ariz., 1964-67; pres. Hawaii Literary Arts Coun., Honolulu, 1982. Robert Frost fellow Middlebury Coll., 1960; recipient Am. Film Mag. award for filmmaking Hawaii Internat. Film Festival, 1990, Grawemeyer award edn., 1993. Mem. Am. Ednl. Rsch. Assn., Am. Anthropol. Assn. Episcopalian. Avocations: tennis, painting. Office: 560 N St SW Apt N702 Washington DC 20024-4621 E-mail: tharp@ucsc.edu.

THARP, STEPHEN JOHN, organist, pianist, artist; b. Chgo., Apr. 12, 1970; s. Michael John and Arlene Erna (Scheer) Tharp; m. Maria Helena Vieira Dacosta Catarro, Oct. 1, 2004. BA in Music Performance magna cum laude, Ill. Coll., Jacksonville, 1992; MusM in Music Performance, Northwestern U., Chgo., 1994. Cert. performance Internat. Acad. Organists, The Netherlands, 1990. Asst. organist Christ Ch., Des Plaines, Ill., 1984—88; organist The Edgebrook Ch., Chgo., 1984—88, First Presbyn. Ch., Jacksonville, 1988—90, First United Meth. Ch., Springfield, Ill., 1990—93; prin. organist Alice Millar Chapel, Northwest U., 1993—94; organist, choirmaster Holy Trinity Episcopal Ch., Skokie, Ill., 1994—95; organist, dir. concerts St. Patrick's Cathedral, NYC, 1995—97; assoc. organist St. Bartholomew's Ch., NYC, 1998—2004; artist in residence St. Peter's Episcopal Ch., Perth Amboy, NJ, 2006—07, Grace Episcopal Ch., NYC, 2007—. Guest tchr. Yale U., New Haven, 2001—; guest instr. Westminster Choir Coll., Princeton, NJ, 2005—06, Bochum U., Germany, 2004. Musician (solo organ): (CD) Stephen Tharp-Debut in Europe, 2001, Stephen Tharp at Sulpice, Paris, France, 2002, Marcel Dupré: The Stations of the Cross, 2005, The Complete Organ Works of Jeanne Demessieux, 2007; composer: (commissioned musical) Easter Fanfares, 2005, performer more than 1300 concerts including 34 world tours. Mem.: Am. Guild Organists, St. Wilfried Club (NYC). Episcopal. Achievements include being the official organist for the papal event with his holiness Pope Benedict XVI during his apostolic journey to the US in April 2008. Avocations: tennis, wine tasting, films, walking. Personal E-mail: stephen.tharp@yahoo.com.

THARPE, DON I., foundation administrator; b. Jan. 1952; m. Linda Tharpe; children: Justin, Adrienne. BS, Murray State U., 1974, MS, 1975; PhD in Edn. Adminstrn., Va. Polytechnic & State U. Dir. trade and vocational edn. Mo. State Dept. Edn.; with Am. Vocational Assn.; dir. profl. programs Assn. of Sch. Bus. Officials Internat., Reston, Va., 1985—89, acting exec. dir., 1989—90, exec. dir., 1990—2002; exec. v.p., COO Coun. on Founds., Washington, 2002—06; pres., CEO Congl. Black Caucus Found., Inc., Washington, 2005—. Former mem. Nat. Policy Bd. for Ednl. Adminstrn. Contbr. articles to profl. jours. Recipient Disting. Alumnus, Murry State U., 2005. Mem.: Am. Soc. Assn. Execs. (former vice chair, fellow), Greater Washington Soc. Assn. Execs., Alpha Phi Alpha. Office: Congl Black Caucus Found 1720 Massachusetts Ave, NW Washington DC 20036 Office Phone: 202-263-2800. Office Fax: 202-775-0773.

THARPE, FRAZIER EUGENE, journalist; b. Panama City, Fla., Jan. 10, 1941; s. Henry Clayton and Margaret Jane (Jenkins) T.; m. Barbara Ann Hembree, Oct. 30, 1971. BA in Polit. Sci. and History, Vanderbilt U., Nashville, 1963. Reporter Miami (Fla.) News, 1963; reporter U.P.I., Atlanta and Columbia, SC, 1964; pub. relations exec. Atlanta, 1965-69; fin. editor Atlanta Constn., 1969-73. Editl. assoc., columnist, 1974-83, columnist Helpline, ConsumerWatch, 1983-98; editor Homefinder, 1999-2002.

THASE, MICHAEL E., psychiatrist; BS in Psychology, Wright State U.; MD, Ohio State U., 1979. Resident & fellow Western Psychiatric Inst. & Clinic, dir. Depression Treatment & Rsch. Program, 1987—, chief adult psychiatry; prof. psychiatry U. Pitts. Med. Ctr. Editor-in-chief Psychopharmacology Bulletin. Mem.: Am. Psychiatric Assn. (Marie Eldredge award). Office: 3811 O'Hara St Pittsburgh PA 15213-2593 Office Phone: 412-624-1000.*

THATCHER, GEORGE ROBERT, banker, writer, columnist; b. Austin, Pa., Sept. 18, 1922; S. Walter Robert and Roberta Estelle (Bernard) T.; widowed; children: Georgia Anne Thatcher Faneca, Janie Estelle Thatcher Holmes, Walter Wimberly. BA, U. Miss., 1948. Pvt. U.S. Army, 1942, infantry maj., 1948, ret., 1952; ptnr. Rand-Thatcher Advt. Agy., Gulfport, Miss., 1948—67; pres. coast divsn. Magnolia Fed. Bank, Gulfport, 1981-92; councilman City of Gulfport, 1989; hon. canon St. Peter's Cathedral, Likoma Island, Malawi, 1997—; daily columnist The Sun Herald, Biloxi, Miss., 1997—; commentator Pub. Radio Miss., 2006. Author: Misrepresentation in MS, 1954, Beach Walks, 1998, 2d edit., 1999, Beach Walks II, 2000, Scenes From the Beach, 2003, A Decade of Beach Walks, 2008. Chmn. Miss. Arts Commn., 1991-2000. Decorated Bronze Star; named Outstanding Citizen Miss. Coast C. of C., 1998. Mem. Gulfport Rotary Club (pres. 1995-96, Citizen of Yr. 1993, Paul Harris fellow), Century Club (pres.), Gulfport Yacht Club, Coast Tennis Club, Great So. Club. Republican. Roman Catholic. Avocations: tennis, chess, reading, classical music. Home: 1302 2nd St Gulfport MS 39501-2219 Office: Regions Bank 2200 14th St Gulfport MS 39501 E-mail: fishcrow@aol.com.

THATCHER, WAYNE, geophysicist; b. Montreal, Quebec, Canada, May 23, 1942; s. Ralph and Bertha Waldon Thatcher; m. Mary Ellen Farwell; 1 child, Iain. PhD, Calif. Inst. Tech., Pasadena, 1971. Geophysicist US Geol. Survey, Menlo Park, Calif., 1971—. Vis. prof. geophysics Calif. Inst. Tech., Pasadena, 1998. Fellow: Am. Geophys. Union (Whitten medal 2004). Office: US Geol Survey Ms/977 345 Middlefield Rd Menlo Park CA 94025 Business E-Mail: thatcher@usgs.gov.

THATTASSERY, EMIL GEORGE, cardiologist; b. Washington, Mar. 19, 1977; s. Pious and Jacie Thattassery. BS, Johns Hopkins U., 1997; MD, U. Md., 2003; MPH, Columbia U., 2006. Rsch. intern Walter Reed Army Inst. Rsch., Washington, 1993—97; software engr. Genesis Med. Tech., Balt., 1998—99, Trilogy Software, Austin, Tex., 1999; resident in internal medicine Northwestern Meml. Hosp., Chgo., 2003—06; mem. rapid response team Meml. Sloan Kettering Cancer Ctr., Chgo., 2006—07; cardiology fellow Emory Med. Ctr., Atlanta, 2007—. Contbr. articles to med. jours. Pres. Cir. K, Johns Hopkins U., Balt., 1996—97; pres. student coun. U. Md. Med. Sch., Balt., 2000—01. Mem.: AMA, Tau Beta Pi. Office: Emory Med Ctr Atlanta GA 30308 Personal E-mail: ethat001@hotmail.com.

THAU, WILLIAM ALBERT, lawyer; b. St. Louis, June 22, 1940; s. William Albert and Irene Elizabeth (Mundy) T.; m. Jane Hancock, Sept. 7, 1961; children: William Albert, Caroline Jane, Jennifer Elizabeth. BS in Indsl. Mgmt., Ga. Inst. Tech., 1962; JD, U. Tex., 1965. Bar: Tex. 1965. Ptnr., head of real estate sect. Jenkens & Gilchrist, Dallas, 1965—2002. Chmn. real estate developer/builder symposium S.W. Legal Found, 1975-79; bd. dirs. Southwestern Film Archives, So. Meth. U.; lectr. Practicing Law Inst. Author: Negotiating the Purchase and Sale of Real Estate, 1975, Non-Recourse, 2004, The Source Code, 2006; editor Tex. State Bar Assn. Newsletter on Real Estate, Probate and Trust Law, 1978-81; contbr. articles to Real Estate Rev., 1983—. Bd. dirs. St. Philips Sch., Dallas, 1988, So. Meth. U.; trustee Dallas Can. Acad., 1987-88. Mem. ABA, Tex. State Bar Assn. (chmn. real estate, probate, trust law sect.), Am. Coll. Real Estate Lawyers. Republican. Office: 140 Tanglewood Rd Saint Simons Island GA 31522 Personal E-mail: wthau@aol.com.

THAUNG, U, journalist; b. Nyaung Oo, Myanmar, Oct. 4, 1926; came to U.S., 1977; s. Thar Phan and Daw Oak; m. Mya Mya Sein, Apr. 23, 1957 (div. Apr. 1964); children: Mi Khine, Po Htin, Mi Kyine; m. Tin Tin Win Thaung, Feb. 19, 1971; children: Aung, Min. Student, Rangoon U., 1949. Reporter Burma Times, Rangoon, 1947-50, news editor, 1950-51, chief editor, 1951-57; founder, chief editor Mirror Daily, Rangoon, 1957-64; political prisoner, 1964-67; dep. dir. min. info. Govt. Burma, 1967-77; feature writer The Missourian, Washington, Mo., 1977-81; mgr. Intercontinental Printing, Inc., Pompano Beach, Fla., 1981-93; chief editor New Era Jour., Bangkok, 1993—; editl. cons. Radio Free Asia, Washington, 1997—. Author: Tale of Women, 1954, Plays by Aung Bala, 1960, Music from the Cave and Romance, 1962, Don't Sleep Humors, 1965, As I Heard, 1966, Smart Man, 1966, People's World, 1966, Practical Buddhism, 1967, Go Beyond, 1967, Forget All, 1967, Historical Plays, 1968, He Who Seeks Find, 1968, Tell All I Heard, 1968, Soviet Humors, 1968, On Politics, 1969, From Burma Times to Mirror Daily, 1971, From Mandalay to Moscow, 1975, To Washnigton, 1975, U Ne Win and His Cronies, 1990, General Ne Win's Militarism, 1994, A Journalist, A General and an Army in Burma, 1995, A Journalist and a Queen, 1999, Village of Evil, 1999, To Be Continued, 1999, practical Buddhism, 2002; prodr. 4 screenplays, radio plays; contbr. articles to profl. jours. Named one of 50 Heroes of the past 50 years, Internat. Press Inst., 2000. Buddhist. Avocation: reading. Home: 4959 NW 48th Ter Tamarac FL 33319-3638 E-mail: thaung@prodigy.net.

THAW, DAVID BERNARD, law educator; s. Jack Thaw. BA in Govt. & Politics, U. Md., 2003; BS in Computer Sci., U. Md., College Park, 2003; MA in Polit. Sci., UC Berkeley, Berkeley, Calif., 2004; JD, UC Berkeley Law, Boalt Hall, Calif., 2008; PhD student in Info. Mgmt. & Sys., UC Berkeley, Calif. Cert.: Conn. (attorney-at-law) 2008, NY 2009. Law intern hon. victor marrero, USDJ U.S. Dist. Ct. So. Dist., NYC, 2006; summer assoc. Dewey & LeBoeuf LLP, NYC, 2007; vis. fellow, info. soc. project Yale Law Sch., New Haven, 2008—. Recipient Departmental Honors award, U. Md., 2003; fellowship, UC Berkeley Dept. Polit. Sci., 2003—04, UC Berkeley Sch. Info., 2004—05. Mem.: NY State Bar Assn., Conn. Bar Assn., Phi Beta Kappa, Omicron Delta Kappa, Zeta Psi. Achievements include patents pending for online system for facilitating collaboration among non-technical users. Office: Yale Law Sch PO Box 208215 New Haven CT 06520

THAXTON, JESSIE J., elementary school educator; d. Jesse Edwin and Rebecca Hutto Jordan; children: Kyle Rawls, Jordan Adams. BA, Coker Coll., 1974; M of Elem. Edn., U. S.C., 1990. Tchr. Timmerman Sch., Columbia, SC, 1974—78, 1982—86, Satchel Ford Elem. Sch., 1986—; cooperating tchr. Columbia Coll., 1995—. Mem.: NEA. Republican. E-mail: jthaxton@richlandone.org.

THAYANITHY, VENUGOPAL, biologist, geneticist, researcher; s. Thayanithy and Vijayalakshmi Maniagar; m. Madhumathi Venugopal, Dec. 11, 2003; 1 child, Neya Venugopal. BSc, Madura Coll., India, 1992; MSc, Madurai Kamaraj U., India, 1994, PhD, 2002. Jr. rsch. fellow Madurai Kamaraj U., 1995—97, sr. rsch. fellow, 1997—2000, rsch. assoc., 2000—02; postdoctoral rschr. U. Mass. Med. Sch., Worcester, 2002—. Author (book chapter) Fish Genetics and Aquaculture; referee, peer reviewer: Jour. Fish Biology; contbr. chapters to books. Student voluntary worker Nat. Svc. Scheme, Madurai, 1989—92. Recipient Srinivasan Endowment award for Academic Excellence, Madura Coll., 1991—92; Jr. Rsch. fellow, U. Grants Commn., India, 1995—97, Sr. Rsch. fellow, 1997—2000, Rsch. Assoc. fellow, Indian Coun. Agr. Rsch., 2000—02, Post-Doctoral Rsch. fellow, U. Mass. Med. Sch., 2002—07. Mem.: AAAS (assoc. Excellence in Sci. Program award 2007), Index Copernicus, Comparative Biochemistry and Physiology (hon.; referee, peer reviewer Marine Biotech. and Med. Sci. Monitor jour. 2006), Internat. Brain Rsch. Orgn. (assoc.), Soc. Biol. Chemists India (life), V.O. Chidambaram Hostel Rsch. Scholars (hon.; gen. sec. 1999—2000). Achievements include research in isolated and characterized growth hormone genes of economically important Asian fish species; generated transgenic technology for the Indian major carps; generated fast growing auto-transgenic Indian major carp Labeo rohita by gene manipulation and transgenesis; isolated and studied the transposable elements from economically important Indian fishes. Home: 2000 Knapp St Saint Paul MN 55108 Office Phone: 612-626-2785. Personal E-mail: thayanithy.venugopal@gmail.com.

THAYER, CHARLES JAMES, investment banker; b. Abilene, Kans., Feb. 28, 1944; s. Bruce V. and Neoma (Obermeyer) T.; 1 child, Travis J. Grad., U. Kans., 1967. Exec. v.p., CFO Citizens Fidelity Bank, Louisville, 1977—87; exec. v.p. fin. PNC Bank Corp., Pitts., 1987—89; chmn., mng. dir. Chartwell Capital Ltd., Ft. Lauderdale, Fla., 1989—; interim chmn., CEO Sunbeam-Oster, Providence, 1993. Adv. dir. Louisville Cmty. Devel. Bank, 1997—, Keefe Mgrs., Inc., NYC, 1990-02; chmn. Am. Assn. Bank Dirs., 2007-; bd. dirs. BB&T Bank, Fla., 2004-06, Republic Bank, St. Petersburg, Fla., 1999-04 Trustee Cystic Fibrosis Found., Washington, 1980—; chmn. Cystic Fibrosis Svcs., Washington, 1994-04. Mem. Nat. Assn. Corp. Dirs. (Fla. bd. dirs. 2005). Avocation: sailing. Office: Chartwell Capital Ltd 420 Isle Of Capri Dr Fort Lauderdale FL 33301-2438 Business E-Mail: cjt@chartwellcapital.com.

THAYER, JANE HILLIS, psychologist; b. NYC, June 17, 1930; d. Harold Lee and Ruth Evelyn (Caldwell) Hillis; m. Roger Eugene Thayer, June 16, 1951; children: Peggy, David, Cynthia. BA in Psychology, Cornell U., 1952; MA in Clin. Psychology, George Washington U., 1956, PhD in Clin. Psychology, 1969. Lic. psychologist, D.C. Intern in psychology St. Elizabeth's Hosp., Washington, 1965-66, intern in rsch., 1966-68; staff psychologist Alexandria Cmty. Mental Health Ctr., 1968-71, acting chief psychologist, 1969-70; pvt. practice Washington, 1971—96, Martha's Vineyard, 1999—. Pres. Gestalt Inst., Washington, 1973; exec. bd. Practicing mediator Martha's Vineyard Mediation Program, 1999; cons. in field. Co-author (with Peggy Thayer): Elderescence - The Gift of Longevity, 2005. Mem. APA, Sigma Xi, Psi Chi. Democrat. Office Phone: 508-693-3490. Personal E-mail: rjthayer@earthlink.net.

THAYER, JONATHAN W., energy executive; married; 2 children. BA in History cum laude, Middlebury Coll., Vt.; MBA, Harvard U., Cambridge, Mass. Project officer Uganda AIDS Project, Mukono, 1994—95; positions in fin. SBC Warburg Dillon Read, Inc., Deutsche Bank Securities, Inc.; dir. investor rels. Constellation Energy Group, Inc., Balt., 2002—04, v.p., mng. dir. corp. strategy & devel., 2004—08, treas., 2008, sr. v.p., CFO, 2008—. Eagle scout Boy Scouts America; bd. mem. United Way Ctrl. Md., Family and Children Services Ctrl. Md. Office: Constellation Energy Group 100 Constellation Way Baltimore MD 21202 Office Phone: 410-470-2800.*

THAYER, M. PATRICIA, lawyer; b. 1954; BA magna cum laude, Harvard U., 1976; JD cum laude, Harvard Law Sch., 1979. Bar: Calif., lic.: Supreme Ct., US Patent & Trademark Office. Law clk. to Hon. Mary Johnson Lowe US Dist. Ct. (so. dist.) NY; shareholder Howard, Rice, Nemerovski, Canaday, Falk & Rabkin, San Francisco, 1986—99, Heller Ehrman LLP, San Francisco, 1999—2008; ptnr. Orrick, Herrington & Sutcliffe LLP, San Francisco, 2009—, mem. Internat. Property Group. Chmn. Sedona Conf. on Patent Litigation, 2003—04. Named to Top 50 IP Litigators in Calif., The Daily Jour., 2008, Top 75 Women Litigators in Calif., 2008. Mem.: Assn. Bus. Trial Laywers, State Bar Calif. (former chmn. Intellectual Property Section 1996—97). Office: Orrick Herrington & Sutcliffe LLP 405 Howard St San Francisco CA 94105 Office Phone: 415-773-4575. E-mail: pthayer@orrick.com.*

THAYER, RUSSELL, III, air transportation executive; b. Phila., Dec. 5, 1922; s. Russell and Shelby Wentworth (Johnson) T.; m. Elizabeth Wright Mifflin, June 12, 1947; children: Elizabeth, Dixon, Shelby, Samuel, David. Student, St. George's Sch., 1937-42; AB, Princeton U., 1949. Mgmt. trainee Eastern Air Lines, 1949-52; mgr. cargo sales and service Am. Airlines, Los Angeles, 1952-63; v.p. mktg. Seaboard World Airlines, NYC, 1963-70; sr. v.p. Braniff Airways, Inc., Dallas, 1970-72, exec. v.p., 1972-77, pres., chief oper. officer, 1977-80, vice chmn., 1981-82; dir. (Braniff Airways, Inc.), 1971-82; v.p. Pan Am. World Airways, Inc., NYC, 1982-84, sr. v.p., 1984-88, Airline Econs., Inc., Washington, 1988—, also bd. dirs., 1988—. Dir. Ft. Worth Nat. Bank, 1977-82; vice chmn. Airline Capital Assn; bd. dirs. Kiwi Internat. Airlines, Inc., World Aux. Power Corp. Mem. Trinity Ch. Ushers Guild, Princeton, N.J., 1968—; Trustee Aviation Hall of Fame N.J. Served with USAAF, 1942-45, ETO. Decorated D.F.C., Air medal with 11 oak leaf clusters. Mem. Am. Aviation Hist. Assn., Air Force Assn., Exptl. Aircraft Assn., Nat. Aeros. Assn., Ivy Club (Princeton), Pretty Brook Tennis Club (Princeton), Bay Head (N.J.) Yacht Club, Nassau Club (Princeton), Princeton Club (N.Y.C.), Phila. Club, Delta Psi. Home: Hulfish St Apt 17-I Princeton NJ 08542-3706 Office: Airline Capital Associates Inc 545 5th Ave Rm 1009 New York NY 10017-3655

THAYER, WALTER RAYMOND, retired internist; b. Providence, Apr. 16, 1929; s. Walter Raymond and Esther Veronica (Hulme) Thayer; m. Meredith Marks, 1998; children from previous marriage: Walter, Ida Marie, Peter. BS, Providence Coll., 1950; MD, Tufts U., 1954. Intern R.I. Hosp., Providence, 1955-57; sr. asst. surgeon USPHS/NIH, Bethesda, Md., 1956-58; resident Georgetown U. Hosp., Washington, 1958-59; fellow in gastroenterology Sch. Medicine Yale U., New Haven, 1959-61, rsch. fellow in internal medicine, 1961, from instr. to asst. prof. medicine, 1960-65; from assoc. prof. to prof. medicine Sch. Medicine Brown U., Providence, 1965—2004; prof. emeritus biol. and med. scis. Brown U. Sch. Medicine, Providence, 2005—; ret., 2005. Rschr. Wenner Glen Inst., Stockholm, 1972—73, Mayo Clinic, Rochester, Minn., 1980, Colo. State Coll., Ft. Collins, 1987; mem. Cancer Control Bd., RI, 1976—77; nat. sci. adv. bd. Crohn's and Colitis Found., Inc., 1978—83, rsch. and tgn. awards com., 1978—85, chmn., 1980—85, chmn. med. adv. bd. R.I. chpt., 1983; adv. bd. Nat. Coop. Crohn's Disease Study Group, 1981—83. Editl. reviewer: Gastroenterology, Digestive Disease and Scis.; contbr. articles to profl. jours. Sr. asst. surgeon USPHS, 1956—58. Recipient Humanitarian of Yr. award, New Eng. chpt. Crohn's and Colitis Found., Keen award, Brown U. Sch. Medicine, 2001; fellow NSF, 1972—73. Fellow: ACP (Hamolsky Achievement award, RI Chpt. 2007), Am. Coll. Gastroenterology (gov. R.I. 1996—98); mem.: Providence Med. Soc., R.I. Gastroenterology Soc., R.I. Med. Soc., Am. Fedn. Clin. Rsch., Am. Gastroenterol. Assn. (Clinician of the Yr. award 1999). Avocations: cross country skiing, birdwatching, gardening. Home: 65 Bullocks Point Ave Riverside RI 02915-5318

THÉBERGE, JEAN, biophysicist; b. Rouyn-Noranda, Qué., Can., 1974; s. Félix and Marthe Théberge; m. Melanie Lyn Brimson, May 2007; 1 child, Luc-Étienne Brimson. BSc in Physique, U. Montréal, Que., 1996, MSc in Physique, 1998; PhD in Med. Biophysics, U. Western Ont., London, Can., 2004; postdoc., Harvard Med. Sch., Cambridge, Mass., 2006. Postdoc. rsch. fellow McLean Hosp., Belmont, Mass., 2004—06; physicist St. Joseph's Health Care, London, 2006—. Asst. prof. U. Western Ont., 2006—. Pub. lectr. Librs., London, 2006. Recipient Young Investigator award, NARSAD, 2008—; New Investigator fellowship, Ont. Mental Health Found., 2008—. Mem.: Internat. Soc. Magnetic Resonance Medicine. Achievements include research in longitudinal studies of schizophrenia with high field magnetic resonance spectroscopy. Avocations: astronomy, chess. Office: St Joseph's Health Care 268 Grosvenor St London ON N6A4V2 Canada

THEBNER, LISA ILENE, pediatrician; b. Oct. 1, 1971; BA in Internat. Rels., Tufts U., Medford, Mass.; MD, SUNY Buffalo, 1999. Cert. in pediat. Am. Bd. Med. Specialties. Resident Montefiore Med. Ctr., Bronx; pediatrician NY Presbyn./Weill Cornell, NYC, Montefiore Med. Ctr., Schneider Children's Hosp. at North Shore, Great Neck, NY, West End Pediatrics, NYC. Office: West End Pediatrics 450 West End Ave New York NY 10024 Office Phone: 212-769-3070.

THE EDGE, (DAVID HOWELL EVANS), musician; b. Ireland, Aug. 8, 1961; children: Holly, Aaron, Blue Angel, Cian. Guitarist U2, 1978—. Albums include U2:3, 1979, Boy, 1980, October, 1981, War, 1983, Under A Blood Red Sky, 1983, Unforgettable Fire, 1984, Wide Awake in America, 1985, Joshua Tree, 1987 (Grammy awards for best rock performance by a duo or group with vocals, album of yr., 1988, MTV Music Video award for viewers choice for With or Without You 1987, best performance music video for Where the Streets Have No Name 1989), Rattle and Hum, 1988 (MTV Music Video award for best video from film for When Love Comes to Town with B.B. King 1989, Grammy award for best rock performance by a duo or group with vocal for Desire 1989), Achtung Baby, 1991 (Grammy award for prodr. yr. 1991, MTV Music Video awards for best group video, best spl. effects in a video for Even Better Than the Real Thing 1992), Zooropa, 1993 (Grammy award for alternative album of yr. 1993), Pop, 1997, All That You Can't Leave Behind, 2000 (Grammy awards: album of the year, best pop performance, best rock performance, best rock album, 2001), The Best of 1990-2000, 2002, How to Dismantle an Atomic Bomb, 2004 (Grammy awards: best rock album, album of yr., best rock group performance & song of yr. for Sometimes You Can't Make it On Your Own, best rock song for City of Blinding Lights, 2006), No Line On the Horizon, 2009. Co-founder Music Rising initiative, 2005. U2 named Best-Selling Irish Artist of Yr., World Music Awards, 1993, 1998, 2007, World's Best-Selling Rock Act, World Music awards, 2006; named to VH1: Greatest Artists of Rock & Roll, 1998; co-recipient (with U2) Ambassador of Conscience award, Amnesty Internat., 2005; recipient Brit. Record Industry award for best internat. group, 1988, 89. Achievements include inducted into Rock and Roll Hall of Fame as mem. U2, 2005. Address: Interscope Records 2220 Colorado Ave Santa Monica CA 90404

THEILER, REGAN, obstetrician, gynecologist, educator; b. Osseo, Wis., Oct. 26, 1973; d. Dennis Theiler and Karol Lynne Hausman; life ptnr. Jessica Merryfield. BS, DePaul U., Chgo., 1996; PhD, U. Wis., Madison, 2001, MD, 2003. Resident, ob-gyn. Emory U., Atlanta, 2003—07; asst. prof., ob-gyn. UTMB, Galveston, Tex., 2007—. Contbr. articles to profl. sci. jours. Mem.: AMA, Am. Coll. Ob-Gyn., Am. Soc. Microbiology. Liberal. Avocations: travel, cuisine, fitness. Office: Univ Tex Medical Br 301 University Ave Galveston TX 77555-0587 Office Fax: 409-747-0366. Personal E-mail: rtheiler2000@yahoo.com. Business E-Mail: rntheile@utmb.edu.

THEIN, MAY-WIN L., mechanical engineer, educator; d. San and Wendy Thein. BS in Mech. Engring., Lehigh U., Bethlehem, 1991, MS in Mech. Engring., 1992; PhD in Mech. Engring., Okla. State U., Stillwater, 1999. Campus tutor Lehigh U., 1988—91; kickboxing instr. Matt Randall's Black Belt Acad., Dover, NH, 2004—06; asst. prof. dept Mech. Engring. U. NH., Durham, 1999—2005, aerobics instr., 2000—, assoc. prof. dept. Mech. Engring., 2005—; rsch. asst. CertainTeed Corp., Blue Bell, Pa., 1988—88, asst. engr., 1990—90, BFGoodrich Aerospace, Hatfield, Pa., 1991—91; tchg. asst. Lehigh U., 1991—92, Okla. State U., Stillwater, 1992—97, reach program instr., 1996—96, lectr., 1997—97, rsch. asst., 1997—99. Vice chair student affairs Am. Automatic Control Coun., 2000—02, publicity chair, mem., program com., registration chair, 2006—, newsletter editor, 2006—; program com. Conf. Control Applications, 1999—2000; assoc. editor Internat. Jour. Control and Intelligent Sys., 2002—05. Contbr. articles to numerous profl. jours. (Session Best Paper Award, 2000). Participant, relay life Am. Cancer Soc., Durham, NH, 2006. Fellowship, UK Royal Soc., 2007, Summer Faculty Fellowship, NASA, 2005, grant, NASA Goddard Space Flight Ctr., 2006—, NASA Lunar Surface Nav. grant, 2008, NASA Lunar Navigational Determination Sys. grant, 2008. Mem.: AIAA, IEEE (Control Systems Soc. 2002—06, chair, membership and admissions 2002—06), ASME (chair, grad. student and young profl. com. 2007, Student Travel Grant 2002—05), Soc. Automotive Engrs. Internat., Soc. Women Engrs. (faculty advisor, u. of nh. chpt. 2003), Phi Eta Sigma, Pi Tau Sigma, Tau Beta Pi, Sigma Xi. Avocations: reading, aerobics, sports, puzzles. Office: Univ New Hampshire W117 Kingsbury Hall Durham NH 03824 Office Fax: 603-862-1865. Business E-Mail: mthein@cisunix.unh.edu.

THEIS, PETER FRANK, engineering executive; b. Chgo., Mar. 21, 1937; s. Frank Victor and Hazel (Ericsson) Theis; m. Jill Anne Pendexter, May 9, 1970; children: Juliana, Ethan. BSEE, Yale U., 1958; MBA in Fin., U. Chgo., 1966; JD, Ill. Inst. Tech.-Kent Coll Law, Chgo., 1974; postgrad., U. Stockholm, 1958—59. Bar: Ill. 1975. Engr. ASEA, Ludvika, Sweden, 1959, Signode Corp., Glenview, Ill., 1959-61; importer Internat. Idea, Inc., Chgo., 1961-62; systems analyst Continental Ill. Nat. Bank and Trust, Chgo., 1963-64; sales rep. Honeywell, Inc., Chgo., 1964-68; exec. Morgan Industries, Inc., Chgo., 1968-87; pres. Conversational Voice Techs. Corp., Chgo., Linderhurst, Ill., 1973—91, Theis Rsch., Inc., Gurnee, 1991—. Pres. Conversational Voice Techs. Corp., 1973—91, 1998—; cons. Ill. Tech. Transfer LLC, 1994—; cons., mng. mem. Theis Rsch. & Engring. LLC, 1994—. With N.G. USAF, 1961—66. Mem.: Intellectual Property Creators (bd. dirs. 1993—98), Tech. Exec. Roundtable (bd. dirs. 1992—99). Achievements include patents for voice, telecommunications, speech recognition and turbine engines. Avocations: canoeing, hiking, sailing. Office: Conversational Voice Techs Corp 1914 E Grand Ave Lindenhurst IL 60046 Home Phone: 815-385-5122; Office Phone: 847-265-4901. Personal E-mail: theis@owc.net. Business E-Mail: theis@theisresearch.com.

THEISEN, HENRY J., manufacturing executive; b. 1953; BSChemE, U. Wis. Pres. Curwood Inc., 1998—2003; v.p. ops., pres. high barrier products Bemis Co., Inc., 2002—03, exec. v.p., COO, 2003—07, pres., COO, 2007—08, pres., CEO, 2008—. Bd. dirs. Bemis Co., Inc. Office: Beamis Co Inc One Neenah Ctr 4th Fl Neenah WI 54956 Office Phone: 920-727-4100. Office Fax: 612-376-3150.

THEISMANN, JOE (JOSEPH ROBERT THEISMANN), sportscaster, retired professional football player; b. New Brunswick, NJ, Sept. 9, 1949; s. Joseph James and Olga (Tobias) T.; m. Robin Smith, Dec. 5, 1970 (div.); children: Joseph Winton, Amy Lynn, Patrick James. BA in Sociology, U. Notre Dame, 1971. Quarterback Toronto Argonauts, CFL, 1971-74; quarterback, punt returner Washington Redskins, 1974—78, quarterback, 1978—86; analyst NFL broadcasts CBS, 1987-88, ESPN, 1988—, announcer, Monday Night Football, 2006—07. Pres., CEO JRT Assocs.; tchr. Offense-Def. Football Camp; Superstar participant, 1979-80; mem. Pres.'s Athletic Adv. Com., 1975; active Pres. Nat. Svc. Adv. Com., 1993. Author: Quarter Backing. Mem. corp. bd. Children's Hosp. Nat. Med. Center, Washington; participant benefits for Multiple Sclerosis children's hosps., Armed Forces Christmas benefits. High sch. All-Am. Football, 1967; All-Am. Coll., 1971; Acad.-All-Am.; recipient Brian Picollo award, Bert Bell award, 1982, Cable Ace award, Best Sports Commentator-Analyst, 1994; named NFL MVP, 1983; named to Nat. Football Conf. Pro Bowl Team, 1982-83; Coll. Football Hall of Fame, 2003 Mem. Nat. Football Players Assn. Republican. Methodist. mem. Super Bowl XVII Championship Team, 1983. Office: ESPN 935 Middle St Bristol CT 06010

THEISS, RICHARD EDWARD, electrical engineer, applications engineer; b. Nyack, NY, July 30, 1965; s. Joseph Francis and Lorraine Anita Theiss; m. Janet Grace Heapes, Apr. 9, 1994; children: Steven Richard, Nicole Grace, Andrew Joseph. BSEE, Boston U., 1987; MBA, Iona Coll. Hagen Sch. of Bus., NYC, 1994. Tech. support engr. IPC Automation, Riverdale, NJ, 1987—92; applications engr. LeCroy Corp., Chestnut Ridge, NY, 1992—95, applications engring. supr., 1995—98, product mgr., 1998—2001; sr. applications engr. Boonton Electronics (Wireless Telecom Group Co.), Parsippany, NJ, 2001—05, product mgr., sr. applications engr., 2005—. Lecroy coprorate rep. PXI Sys. Alliance, San Diego, 2000—01. Author: (web seminar) Wireless OEM Design Expo. Coach Monroe Woodbury PTA Basketball, Central Valley, NY, 2002—06; mgr. Monroe (N.Y.) Woodbury Little League, 2004; coach St. Patricks CYO Basketball, Highland Mills, NY, 2005—06. Liberal. Avocations: coaching, running, travel, baseball, football. Home: 7 Country Hollow Highland Mills NY 10930 Office: Boonton Electronics (Wireless Telecom Group Co) 25 Eastmans Rd Parsippany NJ 07054-3702 Business E-Mail: rtheiss@boonton.com.

THEIVAKUMAR, JEYAKUMARY RUBY, lawyer; b. Jaffna, Sri Lanka, Feb. 3, 1960; arrived in US, 1984; d. Sellathurai and Sivapackiam Sivalingam; m. Navaratnam Thevan Theivakumar, June 14; children: Surein, Tharani, Kirrupan. JD, Rutgers U., Newark, NJ, 1987. Cert.: Bklyn. Law Sch. (fgn. lawyer) 1985, bar: NJ 2005. Atty. at law Sri Lanka Law Sch., Colombo, 1984; dir. legal svc. BCC USA, Inc., Monmouth Junction, NJ, 2000—04; pvt. practice Princeton, NJ, 2004—. Mem.: ABA, NJ Bar Assn. Home: 901 Herrontown Rd Princeton NJ 08540 Office: 145 Witherspoon St Ste 10 Princeton NJ 08542 Office Phone: 609-921-7770. Personal E-mail: theivakumar@hotmail.com. Business E-Mail: info@rubyjlaw.com.

THELEN, BRUCE CYRIL, lawyer; b. St. Johns, Mich., Nov. 24, 1951; BA, Mich. State U., 1973; JD, U. Mich., 1977. Bar: NY 1978, Mich. 1980, Ill. 1992. Assoc. Dewey and LeBoeuf LLP, NYC, 1977-80, Dickinson, Wright, Moon, Van Dusen & Freeman, Detroit, 1981-83; ptnr. Dickinson Wright PLLC, Detroit, 1984—. Mem. US Dept. Commerce-Mich. Dist. Export Coun., 1995—. Contbr. articles to profl. jours. Mem. allocation panel, mem. spkrs. bur., chmn. rsch. and info.

svcs. com., mem. strategic planning com. and cmty. leaders coun. United Way Cmty. Svcs., 1987—; mem. Mich. Task Force Internat. Trade, Lansing, 1990, Detroit Com. Fgn. Rels., Greater Detroit-Windsor Japan Am. Soc.; mem. global partnership Mich. Econ. Devel. Corp.; mem. adv. coun. Ctr. Internat. Bus. Edn., U. Mich. Sch. Bus.; mem. JD, LLB adv. bd. U. Detroit, Mercy Sch. Law, U. Windsor Faculty Law. Decorated Order of Merit Germany; named Mich. Internat. Super Lawyer. Mem.: Intellectual Property Owners Assn. (internat. agreements & trade com. mem.), German Am. C. of C. Mich. (pres. 1994—2004, bd. mem. 1994—, chmn. 2004—08), Internat. Inst. Detroit (bd. dirs. 1997—99, v.p. 1999—2000, adv. coun. 2001—), Ill. Bar Assn. (internat. law sect.), Am. Soc. Internat. Law, Internat. Bar Assn. (chmn. fin. aspects internat. sales subcom. 2003—05, vice chmn. internat. sales com. 2006—07, sr. vice chmn. internat. sales com. 2007—), State Bar Mich. (chmn. internat. law sect. 1990—91), NY Bar Assn. (internat. law sect.), Wayne State U. (mem. office Internat. programs, mem. Internat. Bridge Coun. and bd. visitors), Mich. Israel C. of C. (bd. dirs. 1997—2001), German Am. C. of C. Midwest (bd. dirs. 1992—2006), Detroit Regional Chamber (mem. Leadership Detroit VIII program 1986—87, chmn. European mission com. 1991, 1992, mem. export com. 1992—95, mem. exec. com. world trade club and internat. bus. coun. 1992—, chmn. European mission com. 1995, adv. bd. dirs. Detriot Regional Economic Partnership 2007—), French-Am. C. of C. Detroit, Barton Hills Country Club, Detroit Athletic Club, Econ. Club Detroit. Office: Dickinson Wright PLLC 500 Woodward Ave Ste 4000 Detroit MI 48226-3416 Office Phone: 313-223-3624. Business E-Mail: bthelen@dickinsonwright.com.

THELEN, EDMUND, research executive; b. Berkeley, Calif, May 8, 1913; s. Paul and Alice (Arnold) T.; m. Helen Naomi Betton, Oct. 30, 1965; children: Nancy Anne, Joan Arnold Thelen Hanson. BS, U. Calif., Berkeley, 1934. Asst. chemist Certain-Teed Products Corp., Richmond, Calif., 1934-35; chemist O. C. Field Gasoline Corp., Santa Maria, Calif., 1936-41; asst. mgr. Eclipse Pioneer divsn. Bendix Corp., Teterboro, NJ, 1946-47; sr. rsch. chemist Franklin Inst. Rsch. Labs., Phila., 1947-51, mgr. colloids and polymers br., 1951-74, v.p., dir. phys. and life scis. dept., 1974-76, Inst. fellow, sec. com. on sci. and the arts, 1976-82, mem., 1982-2001, emeritus, 2001—. Pres. Safety Surface Corp., 1983-88; mem. Coun. for Delivery of Dental Care, 1970-85; bd. govs. Franklin-Hahnemann Inst. Occupl. and Environ. Health, 1975-80, Mayor's Sci. and Tech. Adv. Com. on Environment, 1973-80; instr. dental medicine Hahnemann Med. Coll. and Hosp., 1964-74; v.p., dir. Pa. Environ. Coun., 1974-85; treas. Home Health Svcs. of Chester County and Vicinity, 1981-86. Co-author: (book) Porous Pavement for Runoff Control, 1978; editor Am. Assn. Ret. Persons, Eastern Chester County newsletter, 1994-97; contbr. papers to tech. publs. Bd. dir. Neighborhood Vis. Nurse Assn., 1987-93. With USN, 1941-45; comdr. USNR, 1941-66. Recipient spl. recognition award Am. Soc. Landscape Archs., 1974. Mem. Franklin Inst., Sierra Club (ea. Pa. group chmn. 1968, Atlantic chpt. vice-chmn. 1971-73, founding chmn. Pa. chpt. 1974), Ret. Officers Assn. (treas. Valley Forge chpt. 1980-85, v.p. 1987, pres. 1988-89, sec. 1994-97), Toastmasters Internat. (dist. gov. 1960-61), Sunday Breakfast Spkr. Club (pres. 1960-61), Sigma Xi, mem., Nat. Resources Defense Coun., Southern Poverty Law Ctr. Home: 658 Davis Ln Wayne PA 19087-5418 Office Phone: 610-687-3958.

THELEN, PHYLLIS B., artist; b. July 28, 1926; d. William James and Mildred Emison (Bonnell) Barnhill; m. Max, Jr. Thelen, Mar. 8, 1952; children: Nancy Rehkopf, Jane Greene, Max, William. BFA, Stephens Coll., Mo., 1946; BA, Conn. Coll., 1948; PhD (hon.), Dominican U., Calif., 2000. Student dir. Calif. state United World Federalists, San Francisco, 1948—50, nat. student dir. NYC, 1950—51; fgn. travel agt. Calif. State Auto (AAA), San Francisco, 1951—52. Dir., pres. Marin Ballet, San Rafael, Calif., 1975—95, Artisan's, Mill Valley, Calif., 1993—95, Art Works Downtown, San Rafael, Calif., 1997—2006. Pres. Cultural Affairs Commn., San Rafael, Calif., 1995—99; gen. plan steering com. City of San Rafael, Calif., 2000—02; mem. Renaissance com. Marin County, Calif. Recipient Hall of Fame award, Woman's Comm., 2000. Avocations: event planning, art. Home: 200 Deer Valley Rd San Rafael CA 94901 Business E-Mail: pbthelen@comcast.net.

THELIN, JOHN ROBERT, historian, educator, researcher; b. West Newton, Mass., Oct. 15, 1947; s. George Willard and Rozalija Katherine (Komarec) T.; m. Anna Sharon Blackburn, June 24, 1978. AB cum laude, Brown U., 1969; MA, U. Calif., Berkeley, 1972, PhD, 1973. Rsch. asst. Brown U., Providence, 1968-69; rschr., lectr. U. Calif., Berkeley, 1972-74; asst. prof. U. Ky., Lexington, 1974-77; asst. dean Pomona Coll., Claremont, Calif., 1977-79; from asst. dir. to rsch. dir. Assn. Ind. Calif. Colls. and Univs., Santa Ana, 1979-81; chancellor prof. Coll. William and Mary, Williamsburg, Va., 1981-93, pres. faculty assembly, 1990-91; prof. higher edn. and philanthropy Ind. U., Bloomington, 1993-96; prof. ednl. policy and history U. Ky., Lexington, 1996—, disting. univ. rsch. prof., 2001—. Vis. prof. grad. sch. Claremont U., 1978—81; vis. scholar U. Calif., Berkeley, 1995; curator Marquandia Soc., 1971—2006; essay rev. editor Rev. of Higher Edn., 1979—91; rsch. cons. NSF, Washington, 1991; mem. faculty senate U. Ky., 1997—; guest faculty Coll. Bus. Mgmt. Inst., 1998—2006; chair social sci. com. Grad. Coun., U.K., 1998—2001; cons. Booz, Allen & Hamilton, 2004—05; rsch. cons. Am. Enterprise Inst., 2005—06; keynote spkr.; spkr. NASPA Nat. Conf., 2007. Author: Higher Education and Its Useful Past, 1982, The Cultivation of Ivy, 1976, Higher Education and Public Policy, 1991, Games Colleges Play, 1994, A History of American Higher Education, 2004; author: (with others) The Old College Try, 1989, One Hundred Classic Books About Higher Education, 2001; assoc. editor (jour.) Higher Edn.: Theory and Rsch., 1983—91, guest columnist Lexington Herald-Leader, 2001. Pres., bd. dirs. United Way, Williamsburg, 1987-89; pres. Friends of Williamsburg Libr., 1989. Grantee Spencer Found., 1989-91, 99-2001, Ky. Humanities Coun., 2003-05, Rsch. grant Aspen Inst., 2008-09; Regents fellow U. Calif., 1972; recipient Outstanding Faculty Rsch. award Coll. of Edn., U. Ky., 2000, Great Tchrs. award U. Ky., 2004, Provost's Tchg. award U. Ky., 2006,Exchange acad. award Nat. Edn. Assn., 2007, Democracy Higher Edn. prize, State Local History Rsch. award Ky. Hist. Soc., 2006; Outstanding Scholar Athlete Alumnus for Ivy League, 2006. Mem. Assn. for Study of Higher Edn. (bd. dirs. 1988-90, keynote spkr. 1994, pres. 1999-2000), Am. Ednl. Rsch. Assn. (Exemplary Rsch. Higher Edn. award 2007), Nat. Coll. Athletic Assn. (rsch. adv. bd. 2007), History of Edn. Soc. (editl. bd. 1988-91), Order of Ky. Cols., Lexington Club, Phi Beta Kappa (Faculty award for advancement of scholarship Alpha of Va. 1986, Alpha of R.I. 1969), Omicron Delta Kappa. Avocations: long-distance running, history of Los Angeles and California, sports history. Home: 1745 Richmond Rd Lexington KY 40502 Office: U Ky Edn Policy Studies Lexington KY 40506-1 Home Phone: 859-269-0125; Office Phone: 859-257-4996. Business E-Mail: jthelin@uky.edu.

THEOBALD, DAVID MARTIN, ecologist, educator; married. PhD, U. Colo., Boulder, 1995. Rsch. scientist Natural Resource Ecology Lab, Ft. Collins, Colo., 1995—2002; asst. prof. Colo. State U., Ft. Collins, 2002—05, assoc. prof., 2005—. Author: (book) GIS Concepts and ArcGIS Methods. David H. Smith Conservation fellowship, Soc. Conservation Biology, 2000—02. Office: Colo State Univ Dept Human Dimensions Fort Collins CO 80523-1480

THEOBALD, EDWARD ROBERT, lawyer; b. Chgo., Feb. 10, 1947; BA, So. Ill. U., 1969; JD, Ill. Inst. Tech., 1974. Bar: Ill. 1974, U.S. Dist. Ct. (no. dist.) Ill. 1974. Asst. state's atty. Cook County, Chgo., 1974-79, supr. felony trial divsn., 1980-81; assoc. Conklin, Leahy & Eisenberg, Chgo., 1977; ptnr. Boharic & Theobald, Chgo., 1981-83, owner, ptnr., 1983—. Legal adv. Sheriff of Cook County, Ill., 1986-89; spl. state's atty. U.S. Dist. Ct. no. dist. Ill., 1989-91, Cook County, Ill., 2002-06; apptd. spl. corp. counsel City of Chgo., 1994. Mem. Parent adv. bd. Downers Grove (Ill.) South H.S., 1992-94. Named Number One Trial Atty. in Felony Trial Divsn. of Office of Cook County State's Atty., Felony Trial Divsn. Suprs., 1979. Mem. ABA (sect. on tort and ins. law, sect. on labor and employment law, chmn. com. on sentencing alternatives young lawyers sect. 1982-83, tort and ins. practice sect., labor and employment law sect.), ATLA, Chgo. Bar Assn. (mem. bd. mgrs. 1985-87, mem. labor and employment law com. 1983—2002, mem. com. on coms. 1990-94, mem. membership com. 1990-95, vice chair judicial evaluation com. 1999-2000), Ill. Bar Assn. Roman Catholic. Office: Three First Nat Plaza 70 W Masdison Ste 2030 Chicago IL 60602 Office Phone: 312-346-9246. Personal E-mail: bears51@aol.com.

THEOBALD, REBECCA BAYLESS, geographer, educator; b. Dayton, Ohio, Aug. 7, 1962; d. George Harold and Charlene Hagberg Bayless; m. Matthew Charles Theobald, May 31, 1986; children: Sarah Rigg, Andrew Alper, Margaret Evelyn. BA, Middlebury Coll., Vt., 1984; MA, U. Colo., Boulder, 2003, PhD, 2007. Assoc. Coletta Brewer & Co., Memphis, 1986—90; coord. Colo. Geog. Alliance, 2008—; asst. prof. adjoint U. Colo., 2008—. Rsch. fellow Assn. Am. Geographers, Washington, 2008. Contbr. articles to profl. jours. Organiser Brussels Childbirth Trust Belgian Schs. Network, 1997—99; co-chair Colo. Springs Dist. Configuration & Use Com., 2007—08; com. mem. Colo. Dept. Edn. Model Content Standards Rev. Com., Denver, 2009; mem. Middlebury Coll. Alumni Assn., 2001—05; mem., pres. Memphis House Inc., 1991—96; mem. Memphis Youth Symphony, 1992—94; chair, pub. rels. com. CASA Pikes Peak Region, Colo. Springs, 2007—. Recipient Dorothy Falk award, U. Colo., 2002; grant, 2002, fellowship, 2005—06, grant, Nat. Geog. Soc., 2009—. Fellow: Salzburg Seminar. Episcopalian. Avocations: travel, cooking. Office: Univ Colo 1420 Austin Bluffs Pkwy Colorado Springs CO 80918 Business E-Mail: rtheobal@uccs.edu.

THEODORE, CRYSTAL, retired artist, educator; b. Greenville, SC, July 27, 1917; d. James Voutsas and Florence Gertrude (Bell) T. AB magna cum laude, Winthrop Coll., 1938; MA, Columbia U., 1942, EdD, 1953; postgrad., U. Ga., 1947. Instr. art Winthrop Coll., 1938-43; prof. art, head dept. Huntingdon Coll., Ala., 1946—52, E. Tenn. State U., 1953-57, Madison Coll., 1967—68; vis. prof. art World Campus Afloat Chapman Coll., Calif., 1967; prof. art James Madison U., Harrisonburg, Va., 1968-83, prof. emeritus, 1983—2009. Contbr. articles to profl. jours.; paintings in regional and nat. art exhbns. Bd. dirs. Rockingham Fine Arts Assn., 1980—85, 1989, Citizens for the Downtown, 1989, Women's Coop. Coun. Harrisonburg and Rockingham County, 1976—79, Valley Coun. of the Arts, 1998—99, Shenandoah Coun. of the Arts, 1996—, pres., 1996—2002; founder OASIS Co-op Gallery, 2000. Lt. topographical intelligence USMC, 1944—46. Gen. Edn. Bd. of Rockefeller Found. fellow, 1952-53; recipient award Carnegie Found. Advancement of Tchg., 1947, 48, 49, 50; Ednl. Found. Program grantee AAUW, 1981-82; rsch. grantee Ednl. Radio and TV Ctr., 1956. Mem.: AAUW (cultural interests rep., nat. dir. 1980—82), Va. Mus., Va. Watercolor Soc., Mensa, Pi Lambda Theta, Eta Sigma Phi, Kappa Pi. Democrat. Lutheran. Home: 150 Bear Wallow Ln Harrisonburg VA 22802-0153

THEODORE, EUSTACE D., educational association administrator, consultant; b. Marietta, Ohio, Aug. 4, 1941; s. Demetrios E. and Nicoletta D. T.; m. Carol Nagy, June 13, 1964; children: Kyle James, Graham Clark. BA, Yale U., New Haven, 1963; MA, Cornell U., Ithaca, NY, 1965, PhD, 1967. Mem. faculty Hollins Coll., Roanoke, Va., 1967-71, Mt. Holyoke Coll., South Hadley, Mass., 1971-72; dean Calhoun Coll., Yale U., New Haven, 1972-81; exec. dir. Assn. Yale Alumni, 1981-97; pres. Coun. for Advancement and Support of Edn., Washington, 1997-2000; prin. eAdvancement.org, 2000—. Mgmt. and ednl. cons., 1965—. Contbr. articles to jours. Office: eAdvancement 1301 21st St NW Washington DC 20036-1503 Home Phone: 202-986-6676; Office Phone: 202-463-7310. Business E-Mail: theodore@eadvancement.org.

THEODORE, JOSE, professional hockey player; b. Sept. 13, 1976; Goaltender Montreal Canadiens, 1995—2006, Colo. Avalanche, 2006—08, Washington Capitals, 2008—. Mem. Team Can., World Cup of Hockey, 2004. Recipient Vezina Trophy, 2002, Hart Meml. Trophy, 2002; named Fredericton's Player of Yr., Am. Hockey League; named to NHL All-Star Game, 2002, 2004. Achievements include being a member of World Cup Champion Team Canada, 2004. Office: Washington Capitals Ste 850 627 N Glebe Rd Arlington VA 22203

THEOFANOUS, THEOFANIS G., engineering educator, consultant; b. Athens, Greece, May 21, 1942; naturalized, US, 1975; s. George T. and Smaro (Voudouris) T.; m. Danae P. Kembe, May 15, 1969; children: George, Lydia. BS in Chem. Engring., Nat. Tech. U., Athens, Greece, 1965; PhD in Chem. Engring., U. Minn., 1969; D in Laaperanta (hon.), U. Finland, 1999. Instr. in chem. engring. U. Minn., Mpls., 1968-69; asst. prof. chem. engring. Purdue U., West Lafayette, Ind., 1969-73, assoc. prof. chem. engring., 1973-74, assoc. prof. nuc. engring., 1974-76, prof. nuc. engring., 1976-85; prof. chem. and nuc. engring. U. Calif., Santa Barbara, 1985—, dir. Ctr. for Risk Studies and Safety, 1985—, prof. mech. and environ. engring., 1994—. V.p. Fauske, Grolmes, Henry & Theofanous, Ltd., Hinsdale, Ill., 1979-81; pres. Theofanous & Co., Inc., Santa Barbara, 1981—; cons. in field. Recipient Ernest Orlando Lawrence Meml. award in nuclear tech., US Dept. of Energy, 1996. Fellow Am. Nuc. Soc.; mem. AIChE, AAAS, NAE. Achievements include finding the mechanism that caused the Sevesco accident; invented a methodology for risk assessment and mgmt. of high-consequence hazzards; contbr. in risk analyses of nuc. reactors and in mitigating the consequence of severe accidents. Office: U Calif Dept Chem Engring Rm 3349 Engineering II Bldg & ERC Santa Barbara CA 93106-5080 Office Phone: 805-893-4900. Office Fax: 805-893-4927. E-mail: theo@theo.ucsb.edu.

THEOHARIDES, THEOHARIS CONSTANTIN, pharmacologist, physician, educator; b. Thessaloniki, Macedonia, Greece, Feb. 11, 1950; s. Konstantinos A. and Marika (Krava) T.; m. Efthalia I. Triarhou, July 10, 1981; children: Niove, Konstantinos. Diploma with honors, Anatolia Coll., 1968; BA in Biology, History of Sci. and Med., Yale U., 1972, MS in Immunology, 1975, MPhil in Endocrinology, 1975, PhD in Pharmacology, 1978; postgrad., Tufts U., Harvard U. Asst. in rsch. biology Yale U., New Haven, 1968—71, asst. in rsch. pharmacology, 1973—78, spl. instr. modern Greek, 1974, 77, exec. sec. univ. senate, 1976—78, rsch. assoc. faculty clin. immunology, 1978—83; asst. prof. biochemistry and pharmacology Tufts U., Boston, 1983—88, co-dir. med. pharmacology curriculum, 1983—85, 1983—85, dir. med. pharmacology, 1985—93, assoc. prof. pharmacology, biochemistry and psychiatry, 1989—94, dir. grad. pharmacology, 1994—2000, prof. pharmacology and internal medicine, 1995—, prof. biochemistry, 2002—. Vis. faculty Aristotelian U. Sch. Medicine, Thessaloniki, 1979; trustee Anatolia Coll., 1984-85; clin. pharmacologist Commonwealth Mass. Drug Formulary Commn., 1985—; trainee internal medicine and allergy Tufts-New Eng. Med. Ctr., 1986-93; co-chmn. neuro-immunology 2d and 3d World Conf. on Inflammation, Monte Carlo, 1986, 89; mem. internat. adv. bd. 4th, 5th, 6th and 7th World Conf. on Inflammation, Geneva, 1991, 93, 95, 97; spl. cons. Min. of Health, Greece, 1993-95; mem. supreme spl. sci. health coun. Hellenic Republic, 1998—; chmn. Internat. Com. to Upgrade Med. Edn. in Greece, 1994; bd. dirs., spl. cons. Inst. Pharm. Rsch. & Tech., Athens, 1994-2002; mem. Supreme Health Bd.; mem. Nat. Pub. Health Coun. Hellenic Republic, 2003—; vis. prof. Athens U., 2006; spl. advisor Allergy Clin. Rsch. Ctr., Ahikon Hosp., Athens U., 2006—. Author books on pharmacology; mem. editorial bd. numerous jours.; contbr. articles to profl. jours.; patentee in field. Recipient Theodore Buyler award, Yale U., 1972, George Papanicoalou Grad. award, 1977, Med. award, Hellenic Med. Soc. N.Y., 1979, 1983, M.C. Winternitz prize in pathology, Yale U., 1980, Disting Svc. award, Tufts U. Alumni Assn., 1986, Spl. Faculty Recognition award, Tufts U. Med. Sch., 1987, 1988, Boston Mayor Menino Cmty. Svc. award, 1998, Oliver Smith award, 1999, Archon of Ecunemical Patriarchate of Christian Orthodox Ch., 2000, George Papnikolase award, 2003. Mem. AMA, AAUP, AAAS, European Acad. Allergology and Clin. Immunology, Am. Acad. Allergy, Asthma, Immunology, Hellenic Biochem. and Biophys. Soc., N.Y. Acad. Scis., Am. Inst. History Pharmacy, Soc. Health and Human Values, Am. Assn. History Medicine, Am. Soc. Cell Biology, Soc. Neurosci., Am. Fedn. Clin. Rsch., Conn. Acad. Arts and Scis., Am. Soc. Pharmacology and Exptl. Therapeutics, Hellenic Soc. Cancer Rsch., Hellenic Soc. Med. Chemistry, Internat. Soc. Immunopharmacology, Am. Soc. Microbiology, Am. Assn. Immunologists, Internat. Soc. History of Medicine, Mass. Med. Soc., N.E. Hellenic Med. Soc. (sec. 1984-85, v.p. 1985-86, 94-96, pres. 1986-87), Hellenic Sci. Assn. Boston (bd. dirs. 1985), Internat. Anatolia Alumni Assn. (sec. 1984-85), Alpha Omega Alpha, Sigma Xi. Achievements include research on mechanisms of release of secretory products: immunopharmacology, membrane functions of polyamines; pathophysiology of mast cells in neuroimmunoendocrine diseases exacerbated by stress such as irritable bowel syndrome, interstitial cystitis, psoriasis, migraines and multiple sclerosis. Home: 14 Parkman St Apt 2 Brookline MA 02446-3802 Office: Tufts U Sch Med 136 Harrison Ave Boston MA 02111-1817 Office Phone: 617-636-6866. Business E-Mail: theoharis.theoharides@tufts.edu.

THEOHARIS, ATHAN GEORGE, history professor; b. Milw., Aug. 3, 1936; s. George A. and Helen M. (Konop) T.; m. Nancy Artinian, Aug. 21, 1966; children: Jeanne, George, Elizabeth. AB, U. Chgo., 1956, AM, 1959, PhD, 1965. Instr. Tex. A&M U., College Station, 1962-64; asst. prof. Wayne State U., Detroit, 1964-68; assoc. prof. CUNY, SI, 1968-69; assoc. prof. history Marquette U., Milw., 1969—76, prof., 1976—2006, emeritus, 2006—. Cons. select com. on intelligence activities U.S. Senate, Washington, 1975-76; cons. Nat. Archives FBI Records Task Force, Washington, 1980-81. Author: Seeds of Repression, 1972, Spying on Americans, 1978, The Boss, 1988, Chasing Spies, 2002, The FBI and American Democracy, 2004, The Quest for Absolute Security, 2007; also authored 14 other books. Mem. bd. dirs. ACLU-Wis., MIlw., 1975—. Recipient hon. mention Gavel award ABA, 1972, Outstanding Reference Source award database user sect. ALA, 1998, Haggerty award for rsch. excellence, 2002; 18 rsch. grants, Eunice Edgar Lifetime Achievement award ACLU, WI, 2006. Fellow Wis. Acad. Scis., Arts. and Letters; mem. Am. Hist. Assn. (nat. com. 1990-92), Orgn. Am. Historians (chmn. nat. com. 1980-82, Binkley-Stephenson award 1979), Am. Polit. Sci. Assn. Democrat. Greek Orthodox. Avocations: playing basketball, fan of professional and college sports. Home: 8527 N Manor Ln Fox Point WI 53217 Office: Marquette U PO Box 1881 Milwaukee WI 53201-1881 Office Phone: 414-288-7217.

THEON, JOHN SPERIDON, meteorologist, researcher; b. Washington, Dec. 12, 1934; s. Lewis and Merope Theon; m. Joanne Edens, July 31, 1965; children: Christopher James, Catherine. BS in Aero. Engring, U. Md., 1957; BS in Meteorology, Pa. State U., 1959, MS, 1962; PhD in Engring. Sci. and Mechanics, U. Tenn., 1985. Aero. engr. Douglas Aircraft Co., Santa Monica, Calif., 1957-58; engr. U.S. Naval Ordnance Lab., White Oak, Md., 1962; rsch. meterologist, 1962-74; head meterology br. NASA Goddard Space Flight Center, Greenbelt, Md., 1974-77; asst. chief lab. Atmospheric Scis., 1977-78, Nimbus project scientist, 1972—78; program scientist Global Weather Rsch. Program NASA Hdqrs., Washington, 1978—82, chief atmospheric dynamics and radiation program, program scientist Spacelab 3 mission, 1982—87; program scientist Tropical Rainfall Measuring Mission, 1984—95; chief climate process rsch. program NASA Hdqrs., 1987—94, exec. sec. interagency task force on observations and data mgmt., 1994—95, cons., 1998—. Cons. Orbital Scis. Corp., 1995—96, Inst. Global Environ. Strategies, 1995—2005, Cal Tech Jet Propulsion Lab., 1997—99, George Washington U., Washington, 2005—. Contbr. articles to profl. jours. With USAF, 1958—60. Recipient Goddard Exceptional Performance award, 1978, Exceptional Performance award, NASA, 1986, Radio Wave award, Ministry of Posts & Telecom. Japan, 1995; named Disting. Alumnus, U. Tenn., 1989. Fellow: Am. Meterol. Soc. Presbyterian. Home and Office: 6801 Lupine Ln Mc Lean VA 22101-1518

THEOPHILOU, THEOPHILOS SOTIRI, mechanical engineer; s. Sotiris and Anna Theophilou; m. Panayiota Antoniou Nicolaou, Aug. 1, 2000. B, Stony Brook U., 2003, MME, 2005, attending, 2009. Mgr. mech. engring. dept. Source Ray Inc., Bohemia, NY, 2008—. Tchr. St. Paraskevi Greek Sch., Greenlawn, NY, 2006—08. Pvt. Inf., 1997—99, Cyprus. Recipient Sr. Design award, Engring. Dept. Stony Brook U., 2003. Achievements include design of new portable X-Ray machines-Systems.

THERIOT, EDWARD C., museum director; BS in Zoology, La. State U., Baton Rouge, 1975, MS in Fisheries Biology, 1978; PhD, U. Mich. Sch. Natural Resources, 1983. V.p. biodiversity and evolution Acad. Natural Scis., Phila.; dir. Tex. Meml. Mus., Tex. Natural Sci. Ctr., Austin; prof. molecular evolution U. Tex., Austin. Nat. bd. dirs. Assn Systematics Collections, 1995—97, past pres. nat. bd. dirs., 1997—99; com. mem. Species Concepts, Systematics Agenda, 2000; adv. panel Nat. Sci. Found. Biol. Databases and Informatics, 2000. Editl. bd. Phycological Soc. Am., 1988—90, assoc. editor, 1991—93, editl. bd. Molecular Phylogenetics and Evolution, 1992—2000. Office: Tex Meml Mus 2400 Trinity St Austin TX 78705-5730 Office Phone: 512-232-2379. Office Fax: 512-471-4794. E-mail: etheriot@mail.utexas.edu.

THERIOT, JULIE, microbiologist, medical educator; BS, MIT, 1988; PhD in Cell Biology, U. Calif. San Francisco, 1993; predoctoral fellow, Howard Hughes Med. Inst., 1988—93; fellow, Whitehead Inst.for Biomedical Rsch., 1993—97. Asst. prof., biochemistry, microbiology and immunology Stanford U. Sch. Medicine, Calif., 1997—. Author: of numerous articles pub. in such acad. jour. as Nature, Proceedings of the Natl. Acad. of Sci. USA, and Jour. of Cell Biology. Named a MacArthur Fellow, 2004. Office: Theriot Lab Beckman Ctr Dept Biochemistry Stanford Univ Med Sch Stanford CA 94305

THERNSTROM, ABIGAIL, federal agency administrator, writer; b. NYC, Sept. 14, 1936; d. Ferdinand and Helen Mann; m. Stephan Thernstrom, Jan. 3, 1959; children: Melanie, Samuel. BA, Barnard Coll., NYC, 1958; MA, Harvard U., Cambridge, Mass., 1961, PhD, 1975. Lectr. Harvard U., Cambridge, Mass., 1975-78; project dir. The Twentieth Century Fund, NYC, 1981-86; vis. lectr. Harvard U., Cambridge, Mass., 1988-89, Boston Coll., 1990; stringer The Economist, London, 1988-92; adj. prof. Sch. Edn. Boston U., 1991—93; sr. fellow The Manhattan Inst., NYC, 1993—2009. Domestic strategy group Aspen (Colo.) Inst., 1992-97; edn. policy com. Hudson Inst., 1994-97; bd. dirs. Inst. for Justice, Washington; adv. bd. Am. Friends the Inst. US Studies, London, 1993-2003; mem. Mass. State Bd. Edn., 1995-2006; commr. US Commn. on Civil Rights, 2001—, vice-chair, 2004—; adj. scholar Am. Enterprise Inst. 2007-. Author: Whose Votes Count?: Affirmative Action and Minority Voting Rights, 1987, School Choice in Massachusetts, 1991, Voting Rights--and Wrongs: THe Elusive Quest for Racially Fair Elections, 2009; co-author: (with Stephan Thernstrom) America in Black and White: One Nation Indivisible, 1997, No Excuses: Closing the Racial Gap in Learning, 2003; editor: A Democracy Reader, 1992; co-editor: Beyond the Color Line: New Perspectives on Race and Ethnicity in America, 2002; contbr. articles to profl. jours. Mem. Citizen's Initiative on Race and Ethnicity, 1998—2002; vice chair U.S. Commn. on Civil Rights, 2004—; mem. bd. advisors U.S. Election Assistance Commn., 2006—. Recipient Anisfield Wolf Book award, 1987, Am. Bar Assn. cert. merit, 1988, Best Policy Book award Polit. Studies Orgn., 1987, Benchmark Book award Ctr. for Judicial Studies, 1987, Disting. scholarship on edn. award Fordham Found., 2007, prize for Outstanding Achievement Bradley Found., 2007. Am. Polit. Sci. Assn. Home and Office: 5920 Woodley Rd Mc Lean VA 22101-3343 Office Phone: 703-237-1599. Business E-Mail: thernstr@fas.harvard.edu.

THERNSTROM, STEPHAN, historian, educator; b. Port Huron, Mich., Nov. 5, 1934; s. Albert George and Bernadene (Robbins) T.; m. Abigail Mann, Jan. 3, 1959; children— Melanie Rachel, Samuel Altgeld. BS, Northwestern U., 1956; A.M., Harvard, 1958, PhD, 1962. Instr. history Harvard U., Cambridge, Mass., 1962-66, asst. prof., 1966-67, prof., 1973-81, Winthrop prof., 1981—2008, Winthrop rsch. prof., 2008—, chmn. com. on higher degrees in history of Am. civilization, 1985-92; prof. Brandeis U., 1967-69, UCLA, 1969-73; Pitt. prof. Am. history and instns. Cambridge U., 1978-79; dir. Charles Warren Ctr. for Research in Am. History, 1980-83. Author: Poverty and Progress, 1964, Poverty, Planning and Politics in the New Boston, 1969, The Other Bostonians, 1973, History of the American People, 1984, 88; co-author: America in Black and White, 1997, Reflections on The Shape of the River, 1999, No Excuses: Closing the Racial Gap in Learning, 2003; editor: Harvard Ency. Am. Ethnic Groups; co-editor: Harvard Studies in Urban History; Cambridge Interdisciplinary Perspectives on Modern History Series, Beyond the Color Line, 2001. Recipient Bancroft prize Columbia U., R.R. Hawkins award Assn. Am. Pub., Faculty prize Harvard U. Press, Waldo G. Leland prize Am. Hist. Assn., Fordham Found. prize Thomas B. Fordham Found., 2007, Bradley prize Harry & Lynde Bradly Found., 2007; Guggenheim fellow, John M. Olin fellow, ACLS fellow, sr. fellow Manhattan inst., 1998—, Nat. Humanities Coun., 2003-08.

THERON, CHARLIZE, actress; b. Benoni, South Africa, Aug. 7, 1975; naturalized, US, 2007; d. Charles and Gerda Theron. Studied dance, Joffrey Ballet, NYC. TV and print ad representative for J'Adore perfume Christian Dior, 2004—. Actress (films) Children of the Corn III, 1995, 2 Days in the Valley, 1996, That Thing You Do!, 1996, The Devil's Advocate, 1997, Trial and Error, 1997, Celebrity, 1998, Mighty Joe Young, 1998, The Astronaut's Wife, 1999, The Cider House Rules, 1999, Reindeer Games, 2000, The Yards, 2000, Men of Honor, 2000, The Legend of Bagger Vance, 2000, Sweet November, 2001, 15 Minutes, 2001, The Curse of the Jade Scorpion, 2001, Trapped, 2002, Waking Up in Reno, 2002, The Italian Job, 2003, Head in the Clouds, 2004, North Country, 2005, Aeon Flux, 2005, In the Valley of Elah, 2007, Battle in Seattle, 2007, Hancock, 2008, actress, prodr. Monster, 2003 (Golden Globe award for Best Dramatic Actress, SAG award for Best Actress, Acad. award for Best Actress), Sleepwalking, 2008, The Burning Plain, 2009, actress (TV films) Hollywood Confidential, 1997, The Life and Death of Peter Sellers, 2004, guest appearance (TV series) Arrested Development, 2005. Messenger of Peace UN, 2008—. Recipient Best Performance by a Human-Female (In Aeon Flux), Spike TV Video Game awards, 2005, Spirit of Independence award, LA Film Festival, 2006; named Woman of Yr., Hasty Pudding Theatrical Soc., 2008; named one of 50 Most Beautiful People, People Mag., 2000. Address: c/o United Talent Agy Ste 500 9560 Wilshire Blvd Beverly Hills CA 90212*

THERON, PETER, mathematics professor; b. Conn. BA in Stats., Princeton U., NJ; MA, U. Wis., Madison, PhD in Math. Stats., math. and computer sci. prof. Beloit Coll., Wis., U. Wis., Whitewater, Madison. Tech. advisor U. Wis.-Whitewater Purple Comet Math Meet; software and website design cons. Republican. Achievements include development of commercial software for the educational and entertainment markets. Mailing: 1021 Sequoia Trail Madison WI 53713

THEROUX, P. J., sociologist, educator; PhD, Columbia U., NYC, 1999. Vis. asst. prof. Renssalaer Poly. U., Troy, NY, 2003—; asst. prof. SUNY, Albany, 2006—. Rsch. grant, NSF, 2006—, fellowship, Spencer Found., 1995—96. Mem.: Am. Soc. Engring. Edn., Am. Ednl. Rsch. Assn. (program chair 2008—09), Am. Sociol. Assn. Office: SUNY Albany 1400 Washington Ave Albany NY 12222

THEROUX, PAUL EDWARD, author; b. Medford, Mass., Apr. 10, 1941; s. Albert Eugene and Anne (Dittami) T.; m. Anne Castle, Dec. 4, 1967 (div. 1993); children: Marcel, Louis; m. Sheila Donnelly, Nov. 18, 1995. BA, U. Mass., Amherst, DLitt, 1988, Trinity Coll., Washington, 1980, Tufts U., 1980. Lectr. U. Urbino, Italy, 1963, Soche Hill Coll., Malawi, 1963-65; faculty English dept. Makerere U., Uganda, 1965-68, U. Singapore, 1968-71; vis. lectr. U. Va., 1972-73. Author: (fiction) Waldo, 1967, Fong and the Indians, 1968, Girls at Play, 1969, Murder in Mt. Holly, 1969, Jungle Lovers, 1971, Sinning with Annie, 1972, Saint Jack, 1973, The Black House, 1974, The Family Arsenal, 1976, The Consul's File, 1977, Picture Palace, 1978 (Whitbread prize for fiction), A Christmas Card, 1978, London Snow, 1980, World's End, 1980, The Mosquito Coast, 1981, The London Embassy, 1982, Half Moon Street, 1984, O-Zone, 1986, My Secret History, 1988, Chicago Loop, 1990, Millroy and the Magician, 1993, My Other Life, 1996, Kowloon Tong, 1997, Collected Stories, 1997, Collected Short Novels, 1998, Hotel Honolulu, 2001, The Stranger at the Palazzo d'Oro, 2003, Blinding Light, 2005, The Elephanta Suite, 2007, A Dead Hand, 2009; (nonfiction) V.S. Naipaul, 1973, The Great Railway Bazaar, 1975, The Old Patagonian Express, 1979, The Kingdom by the Sea, 1983, Sailing Through China, 1983, Sunrise with Sea Monsters, 1985, The White Man's Burden, 1987, Riding the Iron Rooster, 1988, The Happy Isles of Oceania, 1992, The Pillars of Hercules, 1995, Sir Vidia's Shadow, 1998, Fresh Air Fiend, 2000, Nurse Wolf and Dr. Sacks, 2001, Dark Star Safari, 2002; (film script) Saint Jack, 1979, Chinese Box, 1998. Recipient Editorial award Playboy mag., 1972, 76, 77, 79, Lit. award AAAL, 1977, James Tait Black award, 1982, Yorkshire Post Best Novel award, 1982, Thomas Cook Travel Book prize, 1989. Fellow Royal Soc. Lit., Royal Geog. Soc.; mem. AAAL.

THERRELL, BRADFORD LEON, JR., medical researcher; s. Bradford Leon and Winifred Silicox Therrell. BS in Chemistry with Honors, Missi. Coll., Clinton, 1966; MS in Inorganic Chemistry, Fla. State U., Tallahassee, 1969, PhD in Inorganic Chemistry, 1971. Diplomate Am. Bd. Bioanalysis, 2008; cert. high complexity lab. dir. Prof. U. Tex. Health Sci. Ctr., St. Antorio, 1999—. Dir., chem. svcs. divsn tex. dept. health Bur. Labs., Tex., Tex., 1971—99; dir. National Newborn Screening and Genetics Resourse ctr., Austin, Tex., 1999; editl. chief Infant Screening, 1987—; editl. bd. Jour. Med. Screening, 1997—. Editor: (book) Advances in Neonatal Screening. Recipient Robert Guthrie award, Internat. Soc. Neonatal Screening, 2000. Mem.: Am. Coll. Med. Genetics, Internat. Soc. Neonatal Screening (US rep. 2002—, pre. 1999—2002), Assn. Pub. Health Labs., Com. Newborn Screening & Genetics, Alpha Sci, Phi Kappa Phi.

THERRIEN, MICHEL, former professional hockey coach; b. Montreal, Nov. 4, 1963; m. Genevieve Therrien; children: Elizabeth, Charles. Coach Lvaal Titan, Granby Predateurs; 1st head coach Quebec Citadelles, 1999—2000; head coach Montreal Canadiens, 2000—03, Wilkes-Barre/Scranton Penguins (AHL), 2003—05, Pittsburgh Penguins, 2005—09.

THEUS, REGGIE WAYNE, former professional basketball coach, retired professional basketball player; b. Inglewood, Calif., Oct. 13, 1957; m. Elaine Theus; children: Raquel, Reggie, Rhyan. Student, UNLV, 1975—78. Guard Chgo. Bulls, 1978-83, Kans. City Kings, 1983-85, Sacramento Kings, 1985—88, Atlanta Hawks, 1988—89, Orlando Magic, 1989—90, NJ Nets, 1990—91, Ranger Varese, Italy, 1992—93; NBA analyst Turner Sports, ESPN; head coach Am. Basketball Assn. Las Vegas Slam; vol. asst. Calif. State U., LA, 2002—03; asst. coach U. Louisville, 2003—05; head coach N.Mex. State U., 2005—07, Sacramento Kings, Calif., 2007—08. Head coach So. Calif. All-Stars (17-and-under); summer league coach Phila. 76ers, Denver Nuggets. Actor: (TV series) Hang Time, 1995—98; co-star: Best Damn Sports Show Period, 2001. Named to NBA All-Rookie Team, 1979, Ea. Conf. All-Star Team, NBA, 1981, 1983, UNLV Athletic Hall of Fame, 1989.*

THEUT, C. PETER, lawyer; b. Center Line, Mich., July 24, 1938; s. Clarence William and Anna Marie (Martens) T.; m. Judith Fern Trombley, Aug. 4, 1962; children: Elizabeth Anne, Kristin Claire, Peter Christopher, Sarah Nicole. BA, U. Mich., 1960, LLB, 1963. Bar: Calif. 1964, Mich. 1964, U.S. Dist. Ct. (no. dist.) Ohio 1968, U.S. Dist. Ct. (ea. dist.) Mich. 1968. Assoc. Overton, Lyman & Prince, LA, 1963-67; ptnr. Foster, Meadows and Ballard, Detroit, 1968-72, Theut & Schellig, Mt. Clemens, Mich., 1972-80, Hill, Lewis, Mt. Clemens, 1980-88, Butzel, Long, Detroit, 1988—2009, counsel, 2009—. Chmn. Butzel Long Chaina Initiative. Mem. ABA (internat. law sect., TIPS admiralty com.), Mich. State Bar Assn., Detroit Bar Assn., Macomb County Bar Assn., Calif. Bar Assn., Maritime Law Assn. (past chmn. recreational boatial com.), Chaina Bridge LLC(co found.), Global Com. Outreach(co founder), Lex Mundi, Waune State U.(bd. visitor), Mich. Super Lawyer, Detroit Chaina Bus. Assn.(adv. bd.), U. Mich. Museum Art(adv. bd.), North Star Sail Club,. Republican. Home: 579 Glenmoore Dr Ann Arbor MI 48103-9749 Office Phone: 734-302-1022. E-mail: theut@butzel.com.

THEVENIN, ROSE CARINE, history professor; d. Jean and Jacqueline Thevenin. BS in Crimital Justice, State U. Coll. Buffalo, NY, 1990, BA in Am. History; MA in Am. History, U. Miami, Fla, 1993; PhD, Mich. State U., East Lansing, 2001. Asst. prof. history and coll. historian Fla. Meml. U., Miami Gardens, 2001—06, assoc. prof. and coll. historian, 2007—08. Cofounder and coord. academic instns. Fla. Africana Studies Consortium, Miami, 2002—08. Contbr. articles to profl. jour. Coord. academic instns. F.L.A.S.C., Miami, 2002—08. Grantee Nat. Endowment Humanities, 2006; Rockefeller Found. grant, 2007. Mem.: Orgn. Am. Historians, Assn. Black Women Historians (parliamentarian 2005—08), Assn. Study African Am. Life and History, Southern Hist. Assn. (chair minority affairs com. 2008—). Home: 10531 SW 161 Ave Miami FL 33196 Office: Fla Meml Univ 15800 NW 42 Ave Opa Locka FL 33054 Business E-Mail: rtheven@fmuniv.edu.

THIBADEAU, EUGENE FRANCIS, education educator, consultant; b. NYC, May 18, 1933; s. Eugene Servanis and Lillian (Archer) T.; 1 child, Christine. BA, NYU, 1959, MA, 1967, MA, 1968, PhD, 1973. Instr. NYU, NYC, 1968; lectr. in philosophy Dowling Coll., Oakdale, 1968-70; prof. edn. Indiana U. of Pa., 1970—2008, emeritus prof., 2009. Vis. assoc. prof. Adelphi U., Garden City, NY, 1974-75; vis. scholar NYU, 1984-85; vis. prof. Hofstra U., Hempstead, 1974-75, 84, 86, Fudan U., Shanghai, China, 2000; cons. Ctrl. Bur. of Ednl. Visits, London, 1980-81, Commonwealth Spkrs. Bur., Harrisburg, Pa., 1983-85, US Dept. Edn., Washington, 1983-85, Pa. Dept. Edn., Harrisburg, 1988—. Author: Opening Up Edn.-In Theory and Practice, 1976, Curriculum Theory, 1988; rev. editor: Focus on Learning, 1973-77, editor, 1977-84; contbg. editor: Internat. Ency. of Edn., 2d edit., Internat. Ency.of Teaching and Tchr. Edn., 2nd edit., Internat. Ency. of Social and Behavioral Scis.; contbr. articles to profl. jours. Active United Way, Indiana, Pa., 1980—, NAACP, Indiana, 1985—, Red Cross, Indiana, 1985—. Fulbright sr. lectr. Thames Polytechnic, London, 1978-79, Fulbright sr. scholar Janus Pannonius U., Peces, Hungary, 1990-91; foreign expert Shanghai (China) Tchrs. U., 1988; designated faculty rsch. assoc. Inst. for Applied Rsch. and Pub. Policy, Indiana U. Pa., 1989; named Commonwealth Teaching fellow and Cert. Excellence in Teaching, Pa. State Colls. and Univ. Disting. Faculty Awards Com., 1976; recipient Founder's Day award, NYU, 1973, Outstanding Prof. award Ind. U. Pa.-Pa. State Edn. Assn., 1993; nom. to Ctr. for Social and Behavioral Sci., Stanford U., Palo Alto, Calif., 2007. Fellow Am. Philosophy Edn. Soc.; mem. AAUP, ASCD, Am. Ednl. Studies Assn., The S.W. Philosophy Edn. Soc. Avocations: travel, skiing, tennis, reading, chess. Home: 534 Chestnut Ridge Rd Penn Run PA 15765 Home Phone: 724-349-4680. Personal E-mail: gthibadeau@yahoo.com.

THIBAULT, BRUNO, literature and language professor; b. Neuilly sur Seine, France, May 22, 1956; m. Elizabeth Karpovich, Oct. 6, 1984; 1 child, Louis. PhD, U. Paris, 1983, U. Md., Coll. Pk., 1984. Prof. U. Del., Newark, 1987—. Assoc. editor Nouvelles Etudes Francophones, La., 2005—. Contbr. monograph. Fellow: Cahiers Le Clézio (editor 2006—08). Office: Univ Del Jastak-Burgess Hall Newark DE 19716 Business E-Mail: thibault@udel.edu.

THIBAULT, MIKE, professional basketball coach; m. Nanci Thibault; children: Eric, Carly. Grad., St. Martin's U., 1979. Scout NBA LA Lakers, 1978—80, dir. scouting, asst. coach, 1980—82, NBA Chgo. Bulls, 1982—86; gen. mgr., head coach World Basketball League Calgary 88's, 1987—88, Continental Basketball Assn. Omaha Racers, 1989—97; scout NBA Seattle SuperSonics, 1997—98; asst. coach NBA Milw. Bucks, 1998—2002; head coach WNBA Conn. Sun, 2003—. Head coach U.S.A. Nat. team World Championship Qualifying Tournament (gold medal), PR, 1993, Pan Am. Games, 1995; asst. coach U.S.A. Women's Basketball team World Championships, Sao Paolo, Brazil, 2006; asst. coach US Women's Sr. Nat. Basketball Team, Beijing, 2008. Named Coach of Yr., World Basketball League, 1988, Sportsman of Yr., Omaha sportscasters, 1993, WNBA Coach of Yr., 2006. Office: Conn Sun 1 Mohegan Sun Blvd Uncasville CT 06382*

THIBERT, ROGER JOSEPH, clinical chemist, educator; b. Tecumseh, Ont., Can., Aug. 29, 1929; s. Charles and Violet (Hebert) T.; m. Audrey M. Wissler, July 10, 1954; children: Mark Roger, Robert Francis. BA, U. Western Ont., 1951; MS, U. Detroit, 1954; PhD, Wayne State U., 1958; DSc, U. Windsor, 2004. Diplomate: Am. Bd. Clin. Chemistry (past bd. dirs.). Mem. faculty U. Windsor, Itindsor, Ont., Canada, 1953—, prof. chemistry, 1967—94, dir. clin. chemistry, 1972—94, prof. emeritus, 1994—; prof. pathology Med. Sch. Wayne State U., Detroit, 1972-94; assoc. divsn. head, clin. chemistry Detroit Receiving Hosp., Univ. Health Ctr., 1973-94, mem. med. staff, 1973-94. Cons. med. biochemistry Med. Labs. Windsor, Ont., Can., 1995-2000; sci. dir. Med. Labs., Windsor, 2000-2005. Contbr. articles on chemistry, biochemistry, analytical chemistry, clin. chemistry to profl. jours. Recipient Smith Kline award Am. Assn. Clin. Chemistry, 1980, Tchg. award Ont. Confedn. Univ. Faculty Assns., 1990, Beckman Edn. Excellence award Canadian Soc. Clin. Chemists, 1992, Alumni Tchg. award U. Windsor, 1988, Alumni award of merit, 1994, alumni excellence in mentoring award, 2003; Chem. Inst. Can. fellow, 1968—; Nat. Acad. Clin. Biochemistry fellow, 1978—; grantee Natural Scis. and Engring. Rsch. Coun., Can., award Union Carbide, Chem. Inst., Can., 1978. Fellow AAAS, Can. Acad. Clin. Biochemistry; mem. Am. Chem. Soc., Chem. Inst. Can., Assn. Chem. Profession Ont., Am. Assn. Clin. Chemistry, Nat. Acad. Clin. Biochemistry, Can. Soc. Clin. Chemists (Ames award 1988), Ont. Soc. Clin. Chemists, Am. Soc. for Biochemistry and Molecular Biology, Fedn. Am. Socs. Exptl. Biology, Can. Soc. Biochemistry and Molecular Biology, Can. Fedn. Biol. Scis., Can. Soc. for Chemistry, Sigma Xi. Roman Catholic. Home: 4612 Dali Ct Windsor ON Canada N9G 2M8 Office: U Windsor Dept Chemistry/Biochemistry Windsor ON Canada N9B 3P4

THIBIDEAU, CAROLYN C., musician, educator; d. Emery and Elizabeth Cartwright; m. Robert J. Thibideau, Dec. 28, 1958; children: Stephen R., Michael C., Richard D., Peter J. BS, Oakland U., 1974; MusM, U. Mich., 1980. Cert. tchr. Mich., registered music educator Music Educators Nat. Conf. Ch. organist, music dir. West Bloomfield Schs., Mich., 1954—, music educator, 1975—2003. Organizing dir. Cmty. Music Series, Orchard Lake, Mich.; composer, arranger, conductor, performer organ, piano, trumpet; dir. Nat. Exemplary Handbell Program, 1992. Composer (compositions and arrangements) brass quintet and organ, sch. bands, handbell choirs. Music dir., organist 1st Presbyn. Ch., Pontiac, Mich., 1994—. Recipient Tchr. of Yr., West Bloomfield Schs., 1991, Nat. Exemplary Handbells in Edn. award, 1992; finalist Tchr. of Yr., Mich. Dept. Edn., 1992. Mem.: Mich. Edn. Assn., Am. Guild English Handbell Ringers (former Mich. chairperson, clinician, condr., composer), Am. Guild Organists (assoc.; nat. conv. program com. 1980—86, chair writing com. 1990—94, exec. bd. 2005—08, performer). Avocations: music, opera, skiing. Office: Antioch Pub 8593 Cooley Lake Rd Commerce Township MI 48382

THIBODEAU, GARY A., academic administrator; b. Sioux City, Iowa, Sept. 26, 1938; m. Emogene J. McCarville, Aug. 1, 1964; children: Douglas James (dec.), Beth Ann. BS, Creighton U., 1962; MS, S.D. State U., 1967, MS, 1970, PhD, 1971. Profl. service rep. Baxter Lab., Inc., Deerfield, Ill., 1963-65; tchr., researcher dept. biology S.D. State U., Brookings, 1965-76, asst. to v.p. for acad. affairs, 1976-80, v.p. for adminstrn., 1980-85; chancellor U. Wis., River Falls, 1985-2000; sr. v.p. acad. affairs U. Wis. Sys., 2000—01. Mem. investment com. U. Wis., River Falls Found.; trustee W. Cen. Wis. Consortium U. Wis. System; bd. dirs. U. Wis. at River Falls Found.; mem. Phi Kappa Phi nat. budget rev. and adv. comm., Phi Kappa Phi Found. investment comm., comm. on Agrl. and Rural Devel., steering commn. Coun. of Rural Colls. and Univs., Joint Coun. on Food and Agrl. Scis., USDA. Author: Basic Concepts in Anatomy and Physiology, 1983, Athletic Injury Assessment, 2000, Structure and Function of the Body, 2008, Anatomy and Physiology, 2006. Mem. AAAS, Am. Assn. Anatomists, Am. Assn. Clin. Anatomists, Human Anatomy and Physiology Soc., Sigma Xi, Phi Kappa Phi, Gamma Sigma Delta, Gamma Alpha. Office: U Wis 116 N Hall River Falls WI 54022

THIBODEAU, LINDA, state librarian; Dep. dir. Alaska State Libr., Juneau; Alaska State Libr., dir. divsn. librs., archives, & mus., 2008—. Office: State Libr Agys Divsn Librs Archives & Mus PO Box 110571 Juneau AK 99801 Office Phone: 907-465-2911. Office Fax: 907-465-2151. Business E-Mail: linda.thibodeau@alaska.gov.*

THICKE, ALAN, actor; b. Kirkland Lake, Ont., Mar. 1, 1947; s. Brian Thicke; m. Gloria Loring, 1970 (div. 1983); children: Brennan, Robin; m. Gina Tolleson, Aug. 13, 1994 (div. Sept. 29, 1999); 1 child, Carter William; m. Tanya Callau, May 7, 2005. Formerly stand-up comedian, guitarist in rock bands; worked with series Fernwood 2Night (2 Emmy nominations); writer and/or producer for Bill Cosby, Richard Pryor, Kenny Rogers, Olivia Newton-John, Barry Manilow, Anne Murray; musical performer, co-starred with Dionne Warwick at Las Vegas Hilton; writer over 40 TV theme songs; Actor (films) Copper Mountain, 1983, And You Thought Your Parents Were Weird, 1991, Stepmonster, 1993, Betrayal of the Dove, 1993, open Season, 1995, Demolition High, 1996, Anarchy TV, 1998, Caspar Meets Wendy, 1999, Bear With Me, 2000, X-Roads, 2001, Hollywood North, 2003, Carolina, 2003, Raising Helen, 2004, Childstar, 2004, The Surfer King, 2005, Alpha Dog, 2006, A Little Light, 2006, The Goods: Live Hard, Sell Hard, 2009; (TV films) The Point, 1971, Jack: A Flash Fantasy, 1974, Calendar Girl Murders, 1983, Perry Mason: Case of the Shooting Star, 1986, Hitting Home, 1987, Not Quite Human, 1987, 14 Going on 30, 1988, Dance Til' Dawn, 1988, Not Quite Human II, 1989, Jury Duty: The Comedy, 1990, The Trial of Red Riding Hood, 1992, Still Not Quite Human, 1992, Rubdown, 1993, Lamb Chop and the Haunted Studio, 1994, TV's Funniest Families, 1995, Lamb Chop's Special Chanukah, 1995, Windsor Protocol, 1996, Shari's Passover Suprise, 1996, The Secret She Carried, 1996, Shadow of the Bear, 1997, Any Place But Home, 1997, Thunder Point, 1998, Two of Hearts, 1999, Ice Angel, 2000, Growing Pains: Return of the Seavers, 2004; actor, prodr., The Growing Pains Movie, 2000; Actor (TV series) Its Our Stuff, 1969, Time for Living, 1969, The Alan Thicke Show, 1980, Growing Pains, 1985-92, Travelquest, 1992, Hope & Gloria, 1995, Animals Are People Too!, 1999, All New 3's a Crowd, 1999; (TV appearances) America 2-Night, 1978, Masquerade, 1984, The Love Boat, 1984, 1986, The Hitchhiker, 1990, Murder, She Wrote, 1993,

Burke's Law, 1994, The X-Files, 1995, Married...with Children, 1997, The Outer Limits, 1997, EGG, the Arts Show, 2001, 7th Heave, 2001, Animal Miracles, 2001, Son of the Beach, 2001, 2002, Yes, Dear, 2005, Half & Half, 2005; Author: How Men Have Babies: A Pregnant Father's Survival Guide, 1999, How To Raise Kids Who Won't Hate You, 2006 Bd. chancellors Juvenile Diabetes Found., also spokesperson. Recipient 2 Emmy awards; named Man of Yr. Juvenile Diabetes Found., 1988, Internat. Father of Yr. & Parent of Yr.; named Father of Yr. L.A. Father's Day Coun., Father of Yr. Muscular Dystrophy Assn. Avocations: hockey, tennis. Office: Metropolitan Talent Agency 4500 Wilshire Blvd Fl 2 Los Angeles CA 90010-3858

THIEDE, WALTHER, research scientist, consultant, writer; b. Berlin, Dec. 18, 1931; s.Walther and Elisabeth (Nickel) T.; m. Ulrike Schumacher, Aug. 18, 1962 (dec. July 13, 2005) Pharmacist, U. Frankfurt, Germany, 1959; DSc, U. Bonn, Germany, 1964. Sci. del. Far East Asta-Werke AG, Bielefeld, Germany, 1966-68, Kobe/Osaka, Japan, 1968-73; med. dir. Lipha Arzneimittel, Essen, Germany, 1973-75; dir. mktg. and sales Kettelhack Riker Pharma GmbH, Borken, Germany, 1976-79; CEO UCB Chemie GmbH, Kerpen, Germany, 1979-87; dir. sales and med. sci. Weimer Pharm. GmbH, Rastatt, Germany, 1988-94; pvt. rschr. Cologne, 1994—. Author: BLV Nature Guide Birds, 19 edits., 13 fgn. edits., 1976—2006, BLV Nature Guide Waterbirds-Coastal Birds, 7 edits., 6 fgn. edits., 1979—2005, BLV Nature Guide-Birds of Prey and Owls, 1999, 4th edit., 2008, Bird-Life in County Oberbergisches Land, 1965, Birds of Prey, 5 edits., 1986—2006; translator: Bird Migration, 1969, BLV Bird Guide: The Audubon European Guide, 2 edits., 1982, Animal Tracks, 2000; co-editor: Ornithologische Mitteilungen, 1984—97; pub. Ornithologische Mitteilungen, 1998—, mem. editl. bd. Blätter aus dem Naumann-Museum, 1996, Beiträge zur Gefiederkunde and Morphologie der Vögel, 1997—; contbr. articles to profl. jours. Mem.: History Sci. Soc., Saxonian Ornithol. Soc. (hon.). Lutheran. Home and Office: An der Ronne 184 D-50859 Cologne Germany Office Phone: 02234 70584.

THIEL, DAVID BRIAN, physician assistant; b. Cin., July 2, 1956; s. Joseph Lee and Mary Jane (Otting) T. BA, Wabash Coll., Crawfordsville, Ind., 1978; AS with honors, Kettering Coll. Med. Arts, 1980. Cert. physician asst. Resident Los Angeles County-U. So. Calif. Med. Ctr., LA, 1985-86; physician asst. in orthopedic surgery Ketchikan, Alaska, 1980-85; physician asst. in phys. medicine and electrodiagnostic medicine New Orleans, 1987—2004; physician asst. USCG, 2004—. In-svc. lectr. HealthSouth Rehab., Harahan, La., 1990—. Tannenbaum scholar, 1974-78; recipient Orchid award Paphiopedilum Mystic Jewel, David's Dream, Highly Commended Cert. Am. Orchid Soc., 2003. Fellow: Sigma Xi (numerous Orchid awards); mem.: Internat. High IQ Soc. Republican. Avocations: swimming, skiing, sailing, orchid growing, bicycling. Address: 106 Sawmill Crrek Rd Pearl River LA 70452 E-mail: cynicno@hotmail.com.

THIEL, GLENN R., finance educator; s. Gerald Albert and Dorothy Ann Thiel; m. Lynn Marie Niklas, Mar. 17, 1984; 1 child, Deborah Rightmeyer. BS in Bus. Adminstrn., Duquesne U., Pitts., 1968, MEd in Secondary Sch. Admin., 1977; PhD in Pub. Adminstrn., U. Pitts., 2002. Cert. in bus. edn. U. Pitts., 1972. Secondary sch. asst. prin. Armstrong Babcock Sch. Dist., Kittanning, 1979—82; assoc. prof. mgmt. Robert Morris U., Moon Township, Pa., 1983—2005, assoc. prof. org. studies Pitts., 2005—, dept. head org. studies, 2006—07. Union pres. Robt. Morris Fedn., Pitts., 1990—2005. With US Army, 1969—70, Anniston, Ala., Frankfort, Germany. Conservative. Roman Catholic. Avocations: gardening, golf, walking. Office: Robert Morris Univ 600 Fifth Ave Pittsburgh PA 15219 Business E-Mail: thiel@rmu.edu.

THIEL, PETER ANDREAS, hedge fund manager; b. Frankfurt, Germany, 1967; s. Klaus and Susanne Thiel. BA in Philosophy, Stanford U., Calif., 1989; JD, Stanford Law Sch., 1992. Law clk. to judge J.L. Edmondson US Ct. Appeals (11th cir.); securities law atty. Sullivan & Cromwell; derivatives trader CS Fin. Products; founder, head Thiel Capital Mgmt. LLC, 1996; chmn., CEO Confinity, Inc; co-founder, chmn., CEO PayPal, Inc., 1998—2002; founder, pres., chmn. investment com. Clarium Capital Mgmt., LLC, 2003—; mng. ptnr The Founders Fund, 2005—. Bd. dirs. Facebook, Inc., 2004—, Powerset, Inc., 2006—, Pacific Rsch. Inst., Udorse, Inc., XOOM, Inc., The Ind. Inst.; chmn. bd. dirs. PropertyView Solutions, Inc.; mem. sci. adv. bd. Epoch Innovations, Inc.; mem. investment com. fbFund, L.P. Co-author (with David O. Sacks): The Diversity Myth: Multiculturalism' and the Politics of Intolerance at Stanford, 1998; exec. prodr.: (films) Thank You for Smoking, 2006. Bd. visitors Stanford Law Sch.; bd. dirs. Hoover Inst., Stanford. Recipient Herman Lay award for entrepreneurship, 2006; named one of 250 Most Disting. Leaders Under 40, World Econ. Forum, 2007. Libertarian. Avocation: chess. Office: Clarium Capital Management LLC 1 Letterman Dr Ste 400 San Francisco CA 94129-1495 Office Phone: 415-248-5140. Office Fax: 415-248-5141. Business E-Mail: peter@clariumcapital.com.*

THIEL, PHILIP, retired design educator; b. Bklyn., Dec. 20, 1920; s. Philip and Alma Theone (Meyer) T.; m. Midori Kono, 1955; children: Philip Kenji, Nancy Tamiko, Susan Akiko, Peter Akira (dec.) BSc, Webb Inst. Naval Architecture, 1943; MSc, U. Mich., 1948; BArch, MIT, Cambridge, 1952. Registered arch., Wash. Instr. naval architecture MIT, Cambridge, 1949—50; instr. architecture U. Calif., Berkeley, 1954—56, asst. prof., 1956—60; assoc. prof. U. Wash., Seattle, 1961—66, prof. visual design and experiential notation, 1966—91; guest prof. Tokyo Inst. Tech., 1976—78; vis. prof. Sapporo Sch. Arts, Japan, 1992—98. Lectr., US, Can., Japan, Norway, Denmark, Sweden, Eng., Austria, Switzerland, Peru, Bolivia, Korea; cons. FAO, Rome, 1952; co-founder Environment and Behavior, 1969; founder Ctr. for Exptl. Notation, Seattle, 1981 Author: Freehand Drawing, 1965, Visual Awareness and Design, 1981, People, Paths and Purposes, 1997; patentee in field Soc. Naval Architects and Marine Engrs. scholar, 1947; Rehmann scholar AIA, 1960; grantee NIMH, 1967, Nat. Endowment for Arts, 1969, Graham Found., 1995 Mem. Soc. Naval Archs. and Marine Engrs. (assoc.), Phi Beta Kappa, Sigma Xi

THIEL, ROBB G., musician, director; m. Kris K. Thiel; children: Abby L., Kylie K. Shedd. BME, U. Evansville, Indiana, 1979; MSE, Ind. U., South Bend, 1989. Bands dir. St. Joseph's Coll., Rensselaer, Ind., 1993—, Knox Cmty. Schs., Ind., 1984—93, Winamac HS, Ind., 1983—84, North Miami Cmty. Sch., Denver, 1979—83. Recipient Educator of Yr., Ind. Music Educators Assn., 2007. Fellow: St. Joseph's Coll.; mem.: Cath. Band Dirs. Assn., Ind. Bandmasters Assn., Percussive Arts Soc., Alpha Lambda Delta. Home: 705 W Charles St Rensselaer IN 47978 Office: Saint Joseph's Coll US 231 S PO Box 942 Rensselaer IN 47978 Office Phone: 219-866-6203. Office Fax: 219-866-6100. Business E-Mail: robbt@saintjoe.edu.

THIELE, GLORIA DAY, librarian, small business owner; b. LA, Sept. 4, 1931; d. Russell Day Plummer and Dorothy Ruby (Day) Plummer Thi; m. Donald Edward Cools, June 13, 1953 (div.); children: Michael, Ramona, Naomi, Lawrence, Nancy, Rebecca, Eugene, Maria, Charles. MusB, Mt. St. Mary's Coll., LA, 1953. Libr. asst. Anaheim (Calif.) Pub. Libr., 1970-73, head Biblioteca de la Comunidad, 1973-74, children's libr. asst., 1974-76, children's br. specialist, 1976-78, children's libr., 1978-81; head children's svcs. Santa Maria (Calif.) Pub. Libr., 1981—85; cons. Organizationsl Ch.-Sch. Libr., LA, 1980; owner, founder Discovery Garden, Grass Valley, Calif., 1989-93. Guest lectr. children's lit. Allan Hancock Coll., Santa Maria, 1981-85; cons. children's libr. programs, 1986—; profl. storyteller, 1989—. Contbr. poems to Amherst Soc.'s Am. Poetry Ann., 1988. Libr. liaison Casa Amistad Cmty. Svc. Group, Anaheim, 1973-74; mem. outreach com. Santiago Libr. System, Orange County, 1973-74, mem. children's svcs. com., 1971-81; mem. Cmty. Svcs. Coord. Coun., Santa Maria, 1982-85; chair children's svcs. com. Black Gold Libr. System, 1983-84; Allegro Alliance vol. for music in mountains, 1994-98; vol. Oasis Sr. Ctr., 1998-2002; mem. steering com. Cmty. Svcs. Dist. Status, Orcutt, 1999-2002; rep. 4th supervisorial dist. adv. com. Santa Barbara County Libr., 1999-2002. Mem. So. Calif. Coun. Lit. for Children and Young People, Kiwanis (sec., publicity chair, newsletter editor 1996-98, sec. Orcutt 1999-2000, Central Coast Winds & Waves, 2000—, bd. dirs. 2000-2001), Orcutt Friends of Libr. (v.p. 1999-2000, pres. 2000), P.E.O. Sisterhood (rec. sec. chpt. VZ 2002-03, corr. sec. chpt., 2007-08), Delta Epsilon Sigma, Grass Valley. CA (Disting. Svc. award, 1978-98, Hixon medal, 1999). Republican. Roman Catholic.

THIELE, HOWARD NELLIS, JR., lawyer; b. Dayton, Ohio, June 22, 1930; s. Howard Nellis and Irma Laura (Scheibe) T.; m. Alma Kuhn, Oct. 14, 1995; children: Leslie, Howard III, Craig. AB, Miami U., Oxford, Ohio, 1952; JD with distinction, U. Mich., 1955. Bar: Ohio 1955. Assoc., ptnr. Smith & Schnacke, LPA, Dayton, Ohio, 1957-89; ptnr. Thompson, Hine & Flory, Dayton, 1989-95; ret., 1995. Pres. Dayton Art Inst., 1981-85; bd. dirs. Dayton Area chpt. ARC, 1983—, 1st vice chmn., 1990-91, chmn., 1992-94. Capt. USAF, 1955-57. Mem.: Phi Beta Kappa, Order of the Coif. Republican. Lutheran.

THIEMANN, RONALD FRANK, dean, religious studies educator; b. St. Louis, Oct. 4, 1946; s. Frank Joseph and Marie Magdalene (Graeser) T.; m. Beth Arlene Barkow, June 15, 1968; children: Sarah Elizabeth, Laura Kristen. BA magna cum laude, Concordia Sr. Coll., Fort Wayne, Ind., 1968; MDiv, Concordia Sem., St. Louis, 1972; MA, Yale U., 1973, MPhil, 1974, PhD, 1976; postgrad., Eberhard-Karls Universitat, Tubingen, W.Ger., 1974-75. Asst. prof. dept. religion Haverford Coll., Pa., 1976-82, assoc. prof. dept. religion Pa., 1982-85, prof. dept. religion Pa., 1985-86, acting provost Pa., 1985, acting pres. Pa., 1986; dean Div. Sch. Harvard U., Cambridge, Mass., 1986-98, John Lord O'Brian prof. divinity, 1986-98, prof. theology, religion & soc., 1998—2005, faculty fellow Hauser Ctr., JFK Sch. Govt.; Benjamin Bursey prof. theology, 2006—; faculty assoc. Weatherland Ctr. Internat. Affairs, 2006—. Vis. prof. honors program Villanova U., 1981; vis. asst. prof. Luth. Theol. Sem., Phila., 1977; mem. Ctr. Theol. Inquiry, Princeton, N.J., 1982-83; mem. consultation on Christianity and Marxism, U.S.A. nat. com. Luth. World Fedn., 1979-83, mem. consultation on civil religion, 1983-86, mem. consultation on problem of common good, 1985-88; bd. dirs. Trinity Press Internat.; mem. exec. com. Assn. Theol. Schs., 1994-2000; faculty mem. Hanser Ctr. JFK Sch. Govt. Harvard U., 1998—. Author: Revelation and Theology, 1985, Constructing a Public Theology: The Church in a Pluralistic Culture, 1991, Religion in Public Life: A Dilemma for Democracy, 1995, Who Will Provide? The Changing Role of Religion in American Social Welfare, 2001; editor: The Legacy of H. Richard Niebuhr, 1991, Why Are We Here? Everyday Questions and the Christian Life, 1998, Where Shall My Wandering Soul Begin: The Landscape of Evangelical Piety and Thought, 2000; mem. editl. bd.: Dialog, 1987—; contbr. numerous articles to profl. jours. Mem. bd. trustees Buckingham Browne & Nichols Schs., 1988-90; mem. task force on theol. education, Evang. Luth. Ch. in Am., 1989-91, task force on Luth.-Reformed Conversations, Evang. Luth. Ch. Am., 1988-92. Recipient Disting. Teaching award Lindback Found., 1982, Lilly Scholars award, 1998-99; Mellon Found. fellow, 1982-83; Deutscher Akademischer Austauschdienst fellow, 1974-75. Mem. Am. Acad. Religion, (chmn. narrative interpretation and theology group 1982-86), Soc. Christian Ethics, Am. Theol. Soc. Avocations: tennis, squash, piano. Home: 186 Shadyside Ave Concord MA 01742-2740 Office: Harvard Div Sch 45 Francis Ave Cambridge MA 02138-1911

THIEME, JEAN LOUISE, retired art association administrator; b. Greenville, Ohio, May 9, 1926; d. William Edward and Dorothy Coppock Hole; m. Walter Irving Thieme, June 18, 1948; foster children: Ilona Jekabsons Reif, Gracie Hill Ratliff children: Michael Alan, Rebecca Louise, Susan Kathleen. AB in Chemistry, U. Mich., Ann Arbor, 1947; cert. in mgmt., Radcliffe Coll., Cambridge, Mass., 1948; postgrad., Earlham Coll., Richmond, Ind. Trustee Migrant Health Bd., Greenville Ministerial Assn., Ohio, 1970—73; exec. dir. Migrant Health Clinic (later Family Health Svcs.), Greenville, 1973—81, Darke County Ctr. Arts, Greenville, 1982—90; trustee Ctr. Arts Bd., Jackson, Wyo., 1997—2007. Editor: This is Darke County, 1982. Organizer FISH emergency phone svc., 1975—2006; trustee The Brethren's Home, Greenville, 1982—90, H.O.P.E. Found. of Darke County, 1990—2002; bd. internat. studies U. Wyo., 2001—05; mem. design com. Downtown Greenville, Inc., 2001—06; trustee Offsquare Theatre Co., Jackson, 2006—; organizer design and financing Traffic Cir., Greenville, 2005. Recipient Citizenship award, VFW, Greenville, 1981, Svc. to Mankind award, Greenville Sertoma Club, 1984. Episcopalian. Avocations: family reunions, gardening, reading, travel, performing arts. Home: 3565 Hollansburg Sampson Rd Greenville OH 45331 also: PO Box 3858 Jackson WY 83001 Home Phone: 937-547-9766. Personal E-mail: thieme@bresnan.net.

THIER, HERBERT DAVID, director, retired academic administrator; b. NYC, Feb. 27, 1932; s. Benjamin and Hannah (Greenberg) T.; m. Marlene Bach, Dec. 19, 1954; children: Maura, Lynne, Holli. BA, SUNY, 1952, MA, 1954; Ed.D., NYU, 1962. Tchr., sci. coord., sch. adminstr., NY, NJ; asst. supt. pub. schs. Falls Church, Va., 1962—63; mem. rsch. faculty, asst. dir. sci. curriculum improvement study Lawrence Hall of Sci. U. Calif. at Berkeley, 1963—, 75, assoc. dir., 1974—80, dir. R & D work for the blind, 1969—82, co-dir. biology instructional strategies project, 1972—75, health activities project, 1975—78; head author team Delta Edn. sci. curriculum improvement study elem. sch. sci. program, 1978—86; dir. Sci. Activities for Visually Impaired Project, 1976—79, Sci. Enrichment for Learners with Phys. Handicaps Project, 1978—86, Risk and Youth Smoking Project, 1980—87, Math. Reasoning Improvement Study, 1980—84, Calif. Earthquake Edn. Program, Sci. Edn. Pub. Understanding Program, 1984—2003, founding dir., 2003—, ret.; co-dir. Edn. and Pub. Outreach BioMars project U. Calif., Berkeley, 2004—09; dir. NSF, Cmty. Oriented STEM Edn. Project, 2009—; adv. bd. mem., Ctr. Biophotonics Sci. and Tech. U. Calif., Davis. Cons. various sch. systems, univs.; sci. con., Norway, Germany, Sweden, summer 1980; UNESCO cons. Israel Elementary Sci. Project Tel Aviv U., summer, 1970; cons. Orgn. Am. States, Trinidad, 1975, Jamaica, 1976; vis. prof. Simon Fraser U., Vancouver, B.C., Can., summer, 1972, Tel Aviv U., Israel, summer, 1974, Ben-Gurion U., Israel, summer, 1977, 78, Weizman Inst. Sci., Israel, summer 1982—; co-prin. investigator edn. and pub. outreach component BioMars project NASA Astrobiology Inst., U. Calif., Berkeley; cons. mech. and aerospace engring. dept. U. Va. Author: A New Look at Elementary Science, 1967, Teaching Elementary Science, A Laboratory Approach, 1970, Developing Inquiry-Based Science Materials-A Guide for Educators, 2001; contbg. author: New Trends in Integrated Science Teaching, Vol. II, 1973, Vol. III, 1974, UNESCO Handbook for Science Teachers, 1980; Contbr. numerous articles to profl. jours. Recipient Disting. Svc. award, NSTA, 1994, Sr. Fulbright award, Chinese U. Hong Kong, 2004, Weizmann Inst., Israel, 2007. Democrat. Jewish. Achievements include development of a science instructional program on sustainable and renewable energy for the Hong Kong secondary schools. Home and Office: 142 Hodges Dr Moraga CA 94556-2531 Office Phone: 925-376-6892. Business E-Mail: thier@berkeley.edu. *Public education is fundamental to the continued growth and development of a free democratic society. Science education with its emphasis on evidence and analysis is critical to developing an informed electorate. It is a privilege to be able to develop science education materials which contribute to this goal.*

THIER, SAMUEL OSIAH, physician, educator; b. Bklyn., June 23, 1937; s. Sidney and May Henrietta Thier; m. Paula Dell Finkelstein, June 28, 1958; children: Audrey Lauren, Stephanie Ellen, Sara Leslie. Student, Cornell U., 1953—56; MD, SUNY, Syracuse, 1960, DSc (hon.), 1987, Tufts U., 1988, George Washington U., 1988, Mt. Sinai Sch. Med., 1989, Hahnemann U., 1989; DSc (hon.), U. Pa., 1994, Dartmouth Coll., 1996; LHD (hon.), Rush U., 1988, Va. Commonwealth U., 1992, Med. Coll. Pa., 1992; LHD (hon.), Brandeis U., 1994. Diplomate Am. Bd. Internal Medicine. Intern Mass. Gen. Hosp., Boston, 1960—61, asst. resident, 1961—62, sr. resident, 1964—65, clin. and research fellow, 1965, chief resident, 1966; clin. asso. Nat. Inst. Arthritis and Metabolic Diseases, 1962—64; from instr. to asst. prof. medicine Harvard U. Med. Sch., 1967—69; prof. medicine, health care policy Harvard Med. Sch., 1994—2007; asst. in medicine, chief renal unit Mass. Gen. Hosp., Boston, 1967—69; asso. prof., then prof. medicine U. Pa. Med. Sch., 1969—72, vice chmn. dept., 1971—74; assoc. dir. med. svcs. Hosp. U. Pa., 1969—71; David Paige Smith prof. medicine Yale U. Sch. Medicine, 1978—81, Sterling prof. medicine, 1981—85, chmn. dept., 1975—85; pres. Inst. Medicine NAS, Washington, 1985—91; pres., Univ. prof. Brandeis U., Waltham, Mass., 1991—94; pres. Mass. Gen. Hosp., Boston, 1994—97, Ptnrs. HealthCare Sys., Inc., Boston, 1994—96, 1997—2002, CEO, 1996—2002; emeritus prof. Medicine Health Care Policy Harvard Med. Sch., 2008—. Chief medicine Yale-New Haven Hosp., 1975—85, trustee, 1978—85; bd. dirs. Conn. Hospice, Inc., 1976—82; dir. Am. Bd. Internal Medicine, 1977—85, exec. com., 1981—85, chmn., 1984—85. Mem. editl. bd.: New Eng. Jour. Medicine, 1978—81; contbr. articles to med. jours. Mem. adv. com. to the dir. NIH, 1980—85. With USPHS, 1962—64. Recipient Christian R. and Mary F. Lindback Found. Disting. Tchg. award, 1971. Mem.: ACP (bd. regents 1982—85), Interurban Clin. Club, Assn. Am. Physicians, Assn. Profs. Medicine, Internat. Soc. Nephrology, Am. Physiol. Soc., Am. Soc. Nephrology, Am. Fedn. Clin. Rsch. (pres. 1976—77), John Morgan Soc., Assn. Am. Med. Colls. (adminstrv. bd. coun. acad. socs.), Alpha Omega Alpha. Home: 99-20 Florence St # 8 Chestnut Hill MA 02467-1927

THIERER, MARK A., retail executive; MBA in Mktg., U. Minn. With IBM; v.p corp. accounts CaremarkRx, exec.; pres. Physicians Interactive Allscripts, Inc.; pres., COO SXC Health Solutions Corp., pres., CEO, bd. dirs., 2008—. Adv. bd. Scribe Healthcare Technologies. Office: SXC Health Solutions Corp 2441 Warrenville Rd, Ste 610 Lisle IL 60532-3642 Office Phone: 630-577-3100.*

THIES, RICHARD LEON, lawyer, director; b. Nov. 7, 1931; s. Arnold C. Thies and Wilma J. (Pattison) Player; m. Marilyn Lucille Webber, June 15, 1954; children: David, Nancy, Susan, John, Anne. BA, U. Ill., 1953; JD, 1955. Bar: Ill. 1955, U.S. Dist. Ct. (ea. dist.) Ill. 1958, US Ct. Appeals (7th cir.), U.S. Supreme Ct. 1986. Instr. engring. law U. Ill., Urbana, 1955-56; ptnr. Webber & Thies, P.C., Urbana, 1958—. Past mem. Urbana Park Dist. Bd.; bd. dirs., past mem. Nat. Acad. Arts, Champaign-Urbana Urban League; past bd. dirs., past pres. Salvation Army, Champaign County. Served as 1st lt. USAF, 1956-58. Fellow Am. Bar Found (chair 1993-94), Ill. State Bar Found.; mem. ABA (ho. of dels. 1984-2005, 2007-, bd. govs. 1988-91, exec. com. 1990-91, state del. 1993-2005), Am. Bar Retirement Assn. (bd. 1992-2000, chair 1997-99), Am. Law Inst. Ill. Bar Assn. (various offices, pres. 1986-87), Bar Assn. Ctrl. and So. Fed. Dists. Ill. (pres., co-founder, bd. dirs. 2001—), Champaign County Bar Assn. (v.p.), Urbana C. of C. (pres.), Urbana Country Club, Kiwanis (pres. Champaign-Urbana). Democrat. Presbyterian. Office: Webber & Thies PC 202 Lincoln Sq PO Box 189 Urbana IL 61803-0189 Office Phone: 217-367-1126. Business E-Mail: rthies@webberthies.com.

THIESFELDT, SHEILA M., artist, educator, small business owner; b. San Juan, San Juan, Puerto Rico, Aug. 14, 1973; d. Edmund Thiesfeldt and Margarita Gonzalez. BFA, Jersey City State Coll., Jersey City, New Jersey, 1998. Art tchr. Art Ctr. No. Nj, New Milford, NJ, 1998—2001; camp art dir. Overpeck Riding Acad., Leonia, NJ, 1998—2001, camp dir., 2002—, bus. owner after sch. art sch., 2001—. Exhibited in group shows, N.J., P.R. Established Equine Art program, Leonia, NJ. Avocations: skiing, horseback riding. Office: Overpeck Fine Art 40 Fort Lee Road Leonia NJ 07605 E-mail: start125@aol.com.

THIESSEN, DELBERT DUANE, psychologist; b. Julesberg, Colo., Aug. 13, 1932; s. David and Eva Peters (Wetherby) T.; children: Trevor, Theron, Kendell Courtney. BA in Psychology with distinction, San Jose State Coll., Calif., 1958; PhD, U. Calif., Berkeley, 1963. Extension instr. U. Calif., La Jolla, fall 1964; asst. sect. med. psychology, divsn. psychiatry and neurology Scripps Clinic and Research Found., La Jolla, 1962-65; faculty U. Tex., Austin, 1965-2000, prof. psychology, 1971-2000, prof. emeritus Austin, 2000—. Rsch. cons. NIMH. Author: Gene Organization and Behavior, 1972, The Evolution and Biochemistry of Aggression, 1976, Bitter-Sweet Destiny: The Stormy Evolution of Human Behavior, 1996, Universal Desires and Fears: The Deep History of Sociobiology, 1997, Survival of the Fittest: The Darwinian Diet and Exercise Program, 1998, Night of the Dagger: A Historical Voodoo Novel, 2005; contbr. articles and chpts. to books. With AUS, 1952-54, Korea. Fellow USPHS, 1960-61; recipient Career Devel. award NIMH, 1967-72, grantee, 1967-78; grantee Russel Sage Found., NSF, U. Tex. Rsch. Inst. Fellow AAAS, APA; mem. Alumni Assn. Roscoe B. Jackson Meml. Lab., Am. Genetic Assn., Psychonomic Soc., Animal Behavior Soc., Southwestern Psychol. Assn., Behavior Genetics Assn., Sigma Xi, Phi Kappa Phi, Psi Chi. Home Phone: 512-581-0158; Office Phone: 512-461-2385. Personal E-mail: wolf@delthiessew.com. Business E-Mail: wolf@delthiessen.com.

THIESSEN, MARC A., journalist, former federal official; b. Jan. 1967; AB in Polit. Sci., Vassar Coll., 1989; studied at, US Navel War Coll. Rsch. assoc. Black, Manafort, Stone & Kelley, 1989—91, dep. dir. comm., 1991—93; press. sec. Huffington for Senate, 1994; asst. to pres. Empower America, 1993—94; press spokesman, sr. policy advisor US Senate Com. of Fgn. Rels., 1995—2001; chief speechwriter to sec. US Dept. Defense, 2001—04; spl. asst. to Pres., sr. speechwriter The White

House, 2004—05, spl. asst. to Pres., dep. dir. speechwriting, 2005—06, dep. asst. to Pres., dep. dir. speechwriting, 2006—08, asst. to Pres for speechwriting, chief speechwriter, 2008—09. Mem. Coun. on Fgn. Rels. Contbr. articles to Wall St. Jour., Washington Post, LA Times, Weekly Standard, Nat. Review, NY Post, NY Times, Fin. Times, Fgn. Affairs, Nat. Interest, USA Today. Republican.*

THIGPEN, ALTON HILL, transportation executive; b. Kinston, NC, Feb. 3, 1927; s. Kirby Alton and Alice (Hill) T.; m. Rebecca Ann Braswell, May 16, 1953; children: David Alton, Jennifer Ann, Steven Roy. BS in Indsl. Engring., N.C. State U., 1950. With Assoc. Transport, Inc., Burlington, NC, 1950-71, engr., 1950-57, asst. terminal mgr. Phila., 1957-58, terminal mgr. Knoxville, Tenn., 1959, regional mgr. Valley region, 1960-62, South region, 1962-68, v.p.,dir. So. divsn., 1968-71; v.p. R.S. Braswell Co. Inc., Kannapolis, NC, 1971-80, pres., 1980—, Hartford Motor Inn Inc., North Myrtle Beach, SC, 1982—, A.T. Developers, Inc., North Myrtle Beach, 1983-97. Pres. Cherokee 2 Inc., Shelby, N.C., 1986-95, bd. dirs.; bd. dirs. Wachovia Bank, Earl Ownsby Studios Inc., Shelby. Bd. regents Berkshire Christian Coll., Lenox, Mass., 1975—; mem. adv. bd. Salvation Army, chmn. adv. bd., 1997-99. Served with USNR, 1945-46. Mem. Motor Carriers Va. (pres. 1967-68), N.C. Motor Carriers Assn. (dir. 1968-), Masons (32d degree), Lions, Sigma Chi, Tau Beta Pi. Mem. Advent Christian Ch. Office: PO Box 1197 Kannapolis NC 28082-1197 Home: 6131 Pagemont Rd Kannapolis NC 28081-8790 Home Phone: 704-932-2107; Office Phone: 704-933-2269.

THIGPEN, JAMES TATE, oncologist, educator; b. Columbia, Miss., June 8, 1944; m. Louisa Berdie Kessler, June 14, 1969; children: Monroe Tate, James Howard, Samuel Calvin, Richard Allen, David Albert. BS, U. Miss., 1964, MD, 1969. Cert. Am. Bd. Internal Medicine, Oncology Subspecialty Bd. Am. Bd. Internal Medicine, Hematology Subspecialty Bd. Am. Bd. Internal Medicine. Intern Strong Meml. Hosp., U. Rochester, NYC, 1969-70; resident U. Miss. Sch. Medicine, 1970-71, prof., dir. divsn. med. oncology dept. internal medicine, 1973—. Nat. med. del. from Miss. Am. Cancer Soc., 1983-85, nat. pub. issues com., 1983-85; cancer clin. investigations rev. com. Nat. Cancer Inst., 1990-95, chmn., 1993-95. Nat. bd. govs. ARC, 1981-87. Fellow divsn. hematology/oncology dept. medicine, 1971-73. Fellow ACP; mem. AMA, Miss. Med. Assn., Ctrl. Med. Soc., Jackson Acad. Medicine, Miss. Acad. Scis., SW Oncology Group, Gynecologic Oncology Group (group vice chmn. sci. 1988—), Am. Fedn. Clin. Rsch., Am. Assn. Cancer Edn., Am. Soc. Clin. Oncology, Am. Assn. cancer Rsch., Am. Soc. Hematology, Soc. Gynecologic Oncologists, Soc. Assn. Oncology (pres. 1988-90), Am. Radium Soc., Optimists (internat. v.p. 1983-84, internat. pres. 1990-91). Republican. Baptist. Home: 3601 Kings Hwy Jackson MS 39216-3322 Office: Univ Physicians 2500 N State St Jackson MS 39216-4500 Office Phone: 601-984-5590. Personal E-mail: jtthigpen@att.net.

THIGPEN, RICHARD ELTON, JR., retired lawyer; b. Washington, Dec. 29, 1930; s. Richard Elton and Dorathy (Dotger) Thigpen; m. Nancy H. Shand, Dec. 15, 1951; children: Susan B., Richard M. AB, Duke U., 1951; LLB, U. N.C., 1956. Bar: NC 1956, U.S. Ct. Appeals (4th cir.) 1960, U.S. Ct. Appeals (5th cir.) 1960, U.S. Ct. Appeals (10th cir.) 1974, U.S. Tax Ct. 1958, U.S. Ct. Claims 1978, U.S. Supreme Ct. 2003. Lawyer FTC, Washington, 1956-58, Thigpen & Hines, Charlotte, NC, 1958-84, Moore & Van Allen, Charlotte, 1984-88, Poyner & Spruill, Charlotte, 1988-93; gen. counsel Richardson Sports, 1994-98; ret. Bd. dirs. OrthoCarolina Rsch. Inst., 2001—08, dirs. emeritus; bd. dirs. Charlotte-Mecklenburg YMCA, 1964—88, Heineman Med. Rsch. Ctr., Charlotte, 1970—, Charlotte C. of C., 1982—85. Lt. USNR, 1951—53. Fellow: Am. Coll. Tax Counsel (regent 1989—95, vice chmn. 1992, chmn. 1993—94); mem.: ABA, Sports Lawyers Assn. (bd. dirs. 1995—2007, pres. 2003—05, dir. emeritus 2007—), N.C. Bar Assn. (chmn. tax sect. 1976—80, pres. 1988—89), N.C. State Bar. Avocations: golf, travel. Personal E-mail: thigpenhouse@carolina.rr.com.

THIMMIG, DIANA MARIE, lawyer; b. Germany, May 5, 1959; BA cum laude, John Carroll U., 1980; JD, Cleve. State U., 1982. Bar: Ohio 1983, U.S. Dist. Ct. (no. dist.) Ohio 1983, U.S. Ct. Appeals (6th cir.) 1983, U.S. Supreme Ct. 1983, U.S. Ct. Appeals (3d cir. 1996); cert. Am. Bankruptcy Bd. for Consumer and Bus. Bankruptcy. Ptnr. Roetzel & Andress, Cleve. Contbr. articles to profl. jours. Trustee Geauga United Way Svcs. Coun., 1992-96, Altenheim, 1992-97, Internat. Svcs. Ctr., 1998-04, trustee Cuyahoga County Bar Assn., 1995-08, pres., 2005-06; trustee Legal Aid Soc., 1998-2006, pres., 2003-05.trustee Cuyahoga County Bar Found., 2001-08; hon. coun. Fed. Repub. Germany, 1998-. Recipient Elsa Pavlik Vol. of Yr. award, Women's City Club Cleve., 1990, Trustee award for Outstanding Svc., Legal Aid Soc. Cleve., 2001, Pres. award, Ohio Legal Assistance Found., 2004, Day Weiner award, Cuyahoga County Bar Found., 2005; named an Ohio Super Lawyer, Law and Politics Mag., Cin. Mag., 2004, 2005, 2006, 2007, 2008; named to Order of Merit, Fed. Repub. Germany, 2008. Mem. Fed. Bar Assn., Cleve.-Met. Bar Assn. (Vol. of Yr. 2008), Ohio State Bar Assn. Office: Roetzel & Andress 1375 East Ninth St One Cleveland Ctr Ninth Floor Cleveland OH 44114 Office Phone: 216-696-7078. Business E-Mail: dthimmig@ralaw.com.

THINESEN, PAMELA KAY, biology faculty; d. Philip Leslie and Inez Mae Thinesen; 1 child, Jacob Philip. BA in Biomed. Sci., St. Cloud State U., 1983; MS in Biology, Portland State U., 1989. With, biology faculty Century Coll, White Bear Lake, Minn., 2000—. Office: Biology Faculty Century Coll White Bear Lake MN 55110 Business E-Mail: pamela.thinesen@century.edu.

THIRLBY, OLIVIA, actress; b. NYC, Oct. 6, 1986; Attended, Royal Acad. Dramatic Art, London. Tng. Shakespearian acting Am. Globe Theatre, NYC. Actress (films) United 93, 2006, Unlocked, 2006, Snow Angels, 2007, Juno, 2007, Love Comes Lately, 2007, The Secret, 2007, The Wackness, 2008, Eve, 2008, Uncertainty, 2008, Arlen Faber, 2009, Breaking Upwards, 2009, What Goes Up, 2009. Office: c/o Mgmt 360 9111 Wilshire Blvd Beverly Hills CA 90210

THIRLBY, RICHARD COLLER, surgeon; b. Traverse City, Mich., Aug. 30, 1952; s. Richard Leeson Thirlby; m. Patricia Rosso, July 17, 1976; children: Marjorie Rose, David Ryan. BA, Dartmouth U., Hanover, NH, 1974; MD, U. Mich., Ann Arbor, 1978. Contbr. articles to profl. jours. Mem.: ACS (pres. Wash. State chpt. 2003—04), Am. Bd. Surgery (bd. dirs. 2006—), Western Surg. Assn. (pres. 2005—06). Office: Virginia Mason Med Ctr 1100 9th Ave Mailstop C6-GSUR Seattle WA 98111

THIRSK, ROBERT BRENT, astronaut; b. New Westminster, BC, Can., Aug. 17, 1953; m. Brenda Biasutti; 3 children. BSc in Mech. Engring., U. Calgary, 1976; MSc in Mech. Engring., MIT, 1978; MD, McGill U., 1982; MBA, MIT, 1998. Resident Queen Elizabeth Hosp., Montreal, Canada, 1982—83; astronaut Can. Astronaut Program, 1984—; sabbatical yr. Victoria, B.C., Canada, 1994—95; chief astronaut Can. Space Agy., 1993—94; astronaut NASA, Houston, 1998—. Dir. Can. Found. Internat. Space U., 1992—; crew comdr. CAPSULS mission, 1994; astronaut Space Shuttle mission STS-78, 1996; crew comdr. NEEMO 7 undersea mission, 2004; backup astronaut STS-41G space shuttle mission, 1984, Soyuz 10 S taxi mission, 2005. Recipient Disting. Alumni award, U. Calgary, 1985. Mem.: Coll. Physicians and Surgeons B.C., Coll. Physicians & Surgeons Ontario, Aerospace Med. Assn., Can. Aeronautics & Space Inst., Can. Coll. Family Physicians, Assn. Profl. Engrs. Ontario (Gold Medal award 1997). Avocations: hockey, squash, playing the piano. Office: Astronaut Office CB NASA Johnson Space Center Houston TX 77058

THIRUMALAI, DEVARAJAN, physical sciences researcher, educator; b. Madras, India, June 6, 1956; s. Sadagopan and Saranayaki Thirumalai; m. Cynthia Kahl, Apr. 15, 1982; children: Alexandra, Samuel. BS, Indian Inst. Technology, Kampur, India, 1977; PhD, U. Minn., 1982. Postdoctoral rsch. fellow Columbia U., NYC, 1982-85; prof. U. Md., College Park, 1985—. Guest worker NIST, Gaithersburg, Md., 1990—. Contbr. more than 100 rsch. papers to profl. jours. Named Presdl. Young investigator NSF, 1987; Alfred P. Sloan fellow Sloan Found., Home: 9220 Clematis Ct Gaithersburg MD 20882-3818 Office: U Md Inst For Phys Sci & Tech College Park MD 20742-0001

THIRUPPUKUZHI, SRIKANTH VANKEEPURAM, electronics engineer; PhD, Purdue U., Ind., 1997. Prin. staff engr. Motorola, Libertyville, Ill., 2003—08, disting. mem. tech. staff, 2008—. Office: Motorola Inc 600 North US Hwy 45 Libertyville IL 60048 Business E-Mail: w18363@motorola.com.

THIRUVANAMALAI, VALARMATHI MANI, pathologist, educator; s. Mani Manickkam Thiruvanamalai and Thulasi Bai Mani. BS, U. Madras, India, 1984, MBBS, 1989; MD, U. Madras, 1994; PhD, All-India Inst. Med. Scis., New Delhi, 2003. Compulsory rotary residential internships Kilpauk Med. Coll., U. Madras, 1989—90; immunopathologist Cancer Inst., WIA, Adyar, Tamil Nadu, 1994; asst. prof. pathology Sri Ramachandra Med. Coll. & Rsch. Inst., Madras, 1995—97; post MD, MS tng. in med. biotech. All-India Inst. Med. Scis., New Delhi, 1997—98, rsch. assoc., 1999—2003; vis. scientist Ctr. Cancer Rsch., Nat. Cancer Inst., Bethesda, Md., 2004—06; postdoc. rsch. assoc. U. SC, Columbia, 2006—07, rsch. asssoc., 2007—08, rsch. asst. prof., Sch. Medicine, 2008—. Recipient Award, NIH, 2004; Sr. Rsch. Fellowship, Indian Coun. Med. Rsch., 1992—94, Fellowship, Dept. Biotech., Govt. India, 1997—98, Vis. fellowship, NIH, 2004—06. Mem.: Am. Soc. Investigative Pathology, Am. Assn. Cancer Rsch., Tissue Engring. and Regenerative Medicine Internat. Soc., Internat. Soc. Stem Cell Rsch. Office: SOM Univ SC 6439 Garners Ferry Rd Columbia SC 29209 Office Fax: 803-733-3212. Business E-Mail: valarmathi.thiruvanamalai@uscmed.sc.edu.

THIRY, KENT J., health products executive; BA in Polit. Sci., Stanford U., 1978; MBA with honors, Harvard U., 1983. Sr. cons. Andersen Consulting, 1978-81; ptnr., v.p. Bain & Co., 1983—91; pres., COO Vivra, Inc., San Francisco, 1991-92, pres., CEO, 1992-97; chmn., CEO Vivra Holdings Inc., 1997—99, Da Vita Inc., El Segundo, Calif., 1999—. Dir. Oxford Health Plans, 1998—2004, chmn., 2002—04. Bd. dirs. Vol. Ctr. San Mateo County. Mem. Phi Beta Kappa. Office: 601 Hawaii St El Segundo CA 90245-4814*

THISSELL, JAMES DENNIS, physicist; b. Lincoln County, SD, June 1, 1935; s. Oscar H. and Bernice G.J. (Olbertson) T. BA cum laude, Augustana Coll., 1957; MS, U. Iowa, 1963. Rsch. physicist U. Iowa, Iowa City, 1958-64; engr. McDonnell Douglas, St. Louis, 1965-66; scientist E.G. & G., Inc., Las Vegas, Nev., 1967-68; engr. Bendix Field Engring. Corp. Ames Rsch. Ctr., Moffett Field, Calif., 1970-77, Lockheed Missiles and Space Co., Sunnyvale, Calif., 1978—2002. Mem. AIAA, AAAS, IEEE, Am. Phys. Soc., Am. Geophys. Soc., Sigma Xi. Republican. Lutheran. Home: 38475 Jacaranda Dr Newark CA 94560-4727

THISTLETHWAITE, DAVID RICHARD, architect; b. Burlington, Iowa, Aug. 24, 1947; s. Robert and Nona (Binder) T.; m. Carol Anne Armstrong, Aug. 22, 1970. BArch, Iowa State U., 1971. Registered arch., Calif., 1979, Minn., 1975; registered Nat. Coun. Archtl. Registration Bds., 1978; cert. Health Care arch., Am. Coll. Healthcare Archs., 2000. Designer Morrison Architects, St. Paul, 1971-73, Times Architects, Mpls., 1973-74; project architect Bentz/Thompson Assocs., Mpls., 1974-77; project mgr. Setter Leach Lindstrom, Mpls., 1977-78; project architect Wurster Bernardi Emmons, San Francisco, 1978-79, Strotz & Assocs., Tiburon, Calif., 1979-81, Hood Miller Assoc., San Francisco, 1981-84; prin., ptnr. R S T Architects, San Francisco, 1984-88; prin. Thistlethwaite Archtl. Group, San Francisco, 1988—2007; v.p., prin. HGA Archs. & Engrs., Inc., 2007—. Contbr. articles to profl. jours. Mem. AIA (nat. profl. devel. com. 1983-86, treas. San Francisco chpt. 1985-86, chmn. Calif. coun. health facilities com. 1994-96, chmn. design com. Acad. Architecture for Health, 1994-96, Calif. coun. ins. bd. trustees 1988-2002, Calif. coun. legis. com. 1996-98) Am. Coll. Healthcare Archs. (mem. pub. rels. com. 2004-05), Am. Soc. Healthcare Engring., Design Profls. Safety Assn. (bd. dirs.). Office Phone: 415-814-6910.

THOBURN, ELISABETH Z., humanities educator; b. Dresden, Germany, July 30, 1959; MA in Art History, U. Mich., Ann Arbor, 1994. Prof. Washtenaw CC, Ann Arbor, Mich., 1994—. Travel scholarships, Fulbright-Hayes, NEH, 2001, 2004. Avocations: travel, reading. Office: Washtenaw CC 4800 E Huron River Dr Ann Arbor MI 48108 Business E-Mail: ezt@wccnet.edu.

THODE, EDWARD FREDERICK, chemical engineer, educator; b. NYC, May 31, 1921; s. E. Frederick and Kathleen V. (McGowan) T.; m. Isobel Zoeller, May 27, 1944 (dec. Dec. 19, 2007); children: Karen (Mrs. Paul M. O'Neil), Stephen Frederick, Jonathan Edward. S.B., M.I.T., 1942, S.M., 1943, Sc.D., 1947. Registered profl. engr., Maine, N.Mex. Chem. engr. Boston Woven Hose & Rubber Co., Cambridge, Mass.; asst. prof. chem. engring. U. Maine, Orono, 1947-49, asso. prof., 1949-54; sr. research engr. 3M Co., St. Paul, 1954-55; research asso., faculty mem. Inst. Paper Chemistry, Appleton, Wis., 1955-63, mgr. dept. engring. computer and computer ctr., 1959-63; prof. chem. engring. N.Mex. State U., Las Cruces, 1963-74, head dept. chem. engring., 1963-74, prof. mgmt., 1974-86, prof. emertus chem. engring. and mgmt., 1986—. Cons. Am. Cyanamid Co., IBM, Gen. Elec. Co., Bell Telephone Labs.; affiliate staff mem. Los Alamos Sci. Lab., 1965-90; propr. EIT Cons., 1972-91. Contbr. numerous articles to profl. jours. Mem. exec. bd. Yucca council Boy Scouts Am., 1968-72; dir. Mesilla Park Heritage Assn., 1988-93, sec., 1988-89, v.p., 1990, pres. 1991; treas. Mesilla Valley Conf. Chs., 1989; vestryman, lay reader, lay eucharistic minister, warden, 1970, 71, 87, 93, 94. Recipient Disting. faculty award N. Mex. State U., 1981, 83 Mem. AIChE (chmn. Rio Grande sect. 1990), Am. Soc. Engring. Edn., Masons, Lions, Sigma Xi, Tau Beta Pi, Beta Gamma Sigma, Phi Kappa Phi. Republican. Episcopalian. Home: 3045 Buena Vida Cir # E320 Las Cruces NM 88011-9120 Business E-Mail: ethode@nmsu.edu. *To discover God's will for our lives is difficult; the search is worth the effort.*

THODESEN, CARL CHRISTIAN, civil engineer; b. Cairo, Apr. 16, 1980; s. Terje Thodesen and Lilian Jean Garbouchian; m. Bridget O'Brien Gilles, Nov. 22, 2008. PhD in Civil Engring., Clemson U., SC, 2008. EIT SC, 2003. Rsch. asst. Asphalt Rubber Tech. Svc., Clemson, 2005—08; sr. civil engr. ECOPATH Industries, Scottsdale, Ariz., 2008—. Contbr. articles to profl. jours., chapters to books. Mem.: Assn. Asphalt Paving Technologists, Chi Epsilon. Achievements include development of statistical models for determining high temperature properties of crumb rubber modified asphalt. Personal E-mail: cthodesen@gmail.com.

THOGERSON, MARK T., biology professor, consultant; s. Dolliver D. and Ruth M. Thogerson. PhD, Mich. State U., East Landsing, 1993. Vis.-adj. prof. Grand Valley State U., Allendale, Mich., 1994—2003, vis. prof., 2006—; application devel. Meijer Stores, Inc., Walker, Mich., 1997—2001; instr. Muskegon CC, Mich., 2003—06. Pvt. practice, Muskegon, Mich., 1998—. Scrimshaw and ivory work. Mentor Reeths-Puffer Neighborhood Assn., Muskegon, Mich., 2003—05. Recipient Hon. Mention, North Am. Benthological Soc., 1991. Independent. Lutheran. Avocations: gardening, woodworking, photography, backpacking, canoeing. Office: Biology Dept Grand Valley State Univ Allendale MI 49401 Business E-Mail: thogersm@gvsu.edu.

THOM, RICHARD DAVID, retired electronics executive; b. St. Louis, Oct. 4, 1944; s. Reginald James and Vlasta (Koukl) T.; m. Linda Marie Hunt, Sept. 9, 1967; children: Elizabeth Marie, Robert James. BS in Physics, U. Mo., Rolla, 1967; MSEE, UCLA, 1971. Co-op engr. McDonnell Aircraft Corp., St. Louis, 1962-67; head advanced tech. group IR systems dept., aerospace group Hughes Aircraft Co., Culver City, Calif., 1967-72; mem. tech. staff Santa Barbara Rsch. Ctr., Hughes Aircraft Co., Goleta, Calif., 1972-76, asst. mgr. R&D Lab., 1976-80, mgr. advanced applications, 1980-83, chief engr., 1984-86, chief scientist, 1986-90, dir. tech., 1990-95; tech. program exec. Hughes Aircraft Co., Goleta, Calif., 1995-98; asst. mgr. Raytheon Santa Barbara Rsch. Ctr., Goleta, Calif., 1998-99; ret. Contbr. articles to profl. jours.; patentee in field. Recipient Hughes Group Patent award for pioneering contbns. in infrared detector tech., 1990. Mem. IEEE, Tau Beta Pi, Sigma Pi Sigma, Delta Sigma Phi. Republican. Avocations: freelance travel writing and photography, specializing in railway travel around the world. Home: 38 Fawn Run Pl PO Box 326 Coupeville WA 98239-0326 Home Phone: 360-678-1444. Personal E-mail: richthommail@aol.com.

THOMAN, G. RICHARD, corporate financial executive; b. Tuscaloosa, Ala., June 25, 1944; s. Richard S. and Evelyn (Zumwalt) Thoman; m. Wenke Helina Brier, Aug. 25, 1966 (div. Dec. 1987); children: Camille, Alexis; m. Lynn Susan Bendheim, Sept. 16, 1989; children: Kylie, Max, Amy, Eric. BA with honors, McGill U., 1966; MA, Grad. Inst. Internat. Studies, Geneva, 1968; MA in Internat. Econs., Tufts U., 1967, MA in Law and Diplomacy, 1969, PhD in Internat. Econs., 1971. Exec. trainee Citicorp, NYC, 1968-69; sr. fin. analyst Exxon Corp., NYC, 1970-72; sr. assoc. McKinsey and Co., NYC and Paris, 1972-79; exec. v.p., CFO Am. Express Travel Related Svcs., NYC, 1979-85, pres., Travel Related Svcs. Internat., 1985-89, chmn., CEO, 1989-92; pres., CEO Nabisco Internat. RJR Nabisco, Inc., NYC, 1992-94; sr. v.p., group exec. IBM Corp., Somers, NY, 1994-95, sr. v.p., CFO Armonk, NY, 1995-97; pres., COO Xerox Corp., 1997-99, pres., CEO, 1999-2000, also bd. dirs.; pvt. investor; sr. advisor Evercore Ptnrs., NYC, 2001—02; mng. ptnr. Corporate Perspectives, NYC, 2002—; adj. prof. Columbia U., 2003—; vis. prof. Fletcher Sch., 2005—. Bd. dirs. Schneider Group, Paris; mem. US adv. bd. INSEAD. Bd. dirs. Americas Soc., NYC, 1990—, French-Am. Found.; bd. advisors Fletcher Sch. Law and Diplomacy, Tufts U., Medford, Mass., 1990—; chmn. Internat. Mgmt. Coun., Fletcher Sch. Law and Diplomacy, Tufts U., Mass.; mem. adv. bd. Sch. Mgmt. McGill U., Montreal, Bus. Coun. Recipient Legion of Honors, Govt. of France, 1992. Mem.: Trilateral Commn., Coun. on Fgn. Rels., River Club, Links Club. Avocations: tennis, reading, jogging, travel. Office: Corp Perspectives 126 E 56th St Fl 9 New York NY 10022 Home Phone: 203-661-9505; Office Phone: 212-813-0323.

THOMAN, MARK EDWARD, pediatrician; b. Chgo., Feb. 15, 1936; s. John Charles and Tasula Mark (Petrakis) T.; m. Theresa Thompson, 1984; children: Marlisa Rae, Susan Kay, Edward Kim, Nancy Lynn, Janet Lea, David Mark. AA, Graceland Coll., 1956; BA, U. Mo., 1958, MD, 1962. Diplomate Am. Bd. Pediat., 1967, Am. Coll. Toxicology (examiner), 1975-90. Intern U. Mo. at Columbia, 1962—63; resident in pediat. Blank Meml. Children's Hosp., Des Moines, 1963—65; cons. in toxicology USPHS, Washington, 1965—66; chief dept. pediat. Shiprock (N.Mex.) Navajo Indian Hosp., 1966—67; dir. N.D. Poison Info. Ctr.; also practice medicine specializing in pediat. Quain & Ramstad Clinic, Bismarck, ND, 1967—69; dir. Iowa Poison Info. Ctr., Des Moines, 1969—99; mem. pediat. exec. com. Broadlawns Med. Ctr., Des Moines, 1969—2000, pres. med. staff, 2000—02. Accident investigator FAA, 1976—2005, sr. aviation examiner, 1977—2000; lectr. aviation seminars, 1977—2007; mem. faculty Des Moines U., 1969—2005, dir. cystic fibrosis clin., 1973—82; dir. Mid-Iowa Drug Abuse Program, 1972—76; mem. med. adv. bd. La Leche League Internat., 1965—; chief med. officer Broadlawns Med. Ctr., Des Moines, 2000—02; sci. rev. panel Nat. Libr. Medicine, 2003—; med. cons., med. exam. Social Security Adminstrn., Office Disability Adjudication and Review, 2003—; cons. in field. Editor-in-chief AACTION, 1975-90; monthly columnist Aviation Medicine Twin and Turbine Mag., 2005-06. Bd. dirs. Polk County Pub. Health Nurses Assn., 1969-77, Des Moines Speech and Hearing Ctr., 1974-79, Ecumenical Coun. Iowa, 1990-99; bd. govs. Mo. U. Sch. Medicine Alumni, 1988-, pres. bd. govs.; pres. parish coun. Greek Orthodox Ch., 2007-09. With USMCR, 1954-59; lt. comdr. USPHS, 1965-67; capt. USNR, 1988-96, ret. 1996; dir. Dept. Health Svcs. USNR. Recipient N.D. Gov.'s award of merit, 1969, Cystic Fibrosis Rsch. Found. award, 1975, Am. Psychiat. Assn. Thesis award, 1962. Fellow Am. Coll. Med. Toxicology (diplomate 1996), Am. Acad. Clin. Toxicology (trustee 1969-90, pres. 1982-84); mem. AMA (del. 1970-88), APHA, NRA (life), Assn. Am. Physicians & Surgeons (chief of staff, pres. Broadlawns Polk County Med. Ctr. 2000-02), Polk County Med. Soc., Iowa State Med. Assn., Aerospace Med. Assn., Res. Officers Assn., Civil Aviation Med. Assn., Soc. Adolescent Medicine, Inst. Clin. Toxicology, Internat. Soc. Pediat., Am. Acad. Pediat. (chmn. accident prevention com. Iowa chpt. 1975-2000), Cystic Fibrosis Club, Am. Assn. Poison Control Ctrs., Am. Coll. Physician Execs., U.S. Naval Inst., Flying Physicians Club, Aircraft Owners and Pilots Assn, Nat. Pilots Assn. (Safe Pilot award), Aerospace Med. Assn. Republican. Greek Orthodox. Home: 5355 Crane Ave E Port Orchard WA 98366 Office Phone: 360-871-2219. Office Fax: 360-871-4436. Personal E-mail: paro1795@aol.com.

THOMAN, ROY EDWARD, political scientist, educator; b. Evansville, Ind., Mar. 11, 1938; s. Joseph Henry and Nell Yates Thoman; m. Judith Ann Schiff, May 20, 1967 (div. Apr. 18, 1985); 1 child, Mark; m.

Jan Brister, May 21, 2005. BA magna cum laude, U. Evansville, 1960; MA, Ind. U., 1964; PhD, U. Ky., 1967. Asst. prof. West Tex. A&M U., Canyon, 1968—70, assoc. prof., 1970—76, prof., 1976—. Contbr. articles to profl. jours.; consulting editor World Affairs, 1979—82. Recipient scholarship medal, Pi Gamma Mu, 2000, endowed scholarship in his name, Phi Eta Sigma, 2000; grantee, Tex. Ednl. Assn., 1972—75. Mem.: KC, Am. Polit. Sci. Assn. Republican. Roman Catholic. Office: West Tex A&M U WT Box 725 Canyon TX 79016 Home: 3816 Doris Dr Amarillo TX 79109-5505 Office Phone: 806-352-6140. Business E-Mail: rthoman@mail.wtamu.edu.

THOMAS, ANN VAN WYNEN, retired law educator; b. The Netherlands, May 27, 1919; arrived in U.S., 1921, naturalized, 1926; d. Cornelius and Cora Jacoba (Daansen) Van Wynen; m. A. J. Thomas, Jr., Sept. 10, 1948. AB with distinction, U. Rochester, NY, 1940; JD, U. Tex., 1943; degree, So. Meth. U., Dallas, 1952. US fgn. svc. officer, Johannesburg, London, The Hague, Netherlands, 1943-47; rsch. atty. Southwestern Legal Found. So. Meth. U. Sch. Law, Dallas, 1952-67, asst. prof. polit. sci., 1968-73, assoc. prof., 1973-76, prof., 1976-85, prof. emeritus, 1985—. Author: Communism versus International Law, 1953, Non-Intervention - The Law and Its Import in the Americas, 1956, OAS: The Organization of American States, 1962, International Legal Aspects of Civil War in Spain, 1936-1939, 1967, Legal Limitations on Chemical and Biological Weapons, 1970, The Concept of Aggression, 1972, An International Rule of Law - Problems and Prospects, 1974, Presidential War Making Power: Constitutional and International Law Aspects, 1981; author: (with A. J. Thomas, Jr.) International Treaties, 1950; author: What I did in World War 2, 2007. Chmn. time capsule com. Grayson County Commn. Tex. Sesquicentennial, 1986—88; co-chmn. Grayson County Commn. Bicentennail US Constn., 1988—93, Grayson County Commn. Millenium, 1997—; co-chmn. com. Grayson County Sesquicentennail, 1994—97. Recipient Am. medal, Nat. DAR, 1992. Mem.: Grayson County Bar Assn., Am. Soc. Internat. Law, Tex. Bar Assn. Home: Spaniel Hall 374 Coffee Cir Pottsboro TX 75076-3164

THOMAS, ANNE C., nursing researcher, nurse practitioner; b. Detroit, Nov. 13, 1961; d. Delwyn Robert and Euella Elizabeth (Keats) Thomas; m. Matthew T. Joyal, Dec. 31, 1988; children: Eric Matthew, Nathan Alexander, Lauren Elizabeth. BSN, U. Tex., Arlington, 1984, MSN, 1987; PhD, Tex. Woman's U., 1994. Cert. SLESH course leader Arthritis Found., cancer detection M.D. Anderson Tumor Inst., breast self-exam. trainer Am. Cancer Soc. Oncology staff nurse St. Paul Med. Ctr., Dallas, 1984; nurse educator St. Paul Med. Ctr./Arthritis Ctr., Dallas, 1987-92; specialist primary care program U. Tex. Sch. Nursing, Arlington, 1988-93; nurse practitioner John Peter Smith Hosp., Ft. Worth, 1992-94; asst. prof., coord. family nurse practitioner track Sch. Nursing Ind. State U., Terre Haute, 1994—; nurse practitioner Riley (Ind.) Family Medicine, 1994—. Contbr. articles to profl. jours. Chair skin cancer com., skin cancer edn. com. co-chair, mem. speaker's bur. Am. Cancer Soc., Dallas; 1st v.p., program dir., chair strategic planning com., bd. dirs. Lupus Found., Dallas. Recipient Disting. Svc. award Arthritis Found., 1989, Disting. Faculty award U. Tex.-Arlington Sch. Nursing, 1994; Am. Cancer Soc. rsch. grantee. Mem. Arthritis Health Professions Assn. (North Tex. chpt., program chair, pres.-elect, pres.; nat. newsletter corr. 1990; editorial asst. chpt. newsletter Dallas chpt. 1989, 90), Tex. Nurses Assn., ANA, Am. Acad. Nurse Practitioners, Gerontol. Soc. Am. Office: Ind State U Sch Nursing 8th And Chestnut Sts Terre Haute IN 47809-0001 Home: 1200 Arms St Apt 14 Marshall MI 49068-1088

THOMAS, AUGUSTA READ, composer; b. Glen Cove, NY, Apr. 24, 1964; d. James Augustus and Susan (Norton) T.; m. Bernard Rands, Sept. 4, 1994. MusB, Northwestern U., 1987; MusM, Yale U., 1988; advanced diploma, Royal Acad. Music, London, 1989. Assoc. prof. music composition Eastman Sch. Music, Rochester, NY; Wyatt prof. music Northwestern U.; composer-in-residence Chgo. Symphony Orch., 1997—2006; dir. contemporary music Tanglewood Music Festival, 2009. Bd. dirs. Am. Music Ctr., 2000—08, chair bd., 2005—08. Composer: (opera) Ligeia, Love Songs, 1997, Words of the Sea, 1996, Spirit Musings, 1997, Chanson, 1997; orchestral and chamber music works recorded by numerous musicians and orchestras, including the NY Philharmonic, Phila. Orch., Boston Symphony, Cleve. Orch., Nat. Symphony, Chgo. Symphony Orch., Dallas Symphony, Aspen Music Festival, Tanglewood Music Festival, Chanticleer, Eroica Trio, Stonybrook Contemporary Music Ensemble, San Francisco Contemporary Chamber Players, Network for New Music, many others, performed by condrs. including Pierre Boulez, Mstislav Rostropovich, and Seiji Ozawa. Fellow Guggenheim Found., 1989, Tanglewood Music Ctr., 1989, 1987, 1986, Rotary Internat., 1988-89, NY State Coun. for Arts, 1996, Chamber Music Am., 1996, Nat. Endowment for Arts, 1994, 1992, 1988; Kate Neal Kinley fellow U. Ill., 1989, Bunting fellow Radcliffe Coll., 1990, Jr. fellow Harvard U., 1991-93; recipient Pullen Meml. prize, Royal Acad. Music, 1989, Barlow Endowment Commn., 1989, Naumburg Found. Commn., 1990, Third Century award, US Office of Copyrights and Patents, 1990, Rudolph Nissim award, ASCAP, 1992, Orchestral Music prize, Ind. State U., 1993, Internat. Prize of Henru Dutilleux, France, 1993, Internat. Orpheus prize for opera, 1994, Fromm Found. Commn., 1996, 1992, many others. Mem. AAAL (Charles Ives scholar, 1989, Charles Ives fellow, 1994, Acad. award in Music, 2001), Sigma Alpha Iota (hon.). Mailing: PO Box 769 Lee MA 01238 Office Phone: 312-566-0522, 413-623-5263. E-mail: art24gusty@aol.com.*

THOMAS, BARBARA L., not-for-profit executive; 2 children. With CBS. Named one of Most Influential Black Americans, Ebony mag., 2006; named to Power 150, 2008. Mem.: Nat. Black MBA Assn. (life; pres. Boston Chpt., v.p. fin. and administrn., CFO, interim pres., CEO 2003—04, pres., CEO 2004—). Office: NBMBAA Ste 1400 180 N Michigan Ave Chicago IL 60601 Office Phone: 312-236-2622. Office Fax: 312-236-0990.

THOMAS, BEVERLY IRENE, special education educator, counseling administrator, educational diagnostician; b. Del Rio, Tex., Nov. 12, 1939; d. Clyde and Eve Whistler; m. James Thomas, Jan. 28, 1972; children: Kenneth (dec.), Wade, Robert, Darcy, Betty Kay, James III, Debra, Brenda, Michael. BM summa cum laude, Sul Ross State U., 1972, MEd in Music, 1976, MEd in Counseling, 1992, MEd in Mid. Mgmt., 1996. Cert. music, 1972, elem. edn., 1974, music edn., 1976, learning disabilities, 1976, spl. edn. generic, 1976, ednl. diagnosis, 1976, ednl. counseling, 1996, spl. edn. counseling and mid. mgmt., 1995, anger resolution therapist, 1995; cert. correctional justice addictions profl.; lic. chem. dependency counselor, 2006. Tchr. Pecos-Barstow-Toyah Ind. Sch. Dist., 1974—92, 1999—2000; edn. diagnostician West Tex. State Sch., Tex. Youth Commn.; tchr. spl. edn. and enhanced 5th grade Pecos-Barstow-Toyah Ind. Sch. Dist., 1999-2000; youth counselor Tex. Workforce Ctr., Pecos, 2000; substance abuse counselor Reeves County Detention Ctr., 2001—; LCDC Clover House Inc, 2004—. Gifted-talented coordinator 5th grade, Pecos-Barstow-Toyah Ind. Sch. Dist., 1999-2000. Mem. AAUW, ASCD, NEA, MENSA, Assn. for Children with Learning Disabilities (local sec. 1974), Tex. State Tchrs. Assn. (treas. 1991-94), Tex. Ednl. Diagnosticians Assn., Tex. Profl. Ednl. Diagnosticians, Reeves County Assn. of Children with Learning Disabilities, Nat. Coun. Tchrs. of Maths., Nat. Coun. Tchrs. English, Learning Disabilities Assn., Nat. Coun. for Geog. Edn., Learning Disabilities Assoc., Tex., Coun. for Exceptional Children, Tex. Counseling Assn., Am. Correctional Assn., Alpha Chi, Kappa Delta Pi, Chi Sigma Iota. Personal E-mail: beverlythomas@valornet.com.

THOMAS, BILL (WILLIAM MARSHALL THOMAS), Former United States Representative from California; b. Wallace, Idaho, Dec. 6, 1941; s. Virgil and Gertrude Thomas; m. Sharon Lynn Hamilton, Jan. 1968; children: Christopher, Amelia. Student, Santa Anna CC, 1961; BA, San Francisco State U., 1963, MA, 1965. Mem. faculty Bakersfield (Calif.) Coll., 1965-74, prof. Am. govt., 1965-74; mem. Calif. State Assembly, 1974-78, US Congress from 22nd Calif. dist. (formerly 21st), 1979—2007; chmn. US House Oversight Com., 1995-2001, US House Adminstrn. Com., 1995—2001, US House Ways & Means Com., 2001—07, US House Joint Com. on Taxation, 2001, 2003—07; vis. fellow Am. Enterprise Inst., 2007—; sr. adv. fed. govt. rels. section Buchanan Ingersoll & Rooney PC, 2007—. Mem. del. to Soviet Union, by Am. Council Young Polit. Leaders, 1977; chmn. Kern County Republican Central Com., 1972-74; mem. Calif. Rep. Com., 1972-80; del. Republican Party Nat. Conv., 1980, 84, 88; mem. Rep. Leader's Task Force on Health Care Reform; vice chmn., US Financial Crisis Inquiry Commn., 2009- Recipient James Madison award Am. Library Assn. 1993, Legis. Svc. award, Pharm. Care Mgmt. Assn., 2000, Congl. award, Small Bus. Coun. Am., 2001 Republican. Baptist. Office: Buchanan Ingersoll & Rooney PC 1750 K St Nw Washington DC 20006-2305 E-mail: bill.thomas@bipc.com.*

THOMAS, BRIAN C., legislative staff member; Sr. legis. asst. to Rep. Charlie Norwood US House of Reps., Washington, 2000—01, chief of staff to Rep. Jeb Hensarling, 2003—04, chief of staff and press sec. to Rep. Kenny Marchant, 2005—; legis. dir. to Senator Chuck Hagel US Senate, Washington, 2001—03. Republican. Office: Office of Rep Kenny Marchant 1037 Longworth House Office Bldg Washington DC 20515-4324 Office Phone: 202-225-6605. Office Fax: 202-225-0074. Business E-Mail: brian.thomas@mail.house.gov.*

THOMAS, BRIAN CHESTER, retired state legislator, engineer; b. Tacoma, May 19, 1939; s. Ralph R. and Katheryne Thomas; m. Judith Lynn Adams, Feb. 20, 1965; children: Jeffrey, Kyle, Cheryl. BS in Engring., Oreg. State U., 1961; student in Law, U. Wash., 1968—70; MBA, Pacific Luth. U., 1979. Civil engr. U.S. Coast Guard, Seattle, 1962-63, ops. officer Astoria, Oreg., 1964-65; sr. sales engr. Puget Sound Energy, Bellevue, Wash., 1965—70; mgr. market rsch. Puget Sound Power & Light Co., Bellevue, Wash., 1971-80, rsch. adminstr., 1981-89, prin. engr., rsch. dir., 1989-97; mem. Wash. Ho. of Reps., Olympia, 1993-2001, mem. forecast coun., 1996-2001, mem. joint select com. on edn. restructuring, 1995-2001, chmn. fin. com., 1995-2001, chmn. Sch. Constrn. Task Force, 1998-99, energy, utilities com., 1999-2001, mem. Edn. Com., 1999-2001. Chair EEI Rsch. Mgmt. Com., 1988-89, EPRI Renewable Com., Palo Alto, Calif., 1989-90; adv. bd. Nat. Renewable Energy Lab., Golden, Colo., 1990-93; mem. adv. bd. sch. elec. engring. Oreg. State U., Corvallis, 1991-97; dep. dir. region 10 U.S. Dept. Transp. Emergency Orgn., Seattle, 1989-93. Bd. dirs. Issaquah (Wash.), Sch. Dist., 1989-93, pres. 1992; trustee Mcpl. League of King County, 2000-03; pres. Friendship Force of Seattle, 2002. Capt. USCGR, 1961-84, ret Master: Knights St. Andrew; mem.: Issaquah Rotary (pres. 1982—83), Preston Aboretum (pres. 1999—2002, dir.), Navy League, Scottish Rite and York Rite, past master: Myrtle Lodge 108 F&AM, Wash. (sec. & treas.), Royal Order of Scotland, Phi Sigma Kappa. Republican/Libertarian. Home: 14715 182nd Pl SE Renton WA 98059-8028

THOMAS, BROOKS, publishing executive, director; b. Phila., Nov. 28, 1931; s. Walter Horstman and Ruth Sterling (Boomer) Thomas; m. Galen Pinckard Clark, Apr. 15, 1969 (div. 1973); m. Kiono Tucciarone, Oct. 7, 2004. BA, Yale U., 1953, LLB, 1956; grad. Advanced Mgmt. Program, Harvard U., 1973. Bar: Pa. 1957, N.Y. 1960. With law firm Winthrop, Stimson, Putnam & Roberts, NYC, 1960—68; sec., gen. counsel Harper & Row, Pubs., Inc., NYC, 1968—69, v.p., gen. counsel, 1969—73, exec. v.p., 1973—79, COO, 1977—81, pres., 1979—87, CEO, 1981—87, chmn. bd., 1986—87; sterling fellow, 2008. Chmn. bd. dirs. Harper & Row, Ltd., London, 1973—87; bd. dirs. Harper & Row, Pty. Ltd., Australia, Harla S.A. de C.V., Mexico, Harper & Row Pubs. Asia, Pty. Ltd., Singapore. Trustee Outward Bound USA, 1980—, vice chmn., 1983—84, chmn., 1984—87; bd. dirs. Nat. Book Awards, 1985—87, chmn., 1986—87; bd. dirs. Outward Bound Internat., 1997—2003, Outward Bound Expenditionary Learning, 2000—; pres., bd. dirs. Butterfield House, 1968—72; trustee, bd. dirs. RADG, Inc., 1987—89; bd. dirs. Thomason Island Outward Bound Edn. Ctr., 1987—96, Colo. Outward Bound Sch., 1990—96, bd. govs., 1996—; bd. dirs. Young Audiences, Inc., 1977—, chmn., 1985—, Vail Valley Inst., 1989—; trustee Episcopal Acad., 2000—, sec., 2002—; mem. devel. bd. Yale U., 1985—89, adv. bd. Sch. Orgn. and Mgmt., 1987—96. Lt. (j.g.) USNR, 1956—59. Sterling fellow, 2008. Mem.: ABA, Assn. Am. Pubs. (bd. dirs. 1980—85, chmn. 1983—85), Assn. Bar City of N.Y., Century Assn. (N.Y.C.), Yale U. Alumni Assn. (law sch. rep. 1980—83), Coun. Fgn. Rels., Essex Yacht Club (Conn.), N.Y. Yacht Club (N.Y.C.), Univ. Club (N.Y.C.), Yale Club (N.Y.C.), Merion Cricket Club (Phila.). Home: 5 Tudor City Pl New York NY 10017-6853 also: 141 Saybrook Rd Essex CT 06426-1412

THOMAS, BYRON ANDREW, lawyer; b. Salem, Oreg., Aug. 31, 1947; s. Byron K. and Mary Barbara (Neidig) T. BA, Tex. Tech. U., 1969, JD, 1976. Bar: Tex. 1976, D.C. 1979, U.S. Ct. Appeals (5th cir.) 1978, U.S. Ct. Appeals (d.C. cir.) 1979. Assoc. Butler, Binion, Rice, Cook & Knapp, Houston, 1976-80; pvt. practice Tyler, Tex., 1980-82; exec. v.p. La. Intrastate Gas Corp., Alexandria, 1982-86; v.p., counsel Celeron Corp., Lafayette, La., 1984—85; v.p. Tenngasco Corp., Houston, 1986-87; pvt. practice Houston, 1987—. Mng. editor Tex. Tech. Law Review, 1976. Chmn. Delia Stewart Dance Co., Houston, 1988. Capt. U.S. Army, 1969-73, Korea. Lutheran. Home and Office: 2407 Wroxton Rd Houston TX 77005-1435

THOMAS, CAROL GUGGENHEIM, history professor, writer; b. Oak Park, Ill., Aug. 11, 1938; d. Gordon Francis and Helen Lee Guggenheim; m. Richard R. Johnson, Oct. 22, 1976; 1 child, Mary Susan Johnson. BA, Carleton Coll., 1960; MA, Northwestern U., 1961, PhD, 1965. Lectr. U. Wash., Seattle, 1964—65, asst. prof. history, 1966—70, assoc. prof. history, 1971—80, prof. history, 1981—. Mem., chair U. Book Store Bd. Trustees, Seattle, 1979—99; grant rev. com. NEH, Fulbright Hays; chair European Studies, 2004—09, Hellenic Studies, 2005—; presenter in field. Author: Alexander the Great in His World, 2006; mem. editl. bd. Jour. Warring States, 2005—, Ancient History Bulletin, 2003—; contbr. articles to profl. jours. Lectr. Naval War Coll.; mem. Wash. Commn. Humanities, 1979—83. Fellow, Am. Coun. Edn., 1979—80. Mem.: Assn. Ancient Historians (pres. 1993—99), Soc. Promotion Hellenic Studies, Hist. Soc. (mem. editl. adv. bd. 2005—). Avocations: travel, hiking. Office: U Wash Dept History Box 353560 Seattle WA 98195 Business E-Mail: carolt@u.washington.edu.

THOMAS, CAROLE LESNIAK, retired music educator; d. Stanley Joseph and Mae Ann Lesniak; m. Dennis Michael Thomas, Sept. 9, 1978; 1 child, Barbara Anne Kopp. BS in Edn., No. Ill. U., DeKalb, 1964; MusM, U. Ill., Champaign-Urbana, 1966, MS in Music Edn., 1968. Cert. music tchr. Music Tchrs. Nat. Assn. Music edn. specialist Kenwood Elem. Sch., Champaign, Ill., 1967—68; music instr. U. Ill., Urbana, 1968—70; piano instr. U. Iowa, Iowa City, 1970—72, asst. prof. piano, 1972—77, assoc. prof. piano, 1977—2002, emerita assoc. prof., 2002—. Head piano Sch. Music U. Iowa, 1992—2000; performer, presenter Nat. Conventions Music Tchrs. Nat. Assn., Denver, NYC, Little Rock, Ark., DC, 1975—94. Grantee Iowa Arts Coun. Grant, 1986—87, 1991—94. Mem.: Iowa City Ind. Piano Tchrs. (v.p. 2009—), Music Tchrs. Nat. Assn. (chmn. West Ctrl. Divsn. Collegiate Artist Auditions 1975—77), Iowa Music Tchrs. Assn. (state group piano chmn. 1978—91, pres. East Ctrl. Assn. 1991—93, chair state convs.), Iowa Fedn. Music Clubs (adv. bd. 2003—07), Pi Kappa Lambda (chpt. pres. 1977—79), Sigma Alpha Iota (chpt. advisor 1972—, pres. Iowa City alumnae chpt. 2005—07). Republican. Roman Catholic. Avocations: reading, sewing, knitting. Home: 1614 13th St Coralville IA 52241 Business E-Mail: carole-thomas@uiowa.edu.

THOMAS, CHARLES EDWARD, engineering educator; b. Zanesville, Ohio, May 29, 1956; s. Chuck and Gloria Thomas; m. Kimberly Ann Koenig, Feb. 28, 1979; children: Amber Marie Thomas-Theriot, Christopher Michael, Stephen Aaron, Allisa Kindel Thomas-Latham, Alaura Caitlin Thomas-Dumont, Adam Kimball. BA, Western Ill. U., Macomb, 1994; MS, U. Tex., Tyler, 1997; PhD, Tex. A & M U., Coll. Sta., 2002. Tng. mgr. Exxon Chem., Baytown, Tex., 1981—93; dept. chair Lee Coll., Baytown, 1994—. Author: (textbook) Safety, Health & Environment, Introduction to Process Technology, Process Technology Equipment & Systems, Process Troubleshooting. Conservative. Mem. Lds Ch. Avocation: writing. Home: 2188 Fm 2797 Dayton TX 77535 Office: Lee Coll PO Box 818 Baytown TX 77522-0818 Office Fax: 281-425-6877. Personal E-mail: cethomas2@earthlink.net. Business E-Mail: cthomas@lee.edu.

THOMAS, CHARLES HILL, geneticist, educator; b. Dexter, Ga., Jan. 31, 1922; s. Charlie Shepard and Annie Grace (Hill) T.; m. Inez Myers, Jan. 3, 1945; children: Diane Cheryl Thomas Howell. BSA, U. Ga., 1952, MSA, 1953; PhD, N.C. State U., Raleigh, 1956. Asst. prof. Miss. State U., Mississippi State, 1956-58, assoc. prof., 1958-66, prof., 1966-87, prof. emeritus in genetics, 1987—, coord. genetics program, 1969-87, advisor gen. agr., 1969-87. Cons. in genetics. Mem. Poultry Sci. Assn., Blue Key, Kiwanis, Phi Kappa Phi, Alpha Zeta, Gamma Sigma Epsilon, Gamma Sigma Delta. Baptist. Avocations: photography, basketball, football. Home: 13839 Highway 25 N Sturgis MS 39769-9486

THOMAS, CHRISTOPHER YANCEY, III, surgeon, educator; b. Kansas City, Mo., Oct. 27, 1923; s. Christopher Yancey and Dorothea Louise (Engel) T.; m. Barbara Ann Barcroft, June 27, 1946; children—Christopher, Gregg, Jeffrey, Anne Student, U. Colo., 1942-44; MD, U. Kans., 1948. Diplomate Am. Bd. Surgery. Intern U. Utah Hosp., Salt Lake City, 1948-49; resident in surgery Cleve. Clinic Found., 1949-52; pvt. practice specializing in surgery Kansas City, Mo., 1954-89. Mem. staff St. Luke's Hosp., chief surgery, 1969-70; mem. staff Children's Mercy Hosp.; clin. prof. surgery U. Mo., Kansas City Med. Sch.; pres. St. Luke's Hosp. Edn. Found., 1977-83, Med. Plaza Corp., 1977-79; pres. Midwest Organ Bank, 1977-82. Editor IMTRAC investment adv. letter, 1978-2000. Served to capt. M.C., U.S. Army, 1952-54 Fellow ACS; mem. AMA, Southwestern Surg. Congress, Central Surg. Assn., Mo. State Med. Soc., Kansas City Surg. Soc. (pres. 1968), Jackson County Med. Soc. (pres. 1971) Clubs: Kansas City Country. Republican. Methodist. Home: 50 Coventry Ct Shawnee Mission KS 66208-5225 Personal E-mail: christhomas5452@sbcglobal.net.

THOMAS, CLARA MCCANDLESS, retired literature educator; b. Strathroy, Ont., Can., May 22, 1919; d. Basil and Mabel (Sullivan) McCandless; m. Morley Keith Thomas, May 23, 1942; children: Stephen, John. BA, U. Western Ont., London, 1941, MA, 1944; PhD, U. Toronto, 1962; DLitt (hon.), York U., 1986, Trent U., 1991; LLD (hon.), Brock U., 1992. Instr. English U. Western Ont., London, 1947-61, U. Toronto, 1958-61; asst. prof. English York U., Toronto, 1961-68, prof., 1969-84, prof. emeritus, Librs. Can. Studies Rsch. fellow, 1984—; acad. adv. panel Social Scis. and Humanities Research Council, 1981-84; mem. Killam Awards Selection Bd., 1978-81; rsch. fellow York U. Librs. Can. Studies, 1984—. Author biography of Anna Jameson, 1967, of Egerton Ryerson, 1969, of Margaret Laurence, 1969, 75, (with John Lennox) of William Arthur Deacon, 1982; Literary criticism (Can.), 1946, 72, 94, Memoir, 1999; mem. editl. bd. Literary History of Can., 1980—, Collected Works of Northrop Frye, 1993—. Recipient Internat. Coun. of Can. Studies prize No. Telecom, 1989; grantee Can. Coun., 1967, 73, Social Sci. and Humanities Rsch. Coun. Can., 1978-80, Clara Thomas Archives and Spl. Collections, York U., 2005. Fellow Royal Soc. Can.; mem. Assn. Can. Univs., Tchrs. English (pres. 1971-72), Assn. Can. and Que. Lit., Bus. and Profl. Women's Club, Assn. for Can. Studies. New Democratic. Office: York U 305 Scott Libr 4700 Keele St North York ON Canada M3J 1P3 Personal E-mail: cthomas1@execulink.com.

THOMAS, CLARENCE, United States supreme court justice; b. Pin Point, Ga., June 23, 1948; s. M.C. Thomas and Leola Anderson (Williams); m. Kathy Grace Ambush, 1971 (div. 1984); 1 child, Jamal Adeen; m. Virginia Lamp, May 30, 1987. Student, Immaculate Conception Sem., 1967—68; BA cum laude, Holy Cross Coll., 1971; JD, Yale U., 1974. Bar: Mo. Asst. atty. gen. State of Mo., Jefferson City, 1974—77; legal counsel Monsanto Company, St. Louis, 1977—79; legislative asst. to Senator John C. Danforth US Senate, Washington, 1979—81; asst. sec. for civil rights US Dept. Edn., Washington, 1981—82; chmn. EEOC, Washington, 1982—90; judge US Ct. Appeals (DC circuit), Washington, 1990—91; assoc. justice US Supreme Ct., Washington, 1991—. Mem. bd. trustees Holy Cross Coll.; bd. advisors DC Cases. Author: My Grandfather's Son: A Memoir, 2007. Named to Power 150, Ebony mag., 2008. Mem.: Internat. Churchill Soc. Roman Catholic. Office: US Supreme Court One First St NE Washington DC 20543-0001*

THOMAS, CLAUDEWELL SIDNEY, psychiatrist, educator; b. NYC, Oct. 5, 1932; s. Humphrey Sidney and Frances Elizabeth (Collins) T.; m. Carolyn Pauline Rozansky, Sept. 6, 1958; children: Jeffrey Evan, Julie-Anne Elizabeth, Jessica Edith. BA, Columbia U., 1952; MD, SUNY, Downstate Med. Ctr., 1956; MPH, Yale U., 1964. Diplomate Nat. Bd. Med. Examiners, Am. Bd. Psychiatry. From instr. to assoc. prof. Yale U., New Haven, 1963-68, dir. Yale tng. program in social community psychiatry, 1967-70; dir. div. mental health service programs NIMH, Washington, 1970-73; chmn. dept. psychiatry UMDNJ, Newark, 1973-83; prof., chmn. dept. psychiatry Drew Med. Sch., 1983—93, chmn. dept. psychiatry, 1983-93; prof. dept. psychiatry UCLA, 1983-94, vice chmn. dept. psychiatry, 1983-93, prof. emeritus dept. psychiatry, 1994—; med. dir. Tokanui Hosp., TeAwamutu, N.Z., 1996. Cons. A.K. Rice Inst., Washington, 1978—80, SAMSA/PHS Cons., 1991—99, L.A.

County Homeless Outreach Program, 2001—04; mem. LA County Superior Ct. Psychol. Panel, 1991—97; cons. psychiatrist L.A. County AB2034 Homeless Outreach Program (Skid Row Dual Diagnoses), 2001—04. Author: (with B. Bergen) Issues and Problems in Social Psychiatry, 1966; editor (with R. Bryce LaPorte) Alienation in Contemporary Society, 1976, (with J. Lindenthal) Psychiatry and Mental Health Science Handbook; mem. editl. bd. Adminstrn. Mental Health. Bd. dirs. Bay Area Found., 1987—. Served to capt. USAF, 1959-61. Fellow APHA, Am. Psychoanalytic Assn. (hon.), Am. Psychiat. Assn. (disting. life), NY Acad. Sci., NY Acad. Medicine; mem. Am. Sociol. Assn., Am. Coll. Mental Health Adminstrs., Am. Coll. Psychiatrists (emeritus), Sigma Xi. Avocations: tennis, racquetball, violin, piano. Office: 30676 Palos Verdes Dr E Palos Verdes Peninsula CA 90275-6354 Personal E-mail: cysid32@ucla.edu, cst240@columbia.edu. *Personal philosophy: Integrity sooner or later calls upon courage. If courage is not home integrity goes away.*

THOMAS, COLIN GORDON, JR., surgeon, medical educator; b. Iowa City, July 25, 1918; s. Colin Gordon and Eloise Kinzer (Brainerd) T.; m. Shirley Forbes, Sept. 14, 1946 (dec.); children: Karen, Barbara, James G., John F. BS, U. Chgo., 1940, MD, 1943. Diplomate Am. Bd. Surgery. Intern U. Iowa Hosp., 1943-44, resident surgery, 1944-45, 47-50; assoc. in surgery U. Iowa Med. Sch., 1950-51, asst. prof., 1951-52; mem. faculty U. N.C. Med. Sch., Chapel Hill, 1952—, prof. surgery, 1961—, Byah Thomason Doxey-Sanford Doxey prof. surgery, 1982—, chmn. dept., 1966-84, chief div. gen. surg., 1984-89, part-time prof., 1991—. Contbr. surg. texts, numerous articles to med. jours. Served to capt., M.C. AUS, 1945-47. Recipient Prof. award U. N.C. Sch. Medicine, 1964, Disting. Svc. award U. Chgo., 1982, Med. Alumni Disting. faculty award U. N.C., 1984; Berryhill lectr. U. N.C., 1989; recipient Fleming Fuller award U. N.C. Hosps., 1994. Mem. AMA, ACS (Disting. Leadership award N.C. chpt. 1990), AAUP, Am. Thyroid Assn., Am. Assn. Cancer Research, Am. Assn. Endocrine Surgeons (pres. 1989-90), Soc. Univ. Surgeons, So. Surg. Assn. (v.p. 1989-90), N.Y. Acad. Scis., Halsted Soc., Am. Surg. Assn., Womack Surg. Soc. (pres. 1981-83), Soc. Internationale de Chirurgie, Soc. Surgery Alimentary Tract, N.C. Surg. Assn., Internat. Assn. Endocrine Surgeons, Kiwanis (pres. Tarheel Golden Kiwanis 2004), Alpha Omega Alpha. Episcopalian (warden 1961-62). Home: 621 Cedars Club Cir Chapel Hill NC 27517 Office: Univ NC Chapel Hill 4005 Burnett-Womack CB 7228 Chapel Hill NC 27599-7228 Business E-Mail: cqt@med.unc.edu.

THOMAS, CRISTINA URDANETA, chemical engineer, researcher; b. Maracaibo, Venezuela, May 11, 1960; d. Gilberto Urdaneta Besson and Maria Teresa Finol; m. Scott D. Thomas, June 2, 1990; children: Daniel J., Marcella N., William S. PhD in Chem. Engring., U. Mass., Amherst, 1992; Licenciado in Chemistry, U. del Zulia, Maracaibo, 1998; Licenciado in Math., U. Nat. Abierta, Caracas, Venezuela, 1999. Vis. rschr. IBM Corp., Kingston, NY, 1985—87; sys. engr. Maraven SA, Lagunillas, Venezuela, 1985; rsch. specialist 3M Co., Maplewood, Minn., 1992—2003, lab. mgr. & DFSS black belt, 2003—. Indsl. advisor MRSEC-U. Wis., Madison, 2009—. Contbr. scientific papers to numerous publs. Chair St Croix Montessori, Stillwater, Minn., 1999—2004. Mem.: Am. Chem. Soc. Achievements include patents in field. Home: 2320 Periwinkle Ave N Stillwater MN 55082 Office: 3M Co Maplewood MN 55144-1000 Personal E-mail: cuthomas@comcast.net. Business E-Mail: cuthomas@mmm.com.

THOMAS, DANIEL EDWARD, bishop; b. Phila., June 11, 1959; s. Francis P. and Anna M. (Weber) Thomas. Grad., St. Charles Borromeo Sem., Wynnewood, Pa.; STL, Pontifical Gregorian U., 1989. Ordained priest Archdiocese of Phila., 1985; parochial vicar St. Joseph's Parish, Aston, Pa., 1985—87; official Congregation for Bishops, Rome, 1990—2005; named monsignor, 2005; pastor Our Lady of the Assumption Parish, Strafford, Pa., 2005—06; ordained bishop, 2006; aux. bishop Archdiocese of Phila., 2006—. Roman Catholic. Office: Office of the Auxiliary Bishop 222 N 17th St Philadelphia PA 19103 Office Phone: 215-587-3600. E-mail: bthomas@adphila.org.

THOMAS, DANIEL FOLEY, retired diversified financial services company executive; b. Washington, Aug. 24, 1950; s. Richard Kenneth and Margaret (Foley) T.; m. Barbara Jane Clark, June 30, 1973; 1 child, Alison Clark. BS in Acctg., Mt. St. Mary's Coll., 1972. CPA, Va. Auditor Deloitte & Touche, Washington, 1972-74; various fin. positions Comm. Satellite Corp., Washington, 1974-78, asst. treas., 1984-85, treas., 1986-87, contr., 1987-89, Comsat Telesystems, Washington, 1978-79; mgr. acctg. and taxes Satellite Bus. Systems, McLean, Va., 1979-81, treas., 1981-84; v.p. fin. Comsat Tech. Products, Inc., Washington, 1985-86, Comsat Video Enterprises, Inc., Washington, 1989-90; exec. v.p. Leasetec Corp., Boulder, Colo., 1990—2002; ret., 2002. Instr. acctg. Colo. State U., 2003—, U. Colo., 2003—. Active cmty. svc. activities. Mem. AICPA, Va. Jaycees (life), Great Falls Jaycees (pres. 1978). Roman Catholic. Avocations: running, golf. Home: 36495 Peak to Peak Hwy Nederland CO 80466 Office Phone: 303-808-1181. E-mail: dfthomas@aol.com.

THOMAS, DAVID ALBERT, law educator, director; b. LA, Feb. 4, 1944; s. Albert Rees and Betty Lou (Adams) T.; m. Paula Rasmussen, Aug. 7, 1967; children: Rebecca, David R., John H., Matthew A., Susannah, Amanda, Christina, Erin. BA, Brigham Young U., 1967; JD, Duke U., 1972; MLS, Brigham Young U., 1977. Jud. clk. U.S. Dist. Ct. Utah, Salt Lake City, 1972-73; pvt. practice, 1973-74; asst. prof. Law Sch. Brigham Young U., Provo, 1974-76, dir. law libr. Law Sch., 1974-90, assoc. prof. Law Sch., 1976-79, prof. Law Sch., 1979—, Rex E. Lee endowed chair, prof. law, 2005—. Accreditation site insp. ABA, Chgo., 1978—. Author: Utah Civil Procedure, 1980, (with others) A Practical Guide to Disputes Between Adjoining Landowners, 1989, Utah Civil Practice, 1992, 6th edit., 2007, (with others) Thomas and Backman on Utah Real Property Law, 1999, 2d edit., 2005; prin. author, editor-in-chief: Thompson on Real Property, Thomas Edition, 15 vols., 1994; contbr. articles to profl. jours. With U.S. Army, 1969-71, Vietnam. Mem. ABA (mem. sect. coun., chmn. real property trust and estate sect.) Office: Brigham Young U Law Sch Provo UT 84602 Business E-Mail: david_thomas@byu.edu.

THOMAS, DAVID JOSEPH, literature and language professor; b. Washington, Pa., Jan. 15, 1955; s. Carl Gene and Helen Ann Thomas; m. Edye Lee Heller, Aug. 7, 2003; 1 child, James Dylan. PhD, W.Va. U., Morgantown, 2001. Prof., English West Liberty State Coll., W.Va., 1985—. Bd. dir. Wheeling Human Rights Commn., W.Va., 1997—2005. Named Prof. of Yr., West Liberty State Coll., 1991—92, 1993—94, 1997—98. Home: 25 Walnut Ave 1 Wheeling WV 26003-5726 Office: West Liberty State Coll Rt 88 West Liberty WV 26074-0295 Home Phone: 304-233-8453; Office Phone: 304-336-8189. Office Fax: 304-336-8199. Personal E-mail: drwavydavy@comcast.net. Business E-Mail: thomasdj@westliberty.edu.

THOMAS, DAVID LINDSEY, lawyer, member of former state board education former state senator; b. Washington, Jan. 14, 1962; s. Lindsey Kay and Nancy Ruth Thomas; m. Lynn Stosich Thomas, Apr. 21, 1987; children: Tyler, Tristan, Richard, Gwendolyn. BS in Fin., Brigham Young U., Provo, UT, 1986; JD, Coll. William and Mary, Williamsburg, Va., 1990. Vice chmn. Utah Comm. Agy. Network, West Valley City, Utah, 1996—2006; chief civil dep. Summit County Atty., Utah, 1996—; state senator, 2002—06, Utah State Bd. Edn., 2008—; vice chair State Bd. Edn. Finance Com. Mem. Utah Tech. Commn., 2002—06; former chmn. standing commn. edn. Utah State Senate, Salt Lake City, former chmn. judiciary interim com., former chmn. exec. offices and criminal justice appropriations com. Contbr. articles to law jours. Planning commr., South Weber, Utah, 2000; city councilman, 2001—02, 2007—. Maj. US Army, 1990—99. Recipient Profl. Merit award, ABA, 1991, Exec. Dirs. award, Utah Sheriff's Assn., 2005, Exec. award for merit, Dept. Pub. Safety, 2006. Mem.: Nat. Assn. Bond Attys. Business E-Mail: dthomas@cosimanct.ut.us.

THOMAS, DAVID LLEWELLYN, physician; b. Clinton, Iowa, June 11, 1948; s. Marvin Llewellyn and Marjorie Emma (Mayer) Thomas; m. Sheryl L. Miller, 2002; children: Tana, Paige, Drew, Aleksandr. BA in Zoology, U. Iowa, 1970, MD, 1974. Diplomate Am. Bd. Family Practice, cert. added qualification in geriatric medicine. Resident in family medicine U. Ill., Rockford, 1977; pvt. practice Marshalltown, Iowa, 1977—; family physician McFarland Clinic, PC, Marshalltown, 1994, also bd. dirs., v.p., 1995—98, treas., 1999—. Clin. lectr. U. Iowa Coll. Medicine, Iowa City, 1981—2007, adj. clin. asst. prof., 2007—; med. dir. Iowa Found. Med. Ctr., 1992—. Bd. dirs. Iowa Found. Med. Care, Des Moines, 1986—2001, Iowa Ctrl. Agrl. Safety and Health, 1995—97; trustee Marshalltown Med. and Surg. Ctr., 1998—2003. Mem.: Am. Health Quality Assn. (bd. dirs. 1995—2005, v.p. 1997—2000, pres. 2000—03). Republican. Episcopalian. Office: McFarland Clinic 303 Nicholas Dr Ste 1 Marshalltown IA 50158-4443 Office Phone: 641-752-0099. Business E-Mail: dthomas@mcfarlandclinic.com.

THOMAS, DEB, toy company executive; Grad., Providence Coll. With KPMG Peat Marwick, LLP; v.p., asst. contr. Hasbro Inc., 1998—2003, contr., 2003, sr. v.p., 2003—09, head, corp. fin., 2007—09, CFO, 2009—. Office: Hasbro Inc 1027 Newport Ave Pawtucket RI 02862 Office Phone: 401-431-8697. Office Fax: 401-727-5544.*

THOMAS, DONALD LEE, construction technology educator; b. Hampton, Va., Jan. 28, 1964; s. Lloyd Jene Thomas Sr. and Elsie Marie Thomas, Senior. Cert. in project planning and cost estimating, Old Dominion U., 1989, cert. in purchasing and supply chain mgmt., 2002; B in Mgmt., Calif. Coast U., Santa Ana, 2006; cert. in Paralegal studies, Old Dominion U., Ctr. for Global Bus. & Exec. Edn., Norfolk, Virginia, 1993—93. Cert. quality assurance sys. Def. Logistics Agency, in bus. info. tech. No. Va. Cmty. Coll., 2000, in paralegal studies Va., 1993. Quality assurance specialist Def. Logistics Agy., Richmond, Va., 2001—; instr. constrn. tech. No. Va. CC, Woodbridge, Va., 2000—, Germanna CC, Fredericksburg, Va., 2002—; bldg. inspector nat. office IRS, Washington. Mem. Treasury Taxpayer Advocacy Panel, 2009—. Author: (instrn. manual) Reading Construction Prints, Student Supplement. Mem.: Green Bldg. Inst., Am. Solar Energy Soc., DC Area Inventor Assn., Intellectual Property Owners Assn. (corr.; apptd. com. mem. small bus. affairs 2004—06). Achievements include invention of building energy saving equipment; solar technology; patents for portable photovoltaic window system; authority in workforce development and training. Office Phone: 757-593-1005. Personal E-mail: printreaders@hotmail.com.

THOMAS, DOROTHY, indexing consultant, writer; b. N.Y.C., Mar. 3, 1923; d. Hyman and Clara (Lond) Fisch; student Hunter Coll., 1940-43; cert. N.Y. U. Sch. Bus., 1944; m. Sidney Thomashower, Sept. 2, 1944; children: William Jay, James Evan. Personnel troubleshooter W.P.B., 1943; employment mgr. Emerson Radio & Phonograph Corp., 1943-47; editor, author, 1947—; indexer, cons., N.Y.C., 1960—; biographer, lectr., radio producer and moderator; specialist in history of women in legal profession; dir. spl. projects Found. Continuing Legal Edn.; dir. Documentation Abstracts Inc., lectr. colls., clubs, orgns. Active legis. reform and women's movement; mem. Nat. Women's Polit. Caucus, NOW. Mem. AFTRA, Am. Soc. Indexers (pres. elect 1982-83, pres. 1983-84, dir.), Coalition of Labor Union Women, Friends of Columbia Libraries, Friends of Schlesinger Library of Harvard U., N.Y. Hist. Soc. Ind. Democrat. Club: Women's City (N.Y.C.). Author: Women Lawyers 2009, U.S., 1957; Women, The Bench and The Bar; contbr. articles and biographies to Notable American Women, 1607-1950, 1971, Law Book Indexing, 1983; author: Wigmore on Evidence, Vol. XI, 1985, also other indexes and tables. Home and Office: 123 W 74th St New York NY 10023-2209

THOMAS, DWIGHT REMBERT, writer; b. Savannah, Ga., Dec. 8, 1944; s. Huguenin and Alma (Sanders) Thomas. BA in English with honors, Emory U., 1967; PhD in Am. Lit., U. Pa., 1978. Fellow English dept. U. Pa., Phila., 1971-78; writer Savannah, 1979—. Cons. Film Odyssey, Washington, 1988—89. Author: (book) The Poe Log: A Documentary Life of Edgar Allan Poe, 1987. Dir. Edgar Allan Poe Mus., Richmond, 1988—96. With US Army, 1969—71. Mem.: MLA, Am. Med. Writers Assn., Mensa (treas. Savannah area 1985—88, local sec. 1989—90), Phi Beta Kappa. Roman Catholic. Avocations: German language, current cinema, bicycling. Home: 7 E Gordon St Savannah GA 31401-4925

THOMAS, DYNDA A., lawyer; b. Springfield, Ill., 1959; BA magna cum laude, Miami U., 1982; JD, U. Cin., 1986. Bar: Ohio 1986. Ptnr. Squire, Sanders & Dempsey LLP, Cleve., co-chmn., Project Fin. Practice Group. Mem.: ABA (global infrastructure com., Pub. Utility, Comm. & Transp. Law Sect.), Cleve. Bar Assn. (Real Property, Probate & Trust Law Sect.). Office: Squire Sanders & Dempsey LLP 4900 Key Tower 127 Public Sq Cleveland OH 44114-1304 Office Phone: 216-479-8583. Office Fax: 216-479-8780. Business E-Mail: dthomas@ssd.com.

THOMAS, EDWARD DONNALL, internist, hematologist, retired medical educator; b. Mart, Tex., Mar. 15, 1920; m. Dorothy Martin; 3 children. BA, U. Tex., 1941, MA, 1943; MD, Harvard U., 1946; MD (hon.), U. Cagliari, Sardinia, 1981, U. Verona, Italy, 1991, U. Parma, 1992, U. Barcelona, Spain, 1994, U. Warsaw, Poland, 1996, U. Jagiellonski, Cracow, Poland, 1996. Lic. physician Mass., N.Y., Wash., diplomate Am. Bd. Internal Medicine. Intern in medicine Peter Bent Brigham Hosp., Boston, 1946—47, rsch. fellow hematology, 1947—48; NRC postdoctoral fellow in medicine dept. biology MIT, Cambridge, 1950—51; chief med. resident, sr. asst. resident Peter Bent Brigham Hosp., 1951—53, hematologist, 1953—55; instr. medicine Harvard Med. Sch., Boston, 1953—55; rsch. assoc. Cancer Rsch. Found. Children's Med. Ctr., Boston, 1953—55; physician-in-chief Mary Imogene Bassett Hosp., Cooperstown, NY, 1955—63; assoc. clin. prof. medicine Coll. Physicians and Surgeons Columbia U., NYC, 1955—63; attending physician U. Wash. Hosp., Seattle, 1963—90; prof. medicine Sch. Medicine U. Wash., Seattle, 1963—90, head divsn. oncology Sch. Medicine, 1963—85, prof. emeritus medicine Sch. Medicine, 1990—; dir. med. oncology Fred Hutchinson Cancer Rsch. Ctr., Seattle, 1974—89, assoc. dir. clin. rsch. programs, 1982—89, mem., 1974—. Mem. hematology study sect. NIH, 1965—69; mem. bd. trustees and med. sci. adv. com. Leukemia Soc. Am., Inc., 1969—73; mem. clin. cancer investigation rev. com. NCI, 1970—74; 1st ann. Eugene C. Eppinger lectr. Peter Bent Brigham Hosp. and Harvard Med. Sch., 1974; Lilly lectr. RCP, London, 1977; Stratton lectr. Internat. Soc. Hematology, 1982; Paul Aggeler lectr. U. Calif., San Francisco, 1982; 65th Mellon lectr. U. Pitts. Sch. Medicine, 1984; Stanley Wright Meml. lectr. Western Soc. Pediat. Rsch., 1985; Adolfo Ferrata lectr. Italian Soc. Hematology, Verona, Italy, 1991. Mem. editl. bd. Blood, 1962—75, 1977—82, Transplantation, 1970—76, Proc. of Soc. for Exptl. Biology and Medicine, 1974—81, Leukemia Rsch., 1977—87, Hematological Oncology, 1982—87, Jour. Clin. Immunology, 1982—87, Am. Jour. Hematology, 1985—, Bone Marrow Transplantation, 1986—. With US Army, 1948—50. Recipient A. Ross McIntyre award, U. Nebr. Med. Ctr., 1975, Philip Levine award, Am. Soc. Clin. Pathologists, 1979, Disting. Svc. in Basic Rsch. award, Am. Cancer Soc., 1980, Kettering prize, GM Cancer Rsch. Found., 1981, Spl. Keynote Address award, Am. Soc. Therapeutic Radiologists, 1981, Robert Roesler de Villiers award, Leukemia Soc. Am., 1983, Karl Landsteiner Meml. award, Am. Assn. Blood Banks, 1987, Terry Fox award, Can., 1990, Internat. award, Gairdner Found., 1990, Hong Kong prize, N.Am. Med. Assn., 1990, Nobel Prize in Medicine, 1990, Presdl. medal of sci., NSF, 1990, Lifetime Achievement award, Am. Soc. Blood and Marrow Transplantation, 2004. Mem.: NAS, Soc. Exptl. Biology and Medicine, Western Assn. Physicians, Swiss Soc. Hematology, Internat. Soc. Hematology, Internat. Soc. Exptl. Hematology, Am. Soc. Hematology (pres. 1987—88, Henry M. Stratton lectr. 1975), Am. Soc. Clin. Investigation, Am. Soc. Clin. Oncology (David A. Karnoksky Meml. lectr. 1983), Am. Fedn. Clin. Rsch., Assn. Am. Physicians (Kober medal 1992), Am. Assn. Cancer Rsch., Academie Royale de Medicine de Belgique (corr.), Nat. Acad. Medicine Mex. (hon.), Royal Coll. Physicians and Surgeons Can. (hon.), Swedish Soc. Hematology (hon.). Office: Fred Hutchinson Cancer Ctr 1100 Fairview Ave N D5-100 PO Box 19024 Seattle WA 98109-1024

THOMAS, ELLEN LOUISE, school system administrator; b. Doylestown, Pa., Nov. 30, 1940; d. Edward Martin and Evelyn Graham (Axenroth) Happ; m. Eugene Greene Leffever, June 30, 1963 (dec. Nov. 1978); children: Eugene Greene II, Jeanette Ellen Dellaripa; m. William Dewey Thomas, Sept. 15, 1981; 1 child, Jeremiah David. BA in Edn., Immaculata Coll., Pa., 1962; postgrad., Pa. State U., 1962-67. Pvt. practice tutor, Doylestown, 1958-65; tchr. Cen. Bucks Sch. System, Doylestown, 1962-65; adminstr. The Curiosity Shoppe, Doylestown, 1965—, The Toddler Ctr., Doylestown, 1979—; exec. dir. Camp Curiosity, Doylestown, 1984—, Thomas Lea Equestrian Ctr., Doylestown, 1988—. Tchr. trainer Confortunity of Christian Doctrine, Doylestown, 1965-78; cons. early childhood Am. Sch. in Hong Kong, 1981-84; lectr. in early childhood Bucks County Community Ctr., Newtown, Pa., 1978-90; workshop facilitator Head Start, Phila., 1990; cons. day care Cen. Bucks C. of C., Doylestown, 1989-90; ednl. coord. Forest Grove Presbyn. Ch., 1984-90. Mem. U.S. C. of C., Washington, Bucks County C. of C., Doylestown, Nat. Fedn. of Ind. Bus., Washington; children's ministry coord. Jesus Focus Ministry, 1995—; trainer Pa. Child Care, 1995—; past pres. Pa. Day Camp Assn., 1998-2001; Sunday sch. tchr. Hilltown Bapt. Ch., 1995-2000; mem. Am. Camping Assn., 1994-, Plumstead Christian Sch. Bd., 1995-2001; varsity tennis coach Plumstead Christian Sch.-boys, 1998-2004, girls, 2001-2007; children's chmn. Central Bucks Village Fair, 2001-03; mem. Quality Child Care Coun., Pa. Keystone Stars; bd. dirs., ednl. chair Plumstead Christian Sch., 2002-05. Mem. ASCD, Assn. for Childhood Edn. Internat., United Pvt. Acad. Schs. Assn., Bucks County Assn. Edn. Young Children (pres. 1974-78). Office: The Curiosity Shoppe 4425 Landisville Rd Doylestown PA 18901-1134 E-mail: FaxThomdew@aol.com.

THOMAS, ELLIOTT GRIFFIN, bishop emeritus; b. Pitts., July 15, 1926; Ordained priest Diocese of St. Thomas, VI, 1986; ordained bishop, 1993; bishop Diocese of St. Thomas, VI, 1993-99. Roman Catholic. Office: PO Box 301825 Charlotte Amalie VI 00803-1825 Office Phone: 340-776-3166. Office Fax: 340-774-5816. E-mail: chancery@islands.vi.

THOMAS, ESTHER MERLENE, elementary and adult education educator; b. San Diego, Oct. 16, 1945; d. Merton Alfred and Nellie Lida (Von Pilz) T. AA with honors, Grossmont Coll., 1966; BA with honors, San Diego State U., 1969; MA, U. Redlands, 1977. Cert. elem. and adult edn. tchr.; cert. in crosscultural lang. and acad. devel., English lang. devel. Tchr. Cajon Valley Union Sch. Dist., El Cajon, 1969—; sci. fair coord. Flying Hills Sch. Tchr. Hopi and Navajo Native Americans, Ariz., Utah, 1964-74, Goose and Gander Nursery Sch., Lakeside, Calif., 1964-66; dir., supt. Bible and Sunday schs. various chs., Lakeside, 1961-87; mem. sci. com., math. coun. Cajon Valley Union Sch. Dist., 1990-91, libr. com., 1997-98. Author: Individualized Curriculum in the Affective Domain; co-author: Campbell County, The Treasured Years, 1990; songwriter: songs Never Trouble Trouble, Old Glory, Jesus Is Our Lord, Daniel's Prayer, There Lay Jesus, God's Hands, Washing Machine Charlie, Playmates, The Kid in the Hall, Spring Time on the Blue Ridge, Christ's DNA, If You Need Me, Chances (Four Star award, 2003), Blame, The Star of Bethlehem, Where the Eagle Flies, Born to Win, Happy Birthday Dear Jesus, Christmas Lights, Walk the Line, You Don't Know What Repentance Is, I'm Asking You, Clear the Path Lord, Aqua Forte, In the Volume of the Book, Home is Where the Heart Is, You Don't Even Know Who I Am, No Place to Cry, To Walk With God, Ixnay, If You Never Loved Me, for Columbine Records Corp., Life of A Single Woman, Take This Pain Away, We Can Keep In Touch, Let Me Know, A Letter Is A Letter, The Battle, 2004; contbr. articles to profl. jours., newspapers, chpts. to books. Tem. U.S. Senatorial Club, Washington, 1984—, Conservative Caucus, Inc., Washington, 1988—, Ronald Reagan Presdl. Found., Ronald Reagan Rep. Ctr., 1988, Rep. Presdl. Citizen's Adv. Commn., 1989—, Rep. Platform Planning Com., Calif., 1992, at-large del. representing dist. #45, Lakeside, Calif., 1992, 1995—, Am. Security Coun., Washington, 1994, Congressman Hunter's Off Road Adv. Coun., El Cajon, Calif., 1994, Century Club, San Diego Rep. Century Club, 1995; mem. health articulation com. project AIDS, Cajon Valley Union Sch. Dist., 1988—, Recruit Depot Hist. Mus., San Diego, 1989, Citizen's Drug Free Am., Calif., 1989—, The Heritage Found., 1988—; charter mem. Marine Corps Mus.; life mem. San Diego Aerospace Mus.; mem. Lakeside Centennial Com., 1985-86; hon. mem. Rep. Presdl. Task Force, Washington, 1986; del. Calif. Rep. Senatorial Mid-Term Conv., Washington, 1994; mus. curator Lakeside Hist. Soc., 1992-93, life mem.; mem. Rep. Nat. Com., Washington, 2003 Recipient Outstanding Svc. award PTA, 1972-74, Outstanding Tchr. award KYXY Radio, San Diego, 1999, Dream Classroom award KSWB-TV, San Diego, 2005; recipient Hats Off to Tchr. award, San Diego Bd. Edn., 1989, others; nominee Cajon Valley Edn. Found. Stars, 2009, Calif. Mem. NRA, Tchrs. Assn., Calif. Tchrs. Assn., Cajon Valley Educators Assn. (faculty advisor, rep. 1980-82, 84-86, 87-88), Nat. Trust for Hist. Preservation, Christian Bus. and Profl. Women, Trust for Hist. Preservation, Nat. WWII Memml. (life, charter), Ridgecrest Golden Terrace Park Assn. (pres. 1998-99), Capitol Hill Women's Club, Am. Ctr. for

Law and Justice, Internat. Christian Women's Club (Christian amb. to Taiwan, Korea, 1974). Independent. Avocations: travel, vocal music, piano, guitar. Office: Flying Hills Elem Sch 1251 Finch St El Cajon CA 92020-1433

THOMAS, ETAN, professional basketball player, poet; b. Harlem, NY, Apr. 1, 1978; s. Deborah Thomas; m. Nichole Oliver; children: Malcolm, Imani. BS in Bus. Mgmt., Syracuse U., NY, 2000. Ctr. Washington Wizards, 2001—09, Minn. Timberwolves, 2009, Oklahoma City Thunder, 2009—. Political spkr. and activist. Author: (volume of poetry) More Than An Athlete, 2005; contbr. articles to The Huffington Post. Named Defensive Player of Yr., Big East Conf., 2000, First Team All-Conf., 2000. Office: Oklahoma City Thunder 100 W Reno Rd Oklahoma City OK 73102*

THOMAS, EUGENE, social worker; b. Danville, Ill., Feb. 23, 1933; s. John and Anna (Tate) T. BS, Eastern U., Charleston, Ill., 1954; MS, U. Ill., 1958; MA, U. Chgo., 1971. Lic. social worker, Ill. Tchr. Chgo. Bd. Edn., 1959-61; case worker Dept. Pub. Aid, Chgo., 1961-69; psychotherapist Evanston (Ill.) Family Counseling Svc., 1974-82, Evanston Hosp. Evaluation Ctr., 1975-76; sch. social worker Evanston Sch. Dist. 65, 1971—. Field instr. social work U. Chgo., U. Ill., Jane Addams Sch. Social Work, Loyola U., 1976—. Mem. adv. bd. Jane Addams Sch. Social Work, 1989—). With U.S. Army, 1955-57. Danville (Ill.) High Sch. scholar, 1950. Mem. NASW (co-chmn. coun. sch. social workers 1979-80), Ill. Assn. Sch. Social Workers (co-chmn. profl. practice com. 1975—), Acad. Cert. Social Workers, Lic. Clin. Social Work, Nat. Conf. Social Welfare, Nat. Black Child Devel. Inst. Democrat. Home: 8847 S Dante Ave Apt 3 Chicago IL 60619-7111 Office: Evanston Sch Dist 65 1314 Ridge Ave Evanston IL 60201-4132

THOMAS, FAYE EVELYN J., elementary and secondary school educator; b. Summerfield, La., Aug. 3, 1933; d. Reginald Felton and Atlee (Hunter) Johnson; m. Archie Taylor Thomas, Sept. 8, 1960; 1 child, Dwayne Andre. BA, So. U., 1954; student, Tuskegee Inst., 1958, student, 1969, U. Detroit, 1961, student, 1962, student, 1963, Ctrl. Mich. U., 1965; MS, U. Ctrl. Ark., 1971, Cleve. State U., 1979. Tchr. Cullen (La.) Elem. Sch., 1957; tchr. English and social studies Charles Brown H.S., Springhill, La., 1957—70; tchr. English, Upward Bound Program, Grambling State U., 1968; tchr. English, Springhill H.S., 1970; elem. intermediate tchr. Riveredge Elem. Sch., Berea, Ohio, 1971—93; tchr. 7th grade English, Ford Mid. Sch., 1993—94. Tchr. asst. elem. coun. curriculum and instrn. Berea Sch. Dist., 1984—85. Author: When the Time Is Right, Move On, 2002, A Journey to the Mountain Top, 2003. Program dir. teen pregnancy prevention program First Bapt. Ch., Cullen, La., 2003—04. Grantee, EDPA, 1970—71, Internat. Paper Found., 1958, 1960, NDEA, 1965; scholar Martha Holden Jennings scholar, 1984—85. Mem.: ASCD, NEA, N.E. Ohio Tchrs. Assn., Berea Edn. Assn., Ohio Edn. Assn., Ohio Motorists Assn., Charles Brown Soc. Orgn. (trustee 1984—), Black Caucus NEA, People United to Save Humanity, Toastmasters, Order Eastern Star. Democrat. Baptist. Office: 311 Henrietta White Blvd Springhill LA 71075-8407

THOMAS, FELTON, JR., library director; b. 1966; BA in Psychology, U. Nevada, Las Vegas, 1990; MLIS, U. Hawaii, Manoa, 1993; student, Simmons Coll., Boston. Grad. Urban Libr. Coun. Exec. Leadership Inst. Regional br. svcs. dir. Las Vegas-Clark County Libr. Dist., 2004—08; dir. Cleve. Pub. Libr., 2009—. Named a Mover & Shaker, Libr. Jour., 2002. Office: Cleve Pub Libr 325 Superior Ave NE Cleveland OH 44114 Office Phone: 216-623-2800. Office Fax: 216-623-7015.*

THOMAS, FORSTHUBER G., immunologist, educator; MD., U. Tubingen, Germany, 1987. Diplomate surgical and clinical pathology Am. Bd. Pathology, 1998. Prof. U. Tex., San Antonio, 2005—. Achievements include research in epitope spreading, neonatal Th2 immune deviation.

THOMAS, FRANK NELSON, family therapist; b. Volga, SD, Nov. 9, 1953; s. Marlys D. (Hagen) T.; m. Lori Rae Watchorn, Aug. 21, 1976; 1 child, Allison Leigh. BS summa cum laude, U. S.D., 1975; postgrad., St. Paul's Sem., 1976-77; MDiv summa cum laude, N.Am. Bapt. Coll., 1980; PhD, Tex. Tech. U., 1988; postgrad., U. Nebr., 1982—. Cert. marriage and family therapist, Wash., Tex. Instr. and family therapist Tex. Tex. U., Lubbock, 1983-88, project coord., therapist, Adolescent Drug Treatment Program, 1985-88; dir. outpatient svcs. Willow Creek Hosp., Arlington, Tex., 1988-89; asst. prof., grad. faculty mem. Tex. Women's U., Denton, 1989—. Co-founder The Genesis Found., Inc., Ft. Worth, 1990—; cons., affiliate Willow Creek Hosp., Arlington, 1989—. Author: (with others) Eating Disorders, 1987, (with others) Family Therapy Sourcebook, 1987; contbr. articles to profl. jours. Mem. Mental Health Assn. of Tarrant County, Ft. Worth, 1989-90, Interprofl. Mental Health Liaison Com. of Tex., 1988-91; advisor Assessment Ctr. of Tarrant, Ft. Worth, 1989-90. Mem. Am. Assn. for Marriage and Family Therapy (cert.), Tex. Assn. for Marriage and Family Therapy (exec. dir. 1985-91, Svc. award 1987, Commendation 1991), Phi Kappa Phi. Democrat. Baptist. Avocations: music, outdoor recreation, hiking, aerobic walking. Office: Tex Assn Marriage Family Therapy PO Box 331083 Fort Worth TX 76163-1083

THOMAS, FRANKLIN AUGUSTINE, lawyer, consultant; b. Bklyn., May 27, 1934; s. James and Viola (Atherley) T.; div.; children: Keith, Hillary, Kerrie, Kevin. BA, Columbia U., 1956, LL.B., 1963; LL.D. (hon.), Yale U., 1970, Fordham U., 1972, Pratt Inst., 1974, Pace U., 1977, Columbia U., 1979, New School U., 2002. Bar: N.Y. 1964. Atty. Fed. Housing and Home Finance Agy., NYC, 1963-64; asst. US atty. (so. dist.) NY US Dept. Justice, 1964-65; dep. police commr. for legal matters NYC, 1965-67; pres., CEO Bedford Stuyvesant Restoration Corp., Bklyn., 1967-77; pres. The Ford Found., 1979-96; cons. TFF Study Group, 1996—2005, The Study Group, 2005—. Bd. dirs. Citibank, N.A., 1970-98, Citigroup Inc., 1998-2009, ALCOA Inc., 1977-; chmn. The September 11th Fund, 2001-06 Trustee Columbia U., 1969-75. Served with USAF, 1956-60. Recipient LBJ Found. award for Contbn. to Betterment of Urban Life, 1974, Medal of Excellence Columbia U., 1976, Alexander Hamilton award Columbia U., 1983

THOMAS, FREDERICK BRADLEY, lawyer; b. Evanston, Ill., Aug. 13, 1949; s. Frederick Bradley and Katherine Kidder (Bingham) T.; m. Elizabeth Maxwell, Oct. 25, 1975; children: Bradley Bingham, Stephens Maxwell, Rosa Macaulay. AB, Dartmouth Coll., 1971; JD, U. Chgo., 1974. Bar: Ill. 1974. Law clk. to hon. judge John C. Godbold U.S. Ct. Appeals (5th cir.), Montgomery, Ala., 1974-75; assoc. Mayer Brown LLP, Chgo., 1975—80, ptnr., 1981—. Bd. trustees La Rabida Children's Hosp., 1990—; bd. mgrs. YMCA Met. Chgo., 2002—. Mem.: ABA, Chgo. Coun. Lawyers. Republican. Episcopalian. Office: Mayer Brown LLP 71 South Wacker Dr Chicago IL 60606-4637

THOMAS, GARY LYNN, information technology executive; b. Port Vue, Pa., May 15, 1942; s. Willis L. and Luella M. (Rorabaugh) T.; m. Sharen A. Gibbons, May 13, 1967; children— Gregory Scott, Tara Elizabeth. BS in Bus. Adminstrn, Pa. State U., 1964; grad., Sch. Bank Adminstrn., U. Wis., 1973. CPA, Pa. Sr. auditor Arthur Andersen & Co., Los Angeles and Pitts., 1964-69; v.p. and dep. comptroller Pitts. Nat. Bank, 1969-77; v.p. and treas. Md. Nat. Corp., Balt., 1977-80; v.p., mgr. corp. fin. div. Md. Nat. Bank, Balt.; exec. v.p. adminstrn. Peterson, Howell & Heather, Hunt Valley, Md., 1980-82; v.p. fin. Am. TeleServices, Inc, a Metromedia co., Balt., 1983-85; chief fin. officer First Cellular Group, Inc., Balt., 1985-88, Schelle, Warner, Murray & Thomas, Inc., Balt., 1988—95. Mng. dir. Schelle Cellular Group, Inc., 1989—; pres. Ruxton Capital Group, Inc., 1989-95; chief fin. officer Am. Personal Communications, Inc., Balt. and D.C., 1990-98; adj. instr. Sch. Bank Adminstrn., U. Wis., 1975-80; speaker 14th ann. Bank Tax Inst., 1978. Mem. adv. bd., fin. com. St. Joseph Hosp., Balt., 1979-1982; bd. dirs. industry luncheon club Towson State U., 1980-1985. Served with USAR, 1965-1971. Inducted into McKeesport H.S. Hall of Fame, 1994. Mem. AICPA, Pa. Inst. CPAs, Md. Assn. CPAs (prior chmn. mems. in industry com.), Greater Naples Leadership Program, Conservancy SW Fla.(bd. dir., treas.). Independent. Methodist. Home: 575 18th Ave S Naples FL 34102-7536

THOMAS, GEORGE LEO, bishop; b. Anaconda, Mont., May 19, 1950; s. Mary (Cronin) and George Thomas. BA, Carroll Coll., 1972; MDiv, St. Thomas Sem., Bothell, Wash.; MS in Counseling & Cmty. Mental Health, U. Wash., 1983, PhD, 1986. Ordained priest Archdiocese of Seattle, 1976, chancellor, vicar gen., 1987—99, aux. bishop, 2000—04; assoc. pastor Holy Family Parish, Kirkland, Wash., St. James Cathedral, Seattle; parish adminstr. Sacred Heart Parish, Bellevue, Wash.; with Holy Innocents Mission, Duvall, Wash.; ordained bishop, 2000; bishop Diocese of Helena, Mont., 2004—. Chancellor, bd. trustees Carroll Coll., Helena, Mont., 2004—; bd. dirs. Found. Cath. Diocese of Helena, Cath. Soc. Svcs. for Mont., Cath. Relief Svcs. Recipient Gordon C. Lee award, U. Wash., 1986. Mem.: US Conf. Cath. Bishops (comm. com., comm. subcommittee policy & practices, ad hoc com. for Native Am. Catholics), Mont. Assn. Churches (bd. dirs.), Mont. Cath. Conf. (bd. dirs.). Roman Catholic. Office: Diocese of Helena PO Box 1729 Helena MT 59624-1729 Office Phone: 406-442-5820.

THOMAS, GERALDINE HOGE, elementary school educator; b. Eveleth, Minn., Apr. 8, 1937; d. Robert and Dora (Tassi) Rajacich; m. Gregg LeRoy Hoge, Sept. 15, 1963 (div. Feb. 1972); 1 child, Sheryl Maurine; m. Lance Edward Thomas, March 27, 2007. BS, U. Minn., 1959; MA with honors, Pepperdine U. Cert. elem. tchr., Calif. Tchr. Chaska Pub. Schs., Minn., 1959-60, Minnetonka Pub. Schs., Minn., 1960-62, Norwalk La Mirada Pub. Schs., Calif., 1962-64, Culver City Unified Sch. Dist., Calif., 1966—2000. Fellow Culver City Guidance Clinic Guild, 1981-89; mem. Calif. State Rep. Ctrl. Com., Sacramento, 1986-90, 92-94, L.A. County Rep. Ctrl. Com., 1987—; vice chmn. 49th Assembly Dist. Ctrl. Rep. Com., Culver City, 1988—; bd. dirs. Selective Svc. Sys., Culver City, 1993—; mem. Santa Monica Rep. Women Federated, 2006—. Named Tchr. of the Yr. Elks Lodge, 1982; grantee, 1988-89. Fellow Am. Fedn. Tchrs.; mem. Internat. Platform Assn., Calif. Fedn. Tchrs., Culver City Fedn. Tchrs. (v.p. 1978-79), Alpha Delta Pi (historian 1956-59), Delta Kappa Gamma. Republican. Avocations: travel, gardening, walking. Office: Culver City Unified Sch 4034 Irving Pl Culver City CA 90232-2810 Personal E-mail: gerithomas@peoplepc.com.

THOMAS, GREGG DARROW, lawyer; b. Jacksonville, Fla., July 31, 1951; BA magna cum laude, Vanderbilt U., 1972; JD with honors, U. Fla., 1976. Bar: Fla. 1976, D.C. 1978. Law clk. U.S. Dist. Ct. (mid. dist.) Fla., 1976-79; mem. firm Holland & Knight, Tampa, Fla., 1979—2006, ptnr., 1983—2006, Thomas & LoCicero PC, Tampa, 2006—. Exec. editor U. Fla. Law Rev., 1975-76. Bd. dirs. Vol. Lawyer's Resource Ctr., 1990-95; trustee Tampa Mus. of Art, 1993—, vice chmn., 1998, chair, 1999-2001. Mem. ABA (mem. forum com. comm. law 1983—), Am. Judicature Soc., Fla. Bar (co-chair Fla. bar media and comm. com. 1987-88, mem. grievance com. 1988, chmn. 1989-91), Fla. Bar Found. (mem. legal assistance to poor com. 1988-91), Hillsborough Bar Assn., D.C. Bar, Phi Beta Kappa. Office: Thomas & LoCicero PC 400 N Ashley Dr Ste 1100 Tampa FL 33602 Office Phone: 813-984-3060. Business E-Mail: gthomas@tlolawfirm.com.

THOMAS, HARRY K., JR., former federal agency administrator; b. 1956; m. Ericka O. Smith-Thomas; 1 child, Casey Merie Eunice. Grad., Coll. Holy Cross, 1978; postgrad., Columbia U. With U.S. Fgn. Svc., New Delhi, Harare, Kaduna, and Lima, 1984; staff asst. to asst. sec. for African affairs US Dept State; spl. asst. to under sec. polit. affairs US Dept. State; dep. dir. to dir. Ops. Ctr. US Dept State, sr. watch officer; dir. for South Asia NSC, Washington, 2001—02; US amb. to Bangladesh US Dept. State, Dhaka, Bangladesh, 2003—05, exec. sec. Office of the Sec. Washington, 2005—07, dir. gen. Fgn. Svc., 2007—09. Recipient Arnold Raphel award, US Dept. State.*

THOMAS, HAZEL BEATRICE, state official; b. Franklin, Tenn. d. William Henry Fuller and Mattie Betty (Covington) Fuller Young; m. Charles B. Thomas (dec. 1969); children; Charles Bradford Jr., Deborah Carlotta (dec.). BA, Fisk U., 1946; MA, Tenn. State U., 1972. Cert. elem. and secondary tchr., Tenn. Tchr. elem. Met.-Nashville Sch., 1954—87; rsch. assoc. Johns Hopkins U., Balt., 1978—79, Marquette U., Milw., 1979—86; exec. asst. to commr. edn. Tenn. Dept. Edn., Nashville, 1987—. Cons. Peer Mediated Learning System, Nashville, 1980-82; instr. Met. Sch. Tchr. Ctr., Nasvhville, 1985-87; mem. tech. assistance team for high sch. that work, So. Regional Edn. Bd., 1998-99; nat. disseminator student team learning rsch. project, Johns Hopkins U., 1978-1979. Author training modules Substitute Teaching, Tchr. Aides. Pres. Davidson County Dem. Women, Nashville, 1985-87; v.p. Tenn. Fedn. Dem. Women, 1989-91, pres., 2001—; pres. elect Nashville Women's Polit. Caucus, 1991—; pres. Tenn. Women's Polit. Caucus 1994-95; mem. adminstrv. com. of bd. Nat. Women's Polit. Caucus, 1993-95, v.p., 1995—, v.p. edn. and tng., 2001—; mem. Tenn. Leadership, Inc., 1992—; spkr., polit. trainer U.S. Info. Agy., Nairobi, Kenya, 1997; mem. exec. bd. Citizen's Com. for Ann. Gov.'s Prayer Breakfast, 1992—; mem. exec. com. Tenn. Dem. Party, 2001—; chmn. edn. com. Bellevue C. of C.; pres. Tenn. Fedn. Dem. Women, 2001-03; v.p. Nat. Fedn. Dem. Women, 2002-05, 3d v.p., 2005—; mem. pub. edn. and govt. com. Metro. Govt. Nashville, Tenn., 2002-03; apptd. to pub. ednl. and govtl. access oversight com. Nashville Mayor Purcell, 2003—; apptd. to pub. edn. govt. com. Metro Nashville City Coun., 2002 Recipient Svc. to Edn. and Teaching Profession award Nat. Coun. Negro Women, 1988; Nat. Def. Edn. Act scholar, 1965, 67. Mem. Am. Bus. Womens Assn. (charter), Tenn. Edn. Assn. (pres. dept. classroom tchr. 1974-75, state dept. affiliate, pres. 1988-Ed. c90), Bellevue C. of C. (bd. govs. 1990-91, edn. chair 2002-03), Assn. Classroom Tchrs. (pres. S.E. region 1975-76), Met. Nashville Edn. Assn. (exec. bd. 1971-77), Bellevue Sertoma Club (life, pres. 1990-91), Nat. Women's Polit. Caucus (v.p. 1995—), Nat. Assn. Dem. Women (v.p., 2003-05, named Woman of Distinction for Tenn., 2002, 03), Nat. Fedn. Dem. Women (v.p. 2003). Baptist. Avocations: reading, bridge. Office: Tenn Dept Edn Andrew Johnson Tower 710 James Robertson Pkwy Nashville TN 37243-1219 Office Phone: 615-532-5740. E-mail: hazel.thomas@state.tn.us.

THOMAS, HELEN AMELIA (MRS. DOUGLAS B. CORNELL), editor-in-chief, former White House correspondent; b. Winchester, Ky., Aug. 4, 1920; d. George and Mary (Thomas) T.; m. Douglas B. Cornell. BA, Wayne State U., 1942; BA in Law, Mount Vernon Coll., 1999; LHD, Wayne State U., 1974, U. Detroit, 1979; LLD, Ea. Mich. State U., 1972, Ferris State Coll., 1978; LLD (hon.), Brown U., 1986, St. Bonaventure U., 1988, Franklin Marshall U., 1989, No. Mich. U., 1989, Northeastern U., 1990, Skidmore Coll., 1992, Susquehanna U., 1993, Sage Coll., 1994, U. Mo., 1994, Franklin Coll., 1995, Mich. State U., 1996, Potsdam U., 1998, A. Willenberg Univ., 1999, Milliken U., 2002, Am. U. Beirut, 2003, Western Ky. U., 2005, Cabrini Coll., 2005; LittD (hon.), Ohio Dominican U., 2004; LLD (hon.), Ind. Tech. U., 2007, Sienna Coll., 2007; ddegree (hon.), U. Ky., 2009; degree (hon.), NYU. With United Press Radio, UPI, 1943-2000, wire svc. reporter Washington, 1943-74; White House corr. Washington, 1970; White House bur. chief UPI, Washington, 1974-2000; columnist Hearst Newspapers, 2000—. Author: Dateline White House, Front Row at the White House: My Life and Times, 1999, Thanks for the Memories Mr. President: Wit and Wisdom from the Front Row at the White House, 2002, Watchdogs of Democracy?: The Waning Washington Press Corps and How It Has Failed the Public, 2006; columnist Hearst Newspapers. Recipient Woman of Yr. in Comm. award, Ladies Home Jour., 1975, 4th Estate award, Nat. Press Club, 1984, Journalism award, U. Mo., Al Newharth award, 1990, Ralph McGill award, 1995, Lifetime award, Internat. Media Found., Internat. Women's Press Found., 1996, Lowell Thomas award, Marist Coll., 2001, Kahlil Gibran award, 2003, NOW award, 2003, Torch Bearer award, Planned Parenthood award, Physician Social Responsibility award, Utah Am. Women of Yr., 2004, Eleanor Roosevelt Legacy award, 2004, Lifetime Achievement award, Glamour mag., Lifetime award, Washington Press Found., 2007, Edward R Murrow award, 2009; named one of 25 Most Influential Women in Am., World Almanac. Mem. Women's Nat. Press Club (pres. 1959-60, William Allen White Journalism award), Am. Newspaper Women's Club (past v.p.), White House Corrs. Assn. (pres. 1976, Helen Thomas Lifetime Achievement award 1998), Nat. Newspaper Assn. (Lifetime award 2002), Gridiron Club (pres. 1993), Sigma Delta Chi (fellow, Hall of Fame), Delta Sigma Phi (hon.), AARP (Lifetime award 2007), Anti-Discrimination Comm. (Lifetime Achievement award, 2009) Achievements include research in women's representation in the fields of journalism and politics, and in clubs and organizations; the first women officer of the National Press Club, the White House Correspondents Association, and first women member of the Gridiron Club; has covered nine presidents; only woman print journalist to go on President Nixon's historic trip to China and traveled with presidents Ford, Carter, Reagan, Bush, Sr., Clinton, & Bush; first female White House chief of a wire service in 1974; considered the "dean of Washington press corps" and she was allowed to ask the first question at the presdl. conferences; referred to as "The First Lady of the Press"; covered every presdl. econ. summit until 1999. Office: Hearst Corp 959 8th Ave New York NY 10019 Office Phone: 202-263-6437. Business E-Mail: helent@hearstdc.com.

THOMAS, HERBERT CUSHING, JR., physician, educator; b. Charlotte, NC, Oct. 6, 1941; s. Herbert Cushing and Doris (Roberts) T.; m. Laureen Thompson, June 9, 1961 (div. 1983); children: Steven, Michael; m. Catherine Anne Campbell, Feb. 11, 1989. BA, U. Colo., 1963, MD, 1967; MS, U. Wash., 1976. Resident in surgery Swedish Hosp., Med. Ctr., Seattle, 1972-73; resident in otolaryngology U. Wash., Seattle, 1973-77; fellowship in otology Ear Rsch. Inst., LA, 1977-78; pvt. practice Seattle, 1978—2007. Attending physician Seattle Children's Hosp. and Med. Ctr., Seattle, 1985—, pres. med. staff, 1991-92; pres. Surg. Specialists, Inc., Seattle, 1988-90; dir. Pacific Northwest Otolaryngology, 1978-2007. Capt. USN, 1963-84, USNR, ret. Mem. AMA, Am. Acad. Otolaryngology, Wash. State Med. Soc., King County Med. Soc., Seattle Surg. Soc., N.W. Acad. Otolaryngology, Old Antarctic Explorers Assoc. Avocations: travel, skiing, wine collecting, food and wine, photography. Office: 4800 Sand Point Way NE Seattle WA 98105 Office Phone: 206-987-2105. Personal E-mail: hct392@aol.com.

THOMAS, HOWARD, business educator; b. Jan. 31, 1943; BSc, London U., 1964, MSc, 1965; MBA, U. Chgo., 1966; PhD, Edinburgh U., Scotland, 1970; DSc, Edinburgh U., 2007. From prof. dept. bus. adminstrn. to dean emeritus U. Ill., Urbana-Champaign, 1980—2001, dean emeritus Commerce and Bus. Adminstrn., 2001—; dean Warwick Bus. Sch. U. Warwick, Coventry, U.K., 2000—. Vis. prof. MIT, 1986-87, Northwestern U., 1990. Office: Univ Warwick Warwick Bus Sch Coventry CV4 7AL England Office Phone: 011-44-2476-524534. E-mail: Howard.Thomas@wbs.ac.uk.

THOMAS, HOWARD PAUL, civil engineer, consultant; b. Cambridge, Mass., Aug. 20, 1942; s. Charles Calvin and Helen Elizabeth (Hook) T.; m. Ingrid Nybo, Jan. 4, 1969; children: Kent Michael, Lisa Karen, Karina Michelle. BS in Engring., U. Mich., 1965, MS in Engring., 1966. Registered profl. engr. Alta., 2008; Calif., 1969, Alaska, 1976, BC, 2007, Ont., 2009. Engr. Ove Arup & Ptnrs., London, 1966-67; project engr. Woodward-Clyde Cons., San Francisco, 1967-73, assoc. Anchorage, 1975-89; spl. cons. Cowiconsult Cons., Copenhagen, 1973-75; prin. engr. Harding-Lawson Assocs., Anchorage, 1989-90; v.p., chief engr. EMCON Alaska, Inc., Anchorage, 1991-94; gen. mgr. Internat. Tech. Corp., Anchorage, 1994-96; assoc. GeoEngrs., Inc., Anchorage, 1996—2002; sr. technologist CH2M Hill, Anchorage, 2001—06, Vancouver, BC, 2006—; mem. Anchorage Mayor's Geotech. Adv. Commn., 1997—2003. Chmn. Nat. Tech. Coun. Cold Regions Engring., 1988-89, chmn. com. program and publs., 1982-84; chmn. 4th Internat. Conf. Cold Regions Engring., Anchorage, 1986; liaison NAS/Nat. Rsch. Coun. Polar Rsch. Bd., 1989-99. Contbr. articles to profl. jours. Named Alaskan Engr. of Yr., 1986. Fellow ASCE (life) (pres. Anchorage chpt. 1985-86, chair mgmt. group A 1996-97, pres. Alaska sect. 1998-99, mem. nat. policy com. 2005—08, Harold R. Peyton award 2002); mem. Internat. Soc. for Soil Mechanics and Geotech. Engring., Cons. Engrs. Coun. Alaska (pres. 1989-90), Am. Cons. Engrs. Coun. (nat. dir. 1990-91), Project Mgmt. Inst. (v.p. Alaska chpt. 1991-95), Can. Geotechnical Soc., Toastmasters (pres. Anchorage club 1984), Sons of Norway (pres. Anchorage lodge 2000-02). Lutheran. Avocations: french horn, travel, classical music. Mailing: 8880 202d St Ste 320 Langley BC Canada V1M 4E7 Business E-Mail: hthomas@ch2m.com.

THOMAS, IRV, writer, journalist; b. San Francisco, Apr. 14, 1927; s. David Goldstein and Minnie Resnick; m. Vivian Laura Allen, Nov. 30, 1956; life ptnr.: Alice Joy (dec. Dec. 2006). BA, U. Wash., 1990. Pub./editor Black Bart Brigade/Yin Times, Canyon, Calif., 1971-83; editor Earthstewards jour./newsletter, Bainbridge Island, Wash., 1985-89; pub./editor Ripening Seasons Jour., Seattle, 1995—2003, IRV'S Scrapbook Jours. Newsletter, Seattle, 2007—. Tchr., workshop organizer Finding a Way Out, San Francisco, 1971-75; presenter World Futurist Conf., Toronto, Ont., 1980, Assn. for Humanistic Psychology Conv., Estes Park, Colo., 1976, Calif. Libr. Assn. Conv., Disneyland, 1972. Author, illustrator: Innocence Abroad, 1994, rev. edit., 2001, Derelict Days..., 2004, A Seasoned Life, 2006; contbr. anthology: Alternative Papers, 1982; contbr. articles to profl. jours. Housing activist Seattle Sr.

Housing Program Advocates, 1996-99; co-founder Afterlife.org, 2001. Avocation: hitchhiking. Home: 6545 Ravenna Ave NE #307 Seattle WA 98115 Personal E-mail: irvthom1@comcast.net.

THOMAS, ISIAH LORD, III, men's college basketball coach, retired professional basketball player; b. Chgo., Apr. 30, 1961; s. Isiah Lord and Mary Thomas; m. Lynn Kendall, July 19, 1985; children: Joshua, Lauren. BA in Criminal Justice, Ind. U., 1987. Profl. basketball player Detroit Pistons, 1981—94, ret., 1994; pres. NBA Players Assn., 1989—94; v.p. Toronto Raptors, 1994—97, co-owner, exec. v.p. basketball ops., 1994—98; sportscaster NBC Sports, NYC, 1997—2000; owner, chmn., CEO Continental Basketball Assn., 1999—2001; founder Enlighten Sports, Inc., 1999—; head coach Ind. Pacers, Indpls., 2000—03, NY Knicks, 2006—08, pres. basketball ops., 2003—08, cons., 2008—09; head basketball coach Fla. Internat. U. Golden Panthers, 2009—. Mem. US Olympic Basketball Team (did not compete), 1980; founder Isiah Thomas Found. Actor: (films) Hoop Dreams, 1994, Forget Paris, 1995. Recipient Gold medal, Pan-Am. Games, 1979, All-Star Team MVP award, 1984, 1986, J. Walter Kennedy Citizenship award, NBA, 1987, NBA Playoff MVP award, 1990, Pres. Cabinet medal, U. Detroit Mercy, 1992; named Michiganian of the Yr., 1985, NBA Finals MVP, 1990, Father of Yr., Nat. Father's Day Com., 2004; named one of The 100 Most Powerful People in Sports, The Sporting News, 1999, 100 Most Influential Minorities in Sports, Sports Illustrated, 2003—04; named to NBA All-Rookie team, 1982, All-Star Team, 1982—93, All NBA First Team, 1984, 1985, 1986, Naismith Meml. Basketball Hall of Fame, 2000. Achievements include member of the NBA Championship winning Detroit Pistons, 1989, 1990. Office: Fla Internat Univ Athletics 11200 SW 8th St Miami FL 33199*

THOMAS, J. MARK, sociologist, educator, minister; b. Ft. Worth, Dec. 20, 1947; s. Jacob Gillespie and Eleanor Rose (Geivett) T.; m. Jacquelyn Higby, Sept. 2, 1978; children: Megan Lane, Drew Martin. BA, Tex. Christian U., 1971, MDiv, 1974; PhD, U. Chgo., 1983. Ordained to ministry United Ch. of Christ, 1974. Asst. prof. philosophy and religion, chaplain Drury Coll., Springfield, Mo., 1983-85; adj. asst. prof. religion, chaplain Ripon (Wis.) Coll., 1985-87; vis. asst. prof. philosophy and religion Beloit (Wis.) Coll., 1987-89; sr. rsch. fellow Au Sable Inst. Environ. Studies, Mancelona, Mich., 1989—. Sociology instr., chair dept. social sci. Madison Area Tech. Coll., mem. Faculty Exchange to Holland, 2007, lectr. Oxford U. Oxford Round Table, 2008 Author: Ethics and Technoculture, 1987, (with others) Being and Doing, 1987, Philosophy and Technology, Vol. 10, 1990, Religion in the New Millennium, 2001, Encyclopedia of Science, Technology and Ethics, 2005, Classroom Activities For Introductory Sociology Courses, 2008; editor: Paul Tillich, The Spiritual Situation in Our Technical Society, 1988, God and Capitalism, 1991, Religion in the New Millennium, 2001. Chmn. planning com. Congress of Sci., Tech. and Religion for the Parliament of World Religion, 1993. Recipient Disting. Tchr. Yr., Madison Area Tech. Coll., 1999. Mem. Midwest Sociol. Soc., Communitarian Network. Democrat. Mem. United Ch. of Christ. Home: 816 Lincoln St Madison WI 53711-2163 Office: Madison Area Tech Coll Downtown Edn Ctr 211 N Carroll St Madison WI 53703-2211 E-mail: jmarkthomas@charter.net.

THOMAS, J. REGAN, plastic surgeon, educator; B, Drury U., Springfield, Mo., 1968; MD, U. Mo. Sch. Medicine. Cert. Am. Bd. Facial Plastic/Reconstructive Surgery, Am. Bd. Otolaryngology. Intern Yale U. Med. Ctr.; residency in otolaryngology, head & neck surgery U. Missouri Sch. of Medicine, fellowship in facial plastic and reconstructive surgery; Francis Lederer prof. and dept. head, otolaryngology, head & neck surgery U. Ill. Med. Ctr., Chicago, 2004—; plastic surgeon Facial Plastic Surgery Ctr., 2004—. Fomer pres. Am. Bd. Facial Plastic/Reconstructive Surgery, Am. Acad. Facial Plastic and Reconstructive Surgery; mem. bd. dirs. Am. Acad. Otolaryngology-Head & Neck Surgery. Mem. editl. bd.: Archive Facial Plastic Surgery; editor: Facial Plastic Surgery Clinics; contbr. more than 100 articles to profl. jours. Recipient Schoenrock award, Am. Bd. Facial Plastic/Reconstructive Surgery, William Wright award, Am. Acad. Facial Plastic and Reconstructive Surgery, John Dickinson Teacher of Yr. award, Disting. Alumni award, Drury U., 1993; named one of Best Doctors in America. Office: Facial Plastic Surgery Ctr 60 E Delaware Pl Chicago IL 60611 also: U Ill Med Ctr Eye and Ear Inst 1855 W Taylor St 3d Fl Chicago IL 60612*

THOMAS, JACOB EARL, retired physicist; b. Seattle, Sept. 7, 1918; s. Jacob Earl and Ursula May (Johnson) T.; m. Margaret Louise Johnston, June 15, 1977; children— Richard Bruce, Jacob Earl, John Calvin, James Hayden, Denise May Thomas Pratt, Stillman Jefferson. AB, Johns Hopkins U., 1939; PhD, Calif. Inst. Tech., 1943. Group leader rocket devel. Calif. Inst. Tech., Pasadena, 1942-45; group leader Manhattan Project, U. Calif., Los Alamos, 1945-46; asst. prof. elec. engring. M.I.T., Cambridge, 1946-51; mem. tech. staff Bell Telephone Labs., Murray Hill, NJ, 1951-52; group leader M.I.T. Lincoln Labs., Lexington, 1952-55; prof., chmn. dept. physics Wayne State U., Detroit, 1955-59; dir. research Sylvania Electric, Woburn, Mass., 1959-62; mgr. solid state devel. IBM, Poughkeepsie, NY, 1962-64; mgr. new product devel. Gen. Instrument Co., Newark, 1964-67; v.p. Carman Sapphire Co., Reseda, Calif., 1967-70; cons. Warnecke Electron Tubes, Des Plaines, Ill., 1970-71; dir. components research Victor Comptometer Co., Des Plaines, 1971-75; mgr. advanced devel. NCR Corp., Ithaca, NY, 1975-84. Cons. pvt. cos. and govt. agys. Contbr. articles to sci. jours.; patentee in field. Active S.E. Asian refugee resettlement program. Recipient Service award U.S. Office Sci. Research and Devel., 1946 Fellow: IEEE (Millennium medal), Am. PHys. Soc.; mem.: Tau Beta Pi, Phi Beta Kappa, Sigma Xi. Democrat. Presbyterian. Home: 323 Savage Farm Dr Ithaca NY 14850-6503 E-mail: ethomas4@twcny.rr.com.

THOMAS, JACQUELYN MAY, librarian; b. Mechanicsburg, Pa., Jan. 26, 1932; d. William John and Gladys Elizabeth (Warren) Harvey; m. David Edward Thomas, Aug. 28, 1954; children: Lesley J., Courtenay J., Hilary A. BA summa cum laude, Gettysburg Coll., Pa., 1954; postgrad., U. NC, Chapel Hill, 1969; MEd, U. NH, Durham, 1971. Libr. Phillips Exeter Acad., Exeter, NH, 1971-77, acad. libr., 1977—. Chair governing bd. Child Care Ctr., 1987-91; chair Com. to Enhance Status of Women, Exeter, 1981-84; chair Loewenstein Com., Exeter, 1982—; pres. Cum Laude Soc., Exeter, 1984-86; James H. Ottaway Jr. prof., 1990—; mem. bldg. com. Exeter Pub. Libr., 1986-88; chair No. New Eng., Coun. for Women in Ind. Schs., 1985-87; chmn. Lamont Poetry Program, Exeter, 1984-86. Editor: The Design of the Library: A Guide to Sources of Information, 1981, Rarities of Our Time: The Special Collections of the Phillips Exeter Academy Library; pub.: Memorial Minutes, Phillips Exeter Academy, 1936-2002, Friends of the Academy Library, Collected Letters Book, Class of 1945 special collections brochure, Class of 1945 Library Brochure, 2009, other Phillips Exeter materials. Libr. trustee, treas. Exeter Day Sch., 1965-69; bd. Exeter Hosp. Vols., 1954-59; mem. Exeter Hosp. Corp., 1978—; bd. dirs. Greater Portsmouth Cmty. Found., 1990—; active AAC&U, On Campus with Women, Wellesley Coll. Ctr. for Rsch. on Women; mem. People to People Amb. Program, sch. and youth svcs. libr. del. to People's Rep. China, 1998. Grantee N.H. Coun. for Humanties, 1981-82, NEH, 1982; recipient Lillian Radford trust award, 1989. Mem. ALA, Internat. Assn. Sch. Librs., New Eng. Libr. Assn., NJ, Ednl. Media Assn., New Eng. Assn. Ind. Sch. Librs., Am. Assn. Sch. Librs. (chmn. non-pub. sch. sect.), Phi Beta Kappa. Office: Class of 1945 Libr Phillips Exeter Acad 20 Main St Exeter NH 03833-2460 Home: 17 Eagle Dr Newmarket NH 03857 Office Phone: 603-777-3328. Office Fax: 603-777-4389. Business E-Mail: jthomas@exeter.edu.

THOMAS, JEFFREY CONE, financial executive, consultant; b. New Orleans, Oct. 10, 1941; s. Eads Poitevent and Virginia Lee (King) T.; m. Brenda Gayle Ballard, June 7, 1969 (div. Mar. 1972). BA, La. State U., 1965. CLU; ChFC; CFP; CFS. Mgmt. trainee Am. Bank and Trust Co., Baton Rouge, 1965—68; supr. Travelers Ins. Co., Baton Rouge, 1968—71; dist. dir. Conn. Gen. Life Ins. Co., Baton Rouge, 1971—74; pres., CEO Pension & Profit Sharing Cons., Baton Rouge, 1974—77; pres. Fin. Advisor & Cons., Baton Rouge, 1977—. Adj. instr. adult eve. classes Coll. Fin. Planning, 1987-92; cons. Ethyl Corp., Baton Rouge, 1982, Dow Chem., Plaquemine, La., 1986. Vol. ARC, Baton Rouge, 1965—69; mem. adminstrv. bd. First Meth. Ch., Baton Rouge, 1987—89. Avocations: golf, tennis, fishing, gardening. Office: Fin Advisor & Cons PO Box 65238 Baton Rouge LA 70896-5238 Office Phone: 225-293-1035.

THOMAS, JEREMIAH LINDSAY, III, lawyer; b. Wilmington, Del., June 20, 1946; s. Jeremiah Lindsay Jr. and Dorothy Eleanor (Conway) T.; m. Clara Ewing Ruthrauff, Oct. 17, 1981; children: Catherine Ewing, Lindsay Barlow. BA, U. Va., 1968, JD, 1972. Bar: N.Y. 1973. Assoc. Simpson Thacher & Bartlett, NYC, 1972-79, ptnr., 1979—. Mem.: ABA, Met. Golf Assn. (legal counsel 1984—, exec. com. 1992—98, dir. Found. 1992—98), Assn. Bar of City of N.Y., N.Y. State Bar Assn. Office: Simpson Thacher & Bartlett 425 Lexington Ave Fl 28 New York NY 10017-3954 Office Phone: 212-455-7110. Business E-Mail: jthomas@stblaw.com.

THOMAS, JERRY ARTHUR, retired soil scientist; b. Logansport, Ind., Mar. 5, 1942; s. Purnal Kidd and Dorothy Helen (Smith) T.; m. Virginia Amy York, Oct. 17, 1964; 1 child, Charles Edward. BS in Agronomy and Soil Chemistry, Purdue U., 1965; MS in Soil Fertility, Pa. State U., 1968. Libr. chemistry dept. Purdue Univ., West Lafayette, Ind., 1963, tech. aid USDA, ARS, agronomy dept., 1963-65; grad. teaching asst. agronomy dept. Pa. State U., University Park, 1965-67; soil scientist USDA Soil Conservation Svc., Indpls., 1967-85, Ind. State Bd. Health, Indpls., 1985—2009. Com. mem. Ind. State 4-H Rabbit com., West Lafayette, 1976-2000. Author publs. in field including Classification of the Sloping Soils of the West Baden Group in Monroe County, Ind., 1978, Soil Survey of Monroe County, Ind., 1981, Soil Survey of Lawrence County, Ind., 1985, Availability of Conservation Tillage Planting Systems for Northwestern Ind., 1985. Asst. scoutmaster Boy Scouts Am., Rensselaer, Ind., 1982-92. Recipient Innovative award Coun. State Govts., 1988; named Environ. Health Specialist of Yr., Environ. Health Assn., 1993. Mem. Am. Soc. Agronomy, Soil Sci. Soc. Am., Soil and Water Conservation Soc. Am., Ind. Acad. Sci., Ind. Assn. Profl. Soil Classifiers, Ind. Environtl. Health Assn., Masons, Eastern Star. Mem. Christian Ch. (Disciples Of Christ). Home: 301 S Park Ave Rensselaer IN 47978-3037 Business E-Mail: mar1942@nwiis.com.

THOMAS, JIMI ELIZABETH, elementary school educator; b. Kinston, NC, Oct. 15, 1947; d. Charles L. and Mildred Elizabeth; 1 child, Stephanie Elizabeth. BS in Elem. Edn., Old Dominion U., Norfolk, Va., 1970, MS in Elem. Edn., 1977, degree in Adminstrn. and Supervision, 1984, PhD in Urban Svcs., 1986. Cert. elem. edn. tchr. grades K-7 Va., social studies tchr. grades 5-8 Va. Sixth grade tchr. Lindenwood Elem., Norfolk, Va., 1970—71; fifth grade tchr. Bayview Elem., Norfolk, Va., 1974—76; English and reading instr. Wahiawa CC, Wahiawa, Hawaii, 1977—79, St. Louis HS, Honolulu, 1979—80; eighth grade English and history tchr. Dept. Def., Gaeta, Italy, 1982—83; drug intervention specialist VBCPS, Va. Beach, Va., 1986—87, drug edn. coord., 1987—89; eighth grade civics tchr. Brandon Mid. Sch., Va. Beach, Va., 1989—. Va. and US history tchr. Open Campus HS, Va. Beach, Va., 1998; adj. faculty reading edn. Old Dominion U., 2004—; tchr. mentor City of Va. Beach, 2005—, student tchr. supr., 2005—; presenter in field. Recipient Project Citizen award, Va., 2002. Mem.: Nat. Coun. History Educators, Profl. Assn. Tchrs., Longstreet Soc., Civil War Roundtable. Achievements include design of sixth, seventh and eighth grade social studies remedial program with focus on standards of learning in Virginia. Home: 5048 Clairmont Ct Virginia Beach VA 23462 Personal E-mail: jethomas1@verizon.net.

THOMAS, JIMMY LYNN, retired treasurer; b. Mayfield, Ky., Aug. 3, 1941; s. Alben Stanley and Emma Laura (Alexander) T.; m. Kristin H. Kent, Oct. 1986; children: James Nelson, Carter Danforth. BS, U. Ky., 1963; MBA, Columbia U., 1964. Fin. analyst Ford Motor Co., Detroit, 1964-66; asst. treas. Joel Dean Assocs., NYC, 1966-67; asst. contr. Trans World Airlines, NYC, 1967-73; sr. v.p. fin. svcs., treas. Gannett Co., Inc., Arlington, Va., 1973-98. Bd. dirs. HSBC, Rochester, Tremont Ptnrs. Fundraiser United Negro Coll. Fund; bd. trustees, treas. Harley Sch., Rochester, N.Y.; bd. overseers Strong Meml. Hosp., Rochester; bd. govs. Genesee Hosp., Rochester; bd. dirs. Arlington Cmty. Found., Nat. Press Club Bldg., Washington. With U.S. Army, 1966-72. Ashland Oil Co. scholar, 1959-63, McKinsey scholar 1964; Samuel Bronfman fellow, 1963-64. Mem. Nat. Assn. Corp. Treas., U. Ky. Alumni Assn., Columbia U. Alumni Assn., Country Club of Rochester, Genessee Valley Club, Beta Gamma Sigma, Omicron Delta Kappa, Sigma Alpha Epsilon. Democrat. Mem. Christian Ch. (Disciples Of Christ). Home: 9700 Jennings Rd Eden NY 14057-9518 Office Phone: 716-992-9935.

THOMAS, JOAB LANGSTON, retired academic administrator, biologist, educator; b. Holt, Ala., Feb. 14, 1933; s. Ralph Cage and Chamintney Elizabeth (Stovall) Thomas; m. Marly A. Dukes, Dec. 22, 1954; children: Catherine, David, Jennifer, Frances. AB, Harvard U., 1955, MA, 1957, PhD, 1959; DSc (hon.), U. Ala., 1981; LLD (hon.), Stillman Coll., 1987; LHD (hon.), Tri-State U., 1994; LHD (hon.), N.C. State U., 1998. Cytotaxonomist Arnold Aboretum, Harvard, 1959—61; prof. biology U. Ala., University, 1966—76, 1988—91, asst. dean Coll. Arts and Scis., 1964—65, 1969, dean for student devel., 1969—74, v.p., 1974—76, dir. Herbarium, 1961—76, dir. Arboretum, 1964—69, pres. Tuscaloosa, 1981—88; chancellor N.C. State U., Raleigh, 1976—81; pres. Pa. State U., University Park, 1990—95, pres. emeritus, 1995. Intern acad. adminstrn. Am. Coun. on Edn., 1971. Author: A Monographic Study of the Cyrillaceae, 1960, Wildflowers of Alabama and Adjoining States, 1973, The Rising South, 1976, Poisonous Plants and Venomous Animals of Alabama and Adjoining States, 1990. Bd. dirs. Internat. Potato Ctr., 1977—83, chmn., 1982—83; bd. dirs. Internat. Svc. for Nat. Agrl. Rsch., 1985—91. Recipient Ala. Acad. Honor, 1983, Palmer Mus. Art medal, Coll. Pres.'s award, All-Am. Football Found., 1997, Spl. Recognition award, Assn. for Continuing Higher Edn., 1998; named Citizen of Yr., City of Tuscaloosa, 1987. Mem.: Golden Key, Phi Kappa Phi, Omicron Delta Kappa (Laurel Crowned Circle award 2001), Sigma Xi, Phi Beta Kappa. Office: Univ Ala 413 Sci Collections Bldg Tuscaloosa AL 35487-0001 Home Phone: 205-554-7875; Office Phone: 205-348-1850. Business E-Mail: jlthomas@dbtech.net.

THOMAS, JOAN E., music educator; MusM, Columbus State U., Ga.; MS n Edn., Troy Stat U., Phenix City, Ala., 1998—2000. Cert. tchr. State of Ga. Dir. of choral activities Upson-Lee H.S. and Upson-Lee Mid. Sch., Thomaston, Ga., 1982—2002; min. of music First Presbyn. Ch., Thomaston, Ga., 1996—2000; grad. asst. Columbus State U., 2002—04; min. of music First United Meth. Ch., Thomaston, 2004—; dir. of choral activities Pike County Schs., Zebulon, Ga., 2004—. Home: 2 Thomas Way Thomaston GA 30286 Personal E-mail: jethomas@windstream.net. E-mail: thomasj@pike.k12.ga.us.

THOMAS, JOE CARROLL, retired human resources director; b. Belmont, NC, Nov. 2, 1931; m. Ruth Stone, June 17, 1951; children: Joe(dec.), Jerry, Angela. BA, Belmont Abbey Coll., 1954; MS, Cornell U., 1961; postgrad., U. NC, 1985. Diplomate in profl. counseling Informational Acad. Behavioral Medicine Counseling and Psycho Therapy Inc.; cert. Sr. Profl. in Human Resources. Terr. salesman Gen. Foods Corp., Charlotte, NC, 1954—59, adminstrv. asst. to dist. mgr. Atlanta, 1960, mgr. terr. sales San Antonio, 1962; asst. dir. personnel textiles divsn. Kendall Co., Charlotte, NC, 1962-64; dir. personnel S.E. region Gifford Hill & Co., Charlotte, 1964-71; dir. mgmt. svcs. Ervin Industries, Charlotte, 1971-75; v.p. indsl. rels. Crompton & Knowles, Charlotte, 1975-76; exec. v.p., dir. human resources Barclays Group Inc., Charlotte, 1976-97; ret., 1997. Mem. adv. coun. Sch. Bus., Western Carolina U., Cullowhee, NC, 1980-84; mem. bd. arbitrators Fin. Industry Regulatory Authority, 2001; bd. adv. Belmont Abbey Coll., 2005 Vice chmn. bd. trustees Belmont Abbey Coll., 1982-88; chmn. fundraising campaign Charlotte chpt. Am. Heart Assn., 1984; mem. bd. visitors mercy Hosp., Charlotte, 1984-87; bd. dirs. mercy Health Svcs., Charlotte, 1988-96; bd. dirs. Jr. Achievement Charlotte, 1985-88, INROADS divsn. Charlotte, Inc., 1987-88; bd. visitors Johnson C. Smith Univ., 1989-92 Mem. Soc. Human Resource Mgmt., Employers Assn. (bd. dirs. 1993-99, exec. com. 1995-99), Charlotte Athletic Club (pres. 1982-83), Charlotte Rotary, Charlotte C. of C. (bd. advisors 1992-97, Aldersgate bd. advisors 2000—, Aldersgate bd. dirs. 2003—, bd. dirs. chair-elect 2005-2006, chmn. bd. dirs. 2007). Republican. Personal E-mail: carrolleth@aol.com.

THOMAS, JOHN, professional sports team executive; Grad. in Bus., U. Minn. With KSTP-TV, Mpls./St. Paul, KFAN Sports Radio, Maj. League Baseball Seattle Mariners, NHL Minn. North Stars, NBA Minn. Timberwolves, NBA Rockets, WNBA Comets and Arena Football League Thunderbears, Houston, 1994—99; pres. Maloof Sports & Entertainment (NBA Kings, WNBA Monarchs and ARCO Arena), Sacramento, 1999—. Bd. dirs. Sacramento Conv. and Visitors Bur., Sacramento Metro Chamber, Valley Vision's Leadership Coun. Office: Sacramento Kings ARCO Arena 1 Sports Pky Sacramento CA 95834-2301*

THOMAS, JOHN ARLEN, pharmacologist, educator, science administrator; b. LaCrosse, Wis., Apr. 6, 1933; s. John M. and Eva Hazel (Nelson) T.; m. Barbara A. Fisler, June 22, 1957; children: Michael J., Jane L. BS in Sci. Edn., U. Wis., 1956; MA in Physiology, U. Iowa, 1958, PhD in Physiology, 1961. Diplomate Am. Acad. Toxicologic Sci. Instr. U. Iowa, Iowa City, 1961; asst. prof. U. Va., Charlottesville, 1961-64; assoc. prof. Creighton U., Omaha, 1964-67, W.Va. U., Morgantown, 1968-69, prof. pharmacology, 1970-80; asst. dean W.Va. Sch. Medicine, Morgantown, 1973-75, assoc. dean, 1973-80; v.p. corp. rsch. Baxter Internat. Travenol Labs., Round Lake, Ill., 1980-87; v.p. acad. svcs. U. Tex. Health Sci. Ctr., San Antonio, 1988-99, prof. emeritus pharmacology dept. toxicology, 1988—; prof. Ind. U. Sch. Medicine, 2005—. Chmn. expert adv. com. Can. Network Toxicol. Ctr., 1999-02; sci. adv. bd. USAF, 2002-05, FDA, 2003—08; adj. prof. pharmacology Ind. U. Sch. Medicine, Indpls., 2005; cons. to NIH, Inst. of Medicine, NRC, NAS. Author (with M.G. Mawhinney): Synopsis of Endocrine Pharmacology, 1978; author: (with E.J. Keenan) Principles of Endocrine Pharmacology, 1986; editor (with others): Basic and Clinical Toxicology of Lead, 1985; editor: Endocrine Toxicology, 1985, 1996, Drugs Athletes & Physical Performance, 1988, Biotechnology and Safety Assessment, 1993; editor: (with Laurie A. Myers) Biotechnology and Safety Assessment 2d edit., 1981; editor: (with Roy L. Fuchs) Biotechnology and Safety Assessment, 3d edit., 2002; editor: Endocrine Methods, 1996, Toxic Substances Mechanism Jour.; contbr. articles to profl. jours. Sgt. U.S. Army, 1951-53. Recipient Cert. Svc. US EPA, 1977, Commn. Spl. citation FDA, 2006, Advis Commn. Svc. award FDA, 2007; named Outstanding Tchr., W.Va. U., 1971, 73, 79, Outstanding alumnus U. Wis., La Crosse, 1978, Disting. Alumni, U. Iowa, 1997, Adv. Com. Svc. award FDA, 2007; named to Hall of Excellence-LaCrosse, 2002. Fellow Acad. Toxicol. Sci. (pres. 2001); mem. Endocrine Soc., Soc. Toxicology (councilor, Merit award 1998), Am. Soc. Pharmacology and Exptl. Therapeutics, Am. Coll. Toxicology (councilor, pres., disting. fellow 2004, Disting. Svc. award), Teratology Soc., Am. Acad. Vet. Pharmacology, Am. Chem. Soc. (pres. chem. toxicology pathology), Tex. Soc. Biomed. Rsch. (bd. sci. advisors 1989-99, Disting. Svc. award 1996), Russian Acad. Med. Sci. (fgn. fellow-elect 1995). Home and Office: 7258 Pymbroke Cir Fishers IN 46038 Home Phone: 317-845-5224. Personal E-mail: jat-tox@sbcglobal.net.

THOMAS, JOHN EDWARD, educational consultant; b. Alliance, Ohio, Jan. 14, 1948; s. William Joseph and Betty Rowland Thomas; m. Teresa Ann Hively, June 27, 1970; children: Brett, Trisha, Kristopher. BS, Bowling Green State U., Ohio, 1971; MEd, U. Akron, Ohio, 1978, postgrad., 1987. Cert. supt. Ohio, English, history, political science, earth science Ohio, Md. Tchr. English Robert E. Peary H.S., Rockville, Md., 1971—76; curriculum supr. Stark County Dept. Edn., Louisville, Ohio, 1977—79, mgr. Instrnl. Computer Ctr., 1979—82; elem. prin. M.I. Day Elem., Minerva, Ohio, 1982—88; supt. Crestview Local Schs., Columbiana, Ohio, 1988—91, Alliance City Schs., 1992—97, Delaware City Schs., Ohio, 1997—2003; ednl. cons., 2003—; adj. instr. Mt. Vernon Nazare U. Grad. Program, 2008; tchr. Tech. Ednl. Leaders, Ohio Tech. Commn. Contbg. author: The Power of Public Persuasion, 2000. Mem. Delaware/Morrow Mental Health Bd., 2003—, Cen. Ohio Symphony Bd., Delaware, 2001—05. Recipient Promising Tech. Innovation award, Nat. Assn. Secondary Sch. Prins., 1999—2000. Mem.: Buckeye Assn. Sch. Adminstrs. (Leadership award 2003, Tech. Leadership award 2003), Am. Assn. Sch. Adminstrs. (Pres.'s Tech. Leadership award 2003), Delaware Lions Club (membership chair 2000—), Delaware Rotary Club (treas. 2004—), Phi Delta Kappa. Avocations: hiking, bicycling, camping, white-water rafting, canoeing, travel. Home and Office: 2505 Panhandle Rd Delaware OH 43015

THOMAS, JOHN HOWARD, astrophysicist, mechanical engineer, educator; b. Chgo., Apr. 9, 1941; s. William Whitney and Dorothy Loretta (Derris) T.; m. Lois Ruth Moffit, Aug. 11, 1962; children: Jeffrey, Laura. BS in Engring. Sci., Purdue U., 1962, MS in Engring. Sci., 1964, PhD in Engring. Sci., 1966. Lic. profl. engr., NY. NATO postdoctoral fellow U. Cambridge, Eng., 1966-67; asst. prof. mech. and aerospace sci. U. Rochester, 1967-73, assoc. prof., 1973-81, prof., 1981—, prof. astronomy, 1986—, assoc. dean for grad. studies Coll. Engring. and Applied Sci., 1981-83, univ. dean grad. studies, 1983-91. Vis. astronomer Nat. Solar Obs., Sunspot, N.Mex., 1971, 81; vis. scientist Max-Planck Inst. for Physics and Astrophysics, Munich, 1973—74, High

Altitude Obs., Boulder, Colo., 1985; vis. fellow Worcester Coll., vis. prof. dept. theoretical physics U. Oxford, England, 1987—88; affiliate scientist Nat. Ctr. for Atmospheric Rsch., Boulder, 1989—; vis. prof. Rsch. Ctr. for Theoretical Astrophysics U. Sydney, 1991, Sch. Math. and Stats., 1993; vis. fellow Clare Hall, vis. prof. dept. applied math. and theoretical physics U. Cambridge, England, 2002, sr. fellow Isaac Newton Inst., 04; prin. investigator NASA, NSF, USAF, Office Naval Rsch. Author: Sunspots and Starspots, 2008; editor: Physics of Sunspots, 1981, Sunspots: Theory and Observations, 1992; assoc. editor Astrophys. Jour., 1993—96, sci. editor, 1996—2002, author articles on astrophysics, solar physics and fluid dynamics. NSF fellow, 1963-66; Guggenheim fellow, 1993-94. Fellow AAAS, Am. Phys. Soc., Royal Astron. Soc. (UK); mem. Am. Astron. Soc. (chair solar physics divsn. 1995-97), Internat. Astron. Union, Am. Geophys. Union, Sigma Xi, Tau Beta Pi, Sigma Delta Chi.

THOMAS, JOHN THIEME, management consultant; b. Detroit, Aug. 21, 1935; s. John Shepherd and Florence Leona (Thieme) T.; m. Ellen Linden Taylor, June 27, 1959; children: Johnson Taylor, Evan Thurston. BBA, U. Mich., 1957, MBA, 1958. Mfg. dept. mgr. Procter & Gamble Co., Cin., 1958-60, brand mgr., 1960-63; sr. cons. Glendinning Cos. Inc., Westport, Conn., 1964-66, v.p. London, 1967-69, exec. v.p. Westport, 1970-74, also bd. dirs.; exec. v.p., chief operating officer Ero Industries, Chgo., 1974-76; v.p. Lamalie Assocs. Inc., Chgo., 1977-81; pres. Wilkins & Thomas Inc., Chgo., 1981-87; ptnr. Ward Howell Internat., Chgo., 1987—, mng. dir., cons. practice, 1992-98, chief of staff, 1995-98; also bd. dirs.; cons. ret. LAI Ward Howell, Chgo., 1999—, El Jefe, Thomas Ent. Inc., 1989—. Exec. dir. Procter & Gamble Mktg. Alumni Assn., Chgo., 1981—. Pub. Procter & Gamble Mktg. Alumni directory, 1981—; author articles in profl. jours. Chmn. bd. dirs. Winnetka Youth Orgn., Ill., 1986—2005; chmn. United Way Winnetka, 2001—, United Way North Shore; bd. dirs., exec. com. No. Ill. Girl Scouts Coun., 2002—; mem. planning commn. City Winnetka, 2003—05, 2007—; selector Winnetka Town Coun., 1978, 1980, 1984, Winnetka Zoning Bd., 2002—04, 2006—; selector com., chmn. Winnetka Caucus Exec. Com., 1997—2001; commr. Winnetka Pks., 2005—. Mem. Nat. Assn. Corp. & Profl. Recruiters, Assn. Exec. Search Cons., Am. Soc. Pers. Adminstrn. Clubs: Fairfield (Conn.) Hunt (treas. 1971-74). Avocations: gardening, music, tuba. Home and Office: 525 Ash St Winnetka IL 60093-2601 Office Phone: 847-446-5401. Personal E-mail: pngalumni@aol.com.

THOMAS, JOHN VAL, architect; b. San Diego, Feb. 26, 1943; Grad arch., Rice Univ., Houston; MArch, MCP, U. Pa. Prin. Val Thomas, Inc., Seattle, 1985—; devel. mgr. Pike Pl. Market Preservation and Devel. Authority, Seattle, 1974. Cons. ptnr. Cardwell/Thomas & Assoc., Seattle. Conversion, W. Queen Anne Sch. (Award for Excellence, Nat. Endowment for the Arts). Fellow: Am. Inst. Arch.; mem.: Housing Comm. of the Greater Seattle Chamber of Commerce, Univ. of Wash. Profl. Coun. for the Sch. of Urban Planning, Seattle Planning Commission (chrmn.). Democrat. Episcopalian. Achievements include development of Thomas Incorporated; headed the development team for the new headquarters building of the Fremont Public Association on North 45th Street. Avocations: skiing, aerobics, painting, gardening. Office: STE 420 2025 1ST Ave Seattle WA 98121-2176 Office Phone: 206-621-1221.

THOMAS, JOYCE CAROL, author, educator; b. Ponca City, Okla., May 25, 1938; children: Monica, Gregory, Michael, Roy. BA, San Jose State Coll., Calif., 1966; MS, Stanford U., 1967. Asst. prof. San Jose State Coll., 1969—72, reading prog. dir., 1979—82, prof., 1982—83; tchr. Contra Costa Coll., Calif., 1973—75; prof. St. Mary's Coll., Moraga, Calif., 1975—77; prof. English U. Tenn, 1989—. Vis. prof. English Purdue U., West Lafayette, Ind., 1984. Author: Bittersweet, 1973, Crystal Breezes, 1974, Blessing, 1975, Black Child, 1981, Inside the Rainbow, 1982, Marked by Fire, 1982 (Before Columbus Book award, 1982, Best Book for Young Adults, ALA, 1982, Nat. Book award, 1983), Bright Shadow, 1983, Water Girl, 1986, The Golden Pasture, 1986, Journey, 1988, A Gathering of Flowers: Stories About Being Young in America, 1990, When the Nightingale Sings, 1992, Brown Honey in Broomwheat Tea: Poems, 1993, Gingerbread Days: Poems, 1995, Cherish Me, 1998, I Have Heard of a Land, 1998 (Notable Book award, ALA, 1999, Tchr.'s Book award, Internat. Reading Assn., 1999), You Are My Perfect Baby, 1999, Hush Songs: African-American Lullabies, 2000, The Bowlegged Rooster: And Other Tales That Signify, 2000, House of Light, 2001, A Mother's Heart, A Daughter's Love, 2001, The Gospel Cinderella, 2001, The Blacker the Berry: Poems, 2001, Crowning Glory: Poems, 2002, (plays) A Song in the Sky, 1976, Look! What a Wonder!, 1976, Magnolia, 1977, Ambrosia, 1978, When the Nightingale Sings, 1991. Recipient Arrell Gibson Lifetime Achievement award, Okla. Ctr. For the Book, 2001; named Okla. Poet Laureate, 1996—2000. Office: Tenn Authors Project UT Lib
rs Knoxville TN 37996 Personal E-mail: JCTauthor@aol.com.*

THOMAS, KEITH VIVIAN, historian, former college president; b. Wick, Glamorgan, U.K., Jan. 2, 1933; s. Vivian Jones and Hilda Janet Eirene (Davies) T.; m. Valerie June Little, Aug. 16, 1961; children: Emily Joanna, Edmund Vivian. MA, Oxford U., Eng., 1959; LLD (hon.), Williams Coll., 1988, Oglethorpe U., 1996; DLitt (hon.), U. Kent, 1983, U. Wales, 1987, U. Sheffield, 1992, U. Cambridge, U. Hull, 1995, U. Leicester, 1996, U. Sussex, 1996, U. Warwick, 1998, U. London, 2006. Fellow All Souls Coll., Oxford, 1955-57, 2001—; fellow and tutor St. John's Coll., Oxford, 1957-85; reader in modern history U. Oxford, U.K., 1978-85, prof. modern history, 1986; pres. Corpus Christi Coll., Oxford, 1986-2000; pro vice-chancellor Oxford U., 1988-2000; vis. prof. La. State U., 1970, vis. fellow, 1978; Lawrence Stone vis. prof. Princeton U., 2001, Kratter U.; prof. Stanford U., 2004; vis. fellow Heynen Ctr., Columbia U., 2008. Del. Oxford U. Press, 1980-00, chmn. fin. com., 1988-00. Author: Religion and the Decline of Magic, 1971 (Wolfson prize 1972), Rule and Misrule in the Schools of Early Modern England, 1976, Age and Authority in Early Modern England, 1976, Man and the Natural World, 1983, The Perception of the Past in Early Modern England, 1984, History and Literature, 1989, Changing Conceptions of National Biography, 2005; editor: (with Donald Pennington) Puritans and Revolutionaries, 1978, Opus Books, Past Masters series, The Oxford Book of Work, 1999, (with Andrew Adonis) Roy Jenkins: A Retrospective, 2004; cons. editor: Dictionary of National Biography 1986-90, 1996; chmn. supervisory com., Oxford Dictionary Nat. Biography, 1999-2004, 2008; mem. editl. bd. Past and Present, Ecumene, Prometeo; contbr. chpts. to books, articles to profl. jours. Mem. rev. com. Export of Works of Art, 1989—92; trustee The Nat. Gallery, London, 1991—98, The Brit. Mus., London, 1999—2008; mem. Royal Commn. Hist. Manuscripts, London, 1992—2002, Econ. and Sci. Rsch. Coun., London, 1985—90. With Royal Welch Fusiliers, 1950—52. Decorated knight bachelor (Eng.), cavaliere officiale Ordine al Merito della Repubblica Italiana; hon. fellow Balliol Coll., Oxford U., 1984—, St. Johns Coll., 1986—, Corpus Christi Coll., 2000—. Fellow Brit. Acad. (pres. 1993-97), Royal Hist. Soc. (literary dir. 1970-74, v.p. 1980-84, hon. v.p. 2001-); mem. Am. Acad. Arts and Scis. (fgn. hon. mem.), Academia Europaea. Avocation: visiting secondhand bookshops. Address: All Souls Coll Oxford OX1 4AL England E-mail: keith.thomas@all-souls.ox.ac.uk.

THOMAS, KENNETH GLYNDWR, mining executive; b. Llanelli, Wales, June 25, 1944; arrived in Can., 1980; m. Elizabeth June Hickman, Sept. 25, 1976; children: Louise June, Kelly Jane. BSc in Metallurgy, U. Wales, Cardiff, 1970; MSc in Mgmt. Sci., U. London, 1971; PhD in Tech. Sci., U. of Delft, The Netherlands, 1994. Chartered engr., U.K.; registered profl. engr., Ont., Can. Metallurgist Brit. Steel Corp., Wales, 1959-67, Anglo Am. Corp., Kitwe, Zambia, 1971-75, plant supt. Klerksdorp, South Africa, 1975-80; design metallurgist Kilborn Engring., Toronto, Ont., 1980-85; mill supt. Giant Yellowknife (Can.) Mines Ltd., N.W.T., 1985-87; sr. v.p. metallurgy and constrn. Barrick Gold Corp., Toronto, 1987-95, sr. v.p. tech. svcs., 1995-2001; mng. dir. mining and mineral processing Hatch, Mississauga, Ont., 2001—02; mng. dir. We. Australia, 2002—03; COO, exec. v.p. ops. Crystallex Internat. Corp., Toronto, 2003—05; mng. dir. Hatch, Mississauga, 2006—. Contbr. articles to tech. jours.; co-patentee in field. Fellow Inst. Materials, Minerals & Mining (U.K.), Can. Inst. Mining, Metallurgy and Petroleum (Mill Man of Yr. award 1990, Airey award 1999, Selwyn G. Blaylock medal 2001), Can. Inst. Mining and Metallurgy. Home Phone: 905-896-8608; Office Phone: 905-403-3980. Personal E-mail: kenthomas@rogers.com.

THOMAS, LATASHA R., alderwoman; m. Timothy Thomas; children: Victoria, Timothy III. Law clk. Cir. Ct. Judge Odas Nicholson, City of Chgo. Corp. Counsel; staff atty. CARPLS; pvt. practice atty. Chgo., 1994—97; assoc. dir. children services divsn. Dept. Human Services, Chgo., 1997—2000, dir. intergovernmental rels., 2000; alderwoman, 17th ward Chgo. City Coun., 2000—. Chair edn. com. Chgo. City Coun., vice chair human rels. com. Office: 7811 S Racine Ave Chicago IL 60620 also: 121 N Lasalle St Rm 305 Chicago IL 60602 Office Phone: 773-723-0908, 312-744-7738. Business E-Mail: ward17@cityofchicago.org.*

THOMAS, LATTA ROOSEVELT, religious educator, clergy; b. Buffalo, SC, Oct. 12, 1927; s. Pickett Roosevelt and Alsie (Crenshaw) T.; m. Bessie Mae Lowery, July 22, 1958; children: Latta R. Jr., Ronald Jerome. AA, Friendship Union Coll., 1949; BA, Benedict Coll., 1951; BD, Colgate Rochester Sem., 1955; M of Sacred Theology, Andover Newton Sem., 1966, DMin, 1973. Ordained to ministry, Bapt. Ch., 1955. Pastor Monumental Bapt. Ch., Elmira, N.Y., 1952-63, Mount Olive Bapt. Ch., Newport, R.I., 1963-65; tchr., coll. minister Benedict Coll., Columbia, S.C., 1965-85, chair religion dept., 1980-95; pastor Ridge Hill Bapt. Ch., Ridge Spring, S.C., 1967-74, Lockhart Bapt. Ch., Saluda, S.C., 1968-74, Second Calvary Bapt. Ch., Columbia, S.C., 1975-96; prof. religion, dean of chapel Morris Coll., Sumter, S.C., 1996-2000. Mem. Greater Columbia Cmty. Rels. Coun., 1979-97, Martin Luther King Jr. Meml. Found., Columbia, 1987-96, Friendship Ctr. Bd., Columbia; faculty rep. Benedict Coll. Bd., Columbia, 1973-75; adj. prof. Black ch. studies Columbia Coll., SC, 2004-05; adj. prof. Black and liberation theology Lutheran Theol. So. Sem., Columbia, SC, 2004. Author: (book) Biblical Faith and the Black American, 1976, The Biblical God and Human Suffering, 1987, (meditations) Upper Room Disciplines. Committeeman Richland County Dem. Party, Columbia. Recipient Disting. Svc. as bd. mem. award Benedict Coll. Trustee Bd., 1974-5, Citation for work as chmn. Greater Columbia Cmty. Rels. Coun., 1983, Seminar cert. U.S. Ednl. Found. of India, Madras, 1990, Govs. Disting. Prof. award S.C. State Dept. Edn., 1995, 30 Yrs. Dedicated Svc. award Benedict Coll., 1995. Mem. Columbia Coalition of Blacks and Jews (convenor 1993-94), Am. Bapt. Chs. of South (moderator 1990-96, Plaque 1996), NAACP (pres. Eomira N.Y. br. 1955-63, Plaque 1971). Democrat. Baptist. Avocations: hutning, fishing, researching history. Home: 711 Isaac St Columbia SC 29203-5023

THOMAS, LAWRENCE ELDON, mathematics professor; b. Columbus, Ohio, Mar. 15, 1942; s. Bertram D. and Glorian (Butler) T.; m. Rebecca Nolan, June 13, 1970; children: David Nolan, Kathleen Rebecca. BS, U. Mich., 1964; PhD, Yale U., 1970. Rsch. asst. math. dept. Swiss Fed. Inst. Tech., Zurich, 1970-72; rsch. asst. physics dept. U. Geneva, 1972-74; asst. prof. math. U. Va., Charlottesville, 1974-76, assoc. prof., 1976-82, prof., 1982—, chmn. dept., 1989-93. Contbr. articles on theory of Schrodinger operators, statis. mechanics and stochastic processes to profl. jours. Mem. Am. Math. Soc., Am. Physics Soc., Internat. Nat. Math. Physics, Phi Beta Kappa. Avocations: sailing, tennis. Office: U Va Dept Math Cabell Dr Charlottesville VA 22903

THOMAS, LEONA MARLENE, retired healthcare educator; b. Rock Springs, Wyo., Jan. 15, 1933; d. Leonard H. and Opal (Wright) Francis; children: Peter, Paul, Patrick, Alexis. BA, Govs. State U., University Park, Ill., 1982, MHS, 1986; cert. med. records adminstrn., U. Colo., 1954. Asst. prof. Chgo. State U., 1984—, acting dir. health info. adminstrn. program, 1991-92; acting dir. health info. Internat. Coll., Naples, Fla., 1994; dir. Chgo. State U., 1994—2008. Chairperson dept. health info. adminstrn. Chgo. State U., 1994—2008. Mem. adv. com. Wellness Ctr., mem. adv. com. occupl. therapy program Chgo. State U. Mem. Assembly on Edn., Am. Health Info. Mgmt. Assn., APHA, Chgo. and Vicinity Med. Records Assn., Ill. Assn. Allied Health Profls., Gov.'s State Alumni Assn. Democrat. Methodist. Home: 6340 Americana Dr Apt 1101 Willowbrook IL 60527 Personal E-mail: lmthomas@msn.com.

THOMAS, LINDSEY KAY, JR., research ecology biologist, educator, consultant; b. Salt Lake City, Apr. 16, 1931; s. Lindsey Kay and Naomi Lurie (Biesinger) T.; m. Nancy Ruth Van Dyke, Aug. 24, 1956; children: Elizabeth Nan Thomas Cardinale, David Lindsey, Wayne Hal, Dorothy Ann Thomas Brown. BS, Utah State Agrl. Coll., Logan, 1953; MS, Brigham Young U., Provo, Utah, 1958; PhD, Duke U., Durham, NC, 1974. Park naturalist Nat. Capital Pks., Nat. Pk. Svc., Washington, 1957—62, pk. naturalist (rschr.) Region 6, 1962—63, rsch. pk. naturalist Nat. Capital Region, 1963—66; rsch. biologist S.E. Temperate Forest Pk. Areas, Washington, 1966, Durham, NC, 1966—67, Great Falls, Md., 1967—71, Nat. Capital Pks., Great Falls, 1971—74, Nat. Capital Region, Triangle, Va., 1974—93, Washington, 1985—93; rsch. biologist, Patuxent Environ. Sci. Ctr. Nat. Biol. Svc., Washington, Triangle, 1993—96; resource mgmt. specialist Balt.-Washington Pkwy., Greenbelt, Md., 1996, Nat. Capital Parks-East, 1996—98; rsch. ecologist emeritus and cons. Nat. Capital Region, Nat. Park Svc., 1998—. Bd. dirs. Prince William County Svc. Authority, Va., 1996-2004; adj. prof. George Mason U., Fairfax, Va., 1988—, George Washington U., Washington, 1992-98; instr. US Dept. Agr. Grad. Sch., 1964-66; aquatic ecol. cons. Fairfax County Fedn. Citizens Assns., Va., 1970-71; guest lectr. Washington Tech. Inst. (now U. DC), 1976. Contbr. articles to profl. jours. Wildlife mgmt. cons. Girl Scouts Am., Loudoun County, Va., 1958; preservation and mgmt. cons. McAteean Magnolia Bogs, Save Araby, Mattawoman and Mason Springs in Charles County, Md., 2002-06, Nat. Resources Divsn., Arlington County, Va., 2004—; asst. scoutmaster, scoutmaster, merit badges counselor Boy Scouts Am., 1958—, Scouters Tng. award, 1961. Recipient Incentive awards Nat. Park Svc., 1962, Superior Performance award, 1989; rsch. grantee Washington Biologists' Field Club, 1977, 82. Mem.: AAAS, Md. Native Plant Soc., Nat. Trust for Historic Preservation, Washington Biologists' Field Club, So. Appalachian Bot. Soc., Soc. for Early Hist. Archaeology, The Nature Conservancy, George Wright Soc., Ecol. Soc. Am., Bot. Soc. Washington, Sigma Xi. Mem. Lds Ch. Home: 13854 Delaney Rd Woodbridge VA 22193-4654 Office: Prince William Forest Park 18100 Park Hdqrs Rd Triangle VA 22172

THOMAS, LIZANNE, lawyer; BA, Furman U, 1979; JD, Washington & Lee, 1982. Bar: Ga. 1982. Ptnr. mergers and acquisitions practice Jones Day, Atlanta, firmwide adminstrv. ptnr., 2003—07, ptnr. in charge Atlanta office, 2008—. Lectr. corp. fin. U. Calif., Berkeley and Davis; pres. Law Alumni Assn. Washington and Lee U., 2001—02; bd. dirs. Krispy Kreme Doughnuts, 2004—. Recurring panelist Directors' Inst. of the Conf. Bd. Bd. trustees Furman U.; exec. bd. dirs. Atlanta C. of C. Mem.: State Bar of Ga. Office: Jones Day 1420 Peachtree St NE Ste 800 Atlanta GA 30309-3053 Office Phone: 404-581-8411. Office Fax: 404-581-8330. Business E-Mail: lthomas@jonesday.com.

THOMAS, LOIS C., musician, educator, religious organization administrator, composer; b. Ft. Worth, Oct. 15, 1932; d. Walter Scott and Margaret Alice Dawn Cook; m. Richard Wallace Thomas, Nov. 5, 1988. BA in Organ Performance, Tex. Christian U., 1966; postgrad., SWBT Sem. Cert. profl. instr. piano, organ theory. Organist Western Hills Bapt. Ch., Ft. Worth, 1959-69, 1st Ch. of Christ, Scientist, Ft. Worth, 1969-84, First Congl. Ch., Ft. Worth, 1985-87; organist, dir. Anglican Ch. St. Charles the Martyr, Grand Prairie, Tex., 1989—99; organist, dir., assoc. rector Anglican Ch. St. Raphael, the Archangel, Grand Prairie, 2002—04. Deacon United Cath. Ch., 1996; priest Communion Evang. Episcopal Chs., 1997; fin. officer USCG Aux., Grapevine, Tex., 1989—95, sec., Grand Prairie, Tex., 1995. Commd.: hymnal Diocese St. Paul, the Apostle, 2000. Mem.: Music Tchr.'s Nat. Assn., Tex. Music Tchr.'s Assn., Arlington Music Tchr.'s Assn. (phone com.), Am. Guild Organists (phone com., svc. playing cert.). Home: 1501 Connally Ter Arlington TX 76010-4514

THOMAS, LOUIS JOSEPH, dean, management educator; b. Barnesville, Ohio, Jan. 16, 1942; s. Louis Ward and Mary Elizabeth (Tipton) Thomas; m. Margaret Leah Gilboy, June 25, 1966; children: Molly, Douglas. BS, Carnegie-Mellon U., 1964; MPhil, Yale U., 1967, PhD, 1968. Chem. engr. Eastman Kodak Co., Rochester, NY, 1963—64; asst. prof. prodn. and quantitative analysis Johnson Grad. Sch. Mgmt., Cornell U., Ithaca, NY, 1967—72, assoc. prof., 1972—77, prof. ops. mgmt., 1977—, dir. exec. edn. programs, 1979—91, dir. exec. devel. program, 1979—2000, Nicholas H. Noyes prof. mfg., 1985—2007, assoc. dean academic affairs, 1996—97, 2002—07, Anne and Elmer Lindseth dean, 2007—. Vis. prof. Stanford U., Calif., 1973, U. Cath. Louvain, Belgium, 1979, Belgium, 82, Belgium, 89, Belgium, 95, GSBA Zurich, 1992, 95; cons. IBM, GTE, AT&T. Co-author: Operations Management, 1985, Cases in Operation Management, 1988; contbr. articles to profl. jours. Recipient Excellence in Teaching award, Justice Found., 1974; grantee NSF, 1982. Mem.: Am. Prodn. and Inventory Control Soc., Inst. Indsl. Engrs., Ops. Research Soc. Am., Inst. Mgmt. Sci. Avocations: sports, music. Home: 137 Eastlake Rd Ithaca NY 14850-9700 Office: Johnson Grad Sch Mgmt Cornell U 348 Sage Hall Ithaca NY 14853-6201 Office Phone: 607-255-4854. E-mail: ljt3@cornell.edu.*

THOMAS, LOWELL, JR., writer, retired military officer, state senator; b. London, Oct. 6, 1923; s. Lowell Jackson and Frances (Ryan) T.; m. Mary Taylor Pryor, May 20, 1950; children: Anne Frazier, David Lowell. Student, Taft Sch., 1942; BA, Dartmouth Coll., 1948; postgrad., Princeton Sch. Pub. and Internat. Affairs, 1952. Asst. cameraman Fox Movietone News, S.Am., 1939, Bradford Washburn Alaskan mountaineering expdn., 1940; illustrated lecturer, 1946—; asst. economist, photographer with Max Weston Thornburg, Turkey, 1947, Iran, 1948; film prodn. Iran, 1949; Tibet expdn. with Lowell Thomas, Sr., 1949; field work Cinerama, S.Am., Africa, Asia, 1951-52; travels by small airplane with wife, writing and filming Europe, Africa, Middle East, 1954-55; mem. Rockwell Polar Flight, first flight around the world over both poles, Nov., 1965; mem. Alaska State Senate, 1967-74; lt. gov. State of Alaska, 1974-79; owner Talkeetna Air Taxi, Inc., air contract carrier, Anchorage, Alaska, 1980-94. Producer series of films Flight to Adventure, NBC-TV, 1956; producer, writer TV series High Adventure, 1957-59; producer documentary film Adaq, King of Alaskan Seas, 1960; producer two films on Alaska, 1962, 63, film on U. Alaska, 1964, South Pacific travel documentary, 1965, film on Arctic oil exploration, Atlantic-Richfield Co., 1969. Author: Out of this World, A Journey to Tibet, 1950, (with Mrs. Lowell Thomas, Jr.) Our Flight to Adventure, 1956, The Silent War in Tibet, 1959, The Dalai Lama, 1961, The Trail of Ninety-Eight, 1962, (with Lowell Thomas Sr.) More Great True Adventures, 1963, Famous First Flights that Changed History, 1968. Past pres. Western Alaska coun. Boys Scouts Am.; bd. dirs. Anchorage unit Salvation Army, Alaska Conservation Found. 1st lt. USAAF, 1943-45. Mem. Nat. Parks and Conservation Assn. (bd. dirs.), Alaska C. of C., Aircraft Owners and Pilots Assn. Clubs: Explorers, Marco Polo, Dutch Treat (N.Y.C.); Rotary, (Anchorage), Press (Anchorage); Dartmouth Outing; American Alpine. Address: 10800 Hideaway Lake Dr Anchorage AK 99507-6139

THOMAS, LUCILLE COLE, librarian; b. Dunn, NC, Oct. 1, 1921; d. Collie and Minnie (Lee) Cole; m. George Browne Thomas, May 24, 1943; children: Ronald C., Beverly G. BA, Bennett Coll., 1941; DHL (hon.), Benentt Coll., 1996; MA, NYU, 1955; MS, Columbia U., 1957. Tchr. Bibb County Bd. Edn., Macon, Ga., 1947—55; libr. Bklyn. Pub. Libr., 1955—56, NYC Bd. Edn., Bklyn., 1956—68, supr. librs., 1968—77, dir. elem. sch. librs., 1977—83; program dir. Weston Woods Inst., Weston, Conn., 1984—85; adj. prof. libr. sci. Queens Coll., CUNY, 1986—89. Founder Sch. Libr. Media Day, NY State, 1973; del. NY Gov's. Conf. on Librs., 1978, White House Conf. Libr. and Info. Svcs., 1979; trustee NY Met. Ref. and Rsch. Libr. Agy., NYC, 1979—83; hon. del. White House Conf. Libr. and Info. Svcs., 1991; coord. UNESCO/Internat. Assn. Sch. Librarianship Book Program for devel. countries, 1980—89; adv. bd. Regents' Adv. Council on Learning Tech., Albany, NY, 1982—88; cons. Putnam Pub. Group, NYC, 1983; 1st v.p. Schomburg Corp., 1983—85; bd. examiners NY City Bd. Edn., 1983—91; founder Nat. Sch. Libr. Media Month, 1985; liaison Freedom to Read Found., 1986—88; adj. prof. libr. sci. St. John's U., 1986; reviewer U.S. Office Ednl. Rsch. & Improvement, 1988—90; adj. prof. libr. sci. Pratt Inst., 1989; mem. libr. sect. Nat. Martin Luther King, Jr. Commn., 1990—95; bd. dirs NY is Book Country, 1991—96; chair seminar for librs. from devel. countries, Barcelona, 1993; trustee Bklyn. Pub. Libr., 1993—, v.p., 2000—03, pres., 2003—06, chair audit com., 2006—08; mem. Luhrsry Ops. Com, 2006—. Contbr. articles to profl. jours.; editor: Insight, 1974, Cultural Heritage Through Literature, 1993. Del. World Conf. on Edn. for all in Jamtien, Thailand, 1990; treas. Bklyn. Home for Aged Commn., 1967—2007; adv. bd. Books Kids, 1989—; pres. bd. trustees St. Mark's Day Sch., 2001—; trustee Leroy Merritt Humanitarian Found., 2005—09; vestry mem. St. John's Episcopal Ch., Bklyn., 1988—90, chair stewardship com., 1987—90; active St. Mark's Ch., Bklyn., 1960—. Recipient Disting. Alumna award, Bennett Coll., 1981, Edn. award, Bus. and Profl. Women's Club, 1983, Achievement award, Columbia U. Sch. Libr. Svcs., 1987, Grolier Found. award, 1988, Disting. Pub. Svc. award, SUNY, Albany, 1989, Cmty. Svc.

award, North Queens, NY, 1993, Disting. Svc. award, St. Mark's Ch., 2003, Achievement award, Consortium of Doctors, 2004, NY Black Librs., 2004, citation, Bklyn. Borough Pres., 2005, Letter of Commendation, First Lady Laura Bush, 2005, Faithful Servant award, Concord Bapt. Ch., 2006, Dedicated Svc. honoree, Bklyn. Pub. Libr., 2006, Freedom to Read Found. award, 2007; named Woman on the Move, State Sen. Carl Andrews, 2003; honoree, Bennett Coll. Alumnae, 2006. Mem.: ALA (hon.; councilor 1980—91, exec. bd. 1984—91, direction and rev. com. 1985—91, chair nominations and spl. assignments com. 1987—88, chair Hqtrs. Libr. Rev. Accountability Com. 1987—88, exec. bd. found. 1987—89, pers. com. 1988—89, chair ALA/AASL disting. svc. award com. 1989—90, disaster relief com. 1989—91, chair rev. com. of office for rsch. 1990—91, AASL/SIRS Disting. Libr. Svc. award sch. adminstrs. com. 1990—91, chair rsch. rev. com. 1990—91, AASL internat. rels. com. 1990—94, internat. com. 1991—95, councilor 1993—2002, hon. mem. 2003, mem. intellectual freedom com., assn. trustees 2005—, amb. 2008, Disting. Svc. award Black Librs. Caucus 1992, Trailblazer's award Libr. Black Caucus 1995), Bklyn. Pub. Libr. (hon. 12 ann. gala 2008), Bklyn. Home Aged (bd. dirs. 2008), Weeksville Cir. Giving, NY Libr. Assn. (pres. sch. libr. media sect. 1972—73, v.p. 1976—77, pres. 1977—78, appreciation cert. 1983, oustanding achievement award 1984, achievement award 1988), Internat. Assn. Sch. Librarianship (pres. 1989—95), Internat. Fedn. Libr. Assn. (sec. 1985—96, chair sch. librs. sect. 1989—93, ofcl. rep. UN and UNICEF 1991—94, chair planning and implementation com.), NYC Sch. Librs. Assn. (pres. 1970—72, chair sch. librs. of NY Libr. Assn. sect. 1989—93), Bklyn. Pub. Libr. (hon.), Bklyn. Hist. Soc. (named one of outstanding women of Bklyn. 1985), Schomburg Commn. (1st v.p. 1986—90), Women's City of NYC Club (bd. dirs. 1986—2000, vice chmn. 1987—89, chair edn. com. 1989—92, v.p. 1992—93), NY Libr. Club (life; v.p. 1976—77, pres. 1977—78), Kappa Delta Pi Internat. Hon. Soc., Alpha Kappa Alpha (Pi Phi Omega chpt. parliamentarian 1990—92, v.p. 1990—94, 1992—94, pres. 1994—98, co-coord. North Atlantic region 1996—2000, mem.-at-large 2004—07, Pi Phi Omega chpt. 2nd v.p., chair membership com. 2007—08, 1st v.p. P. Phi Omega Club 2009—, v.p. 2009—, Del. Centennial 2008). Democrat. Avocation: reading. Home: 1184 Union St Brooklyn NY 11225-1512 Personal E-mail: lucillecthomas@verizon.net.

THOMAS, LYNNE M., academic librarian, researcher, blogger; b. Southbridge, Mass., Oct. 8, 1974; d. William I. and Marie A. Fors; m. Michael D. Thomas, Feb. 12, 2000; 1 child, Caitlin R. BA, Smith Coll., Northampton, Mass., 1996; MS Libr. and Info. Sci., U. Ill., Champaign, 1999; MA English and Am. Lit., Northern Ill. U., DeKalb, 2006. Catalog libr., Rare Book Team Yale U., New Haven, 1999—2003; head, Rare Books & Spl. Collections Northern Ill. U. Librs., 2004—. Mem.: ALA. Liberal. Office: Northern Ill Univ Founders Meml Libr 402A Dekalb IL 60115 Office Fax: 815-753-9803. Business E-Mail: lmthomas@niu.edu.

THOMAS, LYNNELL L., language educator; d. Leonard and Sargiena Thomas. BA, Wash. U., St. Louis, 1993; MLA, Tulane U., New Orleans, 1997; PhD, Emory U., Atlanta, 2005—05; MA, Emory U., 2005. Asst. prof. U. Mass., Boston, 2005—. Contbr. chapters to books, articles to profl. jours. Mem.: MLA, Am. Studies Assn.

THOMAS, MALAYILMELATHETHIL, minister, English language educator; b. Chengannur, Kerala, India, Jan. 26, 1932; came to U.S. 1959; s. Malayilmelathethil Thomas and Rachel (Thomas) Koruthu. BA, Kerala U., 1952; BD, Serampore U., Calcutta, 1956; MTh, Princeton Theol. Sem., NJ, 1960; MA, Morehead State U., Ky., 1961; EdD, U. Tulsa, Okla., 1964. Prin. St. George Mid. Sch., Kizharalloor, Kerala, India, 1952-53; tchr. Catholicate H.S., Pathanamthitta, 1956-59; asst. prof. English Morehead State U., 1964-65, assoc. prof. English, 1965-67, prof. English, 1967-94, prof. emeritus, 1994—; pastor St. Gregorios Orthodox Ch., Oak Park, Ill., 1994—. Mem. MLA, Ky. Philol. Soc., Coll. Composition and Communication, Nat. Coun. Tchrs. English, Phi Kappa Phi, Phi Delta Kappa, Kappa Delta Pi. Democrat. Mem. Indian Orthodox Ch. Avocations: travel, cooking, gardening. Office: 1121 N Humphrey Oak Park IL 60302 Office Phone: 708-848-4120. Personal E-mail: frmkthomas@yahoo.com.

THOMAS, MARK FRANCIS, history professor, economics professor, researcher; b. Hampton Ct., Middlesex, England, Nov. 17, 1954; s. Francis and Irene Betty Thomas; m. Victoria Desiree Herzfeld; children: Emma Gabrielle, Adam Hewlett. BA in History and Economics, Oxford U., England, 1973—76, MA, 1976, PhD in Modern History, 1984; MA in Economics, Cornell, Ithaca, 1979. Asst. to assoc. prof., history U. Va., Charlottesville, 1982—, prof. history and economics, 2004—. Vis. fellow All Souls Coll., Oxford, 1996—97; rsch. fellow Australian Nat. U., Canberra, Australia, 1984—85, 1993, 95, 2008; vis. fellow Clare Hall, Cambridge, United Kingdom, 1988—89; fellow commoner Queen's Coll., Oxford, 2000—08; faculty fellow history John M OLin Found., NYC, 1987—88. Co-editor: (academic book) Income Distribution in Historical Perspective, The Economic Future in Historical Perspective; editor: The Disintegration of the World Economy between the Wars; co-editor: Capitalism in Context; co-author: Making History Count; contbr. articles to profl. jours. (T S Ashton Prize, Econ. History Soc., 1984, Cole Prize, Econ. History Assn., 2004). Mem.: Econ. History Assn. (Alexander Gerschenkron prize 1984), Econ. History Soc. Office: Univ of Va Randall Hall Charlottesville VA 22904 Business E-Mail: mark.thomas@virginia.edu.

THOMAS, MARK P., conductor, educator; b. Sellersville, Pa., Jan. 6, 1961; s. Russell C. and Pearl Thomas; m. Eileen Brown Thomas; children: Parker M., Pryce M., Peyton M. BS in Music Edn., West Chester U., Pa., 1984; MS in Telecom. (music), Kutztown U., Pa., 1989; EdD, Walden U., 2007. Music dir. and condr. Schuylkill Choral Soc., Pottsville, Pa., 1986—; music dir. St. John's Luth. Ch., Spinnerstown, Pa., 1988—92; instr. performing arts Bucks County CC, Newtown, Pa., 1989—92; sr. high music dir. So. Columbia Sch. Dist., Catawissa, Pa., 1992—99; supr. music Upper Perkiomen Sch. Dist., Pennsburg, Pa., 1999—; educator music and humanities, dir. univ. choir Pa. State U., Schuylkill Haven, Pa., 2000—; artistic dir. and condr. Choral Arts Soc. of Upper Perkiomen Valley, Red Hill, Pa., 2001—08, Schuykill Symphony Orch., Pottsville, 2008—. Guest condr. Allentown Diocese Music Festival, Tamaqua, Pa., 2002, Ocean Grove Choral Festival Choir, Ocean Grove, NJ, 1998—2001, Schuylkill County Choral Festival, Pine Grove, Pa., 1996. Music dir. and conductor (recordings) Holiday Favorites, 2004, Celtic Celebration, 2007; guest artist: NY Pops, 2005, guest condr.: Prague Symphony Orch., 2006. Mem.: Am. Choral Director's Assn., Pa, Music Director's Assn., Music Educator's Nat. Conf., Columbia Montour County Choral Festival (originator 1996), St. Mark's Luth. Ch., Kappa Kappa Psi (originator 1982). Office: Schuylkill Choral Soc 1440 Mahantonge Street Pottsville PA 17901 Personal E-mail: mpt10@psu.edu.

THOMAS, MARLIN ULUESS, industrial engineer, academic administrator, educator; b. Middlesboro, Ky., June 28, 1942; s. Elmer Vernon and Helen Lavada (Banks) T.; m. Susan Kay Stoner, Jan. 18, 1963; children: Pamela Claire Thomas Davis, Martin Phillip. BSE, U. Mich., Dearborn, 1967; MSE, U. Mich., Ann Arbor, 1968, PhD, 1971. Registered profl. engr., Mich. Asst. and assoc. prof. dept. ops. rsch. Naval Postgrad. Sch., Monterey, Calif., 1971-76; assoc. prof. systems design dept. U. Wis., Milw., 1976-78; mgr. tech. planning and analysis vehicle quality-reliability Chrysler Corp., Detroit, 1978-79; prof. dept. indsl. engring. U. Mo., Columbia, 1979-82; prof. indsl. engring., chmn. dept. Cleve State U., 1982-88, acting dir. Advanced Mfg. Ctr., 1984-85; prof., chmn. indsl. engring. Lehigh U., Bethlehem, Pa., 1988-93; prof., head Sch. Indsl. Engring. Purdue U., West Lafayette, Ind., 1993-98; dir. Inst. Interdisciplinary Engring. Studies, West Lafayette, 1998—. Program dir. NSF, Washington, 1987-88. Contbr. numerous articles on indsl. engring. and ops. rsch. to profl. jours. With USN, 1958-62; capt. USNR, 1971—. Named Outstanding Tchr., U. Mo. Coll. Engring., 1980, Coll. Man of Yr, Cleve. State U. Coll. Engring., 1985, Disting. Alumnus of Yr., U. Mich.-Dearborn, 1996, Engr. Excell Engagement Svc. award, Purdue U., 2003, IIE Holzman Disting. Educator award, 2004. Fellow Inst. Indsl. Engrs. (past pres., recipient Frank Groseclose Medallion award, 2005), Am. Soc. for Quality, Inst. for Ops. Rsch. and Mgmt. Scis.; mem. Am. Soc. for Engring. Edn., Am. Indian Sci. and Engr. Soc., VFW, Seabee Vet. Am. Office: Sch Indsl Engring Purdue Univ 315 N Grant St West Lafayette IN 47907-2023 Home Phone: 765-497-4586. Office Fax: 765-494-1299. Business E-Mail: muthomas@ecn.purdue.edu.

THOMAS, MARY ANN MCCRARY, counselor, school system administrator; b. Washington, Feb. 11, 1935; d. Frank Robert and Mary (Davison) McCrary; m. John Ralph Thomas, Sept. 30, 1961; children: Robert Davison, John Shannon, Kristen Aldridge. BA, U. Calif., Berkley, 1956; MA, UCLA, 1959. Cert. tchr., Calif. Supr. Pacific Bell, San Francisco, 1962-67; advisor gifted, talented San Rafael (Calif.) City Schs., 1973—, counselor, 1973—, dir. student affairs, 1982—. Pres. San Rafael PTA Coun., 1981-84, outstanding svc. award, 1983, 86, 89, San Rafael High Sch. Site Coun., 1985; pres. bd. dirs. Marin Wildlife Ctr., 1979-85. Recipient Golden Bell award, Marin Community Found., 1987, Outstanding Student Activities program state award, 1992; named Pub. Schoolmaster of Yr., 1993. Mem. Calif. Assn. Gifted, Calif. Assn. Tchrs. English. Republican. Episcopalian. Avocations: reading, gardening. Office: Davidson Mid Sch 280 Woodland Ave San Rafael CA 94901-5097

THOMAS, MARY LEE, property manager; d. Louis and Virgie Mae Bedford; children: Tamara Simone Times, Bobbi Makeda. A in Liberal Arts, S.W. Ill. Coll., 2003; B in Bus. Adminstrn., Lindenwood U., 2005. Mgmt. intern program East St. Louis Housing Authority, 1992, cert. earned income dissallowance specialist Nan Mckay And Assoc., 2003, pub. housing rent calculation specialist Nan Mckay And Assoc., 2004, universal phys. condition stds. specialist Nan McKay & Assocs., 2005, project based mgmt. essentials specialist Nan McKay Assocs., 2006. Property mgr. East St. Louis (Ill.) Housing Authority, 1990—2004, asset mgr., 2004—. Mem.: Nat. Assn. Housing Redevelopment Orgn. (cert. pub. housing mgr. 1992). Democrat. Baptist. Achievements include received award for providing inspiration to co-workers and residents by singing at various functions within the housing authority and the community. Avocations: singing, cycling, walking, tae-bo, skating. Home: 718 Country Meadow Ln Belleville IL 62221 Office: E St Louis Housing Authority Phoenix Cts Mgmt Office 7750 Marybelle Ave East Saint Louis IL 62203 Business E-Mail: mthomas@elsha.org.

THOMAS, NANCY HINCKLEY, special education educator; b. LA, Mar. 7, 1939; d. Barton Armin and Helen (Ferguson) Hinckley; children: Gregory Dean, Garold Daniel, Deanna Nancy, Barton William, Deborah Hinckley, Bryan Joseph. AB, Stanford U., Calif., 1959. Resource Specialist Calif. Dept. head K-Mart Corp., Petaluma, Calif., 1982—89; spl. edn. tchr. R-House, Santa Rosa, Calif., 1994—2005; resource specialist St. Rose Sch., 2005—. Resource specialist St. Rose Sch., Santa Rosa, Calif., 2005—07. Mem.: AAUW (treas. 1965—67), Commonwealth Club, Nat. Trust Hist. Preservation. Avocations: reading, gardening. Home: 724 Bassett St Petaluma CA 94952 Home Phone: 707-762-1589.

THOMAS, OLIN C., secondary school educator; b. Newton, Miss., Sept. 27, 1955; s. Mary F. Thomas; m. Janet L. Fetner, Dec. 29, 1981; children: Benjiman C., Olin G., Daniel L., David E. AS, NE La. U., Monroe, 1976. Supr. carpentry dept. Meridian Pub. Schs., Miss., 1990—97; constrn. trades instr. Meridian CC, 1997—, student advisor, 1997—2008. Youth leader, Sunday sch. tchr. Decatur United Meth. Ch., Miss., 1982—2008; leader Boy Scouts America, Decatur, 1989—2008. Recipient Silver Beaver award, Boy Scouts America, 2002, T.J. Harris award, Meridian CC, 2003. Mem.: Skills USA (advisor 1997—2008). Methodist. Avocations: hunting, fishing, gardening, woodworking. Office: Meridian CC 910 Hwy 19 N Meridian MS 39307

THOMAS, OUIDA POWER, music educator; b. Louisville, Miss., Nov. 25, 1939; d. Robert Alvin and Mavis (Simpson) Power; m. Charles Victor Thomas, Aug. 4, 1962; children: Karla Victoria, Sylvia Katharine Thomas White, Charles Gregory. BS in Bus. Edn. with highest honors, Miss. State U., Starkville, 1963; M Music Edn., Delta State U., 1993; postgrad., U. Memphis, 1996—. Nat. cert. tchr. of music. Ind. music tchr. piano and organ, Grenada, Miss., 1963—; classroom gen. music tchr. Kirk Acad., Grenada, 1977-87. Adjudicator auditions Federated Music Clubs, Oxford, Miss., 1990—99. Accompanist musical prodns. Grenada Fine Arts Playhouse, 1979-81; organist, choirmaster All Saints' Episcopal Ch., Grenada, 1977—; mem. music and liturgy com. Episcopal Diocese of Miss., 1996-99. Mem. Am. Guild Organists, Nat. Guild Piano Tchrs. (chmn. local auditions 1977—, adjudicator auditions 1993—), Music Tchrs. Nat. Assn. (cert. in piano and organ), Miss. Music Tchrs. Assn. (cert. in piano and organ, exec. bd. 1993-94, state chair pre-coll. student activities 1995-96, chair state cert. 1999-2000, adjudicator auditions 1993—), Grenada Area Music Tchrs. Assn. (v.p. 1995—). Avocations: gardening, needlecrafts. Home: 1985 Wooded Dr Grenada MS 38901-4073 Personal E-mail: opthomas@cableone.net.

THOMAS, OWEN D., diversified financial services company executive; b. June 1961; BS, U. Va., 1983; MBA, Harvard U. Joined Morgan Stanley, 1987; mgr. real estate investing bus. Morgan Stanley Real Estate, 1994—95, mng. dir., 1995—2000, head real estate, 2000—05; acting pres. Morgan Stanley Investment Mgmt., 2005, pres., COO investment mgmt., chmn., 2005—08; head global asset mgmt. bus., CEO Morgan Stanley Asia, Hong Kong, 2008—. Trustee, exec. com. mem. Urban Land Inst. Mem.: Real Estate Roundtable, Pension Real Estate Assn. (vice chmn.). Office: Morgan Stanley 3 Exchange Sq, 30th Fl Hong Kong Office Phone: +852 2848 5200. Office Fax: +852 2845 1012.

THOMAS, PATRICIA ANNE, retired law librarian; b. Cleve., Aug. 21, 1927; d. Richard Joseph and Marietta Bernadette (Teevans) T. BA, Case Western Res. U., 1949, JD, 1951. Bar: Ohio 1951, U.S. Supreme Ct. 1980. Libr. Arter & Hadden, Cleve., 1951-62; asst. libr., libr. IRS, Washington, 1962-78; libr. dir. Adminstrv. Office U.S. Cts., 1978-93; ret., 1993. Mem. Am. Assn. Law Librs., Soc. D.C. (pres. 1967-69), Soc. Benchers (Case Western Res. Law Sch.)

THOMAS, PATRICK ROBERT MAXWELL, oncologist, educator, academic administrator; b. Exmouth, Devon, Eng., Feb. 23, 1943; came to U.S., 1976; s. Christopher Codrington and Aileen Daphne (Gordon) T.; m. Linda Sharon Rich, June 23, 1986 (dec. 1987), m. Geraldine M. Jacobson, Mar. 2, 1996 (div. 1999); m. Frances Aquino, Feb. 19, 2005. Diploma in biochemistry, London U., 1965, MB, BS, 1968. Lectr. Inst. Cancer Rsch., London, 1974-76; assoc. chief clinician Roswell Park Meml. Inst., Buffalo, 1976-79; asst. prof. Washington U., St. Louis, 1979-83, assoc. prof., 1983-89, prof., 1989-90; prof., chmn. Temple U., Phila., 1991-98; radiation oncologist Pinellas (Fla.) Radiation Oncology Assocs., 1998—2003; prof. radiation oncology Pa. State U., Pa., 2006—. Extramural bd. PDQ, Bethesda, Md., 1989—; mem. in-svc. exam. com. Am. Coll. Radiology, Reston, Va., 1990-97; examiner Am. Bd. Radiology, Louisville, 1990—. Mem. editl. adv. bd.: Med. and Pediatric Oncology, 2002—. Fellow: Royal Coll. Physicians of London, Am. Soc. Radiation Oncologists, Am. Coll. Radiologists; mem.: Pediat. Radiation Oncology Soc. (founding sec.), Internat. Soc. Pediat. Oncology (sci. com. 2000—). Office: 500 University Dr MC H063 Hershey PA 17033 Business E-Mail: pthomas2@psu.edu.

THOMAS, PAUL D., metal products executive, human resources specialist; V.p. Alcoa, Inc., Pitts., 1998—2004, pres. engineered products, 1998—2001, pres. mill products, 2001—03, group pres. N.Am. fabricated products, 2003—04, exec. v.p., 2004—, exec. v.p. people, ABS and culture, 2004—06, exec. v.p., group pres. packaging & consumer products, 2006—. Bd. dirs. Aloca Found., Aluminum Assn., Inc. Office: Alcoa Inc 201 Isabella St Pittsburgh PA 15212-5858 Office Phone: 412-553-4545.

THOMAS, PAUL LINDSLEY, composer, musician, director; b. NYC, Mar. 18, 1929; s. Richard Banks and Virginia Bartholomew (Carrington) T.; m. Joyce Robertshaw, Sept. 3, 1955; 1 child, Craig Carrington. BA, Trinity Coll., Hartford, Conn., 1950; diploma, Am. Conservatory, Fontainbleau, France, 1954; MusB, Yale U., 1957, MusM, 1958; D of Musical Arts, U. North Tex., 1979. Organist, choirmaster St. George's-by-the-River, Rumson, NJ, 1950-55, St. James Episcopal Ch., West Hartford, Conn., 1955-60; organist Wesleyan U., Middletown, Conn., 1958-60; dir. Apollo Glee Club, Yale U., New Haven, 1958-60; instr. in organ So. Meth. U., Dallas, 1960-65; music dir., organist St. Michael and All Angels Ch., Dallas, 1960-97, composer in residence, music dir. emeritus, 1997—; music dir. Trinity Epis. Ch., Dallas, 1998—. Chmn. liturgy and music commn. Episcopal Diocese of Dallas, 1992—98. Composer (opera) Everyman, 1986; composer ch. anthems and organ music. Named Canon of Ch. Music, Episcopal Diocese of Dallas, 1980; recording grantee Stemmons Found., Dallas, 1995; Joyce and Paul Thomas Music Wing named in his honor St. Michael and All Angels, Dallas, 1994. Fellow Am. Guild Organists (dean Dallas chpt. 1967-69, gen. chmn. nat. conv. 1972, nat. coun. 1972-75); mem. Assn. Anglican Musicians, Am. Choral Dirs. Assn. Republican. Episcopalian. Home: 6822 Northwood Rd Dallas TX 75225-2538 Office: Trinity Episcopal Ch 12727 Hillcrest Rd Dallas TX 75230-2007

THOMAS, PAUL MILTON, retired science educator; b. Sligo, Pa., Dec. 1, 1929; s. Milton Ivan and Maude Hazel Thomas; m. Dorothy Marie McGinnett; 1 child, Mona Lee Callahan. BA, Allegheny Coll., 1958; MA, U. Mich., 1959, MS, 1962, PhD, 1964; DMin, Drew U., 1980. Instr. biology Houghton Coll., NY, 1959—62; asst. prof. Point Loma Coll., San Diego, 1964—66; rsch. fellow Calif. Inst. Tech., Pasadena, 1967—68; vis. prof. Johns Hopkins U., Balt., 1968; prof., chmn. dept. biology Edinboro U., Pa., 1968—90; pastor United Ch. of Christ, Greensburg, 1995—. Vis. scholar Harvard U., Cambridge, Mass., 1993. Contbr. articles to profl. jours.; author: (books) W. Edwards Deming: Improving Quality in Colleges and Universities, Easter Urges Us to Look at Death, A Christian Looks at Death, Pennsylvania Fish Commission, Fishes of Erie County, Fishes of Pymatuning. Mem. Sch. Bd., Union City, Pa., 1969—75. Mem.: Audubon Soc., Sigma Xi, Phi Kappa Phi. R-Consevative. United Church Of Christ. Avocations: hiking, world traveling. Home: 87 West High St Union City PA 16438-1239 Home Phone: 814-438-7074.

THOMAS, PHELAN R., dentist; DDS, U. Mo., Kansas City, 1985. Diplomate Am. Bd. Aesthetic Dentistry. Pvt. practice Iowa Ctr. Cosmetic Dentistry, West Des Moines, Iowa. Spkr. in field. Contbr. articles to profl. jours. Mem.: ADA, Nat. Dental Assn., Acad. Gen. Dentistry, Am. Acad. Cosmetic Dentistry. Office: 4100 University, Ste 105 West Des Moines IA 50266 Office Phone: 515-223-8800. Office Fax: 515-223-1437. E-mail: drthomas@iowasmiles.com.

THOMAS, PHILIP JORDAN, science educator; b. Mitchell, SD, Jan. 17, 1957; s. Nancy Bell Thomas; m. Betsy Bodi Thomas, July 16, 1983; children: Bennett Lewis, Weston Philip. BS, Columbia U. SEAS, NY, 1979; PhD, U. SD, Vermillion, 1988. Psotdoc. fellow Johns Hopkins U. Sch. Medicine, Balt., 1988—93; prof. U. Tex. Southwestern Med. Ctr., Dallas, 1993—. Sci. founder Reata Pharmaceuticals, Irving, Tex., 2003—; sci. advisor Cystic Fibrosis Found., Bethesda, Md., 2001—, Dystonia Med. Rsch. Found., Chicago, 2008. Recipient Bioenergetics award, Biophysical Soc., 1991, Posdoc. Rsch. award, Johns Hopkins U., 1992, Established Investigator award, Am. Heart Assn., 1998, MERIT award, Nih Niddk, 2008. Achievements include first to established protein folding as a basis of human disease; patents for methods for discovery of correctors of protein folding defects; discovery of mechanochemical reaction cycle of ABC transporters,role of the proteasome in Parkinson Disease, Endoproteolytic Activity Of The Proteasome. Office: Univ Texas Southwestern MedicaC 6001 Forest Pk Dallas TX 75390-9040 Business E-Mail: philip.thomas@utsouthwestern.edu.

THOMAS, PHILIP STANLEY, economist, educator; b. Hinsdale, Ill., Oct. 23, 1928; s. Roy Kehl and Pauline (Grafton) Thomas; m. Carol Morris, Dec. 27, 1950 (dec. July 30, 2007); children: Lindsey Carol, Daniel Kyle, Lauren Louise, Gay Richardson. BA, Oberlin Coll., 1950; MA, U. Mich., 1951, PhD, 1961; postgrad., Delhi U., 1953—54. Instr. U. Mich., 1956-57; asst. prof. Grinnell (Iowa) Coll., 1957-63, assoc. prof., 1963-65; assoc. prof. econs. Kalamazoo Coll., 1965-68, prof. econs., 1968-94, prof. emeritus, 1994—. Econ. advisor Pakistan Inst. Devel. Econs., 1963—64, USAID, 1965—68, 1971, Planning Commn., Pakistan, 1969—70, Ctrl. Bank Swaziland, 1974—75, Ministry Planning, Kenya, 1980—81, 1983—85, 1986—88, Ministry Fin., Swaziland, 1990, Kenya, 91, 92, Ministry Indsl. Devel., Sri Lanka, 1997, Res. Bank Malawi, 1998—99, Jordan-U.S. Bus. Partnership, 2000—01. Contbr. articles to profl. jours. Mem. alumni coun. Oberlin Coll., 1961—63, 1974—76, 1983—86, 1995—2001, treas. alumni coun., 2004—06, exec. bd. mem alumni coun., 2007—09. With AUS, 1954—56. Fellow Overseas, Ford Found., 1953—54; scholar Fulbright. Mem.: Am. Econs. Assn., Phi Beta Kappa. Home and Office: 313A S Shabwasung St Northport MI 49670-9604 E-mail: pcmthomas@charter.net.

THOMAS, RALPH CHARLES, III, attorney; b. Roanoke, Va., Apr. 10, 1949; s. Ralph C. Jr. and Dorothy (Easley) T. BA, U. Calif., Berkeley, 1975; JD, Harvard U., 1978. Assoc. Bergson, Borkland, Margolis & Adler, Washington, 1978-80; sr. ptnr. Thomas, John & Everett, Washington, 1980-85; clin. instr. in Law Sch. George Washington U., Washington, 1982-83; exec. dir. Nat. Assn. Minority Contractors, Washington, 1985-92; assoc. adminstr. for small/disadvantaged bus. utilization NASA, Washington, 1992—2005; counsel Buchanan Ingersoll & Rooney PC, 2005—; ptnr. Barton Baker Thomas & Tolle LLP, 2008—. Adj. instr. U. Va., Charlottesville, 1989—91; chmn. Fed. Small Bus. Dirs. Interagy. Coun., 2001—03; bd. dirs. Sr. Execs. Assn., 2002—05; solicitor Bar Eng. & Wales, 2009. Author: Extreme Flashbacks, 1997; contbr. articles to profl. jours. Mem. Pres.'s Interagy. Working Group on Minority Bus. Devel., 1995. Staff sgt. USAF, 1967-71, Vietnam. Recipient Spl. Honor award, World Assn. Small and Medium Enterprises, 1999, Presdl. Rank for Disting. Exec. award, 2001, Minority Bus. Entrepreneur Adv. of Yr. award, Asian Enterprise mag., 2004, Man of Yr. award, Minority Enterprise Adv. Mag., 2005. Mem. Fed. Bar Assn. (chair govt. contracts sect. 2002-03).

THOMAS, RANDAL J., cardiologist; b. Salt Lake City, May 24, 1958; MD, George Washington U., 1986. Cert. Internal Medicine, 1989. Intern in internal medicine Ga. Bapt. Med. Ctr., Atlanta, 1986—87, resident, 1987—89; fellow in preventive cardiology, Robert Wood Johnson clin. scholar Stanford U.; assoc. prof. medicine Mayo Clinic, Rochester, Minn., dir. cardiovascular health clinic. Office: Mayo Clinic 200 First St SW Rochester MN 55905*

THOMAS, REGENA L., former state official; b. Clinton, Ky., Oct. 31, 1957; BA in U. Studies, Morehead State U. Cons. Dem. Gov.'s Assn.; legislative analyst Legislative Research Commn., KY State Legislature, 1980—85; ptnr. IEM Mesage mgmt., Inc.; served Torricelli for Senate, 1996, McGreevey for Gov., 1997, Corzine for Senate, 2000; sec. state State of N.J., Trenton, 2002—06. Prin. liaison non-govtl. orgns., key Dem. constituencies; dep., dir. Constituent Svcs. Govt. Dist. Columbia; legis. analyst Legis. Rsch. Commn. Ky. State Legislature; with Nat. Rainbow Coalition and its founder, Rev. Jesse L. Jackson.

THOMAS, RICH L., secondary school educator; b. St. Charles, Mo., Feb. 16, 1980; s. Richard and Rebecca Thomas; m. Kristin Thomas. BS, N.W. Mo. State, Maryville, 2003; MA, S.W. Mo. State U., Cape Giradia, 2007. Cert. secondary edn. Mo. Instr. agr. edn. Jefferson City HS, Mo., 2003—04; head instr. agr. edn. Advance HS, Mo., 2004—. Blood dr. coord. ARC; bell ringer Salvation Army. Named one of Top 50 Agr. Tchr., Indpls., 2005, Top 30 Agr. Tchr., Mo., 2005. Mem.: Mo. State Tchr. Assn., Nat. Assn. Agr. Educators, Mo. Agr. Tchr. Assn. (local pres.). Avocations: golf, fishing. Office: Advance Pub Schs 201 E School St Advance MO 63730

THOMAS, RICHARD STEPHEN, construction executive; b. Mason City, Iowa, June 5, 1949; s. H. Idris and Mildred (Keen) T.; m. Pamela Jane Chipka, Sept. 11, 1982. AA, No. Iowa C.C., 1969; BA, U. No. Iowa, 1971, BLS, 1991; MBA, U. Calif., Berkeley, 1991. Cost acct. Boise Cascade, Mason City, Iowa, 1971-72, cost acct. mgr. Shippensburg, Pa., 1973-74; staff acct. Grumman Corp., Williamsport, Pa., 1974-76; acctg. mgr. Pullman Power Products, Williamsport, 1976-79; treas, controller Schweizer Dipple Inc., Cleve., 1979-87; treas., corp. controller Langenau Mfg. Co., Cleve., 1987-92, chief fin. officer, 1987-92; sec.-treas. World Trade Wins Inc., Cleve., 1987-92; v.p. fin. and CFO Norris Bros. Co., Inc., Cleve., 1992—. Mem. employer adv. com. Ohio Job Svc., Greater Cleve. Growth Assn., Westlake Ohio Sch. Bd. Mem. Inst. Mgmt. Accts. (contr.'s coun. 1985), Constrn. Fin. Mgmt. Assn. (pres. 1995-2002, state dir., nat. dir.), Am. Coun. for Constrn. Edn. (fin. comm. 1997-98), Constrn. Industry Liason Comm. (chmn.), Cleve. Treas.'s Assn., Cleve. Engring. Soc., Associated Builders and Contractors, Constrn. Employers Assn., Cleve. World Trade Assn., Masons (local treas. 1984), York Rite Bodies, City Club of Cleve., U. Club, Cleve. Athletic Club, Phi Beta Lambda. Republican. Avocations: skiing, photography, sailing. Home: 1663 Settlers Reserve Way Westlake OH 44145-2042 Office: Norris Bros Co Inc 2138 Davenport Ave Cleveland OH 44114-3791 Office Phone: 216-771-2233. Business E-Mail: rthomas@norrisbr.com. E-mail: rsthomas49@sbcglobal.net.

THOMAS, RICK W., school system administrator; s. Paul and Barbara Thomas; m. Sharon LeAnn Thomas, June 9, 1984; children: Michelle, Crystal. BS, Okla. State U., Stillwater, 1983, Specialist in Edn., 2002; MEd, Northwestern State U., Tahlequah, Okla., 1995. Tchr., coach Sperry Pub. Schs., Okla., 1984—93, Owasso Pub. Schs., Okla., 1993—95, adminstrn. prin., 1995—2000; asst. supt. Oologah Talala Pub. Schs., Okla., 2000—04, supt., 2004—. Mem.: Okla. Assn. Sch. Adminstrs., Coop. Coun. Okla. Sch. Adminstrs., Oolagah C. of C. (bd. dirs. 2004—). Democrat. Mem. Assemblies Of God. Avocations: soccer, church activities. Office: Oolagah Talala Pub Schs Po Box 189 Oologah OK 74053 Office Phone: 918-443-6080.

THOMAS, RITCHIE TUCKER, lawyer; b. Cleve., Aug. 12, 1936; s. Myron F. and Marjorie (Ritchie) T.; m. Elizabeth Blackwell Hanes Main, Jan. 1, 1994. BA, Cornell U., 1959; JD, Case-Western Res. U., 1964. Bar: Ohio 1964, U.S. Dist. Ct. (no. dist.) Ohio 1964, U.S. Ct. Appeals (D.C. cir.) 1971, U.S. Ct. Appeals (fed. cir.) 1973, U.S. Ct. Fed. Claims 1973, U.S. Ct. Internat. Trade 1976, U.S. Ct. Appeals (9th cir.) 1985. Assoc. office of gen. counsel U.S. Tariff Commn., Washington, 1964-67; assoc. Squire, Sanders & Dempsey, Cleve., 1967-69, Cox, Langford & Brown, Washington, 1969-74; ptnr. Squire, Sanders & Dempsey, Washington, 1974—. Mem. exec. com. Meridian House Internat., Washington, 1977-94. Assoc. editor Western Res. U. Law Rev., 1964; columnist Commerce Germany; contbr. articles to profl. jours. Mem. Waring Prize Com., Western Res. Acad., 1996—; mem. Bretton Woods Com., Washington, 2003— Recipient Book award West Pub. Co., 1964 Mem. Fed. Bar Assn., D.C. Bar Assn., Belgian American Assn. (v.p. bd. dirs. 1989—), Am. C. of C. (Washington rep. 1984—), Order of Coif. Home: 6700 Bradley Blvd Bethesda MD 20817-3045 Office: Squire Sanders & Dempsey 1201 Pennsylvania Ave NW 1201 Pennsylvania Ave NW # 5 Washington DC 20004-2401 Business E-Mail: rtthomas@ssd.com.

THOMAS, ROB (ROBERT KELLY THOMAS), singer, songwriter; b. Landstuhl, Germany, Feb. 14, 1972; m. Marisol Maldonado, 1999; 1 child from previous relationship, Maison Avery William. Co-founder, band mem. Tabitha's Secret, 1993—95; lead singer, pianist Matchbox Twenty, 1996—. Singer: (albums) (Matchbox Twenty) Yourself or Someone Like You, 1996, Mad Season, 2000, More Than You Think You Are, 2002, Exile on Mainstream, 2007, (solo) Something to Be, 2005, (songs) Smooth (with Carlos Santana), 1999 (Grammy awards: Record of the Year, 1999, Song of the Year, 1999, Best Pop Collaboration with Vocals, 1999); vocals: (albums) The Great Divide (with Willie Nelson), 2002, background vocals: (albums) Goddess in the Doorway (with Mick Jagger), 2001, Broken Promises (with Rusty Truck), 2003; prodr.: (films) My Secret Record, 2007. Recipient Starlight award, Songwriters Hall of Fame, 2004. Office: c/o Rob Light Creative Artists Agy 2000 Ave of the Stars Los Angeles CA 90067

THOMAS, ROBERT EGGLESTON, retired manufacturing executive; b. Cuyahoga Falls, Ohio, July 28, 1914; s. Talbott E. and Jane S. (Eggleston) T.; 1 child, Barbara Ann. BS in Econs, U. Pa., 1936. Asst. to gen. mgr., sec., mgr. r.r. investments Keystone Custodian Funds, Boston, 1936-53; v.p. Pennroad Corp., NYC, 1953-59; chmn. exec. com., dir. M.-K.- T. R.R., 1956-65; mem. exec. com. MAPCO Inc., 1960-84, dir., chief exec. officer, 1960-80, pres., 1960-76, chmn. bd., 1973-84. Adv. bd. BancOkla. Corp. Mem.: Newcomen Soc., Nat. Mining Assn. (hon. dir.), Am. Petroleum Inst. (hon. dir.), Desert Horizons Country Club (Indian Wells, Calif.), San Diego Yacht Club, Summit Club (Tulsa), So. Hills Country Club (Tulsa), Chgo. Club. Episcopalian. Office: Williams Cos PO Box 4679 Tulsa OK 74159-0679 Home Phone: 918-749-2113; Office Phone: 918-573-8100. E-mail: Robert.Thomas@williams.com.

THOMAS, ROBERT PAIGE, lawyer; b. Columbus, Ohio, July 31, 1941; s. Charles Marion and Elsie (Cavanaugh) T.; children: Paige Cason, Park Cavanaugh. B.A., Vanderbilt U., 1963, M.A., 1965, J.D., 1970. Bar: Tenn. 1970, U.S. Dist. Ct. (mid. dist.) Tenn. 1970, U.S. Ct. Appeals (6th cir.) 1977. Assoc. Bradley Arant Boult Cummings LLP, Nashville, 1970-74, ptnr., 1974—, mng. ptnr., 1977-84, Bradley Arant Boult Cummings, 2009-. chmn. Tenn. Dem. Party; Mem. Bill Clinton's Nat. Fin. Com.; fin. chmn. Sen. Jim Sasser. Mem. ABA, Tenn. Bar Assn., Nashville Bar Assn. Democrat. Episcopalian. Clubs: Yale of N.Y.C.; Belle Meade Country. Office: PO Box 340025 Nashville TN 37203 Home Phone: 615-383-1907; Office Phone: 615-252-2314. Business E-Mail: bthomas@babc.com.

THOMAS, ROBERT R., state supreme court justice; b. Rochester, NY, Aug. 7, 1952; m. Maggie Thomas; 3 children. BA in govt., U. Notre Dame, 1974; JD, Loyola U., 1981. Cir. ct. judge DuPage County, 1988, acting chief judge, 1989—94; judge Appellate Ct. Second Dist., 1994—2000; justice Ill. Supreme Ct., 2000—, chief justice, 2006—08. Recipient NCAA Silver Anniversary award, 1999; named to Academic All-Am. Hall of Fame. Mem.: DuPage County Bar Assn., Acad. All-Am. Hall of Fame (life NCAA Silver Ann. Award 1999). Republican. Office: Illinois Supreme Ct 160 N LaSalle St Chicago IL 60601*

THOMAS, ROGER MERIWETHER, lawyer; b. Hartford, Conn., Feb. 28, 1930; s. Frederick Metcalf and Helen Meriwether (Lewis) T.; m. Mary Dorothea Wyman, Dec. 4, 1965; children— Donald Wyman, Helen Dorothea. AB, Princeton U., 1952; LL.B., Va. U., 1957; LL.M., Boston U., 1964. Bar: N.Y. 1958, Mass. 1960, U.S. Dist. Ct. (Mass) 1965, U.S. Tax Ct. 1965, U.S. Supreme Ct. 1967. Assoc. Angulo, Cooney, Marsh & Ouchterloney, NYC, 1957-60; assoc., then ptnr. Gaston & Snow, Boston, 1960-91; counsel Condit & Assocs., P.C., Boston, 1992-94. Outline author and lectr. Mass. Continuing Legal Edn., Inc., Boston; past panelist New Eng. Law Inst. Estate Planning Forums, Boston. Trustee Buckingham Browne & Nichols Sch., Cambridge, Mass., 1967-69. 1st lt. U.S. Army, 1952-54, Korea. Mem. Am. Coll. Trust and Estate Counsel, Boston Bar Assn., Mass. Bar Assn. Avocations: reading, sports, old movies. Home: 40 Byron Rd Weston MA 02493-2229

THOMAS, ROGER WARREN, lawyer; b. South Weymouth, Mass., Sept. 17, 1937; s. Clement Rogers and Beatrice (Merritt) T.; m. Maria Sava Brenner, July 5, 1968; children: Caroline, Andrew, Phillip. BA, U. NH, Durham, 1959; postgrad. (Rotary Internat. fellow), Free U. Berlin, 1960; LLB (Root-Tilden scholar), NYU, 1963, LLM (Ford Found. grantee), 1965; postgrad., U. Chile, Santiago, 1965. Bar: NY 1964. Assoc. Cleary, Gottlieb, Steen and Hamilton, NYC, 1965-66, 69-74, partner, 1974—, sr. counsel, 2008—. Mem. Harvard-Chile Tax Reform Project, 1966-68, head project in Chile, 1968-69; cons. to UN, Santiago, 1969; adj. prof. taxation NYU, 1974-96. Co-author: El Impuesto a la Renta, 1969. Bd. dirs. Spanish Repertory Theatre, Fundacion Chile, Santiago; dir. UNH Found., Friends of Cath. U. Mem. N.Am.-Chilean C. of C. (pres. 1984-96), Am. Soc., Coun. of Am., Knickerbocker Club. Home: 1150 5th Ave New York NY 10128-0724 Office: 1 Liberty Plz New York NY 10006-1404 Business E-Mail: rthomas@cgsh.com.

THOMAS, RONALD L., science educator, director; s. Preston Clarence and Evelyn Thomas; m. Martha Warren Thomas, Mar. 25, 1989. BS in Architecture, U. Okla., Norman, 1967; MFA in Mgmt., Antioch U., Seattle, 1995. Cert. planners Am. Planning Assn., 1989. Prin. DC Collaborative and Thomas & Means Assoc., Washington, 1973—91; pres. Cmty. Design Exch., Washington, 1978—97, Ron Thomas & Co., Chgo., 2008—; assoc. prin. Jones and Jones, Seattle, 1991—97; exec. dir. Sustainable Racine, Wis., 1997—2000, Northeastern Ill. Planning Commn., Chgo., 2000—08; adj. prof., planning U. Ill. Chgo., 2006—. Co-chair Campaign Sensible Growth, Chgo., 2000—07; exec. dirs. bd. mem. Nat. Assn. Regional Couns., Washington, 2001—08; midwest adv. bd. Nat. Trust Hist. Preservation, Chgo., 2004—; com. co-chair Ill. Broadband Initiative, Chgo., 2008; sci. & tech. sustainability sub-com. mem. US EPA, Washington, 2009—. Prodr.: (numerous urban planning-electronic town meetings) (Regional Emmy award, 1999); author: (book) Taking Charge: How Communities Are Planning Their Futures; designer (edn. for elected ofcls.) Cities by Design, Urban Environmental Design Program (NEA Fed. Design award, 1982); contbr. articles. Editor Am. Planning Assn. Regional Divsn. Newsletter, Chgo., 2007—09. Recipient Nat. award, Am. Planning Assn., 2001, 2007, Harry Chaddick Disting. Pub. Svc. award, Lambda Alpha Internat. Ely Chpt., 2007, Pub. Recognition award, Am. Soc. Landscape Archts., Ill., 2007. Mem.: Cliff Dwellers Club. Achievements include first to introduce vision and strategic planning in urban and television and technology tools. Avocations: cooking, travel. Office: Ron Thomas & Co 6631 N Maplewood Ave Chicago IL 60645 Business E-Mail: ronthom@ronthomasco.com.

THOMAS, SARA ALICE FOLGER, school librarian, curator; b. Crossville, Tenn., June 23, 1935; d. Dagnall Frank and Genevieve Morrow Folger; m. Bruce Lorrey Thomas, Mar. 18, 1961; children: Richard Folger, Alice Lorrey Thomas Cervantes. Student, Ga. State Coll. Women, Milledgeville, 1952—54; BA in Sociology, U. NC, Chapel Hill, 1956; cert. tchr., Youngstown State U., Ohio, 1983, MEd, 1992. Dir. teenage program YWCA, Providence, 1956—58, program dir. Pitts., 1958—63; co-founder, pres. Children's Sch. Wash., Pa., 1970—76; ednl. aide Warren City Schs., Ohio, 1978—82; outreach organizer Campfire Assn., Warren, 1979; elem. sch. libr. Niles City Schs., Ohio, 1983—2000; curator Sutliff Mus., Warren, 2006—. Editor TELMA Tattler, Trumbull Ednl. Libr. Media Assn., Warren, 1983—2008. Docent Butler Inst. Am. Art, Youngstown, 2001—04; mem. comm. adv. panel Warren City Schs., 2004—06; libr. 1st Presbyn. Ch. Warren, 2000—07; bd. dirs. Friends of McKinley Meml. Libr., Niles, 1990—2000, Warren Chamber Orch., 1980—82. Mem.: YWCA (pres. Wash. PA chpt. 1974—76, bd. dirs. 1977—80), AAUW (officer Warren chpt. 1992—94), Ch. and Synagogue Libr. Assn. NE Ohio (bd. dirs. 2001—05), Monday Afternoon Study Club (sec. 2005—), Warren Book Club, Lit. Club. Avocations: art, gardening, travel, reading, storytelling. Home Phone: 330-399-6766; Office Phone: 330-399-8807 ext. 121. Personal E-mail: bthomass@aol.com.

THOMAS, SARAH ELAINE, music educator; b. Little Rock, Aug. 8, 1947; d. William and Madie Murle (Stout) Collins; m. Gary Wayne Thomas Aug. 8, 1970 (dec. Nov. 1991). MusB in Edn., U. N. Tex., 1970; M in Ednl. Adminstrn., Dallas Bapt. U., 1997. Cert. tchr.-all-levels, Tex., prin. Music tchr. Winnetka Elem., Dallas, 1970-82, L. K. Hall Elem., Dallas, 1982-94, Kleberg Elem., Dallas, 1994—2001, Pleasant Grove Elem., 2001—05; supr. elem. fine arts Lincoln Instrnl. Ctr., 2005—07; dir. fine arts Dallas Ind. Sch. Dist., 2007—. Staff. devel. presenter Dallas Ind. Sch. Dist., 1977-97, 97-2005; workshop presenter Tex. Arts Coun., Austin, 1990-94. Bd. dirs. Dallas PTA, 1980-82; bd. dirs. Dallas All-City Elem. Choir, chair, 1991-2007, dir., 1999-2004. Named Class Act Teacher, Sta. KDFW-TV, Dallas, 1992. Mem. PTA (life), Am. Fedn. Tchrs., Tex. Music Educators Assn., Delta Kappa Gamma, Dallas Music Educators Assn. (v.p. 1992), Am. Orff-Schulwerk Assn., Music Educators Nat. Conf., Rotary (Svc. Above Self award 2003). Avocations: cooking, sewing, gardening, travel. Home: 2407 Norwich Ct Arlington TX 76015-3262 Office: Enrichment Curriculum Instruction 3434 S RL Thornton Frwy Dallas TX 75224 Personal E-mail: elainethomas3@tx.rr.com. Business E-Mail: elthomas@dallasisd.org.

THOMAS, SCOTT E., lawyer, former commissioner; b. Buffalo, Wyo., Mar. 5, 1953; s. Ralph E. and Bonnie E. Thomas; m. Elena W. King, Apr. 28, 1984. BA, Stanford U., 1974; JD, Georgetown U., 1977. Bar: D.C. 1977, U.S. Ct. Appeals (9th cir.) 1980, U.S. Supreme Ct. 1981. Atty. Office of Gen. Counsel, Fed. Election Commn., Washington, 1977-80; asst. gen. counsel for enforcement Fed. Election Commn., Washington, 1980-83, exec. asst. to commr., 1983-86, commr., 1986—2006, vice chmn., 1992, 1998, chmn., 1987, 1993, 1999, 2005; of counsel Pub. Policy & Law Group Dickstein Shapiro Morin & Oshinsky LLP, Washington, 2006—. Mem. D.C. Bar Assn. Office: Dickstein Shapiro Llp 1825 I St NW Frnt 1 Washington DC 20006-5411 E-mail: ThomasS@dsmo.com.

THOMAS, SEAN MICHAEL, journalist, writer; b. Jakarta, Indonesia, Sept. 11, 1974; s. Richard Keith and Lynne Warrem Thomas. Arts Diploma, Interlochen Arts Acad., MI, 1992. Reporter WFTX Fox 4 News, Cape Coral, Fla., 2003—06, KMPH Fox 26 News, Fresno, Calif., 2006—07, KSEE 24 News, Fresno, 2007—; writer Fresno Mag., 2006—. Bd. dir. ARC, Richmond, Ind., 1995—98. Author (illustrator): (children's book) Sedikit-Sedikit Menjadi Bukit: Little by Little We Climb the Mountain. Recipient Interlochen Faculty Achievement award, Interlochen Ctr. arts, 2003, Golden Rule award, City of Cape Coral, 2005, 2006, Award, AP, 2004, Logo Design award, Jakarta Internat. Sch., 2001. Mem.: Internat. Brotherhood Elec. Workers. Avocations: writing, drawing, singing, swimming, travel. Office Fax: 559-454-2496. Personal E-mail: sparkyint@aol.com. Business E-Mail: seant@ksee.com.

THOMAS, SHANNON LAWSON, academic administrator, educator; d. Arra Lightner Lawson; m. Eddie Walden Thomas, June 30, 1979; children: Shadrin Vandell, Jasil Conrad. BA, Hampton U., Va, 1973; MS, U. Tenn., Knoxville, 1975. Psychology instr. Wallace CC, Dothan, Ala., 1975—2000, coord. academic programs, 2000—. Mem. Alfred Saliba Family Svcs. Ctr., Dothan, 2007—08. Recipient Outstanding Cvic Involvement Award, Dothan Jaycees, 1988. Mem.: Delta Sigma Theta Sorority (pres. 1992—96). Baptist. Avocation: organist. Office: Wallace CC 1141 Wallace Dr Dothan AL 36303 Personal E-mail: attdhn@aol.com. Business E-Mail: sthomas@wallace.edu.

THOMAS, SIDNEY, fine arts educator, researcher; b. NYC, Dec. 21, 1915; s. Hyman and Rose (Samilowitz) T.; m. Rae Dinkowitz, May 26, 1940; children: David Phillip, Deborah Rose. BA, CCNY, 1935; MA, Columbia U., 1938, PhD, 1943. Tutor in English CCNY, NYC, 1939-43; instr. English Queens Coll., NYC, 1946-54; self-employed as editor, 1954-58; asst. editor Merriam-Webster, Springfield, Mass., 1958-61; assoc. prof. fine arts Syracuse U. (N.Y.), 1961-66, prof., 1966-85, prof. emeritus, 1985—, dir. humanities doctoral program, 1964-72, chmn. dept. fine arts, 1969-73. Bibliographer Shakespeare Assn., N.Y.C., 1949-54 Author: The Antic Hamlet, 1943; co-editor: The Nature of Art, 1964; editor: Images of Man, 1972. Served to sgt., inf. U.S. Army, 1943-45, ETO. Research fellow Folger Shakespeare Library, Washington, 1947-48 Mem.: AAUP (pres. Syracuse U. chpt. 1974), ACLU, MLA (life), Shakespeare Assn. Am., Phi Beta Kappa. Office: Syracuse U Dept Fine Arts Syracuse NY 13210

THOMAS, SIDNEY R., federal judge; b. Bozeman, Mont., Aug. 14, 1953; m. Martha Sheehy. BA in Speech-Comm., Mont. State U., 1975, JD cum laude, 1978; D (hon.), Rocky Mountain Coll., 1998. Bar: Mont. 1978, US Dist. Ct. Mont. 1978, US Ct. Appeals (9th cir.) 1980, US Dist. Ct. (9th cir.) 1980, US Ct. Fed. Claims 1986, US Supreme Ct. 1994. Shareholder Moulton, Bellimgham, Longo and Mather, P.C., Billings, Mont., 1978—96; judge US Ct. Appeals (9th cir.), Billings, 1996—. Adj. instr. Rocky Mountain Coll., Billings, 1982—95. Contbr. articles to profl. jours. Recipient Gov.'s award for Pub. Svc., 1978, Outstanding Faculty award, Rocky Mountain Coll., 1988. Mem.: ABA, Yellowstone County Bar Assn., State Bar Mont. Office: US Ct Appeals Ninth Circuit PO Box 31478 Billings MT 59107-1478*

THOMAS, SONIA, provider specialist, trainer; children: Shawn, Sarah, Jenny. B in Bus. & Mgmt., Marylhurst U., Oreg., 2006. Program dir. Camp Fire USA Mt Hood Coun., Gladstone, Oreg., 1998—2005; provider specialist Clackamas ESD, Edn. Svc. Dist. Pub. Edn. Agy., Oreg., 2006—. Tng. facilitator Oreg. Forestry Edn. Program, Corvallis, 1995—. Early childhood planning team Clackamas County Commn. Children & Families, Oregon City, Oreg., 2000—05; mem. governing coun. Oreg. Assn. Edn. Young Children, Portland, 1998—2006; area svc. team program specialist Camp Fire USA Mt. Hood Coun., Gladstone, 1995—2004; group leader Advocates Women Sci., Engring., and Math., Portland, 2000—03. Scholar, Alpha Xi Zeta Chpt., CCC, 2004; Margaret Thiele Petti Endowed scholar, Clackamas C.C., 2002—03, Ida M. Crawford scholar, Oreg. Student Assistance Commn., 2002—03, Jim "Rusty" Painter Bus. scholar, Clackamas C.C., 2003, Bill Ryan Bus. Meml. scholar, Oreg. Student Assistance Commn., 2003—04, Ford Family scholar, Ford Family Found., OSAC, 2004—06, Barbara Sue Seal scholar, Marylhurst U., 2005. Mem.: Nat. Afterschool Assn. (assoc.), Assn. Supervision and Curriculum Devel. (assoc.), Oreg. Assn. Edn. Young Children (assoc.; governing coun. 2002—08), Oreg. Sch. Age Coalition (assoc.; mem. at large 2004—06), Phi Theta Kappa (assoc.; v.p. leadership 2003—04). Avocations: hiking, travel, rock climbing. Office: Clackamas ESD 13455 SE 97th Ave Clackamas OR 97015 Office Phone: 503-675-4104.

THOMAS, STEPHEN PAUL, lawyer; b. Bloomington, Ill., July 30, 1938; s. Owen Wilson and Mary Katherine (Paulsen) T.; m. Marieanne Sauer, Dec. 7, 1963 (dec. June 1984); 1 child, Catherine Marie; m. Marcia Aldrich Toomey, May 28, 1988; 1 child, Ellen Antonia. BA, U. Ill., 1959; LLB, Harvard U., 1962; MLA, U. Chi, 2008. Bar: Ill. 1962; cert. naturalist Morton Arboretum, 2001, treekeeper Openlands Found., 2004. Vol. Peace Corps, Malawi, Africa, 1963-65; assoc. Sidley Austin LLP, Chgo., 1965-70, ptnr., 1970-2000; mem. Barrister's Big Band and Scales of Justice Jazz Ensemble; founder Beverly All Stars Band. Lectr. on law Malawi Inst. Pub. Adminstrn., 1963-65. Pres. Hyde Park-Kenwood Cmty. Conf., Chgo., 1988-90; life trustee Chgo. Acad. for Arts, chmn., 1992-97; life trustee Union League Civic and Arts Found., Chgo., 1999—. Recipient Paul Cornell award Hyde Park Hist. Soc., 1981. Mem. ABA, Chgo. Bar Assn., Chgo. Fedn. Musicians, Ill. State Hist. Soc., Union League Club Chgo., Chgo. Lit. Club (pres. 2007-), Ill. Geog. Soc, Natural Areas Assoc. Democrat. Roman Catholic. Avocations: jazz piano playing, naturalist studies. Home: 9756 S Longwood Dr Chicago IL 60643-1610 Office: Sidley Austin LLP One S Dearborn St Ste 900 Chicago IL 60603 Office Phone: 312-853-7516. Business E-Mail: sthomas@sidley.com.

THOMAS, SUZANNE, educational consultant; PhD, U. Fla., Gainesville, 1995. Project cons. Columbus Orgn., King Prussia, Pa., 2000—07. Mem.: Am. Assn. Intellectual Disabilities.

THOMAS, TERESA ANN, retired microbiologist, educator; d. Sam Charles and Edna Thomas. BS cum laude, Coll. Misericordia, Dallas, Pa., 1961; MS in Biology, Am. U., Beirut, 1965; MS in Microbiology, U. So. Calif., LA, 1973; cert. in ednl. tech., U. Calif., San Diego, 1998. Cert. Special Dist. Leadership Acad. Calif. Special Dist. Assn., 2008. Tchr., sci. supr., curriculum coord. Meyers H.S., Wilkes-Barre, 1962-64, Wilkes-Barre Area Pub. Schs., 1961-66; rsch. assoc. Proctor Found. Rsch. in Ophthalmology U. Calif. Med. Ctr., San Francisco, 1966-68; instr. Robert Coll. of Istanbul, Turkey, 1968-71, Am. Edn. in Luxembourg, 1971-72, Bosco Tech. Inst., Rosemead, Calif., 1973-74, San Diego C.C. Dist., 1974-80; prof. microbiology and ecology Sch. Math Sci. and Engring. Southwestern Coll., Chula Vista, Calif., 1980—2005, prof. emeritus, 2005—. Pres. acad. senate, 1984-85, del., 1986-89; chmn., coord., steering com. project Cultural Rsch. Ednl. and Trade Exch., 1991-2000, Southwestern Coll.-Shanghai Inst. Fgn. Trade; coord. great tchg. seminar Southwestern Coll., 1987, 88, 89, coord. scholars program, 1988-90, mem. Vecinos Baja Studies EcoMundo team internat. program, mem. steering com.; exec. com. Acad. Senate for Calif. C.C.s, 1985-86, Chancellor Calif. C.C.s Adv. and Rev. Coun. Fund for Instrnl. Improvement, 1984-86; co-project dir. statewide, coord. So. Calif. Biotech. Edn. Consortium, 1993-95, steering com., 1993-98; adj. asst. prof. Chapman Coll., San Diego, 1974-83, San Diego State U., 1977-79; chmn. Am. Colls. Istanbul Sci. Week, 1969-71; adv. bd. Chapman Coll. Cmty. Ctr., 1978-81; cons. sci. curriculum Calif. Dept. Edn., 1986-89; pres. Internat. Rels. Club, 1959-61; mem. San Francisco World Affairs Coun., 1966-68, San Diego World Affairs Coun., 1992—; v.p. Palomar Palace Estates Home Owners Assn., 1983-85, pres., 1994-99, 2003-2004, v.p., 1999—; mem. Rsch. Conf. on Undergrad. Microbiology Edn., Conn. Coll., 1999; bd. dirs. US Orgn. Med. Ednl. Needs, US Internat. Boundary and Water Commn. Citizens Forum Bd., 2001-08; mem. South Bay Networking Group, 2005-07; dir. South Bay Irrigation Dist., 2006—, v.p. 2007-08, pres. 2009-; governing bd. dir. Sweetwater Authority, 2006—; appt. mem. water quality com. Assn. Calif. Water Agencies, 2008—, prin. Sweetwater Unified Sch. Dist., 2009, chmn. SWA Ops. Com., 2009-. Past emeritus mem. editl. rev. bd., adv. bd.: Jour. Coll. Sci. Tchg. Commr. Internat. Friendship Commn., Chula Vista, 1985-95, vice chmn., 1989-90, chmn., 1990-92; mem. US-Mex. Sister Cities Assn., nat. bd. dirs., 1992-94, gen. chair 30th nat. conv., 1993; founding pres. Chula Vista-Odawara Sister Cities Assn., 1992—; mem. City of Chula Vista Resource Conservation Commn., 1996-05, chmn. 2002-04; mem. Chula Vista Bd. Ethics, 1999-2000, County San Diego Solid Waste Hearing Panel, 2000-05; co-organizer Chula Vista People-to-People Sister City Dels. to Odawara City, Japan, 1991, 94, 99; cmty. adv. com. San Diego Mus. Man, 2000-03; steering com. Chula Vista Gen. Plan Update, 2002-05; mem. vision 20/20 com. Chula Vista Environ., Open Space & Sustainable Devel., 2002-05; del. citizens adv. com. Port of San Diego & City Chula Vista Bayfront Master Plan, 2003—2008; mem. Calif. Local Govts. Commn., 2005—; docent Bonita Mus. & Cultural Ctr., 2006—. Grantee Pa. Heart Assn., 1962; fellow NSF, 1965, USPHS, 1972-73; recipient Nat. Tchg. Excellence award Nat. Inst. Staff and Orgnl. Devel., 1989; named Southwestern Coll. Woman of Distinction, 1987, Hon. Coach Southwestern Coll. Ladies Basketball Apaches, 2001, Jaguars Basketball Team, 2003, Chula Vista Environmentalist of Yr., 2005, 50th Anniversary Cir. Dist. Vol. award Sister Cities Internat., 2006. Mem.: NIH (mentor Bridges to the Future program Southwestern Coll. and San Diego 1993—98, steering com.), NSTA (life; coord. internat. honors exch. lectr. competition 1986, internat. com.), NEA (life), Crossroads II, Endow Chula Vista Found. (founding mem. 2008—), Japanese Coord. Coun. San Diego, Bonita Bus. Profl. Assn., Southwest Chula Vista Civic Assn. (founding steering com. mem. 2006—), Faculty Assn. Calif. CC's (state policy com. 2003—05), Am. Soc. Microbiology Southern Calif. (So. Calif. Microbe-Discovery Team 1995—99, mem. emeritus 2007—), Northwest Chula Vista Civic Assn. (assoc.), Calif. Sci. Tchrs. Assn. (life), Calif. Tchrs. Assn. (life), Nat. Assn. Biology Tchrs. (life), Calif. Spl. dist. Assn. (Spl. Task Forces Com.), Am. U. Beirut Alumni and Friends of San Diego (1st v.p. 1984—91), Chula Vista C. of C., South Bay Water Conservation Garden, Assn. Calif. Water Agys. (Water Quality Com.), Am.-Lebanese Assn. San Diego (1st v.p. 1984—91, pres. 1988—93, chmn. scholarship com. 2009—), Japan Soc. San Diego and Tijuana (life), Japanese Am. Hist. Soc. (life), Chula Vista Nature Ctr. (life), San Diego Yokohama Sister Cities Assn. (life), Congress History (life), San Diego Zool. Soc., Am. Lebanese Syrian Ladies Club (life; pres. 1982—83), Lions Internat. (Melvin Jones fellow for humanitarian svc. bull. editor 1991—93, 2d v.p. 1992—93, 1st v.p. 1993—94, editor Roaring Times Newsletter 1993—94, chmn. dist. internat. rels. and cooperations com. 1993—95, pub. rels. 1997—98, S.W. San Diego County v.p. 2006—07, Best Bull. award 1992—93, Southwest San Diego County Lion of Yr. award 2002, 2006), Delta Kappa Gamma (Gamma Omicron chpt. corr. sec. 2006—07, Outstanding Pub. Svc. award, Gamma Omicron chpt. 2003, liaison Learning Is For Everyone), Sigma Phi Sigma, Kappa Gamma Pi (pres. Wilkes-Barre chpt. 1963—64, pres. San Francisco chpt. 1967—68), Alpha Pi Epsilon (hon.; advisor Southwestern Coll. chpt. 1989—90, founder), Phi Theta Kappa (hon.). Home Phone: 619-427-3181; Office Phone: 619-425-4564. Personal E-mail: terrythomas4water@cox.net. Business E-Mail: tthomas@sweetwater.org.

THOMAS, TIM, professional basketball player; b. Paterson, NJ, Feb. 26, 1977; Student, Villanova U., Pa., 1997. Forward Phila. 76ers, 1997—99, Milw. Bucks, 1999—2004, NY Knicks, 2004—05, 2008—09, Chgo. Bulls, 2005—06, 2009, Phoenix Suns, 2006, LA Clippers, 2006—08, Dallas Mavericks, 2009—. Named All-Rookie 2nd Team, 1997—98. Office: Dallas Mavericks 2909 Taylor St Dallas TX 75226*

THOMAS, TIM, professional hockey player; b. Flint, Mich., Apr. 15, 1974; Grad., U. Vt., 1997. Goaltender Boston Bruins, 2002—03, 2005—, Providence Bruins (Am. Hockey League), 2003—04. Recipient Vezina Trophy, 2009; co-recipient William M. Jennings Trophy, 2009; named NHL Goalie of Yr., Sporting News, 2009; named to East Second All-Am. Team, NCAA, 1995, East First All-Am. Team, 1996, NHL All-Star Game, 2008, 2009, All-NHL Team, Sporting News, 2009, First All-Star Team, NHL, 2009. Office: Boston Bruins TD Banknorth Garden 100 Legends Way Boston MA 02114*

THOMAS, TIMOTHY FRANKLIN, secondary school educator; b. Ironton, Ohio, Dec. 22, 1960; s. James Franklin and Mariam Lou Thomas. BEd, Ohio U., Athens, 1996—99. Cert. secondary social studies tchr. Ohio, 2003. Cross country coach Ironton HS, Ohio, 1982—, track and field coach, 1983—, social studies tchr., 1999—. Basketball coach Ironton HS, 2000—02. Contbr. poetry anthology, 2003. Mem. Benevolent & Protective Order of Elks, 1983—. Mem.: Ohio HS Athletic Assn. (athletics ofcl. 1983—), SE Ohio Track Coaches Assn. (assoc.; pres. 2002—04, Track & Field Coach Yr. award 1993—95), Ohio Assn. Track & Cross Country Coaches (assoc. Dist. Track & Field Coach of Yr. award 1994—95), Ohio Edn. Assn. (assoc.), Nat. Coun. Social Studies (assoc.), US Track & Field (assoc.), Phi Alpha Theta (assoc.), Kappa Delta Pi (assoc.). Office: Ironton HS 1701 S 7th St Ironton OH 45638 Office Fax: 740-533-6027. Business E-Mail: tthomas_ic@scoca-k12.org.

THOMAS, TIMOTHY WAYNE, mathematics educator, athletic director; b. Ft. Wayne, Ind., Nov. 5, 1949; m. Ann Kingsley McDowell, May 29, 1071; children: Joshua McDowell, Aaron Joseph. BA, Tarkio Coll., Mo., 1971; MA, Emporia State U., Kans., 1975. Cert. tchr. Iowa, 1978, athletic adminstr. NIAAA, 2001. Math. instr. Galva-Holstein Schs., Holstein, Iowa, 1990—2007, athletic dir., 1999—. Pres. Iowa Assn. Track Coaches, Ames, Iowa, 2003—05; sr. dir. NW Iowa Iowa HS Athletic Dirs. Assn., Des Moines, 2007—. Huddle leader Fellowship Christian Athletes, Holstein, Iowa, 1996—. None NONE, None. Recipient Regional Class 1-A Track Coach of the Yr., IATC, 2001; named NW Iowa Mid. Sch. Athletic Dir. of Yr., 2006, NW Iowa Athletic Dir. of Yr., 2007. Mem.: NEA, Nat. Coaches Assn., Iowa Assn. Track Coaches (Regional Class 1-A Cross Country Coach of Yr. 1992, 1994—95, 1997, 1999, 2005, 2007—08), Nat. Interscholastic Athletic Adminstrs. Assn. Protestant.

THOMAS, TOM, retired plastics company executive; b. Malang, Java, Indonesia, Feb. 15, 1932; arrived in Can., 1954; s. Ferdinand and Elfrieda Emma (Macht) T.; m. Jannie Chine Sneep, Jan. 19, 1956; children: Gregory John, Renée Sonja Elfrieda, Michael Grant, Thomas. Grad. high sch., The Hague, Holland. Jr. mgr. Lever Bros. Ltd., Toronto, Ont., Canada, 1954-60; sr. mgr. Impac & Somerville Plastics, Toronto, Ont., Canada, 1960-64; founder, C.E.O. Can. Cup Inc., Toronto, Ont., Canada, 1964—, also bd. dirs., 1964-93; ret., 1993. Inventor in field. Trustee Fraser Inst., Vancouver, B.C., Can., 1977-93; gov. Massey and Roy Thomson Hall, Toronto, 1991-92; bd. dirs. Toronto Symphony, 1986-92, mem. Maestro's Club, 1984, mem. pres.'s coun. Can. Opera Co., 1980, adv. coun. Toronto Symphony, 1995-2000, pres. Coun. Can. Opera, 1980-95. Avocations: sailing, history, classical music, chess.

THOMAS, WAYNE LEE, lawyer; b. Sept. 22, 1945; s. W. M. and June F. Thomas; m. Patricia H. Thomas, Mar. 16, 1968; children: Brigitte Elisabeth Williams, Kate Adelaide Culpepper. BA, U. Fla., 1967, JD cum laude, 1971. Bar: Fla. 1971, U.S. Supreme Ct. 1975, U.S. Ct. Appeals (5th cir.) 1975, U.S. Ct. Appeals (11th cir.) 1981, U.S. Ct. Claims 1976, U.S. Dist. Ct. (mid. dist.) Fla. 1973, U.S. Dist. Ct. (so. dist. trial bar) Fla. 1975; cert. mediator and arbitrator. Law clk. U.S. Dist. Ct. (mid. dist.) Fla., 1971—73; assoc. Trenam, Simmons, Kemker, Scharf, Barkin, Frye & O'Neill, PA, Tampa, 1973—77, ptnr., 1978—81; founder, pres. McKay & Thomas, PA, Tampa, 1981—89; ptnr. Carlton, Fields, Ward, Emmanuel, Smith & Cutler, PA, 1989—95; pvt. practice Tampa, 1995—2008; ptnr. Akerman Senterfitt, 2008—. Bd. mem. State of Fla. 13th Jud. Cir. Indigent Svcs. Com., 2006—07. Mem. ABA, Fla. Bar (chmn. sect. gen. practice 1981-83, ethics com., vice chmn. unauthorized practice law com. 1994-98, 2000-04, chmn. 2004-06, vice chmn. fed. practice com. 1995-96, chmn. 1996-97, bd. bar examiners 1986-91, chmn. 1990-91, chmn. unauthorized practice law com. 13A 1998-2001), Nat. Conf. Bar Examiners (multistate profl. responsibility exam. policy com. 1994-2004), Hillsborough County Bar Assn. (chmn. grievance com. 1985-86), J.C. Cheatwood Am. Inn of Ct. (pres. 2007-08), Order of Coif, Fla. Blue Key, Phi Kappa Phi, Omicron Delta Kappa. Democrat. Office: Akerman Senterfitt 701 E Jackson St Ste 1700 Tampa FL 33602 Business E-Mail: wayne.thomas@akerman.com.

THOMAS, WILLIAM SCOTT, lawyer; b. Joliet, Ill., Aug. 16, 1949; AB, Stanford U., Calif., 1971; JD, U. Calif., Hastings, 1974; LLM in Taxation, Golden Gate U., 1981. Bar: Calif. 1975, US Dist. Ct. (no. dist. Calif.) 1975, US Tax Ct. 1982. Tax editor Internat. Bur. Fiscal Documentation, Amsterdam, 1974-75; tax atty. Chevron Corp., San Francisco, 1975-77; assoc. to ptnr. Brobeck, Phleger & Harrison, San Francisco, 1978—2003; ptnr. Morgan Lewis & Bockius, San Francisco, 2003—07, Dickenson, Peatman & Fogarty, Napa, Calif., 2007—. Named one of Top 100 Attys., Worth mag., 2005—07. Mem. ABA (taxation sect.), Calif. Bar Assn. (exec. com. taxation sect. 1984-89, chmn. 1987-88). Office: Dickenson Peatman & Fogarty 809 Coombs Napa CA 94559 Office Phone: 707-252-7122. Office Fax: 707-255-6876. Business E-Mail: sthomas@dpf-law.com.

THOMAS, ZACH MICHAEL (ZACHARY MICHAEL THOMAS), professional football player; b. Pampa, Tex., Sept. 1, 1973; m. Maritza Thomas. BS in Exercise Sci., Tex. Tech. U., 1996. Linebacker Miami Dolphins, 1996—2008, Dallas Coyboys, 2008, Kansas City Chiefs, 2009—. Opened health and fitness club Zach's Club 54, Amarillo, Tex. Mem. Crunch on Paralysis team. Named Am. Football Conf. Defensive Rookie of Yr., 1996, 1st Team All-Pro, AP, 1998, 1999, 2002, 2003, 2006; named to Am. Football Conf. Pro-Bowl Team, NFL, 1999—2003, 2005, 2006, Tex. Tech. U. Red Raiders Hall of Fame, 2006. Avocations: weightlifting, basketball. Office: Kansas City Chiefs One Arrowhead Dr Kansas City MO 64129 Office Phone: 972-556-9900.*

THOMASCH, ROGER PAUL, lawyer; b. NYC, Nov. 7, 1942; s. Gordon J. and Margaret (Molloy) T.; children: Laura Leigh, Paul Butler. BA, Coll. William and Mary, 1964; LLB, Duke U., 1967. Bar: Conn. 1967, Colo. 1974. Assoc. atty. Cummings & Lockwood, Stamford, Conn., 1967-70; trial atty. U.S. Dept. Justice, Washington, 1970-73; ptnr. Roath & Brega, Denver, 1975-87; mng. ptnr. Denver office of Ballard, Spahr, Andrews & Ingersoll LLP, 1987—, chmn. litigation practice, 2005—. Vis. assoc. prof. of law Drake U. Sch. Law, Des Moines, 1973-74; frequent lectr. in field, U.S. and Can.; adj. faculty mem. U. Denver Coll. Law, 1976-80. Recipient Leland Forrest Outstanding Prof. award, Drake U. Sch. Law, 1973. Fellow Am. Coll. of Trial Lawyers, Am. Bar Found., Colo. Bar Found.; mem. ABA, Colo. Bar Assn., Denver Country Club, Univ. Club. Office: Ballard Spahr Andrews & Ingersoll LLP 1225 17th St Ste 2300 Denver CO 80202-5535 Home Phone: 303-744-8434; Office Phone: 303-299-7301. E-mail: Thomasch@BallardSpahr.com.

THOMAS-GREENFIELD, LINDA, United States Ambassador to Liberia; BA in Polit. Sci., La. State U.; MA in Polit. Sci., U. Wis. Lectr. in polit. sci. Bucknell U., Lewisburg, Pa.; joined US Fgn. Svc., 1982; fgn. svc. assignments US Dept. State, Nigeria, The Gambia, Kenya, Jamaica, Pakistan, Switzerland, with Bur. Population, Refugees and Migration Washington, with Office the Dir. Gen. the Fgn. Svc., mem. & pres., sr. seminar, 2003—04, dep. asst. sec., Bur. Population, Refugees and Migration, 2004—06, prin. dep. asst. sec., Bur. African Affairs, 2006—08, US amb. to Liberia Monrovia, 2008—. Recipient Warren Christopher award for outstanding achievement in global affairs, 2000, Presdl. Meritorious Svc. Award, US Dept. State, 2007, Superior, Meritorious and Performance awards. Office: DOS Amb 8800 Monrovia Pl Washington DC 20521-8800*

THOMAS-HARRIS, YVONNE ANITA, writer, poet; b. Millington, Tenn., Aug. 27, 1964; d. William Albert and Romelia Louise (Rich) Thomas; m. Gregory Harris; children: Antonio Dewayne James, Trishanna Renea, Chantell S. Harris, Ashley K. Harris, Gregory Juwan Harris. Cert., Morris & McDaniel Sch., Memphis, 1987, ITT Career Tng. Ctr., 1991; diploma, Jefferson Bus. Coll., Memphis, 1988; attended, Southwest Tenn. C.C., 2005; attneded, World Harvest Bible Coll., 2006. Security guard Ringling Bros. and Barnum Bailey, Washington, 1986; mental health tech. S.E. Mental Health Ctr., Memphis, 1987; nursing asst. St. Peters Villa, Memphis, 1987; profl. model Memphis, 1990; housekeeper Econo Inn, Millington, 1990; med. asst. Primary Med. Care, Inc., Memphis, 1991; receptionist, supr. H & R Block, Memphis, 1991—; adminstrv. asst. Perea Presch., Memphis, 2006; prin., sec. UT Health Sci. Ctr., Coll. of Dentistry, 2006. Med. office asst./receptionist psychiatry dept. U. Tenn. Med. Group, 1996. Contbr. poems to World Treasury of Golden Poems, 1990, Poetic Voices of America, 1992, Shadows and Light, 1996; songwriter Cream High Records, Blue Time Blues, 1986, A Surrender to the Moon, 2005. Sec. Project Amos, Memphis, 1989; vol. Dept. Human Svcs., Memphis, 1988. Mem.: ADEA. Democrat. Avocations: quilting, photography, drawing, crafts. Home: 3815 Kerr Rd Millington TN 38083 Home Phone: 901-873-0614; Office Phone: 901-527-8344. Personal E-mail: yvonneharris64@yahoo.com. Business E-Mail: yvonhrr5@aol.com.

THOMAS-HOUSTON, MARILYN MILLER, anthropologist, educator; d. John Wesley Miller and Vivian Edwards Miller; children: Carl Edward Thomas, Kelvin Thomas, Michael Thomas. MA in Southern Studies, U. Miss., Oxford, 1989, BFA in Theater Arts, 1989; Grad. in Media & Culture, NY U., NYC, MA in Anthropology, MPhil in Cultural Anthropology, PhD in Anthropology, 1997. Profl. entertainer in fields, NYC, 1963—81; program coord. Afro-Am. studies U. Miss., 1989—90, rsch. assoc. & instr., 1994—95; tchg. & grad. asst. NY U., 1990—94; vis. asst. prof. anthropology SC. State U., Orangeburg, 1995—96; asst. prof. anthropology & African Am. studies U. SC., Columbia, 1996—2001, U. Fla., Gainesville, 2001—, assoc. dir. African Am. studies, 2002—03, interim dir. African Am. studies, 2003—04; vis. prof. anthropology Dalhousie U., Halifax, Nova Scotia, Canada, 2007—08. Pres. For My People Prodns. Inc., Gainesville, 2005—. Actor: (plays) Slaveship; contbr. articles to profl. jours. Mem. Gainesville Chpt. NOW, Fla., 2005—08; treas. Soc. Visual Anthropology, Arlington, Va., 2002—04; adv. bd. mem. Glory Day, NYC, 2006—08; web designer & master Assn. Black Anthropologists, Arlington, 2006—09. Recipient award, DSR-TKA, 1986; fellowship, NSF, 1990—93, Fulbright, 2007—08. Mem.: Nat. Coun. Black Studies, Soc. Visual Anthropology, Soc. Applied Anthropology, Assn. Black Anthropologists, Am. Anthrop. Assn., Assn. Study African Am. Life & History, Golden Key, Phi Kappa Phi. Avocations: singing, travel, piano. Office: Univ Fla PO Box 117305 Gainesville FL 32611 Office Fax: 352-392-6929. Business E-Mail: thomas-houston@fmpp-inc.org, marilynm@ufl.edu.

THOMASHOW, STEVEN ROY, military and intelligence officer; b. Bronx, NY, Jan. 27, 1957; s. Isaac Tom and Dorothy (Cuillino Bodsky) T. Accredited, U.S. Mil. Acad. Commd. United States of the World, adm., with spl. ops., 1988—; served with Israeli War USN, served with Gulf War. Recipient Pres. Nat. Medal of Patriotism; named to Am. Police Hall of Fame, 1996. Fellow Nat. Law Enforcement Acad. (hon.); mem. Am. Fedn. Police. Avocations: Karate (black belt), torah studies, boxing, reading. Home and Office: United States of the World Recon One 4644 Myrtle Ln West Palm Beach FL 33417-5316 Office: 4644 Myrtle Ln West Palm Beach FL 33417-5316 Home Fax: 561-640-4359.

THOMAS-LÖWE, CHRISTINE L., small business owner; d. Alfred Joseph Thomas and Loyce Mae Argo (Thomas); m. Scott H. Lowe, Feb. 8, 1997. BA Edn., Western Ky. U., Bowling Green, 1972; MPS in Pub. Adminstrn., Western Ky. U., 1982; MS in Data Processing & Mgmt. & Info. Sys., Amber U., Garland, Tex., 1985. Bus. analyst and ISO internal auditor ADP, Coppell, Tex., 2000—03. Software QA tester and documentation specialist IBM, Dallas, 1997—2000; prin. owner River City Alternative Care, 1997—2000. Composer: (opera) Soldato Del Destino (Soldier of Destiny), 2003—06; author: (screenplay) Soldato Del Destino, 2007; performer: (opera excerpts) Lyon Cmty. Orch., 2004, Owensboro Youth Symphony, 2007, Lyon Cmty. Orch. Mem.: Am. Mensa (assoc.). Roman Catholic. Home and Office: River City Alternative Care 2020 York Dr Owensboro KY 42301-3436 Personal E-mail: lowes@bellsouth.net.

THOMASON, CHRISTIA R., librarian; b. Bloomington, Ind., July 11, 1966; d. David Enfield Thomason and Susanne Bunger; life ptnr. Cristy Lynn Brown, Feb. 26, 1996. MLS, Ind. U., Bloomington, 1994. Libr. technician III Ind. U. Cook Music Libr., 1995—97; head, music tech. svcs. and digital a/v reserves UNC Sch. Arts, Winston-Salem, 1997—. Contbr. presentations. Mem.: Music Libr. Assn. (Best Chpt. award 2006). Liberal.

THOMASON, JAMES BRANT, history professor; b. Honolulu, Dec. 22, 1967; s. Donald R. and Linda J. Thomason; 1 child, Sarah C. MA, U. Ala., Tuscaloosa, 1994. History instr. Marion Mil. Inst., Ala., 1997—. Named Tchr. of Yr., Marion Mil. Inst., 2003.

THOMASON, MICHAEL V.R., retired history professor; b. West Palm Beach, Fla., June 20, 1942; s. Milton Vincent and Carolina Virginia Thomason; m. Marilyn Joan Heinzig, Dec. 28, 1964; children: Caroline Virginia Pryor, Catharine Ann Aunc. BA, U. South, Sewanee, Tenn., 1964; MA, Duke U., Durham, NC, PhD, 1968. Cert. archivist Soc. Am. Archivists, 1995. Dir. and founder, archives U. South Ala., Mobile, 1978, prof., history, 1978, prof. emeritus, history, 2006—. Pres. Ala. Hist. Assn., Auburn, 2001, Gulf South Hist. Assn., Hammond, La., 2005—06. Author: (book) Mobile:American River City, Mobile: Life and Times of a Great Southern City, Trying Times:Alabama Photographs, 1917-1945, To Remember a Vanishing World: D.L. Hightower's Photographs of Barbour County, Alabama 1930-1965, The image of Progress: Alabama 1871-1917, 1978, Mobile: the New History of Alabama's First City, 2001; archtl. photography, From Fort to Port: An Architectural History of Mobile:, contbg. editor profl. jours. With Mobile Hist. Devel. Commn, 1983. Fellowship, Woodrow Wilson Found. Mem.: Gulf South Hist. Assn. (pres., bd. mem. 1985—), Soc. Ala. Archivists (pres. 1985—87), Phi Beta Kappa. Roman Catholic. Home: 1548 Deerwood Dr E Mobile AL 36618 Personal E-mail: jawa1@zebra.net.

THOMASON, SANDRA LEE, elementary school educator; d. Eugene LeRoy Ducat and Jean Frances Miller-Ducat; 1 child, Eric Christopher. EdB, U. Toledo, 1968, MEd, 1974. Permanent Tchg. Cert. Ohio State Dept. Edn., 1993, Reading Cert. K-12 Ohio State Dept. of Edn., 1993. Primary edn. tchr. Wash. Local Schs., Toledo, 1968—75, Sylvania (Ohio) schs., 1985—2000; vis. prof. U. Toledo, 1999—2003; reading instr. Ohio State Dept. of Edn., Perrysburg, Ohio, 1999—2003, Sylvania, 1999—2003, Toledo, 1999—2003; guest tchr. Lourdes Coll., Sylvania, Ohio, 2000; literacy specialist Sylvania Schs., 2000—03; reading cons., tchr., trainer NW Ohio Regional Profl. Devel. Ctr., Toledo, 2000—03; literacy support tchr., mid. sch. Olentangy Local Schs., Powell, Ohio,

2003—. Program adminstr. Summer Fun Summer Play Sch., Toledo, 1979; literacy specialist Ohio State Dept. of Edn., 1999—2003; counseling support group leader U. Toledo Counseling Ctr., 1982—84; youth enrichment seminar tchr. Sylvania Schs., Sylvania, 1996—97, 1996—97; spkr. Lourdes Coll., 1997—98; presenter, integrated curriculum with a lit. base, k-4 Patrick-Henry Local Schs., Deshler, Ohio, 1995—96; cons. in field. Dir.: (exhbn.) Developmentally Appropriate and Integrated Activities Across the Curriculum; contbr. articles to popular mags. Sect. leader Toledo 20/20 City Initiative. Mem.: ASCD, Ohio Coun. of the Tchrs. Lang. Arts, Internat. Reading Assn., Pi Lambda Theta (hon.), Phi Delta Kappa (hon.). Achievements include development of curriculum for primary grade children, balanced literacy curriculum for elementary and middle school students; design of edn. programs for summer sch. students in presch. and primary grades. Office: Olentangy Local Schs 814 Shanahan Rd Ste 300 Lewis Center OH 43035 Business E-Mail: sandra_thomason@olentangy.k12.oh.us.

THOMASON, SARAH GREY, linguistics educator; b. Evanston, Ill., Nov. 28, 1939; d. Arthur L. and Marion (Griswold) Grey; m. Richmond Hunt Thomason, Nov. 25, 1967; children: Lucy Grey, Jennifer Marion. BA in German, Stanford U., 1961; MA in Linguistics, Yale U., 1965, PhD in Linguistics, 1968; postgrad, U. Freiburg, Germany, 1961-62, Ind. U., 1964, U. Novi Sad, Yugoslavia, 1965-66. Instr. linguistics U. Pitts., 1967-68, asst. prof. linguistics, 1973-78, assoc. prof. linguistics, 1978-86, prof. linguistics, 1986—. Lectr. Russian and Slavic Linguistics, Yale U., New Haven, 1968-72; vis. lectr. U. Ill., Champaign-Urbana, 1969, Ohio State U., Columbus, 1993; vis. asst. prof. linguistics U. Pitts., 1972-73, mem. numerous univ. coms.; presenter, cons. in field. Author: (with Terrence Kaufman) Language Contact, Creolization, and Genetic Linguistics, 1988; author (with others) Current Progress in Historical Linguistics, 1976, Historical Morphology, 1980, International Handbook of Bilingualism and Bilingual Education, 1988, Thought Experiments in Science and Philosophy, 1991, Africanisms in Afro-American Language Varieties, 1993; assoc. editor Language, 1983-85, editor, 1988—; edit. bd. dirs. Jour. Pidgin and Creole Langs., 1989—; contbr. articles and book revs. to profl. jours. Vol. linguistic cons. Salish-Kootenai Confederated Tribes, St. Ignatius, Mont., 1981—; vol. tchr. State Correctional Inst. Pitts., 1993—. Woodrow Wilson fellow Yale U., 1962-63, McCormick fellow, 1963-65, NDEA Title VI fellow, 1965, 66-67, Summer Linguistics fellow Am. Coun. Learned Socs., 1964; Faculty Rsch. grantee U. Pitts., 1974, 79, Travel grantee, 1978. Mem. AAAS (chair sect. on linguistics and lang. scis. 1996), Soc. Study Indigenous Langs. of the Ams., Soc. for Pidgin and Creole Linguistics. Democrat. Avocation: sketching. Office: U Pitts Dept of Linguistics Pittsburgh PA 15260

THOMAS-PATTINSON, ROBERT See **PATTINSON, ROBERT**

THOMAS RATTAY, KARYL, state agency administrator, public health service officer; BA in Zoology and Premedicine, Ohio Wesleyan U., Delaware, Ohio, 1987; MD, Med. U. Ohio, 1992; MSc in Epidemiology, U. Md., 2001. Cert. in preventive medicine, pediatric preventive medicine physician, pediatrician. Residency in pediat. Georgetown U., Washington; resident U. Md.; pvt. practice pediatrician; sr. pub. health advisor to the surgeon gen. US Dept. Health and Human Services, Washington, asst. sec. health, Office Disease Prevention and Health Promotion, 2001—04; sr. policy and program analyst Nemours Health & Prevention Services, 2004—09; assoc. faculty, dept. population, family and reproductive health Johns Hopkins Bloomberg Sch. Pub. Health, Balt., 2007—; clin. care weight mgr. Alfred I. Dupont Hosp. for Children, Wilmington, Del., 2008—09; dir., divsn. pub. health Del. Dept. Health and Social Services, 2009—. Mem. USDA/HHS Dietary Guidelines Adv. Com.; faculty Del. Sch. Dist. Learning Collaborative. Contbr. articles to profl. jours. Active Pres. Healthier US Initiative; chairwoman Del. Primary Care Initiative on Childhood Overweight. Office: Del Divsn Pub Health Jesse Cooper Bldg 417 Federal St Dover DE 19901 Office Phone: 302-744-4700. Office Fax: 302-739-6659.*

THOMAS-RAZZA, CONSTANCE, retired elementary school educator; b. Balt., Dec. 28, 1935; d. Arthur and Bertha Crippen Thomas; m. Joseph C. Razza, Jr., Oct. 29, 1968; children: Joseph C. Razza III, Constance Miriam Razza, Renata Joy Razza; m. Garnett George Adams, 1962 (div. 1968). BA, Coppin State Tchrs. Coll., Balt., 1957, U. Mich., Ann Arbor, 1962. Cert. tchr. Balt., Md., 1957, Washington, DC, 1962. Tchr. Balt. City Pub. Schs., 1957—62, DC Pub. Schs., 1962—96; tchr. ESL Peace Corps, Cape Verde, West Africa, 2000—02. Lectr. Am. U., Washington, 1973. Author: (book) My Mother's Love Life, 1998; prodr.: (theatre) Spedjo, 2001. Sec. LeDroit Park Civic Assn., Washington, 1990, 2005; vol. Smithsonian Instn., Washington, 1996—98; protestor No War on Cuba, 2002—. Named Outstanding Newsletter Publisher, DC Fedn. Civic Assns., 1986, Outstanding Educator, Potomac LINKS, 2005. Democrat. Buddhist. Avocations: beading, writing, gardening. Home: 501 T St NW Washington DC 20001 Personal E-mail: ctrazza05@verizon.net.

THOMASSON, DAN KING, newspaper executive, columnist; b. Shelbyville, Ind., Dec. 22, 1933; s. Hubert Lee and Mary Margaret (King) T.; m. Laqueta Forducey, Sept. 7, 1958; children: Scot, Lisa, Sean, Patrick. BS, Ind. U., 1956; postgrad., Colo. U., 1959. Reporter, editor Indpls. Star, 1956; reporter Lawton (Okla.) Constitution, 1957-58, The Rocky Mountain News, Denver, 1959-64; corr. Scripps Howard Newspapers, Washington, 1964-74, asst. mng. editor, 1974-76; mng. editor Scripps Howard News Svc., Washington, 1976-80, editor, 1980—; v.p. news Scripps Howard Newspapers, Cin., 1986—; v.p. E.W. Scripps Co., 1996—. Weill vis. prof. Ind. U., 1999; vis. prof. Hampton U., 2000. Pres. Raymond Clapper Found., Washington, 1980-2004; bd. dirs. Scripps Howard Found., Cin., 1987-2003, v.p., 1994; trustee Franklin Coll., 1990—; mem. nat. adv. com. E.W. Scripps Sch. Journalism, 1990, Ohio U., 1990, Nat. Pub. Affairs Coun., Ind. U., 1990—; bd. visitors Inst. Polit. Journalism Georgetown U., 1990—. With U.S. Army, 1956-58. Named Man of Yr., Shelbyville, Ind. C. of C., 1970, Washington Journalism Hall of Fame, 1993; elected Ind. Acad., 1993; named to Ind. Journalism Hall of Fame, 1997; Presdl. fellow Trinity Coll., Hartford, 2000; media fellow Hoover Instn., 2001, 2002, 2003 Mem. Am. Soc. Newspaper Editors, White House Corrs. Assn., Gridiron Club of Washington, Overseas Press Club, Nat. Press Club, Univ. Club of Washington, Washington Golf and Country Club (Arlington, Va.), Bohemian Club (San Francisco), Sigma Delta Chi. Home: 3729 Morningside Dr Fairfax VA 22031-3317 Office: Scripps Howard 1090 Vermont Ave NW Ste 1000 Washington DC 20005-4906 Business E-Mail: thomassondan@aol.com.

THOMASSON, EMILY, mathematics educator; b. Hayti, Mo., July 1, 1966; d. Jan Jackson; m. Ray Thomasson, June 20, 1989; 1 child, Rick Jackson. BS in Math., Ark. State U., Jonesboro, 1995, MS in Math., 1997, edn. specilist degree in Curriculum and Instr., 2006. Cert. tchr. in secondary math. Ark., 2000. Tchr. math. East Jr. HS, Blytheville, Ark., 1997—2000, Blytheville HS, 2000—; math. dept. chair Rivercrest HS, 2008—. Chmn. math. dept. Blytheville HS, 2003—05. Mem.: Nat. Coun. Tchrs. Math. Office: Blytheville HS 600 North 10th Blytheville AR 72315 also: Rivercrest HS 1700 W State Hwy 14 Wilson Wilson AR 72395 Personal E-mail: ethom@sbcglobal.net. Business E-Mail: ethom@bps.k12.ar.us.

THOME, JIM, professional baseball player; b. Peoria, Ill., Aug. 27, 1970; s. Chuck and Joyce; m. Andrea Pacione, Nov. 7, 1998; children: Lila Grace, Landon. Student Illinois Central College. First baseman, designated hitter Cleve. Indians, 1991—2002, Phila. Phillies, 2003—05, Chgo. White Sox, 2006—09; pinch hitter LA Dodgers, 2009—. Hon. co-chmn. United Way Softball Slam. Recipient Roberto Clemente award, 2002, Lou Gehrig Meml. award, 2004; named to Am. League All-Star Team, 1997—99, Nat. League All-Star Team, 2004, 2006. Achievements include leading the American League in: walks, 1997, 1999, 2002; leading the National League in: home runs (47), 2003; hitting 400th career home run, June 13, 2004; hitting 500th career home run, September 16, 2007. Avocations: cooking, hunting, fishing. Office: LA Dodgers Dodger Stadium 1000 Elysian Pk Ave Los Angeles CA 90012*

THOMLINSON, VIVIAN AYTES, literature and language professor; married. BS in English and Polit. Sci., Tex. A&M U., Commerce, 1976; MA in English, Tex. Women's U., Denton, 1982, PhD in English, 1986. Tchr. North Tex. Coll., Gainseville, Prince George's CC, Largo, Md., US Army's Command and Gen. Staff Coll., Ft. Leavenworth, Kans.; faculty mem. Cameron U., Lawton, Okla., 1986—94, faculty mem. to assoc. prof. English, 1998—. Dir. composition Dept. English, Fgn. Langs. and Journalism Cameron U., 1987—94, 1999—2001, campus coord. writing across the curriculum. Contbr. articles to profl. jours. Recipient US Prof. of Yr. award, Carnegie Found. for Advancement of Tchg. and Coun. for Advancement and Support of Edn., 2006. Mem.: Okla. Coun. Tchrs. of English (coll. chair Exec. bd.). Office: Cameron U Dept English & Fgn Langs 637 S Shepler 2800 W Gore Blvd Lawton OK 73505-6377 Office Phone: 580-581-2545. Office Fax: 580-581-2572. E-mail: viviant@cameron.edu.

THOMOPOULOS, MICHAEL, music educator; b. Lowell, Mass., Apr. 24, 1953; s. George and Doris Thomopoulos. MusB, The New Eng. Conservatory of Music, Boston, 1975; MusM, The Juilliard Sch., NYC, 1977. Founder, music dir. Palisades Chamber Players, Ft. Lee, NJ, 1979—. Founder, dir., tchr. Palisades Sch. Music. Recipient Morris Loeb Meml. prize, Internat. Concert Artist Guild, 1977. Avocations: private piloting, scuba diving, politics, travel. Office: The Palisades Sch of Music 196 Washington Ave Fort Lee NJ 07024 Office Fax: 201-944-1311. Personal E-mail: mthomopoulos@yahoo.com.

THOMOPULOS, GREGS G., consulting engineering company executive; b. Benin City, Nigeria, May 16, 1942; s. Aristoteles and Christiana E. (Ogiamien) Thomopulos; m. Patricia Walker, Sept. 4, 1966 (div. 1974); 1 child, Lisa; m. Mettie L. Williams, May 28, 1976; children: Nicole, Euphemia. BSCE with highest distinction, U. Kans., 1965; MS in Structural Engring., U. Calif., Berkeley, 1966; PhD (hon.), Teikyo Marycrest U., 1996. Sr. v.p. internat. div. Stanley Cons., Inc., Muscatine, Iowa, 1978-84, sr. v.p. project divsn., 1984-87; pres., CEO Stanley Consultants, Inc., Muscatine, Iowa, 1987—2007, chmn., CEO, 2007—; exec. v.p. SC Co., Inc., Muscatine, 1992-98; pres., COO, 1998-99; pres., CEO, 2000—08; pres., CEO, chmn., 2008—; also bd. dirs. SC Co., Inc., Muscatine; chmn., CEO Stanley Environ., Inc., Chgo., 1991—, also bd. dirs.; chmn., CEO SC Power Devel., Inc., 1992—. Chmn., CEO Stanley Design-Build, Inc., 1995—; bd. dirs. Stanley Cons., Inc., Muscatine, Wellmark, Inc., Blue Cross Blue Shield Iowa & S.D., 1999—2008; mem. adv. bd. U. Kans. Sch. Engring., 2002—; mem. industry adv. panel US Dept. State, 2006—07. Mem. adv. bd. Coll. Engrng. U. Iowa, 1992-2000, Hydraulics Inst., U. Iowa Belin-Blank Ctr, 2008-; 2000-06, mem. bd. dirs. U. Iowa Found., 2008-. Fellow ASCE, Am. Coun. Engring. Cos. (vice chair., mem. exec. com.); mem. NSPE, Internat. Fedn. Cons. Engrs. (pres. elect, mem. exec. com.), 33 Club (pres. 1987), Rotary. Presbyterian. Avocations: tennis, computers, music. Home: 75 Shagbark Ct Iowa City IA 52246-2786 Office: Stanley Cons Inc 225 Iowa Ave Muscatine IA 52761-3765 Personal E-mail: thomopulos@home.com. Business E-Mail: thomopulosg@stanleygroup.com.

THOMPSON, ALAN ERIC, economics professor; b. Sept. 16, 1924; s. Eric Joseph and Florence Thompson; m. Mary Heather Long, 1960; 4 children. MA, U. Edinburgh, 1949, MA with 1st class honors, 1951, PhD, 1953. Asst. in polit. econ. U. Edinburgh, 1952-53, lectr. econs., 1953-59, 64-71; prof. econs. of govt. Heriot-Watt U., Edinburgh, 1972—. Adviser to Scottish TV, 1966-76; Scottish gov. BBC, 1976-79; vis. prof. Grad. Sch. Bus., Stanford U. (Calif.), 1966, 68; chmn. adv. bd. econs. edn. Esmee Fairbairn Rsch. Project, 1970-76. Author: (with others) Development of Economic Doctrine, 1980; contbr. articles to profl. jours. M.P. Labour Party, Dunfermline, 1959-64; mem. Scottish Com. Pub. Schs. Commn., 1969-70; mem. Joint Mil. Edn. Com. Edinburgh and Heriot-Watt Univs., 1975—, local govt. boundary commn. for Scotland, 1975-82; chmn. No. Offshore Resources Study, 1974-84; chmn. bd. govs. Newbattle Abbey Coll., 1980-82; bd. govs. Leigh Nautical Coll., 1981-87; trustee Bell's Nautical Trust, 1981-87; parliamentary adviser Pharm. Gen. Coun., 1985-2000; bd. dirs. Scottish AIDS Rsch. Found., 1992-2006; adv. Robert Burns Meml. Trust, 1995—99; advisor Robert Burns Meml. Trust, 1995-2000. With Brit. Army, WWII. Carnegie Rsch. scholar, 1951-52. Fellow Royal Soc. Arts, Soc. Antiquaries (Scotland); mem. Assn. Nazi War Camp Survivors (v.p. 1960—), Edinburgh Amenity and Transport Assn. (pres. 1970-75), New Club.

THOMPSON, ALAN S., federal agency administrator, military officer; BA, UCLA, 1976; MBA, Univ. Fla. Commissioned as ensign US Navy, 1976; asst. supply officer USS David R. Ray (DD 971), 1977—79; supply officer USS Chandler (DDG 996), 1981—83, USS Dwight D. Eisenhower (CVN 69), 1993—95; comdr. naval air force U.S. Pacific Fleet; comdr. US Naval Air Station, Miramar; staff officer Office of the Chief of Naval Ops.; commdg. officer Fleet & Indsl. Supply Ctr., Norfolk, Va.; fellow CNO Strategic Studies Group; comdr. def. supply ctr. Def. Logistics Agy., Columbus, Ohio, 2001—03; dir. supply ordnance & logistics ops. div. Office of the Chief of Naval Ops.; comdr. & chief of supply corps. Naval Supply Sys. Command; vice adm., dir. Defense Logistics Agy., US Dept. of Def., Fort Belvoir, Va., 2008—. Decorated Disting. Svc. medal, Def. Superior Svc. medal, Legion of Merit (3), Meritorious Svc. medal (4), Navy Commendation medal (2), Navy Achievement medal. Office: Defense Logistics Agy 8725 John J Kingman Rd Fort Belvoir VA 22060 Office Phone: 703-767-1152.*

THOMPSON, ANTHONY WAYNE, metallurgist, educator, consultant; b. Burbank, Calif., Mar. 6, 1940; s. William Lyman and Mary Adelaide (Nisbet) T.; m. Mary Ruth Cummings, Aug. 24, 1963; children: Campbell Lyman, Michael Anthony. BS, Stanford U., 1962; MS, U. Wash., 1965; PhD, MIT, 1970. Research engr. Jet Propulsion Lab., Pasadena, Calif., 1962-63; mem. tech. staff Sandia Labs., Livermore, Calif., 1970-73, Rockwell Sci. Ctr., Thousand Oaks, Calif., 1973-77; assoc. prof. Carnegie Mellon U., Pitts., 1977-79, prof., 1980-94, dept. head, 1987-90; staff scientist Lawrence Berkeley Lab., Berkeley, Calif., 1994-99; rsch. engr. U. Calif., Berkeley, Calif., 1995—. Vis. scientist U. Cambridge, Eng., 1983, Risø, Denmark, 1987, U. Calif., 1991; cons. Sandia Labs., 1977—1998, GE, 1988-2000. Editor: Work Hardening, 1976, Metall. Transactions, 1983-88, Signature Press Book Pubs., 1993-; co-editor: Hydrogen in Metals, 1974, Hydrogen Conf. Proc., 1976, 81, 89, 94, 2002; mem. editl. bd. Internat. Metals Revs., 1980-88; contbr. articles to profl. jours. Overseas fellow Churchill Coll. Cambridge U., 1982 Fellow Am. Soc. Metals; mem. Clubs: Sierra, Nat. Model R.R. Assn. Democrat. Home: 2906 Forest Ave Berkeley CA 94705

THOMPSON, BARBARA STORCK, state official; b. McFarland, Wis., Oct. 15, 1924; d. John Casper and Marie Ann (Kassabaum) Storck; m. Glenn T. Thompson, July 1, 1944; children— David C., James T. BS, Wis. State U., 1956; MS, U. Wis., 1959, PhD, 1969; L.H.D. (hon.), Carroll Coll., 1974. Tchr. pub. schs., West Dane County, Mt. Horeb, Wis., 1944-56; instr. Green County Tchrs. Coll., Monroe, Wis., 1956-57; coordinator curriculum Monroe Pub. Schs., 1957-60; instr. U. Wis., Platteville, 1960; supr. schs. Waukesha County Schs., Wis., 1960-63, supt. schs., 1963-65; prin. Fairview Elem. Schs., Brookfield, Wis., 1962-64; adminstrv. cons. Wis. Dept. Pub. Instrn., Madison, 1964-72, state coordinator, 1971-72; instr. U. Wis., Madison and Green Bay, 1972; supt. pub. instrn. Madison, Wis., 1973—81. Mem. Wis. State Bd. Vocat. Edn., 1973-81, Wis. Edn. Comm. Bd., 1973-81, Univ. Wis. Sys. Bd. Regents, 1973-1981. Author: A Candid Discussion of Critical Issues, 1975; mem. editorial bd.: The Education Digest, 1975—; contbr. articles to profl. jours. Mem. White House Conf. Children, 1970, Gov.'s Com. State Conf. Children and Youth, 1969-70, Manpower Council, 1973-81; bd. dirs. Vocational, Tech. and Adult Edn., 1973-81, Ednl. Communications, 1973-81, Higher Edn. Aids, 1973-81, Agy. Instructional TV, 1975-81; mem. nat. panel on SAT score decline; bd. regents U. Wis., 1973-81, U.S. office f Edn. Visiting Sch. Team - England, GErmany, Sweden, Poland, Iran, Syria, India, and Japan. Recipient State Conservation award Madison Lions CLub, 1956; Waukesha Freeman award, 1961 Mem. ASCD, NEA, Nat. Coun. Adminstrv. Women in Edn. (named Woman of Year 1974), Nat. Coun. State Cons. in Elem. Edn. (pres. 1974-75), Wis. Assn. Sch. Dist. Adminstrs., Wis. ASCD, Southwestern Wis. ASCD, Southeastern Wis. ASCD (mem. exec. coun. 1972-73), Dept. Elem. Sch. Prins., Wis. Elem. Sch. Prins. Assn., Wis. Edn. Assn. (pres. local chpt. 1970-71); life mem. So. Wis. Edn. Assn., Wis. Ednl. Rsch. Assn., Dept. Elem.-Kindergarten-Nursery Edn., Assn. Childhood Edn. Internat., Assn. Childhood Edn., Coun. Chief State Sch. Officers, Edn. Commn. States, Nat. Coun. State Cons. in Elem. Edn. (pres. 1974-75), Am. Assn. Sch. Dist. Adminstrs. (chmn. policy com. 1963-81), Madison Ctrl. Internat. Lions Club, U. Wis. Alumni Orgn. (Sarasota, Fla. and Madison), U. Wis. League (Madison chpt.), Delta Kappa Gamma, Pi Lambda Theta. Office: Apt 123 325 S Yellowstone Dr Madison WI 53705-4301 also: 1700 3rd Ave W Apt 1007 Bradenton FL 34205-5937

THOMPSON, BENNIE G., United States Representative from Mississippi; b. Bolton, Miss., Jan. 28, 1948; m. London Johnson; 1 child, BendaLonne. BA in Polit. Sci., Tougaloo Coll., Miss., 1968; MS in Ednl. Adminstrn., Jackson State U., Miss., 1972; grad., U. So. Miss. Alderman, Bolton, Miss., 1969—73; mayor, 1973—79; supr. Hinds County, Miss., 1980-93; mem. US Congress from 2nd Miss. Dist., 1993—; chmn. US House Homeland Security Com., 2007—. Presdl. appointee Nat. Coun. Health Planning and Devel. Bd. trustees Tougaloo Coll.; bd. dirs. So. Regional Coun., Housing Assistance Coun. Named one of 100 Most Influential Black Americans, Ebony mag., 2006; named to Power 150, 2008. Mem.: Miss. Assn. Black Suprs. (founding mem.), Miss. Assn. Black Mayors (founding mem.). Democrat. Methodist. Office: US Congress 2432 Rayburn House Office Bldg Washington DC 20515-0001 also: 107 W Madison St Bolton MS 39041 Office Phone: 202-225-5876. Office Fax: 202-225-5898. E-mail: thompsonms2nd@mail.house.gov.*

THOMPSON, BERNIDA LAMERLE, principal, consultant, educator; b. Tuskeegee, Ala., July 5, 1946; d. Berry James Sr. and Doris LaMerle (Askey) T.; m. Rolando Amerson, June 15, 1968 (div. Aug. 1988); children: Afriye Amerson, Mwando Amerson. BS in Elem. Edn., Cen. State U., 1968; MEd in Adminstrn. and Curriculum, Miami U., Oxford, Ohio, 1971; EdD in Early and Mid. Childhood Edn., Nova U., 1992. Classroom elem. sch. tchr. Dayton Pub. Schs.; asst. prin., intern St. James Cath. Sch., Dayton, Ohio; tchr. St. Augustine Cath. Sch., Washington; sci. resource tchr. D.C. Pub. Schs., Washington; founding tchr., prin. Roots Activity Learning Ctr., Washington, 1977—, Roots Pub. Charter Sch., 1999—. Multicultural advisor HBJ 1992 Reading Textbook. Author: Black Madonnas and Young Lions a Rite of Passage for African American Adolescents, 1992, rev. edit., 1998, Africentric Interdisciplinary Multi-Level Hands On Science, 1994, rev. edit., 2001; contbr. articles to profl. jours. Mem. Nat. Assn. Edn. Young Children, World Coun. Curriculum Instrn., Coun. Ind. Black Inst., Inst. Ind. Edn., Nat. Black Child Devel. Inst. Office: Roots Pub Charter Sch 15 Kennedy St NW Washington DC 20011-5201 Home Phone: 202-829-5941; Office Phone: 202-882-8073. Business E-Mail: bthompson@rootspcs.org.

THOMPSON, BERT ALLEN, retired librarian; b. Bloomington, Ind., Dec. 13, 1930; s. James Albert and Dorothy Fern (Myers) T.; m. Martha Ellen Palmer; children— John Carter II, Anne Palmer, Paul Julian. BS, Ball State Tchrs. Coll., 1953; AM, Ind. U., 1960; certificate in archival adm., U. Denver, 1967. Tchr., libr. Ind. pub. schs., 1953-55; ref. asst. Indpls. Pub. Libr., 1956-59; head ref. svc. Mankato (Minn.) State U., 1959-61; instr. Grad. Libr. Sch. No. Ill. U., Dekalb, 1961-63; dir. libs., asst. prof. ednl. media U. Nebr. at Kearney, 1963-69; dir. libr. svc. Benedictine U., Lisle, Ill., 1969-90, spl. collections libr., 1990-92. Mem. exec. bd. Ill. regional Libr. Coun., 1976-79. Recipient 1st Melvin R. George LIBRAS award for Outstanding Svc. to Libr. Cooperation, 1993. Mem. Ill. (de Lafayette Reid Research scholar 1976), Cath. Libr. Assn. (treas. Ill. chpt. 1973-75, nat. sec.-treas. coll./univ. sect. 1981-85, nat. bd. dirs. 1987-93), Nebr. Libr. Assn. chmn. coll. and univ. sect. 1963-64) Episcopalian. Home: 1808 Caxton Dr Wheaton IL 60189-6140 Home Phone: 630-665-3540.

THOMPSON, BETTY JANE, retired small business owner; b. Ladysmith, Wis., Nov. 18, 1923; d. Edward Thomas and Mayme Selma (Kratwell) Potter; m. Frederick Sturdee Thompson, Apr. 19, 1945 (div. Apr. 1973); children: Denise Alana, Kent Marshall; m. J.R. Critchfield, Feb. 14, 1977 (div. 1989). Student, Jamestown Coll., ND, 1946-47, U. Calif., Long Beach, 1964-69; AA, Orange Coast Coll., 1976; postgrad., Monterey Peninsula Coll., 1979-80; SBA Cert., Hartnell Coll., 1982. Cert. fashion cons. Owner, mgr., buyer Goodview (Minn.) Food Mart, 1947-50; dist. mgr. Beauty Counselor of Minn., Winona County, 1951-61; Boy Scout liaison J.C. Penney Co., Newport Beach, Calif., 1969-72; dept. mgr. and buyer boyswear At Ease, Newport Beach, 1972-77; mgr. Top Notch Boys Wear, Carmel, Calif., 1977-83, buyer, 1984-88; owner, mgr. Top Notch Watch, Sun City, Ariz., 1989-95; editor H&R Block, 1995-98; employee Wells Fargo and Co., 1998—2004; ret., 2004. V.p., chmn. Don Loper Fashion Show, 1967, pres., 1968, bd. dirs., 1969. Co-editor Aux. Antics mag., 1965. Vol. fundraising leadership Family Svc. Assn., Orange County, Calif., 1962-68, other orgns.; chmn. publicity, study group, Sunday sch. tchr., Congl. Ch., Winona, Minn.,

1956-58, fellowship pres., Santa Ana, Calif., 1963-65; pres. Goodview Civic Club, 1948; mem. Wells Fargo and Co. Bank Silver Bullets, Sr. Citizens of the Sun Cities, Phoenix, 1998-2000; counselor AARP Tax Aide, 1997—; moderator Congrl. Christian Fellowship, 1999-2001; sec. Tont Ct. Condominium, 1998-2004. Recipient Athena award Panhellenic Assn. Orange City, Calif., 1968, El Camino Real Dist. Svc. award Orange Empire coun. Boy Scouts Am., Baden-Powell award, Outstanding Leadership award, El Camino Real Dist., Calif., 1972. Ringling North award, 1949; named Outstanding Svc. Vol. Family Svc. Assn., 1969. Mem. Carmel Bus. Assn. Avocations: genealogy, photography, ballroom dance, bicycling, skiing. Home and Office: 10048 W Hawthorn Dr Sun City AZ 85351-2829 E-mail: tbjtonto@aol.com.

THOMPSON, BIRGIT DOLORES, civic worker, writer; b. Jamestown, NY, Apr. 7, 1930; d. Oscar Einar and Karin Johanna (Videll) Wolff; m. William Andrew Thompson, Jan. 26, 1952 (div. June 1978); children: William A., Christina A., Michael J., Timothy A., Kathleen S., Jeffrey B. AB summa cum laude, SUNY, Fredonia, 1974. Exec. dir. Fenton Hist. Ctr., Jamestown, 1975-82; fin. dir. Amicae, Inc., Fredonia, 1983-90; office mgr. JEM Counseling Ctr., Jamestown, 1990-93; resource/info. person Audubon Nature Ctr., Jamestown, 1993—. Author: Illustrated History of Jamestown and Chautauqua County, 1983, Jamestown Audubon Society 50th Year History; musician Jamestown String Quartet, violist local orchestras, 1970-2000; contbr. articles to newspapers. Historian City of Jamestown, 1978—; bd. dirs., chair scholarship com. Mozart Club, 2001—05; play selection com. Lucille Ball Little Theatre of Jamestown, 1976—, pit orch.; mem. steering and fin. coms. Underground Railroad Tableau Project; v.p., bd. trustees Unitarian Universalist Congregation Jamestown; bd. dirs. Jamestown YWCA, Chautauqua Regional Youth Symphony, pres., 1996—2001; com. mem. Jamestown Audubon Soc., newsletter editor, 1982—98. Recipient Women of Achievement award in civic category, YWCA, 2004, Friend of Edn. award, Delta Kappa Gamma Internat. Kappa Chpt., 2006. Mem. AAUW (Jamestown)(bd. coms., 1982-2004, cir. distinction, 1982-, chmn. What's New Fair Jamestown 1988-94, pub. policy chair 1995—, bd. dirs. coms., 1982-2002, pres. 1988-92, co-pres. 2000-06, v.p. membership 2006—, named gift award 1987), Interclub Coun. Jamestown (treas. 1998—, Woman of Yr. award 1992). Avocations: museums, concerts, reading, gardening. Home: 13 Lamont St Jamestown NY 14701-2021 Personal E-mail: musicat2@gmail.com.

THOMPSON, BRADFORD, mathematics professor; married. MS in Math., Jacksonville State U., Ala., 1995. Math. instr. NWSCC, Muscle Shoals, Ala., 2006—. Office: NWSCC Box 44 800 George Wallace Blvd Muscle Shoals AL 35661

THOMPSON, BRIAN JOHN, academic administrator, optics scientist, educator; b. Glossop, Eng., June 10, 1932; came to U.S., 1962; s. Alexander William and Edna May (Gould) T.; m. Joyce Emily Cheshire, Mar. 31, 1956; children: Karen Joyce, Andrew Derrick. B of Sci. Tech., U. Manchester, Eng., 1955, PhD, 1959. Demonstrator in physics dept. tech. U. Manchester, 1955-56, asst. lectr. dept. tech., 1957-59; lectr. physics U. Leeds, England, 1959-62; sr. physicist Tech. Optics, Inc., Burlington, Mass., 1963-65, dir. dept. optics, 1966-67; mgr. tech. ops. west, tech. dir. Beckman and Whitley, Mountainview, Calif., 1967-68; prof. Inst. Optics U. Rochester, NY, 1968-94, dir. Inst. Optics NY, 1968-75, dean Coll. Engring. and Applied Scis. NY, 1975-84, Wm. F. May prof. engring. NY, 1982-85, provost NY, 1984-94, provost emeritus, prof. of optics emeritus, Disting. U. prof. NY, 1994—. Editor Optics and Laser Tech., 1969-96; assoc. editor: Optical Engring., 1972-76, Optics Comm., 1978-86; editor Optica Acta, 1981-85, Optical Scis. and Engring. Series, vols. 1-148, 1980—; mem. editl. bd. Laser Focus, 1970-84, Particle Characterization, 1984-95, Optics and Lasers in Engring., 1985, Milestone Series of Selected Papers, vols. 1-182, 1985-2006, Optical Engring., 1991-98; chmn. adv. bd. Marquis Who's Who Directory Optical Scientists and Engrs., 1983-86; contbr. articles to profl. jours. With Brit. Army, 1950-52. Fellow: Inst. Physics and Phys. Soc. (Gt. Britain), Optical Soc. Am. (bd. dirs. 1969—72, exec. com. 1970—73, assoc. editor jour. 1966—77), Soc. Photo-Optical Instrumentation Engrs. (life; pres. 1974—76, editor jour. 1991—98, Pres.'s award 1967, Pezzuto award 1978, Kingslake medal 1978, Gold medal 1986, Dir. award 1998); mem.: AAAS, Am. Phys. Soc. Home and Office: 9 Esternay Ln Pittsford NY 14534-1014 Office Phone: 585-461-0739.

THOMPSON, CHARLES MURRAY, lawyer; b. Childress, Tex., Oct. 13, 1942; s. Walter Lee and Lois S. (Sheehan) T.; children: Murray, McLean. BS with honors, Colo. State U., Ft. Collins, 1965; JD cum laude, U. SD, Vermillion, 1969, LLD (hon.), 1995. Bar: SD 1969, US Dist. Ct. SD 1969, US Ct. Claims 1989, US Ct. Appeals (8th cir.) 1972, US Supreme Ct. 1973. Ptnr. May, Adam, Gerdes & Thompson, Pierre, SD, 1969—. Bd. dirs. Bank West, Pierre, SD; past pres., dir. Delta Trust, 1997-2002; spkr. in field. Editor S.D. Law Rev., 1969 Pres. SD Coun. Sch. Attys., 1984-86. Fellow Am. Bar Found. (chmn. 1991-92, bd. dirs. 1989-92), Coll. Law Practice Mgmt., Am. Coll. Trial Lawyers; mem. ABA (ho. of dels. 1978-2002, bd. govs. 1983-86, standing com. on fed. judiciary (2004-06), Ctr. for Racial & Ethnic Diversity, 2009-, ATLA, Am. Bd. Trial Advs., Am. Counsel Assn., Am. Judicature Soc. (bd. dirs. 1981-85), Am. Bar Endowment (bd. dirs. 1991-2006, dir. emeritus 2006-, pres. 2000-02), AEFC (Pension Plan Bd., 1987-90, 2005-), Nat. Conf. Bar Pres.'s (exec. coun. 1986-94, pres. 1992-93), State Bar S.D. (pres. young lawyers sect. 1974-75, pres. 1986-87), SD Bar Found. (pres. 1991), SD Trial Lawyers Assn. (pres. 1980-81), Jackrabbit Bar Assn. (chancellor 1981-82, ABA, Am. Bar Endowment, Am. Bar Found., Nat. Jud. Coll. pension bd., 1987-90, adminstrv. com., 2005-), SD Cmty. Found., Kiwanis (pres. local club 1977). Democrat. Avocations: flying, ranching. Home and Office: PO Box 160 Pierre SD 57501-0160 Office Phone: 605-224-8803.

THOMPSON, CHARLOTTE ELLIS, pediatrician, educator, writer; d. Robert and Ann Ellis; divorced; children: Jennifer Ann, Geoffrey Graeme. BA, Stanford U., 1950, MD, 1954. Diplomate Am. Bd. Pediat. Intern Children's Hosp., San Francisco, 1953-54; resident UCLA, 1960-61, L.A. Children's Hosp., 1962-63; pvt. practice La Jolla, Calif., 1963-75; dir. Muscle Disease Clinic Univ. Hosp.-U. Calif. Sch. Medicine, San Diego, 1969-80, asst. clin. prof. pediat., 1969—; founder, dir. Ctr. for Handicapped Children and Teenagers, San Francisco, 1981—2004. Cons. U.S. Naval Hosp., San Diego, 1970-91; dep. dir. Santa Clara County Child Health and Disability, Santa Clara, Calif., 1974-75; dir. Ctr. for Multiple Handicaps, Oakland, Calif., 1976-81; co-dir. Muscle Clinic Children's Hosp., San Diego, 1963-69; dir. muscle program U. Rochester, 1957-60. Author: Raising a Handicapped Child: A Helpful Guide for Parents of the Physically Disabled, 1986, 4th edit., 1991, rev., expanded edit., 2000, Allein leben: Ein umfassendes Handbuch für Frauen, 1993, Making Wise Choices: A Guide for Women, 1993, Raising a Child with a Neuromuscular Disorder, 1999, Raising A Handicapped Child, 1999, 101 Ways To The Best Medical Care, 2006, Grandparenting a child with special needs Jersica Kingsley, 2009; contbr. articles to med. jours., including Clin. Pediat., New Eng. Jour. Medicine, Neurology, Jour. Family Practice, Mothering, Jour. Pediatric Orthopedics, Pediatrician, Am. Baby, Pediatric News, Grandparenting a Child with Special Needs, 2009, also chpts. to books. Mem. Calif. Children's Svc. Com., 1977—. Fellow: Am. Acad. Pediat. Avocations: tennis, ice skating, opera. Office: 8070 La Jolla Shores Dr # 514 La Jolla CA 92037-3296 Office Phone: 858-456-2105. Personal E-mail: cetmd@earthlink.net.

THOMPSON, CHRISTOPHER, legislative staff member; B in Polit. Sci., U. Calif., Santa Barbara. Legis. asst., Rep. Julian Dixon US House of Reps., Washington, 1998—2002; legis. asst., Senator Dianne Feinstein US Senate, Washington, 2002—06, legis. dir., Senator Dianne Feinstein, 2006—08, chief of staff to Senator Dianne Feinstein, 2008—. Democrat. Office: 331 Hart Senate Office Bldg Washington DC 20510-0504 Office Phone: 202-224-3841. Business E-Mail: chris_thompson@feinstein.senate.gov.*

THOMPSON, CHRISTOPHER C., gastroenterologist; Staff Dana Farber Cancer Inst., Children's Hosp. Boston; instr. Harvard Med. Sch.; dir. devel. endoscopy Brigham & Women's Hosp. Office: 75 Francis St Boston MA 02115 Office Phone: 617-732-5500.*

THOMPSON, CLIFTON C., retired chemistry professor, academic administrator; b. Franklin, Tenn., Aug. 16, 1939; s. Clifton C. and Ruby M. Thompson; m. Sarah Ellen Gaunt, Dec. 1, 1978; children: Brenda Kay, Victoria Lea. BS, Middle Tenn. State U., 1961; PhD, U. Miss., 1964. Asst. prof. Rutgers U., New Brunswick, NJ, 1965, Marshall U., Huntington, W.Va., 1965-66; assoc. prof. Middle Tenn. State U., Murfreesboro, 1966-68, U. Memphis, 1968—74; prof. chemistry, dept. head, dean Coll. Sci. and Math., dir. Ctr. for Sci. Rsch., assoc. v.p. for grad. studies and rsch. Mo. State U., Springfield, 1974-96, prof. emeritus, 1996—; prof. chemistry Cen. Mich. U., Mt. Pleasant, 1996-98. Rsch. assoc. U. Tex., Austin, 1964-65; rschr. Oak Ridge Nat. Lab., 1968; cons. Mid-South Research Assocs., Memphis, 1969-71; mem. med. tech. rev. com. Nat. Accrediting Agy. for Clin. Lab. Sci., Chgo., 1974-80; vis. prof. So. Ill. U., Carbondale, 1995. Author: Ultraviolet-Visible Absorption Spectroscopy, 1974; contbr. articles to profl. jours. Mem. health care com. Springfield C. of C., 1978-79, mem. econ. devel. com., 1983-89; bd. dirs. United Hebrew Congregation, Springfield, 1983-86, United Hebrew Found., Inc., 1994-96. NSF fellow, 1961-64; Sigma Xi grantee-in-aide, 1970; NSF sr. fgn. scientist grantee, 1971; NSF coop-coll. sch. sci. grantee, 1972; Higher Edn. Applied Projects grantee, 1987-90. Mem.: Royal Soc. Chemistry, Am. Chem. Soc., Phi Kappa Phi, Sigma Xi. Office: Mo State U Dept Chemistry Springfield MO 65804

THOMPSON, CRAIG SNOVER, corporate communications executive; b. Bklyn., May 24, 1932; s. Craig F. and Edith (Williams) T.; m. Masae Sugizaki, Feb. 21, 1957; children: Lee Anne, Jane Laura. Grad., Valley Forge Mil. Acad., 1951; BA, Johns Hopkins U., 1954. Newspaper and radio reporter Easton (Pa.) Express, 1954-55, 57-59, Wall St. Jour., 1959-60; account exec. Moore, Meldrum & Assocs., 1960; mgr. pub. relations Cen. Nat. Bank of Cleve., 1961-62; account exec. Edward Howard & Co., Cleve., 1962-67, v.p., 1967-69, sr. v.p., 1969-71; dir. pub. relations White Motor Corp., Cleve., 1971-76; v.p. pub. relations No. Telecom Inc., Nashville, 1976-77, White Motor Corp., Farmington Hills, Mich., 1977-80, v.p. corp. communications, 1980-81; dir. exec. communications Rockwell Internat. Corp., Pitts., 1981-86, El Segundo, Calif., 1986-91, Seal Beach, Calif., 1992-97, sr. communications exec., 1997; pres. Craig S. Thompson. Inc., 1997—. Bd. dirs. Shaker Lakes Regional Nature Center, 1970-73. Served to 1st lt., inf. U.S. Army, 1955-57. Mem. Pub. Rels. Soc. Am. (accredited), Alumni Assn. Valley Forge Mil. Acad. (bd. dirs. 1988-94).

THOMPSON, DANIEL EMERSON, vending machine service company executive; b. Fairbanks, Alaska, Jan. 24, 1947; s. George Edmond and Emma Jean (Burns) T.; m. Yvette Clarice Brazeau, Aug. 16, 1980. Student, U. Notre Dame, 1965-67. Vice-pres. Music Inc., Fairbanks, 1965—67, pres., 1967—81, 1987—, sec., 1984—87; pres. Vend Inc. (doing bus. as Vend Alaska-Anchorage), Anchorage, 1984—. Bd. dirs. Music Inc., Fairbanks, Vend Inc., Anchorage, Denali State Bank, Fairbanks; ptnr. Thompson Investment Co., Fairbanks, 1976—. With Monroe Found., Fairbanks, 1991-2000, North Star Dance Found., 2002—; vocatonal edn. adv. com. Fairbanks North Star Borough Sch. Dist., 1993-2009. Mem. Amusement Music Operators Am., Nat. Automatic Merchandising Assn., N.W. Automatic Vending Assn. (bd. govs. 1983—), Rotary, Fairbanks C. of C. Roman Catholic. Office: 1810 Burgess Ave Fairbanks AK 99709-5516

THOMPSON, DANIEL RAY, statistician, consultant; b. Washington, Nov. 15, 1951; s. Conrad Warden and Virginia Thompson; m. Laura Jean Peck, Dec. 10, 1978; 1 child, Brett Wesley. BS in Forestry, Va. Tech, Blacksburg, Va., 1975; MPH, U. South Fla., Tampa, 1989. Forester ITT Rayonier, Lake City, Fla., 1975—78, Boyd Foresters, Tallahassee, 1978—80; statistician Fla. Dept. Health and Rehabilitative Svcs., Tallahassee, 1980—83; computer systems analyst Fla. Dept. Health, Tallahassee, 1983—97, chronic disease epidemiology program adminstr., 1997—2001, pub. health statistician, 2001—. Office: FL Dept Health 4052 Bald Cypress Way Bin A-13 Tallahassee FL 32399-1723 Business E-Mail: dan_thompson@doh.state.fl.us.

THOMPSON, DARLENE BENNETT, realtor, musician; b. Simpson, La., June 28, 1931; d. Odis Pharon and Carrie Josephine (Knight) Blackwell; m. Elmo Bennett (dec.); children: Debra Kathleen Bennett, Eric Blane Bennett, Denise Darlene Bennett; m. Mitchell Glenn Thompson, Dec. 28, 1990. BS, Northwestern State U., Natchitoches, La., 1952, EdM, 1959, MusM, 1963, EdD, 1981. Tchr. K-12 Vernon Parish Sch. Bd., Leesville, La., 1952—82; dir. alternative sch. Vidor (Tex.) Ind. Sch. Dist., 1982—85; reading specialist Burkville (Tex.) Ind. Sch. Dist., 1986—2000; realtor ERA Broker, Leesville, 2003—. Dir. music Simpson Ch. of God, Simpson Assembly of God; organist Pok Episcopal Ch., St. Michael's Cath. Ch. Mem.: Ret. Tchrs. La., Piano Tchrs. La., Music Educators La., Pilot Club Leesville, Phi Delta Kappa. Home: 554 Alexandria Hwy Leesville LA 71446

THOMPSON, DARREL L., legislative staff member; b. Balt. m. Britt Thompson. BA in Polit. Sci. cum laude, Morgan State U., Balt.; MPA, Harvard U. John F. Kennedy Sch. Govt., Mass. Fin. services dir. Dem. Congl. Campaign Com., 1998, co-dir., base vote operation, 2000; sr. policy advisor, dir. mem. services, Rep. Richard Gephardt US House of Reps., Washington, 1999—2003; dep. exec. dir. US House Dem. Caucus, 2000; nat. policy advisor, fin. chief of staff Rep. Richard Gephardt's Presdl. Campaign, 2004; chief of staff Barack Obama's Senatorial Campaign, 2004; sr. advisor to Senator Harry Reid US Senate, Washington, 2005—, interim chief of staff to Senator Roland Burris, 2009. Cons., Congl. campaigns on fundraising, campaign ops. and voter turnout; mgr. and mem. sr. staff on legis., Congl. and gubernatorial campaigns. Democrat. Office: 522 Hart Senate Office Bldg Washington DC 20510 Office Phone: 202-224-3542. Business E-Mail: darrel_thompson@reid.senate.gov.*

THOMPSON, DAVID, publishing executive; b. 1952; m. Jane Thompson; children: Kathryne, Jeffrey, Robyn. Grad., U. Ctrl. Okla., 1973. Mem. retail adv. sales staff The Oklahoman, Oklahoma City, 1974, mgr. phone room classified adv. dept., asst. adv. dir., 1986, dir. adv., 1987—2001, pres., pub., 2003—; pres. OPUBCO Comm. Group, 2007—; mgr. adv. Colo. Springs Sun, 1977—86; v.p. adv. Charlotte Observer, 2001—03. Mem. bd. Carolina Regional Partnership; mem. Mecklenburg Coun., exec. bd. dirs. Last Frontier Coun. Boy Scouts Am., pres. Last Frontier Council, 2006; with Charlotte C. of C.; chmn. elect YMCA, Oklahoma City; mem. bd. Ind. Coll. Found.; chmn. econ. develop. dept. C. of C.; mem. bd. Oklahoma City C. of C., State C. of C., Okla. Health Ctr. Found., Allied Arts, State Fair of Okla., Oklahoma City Pub. Schs. Found., Okla. Bus. Roundtable, Okla. Bus. & Edn. Coalition. Mem.: So. Newspaper Pubs. Assn., Newspaper Assn. Am., Kiwanis (pres.). Office: Oklahoman PO Box 25125 Oklahoma City OK 73125 also: The Oklahoman 9000 N Broadway Oklahoma City OK 73114

THOMPSON, DAVID ALFRED, industrial engineer; b. Chgo., Sept. 9, 1929; s. Clifford James and Christobel Eliza (Sawin) T.; children: Nancy, Brooke, Lynda, Diane, Kristy. B.M.E., U. Va., 1951; BS in Indsl. Engring, U. Fla., 1955, MS in Engring, 1956; PhD, Stanford U., 1961. Registered profl. engr., Calif; cert. profl. ergonomist; bd. cert. diplomate in forensic engring. Research asst. U. Fla. Engring. and Industries Exptl. Sta., Gainesville, 1955-56; instr. indsl. engring. Stanford U., 1956-58, acting asst. prof., 1958-61, asst. prof., 1961-64, asso. prof., 1964-72, prof., 1972-83, prof., asso. chmn. dept. indsl. engring., 1972-73, prof. emeritus, 1983—; clin. faculty occupational medicine U. Calif. Med. Sch., San Francisco, 1985—; pres., chief scientist Portola Assocs., Palo Alto, Calif., 1962—97, Incline Village, Nev., 1997—; prin. investigator NASA Ames Rsch. Ctr., Moffatt Field, Calif., 1974-77. Cons. Dept. State, Fed. EEO Commn., maj. U.S. and fgn. cos.; cons. emergency commn. ctr. design Santa Clara County Criminal Justice Bd., 1974, Bay Area Rapid Transit Control Ctr., 1977, Govt. of Mex., 1978, Amadahl Corp., 1978-79, Kerr-McGee Corp., 1979, Chase Manhattan Bank, 1980, St. Regis Paper Co., 1980-82, Pacific Gas & Electric, 1983-85, Pacific Bell, 1984-86, 89-93, IBM, 1988-91, Hewlett-Packard, 1990-91, 98-99, Reuter's News Svc., 1990-92, Safeway Corp., 1992-94, New United Motors Mfg., 1993-95, Sun Microsys., 1993-94, Microsoft, 1995-00; mem. com. for office computers Calif. OSHA. Dir., editor: documentary film Rapid Answers for Rapid Transit, Dept. Transp., 1974; mem. editorial adv. bd. Computers and Graphics, 1970-85; reviewer Indsl. Engring. and IEEE Transactions, 1972-86; contbr. articles to profl. jours. Served to lt. USNR, 1951-58. HEW grantee, 1967-70 Fellow Nat. Assn. Forensic Engrs.; mem. IEEE, Am. Inst. Indsl. Engrs., Human Factors and Ergonomics Soc., Am. Soc. Safety Engrs., Soc. Forensic Engrs. and Scientists, Am. Assn. Forensic Scientists. Home: PO Box 6685 Incline Village NV 89450-6685 Address: PO Box 6088 Incline Village NV 89450-6088 Office Phone: 775-833-3304. Personal E-mail: davidthompson@pyramid.net. Business E-Mail: davidthompson@humanfactors.org.

THOMPSON, DAVID BERNARD, bishop emeritus; b. Phila., May 29, 1923; Ordained priest Archdiocese of Phila, 1950; ordained bishop, 1989; coadjutor bishop Diocese of Charleston, SC, 1989-90, bishop SC, 1990—99. Pub. New Cath. Miscellany, Charleston, SC. Recipient Bishop John England award, Cath. Press Assn., 1997. Roman Catholic. Office: Diocese of Charleston 119 Broad St Charleston SC 29401-2435 Mailing: 4479 Downing Pl Mount Pleasant SC 29466

THOMPSON, DAVID M., computer software company executive; b. NJ; married; 2 children. Bachelors in Engring., Masters in Engring., Cornell U. With Digital Equipment Corp.; dir. software devel. Concord Comm.; with Microsoft Corp., 1990—, corp. v.p. Windows Server product group, 2000—04, corp. v.p. Microsoft Exch. group, 2004—07, corp. v.p. Microsoft Online, 2007—. Avocations: skiing, snowboarding, bicycling, hiking. Office: Microsoft Corp Microsoft Online 1 Microsoft Way Redmond WA 98052-6399*

THOMPSON, DAVID RENWICK, federal judge; b. 1930; BS in Bus., U. So. Calif., 1952, LLB, 1955. Pvt. practice Thompson & Thompson (and predecessor firms), 1957—85; judge US Ct. Appeals (9th cir.), 1985—98, sr. judge, 1998—. With USN, 1955—57. Mem.: ABA, Am. Bd. Trial Lawyers (sec. San Diego chpt. 1983, v.p. 1984, Pres. 1985), San Diego County Bar Assn. Office: US Ct Appeals 940 Front St Rm 2193 San Diego CA 92101-8919*

THOMPSON, DAVID RUSSELL, engineering educator, dean; b. Cleve., Apr. 4, 1944; s. Dwight L. and Ella Caroline (Wolff) T.; m. Janet Ann Schall, Aug. 27, 1966; children: Devin Mathew, Colleen Michelle, Darin Michael. BS in Agrl. Engring., Purdue U., 1966, MS in Agrl. Engring., 1967; PhD in Agrl. Engring., Mich. State U., 1970. Asst. prof. agrl. engring., food sci. and nutrition depts. U. Minn., St. Paul, 1970-75, assoc. prof., 1975-81, prof., 1981-85; prof. agrl. engring., head dept. Okla. State U., Stillwater, 1985-91, assoc. dean Coll. Engring., Architecture and Tech., 1991—. Engr. ops. dept. Green Giant Co., La Sueur, Minn., 1978-79; reviewer Colo. State U., Coop. State Rsch. Svc., USDA, Ft. Collins, 1989, foods, feeds and prodn. cluster U. Mo., Columbia, 1989, 93, dept. agrl. engring. Pa. State U., University Park, 1990, Tex. A&M U., College Station, 1992, Utah State U., Logan, 1993, USAF, Tyndall, Fla. and San Angelo, Tex., 1994-95, 97, Wash. State U., Pullman, 1995, U. Ga., Athens, 1996, S.D. State U., 1997, U. Fla., 1998, U. Del., 1998, U. Neb., 1999, U. Wis., 2000, U. Idaho, 2001, Rutgers U., 2003, Lake Superior State U., Sault St. Marie, 2003, Auburn U., 2004, U. Tenn., 2005, Western New Eng. Coll., 2005, So. Ill. U., Carbondale, 2006, St. Petersburg Coll., 2006, U. of the Pacific, 2006, U. New Orleans, 2007, Tex. Tech. U., 2007, Eastern Ky. U., 2008, Sultan Qaboos U., 2008, U. Louisville, 2009, U. San Martín Porres, 2009, others; reviewer USDA, 1983; vis. scholar Va. Poly. Inst. and State U., Blaksburg. Author: The Influence of Materials Properties on the Freezing of Sweet Corn, 1984, Mathematical Model for Predicting Lysine and Methionine Losses During Thermal Processing of Fortified Foods; contbr. over 50 articles to profl. jours. including Jour. Food Sci. Fellow Am. Soc. Agrl. Engrs. (divsn. chmn. 1976-77, bd. dirs. 1981-84, 87-89, v.p. 1994-98, stds. coun. chmn. 1997-98, Farm and Indsl. Equip. Inst., Young Rschr. award 1983, Pres.'s citation 1989, 98); mem. ASHRAE, NSPE (chair Okla. mid-north sect. 1994-95), Okla. Soc. Profl. Engrs. (v.p. 2000-01), Inst. Food Technologists (program com. 1982-85, state officer 1987-89), Am. Soc. Engring. Edn. (chair Midwest sect. 1994-95), Engring. Accreditation Commn. ABET Inc., Sigma Xi, Phi Kappa Phi, Tau Beta Pi, Alpha Epsilon, Phi Eta Sigma, Gamma Sigma Delta. Office: Okla State U Coll Engring Arch & Tech 201 Adv Tech Rsch Ctr Stillwater OK 74078-5010 Home Phone: 405-377-5263; Office Phone: 405-744-5140. Business E-Mail: dthomps@okstate.edu.

THOMPSON, DAVID WALKER, astronautics company executive; b. Phila., Mar. 21, 1954; s. Robert H. and Nancy S. (Walker) T.; m. Catherine K. Ahulii, April 16, 1983. BS in Aeronautics and Astronautics, MIT, 1976; MS, Calif. Inst. Tech., 1977; MBA, Harvard U., 1981. Project engr. Jet Propulsion Lab., Pasadena, Calif., 1976; aerospace engr. NASA, Houston, 1977, project mgr. Huntsville, Ala., 1977-79; spl. asst. to pres. Hughes Aircraft Co., Los Angeles, 1981-82; co-founder, pres., chief exec. officer Orbital Scis. Corp., Dulles, Va., 1982—. Cons. Rockwell Internat., Thousand Oaks, Calif., 1980-81, Rand Corp., Santa

Monica, Calif., 1982. Recipient Nat. award Space Found., Houston, 1981, Nat. Medal Tech. U.S Dept. Commerce Tech. Adminstrn., 1991, Nat. Air and Space Mus. Trophy, 1990, George M. Low Space Transportation award, Am. Inst. Aeronautics and Astronautics, 1994, World Tech. award for Space, Economist Mag.; fellow Hertz Found., 1976, NSF fellow, 1976, Rockwell Internat. fellow, Harvard U. fellow, 1979; named Va. Industrialist Yr., 1991, Satellite Exec. of Yr., Satellite Mag., 1990, High-Tech. Entrepreneur Yr. Fellow AIAA (assoc., Young Engr./Scientist Yr. award 1984, George M. Low Space Trans. award 1994), Am. Astronautical Soc., Royal Aeronautical Soc.; mem. Nat. Space Club, Internat. Acad. Astronautics, NAE. Office: Orbital Sciences Corp 21839 Atlantic Blvd Sterling VA 20166-6850

THOMPSON, DAYLE ANN, small business owner, consultant; b. Grand Forks, ND, Jan. 6, 1954; d. Duane Theodore and Anna Mae (Desautel) T.; m. Michael Gary Sciulla, Aug. 6, 1977 (div. Sept. 1980); m. Manfred Hans von Ehrenfried II, June 11, 1982. Secretarial degree, Aaker's Bus. Coll., Grand Forks, 1973; Masters Cert. in Project Mgmt., George Washington U., 1995. Receptionist U.S. Rep. Norman F. Lent U.S. Ho. of Reps., Washington, 1973-74; office mgr., personal sec. U.S. Rep. Les AuCoin, U.S. Ho. of Reps., Washington, 1975-78; bus. mgr., bookkeeper Virgin Islands Post, St. Thomas, 1978; office and pers. mgr. Internat. Energy Assocs. Ltd., Washington, 1978-82; program support mgr. MSI Svcs. Inc., Washington, 1982-84; pres., treas., chief exec. officer Tech. and Adminstrv. Svcs. Corp., Washington, 1984-2000; acctg. mgr. Carolyn Kinder, Inc., Clearwater, Fla., 1997—2002; mgmt. and acctg. sys. cons. St. Petersburg, Fla., 2000—04; pres. Get Taxes Back, Inc., Lago Vista, 2004—. Hosp. vol. ARC, Arlington, Va., 1987. Recipient Group Achievement award NASA, 1984, 93, Commendation Letter, NASA, 1985, 87, 88, 91, 93, 94, Small Bus. Prime Contractor of Yr. award Small Bus. Adminstrn. Region 5, 1994, Adminstr. award for Excellence. Mem. Washington Space Bus. Roundtable (sponsor-benefactor 1990-92). Republican. Roman Catholic. Avocations: boating, fishing, reading. Home and Office: 3102 Point Cove Lago Vista TX 78645 Personal E-mail: daylethompson@sbcglobal.net.

THOMPSON, DEAN M., II, knowledge management and learning executive; BA, U. NC, Greensboro. Dir. mktg. and MIS Stockton Bates LLP, Phila., 1992—99; chief operating officer, co-founder MoveMedia, Inc., Norristown, Pa., 1999—2000; v.p. strategic devel. Wired Vines, Inc., Plymouth Meeting, Pa., 2000; dir. mktg. and comm. Cmty. Options, Inc., Princeton, NJ, 2003—06. CEO Knowledge Shark, Trenton, NJ, 2000—; bd. adv. Practice Devel. Inst., Inc., Pub. Interest Law Ctr., Phila.; internetchief knowledge officer JH Cohn LLP, Roseland, NJ, 2006—; with Act KM Behaviour Change NOCM Braintrust CXO Cmty. Innovation People Network. Mem.: Legal Mktg. Assn., Assn. Acctg. Mktg., Am. Mktg. Assn.

THOMPSON, DEBORAH G., secondary school educator; d. Gallagher; children: James, Amy L Thomas, Michael A. BA, U. of Ala.-Birmingham, 1977; MEd, U. Montevallo, Ala., 1988; Edn. Specialist, U. Montevallo, 1990—91. Cert. tchr. Ala., 2005, Ga., 2005. Tchr. Shelby County Bd. of Edn., Columbiana, Ala., 1977—. English instr. Jefferson State C.C., Birmingham, 2000—03. Named Nat. Tchr. of the Yr., Chadwick's of Boston, 2001, Tchr. of the Yr., Thompson H.S., 2001. Mem.: Ala. Edn. Assn. (assoc.; assn. rep. 1995—2003).

THOMPSON, DENNIS FRANK, political science professor, consultant; b. Hamilton, Ohio, May 12, 1940; s. Frank and Florence (Downs) T.; m. Carol Thompson, June 22, 1963; children: Eric, David. BA, Coll. William and Mary, Williamsburg, Va., 1962, LHD (hon.), 1990; BA, Oxford U., 1964, MA, 1968; PhD, Harvard U., Cambridge, Mass., 1968. Instr. govt. Harvard U., Cambridge, Mass., 1967-68, Alfred North Whitehead prof., 1986—, founding dir., univ. ctr. ethics and the professions (now Edmond J. Safra Found. Ctr. for Ethics), 1986—2007, assoc. provost, 1996—2002, sr. advisor to the pres., 2002—05, prof. pub. policy, John F. Kennedy Sch. Govt.; prof. politics Princeton U., NJ, 1968—75, prof., 1975—86, chmn. dept. politics, 1976—79, 1982—83. Cons. to spl. counsel US Senate Select Com. on Ethics, 1990-91, US Dept. HHS, 1980, FDA, 1993. Author: The Democratic Citizen, 1970, John Stuart Mill and Representative Government, 1976, Political Ethics and Public Office, 1987 (Gladys M. Kammerer award, 1987), Ethics in Congress, 1995, (with A. Gutmann) Democracy and Disagreement, 1996, Ethics and Politics: Cases and Comments, 4th edit., 2005, Just Elections, 2002, (with A. Gutmann) Why Deliberative Democracy, 2004, Restoring Responsibility, 2005; mem. editl. bd. Polit. Theory, 1974—, Philosophy and Pub. Affairs, 1971—, Am. Polit. Sci. Rev., 1985-88; contbr. articles to profl. jours. Trustee Smith Coll., 1994-2004. Fellow Am. Acad. Arts and Scis.; mem. Am. Soc. Legal and Polit. Philosophy (v.p. 1977-80, pres. 1986-89). Office: Harvard Univ Dept Govt CGIS K422 1737 Cambridge St Cambridge MA 02138-5801 Business E-Mail: dennis_thompson@harvard.edu.*

THOMPSON, DENNIS PETERS, plastic surgeon; b. Chgo., Mar. 18, 1937; s. David John and Ruth Dorothy (Peters) T.; m. Virginia Louise Williams, June 17, 1961; children: Laura Faye, Victoria Ruth, Elizabeth Jan. BS, U. Ill., 1957, BS in Medicine, 1959, MS in Physiology, 1961, MD, 1961. Diplomate Am. Bd. Surgery, Am. Bd. Plastic Surgery. Intern Presbyn.-St. Lukes Hosp., Chgo., 1961—62; resident in gen. surgery Mayo Clinic, Rochester, Minn., 1964—66, fellow in gen. surgery, 1964—66; resident in gen. surgery Harbor Gen. Hosp., LA, 1968—70; resident in plastic surgery UCLA, 1971—73, clin. instr. plastic surgery, 1975—82, asst. clin. prof. surgery, 1982—97, assoc. clin. prof. plastic surgery, 1998—2008; clin. prof. Plastic Surgery, 2009—. Practiced medicine specializing in plastic and reconstructive surgery, LA, 1974-78, Santa Monica, Calif., 1978—2008; chmn. plastic surgery sect. St. John's Hosp., 1986-91; staff Olive View Hosp., 1982—, St. John's Hosp., 1982-2008; chmn. dept. surgery Beverly Glen Hosp., 1978-79; pres. Coop. of Am. Physicians Credit Union, 1978-80; bd. dirs. Coop. Am. Physicians, 1980-97, chmn. membership devel. com., 1983-97, treas., 1985-97. Contbr. articles to med. jours. Moderator Congl. Ch. of Northridge (Calif.), 1975-76, chmn. bd. trustees, 1973-74, 80-82; bd. dirs. L.A. Bus. Coun., 1987-90. Am. Tobacco Inst. rsch. grantee, 1959-60. Fellow ACS; mem. AMA (Physicians Recognition award 1971, 74, 77, 81, 84, 87, 90, 93, 96, 99, 2002, 05), Calif. Med. Assn., L.A. County Med. Assn. (chmn. bylaws com. 1979-80, chmn. ethics com. 1980-81, 2000-01, sec.-treas. dist. 5 1982-83, program chmn. 1983-84, pres. 1985-86, councilor 1988-96, 2001-03, councilor-at-large 2004-08, v.p. 1999-2000), Pan-Pacific Surg. Assn., Am. Soc. Plastic Surgeons, Calif. Soc. Plastic Surgeons (chmn. bylaws com. 1982-83, chmn. liability com. 1983-85, councilor 1988-91, sec. 1993-95, v.p. 1995-96, pres.-elect 1996-97, pres. 1997-98), L.A. Soc. Plastic Surgeons (sec. 1980-82, pres. 1982-97), Lipoplasty Soc. N.Am., UCLA Plastic Surgery Soc. (treas. 1983-84, v.p. 1996-98, pres. 1998-2003, 2005), Am. Soc. Aesthetic Plastic Surgery, Internat. Soc. Clin. Plastic Surgeons (bd. dirs. 1999-2006, pres. 2004-06), Am. Assn. Accreditation of Ambulatory Surg. Facilities (bd. dirs. 1995-97, 2002-09, ofcl. observer to AMA ho. of dels. 1999-2009), Western L.A. Regional C. of C. (bd. dirs. 1981-84, 86-89, chmn. legis. action com. 1978-80), Phi Beta Kappa, Alpha Omega Alpha, Nu Sigma Nu, Phi Kappa Phi, Delta Sigma Delta, Omega Beta Pi, Phi Eta Sigma. Republican. Business E-Mail: dthompson@dslextreme.com.

THOMPSON, DON, food products executive; m. Elizabeth Thompson; children: Xavier, Maya. BSc in elec. engring., Purdue U. Engr. specialist, def. systems divsn. Northrop Corp., Rolling Meadows, Ill.; restaurant systems engr. McDonald's Corp., 1990—91, project mgr., 1991—93, staff dir., then dir. ops. for Denver region, 1993, regional v.p., San Diego region, 1998, sr. v.p., restaurant support officer, Midwest divsn., 1998—2000; pres., Midwest divsn. McDonald's USA, 2000—01; pres., West divsn. McDonald's Corp., 2001—04, exec. v.p. restaurant Solutions, 2004—05, exec. v.p., COO McDonald's USA, 2005—06, pres. McDonald's USA, 2006—. Named to Power 150, Ebony mag., 2008. Office: McDonald's Corp McDonald's Plaza Oak Brook IL 60523

THOMPSON, DONALD RAYMOND, film producer, playwright; b. Long Beach, Calif., Oct. 19, 1956; s. Norman Allen and Margie Ann Thompson; m. Diana Misa Takata, June 24, 1984. BA, MA, U. Calif., LA, 1984. Dir.(prodr., writer): (films) Clouds (Best New Dir. award Bklyn. (N.Y.) Internat. Film Festival, 1999); co-prodr.: Singing The Bones (named Ofcl. Selection, Montreal (Can.) Internat. Film Festival, 2001), Through The Hollow Bamboo: Tibet In Song; author: (plays) Democracy: A Work In Progress, Tibet Does Not Exist, L.A. Book Of The Dead; co-editor: Your Life Is A Movie: The Best of SolPix, 2002-2005. Mem.: Ind. Feature Project. Democrat. Office: nextPix Productions LLC 295 Greenwich Street #348 New York NY 10007 Office Fax: 212-658-9627; Home Fax: 212-658-9627. Business E-Mail: don@nextpix.com.

THOMPSON, DOROTHEA KATHLEEN, microbiologist; b. Bellefonte, Pa., May 25, 1963; d. Charles Carr and Deborah Ann (Evenson) T. BA in English and Microbiology, U. Tenn., 1986; MS in Microbiology, Va. Polytechnic Inst./State U., 1989; MA in English, Pa. State U., 1992; PhD in Microbiology, Ohio State U., 1997. Grad. rsch. asst. dept. anaerobic microbiology Va. Tech., Blacksburg, 1986-89; grad. tchg. asst./lectr. dept. English Pa. State, University Park, Pa., 1990-92; grad. rsch. and tchg. assoc. dept. microbiology Ohio State, Columbus, 1992-97; ORISE postdoctoral fellow FDA/CBER divsn. bacterial products, Rockville, Md., 1998—99; rsch. assoc. environ. scis. divsn. Microbial Genomics Group, Oak Ridge Nat. Lab., Tenn., 1999—2002; rsch. staff scientist Oak Ridge Nat. Lab., 2002—05, group leader microbial ecology and functional genomics group, 2004—05; prof. dept. biol. scis. Purdue U., 2005—. Tchg. asst. Howard Hughes Scholars Inst. in Genetics, University Park, 1992; vice-speaker Va. Tech. Grad. Student Assembly, Blacksburg, 1987-88; grad. student rep. Coun. on Rsch. and Grad. Studies, Columbus, 1993-94; departmental del. Ohio State Coun. Grad. Students, 1993-94. Contbr. articles to profl. jours. Mem. Am. Soc. Microbiology, Phi Beta Kappa, Phi Kappa Phi. Avocations: world travel, hiking, creative writing. Home: 3318 Reed St West Lafayette IN 47906-5102 Office: Purdue U Dept Biol Scis 915 W State St West Lafayette IN 47907-2054 Home Phone: 865-588-6744, 765-463-0301; Office Phone: 765-496-8301.

THOMPSON, DOUGLAS C., engineer; b. Scottsdale, Ariz., Feb. 28, 1974; s. Douglas and Beverly Thompson; m. Gabriela Cruz Thompson, June 5, 2004. PhD, Ariz. State U., Tempe, 2008. Rsch. assoc. Ariz. State U., 2004—08; sr. process engr. Microsemi Corp., Bend, Oreg., 2008—. Contbr. articles to profl. jours. Mem.: Materials Rsch. Soc. Achievements include patents pending for microwave induced ion cleave and patternless transfer of semiconductor films. Office: Microsemi Corp 405 SW Columbia St Bend OR 97702 Personal E-mail: douglas.c.thompson@gmail.com. Business E-Mail: dthompson@microsemi.com.

THOMPSON, ED, state agency administrator, public health service officer, epidemiologist, educator; BA, Millsaps Coll.; MD, U. Miss. Sch. Medicine; MPH, Johns Hopkins U. Sch. Hygine and Pub. Health. Lic. Miss. State Bd. Med. Licensure, 1979, cert. in pub. health and gen. preventive medicine Am. Bd. Preventive Medicine, 1991. Clinician, dep. chief disease control Miss. State Dept. Health, 1982—85, state epidemiologist, 1983—93, chief bur. preventative health services, 1985—93, state health officer, 1993—2002, 2007—; dep. dir. pub. health services Centers for Disease Control, dir. pub. health practice; prof. medicine U. Miss. Sch. Medicine, Jackson, 2006—. Mem. exec. com. Coun. State and Territorial Epidemiologists, 1988—93, pres., 1992—93; mem. exec. com. Assn. State and Territorial Health Officials, 1998—2001, pres., 1998—99; mem. Adv. Com. on Immunization Practices; mem. adv. com. to dir. Centers for Disease Control; mem. Sec.'s Adv. Coun. for Pub. Health Preparedness. Mem.: AMA, Miss. Pub. Health Assn., Miss. State Med. Assn., Am. Pub. Health Assn. Office: Miss State Dept Health 570 E Woodrow Wilson Dr Jackson MS 39216 Office Phone: 601-576-7634.*

THOMPSON, EDLEECA PAYNE, humanities educator; d. Harold Leonard and Thelma Daniels Thompson. BA, BFA, U. Tex., Austin, 1980; MFA, U. N.Tex., Denton, 1984; MA, Southern Meth. U., Dallas, 1999. Asst. Curator & staff photographer African Am. Mus., Dallas, 1983—84, Curator exhbns. & Collections, 1991—96; Quality Control Mgr. Barry's Camera & Video, Dallas, 1985—89; adj. instr. art history & Art appreciation, Collin County Cmty. Coll., Plano, Tex., 1999—2002, Eastfield Coll., Mesquite, Tex., 1999—2002; adj. instr. photography Mt. View Coll., Dallas, 1991—99; instr, Photography, South Dallas Cultural Ctr., Tex., 1997—2001; adj. instr. photography history Tex. A&M U. Commerce, Tex., 1999—2001; prof. humanities & cultural Studies, Brookhaven College, Dallas, 2002—; photographer Tex. Black Photographers, 2007. Exhibitions include photography Ceramics, 14th Southwest BlackArt Exhbn., Breaking into the Mainstream:. Mem St. John Bapt. Ch., Grand Prairie, Tex., 1986—99; dir. Thompson Daniels Archives, Dallas, 2001—09. Recipient Merit award, Junior Black Acad. Arts & Letters, Dallas, 1980, Purchase award, U. North Tex., 1984; rsch. fellowship, Comparative Analysis Four African Am. Mus. Smithsonian Inst. Washington DC, 1994. Mem.: ASCD, Faculty Coun. Brookhaven Coll. Dallas, Cmty. Coll. Humanities Assn., Nat. Inst. Staff Orgnl. Devel., Assn. Humanities Edn. Office Phone: 972-860-4236. Business E-Mail: ethompson@dcccd.edu.

THOMPSON, EDWARD IVINS BRADBRIDGE, biological chemistry and genetics educator, endocrinologist; b. Burlington, Iowa, Dec. 20, 1933; s. Edward Bills and Lois Elizabeth (Bradbridge) T.; m. Lynn Taylor Parsons; children: Elizabeth Lynn, Edward Ernest Bradbridge. BA with distinction, Rice U., 1955; postgrad., Cambridge U., 1957-58; MD, Harvard U., 1960. Intern The Presbyn. Hosp., NYC, 1960-61, asst. resident internal medicine, 1961-62; rsch. assoc. Nat. Inst. Mental Health, NIH, Bethesda, Md., 1962-64; rsch. scientist Nat. Inst. Arthritis and Metabolic Diseases, NIH, Bethesda, Md., 1964-68, Lab of Biochemistry, Nat. Cancer Inst., NIH, Bethesda, Md., 1968-73, sect. chief, 1973-84; prof., chmn. dept. human biol. chemistry and genetics U. Tex. Med. Br., Galveston, 1984—2003, I.H. Kempner prof., 1984—2005, prof. internal medicine, 1984—, interim dir., Sealy Ctr. for Molecular Sci., 1996—2003, prof., dept. biochem. & molecular biology, 2003—, J.P. Saunders prof., 2006. UNESCO vis. expert Inst. Genetics, Hungarian Acad. Sci., Szeged, Hungary, 1976; attending physician Nat. Naval Med. Ctr., Bethesda, 1978-80; chmn. hormones and cancer task force NIH, Bethesda, 1978-80; co-chmn. Gordon Rsch. Conf., 1980; mem. adv. com. on Biochem. and Chem. Carcinogenesis, Am. Cancer Soc., 1982-86; mem. revision com. Endocrinology adv. panel U.S. Pharmacopoeial Conv., Inc., 1980-85; mem. coun. for clin. investigation and rsch. awds., Am. Cancer Soc., 1989-93; bd. sci. overseers Pennington Nutrition Rsch. Ctr. La. State U., 1991-98; Fulbright prof., Marburg, Germany. 1992-93; mem. edn. bd. Am. Med. and Grad. Depts. Biochemistry, 1999-2003; co-organizer FASEB Summer Conf., 2006. Co-editor Gene Expression and Carcinogenesis in Cultured Liver, 1975, Steroid Receptors and the Management of Cancer, 1979, DNA: Protein Interactions and Gene Regulation; other vols. in field; assoc. editor Cancer Rsch. jour., 1976-86; corr. editor Jour. Steroid Biochemistry, 1977-85; founding editor-in-chief Molecular Endocrinology Jour., 1985-92; editor-in-chief Endocrine Reviews, 2001-05; mem. editl. bd. Steroids, 1995—, Molecular Endocrinology, 1998; sect. editor: Handbook of Cell Signalling, 2004, 05; contbr. over 250 sci. articles to profl. jours. Mem. troop com. Girl Scouts U.S., Rockville, Md., 1970-76; mem. PTA, Rockville, 1967-77, Wilderness Soc., Washington, 1964-75; initiator sci. edn. liaison program Galveston Pub. Schs., 1991; mem. pres.'s cabinet U. Tex. Med. Br. Served as med. dir. USPHS, 1962-84. Grantee NIH, Walls Rsch., Nat. Inst. Diabetes and Digestive and Kidney Diseases, Nat. Cancer Inst.; Am. Cancer Soc. scholar, 1992-93; Fulbright scholar; named Disting. alumnus Rice U., 2001; honored Signalling Life and Death Symposium, 2004; recipient J.G. Sinclair award Sigma Xi, 1997, Educator award Endocrine Soc., 2004; finalist 4th Pl. age group triathlon Sr. Olympics, 2005, fellow Am. Assn. Advi Sci., 2005. Mem.: SW Environ. Mutagen Soc., Am. Coll. Med Genetics (affiliate), Am. Soc. Microbiology, Endocrine Soc., Am. Soc. Biol. Chemists, Am. Assn. Cancer Rsch., Am. Soc. Cell Biology, Pres.'s Clubs of Rice U. and U. Tex. Med. Br., Harvard Club, Bar Harbor Yacht Club, Phi Kappa Phi, Alpha Omega Alpha, Phi Beta Kappa. Achievements include patent on anti-tumor activity of a modified fragment of glucocorticoid receptor. Office: U Tex Med Br Dept Biochem & Molecular Biology Galveston TX 77555-1068 Office Phone: 409-772-3367. Business E-Mail: bthompso@utmb.edu.

THOMPSON, ELIZABETH ALISON, mathematics professor; b. Oxford, Eng., May 22, 1949; d. Edward Crossley and Octavia Bridget Noble Thompson. BA, U. Cambridge, Eng., 1970, diploma in Math. Stats., 1971, PhD, 1974, DSc, 1988. Cert. in postdoc. studies Stanford U., Calif., 1975. Rsch. fellow King's Coll., Cambridge, 1975—78; lectr. Cambridge U., 1976—85; ofcl. fellow, dir. studies math. Newnham Coll., Cambridge, 1981—85; prof. U. Wash., Seattle. Contbr. articles to numerous sci. jours. Recipient Jerome K. Sacks award, Nat. Inst. Statis. Scis., 2001, Weldon prize, U. Oxford, 2001, Merit award, NIGMS, 2008—; named Fisher Lectr., COPPS, 1994, Neymann Lectr., Inst. Math. Stats., 1998, Fisher Meml. Lectr., R. A. Fisher Soc., Eng., 2006; fellowship, Giggenheim Found., 2002—03. Mem.: NAS, Internat. Statis. Inst., Am. Acad. Arts and Scis. Office: Univ Wash Dept Stats PO Box 354322 Seattle WA 98195-4322 Business E-Mail: eathomp@u.washington.edu.

THOMPSON, EMMA, actress; b. London, Apr. 15, 1959; d. Eric Thompson and Phyllida Law; m. Kenneth Branaugh, Aug. 20, 1989 (div. Oct. 1995); m. Greg Wise, July 29, 2003, 1 child Gaia Romilly Wise. Student of English, Cambridge U., Eng. Performances include: (films) Henry V, 1989, The Tall Guy, 1989, Dead Again, 1991, Impromptu, 1991, Howard's End, 1992 (Acad. award for best actress 1993), Peter's Friends, 1992, Much Ado About Nothing, 1993, The Remains of the Day, 1993 (Acad. award nominee for best actress 1993), In the Name of the Father, 1993 (Acad. award nominee for best supporting actress 1993), My Father, the Hero, 1994, Junior, 1994, Carrington, 1995 (Best Actress award Nat. Bd. Rev. 1995), Sense and Sensibility, 1995 (Golden Globe award nominee for best actress in film 1996, Acad. award nominee for best actress 1996), Winter Guest, 1996, Primary Colors, 1998, Judas Kiss, 1998, Maybe Baby, 2000, Treasure Planet (voice), 2002, Love Actually, 2003, Imagining Argentina, 2003, Harry Potter and the Prisoner of Azbakan, 2004, Nanny McPhee, 2005, Stranger Than Fiction, 2006, Harry Potter and the Order of the Phoenix, 2007, Brideshead Revisited, 2008, Last Chance Harvey, 2008; (TV films) Al Fresco, Up For Grabs (a.k.a. Sexually Transmitted), Tutti Frutti, Fortunes of War, 1987, Cheers, 1991, Wit, 2001; (miniseries) Angels in America, 2003; (London stage) Me and My Girl, Look Back in Anger; also writer screen adaptation: Sense and Sensibility (Jane Austin), 1995 (Best Screenplay award NY Film Critics 1995, LA Film Critics 1995, Boston Film Critics 1995, Golden Globe award for best adapted screenplay 1996, Acad. award for best adapted screenplay 1996, BAFTA Best Actress award 1996), Nanny McPhee, 2005. Active in Footlights Theatrical Group, Cambridge, Eng. Office: William Morris Agy 151 S El Camino Dr Beverly Hills CA 90212-2775*

THOMPSON, EVA M., humanities educator; d. Larry and Lula Bea Thompson; children: Montayna Rosebud, Jamal Anwar Mebane. PhD, Ohio State U., Columbus, 1995. Tchg. asst. Ohio State U., 1992—95; asst. prof. Kennesaw State U., Ga., 1995—2004, assoc. prof., 2004—; instr. Winston-Salem State U., NC, 1995—98. Cons. Franklin County Schs., Columbus, 1992. Contbr. columns in newspapers. Recipient award, Mu Xi Chpt. Alpha Kappa Mu Honor Soc., 1992, Chancellor's award, U. Sys. Ga., 1999, Post-Tenure Faculty Enhancement Leave Funding award, Kennesaw State U., 2005—06; HSS Humanities fellowship, 2007. Office: Kennesaw State Univ 1000 Chastain Rd #2701 Kennesaw GA 30144-5591 Office Phone: 770-499-3625. Office Fax: 770-423-6524. Business E-Mail: ethompso@kennesaw.edu.

THOMPSON, EWA M., foreign language educator; b. Kaunas, Lithuania; came to U.S., 1963; d. Jozef and Maria Majewski; m. James R. Thompson. BA in English and Russian, U. Warsaw, Poland, 1963; MFA in Piano, Sopot Conservatory Music, 1963; MA in English, Ohio U., 1964; PhD in Comparative Lit., Vanderbilt U., 1967. Instr. Vanderbilt U., Nashville, Tenn., 1964-67; asst. prof. Ind. State U., Terre Haute, 1967-68, Ind. U., 1968-70, Rice U., Houston, 1967-73, assoc. prof., 1974-79, prof., 1979—, chair, 1987-90; assoc. prof. U. Va., Charlottesville, 1973-74. Cons. NEH, 1973—, The John D. and Catherine T. MacArthur Found., The John Simon Guggenheim Found., U.S. Dept. Edn.; vis. cons. Tex. A&M U.; seminar dir. NEH Summer Inst., Southeastern La. U., 1990; chair Russian lit. conf. Rice U., 1989; lectr. various colls. and univs. Author: Russian Formalism and Anglo-American New Criticism: A Comparative Study, 1971, Witold Gombrowicz, 1979, Polish transl., 2002, Understanding Russia: The Holy Fool in Russian Culture, 1987, Chinese transl. 1995, 2nd Chinese edit. 1998, The Search for Self-Definition in Russian Literature, 1991, Imperial Knowledge: Russian Literature and Colonialism, 2000, Polish transl., 2000, Ukrainian transl., 2006; editor the Sarmatian Rev., 1988—; contbr. articles to profl. jours., chpts. to books. Recipient Silver Thistle award Houston's Scottish Heritage Found, 1988; Mellon grantee, 1990, Rice U. grantee, 1990, Internat. Rsch. and Exchanges Sr. Scholar grantee, 1991; Hoover Inst. fellow, 1988; Vanderbilt U. scholar, 1964-67, Will Herberg award, ISI, 2003, K. Turzanski Found. award, 2004. Roman Catholic. Personal E-mail: sarmatianreview@yahoo.com.

THOMPSON, FRANCES MCBROOM, mathematics professor, writer; BS in Edn., Abilene Christian U., Tex., 1963; MA, U. Tex., Austin, 1967; EdD, U. Ga., Athens, 1973. Math. cons., tchr., 1963—84; math. prof. Tex. Woman's U., Denton, 1984—. Author: (tchr. resource books) Hands on Math for Grades 4-8, 1994, Hands on Algebra for Grades 7-12, 1998, Math Proficiency Lessons and Activities, Fourth Grade, 2003, Math Essentials, Middle School Level, 2005, Math Essentials, High School Level, 2005, Math Essentials, Elementary School Level, 2007. Bible class coord.; tchr., 1982—95. Recipient Mary Mason Lyon Jr. Faculty award, Tex. Woman's U., 1992, Alumni Citation for achievement, Abilene Christian U., 1998, Grover C. Morlan Outstanding Educator award, 2005, Distinction in Svc. award, Tex. Woman's U., 2006. Mem.: Rsch. Coun. for Math. Learning, Tex. Coun. Tchrs. Math., Tex. Assn. Suprs. Math., Math. Assn. Am., Nat. Coun. Tchrs. Math. Office: Tex Woman's U PO Box 425886 Denton TX 76204-5886 Business E-Mail: fthompson@twu.edu.

THOMPSON, FRED, public relations executive, former medical association administrator; BA, Mich. State U., East Lansing. Mgmt. positions Burson-Marsteller Pub. Rels., Manning Selvage & Lee; pres., COO Jane Goodall Inst., 2001—05; pres., CEO Am. Liver Found., NYC, 2005—07; pres. pub. rels. divsn. Creative Partners LLC, 2007—. Bd. dirs. Real Sch. Gardens; chmn. Ctr. Non-profit Growth. Recipient Silver Anvil award (five), Pub. Rels. Soc. Am. Office: Creative Ptnrs One Stamford Landing Stamford CT 06902 Office Phone: 203-705-9200.*

THOMPSON, FRED DALTON, actor, former United States Senator from Tennessee; b. Sheffield, Ala., Aug. 19, 1942; s. Fletcher and Ruth Thompson; m. Sarah Elizabeth Lindsey, Sept. 12, 1959; children: Tony, Daniel, Elizabeth Betsy Panici(dec.); m. Jeri Kahn, June 29, 2002; 1 child, Hayden Victoria. BS, Memphis State U., 1964; JD, Vanderbilt U., 1967. Asst. U.S. atty. (mid. dist.) Tenn. US Dept. Justice, 1969-72; minority counsel US Senate Select Com. on Presdl. Campaign Activities (Watergate Com.), 1973-74; pvt. practice, 1975-94; spl. counsel to Gov. State of Tenn., 1980; spl. counsel US Senate Fgn. Rels. Coms., 1980—81, US Senate Intelligence Com., 1982; atty. Arent, Fox, Kintner, Plotkin & Kahn, 1991-94; US Senator from Tenn., 1994—2003. Chmn., US Senate Govtl. Affairs Com., 1997-2001, Internat. Security Adv. Bd., US Dept. State, 2005-07; vis. fellow Am. Enterprise Inst., mem. US-China Econ. & Security Review Commn. Actor: (films) Marie: A True Story, 1985, No Way Out, 1987, Feds, 1988, Fat Man and Little Boy, 1989, The Hunt for Red October, 1990, Days of Thunder, 1990, Die Hard 2: Die Harder, 1990, Flight of the Intruder,1991, Class Action, 1991, Necessary Roughness, 1991, Curly Sue, 1991, Cape Fear, 1991, Aces: Iron Eagle III, 1992, Thunderheart, 1992, White Sands, 1992, Born Yesterday, 1993, In the Line of Fire, 1993, Baby's Day Out, 1994, Download This, 2002, (voice only) Racing Stripes, 2005; (TV movies) Unholy Matrimony, 1988, Bed of Lies, 1992, Stay the Night, 1992, Day-O, 1992, Keep the Change, 1992, Barbarians at the Gate, 1993,(voice only) Rachel and Andrew Jackson: A Love Story, 2001, Evil Knieval, 2004, Looking for Comedy in the Muslim World, 2005; (TV series) Law & Order, 2002-07; (TV appearances) Wiseguy, 1988, China Beach, 1989, Roseanne, 1989, Matlock, 1989, Sex & the City, 2000, Law & Order: Special Victims Unit, 2003-2006, Law & Order: Trial By Jury 2005-2006, Law & Order: Criminal Intent, 2005, Conviction 2006; author: At That Point in Time: The Inside Story of the Senate Watergate Committee, 1975. Mem.: Coun. Fgn. Rels. Republican. Office: William Morris Agy 1325 Ave of the Americas New York NY 10019

THOMPSON, GEORGE ALBERT, geophysicist, educator; b. Swissvale, Pa., June 5, 1919; s. George Albert Sr. and Maude Alice (Harkness) T.; m. Anita Kimmell, July 20, 1944; children: Albert J., Dan A., David C. BS, Pa. State U., 1941; MS, MIT, 1942; PhD, Stanford U., 1949. Geologist, geophysicist U.S. Geol. Survey, Menlo Park, Calif., 1942-49; asst. prof. Stanford (Calif.) U., 1949-55, assoc. prof., 1955-60, prof. geophysics, 1960—, chmn. geophysics dept., 1967-86, chmn. geology dept., 1979-82, Otto N. Miller prof. earth scis., 1980-89, dean sch. earth scis., 1987-89. Part-time geologist US Geol. Survey, Menlo Park, 1949-76; cons. adv. com. on reactor safeguards Nuclear Regulation Commn., Washington, 1974-94; mem. bd. earth sci. NRC, 1986-88, vice chmn. Yucca Mountain Hydrology-tectonics panel NRC, 1990-92; mem. sr. external events rev. com. Lawrence Livermore Nat. Lab., 1989-93; mem. exec. com. Inc. Rsch. Inst. for Seismology, Washington, 1990-92; mem. Coun. on Continental Sci. Drilling, 1990-94; cons. Los Alamos Nat. Lab. on volcano-tectonic processes, 1993-96, S.W. Rsch. Inst., 1993; chair com. to review sci. issues NRC, Ward Valley, Calif., 1994-95; mem. panel on probabalistic volcanic hazard analysis Geomatrix Cons., Inc., 1995-96, 2005— Author over 100 research papers. With USN, 1944—46. Recipient John Wesley Powell award US Geol. Survey, 1999; NSF postdoctoral fellow, 1956-57, Guggenheim Found. fellow, 1963-64 Fellow AAAS, Geol. Soc. Am. (coun. mem. 1983-86, George P. Woollard award 1983, v.p. 1995, pres. 1996, Penrose Medal, 2008), Am. Geophys. Union; mem. NAS (chair geology sect. 2000-03), Seismol. Soc. Am., Soc. Exploration Geophysicists. Avocation: forestry. Home: 421 Adobe Pl Palo Alto CA 94306-4501 Office: Stanford U Geophysics Dept Stanford CA 94305-2215 Home Phone: 650-493-3230; Office Phone: 650-723-3714. Business E-Mail: gathomps@stanford.edu.

THOMPSON, GEORGE FLETCHER, editor, publishing executive; b. Denver, Jan. 4, 1954; s. Richard Potter and Alasee Payne Thompson; m. Cynthia Ann Roberts, Sept. 2, 1978; 1 child, Haley Ellen. Student, U. Pa., Phila., 1971—73; BA in English, U. Ala., 1977; MA in Landscape Architecture, U. Wis., Madison, 1990. Acquisitions editor Johns Hopkins U. Press, Balt., 1984—89; founder & dir., thirteen book series, 1989—; founder and pres. Ctr. for Am. Places, Santa Fe and Staunton, Va., 1990—2007; dir. Ctr. Am. Places Columbia Coll., Chgo., 2007—. Editor: Landscape in America (Notable Book of 1995); co-editor: Ecological Design and Planning, 1997, 2007; dir.(founder): (book series) My Kind of Series, 2008; co-author: Registered Places of New Mexico, 1995, Beyond the Great Divide, 1992; editor, curator: Chicago Portfolio: Where Geography and Photography Meet, 2006. Recipient Publs. award, Assn. Am. Geographers, 2000, Publs. citation, Vernacular Architecture Forum, 2002, Comm. award, Coun. Educators in Landscape Architecture, 2005. Mem.: Sigma Lamda Alpha. Independent. Avocations: reading, gardening, travel, photography, music. Office: Columbia Coll Chgo 600 S Michigan Ave Chicago IL 60605-1996 Office Phone: 312-369-6943. Office Fax: 540-886-5263. Business E-Mail: editors@americanplaces.org.

THOMPSON, GEORGE KENNEDY (KEN THOMPSON), retired bank executive; b. Rocky Mount, NC, Nov. 25, 1950; s. Maynard and Stacy Kennedy Thompson; m. Kathylee B. Thompson; 3 children. BA in Am. Studies, U.N.C., Chapel Hill, 1973; MBA, Wake Forest U., 1975. With First Union Corp., Charlotte, NC, 1976—2001, head S.E. divsn., mgr. mid. market dept., mgr. N.Y. loan prodn. office, pres. First Union-Ga., sr. v.p., head human resources, pres. First Union-Fla., vice chmn. corp., head global capital markets, 1998—99, pres., CEO, 1999—2001, Wachovia Corp. (merger of First Union and Wachovia Corp.), 2001—08, chmn., 2001—08; sr. adv. Aquiline Capital Partners, 2009—. Bd. dirs. Hewlett Packard Co., 2006-, N.Y. Clearing House; mem. Fin. Services Roundtable Fin. Svcs. Forum, chmn.-elect. Bd. visitors U. N.C., Chapel Hill, Babcock Grad. Sch. Mgmt., Wake Forest U.; bd. dirs. N.C. Blumenthal Performing Arts Ctr., Charlotte Latin Sch., United Way, Charlotte, Teach for America, Carolinas Healthcare Systems, Charlotte Inst. Tech. Innovation; mem. met. bd. YMCA, chmn. bd. Foundation for the Carolinas Morehead scholar U. N.C. Office: Aquiline Capital Partners LLC 535 Madison Ave New York NY 10022*

THOMPSON, GEORGE LEE, retail executive, consultant; b. Denver, June 12, 1933; s. George H. and Frances M. (Murphy) Thompson; m. Patricia M. Mackenzie, Sept. 25, 1993; children: Shannon, Tracy, Bradley. BS in Bus., U. Colo., 1957; degree in Advanced Mgmt., NYU, 1969. With GTE Sylvania, Danvers, Mass., 1957-65, nat. sales mgr., 1965-67, mktg. mgr., 1967-68; v.p. sales entertainment products Batavia, NY, 1968-73; dir. corp. mktg. Stamford, Conn., 1973-74; v.p. mktg. Servomation Corp., NYC, 1974-76, exec. v.p., 1976-78, Singer Co., Edison, NJ, 1978-81, pres., 1981-83; pres. consumer products SCM Corp., NYC, 1983-86; pres., CEO Smith-Corona Corp., New Canaan, Conn., 1986-89, chmn., CEO, 1989-95; chmn. Mackenzie-Thompson Assocs., Essex, Conn., 1995—. Bd. dirs. Vol. Products, Inc.; chair Sweet P's, Essex, Conn., 1998—; dir. Conn. State Tourism Coun., 2003-, exec. com. mem, 2007-. Chmn. Standards Com. U.S. Dept. Commerce; mem. bus. alumni adv. coun. U. Colo., 1989—94; mem. bd. overseers Sch. Bus. U. Conn., 1993—96; mem. Pres.'s Export Coun., 1991—93; mem. bd. advisors Jr. League; chmn. Essex Econ. Devel. Commn., Conn., 2008; chmn. Main Street renovation com. City of Essex; bd. dirs. Internat. Tennis Hall of Fame, Am. Jr. Golf Found., 1986—89, Am. Jr. Golf Assn., 1986—2000, United Way of New Canaan, 1989—93; pres. Essex Bd. Trade, 2005—. Recipient Disting. Bus. Alumni award, U. Colo., 1990. Mem. Computer and Bus. Equipment Mfg. Assn. (bd. dirs. 1992-94), Sales and Mktg. Execs. Internat. (trustee), Am. Mgmt. Assn. (trustee, exec. com. chmn., gen. mgmt. coun. 1989-99), St. John Assn. (bd. dirs., pres. 1983-93), Woodway Country Club, Club at Seabrook Island, Wilton Riding Club (bd. govs. 1980-83), Navesink Country Club (bd. govs. 1983-86), Harbour Ridge Yacht and Country Club, Essex Yacht Club, Chi Psi. Episcopalian. Office: Mackenzie Thompson Assocs 51 Main St Essex CT 06426-1150 also: Sweet P's LLC Griswold Sq Essex CT 06426 Home Phone: 860-767-8201; Office Phone: 860-767-7805. Personal E-mail: leethompson51@sbcglobal.net.

THOMPSON, GERALD EVERETT, economics professor; b. Leland, Iowa, Feb. 22, 1924; s. Gilbert Theodore and Clara Marie (Charlson) T.; m. Betty Phyllis Collman, Aug. 26, 1950; 1 child, David Forsyth. BA, U. Iowa, 1947, MA, 1948, PhD, 1953. Asst. prof. econs. U. Toledo, Ohio, 1950-54; from asst. to full prof. econs. U. Nebr., Lincoln, 1954—; vis. assoc. prof. statis. U. Mich., Ann Arbor, 1965-66. Author: Linear Programming, 1971, Statistics for Decisions, 1972, Management Science, 1976, Microeconomics, 2001. 1st lt. U.S. Army Air Corps. Harvard U. Faculty fellow Ford Found., Cambridge, Mass., 1959-60. Mem. Am. Econs. Assn., Am. Statis. Assn. Home: 927 Ashworth Rd Apt 102 West Des Moines IA 50265

THOMPSON, GERALDINE KELLEHER RICHTER, retired orthopedist; b. Tokyo, Aug. 22, 1948; (parents Am. citizens); d. Edward Elkins and Marguerite Geraldine Kelleher; m. Wayne Wray Thompson, Dec. 30, 2000; m. Paul S. Richter (div.); children: Karl Kelleher Richter, Brian Kelleher Richter, Kelly Kelleher Richter. BA with high honors, Wellesley Coll., Mass., 1969; MD, Georgetown U., Washington, 1973. Intern internal medicine Georgetown U. Hosp., Washington, 1973—74, residency orthop. surgery, 1974—78; pvt. practice orthop. surgery Fairfax and Manassas, Va., 1978—2002; assoc. prof. orthop. surgery Georgetown U., Washington, 1978—2002; fellow Am. Acad. Orthop. Surgery, 1981—2001. Pres. Prince William Med. Soc., 1999—2000. Parent leader Boy Scouts Am., 1990—99; mem. parents assn. St. Albans Sch., Washington, Nat. Cathedral Sch. Girls. Fellow: Am. Acad. Orthop. Surgeons; mem.: Wellesley Literary Cir., AOA, Sigma Xi, Phi Beta Kappa. Avocations: art history, literature, cultural history, history of medicine. Home: 908 Deer Road Bryn Mawr PA 19010

THOMPSON, GLENN W., JR., United States Representative from Pennsylvania, former health facility administrator; b. Bellefonte, Pa., July 27, 1959; m. Penny Thompson; children: Parker, Logan, Kale. BS in Therapeutic Recreation, Pa. State U., 1981; MEd in Health Sci., Therapeutic Recreation, Temple U., Phila., 1998. Lic. nursing home adminstr., Marywood U., 2006. Residential services aide Centre Crest Nursing Home, 1977—80, Hope Enterprises, 1981—82; recreational therapist The Williamsport Hosp., 1986—95; rehabilitation services mgr. Susquehanna Health Services, 1995—2009; mem. US Congress from 5th Pa. Dist., 2009—. Dir., pres. Pa. Therapeutic Recreation Soc.; dir. Pa. Head Injury Found.; tech. expert mem., inpatient rehab Ctrs. Medicare and Medicaid Services; adj. faculty Cambria County CC, 1997—99; bd. mem., treas. Am. Therapeutic Recreation Assn., 1997—2000, pres., 1998—2003; bd. mem. Workforce Investment Bd., 2002—07; mem., internat. adv. coun. Commn. the Accreditation Rehabilitation Facilities, 2006—08. Mem. Bellefonte Intervally C. of C., 1977—2000; scoutmaster Howard Boy Scout Troop 353, 1981—2008; pres., fire fighter, EMT, rescue technician Howard Vol. Fire Co., 1982—2008; mem. Bald Eagle Area Sch. Bd., 1990—96; sr. v.p. Juniata Valley Boy Scout Coun., 2005—07, pres., 2007—; alt. del. Rep. Nat. Convention, 2004; chair Centre County Rep. Party, 2002—; mem. Howard First United Ch. of Christ; bd. mem. Pvt. Industry Coun. Centre County, 1999—2000; bd. mem. vice-chair Pvt. Industry Coun. Ctrl. Corridors, 2000—08. Mem.: Pa. Rural Devel. Coun., Pa. Rural Health Assn., Leadership Centre County (grad. 2006), Rep. Governors Club. Republican. Protestant. Office: US Congress 124 Cannon House Office Bldg Washington DC 20515-3805 also: Dist Office 3555 Benner Pike Ste 101 Bellefonte PA 16823 Office Phone: 202-225-5121, 814-353-0215. Office Fax: 202-225-5796, 814-353-0218.*

THOMPSON, GORDON, JR., federal judge; b. San Diego, Dec. 28, 1929; s. Gordon and Garnet (Meese) T.; m. Jean Peters, Mar. 17, 1951; children— John M., Peter Renwick, Gordon III. Grad., U. So. Calif., 1951, Southwestern U. Sch. Law, Los Angeles, 1956. Bar: Calif. 1956. With Dist. Atty.'s Office, County of San Diego, 1957-60; partner firm Thompson & Thompson, San Diego, 1960-70; U.S. dist. judge So. Dist. Calif., San Diego, 1970—, chief judge, 1984-91, sr. judge, 1994—. Mem. ABA, Am. Bd. Trial Advocates, San Diego County Bar Assn. (v.p. 1970), San Diego Yacht Club, Delta Chi. Office: US Dist Ct 940 Front St San Diego CA 92101-8994 Office Phone: 619-557-6480.

THOMPSON, GREGORY LEE, social sciences educator; b. Huntington Park, Calif., June 14, 1946; s. Karl Windsor and Virginia Alice (Hanna) T. AB in Geography, U. Calif., Davis, 1968; M of City Planning, U. Calif., Berkeley, 1970; PhD in Social Scis., U. Calif., Irvine, 1987. Transp. planner City of Edmonton (Alberta) Transit Sys., 1970-72; transp. analyst Can. Transport Commn., Ottawa, Ontario, 1972-73; transp. coord. City of Berkeley (Calif.) Planning Dept., 1973-74; sr. transp. planner San Diego County, 1974-77, Met. Transp. Devel. Bd., San Diego, 1977-80; sr. cons. Mass Transit, Calif. Assembly, Sacramento, 1980-81; rsch. fellow Hagley Mus. & Libr., Wilmington, Del., 1987-88; asst. prof. Fla. State U., Tallahassee, 1988-94, assoc. prof., 1994—2003, prof., 2003—. Author: The Passenger Train in the Motor Age: California 1910-1941, 1993; contbr. articles to profl. jours. Organizer, pres. Citizens of Rail Calif., San Diego, 1976—80. Named Advanced Rsch. fellow Andrew W. Mellon/NEH, 1987-88, Disting. Student scholar Sch. Engring. U. Calif., Irvine, 1983. Mem. Am. Planning Assn. (sect. dir. San Diego), Soc. for History of Technology, Econ. History Assn., Bus. History Assn., Planning History Assn., Am. Inst. Cert. Planners. Democrat. Avocations: photography, swimming. Home: 418 E Georgia St Tallahassee FL 32301 Office: Fla State U Dept Urban Regional Pl Tallahassee FL 32306 Office Phone: 850-644-8514.

THOMPSON, GREGORY LYNN, secondary school educator; b. Joliet, Ill., July 12, 1960; s. Adolph and Wessie Mae Thompson; children: Devin Gregory, Megan Christine, Jaylin Marie. BBA, U. St. Francis, Joliet, Ill., 2004, MEd, 2005, U. Aurora, Ill., 2008. Chem. operator Flint Hills Resources, BP Amoco, Channahon, Ill., 1989—2004; head sophmore basketball coach Joliet Ctrl. HS, Joliet, Ill., 2005—08, substitute dean, 2006—08, mem. sch. improvement com., 2009. Co-leader, dist. wide strategic plan com. Joliet Twp. HS, Ill., 2008. Home: 4208 White Tail Ct Joliet IL 60431 Office: Joliet Twp Dist 201 E Jefferson Joliet IL 60432 Business E-Mail: gthompson@gths.org.

THOMPSON, HAROLD LEE, lawyer; b. Dayton, Ohio, Feb. 17, 1945; s. Harold Edward Thompson and Johnita Dorothy (Cox) Metcalf; children: Aishah T., Aliya S. BS in Acctg., Cen. State U., Wilberforce, Ohio, 1967; JD, U. Conn., 1972. Bar: Ohio 1975, US Dist. Ct. (so. dist.) Ohio 1975, DC 1976, US Ct. Appeals (4th cir.) 1990, US Supreme Ct. Acct. Communication Satellite Corp., 1968-69; atty. Ohio State Legal Service, Columbus, Ohio, 1972-74; of counsel Ohio Indsl. Commn., Columbus, 1974-76; sole practice Columbus, 1976—; ptnr. Jones & Thompson, Columbus, 1984-88; prin. H. Lee Thompson Co. L.P.A., Columbus, 1988—; pres. toys and clothing H. Lee Toy Co., Columbus, 1988—. Adj. prof. law Columbus State Coll., 1989; instr. Acad. Ct. Reporting, 1989; adj. prof. tax and prins. of acctg. Bliss Coll., 1990-91. 2nd v.p. NAACP, Columbus, Ohio. Reginald Heber Smith fellow US Fed. Ct., 1972. Mem. Inst. (exec. mem. birth trauma litig. group), Ohio Conf. NAACP (bd. mem.), Ohio Bar Assn., Am. Coll. Legal Medicine, Ohio Acad. Trial Lawyers (trustee, mem. exec. com.), Am. Bd. Forensic Examiners, Franklin County Trial Lawyers Assn., Trial Lawyers Pub. Justice, Am. Assn. for Justice (chair profl. negligence sect. 2000), Am. Trial Lawyers Assoc. (Top 100 Trial Lawyers, 2007, 08), Frontiers Internat., Columbus Met. Club. Roman Catholic. Avocations: reading, music, jogging. Office: 85 E Gay St Ste 810 Columbus OH 43215-3118 Office Phone: 614-461-9000. Personal E-mail: thomlaw@msn.com.

THOMPSON, HEATH, media consultant; Dir. Gov. Bush SC Rep. Primary win, 2000; chief of staff Gov. Bob Peeler, SC; gen. cons. Norm Coleman US Senate win, 2002; cons. Jim DeMint US Senate win, 2004; regional polit. dir. Bush/Cheney 2004 re-election campaign; ptnr., sr. strategist Scott Howell & Co., Dallas. Republican. Office: Scott Howell & Co 208 N Market St Ste 225 Dallas TX 75202*

THOMPSON, HERBERT ALDEN, microbiologist, public health scientist; s. Otto Anous and Carmen Louise Thompson; m. Donna Rae Burrhus, June 13, 1964; 1 child, Bradley Alden. BA, Drake U., Des Moines, 1964; MA, Drake U., 1966; PhD, U. Kans., Lawrence, 1971. From asst. to full prof. W.Va. U., Morgantown, 1976—2000; microbiologist Ctrs. for Disease Control and Prevention, Atlanta, 2000—02, chief viral and rickettsial zoonoses br., 2002—06; retired, 2006. Contbr. articles to profl. jours. Pres., treas., newsletter editor Trout Unlimited, Morgantown, 1982—88. Recipient MacLachlan award, W.Va. U. Sch. Medicine; named Outstanding Tchr., W.Va. U., 1980; grantee, NIH, 1997—99, NSF, 1980—86. Mem.: Am. Biol. Safety Assn. (corr.), Am. Soc. Rickettsiology (corr.), Soc. Gen. Microbiology (corr.), Sigma Xi (corr.). Avocations: physical fitness, physical rehabilitation, fly fishing, carpentry, astronomy.

THOMPSON, HERBERT GEORGE, JR., economics professor, consultant; b. Akron, Ohio, May 31, 1947; s. Herbert George and Dorothy Mae Thompson. BS, U. Akron, Ohio, 1972, MA, 1974; PhD, U. Ga., Athens, 1989. Dir., economics and planning Pub. Utilities Staff Miss., Jackson, 1991—93; sr. economist L.R. Christensen Asso., Madison, Wis., 1993—98; dir., integrated resource planning Md. Pub. Svc. Commn., Balt., 1998—2001; sr. economist Nev. Pub. Svc. Commn., Carson City; assoc. prof. Ohio U., Athens. Assoc. editor Telecom. Jour., Athens; pres. Transp. and Pub. Utilities Group Am. Econ. Assn., San Francisco, 2009—. Author numerous journals in economics, telecom. Rep. coll. comm. Coun. Rsch., Scholarship and Creative Activity, Athens, 2008—. SP5 US Army, 1967—70, Vietnam. Mem.: Internat. Telecom. Soc., Am. Econ. Assn., Transp. and Pub. Utilities Group (president-elect; pres. 2008—). Liberal. Home: 11723 Channingway Blvd The Plains OH 45780 Office: 281 Lindley Hall Athens OH 45701 Personal E-mail: hthomps6@columbus.rr.com. Business E-Mail: thompsh3@ohio.edu.

THOMPSON, HOLLEY MARKER, lawyer, marketing professional, consultant; b. Jamestown, NY, Jan. 30, 1947; d. Burdette James and Mary Marker; m. Lawrence D. Thompson; children: Jennifer Kristen Simos, Kendra Elise Blair, Jennifer Lynn, Stephanie Lynn. AAS, Jamestown C.C., 1966; BS, Ohio U., 1969; MA, W.Va. U., 1974, JD, 1980. Bar: W.Va. 1980, U.S. Dist. Ct. (so. dist.) W.Va. 1980, Pa. 1982, U.S. Dist. Ct. (we. dist.) Pa. 1982. Tchr. math. various pub. schs., Santa Ana (Calif.), Lakewood (NY) and Morgantown (W.Va.), 1970-77; atty. for students W.Va. U., Morgantown, 1980; assoc. libr., lectr. W.Va. U. Coll. Law, Morgantown, 1980-83; assoc., libr. Jackson, Kelly, Holt & O'Farrell, Charleston, W.Va., 1983-86; cons. Hildebrandt, Inc., Somerville, NJ, 1986—94; sr. v.p. mktg. and preference markets LexisNexis, Dayton, Ohio, 1994—2006; ptnr. Sterling Group 925, Springboro, Ohio, 2006—. Spkr. in field. Contbr. articles to profl. jours. Business E-Mail: holleymthompson@tsg925.com.

THOMPSON, HORACE A., III, (TOPPER THOMPSON), commissioner, lawyer; b. New Orleans, 1942; m. Susan Thompson; children: Clarke, Jeffery. BA, Tulane U., 1965, JD, 1968. Bar: La. 1968, Miss. 1998, Ark. 1988, US Ct. Appeals (5th cir.) 1979, US Supreme Ct. 1977, US Dist. Ct. (ea., we. and mid. dists.) La. 1968. Adminstrv. leader labor and employment law sect. Jones, Walker, Waechter, Poitevent, Carrere & Denegre LLP; founding ptnr. McCalla, Thompson, Pyburn, Hymowitz & Shapiro, LLP, 1976—2001; ptnr., co-chair labor and employment law practice group Watkins Ludlam Winter & Stennis, P.A., 2001—06; commr. Occupational Safety and Health Rev. Commn., Washington, 2006—, chmn., 2007—, OJWRC, 2007—; mem. OSHRC, 2006—. Fellow: Am. Coll. Labor Rels. and Employment Lawyers; mem.: ABA, La. Bar Assn., Miss. Bar Assn., New Orleans Met. Safety Coun., La. Assn. Bus. and Industry, La. Restaurant Assn. Office: One Lafayette Ctr 1120 20th St 9th Fl Washington DC 20036-3457 Office Phone: 202-606-5390, 228-864-3094. Office Fax: 202-606-5050, 228-864-0516. E-mail: tthompson@watkinsludlam.com.

THOMPSON, HUGH P., state supreme court justice; b. Montezuma, Ga., July 7, 1943; married; 2 children. JD, Mercer U., 1969. Bar: Ga. 1970. Pvt. practice, Milledgeville, Ga., 1970—71; judge Recorder's Ct. of Milledgeville, 1971—79, Baldwin County Ct., 1973—78, Superior Ct. of Ga., 1979—94; chief judge Ocmulgee Jud. Cir., 1987—94; justice Ga. Supreme Ct., Atlanta, 1994—. Instr. bus. law Ga. Coll., 1971—72; pres. Coun. Superior Ct. Judges, 1993—94. Communicant St. Stephen's Episcopal Ch. Recipient Disting. Svc. award, Baldwin County Jaycees, 1972, Outstanding Alumnus award, Mercer U. Law Sch., 1994, Disting. Svc. award, Ga. Coll. and State U., 2002; named Outstanding Young Man of Baldwin County, 1972. Mem.: ABA, Bleckley Inn of Ct., Ga. Bar Found., State Bar Ga., Charles Longstreet Weltner Family Law Inn of Ct., Old War Horse Lawyers Club, Lawyers Club Atlanta. Avocations: hunting, gardening, golf, fishing. Office: Supreme Ct Ga State Judicial Bldg 244 Washington St SW Rm 572 Atlanta GA 30334-9007*

THOMPSON, IOLA POINTER, choreographer, educator; d. Will Kelly and Lucille Allen Pointer. AA, Malcolm X Coll., Chgo., 1973; BA, Columbia Coll., Chgo., 1975; MA, Northwestern U., Evanston, Ill., 1977; EdM, Tchrs. Coll., Columbia U., NYC, 1988, EdD, 1991. Cert. in ballroom dance instr. Fred Astaire Ballroom Dance Sch., 1978. Adj. instr. Northwestern U., Evanston, 1976—77; English & dance instr. Joseph's Westside Cmty. Acad., Chgo., 1977; adj. lectr. Medgar Evers Coll., CUNY, Bklyn., 1982—84, instr., 1984—92, asst. prof., 1992—2002, assoc. prof., 2002—; chairperson, dept mass communication Creative & Performing Arts and Speech, 2001—07. Ballroom dance instr. Fred Astaire Dance Sch., NYC, 1978, Dale Dance Sch., NYC, 1978—84; asst. ballroom dance instr. Dance Theater Harlem, NYC, 1993. Choreographer (dance) (Merit award, 1995, Recognition award, Dancer of Yr., 1973, First Pl., 1982, award, 1992). Sec. Jonah Village, 2002—08. Recipient Outstanding Svc. award, Student Govt. Assn., 1985, 1987; named Top Tchr. award, 1980. Mem.: AAUP, AAHPERD, Dance Educators Am., Nat. Dance Assn. AAHPERD, Nat. Brotherhood Skiers, Jersey Ski & Sport, Inc., Kappa Delta Pi. Democrat. Avocations: travel, skiing. Office: Medgar Evers Coll CUNY 1650 Bedford Ave Brooklyn NY 11225 Business E-Mail: ithompson@mec.cuny.edu.

THOMPSON, JACK EDWARD, mining company executive; b. Central City, Nebr., Nov. 17, 1924; s. Ray Elbert and Bessie Fay (Davis) T.; m. Maria del Carmen Larrea, May 8, 1948; children: Jack Edward, Ray Anthony, Robert Davis. Student, Northwestern U., 1942-43, Colo. Sch. Mines, 1943-45, D of Engring. (hon.), 1993. V.p. Cía. Química Comercial de Cuba S.A., 1946-60, Cía. de Fomento Químico S.A., 1946-60; with Newmont Mining Corp., NYC, 1960-86, asst. to pres., 1964-67, v.p., 1967-71, dir., 1969-86, exec. v.p., 1971-74, pres., 1974-85, vice chmn., 1985-86, cons., 1986-90. Chmn. bd. trustees Minerals Industry Ednl. Found. Recipient Distinguished Achievement medal Colo. Sch. Mines, 1974 Mem. AIME, Mining and Metall. Soc. Am., Mining Found. of S.W. (past pres., bd. govs.), Tucson Country Club. E-mail: rayonera@aol.com.

THOMPSON, JAMES ALEXANDER, JR., lawyer; b. Providence, July 18, 1945; s. James Alexander and Agnes Florence (Bainton) T.; m. Cheryl Ann Martin, Mar. 6, 1971; children: Scott Alexander, Jeffrey Martin. BA, U. Pa., 1967; JD, George Washington U., 1973. Bar: Mass. 1974, D.C. 1983, Conn. 1989. Atty.-advisor Region 1 U.S. EPA, Boston, 1974-76, asst. regional counsel Region 1, 1976-79, regional counsel Region 8 Denver, 1979-82; ptnr. Wickwire, Gavin & Gibbs, P.C., Washington, 1982-86, Pepe & Hazard, Hartford, Conn., 1986-94; exec. com. and EHS Dewey & LeBoeuf LLP, Conn., 1994—, Wash. Mem. exec. com. Dewey & LeBoeuf LLP, co-chmn. nat. and internat. environ. health and safety practice group. Contbg. author: Environmental Law and Planning, 1973. Soccer coach Hartwell Sports Club, Glastonbury, Conn., 1986—89; basketball coach Youth Basketball Assn., Glastonbury, 1990; chmn. bd. trustees Talcott Mountain Sci. Ctr., Avon, Conn., 1991—2003. 1st lt. US Army, 1969—73. Mem. ABA (natural resources sect.), Conn. Bar Assn. (environ. quality sect.). Avocations: running, skiing, tennis, architecture. Office Phone: 202-346-7822. Office Fax: 860-293-3555. Business E-Mail: jthompso@llgm.com, jthompson@dl.com.

THOMPSON, JAMES E., lawyer, food products executive; BA, U. Mich., 1983, JD, 1986. Bar: Ill., DC. Law clk. stagiaire Court of Justice of European Communities, Luxembourg; atty. Jones, Day, Reavis & Pogue, 1987—95; chief legal officer innovations bus. unit Alticor, Inc., assoc. gen. counsel internat. legal dept.; group v.p., gen. counsel, sec. McLeodUSA Inc.; sr. v.p., gen. counsel, sec. Chiquita Brands Internat., Inc., 2006—. Office: Chiquita Brands Internat Inc Chiquita Ctr 250 E Fifth St Cincinnati OH 45202 Office Phone: 513-784-8000. Office Fax: 513-784-8030.

THOMPSON, JAMES LEE, lawyer; b. LI, NY, Sept. 9, 1941; s. Robert Luther and Marjorie Emma (Jones) T.; m. Diana Dill Stevenson, June 29, 1963; children: James C., Thomas J. BA, Yale U., 1963; JD, U. Va., 1966. Bar: Va. 1966, Md. 1966, U.S. Ct. Mil. Appeals 1968, U.S. Dist. Ct. Md. 1972, U.S. Supreme Ct. 1978. Ptnr. Miller & Canby, Rockville, Md., 1970—, head litigation, 1975—. Mem. jud. conf. U.S. Ct. Appeals (4th cir.). Mem. Thousand Acres Assn., Deep Creek Lake, Md., 1985-87. Capt. JAGC, USMC, 1966-70. Decorated D.S.M. Fellow Am. Coll. Trial Lawyers; mem. ABA, Md. State Bar Assn. (bd. govs. 1975, 78, 79, 83, 89, 94, sec. 1995, pres. 1999-00), Montgomery County Bar Assn. (pres. 1987-88, Cert. of Merit 1985), Nat. Conf. Bar Pres., Md. Bar Found., Montgomery County Bar Found. (pres. 1988-89), Loophole Club (pres. 1978-79), Phi Delta Phi. Democrat. Episcopalian. Avocations: sailing, skiing, tennis, golf, gardening. Office: Miller & Canby 200 Monroe St Ste B Rockville MD 20850-4423 Home: 18516 Boysenberry Dr Apt 204 Gaithersburg MD 20879-3670 Home Phone: 301-216-5591; Office Phone: 301-762-5212. Business E-Mail: jlthompson@mmcanby.com.

THOMPSON, JAMES ROBERT, JR., lawyer, former governor; b. Chgo., May 8, 1936; s. James Robert and Agnes Josephine (Swanson) Thompson; m. Jayne Carr, 1976; 1 child, Samantha Jayne. Student, U. Ill., Chgo., 1953-55, Washington U., St. Louis, 1955-56; JD, Northwestern U., 1959. Bar: Ill. 1959, US Supreme Ct. 1964. Asst. state's atty., Cook County, Ill., 1959-64; assoc. prof. law Northwestern U. Law Sch., 1964-69; asst. atty. gen. State of Ill., 1969-70; chief criminal divsn., 1969; chief dept. law enforcement and pub. protection, 1969-70; 1st asst. U.S. atty. (No. dist.) Ill. US Dept. Justice, 1970-71, U.S. atty., 1971-75; counsel Winston & Strawn LLP, Chgo., 1975-77, ptnr., 1991—, chmn., CEO, 1993—2006, chmn. exec. com., 1991—2006, head gov. rels. practice; gov. State of Ill., Springfield, Ill., 1977-91. Chmn. Rep. Govs. Assn., 1982, Nat. Govs. Assn., Midwest Govs. Assn., Coun. Gt. Lakes Govs., 1985, Pres.' Intelligence Oversight Bd., 1989—93; adv. bd. Fed. Emergency Mgmt. Agy., 1991—93; bd. govs. Chgo. Bd. Trade; mem. ABA Commn. on Separation of Powers & Jud. Independence, 1996—97; commr. The Nat. Commn. on Terrorist Attacks Upon the U.S. (The 9-11 Commn.), 2002—04; bd. dirs. FMC Tech., Inc., Navigant Cons. Inc., Maximus, Inc., John Bean Techs., Inc. Co-author: Cases and Comments on Criminal Justice, 1974, Criminal Law and Its Administration. Bd. dirs. Civic Com. Mem.: ABA, Chgo. Bar Assn., Ill. Bar Assn. Republican. Office: Winston & Strawn LLP 35 W Wacker Dr Ste 4200 Chicago IL 60601-9703 Home Phone: 312-640-0420; Office Phone: 312-558-7400. Office Fax: 312-558-5700. Business E-Mail: jthompson@winston.com.

THOMPSON, JAMES WILLIAM, lawyer; b. Dallas, Oct. 22, 1936; s. John Charles and Frances (Van Slyke) Thompson; m. Marie Hertz, June 26, 1965 (dec. 1995); children: Elizabeth, Margaret, John; m. Linda Ball Dozier, May 2, 1998. BS, U. Mont., 1958, JD, 1962. Bar: Mont. 1962; CPA, Mont. Acct. Arthur Young & Co., NYC, 1959; instr. bus. adminstrn. Ea. Mont. Coll., Billings, 1959-60, U. Mont., Missoula, 1960-61; assoc. Cooke, Moulton, Bellingham & Longo, Billings, 1962-64, James R. Felt, Billings, 1964-65; asst. atty. City of Billings, 1963-64, atty., 1964-66; ptnr. Felt, Speare & Thompson, Billings, 1966-72, McNamer, Thompson & Cashmore, 1973-86, McNamer & Thompson Law Firm PC, 1986-89, McNamer, Thompson, Werner & Stanley, P.C., 1990-93, McNamer Thompson Law Firm PC, 1993-98, Wright Tolliver Guthals Law Firm PC, Billings, Mont., 1999—2003, Guthals Hunnes Reuss Thompson PC, Billings, 2004—07, Thompson Law Firm PLLC, Billings, 2007—. Bd. dirs. Associated Employers of Mont., Inc., 1989—98; mem. adv. coun. Sch. Fine Arts, U. Mont., 1997—2001. Mem. Billings Zoning Commn., 1966—69; v.p. Billings Cmty. Action Program (now Dist. 7 Human Resources Devel. Coun.), 1968—70, pres., 1970—75, bd. trustees, 1975—; mem. Yellowstone County Legal Svcs. Bd., 1969—70, City-County Air Pollution Control Bd., 1969—70; pres. Billings Symphony Soc., 1970—71; bd. dirs. Billings Studio Theater, 1967—73, United Way Billings, 1973—81, Mont. Inst. Arts Found., 1986—89, Downtown Billings Assn., 1986—90, Billings Area Bus. Incubator, Inc., 1991—94, Found. of Mont. State U, Billings, 1992—98, Our Mont., Inc., 1997—, pres., 2000—; bd. dirs. Rimrock Opera Co., 1998—, treas., 1998—2002; mem. Billings Transit Commn., 1971—73, City Devel. Agy., 1972—73; bd. ethics City of Billings, 2001—06, chmn., 2006; Diocesan Exec. Coun., 1972—75. Mem. ABA, Am. Acad. Estate Planning Attys., Nat. Acad. Elder Law Attys., State Bar Mont., Yellowstone Area Bar Assn. (bd. dirs. 1983-87, pres. 1985-86), Elks, Kiwanis (pres. Yellowstone chpt. 1974-75), Sigma Chi (pres. Billings alumni assn. 1963-65). Episcopalian. Home: 123 Lewis Ave Billings MT 59101-6034 Office: Thompson Law Firm PLLC Profl Ctr 176 S 32nd St W Ste 4 Billings MT 59102-6867 Office Phone: 406-294-4230. Personal E-mail: jwtldt@aol.com.

THOMPSON, JAN NEWSTROM, art historian, educator; b. Buffalo, Mar. 19, 1947; d. Marvin William and Nadene (Newstrom) T.; m. Paul L. Goldstein, Aug. 28, 1977; 1 child, Elizabeth Esther Thompson Goldstein. BFA, SUNY, Buffalo, 1968, MA, 1971, Rutgers U., New Brunswick, NJ, 1974, PhD, 1980. Instr. art history Canisius Coll., Buffalo, 1973-74; instr. art history, studio art Union Coll., Cranford, N.J., 1974-77; instr. art history Santa Clara (Calif.) U., 1977-94, San Jose (Calif.) U., 1988—, San Francisco Museum of Modern Art, 1987. Author: Frank Duveneck: Lost Paintings Found, 1987, Theodore Wores: An American Artist in Meiji, Japan, 1993. Mem. adv. bd. No. Calif. Coun. of Nat. Museum of Women in the Arts, 1995—; trustee Triton Museum of Art, Santa Clara, 1980-90. Mem. Coll. Art Assn. Am. Avocations: equestrian sports, dressage. Office: San Jose Stat U Dept of Art and Design 1 Washington Sq San Jose CA 95192-0001

THOMPSON, JAYNE MARIE, literature and language professor; b. Upper Darby, Pa., Jan. 10, 1967; d. Douglass M. Parson and Margaret M. Taggart; m. John Thompson, Aug. 31, 2002. MA in English, West Chester U., Pa., 1993. Sr. lectr. writing Widener U., Chester, 1996—. Book club leader, tutor Chester Edn. Found., 2003—08; tutor Achievement Program, Chester, 2008. Office: Widener Univ One University Pl Chester PA 19013 Business E-Mail: jmthompson@mail.widener.edu.

THOMPSON, JEAN TANNER, retired librarian; b. San Luis Obispo, Calif., June 15, 1929; d. Chester Corey and Mildred (Orr) T.; 1 child, Anne Marie Miller Student, Whitworth Coll., Spokane, Wash., 1946-49; AB, Boston U., 1951; postgrad., U. Wis., Eau Claire, 1964-67; MSL.S., Columbia U., 1973; Ed.M., U. Va., Charlottesville, 1978. Asst. social sci. librarian Univ. Libraries Va. Polytechnic Inst. and State U., Blacksburg, 1973-77, head social sci. dept. Univ. Libraries, 1977-83; head reference dept. Meml. Library U. Wis., Madison, 1983-86, asst. dir. reference and info. svcs., 1986-91, ret. Contbg. editor: ALA Guide to Information Access, 1994; mem. editorial bd. RQ, 1984-89. Mem. ALA, Assn. Coll. and Research Libraries (edn. and behavioral sci. sect. vice chmn. 1985-86, chmn. 1986-87), Wis. Library Assn., Wis. Assn. of Acad. Librarians. Presbyterian. Home: 4929 High Grove Rd Tallahassee FL 32309-2957 Personal E-mail: souterj9@embarg.com.

THOMPSON, JERRY E., oil industry executive; BS, Colo. Sch. Mines. V.p. refining CITGO Petroleum Corp., 1987—98, sr. v.p., 1998—2003, COO, 2003—06; pres., CEO TEPPCO Partners LLP, Houston, 2006—. V.p., past chmn. Nat. Petrochemical & Refiners Assn.

THOMPSON, JEWEL TAYLOR, music educator; b. Kinsale, Va., Oct. 27, 1935; d. Waverly Edward and Ella Joyce (Holman) Taylor; m. Leon Everette Thompson, June 10, 1961 (dec. June 1983); children: Sonca Patrice, Miya Kateri. BS, Va. State U., 1956; MA, Eastman Sch. of Music, 1960, PhD, 1982. Asst. prof. Va. State U., Petersburg, 1960-62, W.Va. State Coll., Institute, 1967-68, W.Va. Inst. Tech., Montgomery, 1968-72; adj. asst. prof. Hunter Coll., CUNY, 1972-85, asst. prof., 1985-90, assoc. prof., 1990-96, prof., 1997—. Organist Abyssinian Bapt. Ch., N.Y.C., 1978-83, minister of music, choirmaster, 1983-2007; ea. area music dir. Links, Inc., 1995-2003, nat. music dir., 2004—06. Author: Samuel Coleridge-Taylor, 1994; composer and arranger numerous compositions; contbr. Internat. Dictionary of Black Composers, 1999. Scholarship selection com. United Negro Coll. Fund; chair art program Links, Inc., 1989-93; music dir. at area and nat. levels; mem. Am. Music Ctr., Inc. Recipient Hunter Coll. Presdl. award for excellence in svc., 1998, Outstanding Ministry award, Coun. Chs. of NYC, 2005, Diamond of Faith, Abyssinian Bapt. Ch., 2007; named Dame of Honour, Knights of Malta, 1982; Hattie M. Strong Found. fellow, 1959—60, Ford Found. fellow, 1974—77, Prince Hall Masons grantee, 1977—78. Mem. ASCAP, Am. Women Composers, Inc., Music Theory Soc. N.Y. State. Avocations: travel, art. Office: CUNY Hunter Coll 695 Park Ave New York NY 10065-5024 Home Phone: 201-488-2617; Office Phone: 212-650-3608. Personal E-mail: jt1425@aol.com.

THOMPSON, JILL LYNETTE LONG, former congressman; b. Warsaw, Ind., July 15, 1952; m. Don Thompson, 1995. BBA, Valparaiso U., 1974; MBA, Ind. U., 1978, PhD, 1984. Asst. instr., lectr. Ind. U., Bloomington, 1977—80; asst. prof. Valparaiso U., 1981—88; mgmt. cons. Campbell and Pryor, 1985-86; mem. US Congress from 4th Ind. Dist., 1989-95, mem. agrl. com., vets. affairs com.; under sec. for rural devel. USDA, Washington, 1995—2001; CEO Nat. Ctr. for Food & Agrl. Policy, Washington, 2003—08. Adj. prof. Indiana U.-Purdue U. Ft. Wayne, 1987-89; Manchester Coll., 2002-03 asst. prof. Valparaiso U. Councilwoman City of Valparaiso, Ind., 1984-86; chair Congrl. Rural Congress. Fellow: Inst. of Politics. Democrat. Methodist.*

THOMPSON, JO(AN), anthropologist; b. Colo. B in Psychology and Sociology, Wittenberg Univ., Ohio, 1978; M in Anthropology, Univ. Colo., 1992; PhD in Biological Anthropology and Primatology, Univ. Oxford, Eng., 1997. Founder, dir. Lukuru Wildlife Research Project, Democratic Republic of Congo, 1992—98; fund-raiser LWRP, Colo. (due to unrest in DRC). Named an assoc. laureate, Rolex award for Enterprise, 2004. Achievements include 13 years of conducting biological field rsch., community-based conservation and wildlife edn. in the Dem. Republic of the Congo on behalf of human and primate populations, particularly bonobos. Home: PO Box 1635 Marion OH 43301-1635 Business E-Mail: jat434@aol.com.

THOMPSON, JOAN HULSE, political science professor; BA, Gettysburg Coll., 1971; MA, Johns Hopkins U., 1972, PhD, 1978. Asst. prof. Luther Coll., Decorah, 1979—86; asst. prof. & co-chair Arcadia U., Glenside, Pa., 1986—92, assoc. prof. & co-chair, 1992—. Program asst. Internat. Orgn. Recruitment, UNESCO liaison Office, 1972—73; vis. asst. prof. Union Coll., Schenectady, NY, 1978—79. Contbr. articles to profl. pubs. & conf. presentations. Vol. Polit. Campaign Judy Lewis Abington Sch. Bd., 1992—94; sunday sch. tchr. Abington Presbyterian Ch., 1991—92. Congressional fellowship, APSA, 1985—86, Fellowship, AAUW, 1983. Mem.: Pa. Polit. Sci. Assn. (exec. bd. 1987—90), Women's Caucus Polit. Sci., Am. Polit. Sci. Assn., Phi Kappa Phi, Pi Sigma Alpha. Office: Polit Sci Dept Arcadia Univ 450 S Easton Rd Glenside PA 19038 Business E-Mail: thompson@arcadia.edu.

THOMPSON, JOANN, Alderwoman; Former correctional officer Cook County Dept. Corrections, Chgo.; alderwoman, 16th ward Chgo. City Coun., 2007—. Office: 5335 S Western Blvd Chicago IL 60609 also: City Hall 121 N La Salle Rm 300 Office 20 Chicago IL 60602 Office Phone: 773-434-3399, 312-744-3184. Office Fax: 773-434-3889. E-mail: JoAnn.Thompson@cityofchicago.org.*

THOMPSON, JOCELYN PHARR, organist, director, educator; b. Peekskill, NY, Mar. 30, 1956; d. Ernest Eugene and Jonsie (Crawford) Pharr; m. Sherman Bradford Thompson, Oct. 12, 1985. MusB, U. NC, Greensboro, 1978, MusM in Edn., 1980, M in Spl. Edn., 1986. Cert. K-12 music, K-12 in spl. edn. Tchrs. aide Clay St. Elem., Gastonia, NC, 1980—81; tchr. Eckerd Family Youth Alternatives, Candor, NC, 1981—85, ednl. coord., 1985—89; choral tchr. Providence Sr. HS, Charlotte, NC, 1989—94; asst. dir., prin. accompanist Carolina Voices, 1994—2001, dir. mainstage choir, 2001—02; asst. dir. music Meml. Presbyn. Ch., 1990—96, dir. music, organist, 1996—; choral tchr. West Charlotte Sr. HS, 1992—. Asst. dir., accompanist Charlotte Contemporary Ensemble, Charlotte, 2002—; dir. Martin Luther King Mass Choir, Gaston County Orgn. for Cmty. Concern, 1997—. Mass choir dir. Nat. Bapt. Conf., Charlotte, 2001, World Gathering Presbyn. Women, Louisville, 2003—. Recipient Cmty. Svc. award, Black Women's Caucus, Charlotte, 2002, Heritage award, Cultural Calendar, Charlotte, 2001, Person of Tear, Gaston County Orgn. for Cmty. Concern, NC, 2005. Mem.: Am. Music Choral Dirs. Assn., Music Educators Nat. Conf., Links Inc., Alpha Kappa Alpha. Democrat. Avocations: reading, tennis, piano, movies. Office: West Charlotte Sr HS 2219 Senior Dr Charlotte NC 28216

THOMPSON, JOE D., physicist; BS in Physics, 1969, PhD in Physics, 1975. Postdoctoral Cryogenics Group Los Alamos Nat. Lab., N.Mex., 1975—77, tech. staff mem. Condensed Matter and Thermal Physics Group, 1977—2001, dep. group leader, 1989—92, group leader, 1992—2001, Lab. fellow, 2001—. Fellow: AAAS, Am. Phys. Soc. Office: Los Alamos Nat Lab MSK-764 PO Box 1663 Los Alamos NM 87545

THOMPSON, JOHN, III, men's college basketball coach; b. Mar. 11, 1966; s. John Thompson; m. Monica Thompson; children: Morgan, John Wallace, Matthew. Grad. in Politics, Princeton U., NJ, 1988. Asst. coach Princeton U. Tigers, NJ, 1995—2000, head coach, 2000—04, Georgetown U. Hoyas, Washington, 2004—. Recipient Fritz Pollard Male Coach of Yr. award, Black Coaches Assn., 2006. Achievements include leading the Princeton Tigers to three Ivy League Championships as head coach. Office: Men's Basketball Georgetown U Athletic Dept McDonough Gym Washington DC 20057

THOMPSON, JOHN ALBERT, JR., dermatologist; b. Austin, Tex., June 5, 1942; s. J. Albert Sr. and Elizabeth (Brady) T. BA, Georgetown U., 1963; MD, Bowman Gray Sch. Medicine, 1967; Dermatology Fellowship, U. N.C., 1971-73. Diplomate Am. Bd. Dermatology. Resident in internal medicine N.C. Baptist Hosp., Winston-Salem, NC, 1967-69; resident in dermatology N.C. Meml. Hosp., Chapel Hill, NC, 1971-73; pvt. practice Charlotte, NC, 1974—; clin. prof. dermatology Dept. Dermatology, U. N.C. Sch. Medicine, Chapel Hill, 1974—. Author profl. papers. Lt. comdr. USNR, 1969-71, Vietnam. Mem. Am. Acad. Dermatology (chmn. subcom. for sch. health edn. 1976-79, task force--nat. health ins.), Carolinas-Va. Dermatology Assn. (adv. bd. council rep. 1976-79), Charlotte Dermatology Assn., Mecklenburg County Med. Soc., N.C. Med. Soc., North Am. Clin. Dermatology Soc. Southern Med. Assn., Southeastern Consortium for Continuing Dermatol. Edn. (steering com. 1983—2003), South Cen. Dermatol. Congress (organizing com. 1982-86), Am. Soc. Dermatol. Surgery, Am. Dermatol. Soc. Allergy and Immunology, Am. Soc. Laser Medicine and Surgery, Inc. Democrat. Episcopalian. Home: 2633 Richardson Dr Apt 8A Charlotte NC 28211-3346 Office: Dermatol Laser Ctr Dermatologic Laser Ctr 2310 Randolph Rd Charlotte NC 28207-1526 Office Phone: 704-376-9849.

THOMPSON, JOHN GRIGGS, mathematician; b. Ottawa, Kans., Oct. 13, 1932; BA, Yale U., 1955; PhD, U. Chgo., 1959; degree (hon.), Yale U., 1980, U. Chgo., 1985, U. Oxford, 1987. Asst. Harvard U., Cambridge, Mass., 1961-62; prof. U. Chgo., 1962-68; fellow Univ. Coll., Cambridge, Eng., 1968-70; Rouse Ball prof. math. Cambridge U., England, 1970—73; grad. rsch. prof. U. Fla., 1993—. Recipient Fields medal Internat. Congress Mathematicians, 1970, Cole prize Am. Math. Soc., Sr. Berwick prize London Math. Soc., 1982, Wolf prize in math. Wolf Found., Israel, 1992, Pioncaré prize, 1992, Nat. Medal Sci., 2000; co-recipient Abel prize, Norwegian Acad. Sci. and Letters, 2008. Fellow: Royal Soc. London. (Sylvester medal 1987); mem.: NAS. Achievements include solution of one of the conjectures of Frobenius; major contributions to coding theory. Office: Math Dept Univ Fla 358 Little Hall PO Box 118105 Gainesville FL 32611-8105 Office Phone: 352-392-0281 ext. 228. E-mail: jthompso@math.ufl.edu.

THOMPSON, JOHN WENDELL, information technology executive; b. Ft. Dix, NJ, Apr. 24, 1949; s. John H. and Eunice Thompson; m. Sandi Thompson; children: John E., Ayanna. BBA, Fla. A&M U., 1971; MBA in Mgmt. Sci., MIT's Sloan School Mgmt., 1982. Sales rep. IBM Corp., 1971—75, branch office mgr., 1975—79, regional adminstrv. asst., regional mktg. dir., 1980—84, asst. to CEO, 1984, dir. Midwest ops., 1990—93, head mktg. US ops., 1993, gen. mgr. personal software products, 1994—98, gen. mgr. IBM Americas, 1997—99; chmn., CEO Symantec Corp., Cupertino, Calif., 1999—2009, chmn., 2009—. Bd.

dirs. Symantec Corp., 1999—, United Parcel Svc., Inc. (UPS), 2000—, Seagate Tech., 2004—; mem. Nat. Infrastructure Adv. Com., Washington, 2002—; chair Silicon Valley Blue Ribbon Task Force on Aviation Security & Tech. Chmn. Fla. A&M U. Cluster; Ill. Gov's human resource adv. coun. Named one of 50 Who Matter Now, CNNMoney.com Bus. 2.0, 2006; named to Power 150, Ebony mag., 2008. Office: Symantec Corp 20330 Stevens Creek Blvd Cupertino CA 95014*

THOMPSON, JON L., retired oil industry executive; BS in Geology, MS in Geology, U. Fla. Geologist Exxon Co. U.S.A., New Orleans, 1962; v.p. Exxon Corp., 1992—99; pres. Exxon Exploration Co., 1992—99; v.p. ExxonMobil Corp., 2000—; pres. ExxonMobil Exploration Co., 2000—. Office: ExxonMobil Exploration Co Ste 1241 233 Benmar St Houston TX 77066-3105

THOMPSON, JOSEPH C., museum director; married; 1 child. BA, Williams Coll., 1981; MA in Art History, U. Pa., 1986, MBA, 1987. Preparator, exhibitions designer Williams Coll. Mus. Art, 1982; James Webb fellow Smithsonian Inst., Washington, 1984; lectr. contemporary art Williams Coll. & U. Pa., 1988—90; founding dir. Mass. Mus. Contemporary Art (MASS MoCA), North Adams, 1988—. Annenberg Fellow, Morganthau Fellowship. Office: Mass Mus Contemporary Art 1040 MASS MoCA Way North Adams MA 01247

THOMPSON, JOSIE, nurse; b. Ark., Apr. 16, 1949; d. James Andrew and Oneda Fay (Watson) Rhoads; m. Mark O. Thompson, Feb. 14, 1980. Diploma, Lake View Sch. Nursing, 1970; student, Danville C.C., 1974-75, St. Petersburg Jr. Coll., 1979. RN Ill., Wyo., cert. Devel. Disabilities Divsn., N.Y. Staff nurse St. Elizabeth Hosp., Danville, Ill., 1970-78, Osteo. Hosp., St. Petersburg, Fla., 1980-81, Wyo. State Hosp., Evanston, 1981-83, Wyo. Home Health Care, Rock Springs, 1984—, adminstr., 1986-95; pres. Home Health Care Alliance Wyo., 1991-92; staff nurse home health Interim Health Care, Cheyenne, Wyo., 1996-97; staff nurse Rocky Mountain Home Health Care, Green River, Wyo., 1997—, dir. nursing, 2000-01; staff nurse Sageview Care Ctr., 2001, S.W. Wyo. Rehab. Ctr. for Mentally and Physically Handicapped Persons, Rock Springs, Wyo., 2001—03, SW Rehab. Ctr., 2006—08; pvt. practice Wyo., 2004—06, Sageview Care Ctr., 2009. Mem. nursing program adv. bd. Western Wyo. C.C.; mem. Coalition for the Elderly, Spl. Needs Com. Sweetwater County, 1992-93. Home: PO Box 1154 Rock Springs WY 82902-1154 Home Phone: 307-362-3144; Office Phone: 307-350-7827. Personal E-mail: goldbar@sweetwater.net.

THOMPSON, KATHY C., bank executive; 2 children. From. sr. v.p. to exec. v.p. Stock Yards Bancorp Inc., Louisville, 1992—96, exec. v.p.; sr. v.p., dir. trust co., dir. sales, services and mktg. Stock Yards Bancorp Inc. Active Home of the Innocents. Named No. 3 Fast Tracker in the Industry, US Bankers mag., 2003; named one of 25 Women to Watch, 2007. Office: Stock Yards Bancorp Inc 1040 East Main St Louisville KY 40206

THOMPSON, KEITH F. MACKECHNIE, geochemist, consultant; b. Romford, Eng., Mar. 16, 1933; arrived in US, 1960; s. Alexander William and Rose Mary Thompson; m. Carol J. Hinkley, Oct. 7, 1961 (div. July 21, 1979); children: Kathryn, Gregory, Rebecca, Gwendolynne, Monica; m. E. Jo Jones, Oct. 3, 1981. BSc, U. Manchester, Eng., 1955; PhD, MIT, Cambridge, Mass., 1966. Geologist Iraq Petroleum Co., Basrah, 1955—59; geochemist Sinclair Rsch. Inc., Tulsa, 1966—69; rsch. assoc. geochemist ARCO Oil and Gas Co., Plano, Tex., 1969—85; assoc. rsch. scientist Tex. A&M U., College Station, 1985—89; rsch. geochemist Brit. Petroleum Co., Ltd., Houston, 1989—93; rsch. geochemist, cons. Petroleum Geochem. Data, Dallas, 1993—. Owner, pres. Petrosurveys, Inc., Dallas, 1992—2002; guest scientist Geoforschungszentrum, Potsdam, Germany, 2003; cons. in field. Contbr. 22 papers to profl. publs. Recipient Energy Related Inventions award, US Dept. Energy, 1995—97. Fellow: Geol. Soc. London; mem.: European Assn. Organic Geochemists. Roman Catholic. Achievements include research in light hydrocarbons; elucidation of petroleum generative reactions; described evaporative fractionation (generation of gas-condensates); patents for offshore petroleum exploration system. Home: 7747 Royal Ln Dallas TX 75230 Office: Petroleum Geochemical Data PO Box 671264 Dallas TX 75367-1264

THOMPSON, KENNETH, software engineer; b. New Orleans, 1943; BSEE, U. Calif., Berkeley, 1965, MSEE, 1966. With Computer Scis. Rsch. Ctr. Bell Labs/Lucent Technologies, Murray Hill, NJ, 1966—2000; disting. mem. tech. staff Bell Labs/Lucent Techs, Murray Hill, NJ; fellow Entrisphere, Inc. Vis. prof. U. Calif., Berkeley, 1975—76, U. Sydney, Australia, 1988. Recipient Fellow award, Computer History Mus., 1997, Emmanuel R. Piore award, IEEE, Richard Hamming medal, Harold Pender Award, Sch. Engring. and Applied Sci., U. Pa., 2003; co-recipient U.S. Nat. Medal of Tech., 1999, C&C prize, NEC, 1989; named Bell Labs Fellow, 1983. Mem.: Assn. Computing Machinery (Turing award and software sys. award 1983), NAE, NAS, IEEE Computer Soc. (Tsutomu Kanai award 1999). Achievements include patents for computer technology; research in operating systems, programming languages, software for voice and data communications, security, computer games and digital music distribution; co-developer of UNIX operating system in 1969; with J.H. Condon was involved with the development of Belle, a chess computer, which won the US and World Computing Chess Championships in 1980.

THOMPSON, KIRK, transportation executive; CPA, Ark. With J.B. Hunt Transport Svcs., Inc., Lowell, Ark., 1973-78, v.p. fin., 1979-84, exec. v.p., CFO, 1984-85, pres., COO, 1986-87, pres., CEO, 1987—. Office: JB Hunt Transport Svcs Inc 615 JB Hunt Corporate Dr Lowell AR 72745*

THOMPSON, LARRY DEAN, lawyer, former federal agency administrator, food products executive; b. Hannibal, Mo., Nov. 15, 1945; s. Ezra W. and Ruth L. (Robinson) T.; m. Brenda Anne Taggart, June 26, 1970; children: Larry Dean, Gary E. BA cum laude, Culver-Stockton Coll., Canton, Mo., 1967; MA, Mich. State U., 1969; JD, U. Mich., 1974. Bar: Mo. 1974, Ga. 1978. Indsl. rels. rep. Ford Motor Co., Birmingham, Mich., 1969-71; atty. Monsanto Co., St. Louis, 1974-77, King & Spalding, Atlanta, 1977-82, ptnr., 1986—2001; U.S. atty. (no. dist.) Ga. U.S. Dept. Justice, 1982-86; dep. atty. gen. U.S. Dept Justice, Washington, 2001—03; sr. fellow Brookings Instn., Washington, 2003—04; sr. v.p. govt. affairs, gen. counsel, sec. PepsiCo, Inc., Purchase, NY, 2005—. Mem. 11th Cir. Commn. on Lawyer Qualifications and Conduct; ind. counsel HUD investigation, 1995, visiting prof., U. Ga Sch. of Law, 2004; mem. Ga. Bd. Bar Examiners; bd. dirs. Delta Air Lines Inc., 2003-. Editor: Jury Instructions in Criminal Antitrust Cases 1976-80, 1982. Chmn. Atlanta Urban League; mem. Ga. Bd. Edn., 1997; bd. dirs. Ga. Rep. Found. Recipient Outstanding Achievement award FBA, 1992. Mem. ABA, Nat. Bar Assn. Republican. Presbyterian. Office: PepsiCo Inc 700 Anderson Hill Rd Purchase NY 10577*

THOMPSON, LARRY FLACK, nanotechnology and semiconductor process company executive; b. Union City, Tenn., Aug. 31, 1944; s. Rufus Russell and Polly (Flack) T.; m. Frank O. Wilson, Mar. 1, 1991; children: Anthony Scott, Russell Allen. BS, Tenn. Tech. U., Cookeville, 1966; MS, Tenn. Tech. U., 1968; PhD, U. Mo., Rolla, 1970. Mem. tech. staff Bell Labs., Murray Hill, N.J., 1971-80; dept. head AT&T Bell Labs., Murray Hill, N.J., 1981-94; v.p. product devel., chief tech. officer Integrated Solutions, Inc., Austin, Tex., 1994-97; pres. Ultrabeam Lithography, 1997—2002, Ultrabeam Lithography Inc. (divsn. of Ultratech Stepper), 1999—; CEO, N.J. Nanotech. Consortium, 2002—. Mem. adv. coun. dept. chem. engring. Cornell U., Princeton U.; chmn. adv. com. to divsn. of chem., biochem. and thermal engring. NSF. Author: Introduction to Microlithography, 1993, 98; patentee in field. Recipient SEMI award for N. Am., 1997. Mem. NAE, Am. Chem. Soc. (bd. dirs. 1993-96, Indsl. Chemistry award 1993, Roy W. Tess award 1993), Am. Inst. Chem. Engring. Avocations: gardening, hunting. Home: 1178 Hidden Creek Dr Dripping Springs TX 78620-4634 E-mail: larry@ipsslp.com.

THOMPSON, LAURA, theater producer; d. D Thompson. BBA Decision Scis., Ga. State U., Atlanta, 1993; MS in Tech. Mgt., Mercer U., Atlanta, 1995; PhD in Bus. Admin. Info. Sys., Argosy U., Sarasota, Fla., 2007. Exec. prodr. AMC World, LLC, Decatur, Ga., 1998—. Prodr.: (albums) (music cd) God's Offer (Gospel Choice award, 1999), singer; composer: (songs) (music cd) Garage Gospel; actor: (plays) Oops, There It Is, God's Trying to Tell You Something. Adv. bd. mem. computer,IT Malix Coll. Online, Atlanta, 2008—; chief ops. officer Thompson Family Found., Decatur, 2008—; advisor Shanti - A Peace, Atlanta, 2008—. Achievements include research in globalization and its impact on music marketing and distribution.

THOMPSON, LAURA ANN MOBLEY, music educator; d. George Green Mobley and Geradine Boatner Phyllis Wright; m. James Christopher Thompson, Aug. 20, 1974; 1 child, Lauren Suzanne. ArtsD in Vocal Pedagogy, U. Miss., Oxford, 2003. Instr. U. La., Monroe, 1998—2003, La. Tech. U., Ruston, 1989—98, asst. prof., 2003—. Musician performer. Grant, La. Tech U., 2008. Mem.: Nat. Assn. Teachers Singing (treas. north dist. La. 1998—2008), Pi Kappa Lambda, Gamma Beta Phi, Phi Kappa Phi. Methodist. Avocations: hiking, gardening. Home: 1971 Hwy 546 West Monroe LA 71292 Office: La Tech Univ Howard Ctr #331 Ruston LA 71272 Office Fax: 318-257-4571. Business E-Mail: laurat@latech.edu.

THOMPSON, LAWRENCE BIGELOW, lawyer; b. NYC, Mar. 29, 1936; s. D.G. Brinton and Anne Harrison (Bigelow) T.; m. Louise Meredith Blanchard, Mar. 5, 1938; 1 child, Elizabeth. BA, Yale U., 1958; LLB, Harvard U., 1962. Assoc. Emmet Marvin & Martin LLP, NYC, 1962-69, ptnr., 1969—2006, sr. counsel, 2007—. Office: Emmet Marvin & Martin LLP 120 Broadway Fl 32 New York NY 10271-3291 Office Phone: 212-238-3004. Business E-Mail: lthompson@emmetmarvin.com.

THOMPSON, LOIS JEAN HEIDKE ORE, psychologist; b. Chgo., Feb. 22, 1933; d. Harold William and Ethel Rose (Neumann) Heidke; m. Henry Thomas Ore, Aug. 28, 1954 (div. May 1972); children: Christopher, Douglas; m. Joseph Lippard Thompson, Aug. 3, 1972; children: Scott, Les, Melanie. BA, Cornell Coll., Mt. Vernon, Iowa, 1955; MA, Idaho State U., 1964, EdD, 1981. Lic. psychologist, N.Mex. Tchr. pub. schs. various locations, 1956—67; tchr., instr. Idaho State U., Pocatello, 1967—72; employee/orgn. devel. specialist Los Alamos Nat. Lab., N.Mex., 1981—84, tng. specialist N.Mex., 1984—89, sect. leader N.Mex., 1989—93; pvt. practice indsl. psychology and healthcare, Los Alamos, 1988—. Sec. Cornell Coll. Alumni Office, 1954-55, also other orgns.; bd. dirs. Parent Edn. Ctr., Idaho State U., 1980; counselor, Los Alamos, 1981-88. Editor newsletter LWV, Laramie, Wyo., 1957; contbr. articles to profl. jours. Pres. Newcomers Club, Pocatello, 1967, Faculty Womens Club, Pocatello, 1968; chmn. edn. com. AAUW, Pocatello, 1969. Mem.: APA, N.Mex. Soc. Adlerian Psychology (pres. 1990, treas. 1991—97, bd. dirs. 1996—), N.Mex. Psychol. Assn. (bd. dirs. divsn. II 1990, 1999, sec. 1988—90, chmn. 1990, 1999—2000). Mem. Lds Ch. Avocations: racewalking, backpacking, skiing, tennis, biking. Home and Office: 340 Aragon Ave Los Alamos NM 87544-3505 Personal E-mail: thompsonlj@cybermesa.com. *Honesty, dependability, spiritual inspiration, and always doing our best are ingredients that lead to a successful and happy life.*

THOMPSON, LONNIE G., glaciologist, educator; b. Gassaway, W.Va., July 1, 1948; m. Ellen Mosley-Thompson. BS in Geology, Marshall U., 1970; MS in Geology, Ohio State U., 1973, PhD in Geology, 1976. Rsch. sci. Byrd Polar Rsch. Ctr. Ohio State U., 1976, assoc. prof., dept. geological sciences, 1991, prof., dept. geological scis., 1994, univ. disting. prof., dept. geological scis., 2002. Field team leader and other roles of several field rsch. expeditions, 1973—; mem. US Ice Core Working Group, 1986—89; mem. sci. adv. panel for the climate change data and detection program NOAA Climate and Global Change Program, 2001—04; co-dir. academics Tibetan Palteau Rsch. Inst., Beijing, 2005; mem. review com. Canadian Found. for Climate and Atmospheric Scis., 2004—05; mem. exec. review com. Canadian Polar Climate Stability Network, 2005—; chmn., external review com. Environ. Sciences Grad. Prog., Sch. Natural Resources, 2005; sci. advisor, climate and water initiative Ohio State U., Coll. Math & Phys. Scis., 2005. Contbr. articles to profl. jours.; mem. internat. editl. adv. bd. Interdisciplinary Journal-The Holocene, 1990—, mem. editl. bd. Geology, 1994—, Quaternary Science Review, 2000—. Recipient John Marshall medal for Civic Responsibility, Marshall U., 2002, Vega medal, Swedish Soc. for Anthropology and Geography, 2002, Common Wealth award for Sci. and Invention, 2002, Dr. A.H. Heineken Prize for Environ. Sciences, Royal Netherlands Acad. Arts and Scis., 2002, Tyler prize, The World prize for environ. achievement, 2005, 2005 Nat. Medal Sci., NSF, 2007; co-recipient (with wife) Disting. Explorer award, Roy Chapman Andrews Soc., Beloit Coll., Wis., 2007; named one of America's Best in Sci. and Medicine, CNN and Time Mag., 2001; several grants from NSF, NASA, NOAA and Nat. Geodetic Survey. Fellow: AAAS, Am. Geophysical Union; mem.: Internat. Glaciological Soc. (mem. adv. bd. 1999—), Am. Philos. Soc., NAS, Phi Beta Kappa (Epsilon of Ohio, elected alumni mem.), Phi Kappa Phi. Office: Ohio State U Sch Earth Scis 275 Mendenhall Lab 125 S Oval Mall Office SC 082C & OR 102 Columbus OH 43210 Office Phone: 614-292-6652. Office Fax: 614-292-4697. E-mail: thompson.3@osu.edu.

THOMPSON, LORING MOORE, retired academic administrator, writer; b. Newton, Mass., Feb. 17, 1918; s. Henry E. and Ella (Gould) T.; m. Pearl E. Judiesch, Dec. 30, 1949 (dec. May 2002); children: Bruce C., Douglas P. (dec.). BS in Indsl. Engring, Northeastern U., 1940; MS, U. RI, 1947; PhD, U. Chgo., 1956. Instr. U. RI, 1946; asst. to pres. Assn. Colls. Upper NY, 1947-49; assoc. prof. U. Toledo, 1952-59, asst. dean acad. adminstrn., 1958-59; dir. univ. planning Northeastern U., Boston, 1959-63, dean adult programs, 1964-66, v.p. planning, 1967-80, emeritus, 1980—2009; faculty assoc. continuing edn. Ariz. State U., 1982-84. Cons. in field. Author: (with others) Business Communication, 1949; contbr. articles to profl. jours. Bd. dirs. Back Bay Assn., Boston, 1961-63, v.p., 1963; trustee Huntington Gen. Hosp., Boston, 1970-80; mem. Fenway Project Area Com., 1973-76; mem. Mass. conf. ch. and edn. com. United Ch. of Christ, 1972-78, chairperson, 1973-74, mem. task force on ch. growth, 1978-80; mem. Chandler Area Coun., 1988-89; sec. Interfaith Coun. Greater Sun Lakes, 1993-96. Lt. USNR, 1942-45. Mem. Inst. Noetic Scis., Tau Beta Pi. Home: 25408 S Sedona Dr Sun Lakes AZ 85248-6636 Home Phone: 480-895-0370.

THOMPSON, LOUIS MILTON, JR., public investor relations consultant; b. Bryan, Tex., Sept. 21, 1938; s. Louis Milton and Margaret (Stromberg) T.; m. Anne Strand, Aug. 5, 1961 (div. Feb. 1992); children: Louis Milton III, Eric Norman, Christopher Scott, Mary Margaret, Mary Elizabeth; m. Laura Russell, Nov. 28, 1992; children: Emily Allan, Helen Aubrey. BS, Iowa State U., 1961, MS with honors, 1969. News editor, anchor Sta. WOI-TV-AM-FM, Ames, Iowa, 1960-61; commd. 2d lt. U.S. Army, 1961, resigned, 1974; advanced through grades to lt. col. USAR, 1981; asst. press sec. The White House, Washington, 1974-75; asst. to pres. Am. Enterprise Inst., Washington, 1975-76; dir. pub. affairs Nonprescription Drug Mfrs. Assn., Washington, 1976-78; sr. v.p. Nat. Assn. Home Builders, Washington, 1978-82; pres., CEO, Nat. Investor Rels. Inst., Vienna, Va., 1982—2006; ptnr. Genesis Inc., 2006—07; managing. dir. Kalorama Ptnrs. LLC, 2006—; ptnr. Beacon Advisors, 2009—. Individual investor adv. com. NY Stock Exch., NYC, 1990—92, NYC, 2004—; new founds. working group Harvard U. John F. Kennedy Sch., Cambridge, Mass., 1992—94; consumer affairs adv. com. SEC, Washington, 1996—99; chmn. adv. coun. Greenlee Sch. Journalism and Comm., Iowa State U., Ames, 2005—09, liberal arts and scis. dean's coun., 2001—07. Author: The Handbook of Investor Relations, 1989; contbr. articles to profl. jours. Va. chmn. U.S. Equestrian Team, Gladstone, NJ, 1978—82; dressage judge Am. Horse Shows Assn., Lexington, Ky., 1979—86; bd. dirs. Nat. Coun. Econ. Edn., 2001—04. Recipient Disting. Svc. award, Investment Edn. Inst., 1987, Investor Rels. Mag. and Barron's lifetime achievement award, 2000, J.W. Schwartz award, Iowa State U., 2001. Mem. Investor Rels. Assn., Internat. Investor Rels. Fedn., Am. Hanoverian Soc. (disting. mem., pres. 1988-94), Univ. Club, Phi Kappa Phi. Avocations: equestrian sports, golf, wine collecting, breeding horses. Home and Office: Home Again Farm 11539 Spicers Mill Rd Orange VA 22960-2103 Home Phone: 540-672-0485.

THOMPSON, MACK EUGENE, historian, educator; b. Burley, Idaho, Feb. 24, 1921; s. Eugene and Nora (McFate) T.; m. Helen Goldhamer, Oct. 30, 1945. AB, Queen's Coll., CUNY, 1948; MA, Brown U., 1951, PhD, 1955. Instr. history Brown U., 1954-55; asst. prof. Calif. Inst. Tech., 1955-56, U. Calif. at Riverside, 1956-62, asso. prof., 1962-66, prof., 1966-77; emeritus prof., 1977—; chmn. div. humanities U. Calif. at Riverside, 1961-63, asso. univ. dean acad. planning, 1965-66, dean, div. undergrad. studies, 1971-74; exec dir. Am. Hist. Assn., Washington, 1974-81. Chmn. editorial bd. Experiment and Innovation: New Directions in Edn., U. Calif., 1966-68 Author: The Ward-Hopkins Controversy and the American Revolution in Rhode Island: An Interpretation, 1959, Moses Brown, Reluctant Reformer, 1962, Causes and Circumstances of the Du Pont Family's Emigration, 1969. Bd. dirs. Harry S. Truman Libr. Inst., 1974-81. With AUS, 1942-45. Home: 1378 River Oaks Ct Oldsmar FL 34677-4828

THOMPSON, MARK R., museum director; BA in English, Dickinson Coll., 1975; JD, Am. U., 1979; MA, U. Del., 2004. Cert. in mus. studies U. Del., 2004. Trial lawyer, 1979—2001; exec. dir. Portland Harbor Mus., Maine, 2004—. Office: Portland Harbor Mus Fort Road - SMCC Campus South Portland ME 04106 Office Phone: 207-799-6337. Office Fax: 207-799-3862. E-mail: director@portlandharbormuseum.org.

THOMPSON, MARK S., electronics executive; BS in Chemistry, SUNY; PhD in Inorganic Chemistry, Univ. NC. V.p. OEM group Raychem Electronics; v.p., gen. mgr. power components divsn. Tyco Electronics; CEO Big Bear Networks, 2001—04; exec. v.p. mfg. and tech. group Fairchild Semiconductor Corp., Portland, Maine, 2004—05, pres., CEO, dir., 2005—08, chmn., pres., CEO, 2008—. Bd. dir. Big Bear Networks. Office: Fairchild Semiconductor Corp 82 Running Hill Rd South Portland ME 04106 Office Phone: 207-775-8100.

THOMPSON, MARTIN CHRISTIAN, retired news executive; b. Council Bluffs, Iowa, Oct. 25, 1938; s. Ross Kenneth and Mary Ellen (Pierce) T.; m. Janet Ann Morrow, Aug. 4, 1962; children: Chris Michael, Sean Martin. BA in Comms., U. Wash., 1960. Newsman Sta. KEDO, Longview, Wash., 1960-61; news dir. Sta. KREW, Sunnyside, Wash., 1961-66; newsman AP, Seattle, 1966-68, corr. Reno, 1968-70, newsman San Francisco, 1970-72, news editor, 1972-75, chief of bur. San Francisco, 1975-86, Los Angeles, 1986-88, mng. editor NYC, 1989-92, dir. state news, 1992—2003; ret., 2003. Methodist.

THOMPSON, MARY CECILIA, nurse midwife; b. Georgetown, Guyana; came to the U.S., 1977; d. John Alexander and Monica Eileen (Thorne) T. RN, Southend-on-Sea Sch. Nursing, Essex, Eng., 1973; cert. midwife, Basildon & Thurrock Sch., Essex, Eng., 1975; perinatal nurse practitioner, Cmty. Gen. Hosp., Syracuse, NY, 1986; cert. nurse midwife, Frontier Sch. Midwifery, Hyden, Ky., 1990. Cert. nurse midwife. Staff nurse pediatric unit Rochford Hosp., Essex, 1973-74; staff midwife Basildon & Orsett Maternity Units, Essex, 1975-76, St. Peter's Hosp. Chertsey, Surrey, Eng., 1976-78; staff nurse pediatric critical care SUNY Health Sci. Ctr., Syracuse, 1978-82; staff nurse pvt. duty nursing Med. Pers. Pool, Syracuse, 1982-83; staff nurse labor and delivery Cmty. Gen. Hosp., Syracuse, 1983-86, perinatal nurse practitioner, 1986-90; pvt. practice cert. nurse midwife Syracuse, 1990—. Mem. AWHONN, Am. Assn. Nurse Practitioners, Am. Coll. Nurse Midwives. Roman Catholic. Avocations: embroidery, reading, tennis, music, travel. Home: 4904 Razorback Run Syracuse NY 13215-1347 Office: Choices West Med Ctr West W Genesee St Camillus NY 13031-2238

THOMPSON, MARY EILEEN, chemistry professor; b. Mpls., Dec. 21, 1928; d. Albert C. and Blanche (McAvoy) T. BA, Coll. St. Catherine, 1953; MS, U. Minn., 1958; PhD, U. Calif., Berkeley, 1964. Tchr. math. and sci. Derham Hall H.S., St. Paul, 1953-58; mem. faculty Coll. of St. Catherine, St. Paul, 1964-69, prof. chemistry, 1969-2000, chmn. dept., 1969-90, prof. emerita, 2000—. Project dir. Women in Chemistry, 1984-98. Contbr. articles to profl. jours. Named one of 100 persons honored, Coll. St. Catherine's 100th Anniversary. Mem. AAAS, Am. Chem. Soc. (chmn. women chemists com. 1992-94, award for encouraging women into chem. scis. careers 1997), Coun. Undergrad. Rsch. (councillor 1991-96), N.Y. Acad. Scis., Chem. Soc. London, Sigma Xi, Phi Beta Kappa (senator 1997-2003). Democrat. Roman Catholic. Achievements include research interests in Cr(III) hydrolytic polymers, kinetics of inorganic complexes, Co(III) peroxo/superoxo complexes. Home: 1870 Randolph Ave Saint Paul MN 55105-1736

THOMPSON, MARY ELIZABETH, retired application developer; d. William Reid Jones and Mildred Faye King; 1 child, Barbara Chancee Craig. BFA, U. Kans., 1963; MA in Edn., U. St. Mary, 1995. Cert. in computer programming and ops. Ga., 1980; supr. devel. program for higher edn. 2005. Art dir. Quantico Va. Dependents Sch. Sys., Quantico, Va., 1964—65, Camp LeJeune NC Dependents Sch. Sys., Camp Lejeune, NC, 1965—67; computer programmer analyst Bank of the South, Atlanta, 1980—82, Hanes Corp., Atlanta, 1982—82; computer programming instr. Cobb County Cmty. Sch. Sys., Marietta, Ga., 1983—83; computer info. sys. instr. Johnson County C.C., Overland Park, Kans., 1987—88; computer info. sys. sr. prof. DeVry U., Kansas City, Mo., 1988—2007, suprv. devel. program, 2005—07; ret., 2007. Kansas designer craftsman show, (Charles Rombold Art Award, 1963), philharmonic showhouse book. Mem. Jr. Women's Philharm. Assn., Kansas City, Mo., 1970—73; chairperson Alpha Phi Help Lick Heart Disease, Kansas City, Mo., 1974; mem. Jr. League of Johnson County, Overland Park, Kans., 1998—99, Philanthropic Ednl. Orgn., Overland Pk., Kans., 2009. Recipient New Prof. Prime Addition award, DeVry U., 1988, Mo. Governor's award for Excellence in Tchg. and Performance Excellence in Edn., The State of Mo., 2004. Mem.: Kans. City Profl. Devel. Coun., Micro Focus User Group, Faculty Assessment Adv. Coun., Assn. Info. Tech. Profls., Alpha Phi Sorority. Achievements include development of innovative stratagies for teaching computer languages online; research in student teamwork in the classroom. Home: 10801 W 115th St Overland Park KS 66210

THOMPSON, MELINDA L., theologian; PhD, Luther Sem., St. Paul, 2005. Dir. distance edn. U. Dubuque Theol. Sem., Iowa, 2005—. Office: Univ Dubuque Theol Sem 2000 University Ave Dubuque IA 52001

THOMPSON, MICK, state banking agency administrator; b. Oct. 11, 1976; BA, Southeastern Okla. State U., Durant; MEd, Northeastern State U., Tahlequah, Okla.; grad. in Banking, U. Colo., Boulder. Exec. v.p. Ctrl. Nat. Bank, Poteau, Okla., 1977—90; dir. legis. and govtl. rels. Okla. Gov.'s Office; commr. Okla. State Banking Dept., Oklahoma City, 1992—. Mem. Okla. House Reps., Poteau, 1976—84, chmn. banking and fin. com., mem. appropriations and budget com., majority floor leader, 1983—84; pres. Okla. Cmty. Bankers Assn., 1988—90; bd. dirs. UICI, North Richland Hills, Tex., 2004—. Mem. adv. coun. Southeastern Okla. State U. Bus. Sch., Durant; adv. to bd. trustees U. Colo. Grad. Sch. Banking, Boulder. Mem.: Conf. State Bank Suprs. (chmn. 2003). Republican. Office: Okla State Banking Dept 4545 N Lincoln Blvd Ste 164 Oklahoma City OK 73105-3403 Office Phone: 405-521-2782. Office Fax: 405-522-2993. E-mail: rmt1@onenet.net.*

THOMPSON, MIKE (C. MICHAEL THOMPSON), United States Representative from California; b. Jan. 24, 1951; s. Charles Thompson and Beverly (Forni) Powell; m. Janet Thompson, Mar. 8, 1982; children: Christopher, Jon. BA in Political Sci., Calif. State U., Chico, 1982, MA in Pub. Adminstrn., 1996. Owner, maintenance supr. Beringer Winery; mem. Calif. State Senate, 1991—98, U.S. Congress from 1st Calif. dist., 1999—; mem. armed svcs. com., agr. com. Former chair select com. Calif. Wine Industry; former chair budget com. Calif. Senate, former vice chair natural resources com.; instr. Army Airborne Sch.; instr. pub. adminstrn. and state govt. San Francisco State U., Calif. State U., Chico. Co-founder, co-chair Congl. Wine Caucus; co-vice chair Congl. Sportsmen's Caucus; mem. New Dem. Coalition, Blue Dog Coalition. Staff sgt. US Army, Vietnam. Decorated Purple Heart, US Army; recipient Disting. Svc. award, Calif. State Assn. Counties, Calif. Assn. Hosps., Legis. Leadership award, Calif. Assn. Health Svcs., 1994, Disting. Svc. award, Aids Project LA, 1995, Outstanding Senator award, Planned Parenthood Affiliates Calif., 1996; named Legislator of Yr., Calif. Abortion Rights Action League, Calif. Assn. Persons with Handicaps, Police Officers Rsch. Assn. Calif., Disabled in State Svc., 1994, Senator of Yr., Calif. Assn. Homes & Svcs. for Aging, 1995, Outstanding Senator of Yr., Calif. Sch. Bds. Assn., 1996, Calif. Profl. Firefighters, 1996. Mem.: Calif. Faculty Assn., Bus. & Profl. Women's Assn., Vietnam Vets. of America, Am. Legion, Native Sons of Golden West, Sons of Italy. Democrat. Roman Catholic. Office: US Ho Reps 231 Cannon Ho Office Bldg Washington DC 20515-0501 Office Phone: 202-225-3111. Office Fax: 202-225-4335.*

THOMPSON, NEIL DANIEL, retired lawyer; b. Calexico, Calif., Feb. 21, 1935; s. Francis Marion Thompson and Leah Harriet Howell. AB with honors, UCLA, 1957; PhD, Columbia U., 1963; LLB, Harvard U., 1963. Bar: NY 1964, US Dist. Ct. (so. dist.) NY 1965, US Customs Ct. 1967, US Ct. Appeals (2d cir.) 1971, US Supreme Ct. 1973. Assoc. Jas. Maxwell Fassett, NYC, 1964-65, Doman & Ablondi, NYC, 1965-69, Pollack & Kaminsky, NYC, 1969-80; pvt. practice NYC, 1980-86; rsch. cons. Salt Lake City, 1986—. Author: Family of Bartholomew Stovall, 1993; editor The Genealogist, 1980-96; contbr. articles to profl. jours. Trustee Bd. for Cert. of Genealogists, 1977-89, pres., 1983-86. Fellow Am. Soc. Genealogists (pres. 1992-95), Soc. Genealogists (London), Utah Geneal. Assn. (bd. dirs. 1988-89); mem. Phi Beta Kappa, Phi Mu Alpha. Mem. LDS Ch. Avocations: music, stamp collecting/philately, book collecting. Home: 255 N 200 W Salt Lake City UT 84103-4545 Office Phone: 801-521-4732. Personal E-mail: gryphon801@aol.com.

THOMPSON, NELS F., biology professor; b. Manitowoc, Wis., Aug. 16, 1938; s. George William and Ethel Edna Thompson; m. Bonnie L. Wiesman, Jan. 21, 1961; children: Nathan David, Eric John, Dana Mathew, Ryan Mark. MS, U. Wis., Milw., 1970. Biology instr. Owatonna HS, 1970—99; biology prof. Riverland CC, Austin, Minn., 1999—. Coun. mem., pres. First Luth., Hope, Minn., 1971—91. Sgt. USN, 1956—59, Various states. Recipient Good Conduct medal, USN, 1959. Lutheran. Avocations: birdwatching, travel.

THOMPSON, N(ORMAN) DAVID, insurance company executive; b. Rockville Centre, NY, July 30, 1934; s. Norman J. and Laurel H. (Johnson) T.; m. Joyce L. Angeletti, June 7, 1958; children: John L., Jennifer L., Sarah S. BA with distinction, Wesleyan U., 1956; LLB, Columbia U., 1959; postgrad., Harvard U., 1973. Bar: N.Y. Pvt. practice law, NYC, 1961-62; corp. sec. Gen. Reins. Corp., NYC, 1964-69, v.p. Greenwich, Conn., 1969, v.p., gen. counsel, sec., 1976-77; exec. v.p. N.Am. Reins. Corp., NYC, 1977-78, pres., 1978-92; chmn., CEO Swiss Reins. Am. Corp. (formerly N.Am. Reins.), 1992-95, Swiss Re Am. Holding Corp. (formerly SwissRe Holding Co.), 1992-97; chmn. SwissRe Group Cos. (U.S.), 1992-95. Dir. Nat. Legal Ctr. for Pub. Interest, chmn., 1992-95; trustee Coll. Ins., 1992, 98. With U.S. Army, 1959-60. Mem. Reins Assn. Am. (chmn. 1982-83), Nat. Assn. Casualty and Surety Execs. (pres. 1986-87), Am. Arbitration Assn. (bd. dirs., chmn. fin. com. 1992-93), Am. Inst. Property and Casualty Underwriters (trustee, 1992-98), Univ. Club (N.Y.C.), Saugatuck Harbor Yacht Club (Westport, Conn.). Home: 47 Kettle Creek Rd Weston CT 06883-2208

THOMPSON, NORMAN WINSLOW, surgeon, educator; b. Boston, July 12, 1932; s. Herman Chandler and Evelyn Millicent (Palmer) T.; m. Marcia Ann Veldman, June 12, 1956; children: Robert, Karen, Susan, Jennifer. BA, Hope Coll., Holland, Mich., 1953; MD, U. Mich., 1957; MD (hon.), U. Linköping, Sweden, 1995. Diplomate Am. Bd. Surgery. From intern to prof. emeritus surgery U. Mich., Ann Arbor, Mich., 1957—2001, prof. emeritus surgery, 2001—. Contbr. articles to profl. jours. Trustee Hope Coll., 1973-88. Fellow Royal Australasian Coll. Surgeons (hon.), Royal Coll. Physicians and Surgeons of Glasgow; mem. ACS (gov. 1979-85), Ctrl. Surg. Assn., Western Surg. Assn. (1st v.p. 1992-93, pres. 1994-95), F.A. Coller Surg. Soc. (pres. 1986), Am. Surg. Assn., Am. Thyroid Assn., Soc. Surg. Alimentary Tract, Internat. Assn. Endocrine Surgeons (pres. 1989-91), Internat. Soc. Surgeons (v.p. 1995—), Am. Assn. Endocrine Surgeons (pres. 1980-81, 81-82), Royal Soc. Medicine, Brit. Assn. Endocrine Surgeons, Spanish Assn. Surgeons (hon.), Assn. French Endocrine Surgeons, Scandanvian Surg. Soc., Soc. Surg. Oncology, Turkish Assn. Endocrine Surgeons, European Soc. Endocrine Surgeons (hon.), Spanish Soc. Surgeons (hon.), European Surg. Assn.(hon.), Alpha Omega Alpha. Home: 465 Hillspur Rd Ann Arbor MI 48105-1048 Office: Surgery Emeritus Faculty 1327 Jones Dr Ste 201 Ann Arbor MI 48105 Office Phone: 734-998-0167. Office Fax: 734-998-0173. Business E-Mail: normant@med.umich.edu.

THOMPSON, PAMELA PADWICK, public relations executive; b. Columbus, Ohio, June 13, 1943; d. Frank John and Tiami Judith (Padwick) T.; stepfather, James William Bampton; m. Fairman Rogers Thompson, Jan. 10, 1942; children: Ryder McNeal, Darby McNeal. BA, U. Louisville, 1994; MA, U. Dayton, 1998. Ptnr. Crutcher, Kelly and Assocs., Louisville, 1979-83; owner Transl. Co., Louisville, 1981-83, Technigraphics, Louisville, 1984-87; v.p. dir. individual support Grtr. Louisville Fund for the Arts, Louisville, 1989-92; v.p. comms. John Templeton Found., Radnor, Pa., 1997—. Adj. prof. U. Louisville, 1997. Contbr. articles to profl. jours. including Small Group Behavior. Chair pub. rels. com. Keene Valley Libr., 2000-01; bd. dirs. Louisville Nature Ctr., 1996-97; mem. ad hoc com. State Ky. Biodiversity Coun., Louisville, 1996-97; city commr. City of Rolling Fields, Louisville, 1991-94; alliance bd. dirs. J.B. Speed Art Mus., Louisville, 1986-92. Mem. APA, Soc. for Consumer Psychology, Pub. Rels. Soc. Am., Jr. League Phila., Cosmo. Club Phila., Ausable Club. Episcopalian. Avocations: hiking, gardening, tennis, travel. Home: 4 Porter Ln Rose Valley PA 19086 Office: John Templeton Foundation 300 Conshohocken State Rd Ste 500 Conshohocken PA 19428-3801 Office Phone: 610-941-5194. Fax: (610) 687-8961. Business E-Mail: pthompson@templeton.org.

THOMPSON, PATRICK S., lawyer; b. Muskegon, Mich., July 24, 1967; BA with high honors, U. Mich., 1989; JD, Harvard Law Sch., 1992. Bar: Calif. 1992. Ptnr., antitrust, telecom., complex litig. Pillsbury Winthrop LLP, San Francisco; ptnr. Goodwin Procter LLP, 2006—. Editor: Antitrust Law Jour., 1996—2002. Vice chair, conservatory com. Am. Conservatory Theater; sec., bd. trustees Grace Cathedral; chmn. bd. dirs. Calif. Pacific Med. Ctr., 2003—04, dir., 1996—2004; sec., bd. trustees Am. Conservatory Theater; bd. dirs. Francis of Assisi Cmty. Named one of Am. Top Black Attys., Black Enterprise, 2003, Top 20 Lawyers Under Age 40, Daily Jour., Calif., 2004, N. Calif. Super Lawyers, 2004—05. Mem.: ABA (mem. antitrust section, mem. editl. bd. Antitrust Source, liaison to commn. racial and ethnic diversity in legal profession), State Bar Calif. (vice chair, exec. com. antitrust and unfair competition section 2005). Office: Goodwin Procter LLP 101 Calif St San Francisco CA 94111 Office Phone: 415-733-6068. Office Fax: 415-677-9041. Business E-Mail: pthompson@goodwinprocter.com.

THOMPSON, PAUL MICHAEL, lawyer; b. Dubuque, Iowa, Aug. 30, 1935; s. Frank W. and Genevieve (Cassutt) T.; m. Mary Jacqueline McManus, Jan. 30, 1960; children: Anne, Tricia, Paul, Tim, Jim. BA magna cum laude, Loras Coll., 1957; LLB, Georgetown U., 1959. Bar: Iowa 1959, DC 1959, Va. 1966. Atty. appellate ct. br. NLRB, Washington, 1962-66; assoc. Hunton & Williams, Richmond, Va., 1966-71, ptnr., 1971—. Adj. prof. The T.C. Williams Sch. Law U. Richmond; adj. prof. law sch. Coll. William and Mary Sch. Law. Served with JAGC, USAF, 1960-62. Mem. ABA, Va. State Bar, Va. Bar Assn., Internat. Bar Assn., Commonwealth Club. Roman Catholic. Office: The TC Williams School Law University of Richmond Richmond VA 23173 Office Phone: 804-289-8856. Personal E-mail: thompmerrypoint@comcast.net. Business E-Mail: pthomps3@richmond.edu.

THOMPSON, PAUL WARWICK, museum director; married; 2 children. B, U. Bristol, 1980; M, U. East Anglia, 1984, D, 1987. English tchr. St. Bede's Sch., Eastbourne, England; scriptwriter, rschr. Design Coun., 1987—88; curator contemporary design Design Mus., 1988—90, curator London, 1990—92, dir., 1992—2000, Cooper-Hewitt Nat. Design Mus., NY, 2001—09; rector Royal Coll. Art, London, 2009—. Office: Cooper-Hewitt Nat Design Mus 2 E 91 St New York NY 10128-9990 Office Phone: 212-849-8400, 212-849-8370, 44 207590 4101. Business E-Mail: thompsonp@si.edu, paul.thompson@rca.ac.uk.

THOMPSON, PHILIP C., lawyer, investment advisor, private equity fund manager, educator, journalist; b. Balt., Oct. 21, 1945; s. Earl Clinton and Virginia Thompson; m. Julie Ann Young, June 10, 1948; children: Kathryn Adair, Julia Hamilton, Philip Clinton Jr. BA, Washington and Lee U., 1967, BS, 1968, JD, 1971. Bar: Ga. 1973, US Dist. Ct. (ea. dist.) Ga. (judicial clk.) 1973. Law clk. to Hon. Walter E. Hoffman US Dist. Ct. (ea. dist.) Va., 1971—72; ptnr. Jones, Day, Reavis & Pogue, Atlanta, 1973—86, Dow, Lohnes & Albertson, Atlanta, 1986—95, Arnall, Golden, Gregory LLP, Atlanta, 1995—2004, Duane Morris LLP, Atlanta, 2004—. Adj. prof. Emory U. Goizueta Bus. Sch., Atlanta, 2003—05, Ga. State Robinson Coll. Brave, Atlanta, 2007—09; bd. trustee Robinson Coll. Bus., 2009—. Capt. US Army, 1972—73. Mem.: Capital City Club. Republican. Reformed Anglican. Avocations: youth programs, prison ministry, golf, tennis, chess. Office: Duane Morris LLP 1180 W Peachtree St Ste 700 Atlanta GA 30309-3448 Office Phone: 404-253-6920. Business E-Mail: pcthompson@duanemorris.com.

THOMPSON, PHILIP DOUGLAS, federal agency administrator, educator; b. Berea, Ky., Sept. 11, 1923; s. Jamie Campbell and Julia Meta (Hatcher) Thompson; m. Lois Marie Coldiron, Sept. 10, 1949; children: Julia-Anna Thompson Marsden, Philip Douglas Thompson Jr. BA in Philosophy & Psychology, U. Ky., 1954, postgrad., 1954—55. Adminstr. aide U.S. mil. dist. U.S. Army, Lexington, Ky., 1957—58; pers. mgmt. insp. Civil Svc. Commn., Cinn., 1959—60; pers. officer IRS, Washington, 1960—64; dir. tng. Fed. Water Pollution Control, Washington, 1964—67, Dept. Interior, Washington, 1967—68; dir. tng., programs and personnel Fed. Power Commn., Washington, 1968—69; dir. exec. devel. Dept. Energy, Washington, 1979—81. Elder Presbyn. Ch., clk. of session; mem. Jr. C. of C. Sgt. US Army, 1942—45, Scotland. Fellow: Soc. Antiquarians; mem.: DAV, VFW, U. Ky. Alumni Assn. (pres. 1977—78), Jr. C of C, Am. Soc. Tng. & Development, Argyll Ednl. Soc. (pres., chmn. bd.), St. Andrews Soc. (pres. 1996—97, bd. trustees 1999—), Vets. Invasion of France Omaha Beach, Mil. Order of Purple Heart, Vets. Battle of Bulge, Sons of Revolution, Am. Legion, Order of Ky. Col. (hon.). Presbyterian. Avocations: violin, clocks, making furniture. Personal E-mail: corblyn@aol.com.

THOMPSON, PHYLLIS D., Associate Judge, DC Court of Appeals, lawyer; b. Washington, Oct. 1, 1952; BA in Anthropology, with distinction, George Washington U., 1974; MA in Religion (focus in Ethics), Princeton U., 1976; JD with high honors, George Washington U., 1981. Bar: DC 1981. Instr., lectr. Georgetown U., Washington, 1977-81; joined Covington & Burling, Washington, 1982—, now ptnr., fed. benefits programs practice group; assoc. judge DC Ct. Appeals, Washington, 2006—. Instr. & lectr. - Theology Dept. Georgetown U., Washington, 1977—81. Co-author (with Susan L. Burke): Analysis Has Its Privileges: Compliance Rev. May Be Protected From Discovery, 1999. Mem.: Am. Health Lawyers Assn., DC Bar Assn. (steering com. affairs divsn.). Office: DC Ct of Appeals Moultrie Courthouse 500 Indiana Ave NW Washington DC 20001 Office Phone: 202-662-5668, 202-897-2781. Office Fax: 202-662-6291. Business E-Mail: pthompson@cov.com.*

THOMPSON, RALPH GORDON, retired federal judge; b. Okla. City, Dec. 15, 1934; m. Barbara Irene Hencke, Sept. 5, 1964; children: Lisa, Elaine, Maria. BBA, U. Okla., 1956, JD, 1961. Bar: Okla. 1961. Spl. agt. Office of Spl. Investigations, USAF, 1957—60; ptnr. Thompson, Thompson, Harbour & Selph (and predecessors), Oklahoma City, 1961-75; judge U.S. Dist. Ct. for Western Dist. Okla., Oklahoma City, 1975—2008; chief judge U.S. Dist. Ct. (we. dist.) Okla., 1986-93. Mem. Okla. Ho. of Reps., 1966-70, asst. minority floor leader, 1969-70; spl. justice Supreme Ct. Okla., 1970-71; tchr. Harvard Law Sch. Trial Advocacy Workshop, 1981-2008; apptd. by chief justice of U.S. to U.S. Fgn. Intelligence Surveillance Ct., 1990-97; elected to jud. conf. of the U.S., 1997; apptd. to Edward J. Devitt Disting. Svc. Justice award selection com., 1997-99; apptd. by chief justice of U.S. to exec. com. of Jud. Conf. of the U.S., 1998-2000; coord. Long Range Planning for Fed. Judiciary, 1999-2000. Co-author: Mr. Integrity, Bryle Harlow, Counsellor to Presidents, Bob Burke and Ralph G. Thompson, 2000. Rep. nominee for lt. gov., Okla., 1970; chmn. bd. ARC, Oklahoma City, 1970-72; chmn., pres. Okla. Young Lawyers Conf., 1965; mem. bd. visitors U. Okla., 1975-78, U. Okla. Honors Coll., 2007—. Lt. USAF, 1957-60, col. Res., ret. Decorated Legion of Merit; named Oklahoma City's Outstanding Young Man, Oklahoma City Jaycees, 1967, Outstanding Young Oklahoman, Okla. State Jr. C. of C., 1968, Outstanding Fed. Trial Judge, Okla. Trial Lawyers Assn., 1980; recipient Regents Alumni award U. Okla., 1990, Disting. Svc. award, 1993, Jour. Record Pub. Co. award for Disting. Svc., 2001, Humanitarian award Oklahoma City Pub. Schs. Found., 2003; inducted Okla. Hall of Fame, 1995, Fellow Am. Bar Found.; mem. ABA, Fed. Bar Assn., Okla. Bar Assn. (chmn. sect. internat. law and gen. practice 1974-75), Oklahoma County Bar Assn. (Jud. Svc. award 1988), Jud. Conf. U.S. (com. on ct. adminstrn. 1981-89, com. on fed.-state jurisdiction 1988-91), U.S. Dist. Judges Assn. 10th Cir. (pres. 1992-94), Rotary (hon.), Order of Coif, Am. Inns of Ct. (pres. XXIII 1995-96), Phi Beta Kappa (pres. chpt. 1985-86, Phi Beta Kappa of Yr. 1991), Beta Theta Pi, Phi Alpha Delta, Nat. Conf. of Commrs. on Uniform State Laws, Judge Fed. Arbitration Inc.; mem. bd. of visitors, U. Oklahoma Honours Coll., U. Oklahoma Coll. of Law. Episcopalian.

THOMPSON, RALPH NEWELL, former chemical corporation executive; b. Boston, Mar. 4, 1918; s. Ralph and Lillian May (Davenport) T.; m. Virginia Kenniston, Jan. 31, 1942; children: Pamela, Nicholas, Diana. BS, MIT, 1940. Research engr. Middlesex Products Co., Cambridge, Mass., 1940-42; tech. dir. Falulah Paper Co., Fitchburg, Mass., 1945-48; staff engr. to v.p., div. gen. mgr. Calgon Corp., Pitts., 1948-70; v.p. mktg., corp. devel. Pa. Indsl. Chem. Corp., Clairton, 1970-74; gen. mgr. chem. div. Thiokol Corp., Trenton, NJ, 1974-76, group v.p.-chem. Newtown, Pa., 1976-82; marine artist, specializing in lighthouses and historic sailing vessels, 1982—. Dir. Mulford Co. Inc., Mass., 1956-82, Thiokol Can. Ltd., 1975-82, Thiokol Chems., Ltd., Eng., 1976-82, Toray Thiokol Co. Ltd., Japan, 1976-82, Nisso-Ventron K.K., Japan, 1977-82, S.W. Chem. Services Inc., Tex., 1978-82, S.W. Plastics Europe (S.A.), Belgium, 1978-82, Dynachem. Corp., Calif., 1979-82, Carstab Corp., Ohio, 1980-82 Patentee in field. Mem. Mt. Lebanon (Pa.) Civic League, 1950-74. Served with USNR, 1942-45. Recipient Goodreau Meml. Fund medal in chemistry, 1936 Fellow Am. Inst. Chemists; mem. TAPPI (contributor monograph series 1950-65), N.Y. Acad. Scis., Soc. Chem. Industry, Nat. Maritime Soc., Am. Soc. Marine Artists, Mil. Order World Wars, Pa. Soc., Soc. Descs. Colonial Clergy. Republican. Presbyterian.

THOMPSON, RAYMOND HARRIS, retired anthropologist, educator; b. Portland, Maine, May 10, 1924; s. Raymond and Eloise (MacIntyre) T.; m. Molly Kendall, Sept. 9, 1948; children: Margaret Kelsey Luchetta, Mary Frances. BS, Tufts U., 1947; A.M., Harvard U., 1950, PhD, 1955. Fellow div. hist. research Carnegie Instn., Washington, 1950-52; asst. prof. anthropology, curator Mus. Anthropology, U. Ky., 1952-56; faculty U. Ariz., 1956-97, prof. anthropology, 1964—, Riecker Disting. prof., 1980-97, head dept., 1964-80; emeritus, 1997; dir. Ariz. State Mus., 1964-97; emeritus, 1997. Mem. adv. panel program in anthropology NSF, 1963-64, mem. mus. collections program, 1983-85; mem. NSF grad. fellowship panel Nat. Acad. Scis.-NRC, 1964-66; mem. research in nursing in patient care rev. com. USPHS, 1967-69; com. on social sci. commn. edn. in agr. and natural resources Nat. Acad. Scis., 1968-69; mem. anthropology com. examiners Grad. Record Exam., 1967-70, chmn., 1969-70; mem. com. recovery archaeol. remains, 1972-77, chmn., 1973-77; collaborator Nat. Park Service, 1972-76; mem. Ariz. Hist. Adv. Commn., 1966-97, chmn., 1971-74, chmn. hist. sites rev. com., 1971-83; mem. editl. bd. Science, 1972-77; chmn. Ariz. Humanities Council, 1973-77, mem., 1979-85; adv. bd. Ariz. Hist. Recors, 1976-84; mem. research review panel for archaeology NEH, 1976-77, mem. rev. panel mus., 1978, Ariz. Archaeology Adv. Commn., 1985-97; cons. task force on archaeology Adv. Council on Historic Preservation, 1978; editl. advisor, Jour. of the Southwest. Author: Modern Yucatecan Maya Pottery Making, 1958; editor: Migrations in New World Culture History, 1958, When is a Kiva, 1990. Trustee Mus. No. Ariz., 1969-84, 86-90; bd. dirs. Tucson Art Mus., 1974-77; cons. Nat. Mus. Act Coun., 1984-86. Served with USNR, 1944-45, PTO. Recipient Pub. Svc. award, Dept. Interior, 1990; named Raymond H. Thompson award in his name, Dept. Anthrop., U. Ariz., 2006. Fellow AAAS (chmn. sect. H 1977-78), Tree-Ring Soc., Am. Anthrop. Assn. (Disting. Svc. award 1980); mem. Soc. Am. Archaeology (editor 1958-62, exec. com. 1963-64, pres. 1976-77, disting. svc. award 1998), Am. Soc. Conservation Archaeology (Conservation award 1980), Seminario de Cultura Maya, Am. Assn. Museums (accreditation vis. com. 1972, 82-90, cons. mus. assessment program 1983-89, repatriation task force 1987, steering com. mus. data collection program 1988-93), Internat. Coun. Museums (assoc.), Coun. Mus. Anthropology (dir. 1978-79, pres. 1980-83), Assn. Sci. Mus. Dirs. (sec.-treas. 1978-80), Ariz. Acad. Sci., Ariz. Archaeol. and Hist. Soc. (Byron Cummings award 1993), Mus. Assn. Ariz. (pres. 1983, 84), Phi Beta Kappa, Sigma Xi. Office: Univ Ariz Ariz State Museum Tucson AZ 85721-0026

THOMPSON, RICHARD FREDERICK, psychologist, neuroscientist, educator; b. Portland, Oreg., 1930; s. Frederick Albert and Margaret St. Clair (Marr) T.; m. Judith K. Pedersen, May 22, 1960; children: Kathryn M., Elizabeth K., Virginia St. C. BA, Reed Coll., 1952; MS, U. Wis., 1953, PhD, 1956. Asst. prof. med. psychology Med. Sch. U. Oreg., Portland, 1959-63, assoc. prof., 1963-65, prof., 1965-67; prof. psychobiology U. Calif., Irvine, 1967-73, 75-80; prof. psychology Harvard U., Cambridge, Mass., 1973-74, Lashley chair prof., 1973; prof. psychology, Bing prof. human biology Stanford U., Palo Alto, Calif., 1980-87; Keck prof. psychology and biol. scis. U. So. Calif., LA, 1987—, dir. neuroscience program, 1989—2001. Mem. Nat. Sci. Bd., 2006—. Author: Foundations of Physiological Psychology, 1967, (with others)

Psychology, 1971, Introduction to Physiological Psychology, 1975; Psychology editor (with others), W.H. Freeman & Co. publs., chief editor, Behavioral Neurosci., 1983—; editor: Jour. Comparative and Physiol. Psychology, 1981-83; regional editor: (with others) Physiology and Behavior; contbr. (with others) articles to profl. jours. Recipient Rsch. Scientist Award, Nat. Institutes of Mental Health, D.G. Marquis Behavioral Neurosci. Award, 1999. Fellow AAAS (John P. McGovern Award, 1999), APA (Disting. Sci. Contbn. award 1974, governing coun. 1974—), Soc. Neurosci. (councilor 1972-76); mem. NAS, Am. Acad. Arts and Scis., Internat. Brain Rsch. Orgn., Am. Philos. Soc., Psychonomic Soc. (gov. 1972-77, chmn. 1976), Am. Psychol. Soc. (pres. 1994-96), Western Psychol. Assn. (pres. 1994-95), Soc. Exptl. Psychology (Warren medal). Office: Univ of So Calif Neuroscis Program HNB 122 Univ Park Los Angeles CA 90007 Office Phone: 213-740-7350. Business E-Mail: thompson@usc.edu.

THOMPSON, RICHARD LEON, pharmaceutical executive, lawyer; b. Rochester, NY, Dec. 5, 1944; s. Leslie L. and Marion (Cosad) T.; m. Catherine Jean Terry, July 6, 1974; children: Kristin Anne, Catherine Elizabeth. AB cum laude, SUNY, Albany, 1966; MA, Syracuse U., 1967; JD, Cath. U., 1975. Staff dir., counsel U.S. Ho. of Reps., Washington, 1973-78; dir. Abbott Labs., Washington, 1978-83; v.p. Squibb Corp., Washington, 1983-89, Bristol-Myers Squibb Corp., Washington, 1989—2001, sr. v.p. policy and govt. affairs, 2001—. Chmn. legis. adv. com. Proprietary Assn., Washington, 1984; bd. dirs. Bus. Govt. Rels. Coun. Mem. com. on changing enrollments Fairfax (Va.) County Pub. Sch., 1983-84, supts. adv. com., 1984-85, mem., 1988-98; mem. Fed. City Coun., 1992; chmn. legis. com. P.R.-U.S.A. Found., 1985-95; co-chair Edn. in 2010; bd. dirs. D.C. Hospice, Bryce Harlow Found., 1990-95; bd. dirs. Ford Theater, 2000—, chmn., 2003-06; chmn. governance com. Meridian Internat. Ctr., 2000-02 1st lt. U.S. Army, 1968-69, Vietnam. Named one of Outstanding Young Men of Am., Jaycees, 1976. Mem. ABA, D.C. Bar Assn., Pharm. Mfrs. Assn. (chmn. Washington reps. com.1988), Congl. Country Club, City Club. Office Phone: 202-783-8609.

THOMPSON, RICHARD THOMAS, academic administrator; b. Buffalo, Oct. 11, 1939; m. Nancy A. Streeter, Aug. 29, 1959; children: Elizabeth Thompson Grapentine, Richard Thomas Jr., David Bryant. BA, Ea. Mich. U., 1961, MA, 1963; LLD (hon.), Walsh Coll., 2000. Cert. tchr. Mich. Tchr. Warren Consol. Sch., Mich., 1961—66; dean, pres. Highland Lake campus Oakland C.C., Union Lake, 1966—75, pres. Orchard Ridge campus Farmington, 1975—84, v.p. Bloomfield, 1984—88, vice chancellor, 1988—91, pres. Auburn Hills campus, 1995—96, chancellor, 1996—2004, chancellor emeritus, 2004. Arbitrator Better Bus. Bur., Detroit, 1987—96; bd. dirs., past chair Providence Hosp., Southfield; cons. examiner North Ctrl. Assn. Higher Learning Commn., 1988—2004. Contbr. articles to profl. jours. Pres. Oakway Symphony Orch., Livonia, Mich., 1981—85; chair Oakland Literacy Coun., Pontiac, 1988—2002. Recipient Leadership award, Oakland County C. of C., 1987, Tricounty Disting. Svc. award, Detroit Coll. Bus., 1996, Shirley B. Gordon award Distinction, Phi Theta Kappa Internat., 2001. Mem.: Watershed Ctr. Grand Traverse Bay (chair), Phi Delta Kappa. Home: 6868 W Harbor Dr Elk Rapids MI 49629

THOMPSON, RICK, computer software company executive; married; 2 children. BA, Bates Coll., 1981. Product mgr. for Microsoft Mouse Microsoft Corp., 1987—91, gen. mgr. Microsoft hardware, 1991—96, v.p. Microsoft hardware, 1996—99, with Xbox team, 1999—2000, corp. v.p. Windows Client extended platform divsn., 2002—06, corp. v.p. Windows Live advt. & monetization platforms, 2006—08, corp. v.p. Zune, 2008—; CFO, v.p. product devel. Go2Net Inc., 2000—02. Owner Seattle Chocolates; co-owner Ferrari of Seattle. Office: Microsoft Corp 1 Microsoft Way Redmond WA 98052-6399

THOMPSON, ROBERT ALLAN, aerospace engineer; b. Cleve., June 10, 1937; s. Roy Henry and Viola Alverta (Nehls) T.; m. Louise Alberta Saari, Nov. 27, 1970. BSEE, Case Western Reserve U., 1958; postgrad. studies, Cleve. State U., 1959, John Marshall Law Sch., 1970; PhD, Union Inst., 1979. Registered profl. engr., Ohio, Wis., Conn., R.I. Tchr. Cleve. Bd. Edn., 1958-65; rsch. engr. Sohio Satellite Tracking Sta., Standard Oil Rsch. Lab., Cleve., 1958-63, acting dir., 1964-65; dir. Warrensville Hghts. (Ohio) Planetarium and Space Sci Program, 1964-65; tchr. spl. programs faculty Case Inst. Tech., Cleve., 1965; dir. planning phase sci. divsn. Cleve. Supplementary Edn. Ctr., 1965-66; dir. James A Lovell Regional Space Ctr., Milw., 1967-73; engring. and edn. cons. Chgo., 1973-78, Mystic, Conn., 1978—; pres., chmn. bd. Spatial-world Corp., 1982—. Chmn. secondary math. curriculum com. Cleve. Pub. Schs., 1963-64; mem. Wis. Aerospace Edn. Com., 1968-71; lectr. U. Wis., Milw., 1968-71; sec. Friends of Space Ctr., 1968-75. Author: The New Egoshell: An Individualized Space Age Realty; co-author (with L. Thompson) Egoshell-Planetary Individualism Balanced within Planetary Interdependence, 1987; contbr. articles to profl. jours. Kiwanian faculty adv. Collinwood Key Club, 1959—64. Recipient Leadership award, NE Cleve. Kiwanis, 1961; Goodwin Watson fellow, Union Inst., 1978—79. Fellow: Brit. Interplanetary Assn.; mem.: AIAA (chmn. Wis. sect. 1969—70, sr. mem. Conn. sect., coun. 1984—85, disting. lectr. 1987—89), AAAS, IEEE (sr. life) (chmn. membership com. Cleve. sect. 1965—66, exec. com.), Cleve. Astron. Soc. (exec. com. 1966—67), Cleve. Engring. Soc., Inst. Planetary Egology (pres. 1988—), Union Inst. Alumni Assn., Case Alumni Assn. Home: PO Box 624 Mystic CT 06355-0624 Office: PO Box 2001 Mystic CT 06355-0624 Personal E-mail: egoshell@aol.com.

THOMPSON, ROBERT LEE, agricultural economist, educator; b. Canton, NY, Apr. 25, 1945; s. Robert M. and Esther Louise (Weatherup) T.; m. Karen Hansen, Aug. 9, 1968; children— Kristina Marie, Eric Robert. BS, Cornell U., Ithaca, NY, 1967; MS, Purdue U., West Lafayette, Ind., 1969, PhD, 1974; LLD, Dalhousie U., 1999; DSc honoris causa, Pa. State U., 1999. Vol. agriculturalist Internat. Vol. Service, Pakse and Vientiane, Laos, 1968-70; vis. prof. Fed. Univ. Vicosa, Brazil, 1972-73; prof. Purdue U., West Lafayette, Ind., 1974-93, dean of agr., 1987-93; rsch. scholar Internat. Inst. for Applied Systems Analysis, Laxenburg, Austria, 1983; sr. staff economist Coun. Econ. Advisers, Washington, 1983-85; asst. sec. econs. U.S. Dept. Agr., Washington, 1985-87; pres., CEO Winrock Internat. Inst. Agrl. Devel., 1993-98; sr. advisor World Bank, Washington, 1998-99, dir. rural devel., 1999—2002; sr. advisor Ctr. for Strategic and Internat. Studies, 1998—99, Nat. Ctr. for Food and Agr. Policy, Washington, 2003—07; Gardner endowed chair agr. policy U. Ill., Urbana, 2004—. Vis. prof. Econ. Rsch. Svc., USDA, 1979-80; chmn. adv. coun. Nat. Ctr. Food and Agrl. Policy, Washington, 1987-92; mem. Ind. Commn. on Agr. and Rural Devel., 1989-93, Nat. Commn. on Agrl. Trade and Export Policy, 1985-86, Nat. Commn. Internat. Trade, Devel., and Cooperation, 1996-97; mem. bd. agr. NRC, 1987-92; mem. Internat. Policy Coun. on Agr. and Trade, 1987—, chmn., 2000-06; mem. USDA Joint Coun. on Food and Agrl. Scis., 1994-96; bd. dir. Land O'Lakes, 2006-, Nat. Coop. Bank, 1985-97, PSI Energy & PSI Resources, 1987-94, Vigoro Corp., 1993-96, Terra Industries, 1997-98; advisory bd. mem. Rabobank N. Am. Agribus., 1998-2003; mem. agrl. policy adv. coun. trade, USDA and US Trade Rep., 2005-. Contbr. numerous articles to profl. publs. Author monographs, book chpts. Bd. dirs. Ind. 4-H Found., Ind. Inst. Agr. Food and Nutrition, 1987-93, Inst. for Sci. in Soc., 1991-93, USDA Grad. Sch., Washington, 1985-87; mem. nat. adv. coun. Minorities in Agr., Natural Resources and Related Sci.; bd. dirs. Farm Found., 1987-92, chmn. 1991-92. Recipient Agrl. Rsch. award Purdue U., 1983, Outstanding Alumni award Cornell U., 1988, Superior Svc. award USDA, 1989, Justin Smith Morrill award, 1995, Nat. 4-H Alumni award, 1992, Chgo. Farmers Agriculturalist of Yr. award, 1992, Bob Pim Agrl. Vision award Nat. Forum Agr., 1997; named Humanitarian of Yr., Am. Coll. Nutrition, 1999. Fellow AAAS, Am. Agrl. Econs. Assn. (editl. coun. 1983-85, 2005-07, quality com. award 1979, 91, 93); mem. Internat. Agribus Mgmt. Assn., Am. Econ. Assn., Internat. Assn. Agrl. Economists (pres. 1993-96), Coun. Fgn. Rels., Chgo. Coun. on Global Affairs, Bretton Woods Com., Royal Swedish Acad. Agr. and Forestry (fgn.), Ukrainian Acad. Agrl. Scis., Sigma Xi, Alpha Gamma Rho, Alpha Zeta (Centennial Honor Role award 1997), Gamma Sigma Delta. Republican. Avocation: foreign language study. Office: 412 Mumford Hall MC-710 1301 W Gregory Dr Urbana IL 61801-3608 Office Phone: 217-333-1313. Business E-Mail: rlt@uiuc.edu.

THOMPSON, RODGER IRWIN, astrophysicist, educator; s. William Berle and Pearle Jean Thompson. BS, MIT, Cambridge, PhD, 1970. Prof. astronomy Steward Obs. and Dept. Astronomy, Tucson, 1970—. Mem. hubble space telescope sci. working group NASA, Washington, 1985—92, mem. astrophysy. coun., 1986—89; mem. hubble space telescope users com. Space Telescope Sci. Inst., Balt., 1992—99; bd. dir. large binocular telescope corp. Large Binocular Telescope Corp., Tucson, 2007—. Contbr. articles to numerous sci. jours. (Mulhmhan award, 2003, Nat. Resource award, 2001). Mem.: Astron. Soc. Pacific, Am. Phys. Soc., Internat. Astron. Union, Am. Astron. Soc. Achievements include serving as principal investigator in the development near infrared camera and multi-object spectrometer (NICMOS) for the hubble space telescope. Office: Univ Ariz Steward Observatory Tucson AZ 85721 Business E-Mail: rthompson@as.arizona.edu.

THOMPSON, ROGER ROY, history professor; b. Mpls., Sept. 18, 1952; s. Lloyd Robert and Nancy Middleton Thompson; m. Melissa Jane Walt, Aug. 12, 1979. BA, Stanford U., Calif., 1979; PhD, Yale U., New Haven, 1985. Vis. asst. prof. history MIT, Cambridge, 1987, U. Wash., Seattle, 1993—94, Stanford U., Calif., 1999—2003, Western Wash. U., Bellingham, 2003—06, Dartmouth Coll., Hanover, NH, 1995—96; assoc. prof. Western Wash. U., Bellingham, 2006—; asst. prof. U. Md. Coll. Pk., 1988—95; temp. lectr. chinese studies U. Cambridge Faculty Oriental Studies, England, 1996—98; vis. asst. prof. history & east Asian studies Colby Coll., Waterville, Maine, 1998—99; a a. Chair history Western Wash. U., 2006—07. Contbr. articles to profl. jours. With USAF, 1970—74, Tex., Md., Thailand, ND. Fellow History Christianity fellowship, Henry Luce Found., 1987—88; Chiang Ching kuo Found. fellowship, Am. Coun. Learned Socs. & Social Sci. Rsch. Coun., 1991—92, Postdoc. fellowship, John K. Fairbank Ctr., 1986—87, Andrew W. Mellon Young China Scholar fellowship, Am. Coun. Learned Socs., 1985—86, fellowship, Social Sci. Rsch. Coun., 1982—84. Mem.: Assn. Asian Studies. Office: Western Washington Univ History 516 High St Bellingham WA 98225-9061 Office Fax: 360-650-7789.

THOMPSON, RONALD EDWARD, lawyer; b. Bremerton, Wash., May 24, 1931; s. Melville Herbert and Clara Mildred (Griggs) T.; m. Marilyn Christine Woods, Dec. 15, 1956; children: Donald Jeffery, Karen, Susan, Nancy, Sally, Claire BA, U. Wash., 1953, JD, 1958. Bar: Wash. 1959. Asst. city atty. City of Tacoma, 1960—61; pres. firm Thompson, Krilich, LaPorte, West & Lockner, P.S., Tacoma, 1961—99. Judge pro tem Mcpl. Ct., City of Tacoma, Pierce County Dist., 1972—, Pierce County Superior Ct., 1972—. Chmn. housing and social welfare com. City of Tacoma, 1965-69; mem. Tacoma Bd. Adjustment, 1967-71, chmn., 1968; mem. Tacoma Com. Future Devel., 1961-64, Tacoma Planning Commn., 1971-72; bd. dirs., pres. Mcpl. League Tacoma; bd. dirs. Pres. Tacoma Rescue Mission, Tacoma Pierce County Cancer Soc., Tacoma-Pierce County Heart Assn., Tacoma Grand Cinema, Tacoma-Pierce County Coun. for Arts, Econ. Devel. Coun. Puget Sound, Tacoma Youth Symphony, Kleiner Group Home, Tacoma C.C. Found., Pierce County Econ. Devel. Corp., Wash. Transp. Policy Inst.; Coalition to Keep Wash. Moving, precinct committeeman Rep. party, 1969-73. With AUS, 1953-55; col. Res. Recipient Internat. Cmty. Svc. award Optimist Club, 1970, Patriotism award Am. Fedn. Police, 1974, citation for cmty. svc. HUD, 1974, Disting. Citizen award Mcpl. League Tacoma-Pierce County, 1985; named Lawyer of the Yr. Pierce County Legal Secs. Assn., 1992. Mem. ATLA, Am. Arbitration Assn. (panel of arbitrators), ABA, Wash. State Bar Assn. (Local Hero award 2002), Tacoma-Pierce County Bar Assn. (sec. 1964, pres. 1979, mem. cts. and judiciary com. 1981-82), Wash. State Trial Lawyers Assn., Tacoma-Pierce County C. of C. (bd. dirs., exec. com., v.p., chmn.), Downtown Tacoma Assn. (com. chmn., bd. dirs. exec. com., chmn.), Variety Club (Seattle), Lawn Tennis Club, Tacoma Club, Optimist (Tacoma, internat. pres. 1973-74), Phi Delta Phi, Sigma Nu. Roman Catholic. Home: 3101 E Bay Dr NW Gig Harbor WA 98335-7610 Office: PO Box 2091 4423 Point Fosdick Dr Ste 312 Gig Harbor WA 98333-4091 Office Phone: 253-853-7449. Personal E-mail: retpllc@att.net.

THOMPSON, RONALD L., finance company executive, former manufacturing company executive; BBA, U. Mich.; MS, PhD, Mich. State U. Chmn., CEO Evaluation Techs., Inc.; chmn. bd. dirs., pres. GR Group Inc., 1980—93; chmn., CEO Midwest Stamping & Mfg. Co. (subs. of GR Group Inc.), Bowling Green, Ohio, 1993—2005. Bd. trustee, Teachers Ins. & Annuity Found. Coll. Retirement Equities Fund (TIAA-CREF), 1995-, chmn., 2008-; bd. dirs., Chrysler Group LLC, 2009- Recipient Nat. Minority Entrepreneur of Yr. award U.S. Dept. Commerce, 1989, Disting. Svc. to Edn. award Harris-Stowe State Coll., 1991, disting. Cmty. Svc. award So. Ill. U., Edwardsville, 1990. Office: TIAA-CREF PO Box 1259 Charlotte NC 28201*

THOMPSON, RONELLE KAY HILDEBRANDT, library director; d. Earl E. and Maxine R. (Taplin) Hildebrandt; m. Harry Floyd Thompson II, Dec. 24, 1976; children: Clarissa, Harry III. BA in Humanities magna cum laude, Houghton Coll., 1976; MLS, Syracuse U., 1976; postgrad., U. Rochester, 1980-81; cert., Miami U., 1990. Libr. asst. Norwalk (Conn.) Pub. Libr., 1977; elem. libr. Moriah Ctrl. Schs., Port Henry, NY, 1977—78; divsn. coord. pediat. gastroenterology and nutrition U. Rochester (N.Y.) Med. Ctr., 1978—81, cons., pediat. housestaff libr. com., 1980—81; dir. Medford Libr. U. S.C., Lancaster, 1981—83; dir. Mikkelsen Libr., Libr. Assocs., Ctr. for Western Studies, mem. libr. com. Augustana Coll., Sioux Falls, SD, 1983—, adminstrv. pers. coun., 1989—94, 1997—2004. Presenter in field. Contbr. articles to profl. jours. Mem. S.D. Symphony; advisor pers. dept. City of Sioux Falls. Recipient leader award YWCA, 1991; Gaylord Co. scholar Syracuse U., 1976; named S.D. Libr. of Yr., 1998. Mem. ALA, AAUW, Assn. Coll. and Rsch. Librs. (nat. adv. coun. coll. librs. sect. 1987—), Mountain Plains Libr. Assn. (chair acad. sect., nominating com. 1988, pres. 1993-94), S.D. Libr. Assn. (chair interlibr. coop. task force 1986-87, pres. 1987-88, chair recommended minimum salary task force 1988, chair local arrangements com. 1989-90, 2002-03), S.D. Libr. Network (adv. coun. 1986—, exec. com. 1992-96, 1998-2000, 2006-, chair adv. coun. 1994-96, 98-2000, 2006-). Office: Augustana Coll Mikkelsen Libr 29th & Smt Sioux Falls SD 57197-0001 Office Phone: 605-274-4921. Business E-Mail: ronelle.thompson@augie.edu.

THOMPSON, RYAN D., legislative staff member; Intern, Senator James Inhofe US Senate, Washington, 2002, dep. press. sec., Senator James Inhofe, 2003—04, press sec., Senator James Inhofe, 2004—07, chief of staff to Senator James Inhofe, 2007—. Republican. Office: 453 Russell Senate Office Bldg Washington DC 20510-3603 Office Phone: 202-224-4721. Business E-Mail: ryan_thompson@inhofe.senate.gov.*

THOMPSON, SAMUEL D., state legislator; b. Mobile, Ala., July 31, 1935; m. Jacqueline Thompson; 3 children. BS in Chemistry & Math, U. Ark., Little Rock, 1960; PhD in Phys. Chemistry, La. State U., 1965. Resident scientist E.I. duPont de Nemours, 1965—68, J.P. Stevens & Co., 1968—71; dir. NJ State Dept. Health, 1972—94, NJ Turnpike Authority, 1995—97; mem. Dist. 13 NJ State Assembly, 1998—, asst. rep. leader, 2004—05. Chmn. Old Bridge Rep. Twp. Com.; co-chmn. Middlesex County Rep. Com., 1976—94; mem. Old Bridge Twp. Planning Bd., 1983. With US Army, 1955—57. Legislator of the Year, New Jersey State Nurses Association, 2000; Legislator of the Year, New Jersey Association Health Rec Dance & Physical Ed, 2000; Legislator of the Year, Garden St Pharmacy Owners, New Jersey State Pharmacists Association, 2001; Legislator of the Year, New Jersey Rec & Parks Association; Legislator of the Year, New Jersey State VFW. Republican. Baptist. Office: 725 Hwy 34 Matawan NJ 07747 Office Phone: 732-583-5558. Office Fax: 732-583-4039. Business E-Mail: asmthompson@njleg.org.

THOMPSON, SANNA J., medical educator; b. Logan, Utah, Feb. 18, 1955; d. Clifton Welby and Elvaletta Zollinger Johnson; m. Donald Hughes, Nov. 2, 1996; children: Shannel Larsen, Chad D. Larsen, Benjamin P. Larsen, Jeremy C. Larsen, Joshua J. Larsen. PhD, Wash. U., St. Louis, 1998. Asst. prof. State U. Buffalo, 1998—2001, U. Tex., Arlington, 2001—03, assoc. prof. Austin, 2003—. Program evaluator Travis County Health and Human Svcs., Austin, 2007—. Grantee, NIH, Nat. Inst. Drug Abuse; Tng. fellowship, NIMH, 1995—97. Office: Univ Tex Austin 1717 W 6th St Ste 295 Austin TX 78703 Business E-Mail: sannathompson@mail.utexas.edu.

THOMPSON, SCOTT L., automotive executive; BBA, Stephen F. Austin State U. CPA. Exec. v.p., oper. and fin. KSA Ind., Inc., 1991—96; sr. v.p., CFO, treas. Group1 Automotive, Houston, 1996—2002, exec. v.p., CFO, treas., 2002—05; sr. exec. v.p., CFO Dollar Thrifty Automotive Group, Tulsa, Okla., 2008, pres., CEO, 2008—. Bd. dir. Dollar Thrifty Automotive Group, Conn's Inc.; non-exec. chmn. Houston Wire & Cable Co.; bd. dir. UAP Holding Co., 2007—08. Mailing: Dollar Thrifty Automotive Group PO Box 35985 Tulsa OK 74135-0985*

THOMPSON, SHIRLEY WILLIAMS, mathematics professor; b. Laurens, SC, Oct. 12, 1941; d. Spellman and Lula Mae S.R. Williams; m. Joseph Earl Thompson, Nov. 27, 1969; children: Shirley Elizabeth Thompson Marshall, Joseph Earl Jr., Amber Gale Thompson Ramsey. BS, Johnson C. Smith U., Charlotte, NC, 1963; MEd, U. NC, 1971; MS, Atlanta U., 1988; PhD, Ga. State U., Atlanta, 1980. Adminstrv. specialist Ga. State U., Atlanta, 1976—77; asst. prof. math. Morehouse Coll., Atlanta, 1980—84, assoc. prof. math., 1984—. Bd. dir. Nat. Assn. Mathematicians, Balt., 1996—2000, Excellence in Edn. Barry Goldwater Scholarship, Phoenix, 1990—; program rev. com. Presdl. Scholars, Washington, 1995—. Field reader Jack Kent Cooke Found., Washington, 2002—. Mem.: Math. Assn. Am., Beta Kappa Chi, Pi Mu Epsilon, Kappa Delta Psi. Presbyterian. Achievements include first to receive master's degree in mathematics from U. NC. Avocations: travel, reading, art history. Home: 4793 Carlene Way SW Lilburn GA 30047 Office: Morehouse Coll 830 Westview Dr Atlanta GA 30314 Business E-Mail: sthompson@morehouse.edu.

THOMPSON, STEPHEN C., research scientist; AB, Kenyon Coll., Gambier, Ohio, 1974; PhD in Physics, Case Western Res. U., Cleve., 1978. Tech. and mgmt. position increasing responsibility Naval Sys. Divsn., Westinghouse Electric Corp., Cleve., 1978—95; dir. rsch. Knowles Electrocincs LLC, Itasca, Ill., 1995—2005; sr. scientist and prof. acoustics Pa. State U., State Coll., 2005—. Contbr. articles to profl. jour. Fellow: Acoustical Soc. America (mem. exec. bd. 2005—08, Sci. Writing award 2003). Office: Applied Rsch Lab PO Box 30 State College PA 16804

THOMPSON, STEVE CHARLES, engineer; b. Mesa, Ariz., Dec. 22, 1976; s. Charles Edward and Wanda Laverne Thompson; m. Laura Shannon Greenig, Jan. 12, 2005; 1 child, Charlize Lorin. PhD, U. Calif., San Diego, 2005. Rschr. U. Calif., La Jolla, 2001—05, postdoc. scholar, 2005—06; sr. engr. Acorn Tech., La Jolla, 2007—. Mem.: IEEE. Achievements include development of digital wireless communication networks & devices. Avocations: yoga, surfing. Home: 4149 Caminito Davila San Diego CA 92122 Office: Acorn Tech 1200 Prospect St Ste 475 La Jolla CA 92037 Business E-Mail: steve@elsteve.com.

THOMPSON, STEVEN BRUCE, music educator, director; b. Warwick, RI; m. Carol Jeanne Pace; children: Eric Daniel, Megan Renae. ArtsD in Instrumental Conducting, U. Northern Colo., Greeley, 1994; MusM in Trumpet Performance, Peabody Inst. Johns Hopkins U., Balt., 1981; MusB in Edn., Wheaton Coll. Conservatory, Wheaton, Ill., 1975. Band and choir dir. Emmons HS, Minn., 1976—79, Nonnewaug HS, Woodbury, Conn., 1980—82, Randolph HS, Minn., 1982—86; asst. prof. instrumental music Waldorf Coll., Forest City, Iowa, 1986—2002; prof. instrumental music Bethel U., St. Paul, 2002—. Avocations: fishing, skiing, jazz. Office: Bethel Univ 3900 Bethel Dr Saint Paul MN 55112 Business E-Mail: s-thompson@bethel.edu.

THOMPSON, SUSAN A., communications educator; b. Birmingham, Ala., Nov. 4, 1957; d. William A. and Ruth C. Thompson. AB in Journalism, U. Ala., Tuscaloosa, 1980, MA in Journalism, 1995, PhD in Mass Communication, 2002. Staff writer Decatur Daily, Decatur, Ala., 1980—81; pubs. editor BMC Montclair, Birmingham, 1984—86; journalist, news editor Jefferson Advertiser, Trussville, 1986—89; adminstrv. asst. UAB, Birmingham, 1990—94; rsch. asst. U. Ala., Tuscaloosa, 1995—2002; asst. prof. communication arts U. Montevallo, 2002—. Co-author (with Jay Black and Jennings Bryant): (textbooks) Introduction to Media Communication, 5th Ed., 1998; co-author: (with Jennings Bryant) Fundamentals of Media Effects, 2002, Fundamentals of Media Effects (Russian edition), 2004, Fundamentals of Media Effects (Chinese Edition), 2006; author: (book) The Penny Press, The Origins of the Modern News Media, 1833-1861, 2004; contbr. articles to profl. pubs., chapters to books. Recipient Newswriting award, AP Ala., 1981, Third Pl. for PR mag., Ala. Hosp. Assn., 1986, Favorite Prof. award, Chi Omega, 2003, 2006. Mem.: Am. Journalism Historians Assn., Assn. for Educators in Journalism and Mass Communication, SE Journalism Conf., Phi Kappa Phi, Kappa Tau Alpha. Episcopalian. Avocation: painting.

THOMPSON, SYDNOR, JR., (CHARLES WILLIAM SYDNOR THOMPSON JR.), lawyer, mediator, arbitrator; b. Balt., Feb. 18, 1924; s. Charles William Sydnor Thompson and Helen Josephine Layne; m. Harriette Line, June 2, 1947; children: Darcy T. Howard, Charles William Sydnor III, Harriet T. Moore, Brenneman L., Mary Katherine Line T. Kelly. AB, Syracuse U., 1947; LLB, Harvard U., 1950; student, St. Andrews U., Scotland, 1945, Manchester U., Eng., 1950, London Sch. Econs., 1951. Cert.: NC Dispute Resolution Commn. (mediator), EEOC, Am. Arbitration Assn. (arbitrator), Fin. Industry Regulatory Authority. Assoc. Davis Polk & Wardwell, NYC, 1951—54; ptnr. Parker Poe Thompson Bernstein Gage & Preston, Charlotte, NC, 1954—94; judge NC Ct. Appeals, Raleigh, NC, 1994; of counsel Parker, Poe, Adams & Bernstein, LLP, Charlotte, 1995—; assoc. Mediation, Inc., Winston-Salem, NC, 1995—. Author: The Sydnor Family Saga, 2000, A Collection of Ad Hominem Verse, 2002, Sydnor Knows the Answer: A Memoir, 2006; contbr. articles to law revs. Pres. Charlotte Symphony Orch., 1958—61, Charlotte Opera Assn., 1971—75; vice chair NC Arts Coun., Raleigh, 1981—84; pres. Mecklenburg Ministries, 1987—89, Wing Haven Found., 2001—02; chmn. Mecklenburg County Dem. Party, 1977—81. With US Army, 1943—46, ETO. Decorated Bronze star; Fulbright scholar, 1950, 1951. Master: William H. Bobbitt Inn of Ct.; mem.: ABA (chmn. circuits subcom. 1977—95), Mecklenburg Bar Assn. (pres. 1990), NC Bar Assn. (chmn. appellate rules study com. 1989—91, chmn. local bar svcs. com. 1991—93), Old Catawba Soc., Horace Williams Philosophy Club, English Speaking Union, Charlotte City Club, Sporadic Book Club, Charlotte Country Club. Avocations: genealogy, writing, tennis, acting. Office: Parker Poe Adams & Bernstein LLP Ste 3000 401 S Tryon St Charlotte NC 28202 Office Phone: 704-372-9000. Business E-Mail: sydnorthompson@parkerpoe.com.

THOMPSON, TED CLARENCE, professional sports team executive, retired professional football player; b. Atlanta, Tex., Jan. 17, 1953; BBA, So. Meth. U., Dallas, 1975. Linebacker Houston Oilers, 1975—84; asst. dir. pro pers. Green Bay Packers, 1992, dir. pro pers., 1993—97, dir. player pers., 1997—99, exec. v.p., gen. mgr., dir. football ops., 2005—; v.p. football ops. Seattle Seahawks, 2000—04. Recipient George Young NFL Exec. of Yr. award, The Sporting News, 2008. Avocation: golf. Office: Green Bay Packers Lambeau Field Atrium 1265 Lombardi Ave Green Bay WI 54304*

THOMPSON, TERENCE WILLIAM, lawyer; b. Moberly, Mo., July 3, 1952; s. Donald Gene and Carolyn (Stringer) T.; m. Caryn Elizabeth Hildebrand, Aug. 30, 1975; children: Cory Elizabeth, Christopher William, Tyler Madison. BA in Govt. with honors and high distinction, U. Ariz., 1974; JD, Harvard U., 1977. Bar: Ariz. 1977, U.S. Dist. Ct. Ariz. 1977, U.S. Tax Ct. 1979. Assoc. Brown & Bain P.A., Phoenix, 1977-83, ptnr., 1983-92, Gallagher and Kennedy, P.A., Phoenix, 1992—. Legis. aide Rep. Richard Burgess, Ariz. Ho. of Reps., 1974; mem. bus. adv. bd. Citibank Ariz. (formerly Great Western Bank & Trust, Phoenix), 1985-86. Mem. staff Harvard Law Record, 1974-75; rsch. editor Harvard Internat. Law Jour.,1976; lead author, editor-in-chief: Arizona Corporate Practice, 1996—; contbr. articles to profl. jours. Mem. Phoenix Mayor's Youth Adv. Bd. 1968-70, Phoenix Internat.; active 20-30 Club, 1978-81, sec. 1978-80, Valley Leadership, Phoenix, 1983-84, citizens task force future financing needs City of Phoenix, 1985-86; exec. coun. Boys and Girls Clubs of Met. Phoenix, 1990-2000, sr. coun. 2000—; bd. dirs. Phoenix Bach Choir, 1992-94; deacon Shepherd of Hills Congl. Ch., Phoenix, 1984-85; pres. Maricopa County Young Dems., 1982-83, Ariz. Young Dems., 1983-84, sec. 1981-82, v.p. 1982-83; exec. dir. Young Dems. Am., 1985, exec. com. 1983-85; others. Recipient Best of Ariz. State Bar, Ariz. Bus. Jour., 2004. Fellow Ariz. Bar Found.; mem. State Bar Ariz. (vice chmn. internt. law sect. 1978, sec. securities law sect. 1990-91, vice chmn. sect. 1991-92, chmn.-elect 1992-93, chmn. 1993-94, exec. coun. 1988-96, sec. bus. law sect. 1992-93, vice chmn. 1993-94, chmn. 1994-95, exec. coun. 1996-98, 07-), Nat. Assn. Bond Lawyers, Nat. Health Lawyers, Selden Soc., Greater Phoenix Black C. of C. (bd. dirs. 1999-2001), Blue Key, Phi Beta Kappa, Phi Kappa Phi, Phi Eta Sigma. Home: 202 W Lawrence Rd Phoenix AZ 85013-1226 Office: Gallagher & Kennedy PA 2575 E Camelback Rd Phoenix AZ 85016-9225 Home Phone: 602-248-8237; Office Phone: 602-530-8515. Business E-Mail: twt@gknet.com.

THOMPSON, TERRY LAMAR, orthopedist, educator; b. Clinton, SC, Aug. 03; m. Audrey Kelly Robinson, May 5, 2001. MD, Howard U., Washington, 1983. Cert. Am. Bd. Orthopaedic Surgery, 1991. Prof. Dept. Orthopaedic Surgery, Howard U. Coll. Medicine, 1989—, chmn., 1989—. None. Dir. Am. Bd. Orthopaedic; mem. J. Robert Gladden Orthopaedic Soc., Chgo., 2002—08. Fellow: Am. Acad. Orthopaedic Surgeons; mem.: Am. Orthopaedic Assn., Am. Orthopaedic Soc. Sports Medicine, Cosmos Club. Office: Howard Univ 2041 Georgia Ave NW Washington DC 20060 Office Fax: 202-865-4904. Business E-Mail: tthompson@howard.edu.

THOMPSON, THELMA BARNABY, university president, classical languages educator; b. Balaclava, Jamaica, West Indies, July 22, 1940; d. Claude Noel and Elaine Jordan (Robertson) Barnaby; m. Winston Lloyd Thompson, June 15, 1976; 1 child, Lisa Valdeen. BA, Howard U., DC, 1970; MA, Howard U., 1972, PhD, 1978; diploma, Bethlehem Tchrs. Coll., Malvern, Jamaica, West Indies, 1960. Lectr. CUNY, 1972—74; asst. prof. Bowie (Md.) State Coll., 1974—76; assoc. prof., asst. chmn. English dept. U. DC, Washington, 1976—88, assoc. dean, 1988—90; dean Sch. Arts and Letters Norfolk State U., 1990—98, v.p. acad. affairs, 1998—2002; pres. U. Md. Ea. Shore, Princess Anne, 2002—. Author: The Seventeenth Century English Hymn; also articles. Recipient Bethlehem Coll. Medal of Distinction, scholarship and grad. fellowship, award for outstanding accomplishment in field of edn., Howard U., 2005, Best of St. Bess award, Jamaica, West Indies, 2003, Govs. award creativity and innovation in edn., 2006, 100 Most Important Blancks Tech. award, 2007; named one of Md.'s 100 Outstanding Women, 2004, Women Shaping the World, Essence Mag., 2005, top 100 in Md. Tech. Black Engrs. award. Mem. MLA, Coll. Lang. Assn., South Atlantic MLA, Middle Atlantic Writers, Phi Beta Kappa, Phi Delta Kappa (award for disting. svc. and commitment to excellence in edn. 1991). Achievements include extensive outreach work in Africa and the Caribbean. Office: U Md Eastern Shore JT Williams Hall Rm 2107 Princess Anne MD 21853 Office Phone: 410-651-6101. Business E-Mail: tbthompson@umes.edu.

THOMPSON, THEODORE ROBERT, pediatric educator; b. Dayton, Ohio, July 18, 1943; s. Theodore Roosevelt and Helen (Casey) J.; m. Lynette Joanne Shenk; 1 child, S. Beth. BS, Wittenberg U., 1965; MD, U. Pa., 1969. Diplomate Am. Bd. Pediatrics (Neonatal, Perinatal Medicine). Resident in pediat. U. Minn. Hosp., Mpls., 1969—72, chief resident in pediat., 1971—72, fellow neonatal, perinatal, 1974—75, asst. prof., 1975—80, dir. divsn. neonatology and newborn intensive care unit, 1977—91, assoc. prof., 1980—85, prof., 1985—, co-dir. Med. Outreach, 1988—91, med. dir. med. outreach, 1991—2000, assoc. chief pediat. svcs., 1988—2003, assoc. head pediat. edn. and cmty. programs, 2003—04, assoc. head cmty. affairs, 2004—; med. dir. outreach, bd. dirs. U. Minn. Physicians, 1992—2008. Med. exec. com., sec.-treas. U. Minn. Med. Ctr., Fairview, 2002—04, chief of staff elect, 2004—07, chief of staff, 2007—09, past chief staff, 2009—. Editor: Newborn Intensive Care: A Practical Manual, 1983. Bd. dirs. Life Link III, St. Paul, 1987—; cons. Maternal and Child Health, Minn. Bd. Health, 1975-94; bd. dirs. Minn. Med. Found., 1995-99. With USPHS. 1972-74. Recipient Advocacy award, U. Minn. Med. Sch., Pres.'s award for outstanding svc., U. Minn., Alumni Catalogs award, Wittenberg U., 2005, Disting. Svc. award, Minn. Chpt. Acad. Pediatry, 2009. Fellow: Am. Acad. Pediats.; mem.: Acad. Med. Educators, Gt. Plains Orgn. for Perinatal Health Care (Sioux Falls, SD Kunshe award 1989). Lutheran. Office: MMC 39 420 Delaware St SE Minneapolis MN 55455-0374 Business E-Mail: thomp005@umn.edu.

THOMPSON, TIMOTHY LEWIS, lawyer; b. Stamford, Conn., Feb. 28, 1948; s. Elbert Paul and Carol Lewis Thompson; m. Elizabeth Anne Wasik, June 3, 1973; children: Andrew Austin, Charles Erling, Nicholas James, Daniel Raymond. Diploma, Phillips Acad., Andover, Mass., 1967; BA, Columbia U. Columbia Coll., NYC, 1971; JD, George Washinton U., DC, 1974. Bar: NY 1975. Assoc. McCanliss & Early, NYC, 1974—82, ptnr., 1982—. Dir. Adirondack Explorer, Saranac Lake, NY, 2005—; trustee Harding Ednl. and Charitable Found., NYC, 1990—; pres., trustee Montauk Club, Bklyn., 2004—; sec., trustee Down Town Assn., NYC, 1996—. Mem.: ABA, NY State Bar Assn., Oneita Boat Club. Avocations: sailing, viola, violin. Office: McCanliss & Early 88 Pine St New York NY 10005 Business E-Mail: tthompson@mccanliss.com.

THOMPSON, TINA MARIE, professional basketball player; b. LA, Feb. 10, 1975; 1 child. B in Sociology, U. So. Calif., LA, 1997. Forward Houston Comets, 1997—; forward (off-season) Rovereto Basket, Italy, 2001—02, Women's Korea Basketball League Kumho Falcons, Republic of Korea, 2003, Nat. Women's Basketball League Houston Stealth, 2003. Mem. USA Basketball Women's Sr. Nat. Team, Athens, Greece, 2004, Beijing, 08. Recipient Gold medal, women's basketball, Athens Olympic Games, 2004, Beijing Olympic Games, 2008; named All-Star Game MVP, WNBA, 2000; named to All-WNBA First Team, 1997, 1998, Western Conf. All-Star Team, WNBA, 1999, 2000, 2001, 2002, 2003, 2006, 2007. Achievements include becoming the number 1 draft pick in 1997, the first WNBA draftee in the history of the league; being a member of WNBA Championship winning Houston Comets, 1997, 98, 99, 2000. Office: Houston Comets 1730 Jefferson St Houston TX 77003-5028

THOMPSON, TOMMY (THOMAS GEORGE THOMPSON), lawyer, former United States Secretary of Health and Human Services; b. Elroy, Wis., Nov. 19, 1941; s. Allan and Julia (Dutton) T.; m. Sue Ann Mashak, 1969; children: Kelli Sue, Tommi, Jason. BS in Polit. Sci. and History, U. Wis., 1963, JD, 1966. Polit. intern U.S. Rep. Thomson, 1963; legis. messenger Wis. State Senate, 1964-66; sole practice Elroy and Mauston, Wis., 1966-87; mem. Wis. State Assembly from Dist. 87, 1966-87, asst. minority leader, 1972-81, floor leader, 1981-87; self-employed real estate broker Mauston, 1970—; gov. State of Wis., 1987-2001; sec. U.S. Dept. Health & Human Services, Washington, 2001—05; pres. Logistics Health Inc., 2005—; ptnr. Akin Gump Strauss Hauer & Feld LLP, 2005—; independent chmn, sr. adv. Deloitte Ctr for Health Solutions Deloitte & Touche USA LLP, 2005—; nat. health policy adv. US Preventive Medicine, Dallas, 2008—. Alt. del. Rep. Nat. Conv., 1976; chmn. Intergovtl. Policy Adv. Commn. to U.S. Trade Rep.; chmn. Nat. Govs. Assn., 1995-96, mem. nat. govs. assn. exec. com., AGA Med. Corp.; chmn. bd. dirs., Amtrak, 1998-2001; mem. bd. dirs. C.R. Bard, Inc., 2005-, Certere Corp., 2005-; pres. Logistics Health, 2005-. Served with USAR. Recipient med. award for Legis. Wis. Acad. Gen. Practice, Thomas Jefferson Freedon award Am. Legis. Exchange Coun., 1991, Most Valuable Pub. Official award City and State Mag., 1991, Governance award Free Congress Found., 1992, Governing Mag. Public Ofcl. of the Year, 1997, recipient Horatio Alger award, 1998, USA Mex. C of C, Good Neighbor award., 1999. Mem. ABA, Wis. Bar Assn., Rep. Govs. Assn., Phi Delta Phi. Republican. Roman Catholic. Office: Akin Gump Robert Stauss Bldg 1333 New Hampshire Ave NW Washington DC 20036-1564*

THOMPSON, WADE FRANCIS BRUCE, manufacturing executive; b. Wellington, New Zealand, July 23, 1940; came to US, 1961, naturalized, 1990. m. Angela Ellen Barry, Jan. 20, 1967; children: Amanda and Charles (twins). B in Commerce, Cert. Acctg., Victoria U., Wellington, 1961; MSc, NYU, 1963; PhD of Commerce (hon.), Victoria U., 2007. Dir. diversification Sperry & Hutchinson, NYC, 1967-72; v.p. Textar Corp., NYC, 1972-77; chmn. Hi-Lo Trailer Co., Butler, Ohio, 1977—2003; chmn., pres., CEO Thor Industries Inc., Jackson Center, Ohio, 1980—. Trustee Mystic Seaport Mus., Conn., 1984—; trustee Wade F.B. Thompson Charitable Found. Inc., 1985—, Mcpl. Art Soc., NYC, 1993—, Seventh Regiment Armory Conservancy, NYC, 1997—; founder The Drive Against Prostate Cancer. Recipient Oliver R. Grace award for Disting. Svc., Cancer Rsch. Inst., 2007, Jacqueline Kennedy Onassis award for Oustanding Contbn. to NYC, Mcpl. Art Soc., 2007, Frederick Law Olmsted award, 2009. Mem. Union Club (NYC). Avocations: tennis, collecting contemporary art. Office: Thor Industries Inc PO Box 629 Jackson Center OH 45334-0629

THOMPSON, WAYNE WRAY, historian; b. Wichita, Jan. 30, 1945; s. Clarence William and Elaine Maxine (Wray) T.; m. Lillian Evelyn Hurlburt, June 28, 1969 (div. 1999); m. Geraldine Kelleher Richter, Dec. 30 2000. BA, Union Coll., Schenectady, 1967; student, U. St. Andrews, Scotland, 1965-66; PhD, U. Calif., San Diego, 1975. Historian USAF, 1975—2004, Checkmate Air Campaign Planning Group, 1990—2004; sr. hist. advisor Gulf War Air Power Survey, 1991-93. Contbr. Congress Investigates (Arthur M. Schlesinger Jr. and Roger Bruns, editors), 1975; editor Air Leadership, 1986; contbr. War in the Pacific (Bernard Nalty, editor), 1991; contbr.: Winged Shield, Winged Sword, 1997; author: To Hanoi and Back, 2000. Served with AUS, 1971-72. Mem. Am. Hist. Assn., Orgn. Am. Historians, Air Force Hist. Found., Air Force Assn., Soc. Historians Am. Fgn. Rels., Soc. Mil. History, US Commn. Mil. History, World History Assn., Phi Beta Kappa, Cosmos Club (Washington). Home: 908 Deer Rd Bryn Mawr PA 19010

THOMPSON, WENOKA SHENAILE, television producer, writer; b. Laurel, Miss., July 23; d. Earnest Lee and Bettie Louise Thompson. Student, U. Md., 1995—. Talk show host, prodr. Sta. WXXV Fox 25, Gulfport, Miss., 1991—93; master control operator, jr. acct. Sta. WBDC, Washington, 1993—98; asst. prodr. Am.'s Voice, Washington, 1999—2000; prodr. WTOP News, CBS, Washington, 2000—05; exec. prodr., host Mother-to-Mother Show at Fox News Radio-WMET, 2005—. Pres. Sarah Elizabeth Co., Hyattsville, Md., 1998—; asst. prodr. Sta. NPR-WAMU, Washington, 1999. Author: John John's Adventure Book Series, 2002, (poem) Love Clearly Defined, 1987. Mem.: Sailing Club Washington, Phi Theta Kappa. Achievements include trademark for 1960's tee-The End of an Era. Avocations: golf, chess, sailing, tennis, photography. Office Phone: 301-853-1723. Personal E-mail: mothertomothershow@yahoo.com.

THOMPSON, WILLARD SCOTT (W. SCOTT THOMPSON), social sciences educator; b. Providence, Jan. 1, 1942; s. Francis Willard and Loretta Bell Thompson; m. Phyllis Anina Nitze, Dec. 28, 1968 (div. May 1984); children: Phyllis Elizabeth Pratt, Nicholas Edwin Scott, Heidi Alexandra Nitze Saunders; m. Luisito S. Pangilinam, Aug. 13, 2007. BA with honors, Stanford U., 1963; PhD, Oxford U., Eng., 1967. Assoc. profl. internat. politics Fletcher Sch. Law and Diplomacy, Medford, Mass., 1967—75; asst. to sec. of def. Dept. Def., Washington, 1975—76; assoc. dir. U.S. Info. Agy. U.S. Govt., Washington, 1981—84; rsch. adj. prof. internat. politics Fletcher Sch. Law and Diplomacy, Medford, Mass., 2001—, prof. emeritus, 2007—. Vis. prof. Asian Inst. Mgmt., Manila, 2001—; chair Universal Trading and Investment Co., Boston, 1993—. Author: Ghana's Foreign Policy, 1969; co-author (with Nicholas Thompson): The Baobab and The Mango Tree, 2000, The Philippines in Crisis, 1992, Democracy and Discipline the Philippine Presidency of Fidel V. Ramos; contbr. articles to profl. jours. Co-chair Ams. for Effective Pres., Boston, 1980, Mass. Tomorrow, Boston, 1972—78; pres. Inst. Internat. Rels., Stanford U., 1962—63. Rhodes scholar, 1963, Fulbright fellow, Manila, 1989, Danforth fellow, 1965—67, White House fellow, 1975—76. Mem.: Coun. on Fgn. Affairs, Internat. Inst. for Strategic Studies. Avocations: gardening, films, marathons, writing fiction. Office: Policy Ctr Asian Inst Mgmt Paseo de Roxas Makati Philippines Address: Villa Kusuma Seri Sukuwati, Bali Indonesia Home: 1113 Bataan St Guadalupe Makati City Philippines Office Phone: 011-63-2-882-4841. Personal E-mail: thompsonwscott@gmail.com.

THOMPSON, WILLIAM ANCKER, intramural-recreational sports director, educator; b. Syracuse, NY, Apr. 26, 1931; s. Frederick Howe Thompson and Ellen (Ensten) Ancker; m. Sally Whitmer; children: Cary, Paige. BS, Springfield Coll., Mass., 1953; MA, Calif. State U., Long Beach, 1960; postgrad., U. So. Calif., LA, 1961-62. Phys. dir. Wendell P. Clark Meml., Winchendon, Mass., 1956-57; dir. intramural/recreational sports Long Beach City Coll., 1958-96, dir. intramural/recreational sports emeritus, 1996—; with promotion and sales div. Calif. Sports, Inc. (L.A. Lakers, Kings), L.A. and Inglewood, 1960-76, v.p. sales, 1970-71. Co-author: Modern Sports Officiating, 1974, 5th rev. edit., 1993. 1st lt. USMC, 1954-56, Korea. Mem. Nat. Intramural-Recreational Sports Assn. (v.p. 1974-76, pres. 1976-77, Honor award 1980), Old Ranch Country Club. Avocations: swimming, golf, writing, reading, avocado growing.

THOMPSON, WILLIAM COLRIDGE, JR., (BILL THOMPSON), city official; b. Bklyn., July 10, 1953; s. William Colridge and Elaine Thompson; m. Angela Jeter (div. 1984); 1 child, Jennifer; m. Sylvia G. Kinard (div. 2006). BA in Polit. Sci., Tufts U., 1974; LHD (hon.), Mercy Coll., 1998, Long Island U., 2004. Chief of staff to Congressman Frederick W. Richmond US Congress, Bklyn., 1974—82; dep. borough pres. Bklyn., 1983—92; sr. v.p. George K. Baum & Co., 1993—94; Bklyn. rep. NYC Bd. Edn., 1994—96, pres., 1996; comptr. NYC, 2002—. Cons. investment banking svcs. to states, muncipalities and pub. benefit corps. in N.Y., Health Care industry, non-profit orgns. Bd. dirs. Bedford Stuyvesant Restoration Corp., City Parks Found., Bklyn. Union Gas Co; trustee Tufts U. Recipient Ann Vanderbilt award for Achievement, Partnership for Children, Inc., 1998, Brotherhood award, 100 Black Men, Inc., 2002, Disting. Svc. award, Fedn. African Am. Civil Svc. Organizations Inc., 2002, Pillar of Justice award, Respect for Law Alliance, Inc., 2003, Ednl. Leadership award, NYC Outward Bound Ctr., 2003, Tree of Life award, Jewish Nat. Fund, 2003, Edgar F. Allen Polit. Svc. award, Easter Seals, 2005. Office: Office of the Comptroller c/o Karen Crowe 1 Centre St Room 526 New York NY 10007 Fax: 718-935-3157.*

THOMPSON, WILLIAM DAVID, minister, educator; b. Chgo., Jan. 11, 1929; s. Robert Ayre and Mary Elizabeth (McDowell) T.; m. Linda Brady Stevenson, Nov. 2, 1968; children: Tammy, Kirk, Lisa, Rebecca, Gwyneth. AB, Wheaton Coll., Ill., 1950; BD, No. Bapt. Sem., 1954; MA, Northwestern U., 1955, PhD, 1960. Ordained to ministry Am. Baptist Ch., 1954. Instr. speech Wheaton Coll., 1952-55; pastor Raymond Baptist Ch., Chgo., 1956-58; assoc. prof. homiletics No. Bapt. Sem., Chgo., 1958-62; mem. faculty Eastern Bapt. Sem., Phila., 1962-87, prof. preaching, 1969-87; minister 1st Bapt. Ch., Phila., 1983-90. Pres. Thompson Comm., 1988-98, prin. The Spirited Workplace, 1998—, Thompson Properties, 1999-. Author: A Listener's Guide to Preaching, 1966, Recent Homiletical Thought, 1967, Dialogue Preaching, 1969, Preaching Biblically, 1981, Listening on Sunday for Sharing on Monday, 1983, Philadelphia's First Baptists, 1989, Public Speaking for Pleasure and Profit, 1997, On the Job Prayers, 2005; editor Abingdon Preachers Libr., 12 vols., Essence of Public Speaking series, 10 vols. Mem. Phila. Hist. Commn., 1984-92, Ctr. for Baptismal Living Bd., 1999-, Singing City Bd., 2003-. Vis. fellow Cambridge U., 1968-69. Mem. Nat. Speakers Assn., Mid-Atlantic Speakers Assn. (pres. 1995), Acad. Homiletics (pres. 1973, Lifetime Achievement award 2005), Religious Speech Comm. Assn. (v.p. 1983, pres. 1984), Union League Club, Wheaton Coll. Scholastic Honor Soc., Am. Composers Forum (Competition winner, 2008). Democrat. Home: 765 Ormond Ave Drexel Hill PA 19026-2417

THOMPSON, WILLIAM MOREAU, radiologist, educator; b. Phila., Oct. 20, 1943; s. Charles Moreau and Aileen (Haddon) T.; m. Thompson Coopon Saudraliez, Oct 20, 2007; children: Christopher Moreau, Thayer Haddon. BA, Colgate U., 1965; MD, U. Pa., 1969. Diplomate Am. Bd. Radiology. Intern Case Western Res. U., Cleve., 1969-70; resident in radiology Duke U., Durham, NC, 1972-75, from asst. prof. Med. Ctr. to prof., 1975—2001, prof. radiology Med. Ctr., 2001—, The Reed and Martha Rice Disting. prof. radiology Med. Ctr., 2004—06; chmn. Dept. Radiology U. Minn. Hosp. and Clinic, Mpls., 1986-2000, Vilhelmina and Eugene Gedgared chair radiology, 1986—2001, prof. radiology, dir. imaging rsch., 2000-01. Contbr. chpts. to books and articles to profl. jours. Served with USPHS, 1970-72. Recipient James Picker Found. Scholar in Acad. Medicine award, 1975-79, Disting. Scientist award, Armed Forces Inst. Pathology, Washington, 2001-02; R & D grantee VA, 1977-86. Fellow Am. Coll. Radiology; mem. AMA, Radiology Soc. N.Am. (program chmn. 1994-97), Minn. Med. Soc., Am. Roentgen Ray Soc., Assn. Univ. Radiologists (pres. 1989-90, Gold medal 2001), Soc. Gastrointestinal Radiology (pres. 1994-95, Cannon medal 2001), Assn. Program Dirs. (pres. 1995, Achievement award 2001), Soc. Chairs of Acad. Radiology Depts. (pres. 1997-98), Sigma Xi. Republican. Presbyterian. Office: PO Box 3808 Durham NC 27702-3808 Home: 1033 Marilee Glen Ct Durham NC 27705 Office Phone: 919-684-7448, 919-684-7442. Business E-Mail: thomp132@nc.duke.edu.

THOMPSON, WILLIAM TRAVIS, physicist; s. Robert Travis Thompson. PhD, Naval Postgrad. Sch., Monterey, Calif., 1994. Meteorologist Naval Environ. Prediction Rsch. Facility, Monterey, Calif., 1981—92; atmospheric physicist Naval Rsch. Lab., Monterey, 1992—. Contbr. articles to profl. jours. Mem.: Am. Meteorol. Soc. (club pres., v.p., conf. co-chair). Office: Naval Rsch Lab 7 Grace Hopper Ave Monterey CA 93943 Business E-Mail: william.thompson@nrlmry.navy.mil.

THOMPSON, WINSTON MARK OBED, entomologist, consultant, writer; s. Samuel Frendo and Iris Agatha Thompson. BSc, U. Guyana, S.Am., 1989; M of Agr., Oreg. State U., 1994; PhD, U. Greenwich, Eng., 2001. Rsch. asst. Nat. Agrl. Rsch. Inst., Georgetown, Guyana, 1989—92, rsch. scientist virology, 1994—98, rsch. scientist, 2001—03; rsch. fellow Internat. Inst. for Biol. Control, Curepe, Trinidad and Tobago, 1991, Caribbean Agrl. R&D Inst., Bridgetown, Barbados, 1991; lectr. entomology Guyana Sch. Agr., Georgetown, 1995—98; pvt. cons. and author Bellevue, Wash., 2004—. Keynote spkr. Ministry of Agr., Guyana, 1989—90; nat. agrl. rsch. inst.'s rep. Guyana's Vegetable Quality Assurance Com., Georgetown, 1996—98; mem. rev. team Caribbean Jour. Agr. and Natural Resources, Georgetown, 1997—98, Internat. Jour. Tropical insect Sci., 2005—. Contbr. articles to profl. jours. V.p. Ebenezer Luther League, New Amsterdam, Berbice, Guyana, 1983—83; music dir. Ebenezer Music Group, New Amsterdam, Berbice, Guyana, 1995—98. Recipient Pub. Svc. Ministry award, Govt. Guyana, 1985-1989, 9 Acad. awards, U. Guyana, 1986-1989; Commonwealth scholar, Assn. of Commonwealth Univs., 1998-2001; FAO of UN fellow, 1992-1994. Mem.: Guyana Assn. Profl. Agriculturists, Entomol. Soc. Am., Internat. Soc. for Pest Info. (corr.). Achievements include research recognized by other professionals; research recognized by the United States Dept. of Justice as an Alien of Extraordinary Ability for the O visa; a visa category exclusive for nobel prize winners or persons of international acclaim; research recognized by the Food and Agricultural Organization of the United Nations in 1995 as the only Plant Virologist In Guyana, South America; research recognized and selected by the Inter-American Institute for Cooperation on Agriculture to participate in a Caribbean Regional Workshop on Citrus Budwood Certification. Avocations: reading, guitar, piano. Office: PO Box 7226 Bellevue WA 98008 Personal E-mail: winston_thompson@hotmail.com.

THOMPSON, ZACHARY, city health department administrator; AS, El Centro Coll.; BS in Social Work, U. Tex., Arlington; MS, Amberton U., Garland, Tex. With W. Dallas Cmty. Ctr.; dep. dir. Dallas Co. Dept. Health and Human Svcs., Dallas, 1997—2004, dir., 2004—. Office: Dallas Co Dept Health and Human Svcs 2377 N Stemmons Fwy Dallas TX 75207-2710*

THOMPSON CORNWALL, LONIETA AURORA, music educator, consultant; b. Newark, June 13, 1944; d. Wilmore and Hattie Stewart Thompson; children: Arminta Morant Cornwall, Ronald Pearson Cornwall Jr. MusB, MusM, Manhattan Sch. Music, NYC, 1966; SMM, Union Theol. Sem., Sch. Sacred Music, NYC, 1973; EdD in Coll. Tchg. of Music, Columbia U., NYC, 2006. Music tchr. Bd. Edn., NYC, 1966—70; asst. prof. music Shaw U., Raleigh, NC, 1984—; adj. prof. Worship and Liturgy, Shaw Div. Sch., 2008—. Organist Abyssinian Bapt. Ch., NYC, 1965—68; dir. music Holy Trinity Luth. Ch., Hollis/Queens, NY, 1970—75; min. music First Bapt. Ch., Raleigh, NC, 1981—95; organist Christian Faith Bapt. Ch., Raleigh, 1999—2001; dir. music First Ref. Ch. of Cary, Cary, NC, 2001—. Composer: (musical score) Canticles for the Soul, Hebrews 25 Let us Encourage One Another, 2004, The African American Art Song: A Continuum In the Art of Song, 2006; presentor Nat. Assn. Negro Mus., 2006; contbr. scientific papers. Participant US EPA, Raleigh, NC, 2002, NC State Workers/ Dr. Martin Luther King Holiday Observance, Raleigh, NC, 2000—09; missionary to Zambia, South Africa Operation Reachback, Redlands, Calif., 2000; chair Gethsemane Seventh-day Adventist Ch. Sch., Raleigh, NC, 1995—2000; choir master Gospel Extravaganza for NC Symphony, 2007—08; musical cons. Dr. Martin Luther King Celebration Com., Raleigh, 1995—2004. Recipient H.B. Caple Humanitarian award, The Shaw Players/Shaw U., 1997—98, Shaw U. Char Tour-Prague and Budapest, 2008, The Crystal award, Women's Ministries/South Atlantic Conf. of Seventh-day Adventists, 1999, Lamplighter -Music Outreach award, Radio One-Hunter Industries, 2002. Mem.: Assoc. Ctr. Blsck Music Rsch., Nat. Assn. Study Performance of African Am. Music, Nat. Assn. Tchrs. of Singing, Nat. Assn. Negro Musicians, Raleigh Chamber Music Guild (bd. dirs. 1994—95, 2006—07), N.C. Bach Festival (bd. dirs. 1990—94), Am. Guild of Organists, Alpha Chi. Seventh-Day Adventist. Avocations: writing (liturgies), walking, travel. Home: 2304 Foxtrot Rd Raleigh NC 27610 Office: Shaw Univ 118 East South St Raleigh NC 27601 Home Phone: 919-828-5476; Office Phone: 919-546-8412. Personal E-mail: lonieta@aol.com.

THOMPSON-STANTON, MARY JEAN, communications educator; b. Kirksville, Mo., Feb. 19, 1959; d. Perley and Letha L. (Pinson) Thompson; m. Larry Stanton, June 14, 1981; children: Lucas, Caitlin. BA in English/Speech-Theatre, NE Mo. State U., 1980; MA in Comm. Studies, U. Iowa, 1990. Cert. secondary sch. tchr., Mo., Iowa. Secondary lang. arts tchr., Brashear, Mo., 1980—81; presch. tchr. Montessori Sch. Iowa City, 1985-86; speech/theatre tchr. Muscatine CC, Iowa, 1987-88; grad. instr. dept. rhetoric U. Iowa, 1988-89, grad. instr. dept. comm. edn., 1989-90; instr. writing and speech comm., dir. acads. Mt. Mercy Coll., Cedar Rapids, Iowa, 1990—. Author: (poetry) Epiphany, Radiant Resurrection, Distance. Mem. Ctrl. States Comm. Assn., Iowa Devel. Edn. Assn., Midwest Coll. Learning Ctr. Assn., Nat. Assn. for Devel. Edn., Speech Comm. Assn., Conf. Mercy Higher Edn., Iowa Transition Innitiative for Higher Edn., Gov's. Coun. for People with Disabilities, Sigma Tau Delta. Home: 412 3rd Ave S Mount Vernon IA 52314-1715 Office: Mount Mercy Coll 1330 Elmhurst Dr NE Cedar Rapids IA 52402-4763

THOMS, DAVID MOORE, lawyer; b. NYC, Apr. 28, 1948; s. Theodore Clark and Elizabeth Augusta (Moore) T.; m. Susan Rebecca Stuckey, Dec. 16, 1972. BA, Kalamazoo Coll., 1970; M in Urban Planning, Wayne State U., 1975, LLM in Taxation, 1988; JD, U. Detroit, 1979. Bar: Mich. 1980, NY 1995. Planner City of Detroit, 1971-75; atty. Rockwell and Kotz, P.C., Detroit, 1980-87; pvt. practice David M. Thoms & Assocs., P.C., Detroit, 1987—2002, Miller Canfield Paddock and Stone, P.L.C., 2002—. Adj. assoc. prof. Madonna U., 1993—; presenter NYU Tax Inst. Editor Case and Comment U. of Detroit Law Rev., 1978-79. Mem. program com. Fin. and Estate Planning Coun. Detroit, 1980—; mem. adv. bd., chmn. nominating com., mem. exec. com. Met. Detroit Salvation Army, 1980—, sec.-treas., vice chmn., 1994-95, chmn., 1995-96; bd. dirs. bylaws and property com., mem. nominating com., devel. com., exec. com. Mich. chpt. ARC; bd. dirs. L'Alliance Française de Grosse Pointe, 1980-2004, 05—, pres., 1985-88, 94-95; bd. dirs. French Festival of Detroit, Inc., 1986-89, 91-94, pres.; bd. dirs. Fedn. of Alliances Françaises, 1989-95, 97-2002, 2007—, past treas., v.p., chmn. fin. com., pres., 2000-01, treas. 2007-09; bd. dirs. Vis. Nurse Assn., 2003—, sec., 2004—; bd. dirs. Detroit Symphony Orch. Hall, Inc., 1996-97, dir. Am. Soc. French Academic Palms, 2008-; trustee Kalamazoo Coll., 1993-97, mem. exec. com., 1995-97; Mich. Colls Found., 2004-, sec., 2009-, Whitney Fund, Henry M. Seldon Chairtable Trust, 2004 (sec. 2006-); dir. vis. com. European art DIA, 1995-97. Decorated officier Ordre des Palmes Academiques, knight Order of Salvador (Salvador Dali Mus.); recipient Prix Charbonnier; Burton scholar U. Detroit, 1979; named to Best Lawyers in Am., 2005, 06, 07, 08, 09, MI Superlawyers, 2004-. Mem. ABA (chmn. subcom. on probate and estate planning, mem. charitable trust com.), Fed. Bar Assn., Oakland County Bar Assn., Detroit Bar Assn., State Bar Mich., NY Bar Assn., Bar Assn. of City of NY, Am. Planning Assn. (Mich. chpt.), The Grosse Pointe Club. Mem. United Church of Christ. Avocations: tennis, architecture, music, travel, art history. Office: 840 W Long Lake Rd Ste 200 Troy MI 48098 Office Phone: 248-267-3242. Business E-Mail: thoms@millercanfield.com.

THOMS, JEANNINE AUMOND, lawyer; b. Chgo. d. Emmett Patrick and Margaret (Gallet) Aumond; m. Richard W. Thoms; children: Catherine Thoms, Alison Thoms. AA, McHenry County Coll., 1979; BA, No. Ill. U., 1981; JD, Ill. Inst. Tech., 1984. Bar: Ill. 1984, U.S. Dist. Ct. (no. dist.) Ill. 1984, U.S. Ct. Appeals (7th cir.) 1985; cert. mediator 19th Jud. Cir. Ill. Assoc. Foss Schuman Drake & Barnard, Chgo., 1984-86, Zukowski Rogers Flood & McArdle, Crystal Lake and Chgo., 1986-92, ptnr., 1992—2006; pvt. practice, 2007—. Arbitrator 19th Jud. Ct. Ill., 1991—. Mem. women's addv. coun. to Gov. State of Ill.; mem. adv. coun. McHenry County Mental Health Bd., 1991—98, v.p., 1993—94, pres., 1995—98; mem. governing coun. Advocate Good Shepherd Hosp., Barrington, Ill., 2001—; mem. adv. com. Adv. Found., 2003—07, McHenry County Cmty. Found., 2004—, mem. grant com. Named one of Ill. Super Lawyers, 2005. Mem.: LWV, Acad. Family Mediators (cert.), McHenry County Bar Assn., Ill. State Bar Assn. (coun. trust and estates sect. 2000—01, Ill. legis. dist. scholarship com. 2001—), Phi Alpha Delta. Office: 101 N Virginia St Ste 150 Crystal Lake IL 60014-4126

THOMS, NORMAN WELLS, retired cardiovascular and thoracic surgeon; b. Bahrain, Nov. 5, 1934; (parents Am. citizens); m. Anna J. Holmes, June 22, 1962; 3 children. BA, Oberlin Coll., 1955; MD, U. Mich., 1959. Diplomate Am. Bd. Surgery, Am. Bd. Thoracic Surgery. Intern Blodgett Meml. Hosp., Grand Rapids, Mich., 1959-60; resident in gen. surgery Detroit Gen. Hosp., 1960-62, 66-68, resident in thoracic surgery, 1968-70; instr. surgery Wayne State U. Sch. Medicine, Detroit, 1968-70, asst. prof., 1970-74, assoc. prof., 1974-75; pvt. practice Topeka, 1975—2003; active staff Lawrence Meml. Hosp., 2003—06; ret., 2006. Contbr. articles to profl. jours. Officer M.C., U.S. Army, 1962-64. Recipient Regents' award for best sci. exhibit Am. Coll. Chest Physicians, 1972, Bal Jeffrey award Stormont-Vail Found., 1995. Fellow ACS; mem. Kans. Med. Soc., Shawnee Century Med. Soc., Soc. Thoracic Surgeons, Wayne State Surg. Soc. E-mail: normthomsmd@netzero.com.

THOMSEN, LINDA CHATMAN, lawyer, former federal agency administrator; b. 1954; d. William C. Chatman; m. Steuart Hill Thomsen, Oct. 16, 1982. BA, Smith Coll., 1976; JD, Harvard U., 1979. Assoc. Davis Polk & Wardwell LLP, Washington, 1979—83, NYC, 1985—89, counsel, 1989—95; asst. US atty. Dist. Md. US Dept. Justice, 1983—85; asst. chief litigation counsel US Securities & Exchange Commn. (SEC), Washington, 1995—97, asst. dir. divsn. enforcement, 1997—2000, assoc. dir., 2000—02, dep. dir., 2002—05, dir., 2005—09; ptnr. Davis Polk & Wardwell LLP, Washington, 2009—. Named one of 50 Women to Watch, The Wall St. Jour., 2005, 2006. Office: Davis Polk & Wardwell LLP Ste 1000 E 1300 I St NW Washington DC 20005 Office Phone: 202-962-7125. Office Fax: 202-962-7098. E-mail: linda.thomsen@davispolk.com.*

THOMSON, ALEXANDER BENNETT, JR., financial planner, tax and management consultant; b. Wyandotte, Mich., Sept. 1, 1954; s. Alexander Bennett and Norma Lee (Fields) T.; 1 child, Luis Joaquin Elizondo-Thomson; m. Carol Michaelsen, Oct. 07, 2002; student Eastern Mich. U., 1972-74, Kalamazoo Coll. 1975-77; MA, Antioch Sch. Law, 1983. Cert. fin. planner; chartered life underwriter, fin. cons.; investment adviser, health underwriter, enrolled agt. Pres. Thomson Mgmt. Group, Inc., Washington, 1977—; budget dir. The White House Conf. on Small Bus., 1979; asst. treas. Kennedy for Pres. Com. 1980, nat. scheduler, Geraldine A. Ferraro, 1984. Mem. Inst. Cert. Fin. Planners, Internat. Assn. Fin. Planners, Nat. Assn. Tax Profls. Democrat. E-mail: al@thomsonmanagement.com.

THOMSON, AUDREY SHIRE, volunteer; b. Paterson, NJ, Nov. 21, 1929; d. Gerald John Shire, Maybelle Conover; m. Norman B. Thomson, Oct. 17, 1954 (div. May 1985); children: Norman B., Christine de Armas, Scott B. BA, Coll. of St. Elizabeth, Morristown, NJ, 1950; MPA, NYU, 1990. Jr. pharmacologist Hoffman LaRoche, Nutley, NJ, 1950—55; exec. asst. Am. Cancer Soc. Nat. Office, NYC, 1983—86; exec. asst. to pres. United Fedn. Tchrs., NYC, 1986—89; asst. to pres. Grand Ctrl. Partnership, NYC, 1990—93, 34th St. Bus. Improvement Dist., NYC, 1990—93, Bryant Park Restoration Corp., NYC, 1990—93; asst. to founding ptnr. Edison Project, NYC, 1992—93. Mgr. first night events Pierpont Morgan Libr., NYC, 1992—93. Editor: (newsletter) Mus. Pieces, 1978—81; contbr. articles to profl. jours. Fundraiser Coll. of St. Elizabeth, 1995—2000, capital campaign com., steering com., 2003—08, class chmn., 2003—08; vol. Ga. Radio Reading Svc., 2004—08. Mem.: AAUW (program organizer 1994—2004, bd. dirs., ednl. equity chmn., fundraising chmn. 1994—2004, fundraiser task force 2002—04, Eleanor Roosevelt Ednl. Found. award 1999, Platinum award 1997—2001, Rosborough Meml. award, Silver award 2002). Roman Catholic. Avocations: reading, sewing. Home: 6206 Waters Ave Unit 212 Savannah GA 31406-2768

THOMSON, BASIL HENRY, JR., lawyer; b. Amarillo, Tex., Jan. 17, 1945; m. Margaret Shepard, May 4, 1985; children: Christopher, Matthew, Robert. BBA, Baylor U., 1968, JD, 1973. Bar: Tex. 1974, U.S. Ct. Mil. Appeals 1974, U.S. Supreme Ct. 1977, U.S. Dist. Ct. (we. dist.) Tex. 1988, U.S. Ct. Appeals (fed. cir.) 1990. Oil title analyst Hunt Oil Co., Dallas, 1971-73; atty., advisor Regulations and Adminstrv. Law divsn. Office of Chief Counsel USCG, Washington, 1973-77; dir. estate planning devel. dept. Baylor U., Waco, Tex., 1977-80, gen. counsel, 1980—2002; ret., 2002; assoc. gen. counsel So. Meth. U., Dallas, 2002—. Adj. prof. law Baylor U.; lobbyist legis. Ind. Higher Edn., 71st Session of Tex. Legislature; mem. legis. com. Gov.'s Task Force on Drug Abuse; dir. govtl. rels. Baylor U.; spkr. at meetings of coll. and univ. adminstrs.; assisted in drafting legis. for Texan's War on Drugs Tex. Legislature; mem. legal adv. com. United Educators Ins. Risk Retention Group, 1994-96, asst. area dir. US naval Acad. Active Longhorn Coun. Boy Scouts of Am.; vice chair planning and zoning commn. City of Woodway, 2004—, mem. bd. adjustment, 1998—2004; bd. dirs. Heart of Tex. Coun. on Alcohol and Drug Abuse, 1987—91. Recipient Pres.'s award Ind. Colls. and Univs. of Tex., 1994, Dist. award of merit Boy Scouts Am. Fellow Coll. State Bar Tex.; mem. ABA, FBA, Nat. Assn. Coll. and Univ. Attys. (fin., nominations and elections comms. 1994-95, bd. dirs. 1988-91, 2000—, pres. 2004-05), Nat. Assn. Ind. Colls. and Univs. (mem. legal svcs. rev. panel), Tex. Bar Assn., Waco Bar Assn., McLennan County Bar Assn., Owners Assn. of Sugar Creek, Inc. (bd. dirs. 1991-95). Baptist. Avocations: backpacking, running, environmental concerns, historical reinactment. Home: 100 Sugar Creek Pl Waco TX 76712-3410 Office: So Meth U PO Box 750132 Dallas TX 75275-0137 Home Phone: 254-772-7706; Office Phone: 214-768-3233. Business E-Mail: bthomson@smu.edu.

THOMSON, DAVID KENNETH ROY, publishing executive; s. Kenneth Thomson; 3 children. Grad., Upper Can. Coll.; MA in Hist., U. Cambridge Selwyn Coll., 1978. With Hudson's Bay Co.; pres. Zellers and Simpsons, 1980—90; dep. chmn. Woodbridge Co. Ltd., 1990—; mem. bd. dirs. The Thomson Corp., Toronto, 1988—, chmn., 2002—. Named one of Top 200 Collectors, ARTnews Mag., 2004—, World's Richest People (with family), Forbes Mag., 2007, 2008. Avocation: Collector of Constable; Italian Futurism; Contemporary art. Office: Thomson Corp Toronto-Dominion Bank Tower, 66 Wellington St W Toronto ON M5K 1A1 Canada Office Phone: 416-360-8700.

THOMSON, DONALD ARTHUR, education educator; b. Detroit, Apr. 9, 1932; s. Arthur and Theresa Rita (Stasin) T.; m. M. Jenean Gruner, Apr. 6, 1957; children: Erin, Kurt, Lisa, Madelon. BS, U. Mich., 1955, MS, 1957; PhD, U. Hawaii, 1963. Asst. prof., curator of fishes & dir. mar. sci. to prof. U. Ariz., Tucson, 1963-98, prof. emeritus, 1998—. Author: Reef Fishes of the Sea of Cortez, 2000, Fishwater's Guide to the Gulf of Calif., 1976, Tide Calendar for the Northern Gulf of Calif., 1967-2003; contbr. articles to profl. jour. Democrat. Avocations: photography, fly fishing, aquaria, dogs, electronics. Office: Dept Ecol/Evol Biol Univ Ariz Tucson AZ 85721-0001 E-mail: dat@u.arizona.edu.

THOMSON, GERALD EDMUND, physician, educator; b. NYC, 1932; s. Lloyd and Sybil (Gilbourne) T.; m. Carolyn Webber; children: Gregory, Karen. MD, Howard U., 1959; DSc (hon.), Morehouse Med. Coll., 1997. Diplomate Am. Bd. Internal Medicine (bd. govs. 1985-92, exec. com. 1988-91, chmn.-elect 1990-91, chmn. 1991-92). Resident in medicine SUNY-Kings County Hosp. Center, 1959-62, chief resident, 1962-63, NY Heart Assn. fellow in nephrology, 1964-65, asst. vis. physician, 1963-70, clin. dir. dialysis unit, 1965-67; practice medicine specializing in internal medicine NYC, 1963-64; attending physician SUNY Med. Bklyn. Hosp., 1966-70; instr. in medicine SUNY, Bklyn., 1963-68, clin. asst. prof. medicine, 1968-70; asso. chief med. services Coney Island Hosp., Bklyn., 1967-70; attending physician Presbyn. Hosp., 1970—; dir. nephrology Harlem Hosp. Center, NYC, 1970-71, dir. med. services, 1971-85, pres. med. bd., 1976-78; assoc. prof. medicine Columbia Coll. Physicians and Surgeons, 1970-72, prof., 1972—, Samuel Lambert prof. medicine, 1980—, Robert Sonneborn prof. medicine, 1997—; exec. v.p. for profl. affairs, chief of staff Columbia-Presbyn. Med. Ctr., 1985-90; sr. assoc. dean Coll. Physicians and Surgeons, Columbia U., NYC, 1990—2003. Mem. Health Rsch. Coun. City NY, 1972-75; mem. med. adv. bd. NY Kidney Found., 1971-82; mem. Health Rsch. Coun., State NY, 1975-81; mem. hypertension info. and edn. adv. com. NIH, 1973-74, NY State Adv. Com. on Hypertension, 1977-80; com. on non-pharm. treatment of hypertension Inst. of Medicine, Nat. Acad. Scis., 1980; mem. med. adv. bd. Nat. Assn. Patients on Hemodialysis and Transplantation, 1973-83; mem. adv. bd. Sch. Biomed. Edn., CUNY, 1979-83, Med. News Network, 1993-95; mem. com. on mild hypertension Nat. Heart and Lung Inst., 1976, mem. clin. trials rev. com., 1980-85, mem. rev. panel, 1979; bd. dirs. NY Heart Assn., 1973-81, chmn. com. high blood pressure, 1976-81; bd. dirs. Primary Care Devel. Corp.; chmn. com. hypertension NY Met. Regional Med. Program, 1974-76; mem. adv. com. Heart and Hypertension Inst. of NY State, 1984; mem. NY Gov.'s Health Adv. Coun., 1981-84, pub. Health Coun., NY, 1983-95, Joint Nat. Com. High Blood Pressure NIH, 1983-84, 87-88, mem. rev. panel hypertension detection and monitoring bd. study cardiovasc. risk factors in young Nat. Heart, Lung and Blood Inst., 1984-90; mem. panel on receiving and withholding med. treatment ACLU, 1984-88; mem. Grad. Med. Edn. Commn., State of NY, 1984-86, mem. Commn. on End-State Renal Disease, 1985, 89-90; pres. Washington Heights-Inwood Ambulatory Care Network Corp., 1986-91; bd. dirs. Primary Care Devel. Corp., 1993-98. Mem. adv. bd. Jour. Urban Health, 1974-80, Med. News Network, 1993-94. Chmn. ad hoc com. on access to nursing homes Pub. Health Coun. State of NY, 1982-96; pres. Washington Heights-Inwood Ambulatory Care Network Corp., 1986-91; mem. Mayor's Commn. Health and Hosps. Corp.; dir. Harlem Ctr. for Health Promotion and Disease Prevention, 1993-95. Recipient Nat. Med. award Nat. Kidney Found., NY, 1984, Outstanding Alumnus award Howard U., 1987, Disting. Alumnus award, 1998, Dean's Outstanding Tchg. award Coll. Physicians and Surgeons Columbia U., 1986, Columbia U. Pres. award Outstanding Tchg., 2002, Nickens award, Soc. General Internal Med., 2004. Mem: AAAS, ACP (master, Gov.'s coun. downstate region 1982-89, chmn. com. health pub. policy NY chpt. 1982-89, health care professions com. 1987-90, bd. regents 1990-97, chmn. nat. health and pub. policy com. 1993-94, pres.-elect 1994-95, pres. 1995-96), NY Acad. Medicine (mem. com. medicine in soc. 1974-76, chmn. com. medicine in soc. 1997-98, bd. trustees, 2000-2007, sec., 2003-07), NY Soc. Nephrology (pres. 1973-74), Am. Fedn. Clin. Rsch., Federated Coun. for Internal Medicine (chmn. 1991-92, 95-96), Soc. Urban Physicians (pres. 1972-73), Am. Soc. Artificial Internal Organs (adv. bd., 1998-2002, chmn. bd. trustees, 2002-), Assn. Program Dirs. in Internal Medicine, Pub. Health Assn. NYC (dir. 1983-86), Inst. Medicine (chmn., bd. dirs., 2003-), Physicians for Social Responsibility of NY (dir. 1983), Physicians Human Rights (bd. trustees, 2005-) Assn. Acad. Minority Physicians (pres. 1988-90), Inst. Medicine, Nat. Acad. Scis. (chmn. com. on review of NIH strategic plan on health disparities, 2004-06). Home and Office: Premium Pt New Rochelle NY 10801-5327 Business E-Mail: get1@columbia.edu.

THOMSON, HELEN LOUISE, artist; b. Lewiston, Ill., Nov. 28, 1928; d. Clyde Arthur Pomeroy and Myrtle Lynch Cluney; m. William Edward Thomson, 1950; children: Persephone Ann, Lucinda Renee, Cynthia Louise. Student, Western Ill. U., Macomb, 1972, 78, 85, U. Ill., 1972; diploma, North Light Art Sch. Artist, Table Grove, Ill., 1970—. Adj. prof. Western Ill. U., Macomb, 1985—94; mem. spkrs. roster Spoon River Coll., Canton, Ill., 1986—94; exec. dir. Two Rivers Arts Coun., Macomb, 1985—94. Exhibitions include in numerous one woman and group exhbns.; contbr. art to calendars. Officer PTA, Table Grove, 1957—85; pres. Fulton County Arts Coun., Canton, 1973—83, Spoon River Coll. Found., Canton, 1979—85; mem. adv. panel Ill. Arts Coun., Chgo., 1980—83; bd. dirs. regional arts adv. coun. Western Ill. U., 1978—85. Recipient Ruth Watts Svc. award, Performing Arts Soc., Western Ill. U., 1994, award, Two Rivers Arts Coun., 1994. Mem.: Table Grove Christian Ch. (moderator 1999—2008), Galesburg Civic Art Ctr. (exhbn. awards), Ill. Watercolor Soc., Ill. Art League (exhbn. awards), PEO Sisterhood (pres., sec., chaplain, v.p.). Avocations: antiques, antique dolls, family history. Home: 404 S Broadway St PO Box 163 Table Grove IL 61482-0163

THOMSON, JAMES ALAN, think-tank executive; b. Boston, Jan. 21, 1945; s. James Alan and Mary Elizabeth (Pluff) T.; m. Darlene Thomson; children: Kristen Ann, David Alan. BS, U. NH, 1967, DSC (hon.), 2007; MS, Purdue U., 1970, PhD, 1972, DSc (hon.), 1992; LLD (hon.), Pepperdine U., 1996. Research fellow U. Wis., Madison, 1972-74; systems analyst Office Sec. Def. US Dept. Def., Washington, 1974-77; staff mem. Nat. Security Council, The White House, Washington, 1977-81; v.p. The RAND Corp., Santa Monica, Calif., 1981-89, pres., CEO, 1989—. Bd. dirs. L.A. World Affairs Coun., AK Steel Holding Corp., Object Reservoir. Contbr. articles to profl. jours. and chpts. to books. Mem. Internat. Inst. for Strategic Studies (coun. 1985-99), Coun. Fgn. Rels. Office: The RAND Corp 1776 Main St Santa Monica CA 90401-3297 Office Phone: 310-451-6936. Business E-Mail: thomson@rand.org.

THOMSON, JAMES ALEXANDER, molecular biologist, educator; b. Oak Park, Ill., Dec. 20, 1958; married; 2 children. BSc in Biophysics, U. Ill., Champaign, 1981; DVM magna cum laude, U.Pa., 1985, DS in Molecular Biology, 1988. Diplomate Am. Coll. Veterinary Pathologists. Postdoctoral rsch. fellow, Nonhuman Primate In Vitro Fertilization and Exptl. Embryology Oreg. Regional Primate Ctr., 1989—91; joined U. Wis., Madison, 1991, resident, veterinary pathology, Wis. Regional Primate Ctr., 1991—94, assoc. veterinarian, asst. scientist, Wis. Regional Primate Ctr., 1992—95, chief pathologist, Wis. Regional Primate Rsch. Ctr., 1995—; asst. prof., dept. anatomy U. Wis. Med. Sch., 1999—2001; scientific dir. WiCell Rsch. Inst., Madison, Wis., 1999—; John D. McArthur Prof., dept. anatomy U. Wis. Sch. Med. and Pub. Health, Madison, 2002—. Adj. prof., molecular, cellular, and develop. biology dept. U. Calif., Santa Barbara, 2007—; dir., regenerative biology Morgridge Inst. for Rsch. Contbr. articles to profl. sci. jours. Recipient Ill. Gen. Assembly award, 1978, Eastman Kodak award in biol. scis., 1979, C.L. Davis award for Student Scholarship in Veterinary Pathology, 1994, Golden Plate award, Am. Acad. Achievement, 1999, Hall of Fame award for Scientific Achievement, 15th Ann. Conf. Biotechnology CEO's, 2001, World Tech. award, 2002, LIFE Internat. Rsch. award, 2002, Frank Annunzio award, Christopher Columbus Fellowship Found., 2003, Outstanding Achievement award, Am. Coll. Veterinary Pathologists, 2003, Disting. Service award for enhancing edn. through biol. rsch., Nat. Assn. Biology Tchrs., Inc., 2005, Nathan R. Brewer Sci. Achievement award, Am. Assn. Lab. Animal Sci., 2006, Lois Pope award Ann. LIFE Internat. Rsch. award, 2002; named Man of Yr., Madison Mag., 2001; named a Nat. Merit Scholar, 1977, finalist for World Tech. award in health and medicine, The Economist, London, 1999; named one of The Most Intriguing People, People Mag., 2001, 18 Scientists representing America's Best in Science and Medicine, TIME Mag., 2001, The 100 Most Influential People in the World, TIME mag., 2008; fellow Wis. Acad. Scis., Arts, and Letters, 2002; NSF Undergraduate Rsch. Participation Fellow, Princeton U., 1979, Summer Fellow, Friedrich Miescher Inst., Basel, Switzerland, 1981, Veterinary Med. Scientist Tng. Program Fellow, U. Pa. Sch. Veterinary Medicine, 1981—87. Mem.: Soc. for Devel. Biology, Internat. Soc. for Stem Cell Rsch., Am. Coll. of Veterinary Pathologists, Phi Zeta, Phi Beta Kappa. Achievements include first to isolate and culture nonhuman primate embryonic stem cells in 1995, and human ES cells in 1998; lab had reported determining a method to modify human skin cells in such a way that they appear to be embryonic stem cells without using a human embryo in 2007. Office: Univ Wisconsin Genome Ctr of WI 425 Henry Mall Rm 4420 Madison WI 53715 Office Phone: 608-263-3585. Office Fax: 608-265-8984, 608-263-3517. E-mail: thomson@primate.wisc.edu.*

THOMSON, JOHN ANSEL ARMSTRONG, biochemist; b. Detroit, Nov. 23, 1911; s. John Russell and Florence (Antisdel) T.; m. June Anna Mae Hummel, June 24, 1938; children: Sheryll Linn, Patrisha Diane, Robert Royce. AA, Pasadena City Coll., Calif., 1935; AB cum laude, U. So. Calif., 1957; BGS (hon.), Calif. Poly. State U., 1961; MA, PhD, Columbia Pacific U., 1978-79; DA, Internat. Inst. Advanced Studies, Clayton, Mo., 1979. Cert. secondary tchr., Calif. Chemist J.A. Thomson Bio-Organic Chemist, LA, 1938, Vitamin Inst. (formerly J.A. Thomson Bio-Organic Chemist), L.A. and North Hollywood, Calif., 1939—. Vocat. edn. instr. U.S. War Manpower Commn., 1943-44; chmn. activities coun. World Coun. of Youth, L.A., 1932; pres. Coun. of Young Men's Divsns. Athletic Commns., YMCA Pasadena area, 1931, chmn. exec. coun., 1932; dist. officer Boy Scouts Am., San Fernando Valley coun., 1954-64, del. to nat. conf., 1959, and others. Author: (booklets) Whose Are the Myths?, 1949, Open Eyes, Illegalize Agency Abuses, 1968, Non-toxic Vitamins-hormones Answers to Environmental, Public Problems, 1972, Lobby Interest Goals to Sequester Nutrients Among Those Rarely Educated in Them, 1973, Support of Pressures to Homeostasis, Normality, 1990, Minimization of Toxics in Agriculture, 1991, Need for Recognition and Reversal of Rapid Decline of Heritage of American and World Children 1995, 1996; contbr. articles to jours. Instr. United Methodist Ch. nat. seminar for profls., Nashville, Tenn., 1983, admin bd., 1952-; chmn. commn. ch. and soc., 1986—, First United Meth. Ch., North Hollywood; mem. United Meth. Men; hon. life, Purdue U. Conf., pres. 1979-1980, program leader, lectr. 1982 Rep. county ctrl. Com. L.A. County, 1941-50, chmn. 63d assembly dist., 1948-50, Rep. state ctrl. com., Calif. 1948-50. Recipient Sci. and Industry award San Francisco Internat. Expn., 1940, various scouting leadership awards Boy Scouts Am., Civic Svc. award State of Calif., 1949, others. Mem. AAAS (life), Am. Inst. Biol. Scis., NY Acad. Scis., Am. Hort. Soc., Am. Chem. Soc., Internat. Acad. Nutrition and Preventive Medicine, Am. Forestry Assn., Garden Writers Assn. Am., Profl. Grounds Mgmt. Soc., Internat. Soc. Hort. Sci., Nat. Recreation and Parks Assn., Natural Products Assn. (Pioneer Svc. award 1970), Nat. Health Fedn. (life), Nat. Resources Def. Coun., Lawn and Garden Mktg. aand Distbn. Assn. (Lifetime Achievement award 2006), Am. Nursery and Landscape Assn., Calif. Assn. Nurseries and Garden Ctrs., China Soc. So. Calif. (pres., 1990-1991), Com. for Nuc. Responsibility, Inst. for Health Freedom, Internat. Union of Pure and Applied Chemistry, Perennial Plant Assn., So. Calif. Pub. Health Assn., Tree Care Industry Assn., Universal City-North Hollywood C. of C., Sierra Club, Soc. Colonial Wars (life), Kiwanis (projects panelist internat. confs. 1987, 91, pres. N. Hollywood club 1996-97), Friends of the Earth, Amnesty Internat., U. So. Calif. Gen. Alumni Assn. (life), Life Extension Found., Am. Assn. for Health Freedom, Union of Concerned Scientists, US C. of C., Am. Acad. of Anti-Aging, Ariz. Nursery Assn., Assn. Zoological Horticulture, Better Bus. Bur., Health Sci. Inst., League Conservation Voters, Nat. Audubon Assn., Nat. Tropical Bot. Garden, NC Turf & Landscape Coun., Pesticide Action Network, SC Hort. Soc., Western Nursery & Landscape Assn. Republican. Achievements include origination of a high proportion of known uses for horticultural hormones, with first products, many of them via solely-invented and produced Horms 4, 1 and 2, Superthrive, Cutstart and Seedyield, multiple vitamins-hormones, distributed worldwide; development of highest known efficacies in plant activating, reviving, transplanting, growing, perfecting, rooting and seed invigoration; creation of water-miscible multiple vitamins powder Auzon, for humans; creation of more than 300 other formula products. Office: Vitamin Inst 12610 Saticoy St S North Hollywood CA 91605-4313

THOMSON, KEITH STEWART, biologist, author; b. Heanor, Eng., July 29, 1938; s. Ronald William and Marian Adelaide (Coster) T.; m. Linda Gailbreath Price, Sept. 27, 1963; children: Jessica Adelaide, Elizabeth Rose. B.Sc. with honors, U. Birmingham, Eng., 1960; A.M., Harvard U., 1961, PhD (NATO fellow), 1963. NATO postdoctoral fellow Univ. Coll., London U., 1963-65; asst. prof. to prof. biology Yale U., 1965-87, dean Grad. Sch., 1979-87; dir. Peabody Mus. Natural History, 1976-79; pres. Acad. Natural Scis., Phila., 1987-95; disting. scientist-in-residence New Sch Social Rsch., NYC, 1996-98; prof., dir. Mus. Natural History Oxford U., 1998—2003, prof. emeritus, 2003—; sr. rsch. fellow Am. Philos. Soc., Phila., 2003—. Dir. Sears Found. Marine Rsch. and Oceanographic History; hon. rsch. fellow Australian Nat. U., 1967; trustee, mem. corp. Woods Hole Oceanographic Inst.; bd. dirs. Wistar Inst., Ctrl. Phila. Devel. Corp., Wetlands Inst., Phila. Cultural Alliance, Charles Darwin Trust; rschr. in vertebrate evolution. Mem. editl. bd. Paleobiology, Jour. Morphology, 1988, Aspects of Lower Vertebrate Evolution, 1968, Origin of Terrestrial Vertebrates, 1968, Saltwater Fishes of Conn., 1971, 88, Priorities and Needs in Systematic Biology, 1981, Morphogenesis and Evolution, 1988, Living Fossil, 1991, The Common But Less Frequent Loon and Other Essays, 1993, HMS Beagle, 1995, 2003, Treasures on Earth, 2002, Before Darwin: Reconciling Science and Religion, 2005, Fossils, A Very Short Introduction, 2005, The Legacy of the Mastodon, 2008. Fellow Linnean Soc. London, Zool. Soc. London; mem. Soc. Vertebrate Palaeontology, Sigma Xi.

THOMSON, MICHAEL J., oil industry executive; V.p. Sunoco, Inc., sr. v.p., 2008—; exec. v.p., COO SunCoke Energy, Inc., pres., 2008—. Office: Sunoco Inc 1735 Market St Ste LL Philadelphia PA 19103-7583 Office Phone: 215-977-3000. Office Fax: 215-977-3409.*

THOMSON, PAUL RICE, JR., lawyer; b. Syracuse, NY, Dec. 28, 1941; s. Paul Rice and Marcella Elizabeth (Shea) T.; m. Elizabeth Ann Cutcliff, Aug. 21, 1965; children: Paul R. III, Pamela Judeth. BA in History, Va. Mil. Inst., 1963; JD, Washington and Lee U., 1966. Bar: Va. 1966, US Dist. Ct. (we. dist.) Va. 1966, US Ct. Mil. Appeals 1967, US Ct. Appeals (4th cir.) 1972, US Ct. Appeals (11th cir.) 2004. Assoc. Clement, Wheatley, Winston & Ingram, Danville, Va., 1969-71; asst. US atty. Western Dist. Va., Roanoke, 1971-75, US atty., 1975-79; gen. counsel natural resources The Pittston Co., Lebanon, Va., 1980—87; dep. asst. adminstr. EPA, Washington, 1987—90; ptnr. Woods Rogers PLC, Roanoke, Va., 1990—. Pres. Roanoke Valley Law Enforcement Coun., 1975-76; mem. Fed.-State Law Enforcement Coun., 1975-79; trustee Ea. Mineral Law Found., Pitts., 1980-82; adj. prof. Washington & Lee U., 1981-99. V.p. Danville Jr. C. of C., 1971. Capt. JAGC USMC, 1966—69. Recipient Spl. Achievement award Dept. Justice, 1974, Silver Beaver award, Boy Scouts Am., Blue Ridge Mountains Coun., 2004. Mem. ABA, Va. Bar Assn., NRA, Trout Unltd. Roman Catholic. Avocations: fly fishing, bird hunting, raising labrador retreivers. Office: Woods Rogers PLC 10 S Jefferson St Roanoke VA 24011 Office Phone: 540-983-7742. Business E-Mail: thomson@woodsrogers.com.

THOMSON, ROBERT JAMES, editor; b. Melbourne, Australia, Mar. 11, 1961; s. Jim and Gen Thomson; m. Wang Ping, 1992; 2 children. BA in Journalism, Royal Melbourne Inst. Tech. Fin. and gen. affairs reporter to Sydney corr. The Herald, Melbourne, 1979—83; sr. features writer Sydney Morning Herald, 1983—85; corr. Fin. Times, Beijing, 1985—89, Tokyo, 1989—94, fgn. news editor London, 1994—96, asst. editor, editor Weekend FT, 1996—98, mng. editor US edit. NYC, 1998—2002; editor The Times, London, 2002—07; pub. The Wall St. Jour., NYC, 2007—08, mng. editor, 2008—; editor-in-chief Dow Jones & Co., 2008—. Author: The Judges: A Portrait of the Australian Judiciary, 1986; co-author: The Chinese Army, 1990; editor: True Fiction, 1998. Named US Bus. Journalist of Yr., TJFR, 2001; named one of 25 Leaders Reshaping NY, Crain's NY mag., 2008. Avocations: tennis, reading, movies. Office: The Wall St Jour 1211 Ave of the Americas New York NY 10036*

THOMSON, ROGER F., lawyer; b. Detroit, Apr. 4, 1949; m. Carol M. Barger. BA, Miami U., Oxford, OH, 1971; JD, So. Meth. U., Dallas, 1974. Bar: Tex. 1974, US Dist. Ct. No. Dist. Tex., US Ct. Appeals 5th Cir. Legal counsel S&A Restaurant Corp., Dallas, 1978—80, corp. counsel, 1980—82, v.p., gen. counsel, 1982—83, v.p., gen. counsel, sec., 1983—84, sr. v.p., gen. counsel, sec., 1984—85, exec. v.p., gen. counsel, sec., 1985—88; sr. v.p., gen. counsel Burger King Corp., Miami, Fla., 1988—93; sr. v.p., gen. counsel, sec. Brinker Internat. Inc., Dallas, 1993—94, dir., 1993—95, exec. v.p., gen. counsel, sec., 1994—, chief adminstrv. officer, 1996—. Mem.: State Bar Tex. Office: Brinker Internat Inc 6820 LBJ Fwy Dallas TX 75240

THOMSON, ROSS DAVID, economics professor; b. Detroit, Sept. 21, 1948; s. Foster Charles and Ramona Rita Thomson; m. Floria Behbin; 1 child, Justin Armin. BA, Ariz. State U., Tempe, 1970; PhD, Yale U., New Haven, Conn., 1976. Asst. prof. economics New Sch. Social Rsch., NYC, 1976—91; assoc. prof. to dean U. Vt., Burlington, 1995—2002. Author: (book) The Path to Mechanized Shoe Production in the United States, Structures of Change in the Mechanical Age; contbr. articles to profl. jour. Sec., v.p., acting pres., chief negotiator United Academics, AFT-AAUP, Burlington, 2002—08. Grant, Sloan Found., 1991—94, NSF, 1970—76. Mem.: Bus. History Conf., Econ. History Assn., Golden Key Nat. Honor Soc. Achievements include design of teacher-advisor program at university of Vermont. Avocations: hiking, jazz. Office: Univ VT Economics Dep't Old Mill Bldg 342 Burlington VT 05405 Business E-Mail: ross.thomson@uvm.edu.

THOMSON, THYRA GODFREY, former state official; b. Florence, Colo., July 30, 1916; d. John and Rosalie (Altman) Godfrey; m. Keith Thomson, Aug. 6, 1939 (dec. Dec. 1960); children— William John, Bruce Godfrey, Keith Coffey. BA cum laude, U. Wyo., 1939. With dept. agronomy and agrl. econs. U. Wyo., 1938-39; writer weekly column Watching Washington pub. in 14 papers, Wyo., 1955-60; planning chmn. Nat. Fedn. Republican Women, Washington, 1961; sec. state Wyo. Cheyenne, 1962-86. Mem. Marshall Scholarships Com. for Pacific region, 1964-68; del. 72d Wilton Park Conf., Eng., 1965; mem. youth commn. UNESCO, 1970-71, Allied Health Professions Council HEW, 1971-72; del. U.S.-Republic of China Trade Conf., Taipei, Taiwan, 1983; mem. lt. gov.'s trade and fact-finding mission to Saudi Arabia, Jordan, and Egypt, 1985 Bd. dirs. Buffalo Bill Mus., Cody, Wyo., 1987—; adv. bd. Coll. Arts and Scis., U. Wyo., 1989, Cheyenne Symphony Orch. Found., 1990—. Recipient Disting. Alumni award U. Wyo., 1969, Disting. U. Wyo. Arts and Scis. Alumna award, 1987, citation Omicron Delta Epsilon, 1965, citation Beta Gamma Sigma, 1968, citation Delta Kappa Gamma, 1973, citation Wyo. Commn. Women, 1986; named Internat. Woman of Distinction, Alpha Delta Kappa, Keith and Thyra Honors Convocation in her honor Coll. of Arts and Scis. U. Wyo., 1997. Mem. N.Am. Securities Adminstrs. (pres. 1973-74), Nat. Assn. Secs. of State, Council State Govts. (chmn. natural resources com. Western states 1966-68), Nat. Conf. Lt. Govs. (exec. com. 1976-79) Republican. Home: 3102 Sunrise Rd Cheyenne WY 82001-6136

THOMSON, TODD STUART, investment company executive; b. Stanford, Calif., Jan. 30, 1961; s. Scott Dayton and Margaret Elaine (Guice) T.; m. Melissa Kay McKeithen, May 22, 1988. BA in Economics, Davidson Coll., 1983; MBA with distinction, U. Pa., 1987. Cons., sr. cons. Booz Allen & Hamilton, Bethesda, Md., 1983-85; cons., mgr. Bain & Co., Boston, 1986-91; sr. v.p. strategic planning & bus. devel. GE Capital Sevices, 1996—98; sr. v.p. strategy & bus. devel. Citigroup Inc., NYC, 1998, CEO Global Pvt. Bank, 1998—2000, exec. v.p. fin., ops. & strategy, CFO, 2000—04, chmn., CEO, Citigroup Global Wealth Mgmt. Divsn., 2004—07; founder, CEO Headwaters Capital, LLC, 2007—. Bd. dirs. World Resources Inst. Bd. trustees Davidson Coll., Wharton Grad. Exec. Bd.; chmn. Wharton Leadership Advisory Bd.; bd. dirs. NYC Acad. Fin. Mem.: Econ. Club NY.

THOMSON, VIRGINIA WINBOURN, humanities educator, writer; b. Oakland, Calif., Aug. 6, 1930; d. Harry Linn and Jennie Cook (Vineyard) Thomson. AA, San Mateo Coll., 1949; BA, San Jose State Coll., 1951; MA, U. Calif., Berkeley, 1952. Cert. secondary tchr. Calif. Tchr. social sci. Capuchino H.S., San Bruno, Calif., 1952—54, Watsonville H.S., Calif., 1954—87. Saleswoman, storyteller Home Interiors, San Mateo, 1963—64. Author: The Lion Desk, 1965, Short Talks Around the Lord's Table, 1985, Lawson's Castle, 2001, The Battle for the Spirits of Mankind, 2008, numerous poems. Mem.: AAUW (life), Nat. Geog. Soc. (life), Calif. Alumni Assn. (life), Calif. Writer's Club (life), Homer Honor Soc., Internat. Poets, Phi Alpha Theta. Republican.

THOMSON, WILLIAM, economics professor; PhD in Economics, Stanford U., Calif., 1976. Asst. prof. U. Minn., 1976—82, assoc. prof. economics, 1982—83, U. Rochester, NY, 1983—85, prof. economics, 1985—. Elected pres. Social Choice & Welfare Soc., 2004—06. Recipient award, U. Rochester. Office: Dept Economics Univ Rochester Rochester NY 14618

THOMSON, WILLIAM ENNIS, music theorist, author; b. Ft. Worth, May 24, 1927; s. William Tell and Ruby Florence (Schwarz) Thomson; m. Elizabeth Anne Everett, Sept. 11, 1948; children: Carol Anne, Mark William, Laurie Elizabeth, John Everett. MusB, North Tex. State U., 1948; MusM, 1949; PhD, Ind. U., 1952. Prof. music Sul Ross State U., Alpine, Tex., 1951—60, Ind. U., Bloomington, 1961—69, Kulas prof. Case Western Res. U., Cleve., 1969—73; dir. grad. studies U. Ariz., Tucson, 1973—75; chmn. dept. and Ziegle prof. SUNY-Buffalo, 1975—80; dean sch. music U. So. Calif., L.A, 1980—86, prof. emeritus, 1992. Mem. music panel Nat. Endowment for Arts, Washington, 1970—74; policy com. Contemporary Music Project, Washington, 1963—73; cons. N.Y. State Arts Coun., 1976—80; editor and cons. Hawaii Music Project, 1969—; assoc. editor Music Perception; v.p. bd. dirs. Buffalo Philharmonic, 1978—80; mem. bd. dirs. Pasadena Chamber Orch., 1980—82; trustee Young Musicians Found., LA, 1981—. Author: Introduction to Music Reading, 1965, Advanced Music Reading, 1969, Introduction to Music as Structure, 1971, Music for Listeners, 1979; co-author: Materials and Structure of Music, 1963—65, Schoenberg's Error, 1990. With USN, 1945—46. Named Outstanding Educator, Case Western Res. U., 1971, U. Ariz., 1974; Composer-in-residence grant, Ford Found, 1960—61. Office: U So Calif Sch Music Los Angeles CA 90089-0001

'T HOOFT, GERARDUS (GERARD), physicist, researcher; b. Den Helder, The Netherlands, July 5, 1946; s. Hendrik 't Hooft and Margaretha Agnes (van Kampen) t' Hooft; m. Albertha Anje Schik, July 1, 1972; children: Saskia Anne, Ellen Marga. Student, Utrecht U., The Netherlands; doctoraalexamen Theoretical Physics, Rijksuniversiteit Utrecht, The Netherlands, 1969, PhD, 1972; DSc (hon.), U. Chgo., 1981, U. Louvain, 1996, U. Bologna, 1998, Eurasian U., Astana, Kazakjstan, 2000, U. Western Cape, South Africa, 2001; D Humane Letters honoris causa, Hofstra U., 2001; Doctorat de Scences honoris causa, U. Mediterranee, 2001; Dsc honoris causa, Ohio State U., 2003; Doctorate (hon.), U. Sci. and Tech. China, 2004. Fellow European Ctr. Nuc. Rsch., Geneva, 1972—74; lectr., asst. prof. physics U. Utrecht, The Netherlands, 1974—77, prof., 1977—. Loeb lectr. Harvard U., Cambridge, Mass., 1976; Fairchild disting. scholar Calif. Inst. Tech., Pasadena, 1981; assoc. etranger Acad. des Scis., Paris, 1995; guest prof. Boston U., 1998, Duke U., 1989; hon. prof. Nanjing U., China, 2002, Zhejiang U., China, 2004. Assoc. editor Nuc. Physics B; contbr. articles to profl. jours. Decorated officer Legion of Honor France, comdr. Order Ned. Leeuw; recipient Dannie Heineman prize, Am. Phys. Soc., 1979, Am. Inst. Physics, N.Y.C., 1979, Wolf prize in physics, Wolf Found., Israel, 1981, Piou XI medal, Pontifica Accademia delle Sci. John Paul II, Vatican City, 1983, Spinoza premium, NWO, 1995, Franklin medal, Phila., 1995, Gian Carlo Wick commn. medal, Lausanne, 1997, HEP prize, European Phys. Soc., 1999, Nobel prize in physics, 1999, Osker Kein Silver medal, Royal Acad. Sweden, 1999, Hon. medal, Astana, Kazakhstan, 2000. Mem.: Academie des Scis. Paris, Koninlijke Nederlandse Academie voor Wetenschappen (Lorentz medal 1986), Am. Acad. Arts and Scis. (hon.), U.S. Nat. Acad. Scis. (assoc.). Office: Spinoza Inst Leuvenlaan 4 PO Box 80 195 NL3508TD Utrecht Netherlands also: Inst for Theoretical Physics Universiteit Utrecht Leuvenlaan 4 3584 CC Utrecht Netherlands E-mail: g.thooft@phys.uu.nl.

THOR, BRAD, writer; b. Chgo., 1969; BA in Creative Writing, U. So. Calif. Creator, prodr., writer, host for Pub. TV series Traveling Lite; founder Thor Entertainment. Mem. Analytic Red Cell Prog. Dept. Homeland Security; appearances as nat. security expert include FOX News Channel, CNN, CNN Headline News, ABC, CBS, NBC, PBS. Author: (novels) The Lions Of Lucerne, 2001, Path of the Assassin, 2003, State of the Union, 2004, Blowback, 2005, Takedown, 2006, The First Commandment, 2007, The Last Patriot, 2008 (Publishers Weekly Bestseller, #1 NY Times bestseller), The Apostle, 2009 (Publishers Weekly Bestseller). Avocations: fishing, hunting, travel, water-skiing, hiking. Mailing: c/o Atria Books 1230 Ave Americas 13th Fl New York NY 10019 Office Phone: 212-698-7000.*

THOR, LINDA M., college president; BA, Pepperdine U., 1971, EdD, 1986; MPA, Calif. State U., LA, 1980. Dir. pub. info. Pepperdine U., Los Angeles, 1971-73; pub. info. officer L.A. C.C. Dist., 1974-75, dir. comm., 1975-81, dir. edn. svcs., 1981-82, dir. high tech., 1982-83, sr. dir. occupl. and tech. edn., 1983-86; pres. West Los Angeles Coll., Culver City, Calif., 1986-90, Rio Salado Coll., Phoenix, 1990—. Contbr. articles to profl. jours. Active Continuous Quality Improvement Network for Cmty. Colls., 1991—; mem. Ariz. Gov.'s Adv. Coun. on Quality, 1992—97; pres. Ariz. Cmty. Coll. Pres.'s Coun., 1995—96; bd. dirs. Coun. for Adult and Experiential Learning, 1990—2005, C.C. Baccalaureate Assn., 2000—, Ariz. Town Hall, 2005—, Nana's Children Mental Health Found., 2003—, Friends of Pub. Radio Ariz., Ariz. Quality Alliance, 2008—. Recipient Delores award, Pepperdine U., 1986, Alumni Medal of Honor, 1987, Outstanding Achievement award Women's Bus. Network, 1989, Shirley B. Gordon award of distinction, Phi Theta Kappa Internat. Honor Soc., 2000, Paul A. Elsner Excellence in Leadership award, Chair Acad., 2003, Pioneer award, CC Baccalaureate Assn., 2007, Disting. Alumni award, Calif. State U., LA Coll. Natural Soc. Scis., 2007; named Woman of the Yr., Culver City Bus. and Profl. Women, 1988, Pacesetter of Yr., Nat. Coun. Mktg. and Pub. Rels., 1998. Office: 2323 W 14th St Tempe AZ 85281-6950 Business E-Mail: linda.thor@riomail.maricopa.edu.

THOR, PAUL VIETS, computer science educator; b. Schenectady, NY, Mar. 10, 1946; s. Donald D. and Eleanor B. (Viets) T.; m. Barbara K. Nelson, Mar. 27, 1982 (div. Dec. 1993). BSME, U. Denver, 1968; MS in Engring. Mgmt., UCLA, 1976; MS in Computer Sci., George Mason U., 1993; DCS, Colo. Tech. U., 1999. Engr. Martin Marietta Corp., Denver, 1968-69; commd. 2d lt. USAF, 1969, advanced through grades to maj.,

1982; pilot trainee USAF-Williams AFB, Phoenix, Ariz., 1970-71; pilot C141A 15 MAS-Norton AFB, San Bernardino, Calif., 1971-75, pilot C141B, 1981-84; communications and computer officer 2044 CG-Pentagon, Washington, 1977-81; air field mgr. 18TFW-Kadena AB, Okinawa, Japan, 1984-86; pilot C12 1402 MAS-Andrews AFB, Washington, 1986-87; comm. and computer officer 7 Comm. Group-Pentagon, Washington, 1987-89; cons. George Mason U., Fairfax, Va., 1990-93; pvt. practice cons. Colorado Springs, Colo., 1993—. Wing flight examiner 63 MAW-Norton AFB, San Bernardino, 1981-84; acquisitions officer 7th Comms. Group-Pentagon, 1987-89; assoc. prof. computer sci. Colo. Tech. U., Colorado Springs, 1993-2001, prof., 2001—. Mem. Computer Soc. of IEEE, Assn. Computer Machinery, Air Force Assn. (life), Mil. Officers Assn. of Am. Avocations: personal computers, woodworking, crafts, photography, book collector. Office: Colo Tech U 4435 N Chestnut St Colorado Springs CO 80907-3812 Personal E-mail: pvthor@earthlink.net. Business E-Mail: pthor@coloradotech.edu.

THORBECKE, ERIK, economics professor; b. Berlin, Feb. 17, 1929; s. William and Madelaine (Salisbury) T.; m. Charla J. Westerberg, Oct. 17, 1954; children: Erik Charles, Willem, Jon. Student, Netherlands Sch. Econs., Rotterdam, 1948-51; PhD, U. Calif., 1957; doctorate (hon.), U. Ghent, 1981. Asst. prof. econs. Iowa State U., 1957-60, assoc. prof., 1960-63, prof., 1963-73, Cornell U., 1974—, chmn. dept. econs., 1975-78, H.E. Babcock prof. econs. and food econs., 1978—. Econ. adviser Nat. Planning Inst., Lima, Peru, 1963-64; asso. asst. adminstr. for program policy AID, Washington, 1966-68, mem. research advisory com., 1976-81; sr. economist world employment program Internat. Labor Office, Geneva, 1972-73; vis. prof. Erasmus U., Rotterdam, 1980-81; mem. com. on internat. nutritional programs NRC-NAS, 1979-81; dir. program on comparative econ. devel., Cornell U., 1988—; sr. rsch. fellow USAID Inst. Policy Reform, 1990—. Author: The Tendency Towards Regionalization in International Trade, 1960, (with Irma Adelman) Theory and Design of Economic Development, 1966, (with K. Fox, J. Sengupta) Theory of Quantitative Economic Policy, 1968, Role of Agriculture in Economic Development, 1968, (with G. Pyatt) Planning Techniques for a Better Future, 1976; (with J. Defourny) Structural Path Analysis and Multiplier Decomposition within a Social Matrix, 1984, (with J. Foster, J. Greer) A Class of Decomposable Poverty Measures, 1984, (with J. Lecaillon, C. Morrisson) Economic Policies and Agricultural Performance of Low Income Countries, 1987, Planning Techniques for Social Justice In: The Balance between Industry and Agriculture in Economic Development, vol. 4, 1989, (with I. Adelman) The Role of Institutions in Economic Development, Special Issue of World Development, 1989, (with others) Adjustment and Equity in Indonesia, 1992, (with D. Berrian) Budgetary Rules to Minimize Societal Poverty in a General Equilibrium Context, 1992, (with T. van der Pluijm) Rural Indonesia: Socio-economic Development in a Changing Environment, 1993, (with A. de Janvry and E. Sadoulet) Impact of State and Civil Institutions on the Operation of Rural Market and Non-Market Configurations In: State, Market and civil Organizations: New Theories, New Practices, and Their Implications for Rural Development, 1995, (with A. Parikh) Impact of Rural Industrialization on Village Life and Economy: A Social Accounting Matrix, 1996, (with H-S Jung) A Multiplier Decomposition Method to Analyze Poverty Alleviation, 1996, (with others) Methods of Interregional and Regional Analysis, 1998, (with H. Wan) Taiwan's Development Experience: Lessons on Roles of Government and Market, 1999, (with C. Charumilind) Economic Inequality and its Socio-economic Impact, 2002, (with M. Nissanke) Impact of Globalization on the World's Poor; contbr. articles to profl. jours. Mem. Am. Econ. Assn., Am. Assn. Agrl. Econs. (Nat. award for best pub. research 1970) Office: Cornell U 3M11 MVR Ithaca NY 14853 Office Phone: 607-255-2066. Business E-Mail: et17@cornell.edu.

THOREEN, MARY LOUISE, elementary school educator, consultant; b. Ft. Walton Beach, Fla., Oct. 3, 1959; d. James Leonard and Norma Jean Thoreen; m. James L. Young, June 14, 1997. BS in Math., Fla. State U., 1981, MS in Higher Edn., 1982. Cert. early adolescence math. Nat. Bd. for Profl. Tchg. Stds., 1999, math. grades 6-12 Fla., 2002, math. grades 5-9 Fla., 2002, gifted edn. Fla. Dir. student activities Mars Hill (N.C.) Coll., 1982—84; program dir. Va. Tech, Blacksburg, 1984—87; asst. dir. U. Ctr. U. South Fla., Tampa, 1987—89; consulting analyst The Omnia Group, Tampa, 1989—94; math. tchr. Sch. Dist. Hillsborough County, Tampa, 1994—. On-air tutor math. homework hotline The Edn. Channel, Tampa, 2004—. Recipient Nat. Educator award, Milken Family Found., 2003; finalist Dist. Tchr. of Yr., Sch. Dist. Hillsborough County, 1999. Mem.: Nat. Coun. Tchrs. Math., Phi Delta Kappa. Lutheran. Avocations: hiking, bicycling, music. Personal E-mail: tampathor@aol.com.

THORELLI, SARAH V., economist, researcher; b. Atlanta, Dec. 30, 1922; m. Hans B. Thorelli; children: Irene, Tom. AB, U. Ga., 1944; MA, U. Ala., 1945; Ph.Lic., U. Stockholm, 1954. Free-lance researcher and scholar; v.p. Intopia, Inc. Cons. FTC, NSF, Sears, Roebuck and Co.; ofcl. translator legal documents Swedish Fgn. Office, Stockholm; intelligence rsch. analyst U.S. Dept. State; overseas rep. Equifax Co.; account exec. J. Walter Thompson Advt. Agy., NYC. Co-author: Consumer Information Handbook: Europe and North America, Consumer Information Systems and Consumer Policy; contbr. articles to profl. jours. Mem. Ind. U. Women's Club, AAUW, Network Career Women, Local Coun. Women, Psi Iota Xi. Home and Office: 2604 E 2nd St Apt F Bloomington IN 47401-5351 Office Phone: 812-333-3174.

THOREN-PEDEN, DEBORAH SUZANNE, lawyer; d. Robert Roy and Marguerite Natalie (Geoghegan) Thoren; m. Steven E. Peden, Aug. 10, 1985. BA in Philosophy, Polit. Sci./Psychology, U. Mich., 1978; JD, U. So. Calif., 1982. Bar: Calif. 1982. Assoc. Bushkin, Gaines & Gaims, LA, 1982-84, Rutan & Tucker, Costa Mesa, Calif., 1984-86; sr. counsel First Interstate Bancorp, LA, 1986-96; ptnr. Pillsbury Winthrop LLP, LA, 1996—; asst. gen. counsel CarsDirect.com; gen. counsel CD1 Financial.com; gen. counsel, sr. v.p., chief privacy officer PayMyBills.Com, 2000; ptnr. Pillsbury Winthrop LLP, 2000—; (Pillsbury Winthrop LLP merged with Shaw Pittman LLP, 2005); ptnr., corp. & securities dept., co-chair, consumer and retail industry team Pillsbury Winthrop Shaw Pittman LLP, Los Angeles, 2005—. Lectr. on e-commerce, privacy Bank Secrecy Act and Ethics, Office of Fgn. Assets Control. Supervising editor U. So. Calif. Entertainment Law Jour., 1982-83, Entertainment Publishing and the Arts Handbook, 1983-84; contbr. articles to profl. jours. Mem. ABA (past vice-chmn. compliance exec. com., money laundering task force, privacy task force, co chmn. BSA staff commentary com.), Calif. Bankers Assn. (regulatory compliance com., co-chmn. regulatory compliance conf., past ex-officio mem. state govt. rels. com., co-vice chmn., vice-chmn., Regulatory Compliance Profl. award 1997, Frandzel award for outside counsel 2001, award 2001), Calif. State Bar Assn. (chmn., consumer fin. com.). Avocations: horseback riding, travel, reading, skiing. Office: Pillsbury Winthrop Shaw Pittman LLP Ste 2800 725 S Figueroa St Los Angeles CA 90017-5443 Office Phone: 213-488-7320. Office Fax: 213-629-1033. Business E-Mail: deborah.thoren-peden@pillsburylaw.com.

THORGEIRSSON, SNORRI SVEINN, medical researcher; b. Iceland, Dec. 1, 1941; came to U.S., 1972, naturalized, 1980; d. Thorgeir Jonsson and Sigurlina Sigujonsdottir; M.D., U. Iceland, 1968; Ph.D., U. London, 1971; m. Unnur Thorgeirsson, Sept. 5, 1969; children— Sif, Christian. Intern, Univ. Hosp., Reykjavik, Iceland, 1968-69; registrar, research fellow dept. clin. pharmacology Royal Postgrad. Med. Sch., London, 1969-71; vis. fellow Lab. Chem. Pharmacology, Nat. Heart and Lung Inst., NIH, Bethesda, Md., 1972-73, vis. scientist sect. devel. pharmacology, Neonatal and Pediatric Medicine br. Nat. Inst. Child Health and Human Devel., 1974-75, chief sect. on molecular toxicology devel. pharmacology br., 1975-76; head biochem. pharmacology sect. Lab. Chem. Pharmacology, Nat. Cancer Inst., 1976-81, chief Lab. Exptl. Carcinogenesis, 1981—, also head Cellular and Molecular Biology Sect.; mem. Chem. Selection Working Group, 1978—; mem. Com. on Occupational Carcinogenesis, 1979; mem. com. on amines Nat. Acad. Scis., 1979-80; co-chmn. Internat. Conf. on Carcinogenic and Mutagenic N-Substituted Aryl Compounds, NIH, Bethesda, 1979; preceptor Pharmacology Research Assoc. Program, Nat. Inst. Gen. Med. Scis., 1977—; mem. biol. response modifiers decision network com. Nat. Cancer Inst., 1980; lectr. in field. Mem. Am. Assn. Cancer Research, AAAS, Am. Soc. Exptl. Pharmacology and Exptl. Therapeutics, Am. Chem. Soc., NY Acad. Scis., Environ. Mutagen Soc., Soc. Toxicology, European Assn. Cancer Research. Contbr. numerous articles, chpts. to profl. publs.; research in mechanisms of chem. carcinogenesis, control of differentiation in neo-plastic cells. Office: Nat Cancer Inst Lab Exptl Carcinogenesis Bldg 37 Rm 4146A1 37 Convent Dr Bethesda MD 20892-4262 Office Phone: 301-496-1935. Office Fax: 301-496-0734. E-mail: snorri_thorgeirsson@nih.gov.*

THORIN, SUZANNE E., dean, university librarian; BA in music edn., N. Park Coll., Chgo., 1963; MA in music history, lit., Univ. Mich., 1964, MLS, 1968. With Libr. Cong., Washington, 1980—96, chief of staff, 1992—96; Ruth Lilly univ. dean of univ. libr. and assoc. v.p. digital libr. devel. Ind. Univ., 1996—2005; univ. libr., dean of libr. Syracuse Univ., 2005—. Office: Dean of Libr Syracuse Univ 223 D S Bird Libr 2573 Syracuse NY 13244 Office Phone: 315-443-2573. Business E-Mail: sethorin@syr.edu.

THORINGTON, RICHARD WAINWRIGHT, biologist; b. Phila., Dec. 24, 1937; AB, Princeton U., 1959; MA, Harvard U., 1963, PhD, 1964. Primatologist Harvard U. Regional Primate Ctr., Southborough, Mass., 1964-69; curator of mammals Smithsonian Instn., Washington, 1969—. Trustee Del. Mus. Natural History, Wilmington, 1957—. Fellow AAAS; mem. Am. Soc. Mammalogists (dir.). Office: Smithsonian Instn Nhb 399 Mrc 108 Washington DC 20013-7012 Business E-Mail: thoringtonr@si.edu.

THORMODSGARD, DIANE L., bank executive; b. 1950; m. Gaylord Thormodsgard; 2 children. BA in Math., Econ. & Acctg., Luther Coll.; MBA, U. Minn. Controller, asst. treas. First Bank System (now US Bancorp), 1978, sr. v.p., regional cmty. banking, 1985—89, sr. v.p. ops., 1989—93, sr. v.p., treas., chief adminstr. officer, 1993—95, sr. v.p., chief adminstr. officer Corp. Trust, 1995—99, pres., corp. trust., inst. trust and custody svcs., 1999—2007, vice chmn., head wealth mgmt., 2007—. Bd. mem. St. Paul C. of C., St. Paul Chamber Orch., Minn. Ch. Found., Ctrl. Corridor Partnership; mem. Luth. Social Services Fin. Com.; bd. trustees The Mpls. Found., 2008—. Named one of The Top 15 Women in Fin., Finance & Commerce, 2005, 25 Most Powerful Women in Banking, US Banker, 2006—08. Mem.: Am. Inst. Cert. Pub. Accountants, Minn. Soc. Cert. Pub. Accountants. Office: US Bancorp US Bancorp Ctr 800 Nicollet Mall Minneapolis MN 55402 Office Phone: 612-303-7936. E-mail: diane.thormodsgard@usbank.com.*

THORN, CHARLES BEHAN, physics professor; b. Washington, Ind., Aug. 14, 1946; s. Charles Behan and Willoughby Allen Thorn; m. Mary Ann Furman, Jan. 2, 1979; children: Alexandra Maria, Jessica Stephanie. PhD, U. Calif., Berkeley, 1971. Asst. prof. physics MIT, Cambridge, 1973—78, assoc. prof. physics, 1978—80; prof. physics U. Fla., Gainesville, 1980—. Recipient Jesse W. Beams medal, Southeastern Sect. Am. Phys. Soc., 2005; fellow, Woodrow Wilson Found., 1968, NSF, 1968—71, 1972, Alfred P. Sloan Found., 1974—78. Fellow: Am. Phys. Soc. Achievements include research in quantum dynamics of a massless relativistic string; proof of no ghost theorem for dual resonance models; MIT bag model of strongly interacting particles. Office: Univ FL PO Box 118440 Gainesville FL 32611-8440 Business E-Mail: thorn@phys.ufl.edu.

THORN, RODNEY KING, professional sports team executive, retired professional basketball player; b. Princeton, W.Va., May 23, 1941; m. Peggy Thorn; children: Jonathan, Amanda, Jessica. Student, W.Va. U.; BA in Polit Sci., U. Wash., Seattle; degree (hon.), W.Va. U. Player NBA Balt. Bullets, 1963—64, NBA Detroit Pistons, 1964—65, NBA St. Louis Hawks, 1965—67, NBA Seattle SuperSonics, 1967—71, asst. coach, 1971—73, Am. Basketball Assn. NY Nets, 1973—75, NBA NY Nets, 1976—78; head coach Am. Basketball Assn. St. Louis Spirits, 1975—76; gen. mgr. NBA Chgo. Bulls, 1978—85, interim head coach, 1982; v.p. basketball ops. NBA, NYC, 1985—2000; pres. NBA NJ Nets, East Rutherford, 2000—. Chair Sr. Men's Basketball com. USA Basketball, 1992—2000. Bd. dirs. W.Va. U. Named NBA Exec. of Yr., 2002. Office: NJ Nets Nets Champion Ctr 390 Murray Hill Pky East Rutherford NJ 07073-2109 Office Phone: 201-935-8888. Office Fax: 201-935-1088.*

THORN, SHANNON H., hospital administrator, consultant; s. Dianne Hayes Thorn; m. Angela Nicole Mann, May 27, 1997; 1 child, Colin Hayes. BA, NE La. U., Monroe, 1993, MA, 1995. Program dir. Tallulah Correctional Ctr. Youth, La., 1995—97; psychol. assoc. Pinecrest Devel. Ctr., Pineville, La., 1997—2001; assoc. adminstr. Pinecrest Supports and Svcs. Ctr., Pineville, 2001—. Cons. Independant Consulting, Pollock, La., 2007—. Contbr. scientific papers. Mem.: Assn. Positive Behavior Supports. Home: 302 Ferguson Loop Pollock LA 71467 Office: Pinecrest Supports and Svcs Ctr PO Box 5191 Pineville LA 71361

THORN, SUSAN HOWE, interior designer; b. Washington, Apr. 22, 1941; d. James Bennett Cowdin and Lois (Fiesinger) Howe; m. William D. Thorn, June 22, 1963; children: Melissa Ann, William David. Cert. lighting design, Parsons Sch. Design, NYC, 1975—77; BA, Syracuse U., NY, 1962; AB, NY Sch. Interior Design, NYC, 1995. Owner, designer Susan Thorn Interiors, Inc., Cross River, NY, 1965—. Designer total bldg. Cooper Labs, Bedford Hills, NY, 1973, total redesign Nycrest Corp., Cold Spring, NY, 1973-75, showrooms, model rooms stylist and coordinator France Voiles Co. Inc., NYC, 1976, total design new corp. hdqrs. in Gen. Dynamics Bldg. (with Marjorie Borradaile Helsel), Robert E. Eastman Co., NYC, 1967, Cummin & Friedland Capital Corp., 1982; designer offices, stores, employee areas comml., public, residential clients, including Waccabuc Country Club, NY, 1969, S. Salem Libr., NY, St. Vincent's Hosp., NYC, 1996; instr. adult edn. dept. John Jay High Sch.; spkr. civic orgns. Mem. Am. Soc. Interior Designers (profl.), Internat. Assn. Lighting Designers (assoc.), Decorators Club, Waccabuc Country Club. Episcopalian. Home: PO Box 187 Cross River NY 10518 Home Phone: 914-763-1210; Office Phone: 914-763-5265. Office Fax: 914-763-9041. Personal E-mail: thorninteriors@earthlink.net.

THORN, TERENCE HASTINGS, energy executive, consultant, writer; b. Takoma, Md., July 6, 1946; s. John Hastings and Norine R. (Freytag) T.; m. Judith Carol Bailey, Aug. 15, 1970; children: Kristin Lynn, Matthew Hastings. BA, U. Md., 1969, MA, 1973. Dir. congl. rels. Am. Gas Assn., Arlington, Va., 1975-79; dir. govt. rels. J. Walter Thompson Co., Washington, 1979-81; v.p. govt. rels. Houston Natural Gas Co., Washington, 1981-85; exec. v.p., chmn. bd. Mojave Pipeline Co., Houston, 1986-89; pres., CEO Transwestern Pipeline Co., Houston, 1993—; sr. v.p., exec. mgmt. com. bd. Enron Corp., Houston, 1993-98, exec. v.p. internat. govt. rels. and environ. affairs, 1998—2001, mng. dir. Middle East, 2001; cons. Houston Tex. Energy, Environment, Tech.; pres. JKM Cons., Houston, 2001—. Cons. in field. Contbr. articles to profl. jours. Bd. dirs. Houston Pops, 1989-90, Pin Oak Charities, Houston, 1991-93, Greater Houston chpt. YMCA, 1994; city alderman, 1992-93; mem. Hermann Soc., 1993—, Energy Industry Sector Adv. Com. U.S. Dept. Commerce; prin. liason Pres.'s Coun. Sustainable Devel.; chmn. internat. com. Bus. Coun. of Sustainable Devel.; mem. adv. com. Commn. for Environ. Cooperation; trustee Tomas Rivera Policy Inst.; chmn. Internat. Gas Ctr. Mem. Pacific Coast Gas Assn. (chmn. 1994-95), Internat. Gas Union (chmn. com. 9), U.S. C. of C. (mem. internat. policy com.), Coun. of the Ams. (adv. com.), Wildlife Conservation Soc. (trustee), Nature Conservancy (trustee, bd. Greater Houston area for smog prevention, industry profl. for clean air). Avocation: international energy development writing.

THORNBERRY, MAC (WILLIAM MCCLELLAN THORNBERRY), United States Representative from Texas; b. Clarendon, Tex., July 15, 1958; m. Sally Thornberry; 2 children. BA in Hist., summa cum laude, Tex. Tech U., Lubbock, 1980; JD, U. Tex. Law Sch., 1983. Legis. coun. Staff of US Rep. Tom Loeffler of Tex., 1983-85; chief of staff Staff of US Rep. Larry Combest of Tex., 1985-88; dep. asst. sec. legis. affairs US State Dept., 1988-89; def. atty. Peterson, Farris, Doores & Jones, Amarillo, Tex., 1989-94; mem. US Congress from 13th Tex. dist., 1995—, mem. armed svcs. com., permanent select com. on intelligence, chair oversight subcommittee. Mem.: Southwestern Cattle Raisers Assn., Tex. Cattle Raisers Assn. Republican. Presbyterian. Office: US Ho Reps 2457 Rayburn Ho Office Bldg Washington DC 20515-4313 Office Phone: 202-225-3706.*

THORNBRO, WILLIAM GRADEN, writer; b. Muncie, Ind., July 8, 1952; s. William Wesley Thornbro and Bonnie Ather (Marcum) Davis; m. Janice Kay Waters, Aug. 7, 1976; children: Christopher Wesley, Nicholas Dale. BS, Ball State U., 1978. Author: (book) An Uncertain Justice, A Question of Conspiracy, A Midsummers Dream and other Poems, The Return of Winter. Mem.: Acad. Am. Poets, Planetary Soc., Sierra Club. Democrat. Avocations: reading /research, gardening. Home: 212 S Pasture Ln Muncie IN 47304-4120 Personal E-mail: wmthornbro@sbcglobal.net.

THORNBURG, FREDERICK FLETCHER, lawyer executive, educator; s. James F. and Margaret R. (Major) T.; children: James Brian, Charles Kevin, Christian Sean, Christopher Herndon; m. Patricia J. Malloy, Dec. 4, 1981. AB, DePauw U., 1963; postgrad., U. Notre Dame, 1965; JD magna cum laude, Ind. U., 1968. Bar: Ind. 1968, U.S. Tax Ct. 1970, U.S. Ct. Appeals (7th cir.) 1970, U.S. Supreme Ct. 1971. Tchr., coach U.S. Peace Corps, Colombia, 1963-65; law clk. to chief judge U.S. Ct. Appeals (7th cir.), 1968-69; assoc. Thornburg, McGill, Deahl, Harman, Carey & Murray Barnes & Thornburg, South Bend, 1969—75; ptnr. Thornburg, McGill, Deahl, Harman, Carey & Murray, South Bend, 1975-80; v.p. systems and svcs. group The Wackenhut Corp., Coral Gables, Fla., 1981-82, sr. v.p. adminstrn., 1982—88, exec. v.p., 1986-88, also bd. dirs.; pres. Wackenhut Internat. Corp. and Wackenhut Svcs., Inc.; v.p., legal counsel St. Thomas U., 1988-90, adj. prof. law, 1989-90; pres., CEO PropServ, Inc., 1991-94; CEO Practice Resources Corp., 1996-97; CEO, of counsel Stephens, Lynn, Klien & McNicholas, P.A., 1998-2000; dean CAU Bus. Sch., 2006—07. Cons. MSC, Am. Tel. Corp.; legal and mgmt. cons., mem. bd. advisors Publix Supermarkets, Inc., 1994—95, St. Thomas U., 1990—95, 2001—06; bd. dirs., mem. exec. com., trustee RFBD, Inc.; bd. dirs. YEI, Inc., 2006—07, Carlos Albizu U. Found., 2002—09; trustee U. Cmty. Hosp. Found., 1991—94; adj. prof. bus. St. Mary's Coll., 1975—78; vis. prof. CTA, 1985—95; vice chmn., pvt. sec. adv. coun. Fla. Sec. of State, 1985—90; chair ethics com. Miami-Dade County Pub. Schs., 2002—; legal and mgmt. cons., mem., chair bd. advisors WLRN-PBS Radio and TV, 2003—; adj. prof. bus. St. Thomas U. Law Sch., 1999—2000, Carlos Albizu U., 2004; sec. Assoc. editor in chief Ind. Law Jour., 1967-68; contbr. articles to legal and bus. jours. Mem. Civic Ctr. Found., 1976—80; pres. Jaycees, 1974; trustee RFD&D, Inc.; former bd. dirs. Michiana YMCA, Channel 34, Symphony Orch. Assn., 1974—80, Boy Scouts of U.S.A., 2000—02; bd. dirs., mem. exec. com. Doral and West Airport C. of C.; bd. dirs. Miami-Dade (Fla.) County Ethics Coalition; bd. dirs., sec. New World Sch. Theaets, 2008—, Miami Dade Sch. Sys. Audit & Fin. Com., New World Sch. the Arts Found., 2008—. Fulbright selectee, Halleck scholar. Mem. ABA, Ind. Bar Assn., Greater Miami C. of C. (former corp. rep. trustee), Doral Park Golf and Country Club (bd. dirs., pres. 2004-06), Order of Coif, Phi Delta Phi, Alpha Delta Sigma, Lambda Phi Gamma Delta (Disting. ED Alumni award) Office: 10005 NW 52nd Ter Miami FL 33178-2608 Home Phone: 305-591-1898; Office Phone: 305-987-2402, 305-591-1898. Office Fax: 305-591-6560.

THORNBURG, GARRETT, JR., finance company executive; BA, Williams Coll.; MBA, Harvard Univ. CFO NY State Urban Develop. Corp.; limited ptnr., founding mem. pub. fin. dept. Bear Stearns & Co., NYC; sole dir. Thornburg Investment Mgmt. Inc., 1982—, Thornburg Securities Corp.; founder, chmn., CEO Thornburg Mortgage Inc., Santa Fe, 1993—2007, founder, chmn., 2007—. Bd. gov. Investment Co. Inst., Nat. Assn. REIT Inc. Bd. mem. Nat. Dance Inst. N. Mex.; trustee Coll. Santa Fe. Office: Thornburg Mortgage Inc Ste 302 150 Washington Ave Santa Fe NM 87501

THORNBURG, JOHN N., literature and language professor; b. East Chgo., Ind., Oct. 30, 1946; s. Charles C. and Lillian H. (Coleman) Thornburg; m. Jane E. Harvey, Apr. 26, 1972; 1 child, Ellen E. BA, Purdue U., West Lafayette, Ind., 1973; MA in English, Ind. U., Bloomington, 1982, MA in English & Creative Writing, 1994. Prof. English & Creative Writing San Jacinto Coll. Ctrl. Campus, Pasadena, Tex., 1990—. Author: (play) The Lion's Tamer. With Med. Corpsman US Army, Korea and Okinawa. Recipient Polymnia prize, Purdue U., 1973; grant, NEH, 1989. Home: 1002 Baronridge Dr Taylor Lake Village TX 77586 Office: San Jacinto Coll Ctrl 8060 Spencer Hwy Pasadena TX 77505 Office Fax: 281-474-2769. Business E-Mail: john.thornburg@sanjac.edu.

THORNBURG, LACY HERMAN, federal judge; b. Charlotte, NC, Dec. 20, 1929; s. Jesse Lafayette and Sarah Ann (Ziegler) T.; m. Dorothy Todd, Sept. 6, 1953; children— Sara Thornburg Evans, Lacy Eugene,

Jesse Todd, Alan Ziegler. AA, Mars Hill Coll., 1950; BA, U. N.C., 1951, JD, 1954. Bar: U.S. Dist. Ct. (we. dist.) N.C. Practiced law, Webster, NC, 1954-67; superior ct. judge State of N.C., 1967-83, atty. gen Raleigh, 1985-92; emergency judge N.C. Superior Ct., Webster, 1993-94; mem. Nat. Indian Gaming Commn., 1994-95; judge U.S. Dist. Ct. for N.C., Asheville, 1995—. Mem. staff Congressman Taylor, Sylva, NC, 1960, Congressman David Hall, Sylva, 1959-60; mem. N.C. Ho. of Reps., 1961-65; mem. NC Cts. Commn., NC Criminal Code Commn., Capital Planning Commn., Raleigh Chmn. Jackson County Bd. of Health, Sylva, 1965-84; commr. Tryon Palace, New Bern, N.C. Served with U.S. Army, 1947-48. Mem. Lions, Masons, Shriners. Democrat. Avocations: fly fishing, skeet shooting. Office: US Dist Ct 200 US Courthouse 100 Otis St Asheville NC 28801-2611 Office Phone: 828-771-7250. Business E-Mail: lacythornburg@ncwd.uscourts.gov.

THORNBURGH, DANIEL ESTON, retired university administrator, journalism educator; b. Terre Haute, Ind., Sept. 17, 1930; s. Lester D. and Dorothy (Green) T.; m. Adrianne Ames, Aug. 11, 1956; children: Debra Kay Thornburgh Considine, Stewart Beckett, Malcolm Noble. BS, Ind. State U., 1952; MA, U. Iowa, 1957; EdD, Ind. U., 1980. Reporter Terre Haute Star, 1952; publicity dir. Simpson Coll., Indianola, Iowa, 1955; info. dir. Marshall U., Huntington, W.Va., 1957—59, Ea. Ill. U., Charleston, 1959—65, chmn., prof. journalism, 1965—84, dir. univ. rels., 1992; ret. Vis. prof. U. Hawaii, 1982—83, U. Fla., 1993—94, Millikin U., 1996; mem. Gov.'s Coun. Health and Phys. Fitness, 1987—2003; pub. Casey Banner Times, Ill., 1967—69. Editor: (with others) Interpretative Reporting Workbook, 1982. Mem. Charleston City Coun., 1973-77; active Ill. Recreation Coun., Springfield, 1979-85; pres. Coles Hist. Soc., Charleston, 1972-74, 1992, trustee, 2004-06; pres., trustee Five Mile House Found., 1998—; trustee Lincoln and Sargent Farm Found., 1999-2004; chmn. higher edn. and campus min. com. Meth. Ch., 2000-02. With US Army, 1952—54. Named Outstanding Advisor, Coun. Coll. Publs. Advisors, 1971. Mem. Charleston C. of C. (Area Man of Yr. award 1971), Assn. Edn. Journalism and Mass Comm., Pub. Rels. Soc. Am., Soc. Profl. Journalists, Coun. Advancement and Support Edn. (Ea. Ill. U. PRSSA chpt.), Assn. Preservation Hist. Coles County (Merit award 2003), Masons (Cmty. Builder award 1997), Elks, Rotary (pres. Charleston 1976-77, dist. gov. 6490 2000-01, dist. Hall of Fame 2004, pres. chpt. Charitable Found. 2004-06), Ea. Ill. U. Found., Charleston Country Club. Methodist. Avocation: writing. Home: 1405 Buchanan Ave Charleston IL 61920-2924 Personal E-mail: adthorn@consolidated.net.

THORNBURGH, DICK (RICHARD LEWIS THORNBURGH), lawyer, former United States Attorney General; b. Pitts., July 16, 1932; s. Charles Garland and Alice (Sanborn) T.; m. Virginia Walton Judson, Oct. 12, 1963; children: John, David, Peter, William. B in Engring., Yale, 1954; LLB, U. Pitts., 1957; 32 degrees (hon.). Bar: Pa. 1958, US Supreme Ct. 1965, DC 1998. Atty. KL Gates LLP, Pitts., 1959-69, 77-79, 87-88, 91-92, 94—; counsel KLL Gates LLP, Washington; US atty. (we. dist.) Pa. US Dept. Justice, Pitts., 1969-75, asst. atty. gen. criminal divsn. Washington, 1975-77; gov. Commonwealth of Pa., Harrisburg, 1979-87; dir. Inst. Politics John F. Kennedy Sch. Govt., Harvard U., 1987-88; atty. gen. US Dept. Justice, Washington, 1988-91; under-sec.-gen. for adminstrn. & mgmt. UN, NYC, 1992-93. Del. Pa. Constl. Conv., 1967-68; vice-chair World Com. on Disability; bd. dirs. Nat. Mus. Indsl. History, Gettysburg Found. Author: (autobiography) Where the Evidence Leads: The Autobiography of Dick Thornburgh, 2003. Emeritus trustee U. Pitts.; life trustee Urban Inst. Recipient Spl. Medallion award, Drug Enforcement Adminstrn., 1973, Americanism Award, Anti-Defamation League of B'nai B'rith, 1980, Citation for Leadership in Victim Assistance, Nat Orgn for Victim Assistance, 1980, Disting. Svc. medal, Am. Legion, 1992, Wiley E. Branton Award, Washington Lawyers' Com. Civil Rights and Urban Affairs, 2002, Lifetime Achievement Award, Am. Lawyer Mag., 2006; co-recipient Henry Betts Award, Nat. Assn. Persons with Disabilities, 2003. Fellow Am. Bar Found.; mem. Coun. Fgn. Rels., Am. Law Inst. Republican. Office: K&L Gates LLP 1601 K St NW Washington DC 20006-1600 Office Phone: 202-778-9080. Office Fax: 202-778-9100.*

THORNBURGH, RON E., Secretary of State, Kansas; b. Burlingame, Kans., Dec. 31, 1962; m. Annette Thornburgh; 2 children. BA in Criminal Justice, Washburn U., 1985. Dep. asst. sec. state to asst. sec. state State of Kans., Topeka, 1985-87, asst. sec. state, 1991-95, sec. state, 1995—. Vice chairperson blue ribbon panel on ethical conduct State of Kans., 1989. Mem. Kids Voting Kans. Exec. Com.; mem. adv. com. United Way. Toll fellow Henry Toll Fellowship Prog., 1995, Digital Govt. Agent of Change award, MIT, 2002, Lee Ann Elliott Election Excellence award, Kids Voting USA, 2004. Mem. Washburn U. Alumni Bd., 20/30 Club Internat. Republican. Methodist. Office: Office Sec State Memorial Hall First Floor 120 SW 10th Ave Topeka KS 66612-1504 Office Phone: 785-296-4575. Office Fax: 785-368-8033.

THORNBURY, JOHN ROUSSEAU, radiologist, physician; b. Cleve., Mar. 16, 1929; s. Purla Lee and Gertrude (Glidden) T.; m. Julia Lee McGregor, Mar. 20, 1955; children: Lee Allison, John McGregor. AB cum laude, Miami U., Oxford, Ohio, 1950; MD, Ohio State U., 1955. Diplomate: Am. Bd. Radiology. Intern Hurley Hosp., Flint, Mich., 1955-56; resident U. Iowa Hosps., Iowa City, 1958-61; instr., asst. prof. radiology U. Colo. Med. Center, Denver, 1962-63; practice medicine specializing in radiology Denver, 1962-63, Iowa City, 1963-66, Seattle, 1966-68, Ann Arbor, Mich., 1968-79, Albuquerque, 1979-84, Rochester, NY, 1984-89, Madison, Wis., 1989-94. Mem. staff U. Wis. Hosp., Madison; prof. radiology, chief sect. body imaging, U. Wis. Med. Sch., 1989-94, prof. emeritus, 1994—; asst. prof. radiology U. Iowa Hosps., 1963-66, U. Wash. Hosp., Seattle, 1966-68; assoc. prof. radiology U. Mich. Med. Ctr., 1968-71, prof., 1971-79, chief uroradiology sect., 1971-79; prof. radiology, chief divsn. diagnostic radiology Sch. Medicine, U. N.Mex., 1979-84; prof. radiology U. Rochester Sch. Medicine, 1984-89, acting chmn., 1985-87; chmn. sci. com. on efficacy studies Nat. Coun. on Radiation Protection, 1980-95; rapporteur/mem. sci. group on indications/limitations of x-ray diagnostic procedures WHO, 1983; cons. com. on efficacy of magnetic resonance nat. health tech. adv. panel Australian Inst. Health, 1986; invited U.S. cons. MRI program, U. Med. Ctr., Nijmegen, The Netherlands, 1992; mem. planning group Low Back Pain Collaboratives and Nat. Congress, Inst. for Health Care Improvement, 1997-98; mem. methodologic rsch. issues working group NIH and Pub. Health Svc.-Office of Women's Health, 1998; cons., spkr. Royal Australasian Coll. Radiologists, Melbourne, Australia, 1997; cons. tech. assessment and outcomes rsch., 1994—; cons. in tech. assessment and outcomes rsch. to dept. neuroradiology Loma Linda Med. Ctr., 2002-; cons. to Am. Soc. Neuroradiology, 1995-2000; lectr. in field. Co-author/cons. Clin. Efficacy Assessment Project, Am. Coll. Physicians, 1986-89; assoc. editor: Yearbook of Radiology, 1971-82; mem. editl. bd.: Contemporary Diagnostic Radiology, 1977-84, Urologic Radiology, 1977-84 Bd. dirs. Sally Jobe Found., Denver, 1996—. Capt., M.C. USAF, 1956-58. Recipient Dist. Svc. award Am. Bd. Radiology, 2000, Alumni Achievement award Ohio State U. Coll. Medicine, 2000, Gold medal Assn. Univ. Radiologists, 2002, Gold medal Soc. Uroradiology, 2005; grantee Agy. Health Care Policy and Rsch., 1986-91, U. Rochester, 1986-89, U. Wis., Madison, 1989-91 Fellow Am. Coll. Radiology (mem. emeritus); mem. Am. Coll. Radiology Imaging Network (outcomes and quality of life subcom., urology com., NIH, 1999-2002), Soc. Uroradiology (pres. 1976-77, dir. 1977-79, gold medal 2005), Assn. Univ. Radiologists (pres. 1980-81), Radiol. Soc. N.Am., Am. Roentgen Ray Soc. (Caldwell medal 1993), Soc. for Health Svcs. Rsch. in Radiology (adv. com. to bd. dirs. 1998—), Colo. Radiol. Soc., Phi Beta Kappa, Delta Tau Delta, Omicron Delta Kappa, Phi Chi. Episcopalian. Home: 1340 Forest Park Cir #16 Lafayette CO 80026 *"Mooring Post" relationships and sharing have been essential to success and achievements in my multi-disciplinary research. "Mooring Post" persons range from expert mentors and stellar colleagues, to the bedrock of a loving and supportive family. Further, to me, Rule One in medicine has always been, "The patient comes first.".*

THORNDIKE, ANN M., microbiologist, educator; b. Grand Island, Nebr., Oct. 17, 1952; d. J. Harley and Lucille Marie Thorndike. Degree in Microbiology, U. Nebr., Lincoln, 1974; degree in Med. Tech., U. Nebr. Med Ctr., Omaha, 1975. Cert. med. techhnologist Nat. ASCP, 1974. Microbiologist & med. technologist St. Francis Med. Ctr., Grand Island, 1975—2006; instr., MLT program Ctrl. CC, Hastings, Nebr., 2006—. Treas. Chpt. EH P.E.O. Nebr., Grand Island, 2002—09. Mem.: ASCP. Independent. Episcopalian. Avocations: golf, art, reading. Home: 2813 Lakewood Cir Grand Island NE 68801 Office: Ctrl CC E Hwy 6 PO Box 1024 Hastings NE 68902-1024 Office Fax: 402-460-2138. Business E-Mail: athorndike@cccneb.edu.

THORNDIKE, EDWARD HARMON, physicist; b. Pasadena, Calif., Aug. 2, 1934; s. Edward Moulton and Louise (Harmon) T.; m. Elizabeth H. Wenger, Sept. 8, 1955; children: Susan Lee, Patricia Lynn, Edward Harmon Jr. AB, Wesleyan U., Middletown, Conn., 1956; MS, Stanford U., 1957; PhD, Harvard U., 1960. Rsch. fellow Harvard U., Cambridge, Mass., 1960-61; mem. faculty U. Rochester, NY, 1961—, asso. prof. physics, 1965-72, prof., 1972—. Vis. prof. U. Geneva, 1969-70; vis. scientist CERN, Geneva, 1969-70; mem. adv. coun. Ctr. Environ. Info., Rochester, 1974-93; mem. adv. com. Stanford Linear Accelerator Ctr. Exptl. Program, 1987-89; mem. vis. com. for Fermilab, Univs. Rsch. Assn., 1993-95. Author: Energy and Environment, a Primer for Scientists and Engineers, 1976; contbr. articles to profl. jours. Recipient W.K.H. Panofsky prize, 1999; NSF fellow, 1970, Guggenheim fellow, 1987-88. Fellow Am. Phys. Soc. Office: U Rochester Dept Physics/Astronomy Rochester NY 14627

THORNE, CHARLES HEDGES MCKINSTRY, plastic surgeon; b. Oakland, Calif., Oct. 27, 1952; BA in Biophysics and Biochemistry, Yale Coll., 1974; MD, UCLA Sch. Medicine, 1976—81. Cert. Am. Bd. Surgery, 1987, Am. Bd. Plastic Surgery, 1991. Peace Corps volunteer, Ghana, 1974—76; intern Mass. Gen. Hosp., 1981—82, resident in plastic surgery, 1982—86, NYU Med. Ctr., 1986—88, fellow in craniofacial surgery, 1988—89, dir., Plastic Surgery Residency Prog., 1989—98, dir., Ctr. for Ear Anomalies, 1990—; exec. chief resident Inst. Reconstructive Plastic Surgery, 1987—88; co-dir. Ctr. for Craniofacial Prosthetics, 1992—; chief, Plastic Surgery Svc. Bellevue Hosp., 1992—2003; prog. dir., Cosmetic Surgery Manhattan Eye and Ear Hosp., 1998—99; assoc. prof., Dept. Surgery NYU Sch. Medicine; private practice in plastic surgery NYC; assoc. attending surgeon NYU Med. Ctr., Bellevue Hosp. Ctr., Manhattan Eye Ear & Throat Hosp. Mem. exec. com., NYU Med. Bd., 1994—96, Surgical House Staff Com., 1989—97, Oper. Rm. Com., NYU, 1990—98, Oper. Rm. Com., Bellevue Hosp., NYU, 1993—98, Exec. Com., NYU Assn. Attending M.D.'s, 1995—98; mem., Credentials Com. Manhattan Eye, Ear and Throat Hosp., 1998—99, mem., Quality Assurance Com., 1998—99, bd. mem., Surgeon Directors, 2000—; mem. LCME Faculty Com., NYU Sch. Medicine, 1999, Curriculum Com., NYU Sch. Medicine, 2002, Adv. Bd., Forward Face; sr. examiner Am. Bd. Plastic Surgery, 2002—. Assoc. editor (journals) Journal of Cranio-Maxillofacial Trauma, 1995—2001, Journal of Plastic and Reconstructive Surgery, 2000—. Vol. Peace Corps, Ghana, 1974—76. Recipient First prize, Am. Soc. Maxillofacial Surgeons, 1990, 1992, NY Regional Soc. Plastic Surgery, 1990, Tchr. of Yr. award, Inst. Reconstructive Plastic Surgery, NYU Med. Ctr., 1993—94, 1997—98, 1999—2000. Mem.: Northeastern Soc. Plastic Surgeons (trustee 2004—07, parliamentarian 2000—01, bd. mem.-at-large 2001—03, pres. 2002—03), Internat. Soc. Craniomaxillofacial Surgeons, Forum for Academic Plastic Surgeons (pres. 1996—97), Am. Soc. Plastic Surgeons, Am. Soc. Craniofacial Surgery, Am. Soc. Aesthetic Plastic Surgery (bd. dir. 2007—, parliamentarian 2006—07), AMA, Am. Coll. Surgeons, Am. Cleft Palate Assn., Am. Assn. Plastic Surgeons. Office: 812 Park Ave New York NY 10021 also: NYU Med Ctr 550 First Ave New York NY 10016 Office Phone: 212-794-0044. Office Fax: 212-772-1326. Business E-Mail: thornc01@popmail.med.nyu.edu.

THORNE, DAVID HOADLEY, United States Ambassador to Italy and San Marino; b. NYC, Sept. 16, 1944; s. Landon K. and Alice (Barry) T.; m. Rose O'Neil Geer, June 26, 1971; children: William Winslow, Emma O'Neil. BA in Am. History, Yale U., 1966; MA in Journalism Sci., Columbia U., 1971. Founding ptnr. Marttila, Payne, Kiley & Thorne, Boston, 1973-78; ptnr. Raymond Cattle Co., Boston, 1978-83; pres. Rising Star Associates, Boston; ptnr. Monaghan Thorne Partners, NYC, Boston; pub. New Age Jour., Boston; co-founder, vice chmn. Adviser Investments, Inc., Newton, Mass., 1994—2009; US amb. to Italy & San Marino US Dept. State, Rome, 2009—. Editor: The New Soldier, 1971. Pres. Inst. Contemporary Art, Boston, 1975-84, Interface Found., Watertown, Mass., 1989—; trustee Action for Children's TV, Boston, 1980-88. Lt. USNR, 1966-70, Vietnam. Office: US Embassy 9500 Rome Pl Washington DC 20521*

THORNE, FRANCIS, composer; b. Bay Shore, NY, June 23, 1922; s. Francis Burritt and Hildegarde (Kobbé) T.; m. Ann Cobb, Dec. 9, 1942; children: Ann Boughton (Mrs. William F. Niles), Wendy Oakleigh (Mrs. William H. Forsyth, Jr.), Candace Kobbé (Mrs. Anthony M. Canton). BA in Music Theory, Yale U., 1942. Founder, pres. Thorne Music Fund, Inc., 1965-75; pub. Edward B. Marks Music Corp., 1963—, Gen. Music Pub. Co., 1971—, G. Schirmer/AMP, 1985—, Theodore Presser Co., 1989—. Exec. dir. Lenox Arts Ctr., 1972-76, Am. Composers Alliance, 1975-85; co-founder, pres. Am. Composers Orch., 1976— Composer: Elegy for Orch., 1964, Burlesque Overture, 1966, Lyric Variations for Orch., 1967, Symphony No. 1, 1963, No. II, 1966, No. III, 1970, No. IV, 1977, Fortuna, 1961-62, Liebesrock, 1969, Sonar Plexus, 1969, Six Set-Pieces, 1969, Contra Band Music, 1970, Antiphonies, 1970, Simultaneities, 1971, Quartessence, 1971, Fanfare, Fugue and Funk, 1972, Lyric Variations II, 1972, Piano Sonata, 1972, Lyric Variations III, 1973, Cantata Sauce, 1973, Evensongs, 1973, Cello Concerto, 1974, Piano Concerto, 1974, Violin Concerto, 1975, String Quartet 1, 1960, 2, 1967, 3, 1976, 4, 1983, Spoon River Overture, 1976, Grand Duo, 1976, Five Set Pieces, 1976, Love's Variations, 1976, Pop Partita, 1978, The Eternal Light for Soprano and Orchestra, 1979, Divertimento for Flute, Strings and Percussion, 1979, Lyric Variations IV for Solo Violin, 1980, Divertimento 2 for Bassoon and Stringed Instruments, 1980, Eine Kleine Meyermusik, 1980, Gems From Spoon River, 1980, Lyric Variations No. 6 for solo clarinet, 1981, Divertimento No. 3, 1982, Praise and Thanksgiving, 1983, Lyric Variations No. 5 for Orch., 1980-81, Symphony No. 5, 1984, Concerto Concertante, 1985, Rhapsodic Variations, No. 2, 1985, Humoresque for Orch., 1985, Rhapsodic Variations No. 3 for Oboe and Strings, 1986, The Affirming Flame for Soprano and Chamber Ensemble, 1987; seven simple syncopations for Piano solo, 1987, Rhapsodic Variations No. 4 For Viol Solo, 1987, Rhapsodic Variations No. 5 for Violins and Piano, 1988, Money Matters for Tenor and Chamber Ensemble, 1988, Piano Concerto No. 3, 1989, Remembering Dizzy for Brass Quintet, 1990, Pop Partita No. 2 for woodwinds and strings, 1991, Mario and The Magician, opera after Thomas Mann, in Prologue and 1 Act, 1991, Symphony No. 6 for Strings, 1992, Symphony No. 7 Along the Hudson for chorus and orch., 1994, Cello Concerto No. 2, 1995, Echo for Soprano and Mixed Chorus, 1996, Clarinet Concerto, 1997, Rhapsodic Variations No. 7 for Solo Piano, 1998, Lyric Variations No. 8, 1999, Flash Dances for Orchestra, 1999, Oboe Concerto, 1999-2000, SONG To Mark Stand's Poem, 2000, Concerto for Orchestra, 2000-01, The Four Seasons, for mezzo and string trio, 2002, Triple Concerto for English Horn, Bass Clarinet, Viola and Orchestra, 2004, Lyric Variations No. 9 for Solo Piano, 2004, Songs and Dances for Orchestra, 2005, The Four Seasons, 2006, Three Poems of Robert Fitzgerald, 2007; Solo Instruments Show: Horn, 2007, Strumpet, 2007, Violin, 2007, VI-OH-LA-LA, 2007, Mello Cello, 2007, Double Bass Hitt, 2007; recs. on Composers' Recs., Inc., Serenus, Owl, Louisville Opus One and New World Trustee Am. Symphony Orchestra League, Manhattan Sch. Music, Am. Music Center, MacDowell Colony, Walter W. Naumburg Found., Contemporary Music Soc., Theater Devel. Fund, Group for Contemporary Music., Am. Brass Quintet. Lt. USNR, 1942-45. Nat. Endowment Arts grantee, 1966, 73; fellow, 1976, 79; Nat. Inst. Arts and Letters grantee, 1968; N.Y. State Arts Council ballet commn., 1973 Mem. AAAL, BMI, Contemporary Music Soc. (bd. dirs.), Am. Composers Alliance, League Composers. Clubs: Century Assn. (N.Y.C.). Home: Geer Village #104 77 S Canaan Rd Canaan CT 06018 Office Phone: 860-824-2650. Business E-Mail: aco@americancomposers.org. *Having spent ten years as a businessman, I have been privileged to serve my composer colleagues as an administrator for musical organizations. The practical experience has also served me well as a creative artist in having instilled the virtues of discipline. Serving music as composer and administrator gives the highest sense of satisfaction, from participating in this life-giving world in a total comprehensive way.*

THORNE, JAMES DANA, astronautical engineer, researcher; b. Fairbanks, Alaska, Feb. 15, 1962; s. James Dale and Doris Jean Thorne; BS in Aero & Astronautical Engring., Purdue U., West Lafayette, Ind., 1984; MS in Astronautical Engring., Air Force Inst. Tech., Wright-Patterson AFB, Ohio, 1989, PhD in Astronautical Engring., 1996. Astronautical engr. USAF, Arlington, Va., 1984—2005; rsch. staff mem. IDA, Alexandria, Va., 2005—. Rep. Bluemont Civic Assn., Arlington, 2006—08. Lt. col. USAF, 1984—2005, Pentagon, Arlington. Recipient Rsch. award, Air Force Inst. Tech., 1989. Mem.: Am. Astronautical Soc. Achievements include discovery of time explicit series solution of Lambert's classical orbit determination problem. Avocations: tennis, music. Business E-Mail: james.thorne7@verizon.net.

THORNE, JOHN WATSON, III, advertising and marketing executive; b. Washington, Jan. 16, 1934; s. John Watson, Jr. and Mary Washington (Tucker) T.; m. Joan Kramer Vail, Mar. 2, 1957; children: Vail Tucker, Tracy Tucker, John Watson, IV. BA in Polit. Sci., George Washington U., 1955; MA in Sociology, The New Sch. U., NYC, 1974. Asst. account exec. Young & Rubicam, Inc., NYC, 1957-59; advt. mgr. GE, Decatur, Ill., 1959-63; dir. advt. promotion Brand Names Found., NYC, 1963-66; account exec. Tatham-Laird & Kudner (advt.), NYC, 1966-67; v.p., mgmt. supr. Wells, Rich, Greene, Inc., NYC, 1973-76; v.p., account supr. Batten, Barton, Durstine & Osborn, Inc., NYC, 1967-73, sr. v.p., mgmt. supr., 1976-81, exec. v.p., 1981-87, also dir., mem. oper. com.; chmn. Thorne & Assocs., Newtown, Pa., 1987—; pres., CEO Telerx Mktg., Spring House, Pa., 1991-95; chmn., CEO Alliance Mktg. Svcs. Group, Inc., Jamison, Pa., 1995—2004, Alliance Healthcare Info., Inc., Ivyland, Pa., 2004—09. Mem. bus. program com. Proprietary Assn., Washington; adj. prof. advt. Syracuse (N.Y.) U. Pres. Hastings-on-Hudson (N.Y.) Bd. Edn.; bd. dirs. Young Concert Artists, N.Y.C.; mem. comm. coms. Nat. Urban League, Carnegie Hall. Served as 1st lt. USMCR, 1955-57. Mem.: Lotos Club (NYC), Buckingham Racquet Club. Republican. Roman Catholic. Home: 100 Stoney Brook Rd Newtown PA 18940-2506 Office: Thorne & Associates 336 E 50th St Ste 3A New York NY 10022

THORNE, NATHAN C., investment company executive; BA, Yale Univ. Joined Merrill Lynch, NYC, 1984, head high yield fin, & restructuring group, head corp. fin., high yield fin. & real estate, head. internat pvt. equity, vice chmn. global pvt. equity, sr. v.p., pres. global pvt. equity, 2002—. Office: Merrill Lynch 4 World Fin Ctr 250 Vesey St New York NY 10080

THORNE, RICHARD MANSERGH, physicist; b. Birmingham, Eng., July 25, 1942; s. Robert George and Dorothy Lena (Goodchild) T.; children: Peter Baring, Michael Thomas, Thomas Mansergh. BSc, Birmingham U., 1963; PhD, MIT, 1968. Grad. asst. M.I.T., 1963-68; asst. prof. dept. atmospheric scis. UCLA, 1968-71, asso. prof., 1971-75, prof., 1975—, chmn. dept., 1976-79. Vis. fellow St. Edmund's Coll., Cambridge (Eng.) U., 1986-87, 92; cons. NATO Adv. Group for Aerospace R&D, 1973, Jet Propulsion Lab., Aerospace Corp. Contbr. articles to profl. jours. Recipient numerous grants NSF, NASA, NATO, Jet Propulsion Lab.; Fulbright scholar, 1963-70; fellow Royal Norwegian Coun. for Sci. and Indsl. Rsch., 1973, sr. vis. fellow U. Sussex, 1979-80, rsch. fellow Royal Soc. London, 1986-87. Fellow Am. Geophys. Union; mem. Internat. Union Radio Scis. Home: 10390 Caribou Ln Los Angeles CA 90077 Office: UCLA Dept Atmospheric and Oceanic Scis Los Angeles CA 90095-1565 Business E-Mail: rmt@atmos.ucla.edu.

THORNE, WILLIAM ALBERT, retired lawyer; b. Chgo., Feb. 20, 1924; s. William A. and Irma J. Thorne; m. Elizabeth Lee Douglas, June 19, 1948; children: Deborah, Elizabeth Ann, Margaret, Doulgas. JD, Valparaiso U., 1949. Bar: Ind. 1949, U.S. Dist. Ct. (no. and so. dists.) Ind. 1949, U.S. Supreme Ct. 1960. Pvt. practice, Elkhart, Ind., 1949-63; ptnr. Thorne Grodnik, LLP, Elkhart, 1963-95; of counsel Thorne.Grodnik, LLP and predecessor, Elkhart, 1995—2002; ret., 2002. Chmn. City of Elkhart Pks. and Recreation Bd., 1971—75, Elkhart Bd. Water Works, 1975—83, No. Ind. Conf. United Meth. Ch., Bd. Higher Edn. and Campus Ministry, 1994—2000; bd. vis. Valparaiso U. Law Sch., 1990—96; trustee Meth. Theol. Sch., Ohio, 1993—2003. With US Army, 1943—46. Named a Disting. Hoosier, Gov. Joseph Kernan, 2005. Fellow: Ind. State Bar Assn. (chmn. bankruptcy sect. 1985—86, bd. govs. 1987—88). Democrat. Avocations: golf, reading. Personal E-mail: thollaw@msn.com.

THORNELOE, KEVIN S., biologist; b. Quebec, Can. PhD, U. Calgary, Alberta, 2001. Sr. rsch. biologist Merck Rsch. Labs., Rahway, NJ, 2004—06; postdoc. fellow U. Vt., Burlington; investigator GlaxoSmithKline Pharm., King of Prussia, Pa., 2006—. Recipient Inst. Aging Spl. Recognition award, Can. Insts. Health Rsch., 2003, Boehringer

Ingelheim Postdoc. award, Pharmacological Soc. Can., 2004; Postdoc. fellowship, Heart & Stroke Found. Can., 2001, Med. Rsch. fellowship, Alta. Heritage Found., 2002, fellowship, Can. Insts. Health Rsch., 2003. Mem.: Am. Physiol. Soc. Office: GlaxoSmithKline Pharm 709 Swedeland Rd King Of Prussia PA 19406

THORNER, JEREMY W., biology professor; Prof., molecular and cell biology, William V. Power chair, biology Univ. Calif., Berkeley. Med. sci. adv. bd. Lowe Syndrome Assn. Fellow: Am. Acad. Arts & Scis.; mem.: Am. Soc. Biochemistry and Molecular Biology, Am. Soc. For Cell Biology. Office: Dept Molecular & Cell Biology Univ Calif MC 3202 526 Barker Berkeley CA 94720 Office Phone: 510-642-2558. Business E-Mail: jthorner@berkeley.edu.

THORNHILL, ARTHUR H., JR., retired publishing executive; b. Boston, Jan. 1, 1924; s. Arthur Horace and Mary Josephine (Peterson) T.; m. Dorothy M. Matheis, Oct. 28, 1944; children: Sandra Susanne Thornhill Brushart, Arthur Horace. AB magna cum laude, Princeton U., 1948. With Little, Brown & Co., Inc., Boston, 1948-88, v.p., 1955-58, gen. mgr., 1960-87, chief exec. officer, pres., 1962-87, chmn. bd., 1970-87; chmn., pres., dir. Little, Brown & Co. (Can.), Ltd., 1955-84; v.p. Time, Inc., 1968-87; vice chmn. Time-Life Books, Inc., 1976-86. Mem. adv. council history dept. Princeton U., 1964-85; trustee, treas. Princeton U. Press, 1972-85; chmn. N.Y. Graphic Soc., 1974-79. Trustee Bennington Coll., 1969-76; fellow emeritus Ctr. for Creative Photography U. Ariz.; bd. dirs. Am. Book Pubs. Council, 1964-67. Served to 1st lt. USAAF, World War II. Decorated Air medal; recipient Princeton U. Press medal, 1985, Disting. Alumni award Dwight-Englewood Sch., 1998. Mem. Assn. Am. Pubs. (bd. dirs. 1978-81), Edgartown Yacht Club, Edgartown Reading Room (pres. 1990-92), Union Club (N.Y.C.), Princeton Club (N.Y.C.), Century Club (N.Y.C.), Publs. Lunch Club (N.Y.C.)(pres. 1969-70), St. Botolph (Boston). Home: Apt 5303 250 Pantops Mountain Rd Charlottesville VA 22911-8703

THORNHILL, HARLEN WEBSTER, retired aircraft engineer; b. Syracuse, NY, June 10, 1932; s. Harlan Alva and Golda Doan Thornhill; m. Earlene Allday Thornhill, Aug. 11, 1956 (div. Feb. 22, 1977); children: Sheryl, David(dec.), Mark, James, Patricia; m. Patricia Scott Hayes Thornhill, Aug. 20, 1977 (dec. Sept. 16, 2008); stepchildren: Henry, Patricia, William. BS in Profl. Aeronautics, Embry Riddle Aero. U., Daytona Beach, Fla., 1978, MS in Aviation Mgmt., 1985. Airframe and powerplant lic. FAA. Aircraft maintenance staff Syracuse Aircraft Sales, 1950—51; flight mechanic Carrier Corp., Syracuse, 1961—64; aircraft mechanic, foreman Eastern Airlines, various locations, 1964—87; aircraft maintenance/engring. staff Continental Airlines, Houston, 1987—97; aircraft maintenance staff Brit. Internat. Aviation, Conroe, Tex., 2000—. Vice comdr. Am. Legion, The Woodlands, Tex., 1987. With USN, 1951—59, ETO, with USAF, 1959—73, Korea, Vietnam. Mem.: AARP, VFW, NRA, VPB-111/ VP-21 Alumni Assn., Pulaski NY Ctrl. Sch. Alumni Assn., Continental Airlines Retiree Assn., Eastern Airlines Retiree Assn., Am. Mil. Soc., Air Force Assn., Air Force Sgts. Assn., Non-Commd. Officers Assn., Nat. Assn. Uniform Svcs., Tex. State Rifle Assn., 174th Alumni Assn. (NYANG), Embry Riddle Aero. Univ. Alumni Assn., Am. Legion, Ret. Enlisted Assn., N.Am. Hunting Club, Alpha Eta Rho. Republican. Avocations: hunting, fishing, bowling.

THORNLOW, CAROLYN, law firm administrator, consultant; b. Kew Gardens, NY, May 25, 1954; 1 child, Johanna Louise Ramm. BBA magna cum laude, Baruch Coll., 1982. Gen. mgr. Richard A. Ramm Assocs., Levittown, N.Y., 1972-78; adminstr. Tunstead Schechter & Torre, NYC, 1978-82, Cowan Liebowitz & Latman, P.C., NYC, 1982-84, Rosenberg & Estis, P.C., NYC, 1984-85; contr. Finkelstein, Borah, Schwartz, Altschuler & Goldstein, P.C., NYC, 1986-92; pres. Concinnity Svcs., Hastings, N.Y., 1984—. Instr. introduction to law office mgmt. seminars Assn. Legal Adminstrs., NYC, 1984. Editor: The ABA Guide to Professional Managers in the Law Office, 1996; contbr. numerous articles to profl. jours. Mem. ABA (bd. dirs. law practice mgmt. div. 2000-01), N.Y. Assn. Legal Adminstrs. (v.p. 1982-83), Internat. Assn. Legal Adminstrs. (asst. regional v.p. 1983-84, regional v.p. 1984-85), Nat. Soc. Tax Profls. (cert. tax profl.), Am. Mgmt. Assn., Inst. Cert. Profl. Mgrs. (cert.), ABA, Inst. Cert. Mgmt. Accts., Mensa, Beta Gamma Sigma, Sigma Iota Epsilon. Home and Office: Concinnity Svcs 109 Washington Ave Hastings On Hudson NY 10706 Home Phone: 914-478-4545; Office Phone: 914-478-9000. Business E-Mail: cthornlow@concinnityservices.com, lawbucks@aol.com, crtinny@aol.com.

THORNSBERRY, CLYDE, microbiologist; b. Pippa Passes, Ky., June 20, 1930; s. Columbus B. and Ollie Mae (Sparkman) T.; m. Glenda L. Martin, May 13, 1952; children: Teresa, David, Robert. BS, U. Ky., Lexington, 1958, PhD, 1966. Chief Antimicrobial Investigations Br. Ctrs. for Disease Control, Atlanta, 1966-89; dir. Inst. for Microbiol. Rsch., Franklin, Tenn., 1989-93, Focus BioInova, Inc., Franklin, 1993—; dirt. Eurofins Medinet, Inc., Franklin. Lectr. in field; chmn., vice-chmn. Intersci. Conf. Anti-Agts., Washington, 1989-94; adv. bd. several pharm. cos., 1980—. Contbr. articles to profl. jours. Recipient awards USPHS, Washington, 1982, 87. Fellow Infectious Disease Soc. of Am.; mem. Am. Soc. Microbiology (BD award for Rsch. in Clin. Microbiology 2003), Am. Acad. Microbiology, NY Acad. Scis., WHO Coms. on Antibiotics, Nat. Com. Clin. Lab. Stds. Democrat. Achievements include patent-use of antimicrobial agts. to sterilize tissue for implanting; study of antimicrobials, antimicrobial resistance, and in vitro testing of antimicrobial activity; lab. was designated a WHO lab. for antimicrobial agts. Home: 5182 Waddell Hollow Rd Franklin TN 37064-9436 Office: Eurofin Medinet Inc 5182 Waddell Hollow Rd Franklin TN 37064 Office Phone: 615-794-7011. Business E-Mail: clyde.thornsberry@eurofinsmedinet.com.

THORNTON, AL, professional basketball player; b. Perry, Ga., Dec. 7, 1983; s. Alford and Philomenia Thornton. B in Sociology, Fla. State U., Tallahassee, 2007. Forward LA Clippers, 2007—. Named to NBA All-Rookie First Team, 2008. Office: LA Clippers 1111 S Figueroa St Ste 1100 Los Angeles CA 90015*

THORNTON, ANITA LYN, family nurse practitioner; b. Toccoa, Ga., Dec. 22, 1960; BS in Biology, Ga. Coll., Milledgeville, 1982; Diploma in Nursing, Ga. Bapt. Hosp. Sch. Nursing, Atlanta, 1986; BS in Nursing, Med. Coll. Ga., Augusta, 1989; MS in Nursing, Ga. State U., Atlanta, 1996; Post M in FNP, North Ga. Coll. & State U., Dahlonega, 2002. FNP, ANCC, 2002, AANP, 2002. Asst. prof. North Ga. Coll. & State U., 2003—08, fnp, 2007—08; FNP Dr. Nursing Practice, MCG, 2009. Mem.: Am. Acad. Nurse Practitioners, ANA, Sigma Theta Tau. Achievements include research in cardiovascular risk assessment in underserved appalachian women. Home: 78 Slade Creek Ct Toccoa GA 30577 Office: North Georgia Coll & State University Sunset Cir Dahlonega GA 30597 Personal E-mail: althornton@windstream.net. Business E-Mail: althornton@ngcsu.edu.

THORNTON, ARLAND, sociologist, educator; b. Boise, Idaho, July 18, 1944; s. Lavar and Alzina Thornton; m. Shirley Dray; children: Richard, Blake, Rebecca, Amy. PhD, U. Mich., 1975. Rsch. prof. Survey Rsch. Ctr., U. Mich., Ann Arbor, 1975—; prof. sociology U. Mich., Ann Arbor, 1977—; rsch. prof., dir. Population Studies Ctr., U. Mich., Ann Arbor, 1983—. Mem. population rsch. subcommittee Nat. Inst. Child Health and Human Develop., Bethesda, 1996—2000; mem. Family and Child Well-Being Rsch. Network, Nat. Inst. Child Health and Hum Devel., Bethesda, 1993—99. Author: (book) Social Change and the Family in Taiwan, 1994 (Otis Dudley Duncan Book award and Goode Disting. Book award, 1995), Reading History Sideways: The Fallacy and Enduring Impact of the Developmental Paradigm on Family Life, 2005 (Goode Distng. Book award, 2007), (book) Marriage and Cohabitation, 2007 (Outstanding Publ. award Am. Sociological Assn., 2008); editor: Ties That Bind, 2000, The Well Being of Children and Families: Research and Data Needs, 2001; author: International Family Change: Ideational Perspectives, 2008; contbr. articles to profl. jours. and chpts. to books. Lt. (j.g.) U.S. C.G., 1968—71. Recipient MERIT award, National Inst. Child Health and Human Devel., 2001, Outstanding Publication award, Am. Sociological Assn., 2008. Mem.: Nat. Coun. on Family Rels., Am. Sociol. Assn. (various offices in population, family, and children sects., Disting. Career award family sect. 2000), Population Assn. Am. (pres. 2001). Avocations: bicycling, hiking, travel, sports. Office: U Mich Inst for Social Rsch Ann Arbor MI 48106 Office Phone: 734-763-1500.

THORNTON, BILLY BOB, actor, film producer; b. Hot Springs, Ark., Aug. 4, 1955; s. Billy Ray and Virginia Thornton; m. Melissa Lee Gatlin, 1978 (div. 1980); 1 child; m. Toni Lawrence, 1986 (div. 1988); m. Cynda Williams, 1990 (div. 1992); m. Pietra Dawn Cherniak, Feb. 18, 1993 (div. Apr. 1997); 2 children; m. Angelina Jolie, May 5, 2000 (div. May 27, 2003); 1 child. Actor: (films) For the Boys, 1991, Indecent Proposal, 1993, Tombstone, 1993, On Deadly Ground, 1994, Floundering, 1994, Dead Man, 1995, The Winner, 1996, A Gun, A Car, A Blonde, 1997, U-Turn, 1997, A Thousand Miles, 1997, The Apostle, 1997, Primary Colors, 1998, Homegrown, 1998, Armageddon, 1998, A Simple Plan, 1998, Pushing Tin, 1999, The Last Real Cowboys, 2000, South of Heaven, West of Hell, 2000, Monster's Ball, 2001, Bandists, 2001, The Man Who Wasn't There, 2001, Waking up in Reno, 2002, The Badge, 2002, Intolerable Cruelty, 2003, Love Actually, 2003, Levity, 2003, Bad Santa, 2003, The Alamo, 2004, Friday Night Lights, 2004, Bad News Bears, 2005, The Ice Harvest, 2005, School for Scoundrels, 2006, The Astronaut Farmer, 2007, Mr. Woodcock, 2007, Eagle Eye, 2008, The Informers, 2009; dir., actor, writer (films) Sling Blade, 1996 (Acad. award Best Adapted Screenplay), Daddy and Them, 2001, dir., prodr. All the Pretty Horses, 2000, actor, writer One False Move, 1992, The Gift, 2000, (screenplays) Trouble Bound, 1993, Some Folks Call It a Slingblade, 1994, A Family Thing, 1996; actor: (TV films) The Man Who Broke 1,000 Chains, 1987, Circus, 1988, Out There, 1995, Don't Look Back, 1996; (TV series) The Outsiders, 1988, Hearts A Fire, 1992; TV appearances include Matlock, 1987, Evening Shade, 1990, Knots Landing, 1990, Ellen, 1997, (voice) King of the Hill, 1998; musician: (albums) Private Radio, 2001, The Edge of the World, 2003, Hobo, 2005, Beautiful Door, 2007. Office: Rogers Cowan 8687 Melrose Ave Ste G700 West Hollywood CA 90069-5721

THORNTON, BRIAN, communication educator, researcher; b. Eglin AFB, Fla., Mar. 10, 1953; s. Daniel and Alice T.; m. Ellen Dyer Thornton, Sept. 7, 1983. BA in Journalism, U. Hawaii, Honolulu, 1983; MS in Mass. Comm., Wichita U., Kans., 1986; PhD in Mass. Comm., U. Utah, Salt Lake City, 1994. Reporter Hawaii Observer, Honolulu, 1973-77, West Hawaii Today, Kona, 1978, Sun Press Newspapers, Kaneohe, Oahu, Hawaii, 1978-79, Maui News, Wailiku, Maui, Hawaii, 1979-83, Wichita (Kans.) Eagle, 1983-84; journalism instr. Butler County C.C., Eldorado, Kans., 1986-87, Wichita (Kans.) State U., 1987-90; teaching fellow, grad. student U. Utah, 1990-94; asst. prof. Midwestern State U., Wichita Falls, 1994—. Contbr. articles to profl. jours. Fellow Am. Soc. Newspaper Editors, Poynter Inst. Journalism Workshop, Assn. for Edn. in Journalism and Mass Comm. Avocations: Karate, tai-chi, blues guitar. Home: 6 Miller Ct Dekalb IL 60115-2311 Office: Midwestern State University 3410 Taft Blvd Wichita Falls TX 76308-2096

THORNTON, CHARLIE MAE, secondary school educator; b. Idabel, Okla., Oct. 7, 1947; d. Juanita Cotton; children: Kimberly, Joel. BA in English Edn., East Cen. State U., Ada, Okla., 1968; MEd, Northeastern State U., Tahlequah, Okla., 1979. Cert. reading specialist Okla. Tchr. 6th grade reading Tulsa Pub. Schs., Okla., 1973—. 6th grade team leader, coord. mid. years program coord. Tulsa Pub. Schs. Contbr. articles to profl. jours. Recipient Excellence Edn. award, Wilson Mid. Sch., 2002—03; named Tchr. of Yr., 2006—07, Tchr. of Today, Masonic Fraternity of Okla. Mem. NEA, Internat. Reading Assn., Okla. Reading Assn., Okla. Edn. Assn., Tulsa County Reading Coun., Tulsa Classroom Tchrs. Assn., Alpha Kappa Alpha, Phi Delta Kappa Democrat. Mem. Ch. Of Christ. Avocation: reading. Home: 2205 W Reading Pl Tulsa OK 74127-2238 Office: Wilson Mid Sch 1127 S Columbia Tulsa OK 74104 Business E-Mail: thornch@tulsaschools.org.

THORNTON, CLARENCE GOULD, electronics executive, civilian military employee; b. Detroit, Aug. 3, 1925; s. Lorenzo C. and Violet (Gould) T.; m. Gloria Fuchs, June 18, 1949; children: Susan Carol, Richard Scott. BS, U. Mich., 1949, MS, 1950, PhD, 1952. Project engr. Sylvania Electric Co., Woburn, Mass., 1951-52; sect. head to dir. Semiconductor div. Philco Corp., Lansdale, Pa., 1952-60; dir. R&D Philco Corp., Blue Bell, Pa., 1960-72; dir. Electronics Technology and Devices Lab., U.S. Army, Fort Monmouth, NJ, 1972-92; directorate exec. Army Rsch. Lab., 1992-95. Mem. Commn. on Engring. and Tech. Sys. Bd. on Army Sci. and Tech., Nat. Rsch. Coun., 1995—; sci., tech., bus. cons. 1995—; vol. lab. dir. emeritus U.S. Commn. Electronics Rsch., Devel. and Engring. Ctr., 2003-05. Contbr. articles to profl. jours.; patentee in field of electronics. Mem. Colts Neck Bd. Health, 1974-79. Served with USN, 1944-46. Recipient Local Svc. award Boy Scouts Am., 1963, Sci. Conf. award Dept. Army, 1976, Rsch. and Devel. Achievement award, 1976, Lab. of Yr. award, 1980, 83, 88, Lab. Excellence award, 1981, 85, 86, Sr. Exec. award, 1980-93, Gold medal Armed Forces Comms. and Electronics Assn., 1983, Handicapped Adv. Coun. award of achievement, 1985, Exceptional Civilian Svc. medal Dept. Army, 1985, Presdl. Rank award of Meritorious Svc., 1986, Presdl. Rank award of Disting. Sr. Exec., 1987, Crozier award, 1990, Superior Civilian Svc. medal, 1995, Exceptional Civilian Svc. medal, 1995. Fellow IEEE (Centennial medal 1994, Third Millennium medal 2000, Engring. Leadership Recognition award 1994, Joint Logistics Comdrs. award 1994); mem. AAAS, Nat. Def. Indsl. Assn., Assn. U.S. Army, Armed Forces Electronics Assn., Sr. Execs. Assn. (Exec. Achievement award 1994), Am. Defense Preparedness Assn., Alpha Chi Sigma, Phi Kappa Phi, Phi Lambda Upsilon. Mem. Reformed Ch. Home: 28 Glenwood Rd Colts Neck NJ 07722-1015 Office: AMSRL-EP Fort Monmouth NJ 07703

THORNTON, D. MCCARTY (MAC), lawyer; b. Wilmington, Del., Sept. 6, 1947; m. Molly F. Carr, July 7, 1996. BA, Stanford U., 1969, JD with high honors, 1972. Bar: Calif. 1973, DC 1973, US Supreme Ct. 1977. Trial atty. Bur. Consumer Protection FTC, Washington, 1972-78, dep. asst. dir., 1978; prosecutor fraud sect., criminal divsn. US Dept. Justice, Washington, 1978-82; assoc. Cole & Corette, Washington, 1982-83; chief of litigation Office of Insp. Gen., US Dept. HHS, Washington, 1983-90, chief counsel to Insp. Gen., 1990—2002; ptnr., health care group Sonnenschein Nath & Rosenthal LLP, Washington, 2003—. Founder, chmn. bd. W.Va. Rivers Coalition, Elkins, 1989-97. Mem. The Potomac Conservancy (founder, chair 1992-95, vice chair 1995-99), Am. Health Lawyers Assn. (bd. dirs. 1991-97), Health Care Compliance Assn. Avocation: whitewater kayaking. Office: Sonnenschein Nath & Rosenthal LLP Ste 600 East Tower 1301 K St NW Washington DC 20005 Office Phone: 202-408-6432. Office Fax: 202-408-6399. Business E-Mail: mthornton@sonnenschein.com.

THORNTON, EDMUND B., philanthropist; b. Chgo., Mar. 9, 1930; s. George A. and Suzanne W. Thornton; children from previous marriage: Thomas, Jonathan, Susan, Amanda; m. Susan Feldhaus; 1 child, Taylor. BA, Yale U., 1954. With No. Trust Co., Chgo., 1957-59; asst. sec., asst. treas. Ottawa Silica Co., Ill., 1959-61, v.p. corp. devel. Ill., 1961-62, pres., CEO Ill., 1962-75, chmn. bd., CEO Ill., 1975-83, chmn. bd. Ill., 1983-86; dir., v.p. Ottawa Nat. Bank, 2007—. Contbr. articles to profl. jours. Del. Rep. Nat. Conv., 1964-88, precinct committeeman, 1978-92; chmn. LaSalle County Rep. Ctrl. Com., 1980-92, Ill. and Mich. Canal Nat. Heritage Commn., 1985-2004; pres. Ottawa Silica Co. Found., Edmund B. Thornton Found., Ottawa, 1986—. 1st lt. USMC, 1954—56. Recipient Conservation Svc. award U.S. Dept. Interior, 1973. Mem. NRA (life), Nat. Assn. Mfrs., U.S. C. of C., Nat. Indsl. Sand Assn. (dir. 1968-73), Ill. Mfrs.' Assn. (dir. 1969-75, chmn. 1975), Ill. State C. of C. (dir. 1972-78), Explorers Club, U. Club Chgo., Chgo. Club, Raquet Club, Adventurers Club, Elks. Republican. Congregationalist. Home: PO Box 1 Ottawa IL 61350-0001 Office: PO Box 949 Ottawa IL 61350-0949 Office Phone: 815-434-6664.

THORNTON, EDWARD RALPH, chemistry professor; b. Syracuse, NY, July 19, 1935; s. Ralph Olin and Edna Rosamund (Hettinger) T.; m. Elizabeth Dee Kaplan, Feb. 18, 1969; 1 dau., Cara Emily. BA, Syracuse U., 1957; PhD (NIH predoctoral fellow), M.I.T., 1959. NIH postdoctoral fellow MIT, 1959-60; NIH Postdoctoral fellow Harvard, 1960-61; asst. prof. chemistry U. Pa., Phila., 1961-65, assoc. prof., 1965-69, prof., 1969—. Author: Solvolysis Mechanisms, 1964. NIH, NSF, Petroleum Research Fund grantee. Mem. ACLU, Am. Chem. Soc. (9th Phila. sect. award 1970), Common Cause, Sierra Club, Phi Beta Kappa, Sigma Xi, Phi Kappa Phi, Phi Lambda Upsilon, Sigma Pi Sigma, Pi Mu Epsilon. Democrat. Home: 7 Swarthmore Pl Swarthmore PA 19081-1023 Business E-Mail: ert@sas.upenn.edu.

THORNTON, ELAINE SERETHA, oncology clinical nurse specialist; b. NYC, Mar. 25, 1967; d. Jerry Richard and Shelia (Beckford) T. BS, Syracuse U., 1990; MSN, Columbia U., 1997. Cert. in gerontology. Staff nurse, clin. nurse I New Rochelle Hosp. Med. Ctr., NY, 1990-92, staff nurse, clin. nurse II, 1993-96, staff nurse drug and alcohol detoxification unit, 1996-97, oncology clin. nurse specialist, 1997-99; breast svc. coord. Robert and Helen Appell Comprehensive Breast Svc., 1997-99; nurse educator III Dept. Vets. Affairs/NY Harbor Health Care Sys., NYC, 1999—; oncology clin. nurse specialist Wyckoff Heights Med. Ctr., 2002—, also assoc. dir. nursing medicine oncology, nurse adminstr., 2004—. RN lab. asst. Sch. Nursing Coll. New Rochelle, 1992-97; adj. prof. Coll. New Rochelle, Borough Manhattan CC, NYC, 1995-97, adj. asst. prof. Iona Coll. Sch. Nursing, New Rochelle, adj. assoc. prof., 1998; vol. Am. Cancer Soc.; with Novartis Pharm. Sprks. Bureau, 1997-. Vol. Cancer Info. Svc., NYC, 1991-92, Clinton/Gore Presdl. campaign, 1992; mem. Sen. John McCain NY State Adv. Com., 2007; vol. providing cancer screening, blood pressure screening Pelham Sr. Ctr., NY, 1992; pub. info. rep. to economically disadvantaged Am. Cancer Soc., bd. dirs. Westchester divsn., 1993-95, 95-97, pres. So. unit; organizer 1st & 2d ann. Cmty. Health Fair, New Rochelle. Recipient Orthobiotech. Spkrs. Bur. Quality of Life award, Pub. Educator award Westchester divsn. Am. Cancer Soc. Mem. Oncology Nursing Soc. (Hudson Valley chpt., nominating com. 1992-93, treas. 1993-94, pres. elect Hudson Valley chpt. 1995-97), Oncology Nursing Soc. (corr., pres. Hudson Valley chpt. 1998-2000), CTME (nat. membership). Republican. Office: 108 Sagamore Rd Apt 1J Tuckahoe NY 10707-4024

THORNTON, FELICIA D., food service company executive; BSc Econs., Santa Clara U.; MBA Corp. Fin., Mktg., U. So. Calif. V.p., corp. planning and acctg. Ralphs Grocery Co., v.p., admin., 1998, group v.p., fin. and adminstrn., 1999—2001; group v.p. retail ops. Kroger Co., 2000—01; exec. v.p., CFO Albertson's, Inc., 2001—.

THORNTON, GIRARD B., JR., (JERRY), elementary school educator; m. Susan Thornton; 1 child, Katee. BA, Wash. Univ., St. Louis, 1970; MA, 1996. Cert. in early and mid. childhood/phys. edn. Nat. Bd. Tchg. Standards, 2004. Tchr., 1970—75; owner summer camp, 1975—95; phys. edn. tchr. Francis Howell Sch. Dist., Mo., 1995—. Recipient The I CAN Learn-NEA Foundation awards for Teaching Excellence, 2007; named Mo. Tchr. of Yr., 2006. Mem.: Mo. Nat. Edn. Assn. Office: Warren Elem Sch 141 Weiss Rd Saint Peters MO 63376 Business E-Mail: Jerry_Thornton@fhsd.k12.mo.us.

THORNTON, GLENDA ANN, librarian; b. Chickasha, Okla., Aug. 11, 1949; d. G. Van and Clara Maude (Lister) Long; m. Phillip Wynn Thornton, Sept. 18, 1970; children: Edward D., Jonathan C. BA, U. Okla., 1971, MLS, 1973; PhD, U. North Tex., 1993. Reference libr. Aurora (Colo.) Pub. Libr., 1974-75; tech. svcs. libr. Adams State Coll., Alamosa, Colo., 1975-80; collection devel. libr. Henderson State U., Arkadelphia, Ark., 1980-85, acting dir. libr., 1984; head material acquisitions libr. U. North Tex., Denton, 1985-91; assoc. dir. libr. svc. Auraria Libr. U. Colo., Denver, 1991—98; dir. Cleve. State U. Libr., 1998—. Co-author: AHE Vendor Directory, 1988; editor: Collection Management, vols. 26-27, 2000-03, mem. editl. bd. vol. 28, 2004—, revs. editor vol. 29, 2005—; revs. editor Tech. Svcs. Quar., 1997—; contbr. articles to profl. jours. Mem. Ohio LINK Libr. Adv. Coun., 1998—. Mem. ALA, Libr. Adminstrn. and Mgmt. Assn., Assn. Coll. and Rsch. Librs., Acad. Libr. Assn. Ohio, Cleve. Area Met. Libr. Assn. (bd. dirs. 2002-06), Beta Phi Mu. Avocation: gardening. Office: 2121 Euclid Ave RT 501 Cleveland OH 44115-2214 Office Phone: 216-687-2475. Business E-Mail: g.thornton@csuohio.edu.

THORNTON, J. RONALD, technology consultant; b. Fayetteville, Tenn., Aug. 19, 1939; s. James Alanda and Thelma White (McGee) T.; m. Mary Beth Packard, June 14, 1964 (div. Apr. 1975); 1 child, Nancy Carole; m. Martha Klemann, Jan. 23, 1976 (div. Apr. 1982); 1 child, Trey; m. Bernice McKinney, Feb. 14, 1986; 1 child, Paul Leon. BS in Physics and Math., Berry Coll., 1961; MA in Physics, Wake Forest Coll., 1964; postgrad., U. Ala., 1965-66, Rollins Coll., 1970. Rsch. physicist Brown Engring. Co., Huntsville, Ala., 1963-66; sr. staff engr. Martin Marietta Corp., Orlando, Fla., 1966-75; dep. dir. NASA, Washington, 1976-77; exec. asst. Congressman Louis Frey, Jr., Orlando, 1978; pres.

Tens Tec, Inc., Orlando, 1978-79; dir. So. Tech. Applications Ctr. U. Fla., Gainesville, Fla., 1979—2002. Bd. dirs., treas. North Fla. Tech. Innovation Ctr., 1994—2004; mem. light wave tech. com. Fla. High Tech. and Indsl. Coun., Tallahassee, 1986—93, NASA Tech. Transfer Exec. Com., Washington, 1987—, Javits Fellowship Bd., Washington, 1986—91, Gov.'s New Porduct Award Com., Tallahassee, 1988—94, Fla. K-12 Math., Sci. and Computer Sci. Edn. Quality Improvement Adv. Coun., 1989—94, Fla. Sci. Edn. Improvement Adv.Com., 1991—92; bd. dirs. North Fla. Enterprise Corp., 2001—04. Pres. Orange County Young Rep. Club, Orlando, 1970-71; treas. Fla. Fedn. Young Reps., Orlando, 1971-72; chmn. Fla. Fedn. Young Reps., Orlando, 1972-74; pres. Gainesville Area Innovation Network, 1988-89; mem. Berry Coll. Alumni Coun., 2006—. Named Engr. Exhibiting Tech. Excellence and Accomplishment ctrl. Fla. chpt. Fla. Engring. Soc., 1975, Achievement award NASA, 1977; named to Berry Coll. Hall of Fame, 2005. Mem. IEEE, Soc. Mfg. Engrs., Tech. Transfer Soc. (pres. 1999, bd. dirs. 1996—2001, Thomas Jefferson award 1999), Nat. Assn. Mgmt. and Tech. Assistance Ctrs. (bd. dirs. 1988, pres. 1992). Republican. Avocations: music, travel, reading, golf. Home and Office: 17829 NW 20th Ave Newberry FL 32669-2143 Office Phone: 352-472-6026. Personal E-mail: ronthornton@cox.net.

THORNTON, JAMES F., plastic surgeon, former military officer; b. Orange, NC, Jan. 4, 1961; m. Katherine Thornton; 5 children. BA, Austin Coll., 1982; MD, Univ. Tex. Southwestern Med. Ctr., 1989. Cert. Am. Bd. Plastic Surgery, 2000. Intern Univ. Tex. Southwestern Med. Ctr., 1989—90, resident in surgery, 1993—97; fellow in plastic surgery Emory Univ., 1997—99; assoc. prof. Univ. Tex. Southwestern Med. Ctr., Dallas, 2000—; staff mem. Parkland Meml. Hosp., Zale Lipshy Univ. Hosp., Children's Med. Ctr., St. Paul Med. Ctr. Comdr., flight surgeon Air Training Wing USN, & USNR. Decorated Navy & Marine Corps Commendation Medal, Nat. Defense Medal Dept. of the Navy; recipient Armed Forces Reserve Medal with M device, 2003; named a Top Doctor - Plastic Surgery, Redbook Mag., 2001. Fellow: Am. Coll. Surgeons; mem.: AMA, Tex. Med. Assn., Dallas County Med. Soc., Am. Soc. Plastic Surgeons, AO No. Am. Maxillofacial Faculty, Am. Soc. Maxillofacial Surgeons, Jurkiewicz Soc., Parkland Surgical Soc. Office Phone: 214-645-3113. Office Fax: 214-645-3140. Business E-Mail: james.thornton@utsouthwestern.edu.

THORNTON, JOE, professional hockey player; b. London, Ont., Can., July 2, 1979; Center Boston Bruins, 1997—2005, HC Davos, Switzerland, 2004—05, San Jose Sharks, 2005—. Mem. Team Can., World Championships, 2001, 05, Team Can., World Cup of Hockey, 2004, Team Can. Olympic Games, Torino, Italy, 2006. Recipient Art Ross Trophy, 2006, Hart Meml. Trophy, 2006; named to Second All-Star Team, NHL, 2003, 2008, First All-Start Team, 2006, NHL All-Star Game, 2002—04, 2007, 2008, 2009. Achievements include being a member of World Cup Champion Team Canada, 2004. Office: c/o San Jose Sharks 525 W Santa Clara St San Jose CA 95113*

THORNTON, JOHN LAWSON, economics professor, former diversified financial services company executive; b. 1954; AB in History, Harvard U., 1976; BA, MA in Jurisprudence, Oxford U., 1978; MPPM, Yale U., 1980. With Goldman Sachs Group, Inc., 1980—88, ptnr., 1988—95; co-CEO Goldman Sachs Internat., 1995—96; chmn. Goldman Sachs Asia, 1996—98; pres., co-COO Goldman Sachs Group, Inc., 1999—2003, sr. adv., 2003—; spl. adv. on China to Pres. Richard C. Levin Yale U., 2003; prof., dir. Global Leadership prog. Tsinghua U., Beijing, 2003—; non-exec. chmn. HSBC North America Holdings, Inc., 2008—. Bd. dirs. Ford Motor Corp., 1996—, Intel Corp., 2003—, News Corp., 2004—, China Netcom, 2004—, HSBC North America Holdings, Inc., 2008—. Trustee Brookings Institution, 2000—, chmn., 2003—; trustee, bd. pres. Hotchkiss Sch.; trustee Asia Soc., China Inst., Eisenhower Fellowships, Morehouse Coll., Tsinghua U. Sch. Econ. & Mgmt., The Hotchkiss Sch.; mem. advisory bd. Yale Univ. Sch. Mgmt. Mem.: Asia Soc., Coun. Fgn. Rels. Office: Tsinghua U Beijing 100084 China*

THORNTON, JONATHAN MILLS, history professor; b. Montgomery, Ala., Oct. 27, 1943; s. Jonathan Mills and Priscilla Marks Thornton; m. Brenda Booth, Jan. 5, 1985. BA, Princeton U., NJ, 1966; MPhil, PhD, Yale U., New Haven, 1974. Instr. U. Ill., Chgo., 1971—74; asst. prof. U. Mich., Ann Arbor, 1974—77, assoc. prof., 1977—82, prof. history, 1982—. Fellow Woodrow Wilson Internat. Ctr. Scholars, Washington, 1994—95; Pitt prof. Am. history Cambridge U., England, 2007—08. Author: (history books) Politics and Power in a Slave Society: Alabama, 1800-1860 (John H. Dunning prize, Am. Hist. Assn., 1978), Dividing Lines: Municipal Politics and the Struggle for Civil Rights in Montgomery, Birmingham and Selma (Liberty Legacy Found. prize, Orgn. Am. Historians, 2003). Danforth Found. fellow, 1966—74, Guggenheim Found. fellow, 1978—79. Home: 564 Galen Cir Ann Arbor MI 48103 Office: Univ Mich Dept History Ann Arbor MI 48109

THORNTON, JOSEPH SCOTT, research and development company executive, materials scientist; b. Sewickley, Pa., Feb. 6, 1936; s. Joseph Scott and Evelyn (Miller) T.; divorced; children: Joseph Scott III, Chris P. BSME, U. Tex., 1957, PhD, 1969; MSMetE, Carnegie Mellon U., 1962. Engr. Walworth Valve Co., Boston, 1958; metall. engr. Westinghouse Astronuclear Lab., Large, Pa., 1962-64; instr., teaching assoc. U. Tex., Austin, 1964-67; group leader Tracor Inc., Austin, 1967-69, dept. dir., 1973-75; dept. mgr. Horizons Rsch., Inc., Cleve., 1969-73; chmn., chief exec. officer Tex. Rsch. Internat., Inc. (formerly Tex. Rsch. Inst., Inc.), Austin, 1975—. Contbr. numerous tech. papers to profl. publs.; editor: WANL Materials Manual, 2 vols., 1964; patentee in field. Founder, chmn., program dir. Cmtys. Recovery 501 (c) Social Profit Corp., Austin, 2004—. Recipient IGS award, 2002; fellow Alcoa, Austin, 1964, RC Baker Found., 1967. Mem.: ASTM, Internat. Geosynthetics Soc. (award 2002), Adhesion Soc., Am. Soc. Metals Internat. (exec. com. 1965—66). Office: Tex Rsch Internat Inc 9063 Bee Caves Rd Austin TX 78733-6201 Office Phone: 512-263-2101. E-mail: jst@tri-intl.com.

THORNTON, KIRTLEY ELLIOTT, psychologist; b. St. Louis, May 24, 1946; s. Maxine Thornton; m. Monika Polte, Feb. 21, 1987. PhD, New Sch. Social Rsch., NYC, 1980. Contbr. scientific papers. Mem.: Quantitative EEG Bd. (sec. treas. 1998—2009). Achievements include patents for QEEG parameters of effective cognitive function. Office: Ctr Health Psychology 2 Ethel Rd Edison NJ 08817 Office Fax: 732-662-7460. Business E-Mail: ket@chp-neurotherapy.com.

THORNTON, MICHAEL B., federal judge; b. Hattiesburg, Miss., Feb. 9, 1954; BS in Acctg., Southern Miss U., 1976, MS in Acctg., 1977; MA in English Lit., U. Tenn., 1979; JD, Duke U., 1982. Bar: DC 1982. Law clk. to Honorable Charles Clark US Ct. Appeals (5th circuit), 1983—84; assoc. Sutherland, Asbill & Brennan, Washington, 1982—83, Miller & Chevalier, Washington, 1985—88; tax counsel US House Com. on Ways & Means, Washington, 1988—93, chief minority tax counsel, 1995; atty. advisor US Dept. Treasury, Washington, 1995, dep. tax legislative counsel Office Tax Policy, 1995—98; judge US Tax Ct., Washington, 1998—. Mem. editl. bd. Duke U. Law Journal, 1981—82. Recipient Treasury Secretary's Annual award, US Dept. Treasury, 1997, Meritorious Svc. award, 1998. Mem.: Order of the Coif. Office: US Tax Ct 400 2nd St NW Washington DC 20217-0001*

THORNTON, PETER A., engineering educator, consultant; b. Troy, NY, Feb. 16, 1941; s. Alan F. and Elizabeth M. Thornton; m. Ellen M. Harmon, June 21, 1969; children: Kelly E. Stone, Kathleen A. Griffin, Jennifer E. Saunders. AS in Engring. Sci., Hudson Valley CC, Troy, 1967; BS in Materials Engring., Rensselaer Poly. Inst., Troy, 1969, MS, 1982. With, constrn. materials testing Benderson Lab., Troy, 1965; constrn. insp. George A. Fuller Co. Consulting Engrs., Albany, NY, 1966; materials engr. Benet Lab., Watervliet, NY, 1969—89, br. & divsn. chief, 1989—99; adj. prof. Hudson Valley CC, Troy, 1975—. Engring. materials cons. INTERTECH, Troy, 1972—, Elmhurst Rsch. Inc., Albany, 2005—; adv. bd. Edison Welding Inst., Columbus, Ohio, 1988—92, Engring. Rsch. Ctr. Net Shape Mfg. Ohio State U., Columbus, 1988—96; vis. lectr. Ohio State U., Columbus, 1988—92, NC A&T State U., Greensboro, 1989—91; lectr. Union Coll. Summer Tech. Inst., Schenectady, NY, 1992—94. Author: (book) Engineering Aspects of Product Liability, Fundamentals of Engineering Materials; contbr. chapters to books. Charter mem. St. Clements Sch. Bd. Edn., Saratoga Springs, NY, 1985—88. E-5 USN, 1960—64, USS Krishna ARL-38, USS Ruchamkin APD-89. Recipient R&D Achievement award, US Army, 1983, Spl. award, Fed. Lab. Consortium, 1988, Hammer award, US V.P., 1999. Achievements include development of calcium injection to gunsteel for shape control of non-metallic inclusions; hot isostatic pressed atomized steel powder to ordnance components.

THORNTON, RICHARD C., history professor; PhD, U. Wash., Seattle, 1966. Prof. history and internat. affairs George Washington U., Washington, 1967—2008. Author: (history) The Reagan Revolution, III: Defeating the Soviet Challenge; contbr. articles to profl. publs. Lt. col. USAF, 1975—85, Pentagon. Fellow, US Govt., 1961—66. Mem.: Phi Beta Kappa (pres., GWU chpt. 1987—88). Business E-Mail: rthornto@gwu.edu.

THORNTON, RITA LOUISE, environmental scientist, lawyer; d. Donald Everett Thornton and Itasker Frances Edmonds-Thornton. BS, Monmouth U., 1973; JD, Seton Hall U., 1993; PhD, N.J. Inst. Tech., 2006. Cert.: (conflict resolution negotiator); pub. mgr. NJ. Toxicologist Johnson & Johnson Ethicon, Somerville, NJ, 1973—81; distributor ednl. film MGM/United Artists Entertainment, NYC, 1981—83; chmn. Dept. Sci. Vail-Deane Sch., Mountainside, NJ, 1983—88; rschr. Reheis Chem. Co., Berkeley Heights, NJ, 1988—90; specialist hazardous site mitigation NJ Dept. Environ. Protection, Trenton, 1990—97, environ. justice adminstr., rule mgr., 1997—99, supr. environ. specialist, 1999—, sect. chief, waste mgmt., 2005—. Founder, CEO Thornton Sisters Found., Inc., Atlantic Highlands, 1991—; exec. dir. Environ. Justice and Equity Cmty. Based Teamwork, Inc, Atlantic Highlands, 1999—; adj. prof. NJ Inst. Tech., Newark, 2003. Co-author: A Suitcase Full of Dreams, 1996; author (editor): New Jersey Solid and Hazardous Waste Transporter Quick Access Guide Book, 2000—05. Recipient Nat. Minority Role Model in Sci. award, Nat. Sci. Inst. and Minority Access, Inc., 2006; grantee, US Environ. Protection Agy., 1998, 2000; fellow, Alliance Grad. Edn. and Professorale, 2001—06. Mem.: Soc. Women Environ. Profls., Nat. Honor Soc., Alpha Epsilon Lambda. Business E-Mail: rita.thornton@dep.state.nj.us.

THORNTON, ROLAND, telecommunications industry executive; married; 3 children. BSBA, Ind. U.; grad. student in Info. Systems, U. Ill. Co-founder Acquired Knowledge, Ltd.; v.p. customer ops. Ameritech; v.p. interconnection svcs. SBC; sr. v.p. customer svc. ops. Wholesale Markets Qwest Comm. Internat., Inc., exec. v.p. wholesale markets, 2004—. Bd. dirs. Rotary Internat., 2007—, Food Bank of the Rockies, Colo. Black C. of C., chmn. Mem.: Rotary Club Denver (mem. world coun. com.). Office: Qwest Comm Internat Inc 1801 California St Denver CO 80202 Office Phone: 303-992-1400. Office Fax: 303-896-8515.

THORNTON, THOMAS NOEL, former publishing executive; b. Marceline, Mo., Apr. 23, 1950; s. Bernard F. and Helen F. (Kelley) T.; m. Cynthia L. Murray, Nov. 26, 1971; children: T. Zachary, Timothy. B.J., U. Mo., 1972. Asst. to editor Universal Press Syndicate, Kansas City, Mo., 1972, v.p., 1974, dir. mktg., 1976; v.p., dir. mktg. Universal Press Syndicate and Andrews McMeel Pub., Kansas City, 1976-87; pres., COO Andrews McMeel Pub., 1987—2002, pres., CEO, 2003—05. Bd. dirs. Andrews McMeel Universal. Business E-Mail: tthornton@amuniversal.com.

THORNTON, YVONNE SHIRLEY, obstetrician, writer, musician; b. NYC, Nov. 21, 1947; d. Donald E. and Itasker F. (Edmonds) T.; m. Shearwood McClelland, June 8, 1974; children: Shearwood III, Kimberly Itaska. BS in Biology, Monmouth Coll., 1969; MD, Columbia U., 1973, MPH, 1996; DSc (hon.), Tuskegee U., 2003. Diplomate Am. Bd. Ob-gyn. Resident in ob-gyn Roosevelt Hosp., NYC, 1973-77; fellow maternal-fetal medicine Columbia-Presbyn. Med. Center, NYC, 1977-79; commd. lt. comdr. M.C. USN, 1979; asst. prof. ob-gyn Uniformed Svcs. U. Health Scis., 1979-82; assoc. prof. Cornell U. Med. Coll., NYC, 1989-92; dir. clin. svcs. dept. ob-gyn N.Y. Hosp.-Cornell Med. Center, 1982-88; asst. attending N.Y. Lying-In Hosp., 1982-89; assoc. clin. prof. ob-gyn. Columbia P&S, 1995-98, assoc. clin. prof., 2001—02; clin. prof. ob-gyn. U. Medicine and Dentistry N.J., 1998-2000, Med. Coll. Cornell U., 2003—05, NY Med. Coll., 2008—. Dir. Chorionic Villus Sampling Program, 1984-92; dir. perinatal diagnostic testing ctr. Morristown Meml. Hosp., 1992-2000, divsn. maternal-fetal medicine St. Luke's Roosevelt Hosp. Ctr., 2000-02; vice chair ob-gyn, dir. maternal-fetal medicine, Jamaica Hosp. Med. Ctr., 2002-05; staff Nat. Naval Med. Ctr., Bethesda, Md.; saxophonist Thornton Sisters ensemble, 1955-76; vis. assoc. physician The Rockefeller U. Hosp., 1986-96; prof. clinical OB/GYN Cornell U. Med. Coll., 2003-05; examiner Am. Bd. Ob-Gyn, 1997—; vice chmn. Dept. Ob-Gyn. Jamaica Hosp. Med. Ctr.; bd. dirs. Integra Med Am., 2006, perinatal cons. Westchester Med. Ctr., Valhalla, NY, 2007-. Author: The Ditchdigger's Daughters, 1995, (named best books for young adults ALA, Excellence in Lit. award, NJ Edn. Assn., One Book NJ, NJ Libr. Assn., 2006, nominated Pulitzer Prize 1995) Primary Care for the Obstetrician and Gynecologist, 1997, Woman to Woman, 1997. Bd. dirs. Fair Housing Coun. Northern NJ, 1985—. Recipient Excellence in Literature award, NJ Edn. Assn., 1996, winner Daniel Webster Oratorical Competition, Internat. Platform Assn., 1996; nominated Pulitzer Prize, 1995. Fellow: ACOG, ACS; mem.: AMA, Am. Fedn. Musicians, Soc. Maternal-Fetal Medicine, Assn. Women Surgeons, NY Acad. Medicine. Democrat. Baptist. Office Phone: 201-570-8181. Business E-Mail: thornton@carroll.com.

THORP, BENJAMIN A., III, retired paper company executive; b. Albany, NY, May 31, 1938; s. Benjamin A. Jr. and Anna C. (Head) T.; m. Barbara Sue Tellock, Aug. 1, 1964 (div. Mar. 1986); 1 child, Benjamin A. IV; m. Laurie Diane Murdock, Oct. 25, 1987. Student in elec. engring., Rensselaer Poly. Inst., 1956-61, postgrad. in mgmt., 1967-68; BS in Physics, U. Md., 1964; postgrad. in engring., U. Bridgeport, 1966; postgrad. in mktg., U. Tenn., 1970. Product devel. mgr. Huyck Formex div. Huyck, Greenville, Tenn., 1969-71, mktg. mgr., 1971-73, v.p., gen. mgr., 1973-75, Huytech Systems div., Wake Forest, NC, 1975-78; v.p., dir. research Huyck Corp., Rensselaer, NY, 1978-80; pres. Benjamin A. Thorp Inc., Albany, 1980-82, POYRY-BEK Inc., Raleigh, NC, 1982-84; v.p. engring. BE&K Inc., Birmingham, Ala., 1984-85, James River Corp., Richmond, Va., 1985—95; v.p. mfg. tech. Chesapeake Corp., Richmond, Va., 1996-97; dir. pulp and paper engring. Ga. Pacific, Atlanta, 1998—2004, ret., 2004; pres. Flambeau River Biorefinery, 2006—07, renewable energy cons., 2004—. Mem. exec. com. Pulp and Paper Found. Bd., Ga. Inst. Tech., 1991-95, pres., 1993-95; mem. indsl. adv. bd. Forest Web.com, 2000—, Peregrine Energy, Greenville, SC, 2002-08; chmn. bd. Besicorp.-Empire Newsprint LLC, 2004-07; bd. dirs. K.P. Products. Co-author: Pulp and Paper Energy Best Practice Guidebook, 2d edit., 2006; tech. editor Paper Machine Operations, Vol. 7, 3d edit., 1991; contbr. more than 200 articles to profl. jours.; patentee in field. Bd. dirs. Richmond Math. and Sci. Ctr., 1987-93, Sic. Mus. of Va. Found., 1989-98; chmn. papermaking project adv. com. Inst. Paper Sci. and Tech., 1990-94. Fellow TAPPI (chmn. papermakers com. 1984-86, vice chmn. paper and bd. divsn. 1988-90, chmn. 1990-92, bd. dir., Leadership award 1994); mem. Paper Industry Mgmt. Assn. (pres. 1996-97, chmn. bd. trustees 1999—2003, Glen T. Rinnegar award 1999), PIMA-CPBIS Mgmt. Excellence award 2003, Exptl. Aircraft Assn., Meadowbrook Estates Civic Assn. (bd. dirs. 1996-98, pres. 2003-04), Meadowbrook Country Club (bd. dirs. 2005-08). Presbyterian. Personal E-mail: bathorp@comcast.net.

THORP, EDWARD OAKLEY, investment management company executive; b. Chgo., Aug. 14, 1932; s. Oakley Glenn and Josephine (Gebert) T.; m. Vivian Sinetar, Jan. 28, 1956; children: Raun, Karen, Jeffrey. BA in Physics, UCLA, 1953, MA, 1955, PhD in Math., 1958. C.L.E. Moore instr. MIT, Cambridge, Mass., 1959—61; asst. prof. N.Mex. State U., 1961—63, assoc. prof. math., 1963—65, U. Calif., Irvine, 1965—67, prof. math., 1967—77, prof. fin., 1977—82, regents lectr., 1992—93; gen. ptnr. Edward O. Thorp & Assocs., LP, Newport Beach, 1989—. Vis. prof. UCLA, 1991; chmn. Oakley Sutton Mgmt. Corp., Newport Beach, Calif., 1972-91; mng. gen. ptnr. Princeton/Newport Ptnrs., Newport Beach, 1969-91, OSM Ptnrs., MIDAS Advisors, Newport Beach, 1986-89; gen. ptnr. Ridgeline Ptnrs., Newport Beach, 1994-2002; portfolio mgr., cons. Glenwood Investment Corp., Chgo., 1992-94; prin., cons. Grosvenor Capital Mgmt., Chgo., 1992-93; pres. Noesis Corp., 1994-2002, UCI Found. Bd., 2004—. Author: Beat the Dealer: A Winning Strategy for the Game of Twenty-One, 1962, rev. edit., 1966, Elementary Probability, 1966, The Mathematics of Gambling, 1984; co-author: Beat The Market, 1967, The Gambling Times Guide to Blackjack, 1984; columnist Gambling Times, 1979-84, Wilmott 2002—. Grantee NSF, 1954-55, 62-64, Air Force Office Sci. Rsch., 1964-73. Fellow NSF, Inst. Math. Stats.; mem. Phi Beta Kappa, Sigma Xi. Avocation: astronomy. Office: Edward O Thorp & Assocs LP 610 Newport Center Dr Ste 1240 Newport Beach CA 92660-6436

THORP, H. HOLDEN, academic administrator, chemistry professor; b. Aug. 16, 1964; m. Patti Worden Thorp; children: John, Emma. BS in Chemistry, U. NC., 1986; PhD in Chemistry, Calif. Inst. tech., 1989. Postdoctoral assoc. Yale U., 1989—90; asst. prof., dept. chemistry NC State U., 1991—93; vis. asst. prof., dept. chemistry U. NC, Chapel Hill, 1993, asst. prof., dept. chemistry, 1993—95, assoc prof., dept. chemistry, 1996—99, prof., dept. chemistry, 1999—2005, Kenan prof. chemistry, 2005—, chair dept. chemistry, 2005—, dean, Coll. Arts & Scis., chancellor, 2008—. Cons. Burroughs-Wellcome Co., 1993—96, Clinical Micro Sensors, 2003—05, Firelake Capital, 2005, Osmetech, Inc., 2005—; vice chair undergrad. studies U. NC, 1995—2000, mem. Lineberger Comprehensive Cancer Ctr., 1997—; founder, bd. dir., chmn. sci. adv. bd. Xanthon Inc., 1996—2002, pres., 2002—05; mem. sci. adv. bd. Novalon Pharmaceutical Corp., 1996—99, MaxCyte Inc., 2004—; mem. NASA Advanced Monitoring & Control Peer Rev. Com., 2000; mem. Metallobiochemistry study sect. NIH, 1999, mem. spl. panel on SBIR & STTR grants, 2001—03; dir. Morehead Planetarium & Sci. Ctr., 2001—05; mem. bd. dirs. NC Ctr. for Sci., Math. & Tech. Edn., 2002—; faculty dir. fundraising Carolina Phys. Sci. Complex, 2003—; chmn. com. sci. in pub. interest Sigma Xi, 2004—07; co-founder, mem. sci. adv. bd. Viamet Pharms., 2005—; lectr. in field. Exec. prodr.: (planetarium shows) Star of Bethlehem, 2002, Life in the Universe, 2003, Magic Tree House Space Mission, 2004, Extinction!, 2005; (documentaries) DNA: The Secret of Life, 2003; co-editor: Bioinorganic Chemistry issue, Current Opinion on Chem. Biology, 2005; contbr. articles to profl. jours., columns in newspapers. Recipient Camile & Henry Dreyfus New Faculty award, 1990, Presdl. Young Investigator award, NSF, 1991, Camile Dreyfus Tchr.-Scholar award, 1995, Ruth & Philip Hettleman prize, 1996, Tanner award, 1998, CED Life Sci. Tech. of Yr. award, 2000; named Disting. Young Alumnus, U. NC Gen. Alumni Assn., 2002; named one of Small Bus. Top Innovators, Fortune Mag., 2001; David & Lucille Packard fellow, 1991, Alfred P. Sloan fellow, 1996. Mem.: Order of the Golden Fleece (hon.). Office: U NC / Office of Chancellor 103 S Bldg Campus Box 9100 Chapel Hill NC 27599-9100 Office Phone: 919-962-1365. Office Fax: 919-962-1647. E-mail: holden@unc.edu, chancellor@unc.edu.*

THORP, JAMES SHELBY, electrical engineering educator; b. Kansas City, Mo., Feb. 7, 1937; s. Joseph Chester and Ruth Vefe (McNamara) T.; m. Barbara Anne Curit, June 27, 1959 (div. July 1976); children: Jeffrey Barton, Elizabeth Anne; m. Christine Annette Moore, Aug. 10, 1980 (div. 1995); children: Gregory, William. BEE, Cornell U., 1959, MS, 1961, PhD, 1962. Asst. prof. Cornell U., Ithaca, NY, 1962-66, with, 1962—2004, assoc. prof., 1966-75, prof., 1975—94, assoc. dir. Sch. Elec. Engring., 1991-94, dir. Sch. Elec. Engring., 1994, Charles N. Mellowes prof. engring., 1994—2001; faculty intern Am. Electric Power Svc. Corp., NYC, 1976-77; fellow Churchill Coll., U. Cambridge, 1988; Hugh P. and Ethey C. Kelley prof. elec. and computer engring. Va. Polytechnic and State U., Blackburg, Va., 2004—, dept. head, Bradley Dept. Elec. and Computer Engring., 2004—. Cons. Am. Electric Power Svc. Corp., 1977-83, Dowty Control Techs., Boonton, N.J., 1988—. Author: Computer Relaying for Power Systems, 1988; assoc. editor IEEE Transactions on Circuits and Sys., 1985-87; editor IEEE Transactions on Power Delivery 1998-2001, mem. editl. bd.; contbr. chpts. to books, articles to profl. jours. Co-recipient Benjamin Franklin medal in Elec. Engring., Franklin Inst., 2008. Fellow IEEE (Power Engring. Soc. Outstanding Power Engring. award, Career Svc. award, mem. power sys. relaying com.), NAE, Eta Kappa Nu, Tau Beta Pi and Sigma Xi Achievements include patents in field. Avocation: golf. Office: Va Tech 302 Whittemore Hall (0111) Blacksburg VA 24061 Office Phone: 540-231-6646, 540-231-3363. Business E-Mail: jsthorp@vt.edu.

THORP, JOHN MERCER, JR., physician; b. Rocky Mountain, NC, Aug. 31, 1957; BA in Zoology, U. NC, Chapel Hill, 1979; MD, East Carolina Univ., 1983. Intern Univ. NC Sch. Medicine, Chapel Hill, 1983, resident ob-gyn., 1983-87, fellow maternal-fetal medicine, 1987-89, clin. asst. prof., divsn. maternal-fetal medicine, dept. ob-gyn., 1989—90, asst. prof., divsn. maternal-fetal medicine, dept. ob-gyn., 1990—95, assoc. chair, dept. ob-gyn., 1995—99, assoc. prof., divsn. maternal-fetal medicine, dept. ob-gyn., 1995—2000, co-dir., Inst. Generalist Physician,

1999—2000, sr. rsch. fellow, Cecil G. Sheps Ctr. for Health, Svcs. Rsch., 1999—, co-dir., NC program for women's health rsch., Cecil G. Sheps Ctr. for Health Svcs. Rsch., 1999—2004, prof., dept. ob-gyn., 2000—, Hugh McAllister Disting. prof. ob-gyn, dept. ob-gyn., 2001—, interim and dep. dir., Ctr. for Women's Health Rsch., Cecil G. Ships Ctr. for Health Svc. Rsch., Dept. Epidemiology, Sch. Pub. Health, Dept. Ob-gyn, 2004—. Med. dir., HORIZONS Perinatal Substance Abuse Program U. NC, Chapel Hill, 1993—; adj. prof., dept. epidemiology, sch. pub. health and tropical medicine Tulane U., 2003—; adj. prof., dept. epidemiology, sch. pub. health U. NC, Chapel Hill, 1999—2004, Chapel Hill, 2004—, fellow, Carolina Population Ctr., 2003—, dir., biomedical core, Carolina Population Ctr., 2004—. Contbr. several articles to profl. jours. Recipient NC Divsn. Mental Health Develop. Disabilities and Substance Abuse Recogntion award for Outstanding Svc. to Women and Children, 1999, Perinatal Health Model of Excellence NC Dept. Health and Human Svcs. in Conjunction with the March of Dimes, 1999; named Mcallister Disting. Prof. Ob-gyn., 2002. Fellow: Am. Gynecological and Obstetrical Soc.; mem.: Soc. for Maternal-Fetal Medicine, Assn. Professors Gynecology and Obstetrics, Soc. Gynecologic Investigation, South Atlantic Assn. Ob-gyn., Am. Fertility Soc., Am. Coll. Ob-gyn. Office: Dept Ob-Gyn 4012 Old Clinic Bldg CB #7570 Chapel Hill NC 27599-7570 Office Phone: 919-843-7850. Office Fax: 919-843-6938. Business E-Mail: thorp@med.unc.edu.*

THORPE, CARLON JUSTINE, engineering and operations executive; b. Siloam Springs, Ark., May 26, 1960; d. Robert F. and Jean (Caroom) Toenges. BS in Indsl. Engring., U. Ark., 1982; MBA, Houston Bapt. U., 1988. Registered profl. engr., Tex. Supr. codes and regulatory compliance Tex. Ea., Houston, 1982-85, supr. ops. spl. projects, 1985-87, mgr. project devel., 1987-90; dir. spl. projects, tech. asst. to pres. Enron, Houston, 1990-91, dir. throughput engring., 1991-92, project dir., 1992-95; v.p. engring. So. Union Gas Co., Austin, Tex., 1995-96; v.p. ops. Mo. Gas Energy, Kansas City, Mo., 1996-99; gen. mgr. Shell Tech. Ventures, Houston, 1999—2002. Mem.: NSPE, Tex. Soc. Profl. Engrs. Baptist. Home: 5334 Indian Shores Ln Houston TX 77041-4298

THORPE, JANET CLAIRE, judge; b. Bklyn., Dec. 8, 1953; d. Burton Walter and Phyllis Claire (Read) T.; m. David Frank Palmer, Aug. 26, 1978 (div. Aug. 1988); children: Katherine Elaine, Jennifer Claire; m. James Francis Box, June 29, 1991; children; Melissa Richelle, Maergrethe Cashel. Student, Boston U., 1972-74; BA in Polit. Sci. & History with honors, Union Coll., 1975; postgrad., Western New Eng. Sch. Law, 1975-76; JD, Emory U., 1978. Bar: Ga. 1978, U.S. Ct. Appeals (5th and 11th cirs.) 1978, 80, Fla. 1987, U.S. Dist. Ct. (mid. dist.) Fla. 1987. Law clk. to judge U.S. Dist. Ct., Atlanta, 1978; regional atty. Comptroller of Curency, Atlanta, 1978-80; assoc. corp. counsel Trust Co. Ga., Atlanta, 1980-86; dir. Trusco Properties, Inc., Atlanta, 1981-86; gen. counsel, corp. sec. SunTrust Banks Fla., Inc., Orlando, 1986-2000; gen. counsel SunTrust Bank N.A., Orlando, 1986-2000; group v.p. SunTrust Banks, Inc., 1995-2000; cir. ct. judge State of Fla. (9th cir.), Orlando, Fla., 2000—. Mem. Coun. Battered Women, Atlanta, 1983-86, bd. dirs., 1986; bd. visitors Cornell Mus. Fine Art, Rollins Coll., 1990-96; mem. bd. zoning variances City of Orlando, 1996-99; bd. dirs. Orange County Cmty. Alliance, 2000-03. Mem. Ga. Bar Assn., Fla. Bar Assn., Assn. Bank Holdings Cos (lawyers com. 1983-90), Am. Corp. Counsel Assn. (bd. dirs. ctrl. Fla. chpt. 1991-99), Am. Diabetes Assn. (bd. dirs. Fla. chpt. 1989-97), Leadership Orlando. Episcopalian. Avocations: gardening, child rearing, house renovation, photography. Office: Orange County Courthouse 425 N Orange Ave Orlando FL 32801

THORPE, JASON M., non-profit organization director; b. 1982; Dir., cmty. edn. and outreach Open-Inn Inc. Bd. co-chair Western States Youth Services Network; mem. Ariz. Statewide Devel. Taskforce, Wingspan award com.; co-chair, bd. of incorporators Porch Light Found. Nat. Safe Place adv. bd. mem. YMCA; official organizer Tucson V-Day. Named one of 40 Under 40, Tucson Bus. Edge, 2006. Office: Open Inn Inc PO Box 5766 Tucson AZ 85703-0766 Office Phone: 520-670-9040.

THORPE, MARION DENNIS, JR., former state agency administrator; b. Durham, NC, Aug. 29, 1964; BS in Psychology, Duke U., Durham; M in Health Policy and Adminstrn., U. NC, Chapel Hill, MD. Chief med. officer Syndeos Corp., Inc., Celebration, Fla., 2002; chief med. officer Agy. Health Care Adminstrn. State of Fla. Vice- chmn. Quantum Grp. Palm Beach County, Fla.; mem. Black Rep. Caucus; del. Fla. Med. Assn., Tallahassee, Healthy Fla. Found.; chmn. Medicaid Reform Advocates Coalition, Care Broward; founding mem. State-Wide HMO Report Card Panel. Expert on-air homeland security analyst CBS News Miami. Polit. dir. Young Reps., Miami. Mem.: Nat. Black Rep. Assn., Jerome Gray Republican Club. Republican. Mailing: PO Box 546017 Miami FL 33154*

THORSEN, DENISE, language educator; m. Marc Thorsen, Sept. 17, 1966; children: Eric, Pierre. MA in French Lang. and Lit., U. Ill., Chgo., 1988. Cert. tchr. State Ill., 1985. Tchr. Sch. Dist. 203, Naperville, Ill., 1986—2005, Elgin CC, Ill., 2002—08. Home: 919 Thornwood Ct Saint Charles IL 60174

THORSEN, MARIE KRISTIN, radiologist, educator; b. Milw., Aug. 1, 1947; d. Charles Christian and Margaret Josephine (Little) T.; m. James Lawrence Troy, Jan. 7, 1978; children: Katherine Marie, Megan Elizabeth. BA, U. Wis., Madison, 1969; MBA, George Washington U., Washington, 1971; MD, Columbia Coll. Physicians and Surgeons, 1977. Diplomate Am. Bd. Radiology. Intern. Columbia-Presbyn. Med. Ctr., NYC, 1977-78, resident dept. radiology, 1978-81; asst. prof. radiology Med. Coll. Wis., 1982-84, assoc. prof., 1984-89, prof., 1989-94; dir. computed tomography Waukesha Meml. Hosp., 1994—, Oconomowoc Meml. Hosp., 1994—. Contbr. articles to profl. jours. Fellow, Med. Coll. Wisc., Milw., 1981—82. Fellow Am. Coll. Radiology, Radiol. Soc. N. Am., Wis. Radiologic Assn. (v.p., 2005, pres., 2007). Office Phone: 262-928-2400.

THORSEN, NANCY DAIN, retired real estate broker; b. Edwardsville, Ill., 1944; d. Clifford Earl and Suzanne Eleanor (Kribs) Dain; m. David Massie, 1968 (div. 1975); 1 child, Suzanne Dain Massie; m. James Hugh Thorsen, May 30, 1980. BSc in Mktg., So. Ill. U., 1968, MSc in Bus. Edn., 1975; grad., Realtor Inst., Idaho, 1983. Cert. residential and investment specialist, fin. instr., luxury home mktg. specialist, 2004; designated real estate instr. State of Idaho; accredited buyer rep. Personnel officer J.H. Little & Co. Ltd., London, 1969-72; instr. in bus. edn. Spl. Sch. Dist. St. Louis, 1974-77; mgr. mktg./ops. Isis Foods, Inc., St. Louis, 1978-80; asst. mgr. store Stix, Baer & Fuller, St. Louis, 1980; assoc. broker Century 21 Sayer Realty, Inc., Idaho Falls, Idaho, 1981-88, RE/MAX Homestead Realty, 1989—2009. Spkr. in field; real estate fin. instr. State of Idaho Real Estate Commn., 1994; founder Nancy Thorsen Seminars, 1995; pres. S.E. Idaho Women's Coun. of Realtors, 2006 Bd. dirs. Idaho Vol., Boise, 1981-84, Idaho Falls Symphony, 1982; pres. Friends of Idaho Falls Libr., 1981-83; chmn. Idaho Falls Mayor's Com. for Vol. Coordination, 1981-84; power leader Power Program, 1995; mem. Mtn. River Valley Red Cross, chair capital campaign, cmty. gifts chair ARC. Recipient Idaho Gov.'s award, 1982, cert. appreciation City of Idaho Falls/Mayor Campbell, 1982, 87, Bus. Women of the Yr. award C. of C., 1998, Gifar Anne Alexander award Greater Idaho Falls Assoc. of Realtors, 2007; named to Two Million Dollar Club, 1987, 88, Four Million Dollar Club, 1989, 90, Top Investment Sales Person for Eastern Idaho, 1985, Realtor of Yr. Idaho Falls Bd. Realtors, 1990, Outstanding Realtors Active in Politics, Women of Yr. Am. Biog. Inst., 1991, Profiles of Top Prodrs. award Real Estate Edn. Assn., Above the Crowd award 1997; named Western Region Power Leader, Darryl Davis Seminars, Lifetime Achievement award Idaho Falls Assn. Relators, 2008 Mem. Nat. Spkrs. Assn., Idaho Falls Bd. Realtors (chmn. Orientation 1982-83, chmn. edn. 1983, chmn. legis. com. 1989, 95—, chmn. program com. 1990, 91), Idaho Assn. Realtors (pres. Million Dollar Club 1988-2001, edn. com. 1990-93, Mem. of Yr. 1991), Idaho Women's Coun. Realtors (Mem. of Yr. 2006, 2007), Am. Bus. Women's Assn., So. Ill. U. Alumni Assn., Idaho Falls C. of C. (Bus. Woman of the Yr.-Professions, 1997), newcomers Club, Civitan (pres. Idaho Falls chpt. 1988-89, Civitan of Yr. 1986, 97, Outstanding Pres. award 1990, Hall of Fame 1998), Real Estate Educators Assn. Office: RE/MAX Homestead Inc 1301 E 17th St Ste 1 Idaho Falls ID 83404-6273 E-mail: thorsen@srv.net.

THORSON, ALAN GLEN, surgeon; b. Omaha, June 20, 1952; s. E. Wallace and Vendela Marie (Havenstein) T.; m. Nancy Lois Maricle, Apr. 18, 1981; children: Alicia Marie, Scott Alan, Katherine Elizabeth. BS in Agrl. Econs., U. Nebr., 1974, BA in Internat. Rels., 1976; MD, U. Nebr., Omaha, 1979, cert. gen. surgery, 1984. Diplomate Am. Bd. Med. Examiners, Am. Bd. Surgery, Am. Bd. Colon and Rectal Surgery. Intern gen. surgery U. Nebr. Hosp., Omaha, 1979-80, resident gen. surgery, 1980-84; fellow colon and rectal surgery U. Minn., Mpls., 1984-85; sec. Colon and Rectal Surgery, Inc., Omaha, 1987-89, v.p., 1989—2008, pres., 2008; clin. asst. prof. surgery U. Nebr. Coll. Medicine, Omaha, 1985-93, clin. assoc. prof., surgery, 1993—2009, clin. prof. surgery, 2009—; clin. asst. prof. surgery Creighton U. Sch. Medicine, Omaha, 1986-88, asst. prof. surgery, 1989-92, assoc. prof. surgery, 1992—2002, program dir. sect. colon and rectal surgery, 1988—, clin. assoc. prof. surgery, 2002—09, clin. prof., 2009—. V.p. Todd Valley Farms, Inc., Mead, Nebr., 1988—; med. advisor United Ostomy Assn., Omaha chpt., 1986—; assoc. examiner Am. Bd. Colon and Rectal Surgery, 1993-96, mem 1998-2005, pres. 2004-05, CARES(chair, Nebr., 2003-) Contbr. articles to profl. jours., chapters to medical textbooks. Trustee Nebr. satellite Crohn's Colitis Found. of Am., 1992—93, med. adv. bd. Nebr. satellite, Rocky Mt. chpt., 2007—08, med. adv. bd. Nebr. chpt., 2008—; pres. Met. Omaha Med. Soc., 1999—2000, Nebr. Med. Assn., 2003—04, Met. Omaha Med. Assn., 2006—; 1st v.p. St. Andrews United Meth. Ch., 2008; pres. elect Am. Cancer Soc., 2009; mem. adminstrv. bd. Faith Westwood United Meth. Ch., Omaha, 1988—92; active health ministries St. Andrews United Meth. Ch., Omaha, 2006—; bd. dirs. Nebr. divsn. Am. Cancer Soc., 1991—96, pres. Nebr. divsn., 1995—96, sec. Heartland divsn., 1998—99, vice chair Heartland divsn., 1999—2000, chmn. Heartland divsn., 2000—03, chief med. office High Plains divsn., 2005—07, pres. Cancer Action Network, 2004—06, 2d v.p. Nat. Bd., 2007—, 1st v.p. Nat. Bd., 2008, nat. bd. pres., 2009—. Fellow ACS, Am. Soc. Colon and Rectal Surgeons (treas. 2007—), Southwestern Surg. Congress (sec.-treas. 1999-2005, v.p 2005-06, pres. elect., 2006-07, pres. 2007-08), Soc. Surg. Oncology; mem. AMA, Am. Soc. Colon Rectal Surgeons (treas. Rsch. Found. 2007-), Am. Soc. Gastrointestinal Endoscopy, Soc. Surgery Alimentary Tract, Soc. Am. Gastrointestinal Endoscopic Surgeons, Wilderness Med. Soc., Nebr. Med. Assn. (pres. 2003-04), Omaha Midwest Clin. Soc., Assn. Program Dirs. for Colon and Rectal Surgery (pres. 1996-99), Am. Assn. Clin. Anatomists, Met. Omaha Midwest Soc. (pres. 1999-2000, sec., treas. found. 2005—). Avocations: swimming, backpacking, landscape painting in oil. Office: Colon and Rectal Surgery 9850 Nicholas St Ste 100 Omaha NE 68114 Office Phone: 402-343-1122.

THORSON, CONNIE CAPERS, library educator; b. Dallas, July 25, 1940; d. Ewing Ashby and Constance (Romberg) Capers; m. James Llewellyn, June 6, 1970. BA, U. Ark., 1962, MA, 1964; PhD, U. N.Mex., 1970; MS in Library Sci., U. Ill., 1977. Instr. English S.E. Mo. State U., Cape Girardeau, 1963-67; with U. N.Mex., Albuquerque, 1970-71, 79-95, acquisitions libr., 1980-94, head reference, 1994-95, assoc. prof. libr., 1984-90, prof., 1990-95, prof. emerita, 1995—; prof., libr. dir. Allegheny Coll., Meadville, Pa., 1995—2000, ret., 2000—; Fulbright sr. scholar Belarus, 2005—06. Author: The RFP Process: Effective Management of the Acquisition of Library Materials, 1998; editor: A Million Stars, 1981, Pocket Companion for Oxford, 1989. Scholar, Fulbright Found., 2005—. Mem. South Cen. Soc. for 18th Century Studies (pres. elect 1988-89, pres. 1989-90, 2002-2003), Modern Lang. Assn. Am., Am. Soc. for 18th Century Studies, ALA. Avocations: travel, reading, walking.

THORSON, ERIC MINES, federal agency administrator; b. L.A., Dec. 8, 1944; m. Susan Lynn White. BS, USAF Acad., 1967; attended, U. So. Calif. Masters Program in Aerospace Ops., 1969—70. Pres. Executive Aviation Services, 1973—75; dep. asst. sec. Dept. Air Force, US Dept. Def., 1985—89, acting asst. sec., 1989; chief investigator permanent subcom. US Senate, 1995—97, spl. asst. to Rep. leader; pres. Eric M. Thorson & Associates, LLC, 1998—2005; sr. adv. for investigative ops. & agy. planning US Office Pers. Mgmt.; insp. gen. Small Bus. Adminstrn., 2006—08, US Dept. Treasury, 2008—. Pres., chmn. Assn. of Graduates (AOG), 1989—91, dir. reunification com., 2004—05. Served with USAF. Decorated Disting. Flying Cross, Air medal (4), Meritorious Svc. medal, Armed Forces Expeditionary medal, Republic of Viet Nam Campaign medal, Viet Nam Svc. medal, Air Force medal for Exceptional Civilian Svc.; recipient Nat. Def. Svc. medal. Office: US Dept Treasury 1500 Pennsylvania Ave NW Rm 1221 Washington DC 20220*

THORUD, JEFFREY SCOTT, lawyer, legal studies director; b. Natrona Heights, Pa., Sept. 14, 1964; s. Carol Jean Guman. BA in Speech Comm., Edinboro U., Pa., 1989; MPA, Marywood U., Scranton, Pa., 1993; JD, Thomas Jefferson Sch. Law, San Diego, 1998; cert. in Intl. Human Rights Law, Oxford U., England, 1996. Prof. Kelsey-Jenney Coll., San Diego, 1998—2002; acquisitions assoc. Teligent Comm., 1999—2000; acquisitions mgr. Qwest Comm., 2000—02; pres. Oxford Pacific Lending, 2002—. Dir. Utility Incentive Corp., San Diego; adv. bd. mem. Kelsey-Jenney Coll., 2000—01; dir. legal studies Maric Coll., 2003—, adv. bd. mem., 2003—; pres. Oxford Holdings, LLC, 2004—. Contbr. articles to profl. jours. Mem.: Pi Kappa Delta, Alpha Phi Sigma. Office: Maric Coll 9055 Balboa Ave San Diego CA 92123 Business E-Mail: jthorud@mariccollege.edu.

THOULESS, DAVID JAMES, retired physicist, educator; b. Bearsden, Scotland, Sept. 21, 1934; arrived in U.S., 1979, naturalized, 1994; s. Robert Henry and Priscilla (Gorton) T.; m. Margaret Elizabeth Scrase, July 26, 1958; children: Michael, Christopher, Helen. BA, U. Cambridge, Eng., 1955, ScD, 1986; PhD, Cornell U., 1958. Physicist Lawrence Berkeley Lab., Calif., 1958-59; rsch. fellow U. Birmingham, England, 1959—61, prof. math. physics, 1965—78; lectr., fellow Churchill Coll. U. Cambridge, England, 1961—65; prof. physics Queen's U., Kingston, Ont., Canada, 1978; prof. applied sci. Yale U., New Haven, 1979-80; prof. physics U. Wash., Seattle, 1980—2003; ret. Author: Quantum Mechanics of Many Body Systems, 2d edit., 1972, Topological Quantum Numbers in Nonrelativistic Physics, 1998. Recipient Maxwell medal Inst. Physics, 1973, Holweck prize Soc. Francaise de Physique-Inst. Physics, 1980, Fritz London award for Low temperature physics, Fritz London Meml. Fund, 1984, Wolf prize in physics, Wolf Found., Israel, 1990, Paul Dirac medal Inst. Physics, 1993, Lars Onsager prize Am. Phys. Soc., 2000; Edwin Uehling disting. scholar U. Wash., 1988-98. Fellow: Royal Soc.; mem.: NAS. Office: U Wash PO Box 351560 Seattle WA 98195-1560 Business E-Mail: Thouless@u.washington.edu.

THOYER, JUDITH REINHARDT, lawyer; b. Mt. Vernon, NY, July 29, 1940; d. Edgar Allen and Florence (Mayer) Reinhardt; m. Michael E. Thoyer, June 30, 1963; children: Erinn Thoyer Rhodes, Michael John. AB with honors, U. Mich., 1961; LLB summa cum laude, Columbia U., 1965. Bar: N.Y. 1966, D.C. 1984. Law libr. U. Ghana, Accra, Africa, 1963-64; assoc. Paul, Weiss, Rifkind, Wharton & Garrison, NYC, 1966-75, ptnr., 1975—. Mem. TriBar Opinion Com., 1995—. Bd. visitors Law Sch. Columbia U., N.Y.C., 1991—; bd. dirs. Women's Action Alliance, N.Y.C., 1975-89, pro bono counsel, 1975-97; mem. Women's Coun. Dem. Senatorial, campaign com., 1993-97; organizing com. Alumnae Columbia Law Sch., 1996—. Recipient medal for excellence, Columbia Law Sch., 2003. Fellow NY Bar Found. (elected 2008); mem. N.Y. County Lawyers Assn. (mem. securities and exchs. com. 1976-98), Assn. of Bar of City of N.Y. (mem. securities regulation com. 1976-79, mem. recruitment of lawyers com. 1980-82, mem. com. on mergers, acquisitions and corp. control contests 1996-2007). Home: 1115 5th Ave Apt 3B New York NY 10128-0100 Office: Paul Weiss Rifkind Et Al 1285 Ave of Americas New York NY 10019-6028

THRALL, ARTHUR ALVIN, artist, educator; b. Milw., Mar. 18, 1926; s. Irving and Helen (Fabich) T.; m. Winifred Rogers, 1960; children: Grant, Wade, Sara, Jay. BS, Milw. State Tchrs. Coll., 1950; MS, U. Wis., Milw., 1954; postgrad. (fellow), U. Ill., 1954-55. Tchr. art Lincoln Jr. High Sch., Kenosha, Wis., 1951-54; asst. prof. SUNY, Geneseo, 1955-56; assoc. prof. Milw.-Downer Coll., 1956-64; prof., Farrar-Marrs prof. fine arts Lawrence U., Appleton, Wis., 1964-90, prof. emeritus, 1990—. One-man shows include Smithsonian Instn., 1960, U. Dubuque, Iowa, 1993, Mt. Mary Coll., Milw., 1994, St. Norbert Coll, De Pere, Wis., 1995, Cardinal Stritch U., Milw., 1998, also others; group shows include Corcoran bienials, Washington, 1951, 53, 55, 57, 62, Bklyn. Mus. annuals, Mus. Modern Art, N.Y.C., NAD, N,Y,C, Audubon Artists, N.Y.C., 1985, S.A.G.A., N.Y.C., 1985, Charles Allis Art Mus., Milw., 1996, Miller Art Ctr., Sturgeon Bay, Wis., 1997, Elvehem Mus. Art, Madison, Wis., 1998, 99, Fairfield Gallery, Sturgeon Bay, Wis., 2001; represented in permanent collections Tate Gallery, Victoria and Alberta Mus., Brit. Mus., all London, Phila. Mus., Seattle Mus., Art Inst. Chgo., Bklyn. Mus., others. Served with U.S. Army, 1944-46, ETO. Recipient Bklyn. Mus. print awards 1952, 64; Pa. Acad. Arts award 1960; NAD awards 1956, 68); Louis Comfort Tiffany fellow, 1963 Mem. AAUP, Boston Printmakers (awards 1963, 65), Soc. Am. Graphic Artists (awards 1951-52, 60, 78, 2000), Audubon Artists Inc. (award 1977) Home: 4225 N Woodburn St Milwaukee WI 53211-1504

THRALL, GORDON FISH, publishing executive; b. Jamestown, NY, July 28, 1923; s. Clyde Lowell and Beulah Mae (Fish) Thrall; m. Betty Jane Roberts Thrall, Sept. 24, 1964 (dec. May 28, 2005); 1 child, Jenifer Jane. AB in History & Polit. Sci., Alfred U., 1949; JD, Baylor U., 1953. Bar: Tex. 1953, US Supreme Ct. 1957, DC 1958, US Ct. Appeals (DC cir.) 1958, US Ct. Mil. Appeals 1958, US Dist. Ct. (ea. dist.) Tex. 1976, US Ct. Appeals (5th cir.) 1986. Law clk. US Dist. Ct. (ea. dist.) Tex., 1953—54; asst. prosecutor Dallas County Dist. Atty., 1954—55; assoc. firm Phinney & Hallman, Dallas, 1955—56; asst. Tex. Atty. Gen., 1957; adviser, examiner ICC, Washington, 1957—59; asst. gen. counsel Tex. State Bar, Austin, 1959—61; county atty. Reagan County, Big Lake, Tex., 1961—72; ptnr. Norman, Thrall, Angle, Guy & Day LLP, Jacksonville, Tex., 1972—2002; v.p. Heflin & Thrall Lang. Publs. Inc., 2002—. Mem. exec. com. Tex. Bapt. Gen. Conv., 1965—70, adminstrv. bd., 1991—95; deacon Southern Bapt. Ch.; chmn. Permian Basin Dist. Concho Valley Coun. Boy Scouts America, Big Lake, 1965—66, Jacksonville United Fund Drive, 1987, pres., 89, Cherokee County Health Facilities Devel. Corp., 1982—; v.p., bd. dirs. Travis Towers Retirement Facility, Jacksonville, 1980—2003; co-trustee Summers A. Norman Found., 1988—2002; mem. Nan Travis Meml. Hosp. Found. Bd., 1994—; pres. bd. visitors Jacksonville Coll., 1998—2003. Mem.: Jacksonville C. of C. (pres. 1979), Big Lake C. of C. (pres. 1963, 1967), Tex. Bar Found., Tex. State Bar (vice chmn. UPL com. 1964), Masons (32 Degree award), Big Lake Lions (pres. 1969), Kiwanis (pres. 1978, lt. gov. divsn. 34 1982), Cherokee Country Club (dir. 1981—83). Republican. Home: 702 Fort Worth St Jacksonville TX 75766-2610 Office: Heflin and Thrall Lang Publs Inc PO Box 1724 Jacksonville TX 75766 Office Phone: 903-586-2445. Business E-Mail: jheflin@language-publications.com.

THRALL, GRANT IAN, geography educator, software developer-consultant; b. San Gabriel, Calif., June 29, 1947; s. William Herman and Carolyn May (Brown) T.; m. Susan Mary Elshaw, July 16, 1977. BA, Calif. State U., Los Angeles, 1970; MA, Ohio State U., Columbus, 1972, PhD, 1975. Asst. prof. McMaster U., Hamilton, Ontario, Can., 1975-78; assoc. prof. SUNY, Buffalo, 1978-83; prof. U. Fla., Gainesville, 1983—. Vis. disting. prof. San Diego State U., 1990; pres., co-founder Spatial Decisions and Analysis, Gainesville, 1992—; cons. Gainesville Regional Utilities, 1988, real estate market analysis and geog. info. sys. to numerous cos. throughout U.S., 1985—; vice chmn. Task Force on Countywide Land Use Plan, Alachua County, Fla., 1987-90; advisor various Fla. cities on geog. inf. sys., econ. devel. and land use plans; chmn. bd. dirs. Downtown Gainesville Redevel. Agy. Author: Land Use and Urban Form, 1987, Spatial Diffusion, 1988; editor: Scientific Geography Series, 10 vols., 1984—; assoc. editor Computers, Environ. and Urban Sys.; mem. editl. bd., columnist Geog. Info. Sys.; co-editor Jour. Real Estate Lit., 1991—; contbr. articles to profl. jours. and newspapers. Mem. Visions 2000, Alachua County, Fla., 1987-89. Fellow Weimer Sch. for Advanced Studies in Real Estate and Land Econs., 1990—; receipient rsch. grants various pvt. firms, pub. agys., U.S. Army, Homer Hoyt Inst., Washington. Mem. Am. Economic Assn., Assn. of Am. Geographers (Math. Models and Quantitative Methods Specialty Group chmn. 1982-84), Regional Sci. Assn., Canadian Assn. of Geographers, Am. Real Estate Soc., Nat. Assn. Realtors (grantee). Avocations: scuba diving, skiing, sports cars. microcomputers. Office: U Fla 3121 Turlington Gainesville FL 32611 Home: 8703 SW 38th Ave Gainesville FL 32608-8695

THRALL, JAMES HUNTER, radiologist, educator; b. Ann Arbor, Mich., 1943; BA, U. Mich., Ann Arbor, 1964, MD, 1968. Intern Walter Reed Army Med. Ctr., Washington, 1968-69, resident in radiology, 1969-72, fellow in nuclear medicine, 1972-73, asst. chief nuclear med. svc. dept. radiology, 1973-75; asst. prof. radiology and nuclear medicine U. Mich., Ann Arbor, 1975-78, assoc. prof., 1978-81, prof., 1981-83; chmn. radiology dept. Henry Ford Hosp., Detroit, 1983; Juan M. Taveras prof. radiology Harvard Med. Sch., Cambridge, Mass., 1988—, chmn. dept. radiology; radiologist-in-chief Mass. Gen. Hosp., Boston, 1988—. Cons. nuclear medicine Ann Arbor VA Hosp.; chmn. bd. dirs. Mobile

Aspects; co-founder, bd. chmn. WorldCare Ltd., 1992; chair exec. com. Harvard Depts. Radiology; hon. lectr. European Soc. Radiology, 2008. Contbr. articles to profl. jours.; mem. editl. bd.: Jour. Nuc. Medicine, Internat. Jour. Cardiac Imaging, Investigative Radiology, Jour. the Am. Coll. Radiology. Bd. trustees Mass. Gen. Physicians Orgn., Rsch. and Edn. Found. the Radiol. Soc. North America; bd. councilors Soc. Chiefs Academic Radiology Depts.; chair internat. medicine com. Mass. Gen. Hosp.; mem. Am. Coll. Radiology Found. Maj. M.C. US Army, 1968—75. Recipient Excellence of Leadership award, Diagnostic Imaging mag. Fellow: Am. Coll. Radiology (chmn. bd. chancellors 2008—, mem. Web site adv. com., past chmn. commn. on molecular imaging); mem.: Radiol. Soc. North America (Gold medal 2007), Am. Roentgen Ray Soc. (past. pres., Gold medal 2007). Office: Mass Gen Hosp 14 Fruit St PO Box 9657 M2-FND 216 Boston MA 02114*

THRASH, PATRICIA ANN, retired educational association administrator; b. Grenada, Miss., May 4, 1929; d. Lewis Edgar and Weaver (Betts) T. BS, Delta State Coll., 1950; LHD (hon.), Delta State U., 2007; MA, Northwestern U., Evanston, Ill., 1953, PhD, 1959; cert. Inst. Edn. Mgmt., Harvard U., Cambridge, Mass., 1983; EdD (hon.), Vincennes U., Ind., 1997; LHD, Drake U., Des Moines, 1997, Adrian Coll., Mich., 1998; LHD (hon.), Delta State U., Cleveland, Miss., 2007. Tchr. high sch. English, Clarksdale, Miss., 1950-52; head resident Northwestern U., 1953-55, asst. to dean women, 1955-58, asst. dean women, 1958-60, lectr. edn., 1959-65, dean women, 1960-69, assoc. prof. edn., 1965-72, assoc. dean students, 1969-71; asst. exec. sec. Commn. on Instns. Higher Edn., North Central Assn. Colls. and Schs., 1972-73, assoc. exec. dir., 1973-76, assoc. dir., 1976-87, exec. dir., 1988-96; exec. dir. emeritus, 1997—. Adv. panel Am. Coun. on Edn., MIVER program evaluation mil. base program, 1991-94; nat. adv. panel Nat. Ctr. Postsecondary Tchg., Learning & Assessment, 1991-95. Author (with others): Handbook of College and University Administration, 1970; editor Jour. Northwestern U. Inst. for Learning in Retirement, 2000-02, 2008-, course coord., 2000—; contbr. articles to ednl. jours. Bd. dirs. Delta State U. Found., 2000-02. Mem. Nat. Assn. Women Deans and Counselors (v.p. 1967-69, pres. 1972-73), Ill. Assn. Women Deans and Counselors (sec. 1961-63, pres. 1964-66), Am. Coll. Pers. Assn. (editl. bd. jour. 1971-74), Coun. Student Pers. Assns. in Higher Edn. (program nominations com. 1974-75, adv. panel Am. Coll. Testing Coll. Outcome Measures project 1977-78, staff Coun. on Postsecondary Accreditation project for evaluation nontraditional edn. 1977-78, mem. editl. bd. Jour. Higher Edn. 1975-80, guest editor Mar.-Apr. 1979, co-editor NCA Quar. 1988-96, vice-chair regional accrediting dirs. group 1993, exec. com. Nat. Policy Bd. for Higher Edn. Inst. 1993-95), Mortar Bd. (hon.), Phi Delta Theta, Pi Lambda Theta, Alpha Psi Omega, Alpha Lambda Delta. Methodist. Home: 2337 Hartrey Ave Evanston IL 60201-2552 Personal E-mail: patsy1941@comcast.net.

THRASHER, FAY C., clinical psychologist; b. Wynne, Ark., Dec. 17, 1935; d. Andrew J. and Joy M. (Charles) Thrasher; children: Jeffrey K. Mitchell, Sidney J. Guidroz Jr. MEd, McNeese State U., 1963; MA, La. State U., 1967, PhD, 1970. Lic. psychologist. Chief psychologist Cmty. Mental Health, Lake Charles, La., 1970-73; clin. psychologist VA Hosp., Salisbury, NC, 1973-76; chief psychologist VA Opt Clinic, San Antonio, 1976-77, Alvin C. York VA Med. Ctr., Murfreesboro, Tenn., 1977-87; clin. psychologist VA Med. Ctr., Alexandria, Va., 1990-95, chief psychologist, 1995—. Bd. dirs. Oasis Ministry, Pineville, La.; cons. to freedom cons., 1996—; bd. dirs. New Beginning Acad., Alexandria, treas., 1997—; cons. Bunkie Adolexcent Ctr., Bunkie Gen. Hosp., 1993—97. Chmn. Combined Fed. Campaign, Murfreesboro, 1985—86. Mem.: APA, Am. Coll. Forensic Examiners, Nat. Register. Avocations: bridge, antiques, art, music. Home: 303 Rain Tree Pl Pineville LA 71360-5472 Office: Freedom Counseling Ctr 2809 Donahue Ferry Rd Pineville LA 71360-4513 Office Phone: 318-473-0010 2626. Personal E-mail: drfay@suddenlink.net.

THRASHER, J. BRANTLEY, urologist; MD, Med. U. SC. Diplomate Am. Bd. Urology. Intern Walter Reed Army Med. Ctr.; resident Fitzsimons Army Med. Ctr.; fellow Duke U. Med. Ctr.; program dir. urology residency program Madigan Army Med. Ctr.; prof. & William L. Valk chair. urology. U. Kans. Med. Ctr., 1998—, co-dir. operative svcs. Presenter in field; prin. investigator on numerous clin. and lab. rsch. protocols; co-investigator or collaborator in rsch. funded by CDC and Dept. of Def. Assoc. editor The 5-Minute Urology Consult, coord. editor Prostate Cancer Journal, Prostate Diseases Journal, Practical Reviews in Urology, specialty editor Journal of Urology, mem. editl. adv. bd. Journal of American Family Physician, mem. editl. coun. Urology Times, sect. editor, Cancer Prevention Seminars in Urologic Oncology; contbr. several articles to peer-reviewed jours. Named one of America's Top Physicians in Urologic Oncology, Consumer's Rsch. Coun., 2003, 2006, 2007, Best Doctors in America, Best Doctors Consortium, 2002—06; named to Best Doctors list, Ingram's Bus. Mag., 2003, 2004, Best Doctors, Kansas City Mag., 2002, 2007. Fellow: ACS (chmn. metropolitan Kansas City com. on applicants); mem.: Soc. Urologic Oncology (exec. bd. and chmn. fellowship com.), Am. Urological Assn. (Kansas state rep. to bd. dirs. of the South Ctrl. sect.). Office: University of Kansas Medical Center 3901 Rainbow Blvd Kansas City KS 66160*

THRASHER, ROSE MARIE, critical care and community health nurse; b. Urbana, Ohio, Jan. 19, 1948; d. Jesse and Anna Frances (Clark) T. Student, Mercy Med. Ctr. Sch. Med. Tech., 1966—67, Wittenberg U., Springfield, Ohio, 1969—70; BSN, Ohio State U., 1974, BA in Anthropology, 1994, BA in Art History, 1997, BA in Geography, 2002, postgrad. in Nursing, 2005—09, MSN, 2009. RN, Ohio; bd. cert. cmty. health nurse ANA; cert. provider BCLS and ACLS, Am. Heart Assn., CCRN, AACN; cert. asthma mgmt. edn. Am. Lung Assn. Ohio. Critical care nurse Staff Builders Health Care Svc., Oakland, Calif., 1975—76, 1981—85; supr., case mgr. and home health nurse passport and intermittent care programs Interim Health Care (formerly Med. Pers. Pool), Columbus, Ohio, 1976—77, 1985—2004; pub. health nurse Columbus Health Dept., 1977—78, Vis. Nurse Assn., Atlanta, 1978, Planned Parenthood, Columbus, Ohio, 1979—80; critical care nurse VA Med. Ctr., San Francisco, 1981; chart reviewer Interim Health Care Support Svc., Columbus, 1996—98; IRP nurse Ohio State U. Hosps. East, 1999—2003; ind. home health nurse, provider med. svcs. State of Ohio Dept. Human Svcs., 1999—2005; home health nurse Interim Health Care, Newark and Pataskala, Ohio, 2004—, case mgr., 2007—08; ind. contractor for people with disabilities WOHL Comm. Svcs. Inc., Gaithersburg, Md., 2007—08, Ohio Jobs and Family Svc.; RN Med. Health Sys., Columbus, Ohio, 2008—. Acad. scholar Wittenberg U., Ohio State U. Mem. AACN, ANA (coun. cmty. health nursing), AAUW, AAAS, Internat. Union Anthrop. and Ethnol. Scis., NY Acad. Scis., Ohio Nurses Assn., Intravenous Nurses Soc., Ohio State U. Alumni Assn., Am. Anthrop. Assn., Midwest Art History Soc., Coll. Art Assn., Nat. Mus. Women in Arts, Nat. Women's Hall of Fame, Ohio Acad. Sci., Ohio State U. Coll. of Nursing Alumni Soc. Business E-Mail: thrasher.2@osu.edu.

THREADGILL, HENRY, musician; b. Feb. 15, 1944; Bachelor's in music, Am. Conservatory Music; attended, Governors State U., Ill. Active in Assn. Advancement of Creative Musicians, Chgo.; mem. Muhal Richard Abrams' Experimental Band; toured with Jo Jo Morris, 1965—67; mem. jazz trio Reflection, 1971—75, Air, 1975—. Albums include: X-75, Vol. 1, 1979, When Was That?, 1982, Just the Facts and Pass the Bucket, 1983, Subject to Change, 1984, You Know the Number, 1986, Easily Slip into Another World, 1987, Rag, Bush and All, 1988, Spirit of Nuff...Nuff, 1990, Live at Koncepts, 1991, Too Much, Sugar for a Dime, 1993, Song out of My Trees, 1993, Carry the Day, 1994, Makin' a Move, 1995, Where's Your Cup, 1996, Everybody's Mouth's a Book, 2001, Up Popped the Two Lips, 2001; albums with Air include: Air Song, 1975, Live Air, 1976, Morning Prayer, 1976, Nonaah, 1976, Air Time, 1977, Open Air Suite, 1978, Air Lore, 1979, Air Mail, 1980, Air Show No. 1, 1986, Air Song, 2002; other albums include: Ming, 1980, Memory Serves, 1981, Amarcord Nino Rota, 1982, Rhythm Killers, 1987, Third Power, 1991, So Many Stars, 1993, Deconstruction, 1993, Darn It!, 1994, Blues in the East, 1994, Novus Sampler,1995, numerous others; worked with Air, Bill Laswell, George Lewis, Paul Haines, Fred Hopkins, Bahia Black, Material, Nino Rota, The Jungle Brothers, Tony Trischka, Bernie Worrell, Chet Baker, others. Fellow US Artists, 2008. Office: c/o Sony Music 550 Madison Ave New York NY 10022-3211*

THREATS, TRAVIS T., speech-language pathologist; b. Kansas City, Kans., Nov. 13, 1960; s. Johnny and Edna Threats; m. Susan Colbert, Aug. 1, 1986. BS summa cum laude, Kans. State U., 1982; MA, U. Ill., 1984; PhD, Northwestern U., 1988. Cert. CCC-SP. Speech-lang. pathologist Easter Seals, Chgo.; clin. profl. assoc. InSpeech, Inc., Valley Forge, Pa.; speech-lang. pathologist, InterRehab bus. mgr. Marianjoy Rehab. Ctr., Wheaton, Ill. CIC Minority Doctoral fellow, Univ. fellow Northwestern U.; McMillan scholar. Mem. Am. Speech-Lang.-Hearing Assn., Nat. Black Assn. for Speech, Lang. and Hearing, Ill. Speech Hearing Assn., Chgo. Speech and Hearing Assn., Phi Kappa Phi. Home: 13700 Fairhill Rd Apt 411 Cleveland OH 44120-1275

THREEFOOT, SAM ABRAHAM, physician, educator; b. Meridian, Miss., Apr. 10, 1921; s. Sam Abraham and Ruth Frances (Lilienthal) Threefoot; m. Virginia Rush, Feb. 6, 1954; children: Barbara Jane Stockton Mattingly, Ginny Ruth Threefoot Lindberg, Tracyann Threefoot Esenstad, Shelley Ann Cowan. BS, Tulane U., New Orleans, 1943, MD, 1945. Diplomate: Am. Bd. Internal Medicine. Intern Michael Reese Hosp., Chgo., 1945-47; asst. vis. physician Charity Hosp. New Orleans, 1947-50, vis. physician, 1950-57, sr. vis. physician, 1957-69, cons., 1969-70, 76-91; clin. asst. dept. medicine Touro Infirmary, New Orleans, 1953-56, jr. asst., 1956-60, sr. asst., 1960-63, dir. med. edn., 1953-63, dir. research, 1953-70, sr. dept. medicine, 1963-70; fellow dept. medicine Tulane U., 1947-49, instr., 1948-53, asst. prof., 1953-59, asso. prof., 1959-63, prof., 1963-70, 76-91, prof. emeritus, 1991—, asst. dean, 1979-91, adj. prof. emeritus Sch. Pub. Health & Tropical Medicine, 1993—; chief of staff VA Hosp. (Forest Hills div.), Augusta, Ga., 1970-76; asso. chief staff VA Hosp., New Orleans, 1976-79, chief of staff, 1979-91, cons., 1991—97; asst. dean Med. Coll. Ga., 1970-76, prof. medicine, 1970-76. Cons. physician Lallie Kemp Charity Hosp. Independence, La., 1951-53 Editor: Lymphology, 1967-70, sr. mem. editl. bd.; Contbr. articles profl. jours. Served with AUS, 1943-45. La. Heart Assn. grantee, 1953-55; John A. Hartford Found. grantee, 1956-74; Am. Heart Assn. grantee, 1959-61; USPHS grantee, 1953-66 Fellow ACP, Am. Coll. Cardiology, NY Acad. Sci.; mem. Am. Heart Assn. (v.p. 1970, fellow council on circulation), Central Soc. Clin. Research, So. Soc. Clin. Investigation (pres. 1967), AAAS, Internat. Soc. Lymphology, Soc. Exptl. Biology and Medicine, Soc. Nuclear Medicine, Microcirculatory Conf., Inc., Am. Fedn. Clin. Research, La. Heart Assn. (pres. 1967), Nat. Assn. VA Chiefs of Staff (pres. 1987-88), Phi Beta Kappa, Sigma Xi. Jewish. Home: 1750 St Charles Ave Unit 616 New Orleans LA 70130 Office Phone: 504-524-3668. Personal E-mail: threefoot@bellsouth.net. *I am one of those fortunate individuals who has been able to approach goals set early in life. Although my achievements are far short of my aspirations, at least I have had the opportunity. In dealing with both people and things, I have always felt that no detail was too small to receive attention.*

THREET, JOHN T., principal; m. Kay Moore. BS in Elem. Edn., U. Tex., Austin, 1979; MS in Edn., Houston Bapt. U., Tex., 1989. Cert. tchr. elem. edn. State Bd. Educator Cert., Tex., 1979, tchr. kindergarten State Bd. Educator Cert., Tex., 1979, tchr. English 6-8 State Bd. Educator Cert., Tex., 1985, mid-mgmt. State Bd. Educator Cert., Tex., 1989. Tchr. 2nd grade Brill elem. sch. Klein Ind. Sch. Dist., Spring, Tex., 1979—80; tchr. English Welch mid. sch. Houston Ind. Sch. Dist., 1984—90, asst. prin. DeChaumes elem. sch., 1990—92, asst. prin. Garcia elem. sch., 1993—93, prin. Stevens elem. sch., 1993—96, prin. West. U. elem. sch., 1996—. Chmn. bd. elders Meml. Luth. Ch., Houston, 2004—06. Named Outstanding Grad. Student in Edn., Houston Bapt. U. Kappa Delta Pi, 1988, Elem. Prin. of Yr., Ctrl. Dist., Houston Ind. Sch. Dist., 2002, 2003. Mem.: Houston Assn. Sch. Administrs. (pres. 2001—02), Coun. Young Children, Internat. Reading Assn., Nat. Coun. Tchrs. Math., Nat. Assn. Elem. Sch. Prins. Lutheran. Office: West Univ Elem Sch 3756 Univ Blvd Houston TX 77005

THRELKELD, RICHARD DAVIS, retired broadcast journalist; b. Cedar Rapids, Iowa, Nov. 30, 1937; s. Robert M. and Lou Jane (Davis) T.; m. Sharon A. Adams, June 11, 1960 (div. 1983); children: Susan Anne, Julia Lynn; m. Betsy Aaron, May 15, 1983. BA, Ripon Coll., 1959, LHD (hon.), 1989; MS in Journalism, Northwestern U., 1961. Editor Sta. WHAS-TV, Louisville, 1961; reporter Sta. WMT-TV, Cedar Rapids, Iowa, 1961-66; corr. CBS News, NYC and San Francisco, 1966-82, nat. corr., 1989-96, Moscow corr., 1996-98, ret., 1998; chief corr. ABC News NY, NYC, 1982-89. Author: Dispatches From the Former Evil Empire, 2001; corr.: TV news report Rhodesia Remembered, 1980 (Overseas Press Club Award), Lebanon-Grenada, 1983 (Overseas Press Club Award), Vietnam Remembered, 1985 (Emmy Award); TV news documentary Defense of America, 1981 (Emmy Award); TV news series Status Reports, 1984 (Alfred I. Dupont-Columbia U. Award). Named to Hall of Achievement, Medill Sch. Journalism, Northwestern U., 2004; CBS News Fellow, 1964. Mem.: Soc. Profl. Journalists. Home: # 33 Robins Way East Hampton NY 11937 Personal E-mail: threlkeld37@gmail.com.

THRESHER, MARK R., insurance company executive; B in Acctg., Otterbein Coll., Westerville, Ohio. With KPMG LLP; v.p., treas. Nationwide Fin. Svcs., Inc., 1996, sr. v.p., CFO, pres., COO Fin., 2004—. Trustee Otterbein Coll., mem. investment and audit coms.; mem. Ctr. of Sci. and Industry (COSI) Columbus Adv. Coun. Mem.: AICPA, Fin. Svcs. Roundtable, Am. Coun. Life Insurers (mem. exec. roundtable com., mem. retirement & fin. security steering com.), Assn. Ohio Life Ins. Cos. Office: Nationwide Fin Svcs Inc One Nationwide Plz Columbus OH 43215-2220

THRO, WILLIAM EUGENE, lawyer, professor, university administrator; b. Elizabethtown, Ky., Nov. 8, 1963; s. Ernest Guernsey and Joan (Young) T.; children: Sandra Lucinda Grace Edwards-Thro, William Thomas Daniel Edwards-Thro, Noah Christopher James Edwards-Thro.; m. Julie Urback, Sept. 04, 2004. BA, Hanover Coll., Ind., 1986; MA, U. Melbourne, Australia, 1988; JD, U. Va., Charlottesville, 1990. Bar: Ky. 1990, Colo. 1991, Va. 1998, US Dist. Ct. (we. dist.) Ky. 1990, US Dist. Ct. Colo. 1991, US Ct. Appeals (6th and 10th cirs.) 1991, US Ct. Appeals (3d cir.) 1993, US Supreme Ct. 1993, US Ct. Appeals (4th cir.) 1997, US Dist. Ct. (ea. dist.) Va. 1998, US Dist. Ct. (we. dist.) Va. 1998, US Ct. Appeals (DC cir.) 1999, US Bankruptcy Ct. (ea. and we. dists.) Va. 1999, US Dist. Ct. (ea. dist.) Ky. 2003, US Dist. Ct. (no. dist.) Ill. 2003, US Ct. Appeals (7th cir.), 2005, US Ct. Appeals (8th cir.), 2006. Jud. clk. Judge Ronald E. Meredith, US Dist. Ct. (we. dist.) Ky., Louisville, 1990-91; asst. atty. gen. State of Colo., Denver, 1991-97, Commonwealth of Va., Richmond, 1997—99; gen. counsel Christopher Newport U., Newport News, 2000—04, u. counsel, 2008—, asst. prof. govt., 2008—; dep. state solicitor gen. Commonwealth Va., 2002—04, state solicitor gen., 2004—08. Author: Why You Cannot Sue State U: A Guide to Sovereign Immunity, 2001, 2d edit., 2007; co-author: Race Conscious Admissions and Financial Aid After the University of Michigan Decisions, 2004; co-editor: The NACUA Handbook for Lawyers New to Higher Education, 2003, 2d edit., 2007, 3rd edit 2009, Free Speech in Higher Education, 2008; mem. editl. bd. Coll. and Univ. Law, 2000—, vice chair, 2004-05, chair, 2005-08; mem. editl. bd. Encyclopedia of Edn. Law, 2005-08, Internat. Jour. Edn. Reform, 2008-; adv. bd. mem. Ency. Higher Edn. Law, 2008-; mem. author's com. West's Edn. Law Reporter, 1992-2007, mem. editl adv. com., 2007-; contbr. articles to profl. jours. Mem. LaCrosse Presbyn. Ch.; elder Presbyn. Ch. USA, 2007—; gen. counsel adv. bd. NCAA, 2001—04. Recipient Best Brief award, Nat. Assn. of Attys. Gen., 2003—04, Hardin County Sch. Disting. Alumni award, 2004; fellow, Nat. Assn. Coll. U. Attorneys, 2007; scholar U.S. Senate Youth scholar, Hearst Found., 1982, Harry S Truman scholar, Truman Scholarship Found., 1984, Rotary Internat. Ambassadorial scholar, Melbourne, 1987. Mem.: Va. Bar Assn., South Africa Edn. Law Assn., Edn. Law Assn., Nat. Assn. Coll. and U. Attys., Ky. Bar Assn., Federalist Soc., Nat. Eagle Scout Assn., Hon. Order of Ky. Cols. Republican. Presbyterian. Office: 1 University Pl Newport News VA 23606 Office Phone: 757-594-7571. Personal E-mail: withro@cox.net. Business E-Mail: wthro@cnu.edu.

THROCKMORTON, PETER EUGENE, retired organic chemist, consultant; b. St. Paul, Jan. 20, 1927; s. James and Carla Margaret (Strim) T.; m. Phyllis Marie McGrew, June 30, 1948; children: Ann Marie, Carla Louise, Peter Eugene Jr. BSChemE, U. Minn., 1948, MS in Chemistry, 1955; PhD in Organic Chemistry, Kansas State U., 1960. Rsch. engr. Tainton Products Co., Balt., 1948-49; mfg. rsch. engr. Glenn L. Martin Aircraft Co., Middle River, Md., 1949-52; rsch. chemist Gen. Mills Rsch., Inc., Mpls., 1952-56; petroleum fellow Petroleum Rsch. Inst. Kans. State U., Manhattan, 1957-58; assoc. chemist Midwest Rsch. Inst., Kansas City, Mo., 1960-65; sr. rsch. chemist Archer-Daniels-Midland Co., Mpls., 1965-67; sr. rsch. chemist II Ashland Chem. Co. (formerly Archer-Daniels-Midland Co.), Columbus, Ohio, 1967-86; prin. Throckmorton Cons., Plain City, Ohio, 1986-95; cons. Teltech, Inc., Mpls., 1991-96; ret. Assoc. chmn. 15th Ann. Kansas City Chemistry Conf., 1963; mem. People's Republic China-U.S. Sci. Exchange Program, Beijing and Shanghai, 1984. Contbr. over 27 articles to profl. jours. including Modern Plastics, Jour. Am. Chem. Soc., Jour. Elastoplastics, Jour. Am. Oil Chemists Soc., Inorganica Chimica Acta. Recipient Best Paper award Reinforced Plastics Div. of Soc. Plastics Industry, 1963. Fellow Am. Inst. Chemists (bd. dirs. 1987-89); mem. AAAS, Am. Chem. Soc. (chmn. tech. program Columbus sect. 1979-80), Am. Oil Chemists Soc. (editl. reviewer 1986-91), Sigma Xi, Phi Lambda Upsilon. Democrat. Achievements include 17 patents, including patent for trimethylene sulfide chemical derivative that when chemically reacted into a well-known plastic provided a substance highly resistant to deterioration by strong radiation, such as gamma rays; derivation of new, effective, very biodegradable surfactants from cornstarch and a fatty substance; novel, highly effective palladium-lead acetate complex oxidation catalyst for aromatics; new blend of melamine and polyol chemicals for fire retardant plastic. Home: 114 Colchester Drive Normal IL 61761-2775 Personal E-mail: petethrk@hotmail.com.

THROCKMORTON, WARREN, psychology professor, consultant; b. Portsmouth, Ohio, 1957; s. Earl A. and Lillian Throckmorton; m. Deborah Sanderlin; children: Sarah Hipps, Anna, Emma, Levi. PhD, Ohio U., Athens, 1992. Cert. profl. clin. counseling Ohio, 1984. Assoc. prof. psychology Grove City Coll., Pa., 1994—; fellow psychology & pub. policy Ctr. Vision & Values, Grove City, 2005—. Mem., govt. relationship com. ACA, Alexandria, Va., 1995—97; editor WThrockmorton.com, Grove City, Pa., 2004—09. Prodr.: (documentaries) I Do Exist. Leader Fellowship Cmty. Ch., Grove City. Recipient Alumni of Yr., Ohio U. Counselor Edn. Dept, 1997. Mem.: Am. Mental Health Counselors Assn. (life; newsletter 1994—96, pres. 1997—98, Chair. Ethics Com., Counselor of Yr. award 1991). Avocations: writing, backgammon. Office: Grove City Coll 100 Campus Drive Grove City PA 16127 Personal E-mail: warrenthrockmorton@gmail.com.

THRODAHL, MARK CRANDALL, medical products executive; b. Charleston, W.Va., Mar. 31, 1951; s. Monte Cordon and Josephine (Crandall) T.; m. Sudie Kenton, Oct. 21, 1978; children: Mary Elizabeth, Anne Katherine, Andrew Kenton. AB, Princeton U., 1973; MBA, Harvard U., Boston, 1975. Various positions Mallinckrodt, Inc., St. Louis, 1975-88; dir. corp. planning Becton Dickinson & Co., Franklin Lakes, NJ, 1988-91, pres. Nippon Becton Dickinson Tokyo, 1991-94, sector pres. Franklin Lakes, 1994-95, sr. v.p., 1995-2001; CEO Consort Med., London, 2001—. Mem. Old Warson Country Club, Ivy Club. Republican. Episcopalian. Home: 38 Carteret Rd Allendale NJ 07401-1850 Office: PO Box 708 Warsaw IN 46581-0708 Business E-Mail: mark.throdahl@gmail.com.

THRONER, GUY CHARLES, JR., aerospace engineering executive, scientist, inventor, consultant; b. Mpls., Sept. 14, 1919; s. Guy Charles and Marie (Zechar) T.; m. Jean wellington Holt, Dec. 5, 1943; children— Richard, Carol Anne, Steven. BA in Sci., Oberlin Coll., 1943; postgrad., UCLA, 1960-61. Registered profl. engr., Calif. Br. head Naval Weapon Ctr., China Lake, Calif., 1946-53; mgr. ordnance div., mgr. weapon systems div. Aerojet Gen. Corp., Azusa, Calif., 1953-64; v.p., div. mgr. FMC Corp., San Jose, Calif., 1964-74; research dir. Vacu Blast Corp., Belmont, Calif., 1976-78; v.p., devel. mfg. Dahlman, Inc., Braham, Minn., 1978-79; mgr. ordnance systems & tech. Battelle Meml. Inst., Columbus, Ohio, 1979—86; pres. Guy C. Throner & Assocs., tech. and mgmt. cons., 1986—96; aerojet gen. v.p. Kirby Steel Co.; v.p. mgr. Def. Tech. Devsn. FMC Corp.; designer Ship Salvage Equipment. Dir. Omron Corp. Am., Chgo., 1976-77 Inventor, patentee indls., med. and mil. systems design, contbr. articles to tech. papers. Served as officer USNR, World War II Recipient Am. Order St. Barbara medal U.S. Army Arty, 1983, IR-100 award Indsl. Rsch. Mag., Chgo., 1971, Congl. Commendation, 1985, Commendation, State of Ohio Ho. of Reps., 1995, also various commendations. Mem. AIAA, ASME, Am. Def. Preparedness Assn. (Bronze medal 1974, Simon Silver medal 1985), Naval & Marine Corps Explosive Ordnance Disposal Assn., Lake Wildwood Country Club, RESA Avocations, Sigma Xi. Republican. Achievements include outstanding contribution in the fields of weaponry and explosive ordnance; 27 patents; research in aircraft armament, guns ammunition, rockets, warheads, mines, explosives, pyrotechnics and fuzes for the army, navy, airforce, FBI and Private industry; development of application of explosive and propellant powered devices which are now recognized as standard missile components; implosion atomic bomb. Avocations: astronomy, photography, golf, music, computers. Home and Office: 3939 Walnut Ave #152 Carmichael CA 95608 Personal E-mail: jeannguy@comcast.net.

THROWER, RANDOLPH WILLIAM, lawyer; b. Tampa, Fla., Sept. 5, 1913; s. Benjamin Key and Ora (Hammond) T.; m. Margaret Munroe, Feb. 2, 1939; children: Margaret MacCary, Patricia Barmeyer, Laura (Mrs. David T. Harris, Jr.), Randolph William, Mary (Mrs. George B. Wickham). Grad., Ga. Mil. Acad., 1930; BPh, Emory U., 1934, JD, 1936. Bar: Ga. bar 1935, D.C. bar 1953. Partner Sutherland, Asbill & Brennan, Atlanta, Washington, 1947-69, 71—. Commr. internal revenue, 1969-71; Lectr. bar, legal meetings; spl. agt. FBI, 1942-43; mem. Arthur Andersen & Co. Bd. of Rev., 1974-80, Nat. Council on Organized Crime, mem. exec. com., 1970-71 Past pres. Ga., Met. Atlanta mental health assns.; chmn. City of Atlanta Bd. Ethics 1981-93; past trustee Emory U., Clark Coll.; past chmn., trustee Wesleyan Coll.; bd. govs. Woodward Acad.; past chmn. bd. visitors Emory U. Served as capt. USMCR, 1944-45. Mem. Atlanta Legal Aid Soc. (past pres.), Emory U. Alumni Assn. (past pres.), ABA (chmn. spl. com. on survey local needs 1971-78, past chmn. sect. taxation, mem. ho. of dels. 1964-66, 74-89), Ga. Bar Assn., Atlanta Bar Assn. (past pres.), Am. Bar Found. (dir. 1980-88, pres. 1986-88, medal 1993), Am. Law Inst., Atlanta Lawyers Club (past pres.), U.S. Claims Ct. Bar Assn. (pres. 1987-88), Phi Delta Phi. Clubs: Commerce (Atlanta), Capital City (Atlanta), Piedmont Driving (Atlanta). Republican. Methodist. Home: 2240 Woodward Way NW Atlanta GA 30305-4043 Office: Sutherland Asbill & Brennan Ste 2300 999 Peachtree St NE Atlanta GA 30309 Office Phone: 404-853-8149. Business E-Mail: randolph.thrower@sablaw.com, randolph.thrower@sutherland.com.

THUEME, WILLIAM HAROLD, secondary school educator, counselor, travel coordinator; b. St. Clair, Mich., Sept. 4, 1945; s. Harold Arthur and Delphine Betty (Buhl) Thueme; m. Katheen Koning, May 8, 1971; children: Benjamin William, Rebecca, Jeffery William, Sarah; m. Nora Thueme. Student, Port Huron Jr. Coll., 1963-64; BA, Mich. State U., 1967, MA, 1969; PhD in Counseling, Progressive Universal Life Ch., 1993, PhD in Motivation, 1997, PhD in Paranormal Psychology, 1997, PhD in Psychometrics, 1999; postgrad., Oakland U., 1971, San Francisco State U., 1975, U. Hawaii, 1975; student, Spring Arbor Coll., 1968; PhD in Reading Edn., U. Mich., 1977; PhD (hon.), Aspen U., 2003. Cert. tchr., Mich. Ordained min. Universal Life Ch. Tchr. pub. schs., Charlotte, Mich., 1967-69, Ann Arbor, Mich., 1969—. Fgn. travel coord.-Ambs. Abroad Program, Amsterdam, The Netherlands, 1968—; regional driver coord. for Southeastern Mich. Avis Rent-a-Car, 1983—; travel coord. domestic and fgn. Go Ahead Tours; worldwide travel coord. Air, Land and Sea Cruises. Active UN Children's Found., Mich. Sheriffs Ednl. Found., Feed the Children, Woods Rd. Assn., Normal Pk. Neighborhood Assn., US Legal Found., Found. for Nicaraguan Democracy, Habitat for Humanity Internat. (charter), Carter Ctr., Nat. Coun. Better Edn., participant Skyhook II Project; coord. Mich. Fraternal Order of Police BBB, Ea. Mass.; elections coord. Eaton County Rep. Party, Mich., 1968, nat. com., 1968—, nat. senatorial com.; troop com. Coun. Boy Scouts Am., Ypsilanti, merit badge counselor, 1988-89, cub scout summer camp instr.; Internat., Incorp. (life mem.). Shore Nat. Network of Poet's Soc. Wolverne Coun., 1987; coach of the angels Ypsilanti Am. Little League, 1988; parent adv. bd. The Childrens Devel. Lab. Ea. Mich. U., 1988-89; active Mich. United Conservation Clubs, Big Bros. Am., Charlotte, Mich., Human Rights Watch, Nat. Security Caucus US, 1988—, Heritage Found., 1988—, ofcl. sponsor Mandate for Leadership III, Policy Strategies for 1990's Project, Project Save Our Schs., 1988—, Citizens United for Better Edn., World Awareness, Inc., Group 61 Amnesty Internat., Legal Affairs Coun., Coun. for Inter-Am. Security, Am. Inst. for Econ. Rsch., Nicaraguan Resistance Edn. Found., Nat. Right to Work Legal Def. Found., Citizens Against Govt. Waste, Citizens Commn. for Ethics in Govt., Citizens for Decency Through Law, Inc., Nat. Consumers League, Participating Parents for Progress in Ypsilanti Pub. Schs.; parents adv. bd. Chapelle Elem. Sch., Ypsilanti, 1989-90, West Mid. Sch., Ypsilanti, 1991-92, Ypsilanti Pub. Schs., 1990—, Ypsilanti HS; charter sponsor Victory over Communism Project; nominated charter mem. Presdl. Task Force; participant Imperial Congress: Crisis in the Separation of Powers Project, line-item veto project Heritage Found., 1989, campaign to revise medicare catastrophic coverage law project Nat. Assn. Uniformed Svcs., 1989, repeal of catastrophic coverage act program Conservative Caucus Inc., 1989, Srs. Coal. Against the Tax, 1989; nat. adv. coun. Citizens Com. for Right to Bear Arms; jr. and sr. choir, Sunday sch. tchr. St. Paul's Luth. Ch., 1959-64 (Perfect Attendance award 8 yrs.), Marine city, Mich., 1960-63; youth Sunday sch. tchr., dir. youth min. coun. Lawrence Ave. Meth. Ch., Charlotte, Mich., 1967-69; assoc. mem. for Gentlemen of All Ages Second Amendment Sisters, 2003, Internat. Amb. Goodwill World Peace and Diplomacy Forum, founding cabinet, life mem., 2003, amb., 2004; senator seat for lifetime term World Nations Congress; vol. The Ctrl. Intelligence Agy., The USA, 1967-06, Homeland Security USA, 2005-. Recipient Spl. Recognition award Richard Nixon, 1968-79, Gerald Ford, 1974-76, Ronald Reagan, 1971-88, George Bush, 1988-92, Spl. Recognition award Reagan Presdl. Campaign, 1981, Bush Presdl. Campaign, 1988, Citizen of Yr. award Citizens Com. for Right to Bear Arms, 1988, cert. recognition US Justice Found., 1991, Hale Found., Am. Security Coun. 30th Anniversary Spl. Recognition cert., cert. appreciation 2d Amendment Found., 1988, Appreciation of Devoted and Valuable Svc. award Chapelle Elem. Sch., 1988-89, Merit Badge, Wolverine Coun.; Internat. Peace prize, United Cultural Conv., 2002, Outstanding contbns. to Literacy, Edn., Humanitarians and Peace, 2002, World medal of Freedom for hope, freedom and peace, 2006; letters from First Lady Nancy Reagan, First Lady Barbara Bush, Mich. Gov. John Engler, Nelson Mandella, Tchg. Excellence award, Cmty. Svc. award, Global Rels. award, 2002, others. Mem. NEA, NRA (life, endowment), Am. Inst. for Econ. Rsch., Lincoln Inst. for Rsch. Edn., United Conservatives of Am. (participant citizens against the catastrophic health act tax 1989), Mich. Edn. Assn., Internat. Reading Assn., Mich. Sheriffs Assn. (assoc.), Police Marksmanship Assn., Washtenaw Reading Coun., Southeastern Mich. Reading Assn., Mich. Reading Assn., Mich. ASCD, Ann Arbor Edn. Assn., Am. Security Coun., Am. Def. Inst., Found. for Christian Living, Am. Family Assn., Nat. Geog. Soc., Am. Film Inst., Internat. Freelance Photographers Orgn. (life, profl. photographer), Taxpayers Edn. Lobby, Gun Owners Am., Nat. Assn. Federally Lic. Firearms Dealers, Nat. Consumers League, Conservative Caucus, Inc., Ams. for Freedom, Tri-County Sportsman League, Mich. United Conservation Clubs, Mich. State U. Alumni Assn. (Blue Water chpt.), Mich. State U. Coll. Comm. Arts Alumni Assn., Cruise Lines Internat. Assn., Internat. Air Transport Assn., US Tour Operators Assn. of One Million Dollar Consumer Protection Plan, Mich. State U. Coll. Social Sci. Alumni Assn., Inventors Assistance League (life), San Francisco State U. Alumni Assn., Shore Nat. Network Poets Soc. (life), Group Leaders Am., Group Travel Bus. Inst., Ft. Gratiot, Lions Club (v.p. 1998—), Lions Club Internat., Washtenaw Sportsmen's Club (Ypsilanti), Internat. Optimist Club (v.p. Ann Arbor chpt., bd. dirs. 1975-78), Port Huron Noon Optimist Club, Judo Black Belt Fedn. Am. (asst. coach US judo team at worldwide Olympics, Atlanta), Sigma Alpha Eta. Evangelican Lutheran. Home and Office: 7238 Rachel Dr Ypsilanti MI 48197-2935 Office Phone: 800-381-5111. Personal E-mail: whthueme@yahoo.com.

THUESEN, GERALD JORGEN, industrial engineer, educator; b. Oklahoma City, July 20, 1938; s. Holger G. and Helen S. T.; m. Harriett M. Thuesen; children: Karen T. Hannah, Dyan T. Jacobus. BS, Stanford U., 1960, MS, 1961, PhD, 1968. Engr. Pacific Tel. Co., San Francisco, 1961-62, Atlantic Richfield Co., Dallas, 1962-63; asst. prof. indsl. engring. U. Tex., Arlington, 1963, 67-68; assoc. prof. indsl. and sys. engring. Ga. Inst. Tech., Atlanta, 1968-76, prof., 1976-96, prof. emeritus, 1996—. Author: Engineering Economy, 4th edit., 1971, 9th edit., 2001, Economic Decision Analysis, 1974, 3rd edit., 1998; assoc. editor: The Engring. Economist, 1974-80, editor, 1981-91. NASA/Am. Soc. Engring. Edn. summer faculty fellow, 1970. Fellow Inst. Indsl. Engrs. (dept. editor Trans. 1976-80, v.p. publs. 1979-80, divsn. dir. 1978-80, Wellington award 1989, Publs. award 1990, bd. trustees 1979-81), Am. Soc. Engring. Edn. (bd. dirs. 1977-79, Eugene L. Grant award 1977, 91); mem. Sigma Xi. Office: Ga Inst Tech Sch Indsl & Sys Engring Atlanta GA 30332-0205 Business E-Mail: gthuesen@isye.gatech.edu.

THULEAN, DONALD MYRON, symphony conductor; b. Wenatchee, Wash., June 24, 1929; s. Elmer Edward and Mary (Myron) T.; m. Meryl Mary Parnell, Mar. 17, 1951; children: Dorcas Marie, Mark Myron, William Norton. BA, U. Wash., 1950, MA in Music, 1952; Mus.D. (hon.), Whitworth Coll., 1967. Faculty Pacific U., 1955-62; dean Pacific U. (Sch. Music), 1957-62. Assoc. conductor Portland (Ore.) Symphony, 1961-62, conductor, music dir. Spokane Symphony, 1962-84; v.p. profl. and artistic svcs. Am. Symphony Orch. League, 1983-99, condr. emeritus, 1998—; asst. conductor Seattle Symphony, 1966-69, chorus master, Aspen Music Festival, 1957-61; artistic cons. Title III project in performing arts, Wash., 1966-68, music dir. Tamarack Music Festival, 1971. Bd. dirs. Seattle Symphony, 2000-06, Seattle Youth Symphonies, 2002--; mem. vis. com. U. Wash. Sch. Music, 2000—. Served with AUS, 1953-55. Unitarian (trustee). Office Phone: 206-790-1632. Personal E-mail: thulean2@comcast.net.

THULL, TOM (JOHN THOMAS THULL), state banking agency administrator; m. Shelley Thull. Grad. in Agr. Edn., Kans. State U., 1975. Loan specialist; v.p. Midland Nat. Bank, Ctrl. Bank & Trust; pres. Ctrl. Nat. Bank, Newton, Kans.; mayor Town of North Newton; mem. Kans. House Reps. from Dist. 72, 2003—07; commr. Office of State Bank Commr., Kans., 2007—. Pres. Harvey County Bankers Assn., Harvey County Econ. Devel. Coun.; dir. Newton C. of C.; mem. adv. bd. Bethel Coll. Democrat. Office: Office of State Bank Commr 700 Jackson Ste 300 Topeka KS 66603 Office Phone: 785-296-2266. Office Fax: 785-296-0168. E-mail: tom.thull@osbckansas.org.*

THUMA, HOLLY DIANE, performing arts educator; d. Theadore Everett and Gennevieve Elizabeth Thuma; m. Larry John Meyers, Sept. 20, 1986; children: Callie Marion, Charlie Will Meyers. BFA, NYU Sch. Arts, NYC, 1979; MFA, U. Pitts., 2002. Acting & voice & speech tchr. Point Pk. U., Pitts., 2003—05, Carnegie Mellon U., Pitts., 2007; tchg. artist in residence U. Pitts., 2005—. Creative dramatics dir. Pitts. Pub. Theatre, 1991—2003; story teller Healy Heartwood Story Bus, Pitts., 2000—03; dir. performance & edn. Hope Acad., Pitts., 2003—06. Dir.: Macbeth Redux, Romeo & Juliet with Violin, Brundibar; actor: Sexes: the Marriage Dialogues, Hard Times, (Jewish theater) The Sisters Rosensweig, (ind. films) No Pets, Daddy Cool, (symphony orch.) An Evening of Pops, (ballet theatre) Juliet & Her Romeo, (theatres) A Christmas Carol, Spendour. Mem.: Am. Fedn. Film & TV Actors, Sceen Actors Guild, Actors Equity Assn. Office: Univ Pitts Pittsburgh PA 15219 Business E-Mail: owlpost@pitt.edu.

THUMM, UWE, physics professor; b. Freiburg, Germany, Apr. 4, 1959; s. Manfred and Hildegard Thumm. Diploma in Physics, U. Freiburg, 1985, PhD, 1989. Prof. physics Kans. State U., Manhattan, 1992—; rsch. dir. Advanced Photonics, Bruckmuehl, Germany, 2000—01. Recipient Profl. award, Kans. State U., 2008. Mem.: Am. Phys. Soc. Achievements include research in atomic, molecular, optical, surface physics. Avocations: piano, skiing, tennis. Home: 2347 Grandview Dr Manhattan KS 66502 Office: Kans State Univ Dept Physics Manhattan KS 66506

THUNE, JOHN RANDOLPH, United States Senator from South Dakota; b. Murdo, SD, Jan. 7, 1961; m. Kimberley Jo Weems, 1984; children: Brittany, Larissa. BBA, Biola U., Calif., 1983; MBA, U. SD, 1984. Legis. asst. to Senator James Abdnor US Senate, 1985-87; dep. staff dir. to the ranking rep. Senate Small Bus. Com., 1987-89; exec. dir. South Dakota Rep. Party, 1989-91; dir. railroad divsn. State of SD, 1991-93; exec. dir. SD Mcpl. League, 1993-96; founder The Thune Group LLC; mem. US Congress from S.D., 1997—2003; US Senator from SD, 2005—. Mem. US Senate Armed Services Com., US Senate Agrl. Nutrition & Forestry Com., US Senate Commerce, Sci. & Transp. Com., US Senate Small Bus. & Entrepreneurship Com.; vice chmn. US Senate Republican Conf., 2009; chmn. US Senate Republican Policy Com. (RPC), 2009—. Republican. Protestant. Avocations: basketball, pheasant hunting. Office: US Senate 383 Russell Senate Office Bldg Washington DC 20510 also: District Office 320 North Main Ave Sioux Falls SD 57104-6056 Office Phone: 202-224-2321, 605-334-9596. Office Fax: 202-228-5429, 605-334-2591.*

THURAI, MERHALA, research scientist; b. Jaffna, Sri Lanka, Jan. 6, 1960; d. Jeevaratnam Victor and Sornagandhimalar Thurai-Rajasingam. BSc (hon.), Imperial Coll., U. London, Eng., 1980; PhD, King's Coll., U. London, 1985. Cert. Chartered Engr., Inst. Elec. Engring., 1997. Sr. rsch. fellow Nat. Inst. Info. and Comm. Tech., Tokyo; sr. sci. officer Rutherford Appleton Lab., Chilton, Didcot, Oxon, England, 1986—2001; sr. rschr. Colo. State U., Fort Collins, 2004—. Cons. Gematronik - Selex, Neuss, Germany, 2004—. Contbr. articles to profl. jours. Del. ITU-R propagation study group, 2004—08. Recipient Best Radiowave Propagation paper, 1997. Mem.: IEEE. Achievements include research in experimentally derived drop shapes in rain; the effect of rain microstructure on radiowave propagation; using rain microstructure information to improve rain estimations from weather radars. Avocation: travel. Office: Colorado State Univ Dept Elec Engring Fort Collins CO 80523 Office Phone: 1-970-491-7678. Personal E-mail: thurai@theiet.orgn. Business E-Mail: merhala@engr.colostate.edu, thurai@iee.org.

THURBER, PETER PALMS, lawyer; b. Detroit, Mar. 23, 1928; s. Cleveland and Marie Louise (Palms) T.; m. Ellen Bodley Stites, Apr. 16, 1955; children: Edith Bodley, Jane Chenoweth, Thomas, Sarah Bartlett. BA, Williams Coll., 1950; JD, Harvard U., 1953. Bar: Mich., 1954. With Miller, Canfield, Paddock and Stone, Detroit, 1953-93, of counsel, 1994—. Trustee McGregor Fund, Detroit, 1979-2003. Bd. dirs. Detroit Symphony Orch., Inc., 1974-93; trustee Community Found. for Southeastern Mich., 1990-2000, Coun. Mich. Founds., 1991-2000. With U.S. Army, 1953-55. Fellow Am. Bar Found.; mem. Clubs: Country of Detroit (Grosse Pointe Farms, Mich.). Roman Catholic. Avocations: reading, travel, sports. Home: 28 Provencal Rd Grosse Pointe Farms MI 48236-3038

THURM, DAVID AARON, publishing executive; b. Winslow, Ariz., Dec. 5, 1953; s. Richard Henry and Evelyn Joyce (Boches) T.; m. Andrea Granoff, Mar. 29, 1981; children: Amanda Margot, Matthew Charles, James Richard. AB, Harvard U., 1975; JD, NYU, 1978. Bar: NY 1979, US Dist. Ct. (So. and Ea. Dists.) NY 1979. Assoc. Rogers & Wells, NYC, 1978-81; atty. The NY Times Co., NYC, 1982-87, sr. atty., 1988-89, dir. adminstrn., 1988—90, exec. dir. project devel., 1991—95, v.p. prodn., 1995—99; COO NY Times Digital, NYC, 1999—2000; v.p. real estate develop. The NY Times Co., NYC, 2000—, chief information officer, 2004—08; sr. v.p. ops. NY Times, 2008—. Office: The New York Times College Scholarship P 230 W 41st St Ste 1300 New York NY 10036-7207

THURMAN, ANDREW EDWARD, lawyer; b. Raleigh, NC, May 11, 1954; s. William Gentry and Peggy Lou (Brown) T.; m. Patricia Thurman, May 19, 1979 (dec. 1989); children: Gentry Brown, Harrison Beauchamp, Andrew Guilford; m. Tracy Fletcher, Nov. 16, 1991; 1 child, Spencer Lee. BA, Columbia U., 1976; JD, Coll. William and Mary, 1979; MPH, U. Okla., 1984. Bar: Va. 1979, Okla. 1980, US Ct. Appeals (10th cir.) 1981, US Supreme Ct. 1985, Pa. 1988. Staff atty. Dept. of Human Svcs., Oklahoma City, 1979—80; counsel State of Okla. Tchg. Hosps., Oklahoma City, 1980—84; mem. Miller, Dollarhide, Dawson & Shaw, Oklahoma City, 1984—87; ptnr. Berkman, Ruslander, Pohl, Lieber & Engel, Pitts., 1988—89; of counsel Buchanan Ingersoll, Pitts., 1989; sr. v.p. and gen. counsel Forbes Health Sys., Pitts., 1989—96; sr. counsel Allegheny Health Edn. & Rsch. Found., Pitts., 1997—98; dep. gen. counsel Allegheny U. Hosps. West, 1998—99; asst. gen. counsel We. Pa. Allegheny Health Sys., 1999—2002; assoc. prof. Carnegie-Mellon U., 2000—; pvt. practice, 2002—; assoc. prof. U. Pitts., 2003—, assoc. dir. consortium ethics program, 2004—; asst. prof. Am. U. Caribbean, 2003—06. Pres. Coun. Neighborhood Assns., Oklahoma City, 1984, Lincoln Terr. Neighborhood Assn., Oklahoma City, 1984; trustee Rader Trust, Oklahoma City, 1980—; treas. Bd. dirs. State Okla. Tchg. Hosps. Found., Oklahoma City, 1984-87, Newman Meml. Hosp., 1983-87, Willowview Hosp., Spencer, Okla., 1985-87, Allegheny U. Med. Ctrs., Allegheny U. Med. Ctr./Cannonsburg Ambulance Svc., 1997—, Allegheny U. Hosps. West, 1998—, Diversified Health Group, 1998-99, Allegheny Med. Practices Network, 1999—, Allegheny Speciality Practice Network, 1999—; chair Hosp. Coun. Western Pa. Ethics Task Force, 1993-2000. Fellow Am. Health Lawyers Assn.; mem. St. Anthony Hall Club NYC (pres. 1976), Pitts. Athletic Assn. Democrat. Presbyterian. Avocation: reading detective novels. Home: 910 N Negly Ave Pittsburgh PA 15206 Office: 1151 Freeport Rd # 391 Pittsburgh PA 15238 Office Phone: 412-567-2106. E-mail: andy@thurmanhealthlaw.com, thurms79@gmail.com.

THURMAN, CYNTHIA DENISE, former human services administrator, writer; b. Ft. Myers, Fla., Mar. 14, 1970; children: Asia Naikee Garcia, Jai'ya Ja'V-ae Armani. Residential care coord. Sandy Pk. Redevelopment Ctr., North Fort Myers, Fla., 2001—08; human services worker Gulf Coast Ctr., Ft. Myers, 2003—08. Author: (poem) Soon. Recipient Shakespare Trophy of Excellence, Famous Poets Soc., 2004.

THURMAN, KAREN L., political organization administrator, former congresswoman, lobbyist; b. Rapid City, SD, Jan. 12, 1951; d. Lee Searle and Donna (Altfillisch) Loveland; m. John Patrick Thurman, 1973; children: McLin Searl and Liberty Lee. AA, Santa Fe CC, Gainesville, Fla.; BA, U. Fla., Gainesville, 1973. Mem. Dunnellon City Coun., Fla., 1975—83; mayor City of Dunnellon, 1979-81; mem. Monroe Regional Med. Ctr. Governancy Com., Comprehensive Plan Tech. Adv. Com., Fla. State Senate, 1983—93, US Congress from 5th Fla. dist., 1993—2002, mem. ways and means com., agrl. com., 1996—2002; lobbyist eAppeals, Miami, 2004—, Freedom Healthcare, Hollywood, 2004—; chairwomen Fla. Dem. Party, Tallahassee, 2005—. Del. Fla. Dem. Conv., Dem. Nat. Conv., 1980; mem. Regional Energy Action com. Recipient Svc. Above Self award Dunnellon C. of C., 1980, Regional Coun. Appreciation for Svc. award. Mem. Dunnellon C. of C. (dir.), Fla. Horseman's Children's Soc. (charter). Democrat. Episcopalian. Office: Fla Dem Party 214 S Bronough St Tallahassee FL 32301 Office Phone: 850-222-3411. Office Fax: 850-222-0916.*

THURMAN, ROBERT KENNETH, retired military officer; b. Cashmere, Wash., July 9, 1914; s. Robert LeRoy and Lucille May Thurman; m. Mary Frederick Steber, Jan. 3, 1997; children: Mark Steber, Julie Goss, Bill Steber, Michael Steber; m. Vera Mary Marotta, Aug. 10, 1945 (dec. Nov. 13, 1994); 1 adopted child, Robert LeRoy 1 child, Frank J. (dec.). With USN, 1927—35, comdr., 1941—63, Salvage Diving Sch., Bayonne, NJ, 1954—57; sailor Second Mate Merchant Marine, 1935—41; ops. mgr. Merret, Chapman and Scott, NYC, 1963—95. Operational boss Antarctic Operation, 1960—63. Mem.: Sabbar Shriners (noble 2003—06), Wally Byam Caravan Club Internat., Wenatchee Riverside Lodge, Aaron Lodge. Republican. Roman Catholic. Avocations: amateur radio, travel. Home: 1008 E Simmons St Tucson AZ 85719

THURMAN, UMA, actress; b. Boston, Apr. 29, 1970; d. Robert and Nena (von Schlebrugge) T.; m. Gary Oldman, Oct. 1990 (div. 1992); m. Ethan Hawke, May 1, 1998 (div. July 20, 2004); children: Maya Ray, Roan. Spokesperson Lancome cosmetics, 2000. Actress: (films) Kaze no tani no Naushika, 1984, Kiss Daddy Good Night, 1988, Johnny Be Good, 1988, Dangerous Liaisons, 1988, The Adventures of Baron Munchausen, 1988, Where the Heart Is, 1990, Henry and June, 1990, Final Analysis, 1992, Jennifer Eight, 1992, Mad Dog and Glory, 1993, Even Cowgirls Get the Blues, 1993, Pulp Fiction, 1994 (Acad. award nom. Best Supporting Actress), A Month By the Lake, 1995, The Truth About Cats and Dogs, 1996, Beautiful Girls, 1996, Batman & Robin, 1997, Gattaca, 1997, Avengers, 1998, Les Miserables, 1998, Vatel, 1999, Sweet and Lowdown, 1999, Vatel, 2000, Tape, 2001, Chelsea Walls, 2001, Kill Bill: Volume 1, 2003, Paycheck, 2003, Kill Bill: Volume 2, 2004, Be Cool, 2005, Prime, 2005, The Producers, 2005, My Super Ex-Girlfriend, 2006, The Life Before Her Eyes, 2007, The Accidental Husband, 2008; TV movies include Robin Hood, 1991, Duke of Groove, 1996, The Golden Bowl, 2000, Hysterical Blindness, 2002 (also exec. prodr., Golden Globe for Best Performance by an Actress). Bd. dirs. Room to Grow. Named a knight in the Order of Arts & Letters, France, 2006.

THURMOND, GEORGE MURAT, judge; b. Del Rio, Tex., Oct. 22, 1930; s. Roger H. and Day (Hamilton) T.; m. Elsiejean Davis, June 27, 1959; children: Carolyn Day, Georganna, Sarah Gail. BA, U. of the South, 1952; JD, U. Tex., 1955. Bar: Tex. 1955. Ptnr. Montague & Thurmond, Del Rio, 1955-69; judge Tex. Dist. Ct. (63rd dist.), Del Rio, 1970-2000, sr. judge, 2000—. Presiding judge 6th Adminstrv. Region, Del Rio, 1983-87; chmn. jud. sect. State Bar Tex., 1988-89. Staff: U. Tex. Law Review, 1955. Rep. Tex. Ho. of Reps., 1955-58. Mem.: ABA, Fifth US Ct. Appeals, Tex. Bar Assn. Republican. Anglican. Avocations: exercise, traditional jazz, model railroading. Office Phone: 830-775-3710. Business E-Mail: gthurmand@stx.rr.com.

THURMOND, J. STROM, JR., lawyer, former prosecutor; b. SC, Oct. 18, 1972; s. Strom and Nancy Thurmond; m. Heather Holland, 1998; 1 child, Strom III. BA in English, U. S.C., 1995, grad. in Law, 1998. Bar: S.C. Ptnr. Strom, Young & Thurmond, LLP, Columbia, SC, 1998—99; asst. solicitor S.C. 2d Jud. Cir., 1999—2001; U.S. atty. Dist. SC US Dept. Justice, 2001—05; ptnr. Smith, Massey, Brodie, and Thurmond LLP, 2005—. Chmn. dist. law enforcement coordinating com. Dist. S.C., mem. atty. gen.'s adv. coun. violent crime subcom.

THURSBY, JACQUELINE SCHUSTER, literature and language professor, director; b. St. Louis, Oct. 13, 1940; d. Clarence Edward and Juanita Richardson Schuster; m. Charles Denny Thursby, Dec. 26, 1959; children: Michelle Thursby Archibald, Christopher Young, Valerie Thursby Hatch, William Jenner. PhD, Bowling Green State U., Ohio, 1994. Adj. prof., English & Am. history Idaho State U., Pocatello, 1994—96; prof., English & folklore Brigham Young U., Provo, Utah, 1996—, chair, William Wilson Folklore archive bd., 2005—08, dir., secondary English edn., 2009—. Author: (books) Mother's Table Father's Chair: Cultural Narratives of Basque American Woman, Begin Where You Are: Nurturing Relationships with Less-Active Family and Friends, Funeral Festivals in America: Rituals for the Living, (book) Story: A Handbook, Foodways and Folklore: A Handbook; contbr. articles to jours. Com. mem. LDS Women's Conf., Provo, 2004—06; sec. Utah Cultural Arts Alliance, Salt Lake City, 2004—05. Recipient Presdl. Svc. award, Utah Coun. Tchrs. English and Lang. Arts, 2001—02, English Dept. Tchg. award, Brigham Young U., 2003. Mem.: Internat. Soc. Folk Narrative Rsch., Am. Culture Assn., Am. Folklore Soc., Phi Kappa Phi (Disting. Lectr. award 2006).

THURSTON, BONNIE BOWMAN, religious studies educator, minister, poet; b. Bluefield, W.Va., Oct. 5, 1952; d. Ernest Venoy and Eleanor Sabina (King) Bowman; m. Burton Bradford Thurston, May 29, 1980 (dec. Nov. 1990). BA summa cum laude, Bethany Coll., 1974; MA, U. Va., 1975, PhD, 1979; postgrad., Harvard Div. Sch., 1983, Eberhard Karls U., Germany, 1983—84, Ecole Biblique, Jerusalem, 1993. Ordained to ministry Disciples of Christ Ch., 1984. Instr., asst. dean U. Va., Charlottesville, 1979—80; adj. prof. Wheeling Coll. (now Wheeling Jesuit U.), W.Va., 1980—81, assoc. prof., chair dept. theology, 1985—95; asst. prof. Bethany Coll., W.Va., 1981—83; assoc. prof. N.T. Pitts. Theol. Sem., 1995—99, William F. Orr prof., 1999—2002. Vis. scholar Harvard U. Div. Sch., Cambridge, Mass., 1983; tutor Inst. Study of Christian Origins, Tubingen, Germany, 1983—85. Author: (books) The Widows, 1989, Wait Here and Watch, 1989, Spiritual Life in the Early Church, 1993, Women in the NT, 1998, To Everything a Season, 1999, Preaching Mark, 2002, Philippians and Philemon, 2005, Religious Vows, the Sermon on the Mount, And Christian Living, 2006, The Spiritual Landscape of Mark, 2008, For God Alone: A Primer on Prayer, 2009, (books of poetry) The Heart's Land, 2001, Hints and Glimpses, 2004; contbr. articles to profl. jours., poetry to jours. Mem.: Soc. for the Study of Christian Spirituality, Disciples Hist. Soc., Soc. for Buddhist-Christian Studies, Internat. Thomas Merton Soc., Soc. Bibl. Lit., Cath. Bibl. Assn. Avocations: gardening, music, cooking. Office: PO Box 2258 Wheeling WV 26003

THURSTON, DONALD ALLEN, broadcast executive; b. Gloucester, Mass., Apr. 2, 1930; s. Joseph Allen and Helen Ruth (Leach) T.; m. Oralie Alice Lane, Sept. 9, 1951; children: Corydon Leach, Carolie Lane. Grad., Mass. Radio and Telegraph, 1949; HHD (hon.), North Adams State Coll., Mass., 1977; LHD (hon.), Emerson Coll., 1995. Announcer, engr. Sta. WTWN, St. Johnsbury, Vt., 1949-52; v.p., gen. mgr. Sta. WIKE, Newport, Vt., 1952-60; v.p., treas., gen. mgr. Sta. WMNB, North Adams, 1960-66; pres., treas. Berkshire Broadcasting Co., Inc., North Adams, 1966—2003. Bd. dirs. Broadcast Capital Fund, Inc., 1980-96, chmn. bd., 1981-89; bd. dirs. Broadcast Music, Inc., NYC, 1990-2005, chmn. bd., 1994-97. Pres. No. Berkshire Indsl. Devel. Corp., 1965-67; commr. Mass. Cmty. Antenna TV Commn., 1972-74; trustee Mass. Coll. Liberal Arts, 1991-2001, vice chmn. bd. trustees, 1993-96, chmn., 1996-2001. Recipient Laymen's award Vt. Tchrs. Assn., 1958; Laymen's award Mass. Tchrs. Assn., 1962; Abe Lincoln Merit award So. Baptist Radio and TV Commn., 1975; named Man of Yr. Vt. Assn. Broadcasters, 1978 Mem. North Adams C. of C. (Hayden award 1967, pres. 1964-67), Nat. Assn. Broadcasters (dir. 1965-69, 73-77, chmn. radio 1976-77, chmn. bd., chmn. exec. com. 1977-79, Disting. Svc. award 1980), Mass. Broadcasters Assn. (pres. 1964, Disting. Svc. award 1964, 71, 78), Taconic Golf Club (Williamston, Mass.; bd. dirs. 1975-89). Republican. Methodist. Office: 61 Main St PO Box 386 North Adams MA 01247-0386 *My goals have been to better my community, profession and life in general because I was a positive participant, and to provide independence, a sense of responsibility and a love of humanity for my family.*

THURSTON, JACQUELINE BEVERLY, retired artist, writer, educator; b. Cin., Jan. 27, 1939; d. John O. and Frances Beverly Thurston; children: Mark, Beverly Thurston Baller. BFA in Painting, Carnegie-Mellon U., 1961; MA in Painting, Stanford U., 1962. Prof. emeritus San Jose State U., Calif., 1965—2009. Co-author: Optical Illusions, 1965; one-woman shows include Susan Spiritus Gallery, 1995, San Jose Mus. Art, 2005, Triangle Gallery, 2005. Fellow Nat. Endowment for the Arts, 1976, 78; Fulbright scholar, Egypt, 2006. Avocation: gardening.

THURSTON, KATHY LYNN, paralegal; b. Indpls., Dec. 3, 1957; d. G. Weldon and Juanita J. (Trotter) Johnson; m. Harold O. Thurston, Jr., June 21, 1977; 1 child, Jonathan Grant Much; 3 stepchildren: Kate Elizabeth Thurston, Jennifer Leigh Thurston, Abigail Ann Thurston. BA, Ind. U., 1980. Paralegal, office mgr. Johnson, Hall & Lawhead P.C., Indpls., 1983—96, Johnson, Lawhead, Buth & Pope, P.C., 1996—99, G. Weldon Johnson, Atty. Law, 2000—04; paralegal Hall, Render, Killian, Heath & Lyman PC, 2004—. Mem. Ind. Paralegal Assn. (chmn. continuing legal edn. 1990-92, chmn. probate and tax sect. 1990—2005, 2008-, pres. 1992-93, Para-Potential award 1991, Paralegal of Yr. award 1995, Lifetime Achievement award 2000), Indpls. Bar Assn. (charter paralegal com., chmn. 1993, 94, mem. exec. com. 1993-2005, Paralegal of Yr. award 2000). Office: Hall Render Killian Heath & Lyman PC One American Sq Ste 2000 Indianapolis IN 46282

THURSWELL, GERALD ELLIOTT, lawyer; b. Detroit, Feb. 4, 1944; s. Harry and Lilyan (Zeitlin) T.; m. Lynn Satovsky, Sept. 17, 1967 (div. Aug. 1978); children: Jennifer, Lawrence; m. Judith Linda Bendix, Sept. 2, 1978 (div. May 1999); chldren: Jeremy, Lindsey. LLB with distinction, Wayne State U., 1967. Bar: Mich. 1968, N.Y. 1984, D.C. 1985, Colo. 1990, Ill. 1992, U.S. Dist. Ct. (ea. dist.) Mich. 1968, U.S. Ct. Appeals (6th cir.) 1968, U.S. Supreme Ct. 1994, U.S. Dist. Ct. (western dist.) Mich. 2004. Student asst. to U.S. Atty. Eas. Dist. Mich., Detroit, 1966; assoc. Zwerdling, Miller, Klimist & Maurer, Detroit, 1967-68; st. prnt. The Thurswell Law Firm, Southfield, Mich. Arbitrator Am. Arbitration Assn., Detroit, 1969—; mediator Wayne County Cir. Ct., Mich., 1983—, Oakland County Cir. Ct. Mich., 1984—, also facilitator, 1991; twp. atty. Royal Oak Twp., Mich., 1982—; lectr. Oakland County Bar Assn. People's Law Sch., 1988. Pres. Powder Horn Estates Subdivsn. Assn., West Bloomfield, Mich., 1975, United Fund, West Bloomfield, 1976. Arthur F. Lederly scholar Wayne State U. Law Sch., 1965; Wayne State U. Law Sch. grad. profl. scholar, 1965, 66; named Super Lawyer Law and Politics Mag., 2006-08, Super Lawyer Mich., 2006, 2007, 2008; named one of Best Lawyers America, 2009. Mem. ATLA (treas. Detroit met. chpt. 1986-87, v.p. 1989-90, pres. 1991-93), Mich. Bar Assn. (investigator/arbitrator grievance bd., atty. discipline bd., chmn. hearing panel), Mich. Trial Lawyers Assn. (legis. com. on govtl. immunity 1984, exec. bd. 2004-, PAC 2004), Jud. Qualifications Com., Mich. Assn. Justice, Detroit Bar Assn. (past panel pub. adv. com. jud. candidates), Oakland County Bar Assn. Office: The Thurswell Law Firm 1000 Town Ctr Ste 500 Southfield MI 48075-1221 Office Phone: 248-354-2222.

THUSWALDNER, GREGOR, literature and language professor; PhD, U. NC, Chapel Hill. Asst. prof. German Gordon Coll., Wenham, Mass., 2003—08, assoc. prof. German and linguistics, 2008—. Contbr. articles to profl. jours. Recipient Disting. Jr. Faculty award, Gordon Coll., 2006. Office: Gordon Coll 255 Grapevine Rd Wenham MA 01984 Business E-Mail: gregor.thuswaldner@gordon.edu.

THWAITES, CHRISTIAN WILLIAM, investment company executive; b. Woking, Eng., Dec. 6, 1957; s. Peter Trevenan Thwaites and Ellen Theresa King; children: Erik, Matthew. BA with honors, U. London, 1981; MBA, Harvard U., Cambridge, Mass., 1988. Fund mgr. Samuel Montagu, London, 1981—86; mktg. exec. Aetna Inc., Hartford, Conn., 1988—96; chief mktg. officer Am. Skandia, Shelton, Conn., 1996—2001; pres., CEO Skandia Global Funds, London, 2001—04, Sentinal Asset Mgmt., Montpellier, Vt., 2005—. Dir. Sentinel Funds, Boston, 2005—. Mem.: Soc. Investment Analysts. Office: Sentinel Asset Mgmt 1national Life Dr Montpelier VT 05604 Home: 561 Golf Course Rd South Burlington VT 05403-7506

THWIN, SOE SE, medical researcher; MSc, U. Washington, Seattle, 1992; PhD, Boston U., 2007. Bio statistician Boston U. Med. Ctr., 2001—, VA Boston Health Care Sys., 2008—. Achievements include development of automated data collection system. Office: Boston Univ Med Ctr 88 E Newton St Robinson-2 Geriat Boston MA 02118

T.I., See HARRIS, CLIFFORD JR.

TIAHRT, TODD (W. TODD TIAHRT), United States Representative from Kansas, former state senator; b. Vermillion, SD, June 15, 1951; s. Wilbur E. and Sara Ella Marcine (Steele) Tiahrt; m. Vicki Lyn Holland, Aug. 14, 1976; children: Jessica, John, Luke. Student, SD Sch. Mines & Tech., Rapid City, 1969-72; BA, Evangel Coll., Springfield, Mo., 1975; MBA, S.W. Mo. State U., 1989. Property estimator Crawford & Co., Springfield, Mo., 1975-78; project engr. Zenith Electronics, Springfield, 1978-81; cost engr. Boeing, Wichita, Kans., 1981-94, proposal mgr., 1991-94; state senator State of Kans., Topeka, 1993—95; mem. US Congress from 4th Kans. dist., Washington, 1995—; mem. appropriations com., 1997—. Chmn. 4th dist. Rep. party, 1990—92; exec. com. Kans. Rep. party, 1990—92, nat. security com., sci. com. Mem.: Delta Sigma Phi. Republican. Office: US Ho Reps 2441 Rayburn Ho Office Bldg Washington DC 20515-1604 Office Phone: 202-225-6216.*

TIAN, FENG, biologist, researcher; m. Hua Xu. PhD, U. Colo., Boulder, 2005. Postdoc. fellow NASA Astrobiology Inst., Boulder, 2006—08; postdoc assoc. MIT, EAPS, Cambridge, 2008—; rsch. scientist U. Colo., 2009—. Recipient Rsch. award, NRC, 2005. Mem.: ISSOL, DPS, AGU. Achievements include research in evolution history of planetary atmospheres.

TIAN, HONGQI, application developer, researcher; arrived in U.S., 2001; s. Tao Tian and Fengkun Li; m. Yan Li; children: Annie Miao, Tony Run. BS, Huazhong U. Sci. Tech., Wuhan, 1982, Master, 1984, PhD, 1989. Rschr. Chiba (Japan) U., 1991—94; sr. rsch. engr. Seiko Instruments Inc., Chiba, 1994—96; sr. software engr. Digital Dispatch Sys., Richmond, BC, Canada, 1997—2000, Digital Control Inc., Kent, Wash., 2001—. Author: (book) Sliding Mode Control, 1994. Mem.: NY Acad. Sci. Achievements include patents for sliding mode control of magnetic bearing sys. Home: 14245 60th St SE Bellevue WA 98006 Personal E-mail: hongqi_tian@hotmail.com.

TIAN, LI, investment company executive, educator; arrived in U.S., 1996; m. Min Shi, Apr. 20, 2001. B in Engring., Tsinghua U., Beijing, 1993; M in Engring., Beijing U. Aeronautics & Astronautics, 1996; MS in Info. Sys., George Mason U., 1999; MBA, U. Chgo. Grad. Sch. Bus., 2008. Cert. sys. engr., database adminstr., solution developer Microsoft; project mgmt. profl. Project Mgmt. Inst. Gen. mgr. multimedia tech. Beijing Feitian Inst. New Tech., 1993—96; software engr. GTSI Corp., Chantilly, Va., 1998; project cons. MCI Comm. Corp., Pentagon City, Va., 1998; supr. systems/infrastructure Airlines Reporting Corp., Arlington, Va., 1998—2006; faculty U. Phoenix, 2002—; founder, CEO Dcom Solutions, Llc, Fairfax, Va., 2001—. Industry advisor and virtual mentor Mgmt. Leadership Tomorrow, NYC, 2005—; dir. Internat. Rsch. Assn., Cambridge, Mass., 2005—; treas. Fairfax Ctr. Recreation Assn., Inc., 2005—; team leader beta program Microsoft, 2001—; v.p. project mgmt. Inst. Diversity SIG, Newtown Sq., Pa., 2005—. Vol. Ctr. Internat. Disaster Info., Arlington, 2003—; pres. Washington organizing com. U.S.-China People Friendship Assn., Fairfax, 2005—. Recipient Software Excellence award, 1996. Mem.: IEEE (sr.), Project Mgmt. Inst., Assn. Computing Machinery (Spl. Interest Group MIS), PA SQL Server, IEEE Control Sys. Soc. (sr.), IEEE Info. Theory Soc. (sr.), IEEE Engring. Mgmt. Soc. (sr.), IEEE Edn. Soc. (sr.), IEEE Computer Soc. (sr.), IEEE Comm. Soc. (sr.). Achievements include development of GTSI.COM, GTSIEXPRESS.COM and MCI ISC Online; C/C++ class libraries for modeling and operation of dimensions and tolerances; computer aided road design system; multimedia general information management software system. Home: 7007 Kilworth Ln Springfield VA 22151-4008 Personal E-mail: ltian01@gmail.com.

TIANO, LINDA V., lawyer, insurance company executive; b. 1957; BA summa cum laude, U. Cin.; JD cum laude, Boston U. Assoc. Epstein Becker and Green, P.C., 1981—90, ptnr., stockholder, 1990—92; v.p. for legal and govt. affairs, gen counsel MVP Health Plan, 1992—95; sr. v.p., gen. counsel Empire BlueCross BlueShield, 1995—2002, WellChoice, Inc., NYC, 2002—05; v.p., dep. gen. counsel for Ea. region & nat. accounts WellPoint, Inc., Indpls., 2005—07; sr. v.p., gen. counsel, sec. Health Net, Inc., Woodland Hills, Calif., 2007—. Office: Health Net Inc 21650 Oxnard St Woodland Hills CA 91367*

TIBAIJUKA, ANNA KAJUMULO, international organization official, advocate, economics professor; b. Muleba, Kagera, Tanzania, Oct. 12, 1950; d. Alexander Bigunila Kajumulo and Aulelia Teyolekelelwa Rwakajuga; m. Wilson Kamuhabwa Tibaijuka, Dec. 27, 1975 (dec.); children: Muganyizi, Kemilembe, Kagemulo, Kankiza. BSc in Agr., U. Dar-Es-Salaam, Tanzania, 1975; MSc in Econs., Swedish Agrl. U., Uppsala, Sweden, 1978, DSc in Econs., 1984; DSc (hon.), U. Coll. London, 2003. Tutorial asst. U. Dar-Es-Salaam, 1975-76, asst. rschr., 1980-81, rsch. fellow, 1981-86, sr. rschr., 1986-94, prof., 1993—98; lectr. Swedish Agrl. U., Uppsala, 1976-79; with UN Conf. on Trade and Devel., Geneva, 1993—2000; under sec. gen., exec. dir. UN-HABITAT, 2002—; dir. gen., Nairobi Hdqs. UN, Kenya, 2006—09. Bd. dirs. UNESCO-ISAB, Paris, 1997—, Conservation Devel. Forum, U. Fla., 1996-97, Tanzania Econ. Policy Devel. and Mgmt Found.; team leader coffee rsch. project, Dar-Es-Salaam, 1986-89; coordinating sec. Social Dimensions Project Planning Commn., Dar-Es-Salaam, 1989-92; spl. coord. at UN conf. on Trade and Devel.; mem., Tanzanian govt. del. to UN summits, including Fourth World Conf. on Women, Beijing, 1995, World Summit for Soc. Devel., Copenhagen, 1995, UN Conf. on Human Settlements, Istanbul, 1996, World Food Summit, Rome 1996. Author: An Economic Analysis of Smallholder Coffee Farms in Tanzania, 1984, The Priority Social Action Programme in Tanzania, 1993; Social Services Crisis of the 1990s, 1998; co-author: (with Frederick Kaijage) Poverty and Social Exclusion in Tanzania, 1996; contbr. articles to profl. jours. Founding chair Tanzania Nat. Women's Coun., Dar-Es-Salaam, 1994—, Barbro Johansson Girls Edn. Trust, 1996—; sec. Muleba Dist. Devel. Assn., 1994-96; convenor Tanzania Local Entrepreneur's Initiative, Dar-Es-Salaam, 1996—; coord. for ea. Africa African Orgns. for Food Security, 1996—. Overseas scholar Swedish Inst., Stockholm, 1981. Mem. Ea. and So. African Econ. Assn., Assn. African Women in R & D. Avocations: gardening, sewing, community development discussion groups. Office: UN-HABITAT PO Box 30030 Nairobi Kenya*

TIBBLE, DOUGLAS CLAIR, lawyer; b. Joliet, Ill., May 26, 1952; BA, DePaul U., 1974; JD, Syracuse U., 1977. Bar: Ill., US Dist. Ct. (no. dist.) Ill., US Ct. Appeals (7th cir.), US Supreme Ct. Ptnr. McDermott, Will & Emery, 1977—95, McBride, Baker & Coles, Oakbrook Terrace, Ill., 1996—2003, Brooks, Adams and Tarulis, Naperville, Ill., 2003—. Mem. ABA, DuPage County Bar Assn., Illinois State Bar Assn. Office: Brooks Adams and Tarulis 101 N Washington St Naperville IL 60540-4511 Office Phone: 630-355-2101. Business E-Mail: dtibble@naperville.com.

TIBBS, MARTHA JANE PULLEN, civic worker, retired social worker; b. Memphis, Feb. 12, 1932; d. John Thomas Jr. and Martha Frances (Gragg) Pullen; m. Eugene Edward Tibbs; children: Martha Katherine, Eugene Edward Jr. BSBA, U. Tenn., 1953; MA Edn., U. Memphis, 1958. Cert. tchr., social worker, Tenn. Tchr. Lausanne Sch., Memphis, 1954-55, Millington H.S., Memphis, 1955-56, Presbyn. Day Sch., Memphis, 1956-57, St. Mary's Episcopal Sch., Memphis, 1958-60; social worker Tenn. Dept. Pub. Welfare, Memphis, 1962-63. Author geneal. works. Mem. Memphis Vol. Svc. Bd., 1963-64; mem. Shelby County Hist. Comm., 1983-97, commr., 1983—; block worker Cancer, Kidney and Heart Fund, Memphis, 1984—; sec., treas. Eastland Presbyterian Ch. Mem.: DAR (past chpt. regent, sec.-treas. regents coun.), AAUW, NEA, Tenn. Geneal. Soc., Tenn. Tchrs. Assn., Colonial Dames of Am., Memphis Scottish Soc., Sovereign Colonial Soc. Ams. Royal Descent, Tenn. State Dames of Ct. of Honor (pres. 2003—05, historian, 1st v.p., nat. def. chmn.), Cleve. Med. Aux. (sec./treas.), West Tenn. Hist. Soc., Chicasaw Dist. DAR Sch. (Tenn. state vice chmn. DAR schs., parliamentarian Zachariah Davies chpt., chmn. Zachariah Davies chpt.), Nat. Registrar Daus. of Founders and Patriots Am. (past Tenn. state registrar 2006—, v.p. Tenn. chpt.), Tenn. State Registrar Founders and Patriots (pres. 2003—), Nat. Soc. Colonial Dames XVII Century (1st v.p., pres. 2003—, 2d v.p. past treas. Chucaqua chpt.), Nat. Soc. So. Dames Am. (historian 2001—02, sec. 2002—, past pres. Memphis chpt., past state pres.), Colonial Dames Am., Tenn. State DAR (transp. chmn. 2001—), Cleve. Jr. Aux., Colonial Order of Crown, Soc. Descendants of Knights Most Noble Order of Garter, Family of Bruce Soc., Planetgenet Soc., Am. Clan Donald Soc., Am. Clan Gregor Soc., Tenn. Soc. Pres. Founders and Patriots of Am., Nat. Soc. Magna Charta Dames and Barons (past state sec. 2000—02, past Magna Carta sec. West Tenn. chpt. 2001—02, treas. West Tenn. chpt. 2002—04), Cleve. Garden Club (past pres.), U. Club Memphis, Early Settlers Shelby County (registrar 1988, bd. dirs. 1992—, sec. 1998—, pres. 2002—), Nineteenth Century Club (newsletter editor 1985—88, sec. 1993—95, corr. sec. 1999—), Racquet Club, Cleve. Women's Club, Alpha Omega Pi. Republican. Presbyterian. Avocations: art, genealogy, computers, dance, tennis. Home: 2008 Massey Rd Memphis TN 38119-6404 Personal E-mail: mtptmem@aol.com.

TIBERI, PATRICK JOSEPH, United States Representative from Ohio, former state legislator; b. Columbus, Ohio, Oct. 21, 1962; m. Denice Tiberi; 1 child. BA in Journalism, Ohio State U., 1985; HHD (hon.), Capital U., 2005. Realtor ReMax Achievers; asst. dist. mgr. Staff of US Rep. John Kasich; mem. Ohio State Ho. Reps. from Dist. 26, 1993—2001, majority leader; mem. ins. and vets. affairs coms. Ohio Ho. Reps.; mem. US Congress from 12th Ohio dist., 2001—, mem. ways and means com., mem. budget com. Mem. adv. bd. Columbus chpt. ARC, Columbus Italian Cultural Ctr.; pres., co-founder Windsor Terrace Learning Ctr. Recipient Pres.'s award, Northland Cmty. Coun., Commendation award, Vet. Adminstrn., Svc. award, ARC, Watchdog of Treasury award, United Conservatives Ohio, Giving from the Heart award, Ctrl. Ohio Chpt. Alzheimer's Assn. Mem.: Sons of Italy. Republican. Roman Catholic. Office: 3000 Corporate Exchange Dr Ste 310 Columbus OH 43231-7689 Office Phone: 614-523-2555, 202-225-5355. Office Fax: 614-818-0887.*

TIBI, RIGOBERT, seismologist, researcher; MS in Geophysics, U. Mining and Tech., Freiburg, Germany, 1995; PhD in Geophysics, Free U. Berlin, 2000. Rsch. asst. GFZ Potsdam, 1997—2000; rsch. assoc. Wash. U., St. Louis, 2000—04, rsch. scientist, 2004—. Contbr. rsch. articles to profl. jours. Grantee, NSF, 2003—. Mem.: German Geophys. Soc., Am. Geophys. Union. Achievements include discovery of deep-faults interaction and deep earthquakes triggering; ground-breaking research on the origin of deep earthquakes, and the structure and sharpness of upper mantle seismic discontinuities near subduction zones. Avocation: soccer. Office: Washington Univ Dept Earth and Planetary Scis One Brookings Dr CB 1169 Saint Louis MO 63130 Business E-Mail: tibi@wustl.edu, tibi@sewmo.wastl.edu.

TIBURCIO, NELSON JOSE, criminologist, consultant; MA, John Jay Coll. Criminal Justice, NY, 2000; PhD, Grad. Ctr., NY, 2006. Cons. 2nd Chance Enterprises, NYC, 2000—. Contbr. articles to profl. jours. Achievements include research in longitudinal follow-up interviewing.

TIBURZI, PAUL A., lawyer; b. Balt., May 28, 1955; BA, Loyola Coll., 1977; JD with honors, Univ. Md., 1980. Bar: Md. 1980. Law clk. Chief Judge Harrison L. Winter, US Ct. Appeals 4th cir.; ptnr., mng. ptnr. Balt. office DLA Piper US LLP, Balt., chmn. state legis. and pub. policy practice group. Editor in chief Md. Law Rev., 1980; legis. counsel and rep. Md. Tort Reform Coalition, 1992—; mem. Coun. Mgmt. and Productivity; adminstrv. law expert, adv. bd. Rev. Md. Laws. Contbr. articles to profl. jours. Chmn. Md. C. of C. Task Force Md. Public Ethics Law, 0200—; mem. transition team Md. Gov. William Donald Schaefer, 1986; chmn. Commn. to Revise Md. Adminstrv. Procedure Act, 1991—92, Md. State Adv. Coun. Adminstrv. Hearings; mem. Md. Governor's Task Force Self-Insurance, 1987, Md. Governor's Task Force Animal Testing, 1989, Md. Governor's Task Force Procurement Law, 1995—96, Md. Governor's Task Force Regulatory Reform, 2000—01, Md. Gen. Assembly Code Revision Com. Public Ethics Law,

1995, Md. Gen. Assembly Code Revision Com. Pub. Svc. Commn. Law, 1998; bd. dir. Greater Balt. Com., 2006—; corp. sec. and chair governance com. Camden Yards Sports and Entertainment Com., Balt., 2006—. Recipient Leadership in Law award, The Daily Record, 2005; named one of Balt.'s Legal Elite, Balt. SmartCEO mag., 2006, Best Lawyers in Am., 2006. Mem.: Wranglers Law Club, Council on Mgmt. & Productivity, Order of the Coif. Office: DLA Piper US LLP 6225 Smith Ave Baltimore MD 21209-3600 Office Phone: 410-580-4273. Office Fax: 410-580-3001. Business E-Mail: paul.tiburzi@dlapiper.com.

TICE, DIANNE LISA, social services administrator; d. Amos Leon Tice and Annie Mae Mobley; 1 child, Daivd J. AA, N.Fla. Jr. Coll., Madison, 1975; BS in Family & Consumer Sci. Edn., Fla. State U., Tallahassee, 1978; MPA, Fla. Internat. U., Miami, 1996. Cert. tchr. Fla., 1978. Social worker State of Fla., Miami, 1985—87; substitute tchr. Hillsbouorgh County Pub. Schs., Tampa, Fla., 1988—89; recreational leader Miami Dade County Parks and Recreation, 1989—91; job developer Miami Dade County Cmty. Action Agy., 1991—. Vol. Inter-City Youth Coun., Miami, 1998—2001. Recipient Centennial Laureate, Fla. State U., 2005; Delores Auzene fellow, Fla. Internat. U., 1995. Mem.: NAACP, Fla. Assn. Cmty. Action (assoc.), Nat. Assn. Family and Consumer Scis. (assoc.), Nat. Coun. Negro Women, Fla. Internat. U. Alumni Asssn. (assoc.), Fla. State U. Alumni & Boosters Assns. (assoc.), Zeta Phi Beta. Democrat. Avocations: walking, bicycling, board games, jazz, card games. Office: Miami Dade County Cmty Action Agy 17801 Homestead Ave Miami FL 33157 Office Fax: 786-293-4598. Business E-Mail: dtice@miamidade.gov.

TICE, DOUGLAS OSCAR, JR., federal judge; b. Lexington, NC, May 2, 1933; s. Douglas Oscar Sr. and Lila Clayton (Wright) T.; m. Janet N. Capps, Feb. 28, 1959 (div. Sept. 1976); children: Douglas Oscar III, Janet E.; m. Martha Murdoch Edwards, June 8, 1996. BS, U. N.C., 1955, JD, 1957. Bar: N.C. 1957, U.S. Ct. Appeals (4th cir.) 1964, Va. 1970, U.S. Dist. ct. (ea. dist.) Va. 1976, U.S. Bankruptcy Ct. (ea. dist.) Va. 1976. Exec. sec. N.C. Jud. Coun., Raleigh, 1958-59; assoc. Baucom & Adams, Raleigh, 1959-61; trial atty. Office Dist. Coun., IRS, Richmond, Va., 1961-70; corp. atty. Carlton Industries, Inc., Richmond, 1970-75; ptnr. Hubard, Tice, Marchant & Samuels, P.C., Richmond, 1975-87; judge U.S. Bankruptcy Ct. (ea. dist.), Richmond, Norfolk, Alexandria, Va., 1987-99, chief judge, 1999—. Co-author: Monument & Boulevard, Richmond's Grand Avenues, 1996; contbr. articles to profl. jours. Vice pres. Richmond Pub. Forum, 1976-80, com. chmn. Richmond Forum, Inc., 1986-2001; past pres. Richmond Civil War Roundtable, mem., 1965—; bd. dirs. Epilepsy Assn. Va., Inc., 1976-87. Capt. USAR, 1957-66. Fellow Am. Coll. Bankruptcy; mem. ABA, Va. Bar Assn., City of Richmond Bar Assn., Am. Bankruptcy Inst., Nat. Conf. Bankruptcy Judges (bd. govs. 2005—08), So. Hist. Assn., Va. Hist. Soc., Old Dominion Sertoma (pres. Richmond chpt. 1967), Comml. Law League Am., Supreme Ct. Hist. Soc., Am. Inn of Ct., Hist. Soc. of U.S. Dist. Ct. for Eastern Va. (asst. sec., bd. dir. mem. 2006—). Home: 5 Foxmere Dr Richmond VA 23238 Office: US Bankruptcy Ct 1100 E Main St Ste 339 Richmond VA 23219-3538 Home Phone: 804-740-1265; Office Phone: 804-916-2460. Personal E-mail: thetices2@comcast.net. Business E-Mail: douglas_tice@vaeb.uscourts.gov.

TICE, GEORGE A(NDREW), photographer; b. Newark, Oct. 13, 1938; s. William S. and Margaret T. (Robertson) T.; m. Joanna Blaylock, 1958; m. Marie Tremmel, 1960; children: Christopher, Loretta, Lisa, Lynn, Jennifer. DHL (hon.), William Paterson U., 2003. Instr. photography New Sch. Social Research, 1970-98. Photographer (one-man shows) Met. Mus. Art, 1972, Internat. Ctr. Photography, 2002, Newark Mus., 2006, (group shows) Whitney Mus. Am. Art, 1974, Mus. Modern Art, 1979, J. Paul Getty Mus., 2006, (permanent collections) Mus. Modern Art, Met. Mus. Art, Art Inst. Chgo., Bibliotheque Nationale, Nihon U., Tokyo, books include Fields of Peace, 1970, Fields of Peace, reissued, 1998, Goodbye River, Goodbye, 1971, Paterson, 1972, Seacoast Maine, 1973, Seacoast Maine 2nd edit., 2009, George A. Tice Photographs, 1953-73, 1975, Urban Landscapes, 1975, Artie Van Blarcum, 1977, Urban Romantic, 1982, Lincoln, 1984, Hometowns, 1988, Stone Walls, Grey Skies, 1991, George Tice: Selected Photographs, 1953-1999, 2001, George Tice: Urban Landscapes, 2002, Common Mementos, 2005, Paterson II, 2006, Ticetown, 2007. Served with USN, 1956-59. Recipient Grand prix for best photography book of Year Arles, France, 1973; Guggenheim Found. fellow, 1973-74, Nat. Endowment for Arts fellow, 1973—; Bradford fellow, Eng., 1990-91, N.J. State Coun. on the Arts fellow, 1998. Address: 581 Kings Hwy East Atlantic Highlands NJ 07716-2825 Office Phone: 732-706-3585.

TICE, JENNIFER S., music educator; b. Sellersville, Pa., Nov. 28, 1979; d. Barry M. and Cheryl C. Tice. MusM, West Chester U., Pa., 2007. Cert. Kodaly Pa., 2007. Pvt. practice, Yardley, Pa., 2003—; vocal music tchr. Pennsbury Sch. Dist., Fallsington, Pa., 2003—. Music dir. Village Pk. Elem., Fairless Hills, Pa., 2003—. Musician: (songs) (chorus musical dir.) Spring Concerts (Pennsbury Arts Found. grants, 2006). Vol. animal rescue Main Line Animal Rescue, Pa., 2007—. Home: 1654A Trellis Circle Yardley PA 19067-6334

TICE, RAPHAEL DEAN, military officer; b. Topeka, Dec. 4, 1927; s. Arthur Taylor and Mamie (McDonald) T.; m. Eunice Miriam Suddarth, Dec. 23, 1946; children: Karen Ann Tice Claterbos, William Dean. BS in Mil. Sci., U. Md., 1963; MSBA, George Washington U., 1970. Served as enlisted man U.S. Army, 1946-47; commd. 2d lt., 1947; advanced through grades to lt. gen., 1981; platoon leader and co. comdr. 1st Inf. div., W.Ger., 1949-52; co. comdr., regimental adj. 8th Inf. divsn., 1955-56; tng. advisor Vietnam, 1956-57; mem. staff Office of Dep. Chief of Staff for Pers., Dept. Army, 1960-63; chief pers. mgmt. divsn. Office of Under Sec. of Army, 1963-64; plans Officer So. Command, Panama, 1965-67; dep. comdr. 3rd Brig., 4th Inf. Divsn., 1967; comdr. 2nd Bn., 12th Inf. of 25th Inf. divsn., Vietnam, 1968; exec. for pers. procurement Office of Sec. Def. for Manpower and Res. Affairs, 1968-69; comdr. 1st Brig., 1st Inf. divsn., 1970, chief of staff, 1971; dep. dir. mil. pers. mgmt. Dept. Army, 1972-73; comdg. gen. Berlin Brigade, 1974-76; dep. chief of staff personnel U.S. Army Europe, 1976-77; comdg. gen. 3rd. Inf. divsn., 1977-79; dep. asst. sec. def. for mil. pers. and force mgmt. Dept. Def., 1979-85; exec. dir. Nat. Recreation and Pk. Assn., 1986—2001; ret., 2001. Spl. adviser Pres.'s Coun. on Phys. Fitness and Sports; bd. dirs. Sports Pub. LLC, Class 6 Kayak, Inc. Decorated Silver Star, Legion of Merit with 2 oak leaf clusters, Air medal with V and 7 oak leaf clusters, Bronze Star with V, Vietnam Cross of Gallantry with Palm, Purple Heart., Def. Disting. Service medal, Army Disting. Service medal Mem. Assn. U.S. Army, Am. Chess Found. (hon. pres.) Home: 18077 Clendenning Cir Round Hill VA 20141-2580 Home Phone: 540-338-7194. Personal E-mail: ticepunky@aol.com.

TICHENOR, CHARLES BECKHAM, III, operations research analyst; b. Balt., Mar. 10, 1950; s. Charles Beckham II and Suzanne Nelson (Stevens) T.; m. Alison P. Walton, May 29, 1971; 1 child, Charles Beckham IV. BSBA, Ohio State U., 1972; MBA, Va. Tech., 1990; PhD in Bus., Berne U., 1999. Asst. prodn. supr. Champale Products, Norfolk, Va., 1977—80; ops. rsch. analyst IRS, Washington, 1989—93, tech. adv. info. sys. performance mgmt. office, 1999—2000; ops. rsch. analyst Dept. Def., Alexandria, Va., 2000—. Adj. prof. Strayer U., Balt. Lt. col. USAR, ret. Mem. Mensa. Roman Catholic. Avocations: Tae Kwon Do, astronomy. Home: 6207 Cardinal Brook Ct Springfield VA 22152-1516 Office: Def Security Coop Agy 201 12th St S Ste 203 Arlington VA 22202 Personal E-mail: charley_tichenor@hotmail.com.

TICHENOR, WARREN W., United States Ambassador to the United Nations, Geneva; b. Harlingen, Tex., 1960; m. Rhonda Tichenor; 1 child, Warren II. BS, U. So. Calif., LA, 1982. Various positions Tichenor Media Systems, Inc. (later renamed Hispanic Broadcasting Corp.); pres. WW Tichenor & Co., Inc, San Antonio; US amb. to the UN US Dept. State, Geneva, 2006—. Dir., Hispanic campaign George Bush Tex. Gubernatorial Campaign, 1998, George Bush Presdl. Campaign, 2000. Office: US Mission to UN in Geneva Route de Pregny 11 1292 Chambesy Geneva Switzerland*

TIDBALL, CHARLES STANLEY, computer scientist, educator; b. Geneva, Apr. 15, 1928; (parents Am. citizens); s. Charles Taylor and Adele (Desmaison) T.; m. Mary Elizabeth Peters, Oct. 25, 1952. BA, Wesleyan U., Middletown, Conn., 1950; MS (Univ. scholar), U. Rochester, NY, 1952; PhD, U. Wis., Madison, 1955; MD (Shattuck fellow, Van Noyes scholar), U. Chgo., 1958; LHD (hon.), Wilson Coll., Chambersburg, Pa., 1994; DSc (hon.), Hood Coll., Frederick, Md., 1999. Rotating intern Madison Gen. Hosp., 1958-59; physician I Mendota State Hosp., Madison, 1959; asst. rsch. prof. physiology dept. George Washington U. Med. Center, Washington, 1959-63, asso. prof., acting chmn. dept., 1963-64, prof., 1964-65, chmn. dept., 1964-71, Henry D. Fry prof., 1965-84, research prof. med., 1972-80; dir. Office Computer Assisted Edn. George Washington U. Med. Ctr., Washington, 1973-75, dir. Office Computer Assisted Edn. and Svcs., 1975-78; Lucie Stern disting. vis. prof. natural scis. Mills Coll., 1980; prof. edn. George Washington U., 1982-84, dir. ednl. computing tech. program Sch. Edn., 1982-84, prof. computer medicine Med. Ctr., 1984-92, prof. emeritus computer medicine, 1992, prof. neurol. surgery, 1990-92, prof. emeritus neurol. surgery, 1992; civil surgeon Immigration and Naturalization Svc., Dept. Justice, Washington, 1986-89; disting. rsch. scholar, co-dir. Tidball Ctr. for Study Ednl. Environments Hood Coll., Frederick, Md., 1994—. Trustee in residence Skidmore Coll., 1995. Co-author: Consolidated Index to For Thy Great Glory, 1993, Taking Women Seriously, 1999, Jesus, Lazarus, and the Messiah, 2005; editor: (with M. C. Shelesnyak) Frontiers in the Teaching of Physiology: Computer Literacy and Simulation, 1981; mem. editorial bd. Jour. Applied Physiology, 1966-69, Jour. Computer-Based Instrn., 1974-89, Am. Jour. Physiology; assoc. editor The Physiologist, 1979-85; contbr. articles to profl. jours. Trustee Cathedral Choral Soc., 1976-79, Wilson Coll., 1983-92, Everitt-Pomeroy, 1993-96, trustee emeritus, 2009-, Population Reference Bur., 1987-94, 1996-2002, chmn. bd. trustees, 1992-94, sec., 1994-97; lay reader St. Albans Parish, 1965-67, Washington Nat. Cathedral, 1967-94, lay eucharist minister, 1994—, clergy asst., 1968—, homilist, 1977—, info. sys. specialist, 1986-93, vol. mgr. info. sys. program, 1993—; mem. commn. Episcopal Diocese Washington, 1964—; mem. com. mgmt. YMCA Camp Letts, 1968-96, chmn., 1972-75, dir., chmn. Endowment Fund, 1977-96; bd. dirs. Met. YMCA, Washington, 1972-84, trustees coun., 1984-91, fin. com., 1972-93, v.p. internat. program, 1974-75, asst. treas., 1975-77, v.p., treas., 1977-79, vice chmn., 1979-80, chmn., 1980-82, pres. of found., 1991-93; bd. dirs., treas. Woodley Ensemble, 1993-2003; bd. dirs. Mid-Atlantic Region YMCA, 1974-83; bd. dirs., vice-chmn. Cathedral West Condo., 1983-84, chmn., 1984-87, 91-93, fin. com., 1979-94; bd. dirs. Buckingham's Choice Residents' Assn., 2000-02, chmn. resident svcs. com., 2000-02, mem. fin. com., 2004—. Recipient Rsch. Career award USPHS, 1961-63, award Washington Acad. Scis., 1967; named Leader of Yr. award Met. YMCA, Washington, 1974, Red Triangle award, 1976, Service award, 1979; Dakota Indian name Am. Youth Found., 1976; Found. Anniversary award Cathedral Choral Soc., 2007; Rsch. Career Devel. awardee USPHS, 1961-63. Mem. Am. Physiol. Soc. (emeritus). Home: 3200 Baker Cir #I-235 Adamstown MD 21710 E-mail: ctidball@gwu.edu.

TIDBALL, M. ELIZABETH PETERS, physiologist, educator; b. Anderson, Ind., Oct. 15, 1929; d. John Winton and Beatrice (Ryan) Peters; m. Charles S. Tidball, Oct. 25, 1952. BA, Mt. Holyoke Coll., 1951, LHD, 1976; MS, U. Wis., 1955, PhD, 1959; MTS summa cum laude, Wesley Theol. Sem., 1990; DSc (hon.), Wilson Coll., 1973, Trinity Coll., 1974, Cedar Crest Coll., 1977, U. of South, 1978, Goucher Coll., 1979, St. Mary-of-The-Woods Coll., 1986; LittD (hon.), Regis Coll., 1980, Coll. St. Catherine, 1980, Alverno Coll., 1989; HHD (hon.), St. Mary's Coll., 1977, Hood Coll., 1982; LLD (hon.), St. Joseph Coll., 1983; LHD (hon.), Skidmore Coll., 1984, Marymount Coll., 1985, Converse Coll., 1985, Mt. Vernon Coll., 1986. Tchg. asst. physiology dept. U. Wis., 1952—55, rsch. asst. physiology dept., 1958—59; rsch. asst. anatomy dept. U. Chgo., 1955-56, rsch. asst. physiology dept., 1956-58; USPHS postdoctoral fellow NIH, Bethesda, Md., 1959-61; staff pharmacologist Hazleton Labs., Falls Church, Va., 1961, cons., 1962; assoc. in physiology George Washington U. Med. Ctr., 1960-62, asst. rsch. prof. dept. pharmacology, 1962-64, assoc. rsch. prof. dept. physiology, 1964-70, rsch. prof., 1970-71, prof., 1971-94, prof. emeritus, 1994—; asst. dir. M of Theol. Studies program Wesley Theol Sem., 1993-94; disting. rsch. scholar Hood Coll., Frederick, Md., 1994—, co-dir. Tidball Ctr. for Study of Ednl. Environments, 1994—. Lucie Stern Disting. vis. prof. natural scis. Mills Coll., 1980; scholar in residence Coll. Preachers, 1984, Salem Coll., 1985, Wesley Theol. Sem., 1992; Disting. scholar in residence So. Meth. U., 1985; vis. trustee prof. Skidmore Coll., 1995; cons. FDA, 1966-67, assoc. sci. coord. sci. assocs. tng. programs, 1966-67; com. on NIH tng. programs and fellowships NAS, 1972-75; faculty summer confs. Am. Youth Found., 1967-78; founder, dir. Summer Seminars Women Am. Youth Found., 1987-95; cons. for instl. rsch. Wellesley Coll., 1974-75; exec. sec. com. on edn. and employment women in sci. and engrng. Commn. on Human Resources, NRC/NAS, 1974-75, vice-chmn., 1977-82; cons., staff officer NRC/NAS, 1974-75; cons. Woodrow Wilson Nat. Fellowship Found., 1975-99, NSF, 1974-91; bd. mentor Assn. Governing Bds. Univs. and Colls., 1991-2000, Gale Fund for the Study of Trusteeship Adv. Comm., 1992-98; cons. Women's Coll. Coalition Rsch. Adv. Com., 1992-2000; Single Gender Schooling Working Group, US Dept. Edn., 1992-94, Women's Colls. Roundtable, 1998; rep. to DC Commn. on Status of Women, 1972-75; nat. panelist Am. Coun. on Edn., 1983-90; panel mem. Congl. Office Tech. Assessment, 1986-87; fellows selection com., fellows mentor Coll. Preachers, 1992-05. Lead author: Taking Women Seriously: Lessons and Legacies for Educating the Majority, American Council on Education Higher Education Series, 1999; columnist Trusteeship, 1993-95; mem. editl. bd. Jour. Higher Edn., 1979-84, cons. editor, 1984—; mem. editl. bd. Religion and Intellectual Life, 1983—; contbr. articles to profl. jours. Trustee Mt. Holyoke Coll., 1968-73, vice chmn., 1972-73, trustee fellow, 1988—; trustee Hood Coll., 1972-84, 86-92, exec. com., 1974-84, 89-92, trustee emerita, 1997—; overseer Sweet Briar Coll., 1978-85, dir. emerita, 2003—; trustee Cathedral Choral Soc., 1976-90, pres. bd. trustees, 1982-84, hon. trustee, 1991—; trustee Skidmore Coll., 1988—, exec. com., 1993—2009, trustee Bishop Claggett Ctr., 2003-09; governing bd. Cathedral Coll. of Preachers, 1979-85, chmn., 1983-85; governing bd. Protestant Episcopal Cathedral Found., 1983-85, exec. com., 1983-85; bd. vis. Salem Coll., 1986-93; ctr. assoc. Nat. Resource Ctr., Girls Club Am., 1983-90; governing bd. Buckinham's Choice Residents' Assn., 1999-2002; cathedral vol. coun. Washington Nat. Cathedral, 2006-09. Recipient Alumnae medal Honor, Mt. Holyoke Coll., 1971, Outstanding Svc. award, Am. Youth Found., 1975, Valuable Contbns. Gen. Alumni Assn. award, George Washington U., 1982, 1987, Pres.'s medal, 1999, medal Outstanding Achievement, Chestnut Hill Coll., 1987, Lifetime Svc. and Scholarship award, Bd. Women's Coll. Coalition and Nation's Women's Coll. Presidents, 1998, Order of Merit, Cathedral Choral Soc., 2000, Kemball-Cook Trustee award, Skidmore Coll., 2008; named Outstanding Grad., The Penn Hall Sch., 1988; Shattuck fellow, 1955—56, Mary E. Woolley fellow, Mt. Holyoke Coll., 1958—59, postdoctoral fellow, USPHS, 1959—61. Mem. AAAS, Am. Physiol. Soc. (chmn. task force on women in physiology 1973-80, com. on coms. 1977-80, mem. emeritus 1994—), Am. Assn. Higher Edn., Mt. Holyoke Alumnae Assn. (dir. 1966-70, 76-77), Histamine Club, Sigma Delta Epsilon, Sigma Xi. Episcopalian. Home: 4100 Cathedral Ave NW Washington DC 20016-3584 also: 3200 Baker Cir I-235 Adamstown MD 21710 Home Phone: 301-644-1793.

TIDEMAN, T. NICOLAUS, economics educator; b. Chgo., Aug. 11, 1943; s. Robert and Jane Catherine (Schmidt) T.; m. Lisa Nicole Woodside, Jan. 29, 1965 (div. Jan. 1971); m. M.J. Estill Putney, Jan. 19, 1971. BA, Reed Coll., 1965; PhD, U. Chgo., 1969. Asst. prof. Harvard U., Cambridge, Mass., 1969—73; sr. staff economist Pres.'s Coun. Econ. Advisors, Washington, 1970-71; postdoctoral fellow Ctr. for Study of Pub. Choice, Blacksburg, Va., 1973-75; assoc. prof. Va. Tech., Blacksburg, 1975-85, prof. econs., 1985—; pres. Schalkenbach Found., NYC, 1996—2002. Cons. Bur. of the Budget, Washington, 1969, U.S. Treasury, Washington, 1973-75, various law firms, Boston, also Roanoke, Va., 1972-96. Contbr. articles to profl. jours. Recipient Disting. Rsch. in Edn. award Va. Edn. Assn., 1976. Mem. Am. Econ. Assn. (nominating com., 1992), Mt. Tabor Ruritan Club (pres. 1995).

TIDWELL, BETTY DAVENPORT, special education educator; b. Birmingham, Ala., Feb. 15, 1953; d. William Harry and Edna Earl (Staggs) Davenport; children: David, Daniel. Dental technician, Carrer Acad., Atlanta, 1973; BS in Spl. Edn. with honors, Auburn U., 1992, M in Mild Learning Handicapped, 1994. Cert. spl. edn. tchr., Ala. Dental technician Clanton Dental Lab., Ala., 1973—86; tchr. asst. Clanton Elem. Sch., 1988—92, tchr. spl. edn., 1992—; tchr. emotionally conflicted Children's Harbor Sch., Ala.; edn. coord. Cmty. Intensive Treatment for Youth, Clanton, 1994—, program coord., 2006. Sec. Thorsby (Ala.) Band Boosters, 1989-91; parade organizer Thorsby Swedish Heritage Com., 1992-93. Mem. NEA, Ala. Edn. Assn., Coun. for Exceptional Children, Kappa Delta Phi, Phi Kappa Phi. Baptist. Avocations: crafts, playing piano, singing, special olympics. Home: 806 Ware Ave Clanton AL 35045 Personal E-mail: angelinelanton38@yahoo.com, bettytidwell@bellsouth.net. Business E-Mail: btidwell@cityprograms.com.

TIDWELL, JERRY, retail executive; With Pepsi Cola Co., 1974—98, Safeway, Inc., 1998—2000, dir. grocery bus. unit, 2000—01, v.p. milk and beverage mfg., 2001—03, sr. v.p. supply ops., 2003—. Office: Safeway Inc 5918 Stoneridge Mall Rd Pleasanton CA 94588 Office Phone: 925-467-3000. Office Fax: 925-467-3323.*

TIE, JIAN-KE, medical educator; Rsch. asst. prof. U. NC, Chapel Hill, 2006—. Office: Univ NC Chapel Hill Wilson Hall 446 Chapel Hill NC 27599-3280 Home Fax: 919-962-9266. Business E-Mail: jktie@email.unc.edu.

TIEDE, TOM ROBERT, journalist; b. Huron, SD, Feb. 24, 1937; s. Leslie Albert and Rose (Allen) T.; children: Kristina Anne, Thomas Patrick. BA in Journalism, Wash. State U., 1959. Mem. staff Kalispell (Mont.) Daily Interlake, 1960-61, Daytona Beach (Fla.) News Jour., 1961-63; war corr. Newspaper Enterprise Assn., NYC, 1964—. Lectr. in field. Author: Your Men at War, 1965, Coward, 1968, Calley: Soldier or Killer?, 1971, Welcome to Washington, Mr. Witherspoon, 1979, The Great Whale Rescue, 1986, American Tapestry: Eye Witness Accounts of the 1900's, 1988, The Man Who Discovered Pluto, 1990, Fosser, 1994, Self Help Nation, 2001; permanent collections Boston U. Libr. Served as lt., inf. AUS, 1960. Recipient Ernie Pyle Meml. award, 1965; Freedoms Found. award, 1966; George Washington medal, 1972 Mem. Internat. Platform Assn., Sigma Delta Chi, Lambda Chi Alpha. Clubs: Overseas Press, National Press, Nat. Headliners (award 1966 Atlantic City). Roman Catholic. Office: NEA 1090 Vermont Ave NW Washington DC 20005-4905 Personal E-mail: tom-tiede@msn.com.

TIEDEMANN, CHARLES WELCH (CHAD), lawyer; b. Bronxville, NY, Jan. 30, 1956; AB, U. Notre Dame, 1978; JD, Catholic U. Am., 1981. Bar: DC 1981. With Holland & Knight LLP, Washington; former chmn., nat. real estate practice; ptnr. Holland & Knight LLP, Washington, chair, United Way Campaign, chair, Christmas in April House Sponsorship. Mem.: Bldg. Industry Assn. (mem. real estate group, Washington. DC), ABA, DC Bar, U. Notre Dame Alumni Club (Washington, DC). Office: Holland & Knight LLP 2099 Pennsylvania Ave NW Ste 100 Washington DC 20006 Business E-Mail: chad.tiedemann@hklaw.com.

TIEDGE, HENRI, medical educator, researcher; came to U.S., 1986; m. Ellen Hsu. PhD, U. Hannover, Germany, 1986. Asst. prof. SUNY HSCB, Bklyn., 1994—97, assoc. prof., 1997—2002, prof., 2002—. Contbr. chpts. to books, articles to profl. jours. Recipient awards, NIH, NSF, DOD. Mem. Soc. Cell Biology, Soc. for Neurosci. Office Phone: 718-270-1370.

TIEDJE, JAMES MICHAEL, microbiologist, ecologist, educator; b. Newton, Iowa, Feb. 9, 1942; married, 1965; 3 children. BS, Iowa State U., 1964; MS, Cornell U., 1966, PhD in Soil Microbiology, 1968. From asst. prof. to prof. Mich. State U., 1968-78, disting. prof., 1991—; dir. sci. and tech. ctr. microbial ecology NSF, 1988—. Vis. assoc. prof. U. Ga., 1974-75; cons. NSF, 1974-77; vis. prof. U. Calif. Berkeley, 1981-82; mem. biotech. sci. adv. com. EPA, 1986-89, chair sci. adv. coun. GPA, 1988-90. Editor: Applied Microbiology, 1974—, editor-in-chief, 1980-86. Recipient Carlos J. Finley prize, UNESCO, 1993. Mem. AAAS, Am. Soc. Agronomy (Soil Sci. award 1990), Internat. Inst. Biotech., Am. Soc. Microbiology (award in applied and environ. microbiology 1992), Soil Sci. Soc. Am., Ecol. Soc. Am., Internat. Soc. Soil Sci. (chair soil biology divsn.). Achievements include research in dentrification, microbial metabolism of organic pollutants, and molecular microbiol. ecology. Office: Michigan State U Microbial Ecology Ctr 540 Plant & Soil Scis Bldg East Lansing MI 48824-1325

TIEFEL, VIRGINIA MAY, librarian; b. Detroit, May 20, 1926; d. Karl and June Garland (Young) Brenkert; m. Paul Martin Tiefel, Jan. 25, 1947; children: Paul Martin Jr., Mark Gregory. BA in Elem. Edn., Wayne State U., 1962; MA in Library Sci., U. Mich., 1968. Librarian Birmingham Schs., Mich., 1967-68; librarian S. Euclid-Lyndhurst Schs., Cleve., 1968-69; acquisitions-reference librarian Hiram Coll., Ohio, 1969-77;

head undergrad. libraries Ohio State U., Columbus, 1977-84, dir. library user edn., 1978-95, faculty outreach coord., 1995-98. Contbr. articles to profl. jours. Recipient Disting. Alumnus award, U. Mich. Sch. Info. and Libr. Studies, 1993. Mem. ALA (v.p. Ohio sect. 1973-74, pres. 1974-75, Miriam Dudley Bibliographic Instrn. Librarian of Yr. 1986), Acad. Library Assn. Ohio (Outstanding Ohio Acad. Librarian 1984), Assn. Coll. and Research Libraries (chmn. bibliographic instrn. sect. com. on research 1983-84, chmn. com. on performance measures 1984-90). Lutheran. Achievements include Excellence in Teaching award at Ohio State University Libraries established in her honor in 2004. Home: 4711 Oak Bluff Ct Eau Claire WI 54701 E-mail: vtiefel1@aol.com.

TIEFEL, WILLIAM REGINALD, hotel company executive; b. Rochester, NY, Mar. 30, 1934; s. William Reginald and Mary Hazel (Cross) T.; m. Vada Morell, Dec. 30, 1985 (dec. Apr. 1999); m. Norma Gewirz Kline, Nov. 25, 2000. Student, Williams Coll., 1952-54; BA with honors, Mich. State U., 1956; postgrad., Harvard Bus. Sch.; DBA in Hospitality Mgmt. (hon.), Johnson and Wales U. Gen. mgr. Marriott Hotels, Arlington, Va., 1964-65, Saddle Brook, NJ, 1966-69, Newton, Mass., 1969-71, regional v.p. Washington, 1971-80; corp. v.p. Marriott Corp., Washington, 1976-89; exec. v.p. Marriott Hotels and Resorts, Washington, 1980-88; pres. Marriott Hotels, Resorts and Suites, 1988-92; exec. v.p., mem. exec. and growth coms. Marriott Corp., 1988—2002; pres. Marriott Lodging Group, 1992-98; vice chmn. Marriott Internat., 1998—2002; chmn. Ritz-Carlton Hotel Co, 1998—2002, chmn. emeritus, 2002—; dir. Bulgari Hotels and Resorts, 2001—07. Bd. dir. CarMax Inc., 2002—, chmn., 2007—; dir. Lydian Pvt. Bank, 2005—, Lydian Trust Co., 2008—. Bd. visitors Valley Forge Mil. Acad. and Jr. Coll., 1976-79, chmn., 1979, trustee, 1982-92; chmn. Campaign Valley Forge, 1985-88, chmn. com. on trustees, 1989-91, hon. life trustee; trustee Johnson and Wales U., 2002—, Norton Mus. Art, 2004-08, adv. coun. Wilmer Eye Inst., Johns Hopkins U.; trustee Town Palm Beach United Way, Lydian Trust, 2008-, With US Army, 1956. Mem. Am. Hotel and Lodging Assn. (dir. Ednl. Inst., Arthur Landstreet award 1997), Soc. of the Four Arts (Palm Beach), Club Colette (Palm Beach), Cosmos Club (Washington), Tavern Club (NYC). Independent. Roman Catholic. Home: 236 Via Las Brisas Palm Beach FL 33480-3612 E-mail: william.tiefel@ritzcarlton.com.

TIEFENBRUN, JONATHAN, surgeon; b. NYC, Feb. 5, 1943; s. Joseph and Helen (Henkin) Tiefenbrun; m. Susan Kissil, June 19, 1966; children: Michele, Jeremy, Gregory. MD, SUNY, Bklyn., 1966. Diplomate Am. Bd. Surgery. Med. intern Kings County Hosp., Bklyn., 1966—67; resident in surgery Mt. Sinai Hosp., NYC, 1967—73, chief resident in surgery, 1972—73, attending surgeon, 1973, Beth Israel Hosp., NYC, 1981; sr. attending surgeon St. Luke's Roosevelt Hosp., NYC, 1981; dir. clin. rsch. Lifescore Global Network, San Diego, 2001—03; dir. Balboa Nephrology Ultrasound Lab., San Diego, 2003—. Asst. prof. Mt. Sinai Sch. Medicine, NYC, 1973; clin. prof. surgery U. Calif., San Diego, 2003; mem. nat. ultrasound faculty Am. Coll. Surgeons. Contbr. articles to profl. journals. Fellow NIH, 1968—70. Fellow: Nat. Ultrasound Faculty of ACS (instr. clin. ultrasound, cons. dialysis access surgery); mem.: NY Cardiovasc. Soc. Achievements include patents in field; invention of catheters; endovascular grafts; ultrasonic and laser devices; gen. and vascular medicine and surgery diagnostic ultrasound. Avocation: classical guitar. Personal E-mail: susant@tjsl.edu.

TIEFENBRUNN, ALAN JAMES, medical educator; b. St. Louis, Aug. 26, 1948; s. Kenneth Sylvester and Margaret Ann (Smith) T.; m. Sharon Kay Frost, June 3, 1972; children: Theresa, Curtis. AB cum laude, Washington U., St. Louis, 1970, MD, 1974. Intern, resident U. Calif., San Diego, 1974-77; fellow in cardiology Washington U., St. Louis, 1977-79, asst. prof. medicine, 1980-86, assoc. prof. medicine, 1986—2008, prof. medicine, 2008—, asst. prof. radiology St. Louis, 1980—; physician Barnes Hosp., St. Louis, 1980—2008, phyisician, 2008—, prof. medicine, 2008—. Mem. adv. bd. Nat. Registry Myocardial Infarction, 1991—; cons. in field. Contbr. articles to profl. jours. Fellow Am. Coll. Cardiology, Am. Heart Assn. (coun. clin.cardiology), Alpha Omega Alpha. Avocations: skiing, scuba diving, shotgun sports. Home: 6255 Wydown Blvd Saint Louis MO 63105-2306 Office: Washington U Box 8086 660 S Euclid Ave Saint Louis MO 63110-1093 E-mail: atiefenb@im.wustl.edu.

TIELKE, JAMES CLEMENS, retired retail and manufacturing executive; b. St. Helena, Nebr., May 15, 1931; s. Joseph Hubert and Catherine Josephine (Schmidt) T.; m. Betty Merle Adams, Apr. 18, 1953; children: P.J., Michael J., Dawn M. BS in Bus. Adminstrn., U. S.D., 1959, MA in Speech and Econ., 1960. Partner, Tielke Motors, Yankton, SD, 1952-54; owner Ft. Collins Motors, Colo., 1954-56; grad. tchg. asst. U. S.D., 1959-60; corp. buyer and mgr. auto, lawn/garden, paint, electronics Montgomery Ward, Chgo., 1960-77, v.p. mdse. adminstrn., 1978-81; pres. Midwest div. Structured Approaches, Inc., 1981-82; v.p. nat. accounts Dupli-Color Products, Elk Grove Village, Ill., 1983-85; pres. Black Leaf Products Co., 1985-89; v.p. Hysan Corp., Des Plaines, Ill., 1985-89; v.p. ice melter sales Koos, Inc., IMC Vigoro, Kenosha, Wis., 1989-97; pres. J.C. Tielke Assocs., Inc., 1997—2009. Mem. Nat. Ind. Conf. Bd. Pers. Mgmt. Conf., 1966, Am. Mgmt. Assn. Sr. Mgmt. Conf., 1977. Chmn. Chgo. Minority Bus. Opportunities Fair Devel. Commn.; bd. dirs. Chgo. Youth Ctrs., 1979-82. Recipient Honors award U. S.D. Sch. Bus., 1977

TIELMAN, ROB A.P., social sciences educator; b. Hilversum, The Netherlands, Aug. 19, 1946; s. Albert Tielman and Tine Angenent. MA in Sociology, U. Utrecht, Netherlands, 1971; PhD in Social Sci., U. Utrecht, 1982. Mem. acad. staff U. Utrecht, 1971—, head Gay and Lesbian Studies dept., 1982—92, prof. humanist studies, 1987—. Chmn. adv. bd. WHO, Geneva, 1989—93; head humanist tchr. tng. Humanist Ethical Edn., Utrecht, 1993—99; sec. Study Ctr. Pub. Edn., Utrecht, 1994—; sr. advisor pub. edn. Gen. Pedagogic Ctr., Utrecht, 1994—2005; pres. ethics commn. Dutch Inst. Mental Health, Utrecht, 1975—97; pres. Pub. Schs. in the Netherlands, Utrecht, 1989—; v.p. European Platform on Edn., Alkmaar, 1994—2006; rep. of Internat. Humanist Ethical Union UNESCO, Paris, 1989—99, Coun. of Europe, Strasbourg, 1989—; rep. of European Humanist Fedn. EU, Brussels, 1991—99. Author: Homoseksualiteit in Nederland, 1982; editor: Bisexuality and HIV/AIDS, 1991, Third Pink Book, 1993. Sec.-gen. Dutch Gay and Lesbian Assn., Amsterdam, 1971—75; pres. Dutch Humanist Assn., Utrecht, 1977—87, Internat. Humanist Ethical Union, London, 1986—98, Humanist Archives, Utrecht, 1996—, Ctr. for Inquiry in the Low Countries, 2006—, Jopie Huisman Mus., 2006—. Named Knight, Queen of the Netherlands, 1987. Fellow: Internat. Acad. Humanism; mem.: Dutch Gay and Lesbian Profs. (sec. 1998—), European Humanist Profls. (pres. 1993—2000). Dutch Labor Party. Humanist. Avocation: historical topography of the low countries and former Dutch colonies. Office: Universiteit Utrecht Heidelberglaan 2 3584 CS Utrecht Netherlands Office Phone: +31-30-2989167. Personal E-mail: robtielman@yahoo.com.

TIEMSTRA, JOHN PETER, economics professor; b. Chgo., July 15, 1950; s. Peter John and Margaret T.; m. Suzanne Spicer, Dec. 28, 1985; 1 child: Remi Spicer Rakipi. AB, Oberlin Coll., 1971; PhD, MIT, 1975. Asst. prof. econs. Calvin Coll., Grand Rapids, Mich., 1975-81, assoc. prof., 1981-85, prof., 1985—. Vis. prof. Potchefstroom U., South Africa, 1992. Author: Economics: A Developmental Approach, 1999; editor, co-author: Reforming Economics, 1990; contbr. articles to profl. jours. Dean Grand Rapids Am. Guild of Organists, 1990-91; pres. West Mich. Irish Heritage Soc., Grand Rapids, 1988-91, Forest Hills Condo Assn., Cascade, Mich., 1988-2008; organist St. Paul's Episcopal Ch., Grand Rapids, 1990-06, Working Group on Ethics and the Earth, Reformed Ch. in Am., 2002-04. Recipient Thomas F. Divine award, 2009. Mem. Assn. Social Econs. (v.p. 2005, pres.-elect 2006, pres. 2007), Assn. Christian Economists, Am. Econ. Assn., Faith Economic (bd. editor 2008-). Avocation: music. Office: Calvin Coll 1740 Knollcrest Cir SE Grand Rapids MI 49546-4301 Office Phone: 616-526-6192. Business E-Mail: tmst@calvin.edu.

TIEN, JAMES M., dean, engineering educator, consultant; b. NYC, Mar. 27, 1945; s. Yu-Shih Tien and Tien-Lun Li; m. Ellen S. Weston, Aug. 27, 1981; children: Lee, Rex. BEE, Rensselaer Poly. Inst., 1966; SM, MIT, 1967, PhD, 1972. Mem. tech. staff Bell Labs., Holmdel, NJ, 1966-69; rsch. project dir. Rand Corp., NYC, 1970-73; area dir. Urban Sys. Rsch. & Engring., Cambridge, Mass., 1973-75; prin., v.p. Structured Decisions Corp., Cambridge, 1975—; prof. Dept. Elec., Computer, and Sys. Engring. Rensselaer Poly. Inst., Troy, NY, 1977—2007, Yamada Corp. prof., acting chair, 1986—87, founding chair Dept. Decision Scis. and Engring. Sys., 1988, acting dean engring., 1992—94, 1998—99; dean Coll. Engring. U. Miami, 2007—. Fellow AAAS, INFORMS, IEEE (Joseph G. Wohl Oustanding Career award 1998, Major Ednl. Innovation award 2000, Norbert Weiner award), NAE. Office: U Miami Coll Engring PO Box 248294 Coral Gables FL 33124

T'IEN, JAMES SHAW-TZUU, engineering educator; b. Santai, China, Mar. 8, 1942; s. Keh-Ming and Yuan-Chin Tien; m. Sibyl Si-Juang Yang, June 24, 1967; children: Matthew Hua Tien, Joseph Hua Tien. BS in Engring., Nat. Taiwan U., Teipei, 1963; MS, Purdue U., West Lafayette, Ind., 1966; PhD, Princeton U., NJ, 1970. From asst. prof. to full prof. Case Western Res. U., Cleve., 1971—2006, Leonard Case Jr. prof. engring., 2007—; chief scientist on combustion Nat. Ctr. Microgravity Rsch., Cleve., 1998—2005, Nat. Ctr. Space Exploration, Cleve., 2005—06. Co-dir. Case-Ohio Aerospace Inst.-NASA Summer Faculty Fellowship Program, Cleve., 1992. Recipient Pub. Svc. medal, NASA, 2000, Silver Snoopy award, 2004; Daniel and Florence Guggenheim fellow in jet propulsion, Guggenheim Found., 1969. Office: Case Western Res U Dept Mech and Aerospace Engring Cleveland OH 44106

TIEN, JOY GARCIA, mathematics, human development counseling professor; b. Manila, Mar. 03; came to U.S., 1986; d. Armando Lazaro Garcia and Miriam (Garcia) Rorabaugh. BS, Philippines Normal U.; MEd in Math., Millersville U., Pa., 1989, MEd in Counseling, 1991; EdD, Temple U., Phila., 2008. Cert. in secondary sch. counseling Pa. Math & sci. instr. Bethel HS, Manila, 1985—86; grad. admissions asst. Millersville U., 1987—91, instr., counselor coord. Upward Bound, 1991—2001, dir. academic adv., 1998—99; prof., counselor HACC Lancaster Campus, Lancaster, 2001—. Partnership com. mem. Habitat for Humanity, Lancaster, 2001—. Recipient Eugene K. Robb scholarship, 1991, James C. Atty scholarship, 1991, Nat. Sci. and Tech. Authority Dept. Svc. & Tech. scholarship, 1981-85. Mem. ASCD, Nat. Academic Adv. Assn., Am. Math. Assn. Two Yrs. Coll., Pa. Assn. Devel. Editors, Lancaster County Counselors Assn., Assn. Pa. State Coll. and Univs. Faculties. Avocations: volleyball, writing, travel, reading, networking. Office: HACC Lancaster Campus 1641 Old Phila Pike Lancaster PA 17602 Office Fax: 717-358-2951. Business E-Mail: jgtien@hacc.edu.

TIEN, NORMAN C., dean, engineering educator; BS, U. Calif., Berkeley; MS, U. Ill.; PhD, U. Calif., San Diego. Faculty mem. dept. elec. and computer engring. Cornell U., Ithaca, NY; chair dept. elec. and computer engring. U. Calif., Davis, co-dir. Berkeley Sensor and Actuator Ctr. Berkeley; Nord prof. engring. Case Western Res. U., Cleve., 2006—, chair dept. elec. engring. and computer sci., 2006, dean Case Sch. Engring., 2007—. Named Ohio Eminent Scholar in Condensed Matter Physics, Ohio Bd. Regents, 2006. Office: Case Sch Engring 10900 Euclid Ave Cleveland OH 44106 Office Phone: 216-368-3227. E-mail: norman.tien@case.edu.

TIERNAN, BOB (ROBERT TIERNAN), political organization administrator, former state legislator; m. Susan Tiernan; 3 children. BA, Oreg. State U., 1977; JD, Seattle U. Sch. Law, 1980; LLM, Georgetown U., 1983. Mem. Oreg. House of Reps. from 24th Dist., 1993—97, chair Gen. Govt. and Crime and Corrections Com., mem. Judiciary and Labor Com.; pres. Tiernan and Assocs.; chmn. Oreg. Republican Party, 2009—. Founder PayLess Drug. Comdr. USNR. Office: Oreg Rep Party PO Box 25406 Portland OR 97298-0406 Office Phone: 503-595-8881. Office Fax: 503-595-8882.*

TIERNEY, BILL, university athletic coach; m. Helen Tierney; children: Trevor, Brendan, Courtney, Brianne. Grad., SUNY, Cortland. Head coach Great Neck South HS, LI, 1976—80, Levittown HS, Willingboro, NJ, 1980, Rochester Inst. Tech., NY, 1982—85, Princeton Tigers, 1988—2009, Denver Pioneers, 2009—; asst. coach Johns Hopkins U., Balt., 1985—88. Recipient NCAA Divsn. 1 Championship, 1992, 1994, 1996, 1997, 1998, 2001; named Morris Touchstone Divsn. I Coach of Yr., 1992; named to LI Lacrosse Hall of Fame, 1995, NJ Lacrosse Hall of Fame, 1999. Office: U Denver Pioneer Athletics 2199 S Univ Blvd Denver CO 80208*

TIERNEY, BRIAN PATRICK, publishing executive, former advertising and public relations executive; b. Bryn Mawr, Pa., Feb. 21, 1957; s. James Richard and Claire Ella (Springfield) T.; married; 2 children. BA, U. Pa., 1979; JD, Widener U., 1987. Field person Rep. Nat. Com., Washington, 1979-82, dir. incumbent programs, 1979-81, dep. dir. edn., 1981-82; polit. dir. GOPAC, Washington, 1982-83; asst. regional adminstr. Small Bus. Adminstrn., Bala Cynwyd, Pa., 1983-84; pres. Tierney & Co., Phila., 1984-86; pres., CEO Lewis, Gilman & Kynett Pub. Rels., Phila., 1986-89, Tierney Communications (formerly The Tierney Group), Phila., 1989—2000, Tierney & Ptnrs., Phila., 1994—98; chief mktg. officer Advanta Corp., 2004—05; CEO Phila. Media Holdings LLC, 2006—; pub. Phila. Inquirer, Phila. Daily News. Entrepreneur in resident Wharton Sch. Bus., 2002—03; bd. dirs. NutriSystems, Inc., Epitome Sys., RelationServe Media, Inc. Ann. giving chmn. Ingis House for Disabled Persons, Phila.; bd. dirs. Wilma Theater, Phila., Moore Coll. Art and Design, Phila., Sch. Bd. Archdiocese of Phila., Ave. of Arts, Inc., Phila. Police Athletic League, Phila. coun. Boy Scouts Am., fund for Phila., Phila. Festival of Arts, Kimmel Ctr. Performing Arts, Thomas Jefferson U., Greater Phila. C. of C., Episopal Acad., U. Pa. Mus.; chmn. Marian Anderson award City of Phila., Phila. Zool. Soc., regional Performing Arts Ctr., Phila. Mem. ABA, Pa. Bar Assn., Phila. Bar Assn., Pub. Rels. Soc. Am., St. Anthony Club, Union League. Roman Catholic. Avocations: skydiving, gardening. Office: Phila Media Holdings LLC 400 N Broad St Philadelphia PA 19130*

TIERNEY, BRIAN X., utilities executive; m. Beth Tierney; 4 children. BA in History, Boston Coll.; MBA in Fin. and Acctg., U. Chgo. Consumer products industry profl.; electricity trader Enron Corp.; mgmt. positions in pricing energy transactions, market ops., and trading & mktg. Am. Electric Power, 1998—2003, sr. v.p. energy mktg., 2003—05, sr. v.p. comml. ops., 2005—07, exec. v.p. East utilities, 2008—. Bd. dirs. Electric Reliability Coun. Tex., 2001—02. Vol. Peace Corps, Philippines. Office: Am Elec Power 1 Riverside Plz Columbus OH 43215-2372 Office Phone: 614-716-1000.*

TIERNEY, JAMES EDWARD, law educator, former state attorney general; b. Bklyn., Apr. 12, 1947; s. Charles J. and Agnes V. (Quinn) T.; m. Susan Webster, Jan. 26, 1969; children: Adam, Josie, Matthew, Daniel, Kate. BA with highest honors, U. Maine, 1969, JD, 1974. Bar: Maine 1974. Mem. Maine State Ho. Reps., 1972-80, majority leader, 1976-80; atty. gen. State of Maine, 1980-90; cons. state attys. gen., 1994—; lectr. Columbia Law Sch., NYC, 2000—, dir. Nat. State Atty. Gen. Program, 2004—. Bd. dirs. People for the Am. Way, Topsham, Maine, 1991-93; spl. prosecutor investigate Pa. Supreme Ct., 1992-93; mem. bd. commentators Courtroom TV Network. Wasserstein fellow Harvard Law Sch., 1992-93. Mem. Am. Judicature Soc. (bd. dirs.). Office: Columbia Law Sch 435 W 116 St Box B-26 New York NY 10027 E-mail: jtiern@law.columbia.edu.

TIERNEY, JOHN F., United States Representative from Massachusetts, lawyer; b. Salem, Mass., Sept. 18, 1951; m. Patrice Tierney. BA, Salem State Coll., 1973; JD, Suffolk U., Boston, 1976. Ptnr. Tierney, Kalis, and Lucas, North Shore, Mass.; mem. US Congress from 6th Mass. dist., 1997—, mem. com. edn. and workforce, com. gov. reform, permanent select intelligence com. Pres. Salem C. of C. Democrat. Office: US Ho Reps 120 Cannon Ho Office Bldg Washington DC 20515-2106 Office Phone: 202-225-8020. Office Fax: 202-225-5915.*

TIERNEY, KEVIN ALLEN, elementary school educator; b. Castro Valley, Calif., Sept. 23, 1958; s. Robert James and Jacqueline Elizabeth Tierney; m. Karen Naomi Zimmer, Aug. 23, 1987. BA in History, San Francisco State U., 1990; MA in Edn. Curriculum and Instrn., Sacramento State U., Calif., 2002. Cert. profl.clear multiple subject tchg. credential Calif. Tchr. grade 4 Wagner Holt Elem. Sch., Stockton, Calif., 1991—92; tchr. grade 5 Silva Valley Elem. Sch., El Dorado Hills, 1992—98; tchr. history grade 7-8 Rolling Hills Mid. Sch., 1998. Trainer El Dorado County Office Edn., Placerville, Calif., 2001—; mentor trainer Buckeye Union Sch. Dist., Shingle Springs, 2000—. Com. mem. Cemetery Advisor Com., El Dorado County, 2002—07. Named Most Influential Tchr., Oak Ridge H.S. students, 1999, Tchr. of Yr., Rolling Hills Mid. Sch., 2001, 2004, 2005; fellow, Colonial Williamsburg Tchr. Inst., 2001, Eurasia Excellence Tchg. fellow, U.S. Dept., 2004, Japan Fulbright Meml. Fund, 2005, Korean Studies Workshop, The Korea Found., 2007. Mem.: ACLU, Nat. Coun. Soc. Studies. Avocations: banjo, golf, fly fishing. Home: 5001 Gold Crest Ct Camino CA 95709 Office: Rolling Hills Mid Sch 7141 Silva Valley Pkwy El Dorado Hills CA 95762-7862 Office Phone: 530-676-2490 x 377. Business E-Mail: ktierney@buckeyeusd.org. E-mail: katierne@mindspring.com.

TIERNEY, MAURA, actress; b. Boston, Feb. 3, 1965; m. Billy Morrissette, 1994. Student, NYU, Cir. in the Sq. Theatre Sch. Actor: (TV series) 704 Hauser St., —, News Radio, 1995—2000, ER, 2000—09; (TV films) Flying Blind, 1990—, Out of Darkness, —, Student Exchange, —, Crossing the Mob, —, (guest appearance): (TV series) Growing Pains; (TV films) Family Ties; (TV series) Law & Order, The Van Dyke Show,: (films) Dead Women in Lingerie, 1991, The Linguini Incident, 1991, White Sands, 1992, Fly By Night, 1993, The Temp, 1993, Primal Fear, 1996, Primary Colors, 1997, Liar, Liar, 1997, Primary Colors, 1998, Forces of Nature, 1999, Instinct, 1999, Welcome to Mooseport, 2004, Danny Roane: First Time Director, 2006, Semi-Pro, 2008, Baby Mama, 2008; (plays) Some Girl(s), 2006. Office: c/o Creative Artists Agy 9830 Wilshire Blvd Beverly Hills CA 90212

TIERNEY, SUSAN FALLOWS, consulting company executive, former federal agency administrator; b. Phila., July 7, 1951; d. James Albert Fallows & Jean Mackenzie F.; m. John Thomas Tierney, 1983; children: James, Thomas BA in Art History, Scripps Coll., 1973; student, L'Institut d'Etudes Politiques, Paris; MA in Regional Planning & Pub. Policy, Cornell U., 1976, PhD in Regional Planning & Pub. Policy, 1980; LLD (hon.), Regis Coll., 1991. Asst. prof. U. Calif., Irvine, 1978-82; sr. economist Mass. Exec. Office Energy Resources, 1983-84; exec. dir. Mass. Energy Facilities Siting Coun., 1984-88; commr. Mass. Dept. Pub. Utilities, 1988-90, sec. environ. affairs, resources authority, 1991-93; asst. sec. for policy, planning & program evaluation US Dept. Energy, Washington, 1993-95; sr. v.p. Lexecon Inc., 1995—2003; mng. prin. Analysis Group, Inc., Boston, 2003—. Chmn. transmission task force New Eng. Gov.'s Conf. Power Planning Com.; mem. Keystone Project Electric Transmission Ind. Power Prodrs.; bd. dirs. Catalytica Energy Systems, Inc., 2001-07, Renegy Holdings Inc., 2007-, Evergreen Solar Inc., 2008- Contbr. articles to profl. jours. Mem. New Eng. Conf. Public Utility Commrs., Nat. Assn. Regulatory Utility Commrs. (energy conservation gas com.), Electric Power Rsch. (adv. com.). Democrat. Office: Analysis Group Inc 111 Huntington Ave 10th Fl Boston MA 02199 Office Phone: 617-425-8114. Office Fax: 617-425-8001. E-mail: stierney@analysisgroup.com.*

TIERNO, PHILIP MARIO, JR., microbiologist, educator, researcher; b. Bklyn., June 5, 1943; s. Philip M. and Phyllis (Tringone) T.; m. Josephine Martinez, Apr. 2, 1967; children: Alexandra Lorraine, Meredith Anne. BS, Bklyn. Coll. Pharmacy, 1965; MS, NYU, 1974, PhD, 1977. Microbiologist Luth. Med. Ctr., Bklyn., 1965-66; chief rsch. microbiologist hemodialysis unit VA Hosp., Bronx, NY, 1966-70; dir. microbiology divsn. NYU Med. Ctr. Goldwater Meml. Hosp., F.D. Roosevelt Island, 1970-81; assoc. and cons. microbiologist Maimonides Med. Ctr., Bklyn., 1970-79; dir. microbiology dept. Tisch-Univ. Hosp., NYU Med. Ctr., 1981—. Adj. asst. prof. CUNY, 1974—76, Bloomfield (NJ) Coll., 1975—82; clin. prof. microbiology and pathology NYU Med. Sch., 1981—; cons. Office Atty. Gen. NY State, NIH, Coll. of Am. Pathologists, Dept. Health City of NY, 1981—; mem. Mayoral Task Force on Bioterrorism, NYC. Author: The Secret Life of Germs: Observations and Lessons from a Microbe Hunter, 2001, Protect Yourself Against Bioterrorism, 2002, Nuclear, Chemical and Biological Terrorism: Emergency Response and Public Protection, 2003, The Secret Life of Germs: What They Are, Why We Need Them, and How We Can Protect Ourselves Against Them, 2004; contbr. articles to profl. jours., chapters to books. Pres. Flushing Taxpayers Assn., 1973-77; bd. dirs. Comprehensive Health Planning Agy. City of NY, 1974-75, Norwood Bd. Adjustment, NJ, 1978-83, 86-98, Norwood Bd. Edn., 1983-86; chmn. Norwood Environ. Commn., 1986-98; co-founder, bd. dirs. Found. Sci. Rsch. in Pub. Interest, S.I., NY, 1985—. Recipient Leone de San Marcos award, 2005. Mem. AAAS, NY Acad. Scis., Am. Acad. Microbiology, APHA, Am. Soc. Microbiology, Am. Soc. for Clin. Pathology, Optimists (v.p. Norwood 1978-95), Knights of Malta (Knighthood). Office: Tisch Hosp-Microbiology Dept NYU Med Ctr 560 1st Ave New York NY 10016-6402 Office Phone: 212-263-5905. Business E-Mail: philip.tierno@nyumc.org.

TIESENGA, MARVIN FRANCIS, surgeon; b. Slayton, Minn., Apr. 3, 1929; s. Edward Tiesenga and Sieka Drenth-Tiesenga; m. Ardythe Rae Noorlag, Aug. 19, 1955; children: Jane, Edward, Mary, Frederick, Anne. BS, Roosevelt U., 1950; MD, U. Ill., 1954. Diplomate Am. Bd. Surgery. Intern Cook County Hosp., Chgo., 1954, resident gen. surgery, 1957—61; pres. med. staff West Suburban Hosp., Oak Park, Ill., 1986—88, chief surgery, 1989—. Contbr. articles to profl. jours. Mem. Elmhurst Christian Ref. Ch., 1971—. Capt. US Army, 1955—57, Korea. Recipient Number one Dr., Crane's Chgo. Mag., 2004, Ken Douglas award for excellence, Citizens of Oak Park, 2000; named Number one Dr., Crane's Chgo. Mag., 2000, 2001, 2002, 2003. Fellow: ACS; mem.: AMA, SAGES, Chgo. Med. Soc., Ill. Med. Soc., Am. Soc. Breast Surgeons, Am. Soc. Bariatric Surgery, Aux Planes Med. Soc., Christian Med. and Dental Assn. Avocations: boating, travel, history, collecting antique tractors. Office: 1950 N Harlem Ave Elmwood Park IL 60707

TIESI, JOSEPH A., tobacco company executive; Grad., St. Francis Coll., 1980. With PricewaterhouseCoopers, 1980—86; sr. fin. analyst Altria Corp. Svcs., Inc., 1986—90, mgr. fin. reporting and analysis, 1990—95, dir. fin. reporting and analysis, 1995—98, asst. contr. fin. reporting and consolidation, 1998—99, v.p., contr., 1999—. Office: Altria Corp Svcs Inc 120 Park Ave New York NY 10017

TIEZZI, ENZO, physical chemistry educator; b. Siena, Tuscany, Italy, Feb. 4, 1938; s. Quintilio and Lidia (Pulselli) T.; m. Lucia Carli, Sept. 3, 1963; children: Elisa, Giovanna. Degree in chemistry, U. Florence, Italy, 1963; PhD in Chemistry, U. Florence, 1965. Assoc. prof. U. Cagliari, Cagliari, Italy, 1963-66; post-doctoral assoc. Washington U., St. Louis, 1966-67; assoc. prof. U. Florence, 1968-71, U. Siena, Siena, Italy, 1972-80, prof., 1980—, dir. dept. chemistry, 1980-87; MP Italian Parliament, Camera Deputati, Rome, 1987—. Pres. Oikos Internat. Found. Ecol. Econs., Interministering Com. Ambiental Rsch.; co-chmn. 4th Internat. Conf. on Ecosystems and Sustainable Develop., Siena, 2003 and 2004, The Sustainable City. Editor: Tempi Storici, Tempi Biologici (The End of Time), 1984-85, I Limiti dell'energia, 1986, Antolologia Verde, 1987, Bugie, Silenzi, Grida, 1989, Ecological Physical Chemistry, 1991, Il Capitombolo Di Ulisse, 1991, L'Equilibrio, 1995, Ecologia E, 1995, Fermare Il Tempo (The Essence of Time), 1996. Recipient Blaise Pascal medal in Physics and Chemistry, European Acad. Scis., 2003. Mem. Am. Chem. Soc., AAAS, Chem. Soc. (Gt. Britain), Soc. Chimica Italiana, European Acad. Scis. Office: U Siena Dept Chem and Biosys Scis Pian dei Mantellini, 44 53100 Siena Italy

TIFFANY, JAMES ROBERT, JR., physical education educator, physical fitness company executive; b. Winchester, Va., Dec. 17, 1944; s. James Robert and Lois Virginia (Pangle) T.; m. Anne King Tweedy, July 14, 1973; children: Heather Anne, James Bronson. AA in Sci., Montreat-Anderson Jr. Coll., 1964; BA in Religion, Lynchburg Coll., 1966; BS in Phys. Edn., Wake Forest U., 1967, MA, 1972; EdD, Nova U., 1980. Grad. asst., rsch. lab. asst. Wake Forest U., Winston Salem, N.C., 1968; tchr. phys. edn., biology pub. schs., Fairfax County, Va., 1968-74; soccer coach Annandale High Sch. (Va.), 1971-72; cross country coach Lee High Sch., Springfield, Va., 1972-74; dir. phys. edn. and intramurals No. Va. Community Coll. Loudoun Campus, Sterling Va., 1974-83, prof., 1983—; pres. EXER-TRAIL, Inc., 1978-2004; cons. on physical fitness; USTA tennis profl. rating. Pres. Lincoln Community League, 1982; co-founder, adv. Loudoun Meml. 10 Miler, 1979-83; clinician Pres.'s Council on Phys. Fitness and Sports; triathlete, USTA Srs. 4.0 capt. Recipient plaques for outstanding contbns. xerox; Washington Fittest award YMCA and Channel 4, 1984. Mem. AAHPERD, Va. Assn. Health, Phys. Edn. and Recreation, Am. Coll. Sports Medicine, Am. Assn. Fitness Dirs. in Bus. and Industry, Shenandoah Valley Road Runners. St. James Episcopal Ch. Club: Potomac Peddlers. Author: (with R.A. Moss) The EXER-TRAIL Guide, 1980; The EXER-TRAIL Way to Total Physical Fitness, 1983. Office Phone: 703-450-2613. Personal E-mail: jtiff70519@aol.com.

TIFFANY, JOHN, theater director; b. Yorkshire, England, 1971; MA in theatre and classics, Glasgow U., 1994. Literary dir. Traverse Theatre, Edinburgh, 1997—2001; assoc. dir. Paines Plough Theatre Co., London, 2001—05; assoc. dir. new work Nat. Theatre Scotland, Glasgow, 2005—. Dir.: (plays) Perfect Days, 1998, Gagarin Way, 2001, Helmet, 2002, The Straits, 2003, Jerusalem, 2005, Home: Glasgow, 2006, Elizabeth Gordon Quinn, 2006, Black Watch, 2006 (Laurence Olivier award for Best Dir., 2009), The Bacchae, 2007, Be Near Me, 2009. Office: Nat Theatre Scotland Civic House Civic St Glasgow G4 9RH Scotland E-mail: john.tiffany@nationaltheatrescotland.com.*

TIFFANY, JOSEPH RAYMOND, II, lawyer; b. Dayton, Ohio, Feb. 5, 1949; s. Forrest Fraser and Margaret Watson (Clark) T.; m. Terri Robbins, Dec. 1, 1984. AB magna cum laude, Harvard U., Cambridge, Mass., 1971; MS in Internat. Relations, London Sch. Econs., 1972; JD, U. Calif., Berkeley, 1975. Bar: US Dist. Ct. (no. dist.) 1975, US Dist. Ct. (ea. dist.) 1977, US Ct. Appeals (9th cir.) 1982, US Ct. Appeals (fed. cir.) 2004. Assoc. Pillsbury, Madison & Sutro, San Francisco, 1975-82, ptnr., 1983-2001, Pillsbury Winthrop LLP, Palo Alto, Calif., 2001—05, Pillsbury Winthrop Shaw Pittman LLP, 2005—. Mem. ABA (antitrust sect.), Calif. Bar Assn. (antitrust and unfair competition sect.). Office: Pillsbury Winthrop Shaw Pittman LLP 2475 Hanover St Palo Alto CA 94304-1115 Office Phone: 650-233-4644. Business E-mail: joseph.tiffany@pillsburylaw.com.

TIFFORD, ARTHUR W., lawyer; b. Bklyn., July 7, 1943; s. Herman and Dorothy (Kessler) T.; m. Barbara J. Sinreich, Aug. 15, 1965 (dec.); children: Melissa Beth, Alexandra Lynn. BA, CUNY, 1965; JD, Bklyn. Law Sch., 1967. Bar: NY 1967, Fla. 1967, US Dist. Ct. (so. dist.) Fla. 1968, US Ct. Mil. Appeals 1968, US Ct. Appeals (5th cir.) 1971, US Dist. Ct. (mid. dist.) Fla. 1979, US Ct. Appeals (10th cir.) 1979, US Ct. Appeals (1st cir.) 1982, US Ct. Appeals (9th cir.) 1982, US Ct. Appeals (11th cir.) 1981, US Ct. Appeals (fed. cir.) 1985, US Ct. Appeals (4th cir.) 1998, US Claims Ct. 1985, US Tax Ct. 1988, US Dist. Ct. (no. dist.) Fla., 2005. Rschr., mgr. clk. Cravath, Swaine & Moore, NYC, 1967; asst. US atty. US Dept. Justice (so. dist. Fla.), Miami, 1971-72; pvt. practice Miami, 1972—. With USMC, 1968-71, USMCR, 1971-92, ret. col. Mem. ABA, Am. Trial Lawyers Assn., Fla. Trial Lawyers Assn., NY Bar Assn., Fla. Bar Assn., Marine Corps Res. Officers Assn. (pres. Greater Miami chpt. 1978-79, 81-82, 84-85, nat. bd. dirs. 1987-89). Democrat. Avocations: writing, photography, parachuting, scuba diving, running. Home: 9980 SW 128th St Miami FL 33176-5632 Office: 1385 NW 15th St Miami FL 33125-1621 Fax: 305-325-1825. Personal E-mail: tiffordlaw@bellsouth.net. Business E-mail: arthur_tifford@tiffordlaw.com.

TIFFT, WILLIAM GRANT, retired physics professor, scientist; b. Derby, Conn., Apr. 5, 1932; s. William Charles and Marguerite Howe (Hubbell) T.; m. Carol Ruth Nordquist, June 1, 1957 (div. July 1964); children: Jennifer, William John; m. Janet Ann Lindner Homewood, June 2, 1965; 1 child, Amy, stepchildren: Patricia, Susan, Hollis. AB, Harvard Coll., 1954; PhD, Calif. Inst. Tech., 1958. Postdoctoral fellow Australian Nat. U., Canberra, 1958-60; rsch. assoc. Vanderbilt U., Nashville, 1960-61; astronomer Lowell Obs., Flagstaff, Ariz., 1961-64; assoc. prof. U. Ariz., Tucson, 1964-73, prof., 1973—2002, prof. emeritus, 2002—; prin. scientist Sci. Assn. Study of Time in Physics and Cosmology, 2000—. Joint author: Revised New General Catalog, 1973; joint editor: Modern Mathematical Models of Time and Their Applications to Physics and Cosmology, 1997; contbr. over 100 articles to profl. jours. NSF Predoctoral fellow, 1954-58, NSF Postdoctoral fellow, 1958-60; grantee NASA, NSF, ONR, Rsch. Corp. Fellow Am. Astron. Soc.; mem. Internat. Astron. Union, Sci. Assn. Study of Time in Physics and Cosmology (prin. scientist 2000-). Achievements include discovery of redshift quantization and correlations relating to it, including possible variability; first to detect voids in mapping of large scale supercluster structure; investigations of three-dimensional time in cosmology and particle physics. Office: U Arizona Dept Astronomy Tucson AZ 85721-0001

TIFT, MARY LOUISE, artist; b. Seattle, Jan. 2, 1913; d. John Howard and Wilhelmina (Pressler) Dreher; m. William Raymond Tift, Dec. 4, 1948. BFA cum laude, U. Wash., 1933; postgrad., Art Ctr. Coll., LA, 1945-48, U. Calif., San Francisco, 1962-63. Art dir. Vaughn Shedd Advt., LA, 1948; asst. prof. design Calif. Coll. Arts & Crafts, Oakland, Calif., 1949-59; coord. design dept. San Francisco Art Inst., 1959-62. Subject of cover story, Am. Artist mag., 1980, studio article, 1987; one-woman shows, Gumps Gallery, San Francisco, 1977, 1986, 90, Diane Gilson Gallery, Seattle, 1978, Oreg. State U., 1981, Univ. House, Seattle, Frye Art Mus., Seattle, 2000; exhibited in group shows including Brit. Biennale, Yorkshire, Eng., 1970, Grenchen Triennale, Switzerland, 1970, Polish Biennale, Crakow, 1972, Nat. Gallery, Washington, 1973, Madrid Biennale, 1980, U.S.-U.K. Impressions, Eng., 1988; represented in permanent collections, Phila. Mus. Art, Bklyn. Mus., Seattle Art Mus., Library Congress, Achenbach Print Collection, San Francisco Palace Legion of Honor, San Diego Mus. Art, U.S. Art in Embassies. Served to lt. USNR, 1943-45. Mem. Print Club Phila., World Print Council, Calif. Soc. Printmakers, Phi Beta Kappa, Lambda Rho. Christian Scientist. Studio: 4400 Stone Way N Apt 521 Seattle WA 98103-7487

TIGAR, MICHAEL EDWARD, law educator; b. Glendale, Calif., Jan. 18, 1941; s. Charles Henry and Margaret Elizabeth (Lang) T.; m. Pamet Ayer Jones, Sept. 21, 1961 (div. Mar. 1973); children: Jon Steven, Katherine Ayer; m. Amanda G. Birrell, Feb. 16, 1980 (div. Aug. 1996); 1 child, Elizabeth Torrey; m. Jane E. Blanksteen, Aug. 22, 1996. BA in Polit. Sci., U. Calif., Berkeley, 1962, JD, 1966. Bar: D.C. 1967, U.S. Ct. Appeals (2d, 4th, 5th, 6th, 7th, 8th, 9th, 10th, 11th, fed. and D.C. cirs.), U.S. Tax Ct., U.S. Supreme Ct. 1972, N.Y. 1993. Assoc. Williams & Connolly, Washington, 1966-69; editor-in-chief Selective Svc. Law Reporter, Washington, 1967-69; acting prof. law UCLA, 1969-71; pvt. practice law Grasse, France, 1972-74; assoc. William & Connolly, Washington, 1974, ptnr., 1975-77, Tigar & Buffone, Washington, 1977-84; prof. law U. Tex., Austin, 1984-87, Joseph D. Jamail Centennial prof. law, 1987-98; of counsel Haddon, Morgan & Foreman, Denver, 1996-98; prof. law Am. U. Washington Coll. Law, Washington, 1998—2008, prof. emeritus, 2008—; vis. prof. Duke Law Sch., 2006—08, prof. practice law, 2008—. Author: Practice Manual Selective Service Law Reporter, 1968, Law and the Rise of Capitalism, 1977, (with Jane B. Tigar) Federal Appeals: Jurisdiction and Practice, 3d edit., 1999, Examining Witnesses, 1993, Persuasion: The Litigator's Art, 1999, Thinking About Terrorism: The Threat to Civil Liberties in a Time of Nat. Emergency, 2004; contbr. articles to profl. jours. Mem. ABA (vice chair 1987-88, chair elect 1988-89, chair 1989-90 sect. litigation). Avocations: sailing, cooking. Office: Duke Univ Sch Law Sci Dr & Towerview Dr Durham NC 27708 Office Phone: 919-613-8513. Personal E-mail: metigar@gmail.com.

TIGER, LIONEL, social scientist, anthropology consultant; b. Montreal, Que., Can., Feb. 5, 1937; s. Martin and Lillian (Schneider) T.; 1 child, Sebastian Benjamin. BA, McGill U., 1957, MA, 1959; PhD, U. London, 1963. Instr. anthropology U. Ghana, Accra, 1960; asst. prof. dept. anthropology and sociology U. B.C., Vancouver, Canada, 1963—68; assoc. prof. anthropology Rutgers U., New Brunswick, NJ, 1969—74, prof. anthropology, 1974—, Charles Darwin prof. anthropology, 1990—. Cons., rsch. dir. Harry F. Guggenheim Found., N.Y.C., 1972-84; chmn. bd. social scientists U.S. News and World Report, 1986-88; sci. adv. bd. Am. Wine Inst., San Francisco; sr. rsch. assoc. Nat. Inst. Pub. Policy; mem. bd. advisors George Polk Awards, 2004—. Author: Men in Groups, 1969, 3d edit., 2004, (with Robin Fox) The Imperial Animal, 1971, 3d edit., 1998, (with Joseph Shepher) Women in the Kibbutz, 1975, Optimism: The Biology of Hope, 1979, 2d edit., 1994, China's Food, 1985, The Manufacture of Evil: Ethics, Evolution and the Industrial System, 1987; editor: Female Hierarchies, 1978, 2nd edit. 2007, (with Michael Robinson) Man and Beast Revisited, 1992, The Pursuit of Pleasure, 1992, 2d edit., 2000, The Decline of Males, 1999, The Apes of New York, 2003; series editor: Anthropology and Human Nature, 2005; mem. editl. bd. Social Sci. Info., Ethology and Sociobiology jour., Jour. of Social Distress and the Homeless Cultural laureate N.Y.C. Landmarks Found., 1999. Recipient W.I. Susman award for excellence in tchg., 1985, McNaughton prize for creative writing; Guggenheim fellow, 1969, rsch. fellow ASDA Found., 1985, Can. Coun., fgn. area tng. fellow Ford Found., Can. Coun.-Killam fellow for interdisciplinary rsch., Rockefeller fellow Aspen Inst., 1979, H.F. Guggenheim Found. fellow, 1988-89; Inst. for Law and Behavioral Rsch. fellow; Govt. of Que. fellow, 2005-06. Mem. PEN (mem. exec. bd., treas. 1988-91, v.p. 1991-94), Am. Anthrop. Assn., Internat. Humanist Assn. (humanist laureate), Can. Humanists Assn. (hon.), Soc. for Study of Evolution, Century Assn. Home: 248 W 23rd St Fl 4 New York NY 10011-2304 also: PO Box 965 Millbrook NY 12545 Office: Rutgers U 131 George St New Brunswick NJ 08901-1414 Business E-Mail: ltiger@anthropology.rutgers.edu.

TIGERMAN, KATHLEEN, humanities educator; d. Lajos Tigerman and Evelyn Hart-Tigerman; m. Carl Arthur Schlecht, July 7, 2006. PhD, U. Wis.-Milw., 1988. Humanities prof. U. Wis.-Platteville, 1993—. Contbr. articles to anthology (Abughalous award, 2008); exhibitions include First Peoples of the Kickapoo; author (editor): Wisconsin Indian Literature: Anthology of Native Voices. Founder Dancing Waters Permaculture CO-op, 1982. Named one of Tchr. of the Yr., U. Wis. Center-Richland, 1991—92. Office: Univ Wis-Platteville 1 Univ Dr Platteville WI 53818 Business E-Mail: tigerman@uwplatt.edu.

TIGERMAN, STANLEY, architect, educator; b. Chgo., Sept. 20, 1930; s. Samuel Bernard and Emma Louise (Stern) T.; m. Margaret I. McCurry; children: Judson Joel, Tracy Leigh. Student, MIT, Cambridge, 1948-49; BArch, Yale U., New Haven, 1960, MArch, 1961. Archtl. draftsman firm George Fred Keck, Chgo., 1949-50, Skidmore, Owings and Merrill, Chgo., 1957-59, Paul Rudolph, New Haven, 1959-61, Harry Weese, Chgo., 1961-62; ptnr. firm Tigerman & Koglin, Chgo., 1962-64; prin. firm Stanley Tigerman & Assos., Chgo., 1964-82; ptnr. Tigerman Fugman McCurry, Chgo., 1982-88, Tigerman McCurry Archs., Chgo., 1988—. Prof. architecture U. Ill.-Chgo., 1967-71, 80-93, dir. Sch. Architecture, 1985-93; vis. lectr. Yale U., 1974, Cornell U., Ithaca, N.Y., 1963, Cooper Union, 1970, U. Calif. at Berkeley, 1968, Cardiff (Wales) Coll., 1965, Engring. U., Bangladesh, 1967; chmn. AIA com. on design, coordinator exhbn. and book Chicago Architects, 1977; Charlotte Shepherd Davenport prof. architecture Yale U., 1979; architect-in-residence Am. Acad. in Rome, 1980; vis. prof. architecture Harvard U., 1982; William Henry Bishop Chair. prof. architecture Yale U., 1984, Sarrinen prof., 1993; dir. post-professional grad. program U. Ill.-Chgo.; co-founder Archeworks, Design Lab., Chgo., 1993; mem. adv. com. Princeton U., 1997. Prin. works include Ounce of Prevention Educare Ctr., Chgo., Fukuoka Apt. Complex, Japan, Power House, Zion, Ill., Chgo. Children's Adv. Ctr., Holocaust Mus. and Edn. Ctr., Skokie, Ill., Pacific Garden Mission, Chgo.; author: Versus, 1982, Architecture of Exile, 1988, Stanley Tigerman: Buildings and Projects, 1966-89, 1989; contbr. Design of the Housing Site, 1966, Chicago on Foot, 1969, Art Today, 1969, New Direction in American Architecture, 1969, Contemporary Jewelry, 1970, Urban Structures for the Future, 1972, Spaces for Living, 1973, Chicago 1930-70, 1974, Interior Spaces Designed by Architects, 1976, 100 Years of Architecture in Chicago, 1976, 100 Years of Architecture in Chicago, 1986, Mies Reconsidered, 1986, Chicago Architecture 1872-1922, 1988, articles; exhibitions include Venice Biennale, 1976, 1980, Calif. Condition, 1982;, author essay; exhibitions include Chicago Architecture, The New Zeitgeist: In Search of Closure, 1989; author: (catalog) Chicago Architecture, The New Zeitgeist: In Search of Closure, 1989. Pres. Yale Arts Assn., 1969-70; bd. dirs. Bangladesh Found.; adv. com. Yale Sch. Architecture, 1976-2006. Served with USN, 1950-54. Recipient Alpha Rho Chi medal, Yale, 1961, Archtl. Record award, 1970, Masonry award, 1974, Masonry gold medal, 1974, Alumni Art award, Yale U., 1985, Design award for Art Inst. Chgo. Schinkel Exhbn., Am. Soc. Interior Designers, 1995, Humanitarian award, Holocaust Meml. Found. Ill., 2001, Grand award of Excellence, NAHB, 2001, 2003, Recognition award, World Trade Ctr. Meml., 2004, Cultures Achievement award, Univ. Club Chgo., 2004, AIA Topaz medallion, 2007; grantee Advanced Studies in Fine Art, Graham Fedn., 1965. Fellow AIA (chmn. com. design 1976-77, adv. com., Disting. Svc. award Chgo. chpt. 1983, Chgo. Honor awards 1977-79, Nat. Honor award 1982, 84, 87, 91, 98, Nat. Modern Income Housing award 1970, Nat. Homes for Better Living award 1974, 75, Ill. award 1976, Nat. award of Merit 1970, 74, 75, named to Hall of Fame 1990, Disting. Bldg. award for pvt. residence Chgo. chpt. 1991, Chgo. Interior Archtl. Award of Excellence 1981, 83, 87, 91, 92, Nat. Interior Archtl. Award of Excellence 1992-93, Chgo. Disting. Bldg. award 1971, 73, 75, 77, 79, 81, 82, 84, 85, 86, 91, 94, Italian Ceramic Tile Design award 1995, Fukuoka Urban Beautification award 1995, 6 citations of merit Chgo. chpt. 1994, Interior Design award for A.I.C. Schinkel Exhibit 1996, Chgo. Interior Architecture award 1997, Chgo. Chpt. Arch. award 1998, Nat. Interior Architecture award 1998, Louis Sullivan award 2000), Ill./Ind. Masonry Coun. (Silver Award for Excellance in Masonry 2003); mem. Arts Club of Chgo., Yale Club of N.Y.C., Phi Kappa Phi. Office: Tigerman McCurry Archs 444 N Wells St Ste 206 Chicago IL 60610-4522 Office Phone: 312-644-5880. E-mail: tma@tigerman-mccurry.com.

TIGHE, MARY ANN, real estate company executive; b. Aug. 24, 1948; m. Kevin Tighe (div.); 1 child, Aaron; m. David Arthur Hidalgo. BA in Art Hist., Cath. U.; MA in Art Hist., U. Md. Staff mem. Smithsonian Instn.; arts adv. to v.p. Walter Mondale; dep. chmn. Nat. Endowment Arts; v.p. ABC; sales assoc. Edward S. Gordon Inc. (name changed to Insignia/ESG Inc. 1997), 1984, exec. mng. dir. NYC, 1993—99; vice chmn. Insignia/ESG Inc., NYC, 1999—2002; pres., CEO NY Tri-State Region CB Richard Ellis, NYC, 2002—. Dir. Imperial Parking Corp. Bd. dirs. NYC Ballet, Parrish Art Mus., The New 42nd St., Joan's Legacy: The Joan Scarangello Found. to Conquer Lung Cancer. Recipient Woman of Yr., Comml. Real Estate Women NY, 2001, NJ Deal of Yr. award, Nat. Assn. Indsl. and Office Properties, 2002, NY Deal of Yr. award, 2003, Rising Exec. award, Comml. Property News, 2004; named one of The 100 Most Influential Women in NYC Bus., Crain's NY Bus., 2007, The 50 Most Powerful Women in NYC, NY Post, 2008. Mem.: Real Estate Bd. NY (mem. exec. com. bd. govs. 2001—, Robert T. Lawrence Meml. award 1992, Henry Hart Rice Achievement award 1997, Robert T. Lawrence Meml. award 1998, Henry Hart Rice Achievement award 2002, Most Creative Retail Deal of Yr. 2002, Louis Smadbeck Meml. Broker Recognition award 2004, Bernard H. Mendik award for Lifetime Leadership in Real Estate 2009). Office: CB Richard Ellis Grp Inc 200 Park Ave New York NY 10166 Office Phone: 212-984-8128. Office Fax: 212-984-8322. E-mail: maryann.tighe@cbre.com.*

TIGHE, WILLIAM (BILL TIGHE), legislative staff member; b. Scranton, Pa., Dec. 3, 1977; m. Erica Bobrek Tighe, July 3, 2004; 1 child. BA, Bucknell U., Lewisburg, Pa., 2000. Legis. corr., legis. asst for Rep. George Gekas US House of Reps., Washington, 2000—03, sr. legis. asst., 2003—08, dep. chief of staff, legis. dir., chief of staff for Rep. Jim Gerlach, 2008—. Mem.: Capitol Hill Club, Phi Gamma Delta. Roman Catholic. Office: Office of Congressman Jim Gerlach 308 Cannon House Office Bldg Washington DC 20515*

TIGHIOUART, MOURAD, statistician, researcher; b. Algiers, Algeria, Dec. 21, 1964; s. Laid Tighiouart and Rezkia Djaballah; m. Leila Benbahmed, Dec. 20, 2000; children: Rayan, Tara. BS in Math., USTHB, Algiers, 1987; MS in Math., U. Ctrl. Fla., Orlando, 1991; MS in Stats., Fla. State U., Tallahassee, 1998, PhD, 1998. Asst. prof. Utah State U., Logan, 1998—2003; rsch. biostatistician Fox Chase Cancer Ctr., Phla., 2003—04; asst. prof. Emory U., Atlanta, 2004—. Co-dir. biostatistics Winship Cancer Inst., Atlanta, 2004—. Contbr. articles to profl. jours. Mem.: Internat. Bayesian Soc., Soc. Clin. Trials, Am. Statis. Assn. (corr.). Home: 6394 Mimosa Cir Tucker GA 30084 Office: Emory Univ 1365 Clifton Rd Room B 4111 Atlanta GA 30322 Business E-Mail: mourad.tighiouart@emoryhealthcare.org.

TIGUE, VIRGINIA BETH (GINNY), volunteer; b. Owosso, Mich., Sept. 10, 1945; d. Joseph Frederick and Florence Marion Sahlmark; m. Joseph James Tigue Jr., Aug. 12, 1967; children: James Christopher, Molly Elizabeth. BS, cert. in phys. therapy, U. Mich., 1967. Registered phys. therapist, Mich., Calif. Phys. therapist at hosps., rehab. ctrs. and pvt. practice. Co-owner Tigue Property Co.; former co-owner Tex. Toyota of Grapevine. Councilman Pl. 5 City of Colleyville, 1998—2004, mayor pro tem, 2000—04, bond steering com., 1991, master plan revision com., 1997-98, chmn. cmty. ctr. adv. com. 1998; mem. Art Coun. Ft. Worth and Tarrant County Bd., Ft. Worth, 1997-2005, 2007-, co-chair Toast Town, 2007, Tarrant County College Found. Bd., 2001-; founding bd. dirs. Grapevine-Colleyville Ind. Sch. Dist. Edn. Found., 1998-2004; bd. dirs. Colleyville C. of C., 1991—, chmn., 1994; founding chmn. women's adv. bd. Harris Meth. HEB Hosp. 1992-2007, chmn. 2007, bd. trustees, 1999-2007, vice chmn., 2005; bd. Meth. Health Harris Found. 2001-; bd. dirs. Arts Coun. N.E. Tarrant, 1991-98, chmn., 1995-96, Art Coun. Ft. Worth and Tarrant County, 1994-2005, 2008-; bd. dirs. Origins Mus., 1998—, v.p. 2000-2001; bd. dirs. Vol. Ctr. of Tarrant County, 1998-2002, chmn. 2000; bd. dirs. Dallas Mus. Art League, 1999-2000, United Way of Met. Tarrant County, 2000-07, exec. bd. dir., 2002-; bd. dirs. N.E Leadership Forum, 1999—, chmn., 2004; sustaining mem. Dallas Jr. League, 1991—; founding bd. dirs. Tarrant County Coll. Found., 2001—; sr. advisor Nat. Charity League, 1994,; bd. dirs. N.E. Tarrant County divsn. Am. Heart Assn., 1993-94, co-chmn. gala 1997; fund raising chmn. Friends of Colleyville Libr., 1992—;

home tour com. Colleyville Women's Club, 1990, 93, 96, fashion show chmn., 1996; mem. adv. bd. Women's Shelter, 1996-98; mem. Women Leader's Summit, Washington, 1995, 96, 98, 99, 05, 08; mem. Women's Policy Forum, 1999—, Women's Found. of Tarrant County, 2000-, bd. dirs. Safehaven, 2007-, chmn Legancy Woman Luncheon, 2008. Named Most Influential Bus. Woman, The Bus. Press, 1997, Vol. of Yr., City of Colleyville, 1997, Colleyville Citizen of Yr., 2001, Colleyville Rotary Citizen of Yr., 2002; recipient Legacy of Women award The Women's Shelter, 1995, Herman J. Smith Leadership award Colleyville C. of C., 1994, Proclamation as Outstanding Citizen of Colleyville, 1995, Leadership award Northeast Leadership Forum, 2008. Mem. Colleyville Area C. of C. (bd. dirs. 1990-98, pres.-elect 1993, pres. 1994, vice-chmn. membership devel. 1997, vice-chmn. cmty. devel. 1998, 2003, 2005, vice chmn. bus. devel. 2004, Citizen of Yr. 2001, Disting. Leadership award, 2007-, exec. bd. 2003-), Tex. Congress Parents and Tchrs. (hon. life mem.). Republican. Methodist. Avocations: golf, travel, reading, the arts. Home: 4415 Meandering Way Colleyville TX 76034-4513 Personal E-mail: gtigue@hotmail.com.

TIGUE, WILLIAM BERNARD, adult education educator; b. Wilkes-Barre, Pa., Aug. 20, 1945; s. Joseph Francis and Susanna Agatha (Opet) T.; m. Faye Gage Cox, Dec. 10, 1977 (div. 1980); m. Dolores Cruz Arriaga, Apr. 17, 1993. BA, Kings Coll., 1967; MA, East Tenn. State U., 1969; TESOL cert., UCLA, 1997. Reporter Johnson City Press-Chronicle and Knoxville Jour., Tenn., 1968—72; dir. pub. rels. Beech Mountain, NC, 1972—76, Bellemead Devel. Corp., Fla., 1976—80; account exec. Carl Byoir & Assocs., San Francisco, 1980—82; editor internal publs. Crocker Nat. Bank, San Francisco, 1983—84; copywriter acct. exec. Doremus & Co., San Francisco; assoc. publ., sales mgr. Calif. Bicyclist Yellow Jersey Enterprises, San Francisco, 1988; tchr. English, LA County C.C. Dist., 1988—; tchr. adult edn. LA Unified Sch. Dist., 1988—. Mem. Women Educators of So. Calif. Independent. Roman Catholic. Avocations: reading, cooking, minor league baseball. Home: 329 California Ave Apt 8 Santa Monica CA 90403-5014 Office: LA Unifed Sch Dist 333 Beaudry 18th Fl Los Angeles CA 90010 Office Phone: 323-357-6200. Personal E-mail: wbtigue@earthlink.com.

TIHAN, TARIK, pathologist, educator; MD, PhD, U. Istanbul, 1985. Diplomate in anatomic pathology & neuropathology Am. Bd. Pathology, 1996. Asst. prof. Johns Hopkins Med. Instn., Balt., 1997—2002; fellow Meml. Sloan-Kettering Cancer Ctr., NYC, 1994—95; prof. pathology UCSF Med. Ctr., 2002—. Fellow SUNY, Stony Brook, 1995—97. Contbr. to numerous profl. jours. Recipient tchg. award, Johns Hopkins Med. Instn., UCSF sch. medicine. Mem.: Am. Assn. Cancer Rsch., US and Can. Acad. Pathology, Am. Assn. Neuropathologists (v.p. profl. affairs 2005—). Office: UCSF Sch of Medicine 505 Parnassus Ave San Francisco CA 94143 Office Fax: 415-476-7963.

TIJARDOVIC, IVICA, research scientist; b. Sibenik, Croatia, Sept. 1, 1960; s. Stipe and Slavenka Tijardovic; 1 child, Ana. BSc in Navigation, Maritime Faculty, Croatia, 1983, MSc in Tech. Transport, 1989; PhD in Naviagation, Naval Acad., Poland, 1994. Cert. Master Mariner Croatia, 1986, instr. ARPA and bridge team training Norway, 1990. Cadet, officer, capt. Various Maritime Cos., Piran, Sibenik, Croatia, 1979—91; capt. Morton Salt, C.Canaveral, 1998—. Supr. of comml. and tech. mgmt. for ships Shipbuilding Industry, Split, Croatia, 1986—87; asst. of navigation Maritime Faculty, 1987—90, 96, lectr. of navigation, 1990—98, asst. prof. of navigation, 2000. Contbr. more than 100 articles to internat. sci. & profl. jours., 15 books. V.p. World Congress of Arts, Scis. and Commns.; singer first tenor, guitar player Croatia, 1979—. Recipient Unique Contributions to Nav. award, Duke of Edinburgh, 2004; nominee Shipmaster of Yr., Lloyd's List and Nautical Inst., 2004, 2005, 2007. Fellow: UK Royal Inst. Nav. (life); mem.: US Naval Inst., Internat. Order Merit (advisor, hon. deputy dir. gen., amb.), UK Nautical Inst. (life). Achievements include research in navigation, ship stability, GPS, AIS; invention of Star Finder. Avocations: walking, singing, travel. Personal E-mail: ivica.tijardovic@st.t-com.hr.

TIJERINO, JOSE A., foundation administrator; b. Managua, Nicavagua, USA, Sept. 19, 1961; s. Jose A. Tijerino and Mercedes Salerno; m. Dinah T. Simpson, Oct. 4, 2004; children: Grace Mercedes, Antonio Juan, Bella Dog. BS in Journalism, U. Md., 1988. Sr. accounts executive Burson Marsteller, 1990—96; mgr. Nike Inc., Beaverton, Oreg., 1997—98; dir. Fannie Mae Found., Wash., DC, 1998—2001; pres. ceo Hispanic Heritage Found., Wash., DC, 2002—. Home and Office: 2600 VA Ave Nw Ste 406 Washington DC 70037

TIKALSKY, PAUL J., civil engineering educator, structural engineer; s. Lee J. and Marilyn A. Tikalsky; m. Julie A. Tikalsky; children: Peter, Daniel. BS in Civil and Environ. Engring., U. of Wis., 1983; MS in Structural Engring., U. of Tex., 1986, PhD in Structural Materials Engring., 1989. Lic. profl. engr., Calif. Housefellow U. of Wis., Madison, 1981—84, tchg. asst., 1984; rsch. asst. U. of Tex., Austin, 1984—89; from asst. to assoc. prof. Santa Clara U., Calif., 1989—95; consulting engr. TEI and Assocs., Santa Clara, 1989—94; prof. Pa. State U., University Park, 1995—2006; chair and prof. U. Utah, Salt Lake City, 2006—. Prin. engr. Tikalsky Engring. Svcs., Sandy, Utah, 1993—. Contbr. scientific papers to profl. jours. Vice-chair, bd. mem. Habitat for Humanity, San Jose, Calif., 1992—95; dep. dir. Pa. Transp. Inst.; bd. dirs. Stand Together, State College, 1998—2000. Grantee, PennDOT, U.S. Dept. Edn., Pvt. Founds., 1989—2003. Fellow: Am. Concrete Inst. (chair coms., bd. dirs.); mem.: ASTM, ASCE, Engring. Acad. Czech Republic, Sierra Club (life), Chi Epsilon (pres.). Achievements include research in development of 100-year highway program.

TIKEKAR, RAHUL VASANT, computer science educator; s. Vasant and Madhumalati Tikekar; m. Rupali Rahul Khandekar, Nov. 9, 1995; 1 child, Uma. B Engring. in Computer Sci., Bangalore U., India, 1988; MS in Computer Sci., Wayne State U., Detroit, 1990, PhD, 1997. Asst. prof. Augustana Coll., Sioux Falls, SD, 1990—91; mgr. info. systems Thesaurus Linguae Graecae, U. Calif., Irvine, 1997—98; assoc. prof. So. Oreg. U., Ashland, 1998—. Vis. lectr. U. Waikato, Hamilton, New Zealand, 2005; cons. Maharashtra Knowledge Corp. Ltd., Pune, India, 2006. Recipient Best Project award, IEEE Bangalore Chpt., 1988; grantee So. Oreg. U., 1989—2005. Office: So Oreg U Dept Computer Sci Ashland OR 97520-5028 Office Fax: 541-552-6171. E-mail: tikekarr@sou.edu.

TILAAR, HENRY A.R., social sciences educator; b. Tondano, Indonesia, June 16, 1932; s. Kilala and Engelien (Mamuaya) T.; m. Martha Handana, Jan. 12, 1964; children: Bryan, Pingkan, Wulan, Kilala. MA in Edn., U. Indonesia, Jakarta, 1961; MSc in Edn., Ind. U., 1967, EdD, 1969. Prof. State U. Jakarta, 1969—97; mem. staff Nat. Devel. Office (Bappenas), Jakarta, 1970—93, asst. min., 1986-93; prof. U. Jakarta, 1987-98, prof. emeritus, 1997—. Dir. Inst. Mgmt. Devel. U. Jakarta, 1991—; mem. adv. bd. Indonesian Tchrs. Assn.; cons. in field. Author: Education in National Development, 1990, National Education Management, 1992, Indonesian Education Development, 1945-1995, A Policy Study, 1995, Human Resources Development, Vision and Mission for 2020, 1997, Agenda for Education Reform for 21st Century, 1998, Education, Culture, and Civil Society, 1999, New Paradigms of National Education, 2000, National Education Reconstruction, 2001, Social Change and Education, A Transformative Pedagogy for Indonesia, 2002, Power and Education, A Cultural Studies Perspective, 2003, Multicultural Education, 2004, National Education Manifesto, 2005. Chmn. bd. advisors Cath. U., Jakarta, 1995-99; mem. bd. advisors Acad. Mgmt., Jakarta, 1996. Recipient Grand medal of merit Republic of Indonesia, 1998. Mem. Nat. Rsch. Coun., Indonesian Soc. for Advancement of Social Scis., Indonesian Lectrs. Assn. Democrat. Roman Catholic. Avocations: gardening, jogging, watching soccer. Home: Jl Patra Kuningan Utara Blok L-VII No 4 Jakarta Indonesia Office: LPMP State U Jakarta Jl Rawamangun Muka Jakarta DKI Indonesia Business E-Mail: hartilaar@martinaberto.co.id.

TILES, NEAL, broadcast executive; BS in Advt./Mktg., Syracuse U., NY. Account exec. Young & Rubicam, NYC, Foote Cone & Belding, San Francisco; dir. advt. & program mktg. ESPN; sr. v.p. mktg. Fox Sports, 1997—99, exec. v.p. mktg. group, 2000—03; exec. v.p. mktg. DirecTV, 2003—05; pres. G4 Videogame TV, 2005—. Office: G4 Media Inc 5750 Wilshire Blvd Los Angeles CA 90036-3697

TILEWICK, ROBERT, lawyer; b. NYC, Jan. 16, 1956; s. David and Helen (Fogel) T.; m. Susan Dara Tilewick; children: Naomi Seana, Benjamin Solomon. BA, Columbia U., 1977; JD, Temple U., 1985. Bar: N.Y. 1986, Ct. 1993, U.S. Dist. Ct. (so. and ea. dists.) N.Y. 1988, U.S. Ct. Appeals (2d cir.) 1989, U.S. Dist. Ct. Conn. 1991. Systems analyst, cons. Personnelmetrics, Inc., NYC, 1977-80, 81-82; assoc. Cravath, Swaine & Moore, NYC, 1985-87, Paul, Weiss, Rifkind, Wharton & Garrison, NYC, 1987-91, 96-97, Wiggin & Dana, New Haven, Conn., 1991-96, Kalow, Springut & Bressler, NYC, 1997-99, Graham & James, NYC, 1999—. Co-designer race timing system for N.Y.C. Marathon, 1977-82. NIH grantee Marine Biol. Lab., Woods Hole, Mass, 1980. Mem. ABA, N.Y.C. Bar Assn., Conn. Bar Assn., Supreme Ct. Hist. Soc. Avocation: music. Office: 885 3rd Ave New York NY 10022-4834 Office Phone: 206-645-6829. Personal E-mail: rtilewick@msn.com.

TILFORD, TERRY TRENT, translator; b. St. Louis, Oct. 21, 1940; s. Winslow Otis Tilford and Arlye June Twombley; m. Louisa Jane Pringle (div.); 1 child, Heather Elaine. BA in English, Creighton U., Omaha, 1964. Tchr. English Nebr. Pub. Schs., Melbeta, 1964—65; instr. English U. Nebr., Lincoln, 1968—69; regular distbn. clerk US Post Office, Omaha, 1969—78; self employed translator, editor San Francisco, 1979—. Mem.: Internat. Campaign Tibet, Defenders Wildlife, Sierra Club, Eta Sigma Phi, Alpha Sigma Nu. Avocations: reading, linguistics, history.

TILGHMAN, SHIRLEY MARIE, academic administrator, biology professor; b. Toronto, Can., Sept. 17, 1946; 2 children. BSc in Chemistry with honors, Queen's U., Kingston, Ont., 1968; PhD in Biochemistry, Temple U., Phila., 1975; DSc (hon.), Mt. Sinai Coll. Medicine of City Coll. NY, 1994, Queen's U., Kingston, Ont., 2002, Oxford U., 2002, Westminster Choir Coll. Rider U., 2002, Bard Coll., 2002, Dickinson Coll., 2002, Yale U., 2002, Queen's U., 2002, Simon Fraser U., 2002, U. BC, 2002, U. Western Ont., 2003, U. Toronto, 2003, Drew U., 2004, Harvard U., 2004, U. Medicine & Dentistry NJ, 2005, NYU, 2005, Columbia U., 2005, Rutgers U., 2006, Rockefeller U., 2006, Wash. U., 2007, Mills Coll., 2007, Mem. U. Newfoundland, 2007, Ryerson U., 2007, Rensselaer Poly. Inst., Amherst Coll., U. Md., Balt., 2008; postgrad., NIH. Secondary sch. tchr., West Africa, Sierra Leone, 1968—70; Fogarty internat. fellow NIH, Bethesda, Md., 1975—77; mem. Inst. Cancer Rsch., Phila., 1979—86; investigator Howard Hughes Med. Inst., Chevy Chase, 1988—2001; asst. prof., Fels Rsch Inst. Temple U., Phila., 1978—79; prof. molecular biology Princeton U., NJ, 1986—, Howard A. Prior prof. life scis., 1986—2001, chair Coun. Sci. and Tech., 1993—2000, pres., 2001—. Founding dir. Lewis-Sigler Inst. Integrative Genomics, 1998—2003; adj. assoc. prof. human genetics and biochemistry and biophysics U. Pa., 1980—86; adj. prof. Robert Wood Johnson Med. Sch., 1988—2001; mem. sci. adv. bd. Whitehead Inst. for Biomed. Scis., MIT, 1995—2001; founding mem. Nat. Adv. Coun. Human Genome Project Rsch. NIH, 1991—96, adv. coun. dir., 1997—2001; mem. Am. Soc. Cell Biology, Soc. Devel. Biology, Am. Soc. Biochemistry & Molecular Biology, Commn. Life Scis., Nat. Rsch. Coun., 1993—2001, Am. Acad. Arts Scis., 1990, Inst. Medicine, 1995, Foreign Assoc., US Nat. Acad. Scis., 1996, Am. Philos. Soc., 2000; fellow Royal Soc. London, 1995; editl. bd. mem. Genes & Development, 1990—2001, Journal Cell Biology, 1988—91, Molecular & Cellular Biology, 1985—94, editor; executive editor Nucleic Acids Rsch, 1983—91, bd. mem.; chair Nat. Acad. Com., Intellectual property Genomic & Protein Rsch. & Innovation, 2004—05; sci. adv. bd. Ctr. Advanced Biotechnology & Medicine, Rutgers U., 1993—2001; bd. mem. of sci. advisors Roche Inst. Molecular Biology, 1988—94; sci. adv. bd. Oak Ridge Nat. Labs., 1987—91; chair, mem. Molecular Biology Study Sec., NIH, 1983—87, Visiting Com. Cell & Devel. Biology, Harvard Coll., 1990—95; mem. U. Coun. Biol. Scis., Yale Coll., 1990—94; bd. trustees Cold Spring Harbor Lab., 1990—96. Trustee The Jackson Lab., 1994—, Carnegie Endowment Internat. Peace, 2005—, Google Inc., 2005, Rockefeller U., 1999—2001, Cold Spring Harbor Lab.; mem. Pew Charitable Trusts Scholars Prog., Biomedical Scis. Selection Com., Lucille P. Markey Charitable Trust Scholar Selection Com.; trustee King Abdullah U. Sci. & Tech., 2008—. Recipient Pres.'s award disting. tchg., Princeton U., 1996, L'Oréal-UNESCO Internat. Women in Sci. award, 2002, Lifetime Achievement award, Soc. Devel. Biology, 2003, Radcliffe Inst. medal, Harvard U., 2004, Presdl. Medal of Honor, Dillard U., 2006; named one of America's Best Leaders, US News & World Report, 2007. Mem.: NAS, Am. Acad. Arts and Scis., Royal Soc. London, Inst. Medicine, Am. Philos. Soc. Achievements include first to identify the H19 gene in mice, an early example of parental imprinting; research in cloning the first mammalian gene. Office: Princeton U Office of Pres One Nassau Hall Princeton NJ 08544-0001 Office Phone: 609-258-6101.

TILLER, CHARLENE TEITELBAUM, communications educator; b. Richmond, Va., Nov. 7, 1946; d. Milton David and Rhodye Freeman Teitelbaum; children: Ryan Lee, Seth Freeman. BS, East Carolina U., Greenville, 1968; M.A. Ed, East Carolina U., 1971. Lic. in speech pathology Va., 1973; cert. in clin. competence Am. Speech, Lang. and Hearing Assn., 1972. Speech-lang. pathologist Craven County Schs., New Bern, NC, 1969—73, Hanover County Pub. Schs., Ashland, Va., 1973—74, Hopewell Pub. Schs., Va., 1974—90, Charles City County Pub. Schs., Va., 1990—99; pub. speaking tchr. and head forensic coach Hopewell Pub. Schs., 1988—90, Charles City County, 1990—99; prof. communication studies John Tyler CC, Chester, Va., 2001—, chairperson communication studies, theater dept., 2007—09. Mem. planning com. Va. CC Sys. Speech Peer Group, 2005, 07, conf. spkr. / workshop presenter, 2005—07; mem. debate, drama & forensics adv. com. Va. HS League, 1993—98; dir. Va. State Forensics Championship Tournament, Charlottesville, 2001—; mem. speech debate & theatre adv. com. Nat. Fedn. State HS, Indianapolis, 2004—08; coach Hopewell HS, 1987—90, Charles City HS, 1990—99; facilitator Va. Dept. Edn. Oral Lang. Inst., Longwood Coll, Farmville, 1990. Recipient Ptnr. Edn. award, Hopewell Optimist Club, 1986, Outstanding Educator award, Gov.'s Sch., 1990, The Internat. Book of Honor, 1990; named to Va. HS Hall of Fame, Va. HS League & Coaches Assn., 2008. Mem.: Va. Assn. Comm. Arts and Scis. (chairperson of Two-Yr.& CC com. 2007—, Va.'s Secondary Speech Tchr. of Yr. 1995), Va. Assn. Speech, Debate and Drama Coaches (life; pres. conf. com. chairperson & charter mem. 1991—, Life Membership 2008), Nat. Forensic League (life Distinction 1994). Jewish. Office: John Tyler CC 13101 Jefferson Davis Hwy Chester VA 23831 Office Fax: 804-796-4361. Business E-Mail: ctiller@jtcc.edu.

TILLER, WILLIAM ARTHUR, retired science educator, scientific researcher; b. Toronto, Ont., Can., Sept. 18, 1929; arrived in US, 1955; s. Arthur and Vera Eden Emma (Pash) T.; m. Jean Elizabeth Ackroyd, June 28, 1952; children: Andrea, Jeff. BASc, U. Toronto, 1952, MASc, 1953, PhD, 1955. Sr. physicist Westinghouse Rsch. Lab., Churchill Borough, Pa., 1955-64; full prof. dept. materials sci. and engring. Stanford (Calif.) U., 1964-66, dept. chmn., 1966-71, full prof., 1971-92, emeritus prof., 1992—; chmn., chief scientist The William A. Tiller Found. for New Sci., Payson, Ariz., 2000—. Cons. Dupont de Nemours & Co., Wilmington, Del., 1965-90, Memc Materials Co., St. Peters, Mo., 1990-96, Durance & Ditron LLC, Excelsior, Minn., 1995-00; bd. dirs. Astron Antennaco, Washington. Author: Computer Simulation, 1982, Science of Crystallization I, 1991, Science of Crystallization II, 1992, Science and Human Transformation: Subtle Energies, Intentionality and Consciousness, 1997; co-author: Conscious Acts of Creation: The Emergence of a New Physics, 2001, Some Science Adventures with Real Magic, 2005, Psychoenergetic Science: A Second Copernican-Scale Revolution, 2007; contbr. articles to profl. jours. Avocations: psychoenergetics research, walking. Home: 909 S Pinecone St Payson AZ 85541-5731 Office: Stanford U Dept MSE Stanford CA 94305-2205 E-mail: bill@tiller.org.

TILLERSON, REX W., oil company executive; b. Wichita Falls, Tex., Mar. 23, 1952; s. Robert Tillerson; m. Renda St. Clair; 4 children. BS in Civil Engring., U. Tex., Austin, 1975. Joined Exxon Co., U.S.A., 1975, various positions, prodn. dept., 1975—87, bus. devel. mgr., natural gas dept., 1987—89, gen. mgr., ctrl. prodn. divsn., 1989—92; prodn. adv. Exxon Corp., Dallas, 1992; coord., affiliate gas sales Exxon Co. Internat., Florham Park, NJ, 1992—95; pres. Exxon Yemen Inc., Esso Exploration and Prodn. Khorat Inc., 1995—98; v.p. Exxon Ventures Inc., 1998—99; pres. Exxon Neftegas Ltd., 1998—99; exec. v.p. ExxonMobil Devel. Co., 1999—2001; sr. v.p. ExxonMobil Corp., 2001—04, pres., 2004—06, chmn., CEO, 2006—. Mem. adv. coun. Engring. Found., U. Tex. at Austin; bd. dirs. Exxon Mobil Corp., 2004—. Bd. trustee Ctr. Strategic and Internat. Studies; mem. nat. exec. bd. Boy Scouts Am.; mem. exec. bd. Circle Ten Coun.; mem. engring. found. adv. coun. U. Tex. Austin. Named a Disting. Engring. Grad., U. Tex., 2006; named one of The 25 Most Powerful People in Bus., Fortune Mag., 2007, The Global Elite, Newsweek mag., 2008. Mem.: U.S.-Russia Bus. Coun. (dir.), Soc. Petroleum Engrs., Am. Petroleum Inst. Office: ExxonMobil Corp 5959 Las Colinas Blvd Irving TX 75039-2298*

TILLEY, CAROLYN BITTNER, information scientist; b. Washington, July 29, 1947; d. Klaud Kay and Margaret Louise (Hanson) Bittner; m. Frederick Edwin Dudley, June 18, 1985 BS, Am. U., 1975; M.L.S., U. Md., 1976. With NIH, 1965-71; statis. research asst. Health Manpower Edn., Bethesda, Md., 1971-72; tech. info. specialist Nat. Libr. Medicine, Bethesda, Md., 1972-81, head medlars (med. lit. analysis and retrieval sys.) mgmt. sect., 1981—2002, advisor for UMLS support, 2002. Mem. editl. bd. Med. Reference Svcs. Quar. Recipient Merit award NIH, 1984, Rogers award Nat. Libr. Medicine, 1991. Mem. Med. Libr. Assn., IEEE Libr. Adv. Coun. Presbyterian. Avocation: horseback riding. Office: Nat Libr Medicine 8600 Rockville Pike Bethesda MD 20894-0002 Home: 1004 Elm Ave Takoma Park MD 20912-5840

TILLEY, TERRENCE WILLIAM, religious studies educator; b. Milw., Apr. 19, 1947; s. John C. and Audrey A. (Kau) T.; m. Maureen Antonia Molloy, Dec. 27, 1969; children: Elena, Christine. AB, U. San Francisco, 1970; PhD, Grad. Theol. Union, 1976. Asst. prof. theology Georgtown U., Washington, 1976-79; from asst. to assoc. prof. religious studies St. Michael's Coll., Winooski, Vt., 1979-89; from assoc. prof. to prof. religion Fla. State U., Tallahassee, 1989-94; chair, dir. grad. studies, prof. religious studies U. Dayton, Ohio, 1994—. Dir. seminars NEH, 1987, 90, 94. Author: Talking of God, 1978, Story Theology, 1985 (Book of Yr. Coll. Theology oc. 1986), The Evils of Theodicy, 1991, The Wisdom of Religious Commitment, 1995, Postmodern Theologies, 1995; (with Phyllis Zagano) The Exercise of Primacy, 1998; (with P. Zagano) Things New and Old: Essays on the Theology of Elizabeth A. Johnson, 1999, Inventing Catholic Tradition, 2000. NEH fellow, 1987-88. Mem. AAUP, Am. Acad. Religion (co-chair Roman Cath. studies group 1995-2000), Coll. Theology Soc. (conv. dir. 1988-95, pres. 1996-98), Cath. Theol. Soc. Am. (bd. dirs. 1995-97), Soc. Christian Philosophers, Soc. for Philosophy of Religion. Roman Catholic. Office: U Dayton Religious Studies Dept Dayton OH 45469

TILLINGHAST, DAVID ROLLHAUS, lawyer; b. NYC, Feb. 25, 1930; s. Charles Carpenter and Josephine Dorothy (Rollhaus) T.; m. Phyllis Van Horn, Sept. 24, 1955 (div. Jan. 1984); m. Lisa Sewell, Feb. 25, 1984; children: Gregory Barrett Sewell, Lauren Alexa. AB cum laude, Brown U., 1951; LLB cum laude, Yale U., 1954. Bar: N.Y. 1955, Oreg. 1956, U.S. Supreme Ct. 1978. Assoc. Hughes, Hubbard & Reed, NYC, 1954-55, 57-61, ptnr., 1961-62, 65-90; assoc. King, Miller, Anderson, Nash & Yerke, Portland, Oreg., 1955-57; spl. asst. for internat. tax affairs U.S. Dept. Treasury, Washington, 1962-65; ptnr. Chadbourne & Parke, NYC, 1990-99, Baker & McKenzie, NYC, 1999—2009, counsel, 2009—. Adj. prof. Sch. Law, NYU, 1977-87; cons. UN Ctr. on Transnat. Corps., 1978-87; reporter Am. Law Inst. Project on Internat. Aspects of U.S. Income Taxation, 1982-91; cons. to reporters Am. Law Inst. Revision of Restatement of Fgn. Relations Law of U.S., 1982-83. Author: Tax Aspects of Internat. Transactions, 1978, 2d edit., 1984; co-author: Income Tax Treaty Arbitration, 2004; contbr. articles to profl. publs. Mem. transition team Sec. of Treasury W. Michael Blumenthal, 1977. Established David R. Tillinghast lectureship on internat. taxation NYU Sch. Law. Mem.: Tax Forum, Internat. Bar Assn. (vice chmn. com. on taxation bus. law sect. 1984—86), Internat. Fiscal Assn. (v.p. U.S. br. 1983—2000, permanent sci. com. 1983—2000, vice chmn. 1993—95, chmn. 1995—2000), Assn. of Bar of City of N.Y. (chmn. com. on taxation 1981—83). Democrat. Avocation: swimming. Office: Baker & McKenzie 1114 Avenue of the Americas New York NY 10036 Office Phone: 212-891-3526. Business E-Mail: david.r.tillinghast@bakernet.com.

TILLINGHAST, JOHN AVERY, utilities executive; b. NYC, Apr. 30, 1927; s. Charles C. and Dorothy J. (Rollhaus) T.; m. Mabel Healy, Sept. 11, 1948; children: Katherine Brickley, Susan Trainor, Abigail Ryan. BSME, Columbia U., 1948, MS, 1949. With Am. Elec. Power Service Corp., NYC, 1949-79, exec. v.p. engring. and constrn., 1967-72, sr. exec. v.p., vice chmn. engring. and constrn., 1972-79; sr. v.p. tech. Wheelabrator-Frye Inc., Hampton, NH, 1979-83, Signal Advanced Tech. Group, The Signal Cos., Hampton, NH, 1983-85; sr. v.p. Allied-Signal Internat., Hampton, 1985-86, Sci. Applications Internat. Corp., San Diego, 1986-88; pres. TILTEC, Portsmouth, NH, 1987—; CEO, Great

Bay Power Corp., Dover, NH, 1994-97; CEO BayCorp Holdings, Ltd., Dover, 1997-98, chmn. bd. Portsmouth, 1998—99. Patentee generating unit control system. Elder Reformed Ch., 1976-79. Served with USN, 1944-46. Fellow ASME; mem. IEEE, NAE, Sigma Xi, Tau Beta Pi. Office Phone: 603-964-7454. E-mail: jtillinghast@comcast.net.

TILLINGHAST, NANCY, library director; b. Buckhannon, W.Va., Mar. 2, 1946; children: Beth Norman, Mark. BS, W.Va. Univ., 1969; MLIS, Univ. SC, 1991. Asst. libr. Roane County Libr., Spencer, W.Va., 1982—90; children's & pub. services libr. Thomas County Pub. Libr. Sys., Thomasville, Ga., 1991—94, asst. dir., 1994—96, dir., 1996—. Chmn. Libr. Council SW Ga. Tech. Coll., mem. Literacy Council; chmn. Certified Literate Cmty. Prog. Thomas County. Chmn. United Way Thomas County; mem. Family Connections, Hands on Thomas County. Recipient Libr. award, NY Times, 2006, Cmty. Svc. award, Zion Christian Bible Inst.; named Woman of the Yr., Thomasville-Thomas County C. of C., 2007. Mem.: ALA, Pub. Libr. Assn., Ga. Libr. Assn., Rotary. Avocations: gardening, cross stitch, reading. Office: Thomas County Pub Libr Sys 201 N Madison St Thomasville GA 31792 Office Phone: 229-225-5252. Office Fax: 229-225-5258. Business E-Mail: nancy@tcpls.org.

TILLIS, MEL, entertainer, songwriter; b. Tampa, Fla., Aug. 8, 1932; children: Pam, Connie, Cindy, Melvin Jr., Carrie, Hannah. Student, U. Fla. Founder Sawgrass Music, Sabal Music, Tillis Tunes, Sweet Tater Tunes, Nashville; owner, pres. Mel Tillis Theater, Branson, Mo., 1993—2002. Songwriter, Cedarwood Music, Nashville, 20 years, (Named Entertainer of Year, Country Music Assn. 1976), composer over 600 songs recorded by Webb Pierce, Ray Price, Carl Smith, Brenda Lee, Kenny Rogers, Charlie Pride, Burl Ives, George Strait, others; (with The Statesiders) 60 albums including; Mel Tillis and the Statesiders on Stage, Best of Mel Tillis, Love Revival, Welcome to Country, California Road, 1985, American Originals, 1990, Greatest Hits, 1991, Beyond the Sunset, 1993, Great, 1994, The Memory Maker, 1995 Branson City Limits, 1999; co-host (TV series) Mel & Susan Together, 1978, actor (films) W.W. & the Dancekings, 1975, The Villain, 1979, Smokey & the Bandit II, 1980, Cannonball Run, 1981, Cannonball Run II, 1984, Uphill All the Way, 1986, (TV films) Skinflint: A Country Christas Carol, 1979, The Stockers, 1981, Bandit Goes Country, 1994; author: Stuttering Boy, 1986. Served in USAF, 1951-55. Named Comedian of Yr., Country Music Assn., 1971, 1973-77, Entertainer of Yr., 1976, Songwriter of Decade, Broadast Music, Inc., 1999; named to Grand Ole Opry, 2007, Country Music Hall of Fame, 2007; recipient Golden Voice Entertainer award, 2001, Golden R.O.P.E. Songwriter award, 2001, Spl. Citation of Achievement, Broadcast Music, Inc., 2001. Home: PO Box 305 Silver Springs FL 34489-0305 Office Phone: 352-694-4900. E-mail: mmel@meltillis.com.

TILLMAN, AUDREY BOONE, insurance company executive; married; 3 children. BA in Polit. Sci., U. NC, Chapel Hill; JD, U. Ga. Law clk. to Judge Richard C. Erwin US Dist. Ct. NC; assoc. Smith, Helms, Mulliss and Moore, Greensboro, NC, 1990—93; assoc. prof. NC Ctrl. U. Sch. Law; mem. legal dept. AFLAC Inc., Columbus, Ga., 1996—97, second v.p., 1997—2000, v.p., sr. assoc. counsel legal divsn., 2000—01, sr. v.p., dir. human resources, 2001, sr. v.p., dir. corp. svcs. Dir.-at-large Soc. Human Resource Mgmt. Mem. Workforce Devel. Task Force State of Ga. Recipient Corp. Governance award, Celebrating Excellence in Leadership Orgn., Office Depot Visionary award, 2007; named one of Top 100 Blacks in Corp. Am., Black Profls. mag. Mem.: Bar DC, NC State Bar, State Bar Ga. Office: AFLAC Inc 1932 Wynnton Rd Columbus GA 31999 Office Phone: 706-323-3431.

TILLMAN, CELESTINE, chemistry professor; d. Elbert Lee and Lillie Tillman. BS in Liberal Arts and Sci., So. U., Baton Rouge, 1955; MS in Computer Sci., So. U., 1988; MS in Chemistry, Howard U., DC, 1957. Grad. tchg. asst. in chemistry Howard U., 1955—57; chemistry tchr. So. U., 1957—87; asst. prof. chemistry Calif. State U., Long Beach, 1989—92; adj. chemistry lectr. El Camino Coll., Torrance, Calif., 1989—96, Rancho Santiago Coll., Long Beach, 1992—94, LA City Coll., 1992—96; chemistry prof. LA SW Coll., 1996—2008, chemistry prof. emeritus, 2009. Mem.: Top Ladies Distin. Inc., Beta Pi Sigma Inc. (Top Ladies Distingtion), Am. Chem. Soc., Iota Sigma Pi (life), Delta Sigma Theta (life). Baptist. Home Phone: 310-324-9843. Home Fax: 310-324-9843. Personal E-mail: celestinet@sbcglobal.net.

TILLMAN, JUDITH R., federal agency administrator; BA summa cum laude, Glassboro State Coll.; MA in Human Resource Devel., Am. U. Joined Fin. Mgmt. Svc., US Dept. Treasury, 1989, human resources dir., 1992—98, asst. commr. fin. ops., dep. commr., 2006—08, commr., 2008—. Recipient Presdl. Rank Meritorious Exec. Award. Office: Fin Mgmt Svc 401 14th St, SW Washington DC 20227*

TILLMAN, MARY NORMAN, urban affairs consultant; b. Atlanta, Jan. 31, 1926; d. Mary Nellie Shehee; m. James A. Tillman Jr., Apr. 11, 1952; children: James A., Gina G. BA, Morris Brown Coll., 1947; postgrad., U. Minn., 1964, Old Dominion U., 1975—. Asst. bus. mgr. Morris Brown Coll., Atlanta, 1947-53; race rels. and urban affairs cons. Tillman Assocs. Cons. Social Engrs., Atlanta and Syracuse, NY, 1963—, sr. ptnr., treas., from 1965, now pres. Bd. dirs. The Tillman Inst. of Human Rels., Inc.; clin. prof. United Theol. Sem., New Brighton, Minn.; adj. prof. Gordon-Conwell Theol. Sem., South Hamilton, Mass. Author: What is Your Racism Quotient?, 1964, A Common Sense Approach to Racism and Other Exclusivities, 1998, (with James A. Tillman, Jr.) Why America Needs Racism and Poverty, 1972, Black Intellectuals, White Liberals and Race Relations: An Analytic Overview, 1973; What is your Exclusivity Quotient, 1978, A Common Sense Approach to Racism and Other Exclusivities, 2001; contbr. articles to profl. jours. Adv. coun. to urban ministries dept. So. Bapt. Conv., Cmty. Rels. Commn., Atlanta; bd. dirs. Christian Coun. Met. Atlanta, Tillman Inst. Human Rels. Mem. Tidewater Assn. Pub. Adminstrs. (dir.), Am. Acad. Cons., Nat. Black Writers Consortium (v.p.), Joint Ctr. for Polit. Studies. Office: 1765 Glenview Dr SW Atlanta GA 30331-2307 Office Phone: 404-349-3668.

TILLMAN, MASSIE MONROE, mediator, arbitrator, art gallery owner, retired judge; b. Corpus Christi, Tex., Aug. 15, 1937; s. Clarence and Artie Lee (Stewart) T.; m. Karen Wright, July 2, 1993; children: Jeff, Holly. BBA, Baylor U., 1959, LLB, 1961. Bar: Tex. 1961, U.S. Dist. Ct. (no. dist.) Tex. 1961, U.S. Ct. Appeals (5th cir.) 1969, U.S. Supreme Ct. 1969, formerly bd. cert. personal injury trial law: Tex.; cert. hearing examiner Tex. Edn. Agy. Pvt. practice, Ft. Worth, 1961—87; U.S. bankruptcy judge Ft. Worth divsn. No. Dist. Tex., 1987—2001; mediator, arbitrator, 2001—. Author: Tillman's Trial Guide, 1970,-1990, comments editor, case notes editor; mem. editl. bd. Baylor Law Rev., 1960-61. Fellow Tex. Bar Found.; mem. Am. Bd. Trial Advocates (founding mem.), Ft. Worth/Tarrant County Bar (bd. dirs. 1969-70, v.p. 1970-71), Trial Attys. Am., Arbitration Assocs., Coll. State Bar Tex. (alternative dispute resolution sect. ssch. law sect.). Baptist. Avocation: quail hunting. Address: PO Box 20213 Fort Worth TX 76102 Personal E-mail: tillmanmediator@yahoo.com.

TILLMAN, VICKIE A., publishing executive, former financial information company executive; b. 1951; BA in Comm., U. Pitts., 1973, MPA in Fin., 1976. With Standard & Poor's, 1977—2009, exec. mng. dir. pub. fin. ratings dept., exec. v.p. structured fin. ratings, 1994—99, exec. v.p., 1999—2009; sr. v.p. global sustainability bus. devel. The McGraw-Hill Companies, 2009—. Bd. visitors U. Pitts. Grad. Sch. Internat. Affairs, 2003—06. Recipient Disting. Alumna award, U. Pitts. Grad. Sch. Internat. Affairs, 2002. Office: The McGraw-Hill Companies Inc 1221 Ave of the Americas New York NY 10020*

TILLMANN, RICHARD, literature and language educator; b. Washington, Feb. 13, 1951; s. Alfred and Ann Tillmann; 1 child, Kevin. BA, Va. Commonwealth U., Richmond, 1975. Tchr. Frederick County Pub. Schs., Winchester, Va., 1979—. Liberal. Office: Dowell J Howard 156 Dowell J Circle Winchester VA 22603

TILSON, M(ARTIN) DAVID, III, surgeon, scientist, educator; b. Texarkana, Tex., Aug. 25, 1941; s. M. David and Leta (Martin) Tilson; 3 children. BA, Rice U., 1963; MD, Yale U., 1967. Diplomate Am. Bd. Surgery, Nat. Bd. Med. Examiners. Surg. intern Yale U., New Haven, 1967-68; resident in surgery U. New Haven, 1968-72; asst. to assoc. prof. Yale U., New Haven, 1974-83, prof., 1983-89; Ailsa Mellon Bruce prof. surgery Columbia U., NYC, 1989—. Contbr. articles to profl. jours. Maj. USAF, 1972-74. Rsch. grantee, NIH, 1983—94, 1999—2003. Mem. ACS, Soc. Univ. Surgeons, Am. Surg. Assn., Soc. Vascular Surgery, Internat. Soc. Cadiovasc. Surgery, Halsted Soc. Home: 105 Garth Rd B2 Scarsdale NY 10583-2714 Office: St Lukes Roosevelt Hosp 1000 10th Ave New York NY 10019-1192 E-mail: mdt1@columbia.edu.

TILSON, WHITNEY R., investment company executive; b. 1966; married; 3 children. BA in govt., Harvard Coll., 1989; MBA, Harvard Bus. Sch., 1994. Founding mem. Teach for America; co-founder, exec. dir. Initiative for a Competitive Inner City; cons. Boston Consulting Group; founder, mng. partner T2 Partners LLC, 1999—, Tilson Mutual Funds, 1999—. Co-founder ICV Partners; co-founder, chmn., co-editor-in-chief Value Investor Insight; co-founder, chmn. Value Investing Congress; teacher, fin. statement analysis and bus. valuation The Dickie Grp.; mem. bd. Cutter & Buck, Fistula Found.; vice-chmn. KIPP Acad., Thorn Tree Project. Author: (writes regular column) Fin. Times, (articles) Motley Fool and TheStreet.com; co-author: (novels) Poor Charlie's Almanack. Named one of five top investors, SmartMoney's Power 30. Mem.: Young Presidents' Orgn. Achievements include has appeared on CNBC, Bloomberg TV, Lou Dobbs Moneyline and Wall $treet Week, profiled by the Wall Street Journal and the Washington Post, spoken widely on the topics of value investing and behavioral fin. Office Phone: 800-773-3863.

TILSON THOMAS, MICHAEL, conductor, music director; b. LA, Dec. 21, 1944; s. Theodor and Roberta Tilson Thomas. Studies with Ingolf Dahl, U. So. Calif.; student in conducting, Berkshire Music Festival, Tanglewood, Mass.; LLD, Hamilton Coll.; LHD (hon.), D'Youville Coll., 1976. Asst. condr. Boston Symphony Orch., 1969, assoc. condr., 1970-72, prin. guest condr., 1972-74; also Berkshire Music Festival, summer 1970, 74; music dir., condr. Buffalo Philharmonic Orch., 1971-79; prin. guest condr. LA Philharm., 1981—85; music dir., prin. condr. Great Woods Ctr. Performing Arts, 1985-88; founder, artistic dir. New World Symphony, Fla., 1988—; prin. condr. London Symphony Orch., 1988—95, prin. guest condr., 1995—; music dir. San Francisco Symphony, 1995—. Chief condr. Ojai Festival, 1967, dir., 1972—77, condr., dir. NY Philharm. Young People's Concerts CBS-TV, 1971—77, vis. condr. numerous orchs., US, Europe, Japan, rec. artist Sony Classical/CBS Masterworks, 1973—, opera debut, Cin., 1975, condr. Am. premiere Lulu, Santa Fe Opera, 1979, prin. guest condr. Gershwin Festival London Symphony Orch., Barbcan Ctr., 1987; composer: Grace-A Song for Leonard Bernstein, 1988; composer: (for Empire Brass Quintet) Street Song, 1988; composer: (for orch. and narator Audrey Hepburn and New World Symphony) From the Diary of Anne Frank, 1990; co-artistic dir. Pacific Music Festival, 1990—, commd. for Concerts for Life's European premiere UNICEF, 1991, conducted Mozart Requiem, —. Recipient Koussevitsky prize, 1968, Grammy award, Carmina Burana with Cleve. Orch., 1976, Gershwin Live with LA Philharm., 1983, Ditson award, 1994, Am. Music Ctr. award, 2001, Grammy award, Mahler Symphony No. 3 with San Francisco Symphony Orch., 2004, Classic FM Gramophone award for Artist of Yr., 2005, Grammy awards for Best Classical Album and Best Orchestral Performance, Mahler Symphony No. 7 with San Francisco Symphony Orch., 2007; named Musician of Yr., Musical Am., 1970, Condr. of Yr., 1994. Fellow: Am. Acad. Arts and Sciences. Office: 888 7th Ave Fl 37 New York NY 10106-3799 Mailing: Van Walsum Mgmt 4 Addison Bridge Pl London W14 8XP England Office Phone: 212-246-7726.*

TILSWORTH, TIMOTHY, retired environmental/civil engineering educator; b. Norfolk, Nebr., Apr. 6, 1939; s. Brooke and Mildred (Palmer) T.; m. Joanne Novak, Apr. 19, 1966 (div. Jan. 1984); children: Craig Scott, Patrick Joseph; m. Debbie J. May, July 20, 1984. BSCE, U. Nebr., Lincoln, 1966, MSCE, 1967; PhD, U. Kans, 1970. Registered profl. engr., Alaska; diplomate Inst. Hazardous Materials Mgmt. Instr. U. Nebr., Lincoln, 1967; prof. environ. quality and civil engring. U. Alaska, Fairbanks, 1970-94, dir. program environ. quality engring. and sci., 1972-76, 78-94, asst. to pres. for acad. affairs, 1976-78, head dept. civil engring, 1990-91, chmn. grad. coun., chmn. chancellor search com., 1990-91; rschr. Antarctic Rsch. UAF/NSF, 1990—92; prof. emeritus civil engring. and environ. quality engring. U. Alaska, 1994—; co-owner Raven Press Alaska Pub. Co., Fairbanks, 1990—; with NSF Antarctic Rsch. McMurdo, 1991—92. Pres. faculty senate U. Alaska, 1992-93; owner Alaska Arctic Environ. Svcs., Fairbanks, 1972-99, DJT's Shelties Delight, Fairbanks, 1985-99, T2 Antiques, 1994-99; project mgr. superconducting super collider proposal State of Alaska, Fairbanks, 1987-88. Chmn. exec. com. Cowper for Gov. Alaska, Fairbanks, 1986; pres. Alaska Soc. Civil Engrs, 1973—74. 1st lt. Army Nat. Guard, 1964—69, Nebr. Recipient commendation State of Alaska, 1988. Mem. Assn. for Environ. Engring. Profs., ASCE (Outstanding Service award 1975), Am. Water Works Assn. Water Pollution Control Fedn., Fairbanks Golf and Country Club (bd. dirs. 2000-01), Chi Epsilon. Roman Catholic. Home and Office: 1900 Raven Dr Fairbanks AK 99709-6661 E-mail: fftt@uaf.edu.

TILTON, DAVID LLOYD, savings and loan association executive; b. Santa Barbara, Calif., Sept. 21, 1926; s. Lloyd Irvine and Grace (Hart) T.; m. Mary Caroline Knudtson, June 6, 1953; children: Peter, Jennifer, Michael, Catharine. AB, Stanford U., 1949, MBA, 1951. With Santa Barbara Savs. & Loan Assn., 1951-90, pres., 1965-84; now pres. Fin. Corp., Santa Barbara. Trustee, chmn. Calif. Real Estate Investment Trust, 1988. Served with USNR, World War II. Mem. Calif. Savs. and Loan League (dir. 1980), Delta Chi. Home: 630 Oak Grove Dr Santa Barbara CA 93108-1402 Office: Fin Corp Santa Barbara 311 E Carillo St Santa Barbara CA 93101-2761 E-mail: dtilton@earthlink.net.

TILTON, GLENN F., air transportation executive; b. Washington, Apr. 9, 1948; m. Jaqueline Morris; 2 children. BA in Internat. Rels., U. SC, 1970. Sales trainee US mktg. ops. Texaco Inc., Washington, 1970, various assignments, 1970—76, div. supr. mktg. East Brunswick, NJ, 1976—78, area mgr. resale NY divsn. NYC, 1978, asst. to gen. mgr. northeastern region, 1978—79, mktg. mgr. resale Phila. divsn., 1979—81, staff coord. corp. planning and econs. dept. Harrison, NY, 1981—83, v.p., 1989, sr. v.p., 1995—2002; asst. gen. mgr. sales Texaco Europe, 1983—84, gen. mgr. mktg., 1984—87; pres. Texaco Eruope, 1992—94; v.p. mktg. Texaco USA, Houston, 1984—88, pres., 1994—2002, Texaco Refining and Mktg. Inc., Houston, 1988—91; chmn. Texaco Ltd., 1991—92; pres. Texaco Global Bus. Unit, 1997—2001; CEO Texaco, White Plains, NY, 2001; chmn., pres., CEO UAL Corp. and United Airlines, 2002—. Bd. dirs. Abbott Labs., Chgo., Air Transport Assn. Bd. dirs. Internat. Rels. Adv. Coun. Chgo. 2016; bd. trustees Field Mus., Mus. Sci. and Industry; bd. dirs. After Sch. Matters. Mem.: US Travel & Tourism Adv. Bd., Comml. Club Chgo. (mem. civic com.), Exec.'s Club Chgo. (bd. dirs.), Econ. Club Chgo. (bd. dirs.). Achievements include being fluent in English, Spanish and Portuguese. Office: UAL Corp PO Box 66100 Chicago IL 60666

TIMBALAND, (TIMOTHY Z. MOSLEY), recording industry executive, rap artist; b. Norfolk, Va., Mar. 10, 1971; m. Monique Idelett, June 22, 2008; 1 child. Mem. Timbaland & Magoo; founder, pres. Mosely Music Group/Geffen. Singer: (albums) Welcome to Our World, 1997, Tim's Bio, 1998, Indecent Proposal, 2001, Under Construction, Part II, 2003, Shock Value, 2007; prodr. (Jodeci) Diary of a Mad Band, 1993, The Show, The After Party, The Hotel, 1994, (Aaliyah) One in a Million, 1996, Aaliyah, 2001, I Care 4 U, 2002, (Ginuwine) The Bachelor, 1996, 100% Ginuwine, 1999, The Life, 2001, (Missy Elliot) Supa Dupa Fly, 1997, Miss E: So Addictive, 2001, Under Construction, 2002, This is Not a Test!, 2003, The Cookbook, 2005, (Jay-Z) Vol. 2: Hard Knock Life, 1998, Vol. 3: Life & Times of S Carter, 1999, The Blueprint, 2001, The Blueprint 2: The Gift & the Curse, 2002, The Black Album, 2003, (Beck) Mutations, 1998, (Nas) I Am, 1999, Nastradamus, 1999, (Snoop Dogg) The Last Meal, 2000, (Ludacris) Word of Mouf, 2001, Red Light District, 2004, (Limp Bizkit) New Old Song, 2001, (Destiny's Child) This is the Remix, 2002, (Justin Timberlake) Justified, 2002, FutureSex/LoveSounds, 2006, (TLC) 3D, 2002, (Fabolous) Ghetto Fabolous, 2001, Street Dreams, 2003, (Bubba Sparxxx) Dark Days, Bright Nights, 2001, Deliverance, 2003, The Charm, 2006, (Alicia Keys) The Diary of Alicia Keys, 2003, (Lil Kim) La Bella Mafia, 2004, (Brandy) Afrodisiac, 2004, (LL Cool J) The DEFinition, 2004, (Jennifer Lopez) Rebirth, 2005, (Black Eyed Peas) Monkey Business, 2005, (Jamie Foxx) Unpredictable, 2005, (Nelly Furtado) Loose, 2006, (soundtracks) Sprung, 1996, Money Talks, 1997, Dr. Doolittle, 1998, Why Do Fools Fall in Love, 1998, The PJs, 1999, Austin Powers: The Spy Who Shagged Me, 1999, Romeo Must Die, 2000, Nutty Professor II: The Klumps, 2000, Exit Wounds, 2000, Lara Croft: Tomb Raider, 2001, Shark Tale, 2004. Recipient Songwriter of Yr. award, ASCAP, 2008, Grammy award for Best Dance Recording, 2007, Favorite Hip-Hop Song, People's Choice Awards, 2008; co-recipient award for Most Performed Song from Motion Picture, ASCAP, 1999, 2001, 2002; named a Maverick, Details mag., 2007; named to Power 150, Ebony mag., 2008. Office: Mosley Music Group LLC c/o Interscope Geffen A&M Records 2220 Colorado Ave Santa Monica CA 90404 also: c/o Blackground Entertainment 23460 Hatteras St Woodland Hills CA 91367 Office Phone: 818-884-8526.

TIMBERLAKE, JUSTIN RANDALL, singer; b. Memphis, Jan. 31, 1981; s. Randy Timberlake and Lynn Harless. Singer, performer 'N Sync, 1996—2002; solo vocalist, 2002—; chmn. & CEO Tennman Records, LA, 2007—. Launched William Rast clothing line (with Trace Ayala), 2005; restaurant co-owner (with Eytan Sugarman) Destino's, 2006. Singer (with 'N Sync): (albums) N Sync, 1998, Home for Christmas, 1998, No Strings Attached, 2000, Celebrity, 2001; singer: (solo albums) Justified, 2003 (Grammy award, Best Pop Vocal Album, 2003), FutureSex/LoveSounds, 2006 (Favorite Album, Am. Music Awards, 2007), (songs) Cry Me a River, 2003 (Grammy award, Best Male Pop Vocal Performance, 2003), Sexy Back, 2006 (Favorite R&B Song, People's Choice awards, 2007, Grammy award for Best Dance Recording, 2007), My Love, 2006 (Grammy award for Best Rap/Sung Collaboration, 2007, Best Choreography, MTV Video Music Awards, 2007), LoveStoned/I Think She Knows, 2006 (Grammy award for Best Dance Recording, 2008), What Goes Around...Comes Around, 2006 (Best Direction, MTV Video Music Awards, 2007, Grammy award for Best Male Pop Vocal Performance, 2008); actor: (films) Longshot, 2000, Edison, 2005, Alpha Dog, 2006, Southland Tales, 2006, Black Snake Moan, 2006; (films, voice) Shrek the Third, 2007; (films) The Love Guru, 2008; (TV films) Model Behavior, 2000. Founder J. Timberlake Found. Recipient Best Pop Artist & Best Male Artist awards, MTV Europe Music Awards, 2006, Internat. Male Solo Artist, BRIT Awards, 2007, Quadruple Threat of Yr., MTV Video Music Awards, 2007, Male Artist of Yr., 2007, Favorite Male Pop Artist, Am. Music Awards, 2007, Best Male Pop Artist, World Music Awards, 2007, Best-Selling Am. Artist, 2007, Favorite Pop Song, People's Choice Awards, 2008; named Favorite Male Singer, 2008; named one of The World's Most Influential People, TIME mag., 2007, The 100 Most Powerful Celebrities, Forbes-.com, 2008. Avocation: golf. Office: Jive Records 137-139 W 25th St 9th Floor New York NY 10012 also: Tennman Records 101 S Robertson Blvd Ste 205 Los Angeles CA 90048-3209

TIMBILLA, JAMES ABANGAH, entomologist, educator; b. Kumasi, Ghana, Sept. 12, 1960; s. Piiga and Soyienna Abangah; m. Christiana Fosua Timbilla, July 25, 1997; children: Deborah Timbilla, John Timbilla. BSc with honors, 1987; MPhil, KN U. Sci. & Tech., Kumasi, 1997; PhD, Kwame Nkrumah U. Sci. & Tech., Kumasi, 2006. Cert. UN-FAO cons 96, reverend Apostolic Faith Ch., Portland, Oreg., 97. Rschr. & cons. CSIR Crops Rsch. Inst., Kumasi, 1986—2006, dep. head divsn., 1999—2006; instr. Essex County Coll., Newark, 2007—, Middlesex County Coll., Edison, 2008—, County Coll. Morris, Randolph, NJ, 2008—. Contbr. scientific papers. Min. Apostolic Faith Ch., Hempstead, NY, preaching & counseling, 2009—. Recipient award, ISCE, 2005; named Best Agrl. Rschr., Ghana Govt., 1998; Rsch. grant, Brit. Ecol. Soc., 2001, 2006. Mem.: Nat. Biol. Control Com. (dep. coord. 1994—97), African Assn. Insect Scientists, Internat. Soc. Chem. Ecology. Home: 83 E Lawn Dr Teaneck NJ 07666 Office: County Coll Morris 214 Ctr Grove Rd Randolph NJ 07869 Home Fax: 201-837-6736. Personal E-mail: jtimbilla@yahoo.com. Business E-Mail: jtimbilla@ccm.edu.

TIMINS, JULIE KELTER, radiologist; d. Joseph and Viola Kelter; m. William Lupatkin, May 1985. MD, Thomas Jefferson U., Phila., 1971. Cert. in diagnostic and therapeutic Am. Bd. Radiology, 1975, physician Am. Bd. Nuc. Medicine, 1976. Staff radiologist Vets. Adminstrn. Med. Ctr., Lyons, NJ, 1976—84, chair, nuc. medicine, 1979—84; staff radiologist St. Joseph's Hosp. & Med. Ctr., Paterson, NJ, 1984—86, Robert Wood Johnson U. Hosp., New Brunswick, NJ, 1986—95, Morris Imaging Assocs., Morristown U. Hosp., NJ, 1995—96, Christ Hosp., Jersey City, 1997—2008. Cons. diagnostic radiology, Morristown, 1978—2009. Contbr. articles to profl. jours. Fellow: Am. Coll. Radiology (coun. steering com.); mem.: Conf. Radiation Control Program Dirs. (Outstanding Achievement award 2007), Nat. Mammography Quality Assurance Adv. Com., Nat. Coun. Radiation Protection & Measurements (dir. 2007—09, Adv. Com. Svc. award 2008), Radiologic Tech. Bd. Examiners (NJ), Am. Assn. Women Radiologists (exec. com. mem., treas., Pres. award 2006), Radiol. Soc. (NJ) (exec. com. mem., officer, Gold Medal award 2007). Home: 20 Footes Ln Morristown NJ 07960 Office: Hirsch and Ratakonda 290 Madison Ave Bldg #4 Morristown NJ 07960

TIMKEN, WARD J., JR., manufacturing executive; BA, Georgetown Univ.; MBA, Univ. Va. Mgr., Washington office McGough & Assoc. govt. affairs. cons.; with Timken Co., Canton, Ohio, 1992—, corp. v.p., 2000—03, bd. dir., 2002—, exec. v.p., pres. steel group, 2003—05, vice chmn., 2005, chmn., 2005—. Bd. mem. Am. Iron & Steel Inst.; bd. dir. Team NEO, Stark Devel. Bd., Henry & Louise Timken Found.; mem. Ohio Bus. Develop. Council. Bd. dir. Firestone Country Club. Office: Timken Company 1835 Dueber Ave SW Canton OH 44706-0932 Office Phone: 330-438-3000.

TIMKEN, WILLIAM ROBERT, JR., United States Ambassador to Germany, former manufacturing executive; b. 1938; m. Sue Timken; 6 children. BA, Stanford U., Calif., 1960; MBA, Harvard U., 1962. With Timken Co. (formerly The Timken Roller Bearing Co.), Canton, Ohio, 1962—2005, asst. v.p. sales, 1964-65, dir. corp. devel., 1965-68, v.p., 1968-73, vice-chmn. bd., chmn. fin. com., 1973-75, chmn. bd., chmn. fin. com., 1975—2003, non-exec. chmn., 2004—05, also dir.; chmn. Securities Investor Protection Corp., Washington, 2003—05; US amb. to Germany US Dept. State, Berlin, 2005—. Recipient Henry Laurence Gantt medal, ASME, 2003, Woodrow Wilson award, Corp. Citizenship, Adam Smith award, Ellis Island Medal of Honor, Ohio Govs. award; named Ohio Bus. Statesman of Yr., Chevalier French Legion of Honor, Hon. Citizen, Colmar, France. Office: DOS Amb 5090 Berlin Pl Washington DC 20521*

TIMLIN, JAMES CLIFFORD, bishop emeritus; b. Scranton, Pa., Aug. 5, 1927; s. James C. and Helen E. (Norton) Timlin. AB, St. Mary's Sem., Balt., 1948; STB, Gregorian U., Rome, 1950. Ordained priest Diocese of Scranton, Pa., 1951, asst. chancellor, sec., 1966—71, chancellor, 1971—77, aux. bishop, vicar gen., 1976—84, bishop, 1984—2003; asst. pastor St. John the Evangelist Ch., Pittston, Pa., 1952—53, St. Peter's Cathedral, Scranton, 1953—66; ordained bishop, 1976; pastor Ch. of Nativity, Scranton, 1979—84; adminstr. St. Joseph's Ch., Wilkes-Barre, Pa., 2004; rector Villa St. Joseph, Dunmore, Pa., 2004—. Roman Catholic. Address: 1600 Green Ridge St Dunmore PA 18509 Office Phone: 570-343-6170.

TIMLIN, ROBERT J., judge; b. 1932; BA cum laude, Georgetown U., 1954, JD, 1959, LLM, 1964. Atty. Douglas, Obear and Campbell, 1960-61, Law Offices of A.L. Wheeler, 1961; with criminal divsn. U.S. Dept. Justice, 1961-64; atty. U.S. Atty. Office (ctrl. dist.) Calif., 1964-66, Hennigan, Ryneal and Butterwick, 1966-67; city atty. City of Corona, Calif., 1967-70; prin. Law Office of Robert J. Timlin, 1970-71, 75-76; ptnr. Hunt, Palladino and Timlin, 1971-74, Timlin and Coffin, 1974-75; judge Mcpl. Ct., Riverside, Calif., 1976-80, Calif. Superior Ct., Riverside, 1980-90; assoc. justice Calif. Ct. Appeals, 1990-94; judge U.S. Dist. Ct. (ctrl. dist.) Calif., LA, 1994—. Part-time U.S. Magistrate judge Ctrl. Dist. Calif., 1970-74. Served U.S. Army, 1955-57. Mem. Calif. Judges Assn. Office: US Dist Ct Central Distric Calif Western Divsn 312 N Spring St Los Angeles CA 90012

TIMM, DELMAR C., engineering educator, consultant; b. Tipton, Iowa, Aug. 19, 1940; s. John F. Timm and Florence M. Schell; m. Alice Ann Alftine; children: David E., Martha Ann Weno, Gegory S. BS, Iowa State U., Ames, 1962, MS, 1965, PhD, 1967. Engr. Esso Rsch. and Engring., Florham Pk., NJ, 1962—64; prof. U. Nebr., Lincoln, 1967—. Cons. Brunswick Def., Lincoln, 1970—95. Contbr. scientific papers. Home: 2933 Jackson Dr Lincoln NE 68502 Office: Univ Nebr 207 I Othmer Hall Lincoln NE 68588-0643 Business E-Mail: dtimm@unl.edu.

TIMM, DONNA FAYE, librarian; m. Daniel Edward Banks, Dec. 27, 2007. MLS, U. NC, Greensboro, 1978. Head, access svc. LSU Health Sci. Ctr. Libr., Shreveport, La., 2002—03, head, user edn., 2003—. Chair-elect, govtl. rels. com. Med. Libr. Assn., Chigo., 2007—. Webmaster LSU Health Sci. Ctr. Women's Club, Shreveport, 2007—08. Recipient Rsch. award, Med. Libr. Assn., 2006, Ida and George Eliot prize, 2009. Office: LSU Health Scis Ctr 1501 Kings Hwy Shreveport LA 71103 Office Fax: 318-675-5442. Business E-Mail: dtimm@lsuhsc.edu.

TIMMCKE, ALAN EDWARD, colon and rectal surgeon; b. Madison, Wis., July 7, 1949; s. Wesley Eugene Timmcke; m. Teresa Ann Watkins, Dec. 31, 1977; children: Gretchen Kristine, Alan Edward Jr. BS, Dickinson Coll., 1971; MD with honors, Temple U., 1975. Diplomate Am. Bd. Surgery, Am. Bd. Colon and Rectal Surgery; lic. physician, Pa., La., Fla. Intern in surgery Nat. Naval Med. Ctr., Bethesda, Md., 1975-76, resident in gen. surgery, 1976-79; rsch. fellow in colon and rectal surgery Jewish Hosp./Washington U. Med. Ctr., St. Louis, 1985-86, clin. fellow in colon and rectal surgery, 1986-87; asst. in surgery Washington U. Sch. Medicine, St. Louis, 1985-87; staff colon and rectal surgeon Ochsner Clinic, New Orleans, 1987—. Staff surgeon Nat. Naval Med. Ctr., Bethesda, 1979, Naval Regional Med. Ctr., Newport, R.I., 1979-82, dept. colon and rectal surgery Lahey Clinic Med. Ctr., Burlington, Mass., 1984-85; staff surgeon Rumford (Maine) Community Hosp., 1982-84, med. staff v.p., 1983-84; instr. surgery Uniformed Svcs. U. of Health Scis., Bethesda, 1978-79; lectr. in field. Assoc. editor Diseases of the Colon and Rectum, 2002—08; contbr. articles and abstracts to profl. jours. Lt. comdr. M.C., USN, 1975-82. Recipient Harry E. Bacon Found. award for best original paper, 1987; NIH Summer Rsch. fellow, 1972. Fellow ACS, Am. Soc. Colon and Rectal Surgeons; mem. New Orleans Surg. Soc., Surg. Assn. of La., Internat. Soc. Univ. Colon and Rectal Surgeons, Soc. of Am. Gastrointestinal Endoscopic Surgeons, Alpha Omega Alpha. Office: Ochsner Clinic Dept Colon/Rectal Surgery 1514 Jefferson Hwy New Orleans LA 70121-2483 Office Phone: 504-842-4060. Personal E-mail: atimmcke@aol.com.

TIMMERHAUS, KLAUS DIETER, chemical engineering professor; b. Mpls., Sept. 10, 1924; s. Paul P. and Elsa L. (Bever) T.; m. Jean L. Mevis, Aug. 3, 1952; 1 dau., Carol Jane. BS in Chem. Engring, U. Ill., 1948, MS, 1949, PhD, 1951. Registered profl. engr., Colo. Process design engr. Calif. Rsch. Corp., Richmond, 1952-53; extension lectr. U. Calif., Berkeley, 1952; mem. faculty U. Colo., Boulder, 1953-95, prof. chem. engring., 1963—86, assoc. dean engring., 1963—86, dir. engring. rsch. ctr. coll. engring., 1983—86, chmn. aerospace dept., 1983—86, chmn. chem. engring. dept., 1986-89, Patten Chair Disting. prof., 1986-89, presdl. tchg. scholar, 1989—95; ret., 1995. Chem. engr. cryogenics lab. Nat. Bur. Standards, Boulder, summers 1955,57,59,61; lectr. U. Calif. at L.A., 1961-62; sect. head engring. div. NSF, 1972-73; cons. in field. Bd. dirs. Colo. Engring. Expt. Sta., Inc., Engring. Measurements Co. Editor: Advances in Cryogenic Engineering, vols. 1-25, 1954-80; co-editor: Internat. Cryogenic Monograph Series, 1965-. Served with USNR, 1944-46. Recipient Disting. Svc. award Dept. Commerce, 1957, Samuel C. Collins award for outstanding contbns. to cyrogenic tech., 1967, Meritorious Svc. award Cryogenic Engring. Conf., 1987, Disting. Pub. Svc. award NSF, 1984, Exemplary Contbr. award Cryogenic Engring. Conf., 2005; named CASE Colo. Prof. of Yr., 1993, Disting. Lectr., L-T Fan, 2001. Fellow AAAS (v.p. 1985, pres. 1986, Southwestern and Rocky Mountain divsn. Pres.'s award 1989), AIChE (v.p. 1975, pres. 1976, Alpha Chi Sigma award for chem. engring. rsch., 1968, Founders award 1978, Eminent Chem. Engring. award 1983, 2008, W.K. Lewis award 1987, F.J. Van Antwerpen award 1991, Inst. Lecture award 1995), Am. Soc. for Engring. Edn. (bd. dirs. 1986-88, George Westinghouse award 1968, 3M Chem. Engring. divsn. award 1980, Engring. Rsch. Coun. award 1990, Delos Svc. award 1991, Lifetime Achievement award 2008), Cryogenic Soc. Am.; mem. Internat. Inst. Refrigeration (v.p. 1979-87, pres. 1987-95, US nat. commn. 1983-2006, W.T. Pentzer award 1989, hon. co-chair, IIR World Congress, 2003); mem. NAE, Am. Astron. Soc., Austrian Acad. Sci., Cryogenic Engring. Conf. (chmn. 1956-67, bd. dirs. 1967-), Internat. Cryocooler Conf. (bd. dirs. 1980-2006, Outstanding Svc. award, 2006), Soc. Automotive Engrs. (Ralph Teetor award 1991), Sigma Xi (v.p. 1986-87, pres. 1987-88, bd. dirs. 1981-89), Verein Deutscher Ingenieure, Sigma Tau, Tau Beta Pi, Phi Lambda Upsilon. Home: 905 Brooklawn Dr Boulder CO 80303-2708 Business E-Mail: klaus.timmerhaus@colorado.edu.

TIMMERMAN, WILLIAM B., utilities executive, accountant; b. Columbia, SC, Nov. 12, 1946; s. William Bledsoe and Helen (Speissegger) T.; m. Janet Russell, Sept. 15, 1971; children: William III, Catherine Lucille. BA in Pub. Acctg., Duke U., 1968; postgrad., Harvard U., 1990. CPA, N.C. Auditor Arthur Andersen & Co., Charlotte, NC, 1968-78; sr. v.p. Carolina Energies, Inc., Columbia, 1978-82; v.p. S.C. Electric & Gas Co., Columbia, 1982-83, v.p., group exec., 1983-84; chief fin. officer, sr. v.p. SCANA Corp., Columbia, 1984—94, exec. v.p., CFO, contr., 1994—95, pres., 1995—97, COO, 1996—97, chmn., pres., CEO, 1997—. Exec. adv. com. Edison Electric Inst.; acctg. and fin. exec. com. Southeastern Electric Exchange; bd. dir. SCANA Corp., Liberty Corp., Preholding Inc., Palmetto Bus. Forum; past dir. Powertel Inc., SouthernNet/Telecom USA, Wachovia Bank SC, Palmetto Seed Corp.; chmn. bd. Standard Fed. Savs. Bank, Columbia; past chmn. SC Rsch. Authority. Trustee United Way of Midlands, Columbia, 1985—; vice chmn. fin. ARC, Columbia, 1986—; adv. bd. Sch. Bus. U. SC, 1985—, Duke Neighbordhood Partnership; bd. dir. Duke U., the Fuqua Sch.; past dir. Benedict Coll., SC State Ports Authority. Served with USN, 1968-72. Office: SCANA Corp 1426 Main St Ste 100 Columbia SC 29201-2834

TIMMERMANN, ALLAN GILLING, management and economics professor; b. Skovlund, Denmark, Oct. 9, 1964; came to U.S., 1994; son of Viggo Nielsen and Gyda (Gilling) T.; m. Solange Maria Ferreli Fortes, Feb. 1, 1992; children: Henry, Rafaella. MS, London Sch. Econs., 1988; degree in Econs., U. Copenhagen, Denmark, 1991; PhD, U. Cambridge, England, 1992. Lectr. fin. econs. U. London, 1991-94; asst. prof. U. Calif., San Diego, 1994-98, assoc. prof., 1999—2001, prof., 2001—, Atkinson/Epstein Chair mgmt. leadership, 2007—. Cons. Barclay's Global Investors, 1998, IMF, Fed. Res. Bd., European Ctrl. Bank; prof. fin. London Sch. Econs., 1998-99. Dept. editor Jour. of Forecasting, 2000-05; assoc. editor Jour. Bus. and Econ. Stats., 2001—, Jour. Fin. Econometrics, 2003—; contbr. articles to profl. jours. Hellman Faculty fellow, U. Calif., San Diego, 1997; British Coun. scholar, London, 1987; recipient Tress prize U. London, 1993. Mem. Am. Fin. Assn., Ctr. Econ. Policy Rsch. (rsch. fellow), Econometric Soc. Avocations: long distance running, tennis. Office Phone: 858-534-4860, 858-534-0894. Business E-Mail: atimmerm@ucsd.edu.

TIMMINS, GEORGE EMERSON, physics professor; b. Boynton Beach, Fla., Sept. 25, 1969; s. George Murry and Maria Theresa Timmins; life ptnr. Letizia Lisa Torres; children: Reagan Mckayla, Brianna Kalani. MS in Physics, Fla. Atlantic U., Boca Raton, 2002. Physics instr. U. Hawaii - MCC, Kahului, 2005—. Carpenter and design (creation of hi-end homes) Re-Built Ida Lapino's home (In Better Homes and Gardens). Achievements include design of Only Capacitive-based dilatometer to measure sub-milimeter sized sampes; discovery of System that reverses Lenz's Law to reverse the symptoms of: Cancer, Arthritis, Fibromyalgia, Reigns disease; In Process of Developing ocean Turbines to provide unlimited renewable power for the Hawaiian Islands. Personal E-mail: vcrossbsin90@gmail.com.

TIMMINS, ROBERT, biologist; b. West Midlands, Eng., Dec. 30, 1969; m. Nancy Ruggeri; 1 child, Benjamin. MA in Natural Sci., Cambridge U., Eng., 1991. Conservation biologist, Madison, 1996—. Home: 2313 Willard Ave Madison WI 53704

TIMMONS, EVELYN DEERING, pharmacist; b. Durango, Colo., Sept. 29, 1926; d. Claude Elliot and Evelyn Allen (Gooch) Deering; m. Richard Palmer Timmons, Oct. 4, 1952 (div. 1968); children: Roderick Deering, Steven Palmer. BS in Chemistry and Pharmacy cum laude, U. Colo., 1948. Chief pharmacist Meml. Hosp., Phoenix, 1950—54; libr. med. lit. rsch. Hoffman-LaRoche, Inc., Nutley, NJ, 1956—57; staff pharmacist St. Joseph's Hosp., Phoenix, 1958—60; relief mgr. various ind. apothecaries, Phoenix, 1960—68; asst. then mgr., dir. compounding Profl. Pharmacies, Inc., Phoenix, 1968—72; mgr. Mt. View Pharmacy, 1972—76, owner/mgr., 1976—; pres. Ariz. Apothecaries, Ltd., 1976—. Mem. profl. adv. bd., bereavement counselor Hospice of Valley, 1983-96; mem. profl. adv. bd. Upjohn Health Care and Svcs., Phoenix, 1984-86; bd. dirs. Am. coun. on Pharm. Edn., Chgo., 1986-92, v.p., 1988, 89, treas., 1990-91; mem. expert adv. bd. compounding pharms. U.S. Pharmacoepial Conv., 1992—; preceptor U. Ariz., 1965—, Midwestern Coll. Pharmacy, Ariz. Campus, 1998—; chief cons. bioidentical hormone replacement therapy and safety; disease mgmt. specialist; lectr. on NHRT and BHRT. Mem. editl. adv. bd. Internat. Jour. Pharm. Compounding, 1997-2000; author poetry; contbr. articles to profl. jours. Mem. Scottsdale (Ariz.) Fedn. Rep. Women, 1963-68; various other offices Rep. Fedn.; mem. platform com. State of Ariz., Nat. Rep. Conv., 1964; asst. sec. Young Rep. Nat. Fedn., 1963-65; active county and state Rep. coms.; adv. bd. Internat. Jour. of Pharm. Compounding, 1996-2001; fin. chmn. Internat. Leadership Symposium: Women in Pharmacy, London, 1987; treas. Leadership Internat. Women Pharmacy, 1991-2001; mem. founders circle Gladys Taylor McGarey Med. Found., 1996—. Named Outstanding Young Rep. of Yr., Nat. Fedn. Young Reps., 1965, Preceptor of Yr., U. Ariz./Syntex, 1984; recipient Disting. Pub. Svc. award Maricopa County Med. Soc., 1962, Disting. Alumni award Wasatch Acad., 1982, Career Achievement award Kappa Epsilon, 1983, Leadership and Achievement award Upjohn Labs., 1985-86, Outstanding Achievement in Profession award Merck, Sharp & Dohme, 1986, award of Merit Kappa Epsilon, 1988, Disting. Coloradoan award U. Colo., 1989, Vanguard award Kappa Epsilon, 1991, Unicorn award Kappa Epsilon, 1993, Compounding Pharmacist of the Yr. award Profl. Compounding Corp. of Am., 1994, 96, Healing Heart award Gladys Taylor McGarey Found., 1998, 50 Yr. Certificate U. Colo., 2000. Fellow Am. Coll. of Apothecaries (v.p. 1982-83, pres. elect 1983-84, pres. 1984-85, chmn. bd. dirs. 1985-86, adv. coun. 1986-92, Chmn. of Yr. 1980-81, Victor H. Morganroth award 1985, J. Leon Lascoff award 1990), Internat. Acad. of Compounding Pharmacists (bd. dirs. 1993-2000, hon. life fellow 2005); mem. Ariz. Soc. of Hosp. Pharmacists, Am. Pharm. Assn. (Daniel B. Smith award 1990), Ariz. Pharmacy Assn. (Svc. to Pharmacy award 1976, Pharmacist of Yr. 1981, Bowl of Hygeia 1989, 1st Innovative Pharmacy award 1994, 50 Yr. Practice and Membership award 2001), Maricopa County Pharmacy Assn. (pres. 1977, Svc. to Pharmacy award 1977), Am. Soc. of Hosp. Pharmacists, Am. Aircraft Owners and Pilots Assn., Air Safety Found., Nat. Assn. of Registered Parliamentarians, Civinettes (pres. Scottsdale chpt. 1960-61), Kappa Epsilon (recipient Career Achievement award 1986, Vanguard award 1991, Unicorn award 1993). Avocations: flying, skiing, swimming, hiking, writing. Office: Mt View Pharmacy 10565 N Tatum Blvd Ste B-118 Scottsdale AZ 85253-1095 Office Phone: 480-948-7065. Personal E-mail: evelyntimmons@cox.net.

TIMMONS, RICHARD BRENDAN, chemist, educator; b. Sherbrooke, Que., Can., June 23, 1938; s. John Patrick and Muriel (O'Connor) T.; m. Philomena C. Liscio, Aug. 31, 1963; children: Kevin, Gregory, Brenda. B.Sc., St. Francis Xavier U., Antigonish, NS, Can., 1958; PhD, Catholic U. Am., 1962. Postdoctoral fellow Brookhaven Nat. Lab., Upton, N.Y., 1962-64; asst. prof. Boston Coll., 1964-65; asst. prof. chemistry Cath. U. Am., 1965-74; prof. chemistry U. Tex., Arlington, 1977—, chmn. dept., 1977—90, prof. chemistry, 1977—2006, disting. prof., 2007—. NIH spl. sr. fellow, 1972-73 Mem. Am. Chem. Soc., AAAS. Home: 3200 Woodford Dr Arlington TX 76013-1137

TIMMONS, ROBBIE, news anchor; m. Jim Brandstatter. Grad., Ohio State U. Anchor WILX-TV, Lansing, Mich., 1972—76, WJBK-TV, Detroit, 1976—82, WXYZ-TV, Detroit, 1982—. Recipient numerous Emmy awards, Silver Cir. award, Nat. Acad. TV Arts and Scis., 1998, Most Powerful Woman in Mich., 2002. Achievements include being the first woman in the US to anchor TV news at 6 & 11pm. Office: WXYZ-TV 20777 W Ten Mile Rd Southfield MI 48037 Office Phone: 248-827-9413. Business E-Mail: rtimmons@wxyz.com.

TIMMONS, SHARON L., retired elementary school educator; b. South Kansas City, Mo., July 25, 1949; d. Clyde George and Sarah Ethyl (Thrift) Manley; m. Joseph D. Timmons, June 6, 1970; children: Stacia, Matt. BSE, U. Kans., 1972; MA, U. Mo., Kansas City, 1980. Cert. elem., jr. high tchr., Mo; elem. tchr., Kans. Team tchr. elem. Loretto Acad., Kansas City, Mo., 1976—80; team tchr. lead mid. sch. and block schedule programs, 8th grade, Ctr. Sch. Dist. 58, Kansas City, Mo., 1980—94; ret., 1994. Author: (Title II grants) For Indivdualized Math Program, Kansas City Rep. for Scientific Literacy. Mem. NSF, Sigma Kappa

TIMMONS, WILLIAM EVAN, retired consulting firm executive; b. Chattanooga, Dec. 27, 1930; s. Owen Walter and Doris (Eckenrod) T.; m. Mimi Bakshian, Sept. 28, 1966; children: Karen Leigh, Kimberly Anne, William Evan. Grad., Baylor Mil. Acad., Chattanooga, 1949; BS in Fgn. Svc., Georgetown U., 1959; postgrad., George Washington U., 1959-61. Aide to U.S. Senator Alexander Wiley, 1955-62; adminstrv. asst. to U.S. Rep. William Brock, 1963-69; dep. asst. to Pres. Richard M. Nixon, 1969-70, asst., 1970-74; asst. to Pres. Gerald R. Ford, 1974; pres. Timmons & Co. Inc., 1975-86, chmn. exec. com., 1986—2002, 09chmn. emeritus, 2002—09. Mem. Fed. Property Rev. Bd., 1972-75, Pres.'s Trade Adv. Com., 1975-80; U.S. del. to Internat. Conf. on Viet Nam, Paris, 1973. Presdl. appointee U.S.-Japan Adv. Commn., 1983—85; nat. conv. dir. Reagan for Pres. Com., Detroit, 1980, Dallas, 1984, nat. polit. dir., 1980; exec. dir. Tenn. Rep. Com., 1962; mgr. Brock campaigns, 1962, 1964, 1966, 1968; dir. congl. rels. Nixon-Agnew campaign, 1968; coord. Nixon for Pres.; active Rep. Nat. Conv., Miami, Fla., 1968, 1972, dir. Pres. Ford com. Kansas City, 1976; mem. adv. com. Rep. Nat. Com. Conv., New Orleans, 1988, San Diego, 1996; mem. exec. com. Nat. Young Reps., 1965—67; dep. dir. for transition Office of Pres.-Elect, 1980—81; mem. faculty Nat. REp. campaign workshops, 1963—69; sr. adviser Bush for Pres. Com., New Orleans, 1988, Dole for Pres. Com., 1996; mem. adv. com. Bush for Pres., Rep. Nat. Conv., Phila., 2000; adviser Bush-Cheney Transition, 2000—01; bd. dirs. Radio Free Europe/Liberty, 1975—82, Georgetown U. Ctr. Strategic and Internat. Studies, 1982—85. With USAF, 1951—55. Named Outstanding Young Rep. of Year Nat. Rep. Com., 1965; recipient 1970 Ann. Achievement award Georgetown Alumni Club; citation for Disting. Service Baylor Mil. Acad. Alumni Assn., 1970 Mem. Soc. of the Cin., Columbia Country Club, George Towne Club, St. Alban's Tennis Club, Masons (33d degree). Home: 4426 Garfield St NW Washington DC 20007-1142 Personal E-mail: BTimmons@aol.com.

TIMMONS-GOODSON, PATRICIA, state supreme court justice; b. Florence, SC, Sept. 18, 1954; d. Edward and Beulah Timmons; m. Ernest J. Goodson; 2 children. BA, U. NC, Chapel Hill, 1976, JD, 1979. Dist. mgr. US Census, 1979—80; asst. dist. atty. Twelfth Prosecutorial Dist., NC, 1981—83; staff atty. Lumbee River Legal Services, Inc., Fayetteville, 1983—84; dist. ct. judge Twelfth Jud. Dist., NC, 1984—97; judge NC Ct. of Appeals, 1997—2005; assoc. justice Supreme Ct. NC, Raleigh, 2006—. Former co-host and co-prodr. TV program Dimensions of Justice. Mem. ctrl. selection com. Morehead Scholarship; bd. dirs. alumni assn. U. NC. Mem.: ABA (mem. appellate judges conference exec. com.), NC Assn. Black Lawyers, NC Bar Assn. Office: NC Supreme Ct PO Box 2448 Raleigh NC 27602 Office Phone: 919-733-3723.*

TIMMONS-MITCHELL, JANE CHRISTINA, clinical psychologist, researcher, consultant, educator, entrepreneur; b. Indpls., Feb. 11, 1955; d. Gerald Dean and Janet Wilson Timmons; m. Robert Allan Mitchell, May 23, 1981; children: Clare Christina Mitchell, Stephen James Mitchell. PhD, Case Western Res. U., Cleve., 1982. Cert. in psychologist Ohio State Bd. Psychology, 1984. Psychologist, med. staff U. Hosps., Cleve., 1990—2001; assoc. prof. Case Sch. Medicine, Cleve., 2000—01, assoc. clin. prof. psychology dept. psychiatry, 2001—; assoc. dir. evaluation and rsch. Ctr. Innovative Practices, Inst. Study & Prevention Violence, Kent State U., 2006—; adj. prof. Mandel Sch. Pres., CEO Junction Psychol. Svcs. Corp., Cleveland Heights, Ohio, 2001—. Musician: Cleve. Orch. Chorus; singer (Regional Emmy, 2001). Spearhead Build it Now (campaign for the Recreation Ctr.), Cleveland Heights, 1997—99; head coach, speech and debate Cleve. Heights HS, 1999—2004; mem., choir Trinity Cathedral, Cleve., 2008—. Recipient Hon. Mention, SAMHSA, 2005; named Rschr. the Yr., MST, 2006; grantee, Cleveland Heights U., Heights Sch. Dist., 2003—06. Mem.: APA. Liberal. Avocations: music, gardening, baking. Home: 2995 E Overlook Rd Cleveland Heights OH 44118 Office: Kent State Univ Inst Study & Prevention Violence Kent OH 44242 Home Fax: 216-397-1107. Personal E-mail: jtm07@aol.com.

TIMONEY, PETER JOSEPH, veterinarian, educator, virologist, consultant; b. Dublin, June 5, 1941; came to U.S., 1983; s. John Francis and Evelyn Norah (Whittle) T.; m. Katherine Mary Murphy, Sept. 11, 1971; children: Peter, Caroline, Sarah, David. MVB, Nat. U., Dublin, 1964;

MS, U. Ill., 1966; PhD, U. Dublin, 1974. Rsch. assoc. U. Ill., Urbana, 1964-66; rsch. officer Vet. Rsch. Lab., Abbotstown, Ireland, 1966-72; sr. rsch. officer equine diseases sect. Veterinary Rsch. Lab., Abbotstown, Ireland, 1972-79; assoc. prof. diagnostic lab., dept. microbiology Cornell U., Ithaca, NY, 1979-81; sci. dir. Irish Equine Ctr., Johnstown, Ireland, 1981-83; assoc. prof. virology vet. sci. dept. U. Ky., Lexington, 1983-87, prof. virology, assoc. chair for rsch., 1987-89, Frederick Van Lennep chair, 1988—, acting chair, 1989-90, chair, 1990-99, 2002—08. Cons. Daryl Labs., Inc., Santa Clara, Calif., 1981-86, Ft. Dodge (Iowa) Animal Health Lab., 1986-92, 94—. Fellow Royal Coll. Vet. Surgeons, World Equine Vet. Assn. (pres. 1995-99); mem. Am. Assn. Equine Practitioners, Am. Soc. Microbiology, Am. Soc. Virology, U.S. Animal Health Assn. Avocations: reading, gardening. Office: Gluck Equine Rsch Ctr 108 Gluck Ctr Lexington KY 40506-0099 Office Phone: 859-257-4757 8-1094. Business E-Mail: ptimoney@uky.edu.

TIMOTHY, DAVID HARRY, retired biology professor; b. Pitts., June 9, 1928; s. David Edgar and Harriett P. (Stein) T.; m. Marian Claire Whiteley, Sept. 5, 1953; children: Marjory J., M. Elisabeth, David W. BS, Pa. State U., 1952, MS, 1955; PhD, U. Minn., 1956. Asst. geneticist Rockefeller Found., Bogota, Colombia, 1956-58, assoc. geneticist, 1958-61; assoc. prof. N.C. State U., Raleigh, 1961-66, prof., 1966-93, prof. crop sci., botany and genetics emeritus, 1993—; ret. Cons. to fgn. and U.S. govts., also U.S. and internat. sci. orgns.; mem. USDA crop adv. com. on grasses, 1983-87, mem. policy adv. com., sci. and edn. grants program, 1982-84, chief scientist USDA Sci. and Edn. Competetive Rsch. Grants Office, 1985, 86; with Nat. Plant Genetic Resources Bd., 1984-91, vice chmn., 1991; bd. dirs., treas. Genetic Resources Comms. Sys., Inc., 1985-91, pres., 1991-93; mem. bd. on agr. NAS-NRC, work group on U.S. Nat. Plant Germplasm Sys., 1987-89. Co-author monographs; contbr. chpts. to books; contbr. articles to profl. jours. With AUS, 1946-48, PTO. Grantee NSF, 1965, 78, Rockefeller Found., 1968, 69, Pioneer Hi-Bred Internat., 1982, 83. Fellow AAAS (electorate nominating com., sect. O, Agr. 1988-90), Am. Soc. Agronomy, Crop Sci. Soc. Am. (editl. bd. 1982-84, assoc. editor Crop Sci. 1982-84, Frank N. Meyer medal for plant genetic resources 1994). Home: 101 Wee Loch Dr Cary NC 27511

TIMPA, VICKI ANN, government health program administrator; b. Houston, Aug. 20, 1955; d. Edmund Burke and Helen Kanosky Huber; m. John Gerrard Fewel, May 27, 2000; children: Julie Marie Fecht, Anthony Alan. BSN, U. Tex., 1977; MSN in Edn. Adminstrn. and Rsch., Tex. Woman's U., 1990, advanced nurse practitioner, 1993. Cert. ACLS, domestic preparedness for biol.-radiol.-chem. VA, neurosurg. cert., cert. prevention inst. instr.; critical care nurse; cert. Covey trainer, antiques and collectibles appraiser. Team leader cardiopulmonary shock trauma emergency ctr., nurse Ben Taub Emergency Ctr., Harris County Hosp. Dist., Houston, 1977; peritoneal dialysis nurse Parkland Meml. Hosp., Dallas County Hosp. Dist.; emergency rm. and GI lab staff nurse Mesquite Hosp., Tex., 1978—80; nurse Baylor U. Med. Ctr. Hosp. Sys., Dallas, 1980—90; rsch. nurse coord. VA, Dallas, 1990—93; dept. of edn. mgr. Meth. Hosps. of Dallas, 1993; patient health and continuing med. edn. coord., chief ethics cons. VA North Tex. Health Care Sys., Dallas, 1993—. Coord. nat. rsch. studies VA, Dallas, 1990—92, nat. liaison for Nat. Ctr. for Health Promotion and Disease Prevention, Durham, NC, 2002—05, congl. legis. cons., Washington, 2000—; ICU mock code creator and trainer Baylor U. Hosp. Sys., Dallas, 1980—90; cardiopulmonary resuscitation instr. Am. Heart Assn., Dallas, 1989—94, 2009, continuing med. educator, 2007—, coord., 2009; Plain Lang. Act cons. Exec. Br., Washington, 1995—. Contbr. articles to profl. pubs. Sr. v.p. Miracle Wish Found., 2006—. Recipient Unsung Hero award, VA, 1993, Plank award, Nat. Ctr. Health Promotion, 2002—05, Customer Svc. award, VA North Tex. Healthcare Sys., 2007, 2009; named Most Valuable Person, VA Rsch., 1992; named one of Great 100 Nurses award, 1997; Pub. Health grant, VA North Tex. Healthcare Sys., 2007. Mem.: Sigma Theta Tau (fin. and fund raising com. 1993—2001, vice chairperson of bd. dir., Miracle Wish Found. 2006—, Academic Excellence and Rsch. Excellence awards 1993, 2001, Public Health Grant award 2007—). Roman Catholic. Avocations: travel, antiques and collectibles appraising. Home: 1307 High Ridge Dr Duncanville TX 75137 Home Phone: 972-572-5525. Home Fax: 972-572-5525. Personal E-mail: vickiern7@netzero.net.

TIMPERLAKE, EDWARD THOMAS, writer; b. Perth Amboy, NJ, Nov. 22, 1946; s. James Elwood Timperlake Jr. and Joan Dorothy (Conkling) Maurer; m. Barbette Runckel, Aug. 10, 1969 (div. 1993); children: Tara, Kimberly; m. Cathryn Porcelli Gekas, Apr. 8, 2000. BS, U.S. Naval Acad., 1969; MBA, Cornell U., 1977. Commd. 2d lt. USMC, 1969, advanced through grades to lt. col., ret., 1993; asst. venture mgr. Exxon Enterprise, NYC, 1977-78; sect. mgr. T.A.S.C., Arlington, Va., 1978-81; dep. dir. Nat. Dir. Vietnam Vets. Leadership Program, Action Agy., Washington, 1981-83; dir. mobilization plans and requirements Office of Sec. Def., Washington, 1984; campaign staff George Bush for Pres., 1988; asst. sec. Dept. Vets. Affairs, Washington, 1989-93; pres. T-9 Group, 1993-95; profl. staff rules com. U.S. House of Reps., Washington, 1996—99; dir. tech. assessment internat. tech. security Office of the Sec. of Def., The Pentagon, Washington, 2003—09. Author: Year of the Rat, 1998, Red Dragon Rising, 1999, Showdown, 2006; contbr. articles to profl. jours. Mem.: Naval Acad. Alumni Assn., Cornell Club (DC), N.Y. Yacht Club, Army-Navy Club. Home: 1027 22d St Arlington VA 22202

TIN, JAN, economist; b. Phongsaly, Laos, May 15, 1957; s. Tze-bun Tin and Mei-Fong Lo; m. Ming-Lee Twan, Dec. 26, 1986; children: Brian, Christine. BA, Pacific Luth. U., Tacoma, 1981; MA, U. Wis.-Milwaukee, PhD, 1991. Instr. U. Wis., 1987—91; economist, statistician US Dept. Commerce, Washington, 1991—. Buddhist. Home: 6066 Oust Ln Woodbridge VA 22193 Home Phone: 703-878-2764; Office Phone: 301-763-3245.

TINCHER, CHRIS MICHAEL, history professor; b. Bakersfield, Calif., Dec. 31, 1963; s. Sandra L. Tincher; m. Hazel L. Dixon, June 11, 2001; children: Lauryn Marie, Laney Rose. MA in History, Portland State U., Oreg., 1996; MA in Kinesiology, Fresno Pacific U., Calif., 2008. History instr. Coll. Siskiyous, Weed, Calif., 2001—03, West Hills CC, Coalinga, Calif., 2003—. Mem.: Calif. Hist. Soc. Roman Catholic. Home: 360 Buena Vista Dr Coalinga CA 93210 Office: West Hills Community College 300 Cherry Lane Coalinga CA 93210 Office Fax: 559-934-2464; Home Fax: 559-934-0611. Business E-Mail: caltincher@whccd.edu.

TINCHER, LAURA MARIE, literature and language educator, photographer; d. Donald Lee and Lauralee Marian Doerner; m. Bill D. Tincher. BA in English and Journalism, Ind. U., Bloomington, 1978; EdM, MS, Purdue U., Indpls., 1983. Faculty mem. Brownsburg HS, Tenn., 1978—; adj. faculty mem. Vincennes U., Ind., 2002—. Book talk coord. Brownsburg HS, 2001—. Editor: (greeting cards) Moments in Time Photo Greetings, 2002—. Fundraiser Nat. Multiplesclerosis Soc., Indpls.; co-chair Bethel U. M.C. Edn. Comm., Indpls., 2002—04; bd. mem. Brownsburg Edn. Found. Bridging the Classics Grant, Brownsburg Edn. Found., 2001, 2002, 2003. Mem.: NEA, Brownsburg Classroom Tchrs. Assn., Nat. Coun. Tchrs. English, Honor Soc. Methodist. Avocations: reading, needlecrafts, photography.

TINDALL, DONALD JAMES, biological chemistry educator; b. Columbia, SC, May 16, 1944; s. James Samuel and Marjorie Edna (Lesley) T.; m. Judith Minick, Feb. 17, 1967; children: Donald J. Jr., John, Darcy. BS, U. S.C., 1966; MS, Clemson U., 1970; PhD, U. N.C., 1973. Clin. chemist Nat. Naval Med. Ctr., Bethesda, Md., 1966-68; rsch. asst. Clemson (S.C.) U., 1968-70, U. N.C., Chapel Hill, 1970-73; NIH fellow Baylor Coll. Medicine, Houston, 1974-76, instr., 1976-77, asst. prof., 1977-83, assoc. prof., 1983-88; prof. biol. chemistry Mayo Clinic and Found., Rochester, Minn., 1989—. Mem. NIH Biochem. Endocrinology Study sect. Editor Jour. Andrology; mem. editl. bd. Cancer Rsch., Endocrinology, Steroids; contbr. articles to Jour. Biol. Chemistry, Molecular and Cellular Endocrinology, Jour. Clin. Endocrinology and Metabolism, Endocrinology. Asst. scoutmaster Boy Scouts Am., Houston, 1985-88; pres. Jr. H.S. PTO, Houston, 1985, Elem. Sch. PTO, Houston, 1987. Grantee Nat. Inst. Child Health and Human Devel., 1981, NIH, 1985, Nat. Inst. Digestive Disease and Kidney, 1994. Mem. Soc. for Basic Urologic Rsch. (pres. 1993), Am. Soc. Biologic Chemists, Endocrine Soc., Am. Soc. Andrology (editl. bd.), Am. Assn. Cancer Rsch. Achievements include patents in prostate cancer marker, steroids as contraceptives and urogenital sinus derived growth inhibitory factor. Office: Mayo Clinic 200 1st St SW Rochester MN 55905-0002

TINDALL, ROBERT EMMETT, lawyer, educator; b. NYC, Jan. 2, 1934; s. Robert E. and Alice (McGonigle) T.; children: Robert Emmett IV, Elizabeth. BS in Marine Engring., SUNY, 1955; postgrad., Georgetown U. Law Sch., 1960—61; LLB, U. Ariz., 1963; LLM, NYU, 1967; PhD, City U., London, 1975. Bar: Ariz. 1963. Mgmt. trainee GE, Schenectady, NY, Lynn, Mass., Glens Falls, NY, 1955-56, 58-60; law clk. Haight, Gardner, Poor and Havens, NYC, 1961; prin., mem. Robert Emmett Tindall & Assocs., Tucson, 1963—; prof. mgmt. U. Ariz., Tucson, 1969—2003; prof. emeritus, 2003. Vis. prof. Grad. Sch. of Law, Soochow U., China, 1972, Grad. Bus. Ctr., London, 1974, NYU, 1991-96, UCSD, 2005-07; dir. MBA program U. Ariz., Tucson, 1975-81, dir. entrepreneurship program, 1984-86; investment cons. Saudi Arabia, 1981—; lectr. USIA, Eng., India, Mid. East, 1974; lectr. bus. orgn. and regulatory laws Southwestern Legal Found., Acad. Am. and Internat. Law, 1976-80. Actor cmty. theatres, Schenectady, 1955-56, Harrisburg, Pa., 1957-58, Tucson, 1961-71; appeared in films Rage, 1971, Showdown at OK Corral, 1971, Lost Horizon, 1972; appeared in TV programs Gunsmoke, 1972, Petrocelli, 1974; author: Multinational Enterprises, 1975; contbr. articles on domestic and internat. bus. to profl. jours. Served to lt. USN, 1956-58. Fellow Ford Found., 1965-67; grantee Asia Found., 1972-73. Mem. Strategic Mgmt. Soc., State Bar Ariz., Acad. Internat. Bus., SAG, Honourable Soc. of Mid. Temple (London), Phi Delta Phi, Beta Gamma Sigma, Assn. Corp. Growth, Royal Overseas League (London). Home: PO Box 42196 Tucson AZ 85733-2196

TINDER, JOHN DANIEL, federal judge; b. Indpls., Feb. 17, 1950; s. John Glendon and Eileen M. (Foley) T.; m. Jan M. Carroll, Mar. 17, 1984 BS, Ind. U., 1972, JD, 1975. Bar: Ind. 1975, U.S. Dist. Ct. (so. dist.) Ind., U.S. Ct. Appeals (7th cir.), U.S. Supreme Ct. Assoc. Tinder & O'Donnell, 1975; asst. US atty. (so. dist.) Ind. US Dept. Justice, Indpls., 1975-77; ptnr. Tinder & Tinder, Indpls., 1977—82; pub. defender Marion County Criminal Ct., Indpls., 1977-78; chief trial dep. Marion County Pros. Office, Indpls., 1979-82; assoc. Harrison & Moberly, Indpls., 1982-84; US atty. (so. dist.) Ind. US Dept. Justice, Indpls., 1984-87; judge US Dist. Ct. (so. dist.) Ind., 1987—2007, US Ct. Appeals (7th Cir.), 2007—. Adj. prof. Ind. U. Sch. of Law, Indpls., 1980—88; mem. Supreme Ct. Character & Fitness Com., Ind., 1982— Co-founder Turkey Trot Invitational Race, Indpls., 1980 Recipient Cert. of Appreciation award Bur. Alcohol, Tobacco & Firearms, Indpls., 1976; Service award Marion County Prosecutor, Indpls., 1981 Mem. ABA, Ind. State Bar Assn. (dir. criminal justice sect. 1984—), Indpls. Bar Assn., 7th Circuit Ct. Bar Assn., Fed. Bar Assn. Republican. Roman Catholic. Office: US Ct Appeals 301 Fed Bldg 204 S Main St South Bend IN 46601*

TINETTI, MARY E., geriatrician, educator; b. July 31, 1951; BA, U. Mich., 1973, MD, 1978. Cert. Internal Medicine, 1981, Geriatric Medicine, 1988. Resident U. Mich., Mpls., 1978—81; Kaiser gen. medicine and geriatrics fellow U. Rochester and Monroe Hosp., Rochester, NY, 1981—84; prin. investigator Claude D. Pepper Older Americans Independence Ctr. Yale Sch. Medicine, New Haven, 1992—, chief geriatrics divsn., 1994—, dir. Yale Prog. on Aging., 1995—, Gladys Phillips Crofoot prof. medicine, epidemiology and pub. health, 2000—. Recipient Herbert deVries rsch. award, Coun. Aging and Adult Devel., 2009. Mem.: Inst. Medicine. Office: Yale Sch Medicine Geriatrics Sect Internal Medicine Dept 20 York St New Haven CT 06510 Office Phone: 203-688-5238. Office Fax: 203-688-4209. E-mail: mary.tinetti@yale.edu.*

TING, ALBERT CHIA, biomedical engineer, researcher; b. Hong Kong, Sept. 7, 1950; came to U.S., 1957; s. William Su and Katherine Sung T.; m. Shirley Roung Wang, July 30, 1988, (dec. Aug. 2003). BA, UCLA, 1973; MS, Calif. State U., LA, 1975, Calif. Inst. Tech., 1977; PhD, U. Calif., San Diego, 1983. Rsch. asst. Calif. Inst. Tech., Pasadena, 1975-77, U. Calif., San Diego, 1982-83; sr. staff engr. R&D Am. Med. Optics, Irvine, Calif., 1983-86; project engr., rsch. Allergan Med. Optics, Irvine, Calif., 1987-89, sr. project engr., rsch., 1989-92, sr. project engr., engring., 1993-94; bioengr. cons. Pharmacia Iovision, Inc., Irvine, Calif., 1995-97; sr. engr. D & E, 1997, sr. engr., project mgr., 1998-99; rsch. and devel. mgr., surg. Bausch & Lomb, Irvine, 1999—2001; R & D mgr. Visiogen, Inc., Irvine, 2001—02, sr. R & D mgr., 2002—. Contbr. articles to profl. jours. Mem. AAAS, Biomed. Engring. Soc., Assn. for Rsch. in Vision and Ophthalmology, Biomed. Optics Soc. Achievements include invention of med. and optical devices. Office: Visiogen Inc 2 Goodyear Ste B Irvine CA 92618 Office Phone: 949-900-3352. Business E-Mail: ating@visiogen.com.

TING, CHIN-SEN, physics professor; 1 child. PhD in Physics, U. Calif. San Diego, La Jolla, 1970. Postdoc. fellow, physics dept. NYU, NYC, 1970—74; rsch. assoc., physics dept. Brown U., Providence, 1974—76. Prof. physics U. Houston, 1985—. Fellow: Am. Phys. Soc. Office: Dept Physics Univ Houston 4800 Calhoun Houston TX 77204 Business E-Mail: ting@uh.edu.

TING, JAN C., political science professor, lawyer, consultant; b. Dearborn, Mich., 1948; m. Helen Page; children: Margaret, Mary. Grad., Oberlin Coll., 1970; MA in Asian Studies, U. Hawaii, 1972; JD, Harvard U., 1975. Atty. Pepper Hamilton & Scheetz, Phila., 1975—77; joined faculty Temple U. Beasley Sch. Law, Phila., 1977, dir. grad. tax program, 1994—2001, now prof. law; asst. commr. Immigration & Naturalization Svc. US Dept. Justice, Washington, 1990—93. Sr. fellow Fgn. Policy Rsch. Inst., Ctr. for Immigration Studies, Found. for Defense of Democracies; vis. prof. Widener U., Wilmington, Del.; mem. Immigration Adv. Bd. Rudy Giuliani Presdl. Com., 2007—. Contbr. articles to law jours. Former chmn. Del. State Personnel Commn. Named 2003 Asian Am. Law Prof. of Yr., Nat. Asian Pacific Am. Law Students Assn. Republican. Office: Temple U Beasley Sch Law 1719 N Broad St Philadelphia PA 19122 E-mail: janting@hotmail.com.

TING, JOHN M., dean, engineering educator; BEng, McGill U., Montreal, 1975; MS, Calif. Inst. of Tech., Pasadena, 1976; ScD, MIT, Cambridge, Mass., 1981. Registered profl. engr., Calif. Mem. faculty Calif. Inst. Tech., 1981—83, U. Toronto, 1983—90, U. Mass., Lowell, 1990—; dean engring., 2003—. Commr. Lowell Arena and Stadium Commn., 1995—2007. Recipient Pres. Public Svc. award, U. Mass., 2006. Fellow: Am. Soc. Civil Engrs. Office: U Mass Lowell One University Ave Lowell MA 01854 Home: Groton MA 01450

TING, SAMUEL CHAO CHUNG, physicist, researcher; b. Ann Arbor, Mich., Jan. 27, 1936; s. Kuan H. and Jeanne (Wong) Ting; m. Kay Louise Kuhne, 1960 (div.); children: Jeanne Min, Amy Min; m. Susan Carol Marks, Apr. 28, 1985; 1 child, Christopher. BS in Engring., U. Mich., 1959, MS, 1960, PhD in Physics, 1962, ScD (hon.), 1978, Chinese U. Hong Kong, 1987, U. Bologna, Italy, 1988, Columbia U., 1990, U. Sci. and Tech., China, 1990, Moscow State U., 1991, U. Bucharest, Romania, 1993, Nat. Tsinghua U., Taiwan, 2002, Nat. Jiaotong U., 2003, Hong Kong Bapt. U., 2003, Rheinische Westfalsich Technische Hochschule, Aachen, Germany, 2004, Nat. Ctrl. U., 2005, Hong Kong U. Sci. and Tech., 2005. Ford Found. fellow CERN (European Orgn. Nuc. Rsch.), Geneva, 1963; instr. physics Columbia U., 1964, asst. prof., 1965—67; group leader Deutsches Elektronen-Synchrotron, Hamburg, Germany, 1966; assoc. prof. physics MIT, Cambridge, 1967—68, prof., 1969—, Thomas Dudley Cabot Inst. prof., 1977—. Program cons. divsn. particles and fields Am. Phys. Soc., 1970; hon. prof. Beijing Normal Coll., 1987, Jiatong U., Shanghai, 1987, U. Bologna, Italy, 1988. Assoc. editor Nuc. Physics B, 1970, editl. bd. Nuc. Instruments and Methods, Mathematical Modeling; contbr. articles to profl. jours. Recipient Nobel prize in Physics, 1976, De Gasperi prize in Sci., Italian Republic, 1988, Ernest Orlando Lawrence award, U.S. Govt., 1976, Gold medal in Sci., City of Brescia, Italy, 1988, Golden Leopard award, Town of Taormina, 1988, Forum Engelberg prize, 1996, Pub. Svc. medal, NASA, 2001; fellow Am. Acad. Arts and Scis., 1975; hon. fellow, Tata Inst. Fundamental Rsch., Mumbai, India. Fellow: Inst. Fundamental Rsch. Mumbai India (hon.); mem.: NAS, Spanish Acad. Sci. (fgn. mem.), Royal Spanish Acad. Sci. (fgn. mem.), Chinese Acad. Sci. (fgn. mem.), Hungarian Acad. Sci., Deutsche Acad. Naturforscher Leopoldina (fgn. mem.), Russian Acad. Sci., Acad. Sinica, Pakistani Acad. Sci. Achievements include the co-discovery of a subatomic particle--a flavor-neutral meson consisting of a charm quark and a charm anti-quark. Office: MIT Dept Nuclear Sci 51 Vassar St # 44-020 Cambridge MA 02139 E-mail: ting@lns.mit.edu.*

TINGLER, MARLENE JOHANNSEN, music educator, insurance agent; b. St. Louis, Aug. 22, 1948; d. Otto August and Charlotte (Sachse) Johannsen; m. Charles E. Tingler, June 19, 1971; 1 child, Matthew Johannsen. BS in Edn., William Jewell Coll., 1970; studied with Max Rabinovitsj, 1970—73; postgrad., Ctrl. Mo. State U., U. Mo., Kansas City. Cert. ins. Mo.; tchr. Mo. Pvt. violin tchr., St. Louis, Kansas City, 1971—; orch. dir., head dept. Berkeley (Mo.) Sch. Dist., 1971—73, Luth. Sch. Sys., Kansas City, 1989—2002; orch. dir. Parkway Schs., St. Louis, 1974—75; office mgr. Pa. Life Ins., Kansas City, 1976—84; mgr. Liberty (Mo.) Symphony Orch., 1977—85, BTI Ins. Co., Kansas City, 1985—88; v.p. Harry Loves Bess, Kansas City, 1999—. Instr. William Jewell Coll., Liberty, 1978—79; world judge, coach State Bd. Odyssey of the Mind. Musician: Jacksonville (Ill.) Symphony, St. Joseph (Mo.) Symphony, St. Louis Philharm. Recipient Outstanding Svc. award, Liberty Symphony, Hickman Mills, Mo. Sch. Dist. Mem.: Music Educators Nat. Conf., Delta Zeta (music dir. 1968—71), Sigma Alpha Iota (sec. 1968—71). Lutheran. Avocations: computers, travel. Personal E-mail: sniffer4@earthlink.net.

TINGLEY, FLOYD WARREN, retired internist; b. Charlotte, NC, Nov. 22, 1933; s. Floyd Warren Sr. and Janie (Suggs) T.; m. Sandra Carpenter, Aug. 20, 1955 (div. Dec. 1984); children: Sheryl Tingley Hagen, David Alan; m. Johnette Hill, Apr. 5, 1985. BA in English, Emory U., 1955, MD, 1959. Diplomate Am. Bd. Internal Medicine (bd. govs. 1986-92). Intern USAF Hosp., Lackland AFB, Tex., 1959-60; resident in internal medicine Parkland Meml. Hosp., Dallas, 1963-65, fellow in cardiology, 1965-66; pvt. practice specializing in internal medicine Arlington, Tex., 1966-88; med. dir. southwestern region Met. Life Ins. Co., Irving, Tex., 1988-90; regional practice leader William M. Mercer Inc., 1990-91; v.p., sr. med. dir. Provident Life and Accident Co., Chattanooga, 1991-92; v.p., nat. med. dir. Travelers Ins. Cos., Hartford, Conn., 1992-94; sr. v.p., chief med. officer Kemper Nat. Svcs., Plantation, Fla., 1995-2000; med. dir. Mednet Connect, 2005—07, Fairpay Solutions, 2007—. Apptd. Tex. Commn. on Health Care Reimbursement Alternatives, 1987; bd. dirs. Riverside Nat. Bank, Grand Prairie, Tex. Contbr. articles to profl. jours. Pres. Arlington YMCA, 1971; chmn. budget com. Family Services, Ft. Worth, 1973; participant Health Policy Agenda for Am. People, Chgo., 1984-87; trustee Tex. Med. Liability Trust, Austin, 1987-88. Capt. USAF, 1958-63. Fellow ACP (pres. Tex. chpt. 1981); mem. AMA (chmn. sect. coun. internal medicine, 1979-88), Am. Soc. Internal Medicine (pres. 1986-87), Tex. Med. Assn. (treas. 1978-85, alt. del. to AMA 1985-91, commendation 1985), Tarrant County Med. Soc. (pres. Arlington br. 1974, del. to Tex. Med. Assn., Community Svc. award 1983). Presbyterian. Avocations: photography, sailing, gardening, computer hobbies. Home: 2709 Park Place Ct Arlington TX 76016-5891

TINGSTRUM, NANCY ASH, dietitian; d. Howard Wesley and Ruth Hamilton Ash; m. James Frederick Tingstrum, Oct. 22, 1988; 1 child, Michelle Martin Monts; m. Ralph K Martin (div.); 1 child, Noelle Lisa Vail. BS, Penn State U., 1964; MBA, George Mason U., 1988. Registered Dietitian Am. Dietitic Assn., 1972. Hosp. dietician RI Hosp., 1965—66; budget analyst Dept. of Def. Pentagon, Wash., DC, 1982—84, program analyst, 1995—2001, dept. team chief, program analyst, 2001—02; ret., 2002. Recipient Civilian Superior Svc. award, Dept. Army, Pentagon, Achievement medal for Commander's Award. Avocations: reading, exercise, gardening, quilting.

TINGUS, STEVEN JAMES, physiologist, researcher; b. Sacramento, Aug. 19, 1963; s. James George and Joanne Fotene (Kamilos) Tingus. BS in Biol. Sci., U. Calif., Davis, 1985, MS in Physiology, 1990, PhD in Physiology, 1994. Policy analyst Calif. Dept. Health Svcs., 1995—98; dir. resource devel./pub. policy Calif. Found. Ind. Living Centers, Inc., 1998—2001; dir. Nat. Inst. Disability & Rehab. Rsch., US Dept. Edn., Washington, 2001—07; dep. asst. sec. planning & evaluation for disability, aging & long term care policy, HHS, Washington, 2007—09. Recipient Gil Moss award, Nat. Spinal Cord Injury Assn., 2003, Best New Freedom Individual award, Jim Mullen Found., 2003, Commr.'s Spl. Citation award, FDA, 2005, 2007, Isabelle & Leonard Goldenson Tech. and Rehab. award, United Cerebral Palsy Rsch. & Ednl. Found., 2006; named one of 40 Under 40, Sacramento Bus. Jour., 2000. Mem.: AAAS, Am. Assn. Polit. Cons. Republican. Greek Orthodox. Personal E-mail: stingus@earthlink.net.*

TINIANOW, DAN ERIC, communications educator; s. Ralph Irving Tinianow and Eva Eichwald. BA in Communication Studies, Oberlin Coll., Ohio., 1986; MS in TV & Film, Syracuse U., 1990, PhD in Communication, 1993. Jet program Japanese Ministry Edn., Mito, Ibaraki, 1987—88; asst. prof. Austin Coll., Sherman, Tex., 1993—2001; sr. rschr. Jaffe Productions, Valencia, Calif., 2001—01; asst. prof. La Sierra U., Riverside, Calif., 2002—. Vis. assoc. prof. Donghua U., Shanghai, 2006—07; creative dir. Digimedia Design, Riverside, Calif., 2007—. Prodr.: (TV series). Recipient Philo T. Farnsworth award, Nat. Assn. Local Cable Programming, 1985, Stephen H. Coltrin award, Internat. Radio & TV Soc. Found., 2000; fellow, Syracuse U., 1988—90. Mem.: Nat. Assn. Photoshop Profls. Home: 5698 Norwood Ave Riverside CA 92505 Office: La Sierra Univ 4500 Riverwalk Pkwy Riverside CA 92515 Personal E-mail: dantini@gmail.com.

TINKER, THOMAS EATON, retired headmaster; b. Providence, May 24, 1941; s. George Milan and Ruth (Eaton) T.; m. Roslyn May Silverman, Dec. 21, 1968. BA, Columbia U., 1963; MA, Brown U., 1968. English instr. Tabor Acad., Marion, Mass., 1964-66; history instr. Wheeler Sch., Providence, 1967-77; headmaster Broadmeadow Sch., Middletown, Del., 1977-82, St. Paul's Sch., Garden City, N.Y., 1982-89, The Barnard Sch., NYC, 1989-93; assoc. head sch. Trevor Day Sch., NYC, 1993—2003, head sch., 2003—05, ret., 2005. Evaluator Mid. State Assn. Colls. and Schs., Phila., 1978—. Trustee Barnard Sch. Found., 1993—; bd. dirs. Univ. Club L.I., 1984-86. With USAR, 1963-69. Mem. Nat. Assn. Ind. Schs., N.Y. State Assn. Ind. Schs., L.I. Episcopal Sch. Assn. (v.p./treas. 1984-89), Del. Assn. Ind. Schs. (sec. 1978-82). Episcopalian. Avocation: sailing. Home: 9629 Gladiolus Preserve Cir Fort Myers FL 33908-9717

TINKEY, PATRICIA A., literature and language professor; d. Edward W. and Nancy B. Armstrong; m. Larry L. Tinkey, Aug. 10, 1974; children: Penny D. Cruder, Thomas R. BA, Grove City Coll., Pa., 1975; MA in Higher Edn., Geneva Coll., Beaver Falls, Pa., 2002; MS in Edn. in Curriculum and Instrn., Gannon U., Erie, Pa., 2002; ABD, Duquesne U., Pitts., 2003. Cert. prin. Assn. Christian Sch. Internat., 2004. Spanish and French tchr. Grove City Christian Acad., guidance counselor; Spanish and German hs tchr. Karns City Area Sch. Dist., Pa.; Spanish and French hs tchr. New Brighton Area Sch. Dist., Pa.; part-time instr. edn. dept. Geneva Coll., Beaver Falls; prek-12 prin. Warren Christian Sch., Ohio; Spanish and English secondary tchr. Rhema Christian Acad., New Wilmington, Pa., 1994—96; asst. prof. modern lang. and edn. dept. Grove City Coll., 2004—. Evaluator and ednl. cons. Erie Home schoolers Diploma Program, Pa., 1995—, Mason-Dixon Home schoolers Assn. Diploma Program, Pa., 1995—. Contbr. to presentations. Founder Christian Home Sch. Orgn., Grove City, leader; sec. Grove City Area Meals-on-Wheels, vol.; publicity chairperson ARC, Grove City; ch. adminstr. River God, Grove City, sunday sch. tchr.; children's jr. coord. East Main Presbyn. Ch., Grove City, author jr. ch. and sunday sch. curriculum, pres. mother's guild, women's bible study leader, adult and children's sunday sch. tchr.; navigator's discipleship tng. leader Tower Presbyn. Ch., Grove City, sunday sch. tchr., author sunday sch. curriculum, deacon; sunday sch. supt. Living Word Ch., New Wilmington, Pa., house group leader, jr. tchr., asst. planter, cell group leader, ministry through mime and worship sign. Recipient Outstanding Grad. Student award, Gannon U., 2002. Mem.: North Am. Christian Fgn. Lang. Assn., Assn. Supervison and Curriculum Devel., Mortar Bd., Alpha Mu Gamma. Conservative. Avocation: travel. Office: Grove City Coll 100 Campus Dr Grove City PA

TINKHAM, MICHAEL, physicist, researcher; b. Green Lake County, Wis., Feb. 23, 1928; s. Clayton Harold and LaVerna (Krause) T.; m. Mary Stephanie Merin, June 24, 1961; children: Jeffrey Michael, Christopher Gillespie. AB, Ripon Coll., Wis., 1951, Sc.D. (hon.), 1976; MS, MIT, 1951; PhD, 1954; MA (hon.), Harvard, 1966; DSc (hon), ETH Zurich, 1997. NSF postdoctoral fellow at Clarendon Lab., Oxford (Eng.) U., 1954-55; successively research physicist, lectr., asst. prof., asso. prof., prof. physics U. Calif. at Berkeley, 1955-66; Gordon McKay prof. applied physics Harvard U., 1966—, prof. physics, 1966-80, Rumford prof. physics, 1980—, chmn. physics dept., 1975-78. Cons. to industry, 1958—; participant internat. seminars and confs.; mem. commn. on very low temperatures Internat. Union Pure and Applied Physics, 1972-78; vis. Miller rsch. prof. U. Calif.-Berkeley, 1987; vis. prof. Technical Univ., Delft, The Netherlands, 1993. Author: Group Theory and Quantum Mechanics, 1964, Superconductivity, 1965, Introduction to Superconductivity, 1975, 2d edit., 1996; contbr. articles to profl. jours. Served USNR, 1945-46. Recipient award Alexander von Humboldt Found. U. Karlsruhe, W. Ger., 1978-79, Fred E. Saalfeld award for lifetime achievement in sci., Office Naval Rsch., 2005; NSF sr. postdoctoral fellow Cavendish lab.; vis. fellow Clare Hall Cambridge (Eng.) U., 1971-72; Guggenheim fellow, 1963-64 Fellow Am. Phys. Soc. (chmn. div. solid state physics 1966-67, Buckley prize 1974, Richtmyer lectr. 1977), AAAS; mem. Am. Acad. Arts and Scis., Nat. Acad. Scis. Office: Harvard Univ Physics Dept Lyman Lab of Physics 326 Cambridge MA 02138 Home: 6126 SE Grant St Portland OR 97215-4055 Business E-Mail: tinkham@RSJ.harvard.edu.

TINSLEY, EDWARD, small business owner, rancher; m. Meredith Tinsley; children: Edward, Ede. BA in Acctg., U. Tex.; JD, Tex. Tech. U. Law Sch. Cattle rancher Flying W Diamond Ranch; owner Schlotzsky's Sandwich Shops, 1978—91; master franchiser K-BOB's Steakhouses, 1991—. Food svc. cons. US Air Force, 2005. Mem. state exec. com. Republican Party, 2003—; mem. Meth. Ch., Capitan, N.Mex.; bd. mem. Carrie Tingley Children's Hosp. Found., Internat. Braford Cattle Assn.; trustee, vice. chmn. Valles Caldera Bd. Recipient award, US Dept. Def., 2008, Tex. Cattle Feeders Assn., Silver Spoon award; named to N.Mex. 4-H Hall of Fame. Mem.: Nat. Restaurant Assn. (bd. mem. 1996, chmn. bd. 2006—07). Republican. Mailing: PO Box 942 Capitan NM 88316 Office: K-BOB's USA Inc Hdqs 141 E Palace Ave Santa Fe NM 87505 Office Phone: 505-982-3438 ext. 100.

TINSLEY, JEFFREY, Internet company executive; married, June 2003. CEO Intelligent Bus. Concepts; founder, CEO GreatDomains.com; CEO, chmn. Reunion.com, Inc., 2002—08, MyLife.com (merger of Reunion.com and Wink.com), Santa Monica, Calif., 2009—. Chmn. RealtyTracker. Recipient Ernst & Young Entrepreneur of Yr. Award in Greater LA Area, 2009. Office: MyLife.com 2118 Wilshire Box 1008 Santa Monica CA 90403-5784*

TINSLEY, JUDITH ANNE, sonographer, program director; d. John and Beverly Baillio; m. Curtis Dwain Tinsley; children: Shannon, Curtis. AAS in Diagnostic Med. Sonography, Lamar Inst. Tech., Beaumont, Tex., 2002. Cert. ARDMS, in RVT, in RDCS, in ARRT. Program dir. diagnostic-cardiovasc. sonography Lamar Inst. Tech., 2004—. Office: Lamar Inst Tech PO Box 10061 Beaumont TX 77710 also: Sonographer Outpatient Cardiovasc Svcs 2245 Plz 10 Dr Beaumont TX 77710 Business E-Mail: judy.tinsley@lit.edu.

TINSLEY-TALABI, ALBERTA, Councilwoman; m. Bamidele A. Talabi; children: Charles, David, Carla. Grad., Eastern Mich. U. Commr. Wayne County Commn., 1988—90; councilwoman Detroit City Coun., 1994—. Founder, chairwoman Coalition Against Billboard Advert Alcohol & Tobacco, 1988—; founder Mack Alive, Buddies in Bus. Fellow Join Together Fellow, Boston U., Urban Health Initiative. Office: Detroit City Coun Coleman A Young Mcpl Ctr 2 Woodward Ave Ste 1340 Detroit MI 48226 Office Phone: 313-224-1645. Office Fax: 313-224-1787. E-mail: A_Talabi_mb@atwpo.ci.detroit.mi.us.*

TINTIANGCO-CUBALES, ALLYSON GOCE, social studies educator; b. Alameda, Calif., Nov. 29, 1971; d. Alberto and Ester Goce Tintiangco; m. Valentino Christopher Cubales; 1 child, Mahalaya Goce. AA, Ohlone Coll., Fremont, Calif., 1991; BA, U. Calif., Berkeley, 1993; PhD, U. Calif., LA, 2000. Prof., Asian-Am. studies San Francisco State U., 2000—; dir. Pin@y Ednl. Partnerships, San Francisco, 2001—08. Sr. rschr., ednl. equity initiative Cesar Chavez Inst., San Francisco, 2000—; urban fellow Inst. Civic and Cmty. Engagement, San Francisco, 2002—; cons., ethnic studies curriculum San Francisco Unified Sch. Dist., 2007—. Adv. bd. mem. Manilatown Heritage Found., San Francisco, 2002—08; bd. mem. Filipino Cmty. Ctr., San Francisco, 2003—08; dir. Bayshore Childcare Svcs., Daly City, Calif., 2006—08. Recipient Disting. Young Alumnus award, U. Calif., 2006, Cmty. Svc. award, Inst. Civic and Cmty. Engagement, 2008. Mem.: Am. Ednl. Rsch. Assn., Assn. Asian Am. Studies. Achievements include development of Filipino American curriculum. Office: San Francisco State Univ 1600 Holloway Ave San Francisco CA 94132 Business E-Mail: aticu@sfsu.edu.

TINTLE, CARMEL JOSEPH, public relations executive; b. Paterson, NJ, Sept. 25, 1924; s. Herbert J. and Agnes (Merna) T.; m. Alice M. Hayes, Sept. 1, 1948; children: Joseph, Alice Maureen. BS, Fordham U., 1951; postgrad., NYU. Editl. asst. Newsweek mag., NYC, 1946-50; news editor Beverage Retailer Weekly, NYC, 1950-52; city editor Paterson Sunday Eagle, 1950-52; staff writer Carl Byoir & Assocs., Inc., NYC, 1952-59, asst. account exec., 1959-64, assoc. account exec., 1964; account supr. Grey Pub. Rels., Inc., NYC, 1964; v.p. Schenley Affiliated Brands Corp., subs. Schenley Industries, NYC, 1964-72, sr. v.p., 1972-74; v.p. corp. affairs Am. Distilling Co., 1974—80; v.p. Banfi Vintners, Old Brookville, NY, 1980—90; CEO Vinum Comm., Inc., Old Brookville, NY, 1980-90; cons. corp. comm. Banfi Vintners, 1990—2002. Publicity dir., Jumby Bay Island, a Banfi resort property, Antigua, 1985-95. Vol. publicist Assumption Coll. Sis., Mendham, NJ, 2001—. Seaman, officer US Mcht. Marine, 1943-46. Mem. NY Press Club, SAR, KC, St. Patrick Guard of Honor NJ, US Mcht. Marine Vets., Irish-Am. Cultural Inst., Fordham Univ.'s Golden Rams. Home: 14 Potter Ct Upper Montclair NJ 07043-1514

TIO, CELINA, chef; BS, Drexel U. Hotel and Restaurant Mgmt. Chef The Grill Room, Ritz-Carlton Hotel, Phila.; opening chef Spoodles, Walt Disney World, Citricos, Walt Disney World; task force chef Palothe, Walt Disney World's M.S. Magic; chef Narcoosee's; exec. chef The American Restaurant, Kansas City. Host James Beard Dinner, 1995—. Named Chef of Yr., Chef mag., 2005, Best Chef: Mid-West, James Beard Found., 2007; named one of 13 Chefs to Keep Your Eye On, Esquire Mag. Office: The American Restaurant 200 E 25th St Kansas City MO 64108 Office Phone: 816-545-8001.

TIONG, TAMRA A., elementary school educator; BA in English, Santa Clara (Calif.) Univ., 1998; Spl. edn. alt. lic., No. N.Mex. Cmty. Coll., 2003. AmeriCorps Co-tchr./Sch. Garden Coord. New Brighton Mid. Sch., 1998—99; tchr. Hidden Villa Environ. Edn. Program, 1999—2002; spl. edn. tchr. Dulce (N.Mex) Elem. Sch., Jicarilla Apache Indian Reservation, 2002—; after sch. tutor Advantage Tutoring Svc., 2004—05. Named N.Mex. Tchr. of Yr., 2007, Dulce ISD Tchr. of Yr., 2007; finalist Nat. Tchr. of Yr., 2007. Mem.: Phi Sigma Tau, Alpha Sigma Nu, Sigma Tau Delta. Office: Dulce Elem Sch PO Box 590 Dulce NM 87528 Personal E-mail: tammy_tiong@hotmail.com. Business E-Mail: ttiong@dulceschools.com.

TIPLER, FRANK JENNINGS, III, physicist; b. Andalusia, Ala., Feb. 1, 1947; s. Frank Jennings Jr. and Anne (Kearley) T.; m. Jolanta Rokicka; children: Allison Anne, Caroline Nicole. S.B., MIT, 1969; PhD, U. Md., 1976. Rsch. mathematician U. Calif., Berkeley, 1976-79; sr. rsch. fellow Oxford (Eng.) U., 1979; rsch. assoc. U. Tex., Austin, 1979-81; assoc. prof. physics and math. Tulane U., New Orleans, 1981-87, prof., 1987—. Vis. sr. scientist Max-Planck Inst. Astrophysics, Munich, 1987; vis. fellow U. Sussex, Brighton, Eng., 1987; vis. prof. Inst. Astrophysics, Liege, Belgium, 1988, U. Bern, Switzerland, 1988, U. Vienna, Austria, 1992. Author: l'Homme et le Cosmos, 1984, The Anthropic Cosmological Principle, 1986, The Physics of Immortality, 1994, The Physics of Christianity, 2007; editor: Essays in General Relativity, 1980; contbr. articles to profl. jour. Rsch. grantee NSF, 1984, 86. Libertarian. Office: Tulane Univ Physics Dept St Charles ave New Orleans LA 70118 Office Phone: 504-862-3449. Business E-Mail: tipler@tulane.edu.

TIPPETT, ANDRE, retired professional football player; b. Birmingham, Ala., Dec. 27, 1959; m. Janea Lynn Tippett; children: Jenea, Asia, Madison, Coby. Student, U. Iowa, 1979—82. Linebacker New Eng. Patriots, Foxboro, Mass., 1982—93. Named AFC Def. Player of Yr., UPI, 1985, Co-Def. Player of Yr., Newspaper Enterprise Assn., 1985; named to NFL 1980's All Decade Team, NFL Pro Bowl, 1984—88, NFL All Pro Team, 1984—88, U. Iowa Hall of Fame, 2007, NFL Pro Football Hall of Fame, 2008. Office: Pro Football Hall of Fame 2121 George Halas Dr NW Canton OH 44708

TIPPETT, DAVE, former professional hockey coach; b. Moosomin, Sask., Can., Aug. 25, 1961; m. Wendy Tippett; children: Nicole, Natalie. Attended, U. ND, 1981—83. Left wing Hartford Whalers, 1983—90, Washington Capitals, 1990—92, Pitts. Penguins, 1992—93, Phila. Flyers, 1993—94, Houston Aeros, 1994—95, asst. coach, 1995—96, head coach, 1996—99, gen. mgr., 1999; asst. coach LA Kings, 1999—2002; head coach Dallas Stars, 2002—09. Mem. Team Canada, Olympic Games, Sarajevo, 1984, Albertville, France, 92. Achievements include being a member of silver medal Canadian Hockey team, Albertville Olympic Games, 1992.

TIPPING, HARRY A., lawyer; b. Bainbridge, Md., Nov. 2, 1944; s. William Richard and Ann Marie (Kelly) Tipping; m. Kathleen Ann Palmer, July 12, 1969; 1 child, Christopher A. BA, Gannon U., Erie, Pa., 1966; JD, U. Akron, Ohio, 1970. Bar: Ohio. Asst. law dir. City of Akron, Ohio, 1971—72, chief asst. law dir., 1972—74; ptnr. Gillen, Miller & Tipping, Akron, 1974—77, Roderick, Myers & Linton, Akron, 1977—87; prin., COO Harry A. Tipping Co. L.P.A., Akron, 1987—2003; COO Tipping Co. L.P.A., Akron, 2003—; of counsel Stark & Knoll Co., L.P.A., 2006—. Mem. Fairlawn Charter Rev. Commn., Ohio, 1990—; chmn. bd. Assessment Equalization for the City of Fairlawn, 1989, 1990, 1997; chmn. Bd. of Tax Appeals, City of Fairlawn, 1979—81, mem. merger com., 1980—82. With USCGR, 1966—72. Mem.: Am. Arbitration Assn., Fedn. Ins. and Corp. Counsel, Def. Rsch. Inst., Akron Bar Assn., Am. Bd. Trial Advocates (adv.), Firestone Country Club, Catawaba Island Club, Fairlawn Country Club. Republican. Roman Catholic. Office: Stark & Knoll Co LPA 3475 Ridgewood Rd Akron OH 44333-3163 Office Phone: 330-376-3300.

TIPPING, WILLIAM MALCOLM, social services administrator; b. Oak Park, Ill., Mar. 31, 1931; s. William McKinley and Evelyn Amelia (Freier) T.; m. Lois A. Grife, Sept. 18, 1954 (dec. May 1986); children: William, Barbara, Robert; m. Babette J. Cumming, Oct. 10, 1987; children: Christopher Cumming, Courtney Barone. BA, Carleton Coll., Northfield, Minn., 1954. Sales rep. Gen. Mills, Inc., Mpls., 1954-56; account exec. Campbell Mithun, Inc., Mpls., 1956-63, v.p. mgmt., supr. Mpls. and Chgo., 1965-76; account supr., v.p. Lennen & Newell, Inc., NYC, 1963-65; ptnr., mgr. Heidrick & Struggles, Inc., Chgo., 1976-88; exec. v.p., chief exec. officer Am. Cancer Soc., Atlanta, 1988-91; pres. Tipping and McRae, Inc., Atlanta, 1991-93; mng. dir. Ward Howell Internat., Inc., Atlanta, 1993-97. Trustee Carleton Coll., 1986-90; bd. dirs. Nat. Health Coun., N.Y.C., Ga. Conservancy, Families First; mem. fin. com. UICC, Geneva, 1990-91. Recipient Disting. Svc. award Carleton Coll., 1984. Mem. Capital City Club (Atlanta), Quechee (Vt.) Club. Republican. Episcopalian.

TIPPITT, ANN, museum director; m. Alan May. PhD in Anthropology, U. NC, Chapel Hill. Various positions including curator Schiele Mus. of Natural History, 1988—2004, interim dir., 2004—05, dir., 2005—. Mem.: Gastonia Area Amateur Radio Club (pres.). Office: Schiele Mus Natural HIstory 1500 E Garrison Blvd Gastonia NC 28054 Office Phone: 704-866-6902. Office Fax: 704-866-6041. Business E-Mail: annt@cityofgastonia.com.

TIPRE, DNYANESH NISHIKANT, pharmacist, researcher; arrived in US, 2002; s. Nishikant and Sandhya Tipre. BS in Pharmacy, Govt. Coll. Pharmacy, Karad, India, 1995; MS in Pharmacy, Nagpur U., India, 1998; PhD in Pharmacy, U. Mumbai, India, 2002. Rsch. fellow NIH, Bethesda, Md., 2002—06; sch. assoc. scientist Howard U. Hosp., Washington, 2006—. Cons. NIH. Vol. adminstrn. Shiva Vishnu Temple, Greenbelt, Md. Fellow, Fogarty Internat. Ctr., 2002—05. Mem.: Acad. Molecular Imaging (assoc. award 2006). Peace And Freedom. Hindu. Achievements include research in successful inhibition of defluorination of 18F-FCWAY radiotracer in a rat model. Avocations: travel, music. Home: 4604 Crekshore Dr Rockville MD 20852 Office: Howard Univ Hospital 2041 Georgia Ave NW Washington DC 20060 Personal E-mail: dnyanesht@yahoo.com.

TIPSORD, MICHAEL L., insurance company executive; b. Ill. B in Acctg., Ill. Wesleyan U.; JD, U. Ill., Urbana-Champaign. CPA; CLU 1991, CPCU 1995. Asst. tax counsel, 1988; with State Farm Ins. Cos., 1988—, dir. acctg., 1995—96, asst. contr., 1996—97, exec. asst., 1997—98, v.p., asst. treas., 1998—2001, v.p., treas., 2001—02, sr. v.p., CFO, 2002—04, vice chmn., CFO, 2004—. Bd. dir. State Farm Lloyds, Inc., Ins. Placement Svc., Inc., State Farm Investment Mgmt. Corp., State Farm V.P. Mgmt. Corp., State Farm Bank, FSB; trustee State Farm Mutual Fund Trust, State Farm Variable Product Trust, State Farm Assoc.'s Funds Trust, State Farm Ins. Co. Employee Retirement Trust, State Farm Ins. Cos. Savings and Thrift Trust for US Employees; prof., dept. accountancy U. Ill., Urbana-Champaign; bd. dirs. Navigant Consulting Inc., 2009—. Bd. trustees Ill. Wesleyan U. Mem.: Ill. State Bar Assn., ABA. Office: Navigant consulting Inc 615 N Wabash Ave Chicago IL 60611 Office Fax: 312-914-9999.*

TIPTON, CLYDE RAYMOND, JR., communications and resources development consultant; b. Cin., Nov. 13, 1921; s. Clyde Raymond and Ida Marie (Molitor) Tipton; m. Marian Gertrude Beushausen, Aug. 6, 1942 (dec. Aug. 2, 2000); children: Marian Page Ashley, Robert Bruce. BS, U. Ky., Lexington, 1946, MS, 1947. Rsch. engr. Battelle Meml. Inst., Columbus, Ohio, 1947-49, sr. tech. adviser, 1951-62, coord. corp. comm., 1969-73, v.p. comm., 1973-75, asst. to pres., 1978-79, v.p., corp. dir. comm. and pub. affairs, 1979-86; staff mem. Los Alamos Sci. Lab., 1949-51; dir. research Basic, Inc., Bettsville, Ohio, 1962-64; asst. dir. Battelle Pacific N.W. Labs., Richland, Wash., 1964-69; pres., trustee Battelle Commons Co. for Cmty. Urban Redevel., Columbus, 1975-78; cons. bus. comm. and devel. Columbus, 1986—2004. Secretariat US del. 2d Internat. Conf. Peaceful Use Atomic Energy, Geneva, 1958; cons. U.S. AEC in Atoms for Peace Program, Tokyo, 1958, New Delhi, 1959—60, Rio de Janeiro, 1960. Author: (book) How to Change the World, 1982; co-author: Trumpet of the Jubilee, 2001; editor: Jour. Soc. Nondestructive Testing, 1953—57, The Reactor Handbook, Reactor Materials, vol. 3, 1955, vol. 1, 1960, Learning to Live on a Small Planet, 1974. Past pres. Pilot Dogs, United Way Franklin County, Greater Columbus Arts Coun.; bd. dirs. Pilot Guide Dog Found. Inc.; pres. emeritus Arhcs. Soc. Ohio Found. With USAAF, 1943. Named to U. Ky. Engring. Hall of Distinction, 1997; Haggin fellow, U. Ky., 1947, Sr. fellow, Otterbein Coll., 1978, fellow, U. Ky. Fellows Soc., 2008, U. Ky. Coll. Engring. Quadrangle Soc., 2008. Fellow: NSPE (past pres., Outstanding Svc. award 1992); mem.: Ohio Soc. Profl. Engr. (past pres., award of distinction, Uncommon Man award, Outstanding Svc. award 1993, 1998), Am. Soc. Metals, Lions (life), Sigma Xi, Alpha Chi Sigma. Episcopalian. Achievements include patents in field. Home and Office: 756 Branford Rd Troy OH 45373-1140

TIPTON, DEBORAH JO, psychologist; b. Sellersville, Pa., Oct. 13; m. Trevor Tipton, Dec. 29; children: Drew Conrad, Jordan. EdS, Sch. Psychology, Ind., 2006. Cert. NCSP NASP, 2007. Kindergarten tchr. CN Schs., Albion, Ind., 1983—2006; adj. prof. Taylor U., Ft Wayne, 1998—2005; psychologist NEISEC, Kendallville, 2007—. Bd. mem. Common Grace, Kendallville, 2007—, Hand In Hand Adoption Agy., Albion, 2000—. Office: NEISEC 1607 E Dowling St Kendallville IN 46755

TIPTON, JAMES D., retired military officer, education educator; b. Greeneville, Tenn., Jan. 8, 1937; s. P.H. and Ruby Tipton; 1 child, Dennis R. BA in Biology, Tusculum Coll., Tenn., 1958; MS in Logistic Mgmt., Air Force Inst. Tech., Dayton, Ohio, 1973; MS in Edn., Jacksonville State U., Ala., 1994. Cert. tchr. secondary edn. State of Ala., 1994. Commdg. officer U.S. Army, Washington, 1958—91. Adj. faculty Gadson State C.C., Anniston, Ala., 1994—98, Troy State U., Ft. Benning Campus, Ga., 2000—02, Columbus Tech. Coll., Ga., 2004—. Deacon, 1974—76. Col. (o6) US Army, 1984—91, Ft. McClellan, Ala. Decorated Joint Superior Svc. medal, Bronze Star U.S. Army, Legion of Merit, Meritorious Svc. medals (5), Army Commendation medal U.S. Army Chem. Sch. Office: Columbus Tech Coll Manchester Expressway Columbus GA 39104 Home: PO Box 3513 Phenix City AL 36868-3513

TIPTON, JENNIFER, lighting designer; b. Columbus, Ohio, Sept. 11, 1937; d. Samuel Ridley and Isabel (Hanson) T. BA, Cornell U., 1958. Artist in residence Nat. Theater Artist Residency Program at Wooster Group funded by the PEW Charitable Trusts, 1994; adj. prof. lighting Yale U. Sch. of Drama., 1981-. Work includes: Paul Taylor Dance Co., Twyla Tharp and Dancers, Am. Ballet Theater, Jerome Robbins, Dana Reitz, Guthrie Theater, Hartford Stage Co., Murder Among Friends, 1975, Rex, For Colored Girls Who Consider Suicide When the Rainbow is Enuf (Drama Desk award), The Landscape of the Body, Newman Theatre, The Cherry Orchard (Drama Desk award, Tony award 1977), Agamemnon, Beaumont Theatre, Happy End, Martin Beck Theatre, Agamemnon, Delacorte Theatre, 1977, Museum, Public Theatre, Runaways, Public Theatre and Plymouth Theatre, All's Well That Ends Well,

Taming of the Shrew, Delacorte Theatre, After the Season, Academy Festival Theatre, A Month in the Country, Williamstown Theatre Festival, Mikhail Baryshnikov's Don Quixote, Am. Ballet Theatre, Drinks Before Dinner, Public Theatre, The Pirates of Penzance, Public Theatre, 1978, Lunch Hour, 1980, Billy Bishop Goes to War, 1980, The Sea Gull, 1980, Sophisticated Ladies, 1981, The Wake of Jamie Foster, 1982, Uncle Vanya, 1983, Orgasmo Adulto Escapes from the Zoo, 1983, Baby with the Bathwater, 1984, Hurlyburly, 1984, Whoopi Goldberg, 1984, Endgame, 1984, Jerome Robbins' Broadway (Tony award 1989), La Bête, 1991, In the Summer House, 1993, James Joyce's The Dead, 2000, Wrong Mountain, 2000, A Moon for the Misbegotten, 2005 (Conn. Critic Cir. award, outstanding lighting design, 2005). Recipient Chgo.'s Joseph Jefferson award, 1976-77, Obie award 1979, Brandeis U. Creative Arts medal in dance, 1982, Mpls. Kudos award 1983, NY Bessie award 1984, (with Dana Reitz), 1987, Am. Theater Wing award 1989, Commonwealth award in dramatic arts, 1989, Lawrence Olivier award, 1991, Dance Mag. award, 1991, NEA Disting. Theater Artist award 1991, Dorothy and Lillian Gish prize, 2001; Guggenheim fellow, 1986-87, MacArthur Fellow, John D. and Catherine T. MacArthur Found., 2008, US Artists fellow, 2008. Home: 11 W 18th St New York NY 10011-4603*

TIPTON, KENNETH WARREN, retired agricultural administrator, researcher; b. Belleville, Ill., Nov. 14, 1932; s. Roscoe Roy and Martha Pearl (Davis) T.; m. Barbara Adds, Mar. 2, 1957; children: Kenneth Warren Jr., Nancy Tipton O'Neal. BS, La. State U., 1955, MS, 1959; PhD, Miss. State U., 1969. Asst. prof. Agrl. Ctr., La. State U., Baton Rouge, 1959-70, assoc. prof., 1970-75, prof., 1975—, supt. Red River Rsch. Sta., La. Agrl. Expt. Sta. Bossier City, 1975-79, assoc. dir. La. Agrl. Expt. Sta. Baton Rouge, 1979-89, dir. La. Agrl. Expt. Sta., vice chancellor, 1989-96, vice chancellor, dir. emeritus, 1996—; ret., 1996. Com. nine USDA/Coop. State Rsch. Svc., 1986-88; Expt. State Com. Orgn. Policy, 1988-91. Contbr. articles to Agronomy Jour., Jour. Econ. Entomology, Grain Sorghum Conf. Coach baseball program Am. Legion, 1969-74; scoutmaster Boy Scouts Am., Baton Rouge, 1970-75. Capt. USAF, 1955-58. Mem. Am. Soc. Agronomy, Crop Sci. Soc. Am., Coun. Agrl. Sci. Tech., Alpha Zeta, Phi Kappa Phi, Gamma Sigma Delta, Sigma Xi. Achievements include research on inheritance of fiber traits in cotton, resistance of grain sorghum hybrids to bird damage, tannin content of grain sorghum and effects of phosphorus on growth of sorghum. Home: 732 Baird Dr Baton Rouge LA 70808-5916 Personal E-mail: barkentip@aol.com.

TIPTON, NOEL MARTIN, JR., musician, writer, composer; b. Bastrop, La., May 20, 1932; s. Noel Martin Sr. and Agnes (Holt) Tipton; m. Elizabeth Ann Hughes, Sept. 6, 1958; children: Lisa, Noel Martin III, Jennifer Dooling. MusB, Centenary Coll. La., Shreveport, 1950—54; BS, Juilliard Sch. Music, NYC, 1956, MS, 1957; postgrad., Columbia Tchrs. Coll., 1972—73. Cert. group tchg. for piano Columbia Tchrs. Coll., 1983. Founder, co-dir. Tipton Music Studios, Westfield, NJ, 1958—88; assoc. organist, choir dir. St. Paul's Episcop. Ch., Westfield, 1960—86; organist 1st Congl. Ch., Yarmouthport, Mass., 1987—88; mem. piano faculty Cape Cod Conservatory Music and Art, Hyannis, Mass., 1988—95; organist, choirmaster St. Peter's Luth. Ch., Harwich, Mass., 1989—93; dir. music Dennis Union Ch., Mass., 1993—2007; founder, artistic dir., emeritus Eventide Arts, Dennis, 1996—2007; min. music Wellfleet United Meth. Ch., 2007—. Condr. festival Episcop. Ch. Girls Choirs, Trenton, NJ, 1970; founder vol. adult choir St. Paul's Ch., Westfield, 1980—86. Composer: (folk opera) Ballad of Ferdinan', 1972, I Ain't Gonna Dance Alone, 1974, (choral anthem) Christmas Prayer, 1981, (chancel drama) Sassy, 1996, (ballet) The Dance Goes On, 1999, (chancel drama) Anna Howard Shaw Meets Harriet Tubman, 1998; author: Anna Howard Shaw meets Anne Bradstreet, 1998, (plays) G!, 2003; composer Hymns and Emily Dickinson, 1997; author (chorus mag.), 1992; composer; (songs) We Are The People, 1992, Barack Obama & Video, 2008—09; author: (songs) Stephen Foster's Dear Friends & Gentle Hearts, 1996; composer Amherst Sabbath, 2007, Anthem: This Place Our Anchorage, 2009; dir.: (Emily Dickinson Internat. Soc.), 2008. Recipient award, Ella Lyman Cabot Trust, 1995, 1st prize, Shreveport Symphony Orch., Concerto Competition, 1952; grantee, Union County Coun. Arts, 1974, Mass. Found. Humanities, 1996, Cmty. Found. Cape Cod, 1996. Mem.: Am. Guild Organists (sr.). Democrat. Episcopalian. Avocations: writing, painting, poetry. Office: PO Box 1266 Eastham MA 02642 Personal E-mail: netipton@comcast.net.

TIRADO, JANET A., advertising marketing and public relations communications executive; b. SI, NY, Jan. 8, 1971; m. Paul Joseph Tirado, Dec. 11, 2004; children: Matthew James, Cameron Brooke. BA in Prof. Writing and Advt., Barry U., Fla., 1993; MA in Comm., suma cum laude, La Salle U., Phila., 2007. Copywriter, pub. rels. coord. Holy Cross Hosp., Ft. Lauderdale, Fla., 1995, Hadley Rose & Marvel, Inc., Boca Raton, Fla., 1995—96; asst. dir., pub. rels. coord. Bethesda Healthcare Sys., Boynton Beach, Fla., 1996—98; cmty. rels. mgr., physician and patient rels. coord. Tenet Healthcare Sys., Fla., Pa., 2000—02; exec. dir. client svcs., sr. account exec. Keel Comm., Pa., 2002—04; owner & comm. expert Red Envelop Comm., Drexel Hill, Pa., 2004—; comm. specialist Bryan R Lente, 2006—; adj. comm. prof. Del. CC, 2008—. Mem.: Pub. Rels. Soc. America, Del. County Press Club, Women in Comm. Office: Communications Expert 1101 Harper Ave Drexel Hill PA 19026

TIRADO, VICTORIA, language educator; b. Modesto, Calif., Nov. 11, 1968; d. Rafael Flores and Juana Leon; children: Abel, Jorge Rangel, Pablo. MA, Calif. State U., Sacramento, 1995. Prof. Spanish Chaffey Coll., Rancho Cucamonga, Calif., 1999—. Active mem. Hillside Cmty. Ch., Alta Loma, Calif., 2004—08. Mem.: CLTA. Office: Chaffey Coll 5885 Haven Ave Rancho Cucamonga CA 91737 Personal E-mail: vipabejo@yahoo.com. Business E-Mail: victoria.tirado@chaffey.edu.

TIRADOR, GABRIEL, insurance company executive; Asst. contr. Mercury Ins. Group, LA, 1994—96; v.p., contr. Automobile Club Calif., 1997—98; v.p., CFO Mercury Gen. Corp., LA, 1998—2001, pres., COO, 2001—06, pres., CEO, 2007—. Office: Mercury Gen Corp 4484 Wilshire Blvd Los Angeles CA 90010

TIRANA, BARDYL RIFAT, lawyer; b. Geneva, Dec. 16, 1937; s. Rifat and Rosamond English (Walling) T.; m. Anne Prather, June 22, 1985; children by previous marriage: Kyra, Amina. AB, Princeton U., 1959; LL.B., Columbia U., 1962. Bar: DC 1962, Md. 1986, NY 1986, Va. 1986, Pa. 1992. Trial atty. Dept. Justice, 1962-64; assoc. Amram, Hahn & Sundlun, Washington, 1965-68, ptnr., 1969-72; dir., sec. Exec. Jet Aviation, Inc., Columbus, Ohio, 1970-77, Technics, Inc., Alexandria, Va., 1971-77; ptnr. Sundlun, Tirana & Scher, Washington, 1972-77; dir. def. civil preparedness agy. Dept. Def., Washington, 1977-79, mem. armed forces policy coun., 1977-79; chmn. bd. Technics, Inc., San Jose, Calif., 1979-85; of counsel Silverstein and Mullens, Washington, 1982-84, ptnr., 1984-90; pvt. practice law Washington, 1991—. Mem.-at-large DC Bd. Edn., 1970-74; trustee Jimmy Carter Inaugural Trust, Washington, 1977-87; co-chmn. 1977 Presdl. Inaugural Com., 1976-77; mem. exec. adv. coun. Calif. Commn. Indsl. Innovation, 1981-82; pres. China/USA Edn. Fund, Inc., Washington, 1981-2002; trustee The Waltz Group of Washington, 2000-07; dir. Rocky Mountain Inst., Snowmass Colo., 1982-95. Recipient medal for disting. pub. svc. Dept. Def., 1979, Fuess award Phillips Acad., 1991, Svc. Commendation award YWCA of Nat. Capital Area, 1991. Mem. NYC Racquet and Tennis Club, DC Met. Club, Century Assn. (NYC), Nyack Field Club (NY). Home: 3 Washington Ave Nyack NY 10960-4713 Office Phone: 845-358-0007. Personal E-mail: btirana@aol.com.

TIRELLA, LINDA GREY, occupational therapist; d. Charles and Joan Grey; m. Francis Tirella, Sept. 2, 1978; children: Andrew, Terence, Alexis, Ronald, Charles. MS, Boston U., 1976; MHA, Suffolk U., Boston, 2001. Occupl. therapist Tufts Med. Ctr., Boston, Mass., 2001—. Grant, NIH. Home: 10 Collamore Rd Winchester MA 01890 Office: Tufts Med Ctr 800 Washington St Boston MA 02111 Home Fax: 617-636-8388. Business E-Mail: ltirella@tuftsmedicalcenter.org.

TIRONE, BARBARA JEAN, retired health insurance administrator; b. Celina, Ohio, Nov. 19, 1943; d. Vincent James and Theresa Barbara (Goettermoeller) G. BA, Miami U., 1965; MBA, U. Chgo., 1977. Asst. dir. for internat. trade State of Ill., Chgo., Brussels, Hongkong and Sao Paulo, Brazil, 1973-76; dir. office of mgmt. and planning Office Human Devel. Svcs., Chgo., 1976-79; dep. regional adminstr. Health Care Financing Adminstrn., Chgo., 1979-82, regional adminstr., 1982-87, dir. bur. of prog. ops. Balt., 1987-92; dir. health stds. and quality bur. Health Care Fin. Adminstrn., Balt., 1992-96; pres., CEO AdminaStar, Inc., Indpls., 1996-2001; ret., 2002. Recipient Presdl. Disting. Rank award 1988, 94, Presdl. Meritorious Rank award 1987, 92; named Fed. Exec. of Yr., 1987. Home: 11212 Appaloosa Dr Reisterstown MD 21136 Office Phone: 410-833-5570. Personal E-mail: bgtirone@yahoo.com.

TIRRELL, JOHN ALBERT, organization executive, consultant; b. Boston, Feb. 11, 1934; s. George Howard and Helen Sarah (Hitchings) T.; m. Helga Ruth Eisenhauer, Jan. 29, 1966; children: Steffanie Ruth, Sabina Lisette, Monica Susanne. BA in Psychology, King's Coll., Briarcliff Manor, NY, 1961; MEd, U. Ariz., Tucson, 1975. Various positions for several orgns., 1962-68; analyst instrnl.-ednl. systems GE, Daytona Beach, Fla., 1969-72; dir. curriculum and program devel. Brookdale CC, Lincroft, NJ, 1972; dir. learning and faculty resources Pima CC, Tucson, 1972-76; dir. human resources planning and devel. Miami divsn. Cyprus Copper Co., Claypool, Ariz., 1976-79; exec. dir. Calvary Missionary Fellowship, Tucson, 1983-85; interim pastor Saguaro Evang. Ch., Tucson, 1985-86; pastor Midvale Evangelical Ch., Tucson, 1986-87; founder, pres. The Jethro Consultancy, Birmingham, Mich., 1979—88, Tucson, 1979—; v.p. mgmt. svc. AA Gage, Ferndale, Mich., 1987; pastor Desert Hills Bapt. Ch., Tucson, 1993-95. Mem. adv. bd. UIM Internat., Greeley, Colo., 1983-92, mem. fin. com., 1983-94, sec. support svcs. field bd., 1993-01, sec. bus. and devel. field bd., 2002-08, sec., chmn. pers. com., 1997-2008, sec., 1998-2008, bd. dirs., 1993-2008, mem. policy revision com., 2004-08, v.p. internat. bd., 2005-08, mem. search com., 2005-08, vice pres., sec. 2005-08, mem. bus. and devel. bd., chmn. nominating com., 2005-08, interim exec. dir., 2008-09; assoc. faculty mem. Gila Pueblo Campus Ea. Ariz. Coll., Globe, 1978; adj. prof. Montclair State Coll., NJ, 1972; chmn. mgmt. and pers. com. Wildwood Ranch, Inc., Howell, Mich., 1989-92; interim pres., v.p. programs, v.p. devel. Detroit Rescue Mission Ministries, 1990-92; v.p. corp. planning, tng., productivity George Instrument Co., Royal Oak, 1988-89; faculty mem. mgmt., comm., sociology, psychology So. Ariz. and Phoenix campuses U. Phoenix, Tucson and Phoenix, 1997—, area chair for social scis., 2001-04; adj. faculty mem. psychology Pima County CC, 1999-2002. Contbr. articles to profl. jours. Mem. Ariz. Coun. for Econ. Conversion, 1992-94; mem. facilities task force Grace Evang. Free Ch., Birmingham, 1989-90, chmn. bylaws revision com., 1989-90, chmn. property devel. com., 1990-92; interim pastor Desert Hills Bapt. Ch., Tucson, 1992-93; elder 1st Evang. Free Ch., Tucson, 1979-81, 86-87, 97, supt. Sunday sch., 1981-84, supr. adult Sunday sch., 1992-93, chmn. gen. bd., elder bd., 1979-82, short-term missions coord., missions bd., 1992-93; bd. dirs. S.W. Border dist. Evang. Free Ch. Am., 1996-00, mem. comm. com., 1996-01, chmn. comm. com., 1998-99; bd. dirs. Clearing House of Operational Resources for Christian Orgns., Royal Oak, Mich., 1991; bd. dirs. Shadow Roc Homeowners Assn., 1996-98, treas., 1997; v.p. parent-tchr. fellowship Palo Verde Christian Sch., Tucson, 1980-81. Staff sgt. USAF, 1952-56, com. man Precinct 264, Rep. Party, Pima County. Mem. ASTD (treas., Old Pueblo chpt. 1982, bd. dirs.-at-large 1983, Human Resources Devel. award Valley of the Sun chpt. 1977), Birmingham-Bloomfield C. of C. (mem. profl. devel. edn. com. 1987-91, mem. pub. rels. mktg. com. 1989), King's Coll. Alumni Assn. (class gov. 1988-95, 2000-03). Independent. Avocation: Bible teaching. Home and Office: 1205 E Deer Canyon Rd Tucson AZ 85718-1069 Office Phone: 520-544-9750. Personal E-mail: jack.tirrell@comcast.net.

TIRRELL, MATTHEW V., engineering educator, department chairman; b. Phillipsburg, NJ, Sept. 5, 1950; s. Matthew Vincent Tirrell Jr. and Loraine (Wier) Gonsky; m. Pamela LaVigne, Aug. 1993. BS in chem. engring., Northwestern U., 1973; PhD in polymer sci. and engring., U. Mass., 1977. Mem. coop. edn. program Cin. Milacron Chem. Inc., 1970-72; tchg. and rsch. asst. U. Mass., Amherst, 1973-77; asst. prof. U. Minn., Mpls., 1977-81, assoc. prof., 1981-85, prof. chem. engring. and materials sci., 1985—99, Shell disting. chair. chem. engring., 1986-91, Earl E. Bakken Prof. Biomed. Engring., 1993—97, head chem. engring. and materials sci., 1995-99; dir. Biomed. Engring. Inst., 1995-98; dean Coll Engring. U. Calif., Santa Barbara, 1999—2009, Richard A. Auhll Prof., 1999—2009, also prof. materials engring.; venture ptnr. NGEN Partners, LLC; chair Dept. Bioengineering, Coll. Engring. U. Calif., Berkeley, 2009—, Arnold and Barbara Silverman prof. Depts. Bioengineering, Materials Sci. & Engring. and Chem. Engring., 2009—. Mem. adv. panel Grad. Sch. Integrative Sciences and Engring. Nat. U. Singapore, 2003—05, vis. com. chem. and environ. engring., 2003—05; cons. Institut Francais du Petrole, 1982—, Kimberly-Clark Corp., 2000—, Edwards Lifesciences, 2000—, Santa Barbara Tech. Group, 2000—, bd. mem.; editl. adv. bd. Jour. Polymer Sci., Polymer Physics Edit., 1986—2000, Macromolecules, 1987—90, McGraw-Hill Chem. Engring. Series, 1987—98, Jour. Rheology, 1990—, Progress in Polymer Sci., 1992—97, Polymerica Acta, 1992—, Jour. Adhesion Sci. and Tech., 1993—96, Langmuir, 1995—, Current Opinion in Colloid and Interface Sci., 1996—, Oxford Univ. Press, Chem. Engring. Series, 1998—2000, Chemistry of Materials, 1998—, Gordon and Breach, 2000—; editl. bd. Jour. Chem. Physics, 1991—93; US editor Chem. Engring. Sci., 1988—91; assoc. editor Reviews in Macromolecular Sci., 1992—2000, editor, 2000—; Sci. and Tech. Panel U. Calif. Pres.'s Coun. for Nat. Lab. Adminstrn., 2000—; bd. dirs. Cottage Health Sys., Santa Barbara, 2000—; US Chair German-Am. Frontiers of Engring., 1999—. Author: Modeling of Polymerization Processes, 1995. Advisor Camille and Henry Dreyfus Found., 1998—. Recipient Camille and Henry Dreyfus Tchr.-Scholar Award, 1980, George Taylor/IT Alumni Soc. Disting. Rsch. Award, U. Minn. Inst. Tech., 1981, Gordon Starr Outstanding Contribution Award, U. Minn., 1981, Presdl. Young Investigator Award, NSF, 1984, Chancellor's Medal, U. Mass. Amherst, 1987, Alumni Merit Award, Northwestern U., 1997; named Outstanding Young Chem. Engr. of Minn., 1981; Alfred P. Sloan Found. Fellowship, 1982, John Simon Guggenheim Meml. Found. Fellowship, 1986. Fellow AAAS, Am. Inst. Med. and Bio. Engineers, Am. Phys. Soc. (John H. Dillon Medal 1987); mem. NAE, AIChE (editor jour. 1991—2001, inst. lectr. 2001, Allan P. Colburn award 1985, Profl. Progress award 1994, Charles M.A. Stine Award 1996), Am. Chem. Soc., Materials Rsch. Soc., Biomed. Engring. Soc., Controlled Release Soc., Soc. Biomaterials, Soc. Polymer Sci. Japan, Soc. Rheology Avocations: gourmet cooking, movies, distance running. Office: U Calif, Berkeley Dept Bioengineering 306 Stanley Hall #1762 Berkeley CA 94720-1762 Office Phone: 510-642-5833. E-mail: mvtirrell@berkeley.edu.*

TIRRO, FRANK PASCALE, music educator, composer, writer; b. Omaha, Sept. 20, 1935; s. Frank and Mary Carmela (Spensieri) T.; m. Charlene Rae Whitney, Aug. 16, 1961; children: John Andrew, Cynthia Anne. B.M.E., U. Nebr., 1960; M.M., Northwestern U., 1961; PhD, U. Chgo., 1974. Chmn. lab. sch. U. Chgo., Ill., 1961—70; fellow of Villa I Tatti Harvard U., Florence, Italy, 1971—72; lectr. U. Kans., Lawrence, Kans., 1972—73; asst. prof. music Duke U., Durham, NC, 1973—74; dir. Southeastern Inst. Medieval and Renaissance Studies, Durham, NC, 1978—80; chmn., assoc. prof. music Duke U., Durham, NC, 1973—80; prof. Yale U., New Haven, 1980—, dean, 1980—89. Reader, cons. several univ. presses; jurist Parisot Internat. Cello Competition, Sao Paolo, Brazil, 1981. Author: Historia del Jazz Clásico, 2001, Historia del Jazz Moderno, 2001, Jazz: A History, 1977, rev. edit., 1993, Renaissance Choirbooks in the Archive of San Petronio in Bologna, 1986, Living With Jazz, 1996, (with others) The Humanities: Cultural Roots and Continuities, 1980, 7th edit., 2004, The Birth of the Cool of Miles Davis and His Associates, 2008; editor: Medieval and Renaissance Studies No. 9, 1982; mem. editl. bd. Am. Music, Wittenberg Rev.; composer American Jazz Mass, 1960; assoc. editor Am. Nat. Biography, 1994—. Bd. dirs. New Haven Symphony, 1980-89, Neighborhood Music Sch., New Haven, 1982-89, Chamber Orch. New Eng., 1980-82, Ctr. for Black Music Rsch., 1985-91. Recipient Standard Composer award Am. Soc. Composers, Authors and Pubs., 1966, 99, 2000-05, Gustavus Fine Arts medal, 1988, Duke Ellington Fellow medal, 1989, Disting. Alumnus award, U. Nebr., 2006; travel grantee Am. Coun. Learned Socs., 1967; rsch. grantee Duke U., 1978; named to Omaha Ctrl. H.S. Hall of Fame, 2002. Mem. Am. Musicol. Soc. (council 1978-80), Coll. Music Soc. (council 1980-82, mem. exec. bd. 1984-86), Nat. Assn. Schs. of Music, Internat. Soc. Jazz Research, Renaissance Soc. Am., Mory's Club, Yale Club (NYC). Republican. Lutheran. Office: Yale U Sch Music PO Box 208246 New Haven CT 06520-8246 Office Phone: 203-432-5989. E-mail: frank.tirro@yale.edu.

TIRYAKIAN, EDWARD ASHOD, sociologist, educator; b. Bronxville, NY, Aug. 6, 1929; s. Ashod Haroutioun and Keghinee (Agathon) T.; m. Josefina Cintron, Sept. 5, 1953; children: Edmund Carlos, Edwyn Ashod. BA summa cum laude, Princeton U., 1952; MA, Harvard U., 1954, PhD, 1956; PhD (hon.), U. Rene Descartes, Paris, 1987. Instr. Princeton U., 1956—57, asst. prof., 1957—62; lectr. Harvard U., 1962—65; assoc. prof. Duke U., Durham, NC, 1965—67, prof., 1967—2004, chmn. dept. sociology and anthropology, 1969—72, dir. internat. studies, 1988—91, prof. emeritus, 2004—. Vis. lectr. U. Philippines, 1954-55, Bryn Mawr Coll., 1957-59; vis. scientist program Am. Sociol. Assn., 1967-70; vis. prof. Laval U., Quebec City, Que., Can., 1978, Inst. Polit. Studies, Paris, 1992, Free U., Berlin, 1996; summer seminar dir. NEH, 1978, 80, 93, 89, 91, 96; lectr. Kyoto Am. Studies Summer Seminar, 1985, project leader Fulbright New Cent. Scholars Program, 2002-03. Author: Sociologism and Existentialism, 1962, For Durkheim: Essays in Historical and Cultural Sociology, 2009; Editor: Sociological Theory, Values and Sociocultural Change: Essays in Honor of P.A. Sorokin, 1963, The Phenomenon of Sociology, 1971, On the Margin of the Visible: Sociology, the Esoteric, and the Occult, 1974, The Global Crisis: Sociological Analyses and Responses, 1984; co-editor: Theoretical Sociology: Perspectives and Developments, 1970; New Nationalisms of the Developed West, 1985; Rethinking Civilizational Analysis, 2004. Fellow Ctr. for Advanced Study in Behavioral Scis., 1997-98; recipient Fulbright rsch. award, 1955; Ford faculty rsch. fellow, 1971-72, fellow Ctr. for Advanced Study in Behavioral Scis., 1997-98, Disting. New Century scholar Fulbright Scholar Program, 2002-03. Mem. Am. Sociol. Assn., African Studies Assn., Am. Soc. for Study Religion (co uncil 1975-78, pres. 1981-84), Assn. Internationale des Sociologues de Langue Française (v.p. 1985-88, pres. 1988-92), Soc. for Phenomenology and Existential Philosophy, Phi Beta Kappa. Clubs: Princeton, Century Assn. (N.Y.C.). Home: 16 Pascal Way Durham NC 27705-4924 Office Phone: 919-660-5632. Business E-Mail: durkhm@soc.duke.edu. *As the first great educator, Socrates realized it is better to set minds on fire than to set the world on fire. This is what I have sought to do in my academic career.*

TISA, LOUIS S., microbiologist, educator; s. Stephen C. and Edith Tisa; m. Linda Stoxen, July 20, 1985. BS, U. Windsor, Ont., Canada, 1976, MSc, 1976—79; PhD, U. Wis., Madison, 1987. Prof. microbiology U. NH., Durham, 1994—, chair dept. microbiology, 2005—08. Mem.: Soc. Gen. Microbiology, Internat. Soc. Molecular Plant-Microbe Interactions, Internat. Soc. Pharm. Engring., Internat. Symbiosis Soc., Am. Soc. Microbiology (divsn. I chair 2005—08). Office: Univ of NH 46 College Rd Durham NH 03824 Business E-Mail: lst@hypatia.unh.edu.

TISCH, ANDREW HERBERT, diversified holding company executive; b. Asbury Park, NJ, Aug. 14, 1949; s. Laurence Alan and Wilma Zelda (Stein) T.; 2 children. BS, Cornell U., Ithaca, NY, 1971; MBA, Harvard U., 1977. Brand mgr. Lorillard Co., NYC, 1971-75; mgr. operational analysis Loews Corp., NYC, 1977-79, chmn. exec. com., 1998—, co-chmn. (with Jonathan Tisch), 2006—; pres. Bulova Corp., Woodside, NY, 1979—90, bd. dirs., past chmn.; chmn., CEO Lorillard Tobacco Co., NYC, 1990—95. Bd. dir. CNA Fin. Corp., 2006—. Contbr. articles to profl. jours. Mem. fgn. affairs com. Am. Jewish Com., NYC, 1983; bd. dirs. Outward Bound, Inc., Greenwich, Conn., 1983-88; trustee Ctrl. Synagogue, NYC, 1984; gen. chmn. United Jewish Appeal Fedn. Jewish Philanthropies NY, vice chmn. United Jewish Appeal, chmn. Prime Min.'s Coun.; bd. dirs. NY Shakespeare Festival, K12; chmn. Children's Hearing Inst., 1988; bd. mem. NYC Sports Commn.; mem. vis. com. Harvard Bus. Sch.; pres. City Pks. Found.; trustee Wildlife Conservation Soc., PENCIL Inc., NY City Police Found. Mem. 24 Karat Club NY, Century Country Club, Harmonie Club, Plumb Club, Achilles Track Club (bd. dirs.). Avocations: tennis, running. Office: Loews Corp 667 Madison Ave New York NY 10021-8087 Office Phone: 212-521-2000.

TISCH, JAMES SOLOMON, diversified holding company executive; b. Atlantic City, Jan. 2, 1953; s. Laurence A. and Wilma (Stein) T.; m. Merryl Hiat; children: Jessica, Benjamin, Samuel. BA, Cornell U., Ithaca, NY, 1975; MBA, U. Pa. Wharton Grad. Sch., 1976. With Loews Corp., NYC, 1977—; exec. v.p., 1987-94, pres., COO, 1994-99, pres., CEO, 1999—. Chmn., CEO Diamond Offshore Drilling, Inc.; bd. dirs. CNA Fin., Vail Resorts, Inc., Loews Corp. Bd. dirs. Fedn. Employment and Guidance Svc., NYC, 1985; trustee Edn. Broadcasting Corp. 2003-, chmn. 2006; trustee NY Pub. Libr., Mt. Sinai Med. Ctr./NYU Med. Ctr.,

NYC, 1988—; past pres., UJA Fedn. NY; past chmn. Conf. Presidents Major Am. Jewish Orgns., United Jewish Communities; mem. bd. overseers, U. Pa. Wharton Sch. Bus.; mem. exec. com. Partnership for NYC. Mem.: Coun. Fgn. Rels., Phi Beta Kappa. Office: Loews Corp 667 Madison Ave Fl 7 New York NY 10021-8087 Office Phone: 212-521-2000.

TISCH, JONATHAN MARK, hotel company executive; b. Atlantic City, Dec. 7, 1953; s. Preston Robert and Joan (Hyman) T. BA in Polit. Sci., Tufts U., 1976. Cinematographer, prodr. WBZ-TV, Boston, 1976-79; sales mgr. Loews Hotels, NYC, 1980-81, dir. devel., 1981-82, v.p., 1982-85, exec. v.p., 1985-86, pres., 1986—89, CEO, 1989—, chmn.; co-chmn. (with Andrew Tisch) Loews Corp., 2006—. Mem. mgmt. com. Loews Corp.; bd. dirs. NY Giants, 1991—. Author (with Karl Weber): The Power of We: Succeeding Through Partnerships, 2004, Chocolates on the Pillow Aren't Enough: Reinventing The Customer Experience, 2007. Trustee Robert Steel Found., NYC, Gunnery Sch., Washington, Conn., 1983, Tufts U., Medford, Mass., 1986-, Vice Pres.'s Residence Found., 1994; chmn. NYC host com. for Grammys, 1988, 92, 94; bd. dirs. Pediatric AIDS found.; vice chair econ. devel. com. NYC Partnership, 1994—; chmn. NYC & Co., 2002-08 Recipient Disting. Alumni award, Tufts U., 1996. Mem. Am. Hotel and Motel Assn. (officer 1994-97), Travel Bus. Roundtable (chmn. 1995—, conf. chmn. 1995—), Friars Club. Avocations: golf, tennis, skiing. Office: Loews Hotels 667 Madison Ave New York NY 10021-8087 Office Phone: 212-521-2801.

TISCH, WILMA STEIN, foundation administrator; b. Asbury Park, NJ, June 25, 1927; d. Joseph F. and Rose E. (Liebesman) Stein; m. Laurence A. Tisch (dec. 2003); children: Andrew H., Daniel R., James S., Thomas J. BS, Skidmore Coll., Saratoga Springs, NY, 1948, LHD (hon.), 1990, Mt. Sinai Med. Sch. CUNY, NYC, 1990, NYU, 2006. Trustee Blythedal Children's Hosp., Valhalla, NY, 1964-71, Fedn. of Jewish Philanthropies, NYC, 1971—, pres., 1980-83. Trustee Coun. Jewish Fedns., NYC, 1980-87, Jewish Communal Fund, NYC, Am. Jewish Joint Distribution Com., NY, 1986-94, United Way NYC, 1986-2007, Skidmore Coll., 1994—, Carnegie Corp., NYC, 1994-98, WNYC Radio, NYC, 1984—, pres., 1988-93; trustee coun. advisors Hunter Coll. Sch. Social Work, NYC, 1986-97. Mem. NY State Gov.'s Select Com. on Capital Health Care Needs, NYC, 1983, Mayor's Transition Coun., NYC, 1993, Carnegie Coun. on Adolescent Devel., NYC, 1987—97; co-chmn. Task Force on Youth Devel. and Cmty. Programs, NYC, 1990—94; chmn. transition adv. team Parks and Recreation Cultural Affairs, NYC, 1993; mem. policy bd. Sept. 11th Fund, 2001—04. Recipient Louis D. Marshall medal Jewish Theol. Sem., 1980; Milender fellow Brandeis U., 1982. Fellow: Am. Acad. Arts & Sciences. Jewish.

TISCHFIELD, JAY ARNOLD, genetics educator; b. NYC, June 15, 1946; s. Max and Ethel Barbara (Smith) T.; m. Donna Marie Mitchell, Aug. 29, 1978; children: Max Alexander, Samuel Eli, David James. BS, Bklyn. Coll., 1967; MPH, Yale U., 1969, PhD, 1973. Diplomate Am. Bd. Med. Genetics. Asst. prof. Case Western Reserve U., Cleve., 1972-78; assoc. prof., prof. Med. Coll. of Ga., Augusta, 1978-87; prof., dir. div. molecular genetics Ind. U. Sch. Medicine, Indpls., 1987—98; Duncan and Nancy MacMillan prof. and endowed chair, dept. of Genetics Rutgers U., 1999—. Prof. of Pediat. and Psychiatry Robert Wood Johnson Med. Sch., 1998—; mem., Sci. Adv. Bd. Genome Inst. of Singapore; mem. scientific adv. bd. Cancer Inst. NJ; dir., Cell and DNA Repository Rutgers U., NJ, dir., Human Genetics Inst., NJ; dir. Ctr. for Collaborative Genetics Rsch. on Mental Disorders, NJ Ctr. for Excellence for the treatment of Tourette Syndrome and Associated Disorders; chmn. scientific adv. bd. Motif Biosciences, NYC; invited lectr. in field. Contbr. articles to profl. jours. Named Disting. Alumnus, Bklyn. Coll., 1990; NIH postdoctoral fellow, 1967-72; grantee NIH, 1972—, NSF, 1983-85; Elliot Osserman award for Disting. Svc. in Support of Cancer Rsch., Israel Cancer Rsch. Fund, 1994. Mem. Am. Soc. for Human Genetics, Am. Soc. for Microbiology, AAAS (elected fellow, 2007), Sigma Xi, Yale Club of Ind. Achievements include patents in field. Office: Dept Genetics Rutgers State Univ NJ Human Genetics Inst LS136 145 Bevior Rd Piscataway NJ 08854-8000 Office Phone: 732-445-1027. Office Fax: 732-445-1147. Business E-Mail: jay@biology.rutgers.edu.

TISCHLER, GARY LOWELL, psychiatrist, educator; b. NYC, Oct. 30, 1935; s. Louis and Dorothy (Green) T.; m. Judith Post, Aug. 18, 1957; children: Laurie Dee, Marc David, Rachel Mara. AB, Hamilton Coll., 1957; MD, U. Pa., 1961; MS, Yale U., 1975. Intern Kings County Hosp., Bklyn., 1961-62; resident in psychiatry Yale U. Sch. Medicine, New Haven, 1962-65, asst. prof., 1967-70, assoc. prof., 1970-75, prof. psychiatry, 1975-90, chmn. dept. psychiatry, 1986-87; prof., chmn. dept. psychiatry and biobehavioral scis., dir. Neuropsychiatric Inst. UCLA Sch. Medicine, 1990-95; dir. Yale Psychiat. Inst., New Haven, 1978-87; chief psychiatry Yale-New Haven Hosp., 1986-87; clin. dir. Hill-West Haven divsn. Conn. Mental Health Ctr., New Haven, 1968-70, dir., 1970-77; prof. psychiatry UCLA, 1990-95, prof. emeritus, 1996—; prof., exec. vice chair dept. psychiatry, dir. Cornell U. Med. Coll., 1994—2002; dir. Westchester divsn., dir. mental health programs N.Y. Hosp., 1994-99, dir. Payne Whitney Clinic, 1996-97. Study dir. Pres.'s Commn. on Mental Health, Washington, 1977-79; cons. Arthur D. Little Inc., Boston, 1973-75, IBM Corp., Armonk, N.Y., 1986-87; mem. profl. adv. com. Am. Med. Internat., L.A., 1984-86; mem. bd. mental health and behavioral medicine Inst. Medicine, Washington, 1986—, com. on clin. evaluation, 1990-94. Author: Quality Assurance Thru Utilization and Peer Review, 1982; editor: Patient Care Evaluation in Mental Health, 1985, Diagnosis and Classification in Psychiatry, 1987; contbr. articles to profl. jours. Mem. Gov.'s transition staff on mental health, Conn., 1975; vice chmn. Bd. Mental Health State of Conn., 1986. Served to capt. U.S. Army, 1965-67, Vietnam. Fellow Am. Psychiat. Assn., Am. Coll. Mental Health Adminstrn., Am. Assn. for Social Psychiatry, Am. Coll. Psychiatry. Home: 36 Rock Hill Rd Bedford NY 10506-1522 E-mail: glt35@netscape.net.

TISCHMAN, MICHAEL BERNARD, lawyer; b. Elizabeth, NJ, Oct. 8, 1937; s. Nathan and Ann (Goldberg) T.; m. Elinor Cohen, Aug. 16, 1959; children: David F., Susan F. BA, U. Pa., 1959; LLB, Harvard U., 1963; LLM in Taxation, NYU, 1968. Bar: N.J. 1964, Fla. 1979, N.Y. 1984. Law sec. Judge Walter J. Freund N.J. Appellate Div., 1963-64; assoc. Schiff, Cummis & Kent, Newark, 1964-67; ptnr. Cummis, Kent, Radin & Tischman, Newark, 1968-70, Sills, Beck, Cummis, Radin & Tischman, Newark, 1971-87, Sills, Cummis, Radin, Tischman, Epstein & Gross, Newark, 1988—2003; sr. counsel Sills, Cummis & Gross, Newark, 2004—. Panel chmn. fee arbitration com. N.J. Supreme Ct. Dist. Essex County, 1987-91; mem. health law and policy program adv. bd. Seton Hall Law Sch., 1997—. Mem. Mayor's Performing Arts Ctr. Task Force, Newark, 1988-96. Mem. N.J. Bar Assn. (com. on ltd. partnership act revisions 1983-88), Phi Beta Kappa. Home: 8 Wedgewood Way Scotch Plains NJ 07076-2727 Office: Sills Cummis & Gross One Riverfront Pla Newark NJ 07102 Office Phone: 973-643-7000. Business E-Mail: mtischman@sillscummis.com.

TISDALE, DOUGLAS MICHAEL, SR., lawyer; b. Detroit, May 3, 1949; s. Charles Walker and Violet Lucille (Battani) Tisdale; m. Patricia Claire Brennan, Dec. 29, 1972 (dec. Jan. 2004); children: Douglas Michael Jr., Sara Elizabeth, Margaret Patricia, Victoria Claire. BA in Psychology with honors, U. Mich., 1971, JD, 1975. Bar: Colo. 1975, U.S. Dist. Ct. Colo. 1975, U.S. Ct. Appeals (10th cir.) 1976, U.S. Supreme Ct. 1979. Law clk. to chief judge U.S. Dist. Ct. Colo., Denver, 1975-76; ptnr. Brownstein Hyatt & Farber, P.C., 1976—92; shareholder Popham, Haik, Schnobrich & Kaufman, Ltd., 1992—97, dir., 1995—97; ptnr. Baker & Hostetler LLP, Denver, 1997—2002; owner Tisdale & Assocs., Denver, 2002—. Chmn. bd. dirs. Eagle Health Care Ctr., Inc., Colo. Neurol. Inst.; treas. Vail Valley Med. Ctr. City councilman Cherry Hills Village, 2000—08; mayor pro-tem, 2006—08. Roman Catholic. Home: 4662 S Elizabeth Ct Cherry Hills Village CO 80113-7106 Office: Tisdale and Assocs LLC 4662 S Elizabeth Ct Cherry Hills Village CO 80113-7106 Office Phone: 303-832-1800. Business E-Mail: doug@tisdalelaw.com.

TISDALE, SHELBY JO-ANNE, museum director, consultant; b. London, Ontario, Canada, Oct. 25, 1950; d. Edith Ilene St. Clair and George Elgin Tisdale. BA in Anthropology, Southwest Archeology, U. of Colo., Boulder, 1980; MA in Socio-Cultural Anthropology, Mus. Studies, U. of Wash., 1985; PhD in Cultural Anthropology, U. of Ariz., 1997. Mus. cons. Ilwaco Heritage Found., Wash., 1983; asst. collections mgr. Sch. of Am. Rsch., Santa Fe, 1984—85; mus. anthropologist, asst. cur. natural sci. Palm Springs Desert Mus., 1985—87; instr. anthropology U. Calif. Ext., Riverside, 1986—87; chief cur. Millicent Rogers Mus., Taos, 1987—89; tchg. assoc. U. Ariz., 1990—93, summer session faculty, 1991—95; tribal mus tech. asst. cons. Ariz. State Mus., 1991; adj. faculty anthropology Pima C.C., Tucson, 1992—97; mus. planning cons. Cocopah Indian Tribe, Somerton, Ariz., 1993—96; assoc. faculty Ariz. Western Coll., Yuma, 1994; ind. contractor URS/Dames and Moore, 1996, contractor, 1997—2001; cur., native am. art Philbrook Mus. of Art, Tulsa, 1999—2002; exec. dir. Millicent Rogers Mus., Taos, 2002—05; dir. Mus. Indian Arts and Culture/Lab of Anthropology, Santa Fe, 2005—. Mus. planning cons. Ilwaco Heritage Found., Wash., 1983, Cocopah Indian Tribe, Somerton, 1993—97; cons. URS/Dames & Moore, Phoenix, 1997—2001. Contbr. articles to pubs. Mem. Northern N.Mex Cultural Arts Celebration Com., 2002—03, Taos Spring Arts Celebration Com., 2002—05; bd. mem. N.Mex com. Nat. Mus. Women in Arts, 2004—; vol. Peace Corps, 1980—81. Fellow: Soc. for Applied Anthropology; mem.: N.Mex Assn. Museums, Mountain Plains Mus. Assn. (bd. mem.-at-large 2005—), Am. Anthrop. Assn. (assoc.), Coun. for Mus. Anthropology (sec. 1988—90), AAM, Rotary Internat. Avocations: travel, reading, hiking. Office: Mus Indian Arts and Culture/Lab of Anthropology PO Box 2087 Santa Fe NM 87504

TISDELL, RONALD H., toxicologist, consultant; s. H. and L. M. Tisdell; m. Patty A. Tisdell; children: R. Kelly, Kevin Marshall. BS in Genetics, U. Alta., Edmonton, 1972; Degree in Pharmacy, U. Alta., Edmonton Can., 1976; PharmD, U. Tex., San Antonio, 1980. Lic. pharmacist Alta. Coll. Pharmacists, 1975. Toxicologist Tex. State Poison Ctr., Galveston, 1978—87; drug info. & drug utilization dir. U. Alta. Hosp., Edmonton, Alberta, 1987—96; clin. pharmacist, clin. toxicologist, forensic toxicologist, corp. pres., cons., rschr. Toxicology Litig. Consultants, Inc., Georgetown, 1976—. Contbr. scientific papers to profl. jours. Achievements include research in formaldehyde and dichromates; development of decentralized pharmacy services for tertiary care teaching hospital. Office: Toxicology Litigation Consultants Inc 201 Westbury Ln Georgetown TX 78626 Office Phone: 254-760-9721. Office Fax: 512-868-2306. Business E-Mail: rtisdell@toxicologylitigation.com.

TISE, LARRY EDWARD, historian, cultural organization administrator; b. Winston-Salem, NC, Dec. 6, 1942; s. Russell Edward and Lena Irene (Norman) T.; children: Larry Edward, Nicholas Allen, William Zane. AB, Duke U., 1965, M.Div., 1968; PhD (Ford Found. fellow, 1970, Research Triangle fellow, 1971), U. N.C., 1974. Part-time editor John Fries Blair, Pub., Winston-Salem, 1969-72; teaching fellow history dept. U. N.C., Chapel Hill, 1971, instr., 1972-73; dir. hist. publs. N.C. Bicentennial Com., 1973-74; asst. dir. N.C. Div. Archives and History, Raleigh, 1974-75, dir., 1975-81, N.C. State Hist. Preservation officer, 1975-81; exec. dir. Pa. Hist. and Mus. Commn., 1981-87; Pa. State Hist. Preservation officer, 1981-87; dir. Am. Assn. for State and Local History, Nashville, 1987-89; exec. dir. Benjamin Franklin Nat. Meml., Phila., 1989-97; pres., CEO Internat. Congress of Disting. Awards, 1997—. Adj. prof. grad. sch. fine arts U. Pa., 1984-87; vis. prof. Vanderbilt U., 1988-89, Temple U., 1989-91; mem. Nat. Hist. Publs. and Records Commn., 1982-88; Wilbur and Orville Wright disting. prof. history, East Carolina U., 2005-. Author, co-author writings in fields of archives, hist. preservation, hist. sites and museums, history, society, religion; author: The Southern Experience in the American Revolution, 1978, The Monitor: Its Meaning and Future, 1978, Writing North Carolina History, 1979, A House Not Made with Hands, 1966, The Yadkin Melting Pot: Methodism and the Moravians in the Yadkin Valley, 1750-1850, 1968, Proslavery: The Defense of Slavery in America, 1987, A Book About Children, 1992, The American Counterrevolution, 1998, Keep on Running, 1998, Benjamin Franklin and Women, 2000, Conquering the Sky: The Secret Flights of Wright Brother at Kitty Hawk, 2009, Benjamin Franklin, 2004, Hidden Images in the Wright Brothers Photographs, 1900-1911, 2005; gen. editor: writings in fields of archives, hist. preservation, hist. sites and museums, history, society, religion including Winston-Salem in History, 13 vols, 1976; edit. bd. The Public Historian, 1980-86; editor N.C. Hist. Rev., 1974-81, Pa. Heritage, 1981-87, History News, 1987-89, Franklin Gazette, 1989-97; contbr. articles to books, newsletters, publs. Recipient William R. Davie History award, 1979, Herbert L. Feis award, Am. Hist. Assn., 1989, Benjamin Franklin Nat. Meml. awards 1990, Best New Book in History, Ind. Book Pubs., 1999; Nat. Endowment for the Humanities fellow, 1992-93; faculty fellow NASA-Langley Rsch. Ctr., 2000-03. Mem. Am. Hist. Assn. (various coms.), Orgn. Am. Historians (chmn. coms.), So. Hist. Assn., Am. Assn. State and Local History (mem. coun. and coms.), Nat. Assn. State Archives and Records Adminstrs. (pres. 1980-81), Nat. Conf. State Hist. Preservation Officers (bd. dirs. 1976-79, pres. 1979-81), Nat. Coun. on Pub. History (bd. dirs., exec. com. 1979-83, pres. 1983-85), N.C. Hist. Commn. (sec. 1975-81), N.C. Lit. and Hist. Assn. (sec., treas. 1977-81), Pa. Fedn. Hist. Socs. (sec. 1981-87), Friends of Franklin, Inc. (exec. sec. 1989-97). Methodist. Office Phone: 215-765-1311. E-mail: ltise@attglobal.net.

TISHER, CHARLES CRAIG, nephrologist, educator, former dean; MD, Wash. U., St. Louis, 1961. Resident Barnes Hosp., St. Louis, U. Wash. affiliated Hosps., Seattle; fellow in nephrology U. Wash., Seattle; positions at Walter Reed Hosp. and Walter Reed Army Inst. Rsch., Washington; joined faculty Duke U. Sch. Medicine, 1969; prof. medicine and pathology U. Fla. Coll. Medicine, Gainesville, Fla., 1980—, chief divsn. nephrology, hypertension and transplantation, 1980—87, named Ctrl. Fla. Kidney Ctr. Eminent Scholar Chair in Nephrology, 1989, prof. anatomy and cell biology, sr. assoc. dean, 1998—2002, Folke H. Peterson Disting. Professorship, 1999—, dean, 2002—07, assoc. v.p. program devel., 2007—; dir. Ctr. Clin. Trials Rsch U. Fla. Founding asst. editor Kidney Internat. jour.; chmn. med. adv. board Bioavailability Systems Inc., Cocoa Beach, Fla. Recipient Faculty Rsch. Prize in Clin. Scis., U. Fla., 1985. Mem.: Internat. Soc. Nephrology, Am. Soc. Nephrology (pres. 1990—91, jour. editor 1996—2001, John P. Peters Award 2001). Office: U Fla Divsn Nephrology Box J224 JHMHC Gainesville FL 32610 also: U Fla PO Box 100215 Gainesville FL 32610-0215 Office Phone: 352-273-7508. Business E-Mail: tisher@ufl.edu.*

TISHLER, WILLIAM HENRY, landscape architect, educator; b. Baileys Harbor, Wis., June 22, 1936; s. William John and Mary Viola (Sarter) T.; m. Betsy Lehner, Sept. 23, 1961; children: William Phillip, Robin Elizabeth. BS in Landscape Architecture, U. Wis., 1960; M in Landscape Architecture, Harvard U., 1964. Urban planner City of Milw., 1961-62; mem. faculty dept. landscape architecture U. Wis., Madison, 1964—; assoc. Hugh A Dega & Assocs. (Landscape Archs.), 1964-66; prin. Land Plans Inc. (Land and Hist. Preservation Planning Cons.), Madison, 1966—. Advisor emeritus Nat. Trust for Hist. Preservation; bd. dirs. The Hubbard Ednl. Trust. Author: American Landscape Architecture: Designers and Places, 1989, Midwestern Landscape Architecture, 2000, Door County's Emerald Treasure: A History of Peninsula State Park, 2005, Country Life, 2009; contbr. articles to profl. jours. With C.E., U.S. Army, 1960. Recipient Design Arts Program award NEA, 1981, Hawthorn award Friends of The Clearing, 1997, Outstanding Educator award Coun. Educators in Landscape Architecture, 1998; Attingham (Eng.) Program fellow Soc. Archtl. Historians, 1980; Dumbarton Oaks sr. fellow, 1990. Fellow Am. Soc. Landscape Archs. (Horace Cleve. vis. prof. U. Minn. 1993, nat. merit award 1971, 97, 99, honor award 1980, 89, Wis. chpt. Lifetime Achievement award 2000), Coun. Educators Landscape Arch.; mem. Wis. Acad. Arts, Letters and Scis., Pioneer Am. Soc. (Henry Douglas award), Hist. Madison (hon.), Vernacular Architecture Forum (past pres.), Madison Trust for Hist. Preservation, Alliance for Hist. Landscape Preservation (founder), The Clearing Landscape Inst. (founder, dir.), Phi Kappa Phi, Sigma Lambda Alpha, Gamma Sigma Delta, Sigma Nu. Meth. Office: U Wis Dept Landscape Architecture Madison WI 53706 Home: 2999 Woods Edge Way Madison WI 53711 Business E-Mail: wtishler@wisc.edu.

TISHMAN, DANIEL R., construction executive; b. July 1955; s. John L. and Suzanne Weisberg Tishman; m. Sheryl C. Tishman. BS in Ecology and Planning, Evergreen State Coll., Olympia, Wash.; MS in Environ. Studies, Lesley Coll., Cambridge, Mass. With Tishman Realty and Constrn. Corp., 1990, exec. v.p., head NE ops., 1994; chmn., CEO Tishman Constrn., Interiors and Techs. Corp. Vice chair bd. trustees Natural Resources Def. Coun.; mem. adv. coun. Ctr. Biodiversity and Conservation Am. Mus. Natural History; mem. bd. governing trustees Jackson Labs., Bar Harbor, Maine; chmn. NY divsn. Israel Bonds; mem. exec. com. United Jewish Appeal, NY Bldg. Congress; gov. Real Estate Bd. NY. Recipient Zeckendorf award, LI U. (C.W. Post campus), 2003, Humanitarian award, Albert Einstein Coll. Medicine of Yeshiva U., 2003; named one of 40 Under 40, Crain's NY Bus., 1995. Office: Tishman Constrn Corp 666 Fifth Ave New York NY 10103-0256 Office Phone: 212-399-3600. Office Fax: 212-397-1317.

TISHMAN, LYNN P., psychologist, psychoanalyst; b. Yonkers, NY, Apr. 3, 1951; d. Neal and Olga Petrucci; m. Peter V. Tishman, May 31, 1992; stepchildren: Steven, Linda, Anita. AAS in Acctg., Westchester CC, 1971; BA in Psychology summa cum laude, Hunter Coll., 1993; MSW, LCSW with honors, Hunter Sch. Social Work, 1995; PhD in Clin. Psychology, Columbia U., 2007. Lic. massage therapist Swedish Inst., NY, 1980, cert. biofeedback therapist BCIA, 1985, psychoanalyst, psychotherapist, and rschr., adult and child cert. psychoanalyst Psychoanalytic Inst. Postgrad. Ctr., NYC, 2002. Child devel. specialist and rschr. Pacella Parent Child Ctr., NY Psychoanalytic Inst. Mem.: NASW, APA, NY State Psychol. Assn., Assn. Applied Psychophysiology and Biofeedback, Postgrad. Psychoanalytic Soc. Avocations: running, weightlifting, bicycling, sailing.

TISSUE, MIKE, medical educator, respiratory therapist; b. Garfield, Wash., Aug. 24, 1941; s. Altha Lester and Fern Adeline (Willard) T.; m. Marjorie Lena Atkinson, Feb. 24, 1961 (div. June 1991); children: Sue Tipton, Pam Kromholtz, Paul, Donna Leach; m. Mary Emma Napier, Aug. 24, 1998. AAS (4 degrees) with honors, Spokane CC, Wash., 1985; BS in Respiratory Therapy cum laude, Loma Linda U., Calif., 1987; MS in Respiratory Care, Ga. State U., 1999. Registered cardiovasc. invasive specialist; registered cardiac sonographer; registered respiratory therapist-neonatal pediat. specialist; registered pulmonary function technologist, respiratory care practitioner; diplomate sr. disability analyst. Respiratory intern, NICU therapist Loma Linda (Calif.) U. Med. Ctr., 1985-87; educator, therapist Riyadh (Saudi Arabia) Armed Forces Hosp., 1987-91; head dept. respiratory care Security Forces Hosp., Riyadh, 1991-93; asst. prof., dir. clin. edn. respiratory therapy program Morehead (Ky.) State U., 1993-94; program dir. assoc. degree respiratory therapy Chattahoochee Tech. Coll., Marietta, Ga., 1994—98; clin. instr. Ga. State U., Atlanta, 1999-2001; dir. respiratory therapy program Nat. Inst. Tech., Atlanta, 2001—08. Pres., founder Riyadh Cardiorespiratory Soc., 1988-93; rschr. Loma Linda U., 1987, Riyadh Armed Forces Hosp., 1988; instr. and affil.various heart assns. at various times cons. ARC, Tacoma, 1984, instr. standard and advanced first aid, and CPR, Inland Empire chpt., Spokane, 1975-94; instr. first aid San Bernardino/Redlands Svc. Ctr., Loma Linda, 1985-87, Am. Cmty. Svcs. U.S. Embassy, Riyadh, 1987-93, U.S. Mil. Operation Desert Storm, Riyadh, 1991-93; instr. Freedom From Smoking Clinic Program Am. Lung Assn., Calif., 1985-87, Saudi Arabia, 1987-93, Smyrna, Ga., 1994-96; mem. several coms. Chattahoochee Tech. Coll., 1994-98. Contbr. articles to profl. jours. Bd. dirs. Am. Heart Assn., Spokane, 1976-83, chair fin. com., 1981-83; chair programming and spkrs. bur. Am. Lung Assn., Smyrna, Ga., 1994-98, chmn. bd. dirs., 1995-96; sec. Cobb County Cmty. Coun., Marietta, 1995-96, spkr., 1995, v.p., 1996, pres. 1997; vol. Ga. Internat. Cultural Exch., 1995; registry exam. sr. proctor Cardiovasc. Credentialing Internat./Nat. Bd. Cardiovasc. Technologists, Riyadh, 1987-90; commr. Boy Scouts Am., Spokane, 1973-82. Named Citizen of Day, KGA Radio, Spokane, 1983. Mem. AAUP (legis. com. Atlanta 1995-96), Am. Assn. Respiratory Care (therapist-driven protocol rev. com. 1994, ad hoc com. on patient-driven protocol rev. com. 1996, ad hoc com. for sects. rev. 1995-96, job analysis, neonatal pedit. specialist 2002), Applied Measurement Profls., Alliance of Cardiovasc. Profls., Ga. Soc. Respiratory Care (chmn. cardiopulmonary com. 1994-95, edn. com., smoking and health com.), Phi Delta Kappa (pub. rels. com. 1995-96). Avocations: photography, travel. Home: 1881 Arnold Dr SW Austell GA 30106-2907 Personal E-mail: miketissue@hotmail.com.

TITCOMB, CALDWELL, music and theatre historian; b. Augusta, Maine, Aug. 16, 1926; s. Samuel and Lura Elizabeth (Smith) T. AB summa cum laude, Harvard U., 1947, MA, 1949, PhD, 1952. Univ. organist Brandeis U., Waltham, Mass., 1953-70, dir. undergrad. studies music, 1956-84, curator creative arts, libr., 1961-64, co-chmn. music dept., 1977-84, from instr. to prof. music, 1953-88, prof. emeritus, 1988—. Drama critic Harvard Crimson, 1953-82, Bay State Banner, 1975-2006, This Month on Stage, 1996-99, Totaltheater.com, 2000—,

Kay Bourne Arts Report, 2006-, Theartsfuse.com, 2007-; trustee Charles Playhouse, Boston, 1966-71 Editor: The Art of Fine Words, 1965, The Furies (Lucien Price), 1988; co-editor: Varieties of Black Experience at Harvard, 1986, Blacks at Harvard: A Documentary History of African-American Experience at Harvard and Radcliffe, 1993; contbr. articles to profl. jours., ency.; composer stage and film music scores. Bd. dirs. Cambridge (Mass.) Civic Symphony Orch., 1959-70; exec. bd. Mus. Fine Arts Friends Music, Boston, 1959-65; panelist Mass. Commn. Arts and Humanities, 1981-83; mem. selection com. Theater Hall of Fame, 1980—; juror Elliot Norton awards, 1985—; pres. Boston Theater Critics Assn., 1994—. With U.S. Army, 1944-46, PTO; with Mil. Intelligence Res., 1946-50. Mem. AAUP, Coll. Music Soc., Am. Theatre Critics Assn. (charter), New Eng. Theatre Conf. (adv. coun. 1961-81, coll. fellows 1981—), Am. Guild Organists, Am. Musicol. Soc. (coun. 1965-67), Soc. for Ethnomusicology, Eugene O'Neill Soc., Hist. Brass Soc., Signet Soc., Soc. for Am. Music, Phi Beta Kappa (sec. Mu chpt. Mass. 1984—). Avocations: philology, afro-american history and culture. E-mail: caldwell67@aol.com.

TITLE, GAIL MIGDAL, lawyer; b. Waldenberg, Germany; AB, Wellesley Coll.; JD, U. Calif., Berkeley. Bar: Calif. Mng. ptnr. Katten Muchin Rosenman, LLP, LA. Adj. prof. law Loyola U.; head Nat. Entertainment Litigation Practice; former trustee Ctr. for Law in the Pub. Interest, 1976-96; exec. com., bd. Pub. Counsel Law Ctr. & Constl. Rights Found; co-chair USDC Magistrate Selection Com., ctrl. Calif. Named a Woman of Distinction, Women's Lawyer's Assn. LA; named one of 100 Power Lawyers, Hollywood Reporter, 2007. Mem. ABA (litigation sect., forum com. entertainment), Assn. Bus. Trial Lawyers, State Bar Calif. (standing com. pub. interest law 1976—), Beverly Hills Bar Assn., LA Copyright Soc. (trustee). Office: Katten Muchin Rosenman LLP 2029 Century Park E Los Angeles CA 90067 Office Phone: 310-788-4727. Office Fax: 310-712-8427. Business E-Mail: gail.title@kattenlaw.com.

TITS, ANDRE LEON, electrical engineering educator; b. Verviers, Belgium, Apr. 13, 1951; came to U.S., 1977; s. Jean A. and Violet (Delaruwiere) T. MScEE, U. Calif., 1979, PhDEE, 1980. Asst. prof. dept. elec. engring. U. Md., College Park, 1981-85, assoc. prof., 1985-90, prof., 1990—. Vis. lectr. EECS Dept. U. Calif., Berkeley, 1981, rsch. engr., 1981; vis. prof. Lund Inst. of Tech., Sweden, 1988, INRIA, Le Chesnay, France, 1988, Cath. U. of Louvain, Louvain-la-Neuve, Belgium, 1995, Australian Nat. U., Canberra, Australia, 1995; cons. Harris Semiconductor, 1981-84, SEPI, Inc., 1982-84; lectr. in field. Assoc. editor IEEE Transactions on Automatic Control, 1990-93, Automatica, 1994—, Systems and Control Letters, 1991-95; assoc. editor-at-large IEEE Transactions on Automatic Control, 1995-98; editor: Technical Notes and Correspondance, IEEE Transactions on Automatic Control, 1998—; reviewer numerous jours.; contbr. articles to profl. jours. With Belgian Air Force, 1976-77. Grantee NSF, 1982-2001, Westinghouse, 1988, 89, Shell Devel. Co., 1988, Rockewell Internat., 1988, NASA Ames Univ. Consortium, 1988-90, Sun Microsystems, 1986, Honeywell S & RC, 1985, others. Fellow IEEE; mem. Math. Programming Soc., SIAM, AILg, AIM, Achievements include research on optimization theory and control theory. Office: Dept Electrical and Computer Engring U Md College Park MD 20742-0001

TITTERINGTON, LYNDA CAROL, biology professor, researcher; d. Wesley Prestage Titterington and Carolyn Jean Edwards; m. Albert Ernest Weller, Oct. 8, 2000; 1 child, Eric Albert Weller. PhD, Ohio State U., Columbus, 2007. Biologist Nat. Cancer Inst., NIH, Bethesda, Md., 1984; rsch. scientist Ohio State U., 1985—95; sci. edn. specialist Eisenhower Nat. Clearinghouse, Columbus, 1995—2001; biology instr. Columbus State Cc, 1992—; sci. tchr. Veritas Acad., Worthington, Ohio, 2001—. Cons. Eisenhower Nat. Clearinghouse, Columbus, 2001—03. Contbr. chapters to books, articles TO PROFL. SCI. JOURS. Sci. fair judge Ohio Acad. Sci., 1990—2000; advancements chair Boy Scouts Am. (Cub scouts), Upper Arlington, Ohio, 2008—09. Fellowship, NSF, 1999. Mem.: Nat. Assn. Rsch. Sci. Tchg., Nat. Sci. Tchrs. Assn. Achievements include development of time-lapse image analysis system to observe wound healing in endothelial cells. Office: Columbus State CC 550 E Spring St Columbus OH 43215

TITTL, MATTHEW PAUL, medical technician, educator; b. Mpls., June 25, 1973; s. Karl August and Lorna Ruth Tittl; m. Carrie Lee Johnson, May 23, 1998; children: Edward Matthew, Broderick William. MS in Perfusion, Milw. Sch. Engring., 2002. Cert. clin. perfusionist Am. Bd. Cardiovasc. Perfusion, 2002. Clin. perfusionist Midwest Heart Surgery Inst., Milw., 2002—; asst. prof. clin. perfusion Milw. Sch. Engring., 2003—, clin. program dir., 2006—08. Contbr. scientific papers. Fellow: Am. Soc. Extracorporeal Tech. Lutheran. Avocations: golf, softball, bicycling. Home: 8207 S 42nd St Franklin WI 53132

TITUS, ALICE COSTANDINA (DINA TITUS), United States Representative from Nevada, former state legislator; b. Thomasville, Ga., May 23, 1950; m. Thomas Clayton Wright. AB, Coll. William and Mary, 1970; MA, U. Ga., 1973; PhD, Fla. State U., 1976. Lectr. North Tex. State U., Denton; prof. polit. sci. U. Nev., Las Vegas, 1977—2009; mem. Nev. State Senate from Dist. 7, 1989—2009, minority leader, 1993—2008, mem. legis. commn.; mem. US Congress from 3d Nev. Dist., 2009—. Chmn. Nev. Humanities Com., 1984-86; mem. Eldorado Basin adv. group to Colo. River Commn.; active Gov. Commn. Bicentennial of U.S. Constn.; former mem. Gov. Commn. on Aging. Author: Bombs in the Backyard: Atomic Testing and American Politics, 1986, Battle Born: Federal-State Relations in Nevada during the 20th Century, 1989. Mem. Western Polit. Sci. Assn., Clark County Women's Dem. Club, Amer. Pen Women, Aquavision, PEO. Democrat. Greek Orthodox. Office: US Congress 319 Cannon House Office Bldg Washington DC 20515-2803 also: Dist Office 8215 S Eastern Ave Ste 205 Las Vegas NV 89123 Office Phone: 202-225-3252, 702-387-4941. Office Fax: 202-225-2185, 702-837-0728. Business E-Mail: cond.edinatitus.public@mail.hase.com.*

TITUS, BRUCE EARL, lawyer; b. NYC, June 5, 1942; BA, Coll. William and Mary, 1964, JD, 1971. Bar: Va. 1971, D.C. 1972, Md. 1984. Asst. dir. torts br., civil divsn. U.S. Dept. Justice, 1971-82; mem. Jones, Waldo, Holbrook and McDonough, Washington; ptnr. Venable, Baetjer and Howard, LLP, McLean, Va., 1986—97; prin. Rees, Broome PC, Vienna, Va., 1997—. Exec. editor William & Mary Law Review, 1970-71. Mem. ABA, Va. State Bar, D.C. Bar, Fairfax Bar Assn. (pres. 1999-2000), Md. State Bar, Phi Delta Phi, Omicron Delta Kappa. Office: Rees Broome PC 9th Fl 8133 Leesburg Pike Vienna VA 22182-2706 Office Phone: 703-790-1911.

TITUS, JANET CATHERINE, psychologist, researcher; m. Charles Titus Boudreaux; 1 child, Jonathan. PhD, U. Minn., Twin Cities. Rsch. psychologist Chestnut Health Systems, Normal, Ill., 1997—. Sign lang. interpreter St. Patrick's Ch. Merna, Bloomington, Ill., 2005—. Mem.: Am. Psychol. Assn., Toastmasters Club (treas. 2007). Office: Chestnut Health Sys 448 Wylie Dr Normal IL 61761 Business E-Mail: jtitus@chestnut.org.

TITUS, ROGER WARREN, judge; BA, Johns Hopkins U., 1963; JD, Georgetown U., 1966. Bar: Md. 1966, D.C. 1966, U.S. Dist. Ct. Md. 1966, D.C. Dist. 1966, U.S. Ct. Appeals (4th cir.) 1966, U.S. Supreme Ct. 1970. Ptnr. Titus & Glasgow, Rockville, Md., 1966-88, Venable, Baetjer & Howard, Rockville, 1998—2003; judge U.S. Dist. Ct. for the Dist. of Md., Greenbelt, Md., 2003—. Asst. city atty. City of Rockville, 1966-69, city atty., 1970-82; spl. asst. Md. State Bd. of Law Examiners, 1969-72; adj. prof. law Georgetown U., Washington, 1972-78; mem. inquiry com. Atty. Grievance Commn., Annapolis, Md., 1975-80; mem. Trial Cts. Judicial Nominating Commn. Montgomery County, 1979-91; mem. standing com. on rules of practice and procedure Ct. of Appeals of Md., 1989-2003; mem. Appellate Jud. Nominating Commn., 1991-99 Trustee Suburban Hosp., Inc., Bethesda, Md., 1986-2000, chmn. bd., 1997-2000. Fellow: Am. Acad. Appellate Lawyers, Md. Bar Found. (bd. dirs. 1987—93, v.p. 1990—91, pres. 1991—93), Am. Bar Found., Am. Coll. Trial Lawyers; mem.: ABA (del. 1987—95), Montgomery County Bar Assn. (exec. com. 1983—84), Md. Mcpl. Attys. Assn. (pres. 1975), Am. Judicature Soc. (bd. dirs. 1995—2001), Md. Bar Assn. (sec. 1984—87, pres. 1988—89), Nat. Conf. Bar Pres. (mem. exec. coun. 1990—93). Office: US Dist Ct for Dist of Md 6500 Cherrywood Ln Greenbelt MD 20770

TITUS, VICTOR ALLEN, lawyer; b. Nevada, Mo., Sept. 2, 1956; s. Charles Allen and Viola Mae (Cliffman) T.; m. Laraine Carol Cook, Oct. 13, 1974 (div. Feb. 1982); 1 child, Matthew; m. Deborah Diane Carpenter, Apr. 28, 1984; 1 child, Jacquelynn. BS, BA, Ctrl. Mo. State U., 1978; JD, U. Mo., 1981. Bar: N.Mex. 1981, U.S. Dist. Ct. N.Mex. 1981, Mo. 1982, U.S. Ct. Appeals (10th cir. 1983), U.S. Supreme Ct. 1986, Colo. 1989, Ariz. 1995. Lawyer Jay L. Faurot, P.C., Farmington, N.Mex., 1981-83; ptnr. Faurot & Titus, P.C., Farmington, N.Mex., 1983-85; lawyer, sole proprietor Victor A. Titus, P.C., Farmington, N.Mex., 1985—. Arbitrator in civil disputes Alternative Dispute Resolution-Arbitration; liquor lic. hearing officer City of Farmington, 1989-94. Contbr. articles to profl. jours. Adult Behind Youth, Boys & Girls Club, Farmington, 1987—; mem. hosp. adv. bd. San Juan Regional Med. Ctr., Farmington, 1988-93. Recipient San Juan County Disting. Svc. award N.Mex. Bar Assn., 1984; named one of Best Lawyers in Am., 1995-96, 97—; named Southwest Super Lawyers, 2009. Mem. ATLA, Am., N.Mex. Trial Lawyers (bd. dirs. 1983—, pres. 1993-94), State Bar of N.Mex. (disciplinary bd. 1997—2002, specialization com. 1992-98, legal advt. com. 1990), San Juan County Bar Assn. (pres. 1984), Nat. Assn. Criminal Def. Lawyers (life), Colo. Trial Lawyers. Democrat. Avocation: sports. Office: Victor A Titus PC 2021 E 20th St Farmington NM 87401-2516 Home: 6040 Bayhill Dr Farmington NM 87402-5078 Office Phone: 505-326-6503. Business E-Mail: victor@titusmurphylawfirm.com.

TITZE, INGO ROLAND, physics professor; b. Hirschberg, Silesia, Germany, July 8, 1941; came to U.S. 1955; s. Kurt Herrmann and Marta Emma (Bettermann) T.; m. R. Katherine Pittard, July 19, 1969; children: Karin, Michael, Jason, Gregory BSEE, U. Utah, 1963, MS in Elec. Engring. and Physics, 1965; PhD in Physics, Brigham Young U., 1972. Rsch. engr. N. Am. Aviation, Tulsa, 1965-66, Boeing Co., Seattle, 1968-70; lectr. Calif. State Poly. U., Pomona, 1973-74; asst. prof. U. Petroleum and Minerals Dhahran, Saudi Arabia, 1974-76, Gallaudet Coll., Washington, 1976-79; disting. prof. speech sci. and voice U. Iowa, Iowa City, 1979—. Cons. Bell Labs., Murray Hill, N.J., 1977-78; exec. dir. Wilbur James Gould Voice Rsch. Ctr., Denver Ctr. Performing Arts, 1983—; pres. Voice Cons. Inc., 1985—; panelist, site visitor NRC-NAS, 1984—; regular cons. divsn. rsch. grants NIH, 1986—; chmn. task force on voice Nat. Inst. Deafness and Other Comm. Disorders, 1989; adj. prof. Westminster Choir Coll., Princeton, N.J., 1989-94; dir. Nat. Ctr. for Voice and Speech, 1990—. Author: Principles of Voice Production, 1993, The Myoelastic Aerodynamic Theory of Phonation, 2006; editor: Vocal Fold Physiology: Biomechanics, Acoustics and Phonatory Control, 1985, Vocal Fold Physiology: Frontiers in Basic Science, 1992; assoc. editor Jour. of Voice; contbr. articles to profl. jours. Adv. bd. Voice Found., N.Y.C., 1980—; young men's pres. Latter Day Saints Ch. and Boy Scouts Am., Iowa City, 1982— Jacob Javits Neurosci. Investigator grantee NIH, 1984; recipient William and Harriot Gould Found. award, 1983, Claude Pepper award, 1989, Quintant award Voice Found.; 1990, U. Iowa Regents award, 1995; ASHA fellow, 1992, Silver medal Acoustical Soc. America, 2007. Fellow Acoustical Soc. Am. (tech. coun., awards com. 1989, Silver medal 2007), Am. Laryngological Assn. (hon.; award 1996); mem. Am. Speech-Hearing-Lang. Assn., Nat. Assn. Tchrs. Singing (rsch. coun. 1977—, editl. bd. 1986—), Internat. Assn. Rsch. Singing (dir. publs. 1982—), Am. Assn. Phonetic Sics., Internat. Assn. Logopedics and Phoniatrics, Collegium Medicorium Teatri. Republican. Avocations: singing, tennis, home building. Office: Nat Ctr for Voice & Speech Univ of Iowa 330 Wjshc Iowa City IA 52242-1012 Home: 1551 Larimer St No 2301 Denver CO 80202

TITZMAN, DONNA M., energy executive; BBA in Acctg., U. Tex. CPA. Acct. natural gas liquids Valero Energy Corp., San Antonio, 1986—89, various positions with fin. dept., 1989, v.p., treas., 1999—. Office: Valero Energy Corpn PO Box 696000 San Antonio TX 78269-6000*

TIWARI, ATUL, chemist, researcher; b. Itawah, Uttar Pradesh, India, Jan. 28, 1975; s. Devaki Nandan and Savitri Devi Tiwari; m. Anupama Chaturvedi, May 4, 2005. MSc in Chemistry, Kanpur U., 1997; PhD, Macromolecular Rsch. Ctr., 2003. Polymer Scientist R.D.university Jabalpur, 2003. Rsch. fellow Macromolecular Rsch. Ctr., Jabalpur, Madhya Pradesh, India, 1999—2004; asst. rschr. Hawaii Corrosion Lab, Honolulu, 2005—. Postdoctoral rschr. U. Hawaii, Honolulu, 2005—. Fellow, Def. Rsch. Devel. Orgn., 1999, Dept. Sci. and Tech., India, 2001, Hawaii Corrosion Lab., 2004; rsch. assoc., Coun. for Sci. and Indsl. Rsch., India, 2004. Mem.: Materials Rsch. Soc., Electron Microscope Soc. India (life), Soc. Polymer Sci. India (life). Achievements include research in high performance polymers for advance applications. Office: Hawaii Corrosion Lab U Hawaii 2540 Doles St Holmes Hall Rm 302 Honolulu HI 96822 Home: Rainbow Pl 2102 2754 Kuilei St Honolulu HI 96826 Office Fax: 808-956-2373. Personal E-mail: atulmrc@yahoo.com. Business E-Mail: tiwari@hawaii.edu.

TIWARI, BINOD, civil engineer; arrived in U.S., 2003; s. Bhoj Raj and Ratna Kumari Tiwari; m. Manisha Khanal, May 5, 1995. B Engring., Tribhuwan U., 1992; MSc, Niigata U., 2000, PhD, 2003. Head civil engring. divsn. MTEC Cons., Kathmandu, Nepal, 1992—93; transp. engr. HMG/Nepal, Dept. Rds., Kathmandu, 1993—2004; vis. faculty Va. Poly. Inst. and State U., Blacksburg, 2003—. GIS analyst, sys. engr. Nippon Koel Co., Ltd., Tokyo, 2002—03; vis. rsch. fellow Niigata U., 2003—04. Author: (innovative rsch. publ.) Soil Slope Stability and Stabilization (Best Paper award, 2004); chief editor: Jour. Nepal Geotech. Soc., 2002—05, ad hoc reviewer: Jour. Japan Landslide Soc., 2002—04. Recipient Monbusho scholarship for Japanese lang. and rsch., Ministry of Edn., Japan, 1997—98, Monbusho scholarship for M.Sc. study, 1998—2000, Monbusho scholarship for PhD. study, 2000—03, Geotech. Rsch. grant, Sabo Tech. Ctr., Japan, 2003—04, Best Paper award, IPL Workshop on Landslide Mgmt., 2004, Presley Yr. Top prize, Tribhuwan U., 1989, 1991. Mem.: ASCE (assoc.), Internat. Soc. for Soil Mechanics and Geotech. Engring. (corr.), Nepal Geotech. Soc. (corr.; exec. 2002—, chief editor jour. 2002—05), Japan Geotech. Soc. (corr.), Japan Landslide Soc. (corr.; soil strength for reactivated landslides 2002—04, commentator children landslide conf. 2003, ad hoc reviewer jour. 2002—04), Nepal Landslide Soc. (corr.), Nepal Geol. Soc. (corr.), Nepal Engr.'s Assn. (corr.), Nepalese Students' Assn. in Japan (corr.; pres. 2001—02), Niigata Nepal Assn. (corr.; pres. 2001—04), Internat. Students' Assn. in Niigata U. (corr.; pres. 2001—02). Achievements include invention of Residual Shear Strength Estimation Based on Mineralogy. Avocations: travel, writing, soccer, music. Office: Civil Environ Engring Dept Calif State Univ Fullerton CA Home: 9 Sycamore Ln Buena Park CA 90621 Office Phone: 714-278-3968. Office Fax: 714-278-3016; Home Fax: 714-228-9720. Personal E-mail: binodtiwari@gmail.com. Business E-Mail: btiwari@fullerton.edu.

TIWARI, SANDIP, electrical and computer engineering educator; s. Anandilal and Lakshmi Tiwari; m. Mari Lee Wallner; children: Nachiketa Wallner, Kunal Landon. PhD, Cornell U., Ithaca, NY, 1980. Sr. mem. tech. staff MA/COM Inc., Burlington, Mass., 1980—83; rsch. staff mem., mgr. exploratory devices and modeling IBM Rsch. Ctr., Yorktown Heights, NY, 1983—99; prof. elec. and computer engring. Cornell U., 1999—2005, Charles N. Mellowes prof. engring., 2005—. Tech. activity bd. Samsung Electronics, Anvik Corp., Hawthorne, NY, 2000—; adv. bd. DANCHIP - Tech. U. Denmark, Beginning, 2003—; tech. adv. bd. ADC Inc., Lansing, NY, 2004—, Samsung Electronics, 2007—; nat. adv. com. EECS Dept., U. Mich., Ann Arbor, 2004—; adv. bd. Wireless Integrated Microsys. Engring. Rsch. Ctr., Ann Arbor, 2004—, Nanoscale Informal Sci. Edn. Network, Boston, 2004—. Recipient Young Scientist award, Internat. Symposium on GaAs & Related Compounds, 1991, Disting. Alumnus award, Indian Inst. Tech., Kanpur, 2003, Cledo Brunetti award, IEEE, 2007; fellow, 1994, Am. Phys. Soc., 1998. Achievements include invention of nanocrystal memory; research in explanation of surface recombination in compound semiconductor transistors; refractory contacts for compound semiconductors; ultra-low threshold current quantum wire lasers; patents for 32 issued patents. Office: Cornell U 410 Phillips Hall Ithaca NY 14853

TIWARI, TEJPRATAP S. P., epidemiologist; s. Suruj and Rukmin Persaud; m. Rohini Narain, Dec. 19, 1982; 1 child, Ashwini. MBBS, Gandhi Med. Coll., Bhopal, India, 1980; MD, Baroda Med. Coll., India, 1987. Cert. Med. Coun., Guyana, 1982. Govt. med. officer Ministry of Health, Georgetown, Guyana, 1982—84, dep. dir., Medex tng. program, 1983—84, nat. epidemiologist, 1992—99, dir., communicable diseases, 1993—99; epidemic intelligence svc. officer Ctrs. Disease Control and Prevention, Atlanta, 1999—2001, med. epidemiologist, 2001—. Contbr. articles to numerous clin. jours., chapters to books. Recipient Honor award, Nat. Ctrs. Infectious Diseases, CDC, 2002, Spl. Accomplishment award, Nat. Immunization Program, 2005. Mem.: EIS Alumni Assn., Am. Soc. Microbiology. Hindu. Home: 4595 Parkview Walk Dr Lilburn GA 30047 Office: Ctrs Disease Control and Preventive 1600 Clifton Rd NE Atlanta GA 30333 Office Fax: 404-639-8616. Personal E-mail: tiwart@yahoo.com. Business E-Mail: tit2@cdc.gov.

TJARKS, MARK DAMON, playwright, literature and language professor; s. Henry B. Tjarks and Joy Jobson; m. Denise Marie Weiss; children: Kira Ann Watanabe, Aysha Rae Weiss, Maia Dawne, Noah Elijah. BA in English, U. Pa., Phila., 1986; MA in Profl. Writing, U. Southern Calif., LA, 1988; PhD in English, U. Hawaii, Honolulu, 2005. Lectr. Kauai CC, Lihue, Hawaii, 1990—91; assoc. prof. English Hawaii Pacific U., Honolulu, 1992—. Author: (play) Imposter, Off Key, Evil at the Post Office, Ventriloquists (Atherton Found. grant, 2004), The Very Old Mango Man (Kumu Kahua Playwriting Contest Resident prize, 2002). Mem.: Soc. Cinema & Media Studies. Avocation: music. Office: Hawaii Pacific Univ 1188 Fort St Mall Honolulu HI 96813 Personal E-mail: mtjarks@hpu.edu. Business E-Mail: mtjarks@campus.hpu.edu.

TJELTVEIT, ALAN C., psychology professor; b. Red Lodge, Mont., Nov. 1, 1954; s. Otis Alvin and Margaret H. Tjeltveit; m. Maria W. E. Eddy; children: William D., Anna M. PhD, Grad. Sch. Psychology, Fuller Theol. Sem., Pasadena, Calif., 1984. Lic. in psychology Pa., 1990. Asst. prof. psychology Muhlenberg Coll., Allentown, Pa., 1989—95, assoc. prof. psychology, 1995—2003, prof. psychology, 2003—. Group and family therapist Abbott Northwestern Hosp., Mpls., 1984—89; part-time asst. prof. psychology St. Olaf Coll., Northfield, Minn., 1985—88; clin. asst. prof. psychology U. Minn., Mpls., 1987—89; psychotherapist Family and Counseling Svcs. Lehigh Valley, Allentown, 1996—99. Author: (book) Ethics and Values in Psychotherapy; contbr. articles to profl. jours., chapters to books. Office: Muhlenberg Coll Psychology Dept 2400 W Chew St Allentown PA 18104 Office Fax: 484-664-5627. Business E-Mail: tjelt@muhlenberg.edu.

TJIAN, ROBERT TSE NAN, biochemistry educator, medical institution administrator; b. Hong Kong, Sept. 22, 1949; BA in Biochemistry, U. Calif., Berkeley, 1972; PhD in Biochemistry and Molecular Biology, Harvard U., 1976. Staff investigator molecular virology Cold Spring Harbor Lab., NY, 1976-79; asst. prof. biochemistry U. Calif., Berkeley, 1979—82, prof. biochemistry, 1982—, prof. molecular & cell biology. Investigator Howard Hughes Med. Inst., Chevy Chase, Md., 1987—, pres., 2009—; co-founder Tularik, Inc., Calif., 1991; adj. prof. biochemistry & biophysics U. Calif., San Francisco. Contbr. articles to profl. jours. Recipient Pfizer award for enzymology, 1983, Cancer Rsch. award, Milken Family Med. Found., 1988, Lewis S. Rosenstiel award for disting. work in basic med. sci., Brandeis U., 1995, Alfred P. Sloan Jr. prize, GM Cancer Rsch. Found., 1999, Louisa Gross Horwitz prize, Columbia U., 1999, MERIT award, Nat. Cancer Inst., 2004; named Calif. Scientist of Yr., 1994. Mem.: NAS (Monsanto award for molecular biology 1991), Academia Sinica (Taiwan), Am. Philos. Soc., Am. Acad. Arts & Scis. Office: U Calif Dept Molecular & Cell Biology Dept 142 LSA #3200 Berkeley CA 94720-3204 also: Howard Hughes Med Inst 4000 Jones Bridge Rd Chevy Chase MD 20815-6789 Office Phone: 510-642-8258, 301-215-8500. Office Fax: 510-642-0884. Business E-Mail: jmlim@berkeley.edu.*

TJOFLAT, GERALD BARD, federal judge; b. Pitts., Dec. 6, 1929; s. Gerald Benjamin and Sarita (Romero-Hermoso) Tjoflat; m. Sarah Marie Pfohl, July 27, 1957 (dec.); children: Gerald Bard, Marie Elizabeth; m. Marcia Penman Parker, Feb. 21, 1998. Student, U. Va., 1947—50, U. Cin., 1950—52; LLB, Duke U., 1957; DCL (hon.), Jacksonville U., 1978; LLD (hon.), William Mitchell Coll., 2003. Bar: Fla. 1957. Pvt. practice, Jacksonville, Fla., 1957—68; judge 4th Jud. Cir. Ct., Fla., 1968—70, US Dist. Ct. Mid. Dist., Jacksonville, 1970—75, US Ct. Appeals (5th cir.), Jacksonville, 1975—81, US Ct. Appeals (11th cir.), Jacksonville, 1981—, chief judge, 1989—96. Mem. Adv. Corrections Coun. U.S., 1975—87, Jud. Conf. U.S., 1989—96, mem. com. adminstrn. probation sys., 1972—87, chmn., 1978—87; mem. Fed. Jud. Ct. Com. on Sentencing, Probation and Pretrial Svcs., 1988—90; U.S. del. 6th and 7th UN Congress for Prevention of Crime and Treatment of Offenders. Hon. life mem., bd. visitors Duke U. Law Sch., 2000; pres. North Fla. coun. Boy Scouts Am., 1976—85, 2000—01, chmn., 1985—90; trustee Jacksonville Marine Inst., 1976—90, Episc. H.S.,

Jacksonville, 1975—90; mem. vestry St. Johns Cathedral, Jacksonville, 1969—71, 1973—75, 1977—79, 1981—83, 1985—87, 1993, 1995—96, sr. warden, 1975, 1983, 1987, 1991, 1992. With US Army, 1953—55. Recipient Merit award, Duke U., 1990, Fordham-Stein prize, 1996. Mem.: ABA, Am. Judicature Soc., Am. Law Inst., Fla. Bar Assn. Episcopalian. Office: US Courthouse 300 N Hogan St Ste 14-200 Jacksonville FL 32202-4257 Office Phone: 904-301-6570.*

TKAC, JOHN ANTHONY, language educator; b. Garfield Heights, Ohio, Aug. 15, 1981; s. John Thomas and Sandra Marie Tkac. MA in Spanish, Bowling Green State U., Ohio, 2005. Instr. Spanish Bowling Green State U., 2005—06; lectr. Spanish James Madison U., Harrisonburg, Va., 2006—. Avocations: reading, racquetball, travel. Office: James Madison Univ MSC 1802 Harrisonburg VA 22807

TKACH, DIANNE, educator; MS, LI U., NY, 1988. Cert. K-12 tech. Vt., 2007; K-12 libr. educator Vt., 1998. Libr. tech. devel. specialist Burlington Sch. Dist., Vt.; prof. children's young adult lit. U. Vt., Burlington, 2002—. Peer reviewer Dept. Edn., Montpelier, Vt., 2007—. Recipient Burlington Edn. Assn. Hall of Fame, 2007. Mem.: NEA. Russian Orthodox. Avocations: reading, rowing, walking, piano, camping.

TKACHEV, SERGEY NIKOLAYEVICH, geophysicist; b. Izmail, Odessa Region, Ukraine, July 19, 1964; arrived in US, 1994; s. Nikolay Yefimovich and Liliya Ivanovna Tkachev; m. Maria Sarah Simmons, June 19, 1999. MS in Physics, Moscow State U., Russia, 1991; MS in Geology, U. Ill., Urbana, 1997; PhD in Geology and Geophysics, U. Hawaii, Honolulu, 2005. Rsch. physicist Inst. Exptl. Mineralogy Russian Acad. Scis., Chernogolovka, Russia, 1991—2001; rsch. asst. dept. geology U. Ill., Urbana, 1994—96, tchg. asst., 1996—97; rsch. scientist Hawaii Inst. Geophysics and Planetology, Honolulu, 1997—98; rsch. asst. dept. geology and geophysics U. Hawaii, 1998—99, tchg. asst., 2000, rsch. asst., 2000—05; postdoctoral rschr. dept. physics Colo. State U., Fort Collins, 2005—06; postdoctoral assoc. Geophys. Lab., Carnegie Instn., Washington, 2006—; postdoc. dept. physics and astronomy U. Nev., Las Vegas, 2007—. Contbr. scientific papers, articles to profl. jours. Guard platoon sgt. Soviet Air Forces, 1982—84. Recipient Tuition Waiver award, Dean Grad. Divsn. U. Hawaii, 1999; J. Watumull Merit scholar, Dept. Geology and Geophysics U. Hawaii, 2002—03. Mem.: Am. Geophys. Union. Achievements include first to characterize elastic moduli of the novel bulk superhard cubic BC2N phase (the hardest crystalline material after Diamond) by Brillouin scattering; research in situ Brillouin spectroscopic study of a pressure-induced apparent second order transition in a Silicate glass; Brillouin scattering study of pentane at high pressure; new experimental data on ice VI, ice VII and liquid water phase boundaries; characterization of current nonlinearity in semiconductors in weak electric fields; characterization of elastic properties of nc-TiN/a-Si3N4 nanocomposites films by surface Brillouin scattering; micro-Raman spectroscopy and X-ray diffraction studies of atomic-layer-deposited ZrO2 and HfO2 thin films; elastic and structural properties of Alkaline-Calcium Silica Hydrogels; hydrated and anhydrous Na2O-2SiO2 liquid and also glass to 8 GPa using Brillouin scattering; Characterization of Elastic Properties of Superhard Amorphous Carbon Pressure-Synthesized from C60 by Surface Brillouin Scattering; Brillouin spectroscopy studies of surface modes in thin-film Si3N4 on GaAs; determination of sound velocity and attenuation in stable and metastable liquid water to 1.2 GPa by Brillouin spectroscopy. Avocations: racquetball, tennis, hiking, swimming, camping. Home: 12053 Cherokee Park Rd Livermore CO 80536 Business E-Mail: stkachev@soest.hawaii.edu.

TKACHEVA, OLESYA, political scientist; d. Anatoliy Tkachev and Iraida Tkacheva. BA, CUNY, 2001; attending, U. Mich., Ann Arbor, 2002—, MA, 2006. Adminstrv. asst. Leopold Schepp Found., NYC, 1999—2002; rsch. asst. Russell Sage Found., NYC. Contbr. articles to numerous profl. jours. Travel grant, Herbert Hoover Presdl. Libr., 1998. Mem.: Golden Key, Phi Beta Kappa. Avocations: tennis, foreign languages. Home: 2146 81st St Brooklyn NY 11214 Office: Polit Sci Dept Univ Mich 5700 Haven Hall 505 S State St Ann Arbor MI 48109 Business E-Mail: otkachev@umich.edu.

TKACHUK, ANDREI, engineering company executive; b. Chernovtsi, Ukraine, Nov. 18, 1972; s. Vasili and Lyudmila Tkachuk; m. Christina Filley. BS in Physics, No. Ill. U., DeKalb, 1995, MS in Physics, 1997; PhD in Materials Sci. and Engring., U. Ill. Urban-Champaign, 2002. Postdoc. appointment Argonne Nat. Lab., Calif., 2002—05; mgr. nano engrng. Xradia, Inc, Concord, Calif., 2005—. Grad. Rsch. fellowship, Argonne Nat. Lab, 1995—97. Office: Xradia 5052 Comml Cir Concord CA 94520 Business E-Mail: atkachuk@xradia.com.

TKACHUK, KEITH, professional hockey player; b. Melrose, Mass., Mar. 28, 1972; m. Chantel Oster; children: Matthew, Braeden, Taryn. Attended, Boston U., 1990—91. Left wing Winnipeg Jets, 1992—96, Phoenix Coyotes (formerly Winnipeg Jets), 1992—2001, St. Louis Blues, 2001—07, 2007—, Atlanta Thrashers, 2007. Mem. Team USA, World Cup of Hockey, 1996, 2004, USA Olympic Hockey Team, Nagano, Japan, 1998, Salt Lake City, 2002, Torino, Italy, 06. Named NHL Second Team All-Star, 1995, 1998; named to NHL All-Star Game, 1997—99, 2004, 2009. Achievements include being a member of World Cup Champion Team USA, 1996; being a member of silver medal winning USA Hockey Team, Salt Lake City Olympics, 2002. Office: St Louis Blues Hockey Club Scottrade Ctr 1401 Clark Ave Saint Louis MO 63103*

TLAPA, RICHARD JOSEPH, retired priest; b. Cicero, Ill., Feb. 20, 1920; s. Francis Richard Tlapa and Josephine Rose Burianek. BA, U. St. Mary of the Lake, Mundelein, Ill., 1941, MA, 1944; PhD, Calif. Christian U., LA, 1976, Columbia U., San Rafael, Calif., 1986. Ordained priest 1944; lic. radiotelephone and ship radar FCC. Pastoral adminstrn. Archdiocese of Chgo., 1944—89; ret., 1989. Tech. cons. Maritime Electronics, Inc., Chgo., 1955—85; assoc. prodr. Acta Films, Chgo., 1957—60. Author: The New Apostles, 1977, The Priest in the Pew, 1986, Jubilate Deo, 1989; contbr. articles to religious and secular publs. Mem.: Am. Radio Relay League (life), Internat. Soc. for Philos. Enquery (life; diplomate), Mensa (life). Avocations: electronics, Latin-Greek biblical research, photography. Home: 6350 Taft St Merrillville IN 46410

TO, KENNETH KIN WAH, medical educator, researcher; BPharm, Sch. Pharmacy, Chinese U. Hong Kong, 1997, PhD, 2001. Registered pharmacist Pharmacy and Poisons Bd., Hong Kong, 1997. Rsch. assoc. dept. chemistry Chinese U. Hong Kong, 2001—01, asst. prof. Sch. Pharmacy, 2008—; postdoc. fellow Johns Hopkins U., Balt., 2002—03; cancer rsch. tng. fellow Nat. Cancer Inst., Bethesda, Md., 2003—08. Achievements include patents for synergistic combination of demethylcantharidin, a constituent from traditional Chinese medicine, with platinum anticancer agents in human cancers; discovery of the novel mechanisms of antitumor activity of a novel series of platinum-traditional Chinese medicine compounds; research in biochemical difference between HIF1a and HIF2a about their roles in genetic and chromosomal instability; regulation of the multidrug resistance gene by DNA methylation; regulation of multidrug resistance gene ABCG2 by permissive histone modification marks in drug resistant human cancer cells.

TO, STEPHEN EDWARD, editor, writer; b. NYC, July 5, 1963; s. Cho To and Lilly Fong Yee. BA in Biology, Purchase Coll., SUNY, 1985; MBA, Fordham U. Technician specialist Cornell U. Med. Coll., NYC, 1986—88; rsch. biologist Rockefeller U., NYC, 1988—97; mng. med. editor, writer IntraMed Ednl. Group, NYC, 1999—2006, clin. regulatory writer; with Hoffmann-La Roche, Inc., Nutley, NJ, 2006—. Freelance editor Nature Am., NYC, 1998—99. Mem.: Drug Info. Assn., Am. Med. Writers Assn. Avocations: sailing, travel. Home: 1539 Lexington Ave Apt 3E New York NY 10029 Office: Hoffmann-La Roche Inc PDR Drug Reg Affairs 340 Kingsland St Nutley NJ 07110 Personal E-mail: sto1967@aol.com. Business E-Mail: stephen.to@roche.com.

TOAL, JAMES FRANCIS, academic administrator; b. NYC, June 7, 1932; s. John Joseph and Catherine (Whyte) T. MA, St. John's U., 1966; PhD, Fordham U., 1976. Cert. elem. tchr., N.Y. cert. supt., adminstrn. and supervision, English 7-12. Athletic dir., tchr. English St. Francis Prep. High Sch., NYC, 1957-60; tchr. Bishop Ford High Sch., NYC, 1960-66, chmn. dept. English; prin. St. Francis Central Summer High Sch., NYC, 1966-73, St. Francis Prep. High Sch., NYC, 1966-73; exec. v.p., assoc. prof. dept. edn. adminstrn. and supervision Grad. Sch. St. Bonaventure U., NY, 1976-83; pres., prof. Quincy U., Ill., 1983-97; v.p. Siena Coll., Loudonville, NY, 1997—; also bd. trustees. Mem. Springfield Diocesan Bd. of Edn., Provincial Bd. of Edn., Franciscan Friars of Chgo. and St. Louis. Trustee Siena Coll., Loudonville, N.Y., 1977-83; bd. advisors Jamestown Community Coll., Olean, N.Y., 1979-83; bd. dirs. Am. Cancer Soc., Olean, 1981-83; mem. Mental Health Assn., 1981-83; mem. state legis. com. Commn. of Ind. Colls. and Univs., Albany. N.Y., 1980-83; mem. bd. trustees Padua Franciscan High Sch. Grantee Colgate U., 1967; grantee SUNY-Plattsburg, 1968, St. Bonaventure U., 1980 Mem. Am. Coun. on Edn., Associated Colls. of Ill., Ill. Bus. and Edn. Forum, Assn. of Governing Bds., West Ctrl. Ill. Ednl. Telecomm. Corp. (bd. dirs. exec. com., fin. com., pers. com.), Fedn. Ind. Ill. Colls. and Univs. (pub. rels. com.), Mid. States Accrediting Assn. (assoc., evaluation team for higher edn.), Nat. Assn. Secondary Sch. Prins., North Ctrl. Accrediting Assn. (evaluation team for higher edn., chair evaluation team 1986—), Soc. Coll. and U. Planning, Quincy C. of C. (transp. com. 1985-96, computer com. 1996—), Rotary, Univ. Club, KC, Phi Delta Kappa. Office: Siena Coll Office of VP Loudon Rd Loudonville NY 12211

TOAL, JEAN HOEFER, state supreme court chief justice; b. Columbia, SC, Aug. 11, 1943; d. Herbert W. and Lilla (Farrell) Hoefer; m. William Thomas Toal; children: Jean Toal Eisen, Lilla Toal Mandsager. BA in Philosophy, Agnes Scott Coll., 1965; JD, U. S.C., 1968; LHD (hon.), Coll. Charleston, 1990; LLD (hon.), Columbia Coll., 1992, The Citadel, 1999, Francis Marion U., 1999, U. S.C., 2000, Charleston Sch. Law, 2007, Columbia Coll., 2008. Bar: S.C. Assoc. Haynsworth, Perry, Bryant, Marion & Johnstone, 1968—70; ptnr. Belser, Baker, Barwick, Ravenel, Toal & Bender, Columbia, 1970—88; assoc. justice S.C. Supreme Ct., Columbia, 1988—2000, chief justice, 2000—, Converse Coll., 2008. Mem. S.C. Human Affairs Commn., 1972-74; mem. S.C. Ho. of Reps., 1975-88, chmn. house rules com., constitutional laws subcom. house judiciary com.; mem. parish coun. and lector St. Joseph's Cath. Ch.; chair S.C. Juvenile Justice Task Force, 1992-94; chair S.C. Rhodes Scholar Selection Com., 1994; bd. dirs. Nat. Ctr. State Cts., 2005-, chair, 2007-2008; pres. Conf. Chief Justices, 2007-08. Mng. editor S.C. Law Rev., 1967—68. Bd. visitors Clemson U., 1978; trustee Columbia Mus. Art, 1980-85; bd. trustees Agnes Scott Coll., 1996—. Recipient Disting. Svc. award, S.C. Mcpl. Assn., 1980, U. Notre Dame award, 1991, Algernon Sydney Sullivan award, U. S.C., 1991, Agnes Scott Coll. Outstanding Alumna award, 1991, John W. Williams award, Richland County Bar Assn., 1995, Jean Galloway Bissell award, S.C. Women Lawyers Assn., 1995, Margaret Brent Women Lawyers of Achievement award, 2004; named Outstanding Legislator of Yr., Greenville News, 1976, Woman of Yr., U. S.C. Mortar Bd., 1989; named one of Top 25 Doers, Dreamers & Drivers, Govt. Tech. Mag., 2002. Mem. ABA, S.C. Women Lawyers Assn., S.C. Bar Assn., John Belton O'Neall Inn of Ct., Phi Beta Kappa, Mortar Bd., Order of the Coif Office: Supreme Ct SC PO Box 11330 Columbia SC 29211-2456 Business E-Mail: jtoal@sccourts.org.

TOAY, THELMA M., columnist, poet; b. Anamosa, Iowa, Feb. 22, 1915; d. Frank Leroy and Edna May Stoughton; m. John S. Toay; 3 children. Student, St. Lukes Sch. Nursing, Davenport, IA, 1933, Highland Classes Coll., 1966—67; AA in Journalism, N.E. Iowa C.C., Peosta, 1995—97; student, U. Iowa, 2001—03. Contbr. newspapers, Freeport, Ill., 1962—; contbr. Julien's Jour., Dubuque, Iowa, 1995—. Author: Bittersweet, 1979, Places for the Heart - Profiles of Life, 2001. Avocations: theater, music, reading, flower gardening.

TOBACMAN, JOANNE KRAMER, medical educator, researcher; b. Cleve., June 26, 1950; d. Sidney Joseph and Ruth Siebert Kramer; m. Larry Steven Tobacman, June 25, 1972; children: Jeremy Bruce, Jessica Lee, Benjamin David. AB, Harvard U., Cambridge, Mass., 1972; MD, Case Western Res. Sch. Medicine, Cleve., 1976. Diplomate Am. Bd. Internal Medicine, 1991. Med. dir. GEICO, Chevy Chase, Md., 1984—86; asst. prof. internal medicine U. Iowa, Iowa City, 1992—2003; assoc. prof. clin. medicine U. Ill., Chgo., 2003—. Interviewer Harvard U. Schs. and Scholarships Com., Chgo., 2005—08. Mem.: Am. Soc. Biochemistry and Molecular Biology, Am. Physiol. Soc., Am. Gastroent. Assn., Am. Assn. Cancer Rsch. Jewish. Achievements include patents for ELISA for BCL10. Avocations: reading, travel, music, puzzles.

TOBE, BARBARA GAINES, information technology executive; d. Gartrell Jerome and Rosa Lee Gaines; m. Gerome Tobe; children: Erika Monique, Alexis Stephanie. BS, Howard U., DC, 1967. Cert. sys. profl. 1985. Physicist Vitro Labs., Silver Spring, Md., 1967—68; programmer, analyst Control Data Corp., Rockville, Md., 1969—72; computer systems analyst Dept. Health, Edn. & Welfare, DC, 1972—80; computer specialist Nat. Weather Svc., Silver Spring, 1980—2002, info. tech. leader, 2002—. NOAA sch. visitation & Saturday acad. lectr. Nat. Weather Svc., 1980—2000, student intern coord., 1980—2007, EEO coord., 1993—96. Sec. 16th St. Heights Civic Assn., DC, 1996—2002. Recipient EEO Essay Contest Coord. award, NOAA EEO Office, 1996, Adminstr. award, Dept. Commerce/NOAA, 1997, Sustained Superior Performance awards, Dept. Commerce, NOAA. Episc. Achievements include design, development and implementation of the replacement primary and backup telecommunication centers; monitoring and supervising in the design and development of a case tracking system; development of an event tabulation program for a submarine system. Avocations: ballroom dancing, travel, genealogy, movies, reading. Office: National Weather Svc 1325 East West Hwy Silver Spring MD 20910 Personal E-mail: bgwtobe@aol.com.

TOBE, STEPHEN SOLOMON, zoology educator; b. Niagara-on-the-Lake, Ont., Can., Oct. 11, 1944; s. John Harold and Rose T. (Bolter) T.; m. Martha Reller. BSc, Queen's U., Kingston, Ont., 1967; MSc, York U., Toronto, Ont., 1969; PhD, McGill U., Montreal, Que., Can., 1972. Rsch. fellow U. Sussex, Eng., 1972-74; asst. prof. U. Toronto, 1974-78, assoc. prof., 1974-78, prof., 1982—, assoc. dean scis., faculty arts and sci., 1988-93, vice dean faculty arts and sci., 1995-96. Vis. prof. U. Calif., Berkeley, 1981, Nat. U. Singapore, 1987, 1993-94, U. Hawaii, 1988; mem. animal biology grant selection com. Natural Scis. and Engring. Rsch. Coun. Can., 1986-89, chair, 1988-89; lectr. Internat. Congress Entomology, Vancouver, B.C., Can., 1988; cons. in hydroponics. Editor Insect Biochemistry, 1987; mem. editl. bd. Jour. Insect Physiology, 1980—, Physiol. Entomology, 1985—, Life Scis. Advances, 1987—, Gen. and Comparative Endocrinology, 1995—; contbr. chpts. to books and articles to profl. jours. Recipient Pickford medal in comparative endocrinology, 1993; E.W.R. Steacie fellow Natural Scis. and Engring. Rsch. Coun. Can., 1982-84, C. Gordon Hewitt, 1982, Gold medal, Entomol. Soc. Can., 1990. Fellow Royal Soc. Can., Royal Entomol. Soc., Soc. Exptl. Biology. Avocations: amater radio, gardening, hydroponics. Home: PO Box 695 Virgil ON Canada L0S 1T0 Office: U Toronto Dept Cell and Systems Biology 25 Harbord St Toronto ON Canada M5S 3G5 Business E-Mail: stephen.tobe@utoronto.ca.

TOBEN, BRADLEY J.B., dean, law educator; m. Beth Toben; children: John, Sarah Beth. BA in Polit. Sci. with honors, U. Mo., St. Louis; JD with honors, Baylor U., 1977; LLM, Harvard U., 1981. Bar: Tex., Mo. Tchr. Ind. U. Sch. Law, Indpls.; of counsel Dawson & Sodd (Dallas and Corsicana); with faculty Baylor Law Sch., 1983—, dean, 1991—, Gov. Bill and Vara Faye Daniel prof. law, 1991—. Participant in accreditation and membership inspection of law schs. ABA, Assn. Am. Schs. Gov. apptd. Tex. commr. Nat. Conf. of Commrs. on Uniform State Laws. Recipient Disting. Alumni Polit. Sci. Award, U. Mo.-St. Louis; named a Outstanding Young Alumnus, Baylor U., Disting. Alumnus, U. Mo.-St. Louis. Fellow Am. Bar Found., Tex. Bar Found.; mem. State Bar of Tex. (active in bankruptcy specialization cert. program). Office: Baylor U PO Box 97288 Waco TX 76798-7288 Business E-Mail: Brad_Toben@baylor.edu.*

TOBER, BARBARA D. (MRS. DONALD GIBBS TOBER), editor; b. Summit, NJ, Aug. 19, 1934; d. Rodney Fielding and Maude Starkey; m. Donald Gibbs Tober, Apr. 5, 1973. Student, Traphagen Sch. Fashion, 1954-56, Fashion Inst. Tech., 1956-58, N.Y. Sch. Interior Design, 1964. Copy editor Vogue Pattern Book, 1958-60; beauty editor Vogue mag., 1961; dir. women's services Bartell Media Corp., 1961-66; editor-in-chief Bride's mag., NYC, 1966-94; chmn. Mus. Arts and Design; pres. Acronym, Inc., NYC, 1995—, Donald Barbara Tober Found., 1995—. Sec.-treas., dir. Sugar Foods Corp.; adv. bd. Traphagen Sch.; coord. SBA awards; Am. Craft Coun., 1983—, benefit food com. chmn., 1984-87. Author: The ABC's of Beauty, 1963, China: A Cognizant Guide, 1980, The Wedding...The Marriage...And the Role of the Retailer, 1980, The Bride: A Celebration, 1984 Mem. Nat. Council on Family Relations, 1966; nat. council Lincoln Center Performing Arts, Met. Opera Guild; mem. NYU adv. bd. Women in Food Service, 1983; NYU Women's Health Symposium: Steering Com., 1983—. Recipient Alma award, 1968, Penney-Mo. award, 1972, Traphagen Alumni award, 1975, Diamond Jubilee award, 1983, Disting. Women award Northwood U., 1997, Legend award, Pratt inst., 2006, Lifetime Achievement award, 2009, Mus. Arts & Design, 2009 Mem. Fashion Group, Internat. Furnishings and Design Assn. (v.p., program chmn.), Am. Soc. Mag. Editors, Am. Soc. Interior Designers (press mem.), Intercorporate Group, Women in Communications (60 yrs. of success award N.Y. chpt. 1984), Nat. Assn. Underwater Instrs., Pan Pacific and S.E. Asia Women's Assn., Asia Soc., Japan Soc., China Inst., Internat. Side Saddle Orgn., Millbrook Hounds, Golden's Bridge Hounds, Wine and Food Soc., Chaines des Rotisseurs (chargée de press) (bd. dirs.), Dames d'Escoffier, Culinary Inst. Am. Home and Office: 620 Park Ave New York NY 10021-6591

TOBER, NINA, music educator, department chairman; d. William Roerig and Verna Anna Tober; m. Richard Morrison, Dec. 26, 1987. MusB, Chatham Coll., Pitts.; MusM in Voice Performance, U. Colo., Boulder; MusD, Claremont Grad. U., Calif., 1993. Assoc. prof. music Susquehanna U., Selinsgrove, Pa., 1993—. Recipient Minna Kaufmann-Ruud Disting. Performance award; finalist Dist. and Regional, Met. Opera Nat. Coun. Mem.: Nat. Assn. Tchrs. Singing (pres. Allegheny mountain chpt. 2004—06). Office: Susquehanna Univ 514 University Ave Selinsgrove PA 17870

TOBER, STEPHEN LLOYD, lawyer; b. Boston, May 27, 1949; s. Benjamin Arthur Tober and Lee (Hymoff) Fruman; m. Susan V. Schwartz, Dec. 22, 1973; children: Cary, Jamie. Grad., Syracuse U., 1971, JD, 1974. Bar: N.H. 1974, U.S. Dist. Ct. N.H. 1974, U.S. Supreme Ct. 1978, N.Y. 1981. Assoc. Flynn, McGuirk & Blanchard, Portsmouth, NH, 1974-79; pvt. practice Portsmouth, 1979-81, 1992—; ptnr. Aeschliman & Tober, Portsmouth, 1981-91. Lectr. Franklin Pierce Law Ctr., Concord, N.H., 1978-80. Contbr. articles to profl. jours. Mem. Portsmouth Charter Commn., 1976, Portsmouth Planning Bd., 1977-81; del. N.H. Constl. Conv., Concord, 1984; city councilman, Portsmouth, 1977-81. Named Best Lawyers America, 2006—08, New England Superlawyers, 2007—08. Fellow: Internat. Acad. Trial Lawyers, Am. Bar Found. (chmn. ea. region 2003—); mem.: ATLA (gov. 1980—86), ABA (chmn. standing com. on fed. judiciary 2005—06, state del., chmn. tech. and comms. com., chmn. credentials and admissions com., bd. govs. 2008—), N.H. Bd. Bar Examiners, N.H. Trial Lawyers Assn. (pres. 1977), N.H. Bar Assn. (pres. 1988—89, chmn. com. to redraft code of profl. responsibility, Disting. Svc. award 1986, 1994), New Eng. Bar Assn. (bd.dirs. 1988—91). Democrat. Jewish. Avocations: reading, tennis. Home: 55 T J Gamester Ave Portsmouth NH 03801-5871 Office: PO Box 1377 Portsmouth NH 03802-1377 Home Phone: 603-436-4231; Office Phone: 603-431-1003. Business E-Mail: stober@toberlaw.com.

TOBEY, BRIAN, computer software company executive; married; 2 children. BSChemE, U. Calif., Berkeley; Masters in Mfg. Mgmt., Northwestern U., MBA. Prin. A.T. Kearney; v.p. N.Am. Bath & Spa mfg. & supply chain ops. Jacuzzi Brands; gen. mgr. supply chain & info. tech. services Microsoft Corp., 2004, corp. v.p. mfg. & ops., entertainment & devices divsn., 2008—. Office: Microsoft Corp Entertainment & Devices Divsn 1 Microsoft Way Redmond WA 98052-6399*

TOBEY, MARTIN ALAN, cardiologist; b. Dallas, Sept. 24, 1947; s. Nathan Gene and Rose Marcus T.; m. Judith Helane Ross, Mar. 10, 1974; children: Daniel, Rachel. BS with highest distinction, Pa. State U., 1968; MD, Jefferson Med. Coll., 1970. Diplomate Am. Bd. Internal Medicine, Am. Bd. Cardiovascular Diseases, Am. Bd. Interventional Cardiology. Intern Phila. Gen. Hosp., 1970-71; resident in internal medicine Parkland Meml. Hosp., Dallas, 1971-74; fellow in cardiology U. Tex. Southwestern Med. Sch., Dallas, 1976-78; cardiologist Fort Worth Heart, 1978—. Mem. med. bd. Harris Hosp. Meth., Ft. Worth, 1988-90, chmn. cardiology divsn., 1988-90. Author (software) Workshops in Coronary Angioplasty, 1984, Revolution: The New Practice of Medicine, 2006, The Torch, 2007. Major U.S. Army, 1974-76. Fellow Am. Coll. Cardiology (regional rep. Tex. chpt. 1996-98); mem. Am.

Heart Assn., Sc. Cardiovasc. Computed Tomography, Torch Club (Ft. Worth), Soc. Cardiovascular Computed Tomography, Alpha Omega Alpha. Avocations: classical music, computers, photography. Office: Ft Worth Heart 1300 W Rosedale St Fort Worth TX 76104-2802 E-mail: mjtob@charter.net.

TOBEY, WILLIAM HAYWARD, former federal agency administrator; b. Decatur, Ill., Aug. 2, 1959; s. William Robert Jr. and Beverly Joy (Nilson) T.; m. Elizabeth Ness, Oct. 28, 1989; 1 child, Emma Channer. BS, Northwestern U., 1981; M of Pub. Policy, Harvard U., 1984. Presdl. mgmt. intern US Dept. Def., Washington, 1984-85; adv. U.S. Delegation to Nuclear and Space Talks, Geneva, 1985-86; dir. def. policy NSC, Washington, 1986-93; v.p. Smith Barney, NYC; gen. ptnr. Embryon Venture Capital, LLC, 1996; dir. counterproliferation strategy NSC, Washington; dep. adminstr. for def. nuc. nonproliferation Nat. Nuclear Security Adminstrn., US Dept. Energy, Washington, 2006—09; sr. fellow Belfer Ctr. for Sci. & Internat. Affairs, John F. Kennedy Sch. Govt., Harvard U., Cambridge, Md., 2009—. Republican. Lutheran. Avocations: golf, squash, oenology. Office: John F Kennedy School of Government 79 JFK St Cambridge MA 02138 E-mail: william_tobey@ksg.harvard.edu.*

TOBIAS, ANDREW PREVIN, columnist, educator; b. NYC, Apr. 20, 1947; s. Seth D. and Audrey J. (Landau) T. BA, Harvard U., 1968, MBA, 1972. Pres. Harvard Agys. Inc., Cambridge, Mass., 1967-68; v.p. Nat. Student Mktg. Corp., NYC, 1969-70; contbg. editor N.Y. Mag., 1972-77, Esquire mag., 1977-83; columnist Playboy mag., 1982-86; contbr. Time mag., 1989-94, Worth mag., 1995—. Co-host Beyond Wall Street, PBS series, 1997; daily internet columnist, 1996-. Author: The Funny Money Game, 1972, (under pen name John Reid) The Best Little Boy in the World, 1973, Fire and Ice, 1976, The Only Investment Guide You'll Ever Need, 1978, rev. edit., 1996, Getting by on $100,000 a Year and (Other Sad Tales), 1980, The Invisible Bankers, 1982, (software) Managing Your Money, 1984-94, Money Angles, 1984, The Only Other Investment Guide You'll Ever Need, 1987, Kids Say Don't Smoke, 1991, Auto Insurance Alert!, 1993, My Vast Fortune, 1997, The Best Little Boy in the World Grows Up, 1998. Treas. Dem. Nat. Com., 1999—; co-founder Alliance to Revitalize Calif.; bd. mem. Human Right's Campaign. Recipient Gerald Loeb award, 1984, Consumer Fedn. of Am. Media Svc. award, 1993, GLSEN Valedictorian award, 1997, Smith-Weld prize Harvard Mag., 1998. Democrat. Office: Dem Nat Com 430 S Capitol St SE Washington DC 20003*

TOBIAS, GEOFFREY, otolaryngologist, plastic surgeon; b. Paterson, NJ, Dec. 20, 1947; MD, Tufts U., 1973. Intern Tufts New England Med. Ctr., 1973—76; resident Mt. Sinai Hosp., NYC, 1976—78; attending surgeon and instr. Mt. Sinai Hosp. and Sch. Medicine, NYC; assoc. chief head and neck surgery Englewood Hosp., NJ. Mem. sci. adv. bd. Longevity mag. Named one of Top Doctors in NY, NY Mag., 2004. Mem.: Am. Acad. Otolaryngology - Head and Neck Surgery, Am. Acad. Facial Plastic Surgery. Office: 214 Engle St Englewood NJ 07631-2418 also: 815 Park Ave New York NY 10021-3276 Office Phone: 201-567-7966. Office Fax: 201-567-6770.*

TOBIAS, JOSEPH DREW, pediatric anesthesiologist; b. St. Louis, Dec. 16, 1958; s. Sherwin Larue and Georgia Xenos Tobias; m. Julie Ann Turpin, Nov. 3, 2001. BA, U. Mo., Kansas City, 1981, MD, 1983. Diplomate Am. Bd. Pediat., Am. Bd. Anesthesiology, Am. Bd. Pediat. Critical Care, Am. Bd. Anesthesiology Critical Care Medicine, Am. Bd. Anesthesiology Pain Mgmt., cert. Am. Acad. Pain Mgmt. 1990. Chief pediatric anesthesiology, attending pediatric ICU St. Jude Children's Hosp., Memphis, 1990—91; assoc. dir., divsn. pediatric anesthesiology/critical care; assoc. prof. anesthesiology and pediat. Vanderbilt U., Nashville, 1991—95; chief, pediatric anesthesiology/pediatric critical care, prof. anesthesiology and pediat. U. Mo., Columbia, 1995—, vice-chmn., dept. anesthesiology, 2001—. Home: 4112 Compton Rd Columbia MO 65203 Office: U Missouri One Hospital Dr - 3W27G HSC Columbia MO 65212 Business E-Mail: tobiasj@health.missouri.edu.

TOBIAS, PAUL HENRY, lawyer; b. Cin., Jan. 5, 1930; s. Charles H. and Charlotte (Westheimer) T.; 1 child, Eliza L. AB magna cum laude, Harvard U., 1951, LLB, 1958. Bar: Mass. 1958, Ohio 1962. Assoc. Stoneman & Chandler, Boston, 1958-61, Goldman & Putnick, Cin., 1962-75; ptnr. Tobias, Kraus and Torchia, Cin., 1976—. Instr. U. Cin. Law Sch., 1975-77. Author: Litigating Wrongful Discharge Claims, 1987; co-author: Job Rights and Survivor Strategies, a Handbook for Terminated Employees, 1997, Advice to a Young Man at 70; contbr. articles to profl. jours. Mem. Cin. Bd. of Park Commrs., 1973-81, Cin. Human Rels. Commn., 1980-84, Cin. Hist. Conservation Bd., 1990-91. With U.S. Army, 1952-54. Mem. ABA, Nat. Employment Lawyers Assn. (founder), Nat. Employee Rights Inst. (chmn.; editor-in-chief Employee Rights quar. 2000-02), Ohio State Bar Assn., Cin. Bar Assn. (past chmn. legal aid com.), Coll.Employment & Labor Lawyers (bd. dirs.), Phi Beta Kappa. Office: Tobias Kraus Torchia 911 Mercantile Libr Bldg Cincinnati OH 45202 Home: 2412 Ingleside Ave Apt 5b Cincinnati OH 45206-2185 Office Phone: 513-241-8137. Business E-Mail: tkt@tktlaw.com.

TOBIAS, ROBERT MAX, labor leader, lawyer; b. Detroit, Aug. 4, 1943; BA, U. Mich., 1965, MBA, 1968; JD, George Washington U., 1969. Lawyer Nat. Treasury Employees Union, Washington, 1968-70, gen. counsel, 1970-79, exec. v.p. and gen. counsel, 1979-83, pres., 1983-99; disting. adj. prof. pub. adminstrn., dir. Inst. for Study of Pub. Policy Implementation, Am. U., Washington, 1999—, dir. pub. sector exec. edn., 2005—. Lectr. George Washington U. Law Sch., Washington, 1970-90; mem. IRS oversight bd., 2000—. Contbr. articles to law revs. Pres. Fed. Employee Edn. and Asst. Fund, Washington, 1986—. Fellow Nat. Acad. Pub. Adminstrn.; mem. ABA, Soc. for Labor Relations Profls. (1st Annual Union Leader award, 1987), Fed. Bar Assn. Democrat. Episcopalian. Office: Am U Sch Pub Affairs 4400 Massachusetts Ave Washington DC 20016-8070 E-mail: rtobias@american.edu.

TOBIAS, VERONICA ANN (RONI TOBIAS), psychologist; b. Ladysmith, Wis., June 21, 1971; d. Ronald Wayne and Florence Rose Runnheim; m. Trent Joseph Tobias, July 14, 2001; children: Asa Thomas, Ayden Ronald. EdS, U. Wis., Eau Claire, 1996. Sch. psychologist Gilman Sch. Dist., Wis., 1996—99, Coop. Ednl. Svcs. Agy, Turtle Lake, Wis., 1999—2001, Chippewa Falls, Wis., 2001—07, Sch. Dist. Phillips, Wis., 2007—. Mem.: Wis. Sch. Psychology Assn. Roman Catholic. Avocations: walking, bicycling, exercise.

TOBIASSEN, BARBARA SUE, systems analyst, consultant, volunteer; b. Bklyn., Feb. 22, 1950; BA in Math Edn., Rider Coll., 1972; postgrad., Montclair State U., 1973. Cert. secondary tchr., NJ. Math tchr. Westwood (NJ) H.S., 1973-80; programmer Prudential Ins. Co., Roseland, NJ, 1980-81; programmer, analyst Grand Union, Paramus, NJ, 1981-82; cons. Five Techs., Montvale, NJ, 1987-90; project mgr. Info. Sci., Inc., Montvale, 1982-84, cons., project mgr., 1987-90; pres. B. Maxwell Assoc., Inc., Westwood, 1990—; vol. Peace Corps; mem. Peace Corps., 2001—02; tchr. St. Paul's Luth., Accra, Ghana, 2002—03, Ghana, 2002—07, St. Vincent Acad., 2008—. Guest spkr. Info. Sci., Best of Am., Computer Assocs. B.A.C.; dir. ZELCOWA. Contbr. articles to profl. jours. Mem.: APA (v.p. N.J. chpt. 1996). Lutheran. Avocations: travel, reading, gardening, hiking.

TOBIN, ALLEN GERALD (JERRY), science educator; b. St. Louis, July 23, 1940; s. Allen Roy Tobin and Jennie Esther Belcher; m. Ardyce Theresa Stuhr, Dec. 17, 1961; children: Allen Randall, Angela Faye Allee, Theresa Lynn Arasim. BA in Physics with honors, North Tex. State U., Denton, 1968; MA in Physics, U. Oreg., Eugene, 1971; MBA, U. Portland, Oreg., 1980. Electronics technician, reactor operator US Navy, New London, Conn., 1958—65; engring. mgr. Tektronix Inc., Beaverton, Oreg., 1974—86; prodn. engring. mgr. Honeywell Avionics Divsn., Albuquerque, 1986—88; engring. supr. Eldec Corp., Lynwood, Wash., 1988—90; dir. mfg. NEC Am., Hillsboro, Oreg., 1990—93; program mgr. Intel Corp., Hillsboro, Oreg., 1995—2002; math & physic instr. Chemeketa CC, Salem, Oreg., 1971—74, Portland CC, 1983—; math instr. DeVry U., Portland, 2002—. Adj. asst. prof. U. Portland, 1974—83. Author: (management book) Managing Strategically - 101 Creative Tips. Head usher large congregation. St. Matthew Luth. Ch., Beaverton, Oreg., 1977—86. Achievements include design of flexible impedance matching device enabling Tektronix to reliably produce the world's fastest-writing CRT; provided design concept for multi-valued state-of-the-art SMT conductor family for Tektronix. Avocations: swimming, golf. Home: 17643 NW Deerbrook Ct Portland OR 97229 Personal E-mail: atobin465@verizon.com.

TOBIN, BARBARA KAY, minister; b. Davenport, Iowa, Oct. 9, 1943; d. Robert Thomas Myers and Frances Louella Davis; m. Richard James Tobin, Feb. 12, 1966; 1 child, Mary Beth Tobin Peter. B.Humanities, Social Sci. and Edn., Purdue U., 1966; BEd, Ball State U., 1968; MDiv, Colgate Rochester Div. Sch., 1994. Cert. tchr. N.Y., ordained to ministry Presbyn. Ch., 1994. Fgn. lang. tchr. West Irondequoit Schs., Rochester, NY, 1968—93; chaplain Strong Meml. Hosp., Rochester, 1993—94; pastor of visitation First Presbyn. Ch., Pittsford, NY, 1994—96; assoc. pastor Perinton Presbyn. Ch., Fairport, NY, 1995—2000; pastor Irondequoit Presbyn. Ch., Rochester, 2000—. Mem., com. ministry; sec., bd. dirs. Irondequoit Sr. Transp. Ministry, Rochester, 2002—; mem. com. on prep. ministry Genesee Valley Presbytery, 2005—08; leader internat. study tours West Irondequoit Schs., 1983—88; leader student mission trips Perinton Presbyn. Ch., 1991—99; co-convener Irondequoit Ministerial Assn., 2008. Mem. Irondequoit Youth Bureau Adv. Bd., 2004—06. Mem.: N.Y. State Ret. Tchrs. Assn., Purdue U. Alumni Assn. (life; pres.'s coun. 1993—). Presbyterian. Avocations: reading, travel, sailing. Office: Irondequoit Presbyn Ch 2881 Culver Rd Rochester NY 14622 Home Phone: 585-872-5284; Office Phone: 585-266-3370. Personal E-mail: pastorbobbi@rochester.rr.com.

TOBIN, CALVIN JAY, retired architect; b. Boston, Feb. 15, 1927; s. David and Bertha (Tanfield) T.; m. Joan Hope Fink, July 15, 1951; children— Michael Alan, Nancy Ann. B.Arch., U. Mich., 1949. Designer, draftsman Arlen & Lowenfish (architects), NYC, 1949-51; with Samuel Arlen, NYC, 1951-53, Skidmore, Owings & Merrill, NYC, 1953; architect Loebl, Schlossman & Bennett (architects), Chgo., 1953-57, v.p., 1953-57, Loebl, Schlossman & Hackl, 1957—; ret., 1998. Chmn. Jewish United Fund Bldg. Trades Div., 1969; chmn. AIA and Chgo. Hosp. Council Com. of Hosp. Architecture, 1968-76; archtl. cons. Resurrection Healthcare Corp., 1998-. Archtl. works include Michael Reese Hosp. and Med. Ctr., 1954—, Prairie Shores Apt. Urban Redevel., 1957-62, Louis A. Weiss Meml. Hosp., Chgo., Chgo. State Hosp., Ctrl. Cmty. Hosp., Chgo., Gottlieb Meml. Hosp., Melrose Park, Ill., West Suburban Hosp., Oak Park, Ill., Thorek Hosp. and Med. Ctr., Chgo., Water Power Pl., Chgo., Christ Hosp., Oak Lawn, Greater Balt. Med. Ctr., Shriners Hosp. for Crippled Children, Chgo. Hinsdale (Ill.) Hosp., South Chgo. Cmty. Hosp., Chgo., Mt. Sinai Med. Ctr., Chgo., Alexian Bros. Med. Ctr., Elk Grove Village, Ill., Luth. Gen. Hosp., Park Ridge, Ill., Evanston (Ill.) Hosp., Resurrection Med. Ctr., Chgo., New Cook County Hosp., Chgo., also numerous apt., comml. and cmty. bldgs. Chmn. Highland Park (Ill.) Appearance Rev. Commn., 1972-73; mem. Highland Park Plan Commn., 1973-79; mem. Highland Park City Coun., 1974-89, mayor pro-tem, 1979-89; mem. Highland Park Environ. Control Commn., 1979-84, Highland Park Hist. Preservation Commn., 1982-89; bd. dir. Highland Park Hist. Soc., Young Men's Jewish Coun., 1953-67, pres., 1967; bd. dirs. Jewish Community Ctrs. Chgo., 1973-78, bd. dirs., 1989-93; Ill. Coun. Against Handgun Violence, 1989-94; trustee Ravinia Festival Assn., 1990-98; bd. govs. Highland Park Cmty. House, 1994—. With USNR, 1945-46. Recipient Boys Club Medallion award, Boys Club Am., 1968, Disting. Alumni award, Taubman Coll. Architecture and Urban Planning, U. Mich., 2004. Fellow AIA (2d v.p. Chgo. chpt.); mem. U. Mich. Alumni Soc. Coll. Architecture and Urban Planning (bd. govs. 1989-95), U. Mich. Alumni Assn. (bd. govs. 1990-95, v.p. 1993-95, pres. 1997-99, Disting. Alumni Svc. award 1996), Std. Club, Ravinia Green Country Club, Pi Lambda Phi. Jewish. Home: 814 Dean Ave Highland Park IL 60035-4749

TOBIN, CRAIG DANIEL, lawyer; b. Chgo., Aug. 17, 1954; s. Thomas Arthur and Lois (O'Connor) T. BA with honors, U. Ill., 1976; JD with high honors, Ill. Inst. Tech., 1980. Bar: Ill. 1980, U.S. Dist. Ct. (no. dist.) Ill. 1980, U.S. Dist. Ct. (no. dist.) Ind. 1986, U.S. Ct. Appeals (7th cir.) 1986, U.S. Supreme Ct. 1987. Trial atty. Cook County Pub. Defender, Chgo., 1980-82; trial atty. homicide task force Pub. Defender, Chgo., 1982-84; ptnr. Craig D. Tobin and Assocs., Chgo., 1984—. Lectr. Ill. Inst. for Continuing Legal Edn., Cook County Pub. Defender, Chgo., 1983, 92, Ill. Pub. Defender Assn., 1987; instr. Nat. Inst. Trial Advocacy. Recipient award for legal excellence Midwest Comm. Coun., 2002, Leading Am. Lawyer; named to Outstanding Young Men in Am., 1985, Ill. Super Lawyer, Best Lawyer in Am. Mem. ABA, Chgo. Bar Assn., Nat. Assn. Criminal Def. Lawyers. Roman Catholic. Office: Tobin Petkus & Munoz LLC 3 First National Plz Chicago IL 60602 Home: 6622 N Longmeadow Ave Lincolnwood IL 60712-3208 Office Phone: 312-641-1321.

TOBIN, DUKE, professional sports team executive; s. Bill Tobin. Attended, U. Ill.; grad., U. Colo. Quarterback Orlando Predators, Arena Football League, Memphis Pharaohs, Arena Football League; scout Indpls. Colts, 1994—99; scouting dept. Cin. Bengals, 1999—, dir. player pers., 2002—. Office: Cin Bengals One Paul Brown Stadium Cincinnati OH 45202*

TOBIN, GREGORY JOHN, biologist; b. Detroit, July 10, 1948; s. John S. and Angeline M. Tobin; m. Elizabeth E. Kreutzer, July 2, 1983; children: John K., Andrew T. PhD, U. Fla., Gainesville, 1988. Sr. scientist to group leader SAIC, Frederick, Md., 1989—99; sr. scientist Biol. Mimetics, Inc., Frederick, 1999—2007, v.p. to coo, 2007—. Sci. cons. Various, 2007—. Contbr. scientific papers. Bsa adult leader BSA, Frederick, 1999; jazz musician Frederick Com Col Jazz Orch., 2001—. Grant, NIH, 1999 - 2009, DoD, Nat. Pork Bd., 1999—. Mem.: Nat. Found. Infectious Disease. Achievements include patents for vaccine design strategies. Avocations: sports, music, photography, travel, scuba diving. Office: Biol Mimetics Inc 124 Byte Dr Frederick MD 21702

TOBIN, JAMES EDWARD, communications educator, writer; b. Pontiac, Mich., Oct. 4, 1956; s. James Edward and Dorothy Tobin; m. Leesa Erickson Tobin, Aug. 16, 1980; children: Elizabeth Erickson, Claire Melanie. BA, U. Mich., Ann Arbor, 1978, PhD, 1986. Reporter Detroit News, 1986—98; assoc. prof. journalism Miami U., Oxford, Ohio, 2006—. Author: (history) Great Projects: The Building of America. Recipient J. Anthony Lukas Work-in-Progress award, 2000. Personal E-mail: tobinje@muohio.edu.

TOBIN, JAMES MICHAEL, lawyer; b. Santa Monica, Calif., Sept. 27, 1948; s. James Joseph and Glada Marie (Meisner); m. Kathleen Marie Espy, Sept. 14, 1985; children: Kristina Claire, Victoria Elizabeth Joy. BA with honors, U. Calif., Riverside, 1970; JD, Georgetown U., DC, 1974. Bar: Calif. 1974, Mich. 1987. From atty. to gen. atty. So. Pacific Co., San Francisco, 1975-82; v.p. regulatory affairs So. Pacific Comm. Co., Washington, 1982-83; v.p., gen. counsel Lexitel Corp., Washington, 1983-85; v.p., gen. counsel, sec. ALC Comm. Corp., Birmingham, Mich., 1985-87, sr. v.p., gen. counsel, sec., 1987-88; of counsel Morrison & Foerster, San Francisco, 1988-90, ptnr., 1990—2005, Tobin Law Group, P. C., 2006—. Mem. ABA, Calif. Bar Assn., Fed. Comm. Bar Assn. Democrat. Episcopalian. Avocations: carpentry, travel. Home: 17 Reed Ranch Rd Tiburon CA 94920 Office: 1628 Tiburon Blvd Tiburon CA 94920 Office Phone: 415-732-1700. Business E-Mail: jim@tobinlaw.us.

TOBIN, JAMES ROBERT (JIM TOBIN), retired biomedical device manufacturing company executive; b. Lima, Ohio, Aug. 12, 1944; s. J. Robert and Doris L. (Hunt) T.; m. Janet Trafton, Dec. 30, 1971; children: James Robert III, Amanda Trafton. BA in Govt., Harvard U., 1966; MBA, Harvard U. Bus. Sch., 1968. Fin. analyst Baxter Internat., Inc., Deerfield, Ill., 1972-73, internat. contr., 1973-75, mng. dir. Japan, 1975-77, mng. dir. Spain, 1977-80, pres. IV Sys. Divsn., 1981—86, group v.p., 1984-88, exec. v.p. Deerfield, 1988-92, pres., COO, 1992-94, Biogen Inc., 1994-97, pres., CEO, 1997-98, Boston Scientific Corp., Natick, Mass., 1999—2009. Bd. dirs. Applera, Inc., 1999—, Boston Scientific Corp., 1999—2009, BioMedical Sci. Career Program, Curis, Inc. Served to lt. USN, 1968—72. Republican.*

TOBIN, PAUL EDWARD, JR., museum director, retired admiral; b. Detroit, Oct. 24, 1940; s. Paul Edward and Mary Margaret (Atkinson) T.; m. Lynne Dawson Carter, June 12, 1963; children: Mary Elizabeth, Patricia Carter. BS in Naval Sci., U.S. Naval Acad., 1963; MS in Computer Sys., U.S. Naval Postgrad. Sch., 1969. Commd. ensign USN, 1963, advanced through grades to rear adm., 1988; commdg. officer USS Tattnall (DDG-19), 1979-81; chief engr. USS Forrestal (CV-59), 1981-83; commdg. officer USS Fox (CG-33), 1984-86, Surface Warfare Officers Sch., 1986-88; dir. USN Info. Sys. Mgmt., 1988-90; commdr. Surface Group Western Pacific, Subic Bay, The Philippines, 1990-92; asst. chief naval pers. USN, Washington, 1992-94, vice commdr. naval edn. and tng. Pensacola, Fla., 1994-96, Oceanographer of the Navy, 1996-98, ret., 1998; exec. dir., edn. found. Armed Forces Comm. Electronics Assn., Fairfax, Va., 1998—2005; dir. Naval Historical Ctr., Washington, 2005—. Decorated D.S.M., Legion of Merit (4), Bronze Star. Mem. U.S. Naval Inst., Surface Navy Assn., Army Navy Country Club. Presbyterian. Avocations: classical music, running, computers, boating.

TOBIN, THOMAS JOSEPH, bishop; b. Pitts., Apr. 1, 1948; Degree, St. Francis Coll., Loretto, 1969, PhD (hon.), 1997; attended, Gannon Coll., Erie, N.Am. Coll., Rome, Gregorian U., Pontifical Liturgical Inst. San Anselmo. Ordained priest Diocese of Pitts., 1973, adminstrv. sec. to bishop, 1984—87, assoc. gen. sec., 1987—90, vicar gen. & gen. sec., 1990—92, aux. bishop, 1992—95; asst. pastor St. Vitus Parish, New Castle, Pa., 1973—79, St. Sebastian Parish, Ross Twp., Pa., 1979—84; ordained bishop, 1992; bishop Diocese of Youngstown, Ohio, 1996—2005, Diocese of Providence, 2005—. Author: (columns) Without a Doubt (Spl. recognition, Cath. Press Assn., 1998), (books) Without a Doubt: Bringing Faith to Life, 2001. Trustee Pontifical Coll. Josephinum, Columbus, Ohio; mem. episcopal adv. bd. Catholics United for the Faith. Mem.: US Conf. Cath. Bishops (mem. adminstrv. com.). Roman Catholic. Office: Diocese of Providence One Cathedral Sq Providence RI 02903-3695 Office Phone: 401-278-4500.

TOBIS, JEROME SANFORD, physician; b. Syracuse, NY, July 23, 1915; s. David George and Anna (Feinberg) T.; m. Hazel Weisbard, Sept. 18, 1938; children: David, Heather, Jonathan. BS, CCNY, 1936; MD, Chgo. Med. Sch., 1943. Diplomate Am. Bd. Phys. Medicine and Rehab. Intern Knickerbocker Hosp., 1943-44; resident Bronx VA Hosp., 1946-48; med. dir. state fever therapy unit USPHS, Brookhaven, Miss., 1944-46; practice medicine NYC, 1948-70; prof. dir. dept. phys. medicine and rehab. N.Y. Med. Coll., Flower and Fifth Av. Hosps., 1948-61; prof. rehab. medicine Albert Einstein Coll. of Medicine, 1963-70; chief div. rehab. medicine Montefiore Hosp., 1961-70; dir. vis. physician Met., Bird S. Coler hosps., 1952-61; prof., chmn. dept. phys. medicine and rehab. Calif. Coll. Medicine, U. Calif. at Irvine, 1970-82, prof., dir. program in geriatric medicine and gerontology, 1980-86; mem. adv. com. Acad. Geriatric Resource program, 1984-86, 95—. Expert med. com. Am. Rehab. Found., 1961-70; cons. Dept. Health, NYC, Long Beach VA Hosp., 1970—, Fairview State Devel. Ctr., 1976—; adv. coun. phys. medicine and rehab. for appeals com. Calif. Med. Assn., 1971-74, adv. com. U. Calif. Acad. Geriatric Resource Program, 1995—; NIH Internat. Fogarty fellow, hon. lectr., dept. geriat. medicine U. Birmingham, 1979-80; rev. panel musculoskeletal diseases NIH, 1996; rsch. prof. dept. phys. medicine & rehab. U. Calif., Irvine, 1986—, chair med. ethics com., 1986—; mem. Ctr. Health Policy Rsch. U. Calif., Davis, 1996—. Author: (book) Fundamentals of the Stem Cell Debate: The Sci., Religious, Ethical, and Polit. Issues Monroe, K. R., Miller, R. B. and Tobis, J., U. Calif. Press, 2008; mem. editorial bd.: Heart and Lung, 1973-76, Geriatrics, 1975-80, Archives of Phys. Medicine and Rehab, 1958-73. Named Physician of the Year, 1957; recipient Distinguished Alumnus award Chgo. Med. Sch., 1972, Acad. award Nat. Inst. on Aging, 1981-86; named hon. faculty mem. Calif. Zeta chpt. Alpha Omega Alpha, 1981; Leavitt Meml. lectureship Baylor Coll. Medicine, 1983, Griffith Meml. lectureship Am. Geriatric Soc., 1984; Australian Coll. Rehabilitation Medicine, 1984; Jerome S. Tobis Ann. Conf. on Geriatric Medicine established in his name, U. Calif. at Irvine, 1986. Fellow ACP, Am. Coll. Cardiology, Am. Congress Rehab. Medicine (hon.); mem. AMA (mem. residency rev. com. Coun. Med. Edn. 1973), AAAS, Am. Acad. Cerebral Palsy, Am. Acad. Phys. Medicine and Rehab. (Disting. Clinician award 1993), Am. Congress Rehab. Medicine (pres. 1962), Calif. Coun. Gerontology and Geriatrics (bd. dirs. 1980-86, pres. 1985), N.Y. Acad. Medicine, N.Y. Acad. Sci., Orange County Med. Soc., Assn. U. Calif. Irvine (chair emeritae/i 1996-97). Home: 1115 Goldenrod Ave Corona Del Mar CA 92625-1508 Office Phone: 714-456-5626. Personal E-mail: jstobis@uci.edu.

TOBISAWA, HIROSHI, computer game company executive; BA, Hosei Univ., Japan; MBA, Hosei Grad Sch., Tokyo. Head tech. rsch. & develop. PowerPC semiconductor IBM, Japan; mgmt. positions in sales, mktg., & corp. planning Capcom Co. Ltd., Osaka, Japan, 1997—2003, pres. Capcom USA, CE Europe, 2003—, pres., acting CEO Capcom USA and Capcom Entertainment. Office: Capcom USA Inc 800 Concar Dr Ste 300 San Mateo CA 94402-2649 Office Phone: 650-350-6500.

TOBISMAN, STUART PAUL, lawyer; b. Detroit, June 5, 1942; s. Nathan and Beverly (Porvin) T.; m. Karen Sue Tobisman, Aug. 8, 1965; children: Cynthia Elaine, Neal Jay. BA, UCLA, 1966; JD, U. Calif., Berkeley, 1969. Bar: Calif. 1969. Assoc. O'Melveny & Myers, LA, 1969-77, ptnr., 1977—2006, Loeb & Loeb LLP, LA, 2006—. Contbr. articles to profl. jours. Trustee L.A. County Bar Assn., 1983-84. With USN, 1961-63. Fellow Am. Coll. Trust and Estate Counsel; mem. Phi Beta Kappa, Order of Coif. Office: Loeb & Loeb LLP 10100 Santa Monica Blvd Los Angeles CA 90067-4120

TOBY, JACKSON, sociologist, educator; b. NYC, Sept. 10, 1925; m. Marcia Lifshitz, Aug. 1, 1952 (dec. Jan. 1997); children: Alan Steven, Gail Afriat (dec.). BA, Bklyn. Coll., 1946; MA in Econs, Harvard U., 1947, MA in Sociology, 1949, PhD in Sociology, 1950. Rsch. assoc. Lab. Social Relations, Harvard, 1950-51; mem. faculty Rutgers U., 1951—2002, prof. sociology, chmn. dept., 1961-68, prof. sociology emeritus, 2002, dir. Inst. for Criminological Rsch., 1969-94; vis. scholar Am. Enterprise Inst., 2004—. Cons. Youth Devel. Program, Ford Found., 1959-63 Author: (with H.C. Bredemeier) Social Problems in America, 1960, 2d edit., 1971; Contemporary Society, 1964, 2d edit., 1971; contbr. numerous articles to profl. jours., pub. policy jours., N.Y. Times, Wall St. Jour., L.A. Times, Chgo. Tribune, Washington Post, Washington Times, The Weekly Standard, Nat. Rev., Sociol. Rsch. Cons., Pres.'s Commn. Law Enforcement and Adminstrn. Justice, 1966; trustee NAMI-N.J., 1997-2000. Recipient Rsch. Excellence award, Rutgers U. Bd. Trustees, 1984, numerous research grants. Mem. Am. Sociol. Assn., Sociol. Rsch. Assn., Am. Soc. Criminology, Nat. Assn. Scholars. Achievements include spl. research adolescent delinquency in U.S., Sweden, Japan, other countries, on violence and dropouts in Am. public schools. Home: 17 Harrison Ave Highland Park NJ 08904-1813 Office: Rutgers U Dept Sociology Lucy Stone Hall Livingston Campus New Brunswick NJ 08903 Business E-Mail: jtoby@rci.rutgers.edu.

TOCCHET, RICK, professional hockey coach, retired professional hockey player; b. Scarborough, Ont., Can., Apr. 9, 1964; Right wing Phila. Flyers, 1984—92, capt., 1991—92, right wing, 2000—02, Pitts. Penguins, 1992—94, LA Kings, 1994—96, Boston Bruins, 1996—97, Washington Capitals, 1997, Phoenix Coyotes, 1997—2000; asst. coach Colo. Avalanche, 2003—04, Phoenix Coyotes, 2005—06, 2008; assoc. coach Tampa Bay Lightning, 2008, interim head coach, 2008—09, head coach, 2009—. Named to NHL All-Star Game, 1989—91, 1993. Achievements include being a member of Stanley Cup Champion Pittsburgh Penguins, 1992. Office: Tampa Bay Lightning Hockey Club St Pete Times Forum 401 Channelside Dr Tampa FL 33602*

TOCCO, ELAINE KAY, technical expert; b. Columbus, Ohio, May 20, 1957; d. Arthur Gene and Nancy Louise Lanker; m. Peter Joseph Tocco; children: Nicholas, Alexander; 1 child, Zachary. BA, Brescia U., 1981. Program cons. Disability Determination Svcs., Indpls., 1983—98; social ins. specialist Social Security Adminstrn., Balt., 1999—. Webelos leader Boy Scouts Am., Columbia, 1999—2001; coord. support group Multiple Sclerosis Soc., Indpls., 1985—86. Mem.: Nat. Assn. Disability Examiners, Mensa, Psy Chi, Alpha Chi. Roman Catholic. Avocations: reading, gardening. Business E-Mail: elaine.tocco@ssa.gov.

TOD, MARTHA ANN, retired small business owner; b. Nogales, Ariz., Dec. 20, 1927; d. R.T. and Beatrice Martha (Jones) Frazier; m. James William Tod, April 18, 1952; children: James, Bill, Bob, John, Gerry. BA, U. Ariz., Tucson, 1952; postgrad., Ariz. State U., Tempe, 1977. Cert. elem. and spl. edn. tchr. Spl. edn. tchr. Paradise Valley. Schs., Phoenix, 1976-77, Round Valley Schs., Springerville, 1977-88; resort owner Tod's Antler Ridge, Greer, Ariz., 1977—98, ret., 1998. Mem. Title XX Bd., Town Hall; treas. WMC Hosp. Bd. Springerville, 1980; pres. Cocopah PTA Paradise Valley, 1967; former touring docent Phoenix Art Mus.; touring docent Butterfly Lodge Mus., Greer, Ariz. Named Tchr. of Yr. Springerville Rotary, 1985. Mem. Assn. for Children and Adults with Learning Disabilities, Greer Civic Club, Ariz. Archaeology Soc. Avocation: gardening. Home: 450 E Raven Hill Rd Clarkdale AZ 86324-3111 Home Phone: 928-300-4856.

TODARO, PETER M., lawyer; b. Easton, Pa., July 20, 1970; s. James M. and Bernice P. Todaro; m. Tanya M. Masri, Sept. 23, 1995; children: Isabella Marie, James Michael, Sofia Grace. BA in Econs. and Fgn. Affairs, U. Va., Charlottesville, 1992, JD, 1996. Bar: Va. 1996, US Ct. Appeals (4th cir.) 1996, DC 1997, US Ct. Appeals (DC cir.) 1998, US Ct. Appeals (7th cir.) 2001, US Ct. Appeals (3rd cir.) 2001, US Supreme Ct. 2002. Assoc. King & Splading LLP, Washington, 1996—2004; ptnr. King & Spalding LLP, Washington, 2005—. Mem. editl. bd.: Va. Law Rev., 1994—96. Vol. Make-A-Wish Found. of Mid-Atlantic, 2006—, spkr., 2006—. Mem.: ABA (antitrust sect.), Va. Bar Assn., Order of the Coif. Avocation: skiing. Office: King & Spalding 1700 Pennsylvania Ave NW Washington DC 20006 Business E-Mail: ptodaro@kslaw.com.

TODD, CAROL, music educator; b. Paulding, Ohio, Apr. 2, 1942; d. Merle and Glendine Jeffery; m. Larry Todd, Aug. 15, 1964; children: Tara Michelle Lineweaver, Trista Lynn Todt. BS, Bowling Green State U., Ohio, 1963; MA, Ohio State U., 1968. Cert. music tchr. Ohio Edn. Dept., elem. tchr. Ohio Edn. Dept., kindergarten tchr. Ohio Edn. Dept. Music tchr. grades 7-12 Watkins Meml. Sch., Pataskala, Ohio, 1963—64; music tchr. grades 1-12 Licking Heights Sch. Dist., Summit Station, Ohio, 1964—67; music tchr. grades 7-12 Hilliard City Schs., Ohio, 1967—69; music tchr. grades 9-12 Clark-Shawnee Local Schs., Springfield, Ohio, 1982—98; asst. prof. music Cedarville U., Ohio, 1998—2006, Wittenberg U., Springfield, 2000—. Dist. rep. curriculum course study Clark County, Ohio, 1988, Ohio, 93; guest condr. Springfield Symphony All-County Choir, 1992, Ohio Music Educators All-Dist. XII Women's Choir, Dayton, 1997, Clark County All-County Choir Festival, Springfield, 2001; adj. prof. music Clark State C.C., Springfield, 1996—2002; clinician Ohio Music Educators' State Conf., Columbus, Ohio, 2004, Cin., 05. Campaign collector March of Dimes, Springfield, 2000—06; min. music Maumee United Meth. Ch., Ohio, 1972—74; leadership coun. Asbury United Meth. Ch., North Hampton, Ohio, 2000—04; active High Street United Meth. Ch., Springfield, 2004—. Recipient Tchr. Achievement award, Ashland Oil Co., 1993, 1995, 1997, Excellence in Tchg. award, Clark County News Assn., 1997. Mem.: Ohio Ret. Tchrs. Assn., Ohio Music Educators' Assn. (Ohio Music Educator 25+ Years award 1999), Am. Choral Dirs. Assn., Music Educators' Nat. Conf. (student chpt. advisor). Republican. Avocations: tennis, musical theater, singing, camping, bridge. Home: 3985 St James Ct Springfield OH 45502 Office: Wittenberg Univ Music Dept PO Box 720 Springfield OH 45501 Office Phone: 937-327-7341. Office Fax: 937-327-7347. Business E-Mail: ctodd@wittenberg.edu.

TODD, CHRISTOPHER MICHAEL, marketing executive, consultant; b. Waukesha, Wis., Aug. 16, 1970; s. Michael Burgess Todd and Billie Jeanette Koepke. BA in Journalism and Mass Comm., Drake U., Des Moines, 1992. Lic. capt. USCG, 2006, registered Notary Public Fla., 2002. Account mgr. Schneider Comm., Milw., 1993—96; account exec. Entertainment Publs., Deerfield Beach, Fla., 1996—98; sr. mgr. interactive mktg. CBS SportsLine.com, Ft. Lauderdale, Fla., 1998—2000; analyst Jupiter Rsch., NYC, 2000—01; pres. Christopher Todd, Inc., Miami Beach, Fla., 2002—. Mktg. cons. PartyPoker.com, Santo Domingo, Dominican Republic, 2001—06. Flotilla staff officer USCG Aux., Miami, 2006; mem. City of Miami Beach Marine Authority Bd., Fla., Rep. Nat. Com., Washington, 2006. Mem.: US Boating Assn., Miami Beach Yacht Club, Pi Kappa Phi (Beta Delta chpt., pres. 1990—91). Office: Christopher Todd Inc 1521 Alton Rd #628 Miami Beach FL 33139 Business E-Mail: ct@christophertodd.us.

TODD, CHUCK (CHARLES DAVID TODD), news correspondent; b. Apr. 8, 1972; m. Kristian Denny; 2 children. Student, George Washington U. Editor-in-chief The Hotline, Nat. Jour., 1992—2007, co-host webcast series Hotline TV; polit. dir. NBC News, 2007—, chief White House corr., contbg. editor Meet the Press, 2008—. On-air political analyst Morning Joe, Hardball with Chris Matthews, Meet the Press, NBC Nightly News with Brian Williams, Countdown with Keith Olbermann; weekly columnist NationalJournal.com, MSNBC.com; contbg. editor Atlantic Monthly; adj. Johns Hopkins U., Balt. Co-author (with Sheldon Gawiser): How Barack Obama Won: A State-by-State Guide to the Historic 2008 Presidential Election, 2009. Named one of the 50 Most Influential People in Politics, George mag., 2001, Washingtonian Mag.'s 'Best Of' Journalists, 2005. Jewish. Office: NBC News 30 Rockefeller Plaza New York NY 10112*

TODD, DEBRA, state supreme court justice; b. Ellwood City, Pa., Oct. 15, 1957; d. Harry and Blanche McCloskey; m. Steve Todd; 1 child. BA with honors, Chatham Coll., Pitts., 1979; JD, U. Pitts. Sch. Law, 1982; LLM (hon.), U. Va. Sch. Law, 2004. Litig. atty. US Steel Corp., Pitts., 1982—87; trial practice Pitts., 1987—99; spl. master Allegheny County Ct. Common Pleas, Pa., 1989—99; justice Pa. Superior Ct., Pitts., 2000—07, Pa. Supreme Ct., 2008—. Lectr. on trial and appellate practice and procedure. Former bd. mem. Leadership Pitts. Program; bd. mem. Pitts. Action Against Rape, Finnegan Found. Mem.: ABA, Women's Bar Assn., Western Pa., Internat. Assn. Women Judges, Nat. Assn. Women Judges, Am. Judicature Soc., Pa. Bar Assn., Allegheny Bar Assn., Acad. Trial Lawyers, Allegheny County. Democrat. Office: Supreme Court Of Pennsylvania 301 Grant St Ste 1010 Pittsburgh PA 15219-1408*

TODD, DIANNA KAYE, nursing administrator, educator; b. Middletown, Ohio, Jan. 7, 1954; d. Rondle and Frances Louise Adams Lee, Alma Rogers Lee (Stepmother); m. Caleph Lee Todd, Aug. 19, 1988; 1 child, Caleb Michael. Registered nurse, State Ohio Bd. Nursing, 1987. Assoc. nursing Miami U., Middletown, 1987; staff RN psyc unit Middletown Regional Hosp., Ohio, 1987—90; staff RN and supr. Willow Knoll Nursing Ctr., Middletown, 1991, Quaker Heights Friends Home, Waynesville, Ohio, 1993—96; staff RN Otterbein Homes, Lebanon, Ohio, 1991; staff RN psyc unit Ft. Hamilton Hughes Meml. Hosp., Ohio, 1992—93; primary instr. Miami Jacobs Coll., Dayton, Ohio, 1998—99; program coord. and primary instr. Sinclair CC, Dayton, 1999—. Republican. Office: Sinclair CC 444 W 3rd St Dayton OH 45402 Office Fax: 937-512-5180. Business E-Mail: dianna.todd@sinclair.edu.

TODD, JAMES DALE, federal judge; b. Scotts Hill, Tenn., May 20, 1943; s. James P. and Jeanette Grace (Duck) T.; m. Jeanie M. Todd, June 26, 1965; 2 children. BS, Lambuth Coll., 1965; M Combined Scis., U. Miss., 1968; JD, Memphis State U., 1972. Bar: Tenn. 1972, US Dist. Ct. (we. dist.) Tenn. 1972, US Ct. Appeals (6th cir.) 1973, US Supreme Ct. 1975. Tchr. sci., chmn. sci. dept. Lyman High Sch., Longwood, Fla., 1965-68, Memphis U. Sch., 1968-72; ptnr. Waldrop, Farmer, Todd & Breen, P.A., 1972-83; cir. judge div. II 26th Jud. Dist., Jackson, Tenn., 1983-85; judge US Dist. Ct. (we. dist.) Tenn., Jackson, 1985—2008, chief judge, 2001—07, sr. judge, 2008—. Recipient Law & Liberty award, Jackson Madison County Bar Assn., 1988, Lifetime Achievement award Lambuth U., 2001; named Alumnus of Yr. Lambuth Coll. Alumni Assn., 1985 Fellow Tenn. Bar Found.; mem. Fed. Judges Assn. (bd. dirs. 1998-2002), Fed. Bar Assn., Jackson Madison County Bar Assn. (pres. 1978-79), Dist. Judges Assn. of 6th Cir. (pres. 2000-2001). Methodist. Office: US Dist Ct 111 S Highland Ave Jackson TN 38301-6107

TODD, JAMES MARION, retired lawyer; b. Paris, Ky., May 13, 1929; s. Thomas Marion and Ida Saxton (Estes) T.; m. Marjorie Ann Vance, Aug. 22, 1959; children: Thomas Melvin, James M. Jr. AB, U. Ky., Lexington, 1952, JD, 1956. Bar: Ky. 1956. Assoc. S.J. Stallings, Louisville, 1956-57; sole practice Lexington, Ky., 1957-65, 1982-86; ptnr. Todd & Compton, Lexington, 1965-73, Todd & Sherrow, Lexington, 1973-82, Todd & Todd, Lexington, 1986-88, Todd, Hicks & Todd, Lexington, 1988-92, Todd, Bradley & Hicks, Lexington, 1992-93; pvt. practice Lexington, 1993—2002. Vice mayor Lexington-Fayette County Govt., 1978-82; ch. elder. Served in Korean War, ret. as maj. USAF, 1952-54. U. Ky. Fellow. Fellow Ky. Bar Found. (charter, life); mem. Lions (pres. breakfast club 1965-66). Republican. Home: 395 Redding Rd # 28 Lexington KY 40517 Home Phone: 859-263-5502. E-mail: toddyhot@aol.com.

TODD, LEE TROVER, JR., academic administrator, electrical engineer; b. Earlington, Ky., May 6, 1946; s. Lee T. Todd; m. Patricia Brantley; children: Troy, Kathryn. BSEE, U. Ky., 1968; MS, MIT, 1970, PhD in Elec. Engring., 1973. IBM postdoctoral fellow MIT, 1973-74; asst. prof. engring. U. Ky., Lexington, 1974-78, assoc. prof., 1978-87, pres., 2001—; chmn., chief exec. officer DataBeam Corp., Lexington, 1983—2000; v.p. Hughes Display Products, Lexington, 1993—93; sr. v.p. pres. Lotus Devel. Corp., 2000—01. Chmn. Ky. Sci. & Tech. Coun., Lexington, 1987—; mem. Ky. Epscor Com., 1985—, Ky. Acad. Sci., 1988; chair Southeastern Conf. Com. on Academic Initiatives; mem. Cou. of Edn. Commn. Contbr. articles to profl. jours. Chmn., deacon Calvary Bapt. Ch., Lexington, 1989; bd. dirs. Ky. Econ. Devel. Corp., Frankfort, Georgetown Coll., Ky. Named Entrepreneur of Yr., INC mag., 1989; recipient Outstanding Alumnus award U. Ky. Coll. Engring., 1989, Small Bus. of Yr. award Lexington C. of C., U.S. Gt. Tchr. award, 1983; Hertz Found. fellow, 1968-73. Mem. NSF, Ky. Soc. Profl. Engrs. (Award of Achievement 1990), U. Ky. Alumni Assn., Leadership Ky., Louisville Adv. Tech. Coun. Baptist. Achievements include patents in field. Office: Pres Office U Ky 101 Main Building Lexington KY 40506-0032 Office Phone: 859-257-1701. Office Fax: 859-257-1760. E-mail: ltodd@email.uky.edu.*

TODD, LINDA MARIE, nutrition researcher, circulation facilitator, financial consultant, pilot; b. LA, Mar. 30, 1948; d. Ithel Everette and Janet Marie Fredricks; m. William MacKenzie Cook, Jan. 11, 1982 (div. Oct. 1989); m. Robert Oswald Todd, Apr. 8, 1990; 1 child, Jesse MacKenzie Todd. BA in Psychology and Sociology, U. Colo., 1969; student in Psychology, U. No. Colo., 1970; ins. and estate planning courses, 1990—2007, mgmt. tng. programs, 2001—. Pilot lic., weather cert., FCC lic., Calif. life ins. lic., coll. teaching credential; registered with Nat. Assn. Securities Dealers. Counselor Jeffco Juvenile Detention Ctr., Golden, Colo., 1969-71; communications Elan Vital, Denver, 1971-81; legal sec. Fredman, Silverberg & Lewis, San Diego, 1980-82; escrow supr. Performance Mktg. Concepts, Olympic Valley, Calif., 1982-85; mgmt. commn. instr. Sierra Coll., Truckee, Calif., 1986-87; regional mgr. Primerica Fin. Svcs., Reno, 1987-91; air traffic, weather advisor Truckee Tahoe Airport Dist., Calif., 1986-96; circulation mgr. Sierra Sun and Tahoe World Newspapers, 2001—08. Student tour leader, air show organizer Truckee (Calif.) Tahoe Airport, 1986-96; fin. cons. Primerica Fin. Svcs., Truckee, 1987-91; gen. agt. TTS Fin., 1992—2007; co-founder Todd Nutrition, 1995—; co-owner Todd Aero, 1990—; bd. dirs. Pacific Crest Fin. Corp., 1996—. Editor: (newsletter) Communications, 1975. Chorus mem. operas and musicals, 1960s-70s; prodn. crew Lake Tahoe Summer Music Festivals, 2000-03; sec. gen. Arapahoe H.S. Model UN, Littleton, Colo., 1965; del. State Model UN, Colo., 1966; conv. del. Elan Vital, The Ninety-Nines, Inc.; pub. affairs officer CAP. Univ. scholar Littleton (Colo.) Edn. Assn., 1966, flight scholar The Ninety-Nines Inc., Reno, 1990; named Recruiter of Month, Al Williams Primerica, Reno, 1987. Mem. CAP (lt.), Elan Vital, Plane Talkers, The Ninety Nines, Planetary Soc. Avocations: hiking, skiing, swimming, flying, soaring. Home and Office: PO Box 1303 Truckee CA 96160-1303 Personal E-mail: ltodd.1971@gmail.com.

TODD, LORI A., toxicologist, professor; b. Bklyn. BS, Antioch Coll., Yellow Springs, Ohio, 1975; M, Cornell U., Ithaca, NY, 1980; PhD, U. NC, Chapel Hill, 1990. Cert. in CIH ABIH, Mich., 1995. Dep. chief environ. toxicology NYC Dept. of Health, 1981—85; prof. U. NC, 1990—; trainer & coach Legacy Ctr., Morrisville, NC, 2000—. Contbr. scientific papers to profl. jours. (Presdl. Faculty Fellows award, 1994, Mich. Ind. Hygiene Assoc. Outstanding Paper award, 2003); artist (sculpture, painting). Recipient Spl. Emphasis Rsch. Career award, CDC, 1991—94, Young Investigator award, Hoechst Celanese Corp., 1993. Mem.: ACGIH. Office: Legacy Ctr 2200 Gateway Ctr Blvd Morrisville NC 27560 E-mail: lori.todd@thelegacycenter.com.

TODD, MARGARET DONNELLAN, library director; MLS, U. So. Calif., LA; MBA, Pepperdine U., Malibu, Calif. Sr. libr. mgr. Orange Pub. Libr., Calif.; dir. Whittier Pub. Libr., Calif., 1989—2001; county libr. County of LA Pub. Libr., 2001—. Mem.: Calif. Libr. Assn. (pres. 2006—07). Office: County of LA Pub Libr 7400 E Imperial Hwy Downey CA 90241-7011 Office Phone: 562-940-8400. E-mail: mdtodd@gw.colapl.org.

TODD, MATTHEW, school librarian; b. Norwalk, Ohio, Nov. 21, 1970; s. Edward and Nan Leonard Todd. MA, U. Exeter, Eng., 1994, Northwestern U., Ill., 1998; MLIS, U. Wis., Milw., 2002. Asst. prof. Northern Va. CC, Alexandria, Va., 1998—. Mem.: Va. Libr. Assn. (treas. 2007—). Home: 4004 Beecher St NorthWest Washington DC 20007 Office: Northern Virginia CC 3001 North Beauregard St Alexandria VA 22311

TODD, MICHAEL CULLEN, sculptor, painter; b. Omaha, June 20, 1935; s. Patrick Cullen and Helen Lorraine (Round) T.; m. Kathryn Asako Doi, June 16, 1974 (div. 1986); 1 child, Mia Doi; m. Patricia Ann Alexakis, Nov. 29, 1986. B.F.A. magna cum laude, U. Notre Dame, 1957; MA, UCLA, 1959. Exhbns., in Paris, London, N.Y.C., Boston, Detroit, Los Angeles, Washington and San Diego, 1960—; represented in permanent collections, Whitney Mus., Los Angeles County Mus. Art, La Jolla Mus., San Diego, Oakland (Calif.) Mus., Norton Simon Mus., Pasadena, Calif., Met. Mus. Art, N.Y., Hirshhorn Mus., Washington. (Woodrow Wilson fellow 1957-59, Fulbright fellow 1961-63, recipient award Nat. Endowment Arts 1974-75). Address: 2817 Clearwater St Los Angeles CA 90039-2807 Office Phone: 323-662-7458. Personal E-mail: miktod@earthlink.net.

TODD, REEDER ALLEN, pharmacist; s. Rodney Reeder and Debrah Thomas. PharmD, Midwestern U. Glendale, Ariz., 2005. Pharmacy resident U. Va. Health Sys., Charlottesville, 2005—07, drug info. pharmacist, 2007; chief, inpatient pharmacy Brooke Army Med. Ctr., Ft. Sam Houston, Tex., 2007—. Mem. Ctrl. Tex. Soc. Health Sys. Pharmacy, San Antonio, 2009. Capt. US Army, 2007—09, Ft. Sam Houston. Recipient Am. Jour. award, Health Sys. Pharmacy, 2008. Mem.: Am. Soc. Health Sys. Pharmacy (Excellence award 2006). Avocations: running, tennis, golf. Office: Brooke Army Med Ctr 3851 Roger Brooke Rd Fort Sam Houston TX 78234

TODD, ROBERT FRANKLIN, III, oncologist, educator; b. Granville, Ohio, Apr. 16, 1948; m. Susan Erhard, 1977; children: Currier Nathaniel, Andrew Joseph. AB, Duke U., 1970, PhD, 1975, MD, 1976. Diplomate Am. Bd. Internal Medicine. Intern Peter Bent Brigham Hosp., Boston, 1976-77, resident, 1977-78; fellow in oncology Sidney Farber Cancer Inst., Boston, 1978-80; clin. fellow in medicine Harvard Med. Sch., Boston, 1978-81; postdoctoral fellow divsn. tumor immunology Sidney Farber Cancer Inst., Boston, 1979-81; asst. prof. medicine Harvard Med. Sch., Boston, 1981-84; assoc. prof. internal medicine U. Mich., Ann Arbor, 1984-88, assoc. prof. cellular and molecular biology, 1985-88, assoc. dir. divsn. hematology-oncology internal medicine, 1987-91, prof. internal medicine, 1988—, assoc. chair for rsch. dept. internal medicine, 1989-91, assoc. chair dept. internal medicine, 1991-93, chief divsn. hematology-oncology dept. internal medicine, 1993—2007, assoc. v.p. rsch., 1999—2005, Frances and Victor Ginsberg prof. hematology/oncology, 1999—, interim chair, dept. internal medicine, 2007—. Attending physician U. Mich. Hosps., 1984—. Contbr. numerous articles to profl. jours.; patentee in field. Mem.: Assn. Am. Physicians, Am. Soc. Clin. Investigation, S.W. Oncology Group, Ctrl. Soc. Clin. Rsch. (councilor 1997—, pres. 2001—02), Am. Fedn. Clin. Rsch. (councilor midwest chpt. 1986—89), Am. Soc. Hematology (councilor 2005—), Soc. Leukocyte Biology (councilor 1996—99), Am. Soc. Clin. Oncology, Am. Assn. Cancer Rsch., Am. Assn. Immunologists, ACP, Alpha Omega Alpha, Phi Beta Kappa. Office: U Mich Med Sch 1500 E Med Ctr Dr 3101 Taubman Ctr Ann Arbor MI 48109-5368 Business E-Mail: robtodd@umich.edu.

TODD, RONALD GARY, lawyer; b. Spokane, Wash., Dec. 12, 1946; s. Theodore H. and Dorothea I. (Swanson) T.; m. Natalie A., June 16, 1973; children: Russell E., Brian N., David E. AB, Cornell U., 1969; JD, Columbia U., 1972. Bar: NY 1973, US Dist. Ct. (so. and ea. dists.) NY 1975, US Ct. Appeals (2d cir.) 1975, US Supreme Ct. 1976, DC 1993. Atty. Dewey Ballantine, NYC, 1973-79, Simpson Thacher & Bartlett, NYC, 1980-82; atty., ptnr. Golenbock & Barell, NYC, 1982-89; ptnr. Reid & Priest, NYC, 1989—2000; chief counsel J.P. Morgan Title Agy. LLC, 2000—05; v.p., asst. gen. counsel JP Morgan Chase & Co., 2000—05; v.p., Nat. Underwriting Counsel 1st Am. Title Ins. Co. NY, NYC, 2005—. Instr., guest lectr. NYU Sch. Continuing Edn., 1983-90; adv. bd. Commonwealth Land Title and TransAm. Title Ins. Co., NYC, 1992-97. Contbr. articles to profl. jours. Pres., bd. dirs. Seven Bridges Field Club, 1982—85. Mem. ABA (real property sect. 1973—), NY Bar Assn. (real property sect. 1973—), DC Bar Assn. (real property sect. 1992—2006). Avocations: instrumental music, tennis. Office: First Am Title Ins Co NY 633 Third Ave New York NY 10017 Business E-Mail: rgtodd@firstam.com.

TODD, WILLIAM E., United States Ambassador to Brunei Darussalam; m. Ann Buckingham-Todd; 4 children. CPA Va. Dir. planning and resource mgmt., US and Fgn. Comml. Svc. US Dept. Commerce; dir., Office Security and Mgmt. US Dept. Transp.; mem., Sr. Exec. Svc. US State Dept., exec. dir., Bur. Resource Mgmt., prin. dep. asst. sec., dep. asst. sec., exec. dir. and contr., Bur. Internat. Narcotics and Law Enforcement Affairs, 2002—06, COO global ops., Bur. Internat. Narcotics and Law Enforcement Affairs, dep. inspector gen., 2006—08, acting inspector gen., 2008, US amb. to Brunei Darussalam, 2008—. Recipient Bronze medal, Dept. Commerce, 1988, Dir. Gen. Spl. Act award, China, 1996, Meritorious Performance award, US State Dept. Sr. Exec. Svc., 2000—07, Spl. Act Group awards, Iraq/Jordan and Afghanistan, 2004, Presdl. Rank award, 2005. Office: US Embassy PO Box 2991 Bandar Seri Begawan BS8675 Brunei Office Phone: 673-222-0384. Office Fax: 673-222-5293.*

TODD, WILLIAM MILLS, III, literature educator; b. Newport News, Va., Aug. 15, 1944; s. William Mills Todd and Jeanette Todd Gray, Joseph Rockhill Gray (Stepfather); m. Eva Andenaes Todd, June 27, 1968; 1 child, Karen Elizabeth. AB, Dartmouth Coll., Hanover, NH, 1966; MA, U. Oxford, Eng., 1968; PhD, Columbia U., NY, 1973. Prof. slavic and comp. lit. Stanford U., Calif., 1972—88, Harvard U., Cambridge, Mass., 1988—, dean undergrad. edn., 1997—2000. Author: (book) Fiction and Society in the Age of Pushkin (Pushkin medal, MOPRIAL, 2003, Disting. award, AATSEEL, 2005).

TODD, ZANE GREY, retired utilities executive; b. Hanson, Ky., Feb. 3, 1924; s. Marshall Elvin and Kate (McCormick) T.; m. Marysnow Stone, Feb. 8, 1950 (dec. 1983); m. Frances Z. Anderson, Jan. 6, 1984. Student, Evansville Coll., 1947-49; BS summa cum laude, Purdue U., 1951, DEng (hon.), 1979; postgrad., U. Mich., 1965; DHL, U. Indpls., 1993. Fingerprint classifier FBI, 1942-43; electric system planning engr. Indpls. Power & Light Co., 1951-56, spl. assignments supr., 1956-60, head elec. system planning, 1960-65, head substation design div., 1965-68, head distbn. engring. dept., 1968-70, asst. to v.p., 1970-72, v.p., 1972-74, exec. v.p., 1974-75, pres., 1975-81, chmn., chief exec. officer, 1976-89, dir., chmn. exec. com., 1989-94, chief exec. officer, 1981-89; chmn., pres. IPALCO Enterprises, Inc., Indpls., 1983-89, dir., chmn. exec. com., 1989-94; chmn. bd., chief exec. officer Mid-Am. Capital Resources, Inc. subs. IPALCO Enterprises, Inc., Indpls., 1984-89, also bd. dirs., 1984-94. Gen. mgr. Mooresville (Ind.) Pub. Svc. Co., Inc., 1956-60; bd. dirs. Nat. City Bank Ind. (formerly Mchts. Nat. Corp.), 1975-94, Am. States Ins. Co., 1976-94; hon. dir. 500 Festival Assocs., Inc., pres. 1987. Originator probability analysis of power system reliability; contbr. articles to tech. jours. and mags. Past pres. adv. bd. St. Vincent Hosp.; past chmn., bd. trustees Ind. Cen. U. (now U. Indpls.); Nat. and Greater Indpls. adv. bds. Salvation Army, 1984-96; bd. govs. Associated Colls. of Ind., 1979-92. Sgt. AUS, 1943-47. Recipient William Booth award Salvation Army, 1994; named Disting. Engring. Alumnus Purdue U., 1976, Outstanding Elec. Engr. Purdue U., 1992, Knight of Malta, Order of St. John of Jerusalem, 1986. Fellow IEEE (past chmn. power sys. engring. com.); mem. ASME, NSPE, Power Engring. Soc., Ind. Fiscal Policy Inst. (bd. govs.), Ind. C. of C., Indpls. C. of C., Mooresville C. of C. (past pres.), PGA Nat. Country Club, Ulen Country Club, Indpls. Athletic Club (past bd. dirs.), Meridian Hills Country Club (past bd. dirs.), Skyline Club (bd. govs.), Newcomen Soc. (past chmn. Ind.), Rotary, Lions (past pres.), Eta Kappa Nu, Tau Beta Pi.

TODD COPLEY, JUDITH A., engineering educator; b. Wakefield, West Yorkshire, Eng., Dec. 13, 1950; arrived in US, 1978; d. Marley and Joan Mary (Birkinshaw) Booth; m. David Michael Todd, June 17, 1972 (div. June 1981); m. Stephen Michael Copley, Aug. 3, 1984; 1 child, Amy Elizabeth. BA in Materials Sci., Cambridge U., Eng., 1972, MA, PhD in Materials Sci., 1977. Rsch. asst. Imperial Coll. Sci. and Tech., London, 1976-78; rsch. assoc. SUNY, Stonybrook, 1978; rsch. engr. U. Calif., Berkeley, 1979-81; asst. prof. materials sci. and mech. engring. U. So. Calif., LA, 1982—90; assoc. prof. metall. and materials engring. Ill. Inst. Tech., Chgo., 1990-97, assoc. chair mech. materials and aerospace engring., 1995—2001, prof. materials and mech. engring., 1997—2002, assoc. dean rsch. Armour Coll. Engring. and Sci., 2001—02; P.B. Breneman dept. head chair chair dept. engring. sci. and mechanics Pa. State U., University Park, 2002—. Mem. task force Materials Property Coun., NYC, 1979—89; prof. Iron and Steel Soc., 1996—2002; mem. editl. bds. Contbr. articles to profl. jours.; patentee in field. Recipient Brit. Univs. Student Travel award, 1972, Brit. Fedn. Univ. Women award, 1972, Faculty Rsch. award Oak Ridge (Tenn.) Nat. Lab., 1986, Vanadium award British Inst. Materials, 1990; Kathryn Kingswell Meml. scholar, 1972, Julia Beveridge award, IIT, 1998, Cert. Appreciation Am. Soc. Mech. Engrs., 1995, 97, Forging Industry Ednl. Rsch. Found., 1993, Booz-Allen and Hamilton Tchg. and Svc. award, Ill. Inst. Tech., 1996, Mary Ewart Traveling Scholarship, Cambridge U., 1972, Sci. Rsch. Coun. Fellowship and Overseas Travel award, 1972; Presdl. Excellence in Sci., Math. and Engring. mentoring award, NSF, 2006, Presdl. award, PAESMEM, NSF, 2007. Fellow ASM Internat., ASME Internat. (chmn. materials and fabrication com. 1993-97, pressure vessel and piping divsn. membership chair PVP divsn., 1997-2001, assoc. editor Jour. Pressure Vessel and Piping Tech. 1994-2001, exec. com. and publs. chair PVP divsn. 2001-05, v.p. mfg. group 2002-05, tech. program chair, 2004-05, tech. conf. chair 2005-06, divsn. chair 2006-07, Bd. on Women and Miniorites award 1997), Disting. Svc. award 2007), Soc. Engring. Sci. (bd. dirs. 2006—), Assn. Women in Sci., ASM Internat. (chmn. LA chpt. 1986-87, coun. mem. materials sci. divsn. 1984-89); mem. AIME (Rsch. award 1983), ASTM, AAUW, Soc. Women Engrs. (sr.), Electron Microscopy Soc., Electrochem. Soc., Hist. Metallurgy Soc., Nat. Soc. Corrosion Engrs. (Seed grant award 1983), Microbeam Analysis Soc., Soc. Mfg. Engrs. (sr.), Instn. Materials, Chartered (sr.) Engr. Status, Minerals, Metals, Materials Soc. of the Am. Inst. Mining, Metall. Petroleum Engrs., Am. Ceramics Soc., Ill. Microscopical Soc., Soc. Engring. Sci. (mem. bd. dirs.). Avocation: archaeology. Office: Pennsylvania State Univ Dept Engring Sci and Mechanics 212 Earth-Engring Sci Bldg University Park PA 16802-6812 Office Phone: 814-863-0771. Business E-Mail: jtodd@psu.edu.

TODHUNTER, JOHN ANTHONY, toxicologist, consultant; b. Cali, Valle, Colombia, Oct. 9, 1949; s. John Arthur and Teresa Maria (Torres) T.; divorced, 1986; children: Jennifer, Julia; m. Holli Wilson, Apr. 19, 1986; 1 child, Jacqueline Rose. BSc, UCLA, 1971; MSc, Calif. State U., 1973; PhD, U. Calif., Santa Barbara, 1976. Diplomate Am. Bd. Toxicology, Am. Bd. Forensic Examiners. Instr. Calif. State U., LA, 1972-73; rsch. asst. U. Calif., Santa Barbara, 1973-76; fellow Roche Inst. Molecular Biology, Nutley, NJ, 1976-78; asst. prof. Cath. U. Am., Washington, 1978-81, chmn. Biochemistry Program, 1980-81; asst. adminstr. U.S. EPA, Washington, 1981-83; cons. Sci. Regulatory Svcs. Internat., Washington, 1983-91; pres. SRS Internat. Corp., 1991—, SRS Internat. Health Care Group, 1995—; CEO Assura Pharmaceuticals, 2006—. Expert advisor European regional office WHO, Stockholm, 1984; mem. Hazardous Waste Siting Bd., Annapolis, Md., 1980-81. Contbr. articles to profl. jours. Bd. dirs. Reagan Alumni Assn., Washington, 1985—; vol. Am. Cancer Soc., Washington, 1988-93; mem. Presdl. Transition Team, Washington, 1980. U. Calif. Bd. Regents fellow, 1975, B.R. Baker Meml. fellow dept. chemistry U. Calif., Santa Barbara, 1976. Fellow Am. Inst. Chemists (dir. at large 1989-92, vice chmn. bd. 1992); mem. Soc. of Toxicology, Am. Chem. Soc., Soc. for Risk Analysis, N.Y. Acad. Sci. Office Phone: 703-821-3221. Business E-Mail: jtodhunter@assurapharm.com.

TODMAN, MICHAEL A., manufacturing executive; b. St. Thomas, US VI; BSBA, Georgetown U. With Price Waterhouse and Co., Wang Labs., Inc.; dir. fin. UK Whirlpool, 1993—95, gen. mgr. No. Europe to v.p. consumer svcs. Whirlpool Europe, 1993—95, contr. N.Am., 1995—96, v.p. product mgmt., 1996—97, v.p. Sears sales and mktg., 1997—99, sr. v.p. sales and mktg. N.Am., 1999—2001, exec. v.p. N.Am., mem. corp. exec. com., 2001, corp. exec. v.p., pres. Whirlpool Europe, 2001—05, pres. Whirlpool Internat., bd. dirs., 2006—07, pres. Whirlpool No. Am., 2007—. Office: Whirlpool Inc 2000 N M-63 Benton Harbor MI 49022

TODOROFF, CHRISTOPHER M., lawyer, insurance company executive; BA, Rutgers Univ., 1984; JD, Cornell Univ., 1987. Bar: 1988. Law practice in NY & Fla., 1988—95; legal positions through v.p. & sr. corp. counsel Aetna Inc., 1995—2008; sr. v.p., gen. counsel Humana, Louisville, 2008—. Editor: Cornell Law Rev. Office: Humana 500 W Main St Louisville KY 40202*

TODOROV, TZVETAN, scientific researcher; b. Sofia, Bulgaria, Mar. 1, 1939; arrived in France, 1963. s. Todor Todorov Borov and Haritina (Peeva) Todorova; m. Martine Van Woerkens, June 18, 1971 (div. Sept. 1980); 1 child, Boris; m. Nancy L. Huston, May 16, 1981; children: Lea, Alexandre. Grad., U. Sofia, 1961; Doctorat, U. Paris, 1966, Doctorat és lettres, 1970. Research asst. Ecole des Hautes Etudes en Scis. Sociales, Paris, 1964-67; vis. lectr. Yale U., New Haven, 1967-68; sci. researcher Ctr. Nat. de la Recherche Sci., Paris, 1968—. Vis. prof. Columbia U., N.Y.C., 1974, 77, 80, 83, 86, 89; bd. dirs. Ctr. de Recherches sur les Arts et le Langage, Paris. Author: The Fantastic, 1970, Theories of the Symbol, 1977, The Conquest of America, 1982, Literature and Its Theorists, 1984; editor Poetique, 1970-79. Mem. Am. Acad Arts & Scis. (fgn. hon.). Office: CRAL - EHESS 105 Bd Raspail 75006 Paris France

TODOROVA, VALENTINA K., biochemist, educator; arrived in US, 2000, permanent resident; BS, U. Sofia, 1976, MS, 1977; PhD, Bulgarian Acad. Scis., Sofia, 1990. Biologist Inst. Parasitology Bulgarian Acad. Scis., 1978—83, asst. prof. Inst. Parasitology, 1983—93, asst. prof. Inst. Molecular Biology, 1996—2000; vis. scientist U. Glasgow, Scotland, 1993—95; postdoctoral rschr. dept. biochemistry U. Ark. Med. Scis., Little Rock, 2000—02, rsch. asst. prof. dept. surgery, 2002—. Grantee, Susan G. Komen Found., 2006—. Mem.: ASPEN (grantee 2006).

TODREAS, NEIL EMMANUEL, nuclear engineering educator; b. Peabody, Mass., Dec. 17, 1935; s. David and Anna (Gendleman) T.; m. Carol S. Schonberg, June 19, 1958; children: Timothy, Ian. BSM.E., MS, Cornell U., 1958; ScD in Nuc. Engring., MIT, 1966. Asst. prof. dept. nuc. engring. MIT, Cambridge, Mass., 1970-71, assoc. prof., 1971-75, prof., 1975—, Kepco prof. nuc. engring. and prof. mech. engring., 1992—, head dept. nuc. engring., 1981-89. Served to lt. (j.g.) USN, 1958-62. Named Disting. Tchr., Ruth and Joel Spira award MIT Sch. Engring., 1995. Fellow: ASME, Am. Nuc. Soc. (Tech. Achievement award for outstanding contbns. to thermal hydraulics 1994, Arthur Holly Compton award for outstanding educators in nuc. engring. 1995, Henry DeWolf-Smyth award 2005); mem.: Internat. Nuc. Energy Acad., Nat. Acad. Engring., Sigma Xi, Tau Beta Pi, Pi Tau Sigma. Office: MIT Bldg 24 Rm 205 77 Massachusetts Ave Cambridge MA 02139-4307 E-mail: todreas@mit.edu.

TOEDT, D(ELL) C(HARLES), III, lawyer; b. Maxwell AFB, Ala., Nov. 17, 1954; m. Maretta A. Comfort. BA with high honors, U. Tex., 1973, JD, 1981. Bar: Tex. 1982, U.S. Patent and Trademark Office 1983, U.S. Dist. Ct. (so. dist.) Tex. 1984, U.S. Ct. Appeals (fed. cir.) 1984, U.S. Supreme Ct. 1991, Calif. 1996. Atty. Schlanger, Cook, Cohn, Mills & Grossberg, Houston, 1982-83, Arnold, White & Durkee, Houston, 1983-99; v.p., gen. counsel BindView Corp., Houston, 1999—2006; founder Pactix Corp., 2006—. Adj. prof. S. Tex. Coll. Law, 1988—90. Assoc. editor: Tex. Law Rev., 1981—82, author, editor: Licensing Law Handbook: Computer Software Issues, 1987; editor: Law and Bus. Computer Software, 1989—2002; contbr. articles to profl. jours. Served to lt. USN, 1974—79. Mem.: ABA (chmn. computer-related coms. 1985—96, elected mem. coun. sect. intellectual property law 1999—2000). Home Phone: 713-665-2901; Office Phone: 713-893-3925. Personal E-mail: dc.toedt@toedt.com.

TOEDTMAN, JAMES SMITH, journalist, editor; b. Dayton, Ohio, Dec. 1, 1941; s. James Christian and Ella Barnes (Smith) T.; m. Haydee N. Sicart, Aug. 23, 1969; children: Eric, Kristen AB, Coll. Wooster, 1963; postgrad., U. Queensland, Brisbane, Australia, 1964; MSc in Journalism, Columbia U., 1967. Pub. dir. Coll. Wooster, Ohio, 1963, 1965; reporter, city editor, Sunday news editor, mng. editor, Washington Bur. chief Newsday, LI, NY, 1967—79, 1986—2005; exec. editor Boston Herald Am., 1979—82; editor Balt. News Am., 1982—86, AARP Bulletin, 2005—. Co-author: Good Roots, 2006. Recipient Shared Silurian Soc. award, Polk award, Pulitzer Prize, 1970, 92, 97, spl. citation Inter-Am. Press Assn., 1979, Best Editl. award Md.-Del.-D.C. Press Assn., 1984, 86; Rotary Found. fellow, 1964, Internat. fellow Columbia U., 1966-67, Pres. Disting. Svc. award, Flagler Coll., 2009. Mem.: Coll. Wooster Alumni Assn. (pres. 1980—81). Methodist. Home: 2604 Geneva Hill Ct Oakton VA 22124-1534 Office: AARP Bulletin 601 E St NW Washington DC 20049 Home Phone: 703-319-8914; Office Phone: 202-434-3357. Business E-Mail: jtoedtman@aarp.org.

TOENNIES, JAN PETER, research chemical physicist; b. Phila., May 3, 1930; arrived in Fed. Republic Germany, 1957; s. Gerrit and Dita (Jebens) T.; m. Monika Elisabeth Zelesnick; children: Susanne, Annette. BA in Physics, Amherst Coll., Mass., 1952; PhD in Chemistry, Brown U., Providence, 1957; PhD (hon.), U. Gothenburg, 2000; DSc (hon.), Amherst Coll., Mass., 2007. Rsch. asst. Bonn (Fed. Republic Germany) U., 1957-65, dozent, 1965-68; dir., sci. mem. Max Planck Inst. Fluid Mechanics, Göttingen, 1969—98. Adj. prof. Bonn U., 1971—; assoc. prof. Göttingen U., 1971—; vis. Miller Prof. Chemistry and Physics, U. Calif., Berkeley, 2005-06; cons. Uranit GmbH, Jülich, Fed. Republic Germany, 1977-89. Author: Chemical Reactions in Shock Waves, 1964; adv. editor Jour. Chem. Physics, 1973-78; editor monograph series, Springer Series in Chem. Physics, 1979—. Recipient Gold Heyrovsky medal Czechoslovak Acad. Scis., 1991, Alumni citation Brown U., 1988, Hewlett-Packard Europhysics prize for outstanding achievement in condensed matter rsch., 1992, Max Planck prize Deutsche Forschungsgemeinschaft and Alexander Humboldt Soc., 1992, Kotos medal Polish Chem. Soc., 2005, Benjamin Franklin medal in Physics, Franklin Inst., 2006. Fellow Am. Phys. Soc., World Innovation Found.; mem. European Phys. Soc., German Phys. Soc. (sect. chmn. 1977-80, Stern-Gerlach medal 2002, mem. atomic physics sect.), Göttingen Acad. Scis. (corr., Physics award 1964), Coun. European Phys. Soc., Acad. Sciences Czech Republic, World Cultural Coun. (hon.), Deutsche Akademie der Naturforscher Leopoldina. Home: Ewaldstrasse 7 D-37085 Göttingen Germany Office: Max Planck Inst for Dynamics and Self Orgn Bunsenstr 10 D-37073 Göttingen Germany Office Phone: 011495515176382. Business E-Mail: jtoenni@gwdg.de.

TOENSING, VICTORIA, lawyer; b. Colon, Panama, Oct. 16, 1941; d. Philip William and Victoria (Brady) Long; m. Trent David Toensing, Oct. 29, 1962 (div. 1976); children: Todd Robert, Brady Cronon, Amy Victoriana; m. Joseph E. diGenova, June 27, 1981. BS in Edn., Ind. U., 1962; JD cum laude, U. Detroit, 1975. Bar: Mich. 1976, D.C. 1978. Tchr. English, Milw., 1965-66; law clk. to presiding justice U.S. Ct. Appeals, Detroit, 1975-76; asst. U.S. atty. U.S. Atty.'s Office, Detroit, 1976-81; chief counsel U.S. Senate Intelligence Com., Washington, 1981-84; dep. asst. atty. gen. criminal div. Dept. Justice, Washington, 1984-88; spl. counsel Hughes Hubbard & Reed, Washington, 1988-90; ptnr. Cooter and Gell, Washington, 1990-91; ptnr., co-chmn. nat. white collar group Manatt, Phelps and Phillips, Washington, 1991-95; founding ptnr. diGenova & Toensing, Wasington, 1996—. Mem. working group on corp. sanctions U.S. Sentencing Commn., 1988-89; co-chairperson Coalition for Women's Appts. Justice Judiciary Task Force, 1988-92; spl. counsel for Teamsters investigation, U.S. Ho. of Reps., Subcom. on Oversight and Investigations of com. on Edn. and the Workforce, 1997-98. Author: Bringing Sanity to the Insanity Defense, 1983, Mens Rea: Insanity by Another Name, 1984; contbg. author: Fighting Back: Winning The War Against Terrorism, Desk Book on White Collar Crime, 1991; contbr. articles to profl. jours. Founder, chmn. Women's Orgn. To Meet Existing Needs, Mich., 1975-79; chmn. Republican Women's Task Force, 1979-81; bd. dirs. Project on Equal Edn. Rights, Mich., 1980-81, Nat. Hist. Intelligence Mus., 1987-95, America's Talking Legal Analyst, 1995; MSNBC legal analyst, 1998-99. Recipient spl. commendation Office U.S. Atty. Gen., 1980, agy. seal medallion CIA, 1986, award of achievement Alpha Chi Omega, 1992; featured on cover N.Y. Time Mag. for anti-terrorism work, April 1991. Mem. ABA (mem. standing com. on law and nat. security, mem. coun. criminal justice sect., mem. adv. com. complex crimes and litigation, vice chmn. white collar crime com., chmn. subcom. on corp. criminal liability). Office: Ste 737 1776 K St NW Washington DC 20006 Office Phone: 202-289-7701.

TOERGE, LYNN, athletic trainer; b. Pitts., Nov. 11, 1955; d. John Elmer and Mary Ruth Toerge. BS, Ind. State U., Terre Haute, 1981. Athletic trainer, phys. ed. tchr. Hampton Sch. Dist., Allison Park, Pa., 1983—87, cert. athletic trainer, 1983—. EMT, paramedic Ross/West View EMS, Pitts., 1987—97. Mem.: Nat. Athletic Trainers Assn. (licentiate athletic trainer cert.). R-Consevative. Avocations: golf, drawing, weightlifting. Home: 203 Monroe Dr Pittsburgh PA 15229 Office: Hampton Sch Dist 2929 McCully Rd Allison Park PA 15101 Office Fax: 412-486-7050. Personal E-mail: itoerge@comcast.net.

TOEWS, JONATHAN, professional hockey player; b. Winnipeg, Man., Can., Apr. 29, 1988; Attended, U. ND, 2005—07. Center Chgo. Blackhawks, 2007—, capt., 2008—. Mem. Team Can., World Jr. Championships, Vancouver, 2006, Sweden, 07, Team Can., World Championships, Moscow, 2007, Canada, 08. Named to All-Rookie Team, NHL, 2008, NHL All-Star Game, 2009; nominee Calder Meml. Trophy, 2008. Achievements include being a member of Gold Medal Team Canada, World Junior Championships, 2006, 2007, World Championships, 2007. Office: Chgo Blackhawks United Ctr 1901 W Madison St Chicago IL 60612-2459*

TOFEL, RICHARD JEFFREY, non-profit publishing executive; b. NYC; s. Robert Leonard and Carol T.; children: Rachel Straus, Colin Straus. AB, Harvard U., 1979; MPP, JFK Sch. Govt., 1983; JD, Harvard U., 1983. Bar: N.Y. 1984, U.S. Dist. Ct. (so. and ea. dists.) N.Y. 1984, U.S. Ct. Appeals (2d cir.) 1987, U.S. Dist. Ct. (no. dist.) N.Y. 1988, U.S. Supreme Ct. 1990. Assoc. Patterson, Belknap, Webb & Tyler, NYC, 1983—86; exec. dir. Mayor's Commn. Human Svcs. Reorganization, NYC, 1984—85; assoc. Gibson, Dunn & Crutcher, NYC, 1986—89; counsel Dow Jones & Co., NYC, 1989—91, asst. gen. counsel, 1991—92; asst. mng. editor Wall Street Jour., NYC, 1992—95; dir. internat. devel. and adminstrn. Dow Jones & Co., NYC, 1995—97, v.p. corp. comm., 1997—2000, v.p., asst. to publ. Wall Street Jour., 2000—02, v.p., asst. publ. Wall Street Jour., 2002—04; pres. The Internat. Freedom Ctr., World Trade Ctr. site, NYC, 2004—05; v.p., gen. counsel The Rockefeller Found., NYC, 2006—07; gen. mgr. Pro Publica, 2007—. Bd. dirs. Wildcat Svc. Corp. Author: A Legend in the Making: The New York Yankees in 1939, 2002, Vanishing Point: The Disappearance of Judge Crater, and the New York He Left Behind, 2004, Sounding the Trumpet: The Making of John F. Kennedy's Inaugural Address, 2005; contbr. articles to profl. jours. Democrat. Jewish. Office: Pro Publica One Exchange Plaza 23rd Fl New York NY 10006 Office Phone: 917-512-0250. Personal E-mail: dick_tofel@yahoo.com. Business E-Mail: dick.tofel@propublica.org.

TOFF, NANCY ELLEN, book editor; b. Greenburgh, NY, Aug. 29, 1955; d. Ira N. and Ruth (Bluthenthal) T. AB, Harvard U., 1976. Editor, prodr. Music Minus One, NYC, 1973-75; rschr. Time-Life Books, Alexandria, Va., 1976-80; editor, asst. prodr. Time-Life Music, Alexandria, Va., 1980-84; prodn. mgr. Vanguard Recording Soc., NYC, 1984-86; editor Grove's Dictionaries of Music, NYC, 1984-85; v.p., editor-in-chief Chelsea House Pubs., NYC, 1986-89, v.p., dir. book devel., 1990; editl. dir. Julian Messner/Silver Burdett Press, Englewood Cliffs, N.J., 1990-91; editl. dir. children's and young adult books Oxford U. Press, NYC, 1991-98, editl. dir. young adult reference, 1998—2006, v.p., 1999—; exec. editor Acad. Trade Divsn., 2006—. Editorial cons., Music Div. Lib. of Congress, 1983; hist. cons., Dept. of Musical Instruments, Met. Mus. of Art, N.Y.C., 1986. Author: The Development of the Modern Flute, 1979, The Flute Book, 1985, 2d edit., 1996, Georges Barrère and the Flute in America, 1994, Monarch of the Flute: The Life of Georges Barrère, 2005; cons. editor Flutist Quar., 1990-99; contbr. articles to profl. jours.; curator Georges Barrère and the Flute in America, N.Y. Pub. Libr., 1994. Bd. dirs., Radcliffe Coll. Alumnae Assn. 1979-80. Recipient Dena Epstein award Music Libr. Assn., 1997; Sinfonia Found. rsch. grantee, Am. Musicological Soc. grant. Mem. Nat. Flute Assn. (asst. sec. 1988-89, sec. 1989-90, bd. dirs. 1990-92), N.Y. Flute Club (bd. dirs. 1986—, sec. 1991-92, 98-2000, pres. 1992-95, 2008-, 1st v.p. 1995-98). Home: 425 E 79th St Apt 6F New York NY 10075-1011 Office: Oxford U Press 198 Madison Ave New York NY 10016-4341 Business E-Mail: nancy.toff@oup.com.

TOFIGHI NIAKI, ALIASSGHAR, research scientist; married. PhD, Poly. U., Toulouse, France, 1982. Cert. in phys. properties materials, Toulouse, 1975. Dir. rsch. ETEX Corp., Cambridge, Mass., 2000—02, dir., product & process devel., 2002—06, disting. rsch. fellow, 2006—. Achievements include patents for bone substitute materials. Office: ETEX Corp 38 Sidney St Cambridge MA 02139 Business E-Mail: atofighi@etexcorp.com.

TOGASAKI, SHINOBU, computer scientist; b. San Francisco, Aug. 17, 1932; s. Kikumatsu and Sugi (Hida) T.; m. Toshiko Kawaguchi, Nov. 24, 1959; children: John Shinobu, Ann Mariko. BS in Math., Duke U., 1954; postgrad., Stanford U., 1954—56. Math. programmer IBM,

1956—69, DB/DC arch., 1969—72, sr. programmer Palo Alto, Calif., 1970—87, mgr. Palo Alto sys. ctr., 1972—74, risk OS mgr., 1974—82, DB/DC mktg. cons., 1982—87; mgr. applications devel. Service Bur. Corp., Palo Alto, 1961—64, sr. analyst, 1964—68, systems architect devel. lab. San Jose, Calif., 1968-70; CFO. Robin Hood Ranch, Inc., 1976—86; mgr. architecture & strategy Hewlett Packard Corp., Cupertino, Calif., 1987-89, mgr. strategic planning, 1989—93; chief architect MFA Hewlett Packard, 1993—2002; strategic cons., 2002—. Mem. Am. Mgmt. Assn., AAAS, Am. Statis. Assn., Assn. Computing Machinery, Inst. Mgmt. Sci., Sigma Pi Sigma. Home: 2367 Booksin Ave San Jose CA 95125-4705 E-mail: togasaki@alumni.duke.edu.

TOGNINO, JOHN NICHOLAS, diversified financial services company executive; b. NYC, Sept. 20, 1938; s. Gennaro and Catherine (Barbieri) T.; m. Norma Lucille Borrelli, Nov. 7, 1959; children: Katherine Ann, John Nicholas Jr., Michael A. BA in Econs. summa cum laude, Fordham U., 1975. Instnl. sales trader A.G. Becker & Co., NYC, 1970-72; trader Merill Lynch, NYC, 1957-69, instnl. salesman, 1972-74, mgr. over-the-counter sales trading, 1974-83, dir. over-the-counter dept., 1983-87, dir. unlisted trading, 1987-88, mng. dir. non-dollar equities London, 1988-91, mng. dir. global equities NYC, 1991-93; exec. v.p. Charles Schwab & Co., Inc., Jersey City, 1993-96; pres., CEO Security Traders Assn., NYC, 1996-99, EVP NASDAQ, 1999—2001; chmn., CEO Pepper Fin. Group, 2001—. Bd. dirs. Nat. Assn. Security Dealers Automated Quotations Inc. Contbg. author: Market Maker Sponsorship: A Synergistic Package of Services, 1987. Mem. Ardlsey Bd. Edn., 1977—84, pres., 1979; v.p. Ardsley Sch. Dist. Bd., 1978, 1981; trustee, vice chmn. St. Barnabas Hosp., Bronx, 1996—; mem. health sci. adv. coun., Coll. of Phys. and Surgeons Columbia Presbyn. Med. Ctr., 1998—; pres. Ardsley Rep. Club, 1967—68; mem. exec. com. of laity Archdiocese of N.Y.C., 1988; trustee Fordham U., 2000—, chmn. bd. trustees, 2004—; dir. Muscular Dystrophy Assn., 2000—05; bd. dirs. Bus. Coun. for Internat. Understanding, 2000—01. Named Trader of Yr., Security Traders Monthly mag., 1984, Over-the-Counter Man of Yr., Equities mag., 1986; recipient lifetime achievement award Chgo. Stock Exch., 1997. Mem. Nat. Security Traders Assn. (various offices 1981-88, chmn. fin. com. Found. 1992—), Nat. Assn. Security Dealers (bus. conduct com. 1984-86), Security Traders Assn. N.Y. (various offices 1973-83, pres. 1980-81), St. Andrews Golf Club (Hastings, N.Y.), Alpha Sigma Lambda, Alpha Sigma Nu. Independent. Roman Catholic. Avocations: jogging, tennis, golf. Home: Two Stoneleigh Plz Apt 4H Bronxville NY 10708 Office: Pepper Fin Group 547 Sawmiu River Rd Ardsley NY 10502 Home Phone: 914-966-6016; Office Phone: 914-234-4580. Personal E-mail: jntog@aol.com.

TOGNOLI, ERA M., opera company director; married. M in Voice, La Scala, Milan, Italy. Gen. mgr., artistic dir., founder Metro Lyric Opera, Allenhurst, NJ, 1959—. Singer: (Operas) Puccini's Turandot, 1948, Verdi's La Traviata, Puccini's Madame Butterfly.*

TOGO, HISATAKE, research institute administrator; b. Tokyo, Jan. 3, 1931; s. Yoshitora and Noriko (Obayashi) T.; m. Teiko Namba, Feb. 27, 1960; 2 children. BA, Gakushuin U., Tokyo, 1953; Dr.Engring., Tokyo U., 1990. Dir. rsch. Tokyo Met. Govt., 1978-80, dir. comprehensive planning, 1980-85, dep. dir.-gen. urban planning, 1985-87, dir.-gen. pers. commn., 1987-90; exec. dir. Tokyo Inst. Mcpl. Rsch., 1990—2002, dir., sr. rsch. adviser, 2003—06; chmn. bd. dirs. Seijo Gakko Sch., 2003—. Mem. exec. com. World Conf. Met. Governance, Tokyo, 1992-93; lectr., Internat. Christian U., 1993-98; vice chmn. exec. com. 3d Conf. World Capitals, Tokyo, 1992-93; mem. organizing com. Metropolis '96 of World Assn. of Major Metropolises, Tokyo, 1995-96; vis. prof. Seigakuin U., 1998-2004. Author: The Development of Urban Policies, 1986, Tracing Urban Reform Plan of Tokyo, 1993, The Reorganization of London Government and the London Plan, 2004; co-author: The Government of World Cities, 1995; editor: 50 Years of Tokyo Metropolitan Administration, 1995; co-editor: (with London Rsch. Ctr., etc.) The Four World Cities Transport Study, 1999. Mem. City Planning Inst. Japan; mem. world conf. internat. cooperation cities and citizens (tech. comm.), 1997-98. Avocation: classical music. Home: 7-6-2 Kinuta Setagaya-ku Tokyo 157-0073 Japan Office: Seijo Gakko Sch 3-87 Haramachi Shinjuku Tokyo 162-8670 Japan Personal E-mail: htogo@ab.auone-net.jp.

TOIG, RANDALL MARC, obstetrician, gynecologist; b. Pitts., Sept. 19, 1950; s. Harry M. and Florence (Levy) T.; m. Allison Beth Wines, June 9, 1985; 4 children. BS in Zoology and Anthropology, U. Mich., Ann Arbor, 1972; MD, U. Pitts. Sch. Medicine, 1977. Lic. Ill., 1978, diplomate Nat. Bd. Med. Examiners, 1978, Am. Bd. Obstetrics and Gynecology, 1985. Profl. tennis player USTA, 1969—72, 1974—75; intern Rush-Presbyn.-St. Lukes Hosp., Chgo., 1977-78; resident in obstetrics & gynecology Northwestern Meml. Hosp., Chgo., 1978-82, staff mem., 1988—; pvt. practice medicine specializing in ob-gyn Gold Coast Gynecology, Chgo., 1982—; staff mem. Prentice Women's Hosp., 1988—; co-founder Cell Pathways, Inc., 1997, bd. dirs., 1997—99. Instr. clin. obstetrics and gynecology, Northwestern U., Chgo., 1982-88, assoc. prof., 1988-2003, asst. prof., 2003-; cons. Morgan Stanley, 1987-92, Lehman Bros., 1992-97. Bd. dirs. Friends of Prentice Hosp., Chgo., 1986-, Make A Wish Found., Chgo., 1989-; mem. adv. bd. Smart Love Parenting Ctr. Recipient America's Top Doctor award, 2001; named a Top Doctor, Obstetrics & Gynecology-Infertility, Chgo. Mag., 2001—, Top Doctor, Obstetrics & Gynecology, 2004—. Fellow Am. Coll. Ob-Gyn; mem. AMA, Chgo. Med. Soc., Gynecol. Laser Soc., Chgo. Gynecol. Soc., Soc. Laparoendoscopic Surgeons. Avocations: tennis, architecture. Office: Gold Coast Gynecology 680 N Lake Shore Dr Chicago IL 60611-4402*

TOKARCZYK, ROMAN ANDRZEJ, law educator, philosopher, researcher; b. Gródki, Lublin, Poland, Mar. 16, 1942; s. Andrzej Jan and Karolina Rozalia (Dubiel) T.; m. Czestawa Paulina Malec, Apr. 30, 1942; 1 childe Malgorzata. LLM, Mariae Curie Sktodowska U., Lublin, 1966, PhD in Law, 1970. From asst. to prof. Mariae Curie Sktodowska U., Lublin, 1966—90, prof., 1990—. Rsch. assoc. prof. Notre Dame U., 1974; vis. assoc. prof. Harvard U., 1974, 93; dir. dept. faculty law and adminstrn. Mariae Curie Sktodowska U., Lublin, 1979—; dean faculty law and economy Studium Generale Sandomiriense, Sandomierz, Poland, 1996-2000. Author: Contemporary Political Doctrines, 1971, 15th edit., 2008, Law of Birth, Life and Death, 1984, 9th edit., 2009, Comparative Law, 1989, 9th edit., 2008, Philosophy of Law, 1993, 11th edit., 2009, American Law, 1996, 10th edit., 2008, History Philosophy of Law, 1988, 3d edit., 2001, Contemporary Law Cultures, 2000, 7th edit., 2008, The History of Village of Gródki, 1992, 2nd edit., 2000, The History of Town Turobin, 2002, Commands of the Legal Ethics. Book of Thoughts, Norms and Sketches, 3rd edit., 2009, Legal Ethics, 2005, 4th edit., 2008, Anthology of Academic Anecdotes, 2006, 2nd edit., 2009, Biojurisprudence: Foundations of Law for the Twenty-First Century, English & Polish vols., 2008; contbr. more than 670 articles to profl. jours. Mem. Tribunale of State, Warsaw, Poland, 1994. Internat. Rsch. Exch. Bd. scholar, 1974, NATO scholar, 1993; recipeint awards Polish Min. Higher Edn., 1973, 77, 83, others. Mem. Internat. Communal Studies Assn. Israel, U.S. (bd. dirs.), Polish Acad. Medicine, Internat. Soc. Philosophy Law Social Philosophy. Roman Catholic. Avocations: skiing, dance, photography. Home: Dudzinskiego 16 20-815 Lublin Poland Office: Pl Marii Curie Skodowskiej 520-031 Lublin Poland

TOKATLIOGLU, THERESA DIAZ LOPEZ, elementary school educator; b. Joliet, Ill., Dec. 26, 1938; d. Emilio Jimenez and Vicenta (Salazar) Diaz; m. Pilar Lopez, Oct. 5, 1957 (dec. May 1971); children: Amanda(dec.), Armand; m. Bernabe Oscar Lopez Argentina, Aug. 19, 1972 (div.); children: Arturo, Adrianna; m. L. Tokatlioglu. AA in Acctg., Joliet Jr. Coll., 1971; BA in Elem. Edn., U. of St. Francis, Joliet, 1974; post grad., Nat. U. Edn., 1974—75. Cert. elem. edn. tchr., high sch. Spanish tchr., bilingual K-12 tchr. Typist Boy Scouts Am., Joliet, 1955-56; office worker Shepley Motor Express, Joliet, 1956-57; dictaphone operator N.Am. Accident Ins. Co., Chgo., 1957-59; elem. edn. tchr. Harlingen (Tex.) Consol. Schs., 1978—79; tchr. Joliet Pub. Schs. Dist. 86, 1974—. Vice-pres. Parks Sch. PTA, Joliet, 1969-70; vol. Rialto Square Theatre, Joliet,JTHS Choir Alumni Assn. Recipient Life Mem. award PTA, 1989, Book of Recognition award PTA, 1991. Mem.: Nat. Hawaiian Steel Guitar Assn., League United Latin Am. Citizens (sec. 1971—74, Joliet Woman of Yr. award 1975, state conv. Woman of Yr. award 1985), Am. Italian Cultural Soc., Alpha Delta Kappa, Kappa Delta Pi Internat. Democrat. Avocations: reading, dance, art, travel, opera. Office: Pershing Sch Midland and Campbell Joliet IL 60435 Personal E-mail: tere57@aol.com.

TOKOFSKY, JERRY HERBERT, film producer; b. NYC, Apr. 14, 1936; s. Julius H. and Rose (Trager) T.; m. Myrna Weinstein, Feb. 21, 1968 (div.); children: David, Peter; m. Fiammetta Bettuzzi, 1970 (div.); 1 child, Tatianna; m. Karen Oliver, Oct. 4, 1981. BS in Journalism, NYU, 1956, LLD, 1959, M in Am. Lit., 1999. Talent agt. William Morris Agy., NYC, 1953-59, v.p. LA, 1959-64; exec. v.p. Columbia Pictures, LA, 1964-69; v.p. Paramount Pictures, London, 1970; exec. v.p. MGM, London, 1971; pres. Jerry Tokofsky Prodns., LA, 1972-82; exec. v.p. Zupnik Enterprises, LA, 1982-92; pres. Jerry Tokofsky Entertainment, Encino, Calif., 1992—; CEO TKO Comm. Prof. Sch. TV and Film U. So. Calif. Sch. Bus. Prodr. films: Where's Poppa, 1971, Born to Win, 1972, Paternity, 1981, Dreamscape, 1985, Fear City, 1986, Wildfire, 1988, Glengarry Glen Ross, 1992, The Grass Harp, 1995, American Buffalo, 1995, Double Down, 1997, Life on Mars, 1998, John Steinbecks In Dubious Battle, 2004, Puccini, 2004, Daisy Winter, 2005, Gods House of Style, 2005, High Desert, 2005; exec. prodr. Easy Rider, Man for All Seasons, Funny Girl, Oliver, Born Free, Georgy Girl, Professionals. With U.S. Army, 1959, 63, res. 1959-63. Named Man of Yr. B'nai B'rith, 1981; recipient L.A. Resolution City of L.A., 1981. Mem. Variety Club Internat. Avocations: skiing, tennis, golf, chess. Office Phone: 818-990-1724. *Passion for family, life, work, with patience and intelligence and you have a chance to grab that winning ring.*

TOKORO, MARIO, computer scientist; PhD, Keio U., Japan. Pres., sr. rsch. fellow Sony Computer Sci. Labs., Tokyo; sr. v.p. innovation strategy Sony Corp.; prof. faculty sci. & tech. Keio U. Contbr. articles to profl. jours. Office: Sony Computer Sci Labs Takanawa Muse Bldg 3-14-13 Higashi-Gotanda Tokyo 141-0022 Japan also: Faculty Sci and Tech Keio U 3-14-1 Hiyoshi Kohoku-ku Kanagawa 223 Japan Office Fax: 81-3-3448-4273, 81-45-560-1151. E-mail: mario@csl.sony.co.jp, mario@mt.cs.keio.ac.jp.

TOKUHATA, GEORGE K., retired medical educator, epidemiologist, consultant; b. Matsue, Japan, Aug. 25, 1924; arrived in U.S., 1951; s. Yujiro and Hama Tokuhata; m. Sumiko Matsui, June 10, 1949. BA, Keio U., 1950; MA, Miami U., Oxford, Ohio, 1952; PhD, U. Iowa, 1955; Dr.PH, Johns Hopkins U., 1962. Chief epidemiology chronic disease divsn. USPHS, Washington, 1961—64; assoc. prof. preventive medicine U. Tenn., Memphis, 1965—67; dir. rsch. Pa. Dept. Health, Harrisburg, 1968—89; prof. behavioral sci. Pa. State U. Coll. Medicine, Hershey, 1970—95; prof. epidemiology U. Pitts., 1970—90; ret., 1990. Cons. product safety U.S. FDA, Washington, 1970—73; cons. maternal child health rsch. U.S. Children's Bur., 1974—77; cons. rsch. grant svcs. Nat. Cancer Inst., 1982—86. Contbr. chapters to books, articles over 100 articles to profl. jours. Grantee, USPHS, U.S. FDA. Fellow: APHA, Am. Coll. Epidemiology; mem.: Fgn. Policy Assn. (bd.dirs. 1995—2000), Torch Club Internat. (bd.dirs. 1999—2002). Achievements include design of and execution of long-term cohort study of health effects of the Three Mile Island accident - first major episode among all commercial nuclear plants in the US; development of a new method of finding familial aggregation of chronic diseases; first to find genetic role played in lung cancer; research in radiation, stress and health. Avocations: classical music, landscape design, gardening. Home: 410 Rupley Rd Camp Hill PA 17011 Home Phone: 717-763-8939.

TOLAN, PATRICK HENRY, psychology educator; b. Buffalo, May 30, 1953; s. Francis Henry and Phyllis (Smith) T.; children: Meredith, Colleen, Kathryn. BA, Temple U., 1978; MA, U. Tenn., 1980, PhD, 1983. Lic. psychologist, cert. sch. psychologist. Psychol. intern Tufts Med. Sch., Boston, 1981-82; postdoctoral fellow U. Chgo. and Michael Reese Hosp., 1983-85; asst. prof. psychology DePaul U., Chgo., 1985-90; from assoc. to full prof. psychology and psychiatry U. Ill.-Chgo., Chgo., 1990—; dir. rsch. Inst. for Juvenile Rsch., Chgo., 1990—99, dir., 1999—. Contbr. articles to books and profl. jours. Mem. Am. Psychol. Assn., Am. Assn. for Marital and Family Therapy, Soc. for Research on Child Devel., Am. Soc. Criminology. Avocations: music, reading, baseball. Office: Inst Juvenile Rsch 1747 W Rosevelt Rd Chicago IL 60608 Office Phone: 312-413-1893. Business E-Mail: tolan@uic.edu.

TOLAND, CLYDE WILLIAM, historic site director, lawyer; b. Iola, Kans., Aug. 18, 1947; s. Stanley E. and June E. (Thompson) T.; m. Nancy Ellen Hummel, July 27, 1974; children: David Clyde, Andrew John, Elizabeth Kay. BA in History, U. Kans., 1969, JD, 1975; MA in 17th Century English History, U. Wis., Madison, 1971. Bar: Kans. 1975, US Dist. Ct. Kans. 1975, U.S. Supreme Ct. 1980. Atty. Toland and Thompson LLC, Iola, 1975—2006; pvt. practice Iola, 2006—. Mem. exec. com. Friends of Libr., U. Kans., 1977-92, pres., 1988-91, Allen County Hist. Soc., Inc., 1990-95, v.p. 1998-2006, exec. dir., curator, 2006-; founder Ann. Buster Keaton Celebration, Iola, co-chmn., 1993-97; leader restoration Frederick Funston Boyhood Home, 1991-95; Chief planner, remodeling designer Allen County Mus., 2003-05. Recipient Appreciation cert. DAR, 1995, First Cmty. Svc. award Current Event Club, Iola, 1998; co-recipient (with US Sen. Nancy Kassebaum) First Alumni Disting. Achievement award Coll. Liberal Arts and Scis. U. Kans., 1996; Paul Harris fellow Rotary Internat., 1986;. Fellow Kans. Bar Found.; mem. ABA, Kans. Bar Assn. (Outstanding Svc. award 1988), Allen County Bar Assn., U. Kans. Alumni Assn. (Strickland award 1969), Iola Rotary Club (pres. 1985-86, Outstanding Cmty. Svc. plaque 1996), Iola Jaycees, Phi Beta Kappa, Order of Coif, Omicron Delta Kappa (presdl. plaque 1969). Presbyterian. Avocation: historical field trips. Office: PO Box 404 Iola KS 66749

TOLAR, ANNE MELTON, minister, music educator; b. Geneva, Ala., Jan. 17, 1937; d. Ernest Lester and Lovie Hewett Melton; m. Robert F. Tolar, Apr. 21, 1966; children: Robert Jr., William, Sharon Tolar Stone, Ginny Tolar Knight. BA in English & Psychology, U. Ala., 1959; BA in Music/Piano, U. W. Fla., 1960. Teller/bookkeeper 1st Bank & Trust, Pensacola, Fla., 1952—56, collections & loan officer Atlanta; br. office asst. mgr. 1st Fed. Savings & Loan Assn., Atlanta, 1970—73; evangelist, musician, tchr. Fountain of Praise Ministries, St. Pauls, NC, 1972—; presbyter, min. Missionary Ch. Internat., Columbia, SC, 1985—; music tchr. St. Pauls; tchr., musician, pastor Fountain of Praise Ch., Lumberton, NC, 2001—. Judge Mountain Gospel Music; v.p. Fountain of Praise Ministries, Missionary Ch. Internat., Lumberton, NC, 2001—; spkr. in field. Author: (book) Wilt Thou Be Made Whole?, 1988; songwriter: 106 songs and cantatas. Recipient Mother of Yr. award, Fountain of Praise Ch., St. Pauls, N.C., 1998; named Internat. Savings & Loan Speech Contest winner, Atla., 1972. Republican. Mem. Christian Ch. Office: Fountain of Praise Ministries Cedar St Lumberton NC 28358

TOLAR, TRINIDAD URIBE, education educator, director; d. Indalecio and Celia Uribe; m. Michael P. Tolar; 1 child, Adam Michael. Degree in Dentistry, U. Autonoma de Mex., 1983; MA in Edn. Adminstr., N.Mex Highlands U., Las Vegas, 2001; MA in Interdisciplinary Studies, Western N.Mex U., Silver City, 2006. Cert. in elem. edn. with a bilingual endorsement N.Mex, 2003, sch. adminstr. N.Mex, 2003. Elem. tchr. Raton Pub. Schs., N.Mex., 1996—2002; mid. sch. tchr. Aberdeen Pub. Schs., Wash., 2002—03; asst. prof. edn., field experience dir. Western N.Mex U., Silver city, 2004—. Bilingual coord., asst. supt. Res. Schs., N.Mex., 2003—04. Sponsor Amigos Club, Silver City, N.Mex., 2006—09. Mem.: Delta Kappa Gamma Internat. - Theta State (v.p. 2006—). Independent. Office: Western N Mex Univ PO Box 680 Silver City NM 88062 Office Fax: 575-538-6417. Business E-Mail: tolart@wnmu.edu.

TOLBERT, BERNARD, sports association executive; married; 3 children. Student, SUNY, Buffalo. Spl. agt. FBI, Buffalo and NYC, 1980—85, supervisory spl. agt. Intelligence Divsn. Washington, 1985—87, supr. fgn. counterintelligence, counterterrorism and civil rights investigations Western NY area Buffalo, 1987—90, chief counterintelligence and counterterrorism tng. unit Washington, 1990—92, asst. spl. agt. in charge Phila. office, 1992—97, insp. Inspection Divsn. Washington, 1997—98, spl. agt. in charge Buffalo divsn., 1998—2001; security mgr. Coca-Cola Co.; sr. v.p., dir. corp. security HSBC Bank; sr. v.p. security NBA, NYC, 2002—. Bd. mem. United Way, Western NY Pub. Broadcasting, Erie County Youth Bd., Medaille Coll., U. Buffalo Alumni Assn., 100 Club Buffalo and Western NY. Recipient Black Achievers in Industry award, Heroes of Pub. Housing award, Ebony and Ivory award, Presdl. Rank award for Meritorious Achievement, The White House, 2001; named to SUNY Buffalo Athletic Hall of Fame, 1998. Office: NBA Olympic Tower 645 5th Ave Fl 10 New York NY 10022-5986*

TOLBERT, BERT MILLS, biochemist, educator; b. Twin Falls, Idaho, Jan. 15, 1921; s. Ed. and Helen (Mills) T.; m. Anne Grace Zweifler, July 20, 1959; children— Elizabeth Dawn, Margaret Anne, Caroline Joan, Sarah Helen. Student, Idaho State U., 1938-40; BS, U. Calif., Berkeley, 1942, PhD, 1945; postgrad., Fed. Inst. Tech., Zurich, Switzerland, 1952-53. Chemist Lawrence Radiation Lab., Berkeley, 1944-57; faculty U. Colo., Boulder, 1957-89, prof., 1961-89, prof. emeritus, 1989—, assoc. chmn. dept. chemistry and biochemistry, 1980-88. Bd. dirs. Hauser Chem. Rsch., Boulder, 1983-99; dirs. Hauser Inc., Boulder, 1983-99, vis. prof. IAEA, Buenos Aires, Argentina, 1961-62; Biophysicist U.S. AEC, Washington, 1967-68; cons. pvt. cos, govt. agys. Author: (with others) Isotopic Carbon, 1948; contbr. (with others) articles to profl. jours. Fellow AAAS; mem. Am. Chem. Soc., Am. Soc. Biochemistry and Molecular Biology, Radiation Rsch. Soc., Soc. for Exptl. Biology and Medicine. Achievements include rsch. on organic chemistry, including use of isotopes in chemistry and biochemistry, radiation chemistry, radiation effects in protein, intermediary metabolism, metabolism of ascorbic acid, nutritional biochemistry, instrumentation in radioactivity. Home: 444 Kalmia Ave Boulder CO 80304-1732 Personal E-mail: bert.tolbert@colorado.edu.

TOLBERT, CLINTON JAME, army officer, machinist; b. Auburn, Ala., Dec. 22, 1953; s. Clinton and Rosia Love (Fillmore) T.; m. Gloria Jean Fitzpatrick, Sept. 23, 1974; children: Christopher, Mark, Marcella. BS, Tukegee U., 1983; MBA, Troy State U., 1987, MS, 1990; AS in Applied Sci., So. U., Opelika, Ala., 1996. EMT U.S. Army, Fort Benning, Ga., 1972-75; machine operator West Point Pepperll, Inc., Valley, Ala., 1975-82; 1st lt. Army Nat. Guard, Roanoke, Ala., 1982-86, capt., 1986-92, major Montgomery, Ala., 1992-96; machinist Falk Corp., Auburn, Ala, 1996—. Elder Methodist Ch., Auburn, Ala., 1996— Named All- Am. Scholar, U.S. Achievement Acad., Lexington, Ky., 1996; recipient Minority Leadership award, U.S. Achievement Acad., Lexington, 1996. Mem. Nat. Guard Assn. Democrat. Avocations: reading, golf. Home: 989 Fitzpatric Rd Auburn AL 36830

TOLBERT, CORNELIA EMMA, music educator; b. St. Louis, Sept. 15, 1954; d. Cornelius and Morzell Tolbert. BA, St. Louis U., 1977. Cert. instrumental and vocal music tchr. grades K-12 Mo., 1982. Substitute tchr. St. Louis Pub. Schs., 1975—83, piano and voice tchr., 1976—78, vocal music tchr., 1985—95, asst. music tchr., 1997—2001, instrumental music asst. tchr., 2001—; pvt. piano and organ tchr. Ludwig Aeolian Music Store, 1982—85. Music choral dir. Meth. Ch., St. Louis, 1972—, asst. orgn., 1977—2003, pianist, 2003—, children's choir dir., 2005—. Vol. phone bank St. Louis Tchrs. Union, 2004; coord. for United Way St. Louis Pub. Schs., 2004, coord. William L. Clay Scholarship fund, 2004. Recipient Editor's Choice award, Internat. Soc. Poets, 2001, Outstanding Achievement in Poetry, 2007, Am. Guild Organist, 2007, Outstanding Svc. award, St. Louis Pub. Sch., 2008; named to Citizen Amb. Music Edn., 2009. Mem.: Am. Guild Organist, St. Louis Univ. Alumni Assn., Internat. Soc. Poets (Best Poem and Poet award 2008), Am. Fedn. Tchrs., St. Louis Tchrs. Union Local 420, Nat. Music Educators Assn., Mo. Music Tchrs. Assn. Democrat. Methodist. Avocations: bowling, tennis, ping pong/table tennis, writing songs, gardening.

TOLBERT, JOHN LEE, literature and language educator; b. Appalachia, Va., Mar. 22, 1947; m. Nancy Delores Erwin, Oct. 9, 1982; children: Johna Michelle Kinlaw, Rachel Rebekah. BS, East Tenn. State U., Johnson City, 1981, MA, 1990. Multimedia specialist Eastman Chem. Co., Kingsport, Tenn., 1967—99; master chief petty officer US Naval Res., Knoxville, Tenn., 1967—92; asst. prof. Va. Intermont Coll., Bristol, 2002—. Decorated Navy Achievement medal US Navy. Office: Virginia Intermont Coll 1013 Moore St Bristol VA 24201 Business E-Mail: johntolbert@vic.edu.

TOLBERT, PATTI MCCLURE, music educator; b. Rome, Ga., Nov. 28, 1948; d. Marshall McClure and Patti Arp Tolbert. MusD, U. Ga., Athens, 1992. Classroom tchr. McIntosh County Schs., Darien, Ga., 1978—80; instrumental music educator Glynn County Schs., Brunswick, Ga., 1971—75, McIntosh County Schs., Darien, Ga., 1980—88, Oconee County Schs., Watkinsville, Ga., 1994—97; prof. music Ga. Coll. & State U., Milledgeville, 1997—. Profl. musician Hilton Head Orch., SC, Albany Symphony Orch., Ga., Macon Symphony Orch., Ga. Vol. Meals on Wheels, Milledgeville, Ga., 2006—08. Recipient Tchr. of

Yr., Oconee County Mid. Sch., 1995—96, Gene M. Simmons Fellowship award, U. Ga., 1997, Excellence Tchg. award, Ga. Coll. & State U., 2006—07; Fulbright-Hays fellowship, US Dept, 2005. Mem.: MENC History Spl. Interest Rsch. Group (web designer and webmaster 2006—08), Ga. Music Educators Assn. (coll. divsn. chair 2006—08), MENC: Nat. Assn. Music Educators, Tri-M Music. Liberal. Avocations: photography, motorcycling, travel. Home: 106 Shortcut Rd NE Milledgeville GA 31061 Office: Georgia Coll & State Univ Dept Music CBX 66 Milledgeville GA 31061 Business E-Mail: patti.tolbert@gcsu.edu.

TOLCHIN, JOAN GUBIN, psychiatrist, educator; d. Harold and Bella (Newman) Gubin; m. Matthew Armin Tolchin, Sept. 1, 1966; 1 child, Benjamin. AB, Vassar Coll., 1964; MD, NYU, 1972. Diplomate Am. Bd. Gen. Psychiatry, Am. Bd. Child Psychiatry. Rsch. asst. Albert Einstein Coll. Medicine, NYC, 1964-68; instr. psychiatry med. coll. Cornell U., NYC, 1977-78, clin. instr., 1978-86, clin. asst. prof., 1986—2004, clin. assoc. prof., 2004—. Contbr. articles to profl. jours., chapters to books. Fellow: Am. Acad. Psychoanalysis and Dynamic Psychiatry (sec. 1998—2001, pres. elect 2007—08, pres. 2008—), Am. Acad. Child and Adolescent Psychiatry; mem.: AMA, Am. Psychiatric Assn., N.Y. Coun. Child and Adolescent Psychiatry (bd. dirs. 1992—96, pres. 1994—95, bd. advisors 2001—), Alpha Omega Alpha. Office: 35 E 84th St New York NY 10028-0871

TOLCHIN, MARTIN, journalist, writer; b. NYC, Sept. 20, 1928; s. Charles T. and Evelyn (Weisman) Tolchin; m. Susan Jane Goldsmith, Dec. 23, 1965; children: Karen. Student, U. Utah, 1947-49; LL.B., N.Y. Law Sch., 1951. Reporter N.Y. Times, NYC, 1954—94; pub., editor-in-chief The Hill, Washington, 1994—2002; sr. pub., editor The Politico, 2006—08; pub. policy scholar Woodrow Wilson Internat. Ctr. Scholars, 2008—09. Author (with Susan Jane Tolchin): To The Victor, 1971; author: Clout-Woman Power and Politics, 1974, Dismantling America-The Rush to Deregulate, 1983, Buying Into America: How Foreign Money is Changing the Face of Our Nation, 1988, Selling Our Security-The Erosion of American's Assets, 1992, Glass Houses: Congressional Ethics and the Politics of Venom, 2001, A World Ignited: How Apostles of Ethnic, Religious and Racial Hatred Torch the Globe, 2006. Served with U.S. Army, 1951-53. Recipient Schaeffer Gold Typewriter award E.M. Schaeffer Co., 1967; recipient Page One award Newspaper Guild N.Y., 1967, 69, 73, Citizens Budget Commn. award, 1967, Sigma Delta Chi award, 1973, Everett M. Dirksen award for disting. reporting of Congress, 1983; named to Journalism Hall Fame, Soc. Profl. Journalists, 2004. Mem. Nat. Press Club (Washington), Univ. Club. Jewish. Home: 3525 Winfield Ln NW Washington DC 20007-2378 Home Phone: 202-625-7782. Personal E-mail: mtolchin@aol.com.

TOLCHIN, SUSAN JANE, political science professor, writer; b. NYC, Jan. 14, 1941; d. Jacob Nathan and Dorothy Ann (Markowitz) Goldsmith; m. Martin Tolchin, Dec. 23, 1965; 1 child, Karen Rebecca. BA, Bryn Mawr Coll., 1961; MA, U. Chgo., 1962; PhD, NYU, 1968. Lectr. in polit. sci. CCNY, NYC, 1963-65, Bklyn. Coll., 1965-71; adj. asst. prof. polit. sci. Seton Hall U., South Orange, NJ, 1971-73; assoc. prof. polit. sci., dir. Inst. for Women and Politics, Mt. Vernon Coll., Washington, 1975-78; prof. pub. adminstrn. George Washington U., Washington, 1978-98; prof. sch. pub. policy George Mason U., Fairfax, Va., 1998—. Disting. lectr. Indsl. Coll. Armed Forces, 1994. Author: The Angry American: How Voter Rage is Changing the Nation, 1996, 2d edit., 1998; author: (with Martin Tolchin) To the Victor: Political Patronage from the Clubhouse to the White House, 1971, Clout--Womanpower and Politics, 1974, Dismantling America--The Rush to Deregulate, 1983, Buying Into America--How Foreign Money Is Changing the Face of Our Nation, 1988, Selling Our Security--The Erosion of America's Assets, 1992, Glass Houses--Congressional Ethics and the Politics of Venom, 2001, A World Ignited: How Apostles of Ethnic, Religions and Racial Hatred Torch the Globe, 2006. Bd. dirs. Cystic Fibrosis Found., 1982-98; county committeewoman Dem. Party, Montclair, N.J., 1969-73. Recipient Founder's Day award NYU, 1968, Trachtenberg award for rsch. George Washington U., 1998; named Tchr. of Yr., Mt. Vernon Coll., 1978; Dilthey fellow George Washington U., 1983, Aspen Inst. fellow, 1979. Fellow Nat. Acad. Pub. Adminstrn.; mem. Am. Polit. Sci. Assn. (pres. Women's Caucus for Polit. Sci. 1977-78), Am. Soc. Pub. Adminstrn. (chair sect. natural resources and environ. adminstrn. 1982-83, Marshall Dimock award 1997). Democrat. Office: Sch Pub Policy George Mason U 3401 Fairfax Dr Arlington VA 22201 Home Phone: 202-625-7782.

TOLEDO, ANDREW ANTHONY, obstetrician, gynecologist; b. Tampa, Fla., June 24, 1955; MD, U. South Fla., 1979. Diplomate in ob-gyn. and reproductive endocrinology Am. Coll. Ob-Gyn. Intern U. Louisville, 1979-80, resident in ob-gyn., 1980-83, fellow in reproductive endocrinology, 1983-85; active staff Northside Hosp., Atlanta, 1990—, Piedmont Hosp., Atlanta, 1992—; cons. staff Dunwoody (Ga.) Med. Ctr., 1992—; asst. clin. prof. ob-gyn. Emory U. Sch. Medicine, Atlanta. Mem. N.Am. Soc. Pediat. and Adolescent Gynecology, Am. Coll. Ob-Gyn., Am. Fertility Soc., N.Am. Soc. for Adolescent Gynecology. Office: PO Box 28618 Atlanta GA 30358 also: Ste 400 1150 Lake Hearn Dr Atlanta GA 30342 Home Phone: 404-314-1135; Office Phone: 404-355-3232, 404-256-6972. Personal E-mail: fertman790@aol.com. E-mail: andrew.toledo@rba-online.com.

TOLEDO, ISABEL, apparel designer; b. Cuba, 1961; m. Ruben Toledo, 1984. Grad., Fashion Inst. of Tech., NYC, Parsons Sch. of Design. Launched collection Isabel Toledo, 1985—; opened first store The Lab, NYC, 1998; creative dir. Anne Klein Jones Apparel Group, 2006—07. Collaborator (with Ruben Toledo) on various art exhibits including A Marriage of Art and Fashion; designs shown in Victoria & Albert Mus., London, Mode Mus., Antwerp, Fashion Inst. of Tech., Kent State U. Mus., Ohio, Gallery of Mus. of Otis Coll. of Art and Design, Los Angeles. Featured in (books) Isabel Toledo: Fashion from the Inside Out, 2009. Recipient Cooper Hewitt Design award, 2005, Otis Critics' award, Otis Coll. Art and Design, Winnie award, Coty Am. Fashion Critics, award for Artistry of Fashion, Couture Coun., Fashion Inst. America, 2008; named Women's Wear Designer of Yr., Hispanic Designers Inc. Achievements include designing the dress worn by the First Lady duing the 2009 Presdl. Inauguration. Office: Isabel Toledo Ltd 277 5th Ave New York NY 10016 Office Phone: 212-685-0948.*

TOLIA, VASUNDHARA K., pediatric gastroenterologist, educator; b. Kolkata, India; came to U.S., 1975; d. Rasiklal and Saroj (Kothari) Doshi; m. Kirit Tolia, May 30, 1975; children: Vinay, Sanjay. MBBS, Calcutta U., 1968-75. Intern, resident Children's Hosp. Mich., Detroit, 1976-79, fellow, 1979-81, dir. pediat. endoscopy unit, 1984-90, dir. pediat. gastroenterology and nutrition, 1990—2005. Instr. Wayne State U., Detroit, 1981—83, asst. prof., 1983—91, assoc. prof., 1991—97, prof., 1997—2005; adjunct prof. pediat. Mich. State U., 2008—. Mem. editl. bd. Inflammatory Bowel Diseases, 1999-2005, Am. Jour. Gastroenterology, 1999-2005, Rev. World Lit. in Pediatrics, 1999—, AAP Grand Rounds and Therapy, 2006—, Gastroenterology Rsch. and Practice, 2008-; contbr. articles to profl. jours. Named Woman of Distinction, Mich. chpt. Crohn's and Colitis Found. Am., 1991. Fellow Am. Coll. Gastroenterology (chair ad-hoc com. pediat. gastroenterology 1998-2000), Am. Acad. Pediats.; mem. Am. Gastroenterology Assn., N.Am. Soc. Pediat. Gastroenterology and Nutrition, Soc. Pediat. Rsch. Office Phone: 248-568-1500.

TOLICH, NIKOLAI, physicist, educator; MSc., U. Auckland; PhD, Stanford U. Fellow Lawrence Berkeley Nat. Lab.; asst. prof. dept. physics U. Wash. Office: University of Washington Dept Physics Box 351560 Seattle WA 98195 Office Phone: 206-543-4223. Office Fax: 206-543-1493. E-mail: ntolich@u.washington.edu.*

TOLINS, ROGER ALAN, lawyer; b. Bklyn., Jan. 25, 1936; s. Albert and Claire (Rothstein) T.; m. Doris Levine, May 15, 1960; children: Fran, Jonathan. AB with distinction, Dartmouth Coll., 1956; LLB, NYU, 1959, LLM in Taxation, 1961. Bar: N.Y. 1959. Assoc. Brennan, London & Buttenwieser, NYC, 1961-67; ptnr. Goldfeld, Charak, Tolins & Lowenfels, NYC, 1967-74, Tolins & Lowenfels, NYC, 1975—. Guest lectr. in securities law Seton Hall U. Sch. Law, 1989—. With U.S. Army, 1959-60. Mem. ABA (sect. on taxation), N.Y. State Bar Assn. Office Phone: 212-421-1965. E-mail: roger@tolinslowenfels.com.

TOLIVER, HAROLD EARL, retired English language professional; b. McMinnville, Oreg., Feb. 16, 1932; s. Marion E. and Mable A. (Mallery) T.; m. Mary Bennette, June 20, 1954; children: Tricia, Brooks. BA, U. Oreg., 1954; MA, Johns Hopkins U., 1958; PhD, U. Wash., 1961. Asst. prof. Ohio State U., Columbus, 1961-64, UCLA, 1965-66; asst. prof., prof. U. Calif., Irvine, 1966-94. Author: Marvell's Ironic Vision, 1965, Pastoral Forms and Attitudes, 1971, Animate Illusions, 1974, Lyric Provinces, 1985, The Past That Poets Make, 1981, Transported Styles, 1989, Herbert's Christian Narrative, 1993, Orbituary Quilt, 1998, Done in Blood Red Ochre, 2000, Bitterroot, 2000, St. Agnes Letters, 2006, Pageant of the Mortals, 2007, Leave not a Trace, 2009; contbr. to profl. publs. Pvt. first class, U.S. Army, 1954-56. Recipient Guggenheim fellowships, 1964, 76. Avocations: bicycling, tennis. Home: 1405 Skyline Dr Laguna Beach CA 92651-1942 Personal E-mail: hetolive@uci.edu.

TOLK, ANDREAS, computer scientist, researcher; b. Hamm, Germany, Mar. 14, 1964; arrived in US, 2002, permanent resident, 2004; s. Lothar Adolf and Else Anni Hedwig Tolk; m. Andrea Koenig, July 20, 1990; children: Florian, Christopher. MSc in Computer Sci., U. of the Fed. Armed Forces, Germany, 1988, PhD, 1995. Project mgr. Elektroniksystem- Logistik GmbH, Munich, 1995—98; v.p. Industrieanlagen-betriebsgesellschaft, 1998—2002; sr. rsch. scientist Va. Modeling, Analysis & Simulation Ctr., Suffolk, 2002—06; assoc. prof. engring. mgmt. Old Dominion U., Norfolk, Va., 2006—. Maj. German Army, Air Def., 1983—95, Germany. Mem.: Simulation Interoperability Stads. Orgn., Nat. Def. Indsl. Assn., Mil. Operational Rsch. Soc., Am. Soc. Engring. Mgmt., Soc. Modelling and Simulation. Office: Old Dominion U 241 Kaufman Hall Norfolk VA 23529 Business E-Mail: atolk@odu.edu.

TOLK, NORMAN HENRY, physics educator; b. Idaho Falls, Idaho, Jan. 9, 1938; s. Henry and Merle (Ricks) T.; m. Marilynn Ann Neubauer, Dec. 19, 1961; children: Jeffrey S., Bentley J., David H., Rebecca E., Amy C. AB in Physics, Harvard U., 1960; PhD in Physics, Columbia U., 1966. Rsch. physicist Columbia Radiation Lab., NYC, 1966, rsch. assoc., 1966-67, lectr., mem. staff, 1967-68; adj. asst. prof. Columbia U., NYC, 1968-69; mem. tech. staff Bell Telephone Lab., Murray Hill, N.J., 1968-83, Bell Comms. Rsch., Murray Hill, 1984; prof. physics Vanderbilt U., Nashville, 1984—, prof. dept. radiology, 1993—. Adj. prof. physics Fisk U., Nashville, 1991—; cons. Physitron, Inc., Huntsville, Ala., 1993—, Lawrence Livermore Nat. Lab., Livermore, Calif., 1995—. Editor: Inelastic Ion-Surface Collisions, 1977, Desorpion Induced by Elec. Trans., 1983, Atomic Collisions in Solids, 1986; N.Am. editor Radiation Effects and Def./Solids, 1987—; contbr. over 160 articles to profl. jours. Alexander von Humboldt sr. scientist, 1987. Fellow Am. Phys. Soc. Office: Vanderbilt U Dept Physics PO Box 1807 B Nashville TN 37202-1807 Home: 913 Center Ridge Ct Brentwood TN 37027-6541

TOLL, BARBARA ELIZABETH, art gallery director; b. Phila., June 8, 1945; d. Joseph M. and Evelyn Toll BA, Goucher Coll., 1967; MFA, Pratt Inst., 1969. Asst. dir. jr. coun. Mus. Modern Art, NYC, 1969-70; dir. Hundred Acres Gallery, NYC, 1971-76; curator David Rockefeller Collection, NYC, 1975-81; pres., dir. Barbara Toll Fine Arts, NYC, 1981-94, dir., 1994—. Bd. dirs. Corp. Yaddo; curator Focus: Donald Judd Furniture, Parrish Art Mus., Southampton, NY, 1996, Friendships in Arcadia: Writers and Artists at Yaddo in the 90s, 2000, Follies: Fantasy in the Landscape, Parrish Art Mus., 2001, Reconfiguring Space: Blueprints for Art in Gen., 2003. Trustee Ind. Curators Internat.; nat. bd. dirs. ArtTable, 2001—04. Mem.: The Drawing Ctr. (bd. dir. 2008). Avocation: gardening. Office: 138 Prince St New York NY 10012-3135

TOLL, BRUCE ELLIOT, real estate developer; b. Phila., Apr. 29, 1943; s. Albert Arthur and Sylvia Toll; m. Robbi Stern; children: Michelle, Elizabeth, Wendy, Jennifer. BA in Acctg., U. Miami, 1965. Pres., dir., COO Toll Brothers Inc., Horsham, Pa., 1967—98, vice chmn., 1998—; founder, principal BET Investments. Bd. dir. UbiquiTel Inc., Home Builders Assn. Bucks & Montgomery Counties. Twp. commr. Abington Twp., Pa., 1985-87; bd. dirs. Abington Meml. Hosp., Pa. Nursing Home Loan Agy., 1983-91; chmn., past pres. Abington Indsl. Devel. Authority; bd. mem. Ben Franklin Tech Ctr. SE Pa., Phila. Mus. Art. Mem. Nat. Homebuilders Assn., Philmont Country Club, Equity. Republican. Office: Toll Brothers Inc 250 Gibraltar Rd Horsham PA 19044

TOLL, JOHN SAMPSON, retired academic administrator, physics professor; b. Denver, Oct. 25, 1923; s. Oliver Wolcott and Merle d'Aubigne (Sampson) T.; m. Deborah Ann Taintor, Oct. 24, 1970; children: Dacia Merle Sampson, Caroline Taintor. BS with honors, Yale U., 1944; AM, Princeton U., 1948, PhD, 1952; DSc (hon.), U. Md., 1973, U. Wroclaw, Poland, 1975; LLD (hon.), Adelphi U., 1978; PhD (hon.), Fudan U., Peoples Republic China, 1987; LHD (hon.), SUNY, Stony Brook, 1990; LLD (hon.), U. Md., Eastern Shore, 1993. Mng. editor, acting chmn. Yale Sci. mag., 1943-44; with Princeton U., 1946-49, proctor fellow, 1948-49; Friends of Elementary Particle Theory Research grantee for study in France, 1950; theoretical physicist Los Alamos Sci. Lab., 1950-51; staff mem., assoc. dir. Project Matterhorn, Forrestal Rsch. Ctr., Princeton U., 1951-53; prof., chmn. physics and astronomy U. Md., 1953-65; pres., prof. physics SUNY, Stony Brook, 1965-78, U. Md., 1978-88, chancellor, 1988-89, chancellor emeritus, prof. physics, 1989—; pres. Univs. Rsch. Assn., Washington, 1989-94, Washington Coll., Chestertown, Md., 1995—. 1st dir. chancellor's panel on univ. pruposes SUNY, 1970; physics cons. to editl. staff Nat. Sci. Tchrs. Assn., 1957—61; U.S. del., head scientist, secretariat Internat. Conf. High Energy Physics, 1960; mem.-at-large U.S. nat. com. Internat. Union Pure and Applied Physics, 1960—63; chmn. rsch. adv. com. on electrophysics NASA, 1961—65; mem. gov. Md. Sci. Resources Adv. Bd., 1963—65; mem., chmn. adv. panel for physics NSF, 1964—67; mem. N.Y. Gov.'s Adv. Com. Atomic Energy, 1966—70; mem. commn. plans and objectives higher edn. Am. Coun. Edn., 1966—69; mem. Hall of Records Commn., 1979—88; mem., chmn. adv. coun. Princeton Plasma Physics Lab., 1979—85; mem. adv. coun. pres.'s Assn. Governing Bds., 1980—88, So. Regional Edn. Bd., 1980—90; mem. exec. com. Washington/Balt. Regional Assn., 1980—89, Nat. Assn. State Univs. and Land Grant Colls., 1980—88, Ctr. Study of the Presidency, 1983—84; mem. univ. programs panel of energy rsch. bd. Dept. Energy, 1982—83; mem. adv. com. SBHE, 1983—89, Md. Gov.'s Chesapeake Bay Coun., 1985; mem. resource com. state trade policy coun. Gov.'s high tech roundtable Md. Dept. Econ. Devel., 1986—89; chmn. marine divsn. NASULGC, 1986; bd. trustees Aspen Inst. Humanities, 1987—89; mem. commn. higher edn. Middle States Assn. Colls. and Schs., 1987; chmn. adv. panel on tech. risks and opportunities for U.S. energy supply and demand U.S. Office Tech. Assessment, 1987—91, chmn. adv. panel on internat. collaboration in def. tech., 1989—91; mem. Sea Grant rev. panel U.S. Dept. Commerce, 1992—, chair, 1996—97; mem. com. financing higher edn. Nat. Assn. Ind. Colls. and Univs., 1996—98; bd. govs. Chesapeake Bay Maritime Mus., 1996—; dir. Md. Gov.'s Blue Ribbon Citizens Pfiesteria Action Commn., 1997; mem. governing coun. Wye Faculty Seminar, 1997—; dir. Eastern Shore Assn. Coll. Pres., 1998—; mem. bd. dirs. Md. Ctr. Agro-Ecology, Inc., 1999—; vis. prof. Nordic Inst. Theoretical Physics, Niels Bohr Inst., Denmark, U. Lund, Sweden, 1975—76; mem. math. scis. edn. bd. NAS; mem. Higher Edn. Heritage Action Com., 2002—. Contbr. articles to profl. jours. Mem. adv. coun. Del-Mar-Va coun. Boy Scouts Am., 1999—; mem. Higher Edn. Heritage Action Com., 2002—; bd. dirs. Hodson Scholarship Found., 1996, Mid-Shore Cmty. Found., 2002—. Recipient Benjamin Barge prize in math. Yale U., 1943, George Beckwith medal for Proficiency in Astronomy, 1944, Outstanding Citizen award City of Denver, 1958, Outstanding Tchr. award U. Md. Men's League, 1965, Copernicus award govt. of Poland, 1973, Stony Brook Found. award for disting. contbns. to edn., 1979, Disting. Svc. award State of Md., 1981, Silver medal Sci. U. Tokyo, 1994, Internat. Landmark award U. Md., 1994, first recipient Lifetime Achievement award Md. Assn. for Higher Edn., 2000, Chief Exec. Leadership award Coun. for Advancement and Support Edn., 2000; named Washingtonian of Yr., 1985, Citizen of Yr. Chestertown Optimist Club, 1997, John S. Toll Physics Bldg., Univ. Md., 2001; John Simon Guggenheim Meml. Found. fellow Inst. Theoretical Physics U. Copenhagen, U. Lund, Sweden, 1958-59. Fellow AAAS, Am. Phys. Soc., Washington Acad. Scis. (pres. 1995-96), N.Y. Acad. Scis.; mem. NSTA, Am. Coun. Edn. (bd. dirs. 1986-89, NAACP (life), Am. Assn. Physics Tchrs., Fedn. Am. Scientists (chmn. 1961-62), Philos. Soc. Washington, Assn. Higher Edn., Yale U. Sci. and Engring. Assn. (award for disting. contbns. 1996), Cosmos Club, Hamilton St. Club, Baltimore, Univ. Club (Washington and N.Y.), Phi Beta Kappa, Phi Kappa Phi (disting., Marylander of Yr. 2000 award), Sigma Xi (Sci. Achievement award 1965), Omicron Delta Kappa (hon.), Sigma Pi Sigma. Achievements include research on elementary particle theory, scattering. E-mail: johntoll@physics.umd.edu, jtoll2@washcoll.edu. *Throughout my life I have tried mainly to do whatever seemed most important and useful.*

TOLL, ROBERT IRWIN, home construction company executive; b. Elkins Park, Pa., Dec. 30, 1940; s. Albert A. and Sylvia (Steinberg) T.; m. Norma (div.); children: Laurie, Deborah; m. Jane Snyder; children: Rachel, Jacob; stepson, Joshua Goldfein. AB, Cornell U., 1963; LLB cum laude, U. Pa., 1966. Bar: Pa. 1967. Atty. Wolf, Block Schorr Solis-Cohen, Phila., 1966-67; founder Toll Bros. Inc., Huntingdon Valley, Pa., 1967, chmn., CEO, 1967—. Mem. Mayor's Coun. on Housing in Phila.; mem. bd. overseers U. Pa. Law Sch.; mem. real estate coun. Cornell U. Real Estate Coun. Bd. dirs. Pa. Campaign for Choice, Phila., Beth Sholom Synagogue, Elkins Park, Southeastern chpt. ARC, Seeds of Peace, NYC; sponsor Say Yes to Edn., Phila.; mem. bd. trustees Abington Meml. Hosp. Found. Recipient Nat. Housing Quality Award, Nat. Assn. Home Builders, 1995, Bronze Award, CEO of Yr., Fin. World, 1996, Residential Building Industry's CEO Silver Award, Wall Street Transcript, 1996; named Profl. Builder of Yr., Builder Mag., 1988, America's Best Builder, Nat. Assn. Homebuilders and Builder Mag., 1996, Ernst & Young's Master Entrepreneur of Yr. Award, 1996. Mem. Nat. Assn. Home Builders, Philmont Country Club (Huntingdon Valley), Equity Lodge 591. Avocations: racing j/35 sailboats, tennis, skiing. Office: Toll Brothers Inc 250 Gibraltar Rd Horsham PA 19044-2323

TOLL, SHELDON SAMUEL, lawyer; b. Phila., June 6, 1940; s. Herman and Rose (Ornstein) T.; m. Roberta Darlene Pollack, Aug. 11, 1968; children: Candice Moore, John Maitland, Kevin Scott. BA, U. Pa., 1962; MA, Oxford U., Eng., 1964; JD, Harvard U., 1967. Bar: Pa. 1967, Mich. 1972, Ill. 1990, Tex. 1990, U.S. Dist. Ct. (ea. dist.) Pa. 1968, U.S. Ct. Appeals (3d cir.) 1970, U.S. Supreme Ct. 1971, Mich. 1972, U.S. Dist. Ct. (ea. dist.), U.S. Ct. Appeals (6th cir.) 1973, U.S. Ct. Appeals (5th cir.) 1978, U.S. Dist. Ct. (no. dist.) Calif. 1986, U.S. Ct. Appeals (9th cir.) 1987, U.S. Dist. Ct. (ea. dist.) Wis. 1989. Assoc. Montgomery, McCracken et al, Phila., 1967-72; sr. ptnr. Honigman Miller Schwartz and Cohn, Detroit, 1972—2003; prin. Sheldon S. Toll PLLC, Southfield, Mich., 2003—. Panelist Bankruptcy Litigation Inst., N.Y.C., 1984-94. Author: Toll's Pennsylvania Crime Code, 2005, Bankruptcy Litigation Manual, 2004. Bd. dirs. Southeastern Mich. chpt. ARC, Detroit. Mem. Fed. Bar Assn. (past pres. Detroit chpt.), ABA, Pa. Bar Assn., Phila. Bar Assn., Franklin (Mich.) Hills Country Club, Mar-a-Lago Club (Palm Beach, Fla.), Phi Beta Kappa. Democrat. Jewish. Office: Sheldon S Toll PLLC 2000 Town Ctr Ste 2100 Southfield MI 48075 Office Phone: 248-351-5480. Business E-Mail: lawtoll@comcast.net.

TOLL, STEVEN J., lawyer; b. Queens, NY, 1950; BS in Economics, U. Pa., 1972; JD, Georgetown U., 1975. Bar: Va. 1975, Washington, DC 1976. Atty. enforcement and litig. sections Fed. Home Loan Bank Bd., 1975—78; joined Cohen, Milstein, Hausfeld & Toll PLLC, Washington, 1979, mng. ptnr., 1997—. Featured in Washington Bus. Jour., 1996. Named one of 500 Leading Lawyers in Am., LawDragon, 2006. Mem.: Beta Gamma Sigma. Office: Cohen Milstein Hausfeld & Toll 1100 New York Ave NW Ste 500 W Washington DC 20005-3964 Office Phone: 202-408-4600. Office Fax: 202-408-4699.

TOLLE, BRENDA KAY, secondary school educator, computer scientist, consultant; b. Xenia, Ohio, Nov. 30, 1942; d. Charles Wilbur and Agnes Geneva Massie; m. Richard William Davenport, May 16, 1963 (div. June 1965); 1 child, Lee A.; m. Glenn Walker Tolle, Apr. 11, 1970. BS in Edn., Ctrl. State U., 1971; MEd, Wright State U., 1976. Clk., sec. Ctrl. State U., Wilberforce, Ohio, 1964-70; tchr., educator Ohio Soldiers and Sailors Orphans Home, Xenia, 1970-72, Cedarville (Ohio) H.S., 1972—; owner, operator Brenda's Computer Svc., Xenia, 1986—. Tech. coord. Cedar Cliffs Schs., Cedarville, 1992—. Contbr. articles to profl. jours. Bd. dirs. Future Bus. Leaders Am., Ohio, 1976-87; sec. Greene County Uni-Serv/Ohio Edn. Assn., 1988-90, MBRDOWGA Rating, DDWGA Rules Com. With US Army, 1962—63. Mem. NEA, Ohio Edn. Assn., Ohio Bus. Tchrs. Assn., Cedarville Area C. of C. (sec. 1991-95, dir. pub. rels. 1996—), Cedarville Edn. Assn. (pres. 1985-91), Sebastian Hills Golf Club, LLC (jr., bd. dirs. 2001—, mgmt. com.). Republican. Baptist. Avocations: computers, reading, golf.

TOLLE, ECKHART, writer; b. Germany, Feb. 6, 1948; BA, U. London. Rschr. Cambridge U.; counselor, spiritual tchr., London. Author: (books) The Power of Now: A Guide to Spiritual Enlightenment, 1999, Practicing the Power of Now: Essential Teachings, Meditations, and Exercises from The Power of Now, 2001, Stillness Speaks: Whispers of Now, 2003, A New Earth: Awakening to Your Life's Purpose, 2005 (Publishers Weekly bestseller). Achievements include having books translated into 32 languages. Mailing: Eckhart Tolle PO Box 93664 Nelson Park RPO Vancouver BC V6E 4L7 Canada Personal E-mail: DearEckhart@eckharttolle.com.

TOLLEFSEN, DOUGLAS MEYER, medical educator; b. Kearney, Nebr., Feb. 27, 1948; s. Wilmer George and Opal Elizabeth Tollefsen; m. Sherida Elaine Lyman, June 27, 1971; children: Benjamin Lyman, Mark William. BA, Grinnell Coll., Iowa, 1970; MD, Wash. U. Med. Sch., St. Louis, PhD, 1977. Resident U. Colo. Sch. Medicine, Denver, 1977—79; fellow hematology-oncology Wash. U. Med. Sch., St. Louis, 1979—80, asst. prof. medicine, 1980—85, assoc. prof. of medicine, 1985—93, prof. of medicine, 1993—, prof. pathology & immunology, 2005—. Hematology study sect. NIH, 1985—91; editl. bd. mem. Jour. Biol. Chemistry, 1992—96; sci. subcom. mem. Am. Soc. Hematology, 1993—97. Recipient Rsch. Career Devel. award, NIH, 1982—87; Med. Scientist Tng. fellow, Wash. U. Med. Sch., 1972—77. Mem.: Assn. Am. Physicians, Am. Soc. Clin. Investigation, Alpha Omega Alpha. Achievements include discovery of natural anticoagulant protein, heparin cofactor II, and its role in vascular homeostasis; patents for DNA encoding modified heparin cofactor II. Home: 6330 Pershing Ave Saint Louis MO 63130 Office: Washington Univ Med Sch 660 S Euclid Ave Campus Box 8125 Saint Louis MO 63110 Office Phone: 314-362-8830. Business E-Mail: tollefsen@im.wustl.edu.

TOLLEFSON, BEN C., state legislator, retired utilities executive; b. Minot, ND, June 14, 1927; s. Ben K. and Hannah G. (Espeseth) T.; m. Lila R. Adams, Apr. 11, 1949; children: Robb, LuAnn, David, Richard. Student, Minot State U., 1946-48. Advt. salesman Minot Daily News, 1956-57; utility salesman No. States Power Co., Minot, 1957-72, sales mgr., 1972-89; retired, 1989; advisor Ctrl. Venture Capital, Minot, 1990-95; mem. N.D. Ho. of Reps., Bismark, 1984-99, N.D. Senate from 38th dist., Bismark, 2001—. Pres. Minot Jaycees, 1957. Served with USN, 1945-47. Recipient Clara Barton Svc. award Am. Red Cross, 1969; named one of Outstanding Young Men Am., Minot Jaycees, 1958, State Ofcl. Yr., Nat. Assn. Home Builders, 1992. Mem. Kiwanis (Minot lt. gov. 1973, Outstanding Lt. Gov. 1973). Republican. Lutheran. Avocations: hunting, public speaking. Home: 500 Twenty Fourth St NW Minot ND 58701

TOLLEFSON, TERRENCE ALFRED, retired educator and consultant; b. Pontiac, Mich., May 1, 1938; s. Alfred and Iva Denice Tollefson; m. Bonnie Lou Bradley, 1961 (dec. 1990); children: Katherine Marie, Michelle Suzanne Miller, Bradley Alfred. BA in Edn. and Soc. Studies, U. Mich., Ann Arbor, 1961; PhD, U. Mich., 1975; MBA in Mktg., Mich. State U., East Lansing, 1963. Assoc. prof. dept. adult and CC edn. NC State U., Raleigh, 1986—93; prof., interim chair dept. ednl. leadership and policy analysis East Tenn. State U., Johnson City, 1993—2007, prof. emeritus, 2007—08, faculty senate pres., 2003—04. Home: 4100 Prescott Dr Johnson City TN 37601

TOLLENAERE, LAWRENCE ROBERT, retired industrial products company executive; b. Berwyn, Ill., Nov. 19, 1922; s. Cyrille and Modesta (Van Damme) T.; m. Mary Elizabeth Hansen, Aug. 14, 1948; children: Elizabeth, Homer, Stephanie, Caswell, Mary Jennifer. BS in Engring., Iowa State U., 1944, MS in Engring., 1949; MBA, U. So. Calif., 1969; LLD (hon.), Claremont Grad. Sch., 1977. Specification engr. Aluminum Co. Am., Vernon, Calif., 1946-47; asst. prof. indsl. engring. Iowa State U., Ames, 1947-50; sales rep. Am. Pipe and Constrn. Co. (now AMERON), South Gate, Calif., 1950-53, spl. rep. S.Am., 1952-54, 2nd v.p., mgr. Columbian divsn. Bogota, S.Am., 1955-57, divsn. v.p., mgr. Calif., 1957-63, v.p. concrete pipe ops. Monterey Park, Calif., 1963-65, pres. corp. hdqrs., 1965-67; pres., CEO Ameron Inc., Monterrey Park, Calif., 1967-89, CEO, pres. Pasadena, 1989-93, chmn. bd. dirs., 1989-94, ret., 1994. Trustee The Huntington Library, Art Gallery and Bot. Gardens; emeritus mem. bd. fellows Claremont U. Ctr.; bd. gov.'s Iowa State U. Found. Mem. Calif. C. of C. (bd. dirs. 1977-92), Calif. Club (past pres.), Jonathan Club, Bohemian Club, San Francisco Club, Beavers Club (past pres., hon. dir.), Alpha Tau Omega. Republican. Avocations: fishing, hunting, horseback riding, stamp collecting/philately.

TOLLES, BRYANT FRANKLIN, JR., retired history and art history professor; b. Hartford, Conn., Mar. 14, 1939; s. Bryant Franklin and Grace Frances (Ludden) T.; m. Carolyn Coolidge Kimball, Sept. 15, 1962; children: Thayer Coolidge, Bryant Franklin III. BA, Yale U., 1961, MA in Tchg., 1962; PhD, Boston U., 1970. Instr. history King Sch., Stamford, Conn., 1962-63; tchr. history St. George's Sch., Newport, RI, 1963-65; instr., asst. dean Tufts U., Medford, Mass., 1965-71; asst. dir., libr., editor publs. N.H. Hist. Soc., Concord, 1972-74; exec. dir., libr. Essex Inst., Salem, Mass., 1974-84; dir. mus. studies program, prof. history and art history U. Del., Newark, 1984—2006, prof. emeritus, 2006—, chmn. art conservation dept., 1997-2000. Mem. Com. for a New Eng. Bibliography, Inc. Author: New Hampshire Architecture, 1979, Architecture in Salem, 1983, The Grand Resort Hotels of the White Mountains: A Vanishing Architectural Legacy, 1998, Summer Cottages in the White Mountains: The Architecture of Leisure and Recreation, 1870-1930, 2000, Resort Hotels of the Adirondacks: The Architecture of a Summer Paradise, 1840-1940, 2003, Summer by the Seaside: The Architecture of New Eng. Coastal Resort Hotels, 1820-1950, 2008; editor: Leadership for the Future, 1991; contbr. articles and book revs. to profl. jours. Trustee Mt. Washington Obs., NH, Squam Lakes Nat. Sci. Ctr., NH, Humanities Coun. Ford. Found. fellow Yale U., 1962. Mem. Am. Antiquarian Soc., Colonial Soc. Mass., Mass. Hist. Soc., Orgn. Am. Historians, Soc. Archtl. Historians, Soc. Indsl. Archaeology, Am. Assn. Mus., New Eng. Mus. Assn., Am. Assn. State and Local History, Appalachian Mountain Club. Home: 39 Dwinell Dr Concord NH 03301-2513 Home Phone: 603-856-7128. Business E-Mail: bftolles@udel.edu.

TOLLETT, LELAND EDWARD, food products executive; b. Nashville, Ark., Jan. 21, 1937; s. Vergil E. and Gladys V. (Sturgis) Tollett; m. Betty Ruth Blew, June 2, 1961; children: Terri Lynn, Gary Dwayne. BSA, U. Ark., 1958, MSA, 1959. Dir. rsch. Tyson Foods, Inc., Springdale, Ark., 1959—64, gen mgr. prodn., 1965—66, v.p. prodn., 1966—80, COO, 1981—83, pres., COO, 1983—91, CEO, 1991, vice chmn., 1993—95, chmn., CEO, 1995—98, interim pres., CEO, 2009—. Bd. dirs. Tyson Foods, Inc., 1984—2008. Served USAF, 1961—62. Mem.: Nat. Broiler Coun. (bd. dirs. 1979—). Avocations: hunting, golf. Office: Tyson Foods Inc 2210 W Oaklawn Dr Springdale AR 72762-6999*

TOLLEY, AUBREY GRANVILLE, psychiatrist, health facility administrator; b. Lynchburg, Va., Nov. 15, 1924; married. Student, Duke U., 1942—43, U. Va., 1946—48, MD, 1952. Diplomate Am. Bd. Psychiatry and Neurology. Intern St. Elizabeths Hosp., Washington, 1952-53; asst. resident psychiatry U. Va. Hosp., Charlottesville, 1953-54; resident psychiatry VA Hosp., Roanoke, Va., 1955-56; instr. U. N.C. Sch. Medicine, 1956-61, asst. prof., 1961-66, clin. asst. prof. psychiatry, 1966-72, clin. assoc. prof., 1972-76, clin. prof., 1976—; dir. psychotherapy Dorothea Dix Hosp., Raleigh, NC, 1962-67, dir. hosp., 1973-88. Dir. resident tng. John Umstead Hosp., Butner, N.C., 1966-67; dir. profl. tng. and edn. N.C. Dept. Mental Health, Raleigh, 1967-72, asst. dir., 1972-73; prin. investigator USPHS grant, 1957-59; cons. VA Hosp., Fayetteville, N.C., 1957-78; sr. cons., supervising faculty, cmty. psychiatry sect. dept. psychiatry U. N.C. Sch. Medicine, 1971-88; exec. sec. Multiversity Group, 1968-73 Trustee Found. Hope, Raleigh, 1984—. Served with USNR, 1943-46. Recipient The Order of the Long Leaf Pine, State of N.C., 1982. Fellow Am. Psychiat. Assn. (disting. life; assembly rep. N.C. Dist. br. 1969-82, 86-2000, mem. joint commn. on pub. affairs 1984-87, mem. constl. membership com. 1990-96, mem. commn. on subspecialization 1990-94, Warren Williams award 1987), Am. Coll. Psychiatrists (life); mem. AMA, N.C. Med. Soc. (life), Durham-Orange County Med. Soc., N.C. Psychiat. Assn. (pres. 1984-85, Lifetime Disting. Svc. award 1999), N.C. Hosp. Assn. (life), George C. Ham Soc. (Disting. Alumni award 1992). Home and Office: 110 Laurel Hill Rd Chapel Hill NC 27514-4323

TOLLEY, EDWARD DONALD, lawyer; b. San Antonio, Jan. 31, 1950; s. Lyle Oren and Mary Theresa Tolley; m. Beth Dekle Tolley; 1 child, Edward Spencer. BBA, U. Ga., 1971, MBA, 1974, JD, 1975. Bar: Ga. 1975, U.S. Dist. Ct. (5th cir.) 1976, U.S. Supreme Ct. 1978, U.S. Ct. Appeals (11th cir.) 1981. Ptnr. Cook, Noell, Tolley and Bates, Athens, Ga., 1975—. Lectr. various colls., univs., civic and profl. groups. Mem. Family Counseling Assn. of Athens, Inc., mem. Gov.'s Commn. on Criminal Sanctions and Correctional Facilities, 1988-90; past bd. dirs. Am. Cancer Soc.; pres. Clarke County Bd. Edn., 1992-93. Recipient award for cmty. svc. Chief Justice Ga. Supreme Ct., 2000, Lifetime Achievement award, State Bar Ga., 2008. Fellow Ga. Bar Found., Am. Bd. Criminal Lawyers (bd. dirs. 1987, pres. 1996); mem. Fed. Bar Assn. (sec. 1983, treas. 1985, pres. Macon chpt. 1997-98), State Bar Ga. (chmn. law office and econ. com., bd. govs. 1985—, formal adv. opinion bd., Professionalism award 2002), Ga. Trial Lawyers (v.p.), Ga. Assn. Criminal Def. Lawyers (pres. 1985, Indigent Def. award 1983, 88), Athens Bar Assn. (past pres.), Am. Judicature Soc., Order of Barristers (Cmty. Svc. award Chief Justice Ga. Supreme Ct., 2000). Office: Cook Noell et al 304 E Washington St Athens GA 30601-2751 Home Phone: 706-546-9972; Office Phone: 706-549-6111.

TOLLEY, JERRY RUSSELL, academic administrator; b. Goldsboro, NC, Nov. 6, 1942; s. Elva Russell Tolley and Clara (Smith) Tolley-Bunch; m. Joan Morrison, June 8, 1965; children: Jerry R. Jr., Justin Clay. BS, East Carolina U., 1965, MEd, 1966; EdD, U. NC, Greensboro, 1982; exec. mgmt. courses, Duke U. Tchr., coach Fayetteville Sr. HS, NC, 1966; asst. football coach, head track and tennis coach Elon Coll., NC, 1967-77, head football coach, 1977-81, dir. athletic sholarship fund, 1982, dir. corp. and ann. resources, 1983, coordinator Pride II Capital Campaign, 1984, assoc. dir. devel., 1985, officer corp. and major gifts, maj. gifts officer, 1999, dir. ann. giving, 2003; dir Elon Soc., NC, 2008; asst. v.p. tng., nat. dir. tng. & pub. affairs Lab. Corp. of Am., Burlington, NC, 1986—. Author: Intercollegiate History of Athletics and Elon College, 1982, American Football Coaches Guidebook to Championship Football Drills, 1985, 101 Winning Football Drills -From the Legends of the Game, 2003, The Complete Book of Defensive Football Drills, 2005, The Complete Book of Offensive Football Drills, 2005, The Complete Book of Speed and Agility Drils, 2007; co-author: 101 Winning Plays, 1977, Leadership Education: A Source Book, 1989; contbr. articles. Treas. Town of Elon Coll., 1984-87, mayor protem, 1988, mayor, 1990-98, 2006, mayor emeritus, 1998-2006, chmn. recreation commn.; mayor Town of Elon, 2006; convenor City County Govt. Assn., 1987-98, 2006-, Alamance County, NC, 1986—; mem. exec. bd. dir. Cherokee Coun. Boy Scouts Am., 1986, Thomas E. Powell Jr. Biology Found.; pres. Alamance Found.; exec. bd. NC Health & Fitness Found.; bd. visitors Elon Coll.; mem. exec. com. Alamance County Ptnrs. in Edn.; bd. govs. 2 Those Who Care; dir. Alamance Edn. Alliance; bd. dir. Cmty. Found. Greensboro; chmn. Citizens for Schs.; mktg. advisory com. Village of Brookwood; bd. advisors Randolf Bank. Named one of Outstanding Young Men Am., 1980, Internat. Men of Achievement, 1990, Cmty. Leaders Am., 1990, Mayors Hall of Fame, 1995; recipient HHP Centenental Leadership medellian, Dwight D. Eisenhower award Nat. Football Hall of Fame, 1980, 81, Nat. Collegiate Football Championship award Eastman Kodak, Meritorious Svc. award Tom Sawyer-Huck Finn Tennis Classic, 1986, Order of the Long Leaf Pine, 1997, Laurel Wreath award State of NC, 2002, Old North State award, 2007; named Nat. Football Coach of Yr., Nat. Assn. Intercollegiate Athletics, 1980, Elon Coll. Sports Hall of Fame, East Carolina U. Athletic Hall of Fame, 1991, East Carolina U. Ednl. Hall of Fame, 2008, East Carolina U. Centenial Leadership medalian, 2008 Mem.: All-Am. Football Found. (Lifetime Achievement award 2003, Hall of Fame 2009), Coun. Advancement of Edn., Am. Football Coaches Assn. (life), Omicron Delta Kappa, Phi Delta Kappa, Sigma Delta Psi. Avocations: writing, racquet sports, jogging. Home: 1322 Westbrook Ave Elon NC 27244-9358 Office: Elon Univ 2600 Campus Box # 2600 Elon NC 27244-2010 Office Phone: 336-278-7447. Business E-Mail: tolleyj@elon.edu.

TOLLEY, LUKE, chemistry professor; b. Durham, NC, Oct. 08; s. Tolley Dennis and Tolley Ann; m. Andrea Maren Whipple, May 6, 1995; 1 adopted child, Isaac children: Sariah, Isaiah, Elizabeth, Daniel, Benjamin. BS, Brigham Young U., Provo, Utah, 1996; PhD, U. NC, Chapel Hill, 2001. Asst. prof. Southern Ill. U., Carbondale, 2003—09, assoc. prof., 2009—. Contbr. scientific papers to profl. jours. (Innovation award, 2008). Bishop LDS Ch., Carbondale, 2005. Achievements include patents pending for method of detecting analytic-molecule interactions; invention of dynamic isoelectric focusing & anisotropy binding ligand assay. Office: Southern Ill Univ 1245 Lincoln Dr Carbondale IL 62901

TOLLIVER, BRYAN K., psychiatrist, educator; b. Whitesburg, Ky., July 25, 1966; s. James and Doris Tolliver. PhD, U. Ky., Lexington, 1994, MD, 2003. Diplomate Am. Bd. Psychiatry and Neurology, 2008. Postdoc. fellow U. Calif., San Francisco, 1994—99; fellow, addiction psychiatry Dept. Psychiatry, Med. U. SC, Charleston, 2007—08, asst. prof., 2008—. Contbr. articles to numerous profl. jours. Recipient Rsch. Svc. award, Nat. Inst. Drug Abuse, 1995—97, Young Investigator award, Am. Coll. Neuropsychopharmacology, 2007; fellowship, Group Advancement Psychiatry, 2005—07, grant, Forest Labs., 2007—. Mem.: Am. Psychiat. Assn. Office: Med Univ SC 67 President St Charleston SC 29425 Office Fax: 843-792-4817.

TOLLIVER, DOROTHY, library director; b. NYC, Apr. 10, 1937; d. Morris and Rose (Poliner) Lamm; m. Robert F. Tolliver, Sept. 3, 1956; children: Craig Lee, Marc Alan. BA, Ind. U., 1958; MSLS, U. Ill., Champaign-Urbana, 1973. Office: Maui Community Coll 310 W Kaahumanu Ave Kahului HI 96732-1617 Office Phone: 808-984-3583. Business E-Mail: tolliver@hawaii.edu.

TOLLIVER, ELKIN, JR., judge; b. Phila., Jan. 29, 1950; s. Elkin and Vernetta Tolliver; m. Toni Diane Bennett, Oct. 3, 1998; 1 child, Nia B. BA in Polit. Sci., Dickinson Coll., 1970; JD, Villanova U., 1976; LLM in Trial Advocacy, Temple U., 1994. Bar: Pa. 1976, US Dist. Ct. (ea. dist.) Pa. Atty. Broujos & Andrews, Carlisle, Pa., 1976—78, US Dept. HEW, Office Gen. Counsel, Phila., 1978—82, US Dept. Edn., Office Civil Rights, Phila., 1982—85; trial atty. Pub. Defender Assn. Phila., 1985—88, State Workers' Ins. Fund, Phila., 1988—90, Rubinate Jacobs & Saba, Phila., 1990—2000; dist. judge Pa. Judiciary, Delaware County, 2000—. Co-author: (legal digest) Digest & Index of Court Cases of the Pennsylvania State Civil Service Commission, 1975. Office: 26 S Highland Ave Lansdowne PA 19050 Home Phone: 610-716-7171; Office Phone: 610-626-2790. E-mail: elkin.tolliveresq@rcn.com.

TOLLIVER, LISA MARIE, management consultant, educator; AB, Harvard U.; MBA, Columbia U., NYC, 1990; postgrad., Columbia U. Registered arbitrator NASD, 2001, cert. def. contr. US Dept. of Def., homeland security safety. Mgmt. cons. legal dept. AT&T, NYC, 1982—83; mgmt. trainee - regulatory/revenue matters New Eng. Tel. and Telegraph, Boston, 1983—84; asst. staff mgr. regulatory/revenue matters New Eng. Tel. and Tel., Boston, 1984—85; mgr. mktg. and regulatory NYNEX Svc. Co., White Plains, NY, 1985—87; talk show host, prodr. Whitney Radio WVOX, New Rochelle, NY, 2000—; staff mgr. corp. planning NYNEX Svc. Co., White Plains, NY, 1987—88, staff dir. corp. planning, 1988—90; assoc. dir. mktg. and planning for large bus. mkts. NYNEX Telesector Resources Group, White Plains, 1990—92; dir. bus. planning Taco Bell Hdqs. PepsiCO, Irvine, Calif., 1992—93; mgmt. cons. Mitchell Madison Group, NYC, 1997—98; prin. 360 Meridian, LLC, Scarsdale, NY, 1995—. Vol. rschr. of post traumatic stress disorder in WTC bombing victims and hiv/aids patients Anxiety Disorders Clinic, Dept. of Psychiatry at NY Hosp.-Cornell Med. Ctr., NYC, 1993; adj. prof. CUNY Hunter Coll., NYC, 2002—; prof. Met. Coll. NY Sch. for Bus., NYC, 2003—, Keller Grad. Sch. Mgmt., 2004—; lectr. in field. Contbr. articles, poetry to profl. jours. Exec. advisor and instr. Jr. Achievement, Boston, 1983—85; founder Women's Lit. Guild and Self-Empowerment Group of So. Calif., Irvine, 1992—93, LA, 1992—93; mentor Westchester Enterprise Devel. Program, White Plains, NY, 2000—; vol. Silicon Alley Cares, NYC, 2001—03; active Minority Bus. Relief Task Force, Bklyn., 2001—02; co-founder, study group host CoachVille, 2003—; ofcl. ptnr. vets. history project Libr. of Congress, 2003—; pub. rels. and media com. Grace Bapt. Ch., Mount Vernon, NY, 2000—01; vol. radio host, bus. counselor and instr. SCORE Chpt. 306, White Plains, 2000—03; mem. African Am. Leadership Forum, White Plains, 2000—03; bus. mem. Nat. Health and Safety Coun., White Plains, 2000—; co-founder NYNEX Assn. Mgmt. Women, White Plains, 1983—85, Tng. Com. of NYNEX Minority Mgmt. Assn.; pub. rels. com. Westchester Assn. of Women Bus. Owners, White Plains, NY, 2001—03; adv. coun. mem. Nassau Educators Fed. Credit Union, Valley Stream, NY, 2001—04; bd. dirs. Boys and Girls Club, Mt. Vernon, 2004—; entrepreneur mem. Interracial Women's Leadership Round Table, White Plains; open book com. PEN Am. Ctr., NYC; grad. sch. rep. to Columbia APA, Washington, 1994—2003; entrepreneur com. Nat. Black MBA Assn. Westchester/Greater Conn., White Plains, 2001—02. Recipient Svc. award, Nat. Assn. of Minority Contrs. and Turner Constrn., 2001, SCORE Success Story, SCORE, 2001, Phenomenal Woman award, Emmis Comms., 2005; scholar NYNEX Corp. scholar, 1988—90, Minority Student and Gen. scholar, Columbia Tchrs. Coll., 1994, Coleman scholar, US Assn. of Small Bus. Enterprise, 2002—03. Mem.: Orgn. of Women in Trade, Orgn. Devel. Network, N.Y.New Media Assn., Nat. Writers Union, Inst. for Supply Mgmt., Internat. Webmasters Assn. - HTML Writers Guild, Assn. of Black Psychologists, Womens Sports Found., Columbia Women Bus. Owners, U.S. Assn. of Small Bus. and Entrepreneurship, Silicon Alley Entrepreneurs Club, Acad. of Mgmt., Tel. Co. Pioneers (life), Nat. Brotherhood of Skiers, Black Ivy, Nat. Assn. of Black Scuba Divers, Aquatic Voyagers Scuba Club, Columbia Bus. Sch. Alumni Club, Assoc. African Am. Harvard Alumni. Avocations: downhill skiing, scuba diving, sailing, art, travel. Office: 360 Meridian LLC 1 Wolfs Lane PO Box 655 Pelham NY 10803

TOLMACH, JANE LOUISE, community activist, municipal official; b. Havre, Mont., Nov. 12, 1921; d. Robert Francis and Veronica (Tracy) McCormick; m. Daniel Michael Tolmach (Dec.), Sept. 9, 1946; children: James, Richard, Eve Alice, Adam, Jonathan. AB, UCLA, 1943; M in Social Scis., Smith Coll., 1945; JD, S. We. U., LA, 1981. Social worker ARC Field Svcs. Corona Naval Hosp., Norco, Calif., 1945-46; chmn. bd. dirs. Camarillo (Calif.) State Hosp., 1959-68; trustee Oxnard (Calif.) Union High Sch. Dist., 1965-72; mem. state reclamation bd. Calif., 1981-82; mem. bd. govs. Calif. C.C., 1982-87; mem. bd. St. John's Regional Hosp., Oxnard, 1986-89; mem. bd. of assessment appeals County of Ventura, Ventura, Calif., 1992—2002, transp. commr., 2002—05, mem. campaign fin. ethics commn., 2005—09, mem. fin. ethics commn., 2006—. Chmn. fin. com. Ventura County Grand Jury, 1958; mem. Oxnard (Calif.) Planning Commn., 1957-62; exec. mem. So. Calif. Assn. Govts., L.A., 1975-76. Author: Smith Studies, 1945. Chmn. dem. com., Ventura County, 1959-62; alternate or del. Dem. Nat. Convs., 1960, 68, 76, 88, 92, alt. 1956, 64; Women'schm. S. Calif. Dem. Com., 1966-70; nominee state assembly, 36th dist., Ventura, Calif., 1976; elected Oxnard City Coun. 1970-78, mayor, 1973-74. Home: 656 Douglas Ave Oxnard CA 93030-4614

TOLMACHEVA, MARINA ALEKSANDROVNA, academic administrator; Degree, USSR Acad. Scis, Leningrad, 1970. Assoc. dean Wash. State U., Pullman, 1998—2005; pres. Am. U. Kuwait, Salmiya, 2006—. Fulbright fellowship, Translation grant, NEH.

TOLMAN, BRETT L., prosecutor; b. Provo, UT; BA, Brigham Young U., 1994, JD, 1998. Asst. US atty. Dist. Utah US Dept. Justice, Salt Lake City, 2000—03, US atty., 2006—; chief counsel crime and terrorism Senate Judiciary Com., Salt Lake City, 2003—05. Office: US Attys Office 185 S State St Ste 300 Salt Lake City UT 84111 Office Phone: 801-524-5682. Office Fax: 801-524-6924.*

TOLMAN, PHILIP D., lawyer, corporate financial executive; s. G. T. and E. F. Tolman. BA, Syracuse U., NY; JD, Suffolk U. Law Sch., Boston; MA, Harvard U., Cambridge, Mass. Bar: Mass. 1991. V.p. legal and contracts Infinium Software, Hyannis, Mass.; gen. counsel Access Tech (formerly Davox Corp.); lawyer, specialist Perot Sys. Corp., Providence. CAO, prin. CSS. Prodr.(broadcaster): (radio program) Life, Law and the Word; program host, author, prodr. (radio broadcasting) Life Skills. Dir., advisor Lighthouse Ministries. Mem.: ABA, Assn. Corp. Counsel, Wilderness Soc., Harvard Club. Avocations: travel, hiking, horseback riding. Personal E-mail: tolman@fas.harvard.edu. Business E-Mail: philip.tolman@ps.net.

TOLMICH, ANDREA J., music educator, department chairman; d. Andrew John and Jane (Kolka) Podraskie; 1 child, Jennifer. MusB (with distinction), U. Rochester, Eastman Sch. Music, NY, 1969; MS in Edn., Queens Coll. of CUNY, 1974. Cert. highly qualified instrumental music-orch. Mich. & NY, K-12 music Mich., gen. edn. K-6 Mich. Orchestra, gen. music tchr. W. Babylon Jr. High, NY, 1969—70; elem.

and jr. high orch. tchr. Plainedge Pub. Schs., NY, 1970—72; elem. and mid. orch. tchr. Walled Lake Consolidated Schs., Mich., 1972—2008, elem. instrumental music dept. chairman, 1974—94. Solo ensemble festival adjudicator Mich. Sch. Br. and Orch. Assn., Okemos, 2006—. Violist Birmingham Bloomfield Symphony Orch., 1974—86, Craven Cmty. Chorus, 2007—. Mem.: Nat. Edn. Assn., Mich. Edn. Assn., Mich. Am. String Tchrs. Assn., Am. Viola Soc., Mich. Bd. and Orch. Assn. (solo and ensemble adjudicator 2006), Am. String Tchrs. Assn. Avocations: reading, travel, kayaking. Home: 3827 Elizabeth Ave New Bern NC 28562 Personal E-mail: atolmich@gmail.com.

TOLOR, ALEXANDER, psychologist, educator; b. Vienna, Oct. 21, 1928; s. Stanley and Josephine (Kellner) T.; m. Belle Simon, Sept. 2, 1951; children: Karen Beth, Lori Ann, Diana Susan. BA, NYU, 1949, MA, 1950, PhD, 1954. Diplomate Am. Bd. Profl. Psychologists. Grad. asst. NYU, 1950-52; intern Neurol. Inst., NYC, 1952-53, clin. psychologist, 1953-55; sr. clin. psychologist Inst. of Living, Hartford, Conn., 1957-59; dir. psychol. services Fairfield Hills Hosp., Newtown, Conn., 1959-64; clinic dir. Kennedy Center, Bridgeport, Conn., 1964-65; dir. Inst. Human Devel., Fairfield U., 1965-77, assoc. prof. psychology, 1965-68, research prof. psychology, 1968-75, prof. psychology, 1975-89, dir. school psychology div., 1975-77, dir. sch. and applied psychology program, 1982-86, prof. emeritus, 1989—; practice psychology Danbury, Conn., 1960-96; clin. instr. psychology Yale U., 1963-67. Cons. West Haven VA Hosp., 1962-66, Bridgeport Bd. Edn., Silver Hill Found., 1972-75, Fairfield Hills Hosp., 1973-94, Hallbrooke Hosp., 1975-92. Author: (with H.C. Schulberg) An Evaluation of the Bender-Gestalt Test, 1963, (with G.G. Brannigan) Research and Clinical Applications of the Bender-Gestalt Test, 1980, (with M. Deignan) Adjustment Problems in Children, 1984; editor: Effective Interviewing, 1985; adv. editor Jour. Cons. and Clin. Psychology; cons. editor Personality: An Internat. Jour.; contbr. articles to profl. jours. Served to 1st lt. USAF, 1955-57. Fellow Am. Psychol. Assn., Soc. Personality Assessment, Conn. Psychol. Assn. (mem. council 1964, pres. 1984); mem. Eastern Psychol. Assn., Psi Chi, Delta Phi Alpha, Beta Lambda Sigma, Phi Delta Kappa Home: 6 Brittania Dr Danbury CT 06811-2606 Personal E-mail: atbt51@aol.com.

TOLSTEDT, CARRIE L., bank executive; BS in Bus. Adminstrn., U. Nebr.; degree in Banking, U. Wash. From credit tng. program to corp. banking officer United Bank Denver, corp. banking officer; from v.p. corp. banking to sr. v.p. downtown Omaha (Nebr.) retail banking Norwest Bank Nebr., Omaha, 1986—95; sr. v.p. corp. retail FirstMerit Corp., Akron, Ohio, 1995—96, pres., CEO Citizens Nat. Bank and Peoples Nat. Bank, 1996—98, exec. v.p., 1996—98; with Norwest Corp., 1998; regional pres. Ctrl. Calif. Wells Fargo & Co., San Francisco, 1998—2001, exec. v.p. regional banking, 2001—07, sr. exec. v.p. cmty. banking, 2007—. Bd. dirs. The Cmty. Coll. Found. Named one of 25 Most Powerful Women in Banking, US Banker, 2006—08. Mem.: Consumer Bankers Assn. (bd. dirs.), U. Nebr. Alumni Assn. (bd. dirs.), Calif. C. of C. (bd. dirs.). Office: Wells Fargo & Co 420 Montgomery St San Francisco CA 94163*

TOLSTRUP, KIRSTEN, cardiologist, educator; d. Poul-Erik and Aase Tolstrup; life ptnr. Massoud Akhtari; children: Niels Niema Tolstrup Akhtari, Teis Nezam Tolstrup Akhtari. MD, U. Health Scis., Copenhagen, 1993. Diplomate Am. Bd. Internal Medicine, 1998, in cardiovas. disease 2001, cert. in echocardiography NBE, 2003. Asst. dir. cardiac noninvasive lab. Cedars-Sinai Med. Ctr., LA, 2002—; assoc. prof. medicine UCLA Sch. Medicine, 2008—. Named one of America's Top Cardiologists, 2007, Southern Calif. Super Drs., 2008. Fellow: Am. Soc. Echocardiograhy, Am. Coll. Cardiology; mem.: Am. Heart Assn. Office: Cedars-Sinai Med Ctr 8700 Beverly Blvd # 5624 Los Angeles CA 90048 Office Fax: 310-423-8571. Business E-Mail: tolstrupk@cshs.org.

TOM, LAWRENCE, technology executive; b. LA, Jan. 21, 1950; BS, Harvey Mudd Coll., 1972; JD, Western State U., San Diego, 1978; spl. diploma, U. Calif., San Diego, 1991. Design engr. Rockwell Internat., LA, 1972-73, Goodrich Corp. (formerly Rohr, Inc.), Chula Vista, Calif., 1973-76, sr. design engr., 1980, computer graphics engring. specialist, 1980-83, chief engring. svcs., 1989-91, chief engring. quality, 1991-93, project mgr., 1993-98, info. tech. specialist, 1998—2002. Sr. engr. Rohr Marine, Inc., Chula Vista, 1977-79; chief exec. officer Computer Aided Tech. Svcs., San Diego, 1983-87; software cons. Small Systems Software, San Diego, 1984-85; computer graphics engring. specialist TOM & ROMAN, San Diego, 1986-88; dir. Computervision Users Group, 1986-88, vice chmn. 1988-91, pres., 1991-93, exec. chmn., 1992-94; bd. dirs. Exec. Program for Scientists and Engrs.-Alumni Assn. U. Calif., San Diego, 1991—; CFO Global Peregrine Users Group, 2001-03; pres. Art to Art, San Diego, 1994-99; pres. SGL Computer Profls., San Diego, 1999—; ptnr. San Diego Tech. Movers, 2007—; cons. in field. George H. Mayr Found. scholar, 1971, Bates Found. Aero. Edn. scholar, 1970-72. Mem. Nat. Mgmt. Assn. (chpt. v.p.), Aircraft Owners and Pilots Assn., Infiniti Club. Office: 7770 Regents Rd Ste 113-190 San Diego CA 92122-1967 Home Phone: 858-546-9090; Office Phone: 619-985-9850. Business E-Mail: larry.tom@sglpro.com.

TOM, RANDOLPH L., corporate financial executive, lawyer; s. Bell Kam and Choy Mee Tom; m. Linda K. Wong, May 28, 1988; children: Gwendolyn L., Jarrett L. BS, MBA, NYU, 1974, JD, MBA, 1978. Lic. CA, 2007; bar: N.Y. 1978, Calif. 1994, DC 1994. Atty. Fulbright & Jaworski, NYC, 1978—85; gen. counsel AT&E Corp., San Francisco, 1985—91; chmn., CEO Dynasty Capital Svcs. LLC, Moraga, Calif., 1988—; pres. Asia Pacific AT&E Corp., San Francisco, 1989—91; securities ptnr., head Asia Pacific practice Oppenheimer Wolff & Donnelly LLP, Palo Alto, Calif., 1998—2000; chmn. Santa Maria Co. Risk Svcs., 2009—. Adj. prof. sch. law New Coll. Calif., 2007—08. Editor: Dynasty Perspectives; author: (nat. law jour. spl. report) Internet May Offer Access to US Cash; columnist Contra Costa Times/Sun, 2005—06; contbr. bus. plans handbook, hamonids weekley. Bd. dirs. Cmty. Tech. Found. of Calif., San Francisco, 2004—, U. of San Francisco Ctr. for the Pacific Rim, San Francisco, 2004—09. Recipient Gary scholarship, NYU, Book scholarship, Mgmt. Assn., N.Y.C., univ. scholarship, NYU, Law Ctr. scholarship, NYU. Sch. of Law, Marcus Nadler fellowship, Stern Grad. Sch. of Bus., George Baker scholar. Mem.: Beta Gamma Sigma, Phi Alpha Kappa. Office: Dynasty Capital Svcs LLC One Madsen Ct Moraga CA 94556 Office Phone: 925-956-7600. Personal E-mail: rtom@smcrisk.com. Business E-Mail: dynasty@dynastycap.com.

TOM, WILLARD KEN, lawyer; b. Honolulu, Aug. 11, 1952; s. Hing Yee and Marian (Chun) T.; m. Natalie G. Lichtenstein, June 10, 1979; children: Alexander, Joshua. AB cum laude, Harvard U., 1975, JD cum laude, 1979. Bar: DC 1979, US Dist. Ct. DC 1979, US Ct. Appeals (DC cir.) 1983, US Supreme Ct. 1986. Trial atty. US Dept. Justice, Washington, 1979-81; assoc. Sutherland, Asbill & Brennan, Washington, 1981-86, ptnr., 1986-93; counselor to asst. atty. gen. US Dept. Justice, Washington, 1993-95; asst. dir. for policy & evaluation FTC, Washington, 1995—97, dep. bureau dir., 1997—2000, gen. counsel, 2009—; ptnr. Morgan, Lewis & Bockius, Washington, 2000—09. Editl. chair ABA Antitrust Law Devels, 1992; contbr. articles to various profl. jours. Recipient Am.'s Leading Lawyers for Bus., Chambers USA, 2006—09, Best Lawyers in America, 2006—09. Mem. ABA (mem. coun. bus. law sect. 2005-08, antitrust sect. 1992-95, DC Bar (nominations com. 1993), Asian-Pacific Am. Bar Assn. Greater Wash. (bd. dirs. 1983). Office: Fed Trade Commn Office Gen Counsel 600 Pennsylvania Ave NW Washington DC 20580 Office Phone: 202-326-3020, 202-326-3020. Office Fax: 202-326-3198. Business E-Mail: wtom@ftc.gov.

TOMA, RAMSES BARSOUM, food science and nutrition educator; b. Cairo, Nov. 9, 1938; came to U.S., 1968; s. Barsoum Toma Khalil and Fieka (Ibrahim) Gabriel; m. Rosette Toma; children: Narmer, Kamy. BS in Agr., Ain Shams U., Cairo, 1959, MS in Food Tech., 1965; PhD in Food Sci., La. State U., 1971; MPH, U. Minn., 1980. Food inspector Ministry of Food Supplies, Egypt, 1960-67; chemist Crystal Foods, New Orleans, 1968; from asst. prof. to prof. U. N.D., Grand Fork, 1972-84; prof. Calif. State U., Long Beach, 1984—. Mem. trade mission to Mid. East countries for N.D., 1976; cons. to food industries, Long Beach, 1984—; vis. prof. Cairo U., Mansora U.; adj. prof. Ain Shams U., Cairo; bd. dirs. Internat. Cmty. Coun. Contbr. more than 89 rsch. articles to profl. and sci. jours. Mem. Rep. Com., Orange County, Calif., 1984; bd. dirs. St. George Ch.; mem. adv. bd. Orange Coast Coll., Calif. Recipient Outstanding Prof. award, Calif. State U., Long Beach, 2005, Cmty. award, 2006; named Disting. Prof., Calif. State U., 1991, Best Advisor of the Yr., 2001. Fellow Am. Inst. Chemists, Am. Chem. Soc.; mem. Am. Dietitian Assn., Inst. food Tech., Am. Assn. Cereal Chemists, Am. Inst. Nutrition, Internat. Cmty. Coun., Egypt Am. Scholars U.S.A. (v.p. 2002-04), Sigma Xi, Phi Kappa Phi, Phi Beta Delta. Republican. Mem. Christian Ch. Christian Orthodox. Avocations: swimming, fishing. Office: Calif State U 1250 N Bellflower Blvd Long Beach CA 90840-0001 Office Phone: 562-985-4497. Business E-Mail: rtoma@csulh.edu.

TOMAN, MARY ANN, federal official; b. Pasadena, Calif., Mar. 31, 1954; d. John James and Mary Ann Zajec T.; m. Milton Allen Miller, Sept. 10, 1988; 1 child, Mary Ann III. BA with honors, Stanford U., Calif., 1976; MBA, Harvard U., Cambridge, Mass., 1981. Mgmt. cons. Bain and Co., Boston, 1976—77; mgr. brand Procter & Gamble Co., Cin., 1977—79; summer assoc. E.F. Hutton, NYC, 1980; head corp. planning Burton Group, PLC, London, 1981—84; pres., founder Glenclair Ltd., London, 1984—86; pres. London Cons. Group, London, Beverly Hills, Calif., 1987—88; mem. U.S. Presdl. Transition Team, Bus. and Fin., 1988—89; dep. asst. sec. commerce, automotive affairs, consumer goods U.S. Dept. Commerce, Washington, 1989—93; commr., chmn. L.A. Indsl. Devel. Authority, 1993—95; dep. treas. State of Calif., Sacramento, 1995—99. Bd. dirs. US Coun. of Devel. Fin. Agencies, 1994-97. Founder, chair Stanford U. Fundraising, London, 1983-88; chair Reps. Abroad Absentee Voter Registration, London, 1983-88; bd. dirs. Harvard Bus. Sch. Assn., London, 1984-87; vol. Bush-Quayle Campaign, 1988; trustee Bath U., Eng., 1988—; apptd. by Gov. Wilson to State of Calif. Econ. Devel. Adv. Coun., 1994-97, Jobs Tng. Coordinating Coun., 1998-2000; first vice chmn. Rep. Party L.A. County, 1996-99, chmn., 1999—; mem. exec. bd. Coun. Calif. County Chairmen, 1999—; mem. US Presdl. Transition Team, 2000-2001; Rep. candidate for Calif. State Treas., 2002. Named Calif. Mother of Yr., 1997. Mem. Stanford Club U.K. (pres. 1983-88), Harvard Club NY, Harvard Club Washington, Harvard Club Boston, Nat. Assn. of Urban Rep. County Chmn. Roman Catholic. Home: 604 N Elm Dr Beverly Hills CA 90210-3421 Office: PO Box 71483 Los Angeles CA 90071-0483 Home Phone: 310-550-5799; Office Phone: 310-274-4822. Business E-Mail: tomanmail@aol.com.

TOMANY, MARIA-CLAUDIA CHRISTINE, language educator, director; b. Berlin, July 10, 1967; d. Michael Franz and Christine Hess; m. Peter Joseph Tomany; children: Sophia Christina, Rebecca Anthea, Raphael Gerard. PhD, Ludwig-Maxilimilians U., Munich, Germany; Cand. mag., U. Bergen, Norway. Lectr. U. Frankfurt, Germany, 1991—94, Ludwig-Maximilians U., 1994—97; faculty assoc. Ariz. State U., Tempe; asst. prof. and dir. scandinavian studies Minn. State U., Mankato, 2005—. Translator icelandic novels; author: (book) Destination Viking und Orkneyinga Saga. Grantee, Scholarship Found. Germany, 1986—91, State Bavaria, 1986—91. Office: Minn State Univ 227 Armstrong Hall Mankato MN 56001

TOMAR, RICHARD THOMAS, lawyer; b. Camden, NJ, Mar. 4, 1945; s. William and Bette (Brown) T.; children: Lindsay, Leanne Meryl, Daniel Gregory. BA, Columbia U., 1967; JD, U. Pa., 1970. Bar: D.C. 1971, N.J. 1971, Md. 1976. Pvt. practice, Washington, 1971-73; ptnr. Philipson, Mallios & Tomar, P.C., Washington, 1973—89, Margolius, Mallios, Davis, Rider & Tomar, LLP, Washington, 1989—2002; chair comml. litigation Karp, Frosh, Lapidus, Wigodsky & Norwind, PA, Rockville, Md., 2002—. Del. US-Russia Joint Conf. on the Rule of Law, 2007, St. Petersburg, 2007. Mem. D.C. Trial Lawyers Assn. (bd. dirs. 1980-89). Office: Karp Frosh Lapidus Wigodsky & Norwind PA 2273 Research Blvd Ste 200 Rockville MD 20850-3283 Home: 4801 Hampden Ln Apt 304 Bethesda MD 20814-6556 Office Phone: 301-948-3800, 301-948-4800. Office Fax: 301-948-5449. Business E-Mail: rtomar@karpfrosh.com.

TOMAS, ALEJANDRO, photographer; BA, Brooks Inst. Photography, Santa Barbara, Calif., 1979. Sr faculty comml. photography prgm Seattle Ctrl. CC, 1993—. Pres. Nat. Assoc Naval Photographers, Seattle, 2006—; co-founder,past pres., Seattle, 1993—2001; bd. dirs. Blue Earth Alliance, Seattle, 2001—06; edn. chair Am. Soc. of Media Photographers, Seattle, 2003—. Photographers mate 3rd class US Navy, 1972—75, USS Enterprise. Office: Comm Photog Prgm Seattle Central Coll 1701 Broadway Seattle WA 98122 Office Fax: 206-344-4390. Business E-Mail: atomas@sccd.ctc.edu.

TOMASETTI, RICHARD L., structural engineer; BS, Manhattan Coll., 1963, DSc (hon.), 2001; MS in Civil Engring., NYU, 1963. Chmn. Thorton-Tomasetti Group Inc., NYC. Adj. prof. Columbia U. Recipient Engr. of Yr. Award, NY Assn. Consulting Engrs., 2002, Industry Honoree, NY Building Congress, 2003. Mem.: NAE, AIA (hon.). Office: Thornton-Tomasetti Group 51 Madison Ave New York NY 10010 Office Phone: 917-661-7800. Office Fax: 917-661-7801.

TOMASH, ERWIN, retired computer company executive; b. St. Paul, Nov. 17, 1921; s. Noah and Milka (Ehrlich) T.; m. Adelle Ruben, July 31, 1943; children: Judith Sarada Tomash Diffenbaugh, Barbara Ann Tomash Bussa. BS, U. Minn., Minneapolis, 1943; MS, U. Md., College Park, 1950. Instr. elec. engring. U. Minn., 1946; assoc. dir. computer devel. Univac div. Remington Rand Corp., St. Paul, 1947-51; dir. West Coast ops. Univac div. Sperry Rand Corp., LA, 1953-55; pres. Telemeter Magnetics, Inc., LA, 1956-60; v.p. Ampex Corp., LA, 1961; founder, pres. Dataproducts Corp., LA, 1962-71, chmn. bd., 1971-80, chmn. exec. com., 1980-89; chmn. bd., dir. Newport Corp., Irvine, Calif., 1982-94. Founder, trustee, dir. Charles Babbage Found., U. Minn.; dir. and nat. gov. Coro Found., L.A. Served to capt. Signal Corps AUS, 1943-46. Decorated Bronze Star; recipient Outstanding Grad. award U. Minn., 1983. Mem. IEEE (sr., computer entrepeneur award 1988), Am. Soc. for Technion, History of Sci. Soc., Soc. for History of Tech., Assn. Internationale du Bibliophile. Home: 3918 Mainsail Pl Soquel CA 95073

TOMASHEFSKI, JOSEPH FRANCIS, JR., pathologist, educator; b. Wilkes-Barre, Pa., Mar. 26, 1950; s. Joseph Francis and Marguerite Tomashefski; m. Catherine Marie Deane, Mar. 7, 1981; children: Carolyn M. Bohm, Jessica R. Billie, Sarah M. Dobrzykowski, David J., Amy M. BS summa cum laude, Notre Dame U., Ind., 1972; MD, Case Western Res. U., Cleve., 1976. Lic. State Med. Bd. Ohio, 1977, diplomate in anatomic and clin. pathology Am. Bd. Pathology, 1980. Resident, anatomic and clin. pathology Inst. Pathology, U. Hosp. Cleve., 1976—80, New Eng. Deaconess Hosp., Harvard Med. Sch., Boston, 1980—81; rsch. fellow, pulmonary pathology Boston Children Hosp., 1981—82; staff pathologist Cleve. Met. Gen. Hosp., 1982—98; lectr. and course dir. Case Western Res. U., Cleve., 1989—98, prof. pathology, 1999—, academic chair, dept. pathology, Metrohealth Med. Ctr., 2008—; chair, dept. pathology MetroHealth Med. Ctr., Cleve., 1998—. Pulmonary pathology cons. Ohio Thoracic Soc., Columbus, 1983—; com. mem., death rev. com. Nat. Registry for Patients with Alpha-1 Anti-trypsin Deficiency, Cleve., 1989—98; mem., bd. trustees Brittingham Meml. Med. Libr., Cleve., 1999—. Editor: (pulmonary pathology text) Dail and Hammar's Pulmonary Pathology, 3rd edit.; contbr. scientific papers to profl. jours. Recipient John R. Carter Tchg. award, Case Western Res. U. Sch. Medicine, 2004. Mem.: Coll. Am. Pathologists (inspection team leader, lab. accreditation program 1995—), Pulmonary Pathology Soc., Am. Thoracic Soc., US and Can. Acad. Pathology, Ohio Thoracic Soc. (pres. 2000—01, 15 Yr. Svc. award 1997), Cleve. Soc. Pathologists (pres. 1990—91), Phi Beta Kappa Soc. Roman Catholic. Achievements include development of unique bar code identification and electronic data base for tracking deceased bodies on a hospital mortality service; discovery of the first description of embolized crospovidone in the lungs of IV drug abusers; first description of pulmonary eosinophilic vasculitis associated with pneumothorax. Avocations: birdwatching, opera, classical music, travel, literature. Office: MetroHealth Med Ctr 2500 MetroHealth Dr Cleveland OH 44109 Office Fax: 216-778-7112. Business E-Mail: jtomashefski@metrohealth.org.

TOMASHOFF, CRAIG L., magazine editor; b. 1961; BA in Comm., U. Wash., 1982; MA in Mag. Journalism, Northwestern U., Ill., 1985. Assoc. bur. chief People mag., 1988—98; TV prodr. VH1, Late Show with Craig Kilborn; West coast bur. chief TV Guide mag., LA, 2003—08, exec. editor, 2008—. Contbr. articles to mags., newspapers. Office: Macrovision Solutions Corp 18 W 18th St 11th Fl New York NY 10011 Office Phone: 212-524-7000, 800-804-0103. Office Fax: 212-524-7001.*

TOMASIELLO, ALESSANDRO, physicist; b. Torino, Italy, Mar. 6, 1974; Degree in Physics, Scuola Normale Superiore, Pisa; PhD in Math. Physics, Internat. Sch. Advanced Studies, Trieste. Postdoc. fellow Ecole Polytech., Paris, 2001—04, Stanford U., 2004—07, Harvard U., 2007—. Office: Harvard Univ 17 Oxford St Cambridge MA 02138

TOMASKO, EDWARD A., financial planner; b. Stafford Springs, Conn., Sept. 18, 1943; s. Edward A. Sr. and Gertrude Ann (Burr) T.; m. Helen F. Flanagan, Oct. 18, 1969; children: Felicia, Joy. BA, Quinnipac Coll., 1966; MBA, Am. U., 1968. CFP. Direct mktg. & sales Iroquois Brands, Stamford, Conn., 1979-81; owner Tomasko Bus. Cons., Bethel, Conn., 1981-82; v.p. mktg. & consulting Excell Mktg., New Canaan, Conn., 1982; market mgr. Stauffer Chem., Westport, Conn., 1982-85; direct mktg. & sales Folz Vending, LI, NY, 1986; registered rep. Moseley Securities, New Haven, 1987-88, Fahnestock & Co. Inc., Danbury, Conn., 1988-90; prin. Titan Value Equities, Hamden, Conn., 1990—. V.p. bd. govs. Quinnipac Coll.; chmn. pension and ins. commn. Town of Bethel, Conn. Mem.: FPA (pres. So. Conn. chpt. 1993—96, chmn. state conf. 1992—93, adv. coun. 1997—). Republican. Avocations: photography, choir singing. Home: 20 Spring Hill Ln Bethel CT 06801-2726 Office Phone: 203-798-9873. E-mail: edward_a_tomasko@sbcglobal.net.

TOMASKY, SUSAN, electric power industry executive; b. Morgantown, W.Va., Mar. 29, 1953; m. Ron Ungvarsky; 1 child, Victoria. BA cum laude, U. Ky., Lexington, 1974; JD with honors, George Washington U., 1979. Staff mem. House Com. Interstate and Fgn. Commerce, Washington, 1974—76; with Office Gen. Counsel FERC, Washington, 1979—81, gen. counsel, 1993—97; assoc. Van Ness, Feldman & Curtin, Washington, 1981—86; ptnr. Van Ness, Feldman & Curtis, Washington, 1986—93, Hogan & Harts, Washington, 1997-98; sr. v.p., gen. coun., sec. Am. Electric Power Svc. Corp., Columbus, Ohio, 1998—2000, exec. v.p., gen. counsel, sec., 2000—01, exec. v.p., CFO, 2001—06, exec. v.p. Shared Services, 2006—07, pres. AEP Transmission, 2008—. Bd. dir. Fed. Reserve Bank Cleve., 2009—. Staff mem. George Washington U. Law Rev., 1979. Trustee Columbus Symphony Orch., Columbus Sch. for Girls; bd. mem. Columbus Regional Airport Authority, Mount Carmel Health Systems; co-chair Keystone Energy Bd. Mem. Greater Columbus C. of C., Phi Beta Kappa. Office: Am Electric Power Svc Corp 1 Riverside Plz Columbus OH 43215-2373 Office Phone: 614-716-1600.*

TOMASSO, ANTHONY, banker; b. New Haven, Conn., July 3, 1939; s. Anthony Nick and Mary Tomasso; m. Kathy Delahant, July 28, 1951; children: Anthony Jr., Dawn, Krista, Gina, Adriana. Degree in Fin. (hon.), U. Conn., 1957. Cert. in fin. Fla., 1995. Owner Nationwide Comml. Finecial Group LLC, Boca Raton, Fla., 2000—. Dir. mortgage banking coml. lending. None. Office: Nationwide Coml Fin Group LL 4400 N Federal highway Ste 122 Boca Raton FL 33431 E-mail: ttomasso@ncfgcomm.com.

TOMASSON, HELGI, performing company executive, dancer, choreographer; b. Reykjavik, Iceland, 1942; m. Marlene Rizzo; children: Kristinn, Erik. Student, Sigridur Arman, Erik Bidsted, Vera Volkova, Sch. Am. Ballet, Tivoli Pantomime Theatre, Copenhagen; DHL (hon.), Dominican Coll. San Rafael, 1996. With Joffrey Ballet, 1961-64; prin. dancer Harkness Ballet, 1964-70, NYC Ballet, 1970-85; artistic dir. San Francisco Ballet, 1985—, also dir. Bd. dirs. Sch. Am. Ballet; mem. artistic com. NY Choreographic Inst.; mem. adv. panel Nat. Endowment for the Arts. Dancer debut Tivoli Pantomime Theatre, 1958, A Season of Hell, 1967, Stages and Reflections, 1968, La Favorita, 1969, The Goldberg Variations, 1971, Symphony in Three Movements, 1972, Coppelia, 1974, Dybbuk Variations, 1974, Chansons Madecasses, 1975, Introduction and Allegro, 1975, Allegro, 1975, Union Jack, 1976, Vienna Waltzes, 1977, choreographer Theme and Variations, Polonaise, Op. 65, 1982, Ballet d'Isoline, 1983, Menuetto, N.Y.C. Ballet, 1984, Beads of Memory, 1985, Swan Lake, 1988, Handel-a Celebration, 1989, Sleeping Beauty, 1990, Romeo and Juliet, 1994, Prism, 2000, Bartok Divertimento, 2002, Chi-Lin, 2002, Concerto Grosso, 2003, 7 for Eight, 2003. Decorated Knight Order of Falcon Iceland, Comdr. Order of Falcon, Grand Cross Star of the Order of the Falcon, Officer French Order Arts and Letters; recipient Silver medal, Internat. Moscow Ballet Competition, 1969, Golden Plate award, Am. Acad. Achievement, 1992, Dance

Mag. award, 1992, Disting. Citizen, Commonwealth Club Calif., 1991, Lifetime Achievement award, Iceland Theatre Assn., 2009. Office: San Francisco Ballet 455 Franklin St San Francisco CA 94102-4438*

TOMASULO, VIRGINIA MERRILLS, retired lawyer; b. Belleville, Ill., Feb. 10, 1919; d. Frederick Emerson and Mary Eckert (Turner) Merrills; m. Nicholas Angelo Tomasulo, Sept. 30, 1952 (dec. May 3, 1986); m. Harrison I. Anthes, Mar. 5, 1988.(dec. Sep. 22, 2007.) BA, Wellesley Coll., 1940; LLB (now JD), Washington U., St. Louis, 1943. Bar: Mo. 1942, U.S. Ct. Appeals (D.C. cir.) 1958, Mich. 1974, U.S. Dist. Ct. (ea. dist) Mo. 1943, U.S. Supreme Ct. 1954, U.S. Tax Ct. 1974, U.S. Ct. Appeals (6th cir.) 1976. Atty. Dept. of Agr., Office of Solicitor, St. Louis and Washington, 1943-48; chief counsel's office IRS, Washington and Detroit, 1949-75; assoc. Baker & Hostetler, Washington, 1977-82, ptnr., 1982-89, of counsel, 1989, ret., 1989. Sec. S.W. Day Care Assn., Washington, 1971—73; state bd. mem., dir. region IV Fla. Life Care Residents Assn., 2002—04; mem. adv. bd. Brede-Wilkins Scholarship Fund LCRC Found., 2002—. Mem.: ABA, Mo. Bar, Fla. Life Care Residents Assoc. chpt. 125, Village on the Green Residents Assn. (mem. coun. 1998—2000, chair health care com. 1999—2001, chair fin. com. 2004—09, mem. fin. com., chair health care com. 2009), Wellesley Club (Ctrl. Fla.). Episcopalian. Home: 570 Village Pl Apt 300 Longwood FL 32779-6037 Office Phone: 401-788-6698.

TOMASZEWSKI, CHRISTIAN, artist; b. Gdansk, Poland, 1971; MFA, Acad. Fine Arts, Poznan, Poland, 1995; studio program, Irish Mus. Modern Art, Dublin, 2001, Kunstsammlungen Chemnitz, Germany, 2002; internat. studio and curatorial prog., NYC, 2001; AIM program, Bronx. Mus. Arts, 2002. Asst. to Ilya Kabakov, NYC, 1996—2000; vis. artist Am. Acad. Rome, 2001. One-man shows include Kunstforum Ostdeutsche Galerie, Regensburg, Switzerland, 2006, On Chapels, Caves and Erotic Misery, Kunstsammlungen Chemnitz, Germany, 2006, Sculpture Ctr., Long Island City, NYC, 2007, exhibited in group shows at Est Fondazione Querini Stampalia ONLUS, Venice, 2001, Internat. Biennale Contemporary Art, Prague, 2005, Site-Ations Internat., Model Arts and Niland Gallery, Sligo, Ireland, 2005, Migration of Energies Part 1, Gandy Gallery, Bratislava, Slovakia, 2005, Singular, Galleri S.E., Bergen, Norway, 2006, Manipulacje O Ekonomii k'amstwa, Kewenig Galerie, Cologne, Germany, 2006. Recipient Ann. Incentive award, Polish and Slavic Found., Bklyn., 1998; grantee Pollock-Krasner Found., 1999, 2004, Polish Cultural Inst., NYC, 2001, Leube Baustoffe Found., Salzburg, Austria, 2004; fellow John Simon Guggenheim Meml. Found., 2008. Office: Kewenig Galerie Appelhofplatz 21 50667 Cologne Germany*

TOMASZEWSKI, RICHARD PAUL, market representation executive; b. Flushing, NY, Jan. 8, 1958; s. Francis Richard and Agatha Jean (Corsaro) T.; m. Joann L. Turone, Aug. 2, 1980; children: Elizabeth Jean, Annamaria Concetta. BA in Econs. and Polit. sci. cum laude, Union Coll., Schenectady, NY, 1980; MBA in Mktg., Fin., Syracuse U., 1982. Grad. asst. Syracuse (N.Y.) U., 1981; field ops. analyst Ford Motor Co., Charlotte, N.C., 1982-83, zone mgr., 1983-93, mkt. representation specialist Atlanta, 1993-98, nat. employee involvement rep. Atlanta region, 1994-98, mkt. representation mgr., 1998—. Mem. Ford Motor Co. Polit. Action Com., Atlanta, 1993, Cmty. Rels. Com., 1999-2002. Tidmarsh scholar Union Coll., Schenectady, 1977; co-recipient Total Market Representation award, 1997, 99-2005. Mem. Union Coll. Alumni Assn., Syracuse U. Alumni Assn., U.S. Tennis Assn., Atlanta Lawn Tennis Assn., Wynterhall Swim and Tennis Club (chmn. tennis com. 2003-05, co-capt. tennis team 2002-08), Omicron Delta Epsilon, Alpha Mu Alpha. Republican. Roman Catholic. Avocations: tennis, walking, swimming, chess. Office: Ford Motor Co 13010 Morris Rd Ste 500 Corp Ctr 1 Milton GA 30004

TOMAZI, GEORGE DONALD, retired electrical engineer; b. St. Louis, Dec. 27, 1935; s. George and Sophia (Bogovich) T.; m. Lois Marie Partenheimer, Feb. 1, 1958; children: Keith, Kent. BSEE, U. Mo., Rolla, 1958, Profl. EE (hon.), 1970; MBA, St. Louis U., 1965, MSEE, 1971. Registered profl. engr., Mo., Ill., Wash., Ohio, Calif. Project engr. Union Electric Co., 1958-66; dir. corp. planning Gen. Steel Industries, 1966-70; exec. v.p. St. Louis Research Council, 1970-74, Hercules Constrn. Co., St. Louis, 1974-75; dir. design and constrn. div. Mallinckrodt, Inc., St. Louis, 1975-93; ret., 1993. Author: P-Science: The Role of Science in Society, 1972, The Link of Science and Religion, 1973. Active Nat. Kidney Found.; bd. dirs. U. Mo. Devel. Council, St. Louis Artists Coalition, Citizens for Modern Transit; elder Luth. Ch.; v.p. Coun. Luth Chs., St. Louis; adv. com. grad. sch. U. Mo., Columbia, mem. pres.'s role and scope commn.; dir. Coun. Luth. Chs. Greater St. Louis; bldg. com. Humane Soc. Mo.; pres. coun. Luth. Ch. of the Living Christ; bd. dirs. Humane Soc. Mo., 2005; bd. trustees Acad. Sci. St. Louis, 2005. Served with U.S. Army, 1959-61. Recipient award Acad. Elec. Engrs., U. Mo., Rolla, Achievement award Humane Soc. of Mo., Spl. award, 1998, Award of Merit, 2002, Achievement award Order of the Golden Shillaleagh, U. Mo., Rolla, 2004, Legacy Cir. award U. Mo., Columbia, 2004, Connaway Soc. U. Mo., Columbia, 2005, Achievement award 2009. Mem. NSPE (life), IEEE (life, chmn. state govt. activities com. 1990-93), Japan-Am. Soc., AAAS, Profl. Engrs. in Industry, Mo. Soc. Profl. Engrs. (pres. St. Louis chpt., Profl. Engr. in Industry 1989, named to Hall Fame 2005), Profl. Engrs. and Land Surveyors (chmn. Mo. bd. for architects 1989-95), Am. Def. Preparedness Assn., U. Mo. Alumni Assn. (bd. dirs. 1972-78), Engrs. Club (pres. 1985-86), Mo. Athletic Club, Rotary, Sigma Pi. Address: #44 Jamestown Farm Dr Florissant MO 63034-1405 Office: 44 Jamestown Farm Dr Florissant MO 63034-1405

TOMBERLIN, MICHAEL, legislative staff member; Staff asst., Office of the Majority Leader US House of Reps., Washington, legis. analyst, Republican Conf., 2001—04, com. liaison, Republican Conf., 2002, com. rels., Republican Conf., 2003—04, legis. dir., Rep. Louie Gohmert, 2005—06, chief of staff to Rep. Louie Gohmert, 2006—. Republican. Office: 510 Cannon House Office Bldg Washington DC 20515 Office Phone: 202-225-3035. Office Fax: 202-225-1230. Business E-Mail: michael.tomberline@mail.house.gov.*

TOMBLIN, EARL RAY, state legislator, Lieutenant Governor of West Virginia; b. Logan County, W.Va., Mar. 15, 1952; s. Earl and Freda (Jarrell) T.; m. Joanne Jaeger, Sept. 8, 1979; 1 child, Brent Jaeger. BS, W.Va. U.; MBA, Marshall U., Huntington, W.Va.; postgrad., U. Charleston, W.Va.; doctorate (hon.), So. W.Va. Cmty. and Tech. Coll., Mount Gay. Former sch. tchr.; businessman; mem. W.Va. House of Delegates, Charleston, 1974-80; mem. Dist. 7 W.Va. State Senate, Charleston, 1980—, pres., 1995—; lt. gov. State of W.Va., Charleston, 2000—. Chmn. So. Legis. Conf., 1999; vice chmn. Nat. Coun. State Govts., 2004—05, chmn., 2005; mem. exec. com. Nat. Conf. State Legislatures; mem. nat. bd. dirs. Senate Presidents' Forum. Past pres., bd. dirs. Appalachia Ednl. Lab., Inc.; mem. Logan County Devel. Authority. Mem.: Kappa Alpha. Democrat. Presbyterian. Office: Capitol Bldg Rm 227M Bldg 1 Charleston WV 25305 Business E-Mail: senate.president@wvsenate.gov.*

TOMBRELLO, THOMAS ANTHONY, JR., physics professor; b. Austin, Tex., Sept. 20, 1936; s. Thomas Anthony and Jeanette Lilian (Marcuse) T.; m. Esther Ann Hall, May 30, 1957 (div. Jan. 1976); children: Christopher Thomas, Susan Elaine, Karen Elizabeth; m. Stephanie Carhart Merton, Jan. 15, 1977; 1 stepchild, Kerstin Arusha (dec.). BA in Physics, Rice U., Houston, 1958, MA, 1960; PhD, Rice U., 1961; PhD (hon.), Uppsala U., Sweden, 1997. Rsch. fellow in physics Calif. Inst. Tech., Pasadena, 1961-62, 64-65, asst. prof. physics, 1965-67, assoc. prof., 1967-71, prof., 1971—, William R. Kenan Jr. prof., 1997—, tech. assessment officer, 1996—, chair divsn. physics, math. and astronomy, 1998—2008; asst. prof. Yale U., New Haven, 1963. Cons. in field; disting. vis. prof. U. Calif.-Davis, 1984; v.p., dir. rsch. Schlumberger-Doll Rsch., Ridgefield, Conn., 1987-89; mem. US V.P.'s Space Policy Adv. Bd., 1992; mem. sci. adv. bd. Ctr. of Nanoscale Sci. and Tech., Rice U., 1995-2004; bd. dirs. Schlumberger Tech. Corp., Schlumberger Found., 1987-89, Thirty Meter Telescope, 2004-08, Combined Array Rsch. Millimeter Astronomy, 2003-08, Cornell-Caltech-Atacama Telescope, 2007-08, Am. Friends Uppsala U., 2008-. Assoc. editor Nuc. Physics, 1971-91, Applications Nuc. Physics, 1980-89, Radiation Effects, 1985-88, Nuc. Instruments and Methods B, 1993-96; mem. editl. bd. Blue Origin, 2003-07, Applied Minds, 2004—, Arrowhead Rsch., 2005—, Form Factor, 2005—, Trilience Rsch., 2005— Recipient Alexander von Humboldt award von Humboldt Stiftung, U. Frankfurt, Germany, 1984-85; named Disting. Alumnus, Rice U., 1998; NSF fellow Calif. Inst. Tech., 1961-62, A.P. Sloan fellow, 1971-73. Fellow Am. Phys. Soc.; Phi Beta Kappa, Sigma Xi, Delta Phi Alpha. Democrat. Avocations: reading, jogging. Office: Calif Inst Tech Dept Physics Mail Code 200 36 Pasadena CA 91125-0001 Office Phone: 626-395-4581. Business E-Mail: tat@caltech.edu.

TOMBROS, PETER GEORGE, pharmaceutical executive; b. Oak Hill, W.Va., June 12, 1942; s. George P. and Mary Jane (Boliski) T.; m. Ann Riblett Cullen, June 12, 1965. BS, Pa. State U., 1964, MS, 1966; MBA, U. Pa., 1968. Mktg. asst. Pfizer Labs. div. Pfizer Inc., NYC, 1968; asst. product mgr. Pfizer Inc., NYC, 1969, product mgr., 1970-71, group product mgr., 1972-74, v.p. mktg., 1975-80; sr. v.p., gen. mgr. Roerig div. Pfizer Inc., NYC, 1980-86; exec. v.p. Pfizer Pharms. div. Pfizer Inc., NYC, 1986-90, v.p. corp. strategic planning, 1990-94; also corp. officer Pfizer Inc., NYC; ret. pres., CEO Enzon, Inc., Piscataway, 1994—2001, also bd. dirs.; chmn., CEO VivoQuest Inc., 2001—05; dir. Cambrex Corp., East Rutherford; prof., exec. in residence Pa. State U., 2005—. Alumni fellow Pa. State U., 1993; bd. dirs. Alpharma Inc., Bridgewater, NJ, 1995-2008; dir., non-exec. chmn. bd., NPS Pharm., Inc., Bedminster, NJ, bd. dirs.; Protalex, Inc., New Hope, Pa., Pharma Net Devel., Inc., 2007-09, PharmaNet's, 2007-09, non-exec. chmn. bd., 2006-09. Bd. dirs. Dendrite Internat., Bedminster, NJ, 2006-07, Am. Found. Pharm. Edn., North Plainfield, NJ, 1980-01, past chmn.; trustee Fisk U., Nashville, 1986-96, Dominican Coll., Orangeburg, NY, 1987-02; trustee Bklyn. Borough Hall Restoration, 1987-92; mem. corp. devel. com. Cen. Park Conservancy, NYC, 1986-94; bd. dirs. Vote America, 1990; bd. dirs. Cancer Care; chmn. bd. dirs. NJ Tech. Coun., 2001-03. Recipient Disting. Alumnus award, Pa. State U., 2006, Alumni Fellow award. Mem. Pharm. Mfrs. Assn. (past chmn. mktg. steering com., 1986-1992), Links Club, Blind Brook Club, Masons. Avocations: marathon running, golf, tennis, skiing, bridge. Business E-Mail: put10@psu.edu.

TOMCZAK, PATRICIA ANN, dean, archivist; b. Detroit, June 8, 1957; d. Raymond and Veronica Tomczak. BA in History, Wayne State U., 1979; MS in Libr. Sci., Wayne State U., Detroit, 1982. Ref. libr. Quincy Pub. Libr., Quincy, Ill., 1986—88; reference libr. Quincy U., Quincy, Ill., 1988—2000, dean of libr. and info. resources, 2000—. Contbr. digitized, online exhibit, digitized online exhibit. Mem.: Soc. of Am. Archivists, Ill. Libr. Assn., ALA, Colonial Williamsburg Found. Roman Catholic. Avocations: travel, visiting historical sites, reading, theater. Office: Quincy University 1800 College Ave Quincy IL 62301 Business E-Mail: tomczpa@quincy.edu. E-mail: Tomczakp@aol.com.

TOMCZYK, FREDRIC JOHN, brokerage house executive; b. St. Catharines, Ont., Can., June 30, 1955; s. John Fredric and Kathleen (Herculuck) Tomczyk; m. Vicki Tomczyk; children: Ainsley, Trevor, Tyler. BS in Sci., Applied Economics & Bus. Mgmt., Cornell U., Ithaca, NY, 1977. Chartered acct., 1982, fellow chartered acct., 2006. Asst. mgr. Bank of Montreal, 1977—80; audit sr. Coopers & Lybrand, 1981—82; with London Life Ins. Co., 1982—96; pres., CEO London Life Internat., 1996—97, chmn., 1996—97; exec. v.p. core banking & wealth mgmt. TD Canada Trust, 1998—2001, exec. v.p. retail distribution, 2001—02; vice chmn. corp. ops. TD Bank Fin. Group, 2002—06; exec. v.p., COO TD Ameritrade Holding Corp., Omaha, 2007—08, pres., CEO, 2008—. Bd. dirs. TD Ameritrade Holding Corp., 2006—, Robarts Rsch. Inst., Meloche Monnex, Inc., Symcor, Inc.; mem. exec. com. Can. Bankers Assn. Mem. undergraduate bus. program adv. coun. Cornell U.; bd. dirs. The John F. Robarts Rsch. Inst., 2002—07, Meloche Monnex, 2002—07. Office: TD Ameritrade Holding Corp 1 Harborside Fin Ctr Plaza IV-A 9th Floor Jersey City NJ 07311 Office Phone: 201-369-8598. Office Fax: 201-369-5932. Business E-Mail: fred.tomezyk@tdameritrade.com.*

TOMÉ, CAROL BUCHENROTH, consumer home products company executive; b. Jackson, Wyo., Jan. 8, 1957; m. Ramon Tomé. BS in Comm., U. Wyo., 1979; MBA in Fin., U. Denver, 1981. Comml. lender United Bank Denver (now Wells Fargo); dir. banking Johns-Manville Corp.; v.p., treas. Riverwood Internat. Corp., 1992—95, Home Depot, Inc., Atlanta, 1995—2000, sr. v.p. fin., 2000—01, exec. v.p., CFO, 2001—07, exec. v.p. corp. services, CFO, 2007—. Bd. dirs. United Parcel Svc., Inc. (UPS), 2003—, Fed. Home Loan Bank Atlanta, 2008—. Bd. dirs. Girls Inc.; trustee Ga. Substance Abuse Adv. Coun., Home Fund; chair adv. bd. Met. Atlanta Arts Fund. Named one of Next 20 Female CEOs, Pink Mag. & Forté Found., 2006, 100 Most Powerful Women, Forbes mag., 2008. Office: Home Depot Inc 2455 Paces Ferry Rd Atlanta GA 30339-4029*

TOMEI, MARISA, actress; b. Bklyn., Dec. 4, 1964; d. Gary and Patricia Tomei. Student, degree, Boston U.; student, NYU. Actress (films) The Flamingo Kid, 1984, The Toxic Avenger, 1985, Playing for Keeps, 1986, Oscar, 1991, Zandalee, 1991, My Cousin Vinny, 1992 (Acad. award for Best Supporting Actress), Equinox, 1992, Chaplin, 1992, Untamed Heart, 1993, The Paper, 1994, Only You, 1994, The Perez Family, 1995, Four Rooms, 1995, Unhook the Stars, 1996, A Brother's Kiss, 1997, Welcome to Sarajevo, 1997, Slums of Beverly Hills, 1998, Happy Accidents, 2000, The Watcher, 2000, What Women Want, 2000, King of the Jungle, 2000, Dirk and Betty, 2000, In the Bedroom, 2001 (Acad. award nominee, Golden Globe award nominee), Someone Like You, 2001, The Wild Thornberrys Movie (voice omly), 2002, Just a Kiss, 2002, The Guru, 2002, Anger Management, 2003, Alfie, 2004, Loverboy, 2005, Marilyn Hotchkiss' Ballroom Dancing & Charm School, 2005, Factotum, 2005, Danika, 2006, Grace Is Gone, 2007, Wild Hogs, 2007, Before the Devil Knows You're Dead, 2007, War, Inc., 2008, The Wrestler, 2008 (Hollywood Film Festival award for Supporting Actress of Yr., Acad. award nominee, Golden Globe award nominee), (TV series) As the World Turns, 1983—88, A Different World, 1987, (TV films) Only Love, 1998, My Own Country, 1998, (Broadway/Off Broadway plays) Slavs! Thinking About the Longstanding Problems of Virtue and Happiness, 1994, Welcome to Sarajevo, 1997, Wait Until Dark, 1998, Salome, 2003, This Is How It Goes, 2005, Top Girls, 2008. Named Best Supporting Actress (for In the Bedroom), Dallas-Fort Worth Film Critics Assn., Southeastern Film Critics Assn., ShoWest awards, Best Supporting Actress (for The Wrestler), Ctrl. Ohio Film Critics Assn., Fla. Film Critics Cir., Las Vegas Film Critics Soc., Online Film Critics Soc., Phoenix Film Critics Soc., San Diego Film Critics Soc., San Francisco Film Critics Cir. Office: c/o Bella Vita Prodns 8033 W Sunset Blvd Ste 891 West Hollywood CA 90046*

TOMEK, WILLIAM GOODRICH, agricultural economist; b. Table Rock, Nebr., Sept. 20, 1932; s. John and Ruth Genevieve (Goodrich) T. BS, U. Nebr., 1956, MA, 1957; PhD, U. Minn., 1961. Asst. prof. Cornell U., Ithaca, NY, 1961-66, NSF fellow, 1965, assoc. prof. agrl. econs., 1966-70, prof., 1970-99, grad. sch. prof., 2000—, chmn. dept. agrl. econs., 1988-93. Vis. econ. USDA, 1978-79; vis. fellow Stanford U., 1968-69, U. New Eng., Australia, 1988; mem. adv. panel Rev. Agrl. Econs., 1996-98; mem. adv. bd. Rev. Futures Markets, 2005-. Author: Agricultural Product Prices, 2003; editor: Am. Jour. Agrl. Econs., 1975-77; co-editor: Chgo. Bd. Trade Rsch. Symposia, 1993-2001; mem. editl. bd. Jour. Futures Markets, 1992-95; contbr. articles to profl. jours. Served with U.S. Army, 1953-55. Recipient Earl Combs Jr. award Chgo. Bd. Trade Found. Mem. Am. Agrl. Econs. Assn. (pres. 1985-86), Am. Econ. Assn., Econometric Soc., Northeastern Agrl. Econs. Assn., Am. Agrl. Econs. Assn. (awards 1981, 89, 97, fellow), Gamma Sigma Delta (rsch. award 1994). Democrat. Methodist. Office: Cornell U Warren Hall Ithaca NY 14853-7801 Home Phone: 607-257-1753; Office Phone: 607-255-2189. E-mail: wgt1@cornell.edu.

TOMER, BRITTA, orthodontist, educator; b. Denmark; undergraduate studies, DDS, Denmark. Cert. orthodontic specialty U. Calif. San Francisco, 1977. Rsch. fellow, dept. craniofacial anomalies Univ. Calif. San Francisco, 1971—76; pvt. practice in orthodontics San Francisco, 1978—; orthodontist OrthoWorks, San Francisco. Part-time assoc. prof. U. Calif. San Francisco, 1978—. Contbr. articles to numerous profl. jours. Mem.: European Orthodontics Soc., Am. Cleft Palate-Craniofacial Assn., Am. Assn. Orthodontics. Office: OrthoWorks 450 Sutter St Ste 2418 San Francisco CA 94108 Office Phone: 415-982-0990. Office Fax: 415-982-0909.*

TOMICH, JOHN M., biochemistry professor, science administrator; s. Matthew and Mary Ellen Tomich; m. Marilyn G. Seibel; children: Matthew P., Samuel W. BA, U. Conn., Storrs, 1974; MS, Purdue U., West Lafayette, Ind., 1975; PhD, U. Waterloo, Ont., Can., 1980. Postdoc. fellow U. Del., Newark, 1980—83, Calif. Inst. Tech., Pasadena, 1983—87; assoc. prof. Kans. State U., Manhattan, 1992—98, dir. biotech., Proteomics Core Lab, 1992—, prof., 1998—. Asst. prof. U. South Calif. Sch. Medicine, LA, 1992—97; founder, chief sci. officer Nacelle Therapeutics, Inc., Manhattan, 2000—. Author: (textbook) Biology and Society (William L. Stamey Tchg. award, Kans. State U., 2007). Mem.: Am. Chem. Soc., Biophys. Soc., Sigma Xi. Achievements include invention of peptide-based therapeutics. Office: Kans State Univ 141 Chalmers Hall Manhattan KS 66506 Office Fax: 785-532-6297. Business E-Mail: jtomich@ksu.edu.

TOMICH, LILLIAN, lawyer; b. LA; d. Peter S. and Yovanka P. (Ivanovic) T. AA, Pasadena City Coll., 1954; BA in Polit. Sci., UCLA, 1956, cert. secondary tchg., 1957, MA, 1958; JD, U. So. Calif., 1961. Bar: Calif., US Ct. Appeals (9th Cir.) 1978, 2002, US Ct. Appeals (4th Appellate Dist.), 2007. Sole practice, 1961-66; house counsel Mfrs. Bank, LA, 1966; assoc. Hurley, Shaw & Tomich, San Marino, Calif., 1968-76, Driscoll & Tomich, San Marino, Calif., 1976—2005, Conway & Tomich, San Marino, Calif., 2005—. Dir. Continental Culture Specialists Inc., Glendale, Calif. Trustee St. Sava Serbian Orthodox Ch., San Gabriel, Calif. Recipient Episcopal Gramata award Serbian Orthodox Met. of Midwestern Am., 1993, Episcopal Gramata award Serbian Orthodox Bishop of Western Am., 1996, 2002; Charles Fletcher Scott fellow, 1957; U. So. Calif. Law Sch. scholar, 1958. Mem.: ABA, ATLA, Women Lawyers Assn., Los Angeles County Bar Assn., Calif. Bar Assn., Order Mast and Dagger, San Marino C. of C., UCLA Alumni Assn., Town Hall and World Affairs Coun., Pi Kappa Delta, Alpha Gamma Sigma, Iota Tau Tau. Office: 2460 Huntington Dr San Marino CA 91108-2643 Office Phone: 626-287-1248. E-mail: lilliantomich@yahoo.com.

TOMICH-BOLOGNESI, VERA, educator; b. LA; d. Peter S. and Yovanka (Ivanovich) T.; m. Gino Bolognesi, July 12, 1969. AA, John Muir Jr. Coll., Pasadena, Calif., 1951; BA in Polit. Sci., UCLA, 1953, MEd, 1955, EdD, 1960. Cert. secondary tchr., Calif.; cert. secondary sch. adminstrn., Calif.; cert. jr. coll. tchr., Calif. Tchg. asst. dept. edn. UCLA, 1956; tchr., dept. chmn. Culver City (Calif.) Unified Sch. Dist., 1956-91; rschr., writer U.S. Dept. Edn., Washington, 1961, del. to Yugoslavia, 1965; co-owner, exec. Metrocolor Engring., San Gabriel, Calif., 1973—. Cons., Continental Culture Specialists, Inc., Glendale, Calif., 1985-92; rsch. asst. Law Firm of Driscoll & Tomich, San Marino, Calif., 1989—. Author: Education in Yugoslavia and the New Reform, 1963, Higher Education and Teacher Training in Yugoslavia, 1967; screenplay editor 1996—. Bd. trustees St. Sava Serbian Orthodox Ch., San Gabriel, 1975—, mem., 1960—. Recipient Episcopal Gramata, Serbian Orthodox Ch. of Western Am., 1996, 2002; named an Outstanding Young Women of Am., 1966. Mem. NEA (life), Calif. Tchrs. Assn., UCLA Alumni Assn., Alpha Gamma Sigma, Pi Lambda Theta. Home: 100 E Roses Rd San Gabriel CA 91775-2343 Office: Metrocolor Engring 5110 Walnut Grove Ave San Gabriel CA 91776-2026

TOMITA, MASARU, engineering educator, researcher; b. Kitakyushu, Fukuoka, Japan, Mar. 10, 1965; s. Hiroshi and Yoko Tomita; m. Yoko Aikawa Tomita, Oct. 22, 1995; children: Yutaka, Kana C. B in Mgmt., Kyushu Inst. Tech., Fukuoka, 1987, B in Engring., 1991, M in Engring., 1993; PhD in Engring., U. Tokyo, 2003. Sr. rschr. Railway Tech. Rsch. Inst., Tokyo, 1993—; chief rsch. scientist Superconductivity Rsch. Lab. ISTEC, Tokyo, 1998—2002; rsch. scientist MIT, Cambridge, Mass., 2004—. Vis. prof. Keio U., Yokohama, Japan, 2005, Tokyo Women's Med. U., 2005—. Author: Nature 421, 2003. Recipient Director's award, ISTEC, 2000, Nat. Minister's award Edn. and Culture, Sports, Sci. and Tech., 2004, Nat. Minister's award Economy, Trade and Industry, 2004. Mem.: Japan Soc. Applied Physics (program com. applied superconductivity conf.), Cryogenic Assn. Japan. Achievements include research in Bulk superconducting materials for improvement of properties and application of superconductivity; discovery of World record data of trapped field of high temprature superconductors. Avocations: basketball, baseball, tennis, ping pong/table tennis, travel. Office: MIT NW14-3209 170 Albany St Cambridge MA 02139 Home Phone: 781-646-5344. Fax: 617-253-5405. Business E-Mail: tomita@mit.edu. E-mail: tomita@rtri.or.jp.

TOMIYASU, KIYO, retired consulting engineer; b. Las Vegas, Nev., Sept. 25, 1919; s. Yonema and Toyono (Kawamura) T.; m. Eiko Nakamizo, Aug. 31, 1947. BS, Calif. Inst. Tech., Pasadena, 1940; MS, Columbia U., NYC, 1941; M.E.S., Harvard U., Cambridge, Mass., 1947,

PhD, 1948. Instr. Harvard U., 1948-49; head engring. sect. Sperry Gyroscope Co., Gt. Neck, N.Y., 1949-55; with GE, 1955-93; cons. engr. microwave techniques GE Valley Forge Space Ctr., Phila., 1969-93; with Martin Marietta Corp., Phila., 1993-95, Lockheed Martin Corp., Phila., 1995—2005; ret., 2005. Author: The Laser Literature-An Annotated Guide, 1968; articles; patentee in field. Exec. bd. Friendship Hill Civic Assn., Paoli, Pa., 1972-73, pres., 1973. Recipient Steinmetz award Gen. Electric Co., 1977; Mgmt. and Data Systems fellow Martin Marietta Corp., 1993; Lockheed Martin fellow, 2004; established Tomiyasu Meml. ann. scholarship Calif. Inst. Tech., 1977. Fellow IEEE (life, hon. life mem. Microwave Theory and Techniques Soc. 1973, tech. activities bd., awards bd., publs. bd., bd. dirs. div. IV 1985-86, ednl. activities bd. 1987-88, Microwave Career award, 1981, Centennial medal 1984, Millennium medal 2000, established Kiyo Tomiyasu award 2000), Geosci. and Remote Sensing Soc. (hon. life mem. 199; Geosci. and Remote Sensing Outstanding Svc. award 1986, Microwave Disting. Svc. award 1987); mem. Am. Phys. Soc. Home: 890 E Harrison Ave Apt T 30 Pomona CA 91767-2075 Personal E-mail: ektom2@verizon.net.

TOMKA, PETER, diplomat, arbitrator, judge, lawyer; b. Banská, Bystrica, Slovakia, June 1, 1956; s. Ján and Kornélia (Plai) Tomka; m. Zuzana Halgasová, June 30, 1990. Grad., Charles U., Prague, Czechoslovakia, 1979; PhD in Internat. Law, Charles U., 1985. Lectr. Law Sch., Charles U., Prague, 1980-86, assoc. lectr. in internat. law, 1986-91; asst. legal advisor Fed. Ministry of Fgn. Affairs, Czechoslovakia, 1986-90, head pub. internat. law divsn., 1990-91; counsellor, legal advisor Permanent Mission to UN, NYC, 1991-92, amb., dep. permanent rep. of Slovakia, 1993-97, charge d'affaires, 1994-97; legal advisor Ministry Fgn. Affairs, Bratislava, Slovakia, 1997-98, dir. gen. legal and consular affairs, 1998-99; permanent rep. of Slovakia to UN, NYC, 1999—2003; judge Internat. Ct. Justice, The Hague, Netherlands, 2003—, v.p., 2009—; arbitrator Iron Rhine Case, Belgium/Netherlands, 2003—05. Former agt. of Slovakia Internat. Ct. Justice in Gabcikovo-Nagymaros Project Case, Hungary/Slovakia; mem. Permanent Ct. Arbitration, 1994—; chmn. UN Legal Com., 1997; vice chair com. legal advisors Coun. of Europe, 1998—99, chmn. com. legal advisors, 2001—02; mem. UN Internat. Law Commn., 1999—2003, vice chmn., 2000; arbitrator UN Law of the Sea Conv., 2004—, World Bank Internat. Ctr. for Settlement Investment Disputes, 2005—. Office: Internat Ct Justice Peace Palace 2517 KJ The Hague Netherlands Office Phone: (31-70) 3022323.

TOMKINS, CALVIN, writer; b. Orange, NJ, Dec. 17, 1925; s. Frederick and Laura (Graves) T.; m. Grace Lloyd Fanning, Sept. 11, 1948; children: Anne Graves, Susan Temple, Spencer; m. Judy Johnston, Nov. 11, 1961 (div. Feb. 1981); m. Susan Cheever, Oct. 1, 1981; 1 child, Sarah Liley Cheever; m. Dodie Kazanjian, May 28, 1988. BA, Princeton U., 1948. Assoc. editor Newsweek mag., NYC, 1955-57, gen. editor, 1957-59; staff writer The New Yorker, NYC, 1960—. Author: The Bride and The Bachelors, 1965, Merchants and Masterpieces, 1970, Living Well Is the Best Revenge, 1971, Off the Wall, 1980, Post- to Neo-, 1988, (with Dodie Kazanjian) Alex: The Life of Alexander Liberman, 1993, Duchamp: A Biography, 1997, The Lives of Artists, 2008. Bd. dirs. Cunningham Dance Found., N.Y.C., 1963-90. With USN, 1944-46. Guggenheim fellow, 1978 Mem. Authors League Am. Inc., Pen Am. Ctr. Clubs: Century (N.Y.C.). Home: 145 E 74th St New York NY 10021-3225 Office: New Yorker Mag 4 Times Sq New York NY 10036-6561 Business E-Mail: dodietad@aol.com.

TOMKO, EDWIN JOSEPH, lawyer; b. McKeesport, Pa., Oct. 23, 1943; s. John Edwin and Madeline Kusic Tomko; m. Katherine Ramm Tomko, July 11, 1970; children: Alexandra, Stuart. BA, Washington and Jefferson Coll., Washington, Pa., 1965; JD, Vanderbilt U., Nashville, 1968. Bar: Pa. 1968, D.C. 1980, Tex. 1984, U.S. Dist. Ct. (we. dist.) Pa. 1968, U.S. Dist. Ct. (D.C. dist.) 1980, U.S. Dist. Ct. (no., ea. and we. dist.) Texs. 1988, U.S. Ct. Appeals (5th cir.) 2006. Asst. dist. atty. trial divsn. Allegheny County, Pitts., 1969—73; trial atty. Spl. Counsel to the Chief Fraud sect., Criminal divsn. Dept. Justice, Washington, 1973—82; asst. regional adminstr. SEC, Houston, 1982—86, chief Office Criminal Ref., asst. chief litigation counsel Divsn. of Enforcement Washington, 1986—87; dep. chief fraud sect., criminal divsn. Dept. Justice, Washington, 1987—88; ptnr. Doke & Riley, LLP, Dallas, 1988—92, Baker Botts LLP, Dallas, 1993—2001, Akin, Gump, Strauss, Hauer & Feld, Dallas, 2001—03, McManemin & Smith, Dallas, 2003—05, Curran Tomko Tarski LLP, Dallas, 2006—. Mem. Bank Fraud Working Group, Washington, 1987—88, Securities Fraud Working Group, Washington, 1987—88. Mem.: ABA, Dallas Bar Assn., Tex. Bar Assn. Republican. Episcopalian. Office: Curran Tomko Tarski LLP 2001 Bryan St Ste 2050 Dallas TX 75201 Office Phone: 214-270-1400.

TOMLIN, CLAIRE J., aeronautical engineer, educator; b. Southampton, Eng., 1969; BASc in Elec. Engring., U. Waterloo, 1992; MSEE, Imperial Coll., London, 1993; PhD in Elec. Engring. and Computer Sci., U. Calif., Berkeley, 1998. Assoc. prof. dept. aeronautics and astronautics Stanford U., Calif. Courtesy assoc. prof. elec. engring. Stanford U.; assoc. prof. dept. elec. engring. and computer sci. U. Calif., Berkeley. Contbr. articles to sci. jours., chapters to books; co-editor: Hybrid Systems: Computation and Control, 2002. Recipient Zonta Amelia Earhart awards for Aeronautics Rsch., 1996—98, Bernard Friedman Memorial Prize in Applied Math., U. Calif., Berkley, 1998, Career award, NSF, 2000—03, Donald P. Eckman award, Am. Automatic Control Coun., 2003, AIAA Outstanding Teacher Award, Stanford, 2000—01; named one of Top 100 Innovators, MIT Tech. Rev., 2003; MacArthur Fellow, John D. and Catherine T. MacArthur Found., 2006. Office: Stanford U Dept Aeronautics and Astronautics Durand Bldg 496 Lomita Mall Stanford CA 94305-4035 E-mail: tomlin@stanford.edu.

TOMLIN, LILY, actress; b. Detroit, Sept. 1, 1939; Student, Wayne State U.; studied mime with Paul Curtis, studied acting with Peggy Feury. Co-founder Lily Tomlin Jane Wagner Cultural Arts Ctr., LA. Appearances in concerts and colls. throughout U.S.; TV appearances include The Music Scene, 1969-70, Laugh In, 1970-73, Lily Tomlin, CBS Spls., 1973, 81, 82; 2 ABC Spls., 1974, 75, Edith Ann Animated Specials, ABC, 1994, The Magic School Bus, 1994 (voice), Murphy Brown, 1996-98, The West Wing, 2002-06, 12 Miles of Bad Road, 2008, Desperate Housewives, 2008-09; motion picture debut in Nashville, 1975 (N.Y. Film Critics award); also appeared in The Late Show, 1977, Moment by Moment, 1978, The Incredible Shrinking Woman, 1981, Nine to Five, 1980, All of Me, 1984, Big Business, 1987, Shadows and Fog, 1992, The Player, 1992, Short Cuts, 1993, The Beverly Hillbillies, 1993, And the Band Played On, HBO, 1993 (Best Supporting Actress Emmy nominee - Special, 1994, Emmy nominations guest appearance Homicide, 1996), Getting Away with Murder, 1995, The Celluloid Closet, 1995, Blue in the Face, 1995, Flirting With Disaster, 1996, Reno Finds Her Mom, 1997, Get Bruce, 1999, Krippendorf's Tribe, 1998, Tea with Mussolini, 1999, Picking Up the Pieces, 2000, The Kid, 2000, Orange County, 2002, I Heart Huckabees, 2004, A Prairie Home Companion, 2006, (voice) The Ant Bully, 2006, The Walker, 2007, The Pink Panther 2, 2009; exec. prodr. TV series Citizen Reno, 2001; one-woman Broadway show Appearing Nitely, 1977 (Spl. Tony award), The Search for Signs of Intelligent Life in the Universe, 1985 (Drama Desk award, Outer Critics Circle award, Tony award 1986, Cable Ace award); recs. include This is a Recording, And That's The Truth, Modern Scream, On Stage. Recipient Grammy award 1971, 5 Emmy awards for CBS Spl. 1973, 81, Emmy award for ABC Spl. 1975, Emmy award Magic Sch. Bus, 1995, Peabody award Celluloid Closet, 1997, Peabody Edith Ann's Christmas, 1997, Mark Twain Prize for Am. Humor, Kennedy Center, 2003. Office: Lily Tomlin Jane Wagner Cultural Arts Ctr Village at Ed Gould Plz 1125 N McCadden Pl Los Angeles CA 90038-1212*

TOMLIN, MIKE, professional football coach; b. Hampton, Va., Mar. 15, 1972; s. Ed and Julia Tomlin; m. Kiya Tomlin; children: Michael Dean, Mason, Harlyn Quinn. BS in Sociology, Coll. William & Mary, Williamsburg, Va., 1995. Wide receivers coach Va. Mil. Inst. Keydets, 1995; grad. asst. Memphis U. Tigers, 1996; wide receivers coach Ark. State U. Red Wolves, 1997, defensive backs coach, 1998, U. Cin. Bearcats, 1999—2000, Tampa Bay Buccaneers, 2001—05; defensive coord. Minn. Vikings, 2006; head coach Pitts. Steelers, 2007—. Named Motorola NFL Coach of Yr., 2008; named to Boys & Girls Clubs of America Alumni Hall of Fame, 2009. Achievements include member of Super Bowl XXXVII winning Tampa Bay Buccaneers, 2003; head coach of Super Bowl XLIII winning Pittsburgh Steelers, 2009; youngest head coach in National Football League history to lead a team to Super Bowl victory (36 years old), 2009. Office: Pittsburgh Steelers 3400 S Water St Pittsburgh PA 15203-2349*

TOMLIN-HOUSTON, LISA, executive, career coach workforce strategist; b. Bklyn. d. George L. and Joan J. Tomlin; m. Anthony D. Houston, Feb. 2, 1991. BA in Psychology, Oberlin Coll., Ohio, 1987; MEd in Counseling Psychology, Rutgers U., 1990. Career counselor U. Pa., Phila., 1990-93; dir. career svcs. H. John Heinz III Sch. of Public Policy and Mgmt., Carnegie Mellon U., Pitts., 1993-95; mgmt. cons. Ford Found., 1995—97; mgr. undergrad. and MBA recruitment Barclays Capital, 1998—2000; pres. Creative Solutions Strategies, LLC, 2000—02; dir. career svcs. Baldwin-Wallace Coll., Berea, Ohio, 2002—06; pres., owner Houston St. Clair Talent Adv., Cleve., 2006—09; v.p. LeeHecht Harrison, 2009—. Avocations: reading, travel, woman's issues.

TOMLINSON, ALEXANDER COOPER, investment banker, consultant; b. Haddonfield, NJ, May 13, 1922; s. Alexander Cooper and Mary (Buzby) T.; m. Elizabeth Anne Brierley, Jan. 10, 1953 (div.); children: William Brierley, Deborah T. Marple, Alexander Cooper III; m. Margaret L. Dickey, Nov. 15, 1986. BS, Haverford Coll., 1943; postgrad., London Sch. Econs. and Polit. Sci., 1947-48; MBA, Harvard U., 1950; LLD (hon.), Haverford Coll., 1995. With Morgan Stanley & Co., NYC, 1950-76, ptnr., 1958-76, mng. dir., 1970-76; dir., pres. Morgan Stanley Can. Ltd. div., Montreal, Que., 1972-76; chmn. exec. com. First Boston, Inc., NYC, 1976-82, dir., 1976-88; pres. Nat. Policy Assn., Washington, 1982-85; exec. dir. Ctr. for Privatization, Washington, 1985-88; pres. Hungarian-Am. Enterprise Fund, Washington, 1990-93; chmn. Fund for Arts and Culture in Ctrl. and Ea. Europe, 1994-97. Mem. U.S. adv. bd. Que. Hydro, 1984-95. Trustee Incorp. Village, Cove Neck, N.Y., 1958-72, 76-82, Cold Spring Harbor Lab., 1976-87, N.Y. Infirmary-Beekman Downtown Hosp., 1968-82, East Woods Sch., Oyster Bay, N.Y., 1962-70, Nature Conservancy, L.I., N.Y., 1970-82, Salisbury Sch., Conn., 1976-87, Carnegie Found. for Advancement Tchg., 1984-90; bd. mgrs. Haverford Coll., 1979-01; bd. dirs. Nat. Bldg. Mus., 1987-94, Nat. Policy Assn., 1982-90, Decatur House Coun., 1990-94; chmn. Am. Friends Can., Inc., 1982-91, Harvard Bus. Sch. Fund, 1981-83. Lt. USNR, 1943-46. Mem. Coun. on Fgn. Rels., Metropolitan Club (Washington), Links (N.Y.). Home: 3314 P St NW Washington DC 20007-2701

TOMLINSON, CAROL ANN, education educator, writer; d. James M. and Louise Askins Windham. BA, U. SC, Columbia, 1965; MEd, U. Va., Charlottesville, 1973, EdD, 1991. Tchr. Lee County Pub. Schs., Sanford, NC, 1967—68; dir. Clarendon Child Devel. Ctr., Arlington, Va., 1968—70; tchr. and adminstr. Fauquier County Pub. Schs., Warrenton, Va., 1970—90; Parish prof. & chair of ednl. leadership, foundations, and policy U. Va., Charlottesville, 1990—. Author: (books) How to Differentiate Instruction in Mixed Ability Classrooms, The Differentiated Classroom: Responding to the Needs of All Learners, Fulfilling the Promise of the Differentiated Classroom: Strategies and Tools for Responsive Teaching. Recipient Outstanding Tchr. award, Warrenton Jr. HS, 1973, Outstanding Prof., Curry Sch. Edn., U. Va., 1994, All U. Tchg. award, U. Va., 2008; named Tchr. of Yr., Va. Dept. Edn., 1974. Mem.: Nat. Assn. Gifted Children (pres.), Nat. State Tchrs. of Yr. Avocations: literature, writing, travel.

TOMLINSON, J. RICHARD, retired engineering services company executive; b. Newtown, Pa., Mar. 26, 1930; s. Robert K. and Margaret (Wright) T.; m. Barbara Elizabeth Brazill, Apr. 30, 1955; children: Karin Kathleen Tomlinson Pizzitola, Kimberly Ann Tomlinson Donahue. BA, Swarthmore Coll., 1952; postgrad., George Washington U., 1952-53, U. Mich., 1955-57, Drexel Inst. Tech., 1954-57, Am. U., 1965. Mgmt. analyst Dept. State, Washington, 1952-53; with Old Republic Life Ins. Co., Washington, 1953-54; supr. financial analysis Ford Motor Co., Detroit, 1954-61; cons. McKinsey & Co., Washington, 1961-65; v.p. finance, dir. passenger svcs. Reading Co., Phila., 1965-69; v.p. finance Rollins Internat., Inc., 1969-71; exec. v.p. Amtrak, Washington, 1972-74; ptnr. L.T. Klauder and Assocs., 1974-75, 79-83; exec. v.p. Penn Central Transp. Co., 1975-78; pres. LTK Engring. Svcs., 1984-95. Named Man of Month, Phila. C. of C., 1967 Mem. Union League, Aronimink Golf and Country Club, Phila. Aviation Country Club. Home: 451 Inveraray Rd Villanova PA 19085-1139 E-mail: jrt77@aol.com.

TOMLINSON, JAMES FRANCIS, retired news agency executive; b. Long Beach, Calif., Oct. 18, 1925; s. Lilburn Jesse and Margaret (Roemer) T.; m. Sally JoAnne Ryan, Aug. 12, 1967; children—Elizabeth Anne, Victoria Alexandra. BA, U. Va., 1950; student, Harvard U., Grad. Sch. Arts and Scis., 1950-51; grad., Advanced Mgmt. Program, Harvard U., 1977. With A.P., 1951-92, chief bur. Newark, 1957-63, bus. news editor NYC, 1963-67, dep. treas., 1967-68, treas., 1968-87, v.p., 1972-92, sec., 1978-92, asst. to pres., 1987-92. Served with AUS, 1943-46, ETO. Mem. SAR, N.Y. Athletic Club (N.Y.C.), Harvard Club (N.Y.C.), Phi Beta Kappa, Phi Eta Sigma. Home: 222 E 71st St New York NY 10021-5164

TOMLINSON, JANICE MEYER, insurance company executive; b. Axtell, Kans., Apr. 29, 1950; d. Henry Herman and Clara Catherine (Haug) Meyer; m. Thomas Fred Tomlinson, Nov. 24, 1973; 1 child, Ryan Thomas. BA, Marymount Coll., 1972. Underwriter trainee St. Paul Cos., Springfield, Mass., 1972-73; casualty underwriter, then casualty mgr. The Chubb Corp., New Haven, 1973-78, comml. lines mgr. White Plains, NY, 1978-81, New Haven, 1981-85, adminstrv. mgr. NYC, 1985-86, br. mgr. White Plains, NY, 1986-90, nat. mgr. human resources Warren, NJ, 1990—95, Canadian zone officer, chmn., pres. Chubb Canada, 1995—2003, exec. v.p., internat. field ops. mgr. Chubb & Son, 2003—. Instr., Inroads Nat. Tng. Seminar, Lawrence, Kans., 1987. Advisor, FIRST, White Plains, 1986—. Mem. NAFE. Roman Catholic. Office: Chubb & Son Inc 15 Mountain Blvd Warren NJ 07059-5611

TOMLINSON, LADAINIAN, professional football player; b. Rosebud, Tex., June 23, 1979; s. Oliver Tomlinson and Loreane Chappell; m. LaTorsha Tomlinson. BA in Gen. Studies, Tex. Christian U., Ft. Worth, 2001. Running back San Diego Chargers, 2001—. Founder Tomlinson Touching Lives Found., 2005—. Recipient NFL MVP award, AP, 2006, ESPY award, Male Athlete of Yr., ESPN, 2007, ESPY award, Best NFL Player, 2007, ESPY award, Record-breaking Performance, 2007, ESPY award, Like Nothing Else award, 2007, Bart Starr award, 2008; co-recipient Walter Payton Man of Yr. award, 2006; named First Team All-Pro, NFL, 2004, 2006—07, Player of Yr., NBC, 2006, NFL Offensive Player of Yr., AP, 2006, Sportsman of Yr., The Sporting News, 2006; named one of Most Influential People in the World of Sports, Bus. Week, 2007; named to Am. Football Conf. Pro Bowl Team, 2002, 2004—07. Achievements include leading the NFL in: rushing yards, 2003, rushing touchdowns, 2004, 2006, 2007, rushing yards per game, 2006, total touchowns, 2006, points scored, 2006; becoming the first and only player in NFL history to rush for 1000 yards and receive 100 passes in a single season, 2003; reaching 100 career touchdowns faster than any other player in NFL history, 2006; setting the NFL single-season record for: most rushing touchdowns (28), 2006, total touchdowns (31), 2006, points scored (186), 2006; setting the NFL record for consecutive games with a rushing touchdown (18), consecutive multi-touchdown games (8). Office: c/o San Diego Chargers 4020 Murphy Canyon Rd San Diego CA 92123*

TOMLINSON, MARK C., professional society administrator; m. Diane Tomlinson; 1 child, Andrew. Grad., Ferris State U., Mich.; MS in Engring. Bus. Mgmt., Warwick U., Eng., 1998. With Buhr Industries; dir. market planning and mfg. engring. activities Body and Assembly and Machine Tool divsns. Lamb Technicon Machining, v.p.; dir. proposal and estimating Cin./Lamb; dir. membership Soc. Mfg. Engrs., Dearborn, Mich., 2003, mng. dir. membership, 2005, exec. dir., gen. mgr. Mem. tech. adv. com. U. Mich. Engring. Rsch. Ctr. Reconfigurable Sci.; pres. bd. Lighthouse Cmty. Devel.; com. chair Boy Scout Troop 1702, Troy, Mich. Office: Soc Mfg Engrs PO Box 930 Dearborn MI 48121 Office Phone: 313-425-3000. Office Fax: 313-425-3400.

TOMLINSON, SUSAN ELIZABETH, language educator; d. Gershom and Ella Mae Tomlinson. BA, Sarah Lawrence Coll., Bronxville, NY; MA, PhD, Brown U., Providence, RI. Asst. prof. English U. Mass., Boston, 2004—.

TOMLINSON, W. JOHN, physicist, researcher; b. Phila., Apr. 3, 1938; s. W. John and Olive (Greatorex) T.; m. Barbara J. Kellog, June 10, 1961; 1 child, Robin B. Tomlinson Van Buren. SB in Physics, MIT, 1960, PhD in Physics, 1963. Sr. scientist Edgerton, Germeshausen & Grier, Bedford, Mass., 1963; mem. tech. staff Bell Labs., Holmdel, N.J., 1965-81, supr. Allentown, N.J., 1981-83; dist. rsch. mgr. Bell Communications Rsch., Red Bank, NJ, 1984—97; mgr. Optical Component Tech., Jellium, NJ, 1997—99; tech. adv. & fellow JDS Uniphase, NJ, 1999—2004; pres. Jomlinson Consulting LLC, Princeton, NJ, 2004—. Topical editor Applied Optics, 1983-90, Optics Letters, 1991-92. Capt. U.S. Army, 1963-65. Fellow Optical Soc. Am., IEEE. Home: 68 Lovers Ln Apt 1 Princeton NJ 08540-6829 Personal E-mail: tomlins@chucxizon.net.

TOMLINSON, WILLIAM HOLMES, management educator, retired military officer; b. Thornton, Ark., Apr. 12, 1922; s. Hugh Oscar and Lucy Gray (Holmes) T.; m. Dorothy Payne, June 10, 1947 (dec.); children: Jane Axtell, Lucy Gray, William Payne; m. Florence Mood Smith, May 1, 1969 (div.); m. Suzanne Scollard Gill, Mar. 16, 1977. Student, Centenary Coll., Shreveport, LA, 1938—39; BS, US Mil. Acad., West Point, NY, 1943; grad., Field Arty. Sch., 1951, Air Command Staff Coll., 1958; MBA, U. Ala., 1960; MS in Internat. Affairs, George Wash. U., Washington, DC, 1966; grad., US Army War Coll., 1966, Indsl. Coll. Armed Forces, 1968; PhD in Bus. Adminstrn., Am. U., Washington, DC, 1974; grad. Advanced Mgmt. Program, Harvard Bus. Sch., Cambridge, Mass., 1968-69; BAS, U. North Fla., Jacksonville, 1988. Commd. 2d lt. US Army, 1943; advanced through grades to Col., Field Arty. US Army, 1966; combat svc. in Leyte and Cebu Philippines 246 Field Arty. Bn. Americal Divsn., 1945; aide de camp to comdg. gen. Robert Eichelberger 8th US Army, Japan, 1945-48; comdr. Btry A, 319th FA Bn and Btry A, 39th FA Bn, 3d Divsn., Ft. Benning, Ga., 1948—50; exec. officer 34 FA Bn, ops. officer 9th Divsn. Arty. Germany and Ft. Carson, Colo., 1954-57; with ODCSPER, 1960—61, Office of Undersec. Army, The Pentagon, Washington, 1961-64; comdr. 2d Bn. 8th Arty. and 7th Divsn. Arty. UN Comd. South Korea, 1964-65; faculty Indsl. Coll. Armed Forces, Ft. McNair, Washington, 1966-72, U. North Fla., Jacksonville, 1972—2002, prof. mgmt., prof. emeritus, 2002—. Vis. prof. U. Glasgow, Scotland, 1987; vis. lectr. Moscow Linguistics U., Plekhanov Econ. Acad., Ulyanovsk U., Russia, 1993; mem. Nat. Def. Exec. Res., Fed. Emergency Mgmt. Agy., 1976—. Author: Assessment of the National Defense Executive Reserve, 1974; co-author: International Business, Theory and Practice, 1991, Business Policy and Strategy, 2000; contbr. articles to profl. jours. Mem. exec. bd. Jacksonville Campus Ministry, 1991—, pres., 2002-04. Decorated Bronze Star, Legion of Merit, Philippine Liberation medal, Japanese Occupation, Asiatic Pacific with Invasion Arrow; recipient Freedom Found. award, 1967-71, Lifetime Sr. Profl. in Human Resources, Tchg. Incentive award State Univ. Sys., 1994-95. Fellow Soc. Antiquaries Scotland; mem. SAR, Sons Confederate Vets., Soc. Human Resource Mgmt., Acad. Mgmt., Indsl. Rels. Rsch. Assn., Acad. Internat. Bus., European Internat. Bus. Assn., Internat. Trade and Fin. Assn., Exec. Svc. Corp. Bd., Co. Mil. Historians, Nat. Eagle Scout Assn., N.E. Fla. Employee Svcs. Mgmt. Assn. (charter pres. 1987-89), Stewart Soc. Edinburgh (regional commr.), West Point Soc. North Fla. (pres. 1976-77), Mil. Order Stars and Bars (comdr. 1980-90), Army Navy Club, Fla. Yacht Club, Masons, Shriners, Rotary, Beta Gamma Sigma (pres. 1988-89), Kappa Alpha. Presbyterian (elder, trustee). Office: 1890 Shadowlawn St Jacksonville FL 32205-9430 Office Phone: 904-388-1148. Personal E-mail: 1shadow@comcast.net.

TOMLINSON-KEASEY, CAROL ANN, academic administrator; b. Washington, Oct. 15, 1942; d. Robert Bruce and Geraldine (Howe) Tomlinson; m. Charles Blake Keasey, June 13, 1964; children: Kai Linson, Amber Lynn. BS, Pa. State U., University Park, 1964; MS, Iowa State U., Ames, 1966; PhD, U. Calif., Berkeley, 1970. Lic. psychologist, Calif. Asst. prof. psychology Trenton (NJ) State Coll., 1969-70, Rutgers U., New Brunswick, NJ, 1970-72; prof. U. Nebr., Lincoln, 1972-77, U. Calif., Riverside, 1977-92, acting dean Coll. Humanities and Social Scis., 1986-88, chmn. dept. psychology, 1989-92, vice provost for acad. planning and pers. Davis, 1992-97, vice provost for acad. initiatives, 1997-99, chancellor, 1996—2006. Author: Child's Eye View, 1980, Child Development, 1985, numerous chpts. to books; contbr. articles to profl. jours. Recipient Disting. Tchr. award U. Calif., 1986. Mem. APA, Soc. Rsch. in Child Devel., Riverside Aquatics Assn. (pres.). Office: PO Box 2039 Merced CA 95344 Home Phone: 404-321-7433. Personal E-mail: caroltk@yahoo.com.

TOMLJANOVICH, ESTHER M., retired judge; b. Galt, Iowa, Nov. 1, 1931; d. Chester William and Thelma L. (Brooks) Moellering; m. William S. Tomljanovich, Dec. 26, 1957; 1 child, William Brooks Tomljanovich. AA, Itasca C.C., 1951; BSL, St. Paul Coll. Law, 1953, LLB, 1955. Bar: Minn. 1955, U.S. Dist. Ct. Minn. 1958. Asst. revisor of statutes State of Minn., St. Paul, 1957-66, revisor of statutes, 1974-77, dist. ct. judge Stillwater, 1977-90; assoc. justice Minn. Supreme Ct., St. Paul, 1990—98, ret., 1998. Adv. bd. women offenders Minn. Dept. Corrections, 1999—; leadership com. So. Minn. Legal Svcs. Corp., 1999—. Former mem. North St. Paul Bd. Edn., Maplewood Bd. Edn., Lake Elmo Planning Commn.; trustee William Mitchell Coll. Law, 1995—2004, Legal Rights Ctr., 1995—2004, pres., 1999; bd. dirs. Itasca C.C. Found., 1996—, Medica Health Ins. Co., 2001—, vice chair, 2003—. Recipient Centennial 2000 award William Mitchell Coll., Disting. Alumna award, First Ann. Esther Tomljanovich Lifetime Achievement award, 2005, Dept. Corrections Acad. Trial Lawyers, Distinguished Jurist award, 2007; named one of One Hundred Who Made a Difference William Mitchell Coll. Law, One of 100 Most Influential Lawyers of All Time, Law & Politics Mag., 2007. Mem. Minn. State Bar Assn., Bus. and Profl. Women's Assn. St. Paul (former pres.), Minn. Women Lawyers (founding mem.). Home and Office: 8533 Hidden Bay Trail Lake Elmo MN 55042 Home Phone: 612-777-5970; Office Phone: 612-777-5970.

TOMNITZ, DONALD J., construction executive; V.p. RepublicBank Dallas, N.A., Crow Devel. Co.; v.p. various divsns. D.R. Horton, Inc., Fort Worth, Tex., 1983—94, v.p. western region, 1994, pres. homebuilding divsn., 1996—98, exec. v.p., 1998, vice chmn., CEO, 1998—, pres., 2000—. Capt. US Army. Office: DR Horton Inc DR Horton Tower 301 Commerce St Ste 500 Fort Worth TX 76102

TOMONOVICH, KRISTIN L., special education educator; b. St. Paul, Nov. 22, 1966; d. David T. and Karen L. Jensen; m. John J. Tomonovich, Nov. 24, 1990 (div. May 16, 2008); 1 child, Joshua John Joon. MS in Spl. Edn., St. Cloud State U., 2002. Cert. in specific learning disabilities State Minn. Dept. Edn., 2005. Kindergarten spl. edn. tchr. Pharr-San Juan-Alamo Sch. Dist., Tex., 1990—94; kindergarten tchr. Greater YMCA St. Paul, Eagan, Minn., 1994—95; substitute tchr. Winona Sch. Dist., Minn., 1995—97; spl. edn. tchr. Brainerd Ind. Sch. Dist. 181, Minn., 1997—, mentor tchr., 2003—07, math curriculum rep spl. edn., 2007—. Mem.: Brainerd United Educators. Dfl. Lutheran. Avocations: reading, cross stitch, gardening. Office: Forestview Mid Sch 12149 Knollwood Dr Baxter MN 56425 Personal E-mail: corgi@brainerd.net. Business E-Mail: kristin.tomonovich@isd181.org.

TOMOYA, TATSUNO, research scientist; b. Kobe, Hyogo, Japan, 1972; D in Energy Sci., Kyoto U. Asst. U. Tokyo, 1999—2003; rsch. assoc. U. Md., Coll. Pk., 2003—05, asst. rsch. scientist, 2003—. Office: IREAP Univ Md 3337 Ave Williams Bldg Paint Br Dr College Park MD 20742 Business E-Mail: tatsuno@umd.edu.

TOMOZAWA, YUKIO, retired physics professor; b. Iyo-City, Ehime Prefecture, Japan, Sept. 3, 1929; s. Buhei and Tosie Tomozawa; children: Peter Kotaro, Ken Taro. BSc, DSc, Tokyo U., 1956. Asst. Tokyo U. of Edn., Tokyo, 1956—59; rsch. assoc. Cambridge U., England, 1959—60, U. Coll. London, 1960—61, U. Pisa, Italy, 1961—64; asst. prof. physics U. Mich., Ann Arbor, 1966—68, assoc. prof. physics, 1968—72, prof. physics, 1972—2003. Visiting mem. Inst. Advanced Study, Princeton, NJ, 1964—66; vis. prof. physics Kyoto U., Kyoto, 1988—89. Mem.: Am. Phys. Soc. Office: U Michigan Physics Dept 450 Church St Ann Arbor MI 48109-1040

TOMPKINS, CURTIS JOHNSTON, government agency administrator; b. Roanoke, Va., July 14, 1942; s. Joseph Buford and Rebecca (Johnston) T.; m. Mary Katherine Hasle, Sept. 5, 1964; children: Robert, Joseph, Rebecca. BS, Va. Poly. Inst., 1965, MS, 1967; PhD, Ga. Inst. Tech., 1971. Indsl. engr. E.I. DuPont de Nemours, Richmond, Va., 1965-67; instr. Sch. Indsl. and Systems Engring., Ga. Inst. Tech., Atlanta, 1968-71; assoc. prof. Colgate Darden Grad. Sch. Bus. Adminstrn., U. Va., Charlottesville, 1971-77; prof., chmn. dept. indsl. engring. W.Va. U., Morgantown, 1977-80, dean Coll. Engring., 1980-91; pres. Mich. Technol. U., Houghton, 1991—2004, pres. emeritus, univ. prof., 2004—; dir., mem. sr. exec. svc. John A. Volpe Nat. Transp. Sys. Ctr., U.S. Dept. Transp., 2004—. Mem. engring. accreditation commn. Accreditation Bd. for Engring. and Tech., 1981-86; mem. exec. bd. Engring. Deans Coun., 1985-89, vice chmn., 1987-89; mem. engring. adv. com., chmn. of planning com. NSF, 1988-91, chm. Mich. Univs. pres. coun., 1996-98; Pres. Coun. Assn. Governing bds. 1996-2004, Gov's. Workforce Commn., 1996-2002; mem. engring. adv. bd. U. Cin., 1996-99 Author: (with L.E. Grayson) Management of Public Sector and Nonprofit Organizations, 1983, (with others) Maynard's Industrial Engineering Handbook, 1992; contbr. chpt. to Ency. of Profl. Mgmt, 1978, 83. Co-chmn. W.Va. Gov.'s Coun. on Econ. Devel.; bd. dirs. Pub. Land Corp. W.Va., 1980-89, Mich. C. of C., 1997—, vice chmn., 2002—; mem. faculty Nat. Acad. Voluntarism, United Way Am., 1976-91; mem. Morgantown Water Commn., 1981-87, Morgantown Utility Bd., 1987-91, steering com. W.Va. Conf. on Environ., 1985-89, Coun. on Competitiveness, 1998-2004, Mich. Higher Edn. Assistance Authority, The Mich. Higher Edn. Student Loan Authority, 2002-04; chmn. Monogalia County United Way, 1989-90; campaign chmn. Copper Country United Way, 1995-96. Named to Com. of 100 Va. Tech. Coll., Disting. Alumni Acad. dept. indsl. engring. hon. alumnus Mich. Technol. U., 2004; recipient Frank and Lillian Gilbreth Indsl. Engring. award Inst. Indsl. Engrs., 1998. Fellow Inst. Indsl. Engrs. (life mem., trustee 1983-90, pres. 1988-89), Nat. Soc. Profl. Engrs., Am. Soc. Engring. Edn. (pres. 1990-91), Mich. Soc. Profl. Engrs.; mem. Am. Assn. Engring. Soc. (bd. govs. 1987-90, exec. com. 1987-90, sec.-treas. 1989-90), Jr. Engring. Tech. Soc. (bd. dirs. 1988-91), Nat. Soc. for Sci., Tech. and Society (bd. dirs. 1991-94), Internat. Hall of Fame of Sci. and Engring. (hon. trustee), Ga. Tech. Coll. Engring. Disting. Alumni Acad., Ga. Tech. Sch. Indsl. and Sys. Engring. Disting. Alumni Acad., W.Va. U. Dept. Indsl. Engring. Disting. Alumni Acad. (hon.), Mich. C. of C. (bd. dirs 1997-2004), Blue Key (hon.), Sigma Xi, Phi Kappa Phi, Tau Beta Pi, Alpha Pi Mu. Methodist. Home: 199 Coolidge Ave #111 Watertown MA 02472 Home Phone: 617-744-0283. E-mail: curtisj42@yahoo.com.

TOMPKINS, ELLEN BETH, retired elementary school educator; b. Waco, Tex., Mar. 2, 1933; d. Richard Curtis and Amanda Hazel (Gunn) Cobb; m. Robert Edward Tompkins, May 24, 1952 (dec. 2006); children: Donna Lynne Keller, Karen Elaine Palmer, Robert Curtis. BS, Stephen F. Austin U., Nacogdoches, Tex., 1968, MEd, 1976. 1st grade tchr. Pine Tree Ind Sch. Dist., Longview, Tex., 1968—90, 1st grade lead tchr., 1990—93; ret. tchr. Bible Classes. Numerous oil painting;, author math and reading curriculum guides. Ongoing vol to dem and rep. election campaigns. Recipient Outstanding Elem. Regional Conservation Tchr., Tex. Assn. Consservation Dists., 1985; named to Outstanding Elem. Tchr. Am., Washington, 1973. Mem.: PTA, Longview HIst. Mus. Republican. Ch. Of Christ. Avocations: art, writing, gardening.

TOMPKINS, HILARY CHANDLER, lawyer; b. Zuni, N.Mex., 1967; adopted d. Kenneth and Nancy Tompkins; m. Michael Prindle; 1 child, Haley. BA, Dartmouth Coll., Hanover, NH, 1990; JD, Stanford U., Calif., 1996. Tribal ct. adv. Navajo Nation Dept. Justice; law clk. Navajo Nation Supreme Ct., Window Rock, Ariz.; spl. asst. US atty. Ea. Dist. NY, Bklyn.; honor program trial atty. Environment and Natural Resources Divsn. US Dept. Justice, Washington; atty. Sonosky, Chambers Sachse, Endreson & Perry; dep. counsel to N.Mex. Gov. Bill Richardson State of N.Mex., 2003—05, chief counsel to N.Mex. Gov. Bill Richardson, 2005—08; adj. prof. law U. N.Mex., Albuquerque; solicitor US Dept. Interior, Washington, 2009—. Mem. Navajo Nation. Office: US Dept Interior 1849 C St NW Washington DC 20240*

TOMPKINS, JAMES RICHARD, retired special education educator; b. Camden, NJ, Jan. 17, 1935; s. Leo Joseph and Cecelia Nichols; children: Tim, Mark. BA cum laude, Mt. St. Mary's Coll., Emmitsburg, Md., 1959; postgrad., U. Mich., Ann Arbor, 1960; MA, Niagara U., NY, 1961; PhD, Cath. U., Washington, 1971. Coord. unit on edn. of emotionally disturbed Bur. Edn. Handicapped-USOE, Washington, 1966-71; asst. prof. U. NC, Chapel Hill, 1971-72; exec. dir. NC Govs. Advocacy Commn., Raleigh, 1972-74; assoc. prof. spl. edn. Appalachian State U., Boone, NC, 1974—76, acting chair dept. spl. edn., 1975, prof. spl. edn., coord. area of emotional disturbance, 1977—89, prof. dept. lang., reading, exceptionalities, 1990—2004, prof. emeritus, 2004—. Cons. edn. of disturbed children NC Dept. Human Resources; presenter in field. Co-author (with R. Calatta, M. Werts): Fundamentals of Special Education: What Every Teacher Needs to Know, 3d edit., 2005; co-author: (with B.L. Brooks, T.J. Tompkins) Commitment, Unity, Self-Reliance, 2000, Child Advocacy: History, Theory and Practice, 1998; contbr. chapters to books, articles to profl. jours. Recipient Creative Achievement award, Appalachian State U. Coll. Edn., 1995, Outstanding Scholarly Achievement award, 1998—99, 2002—03, 2003, Recognition of Excellence in Supervision Student Tchrs. award, 2002, cert. of Appreciation and resolution, 2004, cert. of Recognition, Richard T. Barker Friends of Libr., 1997—98, 2003—04, 2005—06; named Outstanding Tchr. of Yr., Appalachian State U., 1980. Mem. Coun. Exceptional Children, Coun. Children with Behavior Disorders, Coun. Career Devel., Give Youth a Chance Inc., Arts and Humanities for the Handicapped, NC Coun. Behavior Disorders, N.C. Tchr. Preparation Programs for Emotionally Disturbed Children. Home: 8210 Parkton Gate Rd Huntersville NC 28078 Home Phone: 704-987-9920; Office Phone: 828-262-2107.

TOMPKINS, JOSEPH BUFORD, JR., lawyer; b. Roanoke, Va., Apr. 4, 1950; s. Joseph Buford and Rebecca Louise (Johnston) T.; children: Edward Graves, Claiborne Forbes. BA in Politics summa cum laude, Washington and Lee U., 1971; M Pub. Policy, JD, Harvard U., 1975. Bar: Va. 1975, U.S. Ct. Appeals (D.C. cir.), U.S. Ct. Appeals (5th cir.), 1977, U.S. Supreme Ct. 1977, U.S. Dist. Ct. D.C. 1982, U.S. Ct. Appeals (11th cir.) 1982, U.S. Ct. Appeals (3d cir.) 1983, U.S. Ct. Appeals (6th cir.) 1985, U.S. Ct. Appeals (7th cir.) 1991, U.S. Ct. Appeals (4th cir.) 1993, U.S. Ct. Internat. Trade 1996. Assoc. Sidley & Austin (now Sidley Austin LLP), Washington, 1975-79, ptnr., 1982—; assoc. dir. Office Policy and Mgmt. Analysis criminal divsn. U.S. Dept. Justice, Washington, 1979-80, dep. chief fraud sect. criminal divsn., 1980-82. Contbr. articles to profl. jours. Mem. Va. Bd. Health Professions, Richmond, 1984-92, vice chmn., 1984-86, chmn., 1986-88, 90-91. Mem. ABA (white collar crime com. criminal justice sect. 1980—, chmn. task force on computer crime 1982-92), Va. Bar Assn., D.C. Bar Assn., Phi Beta Kappa, Home: 8146 Wellington Rd Alexandria VA 22308-1214 Office: Sidley Austin LLP 1501 K St NW 8th Fl Washington DC 20005 Fax: 202-736-8711. E-mail: jtompkins@sidley.com.

TOMPKINS, RONALD K., retired surgeon, educator; b. Malta, Ohio, Oct. 14, 1934; s. Kenneth Steidley and Mildred Lillian (Loomis) T.; m. Suzanne Colbert, June 9, 1956; children: Gregory Alan, Teresa Susan, Geoffrey Stuart. BA, Ohio U., 1956; MD, Johns Hopkins U., 1960; MS, Ohio State U., 1968; DSc (hon.), U. Bordeaux, 1995. Diplomate Am. Bd. Surgery. Intern in surgery Ohio State U., 1960-61, resident in surgery, 1964-68, adminstrv. chief resident in surgery, 1968-69, NIH trainee in acad. surgery, instr. physiol. chemistry, 1966-69; asst. prof. surgery UCLA, 1969-73, assoc. prof., 1973-79, prof., 1979-2001, prof. emeritus, 2001—, chmn. basic surg. tng. program, 1970-79, asst. dean student affairs, 1979-82, chief divsn. gen. surgery, 1982-88, chief gastrointestinal surgery, 1986-97, assoc. dean, 1988-91, dir. surg. edn., 1996—2004; ret., 2004. Cons. VA Hosps. Editor-in-chief World Jour. Surgery, 1993-2004. With M.C. USAF, 1961-64. Recipient Disting Alumni award, Ohio U. Arts & Scis., 2001; grantee, NIH, 1968—70, John A. Hartford Found., 1970—79; fellow, Royal Soc. Medicine Eng., 1976—77. Fellow ACS (So. Calif. chpt. pres. 1987); mem. Am. Surg. Assn., Am. Gastroenterol. Assn., Am. Fedn. Clin. Rsch. Am. Inst. Nutrition, AMA, Assn. Acad. Surgery, Pacific Coast Surg. Assn. (recorder 1986-91, pres. 1995), Japan Surgical Soc. (hon.), Soc. Clin. Surgery, Soc. Surgery Alimentary Tract (sec. 1982-85, pres.-elect 1985, pres. 1986, chmn. bd. trustees 1987), Soc. Univ. Surgeons, Societe Internationale de Chirurgie (U.S. chpt. sec. 1990-94, pres. 1996-98), Internat. Biliary Assn. (pres. 1979-81), Internat. HepatoPancreato-Biliary Assn. (hon.), Bay Surg. Soc., LA Surg. Soc. (pres. 1981), Robert M. Zollinger/Ohio State U. Surg. Soc. (pres. 1988-90), Longmire Surg. Soc. (pres. 1997-99), Phi Beta Kappa, Sigma Xi, Alpha Omega Alpha, Delta Tau Delta, Soc. Surg. Alimonary Tract (Founders medal, 2008). Achievements include numerous research publications in gastrointestinal surgery and gastrointestinal metabolism and biochemistry. Home: 309 20th St Santa Monica CA 90402

TOMPSON, MARIAN LEONARD, professional society administrator; b. Chgo., Dec. 5, 1929; d. Charles Clark and Marie Christine (Bernardini) Leonard; m. Clement R. Tompson, May 7, 1949 (dec. 1981); children: Melanie Tompson Kandler, Deborah Tompson Frueh, Allison Tompson Fagerholm, Laurel Tompson Davies, Sheila Tompson Doucet, Brian, Philip. Student public and parochial schs., Chgo. and Franklin Park, Ill. Co-founder La Leche League (Internat.), Franklin Park, 1956, pres., 1956-80, dir., 1956—, pres. emeritus, 1990—; exec. dir. Alternative Birth Crisis Coalition, 1981-85; founder, pres., CEO AnotherLook, Inc., 2001—. Cons. WHO; bd. dirs. N.Am. Soc. Psychosomatic Ob-Gyn, Natural Birth and Natural Parenting, 1981-83; mem. adv. bd. Nat. Assn. Parents and Profls. for Safe Alternatives in Childbirth, Am. Acad. Husband-Coached Childbirth; mem. adv. bd. Fellowship of Christian Midwives; mem. profl. adv. bd. Home Oriented Maternity Experience; guest lectr. Harvard U. Med. Sch., UCLA Sch. Pub. Health, U. Antioquia Med. Sch., Medellin, Columbia, U. Ill. Sch. Medicine, Chgo., U. W.I., Jamaica, U. N.C., Nat. Coll. of Chiropractic, Am. Coll. Nurse Midwives, U. Parma, Italy, Inst. Psychology, Rome, Rockford (Ill.) Sch. Medicine, Northwestern U. Sch. Medicine, NGO Forum/4th World Conf. on Women, Beijing; mem. family com. Ill. Commn. on Status of Women, 1976-85; mem. perinatal adv. com. Ill. Dept. Pub. Health, 1980-83; mem. adv. bd. Internat. Nutrition Comm. Svc., 1980—; bd. cons. We Can, 1984—; exec. adv. bd. United Resources for Family Health and Support, 1985-86; mem. internat. adv. coun. World Alliance of Breast Feeding Action, 1996; mem. US Breastfeeding Com., 2006—; vice chair, 2008-09. Author: (with others) Safe Alternatives in Childbirth, 1976, 21st Century Obstetrics Now!, 1977, The Womanly Art of Breastfeeding, 6th edit., 1997, Five Standards for Safe Childbearing, 1981, But Doctor, About That Shot..., 1988, The Childbirth Activists Handbook, 1983; author prefaces and forwards in 11 books; columnist La Leche League News, 1958-80; columnist People's Doctor Newsletter, 1977-88, mem. adv. bd., cons., 1988-92; assoc. editor Child and Family Quar., 1967—; mem. med. adv. bd. East West Jour., 1980—; also articles. Mem. adv. bd. Shelters for Healthy Environments, 1998—2002. Recipient Gold medal of honor Centro de Rehabilitacao Nossa Senhora da Gloria, 1975, Night of 100 Stars III Achiever award Actors Fund Am., 1990, N.Y. Soc. Ethical Culture Ethical Humanist award, 1999, 100 Women Making a Difference Today's Chgo. Woman, Health Humanity award Svc. Humanity, 2007. Mem. Nat. Assn. Postpartum Care Svcs. (adv. bd.), Chgo. Cmty. Midwives (adv. bd.), World Alliance for Breast Feeding Action (mem. internat. adv. coun. 1997). Office: 957 N Plum Grove Dr Schaumburg IL 60173 Office Phone: 847-869-1278. Personal E-mail: m.tompson@comcast.net. E-mail: mt@anotherlook.org.

TOMS, KATHLEEN MOORE, nurse; b. San Francisco, Dec. 31, 1943; d. William Moore and Phyllis Josephine (Barry) Stewart; m. Benjamin Peskoff (dec. Aug. 2002); children from previous marriage: Kathleen Marie Toms Myers, Kelly Terese Toms Shaver. AA, City Coll., San Francisco, 1963; BPS in Nursing Edn., Elizabethtown Coll., Pa., 1973; MS in Edn., Temple U., 1977; MS in Nursing, Gwynedd Mercy Coll., 1988; grad., US Army War Coll., 1999. RN, Calif. Med.-surg. nurse St. Joseph Hosp., Fairbanks, Alaska, 1963-65, emergency rm. nurse Lancaster, Pa., 1965-69, blood, plasma and components nurse, 1969-71; pres. F.E. Barry Co., Lancaster, 1971—; dir. insvc. edn. Lancaster Osteo. Hosp., 1971-75; coord. practical nursing program Vocat. Tech. Sch., Coatesville, Pa., 1976-77; dir. nursing Pocopson Home, West Chester, Pa., 1978-80, Riverside Hosp., Wilmington, Del., 1980-83; assoc. Coatesville VA Hosp., 1983-89, chief nurse, 1984-89; with VA Ctrl. Office; supr. psychiat. nursing Martinez (Calif.) VA Med. Ctr., 1989-94; assoc. chief nursing svc. edn. VA Northern CA HCS, Pleasant Hill, 1994—; nurse mgr. VA Ctr. Rehab. and Extended Care, Martinez, 1996—; patient health edn. coord. VA No. Calif. Health Care Sys., Martinez, 2000—. Trainee assoc. chief Nursing Home Care Unit, Washington; mem. Pa. Gov.'s Coun. on Alcoholism and Drug Abuse, 1974-76; mem. Del. Health Coun. Med.-Surg. Task Force, 1981-83; dir. Lancaster Cmty. Health Ctr., 1973-76, NSQ Edn/Phe coord VA Northern CA HCS Martinez, 2000-; lectr. in field. Col. Nurse Corps, USAR. Decorated Army Commendation medals (6), Meritorious Svc. medals (2); recipient Cmty. Svc. award Citizens United for Better Pub. Rels., 1974; award Sertoma, Lancaster, 1974; Outstanding Citizen award Sta. WGAL-TV, 1975; U.S. Army Achievement award, 1983, grant Devel. Primary Health Care Ctrs. Coomonwealth, Pa. Mem. Elizabethtown U. Alumni Assn., Temple U. Alumni Assn., Pa. Nurses Assn. (bd. dirs. 1972-76), Sigma Theta Tau, Beta Gamma.Lnacaster Cmty. Health Care Ctr.(founder and dir.), VHAVEIN(pres, 2006-07) Achievements include invention of auto-infuser for blood or blood components. Home: 208 Sea Mist Dr Vallejo CA 94591-7748 E-mail: ktoms007@aol.com.

TOMS, STEVEN A., neurosurgeon, researcher; b. Easton, Md., June 24, 1964; s. Stanley Edward and Rae Flowers Toms; m. Madalina Alexandra Popescu. BA, Brown U., Providence, 1986, MD, 1989; MPH, Johns Hopkins Sch. Pub. Health, Balt., 1992. Diplomate Am. Bd. Neurol. Surgeons, 2003. Asst. prof. Vanderbilt U., Nashville, 1998—2001, Oreg. Health Scis. U., Portland, 2001—02; staff Cleve. Clinic, 2002—07; dir., divsn. neuroscis. Geisinger Health Sys., Danville, Pa., 2007—. Contbr. articles to med. jours. Fellow: ACS. Office: Geisinger Health Sys 100 N Academy Ave Danville PA 17822 Office Fax: 570-271-6663. Business E-Mail: satoms@geisinger.edu.

TOMSIC, PEGGY A., lawyer; b. Price, Utah, Mar. 16, 1953; d. Marjorie R. and Edward L. Tomsic; life ptnr. Lucinda Bateman. JD, U. Utah, Salt Lake City, 1982. Bar: Utah 1982. Mng. shareholder Berman, Tomsic & Savage, Salt Lake City, 1984—2005; mgr., sr. atty. Tomsic & Peck LLC, Salt Lake City, 2005—07. Adj. prof. U. Utah Coll. Law, Salt Lake City, 2002—07. Chmn. fin. com. Caroon for Salt Lake County Maj., 2004. Mem.: David K. Watkiss Inns of Ct. (life). Democrat. Avocations: skiing, golf, hiking, poetry, travel. Office: Tomsic & Peck LLC 136 E South Temple Ste 800 Salt Lake City UT 84111 Office Fax: 801-532-4202. Business E-Mail: ptomsic@tomsiclaw.net.

TON, PAUL, investor, educator; b. Buffalo, Apr. 30, 1926; s. Edward Cornelius Ton and Laura Delia Slotboom; m. Joan Karen Marshall, June 18, 1951 (dec. Dec. 27, 2006); children: Scott, Elizabeth, Robert, John. BS, Union Coll., Schenectady, NY, 1949; MA, Stanford U., Palo Alto, Calif., 1951, U. Denver, 1958, PhD, 1969. Instr. electronics USAF, Denver, 1951—52; tchr. history Denver Pub. Schs., 1952—89; adj. prof. history Metro State Coll., Denver, 1990—2003. Dept. head, Driver Edn. Am. Auto Assn., Denver, 1957—64; dept. chair South H.S., Denver, 1972—77; history cons. Am. Frontier TV series, 1985—87; mng. dir. Westton Prodns., 1995—. Contbg. author (book) The Mining Frontier, 1967, Henry M. Porter, Empire Builder, 1991. Cpl. US Army, 1944—46, PTO, pres. 866 Engr. Aviation Bn. Alumni Assn., 2008—, WW II. Mem.: Western Hist. Assn., Orgn. of Am. Historians, Am. Hist. Assn. Republican. Presbyterian. Avocation: photography. Home: 390 Lansing St Aurora CO 80010 Personal E-mail: forpton@comcast.net.

TONCHI, STEFANO, editor; b. Florence, Italy, Oct. 10, 1959; Classic studies, Liceo Classico Forteguerri, Pistoia, Italy; studied polit. sci., U. Florence, Italy, 1979—84. Co-founder, editor, art dir. Westuff mag., 1984—87; fashion dir. L'Uomo Vogue, 1987—94; creative dir. Self, 1994—96; creative cons. J. Crew, 1996—98; fashion creative dir. Esquire mag, 1998—2003; style editor NY Times mag., 2003—; head style dept. T: The NY Times Style mag., 2004—. Co-curator (exhibition) & co-editor (book) Excess: Fashion & the Underground in the 80s, 2004; co-editor: Total Living: Art, Fashion, Design, Architecture, Communication, 2002; co-curator (exhibition) & co-editor (book) Uniform: Order & Disorder, 2001. Office: NY Times 620 8th Ave New York NY 10018-1618 Office Phone: 212-556-3830, 212-556-7596. Office Fax: 212-556-7618, 212-556-7596. E-mail: tonchi@nytimes.com.*

TONDEL, LAWRENCE C., lawyer; b. NYC, Apr. 9, 1946; s. Lyman Mark and Jean (Basch) Tondel; m. Sharyn A. Smith, Aug. 3, 1974; children: Michael Lawrence, Kathryn Chapman. Student, The Lawrenceville Sch., 1964; AB, Wesleyan U., 1968; JD, U. Mich., 1971. Bar: N.Y. 1972. Assoc. Brown & Wood LLP, NYC, 1971-79, ptnr., 1980-97, sr. ptnr., 1997-2001; ptnr. Sidley Austin LLP, NYC, 2001—. Chmn. Internat. Bus. Commn. Ann. Internat. Forum Offshore Funds, 1993—2000. Trustee Elizabeth Morrow Sch., Englewood, NJ, 1988—93; mem. exec. com. parents com. Washington U., St. Louis, 2000—02. Mem.: ABA, Am. Bar Found., Am. Law Inst. Republican. Roman Catholic. Office Phone: 212-839-5399. Business E-Mail: ltondel@sidley.com.

TONEGAWA, SUSUMU, biology professor; b. Nagoya, Japan, Sept. 6, 1939; arrived in U.S., 1963; s. Tsutoma and Miyoko T. (Masuko) Tonegawa; m. Mayumi Yoshinari, Sept. 28, 1985; children: Hidde, Hanna, Satto. BS, Kyoto U., Japan, 1963; PhD in Molecular Biology, U. Calif., San Diego, 1968. Rsch. asst. U. Calif., San Diego, 1963—64, teaching asst., 1964—68; mem. Basel (Switzerland) Inst. Immunology, 1971—81; Whitehead prof. biology MIT, Cambridge, 1981—94, Picower prof., depts. Brain and Cognitive Scis. and of Biology, 1994—. Investigator Howard Hughes Med. Inst., 1988—; founding dir. Picower Inst. for Learning and Memory, 1994—2006; professorship Amgen, Inc., 1994; dir. RIKEN-MIT Neuroscience Rsch. Ctr. Mem. editl. bd. Immunity; contbr. articles to profl. jours. Decorated Order of Culture Emperor of Japan; recipient Cloetta prize, Switzerland, 1978, Warren Triennial prize, Mass. Gen. Hosp., 1980, Genetics Grand prize, Genetics Promotion Found., Japan, 1981, Avery Landsteiner prize, Gesselschaft fur Immunologie, West Germany, 1981, Asahi prize, Asahi-Shimbun (Asahi Press), Tokyo, Japan, 1982, Louisa Gross Horwitz prize, Columbia U., 1982, V.D. Mattia award, Roche Inst. of Molecular Biology, Nutley, NJ, 1983, Gardiner Found. Internat. award, Toronto, Ont., Can., 1983, Robert Koch Found. prize, Bonn, Germany, 1986, Nobel prize in physiology or medicine, 1987, Bristol-Myers award for Disting. Achievement in Cancer Rsch., 1986; co-recipient Albert Lasker Med. Rsch. award, 1987; named Person with Cultural Merit, Japanese Govt., 1983. Mem.: NAS (fgn. assoc.), Scandinavian Soc. Immunology (hon.), Am. Assn. Immunologists (hon.). Office: MIT Dept Biology Room 46-5285 31 Ames St Cambridge MA 02139 Office Phone: 617-253-6459. E-mail: tonewaga@mit.edu.*

TONELLI, ADRIANO R., cardiologist; m. Sandra Lopez. MD, Cuyo Nat. U., Mendoza, 1996. Cert. physician ECFMG, 2003. Cardiology fellow Fundacion Favaloro, Argentina, 1997—2001; internal medicine resident Lansing, 2003—06; pulmonary & critical care fellow U. Fla., Gainesville, 2006—. Contbr. scientific papers (CHEST Young Investigator award, 2008). Recipient Best Cardiology Resident award, Mich. State U., 2006. Office: Univ FL 1600 SW Archer Rd M452 Gainesville FL 32610 Personal E-mail: adrimatonelli@yahoo.com.

TONELLI, MARK R., cardiologist, educator; b. LA, July 27, 1962; s. Arthur L. and Florence L. Tonelli; m. Kelly A. Clancy, Sept. 26, 1992; children: Clare, Benjamin, Quinn. BA in Philosophy, U. Colo., Boulder, 1984; MD, U. Colo. Health Scis., Denver, 1989; MA Med. Ethics, U. Wash., Seattle, 1996. Diplomate pulmonary diseases Am. Bd. Internal Medicine, 2006, critical care medicine Am. Bd. Internal Medicine, 2007. Assoc. prof. medicine U. Wash., 1996—. Fellow: ACP, Am. Coll. Chest Physicians. Office: Univ Wash 1959 NE Pacific St Box 356522 Seattle WA 98195-6522 Office Fax: 206-685-8673. Business E-Mail: tonelli@u.washington.edu.

TONER, MICHAEL E., lawyer, former FEC commissioner; BA with distinction, U. Va, 1986; MA in polit. sci., Johns Hopkins U., 1989; JD cum laude, Cornell Law Sch., 1992. Bar: DC, Va., US Supreme Court, 4th US Circuit Court of Appeals, US Dist. Courts, DC and Eastern Dist. Va. Assoc. atty. Wiley, Rein, & Fielding, Washington, 1992—96; counsel Dole-Kemp Presidential Campaign, 1996; deputy counsel Rep. Nat. Com., 1997—99, chief counsel, 2001; gen. counsel Bush-Cheney Transistion, 2000, Bush-Cheney 2000 Presidential Campaign, 2000; mem. Fed. Election Commn., 2002—07, chmn., 2006—07; ptnr. Bryan Cave Strategies LLC, 2007—, sr. adv., 2007—, adv., 2007—; ptnr. Bryan Cave LLP, 2007—. Office: Bryan Cave Strategies LLC 700 13th St NW Ste 500 Washington DC 20005 also: Bryan Cave LLP 700 13th St NW Ste 700 Washington DC 20005 Office Phone: 202-508-6000.

TONER, MICHAEL F., journalist; b. LeMars, Iowa, Mar. 17, 1944; s. Francis F. and Mary Ann (Delaney) Toner; m. Patricia L. Asleson, Aug. 28, 1966; children: Susan Michelle, Sharon Lynn. BA cum laude, U. Iowa, 1966; postgrad., U. Okla., Peru; MS cum laude, Northwestern U., 1967. Reporter UPI, Chgo., 1966—67; bur. chief Miami Herald, Key West, Fla., 1967—68, reporter, 1968—69, asst. city editor, 1970—72; sci./environ. writer Miami (Fla) Herald, 1973—84; sci. editor Atlanta Jour. and Constrn., 1984—91, sci. writer, 1991—. Co-author: Florida by Paddle and Pack, 1979; contbr. articles to mags. Recipient Pulitzer Prize for explanatory journalism, 1993, Stanford U. Profl Journalism fellow, 1973. Avocations: photography, swimming, cooking, stamp collecting/philately. Office: Atlanta Jour and Constrn 72 Marietta St NW Atlanta GA 30303-2804

TONEV, THOMAS (TOMA) V., mathematics professor; b. Sofia, Bulgaria, Apr. 5, 1945; children: Daniela, Vassilena. MS, Sofia U., 1969; PhD, Moscow State U., 1973. Adj. prof. Sofia U. - Kliment Ohridski, 1974—88; lectr. Banach Ctr., Warsaw, 1982; sr. rsch. assoc. Inst. Math. and Informatics Bulgarian Acad. Scis., Sofia, 1983—2006; vis. mathematician Internat. Ctr. for Theoretical Physics, Trieste, Italy, 1988—89; vis. prof. U. Toledo, 1989—91; prof. math. U. Mont., Missoula, 1991; vis. prof. Kent State U., Ohio, 1999, U. Wash., Seattle, 2000. Senator Faculty Senate U. Mont., Missoula, 2002—05. Author: Big Planes, Boundaries and Function Algebras, 1992, (textbooks) Function Algebras and Function Spaces, 1995, Topics in Analysis - Banach Algebras of Continuous Functions, 2005; co-author (with E. Lyubenova-Toneva): Continued Fractions, 1989; co-author: (with S. Grigoryan) Shift-Invariant Uniform Algebras on Groups, 2006; editor: Pliska, Studia mathematica bulgarica, vol. 10, 1989, Ctrl. European Jour. Math., 2004, Far East Jour. Math. Scis., 2004, Rocky Mountain Jour. Math., 2006; contbr. over 75 articles to profl. jours. Recipient Rsch. award for Young Mathematicians, Balkan Math. Union, 1975; grantee, NSF, 1992—, IREX, NRC, EPSCOR, Mathematisches Forschungsinstitut, Oberwolfach (Germany), Banach Ctr. (Poland), U. Mont. Fellow: Deutsche Mathematiker-Vereinigung, Union Scientists in Bulgaria; mem.: Union Bulgarian Mathematicians, European Math. Soc., NY Acad. Scis., Mont. Acad. Scis., Math. Assn. Am., Am. Math. Soc., Phi Kappa Phi, Pi Mu Epsilon. Office: U Mont Dept Math 32 Campus Dr Missoula MT 59812 Office Fax: 406-243-2674. Business E-Mail: tonevtv@mso.umt.edu.

TONG, FRANK, science educator; s. You-Tan and Shu-Chin Tong; m. Adriane Seiffert, June 17, 2000; 1 child, Katharine Adriane. PhD, Harvard, Cambridge, Mass., 1999. Asst. prof. Princeton U., NJ, 2000—04, Vanderbilt U., Nashville, 2004—07, assoc. prof., 2007—. Recipient Young Investigator award, Cognitive Neurosci. Soc., 2006, Vision Scis. Soc., 2009; Cognitive Neuroscience grant, McDonnell Found. & Pew Charitable Trusts, 1999—2002, grant, NIH, 2002—06, 2007—, NSF, 2007—. Achievements include research in brain imaging studies of human visual perception, neural decoding and visual mind reading, neural correlates of visual consciousness. Office: Vanderbilt Univ 301 Wilson Hall Nashville TN 37240 Business E-Mail: frank.tong@vanderbilt.edu.

TONG, JOHN, ophthalmic plastic surgeon, pediatric ophthalmologist, educator; Bd. cert.; double fellowship trained. Faculty Jule Stein Eye Inst., LA, 2000; asst. clin. prof. Davis Med. Ctr., Sacramento, 2001—. Faculty mem. UCLA Jule Stein Eye Inst., 2000; lectr. in field. Contbr. chapters to books, articles to profl. jours. Fellow: ACS, Am. Acad. Ophthalmology, Am. Assn. Pediat. Ophthalmology and Strabismus, Am. Acad. Cosmetic Surgery, Am. Soc. Ophthalmic Plastic Surgery. Office: 3900 W 15th St Ste 406 Plano TX 75075 also: 3200 N MacArthur Blvd 200 Irving TX 75062

TONG, KAITY, anchor; m. Patrick Callahan; 1 child. BA, Bryn Mawr Coll.; MA, Stanford U. Street reporter various West Coast radio/tv networks; anchor KCRA, Sacramento, WABC Eyewitness News, WB-11 News at 10/WPIX-TV, NYC. Recipient Exceptional Achievement award, Disting. Woman award, Star award, Edward R. Murrow award, 3 Emmy awards Acitve United Cerebral Palsy, Children's Mus. of Manhattan, Juvenile Diabetes Found., Friends for Life, League for the Hard of Hearing. Office: WPIX-TV/Tribune Co 220 E 42d St New York NY 10017 Business E-Mail: ktong@tribune.com.

TONG, MARY POWDERLY, retired mathematician, educator; b. NYC, May 24, 1924; d. William Joseph and Katherine Colwell Powderly; m. Hing Tong, Aug. 19, 1956; children: Christopher, Mary Elizabeth, William, Jane Frances, James. BA, St. Joseph's Coll., 1950; MA, Columbia U., 1951, PhD, 1969. Instr. math. St. Joseph's Coll., Bklyn., 1951-54, Columbia Univ., NYC, 1954-60; asst. prof. math. Univ. Conn., Storrs, 1960-66; assoc. prof. math. Fairfield (Conn.) Univ., 1966-70; prof. math. William Paterson Coll., Wayne, N.J., 1970-81; ret., 1981. Contbr. articles to profl. jours. Trustee Compehensive Behavioral Health Care, Lynhurst, NJ, 1988—99, pres., 1994—96; mem. Bergen County Mental Health Bd., NJ, 1999—2001. Fellow, NSF, Washington, 1959—60. Mem. Am. Math. Soc., Math. Assn. Am., Am. Phys. Soc., N.Y. Acad. Scis., Delta Epsilon Sigma. Roman Catholic. Home: 725 Cooper Ave Oradell NJ 07649-2334

TONG, SIU WING, computer programmer; b. Hong Kong, May 20, 1950; came to U.S., 1968; BA, U. Calif., Berkeley, 1972; PhD, Harvard U., 1979; MS, U. Lowell, 1984. Rsch. assoc. Brookhaven Nat. Lab., Upton, N.Y., 1979-83; software engr. Honeywell Info. Systems, Billerica, Mass., 1984-85; sr. programmer, analyst Hui Computer Cons., Berkeley, Calif., 1985-88; sr. v.p. devel., chief fin. officer Surgicenter Info. Systems, Inc., Orinda, Calif., 1989-94; sr. sys. specialist Info. Sys. Divsn. Contra Costa County Health Svcs., Martinez, Calif., 1995-97, info. tech. supr. Info. Sys. Divsn., 1997—. Vol. tchr. Boston Chinatown Saturday Adult Edn. Program of Tufts Med. Sch., 1977-79. Muscular Dystrophy Assn. fellow, 1980-82. Mem. AAAS, IEEE, Assn. Computing Machinery, N.Y. Acad. Scis. Home: 17 Beaconsfield Ct Orinda CA 94563-4203 Office: Contra Costa County Health Svcs 595 Center Ave Ste 210 Martinez CA 94553-4634 E-mail: swtong@hsd.cccounty.us.

TONG, TOMMY R., surgeon, pathologist; M.B., B.S.(HK), U. of Hong Kong Med. Sch., Pokfulam, Hong Kong, 1976—81. Diplomate Am. Bd. of Pathology. Surgeon St. Teresa's Hosp., Kowloon, Hong Kong, 1988—; sr. pathologist Princess Margaret Hosp., 1996—2006; with Alumnus Pathology Depts. U. Sask., Mt. Sinai Hosp., Meml. Sloan Kettering Cancer Ctr., NY; pathologist Pathology Med. Group, Bakersfield, Calif., 2006—08; attending pathologist Motefiore Med. Ctr., NY, 2008—; assoc. prof. Albert Einstein Coll. Medicine. Vis. prof. Mt. Sinai Pathology, 1999; invited spkr. Vanderbilt U. Pathology, 2004; asst. prof. Albert Einstein Coll. Medicine, 2009—. Reviewer: Jour. Clin. Microbiology, Jour. Infectious Diseases; reviewer BMJ, JAMA, Lancet Infection Diseases, Lancet Neurology; reviewer: Open Microbiol. Jour.; mem. editl. bd. Jour. Clin. Microbiology, Open Infections Diseases Jour.; mem. editl. bd.: Open Microbiol. Jour., Internat. Jour. Bimed. Scis.; mem. editl. bd. Open Infection Diseases Jour., Recent Patents on Anti-Infective Drug Discovery; contbr. articles to profl. jours. Grantee, Princess Margaret Hosp., 2001, 2001, Innovation and Tech. Commn., the Govt. of the Hong Kong Spl. Adminstrv. Region, 2001, 2003, 2004. Fellow: Am. Soc. of Clin. Pathologists, Coll. of Surgeons of Hong Kong, Royal Australasian Coll. of Surgeons, Coll. of Am. Pathology, Royal Coll. of Surgeons of Edinburgh; mem.: Am. Clin. Soc., Am. Soc. of Cytopathology, US and Can. Acad. of Pathology, NY Acad. of Sciences, Assn. for the Advancement of Sci., Papanicolaou Soc. of Cytopathology. Achievements include patents for electromolecular diagnosis; molecular diagnosis; cervical cancer screening; patents pending for method of collection of upper respiratory clinical sample; novel biochip microarrays. Office: Montefiore Med Ctr Dept Pathology 600 E 233rd St Bronx NY 10466 Office Phone: 718-920-9150. Personal E-mail: tommy.tong@electrobiochip.com, tommyrtongmd@gmail.com.

TONGE, BRUCE JOHN, psychiatrist; b. Melborne, Australia, May 9, 1947; s. JOhn Feltham and Joyce (Bates) Tonge; m. Gera Eleanore Degooijer-Tonge, Oct. 12, 1970 (div. June 1996); m. Avril Vaux Brereton, June 10, 1996; children: Jonathan, Rachel, Claire. MB BS, Monash U., Melbourne, 1970; DPM, Royal Coll. Physicians, London, 1974; MD, U. Melbourne, 1985. Cert. child psychiatrist Vic. Child psychiatrist Austin Hosp., Melbourne, 1976—80, dir. dept. child psychiatry, 1980—87; head dept. psychiatry, prof. child psychiatry Royal Alexandra Hosp. for Children, Sydney, NSW, 1987—89; med. dir., mental health program So. Health, Melbourne, 1990—, head ctr. for devel. psychiatry and psychology, 1990—; prof. and head, dept. psychiatry Monash U., Melbourne, 1992—2006, found. head Sch. Psychology and Psychiatry, 2000—. Chair child psychiatry and tng. com. RANZCP, Melbourne, 1986—91; bd. dirs. Autism Victoria, Melbourne, 1991—2001; mem. com. on mental health and ID WHO, London, 1997—; bd. dirs. Neurosci. Australia, Melbourne, 2003—. Author (18 books on child psychiatry); editor: Handbook of Child Psychiatry, 1990; contbr. 58 chpts. to books, articles to profl. jours.; co-author: Developmental Behaviour Checklist; author: Self-Efficacy Questionnaire for Adolescents, Draw a Dream. Flight lt. RAAF, 1961—70. Recipient Rsch. Excellence prize, Monash U., 2001, Nat. Rsch. prize, Australian Soc. for Study of Learning Disabled, 1998, Julian Katz award, RANZCP, 1998; named Blake Marsh Lectr., Roy Coll. Psychiatrists of Edinburgh, 2005. Mem.: Royal Melbourne Tennis Club. Anglican. Office: Ctr for Developmental Psychiatry Monash Medical Ctr 246 Clayton Rd Clayton VIC 3168 Australia Office Phone: 61-39594-1354. Office Fax: 51-3-9594-6937. E-mail: bruce.tonge@med.monash.edu.au.

TONGSON, KAREN, language educator; b. Manila, Philippines, Aug. 23, 1973; d. James Linder and Elizabeth Katindig Dykes, L. James Dykes (Stepfather). BA in English with honors, UCLA, 1995; PhD, U. Calif., Berkeley, 2003. English and gender studies prof. U. So. Calif., LA, 2005—. Prodr.: (play) The Barber of East L.A. (USC Provost's Arts and Humanities Initiative grant, 2007), (album) No More Blues; co-founder (pop culture website) Oh! Industry; contbr. articles to profl. jours. Recipient Dr. Warren Craig Thompson and Erile R. Thompson prize, UCLA, 1995; Humanities Dissertation fellowship, U. Calif., Berkeley, 2002, Andrew W. Mellon fellowship, Andrew W. Mellon Found., 1999, Postdoc. fellowship, U. Calif. Office Pres., 2003—05, Residential fellowship, U. Calif. Humanities Rsch. Inst., Irvine, 2004, Advancing Humanities and Social Sci. grant, U. So. Calif., 2008—. Mem.: Am. Studies Assn., MLA. Liberal. Office: Univ Southern Calif 3501 Trousdale Pky THH 404 Los Angeles CA 90089-0354 Office Fax: 213-741-0377.

TONGUE, JOHN RICHARD, orthopedist; b. Portland, Oreg., Mar. 1, 1946; s. Thomas H. and Bernice Healy Tongue; children: Christopher John, Lisa Jean Margaret McQuiston, Laura Anne Los. BA, Northwestern U., Evanston, Ill., 1968; MD, St. Louis U., 1972. Diplomate Am. Bd. Orthop. Surgery, 2002. Pvt. practice, Tualatin, Oreg., 1978—; chair Am. Acad. Orthop. Surgeons Communication Skills Mentors Program, Rosemont, Ill., 2001—; bd. dirs. Am. Acad. Orthop. Surgeons, mem., 1998—2001. Clin. asst. prof., orthop. surgery Oreg. Health Scis. U., Portland, Oreg., 1978—; pres. North Pacific Orthop. Soc., Portland, 2006. Treas. Western Orthop. Assn., Towson, Md., 2008—09. Recipient Pub. Svc. award, US Nat. Hwy. Traffic Safety Adminstrn., 1991, Humanitarian award, Am. Acad. Orthop. Surgeons, 2003, Knight, Portland Royal Rosarians, 2008. Mem.: Twentieth Century Orthop. Assn. Avocations: fly fishing, backpacking, skiing. Home: 930 West Point Rd Lake Oswego OR 97034 Office: John R Tongue MD PC 6485 SW Borland Rd Tualatin OR 97062 Office Fax: 503-691-2757.

TONIETTE, SALLYE JEAN, physician; b. Sulphur, La., 1929; d. Eugene Augusta and Sallye (Tanner) T. Student, John McNeese Jr. Coll., 1946-47; BS, La. State U., 1949, tchrs. cert., 1950, MD, 1955. Intern Crawford W. Long Meml. Hosp., Emory U., Atlanta, 1955-56, resident in ob-gyn., jr., sr., chief residencies, 1956-59; practice in ob-gyn. Sulphur, La., 1959—. Mem. med. staff West Calcasieu Cameron Hosp., 1959—. Dir. Calcasieu Parish Cancer Soc., 1963-67. Named Woman of Distinction, Calcasieu Parish Police Jurors, also Bus. and Profl. Women's Club of West Calcasieu, 1969; Queen of Krewe of Cosmos, 1963, Mardi Gras. Fellow Am. Coll. Ob-Gyn.; mem. La. Med. Assn., Calcasieu Parish Med. Soc., La. Wildlife Fedn., Am. Quarter Horse Assn., Assn. Am. Physicians and Surgeons, Bayou Oaks Country Club (v.p., bd. dirs. 1974—), Krewe de Bon Coer, Krewe of Cosmos, Alpha Chi Omega, Beta Tau Mu, Iota Sigma Pi, Phi Theta Kappa, Beta Sigma Phi. Republican. Methodist. Home: 4917 La Paix Dr Sulphur LA 70665 Office: 521 Cypress St Sulphur LA 70663-5049 Home Phone: 337-583-7223; Office Phone: 337-527-7841.

TONIOLI, BRUNO, choreographer, dancer; b. Ferrara, Italy, Nov. 25, 1955; s. Werther and Fulvia Tonioli; life ptnr. Paul Tonioli. Mem. dance co. La Grande Eugene; judge Strictly Come Dancing, 2004—07, Dancing with the Stars, ABC, 2005—. Choreographer (films) Space Riders, 1984, Dancin' Thru the Dark, 1990, Bring Me the Head of Mavis Davis, 1997, Little Voice, 1998, Hotel Splendide, 2000, Me Without You, 2001, Ella Enchanted, 2004, (TV films) The Gathering Storm, 2002, Marple: The Body in the Library, 2004, (TV series) DanceX, 2007, Dance Wars: Bruno vs. Carrie Ann, 2008; actor: (TV miniseries) Oscar, 1985; (films) Absolute Beginners, 1986, What a Girl Wants, 2003.

TONJES, MARIAN JEANNETTE BENTON, education educator; b. Rockville Center, NY, Feb. 16, 1929; d. Millard Warren and Felicia E. (Tyler) Benton; m. Charles F. Tonjes (div. 1965, dec.); children: Jeffrey Charles, Kenneth Warren. BA, U. N.Mex., 1951, cert., 1966, MA, 1969; EdD, U. Miami, 1975. Dir. recreation Stuyvesant Town Housing Project, NYC, 1951—53; tchr. music., phys. edn. Sunset Mesa Day Sch., Albuquerque, 1963—64; tchr. remedial reading Zia Elem. Sch., 1965—67; tchr. secondary devel. reading Rio Grande H.S., 1967—69; rsch. asst. reading Southwestern Coop. Ednl. Lab., 1969—71; assoc. dir., vis. instr. Fla. Ctr. Tchr. Tng. Materials U. Miami, 1971—72; asst. prof. U.S. Internat. U., San Diego, 1972—75; prof. edn. Western Wash. U., Bellingham, 1975—94, prof. emerita, 1994—; dir. summer study at Oriel Coll. Oxford U., England, 1976—93. Reading supr. Manzanita Ctr., 1968; vis. prof. adult edn. Palomar (Calif.) Jr. Coll., 1974; vis. prof. U. Guam, Mangilao, 1989-90; adj. prof. U. N.Mex., 1995—; invited guest Russian Reading Assn., Moscow, 1992; internat. travel adv. Vantage Deluxe Travel, 2002-05; spkr. European Conf. reading, Tallinn, Estonia, 2003, symposium chair World Congress, Manila, 2004, keynote spkr. Am. Reading Forum Sanibel Island, Fla., 2008; cons. in field. Author: (with Miles V. Zintz) Teaching Reading/Thinking Study Skills in Content Classroom, 3rd edit., Secondary Reading, Writing and Learning, 1991, Integrated Content Literacy, 1999, (with Ray Wolpow) Integrated Content Literacy, 5th edit., 2006; invited keynote banquet spkr., Am. Reading Forum, Sanibel, Fla., 2008-. Trustee White Mountain Sch., 2000—06; tour dir. In the Footsteps of Dickens, England, 2001; hon. trustee Lomonosov Sch., Moscow; read by three com. Albuquerque Bus. and Edn. Compact, 1999—2002. Named Alumnae Vol. of Yr., White Mountain Sch., 2006; Tng. Tchr. Trainers grantee, 1975; NDEA fellow Okla. State U., 1969; nominated Profl. Outstanding Alumna McDaniel Coll., 2005. Mem.: Am. Reading Forum, Internat. Reading Assn., PEO (past chpt. pres.), World Congress in Reading Buenos Aires, European Coun. Internat. Schs., European Conf. in Reading, UK Reading Assn., Internat. Reading Assn. (non-print media and reading com. 1980—83, workshop dir. S.W. regional confs. 1982, travel, interchange and study tours com. 1984—86, com. internat. devel. N.Am. 1991—96, Outstanding Tchr. Educator award 1981), Am. Reading Forum (chmn. bd. dirs. 1983—85), Oxonian and Friend of Oriel Coll. (Oxford) (hon.), Circumnavigators, Internat. Soc. Rwy. Travelers, Delta Delta Delta. Presbyterian. Avocations: miniatures, reading, bridge, art, travel, cooking. Business E-Mail: mtonjes@unm.edu.

TONKERY, DAN, Internet company executive; b. Fairmont, W.Va., July 21, 1946; s. Thomas H. and Jean D Tonkery; m. Linda E. Persons, May 2, 1981; children: Andrew D., John C. Fiero, Steven C. Fiero. BA, David Lipscomb U., 1968; MLS, U. Ill., 1970. Pres. The Faxon Co., Westwood, Mass., 1996—2001; vp of bus. devel. EBSCO Info. Services, Birmingham, Ala., 2001—. Founder and prisident TDT Ventures, Morristown, NJ, 1995—96; pres. ceo Readmore Co., NYC, 1986—95; founder, pres. Horizon Info. Svcs., LA, 1984—86; sr. v.p. The Faxon Co., Westwood, Mass., 1982—84; assoc. u. libr. U. Calif., LA, 1979—82; chief tech. svcs. divsn. Nat. Libr. Medicine, Bethesda, Md., 1970—79. Treas. Coun. on Libr. Info. Resources, Washington, 1996—2004. Fellow Pub. Health Svc. fellow, Pub. Health Svc, NIH, 1970. Avocation: golf. Office: EBSCO Info Svcs PO Box 1943 Birmingham AL 35201 Home: 1819 Hardwood View Dr Birmingham AL 35242-7064 Personal E-mail: tonkery@mindspring.com. E-mail: dtonkery@ebsco.com.

TONKIN, HUMPHREY RICHARD, academic administrator, educator; b. Truro, Cornwall, Eng., Dec. 2, 1939; arrived in U.S., 1962; s. George Leslie and Lorna Winifred (Sandry) T.; m. Sandra Julie Winberg, Mar. 9, 1968 (div. 1981); m. Jane Spencer Edwards, Oct. 1, 1983; 1 child, Sebastian George. BA, St. John's Coll., Cambridge, Eng., 1962, MA, 1966; AM, PhD, Harvard U., 1966; DLitt (hon.), U. Hartford, 1999. Asst. prof. English U. Pa., Phila., 1966-71, assoc. prof., 1971-80, prof., 1980-83, vice-provost undergrad. studies, 1971-75, coord. internat. programs, 1977-83, master Stouffer Coll. House, 1980-83; pres. State Univ. Coll., Potsdam, NY, 1983-88, U. Hartford, Conn., 1989-98, prof. humanities, pres. emeritus, 1998—; vis. fellow Whitney Humanities Ctr. Yale U., 1998-99. Vis. prof. English Columbia U., N.Y.C., 1980-81; exec. dir. Ctr. Rsch. and Documentation on World Lang. Problems, Rotterdam and Hartford, 1974—. Editor: (journal) Language Problems and Language Planning; author: (bibliography) Sir Walter Raleigh, 1971, Spenser's Courteous Pastoral, 1972, Esperanto and International Language Problems, 4th edit., 1977, The Faerie Queene, 1989, Lingvo kaj Popolo 2006, (with Jane Edwards) The World in the Curriculum, 1981; editor: Esperanto, Interlinguistics and Planned Language, 1997, Service - Learning Across Cultures, 2004, (with Allison Keef) Language in Religion, 1989, (with Timothy Reagan) Language in the 21st Century, 2003; editor, translator Esperanto: Language, Literature and Community (Pierre Janton), 1993, Maskerado: Dancing Around Death in Nazi Hungary (Tivadar Soros), 2000; contbr. articles to profl. jours. Pres. Pa. Coun. Internat. Edn., 1980-81; bd. dirs. World Affairs Coun. Phila., 1979-83, Zamenhof Found., 1987-94, Hartford Symphony Orch., 1989-98, World Affairs Coun. Conn., 1989-2003, Greater Hartford Arts Coun., 1989-99, Can.-U.S. Found. Ednl. Exchange, 1997-2003, chmn. 1999-2000; bd. dirs. World Learning, 1998-2007; chmn. Coun. Internat. Exch. Scholars, 1988-94, Esperantic Studies Found., 1991-, Internat. Partnership for Svc.-Learning, 1991-96, v.p., 2001-05; bd. dirs. Am. Forum, 1985-2008, chmn., 1998-2003; bd. dirs. Ctr. Applied Linguistics, 2007-. Recipient Lindback award for disting. teaching, 1970; Frank Knox fellow Harvard U., 1962-66; Guggenheim fellow, 1974; Cassandra Pyle Award, NAFSA: Assn. Internat. Educators, 2006. Fellow Acad. Esperanto; mem. Universal Esperanto Assn. (pres. 1974-80, 86-89, rep. to UN 1974-83, hon. com. 1995-), Internat. Spenser Soc. (pres. 1983-84, former dir.), Internat. Acad. Scis. San Marino, Conn. Acad. Arts and Scis., Cosmos Club. Home: 279 Ridgewood Rd West Hartford CT 06107-3542 Office: U Hartford Mortensen Libr 200 Bloomfield Ave West Hartford CT 06117-1599 Office Phone: 860-768-4448. Business E-Mail: tonkin@hartford.edu.

TONKIN, INA LYNN DYER, physician, cardiovascular radiologist, educator; b. Louisville, Apr. 26, 1944; d. Robert S. and Nancy E. (Camp) Dyer; m. Allen K. Tonkin, June 29, 1968; children: Allison Elizabeth-Ann, Kieth Allen. BA, DePauw U., 1966; MD, U. Louisville, 1970. Diplomate Am. Bd. Radiology, 1974; Am. Bd. Vascular Interventional Radiology, 1994; Am. Bd. Pediatric Radiology, 1996. Pediatric intern U. Fla., Gainesville, 1970-71, resident in radiology, 1971-73, fellow in cardiovasc. radiology, 1974-75; asst. prof. U. Ariz. Health Sci. Ctr., Tucson, 1975-77, U. Ala.-Birmingham, 1977-79; assoc. prof. radiology U. Tenn., Memphis, 1979-84, prof., 1984—, prof. pediat., 1985—. Exec. com. LeBonheur Children's Med. Ctr., Memphis, 1981-85, chief med. staff, 1987; disting. scientist Armed Forces Inst. Radiologic Pathology, Washington, 1992-93; prof. radiology & pediat. U. Tenn. Hlth. Sci. Ctr., Memphis; lectr. nat. and internat. Editor: (book) Pediatric Cardiovascular Imaging, 1992; contbr. chpts. to books, rsch. articles to profl. jours. Recipient Disting. Alumnus award U. Louisville Med. Sch., 1999. Fellow Soc. Interventional Radiology, Am. Coll. Radiology, Cardiovasc. Coun. Am. Heart Assn.; mem. Soc. Pediat. Radiology (treas.), Jour. Rev. Club Memphis (sec. 1984, pres. 1985), Soc. Interventional Radiology, N.Am. Soc. Cardiac Imaging (pres. 1991). Methodist. Home: 3415 Chambers Chapel Rd Lakeland TN 38002-9573 Office: LeBonheur Children's Med Ctr 50 N Dunlap St Memphis TN 38103-4909 also: Univ Tenn Health Sci Ctr Prof Radiology and Pediat 50 N Dunlap St Memphis TN 38103-4909 Personal E-mail: drs.tonkin@mindspring.com.

TONKIN, LEO SAMPSON, educational association administrator; b. Suffern, NY, Apr. 2, 1937; s. Leo S. and Ann (Petrone) T. AB, Johns Hopkins, 1959; postgrad., Sch. Advanced Internat. Studies, 1962-63; JD, Harvard, 1962; Dr. Pedagogy, SUNY, 1973. Legis. asst. to US Congressman; then Sen. Charles McC. Mathias, Jr., Md., 1962-63; asso. counsel US Ho. of Reps. Select Com. on Govt. Research, 1964; spl. cons. Ho. Spl. Subcom. on Edn., 1965-66; exec. dir. Commrs. Council on Higher Edn., Washington, 1965-66; pres. Leo S. Tonkin Assos., Inc., 1966—; founder, dir., chmn. bd. Washington Workshops Found., 1967—; pres. Travel Seminars, Ltd., 1999—. Mem. White House Conf. on Edn., 1965, White House Conf. on Youth, 1971; spl. asst. to chmn. U.S. Ho. of Reps. Select Com. on Crime, 1972; mem. bd. plebe sponsors U.S. Naval Acad., 1977—; v.p. London Fedn. Boys' Clubs, 1980—; mem. adv. panel Nat. Commn. for Protection of Human Subjects of Biomed. and Behavioral Research, HEW, 1976-77; bd. dirs. Star Sci., Inc., 1998-2007; nat. adv. coun. Retinitis Pigmentosa Found., 1999—. Contbr. articles to mags. Bd. dirs. Washington Choral Arts Soc., 1971-73, Nat. Coordinating Council on Drug Edn., 1973, Nat. Student Ednl. Fund, 1974—76; chmn. Wall Street Seminar Found., 1978—; chmn. bd. trustees St. Thomas Aquinas Coll., 1966-73, continuing trustee, 1973-78, trustee, chmn. emeritus, 1978—; chmn. bd. trustees City of Phila. Govt. Honors Program; trustee Southeastern U., 1966-73; asso. bd. trustees Immaculata Coll., 1966-73; mem. advisory bd. Pub. Affairs and Govt. Degree Program, Mt. Vernon Coll., 1971-74; bd. dirs. YMCA, Washington, 1969-71. Recipient Americanism award, Freedoms Found. at Valley Forge, 1973. Mem. Johns Hopkins Alumni Assn. Washington (pres. 1969-72), Harvard Law Sch. Alumni Assn. Washignton (exec. com.), Georgetown Club (Washington), City Tavern Club (Washington), Nat. Press Club (Washington), Capitol Hill Club (Washington), Capitol Yacht Club (Washington), Harvard Club (N.Y.C.). Home: 4368 Sunset Ct Warrenton VA 20187-3584 Office: 3222 N St NW Washington DC 20007-2849

TONKO, PAUL DAVID, United States Representative from New York, former state agency administrator; b. Amsterdam, NY, June 18, 1949; BS in Mech. and Indsl. Engring., Clarkson Coll. Tech., 1971. Engr. NY State Dept. Transportation; sr. valuation engr. NY Dept. Pub. Svc.; mem. Montgomery County Bd. Suprs., 1975—83, chair, 1981; mem. NY State Assembly from Dist. 105, Albany, 1983—2007, chmn. energy com., 1992—2007; pres., CEO NY State Rsch. & Devel. Authority, Albany, 2007—08; mem. US Congress from 21st NY Dist., 2009—. Mem. Montgomery County C. of C., Schenectady C. of C.; del. Dem. Nat. Convention, 1988; bd. dirs. Montgomery County Red Cross, Am. Cancer Soc., Montgomery County Unit. Recipient Legis. award, NY State Conf. Mayors, 1991. Mem.: Kiwanas, Elks, Lodge 101, K. of C., Coun. 209. Democrat. Roman Catholic. Office: US Congress 128 Cannon House Office Bldg Washington DC 20515-3221 also: Dist Office O'Brien Fed Bldg Rm 827 1 Clinton Sq Albany NY 12207 Office Phone: 202-225-5076, 518-465-0700. Office Fax: 202-225-5077, 518-427-5107.*

TONN, ELVERNE MERYL, pediatric dentist, dental benefits consultant, forensic odontologist; b. Stockton, Calif., Dec. 10, 1929; s. Emanuel M. and Lorna Darlene (Bryant) T.; m. Ann G. Richardson, Oct. 28, 1951; children: James Edward, Susan Elaine (dec.). AA, La Sierra U., Riverside, Calif., 1949; DDS, U. So. Calif., 1955; BS, Excelsior Coll., 1984; grad., Citizens Police Acad., Manteca, 2003, San Joaquin County Citizens Sheriff's Acad. Cert. lifetime cmty. coll. instr., tchg. credential Calif., 1982; lic. dentist Calif., 1955, diplomate Am. Bd. Quality Assurance and Utilization Rev. Physicians, Am. Bd. Forensic Dentistry, Am. Bd. Spl. Care Dentistry, Am. Bd. for Cert. in Homeland Security, cert. dental cons., forensic cons. Am. Coll. Forensic Examiners, 2004, med. investigator Am. Coll. Forensic Examiners, 2004. Pediat. dentistry intern Childrens Hosp. LA, 1957—59; pediatric dentist, assoc. Walker Dental Group, Long Beach, Calif., 1957-59, Children's Dental Clinic, Sunnyvale, Calif., 1959-61; pediatric dentist in pvt. practice Mountain View, Calif., 1961-72; pediatric dentist, ptnr. Pediatric Dentistry Assocs., Los Altos, Calif., 1972-83; pediatric dentist, ptnr. Valley Oak Dental Group, Manteca, Calif., 1987—2003; from clin. instr. to assoc. prof. Sch. Dentistry, U. Pacific, San Francisco, 1964-84; assoc. prof. Sch. Dentistry, U. Calif., San Francisco, 1984-86. 2pediat. dental cons. Delta Dental Plan, San Francisco, 1985—2002; chief dental staff El Camino Hosp., Mountain View, Calif., 1964—65, 1984—85; dental cons. Interplast program Stanford U. Sch. Medicine, 1973; cert. physician adv. Physicians' Review Network, Phoenix, 2004—; peer review cons. Broadspire Svcs. Inc.; Fla., 2009—; forensic dental cons. San Joaquin County Sheriff/Coroner, 2007—; appt. Weekly columnist Manteca Bull., 1987-92; producer 2 teaching videos, 1986; contbr. articles to profl. jours. Extern, dentist for disabled Long Island Jewish Med. Ctr., 1970. Capt. US Army, 1955—63. Recipient Dr. Willard Fleming Meritorious Svcs. award, Am. Coll. Dentists, 2006. Fellow Am. Coll. Dentists, Internat. Coll. Dentists, Am. Acad. Pediatric Dentistry, Royal Soc. Health, Acad. of Dentistry for Handicapped, Pierre Fauchard Acad., Acad. Dental Materials, Am. Soc. Dentistry for Children (mastership award 2001), Am. Acad. Forensic Scis., Am. Coll. Forensic Examiners; mem. ADA, Internat. Assn. Pediatric Dentistry, Internat. Assn. Dental Rsch., Am. Soc. Forensic Odontology, Fedn. Dentaire Internationale, Am. Assn. Dental Cons., Calif. Dental Assn., Calif. Soc. Dentistry for Children (pres. 1968), Calif. Soc. Pediatric Dentistry, NY Acad. Scis., Calif. Acad. Sci., Rotary Internat. (Paul Harris fellow 1990), Manteca Police Dept. (Badge 2003), Nat. Disaster Med. Svc., Disaster Mortuary Org. Response Team (DMORT region 9), Am. Coll. Med. Quality, Manteca Cert. Emergency Response Team, Calif. State Dental Identification Team, AMA (assoc.). Republican. Avocations: photography, travel, medieval history, anthropology. Home and Office: Tonn Forensic Cons Svcs 2420 Bellchase Dr Manteca CA 95336-5108 Personal E-mail: emtonn@comcast.net.

TONN, ROBERT JAMES, retired entomologist; b. Watertown, Wis., June 23, 1927; s. Harry James and Elise (Foogman) Tonn; m. Noemi C. Tonn; children: Sigrid M., Monica E. BS, Colo. State U., 1949, MS, 1950; MPH, Okla. Med. Sch., 1963; PhD, Okla. State U., 1959. Rsch. assoc La. State U., Costa Rica/New Orleans, 1961-63; dir. Taunton (Mass.) Field Sta., 1963-65; chief PMO unit WHO, various locations, 1965-87; ret., 1987. Adj. prof. parasitology U. Tex., El Paso, 1988—; cons. USAID/VBC, 1987—. Contbr. articles to profl. jours. Mem.: Royal Soc. Tropical Medicine and Hygiene, US/Mex. Border Health Assn., Am. Mosquito Control Assn., Soc. Vector Ecology (pres. 1984), Am. Soc. Tropical Medicine, Masons. Congregationalist. Home: 4247 Winchester Rd Las Cruces NM 88011 also: PO Box 772 Cloudcroft NM 88317 Personal E-mail: tonnapollo@aol.com.

TONON, GIOVANNI, medical researcher; s. Giuseppe Tonon and Adele De Nardi; m. Caniato Tonon, May 29, 1994; children: Daniele, Giuseppe, Jacopo. MD, U. Milan, PhD, 2002. Rsch. fellow Nat. Cancer Inst., Bethesda, Md., 1998—2003; instr. medicine Dana Farber Cancer Inst., Boston, 2003—. Contbr. scientific papers. Recipient Career Devel. award, Spore, 2004—06, Postdoc. Traineeship award, NIH, 1998—2001, Brian D. Novis Rsch. award, Internat. Myeloma Found., 2006; Spl. fellowship, Leukemia and Lymphoma Soc., 2006—. Office: via Olgettina 60 Milan 20132 Italy E-mail: tonon.giovanni@hsr.it.

TONSAGER, DALLAS P., federal agency administrator; b. 1954; m. Sharon Tonsager; children: Keith, Joshua. BS in Agrl., SD State U., 1976. Co-owner Plainview Farm, Oldham, SD; SD state rural devel. dir. USDA, 1993—2001; exec. dir. SD Value-Added Agr. Devel. Ctr., 2002—04; bd. dirs. Farm Credit Sys. Insurance Corp., 2004—; bd. mem. Farm Credit Adminstrn., 2004—; under sec. for rural devel. USDA, Washington, 2009—. Pres. SD Farmers Union, 1988—93; bd. mem. Green Thumb, Inc., 1988—93, Nat. Farmers Union Insurance, 1989—93; mem. adv. bd. Commodity Futures Trading Commn., 1990—93. Former bd. mem. Luth. Social Svcs., SD. Office: USDA 1400 Independence Ave, SW Washington DC 20250 E-mail: Dallas.Tonsager@usda.gov.*

TONTIRUTTANANON, CHANNARONG, electrical engineer, researcher; b. Muang, Surin, Thailand, 1971; B in Engring., Chulalongkorn U., Bangkok, 1992; MS, Auburn U., 1997, PhD, 1998. Instr. Assumption U., Bangkok, 1992—95; grad. rsch. asst. Auburn (Ala.) U., 1995—98; postdoctoral rsch. fellow U. Iowa, Iowa City, 1999; sr. mem. sci. staff Nortel Networks Inc., Richardson, Tex., 1999—. Contbr. articles to profl. jours. Mem.: IEEE, Am. Math. Soc., Phi Kappa Phi, Eta Kappa Nu. Achievements include patents for overload control system and method for a telecommunication system. Business E-Mail: channarong@nortel.com.

TOOBIN, JEFFREY ROSS, writer, legal analyst; b. NYC, May 21, 1960; s. Jerome and Marlene (Sanders) Toobin; m. Amy Bennett McIntosh, May 31, 1986; children: Ellen Frances, Adam Jerome. AB magna cum laude, Harvard Coll., 1982; JD magna cum laude, Harvard Law Sch., 1986. Bar: NY 1987. Law clk. Hon. J. Edward Lumbard, NYC, 1986—87; assoc. counsel Indep. Counsel Lawrence Walsh, Washington, 1987—89; asst. US atty. (ea. dist.) NY US Dept. Justice, Bklyn., 1990—93; legal analyst ABC News, NYC, 1996—2002; staff writer The New Yorker, NYC, 1993—; sr. analyst CNN, NYC, 2002—. Author: Opening Arguments: A Young Lawyer's First Case—United States v. Oliver North, 1992, The Run of His Life: The People v. O.J. Simpson, 1997, A Vast Conspiracy: The Real Story of the Sex Scandal That Nearly Brought Down a President, 2000, Too Close to Call: The Thirty-Six-Day Battle to Decide the 2000 Election, 2001, The Nine: Inside the Secret World of the Supreme Court, 2007 (J. Anthony Lukas Book prize). Recipient Emmy award for coverage of Elian Gonzales custody saga, 2000. Office: The New Yorker 4 Times Sq New York NY 10036-6592 Office Phone: 212-286-5886. Business E-Mail: jeffrey_toobin@newyorker.com.*

TOOKER, GEORGE, painter, printmaker; b. Bklyn., Aug. 5, 1920; s. George Clair and Angela Montejo (Roura) Tooker. BA, Harvard U., 1942; student, Art Students League, NYC, 1943-44. Instr. Art Students League, NY, 1965-68. One-man shows include Edwin Hewitt Gallery, 1951, 1955, Robert Isaacson Gallery, 1960, 1962, Durfacher Bros., 1964, 1967, Hopkins Ctr. Dartmouth Coll., 1967, Fine Arts Mus., San Francisco, 1974, Mus. Contemporary Art, Chgo., 1974, Whitney Mus., NYC, 1975, Indpls. Mus. Art, 1975, DC Moore Gallery, 1997, 1998, 2000, 2007, exhibited in group shows at Ann. Exhbn. Contemporary Am. Painting, Whitney Mus., 1947—50, 1953, 1955—58, 1961, 1963, 1965, 1967, 1969, Cadmus, French & Tooker, the Early Years, 1990, The Am. Century 1900-1950, 1999, Symbolic Realism in Am. Painting, Inst. Contemporary Arts, London, 1950, Ann. Am. Exhbn., Art Inst. Chgo., 1951, 1952, 1954, 1959, Am. Painting, Va. Mus., 1954, 1962, Am. Artists Paint the City, Venice Biennale, 1956, Ann. Exhbn. Painting & Sculpture, Pa. Acad. Fine Arts, 1966, Selected Works on Paper, Marisa Del Re Gallery, NYC, 1982, Contemporary Artists in Vt., Robert Hall Fleming Mus., U. Vt., 1984, Modern Am. Realism, Nat. Mus. Am. Art, Washington, 1987, Men Without Women, Paul Cadmus as Curator, NAD Mus., NYC, 1999, Surrealism USA, 2005, Twentieth-Cent. Am. Art, Nat. Gallery Art, Washington, 2000, Making Choices 1929-55, MoMA, NYC, 2000, Cadmus French Tooker, Columbus (Ohio) Mus. Art, 2001, Am. Tableaux, Miami Art Mus., 2003, Ann. Exhbn., NAD, NYC, 2005, Represented in permanent collections Smithsonian Nat. Mus. Am. Art, Smithsonian Hirshorn Mus., Whitney Mus., Dartmouth Coll., Met. Mus., Walker Art Ctr., Mus. Modern Art, S.C. Johnson & Sons, Inc., Art, USA, Sara Roby Fund Collection Am. Art, Addison Gallery, Ariz. State U. Gallery, Bklyn. Mus., Columbus (Ohio) Mus. Recipient Vt. Gov.'s award for Excellence in Arts, 1983, Nat. Medal Arts, 2007; grantee, Nat. Inst. Arts and Letters, 1960. Mem.: AAAL, NAD (assoc. 1968, academician 1970, Eric Isenbeurger prize 2005). Office: care DC Moore Gallery 724 5th Ave New York NY 10019-4106 Home: 97 Advent Hill Hartland VT 05048-0385 Office Phone: 212-247-2111.

TOOKEY, KEITH R., computer science professor; s. Harvey and Mary Tookey; m. Geraldine Tookey, Aug. 8, 1981. MS, U. Ill., Urbana-Champaign, 1981, U. Wis., Madison, 1990, PhD, 1994. Assoc. prof. Morningside Coll., Sioux City, Iowa, 1981—88; grad. asst. U. Wis., 1987—94; asst. prof. Columbia Coll., Mo., 1994—98; prof. Eureka Coll., Ill., 1998—. Mem. Consortium for Computing in Small Colleges. Nat. jamboree vol. Boy Scouts Am., Fort AP Hill, Va., 2005; cub scout leader Watamalo Dist. Boy Scouts, Wash., Ill., 1998—2005; boy scout adult leader Troop 163, Wash., 2001—; Sunday sch. tchr. Baha'i Faith, Peoria. Mem.: Sigma Xi (life). Independent. Bahai Faith. Office: Eureka Coll 300 Eureka College Eureka IL 61571 Business E-Mail: tookey@eureka.edu.

TOOLE, JAMES FRANCIS, medical educator; b. Atlanta, Mar. 22, 1925; s. Walter O'Brien and Helen (Whitehurst) T.; m. Patricia Anne Wooldridge, Oct. 25, 1952; children: William, Anne, James, Douglas Sean, Lauren, James, Robert, Dean, Tyler, Kyle, Kaitlin, Grace. BA, Princeton U., 1947; MD, Cornell U., 1949; LLB, LaSalle Extension U., 1963; Dr. Honoris Causa, U. Targu Mures, Romania, 1998. Intern, then resident internal medicine and neurology U. Pa. Hosp., London, 1949—55, Nat. Hosp., London, 1955—56; mem. faculty U. Pa. Sch. Medicine, 1959—61; prof. neurology, chmn. dept. Sch. Medicine Wake Forest Bapt. Hosp., 1962—83. Vis. prof. neuroscis. U. Calif., San Diego, 1969—70; vis. scholar Oxford U., 1989; mem. Nat. Bd. Med. Examiners, 1970—76; mem. task force arteriosclerosis Nat. Heart Lung & Blood Inst., 1970—81; chmn. 6th and 7th Princeton confs. cerebrovascular diseases; cons. epidemiology WHO, Japan, 1972, 73, 93, USSR, 68, Switzerland, 74, Côte d'Ivoire, 77; mem. Lasker Awards com., 1976—77; chmn. neuropharmacologic drugs com. FDA, 1979; chair Commn. on Presdl. Disability, 1994—97; cons. NASA, 1966. Author: Cerebrovascular Diseases, 7th edit., Translation into Chinese, Japanese, Portugese, Spanish, German, Russian., 1999; editor: Current Concepts in Cerebrovascular Disease, 1969—73, Jour. Neurol. Sci., 1990—97; mem. editl. bd. Annals Internal Medicine, 1968—75, Stroke, 1972—74; mem. editl. bd. Jour. AMA, 1975—77; mem. editl. bd. Ann. Neurology, 1980—86, Jour. of Neurology, 1985—89. Pres. N.C. Heart Assn., 1976-77. Served with AUS, 1950-51; flight surgeon USNR, 1951-53. Decorated Bronze Star with V, Combat Med. badge. Master: ACP (licentiate); fellow: AAAS (life), Royal Coll. Physicians; mem.: AMA, Am. Acad. Neurology Rsch. Found., Am. Chem. Soc., Soc. for Neurosci., Hungarian Neurol. Soc., Polish Neurol. Soc., N.C. Stroke Assn. (pres. 1999—2001), Nat. Stroke Assn. (bd. dirs. 1993—, exec. com. 1994—, chmn. Commn. on U.S. Presdl. Disability 1994—), Russian Acad. Neurology (hon.), Am. Clin. and Climatol Assn. (life), Assn. Brit. Neurologists (hon.), German Neurol. Soc. (hon.), Austrian Soc. Neurology (hon.), Irish Neurol. Assn. (hon.), Internat. Stroke Soc. (exec. com. 1989—97, program chmn. 1992, pres. 1999—2004), Am. Soc. Neuroimaging (pres. 1992—94), Am. Acad. Neurology (bd. mem. 2004—09), World Fedn. Neurology (sec.-treas. 1982—89, mgmt. com. 1990—98, pres. 1998—2001, chmn. Rsch. and Edn. Found. 1999—2004), Am. Neurol. Assn. (sec.-treas. 1978—82, pres. 1984—85, historian 1988—, archivist 2004), Am. Physiol. Soc., Am. Heart Assn. (chmn. com. ethics 1970—75), Bohemian Club. Home: 1836 Virginia Rd Winston Salem NC 27104-2316 Office Phone: 336-716-2338. Business E-Mail: jtoole@wfubmc.edu.

TOOLE, JOAN TRIMBLE, financial consultant; b. Ipswich, Mass., Apr. 3, 1923; d. Dana Newcomb and Barbara (Campbell) T.; m. John R. Marchi, Dec. 28, 1943 (div. Aug. 1959); children: Jon, Jael, Charis, Peter; m. Kenneth Ross Toole, Apr. 22, 1960 (dec. Aug. 1981); children: Dana O'Keefe, David Campbell. BA, Antioch Coll., Yellow Springs, Ohio, 1946; MS in Fin., U. Mont., 1976; MPA, Harvard U., 1985. Rancher J/J and KJ Ranches, 1955-82; Mont. legis. asst., researcher, 1981-83; cons. Mont. Dept. Revenue, 1985-87, U. Mont. Biol. Sta., 1987-89; pvt. practice, 1987—. State coord. Cranston for Pres., 1983-84; lobbyist Office Pub. Instrn., 1989-90; tax appeals bd. Ravalli County, 1981-84; active Mont. Bd. Natural Resources and Conservation, 1986-90, LWV, Mont. Environ. Info. Ctr., No. Plains Resource Coun.; bd. dirs. Mont. Conservation Voters, 1992—; mem. Lewis & Clark City County Health Bd., 1994-98, treas. Montanans for Coal Trust, 1999-2005, Montanans for Common Sense Mining, 1998-, Mont. Property Owners; bd. dirs. Forever Wild Endowment; vol. money mgmt. Rocky Mountain Devel. Co. Mem. AARP (vol. income tax preparer 1993—), Harvard Club (bd. dirs. ch. schs. and scholarships), Mont. Dem. Womens Club (regional dir.), Sr. Med. Protection Program(RSVP vol.), City-County Hist. Preservation Commn. Democrat. Episcopalian. Home and Office: 211 S Montana Helena MT 59601 Office Phone: 406-439-1729.

TOOMAJIAN, WILLIAM MARTIN, lawyer; b. Troy, NY, Sept. 26, 1943; s. Leo R. Toomajian and Elizabeth (Gundrum) Toomajian; children: Andrew, Philip. AB, Hamilton Coll., 1965; JD, U. Mich., 1968; LLM, NYU, 1975. Bar: N.Y. 1968, Ohio 1978. Mem. firm Cadwalader, Wickersham & Taft, NYC, 1971—77, Baker Hostetler LLP, Cleve., 1977—. Lt. U.S. Coast Guard, 1968—71. Mem.: ABA, Cleve. Tax Club, Cleve. Bar Assn., Ohio Bar Assn. Home: 3582 Lytle Rd Cleveland OH 44122-4908 Office: Baker Hostetler LLP 3200 National City Ctr 1900 E 9th St Ste 3200 Cleveland OH 44114-3475 Business E-Mail: wtoomajian@bakerlaw.com.

TOOMEY, DANIEL E., lawyer; b. Bklyn., Sept. 17, 1942; BA, St. Peter's Coll., 1964; JD, Georgetown U., 1967. Bar: Md., DC, Va., US Supreme Ct., Fed. Cir. Ct. of Appeals, US Dist. Courts. Law clk. Chief Judge Andrew M. Hood DC Ct. Appeals, 1967—68; asst. US atty. US Atty. Office DC, 1968—72; ptnr. Sachs Greenebaum & Tayler, 1972—78, Levin & Toomey, 1978—80, Grove Engelberg and Gross, 1980—84; shareholder Wickwire Gavin, 1984—96; ptnr. Thompson Hine, 1996—2002, Venable, 2002—07, Duane Morris LLP, 2007—. Mem. Washington Bldg. Congress; mem. adv. com. US Ct. Fed. Claims; adj. prof. law Georgetown U. Law Ctr., 1980—2000. Founder, team leader Georgetown/NITA Basic Trial Advocacy Skills Program, 1978—2003; program dir. NITA/DC Adv. Trial Advocacy Program, 2005—; faculty mem. NITA Tchr. Tng. Program, Harvard U., U. San Francisco; mem. We Are Family. Recipient Paul R. Dean award, Georgetown Law Ctr. Alumni Assn., 2007; named a Super Lawyer in Constrn. Litig., Super Lawyers, 2006—09; named to America's Leading Lawyers for Bus., 2009. Fellow: American Coll. Trial Lawyers; mem.: Inst. Pastoral Renewal (bd. mem. 1995—2005), US Attys. Assn. DC (pres. 1977—78, bd. mem.), ABA, Counsellors, Barristers. Office: Duane Morris LLP Ste 1000 505 9th St NW Washington DC 20004 Office Phone: 202-776-5291. Office Fax: 202-478-2873. Business E-Mail: detoomey@duanemorris.com.*

TOOMEY, DAVID CHARLES, lawyer; b. St. Johnsbury, Vt., Aug. 3, 1938; s. Charles Francis and Rosamond Stanwood (Melcher) Toomey; m. Caroline Stuckert, Aug. 17, 1963 (div. Sept. 1973); children: Charles, Christopher; m. Virginia Leigh Wood, Sept. 20, 1980. BA, Yale U., New Haven, 1960; LLB, U. Pa. Law Sch., 1963. Bar: Pa. 1964, US Dist. Ct. (ea. dist.) Pa. 1964, US Ct. Appeals (3rd cir.) 1964, Supreme Ct. Pa., US Supreme Ct. 1964. Assoc. Duane Morris LLP, Phila., 1963—70, ptnr., 1970—98, of counsel, 1999—, mem. ptnrs. bd., 1991—98. Bd. dirs. Cmty. Legal Svcs., Phila., 1972—82, pres., 1980—82, 1995—98; bd. dirs. Buck Hill Falls Co., Pa., 1997—. Contbr. articles to profl. jours. Recipient Champion award, Cmty. Legal Svcs., 1993. Mem.: ABA, Phila. Bar Assn. (bd. govs. 1972—75), Pa. Bar Assn., Def. Rsch. Inst. Republican. Roman Catholic. Avocations: golf, skiing. Office: Duane Morris LLP 30 S 17th St Philadelphia PA 19103-7424 Office Phone: 215-979-1000. Office Fax: 215-689-4456. Business E-Mail: Toomey@duanemorris.com.*

TOOMEY, JEANNE ELIZABETH, animal activist; b. NYC, Aug. 22, 1921; d. Edward Aloysius and Anna Margaret (O'Grady) Toomey; m. Peter Terranova, Sept. 28, 1951 (dec. 1968); children: Peter Terranova (dec.), Sheila Terranova Beasley. Student, Hofstra U., 1938-40; student law sch., Fordham U., 1940-41; BA, Southampton Coll., 1976; post-grad., Monmouth Coll., 1978-79. Reporter, columnist Bklyn. Daily Eagle, 1943-52; with The Fitzgeralds, NBC Radio, NYC, 1952-53; reporter, writer King Features Syndicate, NYC, 1953-55; reporter, columnist N.Y. Jour.-Am., NYC, 1955-61; newsman AP, NYC, 1963-64; stringer; columnist News Tribune, Woodbridge, NJ, 1976-86; editor Calexico (Calif.) Chronicle, 1987-88; editor community sect. Asbury Park (N.J.) Press, 1988; pres., dir. Last Post Animal Sanctuary, Falls Village, Conn., 1989—. Author: Murder in the Hamptons, 1994, Assignment Homicide, 1998. Chmn. com. to establish Wildlife Preserve Hackensack Meadows, NJ, 1968—69. Named Woman of the Yr. N.Y. Women's Press Club, 1960. Mem. Newswomen's Club of N.Y., Overseas Press Club, N.Y. Press Club, Silurians. Roman Catholic. Home: 250 Foreside Rd Falmouth ME 04105-1729 Office Phone: 860-824-0831. Office Fax: 860-824-5460.

TOOMEY, KATHLEEN ELIZABETH, federal agency administrator; b. Aspinwall, Pa., Nov. 21, 1951; AB in biology cum laude, Smith Coll., 1973; MPH, MD, Harvard U., 1979. Diplomate Am. Bd. of Family Practice, Nat. Bd. of Med. Examiners. Resident dept. family medicine U. Wash., Seattle, 1979-82; clin. dir. Alaska Native Hosp., Kotzebue, 1982-85; Pew Health Policy fellow Inst. for Health Policy Studies, U. Calif. Sch. Medicine, San Francisco, 1985-87; Epidemic Intelligence Svc. officer Nat. Ctr. for Prevention Svcs., Ctrs. for Disease Control, Atlanta, 1987-89; legis. asst. on health issues to Senator John Chafee, U.S. Senate, Washington, 1991; asst. to dir. for external rels., 1989-90; state epidemiologist, dir. epidemiology and prevention br. Divsn. of Pub. Health, Ga. Dept. of Human Resources, 1993-97, dir. Atlanta, 1997—2005; dir. coordinating ctr. health promotion Ctr. for Disease Control and Prevention, Atlanta, 2005—. Adj. assoc. prof. in epidemiology Rollins Sch. of Pub. Health, Emory U.; clin. assoc. prof. Morehouse U. Sch. Medicine, Emory U.; mem. Statewide Child Fatality Rev. Panel, 1998; mem. Bd. Health Promotion and Disease Prevention, Inst. of Medicine, 1998—; mem. Tech. Adv. Group on Devolution and Federalism, Nat. Health Policy Forum, George Washington U., 1998—. Mem. task force The Nat. Campaign to Prevent Teen Pregnancy, 1996-99. Fulbright scholar, 1973-74; Public Health award, American Academy Family Physicians, 2003. Mem. Am. Acad. Family Physicians, Am. Pub. Health Assn. (governing coun. Ga. state chpt. rep. 1997-99), Am. Sexually Transmitted Diseases Assn., Assn. State and Territorial Health Ofcls. (exec. com. 1998—), Ga. Acad. Family Physicians, Ga. Pub. Health Assn., Med. Assn. Atlanta, Med. Assn. Ga. (pub. health and preventative health care com. 1997—). Office: Coordinating Ctr Health Promotion 4770 Buford Hwy Atlanta GA 30341-3717 E-mail: ket1@dhr.state.ga.us.*

TOOMEY, PATRICK JOSEPH, former United States Representative from Pennsylvania; b. Providence, Nov. 17, 1961; m. Kris Toomey, 1997; children: Bridget, Patrick Jr. BA in Govt., cum laude, Harvard U., 1984. Investment banking Chem. Bank N.Y.; v.p., dir. U.S. subsidiary British merchant bank; founder Toomey Enterprises, Inc., Allentown, Pa.; mem. US Congress from 15th Pa. Dist., 1999—2005; pres., CEO The Club for Growth, Washington, 2004—09. Bd. dirs. Commonwealth Found., 2007—. Republican. Roman Catholic. Achievements include Toomey Enterprises, Inc., a family restaurant bus., operates 2 Rookies Restaurants located in Allentown and Lancaster, Pa.*

TOOMEY, RICHARD ANDREW, JR., lawyer; b. Portsmouth, NH, Oct. 21, 1944; s. Richard Andrew and Elizabeth Neal (Rylander) T.; m. Jeanne Zurmuhlen; 1 child, Samuel Van Pelt. BA, U. N.H., 1966; JD, NYU, 1969. Bar: N.Y. 1969, Mass. 1989. Atty. VISTA, Mpls., 1969-71; assoc. Carter, Ledyard & Milburn, NYC, 1971-77; v.p., sr. assoc. counsel Chase Manhattan Bank, NYC, 1977-89; gen. coun. Shawmut Bank NA, Boston, 1989-94; dep. gen. coun. Shawmut Nat. Corp., Boston, 1995; group sr. counsel Fleet Fin. Group, Boston, 1996-2000; gen. counsel Fleet Bank NA, Jersey City, 1996—2000; asst. gen. counsel Sovereign Bank, Boston, 2000—05, gen. counsel, 2006—. Mem.: Greater Boston Legal Svcs. (dir.), Cmty. Found. Southeastern Mass., Boston Bar Assn. E-mail: rtoomey@sovereignbank.com.

TOOMRE, ALAR, applied mathematician, theoretical astronomer; b. Rakvere, Estonia, Feb. 5, 1937; came to US, 1949, naturalized, 1955; s. Elmar and Linda (Aghen) T.; m. Joyce Stetson, June 15, 1958; children: Lars, Erik, Anya. BS in Aero. Engring., BS in Physics, MIT, 1957; PhD in Fluid Mechanics, U. Manchester, Eng., 1960. C.L.E. Moore instr. math. dept. MIT, Cambridge, 1960-62, asst. prof. applied math., 1963-65, assoc. prof., 1965-70, prof., 1970—; fellow Inst. for Advanced Study, Princeton, NJ, 1962-63. Contbr. articles to profl. jours. Guggenheim fellow, 1969-70, MacArthur fellow, 1984-89; Fairchild scholar, 1975, Marshall scholar, 1957-60 Fellow AAAS; mem. Am. Astron. Soc. (Dirk Brouwer award 1993), Internat. Astron. Union, Am. Acad. Arts and Scis., Nat. Acad. Scis. Office: MIT 77 Massachusetts Ave Rm 2-371 Cambridge MA 02139-4307 Office Phone: 617-253-4326. Business E-Mail: toomre@math.mit.edu.

TOOMRE, JURI, astrophysicist, educator; b. Kuusalu, Estonia, Aug. 29, 1940; s. Elmar and Linda Toomre; m. Linda Christine Morris, Sept. 15, 1963; children: Derek Kalev, Krista Anar Toomre Johnson. BSc, MIT, Cambridge, Mass., MSc, 1963; PhD, U. Cambridge, 1967. Asst. prof., math. NYU, 1969—71; assoc. prof., astro-geophysics U. Colo., Boulder, 1971—75, prof., astrophysics, & fellow JILA, 1975—. Contbr. articles to profl. jours. Mem.: Am. Astron. Soc. Home: 97 Meadowlook Way Boulder CO 80304-0431 Office: Univ Colo Boulder JILA Tower A606 Boulder CO 80309-0440 Business E-Mail: jtoomre@jila.colorado.edu.

TOORAWA, SHAWKAT M., social studies educator; b. London, Sept. 1, 1963; s. Mahmood Hasham Toorawa and Zubeida Abbasbhai Ebramjee; m. Hawan Bibi Areff Bahemia, Aug. 15, 1991; children: Maryam, Asiya Tanveer Jahan. BA in Oriental Studies with honors, U. Pa., Phila., 1985, AM in Arabic and Islamic Studies, 1988, PhD in Arabic Lit., 1998. Instr. Duke U., Durham, NC, 1989—91; lectr. U. Mauritius, Reduit, 1996—2000; assoc. prof. Cornell U., Ithaca, NY, 2000—. Mgr. Indian Ocean Traders Sdn. Bhd., Kuala Lumpur, Malaysia, 1991—92, Toorawa Exports Ltd., Port Louis, Mauritius, 1993—95. Chmn., editor Hassam Toorawa Trust, Port Louis, 1994. Recipient Perkins prize, Cornell U., 2006; African Humanities Inst. Jr. fellowship, Rockefeller Found., Du Bois Inst., Harvard U., 1999—2000, New Directions fellowship, Mellon Found., 2006—, Sr. fellowship, Am. Inst. Indian Studies, 2006, Vis. scholar, Wolfson Coll., Oxford, Eng., 2006, Vis. fellowship, Oxford Ctr. Islamic Studies, 2007. Mem.: Am. Oriental Soc. (dir. 2004—). Muslim. Office: Cornell Univ Dept Near Eastern Studies 408 White Hall Ithaca NY 14853-7901 Office Fax: 607-255-6450. Business E-Mail: smt24@cornell.edu.

TOOTELL, GEOFFREY MATTHEW BEMIS, economist; s. Geoffrey Howland and Anne Whelan Tootell; m. Catherine Mary O'Neil, Apr. 25, 1987; children: Anne, Catherine, Rosemary. BA, Harvard U., Cambridge, Mass., 1983, PhD, 1989. V.p. and economist Fed. Res. Bank Boston, 1998—2007, dep. dir. rsch., 2008—. Contbr. articles to profl. jour. Home: 16 Canoe River Rd Sharon MA 02067 Office: Fed Res Bank Boston 600 Atlantic Ave Boston MA 02210

TOOTLE, KATHLEEN MALOOF, special education educator; b. Columbus, Ga., July 10, 1973; d. Ted R. and Susan V. Maloof; m. Brian Steven Tootle, Feb. 20, 1999; children: Laney E., Gentry W., Colby M. EdB, Ga. Southern U., Statesboro, 1995; MEd, Augusta State U., Ga., 1998. Spl. edn. tchr. Richmond County Sch. Sys., Augusta, 1995—98, Candler County Sch. Sys., Metter, Ga., 1998—2006; coll. instr. Ga. Southern U., 2006—. Com. chair Vision Com., Metter, 2008—09. Mem.: Coun. Exceptional Children. Home: 8707 Hope Valley Circle Metter GA 30439 Office: Georgia Southern Univ PO Box 8134 Statesboro GA 30460 Business E-Mail: ktootle@georgiasouthern.edu.

TOP, EVA MARIA, science educator; m. Larry Forney. PhD, Ghent U., Belgium, 1993. Docent Ghent U., 2000—03; rsch. assoc. prof. U. Idaho, Moscow, 2001—04, assoc. prof., 2004—08, prof., 2008—. Office: Univ Idaho 252 Life Scis South Moscow ID 83844-3051

TOP, FRANKLIN HENRY, JR., physician, researcher; b. Detroit, Mar. 1, 1936; s. Franklin Henry Sr. and Mary (Madden) T.; m. Lois Elizabeth Fritzell, Sept. 23, 1961; children: Franklin H. III, Brian N., Andrew M. BS, Yale U., 1957, MD cum laude, 1961. Diplomate Am. Bd. Pediatrics. Intern, resident, infectious diseases fellow U. Minn. Hosps., Mpls., 1961—66; commd. officer U.S. Army, advanced through grades to col.; med. officer, dept. virus diseases Walter Reed Army Inst. Research, Washington, 1966—70, chief dept. virus diseases, 1973—76; dir. divsn. communicable diseases and immunology Walter Reed Army Inst. Rsch., Washington, 1976—79, dep. dir., 1979—81, dir. and comdt., 1983—87; chief dept. virology Seato Med. Rsch. Lab., Bangkok, 1970—73; comdr. U.S.A. Med. Rsch. Inst. of Chem. Def., Aberdeen Proving Ground, Md., 1981—83; ret. U.S. Army, 1987; sr. v.p. Praxis Biologics Inc., Rochester, NY, 1987—88; exec. v.p. MedImmune, Inc., Gaithersburg, Md., 1988—2004; sr. v.p. MedImmune Ventures, Gaithersburg, Md., 2004—. Contbr. over 40 articles to med. jours. Decorated Legion of Merit with 2 oak leaf clusters. Fellow Am. Acad. Pediatrics, Infectious Diseases Soc. Am.; mem. AMA, Alpha Omega Alpha. Avocation: ornithology. Office Phone: 301-398-4251. Business E-Mail: topf@medimmune.com.

TOPALOGLU, ZEYNEP, economics professor; b. Kayseri, Turkey, Nov. 19, 1982; d. Umit and Nezihe Topaloglu. BA in Economics, Bogazici U., Istanbul, Turkey, 2004; MA, Hunter Coll., NYC, 2007; PhD, CUNY Grad. Ctr., NYC, 2009. Lectr. Queens Coll., Flushing, NY, 2005—, Baruch Coll., NYC, 2007—. Cons. & rep. IDCNJ, Newark, 2006—. Fellowship, GC Office Provost, 2004—. Master: Turkish Students.

TOPAZI, ANTHONY J., utilities executive; b. 1950; BSEE, Auburn U., Ala. Coop. edn. student Ala. Power Southern Co., 1969, various positions including Western divsn. v.p. and Birmingham divsn. v.p. Ala. Power, sr. v.p. Southern Power, exec. v.p. Southern Co. Generation and Energy Mktg., pres., CEO Miss. Power, 2004—. Bd. dirs. Hancock Bank. Mem. steering com., co-chair econ. devel. work group Blueprint Miss.; chmn. Momentum Miss.; vice chmn. Miss. Partnership for Econ. Devel.; mem. Miss. Gulf Coast Econ. Devel. Coun., Miss. Gulf Coast C. of C., DeToqueville Soc. of United Way of Am.; bd. trustees Nature Conservancy Miss.; bd. dirs. Miss. Econ. Coun., Gulf Coast Cmty. Found., Miss. World Trade Ctr. Office: Miss Power Co 2992 W Beach Blvd Gulfport MS 39501 Office Phone: 866-251-1943.*

TOPEL, DAVID GLEN, agricultural studies educator; b. Lake Mills, Wis., Oct. 24, 1937; BS, U. Wis., 1960; MS, Kans. State U., 1962; PhD, Mich. State U., 1965; DSc (hon.), Szent Istvan U., Godallo, Hungary, 2002. Assoc. prof. animal sci. and food tech. Iowa State U., Ames, 1967-73, prof. animal sci. and food tech., 1973-79, dean Coll. Agr., 1988-2000, dir. agr. and home econs. experiment sta., 1988-2000; prof., head dept. Auburn U., Ala., 1979—88, M.E. Ensminger endowed chair animal sci., 2000—. Cons., presenter, lectr. in field; mem. Gov. of Iowa's Sci. Adv. Coun., 1990-2000, Gov. of Iowa's Livestock Revitalization Task Force, 1993-98; chair Gov.'s Environ. Agr. Com., 1994; mem. Iowa Corn Promotion Bd.; mem. faculty Royal Vet. and Agrl. U., Denmark, 1971-72; vis. prof. Nat. Taiwan U., 1972. Author: The Pork Industry - Problems and Progress, 1968. Secretariat World Food Prize, Iowa State U., Ames, 1991-96. Fulbright-Hays scholar Royal Vet. and Agrl. U., 1971-72; recipient award of merit Knights of Ak-Sar-Ben, 1973, Commr.'s award Agrl. Commr. Republic of China, 1977, disting. Achievement award Block and Bridle Club, 1979, Ala. Cattlemen's Assn.,1 984, Hon. State Farmer Degree, Ala., 1986, Harry L. Rudnick Educator's award Nat. Assn. Meat Purveyors, 1989, USDA Honor award, 1999, Hon. Prof. award Gyöngyös Coll., Hungary, 2000; named hon. prof. Ukrainian State Agrl. U., 1993. Fellow Am. Soc. Animal Sci. (Disting. Rsch. award in meat sci. 1979, Bouffault Internat. Agr. award 2002); mem. Am. Meat Sci. Assn., Inst. Food Tech., Iowa Crop Improvement Assn., Extension and Tchg. (pres. North Ctrl. Region 1992), Nat. Assn. State Univs. and Land-Grant Colls. (chair bd. agr. 1993, mem. commn. on food, environ. and renewable resources 1992-99), Ukrainian Acad. Agrl. Scis., Sigma Xi (Outstanding Achievement award Iowa chpt. 1993), Alpha Zeta, Gamma Sigma Delta (Internat. award). Presbyterian. Avocations: fishing, golf. Office: Iowa State U Coll Agriculture 2374 Kildee Hall Ames IA 50011-0001 Home: 4108 Laura Ct Ames IA 50010 Home Phone: 515-292-7543; Office Phone: 515-294-6304.

TOPEL, ROBERT, economics professor; b. LA, Mar. 24, 1952; married. PhD, U. Calif., LA. Brown prof. economics U. Chgo., 1979—. Founding ptnr. Chgo. Ptnr. LLC. Dir. Ingalls Hosp. & Health Sys., Harvey, Ill., 2000. Fellow: Soc. Labor Economists. Office: Univ Chgo 5807 S Woodlawn Chicago IL 60637

TOPINKA, JUDY BAAR, state official, political organization worker; b. Riverside, Ill., Jan. 16, 1944; d. William Daniel and Lillian Mary (Shuss) Baar; 1 child, Joseph Baar. BS, Northwestern U., 1966. Features editor, reporter, columnist Life Newspapers, Berwyn and LaGrange, Ill., 1966-77; with Forest Park (Ill.) Rev. and Westchester News, 1976-77; coord. spl. events dept. fedn. comm. AMA, 1978-80; rsch. analyst Senator Leonard Becker, 1978-79; mem. Ill. Ho. of Reps., 1981-84, Ill. Senate, 1985-94; treas. State of Ill., Springfield, 1995—; chmn. State Rep. Party, 2002—; candidate Gov. Ill., 2006. Former mem. judiciary com., former chmn. senate health and welfare com.; former mem. fin. instn. com.; former co-chmn. Citizens Coun. on Econ. Devel.; former co-chmn. U.S. Commn. for Preservation of Am.'s Heritage Abroad, serves on legis. ref. bur.; former mem. minority bus. resource ctr. adv. com. U.S. Dept. Transp.; former mem. adv. bd. Nat. Inst. Justice. Founder, pres., bd. dirs. West Suburban Exec. Breakfast Club, from 1976; chmn. Ill. Ethnics for Reagan-Bush, 1984, Bush-Quayle 1988; spokesman Nat. Coun. State Legislatures Health Com.; former mem. nat. adv. coun. health professions edn. HHS; mem., GOP chairwoman Legis. Audit Commn. of Cook County; chmn. Riverside Twp. Regular Republican Orgn., 1994—. Recipient Outstanding Civilian Svc. medal, Molly Pitcher award, Abraham Lincoln award, Silver Eagle award U.S. Army and N.G. Office: Office of Ill State Treasurer 100 W Randolph St Ste 15-600 Chicago IL 60601-3232

TOPLIN, ROBERT BRENT, history professor, television producer; b. Phila., Sept. 26, 1940; s. Maurice Cunningham and Janet Rachel (Belsinger) T.; m. Karin Bendel, Dec. 26, 1996; children: Cassandra, Jennifer. BS, Pa. State U., 1962; MA, Rutgers U., 1965, PhD, 1968. Asst. prof. Denison U., Granville, Ohio, 1968-74, assoc. prof., 1976-78; assoc. prof. and program dir. U. Houston-Clear Lake City, 1974-76; assoc. prof. U. N.C. at Wilmington, 1978-80, prof. history, 1980. Vis. prof. U. N.C.-Chapel Hill, 1983; media advisor NEH; lectr. in field. Project dir.: A House Divided (TV series) U.S.A.; A Television history, Pres.'s in Crisis, The Am. Frontier; author: The Abolition of Slavery in Brazil, 1972, Unchallenged Violence: An American Ordeal, 1975, Freedom and Prejudice: The Legacy of Slavery in the United States and Brazil, 1982, History By Hollywood: The use and Abuse of the American Past, 1996; author: Reel History: In Defense of Hollywood, 2002, Michael Moore's Fahrenheit 9/11: How One Film Divided a Nation, 2006, Radical Conservatism: The Right's Political Religion, 2006; editor: Slavery and Race Relations in Latin America, 1974; editor anthology: American History Through Film, 1983, Ken Burns's The Civil War: Historians Respond, 1996, Oliver Stone's USA: Film, History and Controversy, 2000, Masters at The Movies, 2006; contbg. editor: Jour. Am. History, 1986—2007, Perspectives, Am. Hist. Assoc., 1995 - 2000, 2007-; contbr. articles to profl. jours.; book reviewer various jours.; project dir.: (PBS TV) Denmark Vesey's Rebellion 1982, Solomon Northup's Odyssey, 1984; Charlotte Forten's Mission, 1985; (films) The War to End All Wars, 1985, Lincoln and the War Within, 1992; broadcast appearances on PBS TV, CBS TV, The History Channel, Turner Classic Movie Channel, C-SPAN. Pres. Williston Jr. H.S. PTA; v.p. New Hanover County PTA, New Hanover County Bd. Edn. Grantee or fellow Ford Found., 1967, NEH, 1970, 77-80, 82-89, 90-91, Am. Philos. Soc., 1970m 81, Denison U. Rsch. Found., 1972, Annenberg/Corp. for Pub. Broadcasting, 1983-84; grantee Ill. Humanities Coun., 1991; fellow Am. Coun. Learned Soc., 1991. Mem. Am. Hist. Assn. (tchg. com. 1990-93), Orgn. Am. Historians (mem. com. on radio, TV, film media 1978-80, Erik Barnouw prize 1985, 87-89), Conf. on Latin Am. History (com. on tchg. materials 1978), Erik Barnouw prize com. 1987-88. Democrat. Jewish. Home Phone: 434-989-3564. Business E-Mail: toplinrb@uncw.edu.

TOPLITT, GLORIA H., music educator, actress, vocalist; b. St. Louis, May 22, 1925; d. Wade Fitzgerald Hamilton and Neyneen Farrell Pires; m. James Parnell, 1942 (div. July 1949); 1 child, Dennis James Parnell; m. Abraham Toplitt, Aug. 19, 1968. Student, Guy Bates Post Acad. Dramatic Arts, LA, 1941-43. Stage performer, NYC, 1944-59; dir. entertainment Holland Am. Lines, 1959-61; tchr. voice North Hollywood Conservatory, Calif., 1965-67; pvt. voice tchr. North Hollywood, 1968-95; music specialist outreach program NASA Space Sci. and Tech., Inc., Springfield, Va., 1997—. Dir. Workshop Theatre Program, North Hollywood, 1968—78; coach for impaired voices, North Hollywood, 1968—. Author, composer: Parade of Planets, 1998, Space Challenge, 1999; actor: (plays, N.Y. stage prodns.) appeared as leading lady Oklahoma, Chocolate Soldier, Lend an Ear, Courtin' Time, Showboat, Take Me Along, Auld Lang Syne, Three Musketeers, Carousel, Oh! Captain, Brigadoon, Guys and Dolls, Hit the Deck, Finian's Rainbow, others; voice rec. Songs of Harriet Ware Meml., Smithsonian Instn. Mem. election bd. Office of Voter Registrar, North Hollywood, 1996—98. Avocations: poetry, travel, theater, elderhostel classes, reading. Home: 4405 Carpenter Ave North Hollywood CA 91607-4110

TOPOL, ERIC JEFFREY, academic administrator, cardiologist, educator, geneticist; b. NYC, June 26, 1954; s. Erwin and Susan (Lepp) T.; m. Susan Leah Merriman, May 5, 1979; children: Sarah, Evan. BA with highest distinction, U. Va., 1975; MD with honors, U. Rochester, 1979. Med. resident U. Calif., San Francisco, 1979-82; fellow Johns Hopkins U. Med. Ctr., Balt., 1982-85; asst. prof. U. Mich. Sch. Medicine, Ann Arbor, 1985-87, assoc. prof., 1987-90, prof., 1990; dir. cardiac catheterization labs. and interventional cardiology U. Mich. Med. Ctr., Ann Arbor, 1986-91; chmn. dept. cardiovasc. medicine Cleve. Clinic Found., dir. Ctr. for Thrombosis and Arterial Biology, 1991—2006; founder, provost, chief acad. officer Cleve. Clinic Lerner Coll. Medicine, Case Western Reserve Univ., 2002—05, prof. medicine, 2004—06; prof. genetics Case Western Reserve Univ. Sch. Medicine, 2006; dir., Scripps Translational Sci. Inst. The Scripps Rsch. Inst., 2007—, chief academic officer, Scripps Health, 2007—, sr. cons. divsn. cardiology, Scripps Clinic, 2007—, prof. molecular and exptl. medicine, 2007—, founding dean, Scripps Sch. Medicine, 2008—. Editor: Acute Coronary Intervention, 1988, Textbook of Interventional Cardiology, 1990, 4th edit., 2002, Textbook of Cardiovascular Medicine, 1st and 2d edits.; mem. editl. bd. Circulation, Circulation Rsch., Am. Jour. Cardiology, Coronary Art Disease, Jour. Am. Coll. Cardiology, Brit. Heart Jour.; mem. editl. bd. of several med. publs.; contbr. articles to profl. jours. Recipient Clin. Rsch. Innovator award, Doris Duke Charitable Found., 2003, Andres Gruentzig award, European Soc. Cardiology, 2004. Fellow ACP, Am. Coll. Cardiology (editor jour., Simon Dack award, 2005), Am. Soc. Clin. Investigation, Am. Heart Assn. (mem. coun. on clin. cardiology, coun. on circulation and thrombosis), European Soc. Cardiology; mem. Cen. Soc. Clin. Rsch., Am. Fedn. for Clin. Rsch. (councilor), Assn. Am. Physicians, AMA (Dr. William Beaumont award in Medicine 2002), IOM, NAS, John Hopkins Soc. Scholars. being one of the first scientists to raise doubts about the safety of Vioxx, and was a key witness in lawsuits against Merck & Co. Office: Scripps Translational Sci Inst 3344 N Torrey Plnes Ct La Jolla CA 92037

TOPPER, ELISA FREIDEN, former librarian, consultant; b. Jacksonville, Fla., Aug. 2, 1952; d. Phillp and Gina (Szulc) Freiden; m. Gene Edward Topper, Nov. 22, 1981; children: Samantha Paige, Amanda Leigh. B in Liberal Arts, U. South Fla., 1975; MLS, Fla. State U., 1978; M in Indsl. Rels., Loyola U., Chgo., 1985. Bus. libr. Jacksonville Pub.

Library, 1975-78; career libr. Chgo. Pub. Libr., 1978-81, asst. dir. pers., 1981-83; dir. info. svcs. Jewish Vocat. Svc., Chgo., 1983—95; dir. mem. svcs. Assn. Coll. & Rsch. Librs., 1995; asst. dean Dominican U. Grad. Sch. Libr. & Info. Sci., River Forest, Ill.; dir. Dundee Township Pub. Libr., Ill., 2004—08. Recipient Cert. of Svc. award, Assn. Computer-based Sys. for Career Info., 1995. Mem.: ALA, Spl. Librs. Assn. (chair profl. devel. com. Chgo. chpt.). Avocations: gourmet cooking, travel, theater, public speaking.*

TOPPETA, WILLIAM JOHN, insurance company executive, lawyer; b. NYC, Sept. 18, 1948; s. John Francis and Rita Ann (Carretta) Toppeta. BA, Fordham U., 1970; JD, NYU, 1973, ML, 1977. Bar: NY 1974, US Supreme Ct. 1977. Atty. Met. Life, NYC, 1973-79, asst. v.p., 1979-81, asst. gen. counsel, 1981-82, assoc. gen. counsel, 1982-83, v.p., assoc. gen. counsel, 1983-92; pres., CEO MetLife Can. Ops., 1993-95, sr. v.p., 1995—96, exec. v.p. individual bus., 1998—99; sr. exec. v.p., head of client svcs. Met. Life, 1999, pres. (client svcs), chief admin. officer, 1999—2001; pres. (client svcs.), chief administrative officer Met. Life Inc., 1999—2001; pres. internat. Met. Life Inc., Met. Life, 2001—. Adj. prof. Pace U. Law Sch., White Plains, NY, 1984—, Bklyn. Law Sch., 1985—. Mem. ABA (vice-chairperson com. on trial techniques 1986—), NY State Bar Assn., Assn. Bar of City of NY. Democrat. Roman Catholic. Office: MetLife Inc 200 Park Ave New York NY 10166 E-mail: btoppeta@metlife.com.*

TOPPING, AUDREY RONNING, photojournalist; b. Camrose, Alta., Can., May 21, 1928; arrived in U.S., 1967; d. Chester Alvin and Inga Marie (Horte) Ronning; m. Seymour Topping, Nov. 10, 1949; children: Susan, Karen, Lesley, Robin, Joanna. Student, Augustana Univ., Camrose, 1943-46, Nanking U., China, 1947-48, Berlin Art Sch., 1956-58, U. B.C., 1949-50; D of Arts (hon.), Rider Coll., NJ, 1983; PhD, Yunnan U., Kunming, China; LittD (hon.), Adelphi U., NY, 2009, Wilfred Laurier U., Can., 2009. Freelance journalist N.Y. Times Mag., NYC, 1966—2001; writer, photographer Nat. Geographic, Washington, 1971-79; columnist Earth Times, NYC, 1996—; spl. corr. Houston Chronicle, 1997—2001; photjournalist-at-large Earthuman Mag., 2002—; hon. prof. Yunnan U., 2008. Advisor U.S.-China Arts Exch., 1997—; commentator, writer Great Wall Across The Yangtze (PBS), Homecoming (Chinese TV), 2002; TV scriptwriter China Mission, 1975; hon. prof. journalism Southwestern U., Chongging, China, 2008. Author: Dawn Wakes In the East, 1972, The Splendors of Tibet, 1981, Charlie's World, 2000; A Day in the Life of Can., 1986, two children's books, N.Y. Times, Nat. Geographic, Readers Digest, Time, Life, Geo, Sci. Digest, Earth Times, World Policy Jour., others, exhibitions include Royal Ont. Mus., Toronto, 1980, Hallmark Gallery, NYC, 1973, Overseas Press Cub, 1975, Westchester C.C., 1989, 2004, Libby Gallery, Purchase, NY, 2004, Bhutan UN Embassy, NY, 2004, Hammond Mus., North Salem, 2005, CUNY Grad. Ctr. Gallery, 2006, Adelphi U., NY, 2007, Southwest U., China, 2007, Internat. Ctr. Journalist, 2008, U. Richmond, Va. Recipient Alumni award Augustana Univ. Coll., 1989, Medallion award Westchester C.C., 1989, Greenway Winship award Internat. Ctr. Journalists, 2000, Century Old Photo award Xiangfan China, 2009 Mem.: Coun. of Fgn. Relations, Soc. Woman Geographers, Asia Soc., Fgn. Policy Assn., Fox Meadow Tennis Club, Jr. Fortnightly. Avocations: sculpture, painting, tennis, skiing, exploring. Home and Office: 5 Heathcote Rd Scarsdale NY 10583-4413 E-mail: topaud@aol.com.

TOPPING, SEYMOUR, writer; b. NYC, Dec. 11, 1921; s. Joseph and Anna (Seidman) Topolsky; m. Audrey Elaine Ronning, Nov. 10, 1949; children: Susan, Karen, Lesley, Rebecca, Joanna. BJ, U. Mo., 1943; LittD (hon.), Rider Coll., 1993, Adelphi U., 2009. With I.N.S. (China civil war), 1946-47; with AP, Nanking, 1948—49, corr. Saigon, 1950—51, London, 1952—56, Berlin, 1956—59; mem. staff N.Y. Times, 1959-93, chief corr. Moscow, 1960—63, chief corr. S.E. Asia, 1963-66, fgn. editor, 1966-69, asst. mng. editor, 1969-76, dep. mng. editor, 1976-77, mng. editor, 1977-86; dir. editl. devel. N.Y. Times Regional Newspapers, 1987-93; chmn. New Directions for News, 1990-91; pres. Am. Soc. Newspaper Editors, 1992—93; prof. Grad. Sch. Journalism Columbia U., NYC, 1993—2002, adminstr. Pulitzer Prizes, 1993—2002, Sanpaolo prof. emeritus of internat. journalism, 2002—, pres. emeritus profs., 2004—. Chmn. editl. policy bd. World Policy Jour.; adviser Internat. Ctr. for Journalists, Found. Am. Comm.; pres., internat. adv. bd., Tsinghua U.; juror Pulitzer Prize com.; lectr. in field. Author: Journey Between Two Chinas, 1972, The Peking Letter, A Novel of the Chinese Civil War, 1999, Fatal Crossroads, A Novel of Vietnam 1945, 2005. Spl. advisor to Sec.-Gen. UN to Earth Summit, Rio de Janeiro, 1992; mem. Nat. Com. U.S.-China Rels.; Served with inf. AUS, 1943-46, PTO. Recipient Greenway-Winship award for contbns. to internat. journalism, 2000, Disting. Svc. award, Mo. Sch. of Journalism, 1968, Disting Alumni award, 1993. Mem. Coun. Fgn. Rels., Asia Soc., Am. Soc. Newspaper Editors, Century Assn. Home: 5 Heathcote Rd Scarsdale NY 10583-4413 Personal E-mail: st122@columbia.edu.

TOPSAKAL, ERDEM, science educator; b. Istanbul, Turkey, June 27, 1971; arrived in U.S., 1997; s. Mehmet and Imral Topsakal. PhD, Istanbul Tech. U., 1996. Rsch. scientist U. Mich., Ann Arbor, 2001—03; asst. prof. Miss. State U., 2003—. Recipient Young Scientist award, URSI, 1996, Outstanding Educator award, Miss. State U. Dept. Elec. and Computer Engring., 2005; fellow, NATO, 1997. Mem.: IEEE (sr.), IEEE Antennas and Propagation. Achievements include research in Nanoscale Frequency Selective Surface Design for Near Infrared and Optics; UWB and Multiband Antennas; Design and Analysis; Fast Computational Electromagnetic Tools; Implantable Antennas for Wireless Data Telemetry. Home: Apt 26 M 500 Mallory Ln Starkville MS 39759-7121 Office Fax: 662-325-2298. Business E-Mail: topsakal@ece.msstate.edu.

TOPYAN, KUDRET, finance educator; s. Suayip and Mukadder Topyan; 1 child, Meric. PhD in Economics, CUNY, 1992. Prof. economics & fin. Manhattan Coll., NY, 2007—; chair dept. economics & fin. Sch. Bus. Manhattan Coll., Riverdale, NY, 2003—07. Vis. prof. H.Lehman Coll., Bronx, NY, 1991—92; adj. prof., mba program Rutgers U., NB, NJ, 1998; adj. prof., msc econ. program Hunter Coll., Manhattan, NY, 2008. Contbr. scientific papers to profl. jours. Grantee Gabrial Haugie fellow, Sch. Bus., 1997—98. Mem.: AAUP, We. Econ. Assn., Ea. Econ. Assn., Fin. Mgmt. Assn., Am. Econ. Assn. Home: 110 - 74th St North Bergen NJ 07047 Office: Manhattan Coll School Business Manhattan Coll Pkw Bronx NY 10471-4098 Office Fax: 718-862-8032. Personal E-mail: kudret.topyan@yahoo.com. Business E-Mail: kudret.topyan@manhattan.edu.

TORAN, ERIC JAMES, physical therapist, director; s. Clarence Toran and Hester M. Nation. BS, Fla. A&M U., Tallahassee, 1986; MS, Howard U., Washington, 1992, PhD, 1995. Program dir. Fla. A&M U., Divsn. Phys. Therapy, 2003—. Postdoc. rsch. assoc. U. Nebr. Med. Ctr., Omaha, 1995—96. Recipient award, State Ark. Atty. Gen., 2002. Mem.: Am. Assn. Anatomists. Office: Fla A&M Univ MLK Blvd Tallahassee FL 32311 Personal E-mail: ejtfamue08@comcast.net. Business E-Mail: eric.toran@famu.edu.

TORAN-ALLERAND, C(LAUDE) DOMINIQUE, neuroscientist, neurologist, educator; arrived in USA, 1943, naturalized, 1948; d. Jean-Jacques Allerand and Georgette Elias; m. Edward Alexander Toran, Sept. 23, 1972. AB summa cum laude, Smith Coll., Northampton, Mass., 1955; MD, Albany Med. Coll., NY, 1959; ScD (hon.), Smith Coll., 1998. Diplomate Am. Bd. Neurology & Psychiatry, 1972. Internship Albany Med. Ctr. Hosp., 1959—60, asst. resident medicine, 1960—61; asst. resident neurology Columbia-Presbyterian Med. Ctr., New York Neurol. Inst., NYC, 1961—64; postdoctoral fellowship Columbia U., 1964—68, asst., 1968—69, instr., 1968—69; asst. prof. neurology NYU Med. Sch., NYC, 1969—73; rsch. assoc. Columbia U., 1973—74, asst. prof. neurology, 1974—81, assoc. prof. neurology, 1981—89, prof. neurology, pathology & cell biology, obstetrics & gynecology, 1989—. Contbr. articles to profl. jours. Recipient Otolaryngology prize, 1959, International Photomicroscopy award, Nikon, 1994. Mem.: Soc. Neurosci., Sigma Xi, Phi Beta Kappa. Achievements include research in the role and mechanisms of estrogen action in the developing brain; sexual differentiation of the brain; steroid growth factor interactions in the brain; estrogen signal transduction in the brain; novel estrogen hormones and receptor systems. Office: Columbia Univ 630 W 168th St New York NY 10032 Office Fax: 212-305-2134. Business E-Mail: cdt2@columbia.edu.

TORANZO, NILSA CARIDAD, special education services professional; b. Bklyn., Sept. 8, 1958; d. Claide and Aurea Esther Toranzo; m. Kenneth Antoine Cherry, Oct. 10, 1999. BSc, Fordham U., 1980; MA, NY U, 1983. Edn. evaluator St. Francis de Sales Sch. for the Deaf, Bklyn., 1983—. Contbr. articles. Mem.: Internat. Reading Assn. Avocations: exercise, reading, travel. Office: St Francis de Sales Sch for the Deaf 260 Eastern Pkwy Brooklyn NY 11225 Office Phone: 718-636-4573. Business E-Mail: ntoranzo@sfdesales.org.

TORBETT, DAVID JAMES, religion professor; b. Kingsport, Tenn., Aug. 22, 1964; s. David Jesse and Alice Jones Torbett; m. Jill Faith O'Connell; children: Thomas Robert, Nora Faith. BFA in Dramatic Writing, NY U., 1987; MDiv, Andover Newton Theol. Sch., Newton Ctr. Mass., 1992; PhD, Union Theol. Sem. Va., Richmond, 2002. Cert. ordained mins. United Ch. Christ, 1993. Prof. religious studies Mt. Union Coll., Alliance, Ohio, 2001—07. Prof. religion & history Marietta Coll., Ohio, 2007—. Author: (book) Theology and Slavery: Charles Hodge and Horace Bushnell. Mem. First Congl. Ch., Marietta, 2007—. Mem.: Am. Acad. Religion. Office: Marietta Coll 215 Fifth St Marietta OH 45750

TORBETT, GARY BURL, retired telephone company executive; b. Beaumont, Tex., Sept. 16, 1942; s. John Crittendon and Gladys (Porter) T.; m. Sandra Louise Vessels, Mar. 21, 1972; 1 child, Brooke Sheneen. BSBA, Auburn U., 1971. Mgr. Grayson (Ala.) Tel. Co., 1971-73, McClellanville (S.C.) Tel. Co., 1973-76; mgr. S.E. region comml./mktg. Tel. & Data Systems, Inc., Leesburg, Ala., 1976-81, western region network mgr. Madison, Wis., 1981-89; pres., gen. mgr. Okla. Comm. Systems, Inc., Choctaw, 1989—, also bd. dirs.; Okla./Ark. area mgr. TDS Telecom., 1995. Mem. bd. edn. Ea. Okla. County Tech. Ctr., 1993—2001. With US Army, 1965—67, Korea. Mem. Ind. Tel. Pioneer Assn, Okla. Tel. Assn. (pres. 2000), Choctaw C. of C. (v.p. 1996, pres. 1999), Am. Legion. Methodist. Avocations: golf, walking, reading. Home: PO Box 1029 737 Hearthstone Dr Lake Sherwood MO 63357 Personal E-mail: gartor@centurytel.net.

TORBICA, ZELJKO MARKO, construction executive, educator; arrived in U.S.A., 92; s. Marko and Nadezda Torbica; m. Maria Jovanov, Oct. 30, 1999; children: Talia, Nada, Dara, Djordje. PhD, U. Fla., 1997—97; diploma, U. of Belgrad, 1986. Cert. quality engr., Am. Soc. Quality; project mgmt. profl. Project Mgmt. Inst. Engr. Energoprojekt, Belgrade, Serbia and Montenegro, 1986—92; asst. prof. Minn. State U., Mankato, 1996—2001; constrn. mgmt. educator Fla. Internat. U., Miami, 2001—04; assoc. prof. Roger Williams U., Bristol, RI, 2004—06; dir. devel. CABI Developers, Aventura, Fla., 2006—08; assoc. clin. prof. & program dir. Drexel U., Phila., 2008—.

TORDA, ELINOR A., language educator; MA in Spanish summa cum laude, CSULB, Long Beach, Calif., 2007. Cert. tchr. Calif. Spanish tchr. Escuela Americana, San Salvador, El Salvador, 1998; spanish tchg. assoc. CSULB, Long Beach, 2006—07; spanish adj. instr. Merced Coll., Calif., 2008—; spanish lectr. UC Merced, 2008—. Contbr. scientific papers. Recipient Gabriela Mistral award, Sigma Delta Pi CSULB, 2007.

TORELLI, ANTHONY-ALEXANDER, musician, conductor, educator; b. Providence, Sept. 15, 1962; s. Alexander Augustino and Marie Barbara Torelli; m. Adriana Maritza Ramos, June 9, 2001; 1 child, Alexander James. BS, RI Coll., 1986; M, The Hartt Sch. U. Hartford, 1998; D, U. Montreal, 2003; diploma in ARt, The Hartt Sch. U. of Hartford, 2000. Tchg. Cert. RI Dept. of Edn., 2000. Condr. Bel Canto Opera Co., Cranston, RI, 1988—98; assoc. condr. South County Chamber Singers and Orch., Kingston, RI, 1998—; condr. RI Philharm. Youth Orchs., Providence, 2000—05; music dir. and condr. Norton Singers, Mass., 2003—; music dir., condr. German Am. Cultural Soc. Chorus, Pawtucket, RI; music educator North Providence Sch. Dept., North Providence, RI, 2000—. Cons. Pastime Theater Found., Bristol, RI, 2003—. Opera scholar, Bel Canto Opera Scholarship Found., 1993. Mem.: Am. Fedn. of Tchrs. (assoc.), Am. Fedn. of Musicians (assoc.), Conductors Guild (assoc.), Am. Symphony Orch. League (assoc.). Home: 28 Hamilton RD Cranston RI 02910-6007 Personal E-mail: anthonyatorelli@yahoo.com.

TORETSKY, JEFFREY A., physician, researcher, educator; s. Morris and Corrine Toretsky; m. Elizabeth Rudin Toretsky, May 29, 1988. MD, U. Minn., 1988. Assoc. prof. Georgetown U., Washington, 2002—. Vol. musician Einstein HS, Kensington, Md., 2009. Recipient award, Am. Soc. Clin. Investigators, 2007; grantee Burroughs-Wellcome Clin. Scientist Award in Translational Rsch., Burroughs-Wellcome Found., 2008. Mem.: Am. Soc. Pediatric Hematology, Oncology (ann. program com. mem. 2003—07). Achievements include research in novel therapies for childhood cancer. Avocation: music. Office: Georgetown Univ 3970 Reservoir Rd NRB W307 Washington DC 20057

TORG, JOSEPH STEVEN, orthopaedic surgeon, educator; b. Phila., Oct. 25, 1934; m. Barbara Jane Groenendaal, May 23, 1959; children: Joseph Steven, Elisabeth, Jay Michael. AB, Haverford Coll., 1957; MD, Temple U., 1961. Diplomate: Am. Bd. Orthopaedic Surgeons. Intern San Francisco Gen. Hosp., 1961-62; resident in orthopaedic surgery Temple U. Hosp., Phila., 1964-68, Shriners Hosp. for Crippled Children, Phila., 1966-67; asst. surgeon Episcopal Hosp., Phila., 1968-70; surgeon Shriners Hosp. Crippled Children, 1970-78; mem. staff Temple U. Hosp., 1970-78, instr. orthopaedic surgery, 1968-70, asst. prof., 1970-75, assoc. prof., 1976-78; dir. Center for Sports Medicine and Sci., 1974-78; chief orthopaedic sect. St. Christopher's Hosp. for Children, Phila., 1971-74, mem. staff, 1974—; active staff St. Joseph's Hosp., Phila., 1977—; prof. U. Pa., 1978—, active staff hosp., 1978—; dir. Sports Medicine Center, 1978—; prof. orthopaedic surgery Temple U., 1995. Mem. active staff Children's Hosp., Phila., 1978; med. cons. Pres.'s Coun. on Phys. Fitness and Sports Mem. editl. bd. Sports Medicine, Yearbook of Sports Medicine, Contemporary Orthopaedics, Jour. Clin. Sport Medicine, Am. Jour. Knee Surgery, Orthopaedic Rev.; contbr. articles to profl. jours. Served with M.C. US Army, 1962-64. Recipient Layman Honor award Pa. State Assn. Health, Phys. Edn. and Recreation, 1970, Grad. Honor award, 1975; Commendation of Merit Phila. Public HS Football Coaches, 1974 Fellow Am. Acad. Orthopaedic Surgeons, Am. Coll. Sports Medicine (trustee 1975-78), Phila. Coll. Physicians; mem. AMA, Eastern Orthopaedic Soc., Am. Orthopaedic Soc., Sports Medicine, Phila. County Med. Soc., Phila. Orthopaedic Soc., Pa. State Med. Soc., Pa. State Orthopaedic Soc. Home: 401 Conestoga Rd Wayne PA 19087-4811 Office: Temple U Hospital 6th Floor 3401 N Broad St Philadelphia PA 19140 Office Phone: 215-707-1321. Personal E-mail: torgmd@aol.com. Business E-Mail: torgjs@tuhs.temple.edu.

TORGERSEN, ERIC, literature and language professor; s. John and Louise Torgersen; m. Ann Elizabeth Kowaleski, Sept. 23, 1978; 1 child, Elizabeth Kowaleski. BA, Cornell U., Ithaca, 1964; MFA, U. Iowa, 1969. Lectr., English Haile Selassie I U., Addis Ababa, Ethiopia, 1964—66; instr., English Quincy Coll., 1968—70; prof. English Ctrl. Mich. U., Mount Pleasant, 1970—2008. Author: (poetry book) The Carpenter, At War with Friends, The Door to the Moon, Good True Stories. Recipient Individual Artist award, Mich. Coun. Arts, 1987; Summer fellowship, Ctrl. Mich. U., 1990, Rsch. Professorship fellow, 1988—89. Mem.: Am. Lit. Translators Assn., Assn. Writers & Writing Programs, Acad. Am. Poets. Avocation: art. Home: 8475 Chippewa Trail Mount Pleasant MI 48858 Business E-Mail: torge1e@cmich.edu.

TORGERSEN, PAUL ERNEST, academic administrator, educator; b. NYC, Oct. 13, 1931; s. Einar and Frances (Hansen) T.; m. Dorothea Hildegarde Zuschlag, Sept. 11, 1954; children: Karen Elizabeth, Janis Elaine, James Einar. BS, Lehigh U., 1953, DEng, 1994; MS, Ohio State U., 1956, PhD, 1959. Grad. tchg. asst. Ohio State U., Columbus, 1957, instr., 1957-59; asst. to assoc. prof. Okla. State U., Stillwater, 1959-66; prof., dept. head, dean Coll. Engring. Va. Tech, Blacksburg, 1967-93, pres., 1993-2000, John W. Hancock chair of engring. Dir. Roanoke (Va.) Electric Steel, 1986-2001, Luna Innovations, 2000—, EDD, 1996—. Author 5 books. Mem. Gov. Mark Warner's Commn. on Bd. of Visitor Appts., Richmond, Va., 2002–; So.State Energy Bd., Richmond, 1986-90. 1st lt. USAF, 1953-55. Fellow Am. Soc. Engring. Edn. (Lamme medal 1994), Inst. Indsl. Engring (Frank and Lillian Gibreth award 2001); mem. Nat. Acad. Engring. (coun. 1999--). Avocation: tennis. Office: Va Tech 201 Durham Hall Blacksburg VA 24061-0118 Business E-Mail: tennis@vt.edu.

TORGERSEN, TORWALD HAROLD, architect, consultant; b. Chgo., Sept. 2, 1929; s. Peder and Hansine Malene (Hansen) T.; m. Dorothy Darlene Peterson, June 22, 1963. BS in Archtl. Engring. with honors, U. Ill., 1951. Gargoyle Archtl. hon., SighaJau Engring. hon., Lic. architect Ill., D.C., real estate broker, Ill., interior designer, Ill., pvt. pilot, scuba diver; registered architect Nat. Coun. Archtl. Registration Bds. Ptnr. Coyle & Torgersen Architects-Engrs., Washington, Chgo. and Joliet, Ill., 1955—56; coord. project Skidmore, Owings & Merrill, Chgo., 1956—60; corp. architect, dir. architecture, constrn. and interiors Container Corp. Am., Chgo., 1960—86; prin. in charge of orgn. and adminstrn. Jack Train Assocs. Inc., Chgo., 1987—88; cons. Torwald H. Torgersen, AIA, FASID, Chgo., 1988—. Guest lectr. U. Wis. Capt. USNR, 1951-82, US Naval War Coll., 1967 Recipient Top Ten Design award Factory mag., 1964 Fellow Am. Soc. Interior Designers; mem. AIA, Naval Res. Assn., Rear Admiral, United Air Million Miller, Chgo. Marathon, Ill. Naval Militia, Am. Arbitration Assn., Am. Soc. Mil. Engrs., Paper Industry Mgmt. Assn. (hon.), Sports Car Club Am., Nat. Eagle Scout Assn., 20 Fathoms Club. Home and Office: 4625 Whisper Way Pensacola FL 32504

TORGERSON, LARRY KEITH, lawyer; b. Albert Lea, Minn., Aug. 25, 1935; s. Fritz G. and Lu (Hillman) Torgerson. BA, Drake U., 1958, MA, 1960, LLB, 1963, JD, 1968; MA, Iowa U., 1962; cert., The Hague Acad. Internat. Law, The Netherlands, 1965-69; LLM, U. Minn., 1969, Columbia U., 1971, U. Mo., 1976; PMD, Harvard U., 1973; EdM, 1974. Bar: Minn. 1964, U.S. Dist. Ct. Minn. 1964, Wis. 1970, Iowa 1970, U.S. Dist. Ct. (no. dist.) Iowa 1971, U.S. Tax Ct. 1971, U.S. Supreme Ct. 1972, U.S. Dist. Ct. (ea. dist.) Wis. 1981, U.S. Ct. Appeals (8th cir.) 1981. Asst. corp. counsel 1st Bank Stock Corp. (88 Banks), Mpls., 1963-67, 1st Svc. Corp. (27 ins. agys., computer subs.), Mpls., 1965-67; v.p., trust officer Nat. City Bank, Mpls., 1967-69; sr. mem. Torgerson Law Firm, Northwood, Iowa, 1969-87; trustee, gen. counsel Torgerson Farms, Northwood, 1967—, Redbirch Farms, Kensett, Iowa, 1987—2002, Sunburst Farms, Grafton, Iowa, 1987—, Gold Dust Farms, Bolan, Iowa, 1988—, Torgerson Grain Storage, Bolan, 1988—2008, Indian Summer Farms, Bolan, 1991—, Sunset Farms, Bolan, 1992—, Sunrise Farms, Grafton, 1994—. CEO, gen. counsel Internat. Investments, Mpls., 1983-96, Transoceanic, Mpls., 1987-96, Torgerson Capital, Northwood, 1996—, Torgerson Investments, Northwood, 1984—, Torgerson Properties, Northwood, 1987—, Torgerson Ranches, Sundance, Wyo., 1998-2008, Hawaiian Investments Unltd., Maui, Hawaii, 1998-2008, Internat. Investments Unltd., San Pedro, Belize, 1999-2008. Recipient All-Am. Journalism award Thomas Arkle Clark Outstanding Achievement award, 1958, Dennis E. Brumfield Outstanding Achievement award, 1958, Johnny B. Guy Outstanding Leadership award, 1958; named to Outstanding Young Men of Am., U.S. Jaycees; Hagen scholar, Honor scholar. Mem. ABA, Am. Judicature Soc., Iowa Bar Assn., Minn. Bar Assn., Wis. Bar Assn., Hennepin County Bar Assn., Mensa, Drake Student-Faculty Coun., Drake Student Alumni Coun. (chmn.), Jaycees, Harvard Bus. Sch. Study (pres., exec. com., univ. editor in chief), Psi Chi, Circle K (pres. local chpt.), Phi Alpha Delta, Omicron Delta Kappa (pres. local chpt.), Pi Kappa Delta (pres. local chpt.), Alpha Tau Omega (pres. local chpt., Silver Bullet Outstanding Leadership award, 1965, 66), Pi Delta Epsilon (founder, chpt. pres.), Alpha Kappa Delta, Alpha Scholastic Hon. (U. editor-in-chief), Harvard Bus. Sch. Exec. Com. (U. editor-in-chief). Lutheran.

TORGERSON, LINDA BELLE, music educator; b. Sioux City, Iowa, Dec. 16, 1951; d. Fredric William and Clara Jeanette Wilson; m. Peter Kinsey Torgerson; children: Christopher, Patricia. Diploma, Ctrl. H.S., 1971; MusB Edn., Morningside Coll., 1976; MEd, City U., 1999. Cert. Iowa tchr., tchr. Mont., Washington. Choral dir. First United Meth. Ch., Sioux City, Iowa, 1974—76, First Presbyn. Ch., Kalispell, Mont., 1976—80; pvt. music instr. Self-employed, Kalispell, Mont., 1976—80; music tchr. St. Matthews Sch., Kalispell, Mont., 1976—77; music dir., coord. Flathead County Rural Schools, Kalispell, Mont., 1979—85; music dir. Clarkston Sch. Dist., Wash., 1985—. Treas. Clarkston Edn. Assn., 1988—90, v.p., 1990—92, 2001—03, pres., 1991—92, bldg. rep., 1993—94, 2000—01; sec. Wash. uniserv polit. action com. Wash. Edn. Assn., Olympia, 1992—93; jazz band dir. Lincoln Mid. Sch., Clarkston, 1996—2003; co-director for asotin county teens against smoking Asotin County Devel. Services, Clarkston, 2001—02. Singer (composer): (commercial) Flathead County Milk Music Ad for the Radio, 1978; contbr. articles to profl. jours. Mem. U-Pac bd. for SE Wash. Edn. Assn., Kennewick, Wash., 1992—93. Grantee Dist., Clarkston Sch. Dist., 1994,

1995. Mem.: NEA, SE Wash. Music Educators Assn. (pres. 2002—04), Wash. Music Educators Assn., Music Educators Nat. Conf. Home: 1505 8th St Clarkston WA 99403 Office: Lincoln Mid Sch 1945 4th Ave Clarkston WA 99403 Office Phone: 509-758-5506 x5245. Personal E-mail: torgersons@cableone.net. Business E-Mail: torgersonl@csdk12.org.

TORGERSON, PAUL M., prosecutor; b. Des Moines, Iowa, Aug. 28, 1951; BA, Luther Coll., Decorah, Iowa, 1973; JD, U. Minn. Law Sch., Mpls., 1979. Cert. in pub. acct., Minn., 1975. Sr. acct. Peat Marwick Mitchell & Co., Mpls., 1973—76; chief adminstrv. officer, svp and gen. counsel Fairview Health Svcs., 1999—2005; assoc. Dorsey & Whitney LLP, Mpls., 1979—84, ptnr., 1985—99, sr. ptnr., 2005—. Mem.: Am. Health Lawyers Assn., Minn. Bar Assn. Office: Dorsey & Whitney LLP 50 S 6th St Ste 1500 Minneapolis MN 55402

TORGERSON, WILLIAM T., lawyer, retired electric power industry executive; b. Annapolis, Md., May 29, 1944; s. Theodore A. and Augusta (Melvin) T.; m. Maureen Glynis Reynolds, Apr. 19, 1994; 1 child, John Theodore. AB, Princeton U., 1966; JD with honors, U. Md., 1973. Atty. Hogan & Hartson, Washington, 1973-82; various Potomac Electric Power Co., Washington, 1982-89, v.p., gen. counsel, 1989-94, sr. v.p., gen. counsel, 1994—; vice chmn., gen. counsel Pepco Holdings Inc. (formerly Potomac Electric Power Co.), Washington, 2003—08; vice-chmn., chief legal officer Pepco Holdings Inc., 2008—. Bd. dirs. Leadership Md. Lt. USN, 1966-70, Vietnam. Decorated Bronze Star (2).

TORI, CHRISTOPHER DANTE, psychology professor; b. San Francisco, Oct. 13, 1941; s. Ralph Tori; m. Mary Graves, Aug. 1, 1970. BS, U. Dayton, Ohio, 1964; MA, Calif. State U., San Jose, 1968; PhD, U. Ky., Lexington, 1972. Lic. psychologist Bd. Psychology, Calif., 1970. Clin. psychologist Blue Grass East Comprehensive Care Ctr., Lexington, 1969—71; prof. Alliant Internat. U., San Francisco, 1975—. Cons. Wat Mongkonratanaram, Berkeley, Calif., 1980—. Mem.: Am. Psychol. Assn. Liberal. Buddhist. Office: Alliant Internat Univ 1 Beach St Emeryville CA 94608 Business E-Mail: ctori@alliant.edu.

TORIUMI, DEAN MICHAEL, facial, plastic and reconstructive surgeon, educator; b. Chgo., Ill., 1958; Degree in biology, Knox Coll., 1980; grad., Norwestern U. Med. Ctr.; MD, Rush Med. Coll., 1981. Cert. otolaryngology 1988. Resident, gen. surgery U. Ill., Chgo., 1983—85; resident, otolaryngology Northwestern U. Med. Sch., Chgo., 1985—87; fellowship, facial plastic and reconstruction surgery Tulane Med. Sch., New Orleans, 1988, Va. Mason Med. Ctr., Seattle, 1989; prof., head Div. of Facial Plastic & Reconstructive Surgery U. Ill., Dept. Otolaryngology, Chgo. Co-author: Open Structure Rhinoplasty; contbr. articles various profl. papers, chapters to books. Mem.: Am. Acad. Facial Plastic and Reconstructive Surgery (pres.). Office: U Ill Chgo Coll Medicine Dept Otolaryngology 1855 W Taylor St Rm 242 Chicago IL 60612-7242 Address: 60 E Delaware 900 N Michigan Ave Chicago IL 60611 Office Phone: 312-996-8897. Office Fax: 312-996-1282.

TORKILDSEN, PETER GERARD, former United States Representative from Massachusetts; b. Milw., Jan. 28, 1958; s. Robert Allan and Mary Ellen (Hill) T.; m. Gail Bloomgarden, Jan. 1996. BA, U. Mass., 1980; MPA, Harvard U., 1990. Mem. Mass. House of Reps., 1985-91, US Congress from 6th Mass. dist., 1993-97; pres. Thunder Hill Inc., Peabody, Mass., 1997; commr. Mass. Labor Rels. Commn., Boston, 2001; chmn. Mass. Republican Party, 2007—09. Mem. Danvers Town Meeting, 1983-85, Mass. Rep. State Com., Boston, 1984-93. Mem. Am. Legis. Exchange Council, Mass. Legislator's Assn., Nat. Rep. Legislator Assn. Lodges: Sons of Norway. Republican. Roman Catholic.*

TORME, MARGARET ANNE, public relations executive, management consultant; b. Indpls., Apr. 5, 1943; d. Ira G. and Margaret Joy (Wright) Barker; children: Karen Anne, Leah Vanessa. Student, Coll. San Mateo, 1961—65. Pub. rels. mgr. Hoefer, Dieterich & Brown (now Chiat-Day), San Francisco, 1964-73; v.p., co-founder, creative dir. Lowry & Ptnrs., San Francisco, 1975-83; pres., founder Torme and Lauricella Comm., San Francisco, 1983—. Cons. in comm. Mem. Coun. Pub. Rels. Firms, Jr. League (adv. bd.), Pub. Rels. Orgn. Internat. Office: 847 Sansome St San Francisco CA 94111-2908 Office Phone: 415-956-1791. Business E-Mail: margaret@torme.com.

TORMEY, BRIAN B., environmental geomorphologist, aerial mapping consultant; b. S.I., NY, Oct. 8, 1940; s. Bertram M. and Margaret J. Tormey; m. Judith E. Anderson; children: Jennifer E., Brett B., Blair R., Megan A. AAS in Agrl. Scis., SUNY, Morrisville, 1960; BS in Sci. Edn., Western Conn. U., 1964; postgrad., U. Md., 1964—66, Am. U., Washington, DC, 1965—66; DEd in Earth Scis., Pa. State U., 1980. Earth and space scis. tchr. State College Area Schs., Pa., 1968—81; asst. prof. environ. scis. Pa. State U., Altoona, 1981—92, assoc. prof. environ. scis., 1991—. CEO, cons. StoneView Earth Sys. Rsch., Huntingdon, Pa., 2000—; owner, mgr. Hostetler Airport, Jackson Twp., Pa., 2000—; co-owner StoneView Farm, Huntingdon, 2000—; presenter in field. Editor: (textbook) Field Techniques: Atlantic Barrier System, 1984, (guidebook) Central Appalachian Processes, 1990, Iceland - Hot Spot on the Edge of the Arctic, 1994; contbr. more than 100 papers and presentations. Mem., asst. chmn., chmn. Ferguson Twp. Authority, 1989—99; pres., chmn. bd. dirs. Brett B. Tormey Found. Inc., Huntingdon, 1997—; discipline coord. Environ. Earth Sys. Scis.; mem. exec. bd. Juniata Valley coun. Boy Scouts Am., 2005—; mem. Rep. County Com., Huntingdon County, 2003—; bd. dirs. Pa. Earth Scis. Field Sch. Recipient cert. achievement, Pa. Dept. Edn., 1985. Mem.: Geol. Soc. Am. (mem. ednl. initiatives 1992—96, chmn.), Nat. Assn. Geosci. Tchrs. (mem. coun. 1991—94, 2d v.p. 1991—92, 1st v.p. 1992—93, pres. 1993—94, pres. ea. sect. 1993, Outstanding Earth Scis. Tchr. 1980, Disting. Svc. award 2000), Pa. Sci. Tchrs. Assn. (bd. dirs. 1981—96). Roman Catholic. Achievements include research in glacial/periglacial geomorphology. Avocation: breeding and showing Kerry Blue Terriers. Office: Pa State U Altoona Coll Ivyside Dr Altoona PA 16601 Home: 4916 Standing Stone Rd Huntingdon PA 16652 Business E-Mail: stoneview@pennswoods.net.

TORN, RIP (ELMORE RUAL TORN JR.), actor, theater director; b. Temple, Tex., Feb. 6, 1931; s. Elmore and Thelma (Spacek) T.; m. Ann Wedgeworth, Jan. 15, 1955 (div. 1961); 1 child, Danae; m. Geraldine Page, 1963 (div. June 13, 1987); children: Angelica, Anthony, Jonathan; m. Amy Wright. Grad., Tex. A & M U., 1952. Performances include: (stage) Cat on a Hot Tin Roof, 1955, Orpheus Descending, 1958, Chaparral, 1958 (Theatre World award 1959), Sweet Bird of Youth, 1959, on tour, 1960, Daughter of Silence, 1961, Macbeth, 1962, Desire Under the Elms, 1963, Strange Interlude, 1963, Blues for Mr. Charlie, 1964, The Kitchen, 1966, The Country Girl, 1966, The Deer Park, 1967 (Obie award), The Cuban Thing, 1968, The Honest-to-God Schnozzola, 1969, Dream of a Blacklisted Actor, 1969, The Dance of Death, 1970-71, The Marriage Proposal, 1971, Marriage and Money, 1971, Barbary Shore, The Little Foxes, 1974, The Father, 1975, The Glass Menagerie, 1975, Fever for Life, 1975, Creditors, 1977, Night Shift, 1977, Seduced, 1979, Anna Christie, 1992; (motion pictures) Baby Doll, 1956, A Face in the Crowd, 1957, Time Limit, 1957, Pork Chop Hill, 1959, King of Kings, 1961, Hero's Island, 1962, Sweet Bird of Youth, 1962, Critic's Choice, 1963, The Cincinnati Kid, 1965, One Spy Too Many, 1966, Beach Red, 1967, You're a Big Boy Now, 1967, Beyond the Law, 1968, Sol Madrid, 1968, Coming Apart, 1969, Tropic of Cancer, 1970, Slaughter, 1972, Payday, 1973, Crazy Joe, 1974, Birch Interval, 1976, Maidstone, The Man Who Fell to Earth, 1976, Nasty Habits, 1977, Coma, 1978, The Seduction of Joe Tynan, 1979, First Family, 1980, Heartland, 1980, One Trick Pony, 1980, Jinxed, 1982, Airplane II: The Sequel, 1982, The Beastmaster, 1982, A Stranger is Watching, 1982, Cross Creek, 1983, City Heat, 1984, Misunderstood, 1984, Night Shadows, 1984, Song Writer, 1984, Flashpoint, 1984, Summer Rental, 1985, Beer, 1985, Extreme Prejudice, 1987, Defending Your Life, 1991, Beautiful Dreamers, 1992, Hard Promises, 1992, Robocop 3, 1993, Where the Rivers Flow North, 1994, How to Make an American Quilt, 1995, Down Periscope, 1996, Trial and Error, 1997, Men in Black, 1997, Hercules, 1997, The Mouse, 1997, Senseless, 1998, Wonder Boys, 2000, Men in Black Alien Attack, 2000, Men in Black II, 2002, Rolling Kansas, 2003, Welcome to Mooseport, 2004, Dodgeball: A True Underdog Story, 2004, Eulogy, 2004, Forty Shades of Blue, 2005, Yours, Mine and Ours, 2005, Marie Antoinette, 2006, Zoom, 2006, Bee Movie (voice), 2007, August, 2008; (TV films and miniseries) Two Plays, 1971, The President's Plane Is Missing, 1973, The FBI Versus the Ku Klux Klan, 1975, Song of Myself, 1976, Betrayal, 1976, The Gift of Love, 1978, Blind Ambition, 1979, A Shining Season, 1979, Sophia Loren: Her Own Story, 1980, Rape and Marriage: The Rideout Case, 1980, The Blue and the Gray, 1982, When She Says No, 1984, Dream West, 1986, April Morning, 1988, Sweet Bird of Youth, 1989, By Dawn's Early Light, 1990, Another Pair of Aces: Three of a Kind, 1991, My Son Johnny, 1991, Death Hits the Jackpot, 1991, T-Bone and Weasel, 1992, Dead Ahead: The Exxon Valdez Disaster, 1992, A Mother's Right: The Elizabeth Morgan Story, 1993, The Almost Perfect Bank Robbery, 1996, Seasons of Love, 1998, Passing Glory, 1999, Balloon Farm, 1999, A Vision of Murder: The Story of Donielle, 2000, Maniac Magee, 2003, The Lyon's Denn, 2003; (TV series) The Larry Sanders Show, HBO, 1992-98 (Emmy nominee for best supporting actor 1993, 94, Cable Ace award for best supporting actor 1994), Ghost Stories, 1997 (narrator); dir. plays: The Beard, 1968 (Obie award), Look Away, 1973. Mem. AFTRA, SAG, Actors Equity Assn., Actors' Studio (bd. dirs., prodn. bd., 1st chmn. founding com.), Dirs. Guild Am. Office: 118 S Beverly Dr 504 Beverly Hills CA 90212

TORNEDEN, CONNIE JEAN, banker; b. Tonganoxie, Kans., Sept. 14, 1955; d. Byron Calvin and Edna Jeannette (Keck) Swain; m. Lawrence Dale Torneden, Sept. 18, 1976; 1 child, James Milton. Bus. cert., Kans. City CC, 1974; student, Nat. Compliance Sch., Norman, Okla., 1984; Mortgage Lending Diploma, ABA Am. Inst. Banking, 1997. Adminstrv. sec. to chmn. of bd., pres. First State Bank and Trust, Tonganoxie, 1974-80, asst. cashier, 1981-83, asst. v.p. and compliance officer, 1984-97, bank security officer, 1989-95, loan ops. officer, 1998, loan prodn. specialist, 1999—2002, loan asst., 2002—09, sr. loan asst., 2009—. Lobbyist, treas. 24-40 Hwy. Task Force, Leavenworth, Kans., 1989-91; bd. dirs. sec. Reno Cemetery Assn., Tonganoxie, 1986—; co-founder Tonganoxie Days, chmn., 1986, 88-93, 95—; grad. So. Leavenworth County Leadership Devel., 1991; sec.-treas. Maple Grove Cemetery Assn., 1995—, Reno Twp. Fire Dept., 1996—. Mem. Am. Bus. Women's Assn. (treas. 1986-87, sec. 1997-98, 2001-03, Woman of Yr. award Twilight chpt. 1994, nominee Top Ten Bus. Women, 2005), Mid-Am. Dairymen Assn. (sec. 1978-80), Nat. Assn. Old West Gunfighter Teams (nat. champions 1989, 90), Linwood Grange (5th and 6th degrees 1978), Tonganoxie C. of C. (sec. 1983-86, 92-94, pres. 1986, 88, 89, 96, v.p. 1995, treas. 1997, Mem. of Yr. award 1990, 92, Citizen of Yr. award 2001), Tonganoxie Jaycees (sec. 1991). Democrat. Mem. Soc. Of Friends. Avocations: music, fossil collecting, stamp collecting/philately, coin collecting/numismatics, writing poetry and short stories. Office: First State Bank and Trust PO Box 219 Tonganoxie KS 66086-0219

TORNOW, L. WILLIAM, musician; b. Devils Lake, ND, Feb. 1, 1949; s. E. Edward and Ellen Naomi Tornow. BMus in Pub. Sch. Music, Concordia Coll., Moorhead, Minn., 1971; MA in Music, Trinity U., San Antonio, 1978; DMA in Piano Performance, U. Minn., Mpls., 1983. Artist in residence Cmty. Music Ctr., Fargo, ND, 1978—79; organist Our Saviour's Evang. Luth. Ch., Cannon Falls, Minn., 1984—85, St. George's Episc. Meml. Ch., Bismarck, ND, 1985—86. Composer: Elegy, 1971, Symphony No. 1 for Chamber Orch., 1989, Overture to Spring on Themes of Beethoven for orchestra, 1998, Symphony No. 2 for Piano and Orch., 2002, Symphony No. 3 on Four Hymn Tunes, 2006. Spl. 4 (E-4) US Army, 1971—74, Germany and Tex. Fellow: Nat. Music Tchrs. Assn.; mem.: Am. Guild of Organists. Avocations: fishing, golf. Home and Studio: 1806 Cedar Springs Ln Anacortes WA 98221-3567

TORO, JORGE R., dermatologist, researcher; b. Mayaguez, PR, Dec. 26, 1966; s. Jorge R. Toro and Carmen N. Rodriguez. Degree, Cornell U., Ithaca, NY, 1988; MD, SUNY, Buffalo, 1992. Diplomate Am. Bd. Dermatology, 1997. Rsch. assoc. Nat. Cancer Inst., Bethesda, Md., 1997—2001; prin. investigator Genetic Epidemiology Br., Nat. Cancer Inst., Rockville, Md., 2001—. Comdr. USPHS, 1997—2006. Recipient Juan Finlay award, USPHS, 2002, Dir.'s award, Nat. Cancer Inst., 2005. Fellow: Am. Acad. Dermatology (licentiate Young Investigator Award 2000). Achievements include invention of. Home: 4706 17th ST NW Washington DC 02011 Office: Nat Cancer Inst 6120 Executive Blvd EPS 7012 Rockville MD 20852 Business E-Mail: toroj@mail.nih.gov.

TOROK, KEN, delivery service executive; Grad., NC State U. Delivery driver UPS, Inc., 1975, transp. mgr. UPS Europe, 1994—97, mng. dir. Utah ops., 1998, mng. dir. South Fla. ops., pres. Asia Pacific Region Singapore, 2003—08, pres. global freight forwarding ops., 2009—. Office: UPS, Inc 55 Glenlake Parkway, NE Atlanta GA 30328*

TOROK, MARGARET LOUISE, insurance company executive; b. Detroit, June 22, 1922; d. Perl Edward Ensor and Mary (Seggie) Armstrong; m. Leslie A. Torok, Aug. 14, 1952; 1 child, Margaret Mary Ryan. Lic. Ins. Agy. From ins. agt. to corp. officer Grendel-Wittbold Ins., Southgate, Mich., 1961-72, pres. of corp., 1972—2001. Bd. dirs. Ind. Ins. Agts. of Mich., Lansing, 1984-92, Ind. Ins. Agts. of Wayne County, Dearborn, 1967-2006, pres. 1978. Bd. dirs. So. Wayne County C. of C., Taylor, 1975-2005, CEO, chmn. bd. dirs., 1997-98; bd. dirs. City of Southgate Tax. Increment Fin. Authority Dist. and Econ. Devel. Commn., 1987-2007, YMCA, mem. endowment com., Southgate, 1978, chmn. Leadership, 1980-88; bd. dirs. Downriver Cmty. Alliance, 1990-94; lay chmn. Cath. Svc. Appeal for Archdiocese of Detroit, 1989; co-chair fundraiser Sacred Heart Ch.; com. mem., bd. dirs. New Workforce Devel. Com., gov. appt., charter mem.; hon. chmn. Art Ambience, 2002, bd. dir. Art Ambience, 2009-; mem. Downriver Coun. of the Arts, Island Animal League Shelter, Friends of Detroit River, Grosse Ile Land Conservancy, Grosse Ile Hist. Soc.; bd. dirs. MESC Employers Com., 1991-95, chmn., 1991-95. Recipient Capital award Ind. Ins. Agts. of Mich., 1988, Lifetime Achievement award, Amb. award, 1994, Woman of Yr. AAUW, 1994, Salute to Excellence award Downriver Coun. of Arts, 1993-94, Chmn. of Yr. award MESC Job. Svc. Employers Com., 1991, Robert Stewart award Wyandotte Svc. Club Coun., 1994, Partnership award The Info. Ctr., 1996, W.O. Hildebrand award Mich. Assn. Ins. Agts., 1997; named to Ins. Hall of Fame, Olivet Coll., 1998, award YMCA Found., 2009. Mem.: YMCA, Marge Torok Found., Mich. Assn. Ins. Agts., Grosse Ile Hist. Soc., Arts Alliance, US Power Squadron (mem. 2007), Am. Legion Aux., Down River Coun. Arts, Soroptimist Club of Wyandotte Southgate Taylor (pres. 1984—86, Advancing Status Women award 1988, Soroptimist of Yr. award 1993—94), Wyandotte Yacht Club. Roman Catholic. Office: Grendel Wittbold Agy Inc 12850 Eureka Rd Southgate MI 48195-1344 Office Phone: 734-284-4740.

TORO VARGAS, CIRILO, library director, educator; b. Ponce, PR, Dec. 7, 1947; s. Cirilo del Carmen Toro Toro and María Lydia Vargas Vega; m. Lydia Mercedes Hurtado Mateo; children: Francisco Javier Toro Hurtado, Carlos Javier Toro Hurtado, María del Mar Toro Hurtado, Tania Cristina Toro Hurtado. BA, Pontifical Cath. U. PR, Ponce, 1970, MEd, 1981; MLS, U. PR, San Juan, 1975; PhD, Union Inst. and U., Cin., 1992. Cert. counselor Dept. Health, PR, 2005. Alt. dist. mgr. El Mundo Newspaper, Ponce, 1970; libr. Pontifical Cath. U. PR, 1972—, prof. and mentor, McNair program, 1989—, prof. Grad. Sch. Edn., 1992—, assoc. libr. dir., 2004—; bilingual guidance counselor NYC Bd. Edn., Bklyn., 1988—89; libr. cons. LI U. Libr., Bklyn., 1989; Spanish tchr. LI U., 1989, Berlitz Schs., Ponce, 1971; libr. organizer Peace Corps, Ponce, 1971—72; youth counselor and supr. Youth Working Experiences Program, Ponce, 1971; libr. developer and dir. Ponce Coll. Tech., 1981—83; libr. Ponce Sch. Medicine, 1984—87; rsch. prof. Escuela Graduada del Sur, Ponce, 1986—88; libr. cons. Academia Singer, Ponce, 1990—92; coord. Integrated Model for At-Risk Young People, Sistemas Educativos y Empresariales, Maunabo, 1992; guidance counselor Adminstrn. Juvenile Insts. Commonwealth PR, Ponce, 1995. Author: (book) Mejore su Autoestima en catorce días, Ensayos Variados, Manicomio, Senderos Poéticos, El Turno, Nuevos Surcos, Amaneceres. Mem. Com. Constrn. Ch., Ponce, 1974—90; v.p. Albergue La Providencia, Ponce, 2008. Cpl. US Army, 1971—71, Ft. Jackson, SC. Decorated Nat. Def. Svc. medal US Army; recipient Disting. Leadership award, Am. Biog. Inst., 1987, Rsch. Distinction, Puerto Rcio Libr. Assn., 2004, Ednl. grant, Delta Theta Tau Sorority, 1989, Merit cert., Phi Delta Kappa, 1991. Mem.: ALA, ABESPRI, PR Libr. Assn., ASEGRABCI, Reforma: Bilingual Librs. Home: 4036 Calle Fidela Matheu Las Delicias Ponce PR 00728-3711 Mailing: PO Box 32111 Ponce PR 00732-2111 Personal E-mail: pirata78pr@yahoo.com. Business E-Mail: ctoro@email.pucpr.edu.

TORQUATO, SALVATORE, materials scientist, chemistry professor; b. Falerna, Calabria, Italy, Feb. 10, 1954; came to U.S., 1955; s. Vincent and Palma (Vaccaro) T.; m. Kim Tracey Hoberock, Nov. 8, 1975; children: Michelle, Lisa. BSME, Syracuse U., 1975; MSME, SUNY, Stony Brook, 1977, PhD in Mech. Engring., 1980. Rsch. engr. Grumman Aerospace Corp., Bethpage, NY, 1975-78; rsch. asst. dept. mech. engring. SUNY, Stony Brook, 1978-80; asst. prof. dept. mech. engring. GM Inst., Flint, Mich., 1981-82; from asst. to assoc. prof. depts. mech., aerospace & chem. engring. N.C. State U., Raleigh, 1982-90, prof. depts. mech., aerospace & chem. engring., 1991-92; prof. Civil Engring. Princeton (N.J.) U., 1992-99, prof. chemistry, 2000—. Vis. prof. Courant Inst. Math. Scis., N.Y.C., 1990-91; cons. Eastman Kodak, Rochester, N.Y., 1989—; mem. Inst. Advanced Study, 1998-99. Contbr. articles to profl. jours. Grumman Masters fellow, 1975-77; fellow Guggenheim, 1998; recipient Engring. Rsch. Achievement award Alcoa Co., 1987, Disting. Engring. Rsch. award, 1989, Gustus L. Larson Meml. award, 1994. Fellow ASME Am. Phys. Soc.; mem. Am. Inst. Chem. Engrs., Soc. Engring. Sci. (Charles Russ Richards Meml. award, 2002, William Prager medal, 2004), Soc. for Indsl. and Applied Math. Avocations: racquetball, reading, music. Office: Princeton U Princeton Materials Inst Dept Chemistry Princeton NJ 08544-0001

TORRACO, PAMELA LOUISE, psychotherapist; b. Mineola, NY, Feb. 22, 1944; d. Peter and Willamy King Torraco. BA, Wittenberg U., Springfield, Ohio, 1965; MSW, U. Mich., Ann Arbor, 1967. Psychiatric social worker Henry Ford Hosp., Detroit, 1967—69; prin. social caseworker Detroit Health Dept., 1969—72; group & individual psychotherapist Dr. Reuven Bar-Levav & Assoc., PC, Southfield, Mich., 1971—; social worker Kingswood Hosp., Ferndale, Mich., 1972—75. Presenter, panelist in field, 1975—; pres., faculty mem. The Inst. Individual & Group Psychotherapy, Southfield, 1978—; program chair Mich. Group Psychotherapy Soc., Detroit, 1982—84, pres., Southfield, 1984—86. Contbr. articles to profl. jours. Sec. Bar-Levav Family Found., Southfield, 1999—. Mem.: Mich. Group Psychotherapy Soc., Am. Group Psychotherapy Assn., Nat. Assn. Social Workers. Independent. Jewish. Avocations: hiking, music, travel, languages. Office: Dr Reuven Bar-Levav & Assocs PC 29600 Northwestern Hwy Ste 100 Southfield MI 48034 Office Phone: 248-353-0050. Personal E-mail: pamtor@sbcglobal.net.

TORRANCE, ROBERT MITCHELL, comparative literature educator; b. Washington, May 9, 1939; s. Charles Mitchell and Ayma Jean (Sharpe) T.; m. Mildred D. Fischer, June 14, 1963 (div. July 1991); children: Benjamin Henry, Nicholas Aaron; m. Donna K. Reed, Aug. 24, 1991; stepchildren: Benjamin Reed-Lunn, Rebecca Reed-Lunn. BA Classics and English summa cum laude, Harvard U., 1961; MA in Comparative Lit., U. Calif., Berkeley, 1963; PhD in Comparative Lit., Harvard U., 1970. Asst. prof. comparative lit. Harvard U., Cambridge, 1971-75; assoc. prof. comparative lit. CUNY, Bklyn., 1975-76; prof. comparative lit. U. Calif., Davis, 1976—2001, prof. emeritus, 2001—. Author: The Comic Hero, 1978, Ideal and Spleen, 1987, The Spiritual Quest, 1994; editor: Encompassing Nature, A Sourcebook, 1998; translator: Sophocles, The Women of Trachis and Philoctetes, 1966. Jr. fellow Soc. of Fellows, Harvard U., 1966-69, Humanities Inst. fellow U. Calif., Davis, 1990. Home: 2800 Corona Dr Davis CA 95616-0116

TORRANCE, SAM, professional golfer; b. Aug. 24, 1953; m. Suzanne Danielle; children: Daniel, Phoebe, Anouska. Winner Under-25 Match Play tournament Radici Open, 1972; winner Zamibian Open, 1975, Martini Internat., 1976, Scottish PGA Championship, 1978, 80, 85, 91, 93, 95, Columbian Open, 1979, Australian PGA Championship, 1980, Irish Open, 1981, 95, Spanish Open, 1982, Portuguese Open, 1982, 83, Scandanavian Open, 1983, Tunisian Open, 1984, Benson & Hedges Internat., 1984, Sanyo Open, 1984, Monte Carlo Open, 1985, Italian Open, 1987, 95, German Masters, 1990, Jersey Open, 1991, Kronenborg Open, 1993, Catalan Open, 1993, Honda Open, 1993, British Masters, 1995, Anderson Consulting Match Play, 1996, French Open, 1998. Mem. Double Diamond Team, 1973 (winners), 76, 77, Alpha Dunhill Cup Team, 1985, 86, 87, 89, 90, 91, 93, 95, (winners), 99, Henessy Cognac Cup Team, 1976 (winners), 78, 80 (winners), 82 (winners), 88, World Cup Team, 1976, 78, 82, 84, 85, 87, 89, 90, 91, 93, 95, Ryder Cup Team, 1981, 83, 85 (winners), 87, 89, 91, 93, 95 (winners), 99 (vice capt.), European Ryder Cup capt., 2002, Asahi Glass Four Tours Team, 1985, 91 (capt., winners). Decorated Order Brit. Empire. E-mail: vicky.cuming@imgworld.com.

TORRAS, JOSEPH HILL, pulp and paper company executive; b. Americus, Ga., Nov. 14, 1924; s. Fernando Joseph and Nell Wilson (Hill) T.; m. Mary Ravenel Robertson, Sept. 20, 1952; children: Mary Martin, Fernanda Maria, Joseph Hill. S.B., Yale U., 1948; MBA, Harvard U., 1950; D in Bus. Adminstrn., Piedmont Coll., 1997. Asst. to fin. v.p. Seatrian Lines, Inc., 1950—51; with St. Regis Paper Co., 1951—60, sales mgr. printing papers div., 1956—60; exec. v.p. Brown Co., Boston, 1960—64; pres., chmn. bd. Premoid Corp., West Springfield, Mass., 1964—87; pres. Precon, Inc., Ludlow, 1967—87, Astro Tissue Co., Battleboro, Vt., 1968—72; chmn. bd. Whitman Products, Ltd., West Warwick, RI, 1976—89; pres., CEO, Preco Corp., Amherst, Mass., 1976—98; chmn., CEO Lincoln Pulp & Paper Co., Lincoln, Maine, 1968—2004, Eastern Fine Paper, Inc., Brewer, Maine, 1989—2004, CEO, Shelburne Corp., 1999—; adv. dir. Liberty Mut. Ins. Mem. Mass. Gov.'s Bus. Adv. Coun., 1985—89; devel. bd. Yale U.; bd. govs. Mass. Gen. Hosp., 1985—96; bd. dirs. Mass. Taxpayers Assn., 1976—86; trustee Hist. Deerfield, 1990—2004, Piedmont Coll., Ga., 1991—99; dir. Inst. of World Politics, 1990—. Lt. (j.g.) aviator USNR, 1943—46. Mem. Tissue Paper Mfrs. Assn. (dir. 1963-64), Am. Pulp and Paper Mill Supts. Assn., Salesman's Assn. Paper Industry, NAM (dir. 1981-85), Colony Club, Carolina Yacht Club, Yale Club (NYC). Home: 12 Tradd St Charleston SC 29401 Home Phone: 843-722-4976.

TORRE, GARY JEROME, retired lawyer; b. Oakland, Calif., Oct. 14, 1919; s. Giove M. and Jessie (Garibotto) Torre; m. Carol Desaussiere Goodrich, Dec. 25, 1948; children: Michael Durham, Alicia Hayden, Nicholas Goodrich. BA, U. Calif., 1941, JD, 1948. Bar: Calif. Law clerk Justice William Douglas, Wash., DC, 1948—49; ptnr. Litlick, Geary, Wheat, Adams and Charles, San Francisco, 1949—81; ret., 1981. Lt. USAF, 1942—45. Mem.: Sierra Club (pres., dir. legal defense fund 1968—93). Democrat.

TORRE, JOE (JOSEPH PAUL TORRE), professional baseball team manager; b. Bklyn., July 18, 1940; s. Joseph Sr. & Margaret Torre; m. Ali Torre, Aug. 23, 1987; one child, Andrea Rea; children from previous marriages: Michael, Lauren, Tina. HHD (hon.), Rider U., 2006. Profl. baseball player Milw. Braves, 1960-69, St. Louis Cardinals, 1969-74, NY Mets, 1974-77, player-mgr., 1977-82; mgr. Atlanta Braves, 1982-84, St. Louis Cardinals, 1990-94, NY Yankees, 1995—2007, LA Dodgers, 2008—. TV broadcaster Calif. Angels, 1984—90; co-founder (with Ali Torre) Joe Torre Safe at Home Found., 2002—. Author: (novels) Chasing the Dream: My Lifelong Journey to the World Series, 1997, Joe Torre's Ground Rules for Winners: 12 Keys to Managing Team Players, Tough Bosses, Setbacks, and Success, 1999; co-author (with Tom Verducci): The Yankee Years, 2009 (#1 Publishers Weekly bestseller); actor: (films) Taking Care of Business, 1990, Analyze That, 2002, (voice) Everyone's Hero, 2006. Named Nat. League MVP, 1971, Player of Yr. Sporting News, 1971, Mgr. of Yr. AP, 1982, Am. League Mgr. of Yr., 1996, 1998; named to All-Star Team, 1963-67, 70-73, coach 1997, 1999-2002, 2004; recipient Gold Glove award, 1965, MLB.com's Mgr of Yr. award, 2007; hit for cycle, 1973; winner World Series NY Yankees, 1996, 1998, 1999, 2000. over 1,000 career wins, 2006; four world championships. Office: c/o LA Dodgers Dodgers Stadium 1000 Elysian Park Ave Los Angeles CA 90012*

TORREANO, JOHN FRANCIS, painter, sculptor; b. Flint, Mich., Aug. 17, 1941; BFA, Cranbrook Acad. Art, 1963; MFA, Ohio State U., 1967. Prin. works exhibited in numerous one-man shows including Scott Hanson Gallery, NYC, 1989, Shea & Beker Gallery, NYC, 1989, 90, Susanne Hilberry Gallery, Birmingham, Mich., 1990, Shea & Beker Gallery, 1990, Dart Gallery Chgo., 1990, Hypo Bank, NY, 1992, Post Minimalism 1979-1990 An Extended Harvest Genouese Gallery, Boston, 1990, Painting Between the Paradigms Part IV: A Category of Objects as Yet Unnamed, Penine Hart Gallery, NY, With the Grain: Contemporary Panel Painting, Whitney Mus. Am. Art, Stamford, Conn., 1990, Butler Inst. Am. Art, Ohio, 1999, Feature, Inc., NYC, 2002, 2004; exhibited in group shows including Margo Leavin Gallery, LA, 1990, Laforet Mus., Havajuku, Japan, Pleasure, Hallwalls, Buffalo, NY, 1991, Cleve. Ctr. Contemporary ARt, 1991, Corcoran Gallery, Washington, 1995-96, 2004, AAAL, 2008, many others. Grantee Nat. Endowment for Arts, 1978-79, fellow, 1982-83, 89-90, John Simon Guggenheim Meml. Found., 1991, N.Y. Found. Arts, 1991. Office: 103 Franklin St New York NY 10013-2911 Business E-Mail: jt2@nyu.edu.

TORRENCE-THOMPSON, JUANITA LEE, editor, public relations executive; b. Brockton, Mass., Nov. 08; d. James Lee Torrence and Zylpha Odyselle Mapp-Robinson; m. Hugh Warren Thompson, Dec. 19, 1965; 1 child, Derek Rush. BS in Bus. & Comm., Empire State Coll., Old Westbury, NY, 1983; MA in Comm., Fordham U., 1989. Newsletter editor UN Internat. Sch., 1976-77; pub. rels., editl. asst. Nat. Assn. Theatre Owners, 1979-80; asst. acct. exec. Richard Weiner, Inc., 1984; newsletter editor SUNY Empire State Coll., 1985-87; editor Dorf & Stanton Comm., Inc., 1987-88; pub. rels. exec. pvt. practice, 1988—2006; editor, pub., owner Mobius, The Poetry Mag., 2006—. Adj. prof. pub. rels. Coll. New Rochelle, N.Y., 1997. Author: Spanning The Years, Wings Span to Eternity, Celebrating a Tapestry of Life; poetry columnist, 2004—, (audio book) New York and African Tapestries Poetry Among the Flowers: Queens Meets Asia (Micki Caldwell Nixon Jr. award); contbr. articles, poems, short stories, essays to mags., newspapers, newsletters and children's poetry. Bd. dirs So. Queens Park Assn., Jamaica, N.Y., 1988-91; mem. parent faculty soc. UN Internat. Sch., N.Y.C., 1976-80; pub. rels. cons. UN Coll. Fund, N.Y.C., 1994; mem. Queens Coun. on the Arts. Recipient Feature Article award Writers Digest, 1985, Meritorious Svc. award United Negro Coll. Fund, 1994, Editors Choice award Nashville Newsletter, 1994, 2004, Robins Nest Mag., 1996, First prize NY Pub. Libr. Contest, 1996, Outstanding Achievement award SUNY, Empire State Coll., Old Westbury, Margaret A. Walker Short Story Competition award 1999, 2000, 2d prize in 3 categories Internat. Poetry award Poetry Soc. Mich., HM award in short story competition, award Ky. Poetry Soc. Mem. AAUW, Nat. Assn. Black Journalists, Poetry Soc. Am., Acad. Am. Poets, Black Ams. in Pub., Poets and Writers, Queens Coun. on the Arts, Fresh Meadows Poets. Avocations: travel, theater, films, opera, concerts. Office: PO Box 671058 Flushing NY 11367-1058 Personal E-mail: poetrytown@earthlink.net.

TORRENZANO, RICHARD, public relations executive; BS, NY Inst. Tech., Old Westbury, 1972, LittD (hon.), 1990; postgrad. Exec. Program, Stanford Univ., Calif., 1986. With NY Stock Exch., 1982—90, sr. v.p., mgmt. and exec. com., chief spokesman; sr. v.p., dir. corp. affairs, mgmt. com. SmithKline Beecham, London, 1990—94; chmn., CEO Torrenzano Group, NYC, 1995—. Coord. Pres. Reagan's Bd. Advisors on Pvt. Sector Initiatives, Washington, 1986—89; pvt. sector adv. com. USIA, Washington, 1983—92; coord. program USSR-USA Conf. on Stock Markets, Moscow, 1990, PRC-USA Conf. on Stock Markets, Beijing, 1986; lectr. in field. Contbr. articles to profl. journals. Trustee, mem. exec. com. NY Inst. Tech., 1985—. Decorated knight of Malta, Knight Grand Cross Order of Holy Sepulchre, knight comdr. Order of Sts. Maurice and Lazarus, Royal House of Savoy, knight comdr. jus patronato Sacred Constantinian Order St. George, knight comdr. Royal Order of Francis I, Royal House of Bornone, knight Order of Merit Republic of Italy; recipient Ellis Island Medal of Honor, 1997, Silver anvil, Pub. Rels. Soc. Am. Mem.: Royal Soc. Medicine (London), NY Press Club, Nat. Press Club, Washington, DC. Office: The Torrenzano Group 60 E 42nd St Suit 2112 New York NY 10165-2112 Office Phone: 212-681-1700. Office Fax: 212-681-6961. Business E-Mail: richard@torrenzano.com.

TORRES, ALFREDO GABRIEL, biology professor, researcher; PhD, U. Tex., Austin, 1999. Asst. prof. UTMB, Galveston, Tex., 2003—. Office: UTMB Dept Microbiology and Immunolog 301 University Blvd Galveston TX 77555 Office Fax: 409-747-6869. Business E-Mail: altorres@utmb.edu.

TORRES, ARELIS, elementary school educator; arrived in U.S., 1988; d. José Luis Torres and Elizabeth Gómez. B in Psychology, U. P.R., 1988; EdM, Adelphi U., 1991. Tchr. Pub. Sch. 143, Queens, NY, 1988—99, Pub. Sch. 16, Corona, NY, 1999—. Activist, educator SHARE, NYC, 1996—, translator, 1998—; active SHARE-Latina SHARE, NYC, 1998—; vol. Learning Leaders, NYC, 2000—01. Recipient Citizenship award, N.Y.C. Coun., 2000, The Best of Our Cmty. Svc. award, Comité Noviembre, 2004, Citation in Edn., N.Y.C. Coun., 2004; named Most Valuable Vol., SHARE, 2000. Mem.: NSTA, United Fedn. Tchrs. Avocations: poetry, painting, music, bicycling. Office Phone: 718-505-0140.

TORRES, ART, former political organization administrator, former state legislator; b. LA; children: Joaquin, Danielle. AA, East L.A. C.C.; BA, U. Calif., Santa Cruz; JD, U. Calif. John F. Kennedy tchg. fellow Harvard U., Cambridge, Mass.; mem. Calif. State Assembly, Sacramento, 1973—81, Calif. State Senate, Sacramento, 1982—93; chmn. Calif. Dem. Party, 1996—2009. Chmn. Senate Com. Ins., Claims and Corps., Assembly Health Com., Senate Toxics and Pub. Safety Mgmt. Com., Select Com. Pacific Rim, Senate Spl. Rask Force on New L.A.; founder Calif. EPA; sr. mem. Senate Edn. Com.; author 1992 Immigrant Workforce Preparation Act; mem. Nat. Conf. State Legislatures Coalition on Immigration, Senate Appropriations Com., Senate Energy and Pub. Utilities Com., Senate Govtl. Orgn. Com., Senate Judiciary Com., Senate Natural Resources Com., Senate Transp. Com. Mem. Coun. Fgn. Rels., NY, Nat. Commn. Internat. Migration and Econ. Devel.; participant IVth Nobel Prizewinners Meeting Nova Spes Internat. Found., Vatican, Rome, 1989. Recipient Legislator of Yr. award Calif. Orgn. Policy and Sheriffs, 1990, Outstanding Legislator of Yr. award Calif. Sch. Bd. Assn., 1990, Outstanding Alumnus award U. Calif. Santa Cruz, Dreamer award Boys and Girls Club Am., 1990, Achievement award Latin Am. Law Enforcement Assn., 1992. Democrat. Office: 911 20th St Sacramento CA 95814-3115 Office Phone: 916-442-5707. Office Fax: 916-442-5714.*

TORRES, CYNTHIA ANN, marketing professional; b. Glendale, Calif., Sept. 24, 1958; d. Adolph and Ruth Ann (Smith) T.; m. Michael Victor Gisser, Mar. 11, 1989; children: Spencer Williams Gisser, David Westfall Torres Gisser. AB, Harvard U./Radcliffe Coll., 1980; MBA, Harvard U., 1984. Rsch. assoc. Bain & Co., Boston, 1980-82; assoc. Goldman, Sachs & Co., NYC, 1984-88, v.p., 1988, First Interstate Bancorp, LA, 1989—92; dir. Fidelity Investments Mgmt. Ltd., Hong Kong, 1993-96; pres. Integrity Investments Consultants, Ltd., 1996—99; dir. mktg. Diamond Portfolio Advisors LLC, Santa Monica, Calif., 2000—. Mem. judiciary rev. bd. Bus. Sch. Harvard U., Boston, 1983—84; chair fin. oversight com. Santa Monica-Malibu Unified Sch. Dist., 2008—. Rockefeller Found. scholar, 1976; Harvard U. Ctr. for Internat. Affairs fellow, 1979-80; recipient Leadership award Johnson and Johnson, 1980; by Council for Opportunity in Grad. Mgmt. Edn. fellow, 1982-84. Mem.: Harvard Coll. Fund (vice-chair west coast coun. 2008—), Fin. Women's Assn. Hong Kong (pres. 1997—98), Asia Soc., Acad. Polit. Sci., Harvard Alumni Assn. (nominating com. mem. 2008—, co-chair club com. 2008—09, dir. 2008—, exec. com. mem. 2009—, mem.-at-large), Harvard-Radcliffe Club So. Calif. (pres. 2006—08). Office: Diamond Portfolio Advisors LLC 10940 Wilshire Blvd Ste 600 Los Angeles CA 90024 Personal E-mail: cynthia@cynthiatorres.com.

TORRES, DANIEL FERNANDEZ, bishop; b. Chgo., Apr. 27, 1964; Ordained priest Diocese of Arecibo, PR, 1995; pastor Our Lady of Mount Carmel Parish, Arecibo; ordained bishop, 2007; aux. bishop Archdiocese of San Juan, 2007—. Roman Catholic. Office: Archdiocese of San Juan Calle San Jorge 201 Santurce Apartado 901967 San Juan PR 00902 Office Phone: 787-727-7373. Office Fax: 787-727-7938.

TORRES, DARA, Olympic athlete; b. Jupiter, Fla., Apr. 15, 1967; d. Edward Torres; 1 child. BA in Broadcasting & Communications, U. Fla., 1990. Intern CNN and NBC Sports; commentator TV sports NBC, ESPN, TNT, Fox News, Fox Sports; ret. swimmer, 1992—99, 2000—06; TV reporter Good Morning America, Inside Edition; host Oxygen Sports, Discovery Channel. Olympic team capt., 1992; spokesperson Tae Bo workout tapes. Co-author (with Elizabeth Weil): Age is Only a Number: Achieve Your Dreams at Any Stage in Your Life, 2009. Recipient Gold medal, 400, freestyle medley, LA Olympic Games, 1984, Silver medal 400m medley relay; Bronze medal, 400m freestyle relay, Seoul Olympic Games, 1988, Gold medal, 400m freestyle relay, Barcelona Olympic Games, 1992, Gold medal 400m freestyle relay, 400m medley relay; Bronze medal 50m, 100m freestyle, 100m butterfly, Sydney Olympic Games, 2000, Silver medal, 400m freestyle relay, Beijing Olympic Games, 2008, World Championships, 1986, Gold medal, 100m freestyle, 400m MR, 400m freestyle relay, Pan Pacific Championships, 1987, Kiphuth award, Summer Nationals, 1991, Comeback award; named to Internat. Jewish Sports Hall of Fame, 2005. Jewish. Achievements include winning National Titles in: 50m freestyle (9), 1982-2007, 100m freestyle (5), 1985-2007, 200m freestyle, 1991; first American swimmer to compete in five Olympic Games, 1984, 1988, 1992, 2000, 2008; setting the American record in: 50m freestyle, 100m freestyle. Office: USA Swimming 1 Olympic Plz Colorado Springs CO 80909-5746

TORRES, ESTEBAN EDWARD, former congressman, trade association administrator; b. Miami, Ariz., Jan. 27, 1930; s. Esteban Torres and Rena Baron (Gomez) T.; m. Arcy Sanchez, Jan. 22, 1955; children: Carmen D'Arcy, Rena Denise, Camille Bianca, Selina Andre, Esteban Adrian. Student, East Los Angeles Coll., 1960, Calif. State U., Los Angeles, 1963, U. Md., 1965, Am. U., 1966; PhD (hon.), Nat. U., 1987; DHL (hon.), Whittier Coll., 2001. Chief steward United Auto Workers, local 230, 1954-63, dir. polit. com., 1963; organizer, internat. rep. United Auto Workers (local 230), Washington, 1964; asst. dir. Internat. Affairs Dept., 1975-77; dir. Inter-Am. Bureau for Latin Am., Caribbean, 1965-67; exec. dir. E. Los Angeles Community Union (TELACU), 1967-74; U.S. ambassador to UNESCO, Paris, 1977-79; chmn. Geneva Grp., 1977-78; chmn. U.S. del. Gen. Conf., 1978; spl. asst. to pres. U.S., dir. White House Office Hispanic Affairs, 1979-81; mem. 98th-103rd Congresses from 34th Dist. Calif., 1983-98; mem. appropriations com., subcom. fgn. ops., subcom. transp.; chmn. ho. subcom. coinage; mem. ho. banking com., 1983; mem. ho. small bus. com., 1983. Campaign coord. Jerry Brown for Gov., 1974; Hispanic coord. LA County campaign Jimmy Carter for Pres., 1976; mem. Sec. of State Adv. Group, 1979-81; v.p. Nat. Congress Cmty. Econ. Devel., 1973-74; pres. Congress Mex.-Am. Unity, 1970-71; dir. Nat. Com. on Citizens Broadcasting, 1977; cons. U.S. Congress office of tech. assessment, 1976-77; del to IMF gen. conf., Geneva, 1975, del to U.S. Congress European Parliament meetings, 1984; ofcl. congl. observer Geneva Arms Control Talks; chmn. Congl. Hispanic Caucus, 1987; speaker Wrights Del. to USSR, 1987; Dem. dep. Whip, 1990; chmn. bd. Nat. Latino Media Coun., 1999—. Contbr. numerous articles to profl. jours. Co-chmn. Nat. Hispanic Dems., 1988—; chmn. Japan-Hispanic Inst. Inc.; bd. visitors Sch. Architecture UCLA, 1971-73; bd. dirs. LA County Econ. Devel. Com., 1972-75, Internat. Devel. Conf., 1976-78; chmn. Congrl. Hispanic Caucus, 1985-86; pres. Plaza de la Raza Cultural Ctr., 1972-73, chmn. bd. la Plaza de Cultural Art, 2007—; trustee Am. Coll. Paris, 1977-79; active Calif. Transp. Commn., Sacramento. With AUS, 1949-53, ETO. Recipient Congrl. award Nat. Leadership award 1997; sr. fellow UCLA Sch. Pub. Policy, 2000-05. Mem. Americans for Dem. Action (exec. bd. 1975-77), VFW Post 6315, Pico Rivera, Calif., Am. Legion, Smithsonian Inst. (regent emeritus 1999—), Willy C. Velasqez Inst., Calif. Transp. Commn. Democrat. Home: 1104 Montezuma Way West Covina CA 91791 Personal E-mail: etorres_nlmc@hotmail.com.

TORRES, JOSE (JOEY), mayor; b. 1958; m. Sonia Torres; 3 children. Diploma in Bus., Rutgers U. Cert. in ins. and banking, Pub. Housing Mgr. Nat. Assn. Housing and Redevel. Officials. Purchasing agt. Paterson Housing Authority, Paterson, NJ; mem. Paterson City Coun., NJ, 1990—2004; pres. city council City of Paterson, NJ, 1993—94, mayor. Mem. NJ Motor Vehicles Affordability and Fairness Task Force. Mem.: Nat. Inst. Govt. Purchasing, NJ Planning Bd. Assn. (award for smart growth for the city of Paterson). Conservative. Office: City Hall 155 Market St Paterson NJ 07505

TORRES, MARYELLEN, marketing executive; b. 1966; BA in Indsl. and Labor Rels, U. Mich., Ann Arbor, 1988, MBA in Mktg. and Corp. Strategy, 1993. Cons. Booz Allen & Hamilton Inc., NYC, 1988—89; account exec. Marsh & McLennan, Inc., NYC, 1989—91; mgmt. cons. Andersen Cons., Seattle, 1993—94; product mgr. Sierra On-Line, Inc., Seattle, 1994—96; strategic and product mktg. The Walt Disney Co., Burbank, Calif., 1996—99; v.p. mktg. and product devel. Encore Software, Inc., LA; v.p. corp. devel. Checkout.com, LLC, Beverly Hills, Calif.; v.p. mktg. Fasturn, Inc., Century City, Calif.; dir. brand and visual merchandising Meijer, Inc., Grand Rapids, Mich., 2003—07; v.p. mktg. A.J. Wright, 2007—. Named a Woman to Watch, Advt. Age, 2008. Mailing: TJX Cos Inc Hdqs 770 Cochituate Rd Framingham MA 01701 Office Phone: 508-390-1000. Office Fax: 508-390-2828.*

TORRES, NORMA, state legislator; b. Guatemala; m. Louis Torres; children: Robert, Christopher, Matthew. Former 911 dispatcher City of Los Angeles Police Dept.; councilwoman City of Pomona from Dist. 6, 2000—06; mayor City of Pomona, 2006—08; mem. Dist. 61 Calif. State Assembly, 2008—. Treas. Exec. Com. Nat. Conf. Dem. Mayors. Founder Neighbors for Pomona Com.; bd. mem. Pomonoa Valley Transp. Authority, Tri-City Mental Health, Fairplex Blue Ribbon Com.; vol. Suicide Prevention Ctr., Big Sisters Program, Am. Youth Soccer Org., Boy Scouts Am. Mem.: AFSCME Local 3090. Democrat. Office: Dist 61 PO Box 660 Pomona CA 91769 also: 505 South Garey Ave 2nd Fl Pomona CA 91766 Office Phone: 909-620-2051. Office Fax: 909-620-3707. Business E-Mail: Assemblymember.Torres@assembly.ca.gov.*

TORRES, ROBERT J., JR., Chief Justice, Guam Supreme Court; b. Guam; m. Mary Camacho Torres; 3 children. BBA in Accounting, U. Notre Dame, South Bend, Ind., 1980; JD, Harvard Law Sch. Bar: Guam 1987, Mass. Tax practitioner Lourie and Cutler, Boston, 1985—89; prtnr. Torres Limtiaco Cruz & Sison, 1989—2004; justice Guam Supreme Ct., 2004—, chief justice, 2008—. Former chmn. Guam Ninth Circuit Lawyer Representative Coordinating Com.; former mem. Guam Ninth Circuit Jud. Conference Exec. Com.; mem. Guam Jud. Council, 1990—96; chair U.S. Magistrate Judges Merit Selection Panel for Guam. Player, coach, and match commnr. Federation Internationale de Football Assn., Asian Football Confederation. Mem.: ABA, Guam Bar Assn. (past pres.). Office: Guam Supreme Ct Ste 300 Guam Jud Ctr 120 W OBrien Dr Hagatna GU 96910*

TORRES, RUDY ARNOLD, artist; b. LA, Dec. 21, 1957; s. Benjamin Tiburcio and Josephine Irene Torres. Student, East Los Angeles Coll., 1981—83, Pacific Inst. Comml. Art, 1984—85, Otis Parsons Sch. Design, 1985—86. Artist, co-owner Echo Park Gallery, LA, 1989—91. Exhibitions include Alpha Contemporary Exhibits, L.A., 1983—86, Mac Houston Art Gallery, Pasadena, Calif., 1986, Brand Libr. Art Gallery, Glendale, Calif., 1987, Design Ctr. L.A., 1987, L.A. Photography Ctr., 1987, 1989, L.A. Mcpl. Gallery, 1989, L.A. Art Assn., 1989, Echo Park Gallery, L.A., 1990—91, Boathouse Gallery, 1992, Weingart Gallery, 1992, Arthur Coons Gallery, 1992, Galeria Las Americas, 1992—94, 1996, Art & Barbee Art Gallery, Hollywood, Calif., 1993, Hilles Libr. at Harvard U., 1995, Olvera St. Gallery, L.A., 1996, Palette Des Artists, Pasadena, 1996, Galeria Otravez, East Los Angeles, Calif., 1996, 2001, Long Beach (Calif.) Gallery, 1998, Calif. State U. Fullerton grand Ctrl. Art Ctr., Santa Ana, 2001, Guggenheim Gallery, Chapman U., Orange, Calif., 2001, Showcase North Gallery, Santa Ana, 2001—02, Huntington Beach (Calif.) Gallery, 2002, City of Brea (Calif.) Gallery, 2002, one-man shows include Minus Zero Gallery, Torrance, Calif., 1990, Mary Norton Clapp Libr., Occidental Coll., L.A., 2000, Galeria Rustica, Pomona, Calif., 2002, Fullerton (Calif.) Branch Libr., 2002, Aliso Viejo (Calif.) Libr., 2002—03, exhibited in group shows at Latino Art Mus., Pomona, Calif., 2002—03, Huntington Beach (Calif.) Art Ctr., 2003, 2005, Eagle Rock Cmty. Cultural Assn., LA, 2003, Self Help Graphics, East LA, 2003, 2004, Latino Art Mus., Claremont, Calif., 2004, The Green Door Gallery, Santa Ana, Calif., 2004. Recipient cert. of appreciation for mural in Herman Dist., 14th Dist. City of L.A., 1986. Avocations: body building, swimming, jogging, camping, fishing. Personal E-mail: rudeart@sbcglobal.net.

TORRES, SUSIE APURON, special education educator; b. Dededo, Guam, Apr. 25, 1955; d. Jesus Nededog and Francisca (Apuron) Torres; children: Victor, Brian, Simon. BA, U. Guam, 1989; MEd, Portland U., 1992. Tchrs. aide Bredie Meml. Sch., Tumon, Guam, 1982-87, speech and lang. asst., 1987-89; basic life skills instr. Guam C.C., Mangilalo, 1989-90; community base educator George Washington High Sch., Mangilalo, 1991-92; resource instr. Dededo Middle Sch., 1992—, Astumbo Elem. Sch., 1997—, spl. edn. tchr., 1998—. Presenter in field; rental mgr., 1990—. Adviser 4-H Club, 2002—, del. to Washington nat. conf., 2003. Roman Catholic. Home: 118 Gloria Cir Dededo GU 96929-5300 Office: Astumbo Elem Sch DOE PO Box Agana Heights GU 96910

TORRES, TALANI, performing arts educator; b. Miami, Fla., Jan. 13, 1964; d. Angel Manuel and Lucy Maria Torres; life ptnr. Emmie McMahon; children: Christopher McMahon, Brendan McMahon, Liam McMahon. MFA, U. NC, Greensboro, 2006. Tchg. asst. U. NC, 2003—06; dance faculty Meredith Coll., Raleigh, NC, 2006—. Artistic dir. Miami Children's Dance Ensemble, 1991—2003; co-owner Dance Space, Miami, 1994—2003. Choreographer (contemporary concert dance) (NC Dance Alliance fellowship, 2007). Mem. NC Dance Alliance, Raleigh, 2008—. Recipient Outstanding Tchg. Asst. award, U. NC, 2006. Office: Meredith Coll 3800 Hillsborough St Raleigh NC 27614 Business E-Mail: torresta@meredith.edu.

TORRES-CALDERON, ALVARO MARTIN, language educator; s. Guillermo Torres-Calderon and Soledad Cisneros. PhD, Fla. State U., Tallahassee, 2006. Cert.: U. Lima, Peru (lawyer) 1997, 1998; in romance lang. & Spanish Fla. State U., 2006. Law and adminstrv. cons. Ministerio Transportes Comm., Lima, 1998—99; asst. prof. Spanish North Ga. Coll. & State U., Dahlonega, 2006—. Mem.: MLA, Bd. Lawyers (Lima), Latin-Am. Studies Assn., Circolo Sportivo Italiano (assoc.). Avocations: guitar, music, travel, Tae Kwon Do, poetry. Office: North Ga Coll & State Univ 82 College Cir Dahlonega GA 30597

TORRES CANCEL, LOURDES IVELISSE, philosopher, educator; d. Juan Alberto Torres Gorbea and Olga Julia Cancel Ortiz; m. Michael Lawrence Monaghan; children: Enrico Lorenzo Monaghan-Torres, Elena Ines Monaghan-Torres. PhD, Wayne State U., Detroit, 2006. Instr. Wayne State U., 1994—2006; asst. prof. Marygrove Coll., Detroit, 2006—. Office: Marygrove Coll 8425 West McNichols Detroit MI 48221 Business E-Mail: ltorres@marygrove.edu.

TORRESE, DANTE MICHAEL, prosthodontist, educator; b. Yonkers, NY, Feb. 12, 1949; s. Dante Angelo and Matilda (Dal Lago) T.; m. Camille Patricia DiPaola, Aug. 7, 1982. BS in Biology, Manhattan Coll., 1971; DDS, Columbia U., 1975; prosthodontic cert., NYU, 1983. Resident in dentistry Presbyn. Hosp., NYC, 1975-76; clin. instr. dentistry Columbia U., NYC, 1976-78, asst. clin. prof. dentistry, 1978—; pvt. practice dentistry Yonkers, N.Y., 1976—. Attending dentist Presbyn. Hosp., N.Y.C., 1976-86; lectr. in field. Recipient Am. Acad. Oral Pathology Grad. award 1975, Densply Corp. award for removable prosthodontics, 1975, Psi Omega Scholastic Achievement award, 1975. Fellow Am. Coll. of Dentists, Royal Soc. Health; mem. NRA (life), Yonkers Dental Soc., 9th Dist. State Dental Soc., Invested Baker St. Irregular, Sherlock Holmes Wireless Soc., Single Action Shooting Soc. (life), Yonkers Amateur Radio Club, Westchester Astronomy Club, Exch. Club (sec. 1979—), Three Garridebs of Westchester, Priory Scholars of N.Y.C. Club, Montague Street Lodgers of Bklyn. Club, Omicron Kappa Upsilon. Office: 984 N Broadway Ste 503 Yonkers NY 10701-1308 Office Phone: 914-965-4004.

TORRES FILHO, IVO, medical educator; b. Belem, Pará, Brazil, Apr. 17, 1958; s. Ivo and Vilma Torres; m. Luciana Neves, Aug. 27, 2000; children: Patricia Torres, Rodrigo Torres, Natasha Torres. MD, State U. of Rio de Janeiro, 1981; MSc, Fed. U. of Rio de Janeiro, 1984, PhD, 1988; postgrad., U. Calif.-San Diego, La Jolla, 1994. Lic. physician State U. of Rio de Janeiro, 1981. Instr. State U. of Rio de Janeiro, 1982—84, asst. prof., 1984—88, assoc. prof., 1988—2003, Va. Commonwealth U., Richmond, 2003—. Dir. Microcirculatory Lab, Va. Commonwealth U., Richmond, Va., 2003—. Contbr. over 100 articles and abstracts to profl. jours. Recipient Innovative Instrumentation award, Microcirculatory Soc., Inc, Travel award, Radiation Rsch. Soc., 1993; fellow Postdoctoral fellow, The PEW Charitable Trusts, Fogarty Internat. Ctr. Mem.: Am. Physiol. Soc. (assoc.), Microcirculatory Soc., Inc (assoc.). Office: Virginia Commonwealth University 1101 East Marshall St Rm B1-012 Richmond VA 23298-0695 Office Fax: 804-828-6413. Business E-Mail: itorres@vcu.edu.

TORREY, DAVID LEONARD, investment banker; b. Ottawa, Ont., Can., Oct. 6, 1931; s. Arthur Starratt and Josephine Edith (Leonard) T.; divorced; children: Heather Torrey Murphy, John Winthrop, Diana Bruce (dec.), Arthur Bruce, David Molson. BA in Econs., St. Lawrence U., 1953; diploma, Ivey Sch. Bus., U. Western Ont., 1954. With Pitfield Mackay Ross Ltd., Toronto, Ont., Canada, 1954-84, v.p., 1963-73, sr. v.p., 1973-80, vice chmn., 1980-82, pres., 1982-84, also bd. dirs.; vice chmn. Dominion Securities, Inc., 1984-88, RBC Dominion Securities, Inc., 1988-91. Chmn. Montreal Stock Exch., 1971-73, Phillips Cables Ltd., 1991-96; mem. coun. Montreal Bd. Trade, 1971-72. Chmn. Montreal Downtown YMCA, 1972-74; trustee St. Lawrence U., 1980-92; bd. dirs. Montreal Gen. Hosp. Found. Mem. Investment Bankers Assn. (gov. 1971-72), Securities Industries Assn. (bd. govs. 1972-73), Multiple Sclerosis Can. (past pres., bd. dirs.), Royal Montreal Golf Club, Mt. Royal (Montreal) Club, Toronto Club, Saifish Club Fla. (Palm Beach), Beta Theta Pi. Home: 389 Carlyle Ave Montreal PQ Canada H3R 1T3 Office: PO Box 6001 1 Pl Ville Marie 2E Montreal PQ Canada H3C 3A9 Office Phone: 514-399-9932.

TORREY, RICHARD FRANK, retired utilities executive; b. Saratoga Springs, NY, Dec. 31, 1926; s. Reginald Frank and Marian (Currey) T.; m. Betty Louise Stetson, July 2, 1949; children: Patricia Ann Torrey Kritsberg, Carol Louise Torrey Kress, Barbara Jean Torrey Friedman. BA cum laude, Syracuse U., 1951. News reporter, Syracuse (NY) Post Standard, 1947-51; pub. rels. account exec. Syracuse, 1951-53; home sec. 35th Congl. Dist., Syracuse, 1952-53; exec. sec. to mayor Syracuse, 1954—57; dir. area devel. Niagara Mohawk Power Corp., Syracuse, 1958-66, comml. v.p., Western Divsn. Buffalo, 1966-68, adminstrv. v.p., 1968-72, v.p., gen. mgr., 1972-76, sr. v.p. Syracuse, 1976-88; pres. Can. Niagara Power Co. Ltd., Niagara Falls, Ont., Canada, 1968-88, dir., 1968-89; ret., 1989. Pres., dir. Caragh Investments Ltd., 1981-85; pres. Opinac Investments Ltd., Toronto, 1982-88, bd. dirs., 1982-89; pres. Opinac Energy Ltd., Calgary, Alta., 1983-88, bd. dirs., 1983-89. Pres. Syracuse USO, 1959-61, mem. nat. coun., 1959-62, 68-74; co-chmn. Ctrl. N.Y. Interim Coun. Regional Planning, 1965-66; gen. chmn. Dunbar-Huntington Bldg. Fund, Syracuse, 1963; state campaign chmn. N.Y. Job Devel. Authority, 1961; gen. chmn. United Way of Buffalo and Erie County, 1971; mem. Syracuse U. Corp. Adv. Coun., 1972-76; trustee Elmcrest Children's Ctr., 1962-63, Camp Good Will, Syracuse, 1964-66, Syracuse Area Coun. Chs., 1959-64; bd. dirs. United Way Buffalo and Erie County, 1967-76, Greater Buffalo Devel. Found., Kenmore Mercy Hosp., 1970-76, Crouse Irving Meml. Hosp. Found., 1978-87, Nat. Kidney Found., 1987-89, Bon Secours-Venice (Fla.) Hosp. Found., 1992-98, vice chmn. 1995-96, chmn. 1996-98; bd. dirs. Plantation Cmty. Found., Venice, 1989, pres., 1990-93, pres. emeritus, 1993—; mem. bd. adv. Sisters of St. Joseph, 1967-76; elder Trinity Presbyn. Ch., Venice, 1992-94; assoc. mem. Dewitt Cmty. Ch., Ch. of the Palms, 2006-. With Air Corps US Army, 1944—47, with USAFR, 1947—50. Recipient Syracuse Young Man of Yr. award, 1962, Outstanding Citizen award Buffalo Evening News, 1973, Buffalo Man of Yr. award, 1974. Mem. Empire State (v.p., bd. dirs. 1963-80), Buffalo Area (v.p. 1968-72, bd. dirs. 1968-76, pres. 1972-73, chmn. bd. 1973-74) C. of C., Associated Industries of N.Y. (bd. dirs. 1978-80), Bus. Coun. N.Y. (bd. dirs. 1980-82), Mfrs. Assn. Cen. N.Y. (bd. dirs. 1977-88), Augusta Villa Assn. (bd. dirs. 1989-92), Buffalo Club (past 2d v.p., dir.), Syracuse Century Club (gov. 1980-83), Onondaga Golf Club, Automobile Club Western N.Y.(bd. dirs. 1971-73, pres. 1973), N.Y.S. Automobile Assn. (dir. 1975-76). Presbyterian. Home and Office: 7333 Scotland Way #2303 Sarasota FL 34238 Personal E-mail: dicktorrey@aol.com.

TORREZ, CAROLINE HERMINIA, human resources specialist, director, actress, musician, singer, dancer; d. Philip Hernandez and Lucy Mercedes Rivera; m. Robert Pierre Torrez, June 10, 1995. BA, Calif. State U., Fullerton, 1975. Sec. to exec. dir. Pinto program Calif. State U., Fullerton, 1972—73, oral history interpreter, 1973—75; asst. Spanish tchr. Cerritos Coll., Calif., 1974—75; export parts specialist export dept. C.B.S. Musical Instruments/Fender, Rogers & Rhodes, Fullerton, 1975—77; bilingual interviewer Orange County Housing Authority, Santa Ana, Calif., 1977—79, field rep., 1979—83, mktg. rep., 1983—87; recreation dir. City of Anaheim Parks and Recreation/Let's Play to Grow program/Joseph P. Kennedy Found., Calif., 1983—87; Home Investment Partnership Act coord. Urban County Housing and Cmty. Devel. Orange County, Santa Ana, 1987—99; v.p. internal ops. CHAMP, Inc., Santa Ana, 2000—06; dir. Champ Steel, Santa Ana, 2006—. Musician (viola): Yorba Linda Symphony Orch.; singer (alto, mezzo soprano): So. Calif. Chamber Singers. Charter mem. Brea (Calif.) Jaycee Women, 1980; coach Spl. Olympics City of Anaheim, Calif., 1982—87; coord. Hands Across Am., Orange County, 1986; dist. dir. Region 8 Orange County Jaycees, 1987; pres. Fountain Valley Jaycees, Calif., 1989; mem. Men-On-A-Missions-Eastside Christian Ch.; mem. bd. dirs. Alliance/Mentally Ill, Orange County, 1988—89. Mem.: SAG, Nat. Assn. Exec. Women, Southern Calif. Chamber Singers. Avocations: acting, viola, dance, singing, opera. Office: CHAMP Inc 633 Young St Santa Ana CA 92705

TORREZ, MICHELLE MARIE, artist, educator; b. Denver, Feb. 3, 1956; d. John Thomas and Geri Anne Chestor; children: Gwenevieve Louise, Nicole Michelle. Assocs. Visual Comm. and Advt. Design, Art Inst. Colo., Denver, 1986. Art dir. Mentler and Co., Dallas, 1986—87, Hamilton Sweeney Advt., Denver, 1987—94; owner Studio M, Denver, 1994—98; workshop instr. Art in the Aspens, Colo., 2005—, Taos Painters Workshop, N.Mex., 2005—. Adj. instr. painting Met. State Coll. Denver, 2004—; traveling lectr. US State Dept.-Art in Embassies, Sofia, Bulgaria, 2003; participant Coors Invitational We. Art Exhibit, 2002—05, American Art Invitational, 2007; selected artist Colorado Women's Found., 2007, American Art Collector, 2007. S.W. Art Mag., one-woman shows include Michelle Torrez: One Woman Show, Metaphor - Art in Embassies Calendar, 2003, exhibitions include Colo. Gov.'s Office, 2002—05, Mizel Mus. Show, 2006, Sangre De Cristo Art Ctr. Recipient Colo. ALFIE award for art direction of pub. svc. comml., Denver Advt. Agy., 1991, CLEO award for art direction of pub. svc. TV comml., City of Denver, 1991; named to Hall of Fame, Art Inst. of Colo., 2004; Travel grant, Christian Solidarity Internat., 2005. Mem.: Denver Art Students League (assoc.), Denver Art Mus. (assoc.), Nat. Mus. of Women in the Arts (assoc.), Amnesty Internat. Avocation: humanitarian work.

TORRIE, JANE MARIE, chiropractor, secondary school educator; d. Douglas Edward and Carolyn Cooper Torrie; children: Cecilio Eduardo, Benjamin Lucas. BS in Human Biology, Cleve. Chiropractic Coll., LA, 1985, Dr. in Chiropractic, 1985. Lic. chiropractor Calif., Ariz., N.Mex; cert. tchr. Tex. Pvt. practice as chiropractor, Espanola, N.Mex., 1987—94; tchr. Northwest H.S., Justin, Tex., 1999—. Adj. instr. Tarrant County Coll., Ft. Worth, 2003—. Mem. missions coun. 1st Ch. Nazarene, Denton, Tex., 2001—06. Conservative. Nazarene. Avocation: reading.

TORRUELLA, JUAN R., federal judge; b. San Juan, June 7, 1933; BS in Bus. and Fin., U. Pa., 1954; LLB, Boston U., 1957; LLM, U. Va., 1984; MPA, U. P.R., 1984; MSt, Oxford U., 2003; LLD (hon.), St. John's U., 1995, Roger Williams U., 1995. Judge US Dist. Ct. PR, San Juan, 1974—82, chief judge, 1982—84; judge US Ct. Appeals (1st cir.), San Juan, 1984—, chief judge, 1994—2001. Former mem. jud. conf. com. Adminstrn. Fed. Magistrate Sys., former mem. jud. conf. exec. com.; former mem. jud. conf. com. Internat. Jud. Rels. Mem.: FBA, ABA, PR Bar Assn., DC Bar Assn., Assn. Labor Rels. Practitioners PR and VI. Office: John J Moakley US Courthouse 1 Courthouse Ste 2500 Boston MA 02210*

TORSON, DIANNA MAY, retired small business owner; b. San Diego, Dec. 29, 1940; d. Eugene Henry Torson and Dolores Elaine Seaton; m. John Alexander Barney; children: Patricia Ann Torson Berkland, Kim Elaine Zilverberg, Scott Ruel Randall. BA, S.D. State U., 1988, MA, 1990. Instr. Sinte Gleska U., Mission, SD, 1990—92, chair arts and scis., 1992—94, dean arts and scis., 1994—96; dir. student devel., Native Am. advisor Dakota State U., Madison, SD, 1996—2000; co-owner, v.p. LeadingEducation.com, Brookings, SD, 2000—09. With Humanities Spkrs. Bur., SD Humanities Coun., Brookings, 1990—96; coord., instr. summer teacher's inst. Sinte Gleska U. and S.D. State U., Brookings and Mission, 1992—95; advisor Sinte Gleska Lit. Coun., Mission; coord. Sinte Gleska U. Bush Faculty Devel. Com., Mission, 1993—94. Recorder, editor: narrative non-fiction Salt Camp: HerStory Lakota Living Treasure Ollie Napesni, 2003; contbr. poetry to Leaning Into the Wind, Woven on the Wind, poetry and photography to mags. Mem.: SD Pilots Assn. (sec.), Phi Kappa Phi (life). Democrat. Avocations: horseback riding, walking, bicycling, reading, environmental affairs. E-mail: torsond@itctel.com.

TORTI, FRANK MICHAEL, federal agency administrator; b. 1947; BA, MA, Johns Hopkins U., 1969; MPH, Harvard U., 1973, MD, 1974. Diplomate in internal medicine and med. oncology Am. Bd. Internal Medicine. Asst. prof. medicine Stanford (Calif.) U., 1979-84, clin. assoc. prof. medicine, 1984-86, assoc. prof. medicine, 1986-93; Charles L. Spurr prof. medicine Wake Forest U. Sch. Medicine, Winston-Salem, NC, 1993—2008, dir. Comprehensive Cancer Ctr., 1993—2008, chmn. dept. cancer biology, 1993—2008; prin. dep. commr., first chief scientist FDA, Rockville, Md., 2008—, acting commr., 2009. Chair N.C. Gov.'s Commn. on Cancer Coordination and Control, 1993—2003; mem. study sect. Am. Inst. for Cancer Rsch., Bethesda, Md., 1989—. Recipient MERIT award, NIH. Mem. Am. Assn. for Cancer Rsch., Am. Soc. Clin. Oncology, Am. Soc. Cell Biology, Internat. Soc. Interferon Rsch., Am. Fedn. for Clin. Rsch., Soc. for Biol. Therapy. Office: FDA 5600 Fishers Ln Rockville MD 20857*

TORTOLANI, ANTHONY JOHN, surgeon, educator; b. Eastchester, NY, Oct. 15, 1943; s. Salvatore Paul and Yolanda (Vecciarelli) Tortolani; m. Beth Callahan, Dec. 15, 1967 (dec. Oct. 1993); children: Julia Sue, Paul Justin; m. Katherine Gormley, Sept. 25, 1999. BS, Fordham U., 1965; MD, George Washington Sch. Medicine, 1969. Diplomate Am. Bd. Surgery, Am. Bd. Thoracic Surgery. Chief divsn. cardiovascular & thoracic surgery North Shore U. Hosp., Manhasset, NY, 1978-90, chmn. dept. surgery, 1988-96, chmn. med. bd., 1994-96, chmn. dept. surgery Glen Cove, NY, 1990-96; John D. Mountain chair surgery North Shore U. Hosp.- Cornell U. Med. Coll., Manhasset, 1989-96, program dir. surg. residency program, 1992-96; prof. surgery Cornell U. Med. Coll., NYC, 1993-97, prof. cardiothoracic surgery, 1997-99; mem. staff N.Y. Hosp., NYC, 1997-99; dir., prof. cardiothoracic surgery Jack D. Weiler Hosp./Montefiore Med. Ctr. Albert Einstein Coll. of Medicine, NYC, 1999-2001; prof. clin. cardiothoracic surgery Weill Med. Coll. Cornell U., 2001—. Vice-chmn. NY Presbyn. Cornell Cardiothoracic Surgery Network; chmn. dept. cardiothoracic surgery, NY Meth. Hosp., 2004-; chmn. dept. surgery, 2007-. Active Columbus Citizens Found., N.Y.C. Maj. USAF, 1974-76. Roman Catholic. Avocation: breeding arabian horses. Office: NY Presbyn Hosp 525 E 68th St Rm M-404 New York NY 10021 Business E-Mail: astoltol@meo.cornell.com.

TORTORA, ANNE HALLORAN, music educator, director; married. DMA, U. Hartford, Conn., 2006. Adj. lectr. U. Hartford, 2006—; dir. bands Mt. St. Mary's U., Emmitsburg, Md., 2008—. Merit badge counselor Boy Scouts Am., Uncasville, Conn., 1994—2008. Mem.: Music Educators Nat. Conf., Coll. Band Dirs. Nat. Assn., Pi Kappa Lambda, Sigma Alpha Iota. Roman Catholic. Office: Mt Saint Mary's Univ 163000 Old Emmitsburg Rd Emmitsburg MD 21727

TORTORELLA, JOHN, professional hockey coach; b. Boston, June 24, 1958; Coach Va. Lancers (Atlantic Coast Hockey League), 1986—88; asst. coach Buffalo Sabres, 1989—95; head coach Rochester Am. (Am. Hockey League), 1995—97; asst. coach Phoenix Coyotes, 1997—99, NY Rangers, 1999—2001, head coach, 2009—, Tampa Bay Lightning, 2001—08; analyst TSN, 2008—09. Head coach Team USA, IIHF World Hockey Championship, 2008. Recipient Jack Adams Award, NHL, 2004; named Coach of Yr., Atlantic Coast Hockey League, 1986—87, NHL Coach of Yr., Sporting News, 2004. Achievements include being the coach of Stanley Cup Champion, Tampa Bay Lightning, 2004. Office: NY Rangers Hockey Club 2 Pennsylvania Plaza New York NY 10121*

TORTORELLO, NICHOLAS JOHN, public opinion and market research company executive; b. Maspeth, NY, Dec. 1, 1948; s. John Anthony and Verla Jean (Odel) Tortorello; m. Joan Elizabeth King, Jan. 13, 1973 (div. July 2006); children: Kerry Ann, Jennifer Joan. BA in Polit. Sci. with highest honors, Williams Coll., 1971; M Religious Studies, St. Joseph's Sem., Yonkers, NY, 1988. V.p. Louis Harris & Assocs., NYC, 1971-73, sr. v.p., 1973-79; exec. v.p. DMT Inc., NYC, 1979-83; pres. Tortorello Corp., Pearl River, N.Y., 1983-85; pres. Tortorello group Market Facts Inc.-N.Y., NYC, 1985-86; v.p. Total Rsch. Corp., Princeton, N.J., 1986-88; chmn. Rsch. and Forecasts Inc., NYC, 1989-93; sr. v.p. Roper Starch Worldwide Inc., NYC, 1993-98; pres. Guideline Consulting, NYC, 1998—2002; v.p., gen. mgr. Lieberman Rsch. Worldwide Inc., 2003—04; v.p. Internat. Comms. Rsch., NYC, 2004—06; sr. v.p. The Mktg. Workshop, Inc., 2006—07, Pert Survey Rsch. Inc., Bloomfield, Conn., 2007—. Editor, author Tortorello Trendline, 1983-85, Rsch. and Forecasts Trendline, 1989-91. Trustee Riverdale Country Sch., NY, 1982-90, v.p., 1986-89; trustee Marymount Manhattan Coll., NYC, 1986-88; lectr., tchr. religion St. Anthony's Ch., Nanuet, NY, 1984-86; mem. CARA Bd. Georgetown U., Washington, 1992-98, rsch. adv. coun., 2000—; mem. Hosp. Chaplaincy Bd., 1991-97; v.p. Class of '71, Williams Coll., 2001. Recipient Am. Legion award for leadership, scholarship, honor and svc., 1967, Disting. Alumnus of Yr. award, Riverdale Country Sch., 1984. Mem. Am. Dirs. Inst. (trustee 1984-87), Coun. Am. Survey Rsch. Orgn. (chmn. bd. dirs. 2001, chmn. publs. com. 1991-94, chmn. pub. rels. com. 1995-97, chmn. mktg. and comms. com. 1997-99, bd. dirs., chmn. 1999 ann. conf., chmn. bd. dirs. 1999, chmn. bd. trustees 2001, chmn. nominating com. 2002), Am. Assn. Pub. Opinion Rsch.(Counselor-AT Large, 2004-05), Williams Club. Democrat. Avocations: collecting Lionel trains, collecting stereo equipment, golf, collecting american coins. Office: Pert Survey Rsch Inc 522 Cottage Grove Rd Ste 1 Bloomfield CT 06002-3118 Home Phone: 484-483-7692; Office Phone: 914-907-7926. Personal E-mail: ntortorello@hotmail.com, njtortorello@yahoo.com.

TORTORICI, PETER, marketing executive; b. Dec. 4, 1944; m. Susan Tortorici; 3 children. BA in Polit. Sci, Ohio State U.; JD, St. John's U. Sch. Law. Trial atty., 1974—80; exec. v.p., pres. CBS Entertainment, 1990—95; exec. prodr. Carsey-Werner Productions, 1996—98; pres., CEO Telemundo Network, 1999—99; prodr. Sony Pictures Entertainment, Columbia Tristar TV; pres., exec. prodr. MindShare Entertainment, 2003; pres., CEO GroupM Entertainment. Founder Peter Tortorici Productions. Prodr.: (TV series) Cosby, 1996; exec. prodr.: Grace Under Fire, 1996—98; co-exec. prodr. (TV movie) A Very Married Christmas, 2004; exec. prodr.: (TV series) The Days, 2004; exec. prodr.(writer): (TV series) Significant Others, 2004. Achievements include honors from Advertising Age and Buisness 2.0 Magazine's for innovation, leadership, and accomplishment in the emerging area of branded entertainment. Mailing: c/o WPP Media Grp USA Inc 125 Park Ave New York NY 10017

TORTORIELLO, WILLIAM JOSEPH, pharmaceutical executive; b. Newark, July 24, 1951; s. Anthony George and Emily Carmela Tortoriello; m. Sonia Perez, Aug. 26, 1972; children: William Anthony, Jennifer Marie Schlaudecker, Melissa Ann. BS in Chem. Engring., Newark Coll. Engring., 1973; MS in Mgmt. Engring., NJ Inst. Tech., Newark, 1977. Lic. profl. engring., 1977; operate wastewater treatment facility NJ Dept. Environ. Protection, 1989. Mfg. area head Merck, Rahway, NJ, 1981—86, environ. control. mgr., 1986—88; engring. mgr. Merck Sharp & Dohme Quimica de PR, Barceloneta, 1988—91; dir. site ops. Merck, Whitehouse Sta., NJ, 1991—95, team leader tech. transfer, 1995—99, exec. dir. site ops., 1999—2005; sr. dir. global ops. east Johnson & Johnson Pharm. Rsch. & Devel., Raritan, NJ, 2005—. Co-chair, local emergency planning com. City of Rahway, 1986—88; mem. Lower Gwynedd Indsl. Pact, Lower Gynedd, Pa., 2005—07; president's coun. Gwynedd Mercy Coll., 2007—; dir. on bd. Gateway C. of C., Elizabeth, NJ, 1999—2005; bd. of governors Union County Coll., Union, NJ, 2003—05. Recipient Mgmt. award, Merck Sr. Mgmt., 1981, Merck, 1987, Rahway Ctr. Partnership, 2004, Stds. Excellence, Johnson & Johnson, 2006, Encore, 2007. Mem.: Gateway C. of C. (dir. 1999—2007). Republican. Roman Catholic. Achievements include being featured in Fortune Magazine for designing performance based contracts for site services. Avocations: exercise, golf, reading, camping, piano. Home: 22 Stratton Ct Flemington NJ 08822 Office: Johnson & Johnson PRD 920 US Hwy 202 S Raritan NJ 08869 Office Fax: 908-927-7158. Personal E-mail: bill0298@aol.com. Business E-Mail: wtortori@prdus.jnj.com.

TORVALDS, LINUS BENEDICT, application developer; b. Helsinki, Finland, Dec. 28, 1969; s. Nils and Anna Torvalds; m. Tove Torvalds; children: Patricia Miranda, Daniela Yolanda, Celeste Amanda. MS in Computer Sci., Helsinki U., 1996. Developer Transmeta Corp., Santa Clara, Calif., 1997—2003; fellow Open Source Develop. Labs (OSDL), Beaverton, Oreg., 2003—. Co-author (with David Diamond): (autobiography) Just for Fun: The Story of an Accidental Revolutionary, 2001. Recipient Nokia Found. Award, 1997, Lifetime Achievement Award, Uniforum, 1997, Takeda award, 2001; named One of the Most Influential People in the World, TIME mag., 2004. Achievements include invention of Linux operating system. Office: Osdl 210 Fell St # 16 San Francisco CA 94102-5145

TOSCANO, JAMES VINCENT, medical foundation president; b. Passaic, NJ, Aug. 8, 1937; s. William V. and Mary A. (DeNigris) T.; m. Sharon Lee Bowers; children: Shawn Truelson, Lauren Bjorklund, David Brendan, Dania Toscano Miwa. AB summa cum laude, Rutgers Coll., 1959; MA, Yale U., 1960. Lectr. Wharton Sch., U. Pa., 1961-64;

chief opinion analyst Pa. Opinion Poll, 1962-64; mng. dir. World Press Inst., St. Paul, 1964-68, exec. dir., 1968-72; dir. devel. Macalester Coll., St. Paul, 1972-74; v.p. resource devel. and pub. affairs Mpls. Soc. Fine Arts, 1974-79; pres. Minn. Mus. Art, 1979-81; exec. v.p. Park Nicollet Inst., 1981—2006; corp. sec. Park Nicollet Clinic, 1983-86; sr. v.p. Am. Med. Ctrs., Inc., 1985-87; pres. Mpls. Heart Inst. Found., 2006—. Adj. prof. sch. of mgmt. U. St. Thomas, 1989-01; co-chair prin. practices nonprofit excellence com. MCN, 1994-98, 2004—05; lectr. Grad. Sch. Bus., Hamline U., 2003—. Author: The Chief Elected Official in the Penjerdel Region, 1964; co-author, co-editor: The Integration of Political Communities, 1964. Bd. dirs., exec. com., sec.-treas. World Press Ins., 1972-2007; bd. dirs., chmn. Southside Newspaper Mpls., 1975-79; chmn. com. to improve student behavior St. Paul Pub. Schs., 1977-79; bd. dirs. Planned Parenthood St. Paul, 1965-72, Mpls. Action Agy., 1976-79; emeritus dir. Help Enable Alcoholics Receive Treatment; mem. St. Paul Heritage Preservation Commn., 1979-82, vice chmn., 1981; mem. Citizens Adv. Com. on Cable Comm.; bd. dirs. Minn. Newspaper Found., 1987-92, Minn. Coun. Nonprofits, 1989-95, 1997-2003; bd. mem. Vocal Essence, 1993-96, alt. Minn. Healthcare Commn., 1993-95, mem. Minn. Healthcare Commn., 1995-97, chair task force med edn. rsch. costs, 1994-96. com. med. rsch. edn. costs, 1996-2003; chair, 1996-99; liason health tech adv. com., 1993-97; pres. 2000-03, bd. dirs. Summit Ave Residential Preservation Assn., 2000-06, Skylight Club, Informal Club, bd. dirs. Citizens League, 1980, African-Am. Culture Ctr., 1979-82, Am. Composers Forum, 1981-85, St. Paul Chamber Orch., 1976-80, 83-89, United Theol. Sem., 1985-88; dir. emeritus Minn. Citizens for the Arts; mem. exec. com., chmn. Med. Alley Assn., 1986-96, bd. dirs., 1986-96, task force on tech. assessment Med. Alley, 1992-93; mem. health affairs adv. com. Acad. Health Ctr. U. Minn., 1988-95; bd. dirs. Mother Cabrini House, 1985-92, Minn. Civil Justice Coalition, 1987-91, also chmn.; chmn. Gov.'s Task Force on Health Care Promotion, 1985-86, mem. Gov.'s Com. Promotion Health Care Resources, 1986-87; chmn. bd. Minn. Fin. Counseling Svcs., Inc., 1990-93; mem. task force cost effectiveness Med. Alley, 1994-95; bd. dirs. Meml. Blood Bank, 1995-2001, mem. exec. com., 1996-2001; bd. dirs. Bakken Mus., 1997-2003, Stevens Sq. Cmty. Orgn., 1997-99; bd. dirs. Rainbow Rsch., Inc., 2002—, chmn. bd., 2004-07; bd. dirs. Friends of the St. Paul Libr., 2004-07; bd. dirs., treas. Pub. Arts St. Paul, 2004-2007, Minn. Charities Rev. Coun., 2004-07, chmn., 2007-08; mem. West Summit Neighborhood Adv. Coun., 2004-09; co-chair, 2004-07; mem., chair Alley Found., 2006-, bd. mem. 515 Edn. Found., 2009-. Woodrow Wilson Nat. fellow, 1960. Minn. Charities Rev. Coun. (chair 2007-09). Congregationalist. Address: 1982 Summit Ave Saint Paul MN 55105-1460 Office: Mpls Heart Inst Found 920 E 28th St Ste 100 Minneapolis MN 55407 Home Phone: 651-699-1765; Office Phone: 612-863-3978. Personal E-mail: jvt2@comcast.net. Business E-Mail: jtoscano@mhif.org.

TOSHACH, CLARICE OVERSBY, real estate developer, retired computer company executive; b. Firbank, Westmoreland, Eng., Nov. 21, 1928; came to U.S., 1955; d. Oliver and Nora (Brown) Oversby; m. Daniel Wilkie Toshach, July 30, 1965 (dec. Aug. 1992); 1 child, Duncan Oversby Toshach; 1 child from previous marriage, Paul Anthony Beard. Textile designer Storeys of Lancaster, Eng., 1949-55; owner, operator Broadway Lane, Saginaw, Mich., 1956-70; pres., owner Clarissa Jane Inc., Saginaw, 1962-70, Over-Tosh Computers, Inc. dba Computerland, Saginaw and Flint, Mich., 1983-95; mgr., ptnr. Mich. Comml. Devel. L.L.C., Saginaw, 1995—. Trustee Saginaw Gen. Hosp., 1977-83, Home for the Aged, 1978-80; bd. dirs. Vis. Nurse Assn., pres., 1981-83; bd. dirs. Hospice of Saginaw, Inc., v.p., 1981-83; mem. long range planning com. United Way of Saginaw, 1982-83; cmty. advisor Jr. League of Saginaw, 1982-83; pres. Saginaw Gen. Hosp. Aux., 1972-82, pres., 1976-77.

TOSI, LAURENCE A., III, investment company executive; BA, Georgetown U., Washington, DC, 1990, JD, MBA, Georgetown U., Washington, DC, 1994. Corp. lawyer, NYC; dir. bus. devel. NBC, NYC; head bus. devel., global markets & investment banking Merrill Lynch & Co., NYC, 1999—2002, CFO, bus. fin., 2002—04, fin. dir., prin. acctg. officer, 2004—07, sr. v.p., COO, global markets & investment banking, 2007—08; CFO Blackstone Group., NYC, 2008—. Mem. exec. com. Merrill Lynch & Co., Blackstone Group. Bd. advisors Georgetown U. Wall St. Alliance. Office: The Blackstone Group LP 345 Park Ave New York NY 10154 Office Phone: 212-583-5000.

TOSKES, PHILLIP PAUL, gastroenterologist, educator, researcher; b. Balt., Jan. 4, 1940; s. John F. and Mary R. (Vonelli) T.; m. Patricia A. Sponsel, June 3, 1961; children: Tammy Lynn Price, Tracey Lynn, Steven D. BA, Johns Hopkins U., 1961; MD, U. Md., 1965. Diplomate Am. Bd. Internal Medicine (bd. dirs.), Am. Bd. Gastroenterology. Intern, resident U. Md. Hosp., Balt., 1965-68; fellow in gastroenterology Hosp. U. Pa., Phila., 1968-70; asst. prof. medicine U. Fla., Gainesville, 1973-75, assoc. prof. medicine, 1975-78, prof. medicine, 1978—, dir. divsn. gastro, hepatology, 1978-97, prof., chmn. dept. medicine, 1997—2002. Chief gastro sect. Gainesville VA Med. Ctr., 1973-92; chmn. Nat. Digestive Disease Adv. Bd., Washington, 1992-94. Author chpts. to books. Maj. U.S. Army, 1970-73. Recipient Disting. Achievement award Can. Gastroenterol. Assn., 1982. Fellow ACP (Meade Johnson scholar 1966-68); mem. Am. Soc. Clin. Investigation, Am. Fedn. Clin. Rsch., Am. Gastroenterol. Assn. (pres. 1997-98). Avocations: travel, swimming, boating. Office: U Fla Box 100214 1600 SW Archer Rd Gainesville FL 32610-3001 Home: 202 NW 114th Way Gainesville FL 32607-1122 Office Phone: 352-392-2877. Business E-Mail: toskepp@medicine.ufl.edu.

TOSNEY, KATHRYN W., embryologist, biology educator; b. Burke, SD, Sept. 3, 1946; d. Cyril Emory and Dortha P. (Briese) Wiebelhaus. BS with hons., U. Oreg., 1975; PhD, Stanford U., 1980. MDA postdoct. fellow Yale U., New Haven, Conn., 1980-82; MDA, NIH postdoct. fellow U. Conn., Storrs, 1982-84; asst. prof. biology U. Mich., Ann Arbor, 1984-89, assoc. prof. biology, 1989-95, prof. biology, 1995—, assoc. chair biology, 1990-95. Mem. fed. adv. panels NIH, 1988—. Assoc. editor: Jour. of Morphology, 1985-90, Exp. Neurology, 1997—; contbr. articles to profl. jours. Rsch. grantee NIH, 1985—. Mem. Soc. Neurosci., Soc. Developmental Biology (rep. 1995—, bd. trustees 1996—). Achievements include studies of axonal guidance mechanisms during development. Office: U Mich Biology Dept 830 N University Ave Ann Arbor MI 48109-1048

TOSTE, ANTHONY PAIM, chemistry educator, researcher; b. Mountain View, Calif., June 26, 1948; BS in Chemistry with honors, Santa Clara U., Calif., 1970; PhD in Biochemistry and Chemistry, U. Calif., Berkeley, 1976. Rsch. fellow Cardiovasc. Rsch. Inst., San Francisco, 1977—79; rsch. scientist Battelle Meml. Inst. Pacific N.W. Nat. Lab., Richland, Wash., 1980—88; asst. prof. Mo. State U., Springfield, 1988—94, assoc. prof., 1994—99, prof., 1999—. Cons. Mitsubishi Metal Corp., Tokyo, 1984-87, Dow Chem., Tex., 1994-96; presenter in field. Contbr. articles to jours. in field, cmty. svc. presentations. Bd. dirs. Mid Columbia Arts Coun., Richland, 1987-88, Bot. Soc. S.W. Mo., Springfield, 1997-2002; pres. bd. dirs. Springfield Sister Cities Assn., 1993-96; co-founder, co-leader Internat. Friendship Dels. to Japan, 1996, 99, 2001, 03, 05, 07, 09. Rsch., equipment grantee NSF, 1990; recipient Diverse Cmty. award Sister Cities Internat., Boston, 1996, STA Rsch. fellow, Japan, 1998 Mem. Am. Chem. Soc. (treas. Ozark sect. 1989-91, chmn.-elect 2000, chmn. 2000-01), Am. Nuc. Soc. (Best Poster award 1987), Assn. Ofcl. Analytical Chemists (program chair 1986, 90), Mo. Acad. Sci. (program chair 1997, 2002). Avocations: picture framing, collecting fine art, woodworking, reading, cinema. Home: 2113 E Woodhaven Pl Springfield MO 65804-6767 Office: Mo State U Dept Chemistry 901 S National Ave Springfield MO 65804 Home Phone: 417-883-1051; Office Phone: 417-836-5150. Business E-Mail: anthonytoste@missouristate.edu.

TOSTI, ANNETTE BREWER, artist; b. Indpls., June 20, 1958; d. William Marion and Patricia Davis Brewer; m. Donald Thomas Tosti, Dec. 29, 1989; children: Tabitha Szary, Todd, Rene Foppe, Alicia Anderson, Roxanna LaValley, Brett. BA, U. Montevallo, 1979; BS, U. Ala., 1985; MA, U. of Pacific, 1989; MFA, Calif. Coll. Arts, 1992. One-woman shows include San Francisco Art Commission Gallery, Carnegie Art Ctr. Art Commission Gallery, Turlock, Calif., exhibitions include San Diego Mus. Art, Ctr. Visual Arts, Oakland, Calif., Sonoma Valley Mus. Art, SITE, LA, Claudia Chapline Gallery, Stinson Beach, Calif., Carl Cherry Ctr. Arts, Carmel, Calif., Coos Art Mus., Coos Bay, Oreg., Smith Gallery U. Calif., Santa Cruz, Calif. Coll. Arts, Oakland, AXIS Gallery, Sacramento, Calif., Matrix Gallery, Sacramento, California Crafts Mus., San Francisco, Kellogg Gallery Calif. State Poly. U., Pomona, Di Rosa Preserve, Napa, Calif., San Francisco Art Inst., Sebastapol Ctr. Arts, Calif. Recipient Straw Into Gold award, Coll. of Marin, 1991, Discovery award, Art of Calif. Mag., 1992; grantee, Marin Cmty. Found., 1992; Grad. Rsch. scholar, Western Psychol. Soc., 1988, grad. scholar, Calif. Coll. Arts, 1992. Mem.: Coll. Art Assn. Libertarian. Office: Prime Performance 41 Marinita Ave San Rafael CA 94901 Personal E-mail: annette101@aol.com.

TOSTI, SUSAN MARIE, educational consultant; b. Ft. Dix, NJ, Nov. 10, 1959; m. Louis Joseph Tosti, Aug. 6, 1994; children: Christina Lee Brightbill, Keri Lynn Painter, Jennifer Sue Mulhern, Kevin Daniel Mulhern, Nicholas Louis. BS in Edn., West Chester U., Pa., 1986; MA in Edn., Widener U., Chester, Pa., 1996, EdD in Reading, Lang. Arts, 2006. Cert. reading specialist NJ, 2000, Pa., 1996, spl. edn. NJ, 2000, Pa., 1986. Spl. educator Chichester Sch. Dist., Boothwyn, Pa., 1986—2000; reading specialist Cinnaminson Sch. Dist., NJ, 2000—07, dist. reading supervisor, 2007—; educational cons. Macmillan/McGraw Hill, 2008. Adj. prof. Holy Family U., Phila., 2006—07, Rowan U., 2007—08. Mem.: Internat. Reading Assn. (assoc.). Home: 815 Witherspoon Way Mullica Hill NJ 08062 Business E-Mail: susan_tosti@mcgraw-hill.com.

TOSUN, DUYGU, research scientist; married. PhD, Johns Hopkins U., Balt., 2005. Grad. rschr. elec. and computer eng. Johns Hopkins U., 1999—2005; postdoc. fellow Lab. NeuroImaging, UCLA, 2005—08; assoc. rschr. scientist Ctr. Imaging Neurodegenerative Diseases, UCSF, San Francisco, 2008—. Contbr. scientific papers (François Erbsmann prize, 2005). Home Fax: 415 4018101. Personal E-mail: duygu.tsn@gmail.com.

TOTH, BILL D., literature and language professor; b. Millfield, Ohio, Nov. 2, 1944; s. Orley Zoltan and Helen Vivian Toth; m. Teri Lynn Thompson; 1 child, Tristan Zoltan. BA, MA, Calif. State U., Chico, 1969; PhD, Union Inst. and U., Cin., 1989. English instr. Hocking Coll., Nelsonville, Ohio, 1979—90; prof. English Western N.Mex. U., Silver City, 1991—2008. Writer, editor U. Calif., Davis, 1975—77. Contbr. articles to profl. jours. Mem.: Western Lit. Assn., Assn. Study of Lit. and Environment. Avocations: travel, reading, hiking, skeet shooting. Home: 4 Fawn Ct Silver City NM 88061 Office: Western N Mex Univ PO Box 680 Silver City NM 88062 Business E-Mail: tothb@wnmu.edu.

TOTH, MARIAN DAVIES, educational administrator, writer; b. Gt. Falls, Mont.; d. John and Zetta Allen (Jones) Davies; m. Alfred L. Toth, Apr. 21, 1947; children: Jerry Geza, Christopher Keats, Geoffrey Alfred, Richard Kingsley. BA magna cum laude, Ea. Coll., 1967; MA, U. Pa., 1970, EdD, 1977. Tchr. Internat. Sch., Bangkok, 1961-64; tchr. English Conestoga HS, Berwyn, Pa., 1967-72, vice prin., 1973-77; prin. Juniata Valley HS, Alexandria, Pa., 1978; dir. lang. arts East Brunswick Sch. Dist., NJ, 1978-82; supr. lang. arts and reading Moorestown Sch. Dist., NJ, 1982—; mem. Gov.'s Task Force on Career Edn.; spkr. various groups on writing, speaking and composing including U. Pa., 1981, U. Wis., 1981, Wright State U., 1982; spkr. Villanova U., 1976, 78, Rutgers U., 1980, Fordham U., 1980. Author: Tales from Thailand, 1971, Seven Steps to Career Exploration, 1975, Silver Burdett English, 1984, (with others) Silver Burdett and Ginn English Series, 1984-88, (with others) World of Reading, Parent Partners, 1986. Bd. alumni trustees Ea. Coll., 1978-80. Recipient Superior Teaching award Tredyffrin/Easttown Sch. Dist., 1970, 73, Creative Writing award Atlantic Monthly, 1971, Disting. Pub. award Theta Sigma Phi, 1973; named Outstanding Author, Kutztown State Coll., Pa. Libr. Assn., 1975. Mem. Nat. Pen Women, Nat. Coun. Tchrs. English (lectr. 1987), Nat. Assn. Supervision and Curriculum Devel. (lectr. 1982), Phi Delta Kappa, Phi Lambda Theta. Episcopalian. Home: 680 Wetherby Ln Devon PA 19333-1855 Personal E-mail: alfred_toth@msn.com.

TOTH, MYRA BERNSTEIN, artist, educator; MFA, San Francisco State U., 1968. Painting instr. Marin County Jr. Coll., Mill Valley, Calif., 1966—67; art and ceramics instr. Santa Rosa Jr. Coll., Calif., 1970—71; art prof. Ventura Coll., Calif., 1983—; luster glazes and firing instr. Beatrice Wood Ctr. Arts, Ojai, Calif., 2003—. Art and ceramics instr. Latin Sch., Chgo., 1973—75; instr. Pyramid Sch. Ceramics, Ojai, 1976—87; ceramics instr. Elmhurst Coll., Ill., De Paul U., Chgo., U. Calif. ext., Ojai. Design, construct; dir.: (design and built) Arbol de Amistad, (large ceramic studio and gallery); Represented in permanent collections Deja Vue, Ventura City, Ojai Autobiography, Mus. Ventura County, To Muse, Be Muse, A Muse, Contemporary Ceramics; editor: (ceramic text book) Ceramics by Glenn Nelson; sculpture publ'd in Art and Antiques, Uproot, Do Not Uproot the Pumpkin, documented live videotaped interview, Focus on the Masters Archives, 2007, commissioned bronze sculpture, Mus. Ventura County Children's Garden, 2009. Mem.: Nat'l Coun. Edn. Ceramic Arts, Am. Craft Coun., Tenn. Walking Horse Assn., Calif. Rare Fruit Growers, Ventural County Potters Guild. Achievements include co-founding the first Chicago women's art gallery, ARC, and annual Ojai Studio Art Tour. Avocations: horseback riding, gardening, beekeeping. Personal E-mail: pyramidstudio.com.

TÓTH, PETER PAUL, physician, researcher; b. Torrington, Conn., May 5, 1959; s. John and Ilona Barbara (Bereczky) T.; m. Karen Faye Ireland, June 3, 1989. AB, Princeton U., 1981; PhD, Mich. State U., 1988; MD, Wayne State U., 1992. Cert. Am. Bd. Family Practice, Am. Bd. of Clin. Lipidology. Resident U. Iowa; dir. preventive cardiology Sterling Rock Falls Clinic, Ltd.; chief of medicine CGH Med. Ctr. Clin. assoc. prof. U. Ill. Coll. Medicine, Peoria, So. Ill. U. Sch. Medicine, Springfield; bd. dirs. Midwest Cardiovascular Rsch. Found. Co-author: (textbooks) Handbook of Family Practice, 1997, Comprehensive Management of High Risk Cardiovascular Patients, 2006, Therapeutic Lipidology, 2007, Current Controversies in Dyslipidemia Management, 2007, Practical Lipid Management, 2007; editor-in-chief: Jour. Applied Rsch. Clin. and Exptl. Therapeutics; co-contbr. articles to Pediatrics Jour., Jour. Pediatrics Surgery, Jour. Biol. Chemistry, Arch. Biochem. Biophysics, Comp. Biochem. Physiol., Methods Enzymol., Nutrition, Circulation, Current Opinion in Cardiology, Am. Jour. Cardiology, Current Opinion in Lipidology, Family Practice Recertification, Clin. Therapeutics; sect. editor: Current Atherosclerosis Reports; mem. editl. bd. Future Lipidology, MosbyGenRx, Jour. Clin. Lipidology. Recipient Searle-Donald F. Richardson Meml. Prize, Am. Coll. Ob-Gyn. Fellow: Am. Coll. Chest Physicians, Am. Coll. Cardiology (mem. coun. cardiovascular disease prevention), Internat. Coll. Angiology, Am. Heart Assn. (mem. clin. affairs com.), Am. Acad. Family Physicians; mem.: AMA, AAAS, Am. Bd. Clin. Lipidology (mem. bd. dirs.), Midwest Cardiovascular Rsch. Found. (bd. dirs.), Nat. Lipid Assn. (bd. dirs., bd. dirs. midwest chpt., sec. midwest chpt.), Sigma Xi, Alpha Omega Alpha. Roman Catholic. Achievements include research in mitochondrial respiration, carnitine metabolism, enzymology, spectroscopy, lipidology, heart disease prevention. Home: 17719 Grandview Dr Sterling IL 61081-8564 Office: Sterling Rock Falls Clinic 101 E Miller Rd Sterling IL 61081 Business E-Mail: peter.toth@srfc.com.

TOTH, ROBERT CHARLES, retired journalist; b. Blakely, Pa., Dec. 24, 1928; s. John and Tillie (Szuch) T.; m. Paula Goldberg, Apr. 12, 1954; children: Jessica, Jennifer, John. BS in Chem. Engring., Washington U., St. Louis, 1952; MS in Journalism, Columbia U., 1955; postgrad., Harvard U., 1960-61. Started as engr. in Army Ordnance Dept., 1952—54; reporter Providence Jour., 1955—57; sci. reporter N.Y. Herald Tribune, 1957—62, N.Y. Times, 1962—63; mem. staff Los Angeles Times, 1963—93, bur. chief London, 1965—70, diplomatic corr., 1970—71, White House corr. Washington, 1972—74, bur. chief Moscow, 1974—77, nat. security corr. Washington bur., 1977—93; ret. Cons. opinion poll in U.S. and abroad by Times Mirror Ctr. (now Pew Rsch. Ctr.) for People and Press, 1990, sr. assoc., 1993-98. Co-author: The Dimishing Divide, Religion's Changing Role in American Politics, 2000. Served with USMC, 1946-48. Recipient Overseas Press Club award, 1977, Sigma Delta Chi award, 1977, George Polk award in Journalism for fgn. reporting L.I. U., 1978, Columbia U. Alumni award, 1978, Wienthal award Fgn. Service Inst., Georgetown U., 1986, Edwin N. Hood award Nat. Press Club, 1986; Pulitzer Travelling scholar, 1955; Nieman fellow Harvard U., 1960-61 Mem. Coun. on Fgn. Rels. Home: 21 Primrose St Chevy Chase MD 20815-4228 E-mail: tothrc@aol.com.

TOTH, THOMAS LOUIS, medical educator, director; s. Roger L. and Theoni A. Toth. MD, U. Mo. Kans. City, 1986. Cert. Am. Bd. Ob-Gyn. Assoc. prof. Harvard Med. Sch., Boston, 2003—; dir., vincent, vitro fertilization unit Mass. Gen. Hosp., Boston. Office: MA Gen Hosp Yaw 10 55 Fruit St Boston MA 02114 Office Fax: 617-724-8882.

TOTTEN, PATRICIA A., lawyer; b. Cleve. BA in Philosophy, Eckerd Coll.; MEd, Kent St. U., Ohio; JD, So. Tex. Coll. Law, 1983. Bar: Tex. Former v.p. mktg. Verizon Wireless; former gen. coun. Houston Data Svc. Co.; dep. gen. counsel Enterprise Products Partners L.P, 2002—06; v.p., gen. coun., corp. sec. TEPPCO Partners, L.P., 2006—. Office: TEPPCO 1100 Louisiana St Houston TX 77002

TOTTEN, TINA ROSENE, special education educator; b. Chillicothe, Mo., Sept. 2, 1963; d. Ivan North and Dulcena Elizabeth Dolan; m. James Benton Totten, Nov. 19, 1983; children: Alecia, Jamie. AA, NCMC, Trenton, Mo., 1998; BS in Edn. summa cum laude, MWSU, St. Joseph, Mo., 2001; MS in Edn., William Woods U., Fulton, Mo., 2004. Tchr. spl. edn. J.C. Penney HS, Hamilton, Mo., 2001—04; tchr. elem. spl. edn. SW R-1 Sch., Ludlow, Mo., 2004—06; learning specialist NCMC, Trenton, Mo., 2006—. Recipient Scholastic Key award, MWSU, 1999—2001. Mem.: Mo. DEC. Home: 801 Cora St Mooresville MO 64664

TOTTENHAM, TERRY OLIVER, lawyer; b. Dallas, June 5, 1944; s. Edwin Pier and Ruth Elizabeth (Paris) T.; m. Carolyn Sue Lewis, July 7, 1967; children: Leslie Jo, Dana Elizabeth, Jessica Leigh. Student, Blinn Jr. Coll., 1962-67; BS in Pharmacy with high honors, U. Tex.-Austin, 1967, JD with honors, 1970; LL.M., George Washington U., 1973. Bar: Tex. 1970, U.S. Ct. Mil. Appeals 1971. Assoc. Fulbright, Crooker & Jaworski, Houston, 1970; ptnr. Fulbright & Jaworski LLP, Austin, Tex., 1978—, and head pharmaceutical and med. device litig. group. Mem. faculty South Tex. Coll. Law, U. Houston; vis. prof. med. jurisprudence Baylor U.; vis. prof. health law Tex. Women's U.; adj. prof. law U. Tex. Sch. Law; speaker profl. groups Author: Texas Medical Jurisprudence; editor: Patients Rights Handbook, 1980. Served to capt. USMC, 1971-75. Recipient Gene Cavin award, 1992; named Outstanding Young Lawyer Houston, 1981, Outstanding Young Lawyer Tex., 1981. Fellow Tex. Bar Found. (life, trustee 1986—); mem. Tex. Assn. Def. Counsel, Am. Soc. Law and Medicine, Am. Soc. Pharmacy Law, Tex. Ex-Students Assn. (life), ABA, Nat. Health Lawyers Assn., Am. Acad. Hosp. Attys. (bd. dirs. 1989—), State Bar Tex. (chmn. health law sect., chmn. litigation sect, bd. dirs. 1985-86, chmn. continuing legal edn. com., Cert. of Merit award 1989), Houston Young Lawyers Assn. (dir. 1975-77), Tex. Young Lawyers Assn. (chmn. bd. 1979-80). Democrat. Episcopalian. Office: Fulbright & Jaworski LLP 600 Congress Ave Ste 2400 Austin TX 78701-3271 Office Phone: 512-536-4555. Office Fax: 512-536-4598. Business E-Mail: ttottenham@fulbright.com.

TOTTERDELL, MICHAEL STANDFORTH, education educator, researcher; b. Woodford, Essex, UK, Sept. 21, 1950; s. Patrick Albert Totterdell and Joyce Enid Smith; m. Rebecca Helen Burdge, July 16, 1983. BA in Theology and Philosophy with honors, U. London, 1982, MA in Edn. with distinction, 1988; MID in Hist. Policy Studies, U. Strasbourg, France, 1998. Cert. in edn. U. London, 1983, registered tchr. Gen. Tchg. Coun. Eng., 1983. Tchr. Cheshunt Sch., Hertfordshire, England, 1983—88; sr. tchr. Henrietta Barnett Sch., London, 1988—90; lectr. to course dir., dean Inst. Edn. U. London, 1991—2003; dir., prof. edn. to dean, pro-vice chancellor Inst. Edn. Manchester Met. U., Lancashire, England, 2004—07; prof. edn., pro-vice chancellor and, exec. dean, faculty edn. U. Plymouth, Devon, 2007—. Cons. Brit. Coun., Moscow, 1994, Brit. Coun. and World Bank, Jakarta and Surabaya, Java, Indonesia, 1997, London First and McKinsey, Westminster, 2001—03, Ind. Schools Coun., Westminster, 2003; convenor Anglo-Taiwan seminar Brit. Coun., London/Taipei/Kaoshiung, Taiwan, 1999—2004; expert advisor European Union Tempus Project, Albania, 2009, Kosovo, 09, Macedonia, 09; adv. bd. mem. Royal No. Coll. Music, Ctr. for Excellence in Tchg. and Learning, Manchester, 2005—07, U. Ulster Values in Edn. Rsch. Project, Coleraine, Antrim, 2005—08, Manchester City Bldg. Schs. for Future Programme, Manchester, 2006—07; adv. bd. mem. for tchg. 2012 project Tng. and Devel. Agy. for Schs., Westminster, 2004—06, mem. stakeholders group for tchr. tng. resource bank; mem. Plymouth Local Strategic Partnership Bd.; chair Plymouth WISE Group. Contbr. chapters to books; co-author: Improving Induction: Research-based Test Practice for Schools, 2002. Gov. bd. of govs. Broxbourne JMI Sch., Hertfordshire, England, 1995—97, Bennington JMI Sch., Stevenage, Hertfordshire, England, 2000—02; mem. mgmt. group Manchester Met. U. Spl. Collections, 2004—07; chair, WISE group, mem. LSP exec. & govs. bds. Plymouth Local Strategic Partnership, 2006—. Officer Her Majesty's Armed Forces, 1970—79. Fellow, Churchill Found., 1992; R&D grantee, Tech. and Vocat. Edn. Initiative in Higher Edn., 1992—93. Fellow: Royal Soc. for Encouragement of Arts, Mfg. and Commerce, Inst. Adminstrv. Mgmt.; mem.: European Ednl. Rsch. Assn., Phi Kappa Delta, Higher Edn. Found., Philosophy of Edn. Soc., Univ. Coun. for Edn. of Tchrs. (vice chair 2002—05, chair 2005—08), Am. Ednl. Rsch. Assn., Brit. Ednl. Rsch. Assn., Manchester Lit. and Philos. Soc., Spl. Forces Assn., Country Gentlemans Assn. Non-Partisan. Achievements include government report and systemic research syntheses of liturature on induction of newly qualified teachers. Avocations: travel, walking, gardening, reading, opera. Office: Univ Plymouth Rm 603 6th Fl Rolle Bldg Drake Circus Devon Plymouth PL4 8AA England Home: Sweet Briars 9 Crokers Meadow Bovey Tracey Newton Abbot Devon TQ13 9ML England Office Phone: 44(0)1752 585306. Office Fax: 44(0)1752 585328. Business E-Mail: michael.totterdell@plymouth.ac.uk.

TOTTON, CARL ALLEN, II, psychologist; b. LA, May 10, 1948; s. Carl Allen and Elva T. Student, Calif. State U., 1976, BS in Rehab. Counseling, 1978, MS in Counseling, 1980; PsyD in Clin. Psychology, Pepperdine U., Malibu, Calif., 1998. Cert. sch. psychologist, counselor, Calif.; lic. psychologist, Calif., Diagnostic Ctr. South, 2006-2008; ordained Taoist abbot, 1983. Sch. psychologist Alhambra (Calif.) Sch. Dist., LA, 1990—2006; dir. Taoist Inst., North Hollywood, Calif., 1981—. Faculty mem. Calif. State U., Northridge, 1993-96, SAMRA U. Oriental Medicine, 1996-98; dir., counselor Rehab. Counseling Assocs., North Hollywood, 1981-83; stress mgmt. cons., hypnotherapist; adj. and core faculty Phillips Grad. Inst. Clin. Psychology, 2005—, adj. faculty sch. & clin. psychology, 2006—; bd. advisors Rancho San Antonio Home for Boys, Chatsworth, Calif., 1996—. Author: Comprehensive Guide to Chinese Medicine and Structural Tui Na, Martial Arts Chi Kung, 1997, Pediatric Tui Na, 1998; editor: Tui Na: Chinese Healing and Acupressure Massage, 1984; author, pub., prodr., The Core System for Martial Arts, Health, and Chi Kung, 2005; contbr. articles to mags. Recipient Presdl. Sports award, 1993, 95, 97; elected to US Martial Arts Hall Fame as Grandmaster, 2002. Mem. APA, Calif. Rehab. Counseling Assn. (pres. 1983-84), Assn. Transpersonal Psychology, Nat. Assn. Sch. Psychologists, Calif. Assn. Sch. Psychologists (bd. dirs., 2001-2003, named Outstanding Sch. Psychologist 2000), Calif. Assn. Lic. Ednl. Psychologists (named Lic. Ednl. Psychologist of Yr. 1999), Calif. Assn. Marriage and Family Therapists. Democrat. Office: Taoist Inst 10630 Burbank Blvd North Hollywood CA 91601-2511 Office Phone: 818-760-4219.

TOTTY, TOTTY OKORO, soccer coach; b. Calabar, Cross River, Nigeria, June 26, 1966; arrived in U.S., 1989; s. Joseph Okoro and Rachael Okoro Totty. BS in Bus. Comm., So. NH U., Manchester, 1993, MS in Internat. Bus., 1995. Camp co-dir. John Rootes Soccer Sch., Manchester, 1990—2000; asst. coach women's soccer So. NH U., Manchester, 1995—97; city dir. coaching Amherst Soccer Club, NH, 1996—98; head coach women's soccer Clayton State U., Morrow, Ga., 1998—; state staff coach Ga. Olympics Devel. Program, Atlanta, 2001—. Mem. adv. com. S.E. region NCAA, Hickory, NC, 2001—04; conf. chair Peach Belt Conf. W. Soc. Coaches, Augusta, Ga., 2001—02; mem. Nigerian Nat. Soccer Team. Mem. Global Citizens Cir., 1990—; active Big Brother/Big Sister, Manchester, 1994. Named Rookie of Yr., New Eng. Conf., 1989; named to Hall of Fame, So. NH U., 2000. Mem.: US Soccer Fedn. (youth soccer referee 1998—), Nat. Soccer Coaches Assn. of Am. (All-Am. Soccer Player 1991—93). Independent. Avocations: music, theater, dance, movies, art. Home: 639 Garden Walk Blvd # 336 College Park GA 30349 Office: Clayton State U 2000 Clayton State Blvd Morrow GA 30260 Office Phone: 678-466-4684. Office Fax: 678-466-4699. Business E-Mail: tottytotty@clayton.edu.

TOU, JEN-SIE HSU, biochemistry educator; b. Lai-yang, China, Sept. 17, 1936; came to U.S., 1962; d. Pei-min and Jing-yu (Chang) Hsu; m. Patrick P. Tou, May 29, 1965. BS in Agrl. Chemistry, Nat. Taiwan U., 1959; MS in Biochemistry, Baylor Coll. Medicine, 1964; PhD in Biochemistry, Tulane U., 1968. Rsch. asst. Harvard Med. Sch., Boston, 1964-65; rsch. fellow Tulane U. Med. Sch., New Orleans, 1968-71, instr. biochemistry, 1971-73, asst. prof., 1973-80, rsch. assoc. prof., 1980-88, assoc. prof. biochemistry, 1988—. NIH rsch. fellow, 1972-74, recipient rsch. career devel. award, 1975-80. Mem. Am. Soc. Biochemistry and Molecular Biology. Home: 4641 Ithaca St Metairie LA 70006-2708 Office: Dept Biochemistry Tulane U Med Sch 1430 Tulane Ave New Orleans LA 70112-2699

TOUHILL, C. JOSEPH, environmental engineer; b. Newark, Aug. 27, 1938; s. Charles J. and Caroline A. T.; m. Helen Elizabeth O'Malley, June 11, 1960; children: Gregory Joseph, Stephen Mark, Christopher Alan, Kathleen Elizabeth. BCE, Rensselaer Poly. Inst., 1960, PhD in Environ. Engring., 1964; SM, MIT, 1961; postgrad., U. Wash., 1970. Diplomate Am. Acad. Environ. Engrs. Mgr. water and land resources dept. Battelle Meml. Inst., Richland, Wash., 1964-71; pres. Baker/TSA Inc., Pitts., 1977-90; group sr. v.p. ICF Kaiser Engrs. Inc., Pitts., 1990-94; exec. v.p. EG&G Environ. Inc., Pitts., 1994-97; pres. Touhill Tech. Mgmt. Corp., Jamison, Pa., 1997-99, 2003—; nat. discipline lead for process and environ. engring. Tetra Tech FW, Inc. (formerly Foster Wheeler Environ. Corp.), Langhorne, Pa., 1999—2003. Author: Commercialization of Innovative Technologies, 2008; co-author: Hazardous Materials Spills Handbook, 1982, Hazardous Waste Management Engineering, 1987; editor: Resource Management in the Great Lakes Basin, 1971; mem. editorial bd. Environ. Progress Jour., 1979-93. Trustee Am. Acad. Environ. Engr., 1971-77, 83-86; bd. dirs. Suburban Gen. Hosp., Pitts., 1986-96; vice chmn. Franklin Park (Pa.) Authority, 1977-96, chmn. adv. com., dept. Environ. and energy Engring., Rensselaer Polytech Inst., 1996-98, mem. adv. bd. dept. civil and environ. engring., 2000-06. Recipient fellow award Rensselaer Alumni Assn., 1994; Kappe lectr. AAEE, 1992. Fellow ASCE (life), AIChE (chmn. environ. engring. div. 1977, Inst. fellow 2000), Am. Chem. Soc. (editl. adv. bd. 1975-77), Am. Water Works Assn. (life), Water Environment Fedn. (life). Office: 2269 Sunrise Way Jamison PA 18929 Home Phone: 215-491-5616; Office Phone: 215-491-5617. Business E-Mail: jtouhill@alum.mit.edu.

TOULANTIS, MARIE J., former retail bookseller executive, consultant; BA in Mktg., Pace U., 1981. V.p. Chase Manhattan Bank, NYC, 1987-96, sr. v.p., 1996-97; exec. v.p. fin. to CFO Barnes & Noble Inc., NYC, 1997-99, CFO Barnes & Noble.com, 1999—2001, pres., COO, 2001—02, CEO, 2002—08, cons., 2008—. Bd. dir. Hershey Foods Corp. Adv. bd. Pace U. Lubin Sch. Bus. Office: Barnes & Noble dot com Barnes & Noble Inc 2nd fl 122 Fifth Ave New York NY 10011

TOULMIN, PRIESTLEY, retired geologist; b. Birmingham, Ala., June 5, 1930; s. Priestley and Catharine Augusta (Carey) T.; m. Martha Jane Slason, Aug. 30, 1952 (dec. Jan., 2008); children: Catharine Bosier (Mrs. Robert G. Gibson), Priestley Chewning. AB, Harvard U., 1951, PhD, 1959; MS, U. Colo., 1953. With U.S. Geol. Survey, Washington, 1953-56, 57-89, staff geologist for exptl. geology, 1966, chief br. exptl. geochemistry, 1966-71, geologist geologic div., 1971-89, Reston, Va., 1974-89, ret., 1989; also leader inorganic chemistry team NASA (Viking Project). Adj. prof. Columbia U., 1966; rsch. asso. in geochemistry Calif. Inst. Tech., 1976-77; vis. lectr. Am. Geol. Inst.; dir. petrogenesis and mineral resources program NSF, 1985; bd. dirs., treas. 28th Internat. Geol. Congress, 1985-86 Mng. sci. editor Geochemistry Internat., 1965-68; assoc. editor Am. Mineralogist, 1974-76; contbr. articles to profl. jours. Mem. adv. com. spl. edn., Alexandria, Va., 1977-80. Recipient Exceptional Service medal NASA, 1977; Meritorious Service award U.S. Dept. Interior, 1978 Fellow Geol. Soc. Am., Mineral Soc. Am. (bd. assoc. editors 1974-76), Soc. Econ. Geologists, Explorers Club; mem. AAAS, Geol. Soc. Washington (2d v.p. 1977, councillor 1973-74, 90-91, 1st v.p. 1981, pres. 1982), Am. Geophys. Union, Soc. Mayflower Descs., Jamestowne Soc., S.R., SAR, Soc. Colonial Wars (DC), Aztec Club of 1847, St. Andrews Soc. (Washington), Cosmos Club (pres. 1993-94, found. trustee 1994—, chmn. 1996-2001), Sigma Xi, Sigma Gamma Epsilon. Home: 418 Summers Dr Alexandria VA 22301-2449 Office: PO Box 183 Alexandria VA 22313-0183

TOULOUSE, ROBERT BARTELL, retired college administrator; b. Wellsville, Mo., May 8, 1918; s. Walter Eaton and Emma (Schmidt) T.; m. Virginia Lee Danford, Aug. 7, 1948; children— Samuel Phillip, Robert Bartell. Student, Central Coll., 1935-37; BS, U. Mo., 1939, M.Ed., 1947, Ed.D., 1948. Tchr. sci. and social studies, high sch., Mountain View, Mo., 1939-41; asst. prof. to prof. U. North Tex., 1949-54, dean Grad. Sch., 1954-82, v.p., from 1982; now ret. Contbr. articles profl. jours. State sponsor Future Tchrs. Am. Served from pvt. to lt. col. AUS, World War II. Mem. Assn. Tex. Grad. Schs. (pres.), Assn. Coll. Tchr. Edn. (v.p.), Tex. Assn. Audio-Visual Edn. Dirs. (v.p.), AAUP, NEA, Phi Delta Kappa. Clubs: Kiwanis (pres.). Democrat. Methodist. Home: 3901 Montecito Dr Apt 411 Denton TX 76210-5559

TOUMEY, DONALD JOSEPH, lawyer; BA, Williams Coll., 1978; JD, Yale U., 1981. Bar: N.Y. 1982, D.C. 1985, U.S. Supreme Ct. 1986. Law clk. to judge U.S. Ct Appeals (2d cir.), NYC, 1981-82; spl. asst. to gen. counsel U.S. Dept. Treasury, Washington, 1982-85; assoc. Sullivan & Cromwell, NYC, 1985-90; ptnr., 1990—. Republican. Office: Sullivan & Cromwell LLP 125 Broad St New York NY 10004-2489 Office Phone: 212-558-4077. Business E-Mail: toumeyd@sullcrom.com.

TOUPIN, HAROLD OVID, retired chemical company executive; b. Hibbing, Minn., Jan. 21, 1927; s. Ovid Pascal and Ellen (Holt) T.; m. Edna F. Sallila, Feb. 8, 1948 (div. Feb. 1973); m. Colleen Beverly Lange, Apr. 18, 1981; children: James, Ronald. BS, U. Minn., 1954, MA, 1955, postgrad, 1968; PhD (hon.), Internat. Acad. Color, Las Vegas, Nev., 1982, U. Mont., 1990. Mgr. Firestone Tire Co., East Los Angeles, Calif., 1948-51; dir. vocat. edn. Hopkins (Minn.) Pub. Schs., 1955-75; with research and devel. Power-o-Peat Co., Gilbert, Minn., 1956-67; chief exec. officer, cons. Color Specialties Inc., Mpls., 1976-98; ret., 1999. Pres., founder travel, meeting planners svc. co., 1990; founder internat. office for color specialties, 1994; bd. dirs. Vu-tek Inc., St. Paul, Airport Auto Sales, St. Paul Color Specialties of Nev., Las Vegas, Instant Air Inc., Mpls., Freedom Fin.; cons. Runs Hot Cons. Svc., 1966-75; ptnr. Vermes Jewelry, Mpls., 1956-80; mgr. Pati Pages Womens Roma Royal Fine Perfumes, 1960-62. Contbr. articles to profl. jours. Bd. dirs. Hopkins Jaycees, 1958-60. Served with USAAF, 1944-47. Mem. Am. Assn. Mfrs., Internat. Assn. Color, Nat. Ret. Tchrs. Assn., Am. Assn. Self Employeed, Met. Area Dist. Edn. Instrs. Assn. (pres.), Mpls. C. of C. (Super Bowl com. 1992), Am. Legion, VFW, Lions (sec. Hopkins club 1956-76, bd. dirs.), Sun City West Pioneer Club (chair 2008-09), Am. Newsletter Editor and Historian (bd. dirs. 2008-09). Democrat. Roman Catholic. Avocations: travel, golf, writing. Home Phone: 623-975-7495; Office Phone: 952-892-5971. Personal E-mail: haroldtoupin@peoplepc.com.

TOUPS, KIM G., language educator, department chairman; b. Clinton, Mass., Dec. 18, 1946; d. Ralph Samuel and Lillian Zinser Gulliver; m. Gerard Joseph Toups; children: Michael David, Melissa Anne. BS in Secondary Edn., Loyola U., New Orleans, 1969. Tchg. cert. type A La., 1974. Tchr. Grace King HS, Metairie, La., 1969—70; tchr., English dept. chair Archbishop Chapelle HS, Metairie, 1970—. Acad. leadership team Archbishop Chapelle HS, Metairie, 1988—, faculty rep. bldg. campaign com., 2000—. Recipient 30 Yr. pin for Svc. to Sch., Archbishop Chapelle HS, 2000. Mem.: Nat. Cath. Edn. Assn., Nat. Coun. Tchrs. English. Roman Catholic. Avocations: travel, reading. Home: 13199 State St Hammond LA 70403 Office: Archbishop Chapelle HS 8800 Veterans Blvd Metairie LA 70003 Office Fax: 504-466-3191. Personal E-mail: gerardtoups@charter.net. Business E-Mail: ktoups@archbishopchapelle.org.

TOURIÑÁN LÓPEZ, JOSÉ MANUEL, education educator; b. A Coruña, Spain, Oct. 29, 1951; s. Antonio Touriñán Lousa and Carmen López Marzoa; m. María Teresa Morandeira; children: María Teresa Touriñán Morandeira, Laura Touriñán Morandeira. BA with honors, Sch. Tchr. Edn., A Coruña, 1969; Magister, U. Complutense, Madrid, 1974; BA in Philosophy and Edn. with honors, U. Complutense, 1974, Magister in Pedagogy, 1975, PhD in Pedagogy with honors, 1978. Cert. tchr. Coll. Doctors Edn., 1988. Asst. lectr. Complutense U., 1974—81; asst. prof. U. Santiago Compostela, A Coruña, 1981—88, prof., 1988—, head dept. systematic pedagogy, 1980—82, sec. faculty edn., 1982—83, head dept. theory and history of edn., 1986—88, head rsch. group, 2002—. Sci. policy referee Nat. Assessment Agy., Madrid, 2002—; gen. dir. universities' mgmt. and police rsch. Regional Govt. Galicia, A Coruña, 1990—97; hon. prof. Buenos Aires U., 1993; advisor sec. sci. and tech. Dept. Govt. Presidency, Madrid, 1998—99; gen. mgr. Caixa Galicia Found., A Coruña, 1999—2002; vis. prof. Wayne State U., Detroit, 1992, U. Buenos Aires, 1993, Beijing U., 1994, U. Politécnica Lima, Peru, 1995, Fla. Internat. U., 1998, U. South Fla., 1998, Miami U., Fla., 1998, UNS, 1999, Reikiavick U., 1999; mem. editl. bd. Revista Interuniversitaria Teoría Educación, Revista Bordón, Revista Tecnología y Comunicación Educativas, Revista Aula Abierta, 2003. Author: The Meaning of Freedom in Education, 1979, Education as a Knowledge Aim, 1987, Teaching Staff Statute and Pedagogical Function, 1987, The Development of the Galicia University System, 1991, Improvements in the Galician Universitary System, 1993, Statistical Data of the Galician Universitary System, 1994, 1995, Legal Foundations and Development of the Galician Universitary System, 1995, Total Quality Project for the Development of the Murcian Universitary System, 1996, The Consolidation of the Universitary System and the Scientific Community. Analysis Proposals, 1997, Education and Information Society, 1999, Management of Scientific Policy and Research Resources, 2000, Globalization and Development: a Challenge for Regional Research and development Policy, 2000, E-Education. The Challenge of the Digital Society at the School Place, 2005, Education on Values, Intercultural Education and Education for Peaceful Co-Existence, 2007, Education on Values, Civil Society and Civic Development, 2008; co-author: Theory of Education (in Spanish), 1974, Interculturality and Education for Development, 1999; coordinator (book) Education in Galicia, 1984, Family, Youth and Our Elders. A Proactive Attitude, 2001, Family, Education and Civil Society, 2004. Creator distance edn. net, A Coruña, Spain, 1999—2001; creator bd. dirs. Ctr. Supercomputing Galicia, Santiago de Compostela, 1992—97. Second lt. Army (Universitary scale), 1977—77, Alcazar de Toledo (Madrid - Spain). Decorated Honour Sword Ministry of Army, Mil. Acad. Toledo, Spain; recipient Recognition for collaboration in distance edn., Open U., Chrysler Assoc. Ctr., 1975—80, San José de Calasánz Pedagogical Rsch. prize, Madrid Townhall, 1976, Recognition for Bilingual Edn., Wayne State U., 1991, Recognition, U. Salamanca, Spain, 1996—2000, Golden Insignia, U. Santiago de Compostela, 1998, Silver Medal of Galicia, Regional Govt. Galicia, 1998, Golden insignia, A Coruña U., 2000, Recognition for Cooperation in Distance Edn. Network, CREAD, Caracas, Venezuela, 2000, Recognition for Presidency Bd. Dirs., CESGA, Spain, 2003, Recognition for ednl. rsch. in values, Internacional Assn. Media Sci., 2006, Recognition as Prof. in Doctor's Degree Program Edn. in Values, U. Mex., 2006; fellow, Ministry Edn. and Sci., 1974. Mem.: European U. Continuing Edn. Network (assoc.), Soc. for Internat. Devel. (assoc.), Interamerican Distance Edn. Consortium (assoc.), Am. Ednl. Rsch. Assn. (assoc.), Nat. Soc. Pedagogues (assoc.). Achievements include research in total quality in the Murcian universitary system; strategic planning for ICTs improvement in universitary education; an approach to the deployment of new technologies in education; interactive systems in pedagogical intervention; values in education (using an educational platform that combines Internet and television. Avocations: swimming, travel, reading, walking. Home: República de Argentina 21- 6th Fl A Coruña Santiago de Compostela 15701 Spain Office: U Santiago de Compostela Faculty of Sciences of Education A Coruña Santiago de Compostela 15782 Spain Business E-Mail: josemanuel.tourinan@usc.edu.

TOURKOW, JOSHUA ISAAC, lawyer; b. Ft. Wayne, Ind., Mar. 5, 1947; s. Frederick Rhinehold and Leah Sarah (Schwartz) Tourkow; m. Donna Susan Dubin, Aug. 30, 1970; children: Illana Joy, Lisa Michelle, Benjamin Ahron. Student, Bar Ilan U., Israel, 1968; BS in Indsl. Mgmt., Purdue U., 1970; JD, Ind. U., Indpls., 1973. Bar: Ind. 1973, US Dist. Cts. (no. and so. dists.) Ind. 1973, US Ct. Appeals (7th cir.) 1973. Asst. dep. prosecutor Marion County, Indpls., 1972—73; ptnr. Tourkow, Crell, Rosenblatt & Johnston, Ft. Wayne, 1973—. Bd. dirs. Housing & Neighborhood Devel. Svcs., Inc., Ft. Wayne, 1980—84, Ft. Wayne Redevel. Com., 1983; atty. Ft. Wayne Housing Authority, 1983—87; advisor, atty. Parents Without Ptnrs., Ft. Wayne, 1981—85, Fathers United for Equal Rights, Ft. Wayne, 1980—; pres. Ft. Wayne Jewish Fedn., 2009—. Mem.: ABA, Allen County Bar Assn. (chair family law sect. 2000—02), Ind. Bar Assn. (chair family law 1992—94). Home: 7022 Winchester Rd Fort Wayne IN 46819-1530 Office: Tourkow Crell Rosenblatt & Johnston 203 E Berry Sts Rm 814 Fort Wayne IN 46802 Office Phone: 260-426-0545. Business E-Mail: jtourkow@tcrjlaw.com.

TOURLENTES, THOMAS THEODORE, retired psychiatrist; b. Chgo., Dec. 7, 1922; s. Theodore A. and Mary (Xenostathy) T.; m. Mona Belle Land, Sept. 9, 1956; children: Theodore W., Stephen C., Elizabeth A. BS, U. Chgo., 1945, MD, 1947. Diplomate Am. Bd. Psychiatry and Neurology (sr. examiner 1964-88, 90). Intern Cook County Hosp., Chgo., 1947-48; resident psychiatry Downey (Ill.) VA Hosp., 1948-51; practice medicine specializing in psychiatry Chgo., 1952, Camp Atterbury, Ind., 1953, Ft. Carson, Colo., 1954, Galesburg, Ill., 1955-71; staff psychiatrist Chgo. VA Clinic, 1952; clin. instr. psychiatry Med. Sch., Northwestern U., 1952; dir. mental hygiene consultation service Camp Atterbury, 1953-54, Ft. Carson, 1953-54; asst. supt. Galesburg State Research Hosp., 1954-58, supt., 1958-71; dir. Comprehensive Community Mental Health Ctr. Rock Island and Mercer Counties; dir. psychiat. services Franciscan Hosp., 1971-85; chief mental health services VA Outpatient Clinic, Peoria, Ill., 1985-88; clin. prof. psychiatry U. Ill., Chgo. and Peoria, 1955—96; preceptor in hosp. adminstrn. State U. Iowa, Iowa City, 1958-64; ret., 1996. Councilor, del. Ill. Psychiat. Soc.; chmn. liaison com. Am. Hosp. and Psychiat. Assns., 1978-79, chmn. Quality Care Bd., Ill. Dept. Mental Health, 1995-97. Contbr. articles profl. jours. Mem. Gov. Ill. Com. Employment Handicapped, 1962-64; zone dir. Ill. Dept. Mental Health, Peoria, 1964-71; mem. Spl. Survey Joint Commn. Accreditation Hosps.; chmn. Commn. Cert. Psychiat. Adminstrs., 1979-81; pres. Knox-Galesburg Symphony Soc., 1966-68; bd. dirs. Galesburg Civic Music Assn., pres., 1968-70; chair Knox county United Way Campaign, 1989; pres. Civic Art Ctr., 1990-92. Capt. M.C. AUS, 1952-54. Fellow AAAS, AMA, Am. Psychiat. Assn. (chair hosp. and cmty. psychiatry award bd. 1989-90, dist. life fellow, 2002), Am. Coll. Psychiatrists, Am. Coll. Mental Health Adminstrs.; mem. Ill. Med. Soc. (chmn. aging com. 1968-71, coun. on mental health and addictions 1987-89), chair mental health substance abuse com. 1987-89), Ill. Psychiat. Soc. (pres. 1969-70), Am. Pub. Health Assn., Soc. Biol. Psychiatry, Ill. Hosp. Assn. (trustee 1968-70), Am. Coll. Hosp. Adminstrs., Assn. for Rsch. Nervous and Mental, Am. Assn. Psychiat. Adminstrs. (pres. 1980), Ctrl. Neuorpsychiat. Assn. (pres. 1988-89). Home and Office: 138 Valley View Rd Galesburg IL 61401-8524 Office Phone: 309-344-1177. E-mail: tourlentes@gallatinriver.net. *Feeling useful and needed is the greatest recognition and reward.*

TOURNEY, MICHELE MARIE, archivist, historian; b. Hagerstown, Md., July 13, 1976; BA, Dickinson Coll., Carlisle, Pa., 1998; MS in Libr., Info. Sci., U. Pitts., 2003. Departmental intern Dickinson Coll. Archives & Spl. Collections, Carlisle, 1999—2002, asst. archivist, 2003; grad. student asst. U. Pitts., Sch. Info. Scis., 2002—03; project archivist Nat. Sporting Libr., Middleburg, Va., 2003—04; archivist History Assocs. Inc., Rockville, Md., 2004—07; archivist, historian McGhee Found., Middleburg, 2004—. Contbr. articles to profl. jours. Vol. Peerless Rockville Ltd., 2007. Mem.: Loudoun County Heritage Consortium (mem., mus. emergency support team 2009), Mid-Atlantic Regional Archives Conf. (tech. webmaster, various coms. 2004), Rockville Little Theatre, Phi Beta Kappa. Avocations: music, art, travel, photography, theater. Office: McGhee Found 36276 Mountville Rd Middleburg VA 20117 Office Fax: 540-687-3746. Business E-Mail: mtourney@farmersdelight.org.

TOURNILLON, NICHOLAS BRADY, investment company executive; b. New Orleans, Sept. 1, 1933; s. Samuel C. and Anna Mae (Brady) T.; m. Audrey Nicosia, Dec. 15, 1956; children: Brady, Linda, Tracy, Jeffrey, Gregory, Lori. BA, Southeastern La. U., 1958; MBA, La. State U., 1960. Loan officer Export Import Bank U.S., Washington, 1960-66; adminstrv. asst. to exec. officers Atlantic Gulf & Pacific Co. of Manila, 1966-68; asst. treas. GTE Internat., Stamford, Conn., 1968-76, treas., 1976-86, v.p., 1978-86; pres. GTE Fin. Corp., 1984-86; asst. treas. GTE Corp., 1985-86; chmn., chief exec. officer Am. and Internat. Investment Corp., 1986-98; privatization adv. W/Inti. Exec. Svc. Corp. Ctr. Europe, 1991—94; pres., CEO Definco Ltd., 1998—. Bd. dirs. Nat. Fgn. Trade Coun., Cmty. Answers, Global Access Corp.; mem. internat. adv. bd. Union Trust Co.; White House advisor, regan admin. to US Trade rep., Internat. Trade Fin. Contbr. articles to profl. bus. jours. Past chmn. Conn. Dist. Export Council of US Dept. Commerce; mem. monetary com. U.S. Council Internat. Bus.; bd. dirs. Southeastern La. U. Devel. Served with USNR, 1953-54, Korea. Named Outstanding Alumnus of Yr., Southeastern La. U., 1976 Mem. Soc. Internat. Treasurers, Acad. Internat. Bus., Retired Men's Assn. of Greenwich. Home: Midwood Dr Greenwich CT 06831-4400 Office: Definco Ltd 25 Midwood Dr Greenwich CT 06831-4412 Personal E-mail: ntournillo@aol.com. *Perseverance is* *an often mentioned but never overrated quality— the quality that prevents the substitution of expediency for excellence. Throughout life, persevering effort has been responsible for converting ideas and talents into results and recognition.*

TOURTELLOTTE, CHARLES DEE, internist, rheumatologist, educator; b. Kalamazoo, Aug. 28, 1931; s. Dee and Helen May (Lotz) T.; m. Barbara Richwine, June 25, 1955; children: Daniel DeWitt (dec.), Elizabeth Anne, William Charles, Scott David. AB, Johns Hopkins U., 1953; MS in Biochemistry, MD, Temple U., 1957. Diplomate Am. Bd. Internal Medicine. Intern, resident in medicine U. Mich. Hosp., Ann Arbor, 1957-60; fellow in rheumatology Temple U. Hosp., Phila., 1960-61; fellow in biochemistry Rockefeller U., NYC, 1961-63; faculty Sch. Medicine, Temple U., 1963—, prof. medicine, 1972-97, prof. emeritus, 1997—; chief rheumatology Temple U. Hosp., 1994-97, pres. med. staff, bd. govs., 1984-86. Dir. Greater Delaware Valley Arthritis Control Program, 1974-77; pres. Eastern Pa. chpt. Arthritis Found., 1972-74; mem. active/cons. staff 10 area and regional hosps. Contbr. chpts. to textbooks, articles to profl. jours.; mem. editl. bd.: Arthritis and Rheumatism, 1969-77, 19th-24th Rheumatism Revs, 1969-81. Mem. Haddonfield (N.J.) Bd. Edn., 1968-74, pres., 1974; mem. Borough of Haddonfield Environ. Comm., 1975-87, chmn., 1977-85; mem. Haddonfield Civic Assn., 1963—; South N.J. chmn. Johns Hopkins U. Alumni Schs. Com., 1975-90; trustee Bobby Fulton Meml. Fund, 1979-2008, 1st Presbyn. Ch. of Haddonfield, 1998-2000. With AUS, 1953-61. Helen Hay Whitney Found. fellow, 1962-63; Arthritis Found. fellow, 1963-66 Fellow ACP, Phila. Coll. Physicians, Am. Coll. Rheumatology (founding fellow); mem. Pa. Med. Soc., Phila. County Med. Soc.,(50 yr. mem. 2007) Babcock Surg. Soc., Phila. Rheumatism Soc. (pres. 1968-69), Pa. Rheumatology Soc. (founding pres. 1985-86), N.J. Soc. of Pa., Nat. Huguenot Soc. (surgeon gen. 2002-04), Huguenot Soc. Pa., Temple U. Med. Alumni Assn. (pres. 1997-99), Tavistock County Club (N.J.), Little Egg Harbor Yacht Club, Med. Club of Phila. (bd. dirs., pres. 1998-99), Sixty-five Club of Haddonfield (dir. 2003—), Interfaith Caregivers (trustee 2004-2007), Sigma Xi, Alpha Omega Alpha, Delta Upsilon, Phi Chi. Presbyterian. Home: 6 Lane Of Acres Haddonfield NJ 08033-3505 Office: Temple Univ Hosp Dept Rheumatology Philadelphia PA 19140-5192 Office Phone: 215-707-2000. E-mail: cdtourte@comcast.net.

TOURTELLOTTE, WALLACE WILLIAM, neurologist, educator; b. Great Falls, Mont., Sept. 13, 1924; B in Philosophy, Hutchin's Coll., U. Chgo., 1945; BS in Anatomy, U. Chgo., 1945, PhD in Neurochemical Pharmacology, 1948, MD, 1951. Instr. biochem Neuro pharmacology U. Chgo., 1948—50; intern Strong Meml. Hosp. Straight Medicine U. Rochester Sch. Medicine and Dentistry, NY, 1951—52; resident in neurology U. Mich. Med. Ctr., Ann Arbor, 1954-57, asst. prof. neurology, 1957-59, assoc. prof., 1959-66, prof., 1966-71; disting. prof. UCLA, 1950, prof. dept. neurology, 1971—, vice chmn. dept. neurology, 1971-98, emeritus vice chmn. dept. neurology, 1998; chief neurology svcs. VA Wadsworth, West LA, Calif., 1971-99, emeritus dir. neurology tng. program, 1999—, staff neurologist, neuroscientist, 1999—, Inst. Sci. Info., 1981—99. Vis. assoc. prof. pharmacology Washington U., St. Louis, 1963-64; hon. mem. med. adv. bd. Nat. Multiple Sclerosis Soc., 1968—, So. Calif. Multiple Sclerosis Socs., 1972—; dir. Multiple Sclerosis Rsch. and Treatment Ctr., 1971-, Human Brain and Spinal Fluid Resource Ctr., 1961—; reviewer neuroscientist profl. jours. in field. Co-editor (with Cedric Raines, Henry McFarland): Multiple Sclerosis, Clinical and Pathogenetic Basis, 1997; The Wallace W. Tourtellotte Clin. and Neurosci. Libr., Va. Wadsworth, LA, 1999-; author Post-Lumbar Headache Book, 1967, Quantitative Examination Of human Neurologic Function, 2 vols., 1985. Lt. (j.g.) M.C., USNR, 1952-54. Recipient Disting. Alumni Service award U. Chgo., 1982. Fellow Am. Acad. Neurology (S. Weir Mitchell Neurology Reseach award 1959-); mem. Am. Neurol. Assn. (counselor 1982—, v.p. 1992-), World Fedn. Neurochemistry Commn. (founding mem. 1969), Am. Assn. Neuropathologists, Internat. Soc. Neurochemsitry (founding mem. 1959), Am. Soc. Pharmacology and Exptl. Therapeutics, Am. Soc. Neurochemistry (founding mem.), Soc. Neurosci., Confrerie de la Chaine des Rotisseur, Argentier du Baillage de Los Angeles (vice chanceller, comdr. 1971), Pasadena Wine and Food Soc., Physician Wine and Food Soc., Culinary Club French Cuisine LA. Home Phone: 310-454-7763; Office Phone: 310-268-3536, 310-268-4638. Fax: 310-454-7650. Business E-Mail: wtourtel@ucla.edu.

TOUSSAINT, CLAUDIA S., telecommunications industry executive, lawyer; BA in Econ., U. Calif., Los Angeles; JD, U. Calif. Hastings Coll. Law. Atty. Morrison & Foerster LLP, Sprint Corp., 1997—2003, v.p. corp. governance & ethics, corp sec., 2003—; v.p., corp. sec. & chief ethics officer Embarq Corp., gen. counsel, corp. sec. & chief ethics officer. Named one of Kans. City's Top Women Exec., Ingrams Mag., 2008. Mem.: Soc. Corp. Sec. & Governance (pres. Kans. City Chpt.). Office: 5454 W 110th St Overland Park KS 66211*

TOUSSAINT, ROGER, labor union administrator; b. Port of Spain, Trinidad, Nov. 7, 1956; m. Donna Toussaint; 4 children. Attended, Brooklyn Coll. Cleaner Met. Transp. Authority (MTA), 1984—85, track maintenance worker, 1985; leader Track Div. Transport Workers Union (TWU) Local 100, NYC, 1994, pres., 2001—. Co-founder On Track newsletter. Office: TWU Local 100 80 West End Ave New York NY 10023 Office Phone: 212-873-6000.

TOUSSIENG, YOLANDA, make-up artist; Television work includes: (movies) Fallen Angel, 1981, 1981, Blue de Ville, 1986, (series) Pee-wee's Playhouse, 1986, (mini-series) North and South, Book II, 1986, films include Blue City, 1986, No Man's Land, 1987, Beetlejuice, 1988, Gross Anatomy, 1989, Three Fugitives, 1989, Farewell to the King, 1989, Edward Scissorhands, 1990, Flatliners, 1990, Everybody Wins, 1990, Hoffa, 1992, Batman Returns, 1992, Mrs. Doubtfire, 1993, Rising Sun, 1993, Ed Wood, 1994 (Acad. award for Best Make-up, 1994), Being Human, 1994, Junior, 1994. Office: IATSE Local 706 11519 Chandler Blvd North Hollywood CA 91601-2618

TOUSTER, SAUL, law educator; b. Bklyn., Oct. 12, 1925; s. Ben and Bertha (Landau) T.; m. Helen Davidson, Nov. 23, 1954 (div. 1967); children: Natasha Ann, Jonathan Bach; m. Irene Tayler, Jan. 14, 1978. AB magna cum laude, Harvard U., 1944, JD, 1948. Bar: N.Y. 1949. Practiced in, NYC, 1949-55; prof. law SUNY-Buffalo, 1955-69, asst. to pres., 1966-68, mem. adj. faculty in medicine, edn., psychology, 1964-69; prof. law and social scis. State Coll. at Old Westbury, 1969-71; prof., provost, acad. v.p. CCNY, 1971-73; acting pres. Richmond Coll. City U. N.Y., 1973-74; prof. law CUNY Grad. Sch. also John Jay Coll. of Criminal Justice, 1974-80; prof., dir. legal studies, humanities, professions programs Brandeis U., Waltham, Mass., 1980-93, prof. emeritus, 1993. Legis. cons. N.Y. State Law Rev. Commn., 1956-61; vis. prof. U. Brussels, summer, 1968, Boston Coll. Law Sch., 1994. Author: Still Lives and Other Lives, 1966, Surrealism and the Art of Samuel Bak, in Between Worlds, 2002; editor, author introduction: A Survivors' Haggadah, 1998, Beyond Words: A Holocaust History in Sixteen Woodcuts done in 1945 by Miklos Adler, A Hungarian Survivor, 2001; contbr. articles to legal periodicals. Served to lt. (j.g.) USNR, 1944-46. NEH fellow, 1978; Am. Bar Found. Legal History fellow, 1977-78 Mem. Internat. Inst. Boston (bd. advisors), Phi Beta Kappa. Home: 180 Beacon St Boston MA 02116-1408 E-mail: stouster@mac.com.

TOVESSON, FREDRIK, nuclear scientist; b. Kalmar, Sweden; s. Conny and Kristina Tovesson; m. Jessica Tovesson; children: Tiffany, Oliver. MSc, Orebro U., Sweden, 1999, PhD, 2003. Grad. rsch. fellow IRMM, Geel, Belgium, 2000—03; rsch. staff mem. Los Alamos Nat. Lab., N.Mex., 2004—. Named Innovative Sci. Paper of Yr., Joint Rsch. Ctr., 2002. Business E-Mail: tovesson@lanl.gov.

TOVORNIK, MARY ROSE, physical education educator; d. Darlene G. (Gross) and Albert John Tovornik. MA, U. Conn., Storrs, 1997—2004, ABD, 2002. Cert. athletic trainer Nat. Athletic Trainers Assn., 1997, profl. rescuer in CPR and automated external defibrillator ARC. Grad. asst. athletic trainer football, women's soccer, baseball U. Conn., 1997, asst. athletic trainer football, 2002—04; asst. athletic trainer, asst. prof. Lock Haven U., Pa., 2004—. Site host athletic trainer Big East women's basketball tournament Hartford, Conn. U. Conn., 2004, site host athletic trainer NCAA women's basketball tournament, 04; faculty adv., huddle leader Fellowship of Christian Athletes, Lock Haven, 2005—; clin. instr. Bd. Cert. Athletic Tng.; spkr. in field. Active Susquenhanna Pacers Running Club, Lock Haven, 2005. Grantee Grad. Athletic Tng. award, Conn. Athletic Trainer's Assn., Larry Sutton Post Grad. scholarship, Mid-Atlantic Athletic Trainers' Assn., 1996; fellow, U. Conn., 2000; scholar, Nat. Athletic Trainers' Assn. Rsch. & Edn. Found., 1997. Mem.: ARC (instr.), Nat. Athletic Trainer's Assn. Avocations: running, writing, weightlifting. Home: 100 Mariners Way Apt 202 Port Jefferson NY 11777-1838

TOWBIN, A. ROBERT, investment banker; b. NYC, May 26, 1935; s. Harold Clay and Minna (Berlin) Towbin; children: Minna Joyce Pinger, Abraham Robert Jr., Zachary Harold; m. Lisa Grunow; m. Jacqueline de Chollet (div.). BA, Dartmouth Coll., 1957. With Asiel & Co., NYC, 1958-59; with L.F. Rothschild, Unterberg, Towbin Holdings, Inc. (merged with C.E. Unterberg, Towbin Co.), NYC, 1959-86, vice chmn., 1961-86; mng. dir. Lehman Bros., NY, 1987—94; pres. Russian Am. Enterprise Fund., Moscow, NYC, 1994-95; vice chmn. U.S. Russia Investment Fund, Moscow, NYC, 1995; mng. dir. C.E. Unterberg, Towbin, NYC, 1995—99, co-chmn., 1999—2002; exec. v.p. Stephens, Inc., NYC, 2002—. Bd. dirs. Globecomm Sys. Inc., Intertrust. Hon. mem. NY State Coun. Arts. Mem.: Securities Industry Assn., Nat. Golf Links Am., Century Assn., Chelsea Art Club (London), Antigua Yacht Club, N.Y. Yacht Club (fleet capt. 2007—08), Bond Club N.Y. Office: Stephens Inc 65 E 55th St New York NY 10022 Office Phone: 212-891-1720. Business E-Mail: rtowbin@stephens.com.

TOWE, THOMAS EDWARD, lawyer; b. Cherokee, Iowa, June 25, 1937; s. Edward and Florence (Tow) T.; m. Ruth James, Aug. 21, 1960; children: James Thomas, Kristofer Edward. Student, U. Paris, 1956; BA, Earlham Coll., 1959; LLB, U. Mont., 1962; LLM, Georgetown U., 1965; student, U. Mich., Ann Arbor, 1965—67. Ptnr. Towe, Ball, Enright, Mackey & Sommerfeld, Billings, Mont., 1967—; legislator Mont. House of Rep., Billings, 1971-75, Mont. State Senate, Billings, 1975-87, 91-94. Com. mem. Mont. Senate, 1975—87, 1991—94. Contbr. articles to law revs. Mem. Alternatives, Inc., Halfway House, Billing, 1977-99, pres., 1985-86; mem. adv. com. Mont. Crime Control Bd., 1973-78, Youth Justice Coun., 1981-83; mem. State Dem. Exec. Com., 1969-73; Dem. candidate for Congress, 1976; bd. dirs. Mont. Consumer Affairs Coun., Regl. Cmty. Svcs. for the Devel. Disabled, 1975-77, Rimrock Guidance Found., 1975-80, Vols. of Am., Billings, 1984-89, Youth Dynamics Inc., 1989-96, Zoo Mont., 1985-2001, Inst. for Peace Studies, 1993—, Mont. State Parks Assn., 1993—. Capt. JAGC US Army, 1962—65. Named as one of 100 Most Influential Montanans in 20th Century, Missoulian newspaper, 1999, one of 12 state officials in US as "Stars of the States," Washington Monthly mag., one of 10 best state and local officials in US, Mother Jones mag, Jeanette Rankin Civil Liberties award, ACLU, 2008. Mem. Mont. Bar Assn., Yellowstone County Bar Assn., Billings C. of C. Mem. Soc. Of Friends. Avocation: outdoor recreation. Home: 2739 S Gregory Dr Billings MT 59102-0509 Office: Towe Ball Enright Mackey & Sommerfeld 2525 6th Ave N Billings MT 59101 Office Phone: 406-248-7337. Personal E-mail: t.towe@bresnan.net. Business E-Mail: towe@tbems.com.

TOWER, MOLLIE GREGORY, writer, educator, consultant; b. San Antonio, July 17, 1945; d. Malcolm Russell and Margaret Halm Gregory; children: Debbie Tower Tannert, Sheryl Tower Maklary. MusB, U. Tex., Austin, 1967; MEd, U. Tex., Austin, Tex., 1981. Cert. Texas Music K-12 Tex. Edn. Agy., 1967, Texas Supr. Tex. Edn. Agy., 1981. Elem. music tchr., k - 6 Austin Ind. Sch. Dist., Tex., 1967—78, elem. music coord., 1978—92, coord. of choral and gen. music, k-12, 1992—98; author Glencoe/McGraw-Hill, Woodland Hills, Calif., 1995—, Macmillan/McGraw-Hill Pub. Co., NYC, 1982—96, Silver-Burdett Pub. Co., NYC, 2004—; sr. author arts edn. IDEAS Pub. Co., Norwalk, Conn., 1998—; lectr. Tex. State U., 2006—. Cons. Various sch. dist., 1975—2006; pres. Tex. Music Educators Conf., Tex., 1993—96, Tex. Music Admintrs. Conf., Tex., 1996—97, Tex. Coalition for Music Edn., Tex., 1992—93. Author: (ann. elem. curriculum program) Music Memory Bulletin, 1981—2005, (textbook) Music Reading Charts, Grade One & Grade Two, 1988, Songs in Spanish, Primary and Intermediate, 1989, Musica para todas, primary and intermediate, 1995, Choral Connections, 1997, Experiencing Choral Music, 2005. Host Riverside Symphony Music Memory Contest, Lincoln Ctr., NYC, 1999—, Kansas State U. Music Memory Contest, Manhattan, 2003, Dallas Ind. Sch. Dist. Music Memory Contest, 2006—; v.p., commr. Austin Arts Commn., Austin, Tex., 1985—89. Mem.: Sigma Alpha Iota, Delta Kappa Gamma. Personal E-mail: mtower@realtime.net.

TOWERY, CURTIS KENT, lawyer; b. Hugoton, Kans., Jan. 29, 1954; s. Clyde D. and Jo June (Curtis) Towery. BA, Trinity U., 1976; JD, U. Okla., 1979; LLM in Taxation, Boston U., 1989. Mem. Curtis & Blanton, Pauls Valley, Okla., 1980-81; lawyer land and legal dept. Trigg Drilling Co., Oklahoma City, 1981-82; adminstrv. law judge Okla. Corp. Commn., Oklahoma City, 1982-85; counsel Curtis & Blanton, Pauls Valley, Okla., 1985-88; adminstrv. law judge Okla. Dept. Mines, Oklahoma City, 1985-88, assoc. gen. counsel, 1989-92; contracts and purchasing adminstr., atty. Okla. Turnpike Authority, Oklahoma City, 1992-93; asst. gen. counsel Okla. Corp. Commn., 1993-97; spl. judge City of Oklahoma City, 1997—2000; adminstrv. law judge Okla. Dept. of Labor, 1998, 2002—04; v.p., trust officer Bank One Trust, Oklahoma City, 1998-2000; mgr. Cherokee Capital Holdings, 2000—. Sr. adminstrv. law judge Okla. Corp. Commn., 2003—04; dept. special trustee Office of Special Trustee, dept. interior, 2004—05; asst. gen. counsel Okla. Dept. Labor, 2006—. Assoc. bd. Okla. Mus. Art, 1985—88, Okla. Symphony Orch., 1987—92, Ballet Okla., 1987—92, sec., 1990—91, v.p., 1988—89. Mem.: ABA, Okla. Bar Assn., Tex. Bar Assn., Faculty Ho., Elks, Rotary, Sigma Nu, Phi Alpha Delta. Presbyterian. Avocations: flying, golf, travel, investment analysis. Home: PO Box 18668 Oklahoma City OK 73154

TOWEY, JIM (H. JAMES TOWEY), academic administrator, former federal official; b. 1956; m. Mary G. Towey; children: James Marion, Joseph Marius, Maximilian Marian, John Mariano, Marie Therese. BS with high honors, Fla. State U., 1978, JD, 1981. Legis. dir., legal counsel to Senator Mark O. Hatfield US Senate, Washington; cons. Fed. Welfare Reform Fla. State U., to Fla. Gov. Lawton Chiles and US Senator Bob Graham, 1995—96; sec. Fla. Dept. of Health and Rehabilitative Svcs., 1993; dep. asst. to Pres. The White House, Washington, 2002—05, asst. to Pres., 2005—06, dir. Office of Faith-Based & Cmty. Initiatives, 2002—06; pres. Saint Vincent Coll., Latrobe, Pa., 2006—. Author: (document) Five Wishes. Legal cons. Missionaries of Charity, Order of Mother Teresa, 1985—97, full-time vol. in home for people with AIDS, 1990; founder Aging with Dignity, 1996, pres., 1996—2002. Recipient Pro Ecclesia et Pontifice Papal Cross, His Holiness John Paul II, Archbishop John Carroll Award, Archdiocese of Miami; named one of Fifty Most Influential Christians in Am., Church World mag., Power and Influence Top Fifty of 2005, Non-Profit Times mag. Mem.: KC. Roman Catholic. Office: Saint Vincent Coll Office of Pres 300 Fraser Purchase Rd Latrobe PA 15650-2690*

TOWFIGHI, AMYTIS, neurologist; BS, MIT, Cambridge, 1998; MD, Johns Hopkins Sch. Medicine, Balt., 2002. Diplomate Am. Bd. Psychiatry and Neurology, 2008. Resident neurology Harvard, Mass. Gen. Hosp. and Brigham and Women's Hosp., Boston, 2003—06; fellow vascular neurology UCLA, 2006—07; intern internal medicine Harvard, Mass. Gen. Hosp.; chair dept. neurology Rancho Los Amigos Nat. Rehab. Ctr., Downey, Calif., 2007—, dir. acute neurology unit, 2007—; asst. prof. divsn. stroke and neurocritical care, dept. neurology U. Southern Calif., LA, 2007—. Contbr. articles to sci. jour.

TOWLE, ALEXIS CHARLES (LEX TOWLE), education advocate, director; b. Newburyport, Mass., Mar. 23, 1946; s. Sidney Norwood and Nancy Lois (Roberts) Towle; m. Maryellen Foote, Oct. 19, 1991; children: Ian, Devon. BA, Oundle Coll., Northants, Eng., 1964, Yale U., New Haven, 1968. V.p., trust officer Nat. Shawmut Bank, Boston, 1973-78; v.p., fin. cons. Merrill Lynch & Co., Boston, 1979-82, Kidder, Peabody & Co., Boston, 1983-88; v.p., investment banker Boston Bay Capital, Inc., Boston, 1988-93; dir. devel., campaign Boston Renaissance Charter Sch., 1994-95; pres. Apple Tree Inst. Edn. Innovation, Washington, 1995—2005; dir. Apple Tree Inst. Edn., 2004—; sr. loan officer Bank of America, 2006—. Treas., trustee Stoneridge Montessori Sch., Beverly Mass., 1994-2003; co-founder, trustee Cesar Chavez Charter Sch., Washington, 1998-2000, Washington Math Sci. Charter Sch., 1998-2001, Paul Jr. High Charter Sch., Washington, 1999-2001, Apple Early Literacy Presch., Washington, 2001-03; dir. Apple Tree Early Learning Pub. Charter Sch., 2003-. Author (with others) amendments to D.C. School Reform Act of 1995. Lt USMC, 1968—71, Vietnam. Mem.: Nat. Soc. Fundraising Execs. Republican. Episcopalian. Avocation: skiing. Office Phone: 978-869-2424. Business E-Mail: lex@appletreeinstitute.org.

TOWLE, LELAND HILL, retired federal agency administrator; b. Boston, Mar. 29, 1931; s. Leland and Bertha Mary (Hill) T.; m. Carol Peterson, June 5, 1953; children— Peter Kimball, Gretchen Towle Maynard, Michelle Aurora. BS, U. N.H., 1952; MS, M.I.T., 1953; Cert. in Bus. and Mgmt, U. Calif., Berkeley, 1962. Nuclear chemist Stanford Research Inst., Menlo Park, Calif., 1956-59, community systems economist, economist, nuclear economist, 1959-68, mgr. health scis. research, 1968-74; asst. dir. Nat. Center for Alcohol Edn., Arlington, Va., 1974-75. Cons. Medicine in the Pub. Interest, Washington, 1975, Internat. Ctr. for Alcohol Policies, 1995-98—; vis. scientist Nat. Inst. on Alcohol Abuse and Alcoholism, Rckville, Md., 1975-76, dep. dir. office of program devel. and analysis, 1976-77, assoc. dir. office of program devel. and analysis, 1977-81, dir. internat. and intergovtl. affairs, 1981-95; dir. LHT Assocs., Inc., 1995-98. Contbr. articles to profl. jours. Bd. dirs. Med. Resources Found., Palo Alto, Calif., 1972-73. Served with USAF, 1952-56. Mem. APHA, Sci. Research Soc. Am., Am. Nuclear Soc., Am. Chem. Soc., Colonial Capital Kiwanis Club, Sigma Xi, Phi Kappa Phi. Home: 4260 Corbridge Course Williamsburg VA 23188

TOWLER, BRIAN FRANCIS, petroleum engineer, educator; s. Valentine and Nora Towler; m. Shelley Leonard, Nov. 10, 1979; children: Sarah, Renee Clayton, Adam(dec.). B in Engring., U. Queensland, Australia, 1972, PhD, 1978. Registered profl. engr., Wyo., 1996. Prof. Arco Oil & GHS, 1980—83, Moonie Oil Co., Australia, 1983—88, U. Wyo., Laramie, 1988—. Author: Fundamental Principles of Reservoir Engineering, 2002. Mem.: Soc. Petroleum Engrs. Roman Catholic. Achievements include patents for ultrasonic device to mitigate wax deposition in oil wells. Office: U Wyo Dept 3295 1000 E University Ave Laramie WY 82071 Business E-Mail: towler@uwyo.edu.

TOWLER, EVELYN WHEELER, retired elementary school educator; b. Northport, Mich., June 29, 1924; d. Lennis H. and Caroline Greiner Wheeler; m. Charles F. Towler (dec.); children: Jacquetta Sue, Charles F. Towler Jr. BA in History, BA in English Bible, Bob Jones U., Greenville, SC, 1949; postgrad., U. Fla., 1950—54, Fla. So. Coll., Lakeland, 1966—67, U. S. Fla., 1968, Rollins Coll., Winter Park, Fla., 1970, Fla. Technol. U., 1970—75. Cert. elem. tchr., media specialist Fla. Kindergarten tchr., LaBelle, Fla., 1943—44; primary grades tchr. Spring Lake (Fla.) Elem. Sch., 1950—52; youth dir. Presbyn. Ch., Lakeland, Fla., 1952—54; tchg. prin., co-founder Lakeland Christian Sch., 1954—63; asst. to dean of edn. Fla. So. Coll., Lakeland, 1964—67; tchr., lang. arts coord., media specialist Longwood Elem. Sch., Fla., 1967—85; media specialist, libr. Keswick Christian Sch., St. Petersburg, Fla., 1985—91, ret., 1991. Writer Lifepacs Alpha-Omega Pubs., Tempe, Ariz., 1977. Author: (novels) Under Sheltering Wings, 2001, The Road to Home, 2003, Teach Your Child to Write Creatively, 1985, Chronicles of a Hometown Church, 1993, Visitors Guide to Delightful Dunedin, 1995. Vol. Dunedin Hist. Mus.; mem. Dunedin Hist. Soc., Dunedin Friends of the Libr.; camp counselor Children's Bible Mission; bd. dirs. Dunedin Hist. Soc. Recipient History Maker award, Dunedin Hist. Soc., 2000, Lifetime Vol. Achievement award, 2007; named one of Leaders of Am. Elem. Edn., 1971, Outstanding Elem. Tchrs. of Am., 1973; named to Dunedin Sr. Hall of Fame, 2005. Republican. Avocation: genealogy.

TOWLER, KATHERINE, writer; b. Pontiac, Mich., Sept. 1, 1956; d. Lewis W. Towler and Jane B. Kellogg; m. James A. Sparrell, Sept. 14, 1991. BA in English lit., U. of Mich., Ann Arbor, Michigan, 1974—78; MA in English lit., Middlebury Coll., Middlebury, Vermont, 1980—84; MA in fiction writing, Johns Hopkins U., Baltimore, Maryland, 1981—82. Freelance writer, publications cons. self-employed, Portsmouth, NH, 1987—; mem. faculty MFA Program in Writing, So. NH U., 2006—. Author: (novels) Snow Island, 2002 (Barnes and Noble Discover Great New Writers title, Borders Original Voices title, Booksense selection), Evening Ferry, 2005 (Booksense selection). Fellow George Bennett Fellowship, Phillips Exeter Acad., 1989-1990, Individual Artist Fellowship, NH. State Coun. on the Arts, 2003, Fellowship, Yaddo Artists Colony, 1985, 1983, Va. Ctr. for the Creative Arts, 1987, Working Scholarship, Bread Loaf Writers Conf., 1983. Mem.: Authors Guild, NH Writers Project (assoc.; bd. of trustees 1994—97), PEN New Eng. (assoc.). Avocations: bicycling, gardening, bird watching.

TOWLES, DONALD BLACKBURN, retired publishing executive; b. Lawrenceburg, Ky., Sept. 10, 1927; s. Joseph Sterling and Marjorie (Blackburn) Towles; m. Geraldine Gooch, Dec. 20, 1947 (dec. Nov. 1980); children: Sally Blackburn Towles Clark, Rebecca Neale Towles Brown; m. Julia Mason, Dec. 3, 1981. AB in Journalism, U. Ky., 1948. Asst. dir. publicity, editor In Ky. Mag. Commonwealth of Ky., Frankfort, 1948—55; pub. svc. mgr. Courier-Jour. and Louisville Times Co., Louisville, 1956—66, dir. pub. svc. and promotion, 1966—71, v.p., 1974—92, v.p., dir. circulation, 1971—76, v.p., dir. pub. affairs, 1976—92; ret., 1993. Author: (book) The Press of Kentucky 1787-1994; editor: Newspaper Promotion Handbook, 1983. Chmn. Louisville area chpt. ARC, 1987—89; mem. adv. bd. Salvation Army, 1982—97; elder emeritus Disciples of Christ; chmn. program adv. com. Louisville Devel. Program, 1971—80; bd. dirs. Louisville Med. Ctr., 1982—97; pres. Heritage Corp. Louisville, 1982—85; chmn. Thos. D. Clark Found., 2000—04; adv. bd. Christian Ch. Homes Ky., 1992—96; chmn. Sr. Citizens East, 1996—97. With US Army, 1952—54, Korea. Recipient Cmty. Svc. award, Louisville Devel. Com., 1980; named Outstanding Chpt. Vol., Louisville area ARC, 1993, Outstanding State Vol., 1994; named to Ky. Journalism Hall of Fame, 1992. Mem.: Soc. Profl. Journalists (pres.Louisville chpt. 1991—92), Ky. Press Assn. (pres. 1982, Pres.'s Cup Leadership 1982, Disting. Svc. award 1987), Internat. Newspaper Promotion Area (pres. 1980—82, Silver Shovel 1983), Journalism Alumni Assn. U. Ky. (pres. 1979—94, Outstanding Alumnus award 1976, All-Am. Alumni award 1994). Democrat. Home: 4800 Whitekirk Ct Louisville KY 40222

TOWLES, ELIZABETH W., engineering educator; m. Phillip Towles. BS, Miss. State U., 1993; MS, U. Ala., Birmingham, 1995. Instr. NE State Tech. CC, Blountville, Tenn., 2002—05; instr. engring. tech. Piedmont Tech. Coll., Greenwood, SC, 2005—. Asst. cub master Boy Scouts America, Laurens, SC, 2007—. Mem.: Am. Soc. Engring. Educators. Office: Piedmont Tech Coll 620 N Emerald Rd Greenwood SC 29648

TOWN, TERRENCE CHRISTOPHER, research scientist; b. Cleve., Aug. 31, 1974; s. JoAnn Marie Dobbs and Wayne Henry Town; m. Yvon Xuan Roush. PhD, U. South Fla., 2002. Rsch. assoc. Roskamp Inst., Tampa, Fla., 1997—. Achievements include invention of therapeutic strategies for Alzheimer's disease involving blocking the CD40-CD40L interaction. Business E-Mail: ttown@hsc.usf.edu.

TOWNE, GARY SPAULDING, music educator; b. Burlington, Vt., June 12, 1950; s. Raymond Duane and Janet Spaulding Towne; m. Page Maurice Towne (dec.); children: Jonathan, Andrew. AB, Yale U., 1971; PhD, U. Calif., Santa Barbara, 1985. From asst. prof. to assoc. prof. U. N.D., Grand Forks, 1988—2002, prof., 2002—, dept. chair, 1999—2006. Vis. asst. prof. Middlebury (Vt.) Coll., 1985—88; organist, choirmaster St. Paul's Episcopal Ch., Grand Forks, 1995—2003; choirmaster United Luth. Ch., Grand Forks, 1988—91; dir. Collegium Musicum U. N.D., 1989—99. Contbr. articles to profl. publs.; editor: (book) Opera Omnia Gasparis de Albertis, vol. 1, 1999. Recipient Fulbright scholarship, USIA, 1994—95, Gladys Krieble Delmas fellowship, 1982—83, 1993, Stanley Krebs Meml. prize, U. Calif.-Santa Barbara, 1980, 1985. Mem.: Hist. Brass Soc., Coll. Music Soc., Am. Musicol. Soc., Internat. Musicol. Soc., Am. Motorcyclists Assn. Episcopalian. Avocation: motorcycling. Office: U ND Music Dept Box 7125 Grand Forks ND 58202

TOWNE, JUSTIN, biology professor, researcher; b. Marysville, Calif., Mar. 14, 1969; s. Walter James and Helen Towne. PhD, U. Calif., Davis, 1998. Asst. prof. U. Fla., Gainesville, 1999—2000; assoc. prof. Brigham Young U., Provo, Utah, 2000—. Scoutmaster Boy Scouts Am., Gainesville, 1999—2000. Recipient Golden Beaker award, Petroleum Helicopters Inc., 2007—08. Mem.: Willi Hennig Soc. Achievements include patents for entomopathogenic nematodes for biological control of insect pests. Home: 401 Widb Provo UT 84602 Personal E-mail: ztnemepneditor@gmail.com.

TOWNE, SARAH PATTON, physician; b. Fountain Hill, Pa., Aug. 28, 1953; d. William Frank and Arline Rose (Patton) T. Degree in Nursing, Geisinger Med. Ctr., Danville, Pa., 1973; BS magna cum laude, Kutztown U. Pa., 1988; DO, Phila. Coll. Osteo. Medicine, 1992, MSc in Family Practice, 1995. Diplomate Nat. Bd. Osteo. Med. Examiners. Psychiatric nurse Allentown State Hosp., Pa., 1973-76, NW Inst. Psychiatry, Ft. Washington, Pa., 1976-78; RN, psychotherapist Boulder County Mental Health Ctr., Colo., 1979-85; intern Phila. Coll. Osteo. Medicine, 1992-93, resident in family practice, 1993-95; physician Troup Family Practice, Tex., 1995-97; pvt. practice Denver, 1997—2003. Physician Harleysville Med. Assn., Pa., 1993-95; asst. dean clin. edn., assoc. prof. primary care Touro U. Coll. Osteo. Medicine, Calif., 2003-. Bd. dirs. Boulder County Rape Crisis Team, 1979-81. Faculty Devel. Fellowship, U. Calif. San Francisco, 2004—05. Mem. Am. Osteo Assn., Am. Coll. Osteo. Family Practitioners (bd. cert.). Avocations: reading, gardening, dogs. Home: 151 Thresher Dr Vallejo CA 94591-7814 Office: Touro U - Calif Coll of Osteo Med 1310 Johnson Ln Mare Island Vallejo CA 94592 Office Phone: 707-638-5200. Business E-Mail: stowne@touro.edu.

TOWNES, CHARLES HARD, physics professor; b. Greenville, SC, July 28, 1915; s. Henry Keith and Ellen Sumter (Hard) Townes; m. Frances H. Brown, May 4, 1941; children: Linda Lewis, Ellen Screven, Carla Keith, Holly Robinson. BA, BS, Furman U., 1935; MA, Duke U., 1937; PhD, Calif. Inst. Tech., 1939. Mem. tech. staff Bell Telephone Lab., 1939—47; assoc. prof. physics Columbia U., 1948—50, prof. physics, 1950—61; exec. dir. Columbia Radiation Lab., 1950—52, chmn. physics dept., 1952—55; provost and prof. physics MIT, 1961—66, inst. prof., 1966—67; v.p., dir. rsch. Inst. Def. Analyses, Washington, 1959—61; univ. prof. physics U. Calif., Berkeley, 1967—86, prof. physics emeritus, 1986—94, prof. grad. sch., 1994—. Guggenheim fellow, 1955—56; Fulbright lectr. U. Paris, 1955—56, U. Tokyo, 1956; dir. Enrico Fermi Internat. Sch. Physics, 1963; Richtmeyer lectr. Am. Phys. Soc., 1959; Scott lectr. U. Cambridge, 1963; Centennial lectr. U. Toronto, 1967; Lincoln lectr., 1972—73; Halley lectr., 1976; Krishnan lectr., 92; Nishina lectr., 92; Weinberg lectr. Oak Ridge (Tenn.) Nat. Lab., 1997; Rajiv Gandhi lectr., 97; Henry Norris Russell lectr. Am. Astron. Soc., 1998; dir. Gen. Motors Corp., 1973—86, Perkin-Elmer Corp., 1966—69; mem. Pres.'s Sci. Adv. Com., 1966—69, vice chmn., 1967—69; chmn. sci. and tech. adv. com. for manned space flight NASA, 1964—70; mem. Pres.'s Com. on Sci. and Tech., 1976; rschr. on nuc. and molecular structure, quantum electronics, interstellar molecules, radio and infrared astrophysics; Greenstein lectr., 2009. Author (with A.L. Schawlow): Microwave Spectroscopy; author: Making Waves, 1996, How the Laser Happened. Adventures of a Scientist, 1999; author, co-editor Quantum Electronics, 1960, Quantum Electronics and Coherent Light, 1964, mem. editl. bd. Rev. Sci. Instruments, 1950—52, Phys. Rev., 1951—53, Jour. Molecular Spectroscopy, 1957—60, Procs. NAS, 1978—84, Can. Jour. Physics, 1995—, contbr. articles to sci. publs. Mem. corp. Woods Hole Oceanographic Instn.; bd. mem. Calif. Inst. Tech., Carnegie Instn. Washington, Ctr. for Theology and Natural Scis., Mount Wilson Inst. Decorated officier Légion d'Honneur (France); recipient Stuart Ballantine medal, Franklin Inst., 1962, Thomas Young medal and prize, Inst. Physics and Phys. Soc., Eng., 1963, Nobel prize for Physics, 1964, Disting. Pub. Svc. medal, NASA, 1969, Wilhelm Exner award, Austria, 1970, Niels Bohr Internat. Gold medal, 1979, Nat. medal of Sci., 1982, Berkeley citation, U. Calif., 1986, CommonWealth award, 1993, ADION medal, Obs. Nice, 1995, Mendel award, Villanova U., 1999, Frank Annunzio award, Christopher Columbus Fellowship Found., 1999, Rabindranath Tagore Birth Centenary plaque, Asiatic Soc., 1999, Karl Schwarzschild medal, Astronomische Gesellschaft, 2002, Drake award, SETI Inst., 2003, Templeton prize, 2005, Vannevar Bush medal, 2006; named to Nat. Inventors Hall of Fame, 1976, Engring. and Sci. Hall of Fame, 1983. Fellow: IEEE (life medal of honor 1967), Calif. Acad. Scis., Indian Nat. Sci. Acad., Optical Soc. Am. (Mees medal 1968), Am. Phys. Soc. (pres. 1967, Plyler prize 1977, Frederick Ives medal 1996); mem.: NAE (founders award 2000), NAS (coun. 1968—72, 1978—81, chmn. space sci. bd. 1970—73, Comstock award 1959, Carty medal 1962), N.Y. Acad. Scis., Max-Planck Inst. Physics and Astrophysics (fgn. mem.), Pontifical Acad. Scis., Russian Acad. Scis. (Lomonosov medal 2000, fgn. mem.), Royal Soc. (fgn. mem.), Am. Acad. Arts and Scis., Am. Astron. Soc., Am. Philos. Soc. Achievements include patents for masers and lasers. Office: U Calif Dept Physics 366 Leconte # 7200 Berkeley CA 94720-0001 Office Phone: 510-642-1128. Business E-Mail: cht@ssl.berkeley.edu.

TOWNES, DAVID ANDREW, medical educator; b. Rochester, NY, Mar. 26, 1967; s. Philip Leonard and Marjorie Greenstone Townes. BA in Biology, U. Rochester, 1989; MD, U. Mass., Worcester, 1993; MPH in Health Policy and Adminstrn., U. Ill., Chgo., 1998; diploma, London Sch. Hygiene & Tropical Medicine, 2007. Diplomate Am. Bd. Emergency Medicine, 1997. Clin. instr. attending phyisician, emergency medicine Harvard Med. Sch., Boston, 1999—2000; asst. prof. emergency medicine U. Ill. Coll. Medicine, 2000—01, fellow emergency medicine, 1996—98; assoc. prof., emergency medicine U. Wash. Sch. Medicine, Seattle, 2001—; fellow, epidemic intelligence svc. Ctr. Disease Control & Prevention, Atlanta, 2008—; lt. comdr. USPHS, Atlanta, 2008—. Med. dir. Adventure Med, LLC, Seattle, 2002—. Editor: (book) Expedition and Wilderness Medicine. Office: Univ Wash 1959 NE Pacific St Box 356123 Seattle WA 98195 Business E-Mail: townesd@u.washington.edu.

TOWNS, EDOLPHUS (ED TOWNS), United States Representative from New York; b. Chadbourn, NC, July 21, 1934; m. Gwendolyn Forbes, 1960; children: Darryl, Deidra. BS in Sociology, NC A&T State U., Greensboro, 1956; MSW, Adelphi U., Garden City, NY, 1973; PhD (hon.), NC A&T State U., Shaw U. Tchr. NYC Pub. Schs., Medgar Evers Coll., Bklyn., Fordham U.; asst. adminstr. Beth Israel Med. Ctr., 1965-71; dep. borough pres. Bklyn., NY, 1976-82; mem. US Congress from 11th NY dist., 1983—91, US Congress from 10th NY dist., 1992—; chmn. US House Oversight & Govt. Reform Com., 2009—. Mem. adv. coun. Boy Scouts America; active vol. Salvation Army. With US Army, 1956—58. Recipient Congl. Leadership award, Am. Coll. Nurse-Midwives, 1999; named Home Care Hero, Nat. Assn. Home Care, Legislator of Yr., Am. Acad. Nurse Practitioners, Am. Acad. Physician Assts., Am. Assn. Cmty. Health Ctrs., Nat. Coalition Poison Control Ctrs.; named a Friend of Nat. Parks, Nat. Parks Conservation Assn.; named one of 100 Most Influential Black Americans, Ebony mag., 2006—08; named to Acad. of Distinction, Adelphi U. Mem.: NAACP, Nat. Assn. Social Workers, Kiwanis Club, Phi Beta Sigma. Democrat. Baptist. Office: US Congress 2232 Rayburn House Office Bldg Washington DC 20515-0001 also: 186 Joralemon St Ste 1102 Brooklyn NY 11201 Office Phone: 202-225-5936. Office Fax: 202-225-1018.*

TOWNSEL, A. SYLVIANE, language educator; b. Moule, W.I., France, Dec. 3, 1943; d. Evariste G. and Fanny Yolande (Ferand) Griponne; m. Rdell Townsel, Oct. 23, 1978; 1 child, Timothy. BA, U. Madrid, Spain, 1975; MA, Atlanta U., 1977; PhD, Emory U., 1987. Tchg. asst. Spanish Emory U., Atlanta, 1978-80; instr. French, Spanish Morehouse Coll., Atlanta, 1980-82; translator, sec. Atlanta Legal Aid, 1982-85; instr. Spanish Dekalb Coll., Atlanta, 1986-88, Spellman Coll., Atlanta, 1986—; assoc. prof. French, Spanish Va. State U., 2004—. Author: Donjuanism in Zorrilla and Valle-Inclan, 1987; (monograph) Negritude in French Caribbean Literature, 1991; contbr. articles to profl. jours., chpts. to books including Les Femmes Dans Segou de Maryse Conde, Paris, 1995. Recipient French Prof. award French Govt., Strasbourg, 1990. Mem. Modern Lang. Assn., African Lit. Assn., Assn. Fgn. Lang. Tchrs. NY, Conseil Superieure de Lang. Française. Roman Catholic. Avocations: travel, reading, writing, gardening. Home: 16 Woodmere Dr Apt C Petersburg VA 23805-2121 Office: Va State Univ Petersburg VA 23806 Office Phone: 804-524-5183. Business E-Mail: stownsel@vsu.edu.

TOWNSEND, ALAIR ANE, publishing executive; b. Rochester, NY, Feb. 15, 1942; d. Harold Eugene and Dorothy (Sharpe) T.; m. Robert Harris, Dec. 31, 1970 (div. 1994). BS, Elmira Coll., 1962; MS, U. Wis., 1964; postgrad., Columbia U., 1970-71; doctorate (hon.), Elmira Coll., NY, Pace U., Coll. New Rochelle, Baruch Coll., Polytechnic U., Manhatten. Assoc. dir. budget priorities Com. on Budget, US House of Reps., Washington, 1975-79, dep. asst. sec. for budget HEW, 1979-80, asst. sec. for mgmt. and budget, 1980-81; dir. Office Mgmt. & Budget NYC, 1981-85; dep. mayor for fin. & econ. devel., 1985-89; pub. Crain's NY Bus., NYC, 1989—2006, v.p., 1993—2006, pub. dir., 2006, columnist, 1989—. Bd. overseers Tchrs. Ins. and Annuity Assn.-Coll. Retirement Equities Fund; dirs. adv. coun. M & T Bank; former mem. adv. bd. Ford Motor Credit Corp.; former bd. mem. Armor Holdings Inc., Am. Stock Exch., Fay's, Inc. Former vice-chmn., trustee Elmira Coll.; former mem. Coun. Fgn. Rels.; former chmn. Am. Woman's Econ. Devel. Corp.; former chmn. N.Y.C. Sports Commn.; former chmn. Consol. Corp. Fund of Lincoln Ctr.; bd. dirs. Lincoln Ctr.; vice-chmn. Buffalo Fiscal Stability Auth.; bd. dirs., Greater NY Councils-Boy Scouts of Am.; bd. dirs. Levin Inst. SUNY; fmr. mem., Partnership for NYC; fmr. vice chair, Bus. Coun. NY State. Best Bylined Commentary, Soc. Am. Bus. Editors & Writers, 2007, Alliance of Area Business Publications, 2006; Sara Lee Front Runner Award; Star Award, New York Women's Agenda; Governor's Award for Excellence (Pataki); Directors Emeriti Award, Lincoln Center; Civic Leadership Award, Citizens Union; Elizabeth Cutter Morrow Award, YWCA of New York City; Business Leadership Award, Young Adult Institute; Brotherhood Award, 100 Black Men and Association for a Better New York; Iphigene Ochs Sulzberger Award, Barnard College; Leadership in Business Award, New York Business Group on Health; Franklin Award, Association of Graphic Communications; Women's Achievement Award, Brooklyn Chamber of Commerce; Business Leadership Award, Professional Women in Construction Mem. Women's Forum, Econ. Club NY Office: Crain's NY Bus 711 3d Ave New York NY 10017

TOWNSEND, BRIAN DOUGLAS, paralegal; b. Tokyo, Sept. 22, 1961; s. Thomas and Juanita Evora (Sanford) T.; m. Gloria Ann Wigfall, Aug. 23, 1986; children: Brian D. Jr., Brianna A. BA in Criminology, U. Md., 1983. Legal aide Kirkland & Ellis, Washington, 1984-85; legal asst. to mng. clk. Cadwalader, Wickersham & Taft, Washington, 1985-87; paralegal specialist, Office Chief Counsel US Dept. Transp. Maritime Adminstrn., Washington, 1987-90, US Dept. Treasury, IRS, Washington, 1990-92; litig. support specialist US Dept. Justice, Tax Divsn., Washington, 1992-93; paralegal specialist Resolution Trust Corp., Washington, 1993-95, FDIC, Washington, 1996-98, US Dept. Treasury, OIG, Washington, 1998-99; program specialist FOIA/PA US Dept. Treasury, OFAC, Washington, 1999-2000; mgmt. analyst USDA, Washington, 2000—02; program analyst IRS/OPIP US Dept. Treasury, Washington, 2002—. Avocations: bowling, fishing, swimming, chess, football. Office: US Dept Treasury IRS/OPIP 1111 Constitution Ave NW Washington DC 20224-0002 Personal E-mail: briandouglastownsend@yahoo.com. Business E-Mail: brian.d.townsend@irs.gov.

TOWNSEND, CAROL AGNES, artist, educator; d. Clarence William Townsend and Florence Elizabeth Gonyea; m. Thomas Charles Sist, Oct. 6, 1979 (dec. Sept. 2003). BS, Nazareth Coll. Rochester, NY, 1969; MFA, Ohio U., Athens, 1973. Tchr., dir. art action City Sch. Dist., Sch. #14, Rochester, NY, 1969—71; vis. lectr. Ohio U., Athens, 1973—74; asst. to assoc. prof. Daemen Coll., Amherst, NY, 1974—88; instr. Niagara County CC, Sanborn, 1989—95; lectr. Buffalo State Coll., 1994—99, asst. prof., 2000—02, assoc. prof., 2003—. Dir. internat. ceramics program Daemen Coll., Snyder, NY, 1976, chair dept. art, 1982—86, chair divsn. fine and performing arts, 1986—88; chair dept. design Buffalo State Coll., 2002—05, interim chair dept. design, 2006, 2007—. Exhibitions include 4th Biennial Internat. Craft Exhibit, Tweed Mus., 1977, Necessary Objects:Functional Pottery, Nat. Arts Ctr., St. Petersburg, 2002, Common Clay:Creating Olds and New Ceramics, NCECA Conf., 2004, Made in NY 2006, Schweinfurth Meml. Art Ctr., Young Americans:Clay and Textiles, Mus. Contemporary Crafts, 1977, In Western NY, Albright-Knox Art Gallery, 1979, 27th Chautauqua Nat. Exhbn. Am. Art, 1984, Craft Art 1990/Western NY, Burchfield-Penney Art Ctr., The Kenan Masters, Kenan Ctr., 1995, Contemporary NY State Crafts, NY State Mus., 1999, Craft Forms 2001, Wayne Art Ctr, NY State Craft Biennial, 2001. Post prodn. design cons. Meta Media - documentaries aired on PBS affiliate, Buffalo, 2000—03; artist/designer Herd About Buffalo Project, Roswell Pk. Cancer Insitute and the Burchfield-Penney Art Ctr., Buffalo, 2000—00, Buffalo On Wheels Project for the Burchfield-Penney Art Ctr., Buffalo, 2003—03; mem./cons. Buffalo Diocesan Liturgical Commn., Buffalo, 1977—89; cons. for rennovation St. Joseph U. Ch., Buffalo, 1999—2000. Recipient Kenneth Coe award, Beaux Arts Designer Craftmen, Gallery Fine Art, Ohio, 1974, Disting. Faculty Performance award, Daemen Coll., 1979, Bene award, Modern Liturgy Mag., 1985, 1986, 1988, 1989, First pl., Kenan Ctr., Lockport, NY, 1989, Empire State Craft Alliance, 1990, Master Craftsman award, Kenan Ctr., Lockport NY, 1990, Faculty Excellence Citation, Buffalo State Coll., 1996, Jurors' award, Plain Arts IV Internat. Exhbn., 2002. Mem.: Buffalo Soc. Artists (assoc.; pres. 1992, assoc. v.p. 1991). Avocations: writing poetry, gardening. Office: Buffalo State Coll 1300 Elmwood Ave Buffalo NY 14222 Business E-Mail: townseca@buffalostate.edu.

TOWNSEND, CHUCK (CHARLES H. TOWNSEND), publishing executive; b. Mar. 24, 1945; m. Jill Roosa, Oct. 2008; 2 children. Grad., U. Mich. Pres., pub. Family Cir. Mag., 1986—90; pres., CEO, Women's Mag. Pub. Divsn. NY Times Co., 1990—94; pub. Glamour mag., Condé Nast Publs., NYC, 1994—95, exec. v.p. Condé Nast Publs., 1995—2000, COO, 2000—04, pres., CEO, 2005—; COO, Advance Mag. Group Advanced Publs., NYC, 2001—. Office: Conde Nast Publications Inc 4 Times Sq New York NY 10036-6561*

TOWNSEND, COURTNEY M., surgeon; b. Lubbock, Tex., 1943; MD, U. Tex., Galveston, 1969. Specialty bd. 1 Surgery 1975. Intern U. Tex. Med. Br., 1969—70, resident surgery, 1970—74; fellow surg. oncology U. Calif., LA, 1974—76; staff surgeon, surg. dir. intensive care unit Nat. Naval Med. Ctr., Bethesda, 1976—78; assoc. prof. U. Tex. Med. Br., 1978—83, prof., 1983—95, chair, dept. surgery, 1995—. James IV Surg. Traveller U. Tex. Med. Br., 1986; pres. Am. Pancreatic Assn., 1992—93; mem. Tex. Cancer Coun., 1992—2008; dir. Am. Bd. Surgery, 2000—07. Editor-in-chief: Sabiston Textbook of Surgery: The Biological Basis of Modern Surgical Practice, 16th edit., 18th edit. Recipient Rsch. Career Devel. award, NIH, 1982, Ashbel Smith Disting. Alumnus, 1986. Fellow: ACS (exec. com. 1999—2003, chmn. bd. govs. 2004—05, sec. 2006—); mem.: AMA (residency rev. com. 1999—2003), Am. Surg. Assn. (pres. 2007—08), Am. Bd. Surgery (chair 2006—07), So. Surg. Assn. (sec. 1999—2003, pres. 2003—04). Office: 301 University Blvd Galveston TX 77555-0527

TOWNSEND, FRAN (FRANCES FRAGOS TOWNSEND), former federal official; b. Mineola, NY, Dec. 28, 1961; m. John M. Townsend, 1994; 2 children. BA in Polit. Sci., BS in Psychology, Am. U., Washington, 1982; JD, San Diego U., 1984; student, Inst. Internat. & Comparative Law, London. Asst. dist. atty., Bklyn., 1985—88; atty., US Atty. Office (so. dist.) NY US Dept. Justice, 1988—91, chief of staff to asst. atty. gen. criminal divsn., 1993—95, dir. internat. affairs criminal divsn., 1995—97, acting dep. asst. atty. gen., 1997—98, counsel Office Intelligence Policy & Rev., 1998—2001; asst. comdt. intelligence USCG, US Dept. Homeland Security, 2001—03; dep. asst. to Pres., dep. nat. security adv. for combating terrorism The White House, 2003—04, asst. to Pres for homeland security & counterterrorism, 2004—08; chair Homeland Security Coun., 2004—08. Mem. Fgn. Intelligence Adv. Bd., Washington, 2008—. On-air contbr. CNN, 2008—.*

TOWNSEND, FRANCES (FRAN TOWNSEND), healthcare educator, writer; b. Fort Worth, May 25, 1926; d. Robert Emory Hicks and Ida Belle Hagendoorn; m. William Brice Townsend III; children: William Brice IV children: Mary Townsend Seeley. BA, BS, Tex. Women's U., 1946. Cert. clin. nutritionist Clin. Nutrition Certification Bd., dietitian/nutritionist NY, Addictionolotist Am. Coll. of Addictionology and Compulsive Disorders. Addictionologist RITEcare, Springfield, Mo., 1976—; cons., counselor, holistic health educator Well Body/Well Mind, LLC, Springfield, 1996—; assoc. editor Tree of Light Pub., St. George, Utah, 2000—. Author: (column) Today's Healthy Woman, Wellness Way. Avocations: gardening, jewelry making, birdwatching, writing. Personal E-mail: ftownsend3@mchsi.com.

TOWNSEND, JANE KALTENBACH, biologist, educator; b. Chgo., Dec. 21, 1922; BS, Beloit Coll., 1944; MA, U. Wis., 1946; PhD, U. Iowa, 1950. Asst. in zoology U. Wis., 1944-47, asst., project assoc. in pathology, 1950—53; asst., instr. U. Iowa, 1948-50; rsch. fellow Wenner-Grens Inst. Am. Cancer Soc., Stockholm, 1953—56; asst. prof. zoology Northwestern U., 1956-58; asst. prof. to assoc. prof. zoology Mt. Holyoke Coll., South Hadley, Mass., 1958-70, prof., 1970-93, chmn. biol. scis., 1980-86, prof. emeritus, 1993—; summer investigator Marine Biol. Lab., Woods Hole, Mass., 1993—. Contbr. articles to profl. sci. jours. Fellow AAAS (sec. sect. biol. sci. 1974-78); mem. Am. Assn. Anatomists, Am. Inst. Biol. Scis., Soc. Integrated Comparative Biology, Soc. Exptl. Biology and Medicine, Soc. Devel. Biology, Corp. of Marine Biol. Lab., Sigma Xi, Phi Beta Kappa. Achievements include research in amphibian metamorphosis and immune responses in marine sponges. Office: Mount Holyoke Coll Dept Bio Scis South Hadley MA 01075 Office Phone: 413-538-2124. Business E-Mail: jtownsen@mtholyoke.edu.

TOWNSEND, JOHN MICHAEL, lawyer; b. West Point, NY, Mar. 21, 1947; s. John D. and Vera (Nachman) T.; m. Frances M. Fragos, Oct. 8, 1994; children, James E., Patrick M. BA, Yale U., 1968, JD, 1971. Bar: N.Y. 1972, U.S. Dist. Ct. (so. and ea. dists.) N.Y. 1975, U.S. Ct. Appeals (2nd cir.) 1975, U.S. Supreme Ct. 1975, U.S. Ct. Appeals (8th cir.) 1982, U.S. Ct. Appeals (7th and 10th cirs.) 1986, D.C. 1990, U.S. Dist. Ct. D.C. 1990, U.S. Ct. Appeals (D.C. cir.) 1990, U.S. Ct. Appeals (4th cir.) 1991, U.S. Ct. Appeals (fed. cir.) 2000, U.S. Ct. Appeals (11th cir.) 2001, U.S. Ct. Fed. Claims, 2000, U.S. Ct. Appeals (1st cir.) 2003. Assoc. Hughes Hubbard & Reed, LLP, NYC, 1971-73, 75-80, ptnr., 1980—; assoc. Hughes Hubbard & Reed, Paris, 1973-74. Bd. dirs., chair bd. dirs., law com. Am. Arbitration Assn.; trustee US Coun. Internat. Bus.; panel arbitrators Internat. Ctr. Settlement Investment Disputes, 2008. 1st lt. USAR, 1971-75. Mem. ABA, Am. Law Inst., Internat. Bar Assn. (chair mediation com., 2005-06), Assn. Bar City N.Y., Coll. Comml. Arbitrators, Univ. Club, Yale Club (N.Y.C.). Democrat. Episcopalian. Office: Hughes Hubbard & Reed LLP 1775 I St NW Washington DC 20006-2401 Office Phone: 202-721-4600. Office Fax: 202-721-4646. Business E-Mail: townsend@hugheshubbard.com.

TOWNSEND, JOHN WILLIAM, JR., physicist, retired federal agency administrator; b. Washington, Mar. 19, 1924; s. John William and Elenore (Eby) T.; m. Mary Irene Lewis, Feb. 7, 1948; children: Bruce Alan, Nancy Dewitt, John William III, Megan Lewis; m. JoAnn C. Clayton, Sept. 17, 1996. BA, Williams Coll., 1947, MA, 1949, ScD, 1961. With Naval Research Lab., 1949-55, br. head, 1955-58; with NASA, 1958-68, dep. dir. Goddard Space Flight Ctr., 1965-68; dep. adminstrn. Environ. Scis. Svcs. Adminstrn., 1968-70; asso. adminstr. NOAA, 1970-77; pres. Fairchild Space and Electronics Co., 1977-82; v.p. Fairchild Industries, 1979-85; pres. Fairchild Space Co., 1983-85; sr. v.p. Fairchild Industries, 1985-87; chmn. bd. Am. Satellite Co., 1985, sr. v.p., exec. aerospace group, 1987, exec. v.p., 1987; assoc. dep. adminstr. NASA, 1987; dir. NASA Goddard Space Flight Ctr., 1987-90; ret., 1990. Mem. U.S. Rocket, Satellite Rsch. Panel, 1950-60; chmn. space applications bd. NRC, 1985-87; bd. dirs., trustee Telos Corp., 1990-92; mem. adv. bd. Loral Corp., 1990-92; mem. coms. NRC, 1990—; bd. dirs CTA, Inc., 1990-98. Author numerous papers, reports in field. Pres. town council, Forest Heights, Md., 1951-55. Served with USAAF, 1943-46. Recipient Profl. Achievement award Engrs. and Architects Day, 1957; Meritorious Civilian Service award Navy Dept., 1957; Outstanding Leadership medal NASA, 1962; Distinguished Service medal, 1971, 90; recipient Arthur S. Fleming award Fed. Govt., 1963, Edward A. Flinn III award, 1999. Fellow AIAA, AAAS, Am. Meteorol. Soc.; mem. NAE (com. 1990-93), Am. Phys. Soc., Am. Geophys. Union. (fin. com. 1991-98, Edward A. Flinn III award, 1999), Internat. Astronautical Fedn. (mem., tru stee internat., acad. astronautics), Sigma Xi. Home: 6532 79th St Cabin John MD 20818-1201

TOWNSEND, JULIE RAE, artist, educator; b. Davenport, Iowa, Oct. 26, 1964; d. Richard Earl and Gladys Imogene Crow; m. Kelvin Leroy Townsend, Sept. 26, 1989; children: Stephanie Allisson, Elliott Russell. BFA, St. Ambrose U., Davenport, Iowa, 1983—87, BA in Art Edn. K-12, 2001—02; MA in Spl. Edn., St. Ambrose U., 2008. Cert. tchr. Iowa, 2003. Tchr. Davenport Mus. Art, 2002; spl. edn. tchr. Quad City Arts, Davenport, 2004. Presenter Ea. Iowa Writing Project workshop. Commissions, exhibitions include 1st Presbyn. Ch. (700 sq. ft. mural), Davenport, Dubuque Mus. Art, Tri-Ann. Tri-City Exhbn., Moline's Reher Gallery, Ill., prin. works include Rapunzel's Bad Hair Day (charcoal) (Hon. Mention, 1995), Still Life (drawing) (Scholastic Achievement award, 1982); contbr. articles to profl. jours. Vol. Midcoast Fine Arts, Rock I., Ill., 1995—2003; vol. Friends of Catich St. Ambrose U., Davenport, Iowa, 2003—; leader Girl Scouts (Miss. Valley coun.), Davenport, Iowa, 1997—2003; vol. First Presbyn. Ch., Davenport, Iowa. Recipient 3d Best 2D Artist Quad Cities, River Cities Reader, 2001, 2d Best 2D Artist Quad Cities, 2002; named 1st Best 2D Artist Quad Cities, 2003; grant, Quad City Art Dollars, 2008, William Pritchard III, 2008. Mem.: Eastern Iowa Writing Project Adv. Com., Nat. Assn. Spl. Educators Tchrs. (assoc.), Midcoast Fine Arts (life; vol. various jobs 1996—2003). Home: 1131 E Columbia Ave Davenport IA 52803 Personal E-mail: socokeefe@msn.com.

TOWNSEND, KATHERINE, psychologist, educator; d. Ella L. Bey; 1 child, KaJuan D. Jackson. BA in Psychology, Eastern Ill. U., Charleston, 1994, Specialist in Sch. Psychology, 1998; PhD in Ednl. Psychology, U. Ill., Chgo., 2007. Cert. sch. psychologist Ill. State Bd. Edn., 1998. Recreation leader Chgo. Pk. Dist., Austin Town Hall, 1986; sales assoc. Fayva Shoes, North Riverside, Ill., Chgo., Oak Park, Ill., 1987—88; with USAF, Desert Storm, 1988—96; sales assoc., stock worker J.C.Penney, Mattoon, Ill., 1993—94; case mgr., day camp counselor South Ctrl. Cmty. Svcs., Chgo., 1994; emergency work svcs. ARC, Chgo., 1995; dir., Afro-Am. culture ctr. Minority Affairs, Eastern Ill. U., Charleston, 1995—97; sch. psychologist Chgo. Bd. Edn., Chgo. Pub. Schs., Chgo., 1997—; adj. prof. psychology Wright Coll., City Colls., Chgo., 2008—, Ind. Networking Perspective, 2008—. Chair Nat. Invitational Conf., Washington, 2001; facilitator, teen summit Truth & Deliverance Internat. Ministries, Chgo., 2002. Vol. USAF, Germany, 1990; evaluator, registrar, 1st ann. health fair & symposium Eastern Ill. U., 1993, facilitator, single parents group, 1995—97; participant, vol. Ravinia Music Festival, Lawndale Partnership, Chgo., 2005—07; vol. choreographer Homan Sq. Pk., Chgo. Pk. Dist., 2006; coord. Chgo. Pub. Schs., 2008; foster pet care Kitten care, Chgo., 2008; vol. Capital Campaign Victory Cathedral Worship Ctr., 2008—; cheer leading coach Spl. Needs Sch., Chgo., 2008—; audio technician & choreographer Truth & Deliverance Internat. Ministries, Chgo., 2000—07; mem. African Am. Heritage Com., Charleston, 1995—97. With USAF, 1996, Germany, ND, Chgo. Decorated Achievement medal, USAF. Mem.: U. Ill. Alumni Assn., Chgo. Assn. Sch. Psychologist, Ill. Assn. Sch. Psychologist, Am. Ednl. Rsch. Assn., Nat. Assn. Sch. Psychologist, Internat. Reading Assn., Chgo. Urban League. Avocations: reading, swimming, dancing, travel, exercise. Office: Chgo Bd Edn 125 S Clark St Chicago IL 60603 Office Phone: 773-213-2691. Personal E-mail: katone70@5linx.net. Business E-Mail: ktownsend@cps.edu.

TOWNSEND, KATHLEEN KENNEDY, former lieutenant governor; b. Greenwich, Conn., July 4, 1951; d. Robert F. and Ethel S. Kennedy; m. David L. Townsend; children: Meaghan, Maeve, Kate, Kerry. BA cum laude, Harvard Univ., 1974; JD, U. N.Mex., 1978. Instr. Dundalk Cmty. Coll., 1985-86, Essex Cmty. Coll., 1986-87, U. Pa., 1987-88; exec. dir. Md. Student Svc. Alliance, State dept. of Edn., 1987—93; dep. asst. atty. gen. US Dept. Justice, Washington, 1993-94; lt. gov. State of Md., 1995—2003; pres. Operation Respect, 2003; adj. prof. Georgetown's Sch. of Pub. Policy, 2003. Chair so. region Nat. Conf. Lt. Gov., chair oversight com. Johns Hopkins U., Peabody Inst., 1995-96; nat. adv. bd. Export-Import Bank U.S.; bd. adv. Johns Hopkins U. Sch. Advanced Internat. Studies, Inst. Human Virology U. Md; chair, State House Trust, 1995-2003, Adv. Bd., After-School Opportunity Programs, 1999-, co-chair, Safe Schools Interagency Steering Com., 1999-2003; Delegate, Dem. Party Nat. Conv., 1988, 1996, 2000; chair, Dem. Caucus of Lt. Gov. Editor U. N.Mex. Law Rev.; contbg. articles to profl. jour. and newspapers; author: Failing America's Faithful: How Today's Churches Are Mixing God with Politics and Losing Their Way, 2007 Founder Robert F. Kennedy Human Rights Award; chair Cabinet Coun. Criminal and Juvenile Justice, 1995-2003; chair Cabinet Coun. for Bus. and Econ. Devel.; chair Md. del. Pres. Summit Am. Future, 1997; chair State Sys. Reform Task Force for Children and Youth Reform, 1996, Task Force to study increasing availability of substance abuse programs, 1998-2001, Gov.of the Yr. 2000 Pub. Info.; chair adv. bd. after sch. opportunity programs; co-chair Md. Family Violence Coun.; bd. dir. John F. Kennedy Libr. Found., Nat. Inst. Women's Policy Rsch.; chair external adv. bd. Kennedy Krieger Inst. Early Infant Transition Ctr.; sr. advisor, Appropriations Com., House of Delegates, 1984-85; asst. Atty. Gen., Md., 1985-86; bd. ptnr. Radcliffe Coll. Recipient 4 hon. degrees; Visionary Leadership Award, Healthy Families Am., 2000, Clinton Ctr. Award for Leadership, Dem. Leadership Coun., 2002, Mem., Econ. Devel. Commn., Baltimore County, 1987, Gov. Exec. Coun., Gov. Commn. on Svc. and Volunteerism, 1998-. Democrat.

TOWNSEND, MARJORIE RHODES, aerospace engineer, engineering executive; b. Washington, Mar. 12, 1930; d. Lewis Boling and Marjorie Olive (Trees) Rhodes; m. Charles Eby Townsend, June 7, 1948; children: Charles Eby Jr., Lewis Rhodes, John Cunningham, Richard Leo. BEE, George Washington U., 1951. Electronic scientist Naval Rsch. Lab., Washington, 1951-59; rsch. engr. to sect. head Goddard Space Flight Ctr.-NASA, Greenbelt, Md., 1959-65, tech. asst. to chief systems divsn., 1965-66, project mgr. small astronomy satellites, 1966-75, project mgr. applications explorer missions, 1975-76, mgr. preliminary systems design group, 1976-80; aerospace and electronics cons. Washington, 1980-83; v.p. systems devel. Space Am., 1983-84; aerospace cons. Washington, 1984-90; dir. space systems programs, BDM Internat., Inc., Washington, 1990-91; dir. space applications BDM ESC, Washington, 1991-92; sr. prin. staff mem. BDM Fed., Inc., Washington, 1992-93. Aerospace cons., Washington, 1993—. Patentee digital telemetry system. Decorated Knight Italian Republic Order, 1972; recipient Fed. Women's award, 1973, EUR award for Culture, 1974, Engr. Alumni Achievement award George Washington U., 1975, Gen. Alumni Achievement award George Washington U., 1976, Exceptional Svc. medal NASA, 1971, Outstanding Leadership medal NASA, 1980, Eye-of-the-Needle award NASA, 1991. Fellow IEEE (chmn. Washington sect. 1974-75), AIAA (chmn. nat. capitol sect. 1985), AAAS (coun. del. 1985-88), Washington Acad. Sci. (pres. 1980-81); mem. Internat. Acad. Astronautics, Am. Geophys. Union, Soc. Women Engrs., Wing of Aerospace Med. Assn., Inc. (hon.), George Washington U. Sch. Engring. Applied Sci. Hall Fame (charter mem.), DAR, Daus. Colonial Wars, Mensa, Sigma Kappa, Sigma Delta Epsilon (hon.). Republican. Episcopalian. Home and Office: 3529 Tilden St NW Washington DC 20008-3122 Office Phone: 202-966-2330. Personal E-mail: mrtownsend@aol.com.

TOWNSEND, MILES AVERILL, aerospace and mechanical engineering educator; b. Buffalo, Apr. 16, 1935; s. Francis Devere and Sylvia (Wolpa) T.; children: Kathleen Townsend Hastings, Melissa, Stephen, Joel, Philip. BA, Stanford U., 1955; BS MechE, U. Mich., 1958; advanced cert., U. Ill., 1963, MS in Theoretical and Applied Mechanics, 1967; PhD, U. Wis., 1971. Registered profl. engr., Ill., Wis., Tenn., Ont. Project engr. Sundstrand, Rockford, Ill., 1959-63, Twin Disc Inc., Rockford, 1963-65, 67-68; sr. engr. Westinghouse Electric Corp., Sunnyvale, Calif., 1965-67; instr., fellow U. Wis., Madison, 1968-71; assoc. prof. U. Toronto, Ont., Canada, 1971-74; prof. mech. engring. Vanderbilt U., Nashville, 1974-81; Wilson prof. mech. and aerospace engring. U. Va., Charlottesville, 1981—, chmn. dept., 1981-91. Ptnr., v.p. Endev Ltd., Can. and U.S., 1972—; cons. in field. Contbr. numerous articles on dynamics, design dynamical systems, controls and optimization to profl. jours.; 7 patents in field. Recipient numerous research grants and contracts. Fellow ASME, AAAS; mem. N.Y. Acad. Scis., Sigma Xi, Phi Kappa Phi, Pi Tau Sigma. Avocations: running, reading, music. Home: 212 Alderman Rd Charlottesville VA 22903-1704 Office: U Va Dept Mech and Aerospace Engring Thornton Hall Charlottesville VA 22903-2442 Business E-Mail: mat@virginia.edu.

TOWNSEND, PEGGY (STEPHANIE G.), headmaster; m. J. Michael Townsend III; children: Emily, Charlie. BA in History, U. Conn.; MA in Spanish Language and Lit., Middlebury Coll. Spanish Sch. Tchg. asst. U. Conn.; Spanish tchr. North Mt. Hermon Sch., Taft Sch., Watertown, Conn., dean upper middle class, dir. Modern Languages and Resource Ctr., head Dept. Modern Languages, dir. Summer Sch., dean of faculty, 2001—06; headmaster Pennington Sch., Pennington, NJ, 2007—. Office: The Pennington School 112 W Delaware Ave Pennington NJ 08534 Office Phone: 609-737-1838.

TOWNSEND, TERRY, publishing executive; b. Camden, NJ, Dec. 14, 1920; d. Anthony and Rose DeMarco; m. Paul Brorstrom Townsend, Dec. 8, 1961; 1 child, Kim. BA, Duke U., 1942; LHD (hon.), Dowling Coll., 1991. Dir. pub. rels. North Shore U. Hosp., Manhasset, NY, 1953—68; pres. Theatre Soc., LI, 1967—70, Townsend Comm. Bur., LI, 1970—98; ptnr. L.I. Communicating Svc., Bellport, 1977—. Pub. L.I. Bus. News, 1979-98, pub. emeritus, 1998—; v.p. ParrMeadows Racetrack, Yaphank, N.Y., 1977; mem. Bellport Archtl. Rev. Bd., 1997—. Columnist, writer L.I./Bus., Ronkonkoma, 1970-75. Assoc. trustee North Shore U. Hosp., 1968—; bd. govs. Adelphi U. Friends Fin. Edn., 1978-85; chmn. ann. archtl. awards competition N.Y. Inst. Tech., 1970-83; trustee Dowling Coll., 1984—; trustee L.I. Fine Arts Mus., 1984-85; pub. broadcasting PBS Sta. WLIW TV, Garden City, L.I., N.Y., 1990-93; bd. dirs. Family Svc. Assn. Nassau County, 1982-92; dinner chmn. L.I. 400 Ball, 1987; trustee L.I. Mus. Art, 1994-2003. Recipient Media award 110 Ctr. Bus. and Profl. Women, 1977, Enterprise award Friends of Fin. Edn., 1981, LI Loves Bus. Showcase Salute, 1982, Cmty. Svc. award NY Diabetes Assn., 1983, Disting. Long Islander in Comm. award LI United Epilepsy Assn., 1984, Spl. award Dowling Coll. Spring Tribute, 1989, Disting. Svc. award Episcopal Health Svcs., 1989, Disting. Citizen award Dowling Coll., 1991, Gilbert Tilles award Nat. Assn. Fundraising Execs., 1994, Hadassah Cmty. Svc. award, 1996, Golden rule award Little Village Sch., 1997, Lifetime Achievement award LI Assn., 1998, 2007, Promote LI Achievement award, 1998, Lifetime Achievement award Advancement Commerce & Industry, 1999, Lifetime Achievement award LI Bus. News, 2007; named 1st Lady of LI, LI Pub. Rels. Assn., 1973, LI Woman of Yr. LI Assn. Action Com., 1989; Paul and Terry Townsend Sch. of Bus., Dowling Coll., designated in her honor, 2004, lifetime Achievement award Kidney & Urology Found. America, 2009. Mem.: Bellport Women's Golf Club (pres. 2003—04), Deepdale Golf Club (assoc.). Office: LI Communicating Svcs PO Box 915 Bellport NY 11713-0915 E-mail: terytowns@aol.com.

TOWNSEND, TIFFANY G., psychology professor; d. McEwen L. and Ruthann D. Townsend. BA, Spelman Coll., Atlanta, 1993; MPhil, George Washington U., Washington, 1997, PhD, 1998. Lic. psychologist Washington, 2007, Md., 2008. Asst. prof. psychology Pa. State U., Univ. Pk., 1998—2006, Georgetown U. Sch. Medicine, Washington, 2006—. Clin. psychologist Campbell Psychol. Svcs., Silver Spring, Md., 2008—. Contbr. articles to profl. jours. Exploratory grant, Nat. Inst. Nursing Rsch., 2007—. Mem.: Soc. Rsch. Adolescence, Soc. Cmty. Rsch. and Action (NE regional coord. 2004—07), Assn. Black Psychologists, Delta Sigma Theta Sorority, Inc.

TOWNSEND, WILLIAM JACKSON, lawyer; b. Grayson, Ky., June 4, 1932; s. Robert Glenn and Lois Juanita (Jackson) Townsend. BS, Wake Forest U., Winston-Salem, NC, 1954; student, U. Ky., Lexington, 1957, U. Louisville, 1958; JD, U. NC, Chapel Hill, 1960. Bar: NC 1965. Claims adjuster State Farm Ins. Co., 1963; pvt. practice, Fayetteville, NC, 1965—; pub. adminstr. Robeson County, NC, 1966; dir., treas. Colonial Foods, Inc., St. Paul, NC, 1959—; tax atty. City of Lumberton, 1966-67. Served as 1st lt. U.S. Army, 1954-56. Mem.: Cumberland County Bar Assn., NC State Bar, NC Bar Assn., Scabbard and Blade (pres.), Kiwanis (treas. Fayetteville 1973—82), Delta Theta Phi. Presbyterian. Office: PO Box 584 Fayetteville NC 28302 Office Phone: 910-483-4462.

TOWNSHEND, PETE (PETER DENNIS BLANDFORD TOWNSHEND), musician, composer; b. London, May 19, 1945; s. Cliff and Betty Townshend; m. Karen Astley, May 20, 1968 (dissolved 2009); children: Emma, Aminta, Joseph. Guitarist The Who (formerly The Detours, The High Numbers), 1964—; owner Eel Pie Recording Ltd., 1972—83. Guitarist: (albums with The Who) The Who Sings My Generation, 1965, Happy Jack, 1966, The Who Sell Out, 1967, The Magic Bus: The Who on Tour, 1968, Tommy, 1969, Live At Leeds, 1970, Meaty Beaty Big & Bouncy, 1971, Who's Next, 1971, Quadrophenia, 1973, Odds & Sods, 1974, The Who By Numbers, 1975, Who Are You, 1978, Face Dances, 1981, Hooligans, 1981, It's Hard, 1982, Who's Greatest Hits, 1983, Who's Last, 1983, Who's Missing, 1985, Two's Missing, 1987, Who's Better, Who's Best, 1988, Join Together, 1990, Thirty Years of Maximum R&B, 1994, Live at the Isle of Wight Festival 1970, 1996, My Generation: The Very Best of The Who, 1996, The BBC Sessions, 1999, The Blues to the Bush, 1999, The Ultimate Colllection, 2002, Live at the Royal Albert Hall, 2003, The Who: Then & Now, 2004, Live from Toronto, 2006, Endless Wire, 2006; (soundtracks) The Kids Are Alright, 1979, Quadrophenia, 1979; singer, guitarist: (solo albums) Who Came First, 1972, Secret Policeman's Ball, 1980, Empty Glass, 1980, All the Best Cowboys Have Chinese Eyes, 1982, Scoop, 1983, White City: A Novel, 1985, Another Scoop, 1986, Deep End Live, 1987, The Iron Man: A Musical, 1989, Psychoderelict, 1993, The Best of Pete Townsend, 1996, Cool Walking Smooth Talking, 1996, Pete Townshend Live: A Benefit for Maryville Academy, 1998; (with Ronnie Lane) Rough Mix, 1977; performer (films) Monterey Pop, 1968, Woodstock, 1970, Tommy, 1975, The Kids Are Alright, 1979, The Who Rocks America 1982, 1982, The Rolling Stones Rock 'N' Roll Circus, 1996, Message to Love: The Isle of Wight Festival, 1997, Amazing Journey: The Story of The Who, 2007; musical dir. (film and soundtrack) Tommy, 1975; Broadway musical The Who's Tommy, 1993 (Tony awd.for Best Original Score, 1993, Grammy award for Orginial Cast Recording, 1993, Dora Mayer Moore award, 1994, Olivier award, 1997); author: Horse's Neck, 1985, Pete Townshend: An Autobiography, 1999; co-author (with Des McAnuff) Tommy: The Musical, 1993 Recipient Ivor Novello award for Contribution to British Music, 1982, Lifetime Achievement award, British Phonographic Industry, 1983, BRIT Lifetime Achievement award, 1983, BRIT award for Contribution to British Music, 1983, Internat. Rock Living Legend award, 1991, Q Lifetime Achievement award, 1997, Ivor Novello Lifetime Achievement award, 2001, BMI Pres. award, 2002, BMI TV Music award, 2004, Kennedy Ctr. Honors, John F. Kennedy Ctr. for the Performing Arts, 2008; named to The Rock & Roll Hall of Fame (as mem. of The Who), 1990, VHI Rock Honor, 2008. Office: Mgmt Trinifold 12 Oval Rd Camden London NWI 7DH England

TOY, EUGENE C., gynecologist; b. LA, Dec. 12, 1960; s. Chuck Y. and Grace Y. Toy; m. Terri L. Ligh, July 27, 1985; children: Andrew David, Michael Jonathan, Allison Lillie, Christina Grace. MD, Baylor Coll. Medicine, Houston, 1986. Cert. ABFM, 1991, Am. Bd. Ob-Gyn, 1996. Family physician dir. maternity program Hidalgo County Health Care Corp., Pharr, Tex., 1989—91; dir. primary care Meth. Hosp. Ob-Gyn Residency, Houston, 1995—; dir. ultrasound Meth. Hosp. Houston Ob-Gyn Residency, academic chief and program dir., 2001—, vice chair academic affairs, dept. ob-gyn.; assoc. program dir. St. Joseph Hosp., Houston, 1997—2001; clerkship dir. U. Tex. Med. Sch., Houston, 1999—; dir. maternity program SW Cmty. Health Ctr., Houston, 2001—; vice chmn. academic affairs, dept. ob-gyn. Meth. Hosp. Contbr. scientific papers to profl. publs. Exec. com. Tex. Assn. Ob-Gyn, Austin, 2002—. Recipient Dean's award, U. Tex. Med. Sch., John P McGovern award, 2002, 2008, Herbert and Margaret DuPont Master Clin. Tchr. award, 2007, First prize, Assn. Profs. in Ob-Gyn, 2001—03, First prize in rsch. presentation, 2007; named Best Tchg. Faculty, U. Tex. Med. Sch., 2001—. Fellow: Am. Coll. Ob- Gyn.; mem.: Am. Inst. Ultrasound in Medicine (exec. coun. accreditation 2002—07). Office: Methodist Hosp Ob-Gyn Residency 1819 Crawford St Ste 1708 Houston TX 77002

TOYODA, EIJI, automotive executive; b. Toyota, Aichi, Japan, Sept. 12, 1913; s. Heikichi and Nao T.; m. Kazuko Takahashi, Oct. 19, 1939; children: Kanshiro, Tetsuro, Shuhei, Sonoko. B.M.E., Tokyo U., 1936. Dir. Toyota Motor Corp., Aichi, Japan, 1945—94, mng. dir. Aichi, 1950-53, sr. mng. dir. Aichi, 1953-60, exec. v.p. Aichi, 1960-67, pres. Aichi, 1967-82, chmn. bd. Aichi, 1982-92, hon. chmn. Aichi, 1992—99, hon. advisor Aichi, 1999—. Advisor Towa Real Estate Co., Ltd., 1998—; hon. advisor Genesis Rsch. Inst., Inc., 2004—. Author: Toyota Fifty Years in Motion, 1988. Recipient FISITA medal, 1993, Automotive Hall of Fame award, 1994, James Watt Internat. Gold medal, 1995; named Knight Grand Cordon, Thailand, 2001, Knight Grand Cordon First Class Most Admirable Order Direkgunabhorn, Royal Kingdom Thailand, 2001. Fellow Soc. Automotive Engrs. Japan, Inc. (life 1991-), Inst. Mech. Engrs. (hon. 1995, James Watt Internat. Gold medal 1995); mem. Japan Automobile Mfrs. Assn. (supreme adv. 1980-, pres. 1972-80, chmn. 1972-80), Japan Motor Indsl. Fedn. (adv. 1980), Automobile Rsch. Inst. (pres. 1973-81), Toyota Sch. Found. (chmn. 1979-98, 90-98), Fedn. Econ. Orgns. (Keidanren, vice chmn. 1984-90), Hon. Consul Portugal, Japan Inst. Invention and Innovation, Aichi Sci and Tech. Found. (chmn. 1994-2000). Office: Toyota Motor Corp 1 Toyota-cho Toyota Aichi 471 Japan

TOYODA, SHUHEI, automotive executive; b. Toyota City, Japan, 1947; m. Yoko Toyoda; 3 children. Grad., Tamagawa U.; Doctorate in Tribology, U. Leeds, Eng., 1977. Joined Toyota Motor Corp., 1977—; purchasing supr. Toyota Motor Mfg. UK, Ltd., 1992—96; chief engring. project team Toyota Motor Corp., 1997, bd. dirs., 1998—, dir. (with mng. dir. status), 2001—; chmn. Toyota Motor UK, 2001—; pres., CEO Toyota Motor and Mfg. Engring. Europe S.A./N.V., 2001—, Toyota Motor Europe S.A./N.V., 2002—; dir. with sr. mng. dir. status Toyota Motor UK, 2003—; exec. v.p. Toyota Boshoku Co., 2004—, pres., 2006—. Avocations: backgammon, astronomy. Office: Toyota Boshoku Corp 1-1 Toyoda-Cho Kariya Aichi 448-8657 Japan

TOYODA, TATSURO, automobile company executive; b. June 1, 1929; m. Ayako Toyoda. Student, Tokyo U. With Toyota Motor Corp., 1953—, exec. v.p. in charge internat. ops., 1988-92, pres., 1992-95, vice chmn., 1995-96, sr. advisor, 1996—. Former pres. Nummi jt. venture with GM, 1984-86. Decorated grand cordon Order of Sacred Treasure. Office: Toyota Motor Corp 1 Toyota-cho Toyota 471-8571 Japan

TOYOSHIMA, CHIKASHI, structural biologist, educator; b. Honjo, Akita, Japan, July 17, 1954; BS in Physics, U. Tokyo, 1977, PhD in Biophysics, 1982. Prof. supramolecular structure Ctr. for Bioinformatics U. Tokyo, dir. Inst. Molecular and Cellular Biosciences. Named nat. lectr., Biophysics Soc., 2007. Mem.: NAS (fgn. assoc.). Office: Inst Molecular and Cellular Biosciences University Tokyo Bunkyo-ku Tokyo 113-0032 Japan Business E-Mail: ct@iam.u-tokyo.ac.jp.

TOZER, ELIZABETH FARRAN, interior and floral designer; d. Charles and Irma (Gaenisslen) Farran; m. W. James Tozer Jr., July 30, 1965; children: Farran Tozer Brown and Katherine Tozer Roddy. BFA, Ohio Wesleyan U., Delaware, 1964. Residential and comml. interior and floral designer Elizabeth Farran Tozer Design, NYC, 1982—. Interior design cons. N.Y. Found. for Sr. Citizens, N.Y.C., 1982—; pres. The Flower Svc. Store, N.Y.C., 1972-92; spokesperson Am. Florists Mktg. Coun., 1987; appeared in numerous radio, TV, and newspaper interviews in eleven maj. U.S. cities. Author: The Art of Flower Arranging, 1981; contbr. articles to profl. publs. Chmn. N.Y. Flower Show, 1996; mem. exec. com., mem. nominating com. Mus. of the City of N.Y., 1994—; vice chmn., chmn. nominating com., bd. dirs. N.Y. Found. for Sr. Citizens, 1980-; mem. nominating com. Sch. Am. Ballet, Lincoln Ctr., 1977—; chmn. more than 100 maj. fundraising events in N.Y.C. and Dutchess County, N.Y., 1977—; mem. adv. bd. Nat. Acad. Design, 1999-; chmn. Inst. Ecosys. AldoLeopold Soc., 2001-; trustee Ohio Wesleyan U., 2003-, Inst. Ecosystems, 2004-, Park City Mus. and Horticultural Soc, Park City Com. Sundance, Park City Bd. Utah Opera and Symphony. Recipient award Mcpl. Arts Soc., 1997, award YWCA Acad. Women Achievers, 1995, Pillars of Industry award, Best Srs. Mid-Rise Bldg. award Nat. Assn. Home Builders, 1995, Spl. Merit award Associated Builders and Owners of Greater N.Y., 1993. Mem. N.Y. Hort. Soc. (nominating com.). Avocation: raising miniature horses. Home: 550 Park Ave New York NY 10021-7369

TOZER, JEAN FRAME, gifted and talented educator; d. Thomas Hamiton and Lillian Margaret Frame; children: Michael, Kristen, Scott. BA, Coll. N.J., 1968; Masters Degree, City U., 1998. Health and phys. edn. tchr. Kearny Bd. Edn.; gifted and talented tchr. Brick (N.J.) Twp. Bd. Edn. Bd. dirs. Cape Breton Holding Co., Brick. Mem.: NJGAC. Home: 75 Wind Jammer Ct Bayville NJ 08721-1412

TOZER, WILLIAM EVANS, entomologist, educator; b. Binghamton, NY, July 7, 1947; s. William Evans and Gertrude Genevieve (Lewis) T. BS in Natural Sci., Niagara U., 1969; MS in Biology, Ball State U., 1979; PhD in Entomology, U. Calif., Berkeley, 1986. Cert. C.C. biology and zoology tchr. Calif. Jr. H.S. sci. and English tchr. St. Patricks Sch., Corning, NY, 1969-71; tchg. asst. biology Ball State U., Muncie, Ind., 1974-76; pvt. practice biol. environ. cons. Berkeley, Calif., 1976-79, 86-88; rsch. asst. U. Calf., Berkeley, 1979-86; dept. head edn. and tng. USN Disease Vector Ecology and Control Ctr., Poulsbo, Wash., 1988—2004. Mem., acting chmn. San Francisco Bay Area Mosquito Control Coun., Alameda, 1988-96; chmn. Edn. and Tng. com., 1997-06; com. mem. Armed Forces Pest Mgmt. Bd., Washington, 1994—; bd. dirs. EPA Cert. and Tng. Assessment Group, 2001-05; dept. head USN Environ. Preventive Medicine Unit 5, San Diego, 2007—. Editor (field handbook) Navy Environmental Health Center, 1994; contbr. articles to profl. jours. With U.S. Army, 1971-73. Mem. Am. Entomol. Soc., Sigma Xi. Achievements include first to publish evidence for underwater behavioral thermoregulation in adult insects. Office: USN Environ & Preventive Medicine Unit 5 3235 Albacore Alley San Diego CA 92136 Business E-Mail: william.tozer@med.navy.mil.

T-PAIN, (FAHEEM NAJM), rap artist; b. Tallahassee, Fla., Sept. 30, 1985; Singer: (albums) Rappa Ternt Sanga, 2005, Epiphany, 2007, Stay in the Game, 2008, Thr33 Ringz, 2008, (songs) Buy U A Drank (Shawty Snappin'), 2007 (Top Hot Rhythmic Song, Billboard Year-End Charts, 2007), (with Kanye West) Good Life, 2007 (Grammy award for Best Rap Song, 2008, BET award for Best Collaboration, 2008, MTV Video Music award for Best Spl. Effects, 2008).*

TRABER, PETER GEORGE, medical educator, former academic administrator; b. Johnstown, NY, Apr. 6, 1955; m. K. Bobbi Traber; 2 children. Grad., U. Mich., 1977; MD, Wayne State U. Med. Sch., 1981; completed Mgmt. Devel Program for Physician Exec., Wharton Sch. U. Pa. Resident in internal medicine Northwestern U. Med. Sch., Chgo., fellow in gastroenterology, U. Mich. Sch. Medicine, faculty mem. Ann Arbor, 1987—92; chief gastroenterology U. Pa. Sch. Medicine, 1992—97, T. Grier Miller prof. medicine, 1993—97, Frank Wistar Thomas prof. and chair dept. medicine, 1997—2000, interim dean Phila., 2000; interim CEO U. Pa. Health Sys., Phila., 2000; sr. v.p. clinical devel. & med. affairs & chief med. officer GlaxoSmithKline, 2000—03; pres., CEO, prof. medicine Baylor Coll. Medicine, Houston, 2003—08, exec. dean, 2008—, pres. emeritus, 2008—. Bd. dirs. Tanox Inc., 2004—. Bd. trustees Baylor Coll. Medicine; bd. dirs. Houston Branch Fed. Res. Bank Dallas. Recipient Disting. Alumni award, Wayne State U. Sch. Medicine. Mem.: Assn. Am. Physicians, Am. Soc. Clinical Rsch., Am. Gastroenterologic Assn. Office: Baylor Coll Medicine BCM100 One Baylor Plz Houston TX 77030 Office Phone: 713-798-6363. Office Fax: 713-798-6353. E-mail: pgtraber@bcm.tmc.edu.*

TRABITZ, EUGENE LEONARD, aerospace company executive; b. Cleve., Aug. 13, 1937; s. Emanuel and Anna (Berman) T.; m. Caryl Lee Rine, Dec. 22, 1963 (div. Aug. 1981); children: Claire Marie, Honey Caryl; m. Kathryn Lynn Bates, Sept. 24, 1983; 1 stepchild, Paul Francis Rager. BA, Ohio State U., 1965. Enlisted USAF, 1954, advanced through grades to maj.; served as crew comdr. 91st Strategic Missile Divsn., Minot, SD, 1968-70; intelligence officer Fgn. Tech. Divsn., Dayton, Ohio, 1970-73; dir. external affairs Aero. Systems Divsn., Dayton, 1973-75; program mgr. Air Force Armament Divsn., Valparaiso, Fla., 1975-80; dir. ship ops. Air Force Ea. Test Range, Satellite Beach, Fla., 1980-83; dep. program mgr. Air Force Satellite Text Ctr., Sunnyvale, Calif., 1983-84; ret., 1984; sr. staff engr. Ultrasystems Inc., 1984-86; pres. TAWD Systems Inc., Palo Alto, Calif., 1986-92, Am. Telenetics Co., San Mateo, Calif., 1992—; pres., CEO Enterprise Def. Inst., Inc., San Mateo, 2002—. Cons. Space Applications Corp.; Sunnyvale, 1986-87, Litton Computer Svcs., Mountain View, Calif., 1987-91, Battelle Meml. Inst. Columbus, 1993—. V.p. Bd. County Mental Health Clinic, Ft. Walton Beach, Fla., 1973-75. Decorated Bronze Star. Mem. DAV (life), ASIS Internat., Nat. Def. Indsl. Assn., Armed Forces Comm. and Electronics Assn., Am. Soc. for Indsl. Security Internat., U.S. Space Found. (charter), Air Force Assn. (life), Nat. Sojourners, Masons (32d degree). Avocations: golf, tennis, racketball, sailing, bridge. Home: 4333 Bareback Ct Sparks NV 89436 Personal E-mail: gene@amtelenet.com.

TRABOCCHI, FABIO, chef; b. Osimo, Italy, 1974; Grad., Istituto Alberghiero Panzini, Senigallia, Italy. Kitchen staff mgr. Navalge Moena, Italy; chef de cuisine Byblos, Rimini, Italy; chef Bice Ristorante, Wash., DC, Marabella, Spain, Grissini, London, Floriana, London; owner, exec. chef Maestro, Ritz-Carlton Tyson's Corner, McLean, Va., 2001—07; exec. chef, ptnr. Fiamma, NYC, 2007—. Author: (cookbooks) Cucina of Le Marche: A Chef's Treasury of Recipes from Italy's Last Culinary Frontier, 2006. Recipient Carlton award for London's Best Young Chef, 1999; named Chef of Yr., Restaurant Assn. Met. Wash., 2005, Best Chef: Mid-Atlantic, James Beard Found., 2006; named one of America's Best New Chefs, Food & Wine mag., 2002. Office: Fiamma 206 Spring St New York NY 10012 Office Phone: 212-653-0100.

TRABULSI, JUDY, advertising and marketing executive; b. Houston; d. Richard Joseph and Genevieve (Jamail) T. BS in Comm., U. Tex., 1971. Co-founder GSD&M's Idea City (formerly GSD&M Advt.), Austin, Tex., 1971, exec. v.p., exec. media dir., 1971—2007, chairwoman leadership coun., bd. mem., 2007—. Mem. nat. adv. coun. SBA, Washington, 1994-96; adv. coun. U. Tex. Comm. Sch., Austin, 1996—; adv. mem. 21st Century Dems., 1996; mem. hon. com. Jewish Cmty. Assn. Austin. Office: GSD&M's Idea City 828 W 6th St Austin TX 78703-5420

TRACEY, DENNIS HENRY, III, lawyer; b. NYC, Nov. 8, 1956; s. Dennis Henry Jr. and Mary Catherine (Lunney) T.; m. Marcia Jean Hamelin, July 20, 1985. BA, Cornell U., 1978; JD, NYU, 1981. Bar: N.Y. 1982, U.S. Dist. Ct. (so. and ea. dists.) N.Y. 1982, U.S. Ct. Appeals (4th cir.) 1982. Assoc. Paul, Wells, Rifkind, Wharton & Garrison, NYC, 1981-84; litigation counsel CBS Inc., NYC, 1984; assoc. Davis, Markel & Edwards, NYC, 1984—87, ptnr., 1988—2000, Hogan & Hartson LLP, 2000—, mem. exec. com., 2003—05; mng. ptnr. N.Y. Office, 2004—, US Office, 2007—. Co-chmn. Lawyers' Com. for Reelection of Robert Abrams, N.Y.C., 1982. Mem. ABA, N.Y. City Bar Assn. Office: Hogan & Hartson LLP 875 Third Ave New York NY 10022 Office Phone: 212-918-3524. Office Fax: 212-918-3100. Business E-Mail: dhtracey@hhlaw.com.

TRACEY, MATTHEW SEAN, musician, educator; b. Teaneck, NJ, Feb. 4, 1965; s. Patrick Edward and Kathleen Teresa Tracey; m. Dawn C. Cusimano, Nov. 3, 1990. MusM, Montclair State U., NJ, 1987—89; MusB, William Paterson U., Wayne, NJ, 1983—87. Cert. K-12 tchr. of music NJ, 1987. Musician Ray Sepulveda Orch., New York, 1993—, Tito Nieves Orch., New York; musical dir. Frankie Negron Orch., New York, 1994—96; k-12 music dept. chairperson Ridgefield Pub. Schools, NJ, 1990—; dir. of bands Ridgefield Meml. HS, 1987—. Hon. lifetime mem. Nat. PTA, NJ; mem. Music Educators Nat. Conf., NJ, 1983—, Internat. Assn. of Jazz Educators, NJ, NEA, NJ. Edn. Assn., Music Educators of Bergen County, NJ. Musician: (studio/ recording musician) commericial jingles, Pop, Jazz, Latin recordings; profesional marching drill designer, Drill Designer; composer: (composer/arranger) various works. Recipient World Champion Bushwacker Drum & Bugle Corps, Drum Corps Associates, 1986, 198, 1989, 1990, World Champion-Garfield Cadets, Drum Corps Internat., 1984. Mem.: Nat. PTA (hon. Hon. Lifetime Mem. 2004). Achievements include NJ Governor's Tchr. of the Year. Avocations: music, travel, gastronomy. Office: Ridgefield Memorial High School 555 Walnut street Ridgefield NJ 08657 E-mail: contactus@ridgefieldband.com.

TRACEY, PETER LAKE, lawyer; b. New London, Conn., June 4, 1960; s. Joseph Francis and Patricia Lake Tracey. BA, Yale U., New Haven, Conn., 1986; JD, Pa. State U., Carlisle, Pa., 1989. Bar: Del. 1989, Pa. 1990, DC 2000, US Dist. Ct. Del. 1990, US Dist. Ct. DC 2001, US Ct. Appeals (3d cir.) 1990, US Supreme Ct. 1997. Assoc. Potter Anderson & Corroon LLP, Wilmington, Del., 1989—98, Howrey LLP, Washington, 1998—2000, ptnr., 2001—. Author: Insurance Coverage Law in Delaware, 1996. Moderator First Congl. Ch. United Ch. Christ, Washington, 2004—06; pres. West Ctr. City Day Care, Inc., Wilmington, 1996—98. Mem.: Yale Club (NY). Democrat. Avocations: running, skiing. Home: 1213 New Jersey Ave NW Washington DC 20001 Office: Howrey LLP 1299 Pennsylvania Ave NW Washington DC 20004 Office Fax: 202-383-6610. Business E-Mail: traceyp@howrey.com.

TRACEY, WILLIAM RAYMOND, international management consultant; b. Lancaster, Mass., Dec. 29, 1922; s. James Edward and Pauline (Burgoyne) O'Neill, adopted s. Edward Peter and Josephine (Burgoyne) Tracey; m. Kathleen Lucille Doheny, July 1, 1944; children: William R. Jr., Kevin T., Brian J., Kathleen L., Maura G., Sean M. BS in Edn., Fitchburg State Coll., 1946; EdM, Boston U., 1950, EdD, 1955; diploma, U.S. Army War Coll., 1968. Tchr. Lyman Sch., Ashby, Mass., 1946-47; tchr., prin. D.W. Adams Sch., Ashburnham, Mass., 1947-48; from asst. prof. to prof. of Edn./dir. of tng. Fitchburg (Mass.) State Coll., 1948-58; psychologist U.S. Army Security Agy. Sch., Fort Devens, Mass., 1958-62, ednl. cons., 1962-68, dep. comdt., 1968-82; pres. Human Resources Enterprises of Cape Cod, South Yarmouth, Mass., 1982—. Adj. prof. mgmt. Fitchburg State Coll., 1965-68; cons. ESSO Resources Can., Ltd., 1979-80, Indsl. Tng. & Info. Svcs., Jakarta, Indonesia, Swiss Hotel Assn., Sch. of Hotel Mgmt., Les Roches, Bluche Crans-Montana, Switzerland. Author: Designing Training and Development Systems, 1971, rev., 1984, 92, Human Resource Development Standards, A Self-Evaluation Manual for HRD Managers and Specialists, 1981, Critical Skills: The Guide to Top Performence for Human Resources Managers, 1988, Leadership Skills: Standout Performance for Human Resources Managers, 1990, The Human Resources Glossary: A Complete Desk Reference for HR Executives, Managers, and Practitioners, 1991, 3rd edit., 2004, Human Resources Management & Development Handbook, 2d edit., 1993, HR Words You Gotta Know! Essential Human Resources Terms, Laws, Acronyms and Abbreviations for Everyone in Business, 1994, Training Employees with Disabilities: Strategies to Enhance Learning and Development for an Expanding Part of Your Workforce, 1994, Strands of Memory, 2004, Strands of Memory Revisited, 2009; others; contbr. over 100 articles on evaluation, communication, mgmt., tng. and career devel. to profl. jours. Lt. USN, 1944-46, PTO, lt. comdr., 1982. Decorated Exceptional Civilian Svc. Dept. Army, Meritorious Civilian Svc. Mem. ASTD, Am. Mgmt. Assn., Mass. Schoolmasters Club, Assn. Old Crows (spl. silver medal, 1980), Writers Conf. Cape Cod, Cape Cod Writers Ctr., Soc. Human Resource Mgmt.,Army Historical Found, Internat. Soc. Poets, Assn. U.S. Army, Phi Delta Kappa. Roman Catholic. Avocations: golf, reading. Home and Office: 54 Evergreen St South Yarmouth MA 02664-5612 Home Phone: 508-394-9509; Office Phone: 508-760-1103. Personal E-mail: wtracey@comcast.net.

TRACHTENBERG, ELIZABETH ANNE, geneticist, researcher; BA, U. Calif., Berkeley; MS, PhD, John Burns Sch. Medicine, U.Hawaii, Honolulu. Diplomate Amer. Bd. Histocompat. Immunogenetics, 1995. Dir., immunogenetics & molecular diagnostics lab. Childrens' Hosp. & Rsch. Ctr. Oakland, Calif., 1995—, rsch. scientist, 1995—. Achievements include patents for HLA & KIR genotyping. Office: Children's Hosptl & Rsch Ctr 747 52nd St Oakland CA 94609 Office Phone: 510-450-7685. Business E-Mail: etrachtenberg@chori.org.

TRACHTENBERG, MATTHEW J., arts administrator, financial services executive, philanthropist; b. NYC, June 20, 1958; s. Mark Trachtenberg and Joanne Horne. BA magna cum laude, NYU, 1974; JD, Bklyn. Law Sch., 1977; MBA in Fin., Fordham U., 1982. Bar: NY 1979. Mgmt. trainee Mfrs. Hanover Trust Co., NYC, 1977-78, credit analyst, 1978-79, corp. banking rep., 1979-80, asst. sec., 1980-82, asst. v.p., 1982, v.p., 1982-86, v.p., corp. sec., 1987-92; dir. Mfrs. Hanover Found., NYC, 1987-92; v.p., sec. regional bd. Chem. Bank, NYC, 1992-96, v.p., dep. corp. sec., 1992-96, sec. regional bd., 1992-96, v.p., 1992-96, Chem. Banking Corp., NYC, 1992-96; v.p. asst. corp. sec. Chase Manhattan Bank, NYC, 1996—98; sec. Chase Manhattan Regional Bd., NYC, 1996—98; v.p., sr. pvt. banker PNC Bank, NYC, 1999—2000, Fleet Bank, NYC, 2000—02; mng. dir. First Republic Bank, NYC, 2002—04; sr. v.p. US Trust Co., 2004—06. Bd. dirs., chmn., pres., CEO Nat. Orch. Assn., 2006—; bd. dirs., past pres. USO Met. NY; bd. dirs., treas., chair fin. com. NY Eye and Ear Infirmary; bd. dirs. Continuum Health Ptnrs. Mem.: NY State Bar Assn., Phi Beta Kappa, Pi Sigma Alpha. Avocations: music, fishing, painting, writing. Office Phone: 212-208-4691. Business E-Mail: mtrachtenberg@nationalorchestral.org.

TRACHTENBERG, MICHELLE, actress; b. NYC, Oct. 11, 1985; Actor: (TV series) The Adventures of Pete & Pete, 1994—96, All My Children, 1993—96, Buffy the Vampire Slayer, 2000—03, Six Feet Under, 2004, Robot Chicken, 2006—07, Gossip Girl, 2008—; (films) Harriet the Spy, 1996, Richie Rich's Christmas Wish, 1998, Inspector Gadget, 1999, Can't Be Heaven, 2000, EuroTrip, 2004, Mysterious Skin, 2004, Ice Princess, 2005, Beautiful Ohio, 2006, Black Christmas, 2006, Seventeen Again, 2008, (voice) Dragonlance: Dragons of Autumn Twilight, 2008, 17 Again, 2009; (TV films) Christmas in My Hometown, 1996, A Father's Choice, 2000, The Dive from Clausen's Pier, 2005, The Hill, 2007, (guest appearance): (TV series) Law & Order, 1991, Clarissa Explains It All, 1993, Dave's World, 1996, Meego, 1997, House M.D., 2006, Law & Order: Criminal Intent, 2006. Office: c/o Framework Entertainment Ste C 9057 Nemo St West Hollywood CA 90069*

TRACHTENBERG, STEPHEN JOEL, political science professor, former academic administrator; b. Bklyn., Dec. 14, 1937; s. Oscar M. and Shoshana G. (Weinstock) Trachtenberg; m. Francine Zorn, June 24, 1971; children: Adam Maccabee, Ben-Lev. BA, Columbia U., 1959; JD, Yale U., 1962; M in Pub. Adminstrn., Harvard U., 1966; LHD (hon.), Trinity Coll., 1986, Boston U., 1999, Gratz Coll., 1999; HHD (hon.), U. Hartford, 1989; LLD (hon.), Hanyang U., Seoul, 1990, Richmond Coll., London, 1995, Mount Vernon Coll., 1997, So. Conn. State U., 2001, U. New Haven, 2002, Lyon Coll., Batesville, Ark., 2006, Touro Coll., NYC, 2006; DPA (hon.), Kyonggi U., Seoul, 1994, Sangmyung U., 2004, Dongseo U., Busan, Republic of Korea, 2004; MD (hon.), Odessa State Med. U., Ukraine, 1996. Bar: N.Y. 1964, U.S. Supreme Ct. 1967. Atty. AEC, 1962—65; legis. asst. to Congressman John Brademas of Ind., Washington, 1965; tutor law Harvard Coll.; tchg. fellow edn. and pub. policy John F. Kennedy Sch. Govt., Harvard U., 1965—66; spl. asst. to U.S. edn. commr. Office of Edn., HEW, Washington, 1966—68; assoc. prof. polit. sci. Boston U., 1969—77, assoc. dean, 1969—70, dean, 1970—74, assoc. v.p., co-counsel, 1974—76, v.p. acad. svcs., 1976—77; pres., prof. pub. adminstrn. U. Hartford, Conn., 1977—88, George Washington U., Washington, 1988—2007, pres. emeritus, prof. pub. adminstrn., 2007—; chmn. N.Am. edn. practice Korn/Ferry Internat., 2007—. Mem. joint editl. bd. The Presidency and ACE/Praeger Series on Higher Edn.; mem. Fed. City Coun.; bd. dirs. Consortium of Univs. Washington Met. Area, Riggs Bank, Greater Washington Bd. Trade, Nat. Edn. Telecom. Orgn., Washington Rsch. Libr. Consortium, DC Com. to Promote Washington; exec. adv. coun. SCT Edn. Sys. Contbr. articles to profl. jours. Chmn. nat. svc. task force Am. Jewish Com., 2006; trustee Al-Akhawayn U., Morocco, Com. for Econ. Devel.; active 2001 U.S. Savs. Bonds Vol. Com.; chmn. Md./D.C. Selection Com., 1998—2004, Rhodes Scholarships; mem. Washington Regional Panel for Selection of 2004-05 Class of White House Fellows; chair exec. com. Southeastern Univs. Rsch. Assn.; active D.C. Mayor's Bus. Adv. Coun.; exec. panel Chief Naval Ops.; bd. overseers List Coll. Jewish Theol. Sem. Am.; bd. dirs. D.C. C. of C., Chiang Chen Indsl. Charity Found. Ltd., Hong Kong; chair, pres. council Atlantic 10 Conf.; bd. mem. Bankinter Found. Innovation, 2006. Decorated grand officier du Wissam Al Alaoui King Mohammed VI of Morocco; recipient Myrtle Wreath award, Hadassah, 1982, Scopus award, Am. Friends of Hebrew U., 1984, Human Rels. award, NCCJ, 1987, NAACP award, 1988, Conn. Bar Assn. citation, 1988, Univ. medal of highest honor, Kyung Hee U., Korea, 1990, Martin Luther King, Jr. Internat. Salute award, 1992, Hannah G. Solomon award, Nat. Coun. Jewish Women, 1992, Father of Yr. award, Washington Urban League, 1993, Univ. Pres. medal, Kyonggi U., Korea, 1993, Merit award, Am. Czech and Slovak Assn., 1993, John Jay award, Columbia U., 1995, Spirit of Democracy award, Am. Jewish Congress, 1995, Newcomen Soc. award, 1995, Disting. Achievement medal, Greenberg Ctr. for Judaic Studies U. Hartford, 1995, Humanitarian award, B'nai B'rith, 1996, Disting. Pub. Svc. award, U.S. Dept. of State Sec.'s Open Forum, 1997, Tree of Life award, Jewish Nat. Fund, 1999, High Twelve Internat. Founders award, 2000, Key of Life award, Egypt's Internat. Econ. Forum, 2001, medal of merit, U.S. Dept. Treasury, 2001, Father Yr. award, Am. Diabetes Assn., 2002, Humanitarian award, The Albert B. Sabin Vaccine Inst., 2003, Madison Freedom award, 2004, Humanitarian Award, Sabin Vaccine Inst., 2006, Award of Excellence, Pigskin Club, 2007; named Outstanding Young Person, Boston Jr. C. of C., 1970, Alumnus of Yr., James Madison H.S., Bklyn., 1982, Washingtonian of Yr., Washingtonian Mag., 2000; named one of 100 Young Leaders, Acad. Am. Council Learning, 1978, Fifty Outstanding Alumni Problem Solvers, Harvard's John F. Kennedy Sch. Govt., 1987, The 2002 Forty Forward A, Washington Bus. Forward mag., 2002; named to Wall of Distinction, James Madison HS, 2006; Winston Churchill fellow, Eng., 1969, Hon. Wolcott fellow, 1999, Assoc. fellow, Morse Coll. Yale U. Fellow: Am. Acad. Arts and Scis.; mem.: Bus.-Higher Edn. Forum, Ind. Retail Cattleman's Assn. (adv. coun.), Sr. Soc. Sachems, Coun. Fgn. Rels., Newcomen Soc. U.S. (life; former trustee), Am. Coun. Learned Socs. (assoc.), Internat. Assn. Univ. Pres. (N.Am. coun.), N.Y. Acad. Scis., Am. Assn. Univ. Adminstrs. (pres. 1998—2000, Disting. Svc. award 1996), D.C. C. of C. (named Bus. Leader of Yr. 2005), Am. Coun. for the UN U. (vice chair), Hannibal Club (Ann. award 2004), Nat. Press Club, Cosmos Club, Harvard Club, Tumble Brook Country Club, Univ. Club, George Washington U. Club, Masons (33d degree, Grand Cross pin 2004), Phi Beta Kappa. Office: George Washington Univ Pres Emeritus 805 21st St Ste 600 Washington DC 20052 Home Phone: 202-387-4949; Office Phone: 202-994-9820. Business E-Mail: gwupotu@gwu.edu.

TRACKMAN, PHILIP CHARLES, biochemist, researcher; b. Montclair, NJ, July 15, 1953; s. John C. and Irene (Boveri) T.; m. Susan Kirkpatrick Troxler, Oct. 24, 1979 (div. 2004); children: Louisa, Eric. BA in chem., Coll. of Wooster, 1975; PhD, Boston Univ., 1980; post doctoral rsch., Brandeis Univ., 1980-83. Staff scientist Novo Labs., Wilton, Conn., 1983-85, team leader, 1985-86; rsch. asst. prof. Boston U., 1987—92; asst. prof. Boston U. Goldman Sch. Dental Medicine, Boston, 1992—2000, assoc. prof., 2000—04, prof., 2004—. Contbr. articles to profl. jours. Recipient First award Nat. Inst. Health, 1994, fellowship Am. Cancer Soc., 1981. Mem. Am. Chem. Soc. (assoc.),

Sigma Xi. Protestant. Achievements include first to demonstrate that non-peptidyl amines are substates for lysyl oxidase and used this to develop a new assay. First to clone lysyl oxidase cDNA; first to study lysyl oxidase regulation by growth factors in osteoblastic cells; and in gingival fibrolasts; first to identify intermediates in a methionine salvage pathway; research in regulation of extracellular matrix biosynthesis in mineralized and non-mineralized tissues in health and disease; discovered mechanism of tumor suppressor function of lysyl oxidase; patentee in field. Office: Boston U Goldman Sch Dental Medicine 700 Albany St # 201 Boston MA 02118-2518 Office Phone: 617-638-4076.

TRACT, LARRY SCOTT, construction management consultant; b. Chgo., Apr. 16, 1957; s. Leslie Howard and Barbara Mae Tract; m. Tamra Tract, July 11, 1986; 1 child, Samantha Kathleen. BS, Santa Clara U., Calif., 1979; JD, Thomas Jefferson Law Sch., 1982. Bar: Calif.; cert. tchr. Calif. Law clk., paralegal Escho & Scott, LLP, Esq., Redwood City, Calif., 1984—85; v.p. CCMS, Sacramento, 1986—89, Animal Mech., Inc., Gilroy, Calif., 1989—95, Conservation Documentation Svcs., Santa Clara, Calif., 1986—95; contract adminstr., cons. Lawson Mech., Inc., Sacramento, 1996—99; pres., CEO Larry S. Tract Assocs., Constrn. Mgmt. Svcs., Sacramento, 1999—. Condr. seminars in field; lectr. in field; dispute resolution cons. Bd. dirs. Greater Grandparent Need, 1999—2002, Agewell, 2000; adv. bd. YWCA, 1999—2002, Rep. Congl. Com., 2004—. Recipient Vol. of Yr. award, Greater Grandparent Need, Sacramento Vol. of the Yr., Agewell, 2000, Ronald Reagan Spirit award, Rep. Nat. Com., 2005; named Bus. Mem. of the Yr., RNC Pres.'s Adv. Coun., 2005. Avocations: running, football, sports. Home and Office: Larry S Tract & Associates 8655 Hillmon Ct Sacramento CA 95828

TRACT, MARC MITCHELL, lawyer; b. NYC, Sept. 20, 1959; s. Harold Michael and Natalie Ann (Meyerowitz) T.; m. Sharon Beth Widrow; children: Melissa Hope, Harrison Michael, Sarah Michelle. BA in Biology, Ithaca Coll., 1981; JD, Pepperdine U., Malibu, 1984. Bar: NY 1985, NJ 1985, DC 1986. Assoc. Kroll & Tract, NYC, 1985—90, ptnr., 1990—94, Rosenman & Colin LLP, NYC, 1994—2002, Katten Muchin Rosenman, LLP, NYC, 2002—. Bd. dirs. Rampart Ins. Co., Navigators Group Inc., NYC, MAPFRE Ins. Co., Florham Park, NJ, AXA Art Ins. Corp., NYC, Maya Assurance Corp., NYC. Bd. dirs. Italian Acad. Found. Decorated Order of Merit of Savoy. Mem. ABA, Assn. Bar City of NY, NY State Bar Assn., NJ State Bar Assn., NY County Lawyers Assn., Am. Coun. Germany, Old Westbury Golf and Country Club, Met. Club, Econ. Club NY. Republican.

TRACY, ALLEN WAYNE, management consultant; b. Windsor, Vt., July 25, 1943; s. J. Wayne and Helen (Bernard) T.; m. Karla Noelte, Dec. 14, 1969; children: Tania, Tara. BA, U. Vt., 1965; MBA cum laude, Boston U., 1974. Retail salesman Exxon Corp., Boston, 1965-72; mgr. mfg. Leonard Silver Mfg. Co., Inc., Boston, 1974-78, v.p. ops., 1979-81; pres. OESM Corp., NYC, 1978-81; pres., bd. dirs. Gold Lance Inc., Houston, 1981-91; v.p. ops. Town & Country Corp., 1989-92; sr. v.p. L.G. Balfour Co., 1990-92; asst. to pres. Syratech Corp., Boston, 1993; dir. ops. Goldman-Kolber Co., Inc., Norwood, Mass., 1994; exec. v.p., COO, George H. Fuller & Son Co., Inc., Pawtucket, R.I., 1994-97; COO, BioMatrix Techs., Inc., Lincoln, R.I., 1997-98; mgmt. cons. IPA, Buffalo Grove, Ill., 1998—2006, HGMM, Mason, Ohio, 2006—. Bd. dirs. Verilyte Gold, Inc., L.G. Balfour Co., Inc. Mem. Ashland Bd. Selectmen, 1977-78; chmn. Ashland Study Town Govt. Com., 1976-77; vice chmn. ch. coun. Federated Ch. Ashland, 1979-80, chmn., 1981; bd. dirs. Nottingham Forest Civic Assn., 1886. With U.S. Army, 1965-68. Mem. Nottingham Forest Club (bd. dirs. Houston 1986), Beta Gamma Sigma. Home: 118 Lakeview Dr Nokomis FL 34275 Office: HCMM 4770 Duke Dr Ste 390 Mason OH 45040

TRACY, CRAIG ARNOLD, mathematics educator; b. London, Sept. 9, 1945; s. Robert Craig Tracy and Eileen (Arnold) Isenberg; children: Ingrid A., Elizabeth M. BS in Physics, U. Mo., Columbia, 1967; PhD in Physics, SUNY, Stony Brook, 1973. Research assoc. Inst. Fundamental Studies U. Rochester, NY, 1973-75; research assoc. Inst. Theoretical Physics SUNY, Stony Brook, NY, 1975-78; asst. prof. Dept. Math. Dartmouth Coll., 1978—83, assoc. prof., Dept. Math., 1983—84; prof. Dept. Math. U. Calif., Davis, 1984—, chmn. Dept. Math., 1994—98, Disting. prof., 2003, acting dir. Inst. Theoretical Dynamics, 1989, 1992, 2001—02. Visitor Los Alamos Scientific Lab., 1976, Inst. Math. and Its Applications, Univ. Minn., 1982; vis. rsch. scientist Brookhaven Nat. Lab., 1985; rsch. fellow Inst. Scientific Exch., Torino, Italy, 1986; fall rsch. fellow Rsch. Sch. Physical Sciences Australian Nat. U., 1986; rsch. prof. RIMS Kyoto U., 1991; bd. trustees Mathematical Sciences Rsch. Inst., 1998—2002. Mem. editl. bd. Mathematical Physics, Analysis and Geometry, Progress in Mathematical Physics, The Annals of Probability, 2006; contbr. articles to profl. jours. Named Disting. Prof., U. Calif. Davis, 2003; Woodrow Wilson fellowship, 1967—68, Japan Soc. for Promotion Sci. fellowship, 1991. Fellow: Am. Acad. Arts and Sciences; mem.: Am. Math. Soc., Am. Physical Soc., Soc. Indsl. and Applied Math. (George Pólya prize with Harold Widom 2002, and Am. Math. Soc., Norbert Wiener prize in Applied Math. with Harold Widom 2007). Office: Univ of Calif Dept of Math 3146 Math Sciences Bldg One Shields Ave Davis CA 95616-8633 Office Fax: 530-752-6635. Business E-Mail: tracy@math.ucdavis.edu.

TRACY, DAVID JAMES, chemist, consultant; b. Covington, KY, Jan. 22, 1937; s. Harold Anthony and Margaret Loretta Tracy. PhD, U. Ill., Urbana, 1963. Dir. rsch. Rhodia, Cranbury, NJ, 1990—2000; cons. Tracy Consulting LLC, Ohio, 2000—. Recipient Rosen award, AOCS, 2002. Home: 49 Tall Trees Dr Amelia OH 45102 Home Fax: 513-943-9077. Personal E-mail: davidjtracy@aol.com.

TRACY, ERIN ELIZABETH, obstetrician, gynecologist; b. Phila., June 15, 1966; d. Gerald Paul and Mary Margaret Tracy; m. Eules Hood Tracy, Oct. 28, 2000; children: Shannon Meaghan, Bridget Molly, Kevin Gerald. BS, U. Scranton, Pa., 1988; MD, Georgetown U. Sch. Medicine, Washington, 1992; MPH, Harvard Sch. Pub. Health, Boston, Mass., 1997. Diplomate Am. Bd. Ob-Gyn., 1999. Attending physician Mass. Gen. Hosp., Boston, 1996—; asst. prof. Harvard Med. Sch. Fellow at large Am. Coll. Obstetricians and Gynecologists, Washington, 2004—06. Recipient Charles Montraville Green award, BWH, Robert Montraville Green award, MGH, 2006. Mem.: AMA (women physicians congress governing coun. mem. 2002—, chair). Democrat. Roman Catholic. Office: Mass Gen Hosp Founders 424 Fruit St Boston MA 02114

TRACY, JAMES DONALD, historian, educator; b. St. Louis, Feb. 14, 1938; s. Leo W. and Marguerite M. (Meehan) T.; m. Nancy Ann McBride, Sept. 6, 1968 (div. 1993); children: Patrick, Samuel, Mary Ann; m. Suzanne K. Swan, May 2, 1997. BA, St. Louis U., 1959; MA, Johns Hopkins U., 1960, Notre Dame U., 1961; PhD, Princeton U., 1967. Instr. U. Mich., 1964-66; instr. to prof. history U. Minn., Mpls., 1966—, dept. chmn., 1988-91, Union Pacific prof. early modern history, 2001—04. Vis. prof. U. Leiden, Netherlands, 1987, U. Paris IV, 2001, U. Amsterdam, 2004. Author: Erasmus: The Growth of a Mind, 1972, The Politics of Erasmus: A Pacifist Intellectual and His Political Milieu, 1979, True Ocean Found.: Paludanus's Letters on Dutch Voyages to the Kara Sea, 1980, A Financial Revolution in the Habsburg Netherlands: Renten and Renteniers in the County of Holland, 1515-1565, 1985, Holland Under Habsburg Rule: The Formation of a Body Politic, 1506-1566, 1990, Erasmus of the Low Countries, 1996, Europe's Reformations, 1450-1650, 1999, 2d edit., 2006, Emperor Charles V, Impresario of War, 2002, The Founding of the Dutch Republic: War, Finance and Politics in Holland, 1572-1588, 2008, The Low Countries in the Sixteenth Century: Erasmus, Religion and Politics, Trade and Finance, 2005; editor: Luther and the Modern State in Germany, 1986, The Rise of Merchant Empires: Long Distance Trade in the Early Modern Era, 1350-1750, 1990, The Political Economy of Merchant Empires: Long Distance Trade and State Power in the Early Modern World, 1991; editor: (with T.A. Brady and H.A. Oberman) Handbook of European History in the Late Middle Ages, Renaissance and Reformation, Vol. 1, 1994, Vol. 2, 1995, City Walls: The Urban Enceinte in Global Perspective, 2000; editor: (with T.A. Brady, K.G. Brady and S. Karant-Nunn) The Work of Heiko A. Oberman, 2003; editor: (with Marguerite Ragnow) Religion and the Early Modern State: Views from China, Russia and the West, 2004; editor: (with K.L. Reyerson and T.G. Stavrov) Pre-Modern Russia and Its World: Essays in Honor of Thomas S. Noonan, 2006; co-editor: Jour. Early Modern History, 1997—2000; editor, 2000—; mem. editl. bd. Sixteenth Century Jour., 1979—2000. Guggenheim fellow, 1972-73; NEH summer grantee, 1977, 85; Fulbright rsch. grantee, Belgium, 1979, Netherlands, 1980; resident fellow Netherlands Inst. for Advanced Studies, 1993-94. Mem. Am. Cath. Hist. Soc. (pres. 1999-00), Soc. Reformation Rsch. (pres. 1995-97), 16th Century Studies Conf. (pres. 1985-86). Republican. Roman Catholic. Home: 1320 Riverside Ln Apt 410 Saint Paul MN 55118-1757 Office: Univ Minn History 1116 Heller Hall Minneapolis MN 55455 Home Phone: 651-227-0466; Office Phone: 612-624-0808. Business E-Mail: tracy001@umn.edu.

TRACY, JANET LYNN, psychologist, consultant; b. New Brunswick, NJ, July 25, 1963; BSc, Montclair State U., 1985; MEd, South Orange, NJ, 1988; EdS, Seton Hall U., South Orange, NJ, 1991. Cert. sch. psychologist NJ, profl. counselor NJ. Sch. psychologist Cedar Grave Bd. Edn., NJ, 1991—2001, Hillsborough Bd. Edn., NJ, 2001—, cons., 2002—; profl. counselor Pvt. Practise, Somerset, NJ, 2006—. Cons. Hillsborough HS, 2002—. Sponsor Spl. Olympics, NJ, 2006. Avocations: hiking, bicycling, dance, yoga. Home and Office: Pvt Counseling Practise 46 Franklin St Somerset NJ 08873 Office Phone: 908-285-2864. Office Fax: 732-649-1840. Business E-Mail: jtcacy1840@comcast.net.

TRACY, JIM (JAMES EDWIN TRACY), professional baseball manager; b. Hamilton, Ohio, Dec. 31, 1955; s. Jim Tracy, Sr.; m. Debra Tracy; children: Brian, Chad, Mark. Attended, Marietta Coll. Outfielder Chgo. Cubs, 1980—81; minor league mgr. Peoria Chiefs, 1987—88, Chattanooga Lookouts, 1989—91, Harrisburg Senators, 1993, Ottawa Lynx, 1994; minor league field coord. Cin. Reds, 1992; bench coach Montreal Expos, 1995—98, LA Dodgers, 1999—2000, interim mgr., 2000, mgr., 2001—05, Pitts. Pirates, 2006—07; bench coach Colo. Rockies, 2008—09, mgr., 2009—. Coach Nat. League All-Star Team, 2002, 06. Recipient Disting. Alumnus award, Marietta Coll., 2003; named Eastern League's Mgr. of Yr., 1993; named to Badin HS Sports Hall of Fame, Ohio, Marietta Coll. Sports Hall of Fame. Office: Colo Rockies Coors Field 2001 Blake St Denver CO 80205*

TRACY, PATRICIA ANN KOOP, secondary school educator; b. Chickasaw, Ala., Sept. 28, 1947; d. Augustus Galloway Koop and Mildred (Willingham) Koop Conlon; m. Charles Gerald Tracy, Jan. 24, 1970; children: Charles Gerald Jr., William Todd, Michael Patrick. BS in Edn., U. Ala., 1970; postgrad., Ala. State U., 1988, Troy State U., 1989, U. Ala., 1989, Ala. State U., 1995, Auburn U., 1994. Cert. secondary sci. tchr., elem. tchr. Tchr. sci. St. Bede Sch., Montgomery, Ala., 1986—90, coord. Sci. Fair, head dept. sci., 1986—90; libr., media specialist Our Lady Queen Mercy Sch., 1992—93, libr., media specialist, computer tchr., 1993—94, mem. libr. and media, tchr. earth sci., 1994—98; tchr. Wetumpka Jr. H.S., 1998—2003; tchr. sci., dept. chmn., sponsor sci. club, sponsor math. and sci. bowl competition Eclectic Mid. Sch., Ala., 2003—, coach robotics team, 2006—. Chair sci. dept. Wetumpka Jr. H.S., 2001—03; sponsor Ala. Math. & Sci. Bowl Competition, Bayer/NSF Cmty. Grant, Sci. Club; established reading program for grades K-8 involving parents of K-2 and computers in grades 3-8; developed hands-on approach in media with filmstrip, book tapes, computer games and other games involving cognitive skills; sci. fair co-coord., 1994—; coach Math and Sci. Bowl Eclectic Mid. Sch. and HS. Named one of Tchr. of Yr., Eclectic Mid. Sch., 2007—08. Mem.: Ala. Sci. Tchrs. Assn., Nat. Cath. Edn. Assn., Ala. Edn. Assn., Wetumpka H.S. PTO, Ala. Alumni Assn., Montgomery Cath. H.S. PTO, Ala. Conservancy, Ala. Mus. Natural History, Delta Kappa Gamma, Alpha Xi Delta. Roman Catholic. Avocations: crafts, water sports, reading, gardening, work for cleaner environment. Home: 2424 Trotters Trl Wetumpka AL 36093-2311 Office: 170 S Ann Electric Eclectic AL 36024

TRACY, RICHARD E., medical educator; b. Klamath Falls, Oreg., Apr. 30, 1934; BA, U. Chgo., 1955, MD, PhD, 1961. Diplomate Am. Bd. Anatomic Pathology, Am. Bd. Forensic Pathology. Prof. Sch. Medicine La. State U., New Orleans, 1967, prof. emeritus, 2005—. Office: Sch of Medicine Box P5-1 La State U Health Sci Ctr New Orleans LA 70112 Office Phone: 504-568-6072. Business E-Mail: rtracy@lsuhsc.edu.

TRACY, THOMAS MILES, international health organization official; b. Great Barrington, Mass., July 8, 1936; s. Thomas Paul and Marion (Miles) T.; m. June Betts, June 17, 1967; children: Miles Christopher, Keir Thomas John. BA, Colgate U., 1958; MA, Stanford U., 1959; MBA, Columbia U., 1973. Fgn. service officer Dept. State, Washington, 1960-84; counselor Am. Embassy, Moscow, 1975-78, Bonn, Germany, 1978-79; asst. sec. Dept. State, Washington, 1979-83; chief adminstrn. Pan Am./WHO, Washington, 1983-98; mgmt. cons. Dept. State, 2003—. V.p. Pan-Am. Health and Edn. Found., treas. Trustee, vice chmn. Chelsea Sch., 1988-2004. With U.S. Army, 1959-60. Recipient Superior Honor award Dept. State, 1978 Mem.: Am. Fgn. Svc. Protective Found. (sec., treas.), Am. Fgn. Svc. Protective Assn. (dir. 1988—, v.p. 1997—2005, pres. 2005—), Am. Fgn. Svc. Assn. (dir. 1970—72). Home: 5902 Devonshire Dr Bethesda MD 20816-3416

TRADER, JOSEPH EDGAR, orthopedic surgeon; b. Milw., Nov. 2, 1946; s. Edgar Joseph and Dorothy Elizabeth (Senzig) T.; m. Janet Louise Burzycki, Sept. 23, 1972 (div. Nov. 1987); children: James, Jonathan, Ann Elizabeth; m. Rhonda Sue Schultz, May 26, 1990. Student, Marquette U., 1964-67; MD, Med. Coll. Wis., 1971. Diplomate Am. Bd. Orthop. Surgery. Physician emergency rm. Columbia, St. Joseph's Hosps., Milw., 1972—76; orthop. surgeon, pres. Orthop. Assn., Manitowoc, Wis., 1979—. Mem. exec. com. Holy Family Meml. Med. Ctr., Manitowoc, 1985-96, chief-of-staff, 1994-96, ethics com., 1995—, chair instnl. rev. com. Former pres., bd. dirs. Holy Innocents Mens Choir; county del. State Med. Soc. Charitable Sci. and Edn. Found.; pres., bd. dirs. (trustee), mem. cobia com., pres. bd. dirs. Wis. Maritime Mus. Fellow ACS, Am. Acad. Orthopaedic Surgeons; mem. AMA, Wis. State Med. Soc., Wis. Orthop. Soc., Midwest Orthop. Soc., Am. Coll. Sports Medicine, Orthop. Assn. Manitonoc (pres.), Crown and Anchor, Wis. Maritime Mus. (cobia com. mem., bd. dirs.), Manitowoc Yacht Club, Phi Delta Epsilon, Psi Chi. Roman Catholic. Avocations: singing, tennis, skiing, sailing, golf. Home: 1021 Memorial Dr Manitowoc WI 54220-2242 Office: Orthopaedic Assocs 501 N 10th St Manitowoc WI 54220-4039 Office Phone: 920-682-6376. E-mail: jetrader@comcast.net.

TRAEGER, CHARLES HENRY, III, educator and innovator; b. Fountain Hill, Pa., Sept. 30, 1942; s. Charles Henry Jr. and Dorothy Shelly (Weinberger) T.; m. Carole Lynn DeGraff, Feb. 20, 1972; children: Chad, Erin, Seth, Anna, Claire, Ben. AB, Coll. William and Mary, 1964; JD, Stanford U., 1967. Bar: Calif. 1967, N.Y. 1972, Mass. 1976, Ariz. 1980. Assoc. Milbank, Tweed, Hadley & McCloy, NYC, 1967, 71-76; v.p., gen. counsel Shawmut Corp., Boston, 1976-80, Shawmut Bank of Boston, N.A., 1976-80; assoc. Snell & Wilmer, Phoenix, 1980-83, ptnr., 1983-91; v.p., asst. gen. counsel Bank One Ariz. N.A., Phoenix, 1991-95; assoc. gen. counsel Ariz. State U., Tempe, 1996—2007, assoc. dir. Alliance for Constrn. Excellence, 2007—. Contbr. Stanford Law Rev. Lt. comdr. USNR, 1968-71. Mem. Phi Beta Kappa. Republican. Mem. Lds Ch. Office Phone: 480-965-1418. Business E-Mail: hanktr@asu.edu.

TRAFFORD, ABIGAIL, columnist, editor, writer, public speaker; b. NYC, July 14, 1940; d. William Bradford and Abigail (Sard) T.; children: Abigail Brett Miller, Victoria Brett. BA cum laude, Bryn Mawr Coll., 1962. Researcher Nat. Geog. Soc., Washington, 1964-67; tchr. Hermansberg Mission, Northern Ter., Australia, 1967-68; spl. corr. Time mag., The Washington Post, Houston, 1969-74; writer, asst. mng. editor U.S. News & World Report, Washington, 1975-86; health editor The Washington Post, 1986-00, columnist, 2000—. Vis. scholar Stanford U. Ctr. on Longevity, 2007; spkr. in field. Author: Crazy Time: Surviving Divorce and Building a New Life, 1982, revised edit., 1992, My Time: Making the Most of the Rest of Your Life, 2004. Journalism fellow Harvard Sch. Pub. Health, 1980, 2000; sr. fellow Civic Ventures. Mem. Washington Press Club Found. (bd. mem. 1989—, pres. 1993-95). Home and Office: 2600 Upton St NW Washington DC 20008-3826 Office Phone: 202-966-3516. Business E-Mail: trafforda@washpost.com.

TRAFTON, LAURENCE MUNRO, astronomer, researcher; b. Boston, July 31, 1938; s. Herbert Meara and Vesta Estelle Trafton. BS, Calif. Inst. Tech., 1960, MS, 1961, PhD, 1965. Assoc. scientist Jet Propulsion Lab., Pasadena, Calif., summers 1961-62; project officer Kirtland AFB, Albuquerque, 1968, project scientist, 1968-69; spl. rsch. assoc. dept. astronomy U. Tex., Austin, 1969-72, rsch. scientist dept. astronomy, 1972-93, sr. rsch. scientist McDonald Obs., 1993—. Mem. editl. bd. Icarus, 1976-79, assoc. editor, 1980—. 1st lt. USAF, 1965-68. Fellow AAAS; mem. Am. Astron. Soc. (com. mem. divsn. planetary sci. 1977-80), Internat. Astron. Union. Office: Univ Tex Austin Dept Astronomy Austin TX 78712 Office Phone: 512-471-1476. E-mail: lmt@astro.as.utexas.edu.

TRAGER, DAVID G., federal judge; b. Mt. Vernon, NY, Dec. 23, 1937; s. Sol and Clara (Friedman) T.; m. Roberta E. Weisbrod, May 2, 1972; children: Mara Emet, Josiah Samuel, Naomi Gabrielle. BA, Columbia Coll., 1959; LL.B., Harvard U., 1962. Bar: NY. Assoc. Berman & Frost, 1963-65, Butler, Jablow & Geller, 1965-67; asst. corp. counsel Appeals Div. City of NY, 1967; law clk. to Hon. Kenneth B. Keating NY State Ct. Appeals, 1968-69, law clk. to Hon. Stanley H. Fuld, 1969; asst. U.S. atty. chief, appeals divsn. US Dept. Justice, 1970-72, U.S. atty. (ea. dist. NY) Bklyn., 1974-78; prof. Bklyn. Law Sch., 1972-94, dean, 1983-94; judge US Dist. Ct. (ea. dist.) NY, Bklyn., 1994—2006, sr. judge, 2006—; mem. adv. com. on criminal rules Jud. Conf. US, 2000—. Chmn. Mayor's Com. on Judiciary, 1982-89, NY State Temp. Commn. on Investigation, 1983-90. Mem. NYC Charter Rev. Commn., 1986-89. With USAR, 1962-65, USNR, 1965-69. Mem.: Am. Law Inst., Fed. Bar Coun. (pres. 1986—88). Office: US Courthouse 225 Cadman Plz E Brooklyn NY 11201-1818

TRAGER, LORINDA ADELE, finance educator, legal association administrator; b. Alameda, Calif., Aug. 20, 1946; d. Tedford T. and Melodie A. Trager; children: Brian D. Liebelt, Stacie N. Olsen. BS (hon.), Stanislaus State, CAlf., 1980. Cert. tchg. credential Calif., 1980. Tchr. Lodi Unified Sch. Dist., Calif., 1976—96; instr. San Joaquin Delta Coll., Stockton, Calif., 2001—. Legal adminstrv. asst. Robert K. Kolber, Inc., Stockton, Calif., 2007—. Mem.: Banking and Fin. (adv. com. mem. 1976—). Office: San Joaquin Delta Coll 5151 Pacific Ave Stockton CA 95207

TRAGER, MICHAEL DAVID, lawyer; b. NYC, Feb. 15, 1959; s. Philip and Ina (Shulkin) T.; m. Mariella Gonzalez, Sept. 12, 1987; children: Nicholas, Alexander. BA, Wesleyan U., Middletown, Conn., 1981; JD, Boston U., 1985. Bar: Mass. 1985, Conn. 1986, Fla. 1988, DC 1989. Staff atty. enforcement divsn. SEC, Washington, 1985-87; assoc. Morgan, Lewis & Bockius, Miami, Fla., 1987-88; participating assoc. Fulbright & Jaworski, Washington, 1989-92, of counsel, 1993-94, ptnr., 1995—2004, co-head securities litig. and enforcement, firm, chair corp. dept.; ptnr. Arnold & Porter LLP, Washington, 2005—, chmn. securities enforcement practice. Bd. dirs. Jewish Nat. Fund-Mid-Atlantic Region, Wash., 1993-97; officer Horace Mann PTA, Washington, 1997-99. Mem. ABA (bus. law sect. fed. regulation securities com. and civil litig. and SEC enforcement matters subcom., litig. sect. securities litig. com. and SEC enforcement subcom., class action and derivative litig. com. and securities litig. subcom., task force on SEC's insider trading and selective disclosure rules), Assn. SEC Alumni, Securities Industry Assn. (legal and compliance divsn.), DC Bar (corp., fin. and securities law sect. corp. counsel and planning group for broker-dealer programs 1992-94, broker-dealer regulation com., task force on SEC's proposed insider trading and selective disclosure rules), Mass. Bar, Fla. Bar., Conn. Bar, Bond Market Assn. (litig. adv. com.), Wesleyan U. Club of Washington (chair 2001-04), Wesleyan U. Alumni Assn. (exec. com. 2001-04), Post-classical Ensemble (adv. bd. 2003-05), Children's Law Ctr. (chair Law Firm Sponsors 2004), Wash. Ballet (bd. dirs. 2004-06). Office: Arnold & Porter LLP 555 12th St NW 1153 Washington DC 20004 Office Phone: 202-942-6976. Office Fax: 202-942-5999. Business E-Mail: michael.trager@aporter.com.

TRAGOS, GEORGE EURIPEDES, lawyer; b. Chgo., July 15, 1949; s. Euripedes G. and Eugene G. (Gatziolis) T.; m. Donna Marie Thalassites, Nov. 18, 1978; children: Louise, Gina, Peter. BA, Fla. State U., 1971, JD, 1974. Bar: Fla., U.S. Dist. Ct. (mid., so. dists.) Fla., U.S. Dist. Ct. (we. dist.) Tenn., U.S. Ct. Appeals (5th, 11th cirs.). Legis. aide Fla. Ho. of Reps., 1972-73; tax analyst tax and fin. com., 1973-74; chief, felony asst. states atty. State of Fla., Clearwater, 1974-78; partner firm Case, Kimpton, Tragos & Burke, P.A., Clearwater Beach, 1978-83; chief criminal div. U.S. Atty.'s Office for Middle Dist. Fla., Tampa, 1983-85; lead trial asst. Pres. Organized Crime Drug Enforcement Task Force, Tampa, 1985; sole practice Clearwater, 1985—. Contbr. articles to profl. jours. and frequent lectr. Mem. Clearwater Bar (pres. 1994), Fla. Bar Assn. (chmn. fed. practice com. 1986, chmn. criminal law sect. 2000, chmn. bar evidence com. 1990), Fla. Assn. Criminal Def. Lawyers (pres. 1991), Fla. State U. Alumni Assn. Law Sch. (bd. dirs.), Tampa Bay Fed.

Bar Assn. (v.p. 1989), Clearwater Beach Jaycees (pres. 1979), Fla. U. Gold Key Club (pres. 1972), Ahepa. Mem. Greek Orthodox Ch. Avocations: boating, tennis. Office: 600 Cleveland St Ste 700 Clearwater FL 33755-4158 Office Phone: 727-441-9030. Business E-Mail: george@greeklaw.com.

TRAHAN, KELLY, design educator; d. Hugh and Marlene Falvey; m. Chuck Trahan, July 20, 2002; 1 child, Hugh. BS in Elem. Edn., West Chester U., Pa., 1991; AAS in Comml. Art, Hinds CC, Raymond, Miss., 1998; MEd, Miss. Coll., Clinton, 2006. Graphic artist HMI Practice Resource, Vicksburg, Miss., 1998—2000, MCI, Clinton, 2000—04; graphic design tech. instr. Hinds CC, 2004—07; art and digital design instr. Montgomery County CC, Pottstown, Pa. Recipient X-Emplary Performance award, MCI, 2001, Rebranding award, 2003. Office: Montgomery County CC 101 Coll Dr Pottstown PA 19464 Business E-Mail: ktrahan@mc3.edu.

TRAIN, HARRY DEPUE, II, retired naval officer; b. Washington, Nov. 5, 1927; s. Harold Cecil and May (Philipps) T.; m. Catharine Peck Kinnear, July 8, 1950; children: Louise Lucas, Catharine Philipps, Elizabeth Langdon, Cecilia Spencer. BS, U.S. Naval Acad., 1949. Commd. ensign U.S. Navy, 1949, advanced through grades to adm., 1978; comdr. Cruiser-Destroyer Flotilla 8, 1971-72; dir. internat. security affairs East Asia and Pacific Region Office Asst. Sec. Def., 1972-73; dir. Systems Analysis Div., Office Chief Naval Ops., 1973-74; dir. joint staff Orgn. Joint Chiefs of Staff, 1974-76; comdr. U.S. 6th Fleet, 1976-78; comdr.-in-chief, supreme allied cmdr., atlantic cmd, atlantic fleet US Navy, 1978-82; ret. US Atlantic Fleet and NATO supreme allied comdr. Atlantic, 1982. Mgr. Hampton Rds. Ops. Sci. Applications Internat. Corp., 1989—2006. Mem. Hart-Rudman Commn. Decorated D.S.M. with 3 gold stars, Def. Disting. Svc. medal, Legion of Merit with 3 gold stars, Meritorious Svc. medal, Joint Svcs. Commendation medal, Navy Commendation medal; comdr. Order Republic of Tunisia; Order Naval Merit Brazil; Pedro Campbell medal Uruguay; Order of Pres. of Republic Chile; decorated Portuguese Mil. Order Christ; Netherlands Order Orange-Nassau; German Order Merit; French Legion of Honor; Colombian Naval Order Admiral Padilla; Mex. Order Spl. Merit; sr. fellow Joint Advanced Warfighting Sch., Joint Forces Staff Coll. Mem. U.S. Naval Inst., Coun. on Fgn. Rels., Columbia Country Club, Town Point Club. Home: 401 College Pl Apt 10 Norfolk VA 23510-1130

TRAIN, JOHN, investment advisor, columnist; b. NYC, May 25, 1928; s. Arthur Cheney and Helen (Coster) T.; m. Maria Teresa Cini di Pianzano, 1961 (div. 1976); children: Helen, Nina, Lisa; m. Frances Cheston, July 23, 1977. BA magna cum laude, Harvard U., 1950, MA, 1951. Founder, mng. editor Paris Rev., 1952-54; staff asst. sec. Dept. Army, US Dept. Def., Washington, 1954-56; assoc. de Vegh & Co., 1956-58; chmn. Train, Babcock Advisors (and predecessor firms), NYC, 1958-94, chmn. emeritus, 1995—; co-chmn., then hon. dir. ICAP, S.A., Athens, 1964—; chmn. Montrose Fin. Group, NYC, 1992—; pres. Chateau Malescasse, Lamarque-Margaux, Bordeaux, France, 1970-81; columnist Forbes mag., 1977-83, Harvard mag., 1983-95, Wall St. Jour., 1984—, Worth Mag., Boston, 1991-93, Town and Country mag., 1994-95, Fin. Times, London, 1994—, Strategic Rev., 1998—2002, Am. Spectator, 2002—. Bd. dirs. African Devel. Found., Washington, 1988-94; bd. dirs. Bulgarian-Am. Enterprise Fund, Washington, Genesis Funds, London, Internat. Rescue Com., N.Y.C.; chmn. Train Found., 1988—; bd. govs. East-West Ctr., Hawaii, 1993-96. Author: Dance of the Money Bees, 1973, Remarkable Names, 1977, Even More Remarkable Names, 1979, Remarkable Occurrences, 1978, Remarkable Words, 1980, The Money Masters, 1980, Remarkable Relatives, 1971, Preserving Capital and Making it Grow, 1983, Famous Financial Fiascos, 1984, John Train's Most Remarkable Names, 1985, The Midas Touch, 1987, The New Money Masters, 1989, Valsalva's Maneuver, 1989, John Train's Most Remarkable Occurences, 1990, Wit, 1991, Love, 1993, The Craft of Investing, 1994, Crazy Quilt, 1996, Oriental Rug Symbols, 1997, Investing and Managing Trusts under the New Prudent Investor Rule, 1999, Money Masters of Our Time, 2001, The Olive: Tree of Civilization, 2004, The Orange: Golden Joy, 2006; contbr. articles to profl. publs. Chmn. Italian Emergency Relief Com., 1976-77; pres. Afghanistan Relief Com., 1986-95; trustee Harvard Lampoon, Cambridge, Mass., 1974-90, World Monuments Fund, 1988-92; chmn. Free Elections Project, 1990, Brit. Mus. Nat. Hist. Internat. Trust, 1990-95, The Train Found., 1990—; trustee univ. coun. Am. U. Bulgaria, 1996—; overseer Sch. Govt. and Diplomacy Seton Hall U., NJ. With U.S. Army, 1954-56. Decorated commendatore Ordine del Merito della Repubblica, commendatore Ordine Della Solidarieta, medal Provencia di Udine (Italy); recipient Disting. Grotonian award, 1996, Queen's Birthday honors Order of St. John, 1997. Mem.: Fgn. Policy Assn. (trustee), Internat. Inst. Strategic Studies (London), Coun. on Fgn. Rels., Order Colonial Lords of Manors, Travellers Club (Paris), Beefsteak Club (London), Brook's Club (London), Union Club, Racquet & Tennis Club, Met. Club (Washington), Century Club. Office: 505 Park Ave New York NY 10022

TRAIN, RUSSELL ERROL, environmentalist; b. Jamestown, RI, June 4, 1920; s. Charles R. and Errol C. (Brown) T.; m. Aileen Bowdoin, May 27, 1954; children: Nancy, Emily, Bowdoin, Errol. AB, Princeton U., 1941, LL.D. (hon.), 1970; JD, Columbia U., 1948, LL.D. (hon.), 1970, Bates Coll., 1970, Drexel U., 1970; D.E. (hon.), Worcester Poly. Inst., 1970, U. Md., 1975; Sc.D. (hon.), St. Mary's Coll., 1970, Clarkson Coll. Tech., 1973, Salem Coll., 1975, Southwestern U., 1976, Mich. State U., 1976; D.C.L. (hon.), U. of South, 1973; D public svc., Washington Coll., 1996. Bar: D.C. bar 1949. Atty. staff joint com. on internal revenue taxation U.S. Congress, 1949-53; chief counsel Ways and Means Com., U.S. Ho. of Reps., 1953-54, minority adviser, 1955-56; asst. to sec., head legal adv. staff Treasury Dept., 1956-57; judge U.S. Tax Ct., 1957-65; pres. Conservation Found., 1965-69; also trustee; undersec. Dept. Interior, 1969-70; chmn. Council on Environ. Quality, 1970-73; adminstr. EPA, Washington, 1973-77; sr. assoc. Conservation Found., 1977; pres., chief exec. officer World Wildlife Fund, Washington, 1978-85, chmn. bd., 1985-94, chmn. emeritus, 1994—; chmn. bd. Conservation Found., 1985-90; chmn. Nat. Commn. on the Environment, 1991-93; chmn. Nat. Coun. World Wildlife Fund, Washington, chmn. emeritus. Mem. Washington Nat. Monument Assn., Nat. Water Commn., 1968—69; head U.S. del. UN Conf. Human Environment, 1972; rep. Internat. Whaling Commn., 1972, other internat. confs.; mem. Pres.'s adv. com. on trade and trade negotiations, 1991—93. Author: The Bowdoin Family, 2000, The Train Family, 2000, A Memoir, 2000, Politics, Pollution, and Pandas, 2003. Trustee emeritus African Wildlife Found. Decorated Order of the Golden Ark (The Netherlands); recipient Albert Schweitzer medal, Animal Welfare Inst., 1972, Aldo Leopold medal, Wildlife Soc., 1975, Conservationist of Yr. award, Nat. Wildlife Fedn., 1974, 1986, John and Alice Tyler Ecology award, 1978, Freese award, ASCE, 1978, Pub. Welfare award, Nat. Acad. Scis., 1981, Elizabeth Haub prize in internat. environ. law, 1981, Frances K. Hutchinson medal, Garden Club of Am., 1984, Lindbergh award, 1985, Environ. Law Inst. award, 1986, Presdl. Medal of Freedom, 1991, Heinz Chmns. medal, 2001, Internat. Excellence in Conservation award, Bot. Rsch. Inst., Tex., 2006, Founder's award, St. George's Sch., Newport, RI, 2007. Fellow: AAAS; mem.: Am. Acad. Arts and Scis., Atlantic Coun., Coun. Fgn. Rels. Office: World Wildlife Fund 1250 24th St NW Fl 6 Washington DC 20037-1193 Office Phone: 202-495-4512.

TRAINA, SALVATORE ALBERT, publishing executive; b. Bklyn., Apr. 30, 1927; s. Salvatore and Guilia (LeBarbara) T.; m. Vail Devereux, June 22, 1957; children: Caroline Vail, Robert Brooks. BS, Seton Hall U., 1950; postgrad., Columbia U., 1950-51; MBA, NYU, 1954. Circulation promotion advt. space salesman Fairchild Publs., NYC, 1951-53; Eastern advt. mgr. Modern Bride mag. Ziff-Davis, NYC, 1953-58; advt. mgr. Bride and Home mag. Hearst Mags., NYC, 1958-60, pub. Bride and Home mag., 1960-64; pub. Sports Afield mag., 1964-65, Town and Country mag., 1965-67, Harpers Bazaar mag., 1967-70; pres., chief exec. officer Bartell Media Corp., 1970-74; pres. Ziff-Davis Mag. Network, 1974-76, group v.p., 1976-78; sr. v.p. Ziff-Davis Pub. Co., 1978-81; pres. Ziff-Davis Consumer Mag., 1981-85; exec. v.p. mags. CBS, NYC, 1985; pres. Traina Assocs., NYC, 1985—2000. Mem. Scarsdale Bi-Partisan Com., 1975-78; bd. dirs. Crane Berkeley Assn., 1978-88, pres., 1983-84; mem. nat. bd. dirs., chmn. comms. com., treas. Goodwill Industries of Am., 1979-92, chmn. bd., 1988-92; chmn. bd. trustees Chebeague Island Libr., 1997-2001; pres. bd. dirs. Chebeague Recreation Ctr., 1998-2003; bd. dirs. Chebeague Island Hist. Soc., 2000-08. With USNR, 1945-46. NY State War Svc. scholar, Columbia U. and NYU, 1950. Mem. NYU Grad. Sch. Bus. Adminstrn. Alumni Assn., NYU Alumni Fedn. (comms. com. 1970-73), Union League Club (N.Y.C.). Home: 11 Springettes Rd Chebeague Island ME 04017-9723 E-mail: sunsethill@chebeague.net.

TRAINER, KARIN A., librarian; BA in English, Rutgers U., 1970; grad. work in English, Bryn Mawr Coll.; MLIS, Drexel U., 1972; M in liberal studies, NYU, 1983. Descriptive cataloguer Libraries of Princeton U., 1972—74, catalogue maintenance libr., 1974—78; dir. tech. and automated services NYU Libraries, 1978—83; assoc. univ. libr. Yale U., 1983—96, fellow and freshman advisor Ezra Stiles Coll.; univ. libr. Princeton U., 1996—. Trustee Princeton U. Press. Fellow Rockefeller Coll. Office: Princeton U Libr One Washington Rd Princeton NJ 08544 Office Phone: 609-258-3170. Business E-Mail: ktrainer@princeton.edu.

TRAINES, ROSE WUNDERBAUM, sculptor, educator; b. Monroeville, Ind., Sept. 13, 1928; d. Louis and Leah (Fogel) Wunderbaum; m. Robert Jacob Traines, June 25, 1949; children: Claudia Denise Traines Lang, Monica Rae Traines Martin Student, Ind. State Tchr.'s Coll., 1946—48, Mich. State U., 1948—49; BS, Ctrl. Mich. U., 1951. Lectr. in field. One person shows include Ctrl. Mich. U., Mt. Pleasant, 1964, Alma Artmobile, Mich., 1972, Ctrl. Mich. Homecoming, Mt. Pleasant, 1982, Internat. Inst. Scrap Iron and Steel, Inc., Washington, 1983, Fontainebleau Hotel, Miami Beach, Fla., 1983, Elliott Mus. Art Gallery, Stuart, Fla., 1988, 98, 2006, Walt Kuhn Gallery, Cape Neddick, Maine, 1988, Coll. Club Boston, 1990, Brass Latch Gallery, Montpelier, Ind., 1991, 96, 98, Vero Beach Ctr. Arts, Fla., 1992, Maritime and Yachting Mus., Stuart, 1997, Mid-Mich. Regional Med. Ctr., Healing Arts Gallery, Midland, 1997, Northwood Gallery, Midland, Comerica Bank Art Series, Palm Beach Gardens, 2002, Gallery Five, Tequesta, Fla., 2002, Mich. U. Park Libr. Gallery, 2002, Art Reach Mid. Mich., Mt. Pleasant, 2002, 06, Arthur Glick Jewish Cmty. Ctr., Indpls., 2004, Elliott Mus. Gallery, Stuart, Fla., 2006, 2007, Country Club Orchid Island, Orchid, Fla., 2007; two-person shows include Gallery One, North Palm Beach, 1973, Midland Ctr. Arts, 1976, Springfield Art Mart, Ohio, 1977, Hillel Student Ctr. Gallery-U. Cin., 1993; exhibited in group shows including Saginaw Mus. Art, Mich., 1965, Grand Rapids Mus., Mich., 1966, Kalamazoo Mus., Mich., 1967, Kellogg/Kresge Art Ctr., Mich. State U., East Lansing, 1967, Art Reach Mid-Mich., 1987, Salmagundi Club, NYC, 1988, 91-92, 96, Copley Soc., Boston, 1990, 95, Allied Artists Am., Inc., NYC, 1995-96, Self Family Arts Ctr., Hilton Head Island, SC, 1996-97, Palm Beach Gardens Fla. City Hall, 2003, Palm Beach Gardens Cmty. Ctr., 2003, Chapman Maritime Mus., Salerno, Fla., 2008(Art Reach Treas.award Art Reach Mid-Mich.), HATS Arts Exhbn. CMU, 2009, adult lectr. series vets. Meml. Lib. Mich., 2009; 35 min. DVD Documentary Permanent collections at Dow-Corning Corp. Collection, Midland Ctr. Arts, Elliott Mus., Walt Kuhn Gallery, Coll. Club Boston, Pullen Elem. Sch., Isabella Bank and Trust Co., Ctrl. Mich. U., Blake Libr, Stuart, Stuart Fla. Alma Mich. Pub. Libr., Montpelier Ind. Pub. Libr., La Belle Mgmt. Corp., Morey Bandit Industries, Mich., Ctrl. Mich. Cmty. Hosp., Northwood U., Vets. Meml. Libr., Mt. Pleasant, Pub. Libr., Clare, Mich., Brass Latch Gallery, Montpelier, Ind, Northville (Mich.) Pub. Libr, Norman Cousins, Carl Gerstacker Found., Fannie Traines, Attorney Joe Barberi, Doctor Tom Keating, Olga and Rollie Denison, Claudia and Yaron Lang, Marjorie Fishbain, Kitti Pyne, Donnie Hersee, Doctor Carlos Maldonado, Stuart Fla. Doctor Chris Allen, Mich., pvt. collections, CMU Pk. Lib., Mt. Pleasant, CMU Music Bldg., CMU Power Plant office, CMU UC offices. Tchr. Jewish Sunday Sch., Mt. Pleasant, 1955-70; officer Child and Youth Study Clubs, Mt. Pleasant, 1963-73; mem. City Recreation Commn., Mt. Pleasant, 1963-73, Area Health Planning Coun., Mt. Pleasant, 1974-80; pres., vol. Hosp. Aux. Med. Care, Red Cross Blood Bank, United Fund Cancer Dr., Mt. Pleasant, 1960-80; storyteller pub. libr., Mt. Pleasant, 1957-79 Recipient Northwood U. Artist award, Midland Ctr. for Arts, Mich., 2002. Mem.: Brass Latch Gallery, Art Reach Mid-Mich., Hilton Head Art League S.C. (Lifetime of Creative Excellence award 1998), Copley Soc. Boston (signature), Allied Artists Am. (Merit award 1996, Raymond H. Brumer Meml. award 1999), Nat. Mus. Women in Arts (charter), Salmagundi Club (Philip Isenberg award 1993, Pamela Singleton award 1997, Elliot Liskin Meml. award 1998, Anonymous award 1998, Peters Sculpture Materials award 2001, Alphaeus P. Cole Meml. award 2001, Meml. award 2003). Jewish. Avocations: lecturing, community work, tennis, presenting humorous programs, drums. Home: 1217 North Dr Mount Pleasant MI 48858-3226 Office Phone: 989-773-3873. Personal E-mail: fundametal2@webtv.net.

TRAISMAN, HOWARD SEVIN, retired pediatrician; b. Chgo., Mar. 18, 1923; s. Alfred Stanley and Sara (Sevin) T.; m. Regina Gallagher, Feb. 29, 1956; children: Barry D. Lifschultz, Edward S., Kenneth N. BS in Chemistry, Northwestern U., 1943, MB, 1946, MD, 1947. Intern Cook County Hosp., Chgo., 1946-47; resident in pediat. Children's Meml. Hosp., Chgo., 1949-51, attending physician divsn. endocrinology, 1951—2002; mem. faculty Med. Sch. Northwestern U., Evanston, Ill., 1951—2002, prof. pediat., 1973—2002, pres., 1999—2002; ret., 2002. Author articles in field, chpts. in books. Capt. M.C. AUS, 1943-46, 47-49. Recipient Alumni Merit award, 1995, Northwestern U., Alumni medal, 2005, Ravitch award, 2007. Mem. Am. Diabetes Assn. (Disting. Svc. award 1976), Am. Pediatric Soc., Am. Acad. Pediat., Endocrine Soc., Lawson Wilkins Pediatric Endocrine Soc., AMA, Midwest Soc. Pediatric Rsch., Ill. Med. Soc., Chgo. Pediatric Soc., Chgo. Med. Soc., Inst. Medicine Chgo. Democrat. Jewish. Office: 1325 Howard St Evanston IL 60202-3766 Office Phone: 847-869-4300.

TRAKAS, JAMES PETER, state legislator; b. Cleve., May 5, 1965; BA in Social Behavioral Sci., The Ohio State U., Columbus, 1987. Materials mgr. Allied Color Industries, Inc., 1987—96; councilman-at-large City of Independence, 1992—96; CEO Vivid Polymas Technologies, Inc., 1997—98; rep., dist. 15 Ohio State Ho. Reps., Columbus, 1999—2002, rep., dist. 17, 2003—. Mem. fin. and appropriations com. Ohio State Ho. Reps., mem. rules and ref. com., mem. state govt. com., mem. higher edn. subcom. Chair Rep. Party, Cuyahoga County, 1996—, mem. exec. com. Named one of Outstanding Young Men of Am., 1989. Mem.: Cleve. Mus. Art, Western Res. Hist. Soc., City Club of Cleve., Kiwanis Club, Independence, Order of the AHEPA. Republican. Greek Orthodox. Office: Ohio State House Reps 77 S High St 14th Fl Columbus OH 43215-6111

TRALDI, LORENZO, mathematician, educator; b. Rome, May 22, 1955; arrived in U.S., 1955; s. Giuseppe Alberto Traldi, Ila Dawson Little, Charles Little (Stepfather); m. Sharon Richter; children: Arthur, Matthew, Oliver, Rebecca. BA, CUNY, Flushing, NY, 1976; PhD, Yale U., 1980. Asst. prof. Lafayette Coll., Easton, Pa., 1980—86, assoc. prof., 1986—94, prof., 1994—2001, Marshall R. Metzgar prof. math., 2001—. Contbr. articles and revs. to profl. jours. Grantee, Lafayette Coll., 1983, 1987, 1991, 1996, 1997, 2000—07, USAF Office Sci. Rsch., 1991—92, NSF, 1994, 2001, 2003, 2005, 2008. Mem.: IEEE, Inst. for Combinatorics and its Applications, Am. Math. Soc. Independent. Home: 725 Coleman St Easton PA 18042 Office: Dept Math Lafayette Coll Easton PA 18042 Office Phone: 610-330-5276. Business E-Mail: traldil@lafayette.edu.

TRAMMEL, DENISE, science educator; b. Cin., Oct. 28, 1952; d. Benjamin Thomas and Imogene Gilbert; m. James L. Trammel, June 17, 1972; children: Mindy Rae Trammel Moore, James Thomas. BS in Edn., Miami U., Oxford, Ohio, 1980; MEd, Wright State U., Dayton, Ohio, 1987. Cert. tchr. kindergarten - elem. Ohio, lic. gifted and talented grades 1-12 Ohio. Clk. Goodyear, Sharonville, Ohio, 1971; inventory Wickes Furniture, Sharonville, 1971; sec. order svc. GE, Blue Ash, Ohio, 1971—76; substitute tchr. Kings Mills Sch. Dist. Mason City Schs., Mason, Kings Mills, West Chester, Ohio, 1981—83; tchr. Little Miami Sch. Dist., Morrow, Ohio, 1983—88, Mason City Schs., 1988—. 4th grade sci. chairperson Mason City Schs., 1994—2006, ednl. enrichment for kids in sci., 1996—2006. Named Warren County Conservation Tchr. of Yr., 1998; grantee, Western Row Sch. Mem.: Nat. Sci. Tchr. Assn. Republican. Baptist. Avocations: camping, boating, taking cruises, playing piano.

TRAMMELL, BRADLEY ELLIS, lawyer; b. Opelika, Ala., Jan. 11, 1961; s. Herman Bruce and Laura Elizabeth Trammell; m. Katherine Farrell McClintock, Apr. 11, 1992; children: William McClintock, Henry Ellis. BA cum laude, U. of South, Sewanee, Tenn., 1983; JD, U. Ala., Tuscaloosa, 1989. Bar: Tenn. 1989, Ala. 1991. Acct. exec. Travelers Ins. Co., Plantation, Fla., 1983—86; shareholder Baker, Donelson, Bearman, Caldwell & Berkowitz, Memphis, 1989—, chair Memphis office recruiting com., 2002—06. Campaign chmn. Travelers South Fla. offices United Way, 1984; chmn. ann. ptnrs. campaign Downtown YMCA, Memphis, 1993; jr. warden St. John's Episcopal Ch., Memphis, 2002, vestry mem., 2001—03. Mem.: ABA, Memphis Bar Assn. Young Lawyers (bd. dirs. 1991—93), Memphis Bar Assn., Ala. Bar Assn., Tenn. Bar Assn., Omicron Delta Kappa. Office: Baker Donelson Bearman Caldwell & Berkowitz 165 Madison Ave Ste 2000 Memphis TN 38103 Office Phone: 901-577-2121. Office Fax: 901-557-0781. Business E-Mail: btrammell@bakerdonelson.com.

TRAMMELL, CATHERINE LOUISE, language educator; b. New Castle, Pa., July 31, 1941; d. Russell Karl and Beatrice Willette Muder; m. Richard Louis Trammell, Jan. 10, 1985; children: John Kent, Julia Kate McGill, Mark Edward. BA, Allegheny Coll., Meadville, Pa., 1963; MA, Middlebury Coll., Vt., 1964; Propedeutique, Sorbonne, Paris, 1964; PhD, U. Pitts., 1970. Lectr. French New U. Ulster, Londonderry, Northern Ireland, 1971—72; asst. prof. French Westminster Coll., New Wilmington, Pa., 1977—81; prof. French Grove City Coll., Pa., 1981—. Mem.: MLA, AATF, ACTFL. Home: 151 N Liberty-Plain Grove Rd Grove City PA 16127 Office: Grove City Coll 100 Campus Dr Grove City PA 16127 Business E-Mail: trammellcm@gcc.edu.

TRAMMELL, JERRY POWELL, literature and language educator; s. Fred D. and Virginia Rose Trammell; m. Sandra Lynn Martin, Dec. 31, 1972; children: Lou Ann, Paula Rose Bohannon, Martin Kenley. AB in English, Berea Coll., Ky., 1965; PhD in English, Ohio U., Athens, 1968. Prof. English dept. Ohio U., 1965—73; legislative analyst Ky. Legislature, Frankfort, 1974—78; adminstr. U. Louisville, 1976—81; asst. to the v.p. Ky. State U., Frankfort, 1981—. Author: (novels) Stripping Room; The Shimmering Cage (hon. mention, Tenn. Writers Guild, 2007). Grant, Ohio U., 1972. Avocations: poetry, chess. Office: Ky State Univ Hwy 60 E Frankfort KY 40601 Business E-Mail: jerry.trammell@kysu.edu.

TRAMMELL, KENNETH R., automotive executive; married; 2 children. BBA in acctg., U. Houston. Cert. CPA Tex. Sr. mgr. Arthur Andersen LLP; asst. contr. Tenneco Automotive, 1996—97, corp. contr., 1997—99, v.p., contr., 1999—2003, sr. v.p., CFO Lake Forest, Ill., 2003—. Office: Tenneco Automotive 500 N Field Dr Lake Forest IL 60045

TRAMONTE, MICHAEL ROBERT, retired education educator; AB in Sociology, Boston Coll., 1960; EdM, State Coll. Boston, 1963; Cert. Advanced Edn. Specialization, Boston Coll., 1971; Comprehensive Cert. in Paralegal Studies, Bentley Coll., 1982; EdD in Human Devel. and Edn., Boston U., 1986. Lic. psychologist health svc. provider, ednl. psychologist, cert. social worker, cert. tchr. social studies grades 9-12, moderate spl. needs tchr., sch. psychologist, guidance counselor, sch. psychologist N.H., Mass., nat. ret. sch. psychologist. Substitute tchr. Medford (Mass.) Pub. Schs., 1960-61, jr. H.S. tchr. social studies, 1961-68; instr. psychology and edn. Anna Maria Coll., 1968-69; adj. instr. psychology Mass. Bay C.C., 1972—77, Middlesex C.C., 1977—; sch. psychologist Lowell (Mass.) Pub. Schs., 1970-98; assoc. prof. edn. Rivier Coll., Nashua, NH, 1998—2008; ret., 2008. Adj. prof. edn. Rivier Coll., 1983, 87-98; spkr. in field. Chmn. Medford chpt. Greater Boston Assn. Retarded Children, 1969-70; vol. spkr. support groups Mass. chpt. Nat. Multiple Sclerosis Soc., 1971-88; mem. ARC Disaster Svcs. Human Resources Sys. Recipient certificate, Medford Mental Health Assn., 1968, Medford chpt. Greater Boston Assn. Retarded Children, 1970, Mass. chpt. Nat. Multiple Sclerosis Soc., 1979, Faculty award for secondary edn., Rivier Coll., 1994, Faculty Emeritus award, cert. of recognition, ARC of Mass. Bay, 1999, 2000, 2002, 2005; named Sr. Mary Jane Benoit Outstanding Educator of Yr. award, River Coll., 2008. Fellow: America Acad. Experts in Traumatic Stress.

TRAMONTINE, JOHN ORLANDO, retired lawyer; b. Iron Mountain, Mich., Sept. 21, 1932; s. Orlando F. and Susan M. (Hollar) Tramontine; m. Nancy A. McCabe, July 14, 1956; m. Darby S. Macfarlane, June 30, 2006; 1 child, Margaret A. BSChemE, U. Notre Dame, 1955; postgrad., Georgetown U., 1956—58; LLB, NYU, 1960. Bar: N.Y. 1960, U.S. Dist. Ct. (no. dist.) Ill. 1963, U.S. Dist. Ct. (so. and ea. dists.) N.Y. 1965, U.S. Ct. Appeals (2d and 5th cirs.) 1967, U.S. Supreme Ct. 1970, U.S. Ct. Appeals (8th cir.) 1970, (3d cir.) 1973, (7th cir.) 1976, (fed. cir.) 1979, U.S. Dist. Ct. (we. dist.) N.Y. 1981. Examiner

U.S. Patent Office, 1956-58; patent agt. Arthur, Dry & Dole, NYC, 1958-60; assoc. Arthur, Dry, Kalish, Taylor & Wood, NYC, 1960-62, Wolfe, Hubbard, Voit & Osann, Chgo., 1962-63, Fish & Neave, NYC, 1963-70, ptnr., 1970-2000; ret., 2000. 2nd lt. USMCR, 1955. Fellow Am. Coll. Trial Lawyers, Am. Bar Found.; mem. Assn. of Bar of City of N.Y. (chmn. patent com. 1974-77), N.Y. Intellectual Property Law Assn. (pres. 1985-86), St. Andrews Golf Club (sec. 1981-83). Office: Ropes & Gray LLP 1211 Avenue Of The Americas New York NY 10036-8704

TRAMONTO, RICK, chef; b. Rochester, NY; m. Gale Gand. Grill/saute cook The Scotch & Sirloin; chef Strathallen; garde-mgr. chef Tavern on the Green, NYC, 1985; line cook Gotham Bar & Grill; chef Aurora, The Pump Room, Chgo., Scoozi!, Chgo., 1987, Avanzare, Chgo., Charlie Trotter's, Chgo., 1989, Stapleford Park Hotel, London; owner, chef Trio, 1993—95, Tru, Chgo., 1999—, Brasserie T., Chgo.; ptnr. Cenitare Restaurants, 2005—. Bd. mem. Culinary Vegetable Inst.; mem. nat. bd. chefs Am. Culinary Inst. Recipient Outstanding Svc. award, James Beard Found., 2007; named one of America's Best New Chefs, Food & Wine mag., 1994, Am.'s rising Star Chefs, Robert Mondavi, 1995.

TRAMUTOLA, JOSEPH LOUIS, lawyer, educator; b. Union City, NJ, Mar. 6, 1931; s. Joseph Emil and Elda (Brioli) T.; m. Mary Ann Banull, Sept. 4, 1965; children Karen, Kim, Karla. BA, St. Peter's Coll., Jersey City, 1953; JD, Fordham U., 1959. Bar: N.J. 1961. Atty. Toolan, Haney, Romand, Perth Amboy, N.J.; prof. law Fairleigh Dickinson U., Madison, N.J., 1965—, creator, dir. ednl. program for older persons, 1972-2001, ret., 2001. Pre-legal advisor Silberman Coll. bus., Fairleigh Dickinson U.; cons. Am. Coun. on Edn., Washington, Am. Edn. Assn., Washington, Thomas Edison Coll., Trenton, N.J., Chartered Pub. Underwriters, East Orange, N.J., USDA; adj. faculty U. Mich., dir. Fairleigh Dickinson U. Patent Inst. dir. ednl. seminars on student law; seminar dir. student law, Calif., Ill., Mass., N.Y., Ga. Co-author: Guide Book for Student Rights, Legal Perspective for Student Personal Administration, Legal Overview of the New Student; dir. CPA Law Rev. With U.S. Army, 1955-57. Named Outstanding Educator Outstanding Educators Inc., 1973, 1974, Commendation for Civic Contb. N.J. Legis., 1993. Roman Catholic. Avocations: clock making, gardening, zymology, music, photography. Home: 12 Browning Ct Mendham NJ 07945-3301 Home Fax: 973-543-4049. Personal E-mail: jltramutola@aol.com.

TRAN, HUONG MAI, editor-in-chief; b. Vietnam; Editor-in-chief Việt Nam News, Hanoi, Vietnam, 1999—. Office: Viet Nam News Vietnam News Agy 11 Tran Hung Dao St Hanoi Vietnam Office Phone: 84 4 9332314, 84 903404147. Office Fax: 84 4 9332312. Business E-Mail: vnnews@vnagency.com.vn. E-mail: tmhuong06@gmail.com.

TRAN, JUDITH THUHA, psychiatrist; arrived in US, 1975; d. Phuong Nguyen and Ailien Huynh; children: Christopher Baoquoc, STephen Anhkhoa. BS in Biology, Tex. U., San Antonio, 1990; MD, Temple U., Phila., 1994. Intern Pa. Hosp., Phila., 1995—96, resident, 1996—99, chief resident, 1998—99; asst. dir. Friends Hosp. Crisis Response Ctr., 1999—2000; med. dir. Friends Hosp., 2000—03, Mercy Hosp. Phila. Crisis Response Ctr., 2003—. Recipient Merit award, Pa. Hosp., 1998—99. Mem.: Phila. Psychiat. Soc. (com. mem. 1999), Am. Psychiat. Assn. Avocations: reading, dance, swimming. Office: Mercy Hosp Phila 501 S 54th St Philadelphia PA 19143 Office Phone: 215-748-9525.

TRAN, KHANH T., insurance company executive; BA in Econ. and Polit. Sci., Whittier Coll.; MBA in Fin. and Mktg., UCLA. With United Calif. Bank, Flying Tiger Line, Inc.; asst. treas. Vons Cos., Inc.; treas. Pacific Life Ins. Co., Newport Beach, Calif., 1990—91, v.p., treas., 1991—95, v.p. corp. develop., treas., 1995—96, sr. v.p., CFO, 1996—2001, exec. v.p., CFO, 2001—. Mem.: ACLI (CFO Conf.). Office: Pacific Life Ins Co PO Box 9000 Newport Beach CA 92658-9030

TRAN, LIEN, military officer; s. Nu Ly and Xuan Tran. BS in Biochemistry with honors, UC Davis, Calif., 2003. Postgrad. rschr. UC Davis, 2001—06; 2nd lt. USAF, Sacramento, 2007—. Contbr. scientific papers to profl. jours. Mem.: UC Cal Aggie. Achievements include research in cerebral blood flow. Home: 9548 Meadow Cliff Ct Elk Grove CA 95758 Home Phone: 916-670-6814. Personal E-mail: tjiq@hotmail.com.

TRAN, LONG TRIEU, industrial engineer; b. Saigon, Vietnam, Oct. 10, 1956; arrived in US, 1973; s. Nguyen Dinh and Thiet Thi (Nguyen) Tran; m. Khanh Thi-Hong Phan, Aug. 3, 1988. BSME with honors, U. Kans., 1976; MSME, MIT, 1980; MBA with honors, U. Louisville, 1993. Cert. quality engr., mfg. engr., project mgmt. profl. Tchg. asst. U. Kans., 1975-76, U. Calif., Berkeley, 1977; rsch. asst. Lawrence Berkeley Labs., 1977, MIT, 1977-80; libr. staff Harvard U. Med. Sch. Libr., 1977-78; mem. staff New England Deaconess Hosp., Boston, 1978-80; prodn. programming engr. GE, Cleve., 1980-81, advanced mfg. engr. Louisville, 1981-82, quality sys. engr., 1982-84, quality control engr., 1984-86, sr. quality info. equipment engr., 1986-89, sr. quality indsl. engr., 1990-94, sr. supplier tech. assistance engr., 1995-96, sr. advanced supplier quality engr., 1996-98, program mgr. purchased material quality, 1999, combo blackbelt leader supplier quality, 1999-2000, Six Sigma program mgr., 2000—02, sr. purchased material quality engr., 2003—. Exec. advisor Jr. Achievement, Inc., Louisville, 1983—84; monitor/reader Rec. for Blind, 1994—; fundraiser Dream Factory Inc., 1994—. Vol. NCCJ, 1994—, Clothe-A-Child, 1993—, Dare-To-Care, 1994—, Ronald McDonald House, 1994—. Mem.: ASME, AAAS, Heritage Found., Am. Assn. Individual Investors, Ctr. for Positive Thinking, Cato Inst., Ctr. Positive Thinking, Indsl. Computing Soc. (founding), N.Y. Acad. Scis., Am. Mgmt. Assn., Robotics Internat. (charter), Robot Inst. Am., Am. Prodn. and Inventory Control Soc., Computer and Automated Sys. Assn. (charter), Am. Soc. Quality Control, Instrument Soc. Am. (sr.), Soc. Mfg. Engrs. (sr.), U.S. Libr. Congress Assocs. (founding), Nat. Pks. Conservation Assn. (founding), Assn. Compassion (life), Internat. Platform Assn., PGA Tour Ptnrs. Club, Handyman Club Am. (life), Sigma Xi, Beta Gamma Sigma, Phi Kappa Phi, Tau Beta Pi, Pi Tau Sigma. Republican. Achievements include research in grinding processes and material surface analysis, mfg. project mgmt., supplier quality mgmt. Home: 3642 Windward Way Louisville KY 40220-1818 Office: Gen Electric Co Appliance Park AP1-162A Louisville KY 40225-0001 Home Phone: 502-458-9535; Office Phone: 502-452-7082. Business E-Mail: long.tran@ge.com.

TRAN, NAM VAN, secondary school educator; b. Ben Tre, Vietnam, Nov. 18, 1939; s. Ut Van and Thoi Thi Tran; m. Thu Ngoc Nguyen, June 26, 1969; children: Tawny Thuan Tran Huot, Tim, Scott Toai. Degree in pedagogy, U. Saigon, Vietnam, 1967, BA, 1973. H.s. tchr., Vietnam, 1967—81; with Micrographics Inc., Cerritos, Calif., 1985—92, Catalina Inc., Commerce, Calif., 1992—95; printer Lucky and Happy Inc., San Gabriel, Calif., 1995—2002; bookkeeper Todd and Katie Inc., City of Industry, Calif., 2003—07. Author: Essays on the South Vietnam Literature Before 1975 and on the Vietnamese Poetry in Oversea, 2006; contbr. poetry and essays in mag. and newspapers.

TRAN, NANG TRI, research scientist, electrical engineer, entrepreneur; b. Binh Dinh, Vietnam, Jan. 2, 1948; came to the U.S., 1979, naturalized, 1986; s. Cam Tran and Cuu Thi Nguyen; m. Thu-Huong Thi Tong, Oct. 14, 1982; children: Helen, Florence, Irene, Kenneth. BSEE, Kyushu Inst. Tech., Kitakyushu, Japan, 1973, MSEE, 1975; PhD in Materials Sci./Solid State Device, U. Osaka Prefecture, Sakai, Japan, 1979. Rsch. assoc. U. Calif. Irvine, 1979; engr., rsch. scientist Sharp Electronics, Irvine, 1979-80; sr. rsch. scientist Arco Solar Industries, Chatsworth, Calif., 1980-84; sr. rsch. specialist, group leader 3M Co., St. Paul, 1985-96; sr. staff scientist Imation Corp., Oakdale, Minn., 1996—2007; exec. Khanti Inc., Am. Thin Films Ecosolar, 1996—2007. McKnight disting. vis. prof. Ho Chi Minh Nat. U., U. Minn., Mpls., adj. prof.; cons., lectr. Japan industry mgmt.; reviewer NSF; sr. advisor to Vietnamese univs. Author: (poetry) My Journey; contbr. articles to profl. jours. Mem. tech. com. various internat. confs. Recipient R&D awards, Photonic Cir. Excellence award; fellow, Govt. South Vietnam, Japan, USAID, Rotary Internat., 1968—79. Mem. IEEE (sr.), Japan Soc. Applied Physics, N.Y. Acad. Scis. Achievements include invention of direct digital x-rays for chest and mammography, transparent conducting zinc oxide doped with group III elements which has become the standard electrode material in many thin film solar cells; thin film transistors on flexible substrate; structured phosphors; copper indium diselenide and selenium-based solar cells; roll-to-roll coating, in line patterning; patents in field; research in amorphous silicon solar cells; image sensors; solid state memory; photoconductors; CD; high density data storage media; diamond like carbon evaporated lubricant; transparent conducting oxide films. Office: Univ Minn Inst Tech 200 Union St SE 4-174 D EE C Sci Bldg Minneapolis MN 55455 Office Phone: 612-378-2710. Business E-Mail: tranx051@umn.edu.

TRAN, QUI-PHIET, English educator; b. Dalat, Vietnam, Jan. 6, 1937; came to U.S., 1972; s. But Qui and Anh Nguyen Thi Tran; m. Ngan Vo Thi, Aug. 30, 1963; children: Hung, Thuy, Long, Kien. BA, U. Hue, Vietnam, 1960; MA, U. Tex., 1974, PhD, 1977. English tchr. Votanh H.S., Nhatrang, Vietnam, 1960-64, Petrus Ky H.S., Saigon, Vietnam, 1964-65; instr. English U. Hue, 1965-72, U. Tex., Austin, 1977-78; resource specialist Arlington (Va.) Pub. Schs., 1980-81; asst. prof., then assoc. prof. Schreiner U., Kerrville, Tex., 1982-90, prof. English, 1990—2002, prof. emeritus, 2002—. Document analyst Congl. Info. Svc., Washington, 1979-80; refugee resettlement cons. Ctr. for Applied Linguistics, Washington, 1980-81, Action, U.S. Govt., Washington, 1982; Fulbright lectr. Nat. U. Vietnam, Ho Chi Minh City, 1999-2000. Author: William Faulkner, 1980; contbr. articles to profl. publs. Advisor Vietnamese Parents Assn., Arlington, 1980-81. Grantee Mellon Found., 1983, NEH, 1983, 89, Am. Coun. Learned Socs., 1984-85. Mem. MLA, Fulbright Assn. Avocation: gardening. Home: 15842 Clayton Bend Dr Houston TX 77082-4077 Personal E-mail: qui-phiet.tran@fulbrightmail.org.

TRAN, QUOC-HUNG, psychiatrist; b. Hue, Vietnam, July 12, 1964; s. Qui-Phiet Tran and Ngan T. Vo; m. Thuy-Linh Nguyen, Apr. 26, 1992; children: Minh, Van. BS Summa Cum Laude, Tex. Luth. U., 1984; MD, U. Tex., Galveston, 1991. Lic. Tex. Med. Bd., 1995, General Psychiatry Am. Bd. Psychiatry and Neurology, 1996, Child and Adolescent Psychiatry Am. Bd. Psychiatry and Neurology, 2000. Ind. cons. Carbomedics, Inc., Austin, Tex., 1984; nat. facilitator Asian Pacific Islander Inst., Ctr. of Substance Abuse Prevention, HHS, Washington, 1994—95; pres. Quoc-Hung Tran MD PA, 2001—, Dallas Psychiat. Assocs., Dallas, 2001—. Pres. MinhVan Found., Houston, 1996—; co-founder, dir. VDV Media Corp., Dallas, 2000—; dir. Asian Am. Family Counseling Ctr., Houston, 1995; founder Vietnamese Am. Youth Orgn., 1990—2000. Organizer Vietnamese New Yr. Festival, Houston, 1991—92. Recipient Leadership award, AMA, 1995, Physician Recognition award, 2002; named America's Top Psychiatrist award, Consumers' Rsch. Coun. Am., 2004—05; Minority Rsch. Tng. Mini fellow, Am. Psychiat. Assn., 1994. Mem.: Am. Acad. of Child and Adolescent Psychiatry. Buddhist. Office: Dallas Psychiat Assocs 17736 Preston Rd Ste 100 Dallas TX 75252 Office Fax: 972-248-2012. Business E-Mail: ghtranmd@dallaspsychiatry.com.

TRAN, SON CAO, computer science educator; b. Nam Dinh, Vietnam, July 23, 1962; s. Ung Tat Tran and Lang Thi Nguyen; m. Thanh Thi Hong Nguyen; children: Trang Thu, Tra Thanh. PhD in Computer Engrng., U. Tex., El Paso, 2000. Postdoctoral rschr. Stanford (Calif.) U., 2000—01; asst. prof. N.Mex State U., Las Cruces, 2001—. Office: NMex State U MSC CS PO Box 30001 Las Cruces NM 88003

TRAN, TAMMIE, language educator; MA in Linguistics, Calif State U., Fullerton, 2003. With U. Calif., Irvine, Golden West Coll., Huntington Beach. Recipient Outstanding TESOL Leadership award, Alliant Internat. U., 2006.

TRAN, THOMAS L., health products executive; B in Acctg., Seton Hall U., South Orange, NJ; MBA in Fin., NYU, NYC. V.p. fin., contr. CIGNA Healthcare; CFO Blue Cross and Blue Shield Mass.; sr. v.p., CFO ConnectiCare, Inc.; sr. v.p., CFO Uniprise UnitedHealth Group; pres., COO, CFO Careguide, Inc.; sr. v.p., CFO WellCare, 2008—. Office: WellCare Group 8725 Henderson Rd Renaissance One Tampa FL 33634 Office Phone: 813-290-6200.*

TRANGHESE, MICHAEL A., sports association executive; b. Springfield, Mass. m. Susan Huntemann. Grad., St. Michael's Coll., Winooski, Vt., 1965. Sports info. dir. Am. Internat. Coll., 1965—72, Providence Coll., 1972—79; with Big East Conf., 1979—81, asst. commr., 1981—90, conf. commr., 1990—. Chair NCAA Men's Basketball Com., 1996—2001; former chair Divsn. I-A Commissioners, Collegiate Commissioners Assn., NCAA Men's Basketball Subcom. on TV; lead adminstr. Bowl Championship Series. Recipient Met. award, Nat. Assn. Basketball Coaches, 2002, Vanguard award, Cox Sports TV, 2007; named to Athletic Hall of Fame, St. Michael's Coll., 1996. Office: Big East Conf 222 Richmond St Ste 110 Providence RI 02903

TRANI, EUGENE PAUL, university president, educator; b. Bklyn., Nov. 2, 1939; s. Frank Joseph and Rose Gertrude (Kelly) T.; m. Lois Elizabeth Quigley, June 2, 1962; children: Anne Chapman, Frank. BA in History with honors, U. Notre Dame, 1961; MA, Ind. U., 1963, PhD, 1966. Instr. history Ohio State U., Columbus, 1965-67; asst. prof. So. Ill. U., Carbondale, 1967-71, assoc. prof., 1971-75, prof., 1975-76; asst. v.p. acad. affairs, prof. U. Nebr., 1976-80; prof., vice chancellor acad. affairs U. Mo. Kansas City, 1980-86; prof., v.p. acad. affairs U. Wis. System, 1986-90; pres. Va. Commonwealth U., 1990—; pres. bd. dirs. Va. Biotech Rsch. Park, 1992-97, chmn., 1997—; pres., chmn. VCU Health Sys., 2000—. Vis. asst. prof. U. Wis., Milw., 1969; bd. dirs. Met. Richmond SunTrust Mid-Atlantic Bank, Universal Corp., LandAm. Fin. Group, Inc.; mem. commn. Internat. Edn. Am. Coun. Ed., 1991—; bd. gov. Ctr. Russian Am. Bus., Washington, 1993-98; adv. coun. on Grad. Studies and Rsch., U. Notre Dame, 1994—, NASULGC, 1980—, chair commn. on internat. affairs, 1993-94; vis. prof. Univ. Coll., Dublin, 2002; bd. advisors Inst. for U.S. Studies, U. London, 1993-99; cons. in field. Author, editor: Concerns of a Conservative Democrat, 1968, The Treaty of Portsmouth: An Adventure in American Diplomacy, 1969; (with Donald E. Davis) The First Cold War, 2002; (with David Wilson) The Secretaries of the Department of the Interior, 1849-69, 1975; The Presidency of Warren G. Harding, 3d edit., 1989; contbr. articles to profl. jours., newspapers; book reviewer. Permanent mem. Coun. Fgn. Rels., N.Y.C., 1979—; bd. dirs. Richmond Ballet, 1991-96, NCCJ, Richmond, 1991-94, Va. Spl. Olympics, 1991-96, YMCA of Greater Richmond, 1992—, Richmond Renaissance, 1992-96, 2001—, chmn., 2001—; bd. dirs. Met. Bus. Found., 1992-98, Va. Tech. Fund Found., 1993--, Met. Bus. League, 1994--; mem. U.S. Savs. Bond Vol. Com., chmn. higher edn. area, 1992-93; adv. bd. Greater Richmond chpt. ARC, 1992—; mem. Gov.'s Commn. Info. Tech. in Va., 1998-2000; bd. dirs. Collegiate Sch., 1998—; adv. bd. Black History Archives Project, 1992-96; bd. dirs. Va. Ctr. for Innovative Tech., 1990-96, Capital Area Assembly, 1990-93, Richmond Symphony, 1991-94, Richmond Symphony Coun., 1995—; mem. coun. advisors Christian Children's Fund, 1992-95; mem. Ctrl. Richmond Assn., 1992-96; bd. trustees Va. Hist. Soc., 1994-96, Theatre Va., 1994-97, Richmond Children's Mus., 1994—, World Affairs Coun. of Greater Richmond, 1999-2003; bd. dirs. Sci. Mus. of Va. Found., 1994—, Va. Tech. Fund Found., 1993—, Met. Bus. Hague, 1994—; mem. Gov.'s Biotech. Initiative Adv. Bd., 2002—; bd. dirs. Qatar Found. for Edn. Sci. Comm. Devel., Va. Tech. Fund Found., 1993—. Fellow Russian and East European Inst., 1964-65, Nat. Hist. Publs. Commn., 1969-70, Woodrow Wilson Internat. Ctr. Scholars, 1972-73, So. Ill. U. Sabbatical Leave, 1975-76, Coun. Internat. Exchange Scholars, 1981, U. Mo. Faculty, 1981; grantee U.S. Dept. Interior Rsch., 1965-66, So. Ill. U. Office Rsch. and Projects, 1967-74, Am. Philos. Soc., 1968, 72, So. Ill U. Summer Rsch. 1970, 72, 75, Lilly Endowment, 1975-76, Sloan Commn. Govt. and Higher Edn., 1978, USIA Am. Participants Program, 1984-86, 88, 90; Inst. for U.S. Studies fellow U. London, 1995, fellow commoner St. John's Coll., Cambridge, 1998; recipient Younger Humanist award NEH, 1972-73, Leadership and Achievement award Ctrl. Richmond Assn., 1992, Biotech. Leadership award Va. Biotech. Assn., 1999; recipient Disting. Leadership award, Nat. Assn. Cmty. Leaders, 1994, Richmond Humanitarian award, NCCJ, 1995, Flame Bearer of Edn. award Coll. Fund/UNCF, 1998, Richmond Joint Engrs. Coun. Cmty. Svc. award, 2002; named Style Mag. Richmonder of Yr., 1998, Person of Yr., Fifty Plus Mag., 2004, Crystal Ball Spl. Honoree, Arthritis Found. Ctrl. Va. Chpt., 2005; Hope award, Nat. MS Soc., 2003, others. Mem. Internat. Inst. Strategic Studies, Am. Assn. Advancement Slavic Studies, Orgn. Am. Historians, Soc. Historians Am. Fgn. Rels., Greater Richmond C. of C. (bd. dirs. 1991-96, chmn. 1997-98), Phi Kappa Phi. Roman Catholic. Avocations: reading, travel, basketball, golf. Office: Va Commonwealth U Box 842512 910 W Franklin St Richmond VA 23284-2512 E-mail: etrani@vcu.edu.

TRANI, JOHN M., former consumer products company executive; b. NYC, 1945; B in Aerospace Engring., Bklyn. Poly. Inst., 1966, M in Indsl. Mgmt., Ops. Rsch. With GE, 1978—97; pres., CEO GE Med. Svcs. divsn. GE Co., 1986—97; chmn., CEO Stanley Works, New Britain, Conn., 1997—2003. Home: 30 Stanford Dr Farmington CT 06032 Office Phone: 860-674-3764. E-mail: jmtrani@hotmail.com, john@johnmtranille.com.

TRANQUADA, ROBERT ERNEST, retired internist, educator; b. LA, Aug. 27, 1930; s. Ernest Alvro and Katharine (Jacobus) Tranquada; m. Janet Martin, Aug. 31, 1951; children: John Martin, Katherine Anne, James Robert. BA, Pomona Coll., 1951, DSc (hon.), 2007; MD, Stanford U., 1955; DSc. (hon.), Worcester Poly. Inst., 1985. Diplomate Am. Bd. Internal Medicine. Intern in medicine UCLA Med. Center, 1955—56, resident in medicine, 1956—57; resident Los Angeles VA Hosp., 1957—58; fellow in diabetes and metabolic diseases UCLA, 1958—59; fellow in diabetes U. So. Calif., 1959—60, asst. prof. medicine, 1960—63, assoc. prof., 1964—68, chmn. dept. community medicine, 1967—70; med. dir. Los Angeles County/U. So. Calif. Med. Center, 1969—74; assoc. dean U. So. Calif. Sch. Medicine, 1969—76; regional dir. Central Region, Los Angeles County Dept. Health Services, 1974—76; assoc. dean Sch. Medicine U. Calif., LA, 1976—79; chancellor and dean U. Mass. Med. Sch., 1979—86; dean Sch. Medicine U. So. Calif., 1986—91, prof. medicine, 1986—92, Norman Topping/Nat. Med. Enterprises prof. med./pub. policy, 1992—97; prof. emeritus, 1997—. Mem, chair L.A. County Task Force on Health Care Access, 1992—94. Corporator Worcester Art Mus., 1980—86; mem. Ind. Commn. on L.A. Police Dept., 1991—92; governing bd. LA County Local Initiative Health Authority, 1994—2007, chmn., 2001—05; bd trustees Pomona Coll., 1969—, vice chmn., 1971—79, chmn., 1991—2000, emeritus chmn., 2000—; bd. fellow Claremont U. Ct., 1971—79, 1991—2000; chmn. bd. overseers Claremont U. Consortium, 2000—06, emeritus chmn. bd. overseers, 2006—; vice-chmn., bd. trustees Keck Grad. Inst. Applied Life Scis., 1997—2000, emeritus, 2000—; bd. dirs. Nat. Med. Fellowships, Inc., 1973—2005, chmn., 1980—85; bd. trustees Charles Drew U. Med. and Sci., 1968—79, 1986—95, Orthopaedic Hosp., 1986—91, Barlow Hosp., 1987—89; bd. dirs. Worcester Acad., 1984—86, U. So. Calif. Univ. Hosp., 1988—91, Alliance for Childrens Rights, 1991—95, Cmty. Health Coun., Inc., 1993—, Good Hope Med. Found, 1994—, chmn., 2006—; bd. dirs. Ralph M. Parsons Found., 2000—, vice chmn., 2008—; bd. dirs. Huntington Med. Rsch. Inst., 2006—, Congl. Homes, Inc., Mt. San Antonio Gardens, 2006—; mem. coun. pres. Assn. Governing Bodies Colls. and Univs., 2000—03, chair, 2002—03; bd. trustee Alta Med. Health Svc., 2008—. Fellow Milbank Found., 1967—72. Fellow: AAAS, Am. Antiquarian Soc.; mem.: Inst. Medicine of Nat. Acad. Scis., Calif. Med. Assn., L.A. Acad. Medicine, L.A. County Med. Assn., AMA, Alpha Omega Alpha, Sigma Xi, Phi Beta Kappa.

TRANSOU, LYNDA LOU, advertising art administrator; b. Atlanta, Dec. 11, 1949; d. Lewis Cole Transou and Ann Lynette (Taylor) Putnam; m. Lue Gregg Loso, Oct. 25, 1991. BFA cum laude, U. Tex., 1971. Art dir. The Pitluk Group, San Antonio, 1971, Campbell, McQuien & Lawson, Dallas, 1973-74, Bozell & Jacobs, Dallas, 1974-75; art dir., ptnr. The Assocs., Dallas, 1975-77; art dir. Belo Broadcasting, Dallas, 1977-80; creative dir., v.p. Allday & Assocs., Dallas, 1980-85; owner Lynda Transou Advt. & Design, 1986—. Recipient Merit award, N.Y. Art Dirs. Show, 1980, Gold award, Dallas Ad League, 1980, Silver award, 1980, 1981, 1982, 2 Merit awards, Houston Art Dirs. Club, 1978, Dallas Ad League, 1986, Merit award, Broadcast Designers Assn., 1980, Merit awards, Dallas Ad League, 1978, 1987, Silver award, Houston Art Dirs. Show, 1982, Gold award, Tex. Pub. Rels. Assn., 1985, N.Y. One Show, 1982, Creativity awrd, Art Direction mag., 1986, Print award, Regional Design Annual, 1988, 2 Gold Adrian awards, 1997, Katy award, Dallas Press Club, 2001. Dallas Soc. Visual Comm. (Bronze award 1980, Merit award 1978-86), Delta Gamma (historian 1969-70).

TRAPANE, RUTH, educator, artist; b. Danville, Pa., July 18, 1945; d. Richard L. and Oda M. (Sager) Day; m. Mar. 21, 1965 (div. 1983); children: Michael W., Timothy R.; m. Philip B. Trapane, Aug. 23, 1985; stepchildren: Sean, Philip, Bridget. BS, Bloomsburg U., Pa., 1967, MS, 1975, MA, 1990. Grad. asst. Bloomsburg U., 1989; tchr. Berwick Elem. Sch., Pa., 1967—96, Pa., 1990—. Speaker 1st European Space Art Symposium & Exhibitor, Montrieux, Switzerland, 1992, tour India 6 wks., 1994; space art exhibitor Spaceweek Internat., 1994, Art on Mir Space Station, First Exhibit in Space, 1995-96, Art to the Stars (Ars Ad

Astra) 1996-98, Nova Southeastern U. Author curriculum guides; exhibited in Internat. Encaustic Art Show, Nebr., 1989, Selinsgrove, Pa., 1990 (People's Choice award 1990), Cheney, Wash., 1991, Gagarin Collaboration, Moscow, 1990, 25th Anniversary Apollo, 1994, Harrisburg Capitaol Show, 2008, State Reprentive Art Exhbn., 2008. Mem. Internat. Assn. Astron. Artists, Susquehanna Art Mus., North Mt. Art League. Independent. Avocations: online and mystery computer games, interior design, video authoring. Home: 2211 Shasta Dr Bloomsburg PA 17815-8902 Personal E-mail: rotpbt@verizon.net.

TRAPANI, JOHN G., JR., philosophy professor; b. Maspeth, NY, May 24, 1946; s. Margaret K. Trapani; m. Sherry L. Wheeler; children: Lia Schmitt, Josef, Rachel, Lauren. BA, Boston Coll., Chestnut Hill, Mass., 1968; PhD, St. Johns U., Jamaica, NY, 1984. Prof. philosophy Walsh U., North Canton, Ohio, 1974—, chair, humanities divsn., 1994—2006. Author: (book) Truth Matters. Founder, dir. The John Trapani Big Band, North Canton, 1977. With US Army, 1969—71. Decorated Am. Spirit of Honor; recipient Outstanding Educator of Yr. award, Walsh U., 1990, 1995, Outstanding Tchr. award, Northeast Ohio Coun. on Higher Edn., 2004. Mem.: Am. Jacques Maritain Assn. (nat. pres.). Roman Catholic. Avocations: music, travel, reading, writing. Home: 5664 Linder Circle NE Canton OH 44721 Office: Walsh Univ 2020 E Maple Canton OH 44720 Business E-Mail: jtrapani@walsh.edu.

TRAPP, A. C., retired music educator; b. Chase, La., Dec. 4, 1930; s. A. Clayton and Jessie Mae (Stigall) Trapp; m. Beatrice Horn (separated); children: A. Clayton III, Jonathan L. B in Piano Performance and Vocal Suprervision, Northeast Coll.; M, Northwestern State U., 1961. Music supr. Catahoula Parish, 1957; music tchr. DOD, 1959. Judge Nat. Guild of Piano Tchrs. Exhibitions include Delgado Mus., New Orleans, 1956. Corp. US Army, 1952—54. Named to Hall of Fame, Am. Coll. Musicians, Austin, Tex., 2006. Republican. Episcopalian. Home: 501 S Grand Apt 319 Monroe LA 71201 Personal E-mail: atc124@bellsouth.net.

TRAPP, PETER JARL RUDOLF, investment manager; b. Darlington, Eng., Oct. 5, 1945; arrived in U.S., 1971; s. Jarl Rudolph and Olive Lindsay (Fairley) Trapp; m. Regina Thomas, Sept. 6, 1969 (div. Dec. 1986); children: Sophia Antoinette, Alexander Rudolf, Olivia Henrietta Elizabeth; m. Georgette A. Farkas, June 4, 2005 (div. Sept. 2008). Mi-Lic, Fribourg U., Switzerland, 1971; MBA, Columbia U., 1973. V.p. First Boston Corp., NYC, 1973-78, Goldman Sachs & Co., NYC, 1978—81; mgr. dir. Dean Witter Reynolds Inc., NYC, 1982-84; mgr. dir., exec. officer Marine Midland Bank N.A., NYC, 1985-89; sr. v.p. Gerard Klauer Mattison & Co., NYC, 1990-94; mgr. dir. Needham & Co., NYC, 1994—2003; exec. v.p. Needham Investment Mgmt., NYC, 1998—2003; founding ptnr. Bifrost Ptnrs. LLC and Bifrost Fund LP, White Plains, NY, 2003—. Cadet sgt. Swedish Army, 1968—69. Mem.: Coral Beach (Bermuda), Annabel's (London), The Leash (NY). Avocations: skiing, fishing, shooting, farming. Office: Bifrost Ptnrs LLC 50 Main St Ste 1000 White Plains NY 10606 Home: 525 E 72nd St New York NY 10021 Personal E-mail: pt@bifrostcapital.com.

TRASK, THOMAS EDWARD, religious organization administrator; b. Brainard, Minn., Mar. 23, 1936; m. Shirley Burkhart; children: Kimberly, Bradley, Todd, Tom. BA, North Ctrl. Bible Coll., 1956, DDiv (hon.), 1994. Ordained min. Assemblies of God, 1958. Pastor First Assembly of God, Hibbing, Minn., 1956-60, pastor Vicksburg, Mich., 1960-64; Mich. dist. youth and Sunday sch. dir. Assembly of God, 1964-68; pastor First Assembly of God, Saginaw, Mich., 1968-73, Brightmoor Tabernacle, Southfield, Mich., 1976-88; supt. Mich. Dist. Coun., Dearborn, 1973-76; gen. treas. The Gen. Coun. Assemblies of God, Springfield, Mo., 1988-93, gen. supt., 1993—2007. Co-author: Back to the Altar: A Call to Spiritual Awakening, 1994, Back to the Word, A Call to Biblical Authority, 1996, The Battle: Defeating the Enemies of Your Soul, 1997, The Blessing: Experiencing the Power of the Holy Spirit Today, 1998, The Choice: Embracing God's Vision in the New Millennium, 1999, The Fruit of the Spirit, 2000, Ministry for a Lifetime, 2001. Mem. Assemblies Of God Ch.

TRASVIÑA, JOHN DAVID, federal agency administrator; b. 1958; AB, Harvard U., Cambridge, Mass., 1980; JD, Stanford U. Law Sch., Calif., 1983. Dep. city atty. City of San Francisco, 1983—85; legis. atty. Mex. Am. Legal Def. and Ednl. Fund, 1985—87, pres., gen. counsel, 2006—09; legis. counsel to Senator Paul Simon US Senate, Washington, 1987—93, subcom. gen. counsel & staff dir., Senator Paul Simon, 1993—97; spl. counsel, immigration related unfair employment practices & dep. asst. atty. gen. legis. affairs US Dept. Justice, Washington, 1997—2001; dir. Discrimination Rsch. Ctr., Berkeley, LA; prof. immigration law Stanford U. Law Sch.; asst. sec. for fair housing & equal opportunity US Dept. Housing & Urban Devel. (HUD), Washington, 2009—. Mem. San Francisco Elections Commn.; pres. Harvard Club San Francisco; bd. mem. La Raza Lawyers Assn., CORO No. Calif., Lowell HS Alumni Assn., League Women Voters, Pacific Coast Immigration Mus., Campaign for Coll. Opportunity. Recipient Mexican Am. Legal Def. & Ednl. Fund award for Excellence in the Legal Profession, 2000, Conf. on Asia Pacific Am. Leadership Disting. Svc. award, 2000; named one of The 100 Most Influential Hispanics in the US, Hispanic Bus. mag., 1995. Democrat. Office: US Dept Housing & Urban Devel (HUD) 451 7th St SW Washington DC 20410*

TRATTNER, LAURA V., retired middle school educator; b. Cleve., Oct. 26, 1955; d. Harold and Carol Elaine Trattner. BS in Edn., Bowling Green State U., Ohio, 1977; MA in Edn., Baldwin-Wallace U., Berea, Ohio, 1981. Math. tchr. Parma City Schs., Ohio, 1978—2007; ret., 2007. Grantee 3 mini grants, Parma City Schs., 1995—96. Democrat. Jewish. Avocations: gardening, aquacise, dance. Personal E-mail: ltrattner@roadrunner.com.

TRATTNER, WALTER IRWIN, humanities educator, educator; b. NYC, July 26, 1936; s. Samuel and Minnie T.; m. Joan Driscoll, July 8, 1958; children: Stephen Lawrence, Anne Elizabeth, David Chase. BA, Williams Coll., 1958; MAT, Harvard U., 1959; MS, U. Wis., 1961, PhD, 1964. Asst. prof. history No. Ill. U., DeKalb, 1963-65; from asst. prof. to assoc. prof. history U. Wis., Milw., 1965-72, prof. history, 1972—98, prof. emeritus, 1998—. Author: Homer Folks: Pioneer in Social Welfare, 1968, Crusade for the Children: A History of the National Child Labor Committee, 1970, Social Welfare in America: An Annoted Biography, 1983, Social Welfare or Social Control?: Some Historical Reflections on Regulating the Poor, 1983, Biographical Dictionary of Social Welfare in America, 1986, From Poor Law to Welfare State: A History of Social Welfare in America, 6th edit., 1999; contbr. articles to profl. jours. Recipient numerous grants for rsch. Mem. Am. Hist. Assn., Orgn. Am. Historians, Am. Studies Assn., Nat. Conf. Social Welfare. Avocations: reading, travel, tennis, racquetball, biking. Home: 10639 N Magnolia Dr Mequon WI 53092-5055 Office: Univ Wis Milw Dept History 314 Holton Hall Milwaukee WI 53201

TRAUB, ADAM, librarian; b. Rochester, NY, Nov. 4, 1981; s. Thomas and Helen Traub. Bachelors in English Lit., Nazareth Coll., Rochester, 2004; Masters in Libr. Sci., U. Buffalo, 2005. Assoc. libr. Strong Nat. Mus. Play, Rochester, 2006—07; sys. libr. St. John Fisher Coll., 2007—. Sys. mentor Info. Delivery Svcs. Project, Geneseo, NY, 2007—. Recipient Recognition award, Ctr. Devel. Human Svcs., 2005. Office: St John Fisher Coll 3690 East Ave Rochester NY 14618

TRAUB, BARBARA GELLIS, law librarian; BA, SUNY, Buffalo, 1973, JD, 1978; MLS, LIU, Brookville, NY, 1994. Bar: NY 1978. Assoc. Albrecht, Maguire, Heffern & Gregg, PC, Buffalo, 1978—80; catalog editor White Plains Pub. Libr., NY, 1989—90; indexer, abstracter Towers Perrin, Valhalla, NY, 1990—91; reference libr. Pace U. Sch. Law, White Plains, NY, 1992—97, Columbia U. Sch. Law, NYC, 1998, St. John's U. Sch. Law, Jamaica, NY, 1998—2001, head reference & instrnl. svcs., 2001—. Mem.: Law Libr. Assn. Greater NY, Am. Assn. Law Librs. (chair, recruitment com. 2006—08). Office: St John's Univ Sch Law 8000 Utopia Parkway Jamaica NY 11439

TRAUBER, STEPHEN M. (STEVE TAUBER), investment banker; b. Jan. 20, 1962; m. Leticia F. Tauber. BS in Econ., Managerial Studies, Rice U., 1984; MBA, Northwestern U. With Credit Suisse First Boston, 1988—95; mng. dir. energy group Morgan Stanley, Houston, 1995—2003; vice chmn., global head, energy group UBS Investment Bank, Houston, 2003—. Chmn. Houston Econ. Devel. Adv. Com. Pres. Houston Soc. Performing Arts; bd. dir. Theatre Under the Stars, Hobby Center for the Performing Arts, River Oaks Baptist Sch., Greater Houston Partnership; bd. overseers Jones Bus. Sch., Rice Univ. Named a Top Dealmaker, Dealmaker mag., 2006, Top Rainmaker for energy/power, 2007. Office: UBS Energy Investment Banking 1000 Main St Houston TX 77002 Office Phone: 713-655-0075.

TRAUGER, ALETA ARTHUR, judge; BA in English magna cum laude, Cornell Coll., Iowa, 1968; MAT, Vanderbilt U., 1972, JD, 1976. Tchr., Tenn., Eng., 1970-73; assoc., law clk. Barrett, Brandt & Barrett, P.C., Nashville, 1974-77; asst. U.S. atty., first asst., chief of criminal divsn. Mid. Dist. Tenn., 1977-82, No. Dist. Ill., 1979-80; assoc. Hollins, Wagster & Yarbrough, P.C., Nashville, 1983-84; legal counsel Coll. of Charleston, SC, 1984-85; counsel, ptnr. Wyatt, Tarrant, Combs, Gilbert & Milom, Nashville, 1985-91; judge Tenn. Ct. of the Judiciary, 1987-93; chief of staff Mayor's Office, Nashville, 1991-92; bankruptcy judge U.S. Bankruptcy Ct. (mid. dist.) Tenn., Nashville, 1993-98; dist. judge U.S. Dist. Ct. (mid. dist.) Tenn., Nashville, 1998—. Mem. hearing panel bd. profl. responsibility Tenn. Supreme Ct., 1983-84, mem. adv. com. on rules of civil and appellate procedure, 1989-96; lectr. Vanderbilt U. Sch. Law, 1986-88, mem. Law Sch. alumni bd., 1989-92; master of bench Harry Phillips Am. Inn of Ct., 1990-94; mem. Internat. Women's Forum, 1993—, v.p. Tenn. chpt., 1996-97; trustee Cornell Coll., 1998-2007. Bd. dirs. Nashville Inst. for Arts, 1992-99, Miriam's Promise (adoption agy.), 1995-98, Renewal House, 1996-98; mem. Vanderbilt Law Sch. Nat. Coun., 2004-. Fellow: Nashville Bar Found., Tenn. Bar Found. (life), Am. Bar Found. (life); mem.: FBA (v.p. 1983—84, 1985—86), ABA, Dist. Judges Assn. 6th Cir. (pres. 2008—09), Nat. Conf. Bankruptcy Judges (chmn. ethics com. 1994—98), Fed. Judges Assn., Nat. Assn. Women Judges (liaison to ABA commn. on the status of women in the profession 2000—01), Tenn. Lawyers Assn. for Women (v.p. 1988—89, pres. 1989—90, bd. dirs. 1990—91), Lawyers Assn. for Women (pres. 1982—83, bd. dirs. 1983—84, 1986—88), Nashville Bar Assn. (bd. dirs. 1984, 1989—91). Office: 825 US Courthouse 801 Broadway Nashville TN 37203-3816 Office Phone: 615-736-7143.

TRAUGOTT, ELIZABETH CLOSS, linguist, educator, researcher; b. Bristol, Eng., Apr. 9, 1939; d. August and Hannah M. M. (Priebsch) Closs; m. John L. Traugott, Sept. 26, 1967; 1 child, Isabel. BA in English, Oxford U., Eng., 1960; PhD in English Lang., U. Calif., Berkeley, 1964. Asst. prof. English U. Calif., Berkeley, 1964-70; lectr. U. East Africa, Tanzania, 1965-66, U. York, Eng., 1966-67; lectr., then assoc. prof. linguistics and English Stanford (Calif.) U., 1970-77, prof., 1977—2003, chmn. linguistics dept., 1980-85, vice provost, dean grad. studies, 1985-91, mem. grad. record examinations bd., 1989-93, mem. test of English as a fgn. lang. bd., 1990—92, chmn. test of English as a fgn. lang. bd., 1991—92. Mem. higher edn. funding coun. Eng. Assessment Panel, 1996, 2001, 08. Author: (book) A History of English Syntax, 1972; author: (with Mary Pratt) Linguistics for Students of Literature, 1980; author: (with Paul Hopper) Grammaticalization, 1993, rev. edit., 2003; author: (with Richard Dasher) Regularity in Semantic Change, 2002; author: (with Laurel J. Brinton) Lexicalization and Language Change, 2005; editor (with ter Meulen, Reilly, Ferguson): (book) On Conditionals, 1986; editor: (with Heine) Approaches to Grammaticalization, 2 vols., 1991; series co-editor: Topics in English Linguistics; contbr. articles to profl. jours. Am. Coun. Learned Socs. fellow, 1975—76, Guggenheim fellow, 1983—84, Ctr. Advanced Study Behavioral Scis. fellow, 1983—84. Fellow: AAAS, Brit. Acad. (corr.); mem.: AAUW, MLA, AAUP, Internat. Soc. Linguistics English (pres. 2007—08), Internat. Pragmatics Assn. (bd. dirs. 2000—), Internat. Soc. Hist. Linguistics (pres. 1979—81), Linguistic Soc. Am. (pres. 1987, sec.-treas. 1994—98). Office: Stanford Univ Dept Linguistics Bldg 460 Stanford CA 94305-2150 Business E-Mail: traugott@stanford.edu.

TRAUGOTT, PETER S., television producer, broadcast executive; b. 1964; V.p. Brillstein-Grey TV, 1996—2005, pres., 2005—. Actor: (TV series) Party of Five; (films) Silent Men, 2005; exec. prodr.: (TV series) Numb3rs, Way Downtown, 2002, My Big Greek Fat Life, 2003, The Showbiz Show With David Spade, 2005, Jake in Progress, 2005, Girls on the Bus, 2006, 52 Fights, 2006, Mr. Nice Guy, 2006, Cracking Up, 2006, Sam I Am, 2007, Frangela, 2007, See Jayne Run, 2007. Named a Maverick, Details mag., 2007. Office: Brillstein Grey Entertainment 9150 Wilshire Blvd Ste 350 Beverly Hills CA 90212 Office Phone: 310-275-6135. Office Fax: 310-275-6180.

TRAUNER, GARY, entrepreneur; m. Terry Trauner; children: Benjamin, Aaron. Grad., Colgate U., Hamilton, NY; MBA, NYU Stern Sch. Bus., NYC. V.p. fin. Teton Trust Co., Wyo.; co-founder, CFO OneWest-.net, Wyo., Cell Response Formulation, LLC, Wyo. At-large candidate US House of Reps., 2006; past chmn. Teton County Sch. Dist. #1 Bd. Trustees; chmn. Aspens Water & Sewer Dist.; former vice-chmn. Teton County Pathways Task Force; mem. open range com. Jackson Hole Land Trust. Democrat. Office: Cell Response Formulation LLC PO Box 7396 4115 S Pub Pl Jackson WY 83002 Office Phone: 307-734-7839. Office Fax: 307-734-4667.

TRAURIG, ROBERT HENRY, lawyer; b. Waterbury, Conn., June 9, 1925; s. Samuel and Lillian (Rosengarten) T.; m. Jacqueline Block; children: Madeline Traurig Sackel, Wendy Traurig Perlin. Student, U. Fla.; BBA, U. Miami, Fla., 1947, LLB, 1950. Bar: Fla. 1950, U.S. Dist. Ct. Fla. 1950. Co-founder, ptnr., shareholder environ. land devel. Greenberg, Traurig LLP, (formerly Greenberg Traurig, Hoffman, Lipoff, Rosen & Quentel, P.A.), Miami, 1967—. Pres. Greater Miami Opera, 1987-89. Lt. USNR, 1943-46, 51-52. Recipient Friend of Israel Humanitarian award, Greater Miami Jewish Fedn., 2003; named one of 100 Most Powerful People in Miami, Miami Bus. mag., 2001. Mem. Greater Miami C. of C. (chmn.). Democrat. Jewish. Avocation: avid sports spectator. Office: Greenberg Traurig LLP 1221 Brickell Ave Miami FL 33131-3224 Office Phone: 305-579-0500. Office Fax: 305-579-0717. Business E-Mail: traurigr@gtlaw.com.

TRAUTMAN, DONALD WALTER, bishop; b. Buffalo, June 24, 1936; Attended, Our Lady Angels Sem., Niagara Falls, NY, Cath. U., Washington; Licentiate in Sacred Theology, U. Innsbruck, Austria, 1962; Licentiate in Scripture, Pontifical Biblical Inst., Rome, 1965; DST, St. Thomas Aquinas U., Rome, 1966; LHD (hon.), Canisius Coll., Buffalo, 1977; degree (hon.), Niagara U., 1986. Ordained priest Diocese of Buffalo, 1962, chancellor, 1973, vicar gen., 1974, aux. bishop, 1985—90; adminstr. St. Frances Cabrini Parish, Collins, NY; assoc. pastor Holy Family Parish, Buffalo; instr. St. John Vianney Sem. (now Christ the King Sem.), 1966—73, dean students, rector; ordained bishop, 1985; bishop Diocese of Erie, 1990—. Contbr. articles to The Bible Today. Named a Prelate of Honor, 1975. Mem.: Nat. Conf. Cath. Bishops, US Conf. Cath. Bishops. Roman Catholic. Office: Diocese of Erie 429 E Grandview Blvd Erie PA 16514-0397 Office Phone: 814-824-1120. Office Fax: 814-824-1124.

TRAUTMANN, NANCY E., language educator; d. Ralph F. and Betty Schauer; m. David Trautmann, June 18, 1977. MA in English Lit., Lehigh U., Bethlehem, Pa., 1979. Prof. English Northampton CC, Bethlehem, 1979—. Office: Northampton CC 3835 Green Pond Rd Bethlehem PA 18020

TRAUTMANN, THOMAS ROGER, history professor, anthropology educator; b. Madison, Wis., May 27, 1940; s. Milton and Esther Florence (Trachte) T.; m. Marcella Hauolilani Choy, Sept. 25, 1962; children: Theodore William, Robert Arthur. BA, Beloit Coll., 1962; PhD, U. London, 1968. Lectr. in history Sch. Oriental and African Studies, U. London, 1965-68; asst. prof. history U. Mich., Ann Arbor, 1968-71, assoc. prof., 1971-77, prof., 1977—, Richard Hudson rsch. prof., 1979, prof. history and anthropology, 1984—, chmn. dept. history, 1987-90, Steelcase rsch. prof., 1993-94, dir. Inst. Humanities, Mary Fair Croushore prof. humanities, 1997—2002, Marshall D. Sahlins coll. prof. history and anthropology, 1997—. Author: Kautilya and the Arthasastra, 1971, Dravidian Kinship, 1981, Lewis Henry Morgan and the Invention of Kinship, 1987; author: (with K.S. Kabelac) The Library of Lewis Henry Morgan, 1994; author: (edit. with Diane Owen Hughes) Time: Histories and Ethnologies, 1995, Aryans and British India, 1997; author: (edit. with Maurice Godelier and Franklin Tjon Sie Fat) Transformations of Kinship, 1999, Languages and Nations: The Dravidian Proof in Colonial Madras, 2006, The Clash of Chronologies, 2009; editor: Comparative Studies in Society and History, 1997—2006; contbr. articles on India, kinship and history of anthropology;: The Aryan Debate, 2005. Sr. Humanist fellow NEH, 1984. Mem. Am. Anthrop. Assn., Assn. Asian Studies, Am. Inst. Indian Studies (mem. exec. com. trustee, sr. rsch. fellow in India 1985, 97), Phi Beta Kappa. Office: U Mich Dept History Ann Arbor MI 48109-1003

TRAUTNER, JOHN JAMES, real estate executive; b. Simpson, Minn., Dec. 4, 1935; s. John Sylvester and Oridena Francis (Baker) T.; m. Donna L. Jones, June 1960 (div. Dec. 1969); children: Theresa, Carrie, John; m. Carol Lee Rowberry, July 12, 1974 (div. May 1981); 1 child, Lindsey D.; m. Kathy N. Bucy, July 19, 1992; 1 stepchild, Victor. BA, Anchorage C.C., 1968; BBA, U. Alaska, 1970, MBA, 1998. Masters lic. 100 ton U.S. Coast Guard, lic. comml. pilot. Adminstr., pub. affairs RCA Svc. Co., Anchorage, 1965-70; dir. adminstrn. & pub. rels. Alyeska Resort, Inc., Girdwood, 1970-71; mgmt. cons. State of Alaska, 1972-73; exec. dir. City of Lost River (Alaska), 1973-74; v.p., gen. mgr. C. Bruce Ficke Investments, Girdwood, 1974-76; pres., gen. mgr. Gateway, Inc., Girdwood, 1976-85; CEO Alyeska Mgmt. Svcs., Inc., Girdwood, 1985—. Mem. MD49 Coun. Govs., Fairbanks, Alaska, 1996-97, chmn., 1999-2000; marriage commr. 3d Jud. Dist., Anchorage, 1973-93. Patentee in field. Chmn., mem. Girdwood Bd. Suprs., 1992-95; fire chief Girdwood Fire Dept., 1972-75; chmn. Girdwood Cmty. Coun., 1976-78, Jr.-Inter-Fraternity Coun., Seattle, 1957-58. Sgt. U.S. Army, 1953-64. Melvin Jones fellow, chgo., 1993-94. Mem. N.Am. Nature Photographers Assn., Am. Legion, Lions, Disabled VFW, Alaska Airmens Assn., San Francisco Tennis Club. Republican. Roman Catholic. Avocations: photography, music, art, humanitarianism, flying. Office: Alyeska Mgmt Svcs Inc PO Box 909 Girdwood AK 99587-0909 E-mail: outsidermining@msn.com.

TRAVERSE, LYN D., not-for-profit fundraiser, communications executive; b. Kalamazoo, Mich., May 7, 1952; d. Robert Clinton Traverse and Betty Larue Kemp; m. Jonathan G. Tidd (div.); 1 child, Emily. Student, NYU, 1970—74; BA, U. Conn., 1996. Devel. officer NYU, NYC, 1974—80, U. Hartford, Conn., 1980—83; dir. devel. and comms. Forman Sch., Litchfield, Conn., 1983—88, Ethel Walker Sch., Simsbury, Conn., 1988—96, The Nature Conservancy, Middletown, Conn., 1996—2000, Long Wharf Theatre, New Haven, 2000—03, Haskins Labs., New Haven, 2003—06; campaign dir. Friends Sem., NYC, 2006—. Trustee U. Hartford Art, West Hartford, Conn., 1999—; trustee, treas. Endangered Lang. Fund, New Haven, 2004—. Actor: (films) Plainsong, 1983. Mem. patrons bd. New Haven Free Pub. Libr., 2004—; mem. steering com. Simsbury (Conn.) Land Trust, 1999—2002. Mem.: Alpha Sigma Lamda. Office: Friends Seminary 222 E 16th St New York NY 10003

TRAVIS, JAY A., III, lawyer; b. McComb, Miss., June 8, 1940; s. J.A. and Katharine (Brennan) T., Jr.; m. Judith Thompson, Sept. 8, 1965; children: Kathy, John E., William. BBA, U. Miss., 1962, JD, 1965. Bar: Miss. 1965, US Dist. Ct. (so. dist.) Miss. 1967, US Ct. Appeals (5th cir.) 1970. Assoc. Thompson, Alexander & Crews, Jackson, Miss., 1967-69; ptnr. Butler, Snow, O'Mara, Stevens & Cannada, Jackson, 1969—. Chmn. Miss. Law Inst., 1974; pres. Estate Planning Coun. Miss., 1975-76. Mem. vestry, cathedral warden St. Andrew's Episc. Ch., 1983-87. Capt. JAGC, USAR, 1965-73; bd. dirs U. of Miss. Found., 1999-2007. Fellow Am. Coll. Trust and Estate Counsel (bd. regents, 1994-00, state chmn. 1987-92) Am. Coll. Trust and Estate Counsel Found. (bd. dirs. 2006—), Am. Bar Found.; mem. ABA (fellow young lawyers sect.), Miss. State Bar (pres. young lawyers sect. 1975-76), Miss. Bar Assn. (chmn. estates and trusts sect. 1987-88), Hinds County Bar Assn. (pres. 1988-89), Univ. Club, River Hills Club, Phi Delta Phi. Office: PO Box 22567 Jackson MS 39225-2567 Office Phone: 601-948-5711. Business E-Mail: jay.travis@butlersnow.com.

TRAVIS, JEREMY, academic administrator; b. Worcester, Mass., July 31, 1948; BA in Am. studies cum laude, Yale Coll., 1970; MPA, NYU, 1977, JD cum laude, 1982. Exec. dir. victim/witness assistance project Vera Inst. Justice, 1975—77; exec. dir. NYC Criminal Justice Agy., 1977—79; cons. NYC Bd. Correction, 1979—82; law clk. to Hon. Ruth Bader Ginsburg US Ct. Appeals (DC Cir.), 1982—83; spl. counsel to police commr. NYC Police Dept., 1984—86; spl. counsel to first dep. mayor and asst. dir. law enforcement services, Mayor's Office of Ops. City of NY, 1986, spl. advisor to mayor, 1986—89; chief counsel to subcommittee on criminal justice U.S. Ho. of Reps. Com. on the Judiciary, Washington, 1990; dep. commr. legal matters NYC Police

Dept., 1990—94; dir. Nat. Inst. Justice, US Dept. Justice, Washington, 1994—2000; sr. fellow Justice Policy Ctr., The Urban Inst., Washington, 2000—04; pres. John Jay Coll. of Criminal Justice CUNY, 2004—. Vis. lectr. Yale Coll., 1979; adj. prof. Wagner Grad. Sch. Pub. Svc., NYU, 1985-90; adj. assoc. prof., NY Law Sch., 1992-94; vis. prof., George Washington U., 2004; nat. adv. bd., program on State Crime Prevention Initiatives, Nat. Crime Prevention Coun., 2001-, Join Together program, Robert Wood Johnson Found., 2001-, Nat. H.I.R.E. Network, Legal Action Ctr., 2001-, Ctr. for Rsch. on Criminal and Mental Health, Rutgers U., 2002-; nat. adv. com. on Reclaiming Futures, Robert Wood Johnson Found., 2000-; adv. bd., Ctr. for Cmty. Safety, Winston-Salem State U., 2001-; Aspen Inst. Roundtable on Comprehensive Cmty. Initiatives, 1999-. Rockefeller Fellow, Yale Div. Sch., 1970-71; Marden and Marshall Fellow in Criminal Law, NYU Sch. Law, 1983-84; recipient Disting. Alumnus Award, NYU, 1986, Outstanding Pub. Svc. Award, NY County Lawyers Com., 1992, Edmund S. Randolph Award, US Atty. Gen., 2000, August Vollmer Award, Am. Soc. Criminology, 2002, Gerhard O.W. Mueller Award, Internat. Sect., Acad. Criminal Justice Sciences, 2003, Margaret Meade Award, Internat. Cmty. Corrections Assn., 2003. Mem.: NY State Bar. Office: CUNY John Jay Coll Criminal Justice 899 Tenth Ave New York NY 10019

TRAVIS, LAWRENCE ALLAN, accountant; b. Bloomington, Ill., Sept. 17, 1942; s. Willard Burns and Florence May (Harvey) T.; m. Katy Quinones, Apr. 16, 1965 (div. Feb. 1978); children: Lawrence Allan Jr., Matthew B.; m. Kathleen Lucas, May 20, 1995; stepchildren, Joseph Lucas, Sherry Piper. BS in Bus. Edn., Ill. State U., 1968; MA in Pub. Adminstrn., U. Ill., Springfield, 1976. CPA, Ill. Staff acct. Alexander Grant & Co., Chgo., 1969; internal auditor State Farm Ins., Bloomington, 1969-73; registered rep. Genworth Fin. Securities, 1994—; dep. dir. Ill. Dept. Ins., Springfield, 1973-74, state apptd. ofcl., 1973—74; audit mgr. Ill. Auditor Gen., Springfield, 1974-81; pres. bd. dirs. Lawrence Travis & Co., P.C., CPAs, Virden, Normal, Springfield and Jacksonville, Ill., 1979—. Pres., bd. dirs. Travco, Inc., Virden; v.p., bd. dirs. Ka-Lar Enterprises, Inc., Springfield, Miller Comm., Inc. V.p. bd. dirs. Ill. Common Cause, Springfield. Mem. AICPA, Assn. Govt. Accts., Ill. CPA Soc., Nat. Space Soc., Smithsonian Assocs., World Future Soc. Democrat. Roman Catholic. Avocation: sports. Home: 2409 Idlewild Dr Springfield IL 62704-5403 Office: Lawrence Travis & Co PC 1700 S 1st St Springfield IL 62704-3902 Personal E-mail: lawrencetraviscpa@comcast.net.

TRAVIS, LAWRENCE F., law educator; m. Patricia Ann Palmer, Dec. 29, 1973; children: Lawrence F., Christopher. PhD, SUNY, Albany, 1982. Rsch. analyst Nat. Parole Insts., Hackensack, NJ, 1976—78; rsch. dir. Oreg. State Bd. Parole, Salem, 1978—80; prof. U. Cin., 1980—. Author: (book) Introduction to Criminal Justice. Mem.: Acad. Criminal Justice Scis. (trustee). Office: Divsn Criminal Justice PO Box 210389 Cincinnati OH 45221-0389 Office Fax: 513-556-3303. Business E-Mail: lawrence.travis@uc.edu.

TRAVIS, NIGEL, food service executive; b. Woodford, Essex, Eng., 1950; m. Joanna Travis; 2 children. BA with honors in Bus. Studies, Middlesex U., London. With Kraft, Rolls Royce, Massey Ferguson, Parker Hannifin, Grand Metropolitan PLC; sr. v.p. human resources Burger King, Miami, Fla., mng. dir. Europe, Mid. East and Africa, 1991; v.p. Europe to sr. v.p. Europe Blockbuster, 1994—97, pres. internat., 1997—98; pres. worldwide stores divsn. Blockbuster Inc., 1998—2001, pres., COO, 2001—05; exec. v.p. Papa John's Internat. Inc., Louisville, 2005, pres., CEO, 2005—08; CEO Dunkin' Brands, Inc., Canton, Mass., 2009—. Bd. dirs. Bombay Co., Inc, 2000—, Papa John's Internat. Inc., 2005—08, Lorillard, Inc., 2008—. Office: Dunkin' Brands Inc 130 Royall St Canton MA 02021*

TRAVIS, ROBERT M., lawyer; b. Lyons, Ga., Dec. 12, 1945; BA, Univ. NC, Chapel Hill, 1968; JD, Univ. Ga., 1972. Bar: Ga. 1972. Ptnr., chmn. Litig. Dept. Powell Goldstein LLP, Atlanta. Editor (assoc.): Ga. Law Rev. Vice chmn. bd., chmn. devel. com. YMCA, Ga.; mem. Episcopal Diocese Atlanta Registrar, 1988—90. Mem.: ABA, State Bar Ga., Def. Rsch. Inst., Ga. Def. Lawyers Assn. (pres.), Atlanta Bar Assn., Lawyers Club Atlanta, Bleckley Inns of Ct. (Master), Assn. Trial Lawyers Am. (assoc.), U. NC Alumni Assn. (life), YMCA (vice chmn. bd. Ga. chpt., chmn. devel. com.), Phi Delta Phi. Office: Powell Goldstein LLP 1 Atlantic Ctr 14th Fl 1201 W Peachtree St NW Atlanta GA 30309-3488 Home Phone: 404-315-0089; Office Phone: 404-572-6646. Office Fax: 404-572-6999. Business E-Mail: btravis@pogolaw.com.

TRAVIS, TRACEY THOMAS, retail executive; MBA in Fin. and Ops. Mgmt., Columbia U. With Pepsi, 1987—97; CFO Rexam Beverage Can Ams., 1997—99; v.p. fin., CFO Intimate Brands, Inc., 2001—02; sr. v.p. fin. Ltd. Brands, Inc., Columbus, Ohio, 2003—04; sr. v.p. fin., CFO Polo Ralph Lauren Corp., NYC, 2005—. Bd. dirs. Jo-Ann Stores, Inc. Office: Polo Ralph Lauren Corp 650 Madison Ave New York NY 10022*

TRAVIS, VANCE KENNETH, petroleum business executive; b. Coriander, Sask., Can., Jan. 30, 1926; s. Roy Hazen and Etta Orilla (Anderson) T.; m. Louise Mary, Nov. 30, 1948 (div. 1979); children: Stuart, Shirley, Gordon, Donald, Marian; m. Mildred Elaine, June 29, 1979; stepchildren: Susan, Nancy, Gordon, Sandra, Karen. Chmn. bd. Turbo Resources Ltd., 1970-83, Challenger Internat., 1977-83, Bankeno Mines Ltd., 1977-83, Queenston Gold Mines Ltd., Toronto, Ont., Canada, 1977-84, Health Risk Mgmt. Inc., Mpls., 1984-86, Triad Internat. Inc., 1985—96; dir. Health Resource Mgmt. Ltd., Edmonton, Alta., Canada, 1990-97. Bd. dirs. Vencap Equities Alta. Ltd., Edmonton, 1981-86, L.K. Resources Ltd., Calgary, 1973-84. Mem. Young. Pres.'s Orgn., Calgary, 1964-76, World Pres. Orgn. Recipient Presdl. pin Jr. Achievement, 1963, Best Pitcher award Petroleum Fastball League, 1955. Mem.: Calgary Petroleum Club. E-mail: kentravis@telus.net.

TRAVOLTA, JOHN, actor; b. Englewood, NJ, Feb. 18, 1954; s. Salvatore and Helen (Burke) T.; m. Kelly Preston Sept. 12, 1991; children: Jett (dec. Jan. 2, 2009), Ella Bleu. Actor: (TV series) Welcome Back Kotter, 1975-77; (TV movies) The Boy in the Plastic Bubble, 1976, Chains of Gold, 1991, Eye of an Angel, 1991; (films): Carrie, 1976, Saturday Night Fever, 1977 (Best Actor award Nat. Bd. Rev., 1977, Best Actor Acad. award nominee 1977, Best Actor 1st runner up Nat. Soc. Film Critics 1977, Best Actor 2nd runner up N.Y. Film Critics Circle 1977), Grease, 1978 (Golden Globe World Film Favorite 1978), Moment-By-Moment, 1978, Urban Cowboy, 1980, Blow Out, 1981, Staying Alive, 1983 (Male/Box Office Star of Yr., Nat. Assn. Theatre Owners Show East 1983), Two of a Kind, 1983, Perfect, 1985, The Dumb Waiter, 1987, The Experts, 1989, Look Who's Talking, 1989 (Male/Box Office Star of Yr., Nat. Assn. Theatre Owners ShowEast 1989), Look Who's Talking Too, 1990, The Tender, 1991, Shout, 1991, Look Who's Talking Now, 1993, Pulp Fiction, 1994 (Best Actor Acad. award nominee 1994, Best Actor award nominee Brit. Acad. Film and TV Arts 1994, Golden Globe Best Actor award nominee 1994, Best Actor award nominee SAG 1994, Best Actor award nominee Chgo. Film Critics 1994, Best Actor award nominee Comedy awards 1994, Best Actor award L.A. Film Critics 1994, Best Actor award Stockholm Film Festival 1993, Best Actor award London Film Critics Cir. 1994), Get Shorty, 1995, White Man's Burden, 1995, Broken Arrow, 1996, Phenomenon, 1996, Michael, 1996, Face Off, 1997, Mad City, 1997, She's So Lovely (also exec. prodr.), 1997, Primary Colors, 1998 (Golden Globe nominee), A Civil Action, 1998, General's Daughter, 1999, Battlefield Earth, (also prodr.) 2000, Lucky Numbers, 2000, Swordfish, 2001, Domestic Disturbance, 2001, Basic, 2003, The Punisher, 2004, Ladder 49, 2004, Be Cool, 2005, Lonely Hearts, 2006, Wild Hogs, 2007, Hairspray, 2007, (voice) Bolt, 2008, The Taking of Pelham 1 2 3, 2009; rec. artist album, 1976, 77; author: John Travolta Staying Fit, 1984, Propeller One-Way Night Coach: A Fable for All Ages, 1997. Involved with Fight for Kids. Recipient Best Male Vocalist Billboard award, 1976, Best Male Vocalist award Record World and Music Retail mag., 1976, Best Actor Golden Apple award Cue mag., Juno award Can. Acad. Rec. Arts and Scis., 1978, Golden Apple award 1998, Lifetime Achievement award British Acad. Film and TV Assn., 1998, Chgo. Internat. Film Festival, 1998, Palm Springs Internat. Film Festival, 1999, Alan J. Pakula award U.S. Broadcast Film Critics Assn., 1999,; nominated Best New Male Star Women's Press Club, 1976; named Man of Yr., Hasty Pudding Club, Harvard U., 1981. Office: c/o William Morris Agy 151 El Camino Dr Beverly Hills CA 90212*

TRAXLER, WILLIAM BYRD, JR., federal judge; b. Greenville, SC, May 1, 1948; s. William Byrd and Bettie (Wooten) Traxler; m. Patricia Alford, Aug. 21, 1972; children: William Byrd III, James McCall. BA, Davidson Coll., 1970; JD, U. SC, 1973. Assoc. William Byrd Traxler, Greenville, 1973—75; asst. solicitor 13th Jud. Ct., Greenville, 1975—78, dep. solicitor, 1978—81, solicitor, 1981—85, resident cir. judge, 1985—92; US Dist. judge Dist. of SC, Greenville, 1992—98; judge US Ct. Appeals (4th cir.), Greenville, 1998—, chief judge, 2009—. Recipient Outstanding Svc. award, Solicitors Assn., SC, 1987, Leadership award, Probation, Parole & Pardon Svcs., SC, 1990. Office: US Ct Appeals 300 E Washington St Ste 222 Greenville SC 29601-2431*

TRAYLOR, CHET D., state supreme court justice; b. Columbia, La., Oct. 12, 1945; s. John Hardy and Bernice (Bogan) T.; children: Mary Therese, Leigh Ann, Anna Marie. BA in Govt., N.E. La. State U., 1969; JD, Loyola U. Sch. of Law, 1974. Bar: La. Former La. State Trooper; former investigator La. Dept. of Justice Organized Crime & Racketering Unit; former legal advisor La. State Police Narcotics, Detectives & Intelligence Units; asst. dist. atty. Franklin Parish, 1975—76; judge 5th Jud. Dist. Ct., Franklin, Richland and West Carroll Parishes, La., 1985-97; assoc. justice La. Supreme Ct., 1997—2009. Founding bd. mem. Winnsboro Econ. Devel. Found.; mem. Rocky Mountain Conservation Fund. Military police investigator US Army. Mem. ABA, La. Bar Assn., La. Dist. Judges Assn., NRA (life), Franklin Parish Mental Health Assn. (past bd. dirs.), Winnsboro Lions Club (past bd. dirs.), Greenwings (founder John Adams chpt.). Methodist. Home: 5912 Saint Charles Ave M New Orleans LA 70115

TRAYNHAM, EARLE CAMPBELL, retired economics professor, dean; b. Greenville, SC, Jan. 29, 1944; s. Earle Campbell and Ruth Traynham; m. Patricia Ann Moffitt, Jan. 21, 1967; children: Andrew Britt, Miles Scott. BS, U. SC., Columbia, MBA, 1967, PhD, 1973. Prof. economics U. North Fla., Jacksonville, 1981—2008, assoc. dean, coll. bus. adminstrn., 1983—93, dean, Coggin Coll. Bus., 1993—2003, ECT disting. prof. bus. adminstrn., prof. economics, 2003—08, prof. economics emeritus, dean emeritus, 2008—. Econ. cons., Jacksonville, 1984—.

TRAYNHAM, JAMES GIBSON, chemist, educator; b. Broxton, Ga., Aug. 5, 1925; s. James G. and Eddie Louise (Greer) T.; m. Margaret A. Egert, 1948; children: David F., Peter C.; m. Gresdna A. Doty, 1980. Student, South Ga. Coll., 1942-43; BS, U. N.C., 1946; PhD, Northwestern U., 1950. Instr. Northwestern U., 1949-50; asst. prof. Denison U., 1950-53; mem. faculty La. State U., Baton Rouge, 1953—, prof. chemistry, 1963-88, prof. emeritus, 1988—, chmn. dept. chemistry, 1968-73, vice chancellor for advanced studies and rsch., dean Grad. Sch., 1973-81. Postdoctoral research fellow Ohio State U., 1951-53; oral history cons. Chem. Heritage Found., 1997-2002. Author: Organic Nomenclature: A Programmed Introduction, 1966, 6th edit., 2009; editor: Essays on the History of Organic Chemistry, 1987; contbr. articles to profl. jours. Bd. dirs. Council Grad. Schs. in U.S., 1981. Recipient Petroleum Research Fund-Am. Chem. Soc. Type D award Eidg. Technische Hochschule, Zurich, Switzerland, 1959-60; Charles E. Coates award Baton Rouge sects. Am. Chem. Soc. and Am. Inst. Chem. Engrs., 1965; NATO sr. fellow in sci. Universität des Saarlandes, Saarbrücken, Fed. Republic Germany, 1972; named to Hall of Distinction, La. State U. Coll. Basic Scis., 2007 Mem. Am. Chem. Soc. (past councilor, past chmn. Baton Rouge sect., chmn. divsn. history of chemistry 1988), La. Acad. Sci., Internat. Union Pure and Applied Chemistry (former titular mem. commn. on nomenclature of organic chemistry, sec. 1994-99), Phi Beta Kappa, Sigma Xi, Phi Lambda Upsilon, Phi Kappa Phi (past pres. La. State U. chpt.). Home: 122 Highland Trace Dr Baton Rouge LA 70810-5061 Fax: 225-769-7801. Personal E-mail: jimtraynham@msn.com.

TRAYNHAM, LURENE JONES, retired secondary school educator; b. Yazoo City, Miss., July 11, 1925; d. Thomas McKinley and Olivia Purvis Jones; m. Young Robinson (dec.); m. William H. Traynham (dec.); 1 child, Thomas Jefferson Jones. BS, Alcorn State U., Lorman, Miss., 1947; MEd, U. Ill., Urbana, 1958. Tchr. Madison County Tng. Sch., Canton, Miss., 1947—48, pub. schs., West Point, Miss., 1949—57, 1957—69, West Point High, 1969—71, Caldwell HS, Columbus, Miss., 1971—87; ret., 1987. Mem. dist. adv. bd. New Homemakers Am., Columbus, 1952—72; mem. internat. bd. fgn. students Miss. U. for Women, Columbus, 1978—82; mem. adv. bd. Future Homemakers Am., Jackson, Miss., 1972—87. Organizer Columbus Head Start, 1965. Recipient Cmty. Svc. award, Miss. Union Bapt. Ch., Columbus, 1987, Nat. Bapt. Women's Aux. award, So. Regional Conf., Columbus, 2004, cert. of leadership, Nat. Bapt. Conv., Balt., 2006. Mem.: Columbus Ret. Tchrs. Assn., Gamma Gamma Zeta (chaplain 1994—2006, organizer Amicac 1994, Disting. Dove award 2005). Democrat. Avocations: cooking, sewing, singing, travel, piano. Home: 1602 Martin Luther King Dr Columbus MS 39701

TRAYNOR, J. MICHAEL, retired lawyer; b. Oakland, Calif., Oct. 25, 1934; s. Roger J. and Madeleine (Lackmann) Traynor; m. Shirley Williams, Feb. 11, 1956; children: Kathleen Traynor DeRose, Elizabeth Traynor Fowler, Thomas. BA, U. Calif., Berkeley, 1955; JD, Harvard U., 1960; LLD (hon.), U. SC, Columbia, 2007. Bar: Calif. 1961, U.S. Supreme Ct. 1966. Dep. atty. gen. State of Calif., San Francisco, 1961—63; spl. counsel Calif. Senate Com. on Local Govt., Sacramento, 1963; assoc. firm Cooley Godward Kronish, LLP, San Francisco, 1963—69, ptnr., 1969—2004, sr. counsel, 2005—08. Adviser 2d Restatement of Conflict of Laws revs., 1988, 3d Restatement of Unfair Competition, 1988—95, 3d Restatement of Torts, Products Liability, 1992—98, Apportionment, 1994—99, 3d Restatement of Restitution and Unjust Enrichment, 1997—, Principles World Trade Law, 2008—; lectr. Boalt Hall Sch. Law U. Calif., 1982—89, 1996—98; chmn. Earthjustice Legal Def. Fund (formerly Sierra Club Legal Def. Fund), 1991—92; trustee EarthJustice Legal Def. Fund (formerly Sierra Club Legal Def. Fund), 1974—96. Mem. bd. overseers Inst. for Civil Justice RAND, 1991—97; bd. dirs. Environ. Law Inst., 1991—97, 1999—2005, Ecojustice Can. (formerly Sierra Legal Def. Fund), Canada, 1990—96. 1st lt. USMC, 1955—57, USMCR, 1957—63. Recipient John P. Frank award, 2004. Fellow: Am. Acad. Arts & Scis., Calif. Acad. Appellate Lawyers, Am. Assn. Advancement Sci. (life), Am. Bar Found. (life); mem.: Bar Assn. San Francisco (pres. 1973), Am. Law Inst. (coun. 1985—, pres. 2000—08, chair coun. 2008—). Home: 3131 Eton Ave Berkeley CA 94705-2713 Office Phone: 510-658-8839. Office Fax: 510-658-5162. Personal E-mail: mtraynor@traynorgroup.com.

TRAYNOR, KIRSTEN SHOSHANNA, research scientist; d. Gernot and Sandra Reiners; m. Michael Joseph Traynor. BA in English, Kenyon Coll., Gambier, Ohio, 2001; PhD in Biology, Ariz. State U., Tempe, 2008—. Ceo Image Design, Middletown, Md., 2001—. Photography, An Artist's Palette (First Pl., 2006). German Chancellor scholarship, Alexander von Humboldt Found., 2006—07, Director fellowship, Ariz. State U., 2008—. Office: Arizona State University 550 E Orange St Tempe AZ 85281 Personal E-mail: kirsten@kirstentraynor.com. E-mail: kstraynor@asu.edu.

TRCA, RANDY ERNEST, lawyer; b. Mason City, Iowa, Mar. 29, 1957; s. Ernest Edward and Emily (Hrubes) T. BS, N.W. Mo. State U., 1978; JD, U. Iowa, 1981, MBA, 1982. Bar: Iowa 1981, U.S. Dist. Ct. (no. and so. dists.) Iowa 1982. Pvt. practice law, Iowa City, 1981—. Mem. edn. com. Iowa City C. of C., 1982-88. Mem. Iowa State Bar Assn. Democrat. Roman Catholic. Avocations: golf, swimming, travel, culture. Office: 1232 E Burlington St Iowa City IA 52240-3212 Home: PO Box 3168 Iowa City IA 52244-3168 Home Phone: 319-338-3071; Office Phone: 319-354-8440. Personal E-mail: rtlawfirm@prodigy.net.

TREABA, DIANA OLGUTA, physician; b. Ludus, Romania, Nov. 20, 1966; arrived in US, 1999; d. Constantin and Eugenia Treaba; m. Zoltan Szabolcs Szilagyi, June 22, 2004. MD Summa cum laude, U. Medicine and Pharmacy, Targu-Mures, 1987—93. Diplomate Anatomic Pathology and Clin. Pathology Am. Bd. of Pathology, 2003, Hematology Am. Bd. of Pathology, 2004, Specialist in Anatomic Pathology Ministry of Health and Family/Romania, 1998. Intern dr. Clin. County Hosp., Targu-Mures, Romania, 1994—95; resident in anatomic pathology Dept. of Pathology, Clin. County Hosp., Targu-Mures, Romania, 1995—99; resident in anatomic pathology and clin. pathology Dept. of Pathology, Rush Presbyn. St. Luke's Med. Ctr., Chgo., 1999—2003; fellow in hematopathology Northwestern Meml. Hosp., Chgo., 2003—04; fellow in immunohistochemistry PhenoPath Laboratories, Seattle, 2004—. Fellow: US and Can. Acad. of Pathology; mem.: AMA, Am. Assn. of Clin. Pathologists (licentiate), Coll. of Am. Pathologists (licentiate). Christian Orthodox. Office: Miriam Hosp 164 Summit Ave Providence RI 02906 Business E-Mail: dtreaba@lifespan.org.

TREACY, GERALD BERNARD, JR., lawyer; b. Newark, July 29, 1951; s. Gerald B. Sr. and Mabel L. (Nesbitt) T.; m. Joyce M. Biazzo, Apr. 6, 1974. BA summa cum laude, Rider Coll., 1973; JD, UCLA, 1981. Bar: Calif. 1981, Wash. 1982, D.C. 1995. Tchr. English Arthur L. Johnson Regional H.S., Clark, NJ, 1973—77; with Tax Ct., 2008; assoc. Gibson, Dunn & Crutcher, LA, 1981—82; ptnr. Perkins Coie, Bellevue, Wash., 1982—94, McGuire Woods Battle & Boothe, McLean and Bellevue, 1994—96, Egger, Betts, Austin, Treacy, Bellevue, 1996—98; pvt. practice Bellevue and Poulsbo, Wash., 1998—; of counsel Montgomery Purdue Blankinship and Austin, Seattle, 2000—; founder, mgr., CEO CIBO Group Inc., 2008—. Chmn. bd. dirs. estate planning adv. bd. U. Wash., Seattle, 1990-92; presenter TV Seminar, Where There's a Will, PBS affiliate; founder mgr. ArcLine Consulting, LLC; founder, chmn. CIBO Group. Author: Washington Guardianship Law, Administration and Litigation, 1988, supplemented, 1991, 3d edit. supplemented, 2002-08, Supporting Organizations, 1996, 2d edit., 2002, Community Property, 2005; co-author: The CIBO CEO, 2008. Endowment fund com. Unitd Way, Seattle, 1987—89; exec. com. Wash. Planned Giving Coun., 1993—94, 1996—98; bd. dirs., adv. bd. ARC, Seattle, 1985—89, Arthritis Gift, 1987—89, Seattle Symphony, 1992, Seattle U., 1996; bd. dirs. Morning Light Found., Flow Chart Found., Eastside Lyric Theatre, Kitsap Opera, 2003—04; founder, prodr. West Sound Lyric Theater, 2003—. Mem. Kitsap County Estate Planning Coun., Eastside King County Estate Planning Coun., Order of Coif. Avocations: photography, hiking, classical music, poetry. Office: PO Box 710 Keyport WA 98345 Office Phone: 360-697-4142. E-mail: gbtreacy@aol.com.

TREACY, SANDRA JOANNE PRATT, retired art educator, illustrator; b. New Haven, Aug. 5, 1934; d. Willis Hadley Jr. and Gladys May (Gell) P.; m. Gillette van Nuyse, Aug. 27, 1955; 1 child, Jonathan Todd. BFA, R.I. Sch. Design, 1956; student, William Paterson Coll., 1973-74. Cert. elem. and secondary tchr., N.J. Tchr. art and music Pkwy. Christian Ch., Ft. Lauderdale, Fla., 1964-66; developer Pequannock Twp. Bd. of Edn., Pompton Plains, NJ, 1970-72, tchr. art, 1972-76; vol. art tchr. Person County Bd. of Edn., Roxboro, NC, 1978-80, tchr. art, 1980-91, So. Jr. High Sch., Roxboro, 1989-91, Woodland Elem. Sch., Roxboro, 1989-93; tchr. Helena Elem. Sch., Timberlake, NC, 1991-93, So. Middle Sch., 1980—2007; ret., 2007. Tchr. elem. art Bethel Hill Sch., Roxboro, 1974-79, vol. art tchr., 1979-80; tchr. basic art, vol. all elem. schs. Person County, Roxboro, 1977-80; tchr. arts and crafts, summers 1981-882; tchr. art home sch. So. Mid. Sch., 1981-2005, Person H.S., 1993-94 Artist, illustrator. Mem. Roxboro EMTs, 1979-81; bd. dirs. Person County Arts Coun., 1980-81, 93-95, pres., 1981-82; piano and organ choir accompanist Concord United Meth. Ch., 1981—; leader Morgan Trotters, 1992-94, asst. dir., 1993-96, bd. dirs.; coach, horseback riding for handicapped; Guardian Ad Litem Person County vol., 2008-. Mem. NEA, Nat. Mus. of Women in the Arts (continuing charter), Smithsonian Assocs., N.C. Assn. Arts Edn., N.C. Assn. Educators, N.C. Art Soc. Mus. of Art, Internat. Platform Assn., Womans Club (tchr. Pompton Plains chpt. 1974-79), Person County Saddle Club (rec. sec. 1981-84), Puddingston Pony Club (dist. sec. 1974-75 Montville Twp. chpt.), Roxboro Garden Club (continuing, commr. 1980-82, pres. 1982-84, 2004—, sec. 1993-94, 97-98, v.p. 1993-95), Roxboro Woman's Club (arts dept.) Republican. Avocations: horseback riding, swimming, sailing, reading, playing piano and organ. Home: 1345 Kelly Brewer Rd Leasburg NC 27291-9622 Home Phone: 336-599-0825. Personal E-mail: sjptreacy@embarqmail.com.

TREADWAY, JAMES CRISPIN CURRAN CORBETT, lawyer, brokerage house executive, investor, federal official; b. Anderson, SC, May 21, 1943; s. James C. Treadway and Maxine Hall; m. Susan Pepper Davis, Sept. 6, 1969; children: Elizabeth Pepper Hall, Caroline Worrell Harper Corbett. AB summa cum laude, Rollins Coll., 1964; JD summa cum laude, Washington and Lee U., 1967. Bar: Ga. 1967, Mass. 1968, D.C. 1970. Assoc. Candler, Cox, McClain & Andrews, Atlanta, 1967-68, Gadsby & Hannah, Boston and Washington, 1968-72; ptnr. Dickstein, Shapiro & Morin, Washington, 1972-82; commr. SEC, Washington, 1982-85; ptnr. Baker & Botts, Washington, 1985-87; exec. v.p., chmn. mcht. banking dept., mem. exec. com. Paine Webber Group Inc., NYC, 1987—. Commr. Nat. Study Commn., 1985—87; chmn. Nat. Commn. on Fraudulent Fin. Reporting, 1985—87; chmn. bds. dirs. Washington &

Lee U. Sch. Law, 1992—94; dir. U. So. Calif., Sch. of Acctg. and Fin. Disclosure, 1985—93; mem. planning com. Garret Securities Law Inst., Northwestern U., 1985—92; dir. nat. study commn., 1985—87; spl. expert adviser, witness various U.S. congl. coms.; lectr. in field; bd. dirs. Parnounblon, Inc., Matchel Hatchens Asset Mgmt. Inc., Pomawufter, Inc., Gradgne Inc.; bd. dirs. Miran Banking Ctr. Boston U. Editor-in-chief Wash. & Lee U. Law review, 1966-67. Recipient Wildman Medal Am. Acctg. Assn., 1989. Mem. Mass. Bar Assn., Ga. Bar Assn., D.C. Bar Assn., Chevy Chase (Md.) Club, Bedford (N.Y.) Golf and Tennis Club, City Tavern Club (Washington chpt.), Met. Club (Washington chpt.), Verbank Hunting and Fishing Club (Uniondale N.Y.; dir. 1995—), Order of Coif, Phi Beta Kappa, Omicron Delta Kappa, Omicron Delta Epsilon, Kappa Alpha Order Republican. Roman Cath. Office: PaineWebber Group Inc 1285 Ave of Americas New York NY 10019-6028 Home: 1509 Monk Rd Gladwyne PA 19035 Personal E-mail: irishtopspin@aol.com.

TREADWAY, SANDRA GIOIA, library director; b. Jersey City, Jan. 15, 1950; d. Robert Peter and Essey Grace (Graham) Gioia; m. John David Treadway, Sept. 4, 1976 (div. 2006); 1 child, Robyn Grace. BA in History, Manhattanville Coll., 1971; MA in History, U. Va., 1972, PhD in History, 1978; M in Info. Sci., U. Tenn., 2007. Instr. history Va. Polytech Inst. & State U., Blacksburg, 1976-78; editor Va. State Libr., Richmond, 1978-91, dir. pubs., 1991-96; deputy dir. Libr. Va., Richmond, 1996—2007, dir., 2007—. Author: Women of Mark, 1995; co-author: The Common Wealth: Treasures from the Collections of the Library of Virginia, 1997; co-editor: Dictionary of Virginia Biography, vol. 1, 1999, vol. 2, 2001, vol. 3, 2006. Mdm. bd. St. Mary Sch., Richmond, 1988-96, bd. mem. Richmond History Ctr., 2008-. Mem. Am. Hist. Assn., Orgn. Am. historians, So. Historical Assn., So. Assn. Women Historians (pres. 2002), Va. Hist. Soc., Va. Libr. Assn., Serra Internat. (bd. dirs. 1985—). Roman Catholic. Avocations: reading, travel. Home: 8201 Gaylord Rd Richmond VA 23229-4121 Office: Libr Va 800 E Broad St Richmond VA 23219-8000 Business E-Mail: sandra.treadway@lva.virginia.gov.

TREADWAY-DILLMON, LINDA LEE, actress, stuntwoman, dancer, dispatcher, athletic trainer; b. Woodbury, NJ, June 4, 1950; d. Leo Elmer and Ona Lee (Wyckoff) Treadway; m. Randall Kenneth Dillmon, June 19, 1982. BS in Health, Phys. Edn. & Recreation, West Chester State Coll., 1972, MS in Health and Phys. Edn., 1975; postgrad., Ctrl. Mich. U., 1978; Police Officer Stds. Tng. cert. complaint dispatcher, Golden-west Coll., 1982. Cert. EMT Am. Acad. Orthopaedic Surgeons; in safety edn. West Chester State Coll. Grad. asst., instr., asst. athletic trainer West Chester (Pa.) State Coll., 1972-76; asst. prof., program dir., asst. athletic trainer Ctrl. Mich. U., Mt. Pleasant, 1976-80; police dispatcher City of Westminster, Calif., 1980-89; oncology unit sect. Children's Hosp. Orange County, Calif., 1989-96; control clk. food and beverage Marriott Hotel, Anaheim, 1996—2005. Stuntwoman, actress United Stunt Artists, SAG, L.A., 1982—; dancer Disneyland, Anaheim, Calif., 1988—; contbr. articles to profl. jours. Athletic trainer U.S. Olympic Women's Track and Field Trials, Frederick, Md., 1972, AAU Jr. World Wrestling Championships, Mt. Pleasant, Mich., 1977, Mich. Spl. Olympics, Mt. Pleasant, 1977, 78, 79. Recipient bronze and gold Spirit of Disneyland Resort awards, 1997; named Outstanding Phys. Educator, Delta Psi Kappa, Ctrl. Mich. U., 1980, Outstanding Young Woman of Am., 1984; named to Disneyland Entertainment Hall of Fame, 1995. Mem. SAG, Nat. Athletic Trainers Assn. (cert., women and athletic tng. ad hoc com. 1974-75, placement com. 1974-79, program dirs. coun. 1976-80, ethics com. 1977-80, visitation team 1978-80, 25 Yr. award 1997), U.S. Field Hockey Assn. (player), Pacific S.W. Field Hockey Assn. (player, Nat. Champion 1980, 81, 82), L.A. Field Hockey Assn. (player), Swing Shift Dance Team (dancer). Presbyterian. Avocations: flying, piano, athletics, stitchery, travel. Home: 18073 Scanlan Ct Fountain Valley CA 92708-5865

TREADWELL, ALEXANDER F., foundation executive, former state official; b. London, Mar. 25, 1946; m. Libby, 1970; children: Carrie, Zach. BA, U. NC. Former chmn. Essex County. Rep. Com.; vice chmn. NY State Rep. Party, 1989; sec. of state State of NY, 1995—2001; chmn. NY Rep. Com., 2001—04; NY nat. committeeman Rep. Nat. Com., 2004—; v.p. Clark Found., Cooperstown, NY. Reporter & freelance journalist, Sports Illustrated, writer, Classic Magazine, NY Magazine. Author: The World of Marathons, Stewart, Tabori & Chang, 1987. Pres. Lake Placid Regional Winter Sports Com., 2006—. Served with NY Army Nat. Guard, 1968—74. Republican. Office: NY Rep State Com 315 State St Albany NY 12210 also: Clark Found 19 Main St Cooperstown NY 13326 Office Phone: 607-547-2561.

TREADWELL, DAVID, computer software company executive; b. 1967; s. David R. Treadwell and Carol A. Ritter, Elizabeth S. Treadwell (Stepmother) and Donald E. Williams (Stepfather); m. Lynn Treadwell; children: David, Aiden. BEE, Princeton U., 1989. With Microsoft Corp., 1989—, v.p., .NET devel. platform divsn., corp. v.p. Live Platform services, 2007—. Avocations: marathons, triathlons, photography. Office: Microsoft Corp 1 Microsoft Way Redmond WA 98052-6399

TREANOR, WILLIAM MICHAEL, dean, law educator; b. Morristown, NJ, Nov. 16, 1957; s. William Joseph and Margaret Treanor; m. Allison Derivaux Ames, Oct. 15, 1994; children: William Paul Ames, Katherine Derivaux. BA summa cum laude, Yale U., 1979, JD, 1985; AM in History, Harvard U., 1982. Spl. asst. to dep. commr. U.S. Office Edn., Washington, 1979-80; speechwriter to sec. U.S. Dept. Edn., Washington, 1980; law clk. to Hon. James L. Oakes U.S. Ct. Appeals, 2d Cir., Brattleboro, Vt., 1985-86; spl. asst. to chmn. Com. on Govt. Integrity, NYC, 1987; spl. asst. U.S. atty. U.S. Atty.'s Office, Washington, 1990; assoc. counsel Office of Ind. Counsel, Washington, 1987-90; assoc. prof. law Fordham U., NYC, 1991-98, prof. law, 2001—, dean, 2002—; dep. asst. atty. gen. office of legal counsel U.S. Dept. Justice, NYC, 1998-2001. Vis. prof. Univ. Paris I, Pantheon-Sorbonne, 1998, 2000. Contbr. articles to profl. jours. Mem.: Phi Beta Kappa. Democrat. Office: Fordham Law Sch Dean Office Rm110 140 W 62nd St New York NY 10023 Office Phone: 212-636-6875. E-mail: wtreanor@fordham.edu.*

TREASTER, JOSEPH B(LAND), journalist; s. Ellsworth F. and Anna Katherine (Chalupka) T.; m. Barbara A. Gluck, June 6, 1970 (div. Aug. 1976); m. Barbara J. Dill, Feb. 24, 1990; 1 child, Chloe Qiao Xing. BA, U. Miami, 1965; student, Sorbonne, Paris, 1971, San Francisco de Marroquin, Guatemala, 1988; MS, Columbia U., 1996. Reporter Miami (Fla.) Herald, 1963; staff asst. Saigon bur. New York Times, 1965-67, Vietnam corr., 1968-69, 72-74, reporter, 1969-70, chief Conn. bur., 1970-72, investigative reporter N.J. bur., 1974-75, crime/youth violence writer, 1975-76, rewrite desk and spl. assignments to Washington, L.Am. and Mid. East, 1976-84, chief Caribbean bur., 1984-90, drug policy corr. spl. assignments Latin Am., Mid-East, Europe, Baltic States, 1990-95, fin. writer, 1996—. Freelance corr. Atlantic Monthly, Rolling Stone, The Nation, others; fellow Poynter Inst., St. Petersburg, Fla., 1993, U. Nev. Bus. Journalism, 1995; Knight-Bagehot fellow in econs. and bus. Columbia U., 1995-96; Poynter fellow Yale U., 1975; tchg. assoc., Ga. State U. Internat. Program, 1997-; adj. prof. Baruch Coll., Univ. NY, 2002. Author: Hurricane Force: In the Path of America's Deadliest Storms, 2007, Paul Volcker: The Making of a Financial Legend, 2004; co-author: No Hiding Place: Inside Report on the Hostage Crisis (in Iran), 1981; contbg. author: Ency. Brit., Insight Guide to Caribbean, Youth Violence, 1992, Writing About Business, 2000, The New York Times What's Doing Around the World, 2001, The New York Times Almanac, 2005, 2006. Served with U.S. Army, 1963-65, Vietnam. Recipient Page One award NY Newspaper Guild, 1977, 79; Tom Wallace award Inter-Am. Press Assn., 1980, citation and awards Overseas Press Club Am., 1977, 80, 85, News Analysis award Soc. of Silurians, 1993, Casey medal for meritorious journalism U. Md., 1995, others. Avocations: skiing, sport fishing, running, bicycling, archaeology. Office: New York Times 620 8th Ave New York NY 10018 Office Phone: 212-556-3718. Business E-Mail: treaster@nytimes.com, jbtreaster@aol.com.

TREASTER, MELBA MAUCK, retired educational consultant and educator; b. Langdon, Kans., Dec. 10, 1929; d. Phillip Alvis and Bessie F. (Holmes) Mauck; m. W. Arlen Treaster, Dec.16, 1950 (dec. Nov. 1985); children: Paul Arlen, Andrew Philip. BA in Edn., Sterling Coll., Kans., 1951; MS in Psychology, Emporia State U., 1964. Cert. elem. tchr., reading endorsement, Colo. Elem. tchr. Union Five Sch., Reno County, Kans., 1951-52, Sterling (Kans.) Pub. Schs., 1952-53; kindergarten tchr. Lucas (Kans.) Pub. Schs., 1956—61; elem. tchr. Sunny Grove Sch., Atchison County, Kans., 1963-64; H.S. tchr. English/social studies Atchison County Cmty. H.S., Effingham, Kans., 1964-67; chpt. I tchr./supr. Poudre Sch. Dist., Ft. Collins, Colo., 1967-90; ednl. cons. Ft. Collins, 1990—2000; ret., 2000. Developer, demonstrator Prior Project Nat. Diffusion Network, 1979-81; presentor nat., regional profl. confs. Internat. Reading Assn., 1983-92. Co-author: (videos) Reading Aloud to Children, 1989, Listening to Children Read, 1990. Elder Westminster Presbyn. Ch., Ft. Collins, 1989-91; bd. dirs. Ft. Collins READ-Aloud, 1994-98. Recipient Recognition award Chpt. I/Title I, U.S. Dept. Edn., Washington, 1990. Mem. ASCD, Internat. Reading Assn. (local pres., chair Colo. Commn., 1965-67). Avocations: reading, genealogy, travel. Home: 3414 Seneca St # B Fort Collins CO 80526-4223 Personal E-mail: mltreaster@aol.com.

TREAT, JOHN ELTING, entrepreneur; b. Evanston, Ill., June 20, 1946; s. Carlin Alexander and Marjorie Ann (Mayland) T.; adopted s. Howard Elting Jr.; m. Barbara Laflin, May 27, 1984; children: Charles, Luli, Tyler, Tucker, Mayland. BA, Princeton U., 1967; MA, Johns Hopkins U., 1969. Legis. asst. U.S. Senate, 1966; assoc. ops. officer Office of Sec., U.S. Dept. State, 1971-73; research coordinator Presdl.-Congressional Commn. on Orgn. of Govt. for Conduct of Fgn. Policy, Washington, 1973-74; dir. research trade U.S. Fed. Energy Adminstrn., Washington, 1974-78; dep. asst. sec. U.S. Dept. Energy, Washington, 1979-80; staff mem. Nat. Security Council, 1980-81; sr. v.p. N.Y. Merc. Exchange, NYC, 1981-82, pres., 1982-84; ptnr. Bear Stearns & Co., Los Angeles, 1984-85; exec. pub. Petroleum Intelligence Weekly, NYC, 1985-87; pres. Regent Internat., Washington and The Hague, 1987-89; v.p., ptnr. Booz, Allen & Hamilton, Inc., San Francisco, 1989—2001; chmn. Sanctuary Devel. LLC, 2001—; CEO Treat Mgmt. Co.; sr. ptnr. Smart Alliance Ptnrs. Chmn. spl. gifts Am. Cancer Soc., 1983; chmn. bd. dirs. Mirror Repertory Co., 1987—90; trustee, mem. exec. com., chmn. corp. rels. com. No. Calif. World Affairs Coun.; mem. San Francisco Fgn. Rels. com.; bd. trustees Am. U. of Cairo; trustee Yosemite Nat. Insts., 2001—. With USNR, 1969—71. Decorated AF Commendation medal; Ford Found. European Area Travel grantee, 1972; Woodrow Wilson fellow, 1967; McConnell fellow, 1966 Mem. Coun. Fgn. Rels., Internat. Assn. for Energy Econs. Clubs: Colonial (Princeton, N.J.), St. Francis Yacht Club, Bankers (San Francisco). Democrat. Unitarian Universalist. Office: Smart Alliance Ptnr Continental Grand Plaza 2 400 Continental Blvd Suite 600 El Segundo CA 90245 E-mail: treat_john@bah.com.

TREATMAN, PAUL, retired school system administrator; b. NYC, Nov. 19, 1924; s. Meyer Treatman and Sadie Rosenblum; m. Elaine Cohen (dec.); children: Abbe Jo, Scott. BA, Bkyln. Coll., 1948; MA, NYU, 1949, PhD, 1954. Cert. prin. NY, 1956, supr. schs. NY, 1956, dir. Urban edn. programs NY, 1956, sch. adminstr., supr. NY, 1956, sch. adminstr. NJ, 1990. Tchr. NYC Schs., 1949—56, asst. prin., 1956—62, prin. elem. schs., 1962—71, prin. jr. HS, 1971—73, supt., 1973—82; resident edn, cons. to gov. US VI, 1966—67; adj. assoc. prof. ednl. adminstrn. Pace U., NY, 1973—90, Coll. New Rochelle, NY, 1973—90, St. Johns U., NY, 1973—90. Author: (books) Back to the Trenches, 1993, Haikus for Punsters, 2006, More Haikus for Punsters, 2007, A Haiku/Pun for Everyone, 2008, Haiku PUNishment, 2009. Mem., commr. Monroe Twp. Cultural Arts Com., 2002—04; pres. Ponds Condominium Assn., Monroe Twp., 2002—04, NY Acad. Pub. Edn.; county committeeman Dem. Orgn., Monroe Twp., NJ, 1996—. Pvt. US Army, 1943—45. Decorated Bronze Star US Army, Combat Medic badge; named NYC Educator Yr., Doctorate Assn. NY Educators, 1979. Mem.: Jewish War Vets., Coun. Suprs. and Adminstrs. (pres. 2002—04), Vets. of Foreign Wars, French Legion Honor (Chevalier, Belgian Fourragère), Disabled Am. Vets., Am. Legion Post 522 (vice comdr. 2005—), Am. Mensa (hon.). Democrat. Jewish. Avocations: writing, reading, acting. Home: 219 N Pondview Blvd Monroe Township NJ 08831

TREBILCOCK, JAMES R., marketing executive; m. Janet Trebilcock; children: Scott, Zachary. BA in Mktg., Mich. State U.; MBA, Mich. State U. Eli Broad Grad. Sch. Mgmt. With Big G cereal divsn. Gen. Mills Inc.; various regional sales/mktg. positions Coca-Cola Bottling Co. Consol.; joined as Cherry 7 UP brand mgr. Cadbury Schweppes Americas Beverages, 1987, various positions including dir. promotions, v.p. mktg., sr. v.p. mktg. svcs., then sr. v.p. consumer mktg., 2003—08; exec. v.p. mktg. Dr. Pepper Snapple Group Inc. (formerly Cadbury Schweppes Americas Beverages), 2008—. Office: Dr Pepper Snapple Group Inc Corp Hdqs 5301 Legacy Dr Plano TX 75024 Office Phone: 972-673-7000.

TREBINO, RICK PETER, physicist; b. Boston, Jan. 18, 1954; s. Frederick P. and Theresa C. (Bomba) T.; m. Linda Leigh Hobbs, Aug. 5, 1977. BA, Harvard U., 1977; MS, Stanford U., 1979, PhD, 1983. Rsch. assoc. Stanford (Calif.) U., 1983-86; sr. mem. tech. staff Sandia Nat. Labs., Livermore, Calif., 1986—. Editor: Tunable Solid-State Lasers for Remote Sensing; Generation, Amplification, and Measurement of Ultrashort Laser Pulses; contbr. articles to Jour. Quantum Electronics, Phys. Rev., Optics Letters, Jour. Optical Soc. Am. Recipient Harvard U. fellowship, 1976, IBM fellowship, 1980-81, fellow Achievement Rewards for Coll. Scientists, 1980. Mem. Am. Phys. Soc., Optical Soc. Am., AAAS. Achievements include patents for measuring the intensity and phase pf an ultrashort light pulse, diffraction immunoassay apparatus and method, polysilicon binding assay support and methods; patent pending for improved diffraction binding assay apparatus and biograting therefor. Office: Sandia Nat Labs Org 8354 PO Box 969 Livermore CA 94551-0969

TREBON, THOMAS, academic administrator; m. Scottie Trebon. B magna cum laude, Seattle U.; M, PhD, U. Denver. Tchr., adminstr. Seattle U.; acad. dean Coll. Arts and Scis. Rockhurst Coll., Kansas City; provost, v.p. acad. affairs Sacred Heart U., Trumbull, Conn., St. Norbert Coll., 1995—2001, v.p. acad. affairs, dean; pres. Carroll Coll., Helena, Mont., 2001—. Office Phone: 406-447-4401. Business E-Mail: ttrebon@carroll.edu.

TREBUNSKAYA, ANNA, dancer; b. Russia, 1981; arrived in US, 1998; m. Jonathan Roberts. Profl. & competitive ballroom & Latin dancer; winner USA Amateur Youth Standard Ballroom Championship, 1998, USA Rising Star Latin Championship, 2004, Internat. Grand Ball Championship, World Cup Profl. Rising Star Latin Championship, 2005; finalist Blackpool Rising Star Latin Championship, 2003; profl. dancer Dancing with the Stars, ABC, 2006—.

TRECHSEL, STEFAN, law educator; b. Berne, Switzerland, June 25, 1937; s. Manfred F. and Stefanie E. (Friedlaender) T.; m. Franca J. Kinsbergen, Aug. 18, 1967; children: Charlotte Stefanie, Anna Cristina. BA, Berne U., 1963, JD, 1966; PhD (hon.), N.Y. Law Sch., 1975. Dist. atty., Berne, 1971-75; guest prof. U. Fribourg, Switzerland, 1975-77; prof. U. St. Gallen, Switzerland, 1979-99, U. Zurich, 1999—2004. Author: The Reason for Punishing Participants in Crime, 1967, The European Convention of Human Rights, Its Protection of Personal Liberty and the Swiss Codes on Criminal Procedure, 1974, Swiss Penal Code Short Commentary, 1989, 2d edit. 1997, Human Rights in Criminal Proceedings, 2005; contbr. articles to profl. jours. Active European Commn. Human Rights, Strasbourg, 1975-99, 2nd v.p., 1987-94, pres. 1995-99; judge Internat. Criminal Tribunal, the former Yugoslavia, 2006—. Major Swiss mil. Mem.: Internat. Law Assn., Austrian Inst. Human Rights (bd. dirs. 1987—), Max Planck Inst. Penal Law (bd. dirs. 1984-96), Internat. Penal Law Assn. (bd. dirs. 1984—, pres. Swiss nat. group 1985-2001. Avocations: playing cello, bicycling, literature.

TRECKELO, RICHARD M., lawyer; b. Elkhart, Ind., Oct. 22, 1926; s. Frank J. and Mary T.; m. Anne Kosick, June 25, 1955; children: Marla Treckelo Buck, Mary Treckelo Lucchesi. AB, U. Mich., 1951, JD, 1953. Bar: Ind. 1953, U.S. Dist. Ct. (no. and so. dists.) Ind. Pvt. practice, Elkhart, 1953-70; ptnr. Barnes and Thornburg, Elkhart, South Bend, others, 1971-91, of counsel, 1992—. Sec. Skyline Corp., Elkhart, 1959-94, bd. dirs., 1961-91. Bd. dirs. Elkhart Gen. Hosp. Found., Elkhart Park Found.; co-chmn. Elkhart Constl. Bicentennial Commn. Served with USAF, 1945-46. Mem. ABA, Elkhart City Bar Assn. (pres. 1975), Ind. Bar Assn., Elkhart County Bar Assn., Pres.'s Club (U. Mich.), Christiana Country Club, Michiana Club (chmn., U. Mich. Elbel Scholarship award), Rotary. Republican. Office: Barnes & Thornburg 121 W Franklin St Ste 200 Elkhart IN 46516-3200 Office Phone: 574-293-0681.

TREDWAY, DONALD RAY, endocrinologist, educator; s. George I. and Beulah Ray Tredway; m. Donna Jean Ashby, Sept. 13, 1964; children: Tamara Jean Jensen, Jennifer Lyn. BS, Bowling Green State U., Ohio, 1963; MD, U. Ill. Sch. Medicine, Chgo., 1966; PhD, U. Southern Calif., LA, 1974. Lic. Ill., 1966, diplomate Nat. Bd. Med. Examiners, 1967, lic. Calif., 1968, diplomate Am. Bd. Ob-Gyn, 1973, in reproductive endocrinology by the Am. Bd. Ob-Gyn., 1976, lic. Okla., 1978, Hawaii, 1980, Mo., 1996, Kans., 1996. Dir., divsn. reproductive endocrinology and fellowship program Naval Regional Med. Ctr., Oakland, Calif., 1975—77; assoc. prof., dept. ob-gyn. to chief U. Chgo., 1977—79. Prof. to chmn., dept. ob-gyn. Oral Roberts U., Tulsa, Okla., 1978—80, 1984—88, U. Okla. Tulsa Med. Coll., 1982—84; assoc. dean, coll. counseling and health care Pacific and Asia Christian U., Kailua-Kona, Hawaii, 1980—82; med. dir. Hillcrest Fertility Ctr., Tulsa, 1986—88; prof. to sect. chief, reproductive endocrinology and infertility Loma Linda U., Calif., 1989—94; chmn., dept. ob-gyn. King Fahd N.G. Hosp., Riyahd, Saudia Arabia, 1994—96; asoc. med. dir. to reproductive sci. assoc. IntegraMed, Kansas City, Mo., 1996—97; reproductive endocrinologist Tulsa Ctr. Fertility & Womens' Health, 1997—2000; sr. med. dir. Serono, Inc, Rockland, Mass., 2000—06, v.p. to head rep. health & endocrinology, 2006—08; v.p. to head fertility & endocrinology global clin. devel. unit EMD Serono, Rockland, 2008—. Elder Crossroads Worship Ctr. mem., Weymouth, Mass. Capt med. crops USN, 1964—96, SE & SW Asia. Decorated Viet Nam Svc., Nat. Def. Svc., Meritorious Unit Commendation US Navy, SW Asia; recipient Svc. award, Soc. Gynecologic Investigation, 1995. Fellow: ACOG; mem.: Endocrine Soc., SGI, ASRM. Office: EMD Serono One Tech Pl Rockland MA 02370 Business E-Mail: donald.tredway@emdserono.com.

TREFFERT, DAROLD ALLEN, psychiatrist, writer, hospital administrator; b. Fond du Lac, Wis., Mar. 12, 1933; s. Walter O. and Emma (Leu) T.; m. Dorothy Marie Sorgatz, June 11, 1955; children: Jon, Joni, Jill, Jay. BS, U. Wis., 1955, MD, 1958. Diplomate Am. Bd. Psychiatry and Neurology. Resident in psychiatry U. Wis. Med. Sch., 1959-62, clin. prof. psychiatry, 1965—; chief children's unit Winnebago (Wis.) Mental Health Inst., 1962-64, supt., 1964-79, Ctrl. State Hosp., Waupun, Wis., 1977-78; dir. Dodge County Mental Health Ctr., Juneau, Wis., 1964-74; mem. staff St. Agnes Hosp., Fond du Lac, 1963—; exec. dir. Fond du Lac County Mental Health Ctr., 1979-92. Chmn. Controlled Substances Bd. Wis.; chmn. med. examining bd. State of Wis. Author: Extraordinary People: Understanding Savant Syndrome, 1989, 3d edit., 2006, edits. in U.S., U.K., Italy, Japan, Netherlands, Sweden, Korea, China, Mellowing: Lessons from Listening, 2006; autism cons. (movie) Rainman, 1988. Fellow Am. Coll. Psychiatrists; mem. AMA, Wis. Med. Soc. (pres. 1979-80), Wis. Psychiat. Assn. (pres.), Am. Assn. Psychiat. Adminstrs. (pres.), Alpha Omega Alpha. Home: W 4065 Maplewood Ln Fond Du Lac WI 54937-9562 Office: 430 E Division St Fond Du Lac WI 54935-4560 Office Phone: 920-921-9381. Business E-Mail: daroldt@charter.net. *People often spend too much time regretting what they are not and far too little time savoring that which they are.*

TREFIL, JAMES STANLEY, physicist, researcher; b. Chgo., Sept. 10, 1938; s. Stanley James and Sylvia (Mestek) T.; m. Elinor Pletka; children: James Karel, STefan; m. Jeanne L. Waples, Oct. 17, 1972; children: Dominique, Flora, Tomas; m. Wande T. O'Brien, 2005. BS, U. Ill., 1960; BA, MA, Oxford U., Eng., 1962; MS, Stanford U., 1964, PhD, 1966. Rsch. assoc. Stanford (Calif.) Linear Accelerator Ctr., 1966; Air Force Office Sci. Rsch. postdoctoral fellow CERN, Geneva, 1966-67; asst. prof. physics U. Ill., Urbana, 1968-70; assoc. prof. physics U. Va., Charlottesville, 1970-75, prof. physics, 1975-87, Univ. prof. physics, 1987; C.J. Robinson prof. physics George Mason U., Fairfax, Va., 1987—. Sci. adv. bd. Nat. Pub. Radio; sci. cons. Smithsonian Mag.; tech. cons. Am. Heritage Dictionary; cons. Adler Planetarium. Author: Dictionary of Cultural Literacy, 1988, 2d edit., 1993, Reading the Mind of God, 1989, Science Matters, 1991, 2nd edit., 2009, Facts of Life: Science and the Abortion Controversy, 1992, A Scientist in the City, 1994, The Sciences: An Integrated Approach, 1995, 6th edit., 2009, Edge of the Unknown, 1996, Are We Unique, 1997, Human Nature, 2004, Why Science, 2008; contbg. editor: USA Weekend Principle Science. NSF fellow Stanford U., 1966; recipient Sci. Journalism award AAAS-

Westinghouse, 1983; John Simon Guggenheim fellow, 1987-88; Marshall scholar Oxford U., 1962; recipient Gemant award Am. Inst. Physics, 2007, Sci. Journalism award, 2008. Fellow Am. Phys. Soc., World Econ. Forum. Office: George Mason U 207 E Bldg Fairfax VA 22030

TREFNY, JOHN ULRIC, retired college president; b. Jan. 28, 1942; s. Ulric John and Mary Elizabeth (Leech) T.; m. Sharon Livingston, 1992; 1 child from previous marriage, Benjamin Robin. BS, Fordham U., 1963; PhD, Rutgers U., 1968; doctorate (hon.), Colo. Sch. of Mines, 2006. Rsch. assoc. Cornell U., Ithaca, NY, 1967-69; asst. prof. physics Wesleyan U., Middletown, Conn., 1969-77, Colo. Sch. Mines, Golden, 1977-79, assoc. prof., 1979-85, prof., 1985—, assoc. dean rsch., 1988—90, head physics dept., 1990—95, v.p. for acad. affairs, dean faculty, 1995—2000, pres., 2000—06. Dir. Amorphous Materials Ctr. Colo. Sch. Mines, 1986-90; cons. Solar Energy Rsch. Inst., Golden, Energy Conversion Devices, Troy, Mich., others. Contbr. articles to profl. jours. Mem. Golden Civic Found., Red Rocks CC Found.; bd. mem. Denver region Inst. Internat. Edn. Recipient Tchg. award AMOCO Found., 1984, Friend of Sci. Edn. award, 1990. Avocations: golf, travel. Home: 14268 W 1st Ave Golden CO 80401 Personal E-mail: jtrefny@mines.edu.

TREFOUSSE, HANS LOUIS, history professor; b. Frankfurt, Ger., Dec. 18, 1921; came to U.S. 1936; s. George and Elizabeth (Albersheim) T.; m. Rashelle Friedlander, Jan. 26, 1947; 1 child, Roger Philip. BA, CCNY, 1942; MA, Columbia U., 1947, PhD, 1950. Instr. Adelphi Coll., Garden City, N.Y., 1949-50; from instr. to disting. prof. Bklyn. Coll., 1950-98, emeritus, 1998—; from assoc. prof. to disting. prof. history Grad. Ctr., CUNY, 1961-98, emeritus, 1998—. Author: Andrew Johnson, 1989, Carl Schurz, 1982, Impeachment of a President, 1975, The Radical Republicans, 1969, Thaddeus Stevens, 1997, Rutherford B. Hayes, 2002, First Among Equals, 2005; editor: Twayne's Statesmen and Leaders of the World, 1967-77; editor Anvil Series, 1994-2005 Lt. col. AUS, 1942-45, USAR, ret. Named Disting. Tchr. Bklyn. Coll., 1960; Guggenheim fellow, 1977; ACLS grant, 1981. Mem. Am. Hist. Assn., Soc. Am. Historians, Orgn. Am. Historians, So. Hist. Assn. Democrat. Jewish. Avocations: swimming, travel. Home: 22 Shore Acres Rd Staten Island NY 10305-3912 Office: Bklyn Coll Dept History Brooklyn NY 11210 Personal E-mail: hanst@prodigy.net.

TREFRY, JOHN H., III, chemical oceanographer, educator; b. Boston, Sept. 2, 1947; s. John H. Trefry, Jr. and Phyllis Nelson Trefry; m. Susan E. Page, July 20, 1969; 1 child, Caroline Page Kempf; 1 child, John H. IV. BA, Syracuse U., 1969; MS in Chem. Oceanography, Tex. A&M U., 1973, PhD in Chem. Oceanography, 1977. Asst. prof. Fla. Inst. Tech., Melbourne, Fla., 1978—82, assoc. prof., 1982—87, prof., 1987—. Vis. scientist MIT, Cambridge, Mass., 1987—88. Editor (assoc.): Marine Chemistry. Grant, NSF, 1990—94, NOAA, 1977—85, 1995—2000, US Dept Interior, 1997—. Mem.: Coastal Soc., Outer Continental Shelf Scientific Com., U.S. Dept. of Interior, Minerals Mgmt. Svc., Fla. Acad. Sci. (pres. 2005—07, medalist 2002), Am. Chem. Soc., Am. Geophys. Union. Achievements include first to co-discover deep-sea hydrothermal vents in the Atlantic Ocean; show positive impact of banning lead in gasoline to the Mississippi River and Gulf of Mexico; extensive global research in environmental studies of offshore oil exploration and production. Office: Florida Inst Tech 150 W Univ Blvd Melbourne FL 32901 Office Fax: 321-674-7212. Business E-Mail: jtrefry@fit.edu.

TREFRY, ROBERT J., health facility administrator; b. Springfield, Vt., Mar. 29, 1947; married. Bachelors' degree, Ga. Inst. Tech., 1970; Masters' degree, George Washington U., 1974. With Greater Southeast Community Hosp., Washington, 1973, adminstrv. asst., 1973-74, asst. adminstr., 1974-79; sr. v.p. North Kansas City (Mo.) Community Hosp., 1979-83; exec. v.p., chief exec. officer St. Agnes Hosp., White Plains, NY, 1983-88; exec. v.p., chief operating officer Carle Found. Hosp., Urbana, Ill., 1988-91; exec. v.p., chief oper. officer Bridgeport (Conn.) Hosp., 1991-94, pres., CEO, 1994—; exec. v.p. Yale New Haven Health Sys., 1996—. With U.S. mil. 1970-71. Office: Bridgeport Hosp 267 Grant St Bridgeport CT 06610-2870 Office Phone: 203-384-3478.

TREFZGER, RICHARD CHARLES, surgeon; b. Peoria, Ill., Jan. 27, 1948; s. John Dennis and Marilyn Lestilie (Wilson) Trefzger; m. Nancy Ellen Guy, Dec. 19, 1971; children: Emily Jean, Michael Guy. BS, U. Ill., 1970, MD, 1973. Diplomate Am Bd Surgery. Intern in surgery Med. Coll. Wis., Milw., 1973-74, resident in surgery, 1974-75, Presbyn.-St. Luke's Hosp., Chgo., 1975-78; instr. surgery Rush Med. Coll., Chgo., 1977-78; med. dir. Westminster Village Retirement Ctr., Bloomington, Ill., 1980-84, St. Joseph's Trauma Ctr., Bloomington, 1986-96, BroMenn Regional Trauma Ctr., Normal, Ill., 1994-96; chief surgery Bromenn Regional Med. Ctr., Normal, Ill., 1987-88, 94-96, St. Joseph's Med. Ctr., Bloomington, 1989-91, pres. med. staff, 1991-92. Clin. instr. U. Ill. Coll. Medicine, 1980—2006, clin. asst. prof. surgery, 2006—; chmn. bd. dirs. BroMenn Physician Hosp. Orgn., 1995—96; sec. med. staff BroMenn Regional Med. Ctr., 1998, v.p., 99, bd. dirs., 1999—2002, pres. med. staff, 2000—02. Mem. Ill. State U. Civic Chorale, Normal, 1991—98; bd. dirs. Cmty. Cancer Ctr, Bloomington, 1996—2006, pres., 2000; v.p. ofcl. bd. First Christian Ch., Bloomington, 1981—82, 1999—2002, 2005—06, elder, 1980—; rector Cursillo Christianity, 2001; bd. dirs. Barton Stone Christian Home, Jacksonville, Ill., 1979—82. Fellow: ACS (councilor Ill. chpt. 1986—88, mem. Ill. chpt. com. trauma 1996—2003); mem.: AMA, Ill. Surg. Soc. (gov. 1990—94, v.p. elect 1997, v.p. 1998, pres. elect 1999, pres. 2000, trustee 2001—04), Danvers Cmty. Band-Saxophone, Scottish Rite, Rotary (dir. 1982—85, 1994—99, sec. 1995—96, v.p. 1996—97, pres. 1997—98, band-saxophone, Paul Harris fellow 1989), Masons, Alpha Omega Alpha. Avocations: music, travel. Home: 41 Pendleton Way Bloomington IL 61704-6243 Office: Surg Assocs 1404 Eastland Dr Bloomington IL 61701-3532 Office Phone: 309-663-4351.

TREGEMBA, ROBERT D., telecommunications industry executive; married; 2 children. BS in Civil Engring., U. Kans., Lawrence, 1971. With ops. group Southwestern Bell; several exec. positions including v.p. engring. and planning and v.p. mktg. for local exch. divsn. Sprint Corp.; COO Long Distance US West (now Qwest), 1996; exec. v.p. engring. and ops. Qwest Comm. Internat., Inc., v.p. network svcs., 2004—07, exec. v.p. network ops., 2007—. Office: Qwest Comm Internat Inc 1801 California St Denver CO 80202 Office Phone: 303-992-1400. Office Fax: 303-896-8515.

TREGER, MARJORIE MAE, theater director, educator; d. Susan Mae and Lyle Ronald Hull (Stepfather); m. Stephen Todd Treger, Aug. 28, 1994; children: Jamison Mae, Elias Michael. BA in Theatre, U. Calif., San Diego, 1990; MA in Theatre in Design and Tech., So. Oreg. U., 2008. Acting cert. Am. Conservatory Theatre, 1992, cert. clear single subject tchr. Calif., 1994. Dir. various theatres, San Diego, 1984—; theatre arts dir., educator San Diego Unified Sch. Dist., 1994—. Artistic dir. Second Star Productions, San Diego, 1997—99; visual and performing arts resource tchr. San Diego Unified Sch. Dist., 2007—. Actor: (plays) I Oughta Be In Pictures (Drama-Logue award, Best Actress award, 1987), The Heidi Chronicles (ACT Best Supporting Actress nomination, 2004); dir.: The Crucible (ACT Best Dir. nomination, 2005), Beyond Therapy (ACT Best Dir. nomination, 2006). Mem.: Actors Equity Assn. Avocations: travel, reading, dance, design, writing. Office: San Diego Unified Sch Dist 10410 Treena St San Diego CA 92131 Personal E-mail: mar_treger@yahoo.com. Business E-Mail: mtreger1@sandi.net.

TREGGOR, JOSEF PHILIP, music educator, composer, researcher; b. Hartford, Conn., Dec. 29, 1943; s. Philip Noel and Frances Helen (Hitchcock) Treggor; m. Kumi Sato, Oct. 16, 1993. BM in Music Edn. and Violin/cello, U. Hartford, 1968; MS in Biology, Ctrl. Conn. State U., 1983; postgrad. studies, Columbia Pacific U., Calif., 1996—. Instrumental music tchr. Kellogg Jr. H.S., Newington, Conn., 1968—73; orch. dir. John Wallace Mid. Sch., Newington, 1973—80, Newington H.S., 1973—2002; dir. marine mammal program for gifted and talented Newington, Canton, Bloomfield and East Hartford Schs., Conn., 1978—; prodr., music dir. Newington Musical Prodns., Conn., 1980—2002; string specialist music dept. Ridgefield (Conn.) Pub. Schs., 2003—; sr. scientist Marine Edn. and Rsch. Assocs., Farmington, Conn.; dir. Newington H.S. Marine Program for the Gifted and Talented, Newington, Conn. Contbr. film (NEA award for excellence in broadcasting, 1998); composer: (cantata) Mare Eterna, (cantata for Sept. 11) I Just Called to Say Goodbye (performance in St. Paul's Chapel, NYC, 2002); contbr. articles to profl. jours. Scoutmaster Boy Scouts Am., Newington, 1976—80, mem. eagle bd. rev. Conn., 1979—80; marine mammal stranding responder Mystic Aquarium-Nat. Marine Fisheries Svc., Conn., 2003; venue designer Woodstock (NY) Internat. Film Festival, 2004; pres. The Ridge, Farmington, Conn., 2006; mem. Wild Scenic River Study Comm.; chmn. elect Conservation Commn., Farmington, 2003, chmn. Newington, 1978—81; v.p. Farmington Land Trust, Farmington, Conn., 2008—; coord. Maverick Art Colony Centennial, Woodstock, 2005. Recipient Master Class, Mtislav Rostropovich, Hartt Coll., 1969, Tchr. of Yr. award, Newington Bd. Edn., 1993, Enhancement of Edn. Through Film award, NEA, 1996, CEA Salutes award, Conn. Edn. Assn., 1996, reception, White Ho., 1999—2000, Presdl. Performance, Pres. and Mrs. Clinton, White Ho., 2000, Congl. citation, US Congress, 2000, Spl. Recognition, Newington C. of C., 2001, citations and resolutions, Conn. Gen. Assembly, 1985, 1989, 1993, 1999, 2000, 2002; named Outstanding Educator, Sea Grant Univs., 1994, Outstanding Music Educator, Internat. Music Festivals, 1995; fellow, Marine Biol. Lab., Woods Hole, 1982—83, Ctr. for Coastal Studies, Provincetown, MA, 1984; LI Sound Rsch. grantee, Conn, Dept. Environ. Protection, 1990, 1991, 1993. Mem.: Marine Edn. and Rsch. Assn. (chmn. 1997), Marine Biol. Educators Assn., North Am. Marine Mammal Assn., Conn. Music Educators Assn. (com. chairperson, regional chmn. 1967—98), Nat. Music Educators Assn. (life), Conn. Edn. Assn. (life). Republican. Avocations: hiking, travel, sailing, skiing, bagpipes. Home: 9 Talcott Ridge Rd Farmington CT 06032 Office: Marine Edn and Rsch Assocs 9 Talcott Ridge Rd Farmington CT 06032 Personal E-mail: jtreggor@snet.ner. E-mail: jtreggor@oceaned.org.

TREGUB, ALEXANDER (ALEX TREGUB), electronics engineer; s. Iosif Tregub. PhD, MBA, MSEE, Acad. Sci., Kiev, 1989. Engr., sr engr., scientist Ukrainian Acad. Sci., 1980—89; rsch. engr. Hebrew U. Jerusalem, 1990—93; staff engr. Ameron Inst., LA, 1996—98; vis. scientist U. Calif., San Diego, 1995—96; sr. engr. Kaiser Compositek, Brea, Calif., 1998—2000; Humboldt fellow U. Ulm, Germany; staff engr. Intel Corp., Santa Clara, Calif., 2000—; vis. scholar Stanford U., Calif., 2007. V.p. LA SAMPE Chpt., 1999—2000; chair, founder Bay Area Thermal Analytical Soc.-NATAS affiliate, Santa Clara, 2001—03; organizer internat. symposiums and confs. Contbr. more than 100 articles to profl. publs. Grants, Israeli Ministry of Sci., 1990—92, fellowship, Alexander von Humboldt Found., Germany, 1992. Mem.: ASTM (mem. E37 chpt. 2005—07), NATAS, IEEE (sr.; vice chair Santa Clara LEOS chpt. 2007—), SAMPE, Am. Chem. Soc., NY Acad. Scis. Achievements include patents for electronic industry.

TREIBER, ADAM MARK, lawyer; b. Jersey City, Feb. 25, 1963; s. Glenn and Myra Treiber; m. Caroline Chantal Cowen; children: Joshua, William, Kelsey. BSME, U. Md., College Park, 1986; MME, Cath. U. Am., DC, 1989; MSEE, George Wash. U., DC, 2004, JD with honors, 2001. Registered: USPTO (patent atty.) 2001, bar: Md. 2001, DC 2002, US Ct. Appeals (Fed. cir.) 2001, US Dist. Ct., Md. 2001. Engr. various cos., Md., 1986—99, Kenyon & Kenyon, 1999—2004, Miles & Stockbridge, Tysons Corner, Va., 2004—05; atty. Rothwell, Figg, Ernst & Manbeck, 2005—08, Baker & Hostetler, Washington, 2008—. Chmn. ethics panel Frederick County Bd. Edn., Md., 2005—; treas., bd. trustees Beth Sholom Congregation, Frederick, 1993—2003. Mem.: IEEE, ABA, Am. Intellectual Property Law Assn. Office: Baker & Hostetler LLP Washington Sq Ste 1100 1050 Connecticut Ave NW Washington DC 20036 Business E-Mail: atreiber@bakerlaw.com.

TREIBLE, KIRK, retired academic and foundation administrator; b. Newton, NJ, Mar. 29, 1941; s. William Bryan and Grace Almond T.; 1 cons, Todd. BS, W.Va. Wesleyan Coll.; MBA, W.Va. U.; LLD, LaGrange Coll. Bus. mgr. Parkersburg C.C., W.Va., 1969-71; devel. officer W.Va. Wesleyan Coll., 1972-75, acting treas., 1975-77; v.p. fin. Southwestern U., Georgetown, Tex., 1977-88; pres. Andrew Coll., Cuthbert, Ga., 1998—2002, now pres. emeritus; ednl. cons., 2002—; exec. dir. United Meth. Found. for Comm., 2003—. Bd. dirs. Citizen Bank, Geogetown, Tex., 1978-88; bd. dirs. Regions Bank, Cuthbert, Ga., 1989-99; cons. Nebr. Wesleyan U.; cons. So. Assn. Schs. and Colls. Chmn. adminstrv. bd. First United Meth. Ch., 1983-85, univ. senate; mem. W.I.H. and Lula E. Pitts Found., Peed scholarship Trust, United Meth. Ch. Served with USAF, 1966-69. Mem. Assn. Pvt. Colls. and Univs. Ga. (pres. dir.), Nat. Assn. Schs. and Colls. Methodist. E-mail: ktreible@aol.com.

TREICHEL, DIXIE ANN, writer, composer; b. Oshkosh, Wis., Apr. 30, 1956; d. Leona and Carl Treichel. Student, U. Wis., Oshkosh, 1974—76, Vienna Internat. Music Centre, Austria, 1976—77; BMus in Composition, U. Ill., Urbana-Champaign, 1980; postgrad., U. Chgo., 1987—88. Ind. artistic cons., composer, sound designer, theater technician, tchr. Creative Collaborations, 1980—. Co-founder, artistic dir. Diverse Arts Ensemble, Urbana, 1979—86, Milw., 1979—86, Chgo., 1979—86; pres., festival dir. New Music Chgo., Chgo., 1986—87; producing cons., technician, condr. Phoenix Spring Ensemble, San Francisco, 1990—97; founder, dir., composer Unique Sounds Ensemble, Mpls., 2000. Composer (musician): (exploratory music) Portal, Internat. Exptl. Intermedia Festival, 2000, (interdisciplinary performance) Morphos, Internat. Exptl. Intermedia Festival, 2001; composer: (string quartet) Pointed Quarks (Onyx String Quartet Competition Award, 1997); sound designer (theatrical sound design) Street Car Named Desire (Drama-Logue Award, 1996); prodr.: (interdisciplinary performance) Seeds (Producing Grant, 1980); author: We'd Support Tolerance and Acceptance of All People, 2004; composer: (electro-acoustic music) Inclusive Voices, 7th Ann. New Music Festival. Radio host KFAI, Fresh Fruit, Mpls., 1998—. Recipient Drama-Logue award, Theatrical Sound Design, 1996, Onyx String Quartet Competition award, 1997; fellow Edn. Fellowship, U. Chgo., 1987—88. Mem.: New Music Chgo., Am. Composers Forum, Internat. Assn. Women in Music. Achievements include invention of experimental musical instruments. Avocations: swimming, bicycling, reading, poetry, philosophy. Personal E-mail: dixiet007@yahoo.com.

TREIGER, IRWIN LOUIS, lawyer; b. Seattle, Sept. 10, 1934; s. Sam S. and Rose (Steinberg) T.; m. Betty Lou Friedlander, Aug. 18, 1957; children: Louis H., Karen I., Kenneth B. BA, U. Wash., 1955, JD, 1957; LLM in Taxation, NYU, 1958. Bar: Wash. 1958, D.C. 1982, U.S. Dist. Ct. (we. dist.) Wash., U.S. Ct. Appeals (9th cir.), U.S. Supreme Ct. Assoc. Bogle & Gates, Seattle, 1958—63, ptnr., 1964—99, chmn., 1986—94; ptnr. Dorsey & Whitney LLP, Seattle, 1999—. Trustee Am. Tax Policy Inst., 2004—06. Pres. Jewish Fedn. Greater Seattle, 1993-95; chmn. Mayor's Symphony Panel, 1986, Corp. Coun. for the Arts, 1987-88; pres. Seattle Symphony Found., 1986—; trustee, co-chmn. Cornish Coll. of the Arts, 1990-96, chair elect 2003—; trustee The Seattle Found., 1992—, vice chair, 1999-2003, chair, 2003-05; trustee, sec. Samis Found., 1989—; chmn. King County Baseball Pk. Commn., 1995; chmn. task force tax reform Prosperity Partnership Puget Sound Regional Coun., 2006—. Fellow Am. Coll. Tax Counsel; mem. ABA (chmn. taxation sect. 1988-89, sect. del. 1990-96, bd. govs. 2000-03), Wash. State Bar Assn. (chmn. taxation sect. 1975, co-chmn. nat. conf. lawyers and accts. 1997-2000, 09, ABA Sec.Dist. Svc. award), Greater Seattle C. of C. (chmn. 1993-94), Seattle Rotary (trustee 1998-2000), Seattle Rotary Svc. Found. (v.p. 1995-96, pres. 1996-97). Jewish. Office: Irwin L Treiger 600 University St Ste 3600 Seattle WA 98101-4109 Home Phone: 206-328-8404; Office Phone: 206-386-7511. Business E-Mail: iltreiger@stoel.com.

TREISNER, GEORGE HENRY, JR., vocational educator, electrical contractor, financial advisor and tax consultant; b. NYC, Feb. 26, 1936; s. George H. and Florence (Reade) T.; m. Darlene M. Merkle, Apr. 20, 1974; children: George H. III, Dorothy J., Rolf P. Student, Lehigh U., 1953-54, Am. Inst. Banking, 1954-62, Temple U., 1981-89, Northampton County Area Coll., 1970-72. Lic. elec. constrn. instr., Pa. Various positions Union Bank & Trust Co., Bethlehem, Pa., 1954-62; sales rep., gen. agt. Luth. Brotherhood Life Ins. Soc., Bethlehem, 1962-70; v.p. sales Mgmt. Assocs., Bethlehem, 1970-72; sales rep. Olivetti Corp. Am., Allentown, Pa., 1972-74, Pa. Water Works Co., Horsham, 1974-76; elec. contr. Treisner Elec., Bethlehem, 1972-81; tchr. Bethlehem Area Vocat. Tech. Sch., 1981—; lead tchr. Bethlehem Area Vocat. Tchr. Sch., 1989—; fin. advisor Kades Margolis, Wayne, Pa., 2001—, GWN Securities, Palm Beach Gardens, Fla., 2001—; chmn. The Alliance Aging of United Way Greater Lehigh Valley. Mentor tchr. Bethleham Area Vocat. Tech. Sch., 1988—; coord., trainer Assoc. Bldg. Contrs. Apprenticeship, 1990—; adj. prof. elec. constrn. Northampton County Area C.C., 1984-87. Mem. Pa. Task Force on Violence in Schs., 1994; pres. Northampton City Coun. Educators, Easton, Pa., 1991; chmn. adv. com. on curriculum for tchr. excellence Temple U., 1992; mem. Lehigh Valley 2000 State Action Com., 1994—; Bible tchr., youth advisor Holy Cross Evang. Luth. Ch., Bethlehem, 1974—, pres. congregation coun., 2009; v.p. United Way, 2006—; v.p. labor United Way Greater Lehigh Valley; chmn. Alliance Aging, 2001—, mem. bus. edn. partnership bd., 2001—; pres. Aalliance Pub. Schs., 2000-06. Recipient Disting. Citizenship award, ELKS, 2008. Mem. Vocat. Indsl. Club Am., Am. Vocat. Assn., Nat. Assn. Vocat. Edn. Spl. Needs Pers., Pa. Assn. Vocat. Edn. Spl. Needs Pers., Pa. State Edn. Assn. (bd. dirs., chmn. spl. svcs. 1986-93, del to NEA, v.p. Ea. region 1993—, pres. 1994-2001, mem. task force on sch. violence 1994, mem. edn. reform task force 1994), Pa. Vocat. Assn. (Vocat. Tchr. of Yr. 1991, v.p. 1991), Bethlehem Area Vocat. Tech. Sch. Profl. Assn. (past v.p., treas., chief negotiator, pres. 1991—), Fraternal Ins. Counselors (past pres.). Democrat. Avocations: singing, bible study. Home: 236 E Ettwein St Bethlehem PA 18018-4137 Office: PO Box 1637 Bethlehem PA 18016-1637 Home Phone: 610-866-3824; Office Phone: 800-437-1828 ext. 101. Personal E-mail: treisnerg@juno.com.

TREISTER, GEORGE MARVIN, lawyer; b. Oxnard, Calif., Sept. 5, 1923; s. Isadore Harry and Augusta Lee (Bloom) T.; m. Jane Goldberg, Jan. 24, 1946; children: Laura, Neil, Adam, Dana. BS, UCLA, 1943; LL.B., Yale U., 1949. Bar: Calif. 1950. Law clk. to chief justice Calif. Supreme Ct., 1949-50; law clk. to Assoc. Justice Hugo L. Black U. S. Supreme Ct., 1950-51; asst. U.S. atty. So. Dist. Calif., 1951-53; dep. atty. gen. Calif., 1953; practiced in Los Angeles, 1953—; mem. Stutman, Treister and Glatt, 1953—; instr. U. So. Calif. Law Sch., 1954-98, Stanford U. Law Sch., 1977-81. Mem., former vice chmn. Nat. Bankruptcy Conf., emeritus,2007-; former mem. adv. com. on bankruptcy rules Jud. Conf. U.S. Contbr. articles to profl. jours. Served with USNR, 1943-46. Mem. Am. Law Inst. Home: 1201 Neil Creek Rd Ashland OR 97520-9778 Office: 1901 Ave of the Stars 12th fl Los Angeles CA 90067 Home Phone: 541-488-3100; Office Phone: 800-201-3030.

TREITEL, DAVID HENRY, aviation executive; b. Lynn, Mass., Apr. 22, 1954; s. Henry David and Lotte (Elkeses) T.; m. Madelynn Drimmer, Sept. 1982 (div. Oct. 1988); m. Amy Gail Granowitz, Apr. 18, 1990 (div. July 2007). BA in Econs. with honors, Middlebury Coll., 1976; MBA, Columbia U., 1978. Sr. assoc. Simat Helliesen & Eichner, Inc., NYC, 1980-84, v.p., 1984-88, sr. v.p., 1988-90, exec. v.p., 1990-95; pres. Simat Hellliesen & Eichner, Inc., 1995—, CEO, chmn., 1996—, pres., 2007—; sr. v.p. ICF Internat., 2007—. Co-chair Energy, Climate, Transp. Practice, Milw., 2009—; bd. dirs. Aircraft Fin. Trust, Wilmington, Del., Lease Investment Flight Trust, Wilmington, Castle 2003-1 Trust, Wilmington, Castle 2003-2 Trust, Wilmington, ISTAT Found. Contbr. articles to profl. jours. Mem. The Wings Club (bd. dirs.). Republican. Avocations: golf, tennis, tournament bridge, travel. Office: Simat Helliesen & Eichner 90 Park Ave Fl 27 New York NY 10016-1308

TREJOS, SANDRA ROXANA, economics professor; d. Fernando Trejos and Lidieth Rojas; m. Gustavo Adolfo Barboza, Aug. 8, 1992; children: Sofia M. Barboza, Monica M. Barboza, Eugenia M. Barboza, Isabela M. Barboza. BSc in Economics, U. Costa Rica, 1990; MSc, Okla. State U., Stillwater, 1994, PhD, 2000. Budget analyst Comptrollership Republic Costa Rica, San Jose, 1990—91, economist, 1991—92; tchg. assoc. Okla. State U., 1995—97; faculty U. Costa Rica, 1998—2000, rschr., 1998—2000; vis. faculty Ind. U., Indpls., 2001—03, Purdue U., Indpls., 2001—03; assoc. prof. economics Clarion U., Clarion, 2004—, internat. bus. program coord., 2005—. Contbr. articles to profl. jours. Bd. mem. Guatemalan Student Support Group, Inc., Chapel Hill, NC, 2005—. Named Faculty of Yr., 2007; scholarship, US AID, 1992—94, Several instl. grants, U. State Sys. and Coll. Bus., 2005—, fellowship, Ctr. Internat. Bus. Edn. and Rsch., 2006. Mem.: Am. Assn. Hispanic Economists, So. Econs. Assn., Midwest Econs. Assn., Am. Econ. Assn. Avocations: gardening, reading, interior decorating. Office: Clarion Univ Pa 840 Wood St Clarion PA 16214 Business E-Mail: strejos@clarion.edu.

TRELA, RICHARD JOSEPH, conservator, educator; s. Edward Thomas and Marie Catherine Trela; m. Theresa JoAnn Piteo, July 29, 1972; children: Elizabeth Sarah JoAnn, Victoria Marie. BS in Biology, Cleve. State U., 1972—72, BA in Art, 1975; MA of Conservation of Artistic and Hist. Works, SUNY, Oneonta, New York, 1978. Cert. Advanced Study In

Conservation of Hist. & Artistics Works SUNY. Pvt. practice, Helena, Mont., 1978—84; conservator Coll. of Fine Arts & Comm. Brigham Young U., Provo, Utah, 1984—93; dir. Conservation Ctr. Panhandle-Plains Hist. Mus. West Tex. A&M U., Canyon, Tex., 1993—. Adj. prof. Coll. of Fine Arts and Humanities West Tex. A&M U., 2004—. Grant, MIT Mus. Loan Network, 1997, Amarillo Area Found., 1993, 1994, 1995. Mem.: Western Assn. for Art Conservation, Am. Inst. for Conservation of Hist. & Artistic Works (assoc.). Achievements include research in Developed Conservation Treatment for World War II Bomber Folk Art. Avocations: painting, skating, skiing, swimming, bicycling. Home: 414 Taylor Ln Canyon TX 79015 Office: Conservation Ctr PPHM WTAMU 2503 Fourth Ave Canyon TX 79016 Office Fax: 806-651-2250; Home Fax: 806-655-5630. Personal E-mail: rtrela@mail.wtamu.edu.

TRELEASE, ALLEN WILLIAM, historian, educator; b. Boulder, Colo., Jan. 31, 1928; s. William, Jr. and Helen (Waldo) T.; children: William C. (dec. 1990), Mary E., John A. AB, U. Ill., 1950, MA, 1951; PhD, Harvard U., 1955. Mem. faculty Wells Coll., Aurora, NY, 1955-67, prof. history, 1965-67, chmn. dept. history and govt., 1963-67; prof. history U. NC, Greensboro, 1967-94, head dept., 1984-92, prof. emeritus, 1994—. Author: Indian Affairs in Colonial New York: The Seventeenth Century, 1960, White Terror: The Ku Klux Klan Conspiracy and Southern Reconstruction, 1971, Reconstruction: The Great Experiment, 1971, The North Carolina Railroad, 1849-1871, and the Modernization of North Carolina, 1991, Changing Assignments: A Pictorial History of the U. of N.C. at Greensboro, 1991, Making North Carolina Literate: The University of North Carolina at Greensboro, from Normal School to Metropolitan University, 2003. Mem. Am., So. Hist. assns., Orgn. Am. Historians, Hist. Soc. NC (pres. 1986-87), AAUP, Phi Beta Kappa, Phi Kappa Phi, Phi Eta Sigma, Phi Kappa Psi. Personal E-mail: atrelease@triad.rr.com.

TRELLES, ANA, art educator; d. Ana Trelles and Ana Fernandez, Raul Trelles; children: Ana Valdivia, Kenneth Valdivia, Phillip Valdivia, Raphael Valdivia. MA, U. Ariz., Tucson, 2008. Cert. in art Ariz., 2006. Adj. prof. Pima CC, Tucson, 2002—. Personal E-mail: trellesa@email.arizona.edu.

TREMAYNE, ERIC FLORY, lawyer; b. Washington, Nov. 29, 1945; s. Bertram William and Frances (Lewis) Tremayne; m. Barbara Ann Williams, Sept. 18, 1982. BA, Westminster Coll., 1967; JD, Washington U., St. Louis, 1973. Bar: Mo. 1973, U.S. Dist. Ct. (ea. and we. dists.) Mo. 1973, U.S. Tax Ct. 2003. Assoc. Tremayne, Lay, Carr, Bauer, Clayton, Mo., 1973—77, ptnr., 1978—; prosecuting atty. City of Wildwood, Mo., 1996—2000. Dir. Option Computer Corp., St. Louis. Bd. dirs. YMCA of Ozarks; campaign aide Citizens for Kit Bond, St. Louis, 1972. With US Army, 1968—70. Mem.: Bar Assn. Met. St. Louis, St. Louis County Bar Assn. (pres. 1983—84, Outstanding Young Lawyer 1981), Sports Car Club Am. (instr. 1979—), Beta Theta Pi (v.p. 1978—90). Home: 433 Eatherton Valley Rd Wildwood MO 63005-4103 Office: Tremayne Lay & Coleman LLP 7777 Bonhomme Ave Ste 1600 Clayton MO 63105-1911 Home Phone: 636-532-6608; Office Phone: 314-863-4151. Business E-Mail: etremayne@tremayne.org.

TREMBLAY, ANDRÉ-MARIE, physicist; b. Montreal, Que., Can., Jan. 2, 1953; m. Marié à Guylaine Séguin; children: Noémie, Rachel. BSc, U. Montreal, 1974; PhD, MIT, 1978. With Energie Atomique du Can. Limitée, 1973-74, MIT, Boston, 1974-75, Inst. de Recherche de l'Hydro-Que., 1976, Cornell U., Ithaca, NY, 1978-80; prof. physics U. Sherbrooke, Que., 1980—, dir. Rsch. Ctr. Physics of Solids Que., 1991-99. Cons. Cornell U., 1981, Ohio State U., 1982, IBM, 1984; vis. scientist Cornell U., 1986-87, Yale U., 2003; vis. rsch. physicist Inst. for Theoretical Physics, Santa Barbara, Calif., 1989, 96, 2000, 2002, 2009; vis. scientist Brookhaven (N.Y.) Nat. Lab, 1984; assoc. prof. U. Provence, France, 1982, 83, 97, 99, 2000, 02; Can. Rsch. chair in condensed matter physics, 2000—. Contbr. over 130 articles to profl. publs. Recipient Herzberg medal Can. Assn. Physics, Steacie prize Natural Scis. and Engring. Rsch. Coun., 1987, CAP-CRM prize in Theoretical and Math. Physics, 2001, Urgel-Archaubault prize Assn. francophone pour le savoir, 2003; Killam fellow, 1992-94. Fellow: Royal Soc. Can.; mem.: Can. Inst. Advanced Rsch. Office: Sherbrooke U Dept Physics Sherbrooke PQ Canada J1K 2R1 E-mail: tremblay@physique.usherbrooke.ca.

TREMBLAY, DIANA D., automotive executive; BS in Industrial Adminstrn., Kettering U.; MS in Bus. Mgmt., MIT. With ctrl. foundry GM Corp., Defiance, Ohio, 1977, engr. powertrain divsn., 1983—96, engr. Pontiac Saginaw, Mich., exec.-mfg. Automotive Components Group, 1990—96, dir. labor rels. Detroit, 1996—2000; mfg. dir. Luton Vauxhall Motors Ltd., England, 2000—02; plant mgr. Opel Belgium, Antwerp, 2002; exec. dir. labor rels. GM Corp., 2004—06, v.p. labor rels. GM N.Am., 2006—. Named one of the Most Influential Women in Metro Detroit, Crain's Detroit Bus. mag., 2007; Sloan Fellow. Office: GM Corp PO Box 33170 Detroit MI 48232-5170*

TREMBLAY, MARC, information technology executive; B in Physics Engring., Laval U., Can.; M in Computer Sci., D in Computer Sci., UCLA. Co-arch. UltraSPARC I Sun Microsystems, Inc., chief arch. UltraSPARC II, chief arch. MAJC program, arch. picoJava processor core, sr. v.p., chief tech. officer Microelectronics, Sun fellow. Mem.: IEEE, Assn. Computing Machinery. Achievements include patents in field. Office: Sun Microsystems Inc 4150 Network Cir Santa Clara CA 95054 Office Phone: 650-960-1300.

TREMBLAY, MARC ADÉLARD, anthropologist, educator; b. Les Eboulements, Que., Can., Apr. 24, 1922; s. Willie and Laurette (Tremblay) T.; m. Jacqueline Cyr, Dec. 27, 1949; children: Geneviève, Lorraine, Marc, Colette, Dominique, Suzanne. AB, U. Montreal, 1944, L.S.A., 1948; MA, Laval U., 1950; PhD, Cornell U., 1954; PhD (hon.), Ottawa U., 1982, Guelph U., 1983, U. N. B.C., 1994, Carleton U., 1995, U. Ste. Anne, 1997, McGill U., 1998. Research asso. Cornell U., 1953-56; mem. faculty Laval U., 1956-93, prof. anthropology, 1963-68, 81-93, prof. emeritus, 1994, vice dean social scis., 1968-71, dean Grad. Sch., 1971-79, also mem. univ. council.; pres. Quebec Coun. Social Rsch., 1987-91. Dir. Inuit and Circupolar Study Group Laval U., 1991—93; mem. Nunavik Commn., 1999—2001. Author 25 books and monographs in social scis., about 200 articles., The biographical Memoir of dr Alafonda Hamilton Leighton, 2009. Decorated officer Order of Can., gt. officer Order of Que.; recipient Que. Lit. prize, 1965, Innis-Gerin prize Royal Soc. Can., 1979, Molson prize Can. Coun., 1987, Prix Marcel Vincent ACFAS, 1988, Contbn. exceptionnelle Societé de sociologie et d'anthropolotie, 1990, Esdras Minville award Soc. St.-Jean Baptiste, 1991; named to Internat. Order of Merit, Internat. Biog. Inst., Cambridge, Eng., 1990. Mem. Royal Soc. Can. (pres. 1981-84), Acad. des Scis. Morales et Politiques (sec.), Rsch. Inst. Pub. Policy, Am. Anthrop. Assn. (past fellow), Am. Sociology Soc. (past fellow), Can. Soc. Applied Anthropology, Can. Sociology and Anthropology Assn. (founding pres.), Can. Ethnology Soc. (past pres.), Assn. Can. Univs. for Northern Studies (past pres.), Assn. Internat. Sociology, Societe des savants et sci. Can. (pres. nat. order Quebec 1998-2000). Home: 835 N Orléans St Sainte-Foy PQ Canada G1X 3J4 Personal E-mail: matremgt@globetrotter.net.

TREMBLY, CRISTY, television executive; b. Oakland, Md., July 11, 1958; d. Charles Dee and Mary Louise (Cassidy) T.; m. Roman Ziombra. BA in Russian, German and Linguistics cum laude, W.Va. U., 1978, BS in Journalism, 1978, MS in Broadcast Journalism, 1979; advanced cert. travel, West L.A. Coll., 1982; advanced cert. rec. engring., Soundmaster Schs., North Hollywood, Calif., 1985. Engr. videotape Sta. WWVU-TV, Morgantown, W.Va., 1976—80; announcer, engr. Sta. WVVW Radio, Grafton, W.Va., 1979; tech. dir., videotape supr. Sta. KMEX-TV, LA, 1980—85; broadcast supr. Sta. KADY-TV, Oxnard, Calif., 1988—89; dir. news tech. Sta. KVEA-TV, Glendale, Calif., 1985—89; asst. editor, videotape technician CBS TV Network, Hollywood, Calif., 1989—90; supr. videotape Sta. KCBS-TV, Hollywood, 1990—91, mgr. electronic news gathering ops., 1991—92; studio mgr., engr.-in-charge CBS TV Network, Hollywood, 1992—2001, mgr. transmission and satellite, 1994—, mgr. videotape, 2001, mgr. syndication, 2001, mgr. prodn., 2001—. Radio operator KJ6BX Malibu Disaster Comm., 1987—; coun. mem. L.A. World Affairs 2000—. Prodr. (TV show) The Mountain Scene, 1976-78. Vol. Ch. Coun., L.A. Riot Rebldg., Homeless shelter work, VA Hosps., Mus. docent; sponsor 3 overseas foster children; fundraiser La Mision Orphanage Ensenada Libr. Flying Samaritans, 2000—; L.A. Dist. rep. Calif.-Pacific conf.comm. commn. United Meth. Ch., 2002—; chmn. adminstrv. coun. Malibu United Meth. Ch., 1993—, choir, 1995—, comm. commn. rep., 2002—; sec., mem. adv. com. Tamassee (S.C.) Sch., 1992—; sr. orgn. pres. Children of the Am. Revolution, Malibu, Calif., 1992—; mem. internat. vis. coun. Outstanding Program Resource; mem. L.A. World Affairs Coun., 2000—. Named one of Outstanding Young Women of Am., 1988, Internat. Vis. Coun. Outstanding Pvt. Resource, L.A. County, Outstanding Female Broadcast Engr., Soc. Broadcast Engrs., 2006; recipient Asst. editor Emmy award Young and the Restless, 1989-90, Golden Mike award Radio/TV News Assn., 1991, 92, Pub. Svc. commendation, County of L.A., 1999, cert. leadership, USIA, cert. commendation, City of L.A., 1999. Mem.: DAR (state chair motion pictures, radio and TV, Calif. 1988—90, Mex. 1990—, nat. vice-chair units overseas Mex. 1998—, organizing regent Baja Calif. chpt. 1999—, state conf. chair 2001, state sec. 2001—04, 2001—, nat. vice-chair media awards 2001—, nat. vice-chair chpt. devel. 2004—, state conf. chair 2004—, vice regent Mex. 2004—07, state regent 2007—, Nat. Outstanding Jr. 1993), ATAS (judge local and nat. Emmy awards 1991—, exec. com. on electronic prodn. 1992—, membership com. 1994—96, awards com. 1994—, engring. awards com. 1997—, gov. 2000—, daytime awards com. 2000—, awards com. 2000—, chair tech. com. 2001—, activites com. 2002—, theatre stds. com. 2002—, diversity com. 2004—), Acad. Canadian Cinema and TV, Nat. Broadcasting Soc. (conf. spkr. 2001), Women in Comm., Soc. Profl. Journalists, Women in Film Internat. (com. 1999—), Am. Women in Radio and TV (bd. dirs. So. Calif. chpt. 1984—85, 1993—2000, pres. 1996—97, Genii award 2007), Travelers Century Club (life; program chair 1987—), Mensa (life), Travelers Century Club (life), Beta Sigma Phi. Democrat. Methodist. Avocations: singing, cooking, travel, genealogy, languages. Home: 2901 Searidge St Malibu CA 90265-2969 Office: CBS TV City 7800 Beverly Blvd Los Angeles CA 90036-2188

TREML, VLADIMIR GUY, economist, educator; b. Kharkov, USSR, Mar. 27, 1929; came to U.S., 1950, naturalized, 1953; s. Guy Alexey and Lydia Vladimir (Timofeev) T.; m. Emma Miro, July 12, 1952; children— Irene Treml Cagney, Tatiana, Alexey. BA in Econs, Bklyn. Coll., 1955; MA in Econs, Columbia U., 1956; PhD in Econs, U. N.C., 1963. Dept. supr. Bache & Co., NYC, 1953-58; research asso. Inst. for Social Scis., U. N.C., Chapel Hill, 1958-61; asso. prof. econs. Franklin and Marshall Coll., 1961-66; research asso. Inst. Study USSR, Munich, Germany, 1966-67; prof. econs. Duke U., 1967—; dir. Ctr. for Slavic Studies U.S. Dept. Edn. of Duke U., 1991—. Cons. in field; expert Dept. Commerce, The World Bank, other fed. agys., 1971—; vis. Ford research prof. U. Calif., Berkeley, 1984-85; vis. research prof. U. Hokkaido, Sapporo, Japan, 1985. Author: (with others) Structure of the Soviet Economy, 1972, Input-Output Analysis and the Soviet Economy, 1975, Western Sovietology in the Soviet Union, 1999; contbr. reports to publs. of Joint Econ. Com., U.S. Congress; contbr. articles to profl. publs.; editor: Soviet Economic Statistics, 1972; editor, contbg. author: Studies in Soviet Input-Output Analysis, 1977, Alcohol in the USSR, 1982; contbg. editor: Soviet Economy Jour. Trustee Nat. Council for Soviet and East European Research, Inc., Washington, 1978-84. Served with USMC, 1951-53. Grantee Ford Found., 1972-81, Dept. Def.-Advanced Rsch. Project Agy., 1975-76, Dept. State, 1976-77, Dept. Def., 1985-90, Georgetown U., 1984-86, Olin Found., 1989, Internat. Rsch. and Exch. Bd., 1993-96, Nat. Coun. for Eurasian Rsch., 1996-98; Fulbright fellow Moscow U., 1992. Mem. So. Econ. Assn., Am. Econ. Assn., Assn. Comparative Econ. Studies (exec. com. 1972-74), Am. Assn. Advancement Slavic Studies, So. Conf. on Slavic Studies (pres. 1977-78), Phi Beta Kappa. Democrat. Eastern Orthodox. Home: 3719 Albritton Dr Durham NC 27705-7381 Home Phone: 919-490-5111; Office Phone: 919-684-1800, 919-660-1800. Business E-Mail: treml@econ.duke.edu.

TRENBERTH, KEVIN EDWARD, atmospheric scientist; b. Christchurch, New Zealand, Nov. 8, 1944; came to US, 1977; s. Edward Maurice and Ngaira Ivy (Eyre) T.; m. Gail Neville Thompson, Mar. 21, 1970; children: Annika Gail, Angela Dawn. BSc with honors, U. Canterbury, Christchurch, 1966; ScD, MIT, Cambridge, 1972. Meteorologist New Zealand Meteorol. Service, Wellington, 1966-76, supt. dynamic meteorology, 1976-77; assoc. prof. meteorology U. Ill., Urbana, 1977-82, prof., 1982-84; scientist Nat. Ctr. Atmospheric Research, Boulder, Colo., 1984-86, sr. scientist, 1986—, leader empirical studies group, 1987, head sect. climate analysis, 1987—; dep. dir. climate and global dynamics divsn. Nat. Ctr. Atmospheric Rsch., Boulder, Colo., 1991-95. Joint sci. com. for world climate rsch. programme, com. climate changes and the ocean Tropical Oceans Global Atmosphere Program Sci. Steering Group, 1990-94; mem. Climate Variability and Predictability Sci. Steering Group, 1995—2004, co-chair, 1996-99; joint sci. com. World Climate Rsch. Program, 1999-2006, officer 2002-2006, chair observations and assimilation panel, 2004—, mem. global energy and water cycle experiment, 2007—. Editor: Climate System Modeling, 1992, Earth Interactions, 1996-98; contbr. Intergovernmental Panel on Climate Change, 1990, 92, lead author, 1995, 2001, 07; shared Nobel Peace Prize for IPCC, 2007; contbr. articles to profl. jours. Recipient Disting. Achievement award Nat. Ctr. Atmospheric Rsch., 2003; grantee NSF, NOAA, NASA. Fellow Am. Meteorol. Soc. (editor sci. jour. 1981-86, com. chmn. 1985-87, Editor's award 1989, Jule G. Charney award 2000), AAAS (coun. del. sect. atmosphere and hydrosphere sci. 1993-97), Royal Soc. New Zealand (hon.), Am. Geophys. Union (editor's award 2007); mem. NAS (earth scis. com. 1982-85, tropical oceans global atmosphere adv. panel 1984-87, polar rsch. bd. 1986-90, climate rsch. com. 1987-90, global oceans atmosphere land sys. panel 1994-98, panel on reconciling temperature observations, 1999-2000, com. on global change rsch. 1999-02), Meteorol. Soc. New Zealand. Home: 5697 Pennsylvania Pl Boulder CO 80303 Office: Nat Ctr Atmospheric Rsch PO Box 3000 Boulder CO 80307-3000 Home Phone: 303-443-1446; Office Phone: 303-497-1318. Business E-Mail: trenbert@ucar.edu.

TRENDEL, JILL A., pharmacist, educator; d. Donald K. and Marjorie A. Laytart; m. William F. Trendel, Sept. 26, 1992; 1 child, Jarett Ja. BA, U. Toledo, 1997, PhD, 2001. Postdoc. fellow U. Toledo, 2001—02, rsch. fellow, 2002—05, asst. rsch. prof., 2005—, toxicokinetics instr., 2007—08, reviewer, 2007—. Biology instr. Owens State CC, Toledo, 2008; pharmacology instr. Lourdes Coll., Sylvania, 2008. Contbr. articles to profl. jours., chapters to books. Breast cancer adv. U. Toledo, 2008—. Mem.: Internat. Soc. Interferon Cytokine Rsch., Am. Soc. Cell Biology, Am. Assn. Cancer Rsch. Office: Univ Toledo 2801 W Bancroft Toledo OH 43606 Business E-Mail: jill.trendel@utoledo.edu.

TRENGA, ANTHONY JOHN, federal judge; b. Wilkensburg, Pa., 1949; m. Rita Marie FlorCruz; children: Elizabeth, Anthony. AB, Princeton U., NJ, 1971; JD, U. Va. Sch. Law, 1974. Bar: Va. 1974. Law clerk to Hon. Ted Dalton US Dist. Ct. (we. dist.) Va., 1974—75; assoc. Sachs, Greenebaum & Tayler, Washington, 1975—82, ptnr., 1982—87, Hazel & Thomas, P.C., Fairfax, Va., 1987—98; chmn. litigation dept. Miller & Chevalier Chartered, 1998—2008; judge US Dist. Ct. (ea. dist.) Va., Alexandria, 2008—. Office: US Dist Ct 401 Courthouse Sq Alexandria VA 22314*

TRENHOLM, LAURIE E., horticulturist, educator; b. Rochester, NY; BS, U. Fla., Gainesville, 1994, MS, 1996; PhD, U. Ga., Athens, 1999. Asst. prof. U. Fla., 1999—2005, assoc. prof., 2005—. Pres. Puppy Hill Farm Animal Rescue, Melrose, Fla., 1999—. Recipient Educator award, Turfgrass Prodrs. Internat., 2008. Mem.: Crop Sci. Soc.

TRENNEPOHL, GARY LEE, academic administrator, finance educator; b. Detroit, Dec. 6, 1946; s. Leo Donald and Wilma Mae (Tiesnvold) T.; m. Sandra K. Yeager, June 9, 1968; children: Paige E., Adrienne A. BS, U. Tulsa, 1968; MBA, Utah State U., 1971; PhD, Tex. Tech. U., 1976. Asst. prof. aero. studies Tex. Tech. U., Lubbock, 1972-74; asst./assoc. prof. fin. Ariz. State U., Tempe, 1977—82; prof. U. Mo., Columbia, 1982-86, dir. Sch. Bus., 1984-86; prof., head dept. fin. Tex. A&M U., College Station, 1986-91, assoc. dean Coll. Bus., 1991-93, Peters prof. fin., 1992-95, exec. assoc. dean, 1994-95; dean Coll. Bus. Okla. State U., Stillwater, 1995-99; pres. Okla. State U.-Tulsa, 1999—. Mem. faculty options inst. Chgo. Bd. Options Exch., 1987—; bd. dir. Blue Cross/Blue Shield Okla., Tulsa Econ. Devel. Commn., Tulsa Air and Space Mus. Author: An Introduction to Financial Management, 1984, Investment Management, 1993; assoc. editor Jour. Fin. Rsch., 1983-96; contr. chpts. Encyclopedia of Investments, Options: Essential Concepts; contbr. articles to profl. jours. Capt. USAF, 1968—74. Decorated Commendation medal with oak leaf cluster, Vietnam Svc. medal. Mem. Fin. Mgmt. Assn. (v.p. program 1993, pres. 1993-94). Lutheran. Office: Okla State U Tulsa 700 N Greenwood Ave Tulsa OK 74106-0702 Home Phone: 918-523-8563. Business E-Mail: gary.trennepohl@okstate.edu.

TRENT, B. KEITH, lawyer, energy executive; b. Little Rock, Oct. 16, 1959; m. Lucy Trent; 2 children. BSEE with honors, So. Methodist U., 1981; JD with high honors, U. Tex., 1987. Bar: Tex. 1987, US Ct. Appeals (5th cir.), US Supreme Ct., NC. Reservoir/prodn. engr. Arco Oil & Gas, Houston, 1982; atty. Jackson Walker, Dallas; ptnr. Snell Brannian & Trent, Dallas, 1991—2002; gen. counsel litig. Duke Energy, Charlotte, NC, 2002—05, group v.p., gen. counsel, sec., 2005, group exec., chief devel. officer, 2006, group exec., chief strategy and policy officer Charlotte, NC, 2006—07, group exec., chief strategy, policy and regulatory officer, 2007—09, group exec., pres. comml. bus., 2009—. Mem. exec. com. Internat. Inst. Conflict Prevention & Resolution; bd. dirs. NAM. Editor (assoc.): Tex. Law Rev. Bd. visitors Wake Forest U. Babcock Grad. Sch. Mgmt.; mem. Youth Edn. Coun. United Way of Ctrl. Carolinas. Mem.: Mecklenburg County Bar, NC State Bar, ABA, Assn. Corp. Counsel, Tex. State Bar, Dallas Bar Assn., Houston Bar Assn., Dallas Inn of Ct., Order of the Coif, Tau Beta Pi. Office: Duke Energy 526 S Church St Charlotte NC 28202-1904 Office Phone: 704-594-6200.*

TRENT, CALVIN R., city health department director; BA, MA Edn., Wayne State Univ.; MA, PhD, Univ. Detroit-Mercy. Adminstr. Detroit Pub. Sch. Sys. & Highland Park Cmty. Coll., 1976—92; addictions therapist Vet. Adminstrn. Hosp., Battle Creek; dir. Detroit Counseling Ctr.; dir. substance abuse prevention prog. Detroit Dept. Health & Wellness Promotion, 1998—2009, dir. spl. population health services, 2006, health officer & dir., 2009—. Office: Dept Health & Wellness Promotion Herman Kiefer Complex 1151 Taylor Detroit MI 48202 Office Phone: 313-876-4776.*

TRENT, DARRELL M., ambassador, academic administrator, transportation executive; b. Neosho, Mo., Aug. 2, 1938; s. Clarence Melvin and Edna Ruth T.; children: Darrell Michael, Derek Montgomery, Mercy Ruth. AB, Stanford U., 1961; postgrad., Internat. Law Sch., The Hague, Netherlands, summer 1961, Wharton Grad. Sch. Bus., U. Pa., summer 1962; MBA, Columbia U., 1964. Owner, mgr. Trent Enterprises, Kans. and Mo., 1963-66; pres., CEO N.Am. Carmen, Ltd., Del., 1965-68, Assoc. Stores, Inc., Okla., 1967-69, Plz. Supermarkets, Inc., Kans., 1966-69, Food Svc., Inc., Kans., 1966-69, Supermarkets, Inc., Kans., 1966-69, Acton Devel. Co., Inc., Kans., 1966-81; rsch. writer Nixon for Pres., 1968; staff dir. for pers. Presdl. Transition, 1968-69; commr. Property Mgmt. and Disposal Svc., GSA, 1969; dep. asst. to Pres. U.S., 1969-70; exec. dir. Property Rev. Bd., Exec. Office of Pres., 1969-73; dep. dir. Office Emergency Preparedness, 1970-72, acting dir., 1973; mem. Cost of Living Coun., 1973, Oil Policy Com., 1973; chmn. Joint Bd. Fuel Supply and Fuel Transp., 1973; mem. NSC, 1973; chmn. Pres.'s Adv. Coun. CD, 1973; U.S. mem. NATO Sr. Civil Emergency Planning Com., 1973; sr. rsch. fellow Hoover Inst., Stanford U., 1974-81, 89-94, sr. advisor, 1998—, assoc. dir., 1974-81, bd. overseers, 1985-89; dep. campaign mgr. Citizens for Reagan, 1976; dep. campaign mgr., cons. Reagan for Pres. Com., 1979-80, sr. policy advisor, 1980; dir. Office Policy Coordination, Presdl. Transition, 1980-81; U.S. alt. rep. Nato Com. Challenges of Modern Soc., 1982-83; dep. sec. U.S. Dept. Transp., 1981-82, acting sec., 1982-83; chmn. U.S. del. European Civil Aviation Com., U.S. Amb., 1983-88; chmn. Action Devel. Corp., Inc., 1988—; chmn., CEO Rollins Environ. Svcs., Inc., 1983-88, TEC Systems, Inc., 1990-91, Clean Earth Tech., Inc., 1992-93; amb., sr. adv. Ministry of Transp., Iraq, 2003—04; sr. adv. Sec. Def., 2001—04, Transition on Trans. and Budget, 2000; chmn. Trans Adv. Com., Bush Cheney, 2000. Chmn. Fed. Home Loan Bank Pitts., 1983-91; cons. ACDA, 1974-81, HUD, 1974, Dept. Commerce, 1974-76; bd. advisors Chronicle Info. Svcs., Inc., 1984-87; bd. mem. Continental Materials Corp., 1998—; US dept. def. advisor to sec. SEN Staffing, 2001; CPA sr. advisor, rank of amb. Ministry of Trans., Iraq, 2003-04. Author: The U.S. and Transnational Terrorism, 1980, Transportation: Policy, Goals, Accomplishments, 1984; co-author: Terrorism: Threat, Reality, Response, 1979; contbr. articles to profl. publs. Bd. regents Pepperdine U., 1985-92; bd. dirs. Found. Teach Econs., 1988-90; dep. chmn. Ronald

Reagan Presdl. Found., 1985-88. Mem. Bohemian Club. Republican. Methodist. Office: 1610 S Broadway St Pittsburg KS 66762-5845 Personal E-mail: darrell.trent@att.net, darrell.trent@gmail.com.

TRENT, ELTON ROGER, educational assessment administrator, writer; b. Manchester, Ohio, Nov. 18, 1940; s. Wallace V. and Jessie Alise Trent; m. Margaret Vivian Lloyd, Aug. 5, 1978; m. Barbara Wilson, Sept. 12, 1964 (div. Mar. 1975); children: Stephanie Trent Flowers, Stacy Trent Dick. BA in Social Studies, The Ohio State U., 1962, BS in Edn., 1962, MA in Mid. Ea. History, 1964, PhD in Psychology, 1974. Cert. edn. admistrv. specialist Ohio. From cons. test devel. to exec. dir. Ohio Dept. Edn., Columbus, 1963—99, exec. dir. sch. standards and assessment, 1999—2000, exec. dir. emeritus, 2001—; v.p., ops. and devel. Am. Testronics, Iowa City, 1984—86; freelance cons. in field Columbus, 2001—. Vis. lectr., stats. The Ohio State U., Columbus, 1978—78. Author: Ohio Survey Tests, 1977, Ohio Interest Survey, 1983, Career Survey, 1984; co-author (with Nancy Cole and Dena Waddell): 3 R's Achievement Test, 1981; co-author: (with Edward Roeber) Contracting For Testing Services in Handbook of Test Development, 2006. Recipient Governor's Employee award, Gov., State of Ohio, 1991, Disting. Svc. award, Ohio Ho. Reps. and Ohio Senate, 2000, Governor's Employee award, Gov., State of Ohio, 1995, Pioneer in Edn. award, Ohio Dept. Edn., 2001. Mem.: Nat. Coun. Measurement in Edn. (mem. editl. bd. 1998—2000), Am. Edn. Rsch. Assn. Presbyterian. Avocations: travel, reading, sports. Home: 5301 Hollister Street Columbus OH 43235-7603 Personal E-mail: roger-trent@columbus.rr.com.

TRENT, HENRY GIBSON, JR., insurance company executive, educator; b. Knoxville; s. Henry Gibson Trent and Katherine Cooper Brabson; m. Sophie R. Shadow, May 5, 1956; children: Henry Gibson III, William Shadow. BS in Social Sci. summa cum laude, Tenn. Tech., Cookville, 1949; MA in History, So. Meth. U., Dallas, 1950. Tchr. Putnam Co. Schs., Cookville, Tenn., 1950—52, Baylor Sch., Chattagnooga, 1952—53; ins. claims Crawford and Co., 1953—64; regional claims supt. Great Am. Ins. Co., Atlanta, 1964—69; claims mgr. Home Ins. Co., Atlanta, 1969—81, claims officer; claims cons. Alexander and Alexander, Atlanta, 1981—86, Gay and Taylor, Atlanta, 1987—90; ret. Mem. Blue Goose Assn., 1969—81; pres. Atlanta Claims Mgr. Council, 1979—80. Pres. Freinds of the Libr., Athens, Tenn., 1992—96; chmn. com. Athens (Tenn.) Kiwanis Club, 1993—2003; com. mem. United Way, Athens, Tenn., 1992—2006; chmn. Internat. Co-Arbitration Bd., Atlanta, 1969—81; mem. Nat. Auto Theft Bd., Atlanta, 1980—81. Mem.: Sons of the Revolution, Atlanta Claims Assn. (ret. pres.), So. Loss Assn., MENSA, McMinn Heritage Mus. (life; bd. dirs. 1992—2006). Republican. Episcopalian. Avocations: fishing, gardening, reading, ballroom dancing, hunting. Home: 229 Lynwood Dr Athens TN 57303 Office Phone: 423-745-1261.

TRENT, JUDITH SWANLUND, communication educator; b. Grand Rapids, Aug. 29, 1940; d. Vincent George Swanlund and Evelyn Barrows; m. Jimmie Douglas Trent, Dec. 19, 1969; 1 child, Lawrence Andrew. BS, Western Mich. U., Kalamazoo, 1962; MA, U. Mich., Ann Arbor, 1968, PhD, 1970. Dir. debate U. Mich., Ann Arbor, 1967—69; asst. prof. Youngston State U., Ohio, 1970—71; prof. U. Dayton, Ohio, 1971—84; Am. coun. on edn. fellow U. Cin., 1983—84, assoc. v.p., 1984—2000, prof. dept. comm., 1984—. Co-author (with Jimmie D. Trent and Daniel J. O'Neill): Concepts in Communication, 1973; co-author: (with Jimmie D. Trent) Instructor's Guide to Accompany Concepts in Communication, 1973; co-author: (with Robert V. Friedenberg) Political Campaign Communication: Principles and Practices, 1983, 6th edit., 2008; editor: Communication: Views From The Helm For The Twenty First Century, 1998, Included in Communication: Learning Climates That Cultivate Racial and Ethnic Diversity, 2002; contbr. chapters to books, articles various profl. jours. and book reviews. Mem.: Eastern Comm. Assn. (named a Centennial Scholar 2009, Named Disting. Rsch. fellow 2009), Ctrl. States Comm. Assn. (pres. 1982, Hall of Fame 2006), Nat. Comm. Assn. (pres. 1997, Disting. Svcs. award 2004). Avocations: travel, gardening. Home: 101 Country Club Oxford OH 45056 Office: U Cin Dept Comm Cincinnati OH 45221 Home Phone: 513-523-4484; Office Phone: 513-556-4493. Business E-Mail: judith.trent@uc.edu.

TRENT, ROBERT HAROLD, retired business educator; b. Norfolk, Va., Aug. 3, 1933; s. Floyd Murton and Myrtle Eugenia (White) T.; m. Joanne Bell, Aug. 17, 1951; 1 child, John Thomas BS, U. Richmond, 1963; PhD, U. N.C., 1968. Asst. prof. U. N.C., Chapel Hill, 1968-69; assoc. prof. commerce McIntire Sch. Commerce U. Va., Charlottesville, 1970-74, prof. commerce, 1975-84, Ralph A. Beeton prof. free enterprise, 1985-91; C. & P. Telephone Co. prof. commerce U. Va., Charlottesville, 1991-98, prof. commerce emeritus, 1998—. Co-author: Marketing Decision Making, 1976, 4th edit., 1988; editor: Developments in Management Information Systems, 1974 Mem.: Omicron Delta Kappa, Beta Gamma Sigma. Home Phone: 434-293-3761.

TRENTANELLI, JOHN ANTHONY, educational administrator; b. Cleve., Oct. 18, 1939; s. Frank Joseph and Marie Theresa Trentanelli; m. Barbara Kay Trentanelli, Apr. 30, 1977; 1 child, Angela Rose. BS in Edn., S.E. Mo. State U., 1969; postgrad., Cleve. State U., 1980-81; M. Edn. and Adminstrn., Prarie View A&M U., Tex., 1987. Substitute tchr. Parma (Ohio) Pub. Sch. Dist., 1977-78; social studies tchr., Am. Fedn. Tchrs. rep. Cleve. Pub. Schs., 1978-81; social studies tchr., dept. chmn. Houston Ind. Sch. Dist., 1981-87, asst. prin., 1987-99, Yonkers (N.Y.) Pub. Sch. Dist., 1999—. Editor Galveston Bay Power Squadron, Bay Breeze, 1999. Treas. Galveston Bay Power Squadron, Clear Lake, Tex., 1999. Mem. ASCD, Pi Kappa Alpha (pres. Dist. 15, 1972-73). Avocation: power and sail boating. Office: Lincoln HS 375 Kneeland Ave Yonkers NY 10704 Home: 25 Spring Pond Dr Ossining NY 10562-2036 E-mail: jtrentanelli@yonkerspublicschool.org.

TRENTO, ALFREDO A., thoracic surgeon, educator; b. Padua, Italy, July 3, 1950; MD, U. Padova, 1975. Cert. Am. Bd. Surgery, Am. Bd. Thoracic Surgery. Intern, internal medicine Cittadella Gen. Hosp., Padua, Italy; intern, gen. surgery U. Mass., Worcester, Mass., 1977, fellow, 1982; resident, thoracic surgery U. Mass. Med. Ctr., Worcester, Mass., 1977—82; resident, surgery U. Pitts. Sch. Medicine, Pa., 1983—85, faculty mem.; dir., ECMO Program Children's Hosp. Pitts.; dir., divsn. cardiothoracic surgery Cedars-Sinai Med. Ctr., LA, Estelle, Abe and Marjorie Sanders Endowed Chair, cardiac surgery; prof., surgery, David Geffen Sch. Medicine UCLA Sch. Medicine, Calif. Presenter in field. Contbr. articles to profl. jours., chapters to books. Fellow: ACS; mem.: Western Assn. Transplant Surgeons, Am. Assn. for Thoracic Surgery, Soc. Thoracic Surgeons, Internat. Soc. for Heart Transplantation. Office: Cedars Sinai Med Ctr 8700 Beverly Blvd Ste 6215 Los Angeles CA 90048 Office Phone: 310-423-3851. Office Fax: 310-423-0127. Business E-Mail: alfredo.trento@cshs.org.

TRENTON, PATRICIA JEAN, art historian; m. Norman B. Trenton; children: James Davis, Jeffrey Norman. PhD, U. Calif., 1980. Curator of Am. art Denver Art Mus., 1969—74; Editor Am. Personality Drawing Exhibition Catalog, UCLA, 1976; curator of art Union League Club Chgo., 1981; guest curator Western Am. Art, Palm Spring Desert Mus., 1981—82, Bowers Mus., Santa Ana, Calif., 1984, Southwest Mus., Los Angeles, Calif., 1984, Laguna Art Mus., Laguna Beach, Calif., 1987—91, Autry Mus. Western Heritage, Los Angeles, Calif., 1993—97; art curator Los Angeles Athletic Club, 1982—2001; guest curator San Jose Mus. Art, San Jose, Calif., 2003, Irvine Mus., Irvine, Calif., 2005. Lectr. various profl. conf. Contbr. articles various profl. jours.; Crocker Art Mus., Sacramento, Calif., 1990, Laguna Art Mus., Laguna Beach, Calif., 1990, Dixon Gallery and Gardens, Memphis, Tenn., 1991, Montclair Art Mus., Montclair, NJ, 1991, Gene Autry Western Heritage Mus., 1990, Bowers Mus., 1984, Buffalo Bill Hist. Ctr., Wy., 1983, Palm Springs Desert Mus., 1982. Art adv. bd. Yosemite Exhibition, Autry Mus., 2002—. Recipient Susan Koppleman award, 1995, Caroline Bancroft Hist. prize, Indep. Spirits, 1995, Western Heritage Wrangler award, Nat. Cowboy Hall of Fame and Western Heritage Ctr., 1995, Nat. Am. Publisher's award, U. Okla. Press's Publication, 1983; Rockefeller Fellowship award, UCLA, 1977. Mem.: Mus. Western Art (dir, adv. bd. 1985—87), Am. Mus. Assn., Am. Social Studies, Coll. Art Assn., Los Angeles County Mus. of Art, Am. Art Coun. Steering Com., KCET Women's Coun. Home: 10112 Empyrean Way 303 Los Angeles CA 90067 Office Phone: 818-385-3100 Ext. 125. Personal E-mail: pdtrenton@aol.com.

TREPPER, MYRON, lawyer; b. NYC, Mar. 9, 1943; BA, Hunter Coll., 1965; JD, Bklyn. Law Sch., 1968. Bar: NY 1969; US Dist. Ct. (so., ea. dists.) NY 1971; U.S. Ct. Appeals (2nd, 11th cirs.). Co-chmn. Willkie Farr & Gallagher LLP, NYC. Mem. NY County Lawyers Assn., Assn. of Bar of City of NY Office: Wilkie Farr & Gallagher 787 Seventh Ave New York NY 10019-6018 E-mail: mtrepper@willkie.com.

TREROTOLA, SCOTT OAKLEY, intervention radiologist, division chief; s. Laurence Oakley and Isabell Rhoades Trerotola; m. Kathleen McKenna, Sept. 8, 1984; children: Kaitlyn Mary, Ryan Laurence. BA, Wesleyan U., Middletown, Conn., 1982; MD, U. Pa., Phila., 1986. Diplomate Am. Bd. Radiology, 1991, in interventional radiology Am. Bd. Radiology, 1995, Am. Bd. Radiology, 2005. Attending interventional radiologist Johns Hopkins Hosp., Baltimore, 1992—93; dir., vascular & interventional radiology Ind. U. Med. Ctr., Indpls., 1993—2001; assoc. chair & chief, interventional radiology U. Pa. Med. Ctr., Phila., 2001—. Fellow: Cardiovasc. & Interventional Radiology Soc. Europe, Am. Coll. Radiology, Soc. Interventional Radiology; mem.: Radiol. Soc. N.Am., Am. Soc. Nephrology. Achievements include invention of mechanical thrombectomy device. Office: Hosp Univ Pa 1 Silverstein 3400 Spruce St Philadelphia PA 19104 Office Fax: 215-615-3545.

TRESCOTT, PAUL BARTON, economics professor; b. Bloomsburg, Pa., Nov. 22, 1925; s. Paul Henry and Stella Henrietta (Potts) T.; children by previous marriage: Jeffrey A., Jill V., Andrew B. (dec.); m. Kathleen Colcord, Aug. 15, 1982. BA, Swarthmore Coll., 1949; MA, Princeton U., 1951, PhD, 1954. Reporter Evening Bulletin, Phila., 1948; instr. in econ. Princeton (N.J.) U., 1952-54; asst. assoc. prof. Kenyon Coll., Gambier, Ohio, 1954-67; prof. in econs. Miami U., Oxford, Ohio, 1967-69; prof. in econs., history So. Meth. U., Dallas, 1969-76; prof. in econs. So. Ill. U., Carbondale, 1976—. Vis. prof. in econs. Thammassat U., Bangkok, 1965-67, People's U., Beijing, 1992; vis. prof. in fin. U. Ill., Champaign and Urbana, 1981; acad. adv. commn. to Thailand U.S. Dept. State, Washington, 1968-70. Authors: Money, Banking and Economic Welfare, 1960, 2d edit., 1965, Financing American Enterprise, 1963, rep., 1982, The Logic of the Price System, 1970, Thailand's Monetary Experience, 1971, Jingji Xue: The History of the Introduction of Western Economic Ideas into China, 1850-1950, 2007. Sgt. U.S. Army, 1944-46. Rsch. grantee Brookings Inst., Washington, 1961-62; Fulbright scholar U.S. Govt., Peking U., China, 1983-84, Tech. U., Czestochowa, Poland, 1996. Mem. Am. Econs. Assn., History Econs. Soc. Avocations: music, travel. Office: So Ill U Dept Econs Carbondale IL 62901 Office Phone: 618-536-7746. Personal E-mail: trescott@midwest.net.

TRESNOWSKI, BERNARD RICHARD, retired health insurance company executive; b. Chgo., Oct. 14, 1932; s. Al and Luella (Stewart) T.; m. Beverly Ann Gesmond, Nov. 26, 1955; children: Linda, Judy, Mark, Tom, MaryBeth, David; m. Leanne Patricia Irish, Aug. 1985; 1 child, Megan. BS, U. Mich., 1955; MPH in Hosp. Adminstrn., U. Pitts., 1958; JD, Chgo. Kent Coll. Law, 1998. Bar: Ill. 2000. From 2d asst. adminstr. to asst. adminstr. Albert Einstein Med. Ctr., Phila., 1958-61; rsch. assoc. U. Mich., 1961-62; assoc. adminstr. St. Joseph Mercy Hosp., Pontiac, Mich., 1963-67; sr. v.p. Blue Cross Assn., Chgo., 1967-78, exec. v.p., 1977-78, Blue Cross and Blue Shield Assn., Chgo., 1978-81, pres., 1981-94, ret., 1994. Mem. Health Adminstrs. Study Soc.; staff atty. Legal Assistance Foun. Met. Chgo. Author articles in field. Mem. Am. Hosp. Assn., Am. Coll. Health Care Execs., Am. Pub. Welfare Assn., Health Mgmt. Edn. Assn., Soc. Health Svc. Adminstrs., Internat. Found. Employee Benefit Plans, Internat. Fedn. Vol. Health Svc. Funds. (pres.), Am. Health Planning Assn., Ill. State Bar Assn., Chgo. Bar Assn., The Conf. Bd. Personal E-mail: barneyt65@msn.com.

TRESSEL, GEORGE WALTER, television producer, science educator, consultant; b. Newport, RI, Jan. 23, 1926; s. Walter Eugene and Mary (Sylvia) T.; m. Suzette Saperston (dec. Feb., 1992); 1 child, Paul S. PhB, U. Chgo., 1943, postgrad. studies, 1943-45. Rsch. asst. Dept. Meteorology U. Chgo., 1945-47; prodn. staff WBKB TV, Chgo., 1947-49; mgr. Tressel Studio, Chgo., 1949-59; supr. motion picture unit GE ANPD, Cin., 1959-61; film, TV producer Argonne Nat. Lab., Chgo., 1961-67; dir. comms. rsch. Batelle Meml. Inst., Columbus, Ohio, 1967-76; dir Materials Devel., Rsch., Informal Sci. Edn. Div. Nat. Sci. Found., Washington, 1976-89; project mgr. Children's TV Workshop, NYC, 1989-92; cons. sci. comms. edn. pvt. practice, Rockville, Md., 1992—. Chmn. adv. com. Fernbank Mus. Nat. History, Atlanta, 1982—; tech. adviser Quality Edn. for Minorities, Washington, 1985—, cons. Smithsonian Instn., Washington, 1988—, New Eng. Aquarium, Boston, Ontario Ednl. TV, Toronto, Can., Bronx Zoo. Author: (book) The Future of Educational Telecommunications; contbr. articles to profl. jours., chpts. to books. Past chmn. film adv. panel Ohio Arts Coun., fed. Interagy. Com. on Mus. Support; former mem. bd. dirs. Chgo. Film Coun., Free the Children Trust. Numerous awards from film festivals including Chgo., Atlanta, Edinburgh, Brussels; named to Centennial Honor Roll Am. Assn. Museums, 2006. Fellow AAAS (hon., past chmn. sect. Y), Assn. Sci. and Tech. Ctrs. (hon.); mem. Nat. Assn. Sci. Writers. Avocations: tango, folk dancing. Home: 11121 Powder Horn Dr Potomac MD 20854-2540

TRESSEL, JIM (JAMES PATRICK TRESSEL), college football coach; b. Mentor, Ohio, Dec. 5, 1952; s. Lee and Eloise Tressel; m. Ellen Watson; children: Zak, Carlee, Eric, Whitney. BS cum laude in Edn., Baldwin-Wallace Coll., Berea, Ohio, 1975; MS in Edn., Akron U., Ohio, 1977. Grad. asst. Akron U., 1975; quarterbacks, receivers & running backs coach U. Akron, 1976—78; quarterbacks & receivers coach Miami U., Ohio, 1979—80; quarterbacks coach Syracuse U., NY, 1981—83; quarterbacks, receivers & running backs coach Ohio St. U., Columbus, 1983—85, head coach, 2001—, Youngstown St., 1986—2000. Co-author (with Chris Fabry & John Maxwell): The Winners Manual: For the Game of Life, 2008 (Publishers Weekly Bestseller). Recipient Paul "Bear" Bryant award, Nat. Sportscasters & Sportswriters Assn., 2002; named Ohio Valley Conf. Coach of Yr., 1987, Regional Coach of Yr., Am. Football Coaches Assn., 1987, 1993, Nat. Coach of Yr., 1991, 1994, 2002, Chevrolet Nat. Coach of Yr., 1993—94, 1997, Eddie Robinson Nat. Coach of Yr., Football Writers Assn., 1994, 2002. Mem.: Fellowship Christian Athletes, Am. Football Coaches Assn. Achievements include coaching Ohio St. U. to the 2002 BCS Nat. Championship; leading Youngstown U. to Divsn. I-AA Nat. Championship, 1991, 93, 94, 97. Office: Woody Hayes Athletic Ctr 2491 Olentangy River Rd Columbus OH 43210*

TRESTMAN, FRANK D., distribution company executive, director; b. Mpls., Sept. 3, 1934; s. Saul and Rose (Hyster) T.; m. Carol Lynn Wasserman, Apr. 3, 1960; children— Lisa Ellen, Jill Susan BBA with high distinction, U. Minn., 1955. Exec. v.p., treas. Napco Industries, Inc., Mpls., 1965-74, pres., dir., 1974-84; chmn, CEO Mass Merchandisers, Inc., Hopkins, Minn., 1984-86; pres. Trestman Enterprises, Golden Valley, Minn., 1987—. Bd. dirs. Best Buy Co., Mpls., Western Container Corp., Mpls.; chmn. Avalon Real Estate Group., Mpls., Camir Investment Co., Mpls. Mem. bd. govs. Mt. Sinai Hosp., Mpls., 1978-91, Abbott Northwestern Hosp., 1993-2002; chmn. bd. trustees Mpls. Fedn. Endowment Fund; bd. dirs. Harry Kay Found. With USN, 1957-58. Mem. Oak Ridge Country Club (Hopkins). Office: Trestman Enterprises 5500 Wayzata Blvd Ste 1045 Minneapolis MN 55416-1241 Business E-Mail: frank@trestmanenterprises.com.

TRESTMAN, ROBERT LEE, psychiatrist, educator, administrator; b. New Orleans, June 4, 1953; s. Anschel and Mae (Schwedelson) T.; m. Rosanna Gene Liebman, Oct. 9, 1988; children: Lior Anschel, Morris Elia. BS, Carnegie Mellon U., 1975; PhD, U. Tenn., 1981, MD, 1985. Diplomate Am. Bd. Psychiatry and Neurology., 1990-95; intern, then resident Mt. Sinai Med. Ctr., NYC, 1985-89, rsch. fellow, 1988-90, assoc. in psychiatry, 1988-90, asst. prof. psychiatry, 1990-95, assoc. prof. psycyhiatry, 1995—, dir. rsch. fellowship tng., 1990-95, dep. chmn. dept. psychiatry, 1995—; clin. dir. dept. psychiatry, 1996—; co-dir. outpatient psychiatry Bronx (N.Y.) VA Med. Ctr., 1990-95. Ginsburg fellow Group for the Advancement of Psychiatry, Phila., 1987-89; bd. dirs. Managed Care Innovations, Inc.; founder Personality Disorders Found., 1997—. Co-inventor chainless bicycle transmission. Am. Coll. Neuropsychopharmacology travel fellow, 1993. Mem. Soc. for Biol. Psychiatry, Am. Psychiat. Assn., Assn. for Personality Disorders (pres. 1995-97), Mt. Sinai Ind. Physicians Assn. (co-chair mental health and substance abuse subcom. 1996—). Democrat. Jewish. Avocation: bicycling. Office: Mt Sinai Med Ctr 1 Gustave L Levy Pl # 1230 New York NY 10029-6500

TRETTER, SUE ANN, literature and language professor; b. St. Louis, Mo., Feb. 28, 1951; m. Ronald Alan Pearlman, Jan. 20, 2007; children: Laurie Marie, Lisa Catherine. PhD, St. Louis U., Mo., 1996. Adj. prof. English St. Louis U., 1987—94; prof. Am. studies & English Lindenwood U., St. Charles, Mo., 1994—, advisor, 1995—. Tchg. fellowship, St. Louis U., 1987—94, Scholership, Fulbright, 2009. Mem.: Am. Studies Assn. Avocations: walking, travel, writing, singing. Office: Lindenwood Univ 209 S Kingshighway St Saint Charles MO 63301 Business E-Mail: stretter@lindenwood.edu.

TRETTON, JACK, electronics executive; BS, Providence Coll. Sales position Duracell, Majers Corp.; various positions up to v.p. sales Activision, 1986—91; gen. mgr. sales, product devel., mktg., fin. and operation efforts JVC Musical Industries; dir. sales Sony Computer Entertainment Am., 1995, pres., CEO, 2006—; corp. exec. officer Sony Computer Entertainment Inc. Office: Sony Computer Entertainment Am 919 E Hillsdale Blvd Foster City CA 94404

TRETZ, CHRISTOPHE ROBERT, electrical engineer; b. Strasbourg, France, Mar. 22, 1968; arrived in US, 1991; s. Philippe and Liliane (Gué) T. Diplôme d'Ingénieur, Ecole Nationale Supérieure d'Electronique, d'Electrotechnique, d'Informatique, d'Hydraulique de Toulouse, 1991; MS, Columbia U., NYC, 1992, MPH, 1995, PhD, 1997. Rsch. asst. Columbia U., NYC, 1992—97; adv. engr. IBM Rsch., Yorktown Heights, NY, 1997—2000, mem. rsch. staff, 2000; mem. tech. staff design engr. Advanced Micro Devices, Sunnyvale, Calif., 2000—03; sr. cir. design engr. IBM Engring. and Tech. Svcs., San Jose, Calif., 2003—. Rsch. mentor Semiconductor Rsch. Corp., Durham, NC, 1997—. Mem. IEEE (tech. com. 1996-2001, chair pub. rels. and publicity 2001-02, sr. com. 2001-02, chair short course 2002, exec. com. 2003-06, treas. 2003, chair local arrangement com. 2004, tech. program chair internat. sci. conf., 2005, conf. gen. chair, 2006, mem. adv. com., 2007-). Roman Catholic. Achievements include inventor reduction of hysteresis in soi cmos circuits, method and system to tune integrated circuit, method and system for selecting sizes of components for integrated circuits. Avocations: skiing, golf, wine-tasting, gourmet cooking. Home: 235 Briar Ridge Dr San Jose CA 95123-2667 Office: IBM E&TS San Jose Design Ctr 5600 Cottle Rd Mail Stop F010 San Jose CA 95193 Home Phone: 408-888-3852. Business E-Mail: ctretz@us.ibm.com.

TREUTING, EDNA GANNON, retired nursing administrator, educator; b. New Orleans, Dec. 16, 1925; d. Alphonse Joseph and Clara Josephine (David) Gannon; m. August Raymond Treuting, Sept. 4, 1948 (dec.); children: Keith, Karen Treuting Stein, Madeline Treuting LeBlanc, Jaime Treuting Gonzales, Jay (dec.). Diploma, Charity Hosp. Sch. Nursing, New Orleans, 1946; BS in Nursing Edn., La. State U., 1953; MPH, Tulane U., 1972, DPH, 1978. RN, La.; cert. family nurse practitioner Tulane U. Head nurse premature nursery Charity Hosp., New Orleans, 1946-47, head nurse pediatrics, 1947-49; instr. pediatrics Charity Hosp. Sch. Nursing, New Orleans, 1949-52, 54, instr., LPN, 1953; pvt. duty Touro, Hotel Dieu, New Orleans, 1957-59; instr. maternal and child health La. State U. Sch. Nursing, New Orleans, 1960, 65, 69-71; from instr. to prof., sect. head Tulane Sch. Pub. Health and Tropical Medicine, New Orleans, 1972-83; dean, prof. Our Lady Holy Cross Coll. Nursing Div., New Orleans, 1983-84; chief nurse Dept. Health and Hosp., New Orleans, 1987-94. Region IV nurse practitioner Baylor U., Health Edn. and Welfare, 1974-76; citizen amb. to South Am. People to People, 1979; presentor U. Hawaii Pub. Health and Nursing, 1977; planner, advisor, reviewer continuing edn. U. Tenn., Memphis, 1990-95. Author, editor: Occupation Health Nursing, 1979; sect. head, prin. investigator Practitioner Programs Family and Pediatric, 1973-83; item writer Nurse Practitioners, Community Health and Occupational Nursing, 1974-80; mem. editl. bd. to sci. jours. and Nurse Practitioner Jour., 1974-2005. Pres. Oti-Mrs. Internat., New Orleans, 1955-68; sponsor bd. dirs. Holy Cross H.S. Treuting Scholarship, New Orleans, 1966—; hurricane and disaster nurse ARC, New Orleans, 1966-77; v.p. Pandora Carnival Club, New Orleans, 1968-78; alternate state health dept. Commn. Nursing Supply and Demand by Legislation, 1991-94; planner, presentor La. State Rsch. Day, 1990-92. Named outstanding woman in the mainstream world's fair women of achievement, 1984. Mem. AARP (chpt. 3086 pres. 1999-2009, sr. mem., chpt. pres. 2001—, Mandeville chpt. pres. 2001-, Cmty. Svc. award 2006), New Orleans Dist. Nurses Assn. (First J.B. Hickey Meml. Cmty. award 1985, Great

100 Nurse-First Yr. 1987), La. Pub. Health Assn. (Dr. C.B. White Merritorious Diligent Svc. 1990), La. Nurse Practitioners Assn.(Edna Treuting scholarship named in her honor), Tulane U. Alumni Assn. (past pres.); Tulane Med. Alumni Assn. (past pres.), New Image Club of Mandeville (chmn. 1986-2003), Mandeville Rep. Women, Mandeville Srs., New Image Club (chmn. line dance, co-chmn. trips and travel 1995-2004, Young at Heart, New Image Club (chmn. trips and travel, vice chmn.), Delta Omega (nat. and chpt. past pres.), Sigma Theta Tau, AARP(pres. chpt. 3086, 1999-) Republican. Roman Catholic. Avocations: travel, dance, swimming, photography, reading. Home: 1914 Marlin Dr Mandeville LA 70448-1069

TREVATHAN, EDWIN, neurologist, educator; b. Louisville, Nov. 3, 1956; s. Norman Edwin, Jr. and Joyce Brent (Sawyer) Trevathan; m. Linda Scott, Dec. 31, 1977; children: Scott, Daniel, Luke. BS in Biochemistry and Math., Lipscomb U., 1977; MD, Emory U., 1982, MPH in Chronic Disease Epidemiology, 1982. Diplomate Am. Bd. Psychiatry and Neurology, Am. Bd. Pediat., Am. Bd. Clin. Neurophysiology. Resident in pediats. Yale U. Sch. Medicine, New Haven, 1982-84; resident and fellow in neurology/child neurology Mass. Gen. Hosp., Harvard Med. Sch., Boston, 1984-87; fellow in neurophysiology and epilepsy Boston Children's Hosp., 1986-87; epidemic intelligence officer Ctrs. for Disease Control & Prevention, Atlanta, 1987-89; dir. Children's Epilepsy Ctr., chief neurology Scottish Rite Children's Med. Ctr., Atlanta, 1989-95; ptnr. Child Neurology Assocs., P.C., Atlanta, 1989-95; dir. Comprehensive Epilepsy Ctr. U. Ky. Coll. Medicine, Lexington, 1995-98; dir. Pediat. Epilepsy Ctr. Washington U. Sch. Medicine, St. Louis Children's Hosp., 1998—2007, prof. neurology & pediatrics, 2004—07; neurologist in chief St. Louis Children's Hosp., 2004—07; dir. divsn. pediat. and devel. neurology Washington U. Sch. Medicine, 2004—07; dir. nat. ctr. birth defects and developmental disabilities Ctrs. Disease Control and Prevention, Atlanta, 2007—. Assoc. chief neurology svc. U. Ky. Coll. Medicine, Lexington, 1996—98. Contbr. articles to profl. jours. Bd. dirs., mem. Epilepsy Found. Am., Atlanta, 1991—95; mem. profl. adv. bd. Epilepsy Found. Greater St. Louis, 1999—2003. With USPHS, 1987—89. Fellow: Royal Soc. Medicine (London); mem.: Am. Acad. Neurology, Alpha Omega Alpha. Home Phone: 314-963-0825.*

TREVATHAN, JAMES E., waste management executive; Various sales and mktg. positions Stauffer Chem. Co.; regional v.p. indsl. WM Holdings Waste Mgmt., Inc., 1997—98, gen. mgr. environ. remediation, v.p. sales and mktg. So. Group, 1998—2000, sr. v.p. sales and mktg., 2000—04, sr. v.p. Ea. Group, 2004—07, sr. v.p. So. Group, 2007—.

TREVENA, ANTHONY, legislative staff member; BA in Secondary Edn., Youngstown State U., MBA. Regional rep. 6th Congl. Dist., Ohio; dir. Sportsmen for Strickland campaign, 2006; dep. dir. adminstrn. Ohio Dept. of Natural Resources, 2007—08; chief of staff for Rep. John Boccieri, US House of Reps., Washington, 2008—. V.p. Better Bus. Bur. for the Mahoning Valley; instr. Kent State U., Salem. Office: Office of Congressman John Boccieri 1516 Longworth House Office Bldg Washington DC 20515 Office Phone: 202-225-3876.*

TREVES, SAMUEL BLAIN, geologist, educator; b. Detroit, Sept. 11, 1925; s. Samuel and Stella (Stork) T.; m. Jane Patricia Mitoray, Nov. 24, 1960; children: John Samuel, David Samuel. BS, Mich. Tech. U., 1951; postgrad., U. Otago, New Zealand, 1953-54; MS, U. Idaho, 1953; PhD, Ohio State U., 1959. Geologist Ford Motor Co., 1951, Idaho Bur. Mines and Geology, 1952, Otago Catchment Bd., 1953-54; mem. faculty U. Nebr., Lincoln, 1958—2004, prof. geology, 1966—2004, chmn. dept., 1964-70, 74-89, assoc. dean Coll. Arts and Scis., 1989-96, emeritus, 2004. Curator geology Nebr. State Mus., 1964—; participant expdns. to Antarctica and Greenland, 1960, 61, 63, 65, 70, annually 72-76. Rsch. and publs. on geology of igneous and metamorphic rocks of Idaho, New Zealand, Mich., Antarctica, Nebr., Can., Greenland with emphasis on origin of Precambrian granite complexes and basaltic volcanic rocks. Fulbright scholar U. Otago, New Zealand, 1953-54. Fellow Geol. Soc. Am.; mem. Am. Mineral Soc., Am. Geophys. Union, Sigma Xi, Tau Beta Pi, Sigma Gamma Epsilon. Home: 1710 B St Lincoln NE 68502-1524 Office Phone: 402-472-0872.

TREVINO, JERRY ROSALEZ, retired secondary school principal; b. Bee County, Tex., July 9, 1943; s. Geronimo R. and Hilaria (Rosalez) T.; m. Juanita Escalante, Jan. 1, 1985; 1 child, John-Michael. BA, U. Houston, 1967, MEd, 1974; PhD, Kennedy-Western U., 1988; postgrad., U. Tex., Permian Basin, 1988-92. Cert. tchr., adminstr., supt., Tex. Tchr. N.E. Houston Sch. Dist., 1966-70, pub. rels. officer, 1970-72, asst. prin., 1972-76; tchr. Harris County Dept. Edn., Houston, 1968-72, Austin (Tex.) Ind. Sch. Dist., 1977-87; asst. prin. Tex. Youth Commn., Pyote, 1987-91, prin., 1991-96, ret., 1996. Chair edn. seminar, 24th Internat. Congress, Oxford (Eng.) U., 1997; reader, U.S. Dept. Edn., 1996-97; mentor Austin Ind. Sch. Dist., 1996-98; Title VII project dir. U.S. Dept. Edn., Pyote, 1988-96; instr. Austin C.C., 1980-84, chair, Prin. Coun. for Edn. of Lang. Minority Students, S.W. Ednl. Devel. Lab., Austin, 1994-96; rschr. and ednl. cons. Bentiva Edn. Solutions, 2002—. Editor newsletter The Flyer, 1970-72; contbr. articles to profl. publs. Mem. Cmty. Adv. Coun., Pyote, 1987-96; mem. Tex. Children's Mental Health Plan, Monahans, Tex., 1991-96; mem. planning com. Permian Basin Quality Work Force, Midland, Tex., 1992-96; mem. Supt.'s Coun., Pyote, 1987-96. Named Outstanding Adminstr. of Permian Basin (Golden Apple award) Permian Basin Private Industry Coun., 1994. Mem. ASCD, Nat. Assn. for Bilingual Edn., Order Internat. Ambs., Tex. Assn. Secondary Sch. Prins., Civil Air Patrol, Soc. Leading Intellectuals of the World, Tex. Coun. Humanities, League United L.Am. Citizens, World Acad Letters, Tex. State Hist. Soc. Presbyterian. Avocations: flying, travel, reading, landscaping. Address: PO Box 299 Paige TX 78659-0299 Office Phone: 512-253-0222. Business E-Mail: drjerrytrevino@peoplepc.com.

TREVINO, ROBERTO ROSALEZ, historian, educator; b. Mathis, Tex., Mar. 6, 1948; s. Geronimo Ruiz and Hilaria Rosalez Trevino. BA, Houston Bapt. Coll., 1970; MEd, U. Houston, 1980; PhD, Stanford U., Palo Alto, Calif., 1993. Cert. tchr. Tex. Edn. Agy., 1970. Tchr. and program coord. Houston Ind. Sch. Dist., 1975—85; adj. lectr. U. Houston, 1980—85; asst. prof. history U. Colo., Colo. Springs, 1992—99; assoc. prof. history U. Tex., Arlington, 1999—, asst. dir., ctr. Mex. Am. studies, 1999—. Contbr. to hist. monograph and hist. anthologies. Sgt. USAF, 1971—74. Recipient Galarza prize, Stanford Ctr. Chicano Rsch., 1988, Bert M. Fireman prize, Western Hist. Quar., 1991, T.R. Fehrenback Book award, Tex. Hist. Commn., 2007; Summer Study grant, Inst. Hispanic Culture, Houston, 1970, Becas Para Aztlan grant, U. Houston, 1980, Mellon fellowship, Woodrow Wilson Nat. Found., 1986—90, Ford Dissertation fellow, NRC, 1990—91, Pew Program Religion and Am. History fellow, Yale U., 1994—95, Rsch. grant, Lousville Inst., 1997, Mary M. Hughes Rsch. fellowship, Tex. State Hist. Assn., 2006. Mem.: Immigration and Ethnic History Soc., Tex. Cath. Hist. Soc., Orgn. Am. Historians, Western History Assn. (editl. bd. mem. western hist. quar. 1997—2000), Tex. State Hist. Assn. Office: Univ Tex Arlington 601 S Nedderman Dr Arlington TX 76019 Business E-Mail: trevino@uta.edu.

TREVITHICK, RONALD JAMES, underwriter; b. Portland, Oreg., Sept. 13, 1944; s. Clifford Vincent and Amy Lois (Turner) T.; m. Delberta Russell, Sept. 11, 1965; children: Pamela, Carmen, Marla, Sheryl. BBA, U. Wash., 1966. CLU, CPA, ChFC, accredited estate planner. Mem. audit staff Ernst & Ernst, Anchorage, 1966, 68-70; pvt. practice acctg. Fairbanks, Alaska, 1970-73; with Touche Ross & Co., Anchorage, 1973-78, audit ptnr., 1976-78. Exec. v.p., treas., bd. dirs. Veco Internat., Inc., 1978-82; pres., bd. dirs. Petroleum Contractors Ltd., 1980-82; bd. dirs. P.S. Contractors A/S, Norcon, Inc., OFC of Alaska, Inc., V.E. Systems Svcs., Inc., Veco Turbo Svcs., Inc., Veco Drilling Inc., Vemar, Inc., 1978-82; with Coopers & Lybrand, Anchorage, 1982-85; field underwriter, registered rep. New York Life Ins., 1985-2000, Princor, 2000—, Prin. Fin. Group, 2000—; instr. acctg. U. Alaska, 1971-72; lectr. acctg. and taxation The Am. Coll., 1972, 97, instr. adv. sales Life Underwriters Tng. Coun., 1988-89; bd. dirs. Ahtna Devel. Corp., 1985-86. Divsn. chmn. United Way, 1975-76, YMCA, 1979; bd. dirs., fin. chmn. Anchorage Arts Coun., 1975-78, Am. Diabetes Assn., Alaska affiliate, 1985-91, chmn. bd. 1988-89, chmn. hon. bd. 1992-96, Am. Heart Assn., Alaska affiliate, 1986-87, Anchorage dist. com., 1994-96, treas. 1996-98, Alaska State Youth Soccer Assn.; mem. Anchorage Estate Planning Coun., 1996-2000, treas., 1998-99, sec. 1999-2000. With U.S. Army, 1967-68. Mem. Fin. Execs. Inst. (pres. Alaska chpt. 1981-83), Soc. Fin. Svcs. Profs. (v.p. Alaska chpt. 1993-94, pres. 1994-96), Alaska Assn. Life Underwriters (sec., treas. 1987-90), Alaska Goldstrikers Soccer Club (pres. 1992-93, youth coach 1985-95, Ina K tournament dir. 1992-98), Petroleum Club (treas. 1996-2000), Beta Alpha Psi. Home: 4421 Huffman Rd Anchorage AK 99516-2211 Office: 400 W Tudor Rd PO Box 110798 Anchorage AK 99511-0798 Office Phone: 907-258-5830. E-mail: ron4berta@aol.com.

TREVOR, ALEXANDER BRUEN, information technology consultant; b. NYC, Apr. 12, 1945; s. John B. Jr. and Evelyn (Bruen) T.; m. Ellen Ruth Armstrong, Sept. 21, 1974; children: Anne Wood Roebel, Alexander Jay Bruen. BS, Yale U., 1967; MS, U. Ariz., 1971. Rsch. asst. U. Ariz., Tucson, 1971; systems analyst CompuServe Inc., Columbus, Ohio, 1971-73, dir. systems, 1973-74, v.p., 1974-81, exec. v.p., chief tech. officer, 1981-96, also bd. dirs., 1985-96; pres. Nuvocom, Inc., Columbus, 1996—. Bd. dirs. State Auto Fin. Corp., Columbus. Author (software program) CB Simulator, 1980. Trustee Aviation Safety Inst., Worthington, Ohio. 1st lt. Signal Corps, U.S. Army, 1968-70, Vietnam. Decorated Bronze Star. Mem. IEEE (sr.), SAR (N.Y.), Union Club (N.Y.). Republican. Episcopalian. Home: 1987 My Tern Ct Sanibel FL 33957

TREXLER, EDGAR RAY, minister, editor; b. Salisbury, NC, Sept. 17, 1937; s. Edgar Ray and Eula Belle (Farmer) T.; m. Emily Louise Kees, Aug. 21, 1960; children: David Ray, Mark Raymond, Karen Emily. AB, Lenoir-Rhyne Coll., 1959, LittD, 1978; MDiv, Luth. Theol. So. Sem., 1962; MA, Syracuse U., 1964; student, Boston U., 1960, Luth. World Fedn. Study Project, Geneva, 1977, Luth. World Fedn. Study Project, 1981; LittD (hon.), Midland Coll., 1990; DD, Wittenberg U., 1994. Ordained to ministry United Luth. Ch. Am., 1962; pastor St. John's Luth. Ch., Lyons, NY, 1962-65; features editor Luth. Mag., Phila., 1965-72, assoc. editor, 1972-78, editor, 1978-87, Chgo., 1988-99. Sec. Commn. Ch. Papers, Luth. Ch. Am., 1971-72, mem. staff team comm., 1972-78; chmn. Interch. Features, 1971-76; chmn. postal affairs com. Assoc. Ch. Press, 1983-90, Work Group on New Ch. Periodical, 1985-86; Evangelical Luth. Ch. Am. Cabinet of Execs., 1988-99. Author: Ways to Wake Up Your Church, 1969, Creative Congregations, 1972, The New Face of Missions, 1973, Mission in a New World, 1977, LWF/6, 1978, Anatomy of a Merger, 1991, High Expectations: Understanding the ELCA's Early Years, 1988-2002, 2003; mem. editl. adv. bd. The New World, Roman Cath. Archdiocese of Chgo., 1994-96. Pres. Lyons Coun. Chs., 1964; trustee Lenoir Rhyne Coll., 1975-84, 97-2006. Luth. Theol. So. Sem., 2003—09; vol. Interfaith Assistance Ministries, 2000-07; bd. dirs., 2007-. Recipient Disting. Alumnus award Lenoir-Rhyne Coll., 1991, Disting. Svc. award Newberry Coll., 1992, Bachman award for disting. leadership Luth. Theol. So. Sem., 1993, Mauney Leadership Awd., Luth. Theol. So. Seminary (alumni awd.), 1999, award of merit for editls. Assoc. Ch. Press, 1991, 98, award of merit for articles in mission mags. Assoc. Ch. Press, 1974, hon. life mem., Assoc. Ch. Press, 1999. Mem. Nat. Luth. Editors Assn. (pres. 1975-77). Home: 2504 Carriage Falls Ct Hendersonville NC 28791-1816 E-mail: etrexler@bellsouth.net.

TREZZA, ALPHONSE FIORE, librarian, educator; b. Phila., Dec. 27, 1920; s. Vincent and Amalia (Ferrara) T.; m. Mildred Di Pietro, May 19, 1945; children: Carol Ann Trezza Johnston, Alphonse Fiore. BS, U. Pa., 1948, MS, 1950, postgrad.; LHD (hon.), Rosary Coll., 1997. Cert. libr. Drexel Inst., 1949. Page Free Library, Phila., 1940-41, 45-48, library asst., 1948-49; cataloger, asst. reference librarian Villanova U., 1949-50, instr., 1956-60; head circulation dept. U. Pa. Library, 1950-56; lectr. Drexel Inst. Sch. Library Sci., 1956—60; editor Cath. Library world, 1956-60; exec. sec. Cath. Library Assn., 1956-60; assoc. exec. dir. ALA, exec. sec. library adminstrn. div., 1960-67, assoc. dir. adminstrv. services, 1960—69; dir. Ill. State Library, Springfield, 1969-74; lectr. Grad. Sch. Library and Info. Sci., Cath. U., 1975-82; exec. dir. Nat. Commn. on Libraries and Info. Scis., Washington, 1974-80; dir. intergovt. library Cooperation Project Fed. Library Com./Library of Congress, Washington, 1980-82; assoc. prof. Sch. Library and Info. Studies Fla. State U., Tallahassee, 1982-87, prof., 1987-93, emeritus prof., 1993—. Mem. Ill. Library LSCA TITLE I-II Adv. Commn., 1963-69; mem. network devel. com. Library of Congress, 1977-82; bd. visitors Sch. Library and Info. Sci., U. Pitts., 1977-80; cons. Becker & Hayes, Inc., 1980-84, King Research, Inc., 1981-82; mem. planning com and steering com. Fla. Gov.'s Conf. on Library and Info. Svcs., 1988-91. Nat. chmn. Cath. Book Week, 1954—56; pres. Joliet Diocesan Bd. Edn., 1966—68; auditor Borough of Norwood, Pa., 1958—60; mem. patron's bd. Fla. State U. Sch. Theater, 2000—; bd. mem. Lafayette Oaks Home Assn., 2002—; Dem. committeeman Lombard, Ill., 1961—69; extraordinary min. of Eucharistic Blessed Sacrament Cath. Ch., 1984—, mem. pastoral coun., 2000—. 1st lt. USAF, 1942—45. Decorated Air medal with one cluster; recipient Ofcl. commendation White House Conf. on Libr. and Info. Svc., 1979, citation State Libr. Agys., 1994, Silver award Commn. Libr. Info. Sci., 1996. Mem. ALA (coun. 1973-82, 88-92, mem. exec. bd. 1974-79, chmn. stats. coordinating com. 1970-74, mem. pub. com. 1975-78, 81-83, 87-89, chmn. adv. com. interface, 1979-83, chmn. membership com. 1983-84, chmn. nominating com. 1988-89, mem. legis. com. 1989-91, adv. bd. ALA Yearbook 1976-91, Assn. Specialized and Coop. Library Agys. legis. com., 1987-89, ad hoc com. White House Conf. on Libr. and Info. Svcs. 1989-91, chmn. awards com. 1990-92, Exceptional Achievement award 1981, J.B. Lippincott award 1989, hon. mem. award, 2007), Cath. Library Assn. (life, adv. coun. 1960—), Ill. Library Assn. (chmn. legis.-library devel. com. 1964-69, mem. exec. bd., libr's. citation 1974), Fla. Library Assn. (bd. dirs. 1987-93, pres. 1991-92, intellectual freedom com., chmn. com. on Fla. Librs. publ., editor, publ. com., planning com., 1991, site com.), Continuing Libr. Edn. Network and Exchange (pres. 1982-83), Internat. Fedn. Library Assns. and Institutions (statistics standing com. 1976-85, planning com.), Coun. Nat. Library Assns. (chmn. 1959-61), Assn. Coll. and Research Librarians (pres. Phila. chpt. 1953-55), Drexel Inst. Library Sch. Alumni Assn. (pres. 1955-56, exec. bd. 1956-60, chmn. chief officers State Library Agys. 1973-74), Chgo. Library Club (pres. 1969), Assn. Library and Info. Sci. Edn. (govt. relation com. 1985-87), Drexel U. Alumni Assn. (Outstanding Alumnus award 1963), Kappa Phi Kappa (chpt. pres. 1948), Beta Phi Mu (hon.). Lodges: K.C. Personal E-mail: atrezza@mailer.fsu.edu. *You can't do anything alone. You need support and you need opposition. Opposition provides you with challenge. Challenge brings out the best in you. But most of all you need faith in God.*

TRIANDIS, HARRY CHARALAMBOS, psychologist, educator; b. Patras, Greece, Oct. 16, 1926; s. Christos Charalambos and Louise J. (Nikokavouras) T.; m. Pola Fotitch, Dec. 23, 1966; 1 child, Louisa. B.Engring., McGill U., 1951; M.Commerce, U. Toronto, Ont., Can., 1954; PhD, Cornell U., 1958; Doctorate (hon.), U. Athens, Greece, 1987. Asst. prof. U. Ill., Champaign, 1958-61, assoc. prof., 1961-66, prof. psychology, 1966-97; cons. USIA, 1970-75, NSF, 1968-75; prof. emeritus, 1997—. Author: Attitudes and Attitude Change, 1971, The Analysis of Subjective Culture, 1972, Varieties of Black and White Perception of the Social Environment, 1975, Interpersonal Behavior, 1977, Culture and Social Behavior, 1994, Individualism and Collectivism, 1995, Fooling Ourselves: Self-deception in Politics, Religion and Terrorism, 2009; editor: Handbook of Cross-Cultural Psychology, Vol. 1-6, 1980-81, Handbook of Industrial and Organizational Psychology, Vol. 4, 1994; editorial cons.; Jour. Personality and social Psychology, 1963-71, Jour. Applied Psychology, 1970-79, Sociometry, 1971-74, Jour. Cross-Cultural Psychology, 1974—, others. Chmn. fgn. grants com. Am. Psychol. Found., 1968-90. Sr. fellow Ford Found., 1964-65; Guggenheim fellow, 1972-73; grantee USPHS, 1956-60, 62; grantee Office Naval Research, 1960-68, 80-85; grantee Social and Rehab. Service, HEW, 1968-73; grantee Ford Found., 1973-75; recipient award Interam. Soc. Psychology, 1981 Mem. Soc. for Psychol. Study of Social Issues (pres. 1975-76), Internat. Assn. Cross-Cultural Psychology (pres. 1974-76), Interam. Soc. Psychology (pres. 1985-87), Soc. for Exptl. Social Psychology (chmn. 1972-74), Soc. for Personality and Social Psychology (pres. 1976-77), Internat. Assn. Applied Psychology (pres. 1990-94). Office: 603 E Daniel St Champaign IL 61820-6232 Home: 2008 Eagle Ridge Ct Apt A Urbana IL 61802-8695 Business E-Mail: triandis@uiuc.edu, triands@illinois.edu.

TRIANO, CAROLYN P., special education educator; b. Greenville, Tex., Jan. 24, 1946; d. Vernon Odell and Doris Madeline (Cox) Roland; m. Ronald E. Triano, Aug. 20, 1974; children: David, Steven, Sarah. AA, Lake Tahoe CC, South Lake Tahoe, Calif., 1981; BA in Psychology and English, Sierra Nev. Coll., Incline Village, 1999; MEd in Spl. Edn., U. Nev., Reno, 2001, postgrad., 2006—. Cert. tchr. Nev., Calif. Paralegal Butler Mortgage, Stateline, Nev., Feldman Shaw DeVore, South Lake Tahoe; tchr. Douglas County Sch. Dist., Minden; instr. U. Phoenix; tchr. Washoe County Edn. Dist., Reno. Adj. faculty Truckee Meadows CC, Reno; area chair BSED dept. U. Phoenix online. Mem.: Internat. Reading Assn. Presbyterian. Avocations: gardening, reading. Home: 2260 Dover Dr South Lake Tahoe CA 96150 Personal E-mail: ctriano2@pacbell.net.

TRIANO, JAY, professional basketball coach; b. Niagara Falls, Ont., Can. m. Beth Triano; children: Courtney, Jessica, Dustin. Grad., Simon Fraser U., Burnaby, BC, Can. Player Can. Men's Nat. Basketball Team, 1978—88, asst. coach, 1992—93, head coach, 1998—2004; asst. coach Simon Fraser U. Clansmen, 1985—88, head coach, 1988—95, Can. Men's Jr. Nat. Basketball Team, 1993—94; radio analyst, dir. cmty. rels. Vancouver Grizzlies, 1995—2001; basketball analyst TSN Sports, Toronto, 2001; asst. coach Toronto Raptors, 2002—08, interim head coach, 2008—09, head coach, 2009—. Mem. Can. Men's Olympic Basketball Team, 1980, 84, 88, head coach, 2000. Recipient Gold medal, World Univ. Games, 1983, Coach Mac award, Toronto Raptors, 2005; named to Can. Basketball Hall of Fame, Can. Olympic Hall of Fame, Basketball BC Hall of Fame, Basketball Ontario Hall of Fame, Simon Fraser Athletic Hall of Fame, Niagara Falls Hall of Fame. Achievements include being the first Canadian born and Canadian trained coach in the NBA. Office: Toronto Raptors Air Canada Ctr 40 Bay St Ste 300 Toronto ON M5J 2X2 Canada*

TRIANTAFYLLOU, MICHAEL STEFANOS, engineering educator; arrived in US, 1974, naturalized, 1985; s. Stefanos M. and Penelopi I. (Koutras) T.; m. Joan L. Kimball, Sept. 22, 1985; children: Stefanos R., Kimon K. MS in Ocean Engring., MIT, 1977, MSME, 1977, ScD, 1979. Rsch. assoc. MIT, Cambridge, Mass., 1978-79, asst. prof., 1979-83, assoc. prof., 1983-86, tenured assoc. prof., 1986-90, prof., dir. ocean engrng. testing tank, 1990—, dir. Ctr. Ocean Engring., assoc. dept. head mech. engring., William I. Koch prof. marine tech. Vis. scientist Woods Hole Oceanographic Inst., Mass., 1990—; com. chair MIT/Woods Hole Joint Program in Oceanography. Featured cover Scientific American, Science; contbr. articles to profl. jours. Rsch. grantee, Office Naval Rsch., Office Naval Tech., NSF, Doherty Found. Dept. Commerce, 1979—. Mem. Internat. Soc. Offshore and Polar Engrs. (founding mem.), Soc. Naval Architects and Marine Engrs. (papers com., vice chmn. OC-2 com.), Am. Phys. Soc. Greek Orthodox. Office: MIT 77 Massachusetts Ave Rm 5-323 Cambridge MA 02139-4307 Office Phone: 617-253-9614. Business E-Mail: mistetri@mit.edu.

TRIAY, INÉS R., federal agency administrator; b. 1959; BS in Physical Chemistry magna cum laude, U. Miami, 1980, PhD, 1986. Postdoctoral staff mem. Isotope and Nuclear Chemistry Divsn. Los Alamos Nat. Lab., 1985, head Environ. Sci. and Waste Tech. Group, 1994—99, rep to US Air Force, leader Isotope and Environ. Geochemistry Group, acting dep. dir. Chem. Sci. and Tech. Divsn., 1997—98; mgr. Carlsbad Field Officer US Dept. Energy, N.Mex., 1999, chief operations officer Office of Environ. Mgmt. Washington, 2005—07, prin. dep. asst. sec. Environ. Mgmt. Program, 2007—09, acting asst. sec. for environ. mgmt., 2008—09, asst. sec. for environ. mgmt., 2009—. Contbr. articles to profl. jours. Recipient Presdl. Rank Award, Wendell Weart Waste Mgmt. Lifetime Achievement Award, Dixy Lee Ray Award for Environ. Protection, Am. Soc. Mech. Engineers, Nat. Award for Nuclear Sci., Nat. Atomic Mus. Office: US Dept Energy Forrestal Bldg 1000 Independence Ave, SW Washington DC 20585*

TRIBBLE, DENISE HALL, registrar; b. Cin., Dec. 4, 1953; d. Arthur Lee Hall and Nonie Lee Brandon; m. Dwight Tribble, Sept. 14, 1979 (div. July 21, 2004); children: Dwite V. Tribble Jr., Danielle Joy, Desi Anika. MA, Calif. State U. Dominguez Hills, Carson, 1995. Faculty L.A. City Coll., LA, 1997—, asst. registrar, 1993—. Contbr. book:, singer Pan African People's Orch. Mem. Sisters Of Jazz, LA, 1995—2006. Home: 2325 4th Ave Los Angeles CA 90018 Office: Los Angeles City College 855 No Vermont Ave Los Angeles CA 90029 Office Fax: 323-953-4013. Personal E-mail: denisetri@msn.com. E-mail: tribbldh@lacitycollege.edu.

TRIBBLE, DENNIS ANTHONY, pharmaceutical executive; b. Sacramento, Nov. 16, 1949; s. Willard Bruce and Margaret Nualla Tribble; m. Irina Tsyshevskaya, June 24, 2004; children: Megan Elizabeth Newberg, Molly Kathleen Dyer, Mariya Zuyeva. BS, Muhlenberg Coll., Allentown, Pa., 1971; PharmD, U. Pacific Sch. Pharmacy, Stockton, Calif., 1974. Registered pharmacist State Calif., 1974, State Ill., 1975. Asst. dir., pharmacy Northwestern Meml. Hosp., Chgo., 1975—79; dir., pharmacy Alexian Bros. Med. Ctr., Elk Grove Village, Ill., 1979—86; dir., utilities devel. Health Data Scis. Corp., San Bernardino, Calif., 1986—94; chief med. officer Baxa Corp., Englewood, Colo., 1994—2001; chief pharmacy & tech. officer ForHealth Technologies Inc., Daytona Beach, Fla., 2001—. Instr., nursing pharmacology William Rainey Harper Coll., Palatine, Ill., 1983—86. Mem.: Ill. Coun. Health Sys. Pharmacists (pres. 1981—83, Pres's. award 1982), HIMSS, Am. Soc. Health Sys. Pharmacists (chmn., sect. pharmacy informatics and tech. 2007—). Achievements include invention of 9 patents related to automation of IV admixtures. Office: ForHealth Technologies Inc 790 Fentress Blvd Daytona Beach FL 32114-1214 Business E-Mail: dtribble@fhtinc.com.

TRIBBLE, JOAN LUCILLE (JOAN FARNSLEY TRIBBLE), retired literature and language professor, writer; b. New Albany, Ind., Oct. 8, 1928; d. William Newland and Elsie Lenora Farnsley; m. Robert Samuel Tribble, Oct. 6, 1950; children: Robert Samuel Jr., David Michael, Linda Joyce. BA with honors in English, U. Louisville, 1950, MA in English, 1968. H.s. tchr. Ky. Substitute tchr. Jefferson County Pub. Sch. Sys., Louisville, 1963—66; grad. asst. in English U. Louisville, 1966—67, adj. instr. in English, 1968—68, U. Ky./Jefferson CC, Louisville, 1968—71, from instr. to assoc. prof. English, 1972—88. Author: The Farnsleys of Kentuckiana; contbr. articles to profl. jours. Mem.: The Soc. Ky. Pioneers, Ky. Hist. Soc., So. Ind. Genealogy Soc., Ky. Genealogy Soc., U. Louisville Golden Alumni Soc., The Hon. Order Ky. Colonels, Woodcock Soc. Achievements include development of Diagnostic Placement Test for Students of English as a Second Language; design of Computer Tutorial Programs on English Grammar for Developmental Students. Avocations: genealogy, writing, needlecrafts, water sports. Home: 690 Mason Headley Rd Apt 532 Lexington KY 40504-4007

TRIBE, LAURENCE HENRY, law educator; b. Shanghai, Oct. 10, 1941; s. George Israel and Paulina (Diatlovitsky) Tribe; m. Carolyn Ricarda Kreye, June 20, 1964; children: Mark Alexander, Kerry Katrina. AB summa cum laude in Math., Harvard U., 1962, JD magna cum laude, 1966; LLD (hon.), Gonzaga U., 1980, U. Pacific, 1987, Am. U., 1987, Ill. Inst. Tech., 1988, Colgate U., 1997; LHD (hon.), Hebrew U., 1998. Bar: Calif. 1966, Mass. 1978, US Supreme Ct 1978, US Ct. Appeals DC Cir. 1978, US Ct. Appeals 9th Cir. 1979, US Ct. Appeals 1st Cir. 1980, US Ct. Appeals 2nd Cir. 1982, US Ct. Appeals 3rd Cir. 1991, US Ct. Appeals 4th Cir. 1993, US Ct. Appeals Fed. Cir. 1993. Law clk. to Justice Matthew O. Tobriner Calif. Supreme Ct., 1966-67; law clk. to Justice Potter Stewart US Supreme Ct., 1967-68; exec. dir. tech. assessment panel Nat. Acad. Sciences, Washington, 1968-69; asst. prof. law Harvard Law Sch., Cambridge, Mass., 1968—71, prof., 1972-82, Ralph S. Tyler, Jr. prof. constl. law, 1982—2004, Carl M. Loeb univ. prof., 2004—; cons. Akin Gump Strauss Hauer and Feld LLP, Washington, 2007—. Chief appellate counsel Calif. Nuclear Litigation, 1978-83; spl. dep. atty. gen. Hawaii, 1983-84; cons. NSF, Nat. Endowment Humanities, White House, others; cons. Marshall Islands for drafting new constitution, 1978-79; chmn. Marshall Islands Jud. Service Commn.; cons. Akin Gump Strauss Hauer & Feld. Author: Technology: Processes of Assessment and Choice, 1969, Channeling Technology Through Law, 1973, The American Presidency: Its Constitutional Structure, 1974, American Constitutional Law, 1978, 88, 2000, Constitutional Choices, 1985, God Save this Honorable Court, 1985, Abortion: The Clash of Absolutes, 1990; co-author: Environmental Protection, 1971, The Supreme Ct.: Trends and Development, 1979, 80, 82, 83, 84, On Reading the Constitution, 1991; co-editor: When Values Conflict: Essays on Environmental Analysis, Disourse, and Decision, 1976; contbr. articles to profl. jours. Recipient Beale prize, 1966, Detur prize, 1969, Coif Triennial Book award, 1980, Scribe award, 1980; nat. debate champion, 1961; named one of 100 Most Influential Lawyers in America, Nat. Law Jour., 2006; NSF & Woodrow Wilson Fellow, Harvard U., 1962-63. Fellow Am. Acad. Arts and Sciences; mem. ABA (Silver Gavel Award 1991), ACLU, Phi Beta Kappa. Office: Harvard Law Sch 1563 Massachusetts Ave Cambridge MA 02138 Office Phone: 617-495-4621. Office Fax: 617-495-3383. Business E-Mail: tribe@law.harvard.edu.

TRIBOUILLARD, DANIEL JEAN LOUIS, fashion executive; b. Paris, Jan. 8, 1935; s. Rene and Denise (Begon) T.; m. Nicole Marlhiou, Feb. 22, 1969; children: Nathalie, Virginie. Bachelor, Ecole des Francs Bourgeois, Paris, 1958. Designer, gen. mgr. Leonard, Paris, 1958-86, pres., 1987—. Dir. chambre syndicale Couture Francaise. Mem. Found. Du Futur, Paris, 1986. Decorated Commander Legion of Honor, commdr. l'ordre nat. du Mérite et des Arts et Lettres (France), 1984, chevalier des Palmes Academie fres. Mem.: Maxim's Bus. Avocations: sailing, cooking, growing orchids, painting, collecting asian art objects. Office: Leonard 36 Ave Pierre 1er de Serbie 75008 Paris France Home Phone: 0146477996; Office Phone: 0153678787. Business E-Mail: dtribouillard@leonard.com.

TRIBUS, MYRON, management consultant, educator; b. San Francisco, Oct. 30, 1921; s. Edward and Marie D. (Kramer) T.; m. Sue Davis, Aug. 30, 1945; children: Louanne, Kamala. BS in Chemistry, U. Calif., Berkeley, 1942; PhD in Engring, U. Calif., LA, 1949; DSc (hon.) (hon.), Rockford Coll., Ill., 1965, Oakland U., Mich., 1971. Registered profl. engr., Mass.; cert. trainer Feuerstein's method, 1996. Instr. to prof. engring. U. Calif. at Los Angeles, 1946-61; dir. aircraft icing research U. Mich., 1951-54; dean engring. Thayer Sch. Engring., Dartmouth Coll., 1961-69; asst. sec. sci. and tech. Dept. Commerce, Washington, 1969-70; sr. v.p. tech. and engring. info. tech. group Xerox Corp., Rochester, NY, 1970-74; dir. Center for Advanced Engring. Study, Mass. Inst. Tech., Cambridge, 1974-86; cons. in quality mgmt., 1986—; dir. rsch., co-founder Exergy, Inc., Hayward, Calif., 1987-99. Cons. heat transfer Gen. Electric Co., 1950; cons. Fed. Office Saline Water; tech. adv. bd. Dept. Commerce; adviser to NATO, 1953; mem. Nat. Adv. Com. Oceans and Atmosphere, 1971-72. Author: Thermostatics and Thermodynamics, 1961, Rational Descriptions, Decisions and Designs, 1969; Contbr. articles to profl. jours. Bd. govs. Technion, Haifa, Israel, 1973-84. Served to capt. USAAF, 1942-46. Recipient Thurman H. Bane award Inst. Aero. Scis., 1945, Wright Bros. medal Soc. Automotive Engrs., 1945; Alfred Noble prize Engring. Socs., 1952, Robert Fletcher awrd Thayer Sch. Engring., Dartmouth Coll., 1994; named UCLA Alumnus of Yr., 1972. Mem. ASME, IEEE, NSPE. Office Phone: 850-435-7490. Personal E-mail: mtribus@earthlink.net.

TRICARO, ROBERT COLLET, biologist, editor, poet, educator; s. Robert and Frances Tricaro. BS cum laude, Adelphi Coll., 1959, MA in Ednl. Philosophy, 1961; MS in Biology, Adelphi U., 1966; Writing Program in Creative Writing, Columbia U., 1998; Writing Program in Poetry, U. Mass., 2001. Asst. prof., then assoc. prof. Miami-Dade C.C., Miami, 1965—80; pres. Med. Data Control, Inc., San Francisco, 1980—95; adj. faculty mem. City Coll. San Francisco, 1981—2007; co-editor poetry mag. Mother Earth Internat., San Francisco, 2003—08; bd. dir. Internat. Poetry Museum Project, 2005—08. Cons. in med. mgmt. Author: (book of poetry) Letting Go, 2006; contbr. poetry to lit. jours. Pub. rels. specialist L'Alliance Française, Miami, 1974—78. With US Army, 1954—56. Recipient Svc. award, L'Alliance Française, 1976; biology grantee, NSF, 1963—65. Mem.: Bay Area Poets' Coalition (sec. 2005, bd. mem. 2005—, v.p. 2007). Independent. Luth. Avocations: opera, sports, poetry. Home: 601 Van Ness Ave Unit 22 San Francisco CA 94102

TRICE, DAVID A., oil industry executive; BA managerial sci., Duke Univ.; JD, Columbia Univ. With Roy M. Huffington, Inc., 1980—89; vice-pres., dir., CFO Newfield Exploration Co., 1989—91; CEO, dir. Huffco Group, Inc., 1991—97; chmn, pres., CEO Newfield Exploration Co., Houston, 2000—09, chmn., CEO, 2009—. Mem. bd. dir. Hornbeck Offshore Services, Inc., Grant Prideco, Inc. and NJ Resources. Mem. bd. trustees Houston Museum Natural Sci. Mem.: Independent Petroleum Assn. Am., Domestic Petroleum Coun. Office: Newfield Exploration Co Ste 2020 363 N Sam Houston Pkwy E Houston TX 77060*

TRICE, WILLIAM HENRY, III, lawyer; b. Vicksburg, Miss., Nov. 19, 1946; s. William Henry and Ethel Preston Trice; m. Judy Martha Trice, July 26, 1976; 1 child, William Carl. BA, U. Ark., 1968, JD, 1971. Bar: Ark. 1974, U.S. Dist. Ct. (ea. and we. dists.) Ark., U.S. Ct. Appeals (8th cir.). Staff atty. Ark. Hwy. Dept., Little Rock, 1974—75; dep. pros. atty. 6th Jur. Dist. Ark., Little Rock, 1975—77; atty. Howell Trice Hope & Files, Little Rock, 1977—2005; of counsel Hope Fugua & Cambell P.A., 2005—08; ptnr. Hope Trice & O' Dwyer, 2008—. Atty. Ark. State Bd. Dental Examiners, Little Rock, 1981—, Ark. State Med. Bd., Little Rock, 1989—, Ark. State Bd. Optometry, Little Rock, 2000—. Sr. warden vestry St. Margaret's Episcopal Ch., Little Rock, 1999—2001; lobbiest Dist. Judges Assn. Ark., 2000—02. Lt. col. ret. Ark. Army Nat. Guard. Mem.: Ark. Criminal Def. Lawyers Assn. (pres.), Ark. Trial Lawyers Assn. (bd. govs.), Scottish Rite Freemasonry (venerable master 1995—2001). Democrat. Episcopalian. Office: Hope Trice O'Dwyer 211 Spring St Little Rock AR 72201 Office Phone: 501-372-4144. Business E-Mail: btrice@htolaw.com.

TRICHE, ELIZABETH W., epidemiologist, educator; Asst. prof. med. svcs. Dept. Cmty. Health & Epidemiology Brown U., co-dir. epidemiology grad. program; affiliate Yale Ctr. for Perinatal, Pediatric & Environ. Epidemiology. Office: Dept of Community Health 121 S Main St Box G-S121 Providence RI 02912 Office Phone: 401-863-1987. Office Fax: 401-863-3713. E-mail: elizabeth_triche@brown.edu.*

TRICHE III, CHARLES WALTER, librarian, director; b. Napoleonville, La., Aug. 7, 1948; children: Charles Walter Triche IV, Anne Triche Branagan Elizabeth. PhD, La. State U., Baton Rouge, 1992. Sci. & tech. libr. Clemson U., SC, 1973—76; reference libr. U. Southwestern La., Lafayette, 1976—82, head circulation svcs., 1982—93, assoc. dir. libraries, 1993—97; dir. libraries U. La., 1997—. Contbr. chapters to books. Mem. Civitan Internat., Lafayette. Mem.: MLA (chair 1980—95), ALA, ACRL-La. Chpt., Assn. Coll. & Rsch. Librs., La. Libr. Assn. Democrat. Roman Catholic. Avocations: sailing, skiing, gardening, cooking, travel. Home: 1403 St John St Lafayette LA 70506 Office: Unive La 400 E St Mary Blvd Lafayette LA 70503 Office Fax: 337-482-6399. Business E-Mail: ctriche@louisiana.edu.

TRICHEL, MARY LYDIA, middle school educator; b. Rosenberg, Tex., Feb. 2, 1957; d. Henry John and Henrietta (Jurek) Pavlicek; m. Keith Trichel, Aug. 8, 1981; children: Daniel, Nicholas. BS cum laude, Tex. A & M U., 1980. Cert. tchr., Tex. Social studies tchr. grades 6, 7 and 8 St. Francis de Sales, Houston, 1980-81; English tchr. grades 7 and 8 Dean Morgan Jr. High, Casper, Wyo., 1983-86; English and journalism tchr. grades 9 and 11 Tecumseh (Okla.) High Sch., 1987; English tchr. grade 6 Christa McAuliffe Middle Sch., Houston, 1988-92; tchr. Tex. history grade 7, journalism grade 8 Lake Olympia Middle Sch., Missouri City, Tex., 1991-92; tchr. social studies 6th grade Lake Olympia Mid. Sch. Ft. Bend Ind. Sch. Dist., 1993-96; tchr. social studies 6th grade Atascocita Mid. Sch. Humble Ind. Sch. Dist., 1997—; 6th Grade team leader Tex. Attiance Geographic Edn. Recipient teaching awards. Mem. Nat. Coun. Tchrs. Social Studies, Am. Fedn. Tchrs. Avocations: desktop publishing, scuba diving, travel. Home: 14711 Kings Head Dr Houston TX 77044 Personal E-mail: theaggies4@entouch.net.

TRICHOPOULOS, DIMITRIOS VASSILIOS, epidemiologist, educator; b. Volos, Greece, Dec. 9, 1938; s. Vassilios Konstantinou and Alexandra Dimitrios (Kataropoulou) T.; m. Antonia Athanasiou Polychronopoulou, June 17, 1967. MD, Athens U., Greece, 1963, PhD, 1971; MS, Harvard Sch. Pub. Health, 1968; MD honoris causa, Uppsala U., Sweden, 1994. Diplomate Am. Coll. Epidemiology. Lectr. preventive medicine U. Athens Med. Sch., 1965-67, prof., chair preventive medicine, 1972—2005; lectr. epidemiology Harvard Sch. Pub. Health, Boston, 1969-70, prof. cancer prevention and epidemiology, 1989—; prof., dir. Harvard Ctr. Cancer Prevention, Boston, 1994-97. Chmn. health group Coun. European Union, Brussels, 1988; adj. prof. med. epidemiology Karolinska Inst., Sweden, 1998—. Editor: Teaching Epidemiology, 1992, 2001, Textbook of Cancer Epidemiology, 2002, 08; contbr. numerous articles to profl. jours. Decorated officier Ordre Palmes Academiques (France), Commdr. of Honor, Greece. Mem. Acad. of Athens, Royal Acad. Medicine Belgium (corr., fgn.), Nat. Acad. Medicine France (corr., fgn.), Athens Club. Greek Orthodox. Office: Harvard Sch Pub Health 677 Huntington Ave Boston MA 02115-6096 Office Phone: 617-432-4560. Business E-Mail: dtrichop@hsph.harvard.edu.

TRICHOPOULOS, NIKOLAOS, ophthalmologist; MD, Aristotle U. Thessaloniki Med. Sch., Greece, 1998. Ocular oncology rsch. fellow dept. ophthalmology U. Cin., 2000—01; gen. surgery intern Jewish Hosp., Cin., 2001—02; ophthalmology resident U. Hosp., Cin., 2002—05; ocular oncology fellow Royal Liverpool U. Hosp., England, 2005—06; vitreoretinal and ocular oncology fellow U. Hosp. and Cin. Eye Inst., 2006—08; asst. prof. ophthalmology, retina and ocular oncology svc. Veterans Hosp. and U. Tex. Health Sci. Ctr., San Antonio, 2008—. Fellow: Am. Acad. Ophthalmology. Office: San Antonio Vets Hosp 7400 Merton Minter Blvd San Antonio TX 78229 Office Phone: 210-617-5300.

TRICKETT, DENNIS JAMES, psychology professor; b. Morgantown, W.Va., Aug. 16, 1956; s. Charles Jack and Betty Josephine Trickett; m. Paula Jean Estes, Nov. 1, 1996; children: Sara Trickett Cruz, Christopher Matthew, Allison Marie Adair. EdD, New Orleans Bapt. Theol. Sem., La., 1986. Counselor Cumberland River Comprehensive Care Ctr., Corbin, Ky., 1987—97, dir. substance abuse prevention, 1987—97; prof. psychology U. Cumberlands, Williamsburg, Ky., 1997—, chair psychology, 1997—. Mem.: ACA. Office: Univ Cumberlands 7990 College Sta Dr Williamsburg KY 40769 Business E-Mail: dtricket@ucumberlands.edu.

TRIEB, GUENTHER, retail executive; Various mgmt. positions through v.p. European feminine care bus. unit Procter & Gamble Co., 1984—2008; sr. v.p., pres. Kenmore Craftsman & DieHard Sears Holdings Corp., Hoffman Estates, Ill., 2008—. Office: Sears Holdings Corp 3333 Beverly Rd Hoffman Estates IL 60179*

TRIER, JERRY STEVEN, gastroenterologist, educator; b. Frankfurt, Germany, Apr. 12, 1933; came to U.S., 1938, naturalized, 1943; s. Kurt J. and Alice L. (Cahn) T.; m. Laurel M. Bryan, June 8, 1957; children: Stanley, Jeryl, Stephen. MD, U. Wash., 1957; MA (hon.), Harvard U., 1973. Diplomate Am. Bd. Internal Medicine. Intern U. Rochester, NY, 1957-58, resident in medicine, 1958-59; clin. asso. Nat. Cancer Inst., Bethesda, Md., 1959-61; trainee in gastroenterology U. Wash., Seattle, 1961-63; asst. prof. medicine U. Wis., Madison, 1963-67; asso. prof. U. N.Mex., Albuquerque, 1967-69, Boston U., 1969-73, Harvard U. Med. Sch., Cambridge, Mass., 1973-76, prof., 1976—. Sr. physician Brigham and Women's Hosp.; cons. Dana Farber Cancer Ctr., Nat. Inst. Diabetes and Digestive and Kidney Disease; adv. coun. NIH, 1986-90. Editor: Internal Medicine; mem. editorial bd.; Anatomical Record, 1969-98, Gastroenterology, assoc. editor, 1971-77, mem. editorial bd., 1967-71, 78-83, 93-98, chmn., 1988-93, Am. Jour. Medicine, 1978-87, Current Opinion in Gastroenterology, 1990—; contbr. articles to profl. jours.; contbr. chpts. to books. Served as surgeon USPHS, 1959-61. Recipient Disting. Med. Alumnus award U. Wash., 2004, NIH Merit award, 1988-94; USPHS/NIH grantee, 1963-94. Mem. Am. Soc. Clin. Investigation, Assn. Am. Physicians, Am. Gastroent. Assn. (pres. 1985-86, Julius Friedenwald medal 1999, Disting. Mentor award, 2009), Am. Soc. Cell Biology, Am. Fedn. Clin. Research. Office: Brigham and Women's Hosp 75 Francis St Boston MA 02115-6110

TRIER, WILLIAM CRONIN, retired medical educator, plastic surgeon; b. NYC, Feb. 11, 1922; s. John and Anne (Cronin) T.; m. Kathleen Emily Renz, June 14, 1947; children: William Cronin (dec.), Peter L. (dec.). AB, Dartmouth Coll., 1943; MD, N.Y. Med. Coll., 1947. Diplomate Am. Bd. Surgery, Am. Bd. Plastic Surgery (dir. 1976-82, vice-chmn. 1981-82). Intern St. Agnes Hosp., White Plains, NY, 1947-48, Grasslands Hosp., Valhalla, NY, 1948-49, resident in surgery, 1949-50; commd. lt. (j.g.) USN, 1948, advanced through grades to capt., 1964; asst. med. officer USS Midway and USS Wasp, 1950-52; resident in surgery St. Albans Hosp., LI, NY, 1952-55; fellow plastic surgery Washington U. Barnes Hosp., St. Louis, 1956-58; mem. plastic surgery staff Naval Hosp., St. Albans, 1958-60, chief plastic surgery Phila., 1960-63, Nat. Naval Med. Ctr., Bethesda, Md., 1963-67; asst. prof. surgery, plastic surgery U. NC, Chapel Hill, 1967-69, prof. surgery, plastic surgery, 1976-85, prof. dental ecology Sch. Dentistry, 1976-85; assoc. prof., chief plastic surgery U. Ariz. Coll. Medicine, Tucson, 1969-76; prof. surgery U. Wash. Sch. Medicine, Seattle, 1985-90; ret., 1990. Mem. com. on study evaluation procedures Am. Bd. Med. Specialties, 1981-85, sci. adv. com. Contbr. articles to profl. jours. Bd. dirs., pres. Pima County unit and Ariz. divs. Am. Cancer Soc., 1970-76, bd. dirs. N.C. Div., pres. Orange County (N.C.) unit, 1976-82. Mem. ACS, Am. Assn. Plastic Surgeons (historian 1973-76, v.p. 1984-85, pres.-elect 1985-86, pres. 1986-87), Am. Soc. Plastic and Reconstructive Surgeons, Am. Soc. Aesthetic Plastic Surgery (at large bd. dirs. 1979-81, treas. 1984-87), Am. Soc. Maxillofacial Surgeons, Am. Acad. Pediatrics, Am. Cleft Palate Assn. (pres. 1980-81), Am. Cleft Palate Found. (pres., 1984-90), U.S. Power Squadron, U.S. Coast Guard Auxiliary, Gamma Delta Chi, Alpha Kappa Kappa. Episcopalian. Home: 900 Univ St Apt 1301 Seattle WA 98101-2782 Personal E-mail: wctrier@worldnet.att.net.

TRIGG, JACK WALDEN, JR., retired physician; b. Birmingham, Ala., Apr. 18, 1932; s. Jack Walden Sr. and Florine (Hagood) T.; m. Dorothy Wynne, June 3, 1958; 1 child, James Albert. BS, Va. Mil. Inst., 1953; MD, Med. Coll. of Ala., 1958. Diplomate Am. Bd. Internal Medicine. Cardiology fellowship U. Ala. Birmingham, 1956—57; intern in medicine Duke U. Hosp., Durham, NC, 1958-59; resident in medicine Univ. Hosp., Birmingham, 1959-62; physician So. Med. Group, Birmingham, 1964-98, pres., 1987—96. Pres. med. staff St. Vincent's Hosp., 1986, Southview Group, 1987-1996. Capt. USAF, 1962-64. Fellow ACP; mem. Birmingham Soc. of Internists, Jefferson County Med. Soc., Birmingham Rotary Club. Republican. Episcopalian. Home: 2006 Garden Pl Birmingham AL 35223-1156

TRIGGLE, DAVID JOHN, dean, pharmacist, consultant; b. Eng., Apr. 5, 1935; came to U.S., 1962; s. William John and Maud F. (Henderson) T.; m. Ann M. Jones, Sept. 22, 1959; children: Andrew B., Jocelyn A. BSc in Chemistry, U. Southampton, Eng., 1956; PhD, U. Hull, Eng., 1959. Sch. fellow U. Ottawa, Ont., Can., 1959-61; rsch. fellow U. London, 1961-62; asst. prof. SUNY Sch. of Pharmacy, Buffalo, 1962-65, assoc. prof., 1965-69, prof., 1985-95, chmn. dept., 1971-85, dean, 1985-95, Disting. prof., 1987—, vice-provost for grad. edn., 1995-2001, dean Grad. Sch., 1995-2001, provost, 2000-01, univ. prof., 2000—; pres. Ctr. for Inquiry, Inst. Buffalo. Cons. to pharm. industry, 1980—. Author: Chemical Aspects of Autonomic Nervous System, 1965, Neurotransmitter-Receptor Interactions, 1971, Chemical Pharmacology of the Synapse, 1976; editor: Comprehensive Medicinal Chemistry, 2006. Recipient Volwiler Rsch. Achievement award Am. Assn. Colls. Pharmacy, 1988, 89, George Koepf award Biomed. Rsch. Med. Found. Buffalo, 1994. Fellow AAAS; mem. Am. Chem. Soc., Am. Soc. Pharmacology and Therapeutics (Otto Krayer award 1995), Soc. Neurosci., Brit. Pharmacology Soc., Am. Pharm. Assn., Rho Chi (Rho Chi award 1998). Office: SUNY Sch Pharmacy 126 Cooke Buffalo NY 14260-0001 Business E-Mail: triggle@buffalo.edu.

TRIGGS, ELDON DALE, II, aerospace engineer, educator; s. Ronald Eldon and Teddy Roberta Triggs; m. Lindsay Olivia Nolin, June 1, 2004. MS in Aerospace Engring., Auburn U., Ala., 2002—07. Grad. tchg. asst. Auburn U., 2005—07; instr. Tuskegee U., Ala., 2007—. Cons. Transformational Space, LLC, Reston, Va., 2004—06. With US Army, 1997—2001, Ft. Benning, GA. Office: Tuskegee Univ 324 Chappie James Ctr Tuskegee Institute AL 36088 Business E-Mail: etriggs@tuskegee.edu.

TRIGGS, RAY ELLIS, JR., history educator; b. Whittier, Calif., Aug. 18, 1966; s. Ray Ellis Triggs, Sr. and Tyna Lee Triggs; m. Shauna Marie McMann, June 26, 2004; stepchildren: Dylan McMann, Haley McMann, Tristin McMann. BA in Social Studies, San Diego State U., 1993; tchg. credential, Concordia U., Irvine, Calif., 1993; MS in Reading, Calif. State U., Fullerton, 2004. Reading/lang. arts specialist credential Calif. Commn. Tchg. Credentialing, profl. clear single subject credential Calif. Commn. Tchg. Credentialing. Head counselor Los Posas Children's Ctr., Camarillo, Calif., 1986—89; infant aide Downtown YMCA, San Diego, 1991—92; classroom aide Grace Luth. Sch., Anaheim, Calif., 1992—93; student tchr. Ball Jr. HS, Anaheim, 1993; substitute tchr. Newport Mesa Unified Sch. Dist., Calif., 1993—95; tchr. humanities Costa Mesa HS, Calif., 1996—. Master tchr. Nat. U., Costa Mesa, 2005—06. Recipient History Alive grant, Newport Mesa Schs. Found., 2002. Mem.: NEA,

Reading Educators' Guild, Calif. Tchg. Assn., Phi Kappa Phi. Avocations: reading, travel, mountain biking, skiing. Office: Costa Mesa HS 2650 Fairview Rd Costa Mesa CA 92626-5599 Business E-Mail: rtriggs@nmusd.us.

TRIGIANO, LUCIEN LEWIS, physician; b. Easton, Pa., Feb. 9, 1926; s. Nicholas and Angeline (Lewis) T.; children: Lynn Anita, Glenn Larry, Robert Nicholas. Student, Tex. Christian U., 1944-45, Ohio U., 1943-44, 46-47, Milligan Coll., 1944, Northwestern U., 1945, Temple U., 1948-52. Diplomate Am. Bd. Phys. Medicine & Rehab. Intern Meml. Hosp., Johnstown, Pa., 1952-53; resident Lee Hosp., Johnstown, 1953-54; gen. practice Johnstown, 1953-59; med. dir. Pa. Rehab. Ctr., Johnstown, 1959-62, chief phys. medicine & rehab., 1964-70; fellow phys. medicine & rehab. N.Y. Inst. Phys. Medicine & Rehab., 1962—64; dir. rehab. medicine Lee Hosp., 1964-71, Ralph K. Davies Med. Ctr., San Francisco, 1973-75, St. Joseph's Hosp., San Francisco, 1975-78, St. Francis Meml. Hosp., San Francisco, 1978-83, Rehab. Ctr. Nev., Las Vegas, 1998—2000; pvt. practice Las Vegas, 1998—. Asst. prof. phys. medicine and rehab. Temple U. Sch. Medicine; founder Disability Alert; bd. adv. Sch. Medicine Temple U., 2003—, bd. visitors, 2003; adj. prof. Touro U. Sch. Medicine, Las Vegas, 2005—. Served with USNR, 1944-46. Fellow ACP; mem. AMA, Pa. Med. Soc., San Francisco County Med. Soc., Am. Acad. Phys. Medicine and Rehab., Am. Congress Phys. Medicine, Calif. Acad. Phys. Medicine, Nat. Rehab. Assn., Babcock Surg. Soc. Home and Office: 20 Woodside Dr Easton PA 18042 Office Phone: 610-258-1509. Personal E-mail: lltmdmd@aol.com.

TRIGILIO, JOHN PATRICIO, pastor; s. John Trigilio and Elizabeth Lagner. BA, Gannon U., 1983; MDiv, Mary Immaculate Sem., 1988; PhD, LaSalle U., 1998; ThD, Concordia, 2002. Ordained to priesthood Cath. Diocese of Harrisburg, Pa., 1988. Parochial vicar St. Joseph Cath. Ch., Mechanicsburg, Pa., 1988—91, St. John the Bapt. Cath. Ch., New Freedom, 1991—94, St. Joan of Arc Ch., Hershey, 1995—98, Seven Sorrows BVM Ch., Middletown, 1998—2001, Holy Name of Jesus Ch., Harrisburg, 2001—02; sec. to the tribunal Cath. Diocese of Harrisburg, 1994—95; pastor St. Bernadette Parish, Duncannon, 2002, Our Lady of Good Counsel Ch., Marysville, 2002—. Pres. Confraternity Cath. Clergy, Marysville, 2002—. Author: (book) Catholicism for Dummies, The Everything Bible Book, Women in the Bible for Dummies, John Paul II for Dummies, Catholicism Answer Book: 300 Frequently Asked Questions, (weekly television & radio series on EWTN) Web of Faith, Council of Faith, Crash Course in Catholicism; editor: Sapienta Mag., 1992—2006. Mem.: Fellowship Cath. Scholars (life). Conservative. Roman Catholic. Home and Office: Our Lady of Good Counsel Church 121 William St Marysville PA 17053 Office Fax: 717-957-4247; Home Fax: 717-957-4247. Personal E-mail: fr.trigilio@prodigy.net. Business E-Mail: opus-dei@msn.com.

TRIIPAN, MAIVE, library director; b. Virumaa County, Estonia, Jan. 4, 1942; d. Osvald and Minna (Olesk) Triipan; m. Kalle Dobkevich, Mar. 6, 1971 (div. June 4, 1974); 1 child, Raul. B. of Libr., Tartu U., Tartu, Estonia, 1967. Rsch. mgmt. asst. Libr. of Estonian Acad. Sci., Tallinn, Estonia, 1967-74, asst. dir. rsch. work, 1974-84, dir., 1984—; head PR Astangu Vocat. Rehab. Ctr., Tallinn, 2003. Mem. State Libr. Coun., Tallinn, 1974-87, State Libr. Coun. at Dept. of Culture and Edn., Tallinn, 1989—, Tech. U. Coun., Tallinn, 1993—, Estonian Nat. Libr. Coun., Tallinn, 1994—; fin. mgr. Merelaug, 1998-99; project mgmt. Scis. Dept. Estonian Inst. Pub. Adminstrn.; project mgmr. Style Wear, Tallinn, 2000-01; specialist further edn. Astangu Vocat. Rehab. Ctr., Tallinn, 2000, head dept. IT and staff tng., 2002-, head dept. pub. relationship, 2003. Editl. bd. Estonian Retrospective, 1975; mng. pub. National Bibliography 1525-1940, 1993. Mem. Estonian Librs. Assn. Avocations: literature, music, art. Business E-Mail: maive.triipan@astangu.ee.

TRILLIN, CALVIN, writer, journalist; b. Kansas City, Mo., Dec. 5, 1935; s. Abe and Edyth Trillin; m. Alice Stewart, Aug. 13, 1965 (dec.); children: Abigail, Sarah. BA, Yale U., 1957; DLitt (hon.), Beloit Coll., 1987; LHD (hon.), Albertus Magnus Coll., 1990, U. Mo., 2003; DLitt (hon.), SUNY, 1996, U. NC, 1998, Susquehanna U., 1999; DLitt. (hon.), LI U., 2002. Reporter, writer Time mag., 1960-63; columnist Nation mag., 1978-85; syndicated columnist, 1986-95; columnist Time mag., 1996-2001; staff writer New Yorker mag., 1963—. Trustee NY Pub. Libr. Author: (books) An Education in Georgia: Charlayne Hunter, Hamilton Holmes, and the Integration of the University of Georgia, 1964, Barnett Frummer is an Unbloomed Flower, 1969, U.S. Journal, 1971, American Fried: Adventures of a Happy Eater, 1974, Runestruck, 1977, Alice, Let's Eat: Further Adventures of a Happy Eater, 1978, Floater, 1980, Uncivil Liberties, 1982, Third Helpings, 1983, Killings, 1984, With All Disrespect, 1985, If You Can't Say Something Nice, 1987, Travels with Alice, 1989, Enough's Enough (and Other Rules of Life), 1990, American Stories, 1991, Remembering Denny, 1993, Deadline Poet: My Life as a Doggerelist, 1994, Too Soon to Tell, 1995, Family Man, 1998, Tepper Isn't Going Out, 2001, Feeding a Yen, 2003, About Alice, 2006; author: (comic verse with commentary) Obliviously on He Sails: The Bush Administration in Rhyme, 2004, A Heckuva Job: More of the Bush Administration in Rhyme, 2006; author: Deciding the Next Decides, 2008, Presidential Race in Rhyme, 2008; contbr. articles to jours. and newspapers. Mem.: AAAL. Office: c/o New Yorker 4 Times Sq New York NY 10036-6522 Home Phone: 212-243-3455; Office Phone: 212-286-5651.

TRILLING, GEORGE HENRY, physicist, researcher; b. Bialystok, Poland, Sept. 18, 1930; came to U.S., 1941; s. Max and Eugenie (Walfisz) T.; m. Madeleine Alice Monic, June 26, 1955; children: Stephen, Yvonne, David. BS, Calif. Inst. Tech., Pasadena, 1951, PhD, 1955. Rsch. fellow Calif. Inst. Tech., Pasadena, 1955-56; Fulbright post-doctoral fellow Ecole Polytechnique, Paris, 1956-57; asst. to assoc. prof. U. Mich., Ann Arbor, 1957-60; assoc. to prof. dept. physics U. Calif., Berkeley, 1960-94, prof. emeritus, 1994—. Fellow Am. Phys. Soc., Am. Acad. Arts and Scis.; mem. NAS. Achievements include research in high energy physics. Office: Lawrence Berkeley Nat Lab Berkeley CA 94720-0001 Office Phone: 510-486-6801. Business E-Mail: ght@lbl.gov.

TRILLING, LEON, aeronautical engineering educator; b. Bialystok, Poland, July 15, 1924; came to U.S., 1940, naturalized, 1946; s. Oswald and Regina (Zakhejm) T.; m. Edna Yuval, Feb. 17, 1946; children: Alex R., Roger S. BS, Calif. Inst. Tech., 1944, MS, 1946, PhD, 1948. Rsch. fellow Calif. Inst. Tech., 1948- 50; Fulbright scholar U. Paris, 1950-51, vis. prof., 1963-64; mem. faculty MIT, Cambridge, 1951—, prof. aerospace and astronautics, 1962-94, prof. emeritus, 1994—, mem. coun. on primary and secondary edn., 1992—. Mem. Program in Sci. Tech. and Soc., Engring. Edn. Mission to Soviet Union, 1958; vis. prof. Delft Tech. U., 1974-75; vis. prof. engring. Carleton Coll., 1987. Pres. Met. Com. Ednl. Opportunity, 1967-70, Coun. for Understanding of Tech. in Human Affairs, 1984—. Guggenheim fellow, 1963-64. Fellow AAAS. Home: 180 Beacon St Boston MA 02116-1408 Office: MIT 77 Massachusetts Ave Cambridge MA 02139-4307

TRIMBLE, ANMARIE, language educator, editor; b. Portland, Oreg., Dec. 4, 1966; d. Terrence Paul Trimble and Lauriann Hartley Hodges. MA, Portland State U., 1999. Editor & rschr. 2nd Story Interactive Studios, Portland, 1999—2001; asst. prof. U. Studies, Portland State U., 2001—. Recipient Interactive Design Ann. award, Communication Arts, 2001, John P. Zuercher Champions, Janus Youth Programs, 2005. Office: Portland State Univ 1721 SW Broadway St Portland OR 97201

TRIMBLE, PHILLIP RICHARD, law educator; b. Springfield, Ohio, Nov. 12, 1937; s. Melvin R. and Dorothy T.; m. Stephanie Gardner, July 20, 1963 (div. 1977); children: John, William; m. Valeria Vasilevski, Dec. 21, 2000. BA, Ohio U., 1958; MA, Fletcher U., 1959; JD, Harvard U., 1963. Bar: NY 1964. Legal writing instr. U. Calif., Berkeley, 1963-64; assoc. Cravath, Swaine & Moore, NYC, 1964-70; staff mem. fgn. rels. com. U.S. Senate, Washington, 1971-72; asst. legal adviser Dept. State, Washington, 1973-78; counsel to the mayor NYC, 1978; dep. mayor, 1979; U.S. ambassador Nepal, 1980-81; prof. law UCLA, 1981—2001, vice provost internat. studies, 1999—2000; founding mem. Dalai Lama Found., 2001—. Mem. exec. com. Asia Soc. So. Calif. Ctr., L.A., 1981-94; vis. prof. law Stanford U., 1988-89, U. Mich., 1995-96; U.S. panelist under U.S.-Can. Free Trade Agreement, NAFTA; cons. ACDA, 1989-92. Mem. bd. editors Am. Jour. Internat. Law, 1993-98. Bd. dirs. Milarepa Tibetan Buddhist Ctr., 2001—06, Am. Alpine Club, 1978—80, 1982—85. Fellow Explorers Club. Democrat.

TRIMBLE, PRESTON ALBERT, retired judge; b. Salina, Okla., Aug. 27, 1930; s. James Albert and Winnie Louella (Walker) T.; m. Patricia Ann Beadle; children: Todd, Beth, Amy. BA, U. Okla., 1956, LL.B., 1960. Bar: Okla. 1960. Practice law, 1960; asst. county atty. Cleveland County, Okla., 1960-62; county atty., 1962-67; dist. atty., 1967-79; dist. judge, 1979-91. Spl. instr. S.W. Center Law Enforcement Edn.; cons. prosecution mgmt. Mem. Jud. Council Okla.; chmn. Okla. Corrections Workshop; mem. planning com. Nat. Inst. Crime and Delinquency; mem. com. on multi-agy. problems in criminal justice Appellate Judges Conf. Bd. dirs. Okla. U. Crisis Ctr., 1970—, ARC, Lake Murray Conservation Assn.; trustee Nat. Assn. Pretrial Svc. Agys. Resource Ctr., Sarkeys Found., 1994—. With USNR, 1948-52; col. USAFR. Mem. Okla., Cleveland County bar assns., Nat. Dist. Attys. Assn. (past pres.), Okla. Dist. Attys. Assn. (past pres.), Nat. Coll. Dist. Attys. (bd. regents), Am. Legion, Lions, Amateur Field Trial Clubs Am. (trustee 2002—, v.p. 2005—, pres. Okla. chpt.) Democrat. Roman Catholic. Home: 1886 Trailview Dr Norman OK 73072-6655 Office: 231 S Peters Ave Norman OK 73069-6035 Office Phone: 405-321-8272. Personal E-mail: trimble@coxinet.net. *An elected public official must remember that the people own his position and he only holds it in trust for them.*

TRIMBLE, SANDRA ELLINGSON, lawyer; b. Buffalo, Wyo., May 10, 1952; d. Andrew C. and Edna E. Ellingson; children: Samuel James, Stephen Joseph. BA with highest distinction, Colo. State U., 1974; MEd, Sul Ross State U., 1977; JD cum laude, Georgetown U., 1989. Bar: Md. 1989, D.C. 1990. Contract specialist USAF, Pope AFB, N.C., 1979-81; purchasing rep. Damson Oil Corp., Houston, 1982-86; summer assoc. Fried Frank Harris Shriver & Jacobson, Washington, 1988; law clk. Sullivan & Cromwell, Washington, 1988-89; assoc. Cleary Gottlieb Steen & Hamilton, Washington, 1989-97; of counsel Orrick Herrington & Sutcliffe LLP, Washington, 1997—2002; counsel McKee Nelson LLP, 2002—08; sr. counsel Internat. Fin. Corp., 2008—; adj. law faculty George Washington U. Law Sch. Assoc. notes editor Georgetown Law Jour., 1988-89. Recipient Disting. Achievement in Advocacy award Internat. Acad. Trial Lawyers, 1989; Nat. Merit scholar, 1970; law fellow Georgetown U. Law Ctr., 1987-88. Mem. Phi Beta Kappa. Office Phone: 202-327-2110.

TRIMBLE, STANLEY WAYNE, hydrologist; b. Columbia, Tenn., Dec. 8, 1940; s. Stanley Drake and Clara Faye (Smith) T.; m. Alice Erle Gunn, Aug. 16, 1964; children: Alicia Anne, Jennifer Lusanne. BS, U. North Ala., 1964; MA, U. Ga., 1970, PhD, 1973. Asst. prof. hydrology and geography U. Wis., Milw., 1972-75; from asst. prof. to prof. UCLA, 1975—. Vis. asst. prof. U. Chgo., 1978, vis. assoc. prof., 81, vis. prof. environ. geography, 1990—; vis. prof. U. Durham, England, 1998; vis. lectr. U. London, 1985; hydrologist US Geol. Survey, 1974—84; vis. prof. U. Vienna, 1994, 99; Frost lectr. Brit. Geomorphol. Rsch. Group, Durham, 1994; vis. rsch. lectr. Oxford U., 1995; Fulbright scholar in UK, 95; vis. fellow Keble Coll., Oxford U., 1995, Hatfield Coll., U. Durham, 1998. Author: Culturally Accelerated Sedimentation on the Middle Georgia Piedmont, 1971, Man-Induced Erosion on the Southern Piedmont, 1700-1970, 1974, Soil Conservation and the Reduction, 1982, Sediment Characteristics of Tennessee Streams, 1984, (with A Ward) Environmental Hydrology, 2004 (ASAE Blue Ribbon award); joint editor-in-chief: Catena, 1995-2006; editor: Dekker Encyclopedia of Water Science, 2003-; contbr. articles to profl. jours; editor, Enclopedic Water Sci., 2003-07. 1st lt. 101 Airborne Divsn. US Army, 1963—65. Grantee U.S. Geol. Survey, Washington, 1974-79, Wis. Dept. Natural Resources, Madison, 1978, 82, 93, 94, 95, NSF, Washington, 1976, Agrl. Rsch. Svc. of USDA, Washington, 1972, Nat. Geographic Soc., 1993. Mem.: NAS-NRC (Com. on Watershed Mgmt. 1996—98, Com. on Miss. River and Clean Water Act 2005—07), Brit. Geomorphol. Rsch Group, Soil Conservation Soc. Am., Am. Geophys. Union, Assn. Am. Geographers (Disting. Career award 2006), Sigma Xi. Republican. Avocations: historic houses, documentation and restoration, landscape gardens. Office: UCLA Dept Geography 1255 Bunche Hall Los Angeles CA 90095-1524 Home Phone: 931-363-0457; Office Phone: 310-825-1071. Business E-Mail: trimble@geog.ucla.edu.

TRIMBLE, THOMAS JAMES, retired utilities executive, lawyer; b. Carters Creek, Tenn., Sept. 3, 1931; s. John Elijah and Mittie (Rountree) T.; m. Glenna Kay Jones, Sept. 3, 1957; children: James Jefferson, Julie Kay. BA, David Lipscomb U., 1953; JD, Vanderbilt U., 1956; LLM, NYU, 1959. Bar: Tenn. 1956, Ariz. 1961, U.S. Dist. Ct. Ariz. 1961, U.S. Dist. Ct. D.C. 1963, U.S. Ct. Appeals (10th cir.) 1971, U.S. Supreme Ct. 1972, U.S. Ct. Appeals (9th cir.) 1975. From assoc. to ptnr. Jennings, Strouss & Salmon, Phoenix, 1960-85, mng. ptnr., 1985-87; sr. v.p., gen. counsel, corp. sec. S.W. Gas Corp., Las Vegas, Nev., 1987-96; gen. counsel Primerit Bank, 1987—96, corp. sec., 1990-92; exec. v.p. Energy Ins. Ltd., Bermuda, 1992-94, bd. dirs., 1992-97, pres., 1994—96. Bd. dirs. Energy Ins. Mut. Ltd., 1988—97, vice chmn., 1992—94, chmn., 1994—96. Mem. editorial bd. Vanderbilt U. Law Rev., 1954-56. Mem. Pepperdine U. Bd. Regents, Malibu, Calif., 1981—, sec., 1982-2000, chmn., 2000-04, mem. exec. com., 1982-89, 95—2009; bd. visitors Pepperdine Sch. Law, Malibu, 1982-2008; trustee Okla. Christian U., Oklahoma City, 1994—; pres. Big Sisters Ariz., Phoenix, 1975, bd. dirs., 1970-76; chmn. Sunnydale Children's Home, Phoenix, 1966-69, bd. dirs., 1965-75; pres. Clearwater Hills Improvement Assn., Phoenix, 1977-79, bd. dirs., 1975-80; trustee Nev. Sch. of Arts, 1988-92, chmn., 1989-90. 1st lt. JAGC, USAF, 1957-60. Fellow Ariz. Bar Found. (editl. bd. Jour. 1975-80), Am. Gas Assn. (legal sect. mng. com. 1987-96), Order of Coif, Kiwanis (pres. Phoenix 1972-73), Phi Delta Phi. Republican. Mem. Ch. Christ. Home: 7302 E Berridge Ln Scottsdale AZ 85250 Personal E-mail: ttrimble5@cox.net.

TRIMBLE, VANCE HENRY, retired newspaper editor; b. Harrison, Ark., July 6, 1913; s. Guy L. and Josephine (Crump) T.; m. Elzene Miller, Jan. 9, 1932; 1 dau., Carol Ann. Student pub. schs., Wewoka, Okla. Cub reporter Okemah (Okla.) Daily Leader, 1928; worked various newspapers in Okmulgee, Muskogee, Tulsa and, Okla.; successively reporter, rewrite man, city editor Houston Press, 1939-50, mng. editor, 1950-55; news editor Scripps-Howard Newspaper Alliance, Washington, 1955-63; editor Ky. Post and Times-Star, Covington, 1963-79. Author: The Uncertain Miracle, 1974, Sam M. Walton, 1990, (biography) E.W. Scripps, 1992, Frederick Smith of Federal Express, 1993, An Empire Undone: Rise and Fall of Chris Whittle, 1995, Alice & J.F.B.-The Hundred Year Saga of Two Seminole Chiefs, 2006, Choctaw Kisses Bullets & Blood, 2007; co-author: Happy Chandler Autobiography, 1989; editor: Scripps-Howard Handbook, 1981. Trustee Scripps-Howard Found., 1974-79. Recipient Pulitzer prize for nat. reporting, 1960, Raymond Clapper award, 1960, Sigma Delta Chi award for disting. Washington correspondence, 1960, Frank Luther Mott award for journalism book rsch. U. Mo., 1993; named to Okla. Journalism Hall of Fame, 1974. Mem. Am. Soc. Newspaper Editors, Nat. Press Club (Washington), Press Club (Houston), Wewoka Country Club. Baptist. Home: 25 Oakhurst Rd Wewoka OK 74884-3714 Personal E-mail: vhtrimble@aol.com.

TRIMBLE, WILLIAM CATTELL, JR., retired lawyer; b. Buenos Aires, Feb. 7, 1935; s. William Cattell and Nancy Gordon (Carroll) Trimble; m. Barbara Janney, June 19, 1960; children: William C III, Margery M Kennelly. AB, Princeton U., 1958; LLB, U. Md., 1964. Bar: Md 1965. With firm Ober, Grimes & Shriver, Balt., 1965-87, ptnr., 1970-87, mng. ptnr., 1973-77; counsel Semmes, Bowen & Semmes, Balt., 1987—2000; ret., 2000; mem. Gov.'s Commn. to Revise Annotated Code of Md., 1975-83. Hon consul, Netherlands, 1986—2003; pres. class of 1958 Princeton U.; pres. bd. trustees Valley Sch., 1968—73; trustee Garrison Forest Sch., 1975—95, Gilman Sch., 1980—84. Lt USNR, 1958—61. Mem.: ABA, Md. Bar Assn., Md. Club, Soc. Cin., Greenspring Valley Hunt Club, Colonial Club Princeton. Episcopalian. Personal E-mail: williamtrimble@msn.com.

TRIMI, SILVANA, finance educator; d. Agim and Kudrete Trimi; 1 child, Armela Naco. PhD, U. Nebr., Lincoln, 2001. Prof. acctg. U. Tirana, Albania, 1989—95; rschr. U. Nebr., 1997—2008, assoc. prof. MIS, 2001—. Contbr. articles to profl. jours. Mem.: Decision Scis. Inst., Assn. Computing Machinery. Office: Univ Nebr Lincoln 276 College Business Administration Lincoln NE 68588-0491 Business E-Mail: strimi@unlnotes.unl.edu.

TRIMMIER, CHARLES STEPHEN, JR., lawyer; b. Chgo., June 25, 1943; s. Charles Stephen and Lucille E. (Anderson) T.; m. Rae Wade Trimmier, Aug. 19, 1966; children: Charles Stephen, Hallie Wade. BA, U. Ala., Tuscaloosa, 1965, JD, 1968. Bar: Ala. 1968. From assoc. to ptnr. Rives, Peterson, Pettus and Conway, Birmingham, Ala., 1968-77; pres. TrimmierLaw Firm, Birmingham and Mobile, Ala., Tampa, Fla., 1977—. Gen. counsel Nat. Assn. State Chartered Credit Union Suprs., 1983-2001, Ala. Credit Union League, Fla. Credit Union League, La. Credit Union League; adj. prof. U. Ala. Sch. Law. Editor-in-chief: Ala. Law Rev., 1968. Mem. ABA (bus. and banking law sect., credit union com.), Ala. Bar Assn., Birmingham Bar Assn., Comml. Law League, Ala. Law Inst., Shades Valley Rotary, Shades Valley Jaycees (sec. 1973). Episcopalian. Home: 3819 River View Cir Birmingham AL 35243-4801 Office: Trimmier Law Firm PO Box 1885 Birmingham AL 35201-1885 Home Phone: 205-967-4859; Office Phone: 800-666-3151. Business E-Mail: steve@trimmier.com.

TRIMMIER, ROSCOE, JR., lawyer; b. Charlotte, NC, July 22, 1944; s. Roscoe and Susie Elizabeth (Stitt) T.; divorced; 1 child, Leigh Snowden Merritt. AB, Harvard U., 1971, JD, 1974. Bar: Mass. 1974, U.S. Dist. Ct. Mass. 1975, U.S. Ct. Appeals (1st cir.) 1975, U.S. Supreme Ct. 1978, U.S. Claims Ct. 1983, U.S. Ct. Appeals (D.C. cir.) 2002. Assoc. Ropes & Gray, Boston, 1974-83, ptnr., 1983—, chmn. litigation dept. Mem. hearing com. Bd. Bar Overseers, 1983-89; bd. dirs., v.p. Family Counseling & Guidance Ctr., Inc., Boston, 1980-93; gov. Mus. of Sci., 1981-93; mem. exec. com. Jud. Nominating Commn., 1991-96; gov. Partner's Healthcare, 1992—; Tufts Med. Ctr., 1992—; vice chmn. Mass. Bd. Registration in Medicine, 2001-07. 1st lt. U.S. Army, 1965-68. Fellow: Am. Coll. Trial Lawyers, Mass. Bar Found. (life), Am. Bar Found. (life); mem.: ABA (former chair standing com. on fed. judiciary), Am. Law Inst., Boston Bar Assn., Mass. Black Lawyers Assn. (life), Mass. Bar Assn. Home: 1265 Beacon St Brookline MA 02446-5200 Office: Ropes & Gray 1 International Pl Boston MA 02110-2624 Office Fax: 617-951-7050. Business E-Mail: roscoe.trimmier@ropesgray.com.

TRIMPIN, SARAH, chemistry professor; d. Dieter Karl Trimpin and Marika Elmer. PhD, Max-Planck-Inst. Polymer Rsch., Mainz, 2002. Rsch. assoc. Ind. U., Bloomington, 2007—08; asst. prof. Wayne State U., Detroit, 2008—. Mem.: Am. Soc. Mass Spectrometry. Achievements include development of insoluble, complex materials using mass spectrometry. Office: Wayne State Univ Dept Chemistry 5101 Cass Ave Detroit MI 48202 Office Fax: 313-577-8822. Business E-Mail: strimpin@chem.wayne.edu.

TRINCHET, JORGE, language educator; s. Modesto Trinchet and María Pilar De Francisco; life ptnr. Kim Hynes. BA in English, U. Alcalá de Henares, Madrid, 1995; MA in Spanish, Ill. State U., Normal, 1998, MA in Comm., 2000. Instr. Spanish Murray State U., Ky., 2002—. Dir.: (short film) Reflections, Newsbreak; author: (screenplay) Hungrier. Recipient award, Integrated TV & Video Assn., 2000. Master: Murray Ind. Filmmakers Assn.

TRINCHIERI, GIORGIO, medical researcher; Rschr. Wistar Inst.; dir. Schering Plough Lab. for Immunological Rsch., Dardilly, France; NIH Fogarty scholar Lab for Parasitic Diseases, Nat. Inst. Allergy and Infectious Diseases; dir. Cancer and Inflammation Program, chief Lab. of Experimental Immunology Ctr. Cancer Rsch., Nat. Cancer Inst., NIH, Frederick, Md., 2006—. Office: Nat Cancer Inst at Fredrick Bldg 560, Rm 31-93 PO Box 8 Frederick MD 21701-1201 Office Phone: 301-846-1323. Office Fax: 301-846-1673. E-mail: trinchig@mail.nih.gov.*

TRINDADE, ARVIND JULIUS, internist, researcher; b. Toronto, Ont., Can., July 22, 1980; s. Julius Trindade; m. Anu Lala-Trindade, July 19, 2008. MD, UMDNJ-Robert Wood Johnson Med. Sch., New Brunswick, 2006. Resident, internal medicine Mt. Sinai Med. Ctr., NYC, 2006—, GI fellow, 2009—.

TRINDAL, WESLEY STEELE, mechanical engineer; b. Superior, Wis., July 21, 1925; s. Glen W. and Mabel Elda Thorp (Steele) T.; m. Mary Elizabeth Steger, Aug. 12, 1949; 1 child, Joseph William. BSME, La. State U., 1956. Test and devel. engr. Ford Motor Co., Chrysler Corp., Detroit, 1956-58; prin. engr. vehicles U.S. Army Mobility Equipment Rsch. & Devel. Command, Ft. Belvoir, Va., 1958-82; mech. engr. Radian, Inc., Alexandria, Va., 1982—94. With US Army, 1943—52,

ETO. Mem. Soc. Automotive Engrs., Am. Truck Hist. Soc., Hist. Constrn. Equipment Soc. Avocation: writing. Home: 698 Forest View Rd Edinburg VA 22824-3580 Home Phone: 540-984-8788; Office Phone: 540-984-8788.

TRINDLE, CARL, chemistry educator; b. Des Moines, Aug. 26, 1941; s. James Carl and Lois Marie (Halterman) T.; m. Margaret Louise Rea, Jan. 20, 1962 (div. May 1979); 1 child, John Michael; m. Barbara Ann Body, Apr. 26, 1992, 1 child, Nigel. BA, Grinnell Coll., 1963; PhD, Tufts U., 1967. Postdoctoral fellow Yale U., New Haven, 1967-68; rsch. assoc. Argonne (Ill.) Nat. Lab., 1968-69; asst. prof. U. Va., Charlottesville, 1969-73, assoc. prof., 1973—, asst. dean, 1980-85, dir. studies Monroe Hill Coll., 1986—. Mem. adv. bd. U.Va. Women's Ctr., Charlottesville, 1990—. Mem. editorial bd. Soundings, 1989—, IRIS, 1988—; contbr. articles to profl. jours. NAS/NRC fellow Nat. Acad. Sci., Zagreb, Yugoslavia, 1979, Sesquicentennial fellow U.Va., Haifa, Israel, 1976, Sloan Found. fellow, 1971. Mem. Am. Chem. Soc. (sect. chmn. 1977), Alpha Epsilon Delta, Alpha Chi Sigma, Omicron Delta Kappa, Sigma Xi. Office: University of Virginia 33 McCormick Ave Charlottesville VA 22904 Business E-Mail: cot@virginia.edu.

TRINGALE, ANTHONY ROSARIO, insurance executive; b. Syracuse, NY, Apr. 20, 1942; s. Anthony and Susan Marie Tringale; children: Anthony William, Michael Paul, Mark David, Amber Marie. BSFS, Georgetown U., 1967. CLU. Office mgr. trainee N.Y. Life Ins. Co. No. Va., 1965-66, office mgr. Fairfax, Va., 1966, field underwriter, 1966-68; mgmt. asst. home office N.Y. Life Ins. Co., NYC, 1973, gen mgr. Pitts., 1973-76; gen. mgr. Acacia Mut. Life Ins. Co., Annandale, Va., 1976-83, fin. and ins. planner, mgmt. and mktg. cons., 1983-86; from field rep. to mktg. com. Acacia Mut. Life, Annandale, Va., 1983-86; prin. Benefits-By-Design, Fairfax, Va., 1986—; pres. Acacia Prodn. Clubs, 1984, 86. Mem. steering com. Entrepreneurship Forum, Washington, 1980-; founding bd. mem. Commonwealth Va. DECA Found., 2003-; nat. adv. bd. Entrepreurship Inst., Columbus, Ohio, 1985—; mem. supts. bus. and industry adv. coun. Fairfax County Pub. Schs., 1989-2004, mem. mktg edn. adv. bd., 1980-2004, chmn. 1983-84, 90-91; lectr. in field. Contbr. articles in field of personal and bus. fin. strategies to Md. Bus. Observer, Washington Bus. Jour., NALU's Life Assoc. News; radio host Basically Bus. Sta. WGMS-FM, Washington, 1988-91. Trustee SME-1 Accreditation Inst. U. Memphis, 1990—99, Syracuse U., 1995—99; past liaison rep. Am. Soc. CLUs, Bryn Mawr, Pa., 1988—98; arbitrator Fairfax County Dept. Consumer Affairs; pres., bd. dir., exec. com. The Jeane Dixon Children to Children Found., 1980—; chmn. VIP panel DC, 1988—92, Vt., 1988—92; pres. VIP panel, DC, 1992—94, Va., 1992—94, Birch Pond Homeowners Assn., 1998—2000; bd. dir., exec. com., pres. United Cerebral Palsy of D.C. and No. Va., 1985—2006; pres., adv. bd. Fairfax County Corps of Salvation Army, 1996—2004, Front Royal Corps, 2004—07; pres. United Cerebral Palsy of D.C. and No. Va., 2002; dir. at large Nat. Christopher Columbus Quincentary Jubilee Adv. Bd., 1995—; active Nat. Italian-Am. Found. Coun. of 1000, 1989—; mem. Italian Am. Leaders Com. Venture Clinic; founding vice chmn. Fairfax Orgn. Christians/Jews United in Svc.; lector, extraordinary minister Basilica Nat. Shrine Immaculate Conception, 1980—2003; bd. dirs., v.p. exec. com., chmn. grants com. No. Va. Cmty. Found., 1979—2004; bd. dir. Summer Opera Theater Co., 1996—98, Nat. Cath. Cmty. Found., 1996—97; adv. bd., grants com. No. Va. Cmty Found., 2004—; adv. bd. Salvation Army, Fairfax, Va., 1995—2004, Front Royal Waren County Corps., 2004—07; bd. dirs. edn. and conf. ctr. 4-H, Front Royal, Va., 2007—. Recipient 2000 Crystal award No. Va. Cmty. Found. Mem. No. Va. Soc. CLUs (past pres.), Am. Soc. CLUs, No. Va. Assn. Life Underwriters (treas. 1972, nat. com. 1997-99, Pres.' Cup 1991-92), Assn. Advanced Life Underwriting, Sales and Mktg. Execs. Met. Washington (pres. 1979-80, 95-97, treas. 1989-92, bd. dirs. 1990-2000, sr. v.p. profl. devel. 1993-95, Man of Yr. 2000), Nat. Assn. Life Underwriters (Nat. Mgmt. award Gen. Agts. and Mgrs. Conf. 1976-83, exec. com. 1984-85, life qualifying), No. Va. Estate Planning Coun. (exec. com. 1985-92, pres. 1990-91), Internat. Platform Assn. (trustee, bd. govs. 1990-2002), No. Va. Gen. Agts. and Mgrs. Assn. (pres. 1980-81, dir. 1982-83), Greater Washington Area Health Underwriters, Fairfax County C. of C. (dir. small bus. 1989-90, dir. membership 1990-91, exec. com. dir. at large 1991-92, Small Bus. Adv. of Yr. award 1990), Million Dollar Round Table (life), John Carroll Soc. Ins. Club Washington (pres. 1997-98) Personal E-mail: tonyt33@embargmail.com. E-mail: icg@hughes.net.

TRINGALI, MARIA ROSARIA, language educator; d. Angelo Tringali and Carmela Lo Giudice. Diploma in Classical Lyceum, Augusta-,Siracusa,Italy, 1956; PhD, U. Catania, Sicily, 1961; Grad in Coop. Lit., U. Calif., Berkeley, 1968; Degree in English & Gen. Edn., Monterey Peninsula Coll., 1972. Cert. in English Monterey Inst Internat Studies, 1979. Tchr Carmel Adult Sch., 1974—79, 1994—2008; tchr., history & geography Christan Valley Acad., 1978; adj. prof. Monterey Inst. Internat, 1985—93; lectr., Italian Calif. State U., Monterey Bay, 1996—; asst. prof. Defeuse Lang. Inst., Monterey, 2008—. Coord, Italian langs. Monterey Inst. Internat. Studies, Calif., 1984—90. Treas. Italian-Am. Cultural Ctr., 2005—08. Mem.: Am. Assn. Tchrs. Italian, Nat. Italian. Am. Found. (trustee), OSIA, Am. Council Fgn. Lang., Am. Assn. Tchg. Inst. Democrat. Avocations: walking, reading, music. Home: 291 Watson St Monterey CA 93940 Office: Calif State Univ Monterey Bay 100 Campus Ctr Seaside CA 93955 Business E-Mail: maria_tringali@csumb.edu.

TRINGLE, SARAH TAYLOR, biology professor, department chairman; d. Winton and Edwina Taylor; m. Kevin Patrick Tringle, Oct. 11, 1986. MEd, USM. Biology instr. MGCCC, Perkinston, 1998—2005, sci. dept. chair, 2005—. Office: Miss Gulf Coast CC PO Box 548 Perkinston MS 39573 Business E-Mail: sarah.tringle@mgccc.edu.

TRINKAUS, JOHN WILLIAM, management educator; b. Mt. Vernon, NY, July 17, 1925; s. Bernard and Elsie (Kelly) T.; m. Irene Klimowski, July 31, 1954; children: Joanne Trinkaus Dillon, Robert John, John William. BEE, NYU, 1952, PhD, 1976; MBA, CCNY, 1961. Registered profl. engr., Mass. Engr. Bendix Aviation Corp., Teterboro, NJ, 1947-52, Curtis Wright Corp., Carlstadt, NJ, 1952-53, Sperry Corp., Great Neck, NY, 1953-68; prof. CUNY Baruch Coll., NYC, 1968-81, assoc. dean, 1981-93, prof. emeritus, 1993—. Engring. cons. Electronic Industries Assoc., Washington, 1960-68, USAF, Washington, 1965-68; mgmt. cons. Ford Found., NYC, 1980-82, Interracial Coun. Bus. Opportunity, NYC, 1983-93; vis. disting. prof. St. John's U., NYC, 1993-96. Chmn., rsch. comm. Am. Acad. Profl. Law Enforcement, Mineola, NY, 1978-79; cons. NYC Vol. Urban Con. Group, 1979-84. Sgt. US Army, 1945-46. Recipient 1st prize paper Nat. Fedn. Ind. Bus., Washington, 1992, (Ig)Nobel award, 2003. Home: 1 Linden St New Hyde Park NY 11040-2311 Office: Baruch Coll CUNY 1 Bernard Baruch Way New York NY 10010-5518 Office Phone: 646-312-3693.

TRIO, EDWARD ALAN, lawyer, accountant; b. Newark, N.J., Dec. 29, 1952; s. Edward B. and Dorothy J. (Salvia) T.; m. Patricia Ann Sherwood, June 19, 1982; children: Edward Joseph, Michael John. B.B.A., U. Notre Dame, 1974; J.D., Hamline U., St. Paul, 1977; LL.M. in Taxation with honors, Chgo.-Kent Coll. Law, 1984. Bar: Ill. 1977, U.S. Dist. Ct. (no. dist.) Ill. 1977, U.S. Tax Ct. 1979, U.S. Supreme Ct. 1984. C.P.A. Staff auditor Donald E. Bark, C.P.A., Arlington Heights, Ill., 1972-77; assoc. Graf & Gulbrandsen, Morton Grove, Ill., 1977-80; ptnr. Schneider, Graf & Trio, Morton Grove, 1980-82; tax specialist Deloitte Haskins & Sells, Chgo., 1982-85; assoc. Gould & Ratner, Chgo., 1985-90, ptnr., 1991—. Mem. ABA, AICPA, Ill. State Bar Assn., Chgo. Bar Assn., KC. Roman Catholic. Home: 909 N Derbyshire Ave Arlington Heights IL 60004-5776 Office: Gould & Ratner 222 N La Salle St Ste 800 Chicago IL 60601-1086 Office Phone: 312-236-3003. E-mail: etrio@gouldratner.com.

TRIOLO, RONALD J., research scientist, director; BEE summa cum laude, Villanova U., Pa., 1980; MEE, Drexel U., Phila., MS in Biomed. Engring., PhD in Biomed. Engring., Drexel U., Phila. Prin. investigator Cleve. FES Ctr., Cleve., 1994—; asst. prof. Dept. Orthop. and BioMed Eng., Cleve., 1994—2002, Case Western Res. U., Cleve., 1994—2002, assoc. prof., 2002; dir. Motion Study Lab Louis Stokes Cleve. VAMC, 1999—, Advanced Platform Tech. Ctr., Cleve., 2005—; biosci. staff Dept. Orthop. MetroHealth Med. Ctr., Cleve., 1997—; sr. rsch. scientist Rehab. R&D Svcs. US Dept. Vets. Affairs, Washington, 2002—07, sr. rsch. career scientist Cleve., 2007—. Biomed. engr. and rsch. asst. Moss Rehab. Hosp., Phila., 1981—86; with, Phila. Unit Shriners Hosps. Health Hill Hosp. Children, 1986—94, dir. rsch., Cleve., 1995—96; clin. asst. prof. Dept. Orthop. Surgery, Phila., 1986—94; biomed. engr. VA Med. Ctr., Phila. Recipient Maurice Saltzman award, Mt. Sinai Found., 2004; grant, Spinal Cord Rsch. Found., Paralyzed Vets. America, 2000—01, US Dept. Vets. Affairs, 2001—, NIH, 2003—, US Food & Drug Adminstrn., Office Orphan Product Devel., 2005—07, numerous grants. Mem.: Internat. Functional Elec. Stimulation Soc. (bd. mem. 2002—05), Inst. Elec. and Electronic Engrs., Engring. in Medicine and Biology Soc., Gait and Clin. Movement Analysis Soc., Rehabiliation Engring. Soc. North America (officer 1998—2000), Nat. Spinal Cord Injury Assn., Sci. Rsch. Soc., Am. Spinal Injury Assn., Engring. Honor Soc., Nat. Honor Soc., Elec. Engring. Honor Soc. Achievements include invention of variable rigidity trunk corset; surgical clamp for the installation of an epimysial electrode; a slotted epimysial electrode. Office: Advanced Platform Tech Ctr 10701 E Blvd-151AW/Apt Cleveland OH 44106 Office Fax: 216-707-6420. Business E-Mail: ronald.triolo@case.edu.

TRIPATHI, RAM KISHORE, physicist, researcher; b. Rae Bareli, India, Jan. 1, 1942; arrived in U.S., 1966; s. Shiva Kumar and Devi Mani Tripathi; m. Pushpa Shukla Tripathi, May 26, 1966; 1 child, Sanjay. BS, U. Lucknow, 1961, MS, 1963; PhD, U. Kans., 1970. Asst. prof. U. Ky., Lexington, 1970—71, prof., 1986—87; scientist Kern Forschungsanlage, Juelich, Germany, 1971—73; sr. faculty fellow U. Sussex, Brighton, England, 1973—76; fellow Tata Inst. Fundamental Rsch., Bombay, 1975—78; assoc. prof. Dept. Energy/Inst. Physics, Bhubaneswar, India, 1978—85; prof. U. Tuebingen, Germany, 1980—82, U. Liege, Belgium, 1985—86; radiation physicist NASA Langley Rsch. Ctr., Hampton, Va., 1987—. Contbr. numerous articles to profl. jours. Pres. internat. cultural activities U. Kans., Lawrence, 1966-68. Fulbright fellow USIA, Washington, 1966-70, Sr. NRC fellow NAS, Washington, 1999; grantee NASA, Dept. of Def., Dept. of Energy, NSF. Fellow AIAA (assoc.), Am. Phys. Soc. (life), AAAS, Am. Nuc. Soc. (life), Inst. Physics. Avocations: jogging, travel, anthropology. Home: 13 Natalie Dr Hampton VA 23666-5565 Office: NASA Langley Rsch Ctr Ms 188 E Hampton VA 23681-0001

TRIPATHI, RAMESH CHANDRA, ophthalmologist, researcher, educator; b. Jamira, India, July 1, 1936; came to U.S., 1977, naturalized, 1983; s. Arjun and G. Tripathi; m. Brenda Jennifer Lane, May 20, 1969; children: Anita, Paul. ISc, Lucknow Christian Coll., 1954; MD, Agra U. Med. Coll., 1959; M of Surgery in Ophthalmology, Lucknow U., 1963; PhD, U. London, 1970. Ophthalmic resident in surgery and demonstrator Lucknow U. Med. Coll., Kanpur, 1959—63; asst. surgeon, med. officer in charge casualty dept. Rly Hosp., Delhi, 1963; fellow Univ. Eye Clinic, Ghent, Belgium, 1964; ophthalmic registrar Southwest Middlesex Hosp., 1965-68; Hayward fellow, registrar, chief clin. asst. Inst. Opthalmology and Moorfields Eye Hosp., London, 1968-72; lectr. U. London Inst. Opthalmology, 1968-70; sr. lectr. U. London, 1970-77; cons. ophthalmologist and pathologist Moorfields Eye Hosp., London, 1972-77; prof. ophthalmology U. Chgo., 1977-93, The Coll. prof., 1979-93, sec. dept. ophthalmology, 1977-87, cons. pediatric tumor bd., 1978-80; attending ophthalmologist, attending ocular pathologist, mem. med. staff U. Chgo. Med. Ctr., 1977-93, dir. Eye Pathology Labs., 1977-93; prof. ophthalmology U. S.C., Columbia, 1993—2006, chmn., 1993—98, endowed chair ophthalmology Columbia, 2000—; dir. ophthalmology edn. Richland Mem. Hosp., SC, 1993—98; prof. The Graduate Sch., 1996—2006; adj. prof. pathology and microbiology, 2002—06; emeritus disting. prof., 2006—. Cons., attending ophthalmologist Oak Forest (Ill.) Hosp., 1986-93, dir. ophthalmology resident program, 1986-89, chmn. instnl. rev. bd., 1988; quality assurance com. U. Chgo. Hosp., 1979-93, med. curriculum com. U. Chgo., 1990-93; cons. Nat. Eye Inst. NIH, 1981—, Fight for Sight Rev. Bd., 1990-91; vis. prof. Yeshiva U., NYC, 1973, U. Wurzberg, Germany, 1974, U. Toronto, 1979, Jefferson U., Phila., 1979, Columbia U., NYC, 1981, U. Oxford, Eng., 1984, 86, 89, Nat. Autonomous U. Mex., Mexico City, 1981, Hotel Dieux de Paris, 1975, U. Tex. Med. Br., Galveston, 1990, Kresge Eye Inst. Wayne State U., Detroit, 1991, NY Eye and Ear Infirmary, NYC, 1991, Boston U. Dept. Ophthalmology, New Eng. Eye Ctr., Tufts U., Boston, 1991, Mayo Clinic Dept. Ophthalmology, Rochester, Minn., 1992, others; preceptor MS and PhD degree candidates in ophthalmology and visual sci., U. Chgo., 1977-93, U. SC, 1993—; mem. coun. Ill. Asian-Am. Adv. Com. to Gov. State of Ill., 1989-93; rep. to AMA & Chgo. Med. Soc. from Oak Forest Hosp./Cook County Hosp. Med. Staff, 1987-93, alt. del. Ill. State Med. Soc., 1991-93; del. Bd. Govs. Southeastern Chgo. Med. Soc. from U. Chgo. Hosp. & Clinics, 1991-93; faculty basic and clin. sci. course Am. Acad. Opthalmology, 1991-2003; attending ophthalmologist WBJ Dorn VA Hosp., 1993—2006; vis. prof. Harvard Med. Sch. Eye and Ear Infirmary, Boston, Mass., 1997-. Author: Wolff's Anatomy of the Eye and Orbit, 1997; exec. editor Exptl. Eye Rsch., 1973—2000, sect. editor, 1987—99, mem. editl. bd. Ophthalmic Literature, 1974—76, sect. editor, mem. editl. bd. Cornea, 1981—86, assoc. editor Afro-Asian Jour. Ophthalmology, 1981—93, Drug Devel. Rsch., 1988—92, Lens and Eye Toxicology Rsch., 1989—93, Sci. Rsch. Jour., 1990—; contbr. over 600 articles to profl. jours., over 60 chpts. to books and monographs. Chmn. Med. Coun. Assn. Indians in Am., Chgo., 1983-93, v.p., 1986-88; bd. dirs. Indo-Am. Ophthal. Soc. World Eye Found.; mem. Chgo. Found. for Med. Care, 1977-93; pres. Vision Rsch. Found., 1987—; mem. exec. bd. Assn. Scientists of Indian Origin in Am. Recipient Ophthalmology prize Royal Soc. Medicine London, 1971, Royal Eye London prize Ophthal. Soc. London, 1976, Resolutions Commendation, Ill. State Gen. Assembly, 1987, 88, Outstanding US Citizen award, 1984, Internat. prize Alcon Rsch. Inst., 1987; Med. Rsch. Coun. London grantee, 1972-75, Nat. Eye Inst. USPHS grantee, 1977—; named Litchfield endowed lectr. U. Oxford (Eng.), 1986, Ida Mann Gold medal U. Oxford, 1989, Disting. Physician of Am., 1990. Fellow: ACS (diplomate), Am. Acad. Ophthalmology (sect. 2 fundamentals and principles of ophthalmology 1991—2001, chair and past chair, basic and clin. sci. com., Honor award 1984, sr. honor award 1997), Internat. Coll. Surgeons (diplomate, vice regent U.S. 1984—), Royal Coll. Ophthalmologists London (diplomate), Royal Coll. Pathologists (diplomate), Nat. Acad. Scis. of India (life), Royal Soc. Medicine London (coun. 1973—76); mem.: AAUP, AMA, Ill. Med. Soc. (alternate del.), Internat. Soc. Ocular Toxicology (sec., treas. 1993—97, bd. dirs. 1993—, pres. 1998—2000, founder Hockwin-Green Meml. Endowment Fund 2002), Chgo. Ophthal. Soc., S.C. Ophthal. Soc., Glaucoma Soc., Electron Microscopical Soc. Am., Am. Assn. Ophthalmic Pathologists, Am. Assn. Pathologists, Internat. Acad. Pathologists, Contact Lens Assn. Ophthalmologist, Oxford Ophthal. Soc., Ophthal. Soc. U.S., Assn. for Rsch. Vision and Ophthalmology, Pan-Am. Assn. Ophthalmology, Royal Microscopical Soc., Assn. Eye Rsch. Europe (guest of honor 1974), Indian Med. Assn. U.S.A. (bd. dirs. 1984—85, Disting. Physician award 1987), Chgo. Med. Soc. (v.p. 1993, bd. dirs. Southea. br., pres. 1993), Assn. Indians in Am. (v.p. 1988—90, honor award 1986), Fedn. Am. Soc. Exptl. Biology, Physiol. Soc. London, Royal Coll. Physicians and Surgeons (diplomate, conjoin bd.). Achievements include research in pathophysiology, diagnosis and medical and surgical treatment of various ocular disorders including corneal diseases, glaucoma, cataract, vitreoretinopathy; optic nerve orbital diseases & ocular toxicology; pioneer in the field of aqueous humor and cerebrospinal fluid dynamics, growth factors, contact lens spoilage and fibrinolytic therapy of the eye. Avocations: photography, swimming, scientific and technical exhibits, ethnic and civic service. Office: Univ South Carolina Sch Medicine Dept Opthalmology 4 Medical Pk Ste 300 Columbia SC 29212 Home Phone: 803-749-1164; Office Phone: 803-733-1508. Office Fax: 803-733-3216. Business E-Mail: tripathi@med.sc.edu, ramesh.tripathi@uscmed.sc.edu.

TRIPATHI, SAVARNI, plant pathologist; s. Prabhakar Tripathi; m. Ranjana Tripathi; 1 child, Akshar. BSc with honors, Meerut U., 1991; MSc, Banaras Hindu U., India, 1994; PhD, Indian Agrl. Rsch. Inst., New Delhi, 1998. Rsch. assoc. Indian Agrl. Rsch. Inst., New Delhi, 1998—2000; postdoc. rsch. fellow Nat. Sci. Coun., Taichung, Taiwan, 2000—03; jr. rschr. & UH rsch. cooperator US Dept. Agr. & U. Hawaii, Hilo, Hawaii, 2003—. Mentor USDA, Hilo, 2005—07; editl. bd. mem. Assn. Biotech. & Parmacy, Hyderabad, India, 2009—; examinar Acharya Nagrajuna U., Guntur, India, 2009—; panel judge Hawaii sci. & Engring. Fair, Dept Edn., Hilo, 2009. Contbr. scientific papers. Recipient Best Presentation award, 2008. Achievements include discovery of first time decoded the whole genome sequence of genetically modified tropical fruit crop papaya. Office: USDA Pacific Basin Agrl Rsch Ctr 64 Nowelo St Hilo HI 96720-2788

TRIPATHY, BAISHNAB C., science educator; b. Cuttack, India, Jan. 5, 1952; s. Karunakar and Basant Tripathy; m. Padmabati Mohapatra, July 7, 1981; children: Mukta, Ratna, Beda Byas. BSc, Utkal U., Bhubaneswar, India, 1971, MSc, 1973; PhD, Jawaharlal Nehru U., New Delhi, 1980. Rsch. assoc. Ohio State U., Columbus, 1981—83, U. Ill., Urbana-Champaign, 1984—87; asst. prof. Jawaharlal Nehru U., New Delhi, 1987—95, assoc. prof., 1995—2001, prof., 2001—. Co-prin. scientist Photosynthesis Expt. and Sys. Testing and Operation NASA Space Biology Prog., 2000—03. Author: Photosynthesis. Vol. Tsunami Relief, Chenai, Tamil Nadu, India, 2004—06. Recipient Samanta Chandrasekhar award, Govt. of Orissa, India, 2001, Humboldt Found. fellowship, Humboldt Found. Germany, 1992, sr. associateship, NRC, U.S., 1993—95; fellow Rockefeller Biotech. Ctr. award, Rockefeller Found. U.S., 1990—93. Fellow: NAS, Nat. Acad. Agrl. Scis., Indian Nat. Sci. Acad., Korean Soc. of Horticultural Scis. (editor 2004—07); mem.: Am. Soc. of Plant Biologists, Srivastav Found. Plant Physiology and Plant Molecular Biology (life; v.p. 2006—), Soc. of Plant Biochemistry and Plant Biotech. (life), Orissi Kendra (v.p. 2000—07). Hindu. Achievements include patents for Transgenic plants having resistance to abiotic stress. Avocations: travel, creative art. Home: Jawaharlal Nehru U 28 Dakshinapuram Delhi New Delhi 110067 India Office: Jawaharlal Nehru Univ Sch Life Scis Delhi New Delhi 110067 India Home Phone: 91-11-26742484; Office Phone: 91-11-26704524. Office Fax: 91-11-26742558. Business E-Mail: bctripathy@mail.jnu.ac.in.

TRIPATHY, NIRMAL K., retail executive; Grad., Calcutta Univ.; MBA, Tex. Christian Univ. CPA. Fin. analyst Union Carbide Corp., 1982—83; cons. KPMG Peat Marwick, 1983—87; acct. Price Waterhouse, 1987—89; fin. mgmt. positions Pepsico Inc., 1989—2000; exec. v.p. Macy's Fla., 2002—03, pres., COO, 2003—07; exec. v.p., CFO TJX Companies, Framingham, Mass., 2007—. Office: TJX Companies Inc 770 Cochituate Rd Framingham MA 01701

TRIPENY, PATRICK, architect, educator; BArch, U. Notre Dame, South Bend, 1985; MArch, Calif. Poly. State U., San Luis Obispo, 1991; PhD, U. Mich., Ann Arbor, 1996; MArch, U. Mich., 1996. Registered architect, Calif., 1992. Archtl. intern Kendrick Ritter Spross, San Francisco, 1985—87; project arch. Skidmore Owings and Merrill, Los Angeles, 1987—89; asst. prof. U. Utah, Salt Lake City, 1996—2003, assoc. prof., 2003—07, dir. sch. architecture, 2007—. Conf. chair Assn. Collegiate Sch Architecture, Wash., 2005. Author: (textbook) Simplified Engineering for and Builders, Simplified Design of Concrete Structures, Simplified Design of Steel Structures, Simplified Design of Wood Structures. Mem. partners on edn. Am. Inst. of Steel Constrn., Chgo., 2008—; mem. spl. structures com. ASCE, Reston, Va., 1995—2002, chair spl. structures com., 1999—2002. Recipient New Faculty Tchg. award, Assn. Collegiate Sch. Architecture and Am. Inst. Archtl. Students, 2001, Early Career Tchg. award, U. Utah, 2001.

TRIPLEHORN, CHARLES A., entomologist, educator; b. Bluffton, Ohio, Oct. 27, 1927; s. Murray E. and Alice Irene (Lora) T.; m. Wanda Elaine Neiswander, June 12, 1949 (dec. Nov. 1985); children: Bradley Alyn, Bruce Wayne; m. Linda Sue Parsons, July 11, 1987. B.Sc., Ohio State U., 1949, MS, 1952; PhD, Cornell U., 1957. Asst. prof. entomology U. Del., Newark, 1952-54; teaching asst. entomology Cornell U., Ithaca, NY, 1954-57; asst. prof. entomology Ohio Agrl. Research and Devel. Ctr., Wooster, Ohio, 1957-61, Ohio State U., Columbus, 1961-62, assoc. prof. entomology, 1962-66, prof. entomology, 1966-92, prof. emeritus, 1992—. Econ. entomologist U.S. AID/Brazil, Piracicaba, Sao Paulo, 1964-66; vis. curator Field Mus. Natural History, Chgo., 1974, Can. Nat. Collection, Ottawa, Ont., 1977, Am. Mus. Natural History, N.Y.C., 1982, U. Mich., 1989, U. Ariz., 1989, Nat. Mus. of Natural History, 1998, Cornell U., 1999, Colo. State U., 2000, Brigham Young U., 2000, Miss. State U. Co-author: Introduction to the Study of Insects, 7th edit., 2004. Cubmaster Boy Scouts Am., Wooster, Ohio, 1959-60, scoutmaster, Columbus, 1971-72; football coach Upper Arlington Football Assn., Ohio, 1968-71 Grantee Am. Philos. Soc., 1963, NSF, 1979, 85, 92. Mem. Entomol. Soc. Am. (pres. 1985), Coleopterists Soc. (pres. 1976), Royal Entomol. Soc. London, Entomol. Soc. Washington, Sigma Xi, Gamma Sigma Delta Clubs: Wheaton (pres.). Republican. Methodist. Avocations: sports, music, reading, writing. Home: 3943 Medford Sq Hilliard OH 43026-2219 Office: Mus Biol Diversity Div Insects The Ohio State University 1315 Kinnear Rd Columbus OH 43212-1157 Office Phone: 614-292-6839. Personal E-mail: ctriplhrn@aol.com. Business E-Mail: ctriplhrn.1@osu.edu.

TRIPLETT, E. EUGENE, editor; b. La Jolla, Calif., Mar. 12, 1949; s. Erbin Eugene Triplett and Marjorie Ann (Aldrich) Heath; m. Vannie Carol Crow, July 19, 1968; 1 child, Aaron Eugene. BA in Journalism, Ctrl. State U., 1975. Reporter, columnist The Okla. Jour., Oklahoma City, 1976-80; entertainment editor The Daily Oklahoman, Oklahoma City, 1981-85, asst. city editor, 1985-89, city editor, 1989-99, sr. feature writer, columnist, 1999—. Bd. dirs. Crime Stoppers Oklahoma City; mem. comm. com. Okla. Heart Assn., 1989-92. With U.S. Army, 1969-71, Vietnam. Recipient 1st pl. Feature Writing award Soc. Profl. Journalists, 1987, 97-98, Great Plains Journalism Competition, 2009, 2d pl., 1999-2000. Mem. AP/Okla. News Exec. (pres.-elect 1994-95, pres. 1995-96, 2nd pl. Feature Writing award 1988, 1st pl. Feature Writing award, 2002, 1st pl. Rev. Writing award 2003, 1st Pl. Entertainment Feature, Gt. Plains Journalism Competition, 2009). Democrat. Avocations: collecting recorded music, feature films, vintage tv shows. Home: 8116 NW 118th St Oklahoma City OK 73162-1113 Office: The Daily Oklahoman 9000 Broadway Ext Oklahoma City OK 73114-3799 Office Phone: 405-475-4105. E-mail: etriplett@oklahoman.com, geneoat@cox.net.

TRIPODES, JAMES G., nuclear safety and environmental regulatory affairs professional; b. San Francisco, Mar. 12, 1954; s. George J. Tripodes and Daisy Natsoulas Pimentel; m. Nham T. Tripodes, Nov. 5, 1983. BS in Environ. Planning and Mgmt., U. Calif., Davis, 1978. Registered hazardous substances profl. Nat. Environ. Health Assn.; registered environ. assessor Calif. EPA. Envir. health/safety technician, cyclotron health physicist U. Calif., Davis, 1972-79, health physics mgr. Irvine, 1979-89, assoc. dir. envir. health/safety for envir. reg. affairs, 1989-2001, interim dir. environ. health and safety, 2001—02; dep. dept. head environ. protection Lawrence Livermore (Calif.) Nat. Lab., 2002—03, scientist, 2003—. Co-founder, oversight chmn. Internat. Conf. on Incineration and Thermal Treatment Techs., 1980-2000; prin. investigator, project mgr. U.S. Dept. Energy and Calif. Dept. Health Svcs., 1982-95. Editor: (book and CD-ROM) Proceedings of International Conferences on Incineration and Thermal Treatment Technologies, 1985-2000; guest editor spl. issue: Health Physics Jour., 1991. Mem. govt. affairs coun. Irvine C. of C., 1995—2002; patron Heritage Found., Washington, 1995—, Commonwealth Club of Calif., 2003-; commr. Southwestern Low-Level Radioactive Waste Commn., 2004-05. Fellow Acad. Polit. Sci.; mem. AAAS, ASME, Health Physics Soc. (Elda E. Anderson award 1994), Am. Soc. Quality (sr.), Ctr. Study Presidency and Congress, NY Acad. Scis. Republican. Avocations: fine art and music appreciation, public affairs. Office: Lawrence Livermore Nat Lab PO Box 808 L-019 Livermore CA 94551 Office Phone: 925-424-2875. Business E-Mail: tripodes2@llnl.gov.

TRIPODI, JOSEPH V., beverage company executive; b. Aug. 7, 1955; BA, Harvard U., 1977; MS, London Sch. Econs., 1981. Various mgmt. positions IBM, 1977—81, Mobil Oil Corp., 1981—88; exec. v.p. global mktg. MasterCard Internat., 1989—98; chief mktg. officer Seagram Spirits & Wine Group, 1999—2002, Bank of NY, 2002—03; sr. v.p., chief mktg. officer Allstate Ins. Co., Northbrook, Ill., 2003—07; sr. v.p., chief mktg. & comml. officer Coca-Cola Co., Atlanta, 2007—09, exec. v.p., chief mktg. & comml. officer, 2009—. Bd. mem. Ad Council; past. chmn. Assn. Nat. Advertisers. Trustee Field Mus., Chgo. Named a Power Player, Advt. Age, 2008. Office: The Coca Cola Co 1 Coca Cola Pl Atlanta GA 30313*

TRIPODI, TONY, retired social worker, dean, editor, writer; b. Sacramento, Nov. 30, 1932; s. Nicola and Christina (Grandinetti); m. Roni Roberts, Oct. 28, 1969 (div. 1986); children: Lee Anna, Anthony, David, Stephen; m. Miriam Potocky-Tripodi, July 25, 1998 (div. 2006). AB, U. Calif., Berkeley, 1954, MSW, 1958; D of Social Work, Columbia U., 1963. Rsch. tech. Calif. Dept. Mental Hygiene, Sacramento, 1958-59; rsch. analyst Calif. Youth Authority, Sacramento, 1959-60; from rsch. asst. to asst. prof. Columbia U., NYC, 1962-65; asst. prof. U. Calif., Berkeley, 1965-66; from assoc. prof. to prof. U. Mich. Sch. Social Work, Ann Arbor, 1966-87; assoc. dean prof. U. Pitts. Sch. Social Work, 1987—92; prof., assoc. dir., head doctoral program Fla. Internat. U., 1992—95; prof. Coll. Social Work Ohio State U., 1995—2005, dean Coll. Social Work, 1995—2005, dean and prof. emeritus, 2005—. Rsch. assoc. Bklyn. Coll., 1963-65; editor in chief Social Work Rsch. and Abstracts, NYC, 1980-84; interim assoc. dean U. Mich. Sch. Social Work, Ann Arbor, 1985, 1986, 1987; rsch. cons. Zancan Found., Padova, Italy, 1974-1992, NIMH, Silver Spring, Md., 1989-, Nat. Rsch. Adv. Com., Clinton, Mich., 1988-95; vis. Zellerbach prof. social welfare U. Calif., Berkeley, 2006, vis. Moses prof. social work Hunter Coll., NYC, 2006-07. Author: (with others) Clinical Social Judgement, 1966, Requiem for Torchy, 2003, Tuscan Landscapes, 2005, International Social Work Research, 2006, Research Techniques for Clinical Social Workers, 2007, Eternal Love in St. Patrick's Cathedral, 2007, Love and Hope By the Sea, 2008, My Cane and I, 2009, 23 other books; co-editor: Jour. of Social Work Rsch. and Evaluation: An Internat. Pub., 1998-2005; series editor: Pocket Guides to Social Work Research Methods, Oxford U. Press; contbr. articles to profl. jours. Bd. dirs. Parental Stress Ctr., Pitts., 1987-92, Comm, Rsch. Partners, 2000-05, Asian Am. Comm. Svc., 2000-05, Coun. Public Reps. Assoc., NIH, 2003-, With USNR, 1954-62. Doctoral rsch. fellow Sage Found., NYC, 1960-63; rsch. grantee NSF, 1965-66; Fulbright Hays scholar U.S. Govt., Italy, 1973-74; invited scholar Tilburg U., the Netherlands, 1977; vis. scholar U. Kent, Canterbury, Eng., 1980; named to Hall of Fame Columbia U. Sch. Social Work Alumni Assn. Mem. NASW, Acad. Cert. Social Workers, Coun. Social Work Edn., Soc. Social Work and Rsch. (pres. 1998-2000), Internat. Assoc. Sch. Social Work, WHO (World Health Orgn.), Mensa, Phi Kappa Phi. Home: 1401 Riverpl Blvd Apt 2207 Jacksonville FL 32207 Home Phone: 646-709-8553. Business E-Mail: tripodi.5@osu.edu.

TRIPP, ALAN H., educational association administrator, consultant; AB in Econ. and Internat. Rels., Stanford U., 1985, MBA, 1989. Editor, reporter Wall St. Jour., European edit., Brussels, 1985—86; cons. Boston Consulting Group, San Francisco, 1989—91; founder, CEO, Score! Ednl. Crs., San Francisco, 1992—99, InsideTrack Learning, Inc., San Francisco, 1999—. Bd. chair GreatSchools.net, San Francisco, 2001—. Mem.: Phi Beta Kappa. Office: InsideTrack Inc 150 Spear St San Francisco CA 94105

TRIPP, AMANDA, psychologist; d. David and Amelia Keller; m. Brian Tripp; 1 child, Ethan. MS, Rochester Inst. Tech., NY, 2004. Cert. sch. psychology NY. Sch. psychologist Palmyra Macedon Mid. Sch., NY, 2004—05, Victor Jr. High, 2005—.

TRIPP, LLOYD DALE, research scientist; s. John Ray (Stepfather) and Mary Ellen Spyker; m. Deborah Marie Steinke, Oct. 20, 1987; children: Kevin Alexander, Amy Elizabeth. BA, Capital U., Columbus, Ohio, 1998; MA, U. Cin., Ohio, 2004, PhD, 2007. Supt. aeromedical svc. USAF, Wright-Patterson AFB, Ohio, 1977—98; rsch. scientist Gen. Dynamics, Dayton, Ohio, 1990—2002; engrng. rsch. psychologist Air Force Rsch. Lab., Wright-Patterson AFB, Ohio, 2002—06; tech. integration mgr. 711th Human Performance Wing, Wright-Patterson AFB, Ohio, 2006—. Contbr. chapters to books. Msgt USAF, 1977—98. Recipient Harry G. Armstrong award for Sci. Excellence, Armstrong Rsch. Lab., 1988, Young Investigator award, AsMA Space Medicine Br., 1988, Eric Liljencrantz award, Aerospace Med. Assn., 2002, Paul Bert award, Aerospace Physiology Soc., 2007, Jerome H. Ely Human Factors award, Human Factors and Ergonomics Soc., 2007; named Outstanding Sr. Scientist and Engr. award, Safety and Flight Equipment, 1999. Fellow: Aerospace Human Factors Soc., Aerospace Med. Assn.; mem.: Aerospace Physiologist Soc., Space Medicine, Life Sci. & Biomedical Engrng. Br. (pres. 2006—07). Achievements include patents for in fields. Office: 711th Human Performance Wing 2215 First St Wright Patterson AFB OH 45433 Business E-Mail: lloyd.tripp@wpafb.af.mil.

TRIPP, TYLER J., lawyer; b. Sparta, Wis., May 1, 1978; s. James R. and Julia M. Tripp; m. Jessica R. Tripp; 1 child, Gustaf A.; 1 child, Evelyn E. BS in Polit. Sci. with honors, U. Wis., LaCrosse, 2000; JD, Hamline U., St. Paul, 2003. Bar: Wis. 2003. Assoc. Osborne & Goodman SC, Sparta, Wis., 2003—05; ptnr. Osborne, Goodman & Tripp, Sparta, 2006—. Treas., bd. dirs. Slayton Space and Bike Mus., Sparta, 2005—; bd. dirs., sec. Sparta Boys and Girls Club, 2004—06. Mem.: Monroe County Bar Assn., Kiwanis. Office: Osborne Goodman & Tripp PO Box 420 Sparta WI 54656

TRIPPENSEE, GARY ALAN, retired aerospace executive; b. Jefferson City, Mo., May 23, 1940; m. Concha Elvira Perez, Aug. 18, 1981; children: Jena, Darin. BSME, U. Mo., Rolla, 1962; AA in Bus., Antelope Valley Coll., Lancaster, Calif., 1974. Lic. airframe and powerplant mechanic, FAA; single/multi-engine comml. aircraft lic. land & sea, Inst.; cert. flight instr., instrument. Aircraft flight test engr. McDonnell Douglas, St. Louis, 1965-79; project mgr. NASA/Dryden Flight Rsch. Ctr., Edwards, Calif., 1979—2001, project mgr. F14, 1983-84, project mgr. F15, 1984-85, project mgr. X-29, 1985-91, project mgr. X-31, 1991-92, internat. test. orgn. dir. X-31, 1993-95, project mgr. X-33, 1996-2000, project mgr. X-37, 2000-01, ret., 2001. Mem. Grove City Coun., Okla., 2007; capt. U.S. Army C.E., 1962-65, Vietnam. Recipient Laurels award for aeronautics/propulsion Aviation Week & Space Tech., 1990, 93, Outstanding Alumni award U. Mo.-Rolla, 2002. Mem. EAA, Acad. Mech. Engrs. Avocations: flying, fishing, r/c models. Home: 3410 Callie Dr Grove OK 74344 Office Phone: 918-791-1917.

TRIPPI, JOE, media consultant; b. Calif. m. Kathleen Lash; 3 children. Attended, San José State U. With Doak, Shrum and Assocs., Edward M. Kennedy's presdl. campaign, 1980, Andrea Papandreou for Prime Min. campaign, Greece, 1993, George Papandreou for Prime Min., Greece, 2007, various presdl, senate, congl., gubernatorial, mayoral races; nat. campaign mgr. Howard Dean presdl. campaign, 2004; campaign advisor Tony Blair, 2005, Romano Prodi for Prime Min., Italy, 2006; cons. Action Congress Party, Nigeria, 2007; sr. advisor Senator John Edwards presdl. campaign, 2008; sr. advisor, lead media cons. Joe Trippi Associates, 2008—. Cons. MasterCard, Toyota, DaimlerChrysler, SES Americom, LabCorp, IBM, Lionsgate Films, BestBuy, MSNBC, Wave Systems, Progeny Linux Systems; polit. analyst CBS News; fellow Harvard U. Featureed in NY Times, The New Republic, Fast Company, The Atlantic, The Washington Post, NY Times Mag.; author: The Revolution Will Not Be Televised: Democracy, the Internet and the Overthrow of Everything, 2004. Recipient Rave award, Wired Mag., 2004. Democrat. Office: Trippi Multimedia 606A N Talbot St Ste 303 Saint Michaels MD 21663 Office Phone: 410-745-2003.*

TRIPPLEHORN, JEANNE, actress; b. Tulsa, Okla., June 10, 1963; d. Tommy and Suzanne (Ferguson) T.; m. Leland Orser, Oct. 14, 2000; 1 child August Student, Juilliard Sch. Actress: (theatre off-Broadway) The Big Funk, 1990, 'Tis Pity She's A Whore, 1992; (films) Basic Instinct, 1991, The Firm, 1993, The Night We Never Met, 1993, Reality Bites, 1994, Waterworld, 1995, 'Til There Was You, 1996, Office Killer, 1997, Snitch, 1998, Sliding Doors, 1998, Very Bad Things, 1998, Talk of the Town, 1998, Mickey Blue-Eyes, 1998, Steal This Movie, 2000, Timecode, 2000, Paranoid, 2000, Relative Values, 2000, Dial 9 for Love, 2001, Swept Away, 2002, Word of Honor, 2003, The Moguls, 2005; (TV films) The Perfect Tribute, 1991, Old Man, 1997, My Brother's Keeper, 2002; (TV series) Big Love, 2006-; (TV appearances) The Ben Stiller Show, 1992, Frasier, 2003

TRISCO, ROBERT FREDERICK, church historian, educator; b. Chgo., Nov. 11, 1929; s. Richard E. and Harriet Rose (Hardt) T. BA, St. Mary of Lake Sem., Mundelein, Ill., 1951; STL, Pontifical Gregorian U., Rome, 1955, Hist. Eccl.D., 1962; LHD (hon.), Belmont Abbey Coll., 1992. Ordained priest Roman Catholic Ch., 1954. Faculty Cath. U. Am., Washington, 1959-2000, prof. ch. history, 1975-2000, Kelly-Quinn disting. prof. ch. history, 1999-2000, prof. emeritus ch. history, 2000—. Expert 2d Vatican Coun., 1962-65; pres. Am. subcom. Internat. Commn. Comparative Ch. History, 1978-80, asseseur, 1980—; mem. subcoms. Nat. Conf. Cath. Bishops, 1966-76, 87-92; mem. Pontifical Com. Hist. Scis., 1982—; hon. mem. Accademia di San Carlo (Milan), 1986—; hon. prelate (monsignor), 1992; Protonotary Apostolic Supranumerary, 2005; mem. Internat. Joint Commn. for Theol. Dialogue between Cath. Ch. and Orthodox Ch., 1999-2006; mem. Anglican-Roman Catholic Consultation in U.S., 2002-07; mem. adv. com. Assn. Friends of the Archives of Congregation for Doctrine of the Faith (Holy See), 1999—. Author: The Holy See and Nascent Church in the Middle Western U.S., 1826-1850, 1962, Bishops and Their Priests in the United States, 1988; co-author: A Guide to American Catholic History, 2d edit., 1982; editor: Catholics in America, 1976; editor Cath. Hist. Rev., 1963-2005, assoc. editor, 2005-; co-editor, contbr.: Studies in Catholic History in Honor of John Tracy Ellis, 1985; contbr. articles to profl. jours. Decorated knight Equestrian Order of the Holy Sepulchre of Jerusalem, 1993, knight comdr., 1998. Mem. Am. Hist. Assn., Am. Soc. Ch. History (coun. 1980-82), Am. Cath. Hist. Assn. (exec. sec. 1961—, sec., treas. 1983—2009), Can. Cath. Hist. Assn. Office: Cath U Am Mullen Library Rm 320 Washington DC 20064-0001 Office Phone: 202-319-5079. Business E-Mail: trisco@cua.edu.

TRISTANO, ANTONIO GINO, medical researcher; arrived in U.S., 2003; s. Piero Tristano and Speranza Romano; children: Gianpiero, Fabrizio. MD, Luiz Razetti Sch. Medicine, Caracas, 1991; MS in Biology, Instituto Venezolano de Investigaciones Científicas (IVIC), Caracas, 1997; Specialist in Criminalistics cum laude, U. Inst. Sci. Police, Caracas, 1997; Specialist in Internal Medicine, Luis Razetti Sch. Medicine, Caracas, 2000, Specialist in Rheumatology, 2002. Specialist in Rheumatology Colegio de Medicos del Distrito Metropolitano, 2003, Specialist in Internal Medicine Colegio de Medicos del Distrito Metropolitano, 2001, Medical Assistant Am. Registry of Med. Assistants/Fla., 2004. Rural physician Hosp. de Naiguatá, La Guaira, Vargas, Venezuela; intern Instituto de Clínicas y Urología Tamanaco, Caracas, 1992—93; biology prof. Instituto Universitario de Policía Científica, Caracas, 1996—97; toxicology prof. José Maria Vargas U., Caracas, 1997—97; internal medicine staff in internal medicine program Hosp. Domingo Luciani (U. Hosp.), Caracas, 2002—04; rsch. assoc. NOVA Southeastern U., Ft. Lauderdale, Fla., 2004—. Chief resident internal medicine Internal Medicine Residency Program Domingo Luciani Hosp. (Univrsity Hosp.), Caracas, 1997—98; chief resident rheumatology U. Hosp. of the City of Caracas, 2001—02; mem. soc. interns and residents Domingo Luciani Hosp., Caracas, 1998—2000; presenter in field. Reviewer: So. Med. Jour.; contbr. articles to profl. jours. Vaccination Ministerio de Sanidad y Asistencia Social, Caracas, 1987—87. Scholar, Fundación Gran Mariscal de Ayacucho, 1995—97. Mem.: Venezuelan Assn. Internal Medicine (Spl. Award by thesis 2000), Internat. Reviewers Panel of the Med. Sci. Monitor, Venezuelan Assn. for Pain Studies, Venezuelan Assn. Rheumatology, Internat. Assn. for the Study of Pain, ACP, Am. Soc. Internal Medicine (Award for 1° prize of best paper Pub. 2003). Roman Catholic. Avocations: travel, classical music. Office: NOVA Southeastern U 3200 S University Dr Fort Lauderdale FL 33328 Personal E-mail: mjtristano@cantv.net.

TRISTRAM-NAGLE, STEPHANIE ANN, research scientist, educator; b. NYC, Nov. 21, 1948; d. Edward Wells and Marguerite Ann (Doner) Tristram; m. John Frederick Nagle, Dec. 31, 1980; children; Julia Courtney, Lara Kimberly. BA, Rutgers U., 1970; postgrad., U. Mass., 1972-75; PhD in Comparative Biochemistry, U. Calif., Berkeley, 1981. Clin., research lab. tech. Clin. Assays, Cambridge, Mass., 1972-75; chemistry tutor U. Mass., Boston, 1974-75; lab. asst. U. Calif., Berkeley, 1975-80, teaching asst., reader, 1976-80; postdoctoral research biologist Carnegie Mellon U., Pitts., 1982-86, rsch. biologist, 1986-99, sr. rsch. biologist, 1999—2005, assoc. prof. rsch., biol. physics group, physics dept., 2005—08, rsch. prof., 2008—. Mentor Pitts. Pub. Schs. Sci. Outreach Program, 1995, NSF summer undergrad. rsch. program, 1996, 98, Science-by-Mail, 1992—2002; chair membrane structure and assembly subgroup Biophys. Soc., Long Beach, Calif., 2005; reviewer sci. jours.; judge Sigma Xi Undergrad. Rsch. Symposium, Pa. Jr. Acad. Sci., Pitts. Regional Sci. Fair, also presenter Sigma Xi award. Contbr. chpts. to books, more than 60 articles to profl. jours. Fundraiser Wightman Sch. Preservation Soc., Pitts., 1986-89, 3d Presbyn. Ch., 1983—. Recipient Avanti award in lipids Biophys. Soc., 2003; Samuel & Emma Winters grantee, 1985, 90. Mem. Am. Chem. Soc., Assn. Women in Sci. Biophys. Soc., Sigma Xi (membership sec. CMU chpt. 1990-93, v.p. 1993-94, pres. 1994-95). Democrat. Presbyterian. Achievements include research in thermodynamic and structural studies on biomimetic and biological membranes, using differential scanning calorimetry and dilatometry, density centrifugation and x-ray and neutron diffraction as function of temperature. Office: Carnegie Mellon U Biol Physics Group Physics Dept 5000 Forbes Ave Pittsburgh PA 15213 Office Phone: 412-268-3174. Business E-Mail: stn@cmu.edu.

TRITLE, BRADLEY, health facility administrator; s. Elwin and Donna Tritle; m. Ayako Tritle, Aug. 12, 1989; 1 child, Aisha. BA in Asian Lanaguages, Ariz. State U., Tempe, 1992. Cert. Internat. Assn. Privacy Professionals, Maine, 2008. Broadband devel. mgr. State CIO's Office, Phoenix, 2000—03; sales mgr. Ito Am. Corp., Scottsdale, Ariz., 2003—05; telecom. exec. Cox Comm., C3IP Comm., Phoenix, 2005—06; strategic initiatives mgr. State CIO's Office, Phoenix, 2006—07; exec. dir. Ariz. Health-e Connection, Phoenix, 2007—. Chair Soc. Info. Display Ariz. Chpt., Phoenix, 2003—. Contbr. articles (Governor's Spirit Excellence award, 2002). Connecting ctys. com. Health Record Banking Alliance, Alexandria, Va., 2007—; worship ministry Scottsdale Bible Ch., Ariz., 2003—08; com. chair Ariz. Telecom. Info. Coun., Phoenix, 1998—2004. Recipient Innovation award, Coun. State Governments, 2007. Mem.: Soc. Info. Display, Internat. Assn. Privacy Profls., HIMSS. Conservative. Avocations: running, singing, trombone, reading. Office: Arizona Health-e Connection 810 W Bethany Home Rd Phoenix AZ 85013 Office Fax: 602-288-5132. Business E-Mail: brad.tritle@azhec.org.

TRITLE, LAWRENCE ALAN, history professor; b. Glendale, Calif., Oct. 13, 1946; s. Robert Charles Jr. and Dorothy (Brown) T.; m. Margaret Burlington, Jan. 31, 1970 (dec. Aug. 24, 2000) BA, UCLA, 1968; MA, U. S. Fla., Tampa, 1972; PhD, U. Chgo., 1978. Prof. Loyola Marymount U., LA, 1978—, Marie Chilton chair humanities, 1988. Vis. prof. Loyola U. Chgo., 1981-82, 90-91, UCLA, 1992. Author: Phocion the Good, 1988, From Melos to My Lai. War & Survival, 2000, The Peloponnesian War, 2004, A New History of the Peloponnesian War, 2009; editor: The Greek World in the Fourth Century BC, 1997, Balkan Currents, 1998, Text and Tradition: Studies in Greek History & Histiography, 1999, Crossroads of History Age of Alexander, 2003, Alexander's Empire, From Formulation to Decay, 2007, Alexander the Great: A New History, 2009. Lt. U.S. Army, 1968-71, Vietnam. NEH fellow U. Pa., 1979. Mem. Am. Philol. Assn. (chair com. ancient history 1997-99), Am. Hist. Assn., Assn. Ancient Historians, Soc. Mayflower Descs., Am. Legion. Democrat. Home: 8301 Fordham Rd Los Angeles CA 90045-2559 Office: Loyola Marymount U 1 LMU Dr Los Angeles CA 90045-2699 Office Phone: 310-338-7385. Business E-Mail: ltritle@lmu.edu.

TRITOS, NICHOLAS ANGELOS, internist; b. Athens, Feb. 13, 1965; s. Angelos N. and Catherine G. (Papadopoulos) T. MD, Athens U. Med. Sch., 1989, DSc, 1992. Diplomate Am. Bd. Internal Medicine. Intern New Eng. Deaconess Hosp., Boston, 1992-93, resident in internal medicine, 1993-95; clin. fellow in medicine Harvard Med. Sch., Boston, 1992—; fellow in endocrinology Lahey Clin., Burlington, Mass., 1995-96, Joslin Diabetes Ctr., Boston, 1996—, Beth Israel Deanconess Med. Ctr., Boston, 1996—. Contbr. articles to profl. jours. Mem. AMA, Am. Coll. Physicians, Mass. Med. Soc., Endocrine Soc., Am. Assn. Clin. Endocrinologists. Office: Joslin Diabetes Ctr 1 Joslin Pl Boston MA 02215-5306

TRITSCH, GEORGE LEOPOLD, retired biochemist, educator; BA, NYU, 1948; MS, U. Md., 1951; PhD, Purdue U., 1954. Rsch. assoc. Cornell Med. Coll., NYC, 1954—56, Rockefeller U., NYC, 1956—59; cancer rsch. scientist Roswell Pk. Cancer Inst., Buffalo, 1959—95, cancer. rsch. scientist emeritus, 1995—; from asst. rsch. prof. to prof. emeritus SUNY, Buffalo, 1961—; prof. biochemistry Niagara U., Niagara Falls, NY, 1961—; ret., 1995. Vis. prof. dept. biochemistry Dartmouth Med. Sch., 1968, Purdue Cancer Ctr., W. Lafayette, Ind., 1983; mem. grant rev. panel nat. prostatic cancer project NIH, Bethesda, Md., 1975—85; symposium organizer adenosine deaminase N.Y. Acad. Scis., 1984; invited spkr. in field. Editor, author Axenic Mammalian Cell Reactions, 1969, Adenosine Deaminase, 1985; contbr. articles to profl. jours. Bd. dirs. N.Y. State Health Rsch. Coun., Buffalo, 1975—80. Grantee, USPHS, 1960—90, Am. Cancer Soc., 1961—69. Mem.: Soc. Exptl. Biology, Am. Assn. Cancer Rsch., Am. Soc. Pharmacological and Exptl. Therapeutics, Am. Inst. Nutrition, Am. Soc. Biochemistry and Molecular Biology, Harvey Soc., Sigma Xi, Alpha Chi Sigma, Phi Lambda Upsilon. Avocations: playing piano, water sports.

TRITT, TERRY, physicist; s. Gladius Tritt; m. Penny Bigger; children: Kristin, Mary. PhD, Clemson U., SC, 1985. Rsch. assoc. Naval Rsch. Lab, Washington, 1985—87, rsch. physicist, 1989—96; prof. Clemson U., 1991—. Editor: (jour.) MRS Bulletin: Harvesting Energy through Thermoelectrics: Power Generation and Cooling; author: Thermal Conductivity: Theory, Properties, and Applications. Grantee, DOE, 2004—07. Mem.: Internat. Thermoelectrics Soc. (bd. dirs. 1999—, conf. chmn. and organizer 2005). Achievements include patents for transition metal pentatellurides and transition metal chalcogenide compounds for thermoelectric materials; preparation of Di-Sr-Ca-Cu-O high temperature superconducting layers. Avocations: golf, blue grass musician. Office: Clemson University 118 Kinard Laboratory Clemson SC 29634-0978 Office Fax: 864-656-0805. Business E-Mail: ttritt@clemson.edu.

TRITTEN, JAMES JOHN, retired federal agency administrator; s. James Hanley and Jennie (Szucs) Tritten; m. Kathleen Brattesani (div. 1983); children: Kimberly, James John Jr.; m. Jasmine Clark, Dec. 29, 1990. BA in Internat. Studies, Am. U., 1971; MA in Internat. Affairs, Fla. State U., 1978; AM in Internat. Rels., U. So. Calif., 1982, PhD in Internat. Rels., 1984. Commd. officer USN, 1967, advanced through grades to commdr., 1981; joint strategic plans officer Office Chief Naval Ops., Washington, 1984—85; asst. dir. net assessment Office Sec. Def., Washington, 1985—86; chmn. dept. nat. security affairs Naval Postgrad. Sch., Monterey, Calif., 1986—89; ret. USN, 1989; assoc. prof. nat. security affairs Naval Postgrad. Sch., Monterey, 1989—93; spl. asst. comdr. Naval Doctrine Command, Norfolk, Va., 1993—96; chief policy and plan divsn. US Joint Forces Command, Suffolk, Va., 1996—2001, mem. joint doctrine divsn., 2001—02; chief Def. Threat Reduction U./Def. Threat Reduction Agy., Albuquerque, 2002—09; asst. chief staff Def. Threat Reduction Agy., 2002—09. Cons. Rand Corp., Santa Monica, Calif., 1982—84; with Nat. Security Rsch., Fairfax, Va., 1992, Amerlnd, Alexandria, Va., 1996. Author: (book) Soviet Naval Forces and Nuclear Warfare, 1986, Our New National Security Strategy, 1992 (George Washington Honor medal, 1991), A Doctrine Reader, 1996; contbr. chapters to books, articles to profl. jours. Mem. Adv. Bd. on Alcohol Related Problems, Monterey, 1987—90; bd. dirs., officer Leadership Monterey Peninsula, 1989—92, Carmel Valley (Calif.) Property Owners Assn., 1989—91; commr. Airport Land Use Commn., Monterey County, 1990—93; officer Kiwans Club of Corrales, 2006, Concerned Citizens of Conales, 2008. Decorated Def. Superior Svc. medal Sec. Def., Washington, DC, Meritorious Svc. medal Sec. Navy, Navy Civilian Supr. Svc. medal; recipient Joint Meritorious Civilian Svc. award, Chmn. Joint Chiefs Staff, 1998, Alfred Thayer Mahan award literary achievement, Navy League US, 1986. Mem.: Mil. Ops. Rsch. Soc. (v.p. 1990—91), U.S. Naval Inst. (Silver and Bronze medals), Naval Order U.S., Pi Gamma Mu, Pi Sigma Alpha. Republican. Presbyterian. Avocation: writing. Personal E-mail: jtritten121@comcast.net.

TRITTER, RICHARD PAUL, strategic consultant; b. Boston, Sept. 30, 1945; arrived in Israel, 2001, naturalized; s. Herman Louis and Rose (Greenblatt) T.; children: Melissa Rosanne, Matthew Alexander, Rachel Danielle, Adam Levi. AB, Columbia Coll., NYC, 1967; JD, Northeastern U. Law Sch., Boston, 1976. Bar: Mass. 1977, U.S. Supreme Ct. 1980. Mktg. mgr./cons. Digital Equipment Corp., Merrimack, NH, 1979-86; pres. Video/Demo Ctrs., Inc., Burlington, Mass., 1986-88; v.p. bus. devel. Info. Resources, Inc., Boston, 1988-91; dir. facilitation consulting svcs. Arthur Andersen LLP, Boston, Chgo., 1991-96; consulting dir. Computer Assocs., Inc., Andover, Mass., 1998—2001; bus. cons. Israel, 2001—. Panelist MIT Enterprise Forum, Cambridge, 1983-89; ptnr., mng. dir. Horn of Africa Fishing Partnership, 1998. Author: Control Self-Assessment: Experience, Current Thinking and Best Practices, 1996, Control Self Assessment—A Guide to Facilitation-Based Consulting, 2000; creator software application testing svc. in coop. with KPMG Peat Marwick, Compliance Testing and Verification, 1981. UN rep. Jubaland Relief and Rehab. Soc., Somalia; dir. Save Somalia Livestock Campaign, 1993. Recipient Better Govt. award, Pioneer Inst. for Pub. Policy Rsch., 1991, Israel Yoseftal Prize, Min. Labor, 2003. Achievements include facilitating meetings between opposing clans in the Juba region of southern Somalia; initiated lobster export project with cooperation of Gen. Omar Jess, Col. Ahmed Hashi and other Somali leaders. Mailing: Kibbutz Givat Brener 60948 Givat Brener Israel Home Phone: 011-972-5254-00250. Personal E-mail: oleh77@yahoo.com.

TRITTON, THOMAS RICHARD, former academic administrator, biologist, educator; b. Lakewood, Ohio, Dec. 20, 1947; s. William Frank and Margie Jean (Galbraith) Tritton; m. Louise Meschter Tritton; children: Lara, Christiana. BA, Ohio Wesleyan U., 1969; PhD, Boston U., 1973. Asst. prof. Yale Med. Sch., New Haven, 1975—80; assoc. prof. Yale U., 1980—85; prof. U. Vt., Burlington, 1985—97, vice provost, 1991—97; pres. Haverford Coll., Pa., 1997—2007; pres. and CEO Chem. Heritage Found., 2007—; pres. sci. Kilford nonprofit. Mem. NIH Exptl. Therapeutics Study Sect., 1988—92; bd. dirs. Fox Chase Cancer Ctr., 1997—; bd. trustees Ohio Wesleyan U., 2007—. Editor books; mem. editl. bd.: various profl. jours.; contbr. scientific papers to profl. jours. Mem.: Am. Soc. Biol. Chemists, Am. Assn. Cancer Rsch. (com. mem.). Mem. Soc. Of Friends. Avocations: music, tennis, golf. Home: 200W Washington Sq #2208 Philadelphia PA 19106 Home Phone: 267-324-5646; Office Phone: 215-873-8207, 215-873-8290. Business E-Mail: ttritton@chemheritage.org.

TRIUS, VICENTE, retail executive; Attended, U. Barcelona, 1975—77, Ashridge Coll., 1993, Darden Sch. Bus., 1995, Harvard Bus. Sch., 2001. With Coca-Cola, Del Valle, Hertz; regional dir. ops. Revco Drugstores Inc., Twinsburg, Ohio, 1984—91; mng. dir. Dairy Farm Internat., Madrid, 1991—95; v.p. ops. Internat. Divsn. Wal-Mart Stores, Inc., 1996, pres., CEO Wal-Mart Brazil, 1997, exec. v.p., mem. exec. com., 2008—, pres., CEO Wal-Mart Asia, Internat., 2008—. Office: Wal-Mart Stores, Inc 702 SW 8th St Bentonville AR 72716-8611*

TRIVEDI, ABHISHEK, application developer; s. Nripendra Tripathi and Maryada Trivedi. PhD, U. Calif., San Diego, 2005. Rsch. engr. Transoft Internat. Pvt. Ltd., Bangalore, Karnataka, India, 1999—2001; tech. support engr. Solidworks Inc., Santa Monica, Calif., 2005—07; dist. tech. mgr. Autodesk Inc. (Former Algor Inc.), LA, 2007—. Contbr. scientific papers. Mentoring & fin. contbn. Hope Worldwide, LA. Rsch. grant, Office naval rsch. US Navy, 2001—05, NSF, 2005. Mem.: ASME. Achievements include research in adaptive mesh refinement for simulation of dynamic problems such as shock and impact. Home: 3155 S Barrington Ave #F Los Angeles CA 90066 Home Phone: 858-336-8851; Office Phone: 310-266-2338. Personal E-mail: m1a2t3a@yahoo.com.

TRIVELPIECE, ALVIN WILLIAM, physicist, educator, consultant; b. Stockton, Calif., Mar. 15, 1931; s. Alvin Stevens and Mae (Hughes) Trivelpiece; m. Shirley Ann Ross, Mar. 23, 1953; children: Craig Evan, Steve Edward, Keith Eric. BEE, Calif. Poly. Coll., 1953; MEE, Calif. Inst. Tech., Pasadena, 1955, PhD in Elec. Engring. and Physics, 1958. Fulbright scholar Delft U., Netherlands, 1958—59; asst. prof., then assoc. prof. U. Calif. at Berkeley, 1959—66; prof. physics U. Md., 1966—76; on leave as asst. dir. for rsch. divsn. controlled thermonuclear rsch. AEC, Washington, 1973—75; v.p. Maxwell Labs. Inc., San Diego, 1976—78; corp. v.p. Sci. Applications, Inc., La Jolla, Calif., 1978—81; dir. Office of Energy Rsch., US Dept. Energy, Washington, 1981—87; exec. officer AAAS, Washington, 1987—88; dir. Oak Ridge Nat. Lab., Tenn., 1989—2000; v.p. Martin Marietta Energy Systems, 1989—95, Lockheed Martin Energy Systems, 1995; pres. Lockheed Martin Energy Rsch. Corp., 1996—2000; cons. Sandia Nat. Labs., Albuquerque, 2000—. Head del. joint NAS and Soviet Acad. Scis. mtg. and conf. on energy and global ecol. problems USSR, 1989; chmn. math. scis. ednl. bd. NAS, 1990—93; chmn. coordinating coun. for edn. NRC, 1991—93, chmn. com. small innovative firms in Russian nuclear cities, 2001, chmn. com. on Sci. and Tech. in Kazakhstan, 2006—07; mem. Commn. on Phys. Scis., Math. and Applications, 1993—96, com. on tech. issues related to the comprehensive test ban treaty NAS, 2000—02, Tenn. Sci. and Tech. Adv. Commn., 1993—96, chmn., 1996—99, adv. com. Fedn. Networking Coun., 1992—96; chmn. and pres. Tenn. Tech. Devel. Corp., 1998—2000; workshop chmn. NAS and Russian Acad. Scis., Yekaterinburg, Russia, 2004; founding bd. mem., sec., treas. Am. Coun. on Global Nuc. Competitiveness, 2006—. Author: Slow Wave Propagation in Plasma Wave Guides, 1966, Principles of Plasma Physics, 1973; contbr. articles to profl. jours. Recipient Gold medal for Disting. Svc., US Sec. Energy, 1986, Disting. Assoc. award, 2000, Tenn. Outstanding Svc. commendation, Senate Joint Resolution #530, 2000; named Disting. Alumnus, Calif. Poly. State U., 1978, Calif. Inst. Tech., Pasadena, 1987; fellow Guggenheim, 1966. Fellow: IEEE (Outstanding Engr. award region 3 1995), AAAS, Am. Phys. Soc.; mem.: NAE, AAUP, Global Energy Internat. (mem. internat. award com., prize 2009—), Am. Assn. Physics Tchrs., Am. Nuc. Soc., Nat. Press Club, Capital Hill Club, Tau Beta Pi, Sigma Xi. Achievements include patents in field. Home and Office: 14 Wade Hampton Trail Henderson NV 89052-6635 Office Phone: 702-492-1602. Personal E-mail: awt511@cox.net.

TRIVERS, ROBERT L., bioscience and anthropology educator, evolutionary biologist, sociobiologist; b. Washington, Feb. 19, 1943; children: Jonathan, Natasha, Natalia, Alelia, Aubrey. PhD in Biology, Harvard U., 1965. Faculty Harvard U., 1973—78, U. Calif., Santa Cruz, 1978—94; prof. anthropology and biol. sciences, dept. anthropology Rutgers U., New Brunswick, NJ. Sr. scientist The Rutgers Jamaican Symmetry Project, 1996—. Author: Social Evolution, 1985, Natural Selection and Social Theory: Selected Papers of Robert Trivers, 2002; co-author (with Austin Burt): Genes in Conflict: The Biology of Selfish Genetic Elements, 2006; contbr. articles to profl. publications. Recipient Crafoord prize in Biosciences, Royal Swedish Acad. Sciences, 2007; named one of 100 Greatest Thinkers and Scientists of the 20th Century, Time mag. Achievements include fundamental analysis of social evolution, conflict and cooperation among animals, which laid the foundation for modern sociobiology. Office: Dept Anthropology Rutgers U 131 George St New Brunswick NJ 08901-1414 Office Phone: 732-932-5792. Office Fax: 732-932-1564. Business E-Mail: trivers@rci.rutgers.edu.

TRIVIC, DUSAN NIKOLA, retired research scientist; s. Nikola Stanko and Mileva Dragutin Trivic; 1 child, Nikola Dusan. Diploma in Mech. Engring., U. Belgrade, Serbia, 1964, MSChemE, 1976; PhD, U. NB, Fredericton, Can., 1987. Cert. in plant and equipment in chem. industry: design and calculations, Confederation Brit. Industry, UK, 1973. Project engr. Steam Boiler Factory Termoelektro, Belgrade, 1964—66; sr. project engr. Prva Iskra Baric, Belgrade, 1966—69; head process equipment group Hemijska Industrija Pancevo, Serbia, 1969—82; sr. rsch. scientist Inst. Nuc. Scis.-Vinca, Belgrade, 1988—2005. Contbr. scientific papers (Babcock Energy award, Internat. Inst. Energy, London, 1989). Mem.: Serbian Soc. Heat Transfer Engrs., Serbian Soc. Chem. Engrs., Serbian Soc. Mech. Engrs., OUN (UNESCO cons., UNIDO expert 1982). Achievements include development of three-dimensional mathematical model for prediction of turbulent flow with combustion and radiation within a furnace chamber; new mathematical model and code for radiative heat transfer of particulate media with anisotropic scattering for 2-D rectangular enclosure. Avocations: hiking, classical music, motorcycling, art. Home: Brace Jovanovica 16-A Pancevo 26000 Serbia Personal E-mail: trivic@bisinter.net.

TRKSAK, PAUL M., orthopedist; MD, Loyola Univ. Stritch Med. Sch. Intern North Chgo. VA Hosp.; resident Great Lakes Naval Hosp., Loyola Univ. Med. Ctr., Chgo., Cook County Hosp., Ill.; staff physician Silver Cross Hosp., Joliet, Ill., past chmn., dept. orthopaedic surgery; staff physician Provena St. Joseph Med. Ctr., Hinsdale Hosp., Surg. Ctr., Ill.; pvt. orthopaedic practice Joliet, 1989—99; ptnr. Hinsdale Orthopaedic Associates, SC, 1999—. Mem.: Ill. State Med. Soc., Combine Orthopaedic Specialists. Office: Hinsdale Orthopaedic Assoc 550 W Ogden Ave Hinsdale IL 60521*

TROCCOLI, MARIANO, physicist, researcher, entrepreneur; b. Bari, Italy, Oct. 13, 1974; arrived in USA, 2001, permanent resident, 2005; s. Vito Troccoli and Anna Tanzella. MS in Theoretical Physics, U. Bari, Italy, 1997; PhD in Material Sci. and Photonics, Poly. Bari, Italy, 2001. Post-doctoral mem. tech. staff Bell Labs. Lucent Technologies, Murray Hill, NJ, 2001—03; post doctoral fellow Harvard U., Cambridge, Mass., 2003—; founder and dir. device rsch. and engring. Argos Tech LLC, Santa Clara, Calif., 2006—. Cons. Agilent Technologies, Palo Alto, Calif., 2004—05. Contbr. articles to profl. jours. Recipient Premio Civera, 1989, Young Investigator award, European Material Rsch. Soc., 2001. Mem.: IEEE, APS, OSA. Achievements include patents in field. Avocations: painting, drawing, violin. Office: Argos Tech 3671 Enochs St Santa Clara CA 95051 Personal E-mail: mtroccoli@gmail.com. Business E-Mail: troccoli@deas.harvard.edu.

TROCHTENBERG, DAVID SCOTT, medical educator, director; b. St. Louis, Nov. 19, 1959; married. BA with honors, Brown U., Providence, RI, 1982; MD, Vanderbilt U., Nashville, 1986; MSCI, Meharry Med. Coll., Nashville, 2007. Assoc. prof. Meharry Med. Coll., 2005—, residency program dir., 2006—. Contbr. articles to profl. jours. Steering com. Cultural Diversity Network Chest. Fellow: ACCP, ACP. Achievements include research in asthma disparities. Office: Meharry Med Coll 1005 Dr DB Todd Jr Blvd Nashville TN 37208

TROCKI-VIDELL, CYLA, psychiatrist, healthcare administrator; d. Jack and Mira (Kiejdan) Trocki; m. Jared Steven Videll, Dec. 27, 1969; children: Haviv Elana, Mikhael Alon, Samara Pilar. BA, Temple U., 1968, MA, 1972; postgrad., U. Pa., 1972—74; DO, Phila. Coll. Osteo. Medicine, 1978. Diplomate in med. psychology Am. Bd. Psychol. Spltys., Am. Bd. Forensic Medicine. Pediat. intern Med. Coll. Pa., Phila., 1979—89, resident in psychiatry, 1991—93, fellow in child and adolescent psychiatry, 1993—95; pvt. practice Phila., 1983—91; med. dir., cons. Med-Psych Healthcare Assocs., NJ, 2000—; pvt. practice PR, 1995—. Cons. in field. Contbg. author Women's Future World's Future, 2000; contbr. chapters to books. Mem. Nat. Women's History Mus., Washington, 2005, Med. Women's Delegation to Russia, Latvia and Lithuania; mem. USA/China Joint Conf. on Women's Issues, Med. Women's Delegation, mem. World Conf. on Family Values Singapore, mem. NGO Forum-UN 4th World Conf. on Women Beijing; mem. Am. Med. Polit. Action Com., Washington, 1998—. Recipient Nat. Leadership award, Physicians Adv. Bd., Nat. Rep. Congl. Com., Washington, 2000; named to, Am. Biography Polit. Scientists. Mem.: AAUW, AMA, Phila. County Med. Soc., Am. Med. Women's Assn., Pa. Osteopathic Med. Assn., Med. Women's Internat. Assn., Am. Soc. Law, Medicine and Ethics, Am. Acad. Child and Adolescent Psychiatry, Am. Psychiat. Assn., Pa. Med. Soc. Republican. Jewish. Avocations: art, architecture, dance, politics. Office: Med Psych Healthcare Assocs 408 N Exeter Ave Margate City NJ 08402 Office Phone: 609-823-1989. Office Fax: 609-823-1989.

TRODDEN, MARK, physicist; b. Wigan, Eng., Dec. 13, 1968; s. Michael and Joan (Peterson) T. MA in Math. with honors, Cambridge U., Eng., 1990, Cert. Advanced Study Math. with honors, 1991; MSc in Physics, Brown U., 1994, PhD in Physics, 1995. Undergrad. supr. Cambridge U., 1991-92; teaching asst. dept. physics Brown U., Providence, R.I., 1992-94, rsch. asst., 1994—. Presenter in field. Contbr. articles to profl. jours. Mem. Am. Phys. Soc. Office: U Penn Physics Dept 209 S 33rd St Philadelphia PA 19104-6396

TROEDSSON, MATS H.T., veterinarian; b. Solna, Sweden, Feb. 1, 1950; s. Henrik A.G. and Lenah B.H. Troedsson; children: Christofer G.T., Annika H.M., Niels S.T., Sean M.T. DVM, Royal Vet. Coll., Stockholm, 1975; PhD, U. Calif., Davis, 1991. Diplomate Am. Coll. Theriogenologists, 1993, European Coll. Animal Reproduction, 2002. Prof. equine reproduction U. Minn., St. Paul, 1993—2002; prof. and svc. chief theriogenology U. Fla., Gainesville, 2002—08; prof., chair dept. vet. scis U. Ky., Lexington, 2008—, dir. Maxwell H. Gluck equine rsch. ctr., 2008—. Dir. equine rsch. Minitube Am., Verona, Wis., 2002—. Office: Univ Kentucky 108 Gluck Equine Rsh Ctr Lexington KY 40546-0099 Business E-Mail: m.troedsson@uky.edu.

TROEMEL, JEAN WAGNER-WILLHITE, artist; b. Alma, Mich., May 4, 1921; d. Ralph Baptist and Edna Eleanor (Macomber) Wagner; m. Homer Harvey Willhite, Sept. 23, 1944 (div. 1962); m. Benjamin Henry Troemel, Sept. 21, 1962; children: Linda Lovelace, Benjamin H. Jr. Student, Nat. Cathedral Sch., Washington, 1938—39, Nat. Acad. Design, NYC, 1939—41, Art Students League of NY, 1939—41, Norton Sch. Art, West Palm Beach, Fla., 1942—43, U. N.Mex., Albuquerque, 1948-49. Asst. engr. U. Calif., Los Alamos, N.Mex., 1947-48; artist, 1940—; guest artist St. Augustine Fine Art Galleries, 1950—, Fla. Nat. Guard; tchr., painting Ridge Art Assn., Winter HAven, Fla., 1956-81, Jacksonville Art Mus., Fla., 1966-69, Flagler Coll., St. Augustine, Fla., 1978-81; dir. P.A.S.T.A. Plus Gallery, Inc., St. Augustine, Fla., 1984—2006. Founder, dir. Profl. Artists of St. Augustine, 1984—2006. Represented in permanent collections Basilica Cathedral (Cath.) St. Aug., Episcapol Cathedral, Orlando, Mennello Mus. Am. Art, Orlando, Fla., Subs. Gallery Smithsonian Mus., Washington, Bank of Am., Lightner Mus., Flagler Coll., St. Augustine Hist. Soc., Daytona Art Mus., Air Force Collection, Pentagon, Washington, Coast to Coast, The Mus. Arts & Sci., Dayton, 1998, Picturaing-Florida, others, Picturing in Florida, N. Mex., 2008. Fellow Royal Soc. Art, London. Mem. Fla. Artist Group Inc. (pres. 1975-77, life mem.), Ridge Art Assn. (v.p. 1950-60, hon. life mem., founder 1950), St. Augustine Art Assn. (sec. 1978-81, life mem.), Nat. Mus. Women Artists (charter). Republican. Lutheran. Avocations: travel, designing. Home and Office: 6 South St Saint Augustine FL 32084-5135 Home Phone: 904-824-3187. Personal E-mail: jwtart479@bellsouth.net.

TROFFKIN, HOWARD JULIAN, lawyer; b. Port Chester, NY, Jan. 30, 1937; s. Irving and Frieda Troffkin; m. Rhea Dorothy, May 12, 1963; children: Stephen, Barbara. BS in Chemistry, St. Lawrence U., 1959; postgrad., Columbia U., 1959-60; JD, Georgetown U., 1970. Bar: Va. 1971, D.C. 1972. Rsch. chemist Am. Cyanamid Co., 1961-66, legal trainee, 1966-67, patent agt., 1967-71; assoc. Pennie, Edmonds, Morton, Taylor & Adams, Washington, 1971-77; patent atty. W.R. Grace & Co., Columbia, Md., 1977-86, sr. patent counsel, 1987-98; pvt. practice, 1998—. Patentee in chemistry field. Mem. Willerburn Civic Assn., 1971-75. Served with AUS, 1960-61. Mem. ABA, Va. Bar Assn., D.C. Bar Assn., Washington Patent Lawyers Assn., Md. Patent Law Assn. (pres. 1981-83), Am. Intellectual Property Law Assn., Am. Chem. Soc., Concrete Corrosion Inhibitors Assn. (sec./counsel). Jewish. Avocations: woodcrafting, travel. Home and Office: 7808 Ivymount Ter Potomac MD 20854-3218 Personal E-mail: troffkin@aol.com.

TROGAN, ROLAND BERNARD, composer, educator; b. Saginaw, Mich., Aug. 6, 1933; s. Ricardo Bernardo Trocano and Alicia Archangeli-Trocano; m. Annette Patrice Ellams, Mar. 31, 2001; m. Mona Jane Philpot-Trogan, Feb. 6, 1971 (dec. 2000); m. Barbara Jean Mills-Trogan, July 10, 1955 (div. June 22, 1964); children: Christopher Roland, Timothy Bernard. MusB in Composition, U. Mich., 1954, MusM in Composition, 1955, Dr. of Musical Arts in Composition, 1963. Cert. Am. Fedn. of Musicians Mich., 1948, Broadcast Music Inc. NY, 1966. Performing pianist (live, weekly) WKNX Radio, Saginaw, Mich., 1947—50; assoc. condr., composer-in-residence Saginaw Civic Symphony, 1954—56; fellow English drama U. Mich., Ann Arbor, 1956—59, fellow in music theory, 1956—60; lectr. in music CUNY, 1958—65; dir. music Ecole Francaise, 1967—69, Unitarian Ch., Staten Island, 1967—69; instr. of piano Wagner Coll., Staten Island, NY, 1968; pres. Roland Trogan, Inc. dba Dr. Trogan's Music Sch., Staten Island, 1975—, Patrice Editions, L. L. C., Staten Island, 2003—. Pvt. music instr. to internationally-recognized conductors, soloists, diplomats, and stage and film stars. non-affiliated, NYC, 1963—71; prodr. new music concerts performed by Henry Cowell, Wallingford Riegger, Max Polikoff, Paul Jacobs and Walter Trampler, NYC, 1966—69; featured composer Carnegie Recital Hall pvt. concert, introduced by H. Wiley Hitchcock and sponsored by Sybil Burton, Tom Poston and Harold Rome, NYC, 1968. Composer: (cantata) The Seafarer, 1967, (composition for choir and orch.) Hymn to Spring, 1950, (composition) Sextet for Wind Quintet and Piano, 1951, Elegy for String Quartet and Contralto on poems of Elinor Wiley, 1953, Soliloquey for piano, 1955, Divertimenti for two voices on tone rows, 1955, Incidental music to Bertold Brecht's The Good Woman of Szechuan, 1956, Preludes for Piano, 1957 (pub. in Generation mag., 1951), Sonata for solo violin, 1959, Concerto for Violin and Orchestra, 1963, Fantasy for Piano, 1967, Nocturnes for Piano, 1968, Bagatelles for Piano, 1970, Piano Sonata no 1, 1971, Piano Sonata no 2, 1997, Elegy for piano, 1998, Piano Sonata no 3, 1999, Diptych for piano, 2000, Symphony for Chamber Orchestra, 2001, Two Scenes for Orchestra, 2006 (Louisville Orch. award, 1955), Mas ficciones por Juan Luis Borges, for solo violin, 1951, (performance) Preludes for piano, performed by Don Trusdel at University of Michigan, 1951, Septet for Wind Quintet and Piano, performed by the University of Michigan Wind Quintet and Bruce Wise, pianist, 1953, Elegy for String Quartet and Piano, University of Illinois-Urbana, 1954, The Hat Man, performed in Chicago by the After Dinner Opera Co., and at the Interlochen Music Camp, 1956, Incidental music for Bertold Brecht's The Good Woman of Szechuan, University of Michigan Theatre, 1957, (perfomance) Preludes of Piano, premiered by Paul Jacobs in New York City, 1955, (performance) Divertimenti for two voices on tone rows, University of Michigan, 1959, Sonata for solo violin, premiered by Harold Kohon at Town Hall, New York City, 1955, Two Scenes for Orchestra, performed by Louisville Symphony Orchestra, 1971, Piano Sonata no 1, performed by Richard Woitach at Alice Tully Hall, Lincoln Center, New York City, 1967, The Seafarer, performed by Richard Woitach and William Wiederanders, with a dramatic reading of the text by Jean Sullivan at Carnegie Recital Hall, New York City, 1971, Nocturnes for Piano, performed at Alice Tully Hall, Lincoln Center, New York City, 1971, Bagatelles for piano, performed by Richard Woitach, Alice Tully Hall, Lincoln Center, New York City, 1971, (opera) The Hat Man (Broadcast Music Inc. award, 1954). Rep. Staten Island Mus., 1968. Recipient Fulbright scholarship, Dept. of State, US Govt. (rescinded by Ho. UnAmerican Activities Com.

chmn., Eugene McCarthy), 1954, Young Composer award, Broadcast Music Inc., 1954; grantee, AAAL, 1985—87; fellow Music, U. Mich., 1955—56, English, 1955. R-Conservative. Christian. Avocation: travel. Home: 755 Narrows Rd N Apt #914 Staten Island NY 10304-1542 Office: RTrogan Inc /Dr Trogan's Music School 1861 Victory Blvd Staten Island NY 10314-3517 Office Fax: 718-370-8008. Personal E-mail: mymusicfriend@aol.com.

TROJNIAK, DUANE, marketing executive, consultant; s. Edward and Barbara Trojniak; m. Kim Trojniak; children: Sarah, Michelle, Ashley. PhD, Wayne State U., Detroit, 1991. Asst. prof. U. Detroit Mercy, 1989—91; v.p. RDA Group, Bloomfield Hills, Mich., 1994—. Office: RDA Group 450 Enterprise Ct Bloomfield Hills MI 48302 Business E-Mail: dtrojniak@rdqagroup.com.

TROLANDER, HARDY WILCOX, engineering executive, consultant; b. Chgo., June 2, 1921; s. Elmer Wilcox and Freda Marie (Zobel) T.; m. Imogen Davenport, July 3, 1946 (dec.); children: Megan, Patricia. BS in Engring., Antioch Coll., 1947. Instr. Antioch Coll., Yellow Springs, Ohio, 1947-48; co-founder, CEO Yellow Springs Instrument Co., Inc., 1948-86. Dir., co-founder Cook Design Ctr., Dartmouth Coll., Hanover, N.H., 1975-88; bd. dirs. Dessinier Corp., Yellow Springs, Camax Tool co., Arvada, Colo.; mem. evaluation panel Inst. Basic Stds., Nat. Bur. Stds., 1977-79. Contbr. articles to profl. jours.; patentee in field. Co-founder, trustee Yellow Springs Community Found., 1974-83; trustee Autioch Coll., 1968-74, chmn. bd., 1972-74; trustee Engring. and Sci. Found., Dayton, 1982-96, Engrs. Club Dayton Found., 1994-2005, Engring. and Sci. Hall of Fame, 1994-2002; mem. adv. bd. Coll. Engring. and Computer Sci. Wright State U., 1993-2005; bd. dirs. united Way Greater Dayton Area, 1984-92; small bus. innovative rsch. grant panels Nat. Sci. Found., 1988—. 1st lt. USAF, 1943-46. Named Outstanding Engr., Dayton Affiliate Socs., 1967, 89. Fellow Dayton Engrs. Club, Am. Inst. for Med. and Biol. Engring.; mem. ACLU, Nat. Acad. Engring., Am. Inst. Biol. Scis. (bioinstrumentation adv., coun. 1969-75), Internat. Orgn. of Legal Metrology (tech. advisor, sec. 1975-82), Amnesty Internat. Democrat. Achievements include co-development of melting point of gallium which has become recognized as a primary defining point of the International Temperature Scale. Home and Office: 3 Aspen Ct Yellow Springs OH 45387-1326 Office Phone: 937-767-4551.

TROMBETTA, LOUIS D., medical educator, department chairman; s. Edmund and Flora R Trombetta; m. Mariann E Kuntz, June 3, 1972; children: David R., Damian L. PhD, Fordham U., NYC, 1972. Chmn., dept. pharm. scis. St. John's U., NYC, 1999—. Land preservation Oblong Land Conservancy, Pawling, NY, 1998—. Mem.: Soc. Toxicology. Office: St Johns' Univ 8000 Utopia Pky Jamaica NY 11439 Business E-Mail: trombet@stjohns.edu.

TROMPETTER, AMY CLEMENS, theater director; b. Dayton, Ohio, Jan. 26, 1943; d. Charles Herbert Clemens and Thelma Esther Rothenberg; m. Andy Trompetter. Assoc. prof. Bates Coll., Lewiston, Maine, 1993—95; sr. lectr. Barnard Coll., Columbia U., NYC, 1995—2008; dir., designer Blackbird Theater, Rosendale, NY, 1999—. Dir.: (theater) Wobbly Bucket Brigade People's History, (music theater) Requiem for Anna Politkovskaya, (giant puppet opera) Rossini's The Barber of Seville, Malcolm Williamson's The Happy Prince. Active mem. Amnesty Internat., NYC, 1985—2008, ACLU, NYC, 2001—08, Bread and Puppet Theater, Glover, Vt., 1990—2008. Recipient Emily Gregory Excellence Tchg. award, Barnard Coll., 2006; fellow, Ford Found., 1996—97; fellowship, MacDowell Colony, 1999, Individual Artist grant, Jim Henson Found., 2005. Home: PO Box 518 Rosendale NY 12472 Personal E-mail: at164@columbia.edu.

TRONGALE, NICHOLAS ALBERT, entrepreneur, researcher, educator; s. Nick and Mary Rose Trongale; m. Mary Kathryn Sullivan, Nov. 30, 1980; children: Daniel Louis, Megan Kathryn. BA in Philosophy, Dominican U., River Forest, Ill., 1978; MA in National Security Affairs, US Naval Postgraduate Sch., Monterey, Calif., 1986; MA in Polit. Sci., Stanford U., Palo Alto, Calif., 1994; EdD in Leadership Studies, U. San Diego, 2001; exec. edn. in Leadership, Harvard U., Cambridge, Mass., 2001. Enlisted USN, 1979, advanced through grades to capt., ret., 2001; pres., CEO Pb Solutions, Coronado, 2002—; dean, Coll. Profl. Studies Nat. U. Health Scis., Lombard, Ill., 2007—. Instr. Benedictine U., Ill., 2008—, Roosevelt U., Chgo., 2008—. Author: (research) Changes in Navy Leadership Theory and Practice: Post-Vietnam, China's Defense Moderization, China's Naval Power, Investment Strategy of Information Operations, Implications of Unmanned Air Vehicles for the Future Shape of the Air Force. Bd. dirs. Montini Cath. HS, 2007—. Decorated Legion of Merit; recipient Nat. Leadership award, Nat. Rep. Congl. Com., 2003; named E-2C Hawkeye of Yr., Comdr. Fighter/Airborne Early Warning Wing, Pacific, 1988; Adm. Arthur S. Moreau scholar, USN, 1992, Fed. Exec. Rsch. fellow, RAND Corp., 1996—97. Mem.: DAV (life), VFW (life), Tailhook Assn., Undersea Hyperbaric Med. Soc., Kappa Delta Pi (life). Roman Catholic. Avocations: bass, martial arts, swimming. Personal E-mail: trongale@pbsolutions.us.

TROOBOFF, PETER DENNIS, lawyer; b. Balt., June 22, 1942; s. Benjamin M. and Rebecca (Cohen) Trooboff; m. Rhoda Morss, Aug. 10, 1969; children: Hannah, Abigail. BA cum laude, Columbia U., 1964; LLB cum laude, Harvard U., 1967; LLM, London Sch. Econs., 1968; diploma cum laude, Hague Acad. Internat. Law, Netherlands, 1968. Bar: N.Y. 1968, D.C. 1970. Rsch. assoc. Harvard U. Law Sch., Cambridge, Mass., 1968—69; asst. to exec. editor for The Advocates Sta. WGBH-TV, Boston, 1969; assoc. Covington & Burling, Washington, 1969—75, ptnr., 1975—2007, sr. counsel, 2007—. Lectr., dir. seminars The Hague Acad. Internat. Law, 1972, 82, lectr., 86, mem. curatorium, 1991—; lectr. The Hague Acad. External Program, Beijing, 1987, Harare, 93, Santo Domingo, 2008; lectr. internat. orgns. U. Va. Sch. Law, 1973; lectr. Gen. Course Pvt. Internat. Law, 2008, Gen. Cruse Pvt. Instl. Law, 2008; head US del. 3d Inter-Am. Specialized Conf. Pvt. Internat. Law, La Paz, Bolivia, 1984; mem. US del. Hague Conf. pvt. internat. law, 1993, 96, 1997—, expert US del., 2003—04; arbitrator Internat. Ctr. Settlement Investment Disputes. Editor: Law and Responsibility in Warfare-The Vietnam Experience, 1975; contbr. chapters to books, columns to jours., articles to profl. publs. Frank Knox Meml. fellow. Mem.: Washington Inst. Fgn. Affairs, Internat. Law Assn., Am. Soc. Internat. Law (bd. editors Am. Jour. Internat. Law 1980—92, pres. 1990—92, bd. editors Am. Jour. Internat. Law 1994—2003, chmn. nominating com. 2006—07, hon. editor 2006—), Am. Law Inst., Coun. Fgn. Rels., City Club (Washington), Cosmos Club. Office: Covington & Burling 1201 Pennsylvania Ave NW Washington DC 20004 Office Phone: 202-662-5512. Business E-Mail: ptrooboff@cov.com.

TROOP, PAUL MELVIN, public relations executive, journalist; b. Jersey City, May 13, 1942; s. Bernard Lazarus and Ruth (Weiss) T.; m. Maxine Rubin, Dec. 6, 1970; 1 child, Wendy. BA, U. State of N.Y., 1980. Reporter L.I. Press, Jamaica, NY, 1965-66; political editor Suffolk Sun, Deer Park, NY, 1966-67; asst. news dir. L.I. Network News, Freeport, NY, 1967; asst. editor Am. Sch. & U., NYC, 1967-68; acct. exec. Ruder & Finn, NYC, 1969-70; mng. editor L.I. Comml. Rev., Syosset, NY, 1970; bus. writer Atlanta Jour.-Constn., 1970-78; pres. Fin. Comm. Co., Atlanta, 1978—. Cpl. NJNG, 1965-71. Newspaper Fund scholar, 1961, Banking Sch. of the South fellow, 1975.

TROOSKIN, STANLEY Z., surgeon; b. Linden, NJ, July 24, 1949; s. Martin and Irene Trooskin; m. Estelle Kost Trooskin; children: Stacey, Gerri, Amy. BA, Rutgers U., 1971; MD, U. Pitts., 1975. Diplomate Am. Bd. Surgery, Am. Bd. Surgery, lic. physician Pa., N.J., N.Y. Asst. prof. surgery U. Medicine and Dentistry N.J., Piscataway, 1980—85, assoc. prof. surgery, 1985—89, clin. assoc. prof., 1988—89; prof. surgery SUNY, Bklyn., 1989—92, Med. Coll. Pa., 1993—94, Hahnemann U. Sch. Medicine, 1994, MCP Hahnemann U. Sch. Medicine, 1995—2002, U. Med. and Dentistry NJ-Robert Wood Johnson Med. Sch., New Brunswick, 2002—; chief gen. surgery, chief surgery Robert Wood Johnson U. Hosp., New Brunswick, 2002—. Adj. prof. surgery Drexel U. Sch. Medicine, Phila., 2003—; program dir. gen. surgery residency U. Med. and Dentistry NJ-Robert Wood Johnson Med. Sch., New Brunswick, 2006. Mem. editl. bd.: Trauma Quar., 1989—2002, Trauma Chronicle, 1990—91. Mem.: Am. Surg. Assn. (elected mem. 2008—), Ea. Assn. for Surgery of Trauma, Am. Coll. Surgeons. Achievements include patents in field. Office: Robert Wood Johnson Med Sch 1 RWJ Pl CN 19 MEB 443 New Brunswick NJ 08903 Office Phone: 732-235-7920. Business E-Mail: trooskz@umdnj.edu.

TROP, SANDRA, former museum director; b. Bklyn. BS, NYU. Cert. in arts adminstrn. Harvard U. Dir. Everson Mus. Art, Syracuse, NY, 1995—2007. Advt. copy writer; former adj. prof. Syracuse U., mem. adv. bd. Coll. Visual and Performing Arts; program auditor NY State Coun. on Arts, 1983-84, panelist, 1989-90; field reviwer Inst. Mus. Svcs., 1985-87; Everson Mus. Art del. Internat. Conf. Mus. Mem. founding bd. dirs. Lowe Art Ctr., Syracuse U., Salt City Playhouse, Cmyt. Folk Art Gallery, Syracuse Landmark Theatre; bd. dirs. Key Bank's Syracuse Dist.; mem. Internat. Com. Mus. and Collections of Modern Art, Literacy Vols. Am.; mem. adv. bd. Convention and Visitors Bureau; appointed to Mayor's Commn. on Fin. Planning for City of Syracuse. Mem. Am. Arts Alliance, Am. Assn. Museums, N.E. Regional Mus. Conf.

TROPE, SORRELL, lawyer; b. June 9, 1927; m. Linda Trope. AB, U. So. Calif., 1947, JD, 1949. Bar: Calif. 1949, US Dist. Ct. (so. dist. Calif.) 1949, US Ct. Appeals (9th cir.) 1952, US Bd. Immigration Appeals 1952, US Supreme Ct. 1954, US Ct. Appeals (7th cir.) 1958, cert.: State Bar Calif. Bd. Legal Specialization (family law). Co-founding ptnr. Trope and Trope, LA, 1949—. Judge pro tem LA Superior Ct., 1970—72; chairperson So. Calif. Com. Family Law Commn. of State Senate Jud. Com., 1983; mem. State Assembly Family Law Adv. Com., 1984. Founder Trope and Trope/Harriett Buhai Family Law Fellowship, 1995. Recipient Spencer Brandeis award, LA County Bar, 1998, Ramsey award, Harriett Buhai Ctr. Family Law, 1998. Fellow: Internat. Acad. Matrimonial Lawyers; mem.: ABA, Am. Inns Ct. (bencher emeritus U. So. Calif. Legion Lex chpt. 1985—), Am. Acad. Matrimonial Lawyers, LA County Bar Assn. (mem. exec. com. family law sect. 1980—96, 2000—), Phi Kappa Phi. Office: Trope and Trope 12121 Wilshire Blvd Ste 801 Los Angeles CA 90025 Office Phone: 310-207-8228. Office Fax: 310-870-2726. E-mail: strope@tropeandtrope.com.

TROPEZ-SIMS, SUSANNE, pediatrician, educator; b. New Orleans, Apr. 13, 1949; d. Maxwell Sterling and Ethel (Ross) Tropez; m. James Carnell White, Apr. 10, 1971 (div. 1992); children: Lisa, Janifer, James Carnell; m. Michael Milroy Sims, Feb. 18, 1995. BS, Bennett Coll., 1971; MD, U. N.C., 1975, MPH, 1982. Diplomate Am. Bd. Pediatrics. Resident pediat. N.C. Meml. Hosp., Chapel Hill, 1975—76, 1977—79; pediatrician Darnell Army Hosp., Ft. Hood, Tex., 1976—77; acting dir. pediat. day clinic Wake County Med. Ctr., Raleigh, NC, 1979—82; dir. pediat. day clinic, asst. prof. U. N.C., Chapel Hill, 1982—88; assoc. prof. pediat. La. State U. Med. Ctr., New Orleans, 1988—97; dir. divsn. pediat. emergency rm. La. State U., New Orleans, 1988—89, chief divsn. ambulatory care, 1989—97; chmn. and prof. dept. pediat. Meharry Med. Coll., Nashville, 1997—2005; chair Meharry Med. Svc. Found., Nashville, 2000—02; chair curriculum com. Meharry Med. Coll., Nashville, 2003—, assoc. dean acad. support, 2005—06, assoc. dean clin. svcs., 2006—, Joy McCann prof., 2006—, pediatric clearkship dir., 2005—. Clin. dir. maternal and child health units New Orleans Health Dept., 1992-97, chief divsn. cmty. pediat. and adolescent medicine, 1992-97; pediatrician Shelly Child Devel. Ctr., Raleigh, 1981-88, child med. examiner program, 1979-88; chair sch. health com. local chpt. AAP, 1993-96; mem. Nat. Com. Sch. Health, 1992-99; chair health info. network bd. Nat. Edn. Assn., 2000-02. Contbr. articles to profl. jour. Chair adminstrv. bd. Cornerstone U.M.C., 1993-96, chair edn. com., 1991-92; mem. United Meth. Women, Walnut Terr. Child Devel. Ctr., Raleigh, 1981-83, chmn., 1982-83; chmn. pastor parish com. Longview Ch., Raleigh, 1982-84, 87-88, chmn. membership care com.; chair bd. NEA-Health Info. Network, 2000-02; chair bd. trustees Clark Meml. United Meth. Ch., 2002-06. Fellow preventive medicine, 1979-82, Faculty Devel. fellow U. NC Sch. Medicine, 1985-87. Fellow Am. Acad. Pediatrics (mem. sch. health com.); mem. N.C. Pediatric Soc. (com. child abuse and neglect, adolescent pregnancy), La. Pediatric Soc., Ambulatory Pediatric Assn., Adolescent Pregnancy Coalition United Way, Bennett Coll. Alumnae Assn. Democrat. Office Phone: 615-327-6925, 615-327-5915. Business E-Mail: stsims@mmc.edu.

TROPIN, KENNETH G., hedge fund manager; b. NYC, Aug. 17, 1953; s. Leonard and Ruth (Safron) Tropin; m. Kathleen Tropin, Aug. 6, 1986; children: Nicholas, Kelly. BA, Goddard Coll., Plainfield, Vt., 1974. Fin. cons. Shearson, NYC, 1980-82; sr. v.p. Dean Witter Reynolds, NYC, 1982-89; pres., CEO John W. Henry & Co., Inc., Westport, Conn., 1989—93; founder, chmn. Graham Capital Mgmt., Rowayton, Conn., 1994—. Mem.: Managed Futures Assn. (chmn. 1991). Avocations: golf, skiing, tennis, sculpture. Office: Graham Capital Mgmt LP 40 Highland Ave Norwalk CT 06853 Office Phone: 203-899-3400. Business E-Mail: einfo@grahamcapital.com.*

TROST, BARRY MARTIN, chemist, educator; b. Phila., June 13, 1941; s. Joseph and Esther T.; m. Susan Paula Shapiro, Nov. 25, 1967; children: Aaron David, Carey Daniel. BA cum laude, U. Pa., Phila., 1962; PhD, MIT, Cambridge, 1965; D (hon.), U. Claude Bernard, Lyons, France, 1994, Technion, Israel, 1997. Mem. faculty U. Wis., Madison, 1965—, prof., chemistry, 1969—, Evan P. and Marion Helfaer prof. chemistry, from 1976, Vilas rsch. prof. chemistry; prof. chemistry Stanford U., 1987—, Tamaki prof. humanities and scis., 1990, chmn. dept., 1996—2002; Lord Todd vis. prof. Cambridge U., England, 2002—. Cons. Merck, Sharp & Dohme, E.I. duPont de Nemours.; hon. prof. Shanghai Inst. Organic Chemistry, 2006. Author: Problems in Spectroscopy, 1967, Sulfur Ylides, 1975; editor-in-chief Comprehensive Organic Synthesis, 1991—, ChemTracts/Organic Chemistry, 1993—; editor: Structure and Reactivity Concepts in Organic Chemistry series, 1972—; assoc. editor Jour. Am. Chem. Soc., 1974-80; mem. editl. bd. Organic Reactions Series, 1971—, Chemistry A European Jour., 1995—, Sci. of Synthesis, Houben-Weyl Methods of Molecular Transformations, 1995—; contbr. numerous articles to profl. jours. Recipient Dreyfus Found. Tech.-Scholar award, 1970, 1977, Creative Work in Synthetic Organic Chemistry award, 1981, Baekland medal, 1981, Alexander von Humboldt award, 1984, Guenther award, 1990, Janssen prize, 1990, Roger Adams award, Am. Chem. Soc., 1995, Presdl. Green Univ. Challenge award, 1998, Nicholas medal, 2000, Yamada prize, 2001, ACS Nobel Laureate Signature award, Graduate Ed. Chemistry, 2002, John Scott award, City of Phila., 2004, Nagoya medal, 2008; named Chem. Pioneer, Am. Inst. Chemists, 1983; fellow, NSF, 1963—65, Sloan Found., 1967—69, Am. Swiss Found., 1975—, Zeneca, 1997; scholar Cope scholar, 1989. Mem.: NAS, AAAS, Chem. Soc. London, Am. Acad. Arts and Scis., Am. Chem. Soc. (award in pure chemistry 1977, Roger Adams award 1995, Herbert C. Brown award for creative rsch. in synthetic methods 1999, Nobel Laureate Signature award for grad. edn. in chemistry 2002, Arthur C. Cope award 2004, centenary lectr. 1982). Office: Stanford U Dept Chemistry Stanford CA 94305

TROST, CARLISLE ALBERT HERMAN, retired naval officer; b. Valmeyer, Ill., Apr. 24, 1930; s. Elmer Herman and Luella Caroline (Hoffman) T.; m. Pauline Louise Haley, May 1, 1954; children: Carl, Laura Lee, Steven, Kathleen. Student, Washington U., St. Louis, 1948-49; BS, U.S. Naval Acad., 1953; Olmsted scholar, U. Freiburg, W. Ger., 1960-62. Commd. ensign U.S. Navy, 1953, advanced through grades to adm., 1985; exec. officer U.S.S. Scorpion, 1962-63, U.S.S. Von Steuben, 1963-65; mil. asst. to Dep. Sec. Def., 1965-68; comdg. officer U.S.S. Sam Rayburn, 1968-69; staff Comdr. Sub Force Atlantic, 1969-70; exec. asst. to Sec. Navy, 1970-73; comdr. Submarine Group Five, 1973-74; asst. chief Bur. Naval Personnel, 1974-76; dir. systems analysis div. Office Chief Naval Ops., Washington, 1976-78; dep. comdr.-in-chief U.S. Pacific Fleet, 1978-80; comdr. U.S. Seventh Fleet, 1980-81; dir. Navy program planning Office Chief Naval Ops., 1981-85; comdr.-in-chief U.S. Atlantic Fleet, 1985-86, chief naval ops., 1986-90. Bd. dirs. Lockheed Martin Corp., Gen. Pub. Utility Corp., GPU Nuclear Corp., Bird-Johnson Co., Gen. Dynamics Corp., Precision Components Corp.; chmn. Olmsted Fedn. Trustee U.S. Naval Acad. Found. Decorated Def. D.S.M. with cluster, Navy D.S.M. with 2 clusters, Army D.S.M., Air Force D.S.M., Legion of Merit with 2 oak leaf clusters, Navy Achievement medal; named Outstanding Young Man of Am. Nat. Jr. C. of C., 1964 Mem. U.S. Naval Inst., U.S. Naval Acad. Alumni Assn. (chmn.). Episcopalian. Home: 11 Compromise St Annapolis MD 21401-1806

TROST, EILEEN BANNON, lawyer; b. Teaneck, NJ, Jan. 9, 1951; d. William Eugene and Marie Thelma (Finlayson) Bannon; m. Lawrence Peter Trost Jr., Aug. 27, 1977; children: Lawrence Peter III, William Patrick, Timothy Alexander. BA with great distinction, Shimer Coll., 1972; JD cum laude, U. Minn., 1976. Bar: Ill. 1976, U.S. Dist. Ct. (no. dist.) Ill. 1976, Minn. 1978, U.S. Tax Ct. 1978, U.S. Supreme Ct. 1981. Assoc. McDermott, Will & Emery, Chgo., 1976-82, ptnr., 1982-93; v.p. No. Trust Bank Ariz. N.A., Phoenix, 1993-95; ptnr. Sonnenschein Nath & Rosenthal, Chgo., 1995—2006, K & L Gates LLP, Chgo., 2006—. Mem. Am. Coll. Trust and Estate Coun., Minn. Bar Assn., Internat. Acad. Estate and Trust Law, Soc. Trust & Estate Practitioners, Chgo. Estate Planning Coun., Soc. Trust & Estate Practioners. Roman Catholic. Office: K & L Gates LLP 70 W Madison St #3100 Chicago IL 60602 Office Phone: 312-807-4411. Business E-Mail: eileen.trost@klgates.com.

TROST, GLENN W., lawyer; b. Boston, Mar. 27, 1956; BS, MIT; JD cum laude, Southwestern Univ., 1984. Bar: Calif. 1984, US Dist. Ct. (no. & ctrl. dist. Calif.), US Ct. Appeals (9th & Fed. cir.), Supreme Ct. Calif., Supreme Ct. Colo., US Supreme Ct. 2000. Ptnr. mng. partner LA office Coudert Bros. LLP, LA. Adj. prof. Southwestern Univ. Sch. Law, 1986—91. Office Phone: 213-229-2900. Office Fax: 213-229-2999. Business E-Mail: gtrost@coudert.com.

TROST, LOUIS FREDERICK, JR., banker, financial planner; b. Kans. City, Mo., Dec. 11, 1926; s. Louis Frederick and Roberta Ford (Broadus) T.; m. Ann Horner Tillma, Mar. 23, 1951 (div. Oct. 1978); children: Louis Frederick III, Scott Tillma; m. Charlotte Granville Graham, Nov. 15, 1984. BBA, U. Okla., 1951; postgrad., Northwestern U., 1960, grad. Bell Sys. Execs. program, 1960; grad., Sch. Banking of South, Baton Rouge, 1968, Coll. Fin. Planning, Denver, 1989. Divsn. mgr. South Western Bell Tel. Co., Oklahoma City, 1951—64; sr. v.p. Liberty Nat. Bank & Trust Co., Oklahoma City, 1964—91; pres., CEO Lincoln Nat. Bank, Oklahoma City, 1991—95, vice chmn., 1995—2003, CEO, 2002—03. Dir. Ctrl. Okla. Clearing House Assn., 1993-96; advisor Bapt. Found. Okla., Oklahoma City, 1995-2005, hon. dir. emeritus, 2006—; bd. rep., exec. com. Coun. Fed. Home Loan Banks, Washington, 1998-2001; dir., chmn. housing com. Fed. Home Loan Bank Topeka, 1995-2001; mem. gov.'s Cmty. Devel. Capital Formation Task Force, 1998-2003; cert. fin. planner, 1989-2004; bd. dirs. Great Expectations Found, 2004—; bd.dirs. Educator's Leadership Acad., 2004—05; bd. dirs. Okla. State Capitol Preservation Commn., 2005—. Pres., bd. dirs. Travelers Aid, Oklahoma City, 1962; treas., bd. dirs. Okla. Symphony Orch., 1983—87; pres., bd. dirs. Mental Health Assn., Oklahoma City, 1996; cmty. devel. adv. coun. Fed. Res. Bank Kansas City, 2002—03; dir. exec. com. Omiplex Sci. Mus., 1980—85. Master sgt. US Army, 1945—46, PTO. Named Outstanding Young Man in Oklahoma City, Oklahoma, 1960; named Ky. Col., Gov. of Ky., 1970; recipient letter of commendation Mental Health Assn., 1996. Mem. Ind. Bankers Assn. Am., Okla. Bankers Assn. (sr. mgmt. com. 1995-2003), Oklahoma City Golf and Country Club (bd. dirs. 1989-91), Petroleum Club Oklahoma City (v.p., treas., bd. dirs. 1979-81), The Assocs. (U. Okla.), Faculty Club (bd. dirs.,1968-1970), Masons, Scottish Rite, Shriners, Kiwanis (past pres. Oklahoma City), Assn. U.S. Army, Phi Gamma Delta (treas., bd. dirs. Ednl. Found. 1989-97, Wall of Fame award 1997, Disting. Fiji award 2004, trustee emeritus 2004). Baptist. Avocations: gardening, reading, travel. Home and Office: 1601 Queenstown Rd Nichols Hills OK 73116-5522 Business E-Mail: ltrost@cox.net.

TROST, ROBERT PATRICK, economist; b. Rochester, N.Y., June 7, 1946; s. Wilbert W. and Ada J. (Brady) T.; B.S. in Mech. Engring., U. Detroit, 1969; Ph.D. in Econs., U. Fla. 1977. Research economist CNA, 1977-81; vis. asso. prof. U. S.C., 1980, U. Fla., 1981; prof. Econs. George Washington U., 1981—. Contbr. articles to profl. jours. Served with USMC, 1969-71. Mem. Am. Econ. Assn., Am. Statis. Assn., So. Econ. Assn., Western Econ. Assn. Roman Catholic. Office: Dept Econs 2201 G St NW Washington DC 20037-2704 Office Phone: 202-994-9011. Business E-Mail: trost@emu.edu.

TROSTORFF, DANIELLE M., lawyer; b. Buffalo, Dec. 31, 1951; d. Daniel Michael and D. Anne Lombardo; children: Alex Jr., Lauren. BS, Cornell U., Ithaca, NY, 1973; MSW, Washington U., St. Louis, JD, 1977. Bar: NY 1978, Washington 1978, La. 1981, Tex. 1993, US Supreme Ct. Legal asst. Atty. Michael LoPinto, Ithaca, 1973; intern Pub. Defenders Office, Belleville, Ill., 1974; legal asst. Hon. Betty Friedlander, Ithaca, 1975; with personal trust new bus. dept. Irving Trust Co., 1977—78; staff atty., acting mng. atty. Neighborhood Legal Svcs., Washington, 1978—80; trial atty Govt. of Washington, Office Corp. Counsel, 1980—81; ptnr. Donna D. Fraiche, 1981—84; chair health law sect. Broadhurst, Brook, Mangham & Hardy, New Orleans, 1984—87; ptnr. Brook, Morial, Cassibry, Graiche & Pizza, New Orleans, 1987—91,

Locke Liddell & Sapp, New Orleans, 1991—2004; shareholder Baker, Donelson, Bearman, Caldwell & Berkowitz, New Orleans, 2004—, vice chair health law dept., 2004—06. Adj. prof. Tulane U. Sch. Pub. Health and Tropical Medicine, 1989—93; spkr. in field. Contbr. articles to profl. jours. Mem.: ABA, New Orleans Bar Assn. (co-chair healthcare, biotech. & med. malpractice com. 2002—03, chair healthcare, biotech. & med. malpractice com. 2004), La. Soc. Hosp. Attys. La. Hosp. Assn. (pres. 1983—85, past pres. 1985—86), Am. Coll. Healthcare Execs., Greater New Orleans Women's Healthcare Exec. Network (pres. 1995, 2003—04), Nat. Health Lawyers Assn., Am Acad. Hosp. Attys., Tex. Hosp. Assn., Fed. Bar Assn., Cornell Alumni Admissions Ambassador Network (chair), Tulane U. Women's Assn. Roman Catholic. Avocations: bridge, antiques, skiing, art, travel. Office: Baker Donelson Bearman Caldwell & Berkowitz 201 St Charles Ave #360 New Orleans LA 70170

TROTMAN SCOTT, MICHELLE FRAZIER, special education educator; d. Michael Steven and Jacqueline Renee Frazier; m. Charles Edward Scott, Mar. 8, 2008; m. Anthony Sharone Trotman, May 29, 1999 (div. Jan. 25, 2007); children: Camille Trotman, Tayla Scott, Charlean Scott. BS in Edn., Ohio State U., 1994, MA, 1997, PhD, 2002. Tchr. Columbus Pub. Schs., 1994—99; prin. Millennium Cmty. Sch., 2002—04; supt. Omega Sch. Excellence, Dayton, Ohio, 2004—06; asst. prof. U. West Ga., Carrollton, 2006—. Recipient Charles B. Huelsman award, Ohio State U., Coll. Edn., 2001—02; grant, US Dept. Edn., Office Spl. Edn. and Rehab. Svc., 1999, PEGS grant, Ohio State U., Coll. Edn., 2000. Mem.: AERA, CEC, NAGC, Delta Sigma Theta Sorority, Inc. Office: Univ West Ga 1601 Maple St Carrollton GA 30118 Office Fax: 678-839-6162. Business E-Mail: fraztrot@westga.edu.

TROTT, MENA, application developer; b. 1977; m. Ben Trott. Web-blogger dollarshort.org, 2001; co-founder, pres. Six Apart, Inc., 2004—. Spkr. in field. Named one of People of the Year, PC Mag., 2004, Top 100 Young Innovators, MIT Tech. Review, 2004, Fast 50 for 2004, Fast Company, Most Influential Women in Technology, 2009. Achievements include creator of TypePad and Moveable Type, software tools for publishing weblogs. Office: Six Apart 548 4th St San Francisco CA 94107-1621*

TROTT, STEPHEN SPANGLER, federal judge; b. Glen Ridge, NJ, Dec. 12, 1939; s. David Herman and Virginia (Spangler) Trott; m. Carol C. Trott; children: Christina, Shelley. BA, Wesleyan U., 1962; LLB, Harvard U., 1965; LLD (hon.), Santa Clara U., 1992; LLD (hon.), U. Idaho, 2001. Bar: Calif. 1966, US Dist. Ct. (ctrl. dist.) Calif. 1966, US Ct. Appeals (9th cir.) 1983, US Supreme Ct. 1984. Guitarist, mem. The Highwaymen, 1958—; dep. dist. atty. LA County Dist. Atty.'s Office, LA, 1966—75, chief dep. dist. atty., 1975—79; US dist. atty. Ctrl. Dist. Calif., LA, 1981—83; asst. atty. gen. criminal divsn. US Dept. Justice, Washington, 1983—86; faculty Nat. Coll. Dist. Attys., Houston, 1973—80; chmn. central dist. Calif. Law Enforcement Coord. Com., Houston, 1981—83; coord. LA-Nev. Drug Enforcement Task Force, 1982—83; assoc. atty. gen. US Dept. Justice, Washington, 1986—88; chmn. US Interpol, 1986—88; judge US Ct. Appeals (9th cir.), Boise, Idaho, 1988—2004, sr. judge, 2004—. Trustee Wesleyan U., 1984—87; adv. council Big Brothers, Big Sisters S.W. Idaho, 2001—03; ofcl. photographer World Cup Wrestling Championship, 2003—; bd. dirs., pres. Children's Home Soc., Idaho, 1990—2004. Recipient Gold record as singer-guitarist for Michael Row the Boat Ashore, 1961, Disting. Faculty award, Nat. Coll. Dist. Attys., 1977. Mem.: Am. Coll. Trial Lawyers, Boise (Idaho) Philharm. Assn. (bd. dirs. 1995—, v.p. 1997—99, pre-concert lectr. 1997—, pres. 1999—2003), Idaho Classic Guitar Soc. (founder, pres. 1989—2004), Internat. Brotherhood Magicians, Idaho Racing Pigeon Assn., Magic Castle, Brentwood Racing Pigeon Club (pres. 1977—82), Wilderness Fly Fishers Club (pres. 1975—77). Republican. Office: US Ct Appeals 9th Cir 666 US Courthouse 550 W Fort St Boise ID 83724-0040*

TROTTA, RIC CHARLES, aerospace transportation executive, consultant; b. NYC, Mar. 7, 1942; s. Sigmund Robert and Anita Dolores (La Penna) T.; m. Carolyn Carey Bealle Trotta, May 29, 1965; children: Bradley Charles, Ric Charles Jr., Lauren Carey. Student in elec. engring., U. Va., 1959-62; BA in Physics, NYU, 1966; MBA in Mktg., Hofstra U., 1977; postgrad., Carnegie Mellon U., 1987. Engr. Grumman Aerospace Corp., Bethpage, NY, 1966-68, asst. to v.p., 1968-70, advanced programs mgr., 1970-78, mgr. technology planning, 1978-81, asst. dir. advanced systems, 1981-83; dir. corp. ind., rsch. and devel. Grumman Corp., 1983-86, dir. corp. devel. and resources, 1986-94; pres. Trotta Assoc., Cons. to Govt. and Industry, Centerport, 1994—. Sr. player global war games U.S. Naval War Coll., Newport, RI, 1985—; mem. resources working group Fed. Emergency Mgmt. Agy., Washington, 1991—; vice-chair nat. adv. coun. Fed. Lab. Consortium, 1999—, vice chmn., 2000, chmn., 01; mem. nomination and award selection com. L.I. Tech. Hall of Fame, 2003—; bd. dirs. Beachcomber Ltd., Montauk, NY, pres. bd. dirs., 2005. Author: Industry Independent Rsch. and Devel. Study, 1996, Assessing the Impact of Regulatory and Legislative Changes to the DOD Independent Research and Developement Program, 1997, Maritime Industry Definition and Structure- A Workbook for Assessing Organization Capabilities Versus Industry Needs, 1997; Contbg. author: Public Control of Medical Care, 1978, National Security Assessment of the U.S. Maritime Industry Surveys: Building and Repairing of Ships, Boats and other Marine Platforms, Maritime Research Development and Education, 2000, Nat. Security Assesment of Shipbldg. and Repair Ind., 2001, Assessment of Industry Attitudes on Collaborating with U.S. Department of Defense in Research and Development and Technology Sharing, 2003. Mem. com. on sch. utilization Harborfield Sch. Dist., Greenlawn, 1984; bd. dir. Community Sch., Centerport, NY, 1985. Recipient Community Svc. award, Town of Huntington, N.Y., 1985, Merit award, Chief Naval Rsch., 2000, Outstanding Svc. Award, Fed. Lab. Consortium for Tech. Transfer, 2005. Mem. Nat. Security Indsl. Assn., Electronic Industries Assn., Mine Warfare Assn. (bd. dirs. 1997), Assn. Nat. Def. and Emergency Resources, Sigma Nu (historian 1961). Avocations: fishing, tennis, sailing, cooking. Home and Office: 21 Little Bull Ct Centerport NY 11721-1450 Home Phone: 631-424-0494; Office Phone: 631-424-3700. Personal E-mail: RicTrotta@aol.com. Business E-Mail: RTrotta@TrottaAssociates.com.

TROTTER, CHARLIE, chef; Degree in Polit. Sci., U. Wis., 1982. Owner, chef Charlie Trotter's, Chgo., Trotter's To Go, Lincoln Park, Ill., 2000—, "C", Los Cabos, Mexico, 2004—. Founder Charlie Trotter Culinary Edn. Found., 1999—. Author: Lessons in Excellence, 1999, Kitchen Sessions with Charlie Trotter, 1999, Gourmet Cooking for Dummies, 1999, Great Restaurants of the World: Charlie Trotter's, 2000, Charlie Trotter Cooks at Home, 2000, Charlie Trotter's, 2001, Charlie Trotter's Vegetables, 2001, Charlie Trotter's Seafood, 2001, Charlie Trotter's Desserts, 2001, Charlie Trotter's Meat and Game, 2001, Lessons in Service, 2001, Raw, 2003, Workin' More Kitchen Sessions with Charlie Trotter, 2004, The Cook's Book, 2005, Spa Cuisine; host: (tv series) Kitchen Sessions with Charlie Trotter. Recipient Grand award, Wine Spectator, 1993—, Humanitarian of Yr. award, Internat. Assn. Culinary Professionals, 2005, Outstanding Chef award, James Beard Found., 1999, Chgo.'s Rising Stars Mentor award, StarChefs.com, 2008; named Best Chef: Midwest, James Beard Found., 1992; named to Who's Who in Food & Beverage in Am., 1996. Achievements include being one of 5 heroes to be honored by America's Promise. Office: 816 W Armitage Ave Chicago IL 60614

TROTTER, CORTEZ, city official, former fire commissioner; b. Chgo. First dep. fire commr. Chgo. Fire Dept., fire commr., 2001—06; exec. dir. Office of Emergency Mgmt. and Comm. (formerly Office of Emergency Comm.), 2006—. Apptd. to bd. dirs. Emergency Comm. (911) Bd., 1990—. Recipient Martin Luther King Jr. Excellence in Leadership award, Suburban Human Rels. Com. Office: City Hall 121 N La Salle Chicago IL 60602

TROTTER, DONALD WESLEY, history professor; b. Anniston, Ala., Apr. 3, 1945; s. Donald Wesley and Doris Morrison Trotter; m. Patricia Lee Phillips, June 3, 1967; children: Heather Trotter Hull, Peter Shalom, Benjamin Daniel, Jennifer Ruth, Samuel Wesley, David John, Wendy Love, Rowena Jean. BA, Ga. State Coll., Atlanta, 1967; MDiv, Emmanuel Sch. Religion, Johnson City, Tenn., 1989; PhD, U. Tenn., Knoxville, 1998—98. Ordained minister SW Christian Ch., 1988; cert. comml. pilot FAA, 1969. Adj. prof. history Pellissippi State Tech CC, Knoxville, 1990—; adj. prof. history and bible Johnson Bible Coll., Knoxville, 1999—. Prin. Living Word Acad., Copper Ctr., Alaska, 1976—82; fire support chief Army N.G., Jefferson City, Tenn., 1984—2003; pub. assistance worker DPASS, State Wyo., Sheridan, 1984—86; vice chmn. bd. Red Grade Christian Acad., Sheridan, Wyo., 1984—86; adj. prof. history Roane State CC, Harriman, Tenn., 1998—2003; evening coord. Pellissippi State Tech CC, Knoxville, 1999—; adj. prof. history and religion Tusculum Coll., Knoxville, 2002—. Charter com. chmn. Boy Scouts Am., Knoxville, 1990—97; elder West Towne Christian Ch., Knoxville, 1992—2007. Capt. US Army, 1967—72, Ft. Hood, Vietnam, Ft. Stewart. Decorated Bronze Star medal US Army, Air medal, Army Commendation medal, Army Achievement medal, Commendation Ribbon Tenn. Army N.G., and numerous others. Avocations: gardening, guitar, target shooting, camping. Home: 6901 Greenbrook Dr Knoxville TN 37931 Office: Pellissippi State Tech CC 10915 Hardin Valley Rd Knoxville TN 37933 Personal E-mail: dwtrotter@hotmail.com. Business E-Mail: dtrotter@pstcc.edu.

TROTTER, HERMAN (EAGER), JR., retired music critic; b. Providence, Sept. 25, 1925; s. Herman Eager, Sr. and Shelley Fern (Jones) T.; m. Johanne Marguerite Haberstro, Sept. 22, 1956 (div. Apr. 1996); children: Kim Avery. Holly Anne. Joy Caroline; m. Rosa Spillane Whetzle, July 22, 1996. BA, Yale U., 1946. Pub. utility sec. analyst Mass. Mut. Life Ins. Co., Springfield, 1947-51; sales engr., mgr. Buffalo office B-I-F Industries, Providence, 1951-56; asst. sec. Buffalo Batt and Felt Co, Depew, NY, 1956-68; freelance music critic Buffalo News, 1967—77; account exec. Harold Warner Advt., Buffalo, 1968-77; staff music critic Buffalo News, 1977—2001, music critic emeritus, 2002. Contbr. articles to profl. and popular jours., and to New Grove Dictionary of Music. Program annotator Buffalo Philharm., 1964-70. Lt. (j.g.) USN, 1943-46, PTO. Mem.: Music Critics Assn. (v.p. 1988—93, sec. 1999—2003). Avocations: travel, record collecting. Home: 33 Gates Cir Apt 6C Buffalo NY 14209-1197 E-mail: herros72296@aol.com.

TROTTER, JAMES, physician; b. Springfield, Mo., Jan. 13, 1962; s. W. Y. Trotter. MD, Emory, Atlanta, 1989. Cert. physician Colo., 2008. Physician U. Colo. Health Scis. Ctr., Denver, 1999—2009, Baylor U. Med. Ctr., Dallas, 2009—. Home: 820 S Jackson Denver CO 80209 Office: Baylor Univ Med Ctr 4 Roberts 3500 Gaston Avenue Dallas TX 75246 Office Fax: 214-820-8168; Home Fax: 720-848-2246. Business E-Mail: james.trotter@baylorhealth.edu.

TROTTER, JOE WILLIAM, JR., history professor, writer; b. Vallscreek, W.Va., June 18, 1945; s. Joe William and Thelma Odell Trotter; m. H. LaRue Mack, May 19, 1972. AA, Kendall Coll., 1967; BA, Carthage Coll., 1969; MA, U. Minn., 1978, PhD, 1980. Social studies tchr. Tremper Sr. HS, Kenosha, Wis., 1969—75; adult edn. instr. Gateway Tech. Inst., Kenosha, Wis., 1970—73; instr. dept. history U. Minn., 1977—79, vis. prof. dept. history, 1993; asst. prof. dept. history U. Calif.-Davis, 1981—84, assoc. prof. dept. history, 1984—85, Carnegie Mellon U., Pitts., 1985—89, prof. dept. history, 1990—96, Mellon prof. history, 1996—, head dept. history, 2001—; dir. Ctr. for African-american Urban Studies and the Economy, Pitts., 1995—. Editl. bd. mem. Jour. Urban History, Thousand Oaks, Calif., 1997—, Labor History, London, 1991—2003, Jour. Am. Ethnic History, Piscataway, NJ, 1991—, Pa. History, Middletown, 1987—, Labor, Durham, NC, 2003—, Ohio Valley History, 2002—, Jour. of Am. History, Bloomington, Ind., 1992—95, Pa. History, Middletown, Pa., 1987—. Author: (book) Black Milwaukee: The Making of an Industrial Proletariat, 1915-45, 1985, Coal, Class, and Color: Blacks in Southern West Virginia, 1915-32, 1990, African Americans in Depression and War, 1929-1945, 1995, River Jordan: African American Urban Life in the Ohio Valley, 1998, The African American Experience, 2001; editor: (edited volume) The Great Migration in Historical Perspective: New Dimensions of Race, Class, and Gender, 1991; co-editor: Blacks in the Industrial Age: A Documentary History, 1915-1945, 1996, African Americans in Pennsylvania: Shifting Historical Perspectives, 1997, (book) African American Urban Studies: Perspectives From the Colonial Era to the Present, 2004. Spkr. NAACP, Arlington, Va., 1992, 19th dist., Homewood Brushton, Pitts., 1999; keynote spkr. Lemington Elder Care Svcs/, Pitts., 2002; pres. Kenosha Black Caucus, 1972—74; spkr. Friendship Bapt. Ch., Massillon, Ohio, 2001. Recipient Outstanding Svc. award, Pa. chpt. Nat. Assn. Real Estate Brokers, 1991, Gambrinus award, Milw. Hist. Soc., 1985; grantee, U.S. Dept. Edn. Grant, 2002-05, Ford Found., 1997-99, 2001-2002. Mem.: Labor and Working Class History Assn., Am. Studies Assn., So. Hist. Assn., Pa. Hist. Assn., Pitts. Ctr. for Social History, Urban History Assn., Assn. for the Study of Afro-American Life and History, Am. Hist. Assn., Orgn. Am. Historians. Office: Carnegie Mellon Univ Dept of History 5000 Forbes Ave Pittsburgh PA 15213 Office Fax: 412-268-1019. Business E-Mail: trotter@andrew.cmu.edu.

TROTTER, LESLIE EARL, operations research specialist, educator; b. Muskogee, Okla., Nov. 17, 1943; s. Leslie Earl and Sylvia Helene (Freeze) T.; m. Jomi Tuggle, July 19, 1968 (div. Dec. 1995); children: Colleen Nicole, Eamonn Scott; m. Jeannine Rouch, July 7, 2000. AB in Math., Princeton U., 1965; MS in Indsl. and Systems Engring., Ga. Inst. Tech., 1971; PhD in Ops. Rsch., Cornell U., 1973. Sci. computer programmer Lockheed-Ga. Co., Marietta, 1965-68; computer applications analyst Control Data Corp., Atlanta, 1968-70; postdoctoral rsch. assoc. Math. Rsch. Ctr., U. Wis., Madison, 1973; asst. prof. Yale U. Sch. Orgn. and Mgmt., New Haven, 1974-75; assoc. prof. Cornell U. Sch. Ops. Rsch. and Indsl. Engring., Ithaca, NY, 1975-84, dir. of Sch., 1983—87, 1998—99, prof., 1984—; dir. Advanced Computational Optimization Lab. Cornell Theory Ctr., 1995—2001. Vis. prof. Bonn (Germany) U., 1977-79, math. dept. E.P.F.L., Lausanne, Switzerland, 1984-85, 91-92, 2000, Math. Inst., Augsburg (Germany) U., 1987-88; ind. eng. lab. Ecole Centrale-Paris, 2006-07; vis. cons. Bell Labs., Holmdel, N.J., 1981. Editor optimization area Jour. Ops. Rsch., 1982-87; contbr. numerous articles to profl. jours. Recipient tchg. excellence awards Cornell U., 1977, 81, 93, 94, 98, sr. U.S. scientist award Alexander von Humboldt Found., Germany, 1988; numerous rsch. grants NSF, 1974—, including High Performance Computing and Comms. Grand Challenge award, 1995—01. Mem. Inst for Ops Rsch and Mgmt. Sci., Math. Programming Soc. (treas. 1988-94), Soc. for Indsl. and Applied Math. Avocations: exercise, hiking, music. Office: Cornell U Sch Ops Rsch Engring Rhodes Hall Ithaca NY 14853 Office Phone: 607-255-5360. Business E-Mail: ltrotter@cs.cornell.edu.

TROTTER, LLOYD G., investment company executive, former diversified technology and services company executive; b. Cleveland, Apr. 9, 1945; m. Teri Trotter; 3 children. BBA, Cleve. State U., 1972, PhD (hon.) in Bus. Adminstrn., 2001. Field svc. engr. GE Lighting, 1970; various positions GE, 1970-90; v.p., gen. mgr. mfg. ED&C, 1990-98; sr. v.p. GE, 1998-99; pres., CEO GE Indsl. Sys., 1999—2004; CEO, consumer & indsl. divsn. GE, 2004—06; pres., CEO GE Indsl., 2006—08; vice chmn. GE, 2006—08; mng. ptnr. GenNx360 Capital Partners, 2008—. Started GE African-Am. forum, 1990; bd. dir. NAM, Nat. Action Coun. for Minorities in Engring. (NACME), GE, 2007—, Textron Inc., 2008—. Rep. for GE America's Promise. Named 50 Most Important African-Am. in Tech., USBE&IT and Blackmoney.com, 2004. Avocation: collector of Harlem Renaissance Period art and wine. Office: GenNx360 Capital Partners 300 Park Ave 17th Fl New York NY 10022

TROTTER, SUZANNE MICHELLE, psychologist; b. Pontiac, Mich., Aug. 12, 1967; m. Mark Trotter, May 5, 2001; children: Ian Thomas, Conor Ries. BSc, Siena Heights Coll., Adrian, Mich., 1989; MS, Eastern Mich., Ypsilanti, 1993; MA, Wayne State U., Detroit, 1999. Cert. Sch. Psychologist Dept. Edn. mich., 2007. Behavioral psychologist Cmty. Mental Health, Garden, Mich., 1995—97; psychologist Huron Valley Schs., Highland, 1999—. Youth group leader. Recipient Watch Me, Huron Valley Ednl. Assn. Lutheran. Avocations: Tae Kwon Do, swimming. Personal E-mail: trotters@huronvalley.k12.mi.us.

TROTTER, THOMAS ROBERT, lawyer; b. Akron, Ohio, Apr. 11, 1949; s. Fred and Josephine (Daley) Trotter; m. Martha Kaltenbach, 2003. BA, Ohio U., 1971; JD, Tulane U., 1975. Bar: Ohio 1975, D.C. 2000, U.S. Dist. Ct. (no. dist.) Ohio 1975. Assoc. Squire, Sanders & Dempsey, Cleve., 1975-80; shareholder Buckingham, Doolittle & Burroughs, Akron, 1980—2006; of counsel Vorys, Sater, Seymour and Pease LLP, Akron, Ohio, 2007—. Trustee Cascade Capital Corp., Akron, 1983-2000; chair taxation and legis. com. Greater Akron C. of C., 1988-95; trustee Akron-Summit Solid Waste Mgmt. Authority, 1994-97 Trustee Akron Symphony Orch., 1984-93, trustee Weathervane Cmty. Playhouse, 1996-2003, 06—, pres., 1999-2001. Mem. ABA, Ohio Bar Assn. (chair local govt. law com.), Akron Bar Assn., Nat. Assn. Bond Lawyers, Sigma Alpha Epsilon. Democrat. Home: 180 W Fairlawn Blvd Akron OH 44313 Office: Vorys Sater Seymour and Pease LLP 106 S Main St Ste 1100 Akron OH 44308 also: Vorys Sater Seymour and Pease LLP 2100 One Cleveland Ctr 1375 E Ninth St Cleveland OH 44114-1724 Office Phone: 330-208-1126, 216-479-6107. Business E-Mail: trtrotter@vorys.com.

TROTTER II, ROBERT TALBOT, anthropologist, educator; b. Manhattan, Kans., Feb. 26, 1946; s. Robert Talbot and Virginia Yapp Trotter; m. Sara Ann Knight; children: Hara Jordan Evenson, Robert Talbot Trotter III, David Rockford McEntire Trotter, Shelton Rayne Devlin. BA, U. Nebr., Lincoln, 1968; MA, Southern Meth. U., Dallas, 1972, PhD, 1976. Asst. mgr., comml. office Northwestern Bell Tel. Co., Cedar Rapids, Iowa, 1968—70; asst. prof. Pan Am. U., Edinburg, Tex., 1974—81, asst. dean, Sch. Social Scis., 1978—80, assoc. prof., dept. behavioral scis., 1981—85; prof. and chair, dept. anthropology Northern Ariz. U., Flagstaff, 1985—95, regents' prof., 1995—, chair, instl. rev. bd. (IRB), 2008—, sr. scientist, Interdisciplinary Health Policy Inst., 2008; interagency pers. assignment, divsn. HIV AIDS CTRS. Disease Control and Prevention, Atlanta, 1995—97; dir., office faculty rsch. devel. U. Tex. Pan Am., Edinburg, 1983—85, prof. anthropology, 1984—85; dir. Health Rsch. Alliance Ariz., NAU, 2007; lectr. anthropology U. Tex., Arlington. Cons., rsch. anthropologist, dept. migrant edn. Pa. State, Harrisburg, 1984—87; cons., program on substance abuse WHO, Geneva, 1991—95, cons. internat. classification of impairments, disabilities, handicaps, 1995—2000; cons. rare project, office HIV AIDS policy US Dept. Health and Human Svcs., Washington, 1999—2003; rsch. cons. modeling collaborative partnerships Gen. Motors, Warren, Mich., 2001—06, rsch. cons., ideal plant culture program, 2005—07, rsch. cons., integrated health mgmt. program, 2006—08. Prodr.(dir.): (multi-media exhibit) Don Pedrito Jaramillo, San Antonio, Tex. Inst. Cultures, (dir. editor) (ethnographic film) Los Que Curan. Recipient Highly Commended award, Emerald Club, 2005, Praxis award, Wash. Assn. Practicing Anthropologists, 1983, Jour. Mfg. Tech. Mgmt. award, IAMOT Conf., Wash., 2004, Pres.'s award, Northern Ariz. U., 1994, Martin De La Cruz award, Mexican Acad. Traditional Medicine, 1992, Disting. Faculty award, Pan Am. U., 1985; named one of Outstanding Young Men of America, 1978. Fellow: Am. Anthrop. Assn. (exec. com. bd. dirs. 1988—90, Ethnographic Evaluation award 1989), Soc. Applied Anthropology (bd. dirs. 1988—90); mem.: Cibola Anthrop. Assn. (pres. 1981—82), Golden Key Hon. Soc. (hon.), Nat. Assn. Practice of Anthropology (pres. elect 1986—88), Sigma Xi. Achievements include patents for system and model for performance value based collaborative relationships. Avocations: golf, travel, cooking. Office: Northern Ariz Univ 575 E Pine Knoll Dr Flagstaff AZ 86011 Office Fax: 928-523-9135. Business E-Mail: robert.trotter@nau.edu.

TROTTIER, BRYAN JOHN, professional sports team executive, former professional hockey player and coach; b. Val Marie, Sask., Can., July 17, 1956; s. Eldon J. and Mary (Gardner) Trottier; m. Laura Lynn Theis, July 14, 1976; children: Bryan John, Lindsay Ann. Profl. hockey player NY Islanders, 1975—90, Pitts. Penguins, 1990—92, 1993—94, asst. coach, 1993—97; head coach Portland Pirates (Am. Hockey League), 1997—98; asst. coach Colo. Avalanche, 1998—2002; head coach NY Rangers, 2002—03; exec. dir. player devel. NY Islanders, 2006—. Hockey cons. Right Guard Corp., Phila.; spokesman 1980 Winter Olympics, Lake Placid, NY; former pres. NHL Player's Assn.; owner, operator Bryan Trottier Skating Acad., Port Washington, NY. Recipient Calder Meml. Trophy, 1976, Hart Meml. Trophy, 1979, Art Ross Trophy, 1979, Conn Smythe Trophy, 1980, King Clancy Meml. Trophy, 1989; named NHL Rookie of Yr., Sporting News, 1976, NHL Player of Yr., 1979. Achievements include mem. Stanley Cup Champion, NY Islanders, 1980, 1981, 1982, 1983; mem. Stanley Cup Champions, Pitts. Penguins, 1991, 1992; inducted into Hockey Hall of Fame, 1997. Office: NY Islanders Nassau Veterans Meml Coliseum 1255 Hempstead Turnpike Uniondale NY 11553*

TROTTIER, TRACEY, social studies educator; d. Leo and Barbara Trottier; m. Michael J. Tropea. MPA, U. Ctrl. Fla., Orlando, PhD in Pub. Affairs, 2002. Rsch. assoc. Ctr. Cmty. Partnerships, Orlando, 2003—06; asst. prof. Ind. U. South Bend, 2006—. Contbr. articles in pub.

adminstrn. jours. Funding com. mem. United Way St. Joseph County, South Bend, 2006—08. Mem.: ASPA, Assn. Rsch. Nonprofit Orgns. Voluntary Action. Office: Ind Univ South Bend 1700 Mishawaka Ave South Bend IN 46634-7111

TROTZ, BARRY, professional hockey coach; b. Dauphin, Manitoba), Can., July 15, 1962; Asst. coach U. Manitoba, 1984; head coach, gen. mgr. Dauphin Kings Jr. Hockey Club, 1985-87; head coach U. Manitoba, 1987; chief western scout Washington Capitals, 1988, asst. coach, 1991, head coach, 1992-95, US Team at Am. Hockey League All Star Game, 1996, Nashville Predators, 1997—. Named NHL Coach of Yr., Sporting News, 2007. Office: Nashville Predators 501 Broadway Nashville TN 37203-3932

TROUILLE, MARY SEIDMAN, foreign language educator; b. Chgo., Feb. 23, 1951; d. Nathaniel and Virginia (Crosley) Seidman; m. Guy Andre Nodot, Apr. 5, 1971 (div. Sept. 1977); 1 child, Jennifer Lynn; m. Bruno Jean-Louis Trouille, Apr. 15, 1978; children: David Alexander, Laura Elizabeth. BA in French, Loyola U., Chgo., 1972; MA in French, Northwestern U., Evanston, Ill., 1974, PhD in French, 1988. Editor Scott, Foresman Publs., Glenview, Ill., 1976-83; grad. teaching asst. Northwestern U., Evanston, Ill., 1983-88, lectr. French, 1988-89; lectr. humanities & French U. Chgo., 1990-93; asst. prof. French Ill. State U., Normal, 1993-96, assoc. prof. French, 1996—2002, prof. French, 2002—. Presenter in field. Author: Sexual Politics in the Enlightenment: Women Writers Read Rousseau, 1997, Wife-Abuse in Eighteenth Century France, 2009; mem. editl. bd. Studies in 18th-Century Culture, 2000-2003; Translator: The Writing of Melancholy: Modes of Opposition in Early French Modernism, 1993, Les Lieux de Mémoire, vol. 1, 1998; contbr. chpts. to books and articles to profl. jours. Travel grantee Am. Coun. Learned Socs., 1995; Sch. Criticism & Theory fellow, 1985, Internat. Summer Inst. Semiotic and Structural Studies fellow, 1986. Mem. Am. Soc. Eighteenth-Century Studies (co-chair women's caucus 1995-98, mem. editl. bd. Studies in 18th-Century Culture 2000-03, chair tchg. prize selection com. 2002-03), Clifford Prize Com. (chair 2004-2005, mem. exec. bd. 2007-), Internat. Soc. Eighteenth-Century Studies. Office: Ill State U Dept Fgn Langs Lits and Cultures PO Box 4300 Normal IL 61790-0001 Office Phone: 309-438-3604.

TROUNSON, ALAN OSBOURNE, state agency administrator, embryologist; b. Sydney, Feb. 16, 1946; MSc in Wool and Pastoral Sciences, U. New South Wales, 1971; PhD in Animal Embryology, Sydney U., 1974. Dalgety Research Fellow, ARC Inst. Animal Physiology and Biochemistry U. Cambridge, 1974—76; joined as sr. rsch. fellow by 1984 reader in the dept. of Obstetrics and Gynecology Monash U., 1977—84, dir. Centre Early Devel., 1985, Personal Chair in Obstetrics and Gynaecology/Paediatrics, 1991, Personal Chair as Professor of Stem Cell Sciences, 2003, Emeritus Professor, 2008—; pres. Calif. Inst. Regenerative Medicine, San Francisco, 2008—. Fellow: Royal Coll. Obstetricians and Gynaecologists, Australian and New Zealand Coll. Obstetricians and Gynaecologists (hon.). Achievements include pioneer of human in vitro fertilisation (IVF) and associated reproductive technologies; first IVF birth in Australia in 1980; diagnosis of inherited genetic disease in pre-implantation embryos; discovery and production of human embryonic stem cells and of their ability to be directed into neurones, prostate tissue and respiratory tissue. Office: Calif Inst Regnerative Medicine 210 King St San Francisco CA 94107*

TROUNSTINE, PHILIP JOHN, communications consultant, online publisher; b. Cin., July 30, 1949; s. Henry P. and Amy May (Joseph) Trounstine; children: Jessica, David; m. Deborah Williams, May 1, 1993; children: Amy, Ryan, Patrick Wilkes. Student, U. Vt., 1967-68, Stanford U., 1968-70; BA in Journalism, San Jose State U., 1975. Graphic artist Eric Printing, San Jose, Calif., 1972-75; reporter Indpls. Star, Ind., 1975-78, San Jose Mercury News, Calif., 1978-83, editl. writer Calif., 1983-86, polit. editor Calif., 1986-99; ednl. cons. Teen Recovery Strategies, 1995-99; comms. dir. Gov. Gray Davis, Calif., 1999-2001, comm. cons. Calif., 2001—; dir. Survey and Policy Rsch. Inst. at San Jose State U., 2001—08; editor & pub. Calbuzz.com, 2009—. Co-author: Movers & Shakers: The Study of Community Power, 1981. Creator, writer SPJ Gridiron Show, San Jose, 1981-91. Pulliam fellow, 1975, Duke U., 1991, J.S. Knight fellow Stanford U., 1993-94. Mem. Soc. Profl. Journalists (nat. ethics com. 1993-96), Am. Assn. Pub. Opinion Rsch., Seascape Golf Club. Jewish. Avocations: golf, fishing. Home: 620 Middlefield Dr Aptos CA 95003-3560 Personal E-mail: calbuzzer@gmail.com.

TROUP, GORDON A., health products executive; With Am. Hosp. Supply Corp., Cardinal Distbn., 1991—99, exec. v.p. field ops., 1999—2000; pres. pharm. distbn. and splty distbn. bus. Cardinal Health, Inc., 2000—03, exec. v.p., 2003—, pres. nuclear pharmacy svcs., 2003—08; mem. bd. dirs. Neoprobe Corp., 2008—. Office: Neoprobe Corp 425 Metro Place N Dublin OH 43017

TROUPE, WILLIAM HAROLD, lawyer; b. Quincy, Mass., Aug. 7, 1945; s. George Harold and Elizabeth (Harvey) T.; m. Linda M. Corbett, July 19, 1970; children: Allyson Leigh, Adam Jeremy. BBA, U. Mass., 1967; JD, Suffolk U., 1972. Bar: Mass. 1972, U.S. Dist. Ct. Mass. 1975, U.S. Ct. Appeals (1st cir.) 1975, U.S. Supreme Ct., 1991. New Eng. claims mgr. Greater N.Y. Ins. Co., Boston, 1972-73; ptnr. Lawrence Locke & Assocs., Boston, 1973-84, Wynn & Wynn PC, Boston, 1984-89, Hislop Carney & Troupe, Boston, 1990-98; founding ptnr. Carney & Troupe, Boston, 1999—. Spkr. continuing legal edn. programs. Contbr. numerous articles on worker's compensation to legal jours. Mem. Mass. Bar Assn. (chmn. worker's compensaton com. 1985-87), Boston Bar Assn. Office: Carney & Troupe 5th Fl 10 High St Fl 5 Boston MA 02110-1605 Home Phone: 978-535-4184; Office Phone: 617-426-9797. Personal E-mail: willtrou@aol.com.

TROUSDALE, STEPHEN RICHARD, newspaper editor; b. LA, May 29, 1963; s. Richard Gardner Trousdale and Geraldine Barbara Wisdom. AB, Stanford U., 1985. News editor LA Daily Commerce, 1986—87, edit. page editor, 1987—89, mng. editor, 1989—96; bus. editor Copley LA Newspapers, 1996—97; dep. bus. editor Contra Costa Times, 1997—2000, bus. editor, 2000—07; dep. bus. editor San Jose Mercury News, Calif., 2006—07, bus. editor, 2007—. Mem. Soc. Profl. Journalists (past pres. L.A. chpt.), AP Mng. Editors, Calif. Soc. Newspaper Editors, Soc. Am. Bus. Editors and Writers. Avocation: bicycling. Home: 2335 Valley St Berkeley CA 94702-2133 Office: San Jose Mercury News 750 Ridder Park Dr San Jose CA 95190 Office Phone: 408-920-5800. Business E-Mail: strousdale@mercurynews.com.

TROUT, BRETT JOSEPH, lawyer; b. Des Moines, July 28, 1966; s. Patrick Joseph and Susan Jeanne Trout; children: Griffin William, Lindy Elizabeth. BA, Grinnell Coll., Iowa, 1988; JD, U. Iowa, Iowa City, 1992. Bar: US Patent and Trademark Office 1993, US Ct. Appeals (fed. cir.) 1995, US Supreme Ct. 1995, US Ct. Appeals (DCcir.) 2001, US Dist. Ct. (no. and so. dists.) Iowa 2003, US Ct. Appeals (8th cir.) 2004. Assoc. Davis; Brown, Koehn, Shors & Roberts, P.C., Des Moines, 1992—95; shareholder Shearer, Templer & Pingel, P.C., West Des Moines, Iowa, 1995—98, Brown, Winick, Graves, Gross, Baskerville & Schoenbaum, P.L.C., Des Moines, 1998—2000; founding shareholder Gunderson, Sharp, Trout & Rhein, P.C., Des Moines, 2000—01; pvt. practice Law Offices of Brett J. Trout P.C., Des Moines, 2001—. Chmn. tech. com. Iowa State Bar, Des Moines, 2003—06. Author: Internet Laws Affecting Your Company, Internet Laws Affecting Iowa Companies, yBlawg: The Nuts and Bolts of Lawyer Blogging; co-author: What No One Ever Tells You About Blogging and Podcasting; author (contributing author): (non-fiction book) The E-Business Legal Arsenal; author: (web blog) Blawg IT. Chmn. Clive Bd. Adjustment, Iowa, 2003—07; co-founder Iowa Vol. for Arts, Cedar Rapids, Iowa, 2007. Fellow: Rotary Club (Paul Harris fellow 2002); mem.: Blackstone Inn of Ct., Polk County Bar Assn. (chmn. website com. 2006—07), Iowa State Bar Assn. Office: Brett J Trout PC 516 Walnut Des Moines IA 50309

TROUT, JACOB EUGENE, religious studies educator; b. Lamar, Colo., Jan. 4, 1944; s. Jacob and Esther Belle Trout. MA, Assemblies God Theol. Sem., Springfield, Mo., 1976. Cert. ordained min. Assemblies God - Okla., 1971. Youth pastor deaf ch. Okla. Assemblies God, 1968—70; instr., prof. Ctrl. Bible Coll., Springfield, Mo., 1970—. Home: 1901 E Snider Springfield MO 65803 Office: Ctrl Bible Coll 3000 N Grant #A146 Springfield MO 65803 Personal E-mail: jtrout44@mchsi.com. Business E-Mail: jtrout@cbcag.edu.

TROUT, LINDA COPPLE, former state supreme court justice; b. Tokyo, Sept. 1, 1951; BA, U. Idaho, 1973, JD, 1977; LLD (hon.), Albertson Coll. Idaho, 1999. Bar: Idaho 1977. Atty. Blake, Feeney & Clark, 1978—83; judge magistrate divsn. Idaho Dist. Ct. (2d jud. divsn.), 1983-90, dist. judge Lewiston, 1991-92, acting trial ct. adminstr., 1987-91; justice Idaho Supreme Ct., 1992—2007, chief justice, 1997—2004. Instr. coll. law U. Idaho, 1983, 88; chair Idaho State Supreme Ct. Judicial Education Com. Mem. bd. directors Lewiston City Library, Northwest Children's Home, Lewiston YWCA. Mem. Idaho State Bar Assn., Clearwater Bar Assn. (pres. 1980-81).

TROUT, MAURICE ELMORE, diplomat; b. Clifton Hill, Mo., Sept. 17, 1917; s. David McCamel and Charlotte Temple (Woods) T.; m. Margie Marie Mueller, Aug. 24, 1943; children: Richard Willis, Babette Yvonne. BA, Hillsdale Coll., 1939; MA in Pub. Adminstrn, St. Louis U., 1948, PhD in Polit. Sci, 1950. Joined U.S. Fgn. Service, 1950; assigned Paris, 1950-52, Vienna, 1952-55, London, 1955-59, Vientiane, Laos, 1959-61; with Office Exec. Dir. Bur. Far Eastern Affairs, Dept. State, Washington, 1961-65; Am. consulate gen. Munich, 1965-69; 1st sec., consul Am. embassy, Bangkok, 1969—72; dep. office dir. Bur. Politico-Mil. Affairs, Dept. State, Washington, 1972-75; Dept. State advisor Armed Forces Staff Coll., Norfolk, Va., 1975-77. Bd. dirs. Internat. Sch., Bangkok, 1970-72. Served with USCG, 1939-45; capt. USAFR, 1951-55. Recipient Achievement award, Hillsdale Coll., 1962. Mem. Am. Fgn. Service Assn., Diplomatic and Consular Officers Ret., Delta Tau Delta, Delta Theta Phi, Pi Gamma Mu. Home: 6203 Hardy Dr Mc Lean VA 22101-3114

TROUT, MONROE EUGENE, health facility administrator; b. Harrisburg, Pa., Apr. 5, 1931; s. David Michael and Florence Margaret (Kashner) T.; m. Sandra Louise Lemke, June 11, 1960; children: Monroe Eugene, Timothy William. AB, U. Pa., 1953, MD, 1957; LLB, Dickinson Sch. of Law, 1964, JD, 1969; LLD (hon.), Dickinson Sch. Law, 1996, Bloomfield Coll., 1994, Cumberland Coll., 2003. Intern Great Lakes (Ill.) Naval Hosp., 1957-58; resident in internal medicine Portsmouth (Va.) Naval Hosp., 1959-61; chief med. dept. Harrisburg State Hosp., 1961-64; dir. drug regulatory affairs Pfizer, Inc., NYC, 1964-68; v.p., med. dir. Winthrop Labs., NYC, 1968-70; med. dir. Sterling Drug, Inc., NYC, 1970-74, v.p., dir. med. affairs, 1974-78, sr. v.p., dir. med. affairs, bd. dirs., mem. exec. com., 1978-86; pres., CEO Am. Healthcare Sys., Inc., 1986-95, chmn., 1987-95; also bd. dirs. Am. Healthcare Systems, Inc.; chmn. emeritus Am. Healthcare Sys., Inc., 1995—; interim CEO Cytran Inc., 1996. Chmn. bd. dirs. Cytyc Inc., 1998—2002, Ineed MD, Inc., Am. Excess Ins. Ltd., 1990—95; adj. assoc. prof. Bklyn. Coll. Pharmacy; spl. lectr. legal medicine, trustee Dickinson Sch. Law, 1970—93; trustee Ariz. State U. Sch. Health Adminstrn., 1988—91; mem. rsch. bd. Sterling Winthrop, 1977—86; mem. Joint Commn. Prescription Drug Use, 1976—80; sec. Commn. on Med. Malpractice, HEW, 1971—73, cons., 1974; co-chmn. San Diego County Health Commn., 1992—94. Author, Winter Galley, 2008; mem. editl. bd. Hosp. Formulary Mgmt., 1969-79, Forensic Sci., 1971—, Jour. Legal Medicine, 1973-79, Reg. Tox. and Pharmac, 1981-87, Med. Malpractice Prevention, 1985—; editl. reviewer Annals of Internal Medicine; contbr. articles to profl. jours. Exec. com. White House Mini Conf. on Aging, 1980; mem. Nat. Health Adv. Bd. AAA; chmn. bd. Am. Coll. Legal Medicine Found., 1983—87; mem. N.Y. State Commn. Substance Abuse, 1978—80, Town Coun., New Canaan, 1978—86, vice chmn., 1985—86; trustee Cleve. Clinic, 1971—87, Albany Med. Coll., 1977—86, St. Vincent DePaul Ctr. for the Homeless, 1987—90, U. Calif.-San Diego Thornton Hosp. and Med. Ctr., 1990—97, San Diego Mus. Art, 1996—98, Bapt. Health Sys. Found., Knoxville, 1999—2007; trustee, vice chmn. Morehouse Med. Sch., 1980—89; assoc. trustee U. Pa.; bd. visitors U. Pa. Sch. Nursing, 1988—92; pres. bd. trustees U. Calif. San Diego Found., 1994—97; vice chmn. Med. Commn. for Food and Shelter, Inc.; chmn. Internat. B'nai B'rith Dinner, 1989, 1994; Rep. dist. leader New Canaan, 1966—68; bd. dirs. New Canaan Interchurch Svc. Com., 1965—69, Athletes Kidney Found., Cir. in the Sq. Theatre Inc., 1984—86, Knoxville Symphony Soc., 2001—04, Knoxville Opera Co., 2001—04, East Tenn. Hist. Soc., 2003—04. Recipient Alumni award of merit U. Pa., 1953, Disting. Alumni award Dickinson Sch. Law, 1989, Nat. Healthcare award Internat. B'nai B'rith, 1991, Entrepreneur of Yr. award San Diego, 1994, Horatio Alger award, 1995, Salvation Army Tradition of Caring award, 1996, Civis Universitatus award U. Calif. San Diego, 1997, Gold Medal award, Am. Coll. Legal Medicine, 1999, Bapt. Health Sys. Visionary award, 2002, Knoxville Philanthropist of Yr., 2004, Cumberland Coll. Caring Servant award, 2005; Monroe E. Trout Day named in his honor, Knox County, Tenn., Mar. 13, 2007. Fellow Am. Coll. Legal Medicine (v.p., pres., bd. govs.); mem. AMA (Physician's Recognition awards 1969, 72, 76, 82, 85, 88, 92), Med. Execs. (pres. 1975-76), Delta Tau Delta (Alumni Achievement award 1996, Named to 100 Most Influential Delts of Twentieth Century 2000). Lutheran. Office: 2110 Cove View Way Knoxville TN 37919

TROUTEN, DOUGLAS JAMES, journalist; b. Regina, Sask., Can., Dec. 26, 1959; s. Donald James and Elaine Jane (Terwilleger) T.; m. Elisabeth Mae French, Aug. 15, 1981; children: Luke, David, Tracey. BS, Crown Coll., 1981; postgrad., Wheaton Coll., 1981; MA in Journalism, U. Min., 1999. Editor Minn. Christian Chronicle, Edina, Minn., 1982—; dir. EP News Svc., Edina, 1985—. Radio talk show host KKMS, Eagan, Minn., 1997. Cub scout den leader Boy Scouts Am., Crystal, Minn., 1992—. Mem. Christian Newspaper Assn. (founder, bd. dirs. 1985—), Am. Christian Writer's Inst. (bd. dirs. 1993—), Evangelical Press Assn. (bd. mem. 1999—), Phi Kappa Phi. Office: Minnesota Christian Chronicle 623 Lilac Dr N # A Minneapolis MN 55422-4609

TROUTMAN, GEORGE WILLIAM, geologist; b. Aug. 8, 1949; s. George I. and Ellen G. Troutman; m. Marcia Lyn Roseman, Aug. 14, 1971; children: Nancy, Anthony, Janet, David, Barbara, Jonathan. Student, Murray State U., 1967-68; BS in Geology, Western Ky. U., 1974. Lic. prof. geoscientist Tex. Geophys. engr. Birdwell divsn. Seismograph Svc. Corp., Ohio, Pa., W.Va., 1974-77; geologist Consol. Natural Gas, Clarksburg, W.Va., 1977-79; exloration geologist Mountain Fuel Supply Corp., Denver, 1979-80; regional exploration geologist Al-Aquitaine Exploration, Ltd., Denver, 1980-81; sr. staff geologist Resources Investment Corp., Denver, 1981-82; geol. mgr. Petro-Lewis Corp., MCR, Oklahoma City, 1982-84; pres., geologist Troutman Geol. & Assocs., Edmond, Okla., 1984-2000; geol. advisor Devon Energy, Oklahoma City, 2000—03; sr. staff E&P geologist onshore-we. U.S. Dominion Exploration & Prodn., Inc., Oklahoma City, 2003—05; sr. geologist Forest Oil Corp., Denver, 2005—07; v.p. geoscience Golden Energy LLC, Denver, 2007. With USN, 1968—70. Mem. Am. Assn. Petroleum Geologists (cert.), Soc. Profl. Well Log Analysts, Oklahoma City Geol. Soc. (exec. com. 1985-86, editor Shale Shaker Digest XI 1982-85, treas. 1987-88, v.p. 1988-89, pres.-elect 1996-97, pres. 1997-98), Ardmore Geol. Soc., New Orleans Geol. Soc., Geophys. Soc. Oklahoma City, East Tex. Geol. Soc., West Tex. Geol. Soc., Kans. Geol. Soc., Rocky Mountain Assn. Geologists, Wyoming Geol. Assn., New Mex. Geol. Soc. Republican. Mem. Lds Ch. Office: Golden Energy LLC 1999 Broadway Ste 550 Denver CO 80202 Office Phone: 720-227-2740. Personal E-mail: troutman@geologist.com.

TROUTMAN, HOLMES RUSSELL, lawyer; b. Beckley, W.Va., July 27, 1933; s. Holmes Fielding and Florence Lillo (Wallett) T.; m. Patricia Lee Bullion, Nov. 12, 1954; children: Holmes Russell, Richard Byron, Teresa Lee. AB, Marshall U., 1955; postgrad., Stetson Law Sch., 1955-56; LLB, U. Miami, 1958. Bar: Fla. 1958. Assoc., ptnr. firm Akerman, Turnbull, Senterfitt & Eidson, Orlando, Fla., 1958-62; ptnr. firm Fishback, Davis, Dominick & Troutman, Orlando, 1962-69, Troutman, Williams, Irvin, Green, Helms, and Polich, Winter Park, Fla., 1969—. Spl. city prosecutor, City of Winter Park, 1965, city atty., 1968-72, acting county solicitor, 1967-69; spl. counsel Fla. Turnpike Authority, 1968-70, Fla. Pub. Svc. Commn., 1978-79; mem. Fla. Supreme Ct. Nominating Commn., 1978-82, chmn., 1981-82; chmn. bd. trustees Fla. Supreme Ct. Historical Soc., 2000—. Author: Undiscovered Poems; contbr. articles to profl. jours. Host, prodr. Discussion programs Sta. WFTV, 1968-85. Pres. Friends of Orlando Pub. Libr., 1971-73, Fla. Supreme Ct. Hist. Soc., 1997-99; mem. Orange County Charter Study Commn., 1973-74; chmn. Winter Park Charter Study Commn., 1982-83; chmn. bd. advisors Rollins Coll. Hamilton Holt Sch., 1996-98, chmn. emeritus Hamilton Holt Sch. Bd. Rollins Coll.; pres. Fla. Supreme Ct. Hist. Soc., 1997-99; commencement spkr. Rollins Coll., 1999. Recipient Orlando Jr. C. of C. Good Govt. award, 1969, Marshall U. Alumnus Civic Contbrn. award, 1979, Winter Park C. of C. Good Govt. award, 1985. Mem. ABA (mem. ho. of dels. 1978-80), Am. Acad. Trial Lawyers, Fla. Acad. Trial Lawyers, Fla. Bar (mem. bd. govs. 1972-78, pres. 1977-78), Orange County Bar Assn. (mem. exec. coun. 1966-68, pres. 1968-69, driving force and co-founder Legal Aid Soc. 1969), Orlando Tiger Bay Club (pres. 1988-89). Home: 1600 Barcelona Way Winter Park FL 32789-5615 Office: Troutman Williams Irvin Green & Helms PA 311 W Fairbanks Ave Winter Park FL 32789-5094 Home Phone: 407-620-5009; Office Phone: 407-647-2277. Business E-Mail: rtroutman@troutmanwilliams.com.

TROUTNER, JOANNE JOHNSON, director, consultant, secondary school educator; b. Muncie, Ind., Sept. 9, 1952; d. Donal Russel and Lois Vivian (Hicks) Johnson; m. Lary William Troutner, May 17, 1975. BA in Media and English, Purdue U., West Lafayette, 1974; MS in Edn., Purdue U., 1976. Media spls. Lafayette Sch. Corp., Ind., 1974-77, 81-83, computer resource tchr., 1983-84; media splst. Tippecanoe Sch. Corp., Lafayette, 1984-85, ednl. support, 1985-87, coord. instrl. support, 1988-94, dir. tech. and media, 1994—2007; tchr. English Minot Pub. Schs., ND, 1978-79, media specialist, 1979-81; instr. freshman honors seminar Purdue U., Coll. Tech., 2006—08. Vis. prof. continuing edn. U. SC, Columbia, 1983, U. ND; instr. Purdue U., West Lafayette, pres.'s coun. adv. bd. mem., 2008—, convocations adv. bd. mem., 2008—; software selector Elem. Sch. Libr. Collection. Author: The Media Specialist, The Microcomputer and the Curriculum, 1983, World Desk-Classroom Internet Guide, 1998, The Internet: A Curriculum Oriented Guide, 1998, Curriculum Oriented Guide 7th edit., 2009, 5th edit., 2007, 6th edit., 2008, Using the Internet and Technology to Strengthen Learning in English/Language Arts and Social Studies, 1999, Integrating Technology and the Internet into English and Social Studies Classroom, 2002, 2006, Strengthen Your Classroom with Technology, 2004, 2007, Best of the Best Web Sites, 2007, Best of the Best Web Sites, 2nd edit., 2008—09; materials rev. columnist: Sch. Libr., Media Quar., computer literacy columnist: Jour. Computers Math. and Sci. Tchg., computer software columnist: Tchr. Libr., 1989—, internet columnist:, 1995—; editor: Ind. Computer Educators newsletter. Active Greater Lafayette Leadership Acad. Alumni Group, 1983—; bd. dirs. Lafayette Family Svc. Agy., 1987—89; treas., v.p. Greater Lafayette Mortar Bd. Alumni Group, 2006—; bd. dirs. Tippecanoe County Pub. Libr., trustee, 1990—2000, pres., 1994—95; mem. dean's adv. coun. Sch.-Coll. Edn. Purdue U., 2003—; bd. dirs. Lafayette Adult Reading Acad., 2008—. Recipient Disting. Alumni award, Purdue U. Sch. Edn., 2003. Mem.: ASCD, ALA, Internat. Soc. Tech. Educators, Ind. Computer Educators (bd. dirs. 1986—92, pres. 1990—91), Internat. Coun. Computers in Edn. (interactive video spl. interest group newsletter editor 1986—87), Am. Assn. Sch. Librs. (sec. 1983—84, 2d v.p. 1985—86), Ind. Assn. Media Educators (chmn. computer divns. 1982—84), Phi Beta Kappa, Phi Delta Kappa (v.p. programs 1987—88, v.p. memberships 1988—89, pres. 1989—90), Kappa Delta Gamma. Home: 4001 Penny Packers Mill Rd Lafayette IN 47909-3557 Office Phone: 765-477-7306. Business E-Mail: troutner@mindspring.com.

TROUTT, WILLIAM EARL, academic administrator; b. Bolivar, Tenn., June 13, 1949; s. Jack and Earline (Shearin) Troutt; m. Carole Pearson, Nov. 26, 1970; children: Carole Anne, Jack. BA, Union U., Jackson, Tenn., 1971; MA, U. Louisville, 1972; PhD, Vanderbilt U., 1978. Admissions counselor Union U., 1973—75; asst. dir. Tenn. Higher Edn. Commn., Nashville, 1975—78; sr. assoc. McManis Assocs. Inc., Washington, 1978—80; exec. v.p. Belmont Coll., Nashville, 1981—82, pres., 1982—99, Rhodes Coll., Memphis, 1999—. Chmn. Am. Coun. on Edn. Chmn. Jacob Javits Fellowship Bd., Nat. Assn. Ind. Colls. & Univs., Nat. Commn. Cost Higher Edn. Named one of Nation's Most Effective Coll. Pres., Exxon Found. Study, 1986. Mem.: So. Assn. Colls. and Schs. (commnr. commn. colls. 1986—), Tenn. Ind. Colls. Fund (sec.-treas. 1986—), Tenn. Coun. Pvt. Colls. (chmn.), Nashville Area C. of C. (bd. dirs. 1985—), Rotary. Office: Office of the Pres 2000 N Pkwy Memphis TN 38112-1690*

TROVER, ELLEN LLOYD, lawyer, rancher, art dealer; b. Richmond, Va., Nov. 23, 1947; d. Robert Van Buren and Hazel (Urban) Lloyd; m. Denis William Trover, June 12, 1971; 1 dau., Florence Emma. AB, Vassar Coll., 1969; JD, Coll. William and Mary, 1972. Asst. editor Bancroft-Whitney, San Francisco, 1973-74; owner Ellen Lloyd Trover Atty.-at-Law, Thousand Oaks, Calif., 1974-82; ptnr. Trover & Fisher,

Thousand Oaks, Calif., 1982-89; pvt. practice law Thousand Oaks, Calif., 1989-98; mng. ptnr. The Lloyd-Trover Partnership d/b/a Rancho Ellenita & the Gallery at Rancho Ellenita, Calif., 1998—. Editor: Handbooks of State Chronologies, 1972. Trustee Conejo Future Found., Thousand Oaks, 1978—91, trustee emeritus, 1992—, vice chmn., 1982—84, chmn., 1984—88; pres. Zonta Club Conejo Valley Area, 1978—79; trustee Hydro Help for the Handicapped, 1980—85, Atlantis Found., 1994—; pres. Vista Santa Rosa Assn., 2001—; mem. governing bd. Coachella Valley Mountains Conservancy, 2007—; dir. Riverside County Farm Bur., 2005—; trustee Coachella Valley Mosquito & Vector Control Dist., 2009—. Mem. State Bar Calif., Va. State Bar, Phi Alpha Delta. Democrat. Presbyterian. Home: PO Box 297 Coachella CA 92236 Office Phone: 760-398-8326. Personal E-mail: ranchoellenita@gmail.com.

TROWBRIDGE, JOHN PARKS, physician; b. Dinuba, Calif., Mar. 24, 1947; s. John Parks and Claire Dovie (Noroian) Trowbridge; children: Sharla Tyann, Lyndi Kendyll. AB in Biol. Scis., Stanford U., 1970; MD, Case Western Res. U., 1976; postgrad., Fla. Inst. Tech., 1983-85. Diplomate in Preventive Medicine, Am. Bd. Clin. Metal Toxicology (examiner for bd. 1987—, protocol coun. 1996-98), Am. Bd. Biologic Reconstructive Therapy (examiner for bd. 1994-97), Am. Bd. Anti-Aging Medicine, 1998, Nat. Bd. Med. Examiners. Intern in gen. surgery Mt. Zion Hosp. & Med. Ctr., San Francisco, 1976-77; resident in urol. surgery U. Tex. Health Sci. Ctr., Houston, 1977-78; pvt. med. practice (health recovery unit, pain relief unit, life long health unit) Life Celebrating Health Assn., Humble, Tex., 1978—. Chief corp. med. cons. Tex. Internat. Airlines, Houston, 1981-83; immunology rsch. asst. Stanford U. Med. Ctr., Stanford, Calif., 1967-70; night lab. supr. Kaiser Found. Hosp., Redwood City, Calif., 1971-72; advisor to bd. dirs. Am. Inst. Med. Preventics, Laguna Hills, Calif., 1988-90; sr. aviation med. examiner FAA, 1983-96; invited guest lectr. Taipei Med. U., Taiwan, 2005; lectr., cons. in field. Co-author: The Yeast Syndrome, 1986, Chelation Therapy, 1985, 2d edit., 1990, Yeast Related Illnesses, 1987, Do What You Want to Do, 1996, The Rumble in Humble: Heart Surgery and All That Jazz, 1997, Living Well Past 50: Rejuvenate Your Heart and Arteries, 1998; contbr. Challenging Orthodoxy: America's Top Medical Preventives Speak Out, 1991; weekly radio show host (KBME-AM): Feeling Better...Naturally, with Dr. John Trowbridge, Houston, 2003-2004; contbr. articles to profl. jours. Adv. bd. Tex. Chamber Orchestra, Houston, 1979-80; med. dir. Humble unit Am. Cancer Soc., 1980-81; med. cons. personal fitness program Lake Houston YMCA, 1981-83. Nat. Merit scholar, 1965-69, Calif. State scholar, 1967-69; recipient Resolution of Commendation house of dels., 1974 Am. Podiatry Assn., Spl. Profl. Svc. Citation bd. trustees, 1976, Am. Podiatry Students Assn. Fellow: Am. Coll. Advancement in Medicine (v.p. 1987—89, pres.-elect 1989—91), Am. Soc. for Laser Medicine and Surgery; mem.: AMA, Internat. Acad. Biol. Dentistry and Medicine (bd. dir. 2007—), Advanced Med. Edn. and Svcs. Physician Assn., Am. Bd. Clin. Metal Toxicology (bd. dirs. 2006—, sec. bd. dirs. 2007—, sec. 2007—), Neuro Cranial Restructuring Drs. Assn., Neuro Cranial Reconstruction Rsch. Inst. (pres. 2003-) (pres. 2002—03, rsch. inst. pres. 2003—), Am. Soc. Life Ext. Physicians (founding), Am. Assn. Nutritional Cons., Am. Acad. Thermology, Nat. Health Fedn. (chmn. bd. govs. 1989), Am. Soc. Gen. Laser Surgery, Am. Acad. Environ. Medicine, Legal and Edn. Found. Am. Preventive Med. Assn. (bd. dirs. 1996—99, charter), Am. Preventive Medicine Assn. (bd. dirs. 1992—99, charter), Am. Coll. Preventive Medicine, Internat. Coll. Integrative Medicine (editor newsletter 2000—01, bd. dirs. 2000—, sec. 2002—), N.Am. Cervicogenic Headache Soc., Royal Soc. Medicine (London, sect. orthop.), Soc. for Orthomolecular Medicine, Great Lakes Coll. Clin. Medicine (bd. dirs. 1991—95, med. rsch. instnl. rev. bd., v.p. 1993—94, pres. 1994—95, program chair Advanced Tng. Seminar in Heavy Metal Toxicology 1996—98, bd. dirs. 1999—2000), Huxley Inst. for Biosocial Rsch., Inst. Health Freedom (bd. dirs. 1997—2001), Arthritis Trust Am. (med. adv. bd. 1995—), Internat. Acad. Bariatric Medicine, NY Acad. Scis., Aerospace Med. Assn., Houston Acad. Medicine, Harris County Med. Soc., Tex. Med. Assn., Am. Acad. Anti-Aging Medicine, Assn. Am. Physicians and Surgeons. Avocations: private piloting, computer applications. Office: Life Celebrating Health Assn 9816 Memorial Blvd Ste 205 Humble TX 77338-4206 Home Phone: 281-540-2255; Office Phone: 281-540-2329. Personal E-mail: jptlch@earthlink.net. Business E-Mail: info@healthchoicesnow.com.

TROWBRIDGE, THOMAS, JR., mortgage company executive; b. Troy, NY, June 28, 1938; s. of Thomas and Elberta (Wood) T.; m. Delinda Bryan, July 3, 1965; children: Elisabeth Tacy, Wendy Bryan. BA, Yale U., 1960; MBA, Harvard U., 1965. V.p. James W. Rouse & Co., Balt., 1965-66, Washington, 1966-68, San Francisco, 1968-73, 76-78; pres. Rouse Investing Co., Columbia, Md., 1973-76, Trowbridge, Kieselhorst & Co., San Francisco, 1978-97, CEO, chmn., 1997-2000; ret., 2000. Bd. dirs. Columbia Assn., 1975-76; trustee, treas. The Head-Royce Sch., Oakland, Calif., 1980-84; trustee, pres. Gen. Alumni Assn. Phillips Exeter Acad., 1984-90. Lt. USNR, 1960-63. Mem. SAR, Urban Land Inst., Calif. Mortgage Bankers Assn. (bd. dirs. 1991-98, pres. 1996-97), Mortgage Bankers Assn. Am. (bd. govs. 1993-2000), Naval War Coll. Found., 2000-, Olympic Club, Pacific Union Club, Orinda Country Club (bd. dirs. 2005-09, pres. 2008), LOPC Found. (trustee 2005-09, pres 2009). Republican. Presbyterian. Avocation: golf. Home: 4 Ridge Ln Orinda CA 94563-1318

TROXELL, LUCY DAVIS, management consultant; b. Cambridge, Mass., Apr. 25, 1932; d. Ellsworth and Mildred (Enneking) Davis; m. Charles DeGroat Bader, June 13, 1952 (div. Aug. 1974); children: Christie P. Walker, Mary Bader Montgomery, Charles D. Bader Jr., David Bradford Bader; m. Victor Daniel Shirer Troxell, Aug. 1974. BA, Smith Coll., Northampton, Mass., 1952; grad., Inst. Paralegal Training, Phila. Cert. employee benefit specialist, assoc. in risk mgmt. Paralegal O'Melveny & Myers, LA, 1976-77; acct. exec. Olanie Hurst & Hemrich, LA, 1977-78; asst. to trustee Oxford Ins. Mgmt., LA, 1978-80; dir. corp. svcs., asst. corp. sec. Consolidated Elec. Distbrs., Inc., Westlake Village, Calif., 1980-93; pres. MONMAK LDT, Westlake Village, 1993—. Vol. Friends of the Westlake Village Libr., 2000—, ARC; bd.dirs. Friends of the West Lake Village, 2004—, v.p., 2006, pres., 2007; clk. St. Mathew's Parish Vestry, Pacific Palisades, Calif., 1988, sr. warden, 1989—90; lic. lay eucharistic min. Episcopal Ch.; sustaining bd. dirs. Jr. League, Hartford, Conn., 1952—58, LA, 1952—60; bd. dirs. Smith Coll. Club, Hartford, 1952—58, Nat. Charity League, LA, 1964—68, Theatre Palisades, 1960—74; bd. dirs., treas. HOA Lakeshore Cmty. Assn., 1999—2002, v.p., 2005—. Sophia Smith scholar. Fellow: Risk and Ins. Mgmt. Soc. (program chmn. L.A. chpt. 1985—86), Internat. Soc. Cert. Employee Benefit Specialists (bd. dirs., sec., treas. 1988—89, pres. 1989—90, edn. chmn. L.A. chpt. 1986—88). Republican. Avocations: finance, acting, music, art. Home: 450 Puerto Del Mar Pacific Palisades CA 90272-4233 Office: MONMAK LDT 32001 Viewlake Ln Westlake Village CA 91361

TROXELL, MARY THERESA (TERRY TROXELL), geriatrics services professional; b. Syracuse, NY, Aug. 29, 1950; d. Henry and Mary (McDermott) Flynn; 1 child, Melissa Lee. BSN, U. Pa., 1971. Cert. quality improvement specialsit; cert. gerontol. nurse specialist; cert. case mgr. Supr. neonatal ICU St. Joe's, Syracuse, 1976-79; dir. nursing Hillhaven, Phoenix, 1979-81; quality assurance nurse long term care Maricopa County, Phoenix, 1981-83; dir. nursing Desert Haven Nursing Home, Phoenix, 1983-84; team leader, surveyor health care licensure State of Ariz., Phoenix, 1985-87, program mgr. long term care licensure and certification, 1987-89, program mgr. enforcement and compliance licensure and cert., 1989-91; dir. profl. svcs. Unison Healthcare, Phoenix, 1991-94; v.p. clin. ops. SunQuest Healthcare, Phoenix, 1994-96; sr. v.p. clin. and ancillary ops. Unison Healthcare, 1996-98, exec. v.p. opers., 1998—99, CEO, 1999—2000; COO, v.p. health ops., chief complaince officer Fountains Retirement Cmtys., Tucson, 2000—. Author: (manuals) Licensure Procedures, 1990, Quality Improvement, Restorative Nursing: A Key to Quality, 1992, Director of Nursing Manual, 1996, Clinical Operations Series, 1997. Developer legislation for adult care homes, health care licensure laws State of Ariz., 1990. Mem.: Am. Health Care (v.p. region XI), Gerontol. Nurses Assn., Quality Improvement Nurses Assn., Am. Health Care Assn. (nat. facilitu stds. com. 1992—96, nat. multifacility com. 1993—96, LTC nurses coun. 1995, nat. quality com. 1996—97, regional v.p. region XI adv. com., regional v.p. and bd. dirs.), Ariz. Health Care Assn. (chair legis. com. 1992—94, chair devel./revision nursing facility laws 1992—94). Home: 10224 E Sahavro Scottsdale AZ 85260-6331 Office: Fountains Retirement Cmtys 2020 W Rudasell Rd Tucson AZ 85704

TROXLER, WILLIE THOMASENE, retired elementary school educator; b. Raleigh, NC, Sept. 3, 1925; d. Charles Gilmer Cates and Addie Gaye Long; m. Roger Vernon Troxler, Mar. 18, 1950; children: Bonnie Lynn, Teri. BA, St. Mary's Jr. Coll., Raleigh, 1945; BA in Journalism, U. NC, Chapel Hill, 1947; MA in Lang. Arts, U. NC, Charlotte, 1976. Reporter State Advt. Divsn., NC, 1947—48; assoc. editor Carolina Road Builders Trade Mag., NC, 1948—50; tchr. elem. sch. Salisbury City Schs., NC, 1961—78. Exhibited in group shows at Page Walker Arts and History Ctr., Cary, NC, 1999, Rowan Regional Hosp., Salisbury, 1999, Davidson County Mus. Art, Lexington, NC, 1999, one-woman shows include Depot Visual Arts Ctr., Mooresville, NC, 1997, Rowan Pub. Libr., Salisbury, 1982, Chatham County Hosp., Asheboro, NC, 1982, Salisbury Pub. Sch. Supplementary Ctr. Art Gallery, 1982, Creative Art Gallery, Salisbury, NC, 2009; contbr. poetry to mags. Active Salisbury Symphony Guild; 2d v.p. Rep. Women, Salisbury. Recipient 1st pl. Collage, Rowan County Silver Arts, 2005, 2d pl., Rowan County Art Group, 2005, 1st Pl. Mem. Choice award, Rowan County Art Show, 2005, Gold medal visual divsn., Silver Arts, 2007. Mem.: Stanley County Art Guild, Davidson County Art Guild (Judges Commendation 1986, Pres. Choice Stuffer Myer's Meml. award 1995, Third pl. 1998, First pl. 2002), Mooresville Art Guild, Waterworks Visual Art Works, Watercolor Soc. N.C. (Fifth pl. Fall Show 1997, Merit award Spring Show 1999), Carolina Artist (past pres.). Home: 131 Richmond Rd Salisbury NC 28144-2847

TROY, ANTHONY FRANCIS, lawyer; b. Hartford, Conn., Apr. 16, 1941; children: Anthony John, Francis Gerard II, Silvio Connor A. BA in Govt., St. Michael's Coll., Vt., 1963; LLB, U. Richmond, Richmond, Va., 1966. Bar: Va. 1966, D.C. 1972, U.S. Dist. Ct. (ea. dist.) Va. 1966, U.S. Dist. Ct. (we. dist.) Va. 1967, U.S. Ct. Appeals (4th cir.) 1967, U.S. Supreme Ct. 1969. Asst. atty. gen. Commonwealth of Va., Richmond, 1966-72, atty. gen., 1977-78; assoc. Colson & Shapiro, Washington, 1972-74; ptnr., govtl. law, spl. investigations Troutman, Sanders LLP, Richmond, 1978—, and mem., exec. com. Conard Mattox Disting. adj. prof. chair law U. Richmond Law Sch. Contbr. articles to profl. jours. Trustee Sci. Mus. Va. Fellow Am. Law Found., Va. Law Found. Office: Troutman Sanders LLP 1001 Haxall Point Richmond VA 23219 Home Phone: 804-513-7200; Office Phone: 804-697-1318. Office Fax: 804-698-5162. Business E-Mail: tony.troy@troutmansanders.com.

TROY, DANIEL E., pharmaceutical executive, lawyer; b. Queens, NY, Feb. 7, 1960; s. Bernard A. and Elaine (Gerson) T.; m. Cheryl Suzanne Horowitz, June 16, 1991; children: Aaron Lev, Leora Jordana, Ariel Miriam. BS in Indsl. Labor Rels., Cornell U., 1980; JD, Columbia U., 1983. Bar: NY, DC, US Ct. Appeals (2d cir.), US Ct. Appeals (3rd cir.), US Ct. Appeals (4th cir.), US Ct. Appeals (5th cir.), US Ct. Appeals (6th cir.), US Ct. Appeals (7th cir.), US Ct. Appeals (8th cir.), US Ct. Appeals (9th cir.), US Ct. Appeals (10th cir.), US Ct. Appeals (11th cir.), US Ct. Appeals (DC cir.), US Supreme Ct. Law clk. to Hon. Robert H. Bork US Ct. Appeals (DC Cir.), Washington, 1983-84; assoc. Paul, Weiss, Rifkind, Wharton & Garrison, NYC, 1984-87; atty.-advisor Office of Legal Counsel US Dept. Justice, Washington, 1987—89; ptnr. Wiley Rein & Fielding, Washington, 1990—2001; assoc. scholar Am. Enterprise Inst., Washington, 1996; assoc. gen. counsel, chief counsel US FDA, Washington, 2001—04; ptnr. Sidley Austin Brown & Wood LLP, Washington, 2005—08; sr. v.p., gen. counsel GlaxoSmithKline PLC, 2008—. Lectr. in law Columbia Law Sch., 1987; spkr. in the field. Author: (book) Retroactive Legislation, 1998; contbr. numerous articles to profl. jours.; guest appearances on (TV and Radio) CNBC Bull Session and Inside Bus., CNN Burden of Proof, FOX News and News Talk, CBS Radio Gill Gross Show, (radio) Judy Javis Show. Chmn. telecomms. com. Federalist Soc., Washington, 1996-2000; bd. dirs. Ohr Kodesh Congregation, Chevy Chase, Md., 1995-96; spl. asst. Friends of Giuliani, 1989. Mem. ABA (coun. mem. adminstrv. law sect. 1997-2000). Republican. Jewish.

TROY, NANCY J., art history educator; BA in Art magna cum laude with honors, Wesleyan U., 1974; MA, Yale U., 1976, PhD, 1979. Gallery asst. Waddington Galleries, London, 1973; rsch. asst. Soc. Anonyme Collection, Yale U., New Haven, 1975, tchg. asst. history of art dept., 1975-76; asst. prof. dept. history of art Johns Hopkins U., Balt., 1979-83; asst. prof. dept. art history Northwestern U., Evanston, Ill., 1983-85, assoc. prof., 1985-92, prof., 1992-93, chmn. dept., 1990-92; vis. prof. UCLA, 1994; vis. prof. art history U. So. Calif., LA, 1994-95, prof., 1995—, chmn. dept., 1997—. Scholar-in-residence Getty Rsch. Inst. for History Art and Humanities, L.A., 1993-96, organizer Work in Progress lecture series, 1993-98; series co-editor Histories, Culturs, Contexts, Reaktion Book, London; curatorial coord., spl. cons. to Ilya Bolotowsky Retrospective, Solomon R. Guggenheim Mus., N.Y.C., summers 1972-74; asst. to curator French paintings Nat. Gallery Art, Washington, summer 1975, bd. advisors Ctr. for Advanced Study in VisualArts, 1999-2002; guest curator Yale U. Art Gallery, 1979; mem. fine arts accessions com. and com. on collections Balt. Mus. Art, 1979-82; cons. De Stijl: 1917-1931, Visions of Utopia exhbn. Walker Art Ctr., Mpls., Washington, The Netherlands, 1982; cons. amplifying art program Art Inst. Chgo., 1984-85; mem. vis. com. Harvard U. Art Mus., Cambridge, Mass., 1992-98; lectr., chmn., moderator numerous symposia, 1980—; numerous invited lectures, 1975—, including U. Brighton, Eng., U. London, Middlexex U., London, Royal Coll. Art, London, U. Toronto, Mt. Holyoke Coll., Barnard Coll., Columbia U., Newcomb Coll., Tulane U., Los Angeles County Mus. Art, Art Inst. Chgo., Terra Mus. Am. Art, Chgo., N.C. Mus. Art, Raleigh, McGill U., Montreal, Vassar Coll; mus. projects peer rev. panelist NEH, 1991; peer reviewer Woodrow Wilson Ctr., Washington, 1994, 96; external reviewer dept. art history U. Mich., 1987; bd. dirs. Nat. Com. for History Art, 1998—; peer reviewer for promotion and tenure Boston U., Lake Forest Coll., Middlesex U., Occidental Coll., U. Mo., Columbia, U. Va., 1996-98. Author: The De Stijl Environment, 1983, Modernism and the Decorative Arts in France: Art Nouveau to Le Corbusier, 1991, (exhbn. catalog) Mondrian and Neo-Plasticism in America, 1979; editor-in-chief The Art Bull., 1994-97; editor: (with Eve Blau) Architecture and Cubism, 1997; series co-editor Histories, Cultures, Contexts; mem. editl. bd. Art Bull., 1993—, Grey Room, 1998—; contbr. articles and book revs. to profl. jours., including Decorative Arts Soc. Jour., Design Issues, Art Bull., October, Archithese, Arts mag., Portfolio, Design Book Rev., chpts. to books. Mem. Md. Coun. on Arts, 1981-82; trustee Wesleyan U., 1994-97. Recipient Disting. Alumna award Wesleyan U., 1991, postdoctoral tchg. award Lilly Endowment, 1985, Andrew W. Mellon professorship for advanced study in the visual arts Nat. Gallery Art (declined), 2000-02; Fulbright-Hays grantee, The Netherlands, 1977-78, travel grantee Kress Found., summer 1976, spring 1977, grantee Am. Coun. Learned Soc., summers 1981, 91, 98-99; grantee Graham Found. for Advanced Studies in Fine Arts, 1982, publ. grantee, 1989; grantee NEH, 1982-83, Am. Philos. Soc., 1986, Inst. for Advanced Study Sch. Hist. Studies, 1987, Getty Rsch. Inst. for History Art and Humanities, 1989-90, Zumberge Faculty Rsch. and Innovation Fund, U. So. Calif., 1998-99, Guggenheim Found., 1998-99; AT&T rsch. fellow Northwestern U., 1992-93. Mem. Coll. Art Assn. Am. (nominating com. 1990, bd. dirs. 1992-97, ann. meeting local host com. L.A. 1998-99), Soc. Archtl. Historian (sec. Chgo. chpt. 1984-85, peer reviewer Jour. 1996), Nat. Com. for the History of Art (bd. dirs.), Sterling and Francine Clark Art Inst. (mem. fellowship com.). Office: U So Calif Dept Art History University Park 104 Watt MC 0293 Los Angeles CA 90089-0001

TROY, ROBERT SWEENEY, SR., lawyer; b. Quincy, Mass., Aug. 13, 1949; s. Robert F. and Winifred (Sweeney) T.; m. Sabina Greene, Oct. 12, 1985; children: Robert Sweeney Jr., Michael Francis, Matthew Thomas. AB, Georgetown U., 1971; JD, Boston Coll., 1974. Bar: Mass. 1974, Fla. 1976, U.S. Dist. Ct. Mass. 1976, U.S. Ct. Appeals 1977, U.S. Ct. Mil. Appeals 1982, U.S. Supreme Ct. 1990. Asst. dist. atty. Cape and Islands, Mass., 1974-76; counsel Town of Bourne, Mass., 1978—. Counsel Town of Duxbury, Mass., 1986—, Barnstable County, 1992—. Mem. Mass. Bar Assn. (bd. dels. 1977-80), Barnstable County Bar Assn., Plymouth County Bar Assn., Town Counsel Assn. Home: 150 Nichols Rd Cohasset MA 02025 Office: 90 Route 6A Sandwich MA 02563-5301 Office Phone: 508-888-5700.

TROYER, ALICE KAY, library and computer skills educator; d. Robert Emanuel and Ethel Mae Troyer. BA in English, Eureka Coll., Ill., 1979; MLIS, U. Ill., Urbana-Champaign, 1980, MEd in Elem. Edn., 1990. Mem. Rebecca Caudill Evaluators Com., State Level, Ill., 2006—. Contbr. articles to profl. jours. (Larry Stilgebauer Hon. awards, 2003, Barat Edn. Found. fellowship, 2004). Mem.: Ill. Sch. Libr. Media Assn., Ill. Computing Educators. Office Fax: 847-438-2528.

TROYER, ALVAH FORREST, agricultural products executive, horticulturist; b. LaFontaine, Ind., May 30, 1929; s. Alvah Forrest and Lottie (Waggoner) T.; m. Joyce Ann Wigner, Sept. 22, 1950; children: Anne, Barbara, Catherine, Daniel (dec.). BS, Purdue U., 1954; MS, U. Ill., 1956; PhD, U. Minn., 1964. Rsch. assoc. U. Ill., Urbana, 1955-56; rsch. fellow U. Minn., St. Paul, 1956-58; rsch. sta. mgr. Pioneer Hi-Bred Internat., Inc., Mankato, Minn., 1958-65, rsch. coord., 1965-77; dir. R & D, Pfizer Genetics, St. Louis, 1977-81, v.p. and dir. R & D, 1981-82; v.p. R&D, DEKALB Plant Genetics, 1982-93; cons. Hybrid Seed divsn. Cargill, Mpls., 1993-98; adj. prof. crop sci. dept. U. Ill., 1998—. Rschr. corn breeding, econ. botany, crop physiology, increasing genetic diversity, recent corn evolution. Contbr. articles to numerous publs.; developer of popular corn inbred lines and hybrids. Master sgt. U.S. Army, 1951-53, Korea. Recipient Nat. Coun. Comml. Plant Breeders Genetics and Plant Breeding award, 1992, Outstanding Achievement award U. Minn., 1998, nat. award for agrl. excellence Nat. Agrl. Mktg. Assn., 1999, Siehl prize 2009. Fellow AAAS, Am. Soc. Agronomy, Crop Sci. Soc. Am.; mem. Am. Genetic Assn., Genetic Soc. Am., N.Y. Acad. Scis., CAST, VFW, Masons, Sigma Xi, Gamma Sigma Delta (Award of Merit 1996), Alpha Zeta, Lambda Chi Alpha, Gamma Alpha. Methodist. Home: 611 Joanne Ln Dekalb IL 60115 Business E-Mail: atroyer@uiuc.edu.

TROYER, LEROY SETH, architect; b. Middlebury, Ind., Nov. 23, 1937; s. Seth and Nancy (Miller) T.; m. Phyllis Eigsti, May 24, 1958; children: Terry, Ronald, Donald. BArch, U. Notre Dame, 1971. Founder, pres. LeRoy Troyer and Assocs., South Bend, Ind., 1971; chmn. Troyer Group, Inc. (formerly LeRoy Troyer and Assocs.), Mishawaka, Ind., 1988—. With Lead Devel., Inc.; founder, v.p., sec., Am. Countryside, LLC, Midwest Farmers Market, LLC. Author numerous documents; contbr. numerous papers and articles to publs. Chair Environic Found. Internat., 1970-; bd. dirs. Habitat for Humanity Internat. Americus, Ga., 1987-93, global leadership coun., 2003-07; bd. dirs. Coun. of Christian Colls. and Univs., 1991-96, Habitat for Humanity St. Joseph County, Ind., 1992-99, 2001-, Bethel Coll. 1988-97, 2003-09, bd. chair 2005-08, Evangelicals for Social Action, Wynnewood, Pa., 1997-2003, exec. com., trustee Fourth Freedom Forum Internat., 1996—, vice-chmn., 2005—; chmn., Miracle of Nazareth Internat. Found., trustee 2000-; bd. trustee Fuller Ctr. Housing, Americus, Ga., 2005—, chmn. 2006—. Recipient numerous local, state and nat. awards and honors. Fellow AIA (practice mgmt. com., chmn. 1983-84), Ind. Soc. Archs., Mennonite Econ. Devel. Assn. Internat. (chmn. bd., 1987-91). Avocations: photography, travel, reading, art, woodworking. Home: 1442 Deerfield Ct South Bend IN 46614-6429 Office: The Troyer Group Inc 550 Union St Mishawaka IN 46544-2346 Office Phone: 574-259-9976.

TROYER, THOMAS ALFRED, lawyer; b. Omaha, Aug. 15, 1933; s. Robert Raymond and Dorothy (Darlow) T.; m. Sally Jean Brown, June 28, 1958; children: Kenneth D., Robert C., Virginia D., Thomas C. BA, Harvard U., 1955; JD, U. Mich., 1958. Bar: Colo. 1958, U.S. Ct. Appeals (D.C. cir.) 1967. Assoc. Holme, Roberts, Moore & Owen, Denver, 1958—61; USAF, Denver, 1961-62; trial atty. U.S. Dept. Justice, Washington, 1962-64; legal staff Asst. Sec. Treasury for Tax Policy, Washington, 1964-66; assoc. tax legis. counsel U.S. Dept. Treasury, Washington, 1966-67; mem. Caplin & Drysdale, Washington, 1967—. Pres. Stern Fund, NYC, 1985—86; bd. dirs. Children's Def. Fund, Washington, 1977—, Mineral Policy Ctr., Washington, 1988—2002; trustee Natural Resources Def. Coun., NYC, 1977—2005, Carnegie Corp., NYC, 1983—91, Cmty. Found. Nat. Capital Region, 1992—2000; chair Ctr. for Lobbying in Pub. Interest, Washington. Contbr. numerous articles to profl. jours. Bd. dirs. Common Cause, Washington, 1980-83; mem. Treasury Adv. Commn. on Pvt. Philanthropy and Pub. Needs, Washington, 1976-77; mem. adv. group to Commr. Internal Rev., Washington, 1978-80; mem. com. of visitors U. Mich. Law Sch., Ann Arbor, 1982—; mem. IRS Commr.'s Exempt Orgn. Adv. Group, Washington, 1987-90. Fellow Am. Bar Found., Am. Coll. Tax Counsel; mem. ABA (vice chmn. govt. rels. tax sect. 1989-91, commn. on homelessness and poverty 1992-94), Coun. for Excellence in Govt., Am. Law Inst. Democrat. Home: 5514 Cedar Pkwy Chevy Chase MD 20815-3444 Office: Caplin & Drysdale Chartered 1 Thomas Cir NW Ste 1100 Washington DC 20005-5894 Office Phone: 202-862-5025. Business E-Mail: tat@capdale.com.

TROYER, VERNE, actor; b. Sturgis, Mich., Jan. 1, 1969; m. Genevieve Gallen, Jan. 22, 2004 (div.). Actor: (films) Pinocchio's Revenge, 1996, Men in Black, 1997, Wishmaster, 1997, My Giant, 1998, Fear and Loathing in Las Vegas, 1998, The Wacky Adventures of Ronald McDonald: Scared Silly, 1998; Mighty Joe Young, 1998, Here Lies Lonely, 1999, Instinct, 1999, Austin Powers: The Spy Who Shagged Me, 1999 (Best On-Screen Duo (with Mike Myers) MTV Movie Awards, 2000), Bit Players, 2000, How the Grinch Stole Christmas, 2000, Bubble Boy, 2001, Harry Potter and the Sorcerer's Stone, 2001, Run for the Money, 2002, Austin Powers in Goldmember, 2002, The Love Guru, 2008; (TV series) Jack of All Trades, 2000—01; (TV films) Karroll's Christmas, 2004. Office: c/o Elena Bertagnolli Fonolli Mgmt Inc 11218 Osborne St Lake View Terrace CA 91342

TROZZOLO, ANTHONY MARION, chemistry professor; b. Chgo., Jan. 11, 1930; s. Pasquale and Francesca (Vercillo) T.; m. Doris C. Stoffregen, Oct. 8, 1955; children: Thomas, Susan, Patricia, Michael, Lisa, Laura. BS, Ill. Inst. Tech., 1950; MS, U. Chgo., 1957, PhD, 1960. Asst. chemist Chgo. Midway Labs., 1952-53; assoc. chemist Armour Rsch. Found., Chgo., 1953-56; tech. staff Bell Labs., Murray Hill, NJ, 1959-75; Charles L. Huisking prof. chemistry U. Notre Dame, 1975-92, Charles L. Huisking prof. emeritus, 1992—; asst. dean U. Notre Dame Coll. Sci., 1993-98; P.C. Reilly lectr. U. Notre Dame, 1972, Hesburgh Alumni lectr., 1986, Disting. lectr. sci., 1986. Vis. prof. Columbia U., N.Y.C., 1971, U. Colo., 1981, Katholieke U. Leuven, Belgium, 1983, Max Planck Inst. für Strahlenchemie, Mülheim/Ruhr, Fed. Republic Germany, 1990; vis. lectr. Academia Sinica, 1984, 85; Phillips lectr. U. Okla., 1971; C.L. Brown lectr. Rutgers U., 1975; Sigma Xi lectr. Bowling Green U., 1976, Abbott Labs., 1978; M. Faraday lectr. No. Ill. U., 1976; F.O. Butler lectr. S.D. State U., 1978; Chevron lectr. U. Nev., Reno, 1983; J. Crano lectr. U. Akron, 2000; plenary lectr. various internat. confs.; founder, chmn. Gordon Conf. on Organic Photochemistry, 1964; trustee Gordon Rsch. Confs., 1988-92; cons. in field. Assoc. editor Jour. Am. Chem. Soc., 1975-76; editor Chem. Revs., 1977-84; editorial adv. bd. Accounts of Chem. Rsch., 1977-85; cons. editor Encyclopedia of Science and Technology, 1982-92; contbr. articles to profl. jours.; patentee in field. Fellow AEC, 1951, NSF, 1957-59; named Hon. Citizen of Castrolibero, Italy, 1997; recipient Pietro Bucci prize U. Calabria/Italian Chem. Soc., 1997, UNICO Nat. Marconi Sci. award, 2008, Disting. Alumnus award Ill. Inst. Tech., 2009. Fellow: AAAS (life), Inter-Am. Photochem. Soc., N.Y. Acad. Scis. (chmn. chem. scis. sect. 1969—70, Halpern award in photochemistry 1980), Am. Inst. Chemists (Student award 1950); mem.: Am. Chem. Soc. (lectr., Tex. lectr. 1975, Disting. Svc. award St. Joseph Valley sect. 1979, Coronado lectr. 1980, Pacific Coast lectr. 1981, Coronado lectr. 1993, N.Y. State lectr. 1993, Hoosier lectr. 1995, Ozark lectr. 1995, Rocky Mountain lectr. 1996, Coronado lectr. 1998, Osage lectr. 1998, Rocky Mountain lectr. 2002, SE Tex. lectr. 1996), Sigma Xi. Roman Catholic. Home: 53419 Hansel Ln South Bend IN 46637-5248 Office: U Notre Dame Dept Chemistry-Biochemistry Notre Dame IN 46556-5670 Office Phone: 574-631-5768. Business E-Mail: trozzolo.4@nd.edu.

TRPIS, MILAN, vector biologist, educator; b. Mojsova Lucka, Slovakia, Dec. 20, 1930; came to U.S., 1971, naturalized, 1977; s. Gaspar and Anna (Sevcikova) T.; m. Ludmila Tonkovic, Dec. 15, 1956; children: Martin, Peter, Katarina. MS, Comenius U., Bratislava, 1956; PhD, Charles U., Prague, 1960. Research asst. Slovak Acad. Sci., Bratislava, 1953-56, sci. asst., 1956-60, scientist, 1960-62, ind. scientist, 1962-69; ecologist-entomologist East Africa-Aedes Rsch. Unit WHO, Dar es Salaam, Tanzania, 1969-71; asst. faculty fellow dept. biology U. Notre Dame, 1971-73, assoc. faculty fellow, 1973-74; assoc. prof. med. entomology Johns Hopkins U. Sch. Hygiene and Pub. Health, 1974-78, prof., 1978—, dir. labs. med. entomology. Med. entomology, rsch. assoc. U. Ill., Urbana, 1966-67, Can. Dept. Agr., Lethbridge, Alta., 1967-68; dir. Biol. Rsch. Inst. Am., 1971-79; external dir. rsch. Liberiran Inst. Biomed. Rsch., 1981-89; dir. AID project on transmission of river blindness in areas of Liberia, Sierra Leone, and Cote d'Ivoire; dir. WHO rsch. grant; tech. adv. com. AID Vector Biology and Control Project, 1986-91; dir. Johns Hopkins U./Fed. U. Tech. Akure Onchocerciasis Project in Nigeria, 1991-94, Johns Hopkins U./Orgn. Coordination et de Cooperation pour la Lutte les Grandes Endemies-Pierre Richet Inst. Onchocerciasis Project, Bouakè, Ivory Coast, 1993-96; dir. Johns Hopkins U./Pierre Richet Inst./ORSTOM onchocerciasis project in Ivory Coast, 1993-96; prof.,advisor doctoral students, USA, Can., Africa, Asia, Cen. Am., 1979—. Editor: Jour. Biologia, 1956-71, Jour. Entomol. Problems, 1960-72; zool. sect.: Jour. Biol. Works, 1960-71; contbr. articles to profl. jours. Dir. WHO project on prophylactic drugs for river blindness, Liberia, 1985-87. Recipient Slovak Acad. Sci., 1st prize for research project. Mem. AAUP, AAAS, Am. Inst. Biol. Sci., Am. Mosquito Control Assn., Am. Soc. Parasitologists, Helminthol. Soc. Washington, Am. Soc. Tropical Medicine and Hygiene, Entomol. Soc. Am., Am. Genetic Assn., Soc. of Vector Ecology, N.Y. Acad. Scis., Johns Hopkins U. Tropical Medicine Club, Smithsonian Assocs., Royal Soc. Tropical Medicine and Hygiene, Royal Entomol. Soc. of London, Sigma Xi, Delta Omega (Alpha chpt.). Home: 1504 Ivy Hill Rd Cockeysville MD 21030-1418 Office: Johns Hopkins U 615 N Wolfe St Baltimore MD 21205-2103 Office Phone: 410-955-3475. Business E-Mail: mtrpis@jhsph.edu.

TRUANT, ALLAN L., medical educator, laboratory scientist, health science administrator; b. July 6, 1950; BS, U. Mich., 1971; PhD, U. Oreg., 1977. Fellow Ctrs. for Disease Control, Atlanta, 1977-79; assoc. prof., assoc. dir. Univ. Tex. Med. Br., Galveston, 1979-85; prof., dir. clin. microbiology, immunology and virology lab. Temple U. Hosp. and Sch. Medicine, Phila., 1985—. Inspector Coll. Am. Pathologists, Chgo., 1983—; mem. exam. bd. Am. Bd. Bioanalysis, St. Louis, 1996—. Editor: Manual of Commercial Methods in Clinical Microbiology, 2002. Recipient Rorer award for manuscript excellence Am. Coll. Gastroenterology, 1983. Office: Temple U Hosp and Sch Medicine Broad Ontario Sts Philadelphia PA 19140 Office Phone: 215-707-3415. Business E-Mail: allan.truant@tuhs.temple.edu.

TRUBECK, WILLIAM LEWIS, former diversified financial services company executive; b. Chgo., July 5, 1946; s. G. William and Priscilla Jeanne (Nelson) T.; m. Judith Carpenter Williams, Aug. 17, 1969; 1 child, William Andrew. BA, Monmouth Coll., Ill., 1968; MBA, U. Conn., 1976. Fin. sales mgr. Ford Motor Credit Co., Walnut Creek, Calif. and Stamford, Conn., 1971—74; v.p. Aetna Bus. Credit (Barclays Am. Corp.), East Hartford, Conn., 1974—81; corp. v.p., treas. Armco Inc., Middletown, Ohio and Parsippany, NJ, 1981—88; exec. v.p. fin. and chief fin. officer Northwest Airlines Inc. and NWA Inc., St. Paul, 1989—91; chief fin. and adminstrv. officer White & Case, NYC, 1991—93; sr. v.p., CFO, Honeywell, Mpls., 1993—94; sr. v.p., CFO SPX Corp., Muskegon, Mich., 1997; sr. v.p., CFO, pres. Latin Am. ops. Internat. Multifoods, Mpls., 1997—2000; exec. v.p., CFO Waste Mgmt., Houston, 2000—04, H&R Block Inc., Kans. City, Mo., 2004—07. Bd. dirs. Yellow Roadway, Dynegy, Ceridian Corp. Served to capt. C.E., U.S. Army, 1968-70, Vietnam. Mem. Fin. Execs. Inst., Blue Key, Pi Gamma Mu. Republican. Presbyterian. Avocations: golf, tennis.

TRUBY, BETSY KIRBY, artist, illustrator, photographer; b. Winchester, Va., Nov. 8, 1926; d. Thomas Gomery and Nellie Gray Kirby; m. Frank Keeler Truby, Sept. 4, 1948; children: Thomas Lee, Scott R., Susan Alida. Student, Hiram Coll., 1946—48, Cleve. Sch. Art, 1949, N.Mex. Tech., 1951—54, U. N.Mex., 1960. Asst. dir. Yucca Art Gallery, Old Town Albuquerque, 1970—71. One-woman shows include Hiram Coll., 1987, exhibitions include N.Mex. State Mus., 1964—68, Nat. Art Show, Lawton, Okla., 1974, Nat. League Am. Pen Woman MID-AD-Congress, Phoenix, 1975, Indian Child Pastel, Bardean Gallery, N.Mex., 2004 (2d pl., 2004), commd. by, Congressman Albert G Simms, 1964, Christmas card, Easter Seal Soc., 1969, Cystic Fibrosis Found., N.Mex., 1976—77, PBS TV show, The Creative Process, 1983; jury (show) Nat. Pastel Soc., New Mexico, 2007, (one-woman shows) Gallery South Western Art Old Town, 1978, (two women show) Internat. League Am. Pen Women, Las Vegas, Nev., 1982. Recipient Outstanding Quality recognition, America's Nat. Park, 2007. Mem.: Pastel Soc. N.Mex. (charter mem.), Nat. League Am. Pen Women (v.p. Yucca br. 1978—79, photographer Nat. Biennal Conv. Washington 1992, photographer Yucca br. 1992—, 1st pl. painting 1974, Best of Show 2003, 1st pl. 2003, 2d pl. in pastel State Show, Socorro, N.Mex. 2005), Yucca Art Gallery (charter mem.). Presbyterian. Avocations: boating, swimming. Home and Office: 6609 Loftus Ave NE Albuquerque NM 87109 Office Phone: 505-884-8459.

TRUCANO, MICHAEL, lawyer; b. Washington, May 28, 1945; s. Peter Joseph and Fern Margaret (Bauer) T.; m. Doreen E. Struck, 1969; children: Michael, David. BA, Carleton Coll., 1967; JD, NYU, 1970. Assoc. Dorsey & Whitney, Mpls., 1970-75, ptnr., 1976—2004, head of office, 2000—03, of counsel, 2005—. Office: Dorsey & Whitney LLP Ste 1500 50 S 6th St Minneapolis MN 55402-1498 Office Phone: 612-340-2673. Business E-Mail: trucano.mike@dorsey.com.

TRUCKSIS, THERESA A., retired library director; b. Hubbard, Ohio, Sept. 1, 1924; d. Peter and Carmella (DiSilverio) Pagliasotti; m. Robert C. Trucksis, May 29, 1948 (dec. May 1980); children: M. Laura, Anne, Michele, Patricia, David, Robert, Claire, Peter; m. Philip P. Hickey, Oct. 19, 1985 (dec. May 1993). BS in Edn., Youngstown Coll., 1945; postgrad., Youngstown State U., 1968-71; MLS, Kent State U., 1972. Psychometrist Youngstown (Ohio) Coll., 1946-49; instr. ltd. svc. Youngstown State U., 1968-71; libr. Pub. Libr. Youngstown & Mahoning County, Youngstown, 1972-73, asst. dept. head, 1973-74, asst. dir., 1985-89, dir., 1989-97, NOLA Regional Libr. System, Youngstown, 1974-85. Contbr. articles to profl. jours. Mem. bd. Hubbard Sch. Dist., 1980-85. Mem. ALA, Ohio Libr. Assn. (bd. dirs. 1979-81), Pub. Libr. Assn. Address: 133 Viola Ave Hubbard OH 44425-2062

TRUDEL, MARC J., botanist, educator; PhD, Cornell U. Prof. plant physiology and horticulture Laval U., 1969—2003, prof. emeritus, 2005—, former dean sch. agrl. and food scis., 1983-91, former dir. gen. continuing edn., 1992-97, v.p. devel., 1997—2003. Office: 19 Rue de Liege Saint Jean Sur Richelieu PQ Canada J3B 8N4 E-mail: marc.trudel@plg.ulaval.ca.

TRUDEL, TINA M., psychologist, educator; d. Jean-Claude and Constance Mae Trudel; m. Dorothy Palanza, Oct. 21, 2008. PhD, Fordham U., Bronx, NY, 1996. Cert. psychologist NH, 1998, Va., 2006, RI, 2006. Asst. dir. psychology UCP Nassau County, Roosevelt, NY, 1989—92; rehab. program dir. neuropsychology Highwatch Rehab. Ctr., Effingham Falls, NH, 1992—95; v.p. clin. svcs. Lakeview Neurorehab. Ctr., Effingham, NH, 1996—2005, clin. dir., 1996—99; sr. ptnr. NE Evaluation Specialists, PLLC, Dover, NH, 2001—; site dir., prin. investigator Def. & Vets. Brain Injury Ctr., Va. Neuro Care, Charlottesville, 2005—; pres., chief oper. officer Lakeview Healthcare Sys., Inc., Austin, Tex., 2005—; asst. prof. clin. psychiatry U. Va. Sch. Medicine, Charlottesville, 2006—; gallerist, dir. Colorfield Studios, Provincetown, Mass., 2008—. Chairperson NH Brain & Spinal Cord Injury Adv. Coun., Concord, 1997—2006; chairperson, brain injury long term issues task force Am. Congress Rehab. Medicine, Indpls., 1998—; bd. govs. Am. Acad. Cert. Brain Injury Specialists, Reston, Va., 2001—06; adv. bd. mem. Birchtree Ctr. Children, Autism, Portsmouth, NH, 2002—07; chairperson, ethics com. Brain Injury Assn. America, Reston, Va., 2006—; bd. dirs. NH Spinal Cord Injury Assoc., Salem, NH, 2003—07, N.Am. Brain Injury Soc., Alexandria, Va., 2006—, Blast Injury Inst., Alexandria, Va., 2007—. Contbr. articles to numerous sci. jours. Recipient Ellen Hayes award, Brain Injury Assn. NH, 2003, Founder's award, Brain Injury Assn. America, 2008. Fellow: Am. Bd. Disability Analysts, Am. Coll. Forensic Medicine & Forensic Examiners; mem.: APA, Am. Coll. Rehab. Medicine. Avocations: music, gardening, art, travel. Home: 83 Franklin St Provincetown MA 02657 Office: Lakeview Healthcare Sys Inc 2011 W Rutland Austin TX 78758 Office Fax: 603-297-5684. Personal E-mail: tina.trudel@gmail.com. Business E-Mail: ttrudel@lakeview.ws.

TRUDNAK, STEPHEN JOSEPH, landscape architect; b. Nanticoke, Pa., Feb. 25, 1947; s. Stephen Adam and Marcella (Levulis) T.; m. Arden Batchelder Weill, Sept. 6, 1980. BS in Landscape Arch., Pa. State U., 1970. Jr. landscape arch. Kling Partnership, Phila., 1970-72; mem. landscape arch. firm Keith French Assocs., Washington, 1972-73; head dept. landscape arch. Linganore Ctr. Design, Frederick, Md., 1973-74, Toups and Loiederman, Rockville, Md., 1974-76; project landscape arch. Kaiser Transit Group, So. Calif. Rapid Transit Dist., Dade County Transit Improvement Program, Metro Rail Transit Cons.; v.p. Harry Weese & Assocs., Ltd., Miami, Fla., 1976-84; v.p. landscape arch. Canin Assocs., Orlando, Fla., 1984-87; dir. planning and design Bonita Bay Properties, Inc., Bonita Springs, Fla., 1987-91; prin. Stephen J. Trudnak, P.A. Landscape Arch. and Land Planning, 1991—2006; sr. landscape arch. Johnson Engring., Inc., Ft. Myers, Fla., 2006—. Bd. dirs., v.p. Koreshan State Hist. Site, 1989—94; mem. "not for profit" com. Bonita Springs Cmty. Redevel. Agy., 1994—97; v.p. Bonita Springs Mainstreet Program, 1996, 2000, pres., 1997—98; bd. dirs. Bonita Springs YMCA, 1999—2005, mem. exec. com., 2000—03, chair facilities design task force, 2000—04; del. for Congressman Porter Goss Congl. Small Bus. Summit, 1998, 2000; del. representing Fla. state rep. Carol Green Fla. Small Bus. Summit, 1999. Recipient Alumni Achievement award, Pa. State U., Dept. Landscape Architecture, 2003. Fellow Am. Soc. Landscape Archs. (pres. Fla. chpt. 1983, chpt. adv. bd. 1984-85, elections task force 1986, publs. task force 1987, trustee 1987-89, membership task force, chmn. 1989-90, nat. v.p. chpt. and mem. svcs. 1992-94, non-dues revenue task force 1994-95, ASLA On-Line com. 1997-2005, chair 1999, specifications task force 1998-99, Fla. chpt. ann. vice chair 2009), Nat. Xeriscape Coun. (Fla. steering com.), Nat. Speleol. Soc. SCARAB; mem. Bonita Springs C. of C. (chair beautification com. 1991-92, 94-95, chair awards task force 2000, bd. dirs. 1995-2000, v.p. edn. divsn. 1996-98, vice chmn. cmty. devel. divsn. 1998-99, chmn. tech. com. 2003-04, Affiliate of Yr. 1997, Citizen of Yr. 1999, Charter Class Leadership Bonita Grad. 2000). Office: 2122 Johnson St Fort Myers FL 33901 Office Phone: 239-334-0046. E-mail: strudnak@johnsoneng.com.

TRUE, LAWRENCE, pathologist, educator; s. Edward R. and Alice Richardson True; m. Linda Brown, Aug. 0, 1974. BA, Harvard Coll., Cambridge, Mass., 1967; MD, Tulane U., New Orleans, 1971. Cert. anatomic pathologist Nat. Bd. Med. Specialties. Staff physician US Peace Corps., Kathmandu, Nepal, 1973—75; intern, gen. surgery, med. sch. U. Wash., Seattle, 1971—72, prof., 1991—. Resident pathology U. Colo., Denver, 1976—80; asst. prof. U. Chgo., 1982—84; assoc. prof. Yale U., New Haven, 1984—90. Author: (reference textbook) Diagnostic Immunohistopathology; contbr. scientific papers. Bd. mem. True-Brown Found., Seattle, 2000—. Grant, NIH, 1991—. Mem.: Prods APC (chair coord. coun. 1997—98), Am. Soc. Clin. Pathology (coun. anatomic pathology 1992—96), US-Can. Acad. Pathology (edn. com. mem. 2002—06). Office: Univ Washington 1959 NE Pacific St Box 35-6100 Seattle WA 98195-6100

TRUE, RAYMOND STEPHEN, editor, writer; b. Lowell, Mass., June 29, 1934; s. Sylvester Raymond and Madeline Rose (Farrell) T.; m. Doreen Therese Jambrosek. BA, U. Chgo., 1961, MBA, 1968, postgrad., 1968—69. Commd. 2nd lt. USAF, 1953, advanced through grades to col., 1980; master navigator USAFR, Chgo., 1957—77, dir. ops. Milw., 1977—80, base civil engr., 1980—87, chief planning analyst, 1987—89; regional cons. U.S. Bur. Census, 1970—71; owner Classic Comics Libr., 1990—. Fire marshall Milwaukee County, 1980-87, chmn. membership Res. Officers Assn., Wash. 1975-78. Editor Classics Newsletter, 1971-75; pub. The Platform Rep. Newsmag., 2004—. Precinct committeeman, Libertyville, Ill., 2000—; pres. ROA chpt. 61, 2000-02; chmn. Rep. Assembly Lake County, 2001-; mem. steering com. Ill. Ctr. Rights Coalition, 2004-05, 2007—; mem. Ill. Rep. State Platform Com., 2004; mem. bd. dirs. Project Marriage Initiative. Mem. Air Force Assn., Grad. Sch. Bus. Exec. Coun. U. Chgo. Roman Catholic. Avocations: stamp collecting/philately, antique books, videophile. Address: 839 Terre Dr Libertyville IL 60048-1649 Office Phone: 847-367-5231. Office Fax: 847-367-5497. E-mail: raymon8844@aol.com.

TRUE, ROY JOE, lawyer; b. Shreveport, La., Feb. 20, 1938; s. Collins B. and Lula Mae (Cady) T.; m. Patsy Jean Hudsmith, Aug. 29, 1959; children: Andrea Alane, Alyssa Anne, Ashley Alisbeth. Student, Centenary Coll., 1957; BS, Tex. Christian U., 1961; LLB, So. Meth. U., 1963, postgrad., 1968—69. Bar: Tex. 1963. Pvt. practice, Dallas, 1963—; pres. Invesco Internat. Corp., 1969-70, True & Shackelford and predecessors, 1975—2002; of counsel Shackelford, Melton & McKinley, 2002—. Bus. adviser, counselor Mickey Mantle, 1969-95; dir. The Mickey Mantle Found., 1995-98. Mem. editl. bd. Southwestern Law Jour., 1962-63. With AUS, 1956. Mem. ABA, Dallas Bar Assn., Tex. Assn. Bank Counsel, Phi Alpha Delta. Home: 5837 St Marks Circle Dallas TX 75230 Office: 3333 Lee Pkwy 10th Fl Dallas TX 75219 Home Phone: 214-369-0606; Office Phone: 214-780-1400. Business E-Mail: rtrue@shacklaw.net.

TRUE, WILLIAM L. (BILL TRUE), retired real estate company executive; b. Apr. 1954; s. Cecil True; m. Ruth True. Chmn., CEO Gull Industries, Inc., Seattle. Co-founder Western Bridge Gallery, Seattle; mem. adv. bd. Seattle Arts & Lectures; bd. dirs. Pike Place Market Found., Seattle; mem. Betty Bowen com. Seattle Art Mus., 2004. Named one of Top 200 Collectors, ARTnews mag., 2003—08. Avocation: Collector of Contemporary art. Home: 832 37th Ave E Seattle WA 98112-4326

TRUEBLOOD, HARRY ALBERT, JR., oil industry executive; b. Wichita Falls, Tex., Aug. 28, 1925; s. Harry A. and Marguerite (Barnhart) T.; m. Lucile Bernard, Jan. 22, 1953; children: Katherine T. Astin, John B. Student, Tex. A&M Coll., 1942; BS in Petroleum Engring., U. Tex., 1948. Petroleum engr. Cal. Co., 1948-51; chief engr. McDermott & Barnhart Co., Colo., Tex., 1951-52; cons. petroleum and geol. engr. Denver, 1952-55; pres. Colo. Western Exploration Inc., Denver, 1955-58, Consol. Oil & Gas, Inc., 1958-88, chmn. bd., CEO, 1969-88, Princeville Devel. Corp., 1979-87, pres., 1984-86; chmn. bd., CEO Columbus Energy Corp., 1983-2000; pres., mng. mem. HAT Resources LLC, 2001—. Chmn. bd., CEO, Princeville Airways, Inc., 1979-87; chmn. bd. dirs., pres. CEC Resources, Ltd., 1984-99; bd. dirs. NYTIS Exploration Co. With USNR, 1944-46, ensign, 1949-55. Named to Rocky Mountain Oil and Gas Hall of Fame, 2004. Mem. Soc. Petroleum Engrs. (legion of honor), Am. Petroleum Inst. (25 Yr. Club), World Pres. Orgn., Chief Execs. Orgn. (bd. dirs.), Ind. Petroleum Assn. Am. (exec. com.); Ind. Pet Assn. Mountain States (recipient Wildcatter 2006 award for Lifetime Achievement), 2007 Disting. Grad. Sch. Engring. award, U. Tex., Austin, Disting. Eagle Scout. award, Boy Scouts Am., Natural Gas Supply Assn. (exec. com.), Cherry Hills Country Club, One Hundred Club. Roman Catholic. Office: 1720 S Bellaire St Ste 912 Denver CO 80222-4334 Home: 9039 Ranch River Cir Highlands Ranch CO 80126 Office Phone: 303-300-6792. E-mail: hajtrueblood@yahoo.com.

TRUELOVE, TERRY N., nursing educator; b. LA, Jan. 4, 1962; s. Jesse G. and Jessica Truelove; m. Lori L. Kotarba, Mar. 27, 1997; 1 child, Justin D. ADN, Seattle Ctrl. CC, 1990; BSN, Oakland U., Rochester Hills, Mich., 1997; MS in Nursing, U. Phoenix, San Bernardino, Calif., 2000. Nurse clin. cardiac William Beaumont Hosp., Royal Oak, Mich., 1993—97; nurse educator St. Mary Med. Ctr., Dept. Critical Care, Apple Valley, Calif., 1997—2001, staff nurse, 1997—2002; asst. prof. nursing Victor Valley Coll., Victorville, Calif., 2001—, asst. dir., nursing, 2005—08, chair, nursing dept., 2005—. Musician (composer, performer): (performance) Abbadon. Recipient award, Outstanding Minority Nursing Students, 1990. Independent. Avocations: music, history, sports, art. Office: Victor Valley Coll 18422 Bear Valley Rd Victorville CA 92395 E-mail: truelovet@vvc.edu.

TRUEMAN, CARL RUSSELL, theology studies educator; b. Dudley, West Midlands, Eng., Mar. 18, 1967; s. John Harry and Jean Margaret Trueman; m. Catriona Crichton, July 26, 1990; children: John Daniel, Peter Conor. MA, U. Cambridge, Eng., 1988; PhD, U. Aberdeen, Scotland, 1991. Lectr. theology U. Nottingham, Nottinghamshire, England, 1993—98; sr. lectr. ch. history U. Aberdeen; assoc. prof. hist. theology Westminster Theol. Sem., Glenside, Pa., 2001—05, prof. hist. theology and ch. history, 2005—, v.p. academic affairs and academic dean, 2007—. Office: Westminster Theological Seminary 2960 Ch Rd Glenside PA 19038

TRUEMPER, JOHN JAMES, JR., retired architect; b. Helena, Ark., June 18, 1924; s. John James and Mary Ann (Jacob) T.; m. Julia Clare Wood, Nov. 21, 1956; children: Zachary Wood, John James III, Ann Truemper Rogers. BS in Arch., U. Ill., 1950; DHL (hon.), Lyon Coll., 1995. With archtl. firm Cromwell, Truemper, Levy, Thompson, Woodsmall Inc. (and predecessors), Little Rock, 1950-94, v.p., 1972-74, pres., 1974-81, chmn. bd., 1980-89; ret., 1994. Mem. Ark. Bd. Architects, 1974-82, pres., 1980 Prin. works include Ark. system for edn. and tng. mentally retarded, 1956-78, Winrock Farm, Morrilton, Ark., 1953-58, Ark. State Parks, 1955-75, Ark. Power & Light Co., 1961-89, Lyon Coll., Batesville, 1983-94; author: A Century of Service, 1885-1985, 1985. Pres. Ark. Arts Ctr., 1979, chmn. bd., 1980; mem. Little Rock Bldg. Code Bd. Appeals, 1961-86, chmn., 1971-86; mem. Ark. Hist. Preservtion Rev. Bd., 1987-99; bd. dirs. Little Rock Met. YMCA, 1975-84; pres.Ctrl. YMCA; mem. Friends of Libr. Bd., U. Ark., Little Rock, 1989-99, pres. 1995-97; bd. dirs. Greater Little Rock C. of C.,

1986-88. With USAAF, 1943-46. Recipient Winthrop Rockefeller Meml. award Ark. Arts Center, 1980 Fellow: AIA (pres. Ark. chpt. 1968); mem.: Sigma Chi. Roman Catholic. Home: 6502 Cantrell Rd Little Rock AR 72207-4219

TRUESDALE, JOHN CUSHMAN, federal agency administrator, lawyer; b. Grand Rapids, Mich., July 17, 1921; s. John Cushman and Hazel (Christianson) T.; m. Karin A. Nelson, Feb. 10, 1957; children: John Cushman, Charles N., Margaret E., Andrew C. AB, Grinnell Coll., 1942; MS, Cornell U., 1948; JD, Georgetown U., 1972. Bar: Md. bar 1972, D.C. bar 1973. Field examiner NLRB, Buffalo and New Orleans, 1948-52, adminstrv. analyst Washington, 1952-57, assoc. exec. sec., 1963-68, dep. exec. sec., 1968-72, exec. sec., 1972-77, 81-94, mem., 1977-81, 94, 95, chmn., 1998-2001, labor arbitrator, 1996—98, 2001—; mem. Fgn. Svc. Grievance Bd., 1997—2003. Dir. info., dir. World Data Center/Rockets and Satellites, IGY, Nat. Acad. Scis., Washington, 1957-63 Editor-in-chief: How to Take a Case Before the NLRB, 1997-98, 2002--. With USCG, 1943—46. Recipient Presdl. award Pres. of U.S., 1988. Mem. ABA, Nat. Acad. Arbitrators, D.C. Bar Assn., Assn. Labor Rels. Agys. (pres. 1992-93). Democrat. Congregationalist. Personal E-mail: jctrue@aol.com.

TRUETT, HAROLD JOSEPH, III, (TIM), lawyer; b. Alameda, Calif., Feb. 13, 1946; s. Harold Joseph and Lois Lucille (Mellin) T.; 1 child, Harold Joseph IV; m. Anna V. Billante, Oct. 1, 1983 (dec. June 2000); 1 child, James S. Carstensen; m. Patricia Maynord, Mar. 5, 2002 (dec. Aug. 07, 2009). BA, U. San Francisco, 1968, JD, 1975. Bar: Calif. 1975, Hawaii 1987, US Dist. Ct. (ea., so., no., and cen. dists.) Calif. 1976, Hawaii 1987, US Ct. Appeals (9th cir.) 1980, US Supreme Ct. 1988, US Ct. Fed. Claims, 1995. Assoc. Hoberg, Finger et al, San Francisco, 1975-78, Bledsoe, Smith et al, San Francisco, 1979-80, Abramson & Bianco, San Francisco, 1980-83; mem. Ingram & Truett, San Rafael, 1983-90; prin. Winchell & Truett, San Francisco, 1991—. Lectr. in field. Bd. dirs. Shining Star Found. 1991—, pres., 2001-06, Marin County, Calif.; mem. Marin Dem. Coun., San Rafael, 1983-90, 2002. Lt., aviator USN, 1967-74. Mem. ABA, Hawaii Bar Assn., Calif. Bar Assn. (com. for adminstrn. of justice, conf. of dels.), San Francisco Bar Assn., San Francisco Trial Lawyers Assn., Lawyers Pilots Assn. Roman Catholic. Home: 48 Valley Rd San Anselmo CA 94960 Office Phone: 415-989-9001. Business E-Mail: tim@truettlaw.com.

TRUEX, DOROTHY ADINE, retired university administrator; b. Sedalia, Mo., Oct. 6, 1915; d. Chester Morrison and Madge (Nicholson) T AB, William Jewell Coll., 1936; MA, U. Mo., 1937; EdD, Columbia U., 1956. Asst. dean women N.W. Mo. State U., Maryville, 1939-43, dean women, 1943-45, Mercer U., Macon, Ga., 1945-47, U. Okla., Norman, 1947-69, assoc. prof., 1969-72, dir. rsch. and program devel., 1969-74, prof. edn., 1972-74, dir. grad. program in student pers. svcs., 1969-74; vice chancellor for student affairs U. Ark., Little Rock, 1974-83, alumni specialist, 1983-84, acad. adviser, 1984-87. Exec. bd. N. Cen. Assn. Schs. and Colls., 1977—83. Author: Rich Choices, 1994, A Visit to Spitesville, 1999, The 13th Bridesmaid, 1999, Carved in Stone, 2000, Full Circle, 2002, The Twenty Million Dollar Giveaway, 2001, A Left Handed Chord, 2003, Life with Cheryl, 2005. Mem. Nat. Assn. Women Deans, Adminstrs. and Counselors (pres. 1973-74), So. Coll. Pers. Assn. (pres. 1970), Okla. Coll. Pers. Assn. (pres. 1972-73), William Jewell Coll. Alumni Assn. (pres. 1970-73), Woman's City Club (pres. 2000-2001), Pi Beta Phi, Alpha Lambda Delta, Mortar Bd., Sigma Tau Delta, Cardinal Key, Gamma Alpha Chi, Kappa Delta Pi, Pi Lambda Theta, Alpha Psi Omega, Pi Gamma Mu, Delta Kappa Gamma, Phi Delta Kappa, Phi Kappa Phi. (nat. v.p. 1986-89) Avocation: writing. Home: 14300 Chenal Pkwy Apt 7422 Little Rock AR 72211-5819 Home Phone: 501-227-7989.

TRUINI PALOMBA, MARIA GIUSEPPINA, supreme court lawyer, judge; b. Borbona, Ri-Latium, Italy, Aug. 25, 1935; d. Costanzo and Ezia (Giorgi) Truini; m. Emilio Palomba, Jan. 11, 1964; children: Francesco Maria, Giovanna Palomba. Degree in Law, State U. Rome, 1960. Tchr. State High Sch., Rieti, Italy, 1955-84; local magistrate Rieti, Italy, 1974-86; judge Fiscal Commn., Rieti, Italy, 1974—, Fiscal Commn. Reg. Rome v.p., 1996—. Author: La Cucina Sabina, 1991; contbr. articles to profl. jours. Mem. drug Prevention Assn., L'Aquila, 1979—; hon. guard Nat. Inst. Royal Tombs of Pantheon, Rome, 1980—. Decorated Cavalier of the Merit of the Italian Rep., 1984, Lady of the Order of Chivalry of the Holy Sepulchre of Jerusalem, Grand Master Cardinal, 1990, Lady of the Sovereign and Military Order of the Temple of Jerusalem, 1998; mem. Italian Red cross, 1986—, patroness, 1978; vol. UNICEF. Mem. Nat. Civil Lawyers Union (dist. pres. Rieti, nat. councillor 1990—), Italian Women Jurists Assn. (dist. pres. Rieti and nat. councillor 1990—), Internat. Assn. of Lawyers, Eurojuris Internat. Geie, Italian Acad. Cooking (nat. cons. 1974, dist. del.), Italian Women's Mgmt. Assn., Italian Women's Nat. Coun., Amnesty Internat. Lawyers, Aeroclub (pres. 1992-93), Rotary (councillor 1994-95, pres., 1996-97, 2006-), v.p. FILDIS-IFUW, Rome, 2000—. Avocations: travel, cinema, theater, cooking, volleyball. Home and Office: A Gherardi 70 02100 Rieti Italy Office Phone: 39 746 203077. E-mail: studiolegale@palombatruini.it.

TRUITT, EDWARD RAY, performing arts educator, director; b. Riverside, Calif., Feb. 24, 1956; s. James Thomas and Marilyn Emily Truitt; children: Edward Ray III, David James. BFA in Theatre and Dance, U. Nebr., Lincoln, U. Nebr., Omaha, 1979; MS in Dance, U. Oreg., Eugene, 1996. Soloist Omaha Ballet Co., 1976—81; prin. soloist Santa Barbara Ballet Theatre, Calif., 1981—82, LA Classical Ballet Co., Long Beach, Calif., 1982—83; freelance dancer, choreographer LA, 1982—86; photographer, bus. mgr. Truitt Seeley Photography, Tacoma, 1986—96; grad. tchg. fellow U. Oreg., 1993—96; vis. lectr. Ballet and Co., 1998; ballat master, co-dir. Bringham Young U., Provo, Utah, 1998; lectr., dance Calif. State U., Fresno, Calif., 1998—2000; asst. prof., dance Southern Utah U., Cedar City, 2000—03; artistic dir. Lone Star Ballet Co., Amarillo, Tex., 2003—05; asst. prof. West Tex. A&M U., Canyon, Tex., 2003—, dir., dance, 2003—. Specialist peer rev. com. mem. Fulbright Program, 2006—. Dancer (films) Weekend Pass, (ballets) Energy Unbound, (performance) Carmina Burana, Sleeping Beauty, Romeo and Juliet; actor: (performance) Kiss of the Spider Woman, The Country Wife; dir.: Sarah's Dance; choreographer (performance ballets) K-Suite, The Nutcracker, (ballets) Kinetic Ties (1st Pl. for best Contemporary Ballet and 2nd for best choreography, 2005), Misguided Faith.:, performer associated with various popular shows. Named Tchr. of Yr., Fred Astaire Dance Studio, 1979; Grad. Tchg. fellowship, U. Oreg., 1993—95, Sr. Specialist grant, Fulbright Program, 2003. Mem.: Nat. Assn. Schs. Dance, Am. Coll. Dance Festival Assn., CORPS de Ballet Internat., Internat. Dance Coun., Phi Beta Delta. Office: W Texas A&M Univ WTAMU Box 60747 Canyon TX 79016 Personal E-mail: ertruitt@yahoo.com. Business E-Mail: etruitt@wtamu.edu.

TRUITT, GARY R., lawyer, insurance company executive; b. 1950; BA, U. Pitts.; JD, Duquesne U., Pitts. Sr. v.p., gen. counsel, corp. sec. Highmark Inc., Pitts. Office: Highmark Inc Ste 3112 120 5th Ave Pittsburgh PA 15222*

TRUITT, WILLIAM HARVEY, private school educator; b. Alton, Ill., May 27, 1935; s. Howard Earl and Mary Margaret (Haper) T.; m. Janetha Mitchell, Aug. 5, 1961; children: Joy Elizabeth, Janita Ann. BA, Principia Coll., 1957; MA, So. Ill. U., 1964. Headmaster Forman Schs., Litchfield, Conn.; prin. upper and lower sch. The Principia, St. Louis, headmaster; ret., 1998. Musician: The Worlds Greatest Love Songs, Sing Unto the Lord, A New Song. Mem. NASSP, Mo. Assn. Secondary Prins., St. Louis Ind. Sch. Heads, Mo. Ind. Schs. (pres. 1983-84), Am. Coun. for Am. Pvt. Edn. (v.p. 1983-84), North Cen. Accrediting Assn. (exec. bd. dirs. 1988-91). Office: 4002 Radcliffe Place Ct Wildwood MO 63025 Business E-Mail: bill@billtruitt.com.

TRUJILLO, EVELYN FRANQUIZ, language educator, consultant; d. Alejandro Franquiz and Teotista Valle; m. Juan Luis Trujillo, Nov. 28, 1978; children: Paula Maria, Albert John. MA in Spanish Am. Lit., Dept. Fgn. Langs.; PhD in Spanish Golden Lit., Fla. State U., Tallahassee, 1991. Assoc. prof., spanish Fla. A&M U., Tallahassee, 2002—, chairperson, 2005—08. Exam. cons. Dept. Bus. and Profl. Regulation, Tallahassee, 1997—; faculty cons. Coll. Bd. Advanced Placement Exam. Ednl. Testing Svc., Princeton, NY, 1998—; vol. tchr. Sr. Ctr., Tallahassee, 2005—; devel. com. mem., spanish exam. faculty assessment unit Excelsior Coll., Albany, NY, 2008—. Contbr. articles. Recipient Tchg. Incentive Program award, Fla. A&M U., 1995; named Tchr. of Yr. Mem.: Modern Langs. Assn., Sigma Delta (Advisor award 2005), Nat. Collegiate Hispanic Honor Soc. Independent. Roman Catholic. Achievements include spanish for professional health. Avocations: reading, travel, writing, music. Office: Fla A&M Univ Wanish Way SBI Unit 097 Tallahassee FL 32307

TRUJILLO, J. ROBERTO, virologist; b. Mexico City, July 14, 1963; s. Maria Guadalupe Martinez and Roberto Trujillo; m. Elaine B. Barbella, Nov. 19, 1988; children: Daniel Robert, Jacquelyn Elizabeth. BS summa cum laude, Inst. Art and Scis., Mex., 1980; MD summa cum laude, U. Autonomous State of Mex., 1988; PhD, Harvard U., Boston, 1995. Lic. surgeon Faculty of Medicine, State of Mex., Mex., 1988. Rsch. fellow Harvard U., Boston, 1989—95, rsch. assoc., 1996—98, rsch. assoc. in neurovirology, 1998—2002; sr. scientist fellow Nat. Inst. of Neurol. Disorders and Stroke, Bethesda, Md., 2002—05; chief lab. of neurovirology Inst. of Human Virology, UMBI, U. Md., Balt., 2005—, asst. prof. Baltimore, 2005—; adj. prof. U. Autonomous of Nuevo Leon, Monterrey, Mexico, 2002—. Pres., founder Pan-Am. Soc. for NeuroVirology, Boston, 2000—; NIH reviewer Nat. Inst. of Allergy and Infectious Diseases, Bethesda, Md., 2005; dir. rsch. virology and neuroscience Inst. of Human Virology, UMBI, U. Md., Baltimore, 2005—; com. mem. of faculty and administrs. Harvard Sch. of Pub. Health, Boston, 2003—; instr. Harvard Coll., Cambridge, Mass., 1997—99; supr. Harvard Sch. of Pub. Health, Boston, 1997—2002; sci. advisor U. Autonomous of Nuevo Leon, Monterrey, Mexico, 1998—; prof. advisor biomed. sci. careers program, minority faculty devel. program Harvard Med. Sch., Boston, 2004—; internat. editl. bd. Revista Mexicana de Neurociencia, Mexico City, 2004; reviewer Office of AIDS Rsch., NIH, Bethesda, Md., 2002. Prodr.: (Pan.-Am. symposium programs) Scientific & Graphic Design; contbr. articles to profl. jours. Pres. Pan-Am. Soc. for NeuroVirology, Boston, 2000; mem. Faculty of Medicine, UANL, Monterrey, Nuevo Leon, Mexico, 2000—04; dir. Inst. of Human Virology of Mex., Monterrey, Nuevo Leon, 2005. Recipient A-H Robins of Mex. award, Med. Sch., State of Mex., 1981-83, Outstanding Young Presenter, Govt. of Mex. State, 1987, T32 Tng. award, NIH, 1989-1992, Helena Rubinstein award, Harvard Sch. of Pub. Health, 1996-1999, Key of the City, Acapulco, Mex., 1997, 2000, Group Merit award, Nat. Inst. of Neurol. Disorders and Stroke, 2004, Internat. Prof. award, U. Complutense, Spain, 2005, Key of the City, Chihuahua, Mex., 2005; grantee, NIH, 1999-2002, 2000; Med. scholarship, Med. Sch., State of Mex., 1983-1985, Internat. fellowship, Govt. of Mex. State, 1986-1987. Mem.: AAAS (assoc.), Internat. AIDS Soc., Pan-Am. Soc. Ft. NeuroVirology (pres. 2000), Mexican Acad. of Neurology (assoc.). Achievements include first to Molecular Mimicry in NeuroAIDS; Field of NeuroVirology; research in Mannose Receptor and AIDS Vaccine; design of HIV-1 Neurotropism Movie; development of Latin American Program of Virology; Pan-American Program of NeuroVirology. Avocations: black belt in martial arts, poetry, soccer player. Home: 2308 McCormick Rd Rockville MD 20850 Office: Inst of Human Virology UMBI U Md 725 West Lombard St Baltimore MD 21201 Office Fax: 410-706-1952; Home Fax: 410-706-7453. Business E-Mail: trujillo@umbi.umd.edu.

TRUJILLO, MARC, painter; b. Albuquerque, N.Mex., 1966; BA, U. Tex., Austin, 1991; MFA, Yale. U., 1994. Cartoonist Daily Texan, 1989; instr. drawing and painting Dougherty Arts Ctr., Austin, 1995, Santa Monica Coll., Calif., 2007; instr. printmaking and 2-D design Caldwell Coll., NJ, 1997—98; painting instr. Art Ctr. Coll. Design, Pasadena, Calif., 1999, 2003; drawing instr. Pierce Coll., Woodland Hills, Calif., 2000. Vis. artist U. Calif., Riverside, 2003. One-man shows include Tim Gleason Gallery, NYC, 1994, Contemporary Realist Gallery, San Francisco, 1994, 1995, Hackett-Freedman Gallery, San Francisco, 1997, 1998, 2007, Ruth Bachofner Gallery, Santa Monica, 2000, The Plainness of Plain Things, 2003, Minor Works, Santa Monica Coll., 2007, Drive-Thru, Hackett-Freedman Gallery, San Francisco, 2009, exhibited in group shows at Mexicarte, Austin, 1989, Flood Gallery, U. Tex., Austin, 1990, 10th Anniversary Exhbn., Hackett-Freedman Gallery, San Francisco, 1997, Speculative Terrain, Carnegie Art Mus., Oxnard, Calif., 2004, A View from Here, Judson Gallery Contemporary and Traditional Art, LA, 2008, Invitational Exhbn. Visual Art, AAAL, 2008, Recent Acquisition's, Long Beach Mus. Art, Calif.; composer, music performer: (films) El Mariachi, 1992. Recipient Rosenthal Family Found. award for Painting, AAAL, 2008; fellow Guggenheim Found., 2008. Office: c/o Shelly Farmer Dir Hirschl & Adler Modern 21 E 70th St New York NY 10021 Office Phone: 212-535-8810. Business E-Mail: marc_trujillo@aya.yale.edu.

TRUJILLO, NICHOLAS LEE, science educator; b. Pasadena, Calif., Dec. 14, 1955; s. William Lee and Claudia May Trujillo. PhD, U. Utah, Salt Lake City, 1983. Prof. Purdue U., West Lafayette, Ind., 1982—84, Southern Meth. U., Dallas, 1985—90, Sacramento State U. Author: (books) Cancer and Death: A Love Story in Two Voices, In Search of Naunny's Grave; actor: (film and video) Gory Bateson and The Ethnogs. Office: Sacramento State Univ 6000 J St Sacramento CA 95819 Personal E-mail: nictru@surewest.net.

TRUJILLO, ROBERT, musician; b. Santa Monica, Calif., Oct. 23, 1964; Former band mem. Suicidal Tendencies, Infectious Grooves, Ozzy Osbourne; band mem. Metallica, 2003—. Musician (bassist, also prodr.): (albums) (with Infectious Grooves) Plague That Makes Your Booty Move, 1991, Sarsippius' Ark, 1993; musician: (bassist) Groove Family Cyco, 1994, Mas Borracho, 2000, (with Suicidal Tendencies) Art of Rebellion, 1992, Suicidal for Life, 1994, (with Ozzy Osbourne) Down to Earth, 2001, Live at Budokan, 2002, Ozzman Cometh: Greatest Hits, 2002, (with Metallica) St. Anger, 2003 (Grammy award for Best Metal Performance, 2003), Death Magnetic, 2008 (Grammy award for Best Metal Performance, 2009), (others) Poder Latino, A.N.I.M.A.L., 1998; musician: (bassist, vocals, prodr., engr., mastering) Twelve Piece Band, Project Tru, 1999; musician: (bassist) Christmas That Almost Wasn't, Various Artists, 2001, Metallic Assault: A Tribute to Metallica, Various Artists, 2001, Problem Child, Cyco Mike, 2001, Revolution, Insolence, 2001, 1919 Eternal, Zakk Wylde's Black Label Society, 2001, Degradation Trip, Jerry Cantrell, Vol. 1 & Vol. 2, 2002, Different Shade of Green: Tribute to Green Day, Various Artists, 2003, Prison Cell, Wirebox, 2003, Immaculate Deception: A Tribute to the Music of Madon, 2004, Stairway to Rock (Not Just) A Led Zepplin Tribute, Various Artists, 2004; performer: (TV soundtrack) Osbourne Family Album, 2002. Named to Rock & Roll Hall of Fame (with Metallica), 2009. Office: Elektra Entertainment Group 75 Rockefeller Plaza New York NY 10019-7284*

TRUKSA, JAROSLAV, molecular biologist; b. Slany, Czech Republic, Apr. 30, 1978; s. Jaroslav Truksa and Blanka Truksova; m. Gabriela Jenikova, Sept. 17, 2007; 1 child, Vilem. PhD, Charles U., Prague, Czech Republic, 2001. Cert. sci. rschr. Calif., 2005. Rsch. fellow Czech Acad. Scis., Inst. Molecular Genetics, Dr. Jan Kovar's Lab., Prague, 2001—05; rsch. assoc., dept. molecular & exptl. medicine Scripps Rsch. Inst., Ernest Beutler's Lab., La Jolla, Calif., 2005—. Contbr. articles to sci. publs. Mem.: European Cell Proliferation Soc. Achievements include research in iron metabolism and apotheosis in cancer cells. Office: Scripps Rsch Inst 10550 N Torrey Pines Rd La Jolla CA 92037 Office Fax: 1-858-784-2083. Business E-Mail: jtruksa@gmail.com.

TRUMAN, RUTH DIXON, administrator, writer, lecturer, consultant; b. Ashland, Ky., Oct. 5, 1931; d. Rexford Maitland and Allene G. (Barber) Dixon; BS, Taylor U., 1952; MS, Calif. State U., 1967; PhD in Higher Edn., UCLA, 1978; m. Wallace Leroy Truman, June 5, 1952; children— Mark, Rebecca, Timothy, Nathan. Tchr. Atco (N.J.) Elem. Sch., 1954; tchr. home econs. Chatham (NJ) HS, 1955; counselor, instr. Citrus Coll., Azusa, Calif., 1967-70; dir. counseling Calif. Luth. Coll., Thousand Oaks, Calif., 1971-74; cons. Women's Ednl. Improvement Program, L.A., 1978-80; women's center facilitator Mt. San Antonio Coll., Walnut, Calif., 1981-82; free-lance writer, lectr., cons., 1982-83; coord. Cancer Mgmt. Network, U. So. Calif., 1983, assoc. dir. office cancer info. svc. Norris Comprehensive Cancer Ctr., 1984-85; dir. Cancer Info. Svc. Calif., U. So. Calif., 1985-86; dir. cert. programs Calif. State U., Fullerton, 1986-88, dir. extended edn., program svcs., 1988-90, acting assoc. v.p. extended edn., rsch., 1990-91, dir. program svcs, 1991-92, ret., 1992. Trustee Baker Home for Ret. Ministers, Rowland Heights, Calif., 1982-88; chmn. Com. Status and Role of Women, Calif. Pacific Conf., United Meth. Ch., 1980-82, mem. Bd. Higher Edn., 1983-84; mem. exec. com. Ventura County Council Drug Abuse, 1972-73. Mem. UCLA Doctoral Assn., Phi Delta Kappa. Democrat. Methodist. Author: No. Safe Coll., 2008, To Life! A Book of Poetry and Songs, 2008; Spaghetti From the Chandelier, 1984, Not Of This Fold, 2001; How To Be A Liberated Christian, 1981; Mission of the Church College, 1978; Underground Manual for Ministers' Wives and Other Bewildered Women, 1974. Home: 2259 Barbara Dr Camarillo CA 93012-9379

TRUMBLE, ANGUS A. G., curator, writer; b. Melbourne, Australia, Oct. 6, 1964; arrived in US, 2003; s. Peter Campbell and Helen Borthwick Trumble. BA in Fine Arts and History with honors, U. Melbourne, Australia, 1985, MA, 1992, NYU, NY, 1995. Registered Australian Soc. Indexers, 1993. Aide Office Gov. Victoria, Melbourne, 1987—91; resident tutor fine arts Trinity Coll., Melbourne, 1991—93; assoc. curator European art Art Gallery South Australia, Adelaide, 1996—98, curator European art, 1998—2003; curator paintings and sculpture Yale Ctr. Brit. Art, New Haven, 2003—. Mem. adv. bd. Art and Australia, Sydney, 1998—2002; pres. sr. common rm. Trinity Coll., Melbourne, 1991—92; cons. in field. Author: Bohemian London: Camden Town and Bloomsbury Paintings in Adelaide, 1997, Love and Death: Art in the Age of Queen Victoria, 2001, A Brief History of the Smile, 2004, The Finger, A Handbook, 2009. Recipient Barry Humphries Liberal Arts prize, Melbourne Grammar Sch., 1981, Young Australians award, Queen Elizabeth II Silver Jubilee Trust, 1992; scholar, Fulbright Found., 1994—95. Mem.: Yale Club, Athenæum, London. Episcopalian. Avocations: art, music, reading, perfume. Office: Yale Ctr British Art 1080 Chapel St New Haven CT 06520 Office Fax: 203-432-4538. Business E-Mail: angus.trumble@yale.edu.

TRUMBLE, PAUL, librarian; b. Malone, Ny, Nov. 7, 1957; s. Vernal and Marie Trumble; m. Robert Bauver, June 9, 2004. MLS, U. RI, Kingston, 1989. Head, serials Amherst Coll. Libr., Mass., 1989—. Mem. Human Rights Campaign. Mem.: ALA, NASIG. Liberal. Office: Amherst Coll Libr PO Box 5000 Rts 9 & 116 Amherst MA 01002-5000 Business E-Mail: pmtrumble@amherst.edu.

TRUMBORE, DAVID C., retired building materials executive. consultant; b. Allentown, Pa., Sept. 25, 1950; s. Frank Robert and Madeline Trumbore; m. Linda S. Lerch, Jan. 7, 1975; 1 child, Anna E. Jones. BSChemE, Lehigh U., Bethlehem, Pa., 1972; DSChemE, U. Wash., Seattle, 1979. Pilot plant engr. Firestone Plastics, Pottstown, Pa., 1972—74; advanced & sr. engr. Owens Corning, Granville, Ohio, 1979—84, mgr. asphalt process tech. Summit, Ill., 1984—94, mgr. asphalt tech. lab, 1994—2008, leader asphalt shingle recycling, 2009—. Office: Owens Corning Asphalt Tech Lab 7800 W 59th St Summit Argo IL 60501 Office Fax: 708-496-0976. Business E-Mail: dave.trumbore@owenscorning.com.

TRUMBULL, WILLIAM ERNEST, retired surgeon, educator; b. Portland, Oreg., Mar. 16, 1924; MD, NYU, 1951. Diplomate Am. Bd. Surgery, 1959. Intern L.A. County-Harbor, Torrance, Calif., 1951-52, surg. resident, 1953-58; staff St. John's Hosp.-Health Ctr., Santa Monica, Calif., 1958—88; asst. clin. prof. UCLA, 1960—. Fellow ACS; mem. Calif. Med. Assn., L.A. Surg. Soc., Pacific Coast Surg. Assn. Personal E-mail: wtrumbull@earthlink.net.

TRUMKA, RICHARD LOUIS, labor union administrator; b. Nemacolin, Pa., July 24, 1949; s. Frank Richard and Eola Elizabeth (Bertugli) T.; m. Barbara Vidovich, Nov. 27, 1982; 1 child, Richard L. BS, Pa. State U., 1971; JD, Villanova U., 1974. Bar: US Dist. Ct. (DC) 1974, US Ct. Appeals (3d, 4th and DC cirs.) 1975, US Supreme Ct. 1979. Atty. United Mine Workers America, Washington, 1974-77, 78-79, internat. exec. bd. Dist. 4 Masontown, Pa., 1981-82, internat. pres. Washington, 1982-95, pres. emeritus, 1995—; miner, operator Jones & Laughlin Steel, Nemacolin, Pa., 1977-78, 79-81; sec. treas. AFL-CIO, Washington, 1995—. Bd. dirs. Am. Coal Found.; mem. Nat. Coal Council, 1985; mem., President's Econ. Recovery Advisory Bd., 2009- Trustee Pa. State U. Recipient Labor Responsibility Award, Martin Luther King Ctr. for Nonviolent Social Change, 1990; Gompers-Murray-Meany, Massachusetts AFL-CIO; The Jewish Nat. Fund Tree of Life Award; Humanitarian Award, Sons of Italy Found, 2003 Democrat. Roman Catholic. Office: AFL-CIO 815 16th St NW Washington DC 20006-4145*

TRUMP, DONALD JOHN, real estate developer; b. NYC, 1946; s. Fred C. and Mary Trump; m. Ivana Zelnicek, Apr. 9, 1977 (div. 1991); children: Donald, Jr., Ivanka, Eric; m. Marla Maples, Dec. 30, 1993 (div.

June 8, 1999); 1 child, Tiffany Ariana; m. Melania Knauss, Jan. 22, 2005; 1 child, Barron William. BS in Economics, U. Pa., Wharton Sch. Fin., 1968. Chmn., CEO The Trump Orgn., LLC, NYC, 1980—; chmn. Trump Entertainment Resorts, Inc., Atlantic City, 2005—09; owner Trump Tower, Trump Parc, Trump Palace, Trump Bldg. at 40 Wall St., NYC, Trump Internat. Hotel and Tower, NYC, Chgo., Trump Casino Riverboat, Buffington Harbor, Ind., Trump 29 Casino, Palm Springs, Calif., W. Side Rail Yards devel. as Trump Pl., NYC, Mansion at Seven Springs, Bedford, NY, Mar-a-Lago Club, Palm Beach, Fla.; ptnr.-owner 610 Park Ave. and Trump World Tower, NYC, Trump Park Ave. (formerly Delmonico Hotel), Trump Grande Ocean Resort and Residences, Miami Beach, Fla., Trump Internat. Hotel and Twr., Chgo. Owner Trump Internat. Golf Club, Palm Beach, Trump Nat. Golf Club, Briarcliff Manor, NY, Ocean Trails Golf Course, Palos Verde, Calif., Trump Nat., Bedminster, NJ, Trump Mgmt. Group Modeling/Talent Agy.; pres. Trump Pageants LP, includes Miss Universe, Miss USA and Miss Teen USA.; launched line of men's suits, 2004; launched signature fragrance, Donald Trump The Fragrance, 04; announced launching of Trump University will consist of online courses, CD-ROMS, blogs, consulting services and Learning Annex-type seminars, 05. Author: Trump: The Way to the Top: The Best Real Estate Advice I Ever Received: 100 Top Experts Share Their Strategies, 2004, Trump: The Best Golf Advice I Ever Received, 2005; co-author (with Tony Schwartz): Trump: The Art of the Deal, 1987; (with Charles Leerhsen) Surviving at the Top (renamed Trump: The Art of Survival), 1990, (with Kate Bohner) Trump: The Art of the Comeback, 1997, (with Dave Shiflett) The America We Deserve, 2000, (with Meredith McIver) Think Like a Billionaire: Everything You Need to Know About Success, Real Estate, and Life, 2004, Think Like A Champion — An Informal Education in Business and Life, 2009, (with Robert T. Kiyosaki, Sharon Lechter & Meredith McIver) Why We Want You to Be Rich-Two Men-One Message, 2006, (with Bill Zanker) Think Big and Kick Butt—in Business and Life, 2007, host, exec. prodr. (TV series) The Apprentice, 2004—07, launched Trump World mag., 2004, host on syndicated radio program Trumped!, Premiere Radio Networks, 2004. Com. mem., Celebration of Nations Commemorating 50th Anniversary UN and UNICEF; Co-chmn. N.Y. Vietnam Vets. Meml. Fund; founding mem. constrn. com. Cathedral of St. John the Divine; mem. N.Y. Citizens Tax Coun., Fifth Ave Assn., Realty Found. of N.Y., Met. Mus. of Art's Real Estate Coun.; mem. adv. bd. Lenox Hill Hosp., United Cerebral Palsy; spl. advisor to Pres.'s Coun. on Phys. Fitness and Sports; mem. N.Y. Sportsplex Commn.; chmn. N.Y. citizens com. 78th Ann. NAACP Conv., 1987; grand marshall Nation's Parade, 1995; bd. dirs. Police Athletic League; bd. overseers Wharton Sch.; founding mem. adv. bd. Wharton Real Estate Ctr.; bd. dirs. Fred C. Trump Found.; chmn. Donald J. Trump Found. Recipient Entrepreneur of Yr. award, Wharton Entrepreneurial Club, 1984, Ellis Island Medal of Honor, 1986; named Developer of Yr., Constrn. Mgmt. Assn. Am., 1999, Hotel and Real Estate Visionary of the Century, UTA Fedn., 2000; named one of Forbes' Richest Americans, 2006, The 100 Most Powerful Celebrities, Forbes-.com, 2008; named to Wharton Hall of Fame, Benefactors bd. dirs., Hist. Soc. Palm Beach County, 2003. Achievements include the three-month rebuilding of Wollman Skating Rink in Central Park. Office: The Trump Organization LLC 725 5th Ave Fl 26 New York NY 10022-2520*

TRUMP, IVANKA MARIE, real estate company executive; b. NYC, Oct. 30, 1981; d. Donald and Ivana Trump. Attended, Georgetown U., 2000—02; BS in Economics magna cum laude, U Pa. Wharton Sch. Bus., 2004. Model, 1997—; project mgr., retail devel. divsn. Forest City Enterprises, 2004—05; v.p. real estate devel. & acquisition The Trump Orgn., LLC, NYC, 2005—; designer Ivanka Trump Collection. Bd. dirs. Trump Entertainment Resorts Inc., 2007—09. Appears in (documentaries) Born Rich, 2003, (TV series) The Apprentice, 2006—08. Named one of The 50 Most Powerful Women in NYC, NY Post, 2007, 2008. Jewish. Office: The Trump Organization LLC 725 5th Ave New York NY 10022*

TRUMPBOUR, JOHN, historian, researcher, director; b. Greensboro, NC, Feb. 23, 1959; s. Robert and Virginia Trumpbour. BA, History, Stanford U., Palo Alto, Calif., 1977—82; PhD, History, Harvard U., Cambridge, Mass., 1982—96. Rsch. dir. Harvard Trade Union Program, 1999—, Labor & Worklife Program at Harvard Law Sch., 2002—. Cons. and rschr. African Am. Labor Leaders' Econ. Summit, Cambridge, Mass., 1997—2005, 2008—; rschr. and fellowships com. Sci. & Engrng. Workforce Project at Nat. Bur. of Econ. Rsch., Cambridge, Mass., 2001—; editl. bd. Labor History, London, 2004—. Author: Selling Hollywood to the World: U.S. and European Struggles for Mastery of the Global Film Industry, 1920-1950, 2002 (Allan Nevins prize for Lit. Excellence.); editor: How Harvard Rules, 1989, The Dividing Rhine: Politics and Society in Contemporary France and Germany, 1989; guest editor: Comparative Labor Law and Policy Jour., 2007. Bd. of directors Boston Moblzn., 1999—2001; co-chair Samia Tenants Orgn., Boston, 1996—2000; fellowships com., Rhodes and Marshall scholarships Leverett Ho., Harvard U., 1987—. Recipient Best Essay prize, NAAA Found., 1987, James Birdsall Weter award, Stanford U., Dept. History, 1982; grantee, Sloan Found., 2002; fellow Sawyer fellow, Mellon Found., 1996-97, Belgian Am. Edn. Found. Fellow, Brussels, Belgium, 1989-1990. Mem.: Labor and Working-Class History Assn., Soc. for Historians of Am. Fgn. Rels. Home: 60 Woodstock Avenue #14 Brighton MA 02135 Office: Harvard Law Sch Labor and Worklife Program 125 Mt Auburn St 3d Fl Cambridge MA 02138 Personal E-mail: john_trumpbour@harvard.edu.

TRUNDLE, W(INFIELD) SCOTT, publishing executive newspaper, lawyer; b. Maryville, Tenn., Mar. 24, 1939; s. Winfield Scott and Alice (Smith) T.; m. Elizabeth Latshaw, Oct. 14, 1989; children: Stephen, Allison. BA, Vanderbilt U., 1961, JD, 1967. Bar: Tenn. 1967. Spl. agt. U.S. Secret Service, 1963-66; asso. to partner firm Hunter, Smith, Davis & Norris, Kingsport, Tenn., 1967-72; pub. Kingsport (Tenn.) Times-News, 1972-78; pres. Greensboro (N.C.) Daily News, 1978-80; exec. v.p. Jefferson Pilot Publs., Inc., Greensboro and Clearwater, Fla., 1980-82; v.p., bus. mgr. Tampa Tribune (Fla.), 1982-91; sr. v.p. Hillsborough C.C., 1991-93; publisher Ogden (Utah) Standard Examiner, 1993—2005. Assoc. prof. East Tenn. State U., 1973-77; v.p. spl. projects Sandusky Newspapers, Inc., 2005—; bd. dirs., chmn. Container Recycling Inst., Washington. Trustee Eccles Dinosaur Park and Mus. Found., Ogden, Utah. Mem.: Tenn. Bar Assn. Methodist. Home: 2380 Park Forest Blvd Mount Dora FL 32757 Personal E-mail: scott@thetrundles.com.

TRUOG, WILLIAM EDWARD, III, pediatrician, educator, researcher; b. Kansas City, Mo., Feb. 5, 1947; s. William E. and Virginia (Sylvester) Truog; m. Jill D. Jacobson, July 11, 1992. BA cum laude, Carleton Coll., 1969; MD, U. Chgo., 1973. Intern, resident pediat., chief resident Children's Orthop. Hosp.-U. Wash., Seattle, 1973—76, rsch. fellow neonatology, 1976—78; asst. prof., assoc. prof., prof. pediat. U. Wash., Seattle, 1978—93; prof. pediat. U. Mo. Kansas City Sch. Medicine, 1993—, assoc. chair faculty devel. dept. pediats., 2007—; dir. pulmonary disorders Heartland Ctr., Mercy Hosp., 2008—. Med. dir. infant ICU Children's Orthop. Hosp., Seattle, 1982—91. Author: Critical Care of the Newborn, 1983, 1988; contbr. articles to profl. jours. Recipient Best Doctors in Am., 2009, Sosland Endowed Chair Neonatal Rsch., 2001, Founders award, Midwest Soc. Pediat. Rsch., 2008; named First Physician Scientist, Children's Mercy Hosp., 1993; named to Best Doctors in Am., 2005, 2007; grantee, NIH, 1981, 1984, 1997, 2002. Mem.: Perinatal Rsch. Soc., We. Soc. Pediat. Rsch., Soc. Pediat. Rsch., Am. Pediat. Soc., Am. Thoracic Soc. (grantee 1978). Episcopalian. Office: Children's Mercy Hosp 2401 Gillham Rd Kansas City MO 64108-4619

TRUONG, HOAI-AN, pharmacist, director; b. Saigon, Vietnam, Feb. 13, 1979; s. Xuan Thanh Truong and Thao Phuong Phan. Pre-Pharmacy, The Cath. U. America, Washington, DC, 2001; PharmD, U. Md. Sch. Pharmacy, Balt., 2005; MPH, U. Md. Sch. Medicine, Balt., 2007. Clin. coord., pharmacist Walgreens Pharmacy Patient Care Ctr., Perryville, Md., 2006—07; asst. dir., experiential learning program U. Md. Sch. Pharmacy, 2007—. Profl. devel. com. co-chmn. Md. Pharmacists Assn., Balt., 2006—. Editor: (textbook) Pharmacists & Public Health. Active Md. Pub. Health Assn., 2008—. Mem.: Phi Lambda Sigma Pharmacy Leadership Soc., Am. Assn. Coll. Pharmacy, Am. Pharmacists Assn. Roman Cath. Avocations: writing, running, swimming, travel, languages. Office: Univ MD Sch Pharmacy 20 N Pine St #722 Baltimore MD 21201 Office Fax: 410-706-0988. Business E-Mail: htruong@rx.umaryland.edu.

TRUPE, MARY-ANN, secondary school educator; b. Trenton, NJ, Jan. 6, 1935; d. Norman Louis Green and Jean Hortense Lurvey; m. Robert Arthur Barclay, Nov. 28, 1955 (dec. July 2, 1965); children: Mary Ann, Alison Jean; m. Titus Weidman Trupe, Dec. 30, 1966; children: Amy Suzanne, Sara Diana. BA, Houghton Coll., 1960; French cert., Millersville U., 1981, Spanish cert., 1985; Sign lang. cert., Deaf & Hearing Sch., Lancaster, Pa., 2001. Pvt. elem. reading tchr., 1955—59; tchr. Erlton Elem. Sch., NJ, 1955—59; tchr. French and Spanish lang. St. Joseph Acad., Columbia, Pa., 1981—86; tchr. English Lancaster Cath. H.S., Lancaster, 1991—, chair English dept., 1993—2005. Troop leader Girl Scouts Am., Horseheads, NY, 1967—73; Sunday Sch. tchr. Horseheads Presby. Ch., 1974—77, youth leader, 1975—77. Recipient Nat. Gold Apple Tchr. award, Scholastic, 2001. Mem.: AAUW (pres. 1973—75), Lancaster Lit. Guild. Democrat. Unitarian. Avocations: gardening, painting, reading, travel, writing. Home: 105 Green St Canton MA 02021

TRUPPO, MATTHEW DAVID, biochemical engineer, researcher; b. West Long Branch, NJ, Sept. 12, 1979; s. Jay and Grace Truppo; m. Olivia Pascarella, Mar. 13, 2004. BSChemE, Princeton U., NJ, 2002, degree in Engring. Biology, 2002. Biochemical engr. Merck & Co., Inc., Rahway, NJ, 2002—. Achievements include patents in field. Office: Merck & Co Inc 126 E Lincoln Ave Rahway NJ 07065

TRURAN, JAMES WELLINGTON, JR., astrophysicist, educator; b. Brewster, NY, July 12, 1940; s. James Wellington and Suzanne (Foglesong) T.; m. Carol Kay Dell'Acy, June 26, 1965; children— Elaina Michelle, Diana Lee, Anastasia Elizabeth. BA in Physics, Cornell U., Ithaca, NY, 1961; MS in Physics, Yale U., New Haven, Conn., 1963, PhD in Physics, 1966. Postdoctoral rsch. assoc. NAS-NRC Goddard Inst. Space Studies, NASA, NYC, 1965-67; asst. prof. physics Belfer Grad. Sch. Sci., Yeshiva U., 1967-70; rsch. fellow in physics Calif. Inst. Tech., 1968-69; assoc. prof. Belfer Grad. Sch. Sci., Yeshiva U., 1970-72, prof., 1972-73; prof. astronomy U. Ill., Urbana, 1973-91; sr. vis. fellow, Guggenheim Meml. Found. fellow Inst. Astronomy, U. Cambridge, Eng., 1979-80; trustee Aspen Ctr. Physics, 1979-85, 91-93, 96-99, v.p., 1985-88; assoc. U. Ill. Ctr. for Advanced Study, 1979-80, 86-87; prof. astronomy astrophysics U. Chgo., 1991—; sr. physicist Argonne Nat. Lab., 2003—. Alexander von Humboldt-Stiftung sr. scientist Max-Plank Inst., Munich, Germany, 1986-87, 94; Beatrice Tinsley vis. prof. U. Tex., Austin, 1999; Biermann lectr. in astrophysics, Max-Planck Inst., Munich, 2001. Contbr. articles to profl. jours.; co-editor: Nucleosynthesis, 1968, Nucleosynthesis— Challenges and New Developments, 1985, Nuclear Astrophysics, 1987, Type Ia Supernovae: Theory and Cosmology, 2000, Cosmic Chemical Evolution, 2002; editor: Physics Letters B, 1974-80. Co-recipient Yale Sci. and Engring. Assn. annual award for advancement basic or applied sci., 1980 Fellow AAAS, Am. Phys. Soc.; mem. Am. Astron. Soc., Am. Phys. Soc., Internat. Astron. Union. Home: 210 Wysteria Dr Olympia Fields IL 60461-1202 Office: U Chgo Dept Astronomy Astrophysics 5640 S Ellis Ave Chicago IL 60637-1433 Business E-Mail: truran@nova.uchicago.edu.

TRUS, BENES LOUIS, structural chemist; b. Tyler, Tex., May 9, 1946; s. Joseph N. and Ruthie Trus; m. Susan Evans, Apr. 23, 1972; children: Aaron Baram, Anthony Phillip. BS cum laude with honors, Tulane U., 1968; PhD, Calif. Inst. Tech., 1972. Rsch. chemist NIH, Bethesda, Md., 1980—93, chief imaging processing rsch. sect., 1993—2002, chief imaging scis. lab., 2002—, dep. dir. divsn. computational biosci., 2003—07, acting sci. dir. ctr. info. tech., 2007—, acting dir. divsn., 2007—, acting chief computational biosci. and engring. lab., 2007—. Mem. steering com. NIH wide image processing group, 1984—. Contbr. articles to profl. jours., chpt. to books. Mem. NIH Marathon Team, 1986-88, 1st pl. Marine Corps Marathon, Govt. Team Competition, 1986, 3d pl., 1987, 88, 2d pl. Masters Team, 1993. REcipient Dirs. award NIH, 1987, 94, Spl. Achievement award, 1996, Group Merit award, 1998, 2006; Jane Coffin Childs postdoctoral fellow Calif. Inst. Tech., Pasadena, 1972-75, Rsch. fellow NIH, Bethesda, Md., 1975-77, Sr. Rsch. fellow, 1977-80; Tulane U. scholar and fellow, 1965-68. Mem. Chesapeake Soc. for Microscopy, Microscope Soc. Am., Reston Road Runner Club, Phi Beta Kappa, Sigma Xi. Avocations: music, running, carpentry. Office: NIH Bldg 12A Rm 2033 Bethesda MD 20892-5624

TRUSCOTT, CARL JOSEPH, security firm executive, former federal agency administrator; b. Augusta, Ga., May 21, 1957; married; 1 child. BS in Criminal Justice, U. Del., 1979. Investigator NJ Dept. Law & Pub. Safety, 1980—81; spl. agt. US Secret Svc., US Dept. Treasury, 1981—2004, spl. agt. in charge, Presdl. protective divsn., 2001—03; asst. dir. Office Protective Rsch. US Secret Svc., US Dept. Homeland Security, 2003—04; dir. Bur. Alcohol, Tobacco, Firearms & Explosives US Dept. Justice, Washington, 2004—06; sr. v.p. ASERO Worldwide, 2007—. Recipient Dirs. Life Saving award, 1986, Sr. Exec. Svc. Performance award, 2001, 2002, Spl. award for disting. svc. to the Exec. Office of the Pres., 2002, Presdl. Rank award as Meritorious Exec., 2003. Office: ASERO Worldwide 700 12th St Ste 800 Washington DC 20005

TRUSDELL, MARY LOUISE CANTRELL, retired state educational administrator; b. Chandler, Okla., Oct. 24, 1921; d. George Herbert and Lois Elizabeth (Bruce) Cantrell; m. Robert William Trusdell, Jan. 7, 1943; children: Timothy Lee, Laurence Michael. BA, Ga. So. Coll., 1965; MEd, U. Va., 1974. Dir. specific learning disabilities program Savannah Country Day Sch., Ga., 1960-65; learning disabilities tchr. Richmond pub. schs., Va., 1966-73; dir. New Community Sch., Richmond, 1974-75; dir. Fed. Learning Disabilities Project, Dept HEW, Mid. Peninsula, Va., 1975-76; supr. programs for learning disabled Va. Dept. Edn., Richmond, 1976-86; bd. dirs. Learning Disabilities Council, Richmond, Very Spl. Arts- Va., 1986-91; mem. adv. com. Learning Disabilities Research and Devel. Project, Woodrow Wilson Rehab. Ctr., Fisherville, Va., 1983. Co-editor: Understanding Learning Disabilities: A Parent Guide and Workbook, 1989, 3d edit., 2002. Bd. dirs. Savannah Assn. Retarded Children, 1957-60, Meml. Guidance Clinic, Richmond, 1966-69. Named Tchr. of Yr., Learning Disabilities Ctr., Richmond, 1972. Mem. Orton Dyslexia Soc. (pres. capital area br. 1968-70, nat. bd. dirs. 1970-72, Va. br. 1986-91), Alliance for the Mentally Ill. Cen. Va. (pres. 1991-93). Presbyterian. Avocations: travel, theater, reading.

TRUSKOWSKI, JOHN BUDD, lawyer; b. Chgo., Dec. 3, 1945; s. Casimer T. and Jewell S. (Kirk) T.; m. Karen Lee Sloss, Mar. 21, 1970; children: Philip K., Jennifer B. BS, U. Ill., 1967; JD, U. Chgo., 1970. Bar: Ill. 1970, U.S. Dist. Ct. (no. dist.) Ill. 1970, U.S. Tax Ct. 1977, US Ct. Fed. Claims, 2006. Assoc. Keck, Mahin & Cate, Chgo., 1970-71, 74-78, ptnr., 1978-97, Locke, Lord, Bissell & Liddell, Chgo., 1997—. Author, editor Callaghan's Federal Tax Guide, 1981. Lt., USNR, 1971-74. Mem. ABA, Ill. State Bar Assn., Chgo. Bar Assn. Republican. Unitarian. Avocations: model railroading, stamp collecting/philately. Home: 251 Kimberly Ln Lake Forest IL 60045-3862 Office: Locke Lord Bissell & Liddel/LLP 11/ 5 Wacker Dr Chicago IL 60606 Office Phone: 312-443-0257. Business E-Mail: jtruskowski@lockelord.com.

TRUSSELL, ALICE J., library director, department chairman; b. Kans. City, Aug. 4, 1953; d. Robert Kenneth and Eva A. Mullin; m. John R. Trussell, Oct. 25, 1980; children: Jeanette R. Rogers, David R. AA, Kans. C.C., 1973; BS in Edn., Emporia State U., Kans., 1975; MLS, Emporia State U., 1997. Sci. libr. Kans. State U., Manhattan, 1997—2001, head, fiedler engring. libr., 2001—. Mem.: Am. Soc. Engring. Edn., Internat. Assn. Technol. U. Librs. (governing bd. 2006—08), Sigma XI, Beta Phi Mu (chpt. sec. 2001—). Mem. Christian Ch. Avocations: quilting, sewing, reading. Office: Kans State Univ Librs 137 Hale Libr Manhattan KS 66506-1200 Business E-Mail: alitrus@ksu.edu.

TRUSSELL, CHARLES TAIT, columnist; b. Balt., May 9, 1925; s. Charles Prescott and Beatrice (Tait) T.; m. Woodley Grizzard, Dec. 27, 1953 (div. 1990); children: Galen Tait, Thomas Marshall; m. Nancy Rathbun Billington, Dec. 19, 1990. BA in Journalism, Washington and Lee U., Lexington, Va., 1949. Reporter St. Petersburg (Fla.) Times, also; writer Congl. Quar. News Features, 1951-54; reporter Wall St. Jour., 1954-56, Washington Evening Star, 1956; asso. editor Nation's Business mag., 1956-64, mng. editor, 1964-69; sr. editor Congressional Quar., Inc., 1969-70; dir. pub. relations and advt. Investment Co. Inst., Washington, 1970-72; free-lance writer, real estate investor, 1972-74; v.p. Am. Forest Inst., Washington, 1974-79, sr. v.p., 1980-81; v.p. Am. Enterprise Inst., 1981-86; dir. comms. Constitution Bicentennial Commn., 1986-88; freelance writer, columnist, 1988—. Nat. corr. Clear Mountain Comms.; corr. FrontPagemag.com. Producer: documentary record album The Best of Washington Humor, 1963; author: Beating the Competition, 1992; editor: Successful Management, 1964, (with Paul Hencke) Dear NASA Please Send Me a Rocket, 1964, Timeless Truths for Kids, 2002, Washington Doctor: A Parable on Love & Death. Served with USNR, 1944-46. Recipient Loeb Spl. Achievement award for mags. U. Conn., 1961, Benjamin Fine Journalism award, 1992. Mem. Washington Assembly (exec. com. 1961-65, chmn. 1965), Beta Theta Pi. Home: 2467 Cherry Rd Manistee MI 49660- E-mail: ttrussell@chartermi.net.

TRUSSELL, JACQUELINE, theology studies educator; d. Lula P. Alexander. BA, Roosevelt U., Chgo., 1987; MA, Northeastern Ill. U., Chgo., 1992; MA in Theol. Studies, Harvard Div. Sch., Cambridge, 1998. Adj. prof. Roosevelt U., Chgo., 2001—, St. Xavier U., Chgo., 2003—. Pres. and founder Blackand Christian.com, Chgo., 2000—. Past co chair Harvard Div. Sch. Alums African Descent, Cambridge, Mass., 2004—06. Recipient Black Web award, 2007. Mem.: Am. Acad. Religion, Harvard Club Chgo. Mem. United Ch. Of Christ. Avocation: reading. Personal E-mail: jtrussell3@yahoo.com. Business E-Mail: jtrussel@roosevelt.edu.

TRUSSELL, ROBERT PRESCOTT, special education educator; b. Washington, June 15, 1963; s. Galen Douglas and Edwina Ewin Trussell; m. Carolyn Raynor Raynor, Nov. 28, 1992; children: Nicholas Richard, Adelaide Wyn, William Isaac, Jeremiah Robert. PhD, U. Mo., Columbia, 2006. Spl. edn. tchr. to behavioral specialist Pub. Schs. Tex., Maine, Mo., 1992—2006; asst. prof. U. Tex., El Paso, 2006—. Peace corps vol. Peace Corps, Quayaquil, Ecuador, 1989—91. Home: 1420 Copper Ridge Dr El Paso TX 79912 Office: Univ Texas El Paso 500 W Univ Ave El Paso TX 79968 Personal E-mail: rptrussell@utep.edu.

TRUSSELL, R(OBERT) RHODES, environmental engineer; b. National City, Calif. s. Robert L. and Margaret (Kessing) T.; m. Elizabeth Shane, Nov. 26, 1969; children: Robert Shane, Charles Bryan. BSCE, U. Calif., Berkeley, 1966, MS, 1967, PhD, 1972. With Montgomery Watson Inc. (formerly Mongomery Cons. Engrs.), Pasadena, Calif., 1972—, v.p., 1977, sr. v.p., 1986, dir. applied tech., 1988-92, sr. v.p., dir. corp. devel., 1992—. Mem. com. on water treatment chems. Nat. Acad. Sci., 1980-82, mem. com. 3d part cert., 1982-83, com. on irrigation-induced water quality problems, 1986-88, indirect potable reuse, 1996-98, chmn. com. on drinking water contaminants, 1998—, Am. Water Work Commn. on mixing of water treatment chems., 1988-90; mem. U.S./German rsch. com. on corrosion of water sys., 1984-85, U.S./Dutch rsch. com. on organics in water, 1982-83, U.S./USSR rsch. com. on water treatment, 1985-88, U.S./E.C. Com. Corrosion in Water, 1992-94; mem. Water Sci. and Tech. Bd., 1998—. Mem. jt. editl. bd. Standards Methods for Examination of Water and Wastewater, 1980-89; mem. editl. adv. bd. Environ. and Sci. and Tech., 1977-83; mng. editl. bd. Environ. Sci. and Tech., 2001—; contbr. articles to profl. publs. Mem. AIChE, AEEP, Acad. Environ. Engring. (Kappe lectr. 1999), Nat. Acad. Engrs., Water Works Assn. (editl. adv. bd. jour. 1987-94, EPA SAB com. on drinking water 1988-91, 94—, cons. radon disinfectant by-products, 1993, cons. on disinfection and disinfection by-products 1994, ad hoc sci. adv. com. on arsenic 1995-96), Bd. Sci. Couns. Com. on AS, 1997, Internat. Water Supply Assn. (U.S. rep. to standing com. on water quality and treatment 1990-94, chmn. com. disinfection and mem. sci. and tech. coun. 1994—), Water Environ. Fedn., Internat. Water Quality Assn., Am. Chem. Soc., Nat. Assn. Corrosion Engrs., Sigma Xi. Office: Montgomery Watson 618 Michillinda Ave Ste 200 Arcadia CA 91007-1625

TRUTA, IOAN, protective services official; b. Cluj-Napoca, Romania, Oct. 16, 1969; s. Ioan and Ana Truta; m. Raveca Balatici, Feb. 25, 1995. Degree in Faculty Law, A.I. Cuza Police Acad., Bucharest, Romania, 2005. Cert.: Lic. Juridical Sci. 2005; latent print examnier Internat. Assn. Identification, 2007. Officer Cluj-Napoca Police Dept., 1995—96; crime-scene investigator Cluj Police Dept., 1996—2005; crime scene investigator UN, Prizren, Kosovo, Albania, 2001; sr. criminalist Boston Police Dept., 2005—, instr., 2005—08. Contbr. articles to profl. jours. Crime watcher Crime Watch, West Roxbury, Mass., 2006—08. Warrant officer Army Police, 1995—2002, Romania. Recipient Meritorious Svc. Award, Romanian Jour. Criminalistics, 2003. Mem.: Internat. Assn. for Identification (Cert. Latent Print Examiner 2007). Orthodox. Achievements include research in fingerprints. Avocations: swimming, travel. Office: Boston Police Dept One Schroeder Plaza Boston MA 02120 Personal E-mail: ioan_truta@hotmail.com. E-mail: trutai.bpd@cityofboston.gov.

TRUTOR, GENEVIEVE WILLIAMSON, museum director; b. Benson, Vt., Aug. 26, 1923; d. Clayton John and Caroline Aileen (Walker) Williamson; m. John Trutor, May 4, 1946 (dec.); children: Barry, John W., Elizabeth, William C. Diploma, Rutland Bus. Coll., 1942. Sec. War Prodn. Bd., Washington, 1942—45, Soc. Am. Foresters, Washington, 1945—47; adminstrv. asst. Benson Village Sch., Vt., 1971—89; dir. Benson Lumber Yard Inc., 1963—2002; founder, curator Benson Mus., Benson, 1980—. Lib. commr. Town of Benson, 1959—61; dir. Lower Champlain Housing Corp., 1977—82; mem. Benson's Cmty. Hall Restoration project, 1975—80; chmn. Nat. Bicentennial Celebration, Benson, 1976, State Bicentennial Celebration, Vt., 1977, Benson Bicentennial Celebration, 1980; sec., treas. Benson Health Com., 1961—70; trustee Pub. Funds, 1981—87, 1996—, Bertha R. Franke Scholarship Fund, 1971—79. Republican.

TRUTY, MARK, surgeon; married. BA, U. Chgo.; MSc, MD, Chgo. Med. Sch. Gen. surgeon Mayo Clinic, Rochester, Minn., 2002—. Office: Mayo Clinic 200 First St SW Rochester MN 55905

TRUWIT, JONATHON DEAN, dean; married. MD, Georgetown U., Wash., 1983. Sr assoc. dean for clin. affairs, CMO U. Va HS, Charlottesville, 2002—08, divsn. chief, pulmonary and critical care medicine, 1994—2008. Office: Univ of Va Box 800546 UVA HS Charlottesville VA 22908

TRYBAN, ESTHER ELIZABETH, lawyer; b. Chgo., Aug. 14, 1958; d. Chester Joseph and Lottie Elizabeth (Napora) Tryban. AAS with honors, Elgin CC, Ill., 1977, AS with honors, 1982; BS with honors, Roosevelt U., Chgo., 1986; JD, U. Chgo., 1989. Bar: Ill. 1989, U.S. Dist. Ct. (no. dist.) Ill. 1989, U.S. Ct. Appeals (7th cir.) 1990, U.S. Supreme Ct., 1996. Supr. adminstrv. svcs. law dept. Motorola, Inc., Schaumburg, Ill., 1977-86; staff law clk. U.S. Bankruptcy Ct., No. Dist. Ill., Chgo., 1989-90; sr. counsel City of Chgo., 1990—. Mem. ABA, Nat. Lawyers Guild, Assn. Former Bankruptcy Law Clks, Ill. State Bar Assn., Chgo. Bar Assn. (chair govt. svc. com. 1996-97), Advocates Soc. (pres. Chgo. chpt. 2008-09). Roman Catholic. Avocations: reading, football, travel. Office: City Chgo Dept Law 30 N Lasalle St Ste 900 Chicago IL 60602-2503 Business E-Mail: lw00026@cityofchicago.org.

TRYGSTAD, LAWRENCE BENSON, lawyer; b. Holton, Mich., Mar. 22, 1937; BA, U. Mich., 1959; JD, U. So. Calif., 1967. Bar: Calif. 1968, U.S. Supreme Ct. 1974. Legal counsel Calif. Tchrs. Assn., United Tchrs. L.A., LA, 1968-71; ptnr. Trygstad & Odell, LA, 1971-80; pres. Trygstad Law Corp., LA, 1980—2004; ptnr. Trygstad, Schwab & Trygstad, LA, 2004—. Instr., tchr. negotiation U. Calif.-Northridge; panelist TV shows Law and the Teacher. Bd. dirs. George Washington Carver Found., L.A. Mem. ABA, Calif. Bar Assn., Consumer Attys. Calif.; L.A. County Bar Assn., Nat. Orgn. Lawyers for Edn. Assns., Am. Assoc. Justice, Consumer Attys. L.A., Phi Alpha Delta. Home: 4209 Aleman Dr Tarzana CA 91356-5405 Office: 1880 Century Park E Ste 1104 Los Angeles CA 90067-1609 Office Phone: 310-552-0500. Business E-Mail: ltrygstad@trygstadlawoffice.com.

TRYON, ELIZABETH ANNE, educational association administrator; b. Columbus, Ohio, May 1, 1957; d. Anne Colwell Tryon; m. Ted M. Petith, Sept. 9, 1989; children: Charmaine Elizabeth Tryon-Petith, Clayton Colwell Tryon-Petith, Miles William Tryon-Petith. B of music, U. of Ill., 1987—91. Touring performer/rec. artist Cowboy Jazz, Balt., 1977—81; bassist/vocalist freelance, Champaign, Ill., 1983—92, jazz educator/performer Carbondale, Ill., 1992—99; v.p. of mktg. smartgroove.com, Madison, Wis., 1999—; asst. to dir. of human issues program Edgewood Coll., Madison, Wis., 2004—. Event planner Carbondale Cmty. Arts; WDBX radio, Carbondale, Ill., 1992—98; v.p. for edn. Champaign-Urbana Symphony, Ill., 1990—92; v.p. of edn., exec. bd. Krannert Art Mus. Coun., Champaign, Ill., 1990—92. Composer (performer, producer): (audio recording) Chaos Theory, (audio cd) Mr. Fix-It (hon. mention, 1997); editor: (booklet/cd) The Groove Project; co-editor: (book) The Unheard Voices, 2009; musician: (jazz concert) Whitaker Jazz Festival, St. Louis, Groove Merchants. Cultural arts com. mem. Randall PTO, Madison, Wis., 2003—05; fundraising chair Sinfonia da Camera, Urbana, Ill., 1991—92; campaign worker Feingold for Senate, Madison, Wis., 2004. Recipient Vocalist of the Yr., So. Ill. Music Assn., 1997, Outstanding Vocalist, Elmhurst Coll. Jazz Festival, 1989; named Excellence in Diversity, Edgewood Coll., Madison; Music Edn. Residencies, Dane County Cultural Affairs Commn., 2000—03. Mem.: Wis. Music Educators Assn. Achievements include development of music education method for improvisation. Avocations: ceramics, sailing, swimming, knitting, bicycling.

TRYTHALL, HARRY GILBERT, music educator, composer; b. Knoxville, Tenn., Oct. 28, 1930; s. Harry Gilbert and Clara Hannah (Akre) T.; m. Jean Marie Slater, Dec. 28, 1951 (div. 1976); children: Linda Marie, Karen Elizabeth; m. Carol King, Sept. 19, 1985. BA, U. Tenn., 1951; MusM, Northwestern U., 1952; DMA, Cornell U., 1960. Asst. prof. music Knox Coll., Galesburg, Ill., 1960-64; prof. music theory and composition George Peabody Coll. Tchrs., Nashville, 1964-75; dean Creative Arts Ctr., 1975-81; prof. music W.Va. U., Morgantown, 1975-96; ret., 1997. Vis. prof. U. Federal do Espiritu Santo, Vitoria, Brazil, 1999-2000; adj. prof. Brookhaven Coll., Dallas, 2002-. Author: Principles and Practice of Electronic Music, 1974, Eighteenth Century Counterpoint, 1993, Sixteenth Century Counterpoint, 1994; past mem. editorial bd. Music Educators Jour.; composer orchestral music, chamber and electronic music. With USAF, 1953-57. Personal E-mail: htrythal@yahoo.com.

TRZASKO, JOSHUA DAMON, research scientist; b. Yonkers, Minn., Feb. 4, 1981; s. Joseph A. and Ann E. Trzasko. BS in Elec. and Computer Engring., Cornell U., Ithaca, NY, 2003; PhD candidate in Biomed. Engring., Mayo Grad. Sch., Rochester, Minn., 2003—. Intern Gen. Electric Global Rsch., Niskayuna, NY, 2002; predoc. rschr. Mayo Clinic, Rochester, 2003—. Mem. Rochester Good Food Store Coop., 2008—. Mayo Found. fellowship, Mayo Clinic, 2003—. Mem.: IEEE, ISMRM, SIAM. Libertarian. Achievements include research in compressive sensing methods for magnetic resonance imaging. Home: 5100 Weatherstone Dr NW Rochester MN 55901 Office: Mayo Clinic 200 First St SW Opus 2-149 Rochester MN 55905 Business E-Mail: trzasko.joshua@mayo.edu.

TRZCINSKI, EILEEN, social studies educator, director; d. Floryan Trzcinski and Dorothy Morin; life ptnr. Reinhold Cordella. PhD, U. Mich., Ann Arbor, 1985. Prof. Wayne State U., Detroit, 1994—2008; dir. and prof. Ryerson U., Toronto, Onterio, Canada, 2008—. Dir. Sch. Social Work, Toronto, 2008—.

TRZYNA, THADDEUS CHARLES, academic institution administrator; b. Chgo., Oct. 26, 1939; s. Thaddeus Stephen and Irene Mary (Giese) T.; divorced; 1 child, Jennifer. BA in Internat. Rels., U. So. Calif., 1961; PhD in Govt., Claremont Grad. U., 1975. Vice consul US Govt., Elisabethville, Katanga, Congo, 1962-63, consul Leopoldville, 1963-64, sec. Nat. Mil. Info. Disclosure Policy Com. Washington, 1964-67; pres. Calif. Inst. Pub. Affairs, Claremont, 1969-89, Sacramento, 1989—; sr. assoc. Sch. Politics and Econs., Claremont Grad. U., 1989—; dir. Internat. Ctr. Environment and Pub. Policy, 1990—; rsch. assoc. U. Calif., Santa Cruz, 2009—. Mem. coun. Internat. Union for Conservation of Nature and Natural Resources, 1990-96, chmn. commn. on environ. strategy and planning, 1990-96, world commn. protected areas, 1990—; sr. adv. cities and conservation, 2005—; chmn. Calif. Forum on Hazardous Materials, 1985-88, Calif. Farmlands Project Task Force, 1981-84; cons. U.S. and Calif. State Agys. on Environ. Policy; cons. on devel. of natural resources Univ. for Peace, Costa Rica; lectr. internat. rels. Pomona Coll. Author: The California Handbook, rev. 8th edit. 1999, The Power of Convening, 1990, A Sustainable World, 1995, The Urban Imperative, 2005. Mem. World Acad. Art and Sci., Sierra Club (v.p. 1975-77, chmn. internat. com. 1977-79). Democrat. Office: Calif Inst Pub Affairs PO Box 189040 Sacramento CA 95818-9040 Office Phone: 916-442-2472.

TSABETSAYE, JESSICA L., science educator; b. Gallup, N.Mex., Mar. 30, 1982; d. Belden and Bernice Vicenti Wyaco; m. Shaun H. Tsabetsaye, June 30, 2006. BS in Biochemistry (hon.), U. N.Mex., Albuquerque, 2005. Sci. tchr. Zuni Pub. Sch. Dist., Zuni Pueblo, N.Mex., 2006—. Home: PO Box 1687 Zuni NM 87327

TSACHOURIDIS, VASSILIOS A., electrical and control engineer, researcher; b. Ptolemaida, Kozani, Greece; s. Alexandros and Melli Tsachouridis. Qualified elec. engr. technol. edn., Technol. Edn. Inst. Kavala, Greece, 1995; MSc in Electronic Control Engring., U. Salford, Eng., 1997; PhD, U. Leicester, Eng., 2002. Lectr. in engring. Queens Coll., U. Oxford, 2002—04; rsch. asst. U. Oxford, 2002—04; rsch. fellow City U. London, 2004—07, sr. rsch. fellow, 2007—. Presenter in field. Contbr. chpt. to book and articles to profl. jours. Grantee European Social Fund, 1996, U. Leicester, 1997, 98, 99, 2000. Mem. IEEE (sr.), AIAA (sr.), Soc. Indsl. and Applied Math., Am. Math. Soc., Inst. Engring. Tech., Internat. Fedn. Automatic Control (affiliate). Avocations: reading mathematics, ancient greek philosophy, logic, euclidean geometry, attending conferences. Home: 28th Sydagma 7 Ptolemaida 502 00 Ptolemaida Greece Home Fax: 0030 24630 26844. Personal E-mail: vassilios.tsachouridis@ieee.org.

TSACOUMIS, STEPHANIE, lawyer; b. Aug. 31, 1956; BA magna cum laude, Coll. of William & Mary, 1978; JD, Univ. Va., 1981. Bar: DC 1981, Md. 1982. Of counsel Morrison & Foerster, Washington, 1988—91, ptnr., 1991—96; of counsel, corp. fin. Gibson Dunn & Crutcher LLP, Washington, 1996—2000, ptnr. corp. transactions and securities, 2000—, and co-ptnr.-in-charge DC office. Adj. faculty Georgetown Univ. Law Ctr., 2001—. Sr. editor Va. Jour. of Internat. Law, contributing author Corporate Communications and the Federal Antifraud Rules, 1992, Securities in the Electronic Age, 2001. Mem.: ABA, Md. State Bar Assn., DC Bar, Phi Beta Kappa. Office: Gibson Dunn & Crutcher LLP 1050 Connecticut Ave NW Washington DC 20036 Office Phone: 202-955-8277. Office Fax: 202-530-9613. Business E-Mail: stsacoumis@gibsondunn.com.

TSAI, CHI CHUN, engineering educator; m. Patricia Kn Chi, Jan. 21, 1986; children: Victor W., Wyndham W. PhD, U. Tex. Southwestern Med. Ctr., Dallas, 1991. Asst. tech. dir. Alcon Rsch. Ltd., Fort Worth, Tex., 1988—; adj. prof. U. Tex., Arlington, 2004—.

TSAI, CHRISTINA W., civil engineer, educator; arrived in U.S., 1995; d. Jin-Yi Tsai and Jau-Jr Chen; m. Shih-Ping Ho, Jan. 4, 2001; 1 child, Julianne Y. BS in Civil Engring., Nat. Taiwan U., Taipei, 1995; MS in Civil Engring., U. Ill., Urbana, 1997, MS in Applied Math., 2000, PhD in Civil Engring., 2001. Rsch. scientist Ill. State Water Survey, Champaign, Ill., 2000—01; asst. prof. SUNY, Buffalo, 2002—08, assoc. prof., 2008—. Contbr. articles to profl. jours. Recipient Stout Water Resources Rsch. award, U. of Ill. at Champaign-Urbana, 2000, Career award, NSF, 2005, 2007; grantee, SUNY at Buffalo Interdisciplinary Rsch. and Creative Activities Fund, 2002, Environ. Sci. Inst. SUNY at Buffalo, 2003. Mem.: ASCE (assoc. ExCEED tchg. fellow 2003), Am. Soc. of Engring. Edn., Internat. Assn. of Hydraulic Rsch., Internat. Water Resources Assn., Am. Geophys. Union, Am. Soc. of Women Engineers, Phi Kappa Phi. Avocations: reading, travel. Office: SUNY at Buffalo 233 Jarvis Hall Buffalo NY 14260 Business E-Mail: ctsai4@eng.buffalo.edu.

TSAI, LI-HUEI, pathologist, researcher; b. Taipei, Taiwan, Mar. 18, 1960; m. Lonarto Liong; 1 child, Jessica Liong. PhD, U. Tex. Southwestern, Dallas, 1990. Asst. prof. pathology Harvard Med. Sch., Cambridge, Mass., 1994—99, assoc. prof., 1999—2002, prof., 2002—06, asst. investigator pathology, 1997—2002; prof. Picower Ctr. Learning and Memory MIT, Cambridge, 2006—, assoc. mem. Broad Inst., 2006—; investigator RIKEN-MIT Neuroscience, Cambridge, 2006—, Howard Hughes Med. Inst., Cambridge, 2006—. Contbr. articles to profl. jours. Mem.: Soc. Neuroscience (assoc.). Office: 77 Massachusetts Ave 46-4235a Cambridge MA 02139 Office Fax: 617 324 1657; Home Fax: 617-324-1657. Business E-Mail: lhtsai@mit.edu.

TSAI, MING-HUNG, internist, researcher; s. Tseng-Li Tsai and Chieh-Min Tsai-Chuang; m. Yun-Shing Peng-Tsai; children: Sharon, Ann, Juan-Carlos. MD, Chung-Shan Med. U., Taichung, 1992. Cert. physician Adminstrn. Health, Taiwan, 1992, specialist internal medicine Adminstrn. Health, Taiwan, 1995, specialist gastroenterology Soc. Gastroenterology Taiwan, 1998, specialist gastroenterological endoscopy Soc. Gastroent. Endoscopy Taiwan, 1999, specialist for critical care medicine Taiwan Soc. Critical Care Medicine, 2008. Resident dept. internal medicine Chang Gung Meml. Hosp., Taipei, 1992—95, clin. fellow divsn. gastroenterology, 1995—97, attending physician divsn. gastroenterology, 2001—; rsch. fellow sect. digestive diseases Yale U., New Haven, 1999—2001; asst. prof. Chang Gung U., Taipei, 2005—. Contbr. chapters to books, articles to profl. jours. Recipient Med. Rsch. award, New Century Health Care Promotion Found., Taipei, 2007—08. Mem.: European Assn. Study Liver Disease, Soc. Gastroenterologic Endoscopy, Soc. Gastroenterology, Am. Assn. Study Liver Diease. Achievements include research in the mechanism behind nitric oxide overproduction in early stage of portal hypertension when hyperdynamic circulation is not fully established; the association between adrenal insufficiency and multiple organ failure in patients with liver cirrhosis and severe sepsis and the association between hypolipoproteinemia and severe sepsis in cirrhotic patients; critical care for cirrhotic patients; role of hypolipoproteinemia in patients with liver cirrhosis and severe sepsis. Office: Chang Gung Meml Hosp 199 Tung-Hwa North Rd Taipei 105 Taiwan Office Fax: 886-3-3288662. Business E-Mail: mhtsai@cgmh.org.tw.

TSAI, TSU-MIN, surgeon; b. Taipei, Taiwan, Dec. 15, 1936; arrived in U.S., 1976; m. Fu-Mei Tsai; children: Yi-Yi, Ring-Ring Tsai Tien, Berlin. MD, Taiwan U., 1961. Diplomate with added qualifications in surgery of the hand Am. Bd. Orthopedic Surgeons. Intern Nat. Taiwan U. Hosp., China, 1961-62, resident in urology, surgery and orthopedics, 1964-70; intern U. Louisville, 1976-77, resident in orthopedics, 1977-79; Christine Kleinert fellow in hand surgery U. Louisville Affiliated Hosps., 1976; clin. prof. orthopaedic surg., dir. divsn. hand surgery Louisville Sch. Medicine, 1980—. Presenter in field, including Hand Forum, Paris, 2001, Internat. Fedn. of Socs. for Surgery of Hand, Istanbul, Turkey, 2001, Post Congress Mini-Invasive Conf., Rome, 2001; presenter in field Am. Assn. Hand Surgery, Kauai Island, Hawaii, 2003, LIC Meeting, Jewish Hosp., Louisville, 2003, Am. Assn. Hand Surgery, Palm Springs, 2004, Am. Soc. Reconstructive Microsurgery, Palm Springs, 2004, En Chu Kong Hosp., Taipei, 2004, I-Hou U. E-Da Hosp. Coll. Medicine, Kaoshiung, Taiwan, 2004, Hand Forum, Las Vegas, 2004, 9th Congress of CMASH, Shanghai, 2004, Post IFSSH Congress, Bucharest, 2004; chmn. Dept. Surgery Ho-Ping Hosp., Taipei, 1970—75; disting. vis. prof. Divsn. Plastic and Reconstructive Surgery Washington Hosp. Ctr., 1990; vis. prof. Duke U., Durham, NC, 2001; invited spkr. in field. Contbr. articles to profl. jours. and publs.; editor: (issue) Hand Clinics, 2001. With Nat. Taiwan Armed Svcs., 1963. Fellow: ACS, Am. Acad. Orthopedic Surgeons; mem.: AMA, SICOT Soc., Japanese Orthopaedic Assn., Clin. Orthopedic Soc., Hand Forum, Am. Soc. Surgery of Hand, We. Pacific Orthopedic Assn., Am. Soc. Reconstructive Microsurgery, Internat. Soc. Reconstructive Microsurgery, Ky. Pediat. Soc., Ky. Orthopaedic Soc., Ky. Med. Soc., Jefferson County Orthopaedic Soc., Jefferson County Med. Soc. Avocations: fishing, golf. Office: Kleinert Kutz & Assocs 225 Abraham Flexner Way Louisville KY 40202-1846 Personal E-mail: ttsai@kleinertkutz.com.

TSAI, WEN-YING, sculptor, painter, engineer; b. Xiamen, Fujian, China, Oct. 13, 1928; came to U.S., 1950, naturalized, 1962; s. Chen-Dak and Ching-Miau (Chen) T.; m. Pei-De Chang, Aug. 7, 1968; children: Lun-Yi and Ming Yi (twins). Student, Ta Tung U., 1947-49; BSME, U. Mich., 1953; postgrad., Art Students League N.Y., 1953-57, Faculty Polit. and Social Sci., New Sch., 1956-58. Cons. engr., 1953-63; project mgr. Cosentini Assocs., 1962-63; project engr. Guy B. Panero, Engrs., 1956-60. Creator cybernetic sculpture based on prin. harmonic motion, stroboscopic effects; one-man shows include, Ruth Sherman Gallery, N.Y.C., 1961, Amel Gallery, N.Y.C., 1964, 65, Howard Wise Gallery, N.Y.C., 1968, Kaiser Wilhelm Mus. Haus Lange, Krefeld, Germany, 1970, Hayden Gallery of MIT, Cambridge, Ont. Sci. Centre, Toronto, Can., 1971, Corcoran Gallery Art, 1972, Denise René Gallery, 1972, 73, Musée d'Art Contemporain, Montreal, 1973, Museo de Arte Contemporáneo, Caracas, 1975, Wildenstein Art Center, Houston, 1978, Museo de Bellas Artes, Caracas, 1978, Hong Kong Mus. Art, 1979, Isetan Mus. Art, Tokyo, 1980, Galerie Denise René, Paris, 1983, Nat. Mus. History, Taipei, Taiwan, 1989, Taiwan Mus. of Art, Taichung, 1990, China Nat. Mus. Fine Arts, Beijing, 1997, Centre Georges Pompidou, 2001; one man show: Galerie Denise René, Paris, 2000, Shanghai Art Mus., 2002; represented maj. internat. exhbns., also numerous group exhbns., in permanent collections, Centre Georges Pompidou, Paris; Tate Gallery, London, Albright-Knox Gallery, Buffalo Mus., Addison Gallery Am. Art, Andover, Mass., Museo de Arte Contemporáneo, Caracas, Museo de Bellas Artes, Caracas, Whitney Mus., Chrysler Art Mus., Orlando Sci. Ctr., MIT, Hayden Gallery, Kaiser Wilhelm Mus., Mus. Modern Art, Israel Mus., Jerusalem, Artware, Kunst und Elektronik, Honnover-Messe, Great Exploration-The Hands on Mus., Taiwan Mus. Art, Saibu Gas Mus., Nagoya City Mus., Mus. fü Holographie, Kanagawa Sci. Pk., Hong Kong Sci. Mus., others; commd. works include: fountain at Land Mark, Hong Kong, 1980, water sculpture at Shell Tower, Singapore, 1982, cybernetic upward falling fountains (2), Paris; creator spatial dynamic hydro-cybernetic systems for 42d Internat. Exhbn. Art-La Biennale di Venezia, 1986, Digital Visions-Computers and Art, Everson Mus. of Art, 1987, Contemporary Arts Ctr. Cin., 1987, IBM Gallery of Sci. and Art, N.Y.C., 1988, Phenomena Art Expo, Fukuoka, Japan, 1989, Wonderland of Sci.-Art Kanagawa Internat. Art Sci. Exhbn., Kawasaki, Japan, 1989, Vienna Messe-Wiener Festwochen, 1989, Kanagawa Internat. Art & Sci. Exhbn., Kawasaki, Japan, 1989, Artec 91, Internat. Biennale in Nagoya, Japan, 1991 (Artec Grand Prix winner), Homage à Denise Reñe-Cybernetic Arts, Musée Nat. d'art Modern Ctr. Georges Pompidon, 2001, Shanghai Internat. Biennale for Contemporary Arts, Shanghai Art Mus., 2004; developed concept "5 elements," proposal for new modern sculpture park for Oriental Plz., Beijing, 1996-98; creator first CD-ROM version of cybernetic sculpture, 1995, Info-Art Kwang Ju Internat. Biennale Korea, Osaka Triennale, 1995—, Internet Graphics Gallery, 1995; featured: Art for Tomorrow-The 21st Century, CBS-TV, 1969, Video Variation, WGBH-TV, 1971, Science and Art, Japan TV Man Union, 1982, Art and Sci.-Innovation, Sta. WNET-TV, 1988, The World of Wen-Ying Tsai, Taiwan Pub. TV, 1991. Recipient Soc. Merit award U. Mich., 2001; John Hay Whitney fellow, 1963, MacDowell fellow, 1965, fellow Center Advanced Visual Studies, MIT, 1969, 70. Inventor upward falling fountain, computer mural, multiple light computer array, utilizing environ. feedback control system.

TSALAMATA, VICKY DIMITRIOS, artist, educator, painter, printmaker; b. Athens, Sept. 21, 1948; d. Dimitrios Charalambos Tsalamatas and Helen Antonios Tsalamata-Triantafyllou. Cert. pratique langue Francaise, U. Paris, 1966; diploma in graphic design, Athenian Tech. Inst., Athens, 1969; diploma in fine arts painting, Acad. di Belle Arti, Bologna, Italy, 1973; postgrad., U. Coll. London, 1983, London Coll. Printing, 1983, Slade Sch. Fine Art. Freelance artist, 1983—98; asst. prof. Athens Sch. Fine Arts, 1998—. Invited curator Greek sect. Varosi Mcpl. Mus. Gyor Hungary, 1999, 2001; curator Ctr. Arts Municipality Athens, 1999; invited curator V andVI Internat. Biennial of Drawing and Graphic Arts, Varosi Mcpl. Mus., Hungary; curator Skironio Mus. Polychrome, Athens, 2005. One-woman shows include U. Coll. London, 1983, Bloomsbury Theatre, London, 1983, Hellenic Exhbn. Ctr., 1983, Epoches Gallery, Athens, 1987, Malliotis Cultural Ctr., Boston, 1990, Terracotta Gallery, Thessaloniki, 1993, Antonio Gallery, Athens, 1986, Epoches Gallery, 1987, Stadthalle Deidesheim, Germany, 1993, Adam Galleries, Athens, 1997, Terracotta Gallery, 1998, U. Belgrade, Yugoslavia, 2001, Nadezda Petrovic Gallery, Cacak, Yugoslavia, 2001, Mus. Fine Arts, Alexandria, Egypt, 2001, City Gallery Mesta Bratislava, Slovakia, 2002, Ctr. Expositions et de Conf., Luxembourg, 2003, Mpcl. Mus. Arts, Synagague, Gyor, Hungary, 2007, others, exhibited in group shows at Nicholson Inst. Gallery, Leek, Eng., 1982—83, City Gallery Modern Art, Ljubljana, Slovenia, 1986, 1995, Del Bello Gallery, Toronto, 1986—87, Mcpl. Gallery Art, Kiltsen, 1988, Nat. Mus. Warsaw, Poland, 1988, Nat. Gallery, Athens, 1988, Mus. Fine Arts, Bratislava, 1992, Cultural Ctr., Taejon, 1993, Mus. Fine Arts, Alexandria, 1994, 2003, Lalit Kala Acad., New Delhi, 1994, 2001, City Gallery Contemporary Art, Chamalières, France, 1997, Palace Art El Gezira, Cairo, 1999, 2003, Mcpl. Mus. Sint Niklaas, Belgium, 2001, Mcpl. Gallery Athens, 2002, Greece, 2004, Mcpl. Gallery Hania, 2003—04, Dalarnas Mus., Falun, Sweden, 2004, Nat. Mus. Modern Art, Thessaloniki, Greece, 2003, 2007, 2007, Athens Sch. Fine Arts, Greece, 2004, 2007, Galeried Art Luciciv Schweitzer, Luxemberg, 2007, numerous others, Represented in permanent collections Mcpl. Gallery, Athens, Prefectural Gallery, Greece, Nat. Mus., Belgrade, Kanagawa Prefectural

Gallery, Japan, Mus. Modern Art, Chamalières, France, Mus. Graphic Art, Cairo, Floriean Mus., Carbunari, Romania, Ioanian Ctr. Studies, Athens, others, Sakima Mus., Okinawa, Japan, one-woman shows include Synagogue Mus., 2007, Mcpl. Mus. Art, Gyor, Hungary, 2007, 9th Internat. Biennial Drawing and Graphic Arts, 2007, The Mastezio of Graphic Arts, Gyor, 2007. Juror Chamber Fine Arts Greece, Athens, 1986—89, curator printmaking sector, 1990—92, curator mem. adminstrn. bd., 1992—94, com. for internat. rels., adminstrn. bd., 1996—97. Recipient 1st prize in graphic art, Municipality Serra San Quirico, Italy, 1980, Ministry Culture and House Arts and Letters, Greece, 1985, others, Staff award of Faculty of Fine Arts, U. Belgrade, 1998. Mem.: Artistic Assn., Union Greek Printmakers (founder, adminstrv. com. 1986—), Fedn. Internat. Culturelle Féminine, Internat. Coun. Mil. Mus. Avocations: photography, sports. Home: 235 Vouliagmenis Ave 17237 Athens Greece Office: Athens Sch Fine Arts Printmaking Dept 42 Patission St 10682 Athens Greece Office Phone: 0030+96 33 651. Fax: 0030/210/96 33 651, 0030/210/97 14 322. Business E-Mail: tsalamat@otenet.gr.

TSALIKIAN, EVA, physician, educator; b. Piraeus, Greece, June 22, 1949; came to U.S., 1974; d. Vartan and Arousiak (Kasparian) T.; m. Arthur Bonfield, Apr. 8, 2000. MD, U. Athens, 1973. Rsch. fellow U. Calif. Med. Sch., San Francisco, 1974—76; resident in pediats. Children's Hosp., Pitts., 1976-78, fellow in endocrinology, 1978-80; rsch. fellow Mayo Clinic, Rochester, Minn., 1980-83; asst. prof. U. Iowa, 1983—87, assoc. prof., 1987—2004, prof., 2004—, interim chmn., 2004, vice chmn. clin. affairs, 2005—; dir. pediat. endocrinology dept. pediats. U. Iowa Coll. Med., 1988—; chief staff U. Iowa, 2006—, U. Iowa Hosp. & Clinics. Recipient Young Physician award, AMA, 1977; fellow, Juvenile Diabetes Found., 1978—80, Heinz Nutrition Found., 1980—81. Mem. Am. Diabetes Assn. (bd. dirs. Mid-Am. sect.), Endocrine Soc., Soc. Pediat. Rsch., Am. Pediat. Soc., Lawson Wilkins Soc. for Pediat. Endocrinology, Internat. Soc. Pediat. and Adolescent Diabetes, Midwest Pediat. Endocrino Soc. (pres. 1996-99). Home: 206 Mahaska Dr Iowa City IA 52246-1606 Office: U Iowa Dept Pediatrics 2856 JPP Iowa City IA 52242

TSANG, CHIT-SANG, engineering educator; b. Hong Kong, 1952; came to U.S., 1971; s. Chu-Pang and Siu-Han T.; m. Jiuan-Min Chang, 1979; children: Anita Huey-En, Serena Huey-Ning. BS, La. State U., 1974; MS, Ohio State U., 1976; PhD, U. So. Calif., 1982. Network control engr. RCA Am. Communications Corp., Piscataway, N.J., 1976-77; software engr. Digital Equipment Corp., Maynard, Mass., 1977-79; sr. system engr. Lincom Corp., LA, 1980-88; assoc. prof. Calif. State U., Long Beach, 1988-93, prof., 1993—. Cons. Aerospace Corp., El Segundo, Calif., 1991-94. Deacon 1st Evang. Ch., Glendale, Calif., 1994-98, steward, 1989-96, elder, 1997-2001, Arcadia, Calif., 2001-. Mem. IEEE (sr.), Armed Forces Communications and Electronics Assn., Chinese Christians for Justice (chmn. bd. dirs. 1990—), Tau Beta Pi, Eta Kappa Nu. Avocations: reading, hiking. Office: Calif State U Dept Elec Engring Long Beach CA 90840-0001 Business E-Mail: ctsang@csulb.edu.

TSAO, VIVIAN J., artist, educator; arrived in US, 1974, naturalized; d. Sheng Fen and Wendy (Hsiung) Tsao; m. Raymond Clyde Coreil, June 5, 1976. BA, Nat. Taiwan Normal U., 1973; MFA Painting, Carnegie Mellon U., Pitts., 1976. Art instr. Nat. Taipei U. Edn., 1972—74; corr. in US Hsiung Shih Art Monthly, Taiwan, 1980—96; artist Ceres Gallery, NYC, 1984—; artist in residence Asian Am. Arts Ctr., NYC, 1985—86; adj. asst. prof. fine arts Pace U., NYC, 1990—; artist Biddington's Internet Gallery, NYC, 2000—; art commentator in US United Daily News (Chinese), Taiwan, 2003—. Artist presenter on panel China Inst. Gallery, NYC, 1989; program auditor (art reviewer) N. Y. State Coun. Arts, NYC, 1990—96, mem. jury panel, 1996—99. Author: (Chinese) The Mark of Time: Dialogues with Vivian Tsao on Art in New York, 2003, (essays) Boy on the Rocking Horse: An Introduction to the Art and Life of Eugene Speicher, 2005; exhibitions include Pastel Soc. Am., Butler Inst. Am. Art, Ohio, 2003, Nat Arts Club, NYC, 2003, Am. Acad. Arts and Letters, Bklyn. Mus., Butler Inst. Am. Art, Ohio, Ceres Gallery, NYC, 2005, others, paintings pub. in book 100 New York Painters, 2006. Sponsor student presentations Dyson Coll., Soc. Fellows, Pace U., 1994, 1995, 2000; interpreter internat. symposium Met. Mus. Art, NYC, 1985; judge Employees Art Show N.Y. State Supreme Ct., 1995. Scholarship grantee, Carnegie Mellon U., Pitts., 1975, artist in residence grantee, N.Y. State Coun. Arts. Asian Am. Arts Ctr., 1985—86. Fellow: Soc. Fellows Dyson Coll., Pace U.; mem.: Nat. Arts Club, Coll. Art Assn. Am., Pastel Soc. Am. (Cert. Merit 1981). Avocations: films, music, seashell collecting. Home: 17 Fuller Pl Brooklyn NY 11215-6006 Office: Pace U Dept Fine Arts 41 Park Row New York NY 10038 Personal E-mail: viviantsao@earthlink.net.

TSAPENKO, NIKOLAI EVGENIEVICH, mathematician, educator; b. Nizhniy Novgorod, Russia, May 22, 1953; s. Evgeniy Fedorovich and Laresa Ivanovna (Ivanova) T.; m. Evgenia Viktorovna Patskevich Mar. 1991 (div. June 1996); 1 child, Evgeniy. MS in Radio Physics, Power Engring. Inst., Moscow, 1976; PhD in Math. Physics, Belarusian Acad. Scis., Minsk, 1992. Rsch. assoc. Radio Engring. and Electronics Inst. Acad. Scis., Moscow, 1977-79; postdoctoral Mining Inst., Moscow, 1979-84; asst. prof. Acad. Water-Transport, Moscow, 1985-91; assoc. prof. Power Engring. Inst., Tech. U., Moscow, 1992-95; lectr. State Tech. U., Moscow, 1995—2007, State Mining U., Moscow, 2007—. Author: Analytical Functions and Integral Transformations, 1996, New Relativistic Law of the Motion, 2004, Riccati Equation and Wave Processes, 2008; contbr. articles to profl. jours. Mem. Dem. Choice Russia, 1994. Recipient medal Defender of Free Russia, 1994. Mem. N.Y. Acad. Scis. Avocations: sport, poetry. Home: Malysheva St 26 Bldg 1 Apt 25 109263 Moscow Russia Business E-Mail: nt225@yandex.ru.

TSATSARONIS, GEORGE, mechanical engineering educator, researcher; b. Thessaloniki, Greece, Sept. 22, 1949; arrived in US, 1982; s. Asterios and Chrysoula (Ioannidou) T. Diploma in mech. engring., Nat. Tech. U., Athens, Greece, 1972; MBA, Tech. U. Aachen, Germany, 1976, PhD in Mech. Engring., 1977, habilitation in thermoeconomics, 1985; PhD (hon.), U. Polytech., Bucharest, 2004. From rsch. assoc. to lectr. to sr. staff mem. Inst. of Thermodynamics, Aachen, 1972-82; rsch. prof. Energy & Environ. Engring. Ctr. Desert Rsch. Inst., Reno, 1982-86; prof. mech. engring. Ctr. for Electric Power, Tenn. Technol. U., Cookeville, 1986-94; prof. energy engring. and protection of environ. Tech. U. Berlin, 1994—2005, dir. Inst. for Energy Engring., 1996—2005. Reviewer in field; hon. prof. North China Electric Power U., 1997; co-organizer 21 internat. confs. Author (with A. Bejan and M. Moran): Thermal Design and Optimization, 1996; hon. editor: Internat. Jour. Thermodynamics, 2003—, assoc. editor: Energy, The Internat. Jour., 1986—, Jour. Energy Resources Tech., 1988—95, Energy Conversion and Mgmt., 1995—, Internat. Jour. Applied Thermodynamics, 1998—2002, Internat. Jour. Energy, Environment and Econs., 2000—; contbr. articles to profl. jours. Chmn. exec. com. Internat. Ctr. for Applied Thermodynamics, 1998-2001. Recipient Borchers award, Tech. U. Aachen, 1977, E.F. Obert Best Paper award, ASME, 1994, 1999, James Harry Potter Gold medal ASME, 1998, Calvin Rice Lecture award, 2008. Fellow ASME (chmn. systems analysis com. 1987-90, mem. exec. com. advanced energy sys. div. 1993-97); Greek Soc. Engrs., German Assn. Univ. Profs. Greek Orthodox. Home: Weissdornweg 15 12205 Berlin Germany Office: Tech U Berlin Marchstr 18 10587 Berlin Germany Office Phone: +49 30 314 24776. E-mail: tsatsaronis@iet.tu-berlin.de.

TSAY, CHING SOW, retired anesthesiologist; b. Taipei, Taiwan, 1939; MD, Kaohsiung Med. Coll., Taiwan, 1964. Diplomate Am. Bd. Anesthesiology. Intern St. Vincent's Med. Ctr., Staten Island, NY, 1967-68; resident in anesthesiology St. Joseph Hosp., Joliet, Ill., 1968-69, Washington Hosp. Ctr., 1969-71; staff Cmty. Health Ctr. Branch County, Coldwater, Mich.; ret., 2006. Mem. Am. Soc. Anesthesiologists, Mich. Soc. Anesthesiologists, Internat. Anesthesia Rsch. Soc.

TSAY, RUEY SHIONG, business and statistics educator; b. Nan-tou, Taiwan, Dec. 8, 1951; came to U.S., 1977; s. Chung-Sing and Chu (Lee) T.; m. Teresa Kuan, June 28, 1977; children: Julie L., Richard S., Vicki A. BS, Nat. Tsing-Hua U., Tsing-Chu, Taiwan, 1974; PhD, U. Wis., 1982. Asst. prof. Carnegie Mellon U., Pitts., 1982-86, assoc. prof., 1987-89; prof. bus. and stats. U. Chgo. Bus. Sch., 1990—. Contbr. articles to profl. jours. Grantee Alcoa Found., 1985, NSF, 1987, 89, 91. Fellow Am. Statis. Assn., Inst. Math. Stats., Royal Statis. Soc.; mem. IEEE, Econometric Soc., Internat. Chinese Statis. Assn. (dir. 1991—). Avocation: travel. Home: 1363 E Park Pl Chicago IL 60637-1767 Office: U Chgo Grad Sch Bus 1101 E 58th St Chicago IL 60637-1511

TSCHERNISCH, SERGEI P., academic administrator; BA, San Francisco State U.; MFA in Theatre, Stanford U.; student, San Francisco Actors' Workshop, Stanford Repertory Theatre. Founding mem. Calif. Inst. of Arts, 1969, mem. faculty, assoc. dean Sch. Theatre, dir., 1969-80; prof. dept. theatre U. Md., College Park, 1980-82; dir. divsn. performing and visual arts Northeastern U., Boston, 1982-92; dean Coll. of Comm. and Fine Arts Loyola Marymount U., LA, 1992-94; pres. Cornish Coll. of Arts, Seattle, 1994—. Advisor NEA; mem. com. USIA; cons. to many festivals. Office: Cornish College of the Arts 1000 Lenora St Seattle WA 98121-2718 Office Phone: 206-726-5001. E-mail: stschernisch@cornish.edu.

TSCHERNY, GEORGE, graphics designer; b. Budapest, Hungary, July 12, 1924; s. Mendel and Bella (Heimann) T.; m. Sonia Katz, July 7, 1950; children: Nadia, Carla Student, Pratt Inst., Bklyn., 1947-50. Staff designer Donald Deskey & Assocs., NYC, 1950-53; designer, assoc. George Nelson & Assocs., NYC, 1953-55; pres. George Tscherny, Inc., NYC, 1955—. Instr. Pratt Inst., Bklyn., 1956, bd. advisors, 1979; instr. Sch. Visual Arts, NYC, 1955-64; curriculum cons. Phila. Coll. Art, 1967; Mellon vis. prof. Cooper Union, NY, 1978 Exhibitions include Visual Art Mus., NYC, 1992, La Galerie Blanche, Briey, France, 2007; exhibited in group shows, Germany, 1962-67, Italy, 1974, US, 1975; represented in permanent collections Mus. Modern Art, NYC, Cooper Hewitt Mus., NYC, Libr. of Congress, Washington, Bibliotheque Nat. France, Paris, Kunstgewerbeschule der Stadt Zurich, Graphic Design Archive at Rochester Inst. Tech., School Visual Arts Archive; monograph of work George Tscherny, Minimum Means, Maximum Meaning, 2004; author: Changing Faces, 2004, Where Would the Button be Without the Button Hole?, 2008. Contbr. design svcs. to UN Assn., Sta. WNET Pub. TV, Am. Lung Assn., Peace Corps, Cystic Fibrosis Found., L.I. State Park Commn. With U.S. Army, 1943-46, ETO. Recipient numerous awards, Am. Inst. Graphic Arts medal, 1988, Art Dirs. Club N.Y. (hall of fame 1997), N.Y. Type Dirs. Club, Silver medal Warsaw Biennale, 1976; inducted into Art Dirs. Club Hall of Fame, 1997. Mem. Am. Inst. Graphic Arts (pres. 1966-68), Alliance Graphique Internat. Office: 238 E 72nd St New York NY 10021-4503 Office Phone: 212-734-3277. Personal E-mail: gtscherny@aol.com.

TSCHETTER, RONALD ALLEN, former federal agency administrator; b. Huron, SD, Oct. 4, 1941; m. Nancy Tschetter; 2 children. BA in Psychology & Social Studies, Bethel Coll., 1963. Joined Blyth Eastman Dillon Union Securities, 1970, Dain Rauscher, 1973, pres. pvt. client group, 1991—2001; pres. D.A. Davidson & Co., Great Falls, Mont., 2004—06; dir. US Peace Corps, Washington, 2006—08. Bd. dirs. D.A. Davidson & Co., 2004—06, Community Bank of Plymouth; mem. Nat. Peace Corps Assn., 1993—99, chmn., 1995—98, hon. mem., 2000—03. Vol. cmty. health worker Peace Corps, India, 1966—68. Avocations: hunting, fishing, woodworking.*

TSCHIRHART, JOHN THOMAS, economist, educator; b. NYC, Oct. 23, 1946; s. John A. and Mary Ellen (McManus) T.; children: Deborah, Daniel. BS, Johns Hopkins U., 1970; MS, Purdue U., 1972, PhD, 1975. Instr. Purdue U., West Lafayette, Ind., 1973-75; asst. prof. SUNY, Buffalo, 1975-78; assoc. prof. U. Wyo., Laramie, 1978-81, prof., 1982—. Author: Regulation of Natural Monopolies, 1988; contbr. articles to profl. jours. Midshipman USN, 1964-66. Mem. Am. Econs. Assn. Home: 5887 Obenchain Rd Laporte CO 80535-9729 Office: U Wyo Dept Econs 1000 E University Ave Laramie WY 82071-3985 Office Phone: 307-766-2356.

TSCHOEPE, GARY JOSEPH, retired political science professor; b. New Braunfels, Tex., Jan. 4, 1951; s. Anna Lee Tschoepe; m. Gayle Edwards; 1 child, Tara Lynn Edwards. Degree with honors, SW Tex. U., 1972; PhD in Polit. Sci., U. Houston, 1984—92. Vis. asst. prof. polit. sci. U. Louisville, 1992—93; assoc. prof. polit. sci. and pub. adminstrn. U. Tex.-Pan America, Edinburg, 1993—2003. Sr. rschr. Decision Info. Resources, Inc., Houston, 1995—96. Contbr. articles to profl. jours. Mem.: Am. Polit. Sci. Assn. Business E-Mail: tschoepe@utpu.edu.

TSE, CHARLES YUNG CHANG, pharmaceutical executive, lawyer; b. Shanghai, Mar. 22, 1926; s. Kung Chao and Say Ying (Chen) T.; m. Vivian Chang, Apr. 25, 1955; 1 dau., Roberta. BA in Econs, St. John's U., Shanghai, 1949; MS in Acctg, U. Ill., 1950; JD, N.Y. Law Sch., 1990. Asst. to controller Am. Internat. Group, NYC, 1950-54, asst. mgr. Singapore-Malaysia, 1955-57; with Warner-Lambert Co., Morris Plains, NJ, 1957-86, area mgr. S.E. Asia, 1966-68, regional dir. S.E. Asia, 1968-69, v.p. Australasia, 1970-71, pres. Western Hemisphere Group, 1971-72, pres. Pan Am. Mgmt. Center, 1972-76, pres. European Mgmt. Center, 1976-78, pres. Internat. Group, 1979-86, sr. v.p. corp., 1980-83, exec. v.p. corp., 1984-85, vice chmn., 1985-86. Dir. Foster Wheeler Corp., Livingston, N.J., 1984-98, Superior Telecom., Inc., 1996—, Com. of 100; mem. faculty bus. adminstrn. dept. Fairleigh Dickinson U., 1961-64; pres. Cancer Rsch. Inst., Inc., N.Y.C., 1991-92. Bd. visitors CCNY, 1974-78; trustee Morristown Meml. Hosp. (N.J.), 1982-86; bd. dirs. Bus. Council for Internat. Understanding, 1984-87. Mem. NAM (dir. 1984-86), Assn. of the Bar of the City of N.Y. (mem. Asian affairs com. 1991-2001).

TSE, ELIZABETH SUET HING, computer research engineer; m. George Wing Au. BS, Tufts U., Medford, Mass.; MS, Johns Hopkins U., Balt.; PhD, Stevens Inst. Tech., Hoboken, NJ, 2002. Cert. Mass. State engr. in tng. Network mgmt. sys. engr., NM Divsn. AT&T Network and Computing Svcs. Directorate, Middletown, NJ, 1992—97; network mgmt. sys. and rsch. engr. AT&T Labs., IP Svcs. Planning and Devel. Orgn., 1997—99; VoIP project mgmt. sys. engr. AT&T Labs., IP Bus., Enhanced Access Svcs. Orgn., 1999—2004; sys. engr. AT&T Labs, Unified Voice/VoIP Devel. Orgn., 2004; VoIP arch. & tech. cons. Businessedge Solutions, East Brunswick, NJ, 2005. Reviewer Jour. Sys. Architecture, Elsevier Sci., Amsterdam, 2006—, Inst. Engring. and Tech. Comm., 2006—. Computer engr. CERDEC Software Engring. Directorate USAR, 2005—06, Ft. Monmouth, sr. computer rsch. engr., 2006—. Grant, USAR Comm. Electronic Rsch. Devel. & Engring. Ctr., 2007. Mem.: IEEE (treas. comm. chpt. 2009—). Achievements include patents for methods apparatus for network use optimizatio; dual propagation paths for packets scalable reconficurable reutors, method for reconfiguring a router. Office: USAR CERDEC STCD Bldg 2700 4C-334A Fort Monmouth NJ 07703 Personal E-mail: estagau@yahoo.com.

TSE, FLORENCE, director; arrived in US, 1968, naturalized; d. Ying Yuan Wu and Yueh Fu Ma; m. Peter Chin Sang Tse, Nov. 12, 1967; children: Winona, Perkin, David. BS in Biology, Chinese U. Hong Kong, 1967; MS in Biology, LI U., Bklyn., 1972. Tchr. HS sci. Mary Knoll Sisters Sch., Hong Kong, 1967—68; tchg. fellow biology LI U., NY, 1969—71; asst. to dean of students Queensborough Cmty. Coll., NYC, 1980—83, coord. Asian career devel. project, 1983—91, coord. port of entry program, 1991—97, dir. port of entry program and cmty. outreach, 1997—. Cons. to Asian students Newtown HS, NYC, 1988—89, John Bowne HS, NYC, 1988—89; program coord., China pavilion Flushing Coun. on Culture and Arts, NYC, 1988—92; performance coord., Hong Kong dragon boat festival Hong Kong Econ. and Trade Office, NYC, 1990—95. Mem. Neighborhood Chamber Orch., Bklyn., 1975—82; coord. edn. com. Queens Census Outreach for Chinese, NYC, 1988—90; mem. adv. bd. Flushing Coun. on Culture and Arts, NYC, 1999—2003; vol. exec. dir. Chinese Immigrant Svcs., Inc., NYC, 1989—2004; mem. bd. dirs. Queens Oratoria Soc., NYC, 1999—2002. Recipient Cmty. Svc. award, Flushing Chinese Bus. Assn., 1993, Disting. Asian Am. award, NYC Comptroller's Office, 1993, Outstanding Cultural & Cmty. Leader award, Flushing Coun. on Cultures and Arts, 1997, Edn. and Cultural Promotion Svc. award, Asian Am. Dem. Assn. Queens, Inc., 2003, Everyday Hero award, NY Newsday, 2006, Outstanding Vol. award, Chinese Immigrant Svcs., Inc., 2007, Outstanding Cmty. Svc. award, Chinese Am. Voters Assn., 2009; named Women of Yr., Queens Women Ctr. and Queens Courier, 1995. D-Conservative. Avocations: travel, reading, movies.

TSE, MARIAN A., lawyer; AB, Vassar Coll., 1976; JD, Columbia U., 1979. Bar: Mass. 1979. Ptnr., chair, ERISA/employment benefits practice Goodwin Procter LLP, Boston, mem., diversity com. Bd. dir. Greater Boston Legal Services. Mem.: ABA, Asian Am. Lawyers Assn. Mass., New England Employee Benefits Coun., Boston Bar Assn. Office: Goodwin Procter LLP Exchange Pl 53 State St Boston MA 02109 Office Phone: 617-570-1169. Office Fax: 617-523-1231. Business E-Mail: mtse@goodwinprocter.com.

TSE, PHILIP KUI, airport engineering maintenance consultant; b. Guangzhou, China, May 15, 1934; arrived in Can., 1994; s. Wai-Woon and Yok-Wun (Leung) T.; m. Helen Chow, Jan. 22, 1960; children: Christina Suyen, Elsie Ba-Sai, Tony Yee-Hin, Vanilla Hung. BSc in Archtl. Engring., Union Coll., 1963; postgrad. cert. in strategic planning and mgmt., Calif. State U., Fresno, 1989; postgrad. cert. in project mgmt., Tongji U., Shanghai, 1994. Registered profl. civil engr., Hong Kong; chartered water and environ. mgr., U.K.; chartered environmentalist, U.K. Various positions Public Works Dept., Hong Kong Govt., 1956-71; foreman engring. draughtsman class I, engr.-in-tng., asst. engr. drainage works, roads and drainage office, roads and hwys. new territories region PWD, Hong Kong, 1971-75, asst. engr. develop. and airport divsn., 1975-83, engr. devel. sect., devel. and airport divsn., 1983-88; project engr. airport maintenance, devel. and airport divsn. Engring. Devel. Dept., Civil Engring. Svcs. Dept., Hong Kong, 1988-93; sr. airport engr. Hong Kong Internat. Airport Civil Engring. Svcs. Dept., Civil Engring. Dept., 1993-95; airport diagnostic engring., environ. mgmt. cons., 1963-68. Lectr. Hong Kong Tech. Coll. (now Hong Kong Poly. U.), 1968—; hon. constrn. and devel. cons., adv. bd. Shun Shin Chee Kit Yin Koon Charity Orgn., Hong Kong, 1968—. Fellow ASCE (life); mem. Hong Kong Instn. Engrs., Instn. Pub. Health Engrs. (U.K.), Chartered Instn. Water and Environ. Mgr. (U.K.). Avocations: hiking, swimming, calligraphy, reading, drawing. Home: 913-89 Skymark Dr North York ON Canada M2H 3S6 Home Phone: 416-499-8592; Office Phone: 416-499-8592. Office Fax: 416-499-8592.

TSE, STEPHEN, artist, educator; b. Hong Kong, Oct. 20, 1938; arrived in US, 1959; s. Kwan-Yeung Tse and So-Kwan Chu; m. May Kam, Mar. 23, 2973; 1 child, Lisa. BFA, Washburn U., Topeka, Kans., 1965; MFA, U. Idaho, Moscow, 1967. Prof. emeritus Big Bend Coll., Moses Lake, Wash., 1966—96. One-man shows include U. Idaho Mus. Art, 1966, U. Oreg. Mus. Art, 1977, Kristen Gallery, 1977, 1978, 1980, 1982, 1985, Spokane C.C., 1978, Whatcom Mus. Hist. Art, 1980, Wash. State U., 1983, Prichard Art Gallery, U. Idaho, 1986, 30 group shows. Mem.: Asian Art Coun. Home Phone: 425-465-8388. Personal E-mail: stephenstse@msn.com.

TSEBELIS, GEORGE, political science professor; b. Athens, Greece; s. Panayotis T. and Persefone Karnalaki; children: Alexander, Emily. MA, Nat. Tech. U., Athens, 1975; degree in polit. sci., Institut d'Etudes Politiques de Paris, 1979; PhD in Engring., U. Paris VI, 1979; PhD in Polit. Sci., Wash. U., St. Louis, 1985. Vis. asst. prof. Stanford U., Palo Alto, Calif., 1985—86; asst. prof. Duke U., Durham, NC, 1986-87, UCLA, 1987-89, assoc. prof., 1989-91, prof., 1991—2007; Anatol Rapoport collegiate prof. polit. sci. U. Mich., Ann Arbor, 2007—. Author: Nested Games, 1990, Veto Players, 2002; co-author (with J. Money): Bicameralism, 1997; mem. editl. bd.: Polit. Rsch. Quar., 1991-94, Jour. Theoretical Politics, 1996-, Governance, 1998-, European Union Politics, 1999-, French politics, 2003-; contbr. book chapters, articles to profl. jours. Recipient Pi Sigma Alpha award, 1993, Gregory Luebbert award, 1996; grantee, NSF, 1995—99; fellow, Max Planck Inst., 1991, Hoover Inst., 1992—93; Guggenheim fellow, 1995—96, Russell Sage fellow, 2001. Mem. Am. Polit. Sci. Assn. Avocations: tennis, swimming. Office: Univ Mich Dept Polit Sci 6759 Haven Hall 505 S State St Ann Arbor MI 48109-1045 Office Phone: 734-647-7974. Office Fax: 734-764-3522. E-mail: tsebelis@umich.edu.*

TSENG, DYI-HWA, environmental engineer, educator, dean; m. Dyi-Ming Chu, Mar. 17, 1955; children: Tai-Wei Joy, Tai-Fu. Diploma in civil engring., Taipei Inst. Tech., Taiwan, 1974; MS, Marquette U., Milw., 1978; PhD, Purdue U., West Lafayette, Ind., 1983. Rsch. asst. Marquette U., Milwaukee, Wis., 1977—78, Purdue U., West Lafayette, Ind., 1978—83; assoc. prof. Nat. Ctrl. U., Chung-Li, Taiwan, 1983—89, prof. Dept Civil Engring., 1989—90, prof. Grad. Inst. Environ. Engring., 1990—, chair, 1990—95, assoc. dean Coll. Engring., 1997—99, dean of student affairs, 1999—2004, dean of academic affairs, 2005—06. Recipient Disting. Engring. Prof. award, Chinese Inst. of Engrs., 2005,

Engring. medal, Chinese Inst. of Environ. Engring., 2003. Mem.: Internat. Water Assn. Office: Nat Ctrl U No 300 Chungda Rd Jhongli 32054 Taiwan Office Fax: 883-3-4226944. E-mail: dhtseng@ncuen.ncu.edu.tw.

TSENG, GREG, Internet company executive; AB in Chemistry, Physics & Math., Harvard U. Founder Avivon Inc.; COO Limespot.com LLC; co-founder, CEO Jumpstart Technologies, 2000—05, Tagged.com, San Francisco, 2004—. Co-author: Harvard Entrepreneurs Club Guide to Starting Your Own Business, 1999. Mem.: Harvard Entrepreneurs Club (HEC) (dir. 1998—2000). Office: Tagged Inc 110 Pacific Ave Mall Box #117 San Francisco CA 94111

TSENG, HOWARD SHIH CHANG, economics professor, investment company executive; b. Tainan, Taiwan, Jan. 14, 1935; came to U.S., 1963; s. Picheng and Chaoliu (Wang) T.; m. Evelina M. Young, Dec. 25, 1965; 1 child, Elaine Evelina. BA, Nat. Taiwan U., Taipei, 1957, MA, 1963; PhD, U. Okla., 1972. Chief economist Cooperative Bank Taiwan, Taipei, 1959-61; dir. tax services Bur. Taxation, Govt. Taiwan, Republic China, Taipei, 1961-63; instr. U. Okla., Norman, 1968; asst. prof. Ga. So. U., Statosboro, 1968-71; prof. bus. and econs. Catawba Coll., Salisbury, 1971—2001; adj. prof. San Francisco State U., 2002—, 2002—. Pres. Am. Prudential Investments, Salisbury, 1981-89; pres. Tsengs Investments, 1990—. Author: Investments, 1982; contbr. articles to profl. jours. Coordinator, supporter study mathematically precocious youth Johns Hopkins U., Balt., 1982—; ptnr. World Vision, Calif., 1986-92. Academic research grantee Academia Sinica, Taipei, 1962; Ford Found. fellow, Taipei, 1963. Mem. AAUP, Ea. Econ. Assn., Am. Econ. Assn., Am. Assn. Individual Investors, Taiwan Investment (organizer 1986—), Taiwanese-Am. Assn. Greater Charlotte (pres. 1994-96), Nat. Travel Club. Avocations: antiques, travel, reading. Office: Catawba Coll W Innes St Salisbury NC 28144 Office Fax: 704-637-5724.

TSENG, YANI, professional golfer; b. Taiwan, Jan. 23, 1989; Profl. golfer LPGA, 2007—. Named Rookie of Yr., LPGA Tour, Golf Digest, 2008. Achievements include winning LPGA major championships, LPGA Championship, 2008; becoming the first player from Taiwan and the second youngest player (age 19) to win a LPGA major championship; professional wins also include DLF Women's Indian Open, CN Canadian Women's Tour at Vancouver Golf Club. Avocations: pool, movies. Office: LPGA 100 International Golf Dr Daytona Beach FL 32124 Office Phone: 386-274-6200. Office Fax: 386-274-1099.*

TSERETELI, ZURAB, surgeon; MD, Tbilisi State Med. U., Ga., 1994. Rsch. fellow Emory U. Sch. Medicine, Atlanta, 1999—2001; resident-surgeon Oreg. Health & Scis. U., Portland, Oreg., 2001—02, Med. Coll. Ga., Augusta, 2002—06; fellow- minimally invasive & bariatric surgery U. Mo.-Columbia, 2006—07; gen., minimally invasive & bariatric surgeon Hays Med. Ctr., Kans., 2007—. Mem.: ACS, Soc. Am. Gastrointestinal & Endoscopic Surgeons. Achievements include research in minimally invasive and bariatric surgery. Office: Hays Med Ctr 2500 Canterbury Dr Ste 202 Hays KS 67601

TSIBULSKY, VLADIMIR LVOVICH, psychologist, researcher; b. Moscow, Apr. 19, 1951; arrived in U.S., 1993; s. Lev Nikolaevich Tsibulsky and Anna Sergeevna Subbotovich; m. Svetlana Olegovna Dmitrieva, Feb. 15, 2005; children: Cyril, Veronica, Anastasia, Alice. BS, Moscow State U., 1972, MS, PhD, Moscow State U., 1973. Rsch. scientist Severtsov Inst. Evolutionary Morphology and Ecology Animals, USSR Acad. of Sciences, Moscow, 1973—82; sr. rsch. scientist Lab. Neuropharmacology, Ctrl. Sci. Lab. of USSR Ministry of Health, Moscow, 1982—85, All-Union Sci. Ctr. Narcology USSR Ministry of Health, Moscow, 1985—90; vis. scientist Ctr. Studies Behavioral Neurobiology Concordia U., Montreal, Que., Canada, 1990—92; rsch. asst. prof. U. Cin., 1993—. Grantee, Nat. Inst. Drug Abuse, 2001—05; scholar, Nat. Heart, Lung, and Blood Inst., 1998—2001. Mem.: N.Y. Acad. Scis., Soc. Neuroscience, Pavlovian Physiol. Soc. Orthodox Christian. Achievements include patents for 1 (Silatranyl) Metyl Derivate Lactams possessing Neurotropic activity and the method to produce them. Avocations: travel, reading. Office: U Cin 231 Albert Sabin Way Mail Location 559 Cincinnati OH 45267-0559 Business E-Mail: vladimir.tsibulsky@uc.edu.

TSIEN, ROGER YONCHIEN, chemist, cell biologist; b. NYC, Feb. 1, 1952; s. Hsue Chu and Yi Ying (Li) Tsien; m. Wendy M. Globe, July 30, 1982. AB in Chemistry and Physics, summa cum laude, Harvard Coll., 1972; PhD in Physiology, Churchill Coll., U. Cambridge, Eng., 1977; PhD (hon.), Cath. U., Leuven, Belgium, 1995. Rsch. asst. U. Cambridge, Eng., 1975-78; asst. prof. dept. physiology-anatomy U. Calif., Berkeley, 1981-85, assoc. prof., 1985-87, prof., 1987-89, prof. pharmacology, chemistry & biochemistry San Diego, 1989—. Biological investigator Howard Hughes Med. Inst., Chevy Chase, Md., 1989—; T.Y. Shen vis. prof. medicinal chemistry MIT, 1991; co-founder Aurora Bioscis. Corp., 1994, Senomyx, Inc., 1998; Todd vis. prof. chemistry U. Cambridge, 2003. Contbr. articles to profl. jours., chapters to books. Recipient Lamport prize, NY Acad. Scis., 1986, Javits Neurosci. Investigator award, Nat. Inst. Neurological Disorders & Stroke, 1989, Young Scientist award, Passano Found., 1991, W. Alden Spencer award in Neurobiology, Columbia U., 1991, Artois-Baillet-Latour Health prize, Belgium, 1995, Gairdner Found. Internat. award, 1995, Rsch. prize, Am. Heart Assn., 1995, Pearse prize, Royal Microscopical Soc., 2000, Creative Invention award, Am. Chem. Soc., 2002, Christian B. Anfinsen award, Protein Soc., 2002, Heineken prize for biochemistry/biophysics, Royal Netherlands Acad. Scis., 2002, Max Delbrück Medal, Berlin, 2002, Wolf Found. prize in medicine, Israel, 2004, Keio Med. Sci. prize, Japan, 2004, Perl prize in neurosci., U. NC, 2005, J.Allyn Taylor Internat. prize in medicine, Robarts Inst., Canada, 2005, Lewis S. Rosenstiel award for disting. work in basic med. scis., Brandeis U., 2006, E.B. Wilson medal, Am. Soc. Cell Biology, 2008; co-recipient Nobel Prize in Chemistry, 2008. Mem.: NAS, Inst. Medicine, Am. Acad. Arts & Scis., Phi Beta Kappa. Achievements include design of a green fluorescent protein; development of a biological application of molecules to measure and/or manipulate intracellular calcium, sodium, and hydrogen ions; new methods for microscopic imaging and pharmaceutical high-throughput screening. Office: Tsien Lab HHMI - UCSD CMM West 310 9500 Gilman Dr La Jolla CA 92093-0647 Office Phone: 858-534-4891. Fax: 858-534-5270. E-mail: rtsien@ucsd.edu.*

TSIGE, MESFIN, physicist; PhD, Case Western Res. U., Cleve., 2001. Asst. prof. So. Ill. U., Carbondale, 2005. Office: Southern Ill Univ Carbonda 1245 Lincoln Dr Carbondale IL 62901 Business E-Mail: mtsige@physics.siu.edu.

TSIGELNY, IGOR, research scientist; m. Valentina Kouznetsova. PhD, Inst. Physics and Mechanics, Acad. Sci. Ukraine, 1972—78. Asst. scientist U. Calif., San Diego, 1994—99, assoc. scientist, 2000—07, project scientist, 2007—. Author: Molecular Cybernetics, 1990; editor: Protein Structure Prediction: Bioinformatic Approach, 2002; mng. editor: jour. Analytical Reports in Internat. Edn.; contbr. over 180 articles to profl. jours. Mem.: Biophysical Soc., US Fencing Assn. Achievements include 11 Patents. Business E-Mail: itsigeln@ucsd.edu.

TSIKLAURI, SHALVA, physics professor; b. Tbilisi, Georgia, Apr. 14, 1954; s. Mamuka Tsiklauri and Zina Kherkeladze; m. Karolina Gamsakhurdia; children: Tamar, Nino. PhD, Tbilisi State U., 1986. Asst. prof. City Tech. CUNY, Bklyn., 2006—; faculty Phoenix U., Jersey City, 2006—. Assoc. prof. Tbilisi State U., 1991—2005. Grantee, Investigation Few Nuc. and Hypernuclear Physics, 1993—95. Mem.: Am. Phys. Soc. Achievements include research in property of the quantum dots. Home: 2002 Ave J Apt 4C Brooklyn NY 11210 Office Phone: 718-260-5277. Personal E-mail: shalvats@optimum.net. Business E-Mail: stsiklauri@citytech.cuny.edu.

TSILIGARIDIS, JOHN, education educator, researcher; s. Theodoros Tsiligaridis and Georgia Tsiligaridou; m. Labrini Tziamourani, June 8, 1985; children: Theodoros, Athanasios. BS in Math., U. Ioannina, Greece, 1982; MS in Informatics and Operational Rsch., U. Athens, 1985; PhD in Computer Networks, Nat. Tech. U. Athens, 1994; MPhil in Data Mining, U. Manchester Inst. of Sci. and Tech., Eng., 2000; PhD in Computer Sci. and Engring., U. Buffalo, 2003. Rsch. fellow Pacific NW Nat. Lab., Richland, Wash., 2004; asst. prof. computer sci. Heritage U., Toppenish, Wash., 2004—. Software engr., Athens, 1988—99. Author: (rsch. articles) Computer Communications Jour., Elsevier, Telecommunication Systems Journal, Telecommunications Systems Jour. Mem.: Inst. for Ops. Rsch. and the Mgmt. Scis., Assn. of Computing Machinery, IEEE.

TSIRIKOS, ATHANASIOS IOANNIS, orthopedist, spinal surgeon, educator; s. Ioannis Athanasios Tsirikos and Theodora Tsirikou; m. Victoria Maria Papageorge, June 9, 2001; children: Theodora, John. MD, U. Athens, 1994, PhD, 2007. Resident gen. surgery 411 Gen. Mil. Hosp., Dist. Gen. Hosp. Syros, Greece, 1994—96; resident orthopedics U. Hosp., Athens, 1996—2000; fellow pediat. orthopedics A.I. duPont Hosp. for Children, Wilmington, Del., 2001—02; fellow in spine surgery Gt. Ormond St. Hosp. for Children, Royal Nat. Orthopedic Hosp., Stanmore, England, 2002—03, Royal Infirmary, Royal Hosp. for Sick Children, Edinburgh, Scotland, 2004—05; cons. orthop. and spine surgeon Scottish Nat. Spine Deformity Ctr., Royal Hosp. for Sick Children, Edinburgh, 2005—. Clin. dir. Scottish Nat. Spine Deformity Ctr., Edinburgh, 2006—; hon. clin. sr. lectr. U. Edinburgh, 2006—; presenter in field. Contbr. articles to profl. jours., chapters to books. With Greek Army, 1994—95. Scholar, Greek Orthopedic Soc. Fellow: Royal Coll. Surgeons; mem.: Greek Spine Soc., Scoliosis Rsch. Soc. (Best Clin. Poster Presentation award 2003), European Soc. Sports Traumatology, Brit. Orthopedic Assn., Greek Orthopedic Soc., Brit. Scoliosis Soc. (Best Oral Paper Presentation award 2003, Best Clin. Poster Presentation award 2003, Best Oral Paper Presentation award 2005). Avocations: sports, music, literature, films, travel. Office: Scottish Nat Spine Deformity Ctr Royal Hosp Sick Children Sciennes Rd Edinburgh EH9 1LF Scotland

TSIRPANLIS, CONSTANTINE N., theology, philosophy, classics and history educator; b. Kos, Greece, Mar. 18, 1935; arrived in US, 1957; m. Sophia Pappas, July 12, 1975; children: Kalliope-Chrysoula, Nike. BA, STM, lic. in theology magna cum laude, Halke Theol. Sem., Istanbul, Turkey, 1957; ThM, Harvard U., 1962; ThD, Union Theol. Sem., 1963; MA, Columbia U., 1966, PhD, 1970, Fordham U., 1973; DLitt (hon.), World Acad. Arts and Culture, 1993. Instr., organizer Greek-Am. cmtys., 1958-63; founder, chmn., prof. modern Greek studies NYU, 1963-70; prof. world history NY Inst. Tech. NYC and Delaware County Coll., Media, Pa., 1967-75; disting. prof. theology, sociology, history, ecumenism, Greek studies Union Theol. Sem., Barrytown, NY, 1976-97; chmn., prof. scriptures, patristics, Greek lang., theology St. Sophia Ukraine Orthodox Theol. Sem. Am., Somerset, NJ, 1999—. Chmn., prof. classics Collegiate Sch., NYC, 1967—69; prof. modern Greek lang. and lit. New Sch. Social Rsch., NYC, 1968—70; prof. classical mythology Hunter Coll. CUNY, 1968—70. Author: 51 books, A Short History of the Greek Language, 1966, rev. edit., 1970, rev. augmented edit., 2004, A Modern Greek Reader for Americans, 1967, rev. edit., 1968, A Modern Greek idiom and Phrase Book, 1978, Mark Eugenicus, 1979, N. Cabasilas, 1979, Greek Patristic Theology, 30 vols.; founder, editor: The Patristic and Byzantine Rev., 1981—, pub., editor-in-chief: Hellenism in Am., 40 vols., 1969—; contbr. articles to profl. jours. Decorated medal of Nat. Rebirth 1821 Greece, medals of Byzantine nobility including count, baron, G. Chevalier, Gt. Prior N.Am., medal of Accademia Ferdinandea, medals of Diethnés Hetereia Hellenon Logotechnon. Mem.: Panepistimion Oekoumenikou Ellinismou (pres., founder), Pan-Eureopean Inst. Vyzantinōn Erevnon (pres., founder), Justinianum Oikoumenikon R.C. (pres., founder), Am. Inst. Patristic-Byzantine Studies (pres., founder), Am. Soc. Papyrologists, Hellenic Philog. Assn., N.Am. Patristic Soc., Am. Philos. Assn., Internat. Assn. Byzantine Studies, Am. Acad. Medieval Studies, Am. Philog. Assn., Am. Hist. Assn., Pan Dodecanisian Fedn. US (founder, pres.), Am. Soc. Neohellenic Studies (founder, v.p.), World Acad. Arts and Culture (hon.), Pan-Eureopan Inst. and U. Ecumenical Hellenism. Home and Office: 12 Minuet Ln Kingston NY 12401-6955 Office Phone: 845-336-8797. Office Fax: 845-331-1002.

TSITSIKLIS, JOHN N., electrical engineering and computer science educator; b. Thessaloniki, Greece, 1958; BS in Math., MIT, 1980, BSEE, 1980, MSEE, 1981, PhD in Elec. Engring., 1984. Acting asst. prof. elec. engring. Stanford U., Calif., 1983—84; positions to prof. dept. elec. engring. and computer sci. MIT, Cambridge, 1984—. Acting co-dir. MIT Lab. Info. and Decision Systems, 1996, 97; co-dir. MIT Ops. Rsch. Ctr., 2002—05; vis. rsch. dept. elec. engring. and computer scis. U. Calif., Berkeley; vis. rsch. Inst. Computer Sci., Iraklion, Greece. Contbr. articles to sci. jours.; co-author: Parallel and Distributed Computation: Numerical Methods, 1989, Neuro-Dynamic Programming, 1996, Intro. to Linear Optimization, 1997, Intro. to Probability, 2002. Recipient IBM Faculty Devel. award, 1983, Presdl. Young Investigator award, 1986, Outstanding Paper award, IEEE Control Systems Soc., Bodossaki Found. prize, 1994, Computer Sci. Tech. Sect. prize, Inst. Ops. Rsch. and Mgmt. Scis., 1997. Fellow: IEEE, INFORMS; mem.: NAE. Achievements include patents in field. Office: Dept Elec Engring and Computer Sci MIT 32-D662 77 Massachusetts Ave Cambridge MA 02139-4307 Office Phone: 617-253-6175. Office Fax: 617-253-4308. Business E-Mail: jnt@mit.edu.

TSITVERBLIT, NAFTALI ANATOL, physicist, fluid mechanics engineer, researcher; b. Kiev, Ukraine, Oct. 29, 1963; arrived in Israel, 1987; s. Isaac Avraham and Zoya (Beletsky) T. MSc, Kiev Poly. Inst., 1981-87; PhD, Tel-Aviv U., 1995. Engr. Scientific Rsch. Inst. Robotics, Kiev, 1985-87; postdoc. fellow Lamont-Doherty Earth Obs. Columbia U., Palisades, NY, 1995-97. Tchg. asst., instr. mech. engring. Tel-Aviv U., 1988-94, vis., 1997—; vis. scientist Cornell U., 1994. Co-author: (chpt.) Nonlinear Instability of Nonparallel Flows, 1994; contbr. papers to profl. jours. Woods Hole Oceanographic Inst. fellow, 1996. Mem. AAAS, N.Y. Acad. Sci., Am. Phys. Soc., Am. Geophys. Union. Achievements include discovery of two new mechanisms for convection in double-component fluid systems, resulting from different boundary conditions; mechanism for three-dimensionality of instability disturbances; finite-amplitude steady flows arising from one such a convective mechanism that are disconnected from the conduction state; research in multiplicity of the equilibrium states in laterally heated stably stratified fluid systems and its role in explaining diversity of previous observations in such systems; clarification of nature of the oscillatory instability in confined vortex flows with vortex breakdown and formulation of general method for identification of nature of complex instability mechanisms; identifying mechanisms and their role in various fluid mechanical configurations. Home: 1 Yanosh Korchak St Apt 6 Netanya 42495 Israel Business E-Mail: naftali@eng.tau.ac.il.

TSIVIDIS, YANNIS P., electrical engineering educator; b. Piraeus, Greece, Dec. 22, 1946; came to U.S., 1970. s. Pelopidas I. and Maria (Filippa) T. BS, U. Minn., 1972; MS, U. Calif., Berkeley, 1973, PhD, 1976. Asst. prof. elec. engring. Columbia U., NYC, 1976-81, assoc. prof., 1981-84, prof., 1984—, Nat. Tech. U., Athens, Greece, 1992-95; Charles Batchelor chair prof. Columbia U., NYC, 1998—. Cons. AT&T Bell Labs., Murray Hill, N.J., 1977-88. Author: Operation and Modeling of the MOS Transistor, 1987, 2d edit., 1999, Mixed Analog-Digital VLSI Devices and Technology, 1996; co-editor: Design of Mos VLSI Circuits for Telecommunications, 1985, Integrated Continuous-Time Filters, 1993, Design of Analog-Digital VLSI Circuits for Telecommunications and Signal Processing, 1994; contbr. over 100 articles to profl. jours.; patentee in field. Recipient best paper award European Solid State Cirs. Conf., 1986, Great Tchr. award Columbia U., 1991, Disting. Faculty Tchg. award Columbia Engring. Sch. Alumni Assn., 1998, Presdl. award for outstanding tchg. Columbia U., 2003. Fellow: IEEE (Baker best paper award 1984, Darlington award 1987, Guillemin-Cauer award 1998, 2008, Circuits and Sys. Golden Jubilee 2000, co-recipient L. Winner Outstanding Paper award 2003, Undergrad. Tchg. award 2005, Gustav Robert Kirchhoff award 2007). Office: Columbia Univ Dept Elec Engring New York NY 10027

TSO, TIEN CHIOH, federal agency administrator, agronomist, researcher; b. Hupeh, China, July 25, 1917; came to U.S., 1947, naturalized, 1961; s. Ya Fu and Suhwa (Wang) T.; m. Margaret Lu, Aug. 28, 1949; children: Elizabeth, Paul. BS, Nanking U., China, 1941, MS, 1944; PhD, Pa. State U., 1950; postgrad., Oak Ridge Inst. Nuclear Studies. Supt. exptl. farm Ministry Social Affairs, China, 1944-46; exec. sec. Tobacco Improvement Bur., 1946-47; rsch. chemist Gen. Cigar Rsch. Lab., 1950-51; with USDA, 1952—; prin. plant physiologist crop research div. Agrl. Rsch. Svc./USDA, Beltsville, Md., 1964-66, leader tobacco quality investigations, tobacco and sugar crops research br., 1966-71, chief tobacco lab., 1972-83, sr. exec. service, 1974-83, collaborator, 1984—; exec. dir. Internat. Devel. and Edn. in Agr. and Life Scis., 1984-96, chmn. bd., 1997-2001, hon. chmn. bd., 2001—. Cons. World Bank, Nat. Cancer Inst., Ky. Tobacco Health Rsch. Inst., China Nat. Tobacco Corp., Philippine Tobacco Rsch. Ctr., Philip Morris Tobacco Corp. Author: Physiology and Biochemistry of Tobacco Plants, 1972, Production, Physiology and Biochemistry of Tobacco Plants, 1991, Agriculture in China: 1949-2030, 1998; contbg. author: Ann. Rev. Plant Physiology, Vol. 9, 1958, The Chemistry of Tobacco and Tobacco Smoke, 1972, Toward Less Harmful Cigarettes, 1968, 71, 75, 80; editor: Structural and Functional Aspects of Phytochemistry, 1972, Recent Advances in Tobacco Science, vol. 1, 1975, Agriculture in China: 1949-2030, 1998, Dare to Dream: Vision of 2050 Agriculture in China, 2004, Comfort Ye, My People in My Journey in Science and Life, 2007. Fellow AAAS, Am. Soc. Agronomy (chmn. colloquium on agr. and life scis. in China 1983, 84, 85, 86, 87, 88-89), Am. Inst. Chemists; mem. Am. Chem. Soc., Am. Soc. Plant Physiologists, Phytochem. Soc. N.Am. (pres. 1971, life mem.), Tobacco Chemists Rsch. Conf. (symposium chmn. 1965, 79, chmn. 1975, 83), World Conf. Smoking and Health (sect. chmn. 1967, 71, 75), Tobacco Workers Conf., N.Y. Acad. Scis., Interagy. Smoking and Health Forum (chmn. 1979-83), Nat. Coordinating Com. on Tobacco-Related Rsch., Sigma Xi, Gamma Sigma Delta. Achievements include research in loci of alkaloid formation, biosynthetic pathway, interconversion and fate of alkaloids in tobacco plants, chem. composition as affected by macro and micro elements, homogenized leaf curing, health-related factors including mycotoxins, radioactive elements, air pollutants and phenolics, potential for agricultural self-sufficiency in China in the next century. Home: 3152 Gracefield Rd # 216 Silver Spring MD 20904 Office: Beltsville Agr Rsch Ctr Bldg 005 10300 Baltimore Ave Beltsville MD 20705 Office Phone: 301-504-5422. Personal E-mail: tctso@comcast.net. Business E-Mail: tc.tso@ars.usda.gov. *We are thankful to those fools who dare to dream of something new and seemingly impossible.*

TSONGAS, NIKI (NICOLA S. TSONGAS), United States Representative from Massachusetts, former dean; b. Chico, Calif., Apr. 26, 1946; d. Russell Elmer and Marian Susan (Wyman) Sauvage; m. Paul Efthemios Tsongas, Dec. 21, 1969 (dec. Jan. 18, 1997); children: Ashley, Katina, Molly. BA, Smith Coll., Northampton, Mass., 1968; JD, Boston U., 1988. Vol. Eugene McCarthy for US Pres., 1968; social worker NYC Dept. Welfare; dean external affairs Middlesex Cmty. Coll., Mass., 1997—2007; mem. US Congress from 5th Mass. Dist., 2007—. Mem. Lowell Civic Stadium & Arena Commn.; bd. dirs. The Concord Coalition. Democrat. Greek Orthodox. Office: US Congress 2229 Rayburn House Office Bldg Washington DC 20515 also: 11 Kearney Sq Lowell MA 01852*

TSOTSIS, THEODORE THOMAS, engineering educator; PhD, U. Ill., Urbana, 1978. Robert E. Vivian prof. energy resources U. Southern Calif., LA, 1992—. Office: Univ Southern Calif HEDCO 210 University Pk Los Angeles CA 90089-1211

TSOU, YU-MIN, science administrator, chemistry researcher; b. Ping-Dong, Taiwan, Aug. 28, 1953; arrived in US, 1979; s. Shung-Chu Tsou and Ping-Wen Chen; m. Yah-Lih Chao, Apr. 26, 1980; children: Amy Meng Shuan, Benjamin Jiann. BS in Chemistry, Nat. Tsing-Hua U., Taiwan, 1975; MS in Chemistry, Nat. Taiwan U., 1979; PhD in Chemistry, Calif. Inst. Tech., Pasadena, 1985. Sci. rsch. assoc. U. of Tex., Austin, 1985—86; sr. rsch. chemist Dow Chem. Co., Freeport, Tex., 1986—88, project leader, 1989—93, rsch. leader, 1994—2000; R&D mgr. E-Tek divsn. De Nora Northamerica, Inc, Somerset, NJ, 2001—04; tech. dir. E-TEK divsn. PEMEAS USA, Somerset, 2005—07; head tech, chief scientist BASF Fuel Cell, Inc., Somerset, 2007—. Chief tech. officer for Dept. of Energy program E-TEK divsn. De Nora Northamerica, Inc., Somerset, 2002—05; leading scientist of De Nora for Aqueous Hydrochloric Acid Electrolysis project De Nora NA/Bayer Joint Venture, Somerset, 2001—03; head mfr. and devel. PEMEAS USA, Inc., Somerset, 2006—07. Author: The Key to Understand Lau-Tze Philosophy and Its Practice in Chinese History, (philosophy/history writings) Chinese/Western Philosophy Comparisons; contbr. articles to profl. jours. Fund raiser Calif. Inst. Tech. Alumni Assn., Freeport, 1998. Recipient Electrochem. Soc. New Tech. award, E-TEK, 2005, Dow Chem. Tech. Excellence award, 1990, 1992, 1996. Mem.: Electrochem. Soc. (assoc.). Achievements include development of consistent method to manufacture rhodium catalyst and the rhodium electrode for converting waste hydrochloric acid to chlorine; invention of anode and cathode coating technology and scaling up to mass production; mass production of membrane-cell-assembly with electrode-membrane lamination approach in fuel cell industry; highest performing Pt alloy methanol oxidation anode and Pt oxygen reduction cathode catalysts and supply to customers; poisoning-resistant hydrogen evolution cathode on thin substrates and implemented in zero-gap membrane chlorine cells; novel electrode structure for realizing Pt alloy advantage; first to develop catalysts/gas diffusion electrodes for the pioneering PEMEAS over 160 C high temperature MEA; patents and journal review for electrolysis, fuel cells, electro-catalysts, gas diffusion electrodes, porous electrode structure. Avocations: bridge, swimming, philosophy, poetry, music. Home: 533 Mercer Rd Princeton NJ 08540 Office: BASF Fuel Cell Inc 39 Veronica Ave Somerset NJ 08873 Office Fax: 732-545-5170. Personal E-mail: tsou4507@yahoo.com. E-mail: yu-min.tsou@basf.com.

TSOUCALAS, NICHOLAS, federal judge; b. NYC, Aug. 24, 1926; s. George Michael and Maria (Monogenis) T.; m. Catherine Aravantinos, Nov. 21, 1954; children: Stephanie, Georgia. BSBA, Kent State U., 1949; LLB, N.Y. Law Sch., 1951. Bar: NY 1953. Sole practice, NYC, 1953-55, 59-68; asst. US atty. (So. dist.) NY US Dept. Justice, 1955-59; judge NYC Criminal Ct., 1968-86; acting judge NY Supreme Ct., NYC, 1975-82; judge US Ct. Internat. Trade, NYC, 1986—96, sr. judge, 1996—. Dist. leader Republican Party NY County, NYC, 1961-68; mem. Republican Exec. Com., NYC, 1961-68. Served with USN, 1944-46, 51-52. Recipient Proficiency in Constl. Law award NY Law Sch., NYC, 1951, Man of Yr. award St. Paul Soc., NYC, 1971. Mem. ABA, NY County Lawyers Assn., Fed. Bar Assn., Greek American Lawyers Assn., American Hellenic Ednl. Prog. Assn. Lodges: Parthenon, Masons. Republican. Greek Orthodox. Avocations: basketball, racquetball, stamp collecting/philately, walking, dance. Office: US Ct Internat Trade 1 Federal Plz New York NY 10278-0001*

TSOUKALAS, LEFTERI H., engineering educator, department chairman; arrived in US, 1975; s. Charalambos Theodore and Elpis Tsoukalas; m. Demetra Evangelou; children: Ellia, Constantine, Arete Trisevgeni, Charie Anatole. BSEE, U. Ill., Champaign-Urbana, 1981, MS, 1983, PhD, 1989. Prof. nuc. engring. Purdue U., West Lafayette, Ind., 2000—, head Sch. Nuc. Engring., 2001—06. Cons. Internat. Atomic Energy Agy., Vienna, 2004—05. Author: (book) Fuzzy and Neural Approaches in Engineering, 1997 (Keynote Spkr., 1997). Recipient Consortium for the Intelligent Mgmt. of the Electric Power Grid award, Elec. Power Rsch. Inst., 1999—2003, Best Tchr. award, Purdue U. Sch. Engring., 1997. Fellow: Am. Nuc. Soc. (life); mem.: Nuc. Engring. Dept. Heads Orgn. (chmn. 2004—06). Independent. Greek Orthodox.

TSOURI, GILL R., engineering educator, researcher, consultant; s. Nissim and Shoshana Tsouri; m. Dganit Geier, Sept. 1, 2002; children: Daniel M., Noa O., Ilai A. MSc in Elec. & Computer Engring. with cum laude (hon.), Ben Gurion U., Beer Sheva, Israel, 2004; PhD in Elec. & Computer Engring., Ben Gurion U., 2008. Rsch. & devel. engr. Yitran Comm., Beer Sheva, 1998—2002; tchg. asst. & rsch. fellow Ben Gurion U., 2002—08; cons. SigNexT Wireless, Yavne, Israel, 2006—; asst. prof. Rochester Inst. Tech., NY, 2008—. Mem.: IEEE. Office: Rochester Inst Tech 79 Lomb Memorial Dr Rochester NY 14623 Business E-Mail: grteee@rit.edu.

TSUANG, JOHN, psychiatrist; married. MD, Iowa U., 1987. Dir. ddtp Harbor, U. Calif., LA, Torrance, 2000—. Dir. Dual Diagnosis Treatment Program. Bd. mem. LA Homeless Health Care. Named Psychiatrist of Yr., NAMI, 2005. Mem.: CSAM.

TSUANG, MING TSO, psychiatrist, educator; b. Tainan, Taiwan, Nov. 16, 1931; came to U.S., 1971; s. Ping Tang and Chhun Kuei (Lin) T.; m. Snow Huei S. Ko; children: John, Debby, Grace. MD, Nat. Taiwan U., Taipei, 1957; PhD in Psychiatry, 1965, PhD (Sino-Brit. Fellowship Trust scholar); certs. in epidemiology and stats., population genetics, psychiat. genetics, U. London, 1965; D.Sc. in Psychiat. Genetics and Epidemiology, Faculty of Sci., U. London, 1981. Intern Nat. Taiwan U. Hosp., 1956-57, resident in psychiatry, 1957-61, assoc. prof. psychiatry, staff psychiatrist, 1968-71; collaborating investigator Internat. Pilot Study of Schizophrenia, WHO, 1966-71; vis. assoc. prof. psychiatry Washington U. Sch. Medicine, St. Louis, 1971-72; assoc. prof., staff psychiatrist U. Iowa Coll. Medicine, Iowa City, 1972-75, prof. psychiatry, 1975-82, prof. psychiat. epidemiology, 1978-82; clin. tchr., lectr. to residents, med. students; cons. psychiatrist VA Hosp., Iowa City, 1972-82; prof., vice chmn. sect. of psychiatry and human behavior Brown U., Providence, 1982-85; assoc. med. dir. Butler Hosp., Providence, 1982-85, dir. psychiat. epidemiology research unit, 1982-85; prof. psychiatry Harvard Inst. Psychiat. Epid. and Genetics Harvard U. Med. Sch. and Harvard Sch. Pub. Health; dir. psychiat. epidemiology and genetics Mass. Mental Health Ctr., Boston; chief psychiatry, chmn. Ctr. for Mental Health Brockton-West Roxbury VA Med. Ctr., 1985-94; head and supt. dept. psychiatry Harvard U. at Mass. Mental Health Ctr., 1992—; Stanley Cobb prof. psychiatry Harvard U., 1993—2003; dir. Harvard Inst. Psychiat. Epedemiology and Genetics, 1994—; behavioral genomics prof. dept. psychiatry, dir. Ctr. Behavioral Genomics U. Calif., San Diego, 2003—, behavioral genomics endowed chair, 2007—. Epidemiol. studies rev. com. NIMH, 1976-79, mem., chmn. rsch. scientist devel. rev. com., 1982-86, chmn. epidemiologic studies rev. com., 1989-90, extramural sci. adv. bd., 1990-93; med. rsch. svc. planning coun. Vets. Health Svcs. and Rsch. Adminstrn., VA Cen. Office, 1990-93; vis. prof. psychiatry (Josiah Macy faculty scholar award) Oxford U., Eng., Warneford Hosp., 1979-80; chmn. mental health policy working group, divsn. health and policy rsch. and edn. Harvard U., 1986-87. Author: (with R. Vandermey) Genes and The Mind: Inheritance of Mental Illness, 1980, Schizophrenia: The Facts, 2d edit., 1997, (with S.V. Faraone) The Genetics of Mood Disorders, 1990; co-editor: Schizoaffective Psychoses, 1986, Handbook of Schizophrenia, vol. 3, 1988, Affective and Schizoaffective Disorders, Similarities and Differences, 1990, (with S.V. Faraone and D. Tsuang) Genetics of Mental Disorders: A Guide for Students, Clinicians and Researchers, 1999, (with M. Tohen) A Textbook on Psychiatric Epidemiology, 2d edit., 2002, (with W.S. Stone and S.V. Faraone) Early Clinical Intervention and Prevention in Schizophrenia, 2004, also monographs.; contbr. chpts. to books, numerous articles to profl. jours. Recipient Clin. Rsch. award Am. Acad. Clin. Psychiatrists, 1983, Rema Lapous award APHA, 1984, Stanley Dean award for rsch. on schizophrenia Am. Coll. Psychiatrists, 1989, Lifetime Achievement award Internat. Soc. Psychiat. Genetics, 1995, Taiwanese-Am. award for Achievement in Sci. and Engring., 1995, Gold Medal award Soc. Biol. Psychiatry, 2000, award for rsch. in psychiatry Am. Psychiat. Assn., 2003. Mem. Am. Psychopathol. Assn. (pres. 2005), Internat. Soc. Psychiat. Genetics (pres. 2005—, Lifetime Achievement award 1995), Inst. of Medicine/NAAS, Academia Sinica Taiwan, Sigma Xi. Office: U Calif San Diego Dept Psychiatry Med Tchg FAcility Rm 453 9500 Gilman Dr Mail Code 0603 La Jolla CA 92093-0603 Office Phone: 858-822-2464. Business E-Mail: mtsuang@ucsd.edu. *My constant goal is to do the best work I can, to eschew anxiety about the result, to learn from failure, and to build upon success, not for personal honor but for the good of mankind, as God's servant within a serving profession. Helping others is not possible without self-discipline, self-sufficience, and self-sacrifice; at the same time, helping others strengthens the self for its tasks.*

TSUBAKI, ANDREW TAKAHISA, theater director, educator; b. Chiyoda-ku, Tokyo, Japan, Nov. 29, 1931; s. Ken and Yasu (Oyama) T.; m. Lilly Yuri, Aug. 3, 1963; children: Arthur Yuichi, Philip Takeshi. BA in English, Tokyo Gakugei U., Tokyo, Japan, 1954; postgrad. in Drama, U. Saskatchewan, Saskatoon, Canada, 1958-59; MFA in Theatre Arts, Tex. Christian U., 1961; PhD in Speech & Drama, U. Ill., 1967. Tchr. Bunkyo-ku 4th Jr. High Sch., Tokyo, 1954—58; instr., scene designer Bowling Green (Ohio) State U., 1964—68; asst. prof. speech & drama U. Kans., Lawrence, 1968—73, assoc. prof., 1973—79; vis. assoc. prof. Carleton Coll., Northfield, Minn., 1974; lectr. Tsuda U., Tokyo, 1975; vis. assoc. prof. theatre Tel-Aviv (Israel) U., 1975—76; vis. prof. theatre Mo. Repertory Theatre, Kansas City, Mo., 1976, Nat. Sch. Drama, New Delhi, 1983; prof. theatre, film, east Asian Languages and Cultures U. Kans., Lawrence, 1979—2000, prof. emeritus, 2000—. Dir. Internat. Theatre Studies Ctr., U. Kans., Lawrence, 1971-2000, Operation Internat. Classical Theatre, 1988—; Benedict disting. vis. prof. Asian studies Carleton Coll., 1993; area editor Asian Theatre Jour., U. Hawaii, Honolulu, 1982-94; chmn. East Asian Langs. and Cultures, U. Kans., Lawrence, 1983-90; mem. editl. bd. Studies in Am. Drama, Oxford, Miss., 1985-88. Dir. plays Kanjincho, 1973, Rashomon, 1976, 96, King Lear, 1985, Fujito and Shimizu, 1985, Hippolytus, 1990, Busu and the Missing Lamb (Japan) 1992, Suehirogari and Sumidagawa, 1992, 93, Tea, 1995; choreographed Antigone (Greece), 1987, Hamlet (Germany), 1989, The Resistible Rise of Arturo Ui, 1991, Man and the Masses (Germany), 1993, The Children of Fate (Hungary), 1994, The Great Theatre of the World (Germany); editor Theatre Companies of the World, 1986; contbg. author to Indian Theatre: Traditions of Performance, 1990; contbr. 7 entries in Japanese Traditional plays to the Internat. Dictionary of Theatre, vol. 1, 1992, vol. 2, 1994. Recipient citation, Min. Fgn. Affairs Japan, 2003, Statement of Appreciation, Chmn. and Bd. Dirs. Hiratsuka Internat. Exch. Assn., 2004; named to Order of Sacred Treasure, Govt. of Japan, 2006; World Univ. Svc. scholar, U. Saskatchewan, 1958—59, University fellow, U. Ill., 1961—62, Rsch. fellow, The Japan Found., 1974—75, 1990, Rsch. Fulbright grantee, 1983. Fellow Coll. Am. Theatre (elected 2002); mem. Am. Theatre Assn., Asian Theatre Program (chair 1976-79), Assn. for Asian Studies, Assn. Kans. Theatres., Assn. Kans. Theatres U/C Div. (chmn. 1980-82), Assn. for Theatre in Higher Edn., Assn. for Asian Performance. Democrat. Buddhist. Avocations: ki-aikido (5th dan), photography, travel. Home: 924 Holiday Dr Lawrence KS 66049-3005

TSUBOTA, STUART, biology professor; b. Oak Park, Ill., Sept. 29, 1951; m. Katherine Weston. BS in Biology, U. Notre Dame, Ind., 1973; PhD in Genetics, U. Calif., Berkeley, 1980. Vis. rsch. fellow Princeton U., NJ, 1983—86; rsch. assoc. Cambridge U., England, 1979—83; prof. Coll. Brockport, NY, 2005—. Asst. prof. U. Mich., Ann Arbor, 1986—93; assoc. prof. St. Louis U., 1993—2005. Predoc. fellowship, NIH, 1974—78, Postdoc. fellowship, 1984, Rsch. grant, 1986—91, 2002—07, NSF, 1992—96, Long Term Postdoc. fellowship, European Molecular Biology Orgn., 1982. Mem.: Nat. Profl. Sci. Master's Assn., Genetics Soc. America. Achievements include discovery of highly conserved gene, enhancer of rudimentary; transposable elements, nijinsky and isadora. Office: SUNY 350 New Campus Dr Brockport NY 14420

TSUBOUCHI, DAVID H., Canadian provincial official; BA in English, York U., 1972; LLB, Osgoode Hall Law Sch., 1975; LLD (hon.), Assumption U., Windsor, 2006. Ward 5 councillor Town of Markham, 1988-94; sr. ptnr. Tsubouchi & Nichols & Assocs., 1994-95; progressive conservative mem. Legis. Assembly Ont., 1995—2003; Min. Cmty. and Social Svcs. Ont. Progressive Conservative Govt., 1995-99, Min. Consumer & Comml. Affairs Can., 1996—99, chair cabinet legis. and regulations com., 1996, re-elected mem. Provincial Parliament for Markham, 1999; registrar gen. Province of Ont., 1996, solicitor gen., 1999—2001, chair health and social svcs. policy com., chair mgmt. bd. cabinet, 2001—03, min. culture, 2002—03, min. consumer and comml. relations; cons., coun. Miller Thomson LLP, Toronto, Canada, 2008—. Chmn. planning and devel. com., econ. alliance com., indsl. and corp. devel. com. Markham Hist. Mus.; bd. dirs. Markham Stouffville Hosp.; hon. chair Seneca Coll., Fundraising Campaign. Contbr. articles to Law Gazette. Adv. coun. York U. Sch. Fine Arts; gov. Canadian Internat. Peace Project; campaign chair George Brown Coll. Theatre Arts Sch.; bd. gov., also audit com. York U., 2004—; past dir. Japanese Canadian Cultural Ctr.; bd. dirs. Hitachi Can., Found. Markets Inc., co-chairman; bd. dirs. Asian Coast Devel. Inc. Named Optimist of Yr., 1985-86; recipient Air Can. Heart of Gold award, 1988; granted Coat of Arms, Gov. Gen.'s Office, 1993, award of appreciation, First Nations Chiefs of Police, Ontario Soc. for the Prevention of Cruelty to Animals, Bruce Bryden award for Leadership, York U., 2003, The Queen's Golden Jubilee award, Canadian Horse Racing Industry award of Recognition, Ont. Grape Growers award of Merit, Hon. Patron of the Gardiner Mus. Ceramics, Japanese Cultural Centre award for Leadership; names Invested knight Grand Cross in Holy Order St. Martin de Porres, Invested knight Grand Cross in Holy Military Order St Adrian and St. Sebastian, Invested knight Equestrian Secular and Chapterial Order St Joachim. Mem.: Assumption U. Alumni Assn., Japanese Canadian Cultural Ctr. (hon. chair), Ontario Assn. Former Parliamentarians, Markham Bd. Trade, Sleepy Hollow Golf and Country Club, Albany Club. Office: Miller Thomson LLP 600-60 Columbia Way Markham ON Canada L3R 0C9 Office Phone: 905-415-6716. Business E-Mail: dtsubouchi@millerthomson.com.

TSUI, DANIEL C., electrical engineer, physicist; b. Henan, China, 1939; Diploma, Augustana Coll., 1961; PhD in Physics, U. Chgo., 1967. Rsch. assoc. U. Chgo., 1967—68; mem. technical staff Bell Labs., Murray Hill, NJ, 1968—82; Arthur LeGrand Doty prof. dept. elec. engring. Princeton U., NJ, 1982—. Contbr. articles to profl. jours. Recipient Buckley prize for Condensed Matter Physics, 1984, Benjamin Franklin medal in Physics, 1998, Nobel prize in Physics, 1998. Fellow: AAAS; mem.: NAE, NAS, Materials Research Soc., Am. Physical Soc., IEEE, Acad. Sinica. Achievements include discovery of the fractional quantum Hall effect. Office: Princeton U Dept Elec Engring Rm B 426 PO Box 5263 Princeton NJ 08544-0001 Fax: 609-258-6279. E-mail: tsui@princeton.edu.*

TSUI, LAP-CHEE, academic administrator, molecular genetics educator; b. Shanghai, Dec. 21, 1950; arrived in Can., 1981; s. Jing Lue Hsue and Hui Ching Wang; m. Ellen Lan Fong, Feb. 11, 1977; children: Eugene, Felix. BS, Chinese U. Hong Kong, 1972, MPhil, 1974; PhD, U. Pitts., 1979; DSc (hon.), Chinese U. Hong Kong, 1991; DCL (hon.), U. King's Coll., Halifax, NS, Can., 1991; DSc (hon.), U. N.B., Can., 1991; DLL (hon.), U. St. Francis Xavier, Antigonish, NS, Can., 1994; DSc (hon.), York U., Can., 2001. Postdoctoral investigator Oak Ridge Nat. Lab., Tenn., 1979—80; postdoctoral fellow Hosp. for Sick Children, Toronto, Ont., Canada, 1981—83, geneticist-in-chief, 1996—2002; asst. prof. depts. genetics and med. genetics U. Toronto, Ont., Canada, 1983—88, assoc. prof., 1988—90, prof., 1990—2006, u. prof., 1994—2006, u. prof. emeritus, 2006—; H.E. Sellers chair in cystic fibrosis, 1998—2002; head genetics and genomic biology program, 1998—2002. Chmn. chromosome 7 subcom. Human Gene Mapping Workshop, 1986-97; mem. mammalian genetics study sect. NIH, Bethesda, Md., 1988-93; dir. Cystic Fibrosis Rsch. Ctr., Hosp. for Sick Children Spl. Rsch. Ctr., 1994-2002; scientist Med. Rsch. Coun. Can., 1989-2002; advisor European Jour. Human Genetics, 1992-96, Molecular Medicine Today, 1995—; adj. prof. U. New Brunswick, 2000-2002; vice-chancellor & pres. U. Hong Kong, 2002—. Editor: Cytogenetics and Cell Genetics, 1988-92, Internat. Jour. Genome Rsch., 1990—95, Biochimica et Biophysica Acta, 2002—; assoc. editor: Am. Jour. Human Genetics, 1990-93, Genomics, 1994—; mem. editl. bd. Mammalian Genome, 1990, Clin. Genetics, 1991—, Human Molecular Genetics, 1991-99; communicating editor: Human Mutation, 1991-2002, Molec. Medicine Today, sr. editor: Physiological Genomics, 2000-01; internat. adv. The Chinese Jour. of Medical Genetics, 2000—05; mem. editl. bd. Human Genetics, 2005-09; contbr. over 300 articles to sci. jours. Trustee Edn. Found., Fedn. Chinese Canadian Profls., Toronto, 1987-93; advisor, 1994-. Recipient Paul di Sant Agnese Disting. Achievement award Cystic Fibrosis Found., 1989, Zellers SR. Scientist award, 2001, Gold medal of honor Pharm. Mfrs. Assn. Can., 1989, award of excellence Genetics Soc. Can., 1990, Gairdner Internat. award 1990, Cresson medal Franklin Inst., 1992, E. Mead Johnson award, 1992, Disting. Scientist award The Canadian Soc. Clin. Investigators, 1992, Canadian Conf. medal 1992, Sarstedt Rsch. prize, 1993, Sanremo Internat. award for Genetic Rsch., 1993, J.P. Lecocq prize Inst. de France, 1994, Henry Friesen award The Canadian Soc. for Clin. Investigation and the Royal Coll. of Physicians and Surgeons of Can., 1995, Can. Med. Assn. award of honour, 1996, Jonas Salk award Ontario March of Dimes, 1997, Initiative Cmty. Svc. award Toronto Biotech., 1998, Disting. Scientist award Med. Rsch. Coun., 2000, Killam prize Can. Coun., 2002; named scholar Can. Cystic Fibrosis Found., 1984-86. Fellow Royal Soc. Can., Royal Soc. London, Academia Sinica, Royal Coll. Physicians U.K. (hon.); mem. Human Genome Orgn., Am. Soc. Human Genetics, NAS (fgn. assoc.). Achievements include co-discoverer of cystic fibrosis gene. Office: Vice-Chancellor's Office U Hong Kong Pokfulam Rd Hong Kong Hong Kong Office Phone: 852-2859-2100. Office Fax: 852-2858-9435.

TSUI, SZE-KAI JACK, mathematics educator; b. Quinmin, Yunnan, China, Sept. 12, 1945; came to U.S., 1969; s. Hsin-Ya and Nancy (Wong) T.; m. Jan Yuan Ku, Aug. 23, 1969; children: Philip, Jennifer, Jason. BS, Nat. Taiwan U., 1966, MS, 1968; PhD, U. Pa., 1975. Asst. prof. Oakland U., Rochester, Mich., 1975-82, assoc. prof., 1982-87, full prof., 1987—. Vis. prof. Nat. Taiwan U., Taipei, 1984. Contbr. articles to profl. jours. Dalhousie U. fellow, 1979, Oakland U. fellow, 1977, 80, 85, U. Toronto fellow, 1986-87. Mem. Am. Math. Soc., Math. Assn. Am.

TSUJI, FREDERICK ICHIRO, biochemist, molecular biologist; b. Honolulu, Aug. 23, 1923; s. Kijiro Tsuji and Sadako Moriyama; m. Masako Koga, Mar. 31, 1991. BA, Cornell U., Ithaca, NY, 1946, M in Nutritional Sci., 1948, PhD, 1950. Asst. prof. Duquesne U., Pitts., 1950—52; rsch. asst. Princeton U., 1952—55; rsch. biochemist, head basic sci. rsch. VA Hosp., Pitts., 1955—72; rsch. prof. U. So. Calif., LA, 1972—76; dir. biochemistry program NSF, Washington, 1976—78; rsch. biochemist, prof. U. Calif., San Diego, La Jolla, 1978—. Head dept. enzymes and metabolism Osaka Bioscience Inst., Japan, 1987—93; vis. prof. dept. protein crystallography Institute for Protein Rsch., Osaka U., 1998—99. Administr. grant applications and awards for rsch. in biochemistry NSF, Washington, 1976—78. Grantee, NSF, 1970—2000. Mem.: ACS, Soc. Gen. Physiologists, Am. Soc. Biochemistry and Molecular Bio., Sigma Xi. Achievements include research in chemistry of light production in animals and plants. Avocations: classical music, history of modern physics, literature, art. Office: University California San Diego 9500 Gilman Dr La Jolla CA 92093-0202 Office Phone: 858-534-3197. Office Fax: 858-534-7313. Business E-Mail: ftsuji@ucsd.edu.

TSUJI, TOSHIZO, hospital administrator, educator; b. Kyoto, Jan. 2, 1932; s. Yasujiro and Yuki (Nakamura) T.; m. Yoshiko Taniguchi, Mar. 21, 1977; children: Mari, Toshifumi. MD, Kyoto Prefectural U. Medicine, 1957; DMSc, Kyoto Prefectural U. Medicine, 1964. Intern Kyoto 1st Red Cross Hosp., 1957-58; clin. fellow Kyoto Prefectural U. Medicine, 1959-60, asst. prof., 1971-74, assoc. prof., 1974-97; clin. fellow U. Ala. Med. Ctr., Birmingham, 1964-67, instr. medicine, 1967-68; postdoctoral fellow in molecular biology U. Edinburgh, Scotland, 1968-70; v.p. Kyoto Prefectural Yosanoumi Hosp., Iwataki, 1983—97; pres. Kyoto Prefectural Yosanoumi Blood Ctr., Iwataki, 1974-83; prin. Kyoto Prefectural Nursing Sch., Iwataki, 1988-94; pres., med. juridical person Ohtha Found. Ohta Hosp., Kyoto, 1997—2006; pres., med. juridical person Miyazu Kosei Found., Miyazu Takeda Hosp., Kyoto, 2006—. Mem. WHO, Kyoto, 1983—. Contbr. articles to profl. jours. Recipient med. diploma Japanese Ministry Health and Welfare, 1958; fellow NIH, 1965, European Molecular Biology Orgn., 1968. Fellow Japanese Soc. Internal Medicine, Japanese Soc. Gastroenterology, Japanese Soc. Hepatology; mem. AAAS, NY Acad. Scis. Avocations: golf, tennis, stamp collecting/philately, gardening, music. Home: 988 Uoya Kyoto 626-0015 Japan Office Phone: 0772-22-2157.

TSUJIMOTO, KENZO, computer game company executive; Founder, chmn., CEO Capcom Co. Ltd., Osaka, Japan, 1983—; CEO Capcom USA and Capcom Entertainment. Co-founder Computer Entertainment Assn., Japan, vice chmn., chmn., 2002—. Office: Capcom USA Inc 800 Concar Dr Ste 300 San Mateo CA 94402-2649 Office Phone: 650-350-6500.

TSUJIMOTO, TATSUHIRO, gastroenterologist, researcher; b. Kashihara, Nara, Japan, Dec. 11, 1967; s. Kouzou and Kuniko Tsujimoto; m. Kazuko Hiasa, Feb. 20, 1999; children: Sachika, Yuna. MD, Nara Med. U. Grad. Sch., Kashihara, Japan, 2000. Sr. staff gastroenterology Ishinkai Yao Gen. Hosp., Osaka, Japan, 2000—; asst. prof. gastroenterology Nara Med. U., Kashihara, 2005—. Councilor Japan Gastroent. Endoscopy Soc., 2005—, Japan Soc. Gastroenterology, 2009—. Recipient award, Japan Soc. Ultrasonics in Medicine. Fellow: Japan Soc. Hepatology. Achievements include research in alchohol. Office: Nara Med Univ 840 Shijo Nara Kashihara 634-8522 Japan Personal E-mail: tat-tyan@xa2.so-net.ne.jp. Business E-Mail: tujimoto@naramed-u.ac.jp.

TSUKAMOTO, DANIEL, piano instructor, church organist; b. Encarnación, Itapúa, Paraguay, Apr. 18, 1970; s. Minoru and Yoko Tsukamoto. BA, Asbury Coll., 1994; MusM, U. SD, Vermillion, 1995—2009. Cert. in health insurance Mich., in insurance aflac Mich. Region. Electronic organist Free Meth. Ch., Encarnación, Itapúa, Paraguay, 1982—86; instr. HS orch. Rapid City Ctrl. HS, SD, 1986—88; instr. HS orch. (double bass/cello player) Watertown Sr. HS, SD, 1988—89; instr. coll. orch. (double bass player/cello player) Asbury Coll., Wilmore, Ky., 1989—94; instr. U. orch. (double bass/cello player) U. SD, Vermillion, 1994—95, piano grad. asst., 1994—95; instr. U. orch. (double bass player) SD State U., Brookings, 1996—99; ch. organist Romeo United Meth. Ch., Romeo, Mich., 2000—, piano lesson tchr., 2002—, mem. ch. music com., 2000—, piano accompanist, musical singer (tenor), 2002—03.

Double bass player Rapid City Symphony Orch., SD, 1987—88; all-state orch. SD Pub. Schs., Aberdeen, 1988—88, all-state honor's orch., Brookings, 1989—89, all-state band, Huron, 1989—89; double bass player Pit Orch., Wilmore, Ky., 1989—89; ch. organist for weddings, Mich., 2003—; ch. organist Wedding and Funeral in Ch., 2000. Bell ringer Salvation Army, Watertown, SD; mem. music com. Romeo United Meth. Ch., 2000—; guest min. music First United Meth. Ch.; organist, choir dir. Gross Pointe Wood St. Episcopal Ch., 2008—09. Recipient Faculty Award, Watertown Sr. High, 1988—89, Nat. HS Orchestra award, 1989; named to Nat. Honor Soc., Rapid City Ctrl. HS, 1987. Mem.: Am. Guild Organists (assoc.). Home: 42221 Toddmark Ln Apt 124 Clinton Township MI 48038 Office: Romeo United Methodist Church 280 N Main St Romeo MI 48065 Office Phone: 586-541-4500. Home Fax: 586-412-9015. Personal E-mail: z5aj@sbcglobal.net.

TSUNG, CHRISTINE CHAI-YI, financial executive, treasurer; b. Nanking, China, Mar. 23, 1948; came to U.S., 1970; d. Chi-Huang Tsung and Siao-Tuan Huang. BBA, Nat. Taiwan U., Taipei, 1970; postgrad., Washington U., St. Louis, 1970-71; MBA, U. Mo., 1973. Acct. Capital Land Co., St. Louis, 1972-74; chief acct. Servis Equipment Co., Inc., Dallas, 1974-75; acctg. supr. Calif. Microwave, Sunnyale, 1975-76; budget and sales mgr. Columbia Pictures TV Internat., Burbank, Calif., 1976-77; acctg. mgr. Husquarna, San Diego, 1977-82; sr. acct. City of Poway, Calif., 1982-88, fin. mgr. Calif., 1988-95; pres., CEO China Airlines, 2000—. Pres., treas. Jade Poly Investment, Beverly Hills, Calif., 1989—; cons. assoc. Metro Properties, San Diego, 1989—; cons. Kaohsiung City, Taiwan, 2000—. Tchr. San Diego North County Chinese Sch., 1985-86; v.p. San Diego Chinese Culture Assn., 1982-86, bd. dirs., 1988-90, 93-94. Mem. Assn. Asian Pacific Airlines, Pacific Asia Travel Assn. (exec. bd.), Govt. Fin. Officers Assn. (Cert. of Achievement 1988-94), Calif. Soc. Mcpl. Fin. Officers (standing com. membership devel., Cert. of Award 1988-94), Mcpl. Treas. Assn. U.S. and Can., Taiwanese C. of C. of N.Am. (bd. dirs. 1994-95). Avocations: travel, swimming, tennis, golf, reading. Office: China Airlines 2F 131 Sec 3 Nanking E Rd Taipei Taiwan Home Phone: 882-2-2713-3366; Office Phone: 882-2-2514-5799. Business E-Mail: c_tsung@china.airlines.com.

TSURUMOTO, TOSHIYUKI, orthopaedic surgeon, researcher; b. Kitakyushu, Japan, Nov. 21, 1957; s. Shigeyuki and Yasuyo Tsurumoto, Toshiyuki (Stepfather) and Masako Matsuzaki (Stepmother); m. Misako Tsurumoto, Nov. 22, 1986; children: Tadao, Minako, Naoji. MD, Nagasaki U., Japan, 1984, PhD, 1990. Resident Nagasaki U. Hosp., 1984—85, Seishi-Gakuen Children's Hosp., Miyazaki, Japan, 1985—86; staff orthop. surgery Saga Nat. Hosp., Japan, 1990—92, Kochi Prefectural Seinan Hosp., Shimanto, Japan, 1992—94, Kitakyushu Gen. Hosp., Japan, 1994—97, Nat. Saga Hosp., Japan, 1997—98; asst. prof. Nagasaki U. Sch. Medicine, Japan, 1998—2002, lectr., 2002—07, assoc. prof., 2007—. Achievements include research in nanobacteria-like particles in human arthritic synovial fluids. Office: Nagasaki Univ Sch of Medicine Sakamoto 1-7-1 Nagasaki 852-8501 Japan Office Phone: 81-95-819-7321. Business E-Mail: tsurumot@nagasaki-u.ac.jp.

TSURUTANI, BRUCE TADASHI, physicist; b. Santa Monica, Calif., Jan. 29, 1941; s. Heny Junya Tsurutani and Lucy Ayako Imai; m. Olga Verkhoglyadova, Nov. 5, 2003; children: Amanda S., Emily M. BA in Physics, U. Calif., Berkley, 1963, PhD in Physics, 1972. Rsch. scientist Jet Propulsion Lab., Pasadena, Calif., 1972—85, sr. rsch. scientist, 1985—, mgr. space physics and astrophysics, 1985—87, supr. space plasma physics R. & D., 1987—94; adj. prof. U. Southern Calif., 2003—07. Vis. prof. U. Cologne, Germany, 1993—94, Tech. U. Braunschweig, Germany, 1993—94, Calif. Inst. Tech., Pasadena, Calif., 1996—2001, Kyoto U., 1988, 2005—06; mem. British Antartic Survey Sci. Review Bd., Cambridge, England, 1998—2003. Recipient medal, ALAGE, 2001, Brazilian Space Agy., 1992; fellowship, Von Humbolt Soc., 1993—94. Mem.: Union and Sci. Internat., European Geophysical Union, Am. Geophysical Union (v.p. to pres. 1988—92). Avocations: tennis, hiking. Office: Jet propulsion Lab Inst Tech 4800 Oak Grove Dr Pasadena CA 91109 Business E-Mail: bruce.tsrutani@jpl.nasa.gov.

TSYGAN, LEONID IOSIFOVICH, civil engineer, writer; b. Kiev, Ukraine, Dec. 22, 1938; arrived in U.S., 1979; s. Iosif Haim-Garshevech and Bluma Leybovna Tsygan; m. Emmilia Igorevna Shustova, 1971 (div. 1984); 1 child, Russell; m. Zhanna Iosifovna Polonskaya, 1997; 1 child, Joshua 1 stepchild, Lana Polonskaya. BSCE, Kiev Inst. Hwy. Engring., 1968; computer programmer, Syrit Computer Sch. Sys., NYC, 1983. Sr. engr. State Design Inst. Hwys., Kiev, 1968—78; draftsman King and Gavaris Cons. Engrs. Inc., NYC, 1979—81; designer, draftsman Berger, Lehman Assocs. P.C., Rye, NY, 1982—84; bridge designer E. Pavlo Consulting Engr., NYC, 1984—89; engr. Anuman & Whitney Cons. Engr., NYC, 1990—91; asst. civil engr. N.Y.C. Dept. Transp., NYC, 1992—. Contbr. poetry to anthologies. Alt. del. N.Y.C. Dept. Transp. local 375, chpt. 37, DC 37 AFSCME, AFL-CIO, NYC, 2000—. Co-recipient medal for design of Moscow cable-stay bridge, State Design Inst. Hwys., 1976; named to Poetry's Elite: The Best Poets of 2000. Achievements include test track for road pavement and bridge structure with test material in Willowbrook Park, Staten Island. Home: 510 Brighton Beach Ave Brooklyn NY 11235-6404

TSYKALOV, EUGENE, neuroscientist, researcher; b. Kemerovo, Russia, June 22, 1957; came to U.S., 1991; s. Nickolai and Anna (Lebed) T.; m. Ludmila Trojan, July 7, 1976; 1 child, Anna. MSc, Moscow Inst. Physics and Tech., 1980; PhD, Inst. Higher Nervous Activity and Neurophysiology, Moscow, 1986. Rsch. scientist Inst. Higher Nervous Activity and Neurophysiology, Moscow, 1977—; chief sci. officer Imaging Resource Techs., Inc., Phila., 1992—. Vis. scientist U. Pa., Phila., 1991-92, cons., 1992—. Co-author: Thermoencephaloscopy, 1989; contbr. articles to profl. jours. Mem. IEEE, Am. Acad. Thermology (corr.) Achievements include work as principal creator of TES-thermoencephaloscopy method of visualization of brain activity by infrared radiation, patent for advanced image processing algorithms known as ET Filters. Office: Imaging Resource Techs Inc 5500 Wissahickon Ave Philadelphia PA 19144-5653 Home: 415 Nottingham Ln Collegeville PA 19426 E-mail: etsykalov@hotmail.com.

TU, CHUANYI, space physics educator, researcher; b. Beijing, July 24, 1940; s. Yugong Tu and Nonghua Xiao; m. Jinhua Xiao; children: Fangqiu, Ronghui. Grad., Peking U., Beijing, 1964. Asst. prof. Peking U., Beijing, 1972-78, instr., 1978-92, full prof., 1992—. Prin. investigator rsch. Nat. Natural Sci. Found. China, 1985—. Author: Solar-Terrestrial Space Physics, 1988; first author: MHD Structures, Waves and Turbulence in the Solar Wind, 1995; assoc. editor Jour. Geophys. Rsch.-Space Physics, Am. Geophys. Union, 1990-92. Recipient Tan Kah Kee Sci. award Tan Kah Kee Sci. Award Found., Beijing, 2006, award of Nat. natural sci., Chinese Nat. Sci. and Tech. Com., Beijing, 1989, 2001, Wong Dan Ping Sci. prize Com. of Wong Dan Ping Sci. Prize, Beijing and Hong Kong, 1992, Vikram Sarabhei medal Com. on Space Rsch. Internat. Coun. Sci. Unions, 1992. HoLeung Ho Lee Prize, HoLeung HoLee Found., 2002; rsch. fellow dept. mech. engring., Catholic U. of Am., 1980-81, fellow Max-Planck-Inst. für Aeronomie, Katlenberg-Lindau, Germany, 1988-90. Fellow Third World Acad. Scis.; mem. Chinese Soc. Space Sci., Am. Geophys. Union, Acad. Scis. China (academician 2001—). Office: Dept Geophysics Peking Univ Beijing 100871 China Office Phone: 8610-62767223. Office Fax: 10-62564095. Business E-Mail: chuanyitu@pku.edu.cn.

TU, LAWRENCE P., lawyer, computer company executive; b. NYC, Aug. 23, 1954; AB summa cum laude, Harvard Univ., 1976, JD magna cum laude, 1981; BA, Magdalen Coll., Oxford Univ., 1978. Bar: DC 1983, US Supreme Ct. 1988, Hong Kong 1996. Law clk. Judge Walter R. Mansfield, US Ct. Appeals, 2d cir., 1981—82, Justice Thurgood Marshall, US Supreme Ct., 1982—83; gen. counsel, Asia Pacific Goldman Sachs; spl. asst. to legal adviser U.S. Dept. State, 1985—86; assoc. O'Melveny & Myers LLP, 1986—89, ptnr., 1990—2001, mng. ptnr. Hong Kong office, 1995—2000; exec. v.p., gen. counsel NBC Universal, 2001—04; sr. v.p., gen. counsel Dell Inc., 2004—. Editor (notes): Harvard Law Rev., 1979—81. Rhodes Scholar. Mem.: ABA, Minority Corp. Counsel Assn. Bd., DC Bar. Office: Dell Inc 1 Dell Way Round Rock TX 78682-2244*

TU, LORING WULIANG, mathematics educator; b. Taipei, Taiwan, China, Aug. 17, 1952; came to U.S., 1965; s. Grant Tsuchih and Lillian Lichu Tu. AB, Princeton U., 1974; MA, Harvard U., 1976, PhD, 1979. Hildebrandt asst. prof. U. Mich., Ann Arbor, 1979-81, 82-83; mem. Inst. Advanced Study, Princeton, N.J., 1981-82; asst. prof. Johns Hopkins U., Balt., 1983-86, Tufts U., Medford, Mass., 1986-88, assoc. prof., 1988—. Reviewer Math. Revs., Ann Arbor, 1984-89; referee numerous math. jours. and publs. Author: (with Raoul Bott) Differential Forms in Algebraic Topology, 1982. NSF grantee, 1980-82, Tufts U. faculty fellow, 1988. Mem. Am. Math. Soc., Phi Beta Kappa, Sigma Xi. Office: Tufts U Dept Math Medford MA 02155

TU, YUFENG, business educator; BS in Internat. Bus. Mgmt., U. Md., College Park, 2000, PhD in Mgmt. Sci. and Stats., 2006. Rsch. asst. U. Md.; asst. prof. Tourou U., Cypress, Calif. Contbr. articles to profl. jours. Recipient Outstanding Participation award, FAA Ctr. Excellence, 2005; named one of Top Ten Outstanding Women, Beijing Tech. & Bus. U., 2000; Global Tech. & Mgmt. Consortium fellow, Md., 2005. Mem.: Am. Statis. Assn., Inst. Ops. Rsch. and Mgmt. Scis., Decision Scis. Inst., Nat. Ctr. Excellence Aviation Ops. Rsch.

TUAN, DEBBIE FU-TAI, chemist, educator; b. Kiangsu, China, Feb. 2, 1930; arrived in U.S., 1958; d. Shiau-gien and Chen (Lee) T.; m. John W. Reed, Aug. 15, 1987. BS in Chemistry, Nat. Taiwan U., Taipei, 1954, MS in Chemistry, 1958, Yale U., New Haven, Conn., 1960, PhD in Chemistry, 1961. Rsch. fellow Yale U., New Haven, 1961-64; rsch. assoc. U. Wis., Madison, 1964-65; asst. prof. Kent (Ohio) State U., 1965-70, assoc. prof., 1970-73, prof., 1973—; vis. scientist Yeshiva U., NYC, summer 1966; rsch. fellow Harvard U., Cambridge, 1969-70; vis. scientist SRI Internat., Menlo Park, Calif., 1981; rsch. assoc. Cornell U., Ithica, N.Y., 1983. Vis. prof. Acad. Sinica of China, Nat. Taiwan U. and Nat. Tsing-Hwa U., summer 1967, Ohio State U., 1993, 95. Contbr. articles to profl. jours. Recipient NSF Career Advanced award, 1994—; U. Grad. fellow Nat. Taiwan U., 1955-58, F.W. Heyl-Anon F fellow Yale U., 1960-61, U. Faculty Rsch. fellow Kent State U., 1966, 68, 71, 85; Pres. Chiang's scholar Chinese Women Assn., 1954, 58, Grad. scholar in humanity and scis. China Found., 1955. Mem.: Am. Chem. Soc., Am. Phys. Soc., Sigma Xi. Office: Kent State U Chemistry Dept Williams Hl Kent OH 44242-0001

TUAN, KAILIN, management consultant, educator; b. Hefei, China, Sept. 9, 1925; m. Liau G. Tuan; 1 child, Wayne. BS, Chiao Tung U., Shanghai, 1948; MBA, U. Pa., 1952; PhD, New Sch. for Social Rsch., NYC, 1966. Asst./assoc. prof. Upsala Coll., East Orange, NJ, 1959—74; prof. U. Balt., 1974—77, Temple U., Phila., 1977—93, prof. emeritus, 1993—. Prof., dir. Internat. Ins. Inst., Nankai U., Tianyin, China, 1987—97; hon. prof. various Chinese univs.; lectr. in field; econ. adviser to Taiwan and the Philippines, 1970—73; adviser Ministry of Fin., Taiwan, 1970—90; Far Ea. rep. Internat. Coop. Alliance, 1970; cons. to several maj. U.S. and Brit. ins. and bus. cos., 1970—80. Contbr. articles more than 100 numerous articles to profl. jour. publ. in profl. and academic jour. and bus./ins. mag. USA, UK, Japan, China, Taiwan and other Asian countries; author: Modern Insurance Theory and Edn./Ins. Inst. for Asia and the Pacific, 1972—75, Essays in Risk Management, 1988, The Risk Management Movement, 1999, Studies in the Theory of Risk and Insurance, 1995. Recipient Internat. Friendship award, Chinese Govt., 2000, FLMI Ins. Edn. award, Life Office Mgmt. Assn., 2001, Pres.'s award, Ins. Acctg. and Sys. Assn., 2002. Mem.: Asia-Pacific Risk and Ins. Assn., China Assn. Actuaries (hon. lifetime mem. 2008), U.S. Am.-China C. of C. (founder, bd. dirs.), Am. Risk and Ins. Assn. (bd. dirs. 2009), Internat. Ins. Soc. Avocations: gardening, Go. Office: Temple Univ Dept Risk Mgmt and Ins Philadelphia PA 19122

TUBB, GARY ALAN, humanities educator; b. Wichita, Kans., June 1, 1950; s. Jim Monroe Tubb and Lillian Irene Weierich; m. Mary Elizabeth McGee, Nov. 23, 1979; children: Mathilda Sage McGee-Tubb, Cordelia Dillon McGee-Tubb. BA, MA, Harvard U., Cambridge, Mass., PhD, 1979. Editor, Harvard oriental series Harvard U., Cambridge, 1983—91, chair, dept. Sanskrit & Indian studies, 1983—87, assoc. prof. humanities, dept. Sanskrit & Indian studies, 1985—88; sr. lectr., Sanskrit tchg. indic rsch., religion dept. Columbia U., NYC, 1999—2007; prof., south asian langs. & civilizations U. Chgo., 2007—. Mem.: Am. Oriental Soc., Assn. Asian Studies.

TUBB, JAMES CLARENCE, lawyer; b. Corsicana, Tex. s. Cullen Louis and Sarah Elmore (Chapman) T.; m. Suzanne Alice Smith, Nov. 25, 1954; children: James Richard, Sara Elizabeth, Daniel Chapman. BA, So. Meth. U., 1951, JD, 1954. Bar: Tex. 1954, U.S. Dist. Ct. (no. dist.) Tex. 1955, U.S. Ct. Appeals (5th cir.) 1959, U.S. Supreme Ct. 1978; cert. comml. real estate specialist, 1983; lic. Tex. real estate broker; cert. mediator Dallas Bar Assn. With legal dept. Schlumberger Well Surveying Corp., Houston, 1954-55; claims atty. Franklin Am. Ins. Co., Dallas, 1957-58; ptnr. Vial, Hamilton, Koch, Tubb & Knox and predecessor firm Akin, Vial, Hamilton, Koch & Tubb, Dallas, 1958-84; dir., ptnr. Winstead, McGuire, Sechrest & Minick, Dallas, 1984-90; pvt. practice Dallas, 1990—. Guest lectr. on real estate broker liability Real Estate Ctr., Tex. A&M U., 1987. Mem. bd. deacons Highland Park Presbyn. Ch., Dallas, 1972—78, ruling elder, 1978—84, 1988—91; mem. permanent jud. commn. Grace Presbytery, 1984—90; bd. dirs. Christian Concern Found., 1965—71, Dallas County affiliate Am. Diabetes Assn., 1991—95. With Tex. Air N.G., 1949—51, 1st lt. JAGC, SAC USAF, 1955—57, 1st lt. USAF, ret. Recipient Outstanding Student award Student Bar Assn., 1954. Fellow Tex. Bar Found.; mem. ABA (chmn. comml. law com. gen. practice sect. 1982-84, real estate probate and trust law sect.), Tex. Bus. Law Found., Tex. Bar Assn., Am. Arbitration Assn. (sec. comml. arbitration panelist), Dallas Country Club, Dallas County Rep. Men's Club (sec. 1978-79). Home and Office: 3407 Haynie Ave Dallas TX 75205-1842 Office Phone: 214-232-8964. Personal E-mail: jctubb@sbcglobal.com.

TUBBS, MARY S., curriculum coordinator; m. Ronald James Tubbs, Jr., Mar. 25, 2000. AA in Humanities with honors, Chabot Coll., 1975; BA in Psychology, U. Calif-Berkeley, 1978; MEd with honors, San Francisco State U., 1982. Cert. K-8 tchr., reading K-12 tchr. Calif., Hawaii. Head tchr. Jack & Jill Nursery Kindergarten, San Francisco, 1979—80; kindergarten tchr. St. James Early Childhood Devel. Ctr., San Francisco, 1980—81; substitute tchr. San Francisco Unified Sch. Dist., 1981—82; clin. psychol. asst. State Hawaii, 1982; owner Akamai Tutoring, Kailua, Hawaii, 1988—89; psychol. examiner State Hawaii, Dept. Edn., Windward Oahu, 1983—88, spl. edn. tchr. Waianae, 1989—90, Title I reading coord., 1999—2001, tchr. Kailua, 2001—02, curriculum and standards coord., 2002—; dist. resource, diagnostic prescriptive tchr. State Hawaii, Dept. Edn. Spl. Svcs., Honolulu, 1991—99, title I math. coord., 2005—. Chair Windward Oahu Dist. Sch. Climate Task Force, Kailua, 1986—88; facilitator Tchr. Assistance Team, Nanaikapono E., Hawaii, 1989—90. Recipient Summer Tchg. Trning. scholarship, Whittier Coll., 1971, Am. Bus. Women's scholarship, Alameda Bus. Women, 1978. Mem.: NEA, Hawaii State Tchr. Assn. (dist. rep. 1998), Nat. Assn. Sch. Psychologists, Hawaii Humane Soc., Susan G. Komen Breast Cancer Assn. (sec. 2003—), Reading Club (program creator, facilitator 1995—96, grant 1995). Avocations: reading, German shepherds, remodeling. Office: Mokapu Elem Sch 1193 Mokapu Rd Kailua HI 96734 Office Phone: 808-254-7964.

TUBESING, RICHARD LEE, library director; b. Kansas City, Mo., Nov. 25, 1937; s. Clarence and Letha (Thacker) T. BA, Yale U., 1959; MA, U. Chgo., 1969; MSL, Western Mich. U., 1972. Asst. to dir. U. Louisville, 1972-73; reference libr. Ga. Tech. Libr., Atlanta, 1973-76; head bus. and sci. Atlanta Pub. Libr., 1976-79; libr. dir. Lewis U., Romeoville, Ill., 1979-81; collection devel. coord. U. Toledo Libr., 1981-86; libr. dir. Coll. of the Southwest, Hobbs, N.Mex., 1986-89; libr. dir., dir. libr. sci. program Glenville (W.Va.) State Coll., 1989-99; ret., 1999. Part-time libr. Gilmer Pub. Libr., Glenville, W.Va. Author: Architectural Preservation, 1978, Architectural Preservation and Urban Renovation, 1982. Program coord. Lea County Archaeol. Soc., Hobbs, 1987-89. Lt. j.g. USNR, 1960-63. Mem. W.Va. Libr. Assn., Lea County Libr. Assn. (v.p. 1987-88, pres. 1988-89). Avocation: collecting primitive and peasant art. Home: 351 E Valley Dr Glenville WV 26351-9416

TUBIS, ARNOLD, physics professor; b. Pottstown, Pa., Mar. 28, 1932; s. Joseph and Rose (Nemiroff) T.; m. Charlotte Ida Litman, June 14, 1959; children: Cheryl Lynne Tubis Brown, Eliot Jason. BS in Physics, MIT, 1954, PhD in Physics, 1959. Asst. prof. dept. physics Worcester Poly. Inst., Mass., 1956—60; rsch. assoc. Purdue U., West Lafayette, Ind., 1960—62, asst. prof. physics, 1962—64, assoc. prof., 1964—69, prof. physics, 1969—2000, asst. head dept. physics, 1966—73, head dept. physics, 1988—97, prof. emeritus, 2000—. Chmn. tech. com. Internat. Workshop on Mechanics of Hearing, Boston, 1985; ind. cons. physiol. acoustics and math. edn., 2000—. Author 3 books; editor conf. procs.; contbr. numerous articles to refereed jours. Pres. Congregation Sons of Abraham Synagogue, Lafayette, Ind., 1976-78. Am. Phys. Soc. fellow, 1977; grantee AEC, Deafness Rsch. Found., Dept. Energy, Energy Rsch. and Devel. Adminstrn., NIH, NSF, Office Naval Rsch.; vis. scholar Inst. Nonlinear Sci., U. Calif. San Diego, La Jolla, 2000—. Fellow Acoustical Soc. Am. (tech. com. musical acoustics 1984-89, physiol. and psychol. acoustics 1992-97); mem. Am. Assn. Physics Tchrs., Am. Phys. Soc., Nat. Coun. Tchrs. Math., Assn. Rsch. on Otolaryngology, Calif. Math. Coun., Sigma Xi, Sigma Pi Sigma. Jewish. Avocations: hiking, music, reading, puzzles, origami. Personal E-mail: tubisa@aol.com. Business E-Mail: atu@physics.purdue.edu.

TUBMAN, WILLIAM CHARLES, lawyer; b. NYC, Mar. 16, 1932; s. William Thomas and Ellen Veronica Griffin; m. Dorothy Rita Krug, Aug. 15, 1964; children: William Charles Jr., Thomas Davison, Matthew Griffin. BS, Fordham U., 1953, JD, 1960; postdoctoral, NYU Sch. Law, 1960-61. Bar: N.Y. 1960, U.S. Ct. Appeals (2d cir.) 1966, U.S. Supreme Ct. 1967, U.S. Ct. Customs and Patent Appeals 1971. Auditor Peat, Marwick Mitchell & Co., NYC, 1956-60; sr. counsel Kennecott Corp., NYC, 1960-82, Phelps Dodge Corp., NYC, 1982-85, sec., 1985-95, v.p., 1987-95; pres. Phelps Dodge Found., Phoenix, 1988-95. Author: Legal Status of Minerals Beyond the Continental Shelf, 1966. Scholarship adv. U. Ariz., 1990-92; active Big Bros., Inc., N.Y.C., 1963-73; trustee Phoenix Art Mus., 1989-94; bd. dirs. St. Joseph Hosp. Found., 1994-2003, emeritus, 2003—, chmn., 1994-95; bd. dirs. The Phoenix Symphony, 1994-95. Recipient Disting. Svc. cert. Big Brothers Inc., 1968. Mem.: ABA, N.Y. State Bar Assn. Democrat. Roman Catholic. Home: 8008 N 66th St Paradise Valley AZ 85253-2612 Home Phone: 480-951-0091.

TUCCERI, CLIVE KNOWLES, writer, science educator, consultant; b. Bryn Mawr, Pa., Apr. 20, 1953; d. William Henry and Clive Ellis (Knowles) Hulick; m. Eugene Angelo Tucceri, Sept. 1, 1984 (div. Nov. 1991); 1 child, Clive Edna. BA in Geology, Williams Coll., 1975; MS in Coastal Geology, Boston Coll., 1982. Cert. profl. tchr. in Earth and gen. sci. Head sci. dept. Stuart Hall Sch., Staunton, Va., 1975-77; mem. sci. faculty William Penn Charter Sch., Phila., 1977-79, Tower Sch., Marblehead, Mass., 1982-86, Bentley Coll., Waltham, Mass., 1986-88; adminstrv. dir., co-founder Stout Aquatic Libr. Nat. Marine and Aquatic Edn. Resource Ctr., Wakefield, R.I., 1982-89; sci. faculty Mabelle B. Avery Sch., Somers, Conn., 1989—90; faculty, head sci. dept. MacDuffie Sch., Springfield, Mass., 1992—93; sci. faculty East Hampton (Conn.) Middle Sch., 1993—, sci. team leader, 1994—95, sci. chmn. grades K-12, 1995—. Cons. Addison-Wesley Pub. Co., Menlo Park, Calif., 1986—94, Longmeadow Pub. Schs., Mass., 1989—94; cons. and freelance writer Prentice-Hall Inc., Needham, 1991; cons. web content devel. Conn. Sci. Ctr., 2005—07; mem. edn. adv. com. Mashantucket Pequot Mus. and Rsch. Ctr., 2007—. Co-head class agt. Williams Coll. Alumni Fund, 2000—, vice chair, 2003—06; admissions rep. Williams Coll., 2001—; vol. The Bushnell Ctr. for Performing Arts, 2001—; educator adv. com. Mashantucket Pequot Mus. Rsch. Ctr., 2007; mem. search com. Christ Ch., Middle Haddam, Conn., 2000—01, mem. vestry, 2002—05; bd. dir. People Against Rape, Staunton, 1976—77; bd. mem. Southeastern New England Marine Educators, 2007. Mem.: AAUW (br. pres.-elect 1975—77, v.p. 1985—86, sec. 1986—87, bd. dirs.), NEA, NSTA, Cousteau Soc., Conn. Edn. Assn., Conn. Sci Tchrs. Assn., Conn. Sci. Suprs. Assn., Mass. Environ. Edn. Soc. (bd. dirs. 1985—88), Mass. Marine Educators (bd. dirs. 1983—91, pres. 1987—89, editor Flotsam and Jetsam MA Marine Educators newsletter 1991—97), Southeastern New Eng. Marine Educators (publs. chair Nat. Conf. com., bd. dirs. 2007—), Nat. Mid. Level Sci. Tchrs. Assn., Nat. Marine Edn. Assn. (sec. 1986—87, chpt. rep. 1987 1989), Sigma Xi. Episcopalian. Avocations: renovating old homes, sailing, gardening, reading. Home: 12 Birchwood Dr East Hampton CT 06424-1312 Personal E-mail: ctucceri@aol.com.

TUCCI, JOSEPH M., information technology executive; b. Bklyn., 1947; m. Maureen Tucci. BA, Manhattan Coll., 1968; MBA, Columbia U., 1984. With RCA Corp., 1970—86; pres. U.S. ops. Unisys Corp., 1986-90; exec. v.p. ops Wang Labs., Inc., 1990-93, chmn., CEO Lowell, Mass., 1993—99; dep. CEO Getronics NV, 1999; pres., COO EMC

Corp., Hopkinton, Mass., 2000—01, pres., CEO, 2001—, chmn., 2006—. Bd. dirs. Paychex, 2000—, EMC Corp., 2001—. Office: EMC Corp 176 South St Hopkinton MA 01748

TUCCI, OSCAR MAXIMILLIAN, restauranteur, radio host, writer, philanthropist; b. NYC, Feb. 14, 1979; s. Tucci Carlo Mario and Tucci Julianna Gina. Grad., St. Luke's HS, New Canaan, Conn., 2005. Head designer, owner Maximillian, NYC, 1998—2007, Man by Max, NYC, 1999—2003; v.p. Oscar's Delmonico, Stamford, Conn., 2001—; publicist Tucci Pub. Rels., Florence, Italy, 1999—2005; on-air talent America's Next Top Model with Tyra Banks, NYC, 2003, LA Talk Radio, 2008—; reality star Young, Sexy &., NYC, 2004; interior designer Maximillian Interior Designs, NYC, 2003—; owner, founder Wild Lily Prodns., Stamford, 2007—; v.p. Oscar's Delmonico LLC, Stamford, Conn., 2001—; radio host La. Talk Radio, 2008—. Contbr. book; photography, My Portfolio (Gold Key, 1998), Watermark (Gold medal Winner, 1997). Com. mem. Am. Diabetes Assn., Norwalk, Conn., 2005, Lithuanian Orphanage Fund, Stamford, Conn., 2005—07; internat. com. mem. Boy's Town NY, NYC, 2008; com. mem. Montifiore Children's Hosp., Bronx, NY, 1995—2006; chmn. SOS Children's Villages Fla., Coconut Creek, 2007—08. Named One of NY's Most Eligible Bachelor's, Gotham Mag., 2004. Personal E-mail: max@maxtucci.com. Business E-Mail: delmonicollc@yahoo.com.

TUCCI, STANLEY, actor; b. Peekskill, NY, Nov. 11, 1960; s. Stanley and Joan (Tropiano) Tucci; m. Kate Tucci, 1995 (dec. 2009); children: Camilla, Nicolo Robert, Isabel Concetta. BFA, SUNY, Purchase, 1982. Actor (films) Fear Anxiety and Depression, 1990, Billy Bathgate, 1991, Men of Respect, 1991, In The Soup, 1992, Beethoven, 1992, Prelude to A Kiss, 1992, Undercover Blues, 1993, The Pelican Brief, 1993, Somebody to Love, 1994, It Could Happen to You, 1994, Mrs. Parker and the Vicious Circle, 1994, Jury Duty, 1995, Kiss of Death, 1995, A Modern Affair, 1995, Captive, 1995, The Daytrippers, 1996, Montana, 1997, Life During Wartime, 1997, The Eighteenth Angel, 1997, Deconstructing Harry, 1997, A Life Less Ordinary, 1997, The Imposters, 1998, A Midsummer Night's Dream, 1999, Joe Gould's Secret, 1999, In Too Deep, 1999, The Whole Shebang, 2000, Bull, 2000, Sidewalks of New York, 2001, America's Sweethearts, 2001, Big Trouble, 2002, Road to Perdition, 2002, Maid in Manhattan, 2002, The Core, 2003, The Life and Death of Peter Sellers, 2004, The Terminal, 2004, Shall We Dance?, 2004, (voice) Robots, 2005, Lucky Number Slevin, 2006, Four Las Songs, 2006, The Devil Wears Prada, 2006, The Hoax, 2006, Kit Kittredge: An American Girl, 2008, (voice) Space Chimps, 2008, Swing Vote, 2008, What Just Happened, 2008, (voice) THe Tale of Despereaux, 2008, Julie & Julia, 2009; actor, co-dir., co-prodr. (films) Big Night, 1996 (Ind. Spirit award for best 1st screenplay 1996); actor (TV series) Murder One, 1995, 3 Lbs., 2006-, (TV movies) Winchell, 1998 (Emmy award 1998), Conspiracy, 2001 (Golden Globe award 2001) Recipient Creative Arts Primetime Emmy for Outstanding Guest Actor in Comedy Series, Acad. TV Arts and Scis., 2007. Office: William Morris Agy c/o David Yocum 151 S El Camino Dr Beverly Hills CA 90212-2775*

TUCCI, STEVEN MICHAEL, health facility administrator, physician, recording industry executive; b. NYC, Oct. 5, 1949; s. Louis Alexander and Nina Ida (Cerone) T.; m. Mari E. Koerner, Nov., 1974; children: Alexander, Michael, Lara. BS, Manhattan Coll., 1971; MS, SUNY, Brockport, 1977; PhD, Albany Med. Coll., 1978, MD, 1981. Diplomate Am. Coll. Phys. Medicine and Rehab., Am. Coll. Pain Mgmt.; cert. Nat. Bd. Med. Examiners. Rsch. fellow Birth Defects Inst. N.Y. State Dept. Health, 1976-81; instr. anatomy Albany (N.Y) Med. Coll., 1977-78, rsch. assoc. divns. endocrinology, 1978-81, asst. prof. anatomy, 1978-79, rsch. assoc. dept. anatomy, 1979-81; commd. officer student trainee, extern Nat. Inst. Neurol. and Communicative Disorders and Stroke/NIH, 1981; from intern to resident divsn. phys. medicine and rehabilitation George Washington Univ., 1981-84; staff fellowclin. ctr. dept. phys. medicine and rehabilitation NIH, 1983-84; mem. staff dept. medicine Commonwealth Hosp., Fairfax, Va., 1983-84; mem. med. staff Doctor's Hosp., Sarastota, Fla., 1984, med. dir. phys. medicine and rehab., 1989, med. dir., 1994—; founding med. dir. The Ctr. at Manatee Springs, Bradenton, Fla., 1985-86, The Rehab. Inst. Sarasota, Fla., 1986-88; med. dir. Fawcett Meml. Hosp., Port Charlotte, Fla., 1988—; med. dir. phys. medicine and rehab. Charlotte Community Rehab. Ctr., Port Charlotte, 1988; co-founder Sports, Pain and Rehab. Medicine Assocs., Sarasota and Port Charlotte, 1992; med. dir. Manatee Meml. Hosp., Bradenton, 1993—; pres., CEO Groove Tone Records, Sarasota, 1994-96. Writer: (music) Take Me Down to the Ballgame, 1994, Spell on Me, 1994, On the Road to Nowhere, 1994; contbr. articles, papers to profl. jours. Mem. AMA, USTA, Am. Acad. Phys. Medicine and Rehab., Am. Coll. Sprots Medicine, Am. Congress Rehabilitative Medicine, Am. Soc. Pain Mgmt., Fla. Med. Assn., Fla. Soc. Phys. Medicine and Rehab., Major League Baseball Players Alumni Assn., Rep. Presdl. Task Force, Rep. Senatorial Inner Circle. Republican. Roman Catholic. Avocations: musician, tennis, fishing. Office: Sports and Rehab Medicine 7147 Curtiss Ave Sarasota FL 34231-1207

TUCHI, BEN JOSEPH, retired finance educator; b. Hazleton, Pa., Mar. 2, 1936; s. Joseph Ben and Mary Rose (Marnell) T.; m. Patricia Gail O'Brien, Apr. 8, 1961; children: John J., Matthew P. BS, Pa. State U., 1959, MS, 1962; PhD, St. Louis U., 1970. Instr., asst. prof. St. Francis Coll., Loretto, Pa., 1960-66, 68-69; instr. St. Louis U., 1966-68; asst. prof., assoc. prof., prof. fin. W.Va. U., Morgantown, 1969-76, contr., 1976-80, assoc. v.p., chief fin. officer, 1980-85; sr. v.p. U. Ariz., Tucson, 1985-89; vice chancellor U. N.C., Chapel Hill, 1989-92; sr. vice chancellor, prof. fin. U. Pitts., 1992-96, prof. fin., 1996—. Cons. to numerous univs., mining cos., banks, law firms, Washington, San Diego, Pitts., Charleston, W.Va., Columbus, Ohio, Morgantown, 1970—. Contbr. articles to profl. jours. Bd. dirs. U. N.C. Found. Inc., 1989-90, Rise Inc., Cope Behavioral Svcs. Inc., Arizona Rsch. Pk. Authority, 2006-2008. Recipient Outstanding Tchr. award W.Va. U., 1973; Life Ins. Agy. Mgmt. Assn. fellow, 1963, St. Louis U. fellow, 1968-69; HEW grantee, 1973. Mem. Nat. Assn. Coll. and Univ. Bus. Officers (large instns. com. 1976—, orgn. com. 1988-89), Am. Econs. Assn., Am. Fin. Assn. Avocations: racquetball, golf, reading. Home: 7971 N Tuscany Dr Tucson AZ 85742-4300 Personal E-mail: bentuchi@comcast.net.

TUCHMAN, ALAN, consumer products company executive; V.p. Alliance Entertainment Corp., 1991—96, pres., COO, 2000—05, sr. v.p. strategic planning, 1996—97, pres. AEC One Stop Group, Inc., 1997—2000, pres., COO, 2000—05; exec. v.p., pres. Alliance divsn. Source Interlink Cos., 2005—06, interim co-CEO, 2006—08, pres. distbn., 2008—. Office: Source Interlink Cos 27500 Riverview Center Blvd Bonita Springs FL 34134 Office Phone: 239-949-4450.*

TUCHMAN, AVRAHAM (AVI), physicist, researcher; b. NYC, July 1, 1935; s. Max and Rebecca (Brick) T.; m. Sylvia Crystal, Dec. 26, 1957; children: Davida, Ari, Sima, Pnina. BA, Yeshiva U., NYC, 1956; PhD, MIT, Cambridge, 1963. Scientist, group leader to sect. chief Avco Rsch. and Advanced Devel., Wilmington, Mass., 1963; prin. scientist, staff scientist to prin. staff scientist Avco Systems Div., Wilmington; chief scientist Textron Def. Systems, Wilmington, 1988-93; owner, pres., CEO Added Value Innovations, Brookline, Mass., 1994—. Vis. prof. Weizmann Inst. Sci., Rehovot, Israel, 1974, 78, 82. Contbr. numerous articles to profl. jours. Founder, pres. Kehilla Day Camp of Jewish Community Ctrs., Westwood, Mass., 1975-86; chmn. Brookline Traffic Commn., Mass., 1975-81; pres. Mikvah Rescue Svc., Brighton, Mass., 1969-77; pres. Temple Beth Avraham, Brookline, 1969—. Recpient award for outstanding cantorial artistry Am. Soc. Forktwangers, Detroit, 1970. Fellow AIAA (sr.). Avocations: computers, gardening, homecraft, snowboarding, dowhill racing.

TUCHMAN, PHYLLIS, critic; b. Passaic, NJ, Jan. 4, 1947; d. Jack and Evelyn (Sugarman) T. BA in Fine Arts with distinction, Boston U., 1968; MA, NYU, 1973. Ind. critic, NYC, 1968—. Inst. art hist., Sch. Visual Arts, NY, 1972-75; adj. lectr. art history Hunter Coll., CUNY, NYC, 1976-79; vis. prof. art Williams Coll., Williamstown, Mass., 1981-83; curator Six in Bronze, Williams Coll. Mus. Art and tour, 1985, Big Little Sculpture, Williams Coll. Mus. Art and tour, 1988, Venezuela: The Next Generation, Baruch Col. Gallery, 1990, Drawing Redux, San Jose Mus. Art and tour, 1992, Norte del Sur: Venezuelan Art Today, Philbrook Art Mus., 1997. Author: George Segal, 1983, Venezuela: The Next Generation, 1990; contbr. articles to profl. jours., popular mags. Art Critics grantee NEA, 1978-79; vis. fellow Princeton U., NEH, 1980. Mem. Internat. Assn. Art Critics (Am. sect. pres. 1986-90, v.p. internat. parent body, 89-91), Art Table (bd. dirs. 1984-87, v.p. 1987-88), AICA (v.p. Am. sect. 2004—07), Art Com., Longhouse Reserve, East Hampton. Home: 340 E 80th St New York NY 10075-0927

TUCHMANN, ERIC P., lawyer; m. Cheri Fancsali; children: Isabel, Amelia. BS, U. Wis., Madison, 1988; JD, NY Law Sch., 1994. With Am. Arbitration Assn., 1994—, dir. comml. dept. NY, dir. Internat. Ctr. Dispute Resolution, assoc. gen. counsel, gen. counsel, corp. sec. NYC, 2004—. Office: Am Arbitration Assn 1633 Broadway 10th Fl New York NY 10019-6708 Office Phone: 212-716-5800.

TUCHMANN, ROBERT, lawyer; b. NYC, July 7, 1946; s. Frederick C. and Hildegard (Jung) Tuchmann; m. Naomi R. Walfish, June 1, 1969; children: David, Paul. AB, Oberlin Coll., 1967; JD, Harvard U., 1971. Bar: Mass. 1971, U.S. Dist. Ct. Mass. 1971. Assoc. Hale and Dorr, Boston, 1971-76, jr. ptnr., 1976-80, sr. ptnr., 1980—2004, Wilmer, Cutler, Pickering, Hale and Dorr, Boston, 2004—. Lectr. Mass. Continuing Legal Edn., 1976—99. Pres. Project Bread-The Walk for Hunger, Boston, 1990—98; chair Ctrl. Artery Environ. Oversight Com., 1992—; mem. New Fed. Courthouse Task Force, 1993—99; bd. overseers Rogerson Cmtys., 1995—; co-chair Mayor's Ctrl. Artery Completion Task Force, 2001—; mem. com. Oberlin Coll., 1990. Mem.: Architecture Boston (editl. bd. mem. 2007—), Legal Svcs. Ctr. Harvard Law Sch. (vis. clin. instr. 2008—), Real Estate Bar, Boston Soc. Archs. (bd. dirs. 2004—07), Downtown Boston Transp. Mgmt. Assn. (chmn. 1996—), Boston Bar Assn. (com. chmn. 1977—81), Island Alliance (trustee 1997—2000). Office: Wilmer Cutler Pickering Hale and Dorr LLP 60 State St Boston MA 02109-1816 Home Phone: 617-965-2568; Office Phone: 617-526-6920. Business E-Mail: robert.tuchmann@wilmerhale.com.

TUCK, AMY, former lieutenant governor; b. Starkville, Miss., July 8, 1963; d. Grady William and Mary (Boykin) Tuck. BA in Polit. Sci., Miss. State U., Starkville, 1985; postgrad., Miss. State U., Miss. State U., Starkville, 1992—; JD, Miss. Coll., 1989. Legal asst. Ben. F. Hilburn Jr., Atty. at Law, Starkville, Miss., 1984-85; grad. asst. dept. polit. sci. Miss. State U., Starkville, 1986-87; law clk. Minor Buchanan, Jackson, Miss., 1987-88, Deposit Guaranty Nat. Bank, Jackson, 1988-89; state senator dist. 15 State of Miss., Jackson, 1990-99, lt. gov., 2000—08. Adj. prof. Wood Jr. Coll., Mathiston, Miss., 1990-95. Mem. Oktibbeha County Voter Re-Registration Com., Oktibbeha County Fedn. Dem. Women; bd. dirs. Oktibbeha County Am. Cancer Soc., 1991-92; mem. local rels. com. Children and Family Svcs.; assoc. mem. Nat. Mus. Women in the Arts, 1992-93. Mem. NAFE, Am. Legis. Exch. Com., Am. Soc. Pub. Adminstrs., Nat. Conf. State Legislature, Nat. Order Women Legislators, Miss. State U. Alumni Assn., Starkville Area Bus. and Profl. Women's Club, Oktibbeha County C. of C., Gamma Beta Phi, Pi Sigma Alpha, Omicron Delta Kappa, Phi Delta Phi (vice-magister 1988, historian 1988-89). Democrat. Methodist. Office Phone: 601-359-3200. Office Fax: 601-359-4054. E-mail: ltgov@mail.senate.state.ms.us.

TUCK, GRAYSON EDWIN, real estate agent, gas industry executive; b. Richmond, Va., May 11, 1927; s. Bernard Okly and Erma (Wiltshire) T.; m. Rosalie Scroggs, June 6, 1947; children— Janice Lorrain, Kenneth Edwin, Carol Lynn. BS, U. Richmond, 1950. Payroll clk., cost clk. Gen. Baking Co., Richmond, 1948-51; jr. accountant Commonwealth Natural Gas Corp., Richmond, 1951-55, sr. accountant, 1956-57, accounting supr., 1957-58, asst. treas., 1959-62, asst. sec., asst. treas., 1963-64, treas., asst. sec., 1965-77; treas. Commonwealth Natural Resources, Inc., 1977-81, CNG Transmission Co. subs., 1977-79; sec.-treas. Air Pollution Control Products, Inc., Richmond, 1970-73; asst. treas., asst. sec. Commonwealth Gas Distbn. Corp., Richmond, 1969-79; mgr. taxes and cash mgmt. Commonwealth Gas Pipeline Corp., subs. Columbia Gas System Inc., 1981-86; investor, realtor Bill Eudailey & Co., 1986—. Active Boy Scouts Am., 1965—69; bd. dirs. Henrico Area Mental Health Retardation Svcs., 1983—85; active Elpis Christian Ch., 2001—; deacon Presbyn. Ch., 1958—86, elder, 1986—2001, treas., 1968—70. With USNR, 1945—46. Mem.: Nat. Assn. Accts. (assoc. dir. 1963—64). Home: 2923 Oakland Ave Richmond VA 23228-5827 Office: 9012 Three Chopt Rd Richmond VA 23229 Office Phone: 804-282-7678. Personal E-mail: realtortuck1@comcast.net.

TUCK, JUSTIN LEE, professional football player; b. Kellyton, Ala., Mar. 29, 1983; s. Jimmy Lee and Elaine Tuck; m. Lauran Tuck. B in Mgmt., U. Notre Dame Mendoza Coll. Bus., Ind., 2005. Defensive end NY Giants, 2005—. Named 1st Team All-Pro, AP, 2008; named to Nat. Football Conf. Pro Bowl Team, NFL, 2008. Achievements include being a member of Super Bowl XLII winning New York Giants, 2008. Office: NY Giants Giants Stadium East Rutherford NJ 07073*

TUCK, RUSSELL R., JR., college president emeritus; b. June 9, 1934; m. Marjorie Gay Tuck; children: Russell R. III, Catherine Elizabeth. BS in Chemistry, Union U., 1956; MS in Biology, George Peabody Coll. Vanderbilt U., 1957, PhD in Curriculum and Instrn., 1971; studied, Wash. U., 1960—61. Instr. biology, asst. coordinator Korean Tchr. Edn. Program George Peabody Coll. Vanderbilt U., Nashville, 1957-59; tchr. biology, chmn. sci. dept. University City (Mo.) Sr. High Sch., 1960-63, from asst. prin. to prin., 1963-70; prin. Parkway North Sr. High Sch., St. Louis County, Mo., 1971-78; asst. supt. Parkway Sch. Dist., St. Louis County, 1979-81, assoc. supt., 1981-84; pres. Calif. Bapt. U., Riverside, 1984-94, pres. emeritus, 1994—; assoc. prof. Azusa Pacific U., 1995—2001. Contbr. articles to profl. jours. Bd. dirs. Opera Assn.; pres. Riverside County chpt. ARC, 1989-90; active Bapt. Ch., ch. elder, local hosp. assn. bd., local edn. com.; World Affairs Coun. Mem. Calif. Bapt. Hist. Soc. (bd. dirs.), Calif. Bapt. Devel. Found. (bd. dirs.), Am. Assn. Sch. Adminstrs., Inland Empire Higher Edn. Coun. (pres. 1987-88), Rotary, Kappa Delta Pi, Phi Delta Kappa. Lodges: Rotary. Home: 14000 Chelmsford Dr Gainesville VA 20155

TUCKER, ALAN CURTISS, mathematics professor; b. Princeton, NJ, July 6, 1943; s. Albert William and Alice Judson (Curtiss) W.; m. Amanda Almira Zeisler, Aug. 31, 1968 (div. 1997); children: Lisa, Kathryn, Edward, James; m. Ann K. Hong, Feb. 16, 1997. BA, Harvard U., 1965; MS, Stanford U., 1967, PhD, 1969. Asst. prof. applied math. SUNY, Stony Brook, 1970-73, assoc. prof. applied math., 1973-78, prof. applied math., chmn., 1978-89, SUNY Disting. Teaching prof., 1989—. Vis. asst. prof. math. U. Wis., Madison, 1969-70; vis. assoc. prof. computer sci. U. Calif., San Diego, 1976-77; vis. prof. ops. research Stanford U., 1983-84; cons. Sloan Found., 1981-85; acad. cons. 40 colls. and univs. Author: Applied Combinatorics, 1980, Unified Introduction to Linear Algebra, 1987, Linear Algebra, 1993; assoc. editor Math. Monthly, 1996-2001, Applied Maths. Letters, 1986—; contbr. 45 rsch. articles to profl. jours. Ga. U. Consortium Disting. Visitor, 1982; NSF grantee, 1972-86. Mem. Math. Assn. Am. (chmn. publs. 1982-86, editor Studies in Math. series 1979-86, v.p. 1988-90, chmn. ednl. coun. 1990-96, Disting. Tchr. award 1994, Trevor Evans award 1996, Meritorious Svc. award 2005), U.S. Commn. Math. Instrn., Am. Math. Soc., Ops. Rsch. Soc. Am., Soc. Indsl. Applied Maths., Sigma Xi (chpt. pres. 1987—). Home: 19 Crosby Place Cold Spring Harbor NY 11724-2404 Office: SUNY At Stony Brook Dept Of Applied Math Stony Brook NY 11794-3600 Home Phone: 631-367-1841; Office Phone: 631-632-8365. Business E-Mail: atucker@notes.sunysb.edu.

TUCKER, ALAN DAVID, publisher; b. Erie, Pa., Mar. 9, 1936; s. Meredith LaDue and Monica (Klocko) Tucker; m. Kiyoko Iizuka, Feb. 8, 1963; 1 child, Kumi. AB, Princeton U., 1957. Assoc. editor Hawthorn Books, NYC, 1964-66; editor John Day Co., Inc., NYC, 1966-72; mng. editor David McKay Co., Inc., NYC, 1972-75, v.p., 1975-78, exec. v.p., editl. dir., 1978-84; editl. dir. Fodor's Travel Guides, Inc., NYC, 1978-84; founder, prodr. Penguin Travel Guides and other publs., NYC, 1984-91; gen. editor Berlitz Travellers Guides, NYC, 1991-95; consulting sr. analyst Genesis Group Assocs., Montclair, NJ, 1995—2001; v.p. mktg. strategy Oxygen Advt., Inc., NYC, 1996—; consulting sr. analyst Adis Bus. Intelligence, Langhorne, Pa., 2002. Author: Capitation and Risk Sharing, 1995, Integrated Health Information Systems, 1997, Provider-Sponsored Managed Care, 1998, Convergence in Coordinated Care, 1998; co-author: The Electronic Superhighway 1997-2010: Opportunities for the Healthcare Industry, 1996, Diabetes Disease Management, 1995, 2d edit., 1998, Asthma Disease Management, 1997, 2d edit., 1999, Hypertension Management, 1999, Management of Congestive Heart Failure, 1999, Intelligence Report: Depression, 1999, Intelligence Report: Lung Cancer, 2000, Strategic Audit: Alzheimer's and Parkinson's Disease, 2000, Strategic Audit: Stroke and Multiple Sclerosis, 2000, Asthma Forum, 2001, Osteoporosis Forum, 2001, Psoriasis Forum, 2001, Congestive Heart Failure Forum, 2001, Obesity Forum, 2002, Allergic Rhinitis Forum, 2002, Pain Management Forum, 2002, Handbook of Healthcare Marketing, 2003. With USNR, 1957—60. Mem.: Am. Coll. Healthcare Execs., N.Y. Travel Writers Assn. (past pres.). Home: 186 Riverside Dr New York NY 10024-1007 Office: PO Box 1177 Sharon CT 06069-1177

TUCKER, ALVIN LEROY, retired government official; b. Bklyn., Sept. 7, 1938; s. Alvin Leroy Jr. and Alveria (Klune) T.; m. Jacqueline Twiggs, Aug. 27, 1966; children: Hazel, Pluma, Jacqueline, Alvin. BS, U. Md., 1965. CPA, Md.; cert. internal auditor; cert. govt. fin. mgr.; cert. def. fin. mgr. Auditor Dept. Army, Washington, 1965-67; dep. insp. gen. HUD, Washington, 1986-89; auditor Dept. Def., Washington, 1967-72, budget analyst, 1972-79, dir. tng. and edn., 1979-83, dep. asst. insp. gen., 1983-86, dep. comptr., 1989-94, dep. CFO, 1991-97, chmn. concessions com., 1989-97; sr. mgr. Grant Thornton LLP, Alexandra, Va., 1997—2006, dir., 2006—09; exec. dir. Am. Soc. Mil. Comptrollers, 2009—. Mem. steering com. Joint Fin. Mgmt. Improvement Program, 1990-93; mem. CFO's Coun., 1989-97, chmn. fin. sys. com., 1989-97; mem. Fed. Acctg. Stds. Adv. Bd., 1991-97; chmn. Cert. Def. Fin. Mgr. Commn., 2004-09. With U.S. Army, 1958-61. Recipient Def. medal for disting. civilian svc. with Bronze Palm, 1997, meritorious sr. exec. medal, 1985, 92. Mem.: AICPA, Md. Assn. CPAs, Inst. Internal Auditors, Assn. Govt. Accts. (nat. exec. com. 1993—94), Am. Soc. Mil. Comptrs., Kiwanis (club pres. 1981—82, 1986—87). Avocation: genealogy. Office: 415 N Alfred St Alexandria VA 22314 Office Phone: 703-549-0360 ext. 101.

TUCKER, BEVERLY SOWERS, library and information scientist; b. Trenton, NJ, Dec. 1, 1936; d. Eldon Jones and Verbeda Eleanor (Roberts) Sowers; m. Harvey Richard Tucker, Dec. 27, 1958 (div. Nov. 1983); children: Randall Richard, Brian Alan. BS in Chemistry with distinction, Purdue U., 1958; MS in Geology, No. Ill. U., 1985; MA in Library and Info. Sci., Rosary Coll., 1989. Asst. rsch. librarian CPC Internat., Argo, Ill., 1958-62; chem. patent searcher Chgo., 1962-66; info. specialist C. Berger & Co., Wheaton, Ill., 1986, Amoco Corp., Naperville, Ill., 1987-99; faculty Coll. Du Page, Glen Ellyn, Ill., 1989—; libr. cons. Baxter Healthcare, Round Lake, Ill., 1999—2003; libr. Seyfarth and Shaw, Chgo., 2005—. Mem. Spl. Libraries Assn., Ill. Fedn. Women's Club (treas. 5th dist. 1979-81, Outstanding Jr. Clubwoman award 1979-80), Garden Club Council Wheaton (pres. 1981-82), Wheaton Jr. Woman's Club (pres. 1977-78, Single Parent scholar 1984), Gardens Etc. Club (pres. 1978-79), Alpha Lambda Delta, Delta Rho Kappa, Theta Sigma Phi, Alpha Chi Omega (grantee 1985). Republican. Presbyterian. Avocations: bridge, needlecrafts, gourmet cooking. Home: 1507 Paula Ave Wheaton IL 60189

TUCKER, CORINNA JENKINS, social studies educator; PhD, Pa. State U., State Coll., 1998. Cert. life educator Nat. Coun. Family Rels., 2000. Assoc. prof. family studies U. NH., Durham, 2004—. Recipient Class 1940 Professorship award, U. NH., 2005—08. Office: Univ New Hampshire 215 Pettee Hall Family Studies Dept Durham NH 03824 Business E-Mail: cjtucker@cisunix.unh.edu.

TUCKER, DON EUGENE, retired lawyer; b. Rockbridge, Ohio, Feb. 3, 1928; s. Beryl Hollis and Ruth (Primmer) T.; m. Elizabeth Jane Parke, Aug. 2, 1950; children: Janet Elizabeth, Kerry Jane, Richard Parke. BA, Aurora Coll., 1951; LL.B., Yale, 1956. Bar: Ohio 1956. Since practiced in, Youngstown, Ohio; asso. Manchester, Bennett, Powers & Ullman, 1956-62, ptnr., 1962-73, of counsel, 1973-87; gen. counsel Comml. Intertech Corp., Youngstown, 1973-75, v.p., gen. counsel, 1975-83, also dir., sr. v.p., gen. counsel, 1983-87, sr. v.p., 1987-93; ret., 1993. Solicitor Village of Poland, Ohio, 1961-63; former chmn. bd., pres., trustee United Cerebral Palsy Assn., Youngstown and Mahoning County; trustee Mahoning County Tb and Health Assn.; former trustee, pres. Indsl. Info. Inst.; former pres., trustee Ea. Ohio Lung Assn.; trustee, former chmn. Cmty. Corp.; trustee, former pres. Butler Inst. Am. Art. With USMCR, 1946-48, 51-53. Mem. Ohio Bar Assn., Mahoning County Bar Assn. (pres. 1972, trustee 1970-73), Youngstown Area C. of C. (chmn. bd. dirs. 1979). Methodist. Home: 6005 Martins Point Rd Kitty Hawk NC 27949-3819

TUCKER, EDWIN WALLACE, law educator; b. NYC, Feb. 25, 1927; s. Benjamin and May Tucker; m. Gladys Lipschutz, Sept. 14, 1952; children: Sherwin M., Pamela A. BA, NYU, 1948; LLB, Harvard U., Cambridge, Mass., 1951; LLM, NY Law Sch., 1963, JSD, 1964; MA,

Trinity Coll., Hartford, Conn., 1967. Bar: NY 1955, US Dist. Ct. (ea. and so. dists.) NY 1958, US Ct. Appeals (2d cir.) 1958, US Supreme Ct. 1960. Pvt. practice, NYC, 1955-63; disting. alumni prof. and prof. emeritus bus. law U. Conn., Storrs, 1963—2002. Author: Adjudication of Social Issues, 1971, 2d edit., 1977, Legal Regulation of the Environment, 1972, Administrative Agencies, Regulation of Enterprise, and Individual Liberties, 1975, CPA Law Review, 1985; co-author: The Legal and Ethical Environment of Business, 1992; book rev. editor Am. Bus. Law Jour., 1964-65, adv. editor, 1974—99; co-editor Am. Bus. Jour., 1965-73; editor Jour. Legal Studies Edn., 1983-85, editor-in-chief, 1985-87, adv. editor, 1987—99; mem. editl. bd. Am. Jour. Small Bus., 1979-86, North Atlantic Regional Bus. Law Rev., 1984—2004. With USAF, 1951-55. Recipient medal of excellence, Am. Bus. Law Assn., 1979; named to, U. Conn. Sch. Bus. Hall of Fame, 2007. Mem. Acad. Legal Studies in Bus., North Atlantic Regional Bus. Law Assn. Home and Office: 11 Eastwood Rd Storrs Mansfield CT 06268-2401

TUCKER, GLENN GORHAM, retired educational administrator; b. Des Moines, June 6, 1928; s. Glenn Gorham and Lura Irene (Pettijohn) T.; m. Martha Jean Tucker, Aug. 1948 (div. 1959); children: David Ray, Bruce Neil; m. Beverly Ann Stoup Woodward, Apr. 26, 1968(dec. dec. 15, 2006); children: Elizabeth Jeanne, Robert Heartley. BA, U. No. Iowa, 1952; MEd, U. Fla., 1967, EdS, 1968, EdD, 1969. Sci. tchr. Freeport Bd. Edn., Ill., 1952-58, Sarasota County pub. schs., Sarasota, Fla., 1958-68; assoc. prof. sci. edn. Marshall U., Huntington, W.Va., 1969-73; sci. cons. Coastal Plains Coop. Edn. Svcs., Valdosta, Ga., 1973-79; prin. Suwanee County High Sch., Live Oak, Fla., 1980-83, Charlton County Comp. High, Folkston, Ga., 1983-85; dir. curriculum/instr. Brooks County Bd. Edn., Quitman, Ga., 1985-88 (ret.). Adj. prof. edn. Valdosta State U., Ga., 1985-93; sci./adminstrn./curriculum cons., 1985-93. Author: I'm Sorry I Missed You, 2005, Exile Island, 2005, University Past Time, 2005, I'll See You In Twenty Years, 2006. With USN, 1944-46. U. Fla. fellow, 1966-67, 67-68. Mem. Ga. Sci. Tchrs. Assn., So. Ga. Am. Radio Club (pres.), Phi Delta Kappa (emeritus, past pres.). Avocations: amateur radio, travel, competitive shooting, cabinet work. Home: 5018 Hammock Trl Lake Park GA 31636-3027 Personal E-mail: tuckergg@bellsouth.net.

TUCKER, H. RICHARD, oil industry executive; b. Streator, Ill., Oct. 2, 1936; s. H. L. and Dorothy A. Tucker; m. Cheryl L. Kirk, Jan. 14, 1984; children from previous marriage: Randall R., Brian A. BS in Chem. Engring., Purdue U., 1958; MBA, Northwestern U., 1962. Project engr. crude oil supply Amoco Corp., Chgo., 1958-64, specialist product supply, 1965-66, coord. fgn. crude oil supply, 1967-68; coord. orgn. planning Amoco Internat. Corp., Chgo., 1969-70, Amoco Corp., Chgo., 1970-72, mgr. adminstrv. svcs., 1972-84, mgr. real estate svcs., 1984-86, coord. spl. studies, 1986-89, dir. quality mgmt., 1989-92; mgr. cost mgmt., 1992-94. V.p. Amoco Realty Co., 1984-91, Amoco Devel. Co., 1984-91. Mem. adv. com. Sch. Bd. Wheaton, Ill., 1966; mem. Citizen's Nominating Com., Wheaton, 1972; leader Boy Scouts Am., Wheaton, 1979-82; dir. Oak Brook Colony Condominium Assn., 1992-94. Mem. Westhaven Home Owners Assn. (pres. 1965-67), Phi Eta Sigma, Omega Chi Epsilon, Beta Gamma Sigma, Tau Beta Pi. Avocations: tennis, bridge, hiking.

TUCKER, HELEN WELCH, writer; b. Raleigh, NC, Nov. 1, 1926; d. William Blair and Helen (Welch) Tucker; m. William T. Beckwith, Jan. 9, 1971. BA, Wake Forest Coll., 1946; postgrad., Columbia U., NYC, 1957—58. Reporter Burlington Times-News, NC, 1946—47, Times-News, Twin Falls, Idaho, 1948—49, Idaho Statesman, Boise, 1950—51; copy writer Sta. KDYL, Salt Lake City, 1952—53; copy supr. Sta. WPTF, Raleigh, NC, 1953—55; reporter Raleigh Times, NC, 1955—57; editl. asst. Columbia U. Press, NYC, 1959—60; dir. publicity and publs. N.C. Mus. Art, Raleigh, NC, 1967—70. Author: The Sound of Summer Voices, 1969, The Guilt of August Fielding, 1971, No Need of Glory, 1972, The Virgin of Lontano, 1973, A Strange and Ill-Starred Marriage, 1978, A Reason for Rivalry, 1979, A Mistress to the Regent, 1980, An Infamous Attachment, 1980, The Halverton Scandal, 1980, A Wedding Day Deception, 1981, The Double Dealers, 1982, Season of Dishonor, 1982, Ardent Vows, 1983, Bound by Honor, 1984, The Lady's Fancy, 1991, Bold Impostor, 1991; contbr. (to nat. mags. short stories). Recipient Disting. Alumni Award in Journalism, Wake Forest U., 1971; named Artist of Yr., Arts Coun. Franklin Co., NC, 1992. Anglican. Home: 2930 Hostetler St Raleigh NC 27609-7702

TUCKER, HOWARD MCKELDIN, investment banker, consultant; b. Washington, Apr. 1, 1930; s. Howard Newell and Bessie Draper (McKeldin) T.; m. Julia Spencer Merrell, Feb. 1, 1952 (div. 1975); children: Deborah, Mark, Alexander, H. David; m. Megan Evans, Aug. 17, 1979. BA, U. Va., 1954; postgrad., NYU, 1956; MBA, Stern Sch. CFA. With J.P. Morgan & Co., 1954—61, Mackall & Coe, Washington, 1962—69, Legg Mason & Co., Washington, 1969—79, Govt. Rsch. Corp./Nat. Jour., 1979—82, Potomac Asset Mgmt., 1982—91; ptnr., mng. dir. Capital Insights Group, Washington, 1992—2001; with Skillsmith, LLC, 2002—05. Mem. task force balance-of-payments U.S.Treasury Dept., 1967-72; cons. County Natwest (Washinton Analysis Corp.), 1985-90; bd. dirs. Monarch Enterprises, Inc., Uniflight, Inc., Sci. Mgmt. Assocs., Inc., Jeffrey Bigelow Assocs. USA Nica Wind Power. Author: Literature in Medicine, In Memoriam, Michael Halberstam, M.D., 1984; book reviewer Washington Post; contbr. articles to profl. jours. Dir. Washington Area Coun. Chs., 1962-65; vestryman Christ Episcopal Ch., Georgetown, 1962-65; mem. chpt. Washington Nat. Cathedral, 1966-72; del. Va. Republican Conv., 1968; trustee Nat. Cathedral Sch. for Girls, 1972-78; chmn. Missionary Devel. Fund Episcopal Diocese D.C., 1974; co-dir. Andover-Exeter Washington Intern Program, 1976-86; co-organizer U.S.-German Parliamentary Exchange, 1980-82; observer OECD, 1980-82; spl. overseas visitor Australian Govt., 1982; patron West Europe program Woodrow Wilson Ctr., 1985-86; bd. dirs. Am. Hort. Soc., 1998-2008. With USNR, 1950—56. Mem.: Fin. Analysts Fedn., Washington Soc. Investment Analysts, Nat. Economists Club, Dumplings (Jamestown, RI), Alexandria Seaport Found., Cogswell Soc., Hist. Alexandria Found., Old Dominion Boat Club, Nat. Press Club, Naval and Mil. Club London, Georgetown Visitation Tennis Club, Saints and Sinners Club, Beta Theta Pi. Home: 4 Potomac Ct Alexandria VA 22314-3821 Personal E-mail: hmcktucker@yahoo.com.

TUCKER, J. WALTER, JR., manufacturing executive; Vice chmn. Keystone Consolidated Industries, Inc., Dallas, chmn., 1987—. Office: 3 Lincoln Ctr 5430 LBJ Fwy Ste 1740 Dallas TX 75240-2697 Fax: 972-458-8108.

TUCKER, JAMES L., JR., artist, educator; b. New Eagle, Pa., Mar. 28, 1944; s. James Louis Tucker Sr. and Gueraldine Esther (Johnson) Sawyer. MA, Temple U., 1967, BFA, 1966; postgrad., George Washington U., 1977—79, postgrad., 1982—86. Art instr. continuing edn. Germantown H.S., Phila., 1968—69; chmn. art dept. Woodrow Wilson H.S., Washington, 1969—70; art specialist Gallaudet Coll., Washington, 1970—77; from specialist in the arts to chief arts and humanities program Md. State Dept. Edn., Balt., 1979—2003, coord. fine arts, 2003—. Art instr. Pastorius Elem. Sch., Phila., 1966—69, Emlen Elem. Sch., Phila., 1966—69; steering com. Art Edn. in Md. Schs. Alliance, 1992—; adj. instr. Md. Inst. Coll. Art, George Washington U.; team leader Brazilian curriculum project Ptnrs. of the Americas, 1984—86; arts assessment standing com. Nat. Assessment Ednl. Progress, 1996—97; cons., presenter in field. Editor: Better Fine Arts Edn., 4 vols., 2004. Co-dir. Kenya-Tanzania project Fulbright-Hays Group Projects Abroad, 1989, co-dir. Ghana-Senegal project, 1993, co-dir.Namibia project, 1995; edn. com. Balt. Symphony Orch., 1995—2004; adv. Ctr. for VSA Arts Md., Balt., 1980—2002, bd. dirs., 2002—; Md. Alliance for Arts Edn., Balt., 1980—2002, exec. sec.-treas., 1980—86; bd. dirs. Md. Artist Equity Found., Balt., 1992—2004, v.p., 2002—04. Recipient State of Md. Performance award, Md. State Employee's Conf., 1986, Outstanding Svc. award, Md. Coun. for Dance, 2002, Cert. Achievement, Md. State Bd. Edn., 2003, Nina Wood Collier Arts Champion award, Young Audiences Md.; named Md. State Adminstr. of Yr., State Employees Assn., 1986. Fellow: Nat. Art Edn. Assn. (review panel Art Edn. 1995—97, chmn. nat. conv. Miami Beach 2002, convention task force 2002, J. Eugene Grigsby award 1984, Md. Art Educator award 1987, Ea. Supervision/adminstrn. Art Educator of Yr. 1994, Eastern Region Art Educator of Yr. 1995, Nat. Supervision/adminstrn. Art Educator of Yr. 1997, Disting. Svc. award 2003); mem.: Music Educators Nat. Conf., Nat. Assn. State Dirs. Art Edn. (pres.), Nat. Coun. State Arts Edn. Cons. (founding mem., pres. 1995—97), Md. Music Educators Assn. (exec. bd. dirs., Corwin Taylor award 1997, Hall of Fame 2008), Md. Art Edn. Assn. (dept. edn. rep. 1980—82, dir. supervision/adminstrn. divsn. 1982—86, v.p. programs 1986—88, pres.-elect 1990—92, pres. 1992—94, awards coord. 1994—96, parliamentarian 1996—2000, historian 2000—, officer). Avocations: painting, reading, cooking, travel. Office: Md State Dept Edn 200 W Balt St Baltimore MD 21201-2595 Office Phone: 410-767-0352. Business E-Mail: jtucker@msde.state.md.us.

TUCKER, JONATHAN BRIN, political scientist; b. Boston, Aug. 2, 1954; s. Leonard Walter and Deborah Alice (Brin) T.; m. Karen Fern Fifer, Aug. 27, 1980 (div.). BS in Biology, Yale U., New Haven, Conn., 1975; MA in Internat. Rels., U. Pa., Phila., 1982; PhD in Polit. Sci., MIT, Cambridge, 1990. Mem. bd. editors Scientific Am. mag., NYC, 1976-79; freelance sci. writer Phila., 1979-83; sr. editor High Tech. mag., Boston, 1983-85; arms control fellow U.S. Dept. of State, Washington, 1989-90; def. policy analyst U.S. Congress Office of Tech. Assessment, Washington, 1990-93; fgn. affairs splst. U.S. Arms Control and Disarmament Agy., Washington, 1993-95; sr. policy analyst Presdl. Adv. Com. on Gulf War Vets. Ilnesses, Washington, 1995; sr. fellow James Martin Ctr. Nonproliferation Studies Monterey Inst. Internat. Studies, Calif., 1996—. Vis. fellow Hoover Instn. Stanford (Calif.) U., 1999-2000, U.S. Inst. Peace, Washington, 2002-03, Am. Acad. in Berlin, 2006. Author: Ellie: A Child's Fight Against Leukemia, 1982; editor: Toxic Terror: Assessing Terrorist Use of Chemical and Biological Weapons, 2000, Scourge: The Once and Future Threat of Smallpox, 2001, War of Nerves: Chemical Warfare from World War I to Al-Qaeda, 2006; govt. reports; contbr. articles to profl. jours. Mem. Arms Control Assn. (life, bd. dirs.), Coun. Fgn. Rels. Democrat. Avocations: ballroom dancing, hiking. Office: James Martin Ctr Nonproliferation Studies/MIIS Ste 450 1400 K St NW Washington DC 20005 Office Phone: 202-842-3100. Business E-Mail: jtucker@miis.edu.

TUCKER, KATHERINE LOUISE, elementary school educator; b. Milw., Wis., Oct. 14, 1947; d. William Karl and Margaret Anna Taube; m. Fred Tucker, Aug. 16, 1969 (dec.); 1 child, William Mark. BS, Concordia U., Chgo., 1969, MA, 1983. Tchr. St. Paul's Luth. Sch., Rolling Meadows, Ill., 1969—71, Bethlehem Luth. Sch., Milw., 1970—72; assoc. prof. Concordia U., Mequon, Wis., 1976—89; tchr. Emmaus Luth. Sch., Milw., 1972—81, Walther Meml. Sch., Milw., 1981—89, Redeemer Luth. Sch., Kokomo, Ind., 1989—. Ch. group leader; dir. Mission Possible Luth. Ch. Our Redeemer, Kokomo, 2000—06. Mem.: Alpha Delta Kappa. Lutheran. Avocation: handbell ringing. Home: 5406 Buckskin Dr Kokomo IN 46902

TUCKER, KIMBERLY JOAN, music educator, director; b. Racine, Wis., May 4, 1977; d. Joan Marie and Robert Edward Griswold (Stepfather), Joseph Zoltan and Lilac Kriston (Stepmother); m. Christopher Michael Tucker, Aug. 14, 2004. B in Music Edn., U. North Tex., Denton, 2000; MusM in Instrumental Performance, Tex. A&M U., Commerce, 2007. Asst. band dir. DeSoto West Jr. H.S. and Amber Ter. Intermediate Sch., Tex., 2000—02, head band dir., 2002—05; band tchr. Rockwall ISD, 2005; band dir. Bussey Mid. Sch., Garland, Tex. Sch. rep. DeSoto Dist. Advocacy Com., 2000—02. Recipient Sweepstakes award, U. Interscholastic League Region 20, 2002—04, Beach Within Reach Contest, 2002—04, Sandy Lake Music Festival, 2002—04. Fellow: Alpha Lambda Delta (life); mem.: World Assn. Symphonic Bands and Ensembles, Tex. Flute Soc., Nat. Flute Assn. (corr.), Internat. Clarinet Assn. (corr.), Music Educators Nat. Conf. (corr.), Tex. Bandmasters Assn. (corr.), Tex. Music Educators Assn. (corr.), Sigma Alpha Iota (life; rec. sec. 1998—2000, Sword of Honor 1999). Roman Catholic. Avocations: practicing instruments, singing, sketching. Home: 684 Danielle Ct Rockwall TX 75087 Office: Bussey Mid Sch 1204 Travis St Garland TX 75040 Business E-Mail: ktucker@lonestarwindorchestra.com, kjtucker@garlandisd.net.

TUCKER, LAUREY DAN, lawyer; s. Floyd A. and Harriet Kathleen (Graves) T.; m. Katherine Washburn, June 21, 1958; children: Laurie Tucker Diaz, Dana Tucker Kleine. BSChemE, U. Okla., Norman, 1959, LLB, 1962. Bar: Okla. 1962, Tex. 1972. Patent atty. Phillps Petroleum Co., Bartlesville, Okla., 1964—67, Monsanto Co., St. Louis, 1967—70, patent mgr. Texas City, Tex., 1970—74; ptnr. Hubbard, Tucker & Harris, Dallas, 1974—94, Harris, Tucker & Hardin, Dallas, 1994—97, Locke Purnell Rain Harrell, Dallas, 1997—98, Locke Liddell & Sapp LLP, Dallas, 1999—2006. Past pres. Dallas-Ft. Worth Patent Assn. Capt. USAR, 1959—69, 1st lt. US Army, 1962—64. Mem.: State Bar Tex. (past officer Intellectual Property Law Section), Okla. Bar Assn. Republican. Episcopalian. Avocations: fishing, hunting, travel. Personal E-mail: tucker_dan@sbcglobal.net.

TUCKER, LAURIE A., marketing executive; b. 1957; m. John Tucker; 2 children. BBA, U. Memphis, 1978, MBA, 1983. Fin. analyst FedEx Corp., 1978—83, mgr. pricing, 1983—89, mng. dir. customer automation, 1989, sr. v.p. logistics, electronic commerce and catalog, sr. v.p. corp. mktg., 2000—. Bd. dirs. Iron Mountain, Inc., Boston. FedEx co-chair March of Dimes; mem. United Way Alexis de Tocqueville Soc., 1998—; bd. visitors U. Memphis. Recipient inaugural Diversity Champion award, FedEx Services, Woman of Achievement award, The Women's Project, 2008, Disting. Alumni award, U. Memphis, 2001; named Outstanding Alumna, Fogelman Coll. Bus. and Econ.; named one of Best Marketers, BtoB Mag., 2008. Office: FedEx Corp 942 South South Shady Grove Rd Memphis TN 38120*

TUCKER, LOUIS LEONARD, retired historical society administrator; b. Rockville, Conn., Dec. 6, 1927; s. Joseph and Dora (Conn) T.; m. Beverley Jones, Mar. 27, 1953; children: Mark T., Lance K.; m. Carolyn woollen, Sept. 14, 1996. BA, U. Wash., 1952, MA, 1954, PhD, 1957. Instr. history U. Calif., Davis, 1958; fellow Inst. Early Am. History and Culture, Williamsburg, Va., 1958-60; instr. history Coll. William and Mary, 1958-60; dir. Cin. Hist. Soc., 1960-66; asst. commr., state historian of NY, N.Y State Edn. Dept., 1966-76; also dir. N.Y. State Bicentennial Commn., 1969-76; dir. Mass. Hist. Soc., Boston, 1977-97. Author: Puritan Protagonist, 1962, Cincinnati During Civil War, 1962, Cincinnati's Citizen Crusaders, 1967, Our Travels, 1968, Cincinnati: Students Guide to Local History, 1969, James Allen, Jr.: From Elkins to Washington, 1969, Connecticut's Seminary of Sedition, Yale College, 1974, Clio's Consort: Jeremy Belknap and the Founding of the Massachusetts Historical Society, 1990, The Massachusetts Historical Society: A Bicentennial History, 1791-1971, 1996, Worthington Chauncey Ford: Scholar and Adventurer, 2001. Dir. Shaker Mus., 1967-74; Am. Heritage Co., 1973-75, Ft. Ticonderoga Assn., 1990-97. Served with AUS, 1946-47. Winston Churchill fellow, 1969 Mem. Am. Assn. State and Local History (pres. 1972-74) Home: 328 Harvard St Cambridge MA 02139-2002

TUCKER, MARCUS OTHELLO, judge; b. Santa Monica, Calif., Nov. 12, 1934; s. Marcus Othello Sr. and Essie Louvonia (McLendon) T.; m. Indira Hale, May 29, 1965; 1 child, Angelique. BA, U. So. Calif., 1956; JD, Howard U., 1960; MA in Criminal Justice, Chapman U., 1997; BS in Liberal Arts, Regents Coll., SUNY, 1999. Bar: Calif. 1962, U.S. Dist. Ct. (cen. dist.) Calif. 1962, U.S. Ct. Appeals (9th cir.) 1965, U.S. Ct. Internat. Trade 1970, U.S. Supreme Ct. 1971. Pvt. practice, Santa Monica, 1962-63, 67-74; dep. atty. City of Santa Monica, 1963-65; asst. atty. U.S. Dist. Ct. (Cen. Dist.) Calif., 1965-67; commr. L.A. Superior Ct., 1974-76; judge mcpl. ct. Long Beach (Calif.) Jud. Dist., 1976-85; judge superior ct. LA Jud. Dist., 1985—; supervising judge L.A. County Dependency Ct. LA Superior Ct., 1991-92; presiding judge Juvenile divsn. LA County Juvenile Ct., 1993-94. Asst. prof. law Pacific U., Long Beach, 1984, 86; justice pro tem Calif. State Ct. Appeals (2nd cir.), 1981; mem. exec. com. Superior Ct. of L.A. County, 1995-96. Mem. editl. staff Howard U. Law Sch. Jour., 1959-60; featured on www.thehistorymakers.com. Pres. Community Rehab. Industries Found., Long Beach, 1983-86, Legal Aid Found., L.A., 1976-77; bd. dirs. Long Beach coun. Boy Scouts Am., 1978-92. With U.S. Army, 1960-66. Named Judge of Yr. Juvenile Cts. Bar Assn., 1986, Disting. Jurist Long Beach Trial Trauma Coun., 1987, Honoree in Law Handy Cmty. Ctr., L.A., 1987, Bernard S. Jefferson Jurist of Yr. John M. Langston Bar Assn. Black Lawyers, 1990, Judge of Yr. Long Beach Bar Assn., 1993, Judge of Yr., First Ann. Adoption Cong., 1997, Jurist of Yr., Juvenile Cts. Bar Assn., 1997, Daniel O'Connell award Irish-Am. Bar Assn., 1999, award for Law-Related Edn. Constl. Rights Found./L.A. County Bar Assn., 1992, commendation L.A. County Bd. Suprs., 1994, History Maker in Law award, 2002, Excellence in Cmty. Svc. award Aquarium of Pacific, 2004, Lifetime Achievement award (with Indira Hale Tucker) NAACP, Long Beach Br., 2004; named to Nat. Bar Assn. Hall of Fame, 2002; honored 30 yrs. svc. LA Superior Ct. Resolution, 2004, 30 yrs. jud. svc. Congl. Resolution, 2004. Fellow Internat. Acad. Trial Judges; mem. ABA, Calif. Judges Assn. (chmn. juvenile law com. 1986-87, Svc. award 2001), Langston Bar Assn. (pres. bd. dirs. 1972-73, named to hall of fame 2001), Calif. Assn. Black Lawyers, Santa Monica Bay Dist. Bar Assn. (treas. 1969-71), Am. Inns of Ct., Selden Soc. Avocations: comparative law, travel. Office: 415 W Ocean Blvd Dept 245 Long Beach CA 90802-4512

TUCKER, MARNA S., lawyer; b. Phila., Mar. 5, 1941; BS, U. Tex., 1962; LLB, Georgetown U. Law Ctr., 1965; JD (hon.), U. DC Sch. Law, 1995. Bar: D.C. 1966, Calif. 1969, U.S. Supreme Ct. 1970. Deputy dir. legal svcs. program western region Office Of Econ. Opportunity, 1967-69; spl. asst. to Rep. Allard K. Lowenstein NY, 1969-70; dir. ABA Pro Bono Project, 1971—73; ptnr. to sr. ptnr., family law Feldesman, Tucker, Leifer, Fidell and Bank (now Feldesman Tucker Leifer Fidell LLP), Washington, 1972—. Adj. prof. of law Georgetown U. Law Ctr., 1972; lectr. of law Cath. U., Columbus Sch. Law, 1972-74. Apptd. Bd. Prof. Responsibility, D.C. Ct. Appeals, 1977-83; mem. U.S. Cir. Ct. Com. on Admissions and Grievances, 1979-89, U.S. Jud. Nominating Com. for D.C., 1977-80; bd. regents Georgetown U., 1986-89; bd. visitors, Georgetown Law Ctr., 1994-2000; trustee Ctr. for Law and Social Policy, 1977-99, Pub. Defender Svc. D.C., 1986-92; founding bd. mem., sec./treas., bd. trustee, Nat. Women's Law Ctr., 1981-2005; mem. exec. com. Washington Lawyers Com. for Civil Rights Under Law, 1973—; chair Mayor's Commn. on Violence Against Women, 1996-2002; commr., U.S. Comm. of Child and Family Welfare, 1994. Named Women Lawyer of Yr. Women's Bar Assn. of D.C., 1985; recipient Annual Alumni Achievement award Georgetown Alumni Club, 1986, Alumni Achievement award, Georgetown Law Ctr., 1998, Exceptional Achievement award NAACP Legal Def. and Ednl. Fund, Inc.NOW Intrepid Women award 2008, Washington Com., 1985; named one of 75 Best Lawyers in Washington, Washingtonian Mag., 2002, (several times) Top Divorce Lawyer. Fellow Am. Bar Found. (chair, 1995), Am. Acad. Matrimonial Lawyers, Am. Coll. Trial Lawyers; mem. ABA (house of del. bar del., 1974-80, 1988-2008, state del. 2008-, chmn. commn. on pub. understanding about law 1979-82, chmn. sect. individual rights and responsibilities 1982-83, chmn. standing com. profl. discipline 1987-90, co-chmn. commn. on domestic violence, 1995-97, standing com. fed. judiciary 2007-07, Margaret Brent Women Lawyers of Achievement award, Robert Drinan Disting. Svc. award), ACLU Nat. Capital Area (bd. dirs. 1973-76), Nat. Legal Aid and Defender Assn. (v.p. 1973-77, Nat. Legal Aid and Defender Assn. Annual award, 1993), D.C. Bar (pres. 1984-85, legal ethics com. 1974-76, del. ABA ho. of dels. 1974-91), Nat. Conf. Bar Pres. (pres.-elect, pres. 1991), Women's Forum Washington; chair Fellows Am. Bar Found., 1995-96; bd. mem. Fed. Jud. Ctr. Found. Bd., 1997-, chair, 2000-08. Office: Feldesman Tucker Leifer Fidell LLP 2001 L St NW 2d Fl Washington DC 20036 Office Phone: 202-466-8960. Office Fax: 202-293-8103. Business E-Mail: mtucker@feldesmantucker.com.

TUCKER, MELVIN JAY, education educator, researcher; s. Earle Homer and Florence Gertrude Tucker; m. N. Evelyn Rapalus, June 27, 1953; children: Ann Evelyn Jobson, Ellen Marie Tucker-Cohen, Michael Jay. BA, U. Mass., Amherst, Mass., 1953, MA, 1954; PhD, Northwestern U., Evanston, Il., 1962. Instr. Colby Coll., Waterville, Maine, 1959—60, MIT, Cambridge, Mass., 1960—63; assoc. prof. U. Buffalo, Buffalo, 1963—. Dir. grad. studies, history Univ. Buffalo, 1979—85; fellow Medieval Ctr., SUNY, Binghampton, 1970—77. Author: The Life of Thoms Howard, Earl of Surrey and Second Duke of Norfolk, 1443-1524; co-author: Centering: A Guide to Inner Growth, 2nd ed.; contbr. chapters to books; contbg. editor: History of Childhood Quarterly, 1973—76, Journal of Psycho History, 1976—84. 1st lt. USAF, 1954—56, Japan. Recipient Fulbright Award, Fulbright Commn., 1958-1959, Cert. of Merit, Buffalo & Erie County Hist. Soc., 1974, Cert. of Recognition, Career Planning, U. Buffalo, 2002. Mem.: Assn. for the Bibliography of History (coun. mem. 1982—92), Am. Hist. Assn., North Am. Conf. of Brit. Studies. Roman Catholic. Avocations: walking, movies. Office: History Dept Univ Buffalo 580 Pk Hall Buffalo NY 14260 Business E-Mail: mjtucker@acsu.buffalo.edu.

TUCKER, ROBERT C., JR., materials scientist, consultant; b. Mar. 1, 1935; BS, ND State U., Fargo, 1957; MS, Iowa State U., Ames, 1965, PhD, 1967. Corp. fellow and dir. bus. devel. & strategic R & D Praxair Surface Techs. Inc., Indpls., 1967—98; pres. Tucker Group, LLC,

Wesley Chapel, Fla., 1998—. Cons. Tucker Group, LLC, Wesley Chapel, Fla., 1998—. Contbr. scientific papers. Fellow: ASM Internat. (pres. 2003—04, Thermal Spray Hall of Fame); mem.: Mining & Metall. Soc., Am. Ceramic Soc., ASM Thermal Spray Soc. (pres. 2003—04), Sigma Xi. Achievements include 23 US patents & many foreign derivatives. Office: Tucker Group LLC 5154 Pine Lake Rd Wesley Chapel FL 33543 Business E-Mail: rctucker@aol.com.

TUCKER, ROBERT DAVID, geologist; b. Little Falls, NY, July 18, 1952; s. Stanley and Edith Tucker; m. Julie Diane Morris, June 13, 1992. BS, SUNY, Brockport, 1974; MS, U. Mass., Amherst, 1977; PhD, Yale U., New Haven, 1985. Rsch. scientist Royal Ont. Mus., Toronto, Canada, 1985—92; prof., geology Wash. U., St. Louis, 1992—2007; rsch. scientist US Geol. Survey, Reston, Va., 2007—. Office: US Geol Survey 12201 Sunrise Valley Dr Reston VA 20192

TUCKER, ROBERT DENNARD, health care products executive; b. Tifton, Ga., July 18, 1933; s. Robert Buck and Ethel Margaret (Dennard) T.; m. Peggy Angelyn Smith, June 23, 1957; children: Robert Barron, Jennifer Lee. BBA, Ga. State U., 1958. With sales and sales mgmt. Johnson & Johnson Inc., New Brunswick, NJ, 1958-68; v.p., gen. mgr. ASR Med. Industries, NYC, 1968-72, Howmedica Suture div. Pfizer Inc., NYC, 1972-75; exec. v.p., chief operating officer R. P. Scherer Corp., Detroit, 1976-79; pres., chief operating officer Scherer Sci. Inc., Atlanta, 1980-95, also bd. dirs; chmn., chief exec. officer Scherer Health Care Inc., Atlanta, 1980-95, also bd. dirs. Bd. dirs., pres., CEO Splty. Surgictrs., Inc., Atlanta, 1997—2002; bd. dirs., chmn., CEO Maximum Benefits Co., Atlanta; chmn., CEO Throwleigh Techs., LLC, 1995—; bd. dirs., mem. exec. com. Horizon Med. Products, 2002—05; bd. dirs., chmn compensation com. Averion Internat. Corp., 2006—. Pub: Tuckers of Devon, 1983; author, pub.: Descendants of William Tucker of Throwleigh, Devon. Chmn. bd. Health Industries Mfrs. Assn. polit. action com., Washington, 1983-85; trustee, past pres. Ga. Horse Found., Atlanta; trustee Brenau Coll., Gainesville, Ga., 1985—. Served with Frogmen UDT3 USN, 1951-54, Korea. Decorated Knight of Malta, Imperial Russian Order of St. John; recipient Disting. Service award Brenau Coll., 1987. Mem. Nat. Assn. Mfrs., Health Industries Mfrs. Assn. (bd. dirs. 1979-86, disting. service recognition 1981, 86), Pharm. Mfrs. Assn., Thoroughbred Owners and Breeders Assn. Ky. and Ga. (Man of Yr. 1984). Clubs: Cherokee (Atlanta); Big Canoe (Ga.). Republican. Methodist. Avocations: scuba diving, tennis, genealogy. Home: 548 Persons St Monticello GA 31064 Office: Throwleigh Techs PO Box 220 Ball Ground GA 30107

TUCKER, ROY W., lawyer; b. Buffalo, Aug. 31, 1952; BA in Polit. Sci. & English, with dist. in Polit. Sci., magna cum laude, Kenyon Coll., 1974; JD, SUNY Buffalo, 1979. Bar: NY 1980, Oreg. 1985. Law clk. to Hon. Reid S. Moule Appellate Divsn., NY State Supreme Ct., 1979—80; with Davis Polk & Wardwell, NY, 1980—84; ptnr., mem. exec. com. Perkins Coie LLP, Portland, Oreg. Assoc. editor Buffalo Law Rev., 1977—78, sr. editor, 1978—79. Mem.: Phi Beta Kappa. Office: Perkins Coie LLP 1120 NW Couch St Floor 10 Portland OR 97209-4128 Office Phone: 503-727-2044. Office Fax: 503-727-2222. Business E-Mail: rtucker@perkinscoie.com.

TUCKER, SHIRLEY LOIS COTTER, botanist, educator; b. St. Paul, Apr. 4, 1927; d. Ralph U. and Myra C. (Knutson) Cotter; m. Kenneth W. Tucker, Aug. 22, 1953. BA, U. Minn., 1949, MS, 1951; PhD, U. Calif., Davis, 1956. Asst. prof. botany La. State U., Baton Rouge, 1967-71, assoc. prof., 1971-76, prof., 1976-82, Boyd prof., 1982-95, prof. emerita, 1995—. Adj. prof. dept. biology U. Calif., Santa Barbara, 1995—. Co-editor: Aspects of Floral Development, 1988, Advances in Legume Systematics, Vol. 6, 1994; contbr. numerous articles on plant devel. to profl. jours. Recipient, Outstanding Alumni Achievement award U. Minn., 1999; fellow Linnean Soc., London, 1975—, Fulbright fellow Eng., 1952-53; named to Hall of Distinction La. State U., Baton Rouge, 2006. Mem. Bot. Soc. Am. (v.p. 1979, program chmn. 1975-78, pres.-elect 1986-87, pres. 1987-88, Merit award 1989, Centennial award 2006), Am. Bryological and Lichenological Soc., Brit. Lichenological Soc., Am. Inst. Biol. Scis., Am. Soc. Plant Taxonomists (pres.-elect 1994-95, pres. 1995-96), Phi Beta Kappa, Sigma Xi. Home: 3987 Primavera Rd Santa Barbara CA 93110-1467 Office: U Calif Dept Biology EEMB Santa Barbara CA 93106 Home Phone: 805-898-0908. Business E-Mail: tucker@lifesci.ucsb.edu.

TUCKER, STEFAN FRANKLIN, lawyer; b. Detroit, Dec. 31, 1938; Assoc. in Bus., Flint Jr. Community Coll., 1958; BBA, U. Mich., 1960, JD, 1963. Bar: US Dist. Ct. DC 1964, US Ct. Appeals (DC cir.) 1964, US Ct. Claims 1964, US Tax Ct. 1964. Clk. to judge US Tax Ct., Washington, 1963-64; assoc. Arent, Fox, Kintner, Plotkin & Kahn, Washington, 1964-69, ptnr., 1970-74, Tucker, Flyer & Lewis, Washington, 1975—99, Venable LLP, Washington, 2000—. Profl. lectr. law George Washington U. Nat. Law Ctr., 1970—1990; adj. prof. law Georgetown U. Law Ctr., 1990—; adj. profl. lectr. law U. Miami Law Ctr., 1975-78; mem. adv. com. Ann. Inst. Estate Planning, U. Miami, 1978-91; trustee Mass. Sch. Law, Andover, 1989—, chmn. bd. trustees, 1989-95; mem. visitors com. U. Mich. Law Sch., 1989-2004. Author: Tax Planning for Real Estate Transactions, 1989, semi-ann. supplements; mem. editl. bd. Taxation for Lawyers, 1972-2000; mem. adv. bd. Bur. Nat. Affairs Housing and Devel. Reporter, 1973-76, Mertens on Federal Income Taxation, 1985-2000, The Tax Times, 1986-87; mem. editl. adv. bd. Real Estate Taxation, 1975—, Practical Real Estate Lawyer, 1984—2001. Mem. nat. com. U. Mich. Law Sch. Fund, 1972-78. Named Top Washington Lawyer in Tax Law, Washington Bus. Jour., 2004; named a Leading Lawyer in Real Estate Law, Legal Times, 2003; named one of Top 100 Attys., Worth mag., 2005—06, Leading Real Estate Lawyers in US, Chambers USA: Am. Leading Lawyers for Bus., 2006; named to Best Lawyers in Am., 1987—2007. Mem. ABA (tax sect., chmn. real estate tax problems com. 1977-79, chmn. continuing legal edn. com. 1984-86, coun. mem. 1987-91, vice chmn. com. ops. 1991-93, chair-elect 1997, chair 1998-1999), FBA, D.C. Bar Assn. (taxation divsn., mem. steering com. 1980-82), Nat. Trust Hist. Preservation (mem. com. on legal svcs. 1978-85), Am. Law Inst., Am. Coll. Real Estate Lawyers, 1981-, Am. Coll. Tax Coun., 1995-, Am. Tax Policy Inst. (bd. dirs. 2000-04). Office: Venable LLP 575 7th St NW Washington DC 20004 *I believe that each person has an obligation to share with others, whether through teaching, lecturing or writing, the knowledge and experience gained through his life's work. Such sharing provides a greater reward than monetary gain can ever provide.*

TUCKER, SUSAN, biomathematics and computational biology professor; BA in Math., Smith Coll., Northampton, Mass., 1974; PhD in Math., U. Mich., Ann Arbor, 1980. Prof. bioinformatics and computational biology U. Tex. MD Anderson Cancer Ctr., Houston, 1980—. Contbr. 200 articles to profl. jours. Office: Univ Tex MD Anderson Cancer Ctr PO Box 301402 Houston TX 77230-1402 Business E-Mail: sltucker@mdanderson.org.

TUCKER, THOMAS DEANE, humanities educator; b. Milton, Fla., Sept. 25, 1962; s. Deane Thomas and Dolores Tucker; m. Rana Abigail Smith, July 3, 2004; 1 child, Yvonne. PhD in Humanities, Fla. State U., Tallahassee, 1996. Prof., humanities Chadron State Coll., Nebr., 1998—. Business E-Mail: ttucker@csc.edu.

TUCKER, THOMAS JAMES, retired investment company executive; b. Atlanta, Sept. 5, 1929; s. Thomas Tudor and Carol (Govan) T.; m. Margaret Guerard. BA, U. of the South, 1952. With CIT Corp, NYC, 1957—72; pres., CEO AmSouth Fin. Corp., Birmingham, Ala., 1972—82, chmn. bd., 1982, also dir., 1972—93; exec. v.p. AmSouth Bank N.A., Birmingham, 1982—93, chief credit officer, 1992; prin. Tucker Investments, Birmingham, 1993—2003; ret., 2003. Exec. v.p. AmSouth Bancorp, Birmingham, 1982-93; bd. dirs. Alabanc Properties Corp., Birmingham, chmn., 1991-93; bd. dirs. Birmingham Broadway Series Inc., treas., 1996-97, pres., 1997-99, chmn., 1999-2001; co-founder Garland-Govan Scholarship Fund, Sewanee-U. of the South. Photographer gen. interest mags., 1970—; contbr. articles on credit and leasing to trade jours. Bd. dirs. Birmingham Cmty. Devel. Corp.; chmn. bd., 1990-93. 1st lt. USAF, 1952-56. Mem.: Vulcan Trail Assn., Birmingham Art Mus. Assn., Birmingham Bot. Soc., Friends of Emmt O'Neal Libr., Birmingham Canoe Club (bd. dirs. 1990-96), Photography Guild, Cahaba River Soc. (adv. bd. 1991-92, bd. dirs. 1993-98, v.p. orgnl. devel. 1995-98), Ala. Growth Strategies Task Force, Regional Open Space and Trails Alliance, Manigault Soc., Sewanee Devel. Coun., Order of Purple/Sewanee-U. of the South, Never Failing Succession of Benefactors/Sewanee-U. of the South, Carolynne Scott Writers Group (2d pl. 2006, 3rd pl. 2007, Hackney Short Fiction awards), The Club, Jefferson Club, Silhouettes Club. Episcopalian. Avocations: photography, high altitude hiking, white water canoeing, fiction writing. Office: 6 Office Park Cir Ste 308 Birmingham AL 35223 Home: 415 Club Pl Birmingham AL 35223

TUCKER, THOMAS RANDALL, public relations executive; b. Indpls., Aug. 6, 1931; s. Ovie Allen and Oris Aleen (Robertson) T.; m. Evelyn Marie Armuth, Aug. 9, 1953; children: Grant, Roger, Richard. AB, Franklin Coll., 1953. Grad. asst. U. Minn., 1953-54; dir. admissions registrar Franklin Coll., 1954-57; with Cummins Engine Co., Inc., Columbus, Ind., 1957, dir. pub. rels., 1968-88; pub. rels. cons. Mem. sch. bd. trustees Bartholomew County, Ind., 1966-72, pres., 1968-69; mem. Ind. State Bd. Edn., 1977-89; treas. Bartholomew County Rep. Ctrl. Com., 1960-80; sec. Columbus Learning Ctr. Mgmt. Corp.; hon. trustee Franklin Coll.; trustee Ind. State Mus. Mem. Pub. Rels. Soc. Am., Columbus (Ind.) C. of C. (Cmty. Svc. award 1986), Rotary, Sagamore of the Wabash, Kappa Tau Alpha, Phi Delta Theta, Sigma Delta Chi. Lutheran. Home: 4380 N Riverside Dr Columbus IN 47203-1123 Office: PO Box 3005 Columbus IN 47202-3005

TUCKER, THOMAS WILLIAM, mathematics professor; b. Princeton, NJ, July 15, 1945; s. Albert William Tucker and Alice Judson (Curtiss) Beckenbach; m. Mollie Dalton; children: Thomas John, Emily McDonnell. AB magna cum laude, Harvard U., 1967; PhD, Dartmouth Coll., 1971. Instr. Princeton U., 1971-73; from asst. prof. to prof. math. Colgate U., Hamilton, NY, 1973-83, prof., 1983—, Charles G. Hetherington prof. math., 1994—, chmn. math. dept., 1982-86, acting dean coll., 1991-92, dir. divsn. nat. sci., 1993-96. Vis. assoc. prof. Dartmouth Coll., Hanover, NH, 1978-79; cons. Ednl. Testing Svc., 1973—, Inst. for Def. Analyses, Princeton, 1974-75, 78-79, 84-85; chmn. advanced placement calculus com. Coll. Bd., NYC, 1983-87; pres. Calculus Consortium for Higher Edn., Inc., 1998-2005. Co-author: Topological Graph Theory, 1987; editor: Priming the Calculus Pump, 1990; contbr. numerous articles to profl. jours. NSF grantee, 1976-77, 80-82, 86-88, 89, 90-97. Mem. Math. Assn. Am. (mem., chmn. many coms., v.p. 1990-92), Am. Math. Soc. Home: 21 Hamilton St Hamilton NY 13346-1329 Office: Colgate U Dept Math Hamilton NY 13346 Business E-Mail: ttucker@mail.colgate.edu.

TUCKER, TOM, science and invention writer, literature and language professor; s. Buell and Susie Tucker; m. Diane Sherer; children: Matthew, Joseph, Bonnie. MA, Harvard, Wash. U, Cambridge, St. Louis, 1966. English prof. Isothermal CC, Spindale, NC. Author: Bolt of Fate: Benjamin Franklin and his Electric Kite Hoax, The Eclipse Project, Touchdown: The Development of Propulsion Controlled Aircraft, Brainstorm: The Stories of Twenty American Kid Inventors. Recipient NC Blumenthal Reader award; named Best Non-fiction Book for Young Readers, NCET; fellowship, NASA Dryden, Stanford U., 1999—2000, Bakken Libr. & Mus. Home: 143 S Ridgecrest St Rutherfordton NC 28139 Office: Isothermal CC 286 ICC Loop Rd Spindale NC 28160 Business E-Mail: ttucker@isothermal.edu.

TUCKER, VICKY ROSE, systems analyst, director; b. Evergreen Pk., Ill., July 7, 1963; d. Edwin John and Judy Irene Plys; m. Robert Eugene Tucker II, June 6, 1992; children: Rachel Viola, Robert Eugene III. BS in Biology, Ill. Benedictine Coll., Lisle, 1985; MBA, Lewis U., Romeoville, Ill., 1990. Admission counselor Lewis U., 1985—89, asst. transfer coord., 1989—92, asst. dir. admission, 1990—97, adj. faculty mem., economics dept., 1996—, dir. admission, 1997—2000, dir. enrollment data and analysis, 2000—01, dir. instl. data analysis & assessment, 2001—. Pres., v.p., sec. & instl. rep. positions Assn. Chgo. Cath. Coll. & U., 1986—2000. Recipient Student Laureate Representing award, Ill. Lincoln Acad., Benedictine Coll., 1985, Academic Excellence Award, Lewis U. Grad. Sch. Mgmt., 1990, Rewards & Recognition Profl. Staff Mem. award, Lewis U., 1994, Rewards & Recognition Team award, 1998, 2008; named to Nat. Deans List, Ill. Benedictine Coll., 1984—85; Data & Decisions Workshop grant, Assn. Instl. Rsch. & Coun. Ind. Coll., 2003. Mem.: Ill. Assn. Instl. Rsch., Cath. Higher Edn. Rsch. Consortium, Assn. Instl. Rsch. Home: 2000 Saint Andrews Drive Plainfield IL 60586 Office: Lewis University One University Parkway Romeoville IL 60446

TUCKER, WILLIAM EDWARD, academic administrator, minister; b. Charlotte, NC, June 22, 1932; s. Cecil Edward and Ethel Elizabeth (Godley) T.; m. Ruby Jean Jones, Apr. 8, 1955; children: Janet Sue, William Edward, Gordon Vance. BA, Barton Coll., Wilson, NC, 1953, LLD (hon.), 1978; BD, Tex. Christian U., Ft. Worth, 1956; MA, Yale U., New Haven, Conn., 1958, PhD, 1960; LHD (hon.), Chapman U., Orange, Calif., 1981, Ky. Wesleyan Coll., Owensboro, 1989; DH (hon.), Bethany Coll., W.Va., 1982; DD (hon.), Austin Coll., Sherman, Tex., 1985. Ordained to ministry Disciples of Christ Ch., 1956; prof. Barton Coll., 1959-66, chmn. dept. religion and philosophy, 1961-66; mem. faculty Brite Div. Sch., Tex. Christian U., 1966-76, prof. ch. history, 1969-76, dean, 1971-76, chancellor, 1979-98, chancellor emeritus, 1998—. Pres. Bethany (W.Va.) Coll., 1976-79; dir. RadioShack Corp., 1985-2003, Brown and Lupton Found.; mem. gen. bd. Christian Ch. (Disciples of Christ), 1971-74, 75-87, adminstrv. com., 1975-81, chmn. theol. edn. commn., 1972-73, mem. exec. com., chmn. bd. higher edn., 1975-77; dir. Christian Ch. Found., 1980-83; moderator Christian Ch. (Disciples of Christ), 1983-85 Author: J.H. Garrison and Disciples of Christ, 1964, (with others) Journey in Faith: A History of the Christian Church (Disciples of Christ), 1975; also articles. Bd. dirs. Van Cliburn Found., 1981—; bd. trustees Amon Carter Mus. Mem. Exch. Club, Phi Beta Kappa. Home: 2337 Colonial Pky Fort Worth TX 76109-1030 Office: 777 Taylor St Ste P2-J Fort Worth TX 76102 Office Phone: 817-347-3220. Business E-Mail: w.tucker@tcu.edu.

TUCKER, WILLIAM P., lawyer, writer; b. Kingston, NY, Jan. 26, 1932; s. Philip and Mary (McGowan) T.; m. Dolores F. Beaudoin, June 10, 1961; children: Andrew M., Thomas B., Mary A. BA, Hunter Coll., 1958; JD, St. John's U., 1962. Bar: N.Y. 1962, Fla. 1980, U.S. Dist. Ct. (ea. dist.) N.Y. 1963, U.S. Dist. Ct. (so. dist.) N.Y., 1963, U.S. Cir. Ct. (2d cir.) Ill. Assoc. Mendes & Mount, NYC, 1962-63; ptnr. Cullen and Dykman, Bklyn. and Garden City, NY, Washington, Newark, Hauppauge, 1963-98, Golden, Wexler & Sarnese, Garden City/Purchase/S.I., 1998-2001; pvt. practice, 2001—. Former gen. counsel Broadway Nat. Bank, Wartburg Luth. Svcs., Luth. Ctr. for the Aging, Martin Luther Ter. Apts., Inc., Interfaith Med. Ctr., Roosevelt Savs. Bank, Olympian Bank, GreenPoint Bank, Ridgewood Savs. Bank, Atlantic Liberty Savs., F.A., Bethpage Fed. Credit Union, Mcpl. Credit Union, Lincoln Savs. Bank, Bklyn. Savs. Bank, Met. Savs. Bank, Crossland Savs. Bank, Bushwick Savs. Bank, Anchor Savs. Bank, Episc. Diocese L.I., St. John's Episc. Hosp., Bklyn., Rockaway, Smithtown; former spl. counsel OCI Mortgage Corp., Bklyn C. of C., Downtown Bklyn. Bus. Assn., Bank of N.Y., J.P. Morgan Chase Bank, Fleet Bank, Kraft Credit Union, Apple Bank for Savs., Barclays Bank of N.Y.; chmn. bd. dirs. Broadway Nat. Bank; co-owner Salem-Keizer Volcanoes N.W. League baseball team; former owner Norwich Navigators Ea. League baseball team; former v.p., N.W. Profl. Baseball League; bd. dirs. Bklyn. Sportsplex, Inc.; mem. WWII vets. history com. Libr. of Congress; rschr. U.S. Assassination Archives. Author: DP-or Billy and Jerry in the Promised Land, 1996, Moving Home Plate, 1999, (novels) Excalibur, 2001, With Justice for All, 2003, Kingsway 37, 2008; contbr. articles to profl. jours. Past mem. Selective Svc. Bd. 33; past pres. St. Vincent Ferrer Home Sch. Assn.; del. Diocesan Union Holy Name Socs.; mem. coun. St. John's U.; mem. coun. of regents St. Francis Coll., Bklyn.; bd. dirs. Faith Home Found., St. Joseph's Coll. Served US Army, Korean War. Mem. Am. Coll. Real Estate Lawyers(retired), N.Y. State Bar Assn., Fla. Bar Assn., Savs. Banks Lawyers Assn. Bklyn. (pres.), Suffolk County Bar Assn., Savs. Bank Assn. N.Y. State (law com.), Bklyn. Mcpl. Club (pres.), Knight of Malta, LI Authors Group. Home: 23 Bunker Hill Dr Huntington NY 11743-5705 Office: 775 Park Ave Ste 2 Huntington NY 11743 Office Phone: 631-351-1112. Personal E-mail: wptucker@optonline.net.

TUCKER CHAMBERS, JOHNNIE L., elementary school educator, rancher; b. Crocket County, Tex., Sept. 28, 1929; d. Robert Leo and Lois K. (Slaughter) Tucker; m. R. Boyd Chambers; children: Theresa A., Glyn Robert, Boyd James, John Trox. EdB, Sul Ross State U., Alpine, Tex., 1971. Tchr. 1st and 2d grades Candelaria Elem. Sch., Tex., 1971-73; head tchr. K-8 Ruidosa Elem. Sch., Tex., 1973-77, Candelaria Elem. Sch., 1977—91, tchr. 2d and 3d grades, 1991—93, tchr. pre-kindergarten, kindergarten and 1st grade, 1993—98; acting prin. Candelaria Elem. and Jr. High, 1995—98, head tchr. pre-K to 8th grades, 1996—98, tchr. pre-K, kindergarten, 1st and 2d grades, 1996—99; tchr. pre-K-6 Redford Elem. Sch., Tex., 2001, tchr., 2001—. Mem. sight-base decision making, Presidio, 1991-94; mem. Chihuahuan Desert Rsch. Inst., Alpine, 1982-94, mem. family crisis bd., v.p. Ret. Tchrs. Assn. Leader Boy Scouts Am., Ruidosa and Candelaria, 1973-91, Cub Scout leader, 1973-91; chpt. mem. Sheriffs Assn. Tex., Austin, 1980; bd. dirs. Big Bend Regional Hosp. Dist., 2001—, Family Crisis Ctr. Big Bend Inc., 2006; mem. Ctr. for Big Bend Studies. Recipient awards Boy Scouts Am., 1969, 83, Litter Gitter award, 1994-95. Mem. Tex. State Tchrs. Assn., Tex. Fedn. Rep. Women, The Archaeol. Conservancy, Phi Alpha Theta, Daughters Tex. Republic. Avocations: hiking, camping, anthropology, cave exploring, cooking. Home: PO Box 187 707 E Hancock Alpine TX 79830 Office Phone: 432-229-4707. Office Fax: 432-229-4707. Personal E-mail: jltchambers@yahoo.com. Business E-Mail: johnnieltc@rionet.coop.

TUCKSON, REED V., physician, health insurance company executive; Grad., Howard U.; MD, Georgetown U. Residency & fellowship in internal med. Hosp. Univ. Pa.; commr. pub. health Washington, 1986—90; sr v.p. progs. March of Dimes Birth Defects Found., 1990—91; pres. Charles R. Drew U., LA, 1991—97; sr. v.p. profl. stds. AMA, Chgo., 1998—2000; sr. v.p. consumer health and med. care advancement UnitedHealth Group, Mpls., 2000—06, exec. v.p., head med. affairs, 2006—. Named to Power 150, Ebony mag., 2008. Office: UnitedHealth Grp PO Box 1459 Minneapolis MN 55440*

TUDMAN, CATHI GRAVES, elementary school educator; b. Fresno, Calif., June 24, 1953; d. Robert Eugene and Bettyelou (Seagraves) Graves; divorced; children: Colleen Melissa, Andrew James. BA in Music cum laude, Calif. State U., Fresno, 1978, MA in Communication, 1991. Gen. elem., English, music and gen. sci. teaching credentials, Calif. Founder, coord. Lake Sequoia Symphonic Music Camp, Miramonte, Calif., 1985—; asst. lectr. communications speech dept. Calif. State U., 1988-91, instr. reading ednl. opportunity program summer bridge, 1990, instr. writing ednl. opportunity program summer bridge, 1991, coach, judge Peach Blossom Festival, 1988-91; band dir. Yosemite Mid. Sch., 1991—2004, Mayfair Elem. Sch., 1991—2000, Hidalgo Elem. Sch., 1991-92, 94-96, Balderas Elem., 1992-93, Turner Elem., 1993-96, Burroughs Annex Elem. Sch., 1993-95; art dir. Yosemite Mid. Sch., 2000—04; art dir., physical sci. instr. Ft. Miller Med. Careers Magnet Mid. Sch., 2004—. Instr. comms. dynamics Phillips Coll., Fresno, 1989-90; rsch. assoc. Renshaw Assocs., Fresno, 1989-91; flutist, piccoloist Fresno Philharm. Orch., 1981—, libr., 1985, 2007-, pers. mgr., 1984-85; flute clinician Selmer Corp., Ind., 1988-93; festivals chmn. Cen. Sect. Calif. Music Educators, 1972-82, publicity chmn., 1992-93; pvt. tutor in math., music and social studies; chmn. Fresno Unified Showcase Mid. Sch. Massed Band, 1991, 93. Flute clinician Fresno County Schs., 1980—; founder San Joaquin Valley Instrument Fund, 1984; bd. dirs. Community Concert Series, Fresno County, 1986-88; liaison com. bd. dirs. Fresno Philharm. Orch., 1992-94, mem. bd., 2002-04, edn. com., 2003-05; asst. chair FMCMEA Hon. Band, 1992-93; bd. dirs. Cen. Valley YMCA, 1994-95; music chair Fresno Met. Mus., 1996-97; mem. Yosemite Mid. Sch. Site Coun. 2000-2003, pres., sec., by-laws chair Fresno Arts Coun., bd. dirs. 2002-04, Tree Fresno-Rails to Trails Project, 2000; Great TV auction vol. Valley Pub. TV, 2005; mem. Ft. Miller Mid. Sch. Site Coun., 2007-09. Rsch. grantee Calif. State U., 1991, Cmty. Enrichment grant, 1999-2002; recipient Outstanding Teaching award Internat. Communication Assn., 1991. Mem. Western States Communication Assn., Fresno-Madera Music Educators Assn., Fresno Tchrs. Assn. (dir.-at-large, 2002-05), Calif. Tchrs. Assn. (rep. coun. 2000-2005), Fresno Mus. Club (social chmn. 1992-95) Calif. Music Educators (festival chmn. cen. sect. 1972-82), Sci. & Math. Educators Consortium, Calif. State U.-Fresno Alumnae Assn. (sec. 1982-83, nat. friendship chmn. 1979-81), Blue Key (Tokalon alumni 1978), Phi Kappa Phi, Mu Phi Epsilon (pres., v.p. Phi Chi chpt.). Avocations: quilting, kite making, church musician. Home: 5467 E Saginaw Way Fresno CA 93727-7536 Office: Fort Miller Mid Sch 1302 E Dakota Fresno CA 93704 Office Phone: 559-248-7100. E-mail: cgtudman@att.net.

TUDOR, HELEN E. A., materials engineer, consultant; b. Bucharest, Romania, Sept. 16, 1958; m. Colin C. Harris. PhD in Materials Sci. and Mineral Engring., Columbia U., NYC, 2001. Analysis engr. Grumman Aerospace Corp., Bethpage, 1977—88; tchg. and rsch. asst. MIT, Cambridge, Mass., 1980—83; vis. scientist Matsushita Electric Co., Osaka, Japan, 1983—84; materials engr. Intel Corp., Santa Clara, Calif., 1984—86; rsch. asst. Columbia U., NYC, 1994—2002; rsch. scientist Hosp. Spl. Surgery, NYC, 2002—06; pvt. cons. and advisor, 2006—. Cons. and advisor environ. issues and water decontamination methodologies, 1995—; dir. r&d ShellGen Water Purification Corp., NYC, 1996—2002. Contbr. articles to profl. jours. Sustaining mem. Rockefeller U. Concert Series, NYC, 2002—06. Recipient Presdl. Recognition award, Columbia U., 1997; grantee, MIT and Matsushita Ctrl. Rsch. Labs, Osaka, Japan, 1983—84; STAR fellow, US EPA, 1996—99. Mem.: AAAS, NY Acad. Sci., Am. Chem. Soc., MIT Alumni Assn., Penn Club. Achievements include patents for method for treating contaminated liquids using waste shells; using waste shells; complexed acidic phospholipid-collagen composites for bone induction; patents pending for. Avocations: seashore preservation, classical music, architectural conservation, Japanese art and architecture, wildlife protection. Home: 110 E 57th St New York NY 10022 Business E-Mail: tudorh@alum.mit.edu.

TUDOR, TAMARA, theater educator; d. Richard Edwin and Rosemary Tudor. BS, Ball State U., Muncie, Ind., 1974; MA in Edn., Purdue U., West Lafayette, Ind., 1979. English tchr. Tuttle Jr. High, Crawfordsville, Ind., 1974—78; speech and drama tchr. Clay Jr. HS, Carmel, Ind., 1978—86; drama dir. Carmel HS, Ind., 1986—2007; adj. prof. theatre Ball State U., Muncie, Ind., 2008—; speech and drama instr. Pk. Tudor Sch., Indpls., 2008—. Bd. dir. Ind. State Thespian Exec. Bd., Mishawaka, Ind., 1986—2002. Playwright Snapshots, Christmas in the Land of Oz, Shakespeare on Love, A Cowboy Christmas. Rec. sec. ShadowApe Theatre Co., Indpls., 2005—. Recipient Award, Ednl. Theatre Assn., 1997. Mem.: Phi Kappa Phi. Achievements include development of carmel high school parent support group; American cabaret theatre. Avocations: reading, travel, dominoes, theater, movies. Office: Pk Tudor Sch 7200 N Coll Ave Indianapolis IN 46240 Business E-Mail: ttudor@parktudor.org.

TUDRYN, JOYCE MARIE, professional society administrator; b. Holyoke, Mass., July 27, 1959; d. Edward William and Frances Katherine (Bajor) T.; m. William Wallace Friberger III, Sept. 18, 1982; 1 child, Kristen. BS in Comm., Syracuse U., 1981. Asst. editor Nat. Assn. Broadcasters, Washington, 1981-83; dir. programs Internat. Radio and TV Soc. Found., NYC, 1983-87, assoc. exec. dir., 1988-94; exec. dir. Internat. Radio and TV Soc., NYC, 1994-97, pres., 1997—. Spkr. in field; nat. adv. bd. Alpha Epsilon Rho Broadcasting Soc., 1988-91, 93-94, hon. trustee, 1994-98, officer, 1999-2001; v.p. Corp. for Ednl. Radio and TV, 1988-94; adv. bd. Marist Coll. Sch. Comm., 1999—, Syracuse U. Newhouse Sch. Pub. Comm., 1999—; vice chmn. edn. iEmmy Festival, 1999; guest prof. U. Scranton, 2000. Columnist TV Facts, Figures and Film mag., 1983-88; one-woman photography exhbn. Synchronicity Space, N.Y.C., 1998. Recipient Disting. Edn. Svc. award Broadcast Edn. Assn., 2003; named one of Most Influential Women in Radio, Radio INK Mag., 2003; inducted into Syracuse U. Newhouse Sch. Profl. Wall of Fame Gallery, 2000. Mem. N.Y. Media Roundtable, Gamma Phi Beta. Avocation: photography. Office: Internat Radio and TV Soc Found 420 Lexington Ave Ste 1601 New York NY 10170-1799

TUELL, JACK MARVIN, retired bishop; b. Tacoma, Nov. 14, 1923; s. Frank Harry and Anne Helen (Bertelson) T.; m. Marjorie Ida Beadles, June 17, 1946; children: Jacqueline, Cynthia, James. BS, U. Wash., 1947, JD, 1948; MDiv, Boston U., 1955; MA, U. Puget Sound, 1961, DHS, 1990; D.D., Pacific Sch. Religion, 1966; LLD, Alaska Pacific U., 1980. Bar: Wash. 1948; ordained to ministry Meth. Ch., 1955. Practice law with firm Holte & Tuell, Edmonds, Wash., 1948-50; pastor Grace Meth. Ch., Everett, Wash., 1950-52, South Tewksbury Meth. Ch., Tewksbury, Mass., 1952-55, Lakewood Meth. Ch., Tacoma, 1955-61; dist. supt. Puget Sound dist. Meth. Ch., Everett, 1961-67; pastor 1st United Meth. Ch., Vancouver, Wash., 1967-72; bishop United Meth. Ch., Portland, Oreg., 1972-80, Calif.-Pacific Conf., United Meth. Ch., LA, 1980-92, ret., 1992; interim sr. pastor First United Meth. Ch., Boise, Idaho, 1995; interim supt. Seattle Tacoma Dist., 2004—05. Mem. gen. conf. United Meth. Ch., 1964, 66, 68, 70, 72; pres. coun. of Bishops United Meth. Ch., 1989-90. Author: The Organization of the United Methodist Church, 1970, 11th edit. 2008, (autobiography) From Law to Grace, 2004. Pres. Tacoma U.S.O., 1959-61, Vancouver YMCA, 1968; v.p. Ft. Vancouver Seamens Cnt., 1969-72; vice chmn. Vancouver Human Rels. Commn., 1970-72; pres. Oreg. Coun. Alcohol Problems, 1972-76; trustee U. Puget Sound, 1961-73, Vancouver Meml. Hosp., 1967-72, Alaska Meth. U., Anchorage, 1972-80, Willamette U., Salem, Oreg., 1972-80, Willamette View Manor, Portland, 1972-80, Rogue Valley Manor, Medford, Oreg., 1972-76, Sch. Theology at Claremont, Calif., 1980-92, Methodist Hosp., Arcadia, Calif., 1983-92; pres. nat. div. bd. global ministries United Meth. Ch., 1972-76, pres. ecumenical and interreligious concerns div., 1976-80, Commn. on Christian Unity and intereligious concerns, 1980-84, Gen. Bd. of Pensions,1984-92, Calif. Coun. Alcohol Problems, 1985-88. Jacob Sleeper fellow, 1955. Methodist. Home and Office: 816 S 216th St 637 Des Moines WA 98198-6331 Home Phone: 206-870-8637.

TUELL, STEVEN SHAWN, religious studies educator, minister; b. Est Liverpool, Ohio, Oct. 3, 1956; s. Bernard Earl and Mary Louise Tuell; m. Wendy Louise Rodan, May 30, 1981; children: Sean Michael, Anthony Ryan, Mark Anderson. BA magna cum laude, W.Va. Wesleyan Coll., 1978; MDiv, Princeton Theol. Sem., 1981; PhD, Union Theol. Sem., 1989. Student pastor Siloam and DeBowj United Meth. Chs., Allentown, NJ, 1979—81; pastor Red Hill and Murphytown United Meth. Chs., Parkersburg, W.Va., 1981—85; instr. religious studies Coll. William & Mary, Williamsburg, Va., 1988; asst. prof. Bible and religion Erskine Coll., Due West, SC, 1989—92; asst. prof. religious studies Randolph-Macon Coll., Ashland, Va., 1992—97, assoc. prof. religious studies, 1997—2009, chmn. religious studies, 2003—; assoc. prof. Old Testament Pitts. Theol. Seminary, 2009. Interim pastor Woodlake United Meth. Ch., Midlothian, Va., 1994. Author: The Law of the Temple in Ezek, 1992, 1 and 2 Chronicles, 2001; musician: (albums) Dumbarton's Drums, 1997; author: Ezekiel, 2009, Constituting the Community, 2005, Down in The River, 2007. Mem.: Soc. Biblical Lit. (mem. steering com. 1981—), Amnesty Internat. Democrat. Meth. Office: Pitts Theol Seminary Pittsburgh PA 15206 Office Phone: 804-752-7280. E-mail: stuell@rmc.edu.

TUENGEL, LISA MARIE, elementary school educator; b. Port Townsend, Wash., July 26, 1959; d. Konrad Willi Karl and Jane Marie Schwencke; m. Bradley Marcus Tuengel, Aug. 23, 1987; children: Marcus, Martin, Marie. BA in Elem. Edn., Concordia Coll., Portland, Oreg., 1981; MA in Am. Studies, Pepperdine U., Malibu, Calif., 1992. Profl. edn. cert. continuing tchr. Wash. Tchr., coach Evansville Luth. Sch., Ind., 1981—85, Zion Luth. Sch., Snohomish, Wash., 1985—90; tchr., phys. edn. specialist Snohomish Sch. Dist., 2000—. Sunday sch. tchr., mem. choir Zion Luth. Ch., Snohomish, 1985—. Recipient Athlete of Yr. award, Concordia Coll., 1981; Am. studies fellow, Pepperdine U., 1986—89. Mem.: AAHPERD, Washington Alliance for Health, Phys. Edn., Recreation and Dance (award phys. edn. divsn. 2005). Avocations: sports, photography, knitting. Home: 1610 S Machias Rd Snohomish WA 98290 Office: Machias Elem Sch 231 147th Ave SE Snohomish WA 98290 Office Phone: 360-563-4871. Office Fax: 360-563-4828. E-mail: lisa.tuengel@sno.wednet.edu.

TUERCK, DAVID GEORGE, economist, educator; b. Belleville, Ill., Feb. 11, 1941; s. George Nicholas and Bertha Amollie Tuerck; m. Prema Popat, Nov. 23, 2002; 1 child, John David. BA in Govt., George Wash. U., Washington, DC, 1962, MA in Govt., 1964; PhD, U. Va., Charlottesville, 1966. Dir. Ctr. Rsch. Advt. Am. Enterprise Inst., DC, 1975—77, Econ. Consulting Practice, Coopers & Lybrand, DC, 1977—82; chmn. econ. Suffolk U., Boston, 1982—, prof. econ., 1987—, exec. dir. Beacon Hill Inst., 1991—. Co-author: Foreign Trade and U.S. Policy. Republican. Congregationalist. Avocation: drums. Home: 11 Joan Dr Quincy MA 02169 Office: Suffolk Univ 8 Ashburton Pl Boston MA 02108 Office Fax: 671-994-4279. Personal E-mail: dgtuerck@aol.com. Business E-Mail: dtuerck@beaconhill.org.

TUERK, WILLIAM F., federal agency administrator, lawyer; b. 1949; AB in Govt., U. Notre Dame, 1971; JD, George Washington U., 1978. Bar: D.C. 1978. Legis. analyst US Dept. Treasury, 1974—76; pvt. law practice, 1978—86; atty. US Dept. Veterans Affairs, 1986—91; minority gen. counsel US Senate Com. on Veterans Affairs, 1991—95, gen counsel, 1995—99, chief counsel & staff dir., 1999—2005; under sec. for meml. affairs US Dept. Veterans Affairs, Washington, 2005—. Mil. policeman US Army, 1971—73. Office: US Dept Vets Affairs 810 Vermont Ave NW Rm 400 Washington DC 20420*

TUFANO, PAUL J., telecommunications industry executive; BS in Economics, St. John's U.; MBA in Fin. Acctg. & Internat. Bus., Columbia U. With IBM Corp., 1984—2001; v.p. fin., CFO Maxtor Corp., 1996—98, sr. v.p., CFO, 1998—2001, exec. v.p., COO, 2001—03, pres., CEO, 2003—04; exec. v.p., CFO Solectron Corp., Milpitas, Calif., 2006—07, interim CEO, 2007; exec. v.p., CFO Alcatel-Lucent SA, Paris, 2008—. Bd. dirs. Celestica Asia, 1996—, Maxtor Corp., 2003—04, Amphenol TCS, 2005—, Terradyne Corp., 2005—. Office: Alcatel-Lucent SA 54 rue la Boétie 75008 Paris France*

TUFT, MARY ANN, executive search firm executive; b. Easton, Pa., Oct. 11, 1934; d. Ben and Elizabeth (Reibman) T. BS, West Chester State Coll., Pa., 1956; MA, Lehigh U., 1960. Cert. assn. exec. Nat. trainer Girl Scouts U.S.A., NYC, 1965-68; cons. Nat. League for Nursing, NYC, 1968-69; exec. dir. Nat. Student Nurses Assn., NYC, 1970-85; mem. Commn. on Dietetic Registration, Am. Dietetic Assn., 1981-85; pres. Specialized Cons. Ltd., 1983-85; exec. dir. Radiol. Soc. N.Am., Oak Brook, Ill., 1985-88; pres. Tuft & Assocs., Inc., 1989—. Trustee, Found. of the Nat. Student Nurses Assn., 2001—; adv. bd. Cognitive Neurology and Alzheimer's Disease Ctr. of Northwestern Univ./Feinberg Sch. of Medicine, 2002-; mem. pres.'s adv. coun. Sch. Nursing, Saint Xavier U., 2006—. Bd. dirs. Nurses House, Inc., 1981-85, Chgo. chpt. Am. Friends of Hebrew U., 2000-, nat. bd. Am. Friends of Hebrew U., 2006-; mem. exec. com. Chgo. Sinai Cong., 1987-91, v.p., 1988. Recipient Disting. Alumnus award West Chester State Coll., 1979; Mary Ann Tuft Scholarship Fund named in her honor Found. Nat. Student Nurses Assn.; Kepner-Tregoe scholar, 1966. Mem.: ALA (pub. mem. com. on accreditation 1993—95), Am. Dietetic Assn. (pub. mem. commn. on accreditation for dietetics edn. 2005—08), Specialized Cons. in Nursing (faculty), Continuing Care Accreditation Assn. (bd. dirs. 1983—85), NY Soc. Assn. Execs. (bd. dirs. 1975—78, pres. 1978—79, 1st Outstanding Exec. award 1982), Am. Soc. Assn. Execs. (bd. dirs. 1980—83, trustee for cert. 1980—83, vice chmn. 1983—84), Sigma Theta Tau (hon.). Home Phone: 312-642-7490; Office Phone: 312-642-8889. Business E-Mail: matuft@tuftassoc.com.

TUFT, TOM (THOMAS EDWIN TUFT), investment banker; b. 1947; m. Diane Tuft; 1 child, Erica Brooke. BA, U. Mich., 1969; attended, NYU Grad. Bus. Program. V.p. instl. sales Goldman Sachs Group, Inc., NYC, 1976—85, co-founder Energy Capital Markets, 1985, ptnr., 1986—96, mng. ptnr., 1996—2009, chmn. Equity Capital Markers, 2004—09; chmn. Global Capital Markets Advisory, vice chmn. US Investment Banking Lazard Ltd., NYC, 2009—. Chmn. Roundabout Theatre Co.; v.p. bd. trustees Whitney Mus. Am. Art; bd. dirs. Boys & Girls Harbor, Cancer Rsch. Inst., 2005—; mem. investment com. Wesleyan U. Office: Lazard Ltd 30 Rockefeller Plz New York NY 10112 Office Phone: 212-902-1000. Office Fax: 212-902-3000.*

TUGGLE, DAVID W., pediatric surgeon; b. Tex. BS with highest honors, Abilene Christian U., Tex., 1975; MD, U. Tex. Southwestern Med. Sch., 1979. Diplomate Am. Bd. Surgery, cert. Spl. Competence in Pediat. Surgery and Added Qualification in Surgical Critical Care, lic. Tex., 1979, Okla., 1985. Resident, gen. surgery Parkland Meml. Hosp., Dallas, 1979—82, 1983—84, chief resident, gen. surgery, 1984—85; surgical rsch. fellow U. Tex. Health Sci. Ctr., Dallas, 1982—83; chief resident, pediat. surgery Okla. Children's Meml. Hosp., 1985—87; coord., surgical critical care Children's Hosp. Okla., 1987—; clin. asst. prof., dept. pediat. U. Okla., 1987—, asst. prof. surgery, dept. surgery, sect. pediat. surgery, 1987—92, assoc. prof. surgery, dept. surgery, sect. pediat. surgery, 1992—99, chief, sect. pediat. surgery, dept. surgery, 1995—, prof. surgery, dept. surgery, sect. pediat. surgery, 1999—, Paula Milburn Miller, Children's Med. Rsch. Inst., chair pediat. surgery, 2001—, vice-chmn., dept. surgery, 2002—. Trauma med. dir. Okla. U. Med. Ctr., Level 1 Trauma Ctr., 1999—2001; dir., Extracorporeal Membrane Oxygenation Ctr. Children's Hosp. Okla., 1992—97. Peer-reviewer Archives of Surgery, Journal Pediatric Surgery; contbr. several articles to profl. jours. Recipient Weigelt-Wallace award for exemplary med. care for performing an on-site amputation to free a victim from the debris of the Olka. City bombing, 1995. Fellow: Am. Acad. Pediat. (Spl. Achievement award 1996), Am. Coll. Critical Care Medicine, ACS (com. on trauma 1997—2003, liaison to Am. Acad. Pediat. com. on pediat. emergency 2002—, Okla. Dist. #1 com. on applicants 1994—99, verification review com. 1995—2003); mem.: Okla. Chpt. ACS (vice-pres. 1995—96, pres.-elect 1996—97, pres. 1997—98, Spl. Achievement award 1996), Am. Assn. Surgery of Trauma, AMA, Am. Pediat. Surgical Assn. (critical care com. 1992—93, publications com. 1995—98, trauma com. 1998, chmn. 2004—05), Am. Soc. for Parental and Enteral Nutrition, Am. Trauma Soc., Assn. for Academic Surgery, Ctrl. Okla. Pediat. Soc., Okla. City Surgical Soc., Okla. County Med. Assn., Okla. Organ Sharing Network, Okla. State Med. Assn., Okla. Surgical Assn., Parkland Surgical Soc., Soc. for Critical Care Medicine (sec./treas., surgical sect. 1987—90, chmn. surgical sect. 1991—92), Southwestern Surgical Congress, So. Surgical Assn., Alpha Omega Alpha. Achievements include being part of surgical team who separated what is believed to be the first known American Indian conjoined twins in 2008. Office: U Okla Dept Surgery PO Box 26901 CHO 2B 2403 Oklahoma City OK 73126 Office Phone: 405-271-5922. Office Fax: 405-271-3278. Business E-Mail: David-Tuggle@ouhsc.edu.*

TUGGLE, FRANCIS DOUGLAS, entrepreneur, consultant, management educator, scientist; b. Portsmouth, Va., Jan. 19, 1943; s. Francis Joyner and Florence Eleanor (Dahlgren) T.; m. Mary Ann Tredway, June 3, 1967; children: Wendy Elizabeth, Laura Michelle. SB, MIT, 1964; MS, Carnegie-Mellon U., 1967, PhD, 1971. Prof. bus. adminstrn. and computer sci. U. Kans., Lawrence, 1968-78; Jesse H. Jones prof. mgmt. Rice U., Houston, 1978-90; dean Kogod Coll. Bus. Adminstrn., Am. U., Washington, 1990-96, prof. info. systems and strategic planning, 1996—2002; Robert J. & Carolyn A. Waltos Jr. dean Argyros Sch. Bus. Econs. Chapman U., Orange, Calif., 2002—06, prof., 2006—; founder Family Health Info. Svcs., Inc., Yorba-Linda, Calif., 2006—, Anderson & Tuggle Inc., 2002—; ptnr. Insight Cons., 2006—. Bd. dirs. Equus Total Return Inc., Houston; dir.-at-large Inst. for Ops. Rsch. and Mgmt. Scis., 1995; cons. in field; bd. trustees, Internat U. Creative Leadership Entrepreneurship, Breda, Holland, 2007- Author: How to Program a Computer, 1975, Organizational Processes, 1978. Com. chmn. United Way Tex. Gulf Coast, Houston, 1985-88. Fellow, Ford Found., 1966. Mem. Inst. for Ops. Rsch. and Mgmt. Scis. (bd. dirs. 1995, v.p. 1992-94), Am. Assn. Artificial Intelligence, Assn. for Computing Machinery, Acad. of Mgmt., Sigma Xi, Beta Gamma Sigma, Alpha Kappa Psi. Episcopalian. Avocations: golf, bicycling, jogging, painting, drawing. Home: 20465 Via Torralba Yorba Linda CA 92887 Office: Argyros Sch Bus Econs Chapman U 1 University Dr Orange CA 92866 Office Phone: 714-997-6537. Business E-Mail: tuggle@chapman.edu.

TUHRIM, STANLEY, physician, neurologist; b. NYC, Jan. 26, 1954; m. Betty Jane Mintz, Feb. 8, 1981; 1 child, Richard J. BA in Psychology, Haverford Coll., 1975; MD, Mt. Sinai Sch. Medicine, 1979. Intern U. Pa. Hosp., Phila., 1979-80; resident in neurology Mt. Sinai Hosp., NYC, 1980-83; stroke fellow U. Md. Hosp., 1983-84; asst. prof. dept. neurology U. Md., Balt., 1985-87, Mt. Sinai Hosp., NYC, 1987-90, assoc. prof. dept. neurology, 1991—2001, prof. dept. neurology, 2002—; prof. dept. geriatrics and adult devel. Mt. Sinai Med. Ctr., NYC, 2008—. Contbr. articles to profl. jours. Recipient Tchr.-Investigator award NINCDS, 1984, Bressler Rsch. award U. Md., 1985; NINDS clin. investigator, 1988. Fellow: Am. Heart Assn. (stroke coun.); mem.: Am. Acad. Neurology, Nat. Stroke Assn., Am. Neurol. Soc. Office: Mt Sinai Med Ctr One Gustave Levy Pl PO Box 1137 New York NY 10029-0312

TUINSTRA, TIMOTHY RYAN, engineering educator; b. Kalamazoo, Mich., Sept. 7, 1973; s. Roger Elliot and Ruth Anne Tuinstra; m. Kelly Ann Reitz, July 7, 2002; 1 child, Iain Paul. BSEE, Cedarville U., Ohio, 1996; MSEE, U. Dayton, Ohio, 1998, PhD, 2008. Sr. engr. Gen. Dynamics, Beavercreek, Ohio, 1998—2002; asst. prof. elec. engring. Cedarville U., 2002—. Contbr. articles to profl. jours. Elder Grace Covenant Ch., Beavercreek, 2000—08. DAGSI scholarship, Dayton Area Grad. Studies Inst., 2003—06. Mem.: Inst. Elec. and Electronics Engrs. Achievements include research in investigation of novel techniques for automatically segmenting pulmonary nodules in computed tomography imagery. Home: 1266 Eileen Dr Dayton OH 45434 Office: Cedarville Univ 251 N Main St Cedarville OH 45314

TUITE, GERALD FRANCIS, lawyer, commercial real estate manager; b. Rockford, Ill., Nov. 15, 1928; s. John Christopher and Mildred Tuite; m. Francine Lynn Williams, Aug. 2, 1980; children: Gregory, Gerald F., Michael, Tracy. Degree, Georgetown U., 1955; JD, Chgo. Kent Coll. Law, 1958. Bar: Ill. 1958. Sr. ptnr. Gerald Tuite & Assocs. Law Firm, Rockford, Ill., 1958—; asst. atty. gen. Ill., 1961—68. Spkr. in field. Vice chmn. Dem. Party, Ill., 1961—64, precinct committeeman; candidate State Atty., 1960. Cpl. US Army, 1950—52, Korea. Recipient Svc. to Youth award, City and County Officials Rockford, Ill., 1960, Svc. award, Am. Legion, 1961, AFL-CIO Unions, 1980, 1986. Mem.: ATLA, ABA, Ill. Trial Assn., Ill. Bar Assn. Democrat. Roman Catholic. Avocations: travel, boating, swimming, golf, tennis. Office: Greg Tuite & Assocs 119 North Church St Rockford IL 61101 Home: Embassy Club #604 1717 Gulf Shore Blvd N Naples FL 34102

TUITELE, LUI, retired school system administrator; b. Leone Village; BS in Biology, Truman State U., Mo.; MEd in Secondary Edn., Brigham Young U., EdD in Ednl. Leadership. Classroom tchr., Am. Samoa; high school principal Am. Samoa; asst. dir. edn. Am. Samoa Dept. Edn., dir. edn., 2003—06. Program dir. Goals 2000, Teacher Cert.; dep. dir. Instrnl. Services. Mem.: Am. Samoa Humanities Coun. (chmn.), Bd. Higher Edn., Territorial Planning Commn., Coun. Chief State Sch. Officers.

TUKE, ROBERT DUDLEY, lawyer, educator; b. Rochester, NY, Dec. 5, 1947; s. Theodore Robert and Doris Jean (Smith) T.; m. Susan Devereux Cummins, June 21, 1969; children: Andrew, Sarah. BA with distinction, U. Va., 1969; JD, Vanderbilt U., 1976. Bar: Tenn. 1976, U.S. Dist. Ct. (mid. dist.) Tenn. 1976, U.S. Ct. Appeals (6th cir.) 1976, U.S. Ct. Appeals (4th cir.) 1978, U.S. Ct. Appeals (fed. cir.) 1993, U.S. Supreme Ct. 1986, U.S. Ct. Internat. Trade 1993. Assoc. Farris, Warfield & Kanaday, Nashville, 1976—79, ptnr., 1980—94, Tuke Yopp & Sweeney, Nashville, 1994—99, Trauger, Ney & Tuke, Nashville, 2000—05, Trauger & Tuke, Nashville, 2006—; candidate US Senate, 2008. Adj. prof. law Vanderbilt U. Law Sch., Nashville. Author: (with others) Tennessee Practice, 1992—; editor-in-chief Vanderbilt Law Rev.; contbr. articles to profl. jours. Mem. Tenn. Adoption Law Study Commn., 1993-96, Metro CATV Com.; chmn. Tenn. Dem. Party, 2005-07. Capt. USMC, 1969-73. Decorated Cross of Gallantry; Patrick Wilson Merit scholar. Mem. ABA, Am. Health Law Assn., Nat. Assn. Bond Lawyers, Am. Acad. Adoption Attys. (past pres.), Tenn. Bar Assn., Nashville Bar Assn., Order of Coif. Democrat. Episcopalian. Avocations: rowing, running, bicycling, hiking, travel. Office: 222 4th Ave N Nashville TN 37219-2115 Home Phone: 615-385-2786; Office Phone: 615-256-8585. Business E-Mail: rtuke@tntlaw.net.

TULAFONO, TOGIOLA T.A., Governor of American Samoa; b. Aunu'u Island, American Samoa, Feb. 28, 1947; s. Aitu and Silika (Vaatu'itu'i) T.; m. Maryann Taufaasau Mauga, Sept. 17, 1984; children: Puataunofo, Olita, Cherianne, Emema, Timoteo, Rosie. Grad., Honolulu Police Acad., 1967; BA, Chadron State Coll., 1970; JD, Washburn U., 1975. Bar: Kans., Am. Samoa. Police instr. Am. Samoa Police Dept., Pago Pago, 1967; adminstrv. asst. Sec. of Samoan Affairs, Pago Pago, 1970-71; legal asst. Atty. Gen., Pago Pago, 1971-72; assoc. Law Offices of George A. Wray, Pago Pago, 1975-77; v.p. South Pacific Island Airways, Pago Pago, 1977-79; judge Dist. Ct. of Am. Samoa, Pago Pago, 1979-80; chmn. bd. dirs. Am. Samoa Power Authority, Pago Pago, 1978-80; mem. Am. Samoa Senate, Pago Pago, 1981-85, 89—; pres. Nayram Samoa, Ltd., Pago Pago, 1985-88; lt. gov. Am. Samoa Pago Pago, 1997—2003; gov. Am. Samoa, 2003—. Chmn. Senate Investigation Com., 1993—. Chmn. Bd. Higher Edn., Am. Samoa, 1993—; bd. dirs. Am. Samoa Jr. Golfers' Assn.; deacon Sailele Congrl. Ch. Mem. ATLA, Am. Samoa Bar Assn., Kans. Bar Assn., Samoa Profl. Golfer's Assn. (pres. 1985-87), Am. Samoa Golf Assn. (pres.). Democrat. Congregationalist. Office: Office of the Gov Ter of American Samoa Pago Pago AS 96799 Office Phone: 684-633-4116. Office Fax: 684-633-2269.

TULI, SONAL, medical educator; Diplomate Am. Bd. Ophthalmology, 2001. Asst. prof. U. Fla., Gainesville, 2001—. Fellow: Am. Acad. Ophthalmology. Office: Univ Fla 1600 Swarcher Rd Gainesville FL 32610

TULL, PAMELA M., public relations executive; b. Hutchinson, Kans., July 10, 1953; d. Raymond L. and Marjorie L. McDaniel; 1 child, Megan L. McAdoo. AA, Independence CC, Kans., 1973; BS in Elem. Edn., Emporia State Coll., Kans., 1975, MLS, 1994. Readers aide, bookmobile Topeka Pub. Libr., 1977—80; libr. asst. Mabee Libr., Washburn U., Topeka, 1983—86; part time libr. asst. Sch. Libr. Sys., BDT BOCES, Binghamton, NY, 1987; libr. asst. Four County Libr. Sys., Binghamton, 1987—89; libr. asst., govdocs Washburn U. Law Libr., Topeka, 1990—95; head pub. svcs. Wheat Law Libr., U. Kans., Lawrence, 1995—. Webmaster Kans. Jud. Br., Topeka, 1995—2007. Contbr. articles to sci. publs. Mem.: Mid Am. Assoc. Law Librs. (sec. 2008—). Office: Wheat Law Libr Univ Kans 1535 W 15th Lawrence KS 66045 Office Fax: 785-864-3680. Business E-Mail: ptull@ku.edu.

TULL, THERESA ANNE, retired diplomat; b. Runnemede, NJ, Oct. 2, 1936; d. John James and Anna Cecelia (Paull) T. BA, U. Md., 1972; MA, U. Mich., 1973; postgrad., Nat. War Coll., Washington, 1980. Fgn. svc. officer Dept. State, Washington, 1963, Brussels, 1965-67, Saigon, 1968-70; dep. prin. officer Am. Consulate General, Danang, Vietnam, 1973-75; prin. officer Cebu, Philippines, 1977-79; dir. office human rights, 1980-83; charge d'affaires Am. Embassy, Vientiane, Laos, 1983-86; Dept. State Senior Seminar, 1986-87; ambassador to Guyana, 1987-90; diplomat-in-residence Lincoln U., Pa., 1990-91; dir. office regional affairs, bur. East Asian & Pacific affairs Dept. State, Washington, 1991-93; amb. to Brunei Bandar Seri Begawan, 1993-96. Recipient Civilian Service award Dept. of State, 1970, Superior Honor award, 1977 Mem. Am. Fgn. Svc. Assn., Women's Civic Club. Address: 3500 Boardwalk Apt 726N Sea Isle City NJ 08243

TULL, WILLIS CLAYTON, JR., retired librarian; b. Crisfield, Md., Feb. 22, 1931; s. Willis Clayton and Agnes Virginia (Milbourne) T.; m. Taeko Itoi, Dec. 18, 1952. Student, U. Balt., 1948, Johns Hopkins U., 1956; BS, Towson State Coll., Md., 1957; MLS, Rutgers U., 1962; postgrad., Miami U., Oxford, Ohio, 1979. Editl. clk. 500th Mil. Intelligence Svc. Group, 1952-53; tchr. Hereford Jr.-Sr. H.S., Parkton, Md., 1957-59; aide Enoch Pratt Free Libr., Balt., 1959-61, profl. asst., 1962-64; coord. adult svcs. Washington County Free Libr., Hagerstown, Md., 1964-67; asst. regional libr. Eastern Shore Regional Libr., Salisbury, Md., 1967; br. libr. Balt. County Pub. Libr., Pikesville, Md., 1968-71, asst. area br. libr. Essex, Md., 1971-72, sr. info. specialist Catonsville, Md., 1972-87, on-line supr. Towson, Md., 1988-89, sr. info. specialist Reisterstown, Md., 1989-90; exec. dir. Milbourne and Tull Rsch. Ctr., 1991—2002; ret. Contbr. to profl. and geneal. jours. Mem. Rep. Ctrl. Com. Baltimore County, 1971-72. With U.S. Army, 1949-52. Fellow Nat. Congress Patriotic Orgns.; mem. Freedom To Read Found., Md. Libr. Assn. (chmn. intellectual freedom com. 1969-70), Friends Johns Hopkins U. Librs., Md. Assn. for Adult Edn. (coord. Western Md. region 1965-67), Am. Coun. Trustees and Alumni, Am. Acad. Religion, Ctr. for Theology and the Natural Scis., Metaphys. Soc. Am., Nat. Assn. Scholars, Woodrow Wilson Internat. Ctr. for Scholars, Assn. for Asian Studies, World Future Soc., Freedom House, Internat. Rescue Com., Nature Conservancy, Unitarian Universalist Hist. Soc, Unitarian and Universalist Geneal. Soc. (founder, bd. dirs. 1971-87), Md. Geneal. Soc., Royal Soc. St. George, Jamestowne Soc., Sons and Daus. Pilgrims, Descs. Early Quakers, SAR, Soc. War of 1812, Ancient and Hon. Mech. Co. Balt., Johns Hopkins U. Club, Salisbury U. Pres.'s Club, Rutgers Club, Kappa Delta Pi. Home: 800 Southerly Rd Apt 409 Towson MD 21286-8405 Personal E-mail: towson57rutgers62@gmail.com.

TULLER, MARKUS, geophysicist, educator; b. Bruck, Styria, Austria, Feb. 16, 1967; PhD, U. Natural Resources and Life Scis., Vienna, 1997. Assoc. prof. U. Idaho, Moscow, 2001—07, U. Ariz., Tucson, 2007—. Recipient NSIP Rsch. Advisor award, NASA, 2003. Mem.: SSSA (Soil Physics Early Career award 2003). Office: The Univ Ariz SWES Dept Shantz 38 Rm 526 Tucson AZ 85721 Business E-Mail: mtuller@cals.arizona.edu.

TULLIS, GREGORY EARL, research scientist; PhD, U. Mo., Columbia, 1992. Postdoctoral fellow Princeton U., NJ, 1993—99; rsch. scientist Avigen, Inc, Alameda, Calif., 1999—2000; rsch. asst. prof. U. Mo., 2001—06; assoc. prof. Boston U. Med. Sch., 2006—. Mem. editl. bd. Biomarkers Insights, 2006—. Contbr. articles to profl. jours., chapters to books. Jane Coffin-Childs Rsch. fellow, Jane Coffin-Childs Meml. Fund Med. Rsch., 1993—96. Mem.: AAAS, Internat. Soc. Stem Cell Rsch., Am. Soc. Virology, Am. Soc. Microbiology, Assn. Rsch. Vision and Ophthalmology, Am. Soc. Gene Therapy. Office: Boston U Med Sch 715 Albany St L905 Boston MA 02118 Business E-Mail: tullisg@bu.edu.

TULLY, CATHERINE T., lawyer; b. NY, Aug. 22, 1953; m. Jack Dierks, June 21, 1975; 3 children. BA, Valparaiso U., Ind., 1975; JD, Marquette U., Milw., 1978. Atty. Riordan, Crivello & Carlson, Milw., 1978—83; atty./shareholder Habush Habush & Rottier, Milw., 1983—. Software mgmt. comm. All Saints Cath. Ch., Milw., 1982—, All Saints Gospel Choir, 2007—. Mem.: ABA (mem. adv. panel 2008—), Am. Assn. Justice, Wis. Assoc Justice, Milw. Bar Assn., Wis. Bar Assn. Office: Habush Habush & Rottier SC 777 E Wis Ave Ste 2300 Milwaukee WI 53202 Business E-Mail: ctully@habush.com.

TULLY, DARROW, newspaper publisher; b. Charleston, W.Va., Feb. 27, 1932; s. William Albert and Dora (McCann) T.; m. Victoria Lynn Werner; children: Bonnie Tully Paul, Michael Andrew. Student, Purdue U., 1951; BA in Journalism, St. Joseph's Coll., 1972; PhD in Journalism (hon.), Calumet Coll., Ind., 1975. V.p., gen. mgr. Stas. WDSM-AM-FM and WDSM-TV, Duluth, Minn., 1956-59; bus. mgr. Duluth Herald & News Tribune, 1960-62; gen. mgr. St. Paul Dispatch & Pioneer Press, 1962-66; pub. Gary (Ind.) Post-Tribune, 1966-73; v.p., pub. Wichita (Kans.) Eagle & Beacon, 1973-75; pres. San Francisco Newspaper Agy., 1975-78; exec. v.p., pub. Ariz. Republic & Phoenix Gazette, 1978-85; editor., pub., chief exec. officer Ojai (Calif.) Valley News, 1987-90; pres., pub., CEO Beacon Comms., Acton, Mass., 1990-92; asst. to pres. newspaper divsn. Chronicle Pub. Co., 1992-94. Author: Minority Representation in the Media, 1968. Trustee Calumet Coll. Recipient Disting. Achievement award Ariz. State U., 1982, Disting. Journalist award No. Ariz. U./AP, 1983, 1st Pl. Editorial Writing award Ariz. Planned Parenthood, 1983. Mem. Am. Soc. Newspaper Editors, Soc. Profl. Journalists. Office: 9862 Bridgeton Dr Tampa FL 33626-1802 Office Phone: 813-926-9709. Personal E-mail: dtully1@tampabay.rr.com.

TULLY, MAC, publishing executive; m. Cindy Tully. BA, U. Kans. Pres. & pub. Bradenton Herald, Fla.; v.p. advt., pub. Arlington Star-Telegram, Tex.; corp. v.p. ops. Knight Ridder, 2004; pub. Kansas City Star, Mo., 2005—08; v.p. Bay Area News Group MediaNews Group, 2008—; pres., pub. San Jose Mercury News, 2008—. Bd. dirs. San Jose Silicon Valley C. of C. Recipient John S. Knight Gold medal, Knight Ridder. Office: San Jose Mercury News 750 Ridder Park Dr San Jose CA 95190 Office Phone: 816-234-4490. E-mail: mtully@kcstar.com.*

TULLY, MATHEW B., lawyer; s. Kevin Timothy and Alice Tully; m. Kimberly Jill Tully; 1 child, Kevin T. JD, Bklyn Law Sch., Brooklyn, NY, 1998—2002; BA, Hofstra U., Hempstead, NY, 1993—95; AA, Nassau C.C., Garden City, NY, 1991—93. Bar: NY State (Atty.) 2003. Detective Suffolk County SPCA, 1993—2002; peace officer/investigator Columbia-Greene SPCA, Hudson, NY, 2002—07; fed. law enforcement officer US Dept. Justice, NYC, 1995—2000; atty. Law Office of Mathew B. Tully, Hunter, NY, 2002—, 2002—08; litig. mgr. Morgan Stanley, NYC, 2000—02; chief Schenectady County SPCA, 2007—. Solicitor Supreme Ct. Eng. and Wales, 2008—. Columnist The Army Times Pub. Co., 2006—, (newspaper) The Saratogian, 2008—, host Tully Rinckey Legal Power Hour WGY, 2008—. Mem. NY State Juvenile Justice Adv. Group, Albany, NY, 2000—06, Nassau County Cultural Devel. Commn., Mineola, NY, 1992—2000. Capt., officer, paratrooper US Army, 1995—98, Fort Sill; Seoul, Republic of Korea, officer NY Army NG, 1998—, Latham, NY. Decorated Iraq Campaign medal, Global War on Terrorism Svc. medal; recipient Leadership award, Nat. Bus. Adv. Coun., 2006; named Pro Bono Atty. of Yr., Am.-Arab Anti-Discrimination Com., 2007; named one of Top 40 Under 40, Albany Bus. Rev., 2007, Irish Echo, 2009. Mem.: Res. Officers Assn., NRA, Fraternal Order Police (life), Nat. Press Club, VFW (life). Office: Rinckey PLLC Attys & Counselors at Law 441 New Karner Rd Albany NY 12205 Personal E-mail: mtully@tullylegal.com. E-mail: info@tullylegal.com.

TULLY, ROBERT GERARD, lawyer; b. Dubuque, Iowa, Sept. 7, 1955; s. Thomas Alois and Marjorie May (Fosselman) T. BA, U. Notre Dame, 1977; postgrad., U. Notre Dame, London, summer 1979; JD, Drake U., 1981. Bar: Iowa 1981, U.S. Dist. Ct (no. and so. dists.) Iowa 1981, U.S. Ct. Appeals (8th cir.) 1981, U.S. Supreme Ct. 1986. Assoc. Verne Lawyer & Assocs., Des Moines, 1981-93, Michael J. Galligan Law Firm; ptnr. Galligan, Tully, Doyle & Reid P.C., 1993, Anderson & Tully, Des Moines, 2003—. Bd. dirs. Dubuque Lumber Co., sec., treas., 1984-87; lectr. Nat. Collegiate Mock Trial Drake U., Des Moines, 1984-93, atty., coach, 1985-93; bd. counselors Drake U. Law Sch., 1986-92, 2005—, chmn. alumni rels. com. Contbr. articles to profl. jours. Com. mem. Dubuque County Dem. party, 1976-78, Polk County Dem. party, 1982-83, 87-89, 92—, del. state convs., 1988, chmn. IA Dem. Party, 1999-2007; bd. dirs. nat. Coun. Alcoholism and Other Drug Dependencies for Des Moines Area, pres. 1985-92; mem. nat. commn. on future of Drake U.; Dem. candidate for U.S. Congress 2d Dist., 1998. Fellow Iowa Acad. Trial Lawyers (compiler various profl. publs.); mem. ABA, ATLA (state del. 1991—, bd. govs. 1993-2003, key peron com.), Iowa Bar Assn. (Uniform Jury Instructions rules com., young lawyers sect., com. legal svcs. for elderly chmn. fed. practice com., law related edn. com.), Assn. Trial Lawyers Iowa (pres. 1992-93, pres.-elect 1991-92, v.p. legis. 1988-91, bd. govs. 1985—, Outstanding Key Person 1983-84, 91-92, chmn. key person com. 1985-88), Polk County Bar Assn. (bd. dirs. 1993—, grievance com.), Iowa Citizens Action Network (bd. dirs. 1989-98), Blackstone Inn of Ct., Notre Dame Club of Des Moines (pres. 1981-83), Drake Student Bar Assn. (pres. 1980-81), Phi Alpha Delta. Roman Catholic. Home: 4315 Greenwood Dr Des Moines IA 50312 Office: Anderson and Tully 700 W Towers 1200 Valley West Dr West Des Moines IA 50266-1908 E-mail: tully@andersontullylaw.com.

TULOWITZKI, TROY TREVOR, professional baseball player; b. Santa Clara, Calif., Oct. 10, 1984; s. Ken and Susan Tulowitzki. Grad. in Kinesiology, Calif. State U., Long Beach, 2005. Shortstop Colo. Rockies, 2006—. Shortstop Grand Canyon Rafters (Ariz. Fall League), 2006. Recipient Fielding Bible award, 2007; named Spring Tng. MVP, Colo. Rockies, 2007; named to Topps Maj. League Rookie All-Star Team, 2007. Achievements include reaching the Major Leagues in the shortest time span between draft day and debut in Rockies franchise history (one year, 83 days); turning the 13th unassisted triple play in Major League history, April 29, 2007; setting a new record for the most home runs in a single season by a National League rookie with 20, 2007; leading all Major League shortstops in fielding percentage (.987) and double plays turned (114) during the 2007 season; being a member of the 2004 National League Champion Colorado Rockies; signing the largest contract ever for a player with less than two year experience, 2008. Office: c/o Colo Rockies Coors Field 2001 Blake St Denver CO 80205

TUMA, MYM, sculptor, painter, educator; b. Berwyn, Ill., Sept. 23, 1940; d. William Anthony Thuma and Mabel Otradovec Thuma. BS, Northwestern U., 1959—62; MA in painting and philosophy, Stanford U., 1963—64; post-graduate study under Esteban Vicente, NYU, 1964—65. Cert. art tchr. NY, 1993. Tchr. State of Ill., 1972—73, The Clearing, Ellison Bay, Wis., 1978. Guest lectr. O'Keeffe Centennial Celebration Columbia Coll., SC, 1987, Bklyn. Mus., 1993. Exhibitions include Canyon Road Art Gallery, Sante Fe, 1971, Clayton-Liberatore Gallery, Bridgehampton, NY, 1992, Merchants Bank, So. Hero, Vt., 2005, Madelle H. Semerjian Gallery, Rogers Meml. Libr., 2006, Hampton Art Scene, Quogue Gallery, Quogue Libr., NY, 2009; artist (one-woman shows) Art League, La Grange, Ill., 1987, Edens Gallery, Columbia Coll., 1987, (prin. works) Pastel Drawings and Abstract Sculptured Paintings, (permanent collections) Hirshhorn Mus., Wash., Stanford Mus., Palo Alto, Calif.; author: Awakening the Spirit, 2001, The Shell Theory of the Sculptured Paintings, 2002, The Blue Planets, 2003, O'Keeffe & Me: Abstracts of Our Letters, 2004, Radiant Energy, 2005, God's Architecture: The Spiral-Sphere, 2009. Harley J. Earl scholar, art and arch. dept. Stanford U., 1963—64. Mem.: Nat. Mus. Women in Arts (charter mem.), Coll. Art Assn. Home: PO Box 549 Southampton NY 11969 Office Phone: 631-878-0287. Personal E-mail: okeeffeandme.com.

TUMA, STANISLAV JOSEF, radiologist; b. Mělník, Czech Republic, Mar. 30, 1934; s. Josef and Marta (Panochová) T.; m. Vanda Langrová, May 10, 1954 (div. 1966); children: Zuzana, Ondřej, Magdalena; m. Jitka Fabichová, Nov. 2, 1990. MD, Charles U., Prague, Czech Republic, 1958, cert. pediat. I, 1962, cert. radiology I, 1964, CSc, 1970, cert. radiology II, 1971. Med. registrar Dist. Hosp., Šumperk, Czech Republic, 1958-60, Clinic of Pediat., Prague, 1960-64, X-Ray Dept., Prague, 1964-70; rsch.fellow Pediat. Cardiocenter, Prague, 1970-90; head Clinic Imaging Methods, Prague, 1990-99; head dept. rsch. and edn. Ministry Health Czech Republic, 2000—02. Prof. South Bohemian U., Ceske Budejovice, 2003. Editor: Congenital Anomalies, 1995, Dextrocardia, 1999; contbr. articles to profl. jours. Office: Clinic Imaging Methods U Hosp Motol V Uvalu 84 CZ 150 06 Prague 5 Czech Republic Office Phone: 420-22-443-8101. Business E-Mail: sttuma@volny.cz.

TUMAS, MICHAEL B., lawyer; b. South Bend, Ind., Apr. 25, 1959; BA in Econs., SUNY, Binghamton, 1981; JD, U. Pa., 1984. With Potter Anderson & Corroon LLP, Wilmington, Del., 1984—, mem. firm, 1992—, chmn. corp. group, 2006—. Office: Potter Anderson & Corroon LLP 1313 N Market St Wilmington DE 19801 Office Phone: 302-984-6029. Office Fax: 302-778-6029. E-mail: mtumas@potteranderson.com.

TUMAY, MEHMET TANER, geotechnical engineering educator, researcher, consultant; b. Feb. 2, 1937; arrived in US, 1959; s. Bedrettin and Muhterem (Uybadin) T.; m. Karen Nuttycombe, June 15, 1962; children: Peri, Suna. BSCE, Robert Coll. Sch. Engring., Istanbul, Turkey, 1959; MSCE, U. Va., 1961; postgrad., UCLA, 1963—64; PhD, Tech. U. Istanbul, 1971. Lic. civil engr., La., Ga., SC, Turkish Chamber of Civil Engring. Instr. civil engring. U. Va., Charlottesville, 1961-62; asst. prof. civil engring. U. Louisville, 1962-63; tchg. fellow UCLA, 1963-64; asst. prof. civil engring. Robert Coll. Sch. Engring., Istanbul, 1966-71; assoc. prof. dept. civil engring. Bogazici U., Istanbul, 1971-75; Fugro-Cesco postdoctoral rsch. fellow U. Fla., Gainesville, 1975-76; Ga. Gulf disting. prof. La. State U., Baton Rouge, 1976—2005, prof. emeritus, 2005—. Adv. prof. U. Vicosa, Minas Gerais, Brazil, 1991—, Tongji U., Shanghai, 1991—; dir. geomechanics program NSF, Washington, 1990-94; dir. rsch. La. Transp. Rsch. Ctr., Baton Rouge, 1994-97; assoc. dean rsch. and grad. studies Coll. Engring., La. State U., 1997-2004; maitre de conferences Ecole Nationale des Ponts et Chaussees, Paris, 1980-94; geotech. cons. Sauti, Spa, Cons. Engrs., Italy, 1969-72, SOFRETU-RATP, Paris, 1972-73, D.E.A., Cons. Engrs., Istanbul, 1974-75, BOTEK, Ltd., Istanbul, 1975—, Senler-Campbell Assocs., Louisville, 1979-90, Fugro Gulf-Geogulf, Houston, 1980-83; cons. in field. Contbr. articles to profl. jours. AID scholar, 1975-76, French Ministry External Rels. scholar, 1982. Fellow: ASCE; mem.: ASTM, Transp. Rsch. Bd. of the Nat. Acads, (emeritus), Internat. Soc. Soil Mechanics and Found. Engring., Turkish Chamber Civil Engrs., Turkish Soil Mechanics Group, La. Engring. Soc., Am. Soc. Engring. Edn., Tau Beta Pi, Chi Epsilon, Sigma Xi. Home: 2217 Dove Hollow Dr Baton Rouge LA 70809-1275 Office: La State U Coll Engring Baton Rouge LA 70803-0001 Home Phone: 225-927-7719; Office Phone: 225-578-9165. Business E-Mail: mtumay@eng.lsu.edu.

TUMLINSON, ALEXANDRE REX, biomedical engineer, researcher; b. Spokane, Wash., July 16, 1976; s. Thomas William and Janell Rae Tumlinson; m. Anna Catherine Gradillas, Sept. 29, 2007. BS in Optical Engring., U. Ariz., Tucson, 1998, MS in Optical Sci., 2003, PhD in Biomed. Engring., 2007. Lab asst. Zetetic Inst., Tucson, 1995; student sys. adminstr. U. Ariz., Tucson, 1995—97, grad. rsch. assoc., 2001—07; asst. rsch. scientist Innovative Lasers Corp., Tucson, 1997; jr. applications engr. Opto Power Corp., Tucson, 1998; optical engr. Etec Sys. Corp., Tucson, 1999—2001; guest rschr. Med. U. Viena, 2004—05; rsch. assoc. Cardiff U., Wales, England, 2007—. With peer rev. svc. Nature Protocols, Jour. Biomed. Optics, Optical Comm., Applied Optics. Contbr. articles to sci. jours., chapters to books. Chpt. rec. sec., pres. Eta Kappa Nu, Elec. Engring. Honor Soc., Tucson, 1996—98; vol. Pedal Power Cycling, Cardiff, 2007—08. Fulbright fellowship to Austria, Fulbright Found., 2004—05, fellowship to Austria, Ernst-Mach found., 2004. Mem.: Assn. Rsch. Vision and Ophthalmology, Soc. Photonic and Indsl. Engrs. Achievements include patents for combination lamp assembly; patents pending for optical coherence tomography endoscope utilizing a distally integrated interferometer. Office: Sch Optometry Cardiff Univ Maindy Rd Cardiff Wales CF24 4LU England Business E-Mail: tumlinsonar@cardiff.ac.uk.

TUMLINSON, JAMES H., III, agriculturist; BS in Chemistry, Va. Mil. Inst., Lexington, 1960; MS in Organic Chemistry, Miss. State U., 1966, PhD in Organic Chemistry, 1969. Chemist Boll Weevil Rsch. Lab. USDA-Agrl. Rsch. Svc., State Coll., Miss., 1964-69, rsch. chemist, Insect Attractants, Behavior, and Basic Biology Rsch. Lab. Gainesville, Fla., 1970-72, rsch. leader Ctr. Med., Agrl., and Vet. Entomology, 1972—2003; postdoctoral NY State Coll. Forestry, Syracuse, 1969—70; adj. asst. prof. U. Fla. Inst. Food Agr., Gainesville, 1970—75, adj. assoc. prof., doctoral faculty, 1975—82, adj. prof., doctoral faculty, 1982—; Ralph O. Mumma prof. entomology Pa. State U., U. Pk., 2003—. FAO cons. Nuclear Rsch. Ctr., Demokritos, Greece, 1974; mem. Boll Wevil Pheromone Devel. Group, 1975; rsch. leader Insect Chemistry Rsch. Group, 1983. Recipient Superior Svc. award, USDA, 1975, 1983, Sec. Agrl. award, 1995, award Outstanding Rsch. and Leadership, Agrl. Rsch. Svc., 1979, Disting. Scientist of Yr., 1984, Hall of Fame, 1998, Burdick and Jackson Internat. award, Am. Chem. Soc., 1986, Disting. Lectr. in Life Scis., Boyce Thompson Inst. Plant Rsch., 1998, Kenneth A. Spencer award, 2002, listed in top 1% of environment/ecology citations, ISI Essential Sci. Indicators, 2002, Presdl. Rank award as Meritorious Sr. Profl., USDA, Agrl. Rsch. Svc., 2003, Jean-Marie Delwart Found. prize, 2003; co-recipient Ann. Rsch. award, Fla. Entomol. Soc., 1991, Wolf Found. prize in Agr., Israel, 2008; Agrl. Rsch. Svc. fellowship, Ctr. Insect Sci., U. Ariz., 1989. Fellow Entomol. Soc. Am. (J.E. Bussart Meml. award 1990, Recognition award 2000); mem. NAS, Internat. Soc. Chem. Ecology (v.p. 1997, pres. 1998). Office: Usda Ars 1600 SW 23rd Dr Gainesville FL 32608-1067

TUMMALA, V.M RAO, supply chain management and operations educator; b. Pedalimgala, Andhra Pradesh, India, Sept. 10, 1937; s. Veeraiah and Venkata Subbamma Tummala; m. Parvati V. Yanamadala, May 12, 1955; children: Chandra Sekhara V., Prabhakar, Sreenidhi. PhD, Mich. State U., East Lansing, 1967. Prof. mgmt. sci. U. Detroit, 1967—81; prof. ops. and supply chain mgmt. Ea. Mich. U., Ypsilanti, 1981—. Visitng prof. City U., Hong Kong, 1992—96. Contbr. articles to profl. jours. Pres., and founding sec. Telugu Assn. of N.Am., Detroit, 1979—81. Recipient Outstanding Rsch., Coll. Bus., 1997, 1998, 2002. Achievements include research in field of project risk management, quality management, supply chain management, bayesian decision theory and analytic hierarchy process. Home: 2385 St Francis Dr Ann Arbor MI 48104 Office: Coll Business Ea Mich Univ Ypsilanti MI 48197 Office Fax: 734-487-1941; Home Fax: 734-487-1941. Business E-Mail: rao.tummala@emich.edu.

TUMOLA, THOMAS JOSEPH, lawyer; b. Newton Square, Pa., Jan. 18, 1941; s. Joseph Thomas and Vera P. Tumola; m. Sarabelle Hare, Aug. 19, 1972; children: Thomas Joseph Jr., Cristabel Hill. BS in Economics, Villanova U., 1962; JD, Villanova U. Sch. Law, 1966; Postgraduate, Temple U., 1970—72. Lic.: Pa. 1967, US Ct. Appeals (3rd Cir.) 1967, US Dist. Ct. (ea. dist.) Pa., US Tax Ct. 1971, Supreme Ct. Pa. Law clk. to Hon. Harry E. Kalodner US Ct. Appeals (3rd Cir.), 1966—68; assoc. Clark, Ladner, Fortenbaugh & Young, Phila., 1968—73, ptnr., 1974—96, Duane Morris LLP (formerly Duane, Morris & Heckscher), Phila., 1996—. Mem. advisory task force Revision of Pa. Navigation Commn. Law, 1978. Mem.: ABA, Phila. Bar Assn., Pa. Bar Assn., Italian Am. Chamber of Commerce, Phila. Maritime Soc., Union League, Gamma Phi. Office: Duane Morris LLP 30 S 17th St Philadelphia PA 19103 Office Phone: 215-979-1286. Office Fax: 215-689-4471. E-mail: TJTumola@duanemorris.com.*

TUNE, JAMES FULCHER, lawyer; b. Danville, Va., May 13, 1942; s. William Orrin and Susan Agnes (Fulcher) T.; m. Katherine Del Mickey, Aug. 2, 1969; children: Katherine Winslow, Jeffrey Bricker. BA, U. Va., 1964; MA, Stanford U., 1970, JD, 1974. Bar: Wash. 1974, U.S. Dist. Ct. (we. dist.) Wash. 1974. Assoc. Bogle & Gates, Seattle, 1974-79, ptnr., 1980-99, head comml./banking dept., 1985-93, mng. ptnr., 1986-93, chmn., 1994-99; ptnr. Dorsey & Whitney LLP, Seattle, 1999—2000, Stoel Rives LLP, Seattle, 2001—05, Seattle mng. ptnr., 2001—05; pres., CEO ArtsFund, Seattle, 2006—. Bd. dirs. Keynetics Inc., Boise, Idaho,

Click Sales Inc., Boise, Kount Inc., Boise, Pay-Track Inc., Boise, Puget Sound Bank, Bellevue, Wash.; chmn. Seattle-King City Econ. Devel. Coun., 1992. Chmn. Seattle Repertory Theatre, 1995, Corp. Coun. for the Arts, 2001—02, United Way King County, 2004. Lt. USN, 1964—69, Vietnam. Woodrow Wilson fellow, 1964, Danforth Found. fellow, 1964. Mem. ABA, Wash. State Bar Assn. (lectr. CLE 1976, 78, 84, 99, 02), Seattle C. of C. (vice chmn. City Budget Task Force 1980-82), Greater Seattle C. of C. (trustee 2006—), Ranier Club (trustee 2006—), Seattle Tennis Club, Phi Beta Kappa. Presbyterian. Office: ArtsFund PO Box 19780 10 Harrison St Ste 200 Seattle WA 98109 Home Phone: 206-329-0372; Office Phone: 206-281-9050. Business E-Mail: jimtune@artsfund.org.

TUNG, CHIA-CHI, mathematics professor; BS, Nat. Taiwan U., 1967; PhD, U. Notre Dame, South Bend, Ind., 1973. Prof. Minn. State U., 1990—; wissenschaftlicher mitarbeiter, sonderforschungsbereich theoretische math. U. Bonn, 1980—81. Dickson instr. U. Chgo., 1973—75. Contbr. articles to profl. jours. Mem.: Am. Math. Soc. Achievements include research in singular spaces,value distribution for schubert zeroes. Office: Minn State Univ Mankato MN 56001 Office Phone: 507-389-5909. Business E-Mail: chia.tung@mnsu.edu.

TUNG, KO-YUNG, lawyer; b. Peking, China, Feb. 20, 1947; came to U.S., 1964; s. Hung-Fang T. and Koichiro Tanaka; m. Alison Heydt, Feb. 2, 1975; children: Vanessa, Adrian, Cameron, Gregory. BA, Harvard U., 1970; JD, U. Tokyo, 1972. Bar: NY, 1972. Assoc. Debevoise & Plimpton, NYC, 1973—76; ptnr. Tung, Drabkin & Boynton, NYC, 1976—84, O'Melveny & Myers, NYC, 1985—99; v.p., gen. counsel The World Bank, Washington, 1999—2003; sec.-gen. Internat. Ctr. Settlement Investment Disputes, Washington, 2000—03; sr. counsellor Morrison & Foerster, NYC, 2003—. Adj. assoc. prof. sch. law NYU, 1974—88; vis. lectr. Yale Law Sch., 2003—. Mem. Coun. on Fgn. Rels., N.Y.C., 1986—, The Brookings Inst., 1999, Overseas Devel. Coun., Washington, 1999, The Japan Soc., 1990, Asia Soc., 1994-99, Presl. Commn. U.S. Pacific Trade Investment Policy, 1996-97, Trilateral Commn., N.Y.C., 1990-97; bd. govs. East West Ctr., Honolulu, 1990-99, 2003—, chmn., 1997-99; U.S. Nat. Commn. for Pacific Econ. Cooperation, 1991—; bd. dirs. Asian Am. Legal Def. and Edn. Fund, 1990-99, 2003—; vice chmn. adv. coun. Human Rights Watch/Asia, 1997-99, 2003-. Fellow Harvard Law Sch., 1973. Mem. Am. Law Inst., Am. Arbitration Assn., Internat. Panel Arbitrators, Phi Beta Kappa. Office: Morrison & Foerster 1290 Avenue of the Americas New York NY 10104 Office Phone: 212-468-8055. Business E-Mail: Ktung@mofo.com.

TUNG, ROSALIE L., business educator, consultant; came to U.S., 1975; d. Andrew and Pauline Lam; m. Byron Tung; 1 chlid, Michele BA, York U., 1972; MBA, U. B.C., 1974, PhD Bus. Adminstrn., 1977. Lectr. diploma divsn. U. B.C., 1975, lectr. exec. devel. program, 1975; asst. prof. mgmt. Grad. Sch. Mgmt. U. Oreg., Eugene, 1977—80; assoc. prof. U. Pa., Phila., 1981—86; prof., dir. internat. bus. ctr. U. Wis., Milw., 1986—90; endowed chaired prof. Simon Fraser U., 1991—. Fgn. expert Fgn. Investment Commn., China; vis. scholar U. Manchester (Eng.) Sci. and Tech., 1980; vis. prof. UCLA, 1981, Harvard U., 1988, Copenhagen Bus. Sch., 1995, 97, 2006, 07, Chinese U. Hong Kong, 1997, Peking U., 2001, China Europe Internat. Bus. Sch., 2002-03, U. Auckland, 2006; disting. prof. U. Wis. Sys., 1988-90, Ming and Stella Wong chair internat. bus., 1991— Author: Management Practices in China, 1980, U.S.-China Trade Negotiations, 1982, Chinese Industrial Society After Mao, 1982, Business Negotiations with the Japanese, 1984, Key to Japan's Economic Strength: Human Power, 1984, The New Expatriates: Managing Human Resources Abroad, 1988; editor: Strategic Management in the U.S. and Japan, 1987, International Management in International Library of Business and Management Series, 1994, Internat. Ency. Bus. and Mgmt., 1996, IEBM Handbook of International Business, 1998, Learning from World Class Companies, 2001 Recipient Leonore Rowe Williams award U. Pa., 1990, U. B.C. Alumni 75th Anniversary award, 1990, Advanced Global Competitiveness Rsch. award, 1997, Woman of Distinction in Professions, Mgmt. and Trades award YWCA, Vancouver, 1998; York U. scholar, 1972; U. fellow, Seagram Bus. fellow, H.R. MacMillan Family fellow; Oppenheimer Bros. Found. fellow, 1973-74, U. B.C. fellow, 1974-75, H.R. Macmillan Found. fellow, 1975-77 Fellow Royal Soc. Can., Acad. Mgmt. (bd. govs. 1987-89, v.p. 2001-02, pres. 2003—), Internat. Acad. Cultural Rsch. (founding), Acad. Internat. Bus. (exec. bd., treas. 1985-86), Brit. Acad. Mgmt.; mem. Internat. Assn. Applied Psychology, Am. Arbitration Assn. (comml. panel arbitrators) Roman Catholic. Avocation: creative writing. Office: Simon Fraser U Faculty Bus Adminstrn Burnaby BC Canada V5A 1S6 Business E-Mail: tung@sfu.ca.

TUNKEY, JAMES PETER, security firm executive; b. Newmarket, Ontario, Canada, May 18, 1971; BA, SUNY, Buffalo, 1995; MBA, NYU, 2004. Dir. Kroll Assocs., Wanchai, Hong Kong, 1995—2001, Pinkerton Cons. & Investigations, Hong Kong, 2002—04; COO I-OnAsia, NYC, 2004—. Bd. dirs. Internat. Coun. Life Scis., Washington, 2005—, World Water Ctr., Fredericksburg, Va., 2005—; mem. Internat. Inst. Strategic Studies, London, 2005—. Mem.: Coun. Fgn. Rels., Profl. Risk Mgrs. Internat. Assn. (regional dir. 2006—), ASIS Internat. (assoc.). D-Conservative. Office: I-OnAsia 1603 Lever Tech 69-71 King Yip St Kowloon Kwun Tong 0000 Hong Kong Home: 175 W 85TH St Apt 27A New York NY 10024-2910 Office Fax: 852-2217-4449. Business E-Mail: james@ionasia.com.hk.

TUNNEY, JOHN VARICK, lawyer, former United States Senator from California; b. NYC, June 26, 1934; s. Gene and Mary (Lauder) T.; m. Kathinka Osborne, April 1977; children: Edward Eugene, Mark Andrew, Arianne Sprengers, Tara Theodora. BA in Anthropology, Yale, 1956; JD, U. Va., 1959; student, Acad. Internat. Law, The Hague, Netherlands, 1957. Bar: N.Y. 1959, Calif. 1963, Va. 1963. With firm Cahill, Gordon, Reindel & Ohl, NYC, 1959-60; tchr. bus. law U. Calif., Riverside, 1961-62; practice law Riverside, 1963—; mem. 89th-91st Congresses from Calif. 38th Dist., U.S. Senate from Calif., 1971-77; mem. firm Manatt, Phelps, Rothenberg & Tunney, Los Angeles, 1977-86; chmn. bd. Cloverleaf Group, Inc., Los Angeles, 1986—; gen. ptnr. Sun Valley Ventures, 1994—; pres. JVT Consulting, Inc., 1997—. Chmn. bd. Enterprise Plan, Inc., chmn. bd. Trusted Brands Inc.; bd. dirs. Prospect Group Inc., Garnet Resources Corp., Ill. Central Railroad, The Forschner Group, Inc., Foamex Internat.; bd. dir. Proscpect Group Inc. Polit. commentator Station KABC-TV. Trustee Westminster Sch., St. Matthews Sch.; bd. visitors Loyola Law Sch.; vice chmn. Limited Incomes Housing Corp.; mem. Lawyers Adv. Council. Constl. Rights Found., Citizens Rsch. Found., Commn. on Soviet Jewry. Served to capt. USAF, 1960-63. Chubb fellow Yale U., 1967 Mem. Am. Bar Assn. Democrat. Episcopalian. Office: 1819 Ocean Ave Santa Monica CA 90401-3223

TUNNEY, THOMAS M., alderman, restaurant owner; b. Chgo. B, U. Ill.; M, Cornell U. Sch. Hotel and Restaurant Mgmt., Ithaca, NY. Owner Ann Sather Restaurants, Chgo., 1981—; alderman, 44th ward Chgo. City Coun., 2003—. Former chmn. Ill. Restaurant Assn.; former pres. Lakeview Ctr. Bus. Assn.; founding bd. dir., former chmn. White Crane Sr. Ctr. Office: 1057 W Belmont Ave Chicago IL 60657 also: 121 N Lasalle St Rm 300 Office 14 Chicago IL 60602 also: Ann Sather Restaurant & Catering 909 W Belmont Chicago IL 60657 Office Phone: 773-525-6034, 312-744-3073, 773-348-2378. Office Fax: 773-525-5058. Business E-Mail: ward44@cityofchicago.org, tom@annsather.com.*

TUNNICLIFF, DAVID GEORGE, retired civil engineer; b. Ord, Nebr., Sept. 18, 1931; s. George Thomas and Ada Ellen (Ward) Tunnicliff; m. Elaine Jean Interrante, Oct. 17, 1959 (div.); children: Martha Allison Tunnicliff Loeb, Vivian Jean; m. Joan Elizabeth Duchesneau, Oct. 25, 1975. BS, U. Nebr., Lincoln, 1954; MS, Cornell U., Ithaca, NY, 1958; PhD, U. Mich., Ann Arbor, 1972. Registered profl. engr., Nebr., Mass. Engr. Nebr. Dept. Rds., Lincoln, 1954-60; from asst. prof. to assoc. prof. Wayne State U., Detroit, 1960-67; chief tech. svcs. Warren Bros. Co., Cambridge, Mass., 1967-79; prin., cons. engr. D.G. Tunnicliff, Cons. Engr., Omaha, 1979—2007; ret. Contbr. articles to profl. jours. Rep. precinct del., Detroit, 1965—66. With US Army, 1955—56. Mem.: ASCE, ASTM, Transp. Rsch. Bd. (com. chair 1983—89), Assn. Asphalt Paving Tech. (bd. dirs. 1976—78). Mem. Evangel. Convenant Ch. Home and Office: DG Tunnicliff Cons Engr 9624 Larimore Ave Omaha NE 68134-3038 Office Phone: 402-572-8955. Personal E-mail: dgtnnclff@aol.com.

TUNSTALL, GRAYDON ALLEN, history professor, professional society administrator; b. Laurel, Md., May 29, 1941; s. Graydon Allen and Valance Townsend Tunstall; m. Wendy Marie Tunstall-Werner; 1 child, Graydon Allen III. AB, Dickinson Coll., Carlisle, Pa., 1963; MA, Rutgers U., New Brunswick, NJ, 1967, PhD, 1973. V.p. for advancement St. Johns, The Gt. Book Coll., Santa Fe, 1987—88; vis. prof. European history U. Cin., 1988—90; post-graduate seminar in mil. history US Mil. Acad., West Point, NY, 1991—93; assoc. prof. European history Cedar Crest Coll., Allentown, Pa., 1993—2000; lectr. U. South Fla., Tampa, 2000—. Vis. prof. European history Lafayette Coll., Easton, 1990—93; exec. dir. Phi Alpha Theta History Honor Soc., Tampa, 1994—. Author: Planning for War Against Russia and Serbia: Austro-Hungarian and German Military Strategies, 1871-1914, Blood in the Snow: The Carpathian Winter War 1915; contbr. book, articles to profl. jours. Lectr. Osher Lifelong Learning Inst., U. South Fla., Tampa, 2006—07. 1st lt. US Army, 1963—65. Recipient Superior Tchr. award in the Social Sciences, Lafayette Coll., 1991, 1993. Mem.: Assn. Coll. Honor Socs., The Gt. War Soc., Soc. for Mil. History, Soc. for the Advancement of Habsburg Studies, Orgn. Am. Historians, Am. Hist. Assn., The Hist. Soc. (bd. mem. 2006—07), Western Front Assn. (bd. mem. 2003—07), Assn. for the Study of Hungarian History (bd. mem. 1998—2002), Am. Assn. for the Advancement of Slavic Studies. Office: Univ South Florida 4202 E Fowler Ave SOC 107 Tampa FL 33620-8100 Office Fax: 813-974-8215. Personal E-mail: graydontunstall@yahoo.com. Business E-Mail: tunstall@cas.usf.edu.

TUOHEY, CONRAD GRAVIER, lawyer; b. Bklyn., Dec. 27, 1933; s. James L. and Rose Gravier Tuohey; m. Judith Octavia Jeeves, July 7, 1956; children: Octavia Jeeves, Heather Gravier, Meighan Judith, Caragh Rose. BA, George Washington U., 1957; JD, U. Mich., 1960. Bar: Calif. 1962, N.Y. 1980, D.C. 1980. Dir. Fed. Home Loan Bank, San Francisco, 1980—83; legal cons., counsel Calif. State Senate, 1981—87; counsel Senate Select com. Pacific Rim, 1986—87. Mem. Citizens adv. bd. Orange County Transit com., 1966—68; pres. Friends of Calif. State U., Fullerton, 1969—71, Calif. Alliance Ptnrs. Progress, 1969—72; mem. InterAm. bd. Ptnrs. Alliance Progress, 1969—72; mem. nat. bd. dirs., 1970—72. Contbr. articles to profl. jours. With US Army, 1951—54, leader rifle squad. Decorated Combat Infantryman's badge, Korean Svc. medal with 3 battle stars. Mem.: D.C. Bar Assn., State Bar Calif., Phi Sigma Kappa, Phi Delta Phi. Home and Office: 23391 Rockrose Mission Viejo CA 92692-1686 E-mail: tuohey@lawyer.com.

TUOHEY, MARK HENRY, III, lawyer; b. Rochester, NY, Sept. 27, 1946; s. Mark Henry Tuohey; m. Martha Tuohey; children: Brendan, Sean, Devin. BA in History, St. Bonaventure U., 1968; JD, Fordham U., 1973. Bar: D.C. 1973, U.S. Supreme Ct. 1980, U.S. Ct. Appeals (D.C. cir.) 1974, U.S. Dist. Ct. D.C. 1974, N.Y. 1984. Asst. U.S. atty. U.S. Atty.'s Office, Washington, 1973-77; spl. trial counsel U.S. Dept. Justice, Washington, 1977-79; spl. counsel to U.S. Atty. Gen. Washington, 1979; co-adminstrv. ptnr. Washington office Vinson & Elkins, 2000—04; prin. dep. ind. counsel Whitewater Investigation, 1994-95; spl. counsel D.C. City Coun. Investigation of Met. Police Dept., 1998. Trustee Cath. U. Am., 2002—, Washington Jesuit Acad., 1999—2004, Gonzaga Coll. H.S., 1993—2003. Served to 1st lt. US Army, 1970—71. Named Washingtonian of Yr., Washingtonian Mag., 2006; named one of Best Lawyers in Am., 2003—. Fellow: Am. Bar Found. (bd. dirs. 1980—85), Am. Law Inst., Am. Coll. Trial Lawyers; mem.: ABA (chair standing com. on continuing edn. bar 1980—85, litig. sect. coun. 1980—90, mem. Am. Law Inst./ABA com. continuing profl. edn. 1983—), Corp. Ireland, US (chair 2007—), Bar Assn. D.C. (Lawyer of the Yr. 2001), Jud. Conf. US Ct. Appeals (DC cir.), DC Bar Found. (chair 1998—2003), DC Bar (bd. govs. 1988—94, pres. 1993—94), DC Sports and Entertainment Commission (chair 2003—07). Home: 1655 Kalmia Rd NW Washington DC 20012-1125 Office: Vinson Elkins 950 F St NW Ste 550 Washington DC 20004-1463 Office Phone: 202-639-6660. Business E-Mail: mtuohey@velaw.com.

TUOHY, PATRICIA ANNE, library director, consultant; d. Wilfred J Tuohy; m. Eugene S. Cuny III, 1948; children: Zeke H. Cuny, Kittrick C. Cuny. BA, U. Tex., Austin, 1970, MLS, 1972; MPA, Tex. State U., San Marcos, 1985. Coord., CTLS Austin Pub. Libr., Tex., 1982—2005, br. libr., 1972—77; exec. dir. Ctrl. Tex. Libr. Sys., Inc, Austin, 2005—. Info. coord. Tex. Dept Cmty. Affairs, Austin, 1978—81. Mem.: Tex. Libr. Assn. (mem. 1973—2008). Office: Ctrl Tex Libr Sys Inc 1005 W 41st St Austin TX 78756 Business E-Mail: pat.tuohy@ctls.net.

TUR, CLARISSE, physicist; d. Feyzi and Derman Tur. BS in physics, U. Paris Sud XI, Orsay, 2000; MS in physics, U. SC., Columbia, 2003, PhD in physics, 2005. Postdoc. rsch. assoc. Nat. Superconducting Cyclotron Lab., Mich. State U., East Lansing, 2005—08; applications physicist Saint-Gobain Crystals, Hiram, Ohio, 2008—. Contbr. scientific papers. Recipient Rsch. award, Dept. Physics, U. SC, 2005; Rsch. fellowship, Jefferson Lab. and South Ea. U. Rsch. Assn., 2003—05, Dept. Physics, U. SC, 2001—04. Office: Saint Gobain Crystals 17900 Gt Lakes Parkway Hiram OH 44234

TURAGA, DEEPAK SRINIVAS, electrical and computer engineer, researcher; B in Tech., Indian Inst. of Tech., Mumbai, India, 1997; PhD, Carnegie Mellon U., Pitts., 2001. Sr. mem. rsch. staff Philips Rsch. USA, Briarcliff Manor, NY, 2001—03; sr. rsch. engr. Sony Electronics, San Jose, Calif., 2003—04; rsch. staff mem. IBM T. J. Watson Rsch. Ctr., Hawthorne, NY, 2004—. Author: (book) MPEG4: Beyond Conventional Video Coding, (book chpt.) Fundamentals of Video Compression: H.263 as an example, 35 conf. and jour. papers. Mem.: IEEE (assoc. editor IEEE Transactions on Multimedia 2004—06). Achievements include patents pending for 8 Patents Pending on Multimedia Processing and Compression.

TURBIDY, JOHN BERRY, investor, management consultant; b. Rome, Ga., Oct. 18, 1928; s. Joseph Leo and Louyse (Berry) T.; m. Joan Marsales, Dec. 19, 1958 (dec.); children: John Berry, Trevor Martin; m. Jaquelin Lamond Schulter, June 8, 1996 Grad., Darlington Sch., 1945; BA, Duke U., 1950; postgrad., NYU, 1952, Emory U., 1954-56. Various positions Lockheed Aircraft, Marietta, Ga., 1951-56; gen. mgmt. cons. McKinsey & Co., NYC and London, 1956—62; v.p. adminstrn. ITT Europe, Inc., Brussels, 1963, v.p., group exec. European consumer products, 1963—65, v.p., group exec. for No. Europe, 1965-67; corp. v.p. adminstrn. Celanese Corp., NYC, 1967-68; pres., mng. dir. SIACE, SP.A. subs., Milan, 1968-69; chmn. bd., pres. Vecta Group, Kalamazoo, 1970-74; sr. v.p. corp. devel. IU Internat. Corp., Phila., 1974-78, exec. v.p., 1978-83; pres., chief exec. officer Pitcairn Fin. Mgmt. Group, Jenkintown, Pa., 1984-90; chmn. Office John Turbidy, 1990-95; mng. dir. Friedman, Turbidy & Co., Inc., NYC, 1995—2000. Bd. dirs. Statute of Liberty Ellis Island Found., 1982-2004, chmn. 2003-08. Served with USNR, 1952 Mem. Sea Island Club. Address: 113 Biltmore Saint Simons Island GA 31522 Personal E-mail: jbturb@hotmail.com.

TURCHIN, PETER, biology professor; b. Obninsk, Kaluga, Russia, May 22, 1957; s. Valentin and Tatiana Turchin; m. Olga Turchin. PhD, Duke U., Durham, 1985. Prof. U. Conn., Storrs, 1994—. Author: (book) War and Peace and War: The Rise and Fall of Empires. Office: Univ Conn 75 N Eagleville Rd Storrs Mansfield CT 06269

TURCO, LEWIS PUTNAM, writer, English educator; b. Buffalo, May 2, 1934; s. Luigi and May Laura (Putnam) T.; m. Jean Cate Houdlette, May 29, 1934; children: Melora Ann, Christopher Cameron. BA, U. Conn., Storrs, 1959; MA, U. Iowa, Iowa City, 1962; LHD (hon.), Ashland U., Ohio, 2000, U. Maine Ft. Kent, 2009. Instr. Cleve. State U., 1960-64; asst. prof. Hillsdale Coll., Mich., 1964-65; asst. prof. to full prof. SUNY, Oswego, 1965-96, poet-in-residence, 1995—96, prof. emeritus, 1996. Grad. asst. English, U. Conn., 1959; editl. asst. Writer's Workshop, U. Iowa, 1959-60; vis. prof. SUNY, Potsdam, 1968-69; Bingham Poet in Residence, U. Louisville, 1982; Writer in Residence, Ashland U., 1991; founding dir. Cleve. State U. Poetry Ctr., 1962, program in creative writing arts, SUNY Oswego, 1968. Author: First Poems, 1960, Awaken, Bells Falling: Poems 1959-67, 1968, numerous other poetry books including The Shifting Web: New and Selected Poems, 1989, The Collected Lyrics of Lewis Turco/Wesli Court, 1953-2004, Saturn's Scorge: A Narrative of the Age of Witchcraft in England and New England, 1980-1997; author numerous non-fiction books including The Book of Forms: A Handbook of Poetics, 1968, 3d edit., 2000, Visions and Revisions of American Poetry, 1986, Emily Dickinson, Woman of Letters, 1993, The Book of Literary Terms, 1999, The Book of Dialogue, 2004, A Sheaf of Leaves: Literary Memoirs, 2004, Fantaseers, A Book of Memories, 2005, Fearful Pleasures: The Complete Poems, 1953-2007, others; editor: The Life and Poetry of Manoah Bodman, 1999; contbr. articles to profl. jours. Sec. City of Oswego Charter Revision Commn., 1990-91; active Oswego Opera Theater Chorus, Oswego Festival Chorus, 1986-96. With USN, 1952-56. Recipient scholarship Meriden Record-Jour. Pub. Co., U. Conn., 1957-58, 58-59, Disting. Alumnus award, 1992, Melville Cane award Poetry Soc. Am., 1986, Bordighera Bilingual Poetry prize Sonia Raiziss-Giop Charitable Found., 1997, John Ciardi award for lifetime achievement in poetry Italian-Am., Found., 1999, others; resident fellowships Yaddo Found., 1959, 77, Faculty fellowships Rsch. Found. of SUNY, 1966-67, 69, 71, 73, 78; grant-in-aid, 1969; inducted into Meriden Hall of Fame, 1993, Robert Fitzgerald Prosody award, West Chester U. Poetry Conf., 2008. Home: PO Box 161 Dresden ME 04342-0161 Home Phone: 207-737-2326. Personal E-mail: turco@oswego.edu.

TURCO, MARTY, professional hockey player; b. Sault Ste. Marie, Ont., Can., Aug. 13, 1975; m. Kelly Turco; children: Hailey, Katelyn. B in Physical Edn., U. Mich., 1998. Goaltender U. Mich., 1994—98, Dallas Stars, 2000—. Mem. Team Can., Olympic Games, Torino, Italy, 2006. Recipient Championship Tournament MVP, NCAA, 1998, Roger Crozier Saving Grace Award, NHL, 2001, 2003, Second All-Star Team, 2003, NHL Found. Player Award, 2006; named to Championship All-Tournament Team, NCAA, 1996, 1998, West First All-Am. Team, 1997, NHL All-Star Game, 2003, 2004, 2007. Achievements include being a member of NCAA National Championship Team, University of Michigan, 1996, 1998. Avocations: fishing, golf. Office: c/o Dallas Stars 2601 Avenue of the Stars Frisco TX 75034*

TURCOTTE, DONALD LAWSON, geophysical sciences educator; b. Bellingham, Wash., Apr. 22, 1932; s. Lawson Phillip and Eva (Pearson) Turcotte; m. Joan Meredith Luecke, May 17, 1957; children: Phillip Lawson, Stephen Bradford. BS, Calif. Inst. Tech., 1954, PhD, 1958; M in Aero. Engring., Cornell U., 1955; PhD (hon.), U. Paris, 2005. Asst. prof. aero. engring. U.S. Naval Postgrad. Sch., Monterey, Calif., 1958-59; asst. prof. aero. engring. Cornell U., Ithaca, NY, 1959-63, assoc. prof., 1963-67, prof., 1967-73, prof. geol. scis., 1973-85, Maxwell Upson prof., 1985—2002, chmn., 1981-90; disting. prof. geology U. Calif. Davis, 2003—. Author (with others): Statistical Thermodynamics, 1963, Space Propulsion, 1965, Geodynamics, 1982, Fractals and Chaos in Geology and Geophysics, 1992, Mantle Convection, 2001. Trustee U. Space Rsch. Assn., 1975—79. Recipient Wegener medal, European Union Geosci., 1991, Disting. Alumni award, Calif. Inst. Tech., 1999; sr. postdoctoral rsch. fellow, NSF, 1965—66, Guggenheim fellow, 1972—73. Mem.: NAS, Am. Acad. Arts and Scis., Seismol. Soc. Am., Geol. Soc. Am. (Day medal 1982), Am. Geophys. Union (Charles A. Whitten medal 1995, William Bowie Medal 2003), El Macero Country Club. Home: 27104 Middle Golf Dr El Macero CA 95618 Office: Univ Calif Dept Geology Davis CA 95616 Office Phone: 530-572-6808. Business E-Mail: dlturcotte@ucdavis.edu.

TURCOTTE, ELIZABETH ANNE, art educator; b. Vincennes, Ind., Mar. 4, 1953; d. Pauletta June Woods; 1 child, Emma Su Pin. MFA, Southern Meth. U., 1978. Assoc. prof. Ball State U., Muncie, Ind., 1982—. CEO Corner Stone Ctr. Arts, Muncie, 1999—2003. Recipient Person of Yr., Star Press, 1999. Office: Ball State Univ University Ave Muncie IN 47306

TURCOTTE, JEAN-CLAUDE CARDINAL, cardinal, archbishop; b. Montreal, Que., Can., June 26, 1936; s. Paul-Émile and Rita (Gravel) Turcotte. Lic. theology, Grand Seminaire Montreal; student, U. Cath., Lille, France, 1964—65; DD (hon.), McGill U. Ordained priest Archdiocese of Montreal, Canada, 1959; parochial vicar St. Mathias parish, 1959—61; asst. diocesan chaplain for Christian working youth Archdiocese of Montreal, 1961—64; chaplain Movement of Christian Workers, 1965—67; positions in Office of Clergy Archdiocese of Montreal, 1967—74, dir. parish pastoral care, 1974—81, vicar gen., 1981—82; ordained bishop, 1982; aux. bishop Archdiocese of Montreal, 1982—90, archbishop, 1990—; elevated to cardinal, 1994; cardinal-priest Nostra Signora del SS. Sacramento e Santi Martiri Canadesi, 1994—. Pres. Canadian Conf. Cath. Bishops, 1997—2000; mem. Congregation for the Causes of Saints, Pontifical Council for Social Communications. Mem.: Coun. of Social Commn., Congregation of Causes of Saints. Roman Catholic. Office: 2000 Sherbrooke Ouest Montreal PQ Canada H3H 1G4

TURCOTTE, MARGARET JANE, retired nurse; b. Stow, Ohio, May 17, 1927; d. Edward Carlton and Florence Margaret (Hanson) McCauley; m. Rene George Joseph, Nov. 24, 1961 (div. June 1967); 1 child, Michael Lawrence. Degree, St. Thomas Hosp. Sch. Nursing, Akron, Ohio, 1949. cert. RN Ohio, 1950. Nurse St. Thomas Hosp., 1949-50; pvt. duty nurse, 1950-57; polio nurse Akron Children's Hosp., 1953-54; mem. nursing staff Robinson Meml. Hosp., Ravenna, Ohio, 1958-67, head ctrl. svc., 1963-67; supr. ctrl. svc. Brentwood Hosp., Warrensville Heights, Ohio, 1967-93, infections control nurse, 1982-91; emergency med. technician. Mem. aux. Robinson Meml. Hosp.; vol. Portage County Vis. Nurse Svc. and Hospice; active RSVP, Cozy Christian Quilters. Mem.: St. Thomas Hosp. Alumni Assn., Cozy Christian Quilters. Democrat. Mem. Christian Ch. (Disciples Of Christ). Home: 6615 Cleveland Rd Lot H3 Ravenna OH 44266-4206

TURCZYN, CHRISTINE LILIAN, writer, educator; d. Paul and Bohdanna (Felker) Turczyn. BA, Cornell U., Ithaca, NY, 1982; MA, U. Wis., Milw., 1989; PhD, Binghamton U., 1995. Cert. in grant writing SUNY Tng. Ctr. Asst. editor Scholastic, Inc., NYC, 1985—86; assoc. editor Holt, Rinehart & Winston, NYC, 1991—92; asst. prof. William Paterson U., Wayne, NJ, 1997—2001, Passaic County CC, NJ, 2002—03; instr. Dutchess CC, Poughkeepsie, NY, 2004—07. Mem. scholarship com. Dutchess CC, 2005—06; grad. asst. U. Wis., 1987—89; instr. creative writing Binghamton U., 1992—95; adj. prof. composition Montclair State U., NJ, 1995—96; vis. lectr. creative writing SUNY, New Paltz, 2007. Exhibitions include Reading Objects 2008, Samuel Dorksy Mus. of Art, SUNY, 2008, Botanicals, Still Life and Land Journeys, Betsy Jacaruso Studio, Rhinebeck, NY, 2008; contbr. articles to profl. jours. Recipient 1st prize, Allen Ginsberg Poetry, 1999, Ednl. Opportunity Program Appreciation cert., Dutchess CC, 2005, 2007; grantee, Fulbright Commn., 1982—83; scholar, Harvard U., 1984; Geraldine R. Dodge fellow, Vt. Studio Ctr., 2000, 2002, Writers grant, Vt. Studio Ctr., 2003, Instrn. Improvement grant, Dutchess CC, 2006, Grad. fellowship, Ctr. Twentieth Century Studies. Mem.: Nat. Coun. Tchrs. English, Cornell Club NY, Fulbright Assn. Avocations: swimming, painting.

TUREK, PAUL JOHN, III, construction executive; b. Columbia, SC, Feb. 10, 1964; s. Paul John Jr. and Patricia Veronica (Saluta) T.; m. Emma Lactao, Dec. 24, 1995; children: Samantha Claire, Paul John, Isabella. BS in Civil Engring., Northwestern U., 1986. Registered civil engr., Calif. Constrn. mgr. Brown & Root Inc., Houston, 1990-94; sr. project mgr. Shorenstein Co., San Francisco, 1994-98; v.p. Thompson Brooks, Inc., San Francisco, 1998-2000; pres. Summa III, Inc., San Francisco, 2000—04; sr. assoc. Marx Okubo, San Francisco, 2004—05, v.p. constrn. mgmt. svcs., 2006—. Active Walnut Creek Masters Swim Team. 1st lt. USMC, 1986-90. Avocations: fly fishing, swimming. Home: 2121 Carrol Rd Walnut Creek CA 94596-5714 Office: Marx Okubo 444 Spear St # 205 San Francisco CA 94105 Office Phone: 415-957-9240. E-mail: turekpe@sbcglobal.net.

TUREK, SONIA FAY, journalist; b. NYC, Aug. 2, 1949; d. Louis and Julia (Liebson) Turek; m. Gilbert Curtis, June 18, 1995. BA in English, CCNY, 1970; MSLS, Drexel U., 1972; MS in Journalism, Boston U., 1979. Children's libr. Wissahickon Valley Pub. Libr., Ambler, Pa., 1973; supr. children's svcs. Somerville Pub. Libr., Somerville, Mass., 1973-78; stringer The Watertown (Mass.) Sun, 1979, The Bedford (Mass.) Minuteman, 1979; reporter The Middlesex News, Framingham, Mass., 1979-83, The Boston Herald, 1983, asst. city editor, city editor, 1983-86, asst. mng. editor features, 1986-89, asst. mng. editor Sunday, 1989-93, dep. mng. editor, arts and features, 1993-99, wine columnist, 1984—. Tchr. Cambridge (Mass.) Ctr. for Adult Edn., 1982, 83; adj. prof. Boston U., 1986; travel writer The Boston Herald, 1984-2003. Bd. dirs. Rosie's Place, Boston, 2004—. Avocations: wine and food, travel, sailing. Personal E-mail: sfturek@aol.com.

TURFA, ARTHUR WILLIAM, literature and language professor; b. Pittsburgh, May 28, 1953; s. Alexander and Margaret Elizabeth Turfa; m. Pamela Anne Chesser, June 18, 1983; 1 child, Andrew Martin. BA in German, Pa. State U., U. Pk., 1974; MA, U. Calif., Irvine, 1977; MA in History, Binghamton U., NY, 1996; MDiv, Luth. Sch. Theology, Chgo., 1981; LittD, Drew U., Madison, NJ, 2007. Cert. tchr. SC Dept. Edn., 2008; ordinator Evang. Luth. Ch. Am., 1983. Pastor Redeemer Luth. Ch., Pearisburg, 1981—84, Old Zion Luth. Ch., Phila., 1984—86, Peace Luth. Ch., Las Vegas, N.Mex., 1987—92, St. John's Luth. Ch., Nanticoke, Pa., 1992—96, St. John's Slovak Luth. Ch., Lansford, Pa., 1996—98, St. Mark, Blythewood, SC, 2005—; German and social studies tchr. Espanola Valley Sch. Dist., N.Mex., 1989—92; German history tchr. MMI Prep, Freeland, Pa., 1996—97; German tchr. Weatherly Sch. Dist., Pa., 1998—99, Hazleton Area Sch. Dist., 2000—05; English tchr. Lexington 1 Sch. Dist., 2005—07; English and German tchr. Tri Valley Sch. Dist., Hegins, Pa., 1999—2000, Richland 2 Sch. Dist., Columbia, SC, 2007—. Chaplain USAR Component, 1983—2006. Contbr. articles to profl. jour. Lt. col. US Army, 2004—05, Wuerzburg, Germany. Liberal. Lutheran. Avocations: travel, reading, exercise. Office: Blythewood High Sch 10901 Wilson Blvd Blythewood SC 29016 Business E-Mail: aturfa@bh.richland2.org.

TURIGLIATTO-FAHRNEY, TERRI A., educational association administrator, educator; d. Perry H. Turigliatto and Frances A. Henning; m. Richard S. Fahrney Sr, Sept. 7; children: Elizabeth A. Fahrney, Richard S. Fahrney Jr., Joseph P. Fahrney, Katheryn L. Fahrney, Karaleigh F. Fahrney. BA, U. Dallas, Irving, 1989; MA, U. Mo., St. Louis, 1997; PhD, St. Louis U., 2008. Adj. assoc. prof. Webster U., St Louis, 2002—08; asst. dean and prof. St. Louis U., 2008—. Rsch. fellowship, DAR, 2003. Mem.: Coun. Grad. Sch., Phi Alpha Theta. Democrat. Roman Catholic. Avocations: golf, travel.

TURILLI, M. LOUISE, lawyer; Grad., Oberlin Coll., Ohio; M, U. Cin.; law degree, U. Conn. Sch. Law. Ptnr. east coast law firm; law v.p., asst. sec. NCR Corp.; v.p., assoc. gen. counsel Bellsouth Corp., Atlanta; v.p., dep. gen. counsel Qwest Comm. Internat. Inc., Denver; v.p., gen. counsel Ryerson Inc., Chgo., 2007—. Office: Ryerson Inc 2621 W 15th Pl Chicago IL 60608-1712

TURINO, GERARD MICHAEL, internist, educator; b. NYC, May 16, 1924; s. Michael and Lucy (Arciero) T.; m. Dorothy Estes, Aug. 25, 1951; children: Peter, Phillip, James. AB, Princeton U., 1945; MD, Columbia U., 1948. Diplomate: Am. Bd. Internal Medicine. Intern Columbia U., Bellevue Hosp., 1948-49, asst. resident in medicine, 1949-50; resident in medicine New Haven Hosp., 1950-51; chief resident in medicine Columbia U. div. Bellevue Hosp., 1953-54; sr. fellow N.Y. Heart Assn., 1956-60; career investigator Health Research Council City of N.Y., 1961-71; asst. prof. medicine Columbia U., 1960-67, assoc. prof., 1967-72, prof. medicine, 1973-83, John H. Keating prof. medicine, 1983—; mem. staff Presbyn. Hosp., NYC, 1960—, attending physician, 1983—; dir. med. svcs. St. Lukes-Roosevelt Hosp., NYC, 1983-92; dir. St. Lukes-Roosevelt Hosp. James P. Mara Ctr, 1997. Cons. on sci. affairs Am. Thoracic Soc., 1992—; mem. sci. adv. com. Nat. Heart, Lung, and Blood Inst., Am. Lung Assn., Am. Heart Assn., N.Y. Lung Assn., N.Y. Heart Assn., Alpha, Antitrypsin Found.; mem. staff divsn. med. sci. Nat. Rsch. Coun., Washington; cons. VA Hosp., East Orange, N.J., 1962-67; cons. in medicine Englewood (N.J.) Hosp., Hackensack (N.J.) Hosp.; pres.-elect Am. Bur. Med. Advancement in China, 1994, pres., 1994-2001, chmn., 2001-; chmn. bd. dirs. Chronic Obstructive Pulmonary Disease Found., 2004 Contbr. articles to med. jours. Mem. Bd. Edn., Alpine, N.J., 1960-67; chmn. Chronic Obstructive Pulmonary Disease Found., 2004. Served to capt. USAF, 1951-53. Recipient Joseph Mather Smith prize Columbia U., 1965, Alumni medal, 1983, Silver medal Alumni Assn. Coll. Physicians and Surgeons Columbia U., 1979, gold medal, 1986, Edward Livingston Trudeau medal Am. Lung Assn., 2003, Fellow AAAS; mem. Assn. Am. Physicians, Am. Soc. Clin. Investigation, Harvey Soc., Am. Thoracic Soc. (pres. 1987-88, Edward Livingston Trudeau prize 2003), Am. Fedn. Clin. Rsch., Am. Physiol. Soc. (chmn. steering com. respiration sect.), Am. Heart Assn. (award of merit 1980, Disting. Achievement award 1989, bd. dirs.), N.Y. Heart Assn. (pres. 1981-83, dir.), N.Y. Lung Assn. (dir.), N.Y. Med.-Surg. Soc. (pres. 1995), N.Y. Clin. Soc., Princeton Club (N.Y.C.), Maidstone Club, Devon Yacht Club, Century Assn. Club. Home: 66 E 79th St New York NY 10021-0244 Office: St Lukes Roosevelt Hosp 1000 10th Ave New York NY 10019-1192 Business E-Mail: GMT1@Columbia.edu.

TURINSKY, PAUL JOSEF, nuclear engineer, educator; b. Hoboken, NJ, Oct. 20, 1944; s. Paul J. and Wilma A. (Budig) T.; m. Karen Ann DeLuca, Aug. 29, 1966; children: Grant Dean, Beth Noelle. BS, U. R.I., 1966; MSE, U. Mich., 1967, PhD, 1970; MBA, U. Pitts., 1979. Asst. prof. Rensselaer Poly. Inst., Troy, NY, 1971-73; engr., mgr. nuc. design Westinghouse Elec. Corp., Pitts., 1973—78, mgr. core devel., 1978-80; head dept. nuc. engring. NC State U., Raleigh, 1980—88, 1999—2006, prof., 1980—, dir. Electric Power Rsch. Ctr., 1989—2008; pres. Nuclear Fuel Mgmt. Assocs., 1994—2007. Bd. dir. Quantum Rsch. Svcs.; cons. Electric Power Rsch. Inst., Palo Alto, Calif., 1980-98, Sci. Applications Internat. Corp., 1990-92, US Dept. Energy, 1993; tech. specialist Internat. Atomic Energy Agy., Vienna, Austria, 1982—; mem. nuc. safety rev. bd. Duke Power Co., Charlotte, NC, 1986-2001; cons. Can. Nuc. Safety Commn., 2000-, Western Svcs. Corp., 2006-; mem. nuc. sci. advisory bd. Commissariat l'Energie Atomique, France, 2006-. Author: (with others) CRC Handbook of Nuclear Reactor Calculations, 1986; contbr. more than 100 articles to tech. jours. Recipient Outstanding Tchr. award, NC State U., 1985, RJR award, 2007, Supercomputer award, IBM, 1991, Alcoa Disting. Rschr. award, 1993, E.O. Lawrence award in nuc. tech., U.S. Dept. Energy, 2002, Merit award, Alumni Soc. U. Mich., 2003. Fellow: Am. Nuc. Soc. (chmn. reactor physics divsn. 1987—88, chmn. math. and computer divsn. 1995—96, bd. dirs. 1990—93, Mark Mills award 1971, Eugene E. Wigner Reactor Physics award 2003, Arthur Holly Compton award 2004, Presdl. Citation award 2009); mem.: AAAS (math. com.), Soc. Indsl. and Applied Math., Edison Electric Inst. (Power Engring. Educator award 1992), Am. Soc. Engring. Educators (chmn. nuc. engring. divsn. 1984—85, Glenn Murphy award 1990). Office: NC State U Dept Nuclear Engring PO Box 7909 Raleigh NC 27695-7909 Business E-Mail: turinsky@ncsu.edu.

TURITTO, GIOIA, physician; b. Siena, Italy, Apr. 25, 1957; MD, U. Rome, 1981. Diplomate Am. Bd. Internal Medicine. Resident in internal medicine SUNY Downstate, Bklyn., 1991-92, fellow in cardiology, 1985-87, mem. staff, asst. prof. medicine, 1991-96, assoc. prof. medicine, 1996—. Mem. AMA, Am. Coll. Cardiology, Am. Fedn. for Clin. Rsch. Office: SUNY Health Sci Ctr Box 1199 450 Clarkson Ave Brooklyn NY 11203-2056

TURITZIN, JOHN N., entertainment company executive, lawyer; b. Manhasset, NY, Sept. 5, 1955; m. Barbara Turitzin; children: Allison, David, Emily. Grad., Earlham Coll., 1976; M in Pub. Affairs, Princeton U., 1981; JD, NYU, 1981. Assoc. Cahill Gordon & Reindel, NY, 1981—84; ptnr. Battle Fowler LLP, Stamford, Conn., 1985—2000, Paul, Hastings, Janofsky & Walker LLP, 2000—04; exec. v.p., gen. counsel Marvel Entertainment Inc., NYC, 2004—06, exec. v.p., Office Chief Exec., 2006—. Office: Marvel Entertainment Inc 417 Fifth Ave 11th Fl New York NY 10016 Office Phone: 212-576-4000. Office Fax: 212-576-8517.

TURK, AUSTIN THEODORE, social studies educator; b. Gainesville, Ga., May 28, 1934; s. Hollis Theodore and Ruth (Vandiver) T.; m. Janet Stuart Irving, Oct. 4, 1957 (div. 1977); children: Catherine, Jennifer; m. Ruth-Ellen Marie Grimes, July 27, 1985. BA cum laude, U. Ga., 1956; MA, U. Ky., 1959; PhD, U. Wis., 1962. Acting instr. sociology U. Wis., Madison, 1961-62; from instr. to prof. sociology Ind. U., Bloomington, 1962-74; prof. U. Toronto, Can., 1974-88, U. Calif., Riverside, 1988—, chmn. dept. sociology, 1989-94; interim dir. Robert B. Presley Ctr. for Crime and Justice Studies, 1994-95. Author: Criminality and Legal Order, 1969, Political Criminality, 1982; gen. editor crime and justice series SUNY Press, Albany, 1990-2008; contbr. articles to jours. in field. Mem. Calif. Mus. Photography, 1988—, Citizens Univ. Com., 1990—. Recipient Paul Tappan award Western Soc. Criminology, 1989. Fellow Am. Soc. Criminology (pres. 1984-85); mem. Am. Sociol. Assn. (chair criminology sect. 1975-76), Law and Soc. Assn. (trustee 1982-85), Acad. Criminal Justice Scis. Democrat. Avocations: gardening, reading, swimming, tennis. Office: Dept Sociology U Calif Riverside Riverside CA 92521-0001 E-mail: austin.turk@ucr.edu.

TURK, ELEANOR LOUISE, history professor; b. Charlottesville, Va., Sept. 9, 1935; d. Alan P. and Louise H. (Goodman) Fort; divorced; 1 child, Andrew Kittridge. BA, Ohio Wesleyan U., 1957; MA, U. Ill., 1970; PhD, U. Wis., 1975. Asst. dean Coll. Arts and Scis. U. Kans., Lawrence, 1976—78; asst. dean Sch. Humanities and Social Scis. Ithaca (N.Y.) Coll., 1978-83; from assoc. prof. to prof. history Ind. U. East, Richmond, 1983—2003, prof. history emerita, 2003—, chmn. divsn. Humanities and Social Scis., 1983-87, asst. vice chancellor for assessment, 1993-97, faculty colloquim on excellence in teaching, 1991—, chmn. instnl. self-study com., 1990—92, 1996—97. Cons. North Ctrl. Assn., Higher Learning Commn., evaluator, 1996—2003. Author: The History of Germany, 1999 (Choice Outstanding Acad. Title award, 1999), Issues in Germany, Austria and Switzerland, 2003. Bd. dirs., dep. chair Inst. for Advanced Studies, Ind. U., Bloomington, 1991-92, chair, 1992-94; mem. pres.'s coun. for internat. programs, 1984-2003; pres. Sister Cities of Richmond, Inc., 1987-90, bd. dirs., 1987-92, 95-98; del., panel chair USSR/USA Sister Cities Conf., Tashkent, 1989; bd. dirs., treas. Wayne County Arts Consortium, Richmond, 1986-89. Recipient Excellence in Writing award Kans. State Hist. Soc., 1983, Cmty. Leadership award Richmond YWCA, 1989, John W. Ryan award for Disting. Contbns. to Internat. Programs and Studies Ind. U., 1995; Fulbright scholar Kiel U., Germany, 1957-58, German Landeskunde, 1992. Mem. Soc. for German-Am. Studies, Kans. State Hist. Soc. (life), Phi Beta Kappa, Phi Alpha Theta, Pi Sigma Alpha. Democrat. Unitarian Universalist. Personal E-mail: etathome@yahoo.com. Business E-Mail: eturk@indiana.edu.

TURK, ELIZABETH ANN, music educator; b. NYC, July 10, 1957; d. William Robert Turk, Elizabeth Ann Brittingham. BA in Music and History, Dowling Coll.; MA in German Lang. and Lit., Hofstra U.; MA in European History, SUNY Stony Brook; MA in Music Libr. Sci., Columbia U. Tchg. asst SUNY, Stony Brook, 1986—88; lectr. music Dowling Coll., Oakdale, NY, 1988—91; choral tchr. music Amityville (NY) Pub. Schs., 1991—; dir. theater arts, dir. choral music Miller Pl. HS; theater dir. Amityville HS; music dir. theater prodns. Commack HS South, Carriage House Players Theater Three, Kids for Kids Theater, Inc.; music dir. theater Syosset Mid. Sch., Conn. Sch. Dist., Conn., Jericho H.S. Tchr. vocal music Miller Place Middle Sch., Miller Place, NY, Hewlett Woodmere HS, NY; pvt. tchr. and vocal coach, Massapequa, NY. Singer (soloist): (lead rolls) Rome Opera Festival, 1989, 1990; performer: Tchaikovsky Competition, 1978, 1982, 1986, Idle Hour Gilbert & Sullivan Players, Minn. Opera, 1979, 1980, 1981, L.I. Youth Orch. Summer Tours; dir.: Sleeping Beauty, Sound of Music, Fiddler on the Roof, Little Shop of Horrors, Cinderella, Oliver, numerous others; choreographer Fiddler on the Roof, Sound of Music, Little Shop of Horrors, Oliver, Grease; dir.: 42nd Street, West Side Story, Guys & Dolls, Mikado, HMS Pinafore & Pirates of Penzance, King and I, Best of Broadway. Recipient award for further study, Met. Opera, 1981—90, Herald award for choreography and music dir. Mem.: Suffolk County Music Educators Assn., Music Educators Nat. Assn., Suffolk County Wrestling Assn. (tournament dir. league V 1974—, numerous awards), White Star Triangle (Beloved Queen 1973—74), Order Ea. Star (various offices, assoc. condr.). Home: 90 Clock Blvd Massapequa NY 11758

TURK, JAMES CLINTON, federal judge; b. Roanoke, Va., May 3, 1923; s. James Alexander and Geneva (Richardson) T.; m. Barbara Duncan, Aug. 21, 1954; children: Ramona Leah, James Clinton, Robert Malcolm Duncan, Mary Elizabeth, David Michael. AB, Roanoke Coll., 1949; L.L.B., Washington and Lee U., 1952. Bar: Va. 1952. Assoc. Dalton & Poff, Radford, Va., 1952-53; ptnr. Dalton, Poff & Turk, Radford, 1953-72; state senator from Va., 1959-72; judge U.S. Dist. Ct. (we. dist.) Va., Roanoke, 1972-73, chief judge, 1973—. Dir. 1st & Mchts. Nat. Bank of Radford Mem. Va. Senate, from 1959, minority leader.; Trustee Radford Community Hosp., 1959—. Served with AUS, 1943-46. Mem.: Order of Coif, Omicron Delta Kappa, Phi Beta Kappa. Baptist (deacon). Home: 1002 Walker Dr Radford VA 24141-3018 Office: US Dist Ct 246 Franklin Rd SW # 220 Roanoke VA 24011-2214 Home Phone: 540-639-2055; Office Phone: 540-857-5122. Office Fax: 540-857-5123. Business E-Mail: jamest@vawd.uscourts.gov.

TURK, JAMES CLINTON, JR., lawyer; b. Radford, Va., Oct. 27, 1956; s. James Clinton and Barbara (Duncan) T.; m. Allison Blanding, Oct. 16, 1993; children: Lindsey Leigh, Katherine Alexandra, Alana Rae. BA in Econs., Roanoke Coll., 1979; JD, Samford U., 1984. Bar: Va. 1984, US Dist. Ct. (ea. and we. dists.) Va. 1984, US Bankruptcy Ct. 1985, US Ct. Appeals (4th cir.) 1985, US Supreme Ct. 1988; cert. specialist in civil and criminal trial advocacy Nat. Bd. Trial Advocacy; cert. players agt. Nat. Basketball Players Assn.; cert. players agt./contract advisor NFL. Ptnr. Harrison & Turk, Radford, 1985—. Adj. prof. criminal justice dept. Radford U.; bd. dirs. New River brs. SunTrust Bank, Va. Tech. Found., Intrexon Transcriptional Therapeutics Corp.,2006-07, Synchrony, Inc, 2008-. Sec. Radford Rep. Com., 1984—; fundraising chmn. Am. Heart Assn., Radford, 1986—; bd. dir. New River Valley Workshop, Inc., v.p., 1990-92, pres., 1992-93; bd. dirs. new River CC Ednl. Found.; apptd. chmn. and dir. Va. Student Assistance Authorities by Gov. George Allen, 1994—; escheator City of Radford and Pulaski County; rep. western dist. CJA Panel Atty., Va.; mem. 4th Cir. Jud. Conf., 2000-01; bd. dirs. Va. Tech. Athletic Found. Recipient Bill Geimer Capital Defender award, Va. Capital Case Clearinghouse, 2000—01; named a Va. Super Lawyer, 2006—07, 2007. Mem. ATLA (sustaining, fellow Coll. of Advocacy), Ted Dalton Am. Inn Courts (barrister), ABA, Am. Bd. Trial Adv., Am. Coll. Barristers, Am. Triple Lawyers Assn., Va. Bar Assn. (civil litig. sect. coun. 1991—, criminal litig. sect. coun. 1994—), Nat. Assn. Criminal Def. Lawyers (life; death penalty com. and indigent def. com.), Va. Trial Lawyers Assn., Inn of Cts., Jaycees, Am. Inn of Ct., Rotary. Republican. Roman Catholic. Avocations: weightlifting, golf, travel, flying, scuba diving. Home: 460 Quailwood Dr Blacksburg VA 24060-6724 Office: Harrison And Turk Pc 1007 E Main St Radford VA 24141-1745 Office Phone: 540-639-9056. Personal E-mail: jimturk@aol.com.

TURK, JON BRANDEN, plastic surgeon; b. Bklyn., Jan. 31, 1963; s. Stephen Noel and Sandra (Rich) T.; m. Carolyn Sue Gusoff, Sept. 21, 1991; children, Graham, Amanda BA, Amherst Coll., Mass., 1984; MD, SUNY, 1988. Med. diplomate Am. Bd. Facial Plastic and Reconstructive Surgery. Asst. prof. SUNY Health Sci. Ctr., 1994—; clin. asst. attending Mt. Sinai Hosp., NYC, 1997—; attending physician Lenox Hill & Manhattan Eye & Ear Hosp. Author: (chpt.) Otolaryngological Clinics of North America, 1994. Fellow Am. Acad. Facial Plastic and Reconstructive Surgery, Am. Acad. otolaryngology Heal and Neck Surgery; mem. N.Y. Facial Plastic Surg. Soc. Office: Jon Turk MD 800 5th Ave New York NY 10065-7239 also: 173 Froehlich Farm Blvd Woodbury NY 11797 Office Phone: 516-921-8989.*

TURK, RICHARD ERRINGTON, retired psychiatrist; b. Staten Island, NY, Oct. 6, 1925; s. Richard Jason and Marian (Errington) T.; m. Dec. 30, 1948 (widowed Dec. 23, 1978); children: Stephanie, Jeffrey, Alan. BA, Dartmouth Coll., 1945; MD, Johns Hopkins Med. Sch., 1948. Diplomate Am. Bd. Psychiatry. Intern Highland-Alameda County Hosp., Oakland, Calif., 1948-49; resident Herrick Meml. Hosp., Berkeley, Calif., 1949-50; fellow psychiatry Med. Sch. Harvard U., Boston, 1950-51, 53-54; clin. instr. Med. Sch. U. Calif., San Francisco, 1954—70; pvt. practice psychiatry Berkeley, 1954-85. Pvt. practice, Walnut Creek, Calif., 1972-88; staff Herrick Meml. Hosp., 1954-85, Walnut Creek Hosp., 1972-88, John Muir Meml. Hosp., Walnut Creek, 1972-88. Capt. USAF Res., 1951—53. Mem. AMA, Am. Psychiat. Assn., No. Calif. Psychiat. Assn., Calif. Med. Assn., Alameda-Contra Costa County Med. Assn. Avocations: travel, bicycling, boating, car camping.

TURK, THOMAS LIEBIG, arts consultant; b. Indpls., July 4, 1936; s. Laurel Herbert and Esther Lucille (Liebig) T.; m. Judith Ann Prochnow, July 26, 1969; children: Martisha Emily, Benjamin Edward. AB, DePauw U., 1958; MA, Mich. State U., 1960; cert., Harvard U., 1973. Promotion and publicity dir. Sta. WMSB-TV Mich. State U., East Lansing, 1961, asst. editor news bur., 1962-63, fine arts assoc. producer Sta. WKAR-TV, 1963-68, fine arts producer Sta. WKAR-TV, 1969-81; acting dir. publicity DePauw U., Greencastle, Ind., 1961-62; exec. dir. Cultural Activities Ctr., Temple, Tex., 1981-91, Met. Nashville Arts Commn., 1993—2003, Tennesseans for the Arts, 2003—06; mng. dir. Texarkana (Tex.) Regional Arts & Humanities Coun., 1991-93. Pres. Met. Lansing (Mich.) Fine Arts Coun., 1975-77, Mich. Assn. Comm. Arts Agys., East Lansing, 1979-81; Gov. apptd. mem. Mich. Coun. for Arts, 1979-81; chmn. Mich. Arts Forum, 1980-81; pres. U.S. Urban Arts Fedn., 1999-00; mem. State Arts Action Network Coun., 2005-06. Producer, co-producer: 400 programs for local, nat. and internat. distbn. on pub. TV, 1963-81. Bd. dir. Alias Chamber Music Ensemble, 2006—, Univ. Club Nashville, 2006—. With USAF, 1960. Mem.: Tennesseans for Arts (bd. dirs. 2000—03), Nat. Assembly Local Arts Agys. (bd. dirs. 1979—85), Rotary, Sigma Chi. Episcopalian. Home and Office: 643 Harpeth Trace Dr Nashville TN 37221-3147 Personal E-mail: turktj@comcast.net.

TURKE, PAUL WILLIAM, pediatrician, anthropologist; s. John Franklin and Helen Louise Turke; m. Laura L. Betzig, June 25, 1983; children: Alexa Betzig, Maximilian Turke Betzig. MD, Northwestern U., Evanston, Ill., PhD, 1985. Anthropologist U. Mich., Ann Arbor, 1986—92; pediatrician Turke & Thomashow Pediat., Pc, Ann Arbor, 1999—. Office: Turke & Thomashow Pediat Pc 1821 Stadium Blvd Ann Arbor MI 48103 Personal E-mail: paulturke@gmail.com.

TURKEL, GERALD MICHAEL, social sciences educator; b. Bklyn., Aug. 13, 1945; s. Eli Joseph and Rachel Turkel; m. Kathleen Anne Doherty, Jan. 6, 1977; children: Eli Walter, Helen Julia. PhD, U. Calif., Santa Barbara, 1976. Asst. prof. sociology Fla. Atlantic U., Boca Raton, 1973—74; pres. U. Del., Newark, 2000—06, prof. sociology and legal studies, 1975—. Mem., nat. coun. AAUP, Washington, 1999—2003; commr. New Castle County Ethics Commn., Wilmington, Del. Author: (book) Dividing Public and Private: Law, Social Theory, and Politics, Law and Society: Critical Approaches. Commr. New Castle County Ethics Commn., Wilmington, Del., 2008. Office: Univ Del 314 Smith Hall Newark DE 19716

TURKOGLU, HEDO (HIDAYET), professional basketball player; b. Istanbul, Turkey, Mar. 19, 1979; Basketball player Turkish Profl. League Efes Pilsen, Istanbul, 1996—2000; guard-forward Sacramento Kings, 2000—04, Orlando Magic, Fla., 2004—09, Toronto Raptors, 2009—. Recipient Most Improved Player award, NBA, 2008; named to All-Under the Radar Team, NBA Inside Stuff, 2003—04. Avocations: reading, music, movies, video games. Office: Toronto Raptors Air Can Ctr 40 Bay St Ste 400 Toronto ON Canada M5J 2X2*

TURLEY, JAMES S., corporate financial executive; m. Lynn Turley; 1 child, Jay. BS in Economics and Managerial Studies, Rice U., 1977, MS in Acctg., 1978. With Ernst & Young, Houston, 1977—79, St. Louis, 1979—87, US nat. dir. client services and bus. devel. NYC, 1987—90, coord. ptnr. St. Louis, 1991—93, area dir. entrepreneurial svcs., 1993—94, mng. ptnr. upper midwest area, 1994—98, met. NY area mng. ptnr. NYC, 1998—2000; dep. global chmn. Ernst & Young Internat., NYC, 2000—01, global chmn., 2001—, global CEO, 2003—. Mem. Bus. Roundtable, Com. to Encourage Corp. Philanthropy, Transatlantic Bus. Dialog; co-chmn. adv. council Russia Fgn. Investment. Bd. dirs. Boy Scouts of Am., Catalyst; v.p. bd. dirs. Nat. Corp. Theater Fund; mem. nat. leadership coun. Character Edn. Partnership. Avocations: golf, tennis. Office: Ernst & Young 5 Times Sq New York NY 10036*

TURLEY, LINDA, lawyer; b. Altus, Okla., July 16, 1958; d. Windle and Shirley (Lacey) Turley; 1 child, Lacey. BS, Georgetown U., 1980; JD with honors, U. Tex., 1983. Bar: Tex. 1983; bd. cert. in personal injury trial law. Atty., head product liability dept. Law Offices of Windle Turley, P.C., Dallas, 1986-95; personal injury trial lawyer Turley Law Firm, 2001—05; ptnr. Turley & Stutz, P.C., Dallas, 1997—2001; with Turley Law Firm, 2006—. Mem. task force on Tex. rules of civil procedure Tex. Supreme Ct., 1992-93. Mem. ATLA (bd. govs. 1993-96, chair women trial lawyers' caucus 1989-90, chair product liability sect. 1996-97), Am. Bd. Trial Advocates, Tex. Trial Lawyers Assn. (bd. dirs. 1989—). Office: 1000 Turley Law Ctr 6440 N Central Expy Dallas TX 75206 Office Phone: 214-691-4025. Business E-Mail: lindat@wturley.com.

TURLEY, ROBERT STEVEN, physicist, researcher; b. Monterey Park, Calif., May 8, 1954; s. Robert Starling Jr. and Maurine (Johnson) T.; m. Deon Staffanson, Apr. 22, 1978; children: Robert Staffan, Marin, Carole, Allison, Patrick Ansel, Neil Peter, Lisa. BS summa cum laude, Brigham Young U., 1978; PhD, MIT, 1984. Sr. staff physicist rsch. labs Hughes Aircraft Co., Malibu, Calif., 1975-95; assoc. prof. physics Brigham Young U., 1995—2001, prof., 2001—, dept. chair, 2001—04, assoc. dean, 2004—08. Chmn. 2nd Internat. Conf. on Soft X-rays in the 21st Century. Contbr. articles to profl. jours. Chmn. Conejo dist. com. Ventura County coun. Boy Scouts Am., 1992-95, mem. site coun. Manzanita Elem. Sch., Newbury Park, Calif., 1989-90. Fellow Hughes Aircraft Co., 1979. Mem. Am. Phys. Soc., Am. Assn. Physics Tchrs., Sigma Pi Sigma, Brigham Young U. Alumni Assn. (chmn. Ventura County regional coun. 1990-92). Republican. Mem. Lds Ch. Achievements include patent for Apparatus and Method for Locating the Direction of an Atomic Beam. Office: Brigham Young Univ Dept Physics Astronomy N308 ESC Provo UT 84602

TURLEY, STEWART, retired retail company executive; b. Mt. Sterling, Ky., July 20, 1934; s. R. Joe and Mavis S. Turley; children from previous marriage: Carol Cohen, Karen Shockley; m. Linda A. Mulholland; stepchildren: Kathleen Smiley, Kristine Johnson. Student, Rollins Coll., 1952-53, U. Ky., 1953-55. Plant mgr. Crown Cork & Seal Co., Orlando (Fla.), Phila., 1955-66; mgr. non-drug ops., dir. corporate employee rels. and spl. svcs. Eckerd Corp. (formerly Jack Eckerd Corp.), Clearwater, Fla., 1966-68; v.p. Eckerd Corp., Clearwater, Fla., 1968-71, sr. v.p., 1971-74, dir., 1971-97, pres., chief exec. officer, 1974-96, chmn. bd., 1975-97. Past bd. dirs. WCI Cmtys., Inc., Sprint Corp., Marine Max, Inc., Springs Industries, Inc., Barnett Banks, Inc. Past chmn. U.S. Ski Team Found.; bd. dirs. Vilar Ctr. Found., Vail Valley Found.; bd. visitors Duke U.; bd. dirs. Steadman-Hawkins Sports Medicine Found. Mem. Nat. Assn. Chain Drug Stores (chmn. bd. 1978-79, 88-89), Fla. Coun. 100 (past chmn.), Carlouel Yacht Club, Belleair Country Club, Eagle Springs Golf Club, Kappa Alpha. Office: 1465 S Fort Harrison Ave Ste 201 Clearwater FL 33756-2505

TURLEY MURPHY, DANIEL THOMAS, bishop; b. Chgo., Jan. 25, 1943; Ordained priest Order of St. Augustine, 1968; ordained bishop, 1996; coadjutor bishop Diocese of Chulucanas, Peru, 1996—2000, bishop, 2000—. Roman Catholic. Office: Diocese of Chulucanas Obispado Calle Cuzco 381 Chulucanas Dept de Piuria Peru

TURNAGE, FRED DOUGLAS, retired lawyer; b. Ayden, NC, Sept. 24, 1920; s. Fred C. and Lou (Johnson) T.; m. Margaret Futrell, Aug. 21, 1943 (div. Nov. 1980); children: Betty Lou Griffith, Douglas C.; m. Elizabeth Louisa Turnage, Jan. 23, 1981. Grad. Naval Sch. on Far Eastern Civil Affairs, Princeton U., 1945; LLB, Wake Forest U., 1948, LLD, 1970. Bar: N.C. 1948, U.S. Supreme Ct. 1953, U.S. Dist. Ct. D.C. 1965, U.S. Ct. Appeals (D.C. cir.) 1967, U.S. Ct. Appeals (4th and 7th cirs.) 1979. Trial atty. antitrust div. U.S. Dept. Justice, Kansas City, Mo., 1948-51, sr. trial atty. antitrust div. Washington, 1951-65, spl. asst. to atty. gen., 1965; sr. ptnr. Cleary, Gottlieb, Steen & Hamilton, Washington, 1968—, counsel, 1990—2004, ret., 2004. Lectr. continuing legal edn. courses, 1973-77. Contbr. articles to profl. jours. Bd. Visitors Wake Forest U. Sch. Law, Winston-Salem, N.C., 1980—. Served to 1st lt. AUS, 1942-46. Recipient Disting. Service in Law citation Wake Forest U., 1979. Mem. ABA (antitrust and litigation sects.), Fed. Bar Assn., Adv. Bd. Antitrust Bulletin, Wake Forest U. Alumni Assn. (pres. 1977), Nat. Lawyers Clubs. Methodist. Avocations: fishing, golf, writing.

TURNAGE, JEAN ALLEN, retired state supreme court chief justice; b. St. Ignatius, Mont., Mar. 10, 1926; JD, Mont. State U., 1951; D of Laws and Letters (hon.), U. Mont., 1995. Bar: Mont. 1951, US Supreme Ct. 1963. Former ptnr. Turnage, McNeil & Mercer, Polson, Mont.; former Mont. State senator from 13th Dist.; pres. Mont. State Senate, 1981—85; chief justice Supreme Ct. Mont., 1985-2001. Mem. Mont. State Bar Assn., Nat. Conf. Chief Justices (past pres.), Nat. Ctr. State Courts (past chair). Office: Turnage & Mercer PO Box 460 Polson MT 59860 Office Phone: 406-883-5367. Personal E-mail: jeanturnage@centurytel.net.

TURNAGE, SCOTT E., history professor; b. Spartanburg, SC, Oct. 26, 1951; s. James W. and Joan D. Turnage; m. Charlotte D. Newsome, Feb. 26, 1999; children: Jennifer T. McCarter, Josephine B. MA, U. SC., Columbia, 1993; BA in History, Wofford Coll., 1973. History prof. Midlands Tech. Coll., Columbia, SC, 1993—. Home: 1216 Pine St Cayce SC 29033 Office: Midlands Tech Coll PO Box 2408 Columbia SC 29202 Business E-Mail: turnages@midlandstech.edu.

TURNAU, VIVIAN WILLIAMSON, retired literature and language educator; b. NYC, Apr. 16, 1937; m. Roger William Turnau, Apr. 1 (dec.); children: Theodore Arthur III, Roger Williamson. BA in French Edn., Russell Sage Coll., Troy, NY, 1958; cert. French studies, U. Lausanne, Switzerland, 1959; MA in Spanish, State U. Pa., Millersville, 1995; postgrad., U. NC, Greensboro; PhD, 2009—. Adminstrv. asst. United Way Berks County, Reading, Pa., 1988—90; tchr. Spanish and ESL Reading Area C.C., 1991—93; tchr. French and Spanish Wyomissing Sch. Dist., Pa., 1990—94, Bishop Wood H.S., Warminster, Pa., 1994; tchr. Spanish Salem Acad., Winston-Salem, NC, 1995—96; ret., 1997; tutor YMCA, Winston-Salem, 1999—2006; substitute tchr. Summit Sch., Winston-Salem, 2004—05. ESL instr. Forsyth Tech. CC, adj. prof., 2009—. Exch. fellow, Inst. Internat. Edn., 1958—59, Chancellor's scholar. Mem.: PEO, Outstanding Student Honor Soc., Nat. Scholars Honor Soc. Presbyterian. Avocations: music, reading, needlecrafts. Personal E-mail: vturnau@triad.rr.com.

TURNBAUGH, WILLIAM ARTHUR, archaeologist, educator; b. Williamsport, Pa., June 1, 1948; s. William Hugh and Louise Elizabeth (Muller) Turnbaugh; m. Sarah Ropes Peabody, Oct. 12, 1974. BA in History summa cum laude, Lycoming Coll., 1970, LHD (hon.), 2006; PhD in Anthropology, Harvard U., 1973. Accredited mem. Register Profl. Archaeologists. Curator of archaeology Lycoming County Mus., Williamsport, 1968-70; tchg. fellow, dept. anthropology Harvard U., Cambridge, Mass., 1971-72, asst. to dir. Peabody Mus., 1973-74; asst. prof. anthropology U. R.I., Kingston, 1974-78, assoc. prof. anthropology, 1978-83, prof. anthropology, 1983—2006, prof. emeritus, 2006—. Ind. contracting archaeologist ea. U.S. and Can., 1968—74; dir. U. R.I. Mus., 1975—77; adv. bd. Inst. Conservation Archaeology, Cambridge, 1976—83. Author: Man, Land and Time, 1975, Material Culture of RI-1000, 1984; co-author: Indian Baskets, 1986, rev. edit., 2004, R.F.D. Country!, 1988, Indian Jewelry of the American Southwest, 1988, rev. edit., 2006, Basket Tales of the Grandmothers, 1999, Understanding Physical Anthropology & Archaeology, 1981, 8th edit., 2002; assoc. editor: Historical Archaeology, 1986—2008; contbr. articles to profl. jours., chapters to books. V.p., acting pres. Lycoming County Hist. Soc., Williamsport, 1968—70; designed ofcl. flag Lycoming County, Pa., 1970. Recipient Archie award, Soc. Pa. Archaeology, 1967, J. Alden Mason award, 1988; fellow NSF, 1970—73, Woodrow Wilson Found., 1970—71. Fellow: Explorers Club; mem.: Soc. Hist. Archaeology, Soc. Am. Archaeology, Sigma Xi, Phi Alpha Theta, Phi Kappa Phi. Unitarian Universalist. Avocations: travel, geology, American history. Office: Univ RI Dept Sociol and Anthropol Kingston RI 02881 Business E-Mail: wtu4496u@postoffice.uri.edu.

TURNBULL, CHARLES WESLEY, former governor; b. St. Thomas, VI, Feb. 5, 1935; BS, Hampton U., 1958, MS, 1959; PhD, U. Minn., 1976. Elem., sec. sch. tchr.; prin. Charlotte Amalie H.S.; from asst. commr. to commr. VI Dept. Edn.; prof. history U. VI; gov. US VI, Charlotte Amalie, 1999—2007. Chair VI Bd. Edn., 1996-2000; bd. dirs. U. VI, Roy Lester Schneider Hosp., 1995-98; chmn., Public Fin. Authority, 1999-2007. Democrat. Methodist. Office: PO Box 302265 St Thomas VI 00803

TURNBULL, H. RUTHERFORD, III, lawyer, educator; b. NYC, Sept. 22, 1937; s. Henry R. and Ruth (White) T.; m. Mary M. Slingluff, Apr. 4, 1964 (div. 1972); m. Ann Patterson, Mar. 23, 1974; children: Jay, Amy, Katherine. Grad., Kent (Conn.) Sch., 1955; BA, Johns Hopkins U., 1959; LLB with honors, U. Md., 1964; LLM, Harvard U., 1969. Bar: Md., N.C. Law clk. to Hon. Emory H. Niles Supreme Bench Balt. City, 1959-60; law clk. to Hon. Roszel C. Thomsen U.S. Dist. Ct. Md., 1962-63; assoc. Piper & Marbury (now LDA Piper), Balt., 1964-67; prof. Sch. Govt. U. N.C., Chapel Hill, 1969—80, U. Kans., Lawrence, 1980—. Disting. prof. spl. edn., courtesy prof. law U. Kans. Editor-in-chief Md. Law Rev. Cons., author, lectr., co-founder, co-dir. Beach Ctr. on Disability, U. Kans.; pres. Full Citizenship Inc., Lawrence, 1987-93; spl. staff-fellow U.S. Senate subcom. on disability policy, Washington, 1987-88; bd. dirs. Camphill Assn. N.Am., Inc., 1985-87; trustee Judge David L. Bazelon Ctr. Mental Health Law, 1993-2007, chmn., 2000-05. With US Army, 1960-65. Recipient Nat. Leadership award Nat. Assn. Pvt. Residential Resources, 1988, Internat. Coun. for Exceptional Children, 1996, Am. Assn. on Mental Retardation, 1997, Century award Nat. Trust for Hist. Preservation in Mental Retardation, 1999, Nat. Adv. award Am. Music Therapy Assn., 2002, Leadership award Camphill Assn. N.Am., 2004, Leadership award The Arc of the US, 2004, U. Kans. Gene A. Budig Disting. Tchg. Professorship award, 2005, Nat. award advocacy positive supports Assn. Persons with Severe Handicaps, 2005, Kans.U. Sch. of Edn. Disting. Leadership award, 2005, Burton Blatt award Coun. Exceptional Children, 2006; named Nat. Educator of Yr., The Arc of the U.S., 1982; Pub. Policy fellow Joseph P. Kennedy, Jr. Found., 1987-88. Fellow Am. Assn. on Mental Retardation (pres. 1985-86, bd. dirs. 1980-86); mem. ABA (chmn. disability law commn. 1991-95), U.S.A. Assn. for Retarded Citizens (sec. and dir. 1981-83), Assn. for Persons with Severe Handicaps (treas. 1988, bd. dirs. 1987-90), Nat. Assn. Rehab. Rsch. and Tng. Ctrs. (chair govt. affairs com. 1990-93), Internat. Assn. Sci. Study of Mental Deficiency, Internat. League of Assns. for Persons with Mental Handicaps, Johns Hopkins U. Alumni Assn. (pres. N.C. chpt. 1977-79). Democrat. Episcopalian. Office: U Kans 3111 Haworth Hall 1200 Sunnyside Ave Lawrence KS 66045-7534 Office Phone: 785-864-7600. Business E-Mail: Rud@ku.edu.

TURNBULL, JOHN CAMERON, retired pharmacist, consultant; b. Regina, Sask., Can., Sept. 5, 1923; s. Cameron Joseph and Lillian Irene (Pentz) T.; m. Hazel Evelyn Rockwell, July 31, 1948; children: Lillian Elizabeth, John Rockwell, Jocelyn Hazel. BS in Pharmacy, U. Sask., 1949. Pharmacist with village and city pharmacies, 1945-50; supr. pharm. services Dept. Pub. Health, Sask., Regina, 1950-52; ops. mgr. Nat. Drugs, Ltd., Winnipeg, and Saskatoon, 1953; exec. dir. Can. Pharm. Assn., Toronto, Ont., 1953-78; ret. Sec.-treas., mng. dir. Canadian Pharm. Realty Co. Ltd.; mem. provisional bd. Pharmacare Ltd.; registrar-treas. Pharmacy Examining Bd. of Can., 1963-68, mem. bd., 1963-78; pharmacy cons., dir. drug service Ministry of Health, Barbados, 1979-84; staff assoc. Mgmt. Scis. for Health, Boston, 1984-85; cons. logistics and pharms. USAID, East Caribbean, PanAm. Health Orgn./WHO (Belize, Cen. Am.), 1985—. Chmn. Govt.'s Spl. Com. on Acetylsalicylic Poisonings, 1967; mem. Emergency Health Svcs. Adv. Com.; gen. chmn. Allied Air Forces Reunion, 1995, 96. Served to squadron leader RCAF, 1941-45. Decorated D.F.C., 1944, Order of Can., 1975; recipient Can. Centennial medal, 1967, Queen's Jubilee medal, 1977, Can. 125th Anniversary medal, 1992, John C. Turnbull rsch. ann. award in socio-econs. pharmacy established in his honor Can. Pharm. Assn., 1990. Mem. Fedn. Internationale Pharmaceutique (v.p.), Inst. of Assn. Execs. (hon. life), Conf. of Pharmacy Registrars of Can. (sec.), Commonwealth Pharm. Assn. (coun. 1969-78); hon. mem. Am., Canadian, Saskatchewan, B.C., Alta., Ont., Man., N.S. Pharm. Assns., Sask. Pharm. Assn., Ont. Pharmacists Assn., Canadian Soc. Hosp. Pharmacists, Rho Pi Phi. Mem. United Ch. of Canada. Club: Bayview Country (past dir.). Office: John and Hazel Turnbull 303-15 Barberry Pl Toronto ON Ontario Canada M2K 1G9 Home Phone: 416-222-4086.

TURNBULL, MARJORIE REITZ, educational consultant, state legislator; b. Madison, Wis., July 4, 1940; d. J. Wayne anf Frances H. (Millikan) R.; m. Augustus Bacon Turnbull, Nov. 26, 1965 (dec. Nov. 1991). Student, Agnes Scott Coll., 1958-60; BA, U. Fla., 1962; MA, U. Ga., 1968. Legis. analyst Fla. Ho. of Reps., Tallahassee, 1973-85, staff dir. com. on health and rehab. svcs., 1975-78, exec. asst. to speaker, 1978-80; asst. dir. Devel. Svc. Program Office, Tallahassee, 1980-82; dep. asst. sec. Health Planning State Fla., 1982-84; ind. cons. legis. mgmt. and planning, Tallahassee, 1984-95; ednl. cons., person assoc. Tallahassee C.C. Found.; state rep. legis. mgmt. and planning, Tallahassee, 1994-2000; found. dir. and v.p, Instl. Advancement, Tallahassee CC, 1995—2007. County commr. Leon County, Tallahassee, 1988-94; bd. dirs. Fla. Assn. Counties, Tallahassee, 1993-94, pres. 1994, Tallahassee Symphony Orch., 1992-98, chair State Juvenile Justice Found., 2007-08; mem. Found. Fla. CC; trustee Esward Waters Coll. Named Woman of Yr., AAUW, Tallahassee, 1991, County Champion in the Legislature, Fla. Assn. Counties, 1995, Legislator of Yr., Fla. Assn. Sch. Supts., 1999; recipient Girl Scout Woman of Distinction award, 1999, Disting. Svc. award Fla. Student Assn., 2000, Disting. Citizens award Boy Scout Coun., 2000, Meritorious Achievement award Fla. A&M U., 2000, Legis. Advocacy award Fla. Coalition Against Domestic Violence, 2000, Freedom from Violence Leadership awrd, 2000, Model of Achievement award Tallahassee C.C., 2001. Mem. Rotary (program com. 1992—), Zonta Internat., Fla. Blue Key. Democrat. Presbyterian. Avocations: scuba diving, travel, cultural activities. Home: 3221 E Lakeshore Dr Tallahassee FL 32312-2062 Office: Tallahassee C C 444 Appleyard Dr Tallahassee FL 32304 E-mail: turnbulm@tcc.fl.edu.

TURNBULL, ROBERT B., librarian; b. Northville, Mich., July 1, 1945; s. Bruce Turnbull and Rita Heatley; m. Margaret Coombs, June 16, 1984; 1 child, Andrew. BA, Mich. State U., Lansing, 1967, MA, 1968; AMLS, U. Mich., Ann Arbor, 1970. Retail mgr. Montgomery Wards, Detroit, 1968—69; head libr. U. Guam, Agana, 1971—75, Concord U., Athens, W.Va., 1995—, reader svcs. libr., 1977—, prof., 1977—. Singer: (Operas) Don Giovanni. Libr. cons. vol. Lady Victory Sch., Northville, 1971; vol. mgr. Guam Food Coop., Tamuning, 1972—74, Food For Us Coop. Inc., Athens, 1981—2000; vol. worker Givat Hayim Kibbutz, Hadera, Israel, 1975—76. Mem.: Beta Phi Mu, Phi Eta Sigma. Episcopalian. Office: Concord Univ Vermillion St Athens WV 24712 Office Fax: 304-384-7955. Business E-Mail: turnbull@concord.edu.

TURNBULL, SUSAN W., political organization administrator; m. Bruce Turnbull; children: Joshua, David. BS in Cmty. Svc. magna cum laude, U. Cin.; BS in Interior Design, Marymount U., Arlington, Va.; MS in Urban Studies, U. Md. Principal, interior space planning bus.; various staff positions in US House and Senate Washington; mem. exec. com. Md. Dem. Party, 1990—2004, chairwoman, 2009—; vice chair Montgomery County Dem. Party, Md., 1990—93, chair Md., 1993—94; mem. Dem. Nat. Com., 1992—, mem. exec. com., 1997—2009, chair women's caucus, 1997—2003, nat. chair women's leadership forum, 2002—04, dep. chair, 2003—05, founding co-chair, women's vote ctr., 2005, vice chair, 2005—09; sr. advisor, grant cons. US House of Reps., Washington. Appearances include FOX News Channel, MSNBC; sr. Dem. strategist Women Impacting Pub. Policy; sr. advisor, grant cons. Dem. mems. of Congress. Founding bd. mem. Bolechow Jewish Heritage Soc.; bd. mem. Jewish Social Svc. Agency Met. Washington, Jewish Women's Internat., 2006—, Jewish Coun. Pub. Affairs, 2008—, U. Md. Ctr. Am. Politics and Citizenship, 2008—. Recipient Disting. Svc. award, Md. Dem. Party, 2003, Tikkun Olam Svc. award, Jewish Coun. Pub. Affairs, 2009; named Dem. of Yr., Montgomery County Dem. Party, 2000; named one of Top 10 Women to Watch, Jewish Women's Mag., 2005. Democrat. Office: Md Dem Party 188 Main St Ste 1 Annapolis MD 21401 Office Phone: 410-269-8818. Office Fax: 410-280-8882.*

TURNBULL, THOMAS LEIGH, social studies educator, secondary school educator; b. Bronxville, NY, Mar. 2, 1951; s. Kenneth Hamilton and Carolyn Mays Turnbull; 1 child, Sarah McCurrach. BA, U. Calif., Berkeley, Calif., 1983; MA, San Francisco State U., Calif., 1987. Tchr. San Ramon Valley H.S., Danville, Calif., 1986—87, Ygnacio Valley H.S., Concord, Calif., 1993—94, Acalanes H.S., Lafayette, Calif., 1994—95, Clayton Valley H.S., Concord, 1996—. Home: 10 Park Ave Walnut Creek CA 94595 Office: Clayton Valley High Sch 1101 Alberta Way Concord CA 94521-3799 Office Phone: 925-682-7474.

TURNBULL, VERNONA HARMSEN, retired education educator, counseling administrator; b. Teeds Grove, Iowa, Dec. 6, 1916; d. Henry Ferdinand and Ida Amelia (Dohrmann) Harmsen; m. Alexander Turnbull, Oct. 12, 1961. BA, Cornell Coll., Mt. Vernon, Iowa, 1939; MEd, U. Colo., Boulder, 1947, profl. cert. edn., 1955. Cert. secondary and h.s. tchr. Tchr. English, Latin and phys. edn. Winslow H.S., Ill., 1939-45; dir. women's activities, instr. Trinidad State Jr. Coll., Colo., 1947-53; counselor women, assoc. prof. edn. Western State Coll., Gunnison, Colo., 1953-54; instr., residence counselor Stephens Coll., Columbia, Mo., 1955-61; ret., 1961. Active Salvation Army Aux. Mem. AAUW, AARP (corr. sec. 1986-87), Kena Kampers Camping Club. Avocations: photography, camping, art, dance, baking.

TURNBULL-BRUEHL, JO'ANN HAZEL, special education educator; d. James Andrew and Beatrice Hazel Turnbull; 1 child, Erin Elizabeth Bruehl. BA in Art, Caldwell Coll., NJ, 1968. Cert. art tchr. K-12 NJ, 1970, handicapped tchr. NJ, 1972. Art elem. and secondary tchr. Franklin Twp. Sch. Dist., 1969—71; tchr. Jordan Day Sch., Princeton, NJ, 1974—75; 7th and 8th grade tchr. NJ Tng. Sch. Boys, Skillman, NJ, 1975—81; tchr. Wordsworth Acad., Ft. Wash., Pa., 1983; 7th and 8th grade English tchr. St. Raphael's Sch., Trenton, NJ, 1983—84; per diem and long-term substitute tchr. Neshaminy Sch. Dist., Bucks County, Pa., 1984—85, Pennsbury Sch. Dist., Bucks County, 1984—85; tchr., gen. edn. development program Forensic Psychiat. Hosp., Trenton, 1985, Ancora Psychiat. Hosp., Hammonton, NJ, 1985—86; mid. sch. and HS tchr., jr. high resource ctr. Morrisville Mid./Sr. HS, Pa., 1986—89; spl. edn. tchr. Crockett Mid. Sch., Hamilton Twp., NJ, 1989—. Home: 414 Cedar St Bristol PA 19007 Office: 2631 Kuser Rd Hamilton NJ 08619

TURNDORF, HERMAN, anesthesiologist, educator; b. Paterson, NJ, Dec. 22, 1930; s. Charles R. and Ruth (Blumberg) T.; m. Sietske Huisman, Nov. 24, 1957; children: David, Michael Pieter. AB, Oberlin Coll., 1952; MD, U. Pa., 1956. Diplomate Am. Bd. Anesthesiology. Instr. anesthesiology U. Pa. Hosp., 1957-59; asst. anesthetist med. sch. Harvard U., Mass. Gen. Hosp., Boston, 1961-63; assoc. attending anesthesiologist, asst. dir. dept. anesthesiology Mt. Sinai Hosp., NYC, 1963-70, clin. prof. anesthesiology, 1966-70; prof., chmn. dept. anesthesiology W.Va. U. Sch. Medicine and Med. Ctr., Morgantown, 1970-74, NYU Sch. Medicine, 1974—2000; dir. anesthesiology NYU Tisch Hosp., Bellevue Hosp. Ctr., 1974—2000; pres. med. bd., med. dir. Bellevue Hosp. Med. Ctr., 1990—91, 1997; ret., 2000. Co-author: Anesthesia and Neurosurgery, 2nd edit., 1986, Trauma, Anesthesia and Intensive Care, 1990; contbr. over 200 articles to profl. jours. Lt. M.C., USNR, 1959-61. Fellow Am. Coll. Chest Physicians, Am. Coll. Anesthesiologists (mem. bd. govs. 1977-85, chmn. bd. govs. 1984), N.Y. Acad. Medicine; mem. AMA, Am. Soc. Anesthesiologists, Assn. Univ. Anesthetists, Internat. Soc. Study of Pain, Soc. Acad. Anesthesia Chairmen, Soc. Critical Care Medicine, Soc. Neurosurg. Anesthesia and Neurologic Supportive Care, N.Y. Acad. Scis., N.Y. State Soc. Anesthesiologists. Personal E-mail: hermanturndorf@bellsouth.net.

TURNER, ALICE KENNEDY, editor; b. Mukden, Manchuria; d. William Taylor and Florence Bell (Green) T. BA, Bryn Mawr Coll., 1962. Sr. editor Holiday mag., NYC, 1969-70; assoc. editor Publishers Weekly, NYC, 1972-74; sr. editor Ballantine Books, NYC, 1974-76, New York mag., NYC, 1976-80; fiction editor Playboy mag., Chgo., NYC, 1980—2001, contbg. editor, 2001—. Author: Yoga for Beginners, 1973, The History of Hell, 1993; co-author: The New York Woman's Guide, 1975; editor: Playboy Stories, 1993, The Playboy Book of Science Fiction, 1996; co-editor: Snake's-hands: The Fiction of John Crowley, 2002; editor: Playboy's College Fiction, 2007. Home: 2 Charlton St New York NY 10014-4909 Personal E-mail: aktnyc@gmail.com.

TURNER, ALMON RICHARD, retired art historian, educator; b. New Bedford, Mass., July 28, 1932; s. Louis Alexander and Margaret (Mather) T.; m. Jane Beebe; children: Louis Hamilton, David Alexander. AB, Princeton U., 1955, MFA, 1958, PhD, 1959. Instr. in fine arts U. Mich., Ann Arbor, Mich., 1959-60; from instr. to prof. art and archaeology Princeton U., NJ, 1960-68; prof. fine arts Middlebury Coll., Vt., 1968-74, dean faculty Vt., 1970-74; prof. fine arts, pres. Grinnell Coll., Iowa, 1975-79; prof., dir. Inst. Fine Arts NYU, NYC, 1979-82, dean faculty arts and scis., 1982-85, prof. dept. fine arts, 1985-2000, dir. N.Y. Inst. Humanities, 1986-93, Paulette Goddard prof. in arts and humanities, 1994—2000, prof. emeritus, 2000—. Sec. Princeton Project 55, 2002—06. Author: Vision of Landscape in Renaissance Italy, 1966, 73, (With G. Andres and J. Hunisak) Art of Florence (L'Art de Florence), 1988 (prix 1989), Inventing Leonardo, 1993, Renaissance Florence: The Invention of a New Art, 1997, La Pietra: Florence, a Family, and a Villa, 2002 Bd. dirs. Pinelands Preservation Alliance, 2007—. Mem. Coll. Art Assn., Century Assn., NJ Audubon Soc. (1st v.p. 1990-93, pres. 1993-96), Phi Beta Kappa. Democrat. Unitarian Universalist. Avocations: birding, photography. Home: PO Box 2322 Cape May NJ 08204-7322

TURNER, B. RUSSELL, tax accountant, financial planner, real estate broker; b. Fresno, Calif., Nov. 19, 1948; s. Frank Robert T. and Dorothy Elaine Smith; m. LoRayne A. Haye, Aug. 15, 1984 (div. Aug., 1987); 1 child, Tyler Cayden Turner-Haye (dec.); m. Linda Marie Vanderbeke, Sept. 9, 1990; 1 child, R. Vanderbeke Turner. AA, Fresno City Coll., Calif., 1971; BA in Psychology, Calif. State U., Fresno, 1973; postgrad., Heald Coll., 1982. Counseling cert.; Santa Cruz Suicide Prevention Svc.; neurolinguistics profl. Robbins Rsch. Inst.; Enrolled Agent, CFP®. Constrn. asst. Barry R. Turner Constrn., Corralitos, Calif., 1973-75; substitute tchr. Pajaro Unified Schs., Watsonville, Calif., 1975-77; counselor Suicide Prevention Svc., Santa Cruz, Calif., 1977-79; psychoanalyst HELP Youth Tng. Program, Santa Cruz, 1978—81; law office mgr. Juno Fin. Group, San Diego, 1982-91; tax acct. Turner Fin. Svcs., San Diego, fin. planner, real estate broker, 1992—. Software analyst Intuit, Inc., San Diego, 1996-98. Mem. Nat. Assn. Enrolled Agents, Calif. Soc. Enrolled Agents, San Diego Soc. Enrolled Agents (dir. membership 1992), San Diego Assn. Realtors, Calif. Soc. Tax Cons., SD Nat. Fin. Plan Assoc. Independent. Avocations: holds rokkyu in kenpo kung fu, vegetable gardening. Office: Turner Fin Svcs PO Box 86674 San Diego CA 92138-6674

TURNER, BILLIE LEE, II, geographer, educator; b. Texas City, Dec. 22, 1945; s. Billie Lee and Virgina Ruth Turner; m. Linda Lee Van Zandt; children: Billie Lee III, Victoria Kelly. Attended, Miami U., Oxford, Ohio, 1964—65; BA, U. Tex., Austin, 1968; MA, U. Tex., 1969; PhD, U. Wis., Madison, 1974. Asst. prof. geography U Md. Balt. County, Balt., 1974—75, U. Okla., Nomran, 1975—80, Clark U., Worcester, Mass., 1980—81, assoc. prof. geography, 1981—85, prof. geography, 1985—2008, dir. George Perkins Marsh Inst., 1991—97, prof. environment and sociology, 1995, Milton P. & Alice C. Higgins prof. environ. and soc., 1995—2008, dir. Grad. Sch. Geography, 2004—08, rsch. prof., 2008—; Glibert F. White prof. environ. and soc. Sch. Geographical Scis., Ariz. State U., Tempe, 2008—. Dir. grad. sch. geography Clark U., 1983—88, dir. Marsh Inst., 1991—97, dir. grad. sch. geography, 1997—98, 2004. Author: (book) Beneath the Forest: Prehistoric Terracing in the Rio Bec Region of the Maya Lowlands; editor: (books) Global Land-Use Change: A Perspective from the Columbian Encounter, Land Change Science: Observing, Monitoring and Understanding Trajectories of Change on the Earth's Surface, The Earth as Transformed by Human Action: Global and Regional Changes in the Biosphere over the Past 300 Years; co-editor (with J. Kasperson and R. Kasperson): 1995 Regions at Risk: Comparisons of Threatened Environments; co-editor: (J. Geoghegan and D. Foster) Integrated Land-Change Science and Tropical Deforestation in the Southern Yucatán: Final Frontiers; co-author (with Whitmore): Cultivated Landscapes of Native Middle America on the Eve of Conquest; co-author: (with W. Steffen etal) Global Change and the Earth System: A Planet under Pressure; co-editor (with P. D. Harrison): Pre-Hispanic Maya Agriculture, Pulltrouser Swamp: Ancient Maya Habitat, Agriculture and Settlement in Northern Belize; co-editor: (with S. B. Brush) Comparative Farming Systems; co-editor: (with G. Hyden and R. Kates) Population Growth and Agricultural Change in Africa; co-editor: (with W. Meyer) Changes in Land Use and Land Cover: A Global Perspective. Specialist 5 US Army, 1969—71, Frankfurt, Germany. Recipient Centenary medal, Royal Scottish Geog. Soc., 1996; Guggenheim fellow, Guggenheim Found., 1981—82, fellow, Ctr. Advanced Studies in Behavioral Scis., 1994—2005. Fellow: AAAS, Mass. Acad. Sci.; mem.: NAS. Achievements include research in human-environment relationships, from ancient Maya to sustainability science. Office: Ariz State Univ Sch Geographical Scis PO Box 87014 Tempe AZ 85287-0104 also: Clark U 950 Main St Worcester MA 01610 Office Phone: 480-965-7533. Office Fax: 480-965-8313. Business E-Mail: billie.l.turner@asu.edu.

TURNER, BONESE COLLINS, artist, educator; b. Abilene, Kans. d. Paul Edwin and Ruby (Seybold) Collins; m. Glenn E. Turner; 1 child, Craig Collins. BS in Edn., MEd, U. Idaho, Moscow; MA, Calif. State U., Northridge, 1974. Adj. prof. L.A. Pierce Coll., Woodland Hills, Calif., 1964—. Prof. art Calif. State U., Northridge, 1986-89; adj. prof. L.A. Valley Coll., Van Nuys, 1987-89, Moorpark Coll., Calif., 1988-98, Arrowmont Coll. Arts and Crafts, Gatlinburg, Tenn., 1995-96; advisor Coll. Art and Arch. U. Idaho, 1988—; juror for art exhbns. including Nat. Watercolor Soc., 1980, 91, San Diego Art Inst., Brand Nat. Watermedia Exhbn., 1980, 96-97, prin. gallery Orlando Gallery, Tarzana, Calif.; juror South Bay Watercolor Soc., 2008, Montrose Verdugo Juried Art Exhibit, 2005; tchr. watercolor seminar Dale Chihuly Found., W.Hills, Calif., 2005. Represented in permanent collections Smithsonian Inst., U. Idaho Hartung Performing Arts Ctr., Moscow Idaho Installation, 1994, Olympic Arts Festival, L.A.; one-woman shows include Angel's Gate Gallery, San Pedro, Calif., 1989, Art Store Gallery, Studio City, Calif., 1988, L.A. Pierce Coll. Gallery, 1988, Brand Art Gallery, Glendale, Calif., 1988, 93, 2000, 05, Coos (Oreg.) Art Mus., 1988, U. Nev., 1987, Orlando Gallery, Sherman Oaks, Calif., 1993, 98, 2002, 05, Burbank (Calif.) Creative Arts Ctr., 2000, 07, Village Sq. Gallery, Montrose, Calif., 2002, 05, Pierce Art Gallery, 2005, Calif. Inst. Tech., 2007, La Galeria Gitana San Fernando, Calif, 2009, Of Dreams & Memories, 2009, The Sacred in Art, Birger Sandzen Gallery, Lindsborg, Kans., 2007, Torrance Art Mus., 2008, Springfield Art Mus., Mo., 2003; prin. works in pub. collections include The Smithsonian Inst., Hartung Performing Arts Ctr., Moscow, Idaho, Robert V. Fulton Mus. Art, Calif. State U., San Bernardino, Calif., Springfield (Mo.) Art Mus, Home Savs. and Loan, San Bernardino Sun Telegram Newspapers, Oreg. Coun. for the Arts, Newport, Oreg. Pub. Librs., Brand Libr., Glendale, Calif., Lincoln (Nebr.) Pub. Lib., Indsl. Tile Corp., Lincoln. Recipient Springfield (Mo.) Art Mus. award, 1989, 2002, 1st prize Brand XXVIII, 1998, Glendale, Calif., Butler Art Inst. award, 1989, 1st award in graphics Diamond Jubilee Exhibit/Pasadena Soc. Artists, 2002, Nat. award Acrylic Painters Assn. Eng. and U.S.A., 1996, Ruth Kain award, LA Brewery, 2003. Mem. Nat. Acrylic Painters Assn. of Eng. (award 1996), Nat. Mortar Bd. Soc., Nat. Watercolor Soc. (life, past pres., Purchase prize 1979), Watercolor U.S.A. Honor Soc. (awards), Watercolor West. Avocations: bicycling, music, singing. Personal E-mail: boneseturner@yahoo.com.

TURNER, BRACHA, painter; b. Jerusalem; Exhbns. include 55 solo exhbns. and numerous juried exhbns.: J.F. Kennedy Art Gallery, Montreal, New Eng. Fine Arts Inst., Boston, Internat. Women in the Arts Conf., Beijing, Galerie Everarts, Paris; permanent display of paintings include Hadassah Hdqrs., N.Y., ZOA House, Tel-Aviv, Nat. Coun. of Jewish Women, N.Y., Ichilov Hosp., Tel-Aviv, Office of the Mayor of Jerusalem, Israel, The Bible Mus. Tel Aviv, Office of the Mayor N.Y.C., Rambam Hosp., Haifa, Israel, others; painting reproduced on cards by Hadassah; contbr. drawings to Sara's Daughters Sing, 1989. Home: 330 W 145 St New York NY 10039

TURNER, CHARLES HALL, biomedical engineer, educator; b. Roswell, N.Mex., Nov. 29, 1961; s. Bob Franklin and Mary (Hall) T.; m. Nancy Jo Wieczorek, Mar. 13, 1993. BSME, Tex. Tech. U., 1983; PhD, Tulane U., 1987. Rsch. asst. biomed. engring. Tulane U., New Orleans, 1984-87; dir. biomechanics, asst. prof. oral biology Creighton U., Omaha, 1987-91; prof. biomed. engring. Purdue U., Indpls., 1991—; prof. orthopaedic surgery, dir. orthopaedic rsch. Ind. U., Indpls., 1991—. Contbr. articles to Jour. Biomechanics, Jour. Biomech. Engring., Jour. Materials Sci. Recipient Morris F. Miller award Health Future Found., Omaha, 1987, FIRST award NIH, 1991; Whitaker Found. grantee, 1989. Mem. ASME, Orthopaedic Rsch. Soc., Soc. Biomechanics. Office: IUPUI 1120 South Dr FH 115 Indianapolis IN 46202 Home Phone: 317-259-8276. Business E-Mail: turnerch@iupui.edu.

TURNER, CHRISTOPHER D., pediatrician, director; MD, U. Rochester Sch. Medicine, NY, 1994. Diplomate in pediat. 1997, in hematology oncology Am. Bd. Pediat., 2004. Dir., pediat. neuro oncology program Dana Farber Cancer Inst., Boston, 2001—08, attending, 2008—; med. dir. oncology ARIAD Pharm., Inc., Cambridge, 2008—. Editor: (med. book) Late Effects of Treatment for Brain Tumors. Vol. physician Mass. Med. Res. Corp, Boston, 2006—. Fellow: Am. Acad. Pediat.; mem.: Children's Oncology Group, Soc. Neuro Oncology, Am. Soc. Clin. Oncology. Office: Dana Farber Cancer Inst 44 Binney St Boston MA 02115 Office Fax: 617-632-4897. Business E-Mail: christopher_turner@dfci.harvard.edu.

TURNER, DOROTHY JEAN, school librarian; b. Lakewood, Nj., Feb. 15, 1949; d. Russell Stanley and Jean Horton; m. Charles Terry Turner, Aug. 19, 1972; children: Philip, Andrew. BA, Georgian Ct. U., Lakewood, 1971; MA, U. Denver, 1972. Cert. Colo. Dept. Education. Reference libr. Ocean County Libr., Toms River, NJ, 1972—74; law libr. Colo. Nat. Bank, Pueblo, Colo., 1975—78; br. libr. Pueblo Libr. Dist., 1984—85; educator-media specialist Pueblo City Sch., 1986—. Libr. cons. St. Mary Corwin Med. Ctr., 1983. Contbr. articles to profl. jours. Pres. Jr. League Pueblo, 1984, Chmn.-50th Anniv., 1987. Grant, 3M and Am. Assoc. Sch. Libr., 2002. Mem.: Ark. Valley Chpt. Daughter Am. Revolution (sec. 1998), Delta Kappa Gamma (v.p. 1994). Methodist. Avocations: travel, ballroom dancing. Home: 212 Bridle Trail Pueblo CO 81005 Office: Pueblo City Sch-Heaton Middle Sch 6 Adair Rd Pueblo CO 81001 Personal E-mail: doturner_98@yahoo.com.

TURNER, E. DEANE, lawyer; b. Auburn, NY, Aug. 4, 1928; s. Alfred Edward and Bertha (Deane) T. AB summa cum laude, Princeton U., 1950; LLB cum laude, Harvard U., 1953. Bar: NY 1953. Assoc. Dewey & LeBoeuf LLP and predecessor firms, NYC, 1953-63, ptnr., 1963—, of counsel, 1991—. Treas. Harvard Law Sch. Assn., N.Y.C., 1964-83; elder, trustee Brick Presbyn. Ch., N.Y.C., 1976-2003, pres. bd. trustees, 1988-90; trustee Presbytery N.Y.C., 1993-98, pres. bd. trustees, 1995-98; com. to adminstr. James N. Jarvie Endowment, 1993-2000. Fellow Am. Coll. Investment Counsel (emeritus); mem. Soc. Mayflower Descendants, Soc. Colonial Wars, Union Club, John's Island Club, Phi Beta Kappa. Republican. Home: 1120 5th Ave New York NY 10128-0144 also: 381 Llwyds Ln Johns Island Vero Beach FL 32963 Office: Dewey & LeBoeuf LLP 1301 Avenue Of The Americas New York NY 10019-6022

TURNER, ELIZABETH ADAMS NOBLE (BETTY TURNER), real estate company executive, author; b. Yonkers, NY, May 18, 1931; d. James Kendrick and Orrel (Baldwin) Noble; m. Jack Rice Turner, July 11, 1953; children: Jay Kendrick, Randall Ray. BA, Vassar Coll., 1953; MA, Tex. A&I U., 1964. Ednl. cons., Tex. sales mgr. Noble & Noble Pub. Co., NYC, 1956-67; psychometrist Corpus Christi Guidance Ctr., 1967-70; psychologist Corpus Christi State Sch., 1970-72, dir. programs, asst. supt., 1972, dir. devel. and vol. svc., 1972-76, dir. rsch. and tng., 1977-79; psychologist Tex. Mental Health and Mental Retardation, 1970-79; dir., alumni affairs Corpus Christi State U., 1976—78; pres. Turner Co., 1975-82; mayor pro tem Corpus Christi, 1981-85; mayor, 1987-91; CEO, pres. Corpus Christi C. of C., 1991; pres. Betty Turner Real Estate, 1999—. V.p. bus. and govt. rels. ctrl. and south Tex. divsns. Columbia Healthcare Corp., 1994—99; paternal co-founder Barnes and Noble, NYC. Author: The Noble Legacy. Bd. dirs. Nat. AARP, 2002—04; coord. vols. Summer Head Start Program, Corpus Christi, 1967; chmn. spl. gifts com. United Way, Corpus Christi, 1970; founder Com. 100, Goals for Corpus Christi, Bay Area Sports Assn., Coastal Bend Mayor's Alliance, Mayor's Commn. on Disabled, Mayor's Task Force on Homeless; pres. Mayor's Interagy. Coun.; bd. dirs. USO, Coastal Bend Coun. Govts., Corpus Christi Mus., Harbor Playhouse, Cmtys. in Schs., YWCA, Y-Teen Sponsor, Del Mar Coll. Found., 1998—2005, Tex. A&M at Corpus Christi Pres. Coun., Hispanic C. of C., TAMACC Corp. Ptnrs. Bd., Salvation Army, Jr. League, Coun. Deaf Silent Found., 2001—, Am. Heart Assn., 1999—2000, Bethune Day Care Nursery, 1999—2004, Jr. League Cmty. Adv. Coun., 1999—2000, 21st Century Charter Sch. Bd., 2001—02, Boys and Girls Club Corpus Christi, bd. mem., 2002—05; bd. dirs. Food Bank, bd. pres., 2004—05, Adm. Tex. Navy; mem. Gov.'s Commn. Women, 1984—85, Leadership Tex. Class I, Corpus Christi, Class II; fundraising chair Port Aransas Leadership Cmty. Performing Arts Theater; libr. bd. Port Aransas Charter Rev. Commn.; bd. mem. Port Aransas C. of C., 2009; mem. Corpus Christi City Coun., 1979—91; elder Cmty. Presbyn. Ch., 2004—07; bd. dirs. Southside Cmty. Hosp., 1987—93; mem. strategic planning com. Meml. Hosp., 1992, Tex. Capital Network Bd., 1992—95, Humana Hosp., Physician Relocation and Condo Sales; bd. dirs. Rehab. Hosp., St. David's/Austin and Medth. Healthcare Sys., San Antonio, 1997—99; adv. coun. Sch. Nursing U. Tex., 1998—99; bd. dirs. Gulfway Bank and Pacific Southwest Bank, 1997—2000. Recipient Love award, YWCA, 1970, Y's Women Careers award, 1988, Recognition award, Rotary, 1991, Comdr.'s award for pub. svc., U.S. Army, Scroll Honor award, Navy League, Tex. Hwy Dept., Road Hand award, Tex. Hwy. Commn., Women of Distinction award, Pres. award, Corpus Christi Food Bank, 2008, DAR Cmty. Svc. award, 2009; named Newsmaker of Yr., 1987. Mem.: NAACP (life), Tex. Assn. Realtors, Tex. Bookman's Assn., Tex. Mcpl. League (bd. dirs.), Psychol. Assn. (pres., founder), Tex. Psychol. Assn. (pres., mem. exec. bd.), Jr. League Corpus Christi, Jr. Cotillion Club, Corpus Christi Town Club, Kappa Kappa Gamma, Delta Kappa Gamma (hon.). Home: 403 Blue Heron Dr Port Aransas TX 78373 Home Phone: 361-749-5712; Office Phone: 361-877-1111. Personal E-mail: bettyturner@centurytel.net.

TURNER, ELVIN L., retired school system administrator; b. Springfield, Ohio, Jan. 9, 1938; s. Willie and Jinada (Lawson) T.; 1 child, Anthony; m. Carrie Johnson, Aug. 3, 1972; 1 child, Brenetta Bell. BS in Biology and Chemistry, Knoxville Coll., Tenn., 1962; MEd, U. Cin., 1968; postgrad., Nova U., Ft. Lauderdale, Fla., 1973, Kensington U., Glendale, Calif., 1993—. Cert. secondary prin., tchr., Ohio. Spl. edn. tchr. Cin. Pub. Schs., 1965-69, coord. spl. edn., 1969-72, asst. prin., 1972-78, 1990—93, prin., 1978—90, Kiwanis Club, 1978—79. Part-time adj. prof. Mt. St. Joseph Coll., Ohio, 1987—88; mem. adv. com. Millcreek Psychiat. Ctr. for Children, Cin., 1988—89; bus driver Bristol Village Retirement Cmty., 1997—99; ombudsman Pro-Srs., Cin., 1993—96, Waverly, Ohio, 1997—2005; vol. ombudsman rep. Area Agy. on Aging Dist. Seven, Inc., Portsmouth, Ohio; sec. Bristol Village Residents Assn., 1997; spkr. Rotary Club, Pike County, Waverly, Ohio. Author: numerous internat. poems, 2007. Vol. Ohio Dept Aging, Columbus, 2002—; asst. feeding program Visiting The Sick Ministries; master of ceremonies Black History Month Soul Food Luncheon; elected sec. exec. adv. coun. Bristol Village Nat. Ch. Residencies, Waverly, 1997; bd. deacons New Hope Bapt. Ch., Hamilton, Ohio, 1993; Sunday sch. tchr. Bethel AME Ch., Lebanon, Ohio, 1996; chmn. sick com. Usher Bd.; Bible study course instr. Asbury North United Meth. Ch., Columbus, 2000—01, instr. Vacation Bible Sch., 2000; bd. dirs. Big Bros./Big Sisters, Cin., 1973. Recipient plaque for statewide outstanding sr. vol. radio, TV and newspaper coverage, Independence, Ohio, 2001; named Outstanding Young Man, Montgomery C. of C., 1966. Mem. Assn. Secondary Sch. Adminstrs., So. Law Poverty Ctr. (named to Wall of Tolerance 2004), Knoxville Coll. Alumni Assn., Phi Delta Kappa (pres. U. Cin. chpt. 1970), Alpha Phi Alpha, Internat. Soc. Poet. Avocations: bowling, golf, reading, travel, writing. Personal E-mail: eturner001@insight.rr.com.

TURNER, EUGENE ANDREW, manufacturing executive; b. Bridgeton, NJ, Aug. 7, 1928; s. Benjamin Homer and Pearl Irene (Wolbert) T.; m. Paula Ann Webb, 1987; children: Mary Ann, John-Reed. BA, Rutgers U., 1956; student, Columbia U., 1980. With Owens Ill., 1950-73, regional mgr. West Coast, 1970-73; v.p. adminstrn. Midland Glass Co., Cliffwood, NJ, 1973-76, pres., chief operating officer, 1981-82, also bd. dirs.; v.p., gen. mgr. Anchor Hocking Corp., Lancaster, Ohio, 1976-81; dir. ops. Theo Chem. Labs., Tampa, Fla., 1988-90, Profit Counselors Inc, Sarasota, Fla., 1990-94; pres. Profit Sys. Inc., Oklahoma City, 1994—. Mng. cons. 1987-88; trustee Glass Packaging Inst. Mem. Harbor Island Club, Seaview Country Club, Navesink Country Club. Home: 428 Moody Ave Clovis CA 93619 Office Phone: 405-209-1103. Personal E-mail: gene227@juno.com. *Take time to learn the chosen business then develop credibility by doing what you say you will do.*

TURNER, FRANK MILLER, historian, educator; b. Springfield, Ohio, Oct. 31, 1944; s. Ronald O. and Mary Elizabeth (Miller) T.; m. Margaret Good, Aug. 26, 1967 (div. 1981); m. Nancy Rash, July 29, 1984 (dec. Mar. 1995); m. Ellen L. Tillotson, Aug. 7, 1999. BA, Coll. of William and Mary, 1966; MPhil, Yale U., 1970, PhD, 1971; LHD (hon.), Coll. William and Mary, 1991, Quinnipiac U., 2003, Wilmington Coll., 2007. Asst. prof. Yale U., New Haven, 1971-77, assoc. prof., 1977-82, prof., 1982—, provost, 1988-92, John Hay Whitney prof. history, 1992—, dir., Beinecke Rare Book and Manuscript Libr., 2003—. Author: Between Science and Religion, 1974, The Greek Heritage in Victorian Britain, 1981, Contesting Cultural Authority: Essays in Victorial Intellectual Life, 1993, John Henry Newman: The Challenge to Evangelical Religion, 2002, Reflections on the Revolution in France, 2003; co-author: The Western Heritage, 1979, 83, 87, 91, 94, 97, 2000, 2003, 2006, Heritage of World Civilizations, 1985, 90, 93, 96, 99, 2001, 2004, 2008; editor: John Henry Newman, The Idea of a University, 1996.; contbr. articles to profl. jours. Trustee Conn. Coll., New London, 1996-2006. Guggenheim fellowship, 1983; recipient Brit. Coun. prize Conf. on Brit. Studies, 1982, Yale Press Gov.'s award, 1983. Office: Yale U History Dept PO Box 208324 New Haven CT 06520-8324 Office Phone: 203-432-2959. Business E-Mail: frank.turner@yale.edu.

TURNER, GRACE-MARIE, non-profit organization executive; d. Nell Amelia and Will Seaton Arnett; m. Douglas Kearny Turner, May 19, 2001. BA, U. N.Mex, 1969. Exec. dir. Wash. Psychiat. Soc., Washington, 1982—84; pres. Arnett & Co., Washington, 1984—95; exec. dir. Nat. Commn. on Econ. Growth and Tax Reform, Washington, 1995—96; v.p. The Heritage Found., Washington, 1996—97; founder, pres., trustee Galen Inst., Inc., Alexandria, Va., 1997—. Facilitator Health Policy Consensus Group, Washington, 1993—. Dir. Ethics and Pub. Policy Ctr., Washington, 1998—99. Recipient Numerous Journalistic Writing awards, 1970—82, Outstanding Achievement award for Promotion of Consumer Driven Health Care, Consumer Health World, 2007. Roman Catholic. Avocations: piano, gardening, travel, theater. Office: Galen Institute Inc PO Box 320010 Alexandria VA 22320 E-mail: gracemarie@galen.org.*

TURNER, GWENDOLYN MARIE, band director, musician; b. Dillon, SC, Mar. 25, 1957; d. G. Maurice and Marguerite P. Turner. Student, Winthrop Coll., 1977; BS in Music, U. N.C., Pembroke, 1980. Cert. tchr. N.C. Band dir. Lewis Chapel Mid. Sch., Fayetteville, NC, 1980—2003, Pine Forest Mid. Sch., 2003—, chair art dept., 2006—. Chair N.C. All-State Mid. Sch. Band, Greensboro, 1993—94; condr., clinician Cumberland NC All-County Band, 1984, Cumberland NC All-County Band 1984, 2008, S.E.D.B.A. All-Dist. Band, NC, 1993, U. N.C.-Pembroke Invitational Band, 1995; clarinetist Snyder Meml. Bapt. Ch. Orch., Fayetteville, 1982—, Cumberland Oratorio Singers Orch., Fayetteville, 1991—, Cape Fear Regional Theatre Orch., Fayetteville, 1998—2002, Fayetteville Cmty. Band, 2007—. Named one of Outstanding Young Women of Am., 1987. Mem.: So. Dist. Bandmasters Assn. (v.p., recording sec. 1995—97, pres. 1997—99, treas. 2008—, 2008), Profl. Educators of N.C., N.C. Bandmasters Assn. (Award of Excellence 1998), Music Educators Nat. Conf. Avocations: gardening, reading, needlecrafts, collecting. Office: Pine Forest Mid Sch 6901 Ramsey St Fayetteville NC 28311 Office Phone: 910-488-2711. Personal E-mail: gturner357@hotmail.com.

TURNER, HARRY SPENCER, preventive medicine physician, educator; b. Dayton, Ohio, July 25, 1938; s. Eli and Daphne (Cunagin) T.; m. Jan (Fairley) T.; children: Michael, Mary, Daniel. BA, Manchester Coll., North Manchester, Ind., 1960; MD summa cum laude, Ohio State U., 1963, MS in Preventive Medicine, 1968. Diplomate Am. Bd. Preventive Medicine. Resident in preventive (aerospace) medicine Ohio State U., Columbus, 1966-69, chief resident, 1968-69, clin. asst. prof. dept. preventive medicine, 1969-80, dir. Univ. Health Svc., 1970-80; pvt. practice Dayton, 1980-90; dir. Univ. Health Svc., head team physician U. Ky., Lexington, 1991—2003, prof. preventive medicine and environ. health, 1991—2003, prof. emeritus, 2003, dir. emeritus, 2003; med. dir. Sutton Pl. Behavioral Health, 2003—. Editor: (textbook) History and Practice of College Health, 2002; contbr. articles and papers to profl. jours. and meetings. Bd. dirs. Blue Shield, 1981-86; mem. Cin. Internat. Chorale, 1989-94; mem. Lexington Singers, 1992—2003, Island Chamber Singers, 2005-07. Capt. U.S. Army, 1964-66. Fellow Am. Coll. Preventive Medicine, Am. Coll. Health Assn. (pres. 1980, Ruth Boynton award 1982, Edw. Hitchcock award 1996, Lifetime Achievement award 2003), Alpha Omega Alpha Avocation: music. E-mail: hsturner904@comcast.net.

TURNER, HARRY WOODRUFF, lawyer; b. Blairsville, Pa., May 2, 1939; s. James McKinnie and Dorothy Elizabeth (Tittle) Turner; m. Mary Elizabeth Phelan, Dec. 30, 1972; children: James William, David Woodruff. AB, U. Pitts., 1961; JD, Harvard U., 1964. Bar: Pa. 1965, U.S. Supreme Ct. 1979. Assoc. Kirkpatrick & Lockhart, Gates LLP, Pitts., 1964-71, ptnr., 1971—. Bd. vis. Coll. Arts & Scis. U. Pitts., 1988—2003, chmn. bd. vis. Sch. Info. Scis., 1994—2002, trustee, 1995—2003, bd. visitors Med. Sch., 1995—2002; mem. Fed. Jud. Selection Commn., Pa., 1995—2008, chmn., 1997—2008. Trustee Pitts. Opera, 1993—, pres., 2001—04, 2007—09; trustee, v.p. Torrance (Pa.) State Hosp., 1969—73; chair distbn. com. William L. Benz Found., 1985—; bd. dirs. Am. Heart Assn., Pitts., 1993—2002; mem. Fox Chapel Vol. Fire Dept.; alt. del. Rep. Nat. Conv., Miami, 1968, Houston, 1992, Phila., 2000, Rep. State Com., 1994—; trustee U. Pitts., 1995—2003, Wilson Coll., Chambersburg, Pa., 1978—89, Pitts. Cultural Trust, 2002—04, 2007—09, Foxwall Emergency Med. Svc., 2007—. Mem.: SAR (pres. 1995—96), ABA, Supreme Ct. Hist. Soc., Bar Assn. of Third Cir., Allegheny County Acad. Trial Lawyers, Allegheny County Bar Assn., Internat. Acad. Trial Lawyers, Am. Law Inst., Pa. Bar Assn., Hist. Soc. Western Pa. (trustee 1993—, vice chmn. 1999—2003), U. Pitts. Alumni Assn. (pres. 1991—92), Duquesne Club, Fox Chapel Golf Club. Presbyterian. Office: K & L Gates Henry W Oliver Bldg 535 Smithfield St Ste 535 Pittsburgh PA 15222 Office Phone: 412-355-6478. Business E-Mail: woodruff.turner@klgates.com.

TURNER, HENRY BROWN, finance company executive, director; b. NYC, Sept. 3, 1936; s. Henry Brown III and Gertrude (Adams) T.; m. Sarah Jean Thomas, June 7, 1958 (div.); children: Laura Eleanor, Steven Bristow, Nancy Carolyn. AB, Duke U., 1958; MBA, Harvard U., 1962. Controller Fin. Corp. of Ariz., Phoenix, 1962-64; treas., dir. corporate planning Star-Kist Foods, Terminal Island, Calif., 1964-67; dir., 1st v.p. Mitchum, Jones & Templeton, Los Angeles, 1967-73; asst. sec. Dept. Commerce, Washington, 1973-74; v.p. fin. N-Ren Corp., Cin., 1975-76; v.p. Oppenheimer & Co., NYC, 1976-78; exec. v.p., mng. dir. corporate fin. Shearson Hayden Stone Inc., NYC, 1978-79; sr. mng. dir. Ardshiel Inc., 1980-81, pres., 1981-93, chmn. emeritus, 1994—. Vis. lectr. U. Va. Sch. of Bus.; bd. dirs. MacDonald & Co., Pembrook Mgmt., Inc., Golden State Vitners, Inc., Cellu-Tissue Corp., Rio Verde, Ariz; quarter horse trainer; prof. piano player. Sponsor Jr. Achievement, 1964-67. Served to lt. USNR, 1958-60. Coll. Men's Club scholar Westfield, N.J., 1954-55 Mem. Fed. Govt. Accountants Assn. (hon.), Duke Washington Club, Omicron Delta Kappa.

TURNER, HOWARD, engineering educator, consultant; s. Herbert Mitchell Turner and Dorothy Irwin; m. Carol Lynn Lane, Jan. 4, 1988. BSc, Birkbeck Coll., London, 1968; MSc, McGill U., Montreal, Can., 1970; Grad. Diploma in Photogrammetry, U. Coll. London, 1971; PhD, U. Waterloo, 1975. Cert. in land surveying Calif., 1988, Ind., mrics Royal Inst. Chartered Surveyors, 2005. Land surveyor McConnell Maughan, Oakville, Ontario, Canada, 1977—81; photogrammetrist Can. Marconi, Montreal, Quebec, 1981—82; asst. prof. Purdue U., West Lafayette, Ind., 1983—88; prof. Calif. State Poly. U., Pomona, Calif., 1988—. Cons. Gale Rsch., Farmington Hills, Mich., 1998—98, World Book Ency., Chicago, Ill., 1992, McGraw Hill, Trenton, NJ, 1996, So. Calif. Joint Apprenticeship Com., Walnut, 1989—90, Calif. Found. Land Surveying Edn., Tustin, Calif., 1989—2000, Psomas & Assocs., La., 1990—91, Magellan Sys., San Dimas, Calif., 1991—93, Caltrans, Sacramento, 1992, Earth Vectors, Costa Mesa, Calif., 1993—93, Westech Coll., Pomona, 1994, Kelar Corp., San Diego, 1995, BEA Sys., 1998, Geofon, Diamond Bar, 1998—2000, Psomas & Assocs., Costa Mesa, 1998—2002, Prizm Group, Norco, 2002—04, Marshall Engring., Glendora, 2004—05, Land Design Consultants, Pasadena, 2005—; expert witness Superior Ct.,La., Chatsworth, 2003, Harry J Gerrity Law Office, West Hills, 2005—05, Bruce Graham Law Office, Westlake Village, 2005, Luce Forward Hamilton & Scripps, San Diego, 2006, Thorsnes Bartolotta & McGuire, La Jolla, 2006—07, Robert E. Weiss Law Office, West Covina, Calif., 1992—93; cons. Bentley Systems, Exton, Pa., 2004—06. Recipient Minority Instn. Equipment award, Air Force Office Sci. Rsch., 2001, Curriculam Devel. award, NSF, 2001, DOD Equipment award, Army Rsch. Office, 2006; named Educator of the Yr., Bentley Sys., 2007. Fellow: Inst. Advancement Engring.; mem.: Royal Inst. Chartered Surveyors. Achievements include development of surveying engineering program at Cal Poly Pomona. Office: California State Poly Univ Pomona 3801 W Temple Ave Pomona CA 91768 Office Fax: 909-869-4342. Business E-Mail: hturner@csupomona.edu.

TURNER, HUGH JOSEPH, JR., lawyer; b. Paterson, NJ, Oct. 5, 1945; s. Hugh Joseph and Louise (Sullivan) T.; m. Charlene Chiappetta, Feb. 11, 1983. BS, Boston U., 1967; JD, U. Miami, Coral Gables, Fla., 1975. Bar: Fla. 1975, U.S. Dist. Ct. (so., no. and mid. dists.) Fla. 1975, U.S. Ct. Appeals (11th cir.) 1981, U.S. Supreme Ct. 1984. Tchr. Browne & Nichols, Cambridge, Mass., 1968-72; ptnr. Smathers & Thompson, Miami, Fla., 1981-87, Kelley Drye & Warren, Miami, 1987-93, English, McCaughan & O'Bryan, Ft. Lauderdale, 1993—2001, Redgrave & Turner LLP, Boca Raton, Fla., 2001—03, Akerman Senterfitt, Ft. Lauderdale, 2003—. Chmn. Fla. Bar internat. law sect., 1988-89. Contbg. author book on internat. dispute resolution Fla. Bar, 1989; contbr. articles to profl. jours. Bd. dirs. Japan Soc. South Fla., Miami, 1989-97; mem. Sea Ranch Lakes Village Coun., 1997-2000; mayor Sea Ranch Lakes, 2000-02. Mem.: ABA, Def. Rsch. Inst. Avocation: running. Office: Akerman Senterfitt Ste 1600 350 E Las Olas Blvd Fort Lauderdale FL 33301-2229 Home Phone: 954-942-8073; Office Phone: 954-463-2700. Business E-Mail: hugh.turner@akerman.com.

TURNER, JAMES HILTON, JR., lawyer; b. Chattanooga, Oct. 31, 1946; s. J. Hilton and Helen Cornelia (Herbert) T.; m. Betty Pei-Cheng Lee, Aug. 21, 1971; 1 child, Justin Lee. B.S., Westminster Coll., 1968; M.Div., Yale U., 1972; J.D., Georgetown U., 1975. Bar: D.C. 1979, Pa. 1975. Dir. legal writing program Georgetown U., Washington, 1974-75; counsel, legis. asst. to Rep. Gary Myers, Washington, 1975-77; Republican energy counsel Com. on Sci. and Tech., U.S. Ho. of Reps., 1977-81; dir. govt. relations Internat. Coal Refining Co., Washington, 1981-84; counsel and tech. staff Com. on Sci. and Tech., US Ho. of Reps., 1984-1997, chief Dem. counsel, 1997-2006, chief counsel, 2007-. Trustee strategic planning com. and com. bd., chair adv. bd. dept. sci., tech. and soc. U. Va. Sch. Engring. and Applied Scis.; mem. presdl. adv. bd. Carnegie Mellon U.; mem. bd. dirs. Am. Nat. Stds. Inst., Scientists and Engrs. for Am., treas. Mem. Adv. Bd.: (jour.) Innovations: Tech., Governance, Globalization. Mentor Georgetown U. Law Sch.; bd. dirs. Downtown Cluster Congregations, Accelerating Innovation Found.; treas. bd. dirs. Pediat. AIDS/HIV Care; trustee, session mem. NY Ave. Presbyn. Ch.; vestry mem., outreach com. chair St. Columbia's Episcopal Ch. Recipient Outstanding Svc. award Fed. Lab. Consortium, 1989, Patriot of the Expatriots award Am. Bus. Coun. of Gulf States, 1991, Thomas Jefferson award Tech. Transfer Soc., 1992, Congressional Leadership award, Semiconductor Industry Assn., 1994, Howard Coonley medal Am. Nat. STds. Inst., 1996, Appreciation cert. Am. Math. Soc., 1997, William T. Cavanaugh Meml. award, 2000, Svc. award Va. Engring. Found., 2002, Appreciation award, 2004, Disting. Svc. award Fed. Patent Lawyer Assn., 2001, Melvin R. Green Codes and Stds. medal Am. Soc. Mech. Engrs., 2005, Honor award Nat. Inst. Bldg. Scis., 2006, Ronald L. Brown Stds. Leadership award World Stds. Day Com., 2008. Mem. D.C. Bar Assn., Pa. Bar Assn. Clubs: Georgetown, Yale. Office: Committee on Science 2320 Rayburn HOB Washington DC 20515

TURNER, JAMES LEE, energy executive; b. Muncie, Ind., Aug. 20, 1959; s. Jack Edwin and Nancy Kathleen (Marvin) T.; m. Leah Wakeland, Dec. 26, 1981; 3 children. BS, Ball State U., Muncie, 1981; JD cum laude, Ind. U., Indpls., 1984. Bar: Ind. 1984, US Dist. Ct. (so. dist. Ind.) 1984. Assoc. Bingham, Summers, Welsh & Spilman, Indpls., 1984—90, ptnr., 1990—91; Utility Consumer Counselor State of Ind., 1991—93; prin. Lewis & Kappes, Indpls., 1993—95; with Cinergy Corp., Cin., 1995, v.p. customer svc., 1999—2000, pres. energy delivery bus. unit, 2000—01, CEO regulated bus. unit, 2001—04, exec. v.p., CFO, 2004—05, pres., 2005; group exec., pres. US Franchised Electric and Gas Duke Energy, group exec., pres. and COO US Franchised Electric and Gas, 2007—. Mem. exec. com. Nat. Assn. State Utility Consumer Advs., 1992; bd. dirs. NAM, Electric Power Rsch. Inst. Mem. Ohio State Bd. of Edn., 1999—2004; bd. mem. Cin. Mus. Ctr., Boys & Girls Clubs Greater Cin., Charlotte C. of C., NC, Charlotte Ctr. City Ptnrs. Mem. ABA, (environ. law com., Tort & Ins. Practice Sect.), Ind. State Bar Assn., Indpls. Bar Assn. Def. Rsch. Inst. Clubs: Sierra (Hoosier chpt. Indpls.). Democrat. Office: Duke Energy 526 S Church St Charlotte NC 28202-1904 Office Phone: 704-594-6200.

TURNER, JANA L., real estate company executive; b. 1955; BSBA in Mktg., No. Ariz. U., 1977. Cert. property mgr. Inst. Real Estate Mgmt. Leasing receptionist R&B Comml. Mgmt., LA; pres. Pacific S.W. Region Koll Real Estate Svcs., Newport Beach, Calif., 1990—97; exec. v.p., mgr. western divsn. CB Comml., 1997—98; pres. asset svcs. CB Richard Ellis, 1998—. Bd. dirs. SiteStuff, Inc. Office: CB Richard Ellis 3501 Jamboree Rd Ste 100 Newport Beach CA 92660 Office Phone: 949-809-4057. E-mail: jana.turner@cbre.com.

TURNER, JEAN L., astronomer, educator; AB, Radcliffe Coll., Harvard U., Cambridge, Mass., 1976; PhD, U. Calif., Berkeley, 1984. Prof. UCLA, 1993—2008. Fellow: AAAS; mem.: Union Radio-Sci. Internat., Sigma Xi Soc., Am. Astron. Soc., Phi Beta Kappa.

TURNER, JIM (JAMES W. TURNER), lawyer, former United States Representative from Texas; b. Ft. Lewis, Wash., Feb. 6, 1946; m. Ginny Ward, Oct. 3, 1970; 2 children. BBA, U. Tex., 1968, MBA, JD, U. Tex., 1971. Bar: Tex. 1971, DC 2005. Mayor City of Crockett, Tex., 1989—91; mem. Tex. House Reps. from Dist. 15, 1981—84, Tex. State Senate from Dist. 5, 1991—96; spl. counsel for legis. affairs, exec. asst. to Gov. State of Tex., Austin, 1984—85; mem. US Congress from 2nd Tex. Dist., Washington, 1997—2005; ranking mem. US House Select Com. on Homeland Security, Washington; ptnr. Arnold & Porter LLP, Washington, 2005—. Mem. Econ. Growth, Natural Resources, and Regulatory Affairs subcom., Nat. Security, Internat. Affairs, and Criminal Justice subcom. House Govt. Reform and Oversight Com., Mil. Rsch. and Devel. subcom., Mil. Procurement subcom., ranking mem. Terrorism subcom., House Nat. Security Com.; ptnr. Arnold & Porter LLP, 2005-. Served in US Army, 1970—78. Democrat. Baptist. Office: Arnold & Porter LLP 555 Twelfth St NW Washington DC 20004 Office Phone: 202-942-5181. Office Fax: 202-942-5999. Business E-Mail: jim.turner@aporter.com.*

TURNER, JOHN ANDREW, economist; b. Chgo., July 9, 1949; s. Henry Andrew and Mary Margaret (Tilton) T.; m. Kathleen King Peery, June 21, 1975; 1 child, Sarah. BA, Pomona Coll., Claremont, Calif., 1971; MA, Stanford U., Calif., 1972; PhD, U. Chgo., 1977. Rsch. econ. SSA, Washington, 1976-80, ILO, Geneva, 1996-98, US Dept. Labor, Washington, 1980-96, rsch. econ. Office of Sec., 1999-2000, Pub. Policy Inst., AARP, 2000—06, pension policy cons., 2006—07; dir. Pension Policy Ctr., 2008—. Cons. OECD, Paris, 1989, IMF, 1995, AFL-CIO, 1996; chmn. Internat. Pension Conf., US Dept. Labor, Washington, 1990; adj. prof. George Washington U., 1994-96. Author: Pension Policy for a Mobile Labor Force, 1993, Individual Accounts for Social Security Reform, 2006; editor: Trends in Pensions, 1989 (transl. into Japanese 1991), Pension Policy: An International Perspective, 1991, Trends in Health Benefits, 1993, Private Pension Policies in Industrialized Countries, 1995, Securing Employer-Based Pensions, 1996, Social Security: Development and Reform, 2000. Fulbright scholar Institut de Recherches Economiques et Sociales, France, 1994. Mem. Am. Econ. Assn., Nat. Acad. Social Ins. Methodist. Avocation: travel. Home: 3713 Chesapeake St NW Washington DC 20016-1813 Personal E-mail: jturner47@verizon.net.

TURNER, JOHN FREELAND, former federal agency administrator, state legislator; b. Jackson, Wyo., Mar. 3, 1942; s. John Charles and Mary Louise (Mapes) T.; m. Mary Kay Brady, 1969; children: John Francis, Kathy Mapes, Mark Freeland. BS in Biology, U. Notre Dame, 1964; postgrad., U. Innsbruck, 1964-65, U. Utah, 1965-66; MS in Ecology, U. Mich., 1968. Rancher, outfitter Triangle X Ranch, Moose, Wyo.; chmn. bd. dirs. Bank of Jackson Hole, 1985-89; photo-journalist; mem. Wyo. Ho. of Reps., 1970-74, Wyo. Senate, 1974-89, pres., 1987-89; dir. Fish and Wildlife Svc. US Dept. Interior, Washington, 1989-93; pres. Conservation Fund, Arlington, Va., 1993—2001; asst. sec. for oceans, internat. environ., & scientific affairs US Dept. State, Washington, 2001—05. Exec. adv. Hancock Timber Resource Group, 1993—2001; chmn. rev. com. Argonne Nat. Lab.-West, U. Chgo., 1999—2001; bd. dirs. Land Trust Alliance, 1994—2000, N.E. Utilities, 1995—2001, Internat. Paper Co., Stamford, Conn., 2005—, Ashland Inc., 2006—; chmn. bd. dirs. Inst. Environ. and Natural Resources, U. Wyo., Laramie, 2001—; mem. Nat. Coal Coun., 1995—, Teton Sci. Sch. Bd., Nat. Wetland Forum, 1983, 87; mem. exec. com. Coun. of State Govts.; chmn. Pride in Jackson Hole Campaign, 1986; chmn. steering com. UN Conv. on Wetlands of Internat. Importance, 1990—93; head U.S. delegation Conv. on Internat. Trade Endangered Species. Author: The Magnificent Bald Eagle: Our National Bird, 1971. Named Citizen of Yr. County of Teton, 1984; recipient Nat. Conservation Achievement award Nat. Wildlife Fedn., 1984, Sheldon Coleman Great Outdoors award, 1990, Pres.'s Pub. Svc. award The Nature Conservatory, 1990, Stewardship award Audubon Soc., 1992, Nat. Wetland Achievement award Ducks Unlimited, 1993, Chevron/Times-Mirror Nat. Conservation Leadership award, 1995. Mem. Nat. Wildlife Refuge Assn. (bd. dirs.), Boone and Crocket Club (profl. mem.). Republican. Roman Catholic.

TURNER, JOHN SIDNEY, JR., retired otolaryngologist, educator; b. Bainbridge, Ga., July 25, 1930; s. John Sidney and Rose Lee (Rogers) T.; m. Betty Jane Tigner, June 5, 1955 (dec.); children: Elizabeth, Rebecca, Jan Marie; m. Nina Jones, June 16, 1999. BS, Emory U., 1952, MD, 1955. Diplomate Am. Bd. Otolaryngology. Intern U. Va. Hosp., 1955-56; resident in otolaryngology Duke U. Med. Ctr., 1958-61; prof. otolaryngology Emory U., Atlanta, 1961-95, chmn. divsn., 1961—95; ret. Ear specialist, chief otolaryngology Emory Clinic, 1961-95; area cons. in field U.S. 3d Army, 1962-69; assoc. dir. heart disease control program Fla. Bd. Health, 1956-58; Ga. state chmn. Deafness Rsch. Found., 1968-95; v.p. Clifton Casualty Ins. Co., Atlanta, 1975-95. Mem. internat. editl. bd. Drugs Jour., 1982-2004, Ethicals in Med. Progress, 1982—, Dialogue Jour., 1988-95; mem. editl. bd. Otolaryngolog—Head and Neck Surgery, 1991; contbr. chpts. to books, articles to profl. jours. With USPHS, 1956-58. Recipient Appreciation award Children of Fulton County and Fulton County Health Dept., 1975, Citation for Disting. Svc., Fla. divsn. Am. Cancer Soc., 1957, Lester A. Brown award Ga. Soc. Otolaryngology*Head and Neck Surgery, 1995. Mem. AMA, So. Med. Assn. (chmn. otolaryngology sect. 1974, cert. of appreciation 1974), Am. Acad. Otolaryngology--Head and Neck Surgery (Honor award 1994), Triological Soc. (v.p., chmn. so. sect. 1991—), Am. Acad. Otolaryngic Allergy, Ga. Soc. Otolaryngology (pres. 1973), Med. Assn. Ga., Med. Assn. Atlanta, Assn. Acad. Depts. Otolaryngology, Optimists (pres. Atlanta 1975), Alpha Omega Alpha. Democrat. Methodist. Home Phone: 941-778-6294.

TURNER, JONATHAN SHIELDS, computer science educator, researcher; b. Boston, Nov. 13, 1953; m. Helen Gaddy; 1 child, Gregory. AB, Oberlin Coll., 1977; BS in Computer Sci., Washington U., St. Louis, 1977, BSEE, 1977; MS in Computer Sci., Northwestern U., 1979, PhD in Computer Sci., 1982. Mem. tech. staff Bell Labs., Naperville, Ill., 1977-83; asst. to assoc. prof. computer sci. Washington U., St. Louis, 1983-90, prof., 1990—, chmn. computer sci. dept., 1992-97, Henry Edwin Sever prof. engring., 1994—2006, Barbara J. and Jerome R. Cox Jr. prof. computer sci., 2006—. Adv. NSF, 1990; co-founder Growth Networks. Editl. bd. IEEE/Assn. Computing Machinery Transactions on Networking, 1993; contbr. numerous articles to profl. jours.; patentee in field. Recipient Tech. Devel. award St. Louis, Econ. Coun., 1995. Fellow IEEE (Koji Kobayashi Computers and Comm. award 1994), Assn. Computing Machinery; mem. NAE. Avocations: music, tennis, reading. Office: Computer Sci and Engring Dept Washington U Campus Box 1045 Saint Louis MO 63130-4899

TURNER, KATHLEEN, actress; b. Springfield, Mo., June 19, 1954; m. David Guc, 1977 (div. 1982); m. Jay Weiss, 1984; 1 child, Rachel Ann. Student, Cen. Sch. of Speech and Drama, London, Southwest Mo. State U.; BFA, U. Md., 1977. Broadway debut: Gemini, 1978, Cat on a Hot Tin Roof, 1990, Indiscretions, 1995, Who's Afraid of Virginia Woolf?, 2005 (Evening Standard Best Actress award, 2006), The Third Story, 2009; actress: (films) Body Heat, 1981, A Breed Apart, 1982, The Man With Two Brains, 1983, Crimes of Passion, 1984, Romancing the Stone, 1984, Prizzi's Honor (Golden Globe award for Best Actress, Hollywood Fgn. Press), 1985, The Jewel of the Nile, 1985, Peggy Sue Got Married, (D.W. Griffith award for Best Actress, Acad. award nomination for Best Actress) 1986, (voice only) GoBots: War of the Rock Lords, 1986, Julia and Julia, 1987, Switching Channels, 1988, (voice only) Who Framed Roger Rabbit, 1988, Accidental Tourist, 1988, The War of the Roses, 1989. V.I. Warshawski, 1991, Undercover Blues, 1993, House of Cards, 1993, Serial Mom, 1994, Naked in New York, 1994, Moonlight and Valentino, 1995 A Simple Wish, 1997, (voice only) Bad Baby, 1997, The Real Blonde, 1998, Baby Geniuses, 1999, Lova and Action in Chicago, 1999, The Virgin Suicides, 1999, Prince of Central Park, 2000, Beautiful, 2000, Without Love, 2004, (voice only) Monster House, 2006, Marley & Me, 2008; (TV films) Leslie's Folly, 1994, Friends at Last, 1995, Love in the Ancient World, 1997, Legalese, 1998, Cinderella, 2000; (TV appearances) The Doctors, 1977, (voice only) The Simpsons, 1994, Style and Substance, 1996, (voice only) King of the Hill, 2000, Friends, 2001, Law & Order, 2006, Nip/Tuck, 2006; dir. (films) Leslie's Folly, 1994, (play) Crimes of the Heart, 2008; performed in radio shows with the BBC, 1992, 1993; author: (autobiography) Send Yourself Roses: Thoughts on My Life, Love, and Leading Roles, 2008 Recipient Lifetime Achievement award, Savannah Coll. Art & Design, 2004. Office: ICM care Chris Andrews 8942 Wilshire Blvd Beverly Hills CA 90211-1934*

TURNER, KATHY ANN, special education services professional, director; b. Cinn., May 16, 1962; d. James Robert and Alice Louise Taylor; m. Michael Arcia Turner, Jr., June 1, 1985; children: Joseph Paul, Christopher James, Sarah Alyse. AA, Riverside C.C., 1998; BS in Edn., Lewis Clark State Coll., 2002. Spl. edn. asst. Corona-Norco Unified Sch. Dist., Norco, Calif., 1996—98; direct care provider devel. disabilities Inclusion North, Inc., Grangeville, Idaho, 1998—2000; tech. for tchrs. asst. Lewis Clark State Coll., Lewiston, Idaho, 2000—01; sub. tchr. Prairie Sch., Idaho, 2001—03; specialist devel. disabilities Opportunities Unltd., Inc., 2003—05; psycho social rehab provider Camas Profl. Counseling, 2005—06; spl. edn. tchr. lower Kuskokwim sch. dist. Bethel Regional High Sch., Ark., 2006—07; devel. disabilities dir. Yukon Kuskokwim Health Corp., 2007—. Psychol. social rehab. provider Frontier Journeys, Grangeville, Idaho, 2002—05, 2007—; counselor Hope Pregnancy Ctr., Grangeville, 2003—06, 2007—. Portrait, Liz

(2nd pl. award Idaho County Art Competition, 1998). Daffodil days chmn. Am. Cancer Soc., Corona, Calif., 1995—98; com. mem. Relay for Life, 2005; chmn. Key Coalition. Named Life Woman of the Yr., Norco C. of C., 1995. Mem.: Bethel Art Guild, Coun. for Exceptional Children, Grangeville Elks, Kappa Delta Pi (pres. 2001—03). Republican. Avocations: baking, fishing, sewing, card playing, ballroom dancing. Home: PO Box 1901 Bethel AK 99559 Personal E-mail: imspcl2002@yahoo.com.

TURNER, KEITH WHISNANT, gerontologist, educator; PhD in Geriat., Urban Planning, Health Policy and Adminstrn., U. Cin., 1989. Cert. in mediation, dispute resolution sys. design CDR Assoc., 1995. Dir. Inst. Mediation Aging, Denton, Tex., 1997—2009; assoc. prof. applied gerontology U. North Tex., Denton, 1991—. Contbr. articles to profl. jours. Cons.-advisor Denton County Health Dept. Recipient Svc. award, Tex. Orgn. Residential Care Homes., 2004, Disting. Svc. Lasting Benefit award, North Ctrl. Tex. Coun. Govt., 2008. Mem.: APHA. Office: Univ of North Texas PO Box 310919 Denton TX 76203-0919 Office Fax: 940-565-4370. Business E-Mail: keith.turner@unt.edu.

TURNER, KELLI, diversified media and merchandising company executive; b. 1971; B in Bus., U. Mich., JD, 1997. Registered CPA Ernst & Young, LLP; various investment banking positions Allen & Co., Salomon Smith Barney; joined as v.p. investor rels. Time Warner Inc., 2004, sr. v.p. bus. devel. New Line Cinema, then sr. v.p. ops.; exec. v.p., CFO Martha Stewart Living Omnimedia, Inc., 2009—. Office: Martha Stewart Living Omnimedia Inc 11 W 42nd St New York NY 10036 Office Phone: 212-827-8000. Office Fax: 212-827-8204.*

TURNER, KEVIN (B. KEVIN TURNER), computer software company executive; m. Shelly Turner; 3 children. BS, E. Ctrl. U., 1987. Cashier Wal-Mart Stores, Inc., Ada, Okla., 1985—88, with internal audit dept., 1988—89, bus. analyst info. sys. div., strategy mgr. info. sys. div., dir. info. sys. div., v.p. and asst. chief info. officer info. sys. div., chief info. officer info. sys. div., 2000—03, exec. v.p., 2000, pres. and CEO Sam's Club div., 2002—05; COO Microsoft Corp., Redmond, Wash., 2005—. Recipient inaugural Sam M. Walton Entrepreneur of the Yr. award, 1997, Disting. Alumnus award, E. Ctrl. U., 2003; named one of Top 25 Most Innovative Execs., CRN Mag., 2007; named to CIO Hall of Fame, CIO Mag., 2007. Office: Microsoft Corp 1 Microsoft Way Redmond WA 98052-6399*

TURNER, KRISTA DENISE, director; b. Abingdon, Va., Apr. 10, 1971; d. Patricia B. and Garry L. Shaffer (Stepfather); m. Anthony J. Turner, Dec. 17, 1994; 1 child, Morgan. MEd in Early Childhood, E. Tenn. State U., Johnson City, 2002—05; D in Early Childhood, ETSU. Dir. ETSU Little Buccaneers Student Child Care Ctr., Johnson City, 2001—. Adv. bd. mem. Tenn. Early Childhood Tng. Alliance, Johnson City, 2003. Mem.: NAEYC, Kappa Delta Pi, Gamma Beta Phi. Avocation: knitting. Office: ETSU Little Buccaneers Child Care Ctr Box 70434 Johnson City TN 37614 Office Fax: 423-439-7550. Business E-Mail: turnerk@etsu.edu.

TURNER, LINDA FAY, finance educator; d. Mary S. Turner; 1 child, Diedre LaFay Boozer. BBA, U. Tex., Tyler, 1980; MBA, Old Dominion U., Norfolk, Va., 1981; PhD in Bus. Adminstrn., U. Phoenix, Ariz., 2007. Cert. profl. Human Resource Certification Inst., 2000. Asst. prof. Morrisville State Coll., NY, 1999—2002, assoc. prof., 2002—. Pres. WorkPlace Solutions, Fayetteville, NY, 2003—08. Contbr. articles to profl. jours. Fellow: Oxford U. Round Table Resident Employment Rights and Responsibilities; mem.: Acad. Mgmt., Soc. Human Resource Mgmt. Home: 109 South St Fayetteville NY 13066 Office: Morrisville State Coll Rt 20 Main St Morrisville NY 13408 Business E-Mail: boozerlt@morrisville.edu.

TURNER, LISA PHILLIPS, human resources executive; b. Waltham, Mass., Apr. 10, 1951; d. James Sinclair and Virginia Turner. BA in Edn. and Philosophy magna cum laude, Washington Coll., Chestertown, Md., 1974; AS in Electronics Tech., AA in Engring., Palm Beach Jr. Coll., 1982; MBA, Nova U., 1986, DSc, 1989; PhD, Kennedy Western U., 1990. Cert. sr. profl. in human resources; cert. quality engr.; lic. USCG capt.; lic. pvt. pilot FAA, IFAA lic. airframe and powerplant mechanic, 2004; cert. Black Belt, 2006. Founder, pres. Turner's Bicycle Svc., Inc., Delray Beach, Fla., 1975-80; electronics engr., quality engr. Audio Engring. and Video Arts, Boca Raton, Fla., 1980-81; tech. writing instr. Palm Beach Jr. Coll., Lake Worth, Fla., 1981-82; adminstr. tng. and devel. Mitel Inc., Boca Raton, 1982-88; mgr. comm. and employee rels. Modular Computer Systems, Inc., Ft. Lauderdale, Fla., 1988-89; U.S. mktg. project mgr. Mitel, Inc., Boca Raton, 1990-91; v.p. human resources Connectronics, Inc., Ft. Lauderdale, 1991-93; sr. mgr. human resources Sensormatic Electronics Corp., Boca Raton, 1993-98, dir. human resources, 1998—2001; chief tng. officer and dir. human resources Tyco Fire and Security Svcs., Inc., Boca Raton, 2001—05, Six Sigma black belt, 2005—06; pres. Turner Bus. Svcs., Inc., Hayesville, NC, 2007—. Contbg. author Kitplanes Mag. With USCG Aux. Recipient Human Resources Profl. Excellence award, Soc. Human Resource Mgmt., 1999. Mem. Soc. for Human Resource Mgmt., Internat. Assn. Quality Cirs., Am. Soc. Quality Control, Fla. Employment Mgmt. Assn., Am. Acad. Mgmt., Employment Assn. Fla., Am. Capts. Assn., Citizens Police Acad., Aircraft Owners and Pilot's Assn., Exptl. Aircraft Assn., Fla. Aero. Club. Achievements include being the first female to construct, complete and fly a pulsar XP aircraft. Home and Office: Turner Bus Svcs Inc 559 Brown Arrow Trail Hayesville NC 28904-9277 Home Phone: 828-389-2127; Office Phone: 561-866-0011. Personal E-mail: lisaturner@prodigy.net. Business E-Mail: lisaturner@lisaturner.com.

TURNER, MARK BERNARD, English language educator; b. Kingville, Tex., Mar. 24, 1954; s. James Lloyd and Dell Turner; m. Megan Milar Whalen, June 20, 1987; children: John, Donald, William. BA in English, U. Calif., Berkeley, 1974, BA in Math., MA in English, 1978, MA in Math., 1979, PhD in English Lang. and Lit., 1983. Asst. prof. English U. Chgo., 1983-90; assoc. prof. English U. Md., College Park, 1990-91, prof. English, 1992—. Vis. scholar linguistics and cognitive sci. U. Calif., San Diego, 19931 vis. scholar linguistics Stanford U., 1999. Author: Death is the Mother of Beauty: Mind, Metaphor, Criticism, 1987, Reading Minds: The Study of English in the Age of Cognitive Science, 1991, The Literary Mind, 1996; co-author: (with G. Lakoff) More than Cool Reason: A Field Guide to Poetic Metaphor, 1989; (with F.-N. Thomas) Clear and Simple as the Truth: Writing Classic Prose; (with C. Caccieri, R. Gibbs and A. Katz) Figurative Language and Thought, 1998; mem. editl. bd. Arobase (Jour. des lettres et scis. humaines), Metaphor and Symbol, Psychol. Study of the Arts, Prix du Rayonnement de la langue et de la littérature françaises, 1996; contbr. chpts. to books and articles to profl. jours. Fellow NEH, 1986-87, Nat. Humanities Ctr., 1989-90, John Simon Guggenheim Meml. Found., 1992-93, Ctr. for Advanced Study in the Behavioral Scis., 1994-95, Inst. for Advanced Study, Princeton, 1996-97, Collège de France, 2000. Office: Univ Md Dept English College Park MD 20742-0001

TURNER, MARVIN WENTZ, insurance company executive; b. Lower Marion, Pa., Oct. 17, 1959; s. Gilbert Jr. and Frances (McAlister) T. BBA, Howard U., 1981; postgrad., Temple U., 1984-86; MBA fin./info. sys. mgmt., George Washington U., 1988; JD, Georgetown U., 1998; grad., Dale Carnegie Leadership Inst., Wharton Sch., U. Pa., Kennedy Sch. Govt. Harvard. Registered investment advisor; chartered asset mgr., chartered wealth mgr., fin. specialist Bd. Cert., assoc. bus. continuity profl., NY Bar; cert. fund specialist. Claim advisor Prudential Ins., Fort Washington, Pa., 1982-84; ptnr. Mgmt. Enterprise, Phila., 1984-86; analyst CNA Fin. Group, Washington, 1986-88; mgr. fin. planning analysis Bell Atlantic, Arlington, Va., 1988—93; CFO Local Govt. Ins. Trust, Columbia, Md., 1993—95; mng. dir. Fin Assets Capital LLC, 1995—99; field mgmt. officer US Dept. Housing & Urban Development, 1999—; adj. prof. U. Md. U. Coll., Adelphi, Md., 1997—; CEO Black Arrow Advisors, Inc., 2006—. Adv. bd. mem. Access Washington; ptnr. Target Group Investors, Upper Marlsboro, Md., 1990—; fin. advisor Turner Mgmt. Group, Watkins Park, Md., 1991. Chmn., Kappa Epsilon Lambda Edn. Found. 2008-, Nat. Coun. Adv. Coun., US Small Bus. Adminstrn., Pres. Coun. Future Princeville, NC, White House Conf. Small Bus., White House Conf. Small Livable Cmtys., Washington Telephone Fed. Credit Union; chmn. Compliance & Suprvisory Com., HUD Fed. Credit Union Bd. Dirs.; treas. Cmty. Hope, Interagency Working Group Continuity Operations, Fed. Radiol. Preparedness Coord. Com.; ptnr. The Tucker Group, Cheverly, Md., 1990. Recipient Elizabeth B. Adams Meml. award George Washington U., 1988, minority fellowship, 1987, several fin. and mgmt. awards, honors and designations, Sec. award 2001; named Coun. for Excellence in Govt. Sr. fellow, 2007; HUD Cmty. Builder fellowship 1999. Mem. Nat. Black MBA Assn. (exec. bd. D.C. chpt., treas. 1988-90, v.p. 1992-94), Fin. Exec. Inst., Alpha Phi Alpha, Am. Bar Assn., Nat. Bar Assn., Delta Sigma Pi Profl. Bus., Phi Delta Phi, Internat. Legal Fraternity, NAACP (life), Washington League (life). Office: U Md U Coll 3501 U Blvd E Adelphi MD 20783 E-mail: marvin_turner_esq@yahoo.com.

TURNER, MARY ALICE, curriculum specialist; b. Birmingham, Ala., Aug. 8, 1946; d. Henry and Elzona (Griffin) Johnson; m. Raymond Carver Turner, July 6, 1968; 1 child, Taunya Nicole. BS in Edn., Ala. A&M U., 1968, MEd, 1992. Cert. tchr. home econs. edn., elem. edn., early childhood edn., adminstrn. and supervision 1994. Title I curriculum specialist Huntsville City Schs., Ala., 1969—. Mem. Parent/Sch./Tchr. adv. bd. Ridgecrest Elem. Sch., Huntsville, 1978; tchr. rep. PTA, Rolling Hills Elem. Sch., Huntsville, 1988-93. Recipient Award for Dedicated Svc. Rolling Hills PTA, 1988. Mem. ASCD, NEA, Ala. Edn. Assn., Huntsville Edn. Assn. (sch. rep. 1969-96, mem. budget com., rule and regulations com. review), Ala. Reading Assn., Alpha Kappa Alpha. Democrat. Baptist. Avocations: needlepoint, sewing, reading, public speaking. Home: 213 Lake Carmel Ct Huntsville AL 35811-8005 Office: Terry Heights Elem Sch 2820 Barbara Dr Huntsville AL 35816 Business E-Mail: mturner@hsv.k12.al.us.

TURNER, MICHAEL, professional football player; b. Waukegan, Ill., Feb. 13, 1982; BA, No. Ill. U., DeKalb. Running back San Diego Chargers, 2004—08, Atlanta Falcons, 2008—. Named 1st Team All-Pro, AP, 2008; named to All-Joe Team, USA Today, 2006, Nat. Football Conf. Pro Bowl Team, NFL, 2008. Achievements include leading the NFL in: rushing attempts (376), 2008. Office: Atlanta Falcons 4400 Falcon Pky Flowery Branch GA 30542*

TURNER, MICHAEL DAN, academic administrator; b. Pasadena, Tex., Sept. 14, 1966; s. Daniel Lee and Freda Gayle (Cullie) Turner; m. Lisa Dawn Bowers, July 19, 1997; children: Madison, Megan. AAS, Okla. State U., Okmulgee, 1988; BS, Northeastern State U., 1991, MS, 1998. Univ. rep. Northeastern State U., Tahlequah, Okla., 1995—97, spl. asst. to pres., 1999—2003; dir. admissions and prospective student recruitment 199 Okla. State U., Okmulgee, Okla., 1997—99; v.p. student affairs Rogers State U., Claremore, Okla., 2003—07; pres. Southeastern Okla. State U., Durant, 2008—. Bd. trustees Claremore Pub. Schs. Found; exec. com. mem. Okla. Coun. on Student Affairs. Vol. Okla. Spl. Olympics, 1988—95; event chmn. Am. Cancer Soc., 1997—98; chmn. bd. dirs. Claremore C. of C. Capt. USMC, 1991—97. Named to Outstanding Young Men of Am., 1989. Mem.: Okmulgee Rotary Club, Okmulgee C. of C. (cmty. image and pub. rels. coms. 1997—98), Northeastern State U. Alumni Assn., Okla. State U.-Okmulgee Alumni Assn., Pi Kappa Alpha (chpt. advisor 1995—97). Methodist. Avocations: golf, water-skiing, softball, classic car restoration. Office: Southeastern Okla State U Office of Pres 1405 N 4th Durant OK 74701 Home: 1401 N 6th Ave Durant OK 74701-2724 Office Phone: 580-745-2000.

TURNER, MICHAEL G., history professor; b. Cleve., Mar. 25, 1969; s. Ronald and Christine Turner; m. Jennifer L. Hartman, Oct. 26, 2001; children: Louisa Grace, Henry Ronald. PhD, U. Cin., 1998. Assoc. prof. U. NC, Charlotte, 2002—. Office: Univ NC Charlotte 2701 Univ City Blvd Mooresville NC 28117 Office Fax: 704-687-3349. Business E-Mail: mgturner@uncc.edu.

TURNER, MICHAEL R., United States Representative from Ohio; b. Dayton, Ohio, Jan. 11, 1960; s. Ray and Vivian Turner; m. Lori Turner; 2 children. BS in Polit. Sci., Ohio No. U., Ada, 1982; JD, Case Western Res. U. Sch. Law, 1985; MBA, U. Dayton, Ohio, 1992. Bar: Ohio 1985. Corp. counsel Modern Technologies Corp., Dayton, Ohio; pres. JMD Devel.; mayor Ohio, 1994—2002; mem. US Congress from 3rd Ohio dist., 2003—. Mem. armed svcs. com. US Congress, mem. govt. reform com., mem. vets. affairs com., chmn. federalism and the census subcommittee. Recipient Nat. Legis. Leadership award, US Conf. Mayors, 2005, Restore Am. Hero award, Nat. Trust Hist. Preservation and HGTV, 2005. Mem.: ABA, Am. Corp. Counsel Assn., Ohio Bar Assn., Dayton Bar Assn. Republican. Office: US House Reps 1740 Longworth House Office Bldg Washington DC 20515 Office Phone: 202-225-6465. Office Fax: 202-225-6754.*

TURNER, MICHAEL R., energy executive; BA in Math. with honors, U. Oxford; PhD in Theoretical Physics, U. Southampton. Analyst, quantitative rsch. Schroder Salomon Smith Barney; various mgmt. positions in internat. production ops. Shell Oil, 1981—2009; sr. v.p., global prodn. Hess Corp., 2009—. Former bd. dirs. Aspect Capital Ltd. Office: Hess Corp 1185 Ave of the Americas New York NY 10036 Office Phone: 212-997-8500. Office Fax: 212-536-8390.*

TURNER, MICHAEL STANLEY, astrophysics professor, researcher, science administrator; b. LA, July 29, 1949; s. Paul Joseph and Janet Mary (Lindholm) Turner; m. Terri Lee Shields, Aug. 1978 (div. Sept. 1980); m. Barbara Lynn Ahlberg, Sept. 10, 1988; children: Rachel Mary, Joseph Lucien. BS in Physics, Calif. Inst. Tech., Pasadena, 1971; MS in Physics, Stanford U., Calif., 1973, PhD in Physics, 1978; DSc (hon.), Mich. State U., East Lansing, 2005. Enrico Fermi fellow U. Chgo., 1978-80, from asst. to assoc. prof. physics and astronomy and astrophysics, 1980-85, prof., 1985—, chmn. dept. astronomy and astrophysics, 1997—2003, Bruce V. and Diana M. Rauner Disting. Svc. prof., 1998—; scientist Fermi Nat. Accelerator Lab., Batavia, Ill., 1983—2003, 2006—; asst. dir. US NSF, 2003—06; chief scientist Argonne Nat. Lab., 2007—08. Trustee Aspen Ctr. Physics, Colo., 1984—97, pres., 1989—93, hon. trustee, 2002—; Halley lectr. Oxford U., 1994; Klopsteg lectr. Am. Assn. Physics Tchrs., 1999; Neils Bohr lectr. Copenhagen U., 2001; Marker lectr. Pa. State U., 2002; W. Paul fellow Bonn U., 2000; Houston lectr. Rice U., 2003; Herzfield lectr. Cath. U., 2004; Buhl lectr. Carnegie Mellon U., 2004; Heinrich Hertz lectr. DESY-Germany, 2004; Kaczmarczk lectr. Dexel U., 2004; Buhl lectr. Carnegie Mellon, 2004; Fisher lectr. Brandeis U., 2005; Centennial lectr. Purdue U., 2005; Shaw lectr. So. Ill. U., 2005; Mohler Prize lectr. U. Mich., 2007; Biermann lectr. Max Planck Inst. Astrophysics, 2009. Author: (with E.W. Kolb) The Early Universe, 1990; contbr. over 200 articles to profl. jours. Trustee Ill. Math. Sci. Acad., 1998-2003, Project Exploration, Ill., 2002-03, Fermi Rsch. Alliance, 2006-. Sloan fellow A.P. Sloan Found., 1983-88; recipient Disting. Alumni award Caltech, 2006. Fellow AAAS (chair physics sect. 2003), Am. Acad. Arts and Scis., Am. Phys. Soc. (mem. exec. bd. 1992-94, chmn. publ. oversight com. 1993-94, chmn. nominating com. 1999-2000, Lilienfeld prize 1997, Primakoff lectr., 2003, chair-elect, dir. astrophysics 2007-, mem. governing bd. 2009-), Phi Beta Kappa (nat. lectr. 2002-2003); mem. NAS (NRC astronomy astrophysics survey com. 1998-2000, chair NRC com. Physics of Universe, 2000-02, chair physics sect. 2007-, bd. on physics and astronomy, 2007), Am. Astron. Soc. (Helen B. Warner prize 1984), Internat. Astron. Union, Sigma Xi. Office: U Chgo Astron & Astrophysics Ctr 5640 S Ellis Ave Chicago IL 60637-1433 Office Phone: 630-252-3575. Business E-Mail: mturner@uchicago.edu.

TURNER, NATALIE A., retired consultant; b. Vancouver, BC, Can. d. Walter P. and Jenny (Ferley) Koohtow; m. George M. Turner, Jr. BS, McGill U., 1949. Rsch. asst. in neurophysiology Allen Meml. Inst., Montreal, 1949—51; rsch. asst. Harvard Med. Sch., Boston, 1951—54; chem. program mgr. in r&d, tech. svc. mgr. to Internat. Ops., clearance officer for Latin-Am. and Asia-Pacific companies Gillette Co., Boston, 1954—88; ret., 1989. Technician Red Cross Blood Transfusion Svc., Montreal, 1949; tech. cons. Damon Biotech, Boston, 1988-89, rsch. asst., Harvard Sch. of Pub. Health Co-author rsch. publs. in field. Bd. dirs. Children's Mus. in Easton, Mass., 1989—. Mem. NAFE, Internat. Congress Physiology, Am. Chem. Soc., Soc. Cosmetic Chemists (life, pres. New Eng. chpt., dir. US Nat. Bd., US rep. to Internat. Fedn. Exec. Bd.), New Eng. Women Bus. Owners, Kappa Alpha Theta (life). Avocations: sewing, golf, portraits in fabric and oils.

TURNER, NIESCJA E., physics professor; BA in physics, Rice U., Houston, 1994; PhD astrophysy. planetary & atmospheric sci., U.Colo. Boulder, 2000. Scientist, geophys. rsch. Finnish meteorol. inst., Helsinki, Finland, 2001; asst. prof., physics U. Tex., El paso, 2002—04; asst. prof., physics & space sci. Fla. inst. tech., Melbourne, 2004—. Contbr. articles to prof. jour. Recipient Career award, NSF, 2003. Mem.: Am. geophys. Union. Office: Fla Inst Tech 150 W University Blvd Melbourne FL 32901 Business E-Mail: neturner@fit.edu.

TURNER, NORV (NORVAL EUGENE TURNER), professional football coach; b. LeJeune, NC, May 17, 1952; m. Nancy Turner; children: Scott, Stephanie, Drew. Asst. coach U. So. Calif. Trojans, 1976—84; receivers coach LA Rams, 1985—90; offensive coord. Dallas Cowboys, 1991—93, San Diego Chargers, 2001, Miami Dolphins, 2002—03, San Francisco 49ers, 2006—07; head coach Washington Redskins, 1994—2000, Oakland Raiders, 2004—06, San Diego Chargers, 2007—. Achievements include being a member of Super Bowl Championship winning Dallas Cowboys, 1993, 1994. Office: c/o San Diego Chargers PO Box 609609 San Diego CA 92160*

TURNER, PETER, biopharmaceutical company executive; BSc in Chemistry, Biochemistry and Microbiology, U. Melborne; MBA, Royal Melbourne Inst. Tech. Ops. mgr., plasma products project dir. CSL Bioplasma, bus. unit of CSL Ltd., gen. mgr., 1996—2000; pres., CEO ZLB Bioplasma AG and ZLB Bioplasma, Inc., (the ZLB Bioplasma Group), 2000—04, ZLB Behring, L.C.C. (merger of Aventis Behring and ZLB Bioplasma), King of Prussia, Pa., 2004; pres. CSL Behring, 2004—. Mem.: Plasma Protein Therapeutics Assn. (chmn.). Office: CSL Behring 1020 First Ave PO Box 61501 King Of Prussia PA 19406 Office Phone: 610-878-4155. Office Fax: 610-878-4584.*

TURNER, PHILIP MICHAEL, academic administrator, writer; b. West Acton, Mass., Nov. 26, 1948; s. William Albert and Evelyn Olena (Peterson) T.; m. Lis Jane VanderBeke, Aug. 16, 1969; children: Gabrielle, Adrienne. BS in Edn., Boston State Coll., 1970; MS, U. Wis. at La Crosse, 1972; MSLS, EdD, East Tex. State U., 1977. Tchr. math. Edgewood Jr. High Sch., Merritt Island, Fla., 1969-71; ptnr. Video Guide Prodn. Co., Denver, 1973; libr. media specialist Edison Jr. High Sch., Green Bay, Wis., 1973-76; prof. libr. sci. U. Ala., Tuscaloosa, 1977-88; dean Sch. Libr. and Info. Studies U. North Tex., Denton, 1996—2004; asst. vice chancellor acad. affairs U. Ala. System, 1991-96; assoc. v.p. for acad. affairs for distance edn. U. North Tex., Denton, 1996—2004, vice provost learning enhancement, 2004—. Chair distance edn. adv. com. Tex. Higher Edn. Coordinating Bd., 2004—. Author: Handbook for In-School Media Personnel, 1980, Helping Teachers Teach, 1985, 3d edit., 2003. Vol. Meals on Wheels, Tuscaloosa, 1987-96. Recipient Outstanding Commitment To Teaching award U. Ala. Alumni Assn., 1979, Outstanding Svc. award Ala. Libr. and Media Prodrs., 1987, publ. award Div. Sch. Libr. Media Specialist, 1987, award for mng. info. tech., 1994, Ala. Libr. Assn. Disting. Svc. award, 1996; named Libr. of Yr., Beta Phi Mu, 1991. Mem. ALA (mem. accreditation com. 2000—04), Assn. Sch. Librs. (chair rsch. com. 1987-90, bd. dirs. 1990-94). Unitarian Universalist. Office: U North Tex PO Box 310889 Denton TX 76203-0889 Home Phone: 940-484-8214; Office Phone: 940-565-4462. Business E-Mail: pturner@unt.edu.

TURNER, R. GERALD (ROBERT GERALD TURNER), academic administrator; b. Atlanta, Tex., Nov. 25, 1945; s. Robert B. and Oreta Lois (Porter) T.; m. Gail Oliver, Dec. 21, 1968; children: Angela Jan, Jessica Diane AA, Lubbock Christian Coll., 1966, LLD (hon.), 1985, Pepperdine U., 1989; BS, Abilene Christian U., 1968; MA, U. Tex., 1970, PhD, 1975. Tchr. Weatherford High Sch., Tex., 1968-69; tchr. Lanier High Sch., Austin, Tex., 1969-70; instr. psychology San Antonio Coll., 1970-72; instr. Prairie View A & M U., Tex., 1973-75; asst. prof. psychology Pepperdine U., Malibu, Calif., 1975-78, assoc. prof. psychology, 1978-79, dir. testing, 1975-76, chmn. social sci. div., 1976-78, assoc. v.p. univ. affairs, 1979; assoc. prof. psychology U. Okla., Norman, 1979-84, exec. asst. to pres., 1979-81, acting provost, 1982, v.p. exec. affairs, 1981-84; chancellor U. Miss., University, 1984-95; pres. So. Meth. U., Dallas, 1995—. Pres. Southeastern Conf., 1985-87; trustee Pepperdine U., 1994-95; mem. Pres.'s Commn., NCAA, 1989-92, chmn., 1991-92; mem. Knight Commn. on Intercollegiate Athletics, 1991—; chmn. pres. coun. Miss. Assn. Colls., 1985-86; mem. def. adv. com. Svc. Acad. Athletic Programs, 1992—; bd. dirs. J.C. Penney Co.,Inc., 1995- Author: (with L. Willerman) Readings About Individual and Group Differences, 1979. Contbr. articles to profl. jours. Recipient Outstanding Alumni award Abilene Christian U., 1989; named to New Boston HS Athletic Hall of Fame, 1993. Mem. Young Pres. Orgn.,

Sigma Xi, Beta Alpha Psi, Phi Theta Kappa, Alpha Chi, Phi Kappa Phi. Mem. Ch. of Christ. Avocations: reading, tennis, golf, travel. Office: So Meth Univ Office Of The Pres Dallas TX 75275-0001 Office Phone: 214-768-3300.*

TURNER, RALPH HERBERT, sociologist, educator; b. Effingham, Ill., Dec. 15, 1919; s. Herbert Turner and Hilda Pearl (Bohn) T.; m. Christine Elizabeth Hanks, Nov. 2, 1943; children: Lowell Ralph, Cheryl Christine. BA, U So. Calif., 1941, MA, 1942; postgrad., U. Wis., 1942-43; PhD, U. Chgo., 1948. Rsch. assoc. Am. Coun. Race Relations, 1947-48; faculty UCLA, 1948—, prof. sociology and anthropology, 1959-90, prof. emeritus, 1990—, chmn. dept. sociology, 1963-68; chmn. Acad. Senate U. Calif. System, 1983-84. Vis. summer prof. U. Wash., 1960, U. Hawaii, 1962; vis. scholar Australian Nat. U., 1972; vis. prof. U. Ga., 1975, Ben Gurion U., Israel, 1983; vis. fellow Nuffield Coll. Oxford U., 1980; disting. vis. prof. Am. U., Cairo, Egypt, 1983; adj. prof. China Acad. Social Scis., Beijing, People's Republic China, 1986. Author: (with L. Killian) Collective Behavior, 1957, 2d edit., 1972, 3d edit., 1987, The Social Context of Ambition, 1964, Robert Park on Social Control and Collective Behavior, 1967, Family Interaction, 1970, Earthquake Prediction and Public Policy, 1975, (with J. Nigg, D. Paz, B. Young) Community Response to Earthquake Threat in So. Calif., 1980, (with J. Nigg and D. Paz) Waiting for Disaster, 1986; editl. cons., 1959-62; editor: Sociometry, 1962-64; acting editor: Ann. Rev. of Sociology, 1977-78; assoc. editor, 1978-79, editor, 1980-86; adv. editor: Am. Jour. Sociology, 1954-56, Sociology and Social Rsch., 1961-74; editl. staff: Am. Sociol. Rev., 1955-56; assoc. editor: Social Problems, 1959-62, 67-69; cons. editor: Sociol. Inquiry, 1968-73, Western Sociol. Rev., 1975-79; mem. editl. bd. Mass Emergencies, 1975-79, Internat. Jour. Crit. Sociology, 1974-76, Symbolic Interaction, 1977-90, 95—, Mobilization, 1996—. Mem. behavioral scis. study sect. NIH, 1961-66, chmn., 1963-64; dir.-at-large Social Sci. Rsch. Coun., 1965-66; chmn. panel on pub. policy implications of earthquake predictions Nat. Acad. Scis., 1974-75, also mem. earthquake study del. to Peoples Republic of China, 1976; mem. policy adv. bd. So. Calif. Earthquake Preparedness program, 1987-92, mem. com. social edn. and action L.A. Presbytery, 1954-56. Served to lt. (j.g.) USNR, 1943-46. Recipient Faculty prize Coll. Letters and Scis. UCLA, 1985; Faculty Rsch. fellow Social Sci. Rsch. Coun., 1953-56; Sr. Fulbright scholar U.K., 1956-57; Guggenheim fellow, U.K., 1964-65; Faculty Rsch. lectr. UCLA, 1987, UCLA Emeritus of Yr., 1997. Mem. AAAS (exch. del. to China 1988), AAUP, Am. Sociol. Assn. (coun. 1959-64, chmn. social psychology sect. 1960-61, pres. 1968-69, chmn. sect. theoretical sociology 1973-74, chmn. collective behavior and social movements sect. 1983-84, Cooley-Mead award 1987), Pacific Sociol. Assn. (pres. 1957), Internat. Sociol. Assn. (coun. 1974-82, v.p. 1978-82), Soc. Study Social Problems (exec. com. 1962-63), Soc. for Study Symbolic Interaction (pres. 1982-83, Charles Horton Cooley award 1978, George Herbert Mead award 1990), Sociol. Rsch. Assn. (pres. 1989-90), Am. Coun. of Learned Soc. (exec. com. of coun. 1990-93), UCLA Emeriti Assn. (coun., pres. 1992-93), U. of Calif. Emeriti Assns. (chair-elect 1996-97, chair 1997-98, Panunzio award 2002, Lifetime Svc. award 2007). Home: 1126 Chautauqua Blvd Pacific Palisades CA 90272-3808 Office: UCLA 405 Hilgard Ave Los Angeles CA 90095-9000

TURNER, ROBERT COMRIE, composer; b. Montreal, Que., Can., June 6, 1920; s. William Thomson and Myrtle T.; m. Sara Nan Scott, June 30, 1949; children: Alden, Martin, Carolyn. BM, McGill U., 1943, MusD, 1953; postgrad., Royal Coll. Music, London, 1947—48; MusM, Vanderbilt U., 1950. Sr. music producer Canadian Broadcasting Corp., Vancouver, B.C., 1952—68; lectr. music U. B.C., Vancouver, 1955—57; prof. composition U. Manitoba, Winnipeg, 1969—85, prof. emeritus, 1985—. Composer-in-residence MacDowell Colony, Peterborough, N.H., 1987. Composer: Opening Night: A Theatre Overture, 1955, The Third Day (Easter Cantata), 1962, Symphony for Strings, 1960, Capriccio Concertante, 1975, 3 String Quartet, 1944, 1954, 1975, opera The Brideship, 1967, Trio (transition) for Violin Cello and Piano, 1969, The Phoenix and the Turtle, 1964, Concerto for Two Pianos and Orchestra, 1971, Johann's Gift to Christmas, 1972, Eidolons, 1972, Variations on The Prairie Settler's Song, 1974, From a Different Country, 1976, Lament for Linos, 1978, Amoroso Canto, 1978, Shadow Pieces (after Joseph Cornell), 1981, opera Vile Shadows, 1983, Symphony in One Movement, 1983, Encounters I-IX, 1984, Time for Three, 1985, Playhouse Music, 1986, Concerto for Viola and Orchestra, 1987, Shades of Autumn, 1987, Manitoba Memoir, 1989, Third Symphony, 1990, a Group of Seven, 1991, The River of Time, 1994, House of Shadows, 1994, Four "Last Songs", 1995, Festival Dance, 1997, Diverti-Memento for Chamber Orch., 1997, Premiere of House of Shadows by Winnipeg Symphony, 2006; All-Turner concert, 1989, Canada House, London, All-Turner concert, Victoria, 2003, All Turner concert, Winnipeg, 2005; composer (recordings): Portrait, Robert Turner, 2005, Ovation IV, Robert Turner, 2005, Amoroso Canto, 2008; adjudicator Met. and San Francisco Opera auditions; Bramwell Tovey and The Winnipeg Symphony Orch. premiered The River of Time for SATB chorus and orch. in celebration of Robert Turner's 75th yr., 1996. Bd. dirs. Vancouver Internat. Festival. Recipient Commemorative medal for 125th Anniversary of Confedn. Can., 1993, Queen's Golden Jubilee medal, 2003, Order of Can., 2003, Outstanding Classical Composition award Western Can. Music Alliance, 2004, Manitoba Arts Coun. Award of Distinction, 2008, Heritage award, 2009; nominee Juno award Can. Acad. Recording Arts and Scis., 2004, 05. Mem.: Can. League Composers, SOCAN, SODRAC, Can. Music Ctr. Home: One Evergreen Pl #2602 Winnipeg MB Canada R3L 0E9

TURNER, ROBERT FOSTER, law educator, writer; b. Atlanta, Feb. 14, 1944; s. Edwin Witcher and Martha Frances T. AB, Ind. U., Bloomington, 1968; postgrad., Stanford U., 1972-73; JD, U. Va., 1981, SJD, 1996. Bar: Va. 1982, U.S. Supreme Ct. 1986. Rsch. assoc., pub. affairs fellow Hoover Instn. on War, Revolution and Peace, Stanford U., 1971-74; spl. asst., legis. asst. U.S. Sen. Robert P. Griffin, 1974-79; co-founder, assoc. dir. Ctr. for Nat. Security Law U. Va., Charlottesville, 1981, 87—; sr. fellow, 1985-86; spl. asst. undersec. for policy Dept. Def., 1981-82; counsel Pres.'s Intelligence Oversight Bd., White House, 1982-84; prin. dep. asst. sec. for legis. and intergovtl. affairs Dept. State, 1984, acting. asst. sec., 1984—85; pres. U.S. Inst. Peace, Washington, 1986-87; lectr. in law and in govt. and fgn. affairs U. Va., Charlottesville, 1988-93, assoc. prof., 1993-97, prof., 1997—; Charles H. Stockton prof. internat. law Naval War Coll., 1994-95. Disting. lectr. U.S. Mil. Acad., West Point, 1995. Author: Myths of the Vietnam War: The Pentagon Papers Reconsidered, 1972, Vietnamese Communism: Its Origins and Development, 1975, The War Powers Resolution: Its Implementation in Theory and Practice, 1983, Nicaragua v. United States: A Look at the Facts, 1987, Repealing the War Powers Resolution: Restoring the Rule of Law in U.S. Foreign Policy, 1991, The ABM Treaty and the Senate: Issues of International and Constitutional Law, 1999 (with John Norton Moore) The Legal Structure of Defense Organization, 1986, International Law and the Brezhnev Doctrine, 1987, Readings on International Law, 1995, The Real Lessons of the Vietnamm War, 2005, National Security Law, 2d edit., 2005, (with John Norton Moore and Guy B. Roberts) National Security Law Documents, 1995, 2d edit., 2006, National Security Legal Issues in the Struggle Against Terror, 2009, (with John Norton Moore and Ross A. Fisher) To Oppose Any Foe, 2006; National Security Legal Issues in the Struggle Against Terror 2009. Pres. Endowment of U.S. Inst. Peace, 1986-87; trustee Intercollegiate Studies Inst., 1986-92; bd. dirs. Thomas Jefferson Inst. for Pub. Policy, 1997—; chmn. scholars commn. on Jefferson-Hemings matter Thomas Jefferson Heritage Soc., 2000-01. Capt. US Army, 1969—71, Vietnam. Grantee Hoover Press, 1972, Earhart Found., 1980, 1989-90, Inst. Ednl. Affairs, 1980, Carthage Found., 1980. Mem. ABA (chmn. com. on exec.-congl. rels., sec. internat. law and practice 1983-86, adv. com. on law and nat. security 1984-86, standing com. on law and nat. security 1986-92, chmn. 1989-92, editor ABA Nat. Security Law Report 1992-99), Federalist Soc. (chmn. subcom. on nat. security law 1998—), Com. on the Present Danger, 2005-, Bd. Rsch. Cons., Inst. Fgn. Policy Analysis, Mensa, Am. Soc. Internat. Law, Nat. Eagle Scout Assn., Coun. on Fgn. Rels., Acad. of Polit. Sci. Office: Univ Va Sch of Law Ctr for Nat Security Law 580 Massie Rd Charlottesville VA 22903-1738 Home Phone: 434-978-7838; Office Phone: 434-924-4083. Business E-Mail: bobturner@virginia.edu.

TURNER, ROBERT W., rail transportation executive; married; 2 children. Grad. in Econs., Hiram Coll., Ohio. V.p. pub. affairs Champion Internat. Corp.; sr. v.p. corp. rels. Union Pacific Corp., Omaha, 2000—. Pres. Union Pacific Found.; head Union Pacific RR Mus.; vice chair Omaha Sister Cities Assn.; trustee Nebr. chpt. Nature Conservancy; bd. dirs. US Bank Adv. Bd., Omaha C. of C., Durham Western Heritage Mus. Office: Union Pacific Corp 1400 Douglas St Omaha NE 68179 Office Phone: 402-544-5000.

TURNER, ROGER D., lawyer; b. Madison, Ind., Feb. 3, 1952; BS with highest honors, Purdue Univ., 1973; JD, Univ. Chgo., 1976. Bar: NY 1977. Assoc. Cravath Swaine & Moore LLP, NYC, 1976—83, ptnr., 1983—, head corp. real estate. Mem. Chgo. Law Rev. Mem.: Assn. Bar City NY. Office: Cravath Swaine & Moore LLP Worldwide Plz 825 Eighth Ave New York NY 10019-7475 Office Phone: 212-474-1668. Office Fax: 212-474-3700. Business E-Mail: rturner@cravath.com.

TURNER, SHARON P., dean, dentist, educator; b. Charleston, W.Va., Aug. 8, 1950; d. George Brock and Anna Hopkins Pullen; m. Aubrey Williams Turner, Jr., Feb. 26, 1972; children: Brock Leslie Turner, Martin Gresham Turner, Karen Anna Turner. BA in Biology, Winthrop U., 1971; DDS, U. N.C., 1979; JD, N.C. Ctrl U., 1995. Bar: NC; lic. dentist NC, Oreg., Ky., diplomate Am. Acad. Pain Mgmt. Pvt. dental practitioner Dengler & Turner, Raleigh, NC, 1985-86; asst. prof. of diagnostic scis. U. N.C. Sch. of Dentistry, Chapel Hill, 1986-94, assoc. prof. of diagnostic scis., 1994-98, dir. patient admissions and emergency svcs., 1986-94, dir. dental faculty practice, 1989-98, assoc. dean for adminstrn. planning, 1994-98; dean, prof. dentistry Oreg. Health and Sci. U. Sch. Dentistry, Portland, 1998—2003; dean U. Ky. Coll. Dentistry, Lexington, 2003—. Cons. VA Hosp., Durham, N.C., 1999. Contbg. author: Oral Surgery, 1999. Youth group leader Eno River Unitarian Universalist, Durham, 1996-97, Sunday Sch. tchr., 1997-98; girl scout leader Pines of Carolina Coun., Girl Scouts U.S., Durham, N.C., 1990-94. Named one of Top 25 Visionary Leaders in Dentistry, Am. Student Dental Assn., 1999. Fellow Internat. Coll. Dentists, Am. Coll. Dentists, Am. Coll. Legal Medicine, Piere Fourchard Acad.; mem. ADA, Am. Dental Edn. Assn., Am. Acad. Pain Mgmt., Internat. Assn. Dental Rsch., Intenat. Assn. for Study of Pain, Soc. for Exec. Leadership in Academic Medicine (v.p. 1999-2000, pres. 2000-01, Excellence award 2004), Acad. General Dentistry, Rotary Club Lexington. Avocations: swimming, hiking, singing, reading. Office: U Ky Coll Dentistry Chandler Med Ctr D136 800 Rose St Lexington KY 40536-9707 Business E-Mail: turnersp@uky.edu.

TURNER, STANSFIELD, former CIA director, retired military officer; b. Chgo., Dec. 1, 1923; s. Oliver Stansfield and Wilhelmina Josephine (Wagner) T.; m. Marion Weiss Turner, Sept., 2003. Student, Amherst Coll., 1941-43, DCL, 1975; BS, U.S. Naval Acad., 1946; MA (Rhodes scholar), Oxford U., 1950; degree (hon.), Sierra Nev. Coll., 1984, Roger Williams Coll., 1975; degree in Edn (hon.), Bryant Coll., 1977; degree (hon.), Salve Regina Coll., 1977; LLD, The Citadel, 1980, Pace U., 1980. Ensign USN, 1946, advanced through grades to adm., 1975, ret., 1979; served primarily in destroyers; comdr. U.S.S. Horne, guided missile cruiser, 1967-68; aide to Sec. Navy; comdr. carrier task group 6th Fleet, 1970-71; dir. systems analysis div. Office Chief Naval Ops., Navy Dept., Washington, 1971-72; pres. Naval War Coll., Newport, RI, 1972-74; comdr. U.S. Second Fleet, 1974-75; comdr.-in-chief Allied Forces So. Europe, NATO, 1975-77; dir. CIA, Washington, 1977-81; John M. Olin Disting. prof. nat. security U.S. Mil. Acad., West Point, 1989-90; prof. U. Md. Grad. Sch. Pub. Policy, College Park, 1991—2007; Raymond H. Spruance Disting. Fellow Naval War Coll., Newport, RI, 2000—01. Sr. rsch. fellow Norwegian Nobel Inst., Oslo, Norway, 1995-96; bd. dirs., Chase Investment Counsel Corp.; bd. visitors U.S. Naval Acad., 1996-2000, bd. dir. Monsanto Co., 1981-91, Nat. Life Insurence Co., 1985-92. Author: Secrecy and Democracy, 1985, Terrorism and Democracy, 1991, Caging the Nuclear Genie: An American Challenge to Global Security, 1997, Caging the Genies: A Workable Plan for Chemical, Biological and Nuclear Weapons, 1999, Burn Before Reading: Presidents, CIA Directors, and Secret Intelligence, 2005. Decorated Legion of Merit, Bronze Star; Recipient Nat. Security medal, 1981, Fgn. Policy Assn. medal, 1998. Office: 488 River Bend Rd Great Falls VA 22066 Office Phone: 703-438-8408. Personal E-mail: admturner@aol.com.

TURNER, STEPHEN PARK, philosopher, sociologist, educator; b. Chgo., Mar. 1, 1951; s. Lawrence Lynn and Natalie (Stephens) Turner; m. Kimberly Anne Wills, Apr. 21, 1990; children: Evan Wills, Douglas Carrera. AB, U. Mo., Columbia, 1971, AM in Sociology, 1971, AM in Philosophy, 1972, PhD in Sociology, 1975. Asst. prof. U. South Fla., 1975—80, assoc. prof., 1980—84, prof., dept. sociology, 1984—87, grad. rsch. prof., dept. of sociology, 1987—89; vis. prof. Boston U., 1987; grad. rsch. prof. dept. philosophy U. South Fla., Tampa, Fla., 1989—; dir. Ctr. Social and Polit. Thought, 1994—. Simon hon. prof. U. Manchester, 1996—97; vis. prof. Va. Poly. Inst. and State U., Blacksburg, 1982, U. Notre Dame, 1985. Author: (books) Sociological Explanation as Translation, 1980, The Search for a Methodology of Social Science: Durkheim, Weber, and the 19th Century Problem of Cause, Probability, and Action, 1986, The Social Theory of Practices: Tradition, Tacit Knowledge, and Presuppositions, 1994, Brains/Practices/Relativism: Social Theory after Cognitive Science, 2002, Liberal Democracy 3.0: Civil Society in an Age of Experts, 2003; co-author (with F. Weed): Conflict in Organizations, 1983; co-author: (with R. Factor) Max Weber and the Dispute Over Reason and Value: A Study in Philosophy, Ethics, and Politics, 1984; co-author: (with Jonathan Turner) The Impossible Science: An Institutional Analysis of American Sociology, 1990; co-author: (with Regis A. Factor) Max Weber: The Lawyer as Social Thinker, 1994; editor: The Cambridge Companion to Weber; editor: (with Dirk Käsler) Sociology Responds to Fascism, 1992; editor: Emile Durkheim: Sociologist and Moralist, 1993; co-editor (with M. Wardell): Sociological Theory in Transition, 1986; co-editor: (with Alan Sica) The Disobedient Generation: Social Theorists in the Sixties, 2005; co-editor: (with Mark Risjord) Philosophy of Anthropology and Sociology, 2007; co-editor: (with William Outhwaite) The SAGE Handbook of Social Sci. Methodology, 2007; collaborating editor: jour. Social Studies of Science, 1986—; contbr. articles to profl. jours., NEH fellow, 1991-1992, Swedish Collegium for Advanced Study in Social Scis. fellow, 1992, 1998. Mem.: Soc. Social Studies Sci., Am. Sociol. Assn., Am. Philos. Assn., St. Petersburg Yacht Club. Office: U South Fla Dept Philosophy Tampa FL 33620 Office Phone: 813-974-5549. E-mail: turner@shell.cas.usf.edu.

TURNER, TED (ROBERT EDWARD TURNER III), retired broadcast company executive, philanthropist; b. Cin., Nov. 19, 1938; s. Robert Edward and Florence (Rooney) Turner; m. Judy Nye, 1960 (div. 1964); children: Laura Lee, Robert Edward IV; m. Jane Shirley Smith, June 1965 (div. 1988); children: Beau, Rhett, Jennie; m. Jane Fonda, Dec. 21, 1991 (div. May 22, 2001). Attended, Brown U., 1957—60; DSc in Commerce (hon.), Drexel U., 1982; LLD (hon.), Samford U., 1982, Atlanta U., 1984; D Entrepreneurial Sci. (hon.), Cen. New Eng. Coll. Tech., 1983; D in Pub. Adminstrn. (hon.), Mass. Maritime Acad., 1984; D in Bus. Adminstrn. (hon.), U. Charleston, 1985; BA in Philosophy (hon.), Brown U., 1989, LHD (hon.), 1993; D (hon.), Trinity Coll., 2001. Account exec. Turner Advt. Co., Atlanta, 1961—63, pres., COO, 1963—70; pres., chmn. bd. Turner Broadcasting Sys., Inc. (TBS), Atlanta, 1970—96; chmn. Turner Found. Inc., 1990—; vice chmn. Time Warner Inc. (merger Turner Broadcasting Sys.), 1996—2000; vice chmn., sr. advisor AOL Time Warner (merger of Time Warner Inc. and AOL, Inc.), 2001—03; chmn. Turner Enterprises, Inc., 2003—; owner Atlanta Braves, 1976—. Bd. dirs. Time Warner, 1996—2001, Time Warner Inc. (formerly AOL/Time Warner), 2001—06. Prodr. created two film production companies, Ted Turner Pictures and Ted Turner Documentaries films; co-author (with Bill Burke): (autobiography) Call Me Ted, 2008. Co-founder, co-chair Nuclear Threat Initiative, Washington, 2001—; bd. dirs. Martin Luther King Ctr., Atlanta; donations to a number of non-profit foundations, including Turner Found., Inc., Endangered Species Fund, UN Found. and the Nuclear Threat Initiative. Recipient Outstanding Entrepreneur of Yr. award, Sales Mktg. and Mgmt. Mag., 1979, Salesman of Yr. award, Sales and Mktg. Execs., 1980, Pvt. Enterprise Exemplar medal, Freedoms Found. at Valley Forge, 1980, Communicator of Yr. award, Pub. Rels. Soc. Am., 1981, N.Y. Broadcasters, 1981, Internat. Communicator of Yr. award, Sales and Mktg. Execs., 1981, Nat. News Media award, VFW, 1981, Disting. Svc. in Telecomm. award, Ohio U. Coll. Communication, 1982, Carr Van Anda award, Ohio Sch. Journalism, 1982, Spl. award, Edinburgh Internat. TV Festival, Scotland, 1982, Media Awareness award, United Vietnam Vets. Orgn., 1983, Bd. Govs. award, Atlanta chpt. NATAS, 1982, Spl. Olympics award, Spl. Olympics Com., 1983, Dinner of Champions award, Ga. chpt. Multiple Sclerosis Soc., 1983, Praca Spl. Merit award, N.Y. Puerto Rican Assn. for Cmty. Affairs, 1983, World Telecomm. Pioneer award, N.Y. State Broadcasters Assn., 1984, Golden Plate award, Am. Acad. Achievement, 1984, Outstanding Supporter Boy Scouting award, Nat. Boy Scout Coun., 1984, Silver Satellite award, Am. Women in Radio and TV, Lifetime Achievement award, N.Y. Internat. Film and TV Festival, 1984, Corp. Star of Yr. award, Nat. Leukemia Soc., 1985, Disting. Achievement award, U. Ga., 1985, Tree of Life award, Jewish Nat. Fund, 1985, Bus. Exec. of Yr. award, Ga. Security Dealers Assn., 1985, Life Achievement award, Popular Culture Assn., 1986, George Washington Disting. Patriot award, SAR, 1986, Mo. Honor medal, Sch. Journalism, U. Mo., 1987, Golden Ace award, Nat. Cable TV Acad., 1987, Sol Taishoff award, Nat. Press Found., 1988, Citizen Diplomat award, Ctr. for Soviet-Am. Dialogue, 1988, Chmn.'s award, Cable Advt. Bur., 1988, Directorate award, NATAS, 1989, Paul White award, Radio and TV News Dirs. Assn., 1989, Bus. Marketer of Yr. award, Am. Mktg. Assn., 1989, Disting. Svc. award, Simon Wiesenthal Ctr., 1990, Glasnost award, Vols. Am. and Soviet Life mag., 1990, Cable & Broadcasting's Man of the Century, 1999, Carnegie Medal of Philanthropy, 2001, Bower award for Bus. Leadership, Franklin Inst., 2006; named Yachtsman of Yr. 4 times, Man of the Yr., TIME mag., 1991; named one of 50 Most Generous Philanthropists, Fortune Mag., 2005, Forbes Richest Americans, 2006, The World's Most Influential People, TIME mag., 2009; named to The Promotion & Mktg. Assn. Hall of Fame, 1980, The Nat. Assn. for Sport & Phys. Edn. Hall of Fame, 1986, The Advt. Hall of Fame, 2004, The Jr. Achievement US Bus. Hall of Fame, 2007; won America's Cup in his yacht Courageous, 1977. Mem.: NAACP (life; bd. dirs. Atlanta chpt.), Nat. Cable TV Assn. (Pres.'s award 1979, 1989, Regional Employer of Yr. award 1976), Cousteau Soc., Nat. Audubon Soc., Bay Area Cable Club (hon.). Achievements include launching TBS Superstation concept, CNN, built a portfolio of unrivaled cable TV news and entertainment; launched Nuclear Threat Initiative, opened first Teds Montana Grill. Avocations: sailing, fishing. Office: Turner Enterprises Inc 133 Luckie St NW Atlanta GA 30303 Personal E-mail: info@tedturner.com.*

TURNER, TERRY CAMPBELL, lawyer; b. Salt Lake City, Dec. 12, 1952; s. George Ernest and Bettie Campbell Turner; m. Kim S. Sandberg, June 12, 1975; children: Jared Sandberg, Jonathan Terry, Jacey Turner Miller, Jennifer Turner Evans, Joshua Campbell. BA in Polit. Sci., Spanish, U. Utah, Salt Lake City, 1977; JD, Brigham Young U., Provo, Utah, 1980. Bar: Supreme Ct., Utah 1980, Republic of Bolivia Nat. Bar Assn. 1994, La Paz State Bar Assn., Bolivia 1994, US Ct. Appeals (10th Cir.) 1989, US Supreme Ct. 2004. Atty., ptnr. Day, Barney & Tycksen, Attys., Salt Lake City, 1980—83; pres. & CEO High Andes Mining, S.A., La Paz, 1983—89, Bolivian Copper Chem. Co., S.A., La Paz, 1995—97, Golden Eagle Internat., Inc., Salt Lake City, 1997—, chmn. bd., 1997—; atty., cons. Cordero & Cordero, Attys., La Paz, 1983—97; v.p. & gen. counsel Tipuani Devel. Co., S.A., La Paz, 1989—93, Minas del Glaciar, S.A., La Paz, 1993—95. Dir. Am. Coop. Sch., La Paz, 1995—98. Recipient medal, Gov. La Paz State, 1998. Mem.: Soc. Order Barrister (Order of Barrister 1979), Pi Sigma Alpha (Order 1977). Avocations: running, travel, history, archaeology, anthropology.

TURNER, THOMAS J., engineering company executive; b. Chgo., Apr. 26, 1971; s. Thomas J. Turner and Darlene M. Kaszuk; m. Jamie L. Lacey, Dec. 28, 2001; children: Elizabeth M., Benjamin L. BS in Indsl. Engring., Marquette U., Milw., 1994; M in Project Mgmt., Keller Grad. Sch. Mgmt., Oak Brook, Ill., 1998; MBA, DeVry U., Oak Brook, 2004. Engr./sr. engr. Panduit Corp., Tinley Park, Ill., 1994—2001, asst. chief engr., 2001—03, product devel. mgr. New Lenox, Ill., 2003—05, bus. devel. mgr., 2005—. Sec. bd. dirs. Lacey & Turner Investment, Inc., Peotone, Ill., 2003—06. Contbr. articles to profl. jours. Vol. Mc Kinsey Quarterly Exec. Panel, 2008—. Recipient Exhibitor Excellence award, Graybar Comm Data Tng. Conf., 2007, Advertising Excellence award, Baxter Rsch. Ctr., 2008; finalist Elec. Contracting Products Innovation award, NECA, 2008. Mem.: Pk. Forest Running and Pancake Club (course martial at races, team capt. relays). Office: Panduit Corp 1333 Schoolhouse Rd New Lenox IL 60451

TURNER, TODD, political organization administrator, lawyer; m. Becca Arnold; children: Harper, Cannon. Grad., Ouachita Bapt. U.; JD, U. Ark., Little Rock, 1992. Atty., Arkadelphia, Ark.; chmn. Dem. Party of Ark., 2009—. Contbr. articles to profl. jours. Bd. dirs., exec. com. Ark. Better Bus. Bur.; chmn. Clark County Dem. Com., 2007—. Recipient

Consumer Advocate award, Ark. Trial Lawyers Assn., 2000. Democrat. Office: Ark Dem Party 1300 W Capitol Ave Little Rock AR 72201 Office Phone: 501-374-2361. Office Fax: 501-376-8409.*

TURNER, V(ERAS) DEAN, dean; b. Tompkinsville, Ky., Oct. 19, 1925; s. Hubert B. and Hazel Pearl (Craig) T.; m. Maxine H. Henson, June 30, 1946; children: Sharon Kay, Ruth Diane. BS, Northwestern U., 1946; MA, U. Ill., 1949; PhD, U. Okla., 1968. Instr. dept. math. Moark Bapt. Coll., West Plains, Mo., 1949-51; instr. chair of math. dept. Champaign (Ill.) Jr. H.S., 1953-56; spl. instr. math. U. Okla., Norman, 1965-66; prof. Mankato (Minn.) State U., 1956-73, chairperson, dept. math., 1973-77, dean, 1977-89, dean emeritus, Coll. of Natural Scis., Math, Home Econs., 1989—. Chairperson external affairs subcom. on internat. math. edn. Upper Midwest Danforth Found., 1974-77; cons. Haldingford (Minn.) Sch., Assn. of Math. Tchrs. in Mex., Toluca; faculty senate, fiscal affairs com. Mankato State U., Sch. Arts and Scis. exec. com., curriculum com., dean selection com., chmn. task force on consolidation; mem. Study Group to Peoples Republic of China, 1980; mem. Minn. Coun. of Engring. Deans; mem. State U. Systems task force on admissions requirements. Co-author: Introduction to Mathematics, 1972, Principles of Mathematics, 1972. Comdr. USN, 1944, WWII, Korean War. Mem. Nat. Coun. of Tchrs. of Math., Math. Assn. of Am., Minn. Coun. of Tchrs. of Math., Sch. Sci. and Math. Assn., Phi Delta Kappa (pres. Mankato State U. chpt. 1984-85), Sigma Xi. Republican. Baptist. Home: 1034 Siena Oaks Cir W Palm Beach Gardens FL 33410-5122 E-mail: vturner@aol.com.

TURNER, VICKY JO, music educator; b. Kansas City, Mo., Mar. 17, 1968; d. James Phillip and Virginia Joan Turner. BS in Music Edn., N.W. Mo. State U., 1992. Lic. tchr. Mo., 1993. Music tchr. Linn County Sch. Dist., Purdin, Mo., 1994—96, McDonald County Sch. Dist., Jane and Rocky Comfort, Mo., 1999—2002, Kennett Sch. Dist., Mo., 2002—06, Adrian R-III Sch. Dist., 2006—. Mem. first bapt. choir First Bapt. Ch., Kennett, 2002, Sunday sch. sec. 1st and 2d grade students, 2003. Recipient Cert. of Appreciation, Am. Legion, 1999. Mem.: Mo. Band Dir.'s Assn. (licentiate), Am. Choral Dir.'s Assn. (licentiate), Music Educator's Nat. Conf. (licentiate), Mo. State Tchr.'s Assn. (licentiate). Baptist. Avocations: exercise, singing, birdwatching, hiking, music. Office: Adrian R III Sch Dist Butler MO 64730 Office Fax: 816-297-2980. E-mail: vjturner@netection.net.

TURNER, WILLARD CRAIG, academic administrator; b. Mobile, Ala., Jan. 7, 1947; s. A. C. and Sybil Willard Turner; m. Annette Louise Enloe, Dec. 20, 1969; children: Scott Craig, Shannon Leigh Hays. BA, Baylor U., 1969, MA, 1971; PhD, Tulane U., 1977. Asst., assoc. prof. English Tex. A&M U., Coll. Station, Tex., 1976—85; prof., chair English Miss. Coll., Clinton, 1985—92; exec. v.p., chief academic officer Hardin-Simmons U., Abilene, Tex., 1996—2001, pres., 2001—. Mem., distance edn. adv. com. Tex. Higher Edn. Coordinating Bd., Austin, Tex., 1999—2001; bd. dirs. Ind. Coll., Univ. Tex., 2001—, Assn. Tex. Coll., Univ., 2004—. Editor: Critical Essays on Eudora Welty, Critical Essays on American Humor, The Poet Robert Browning and His Kinsfolk, by His Cousin, Cyrus Mason. Bd. dirs. Abilene (Tex.) C. of C., 2001, United Way of Abilene, 2000—05, Serenity Found. of Tex., Abilene, 2003, Consortium for Global Edn., Atlanta, 2005; bd. govs. Abilene Philharm., 2002—05. Avocations: fishing, reading, motion pictures. Office: Catawba College 2300 W Innes St Salisbury NC 28144 Business E-Mail: cturner@hsutx.edu.

TURNER, WILLIAM WEYAND, writer; b. Buffalo, Apr. 14, 1927; s. William Peter and Magdalen (Weyand) T.; m. Margaret Peiffer, Sept. 12, 1964; children: Mark Peter, Lori Ann. BS, Canisius Coll., 1949. Spl. agt. in various field offices FBI, 1951-61; free-lance writer Calif., 1963—; sr. editor Ramparts Mag., San Francisco, 1967—. Investigator and cons. Nat. Wiretap Commn., 1975; U.S. del. J.F.K. Internat. Seminar, Rio de Janeiro, 1995. Author: The Police Establishment, 1968, Invisible Witness: The Use and Abuse of the New Technology of Crime Investigation, 1968, Hoover's F.B.I.: The Men and the Myth, 1970, Power on the Right, 1971, (with Warren Hinckle and Eliot Asinof) The Ten Second Jailbreak, 1973, (with John Christian) The Assassination of Robert F. Kennedy, 1978, (with Warren Hinckle) The Fish is Red: The Story of the Secret War Against Castro, 1981, updated, expanded, retitled as Deadly Secrets: The CIA-Mafia War Against Castro and the Assassination of JFK, 1992, Rearview Mirror: Looking Back at the FBI, the CIA and Other Tails, 2001, Mission Not Accomplished: How George Bush Lost the War on Terrorism, 2004; contbg. author: Investigating the FBI, 1973; contbr. articles to popular mags.; book reviewer L.A. Times. Dem. candidate for U.S. Congress, 1968. Served with USN, 1945-46. Mem. Authors Guild, Internat. Platform Assn., Press Club of San Francisco. Roman Catholic. Avocation: tennis. Home and Office: 163 Mark Twain Ave San Rafael CA 94903-2820 Office Phone: 415-479-7945. Business E-Mail: fanofjfk@aol.com.

TURNER-RICHARD, LANA R., musician, director, composer; b. Wood River, Ill., Oct. 14, 1952; d. George A. and Grace E. (Brake) Turner; m. Robert Richard, Oct. 27, 1984. MusB in Edn. and Piano Performance, So. Ill. Univ., Edwardsville, Ill., 1974, M in Piano, 1977; doctoral studies in piano, Washington Univ., 1984. Instr. various C.C., St. Louis, 1985—95; accompanist St. Louis (Mo.) Children's Choir; music dir. Summer Playhouse Prodns., Crestwood, 1989—, St. Lucas U.C.C., St. Louis, 1996—. Chmn. auditions Piano Guild, Ill., Mo., 1974—90; judge variuos music festivals U.S., 1971—. Author: (book) Modern Day Prodigal Son, 2007. Worker habitat for Humanity, St. Louis., 2006. Mem.: U.S. humane Soc., Pi Kappa Lambda. Office: St Lucas UCC 11735 Denny Rd Saint Louis MO 63126

TURNER THORNE, CHARLI, women's college basketball coach; d. Jim Turner; m. Will Thorne, May 14, 1994; children: Conor, Liam, Quinn. BA in Psychology, Stanford U., Calif., 1988; MEd, U. Wash., Seattle, 1990. Grad. asst. U. Wash. Huskies, 1988-90; asst. coach, recruiting coord. Santa Clara U. Broncos, Calif., 1990-93; head coach No. Ariz. U. Lumberjacks, Flagstaff, 1993—96, Ariz. State U. Sun Devils, Tempe, 1996—. Bd. dirs. Women's Basketball Coaches Assn. Named Dist. VIII Coach of Yr., Women's Basketball Coaches Assn., 2006. Office: Ariz State U Womens Basketball Carson Ctr PO Box 872505 Tempe AZ 85287-2505 Office Phone: 480-965-6086. E-mail: ASUHoop@asu.edu.*

TURNER VANLYDEGRAF, CLAUDIA BETH, writer, researcher; b. Salinas, Calif., Mar. 19, 1945; d. Prentiss Dixon Hill and Barbara Clayborne, Leonard Francis Balch (Stepfather); m. Robert Michael Turner, May 21, 1966 (div. Aug. 14, 1972); m. Jay Frank VanLydegraf, 1980; children: David Michael Reinhardt, Jeffrey Warren Gregory, Amber Beth Turner. Student, El Camino Coll., 1969—72. Cert. Nev. State Ins. Bd., 1999; Nev. Real Estate Divsn., 1979, notary public load signing agent. Cost, manpower budget analyst Hughes Aircraft Co., Culver City, Calif., 1972—77; auditor No. Nev. Health & Welfare & Pension Plans Adminstrv. Office, Reno, 1980—81; co-owner TV Signal Corp, Cold Springs, Nev., 1981—86; flagger, laborer Laborers Local 169, Reno, 1989—94; jewelry sales assoc. SuperPawn/Camco, Reno, 1994—96; sales, loan assoc. Pioneer Jewelry and Loan, Reno, 1996—97; owner document rsch. firm Coyote Svcs., Cold Springs, 1998—; pub./owner Coyote News, Cold Springs, 1998—2002. Author: Notes from Nobody, 2001. Citizens adv. bd. Washoe County Commn., Cold Springs, 1999—2001; adv. - reporter Cold Springs Cmty. Assoc, 1998—2003; lobbyist Nev. Mem.: UnNamed Writers Group, Ea. Star. Independent. Avocations: genealogy, gemology, antiques, history, art. Home: 17890 Fantail Circle Cold Springs NV 89506 Office: Coyote Services 17890 Fantail Circle Cold Springs NV 89506 E-mail: cltvcoyote@aol.com.

TURNER-WRIGHT, MARIE ANNETTA, retired librarian; b. Indpls., May 13, 1936; d. Clarence and W. Marie Turner; 1 child, Milicent Anne Wright. AB, Ind. U., Bloomington, 1957, MLS, 1971, specialist degree in libr. info. sci., 1986. Adminstrv. asst. childrens svcs. Indpls.-Marion County Pub. Libr., 1971—74, br. libr., 1974—79; assoc. faculty Ind. U. Sch. Libr. and Info. Sci., Bloomington, 1974—84; assoc. libr. Ind. U.-Purdue U. Indpls., U. Libr., Indpls., 1985—2001; adj. faculty dept. English Ind. U.-Purdue U. Indpls., Sch. Liberal Arts, Indpls., 1989—2002; adj. faculty. Martin U., Indpls., 2006—. Vis. asst. libr. Ind. U. -Purdue U. Indpls., U. Libr., Indpls., 1981—82. Author: (bibliography) African-American Archaeology and African Diaspora Archaeology Resources, 2000. Bd. mem. Indpls. Marion County Pub. Libr., 2009—. Recipient Glenn W. Irwin, Jr., MD Experience Excellence Recognition award, Ind. Purdue U., Indpls., 1995, Herbert S. and Va. White Profl. Devel. award, Ind. U. Libraries, 1999, Outstanding Contbn. award, Ind. Purdue U. Black Faculty and Staff Coun., Indpls., 2002; grantee, NEH, 1996, 1998, 2000, Clowes Fund, Inc., 1996, Ind. Humanities Coun., 1996, 1998, Nissan Motors, 2000, Lila Wallace Readers' Digest Fund, 2000—01, Indpls. Found. Libr. Fund and Associated Writing Programs, Cooper Canyon Press, Pubs. of MLA, 2001, Nat. Endowment Arts, 2001. Mem.: ALA (elected coun. mem. 2001—04), Assn. for the Study of African Am. Life and History, Freedom to Read Found., Am. Hort. Soc. Episcopalian. Avocations: African American folklife, gardening, birdwatching. Home: 328 N East St Indianapolis IN 46202 Personal E-mail: mtwright@iupui.edu.

TURNEY, SHAREN JESTER, retail executive, cosmetics executive; b. 1956; BA in Bus. Edn., U. Okla., 1974. With Foley's, 1979—88, Byer Calif. Federated Dept. Stores; sr. v.p., gen. merchandise mgr. Neiman Marcus stores, 1997—98; exec. v.p. merchandising, creative prodn., advt., pub. rels. Neiman Marcus, 1998; pres., CEO Neiman Marcus Direct, 1999—2000, Victoria's Secret Direct, 2000—06, Victoria's Secret Megabrand and Intimate Apparel, 2006—. Campaign chmn. United Way, Dallas; hon. co-chair Children's Hunger Alliance, Ohio, 2006; bd. dirs. Winston Sch., Addison Theater, Columbus Coalition Against Family Violence, Jay H. Retailing Initiative Adv. bd., Wharton Sch., U. Pa. Recipient Fashion Medal Hon. for Fashion Retailing, 1997, Dr. Catherine White Achievement award, HeartShare Human Services, 2005; named to Hall of Fame Bus. Edn., U. Okla., 2005. Office: Victoria's Secret PO Box 16589 Columbus OH 43216-6589*

TURNG, LIH-SHENG, education educator; b. Taiwan, Sept. 21, 1959; MS, Cornell U., Ithaca, NY, 1987, PhD, 1990. Task leader C-MOLD, Ithaca, 1990—2000; prof. U. Wis., Madison, Wis., 2000—; hon. prof. Zheng Zhou U., China, 2006—. Chair prof. SCUT; co-dir. Polymer Engring. Ctr., Madison, Wis., 2001—. Dir., prin. investigator (engring. rsch.) Microcellular Nanocomposites (3M Non-Tenured awards, 2002, 2003). Bd. mem. chair Soc.Plastics Engrs., Injection Molding Divsn., Brookfield, Conn., 2002—, fellow, 2008—, chair, 2002—. Grant, NSF, 2001—, EPA, 2007—. Fellow: ASME. Achievements include research in computer simulation optimization microcelluar injection molding and nanocomposites for injection molding and lightweight, high-performance polymer nanocomposites and tissue engineering scaffolds. Office: Univ Wis 1513 University Ave Madison WI 53706 Office Phone: 608-262-0586. Business E-Mail: turng@engr.wisc.edu.

TURNHAM, JOE (JOSEPH R. TURNHAM), political organization administrator; b. Ala., Oct. 28, 1959; BS in Bus. Adminstrn., Auburn U., 1981. Joined Ala. Contract Sales, Inc., 1981; chmn. Ala. Dem. Party, 1995-98, 2005—; former mem. Dem. Nat. Com., Washington. Founder Ala. League of Environ. Action Voters. Mem. Auburn C. of C., Lee County Habitat for Humanity, Boys and Girls Clubs of Greater Lee County; founding bd. mem. Land Trust of East Ala.; bd. mem. Chattowah Ala. Land Trust; vice chair Redeem the Vote; bd. dirs. Den. for Life of Am. Mem.: Auburn Kiwanis Club (former pres., named Kiwanian of Yr.). Democrat. Office: PO Box 928 Auburn AL 36831-0928 also: Ala Dem Party 501 Adams Ave Montgomery AL 36104 Office Phone: 334-262-2221. Office Fax: 334-262-6474. E-mail: joeturnham@aol.com.*

TURNIPSEED, BARNWELL RHETT, III, journalist, broadcaster, public relations consultant; b. Apr. 6, 1929; s. Barnwell Rhett and L. (Rogers) T.; m. Jane Whitley, June 12, 1982. BA in Journalism, U. Ga., 1950, MA in Journalism, 1960. With Sta. WGGA, Gainesville, Ga., 1943-46; prodn. mgr. Sta WGGA, Gainesville, Ga., 1958-60; with Sta. WRFC, Athens, Ga., 1947-50; program dir. Sta. WKYW, Louisville, 1953, Sta. WGBA, Columbus, Ga., 1953-55; broadcasting cons., 1955—60; sr. corr., sci. editor Voice of Am. Worldwide English, 1960-72; coord. radio-TV pub. affairs HEW, 1972-73; mem. staff Ga. Congressman Phil Landrum, 1974-75; dir. solar energy tech. info. Dept. Energy, Washington, 1975-77, spl. asst., 1977-81; pvt. practice, 1981-88, 94—; instr. West Ga. Coll., Carrollton, 1988-89, 90-94; asst. prof. Brenau Coll., Gainesville, Ga., 1989-90; mgr. WBCX-FM, Gainsville, Ga., 1989—90, WWGC-FM, Carrollton, Ga., 1990-94. Dir. Ga. Broadcasters Annual Awards, 1998—2005. Author: History of Georgia Broadcasting, 1972; prin. corr. Voice of Am. (Peabody award winning space exploration broadcasts, 1969). Symphony Guild rep. Louisville, Columbus, Ga. Jaycees; active symphony and arts devel. Sgt. U.S. Army, 1950-52. Recipient Two Meritorious Svc. awards, USIA; named to Ga. Broadcasters Hall of Fame, 2003. Mem. Nat. Assn. Sci. Writers (life), Aircraft Owners and Pilots Assn., Sigma Delta Chi, Kappa Sigma. Democrat. Methodist. Home and Office: 295 Greenfield Cir Fayetteville GA 30215-2622

TURNLEY, DAVID CARL, photojournalist; b. Ft. Wayne, Ind., June 22, 1955; s. William Loyd and Elizabeth Ann (Protsman) Turnley; m. Karin Nicolette, Apr. 15, 1989. BA in French, U. Mich., 1977; student, Sorbonne, Paris, 1975; DMus (hon.), Keele U., Eng., 1991. Staff photogapher Sliger Home Newspapers, Northville, Mich., 1978—80, Detroit Free Press, 1980—99; European based photographic corr. Detroit Free Press/Black Star Paris, 1988—99; Neiman fellow Harvard U., Boston, 1997—98; internat. exec. prodr. Corbis Sygma, NYC, 1999—. Author: Why Are They Weeping? South Africans under Aparthied, 1988, Beijing Spring, 1989, Moments of Revolution: Eastern Europe, 1990; London Decca Records. Recipient Canon essay award for S. African coverage, 1985, World Press Picture of Yr. award for Earthquake in Armenia, 1988, Robert Capa Gold medal for China, Romania coverage, 1990, Pulitizer Prize for China, E. Europe coverage, 1990.

TURNMEYER, DENISE L., pediatrics nurse, educator; b. Ohskohs, Wis., May 26, 1971; m. Kevin Turnmeyer, Sept. 9, 1994; children: Kayli A., Megan N. MSN, Regis U., Colo., 2007. RN Children's Hosp. Wis.-Fox Valley, Neenah, 2001—; academic instrnl. staff U. Wis., Oshkosh, 2007—. Mem.: Acad. Neonatal Nursing, Wis. Nurses Assn. (nursing practice coun. 2008). Office: Univ Wis-Oshkosh 1100 Algoma Blvd Oshkosh WI 54901 Business E-Mail: turnmeyd@uwosh.edu.

TURNOVSKY, STEPHEN JOHN, economics professor; b. Wellington, New Zealand, Apr. 5, 1941; came to U.S., 1981; s. Frederick and Liselotte Felicitas (Wodak) T.; m. Michelle Henriette Louise Roos, Jan. 21, 1967; children: Geoffrey George, Jacqueline Liselotte. BA, Victoria U., Wellington, 1962, MA with honors, 1963; PhD, Harvard U., 1968. Asst. prof. econs. U. Pa., Phila., 1968-71; assoc. prof. U. Toronto, Ont., Canada, 1971-72; prof. Australian Nat. U., Canberra, 1972-82; IBE disting. prof. econs. U. Ill., Champaign, 1982-87; prof. econs. U. Wash., Seattle, 1987—, chmn. dept., 1990-95; Castor prof., 1993—. Rsch. assoc. Nat. Bur. Econ. Rsch., Cambridge, Mass., 1983-93. Author: Macroeconomic Analysis and Stabilization Policy, 1977, International Macroeconomic Stabilization Policy, 1990, Methods of Macroeconomic Dynamics, 1995, 2d edit., 2000, International Macroeconomic Dynamics, 1997; mem. editl. bd. several jours.; contbr. articles to profl. jours. Fellow Econometric Soc., Acad. Social Scis. in Australia; mem. Soc. Econ. Dynamics and Control (pres. 1982-84, editor Jour. Econ. Dynamics and Control 1981-87, 95-2001), Soc. Computational Econs. (pres. 2004-05). Avocations: skiing, hiking, music. Home: 6053 NE Kelden Pl Seattle WA 98105-2045 Office: Dept Econs U Wash Box 353330 Seattle WA 98195-3330 Office Phone: 206-685-8028. E-mail: sturn@u.washington.edu.

TURNSHEK, DAVID ALVIN, physics and astronomy professor, department chairman; b. Greensburg, Pa., May 17, 1955; s. Alvin and Josephine Marie (Polyfka) Turnshek; m. Diane Elaine Routsis; children: James David, Steven David, Alex David, Matthew David. BS, Villanova U., Pa., 1977; PhD, U. Ariz., Tucson, 1981. Prof. and chair, dept. physics & astronomy U. Pitts., 1988—, edn. pub. outreach, 1988—2008. Contbr. scientific papers to profl. publs. Grants, NSF, NASA, 1980—2008. Mem.: Am. Astron. Soc. Office: Univ Pitts Dept Physics and Astronomy Pittsburgh PA 15260

TURO, JOANN K., psychoanalyst, psychotherapist, consultant; b. Westerly, RI, Feb. 13, 1938; d. Angelo and Anna Josephine (Drew) T. BS in Biology and Chemistry, U. R.I., 1959; MA in Human Rels. and Psychology, Ohio U., 1964; postgrad., NYU, 1966-71, N.Y. Freudian Inst., NYC, 1977-85, Mental Health Inst., 1977-80. Rsch. asst. biochemistry studies on schizophrenia Harvard U. Med. Sch., Boston, 1959-60; indsl. psychology asst. studies on managerial success N.Y. Telephone Co., NYC, 1964-66; staff psychologist Testing and Advisement Ctr. NYU, 1966-70; psychology intern Kings County Hosp., Bklyn., 1970-71; staff psychologist M.D.C. Psychol. Svcs., NYC, 1971-72; clin. dir. Greenwich House Substance Abuse Clinic, NYC, 1973-76; cons. psychotherapist Mental Health Consultation Ctr., NYC, 1977-82; pvt. practice NYC, 1981—. Mental health cons. Bklyn. Ctr. for Psychotherapy, 1976-78; organizing comm.mem., Future Psychoanalytic End., 2006-2007; with Psychoanaltyic Consultation Svcs., 1994—; conf. future psychoanalytic edn., NYC, 2007-; chair task force lic. NY Freudians Inst., 2008-2009. Mem. Internat. Psychoanalytic Assn. (panel discussant 2007, presenter 2007, 09), Soc. for Personality Assessment (cert.), N.Y. Freudian Soc. (co-chmn. grad. com. 1985-86, mem. continuing edn. com. 1986—, pub. rels. com. 1992-93, psychoanalytic consult svc. 1994—, tng. and supr. psychoanalyst 1995—, ethics com. 1999—, tng. analyst panel 2000—, chair 2002-03, presenter 2002, bd. dirs. 2003-06, v.p. 2005-2006), N.Y. Coun. Psychoanalytic Psychotherapists (cert.), Met. Assn. for Coll. Mental Health Practitoners (cert.), Am. Psychoanalytic Assn. (discussion group presenter 2009). Office: 175 W 12th St Apt 15A New York NY 10011-8211 Office Phone: 212-691-2041.

TUROCK, BETTY JANE, retired library and information science professor; b. Scranton, Pa., June 12; d. David and Ruth Carolyn (Sweetser) Argust; m. Frank M. Turock, June 16, 1956; children: David L., B. Drew. BA magna cum laude (Charles Weston scholar), Syracuse U., 1955; postgrad. (scholar), U. Pa., 1956; MLS, Rutgers U., 1970, PhD, 1981. Library and materials coordinator Holmdel (N.J.) Public Schs., 1963—65; story-teller Wheaton (Ill.) Public Library, 1965—67; ednl. media specialist Alhambra Public Sch., Phoenix, 1967—70; br. librarian, area librarian, head extension service Forsyth County Public Library System, Winston-Salem, NC, 1970—73; asst. dir., dir. Montclair (N.J.) Public Library, 1973—76; asst. dir. Monroe County Library System, Rochester, NY, 1978—81; asst. prof. Rutgers U. Sch. Comm., Info. and Libr. Studies, 1981—87, assoc. prof., 1987—93, prof., 1994—, dept. chair, 1989—95, 2002—03, dir. MLS program, 1990—95, 2002—03, assoc. dean, 2002—04, 2004—08, prof. emerita, assoc. dean emerita; pres. Rock Info. Assocs., 2004—09. Vis. prof. Rutgers U. Grad. Sch. Library and Info. Studies, 1980-81; adviser U.S. Dept. Edn. Office of Libr. Programs, 1988-89. Author: Serving Older Adults, 1983, Creating a Financial Plan, 1992; editor: The Bottom Line, 1984-90; contbr. articles to profl. jours. Trustee Raritan Twp. (N.J.) Pub. Libr., 1961—62, Keystone Coll., 1991—, Freedom to Read Found., 1994—97, Librs. for the Future, 1994—97, Fund for Am.'s Librs., 1995; mem. bd. Trejo Found., 1995—, pres., 2009—; trustee Bd. Am. Libr., Paris, 1999—; mem. Bd. Edn. Raritan Twp., 1962—66; ALA coord. Task Force on Women, 1978—80; mem. action coun.; treas. Social Responsibilities Round Table, 1978—82; mem. bd. visitors Johns Hopkins Medicine, 2005—; mem. Nat. Lib. Coun., John Hopkins U., 2007—. Recipient NJ Libr. Leadership award, 1994; named Woman of Yr., Raritan-Holmdel Woman's Club, 1975; Charles Weston scholar Syracuse U., 1955. Mem. AAUP, Am. Soc. Info. Sci., Assn. Libr. and Info. Sci Edn., ALA (pres. 1995-96, pres.-elect 1994-95, exec. bd. 1991-97, coun. 1988-97, Equality award 1998, Lippincott award 2006), Rutgers U. Grad. Sch. Library and Info. Studies Alumni Assn. (pres. 1977-78, Disting. Alumni award 1994), Phi Theta Kappa, Psi Chi, Beta Phi Mu, Pi Beta Phi. Unitarian Universalist. Business E-Mail: bturock@schs.rutgers.edu.

TUROCK, JANE PARSICK, nutritionist; b. Peckville, Pa., Apr. 15, 1947; d. Paul Charles and Elizabeth Dorothy (Mistysyn) Parsick; m. Michael John, July 12, 1968; children: Eric Matthew, Nathan Andrew, J. Seth, Melanie Kay. BS, Marywood Coll., Scranton, Pa., 1969, MS, 1982. Registered dietitian; cert. nutrition specialist. Registered dietitian Jane P. Turock, Scranton, Pa., 1985—; founder and chief dietitian Gastric Bubble, Scranton, Pa., 1986—; prof. Penn State Coll., Scranton, Pa., 1987—; dietitian & presenter WNEP TV Healthwatch, Avoca, Pa., 1988—; dir. & chief dietitian Vascular Inst. of Northeast Pa., Pa., 1989—; owner, mgr. Nutrition...Plus/Fitness Unlimited, Scranton, Pa., 1991—; owner Pauliz Profl. Plz., Olyphant, Pa., 2006—, Sonny's Patching, Inc., 2007. Cons. Home Health Care Assn., Clarks Summit, 1985—; dietitian Clarks Summit, 1985—; founder Nat. Nutrition Month Bakeoff; dir. Camp Jane. Treas. Lackawanna County Med. Soc. Aux., 1974-76, pres., 1979-80, bd. dirs., 1980-81; allocations com. United Way Lackawanna County, 1990—; bd. dirs. Lupus Found., 1995, St.

Francis of Assissi Kitchen, 1995; coord. Gary DiBileo For Mayor Scranton Campaign, 2005. Mem. Am. Dietetic Assn., Northeast Dist. Pa. Dietic Diet Therapy, Consulting Nutritionists in Pvt. Practice, Am. Diabetic Assn., Northeast Womens Network, Allied Wedding Firm. Republican. Roman Catholic. Avocations: skiing, tennis, gourmet cooking, jogging, swimming. Office: 397 N 9th Ave Scranton PA 18504 Personal E-mail: janeturock@excite.com.

TUROK, PAUL HARRIS, composer, commentator, music critic; b. NYC, Dec. 3, 1929; s. Joseph and Esther (Pashman) T.; m. Susan Kay Frucht, Mar. 24, 1967. BA, Queens Coll., NYC, 1950; MA, U. Calif., Berkeley, 1951; MS, Baruch Coll., 1986. Music dir. Sta. KPFA, Berkeley, 1955-56; lectr. CCNY, 1959-63; vis. prof. Williams Coll., Williamstown, Mass., 1963-64; music critic New York Herald-Tribune, 1964-65; critic, columnist Music Jour., New York, 1964-79, Ovation mag., New York, 1980—; critic, contbr. New York Times, 1984—, Sta. WQXR, First Hearing, New York, 1985—. Pub. Turok's Choice, 1990—. Composer musical compositions, premiered Indpls. Symphony, 1971, Louisville Orch., 1973, Cleve. Orch., 1973, Phila Orch., 1976; opera Richard III, 1975, Sousa Overture, 1976, Lanier Songs, 1978, English Horn Quintet, 1982, Cello Sonata, 1984, Organ Toccata, 1984, Tourist Music, 1985, String Quartet No. 4, 1986, Rhapsody for Band, 1987, Piano Dance, 1988, Violin Sonata, 1989, From Sholem Aleichem, 1990, Abac for trumpet and organ, 1990, Partita for three winds, 1991, Concerto for two violins and orchestra, 1991, Piano Trio, 1992, C.C. 6 for bassoon and orchestra, 1992, Fantasy for 4 flutes and piano, 4 hands, 1994, Clap, Cluck, Count: Three Interactive Proverbs for Children and Orchestra, 1995, Sonata No. 2 for Cello and Piano, 1996, Concerto for Piano and Orch., 1997, Canzone Concertante No. 7 for viola, percussion and strings, 1998, Reeling in the Y2K, 1999, Flute Sonata, 2000, Behold, Thou Art Fair, 2001, Sextet for piano and winds, Partita No.3 for English horn, 2002, Variations on a theme by Grieg for 8 trombones, Elegy in Memory of Nathan Schwartz, 2002, C.C. No. 8 for Violin and Orch., String Quartet No. 5, 2003, C.C. No. 9 for Trumpet and Strings, 2003, C.C. No. 10 for Piano and Strings, 2006, Caprice d'Octobre for 3 violins, 2004, Brass Quintet No. 2, 2004, Fanfare for Brass Ensemble, 2005, Sonata for Piano, 2006, 2008, Barbershop Variations for Five Horns, 2006. Served with U.S. Army, 1953-55. Hertz travelling scholar, U. Calif., 1956-58; Grammy nominee 1992, 93. Jewish. Avocations: world travel, computing. Personal E-mail: pturok@verizon.net.

TUROW, SCOTT F., writer, lawyer; b. Chgo., Apr. 12, 1949; s. David D. and Rita (Pastron) Turow; m. Annette Weisberg, Apr. 4, 1971 (div. 2007); 3 children. BA magna cum laude, Amherst Coll., 1970; MA, Stanford U., 1974; JD cum laude, Harvard U., 1978. Bar: Ill. 1978, U.S. Dist. Ct. (no. dist.) Ill. 1978, U.S. Ct. Appeals (7th cir.) 1979. Asst. U.S. atty. US Dept. Justice (no. dist.) Ill., Chgo., 1978—86; ptnr. Sonnenschein Nath & Rosenthal LLP, Chgo., 1986—. E.H. Jones lectr. Stanford U., 1972—75; pres. Author's Guild, 1997—98. Author: (novels) Presumed Innocent, 1987, The Burden of Proof, 1990, Pleading Guilty, 1993, The Laws of Our Fathers, 1996, Personal Injuries, 1999, Reversible Errors, 2002, Ordinary Heroes, 2005, Limitations, 2006, (nonfiction) One L.: An Inside Account of Life in the First Year at Harvard Law School, 1977, Ultimate Punishment: A Lawyer's Reflections on Dealing With the Death Penalty, 2003 (Robert F. Kennedy Book award, 2004); contbr. articles to profl. jours. Mem.: Chgo. Coun. Lawyers, Chgo. Bar Assn. Office: Sonnenschein Nath Rosenthal 233 S Wacker Dr Ste 8000 Chicago IL 60606-6491 E-mail: sturow@sonnenscheim.com.

TUROWSKI, GREGORY, plastic surgeon; MD, Med. U. of Lodz, Poland, 1988; PhD in Surgery, Yale U. Cert. Am. Bd. Surgery, Am. Bd. Plastic Surgery. Internship NY Meth. Hosp., 1990; surg. residency St. Mary's Hosp./Yale Med. Sch.; plastic surgery residency Harvard U. Med. Sch.; fellowship, Gastrointestinal Pathobiology Lab. Yale U. Med. Sch., 1992—93; staff mem. Brigham and Women's Hosp., Boston Children's Hosp., Mass. Gen. Hosp.; pvt. group practice Chgo.; med. dir. New Horizons Ctr. Cosmetic Surgery, 1999—. Faculty mem. Harvard Med. Sch., U. Chgo. Contbr. articles to profl. jours. Named one of Top Doctors, Castle Connolly. Fellow: Am. Coll. Surgeons; mem.: Am. Soc. Plastic Surgeons. Office: New Horizons Ctr for Cosmetic Surgery 9843 Gross Point Rd Skokie IL 60076*

TURPIN, RICHARD E., sales executive; b. Hamilton, Ohio, Aug. 10, 1950; 1 child, Vincent Paul Huntington Turpin. Degree, UCLA, 1972. Dir. sales Pepsico, Hamilton; dir. mktg. Tri-State, Inc., Columbus, Ohio; dir. sales CMR, Inc., Columbus, Ohio, 1985-96; prin., cons. Turpin Assocs., Cin., 1996—; sr. exec. Arch Wireless, 1996—. Vol. Children's Svcs., Columbus, 1994—, Old English Sheepdog Rescue; bd. dirs. EE Homeowners Assn., 2005, 06, 07, 08, 09. Recipient Citizenship award, City of Chgo., 1970, Rosa Parks Wall of Tolerance award, 2004, 2006—08, Rosa Parks Humanitarian award, 2004, 2008. Mem.: Dayton C. of C., Dayton Realtors, Columbus Exec. Sales Assn. (awarded for Vol. Children with AIDS), Columbus C. of C. (com. chmn. 1993—94), Arch Press Club, Metrocall Pres. Club, Pres.'s Club. Jewish. Home: 515 Marshall Rd Middletown OH 45042 Office Phone: 937-313-9218. Business E-Mail: rturpin@cinci.rr.com.

TURQUETTE, ATWELL RUFUS, logician; b. Texarkana, Tex., July 14, 1914; s. Rufus Watson and Dale Cook (Warmack) Turquette; m. Lucille Case Le Roy, June 2, 1937 (dec. Feb. 1956); m. Maxine Harriot Kennedy, Apr. 2, 1958 (dec. Aug. 1992); m. Frances D. Bond, Dec. 27, 1998 (dec. Nov. 2007). BA, U. Ark., 1936; MA, Duke U., 1937; PhD, Cornell U., 1943. Asst. prof. Fla. So. Coll., Lakeland, 1937-38; fellow U. Chgo., 1938-39; assoc. prof. Fla. So. Coll., Lakeland, 1939-40; assistantship, fellow Cornell U., Ithaca, N.Y., 1940-43, instr., 1943-45; asst. prof. U. Ill., Champaign-Urbana, 1945-48, assoc. prof., 1948-52, prof., 1952-75, prof. emeritus, 1975—. Co-author: Many-valued Logics, 1952; contbg. author: Les 265 communications, Congrès International des Mathématiciens, Nice, 1970; editor: Jour. of Symbolic Logic, 1950-68; patentee in field. Duke U. scholar, 1936; U. Chgo. fellow, 1938; grantee NSF, 1968-70, Rockefeller Gen. Edn. Bd., 1954. Mem. Am. Math. Soc., Soc. Indsl. and Appl. Math., Symbolic Logic Assn., London Math. Soc., Calcutta Math. Soc., AAAS, N.Y. Acad. Scis., Am Phil. Assn. Achievements include design for multi-valued circuits, functional completeness and incompleteness results for many-valued logics; minimal axiomatizations for many-valued logics; relating Pascal triangles to Post sets; deciphering Peirce's triadic logic; discovery of quasistrokes and their application to networks. Home: 914 W Clark St Champaign IL 61821-3328

TURRI, JOSEPH A., lawyer; b. Seneca Falls, NY, July 24, 1943; s. Louis Arthur and Assunta (Faiola) T.; m. Susan Ruth Testa, Dec. 29, 1975 (dec.); 1 child, Michael James. BA, SUNY, Buffalo, 1965; JD, Cornell U., 1970. Bar: N.Y. 1971, U.S. Dist Ct. (we. dist.) N.Y. 1971, U.S. Supreme Ct. 1974, U.S. Dist. Ct. (so. dist.) N.Y. 1996, U.S. Ct. Appeals (2d cir.) 1996. Mem. Harris Beach PLLC, Rochester, NY, 1970—, chmn. constrn. law dept., 1992-98, 2002—, 1994-96, pres., 1999—2002. Bd. dirs. Thousand Island Park Corp., N.Y., O'Connell Electric Co.; v.p. Castle Bay Ltd., Rochester, N.Y.; arbitrator Am. Arbitration Assn., Syracuse, 1985—. Bd. dirs. Rochester Downtown Devel. Corp., 1992-97. Named to Best Lawyers in Am. in constrn. law, 2006—09. Mem. N.Y. State Bar Assn., Monroe County Bar Assn., Assn. Gen. Contractors, Met. Forum (trustee). Avocations: horseback riding, antique wooden boats. Home: 21 Evergreen Ln Rochester NY 14618-4719 Office: Harris Beach PLLC 99 Garnsey Rd Pittsford NY 14534 Office Phone: 585-419-8644.

TURRO, NICHOLAS JOHN, chemistry professor; b. Middletown, Conn., May 18, 1938; m. Sandra Jean Misenti, Aug. 6, 1960; children: Cynthia, Claire. BA, Wesleyan U., 1960, DSc (hon.), 1984; PhD, Calif. Inst. Tech., 1963; doctorate (hon.), U. Fribourg, Switzerland, 2004. Instr. chemistry Columbia U., NYC, 1964-65, asst. prof., 1965-67, assoc. prof., 1967-69, prof. chemistry, 1969—, William P. Schweitzer prof. chemistry, 1982—, chmn. chemistry dept., 1981-84, co-chmn. dept. chem. engrng. and applied chemistry, 1997-2000, prof. earth and environ. engrng., 1998—. Author: Molecular Photochemistry, 1965; author: (with A.A. Lamola) Energy Transfer and Organic Photochemistry, 1971; author: Modern Molecular Photochemistry, 1978; co-author (with V. Ramanuothy and J.C. Scaiano): Principles of Molecular Photo Chemistry: An Introduction, 2008; mem. editl. bd.: Jour. Reactive Intermediates, Langmuir and Proceedings of Nat. Acad. Scis., 2004. Recipient Eastman Kodak award for excellence in grad. rsch. pure chemistry, 1973, award, E.O. Lawrence U.S. Dept. Energy, 1983, Porter medal, European Photochem. Soc., Inter-Am. Photochem. Soc., 1994, Havinga medal, Leiden, The Netherlands, 1994, Disting. Alumnus award, Calif. Inst. Tech., 1996, Strahlenchemie preis, Max-Planck-Inst., Mülheim, Germany, 1998, Dir's. award for Tchr.-Scholar, NSF, 2002, Mayor's award excellence in sci. and tech., NYC, 2004; fellow NSF, Alfred P. Sloan Found., Guggenheim fellow, Oxford U., 1985. Mem.: AAAS, NAS (editl. bd. Procs. NAS 2002—), European Photo-Chem. Assn. (Porter medal), Inter-Am. Photochemistry Soc. (award 1991, 1994), N.Y. Acad. Scis. (Freda and Gregory Halpern award in photochemistry 1977), Am. Chem. Soc. (mem. editl. bd. jour. 1984—87, Fresenius award 1973, award for pure chemistry 1974, Harrison Howe award Rochester, N.Y, sect. 1986, Arthur C. Cope award 1986, James Flack Norris award 1987, award in colloid and surface chemistry 1999, Gibbs medal award Chgo. sect. 2000, George C. Pimentel award 2004, Nichols Medal award 2007), Sigma Xi, Phi Beta Kappa. Office: Columbia U 3000 Broadway New York NY 10027-6941 Business E-Mail: njt3@columbia.edu.

TURSHEN, MEREDETH, educator; PhD, U. Sussex, Falmer, Eng., 1975. Prof. Rutgers U., New Brunswick, NJ, 1982—. One-man shows include Ceres Gallery, NYC, Viridian Gallery; author: (nonfiction book) Privatizing Health Services in Africa, Women's Health Movements: A Global Force for Change, (nonfiction) What Women Do in Wartime, The Aftermath. Office: Rutgers Univ 33 Livingston Ave New Brunswick NJ 08901

TURSKA, JOANNA, music educator; d. Marian Turski and Halina Paszkowska; children: Klaudia Natalia Siczek, Konrad Igor Siczek. Degree, Acad. Music, Warsaw. Tchr.'s cert. 1994. Flute instr. Coll. Lake County, Grayslake, Ill. Musician (flutist) solo, chamber music and orchestral performances. Grant, French Govt. Mem.: Musicians Club Women (Farwell award), Chgo. Flute Club, Nat. Flute Assn. Avocations: travel, skiing. Home: 1963 Sprucewood Ln Gurnee IL 60031 Office: Coll Lake County 19351 W Washington St Grayslake IL 60030 Home Phone: 847-672-2779; Office Phone: 847-543-2000. Personal E-mail: joantur@yahoo.com. Business E-Mail: jturska@clcillinois.edu.

TURSO, AIMEE LYNN, music educator; b. New Brunswick, NJ, Mar. 20, 1982; d. Candi Elaine and Thomas Turso. B in Music Edn., West Chester U., 2005. Cert. tchr. Pa., 2005. 4th & 5th grade music tchr. Lakeview Elem., Ridley Sch. Dist., Ridley Park, Pa., 2006; 3rd-5th grade instrumental music tchr. Leedom Elem., Ridley Sch. Dist., Ridley Park, Pa., 2006, Eddystone Elem., Ridley Sch. Dist., Pa., 2006—, kindergarten & 1st grade classroom music tchr., 2007—; 3rd-5th grade instrumental music tchr. Woodlyn Elem. Sch., Ridley Sch. Dist., Pa., 2006—, chorus instr., 2007—; pvt. music instr. Ridley Music Studio, Ridley Park, 2006—. Marching band instr. Wash. Twp. H.S., 2002—04; asst. marching band dir. Garnet Valley H.S., Glen Mills, Pa., 2006—, marching band instr., 2005, indoor drumline dir., 2006—, marching band drill writer, 2007—. Mem.: Sigma Alpha Iota (life; sargent at arms, editor, v.p. membership, v.p. rituals 2001—05, Sword of Honor, Collegiate Leadership award 2004—05). Democrat. Roman Catholic. Office: Woodlyn Elementary Sch 1200 Colson Rd Woodlyn PA 19094

TURTELL, NEAL TIMOTHY, librarian; b. NYC, Nov. 1, 1949; s. Richard Roland and Ann Grace (Glover) T. AB, Fordham U., 1971; MLS, Pratt Inst., 1975. Cataloger-libr. Ford Found., NYC, 1972-75, U.S. Dept. Transp., Washington, 1975-77; spl. projects libr. Smithsonian Instn., Washington, 1977-81; chief catalogue records, 1981-82; asst. dir. tech. svcs. U. Wis., Oshkosh, 1982-83, asst. prof. libr. sci., 1982-83; asst. chief libr. Nat. Gallery of Art, Washington, 1983-87, exec. libr., 1987—. Contbr. to book revs. Libr. Jour., 1972-75, exhbn. catalogue. Bd. trustees Pyramid Atlantic Ctr. for Printmaking and the Art of the Book, Riverdale, Md., 1988—, v.p. bd. trustees, 1991—. Mem. Art Librs. Soc. N.Am., Rsch. Librs. Group (steering com. for art and architecture 1988-89), Assn. Internat. de Bibliophilie, Grolier Club. Office: Nat Gallery of Art 4th & Constitution Ave NW Washington DC 20565-0001

TURTELTAUB, JON, film director; Dir. (films) Think Big, 1990, Driving Me Crazy: Trabbi Goes to Hollywood, 1991, 3 Ninjas, 1992, Cool Runnings, 1993, While You Were Sleeping, 1995, Phenomenon, 1996, Instinct, 1999, dir., prodr. The Kid, 2000, National Treasure, 2004, National Treasure: Book of Secrets, 2007, dir., exec. prodr. (TV series) Jericho, 2006-2007

TURTIL, LAWRENCE CHARLES, psychiatrist; b. NYC, Dec. 30, 1951; s. Joseph Fredric and Estelle Rebecca Turtil. BA cum laude, U. Pa., 1972; MD, Georgetown U., 1977. Diplomate Am. Bd. Psychiatry and Neurology, Am. Bd. Internal Medicine, Am. Bd. Adolscent Psychiatry. Resident in internal medicine Lenox Hill Hosp., NYC, 1977-80, attending physician emergency svc., 1980-81, attending physician dept. psychiatry, 1989-90, asst. chief inpatient psychiatry unit, 1990-94; resident in psychiatry Cornell, N.Y. Hosp., White Plains, 1981-84; attending physician N.Y. Hosp., Westchester div., 1984-85; med. dir. Four Winds Hosp., Katonah, N.Y., 1985-89; pvt. practice NYC & Katonah, N.Y.; attending psychiatrist Manhattan Psychiatric Ctr., NYC, 1994; med. dir. Four Winds Hosp., Katonah, N.Y., 1994-97; med. dir. Psych Sys. Manhattan partial hospitalization Gracie Square Hosp., NYC, 1997—2001; psychiatric cons. Counseling Ctr. Student Health Svcs. Fashion Inst. Tech., 1999—2001, Children's Aid Soc. PINS Diversion Program, 2001—04. Mem. Am. Psychiat. Assn. Office: 40 E 83d St Ste 1E New York NY 10028 Office Phone: 212-734-5482.

TURTURRO, AIDA, actress; b. NYC, Sept. 25, 1962; Grad., State U. NY, New Paltz, 1984. Actor: (films) Life with Mikey, 1993, Money Train, 1995, Sleepers, 1996, Fallen, 1998, Celebrity, 1998, Deep Blue Sea, 1999, Mickey Blue Eyes, 1999, Bringing Out the Dead, 1999, Play It to the Bone, 1999, Crocodile Dundee in Los Angeles, 2001; (TV series) As the World Turns, 1998, The Soprano's, 2000— (Outstanding Performance by an Ensemble in a Drama Series, SAG, 2008); (Broadway plays) A Streetcar Named Desire, 1992, (guest appearance): (TV series) Law and Order, 1990.

TURTURRO, JOHN, actor; b. Bklyn., Feb. 28, 1957; s. Nicholas and Katherine Turturro; m. Katherine Borowitz, 1985; children: Amedeo, Diego. Grad., SUNY, 1978; student, Yale Drama Sch. Worked in regional theater and off-Broadway prodns.: Danny and the Deep Blue Sea; Men Without Dates; Tooth of the Crime; La Puta Vida; Chaos and Hard Times; The Bald Soprano; Of Mice and Men; The Resistable Rise of Arturo Ui, 1991; Waiting for Godot; appeared in Broadway prodn.: Death of a Salesman, 1984; appeared in films: Raging Bull, 1980; The Flamingo Kid, 1984; To Live and Die in L.A., 1985; Desperately Seeking Susan, 1985; Hannah and Her Sisters, 1986; Gung Ho, 1986; Offbeat, 1986; The Color of Money, 1986; The Sicilian, 1987; Five Corners, 1988; Do the Right Thing, 1989; Miller's Crossing, 1990; Men of Respect; Mo Better Blues, 1990; Jungle Fever, 1991; Barton Fink, 1991; Backtrack, 1991; Brain Donors, 1992; Fearless, 1993; Festival, 1991; Being Human, 1994; Quiz Show, 1994; Grace of My Heart, 1994; Search and Destroy, 1995; Unstrung Heroes, 1995; Clockers, 1995; Box of Moonlight, 1996; Girl 6, 1996; The Big Lebowski, 1997; Animals, 1997; The Truce, 1998; Lesser Prophets, 1998; Rounders, 1998; He Got Game, 1998; The Source, 1999; The Cradle Will Rock, 1999; Company Man, 1999; Two Thousand and None, 1999; Oh Brother, Where Art Thou?, 1999; The Man Who Cried, 1999; The Luzhin Defense, 1999; Anger Management, 2003; appeared in films Collateral Damage, 2000, Mr. Deeds, 2002, Secret Passage, 2002, Secret Window, 2004, 2BPerfectly Honest, 2004, She Hate Me, 2004, A Few Days in September, 2006, The Good Shepherd, 2006, You Don't Mess with the Zohan, 2008, Miracle at St. Anna, 2008, What Just Happened, 2008, The Taking of Pelham 1 2 3, 2009, Transformers: Revenge of the Fallen, 2009; actor: (TV films) Monday Night Mayhem, 2002; dir.: (films, debut) Mac; (films) Illuminata, 1998, Thirteen Conversations About One Thing, 2000; actor, dir.: Romance & Cigarettes, 2005; dir.: (plays) A Spanish Play, 2007. Office: c/o Creative Artists Agy 2000 Ave of the Stars Los Angeles CA 90067*

TURULA, JOSEPH, lawyer; Mem. Pompton Lakes Borough Coun., NJ; ptnr. Garcia & Turula, Jersey City. Del. Rep. Nat. Convention, 2008. Republican. Office: Garcia & Turula 3 2nd St # 1201 Jersey City NJ 07302 Office Phone: 201-200-1900.

TUSCHMAN, BOB, broadcast executive; Prodr. Good Morning America ABC News; exec. prodr. Food Network, 1998—99, v.p. programming and prodn., 1999—2005, sr. v.p. programming and prodn., 2005—. Exec. prodr.: 30 Minute Meals (co-recipient Daytime Emmy Award for Outstanding Svc. Show, 2006), Barefoot Contessa, My Country, My Kitchen, Everyday Italian. Office: Food Network 75 Ninth Ave New York NY 10011

TUSCHMAN, JAMES MARSHALL, lawyer; b. Nov. 28, 1941; s. Chester and Harriet (Harris) T.; m. Ina S. Cheloff, Sept. 2, 1967; children: Chad Michael, Jon Stephen, Sari Anne. BS in Bus., Miami U., Oxford, Ohio, 1963; JD, Ohio State U., 1966. Bar: Ohio 1966, U.S. Ct. Appeals (6th and 7th cirs.), U.S. Supreme Ct. Assoc. Shumaker, Loop & Kendrick, Toledo, 1966—84, ptnr., 1970—84; co-founder, chmn. ops. com. Jacobson Maynard Tuschman & Kalur, Toledo, 1985—97; COO Ohio Ferrous Group Omnisource Corp., Toledo, 1998—99, dir. bus. devel. No. Ohio group, 1999—2001; of counsel Barkan & Robon Ltd., Maumee, Ohio, 2002—. Chmn. bd., sec. Tuschman Steel Co., Toledo, 1969-76, Toledo Steel Supply Co., 1969-86; vice-chmn. bd. Kripke Tuschman Industries, Inc., 1977-85; ptnr. Starr Ave. Co., Toledo, 1969-86. Past trustee, chmn. bd. trustees U. Toledo; past trustee, chmn. fin. com., past treas. Maumee Valley Country Day Sch.; past trustee, v.p., treas. Temple B'nai Israel, 1984-88; mem. nat. alumni coun. Ohio State U. Coll. Law; mem., co-chmn. subcom. on structure, governance and fin. Gov.'s Commn, on Higher Edn. and Economy; mem., chmn. bd. Ohio Bd. Regents, chmn. Mayors Task Force Intermodal Transportation Fellow Internat. Soc. Barristers; mem. ATLA, Am. Bd. Trial Advocates, Ohio Bar Assn., Toledo Bar Assn., Ohio Trial Lawyers Assn., Million Dollar Advocates Forum, Zeta Beta Tau, Phi Delta Phi. Home: 2579 Olde Brookside Rd Toledo OH 43615-2233 Office: Barkan & Robon Ltd 1701 Woodlands Dr Maumee OH 43537-4092 Home Phone: 419-536-2557; Office Phone: 419-897-6500. Business E-Mail: jmt.br@bex.net.

TUSIANI, JOSEPH, foreign language educator, author; b. Foggia, Italy, Jan. 14, 1924; came to U.S., 1947, naturalized, 1956; s. Michael and Maria (Pisone) T. Dottore in Lettere summa cum laude, U. Naples, 1947, LittD, 1971; Dottore (hon.), U. Foggia, 2004. Lectr. in Italian lit. Hunter Coll., 1950-62; chmn. Italian dept. Coll. Mt. St. Vincent, 1948-71. Vis. assoc. prof. NYU, 1956-64, CUNY, 1971-83; prof. Herbert H. Lehman Coll., 1971-83; NDEA vis. prof. Italian Conn. State Coll., 1962. Author: Dante in Licenza, 1952, Two Critical Essays on Emily Dickinson, 1952, Poesia Missionaria in Inghilterra ed America, 1953, Sonettisti Americani, 1954, Melos Cordis: Poems in Latin, 1955, Lo Speco Celeste, 1956, Odi Sacre; poems, 1958, The Complete Poems of Michelangelo, 1960, Rind and All, 1962, Lust and Liberty (The Poems of Machiavelli), 1963, The Fifth Season, 1963, (novels) Envoy from Heaven, 1965, Tasso's Jerusalem Delivered, 1970, Boccaccio's Nymphs of Fiesole, 1971, Gente Mia and Other Poems, 1978, (poems in Latin) In Exilio Rerum, 1985, (autobiography) La Parola Difficile, vol. I, 1988, (poems in Latin) Confinia Lucis et Umbrae: La Parola Nuova, vol. II, 1991, La Parola Antica, vol. III, 1992, (poems in Italian) Il Ritorno, 1992, Bronx America, 1992, Annemale Parlante, 1994, Carmina Latina, 1994, La Poceide, 1996, Carmina Latina, vol. 11, 1998, Li Quatte Staggione, 1998, Lu Deddú, 1999, Maste Peppe Cantarine, 2000, Lu Ponte de Sóla, 2001, In Quattro Lingue, 2001, Dante's Divine Comedy (As told for young people), 2001, L'ore de Gesu Bambine (a Christmas play in verse), 2001, La Prima Cumpagnia, 2002, (in Apulian dialect) La Tomba de Patre Pí, 2003, (plays) (in verse) La Cunte de Pasqua, 2003, La Padula (in Apulian dialect, 2004, Lu Scazzamuredde, 2005, Storie dal Gargano, 1955-2005, 2006, (play in verse) If Gold Should Rust, 2009, Sciusce de Vente, 2009, (Latin poems) Fragmenta ad Aemilium, 2009; translator: Pulci's Morgante, 1998. Recipient Greenwood prize for poetry in England, 1956, Outstanding Tchr. award, 1969, cavaliere ufficiale Italian Republic, 1973, Leonardo Covello's educator award, 1980, Leone di San Marco award, 1982, Avis award, 1983, Joseph Tusiani scholarship fund established in his honor at Lehman Coll., 1983, Congl. medal merit, 1984, Progresso medal liberty, 1986, Gold plaque City Hall San Marco, 1986, Outstanding tchr. award Am. Assn. Tchrs. Italian, 1986, Renoir literary award, 1988, Joseph Tusiani, Poet, Translator, Humanist (An Internat. Homage), 1995, Enrico Fermi award, 1995, Fiorello La Guardia award, 1998; Melvin Jones fellow, 1995, Gov.'s award for excellence, 1999, Apulia prize of Regione Puglia, 1999, Gold medal at Rome's Capitol, 2004, Gold medal of Regione Puglia, 2004, prize Italiani nel Mondo, 2004; Joseph Tusiani Found. established at U. Lecce, 1998, NEH, 1998; Silver Lily and the Keys to the City of Florence, 2007. Mem. Poetry Soc. Am. (v.p.), Cath.

Poetry Soc. Am. (dir. 1958, Spirit gold medal 1968) Home: 308 E 72nd St New York NY 10021-4727 *Strange how this continually re-edited Who's Who forces one to work and achieve.*

TUSK, BRADLEY, communications specialist; b. Oct. 3, 1973; Grad., U. Pa.; JD, U. Chgo. Law clk. Office of Spl. Investigations US Dept. Justice; sr. advisor to commr. NYC Dept. Parks and Recreation; comm. dir. for Senator Charles Schumer US Senate; spl. asst. to Mayor Michael Bloomberg, NYC; dep. gov. State of Ill., 2003—06; sr. v.p. Lehman Brothers, 2006—08; campaign mgr. Michael Bloomberg for Mayor 2009, NYC, 2008—. Former adj. prof. Fordham U., NYC. Named one of The 40 under 40, Crain's NY Bus., 2003. Mem.: NY State Bar Assn. Office: Michael Bloomberg for Mayor 2009 111 W 40th St New York NY 10018 Office Phone: 212-768-2009.*

TUSK, CLAUDE M., lawyer; b. NYC, Nov. 11, 1954; AB magna cum laude, Harvard U., 1974, JD magna cum laude, 1977. Bar: NY 1978, US Dist. Ct. (so. and ea. dists.) NY 1978, US Ct. Appeals (2d cir.) 1980, US Ct. Appeals (11th cir.), US Supreme Ct. 1981. Law clk. to Hon. J. Edward Lumbard U.S. Ct. Appeals (2d cir.), 1977-78; atty. Graham & James, NYC; ptnr. Dechert LLP, NYC. Contbr. articles to profl. jour. Mem. ABA, Assn. of Bar NYC, Fed. Bar Coun., Phi Beta Kappa. Editor Harvard Law Review. Office: Dechert LLP 1095 Ave Americans New York NY 10036 Office Phone: 212-698-3612, 212-698-3599. Business E-Mail: claude.tusk@dechert.com.

TUSKA, JON, writer, publishing executive; b. South Milwaukee, Wis., Apr. 30, 1942; s. Andrew and Florence Catherine (Tommet) T.; m. Vicki Piekarski, May 24, 1980; 1 child, Jennifer Lee. BA, Marquette U., 1965. Owner Pers. Cons., Milw., 1969-74; editor, pub. Views & Revs. mag., 1969-75; freelance writer, 1975--91; co-owner, agt. Golden West Literary Agy., Portland, Oreg., 1992—. Adj. faculty MA and tchg. program and undergrads. Lewis and Clark Coll., 1979-88' staff music critic Ovation mag., 1987-89, Fanfare mag., 1989-95; spl. film. cons. Images of Indians, PBS, 1980, Images of Appalachia, PBS, 1984, Mommy, Who's Winning Now? The Cold War in America, Turner, 1986, Say It with Music: Irving Berlin's America, PBS, 1986, Broadway's Eternal Romantics: Lerner and Loewe, PBS, 1988, John Wayne: Standing Tall, PBS, 1989, Big Guns Talk, Turner, 1997; prodr. classical music programs, art and news features and interviews with musicians and motion picture personalities, and film revs. for radio stas. Oreg. Pub. Broadcasting. Author: Philo Vance: The Life and Times of S.S. Van Dine, 1973, The Films of Mae West, 1973, The Filming of the West, 1976, The Detective in Hollywood, 1978, The Vanishing Legion: A History of Mascot Pictures 1927-35, 1982, 2d edit., 1986, Billy the Kid: A Bio/Bibliography, 1983, Dark Cinema: American Film Noir in Cultural Perspective, 1984, The American West in Film: Critical Approaches to the Western, 1985, In Manors and Alleys: A Case-Book on the American Detective Film, 1988, A Variable Harvest: Essays and Reviews in Literature and Film, 1989, Encounters with Filmmakers: Eight Career Studies, 1991, The Complete Films of Mae West, 1992, Billy the Kid: His Life and Legend, 1994, (with Vicki Piekarski) The Frontier Experience: A Reader's Guide to the Life and Literature of the American West, 1984; editor-in-chief (with Piekarski) Ency. of Frontier and Western Fiction, 1983; editor: The Western Story: A Chronological Treasury 1894-1994, 1994, Shadow of the Lariat, 1995, Star Western: Twenty-Two Western Stories from the Golden Age, 1995, The Big Book of Western Action Stories, 1995, (with Piekarski) The Morrow Anthology of Great Western Short Stories, 1997, The First Five Star Western Corral, 2000, Five Star Westerns, 2000, Stories of the Golden West, Book One, 2000, Book Two, 2001, Book Three, 2002, Book Four, 2003, Book Five, 2004, Book Six, 2005, Odyssey to the North: Northwestern Stories, 2003, Stories of the Golden West: Book Seven, 2006. Avocations: reading, classical music, film history, book collecting. Home and Office: 2327 SE Salmon St Portland OR 97214-3943 Office Phone: 503-232-0238. Personal E-mail: jtuska@live.com.

TUSSING, LEWIS BENTON, III, (TONY), secondary education educator, coach; b. Columbus, Ohio, May 23, 1943; s. Lewis Benton and Dorothy (Schueller) T.; m. Monica Kane, Nov. 23, 1974; children: Leith Benton, Ethan Kane. BA, Stetson U., 1966. Cert. educator, Fla., track and field ofcl. Tchr. geography Volusia County Sch. Bd., Deland, Fla., 1966-97; dir. Camp Sparta, Sebring, Fla., 1967-79; adminstrv. asst. Volusia County Schs., Deland, 1983-88. Asst. football coach, head track and swim coach, asst. athletic dir. Deland H.S.; dept. chair Southwestern Mid. Sch., Deltona Mid. Sch., Deland; head track ofcls. U. Fla., Gainesville, 2005-. Mem. mid. sch. task force Volusia County Sch. Sys., Deland, 1997; v.p., pres. Glenwood (Fla.) Civic Assn.; vol. Deland Recreation Dept.; adv. coun. Southwestern Sch., 1997—, sec., 2000—; adv. coun. Deland HS, 1999-2003, v.p., 2000-2002, pres. 2003. Recipient Race Rels. award Greater Union 1st Bapt., Deland, 1990, Svc. award Volusia Coun. Social Studies, Deland, 1993, Vol. of Yr. award United Way, 1998, Vols. in Pub. Schs. (V.I.P.S.), 1999; named Tchr. of Yr., Deltona Mid. Sch., 1994, Southwestern Mid. Sch., 1998, Make A Difference Person of Yr., Pilot Club, 2005, Girls Track and Field Official of Yr., Nat. Fedn. of High Schs., 2006, Girls Track Ofcl. of Yr., Fla. HS Athletic Assn., 2006; named to Deland Sports Hall of Fame, 2003. Mem. NEA (ret.), U.S. Geog. Educators, Fla. Geog. Educators, Fla. Edn. Assn., Volusia County Edn. Assn., USA Track and Field Ofcls., Jaycees (v.p.), Lake Eustis Sailing Club (sec. 2001, 2004—, flying scots bd. 2002—), Optimists (v.p., pres.), Kiwanis (hon., dir. jr. olympics 1962-, bd. dirs. 2007-, v.p. 2008-09, award 2008), Ctrl. Fla. Track Ofcls. Assn. (bd. mem.), Ofcls. Sect. Track Championships (dir. 2009), Fla. HS Athletic Assn. Track Ofcls. Republican. Roman Catholic. Avocations: sailing, stamp collecting/philately, youth work, volunteer work, geography. E-mail: flacoach43@hotmail.com.

TUSSING, MARILEE APPLEBY, music educator; b. Decatur, Ill., Feb. 6, 1953; d. Robert William and Dorothymaie (Mallory) Appleby; m. Donald Tussing, April 17, 1976; 1 child, Torrance Ashley. B in Music Edn., Ill. State U., 1975; M in Music Edn., U. Okla., 1985. Nat. bd. cert. early and mid. childhood music 2004. Music tchr. Shannon Elem., Shannon, Ill., 1976-80, Thompson Schs., Thompson, Ill., 1980-82; Kodaly music specialist Southgate Elem., Moore, Okla., 1982—. Riding instr. Shenandoah Riding Ctr., Galena, Ill. 1977-81, freelance Norman, Okla., 1982—; creator Sooner Pony Club Worksheet Program; founder Southgate String Players; clinician Orgn. Am. Kodaly Educators Conf., Chgo., 2002, Charlotte, NC, 2006. Musician: (band) Traditions, 1999—. Dist. Commr. Sooner Pony Club, 1985—; judge Okla. Kids Talent Search, 1993-96; mem. Moore Assn. Classroom Tchrs. 1982—; pres. Moore Elem. Music Orgn., 1990-91; founder Southgate Entertainer's Club; dir. Am. Kids Celebrity Chorus, 1996-97; mem. Irish Arts Project, 2002—; mem. Comhaltas Ceoltiori Eirhann, 2004—. Recipient Equestrian Event Silver medal Sooner State Games, Okla., 1989; grantee Okla. Found. for excellence in edn., 2006. Mem. Midwest Kodaly Music Educators (bd. dirs. 1983-85), US Pony Club (knowdown judge, 1990-98, tech. del.), US Combined Tng. Assn. (cert. of achievement, 1985, 89, area V adult team mem. award, 1993), Nat. Edn. Assn., Okla. Edn. Assn., Am. Quarter Horse Assn., Orgn. Am. Kodaly Educators, Okla. City Traditional Music Assn., Am. Connemera Pony Soc Republican. Mem. Christian Ch. (Disciples Of Christ). Avocations: skiing, needlepoint, violin, guitar, collecting and reading horse books. Home: 11850 E Rock Creek Rd Norman OK 73026-8155 Personal E-mail: mrstussing@aol.com.

TUTHILL, JOHN G., academic administrator; b. Charlottesville, Va., Aug. 15, 1951; s. William Carroll Tuthill and Mary Wilson Gee; m. Lyudmila Muntyan; children: Alice Bailey, Olga Khakova, Alex Khakov. BA, U. Mich., Ann Arbor, 1972; MA, Columbia U., NYC, 1975; PhD, U. Calif., Berkeley, 1982. Assoc. prof. history U. Guam, Mangilao, 1992—99; dean instrn. Ilisagvik Coll., Barrow, Alaska, 2003—05; v.p. instrn. Coll. Marshall Islands, Majuro, 2000—02, v.p. academic & student affairs, 2005—07; v.p. student learning NW Ark. CC, Bentonville, Ark., 2007—. Fulbright scholar, Ukrainian Cath. U., 2003—04. Office: NorthWest Ark CC One College Dr Bentonville AR 72712 Office Fax: 479-619-4342. Business E-Mail: jtuthill@nwacc.edu.

TUTHILL, OLIVER W., JR., psychologist, consultant, independent film producer, director; b. Orange, NJ, Aug. 8, 1945; s. Oliver W. and Virginia Tuthill. BA in Sociology, Olivet Coll., 1968, BA in Psychology, 1968; MA in Psychology, Antioch U., 2002. Singer, songwriter, Chgo., 1955—72; actor Hollywood, Calif., 1972—84, Universal, Hollywood, 1973—84; pres., profl. spkr. Autumn Tree Prodns., Seattle, 1999—2005; pres. Blue Pony Trail Music, Seattle, 2005—. Pres. 140th St Promotions, Seattle, 1986—88, Blue Wood Films LLC, Seattle, 2003—05; cons. Jr. Achievement, Seattle, 1996—2000; advisor, com. mem. Gov. Blue Ribbon Commn., Seattle, 2000—02. Dir.: (films) Understanding 6 Forms of Emotional, 1999 (Bronze Telly award, 2000, 2003), Dysphoria, 2001 (Best Feature Film, 2001), Children's Rights: Why America Says No, 2004 (4 Bronze Telly awards, 2004); prodr.: (albums) Acoustic Concerto, 2005; prodr.(dir.): (films) Willatuk: The Legend of Seattle's Sea Serpent, featuring Graham Greene, 2006; prodr. (dir.): (films) Child Abuse; prodr.(dir.): (films) Wounded Heart: Pine Ridge Run and The Sioux Featuring Russell Means, 2005 (Bronze Telly award, 2005, Grand Goldie Film award, 2005); dir.: (documentary) Questions for Crazy Horse, (producer, writer): The Right To Bear Arms, 2009. Recipient Media award, Gov. Wash. State, 2002, Horace Mann award, Antioch U., 2003, Silver Plaque, Music Intercom Video Competition, 2001, Silver Telly award for Complex: Life Inside a Section 8 Apt., 2006, Silver Telly award. Mem.: APA (assoc.), Am. Screenwriters Assn., Internat. Documentary Assn., Screen Actors Guild, Broadcast Music Inc. Avocations: sports, swimming, singing, reading, politics. Home: 20044 Bagley Dr N Y304 Seattle WA 98133 Office Phone: 206-364-9202. Personal E-mail: owtuthi@earthlink.net.

TUTOR, RONALD N., construction executive; b. Oct. 13, 1940; BS in Fin., U. So. Calif., LA, 1963. Pres., CEO Tutor-Saliba Corp., Calif.; bd. dirs. Perini Corp., 1997—, COO, 1997—2000, vice chmn., 1998—99, chmn., 1999—, CEO, 2000—. Bd. dirs. Southdown Corp.; mem. adv. com. U. So. Calif. Sch. Engring. Recipient LA Conservancy Preservation award, 1994, Greater LA African-Am. C. of C. Contractor of Yr. award, 1994, US Army C.E. LA Dist. Contractor of Yr. award, 1994, NCCJ Real Estate and Constrn. Industry Humanitarian award, 1992. Mem. Am. Concrete Inst. Office: Tutor-Saliba 15901 Olden St Sylmar CA 91342-1093 also: Perini Corp 73 Mt Wayte Ave Framingham MA 01701

TUTT, KARL FLEMING, literature and language professor; b. Dallas, Feb. 17, 1946; s. Nada Butler Bennett; m. Dawn Rodgers Lamb, Jan. 10, 1996; 1 child, Jane Brittan. BA, Wake Forest U., Winston-Salem, NC, 1968, MEd, 1978. Instr. Waterways Sailing Sch., Wilmington, NC, 1990—96; English tchr. Performance Based Diploma Program, Ft. Pierce, Fla., 2001—. Contbr. articles to profl. jours. and mags. Named Instr. of Yr., Am. Sailing Assn., 1995—96. Independent. Avocations: sailing, music, writing, painting.

TUTTLE, DAVID BAUMAN, electrical engineer; b. NYC, Oct. 25, 1948; s. John Bauman and Charlotte (Root) T.; m. Mildred Suzanne Lamb, May 5, 1973 (div. May 1978); m. Nancy Viola Caraber, Mar. 14, 1981; children: Jason David, John Paul. Student, MIT, 1966—69. Assoc., sr. assoc. programmer IBM Cambridge Sci. Ctr., Mass., 1968-71; staff programmer IBM VM/370 Devel., Burlington, Mass., 1971-76; sr. prin. S/W engr. Digital Equipment Corp., Maynard, Mass., 1976-78; mgr. Cambridge Telecom/GTE Telenet, Burlington, 1978-81; sr. scientist GTE Telenet, Burlington, 1981-84, chief scientist, 1984-85; sr. tech. cons. Prime Computer, Inc., Framingham, Mass., 1985-86, prin. tech. cons., 1986-89; sr. rsch. engr. Ungermann-Bass Inc., Andover, Mass., 1990-91; chief engr. Ungermann-Bass, Inc., Andover, Mass., 1991-93; cons. engr. Augment Sys., Inc., Bedford, Mass., 1993-95; chief tech. officer Augment Systems Inc., Westford, Mass., 1995-97; cons. engr. VideoServer Connections, Inc., Marlborough, Mass., 1997-99; chief engr. NorthStar Internetworking, Waltham, Mass., 1999-2000; project engr. Hammer Techs. Inc., Wilmington, Mass., 2000; prin. engr. Vividon, Inc., Sudbury, Mass., 2000—02, StarBak Comm. Inc., Waltham, 2003, Katana Tech. Inc., Acton, Mass., 2003—04; prin. software engr. Crossbeam Sys. Inc., Boxborough, Mass., 2004—. Strategy forum del. Corp. for Open Systems, McLean, Va., 1986-89, architecture com. mem., 1989, strategy forum nominating com., 1986-87; patent rev. com. Prime Computer, Inc., 1985-89; sole proprietor Viewpoint Cons., Reading, Mass., 1994—. Co-author and editor: 3270 Display System Protocol, 1981, 83, Hotline BSC Access Method, 1970. Donor mem. Smithsonian Inst., Washington, 1980—; Town Meeting mem. Precinct 3, Reading, Mass., 2004—; cmty. planning and develop. commn. Reading, Mass., 2006-. Mem. IEEE, IEEE Computer Soc., Nat. Space Soc. (life mem.), The Cousteau Soc., Assn. for Computing Machinery, Black and Blues of Killington (treas. 1986-89), Mandala Folk Dance Ensemble (dancer 1970-73). Republican. Presbyterian. Achievements include co-invention for a patent in PC configuration fault analysis. Avocations: duplicate bridge, alpine skiing, genealogy. Home: 27 Heather Dr Reading MA 01867-3961 E-mail: dtuttle@acm.org.

TUTTLE, JEREMY BALLOU, neuroscientist; s. John Bauman and Charlotte Marion (Root) T.; m. Sara Jane Stasko, Mar. 23, 1971. AB, U. Rochester, 1969; PhD, Johns Hopkins U., 1977. Postdoctoral fellow U. Conn., Storrs, 1976-79, vis. asst. prof., 1980, asst. prof. in residence, 1981-84; asst. prof. physiology U. Va., Charlottesville, 1984-87, asst. prof. neuroscience, 1987-90, rsch. asst. prof., 1990-93, assoc. prof. urology neuroscience, 1993-98, prof., 1998—. Contbr. articles to Devel. Biology, Science, Jour. Neuroscience, others; mem. editl. bd. Investigative Urology, Jour. Urology, Jour. Hypertension. Chmn. mem. Common Area Planning Comm., 1984-87; pres. bd. Earlysville Forest Homeowner's Assn., 1986-89, Earlysville, Va.; chmn. urology spl. emphasis panel NIH, 1996-2001; chmn. spl. emphasis panel on female pelvic floor disorders Nat. Inst. Child Health and Human Devel., 1999; mem. promotion and tenure com. U. Va., 2004—. U. Rochester Hon. scholar, 1965-69, Regent's scholar for Medicine, 1969, NIH predoctoral fellow, 1971-75, Nat. Rsch. Svc. fellow, 1976-79, Nat. Spinal Cord Injury Found. rsch. fellow, 1979-80; recipient Rsch. Career Devel. award Nat. Inst. Neurol. Disease/NIH, Muscular Dystrophy Assn. Rsch. award, 1990—; Am. Heart Assn. grantee, 1987-89, 90—, fellowship, Fogarty Internat. Ctr. for Rsch. NIH, Japan, 1997. Mem.: AAAS, Am. Soc. Cell Biology, Biophys. Soc., Soc. Neuroscience, Sigma Xi. Achievements include research on NGF dynamics in hypertrophic disease, carbon dioxide transport and chemosensitivity, molecular mechanisms of quantal synaptic transmission, nerve growth factor synthesis by vascular smooth muscle, trophic regulation of motor neurons, neurodegenerative diseases. Office: U Va Med Sch PO Box 801392 Charlottesville VA 22908-1392 Office Phone: 434-924-5634. Business E-Mail: tuttle@virginia.edu.

TUTTLE, KAREN ANN, violist, educator; b. Lewiston, Idaho, Mar. 28, 1920; d. Ray and Eunice Valborg (Nelson) T.; m. Morton Herskowitz; 1 child, Robin Ray Heald. MusB, Curtis Inst. Music, 1944, MusD (hon.), 2005, PhD (hon.) in Music. Ind. violist, 1944—; tchr. viola Curtis Inst. Music, Phila., 1945—. Mem. The Schneider Quartet, Philomusica chamber group; instr. Mannes Coll. Music, Manhattan Sch. Music, Peabody Conservatory Music; faculty Juilliard Sch. Music, ret., 2005, Banff Sch. Arts. Carnegie Hall debut, N.Y.C., 1960. Home: 2132 Pine St Philadelphia PA 19103-6535

TUTTLE, KENNETH LEWIS, retired engineering educator, consultant, researcher; b. Toledo, Oreg., Apr. 4, 1944; s. Martin Lewis and Norma Corinne (Nichols) Tuttle; m. Susanna Anna Maria Woodworth, June 24, 1967; children: Stephanie, Meghan, Lewis. BS, US Naval Acad., 1967; MS, Oreg. State U., Corvallis, 1974, PhD, 1978. Registered profl. engr., Oreg., 1976 (environ. branch added in 1995). Commd. ensign USN, 1967, advanced through grades to lt., 1971, shipboard line officer Norfolk, Va., 1967-69, intelligence officer Tan An, Vietnam, 1970; grad. asst. Oreg. State U., Corvallis, 1971—77; rsch. engr. Weyerhaeuser Co., Tacoma, 1978—81; pvt. practice Federal Way, Wash., 1982-83; assoc. prof. mech. engring. US Naval Acad., Annapolis, Md., 1983—2004, dir. marine propulsion labs., 1984—90, ret., 2004; rschr. and cons. solid fuel rsch. Tuttle Engring., 2004—. Dir. Ocean and Marine Engring. Divsn., Am. Soc. for Engring. Edn., Washington, 1989-91; mem. com. on shipboard pollution control, Nat. Rsch. Coun., Washington, 1994-96; chmn. environ. panel Soc. Naval Arch. and Marine Engrs., Jersey City, 1993-2000; prin. cons. Solid Fuel Rsch., Annapolis, 1984—. Author: Combustion Mechanisms in Wood Fired Boilers, 1978, Review of Biomass Gasification in Progress in Biomass Conversion, 1984, Thermodynamics: A Computer-Based Approach, 2001, 2003; contbr. articles to profl. jours. Mem. Combustion Inst., George C. Marshall Inst. Achievements include development of a prototype for new high compression-ratio vane-in-rotor compressor; pulverized-wood burner and fixed-bed wood gasifier; discovery of the effect of underfire air on particulate emissions; patents in field. Avocations: travel, fishing. Home and Office: 25609 Dog Creek Rd John Day OR 97845 also: 405 Widgeon Way Chester MD 21619 Office Phone: 410-490-9534. Personal E-mail: kentuttle@1967.usna.com, tklewis67@gmail.com.

TUTTLE, RICHARD, artist; b. Rahway, NJ, 1941; BA, Trinity Coll., 1963; DFA (hon.), Calif. Coll. Arts, 2006. One-man shows at Betty Parsons Gallery, N.Y.C., 1965, 67, 68, 70, 72, 74, 78, 82, Galerie Schmela, Dusseldorf, Fed. Republic Germany, 1968, 78, 84, 85, Nicholas Wilder Gallery, N.Y.C., 1969, Albright-Knox Gallery, Buffalo, 1970, Dallas Mus. Fine Arts, 1971, The Helman Gallery, St. Louis, 1971, Mus. Modern Art, N.Y.C., 1972, Galerie Rudolf Zwirner, Cologne, Fed. Republic Germany, 1972, Galerie Yvon Lambert, Paris, 1972, 74, 76, 78, 81, 84, 85, 87, The Clocktower Inst. for Art and Urban Resources, N.Y.C., 1973, Kunstraum Munchen, Munich, 1973, 77, Daniel Weinberg Gallery, San Francisco, 1973, 78, Los Angeles, 1984, Francoise Lambert, Milan, 1973, 78, Galerie Heiner Friedrich, Munich, 1973, 77, Galleria Toselli, Milan, 1974, 85, Galleria Marilena Bonomo, Bari, Italy, 1974, 79, 85, Annemarie Verna Galerie, Zurich, 1974, 79, 81, 84, 87, Barbra Cusack Gallery, Houston, 1974, 75, Nigel Greenwood Inc. Ltd., London, 1974, 77, 82, Wadsworth Atheneum, Hartford, Conn., 1975, Whitney Mus. Am. Art, N.Y.C., 1975, Parsons-Truman Gallery, N.Y.C., 1975, Brooke Alexander Inc., N.Y.C., 1976, Fine Arts Bldg. Gallery, N.Y.C., 1976, Graeme Murray Gallery, Edinburgh, 1976, McIntosh Gallery U. Western Ont., London, Can., 1976, Galleria Ugo Ferranti, Rome, 1977, 78, 79, 81, 82, 83, 84, Kunsthalle Basel, 1977, Young Hoffman Gallery, Chgo., 1978, Bell Gallery Brown U., Providence, 1978, Mus. van Hedendaagse Kunst, Gent, Belgium, 1978, Stedelijk Mus., Amsterdam, 1979, Truman Gallery, N.Y.C., 1979, Centre d'Arts Plastiques Contemporains de Bordeaux, 1979, Centre d'Art Contemporain, Geneva, 1980, Ga. State U. Art Gallery, Atlanta, 1980, Baxter Art Gallery Calif. Inst. Tech., Pasadena, 1980, Baronian-Lambert, Gent, 1981, Mus. de Calais, 1982, Taidemaalariliiton Galleria 4, Helsinki, 1983, Blum Helman Gallery, N.Y.C., 1983, 84, 86, Galerie Hubert Winter, Vienna, 1983, 87, Studio La Citta, Verona, 1984, Galleriet, Lund, Sweden, 1984, Portland (Oreg.) Ctr. for Visual Arts, 1984, Stadtisches Mus. Abteiberg, 1985, Inst. Contemporary Arts, London, 1985, Victoria Miro Gallery, London, 1986, Reinhard Onnasch Galerie, Berlin, 1986, CAPC Mus. d'Art Contemporain, Bordeaux, 1986, Neue Galerie Am Landesmuseum Joanneum, Graz, Austria, 1987, Galerie des Arènes, Nimes, France, 1987, Anders Tornberg Gallery, Lund, 1987, Mary Boone Gallery, NY, 1992, Mus. Fine Arts, Santa Fe, N. Mex., 1995, Calif. State Long Beach Art Mus., 1997, Tomio Koyama Gallery, Tokyo, 2001-2002, Whitney Mus. Am. Art, 2005-06, Jurgen Becker, Hamberg, 2006 various others; exhibited in group shows at San Francisco Mus. Art, 1965, 73, Byron Gallery, N.Y.C., 1965, Ralph Wilson Gallery Lehigh U., Bethlehem, Pa., 1965, 66, Penthouse Gallery Mus. Modern Art, N.Y.C., 1966, 70, 74, 76, 80, Bykert Gallery, N.Y.C., 1968, 71, Austin Art Ctr. Trinity Coll., Hartford, 1968, 70, Pitts. Plan for Art, 1968, 80, Brainerd Art Gallery SUNY at Potsdam, 1968, 82, Corcoran Gallery Art, Washington, 1969, Whitney Mus. Am. Art, N.Y.C. and Fairfield, Conn., 1969, 73, 77, 78, 81, 83, 84, 85, Detroit Inst. Arts, 1969, 76, 79, Paula Cooper Gallery, N.Y.C., 1971, U. N.C., Greensboro, 1969, 75, Galerie Schmela, Dusseldorf, 1972, 82, 85, Galerie Yvon Lambert, 1970, 72, Yale U. Art Gallery, New Haven, 1973, 75, 82, Art Inst. Chgo., 1975, 82, Stedelijk Mus., Amsterdam, 1978, 82, 84, Brooke Alexander Inc., N.Y.C., 1974, 78, 80, 85, Betty Parsons Gallery, N.Y.C., 1979, 83, Centre Nat. d'Art et de Culture Georges Pompidou, Paris, 1981, Daniel Weinberg Gallery, Los Angeles, 1983, N.Y.C., 1984, Kent Gallery, N.Y.C., 1987, Blum Helman Gallery, 1982, 84, 86, 87, Kunsthalle, Bielefeld, Fed. Republic Germany, 1987, Galerie Harald Behm, Hamburg, Fed. Republic Germany, 1987, Holly Solomon Gallery, N.Y.C., 1987, Damon Brandt Gallery, N.Y.C., 1986, 87, Galería Juana de Aizpuru, Madrid, Spain, 1986, 87, Genovese Graphics, Boston, 1987, Madison Art Ctr., Wis., 1987, numerous others; represented in permanent collections Fogg Art Mus., Cambridge, Mass.,Kaiser Wilhelm Mus., Kreefeld, Fed. Republic Germany, Kunsthaus, Zurich, La. Mus. Modern Art, Humlebaek, Denmark, Ludwig Mus., Cologne, Fed. Republic Germany, Met. Mus. Art, N.Y.C., Mus. Nat. d'Arte Moderne, Paris, Staatliche Kunstsammlungen, Kassel, Fed. Republic Germany, Stedelijk Mus., Whitney Mus. Am. Art; subject of retrospective tour The Art of Richard Tuttle, San Francisco Mus. Modern Art, Whitney Mus., etc. Recipient Skowhegan medal for sculpture, NY, 1998, Aachen Art prize, Ludwig Forum fur Internationale Kunst, Germany, 1998, Acad. award in Art, Am. Acad. Arts & Letters, NY, 2003. Fellow: Am. Acad. Arts & Scis. Mailing: c/o Sperone Westwater 415 W 13th St #2 New York NY 10014-1104

TUTTLE, ROBERT HOLMES, former ambassador; b. Calif., Aug. 4, 1943; m. Maria Hummer; children: Tiffany, Alexandra. BA, Stanford U., Calif., 1965; MBA, U. So. Calif., 1968. Asst. to Pres. The White House, Washington, 1982-85, dir. presdl. pers., 1985—89; bd. dirs. Woodrow Wilson Internat. Ctr. Scholars, Washington, 1989—93; mng. ptnr. Tuttle-Click Automotive Grp., Irvine, Calif.; US amb. to UK US Dept. State, London, 2005—09. Mem. bd. Ronald Reagan Presdl. Libr., U. So. Calif. Sch. Comm., LA Mus. Contemporary Art, chmn. bd., 2001—04. Co-chmn. Calif. Rep. Presdl. Campaign, 1980. Republican.*

TUTTLE, SANDIA LOU DEWAIDE, literature and language educator; d. Emil Noel and Lois Lucile DeWaide; m. Dennis C. Tuttle, Aug. 12, 1967; children: Greg, Alexandra. MA in English, San Diego State U., 1967. Cert. in gen. edn. tchg. credential State of Calif., 1965. Instr. Grossmont Coll., El Cajon, Calif., 1986—. Scholarship chmn. Grossmont Cmty. Concert Assn.-Music Scholarship Coun., El Cajon, 1970—2009. Named Outstanding Distance Educator, ITC, 2007. Mem.: Prayers and Sqs. Office: Grossmont Coll 8800 Grossmont Coll Dr El Cajon CA 92020

TUTTLE, WILLIAM MCCULLOUGH, JR., history professor; b. Detroit, Oct. 7, 1937; s. William McCullough and Geneva (Duvall) T.; m. Linda Lee Stumpp, Dec. 12, 1959 (div.); children: William McCullough III, Catharine T., Andrew S.; m. Kathryn Nemeth, May 6, 1995. BA, Denison U., 1959; MA, U. Wis., 1964, PhD, 1967. From mem. faculty to prof. history U. Kans., Lawrence, 1967—2000, prof. Am. studies, 2000—08, John Adams disting. Fulbright chair in Am. history, 2007. Vis. scholar Radcliffe Coll., 1993—94; Charles Warren fellow Harvard U., Cambridge, Mass., 1972—73; sr. fellow Johns Hopkins U., 1969—70; vis. prof. U. S.C., Columbia, 1980; fellow Humanities Ctr. Stanford U., 1983—84; rsch. assoc. U. Calif., Berkeley, Calif., 1986—88. Author: Race Riot: Chicago in the Red Summer of 1919, 1970, 2d edit., 1996, W.E.B. Du Bois, 1973, (with David M. Katzman) Plain Folk, 1982, (with others) A People and A Nation, 1982, 7th edit., 2005, Daddy's Gone to War: The Second World War in the Lives of America's Children, 1993, (with others) World War II and the American Home Front, 2007; contbr. chpts. to books, articles to profl. jours. Dem. precinct committeeman, Lawrence, 1980-90. Lt. USAF, 1959-62. Recipient Merit award Am. Assn. for State and Local History, 1972, Balfour S. Jeffrey Rsch. Achievement award Humanities and Social Scis., 2004, Chancellors Club Career Tchg. award, 2004, Steeples Svc. to Kans. award, 2006; named Outstading Progressive Educator, 2000; Younger Humanist fellow NEH, 1972-73, Guggenheim fellow, 1975-76, NEH fellow, 1983-84, rsch. fellow Hall Ctr., 1990, Kemper fellow for tchg. excellence, 1998; Evans grantee, 1975-76, Beveridge grantee, 1982; NEH grantee, 1986-89. Mem. Soc. Am. Historians (elected), Orgn. Am. Historians, Am. Studies Assn., Assn. for Study of African Am. Life and History, Lawrence Trout Club, Golden Key (hon.), Omicron Delta Kappa, Phi Beta Delta, Phi Gamma Delta. Home: 713 Louisiana St Lawrence KS 66044-2339 Office: U Kans Dept Am Studies Lawrence KS 66045-0001 Business E-Mail: tuttle@ku.edu.

TUTWILER, MARGARET DEBARDELEBEN, diversified financial services company executive, former stock exchange executive; b. Birmingham, Ala., Dec. 28, 1950; d. Temple Wilson and Margaret (DeBardeleben) Tutwiler, II. Student, Finch Coll., 1969-71; BA, U. Ala., 1973. Sec. Ala. Rep. Party, Birmingham, 1974; scheduler Pres. Ford Com., Birmingham, 1975-78; exec. dir. Pres. Ford Com. Ala., Birmingham, 1976; pub. rels. rep. Nat. Assn. Mfrs. for Ala. and Miss., Birmingham and Washington, 1977-78; dir. scheduling George Bush for Pres. Com., Houston and Washington, 1978-80; spl. asst. to Pres. Reagan & exec. to chief of staff The White House, Washington, 1981-85; asst. sec. for pub. affairs & pub. liaison US Dept. Treasury, 1985-88; sr. adv. transition team US Dept. State, Washington, 1988-89, asst. sec. for pub. affairs, spokesman, 1989-92, US amb. to Morocco Rabat, 2001—03, under sec. for pub. diplomacy & pub. affairs Washington, 2003—04; ptnr. Fitzwater & Tutwiler, Inc., Washington, 1993—2001; exec. v.p., comm. & govt. relations NY Stock Exchange, Inc., NYC, 2004—07, NYSE Group, Inc., 2006—07, NYSE Euronext, 2007; sr. v.p. comm., head global comm. & pub. affairs Merrill Lynch & Co., Inc., 2007—. Dep. chmn. Bush-Quayle '88, Washington, 1988. Recipient Woman of Yr. award Wake Forest U., 1986, Alexander Hamilton award, 1988, Am. Ctr. for Internat. Leadership's Marshall award for outstanding leadership Birmingham Sothern's GALA 10, 1991; named to Ala. Hall of Honor. Republican. Episcopalian. Office: Merrill Lynch & Co Inc 4 World Fin Ctr New York NY 10080

TUUK, MARY, diversified financial services company executive; BA, Calvin Coll., Grand Rapids, mich.; MBA, JD, Ind. U. Sr. v.p. Old Kent Fin. Corp.; various exec. positions Fifth Third Bank, Mich., 2001—03; mgr. risk policy group, chief operational risk and compliance officer Fifth Third Bancorp, Cin., 2003—07, sr. v.p., sr. dir. security and risk services, 2007, exec. v.p., chief risk officer, 2007—. Bd. dirs. Fifth Third Bank; mem. adv. bd. Fifth Ward Bancorp's Women's Network. Operatic soprano: Cin. Vocal Arts Ensemble. Active Fine Arts Fund Cin.; bd. trustees Cin. Opera. Named one of 25 Women to Watch, US Banker, 2008. Mem.: Ill. State Bar Assn., mich. Bar Assn. Office: Fifth Third Bancorp Fifth Third Ctr 38 Fountain Sq Plz 13th Fl Cincinnati OH 45263*

TUUL, JOHANNES, physics professor, researcher; b. Tarvastu, Viljandi, Estonia, May 23, 1922; came to US, 1956, naturalized, 1962; s. Johan and Emilie (Tulf) T.; m. Marjatta Murtoniemi, July 14, 1957 (div. Aug. 1971); children: Melinda, Melissa; m. Sonia Esmeralda Manosalva, Sept. 15, 1976; 1 child, Johannes. Elem. Tchg. Credential, Tartu Normal Sch., Estonia, 1941; diploma in Elec. Engring., Stockholm Tech. Inst., 1947; BS, U. Stockholm, 1955, MA, 1956; ScM, Brown U., 1957, PhD, 1960. Tchr. Valuste Elem. Sch., 1941-43; escaped to Finland December, 1943; after Finland surrendered to Russia escaped to Sweden, 1944; instr. Stockholm Tech. Inst., 1947-49; lab. engr. Electrical Prospecting Co., Stockholm, 1949-53; elec. engr. LM Ericsson Telephone Co., Stockholm, 1954-55; rsch. physicist Am. Cyanamid Co., Stamford, Conn., 1960-62; sr. rsch. physicist Bell & Howell Rsch. Ctr., Pasadena, Calif., 1962-65; from asst. to assoc. prof. Calif. State Poly. U., Pomona, 1965-68, chmn. physics and earth scis. dept., 1971-75, prof. physics, 1975-91; prof. emeritus, 1992—. Vis. prof. Pahlavi U., Shiraz, Iran, 1968-70; cons. Bell & Howell Rsch. Ctr., Pasadena, Calif., 1965, Teledyne Co., Pasadena, Calif., 1968; guest researcher Naval Weapons Ctr., China Lake, Calif., 1967, 72; resident dir. Calif. State U. Internat. Programs in Sweden and Denmark, 1977-78. Author: Physics Made Easy, 1974; contbr. articles to profl. jours. Pres. Group Against Smoking Pollution, Pomona Valley, Calif., 1976; foster parent Foster Parents Plan, Inc., Warwick, RI, 1964-2003; block capt. Neighborhood Watch, West Covina, Calif., 1982-84; citizen amb. People to People Internat., 1990—; mem. Physics Edn. Del. to Peoples Rep. China, 1990, 30th Anniversary Caravan to Soviet Union, 1991, Baltic Assist Delegation, 1992, Industry and Sci. Initiative 1 Delegation to Cuba, 2000, Mission in Understanding to Iceland and Greenland, 2002, Global Peace Initiative to Egypt, 2003. Fellow Brown U., 1957-58; rsch. grantee U. Namur (Belgium), 1978, Ctr. Nat. Recherche Scientifique, France, 1979; recipient Humanitarian Fellowship award Save the Children Fedn., 1968, spl. award Travelers' Century Club, 1998. Mem. AAAS (life), NY Acad. Scis., Am. Phys. Soc. Republican. Roman Catholic. Achievements include research in energy conservation and new energy technologies. Personal E-mail: tuuljohannes@hotmail.com.

TUZCU, EMIN MURAT, cardiologist, educator; b. Isparta, Turkey, July 5, 1953; came to U.S., 1985; s. Omer Lufti and Guzide T.; m. Füsun Tuzcu, Apr. 26, 1982; children: Omer C., Hande N. MD, Istanbul Med. Faculty, 1977. Diplomate Am. Bd. Internal Medicine. Intern, resident Istanbul U. Sch. Medicine, 1971—81; fellow in cardiology Cleve. Clinic Found., 1985—89, staff physician, cardiologist, 1992—, prof. medicine, 1992—, vice chmn. Dept. Cardiovascular Medicine; fellow Mass. Gen. Hosp., 1989—91. Contbr. articles to profl. jours. Fellow: ACP, Am. Coll. Cardiology; mem.: Turkish Soc. Cardiology, Soc. Cardiac Angiography and Interventions, Am. Heart Assn. Office: Cleveland Clinic Found 9500 Euclid Ave Cleveland OH 44195-0002 Office Phone: 216-444-8130.

TUZEL, SUZANNE L., psychiatrist; b. Jacksonville, Fla., Aug. 12, 1960; children: Haldun, Kenan. MD, U. Istanbul Med. Sch., 1986. Diplomate bd. cert. in psychiatry and neurology 1992. Chief resident Creedmoor Psychiatric Ctr., Queens Village, NY, 1992—95, chief psychiatrist, 1995—96; chief of psychiatry Pilgrim Psychiatric Ctr., Brentwood, 1997—99, acting clin. dir., 1999—2000, asst. clin. dir., 2000—02; pvt. practice North Shore Psychiatric Cons., Smithtown, 2002—; attending psychiatrist St. Catherine of Siena Med. Ctr., 2002—; med. dir. Huntington Drug and Alcohol Project, 2006—. Addiction fellow North Shore U. Hosp., Manhasset, 2000. Mem.: Am. Acad. Addiction Psychiatry, Am. Psychiatric Assn. Office: 222 Mid Country Rd Smithtown NY 11787 Office Phone: 631-265-6868.

TÜZÜN, ERDEM, neurologist, consultant; b. Istanbul, Marmara, Turkey, Nov. 11, 1971; s. Neriman and Muhsin Burhanettin T. MD, Istanbul Med. Faculty, 1995. Specialist in neurology; med. diplomate. Intern U. Istanbul, 1994-95, resident in neurology, 1995-2000, specialist in neurology, 2000—01; postdoctoral fellow U. Tex. Med. Br., Galveston, Tex., 2002—05; sr. rsch. investigator U. Pa., Phila., 2006—. Sec. Archives of Neuropsychiatry, 1998—2000. Commando Mil. doctor Commando Mil. Hosp., 2000. Recipient 1st degree award, project prize Brain Rsch. Orgn., 1999. Mem. European Neurol. Soc. Achievements include research in measurements of intracavernosal endothelin levels of impotent men, providing evidence for using nitric oxide (antagonist of endothelin) agonist drugs in male erectile dysfunction; detection of ganglioside levels of salivary glands; treatment of congenital penile deformity by a new surgical method; demonstration of the presence of antibodies against voltage-gated potassium channels in patients with limbic encephalitis; identification of the autoimmune etiology of neuromyotonia and demonstration of the role of autoantibodies against thalamic structures as a casual factor for Morvan's syndrome; identification of cytokines and complements as important contributors of pathogenesis in myasthenia gravis. Office: U Pa Dept Neurology 3400 Spruce St Philadelphia PA 19104 Home Phone: 215-735-0767; Office Phone: 215-746-2824. Personal E-mail: drerdem@yahoo.com.

TVEDT, RYAN ROBERT, theater educator; b. Brainerd, Minn., Aug. 25, 1971; s. Ronald and Avis Tvedt; m. Irina Zelenskaya, May 18, 2001 (div. Oct. 10, 2007). BA, Concordia Coll., Moorhead, Minn., 1994; MA, Stony Brook U., NY, 1999. Vol. Americorps Nat. Civilian Cmty. Corps, Denver, 1995—96, Peace Corps, Vladivostok, Primorye, Russia, 1999—2001; legislative corr. US Senator Kent Conrad, Washington, 2001—02; program officer Am. Councils Internat. Edn., Washington, 2002—04; instr. theatre & drama, english as 2nd lang. U. Wis., Madison, 2004—. Fgn. Lang. Area Scholarship-Russian, US Dept. Edn., 2008. Mem.: Am. Soc. Theatre Rsch., Am. Theatre Higher Edn. Office: Univ WI Madison 6173 Vilas 821 Univ Ave Madison WI 53706 Personal E-mail: ryantvedt@earthlink.net. Business E-Mail: tvedt@wisc.edu.

TWAGILIMANA, AIMABLE, language educator, writer; b. Muyira, Butare, Rwanda, Dec. 4, 1961; arrived in U.S., 1992, naturalized, 2006; s. Louis Mudugu and Belancila Nyiragakinga; m. Marie-Rose Nkundimfura, Dec. 26, 1987; children: Leandre Munyana, Raissa Umwari. BA in English, Nat. U. of Rwanda, Butare, 1984, MA in English, 1986; MA in Applied Linguistics, U. of Reading, Berkshire, Eng., 1989; PhD in English, SUNY, Buffalo, 1995. Cert. tchr. h.s. Nat. U. of Rwanda. Lectr. Nat. U. of Rwanda, Ruhengeri, 1986—92; asst. prof. SUNY, Buffalo, 1995—2000, assoc. prof. English, 2000—04, prof., 2004—. Dir. of studies faculty of letters Nat. U. of Rwanda, Ruhengeri, 1991—92. Author: (novel) Manifold Annihilation, 1996, (book) Race and Gender in the Making of an African American Literary Tradition, 1997, In Their Own Voices: Rwandan Refugees Speak Out, 1997, Hutu and Tutsi (The Heritage Library of African People series), 1998, The Debris of Ham: Ethnicity, Regionalism and the 1994 Rwandan Genocide, 2003, Historical Dictionary of Rwanda, 2007; contbr. articles to encyclopedias. Fellow, NEH, 1999, 2003, 2006; scholar, Fulbright Found., 1992—95, Brit. Coun., 1988—89; Fulbright scholar, Cheikh Anta Diop U., Senegal, 2008—. Mem.: MLA, Assn. African Studies Programs (chair 2008—), Assn. Am. Transls., Nat. Coun. Tchrs. English, Nat. Assn. Lit. Critics. Roman Catholic. Home: 68 Fairchild Pl Buffalo NY 14216 Office: SUNY 1300 Elmwood Avenue Buffalo NY 14222 Personal E-mail: twagila12@hotmail.com. Business E-Mail: twagila@buffalostate.edu.

TWAIN, SHANIA (EILLEEN REGINA EDWARDS), musician; b. Windsor, Ontario, Can., Aug. 28, 1965; d. Sharon and Jerry Twain (Stepfather), Clarence Edwards; m. Robert John Lange, Dec. 28, 1993 (separated 2008); 1 child, Eja. Recs. Beginnings, 1989—90, 1999, Shania Twain, 1993, The Woman in Me, 1995 (Acad. Country Music Assn. Award for Album of Yr., 1995, ABC Radio Networks Country Music Award for Female Video Artist of Yr., 1995, Billboard Music Award for Country Album of Yr., 1996, Grammy award for Best Country Album, 1996), These Blues are Mine, 1996, Come on Over, 1997, Star Profile, 1999, Maximum Shania, 2000, Complete Limelight Sessions, 2001, Up!, 2002 (Can. Country Music Assn. Award for Album of Yr., 2003, Billboard Music Award for Country Album of Yr., 2003), Greatest Hits, 2004. Recipient Country Music TV (Europe) Rising Star award, 1993, Am. Music Award for Favorite New Country Artist, 1995, Can. Country Music Assn. Award for female vocalist of yr., 1995, Acad. of Country Music Award for Top New Female Vocalist, 1995, Best Country Album Grammy award, 1995, Blockbuster Entertainment Award for Favorite New Country Artist, 1996, Country Music TV (Europe) award for Female Artist of Yr., 1996, Juno Award for Country Female Vocalist of Yr., 1996, Juno Award for Entertainer of Yr., 1996, World Music Award for World's Best Selling Country Artist, 1996, Favorite New Artist award, Am. Music Awards, 1996, Am. Music Award for Best Female Country Artist, 1997, Juno Award for Country Female Vocalist of Yr., 1997, Juno Award for Internat. Achievement, 1997, Am. Music Award for Favorite Female Country Artist, 1998, Billboard Music Award for Female Artist of Yr., 1998, Country Music Assn. Award for Entertainer of Yr., 1999, Acad. Country Music Award for Entertainer of Yr., 1999, Am. Music Award for Favorite Female Country Artist, 1999, Am. Music Award for Favorite Female Pop/Rock Artist, 1999, Blockbuster Entertainment Award for Favorite Overall Single, 1999, Juno Award for Country Female Vocalist of Yr., 1999, Grammy Award for Best Female Country Vocal Performance (You're Still The One), 1999, Grammy Award for Best Country Song (You're Still The One), 1999, Juno Award for Best Songwriter, 2000, Juno Award for Best Country Female Artist, 2000, Grammy Award for Best Female Vocal Country Performance (Man!I Feel Like A Woman), 2000, Grammy Award for Best Country Song (Come On Over), 2000, Acad. Country Music Award for Entertainer of Yr., 2000, Billboard Music Award for Top County Artist of Yr., 2003, Billboard Music Award for Country Album Artist of Yr., 2003, Juno Fan Choice Award, 2003, Juno Award for Artist of Yr., 2003, Juno Award for Country Rec. Yr. (I'm Gonna Getcha Good), 2003, Can. Country Music Assn. Award for Video of Yr. (I'm Gonna Getcha Good), 2003, Can. Country Music Assn. Award for Female Artist of Yr., 2003, Order of Canada, 2005. Office: Mercury Records 66 Music Sq W Nashville TN 37203-4315 Address: Shore Fire Media c/o Georgette Pascale 32 Court St Fl 16 Brooklyn NY 11201-4404 Office: c/o Q Prime 131 S 11th St Nashville TN 37206

TWARDOWSKI, ZBYLUT JÓZEF, nephrologist, educator; b. Stanisławice, Poland, June 2, 1934; arrived in U.S., 1981; s. Jozef Twardowski and Marianna (Skoczek) Twardowska; m. Halina Anna Nowosielska, Sept. 26, 1958; children: Radomysl M., Przemyslaw W. MD with distinction, Collegium Medicum Univ. Jagelloniensis, Kraków, Poland, 1959; PhD, Med. Acad., Kraków, Poland, 1964; Hab. Dr Med. Sci., Med. Acad., Katowice, Poland, 1975. Teaching asst. Med. Acad., Krakow, 1954-57, intern, 1958—59, resident, 1959—62, assoc. prof. Lublin, Poland, 1977-82, chmn. dept. nephrology, 1977-82; chmn. dept. medicine Hosp. for Miners, Bytom, Poland, 1963-76; assoc. prof. U. Mo., Columbia, 1982-84, prof., 1985—99, prof. emeritus medicine, 1999, dir. outpatient peritoneal dialysis, 1985—99. Cons. Baxter-Travenol, Deerfield, Ill., 1982—. Editor: Peritoneal Dialysis, 1990, Hemodialysis Internat., 1996—2000; assoc. editor: Peritoneal Dialysis Internat., 1990—2000; contbr. articles to profl. jours. Fellow: ACP; mem.: Internat. Soc. for Hemodialysis (founder), Internat. Peritoneal Dialysis Soc., Internat. Soc. Nephrology, Am. Soc. Artificial Internal Organs, European Dialysis and Transplant Assn. (assoc.). Republican. Roman Catholic. Achievements include invention of capillary artificial kidney; catheter for peritoneal dialysis; intravenous catheter for home-dialysis; artificial kidney for daily dialysis. Avocations: swimming, skiing, travel. Office: Univ Mo 5 Hospital Dr CE421 Columbia MO 65212 Office Phone: 573-884-8799. Business E-Mail: twardowskiz@health.missouri.edu.

TWARDUS, SUSAN M., artist, art gallery owner, display designer; d. Joseph R. and Margaret L. Twardus; 1 child, Christopher M. Geoghan. Bd. dirs., treas. Catharine Lorillard Wolfe Art Club, Inc., NYC, 1998—. Awards chmn. Catherine Lorillard Wolfe Art Club, Inc., NYC, 1997—. Prin. works include sculpture Crutch And Burden (Anna Hyatt Huntington Bronze Horses Head Award, 2001), Yesterdays Commodities (CLWAC Corp. Award, 1996), The Winds Of Opportunity (Excalaber Award, 1997). Mem.: Pen And Brush Inc. (Excalaber Award For Sculpture 1997), Catharine Lorillard Wolfe Art Club (bd. dirs. 1998—2004). Achievements include development of Newspaper Sculpture Process And Design. Office: Catharine Lorillard Wolfe Art Club Inc 802 Broadway New York NY 10003 Personal E-mail: papiersun@aol.com.

TWARDY, STANLEY ALBERT, JR., lawyer; b. Trenton, NJ, Sept. 13, 1951; s. Stanley Albert Twardy and Dorothy M. Stonaker. BS with honors, Trinity Coll., 1973; JD, U. Va., 1976; LLM, Georgetown U., 1980. Bar: Conn. 1976, DC 1978, US Supreme Ct. 1979, US Ct. Appeals (2d cir.) 1984. Assoc. Whitman & Ransom, Greenwich, Conn., 1976-77; counsel com. on small bus. US Senate, 1977-79, counsel to Senator Lowell Weicker Jr., 1979-80; ptnr. Silver, Golub & Sandak, Stamford, Conn., 1980-85; US atty. Dist. of Conn., 1985-91; chief of staff Office of Gov. Lowell Weicker, Conn., 1991-93; ptnr. Day Pitney LLP, Stamford, Conn., 1993—. Pres. LCD, 2007—08, bd. dirs., 2007—; chmn.police chief selection panel City of Stamford, 1993—94; mem. nat. alumni exec. com. Trinity Coll., 1985—90, mem. athletic adv. com., 1992—97; chmn. program com. Drugs Don't Work!, 1989—91, bd. dirs., 1989—93, 1994—2000; mem. area adv. com. U. Conn., Stamford, 1993—96, mem. strategic planning mgmt. com., 1993—95; bd. dirs. Rehab. Ctr., 1995—2002, Stamford Health Found., 1995—, Trinity Coll., 1996—2002, Nat. Conf. Cmty. and Justice Fairfield County Region, 1996—2004. Mem.: ABA, Conn. Bar Assn., Phi Beta Kappa. Office Phone: 203-977-7300. Business E-Mail: satwardy@daypitney.com.

TWARK, JILL E., language educator; b. Akron, Ohio, July 9, 1968; d. Allan J. and Charlene R. Twark; m. Arno Forst, June 9, 2000. PhD, U. Wis.-Madison, 2002. Assoc. prof. German East Carolina U., Greenville, NC, 2002—; exec. dir. Friends Greenville Greenways, 2004—. Mem.: MLA, Am. Assn. Tchrs. German, German Studies Assn. Liberal. Avocations: travel, bicycling. Office: E Carolina Univ 3316 Bate Greenville NC 27858 Business E-Mail: twarkj@ecu.edu.

TWEARDY, DAVID JOHN, physician, educator; b. Monessen, Pa., Feb. 12, 1952; s. John Tweardy Sr. and Helen Kotch Tweardy; m. Ruth Falik, Jan. 21, 1982; children: Samuel David, Benjamin John, Daniel James. AB in Chemistry, Princeton U., 1974; MD, Harvard U., 1978. Diplomate Am. Bd. Internal Medicine, 1983, Am. Bd. Infectious Diseases, 1984. Asst. prof. medicine U. Pitts. Sch. Medicine, 1987—93, assoc. prof. medicine, 1993—99; prof. medicine Baylor Coll. Medicine, Houston, 1999—, chief sect. infectious diseases, 1999—. Grantee, NIH, 1997—2005, 2002—, 2004—. Mem.: Am. Clin. and Climatalogical Assn., Assn. Am. Physicians. Home: 3769 Nottingham St Houston TX 77005 Office Phone: 713-798-8918. E-mail: dtweardy@bcm.edu.

TWEEN, DOUGLAS M., lawyer, former prosecutor; b. 1962; BA, Columbia Univ., 1984; JD cum laude, Northwestern Univ., 1989. Bar: NY, Conn. Law clk. Judge William Timbers, US Ct. Appeals 2d Cir.; trial atty. Antitrust Div., U.S. Dept. Justice, 1990—2005; ptnr., Global Antitrust & Global Litigation practices Baker & McKenzie LLP, NYC, 2005—. Moderator Prog. on Cartel Enforcement So. African Competition Com., 2004. Recipient Antitrust Div. Award of Distinction, U.S. Dept. Justice, 2000, Attorney Gen. Disting. Svc. award, 2003. Mem.: Bar of City of N.Y., NY State Bar Assn., ABA. Office: Baker & McKenzie LLP 1114 Ave of the Americas New York NY 10036 Office Phone: 212-626-4355. Office Fax: 212-310-1655. Business E-Mail: douglas.tween@bakernet.com.

TWENHAFEL, NANCY ANN, pathologist, director; d. Marvin Gilbert and Kathleen Ann McDougall Twenhafel. BFA in Painting, Colo. U., 1986, BA in Biology, 1986; DVM, Colo. State Vet. Sch., Ft. Collins, 1992. Diplomate Am. Coll. Vet. Pathologists, 2003. Officer-in-charge Tenn. Valley VSSD, Ft. Campbell, Ky., 64th Med. Detachment Vet. Svc., Baumholder, Germany, 1995—98; pathology resident Armed Forces Inst. Pathology, Washington, 1998—2001; asst. dir., rsch. support coordination US Army Med. Rsch. Inst. Infectious Diseases, Frederick, Md., 2001—; lt. col. US Army, Ft. Detrick, 2001—08. Contbr. articles to profl. jours. Decorated Army Commendation medal, Joint Meritorious

Unit award, Nat. Def. Svc. medal, Global War Terrrorism Svc. medal, Nat. Svc. Ribbon, Oversees Svc. Ribbon. Mem.: Am. Coll. Vet. Pathologists, Am. Quarter Horse Assn., Appaloosa Horse Club Assn., Blue-Ridge Riding Club. Personal E-mail: natwenhafel@aol.com.

TWICHELL, CHASE, poet; b. New Haven, Conn., Aug. 20, 1950; d. Charles P. and Ann (Chase) T. BA, Trinity Coll., Hartford, 1973; MFA, U. Iowa, 1976. Editor Pennyroyal Pr., W. Hatfield, Mass., 1976-84; assoc. prof. English U. Ala., 1984-88; mem. MFA Program in Creative Writing, Warren Wilson Coll., 1999—; editor Ausable Press, 1999—. Asst. prof. Hampshire Coll., 1983-84; co-editor Alabama Poetry Series, 1984-88; lectr. Princeton U., 1990-98; faculty MFA program in creative writing Goddard Coll., 1997-99. Author: (poetry) Northern Spy, 1981, The Odds, 1986, Perdido, 1991, The Ghost of Eden, 1995, (book) Dog Language, 2005; editor: The Practice of Poetry, 1992, The Snow Watcher, 1998, Ausable Press, 1999—; translator The Lover of God, 2003. Recipient Acad. award in lit. Am. Acad. Arts and Letters, 1994; Nat. Endowment for Arts fellow, 1987, 93, Guggenheim fellow, 1990. Business E-Mail: editor@ausablepress.org.

TWIDDY, ELIZABETH, writer, educator; b. Detroit, Nov. 16, 1973; d. Frances Elizabeth and William Twiddy; life ptnr. Edward Ruchalski. BS in Biochemistry and Chemistry, Pa. State U., U. Pk., 1996, degree in English, 1996; MFA in Creative Writing Poetry, Syracuse U., NY, 2005. Lab. rschr. Dartmouth Med. Sch., Hanover, NH, 1997—2000; vis. writing instr. Le Moyne Coll., Syracuse, 2006—. Poetry instr. Downtown Writer's Ctr., Syracuse, 2005—. Author: (poems book) Zoo Animals in the Rain; contbr. articles to profl. jours. Child care worker Children's Home Detroit, 2000—01; tchg. artist Partners Arts Edn., Syracuse, 2005—06. Recipient Shigley award, Pa. State U., Dept. Biochemistry, 1995, Joyce Carol Oates award, 2005. Mem.: MLA, Penn State Alumni Assn., Assn. Writers and Writing Programs, Acad. Am. Poets, Golden Key Nat. Honor Soc. Avocations: music, photography, painting, walking, cooking.

TWIGG, JUDYTH L., political science professor; b. Cumberland, Md., Nov. 9, 1962; d. Richard A. and Sandra K. Twigg; m. William W. Newmann, Aug. 1, 1987; 1 child, Jerelyn. BS, Carnegie Mellon U., 1984; MA, U. Pitts., 1986; PhD, MIT, 1994. Rsch. assoc. Carnegie Mellon U., Pitts., 1989-92; instr. Va. Commonwealth U., Richmond, 1992-95, asst. prof., 1995—2001, assoc. prof., 2001—. Cons. Aries Analytics, Arlington, Va., 1992-98. Contbr. articles to profl. jours. Grantee rsch. grantee, Nat. Coun. for Soviet and East European Rsch., 1997, 2000, Carnegie Corp. N.Y., 2000—; fellow postdoctoral fellow, Social Sci. Rsch. Coun., 1999—2000. Mem. APHA, Internat. Studies Assn., Am. Polit. Sci. Assn., Am. Assn. for Advancement of Slavic Studies. Home: 5333 Stanwood Way Glen Allen VA 23059-6900 Office: Va Commonwealth U Wilder Sch of Govt Pub Affairs 923 W Franklin St # 842028 Richmond VA 23284-9008 Office Phone: 804-828-8051. Office Fax: 804-827-1275. E-mail: jtwigg@vcu.edu.

TWIGG-SMITH, THURSTON, newspaper publisher; b. Honolulu, Aug. 17, 1921; s. William and Margaret Carter (Thurston) Twigg-S.; m. Bessie Bell, June 9, 1942 (div. Feb. 1983); children: Elizabeth, Thurston, William, Margaret, Evelyn; m. Laila Roster, Feb. 22, 1983 (div. Dec. 1994); m. Sharon Smith, Feb. 28, 1996. B.Engring., Yale U., 1942. With Honolulu Advertiser, 1946-2000, mng. editor, 1954-60, asst. bus. mgr., 1960-61, pub., 1961-86; pres., dir., chief exec. officer Honolulu Advertiser, Inc., 1962-93, chmn., 1993-2000. Chmn., dir., CEO Persis Corp., 1962-2002, chmn. Twigg-Smith Group LLC, 2002—. Trustee Honolulu Acad. Arts, The Contemporary Mus., Hawaii, Yale Art Gallery, New Haven. Maj. AUS, 1942-46. Mem. Waialae Country Club, Pacific Club, Oahu Country Club, Outrigger Canoe Club. Office Phone: 808-735-3883. Personal E-mail: ttwiggsmith@aol.com.

TWINAME, JOHN DEAN, minister, human services administrator; b. Mt. Kisco, NY, Dec. 27, 1931; s. C. G. and Constance Jean (Ulmer) Twiname; m. Carolyn Anderson, Aug. 6, 1955; children: Karen, Jeanne, Julia. AB, Cornell U., 1953; MBA, Harvard U., 1957; MDiv, Union Theol. Sem., 1983. Ordained to ministry Presbyn. Ch., 1983. Sales rep. Am. Hosp. Supply Corp., Evanston, Ill., 1957-60, dir. product research, 1961, sales mgr., 1962, asst. to div. pres., 1963, product mgr., 1964, mktg. mgr., 1965-67, mktg. v.p., 1968-69; dep. adminstr. Social and Rehab. Svc., HEW, Washington, 1969-70, adminstr., 1970-73; adminstr. Office Health Cost of Living Coun., 1973-74; pvt. cons. Mott-McDonald Assocs., Inc., Washington, 1974-76, pres., 1976-78; exec. v.p. Am. Health Found., NYC, 1978-81; co-pres. HealthCare Chaplaincy, Inc., NYC, 1983-93, co-chair exec. com., 1993-94, life trustee, 1995—, exec. v.p., 1999—2000. Cons. exec. Coll. Chaplains, 1997; acting sr. min. Green's Farms Congl. Ch., Westport, Conn., 2001—03, pastoral assoc., 2003—. Treas. U.S. com. Internat. Coun. Social Welfare, 1977—80; mem. pres. coun. United Hosp. Fund, 1991—99; voting mem. Empire Blue Cross/Blue Shield, 1994; chmn. bd. dirs. Bauman Bible Telecasts, Inc., 1976—80; sec. bd. dirs. U.S. Coun. Internat. Yr. of Disabled Persons, 1979—81; founding bd. dirs. Am. Paralysis Assn. (formerly Paralysis Cure Rsch.), 1976—83; bd. dirs. Epilepsy Found. Am., 1978—85; chmn. bd. dirs. Chgo. Bus.-Indsl. Project, 1967—68, People to People Com. for Handicapped, 1976—78; bd. dirs. N.Y. Regional Transplant Program, 1988—92, Beck Mack & Oliver Ptnrs. Fund, 2000—05. 1st lt. AUS, 1953—55. Recipient Disting. Svc. award, Coll. Chaplains, 1992, Wholeness of Life award, The Health Care Chaplaincy, Inc., 2003, Disting. Alumnus award, Union Theol. Sem., 2004; Baker scholar, Harvard U. Bus. Sch. Home: 60 East End Ave New York NY 10028 Office: 163 Harbor Rd Southport CT 06890 Office Phone: 203-254-1506.

TWINING, JONATHAN EMERSON, biology professor; s. Lorin Emerson and Rita Twining; m. Julia Elsen Twining, Aug. 20, 1988; 1 child, Jonathan Jared. BS in Biology, Eastern Nazarene Coll., Quincy, Mass., 1984, MEd, 2005; MS in Oceanography, Old Dominion U., Norfolk, Va., 1986. Cert. in tchg. gen. sci. Mass. Dept. Edn., 2001. Environ. scientist RI Analytical, Warwick, 1989—94; project mgr. Environ. Sci. Svcs., Providence, 1994—96; sr. environ. scientist SAGE Environ., Pawtucket, RI, 1996—99, ATC Assocs., East Providence, RI, 2000—01; instr. environ. sci. Eastern Nazarene Coll., Mass., 1997—2001, asst. prof. biology, 2005—; sci. tchr. Remington Mid. Sch., Franklin, Mass., 2001—05. Pres. Marah Internat., Smithfield, RI, 1999—2009; bd. mem. Smithfield Land Trust, RI, 2004—06. Recipient Environ. Merit award, EPA, 1999, Formal Environ. Educator award, New Eng. Environ. Edn. Assn., 2005. Mem.: Assn. Profl. Wildlife Educators. Office: Eastern Nazarene Coll 23 East Elm Ave Quincy MA 02170 Business E-Mail: jonathan.e.twining@enc.edu.

TWISDALE, HAROLD WINFRED, dentist; b. Roanoke Rapids, NC, Apr. 28, 1933; s. James Robert and Elma (Smith) T.; m. Barbara Ann Edmonds, Aug. 2, 1958 (div. Apr. 1974); children: Harold Winfred, Leigh Ann.; m. Frances Jean Winstead, July 1983. BS in Dentistry, U. N.C., 1955, D.D.S., 1958. Individual practice dentistry, Charlotte, NC, 1961—; head, dept. dental prosthetics Meml. Hosp., 1964-66; lectr. dental subjects.; pres., gen. mgr. WCTU-TV, Charlotte Telecasters, Inc., 1967-69, WATU-TV, Augusta, Ga., Augusta Telecasters, Inc., 1968-69, Television Presentations, Inc., Charlotte, 1967-69; partner Twisdale and Steel Assocs., Charlotte, 1965-70; propr. Twisdale Enterprises, Charlotte, 1965-70. Pres. Memphis Telecasters, Inc., 1966-76, Va. Telecasters, Inc., Richmond, 1966—, Durham-Raleigh Telecasters, Inc., Durham, N.C., 1966-70, Gentil Elite, Inc., 1979— Transp. chmn. Miss N.C. Pageant, 1965; v.p. N.C. Jaycees, 1963-64; Trustee Boys Home, Lake Waccomaw, N.C., 1966-67. Served to capt. USAF, 1958-60. Recipient various awards Charlotte Jaycees, 1962-66. Fellow Acad. Dentistry Internat.; mem. ADA, N.C. Dental Found., N.C. Dental Soc., Charlotte Dental Soc. (chmn. various coms. 1961—), Am. Analgesia Soc., Internat. Analgesic Soc. (dir. 1980-85), N.C. Dental Soc. Anesthesiology (v.p. 1983-84), Charlotte Analgesia Study Club (co-founder 1970), N.C. 2d Dist. Dental Soc., Metrolina Dental Soc. (founder 1994, pres. 1994-95), U. N.C. Dental Alumni Assn., Southeastern Analgesia Soc. (founder 1972, pres. 1972-74), Lambda Chi Alpha, Delta Sigma Delta. Republican. Methodist. Office: 3104 Weddington Rd Ste 200 Matthews NC 28105 Home Phone: 704-841-3605; Office Phone: 704-849-2595. Personal E-mail: twisdds@aol.com. *I must give the full credit for any achievement I might have accomplished in life to my mother and father. They not only provided me the means and direction one needs to make even the slightest accomplishment in our mortal life, but most of all, they gave me love, understanding, and a sense of values. These values have never deserted me, nor have they been compromised, even in the darkest hours of depression or during the brightest times of accomplishment. They have been my steady companions.*

TWISS, PAGE CHARLES, geology educator; b. Columbus, Ohio, Jan. 2, 1929; s. George Ransom and Blanche (Olin) T.; m. Nancy Homer Hubbard, Aug. 29, 1954; children— Stephen Ransom, Catherine Grace, Thomas Stuart. BS in Geology, Kans. State U., 1950, MS, 1955; PhD, U. Tex. at Austin, 1959. Mem. faculty dept. geology Kans. State U., Manhattan, 1959-95, prof. emeritus, 1995—, assoc. prof., 1964-69, prof., 1969-95, prof. emeritus Manhattan, 1995—, also head dept., 1968-77. Geologist agrl. research service U.S. Dept. Agr., 1966-68; research scientist U. Tex., Austin, 1966-67 Contbr. articles to profl. jours. Chmn. Manhattan Council Human Relations, 1960-61; vice pres. Riley County Democratic Club, 1970-71; mem. Dem. Precinct Com., Manhattan, 1970-72, 74-80, 96-2004. Served with USAF, 1951-53. Fellow Pan Am. Petroleum Found., 1957-58; Shell Found. fellow, 1958-59 Fellow Geol. Soc. Am. (chmn. south cen. sect. 1972-73, 95, sec.-treas. 1980-89, vice-chmn. 1994-95, chmn. 1995-96); mem. Am. Assn. Petroleum Geologists (geologic maps com. 1968-70), Soc. Sedimentary Geology, Kans. Acad. Sci. (mem. rsch. awards com. 1966-70, assoc. editor 1977-92), Kans. Geol. Soc., W. Tex. Geol. Soc., AAUP (chpt. v.p. 1971-72, chpt. pres. 1972-73), Soc. Phytolith Rsch. (organizing com. 1990-92, mem.-at-large, exec. com. 1992-93, pres.-elect 1993-94, pres. 1994-95, past pres. 1995-96), Sigma Xi, Sigma Gamma Epsilon, Gamma Sigma Delta. Home: 2327 Bailey Dr Manhattan KS 66502-2733 Home Phone: 785-539-6959. Business E-Mail: pctwiss@ksu.edu.

TWITCHELL, THEODORE GRANT, music educator, composer; b. Melrose, Kans., Jan. 26, 1928; s. Curtis and Sarah Frances (Lane) T.; m. Rebecca Janis Goldsmith, Nov. 18, 1989; stepchildren: Ralph Norman, Russell Norman, Dawn Jiricek. AA in Music, L.A. City Coll., 1949; BA in Social Studies, Calif. State U., LA, 1951, MA in Secondary Edn., 1955; EdD in Secondary and Higher Edn., U. So. Calif., LA, 1964. Tchr. Barstow (Calif.) Union High Sch., 1952, Burbank (Calif.) Unified Sch. Dist., 1954-66; dean instrn., dir. evening divsn., dir. summer sessions, 1966-69; pres. Palo Verde Coll., Blythe, Calif., 1969-70; adult tchr. L.A. Unified Sch. Dist., 1977-78; faculty Columbia West U., LA, 1993—. Pvt. English tutor, 1979—. Composer: The Gettysburg Address, Tidewater, The Pride of Monticello, Labor Day March, Valley Forge, Normandy Prayer, Christmas in L.A., L.A., Overture to Tidewater, The Lord Is My Shepherd, The Joy of Snow, Walt Whitman and Friends, over 90 others; contbr. articles to profl. jours.; author: Dear Mr. President, 1982, Courage, Conflict and Love, 1988, The Magnificent Odyssey of Michael Young, 1992; author of poems. With U.S. Army, 1952-53. Recipient Coll. Faculty Senate Award for Achievements for the coll., Palo Verde Coll., Student Body award. Mem. Internat. Poetry Hall Fame, Cmty. Coll. Pres.'s Assn., Am. Assn. Composers, Authors and Pubs., Calif. PTA (hon. life mem.), Rho Delta Chi. Republican. Methodist. Avocations: music, writing, travel, hiking, photography. Business E-Mail: ggoldfish@earthlink.net.

TWITCHELL, THOMAS EVANS, neurologist, educator; b. Springfield, Ohio, Sept. 4, 1923; s. Ernst Albert and Charlotte Marie (Schelling) T.; m. Patricia Ann O'Brien, Nov. 18, 1956; children: Carol, Susan, Mauyra, Evelyn. MD, U. Mich., 1946. Rsch. fellow in neurophysiology Yale U., New Haven, 1947; intern in neurology Boston City Hosp., 1947-48, rsch. fellow in neurology, 1948-49; USPHS rsch. fellow in neurophysiology Yale U., 1949-51; asst. resident in medicine New Eng. Med. Ctr., Boston, 1954, chief resident in neurology, 1954-55, neurologist, 1955-88; instr. neurology Tufts U. Sch. Medicine, Boston, 1955-56, asst. prof. neurology, 1956-62, assoc. prof. neurology, 1963-83, prof., 1983-88, prof. neurology, 1983-88, prof. emeritus, 1988—. Rsch. assoc. in psychology MIT, Cambridge, 1963-77. Served to capt. USAF, 1952-54. Mem. Am. Acad. Neurology, Am. Neurol. Assn. (sr.), Mass. Med. Soc. Avocations: music, philosophy, physics, literature. Home: 54 Longfellow Rd Wellesley MA 02481-5221 Home Phone: 781-235-3128.

TWOMBLY, STEPHEN DOANE, magazine publisher; b. Summit, NJ, July 26, 1953; s. Doane and Betty (Bowers) T.; m. Jean Sawyer. BA summa cum laude, Drew U., 1976. Dist. mgr. McGraw-Hill Publs. Co., NYC, 1978-83; dir. advt. IDG Communications, Peterborough, NH, 1983—84, pub. RUN, 1984—87, pub. AmigaWorld, 1985—88, v.p., 1988-89, exec. v.p., 1989—90, exec. v.p., pub. dir. PCResource, 1989—90; group pub. Consumer/Home Mag., Special Products, 1987-88; pub. dir. PC Resource, 1988—90; exec. v.p., pub. dir. PCResource Cahners Pubs. Co., Newton, Mass., 1990—97; nat. sales mgr. Datamation, 1990—92, assoc. pub., 1993—94; pub. Digital News & Rev., 1994—95, Reseller Mgmt., 1995—97; v.p. sales IDG Channel Svcs. Corp., Framingham, Mass., 1997—98; v.p., pub. New Age Jour. & Body & Soul, 1998—2001; pub. dir. Weider Pubs. Natural Health mag., 2001—03; group pub. Advanstar Comm. Sensors & Frontline Solutions, 2003—04; pub. CMO mag. Internat. Data Group, 2004—06; pub. Boston Globe Media Design New Eng., 2006—. Spkr. in field. Mem. Sigma Phi. Avocations: composing, painting, outdoor sports. Home: PO Box 1365 New London NH 03257 Office: Boston Globe Media Design New England 320 Congress St Boston MA 02210 Office Phone: 617-929-2706.

TWOMEY, KEVIN, retail executive; BA in Econs. and Acctg., St. John's U. Various positions Deloitte & Touche, 1972—89, Fleming Cos., Inc., 1989—2000, dir. planning and analysis to ops. contr. to v.p., contr., 1995—99, sr. v.p. fin., contr., 1999—2000; sr. v.p., chief acctg. officer Rite Aid Corp., 2000—05, exec. v.p., CFO, 2005—08. Office Phone: 717-761-2633.

TWORETZKY, WAYNE, cardiologist; married. MD, U. Stellenbosch, Cape Town, 1988. Diplomate Am. Bd. of Pediat., 2000. Attending in cardiology Children's Hosp. Boston, 1999—. Recipient Fellows Clinic Rsch. award, Soc. Pediatric Rsch.-Pediatric Academic Societies, 1999, Clin. Rsch. award, Am. Heart Assn., 2004. Achievements include development of Is instrumental in developing a fetal cardiac therapy program at Children's Hospital Boston. Home and Office: Children's Hospital Boston 300 Longwood Ave Boston MA 02115 Business E-Mail: wayne.woretzky@cardio.chboston.org.

TYABJI, HATIM AHMEDI, computer systems company executive; b. Bombay, Mar. 12, 1945; arrived in US, 1967, naturalized, 1976; BSEE, Coll. Engring., Poona, India, 1967; MSEE, SUNY, Buffalo, 1969; MBA in Internat. Bus., Syracuse U., 1975; grad. exec. program, Stanford U., 1981; Doctorate (hon.), SUNY. Program mgr. Mohawk Data Scis. Corp., Herkimer, N.Y., 1969-73; pres. Info. Systems Products and Techs. Group, Sperry Corp. (now Unisys Corp.), Roseville, Minn., 1973-86; chmn., pres., CEO VeriFone, Inc., Redwood City, Calif., 1986—98; founding chmn., CEO Saraide, 1998—2000; exec. chmn. Bytemobile Inc., 2001—. Bd. dirs. Best Buy, DepotPoint, Jasper Wireless, Merchant Solutions, TAFMO Ltd.; amb.-at-large Benchmark Capital. Contbr. articles to profl. pubs.; author: Husband, Wife, and Company: An Honest Perspective on Success in Life and Work, 2007. Recipient Disting. Exec. of Yr. award, Acad. Mgmt., 2000, Lifetime Achievement award, Silicon India, Point Of Sale Industry, 2001. Muslim. Avocations: skiing, tennis. Office: Bytemobile Inc 2025 Stierlin Ct Ste 200 Mountain View CA 94043

TYACK, THOMAS MICHAEL, lawyer; b. Columbus, Ohio, June 20, 1940; s. George E. and E. Naomi (Ballard) T.; m. Patricia J. Clark, Sept. 7, 1969; children: Jonathan, Jeffrey, James, Justin. BA cum laude, Ohio State U., Columbus, 1962, Jd, 1965. Bar: Ohio 1965, U.S. Ct. Appeals (6th cir.) 1970, U.S. Supreme Ct. 1970, U.S. Dist. Ct. (so. dist.) Ohio 1972. Ptnr. Tyack, Scott & Colley, Columbus, 1965-79, Tyack Scott & Wiseman, Columbus, 1979-81; prin. Thomas M. Tyack Assocs. Co., L.P.A., Columbus, 1981-90; ptnr. Tyack & Blackmore Co., L.P.A., Columbus, 1991-94; pres. Tyack, Blackmore & Liston Co. LPA, Columbus, 1994—. Bar examiner Ohio Supreme Ct., 1975-80; lectr., legal asst. program Capital U., Ohio, 1977-90. Fellow Am. Coll. Trial Lawyers; mem. ABA, Ohio Bar Assn., Columbus Bar Assn., Franklin Ct. and Trial Lawyers, Assn. Trial Lawyers Am., Ohio Acad. Trial Lawyers, Ohio Acad. Trial Lawyers, Ohio Acad. Criminal Def. Lawyers, NDCDL. Republican. Methodist. Office: 536 S High St Columbus OH 43215-5605 Office Phone: 614-221-1341.

TYAGI, PUNAM, environmental services administrator; d. Nakli Ram and Rajeshwari Tyagi; m. Pawan Tyagi, Feb. 15, 2002; 1 child, Pranshu. PhD, Devi Ahilya U., Indore, M.P., India, 2003. Cert. erosion & sediment control Md. Dept. of Environment, 2008, watershed mgmt. tng. EPA's Watershed Acad., 2008. Postdoc fellow U. Ky., Lexington, 2004—08; environ. compliance specialist Md. Dept. Environment, Cambridge, 2008—. Contbr. scientific papers, articles to profl. jours. Recipient award, AWWA, 2004—06, IAEH, 2005—06; fellow Rsch. fellow, AICTE, New Delhi, 1999—2000, Sr. Rsch. fellow, Indian Coun. Agr. Rsch. Delhi, India., 2000—01, Coun. Sci. & Indsl. Rsch., New Delhi, 2002—03. Achievements include research in multimolecular biomarker approach developed to identify the microbiological pollution sources. Office: Maryland Dept Environment 407 Race St Cambridge MD 21613 Office Fax: 410-221-6317. E-mail: ptyagi@mde.state.md.us.

TYBOUT, ALICE MARIE, educator; b. Ann Arbor, Mich., Dec. 2, 1949; d. Richard Alton and Rita Harris (Holloway) T. B.A. in Bus. Adminstrn., Ohio State U., 1970, M.A. in Consumer Behavior, 1972; Ph.D. in Mktg., Northwestern U., 1975. Academic counselor Coll. Adminstrv. Scis. Ohio State U., 1970-72; research asst. Northwestern U., Evanston, Ill., 1972-74, asst. prof. mktg. and transp., 1975-81, asso. prof., 1981-85, prof., 1985—, J.L. Kellogg research prof. Kellogg Grad. Sch. Mgmt., 1980-81 Buchanan research prof. Kellogg Grad. Sch. Mgmt., 1983-84, Gen. Foods research prof., 1985-86, prof. mktg. J.L. Kellogg Grad. Sch. Mgmt., 1985-88, Harold T. Martin, 1988—; instr. bus. U. Chgo., 1974-75; cons. Am. Bankers Assn., Batus Corp., First Nat. Bank of Chgo., Blue Cross and Blue Shield of Va., Sears Retailing scholar, 1969; bd. dirs. Art Encounter, 1987-89, Old Kent Bank, Chgo., 1989—. Mem. Am. Mktg. Assn., Assn. Consumer Research (treas. 1982, 83, co-chmn. 1982 conf.). Mem. editorial bd. Jour. Mktg., 1979-81, Jour. Bus. Research, 1980—, Jour. Mktg. Research, 1988-90, Jour. Consumer Rsch., 1982-90; Co-editor: Advances in Consumer Research, Vol. 10, Cognitive and Affective Responses to Advertising; contbr. articles to profl. jours. Office: Northwestern U Dept Mktg 2001 Sheridan Rd Dept Mktg Evanston IL 60208-0814

TYBURSKI, CHARLES J., lawyer; b. New Kensington, Pa., Feb. 25, 1934; s. Steven John and Estella Ann Tyburski; m. Nancy Cara Brown, July 20, 1963. BA, Ohio Wesleyan U., Deleware, 1956; JD, The Ohio State U., Columbus, 1964. Bar: 1964, ct. cert. specialist in trust and estate law: 2003. Atty., ptnr. Black, McCuskey, Souers & Arbaugh, Canton, Ohio, 1964—. Dir. Hilscher-Clarke Electric Co., Canton, 1980—2006, Gregory Industries, Canton, 1985—2006; dir. regional bd. KeyBank, N.A., Canton, Ohio, 1990—2002. Nat. coun. The Moritz Coll. Law, Columbus, 1984—; trustee Walsh U., North Canton, Ohio, 1992—2004. Lt. col. USAF, 1956—84. Fellow: Ohio Bar Found. (life). Democrat. Roman Catholic. Avocations: fishing, hunting, gardening, travel, reading. Home: 130 Brookview Cir North Canton OH 44709 Office: Black McCuskey Souers & Arbaugh Ste 1000 220 Market Ave Canton OH 44702

TYBURSKI, JAMES GERARD, surgeon; s. Chester and Elizabeth Tyburski; m. Julie Fleming, May 5, 1990. BS, SUNY, Binghamton, 1983; MD, Upstate Med. Ctr., Syracuse, NY, 1987. Cert. Am. Bd. Surgery, 1993, critical care Am. Bd. Surgery, 1993. Resident surgery Wayne State U. Detroit Med. Ctr., 1987—92, trauma fellow, 1992—94; asst. prof. surgery Wayne State U. Sch. Medicine, Detroit, 1994—2001, assoc. prof. surgery, 2001—07, prof. surgery, 2007—; program dir. Wayne State Dept. Surgery, Detroit, 1997—; chief surgery Detroit Receiving Hosp., 2004—. Recipient Wayne State Faculty Tchg. award, Wayne State U. Sch. Medicine, 2003, 2005. Mem.: Western Surg. Assn., Midwest Surg. Assn., Eastern Assn. for the Surgery of Trauma, Am. Assn. for the Surgery of Trauma, ACS, Alpha Omega Alpha Honor Med. Soc. (life). Office: Detroit Receiving Hosp 4201 St Antoine Ste 4S-13 Detroit MI 48201

TYER, TRAVIS EARL, librarian, consultant; b. Lorenzo, Tex., Oct. 23, 1930; s. Charlie Earl and Juanita (Travis) T.; m. Alma Lois Davis, Nov. 6, 1951; children: Alan Ross, Juanita Linn. BS, Abilene Christian U., 1952; BLS, U. North Tex., 1959; AdM in LS, Fla. State U., 1969, postgrad., 1969-71. Librarian, tchr. pub. schs., Gail, Lubbock, and Seminole, Tex., 1952-61; with Dallas Pub. Library, 1961-66, coordinator young adult services, 1962-66; library dir. Lubbock Pub. Library, 1966, Lubbock City-County Libraries, 1967-68; grad. library sch. faculty-state personnel coordinator Emporia (Kans.) State U., 1971-72; sr. cons. profl. devel. Ill. State Library, Springfield, 1972-80; exec. dir. Great River Libr. Sys., Quincy, Ill., 1980-94; cons. pub. rels. and comm. Alliance Libr. Sys., Quincy, 1994-97; ind. libr. cons., 1997—. Lectr. summer workshops Tex. Woman's U., U. Okla., U. Utah, Fla. State U., U. North

Tex.; adj. faculty U. Mo., 1986-89; cons. in field; mem. adv. com. Ill. State Libr., 1984-87, 93-96; pres. Resource Sharing Alliance West Ctrl. Ill., Inc., 1981-94, sec., 1994-97; pres. Ill. Libr. System Dirs. Orgn., 1992-94. Contbr. articles to library jours. Inductee U. North Tex. Libr. and Info. Sci. Hall of Fame, 1990. Mem. ALA, Ill. Libr. Assn., Ill. Ctr. for the Book, Friends of Librs. U.S.A., U. North Tex. Sch. Libr. and Info. Sci. (life), Friends Lubbock City-County Librs. (life), Ill. Sch. Libr. MEdia Assn. Democrat. Mem. Ch. of Christ. Home and Office: 2008 S Arrowood Ct Quincy IL 62305-8961

TYGRETT, HOWARD VOLNEY, JR., judge, lawyer; b. Lake Charles, La., Jan. 12, 1940; s. Howard Volney and Hazel (Wheeler) T.; m. Linda Lee; children: Carroll Diane, Howard V. III. BA, Williams Coll., 1961; LLB, So. Methodist U., 1964. Bar: Tex. 1964. Gen. atty. SEC, 1964-65; law clk. to chief judge U.S. Dist. Ct. No. Dist. Tex., 1965-67; ptnr. Tygrett & Walker and predecessors, Dallas, 1968-98; state dist. judge, 86th dist. Kaufman County, Tex., 2003—. Bd. dirs. Routh St. Ctr., 1976-83, Theatre Three, 1974-75, Shakespeare Festival, 1978-81, Suicide and Crisis Ctr., 1983-88, Kaufman County Civic Theatre, 2005—, Terrell Christian Acad., 2006-08; bd. dirs. Dallas Ctr. for Developmentally Disabled, pres., 2006-08; chmn. Terrell Hist. Preservation Commn., 2000-03. Mem. Tex. Bar Assn., Civitan (lt. gov. Tex. dist. 1976-77, gov. 1979-80), Terrell Heritage Soc. (v.p. 1999—), Delta Phi, Delta Theta Phi. Episcopalian. Home: 505 Pacific Ave Terrell TX 75160-2073 Office: Kaufman County Courthouse 100 W Mulberry Kaufman TX 75142

TYL, NOEL JAN, retired vocalist, astrologer, writer; b. West Chester, Pa., Dec. 31, 1936; BA, Harvard U., 1958. Bus. mgr. Houston Grand Opera Assn., 1958-60; account exec. Ruder and Finn Pub. Rels., NYC, 1960-62; profl. astrologer, 1970—; editor Astrology Now mag., 1974-79. Pres. Tyl Assocs., Inc. pub. rels. and advt., 1980-89; media spokesman; internat. lectr., locations including U.S., Moscow, London, Oslo, Copenhagen, Berlin, Amsterdam, The Netherlands, Toronto, Ont., Tel Aviv, Bologna. Winner Am. Opera Auditions, 1964; opera singer U.S. and Europe, 1964-80; Wagner specialist; appearances include Vienna State Opera, Düsseldorf, Rome, Milan, Barcelona, N.Y.C. Opera, also throughout U.S.; author: Principles and Practice of Astrology, 12 vols., 1973-75, Teaching and Study Guide, 1976, The Horoscope as Identity, 1974, Holistic Astrology, 1980, Prediction in Astrology, 1991, Synthesis and Counseling in Astrology, 1994, Astrology of the Famed, 1995, Predictions for a New Millennium, 1996, Astrological Timing of Critical Illness, 1998, Creative Astrologer, 1999, Solar Arcs, 2001, Intimacy, Sexuality, and Relationship, 2002, Vocations, 2005. Mem. Astrology's World Orgn./AFAN (presiding officer 1982-98). Home: 15634 N Cholla Dr Fountain Hills AZ 85268-1225 Home Phone: 480-816-0000; Office Phone: 480-816-0000. E-mail: noeltyl@cox.net.

TYLE, CRAIG S., lawyer, investment company executive; b. Syracuse, NY, 1960; BA with high honors, Swarthmore Coll., 1982; JD magna cum laude, Harvard Univ., 1985. Bar: NY 1988, DC 2004. Assoc. Sullivan & Cromwell, NYC, 1982—88; atty. Investment Company Inst., Washington, 1988—97, gen. counsel, 1997—2004; ptnr., asset mgmt. group Shearman & Sterling LLP, Washington, 2004—05; exec. v.p. & gen. counsel Franklin Resources Inc. (Franklin Templeton Investments), San Mateo, Calif., 2005—. Mem. NASDAQ Quality of Markets com., 1997—2003, co-chmn., 2003. Contbr. articles to profl. jours. Mem.: ABA, Assn. Bar City of NY. Office: Franklin Resources Inc 1 Franklin Pkwy San Mateo CA 94403-1906 Office Phone: 202-508-8016. Office Fax: 202-508-8100. Business E-Mail: craig.tyle@shearman.com.

TYLER, ANNE (MRS. TAGHI M. MODARRESSI), writer; b. Mpls., Oct. 25, 1941; d. Lloyd Parry and Phyllis (Mahon) T.; m. Taghi M. Modarressi, May 3, 1963 (dec. Apr. 1997); children: Tezh, Mitra. BA, Duke U., 1961; postgrad., Columbia U., 1962. Author: If Morning Ever Comes, 1964, The Tin Can Tree, 1965, A Slipping-Down Life, 1970, The Clock Winder, 1972, Celestial Navigation, 1974, Searching for Caleb, 1976, Earthly Possessions, 1977, Morgan's Passing, 1980, Dinner at the Homesick Restaurant, 1982, The Accidental Tourist, 1985 (Nat. Book Critics Cir. award 1986), Breathing Lessons, 1988 (Pulitzer Prize for fiction 1989), Saint Maybe, 1991, (juvenile) Tumble Tower, 1993, Ladder of Years, 1995, A Patchwork Planet, 1998, Back When We Were Grownups, 2001, The Amateur Marriage, 2004, (juvenile) Timothy Tugbohom Says No, 2005, Digging to America, 2006; contbr. short stories to nat. mags.

TYLER, CARL WALTER, JR., retired epidemiologist, health science association administrator; b. Washington, Aug. 22, 1933; s. Carl Walter and Elva Louise (Harlan) T.; m. Elma Hermione Matthias, June 23, 1956 (dec. Dec. 1991); children: Virginia Louise, Laureen, Jeffrey Alan, Cynthia T. Crenshaw. AB, Oberlin Coll., 1955; MD, Case-Western Res. U., 1959. Diplomate Am. Bd. Ob-Gyn. Rotating intern Univ. Hosps. of Cleve., 1959-60, resident in ob-gyn, 1960-64; med. officer USPHS, 1964; obstetrician-gynecologist USPHS Indian Health Service, Tahlequah, Okla., 1964-66; epidemic intelligence service officer Bur. Epidemiology, Ctrs. for Disease Control, Atlanta, 1966-67, dir. family planning evaluation div., 1967-80, asst. dir. for sci., 1980-82, acting dir. Ctr. for Health Promotion and Edn., 1982, dir. epidemiology program office, 1982-88, med. epidemiologist Office of Dir., 1988-90, asst. dir. for acad. programs, pub. health practice program office, 1990-97; clin. assoc. prof. ob.-gyn. Emory U. Sch. Medicine, Atlanta, 1997-98. Clin. asst. prof. ob-gyn Emory U. Sch. Medicine, Atlanta, 1966-80, clin. assoc. prof., 1980—, also clin. assoc. prof. preventive medicine and community health, adj. assoc. prof. sociology Coll. Arts and Scis., 1977-90; adj. assoc. prof. pub. health Sch. Pub. Health, 1990—; clin. prof. pub. health and community medicine Morehouse Sch. Medicine, Atlanta, 1990—; mem. Nat. Sleep Disorders Rsch. Commn., 1990—; mem. adv. com. on oral contraception WHO, Geneva, 1974-77, mem. adv. com. maternal and child health, 1982-88; lectr. in field Editor: (monograph) Venereal Infections; assoc. editor: Maxcy-Rosenau Textbook of Public Health and Preventive Medicine, 13th edit., 1992; contbr. articles to profl. jours. Chmn. Dekalb County Schs. com. on instruction programs, subcom. on health, phys. edn. and safety, (Ga.), 1967-68; active Ga. State Soccer Coaches Assn., Atlanta, 1973-79, DeKalb County YMCA Josiah Macy Found. fellow, 1956-58; NIH grantee, 1961-64; recipient Superior Service award, 1974, Meritorious Service medal USPHS, 1984, Disting. Service medal, 1988; Carl S. Shultz Population award APHA, 1976, medal of Excellence Ctrs. for Disease Control, 1984. Fellow Am. Coll. Ob-Gyn (chmn. community health com. 1974-77), Am. Coll. Preventive Medicine, Am. Coll. Epidemiol.; mem. Am. Epidemiologic Soc., Internat. Epidemiologic Assn., Assn. Tchrs, Preventive Medicine (bd. dirs. 1988-89), Am. Pub. Health Assn. (governing council 1976-78), Assn. Planned Parenthood Profls., Population Assn. Am., Sierra Club Avocations: photography, camping.

TYLER, CATHIE ANN, artist, educator; d. Robert Udell Tyler and Lillian Estelle McLean Tyler; 1 child, Russell Warren Spearman. BA in Art Edn., U. North Tex., Denton, 1967, MFA, 1977. Cert. in edn. Tex., 1967. Tchr. wayside mid. sch. ISD, 1967—70, tchr. strickland mid. sch., 1970—77; art instr. Paris Jr. Coll., Tex., 1980—, divsn. chair, fine arts, 1998—. Pres. Tex. Assn. Schs. Art, 2008—. Mem.: Artist Guild Lamar County (pres. 2000—01). Avocation: gardening. Office: Paris Junior Coll 2400 Clarksville St Paris TX 75460 Business E-Mail: ctyler@parisjc.edu.

TYLER, DAVID EARL, veterinary medical educator; b. Carlisle, Iowa, July 12, 1928; s. Guy Earl and Beatrice Virginia (Slack) T.; m. Alice LaVon Smith, Sept. 6, 1952; children: John William, Anne Elizabeth. BS, Iowa State U., 1953, D.V.M., 1957, PhD, 1963; MS, Purdue U., 1960. Instr. dept. vet. sci. Purdue U., 1957-60; asst. prof. dept. pathology Coll. Vet. Medicine, Iowa State U., 1960-63, asso. prof., 1963-66; prof., head dept. pathology and parasitology Coll. Vet. Medicine, U. Ga., 1966-71, head dept. pathology, 1971-79, prof., 1971-91, prof. emeritus, 1991—; ret., 1991. Co-founder internat. vet. pathology slide bank, 1984, co-dir., 1984-98; apptd. discussant Charles L. Davis Found. for Advancement Vet. Pathology, 1977-91. Cub Scout master, 1967-69, scout com. chmn., 1970-72; elder Disciples of Christ Ch., 1968—, chmn. ch. bd., 1973-74, 92-94; mem. citizens com. to County Bd. Edn., 1968-70; bd. dirs. Christian Coll., Ga., 1974-77. With AUS, 1946-48. Recipient Borden award Gail Borden Co., 1956, Norden Disting. Teaching award Norden Labs., 1964, 69, 81, 85, 91, Prof. of Yr. award Coll. Vet. Medicine, Iowa State U., 1965, Outstanding Prof. award Coll. Vet. Medicine, U. Ga., 1970, 76, 80-81, 83, 86, 87-88, 90, Joshia Meigs Teaching award, 1985, Stange award Coll. Vet. Med., Iowa State U., 1987, Phi Zeta Teaching award, 1985, N.Am. Outstanding Tchr. award, 1991, Omicron Delta Kappa Outstanding Prof. award U. Ga., 1981, Harold W. Casey award C.L. Davis Found., 1995. Mem. AVMA, Farm House, Am. Coll. Vet. Pathologists (mem. council 1975-77, exam. com. 1982-85), Am. Assn. Vet. Med. Colls. (chmn. com. teaching-learning materials 1975-77), Nat. Program for Instructional Devel. in Vet. Pathology (adv. com. 1976-77), Aghon, Sigma Xi, Phi Eta Sigma, Alpha Zeta, Gamma Sigma Delta, Phi Kappa Phi, Phi Zeta (chpt. sec.-treas. 1982-84), Omega Tau Sigma. Home: 160 Sunny Brook Dr Athens GA 30605-3348

TYLER, H. RICHARD, physician; b. Bklyn., Oct. 16, 1927; s. Max M. and Beatrice F. T.; m. Joyce Colby, June 17, 1951; children: Kenneth, Karen, Douglas, Lori. AB, Syracuse U., 1947; BS in Medicine, Washington U., 1951, MD, 1951; MA (hon.), Harvard U., 1989. Diplomate Am. Bd. Neurology and Psychiatry. Intern Peter Bent Brigham Hosp., Boston, 1951-52; resident in neurology Boston City Hosp., 1952-54; public health fellow Neurol. Inst., Queen's Sq., London, Salpêtriére, Paris, 1954-55; asst. in pediatrics and neurology Johns Hopkins Hosp., Balt., 1955-56; neurologist Peter Bent Brigham Hosp., Boston, 1956-74; asst. in neurology Harvard Med. Sch., Boston, 1956-59, assoc. in neurology, 1959-61, from instr. to prof., 1961—98, prof. emeritus, 1998—. Sr. physician Brigham and Women's Hosp., Boston, 1974—, dir. neurol. svc., 1979-88. Co-editor: Current Neurology I and II, 1979, 80; mem. editorial bd.: Jour. Neurology, 1979-84, Classics on Neurology and Neurosurgery Libr., 1983; contbr. articles to profl. jours. Trustee Brookline Pub. Libr., 1970-2001, chmn. bd. trustees, 1985-86, 90-91. Served with U.S. Army, 1946-47. Mem. Am. Neurol. Assn.(hon.), Am. Acad. Neurology (hon.), Mass. Med. Soc. Office: 1 Brookline Pl Ste 503 Brookline MA 02445-7224 Office Phone: 617-735-8720. Personal E-mail: Htyler1798@aol.com.

TYLER, JOHN DUKE, psychologist, educator; b. Nashville, Nov. 30, 1943; s. John Duke and Eleanora (Hammond) Tyler; m. Shirley Kay Montgomery; 1 child, Wade McLeod. BA, Vanderbilt U., 1965; PhD, U. Tex., Austin, 1970. Bd. cert. diplomate Am. Bd. Profl. Psychology. Prof. psychology U. ND, Grand Forks, 1970—2006; dir. Family Inst., Grand Forks, 1980—2006; prof. emeritus psychology, 2006—. Dir., Psychol. Svcs. Ctr. U. ND, Grand Forks, 1979—98. Contbr. articles to profl. jours. Fellow: Acad. Clin. Psychology; mem.: APA, N.D. Psychol. Assn. (pres. 1982—83).

TYLER, JOHN EDWARD, III, lawyer; b. Kansas City, Mo. BA, U. Notre Dame, 1986, JD, 1989. Bar: Mo. 1989, Kans. 1990. From assoc. to ptnr. Lathrop & Gage L.C., Kansas City, 1989-99; gen. counsel, sec. Ewing Marion Kauffman Found., Kansas City, 1999—, chief ethics officer, 2004—. Adj. prof. Rockhurst U., Kansas City, 2000—; bd. advisors Nat. Ctr. Philanthropy and Law, NYU, 2003-06; bd. dirs. Kauffman Scholars, Inc., Kansas City, sec., 2003—; bd. dirs. UEP Gulf Coast, Inc., Kansas City, sec., 2006-07, chair 2007-; bd. dirs. Urban Entrepeneur Partnership, Inc., sec., 2006-07, chair 2007-; bd. dirs. Kauffman Innovation Network, Inc., Kansas City, 2005—, chair, 2006—. Co-Author How Publicis Private Philanthropy? Separately Reality from Myth; co-author: How Public is Private Philanthropy? Seperating Myth From Reality, 2009 Contbr. articles to profl. jours. Pres. Genesis Sch., Kansas City, 1995-97; pres. Archbishop O'Hara H.S., Kansas City, 1994-97, bd. dirs.; pres. Sch. Bd. Diocese of Kansas City-St. Joseph, 2002-2004; chmn. tax increment fin. commn. city of Raytown, Mo., 1997-99; bd. dirs. Ctr. for Mgmt. Assistance, Kansas City, pres., 1999-2001. Recipient Bernie Hoffman award Cmty. Svc. Awards Found., 1997; named Man of Yr. Leukemia Soc., Kansas City, 1998, Best of the Bar, Kansas City Bus. Jour., 2004. Mem. ABA, Mo. Bar Assn. (Thomas D. Cochran award for cmty. svc. 1995), Kans. Bar Assn., Kansas City Met. Bar Assn. (Young Lawyer of Yr. 1998). Home: 2420 SW Wintercreek Ct Lees Summit MO 64081-4085 Office: Ewing Marion Kauffman Found 4801 Rockhill Rd Kansas City MO 64110-2046 Office Phone: 816-932-1293.

TYLER, JOHN RANDOLPH, lawyer; b. Canandaigua, NY, Aug. 3, 1934; s. John Randolph and Helen McGregor (Tewinkle) T.; m. Carroll Smith, Apr. 1, 1962 (div. Sept. 28, 1981); children: John R. III, Carroll Barrett; m. Janet MacAdam, June 5, 1982. BA cum laude, Amherst Coll., 1956; JD, Harvard U., 1963. Bar: N.Y. 1983. Assoc. Nixon, Hargrave, Devans & Doyle, Rochester, N.Y., 1963-70, ptnr., 1971-97; ret., 1998. Contbr. articles to profl. jours. Bd. dirs. Geva Theater, 1990-2003, treas., 1993-96, Flower City Habitat, 1992-2003, Fin. Inst., Inc., 2000-09, Bath Nat. Bank, 2002-05; Lt. USNR, 1956-59. Mem. ABA, N.Y. State Bar Assn. (chmn. exec. com. bus. corp. banking sect. 1981-82, ho. of dels. 1984-86, 95-98, opinion com. 1986-98), Chi Psi., Genesee Valley Club (Rochester), Adirondack League Club. Republican. Epicopalian. Avocations: sailing, skiing. Home: 25 Oak Ln Rochester NY 14610-3133 Home Phone: 585-381-0253.

TYLER, LIV, actress; b. Portland, Maine, July 1, 1977; d. Steven Tyler (lead singer: Aerosmith) and Bebe Buell; m. Royston Langdon, Mar. 25, 2003 (separated 2008); 1 child, Milo William. Spokesperson Givenchy Perfume and Cosmetics. Actress (films): Silent Fall, 1994, Heavy, 1995, Empire Records, 1995, Stealing Beauty, 1996, That Thing You Do!, 1996, Inventing the Abbotts, 1997, U-Turn, 1997, Armageddon, 1998, Onegin, 1999 (Best Fgn. Actress, Russian Guild Film Critics, 1999), The Little Black Book, 1999, Cookie's Fortune, 1999, Plunkett & MacLeane, 1999, Dr. T & the Women, 2001, One Night at McCool's, 2001, Lord of the Rings: The Fellowship of the Ring, 2001 (Best Acting Ensemble, Phoenix Film Critics Soc., 2002, 2003), The Lord of the Rings: The Two Towers, 2002, The Lord of the Rings: The Return of the King, 2003 (Best Acting by an Ensemble, Nat. Bd. Review, 2003, Best Acting Ensemble, Broadcast Film Critics Assn., 2004, Outstanding Performance by Cast in a Motion Picture, SAG, 2004), Jersey Girl, 2004, Lonesome Jim, 2005, Reign Over Me, 2007, Smother, 2007, The Strangers, 2008. The Incredible Hulk, 2008; appeared in Aerosmith's music video, Crazy, 1994. Office: c/o Creative Artists Agy 9830 Wilshire Blvd Beverly Hills CA 90212-1804*

TYLER, LLOYD JOHN, retired lawyer; b. Aurora, Ill., May 28, 1924; s. Lloyd J. and Dorothy M. (Curtis) T.; m. Inez Chappell Busener, Feb. 25, 1970; children by previous marriage: Barbara Tyler Miller, John R., Benjamin C., Robert B., Amy C. Tomas. BA, Beloit Coll., 1948; JD, U. Mich., 1951. Bar: Ill. 1951, Mich. 1951. Mem. firm Sears, Streit, Tyler and Dreyer and predecessors, Aurora, 1951-62, Tyler and Hughes P.A., Aurora, 1962-99; ret. Lectr., spkr. on profl. subjects, 1964—. Contbr. chpts. to profl. books, articles to profl. jours. Democratic precinct committeeman, 1954-59; mem. Batavia (Ill.) Sch. Bd., 1959-62. Served with USAAF, 1943-46. Fellow Am. Bar Found.; mem. ABA (ho. of dels. 1975-79), Ill. Bar Assn. (gov. 1970-78, pres. 1978-79, chmn. legis. com. 1980, task force on alternative forms of legal service 1981-82, long range planning com. 1982-88, fed. judiciary appointment com. 1984-90, spl. com. on merit selection 1987—), Ill. Bar Found. (pres. 1972-75), Ill. Inst. Continuing Legal Edn. (dir. 1971-75, 77-79), Ill. Lawyers Polit. Action Com. (trustee 1982—, chmn. 1987-88), Soc. Trial Lawyers Ill., Appellate Lawyers Assn., Phi Beta Kappa, Omicron Delta Kappa. Presbyterian. Home and Office: 701 Fargo Blvd Geneva IL 60134-3227 Office Phone: 630-232-8575.

TYLER, MICHAEL ROBERT, lawyer; b. Hollywood, Calif., May 20, 1956; m. Christine D. von Wrangel. BA in history, UCLA, 1979, MA in history, 1980; JD, Loyola Law Sch., LA, 1983; LLM in comparative law, Fitzwilliam Coll., Cambridge U., 1986. Bar: Calif. 1984. Law clk. to the Hon. Arthur Alcaron US Ct. Appeals (9th Cir.), San Francisco, 1987—88; assoc. Heller Ehrman White & McAuliffe, LA, 1991—95; sr. corp. counsel internat. Northrop Grumman Corp., LA, 1995—2000; v.p., group counsel for Europe, Middle East, and Africa ops. Gateway Inc., London, 2000—02, v.p. law for procurement activities Irvine, Calif., 2002—03, v.p., asst. gen. counsel, 2003—04, sr. v.p., gen. counsel, sec., 2004—05, sr. v.p., chief legal & adminstrv. officer, 2005—07; exec. v.p., gen. counsel Sanmina-SCI Corp., San Jose, Calif., 2007—. Mem.: State Bar Calif. (chair internat. law sect. 1999), ABA (editor-in-chief European Law Bulletin 1989—91, chair European law com. of internat. law and practice sect. 1998). Office: Sanmina-SCI Corp 2700 N 1st St San Jose CA 95134

TYLER, PEGGY LYNNE BAILEY, retired lawyer; b. Seattle, Oct. 15, 1948; d. John Thomas and Doris Mae (Lindgren) Bailey; m. Tom Kenneth Newton, May 25, 1975 (div. 1980); m. Allan Gregory Lambert, Aug. 3, 1980 (div. May 1996); m. Charles Kevin Tyler, Sept. 12, 1997; children: Eli Raven, Joshua Alec. BA in Psychology, Beloit Coll., 1970; MS in Counseling Psychology, Ill. Inst. Tech., 1973; JD, Syracuse U., NY, 1978. Bar: D.C. 1983., Mich., 2009. Mental health specialist Ill. Dept. Mental Health, Chgo., 1971-72; mem. rsch. faculty Cornell U., Ithaca, N.Y., 1973-75; assoc. O'Connor, Sovocool, Pfann and Greenburg, Ithaca, 1978, Dacy, Richin & Meyers, Silver Spring, Md., 1979-81; ins. adminstr. Nat. Assn. Broadcasters, Washington, 1981-86, dir. ins. programs, 1986-90; assoc. gen. counsel Architect of the Capitol, Washington, 1990—2006, ret., 2006. Co-author, editor: Broadcaster's Property and Liability Insurance Buying Guide, 1989. Bd. dirs. Hartford-Thayer Condominium Assn., 1994-2006, pres., 1995-96, sec., 1996-2000, treas., 2000-05. Mem. D.C. Bar Assn. (mem. steering com. of arts entertainment, sports law sect. 1989-90, sect. editor newsletter 1989-90), State Bar Mich. Independent. Jewish. Avocations: antiques, gourmet cooking, ballet. Home Phone: 616-607-9217; Office Phone: 240-216-8287. Business E-Mail: pctyler@charter.net.

TYLER, RALPH SARGENT, III, lawyer; b. Cleve., Feb. 7, 1947; s. Ralph Sargent Jr. and Marion (Clark) T. BA, U. Ill., 1969; JD, Case Western Res. U., 1972; LLM, Harvard U., 1977. Bar: Mass. 1972, Mich. 1973, Ohio 1978, D.C. 1981, Md. 1982, U.S. Dist. Ct. Mass. 1973, U.S. Dist. Ct. (we. dist.) Mich. 1973, U.S. Dist. Ct. (no. dist.) Ohio 1978, U.S. Dist. Ct. D.C. 1981, U.S. Dist. Ct. Md. 1982, U.S. Ct. Appeals (1st, 4th, 6th and D.C. cirs.) 1982, U.S. Supreme Ct. 1981. Atty. Greater Boston Legal Services, 1973-76, Mass. Law Reform Inst., Boston, 1977-78; asst. prof. law Cleve. State U., 1978-80; lectr. law Nat. U. Singapore, 1980-81; asst. atty. gen. State of Md., Balt., 1982-91, chief of litigation, 1986-91, dep. atty. gen., 1991-96; ptnr. Hogan L. Hartson, LLP, Balt., 1996—2004; city atty. Law Dept., Balt., 2004—06; chief counsel Gov. Md., 2007; commr. Md. Insurance, 2007—. Mem. Balt. City Pub. Sch. Bd., 2003—04. Mem. ABA, Md. Bar Assn. Home: 205 Gittings Ave Baltimore MD 21212-2504 Office Phone: 410-468-2090. Office Fax: 410-468-2019. Business E-Mail: rtyler@mdinsurance.state.md.us.

TYLER, RONNIE CURTIS, museum director, art historian; b. Temple, Tex., Dec. 29, 1941; s. Jasper J. and Melba Curtis (James) T.; m. Paula Eyrich, Aug. 24, 1974. BSE, Abilene Christian Coll., TEx., 1964; MA, Tex. Christian U., 1966, PhD (Univ. fellow), 1968; DHL, Austin Coll., 1986. Instr. history Austin Coll., Sherman, Tex., 1967-68, asst. prof., 1968-69; curator history Amon Carter Mus., Ft. Worth, 1969, dir. publications, asst. dir. history and publications, asst. dir. collections and programs, 1984—86, dir., 2006—; prof. history U. Tex., Austin, 1986—2006. Adj. prof. history Tex. Christian U., 1971-72; dir. Tex. State Hist. Assn., 1986-2005; cons. visual materials Western. Am. art. Author: Santiago Vidaurri and the Confederacy, 1973, The Big Bend: The Last Texas Frontier, 1975, The Image of America in Caricature and Cartoon, 1975, The Cowboy, 1975, The Mexican War: A Lithographic Record, 1974, The Rodeo Photographs of John Addison Stryker, 1978, Visions of America: Pioneer Artists in a New Land, 1983, Views of Texas: The Watercolors of Sarah Ann Hardinge, 1852-56, 1988, Nature's Classics: John James Audubon's Birds and Animals, 1992, Audubon's Great National Work: The Royal Octavo Edition of the Birds of America, 1993, Prints of the West, 1994, Alfred Jacob Miller: Artist as Explorer, 1999; (with Paula Eyrich Tyler) Texas Museums: A Guidebook, 1983; editor: (with Lawrence R. Murphy) The Slave Narratives of Texas, 1974, Posada's Mexico, 1979, Alfred Jacob Miller: Artist on the Oregon Trail, 1982, Wanderings in the Southwest in 1855 (J.D.B. Stillman), 1990, Prints and Printmakers of Texas, 1997. Pres. Tarrant County (Tex.) Hist. Soc., 1975-77. Good Neighbor Commn. scholar Instituto Tecnologico Monterrey, Mex., 1967; Am. Philos. Soc. grantee, 1970-71; recipient H. Bailey Carroll award, 1974; Coral H. Tullis award, 1976, Alonso de León medal Sociedad Nuevoleonsa História Geografía y Estadística, 2002. Mem. Am. Antiquarian Soc., Tex. Inst. Letters (Friends of Dallas Pub. Libr. award), Philos. Soc. Tex. (sec. 1990), Phi Beta Kappa. Office: Amon Carter Museum 3501 Camp Bowie Blvd Fort Worth TX 76107-2695 Home Phone: 817-377-1297; Office Phone: 817-989-5095. Business E-Mail: ron.tyler@cartermuseum.org.

TYLER, STEVEN (STEPHEN VICTOR TALLARICO), singer; b. Yonkers, NY, Mar. 26, 1948; s. Victor and Susan (Blancha) Tallarico; 1 child Liv (with Bebe Buell); m. Cyrinda Foxe, Sept. 1, 1978 (div. 1987); 1 child, Mia Abigail; m. Teresa Barrick, May 28, 1988 (div. 2006); children: Chelsea Anna, Taj Monroe D (hon.), Berklee Coll. Music, 2003, U. Mass., 2005. Lead singer Aerosmith, 1970—. Singer: (albums with Aerosmith) Aerosmith, 1973, Get Your Wings, 1974, Toys in the Attic, 1975, Rocks, 1976, Draw the Line, 1977, Live Bootleg, 1978, Night in the Ruts, 1979, Greatest Hits, 1980, Rock in a Hard Place, 1982, Done with Mirrors, 1985, Classics Live!, 1986, Classics Live! Vol. 2, 1987, Permanent Vacation, 1987, Gems, 1988, Pump, 1989, Pandora's Box, 1991, Get a Grip, 1993, Box of Fire, 1994, Big Ones, 1994, Nine Lives, 1997, A Little South of Sanity, 1998, Just Push Play, 2001, Young Lust: The Aerosmith Anthology, 2001, Oh, Yeah!: The Ultimate Aerosmith Hits, 2002, Honkin' On Bobo, 2004, Rockin' the Joint, 2005, Devil's Got A New Disguise, 2006; co-author (with Aerosmith & Stephen Davis): Walk This Way: The Autobiography of Aerosmith, 1997; performer: (films) Sgt. Pepper Lonely Heart's Club Band, 1978, Aerosmith: Live Texxas Jam '78, 1989, Aerosmith: Rockin' the Joint - Live at the Hard Rock Hotel, Las Vegas, 2005; actor: (films) Clubland, 1999, The Polar Express, 2004; appeared in (films) The Decline of Western Civilization Part II: The Metal Years, 1988, voice only (TV appearances) The Simpsons, 1989. Named to The Rock and Roll Hall of Fame (as mem. of Aerosmith), 2001.

TYLER, W(ILLIAM) ED, finance company executive; b. Cleve., Nov. 3, 1952; s. Ralph Tyler and Edith (Green) Kauer; m. Vickie Sue Boggs, Feb. 7, 1976; children: Stacia Leigh, Adam William. BSEE, Ind. Inst. Tech., 1974; MBA, Ind. U., 1977; postgrad., Harvard U., 1981, Baruch U., 1988. From electronic engr. to exec. v.p. R.R. Donnelley & Sons Co., Warsaw, Ind., 1974—95, exec. v.p. & chief tech. officer, 1995—98; CEO, pres. Moore Corp. Ltd., 1998—2001, Willoughby Capitol, Lake Forest, Ill., 2001; CEO Ideapoint Ventures, 2002—. Home: 1000 N Lake Shore Plz Ste 45A Chicago IL 60611 Office Phone: 847-567-7111.

TYLER, WILLIAM HOWARD, JR., advertising executive, educator; b. Elizabethton, Tenn., May 21, 1932; s. William Howard and Ethel Margaret (Schueler) T.; m. Margery Moss, Aug. 31, 1957; children: William James, Daniel Moss. Student, Iowa State U., 1950-52, U. Iowa, 1952; AB in Lit., BJ in Advt., U. Mo., 1958, MA in Journalism, 1966. Advt. mgr. Rolla (Mo.) Daily News, 1958-59; instr. sch. journalism U. Mo., Columbia, 1959-61; copy writer, then v.p. copy dir. D'Arcy Advt. Agy., St. Louis, 1961-67; writer, producer, creative supr. Gardner Advt. Co., St. Louis, 1967-69; sr. v.p., creative dir. D'Arcy, McManus, Masius, St. Louis, 1969-77; exec. v.p., creative dir. Larson Bateman Advt. Agy., Santa Barbara, Calif., 1977-80; v.p. advt. Pizza Hut, Inc., Wichita, Kans., 1980-82; v.p., creative dir. Frye-Sills/Y&R, Denver, 1980; exec. v.p., creative dir. Gardner Advt. Co., St. Louis, 1982-88; exec. v.p., ptnr., creative dir. Parker Group, St. Louis, 1988-91; pres. Tylertoo Prodns., St. Louis, 1991—. Assoc. prof. St. Louis U., 1993-2003, prof., 2003—. Mng. editor St. Louis Advt. Mag., 1992-95. Trustee Blackburn Coll., Carlinville, Ill., 1983—84; bd. advisors U. Mo. Journalism Sch., 1986—91. 1st lt. USMC, 1952—55, Japan, Korea. Recipient Faculty and Excellence Award, 2001, 2002, Outstanding Advisor awards, 1999, 2007; named AAF 9th Dist. Educator of Yr., 1998, 2007. Mem. U. Mo. Alumni Assn. (bd. dirs. 1969-70), Advt. Club Greater St. Louis, Golden Key (hon.), Mensa, Kappa Tau Alpha (hon.). Episcopalian. Office: Saint Louis U Dept Comm Xavier 300 3733 W Pine Blvd Saint Louis MO 63108-3305 Office Phone: 314-977-3190. Business E-Mail: tylerwh@slu.edu.

TYMKOVICH, TIMOTHY MICHAEL, federal judge; b. Denver, Nov. 2, 1956; married; 2 children. BA, Co. Coll., 1979; JD, U. Colo. Sch. Law, 1982. Clk. Co. Supreme Ct., 1982—83; assoc. Davis, Graham, & Stubbs, 1983—89; of counsel Bradley Campbel Carney & Madsen, 1990—91; solicitor gen. Office of Co. Atty. Gen., 1991—96; ptnr. Hale Hackstaff Tymkovich & ErkenBrack, 1996—2003; judge US Ct. of Appeals (10th cir), 2003—. Mem.: ABA, Internat. Soc. Barristers, Colo. Bar Found., Am. Law Inst. Office: Byron White US Courthouse 1823 Stout St Denver CO 80257*

TYNAN, WILLIAM DOUGLAS, psychologist; b. Meriden, Conn., Jan. 14, 1953; s. William Douglas and Frances Tynan; m. Catherine Albergotti, Sept. 18, 1987; children: Philip Douglas, Caroline Frances. PhD, Binghamton U., Binghamton, NY, 1978—83; MS, U. of Conn., Storrs, CT, 1976—78; BA, Boston U., Boston, MA, 1970—74. Diplomate in clin. health psychology Am. Bd. Profl. Psychology, 1994, child & adolescent clin. psychology Am. Bd. Profl. Psychology, 2004; lic. psychologist DE, 2001. Chief health psychologist Nemours Health & Prevention Svcs., Newark, Del., 2008—; psychologist AI du Pont Hosp. Children, Wilmington, Del., 2001—08. Bd. mem. Del. Early Childhood Coun., Newark, 2003—09, Del. Epilepsy Found., Wilmington, 2001—09, Com. Evaluation Head Start, Wash., 2002—06; pres. Am. Acad. Clin. Health Psychology, Chapel Hill, NC, 2007—09; bd. mem. Am. Bd. Clin. Health Psychology, Chapel Hill, NC, 1994—2009, Soc. Pediatric Psychology, Wash., 2001—09. Grant, Health Resources Svcs. Adminstrn. HHS, 2002—. Fellow: APA. Democrat. Achievements include development of co-location model of providing Psychological services in inner city primary care Pediatric offices. Avocations: bicycling, tennis, swimming. Office: Nemours Health & Prevention Svcs 252 Chapman Rd Newark DE 19702 Office Fax: 302-444-9200. Business E-Mail: dtynan@nemours.org.

TYNE, GERALD ROBERT, history professor; s. Gaila Jo Tyne. EdM, Ill. State U., Normal, 1986. Tchr. Streator HS, Ill., 2004—. 4th july com. mem., Streator, 1990—2008. Conservative. Baptist. Home: 1306 Johns Street Streator IL 61364 Office: Streator High School 202 W Lincoln Ave Streator IL Personal E-mail: rob_tyne@hotmail.com.

TYNER, LEE REICHELDERFER, lawyer; b. Annapolis, Md., Mar. 12, 1946; d. Thomas Elmer and Eleanor Frances Reichelderfer; m. Carl Frederick Tyner, Aug. 31, 1968; children: Michael Frederick, Rachel Christine, Elizabeth Frances. BA, St. John's Coll., 1968; MS, U. Wash., 1970; JD, George Washington U., 1975. Bar: DC, US Dist. Ct. (DC), US Ct. Appeals (4th cir., 1st cir., 9th cir., DC cir., 5th cir., 8th cir., 11th cir., 10th cir.), US Ct. Claims, US Supreme Ct. Profl. staff US Senate Commerce Com., Washington, 1970-72; trial atty. Land and Natural Resources div. US Dept. Justice, Washington, 1975-85; atty. Office of Gen. Counsel US EPA, Washington, 1985—. Bd. dirs. Grace Episcopal Day Sch., Silver Spring, Md., 1987-89, vestry Grace Episcopal Ch., 1997-2003, 2004-07, sec., 2004-07; den leader, cubmaster Boy Scouts Am., Silver Spring, 1987-91. Recipient Bronze medals, US EPA, 1988, 1992, 2002, 2003, 2006, 2008. Mem.: Order of the Coif. Episcopalian. Home: 1401 Geranium St NW Washington DC 20012 Office: US EPA 2366A 1200 Pennsylvania Ave NW Washington DC 20460 Personal E-mail: skildpadde@aol.com. Business E-Mail: tyner.lee@epa.gov.

TYNER, MCCOY (ALFRED MCCOY SULAIMON SAUD TYNER), jazz pianist, composer; b. Phila., Dec. 11, 1938; Mem. Art Farmer and Benny Golson's Jazztet, 1959, John Coltrane Quartet, 1960-65; ind. pianist, 1965—. Musician: (albums) (with John Coltrane) A Love Supreme, Live at the Village Vanguard, Coltrane, Meditations, (with Jackie McLean) It's About Time, Echoes of a Friend, Enlightenment, Atlantis, Passion Dance, Together, 4 x 4, 13th House, Dimensions, Just Feelin', Hancock/Jarrett, Key of Soul, McCoy Tyner: The Earthly Trios, Vol. 6, Great Moments with McCoy Tyner, Reevaluations: the Impulse Years, Today and Tomorrow, Live at Newport, McCoy Tyner Live at Newport, 1963, McCoy Tyner Plays Ellington, 1964, Jazz Profile, 1967, Expansions, 1968, Cosmos, 1969, Extensions, 1970, Echoes of a Friend, Song for My Lady, Sahara, Reflections: A Retrospective, 1972, Atlantis, Sama Layuca, 1974, Trident, 1975, Focal Point, Four Times Four, 1976, Supertrios, Inner Voices, 1977, Together, The Greeting, Passion Dance, 1978, Horizon, 1979, 4 X 4, 1980, 13th House, 1981, La Leyenda de la Hora, Looking Out, 1982, Dimensions, 1984, Double Trios, 1986, Bon Voyage, Tribute to John Coltrane, Live at the Musicians Exchange Cafe, What's New?, 1987, Uptown/Downtown, Inception/Nights of Ballads of Blues, Revelations, The Real McCoy, 1988, Live at Sweet Basil, Live at Sweet Basil, Vols. 1&2, Things Ain't What They Used To Be, 1989, Remembering John, Double Exposure, 44th Street Suite, Turning Point, Blue Bossa, Soliloquy, New York Reunion, 1991, Manhattan Moods, Hot Licks: Giant Steps, Journey, Solar, 1993, Prelude & Sonata, 1994, Infinity, Live in Warsaw, 1995, What the World Needs Now: The Music of Burt Bacharach, Autumn Mood, 1997, McCoy Tyner & the Latin All-Stars, New Best One, Music of Burt Bacharach, 1999, McCoy Tyner Honors Jazz Piano Legends of the 20th Century, 2000, Summer Time, 2001, McCoy Tyner Plays John Coltrane: Live at the Village Vanguard, 2001, Port au Blues, 2002, Suddenly, 2002, Land of Giants, 2003, Hip Toe, Modern Jazz Archive, Illuminations, Monk's Dream, Counterpoints: Live in Tokyo, 2004, Latin All Stars, 2006, McCoy Tyner Quartet, 2007, Afro Blue, 2007. Recipient Grammy award for Best Instrumental Jazz Performance, Individual or Group, 1989, 1996, Grammy award for Best Large Jazz Ensemble Performance, 1993, 1995, Jazz Master award, Nat. Endowment for the Arts, 2002. Office: Blue Note Mgmt Group 131 W 3rd St New York NY 10012

TYNER, NEAL EDWARD, retired insurance company executive; b. Grand Island, Nebr., Jan. 30, 1930; s. Edward Raymond and Lydia Dorothea (Kruse) T.; children: Karen Tyner Redrow, Morgan. BBA, U. Nebr., 1956. Jr. analyst Bankers Life Nebr., Lincoln, 1956-62, asst. v.p. securities, 1962-67, v.p. securities, treas., 1967-69, fin. v.p., treas., 1970-72, sr. v.p. fin., treas., 1972-83, pres., chief exec. officer, 1983-87, chmn., pres., chief exec. officer, 1987-88; chmn., CEO Ameritas Life Ins., Lincoln, 1988—95; pres. Net Cons., Paradise Valley, Ariz., 1995—. Bd. dirs. Union Bank & Trust Co. Trustee U. Nebr. Found. Capt. USMC, 1950-54, Korea. Fellow: CFAs. Lutheran. Avocations: tennis, computers. Office: 8225 N Golf Dr Paradise Valley AZ 85253-2716

TYNER, WALLACE EDWARD, agricultural economics educator; b. Orange, Tex., Mar. 21, 1945; s. Richard D. and Jeanne (Gullahorn) T.; m. Jean M. Young, May 2, 1970; children: Davis, Jeffrey. BS in Chemistry, Tex. Christian U., 1966; MA in Econs., U. Md., 1972, PhD in Econs., 1977. Vol. Peace Corps., India, 1966-68, math, sci., engl. skill desk chief Washington, 1968-70; grad. teacher asst. U. Md., Balt., 1971-73; assoc. scientist Earth Satellite Corp., Washington, 1973-74; rsch. assoc. Cornell U., Ithaca, NY, 1974-77; asst. prof., assoc. prof. natural resource econs. and internat. devel. policy Purdue U., West Lafayette, Ind., 1977-84, prof., asst. dept. head, 1983-88, dept. head, 1989—2002. Cons. UN Food and Agrl. Orgn., Rome, Office Tech. Assessment, Washington, U.S. Dept. Interior, Washington, OECD, Paris, World Bank, Washington, USDA, Washington. Author: Energy Resources and Economic Development in India, 1978, A Perspective on U.S. Farm Problems and Agricultural Policy, 1987. Recipient Disting. Policy Contbn. award, Am. Agrl. Economics Assn., 2005. Mem. Am. Assn. Agrl. Economists, Am. Econs. Assn., Internat. Assn. Agrl. Economist, Sigma Xi, Gamma Sigma Delta. Home: 116 Arrowhead Dr West Lafayette IN 47906-2105 Office: Purdue U Krannert Bldg West Lafayette IN 47907-1145 Office Phone: 765-494-0199. Business E-Mail: wtyner@purdue.edu.

TYNES, ALANNA MARIE, biology professor; b. Winter Haven, Fla., Apr. 18, 1963; d. Willie Frank and Edna Denise Minshew; m. Brett Allen Tynes, June 6, 1987; children: Cameron Allen, Christian Allen, Caidyn Isabella Marie, Cassady Olivia Marie. MS, Tex. A&M U., Coll. Sta., 1992. Cert. emergency med. technician Tex., 2005. Prof. biology Lone Star Coll. Tomball, Tex., 1994—. Nutritionist, owner Holistic Goodness, Tomball, 2007—. Office: Lone Star Coll Tomball 30555 Tomball Pky Tomball TX 77375 Business E-Mail: atynes@lonestar.edu.

TYNES, ROBERT DICK, artist, educator; b. Chgo., Jan. 7, 1953; s. Marion F. and Faye Tynes Dick; m. Bette L. Bates, June 13, 1981; children: Alison Hayley, Robin Elizabeth. BA with hons. in Art, Rhodes Coll., Memphis, Tenn., 1975; MFA in Painting, East Carolina U., Greenville, NC, 1981. Lectr. art East Carolina U., 1981—82, Humboldt State U., Arcata, Calif., 1982—84; vis. asst. prof. art U. Hawaii Manoa, Honolulu, 1986—87; artist-in-residence U. NC, Asheville, 1987—91, from asst. prof. to prof. art, 1991—2004, prof. art, 2004—. Dir. S. Tucker Cooke Gallery U. NC, 1994—. Over 20 solo exhbns., over 100 group shows, one-man shows include Fay Gold Gallery, Atlanta, Ga., 2001, Lee Hansley Gallery, Raleigh, NC, 2004, Gallery at Carillon, Charlotte, NC, 2005, Blue Spiral, Asheville, NC, 2006, Represented in permanent collections Charlotte Pub. Arts Commn., IBM Corp., Field Engring. Ctr., Atlanta, Ga. Chair Black Mountain Coll. Mus. and Art Ctr., Asheville, NC, 1993—95; dir. Asheville Area Arts Coun., 1994—2002, sec., 2000—02; dir. Black Mountain Ctr. Arts, NC, 2003—04, sec., 2004. Recipient We. NC Regional Juried Exhbn. 1st prize, Asheville Art Mus., 1993; fellow, Roswell Mus. and Art Ctr., Roswell, N.Mex., 1985, 1991, Ucross Found. Residency Program, Wyo., 1986. Democrat. Unitarian Universalist. Achievements include development of original style of painting juxtaposing abstract brush marks with hyperrealistic trompe l'oeil illusionism; original style of cutout paintings. Avocations: hiking, tennis. Office: Dept of Art Univ of NC Asheville One University Heights Asheville NC 28804 Business E-Mail: rtynes@unca.edu.

TYNG, ANNE GRISWOLD, architect; b. Kuling, Kiangsi, China, July 14, 1920; d. Walworth and Ethel Atkinson (Arens) T.; 1 child, Alexandra Stevens. AB, Radcliffe Coll., 1942; M of Architecture, Harvard U., 1944; PhD, U. Pa., 1975. Assoc. Stonorov & Kahn, Architects, 1945-47; assoc. Louis I. Kahn Architect, 1947-73; pvt. practice architecture Phila., 1973—; adj. assoc. prof. architecture U. Pa. Grad. Sch. Fine Arts, 1968-96. Assoc. cons. architect Phila. Planning Commn. and Phila. Redevel. Plan, 1954; vis. disting. prof. Pratt Inst., 1979-81, vis. critic architecture, 1969; vis. critic architecture Rensselaer Poly. Inst., 1969, 78, Carnegie Mellon U., 1970, Drexel U., 1972-73, Cooper Union, 1974-75, U. Tex., Austin, 1976; lectr. Archtl. Assn., London, Xian U., China, Bath U., Eng., Mexico City, Hong Kong U., 1989, Baltic Summer Sch., Architecture and Planning, Tallinn, Estonia, Parnu, Estonia, 1993, Alicante U., Spain, 1997, Barcelona U., Spain, 1997; panel spkr. Nat. Conv. Am. Inst. Architects, N.Y.C., 1988, also univs. throughout U.S. and Can.; asst. leader People to People Archtl. del. to China, 1983; vis. artist Am. Acad., Rome, 1995; spkr. in field. Subject of films Anne G. Tyng at Parsons Sch. of Design, 1972, Anne G. Tyng at U. of Minn., 1974, Connecting, 1976, Forming the Future, 1977; interview by Robert Kirkbride, Form is Number and Number is Form, 2005; work included in Smithsonian Travelling Exhbn., 1979-81, 82, Louis I. Kahn: In the Realm of Architecture, 1990-94, Mus. Contemporary Art Travelling Exhbn., L.A., 1998—; author, editor: Louis Kahn to Anne Tyng, The Rome Letters 1953-1954, 1997; contbr. articles to profl. publs.; prin. works include Walworth Tyng Farmhouse (Hon. mention award Phila. chpt. AIA 1953); builder (with G. Yanchenko) Probability Pyramid, 1984. Fellow, Graham Found. for Advanced Study in Fine Arts, 1965, 1979—81. Fellow AIA (Brunner grantee N.Y. chpt. 1964, 83, dir., mem. exec. bd. dirs. Phila. chpt. 1976-78, John Harbeson Disting. Svc. award Phila. chpt. 1991); mem. Nat. Acad. Design (nat. academician), C.G. Jung Ctr. Phila. (planning com. 1979-97), Form Forum (co-founder, planning com. 1978-85). Democrat. Episcopalian. Home and Office: 501 Via Casitas Apt 907 Greenbrae CA 94904-1936

TYREE, ALAN DEAN, clergyman; b. Kansas City, Mo., Dec. 14, 1929; s. Clarence Tillman and Avis Ora (Gross) T.; m. Gladys Louise Omohundro, Nov. 23, 1951; children: Lawrence Wayne, Jonathan Tama, Sharon Avis. BA, U. Iowa, 1950; postgrad., U. Mo.-Columbia, 1956-58, U. Mo.-Kansas City, 1961-62. Ordained to ministry Cmty. of Christ, 1947. Appointee min., Lawrence, Kans., 1950-52; mission adminstr. (Mission Sanito), French Polynesia, 1953-64; regional adminstr. Denver, 1964-66; mem. Council Twelve Apostles, Independence, Mo., 1966-82, sec., 1980-82, mem. First Presidency, 1982-92; ret. First Presidency, 1992; pastor East 39th Street Congregation Cmty. of Christ, Independence, 2000—02. Mem. Joint Coun. and Bd. Appropriations, 1966-92; originator music appreciation broadcasts Radio Tahiti, 1962-64, Mission Sanito Radio Ministry, 1960-64; instr. Music/Arts Inst., 1992-2005, Met. C.C.'s, 1994-2005. Editor: Cantiques des Saints French-Tahitian hymnal, 1965, Exploring the Faith: A Study of Basic Christian Beliefs, 1987; mem. editing com.: Hymns of the Saints, 1981; author: The Gospel Graced by a People: A Biography of Persons in Tahiti, 1993, Evan Fry: Proclaimer of Good News, 1995, Priesthood: For Other's Sake, 1996, God: Getting to Know the Unknown, 1998. Bd. dirs. Outreach Internat. Found., 1979-82, mem. corp. body, 1982-92; mem. corp. body Independence Regional Health Ctr., 1982-92, v.p., 1983-92, bd. dirs., 1984-93; mem. bd. publs. Herald House, 1984-92; mem. corp. body Restoration Trail Found., 1982-92; chmn. Temple Art Com., 1988-94; bd. dirs. Independence Symphony Orch., 1992-96, pres., 1995-96; mem. human rels. commn. city of Independence, 1995-97, chmn., 1996-97. Recipient Elbert A. Smith Meml. award for publ. articles, 1968, 72 Mem. Phi Beta Kappa, Phi Eta Sigma. Home and Office: 3408 S Trail Ridge Dr Independence MO 64055 Office Phone: 816-373-8151. E-mail: adtyree@gmail.com.

TYREE, DONALD ANDREW, financial educator, department chairman; b. St. Louis, Nov. 19, 1930; s. Wesley F. and Dena (Krieter) T.; m. Sherry Johnson, Nov. 18, 1978; 1 son, Paul H. (dec.); children by previous marriage: Wesley G., Thomas A. BS, BA, Washington U., St. Louis, 1953, MBA, 1956; PhD in Finance, U. Tex. at Austin, 1959. Research asso. Washington U., 1953; lectr. U. Tex., 1956-59; mem. faculty St. Louis U., 1959—69, prof. fin., 1969—2000, chmn. dept., 1968—80, 1983—95, assoc. dean Sch. Bus. Adminstrn., 1973-74, prof. emeritus, 2000—. Cons. in field. Mem. St. Louis County Ins. Com., 1962-68 Author: Small Loan Industry in Texas, 1960, School Insurance Administration, 1975, Urban Residential Mortgage Financing: Lending Practices in St. Louis, 1979. Served with AUS, 1953-55. Wienhiemer fellow, 1955-56; Tex. Savs. and Loan Assn. fellow, 1956-59 Home: 14 Huntleigh Woods Saint Louis MO 63131-4818 Home Phone: 314-822-7740; Office Phone: 334-232-3800. Business E-Mail: tyreeda@slu.edu.

TYREE, REBECCA YOUNG, music educator; b. Durham, NC, Dec. 29, 1955; d. Barbara J Tyree; 1 child, Stephen Hunter Owen. MusB, Va. Commonwealth U., Richmond, 1978; MusM, U. Md., Coll. Pk. Choral dir., dept. chair Hermitage HS, Richmond; asst. prof, choral music edn. Va. Commonwealth U., 2006—. Artistic dir. and condr. Chamber Chorale Fredericksburg, Va., 1993—2003. Recipient Gilman award, Henrico County Pub. Schs., 2003; named Music Educator of Yr., 2000. Mem.: Music Educators Nat. Conf., Am. Choral Dirs. Assn. (va. chpt. pres. 2007—09).

TYRL, PAUL, mathematics professor, researcher; b. Prague, Czech Rep., Dec. 24, 1951; came to U.S., 1970, naturalized, 1978; s. Vladimir Tyrl and Marta Kocian. BA with honors, N.J. City U., 1977, MA, 1980; EdD, Rutgers U., 1987. Cert. tchr. secondary edn., higher edn. N.J. quality contr. Agfa-Perutz, Munich, 1969—70; technician AT&T, Kearny, NJ, 1970—73; acquisition libr. N.J. City U., 1973—74, supr. post office, 1974—76, dir. math. lab., instr. math., 1976—80; instr. math. Hudson County C.C., NJ, 1980—82, assoc. prof., coord. math., 1982—84; prof., chmn. math., acad. coord., curriculum dir. Sch. New Resources-New Rochelle Coll., NYC, 1984—. Rschr. Rutgers U., New Brunswick, N.J., 1980—; cons. Jersey City Bd. Edn., N.J., 1982—. Contbr. articles to profl. jours. Recipient Commemorative medal of honor, 1986. Mem. AAAS, ASCD, Nat. Coun. Tchrs. Math. (reviewer and referee), N.Y. Acad. Scis., Am. Ednl. Rsch. Assn., Math. Assn. Am., Am. Math. Assn. 2-Yr. Colls., Am. Math. Soc., Am. Mus. Natural History, Nat. Geog. Soc., Nat. Wildlife Fedn., Smithsonian Instn. Roman Catholic. Achievements include research in math. anxiety and math. problem solving.

TYRRELL, COLE BROOKS, music educator; BA, MA, Mich. State U., East Lansing, 1974. Choir dir. Benton Harbor Pub. Sch., Mich., 1969—78, Whitehall Pub. Schs., Mich., 1978—89, South Haven Pub. Schs., Mich., 1989—. Mem. adj. faculty Lake Mich. Coll., Benton Harbor, 1976—78; dir. White Lake Madrigals, Whitehall, 1982—89, Lakeland Choral Soc., St. Joseph, Mich., 1990—2000. Author: (music text) Rhythmic Sight Reading Made Easy, 2000, (music text) Sight Reading: The Fixed Do Method, 2001. Recipient Carolyn Leep scholarship, Mich. Sch. Vocal Music Assn., 1994; named Regional Coach of Yr., Mich. HS Athletic Assn., 1995, Wal-Mart Tchr. of Yr., S.W. Mich. Wal-Mart, 2000. Mem.: Nat. Assn. Tchrs. Singing, Music Educator's Nat. Conf., Am. Choral Dir.'s Assn. (life). Office: South Haven HS 600 Elkenburg St South Haven MI 49090-1999

TYRRELL, GERALD GETTYS, banker; b. Canton, China, Dec. 27, 1938; came to U.S., 1940. s. Gerald Fraser and Virginia Lee (Gettys) T.; m. Jane Haldeman, June 1961 (div. Aug. 1975); children: Gerald F., Jane N., Robert M.; m. Elizabeth Ann Drautman, Mar. 31, 1978. BA, Yale U., 1960; MA, Rutgers U., 1971. Cert. real estate financier. With 1st Nat. Bank of Louisville, 1961—89, sr. v.p., 1975—81, exec. v.p., 1981—89; pres., chmn. Churchill Mortgage Corp., 1975—77; chief fin. cons. City of Louisville Office of Downtown Devel., 1989—2000; exec. v.p. Univ. Group, Consultants for Bus., Prospect, 2000—06, assoc., 2006—08. Vice chmn. bd. dirs. Porcelain Metals Corp., 2001—06; assoc. Venture Resource Bus. Brokers, 2006—; adv. bd. Skyway LLC, 2007—08, chief fin. officer, 2008—, mem., bd. dirs., 2009—. Author: A Positive Approach to Financing Black Business, 1972 Trustee, treas. Patton Mus., Ft. Knox, Ky., 1970—96; mem. exec. bd. Boy Scouts Am., 1983—; bd. dirs. The Louisville Orch., 1984—90, Crane Ho., The Asia Inst., 1988—, pres., 1995—97; bd. dirs., chmn. fin. com. Glassworks Found., Inc., 2001—03; bd. dirs. Thomas Merton Found., 2003—05. Served to capt. US Army, 1960—68. Recipient Disting. Service Ribbon Ky. Nat. Guard, 1966 Mem. Robert Morris Assocs., Nat. Soc. Real Estate Fin. (bd. govs), Soc. Colonial Wars Commonwealth Ky. (treas. 1970-89, sec. 1996-99, gov. 2000-05), Gen. Soc. Colonial Wars (treas.

gen. 2004-07, lt. gov. gen. 2007—), Louisville Country Club, Pendennis Club. Democrat. Avocations: fine wines, tennis. Office Phone: 502-640-5892. Personal E-mail: betsyandgerald@aol.com.

TYSOE, WILFRED TJALKE, chemistry professor; b. Gainsborough, Calif., May 7, 1951; s. Wilfred Morgan Tysoe and Rimke Haven; m. Maria Cristina Justo, July 24, 1983. BSc, U. Manchester, England, 1972; MSc, U. Sydney, 1975; PhD, U. Cambridge, England, 1982. Disting. prof. chemistry UW-Milwaukee, 2007—, prof. chemistry, 1984—2006. Contbr. scientific papers. Rsch. grants, NSF, 1994—2008. Mem.: Am. Chem. Soc. (chair elect 2008—). Avocations: travel, gardening. Office: UW Milwaukee 3210 N Cramer St Milwaukee WI 53211

TYSON, CYNTHIA HALDENBY, academic administrator; b. Scunthorpe, Lincolnshire, Eng., July 2, 1937; came to U.S., 1959; d. Frederick and Florence Edna (Stacey) Haldenby; children: Marcus James, Alexandra Elizabeth. BA, U. Leeds, Eng., 1958, MA, 1959, PhD, 1971; DHL (hon.), Mary Baldwin Coll., 2003, Queens U., Charlotte, 2006. Lectr. Brit. Council, Leeds, 1959; faculty U. Tenn., Knoxville, 1959-60, Seton Hall U., South Orange, NJ, 1963-69; faculty, v.p. Queens Coll., Charlotte, NC, 1969-85; pres. Mary Baldwin Coll., Staunton, Va., 1985—2003, pres. emerita, 2003—; pres. Robert Haywood Morrison Found., 2002—. Pres. adv. cir. Queens U., Charlotte, NC, 2005—09, trustee, 2009—; WDAV radio adv. bd. Davidson (NC) Coll., 2005—. Contbr. articles to profl. jours. Mem. Va. Internat. Trade Commn., Richmond, 1987; trustee Am. Frontier Culture Mus., Va.; mem. Va. Lottery Bd., 1987-94; chair selection com. State of Va. Rhodes Scholarship Competition, 1993-97; bd. dirs. Cmty. Found. Staunton, Augusta County and Waynesboro, 1993-98; mem. adv. bd. WDAV Radio of Davidson Coll., 2005—; mem. pres.'s adv. cir. Queens U. of Charlotte, NC, 2005—. Fulbright scholar, 1959; Ford Found. grantee Harvard U., 1981; Shell Oil scholar Harvard U., 1982. Mem.: Assn. Presbyn. Colls. and Univs. (bd. dirs. 1998), So. Assn. Colls. and Schs. (vice chair 1998, pres.-elect 2001, pres. 2002), Assn. Va. Colls. and Univs. (pres. 1997—98), So. Assn. Colls. for Women (pres. 1980—81), Mary Baldwin Coll. (hon.), Phi Beta Kappa. Republican. Office: Robert Haywood Morrison Found 1373 East Morehead St Ste 2 Charlotte NC 28204-2979

TYSON, JOHN H., food products executive; b. Springdale, Ark., Sept. 5, 1953; s. Don and Jean Tyson; m. Kimberly McCoy; children: John Randal, Olivia Laine. BBA, So. Meth. U., 1975. Complex mgr. N.C. area Tyson Foods, Inc., Springdale, Ark., v.p. mktg. corp. accounts, purchasing mgr., retail sales mgr. N.E. states, pres. beef and pork divsn.; pres., chmn. Tyson Foods Inc., Springdale, 1998-00, pres., chmn., CEO, 2000—01, chmn., CEO, 2001—06, chmn., 2006—. Polit. liaison to Washington and Little Rock Tyson Foods, Inc. Bd. dirs. Area United Way; supporter Farm Aid; vol. activities for well-being and edn. of Ark. children. Named Man of Yr., Ark. Poultry Industry, 1994. Mem.: Ark. Poultry Fedn. (past pres.), Am. Meat Inst., Nat. Assn. Mfrs. Avocations: deep sea fishing, music, golf. Office: Tyson Foods Inc 2210 W Oaklawn Dr Springdale AR 72762-6999

TYSON, JOSEPH JUDE, bishop; b. Moses Lake, Wash., Oct. 16, 1957; BA, U. Wash., 1980, MA, 1984; MDiv, Cath. U. Am., Washington, 1989. Ordained priest Archdiocese of Seattle, 1989; pastor St. Edward, St. George & St. Paul parishes, Seattle; ordained bishop, 2005; aux. bishop Archdiocese of Seattle, 2005—. Roman Catholic. Office: Archdiocese of Seattle 710 9th Ave Seattle WA 98104 Office Phone: 206-382-4560.

TYSON, KATHLEEN HAYHURST, educational association administrator; b. Oakland, Calif., Mar. 6, 1947; d. Amos Ira and Marie Gertrude (Sanchez) Hayhurst; 1 child, Kathryn Elena. BA, San Jose State U., Calif., 1971; MA, St. Mary's Coll., Moraga, Calif., 1995. Cert. tchr. Calif., tchr. learning handicapped Calif., resource specialist Calif., in addiction studies. Tchr. elem. Richmond Sch. Dist., Calif., 1972—79; tchr. learning handicapped Richmond Elem. Sch. Dist., Calif., 1979—81; resource specialist West Contra Costa Sch. Dist., Pinole and Hercules, Calif., 1992—. Software designer Beck Tech., Berkeley, Calif., 1991—92; coord. At Risk Program Dept. Drug and Alcohol, Hercules, Calif., 1994—97; dir. Reading Intervention Program Elem. Schs., Hercules; instr. lang. arts Calif. State U., Hayward San Pablo; ednl. cons., intervention tutor, Orinda; supr. student tchrs. San Francisco State U., Hercules, 2005. Author: (Intervention Program) Star Trak, 1989—92, (Reading Intervention program) Firebear, 1995—2003; editor: (book) Habitats, 1998. Organizer, fund raiser Tsunami Toy Drive Orinda Sch., Hercules, 2005; facilitator, instr. Parent Workshop for At Risk Students, Hercules, 1996—97; literacy trainer staff training workshops Hercules, 1998—99; min. Unity Ch., 1999—, spiritual mentor, 1997—99; amb. People to People, Spokane, Wash., 2000. Recipient You Make a Difference award, Contra Costa County, 1991, Cert. Excellence in Svc., Contra Cost. County, 1992. Mem.: Nat. Alliance Mental Health, Calif. Reading Assn., Coun. Exceptional Children, Calif. Tchrs. Assn. Avocations: gardening, reading, travel, tennis. Office: West Contra Costa Sch Dist 1616 Pheasant Dr Hercules CA 94563

TYSON, KIRK W. M., management consultant; b. Jackson, Mich., July 2, 1952; s. George Carlton and Wilma Marion (Barnes) Tyson; m. Terri Lynn Long, Mar. 25, 2000; 1 child, Gabriel 1 stepchild, Robert. BBA, Western Mich. U., 1974; MBA, DePaul U., Chgo., 1982. CPA, Ill.; cert. mgmt. cons. Bus. cons. Arthur Andersen & Co., Chgo., 1974-84; v.p. cons. First Chgo. Corp., 1984; chmn. Kirk Tyson Internat., 1984-2000; pres. The Perpetual Strategist, Chgo., 2001—; adj. prof. mgmt., Coll. Bus. Wright State U., 2007—. Author: Business Planning, 1982, Business Intelligence: Putting It All Together, 1986, Competitor Intelligence: Manual and Guide, 1990, Competition in the 21st Century, 1996, The Complete Guide to Competitive Intelligence, 1998, 4th rev. edit. 2006. Pres., Chgo. Jr. Assn. Commerce and Industry Found., 1977-79; active Easter Seals Soc., 1977, Am. Blind Skiing Found., 1977-78, Jr. Achievement, 1976-77, United Way Met. Chgo., 1979-80, Urban Gateways, 1975; Rep. precinct committeeman Downers Grove Twp., 1985-88; treas. St. Charles H.S. Football Booster club, 1994-95. Fellow Soc. Competitive Intelligence Profls. (Meritorious award, 2005); mem. Rotary Club, Dayton (asst. dist. gov., 2005-08), Alpha Kappa Psi (Disting. Alumni Svc. award 1974-86, named Alumnus of Yr. 2003) Centerville-Washington Found. (trustee 2007-), Ctr. Innovation Mgmt., Wright State U. (bd. mem. 2008-). Office: The Perpetual Strategist 30 S Wacker Dr Ste 2200 Chicago IL 60606-7456 Office Phone: 312-466-5733. Business E-Mail: kirk.tyson@perpetualstrategist.com.

TYSON, LAURA D'ANDREA, economics professor, former dean; b. Bayonne, NJ, June 28, 1947; m. Erik Tarloff; 1 child. BA, Smith Coll., 1969; PhD, MIT, 1974. Asst. prof. econ. Princeton U., 1974—77; prof. econ. U. Calif., Berkeley, 1977—2001; prof. econ. & bus. adminstrn. Haas Sch. Bus., U. Calif., Berkeley, 1990—2001, 2007—, prof. bus. & pub. policy, 1992—, dean Berkeley, 1998—2001; chmn. Coun. Econ. Advisors Exec. Office of the Pres., Washington, 1993-95; dir. Nat. Econ. Coun., Washington, 1995-96; dean London Bus. Sch., 2002—06; dir. LECG, LLC, Emeryville, Calif., 2007—. Bd. dirs. AT&T Inc., Eastman Kodak Co., 1997—, Morgan Stanley, 1997—, 24/7 Customer, 2007; bd. economists L.A. Times, 1989—92; bd. dirs. Coun. Fgn. Rels., 1997; bd. trustees Brookings Instn., 2003—; econ. viewpoint columnist Business Week mag., 1997—2006; mem. President's Econ. Recovery Advisory Bd., 2009—; bd. dirs. Silver Spring Networks, 2009—. Editor: (with John Zysman) American Industry in International Competition, 1983, (with Ellen Comisso) Power, Purpose and Collective Choice: Economic Strategy in Socialist States, 1986, (with William Dickens and John Zysman) The Dynamics of Trade and Employment, 1988, (with Chalmers Johnson and John Zysman) Politics and Productivity: The Real Story of How Japan Works, 1989, Who's Bashing Whom? Trade Conflict in High Technology Industries, 1992 Mem. Nat. Bipartisan Commn. Future Medicare, 1997—99; chmn. White House Council of Economic Advisers. Named one of 50 Women to Watch, The Wall St. Jour., 2008. Democrat. Office: Silver Spring Networks 555 Broadway St Redwood City CA 94063 Office Phone: 650-298-4200, 650-363-5240.*

TYSON, LUCILLE R., health facility administrator, geriatrics nurse; b. North Wales, Pa., Feb. 14, 1939; d. Edwin Shelly and Marion (Wenhold) Rosenberger; m. Ronald Saylor Tyson, June 29, 1963; children: Bryan, Bruce. AS, Middlesex County Coll.; BA, Wheaton Coll.; MSW, Rutgers U. Cert. gerontol. nurse; lic. social worker; RN. Dir. N.J. Parkinson Info. & Referral Ctr. Robert Wood Johnson U. Hosp., New Brunswick, NJ; human svcs. planner Middlesex County Dept. Human Svcs., New Brunswick; dir., right to know regulations Roosevelt Hosp., Edison, NJ; dir., quality assurance Cen. N.J. Jewish Home for Aged, Somerset, NJ. Mem. Piscataway (N.J.) Twp. Coun., 1990—; mem. rev./appeals com. Middlesex County Dept. Human Svcs., 1992—; bd. dirs. Metlar Ho. Found.; mcpl. dir. Piscataway Rep. Orgn., 1995—; county committewoman Middlesex County Rep. Orgn., 1995—2001; rep. exec. committewoman Greenville County, SC, 2001-. Mem. ANA, NASW, Nat. Soc. DAR, N.J. Nurses Assn., Assn. Quality Assurance Profls. N.J., Geriatric Inst. N.J., Rep. Exec. Comm.

TYSON, NEIL DEGRASSE, astrophysicist, museum director; b. NYC; married; 2 children. BA in Physics, Harvard U., 1980; MA in Astronomy, U. Tex., Austin, 1983; PhD in Astrophysics, Columbia U., 1991; DS (hon.), CUNY, 1997, Ramapo Coll., 2000, Dominican Coll., 2000, U. Richmond, 2001, Bloomfield Coll., 2002. Postdoctoral rsch. assoc. dept. astrophysics Princeton U., 1991—94; staff scientist Am. Mus.-Hayden Planetarium, NYC, 1994—95, acting dir., 1995—96; chair dept. astrophysics Am. Mus. Natural Hist., NYC, 1997—99, Frederick P. Rose dir. Hayden Planetarium, 1996—, rsch. assoc., 2003. Author: Merlin's Tour of the Universe, 1989, Universe Down to Earth, 1994, Just Vis. This Planet, 1998, The Sky is Not the Limit: Adventures of an Urban Astrophysicist, 2000, Death by Black Hole: And Other Cosmic Quandaries, 2007; co-author: One Universe: At Home in the Cosmos, 2000 (Sci. Writing award, Am. Inst. Physics, 2001), Origins: Fourteen Billion Years of Cosmic Hist., 2004; co-editor: Cosmic Frontiers: Astronomy at the Cutting Edge, 2001; contbr. articles to profl. jours., chapters to books. Recipient Medal of Honor, Columbia U., 2001, Disting. Pub. Svc. medal, NASA, award for Pub. Understanding of Sci. & Tech., AAAS, 2007; named Sexiest Astrophysicist Alive, People mag., 2000; named one of 40 under 40, Crain's NY mag., 1996, 25 Leaders Reshaping NY, 2008, The World's Most Influential People, TIME mag., 2007; named to Power 150, Ebony mag., 2007, 2008. Fellow: NY Acad. Scis.; mem.: Nat. Soc. Black Physicists, Internat. Planetarium Soc., Astron. Soc. Pacific, Am. Phys. Soc., Am. Astron. Soc. Office: Hayden Planetarium & Dept Astrophysics Am Mus Natural History Central Park W at 79th St New York NY 10024 Office Phone: 212-769-5912. Office Fax: 212-769-5007. Business E-Mail: tysonwebquery@mac.com.

TYSON, PETER, editor-in-chief; b. Bryn Mawr, Pa., May 25, 1960; s. Noel Jon Tyson and Patricia McCurdy; m. Melissa Banta (div.); children: Olivia, Nicholas 1 stepchild, Christopher Legare. BA in English, Trinity Coll., Hartford, Conn., 1982. Asst. editor Omni Mag., NYC, 1983—86; sr. staff writer Interleaf, Inc., Boston, 1988—89; mng. editor Earthwatch Mag., Watertown, Mass., 1989—96, sr. editor, 1996—98; contbg. editor Tech. Rev. Mag., Cambridge, Mass., 1993—97; editor-in-chief Nova Online, Boston, 1998—. Author: Acid Rain, 1992, Groucho Marx, 1995, Vincent Van Gogh, 1996, The Eighth Continent: Life, Death and Discovery in the Lost World of Madagascar, 2000, 2001; contbr. articles to mags., newspapers. Mem.: New Eng. Sci. Writers, Nat. Assn. Sci. Writers. Avocations: travel, mountaineering, fly fishing, rowing, tennis. Home: 45A Fayerweather St Cambridge MA 02138 Office: WGBH Ednl Found 1 Guest St Boston MA 02135 Office Phone: 617-300-4371. Office Fax: 617-300-1003. Business E-Mail: peter_tyson@wgbh.org.

TYSON, PRISCILLA R., city councilwoman; BS in Bus. Adminstrn., Franklin U., Columbus. V.p. cmty. rels. OhioHealth, Columbus; v.p. cmty. devel. Nat. City; founder, pres. Star Arts Ltd., Columbus, 2005—; councilwoman Columbus City Coun., 2007—, chair recreation & parks com., zoning. com. Mem. pres. Columbus Civil Svc. Commn., 1993—2006; exec. dir. emeritus City Yr. Columbus; human resource dir. Ribway Engrng. Group, Columbus. Bd. dirs. Nat. Black Programming Consortium, Greater Columbus Arts Coun., Opera Columbus, Cmty. Shelter Bd., Phoenix Theatre Circle. Recipient YWCA Women of Achievement award, 1996. Office: Columbus City Coun 90 W Broad St 2nd Fl Columbus OH 43215 Office Phone: 614-645-2933. Office Fax: 614-645-7399.

TYTELL, JOHN, literature educator, writer; b. Antwerp, Belgium, May 17, 1939; arrived in U.S., 1941; s. Charles and Lena (Gano) T.; m. Mellon Gregori, May 28, 1967. BA, CCNY, 1961; MA, NYU, 1963, PhD, 1968. Grad. reader NYU, 1963-67; lectr. Queens Coll., NYC, 1963-68, assoc. prof., 1968-73, 1973-76, prof. English, 1977—; exec. editor Am. Book Rev., 1979—; vis. prof. Rutgers U., 1980, U. Paris, 1983; cons. Nat. Humanities Faculty, Ga., 1978—. Author: The American Experience, 1970, Naked Angels, 1976, 3d edit., 2006, Ezra Pound: The Solitary Volcano, 1987, 2d edit., 2004, Passionate Lives, 1991, The Living Theatre: Art, Exile and Outrage, 1995, Paradise Outlaws: Remembering the Beats, 1999, Reading New York, 2003; contbr. articles to mags. including Am. Scholar, Partisan Rev., Vanity Fair, Fame. Fellow, NEH, 1974. Home: 69 Perry St New York NY 10014-3297 Office: Queens Coll Flushing NY 11367 Office Phone: 718-997-4654.

TYTLER, LINDA JEAN, emergency manager, state legislator; b. Rochester, NY, Aug. 31, 1947; d. Frederick Easton and Marian Elizabeth (Allen) Tytler; m. George Stephen Dragnich, May 2, 1970 (div. July 1976); m. James Douglas Fisher, Oct. 7, 1994. AS, So. Va. Coll., Buena Vista, Va., 1967. Spl. asst. to Congressman John Buchanan, Washington, 1971-75; legis. analyst US Senator Robert Griffin, Washington, 1975-77; ops. supr. Pres. Ford Com., Washington, 1976; office mgr. US Senator Pete Domenici Re-election, Albuquerque, 1977; pub. info. officer S.W. Cmty. Health Svc., Albuquerque, 1978-83; cons. pub. rels. and mktg. Albuquerque, 1983-84; account exec. Rick Johnson & Co., Inc., Albuquerque, 1983-84; dir. mktg. and comm. St. Joseph Healthcare Corp., 1984-88; mktg. and bus. devel. cons., 1987-90; dir. comm. and pub. affairs Def. Avionics Systems Honeywell Inc., 1990-2000, dir. comms., 2000—01; dep. dir. pub. affairs Los Alamos Nat. Lab., 2001—05, group leader emergency response instl. svcs., 2006—. Capt. N.Mex. Mounted Patrol, 1998—2002; bd. dirs. Jobs for N.Mex., N.Mex chpt. ARC, Albuquerque, 1984; chmn. legis. campaign com. Rep. Com.; co-chair del. to China Am. Coun. Young Polit. Leaders, 1988; mem. N.Mex. Ho. of Reps., Santa Fe, 1983—95, vice chmn. appropriations and fin. com., 1985—86, chmn. Rep. Caucus, 1985—88. Recipient award, N.Mex. Advt. Fedn., Albuquerque, 1981, 1982, 1985, 1986, 1987, Honeywell Cmty. Svc. award, 1997. Mem.: N.Mex. Assn. Commerce and Industry (bd. dirs., exec. com. 1996—2002), Am. Mktg. Assn., Soc. Hosp. Planning and Mktg., Nat. Advt. Fedn., Am. Soc. Hosp. Pub. Rels. (cert.). Republican.

TYUS, GORDON, graphics designer, educator; b. Salinas, Calif., Dec. 9, 1966; s. Bobby and Joan Tyus; m. Jamie Aronson. BA in Graphic Comm. magna cum laude, Ea. Wash. U., Cheney, 1989, BS in Design Tech., 1989, MS in Comm., 1993. Instr. tech. graphics Ea. Wash. U., 1990—94; graphic designer City of Spokane, 1991—93; instr. computer aided drafting and design ITT Tech. Inst., Spokane, 1993—96; instr. graphic and interior design Spokane Falls C.C., 1996—97; graphic design specialist Maricopa Assn. Govts., Phoenix, 1997—. Testing coord., cert. proctor Greater Phoenix Mensa, 2005—. Graphic designer (publication) MAG Annual Budget and Work Program (GFOA Disting. Budget Presentation award, 2008), Regional Report: A Resource for Policy Makers in the Maricopa Region (Ariz. Planning Association's Best Regional Plan award, 2005), graphic design and web support (transportation plan public outreach) MAG Regional Transportation Plan (Fed. Hwy. Adminstrn. Leadership award for Regional Transp., 2005), graphic designer (newsletter) MAGAZine (Pub. Rels. Soc. Am. Copper Anvil award Merit, 2001), graphic and web support (domestic violence prevention) Domestic Violence Council Web Site and Safety Plan (Desert Peaks award Public-Private Partnership, 2001), graphic designer (logo, brochure and program) Arizona Alternatives, Clean Fuel for Clean Cities Forum (Valley Forward Environ. Excellence award, 2000), (logo) Safety First. Scholar, Dale Wilson Scholarship Fund, 1985. Mem.: ACLU, Chronic Fatigue Immune Dysfunction Syndrome Assn. Am., Am. Mensa. Avocations: running, video editing, video games, reading. Office: Maricopa Association of Governments 302 N 1st Avenue Suite 300 Phoenix AZ 85003 Home: 4326 E Everett Dr Phoenix AZ 85032 Personal E-mail: gtyus@hotmail.com.

TYZACK, MARGARET, actress; b. London, Sept. 9, 1931; d. Thomas Edward Tyzack and Doris Moseley; m. Alan Stephenson; 1 child. Student, St. Angela's Ursuline Convent, Forest Gate, London, Royal Acad. Dramatic Arts. Appeared in stage productions from 1951, including Who's Afraid of Virginia Woolf (Laurence Olivier award, Actress of Yr., 1981), Lettice and Lovage (Tony award, Dramatic Actress, Supporting or Featured, 1990), The Chalk Garden, 2008 (Laurence Olivier award for Best Actress, 2009_); appeared in films from 1957, including 2001, The Whisperers, A Touch of Love, A Clockwork Orange, Match Point; appeared in TV productions including The Forsythe Saga, The First Churchills (Brit. Acad. Film and TV Arts award, TV-Best Actress, 1969), Cousin Bette, Quatermass, I Claudius, The Young Indiana Jones Chronicles. Recipient Order Brit. Empire in Birthday Honours, 1970.*

TZAMALOUKAS, ANTONIOS HELIAS, nephrologist; b. Athens, Greece, Nov. 1, 1939; s. Helias and Erasicleia Tzamaloukas; m. Rolinda Anita Griffin, Nov. 16, 1974; children: David Griffin, Sheila Ann Case, Erasicleia Anita Schrandt-Tzamaloukas. MD, Athens U., Greece, 1963. Diplomate Am. Bd. Internal Medicine, 1974, in nephrology 1976, 1980, 1987. Asst. prof., U. N.Mex, Albuquerque, 1975—82, assoc. prof., 1982—88; prof. medicine, u. N.Mex. chief, nephrology sect. Raymond G Murphy Va. Med. Ctr., 1988—. Contbr. scientific papers. Mem., Nat. Kidney Found., Albuquerque, N.Mex., 1976—2000. Lt. Greek Air Force, 1964, Greece. Recipient Outstanding Med. Attending award, U. N.Mex Sch. Medicine, 1981, Outstanding Achievement in Renal Medicine award, Nat. Kidney Found. N.Mex., 1992, Spl. Contbn. award, US Nat. Kidney Found., 1996, US Dept. Vet. Affairs, 1996, Outstanding caregiver award, Chaplain svc., Albuquerque Va. Med. ctr., 1998, Spl. Contbn. award, US Dept. Vet. Affairs, 1999, award, U. Mo. Ann. Dialysis Conf., 2007. Fellow: ACP (pres., N.Mex chpt. 2000—01, Internist laureate 2003). Liberal. Greek Orthodox. Achievements include research in fluid ENA electrolyte balance, peritoneal dialysis. Avocations: ballooning, travel, swimming. Office: Raymond G Murphy VA Medical Center 1501 San Pedro SE Albuquerque NM 87108

TZANNETAKIS, TZANNIS, Greek government official; b. Gytheion, Greece, 1927; married; 2 children. Commd. officer, advanced through grades to comdr. Greek Navy, resigned after mil. coup, 1967; arrested and imprisoned 9 mos., exiled 1 yr.; sec.-gen. Greek Nat. Tourist Orgn., Athens; M.P., 1977—; min. pub. works Govt. of Greece, 1980-81; supr. local govt. affairs New Democracy Party, 1982-86, prime min., min. fgn. affairs, 1989, min. nat. def., 1989-90, vice premier, min. culture, 1990-91, dep. prime min., 1992-93. Author: The Greek Agora Public Political Science, 1994, India-Another Way of Life, 1994; translator: Upanishads, 1961, Mani, 1973. Decorated Honor Grand Cross of Greece, Grand Cross Of Luxembourg. Home: Odos Pefkon 25 Kifissia Athens Greece Office: Greek Parliament 10021 Athens Greece Home Phone: 00302108017133; Office Phone: 00302103385374. Business E-Mail: tztz@parliament.gr.

TZENG, JUNG-YING, statistician, researcher; PhD, Carnegie Mellon U., Pitts., 2003. Asst. prof. Dept. Stats. and Bioinformatics Rsch. Ctr., Raleigh, NC, 2003—. Assoc. editor Biometrics. Recipient Umesh Gavasakar Thesis award, Carnegie Mellon U., 2003. Mem.: Am. Statis. Assn. Achievements include research in Statistical methods for studying susceptibility genes for complex traits, Bayes hierarchical modeling. Office Fax: (919)515-7315; Home Fax: (919)515-7315. Business E-Mail: jytzeng@stat.ncsu.edu.

TZIMAS, NICHOLAS ACHILLES, orthopedic surgeon, educator; b. Greece, Apr. 18, 1928; arrived in U.S.A., 1955, naturalized, 1960. s. Archilles Nicholas and Evanthia B. (Exarchou) T.; m. Helen J. (Papastylopoulos), Apr. 22, 1958; children: Yvonne and Christina. MD, U. Athens, Greece, 1952. Intern St. Mary's Hosp., Hoboken, NJ, 1955—86; resident in gen. surgery Misericordia Hosp., NYC; resident in orthopedic surgery Bellevue Hosp., NYC, 1957—60; instr. orthopedic surgery N.Y. U. Sch. Medicine, 1961—63, asst. clin. prof., 1963—65, asso. clin. prof., 1965—71, clin. prof., 1971—. Staff Univ. and Bellevue Hosp.; chief children's orthopedics, 1966; orthopedic cons. Inst. Rehab. Medicine, NYU, 1966, St. Agnes Hosp., White Plains, NY, 1972; advisory com. Bur. Handicapped Children, NYC, 1975; spl. invitations for tchg., Osaka, Japan, 1970, Jerusalem, 1974, São Paolo, Brazil, 1976, Taranto, Italy, 1977, Bari, Italy, 1978, Barquisimeto, Venezuela, 1979, Bogotá, Colombia, 1983, Buenos Aires, Argentina, 1983. Author of articles on spina bifida child mgmt. Served with M.C. Greek Army, 1952-55. Named Ofcl. Knight of Italian Republic, 1979 Fellow Am., Internat. Coll. Surgeons; mem. N.Y. Acad. Medicine, N.Y. State, N.Y. County Med. Soc., Am. Acad. Orthopedic Surgeons, Am. Congress Rehab. Medicine, Am. Acad. Cerebral Palsy. Mem. Greek Orthodox Ch.; Archon of the Ecumenical Patriarchate of Constantinople. Home: 33

Edgewood St Tenafly NJ 07670-2909 Office: 530 1st Ave New York NY 10016-6402 Office Phone: 212-263-7278. Personal E-mail: ntzimas@aol.com. Business E-Mail: nicholasotzimas@med.nyu.edu.

TZITSIKAS, HELENE, retired literature educator; b. Athens, Greece, Apr. 2, 1926; arrived in US, 1944; d. Christos Jean and Evangelia (Chouases) T. BA, Lake Forest Coll., Ill., 1952; MA, Northwestern U., 1954, PhD, 1963. Instr. Rockford (Ill.) Coll., 1962-63, asst. prof., 1963-65; assoc. prof. Hispanic lit. Mich. State U., East Lansing, 1965-71, prof., 1971-91, prof. emerita, 1991—. Author: Santiago Ramón y Cajal-Obra Literaria, 1965, El Pensamiento Español 1898-1899, 1967, Fernando Santiván - Humanista y Literato, 1971, 2d edit., 1985, Dos Revistas Chilenas: Los Diez y Artes y Letras, 1973, El sentimiento ecológico, 1977, La supervivencia existencial de la mujer, 1982, El Quijotismo y la raza en la Generacion de 1898, 1988, Los exiliados argentinos en Montevideo durante la época de Rosas, 1991. Recipient Diana award YWCA, Lansing, Mich., 1988, cert. of employee recognition, 1988. Mem. MLA, AAUP, MLA Am., Am. Assn. Tchrs. Spanish and Portuguese, Univ. Club Mich. State U., Daus. Penelope. Greek Orthodox. Avocations: theater, music, painting, gardening. Office: Mich State U Dept Romance and Classical Langs East Lansing MI 48824 Office Phone: 517-355-8350.

TZIVION, GURI, medical educator; married. PhD, Hebrew U., Jerusalem, 1995. Postdoc. assoc. Mass. Gen. Hosp. & Harvard Med. Sch., Boston, 1995—2000; asst. prof. Tex. A&M U., Temple, 2000—04; assoc. prof. Wayne State U., Detroit, 2004—. Grant, NIH, 2002—08. Office: Wayne State Univ 4100 John R HWCRC-716 Detroit MI 48201 Business E-Mail: tziviong@karmanos.org.

TZYY-JIANN, WANG, science educator; BS in Elec. Engring., Nat. Taiwan U., Taipei, 1992, PhD in Elec. Engring., 1999. Asst. prof. Nat. Taipei U. Tech., Taiwan, 2000—04, assoc. prof., 2005—08, prof., 2008—. Contbr. articles to profl. jours.; reviewer, referee: several profl. jours. Mem.: IEEE. Achievements include research in integrated-optic device, surface-plasmon-resonance biosensor, fiber laser, and optoelectronic device simulation; patents for integrated-optic devices; surface-plasmon-resonance biosensor. Office: Nat Taipei U Tech Inst Electro-Optical Engring No1 Sec3 Chung-Hsiao E Road Taipei 10608 Taiwan Office Fax: 886-2-87733216. Business E-Mail: f10939@ntut.edu.tw.

UBA, ALAN KEITH, pediatrician, educator; b. Oct. 23, 1961; MD, U. Calif., San Francisco, 1988. Cert. in pediat. Am. Bd. Med. Specialties. Intern in pediat. Children's Hosp. at LA, resident in pediat.; assoc. clinical prof. pediat. U. Calif. San Francisco, 1992—. Recipient Chief Residents' Commendation, U. Calif. San Francisco Dept. Pediat., 1992—93, Faculty Tchg. award, 1993; named to Top Docs - the Top 425 Doctors in the Bay Area, San Francisco Mag., 1999, 2005. Office: Dept Pediat U Calif San Francisco Med Sch 505 Parnassus Ave San Francisco CA 94143 Office Phone: 415-353-2790. Office Fax: 415-353-2000, 415-353-2680. Business E-Mail: ubaa@peds.ucsf.edu.

UBBEN, DONALD THOMAS, lawyer; b. Pekin, Ill., May 9, 1946; s. Wilbert Donald and Verna Lanelle (Ducker) U. BA, Furman U., 1968; MA, Baylor U., 1972; JD, U. Va., 1982. Bar: SC 1983, DC Ct. Appeals 1983, US Dist. Ct. DC 1984, US Dist. Ct. SC 1984, US Ct. Appeals (DC, 4th and fed. cirs.) 1984, US Claims Ct. 1984, US Tax. Ct. 1984, Va. 1991. Asst. to sec. for spl. programs HEW, Washington, 1973-75; legis. asst. U.S. Senate, Washington, 1975-77, 81-82; dir. exec. br. liaison U.S. C. of C., Washington, 1977-79. With Legal Svcs. Corp., acting dir. N.Y. regional office, 1984, acting dir. bar rels., 1985; ptnr. Macdonald, McEnerny, Guandolo, Jordan and Crampton, 1985-87; atty. U.S. Dept. of Interior, 1988-91. Del. to county and state Rep. convs., S.C. and Va., 1968-94; alt. delt. Rep. Nat. Conv., 1972, 84, del., 1976; mem. Albemarle County (Va.) Rep. Ctrl. Com., 1981-88, 91-97; precinct capt., 1992-93; bd. dirs. Opera Americana, 1990-92, Va. Ctr. Creative Arts, 2006-; chmn., By-Laws Com., 2007-2008, Alexandria Symphony, 1987-90, mem. exec. com., 1988-1990, chmn. nominating com., 1988-89, chmn. govt. liaison com., 1989-90, mem. long range planning com., 1988-90. Mem. Nat. Rep. Lawyers Assn., Conservative Network (counsel 1986-87), English Speaking Union (bd. dirs. 1992-98, chmn. membership com. 1992-94, chmn. program com. 1994-96, pres. 1996-98), Albemarle County Geneal. Assn., Greencroft Club (bd. dirs. 1992-94, sec. 1993-94, mem. exec. com., 1993-94, chmn. by-laws com.). Republican. Home: PO Box 171 Ivy VA 22945-0171

UBELL, ROBERT NEIL, editor, educator, publishing executive, consultant; b. Bklyn., Sept. 14, 1938; s. Charles and Hilda (Kramer) U.; m. Rosalyn Deutsche, Sept. 24, 1976; children: Jennifer Hayslett, Elizabeth Miller. BA, Bklyn. Coll., 1961; postgrad., Acad. Fine Arts, Rome, Italy, 1959-60, CUNY, 1961-62, Pratt Graphic Arts Workshop, NYC, 1972-73. Assoc. editor Nuclear Industry, Atomic Indsl. Forum, 1962-64; from editor to sr. editor Plenum Pub. Corp., NYC, 1965-70, v.p., editor in chief, 1970-76; editor The Sciences, N.Y. Acad. Scis., NYC, 1976-79; Am. pub. Nature, NYC, 1979-83; founding pub. Nature Biotechnology, 1983; pres., CEO Robert Ubell Assocs., NYC, 1983—97; pres. BioMedNet, Ltd., 1996-97; exec. v.p. Marcel Dekker, Inc., NYC, 1997-99; dir. web-based distance learning Stevens Inst. Tech., Hoboken, NJ, 1999—2001, dean online learning, 2001—03, dean sch. profl. edn., 2004—07; exec. dir. Inst. for the Advancement of Online Learning and Profl. Edn., 2007—09; v.p. Enterprise Learning, Poly. Inst. NYU, 2009—. Instr. MIT, 1987, Columbia U. Coll. Physicians and Surgeons, 1987; mem. Book Industry Study Group, Inc., 1992; mem. vis. com. Nat. Acad. Press, NRC, NAS, 1986; mem. books subcom. Am. Inst. Physics, 1985—91; mem. awards com. Am. Inst. Physics-US Steel Sci. Writing Awards, 1982—83, Corp. Univ. Xchange, 2006; mem. publs. com. Am. Inst. Biol. Scis., 1994, NY Acad. Scis., 1976—97; cons. Lotus Devel. Corp., 1987—89, Coalition for Networked Info., 1995—98, Am. Soc. Addiction Medicine, 2003—04; mem. pub. info. com. NAE, 1989—2002; mem. program com. Soc. Scholarly Pub., 1989—91; mem. rev. panel NSF, 2000, 03, Nat. Sci., Math. and Tech. Edn. Digital Libr., 2007, Internat. Opportunities Scientists and Engrs., 2003, 08, Reform Undergrad. Engring. Edn., 2003, Nat. Digital Libr., 2008; distance learning observer Mid. States Commn. on Higher Edn., 2000—04; chair Sloan Found. Greater NYC ALN Conf., 2002; mem. planning com. Breakthrough Thinking in Online Bus. Edn., 2002—03; mem. adv. panel Nat. Rsch. Inst. on Wireless Tech. in Edn. and Industry, 2002, ABET Adv. Panel, Online Engring., Alliance Expanded Tchr. Preparation CCs; co-host Stevens Views Radio, 2002—06; mem. edn. com. The Scientist, 1987—90; mem. adv. bd. comm. industry network NJ Tech. Coun., 2002—, Sloan Found. Program Com., Sloan C-Conf., 2005—, Sloan Found. Corp. e-Learning, 2003—04, sci. learning through cyber resources, 2007—; prin. investigator Sloan Greater NYC Online Learning Ctr., 2003—05; co-chair Sloan Workshop Corp.-Acad. Online Learning, 2004; mem. adv. task force Nat. Hwy. Inst. Distance Learning Program, 2004, chair, Sloan-C Alliance Adv. Com.; cons. in field; mem. adv. bd. Sci. Learning Through Cyber Resources; v.p. Enterprise Learning Poly. Inst. NY U. Author: (with Marvin Leiner) Children Are the Revolution, 1974; (with Mark Tesoriero) Negotiating Networked Licensing Agreements, 1995, Cost Centers and Measures in the Networked Information Value Chain, 1997, The R&D Economics in the Digital Environment, 1998; editor Nature Directory of Biologicals, 1981, Physics Today Buyer's Guide, 1984-89, virtual Teamwork, 2009; exec. editor: Linguistics: The Cambridge Survey, 1987-88, Pre-Med Handbook, 1986, International Encyclopedia of the Social Sciences, Vol. 19, 1991, Encyclopedia of Astronomy and Astrophysics, 1991, Sci. Am. Triumph of Discovery, 1995, Oxford Encyclopedia of Climate and Weather, 1996; cons. editor ISI Press, 1985-87, Am. Inst. of Physics Book Program, 1986-96; Am. Chem. Soc. Book Program, 1989; cons. pub. Computers in Physics, 1987-91; series editor Masters of Modern Physics, 1991-96, Creators of Modern Chemistry, 1994-95, Sci. Am. Focus, 1995-96; mem. editl. bd. ISI Press, 1986-90, Grants Mag., 1981-85, Nonprofit Mgmt. and Fin., 1980-85; mem. editl. bd. The Sciences, 1980-82; editl. dir. Nutrition Advisor, 1998-99; Innovations in End of Life Care, 1999-2003; editl. advisor Cancer Practice, Am. Cancer Soc., 1997-98, Virtual Teamwork, 2009; contbr. articles to profl. jours. Chief learning Bus. Intelligence Bd., 2008—; chmn. bd. Woodword Sch., 1971—74; mem. adv. com. Children's TV Workshop, 1980, Interpool, Inc., 2006; mem. bd. dirs. Marcel Dekker Inc., 1992—98; v.p. bd. dirs. Parkinson's Walk Found., 2001—, Hekate, 2003—04, Lianyungang Universal Vehicle Mfg. Co., Ltd., 2006—08; exec. dir. Fin. Industry Workforce Responce Taskforce. Mem. AAAS, ASTD, NY Acad. Scis. (mem. publs. com. 1976-97). Office: Stevens Inst Tech Castle Point Hudson Hoboken NJ 07030 Business E-Mail: rubell@poly.edu.

UBERALL, HERBERT MICHAEL STEFAN, physicist, professor emeritus; b. Neunkirchen, Austria, Oct. 14, 1931; arrived in U.S., 1953, naturalized, 1963; s. Michael and Stefanie U.; m. Reyna Tosta, 1981; children by previous marriage: Bernadette Chauvallon, Bertrand. PhD, U. Vienna, Austria, 1953, Cornell U., 1956; PhD (honoris causa), U. Le Havre, France, 1987. Staff mem. Signal Corps Labs., Ft. Monmouth, NJ, 1953-54; research asst. Cornell U., 1954-56; research fellow Nuclear Physics Research Lab., U. Liverpool, Eng., 1956-57; Ford Found. fellow CERN, Geneva, 1957-58; research physicist Carnegie Inst. Tech., Pitts., 1958-60; asst. prof. U. Mich., Ann Arbor, 1960-64; assoc. prof. Cath. U. Am., Washington, 1964-65, prof. physics, 1965-94, prof. emeritus, 1994—2008. Vis. prof. U. Paris VII Jussieu, 1984-85, U. Le Havre, 1990, 92, 94, 96, U. Bordeaux, 1993, 95, U. Aix-Marseille II and Lab. Mech. Acoustics, 1995, Ecole Centrale de Lille, 1997, Tech. U. Denmark, 1998; cons. Naval Rsch. Lab., Washington, 1996-92. Author: Electron Scattering from Complex Nuclei, 1971; co-author: Giant Resonance Phenomena, 1980, Nuclear Pion Photoproduction, 1991; editor: Acoustic Resonance Scattering, 1992; co-editor: Long Distance Neutrino Detection, 1979, Classical and Quantum Dynamics, 1991, Coherent Radiation Sources, 1985, Coherent Radiation Processes in Strong Fields, 1991, Radar Target Imaging, 1994; contbr. 300 articles to profl. jours. Recipient Fgn. medal French Soc. Acoustics, 1996. Fellow (life) IEEE, (life) Am. Phys. Soc., Acoustical Soc. Am., Washington Acad. Scis. (Achievement award 1984); mem. AAUP, Am. Acad. Mech., Electromagnetics Acad., Internat. Union Radio Sci. Personal E-mail: uberallh@msn.com.

UBERTI, JOSEPH P., oncologist, educator; s. Oswald Uberti and Lina Bizzochi; m. Kathryn Uberti; children: Christopher, David. PhD, Wayne State U., Detroit, 1979, MD, 1983. Assoc. prof. medicine U. Mich. Med. Ctr., Ann Arbor, 1994—2004; prof. medicine, co-dir. Barbara Ann Karmanos Cancer Ctr., Detroit, 2004—; asst. prof. medicine Wayne State U., 1989—94, chief, divsn. hematology, oncology, 2008—. Office: Barbara Ann Karmanos Cancer Ctr 4100 John R Detroit MI 48201 Business E-Mail: ubertij@karmanos.org.

UBIÑAS, LUIS ANTONIO, foundation president; b. Bronx, NY, 1963; m. Deborah L. Tolman; 2 children. BA in Govt., magna cum laude, Harvard Coll., 1989; student, Inst. L.Am. Studies, U. Tex., Austin; MBA, Harvard Bus. Sch. Cert. in L.Am. Studeis Harvard Coll. Intern, reporter Wall St. Jour., LA Times; various mktg./strategy roles Booz Allen Hamilton; dir. West coast media practice McKinsey & Co., San Francisco, 1989—2008; pres. Ford Found., NYC, 2008—. Bd. dirs. Bay Area United Way, LEAD Prog. (Leadership Edn. & Devel.); past bd. dirs. Steppingstone Found., Boston. Office: Ford Found 320 E 43rd St New York NY 10017 Office Phone: 212-446-7000, 212-573-5000. Office Fax: 212-446-8575, 212-351-3677.*

UCHIDA, MITSUKO, pianist; b. Dec. 20, 1948; d. Fujio and Yasuko Uchida. Student, Hochschule für Musik, Vienna, Austria. Dame comdr. Order British Empire. Performer: performs with Berlin Philharm., Vienna Philharm., Cleve. Orch., LA Philharm., Chgo. Symphony Orch., London Symphony, NY Philharm., others, recs. include complete piano sonatas and concertos of Mozart, Beethoven's piano concertos, Debussy's Etudes, Schubert Sonatas and Impromptus, Schoenberg Piano Concerto, Carnegie Hall recital series Mitsuko Uchida: Vienna Revisited, 2002—; artist-in-residence Cleve. Orch., 2001—07. Recipient Gramophone award, 2001, Instrumental Award, Royal Philharm. Soc., 2004. Mem. Am. Acad. Arts & Scis. (hon. fgn.), Borletti-Buitoni Trust (trustee), Marlboro Music Festival (co-dir.). Avocation: music. Address: Victoria Rowsell Artist Mgmt Ltd 34 Addington Sq London SE5 7LB England E-mail: management@victoriarowsell.co.uk.

UCHIDA, RICHARD Y., lawyer; b. Mars, Pa., Sept. 18, 1957; s. Henry S. and Sachiko (Sakaguchi) U. BA, Colby Coll., 1979; JD, Franklin Pierce Law Ctr., 1984. Bar: N.H. 1984, U.S. Dist. Ct. N.H. 1984. Reporter, editor Lake Charles (La.) Am. Press., 1979-81; assoc. Rinden Profl. Assn., Concord, NH, 1984-86, Law Offices Raymond P. D'Amante, Concord, 1986—92; ptnr. Crisp, Barrett, Hebert & Uchida, Concord, NH, 1992—. Lectr. Franklin Pierce Law Ctr., Concord, 1985—96, N.H. Liquor Commn., Concord, 1986—92. Overseer Colby Coll., 1997-05, trustee, 2005-. Mem. Assn. Trial Lawyers Am., NH Trial Lawyers, NH Bar Assn. (chmn. pub. info. com. 1987-90, CLE com. 1990, ethics com. 1990, bar news com. 1996-, fin. com. 2003-, pres. 2005), NH Bar Found. (treas. 1999-02, dir. 2003-). Republican. Avocations: golf, hiking. Address: Crisp Barrett Hebert & Uchida PLLC 2 Pillsbury St Ste 502 Concord NH 03301-3549 Office Phone: 603-224-5004.

UCHIN, ROBERT ALLEN, dean, endodontist; b. Phila., Apr. 19, 1933; s. Harry and Doris (Goodman) U.; m. Marlene Florence Neiman; children: Andrew, Richard, Carol. Student, Franklin and Marshall Coll., 1951-53; DDS, Temple U., 1957. Diplomate Am. Bd. Endodontics. Fellow research teaching. dept. endodontics Temple U., Phila., 1959-60, instr. Sch. of Dentistry, 1960-69; co-chmn. endodontic sect. Dade County (Fla.) Dental Research Clinic, 1961-75; founding v.p., chmn. endodontic sect. Broward County (Fla.) Dental Research Clinic, 1974-79; clin. assoc. Sch. of Dentistry U. Fla., Gainsville, 1970; practice dentistry specializing in endodontics Ft. Lauderdale, Fla., 1960—2000; assoc. dean, dir. extramural programs Coll. Dental Medicine, Nova Southeastern U., Ft. Lauderdale, Fla., 1996—2000, dean, 2000—. Chmn. Endodontic sect. Atlantic Coast Research Clinic, 1971-75; vis. lectr. Emory U., 1965, U.N.C., 1970, 72, U. Wash., 1972, U. Pitts., 1974, U. Pa., 1973-89; cons. VA Hosp., Miami, 1968-86, Cen. Office, 1972-84, dir. endodontic residency, 1972-79; bd. dirs., founding chmn. Gold Coast Savs. and Loan Assn. of Fla., 1984-90, Commonwealth Savs. and Loan of Fla., Ft. Lauderdale, 1979-84; adv. dir. Landmark First Nat. Bank, Ft. Lauderdale, 1974-81; vice chmn. Fla. Dental Assn. Services, Inc. Assoc. editor Jour. Endodontics and Traumatology, 1981-89; contbr. numerous articles to profl. jours. Pres., Temple Emanu-El Reform Congregation, Ft. Lauderdale, 1967-69; trustee, Vanguard Sch., Haverford, Pa., 1971-77; bd. dirs., Vanguard Sch., Ft. Lauderdale, 1970-73, Performing Arts Found., Broward County, Fla., 1986-90. Served to capt. USAF, 1957-59. Fellow: Am. Assn. Endodontists (pres. 1976), Internat. Coll. of Dentists, Am. Coll. of Dentists; mem.: Broward County Dental Assn. (pres. 1982), Fla. Dental Assn. (past pres.), Am. Dental Assn. Holding Co. (past pres.), Fla. Assoc. of Endodonties, So. Endodontic Study Group, Am. Dental Assn., Rotary (pres. Ft. Lauderdale 1969—70). Republican. Jewish. Avocations: fly fishing, stamp collecting/philately, orchids. Office: Coll Dental Medicine Nova Southeastern U 3200 S Univ Dr Fort Lauderdale FL 33328 Office Phone: 954-262-7312. Office Fax: 954-262-1782. Business E-Mail: ruchin@nova.edu.

UCHITELLE, LOUIS, journalist; b. NYC, Mar. 21, 1932; s. Abraham and Alice Lee (Cronbach) Uchitelle; m. Joan Eva Shapiro, Oct. 7, 1966; children: Isabel Anne, Jennifer Emily. BA, U. Mich., 1954. Reporter Mt. Vernon Daily Argus, 1955-57; with AP, 1957-80, fgn. corr. and bur. chief San Juan, 1964-67, Buenos Aires, 1967-73; supervising editor AP Newsfeatures, NYC, 1974-76; bus. news editor AP, 1977-80; asst. bus. and fin. editor New York Times, 1980-87, economics reporter, 1987—. Instr. journalism Sch. Gen. Studies Columbia U., 1976—89. Author: The Disposable American: Layoffs and Their Consequences, 2006. Office: New York Times 620 8th Ave New York NY 10018 Home Phone: 914-723-0372; Office Phone: 212-556-1705. Office Fax: 212-556-8762. Business E-Mail: louisu@nytimes.com.

UCHRIN, CHRISTOPHER GEORGE, environmental engineer and scientist; b. South Amboy, NJ, Oct. 27, 1950; s. George Christopher and Annette Rose Marie (Skokan) U.; m. Lisa C. Ferguson, July 31, 1998; 1 child, George Henry. B in Civil Engring., Manhattan Coll., 1972, M. in Environ. Engring., 1974; PhD in Environ. Engring., U. Mich., 1980. Registered profl. engring. N.Y. Environ. engr. U.S. EPA, NYC, 1972-77; Rackham fellow U. Mich., Ann Arbor, Mich., 1977-78, rsch. asst., 1978-80; asst. prof. Rutgers U., New Brunswick, NJ, 1980-86, assoc. prof., 1986-90, prof. environ. sci., 1990—. Chair dept. environ. sci. Rutgers U., New Brunswick, 1991-94, dir. grad. program in environ. sci., 1986-91; co-dir., co-founder Joint PhD Program in Exposure Assessment, Rutgers U. & UMDNJ/Robert Wood Johnson Med. Sch., 1991—, dir. undergrad. curriculum in bioenvironmental engring., 1999—; assoc. editor ASCE Jour. Envoron. Engring., 2008-. Mem. Lebanon Borough (N.J.) Planning Bd., 2003—; elected mem. Hunrerdon County Dem. Com., 2008—. Recipient Excellence in Tchg. award, Cook Coll./N.J. Agrl. Experiment Sta., 2005. Mem. ASCE, Am. Chem. Soc., Water Environment Fedn., Am. Soc. for Materials, Soc. Environ. Toxicology and Chemistry, N.J. Acad. Sci. (pres. 1991-92). Personal E-mail: cuchrin@rci.rutgers.edu.

UCHUPI, ELAZAR, geologist, researcher; b. NYC, Oct. 31, 1928; parents Alfonso and Carmen (Urbizu) U. BS, CCNY, 1952; MS, U. So. Calif., 1954, PhD, 1962. Rsch. asst. U. So. Calif., LA, 1955-62, Woods Hole (Mass.) Oceanographic Inst., 1962-64, assoc. scientist, 1964-79; sr. scientist Woods Hole (Mass.) Oceanog. Inst., 1979-93, sr. scientist emeritus, 1993—, J. Seward Johnson chmn. oceanography, 1989-93. Mem. Gulf of Mexico panel Joint Oceanog. Instns. Deep Earth Sampling, 1972-74; sci. com. Oceanic Rsch. Working Group 41, 1973-74; steering com. U.S. Oceanog. Office Relief Map Worlds' Oceans; site survey panel Joint Oceanog. Instns., 1978-85; compiler geol. maps on ocean margin drilling; adj. rschr. Inst. Exploration, Mystic, Conn., 1997—. Mem. editl. staff Offshore Mag., 1972-74, Marine Geology, 1971-75; co-author 4 books North Atlantic, geology of Atlantic Ocean, and morphology of rocky mems. of Solar Sys. Recipient cert. of recognition Nat. Assn. Geology Tchrs., Inc., and its Crustal evolution Edn. project, 1979, medal editl. adv. bd. Offshore Mag., 1974, Frances P. Shepard award, 1991. Mem. Am. Geophys. Union, Sociedad Geologica de España. Achievements include research in seismic reflection, magnetic and gravity profiles of the eastern Atlantic continental margin and adjacent deep seafloor, Caribbean, Bahamas, Iberian Margins, New England margin, Branefield Trough, South Scotia Ridge, Canary Islands, Red Sea, Persian Gulf, Gulf of Oman, Black Sea, Egyptian Margin, Western Mediterranean, East Pacific Rise, Mohns Ridge, suspended matter and other properities of surface waters of the northeastern Atlantic Ocean, the continental margin off western Africa: Angola to Sierra Leone, Senegal to Portugal, sediments of 3 bays of Baja, Calif.: Sebastian Viscaino, San Cristobal and Todos Santos, characteristics of sediments of the mainland shelf of southern Calif., submarine geology of the Santa Rosa-Cortes Ridge, sediments on the continental margin off eastern U.S., the continental slope between San Francisco and Cedrow Island, Mex., sediments of the Palos Verdes shelf, sediments and topography of Kane Basin, statistical parameters of Cape Cod Beach and eolian sands, basins of Gulf of Mex., structure of Georges Bank, and the continental margin of the Atlantic coast of the U.S. and off west Africa, topography and structure of Northeast Channel, Gulf of Mex., and Cashes Ledge, Gulf of Maine, distribution and geologic structure of Triassic rocks in the Bay of Fundy and the northeastern part of the Gulf of Maine, microrelief of the continental margin south of Cape Lookout, N.C., shallow structure of the Straits of Fla., sub-surface morphology of L.I., Block Island, Rhode Island sounds, and Buzzards Bay, bathymetry of the Gulf of Mex., slumping on the continental margin southeast of L.I., N.Y., woody debris on the mainland shelf off Ventura, southern Calif., the continental margin south of Cape Hatteras, N.C., the Atlantic continental shelf and slope of the U.S., geological structure of the continental margin off Gulf Coast of the U.S., continental margin of West Africa, the Caribbean Canary Islands, margin off northwest Spain. Office: Woods Hole Oceanographic Inst Dept Geology Geophysic Woods Hole MA 02543

UCKO, BARBARA CLARK, writer; b. Cambridge, Mass., Mar. 27, 1945; d. Hugh Kidder and Marie (Folsom) Clark; m. David Alan Ucko, Aug. 13, 1972; 1 child, Aaron Mark. BA in Art History, Oberlin Coll., 1967; MA in English, U. Mo., Kansas City, 1992. Copywriter Bantam Books, NYC, 1974—76; promotion dir. Pocket Books, NYC, 1976—77, Antioch Bookplate, Yellow Springs, Ohio, 1977; instr. composition Sch. of Chgo. Art Inst., Chgo., 1986; mgr. corp. comm. Sprint, Westwood, Kans., 1992—98; pvt. piano tchr. Kansas City, Mo., 1998—2001. Author: (novels) Family Trappings, 1985, Scarlett Greene, 1987, (short stories) Laurel Review, Nit and Wit, Open, Artful Dodge and Chatelaine. Various libr. bds., sch. vol. and hosp. bds. Calif., Mo., Washington D.C. Recipient 1st pl. award, Barbara Storck Short Fiction Competion, U. Mo., 1991, 2d pl., 1992. Mem.: Soc. Midland Authors. Democrat. Avocations: crossword puzzles, piano, walking, reading, painting. Home Phone: 202-337-7982. Personal E-mail: barbara.ucko@verizon.net.

UCKO, DAVID ALAN, science foundation official; b. NYC, July 9, 1948; s. Lawrence L. and Helen H. Ucko; m. Barbara Alice Clark, Aug. 13, 1972; 1 child, Aaron. BA, Columbia Coll., NYC, 1969; PhD, MIT, 1972. Asst. prof. chemistry Hostos C.C., CUNY, Bronx, 1972-76, Antioch Coll., Yellow Springs, Ohio, 1976-79, assoc. prof. chemistry,

1979; rsch. coord. Mus. Sci. and Industry, Chgo., 1979-80, dir. sci., 1981-87, v.p., 1986-87; dep. dir. Calif. Mus. Sci. and Industry, LA, 1987-90; pres. Kansas City (Mo.) Mus., 1990-2000, Sci. City at Union Sta., 1999-2000; exec. dir. Koshland Sci. Mus. and Sci. Outreach, NAS, Washington, 2001—02; pres. Mus. + More LLC, 2002—; program dir. Informal Sci. Edn. NSF, 2003—07, head sci literacy section, 2004—07, dep. dir. divsn. rsch. learning in formal and informal settings, 2007—; guest faculty mus. mgmt. program U. Colo., Boulder, Colo., 2001. Rsch. assoc. and assoc. prof. dept. edn. U. Chgo., 1982—87; adj. staff scientist C. F. Kettering Rsch. Lab., Yellow Springs, Ohio, 1977—79; mem. pub. engagement working group, nanoscale sci. edn. and tech. subcom. Nat. Sci. and Tech. Coun., 2005—. Author: (book) Basics for Chemistry, 1982, Living Chemistry, 2d edit., 1986; contbr. articles to profl. jours.; host, prodr. (radio program) Science Alive!, 1983—87, developer numerous mus. exhibits. Apptd. Nat. Mus. Svcs. Bd., 1996—2003; trustee Mus. Without Walls, 1996—2000, Sci. Pioneers, 2000. Recipient Up and Comers award, Jr. Achievement Mid.-Am., 1992; grantee, NSF, NEH, U.S. Dept. Edn., Ill. Humanities Coun., 1976—88; fellow Woodrow Wilson, 1969, NIH postdoctoral, 1972. Fellow: AAAS (at large sect. Y 1987—93); mem.: Am. Assn. Museums (mus. assessment program adv. com. 2000—03), Assn. Sci. Tech. Ctrs. (publs. com. 1984—94, chmn. 1988—94, ethics com. 1994—95, legis. com., chmn. 1996—2000), Phi Lambda Upsilon, Sigma Xi, Alpha Sigma Nu (hon.). Home: 2528 Queen Anne's Ln NW Washington DC 20037-2148 Office Phone: 703-292-5126.

UDAGAWA, TAKESHI, physicist, researcher; b. Tokyo, May 3, 1932; arrived in U.S., 1970; s. Saheiji Udagawa and Teruko (Yamazaki) Urayama; m. Yukiko Amano, Mar. 20, 1960 (dec. Oct. 1989); children: Yoichi, Taturo; m. Mami Eto, Apr. 15, 1991. BS, Tokyo Inst. Sci., 1957; MS, Tokyo U. of Edn., 1959, PhD, 1962. Instr. Tokyo Inst. Tech., 1962-64; rsch. assoc. Fla. State U., Tallahassee, 1964-66; rsch. fellow Niels Bohn Inst., Copenhagen, 1966-68; assoc. prof. Kyoto (Japan) U., 1968-70; prof. dept. physics U. Tex., Austin, 1970—. Rsch. fellow Kernforschungsanlage, Juelich, Germany, 1981—95. Contbr. articles to profl. jours. Recipient Fgn. Mins. commendation in Commemoration of 150th Anniversary Japan/U.S. Relationship, 2004; Rsch. grantee, Dept. Energy, Washington, 1970—96. Mem.: Japanese Phys. Soc., Am. Phys. Soc. Achievements include contributions to various aspects of nuclear reaction theories. Home: 4018 Amy Cir Austin TX 78759-8146 Office: U Tex Dept Physics Austin TX 78712 Home Phone: 512-795-8191; Office Phone: 512-471-1984. Business E-Mail: udagawa@physics.utexas.edu.

UDALL, JOHN NICHOLAS, JR., medical educator, researcher; b. Washington, Dec. 30, 1940; s. John Nicholas Udall and Sybil Elizabeth Webb; m. Roslyn Iris Udall, Aug. 23, 1967; children: Alexis Swain Schmitt, John Hunt, Caroline Elizabeth Garcia, Leah Catherine Getscher. BS, Brigham Young U., Provo, Utah, 1965; MD, Temple U. Med. Sch., Phila., 1969; PhD, MIT, Cambridge, Mass., 1980. Diplomate Nat. Bd. Med. Examiners, Am. Bd. Pediatrics, Sub-bd. Pediatric Gastroenterology, Am. Bd. Nutrition; lic. physician Calif., Mass., Ariz., La. Prof., chmn. pediat. W.Va. U. Health Scis. Ctr., Charleston Divsn., 2005—. Resident physician Clin. Rsch. Ctr., MIT, 1977-80, prin. investigator, 1980-85; assoc. staff physician Mass. Rehab. Hosp., Boston, 1978-85; asst. in pediatrics Mass. Gen. Hosp., Boston, 1979-86; dir. nutrition support svc. Children's Hosp., Boston, 1983-85, assoc. in medicine/gastroenterology, 1983-86; dir. sect. pediatric gastroenterology U. Ariz. Health Scis. Ctr., Tucson, 1986-92. Contbr. numerous articles to profl. jours., chpts. to books; editorial bd. Mass. Gen. Hosp. Dietary Manual, 1982, Seminars in Pediatric Gastroenterology and Nutrition, 1990—, Healthy Kids: The Magazine for Parents, 1990—, Jour. Pediatric Gastroenterology and Nutrition, 1991—, Nutrition: The Internat. Jour. of Applied and Basic Nutrition Scis., 1993—; editorial adv. bd. Snyder Comms., Rockville, Md., 1990-92; book rev. editor Jour. Pediatric Gastroenterology and Nutrition, 1983-90. With USPHS, 1970-72. Capt. Pub. Health Svcs. US Army, 1970—72, Phila., Miss., Sante Fe, N.Mex. Grantee NIH, 1978-80, 81-83, 83-86, 84-89, 86-89, 1993, Shriners Hosp., 1986-89, Ariz. Disease Control Rsch. Commn., 1988-90, U. Ariz. Small Grants Project, 1988-89, Joseph and Mary Cacioppo Found., 1988-89. Fellow Am. Acad. Pediatrics; mem. Internat. Soc. Supramolecular Biology, N.Am. Soc. for Pediatric Gastroenterology, Soc. for Pediatric Rsch., Am. Burn Assn., AAAS, Am. Soc. Clin. Nutrition (nomination com. 1993), Am. Inst. Nutrition, Western Soc. Pediatric Rsch., Am. Gastroenterol. Assn., Nat. Ileitis and Colitis Found., Am. Soc. Parenteral and Enteral Nutrition, Pima County Pediatric Soc. (sec. 1988), Ariz. Pediatric Soc., Am. Pediatric Soc., Tucson Area Soc. Parenteral and Enteral Nutrition. Mem. Lds Ch. Avocations: jogging, sports, hiking, writing. Office: Women and Children's Hosp 830 Pennsylvania Ave Charleston WV 25302 Office Phone: 304-388-1561. Office Fax: 304-388-1577. Personal E-mail: jnudall@gmail.com. Business E-Mail: judall@hsc.wvu.edu.

UDALL, MARK, United States Senator from Colorado; b. Tucson, July 18, 1950; m. Maggie Fox; children: Jed, Tess. B in Am. Civilization, Williams Coll., Mass., 1972. Course dir., educator Colo. Outward Bound Sch., 1975-85, exec. dir., 1985-95; mem. dist. 13 Colo. Ho. of Reps., 1997—98; mem. US Congress from 2d Colo. dist., Washington, 1999—2008, dep. regional whip; mem. armed svcs. com., resources com., sci. & tech. com., small bus. com., agrl. com.; US Senator from Colo., 2009—. Mem. Dem. Homeland Security Task Force, North Atlantic Treaty Orgn. Parliamentary Assembly, Congl. Fitness Caucus; v.p. Dem. Freshman Class; co-chair Renewable Energy & Energy Efficiency Caucus. Mem. Parkinson's Action Network; bd. dirs. Berger Found. Mem.: Am. Alpine Club. Democrat. Avocation: mountain climbing. Office: Ste 206 8601 Turnpike Dr Westminster CO 80031-7044 also: B40E Dirksen Senate Office Bldg Washington DC 20510 Office Phone: 202-244-5941. E-mail: Senator_Mark_Udall@markudall.senate.gov.*

UDALL, THOMAS S. (TOM), United States Senator from New Mexico; b. Tucson, May 18, 1948; s. Stewart and Lee Udall; m. Jill Z. Cooper; 1 child, Amanda. BA in Govt./Polit. Sci., Prescott Coll., Ariz., 1970; LLB in Internat. Law, Cambridge U., Eng., 1975; JD, U. N.Mex. Sch. Law, 1977. Bar: N.Mex. 1978. Legis. asst. Staff of US Senator Joseph R. Biden of Del., 1973; law clk. to Chief Justice Oliver Seth US 10th Cir. Ct. Appeals, Santa Fe, 1977-78; asst. US atty. criminal divsn. US Atty.'s Office, 1978-81; atty. pvt. practice, Santa Fe, 1981-83; chief counsel N.Mex. Health and Environ. Dept., 1983-84; atty. to ptnr. Miller, Stratvert, Togerson and Schlenker, P.A., Albuquerque, 1985-90; atty. gen., 1991—99; mem. US Congress from 3rd N.Mex. dist., 1999—2009, mem. appropriations com., co-vice chair Native Am. caucus, mem. Bipartisan Rural Caucus; US Senator from NMex., 2009—. Pres. Rio Chama Preservation Trust; mem. N.Mex. Environ. Improvement Bd., 1986—87; bd. dirs. La Compania de Teatro de Albuquerque, Santa Fe Chamber Music Festival, Law Fund, 1991—98. Recipient Leadership award, Nat. Commn. Against Drunk Driving, Legal Impact award, N.Mex. Bar Prosecution Sect., Pub. Svc. award, Nat. Highway Traffic Safety Adminstrn. Mem.: Nat. Assn. Atty. Gens. (pres. 1996). Democrat. Office: US Senate B40D Dirksen Senate Office Bldg Washington DC 20510 Mailing: Ste A & B 3311 Candelaria Ave Albuquerque NM 87107 Office Phone: 202-225-6190. Office Fax: 202-226-1331.*

UDDIN, MOHAMMED RAFIQUE, biology professor; PhD, U. Wales, Eng., 1980. Prof. biology LeMoyne-Owen Coll., Memphis, 1994—; adj. prof. biology Pk. U., Millington, Tenn., 2007—. Assoc. prof. biology Rust Coll., Hollysprings, Miss., 1990. Contbr. scientific papers to publs. (Tchg. Excellence award, 2001). Mem. cmty. adv. bd. Memphis Utility Co., MLGW, Memphis, 1996—2003. Achievements include patents for an US patent on somatic embryogenesis.

UDELSON, JAMES ERIC, cardiologist, educator; b. Dec. 16, 1955; MD, NY Med. Coll., 1981. Cert. Internal Medicine, 1984, Cardiovascular Disease, 1989. Resident Newton-Wellesley Hosp., Mass., 1981—84; fellowship cardiology Nat. Heart Lung and Blood Inst., NIH, Bethesda, Md., 1985—87; assoc. chief Tufts-New England Med. Ctr., Boston, 1989, assoc. chief Divsn. Cardiology, dir. nuclear cardiology, co-dir. Heart Failure Ctr. and Hypertrophic Cardiomyopathy Ctr., dir. Cardiac Imaging Core Lab. Assoc. prof. Tufts U. Sch. Medicine, Boston, 1989—. Assoc. editor Circulation, mem. editl. bd., guest editor Jour. Am. Coll. Cardiology. Mem.: Am. Coll. Cardiology, Am. Soc. Nuclear Cardiology (past pres.). Office: Tufts Med Ctr 800 Washington St Boston MA 02111 Office Phone: 617-636-8066.

UDEVITZ, NORMAN, publishing executive; b. Cheyenne, Wyo., Jan. 22, 1929; s. Jay and Edith (Stienberg) U.; m. Marsha Rae Dinner, Dec. 17, 1960; children: Jane, Kathryn, Andrew. Student, U. Colo., 1946-49. With Cheyenne Newspapers Inc. Cheyenne, 1949-54; editor-pub. Wyo. Buffalo, Cheyenne, 1954-63; account supr. Tilds & Cantz Advt. Agy., LA, 1963-66; exec. v.p. Fitzgerald, Maahs & Miller, LA, 1966-71; staff writer The Denver Post, 1971-88; dir. pubs. Am. Water Works Assn., Denver, 1988-97; ret., 1997. Sgt. USNG, 1950-53. Named Colo.'s Outstanding Journalist, U. Colo., 1977; recipient Pulitzer Prize Gold medal Columbia U., 1986. Mem. Investigative Reporters and Editors Inc., (bd. dirs. 1978-80, 81-83), The Newspaper Guild (McWilliams award 1976, 77). Jewish. Home: 4677 E Euclid Ave Centennial CO 80121-3224

UDEY, MARK C., dermatologist, researcher; B in chemistry, U. Wis., Madison; MD, PhD, Washington U., St. Louis. Med. intern Barnes Hosp., St. Louis, dermatology resident; now chief Dermatology Br. Ctr. Cancer Rsch., Nat. Cancer Inst., NIH. Office: Dermatology Br Ctr Cancer Rsch 10 Center Dr Bldg 10 Rm 12N238 Bethesda MD 20892-1908 Office Phone: 301-496-1741. Office Fax: 301-496-5370. E-mail: udey@helix.nih.gov.*

UDEY, SUSAN S., accounting educator; d. Elmer J. and Mildred Miles Schwiesow; m. Ross A. Udey, Mar. 15, 1986; 1 child, Christopher S. EdB, Wayne State Coll., Nebr., 1979, MEd, 1981; MPA, U. Nebr., Lincoln, 1986, PhD, 1998. Asst. prof. bus. Wayne State Coll., 1991—92; asst. prof. Peru State Coll., Nebr., 1982—86, bus. mgr., 1993—95, v.p. adminstrn. and fin., 1995—2000; prof. bus. Dana Coll., Blair, Nebr., 2001—. Vol. AARP Tax Preparer, Blair, 2003—. Mem. fin. and other coms. First United Meth. Ch., Blair, 2001—08. Office: Dana Coll 2848 College Dr Blair NE 68008 Office Phone: 402-426-7287.

UDOFF, ERIC JOEL, diagnostic radiologist; b. Balt., Oct. 8, 1948; s. Melvin Jerome and Esther (Fisher) U.; m. Ronni Ann Chapin, June 7, 1980; children: Brian Evan, Jonathan Andrew. AB, Washington U., 1969; MD, U. Rochester, 1973. Intern, resident in diagnostic radiology U. Chgo., 1973-77; instr. in cardiovasc. radiology Johns Hopkins U., Balt., 1977-79; radiologist Sinai Hosp., Balt., 1979-86, Mt. Sinai Med. Ctr., Milw., 1986-88, Sinai Hosp., Balt., 1988-90; asst. prof. radiology Johns Hopkins U. Hosp., 1990-91; radiologist North Fulton Regional Hosp., Roswell, Ga., 1991-97; instr. thoracoabdominal imaging U. Va., 1997-98, Radiologist, Diagnostic Imaging Specialists, Atlanta, 1998—. Mem. AMA, Am. Roentgen Ray Soc., Am. Coll. Radiology, Radiol. Soc. N.Am., Ga. Radiol. Soc., Phi Beta Kappa. Avocations: reading, tennis. Office: 6000 Lake Forrest Dr Ste 475 Atlanta GA 30328 Office Phone: 404-459-8440. Personal E-mail: ejurad@yahoo.com.

UDOGU, E. IKE, social sciences educator, researcher; s. Onya Olisa and Cicelia Udogu; m. Ahante A. Diamond; 1 child, Eric. PhD, So. Ill. U., Carbondale, 1980. Prof. Francis Marion U., Florence, SC, 1985—2003; prof. and faculty fellow Appalachian State U., Boone, NC, 2003—. Mem. editl. bd. Collegiate Press, San Diego, 1990-92, cons., 1992—; reviewer Jour. of Third World Studies, Columbus, Ga., 1990—, Can. Rev. of Studies in Nationalism, Charlottetown, Can., 1994—. Sr. co-editor: Internat. Jour. of Asian Studies, 1995, guest editor Jour. Asian & African Studies, 1996; contbr. articles to profl. jours. Polit. analyst, guest speaker Black History Month, CBS-TV-13, Florence, 1988, PBS-Ch. 27, Sumter, S.C., 1991, ABC-TV-15, Florence, S.C., 1992, Kingstree (S.C.) High Sch., 1991; pres. Coalition of Black Networking, Florence, 1990-91. Nat. Endowment Humanities fellow U. Wis., 1983; recipient cert. Outstanding Young Men of Am., 1982, 84, cert. appreciation Senate of the State of S.C., Columbia, 1990, cert. merit Collegiate Press, San Diego, 1991, Minority Recruiter Positive Image award, 1992; named to Athletic Hall of Fame, Appalachian State U., Boone, N.C., 1986., Outstanding Scholars of 21st Century, Internat. Biographical Ctr., Cambridge, Eng., 2000 Mem. Internat. Studies Assn., Internat. Soc. Study European Ideas, African Studies Assn., Assn. Third World Studies, S.C. Polit. Sci. Assn. (bd. mem. 1983-85), S.C. Consortium for Internat. Studies. Avocations: writing fiction, soccer, tennis, jogging. Office: Appalachian State Univ Anne Belk Hall Boone NC 28608-2107 Office Fax: 828-262-2947. Business E-Mail: udoguei@appstate.edu.

UDRY, STEPHEN POTTER, history professor; b. Washington, Oct. 11, 1963; s. William and Dorothy Udry; m. Tsai wei Zhang, May 27, 1989; children: Justin A. Z., Matthew W. Z. PhD, U. Wash., Seattle, 2000. Assoc. prof. Carthage Coll., Kenosha, Wis., 2000—. Office: Carthage Coll 2001 Alford Pk Dr Kenosha WI 53140 Business E-Mail: sudry@carthage.edu.

UDUPI, YATHIRAJ BHAT, software engineer; m. Anupama Rao Karaya. BTech, Indian Inst. Tech. Madras, 2002; MS, NC State U., Raleigh, 2005, PhD, 2008. Grad. rsch. asst. NC State U., 2002—07; software engr. III Cisco Sys. Inc., San Jose, Calif., 2008—. Personal E-mail: ybudupi@gmail.com.

UDVAR-HAZY, STEVEN F., leasing company financial executive; b. Budapest, Hungary, Feb. 23, 1946; came to U.S., 1958. m. Christine L. Henneman, June 7, 1980; 4 children. BA, UCLA, 1968; HHD (hon.), U. Utah, 1990; D (hon.), Emory Riddle Aero. U., 2000. Cert. airline transp. jet pilot. Chmn., CEO Internat. Lease Fin. Corp., Beverly Hills, Calif., 1973—. Bd. dirs. Sky West Inc., St. George, Utah; chmn. bd. dirs. Ocean Equities, Inc. Active Smothsonian's Udvar-Hazy Nat. Air & Spave Mus. Named one of Forbes' Richest Americans, 2000—, World's Richest People, Forbes mag., 2001—. Mem. Wings Club (Achievement to Aviation award 1989). Office: Internat Lease Fin Corp 10250 Constellation Blvd 35th Fl Los Angeles CA 90067 Office Phone: 310-788-1999.

UDWADIA, FIRDAUS ERACH, engineering educator, consultant; b. Bombay, Aug. 28, 1947; arrived in US, 1968; s. Erach Rustam and Perin P. (Lentin) Udwadia; m. Farida Gagrat, Jan. 6, 1977; children: Shanaira, Zubin. BS, Indian Inst. Tech., Bombay, 1968; MS, Calif. Inst. Tech., 1969, PhD, 1972; MBA, U. So. Calif., 1985. Mem. faculty Calif. Inst. Tech., Pasadena, 1972-74; asst. prof. engring. U. So. Calif., LA, 1974-77, assoc. prof. mech., civil, and aerospace engring. and bus. adminstrn., 1977-83, prof., 1983-86, bd. dirs. Structural Identification Computing Facility, prof. engring, bus. adminstrn., maths., 1986—2005, prof. civil engring., aerospace mech. engring., math., info. ops., mgmt., and sys. architecture engring., 2005—. Cons. Jet Propulsion Lab., Pasadena, 1978—, Argonne Nat. Lab., 1982—83, Air Force Rocket Lab., Edwards AFB, Calif., 1984—, Air Force Rsch. Lab., 1990—; vis. prof. applied mechanics and mech. engring. Calif. Inst. Tech., Pasadena, 1993. Author: Analytical Dynamics, A New Approach, 1996; hon. editor: Jour. Math. Ctrl. Sci. and Applications, assoc. editor: Applied Math. and Computation, Applied Mechanics Reviews, Discrete Dynamics Nature and Soc., Jour. Optimization Theory and Applications, Jour. Franklin Inst., Jour. Differential Equations and Dynamical Sys., Nonlinear Studies; assoc. editor Applied Mechanism Revs.; assoc. editor: Jour. Math. Analysis and Applications, Jour. Math. Problems in Engring.; editor: Jour. Aerospace Engring., Advances in Dynamics and Control, 2000; co-editor: Dynamics and Control, 1999; chief editor Dynamical Systems and Control, 2004; hon. editor: Jour. Math. Control and its Applications; mem. adv. bd. Jour. Tech. Forecasting and Social Change; contbr. articles to profl. jours. Bd. dirs. Crisis Mgmt. Ctr. U. So. Calif., LA. Recipient Golden Poet award, 1990; NSF grantee, 1976—. Fellow: ASME, AIAA (Outstanding Achievement award 2007); mem.: ASCE (Outstanding Tech. Contributions award 2006, Richard Torrens award 2008), Seismol. Soc. Am., Soc. Indsl. and Applied Math., Am. Acad. Mechanics, Sigma Xi (mem. Earthquake Engring. Rsch. Inst. 1971, 1974, 1984). Achievements include patents in field; patents for control of nonlinear systems, 2002. Avocations: poetry, piano, chess. Home: 2100 S Santa Anita Ave Arcadia CA 91006-4611 Office: U So Calif 430K Olin Hall University Park Los Angeles CA 90007 Office Phone: 213-740-0495.

UDY, RAE, columnist, writer; b. Ogden, Utah, Mar. 24, 1950; d. Verl Nish Udy and Elizabeth Jones White; m. Steven James Weese, Apr. 9, 1971; children: Nation Verl Weese, Luke Ray Weese. Student, Weber State U., 1968. Columnist Longview News-Jour., Longview, Tex., 1989—; lifestyle editor Marshall News Messenger, Marshall, Tex., 1999—2000. Mem. and past v.p. East Tex. Writers Assn., 1987—; former contbr. Idaho Enterprise, Harleton Happenings. Author: (book) Countdown Cooking, 1993. Mem.: Ladies Aux. of Frat. of Eagles. Democrat. Christian. Avocations: gardening, travel, camping. Office: PO Box 5965 Longview TX 75608 Office Phone: 903-777-2723. Personal E-mail: raeudy@gmail.com.

UEBERROTH, HEIDI J., sports association executive; b. 1965; d. Peter and Virginia (Nicolaus) Ueberroth. BA in English, Vanderbilt U., 1987. With Ohlmeyer Comm., Paris; dir. sales & programming ESPN; dir. internat. mktg. NBA, NYC, 1994—96, head global TV and media distbn. divsn., 1996—, exec. v.p. global media properties and mktg. partnerships, 2000—06, pres. global mktg. partnerships & internat. bus. ops., 2006—. Bd. dirs. Quiksilver, Inc., 2006—. Dir. Ueberroth Family Charitable Found., 1990—; bd. trustees Cancer Rsch. Inst., 2003—; bd. mem. Advt. Coun. Named a Woman to Watch, Advt. Age, 2008; named one of 40 Under 40, Sports Bus. Jour., 2000, 2001, 2002, 20 Most Influential Women in Sports Bus., 2005, The Most Influential People in the World of Sports, BusinessWeek, 2007; named to Advt. Hall of Achievement, Am. Advt. Fedn., 2005. Office: NBA Olympic Tower 645 5th Ave Fl 10 New York NY 10022-5986*

UEBERROTH, PETER VICTOR, sports association executive; b. Evanston, Ill., Sept. 2, 1937; s. Victor and Laura (Larson) U.; m. Virginia Nicolaus, Sept. 1959; children: Vicky, Heidi, Keri, Joe BS in Bus., San Jose State Coll., 1959. Ops. mgr. then v.p. Trans Internat., 1959-62; founder, chmn. Transp. Cons. Internat., 1963-79; pres., mng. dir. LA Olympic Organizing Com., 1979-84; commr. Maj. League Baseball, NYC, 1984-89; mng. dir. Contrarian Group, 1990—; co-chmn. Doubletree Hotels Corp., Phoenix, 1993—; co-owner, co-chmn. Pebble Beach Co., 1999—; dir. McLeodUSA, 2001—; chmn. US Olympic Com., 2004—. Former chmn. Ask Mr. Foster Travel Service; chmn. Colony Hotels, Intercontinental Tours, Inc., First Travel Corp; mem. bd. dirs. California Angels. Ambassadors Internat., Coca-Cola Co., Hilton Hotels Corp. Author: Made in America, 1985 Named Man of Yr., Time Mag. and Sporting News, 1984; recipient Scopus award Am. Friends of Hebrew U., Jerusalem, 1985; named one of Most Influential People in the World of Sports, Bus. Week, 2008. Fellow: Am. Acad. Arts and Scis. Office: Ambassadors Intl Inc 110 S Ferrall St Spokane WA 99202*

UEDA, ATSUKO, educator; b. Tokyo; PhD, U. Mich., Ann Arbor. Asst. prof. U. Ill., Champaign, 2000—04, Princeton U., NJ, 2004—. Office: Princeton Univ 211 Jones Hall Princeton NJ 08544

UEHLEIN, EDWARD CARL, JR., lawyer; b. Boston, May 7, 1941; s. Edward Carl and Elizabeth (Thatcher) U.; m. Judith Taylor, June 16, 1962; children: Christine, Sara. Student, Bowdoin Coll., Brunswick, Maine, 1958-59; BA, Swarthmore Coll., 1962; LLB, Boston Coll., 1965. Bar: Mass. 1965, D.C. 1968. Atty. Nat. Labor Relations Bd., Atlanta, 1965-68; assoc. Morgan, Lewis & Bockius, Washington, 1968-71; exec. asst. to sec. U.S. Dept. Labor, Washington, 1971-73; ptnr. Morgan Lewis & Bockius, Washington, 1973—2001, counsel, 2001—. Sec.-treas. Carlou Corp., Wilmington, Del., 1969-71. Fellow, Ford Found., 1961. Mem. ABA, FBA, D.C. Bar Assn., Belle Haven Country Club, Ballybunion Golf Club, Royal Dornoch Golf Club. Avocations: travel, golf, reading. Office: Morgan Lewis & Bockius 1111 Pennsylvania Ave Washington DC 20004 Office Phone: 202-739-5075. Business E-Mail: ecuehlein@morganlewis.com.

UEHLING, BARBARA STANER, academic administrator; b. Wichita, Kans., June 12, 1932; d. Roy W. and Mary Elizabeth (Hilt) Staner; children: Jeffrey Steven, David Edward. BA, U. Wichita, 1954; MA, Northwestern U., 1956, PhD, 1958; degree (hon.), Drury Coll., 1978; LLD (hon.), Ohio State U., 1980. Mem. psychology faculty Oglethorpe U., Atlanta, 1959-64, Emory U., Atlanta, 1966-69; adj. prof. U. R.I., Kingston, 1970-72; dean Roger Williams Coll., Bristol, RI, 1972-74; dean arts scis. Ill. State U., Normal, 1974-76; provost U. Okla., Norman, 1976-78; chancellor U. Mo.-Columbia, 1978-86, U. Calif., Santa Barbara, 1987-94; mem. Pacific Rim Pub. U. Pres. Conf., 1990-92; exec. dir. Bus. and Higher Edn. Forum, Washington, 1995-97. Cons. North Ctr. Accreditation Assn., 1974-86; mem. nat. educator adv. com. to Comptr. Gen. of U.S., 1978-79; mem. Commn. on Mil.-Higher Edn. Rels., 1978-79, Am. Coun. on Edn., bd. dirs. 1979-83, treas., 1982-83, mem. Bus.-Higher Edn. Forum, 1980-94, exec. com. 1991-94; sr. vis. fellow Am. Coun. Edn., 1987; mem. Commn. on Internat. Edn., 1992-94, vice chair 1993; bd. dirs. Coun. of Postsecondary Edn., 1986-87, 90-93, Meredith Corp., 1980-99; mem. Transatlantic Dialogue, PEW Found., 1991-93; mem. West Coast adv. bd. Inst. Internat. Edn., 2004—. Author: Women in Academe: Steps to Greater Equality, 1979; mem. editl. bd. Jour. Higher Edn. Mgmt., 1986-95; contbr. articles to profl. jours. Bd. dirs., chmn. Nat. Ctr. Higher Edn. Mgmt. Sys., 1977-80; trustee Carnegie Found. for Advancement of Tchg., 1980-86, Santa Barbara Med. Found. Clinic, 1989-94; bd. dirs. Resources for the Future, 1985-94; mem. select com. on athletics NCAA, 1983-84, also mem. presdl. commn.; mem. Nat. Coun. on Edn. Rsch., 1980-82. Social Sci. Rsch. Coun. fellow, 1954-55; NSF fellow, 1956-57; NIMH postdoctoral rsch. fellow, 1964-67; named one of 100 Young Leaders of Acad. Change Mag. and ACE, 1978; recipient Alumni Achievement award Wichita State U., 1978, Alumnae award Northwestern U., 1985, Excellence in Edn. award Pi Lambda Theta, 1989. Mem. Am. Assn. Higher Edn. (bd. dirs. 1974-77, pres. 1977-78), Western Coll. Assn. (pres.-elect 1988-89, pres. 1990-92), West Coast Adv. Bd., Inst. Internat. Edn., Golden Key, Sigma Xi. Personal E-mail: buc2193@mac.com.

UEJO, COLLEEN MISAYE, elementary school educator; b. Honolulu, Oct. 18, 1953; d. Masaichi and Esther Itoyo Uejo. EdB, U. Hawaii, Manoa, 1976, M in Spl. Edn., 1983. Tchr. Liholiho Elem., Honolulu, 1979, Tenrikiyo Preschool, Honolulu, 1976—84, Queen Emma Preschool, Honolulu, 1984—88, Kaimuki Mid. Sch., Honolulu, 1988—99, Linapuni Elem., Honolulu, 1999—. After sch. care staff Waiolani Judd Sch., Honolulu, 1971—76; big sister Big Bros./Big Sisters Hawaii, Honolulu, 1984—88; coach Spl. Olympics, Honolulu, 1988—99. Yonashiro Chojin Kai v.p. Hawaii United Okinawan Assn., Honolulu, 1994. Named Uchinanchu of Yr., Hawaii United Okinawan Assn., 1998, Honolulu Dist. Tchr. of Yr., State Hawaii Dept. Edn., 2006. Mem.: ASCD, Nat. Coun. Tchrs. for Math., Nat. Assn. for the Edn. Young Children, Coun. for Exceptional Children, Phi Delta Kappa Internat. Office: Linapuni Elementary School 1434 Linapuni St Honolulu HI 96819

UFFELMAN, MALCOLM RUCJ, electronics executive; b. Clarksville, Tenn., Oct. 22, 1935; s. Malcolm C. and Margaret Lillian (Davidson) U.; m. Sarah White Barksdale, June 11, 1957; children: Malcolm Rucj Jr., Katharina White, Davidson Barksdale, Jefferson Churchill. BS, Vanderbilt U., 1957; MS, George Washington U., 1963. Engr. Melpar, Inc., Falls Church, Va., 1957-60; v.p. Scope, Inc., Reston, Va., 1960-73; sr. cons. MRI, Inc., McLean, Va., 1973-78; v.p. Racal Communications Inc., Rockville, Md., 1978-80; sr. cons. MRJ, Inc., Fairfax, Va., 1980-82; v.p., gen. mgr., Ctr. Advanced Planning and Analysis E-Systems Inc., Fairfax, 1982-96; US del. NATO Indsl. Adv. Group, 1993—97; v.p. Constellation Comm., Inc., Fairfax, 1996-99; patent agt., 1999—2000; exec. v.p. Contact Corp., 2000—08, bd. dir., 2009—; trustee Camco Fund, 2002—. Contbr. numerous articles to profl. jours.; holder 7 patents in field. Scoutmaster Troop 183 Boy Scouts Am., Oakton, Va., 1973-79; Capt. USAR, 1957-69. Fellow IEEE; mem. Cosmos Club (Washington), Internat. Brotherhood Magicians. Episcopalian. Avocations: sailing, reading, travel, magic, fly fishing. Personal E-mail: rucj@ieee.org.

UFFNER, MICHAEL S., automotive executive; b. Phila., July 18, 1945; s. Ray and Shirley A. (Block) Uffner; m. Marilyn A. Ursomarso; 1 child, Lauren R. BA, MA, U. Pa., Phila., 1971. V.p. Union Park Pontiac, BMW, Honda, Wilmington, Del., 1972-82; pres. Del. Motor Sales Inc., Auto Team Del., Wilmington, 1982—. Mem. manpower tng. adv. com. GM, pres. dealer adv. coun., 1985, mem. dealer policy bd., 1990—91; trustee Christiana Health Care Sys., 2002—. Mem. Wilmington Police Bus. Adv. Coun., 1991—, New Castle County Small Bus. Commn., 1993—; trustee Goldey-Beacom Coll., 2007—; bd. dirs., mem. exec. com. BBB Del., 1992—2007, chmn., 1998—2000. Recipient Quality Dealer award, Time Mag., 1997, numerous other awards. Mem.: Del. Automobile and Truck Dealers Assn. (bd. dirs., v.p. 1992—93, pres. 1994—95), Am. Econ. Assn., Cadillac Motor Car Divsn. Nat. Dealers Coun. (vice chmn. 1989—90, chmn. 1990—91, chmn. DeVille brand com. 1995—97), Tavistock Civic Assn. (pres. 1976—77), US C. of C. (bd. dirs. 1998—2004, chmn. pub. affairs com. 2001—04), Del. C. of C. (chmn. small bus. com. 1991—95, bd. dirs. 1993—, chmn. small bus. alliance 1995—96, mem. exec. com. 1995—, vice chmn. bd. dirs. 1996—99, chmn. bd. dirs. 2000—02), Am. Heart Assn. (bd. dirs. Del. chpt. 1981—98, pres. 1985—86, chmn. 1986—87, v.p., bd. dirs. Nat. Ctr. 1987—90), U. Pa. Alumni Assn. (v.p. Del. chpt. 1978—80, pres. 1980—81), Univ. Whist Club, Ocean City Yacht Club, Hidden Creek Golf Club, Fieldstone Golf Club. Office: 1606 Pennsylvania Ave Wilmington DE 19806-4018

UFFORD, CHARLES WILBUR, JR., lawyer; b. Princeton, NJ, July 8, 1931; m. Isabel Letitia Wheeler, May 20, 1961; children: Eleanor Morris Ufford Léger, Catherine Latourette Ufford-Chase, Alison Wistar Ufford Salem. BA cum laude (Francis H. Burr scholar), Harvard U., Cambridge, Mass., 1953, LLB, 1959; postgrad. (Lionel de Jersey Harvard studentship), Cambridge U., Eng., 1953-54. Bar: NY 1961, US Tax Ct. 1963. Assoc. Riggs, Ferris & Geer, NYC, 1959-61; from assoc. to ptnr. Jackson, Nash, Brophy, Barringer & Brooks, 1961-78; ptnr. Skadden, Arps, Slate, Meagher & Flom, NYC, 1978-92, of counsel, 1993-96. Contbr. articles to legal jours. Trustee Nat. Squash Racquets Ednl. Found., NYC, 1972-81; mem. Princeton Monthly Meeting, Soc. of Friends, clk., 1986-88, 99; mem. exec. com. Friends Com. on Nat. Legislation, 1997-98; bd. dirs. Pennswood Village, 1998-2007, Friends Fiduciary Corp., 1999-. Nat. Intercollegiate Squash Racquets champion, 1952-53; mem. NCAA All-Am. Soccer 1st team, 1952. Fellow Am. Coll. Trust and Estate Counsel (transfer tax study com. 1990-93); mem. ABA, NY Bar Assn. (chmn. trusts and estates law sect. 1984), Assn. Bar City NY, NY State Office of Ct. Adminstrn. (Surrogates Ct. Adv. Com., 1994-96), US Squash Racquets Assn. (hon. life; trustee endowment fund 1994-96), Internat. Lawn Tennis Club U.S.A. (dir. 1982-2005). Personal E-mail: ufford@verizon.net. *Integrity, perseverance, compassion and humor are all very well--but the key is to be blessed by a Divine Improvidence.*

UFIMTSEV, PYOTR YAKOVLEVICH, physicist, electrical engineer, educator; b. Ust'-Charyshskaya Pristan', Altai Region, Russia, July 8, 1931; s. Yakov Fedorovich and Vasilisa Vasil'evna (Toropchina) U.; m. Tatiana Vladimirovna Sinelschikova; children: Galina, Ivan, Vladimir. Grad., Odessa State U., Ukraine, 1954; PhD, Ctrl. Rsch. Inst. Radio Industry, 1959; DSc, St. Petersburg State U., Russia, 1970. Engr., sr. engr., sr. scientist Ctrl. Rsch. Inst. of Radio Industry, Moscow, 1954-73; sr. scientist, head scientist Inst. Radio Engring. & Electronics Acad. Scis., Moscow, 1973-90; prin. engr. Northrop Grumman Corp., 1995—2000; prof. U. Calif., Irvine, 2003—04. Vis. prof., adj. prof. UCLA, 1990—2003; mem. sci. bd. radio waves Acad. Scis., Moscow, 1960—90. Author: Method of Edge Waves in the Physical Theory of Diffraction, 1962, Theory of Edge Diffraction in Electromagnetics, 2003, Fundamentals of the Physical Theory of Diffraction, 2007; contbr. articles to profl. jours. Recipient USSR State Prize, Moscow, 1990, Leroy Randle Grumman medal for outstanding sci. achievement, N.Y.C., 1991, 20th Century Achievement medal, Cambridge, 1996, Hall of Fame medal, Cambridge, 1996. Fellow IEEE; assoc. fellow AIAA; mem. Electromagnetics Acad. (U.S.), A.S. Popov Sci. Tech. Soc. Radio Engring., Electronics & Telecommunication (Russia). Achievements include origination of the Physical Theory of Diffraction, used for design of American stealth aircrafts and ships; for radar-cross-section calculation, and antenna design.

UGALDE, ARANTZA, language educator; b. Elko, Nev., July 6, 1980; d. Agustin Ugarriza and Judy Moses Ugalde; life ptnr. Alicia Diane Eshbach. BA, Boise State U., Idaho, 2003. Spl. lectr. Spanish Boise State U., 2005—07, academic advisor, 2005—08, instr. Spanish, 2007—. Mem.: Boise State Faculty Senate (senator). Personal E-mail: thorndoublemajor@hotmail.com.

UGGAMS, LESLIE, entertainer; b. NYC, May 25, 1943; d. Harolde Coyden and Juanita Ernestine (Smith) Uggams; m. Grahame John Kelvin-Pratt, Oct. 16, 1965; children: Danielle Nicole Pratt, Justice Harolde John Kelvin-Pratt. Student, Juillard Sch. Music, 1961-63; degree (hon.), Jarvis Coll., Tyler, Tex., Wilberforce U., Ohio. Performer: (TV series) Beulah, 1949, Sing Along with Mitch, 1961—64, The Leslie Uggams Show, 1969; co-host (TV series) Fantasy TV, 1982—83 (Emmy award 1983, 1983); performer: (films) Two Weeks in Another Town, Black Girl, 1962, Skyjacked, 1972, Poor Pretty Eddie, 1973, Sizzle, 1981, Harlem, 1993, (TV miniseries) Roots, 1977 (Critics Choice award for best supporting actress, 1977), Backstairs at the White House, 1979, (Broadway plays) Hallelujah Baby, 1967 (Tony award, 1968), Her First Roman Broadway Musical, 1968, Blues in the Night, 1982, Jerry's Girls, 1985, Anything Goes, 1987, King Hedley II, 2001 (nominated Tony award for best actress, 2001), Thoroughly Modern Millie, 2004, On Golden Pond, 2005 (nominated Helen Hayes award for best actress, 2005), (plays) The Old Settler, 1999 (Audelco award for best actress), Thunder Knocking on the Door, 2002 (Audelco award for best actress, 2002), Stormy Weather: Imagining Lena Horne, 2007, The First Breeze of Summer, 2008; author: The Leslie Uggams Beauty Book, 1966. Founding mem. BRAVO chpt. City of Hope, Los Angeles, 1969, treas., 1969—79. Recipient Drama Critics award, Newspaper and TV critics, 1968, Tony award, 1968, Emmy award, 1993; named best singer on TV, 1962—63. Mem.: SAG, NARAS, AFTRA, Actors' Equity Assn. Democrat. Presbyterian. Avocations: needlepoint, knitting, tennis, squash, exercising. Business E-Mail: leslie@leslieuggams.com.

UGHETTA, JAMES C., lawyer; BA, Denison U., 1977; JD, St. John's U., 1981. Bar: NY 1982, NJ 1982, US Dist. Ct. NJ, US Dist. Ct. (ea. dist.) NY, US Dist. Ct. (so. dist.) NY, US Dist. Ct. (no. dist.) NY, US Supreme Ct. Ptnr. Littleton Joyce Ughetta, Park and Kelly, LLP, NYC. Mem.: Product Liability Adv. Coun., Soc. Automotive Engineers, Assn. for the Advancement of Automotive Medicine, Def. Rsch. Inst. Office: Littleton Joyce Ughetta Park and Kelly LLP Oe Manhattanville Rd Purchase NY 10577

UGHETTA, WILLIAM CASPER, lawyer, manufacturing executive, director; b. NYC, Feb. 8, 1933; s. Casper and Frieda (Bohland) U.; m. Mary L. Lusk, Aug. 10, 1957; children: William C., Robert L., Edward F., Mark R. AB, Princeton U, 1954; LLB, Harvard U., 1959. Bar: N.Y. 1959. Assoc. Shearman & Sterling, NYC, 1959-67; asst. sec. Corning Glass Works, NY, 1968-70, sec., counsel NY, 1971-72, v.p., gen. counsel NY, 1972-82, sr. v.p., gen. counsel NY, 1983-98. Bd. dirs. Covance Inc. Lt. (j.g.) USN, 1954-56. Mem. Am. Corp. Counsel Assn. (trustee 1982-85) Home: 261 Llwyds Ln Vero Beach FL 32963

UGOROWSKI, PHILIP BRIEN, nuclear scientist, researcher; s. Felix Joseph and Mary Margaret (Van Tiem) Ugorowski. BA in Physics, Kalamazoo Coll., Mich., 1983, BA in Math, 1983; MS in Rsch. Physics, Mich. State U., East Lansing, 1987; PhD in Exptl. Nuc. Physics, Western Mich. U., Kalamazoo, 2002. Grad. asst. temp. faculty Western Mich. U., 1995—99; vis. faculty mem. Kalamazoo Coll., 1999—2000; postdoctoral rschr. Youngstown State U., Ohio, 2003—05; nuc. rschr., educator Glen Oaks CC, Centreville, Mich. Recipient Tchg. Awards, Western Mich. U., 1995, 1996, 1999. Mem.: Am. Phys. Soc., Am. Mensa. Achievements include research in hafnium controversy using nuclear calorimetry. Avocations: swimming, hiking. Personal E-mail: phil.ugorowski@juno.com.

UGURBIL, KAMIL, radiologist, neuroscientist, educator; b. Turkey, July 11, 1949; AB in physics, Columbia Coll., 1971; MA in chem. physics, Columbia U., 1974, MPhil in chem. physics, 1976, PhD in chem. physics, 1977; PhD (hon.), U. Utrecht, 2005. Fellow Bell Labs., 1977—79; asst. prof. biochemistry Columbia U., 1979—82; assoc. prof. biochemistry U. Minn., 1982—85, prof. radiology, neuroscience and medicine, 1985—2007, dir. Ctr. Magnetic Resonance Rsch., 1991—, Margaret and H.O. Peterson chair neuroradiology, 1996—2003, McKnight presdl. endowed chair prof., 2003—. Dir. Hochfeld Magnetresonanz Zentrum Max Planck Inst. fur Biologische Kybernetik, Tubingen, Germany, 2003—08. Recipient Hammett award, 1976, Irma T. Hirschl Career Scientist award, 1980, Rsch. Career Devel. award, NIH, 1983, Gold medal, Internat. Soc. Magnetic Resonance Rsch., 1996. Fellow: Internat. Soc. Magnetic Resonance in Medicine; mem.: Inst. Medicine, Am. Acad. Arts and Sciences, Soc. Neuroscience. Office: Ctr Magnetic Resonance Rsch U Minn Med Sch 2021 6th St SE Minneapolis MN 55416 E-mail: kamil@cmrr.umn.edu.*

UHDE, THOMAS WHITLEY, psychopharmacology, psychiatrist; s. George Irwin and Maurine U.; m. Marlene Ann Kraus, Oct. 22, 1977; children: Miles August, Katherine Kraus. BS, Duke U., 1971; MD, U. Louisville, 1975. Diplomate Am. Bd. Psychiatry and Neurology. Postdoctoral fellow Yale U., New Haven, 1975-79, chief resident clin. rsch. unit, 1979; rsch. fellow NIMH, 1979-81; pvt. practice in psychiatry Bethesda, Md., 1979-93; clin. adminstr. sect. psychobiology BPB, NIMH, ADAMHA, Bethesda, Md., 1979-80, chief unit on anxiety and affective disorders, 1982-89, chief 3-West clin. rsch. unit, 1980-90, chief sect. on anxiety and affective disorders, 1989-93; asst. clin. prof. Uniformed Svcs. U. Health Scis., Bethesda, Md., 1982-85, assoc. clin. prof. uniformed svcs., 1985-91; attending staff Clin. Ctr. NIH, Bethesda, Md., 1982-93; chmn. dept. psychiatry Detroit Receiving Hosp. and Harper Hosp., 1994-98; psychiatrist in chief Detroit Med. Ctr., 1993—2001; clin. prof. Uniformed Svcs. U. Health Scis. Sch. Medicine, Bethesda, 1991—; chmn. dept. psychiatry and behavioral neuroscis. Wayne State U. Sch. Medicine, Detroit, 1993—2001; prof. dept. pharmacology Wayne State U. Sch. of Medicine, Detroit, 1993—2003, 1999—2001; prof., chair dept. psychiatry Penn State Coll., Hershey, Pa., 2004—, dir. ctrl. Pa. Psychiatric Inst., 2004—, dir. neurosci. rsch. inst., 2004—06. Prof., psychiatry and behavioral neuroscis. dept., Wayne State U. Sch. Medicine, 1993-2003, assoc. dean rsch. and grad. programs, 1999-2001; asst. dean neuroscis., 2001-03; mem. sci. adv. com. Bethesda, Md., 1990; cons. Rsch. Scientist Devel. Rev. Com., HHS, ADAMHA, 1983, Career Devel. Program Awards Com., VA, Washington, 1986, Primary Care Rsch. Program, ADAMHA, 1988; exec. bd. Anxiety Disorders Assn. Am., 1991-93, 99-, chair sci. adv. bd., Rockville, Md., 1991-93; biomed. instr. review bd. Penn State U., 2004-; mem. sci. adv. bd. VA VISN4 MIREXX, 2005-. Editor-in-chief (jour.) Anxiety 1993-1996; Co-editor-in-chief (jour.) Depression and Anxiety 1996-2002; Editor-in-chief (jour.) Depression and Anxiety 2002--; mem. editl. bd. Actualities Medicales Internationales en Psychiatrie, 1983, Jour. Affective Disorders, 1986, Jour. Anxiety Disorders, 1987-95, Biol. Psychiatry, 1998—2001; contbr. more than 300 sci. articles to profl. jours. Sr. asst. surgeon US Pub. Health Svc., 1979—80, surgeon US Pub. Health Svc., 1980—84, sr. surgeon US Pub. Health Svc., 1984—91, med. dir. US Pub. Health Svc., 1991—93. Recipient Ackerly award, Nat. Rsch. Svc. award, A.E. Bennet Neuropsychiat. Rsch. Found. award, Brain, Body & Mind award Uniformed Svc. Univ. Health Sci., Recognition award ADAA; Am. Coll. Neuropsychopharmacology travel fellow; Commendation medal, US Public Health Svc.; Meritous Svc. medal; named disting. lectr., U. Va., Heninger Lectr., Yale, Highly Cited Scientist in Psychology/Psychiatry, ISI. Fellow Am. Psychiatric Assn. (disting.); mem. Am. Coll. Neuropsychopharmacolgoy, Am. Coll. Psychiatry, Am. Soc. of Clin. Psychopharmacology, Internat. Brain Rsch. Orgn., Sleep Rsch. Soc., Biol. Psych. Soc., Am Psych Assoc., Penn Psych. Soc., Anx. Dis. Assoc. Am., Anx. Assoc. Argentina (hon), Am. Assoc. Chair Dept. Psych., Int. Soc. Psychoneurology. Independent. Unitarian Universalist. Avocations: art, piano, hiking, boating. Office: Penn State Coll Medicine Dept Psychiatry PO Box 850 500 University Dr Hershey PA 17033-0850 Office Phone: 717-531-8516. Office Fax: 717-531-6491. Business E-Mail: tuhde@psu.edu.

UHL, CHRISTOPHER MARTIN, lawyer; b. Balt., Feb. 21, 1958; s. Robert Henry and Marie Antoinette (Carosella) U.; m. Gael Anna Evangelista, Feb. 16, 1991; children: Christopher Martin Uhl, Grace Molinari Uhl. BS in Acctg., Northeastern U., Boston, 1989, MBA, 1991; JD, New Eng. Sch. Law, 1992. Bar: Mass. 1993, NY 1993, Md. 2004, US Dist. Ct. Mass. 1993, DC 1994, Maine 1994, US Dist. Ct. DC 1994, US Dist. Maine 1994, Conn. 1995, US Supreme Ct., 1998, US Dist. Ct. (ea. and so. dists.) NY 1999, US Dist. Ct. Conn. 1999, US Ct. Appeals (1st cir.) 2000. Fingerprint technician FBI, Washington, 1976-79; project mgr. various constrn. cos., Balt., 1979-87, Admiral Constrn. Co., Boston, 1987-91; asst. dist. atty. Worcester Dist. Atty.'s Office, Mass., 1992-96; prin. Christopher Uhl, Attorney at Law, Worcester, 1997—. Prof. Becker Coll., Worcester, 1993-97. Bd. dirs. Am. Cancer Soc., Boston, 1990-96; ward coord. Reelect Dist. Atty. Campaign, Worcester, 1994; elected mem. Southborough Rep. Town Com., Southborough Housing Authority, Northborough/Southborough Regional Sch. Com. Named Hon. Mem. Rep. State Com. Republican. Roman Catholic. Roman Catholic. Office: 5 State St Worcester MA 01609-2893 Office Phone: 508-797-9000. Office Fax: 508-797-4210. Business E-Mail: chris@uhllaw.com.

UHL, SCOTT MARK, retired state agency administrator, consultant; b. Balt., July 6, 1950; s. Edward George and Maurine Barbara (Keleher) Uhl; m. Charlene Hughins, Feb. 29, 1988. BA, Lehigh U., 1972. Cmty. systems developer Md. Mental Hygiene Adminstrn., Balt., 1979-82, chief, housing and cmty. support, 1982-89; adminstr., cmty. programs, dep. secretariat pub. health Md. Health and Mental Hygiene, Balt., 1989-95; dep. dir. Md. Devel. Disabilities Adminstrn., Balt., 1995—2007, acting dir., 2007, cons., 2007—. Pres. Waterfields Press, Inc., 1994—2004; mem. CARE adv. bd. Md. Dept. Human Resources, Balt., 1987—94; prin. staff Md. Gov.'s Task Force Long Term Fin. Planning for Individuals with Disabilities, 1991—92. Mem. State Adv. Coun. Adminstrv. Hearings, 1993—97. Recipient Gov's Citation, 1992, 2007. Republican. Home: 2004 Sleepy Hollow Dr Woodbine MD 21797

UHL, SUZANNE M., educator; PhD in Comm. Studies, Regent U., Virginia Beach, Va., 2006. Coll. prof., dept. chair Mt. San Jacinto Coll., Menifee, Calif., 2000—. Office: Mt San jacinto CC 28237 La Piedra Rd Menifee CA 92584-8947

UHLANER, CAROLE JEAN, political science professor; b. Wash., 1950; d. Julius Earl and Vera Kolar Uhlaner; m. David Brownstone; 1 child, Steven Brownstone. AB, Radcliffe Coll., Cambridge, Mass., 1971; MS, Stanford U., Palo Alto, CA, 1972; PhD, Harvard U., Cambridge, 1978. Assoc. prof., polit. sci. U. Calif., Irvine, 1981—; asst. prof., polit. sci. Northwestern U., Evanston, Ill., 1977—81. Bd. mem. PTA, Irvine, Calif., 2002—09. Recipient Best Paper award, Western Polit. Sci. Assn., 1999, Breckinridge prize, Midwest Polit. Sci. Assn., 1985; Presdl. scholar, US Govt., 1968, Vis. Postdoctoral fellowship, Russell Sage Found., 1986—87. Mem.: Western Polit. Sci. Assn. (exec. coun. 1990—93, 1995—98). Achievements include research in political participation, ethnicity and politics, political behavior. Office: Univ Calif Irvine Social Sci Plz 3151 Irvine CA 92697

UHLANER, LORRAINE MARIE, finance educator; b. Washington, July 28, 1953; d. Julius E. and V. Uhlaner; m. Tsale Kirzner, June 25, 2000; children: Osne Kirzner, Arye Kirzner, Raya Kirzner; m. Jack Reynold Hendrickson, Dec. 29, 1978 (div. Apr. 25, 2000); children: Eric Benjamin Hendrickson, Susan Abigail Hendrickson. BS, Harvard U., Cambridge, Mass., 1973; MS, U. Mich., Ann Arbor, 1976; doctorandus, U. Leiden, Netherlands, 1976; PhD, U. Mich., Ann Arbor, 1980. Prof. entrepreneurship Nyenrode Bus. U., Breukelen, Netherlands, 2007—, dir., IMBA program, 2007—. Sr. rsch. fellow Max Planck Inst. Economics, Jena, Germany, 2004—. Office: Nyenrode Bus Univ Straatweg 25 Breukelen 3620AC Netherlands E-mail: l.uhlaner@nyenrode.nl.

UHLENHUTH, EBERHARD HENRY, psychiatrist, educator; b. Balt., Sept. 15, 1927; s. Eduard Carl Adolph and Elisabeth (Baier) Uhlenhuth; m. Helen Virginia Lyman, June 20, 1952; children: Kim Lyman, Karen Jane, Eric Rolf. BS in Chemistry, Yale U., 1947; MD, Johns Hopkins U., 1951. Intern Harborview Hosp., Seattle, 1951-52; resident in psychiatry Johns Hopkins Hosp., Balt., 1952-56, asst. psychiatrist in charge outpatient dept., 1956-61, psychiatrist in charge, 1961-62; chief adult psychiatry clinic U. Chgo. Hosps. Clinics, 1968-76; instr. psychiatry Johns Hopkins U., 1956-59, asst. prof., 1959-67, assoc. prof., 1967-68, U. Chgo., 1968-73, prof., 1973-85, acting chmn., 1983-85; prof. psychiatry U. N.Mex., Albuquerque, 1985-97, prof. emeritus, 1997—, Disting. Univ. prof., 2005—, vice chmn. for edn., 1991-94. Cons. in field; mem. clin. psychopharmacology rsch. rev. com. NIMH, 1968-72, mem. treatment devel. and assessment rsch. rev. com., 1987-88; mem. psychopharmacology adv. com. FDA, 1974-78; adv. group to Treatment of Depression Collaborative Rsch. Program, NIMH, 1978-92; study rev. com. Xanax discontinuation program Upjohn Co., 1988-92, Nat. Adv. Coun. on Drug Abuse, NIDA, 1989-92, Coop. Studies Evaluation Com., VA, 1989-92. Mem. editl. bd. Jour. Affective Disorders, 1978—, Psychiatry Rsch., 1979-96, Behavioral Medicine, 1982—, Neuropsychopharmacology, 1992-95, Exptl. and Clin. Psychopharmacology, 1992-99, Depression and Anxiety, 1992—2008; contbr. articles to profl. jours. Recipient Rsch. Career Devel. award USPHS, 1962-68, Rsch. Scientist award, 1976-81. Fellow: Collegium Internat. Neuro-Psychopharmacologicum, Am. Psychopath. Assn., Am. Psychiat. Assn., Am. Coll. Neuropsychopharmacology (pres. 1986); mem.: Psychiat. Rsch. Soc., Balt.-Washington Soc. Psychoanalysis. Office: Univ N Mex Dept Psychiatry Ctr Psychiatric Rsch MSC 11 6035 Univ New Mex Albuquerque NM 87131-0001 Home Phone: 505-265-0663; Office Phone: 505-272-8876. Business E-Mail: uhli@unm.edu.

UHLER, WALTER CHARLES, government official, writer; b. Lebanon, Pa., Feb. 23, 1948; s. Victor Cornelius and Barbara Jean (Malin) U.; m. Judy Ann Sherk, Aug. 7, 1967 (div. 1984); children: Terry Allen,

Matthew David. Life partner: Carol A. DePrisco. BA in Polit. Sci. cum laude, Pa. State U., 1973, BA in Russian cum laude, 1973, cert. Russian area, 1973, MPA, 1992. Tchg. asst. Pa. State U., University Park, 1975-76; procurement agt. Naval Aviation Supply Office, Phila., 1976-80; contracts adminstr. GSA, Phila., 1980-81; contracting officer Def. Logistics Agy., Phila., 1981-86, corp. contracting officer, 1986-94; chief fin. svcs., 1993—2001; chief of ops. Def. Contract Mgmt. Agy., Lockheed Martin Delaware Valley, 2001—; dir. Def. Contract Mgmt. Agy., Valley Forge, 2006—; regional cons. Def. Logistics Agy., LA, 1985-86, nat. cons. Cameron Station, Va., 1989-90, leader Testing Labs. Privatization Assessment Team Ft. Belvoir, Va., 1997-98. Participant Air Force Intelligence Conf. on Soviet Affairs, Arlington, Va., 1988, Venona Conf., Washington, 1996, Ballistic Missile Def. Conf., Washington, 1998, AP/Harriman Inst. Conf., N.Y.C., 1999, State of the World Forum, N.Y.C., 2000; testified against nat. missile def., Vt. Ho. of Reps., 2002; gave radio interviews on nat. missile def., Vt., Calif., Wis., Radio Free Europe/Radio Liberty, 2002; presenter, 11th ann. Russia-Am. Conf., St. Petersburg, Russia, 2002; spkr. on contracts DOD Conf., Cleve., 1988, on restructuring costs, Memphis, 1994; chmn. Ann. Nat. Conf. Contracting Officers and Auditors, 1987-93; mem. Citizen Amb. Archivists' Del. to Russia and Poland, 1995, Citizen Amb. Del. to China, 1996, Russia and Finland, 1998; prodr., interviewer (with George Enteen) Sergei Vasilievich Utechin's Oral Reminiscences, 1997—; pres, Russian-American Internat. Studies Assn, 2004-. Contbr. articles to profl. publications. Baseball coach Valley Athletic Assn., Bensalem, Pa., 1979-88, basketball coach, 1980-85, coord., 1981; tutor Ctr. for Literacy, Phila., 1991-93, Project GIVE, Phila., 1995-98. Recipient Comdrs. Excellence award Defense Contract Mgmt. Area Ops., 1993. Mem. Am. Assn. for Advancement Slavic Studies, Soc. for Mil. History, Nat. Book Critics Cir., Russian Am. Internat. Studies Assn., Penn State Nittany Lion Club Democrat. Avocations: history, literature, Pennsylvania State University football. Personal E-mail: waltuhler@aol.com.

UHLIG, HARALD, economics professor; b. Bonn, Germany, Apr. 26, 1961; s. Sigmar and Elfriede Uhlig; m. Christine; children: Anjuli Sarah, Jan Peter. PhD in Economics, U. Minn., 1990. Asst. prof. dept. economics Princeton U., NJ, 1990—94; prof. Ctr. Tilburg U., Netherlands, 1994—2000, Humboldt U. Berlin, 2000—07; prof. dept. economics U. Chgo., 2007—. Asst. editor Rev. Econ. Studies, Macroecon. Dynamics, Computational Econ.; editor European Econ. Rev.; contbr. articles to profl. jours. Named to Rev. Econ. Studies Tour, London, 1990; Sloan Dissertation fellow, Sloan Found., Boston, 1989-90; Studienstiftung des Deutschen Volkes study grantee, Bonn, Germany, 1982-85, Fulbright study grantee, Fulbright Commn., Bonn, 1985. Mem. CEPR, Econometric Soc., Am. Econ. Assn., Verein für Socialpolitik. Avocations: cello, middle eastern history, music. Office: Univ Chgo 1126 East 59th St Chicago IL 60637 Office Fax: 773-702-8490. Business E-Mail: huhlig@uchicago.edu.

UHLIR, ARTHUR, JR., retired electrical engineer, academic administrator; b. Chgo., Feb. 2, 1926; s. Arthur and Helene (Houghteling) U.; m. Ingeborg Williams, July 24, 1954; children: Steven, Donald, David. BS, Ill. Inst. Tech., 1945, MSChemE, 1948; SM in Physics, U. Chgo., 1950, PhD in Physics, 1952. Process analyst Douglas Aircraft, Chgo., 1945; asst. engr. Armour Rsch. Found., Chgo., 1945-48; tech. staff Bell Telephone Labs., Murray Hill, NJ, 1951-58; dir. semi- condr. research and devel., mgr. semicondr. div., group v.p. engring. Microwave Assos., Inc., Burlington, Mass., 1958-69; dir. rsch. Computer Metrics, Rochelle Park, NJ, 1969-73; prof. elec. engring. Tufts U., Medford, Mass., 1970-94, chmn. dept. elec. engring., 1970-75, dean of engring., 1973—96. Fellow, AEC, 1949—51. Fellow: AAAS, IEEE; mem.: Am. Phys. Soc., Sigma Xi. Home: 45 Kendal Common Rd Weston MA 02493-2159 Personal E-mail: auhlir@mailaps.org, uhlir2@verizon.net.

UHLMANN, FREDERICK GODFREY, securities trader; b. Chgo., Dec. 31, 1929; s. Richard F. and Rosamond G. (Goldman) U.; m. Virginia Lee Strauss, July 24, 1951; children: Richard, Thomas, Virginia, Karen, Elizabeth. BA, Washington and Lee U., 1951. Ptnr. Uhlmann Grain Co., Chgo., 1951-61; v.p. Uhlmann & Co., Inc., Chgo., 1961-65; sr. v.p. H. Hentz & Co., Chgo., 1965-73, Drexel Burnham Lambert Inc., Chgo., 1973-84; exec. v.p., dir. bus. futures Dean Witter Reynolds Inc., Chgo., 1984-85; sr. v.p., mgr. commodity dept. Bear, Stearns & Co., Inc., Chgo., 1985-88; exec. v.p. Rodman & Renshaw, Inc., 1988-95; sr. v.p. LIT-Divsn. of First Options Inc., Chgo., 1995-98; chmn. Chgo Bd. Trade, Ill., 1973-74; sr. v.p., exec. dir. MAN Financial, 1998—. Ptnr. Uhlmann Price Securities LLC. Bd. dir. Dist. 113 H.S. Found., 1990—, Mt. Sanai Hosp. Inst., Chgo., 1999—. Mem. Nat. Futures Assoc. (dir. 1981-2000, vice chair 1998-2000), Futures Industry Assn. (bd. dir., chmn. 1975-76), Futures Industry Inst. (bd. dir.). Home: 783 Whiteoaks Ln Highland Park IL 60035-3656 Home Phone: 847-432-5122; Office Phone: 847-444-1104.

UHRIG, ROBERT EUGENE, nuclear engineer, educator; b. Raymond, Ill., Aug. 6, 1928; s. John Mathew and Anna LaDonna (Fireman) U.; m. Paula Margaret Schnepf, Nov. 27, 1954; children: Robert John, Joseph Charles, Mary Catherine, Charles William, Jean Marie, Thomas Paul, Fredrick James. BS with honors, U. Ill., 1948; MS, Iowa State U., Ames, 1950, PhD, 1954; grad. Advanced Mgmt. Program, Harvard U., Cambridge, Mass., 1976. Registered profl. engr., Iowa, Fla. Instr. engring. mechanics Iowa State U., 1948-51; assoc. engr., rsch. asst. Inst. Atomic Rsch. (at univ.), 1951-54, assoc. prof. engring. mechanics and nuc. engring., also group leader, 1956-60; prof. nuc. engring., chmn. dept. U. Fla., Gainesville, 1960-68, on leave, 1967-68, dean Coll. Engring., 1968-73, dean emeritus, 1989—; dep. asst. dir. rsch. Dept. Def., Washington, 1967-68; dir. nuc. affairs Fla. Power & Light Co., Miami, 1973-74, v.p. for nuc. affairs, 1974-75, v.p. nuc. and gen. engring., 1976-78, v.p. advanced systems and tech., 1978-86; disting. prof. engring. U. Tenn., Knoxville, 1986—2002, disting. prof. engring. emeritus, 2003—; disting. scientist Oak Ridge Nat. Lab., 1986—2002, disting. scientist emeritus, 2003—. Instr. engring. mechanics US Mil. Acad., 1954-56; rep. Dept. Def. to com. on acad. sci. and engring. Fed. Coun. Sci. and Tech., 1967; chmn. engring. adv. com. NSF, 1972-73; bd. dirs. Engring. Coun. Profl. Devel., 1968-72; mem. commn. edn. for engring. profession Nat. Assn. State Univs. and Land Grant Colls., 1969-72; apptd. mem. adv. com. on reactor safeguards US Nuc. Regulatory Commn., 1997-2001. Author: Random Noise Techniques in Nuclear Reactor Systems, 1970, trans. into Russian, 1974; co-author: (with Lefteri H. Tsoukalas) Fuzzy and Neural Approaches in Engineering, 1997—. Served to 1st lt. USAF. Recipient Sec. of Def. Civilian Svc. award, 1968, Outstanding Alumni award U. Ill. Coll. Engring., 1970, Alumni Profl. Achievement award Iowa State U., 1972, President's medallion U. Fla., 1973; Disting. Achievement citation Iowa State U. Alumni Assn., 1980, Glenn Murphy award Am. Soc. for Engring. Edn., 1992; Named to Hall Disting. Alumni, Aerospace Dept., Iowa State U., 2005. Fellow ASME (life, Richards Meml. award 1969, ASME medal, 2005), AAAS, Am. Nuc. Soc. life, chmn. edn. com. 1962-64, chmn. tech. group for edn. 1964-66, bd. dirs. 1965-68, exec. com. bd. 1966-68); mem. Am. Soc. Engring. Edn. (pres. S.E. sect. 1972-73, chmn. nuc. engring. divsn. 1966-67, 88-89, rsch. award S.E. sect. 1962), John Henry Newman Honor Soc., Sigma Xi, Tau Beta Pi, Phi Mu Epsilon, Pi Tau Sigma, Phi Kappa Phi (Disting. Mem. award 1997). Home and Office: 5221 NW 44th Pl Gainesville FL 32606-4328 Home Phone: 352-367-0374. Business E-Mail: ruhrig@utk.edu.

UICKER, JOSEPH BERNARD, retired engineering company executive; b. Mar. 29, 1940; s. John Joseph and Elizabeth Josephine (Flint) U.; m. Mary Catherine Howze, June 5, 1965 (div. Oct. 1971); children: Patricia, Suzzane; m. Janet Ann Ballman, Sept. 22, 1973 (dec. Feb, 2008) BSME, U. Detroit, 1963, MS, 1965. Registered profl. engr., Mich. Engr. Smith Hinchman & Grylls, Detroit, 1964-72, chief mech. engr. health facilities, 1972-73, asst. dir. health facilities, 1973-75, v.p., dir. mech. engring., 1975-82, v.p., dir. profl. staff, 1983-2000; also bd. dirs.; ret., 2000. Dir. Smith Group, Detroit, 1984-2000. Capt. US Army, 1966—67. Mem. NSPE, ASME, ASHRAE, Soc. Am. Mil. Engrs., Engring. Soc., Athletic Club. Avocations: golf, photography, gardening. Home: 15250 Knolson St Livonia MI 48154-4736 E-mail: juicker@ameritech.net.

UKROPINA, JAMES R., lawyer; b. Fresno, Calif., Sept. 10, 1937; s. Robert J. and Persida (Angelich) Ukropina. AB, Stanford U., 1959, MBA, 1961; LL.B., U. So. Calif., 1965. Bar: Calif. 1966. Assoc. firm O'Melveny & Myers, Los Angeles, 1965-72, ptnr., 1972—80, 1992—2000, of counsel Los Angeles, 2001—; exec. v.p., gen. counsel Santa Fe Internat. Corp., Alhambra, Calif., 1980-84, dir., 1981-86; exec. v.p., gen. counsel Pacific Enterprises, Los Angeles, 1984-86, pres. and dir., 1986-89, chmn. bd. and chief exec. officer, 1989-91; chmn., CEO Directions, LLC, 2002—. Bd. dir. Lockheed Martin Corp., Pacific Life Ins. Co., Trust Co. of West Group, Inc., Ctrl. Natural Resources, Keck Found., Internet Brands. Editor in chief So. Calif. Law Rev, 1964-65. Trustee Stanford U., 1991-2000 Mem. ABA, Calif. Bar Assn., Los Angeles County Bar Assn., Annandale Golf Club, Calif. Club, Beta Theta Pi. Office: O'Melveny & Myers 400 S Hope St Los Angeles CA 90071-2899

ULABY, FAWWAZ TAYSSIR, academic administrator, engineering educator; b. Damascus, Syria, Feb. 4, 1943; came to US, 1964; s. Tayssir Kamel and Makram (Ard) Ulaby; children: Neda, Aziza, Laith. BS in Physics, Am. U. Beirut, 1964; MSEE, U. Tex., Austin, 1966, PhD in Elec. Engring., 1968. With Boeing Co., 1966; asst. prof. elec. and computer engring. U. Kans., Lawrence, 1968-71, assoc. prof., 1971-76, prof., 1976-84; prof. elec. engring. and computer sci. U. Mich., Ann Arbor, 1984—, dir. NASA Ctr. for Space Terahertz Tech., 1988, R. Jamison and Betty Williams Disting. prof. elec. engring. and computer sci., 1993—, v.p. for rsch., 1999—2005; founding provost, exec. v.p. King Abdullah U. Sci. and Tech., 2008—. Author: Microwave Remote Sensing, Vol. 1, 1981, Vol. 2, 1982, Vol. 3, 1986, Radar Polarimetry, 1990. Recipient Kuwait prize in applied scis. Govt. of Kuwait, 1987, NASA Grp. Achievement award, 1990. Fellow IEEE (gen. chmn. internat. symposium 1981, Disting. Achievement award 1983, Centennial medal 1984, Edison medal 2006, Geoscience and Remote Sensing Soc. Edn. award 2006); mem. IEEE Geoscience and Remote Sensing Soc. (exec. editor jour., pres. 1979-81), Internat. Union Radio Sci., NAE. Avocations: flying kites, racketball. Office: U Mich 3228 Elec Engring and Computer Sci 1301 Beal Ave Ann Arbor MI 48109-2122 E-mail: ulaby@eecs.umich.edu.

ULANOFF, LANCE, editor-in-chief; Various editing positions to sr. assoc. editor PC Mag. Ziff-Davis Publ., 1991—98, online editor HomePC mag., 1996—98; sr. online editor Windows Mag., 1998—99; prodr. computing/consumer electronics channels to sr. dir. content Deja.com, 1999—2000; re-launch PC Mag. Ziff-Davis Publ., 2000, editor-in-chief, v.p. content, 2007—. Co-host (weekly podcast) PCMag Radio. Office: PC Mag Ziff Davis Media Inc 28 E 28th St New York NY 10016 E-mail: Lance_Ulanoff@ziffdavis.com.*

ULANOFF, STANLEY M., communications executive; b. Bklyn., May 30, 1922; s. Samuel H. and Minnie (Druss) U.; m. Bernice Mayer, June 15, 1947; children: Roger, Amy Ulanoff Christie, Lisa M. Ulanoff, Dory Ulanoff Kennedy. BA in Journalism, U. Iowa, 1943; MBA in Mktg., Hofstra U., 1955; PhD in Comm., NYU, 1968. Copywriter promotions dept. N.Y. Times, 1946—49; asst. to pres. SUNY, Stony Brook, 1962—64; prof. mktg., head advt., sales promotion & pub. rels. divsn. Baruch Coll. (CUNY), NY, 1964—86; pres. Viewmark Prodns. Inc. d.b.a. Advisions, 1986—. Cons. U.S. Dept. Def., Grosset & Dunlap pubs., Siebel/Mohr, U.S. Postal Svc.; cons, asst. to pres. Compton Advt.; arbitrator N.Y. Stock Exch., Nat. Assn. Securities Dealers; cons. Hasbro Toys. Author or editor 34 books including Handbook of Sales Promotion, also mags., newspaper articles, rsch. papers; prodr. over 200 video documentaries. From pvt. E-1 to brig. gen. U.S. Army, 1942-84. Decorated chevalier Ordre des Palmes Academique, Republic of France, Legion of Merit, Meritorious Svc. medal, USA, Army Commendation medal, Army Achievement medal, U.S. Army, Silver Conspicuous Svc. Cross, Merit medal State of N.Y., 1st prize award Am. Assn. Advt. Agys.; named VIP (Very Important Prof.) Splty. Adv. Assn. Internat. (2); Am. Assn. Advt. Agys. fellow, Eastman-Kodak fellow in film prodn.; Lewis Kleid Direct Mail Advt. scholar. Mem. Mil. Intelligence Res. Soc. (pres.), Res. Officers Assn. (pres.); disting. alumnus, Hofstra Univ. Office: 17 The Serpentine Roslyn NY 11576-1736 Office Phone: 516-621-1603. Fax: 516-801-2501.

ULANOWICZ, ROBERT EDWARD, science educator; s. Edward Stanislaus and Mary Isabel (Bielat) U.; m. Marie Antoinette Chmilewsky, July 1, 1967; children: Anastasia, Peter, Vera. BS, Johns Hopkins U., Balt., 1964, PhD, 1968. Asst. prof. Cath. U. America, Washington, 1968—70; asst. prof., ctr. environ. sci. U. Md., Solomons, 1970—75, assoc. prof., ctr. environ. & estuarine sci., 1975—81, prof., ctr. environ. sci., 1981—2008, prof. emeritus, ctr. environ. sci., 2008—. Mem. sci. com. on oceanographic rsch. UNESCO, 1977-85; mem. panel NRC, Washington, 1987-88; Crafoord symposium speaker Royal Swedish Acad. Scis., Stockholm, 1987. Author: Growth and Development: Ecosystems Phenomenology, 1986; editor: Mathematical Models in Biological Oceanography, 1981, Ecosystem Theory for Biological Oceanography, 1985; contbr. articles to sci. jours. Bd. dirs. Am. Chestnut Land Trust, Port Republic, Md., 1988-93; mem. adv. com. Battle Creek Cypress Swamp, Nature Conservancy, Prince Frederick, Md., 1980-84; mem. Pleasant Peninsula Planning Com., Prince Frederick, 1974; mem. Parker's Creek Watershed Planning Com., Prince Frederick, 1993-94; lector St. John Vianney Ch., Prince Frederick, 1975—. Recipient Frederick C. Hettinger Meml. award Md. sect. Am. Inst. Chem. Engrs., 1964, citation Gov. of Md., 1988. Mem. Atlantic Estuarine Rsch. Soc. (pres. 1980-81), Estuarine Rsch. Fedn. (exec. sec. 1986-87), Washington Evolutionary Systems Soc., Internat. Soc. for Ecol. Modelling, EcoGreen Global Soc. (mem. selection bd. 1990-95), Phi Beta Kappa, Tau Beta Pi. Liberal. Roman Catholic. Avocations: swimming, gardening, flying, history. Office: Dept Biology & Zoology 110 Bartram Hall Univ Fla Gainesville FL 32611-8575

ULATE, ISAI, engineering educator; b. San Jose, Costa Rica, Sept. 1, 1955; s. Humberto Ulate Soto and Rosa Maria Sanchez Padilla; m. Libny Yojana Macario, Nov. 10, 2005; 1 child, Isai Joshua. BSBA, U. Phoenix, LA, 2000, MBA, attending, U. Phoenix, LA, 2008—. Cert. in managing union environ. Disneyland Resort, Anaheim, Calif., 2006, in leading an inclusive environ. 2006, in recognition guide for leaders 2006, in leadership 2006, in career mgmt. 2006, in leading our cast 2006. Gen. mgr. Gear Tech., West Covina, Calif., 1991—92; foreman M & M Machine Tool Co., Huntington Beach, Calif., 1993—98; gen. mgr., owner and founder CNC Dynamics Mfg., Anaheim, 1998—2004; cons. Cerritos Coll., Norwalk, Calif., 1999—, educator, 1999—, Compton CC, Calif., 2007, San Jose City Coll., Calif., 2008—; supr. Performance Machine, La Palma, Calif., 2004—05, acting mfg. engr., 2007—08; reliability mgr. Disneyland Resort, 2005—06. Contbr. scientific papers. V.p. Light of Life, Anaheim, 1990—95; mem. Basic Skill Initiative Adv. Group, San Jose, 2008—09. Mem.: Soc. Mfg. Engrs. Conservative.

ULBRICH, DAVID J., history professor; b. Dayton, Ohio, Mar. 2, 1971; s. Richard W. and Jill G. Ulbrich. BA in History, U. Dayton, Ohio, 1993; MA in History, Ball State U., Muncie, Indiana, 1996; PhD in History, Temple U., Phila., 2007. Instr. history U. Del., Newark, 2001—04, Ball State U., Muncie, Ind., 2004—08, co dir., cantigny first divsn. oral history project, 2008; vis. asst. prof. history Ohio U., Athens, 2008—. Hist. cons. and on-air segment host, echoes war WIPB-TV, Muncie, Ind., 2007. Contbr. articles to profl. jours. Recipient Accessible Tchr. award, Disabled Student Devel., Ball State U., 2007—08, 2 Silver Telly awards, 2008, Robert Debs Heinl award, 2000; named Outstanding Educator, Correctional Edn. Program, Ball State U., 2006—07; John F. Votaw Rsch. fellowship, Ctr. for the Study of Force and Diplomacy, Temple U., 2004—05, Citizenship Program grant, McCormick Found., 2008. Mem.: Marine Corps Assn., Soc. Historians Am. Fgn. Rels., Soc. Mil. History, Sigma Phi Epsilon (pledge edn. 1992). Office: Ohio Univ History Dept Bentley Annex 405 Athens OH 45701 Business E-Mail: ulbrichd@ohio.edu.

ULE, GUY MAXWELL, JR., stockbroker; b. Chgo., Jan. 2, 1940; s. Guy Maxwell and Margaret (Karahuta) U.; m. Angela Joanne Genelli, Nov. 17, 1975. BA, Harvard U., Cambridge, Mass., 1961, MBA, 1967. Analyst, phys. distbn. specialist TWA, NYC and Phila., 1967—69, supr. comml. passenger sales NYC, 1969—71; pvt. practice cons. NYC, 1971—72; mgr. sales mktg. Source Equities, NYC, 1972; ptnr., N.Y.C. office mgr. Daley, Coolidge & Co., 1973—77; v.p., divsn. mgr. Rosenkrantz, Ehrenkrantz, Lyon & Ross Inc., 1977—85, Ingham Becker & Co., Inc., 1985—87; v.p., asst. sec. Meyers, Pollock, Robbins Inc., 1987—89; v.p., Max Ule divsn. Herzog Heine Geduld Inc., 1989—2000; v.p. investments Shields & Co., Inc., 2000—. Pres. Max Ule & Co., Inc., N.Y.C., 1977-2004, Max Ule Advt. & Mktg., Inc., N.Y.C., 1980—; brokerage info. cons. Internet World Wide Web, 1995 Creator first discount brokerage sys. on computer, 1980. Chmn., pres. Assn. in Manhattan for Autistic Children, 1985-86. Lt. USN, 1962-65 Mem.: Racquet Club Phila., Knickerbocker Club, Racquet and Tennis Club. Republican. Episcopalian. Avocations: photography, tennis, travel. Home: 8 Gramercy Park S Apt 5B New York NY 10003-1721 Office: Shields and Co 140 Broadway 44th Fl New York NY 10005 Office Phone: 800-809-1160. Business E-Mail: max.ule@shieldsandco.com.

ULEVICH, NEAL HIRSH, photojournalist; b. Milw., June 18, 1946; s. Ben and Lea Jean (Klitsner) U.; m. Maureen Ann Vaughan, Sept. 25, 1974; children: Jacob Vaughan, Sarah Beatrice. BA in Journalism, U. Wis., 1968. Reporter A.P., 1968-69, photographer, photo editor, 1971-78, Asia photo editor, 1978-83. Freelance writer, Vietnam, Hong Kong, 1969-71; fellow in journalism U. Wis.-Madison, 1971-72 Recipient Pulitzer prize for news photography, 1977. Jewish.

ULFELDER, JAY, political scientist, director; s. John C. Ulfelder and Linda S. Potter; m. Francesca Milliken, Sept. 4, 1994; children: Parker Milliken, August Milliken. PhD, Stanford U., Calif, 1997. Rsch. dir., polit. instability task force Sci. Applications Internat. Corp., McLean, Va., 2001—. Contbr. articles to profl. jours. Mem.: Am. Polit. Sci. Assn., Phi Beta Kappa. Business E-Mail: jay_ulfelder@stanfordalumni.org.

ULICK, SUSAN E., investment company executive; BA, Sarah Lawrence Coll., Bronxville, NY, 1975; MA in Economics, Columbia U., NYC. Energy exec. trainee Mobil Oil; indsl. analyst Sanford C. Bernstein & Co.; analyst, v.p. J.P. Morgan Investment Mgmt., 1987—95, head, US rsch., 1995—97, head, global rsch., 1997—2000, TIAA-CREF Asset Mgmt., 2000—04, sr. mng. dir., head, equity investments, Teachers Advisors, Inc., 2004—08. Named one of Top 20 Nonbank Women in Fin., US Banker, 2007.

ULICNY, GARY R., rehabilitation center executive; BA in Special Edn., UNC Chapel Hill; MA in Special Edn., Appalachian U.; PhD in Behavorial Psychology, U. Kansas. Regional v.p. Learning Services Corp., NH, exec. dir.; adminstrv. dir. rehab. services WakeMed Hosp. System, Raleigh, NC; pres., CEO Shepherd Ctr., Atlanta, 1994—. Mem. Ga. Dept. Cmty. Health, 2005—. Mem.: American Coll. Healthcare Executives, American Congress of Rehab. Medicine (v.p.), Ga. Hosp. Assn. (bd. trustees 2009—, chmn. rehab. council). Office: Shepherd Ctr 2020 Peachtree Rd NW Atlanta GA 30309-1402*

ULLBERG, KENT JEAN, sculptor; b. Gothenburg, Sweden, July 15, 1945; arrived in US, 1974; s. Jean Wilgot and Kerstin Aina (Axelson) U.; m. Veerle Rufina Vermeir, May 5, 1978; children: Robert, Gerald. Diploma in sculpture, Swedish State Sch. Art, 1966. Cert. conservator German Assn. Museology. Curator Nat. Mus. and Art Gallery, Botswana, Africa, 1971-74; curator III Mus. Natural History, Denver, 1974-75. Prin. works include Lincoln Ctr. Eagle, Dallas, 1981, Wind in the Sails, Corpus Christi, Tex., 1983, Genesee Eagle, Mumford, N.Y., 1984, Deinonychus Dinosaurs, Phila., 1987, Whooping Cranes Fountain, Washington, 1989, Swordfish Monument, IGFA Hdqs., Dania, Fla., 1999, Broward Conv. Ctr., Fountain, Ft. Lauderdale, Fla., Rudor Monument, Stockholm, 1991, Monumental Triptych Art Mus. South Tex., 1993, Bird Mountain Telecom. Hdqs., Stockholm, 1994, Christ Monument, Corpus Christi, 1995, Grizzly Bear Monument, Nat. Mus. Wildlife Art, Jackson, Wyo., 1994, King Penguin Monument, Mystic Marine Life Aquarium, Conn., 1997, R.T. Peterson Meml., Cougar Monument San Antonio Zoo, 1998, Otters Monument St. Louis Zoo, 1998, Tex. State Aquarium, 1998, Swordfish Monument, Dania Beach, Fla., 1998, Spanish Bull Monument, Johnson C. Smith U., Charlotte, N.C., 1999, Ram Monum, U. N.C., Chapel Hill, 2001, First Nat. Bank Omaha Can. Geese Monument, 2002, Eagle Monument, Fed. Res. Bank, Houston, 2005, Danzamar, Performing Arts Ctr., Tex. A&M, Corpus Christi, 2005, Chub Cay Marlin Monument, Bahamas, 2006. Recipient Gold medal Tex. Rangers Hall of Fame, 1980, Rungius award Nat. Mus. Wildlife Art, 1996, Prix de West award Nat. Cowboy Hall of Fame, 1998, award for wildlife Autry Nat. Ctr., 2004; named Master Wildlife Artist, 1987. Fellow: NAD (academician 1990, Barnett prize 1995, Speyer prize 1995), Am. Soc. Marine Artists, Nat. Acad. Western Art (gold medal 1981, 1982, 1988, 1995, 1999), Nat. Sculpture Soc. (Percival Dietsch award 1979, gold medal 1983, Silver medal and John Cavanaugh Meml. prize 2002, Hering award 1993, 2008); mem.: Soc. for Wildlife Art of Nations, Allied Artists of Am. (N.Y. Silver medal

1989, mem. assoc. award 2007), Soc. Animal Artists (medal merit 1979, 1980, 1982, 1987, 1996, 2001, E. Haller award 2001, Sponsor award 2002), Explorers Club N.Y.C. Office Phone: 361-851-1600. Personal E-mail: ullberg@sbcglobal.net.

ULLESTAD, CHARLES LEE, humanities educator; s. Harlold Norman and Cleone Maxine Ullestad; m. Susan Eileen Graefe, Dec. 22, 1982; children: Charles Grant, Shannon Noelle, Madalyn Rose, Christopher James. BS in Liberal Studies, Bowling Green State U., Ohio, 1983; MA in History, Calif. State U., Turlock, 1994; MEd, U. Phoenix, Ariz., 2006. Lic. air transport pilot, FAA, 2003. Pilot, lt. col. USAF, Washington, 1983—2007; prof., adj. faculty J.S. Reynolds CC, Richmond, Va., 2007—; tchr. Warwick HS, Newport News, Va., 2008. Decorated Def. Meritorious Svc. medal USAF, Meritorious Svc. medal, Air medal, Aerial Achievement medal, Commendation medals, AF Achievement medal, Combat Readiness medal, Nat. Def. Svc. medal, Afghanistan Svc. medal, Global War on Terrorism Expeditionary medal. Presbyterian. Avocations: travel, golf. Personal E-mail: cullestad@reynolds.edu.

ULLESTAD, MERWIN ALLAN, tax specialist, director; b. Hampton, Iowa, June 29, 1949; s. Allan L. and Georgia E. (Simms) Ullestad; m. Crystal R. Kleppinger, Sept. 17, 1977. BS, Iowa State U., 1971. CPA; PFS Iowa, Tenn., lic. capt. inland waters USCG. Ptnr. Coopers and Lybrand, Des Moines, 1971-83; ptnr. in charge, tax svcs. Touche Ross and Co., Nashville, 1983-89; ptnr. tax svcs. Deloitte & Touche, LLP, Nashville, 1989—2002; mem.-in-charge tax svcs., mgmt. com. Kraft CPAs LLC, Nashville, 2002—. Adj. tax prof. Simpson Coll., 1981—82; sprk. prof. acct. seminar Lipscomb U., 1990—2004. Editor: Abingdon Clergy Income Tax Guide, 1989—98. Sustaining membership capt. Mid. Tenn. coun. Boy Scouts Am., 1985—88; ednl. adv. com. Nashville Health Care Coun., 1998—2002; bd. dirs., exec. com., treas. United Way Mid. Tenn., 1990—96, mem. allocations panel, 1983—89; bd. dirs., mem. exec. com. Am. Cancer Soc., Des Moines, 1977—83, Nashville City Ballet, 1983—85; bd. dirs., chmn. fin. com. Watkins Coll. Art and Design, 1996—2001; bd. dirs. Gilda's Club, Nashville, treas., 1996—2002; trustee, program chmn., sec., pres. Tenn. Fed. Tax Inst., 2001—; bd. dirs., treas. Tenn. chpt. Arthritis Found., 2003—, regional performance oversight com. mem., 2009—. Mem.: AICPA (cert. pers. fin. specialist), Nashville Songwriters Assn. Internat. (fin. cons. to bd. dirs. 1990—97), Nashville Estate Planning Coun. (pres. 1996—99, bd. dirs. 1993—2002), Internat. Assn. Fin. Planning (pres., bd. dirs. Nashville chpt. 1987—90), Iowa Soc. CPAs, Tenn. Soc. CPAs, Nashville C. of C. (mem. econ. devel. com. 1988—90, mem. employment coun. 1999—2002, editor HR notes 2000—01, mem. small bus. coun. 2006—), Seven Seas Cruising Assn., Nashville Tax Club (founding mem.), Nlue Yacht Club, Commonwealth Yacht Club, Nashville City Club, Old Hickory Country Club. Avocations: sailing, hiking, music. Office: 555 Great Circle Rd #200 Nashville TN 37228-1310 Office Phone: 615-782-4281. Business E-Mail: mullestad@kraftcpas.com.

ULLMAN, CHRISTOPHER CHARLES, school librarian, educator; b. Myrtle Point, Oreg., May 24, 1953; s. John Alexander and Joanne Elizabeth Ullman; m. Laurie Kay Birk, Apr. 14, 1973; 1 child, Megan Elizabeth. AA in Liberal Arts summa cum laude, Springfield Coll. Ill., 1982; BA in Philosophy magma cum laude, U. Ill., Springfield, 1988; MA in Philosophy cum laude, Trinity Internat. U., Deerfield, Ill., 1994. Coll. tchr. Christian Life Coll., Mount Prospect, Ill., 1989—, libr., 2001—; coll. tchr. Harper Coll., Palatine, Ill., 1997—. Contbr. chapters to books. Men's ministry leader Christian Life Ch., Mount Prospect, 2002—08. Mem.: Ctr. Bioethics & Human Dignity, Assn. Christian Libr., Evang. Philos. Soc., Soc. Christian Philosophers. Conservative. Mem. Christian Ch. Avocations: tennis, golf, camping, bicycling, gardening. Home: 318 North School St Mount Prospect IL 60056 Office: Christian Life Coll 400 East Gregory St Mount Prospect IL 60056 Office Fax: 847-259-3888. Personal E-mail: christopher.ullman@gmail.com. Business E-Mail: cullman@christianlifecollege.edu.

ULLMAN, EDWIN FISHER, biotechnologist, consultant; b. Chgo., July 19, 1930; s. Harold P. and Jane F. Ullman; m. Elizabeth J. Finlay, June 26, 1954; children: Becky L., Linda J. BA, Reed Coll., 1952; MA, Harvard U., 1954, PhD, 1956. Rsch. chemist Lederle Labs., Am. Cyanamid, Pearl River, NY, 1955-60; group leader ctrl. rsch. divsn. Am. Cyanamid, Stamford, Conn., 1960-66; sci. dir. Synvar Rsch. Inst., Palo Alto, Calif., 1966-70; v.p., dir. rsch. Syva Co., Palo Alto, 1970-95, Behring Diagnostics Inc., San Jose, Calif., 1995-97; sci. cons., 1997—; chief sci. officer Thau MDx, LLC, Santa Barbara, Calif., 2001—02, Adv. DiscoverRx, Corp., Fremont, Calif., 2002—. Mem. various sci. adv. bds.; mem. adv. bd. San Francisco State U. Coll. of Sci. and Engring., 1994-96. Mem. editl. bd. Jour. Organic Chemistry, 1969-74, Jour. Immunoassay, 1979—, Jour. Clin. Lab., Analysis, 1986-87, Jour. Clin. Ligand Assay Soc., 1999-2000; contbr. articles to sci. jours.; patentee in field. NSF predoctoral fellow, 1952-53; U.S. Rubber Co. fellow, 1954-55. Recipient Clin. Ligand Assay Soc. Mallinckrodt award, 1981, Can. Soc. Clin. Chemists Health Group award, 1982, Inventor of Yr. award Peninsula Patent Law Assn., 1987. Fellow AAAS; mem. Am. Chem. Soc., Am. Assn. Clin. Chemistry (Van Slyke award N.Y. sect. 1984, No. Calif. sect. award 1991, Outstanding Contbns. to Clin. Chemistry in Selected Area of Rsch. award 1997, Ann. Edwin F. Ullman award established 1998), Phi Beta Kappa.

ULLMAN, JEFFREY DAVID, computer scientist, educator; b. NYC, Nov. 22, 1942; s. Seymour and Nedra L. (Hart) Ullman; m. Holly E. Ullman, Nov. 19, 1967; children: Peter, Scott, Jonathan. BS, Columbia U., 1963; PhD, Princeton U., 1966; PhD (hon.), U. Brussels, 1975, U. Paris-Dauphine, 1992. Mem. tech. staff Bell Labs., Murray Hill, NJ, 1966-69, cons., 1969-89; prof. elec. engring., computer sci. Princeton (N.J.) U., 1969-79; prof. computer sci. Stanford (Calif.) U., 1979—2003, prof. emeritus, 2003—; CEO Gradiance Corp., 2003—. Mem. computer sci. adv. panel NSF, 1974—77, mem. info., robotics and intelligent sys. adv. panel, 1986—88; mem. exam. com. computer sci. grad. record exam. Endl. Testing Svc., 1978—86; chmn. doctoral rating com. computer sci. N.Y. State Regents, 1989—93, 1998—99; mem. tech. adv. bd. Google, 1998—, Viquity, 1999—2002, Surromed, 1999—, Whizbang Labs, 1999—2002, Quiq, 1999—2002; adv. bd. World Wide Web Consortium, 1998—99; bd. dirs. Junglee, 1996—98, Kirusa, 2001—03, Enosys software, 2000—01, 2002—03; mem. internat. sci. advisory group Nat. Info. & Comms. Tech., Australia, 2003—; chair Nat. Rsch. Coun. for Nat. Inst. Standards and Tech. Info. Tech. Lab., 2007. Author: (book) Principles of Database and Knowledge-Base Systems, 1988, 1989; author: (with A. V. Aho and J. E. Hopcroft) Data Structures and Algorithms, 1983; author: (with A. V. Aho, M. Lam and R. Sethi) Compilers: Principles, Techniques and Tools, 2006; author: (with A. V. Aho) Foundations of Computer Science, 1992, Elements of ML Programming, 1994, 1998; author: (with J. Widom) A First Course in Database Systems, 1997, 2002, 2008; author: (with H. Garcia-Molina and J. Widom) The Complete Book of Database Systems, 2002; author: (with J. E. Hopcroft and R. Motwani) Intro. to Automata, Languages, and Computation, 2006. Guggenheim fellow, 1989. Fellow: Assn. Computing Machinery (coun. 1978—80, Spl. Interest Group Mgmt. Data Contbns. award 1996, Outstanding Educator award 1998, Knuth prize 2000, Spl. Interest Group Mgmt. Data E.F. Codd Innovations award 2006, E. F. Codd Innovation award 2006); mem.: NAE, Spl. Interest Group Mgmt. Data (vice chmn. 1983—95), Computing Rsch. Assn. (bd. dirs. 1994—2001), Spl. Interest Group Automata and Computability Theory (sec.-treas. 1973—75). Home: 1023 Cathcart Way Palo Alto CA 94305-1048 Office: Stanford U Dept Computer Sci 433 Gates Hall 4A-Wing Stanford CA 94305-9040 E-mail: ullman@gmail.com.

ULLMAN, LEO SOLOMON, lawyer; b. Amsterdam, The Netherlands, July 14, 1939; s. Frank Leo and Emily (Konijn) U.; m. Katharine Laura Marbut, Aug. 27, 1960; children: Laura, Susan, Valerie, Frank. AB, Harvard U., 1961; JD, MBA, Columbia U., 1964. Bar: N.Y. 1966, U.S. Ct. Claims 1966, U.S. Tax Ct. 1969, U.S. Customs Ct. 1970. Assoc. Sullivan & Cromwell, NYC, 1965-68; pres., mem. Ullman, Miller & Wrubel and predecessors, NYC, 1970-81; mem. Reid & Priest, 1984-91, of counsel, 1991-92, Schnader, Harrison, Segal & Lewis, NYC, 1993-99; chmn., CEO Cedar Shopping Ctrs., Inc. (NYSE), 1998—. Adj. prof. internat. bus. NYU, 1972-77; lectr., panelist profl. organs. programs. Co-author: Investeringen in Onroerend Goed in de Verenigde Staten, 1982; editor: European Taxation, Internat. Bur. Documentation, Amsterdan, 1964-65; founding editor: Taxation of Private Investment Income in Europe; contbr. articles to profl. publs. Mem. Port Washington (N.Y.) Bd. Edn., 1970-73, pres., 1972-73; bd. dirs. Found. for Jewish Hist. Mus. in Amsterdam, Inc.; bd. dirs. Anne Frank Ctr., U.S.A., chmn., 1994-00; bd. dirs. Cmty. Chest of Port Washington. Served with USMCR, 1959-65; nat. judge Ernst & Young Entrepreneur of Yr. Awards, 2006, 07. Co-recipient Cmty. Svc. award, Port Washington, 1981, Citizen of Yr. award, Cmty. Chest, Port Washington, 2003, Entrepreneur of Yr. award in Greater NY area Ernst & Young, 2005, 06; Harlan Fiske Stone scholar Columbia Law Sch., 1963. Mem. ABA (tax sect. com. U.S. taxation of fgn. persons), N.Y. State Bar Assn. (tax sect. com. internat. trade and investment), Harvard Club, Netherlands Club. Home: Seacoast Ln Sands Point NY 11050-1230 Office: 44 S Bayles Ave Port Washington NY 11050 E-mail: leoullman@aol.com.

ULLMAN, MYRON EDWARD, III, (MIKE ULLMAN), retail executive; b. Youngstown, Ohio, Nov. 26, 1946; s. Myron Edward Jr. and June (Cunningham) U.; m. Cathy Emmons, June 20, 1969; children: Myron Cayce, Denver Tryan, Peter Brynt, Benjamin Kyrk, Kathryn Kwynn, Madylin Ming Yan. BS in Indsl. Mgmt., U. Cin., 1969; postgrad. Inst. Ednl. Mgmt., Harvard U., 1977. Internat. account mgr. IBM Corp., Cin., 1969-76; v.p. bus. affairs U. Cin., 1976-81; White House fellow The White House, Washington, 1981-82; exec. v.p. Sanger Harris div. Federated Stores, Dallas, 1982-86; mgr. dir., chief oper. officer Wharf Holdings Ltd., Hong Kong, 1986-88; chmn., CEO, dir. R.H. Macy & Co. Inc., NYC, 1988-95; dir., deputy chmn. Federated Dept. Stores, Inc.; chmn., CEO DFS Group Ltd., San Francisco, 1995-98, group chmn., 1999-2000; also bd. dirs.; dir. gen., group mng. dir. LVMH, Louis Vuitton Moet Hennessy, Paris, 1999—2002; chmn. DeBeers-LV, 2000—02; dir., chmn., CEO J.C. Penney Co. Inc., 2004—. Mng. dir. Lane Crawford Ltd., Hong Kong, 1986-88; bd. advisors Gt. Traditions Corp., Cin.; chmn. Omni Hotels, Hampton, N.H., 1988; co-chmn. Global Crossing, Ltd., 2002-04; chmn. bd. dirs. Mercy Ships Internat., 1992-; bd. dirs. Starbuck's Coffee Co., 2008-, bd. dirs. Fed. Res. Bank Dallas, Polo Ralph Lauren, 2004-06, Taubman Ctrs., 2002-04, Kendall Jackson Wine Estates, 2001-04, Lucille Packard Found. Children's Health, 2001-04, Segway LLC, 2003-05. Internat. v.p. U. Cin. Alumni Assn., 1980—; bd. dirs. Nat. Multiple Sclerosis Soc., NYC; bd. dirs. Brunswick Sch., Greenwich, Conn., U. Cin. Found., Lincoln Ctr. Devel., Deafness Rsch. Found., 1997-01, Stanford U. Children's Med. Ctr., 2004-04; chmn. exec. coun. U. Calif. Med. Ctr. Found., San Francisco, 2002-, bd. dirs., 1998—. Mem. White House Fellow Alumni Assn., Econ. Club N.Y.C. (bd. dirs., exec. com.), Nat. Retail Fedn. (chmn., bd. dirs., exec. com. 1993—), Pzena Investment Mgmt. (bd. dirs. 2007-08). Republican. Office: JC Penney Corp Inc 6501 Legacy Dr Plano TX 75024-3698 Business E-Mail: mike@meullman.com.

ULLMAN, NELLY SZABO, statistician, educator; b. Vienna, Aug. 11, 1925; came to U.S., 1939; d. Viktor and Elizabeth (Rosenberg) Szabo; m. Robert Ullman, Mar. 20, 1947 (dec.); children: Buddy, Wiliiam John, Martha Ann, Daniel Howard. BA, Hunter Coll., 1945; MA, Columbia U., 1948; PhD, U. Mich., 1969. Rsch. assoc. MIT Radiation Lab, Cambridge, Mass., 1945; instr. Polytechnic Inst. of Bklyn., 1945-63; from asst. prof. to prof. Ea. Mich. U., Ypsilanti, 1963—2002, prof., 2002; ret., 2002. Author: Study Guide To Actuarial Exam, 1978; contbr. articles to profl. jours. Mem. Am. Math. Assn., Am. Assn. Univ. Profs. E-mail: nullman4@emich.edu.

ULLMAN, PIERRE LIONI, retired Spanish literature and language educator; b. Nice, France, 1929; (parents Am. citizens); s. Eugene Paul and Suzanne (Lioni) U.; m. Mary Meade McDowell, June 9, 1956; children: Katherine Meade Turner, Susan Randolph Johnson. BA, Yale U., 1952; AM, Columbia U., 1956; PhD, Princeton U., NJ, 1962. Instr. Rutgers U., New Brunswick, NJ, 1961-63; asst. prof. U. Calif., Davis, 1963-65; assoc. prof. U. Wis., Milw., 1965-69, prof., 1969-94, prof. emeritus, 1994—. Vis. prof. U. Minn., Mpls., 1970-71, U. Mich., Ann Arbor, 1975. Author: Mariano Jose de Larra and Spanish Political Rhetoric, 1971, A Contrapuntal Method for Analyzing Spanish Literature, 1988; translator: The Friend from Kananam: Adventures in the New Guinea Jungle, by Kenneth G. Linton, 2002; contbr. articles to profl. jours. Past pres. U. Wis. Milw. Retired Faculty Assn., 2000-2002. With U.S. Army, 1952-54. Mem. MLA (emeritus), U. Esperanto Assn. (2d prize for drama 1981), Esperanto League for N.Am., Sigma Delta Pi. Address: 1840 N Prospect Ave Milwaukee WI 53202 Personal E-mail: ullmanpl@uwm.edu.

ULLMAN, TRACEY, actress, singer; b. Slough, Eng., Dec. 30, 1959; m. Allan McKeown, 1983; children: Mabel Ellen, John Albert Victor. Student, Itaia Conti Stage Sch., London. Appeared in plays Gigi, Elvis, Grease, The Rocky Horror Show, Four in a Million, 1981 (London Theatre Critics award), The Taming of the Shrew, 1990, The Big Love, (one-woman stage show) 1991; actress: (films) Give My Regards to Broad Street, 1984, Plenty, 1985, Jumpin' Jack Flash, 1986, I Love You To Death, 1990, Household Saints, 1993, Robin Hood: Men in Tights, 1993, I'll Do Anything, 1994, Bullets over Broadway, 1994, Ready to Wear (Prêt-à-Porter), 1994, Everybody Says I Love You, 1996, Panic, 2000, Small Time Crooks, 2000, A Dirty Shame, 2004, (voice only) Corpse Bride, 2005, I Could Never Be Your Woman, 2007, (voice) The Tale of Despereaux, 2008, (TV films) Women of the Night IV, 1995, Once Upon a Mattress, 2004; Brit. TV shows include Three of a Kind, A Kick Up the Eighties, Girls on Top; (TV series) The Tracey Ullman Show, 1987-90 (Emmy award Best Performance, Outstanding Writing, 1990, Golden Globe award Best Actress, 1987), Tracey Takes On, 1996-99 (four Emmys including Outstanding Music, Comedy and Variety Show 1997, Cable Ace award for best comedy variety series 1996), Visible Panty Lines, 2001, Tracey Ullman's State of the Union, 2008-; singer: (albums) You Broke My Heart in Seventeen Places, You Caught Me Out, 1984, Takes on the Hits, 2002. Recipient Brit. Acad. award, 1983, Am. Comedy award, 1988, 90, 91, Emmy award for Best Performance in a Variety/Music Series for "Tracey Ullman Takes on New York", 1994. Office: IFA Talent Agy 8730 W Sunset Blvd Ste 490 Los Angeles CA 90069-2248

ULLOA, LEONOR ALVAREZ DE, language educator; PhD in Latin American Lit. & Culture, U. Ky., Lexington, 1979; MA in Spanish, U. Ky., 1976. Dir. study abroad programs in Mex. and Spain Radford U., 1980—2005, prof. Spanish, 1990—. Editor-in-chief Mountain Interstate Foreign Language Conference Jour.; contbr. articles to profl. latin jours. Recipient Donald Dedmon Profl. Excellence award, Radford U., 1992, Excellence in Tchg., Rsch. & Svc. award, State Coun. Higher Edn. Va., 1993, Orden de los Descubridores, Sigma Delta Pi, 1998, Ted R. & John Dalton Disting. Prof. of Spanish award, Radford U., 1998—2006. Independent. Roman Catholic. Avocations: travel, reading, swimming, music. Office Phone: 540-831-5120. Business E-Mail: lulloa@radford.edu.

ULLRICH, ROBERT ALBERT, academic administrator; b. Port Jefferson, NY, Mar. 25, 1939; s. Albert Herman and Marie Kathryn (Miller) U.; m. Portia M. Little; children: Karl Albert, Eleanor Marie. BS, U.S. Mcht. Marine Acad., 1960; MBA, Tulane U., 1964; D in Bus. Adminstrn., Washington U., 1968. Marine engr. Lykes Bros. Steamship Co., New Orleans, 1960-62; trainee IBM Corp., New Orleans, 1964-65; sr. rsch. officer London Sch. Econs., 1968-69; prof. Vanderbilt U., Nashville, 1969-88; dean Clark U., Worcester, Mass., 1988-96, prof., 1996-98; dean Ithaca (N.Y.) Coll., 1998—2004. Author: Motivation Methods, 1981, Robotics Primer, 1983; co-author: Organization Theory and Design, 1980; editor: The American Work Force, 1984. Lt. j.g. USNR, 1960-66. Mem. Beta Gamma Sigma. Office: 33 Friendship St Jamestown RI 02835 Home Phone: 401-423-0259. E-mail: rullrich1@msn.com.

ULLRICH, ROXIE ANN, special education educator; b. Ft. Dodge, Iowa, Nov. 10, 1951; d. Rocco William and Mary Veronica (Casady) Jackowell; m. Thomas Earl Ullrich, Aug. 10, 1974; children: Holly Ann, Anthony Joseph BA, Creighton U., 1973; MA in Teaching, Morningside Coll., 1991. Cert. tchr. Iowa, cons. in spl. edn. Iowa. Tchr. Corpus Christi Sch., Ft. Dodge, Iowa, 1973—74, Westwood Cmty. Schs., Sloan, Iowa, 1974—80, Sioux City Cmty. Schs., 1987—. Cert. judge Iowa High Sch. Speech Assn., Des Moines, 1975—; supt. Woodbury County Fair; leader 4H Club; mem. Westwood Cmty. Sch. Bd., Sloan, Iowa. Mem.: Sioux City Art Ctr., Sioux City Hist. Assn., Am. Paint Horse Assn., Am. Quarter Horse Assn., Red Hat Soc., M.I. Hummel Club, Phi Delta Kappa. Avocation: horseback riding. Home: PO Box W 819 Brown St Sloan IA 51055

ULMAN, DOUG, foundation administrator; BS in History, Brown U., Providence, 1999. Founder, pres. Ulman Cancer Fund for Young Adults, 1997—, exec. dir., 1997—2001; dir. survivorship, chief mission officer Lance Armstrong Found., Austin, Tex., 2001—07, pres., CEO, 2007—. Mem. exec. bd. Ulman Cancer Fund for Young Adults; founder LIVESTRONG Young Adults Alliance. Chmn., director's consumer liaison group Nat. Cancer Inst., 2005—09. Recipient Austin Under-40 award, healthcare, 2003, Health Care Hero award, Austin Bus. Jour., 2008. Mem.: Am. Soc. Clin. Oncology. Avocations: soccer, running. Office: Lance Armstrong Found 2201 E Sixth St Austin TX 78702*

ULMANIS, GUNTIS, former President of Latvia; b. Riga, Latvia, Sept. 13, 1939; m. Aina Ulmane; children: Guntra, Alvils. Student, Latvian U. Economist, mcpl. employee, Riga, Latvia, 1963-92; dep. Parliament, Riga, 1993; pres. of Latvia, 1993—99. Hon. chmn. bd. Nat. Libr. Support Found.; dir. gen. 2006 Internat. Ice Hockey Fedn. World Championship Organizing Com., 2002-06. Author: (autobiography) You are not Asked Much, (book of photographs) My Time as President. Active CPSU, 1965-89, Union of Farmers of Latvia, 1992-2000. Achievements include facilitating admission of Latvia to Coun. of Europe; declaring moratorium on the execution of the death penalty in Latvia. Office: Office of Pres Pils Laukums 3 LV-1900 Riga Latvia Business E-Mail: eva@president.lv, eva.eihmaw@president.com.

ULMER, FRANCES ANN, academic administrator, retired state official; b. Madison, Wis., Feb. 1, 1947; m. Bill Council; children: Amy, Louis. BA in Econs. and Polit. Sci., U. Wis.; JD with honors, Wis. Sch. Law. Polit. advisor Gov. Jay Hammond, Alaska, 1975-81; former mayor City of Juneau, Alaska; mem. Alaska Ho. of Reps., 1986-94, minority leader, 1992-94; lt. gov. State of Alaska, 1995—2002; U.S. rep. to North Pacific Anadramous Fish Commn., 1994—; disting. prof. U. Alaska, Anchorage, 2003—, dir. Inst. Social and Econ. Rsch., 2004—07, chancellor, 2007—. Office: U Alaska Anchorage Office of Chancellor 3211 Providence Dr, ADM 216 Anchorage AK 99508 Office Phone: 907-786-1437. E-mail: fran.ulmer@uaa.alaska.edu.

ULMER, GENE CARLETON, geochemistry educator, researcher, editorial consultant; b. Cin., Jan. 28, 1937; s. Howard S. and Mildred (Miller) U.; m. Dagmar Ingrid Schröter, Dec. 26, 1959; children—Alexander, Susan Claudia, Erika Dyan, Kirk Brian. BS in Chemistry, U. Cin., 1959; PhD in Geochemistry and Geophysics, Pa. State U., Center Co., 1964. Grad. rsch. asst. Pa. State U., State College, 1959-64; refractory engr. Bethlehem Steel Co., Pa., 1964-69; assoc. prof. geochemistry Temple U., Phila., 1969-74, prof., 1974—2007, chmn. geology dept., 1975-78, prof. emeritus geology, 2007—; contract rschr. on nuc. waste Dept. Energy, 1980—, Rockwell Corp., 1980—; platinum rschr. NSF, Africa and Mont., 1980—; cons. in field. Contbg. editor: High Temperature-High Pressure Techniques, 1971, Hydrothermal Rsch. Techniques, 1987—. Contbr. articles to sci. publs. Patentee diamond synthesis. Twp. advisor Warrington Twp. Planning Commn., 1976; vol. water cons., 1978. Recipient Fulbright award, 1992, Humboldt fellow, 1992-95. Fellow Mineral. Soc. Am. (publs. com. 1976-78); mem. Am. Geophys. Union, Am. Ceramic Soc., Planetological Soc. Am., Phi Beta Kappa, Sigma Xi. Avocations: fishing; camping; photography. Home: 2207 Blackhorse Dr Warrington PA 18976-2100 Home Phone: 215-343-3689. Home Fax: 215-343-0830. Business E-Mail: gulmer@temple.edu.

ULMER, GREGORY LELAND, literature and language professor; b. Sheldon, Iowa, Dec. 23, 1944; s. Walter J. and Lavonne Ulmer; m. Kathleen C. Harlowe, June 1, 1968; children: Tyson H., Leland H. BA, U. Mont., Missoula, 1967; PhD, Brown U., Providence, 1972. Prof. U. Fla., Gainesville, 1972—. Faculty European Grad. Sch., Saas-Fee, Switzerland, 2000—; coord. Fla. Rsch. Ensemble, 2008—. Contbr. scholarly articles. Named Outstanding Undergrad. Tchr., U. Fla., 1990—91, First Herb and Catherine Yardley Term Prof., 1995—96; named to Acad. Disting. Tchg. Scholars, 2006—; Lilly Found. Postdoc. Tchg. fellow, 1979—80, Summer Rsch. grant, Nat. Endowment for Humanities, 1979. Mem.: MLA (adv. com. 2004—07). Home: 3431 NW 12th Ave Gainesville FL 32605 Office: Univ Fla Gainesville FL 32611 Business E-Mail: glue@ufl.edu.

ULMER, WILLIAM H., SR., dentist; b. Wilmington, Del., Sept. 20, 1946; s. Horace Hiate Ulmer and Lillian Palmer Queripel; m. Patricia Ann Kokoszka, July 10, 2004; m. Loreta Harriet Pasquine, June 6, 1970 (div. Oct. 15, 2001); children: Robert John II, William H. Jr., Alison Theresa Kristunas. BS in Biology, Pa. Mil. Coll., 1967; DDS, Fairleigh Dickenson U., Teaneck, NJ, 1971. Cert. forensic dentistry Armed Forces Inst. Pathology, 1990, forensic odontology Northwestern U., 1990. Intern gen. dentistry Del. State Hosp., 1972; dentist Dental Assocs. Del., Hockessin, 1972—. Forensic dentist Office of the Med. Examiner, State Del., Wilmington, 1989—; forensic facial recontruction sculptor Office of the Med. Examiner, State of Del., Wilmington, Del., 1992—; forensic dentist Pa. Dental Identification Team, Harrisburg, 1990—, Dept. Health Dimort Team, 1994—2001; cert. police instr. Del. State Police, Wilmington. Dental surgeon Team Health Care, Towaco, NJ, 2002—03, Jamaica. Recipient Gold medal Weight Lifting, Sr. Olympics, 2006. Master: TaeKwonDo Internat. (4th Degree Black Belt 2006); fellow: Acad. Dentistry Internat., Acad. Forensic Sciences, Acad. Gen. Dentistry; mem.: Surfers Med. Assn., Am. Dental Soc., Del. State Dental Soc. (chmn. emergency response team 1990—2007). Avocations: trumpet, guitar. Office: Dental Associates Of Delaware Hockessin 500 Lantana Dr Hockessin DE 19707-8813 Office Fax: 302-239-3657; Home Fax: 302-239-3657.

UL-MUSTAFA, RAZA, application developer, researcher; s. Ghulam Mustafa and Saleema Bibi; m. Nadia Sheikh, Aug. 14, 2002; children: Affaan Mustafa, Maha Mustafa. B, U. Azad Jammu and Kashmir, Mirpur, Pakistan, 1995; M, Kuwait U., 1999; PhD, Iowa State U., Ames, 2004. Rsch. asst. Kuwait U., 1996—99, Iowa State U., Ames, 2000—04; software engr. Microsoft Corp., Redmond, Wash., 2004—08, program mgr., 2008—. Conf. organizer Iowa State U., 2004, mem. tech. program com., 2004—04. Reviewer: Iowa State U. Rsch. Jour., 2003—07; contbr. articles to profl. jours., chapters to books. Mem.: Tau Beta Pi. Home: 708 142nd pl SE Bellevue WA 98007 Office: Microsoft Corp 1 Microsoft Way Redmond WA 98052

ULRICH, ERIC A., city councilman; b. Queens, NY; BA in Polit. Sci., St. Francis Coll., 2007; Postgraduate, St. John's U. Grad. Sch. Am. Govt. Pres. Our Neighbors Civic Assn. of Ozone Park, Inc.; mem. 23rd Assembly Dist. NY Republican State Com.; councilman Dist. 32 NY City Coun., 2009—. Mem.: Kiwanis Club of Howard Beach, Knights of Columbus, Pi Sigma Alpha. Republican. Office: NY City Council 98-16 Rockaway Beach Blvd Far Rockaway NY 11694 also: 250 Broadway 18th Fl New York NY 10007 Office Phone: 718-318-6411.*

ULRICH, LARS, musician; b. Gentofte, Denmark, Dec. 26, 1963; m. Skylar Satenstein, 1997 (div. 2004); children: Myles, Layne; (one child with Connie Nielsen) Bryce Thadeus Drummer, co-founder Metallica, 1981—. Drummer (albums with Metallica) Kill 'em All, 1983, Ride the Lightning, 1984, Master of Puppets, 1986, The $5.98 E.P.: Garage Days Re-Revisited, 1987, ...And Justice for All, 1988, Metallica (The Black Album), 1991 (Grammy award for Best Metal Performance), Live Sh*t: Binge and Purge, 1993, Kill 'Em All, 1995, Load, 1996, Reload, 1997, Garage Inc., 1998 (Grammy award), S & M, 1999, St. Anger, 2003, Death Magnetic, 2008; (songs with Metallica) One (Grammy award for Best Metal Performance, 1989), Stone Cold Crazy (Grammy award for Best Metal Performance, 1990), Better Than You (Grammy award for Best Metal Performance, 1998), Whiskey in the Jar (Grammy award for Best Hard Rock Performance, 1999), The Call of Ktulu (Grammy award for Best Rock Instrumental Performance, 2000), St. Anger, 2003 (Grammy award for Best Metal Performance, 2003), My Apocalypse, 2008 (Grammy award for Best Metal Performance, 2009); played on compilation albums including Metal Massacre, 1982, The Good, The Bad and The Live, 1990, Rubaiyant: Elektra's 30th Anniversary, 1990, For Those About To Rock: Moscow, 1992, Woodstock '94, 1994, Spawn: The Album, 1997, Woodstock '99, 2000, WCW: Mayhem The Music, 1999, M:I-2, 2000, NASCAR: Full Throttle, 2001, Swizz Beatz Presents G.H.E.T.T.O. Stories, 2002, Biker Boyz Soundtrack, 2003, We're A Happy Family: Tribute to the Ramones, 2003, I've Always Been Crazy: Tribute to Waylon Jennings, 2003. Inducted into Rock & Roll Hall of Fame (with Metallica), 2009. Office: care Metallica Elektra Records 75 Rockefeller Plz New York NY 10019-6908*

ULRICH, PAUL GRAHAM, lawyer, writer, editor; b. Spokane, Wash., Nov. 29, 1938; s. Donald Gunn and Kathryn (Vandercook) U.; m. Kathleen Nelson Smith, July 30, 1982; children: Kathleen Elizabeth Pennington, Marilee Rae Timbrooks, Michael Graham Ulrich. BA with high honors, U. Mont., 1961; JD, Stanford U., 1964. Bar: Calif. 1965, Ariz. 1966, U.S. Ct. Appeals (9th cir.) 1965, U.S. Supreme Ct. 1969. Law clk. judge U.S. Ct. Appeals, 9th Circuit, San Francisco, 1964-65; assoc. Lewis and Roca, Phoenix, 1965-70, ptnr., 1970-85; pres. Paul G. Ulrich P.C., Phoenix, 1985-92, Ulrich, Thompson & Kessler, P.C., Phoenix, 1992-94, Ulrich & Kessler, P.C., Phoenix, 1994-95, Ulrich, Kessler & Anger, P.C., Phoenix, 1995-2000, Ulrich & Anger, P.C., Phoenix, 2000—03, Paul G. Ulrich P.C., 2003—; owner Pathway Enterprises, 1985-91. Judge pro tem divsn. 1, Ariz. Ct. Appeals, Phoenix, 1986; instr. Thunderbird Grad. Sch. Internat. Mgmt., 1968-69, Ariz. State U. Coll. Law, 1970-73, 78, Scottsdale CC, 1975-77, also continuing legal edn. seminars. Author and pub.: Applying Management and Motivation Concepts to Law Offices, 1985; co-editor: Arizona Appellate Handbook, 1978-2000, Working With Legal Assistants, 1980, 81; editor, co-author Future Directions for Law Office Management, 1982, People in the Law Office, 1985-86; co-author, pub.: Arizona Healthcare Professional Liability Handbook, 1992, supplement, 1994, Arizona Healthcare Professional Liability Defense Manual, 1995, Arizona Healthcare Professional Liability Update Newsletter, 1992-99; co-author, editor: Federal Appellate Practice: Ninth Circuit, 1994, 2d edit., 1999, supplement, 2008; contbg. editor Law Office Econs. and Mgmt., 1984-97, Life, Law and the Pursuit of Balance, 1996, 2d edit., 1997; co-author Ariz. Appellate Handbook, 1978-. Mem. Ariz. Supreme Ct. Task Force on Ct. Orgn. and Adminstrn., 1988-89; mem. com. on appellate cts. Ariz. Supreme Ct., 1990-91; bd. visitors Stanford U. Law Sch., 1974-77; adv. com. legal assisting program Phoenix Coll., 1985-95; atty. rep. 9th Cir. Jud. Conf., 1997-2000. With U.S. Army, 1956. Recipient continuing legal edn. award State Bar Ariz., 1978, 86, 90, Harrison Tweed spl. merit award Am. Law Inst./ABA, 1987. Fellow Ariz. Bar Found. (founding 1985—); mem. ABA (chmn. selection and utilization of staff pers. com., econs. of law sect. 1979-81, mem. standing com. legal assts. 1982-86, co-chmn. joint project on appellate handbooks 1983-85, co-chmn. fed. appellate handbook project 1985-88, chmn. com. on liaison with non-lawyers orgns. Econs. of Law Practice sect. 1985-86), Am. Acad. Appellate Lawyers, Am. Law Inst. (life), Am. Judicature Soc. (Spl. Merit citation 1987), Ariz. Bar Assn. (chmn. econs. of law practice com. 1980-81; co-chmn. lower ct. improvement com. 1982-85, co-chmn. Ariz. appellate handbook project 1976-2000), Coll. Law Practice Mgmt., Maricopa County Bar Assn. (bd. dirs. 1994-96), Calif. Bar Assn., Phi Kappa Phi, Phi Alpha Delta, Sigma Phi Epsilon. Democrat. Home and Office: 131 E El Caminito Dr Phoenix AZ 85020-3503 Office Phone: 602-248-9465. Personal E-mail: ulrichpc@aol.com.

ULRICH, PETER HENRY, banker; b. Munich, Nov. 24, 1922; s. Hans George and Hella (Muschweck) U.; m. Carol A. Peek, Oct. 21, 1944; children: Carol Jean Hewes, Patricia Diane (Mrs. Damon Eberhart), Peter James. Student, Northwestern U., 0194—1942, U. Iowa, 1943, Sch. Mortgage Banking, 1954—56. Lic. real estate broker, cert. mortgage banker; cert. rev. appraiser; cert. mortgage underwriter. Escrow officer Security Title Ins. Co., Riverside, Calif., 1946-53; asst. cashier Citizens Nat. Trust & Savs., Riverside, 1953-57; v.p. Security First Nat. Bank, Riverside, 1957-63; sr. v.p. Bank of Calif. (N.A.), LA, 1963-72; pres. Ban Cal Mortgage Co., 1972-74, Ban Cal Tri-State Mortgage Co., 1974-75; pres., dir. Beneficial Std. Mortgage Co., 1976-88; real estate cons., 1988—. Instr. real estate and bus. San Bernardino Valley Coll., Riverside City Coll., Pasadena City Coll. Pres. Residential Rsch. Com. So. Calif., 1965, Riverside Opera Assn., 1956—59, Riverside Symphony Soc., 1959—61; trustee Idyllwild Arts Found., 1957—, pres., 1970—73, sec., 1986—87; mem. adv. bd. Salvation Army, 1959—, vice chmn., 1971—74, chmn., 1975, hon. life mem., 2008; chmn. Harbor Light Com., 1965—68, hon. life mem., 2008, chmn., 2002—; convocator Calif. Luth. U., 1976—80, 1981—83, regent, 1981—90; v.p. Guild Opera Co., 1991—99; bd. dirs. Lark Ellen Lions Charities, 1994—, pres., 1994—; treas. Opera Buffs, 1983—; mem. Arcadia Beautiful Commn., 1989—95, vice chair, 1991—92, chmn., 1992—93; trustee Calif. Luth. Edn. Found., 1989—2001; v.p. Arcadia Tournament Roses Assn., 1997; mem. Arcadia City Coun., 1995—96; trustee Arcadia Pub. Libr., 1997—2005, chair, 1999, 2005; vol. Arcadia Police Dept., 2002—; v.p. ch. coun. Ch. of the Cross, 2003—04, 2006—; bd. dirs. Arcadia Tournament Roses Assn., Am. Heart Assn. Foothill divsn. chair, 1997—99, South Pasadena-Arcadia Adult Reading Ctrs., 1998—2002, pres., 2002; bd. dirs. Arcadia Coordinating Coun., 2005—, 2006; v.p. Arcadia Libr. Found., 2007—. With US Army, 1943—46. Recipient Resolution of Commendation Riverside City Coun., 1963; Resolution of Appreciation LA City Coun., 1968, 1973; named Arcadia Vol. of Yr., 1997. Mem.: Arcadia Lions Found. (v.p. 2007—), Sch. Bond Oversight Com. (arcadia unified sch. dist. 2007—), Arcadia Human Resources Commn., Arcadia C. of C. (dir. 2004—, chmn. legis. affairs com. 2005—, Arcadia C. of C. Svc. award 2007), Assn. Corp. Real Estate Execs. (sec. 1967—71, pres. 1974—75), Inland Empire Mortgage Bankers Assn. (pres. 1962, hon. dir.), So. Calif. Mortgage Bankers Assn. (dir. 1975, 1980—81, v.p. 1982, pres. 1983), Calif. Mortgage Bankers Assn. (sec. 1965, dir. 1972—75, Disting. Svc. award 1997), Mortgage Bankers Assn. Ave. (chmn. Life Ins. Co. com. 1986—87), Lambda Alpha Internat. (historian, dir. 2004—05). Lutheran. Office: 37 E Huntington Dr Arcadia CA 91006-3210 Home: 1420 Santo Domingo Ave Duarte CA 91010-2632 Office Phone: 626-294-1058. Personal E-mail: ulrichgmb@verizon.net. *Being of foreign birth, I particularly appreciate and cherish the American way of life. I am grateful for the opportunities which it has afforded me. I also feel strongly that we who have had the benefit of these opportunities owe something in return to our communities and to our country. I have tried to the best of my abilities to conduct myself and my business affairs in an honorable and forthright manner, thus helping to preserve what I feel is still the best life style in the world.*

ULRICH, ROBERT J. (BOB ULRICH), retired retail executive; b. Mpls., Minn., 1944; 2 children. BA, U. Minn., 1967. With Dayton Hudson Corp., Mpls., 1967—2000, exec. v.p. Target Stores divsn., 1981-84, pres. Target Stores divsn., 1984-87, chmn., CEO Target Stores divsn., 1987-93; chmn, CEO Target Corp. (formerly Dayton Hudson Corp.), Mpls., 2000—08, chmn., 2008—09, chmn. emeritus, 2009—; chmn, CEO Dayton Hudson Corp., Mpls., 1994—2000. Bd. dirs. Dayton Hudson Corp., 1993—2000, Target Corp., 2000—, Yum Brands!, Inc., 1997—2007. Recipient Gold Medal award, Nat. Retail Fedn., 2001; named CEO of Yr., Chief Exec. mag., 2007. Office: Target Corp 1000 Nicollet Mall Minneapolis MN 55403-2467*

ULRICH, THEODORE ALBERT, lawyer; b. Spokane, Wash., Jan. 1, 1943; s. Herbert Roy and Martha (Hoffman) Ulrich; m. Nancy Allison, May 30, 1966; children: Donald Wayne, Frederick Albert. BS cum laude, U.S. Mcht. Marine Acad., 1965; JD cum laude, Fordham U., 1970; LLM, NYU, 1974. Bar: NY 1971, U.S. Ct. Appeals (2d cir.) 1971, U.S. Supreme Ct. 1974, U.S. Ct. Claims 1977, U.S. Customs Ct. 1978, U.S. Ct. Internat. Trade 1981, U.S. Ct. Appeals (5th cir.) 1988, U.S. Ct. Appeals (DC cir.) 1992, Colo. 1993, U.S. Ct. Appeals (10th cir.) 1994. Mng. clk. U.S. Dept. Justice, NYC, 1968-69, law clk. to fed. dist. judge, 1969-70; assoc. Cadwalader, Wickersham & Taft, NYC, 1970—94, ptnr., 1980-94, Popham, Haik, Schnobrich & Kaufman, Ltd., Denver, 1994-96; pvt. practice law Denver, 1996—. Author: Arbitration of Construction Contracts, V, 1991; co-author: Encyclopedia of International Commercial Litigation, 1991; contbg. author: Marine Engineering Economics and Cost Analysis, 1995; author, editor Fordham Law Rev., 1969. Leader Boy Scouts Am., Nassau County, NY, 1984-94, Denver, 1994—. Capt. USCGR, 1965-86. Mem. ABA, Colo. Bar, Denver Bar, Maritime Law Assn., Am. Soc. Internat. Law, Soc. Naval Archs. and Marine Engrs., U.S. Naval Inst., Am. Arbitration Assn. Home and Office: 4300 E 6th Ave Denver CO 80220-4940 E-mail: tnulrich@verizon.net.

ULRICH, WERNER, retired lawyer; b. Munich, Mar. 12, 1931; came to U.S., 1940, naturalized, 1945; s. Karl Justus and Grete (Rosenthal) U.; m. Ursula Wolff, June 28, 1959; children: Greta, Kenneth. BS, Columbia U., 1952, MS (NSF fellow 1952-53), 1953, Dr.Engring. Sci., 1957; MBA, U. Chgo., 1975; JD, Loyola U., Chgo, 1985. Bar: Ill. 1985. With AT&T Bell Labs, Naperville, Ill., 1953-95; head electronic switching dept. AT&T Bell Labs., Naperville, Ill., 1964-68; dir. Advanced Switching Tech., Naperville, 1968-77, head maintenance architecture dept., 1977-81; sr. atty. Intellectural Property Law Orgn., Naperville, 1981-95; pvt. practice Glen Ellyn, Ill., 1995—2007; ret., 2007. Vis. lectr. U. Calif., Berkeley, 1966-67 Inventor of over 20 telecommunications inventions; patentee electronic switching systems. Fellow IEEE; mem. ABA, Ill. State Bar Assn., Tau Beta Pi, Beta Gamma Sigma. Office: 501 Forest Ave Unit 406 Glen Ellyn IL 60137-4175

ULSENHEIMER, DEAN, language educator; b. Cleve., Dec. 20, 1941; s. Lon Sherwood and Mary Dorothy (Kupstas) U.; m. Sharon Lee Williams, Dec. 27, 1963 (div. June 1980); children: Cathi, Chris, Shelley, Scott.; m. Monica Joan Rigo, Aug. 10, 1984. BS in Edn., Ohio U., Athens, 1964; postgrad., John Carroll U., 1969—70, postgrad., 2006—07, Kent State U., 1979. Cert. secondary sch. tchr. Tchr. English South Amherst (Ohio) Schs., 1964-66; project engr. Otto Konigslow Mfg. Co., Cleve., 1966-67; tchr. English Cardinal Schs., Middlefield, Ohio, 1967-80, Shaw High Sch., East Cleveland, Ohio, 1980-92; instr. English Cuyahoga C.C., Cleve., 1980—, Lakeland C.C., Mentor, Ohio, 1984—; owner, cons. DU Power Reading, 2000—. Owner, cons. Power Writing; spkr. Lakeland C.C. Spkrs. Bur., Mentor, 1988—; hon. poetry intern NEH, Hiram Coll., 1977; cons. in field. Author: Easy Writing, 1977, Sentence Analysis, 1977, Communication Problems, 1978, Short Story Starters, 1980. Mem. NEA, Am. Cons. League, Ohio Edn. Assn., Greater Cleve. Growth Assn., Coun. Smaller Bus. Ent. Roman Catholic. Avocations: tennis, golf, phys. fitness. Home and Office: 6691 Morley Rd Concord OH 44077-5924

ULSH, GORDON A., battery manufacturing company executive; BA, Butler Univ. With Ford Motor Corp., 1968—84; v.p. Cooper Industries, 1984—97, exec. v.p., 1997—98; exec. v.p. worldwide aftermarket div. Federal-Mogul Corp., 1998, pres., COO, 1999; ptnr. Ripplewood Equity Partners, 1999—2001; chmn., pres., CEO Fleetpride Inc., 2001—05; pres., CEO, dir. Exide Technologies, Lawrenceville, NJ, 2005—. Mem.: Soc. Mfg. Engineers, Soc. Automotive Engineers.

ULSHEN, MARTIN HOWARD, pediatric gastroenterologist, researcher; b. NYC, Mar. 5, 1944; s. Lawrence F. and Dorothy C. Ulshen; divorced; children: Sarah Powell, Daniel; m. Sue Ellen McRae, Dec. 17, 1988. BA, U. Rochester, 1965, MD, 1969. Diplomate Am. Bd. Pediat., sub-bd. pediatric gastroenterology, 1990. Intern in pediatrics Univ. NC, 1969-70; resident in pediatrics Univ. Colo., 1972-74, fellow in pediat. gastroenterology, 1974-75, Childrens Hosp., Boston, 1975-77; prof. Univ. NC, Chapel Hill, 1977—97; fellow in pediat. gastroenterology St. Mary's Hosp. & Good Samaritan Hosp., W. Palm Beach, Fla., 1996—99, Duke Univ. Med. Ctr., Durham, NC, 1999, prof., division chief pediatric gastroenterology, hepatology & nutrition, 1999—. Assoc. editor Jour. Pediat.; med. editor Pediat. Gastroenterology, Am. Bd. Pediat.; contbr. articles to profl. jours. With USPHS, 1970-72. Office: Duke Univ DUMC 3009 Durham NC 27710 Office Phone: 919-684-5068. Office Fax: 919-684-4836. Business E-Mail: martn.ulshen@duke.edu.

ULSOY, ALI GALIP, engineering educator; b. Kozlu, Zonguldak, Turkey, Aug. 17, 1950; s. Muzaffer and Fatma Emel (Tugsal) U.; m. Susan Kathleen Glowski, Apr. 17, 1975; 1 child, Jessie Elif. BS, Swarthmore Coll., 1973; MS, Cornell U., 1975; PhD, U. Calif., Berkeley, 1979. Teaching and rsch. asst. Cornell U., Ithaca, N.Y., 1973-74, U. Calif., Berkeley, 1975-79, postdoctoral fellow, 1979-80; asst. prof. U. Mich., Ann Arbor, 1980-86; assoc. prof. engring. Bogazici U., Istanbul, Turkey, 1986-87, U. Mich., Ann Arbor, 1986-92, prof., 1992-96, chmn. grad. program, 1987-89, assoc. chair dept. mech. engring., 1992-93, chair program in mfg., 1992-98, William Clay Ford prof. mfg., 1996—, chair dept. mech. engring., 1998—. Vis. rschr. Ford Motor Co. Rsch. Labs., Dearborn, Mich., 1995; dir. NSF Mfg. Ctr., Ann Arbor, 1992—, NSFD Divsn. of Civil and Mech. Sys. Author (book) Microcomputer Applications in Manufacturing, 1989; contbr. articles to profl. jours.; tech. editor ASME Jour. of Dynamic Systems Measurement and Control, 1999-2004. Recipient Rsch. Incentive award Exxon Found., 1984-85, Wood award Forest Products Rsch. Soc., 1979, O. Hugo Schuck Best Paper award, 1994, Southwest Mechs. Lectr., 1995. Fellow ASME and SME (Oldenburger medal, 2008); mem. ASME DSCD (payroler) (Outstanding Investigator award, 2004), ASME JDSMC (Kalman Best Paper award, 2003), ASME DSCD (Leadership award, 2002), IEEE, NAE, Soc. Mfg. Engrs. (Outstanding Young Mfg. Engr. award 1986, A.M. Sargent Progress award, 2008), Am. Soc. Engring. Edn., U. Mich. Rsch. Club, Sigma Xi. Avocations: reading, poetry, soccer, bicycling, canoeing, fishing. Office: U Mich Dept Mech Engring Ann Arbor MI 48109-2125 Office Phone: 734-936-0407. Business E-Mail: ulsoy@umich.edu.

ULSTROM, ROBERT A., retired pediatrician; b. Mpls., Feb. 23, 1923; m. Mary Janet McGrath, 1946 (dec. 1981); 3 children; m. Betty Bernard, 1982 (div. 1985). BS, U. Minn., 1944, MD, 1946; postgrad., Strong Meml. Hosp. Lic. physician, Minn., Calif.; diplomate Am. Bd. Pediatrics with subsplty. in endocrinology (bd. dirs. 1980-86, v.p. 1985, chmn. rsch. and devel. com. 1980-86, tech. adv. com. for devel. of computerized exams. 1983-86), Am. Bd. Emergency Medicine (bd. dirs. 1982-86). Intern, resident in pediats. U. Rochester, 1946-48; instr., asst. prof. U. Minn., Mpls., 1950-53, assoc. prof., 1956-61, prof. pediatrics, 1961-64, 66-90, prof. emeritus, 1990—, mem. Ctr. for German and European Studies, Inst. for Global Studies, 2004—, acting head dept. pediats., 1961—62, assoc. dean Coll. Med. Scis., 1967-70; asst. prof. UCLA, 1953-56, prof., 1964-67, chmn. dept. pediatrics, 1964-67; vis. prof. medicine U. So. Calif., 1982-83, ret. Chief pediats. 97th Gen. Hosp., 1949-50; cons. in pediats. Harbor Gen. Hosp., L.A., 1953-56, 64-67, Mpls. Gen. Hosp., 1956-64, Hennepin County Gen. Hosp., 1967-90, hon. staff, 1990—; Well Child Clinic cons. City of L.A., 1953-56; track physician Donneybrooke Racetrack, Brainerd, Minn., 1968-73; dir. Reg. Ctr. for Metabolic Defects, 1975-79; cons. Ellwood & Assocs., 1986-87; med. legal cons. various plantiffs, 1985-95; mem. med. adv. bd. Group Health, Inc., 1967-90, Diabetes Detection and Edn. Ctr., 1969-71; mem. grants review com. Human Growth Inc., 1974-78; mem. tech. adv. com. on human genetics Minn. State Bd. Health, 1976-90; mem. pers. selection com. NIH, 1979, mem. gen. medicine study sect. NIH, 1964-68; mem. divsn. med. scis. NRC, 1961-64; oral examiner Am. Bd. Pediats., 1970-89; expert witness for prosecution U.S. Fed. Dist. Ct., Mpls., 1994-95; instr. computer course for beginners Elder Learning Inst., Coll. Continuing Edn., U. Minn., 1995—, bd. dirs., 1996-2000, webmaster, author, 1997-2002, v.p., 1998-99, mentor undergrad. students Coll. Liberal Arts, 1992—2004. Mem. edit. bd. Jour. Pediats., 1962-65; contbr. articles to profl. jours. Sec.-treas. Minn. Med. Found., 1967-68. With M.C., U.S. Army, 1948-50. Markle scholar in med. scis., 1954-59; Pew Found. fellow, 1985-86; recipient Wyeth award for med. rsch., 1963. Mem. AAAS, Am. Pediat. Soc., Am. Soc. Clin. Investigation, Ctrl. Soc. for Clin. Rsch., Endocrine Soc., Lawson-Wilkins Pediat. Endocrine Soc. (founding mem., membership com. 1971-75, chmn. 1975), Midwestern Pediat. rsch. Soc. (coun. 1961-64), Soc. for Pediat. Rsch. (NRC rep. 1961-64), Western Soc. for Clin. rsch., Western Soc. for Pediat. Rsch., Alpha Omega Alpha, Phi Rho Sigma. Home: 4616 Sunset Rdg Minneapolis MN 55416-3335 Personal E-mail: ulstr001@tc.umn.edu.

ULTAN, LLOYD, historian, educator; b. Bronx, NY, Feb. 16, 1938; s. Louis and Sophie U. BA cum laude, Hunter Coll., 1959; MA, Columbia U., 1960. Assoc. Edward Williams Coll., Fairleigh Dickinson U., Hackensack, NJ, 1964-74, asst. prof. history, 1974-75, assoc. prof., 1975-83, prof., 1983—. Adj. prof. history H. Lehman Coll. CUNY, 2004-; cons. in field. Editor Bronx County Hist. Soc. Jour., 1964—, Bronx County Hist. Soc. Press, 1981—; author: The Beautiful Bronx, 1920-50, 1979, Legacy of the Revolution: The Valentine-Varian House, 1983, The Bronx in the Innocent Years, 1890-1925, 1985, The Presidents of the United States, 1989, The Bronx in the Frontier Era: From the Beginning to 1696, 1993, The Bronx: It Was Only Yesterday, 1935-65, 1993, Roots of the Republic, Vol. VI, 1996, The Bronx Cookbook, 1997, Bronx Accent: A Literary and Pictorial History of the Borough, 2000, The Birth of The Bronx, 1609-1900, 2000; contbr. Ency. NY City, 1995. Gen. sec. Bronx Civic League, 1964—67; v.p. bd. trustees Bronx County Hist. Soc., 1965—67, 1977—84, curator, 1968—71, pres., 1971—76, historian, 1986—; founding mem., bd. dirs. Bronx Coun. on Arts, 1968—71; chmn. Bronx County Bicentennial Commn., 1973—76, Bronx Borough Pres.'s Bicentennial Adv. Com., 1974—76; vice chmn. Commn. Celebrating 350 Yrs. of the Bronx, 1989; mem. program guidelines com. N.Y.C. Dept. Cultural Affairs, 1976—77; mem. N.Y.C. Com. on Cultural Concerns, 1982—88, N.Y.C. Mayor's Task Force on Spontaneous Memls., 2002; bd. sponsors Historic Preservation com. St. Ann's Ch. Morrisania, 1987—; ofcl. historian Bronx Borough, NY, 1996—; bd. dirs. Nat. Shrine Bill of Rights, Mt. Vernon, NY, 1983—, 91 Van Cortlandt Owners Corp., 1986—. Recipient Fairleigh Dickinson U.

15-Yr. award, 1979, 20-Yr. award, 1984, 25-Yr. award, 1989, 30-Yr. award, 1994, 35-Yr. award, 1999, Outstanding Tchr. of Yr. award, 1994, 40-Yr. award, 2004; named NYC Centennial Historian, 1999, NYC Book award for borough history NY Soc. Libr., 2001; named to Hunter Coll. Alumni Hall of Fame, 1974; NY State Regents Coll. tchg. fellow, 1959. Mem.: AAUP (v.p. Teaneck chpt. 1992—93, sec. coun. of FDU chpts. 1992—93), NY Hist. Soc., Am. Hist. Assn., Sigma Lambda, Alpha Chi Alpha, Phi Alpha Theta. Home and Office: 91 Van Cortlandt Ave W Bronx NY 10463-2712 *Transmitting the heritage of the past to the youth and to the mature adult, either through the spoken or written word, not only ensures that the civilization we inherited will be passed on, it will also warn people about earlier mistakes that should now be shunned and will, hopefully, inspire them to add their own positive contribution. I believe I am continuing to perform this service.*

UM, KI SUNG, research scientist; b. Gongju, Choongnam, Republic of Korea, Apr. 13, 1961; s. Dong Seop Um and Kyung Sook Lee; m. Soon Yi Yang, Apr. 16, 1988; children: Jung Yong, Se Yong. MPH, Yonsei Grad. Sch. Health Sci. and Mgmt., Seoul, 1989; PhD, Kyungpook Nat. U., Daegu, Republic of Korea, 2004. Cert. info. process engr. Human Resources Devel. Svc. Korea. Rschr. Ctr. Bioinformatics Nat. Cancer Inst./NIH, Rockville, Md., 2005—. Maj. Republic of Korea Air Force, 1985—2001. Recipient Sci. award for best paper of yr., Korean Soc. Med. Informatics, 2003; Postdoctoral fellow, Korea Rsch. Found., 2004—05. Mem.: Health Level Seven Inc. (cert. specialist). Achievements include patents for linear streaming algorithm as an HL7 parsing method. Office: Nat Cancer Inst NIH Ctr Bioinformatics 2115 E Jefferson St Ste 5000 Rockville MD 20852 Office Fax: 301-480-4222. Business E-Mail: umkis@mail.nih.gov.

UMANS, ALVIN ROBERT, manufacturing executive; b. NYC, Mar. 11, 1927; s. Louis and Ethel (Banner) U.; m. Nancy Jo Zadek, June 28, 1953 (div.); children: Kathi Lee Umans Lind, Craig Joseph; m. Madeleine Sayer, Sept. 21, 1985; 1 child, Valentine Brett. Student, U. Rochester, NY, 1944—45. Sales mgr. Textile Mills Co., Chgo., 1954-56; regional sales mgr. Reflector Hardware Corp., Melrose Park, Ill., 1956-58, nat. sales mgr., 1959-62, v.p., 1962-65, pres., treas., dir., 1965-92; pres., CEO RHC/Spacemaster Corp., Melrose Park, 1992-97, chmn., CEO, 1997—2003, Commerce Nat. Group, Chgo., 2004—. Past chmn., bd. dirs. Goer Mfg. Co., Inc., Charleston, SC, Morgan Marshall Industries, Inc., Ill., Capitol Hardware, Inc., Ill., Spartan Showcase Inc., Mo.; v.p., dir. Adams Comm., Chgo.; bd. dirs. Monroe Comm., Chgo.; trustee Driehaus Mut. Funds, 1996—, chmn. bd., 2005—; mem. adv. bd. Capsonic Group, Elgin, Ill. Trustee Mt. Sinai Hosp. Med. Ctr., Chgo., 1970—, chmn. bd., 1987-89; trustee Schwab Rehab. Hosp., Chgo., 1987—, chmn. bd., 1987-89; trustee Sinai Health Sys., Chgo., 1993—, chmn., 1995-97; mem. Cook County Bur. Adv. Com., 1994—; bd. dirs. Milton & Rose Zadek Fund, 1965-78; governing bd. mem. Cinema/Chgo., 1988-89. Served with US Army, 1945-46. Mem. Nat. Assn. Store Fixture Mfrs. (dir. 1969-70), World Pres.'s Orgn., Chgo. Pres.'s Orgn. Clubs: Standard (Chgo.). Home: 132 E Delaware Pl Chicago IL 60611-1445 Office: Commerce National Group 980 N Michigan Ave Ste 1175 Chicago IL 60611-4530 Office Phone: 312-654-9150. Office Fax: 312-654-9180. Business E-Mail: arumans@gmail.com.

UMANSKY, DIANE, editor; B in Journalism, U. RI. Corr. Bergen Record; writer various teen publs. including Scholastic; mng. editor Nickelodeon; sr. editor First for Women; editl. dir. MediZine LLC, 1995—. Freelance writer First for Women, SELF, Family Circle, American Health, Harper's Bazaar, Working Mother, Good Housekeeping, Weight Watchers. Recipient Golden Triangle award, Am. Acad. Dermatology, 2003. Office: MediZine 500 Fifth Ave Ste 1900 New York NY 10110 Office Phone: 212-695-2223.*

UMANZOR-YASHIMURA, MARTA A., literature educator; b. San Miguel, El Salvador, Oct. 26, 1943; arrived in US, 1977; d. Rafael Robles and Maria Teresa Umanzor de Robles; m. Carlos Kimio, July 17, 1977 (dec. Aug. 11, 2008); children: Juan Carlos, Gustavo Adolfo, Evelyn Patricia. BA in Law, Nat. U. El Salvador, 1973; MA in Latin Am. Lit., U. Ariz., 1984; PhD in Latin Am. Spanish Lit., 1990. Tchg. Spanish lang & Lit. U. Ariz., Ariz., 1982—90; assst. tchr. St. Michaels Coll., Vermont, 1990—96, assoc. prof., 1996—, chair modern lang., 2007. Spanish minority rep. Health Dept., Vermont, 2000—03. Author: (book) La Vision de la Mujer en la Obrea de Elana Garro, 1996. Mem. Peace & Justice, Burlington, Vermont, 1993—, Pax Christi, Burlington, 1995—, Amensty Internat., 2000—. Recipient Norber A. Kuntz Svc. award, St. Michaels Cmty., 2003, Rev. Gerald Dupont award, Students Assn., 2002. Mem.: Sigma Delta Pi, Golden Key, Delta Epsilon Sigma. Office: St Michaels Coll 384 One Winooski Pk Colchester VT 05439

UMBARGER, GARDNER THOMPSON, III, special education educator, researcher; b. Homestead, Fla., Dec. 21, 1956; s. Gardner Thompson Umbarger and Ann Weaver Sweeny; m. Lynne Judy, Apr. 11, 1992; 1 child, Chloe Emma. BA, Wash. & Lee U., Lexington, Va., 1979; Med, Lynchburg Coll., Va., 1989; PhD, U. Kans., Lawrence, 2000. Info. mgr. Thomas & Fiske, P.C., Alexandria, Va., 1984—86, Verner, Liipfert, et al., Washington, 1986—87; spl. edn. tchr. Laurel Regional Spl. Edn. Ctr., Lynchburg, 1988—95; dir. spl. edn. Big Horn Sch. Dist. 3 & 4, Greybull, Wyo., 2000—02; asst. prof., intervention svcs. Bowling Green State U., Ohio, 2002—. Maj., med. svcs. corps Army Res., 1979—2001. Mem.: Divsn. Devel. Disabilities, Coun. Exceptional Children. Office: Bowling Green State Univ Bowling Green OH 43403 Office Fax: 419-372-8265.

UMBDENSTOCK, RICHARD J., medical association administrator; b. 1950; BA in Politics, Fairfield U., Conn., 1972; MSc in Health Svcs. Adminstrn., SUNY, Stony Brook, 1974; LLD (hon.), Gonzaga U., Spokane, Washington, 2003. Diplomate Am. Coll. Healthcare Execs. Ind. cons. for voluntary hosp. governing boards in US and Can.; pres., CEO Providence Svcs., Spokane, Wash., 1993—2006; chmn. Premier, Inc., Charlotte, NC, 2006; exec. v.p. Providence Health & Svcs. (merger of Providence Svcs. & Providence Health Sys.), 2006; spl. asst. to pres. Am. Hosp. Assn., Inc., Chgo., trustee, 2000—04, chmn.-elect, 2005, chmn., COO, pres.-elect, 2006, pres., 2006—. Mem. nat. bd. advs. Ctr. Healthcare Governance. Author: several books and articles for hosp. bd. audiences, nat. survey reports for Am. Hosp. Assn., Health Rsch. Ednl. Trust, Am. Coll. Healthcare Execs. Office: Am Hosp Assn One North Franklin St Chicago IL 60606-3421 Office Phone: 312-422-3000. Office Fax: 312-422-4796. Business E-Mail: rich@aha.org.*

UMBERG, THOMAS JOHN, lawyer; b. Cin., Sept. 25, 1955; s. John H. and Joan (Jansen) U.; m. Robin Bailey; children: Erin, Brett, Tommy. BA cum laude, UCLA, 1977; JD, U. Calif., San Francisco, 1980. Bar: Calif. 1980, U.S. Dist. Ct. (ctrl. dist.) Calif. 1981, U.S. Dist. Ct. (so. dist.) Calif. 1986, U.S. Ct. Appeals (9th cir.) 1988. Asst. U.S. atty. Ctrl. Dist. Calif., criminal div., LA, 1987—90; mem. Calif. Assembly, Sacramento, 1990—94, 2004—; ptnr. Morrison & Foerster LLP, Irvine, Calif., 1995—97; dep. dir. White House Office Nat. Drug Control Policy, 1997—2000; mng. ptnr.-Orange County Office Morrison & Foerster LLP, Irvine, Calif., 2000—. Adj. prof. law Southwestern U., 1995—97. Military Prosecutor, U.S. Army, Korea, Italy 1980-1985; col. USAR. Mem.: Calif. Coun. Criminal Justice (mem. 1991—95). Roman Catholic. Office: Morrison And Foester 555 W 5TH ST STE 3500 Los Angeles CA 90013-1024 Office Phone: 949-251-7500. Office Fax: 949-251-0900. Business E-Mail: tumberg@mofo.com.

UMBERSON, DEBRA, sociologist, educator; b. Springhill, La., Aug. 8, 1957; children: Eliza Steiker, Aaron Steiker. PhD, Vanderbilt U., Nashville, 1985. Prof. sociolgoy U. Tex., Austin, 1988—, chair sociology, 2000—06. Recipient Nat. Rsch. Svc. award, Nat. Inst. Aging, 1987—89, First Ind. Rsch. & Transition award, 1990—95, award, Sociol. Rsch. Assn., 2008—; named Highly Cited Rschr. Social Sci., Inst. for Sci. Info., 2008. Mem.: Am. Sociol. Assn. (chair, mental health sect. 2006—07). Liberal. Office: Univ Tex 1 Univ Sta A1700 Austin TX 78712-1088 Office Fax: 512-471-1748. Business E-Mail: umberson@prc.utexas.edu.

UMENYIORA, OSI, professional football player; b. London, Nov. 16, 1980; Grad., Troy State U., Ala. Defensive end NY Giants, 2003—. Named First Team All-Pro, NFL, 2005; named to Nat. Football Conf. Pro Bowl Team, 2005, 2007. Achievements include being a member of Super Bowl XLII championship winning New York Giants, 2008. Office: New York Football Giants Giants Stadium East Rutherford NJ 07073*

UMHOEFER, AURAL M., retired dean, educational consultant; b. Wausau, Wis., May 11, 1942; d. Mark John Vladick, Alice Marion Vladick; m. Paul Anthony Umhoefer. MS, U. Wis., Madison, 1965; BA in French, Rosary Coll., River Forest, Ill., 1964—64; AA (hon.), U. Wis., Baraboo, 2006. Head libr. Green Bay ctr. U. Wis., 1965—68, dir. learning resource ctr. Baraboo, 1968—80, dean, campus exec. officer Baraboo/Sauk county campus, 1980—2002, ret., 2002; cons. U. Wis. Sys., 2003—05. Bd. dirs. Wells Fargo, Baraboo; bd. dirs. Hist. Sites Found. Circus World Mus., Baraboo, 1984—90. Bd. dirs. Al Ringling Theatre, Friends of Campus, Inc., Boy Scouts Am., Madison, Wis., 1985—97; devel. coun. St. Clare Hosp., Baraboo, 1993—97. Recipient Outstanding Alumni award, Newman H.S. - Wausau, Wis., 1992, Citation from Senate, State of Wis., 1991, 2002, Pub. Svc. award, Fed. Bur. Prisons, 1991, 2002, Appreciation award, Circus World Mus., 1986, Citation from Govt., State of Wis., 2002; named Outstanding Young Women of Am., 1975, Aural M. Umhoefer bldg. in her honor, U. Wis., Baraboo, 2002. Mem.: AAUW (corp. rep. 1985—97, Wis. Women Leaders in Edn. award 1986, 1989), Wis. Correctional Edn. Assn. (v.p., pres. 1994—98), U. Wis. Alumni Assn. (pres. 1984—86, Spark Plug award 1992), Rotary Internat. (vocat. chair, bd.dirs.). Avocations: cooking, reading, travel, gardening. Home: 700 Effinger Rd Baraboo WI 53913 Office: University of Wisconsin 1006 Connie Rd Baraboo WI 53913 Business E-Mail: aural.umhoefe@uwc.edu.

UMHOLTZ, CLYDE ALLAN, financial analyst; b. Du Quoin, Ill., Dec. 20, 1947; s. Frederick Louis and Opal Kathleen (Beard) U. BS, U. Ill., 1969; MS, U. Miss., 1972; MBA, Memphis State U., 1983, PhD, 1986; Dr of Higher Learning (hon.), London Sch. Econs., 2002. CFA; cert. systems profl., tax practitioner; registered profl. engr.; cert. data processor. Supr. quality control Champion Internat. Corp., Oxford, Miss., 1971-72; mgr. divsn. quality control Cook Industries, Memphis, 1973; engrng. planner Northwest Industries and subs., Memphis, 1974-75; long range planning and analysis W.R. Grace and Co. and subs., Memphis, 1975-78; mgr. planning and analysis Ctr. Nuc. Studies Memphis State U., 1979-83; data processing mgr. Shelby County (Tenn.) Govt., 1983-87, dep. adminstr., 1987—2005, spl. asst. to county exec., 1989—2005, vice chancellor higher edn. commn., 2005—. Adj. prof. U. Tenn., Memphis, 1985—; ptnr. Custom Data Systems Inc., Memphis, 1987—, Western Techs. Inc., Memphis, 1988—; bd. dir. Am. Tech. Inst., Memphis, Am. Info. Cons., Atlanta, Eastgate Corp., Anaheim, Calif., CIPCO Corp., Chgo., Sanford Cons. Group, London, Paris; bd. underwriters Lloyd's of London; diplomate editl. adv. bd. Brent's Peerage, London, Memphis-Amsterdam Gateway Com., Holland, 1997; Goodwill Amb. Am. Ukrainian Trade Alliance, Kiev, 1997—, Asian Econ. Recovery Coun., Tokyo, 1998—; elected to U.S. China Bd. of Trade, 2002; adv. bd. Fed. Res. Bank, Memphis, 1998—; mem. Am.-Japanese Tire Safety Adv. Bd., 2000, Tenn. Commn. on Homeland Security, 2002—; diplomate Multi-Country Healthcare Exch., 2003, Medicare Nat. Study Com., 2003; oversight com. Internat. Energy Prodn. Alliance, 2003, 06; adv. com. OPEC Price Stblzn. Coop., 2004, 06; mem. Internat. Symposium Strategic Energy Resources, 2005, 06, Congressional Com. Social Security Reform, 2005, 06, Citizens' Congl. Ethics Coun., 2006, Emergency Mgmt. Comms. Coordinating Com., 2006, Accreditation Com., Internat. Baccalaureate Edn. Program, 2006, Mid-East Stabilization Planning Conf., 2006; mem. Govt. Ethics Reform Task Force, 2007; internat. bus. cons. McKinsey Co., 2007; bd. Am. Mideast Ednl. and Training Sys.,2008-;Tennessee Task Force Job Creation, 2009; US Congressional Commn. Economic Stimulation & Global Recovery Planning, 2009; cons. in field. Author: Prototyping of Computerized Financial Systems, 3d edit., 1997, Context Analysis in System Design, 2d edit., 1999, The Family Partnership-An Estate Planning Model, 3d edit., 2000, The Use of Chemical Molecules as Computer Switches, 2002, The Science of Plastics, 2007; contbr. articles to profl. jours.; inventor angle trisector. Active presdl. election campaigns, 1968-72, 80-2004, 2008; del. Rep. Nat. Conv., 1996-2004, 2008; mem. Rep. Nat. Com., 2002—; active mayoral campaign, Memphis, 1975, 83, 87, 91, Shelby County, 1990, 94, sheriff's campaign Shelby County, 1990, 94, Mid-South Billy Graham Crusade, 1978; del. So. Govs.' Conf., 1992-93; gov. staff State of Tenn., 1993-94; mem. Mayor's Adv. Com., Memphis, 1991; steering com. Future Memphis, 1992, Arena Football League, Memphis, 1994; active Houston Oilers Relocation Com., 1996; adv. coun. Kordes' Gardens, Hamburg, Germany; study com. Nat. Electoral Coll., 2001; co-chmn. 27th Ann. Pres.'s Dinner, 2002; oversight com. Fin. Acctg. Stds. Bd., 2002—; bd. dirs. West Tenn. Cmty. Found., 2006—, Memphis Biomed. Rsch. Found., 2007—, Resources for the Future, Washington, 2007-; bd. dirs. Internat Commn on Global Warming, 2008- Recipient Oratorical award Optimist Club, 1963, Leadership and Human Rels. award Dale Carnegie Inst., 1977, Disting. Svc. award State of Tenn., 1991; Humanist award Internat. Ethical Union, 2008; NSF fellow, 1970-72. Fellow NAS, Australian Acad. Scis., NY Acad. Scis., Am. Acad. Info. Tech., Nat. Acad. U. Adminstr.; Internat. Enterprise Inst. (hon.); mem. AAAS, AIChE, Am. Mgmt. Assn., Fin. Execs. Inst., Am. Chem. Soc., Assn. MBA Execs., Data Processing Mgmt. Assn., Planning Execs. Inst., Am. Assn. Investment Advisors, U. Ill. Alumni Assn., U. Miss. Alumni Assn., Memphis State U. Alumni Assn., Am. Rose Soc. (accredited life rose judge 1990), Am. Iris Soc., Am. Hemerocallis Soc., Elvis Presley Meml. Soc., Am. Hort. Soc., Internat. Platform Assn., Gt. Am. Pyramid Boosters Memphis, Mensa, Admirals Club, Oxford Club, London Club, Exec. Club Memphis, Petroleum Club Memphis, Olympic Soc. Atlanta, Order of De Molay, Phi Beta Kappa. Baptist. Achievements include patent on fiber optic router; patents for wireless digital x-ray. Home: 3580 Hanna Dr Memphis TN 38128-3451 Office: 100 N Main St Memphis TN 38103-5011 Office Phone: 901-388-3997. Business E-Mail: cau@memphis.gov. E-mail: cau@hannamem.gov.

UMMER, JAMES WALTER, lawyer; b. Pitts., July 16, 1945; s. Walter B. and Rose P. (Gerhardt) U.; m. Janet Sue Young, Dec. 21, 1968; children: James Bradley, Benjamin F. BA, Thiel Coll., 1967; JD, Duke U., 1972. Bar: Pa. 1972. Trust officer Pitts. Nat. Bank, 1972-75; tax atty., shareholder Buchanan Ingersoll P.C., Pitts., 1975-92; prin. Hirtle, Callaghan & Co., Pitts., 1992-93; shareholder Babst, Calland, Clements and Zomnir, Pitts., 1993-99; ptnr. Reed, Smith, Shaw & McClay, Pitts., 2000—03, Rothman Gordon, P.C., Pitts., 2003—. Golf course cons., Orlando, Fla. Trustee Thiel Coll., Greenville, Pa., 1984—, The Childrens' Inst., Pitts., 1984—; mem. bd. visitors Duke U. Div. Sch., 1999—. Fellow Am. Coll. Probate Counsel, Am. Coll. Trust and Estate Counsel; mem. Estate Planning Coun. Western Pa. (pres. 1986-87), Tax Club (Pitts.), Duquesne Club, Rolling Rock Club, Oakmont Country Club. Republican. Presbyterian. Home: 200 Woodland Farms Rd Pittsburgh PA 15238-2024 Office: Rothman Gordon PC 3d Fl Grant Bldg 310 Grant St Pittsburgh PA 15219 Office Phone: 412-338-1105. E-mail: jwummer@rothmangordon.com.

UMMINGER, BRUCE LYNN, government agency administrator, research scientist, educator, consultant; b. Dayton, Ohio, Apr. 10, 1941; s. Frederick William and Elnora Mae Umminger; m. Judith Lackey Bryant, Dec. 17, 1966; children: Alison Grace, April Lynn. BS in Biology magna cum laude with honors, Yale U., 1963, MS, 1966, MPhil, 1968, PhD, 1969; postgrad., U. Calif., Berkeley, 1963—64; cert. univ. adminstrv./mgmt. tng. program, U. Cin., 1975; cert., Fed. Exec. Inst., 1984. Asst. prof. dept. biol. scis. U. Cin., 1969-73, assoc. prof. dept. biol. scis., 1973-75, acting head dept. biol. scis., 1973-75, prof. dept. biol. scis., 1975-81, dir. grad. affairs, 1978-79; program dir. regulatory biology program NSF, Washington, 1979-84, dept. dir. cellular bioscis. divsn., 1984-89, mem. sr. exec. svc., 1984—2006, acting divsn. dir., 1985-87, 88-89, divsn. dir. cellular bioscis. divsn., 1989-91, divsn. dir. integrative biology and neurosci., 1991—99, sr. scientist office integrative activities, office of dir., 1999—2006, cons., 2006—09, The Implementation Group, Washington, 2006—; sr. advisor on health policy Office of Internat. Health Policy Dept. State, Washington, 1988; sr. advisor on biodiversity Smithsonian Instn., Washington, 1993-94. Exec. sec. Nat. Sci. Bd. Com. on Ctrs. and Individual Investigator Awards, 1986-88; rev. panel exptl. program to stimulate competitive rsch. NSF, 1989, Rsch. Improvement in Minority Instns., 1986-87, US-India Coop. Rsch. Program, 1981-82, U.S.-India Exch. of Scholars Program, 1979-81; vice chmn. biotech. rsch. subcom. Fed. Coord. Coun. on Sci. Engrng. and Tech., Office Sci. and Tech. Policy, 1991-94; exec. sec. subcom. biodiversity and ecosystem dynamics, com. on environment and natural resources Nat. Sci. and Tech. Coun., 1994, interag. working group on rsch. misconduct policy implementation, 2000-06; group nat. experts on safety in biotech. OECD, 1988-89; sr. exec. panel Exec. Potential Program, Office Pers. Mgmt., 1988-89; space shuttle proposal rev. panel in life scis. NASA, 1978, rsch. assocs. in space biology award com., 1985-91, chmn. cell and devel. biology discipline working group, space biology program, 1990-91, chmn. gravitational biology panel, NASA Specialized Ctrs. Rsch. and Tng., 1990, chmn. specialized ctrs. rsch. and tng. peer rev. panel NASA, 1995, exec. steering com. in life scis., 1991, gravitational biology facility sci. working group, 1992-95, space sta. biol. rsch. project sci. working group, 1995-96, neurolab. steering com., 1993; panel study biol. diversity, Bd. Sci. and Tech. Internat. Devel. NRC, 1989; exec. sec. adv. planning bd. Nat. Biodiversity Info. Ctr., Smithsonian Instn., 1993-94; adv. screening com. in life scis. Coun. for Internat. Exch. of Scholars, 1978-81; liaison rep. nat. heart, lung and blood adv. coun. NIH, 1979-87, nat. adv. child health and human devel. coun., 1990-99; recombinant DNA adv. com., 1988; liaison rep. agrl. biotech. Rsch. Adv. com., USDA, 1989-94; animal com. Interagy. Rsch., 1984-88; Interagy. working group on Internat. Biotech., 1988-94; chmn. proposal panel in biology Sci. Found. Ireland, 2002, Human Proteomics Site Visit, 2003; cons. U. Nebr., 2007-. Author book chpts. and contbr. articles to profl. jours.; assoc. editor Jour. Exptl. Zoology, 1977-79; editl. adv. bd. Gen. and Comparative Endocrinology, 1982. World mission com. Ch. of the Redeemer, New Haven, 1967-68; Sunday Sch. steering com. Calvary Episcopal Ch., Cin., 1972-73, sr. acolyte, 1972-77, adult edn. com., 1975-76; deacon Faith Presbyn. Ch., Springfield, Va., 1996-99; adv. com. Wakefield H.S., 1991-92, PTA exec. bd., 1991-92; sci. adv. com. Arlington Pub. Schs., 1987-92, adv. coun. on instrn., 1991-92; adv. bd. Campbell Comml. Coll., Cin., 1977-79. Recipient George Rieveschl, Jr. Rsch. award U. Cin., 1973, Presdl. Rank Meritorious Exec. award NSF, 1992; U. Cin. Grad. Sch. fellow 1977—, NSF fellow 1964; Rsch. grant NSF 1971-79. Fellow AAAS (coun. 1980-83, 89-90, program com. for 1989 ann. meeting 1988, chmn.-elect sect. G-Biol. Scis. 1987-88, chair 1988-89, ret. 1989-90); mem. Assn. of Yale Alumni (del. 1990-93), Mory's Assn., Sigma Xi (Disting. Rsch. award U. Cin. chpt. 1973, pres. U. Cin. chpt. 1977-79), Mensa. Home: 205 Helmsdale Dr Chapel Hill NC 27517 Personal E-mail: bruce.u@hotmail.com.

UMPENHOUR, KEN EUGENE, protective services official; b. Dayton, Ohio, Sept. 14, 1928; s. Richard George and Ruby Ann Umpenhour; m. Astrid Helen Byttner (dec.); children: Kathy, Kurt, Kent, Kristopher; m. Janet Elaine Gaffney, July 7, 1997. AS, Sinclair C.C., Edison C.C. Border patrol agt. US Border Patrol, Brownsville, Tex., 1952—53; dep. sheriff Montgomery County, Dayton, Ohio, 1958—68, chief of detectives, 1966—68; auto racer Lotus and Jaguar Autos, Dayton, 1969—74, Can-Am Championship Races, 1970—74; owner Boston Stoker Tobacco Shop, Naples, 1975—86; state corrections officer Fla. Dept of Corrections, Naples, Fla., 1986—95. Dep. sheriff Polk County Sheriff's Office, Bartow, Fla., 1995—97; state trooper Fla. Hwy. Patrol, Lakeland, Fla., 2000—. 1st lt., pilot USAAF, 1945—49. Decorated DFC, Air medals. Mem.: Fraternal Order of Police, Sports Car Club of Am. Avocations: flying, motorcycling, boating. Home Fax: 868-956-3154. E-mail: srgtump@tampabay.rr.com.

UMPHREY, DONALD WAYNE, adult education educator, academic administrator, writer; b. Detroit, Apr. 25, 1946; s. Earl Donald and Mary Evelyn (Phillips) U. BA in English, Lipscomb U., 1969; MA in Mass Comm., Tex. Tech U., 1981; PhD in Communication, U. Tex., Austin, 1986. Reporter The News-Herald Newspapers, Wyandotte, Mich., 1969, news editor, 1969—72; sr. editor All Media Assocs., Dearborn, Mich., 1973-75; reporter and columnist Mellus Newspapers, Lincoln Park, Mich., 1975; dir. pub. info. Lubbock (Tex.) Christian U., 1975-77; asst. prof. Tex. Tech U., Lubbock, 1979-83; asst. instr. U. Tex., Austin, 1983-86; assoc. prof., head dept. advt. Southern Methodist U., Dallas, 1986—93, prof., 1993—2006, prof. emeritus, 2006; pub. Quarry Press, Dallas, 2002—. Info. dir. Tex. Tech Programs Older Tex., Lubbock, 1977-78. Author: The Meanest Man in Texas, 1984, Twelve Steps to a Closer Walk With God, 1992; editor: Under the Influence, 1990; contbr. articles to acad. jours. Named Best Debut Paper Broadcast Edn. Assn., 1989; Recipient Crystal award Dallas Pub. Access, 1994; grantee So. Methodist U., 1991, 92. Republican. Avocations: fishing, mountain climbing. Office: 206 Umphrey Lee Dallas TX 75275-0001 Personal E-mail: quarrypress@msn.com.

UN, KHEANG, political scientist; s. Try Un and Oeun Sae; m. Judy L. Ledgerwood; children: Paul Thomas, Anthony Ly. PhD, Northern Ill. U., DeKalb, 2004. Adj. asst. prof. Northern Ill. U., 2005—08, asst. dir. ctr.

SE Asian studies, 2006—08; vis. rsch. fellow Ctr. Asian Democracy, U. Louisville. Coord., tracking devel. project Leiden U., Netherlands; bd. mem. Build Cambodia, Chgo.; tech. advisor Cambodia Devel. Rsch. Inst., Phnom Penh, cons., 2007—08, World Bank, Phnom Penh, Cambodia, 2006, UK Dept. Internat. Devel., Phnom Penh, 2007. Contbr. articles to profl. jours. Recipient award, U. Hawaii, 1995, Bd. of Regents award, 1996; Rsch. fellowship, Ctr. Khmer Studies, 2007, grant, UK Dept. Internat. Devel., 2008, Build Cambodia, 2008. Mem.: Phi Beta Delta, Assn. Asian Studies (coun. SE asian studies 2008—). Home: 134 Cobblestone Trail Dekalb IL 60115 Office: Northern Ill Univ Dekalb IL 60115 Office Fax: 815-753-1776. Business E-Mail: kun1@niu.edu.

UNAKAR, NALIN JAYANTILAL, biological sciences educator; b. Karachi, Sindh, Pakistan, Mar. 26, 1935; came to U.S., 1961; s. Jayantilal Virshankar and Malati Jaswantrai (Buch) U.; m. Nita Shantilal Mankad; children: Rita, Rupa. BS, Gujerat U., Bhavnagar, India, 1955; MSc, Bombay U., 1961; PhD, Brown U., 1965. Research asst. Indian Cancer Research Ctr., Bombay, 1955-61; USPHS trainee in biology Brown U., Providence, 1961-65; research assoc. in pathology U. Toronto, Ont., Canada, 1965-66; asst. prof. biology Oakland U., Rochester, Mich., 1966-69, assoc. prof., 1969-74, prof., chmn. biology dept., 1974-87, prof., 1974-2000, prof. emeritus, 2000—, adj. prof. biomed. scis., 1984—. Mem. coop. cataract research group Nat. Eye Inst., Bethesda, Md., 1977—; mem. visual scis. study sect. NIH, Bethesda, 1982-86, mem. cataract panel, 1980—. Mem. vis. bd. Lehigh U., Bethlehem, Pa., 1986-89. Grantee Nat. Cancer Inst., NIH, 1967-70, Nat. Eye Inst., NIH, 1976-97. Mem. AAAS, Am. Soc. Cell Biology, Assn. Rsch. in Vision and Ophthalmology, Sigma Xi. Home: 2822 Rhineberry Rd Rochester Hills MI 48309-1912

UNAN, GEORGE VINCENT, adult education educator; b. Bell Island, Newfoundland, Can., July 19, 1920; arrived in U.S., 1958; s. Samuel S. Unan and Ellen A. Kennedy-Unan; m. Myra Lanza Unan, Apr. 3, 1948 (div. July 1974); children: Veronica Gonzalez, Vivien Irving, Valerie Kitto, Venessa Mangione, Vernon A.; m. Gahyle Rich Unan, July 26, 1975; 1 child, Diane Baer. BS, Calif. State U., Long Beach, 1965, MBA, 1967. Cost estimator Hydro Electric Power Commn., Toronto, Ont., Canada, 1950—58; chief acct. Darco Industries, El Segundo, Calif., 1959—62; contr., sec./dir. State Industries, LA, Calif., 1962—68; contr. Direct Image Corp., Monterey Park, Calif., 1968—70, Harrington Indsl. Plastics, LA, 1970—83; CFO Long Beach Conv. Ctr., 1984—86; educator Anaheim (Calif.) Adult H.S. Dist., 1997—. Seminar instr. in field; educator, exploratory seminars U. Sydney, Australia, 1987—96, Nat. U. Buenos Aires, Argentina, 1993, Charles U., Prague, Czech Republic, 1996. Author: Anecdotes and Quintessences From The Holy Bible, 1999. Adv. bd. Orange County, Santa Ana, Calif., 1984—97; mem. oversight com. Orange County Transp. Authority, Santa Ana, 1997—99; chmn., mem. Citizens Adv. Commn., Cypress, Calif., 1985—96. Home: 6424 Anguilla Ave Cypress CA 90630-5308 Office: Anaheim Adult High Sch Dist 1800 Ball Rd Anaheim CA 92804 Office Phone: 714-999-5616.

UNANUE, EMIL RAPHAEL, immunopathologist; b. Havana, Cuba, Sept. 13, 1934; married, 1965; 3 children. B.Sc., Inst. Secondary Edn., 1952; MD, U. Havana Sch. Medicine, Cuba, 1960; MA, Harvard U., 1974. Assoc. exptl. pathology Scripps Clin. and Research Found., 1960-70; intern in pathology Presbyn. Univ. Hosp., Pitts., 1961-62; research fellow in exptl. pathology Scripps Clin. and Research Found., 1962-65; research fellow immunology Nat. Inst. Med. Research, London, 1966-68; from asst. prof. to assoc. prof. pathology Harvard U. Med. Sch., Boston, 1971-74, prof., 1974-77, Mallinckrodt prof. immunopathology, 1977—; prof., chmn. dept. pathology Washington U. Sch. Medicine, St. Louis, 1988—. Recipient T. Duckett Jones award, Helen Hay Whitney Found., 1968, Park-Davis award, Am. Soc. Exptl. Pathology, 1973, Albert Lasker award for Basic Med. Rsch., Lasker Found., 1995, Gairdner Found. Internat. award, 2000. Office: Washington U Sch Medicine Dept Pathology and Immunology Box 8118 Saint Louis MO 63110-1093 Office Phone: 314-362-7440. Office Fax: 314-362-4096. E-mail: unanue@pathbox.wustl.edu.*

UNDAR, AKIF, research scientist, biomedical engineer, educator; b. Istanbul, Turkey, Aug. 3, 1963; arrived in U.S., 1987; s. Fikret and H. Neriman Undar; m. F. Pinar Albayrak; children: Damla, Akifcan. BS, Yildiz U., Istanbul, 1986; MS, S.W. Tex. State U., 1992; MSE, U. Tex., 1994, PhD, 1996. Asst. instr., dir. surg. rsch. U. Tex. Health Sci. Ctr., San Antonio, 1996—97; instr. Baylor Coll. Medicine, Houston, 1997—99, asst. prof. surgery, 1999—2002, assoc. prof., 2002—03; assoc. prof. pediat., surgery & bioengring. Pa. State Coll. Medicine, Hershey, 2003—09, prof. pediat., surgery & bioengring., dir. pediat. Coord. rschr., 2009—. Tchg. asst. U. Tex., Austin, 1994—96; dir. perfusion rsch. Tex. Children's Hosp., Houston, 1997—2001, dir. rsch., 2001—03; presenter, lectr. in field. Mem. editl. bd. Artificial Organ, 2003—, ASAIO Jour., 2004—; contbr. articles to profl. jours. Rsch. grantee, AHA Tex. affiliate, 1998-2000, Tanox, Inc., 1999-2001, NIH, 2000, NHLBI, 2005—, Pa. Health Dept., 2004—. Mem.: ASAIO, AHA (cert. 2000), Internat. Soc. Rotary Blood Pumps, Biomedical Engring. Soc., Internat. Soc. Artificial Organs. Office: Pa State Milton S Hershey Med Ctr Pa State Children's Hosp Dept Pediat 500 University Dr P Box 850 Hershey PA 17033 Office Phone: 717-531-6706. Business E-Mail: aundar@psu.edu.

UNDERBERG, MARK ALAN, lawyer; b. Niagara Falls, NY, July 9, 1955; s. Alan Jack and Joyce Love (Wisbaum) U.; m. Diane Englander, Mar. 22, 1986; children: Andrew Englander, James Englander. BA, Cornell U., 1977, JD, 1981. Bar: N.Y. 1981. Law clk. to chief judge U.S. Ct. Appeals (3d cir.), Wilmington, Del., 1981-82; assoc. Debevoise & Plimpton, NYC, 1982-87; mng. dir., dep. gen. counsel Henley Group, Inc., NYC, 1987-90, mng. dir., gen. counsel, 1990-92; v.p., gen. counsel Abex Inc., Hampton, NH, 1992-95; counsel Paul, Weiss, Rifkind, Wharton & Garrison, NYC, 1998—99, ptnr., 2000—. V.p., gen. counsel Fisher Sci. Internat. Inc., Hampton, N.H., 1991-97, cons. 1997-98. Editor-in-chief Cornell Law Rev., 1980-81. Bd. dirs. Catalog for Giving of NYC. Mem. ABA, Assn. Bar of City of N.Y., Genesee Valley Club, University Club. Office: Paul Weiss Rifkind Wharton & Garrison 1285 Avenue Of The Americas New York NY 10019-6065 Office Phone: 212-373-3368. Business E-Mail: munderberg@paulweiss.com.

UNDERDOWN, DAVID EDWARD, historian, educator; b. Wells, Eng., Aug. 19, 1925; s. John Percival and Ethel Mary (Gell) U. BA, U. Oxford, 1950, MA, 1951, Yale U., 1952; B.Litt., U. Oxford, 1953; D.Litt. hon., U. of South, 1981. Asst. prof. U. of South, Sewanee, Tenn., 1953-58, assoc. prof., 1958-62; then assoc. prof. U. Va., Charlottesville, 1962-68; prof. Brown U., Providence, 1968-85, Munro-Goodwin Wilkinson prof., 1978-85; vis. prof. Yale U., New Haven, 1979, prof., 1986-94, George Burton Adams prof., 1994-96, emeritus, 1996—. Dir. Yale Ctr. Parliamentary History, 1985-96; vis. Mellon prof. Inst. for Advanced Study, 1988-89; vis. fellow All Souls Coll., Oxford, 1992; Ford's lectr. Oxford U., 1992. Author: Royalist Conspiracy in England, 1960, Pride's Purge, 1971, Somerset in the Civil War and Interregnum, 1973, Revel, Riot and Rebellion, 1985, Fire from Heaven, 1992, A Freeborn People, 1996, Start of Play, 2000. Guggenheim fellow, 1964-65, 91-92, fellow Am. Coun. Learned Socs., 1973-74, NEH fellow, 1980-81. Fellow Royal Hist. Soc., Brit. Acad. (corrs.); mem. Am. Hist. Assn. (award for scholarly distinction 2005), Conf. Brit. Studies. Office: Yale U Dept History New Haven CT 06520 Business E-Mail: david.underdown@yale.edu.

UNDERHILL, JACOB BERRY, III, retired insurance company executive; b. NYC, Oct. 25, 1926; s. Jacob Berry, Jr. and Dorothy Louise (Quinn) U.; m. Cynthia Jane Lovejoy, Sept. 9, 1950 (div. Sept. 1962); children: David Lovejoy, Kate Howell Underhill Kerwin, Benedict Quinn; m. Lois Beachy, Nov. 2, 1963 (div. July 1987); m. Betsy F. Ashton, Oct. 17, 1987 (div. Apr. 2007); m. Nancy McDonnell Maloney, June 5, 2007. Grad., Phillips Exeter Acad., 1944; AB, Princeton U., 1950. Editor Courier & Freeman, Potsdam, NY, 1950-53; reporter Democrat & Chronicle, Rochester, NY, 1953-56; chief editorial writer St. Petersburg (Fla.) Times, 1956-59; asso. editor McGraw Hill Publ. Co., NYC, 1959-61, Newsweek, NYC, 1961-63; asst. press sec. to Gov. N.Y., 1963-67; dep. supt., 1st dep. supt. State N.Y. Ins. Dept., 1967-72; v.p., sr. v.p., exec. v.p., dir., vice chmn. bd., pres. N.Y. Life Ins. Co., NYC, 1972-86. Hon. chmn. bd. dirs. Manhattan Eye, Ear and Throat Hosp.; trustee emeritus Nat. Trust for Hist. Preservation. With USNR, 1944-46. Mem. Players Club, Links Club, Piping Rock Club (Locust Valley, N.Y.).

UNDERHILL, PACO, market research and consulting company executive, environmental psychologist; Student, Ehwa U., Seoul, Korea; grad., Vassar Coll., Poughkeepsie, NY, 1975. With Project for Pub. Spaces, NYC, 1975; instr. environ. psychology CUNY, 1977—78; founder, pres., CEO Envirosell, Inc. (formerly Environ. Analysis & Planning Consultants), NYC, 1979—. Bd. dirs. Watt Internat., Toronto, Ont., Canada, 2006—. Author: Why We Buy: The Science of Shopping, 2000, Call of the Mall: The Geography of Shopping, 2004; regular contbr. NPR, BBC Radio, contbr. articles to NY Times, Wall St. Jour., London Times, Christian Sci. Monitor, spkr. in field. Office: Envirosell Inc 907 Broadway 2nd Fl New York NY 10010 Office Phone: 212-673-9100. Office Fax: 212-673-8358. Business E-Mail: paco.underhill@envirosell.com.*

UNDERWEISER, IRWIN PHILIP, mining executive, lawyer; b. NYC, Jan. 3, 1929; s. Harry and Edith (Gladstein) U.; m. Beatrice J. Kortchmar, Aug. 17, 1959; children: Rosanne, Marian, Jeffrey. BA, CCNY, 1950; LL.D., Fordham U., 1954; LL.M., NYU, 1961. Bar: N.Y. 1954. With firm Scribner & Miller, NYC, 1951-54, 56-62; partner firm Feuerstein & Underweiser, 1962-73, Underweiser & Fuchs, 1973-77, Underweiser & Underweiser, 1977—. V.p., sec. Sunshine Mining Co., Kellogg, Idaho, 1965-70, chmn. bd., 1970-78, pres., 1971-74, 77, v.p., 1977-83; vice chmn., dir. Underwriters Bank and Trust Co., N.Y.C., 1969-73; sec., dir. Bus. Consortium Fund, 1994—. Triad Capital Corp. N.Y., 1994—; dir. Anchor Post Products, Inc. Bd. dirs. Silver Inst. Inc., vice chmn., 1998-2001; bd. dirs. Bronx Mus. of the Arts, 1993-2001, Sheltering the Homeless is Our Responsibility, 1993-2001, 02—; gen. counsel, mem. bus. council Friends City Center Music and Drama, N.Y.C., 1966-67; pres. W. Quaker Ridge Assn., 1969-70; treas. Scarsdale Neighborhood Assn. Presidents, 1970-71. Served with AUS, 1954-56. Mem. Am., N.Y. State bar assns., Bar Assn. City N.Y., Phi Beta Kappa, Phi Alpha Theta. Home: 7 Rural Dr Scarsdale NY 10583-7701 Office: 1 Water St White Plains NY 10601

UNDERWOOD, ANTHONY PAUL, lawyer; b. Atlanta, June 25, 1955; s. Paul L. and Charlene B. (Snider) U.; children: Andrew Ryan, Elizabeth Kaitlin, Caroline MacKenzie. BA, U. North Ala., 1977; MA, JD, Samford U., 1980; MS, Johns Hopkins U., 1983; LLM, Judge Adv. Gen.'s Sch., 1994; MS, George Washington U., 2006. Bar: Ala. 1980, U.S. Ct. Mil. Appeals 1981, U.S. Supreme Ct. 1983. Trial atty. U.S. Army, various locations, 1980-87; sr. assoc. Doke & Riley, Dallas, 1987-89; legal counsel, dir. contracts Hughes Aircraft Co., Torrence, Calif., 1989-93; mgr., contracts Hughes Missile Systems Co., Tucson, 1993-95; dir., licensing and regulatory affairs Lockheed Martin Internat. Launch Svcs., San Diego, 1995—2000; prof. bus. Piedmont Coll., Demorest, Ga., 2000—01; chief bus. counsel U.S. Army Space Command, Colorado Springs, Colo., 2001—02; dir. contracts Ball Aerospace and Tech Corp., Boulder, Colo., 2002—07; v.p. contracts SpaceDev, Inc., Louisville, Colo., 2007—08; sr. dir. contracts Express Scripts, Inc., St. Louis, 2008—. Author: A Progressive History of the Young Men's Business Club of Birmingham, Ala.: 1946-70, 1980. Lt. col. USAR, 1977—2003. Mem. ABA (vice chair various coms., pub. contract law sect). Republican. Avocations: church, travel, reading. Office: Express Scripts Inc One Express Way Saint Louis MO 63121

UNDERWOOD, BLAIR, actor, television producer; b. Tacoma, Aug. 25, 1964; s. Frank and Marilyn Underwood; m. Desiree Da Costa, Sept. 17, 1994; 3 children. Student, Carnegie-Mellon U. TV debut The Cosby Show, 1985; actor, prodr.: (films) Straight Out of Compton 2, 2005; actor (films) Krush Groove, 1985, The Second Coming, 1992, Posse, 1993, Just Cause, 1995, Set it Off, 1996, Gattaca, 1997, Deep Impact, 1998, Asunder, 1998, The Wishing Tree, 1999, Rules of Engagement, 2000 (NAACP Image award for sup. actor, 2001), G, 2002, Full Frontal, 2002, Malibu's Most Wanted, 2003, Fronterz, 2004, How Did it Feel, 2004, Do Geese See God?, 2004, Something New, 2006, Madea's Family Reunion, 2006, The Hit, 2007, The Legend of Spyro: Dawn of the Dragon, 2008, Weather Girl, 2009; (TV series) One Life to Live, 1985-86, Downtown, 1986, LA Law, 1987-94, High Incident, 1996, City of Angels, 2000 (NAACP Image award for lead actor, 2001), Fatherhood, 2004, LAX, 2004-05, The New Adventures of Old Christine, 2006-08, In Treatment, 2008, Dirty Sexy Money, 2007-09; (TV movies) The Cover Girl and the Cop, 1989, Murder in Mississippi, 1990, Heat Wave, 1990, Father and Son: Dangerous Relations, 1993, Soul of the Game, 1996, Mistrial, 1996, Mama Flora's Family, 1998, The Golden Blaze, 2005, Company Town, 2006, Covert One: The Hades Factor, 2006; theater credits include Measure for Measure, 1993, El Negro en Peru, The Game of Love and Chance, and Love Letters, Purlie, 2005. Co-founder Artists for a New South Africa, 1989. Recipient Humanitarian Award, Muscular Dystrophy Assoc., LA, 1993; named Artist of the Year, Harvard Found., Harvard U., 2002. Office: William Morris Agency 151 El Camino Dr Beverly Hills CA 90212*

UNDERWOOD, CARRIE MARIE, singer; b. Muskogee, Okla., Mar. 10, 1983; d. Stephen and Carol Underwood. BA magna cum laude, Northeastern State U., 2006. Recording artist RCA Music Group, NYC, 2005—. Singer: (albums) Some Hearts, 2005, Carnival Ride, 2007 (Favorite Country Album, Am. Music Awards, 2008), (songs) Inside Your Heaven, 2005 (Billboard Hot 100 Song of Yr., 2005), Jesus, Take the Wheel, 2005 (Single Record of Yr., Acad. Country Music, Female Video of Yr. & Breakthrough Video of Yr., Country Music TV, 2006, Best Female Country Vocal Performance & Best Country Song, Grammy Awards, 2007), Some Hearts, 2005 (Billboard Album of Yr. & Country Album of Yr., 2006, Album of Yr., Acad. Country Music, 2007, Favorite Country Album, Am. Music Awards, 2007), Before He Cheats, 2006 (Favorite Country Song, People's Choice awards, 2007, Video of Yr., Female Video & Best Video Dir., Country Music TV awards, 2007, Video of Yr., Acad. Country Music, 2007, Single of Yr., Country Music Assn., 2007, Grammy award, Best Female Country Vocal Performance, 2008), Last Name, 2007 (Grammy award for Best Female Country Vocal Performance, 2009). Recipient Top-Selling Country Single of Yr., Billboard Music Awards, 2005, Country Single Sales Artist of Yr., 2005, New Country Artist of Yr., 2006, Female Country Artist of Yr., 2006, Female Billboard 200 Album Artist of Yr., 2006, New Female Vocalist award, Acad. Country Music, 2006, Top Female Vocalist award, 2007, 2008, 2009, Entertainer of Yr. award, 2009, Horizon award, Country Music Assn., 2006, Female Vocalist of Yr. award, 2006, 2007, 2008, Favorite New Breakthrough Artist, Am. Music Awards, 2006, Favorite Female Country Artist, 2007, Favorite Female Singer, People's Choice Awards, 2007, Favorite Country Song, 2009, Best New Artist, Grammy Awards, 2007, Choice Red Carpet Fashion Icon Female, Teen Choice Awards, 2008; named Favorite Female Singer, People's Choice Awards, 2009, Favorite Star Under 35, 2009; named one of Top 25 Entertainers of Yr., Entertainment Weekly, 2007, The 100 Most Powerful Celebrities, Forbes.com, 2008. Baptist. Achievements include winning the fourth season of American Idol on May 25, 2005; inducted into the Grand Ole Opry, 2008. Avocations: guitar, piano. Office: c/o Jeff Frasco Creative Artists Agy 2000 Ave of the Stars Los Angeles CA 90067

UNDERWOOD, CATHERINE H., healthcare association administrator; b. Sept. 02; BS, U. Wis., Stout; MBA, Kellogg Sch. Mgmt., Northwestern U., 1984. Cert. Assn. Exec. Exec. dir. Am. Pain Soc., Glenview, Ill., 1999—, Assn. Mgmt. Ctr., Glenview, Ill., 2002—. Office: Am Pain Soc 3700 W Lake Ave Glenview IL 60025 Office Phone: 847-375-4715. E-mail: cunderwood@connect2amc.com.*

UNDERWOOD, JAN MARIE, language educator; b. Jersey Shore, Pa., Dec. 31, 1964; d. Jerry and June Underwood; life ptnr. Rick Craycraft; 1 child, Sam. BA in English, French, U. Kans., Lawrence, 1986; MA in Comparative Lit., McGill U., Montreal, 1989; MA in Fgn. Lang. & Lit., Portland State U., Oreg., 1998. Cert. TESL Portland State U., 1998. Spanish instr. Portland Comm. Coll. Cascade Campus, Oreg., 1992—, chair Spanish dept., 2005—. Author: (novels) Day Shift Werewolf (award, 2006). Home: 5946 SE Tibbetts Portland OR 97206 Office: Portland CC 705 N Killingsworth Portland OR 97217 Business E-Mail: junderwo@pcc.edu.

UNDERWOOD, JANE HAINLINE HAMMONS, anthropologist, educator; b. Ft. Bliss, Tex., Oct. 30, 1931; d. Frank and Lydia (Williams) Hammons; m. Van K. Hainline, Oct. 20, 1947 (div. 1966); children: Michael K., Susan J.; m. John W. Underwood, July 4, 1968; 1 dau., Anne K. AA, Imperial Valley Coll., 1957; BA, U. Calif., Riverside, 1960; MA, UCLA, 1962, PhD, 1964. Asst. prof. U. Calif., Riverside, 1963-68; research anthropology Yap Islands, 1964, 65-66; prof. anthropology U. Ariz., Tucson, 1968-99, prof. emeritus, 1999—, assoc. dean Grad. Coll., 1979-80, asst. provost for grad. studies, 1980-82, acting dir. Sch. Health Related Professions, 1980-82, asst. v.p. research, assoc. dean Grad. Coll., 1982-87; assoc. Micronesian Area Rsch. Ctr., 1987—. Contbr. articles to profl. jours. Woodrow Wilson fellow, 1960-61; UCR Jr. Faculty fellow, 1968 Fellow AAAS; mem. Am. Assn. Phys. Anthropologists (v.p. 1980-82), Assn. Study Human Biology, Pacific Sci. Assn. (life), Assn. Study Social Biology (bd. dir. 1996-99), Sigma Xi (pres. U. Ariz. chpt. 1991-92). Home: 2228 E 4th St Tucson AZ 85719-5118 E-mail: kammagar@prodigy.net.

UNDERWOOD, JOANNA DEHAVEN, environmental services administrator; b. NYC, May 25, 1940; d. Louis Ivan and Helen (Guiterman) U.; m. Saul Lambert, July 31, 1982; stepchildren: Jonathan Whitty, Katherine Aviva. BA, Bryn Mawr Coll., 1962; Diplome d'etudes de Civilisation francaise with honors, Sorbonne U., Paris, 1965; DS (hon.), Wheaton Coll., 1999. Co-dir. Council on Econ. Priorities, NYC, 1970-73; founder, pres. INFORM, Inc., NYC, 1974—. Bd. dirs. Robert Sterling Clark Found., N.Y.C., Washington, Clean Vehicle Edn. Found.; mem. Dow Environ. Adv. Coun., 1992-96; awards com. Pres.'s Coun. on Environ. Quality, 1991; mem. eco-efficiency task force Pres.'s Coun. on Sustainable Devel., 1995-96. Author (with others) Voices from the Environmental Movement: Perspectives for a New Era, 1991; co-author: Paper Profits, 1971; editor: The Price of Power, 1972; contbr. articles to profl. jours. Former circle of dirs. Planned Parenthood of N.Y.C. Recipient Region II Environ. Achievement award U.S. EPA, 1992, Adminstrs. award, 1992, Recognition award, 1987. Home: 138 E 13th St New York NY 10003-5306 Office: INFORM Inc 120 Wall St Fl 14 New York NY 10005-3904

UNDERWOOD, JOSEPH WARREN, athletic trainer, educator, actor; b. Indpls., Jan. 18, 1953; s. Warren E. Underwood and Kay A. Craft; m. Nancy Nelson, Nov. 16, 1984; 1 child, Jolene. B in speech, theatre, Tenn. Technol. U., Cookeville, 1975; M in sports sci., US Sports Acad., Daphne, Ala., 1987; EdD in Ednl. Leadership, Nova Southeastern U., 2006. Cert. real estate agt. Fla., 1982, athletic trainer Nat. Athletic Trainers Assn., 1990, tchr. Fla., 2003, lic. athletic trainer Fla., 2000. Tchr. earth sci. Miami HS, Fla., 1984—85, tchr. English to Spanish spkrs., 1985—86, tchr. drama, 1986—88, leading learner ARTEC, 1988—; instr. H.S. football rules clinic Greater Miami Athletic Conf., 1995—. Mem. Black history month com. Miami HS, 1994—, chair grant com., 2000—05; state bd. athletic tng. Fla. Dept. of Health, Tallahassee, 2002—; pres. Greater Miami Athletic Conf. Football Ofcls. Assn., Greater Miami Athletic Conf., 2003—; football ofcls. adv. com. Fla. H.S. Athletic Assn., Gainesville, 2005—; state H.S. football championship com. Greater Miami Conv. and Visitors Bur., 2005. Actor: (film) Any Given Sunday, (instructional video series) Wally Word's Word of the Day, (ednl. video series) Words of Wisdom from the Wise Professor (Grant award, 2003), (nat. print advertisement) Cingular Wireless March Madness; writer, voice over (ednl. video) Miami High Centennial Video, prodr., videographer, editor Galapagos Adventures; author, editor: book Today I Made A Difference: A Collection of Inspirational Stories from America's Top Teachers; actor, prodr.: Miami Undercover; actor: (Super Bowl comml.) Budweiser Select, (feature length documentary) Dear Mr. President; (TV series) Miami Vice; dir., tech. advisor for football ofcls. (TV comml.) Mountain Dew, Directed by Spike Lee; actor: (instrl. video series) Billy Joe Bob's FCAT Tips, Nat. ATH Triners Assoc. (award RAP Video, 2009). Student coord. for casted audience MTV Video Music Awards, Miami, 2004—05; vol. Orange Bowl Com. Youth Football Championships, Miami, 1990—2007; prodr. Martin Luther King parade video Dr. Robert Ingram, Sch. Bd. Mem., Miami, 2005; video team Miami Schs. Emergency Response Ops. Drill, 2006; mem. Japan Fulbright Meml. Fund Tchr. Program, 2008, Kenny Kaizens Japan Con Video Series, 2008; campaign vol. Barrera for Sch. Bd., Miami, 2004—06; nat. selection com. Disney Tchr. Awards, Anaheim, Calif., 2006; football ofcl. Greater Miami Athletic Conf., 1990—; ext. com. Pi Lambda Theta Ednl. Assn. Recipient State HS Basketball Championship ring as team's athletic trainer, Miami High Boys Basketball, 1987, 1989—91, 1993, 1996—97, 1998, 2005, Key to City of Miami, Miami Mayor Xavier Suarez, 1987, Four Way Test - Tchr. Fellowship award, Miami Rotary Club, 2002, Tchr. of Yr. award, Miami HS, 2003, 2005, Cert. of Honor, City of Miami, Miami Mayor Manny Diaz, 2004, Disney Tchr. Awards Honoree, Walt Disney Co., 2004, Cert. of Appreciation, Miami City Commn., Commr. Joe Sanchez, 2004, Spl. Recognition Ana Logan Sch. Bd., Miami-Dade County Pub. Schs., 2005, Cancer Rsch. Marathon Honoree, Run for Leukemia/Lymphoma Rsch., 2005, All-Star

Tchr. Team award, USA Today Newspaper, 2005, State HS Basketball Championship ring as team's athletic trainer, Miami High Girls Basketball, 2005, Proclamation for Effective and Creative Tchg., City of Miami City Commn., 2006, Internat. Tchrs. Program to Galapagos, Toyota Motor Co., 2006, Bob Costas award for tchg. writing, Coll. Bd., 2007; named Tchr. of Yr., Miami Mioh Alumni, 2009; named to Nat. Tchrs. Hall of Fame, 2007, Hall of Fame, Adopt a Classroom, 2009; finalist Tchr. of Yr. award, Miami-Dade County Pub. Schs., 2002, Nat. Teachers Hall of Fame, 2006; numerous grants, various granting bodies, 1996—, Industry Focus grant, One Cmty. One Goal, 1999, Doctoral scholarship, Nova Southeastern U., 2005, grant, Best Buy, 2005. Mem.: ASCD, Internat. Honor Soc. of Nova Southeastern U., Phi Gamma Sigma, Vocat.-Tech. Edn. Consortium of States (pilot site sch. coord. 1999—2002), U. Fla. Alliance, Nat. Coun. Tchrs. of English, Nat. Bd. Cert. Tchrs., Athletic Trainers Assn. Fla. (various positions including newsletter editor 1985—92, H.S. Athletic Trainer of Yr. 1995), SE Athletic Trainers Assn., Nat. Athletic Trainers Assn. (various coms. 1986—, Most Creative Video award 2009), Am. Coll. of Sports Medicine, Fla. Film Educators, South Fla. Football Ofcls. Assn. (various coms. 1985—), Fla. Inst. for Film Edn., Am. Youth Football League (game ofcl. 1999—2006), Nat. Assn. Sports Ofcls., Greater Miami Athletic Conf. Football Ofcls. Assn. (various positions including pres. 1985—), So. States Football League Ofcls. Assn. (So. rep. 2004—07, Referee of Yr. 2003), Pi Lambda Theta (ext. com. 2005, music scholarship 2005), Nat. Scholars Honor Soc. Roman Catholic. Avocations: football officiating, travel, writing. Office: Miami HS 2450 SW 1 St Miami FL 33135 Office Phone: 305-649-9800 2265. Business E-Mail: underwoodj@dadeschools.net.

UNDERWOOD, KIRSTEN FEDJE, musician, educator; MusB, Willamette U., 1978; MusM, Boston U., 1981; postgrad., U. Okla., 1998—. Cellist Okla. City Philharm., 1990—96; asst. prof. Cameron U., Lawton, Okla., 1997—. Founder Lawton Cello Club, Okla. Mem.: AAUW, Am. String Tchrs. Assn., Am. Fedn. Musicians, Hardanger Fiddle Assn. Am., Lawton Bus. & Profl. Women, Gamma Beta Phi, Phi Kappa Phi, Mu Phi Epsilon, Pi Kappa Lambda (pres., Theta Sigma chpt. 1999—2004). Office: Cameron Univ Dept of Music & Theatre 2800 W Gore Blvd Lawton OK 73507 E-mail: kirstenu@cameron.edu.

UNDERWOOD, LORAINNE BALLARD, literature and language educator; b. Opelousas, La., Feb. 6, 1940; d. Lawrence James and Vertna Estelle Ballard; m. Albert McThomas Underwood, Jan. 7, 1976 (dec. Aug. 12, 2004); children: Kirk Albert, Antonio McVhea; m. Charles James Taylor (dec.); children: Christopher Charles, Jennifer Vertna. BA in Polit. Sci., So. U., Baton Rouge, 1963; MEd, U. La., 1987. Cert. tchr. Chgo. State U., 1966. Sec. Kraft Foods Divsn., Nat. Dairy Products Corp., Chgo., 1964—65; tchr. Chgo. Bd. Edn., 1965—80, St. Landry Parish Sch. Bd., Opelousas, 1980—2000, Lafayette Parish Sch. Sys., La., 2002—. Fellow mem. The Nature Conservancy, Arlington, Va., 2002—, So. Poverty Law Ctr., 2004—, Nat. Com. to Preserve Social Security, Washington, 2004—, NAACP, Balt., 2004—; organizer, coord. com. to erect a commemorative marker for St. Landry Parish Tng. Sch., 2004—; fellow mem. Dem. Nat. Com., Washington, 2004—; recording sec. Seventh Dist. Bapt. Assn. Women's Aux. and Missionary Soc.; deaconess Little Zion Bapt. Ch. Mem.: La. Fedn. Tchrs./AFT Profl. Educators Group (membership chair 1989—95), La. Ret. Tchrs. Assn. (life). Democrat. Baptist. Avocations: sewing, Bible reading, singing. Home: 1508 Laurent St Opelousas LA 70570

UNDERWOOD, PAUL BENJAMIN, gynecologist, oncologist, educator; b. Greer, SC, Aug. 8, 1934; s. Paul Benjamin and Gladys (Guest) Underwood; m. Peggy Joyce Outen, July 7, 1957; children: Paul Benjamin III, Mary Barton. MD, Med. U. S.C., 1959. Diplomate Am. Bd. Ob-gyn., Am. Bd. Gynecol. Oncology. Intern Med. U. S.C., Charleston, 1959—60, resident, 1960—64; fellow M.D. Anderson Hosp. and Tumor Inst., Houston, 1966—67; asst. prof. U. S.C., Charleston, 1967—70, assoc. prof., 1970—74, prof., 1974—99, staff, dir. gynecology, assoc. dean admissions Med. Sch., 1999—, dir. divsn. gynecol. oncology, 2002; chmn. dept. ob-gyn. U. Va. Sch. Medicine, Charlottesville, 1979-99. Contbr. articles to profl. jours. With USN, 1964—66. Recipient Alumni of Yr. award, Med. U. S.C., 1989. Mem.: Thegos Soc., S.C. Ob-Gyn. Soc., Charlottesville Med. Soc., So. Med. Soc., Felix Rutledge Soc. (pres. 1977), Am. Assn. Ob-Gyn. (sec. 1992—95, pres. 1999—), Soc. Gynecol. Oncologists (mem. coun. 1972—75, v.p. 1977—78, pres. 1983), Am. Coll. Ob-Gyn., Am. Gynecol. Club (pres. 1996), Alpha Omega Alpha. Office: 171 Ashley Ave Charleston SC 29425-0001 Office Phone: 843-792-4026. Business E-Mail: underwp@musc.edu.

UNDERWOOD, PAUL LESTER, cardiologist; b. Knoxville, Tenn., Mar. 23, 1960; MD, Mayo Med. Sch., 1984. Diplomate Am. Bd. Cardiovascular Disease. Intern Henry Ford Hosp., Detroit, 1984-85; resident internal medicine Mayo Grad. Sch. Medicine, Rochester, Minn., 1985-87; fellow in cardiology Cleve. Clinic, 1990-93; fellow in interventional cardiology Iowa Heart Ctr., Des Moines, 1993; dir. emergency medicine, dir. ICU St. Croix Hosp., U.S. V.I., 1987-90; staff N. Phoenix Heart Ctr., Ariz., 2001—07; dir. rsch. Sonoran Health Specialists-Eclipse Clin. Rsch. Assoc., 2007—. Mem. AMA, Nat. Med. Assn., Assn. Black Cardiologists (former pres.), Am. Coll. Cardiology (councilor), Am. Heart Assn. (bd. dirs. Ariz. affiliate), Soc. for Cardiac Angiography and Interventions. Office: Sonoran Health Specialists Eclipse Clin Rsch Assoc 8414 E Shea Bld Ste 103 Scottsdale AZ 85260 Home: 4727 E Berneil Dr Phoenix AZ 85028-5506 Office Phone: 480-767-3877. Business E-Mail: punderwood@sonoranhealth.com.

UNDERWOOD, PAULA KAY, military officer; d. Agnes Josephine Underwood; m. Juan Guillermo Jaramillo Angel, June 11, 1987; 1 child, Paula Alicia Jaramillo-Underwood. BS, U. of Denver, 1973; S.R.N. (State RN), Gloucestershire Royal Sch. of Nursing, Gloucester, Eng., 1977; S.C.M. (State Cert. Midwife), Simpson Meml. Maternity Pavilion, Edinburgh, Scotland, UK, 1978—79; MD, U. of Colo., Denver, 1984; MPH, Harvard U., Boston, 1987; MHA, U.S. Army-Baylor U. Program, San Antonio, Tex., 2001. Cert. healthcare exec. Am. Coll. of Healthcare Execs., 2001. Stewardess Pan Am. Airways, Boston, 1973—74; staff nurse Dilke Hosp., Chepstow, Gloucestershire, England, 1977—78; intern Tripler Army Med. Ctr., Honolulu, 1984—85; gen. med. officer Irwin Army Cmty. Hosp., Ft. Riley, Kans., 1985—86; resident in preventive medicine Walter Reed Army Inst. of Rsch., Washington, D.C., 1987—88; gen. med. officer Irwin Army Cmty. Hosp., Ft. Riley, Kans., 1985—86; chief of preventive medicine 98th Gen. Hosp., Nuernberg, Bavaria, Germany, 1988—90; preventive medicine officer 1st Armored Divsn., Southeast Asia-Gulf War, Iraq, 1990—91; chief of preventive medicine 3rd Combat Support Hosp., Nuernberg, Bavaria, Germany, 1991—93, Evans Army Cmty. Hosp., Ft. Carson, Colo., 1993—96; dep. comdr. for clin. svcs. (chief of the med. staff) Winn Army Cmty. Hosp., Ft. Stewart, Ga., 2001—03; comdr. U.S. Army Med. Rsch. Unit, Rio de Janeiro, Rio de Janeiro, 1997—99; preventive medicine staff officer Office of The Army Surgeon Gen., Falls Church, Va., 2003—04, dep. functional proponent for preventive medicine, 2004—. Residency adv. bd. mem. Walter Reed Army Inst. of Rsch., Washinton, 2004—; chair Joint Preventive Medicine Policy Group, Washington, 2004—; army preventive medicine rep. Armed Forces Epidemiology Bd., Washington, 2003—04. Col. US Army, 1984. Decorated Bronze Star., Meritorious Svc. medal Winn Army Cmty. Hosp., Walter Reed Army Inst. of Rsch., Evans Army Cmty. Hosp., 3rd Combat Support Hosp., Army Commendation Medal; recipient Alumni Assn. award, U.S. Army Baylor U. Alumni Club, 2001, Peter Shaul Peer award, 2001; scholar Acad. scholar, U. of Denver, 1969—73. Fellow: Am. Coll. of Preventive Medicine (cert.); mem.: U.S. Army Baylor U. Alumni Club, U. of Colo. Alumni Assn. (life), Assn. of the U.S. Army (life), VFW (life), Desert Storm Vets. Assn., The Army Hist. Found. (life), Mil. Officers Assn. of Am. (life). Avocations: running, travel, reading. Office: Office of The Army Surgeon General 5111 Leesburg Pike Falls Church VA 22041 E-mail: paula.underwood@otsg.amedd.army.mil.

UNDERWOOD, RICHARD ALLAN, English language educator; b. Plymouth, Mich., Mar. 28, 1933; s. Harold Raymond and Yvonne Clara (Foster) U.; m. Sandra Jane Hayes, Nov. 17, 1962; 1 child, Eric Michael. BA, U. Mich., 1955, MA, 1967, PhD, 1970. Asst. prof. Clemson U., SC, 1970-77, assoc. prof., 1977-84, prof. English SC, 1984—. Author: A Little Bit of Love, 1963, Shakespeare's The Phoenix and Turtle: A Survey of Scholarship, 1974, Shakespeare on Love: The Poems and the Plays, 1985, The Two Noble Kinsmen and Its Beginnings, 1993; translator: En Smula Karlek, 1969, 81; editor: Phoenix with a Bayonet: A Journalist's Interim Report on the Greek Revolution (by Bayard Stockton), 1971. 1st lt. U.S. Army, 1955-57. Fellow Bread Loaf Writers Conf., 1963; vis. scholar Rackham Sch. Grad. Studies, U. Mich., 1983-85, 90-91, 91-92, 92-93, 93-94. Avocation: piano music. Home: 111 Lakeview Cir Clemson SC 29631-1019

UNDERWOOD, RICHARD LEE, educator; b. Hammond, Ind., Jan. 4, 1961; s. Richard H. and Mary L. Underwood; m. Carla M. Disselkoen, June 23, 1989; children: Jordan Richard, Chad Donald, Justin Theodore. BA, Purdue U., West Lafayette Ind., 1983, MA, 1986. Prof. Kirkwood CC, Cedar Rapids, Iowa, 1986—. Named Outstanding Male Advisor, Kirkwood CC, 2001. Mem.: Phi Theta Kappa (v.p. southeast region 2000, Robert Giles Disting. Advisor award 2005). Conservative. Home: 1518 Seminole Ave NW Cedar Rapids IA 52405 Office: Kirkwood CC 6301 Kirkwood Blvd SW Cedar Rapids IA 52404 Office Fax: 319-398-4917. Personal E-mail: rich_61@live.com. Business E-Mail: rich.underwood@kirkwood.edu.

UNDERWOOD, ROBERT LEIGH, venture capitalist; b. Paducah, Ky., Dec. 31, 1944; s. Robert Humphreys and Nancy Wells (Jessup) Underwood; m. Susan Lynn Doscher, May 22, 1976; children: Elizabeth Leigh, Dana Whitney, George Gregory. BS with great distinction, Stanford U., 1965, MS, 1966, PhD, 1968; MBA, Santa Clara U., 1970. Rsch. scientist, project leader Lockheed Missiles & Space Co., Sunnyvale, Calif., 1967—71; spl. asst. for engring. scis. Office Sec., Dept. Transp., Washington, 1971—73; sr. mgmt. assoc. Office Mgmt. and Budget, Exec. Office Pres., 1973; with TRW Inc., LA, 1973—79, dir. retail nat. accts., 1977—78, dir. product planning and devel., 1978—79; pres., CEO OMEX, Santa Clara, Calif., 1980—82; v.p. Heizer Corp., Chgo., 1979—85; pres. No. Capital Corp., Chgo., 1985—86; mng. ptnr. ISSS Ventures, 1986—88; founding ptnr. N.Am. Bus. Devel. Co., Chgo., 1988—; pres., CEO Polymer Corp., Rockland, Mass., 2003—. Trustee Burridge Mut. Funds, 1996—98. Contbr. articles to profl. jours. Sch. bd. Avoca Dist. 37, 1990—99, v.p., 1996—99; adv. bd. Leavy Sch. Bus. and Adminstrn. Santa Clara U., 1995—; adv. com. on indsl. innovation NSF, 1982—96; trustee Kenilworth Union Ch., 2003—; elder Presbyn. Ch., 1978—79. Fellow, NASA, NSF; scholar, Alcoa. Mem.: IEEE, Farmington Country Club (Charlottesville, Va.), Indian Hill Club (Winnetka, Ill.), Union League Chgo., Chgo. Club, Beta Gamma Sigma, Tau Beta Pi, Phi Beta Kappa, Sigma Xi. Home: 59 Woodley Rd Winnetka IL 60093-3748 Office: 135 S La Salle St Chicago IL 60603-4159

UNDERWOOD, ROBYN M., medical researcher; PhD, U. Man., Winnipeg, Can., 2005. Rsch. assoc. Pa. State U., University Pk., 2005—. Office: Pa State Univ Dept Entomology University Park PA 16802 Personal E-mail: underwoodrm@yahoo.com. Business E-Mail: rmu1@psu.edu.

UNDERWOOD, STEVEN CLARK, financial services company executive; b. Arlington Heights, Ill., Dec. 1, 1960; s. Donald William and Mary Frances (Clark) U.; m. Gloria Jean Dec, Sept. 8, 1999. BBA, U. Tex., 1982, MBA, 1987; JD, So. Meth. U., 1985. Bar: Tex. 1985; cert. fin. mgr. Inst. Cert. Mgmt. Accts., 2006, managerial acct. Inst. Cert. Mgmt. Accts., 2006. Sr. fin. analyst CBS, Inc., NYC, 1987—89; assoc. bus. mgr. Supplementary Edn. Group Simon & Schuster, Englewood Cliffs, NJ, 1989—90, bus. mgr. Fearon/Janus/Quercus divsn. Belmont, Calif., 1990—91, pres. Fearon/Janus/Quercus divsn., 1991—92, pres. Globe Fearon divsn. Upper Saddle River, NJ, 1993—96, v.p. bus. devel. NYC, 1997—98; v.p. dir. bus. devel. Secondary Edn. Group, Upper Saddle River, NJ, 1996—97; v.p. sch. markets Troll Comms., Mahwah, NJ, 1998—2001; v.p., contr. Current Med. Directions Divsn., WWP Group, NYC, 2002—06; CFO Bronson & Migliaccio, LLP, Ft. Lee, NJ, 2006—07; v.p. fin. Argus Info. & Adv. Svcs., LLC, White Plains, NY, 2007—. Mem. ABA, Am. Mgmt. Assn. (pres.'s assn.), Assn. Am. Pubs., Inst. Cert. Mgmt. Accts. (cert.), Fin. Exec. Internat., Nat. Eagle Scout Assn., Coll. Bus. Adminstrn. Found., Tex. Bar Assn., Tex. Alumni Assn., U. Tex. Century Club, Alpha Phi Omega, Beta Gamma Sigma, Phi Kappa Phi, Phi Eta Sigma, Golden Key, Ramsey Golf & Country Club. Republican. Methodist. Avocations: sailing, camping. Office: Argus Info & Advisory Svcs LLC 50 Main St Ste 1175 White Plains NY 10606 Home: 45 Ronald Ct Ramsey NJ 07446-2626

UNDIEH, ASHIWEL S., science educator, department chairman; s. Litio I. and Hannah A. Undieh; m. Amaka J. Kanu, Dec. 12, 1987; children: Abegim A., Ashikam O., Ake A., Adaeze A. BPharm, U. Nigeria, Nsukka, 1981; PhD, Med. Coll. Pa., Phila., 1990. Asst. prof. U. Md., Balti., Md., 1994—2000, assoc. prof., 2000—07; prof. & chmn. Thomas Jefferson U., Phila., 2008—. Contbr. articles to profl. sci. jours. Rsch. grants, NIH, 1996—2008. Mem.: AAAS, Am. Assn. Pharm. Scis., Soc. Neuroscience, Am. Assn. Coll. Pharmacy, Am. Soc. Pharmacology & Exptl. Therapeutics. Independent. Avocations: missions, travel, nature. Office: Thomas Jefferson Univ 130 South 9th St Philadelphia PA 19107 Business E-Mail: ashiwel.undieh@jefferson.edu.

UNGAR, BARBARA LOUISE, literature and language professor; d. Frank and Shirley Ruth Ungar; 1 child, Izaak Michael Ungar Savett. PhD in English, CUNY Grad. Ctr., 1995. Adj. asst. prof. City Coll., CUNY, 1987—95; assoc. prof. Coll. St. Rose, Albany, NY, 1995—. Finalist Tupelo prize. Office: Coll St Rose 432 Western Ave Albany NY 12203 Business E-Mail: ungarb@strose.edu.

UNGAR, ERIC EDWARD, mechanical engineer; b. Vienna, Nov. 12, 1926; arrived in U.S., 1939; s. Irwin Isidor and Sabina (Schlesinger) U.; m. Goldie Edna Becker, July 1, 1951; children: Judith Fishman, Susan Green, Ellen Borgenicht, Sharon Ungar Lane. BSME, Washington U., St. Louis, 1951; MS, U. N.Mex., 1954; D.Eng.Sc., NYU, 1957. Aero-ordnance engr. Sandia Corp., Albuquerque, 1951-53; rsch. scientist, asst. prof. NYU, 1953-58; chief cons. engr. Bolt Beranek & Newman, Inc., Cambridge, Mass., 1958-96. Chief engrng. scientist Acentech Inc., Cambridge, 1993—. Co-author: Structure-Borne Sound, 1973, 2nd edit. 1988; contbr. articles to profl. jours., chpts. to books. 1st lt. US Army, 1945—48, ETO. Recipient Lifetime Achievement award, Shock and Vibration Info. Analysis Ctr., 2004. Fellow ASME (life; chmn. design engring. divsn. 1978-80, Centennial medallion 1981, Per Bruel Gold medal for noise control and acoustics 1994), AIAA (assoc.), Acoustical Soc. Am. (pres. 1991-92, Trent-Crede Silver medal 1983); mem. Inst. for Noise Control and Engring. (bd. cert., pres. 1985, Disting. Noise Control Engr. award 2004). Home: 15 Considine Rd Newton MA 02459-3603 Office: Acentech Inc 33 Moulton St Cambridge MA 02138-1118 Home Phone: 617-244-2096; Office Phone: 617-499-8022. E-mail: eungar@acentech.com.

UNGARETTI, RICHARD ANTHONY, lawyer; b. Chgo., May 25, 1942; s. Dino Carl and Antoinette (Calvetti) U.; children: Joy A., Paul R. BS, DePaul U., 1964, JD, 1970. Bar: Ill, 1970, U.S. Dist. Ct. (no. dist.) Ill. 1970, U.S. Supreme Ct. 1980; Cert. Cook County Courts Mediator. Assoc. Kirkland & Ellis, Chgo., 1970-74; ptnr. Ungaretti & Harris, Chgo., 1974—. Mem. ABA, Chgo. Bar Assn., Ill. State Bar Assn., Internat. Coun. Shopping Ctrs., Am. Coll. Real Estate Lawyers, Justinian Soc., Urban Land Inst. (assoc.), Lamda Alpha Avocations: golf, fishing, hunting. Office: Ungaretti & Harris 3500 Three First Nat Plz Chicago IL 60602 Office Phone: 312-977-4430. Business E-Mail: raungaretti@uhlaw.com.

UNGER, BARBARA, poet, writer, retired literature and language professor; b. NYC, Oct. 2, 1932; d. David and Florence (Schuchalter) Frankel; m. Bernard Unger, 1954 (div. 1976); m. Theodore Sakano, 1987; children: Deborah, Suzanne. BA, CCNY, 1955, MA, 1957; advanced cert., NYU, 1970. Grad. asst. Yeshiva U., 1962-63; edn. editor County Citizen, Rockland County, NY, 1960-63; tchr. English N.Y.C. Pub. Schs., 1955-58, Nyack (N.Y.) H.S., 1963-67; guidance counselor Ardsley (N.Y.) H.S., 1967-69; prof. English Rockland C.C., Suffern, NY, 1969—95, ret., 1995. English prof. Rockland C.C., 1995-2003, Rockland Sr. Citizen Program, 2001-2003; poetry fellow Squaw Valley Cmty. of Writers, 1980; writer-in-residence Rockland Ctr. for Arts, 1986. Author: (poetry) Basement, 1975, Impulse Toward Flight, 2008, Learning to Fox Trot, 1989, The Man Who Burned Money, 1980, Inside the Wind, 1986, Blue Depression Glass in Troika One, 1991, (fiction) Dying for Uncle Ray, 1990; co-author (with Lloyd Ultan): (non-fiction) Bronx Accent: A Literary and Pictorial History of the Borough, Hardcover, 2001 (N.Y. Soc. Libr. Book award, 2001, J.M. Kaplan Furthermore grantee, Hermalyn Family Urban History award, 05); author: Paperback, 2006; contbr. Anthology Mag. Verse, Yearbook Am. Poetry, 1984, Anthology Mag. Verse, Yearbook Am. Poetry, 1989, poetry and fiction to more than 75 lit. mags. Mass. Review Denver quarterly NYQ. Ragdale Found. fellow, 1985, 86, 89, SUNY Creative Writing fellow, 1981-82, Edna St. Vincent Millay Colony fellow, 1984, Ragdale, 1986, Djerassi Found. fellow, 1991, Hambidge Ctr. for Creative Arts and Scis. fellow, 1988, Dorset Colony fellow, 2005; NEH grantee, 1975; recipient Goodman Poetry award, 1989, Anna Davidson Rosenberg award Judah Magnes Mus., 1989, Roberts Writing award, 1990, New Letters Lit. awards, 1990; finalist Am. Fiction Competition, 1982, John Williams Narrative Poetry Competition, 1992; honorable mention Chester Jones Nat. Poetry Contest. Mem.: PEN, Assn. Writers and Writing Programs, Poets and Writers. Personal E-mail: barungr@aol.com.

UNGER, DAVID C., journalist; b. Bklyn. AB, Cornell U., 1967; postgrad., U. Wis., Madison, 1967—68; PhD, U. Tex., Austin, 1979. Elem. sch. tchr., Staten Island, Bklyn.; joined NY Times, 1977, now sr. editl. writer, fgn. affairs, mem. editl. bd. Office: Editl Bd NY Times 620 Eighth Ave New York NY 10018 Office Fax: 212-556-3815. Business E-Mail: editorial@nytimes.com.

UNGER, GERE NATHAN, emergency physician, lawyer; b. Monticello, NY, May 15, 1949; s. Jessie Aaron and Shirley (Rosenstein) Unger; m. Alice J. McGowan, July 21, 1990; children: Elijah, Breena, Ari, Sasha, Arlen. JD, Bernadean U., 1979; MD, Inst. Polytecnico, Mexico City, 1986; D Phys. Medicine, Met. U., Mexico City, 1987; postgrad., Boston U., 1993, Harvard Law Sch., 1994-96; LLM in Med. Law, U. Glasgow, 2001. Diplomate Am. Bd. Forensic Examiners, Am. Bd. Med. Legal Analysis Medicine and Surgery, Am. Bd. Forensic Medicine, Am. Bd. Risk Mgmt., Am. Bd. Disability Analysts. Med. dir. Vietnam Vets. Post-Traumatic Stress Disorder Program, 1988-90; emergency rm. physician, cons. in medicaid fraud Bronx (N.Y.)-Lebanon Hosp., 1990—; clin. legal medicine Paladin Profl. Group, P.A., Palm Beach, Fla., 1992-98; pres. Albany Law Jour. Co., Inc., 1998—; jurisconsult Office of Gere Unger, M.D., J.D., 1999—; with Inalienable Rights Project Justice Watchdog Group. Mem. surg. critical care com. Am. Soc. Critical Care Medicine, 1992; mem. peer rev. com. Nat. Inst. Disability and Rehab. Rsch., Office Spl. Edn., U.S. Dept. Edn., 1993; mediator, arbitrator, negotiator World Intellectual Property Orgn., 1994; mem. clin. ethics com. Inst. Medecine Legale et de Medecine Sociale, Strasbourg, France, 1994; mediator, arbitrator World Bank, 2000—. Mem. editl. bd. Am. Bd. Forensic Examiners, 1993, Jour. Neurol. and Orthopaedic Medicine and Surgery, 1993. Comdt. Broward County Marine Corps League, 1995—. With USMC, 1968—72. Fellow: The Cognitive Sci. Soc., Exec. Practice Mgmt., Am. Coll. Forensic Examiners, Internat. Coll. Surgeons (mem. ethics com. 1994, mem. emergency response program eastern region 1994), Am. Acad. Neurol. and Orthopedic Surgeons, Am. Coll. Legal Medicine; mem.: FBA (mem. health com., rep. ABA 1994, chmn. med. malpractice/tort com., liaison to AMA), ATLA (N.Y. state capt. 1992), ABA, N.Y. State Defenders Assn., Nat. Am. Indian Ct. Judges Assn., N.W. Indian Bar Assn., Internat. Assn. Prosecutors, Am. Soc. Investigative Pathology, Internat. Criminal Law Network (The Hague), Internat. Assn. Prosecutors, Internat. Royal Soc. Medicine (London), Nat. Assn. Forensic Econs., Am. Soc. Laser Medicine and Surgery, Kennedy Inst. Ethics, Am. Coll. Physician Execs. (chair forum law and med. mgmt. 1995), Internat. Bar Assn., Nat. Coll. Advocacy. Avocations: flying, boating. Office Phone: 508-759-0009. Business E-Mail: rumpole@justice.com.

UNGER, PAUL WALTER, retired soil scientist; b. Winchester, Tex., Sept. 10, 1931; s. Edwin Herman and Elsie Anna U.; m. Barbara Charlene Dutton Steelman, Sept. 13, 1960; children: Gary Robert, Paula Dianne. BS, Tex. A&M U., 1961; MS, Colo. State U., 1963, PhD, 1966. Soil scientist USDA Agrl. Rsch. Svc., Bushland, Tex., 1965-81, soil scientist/rsch. leader, 1981-87, supervisory soil scientist/rsch. leader, 1987-93, soil scientist, 1993-2000; ret., 2000. Cons. Food and Agrl. Orgn. UN, Rome, 1986. Author and co-author bulls. and articles; co-editor conf. proc., Agronomy Monograph, other publs.; editor Managing Agricultural Residues, 1994; author Soil and Water Conservation Handbook-Policies, Pratices, Conditions, and Terms, 2006, Tillage Systems For Soil and Water Conservation, 1984. With U.S. Army, 1952-55. Recipient Disting. Svc. award Great Plains Agrl. Coun., 1984; named Scientist of Yr., USDA-Agrl. Rsch. Svc., So. Plains Area, 1987. Fellow Am. Soc. Agronomy (emeritus, selection com. 1988-89), Soil Sci. Soc. Am. (emeritus, assoc. editor 1977-82, divsn. chmn. 1986, mem.

selection com. 1994-95, Applied Rsch. award 1991), Soil and Water Conservation Soc. (various local and state offices, photography awards 1990-92); mem. Internat. Soil Tillage Rsch. Orgn., World Assn. Soil and Water Conservation. Lutheran. Avocations: woodworking, gardening, photography. Personal E-mail: pwunger@suddenlink.net.

UNGER, PETER KENNETH, philosophy educator; b. N.Y.C., Apr. 25, 1942; s. Sidney and Naomi (Fein) U.; m. Susan Gill, June 2, 1977; 1 child, Andrew. BA, Swarthmore Coll., 1962 DPhil, Oxford U., Eng., 1966. Instr. U. Wis., Madison, 1965-66, asst. prof., 1966-70, assoc. prof., 1970-72; assoc. prof. NYU, N.Y.C., 1972-75, prof., 1975—. Author: Ignorance, 1975, 2d edit., 2002, Philosophical Relativity, 1984, 2d edition, 2002, Identity, Consciousness and Value, 1990, Living High and Letting Die, 1996, All the Power in the World, 2006, Philosophical Papers, Vols. 1 and 2, 2006; contbr. articles to profl. jours. Guggenheim fellow, 1974, NEH fellow, 1993. Mem. Am. Philos. Assn. Democrat. Home: 100 Bleecker St New York NY 10012-2202 Office: Dept Philosophy NYU 5 Washington Pl New York NY 10003 Office Phone: 212-998-8321, 212-998-8320. E-mail: peter.unger@nyu.edu.

UNGER, RICHARD WATSON, history professor; b. Huntington, W.Va., Dec. 23, 1942; s. Abraham I. and Marion Patterson U.; 1 child, Emily Patterson. BA, Haverford Coll., Pa., 1963; AM, U. Chgo., 1965; MA, Yale U., 1967, MPhil, 1969, PhD, 1971. Prof. dept. history U. B.C., Vancouver, Canada, 1969—. Author: Dutch Shipbuilding Before 1800, 1978, The Ship in the Medieval Economy, 600-1600, 1980, The Art of Medieval Technology: The Image of Noah the Shipbuilder, 1991, Ships and Shipping in the North Sea and Atlantic, 1400-1600, 1997, A History of Brewing in Holland, 900-1900, Economy, Technology and the State, 2001, Beer in the Middle Ages and the Renaissance, 2004; editor: Britain and Poland Lithuania Contact and Comparision from the Middle Ages to 1795, 2008; editor: Cogs, Caravels and Galleons, 1994; co-editor: War at Sea in the Middle Ages and the Renaissance, 2003, Studies in Medieval and Renaissance History, 1978-95; contbr. articles to profl. jours. Trustee Vancouver Maritime Mus., 1979-83, 97-98. Mem. Medieval Assn. Pacific (pres. 1994-96), Econ. History Soc., Soc. Nautical Rsch. Office: U BC Dept History 1297-1873 East Mall Vancouver BC Canada V6T 1Z1 Business E-Mail: richard.unger@ubc.ca.

UNGER, ROGER HAROLD, physician, research scientist; b. NYC, Mar. 7, 1924; s. Lester and Beatrice (Raphael) Unger. BS, Yale U., 1944; MD, Columbia U., 1947; MD (hon.), U. Geneva, 1976, U. Liège, Belgium, 1980. Diplomate Am. Bd. Internal Medicine. Asst. prof. internal medicine U. Tex. Med. Sch., Dallas, 1959—64, assoc. prof., 1964—69, prof., 1969—; dir. Ctr. for Diabetes Rsch., U. Tex. Health Sci. Ctr., Dallas, 1985—2007, Touchstone/West Disting. chair diabetes rsch., 1989—. Sr. med. investigator VA Med. Ctr., Dallas, 1979—99; mem. Nat. Diabetes Adv. Bd., Bethesda, Md., 1985—; mem. adv. coun. Nat. Inst. Diabetes, Digestive and Kidney Diseases, 1990—94. Editor: Glucagon, 1972, Glucagon Physiology etc., 1981; assoc. editor Diabetes, 1979—84, mem. editl. bd., 1975—79, Endocrinology, 1976—81; contbr. articles to profl. jours., chapters to books. With US Army, 1946—48, with USPHS, 1950—52. Recipient Lilly award, Am. Diabetes Assn., 1964, Banting medal, 1975, David Rumbough award, Juvenile Diabetes Assn., 1975, Joslin medal, Harvard U., 1979, Claude Bernard award, European Assn. for Study of Diabetes, 1979, Fred Conrad Koch award, Endocrine Soc., 1983, Maurice Derot prize, Jour. Diabetique, Paris. Mem.: Am. Soc. for Clin. Investigation (emeritus), Assn. Am. Physicians, Am. Acad. Arts and Scis., NAS. Office Phone: 214-648-6742. E-mail: roger.unger@utsouthwestern.edu.

UNGER, SUSAN J., automotive executive; b. Detroit, Apr. 8, 1950; BA in Economics, Mich. State U., 1972; MBA in Fin., Wayne State U., 1976. Fin. analyst, sales and mktg. DaimlerChrysler AG, 1972, various financial positions, fin. dir. product devel. and Jeep/Truck Ops., exec. dir. mgmt. info. sys., 1993, sr. v.p., 1998—, chief info. officer, 1998—. Mem., past pres., Eli Broad Bd., Coll. Bus. Mich. State U.; bd. dir. Cyberstate.org; nat. adv. com. Coll. of Engring. U. Mich.; adv. tech. bd. Oakland U. Recipient Top Am. Woman award, Assn. Woman in Computing, 2003, Pioneer award, Phoenix Hill Women's Mus., 2004, Disting. Svc. Citation, Automotive Hall of Fame, 2006; named 100 Leading Women in N.Am. Auto Industry, Automotive News, 2002, CIO of Yr., Automation Alley, 2002, Salomon Smith Barney, 2002, Disting. Alumnus of Yr., Wayne State U. Sch. Bus. Adminstrn., 2002; named one of Detroit's Most Influential Women, Crain's Detroit Bus., 2002. Mem.: Automotive Womens Alliance, Kleiner Perkins CIO Strategy Exch. Forum. Office: Daimler-Chrysler Corp 1000 Chrysler Dr Auburn Hills MI 48326-2766

UNGER, SYDNEY ELLIOTT, lawyer; b. 1947; BA, U. Chgo., 1968; MBA with distinction, NYU, 1970, JD cum laude, 1974, LLM in Taxation, 1979. Bar: NY 1975, US Tax Ct. 1975, US Ct. Claims 1975, US Dist. Ct. (so. and ea. dists.) NY 1975, US Ct. Appeals (2d cir.) 1975, US Ct. Appeals (fed. cir.) 1982, US Supreme Ct. 1995. Ptnr., chair Tax Dept. Kaye, Scholer LLP, NYC; adj. prof. NY Law Sch., 2005—06. Lectr. in field. Editor, bus. mgr. Ann. Survey Am. Law, 1973-74; articles editor The Tax Lawyer, 1981-84, mng. editor, 1984-87; contbr. articles to profl. jours. Mem. ABA (publications com., chmn. Tax Lawyer subcom., sect. on taxation 1984-87), NY State Bar Assn., Assn. of Bar of City of NY (tax com. 1988-89, taxation of corporations com. 1990-99). Office: Kaye Scholer LLP 425 Park Ave New York NY 10022-3506 E-mail: sunger@kayescholer.com.

UNGERER, JEAN THOMAS (TOMI UNGERER), writer, artist; b. Strasbourg, Alsace, France, Nov. 28, 1931; came to U.S., 1957; s. Théodore and Alice (Essler) Ungerer, Theo and Alice (Essler) Ungerer; m. Deborah Yvonne Wright, Dec. 5, 1971; children: Aria, Pascal, Lukas; m. Miriam Lancaster (div.); 1 child, Phoebe Alexis; m. Yvonne Wright, 1970; children: Aria, Pascal, Lukas. Student, Mcpl. Sch. Decorative Arts, Strasbourg, 1952—53; D honoris causa (hon.), U. Karlsruhe, 2004. Free-lance artist, illus., cartoonist for nat. mags. Illustrator and author of over 140 children's books, cartoon album; author: Erotoscope, The Mellops Go Flying, 1957, Crietor, 1958, Adelaide, 1959, Emile, 1960, Inside Marriage, 1960, Horrible, 1960, Rufus, 1961, Three Robbers, 1962, Snail Where Are You, 1962, Herzinfarkt, 1962, The Mellops Go Underground, 1962, A Child-Phoebe Alexis, 1962, Underground Sketchbook, 1964, One Two Where Is My Shoe, 1964, The Party, 1966, Orlando, 1966, Zeralda's Ogre, 1967, Moon Man, 1967, Ask Me A Question, 1968, The Hat, 1969, The Fornicon, 1969, Compromises, 1969, Beast of Monsieur Racine, 1971, I Am Papa Snap and These Are My Favorite No Such Stories, 1971, No Kiss for Mother, 1972, Spiegelmensch, 1972, T. Ungerer Fairy Tales, 1972, Amerika, 1974, Allumette, 1974, Totempole, 1976, A. Great Song Book, 1978, Babylon, 1979, Politricks, 1979, Far Out Isn't Far Enough, 1984, The Joy of Frogs, 1985; retrospective show Musée des Arts Decoratifs, Louvre, Paris, 1981. Amb. Coun. Europe Childhood and Edn., 2000. Served with Mounted Police, 1953, Sahara. Recipient honors for books N.Y. Herald Tribune; gold medal Soc. of Illustrators, 1960; International Children's Book Prize, Hans Christian Anderson prize, 1998, European Culture award, 1999; Comdr. aux Arts et Lettre, 1984, German Cross of Honor, 1993, Officier de la Legion d'Honneur, 2001 Mem. Franco-German Interministerial Cmty. Office: Conseil de l'Europe 67075 Strasbourg France

UNHJEM, MICHAEL BRUCE, lawyer; b. Fargo, ND, Aug. 22, 1953; s. Kalmer Joseph and Lorelei Mae (Myhra) U.; children: Kaia Mary, David Burges, Kirsten Elizabeth. BA magna cum laude, Jamestown Coll., 1975; JD with distinction, U. N.D., 1978. Bar: N.D. 1978. Pvt. practice, Jamestown, ND, 1978-86; compliance officer Norwest Bank, Jamestown, ND, 1981-84; planned giving officer Jamestown Coll., Anne Carlsen Sch., Jamestown, 1984-86; asst. to pres., gen. counsel Blue Cross Blue Shield of N.D., Fargo, 1986-91, pres., chief exec. officer, 1991—, Pioneer Mutual Life Ins. Co., Fargo, 1997—99, Chmn. bd. dirs. Lincoln Mut. Life & Casualty Ins. Co., Fargo, Noridian Adminstr. Svc., LLC, Fargo, Noridian Ins. Svc., Inc., Fargo; chmn. TriWest HC All, Cass Clay United Way; bd. dirs. Prime Ther, Western Conf. Prepaid Health Plans, Jamestown Coll., Blue Cross Blue Shield Assn. State rep. N.D. Legis. Assembly, Bismarck, 1974-86; mem. Nat. Conf. Commrs. on Uniform State Laws, Chgo., 1981—, chmn., Bismarck, 1982-86; co-chmn. Bush for Pres. Com., 1980, 88, 92; presdl. appointee Nat. Coun. on Disability, Washington, 1990.chmn. ND Caring Found., pres. Mental Health Assn., bd. dirs. Jamestown Hosp. Named Outstanding Young North Dakotan, N.D. Jaycees, 1983; recipient Nat. Excellence in Leadership award State of N.D., 1988, Disting. Leadership award N.D. Psychol. Assn., 1988, Spl. Presdl. Commendation award Am. Psychiatric Assn., 1989, Toastmaster Internat. Comm. and Leadership award, 1992, brand excellence awards, BCBS Assn. Mem. ABA, N.D. Bar Assn., Cass County Bar Assn., Kiwanis, Elks, Masons, Shriners. Republican. Lutheran. Office: Health Integrated Inc 10008 N Dale Mabry Hwy Tampa FL 33618 Office Phone: 813-388-4000.

UNIKEL, EVA TAYLOR, interior designer; b. Hungary; arrived in Can., 1956; came to U.S., 1967; d. Istvan Domolky and Lea Maria (Koszegi) Coan; m. Alan L. Unikel; 1 child, Renee Christine; m. June 26, 1993. BS, So. Ill. U., 1972. Dir. mktg. Lococo Design, St. Louis, 1982-83; project mgr., nat. dir. mktg. hosp. div. Hotel Restaurant Planners div. Profl. Interiors, St. Louis, 1983-87; founder Interior Solutions Inc., Hinsdale, Ill., 1987—. Mem. AIA (assoc.), Nat. Assn. Women Bus. Owners, Am. Soc. Interior Design (chairperson 1984-86), Interior Design Assn. Roman Catholic. Office: 500 E Ravine Rd Hinsdale IL 60521-2449 Home Phone: 630-986-4464; Office Phone: 630-464-9696.

UNIS, RICHARD L., judge; b. Portland, Oreg., June 11, 1928; BS, JD, U. Oreg. Bar: Oreg. 1954, U.S. Dist. Ct. Oreg. 1957, U.S. Ct. Appeals (9th cir.) 1960, U.S. Supreme Ct. 1965. Judge Portland Mcpl. Ct., 1968-71, Multnomah County Dist. Ct., 1972-76, presiding judge, 1972-74; former judge Oreg. Cir. Ct. 4th Judicial Dist., 1977-90; former sr. dep. city atty. City of Portland; assoc. justice Oreg. Supreme Ct., Portland, 1990-96; spl. master US Dist. Ct. House, Portland, 1996—2005. Adj. prof. of local govt. law and evidence Lewis & Clark Coll. Northwestern Sch. Law, 1969-76, 77-96; spl. master supr. La.-Pacific Inner-Seal Siding nationwide class action litig.; faculty mem. The Nat. Judicial Coll., 1971-2000; former faculty mem. Am. Acad. Judicial Edn. Author: Procedure and Instructions in Traffic Court Cases, 1970, 101 Questions and Answers on Preliminary Hearings, 1974. Bd. dirs. Oreg. Free from Drug Abuse; mem. Oreg. Adv. Com. on Evidence Law Revision, chmn. subcom., 1974-79. Maj. USAFR, JAGC, ret. Recipient Meritorius Svc. award U. Oregon sch. Law, 1988; named Legal Citizen of Yr. Oreg. Law Related Edn., 1987; inducted into The Nat. Judicial Coll. Hall of Honor, 1988. Mem. Am. Judicature Soc. (bd. dirs. 1975, Herbert Harley Nat. award 1999), Am. Judges Assn., Multnomah Bar Found., Oregon Judicial Conf. (chmn. Oreg. Judicial Coll. 1973-80, legis. com. 1976—, exec. com. of judicial edn. com., judicial conduct com.), N.Am. Judges Assn. (tenure, selection and compensation judges com.), Dist. Ct. Judges of Oreg. (v.p., chmn. edn. com.), Nat. Conf. Spl. Ct. Judges (exec. com.), Oreg. State Bar (judicial adminstrn. com., sec. local govt. com., com. on continuing certification, uniform jury instrn. com., exec. com. criminal law sect., trial practice sect. standards and certification com., past chmn., among others), Oreg. Trial Lawyers Assn. (named Judge of Yr. 1984). Office: 28338 Hist Colum Riv Hwy Troutdale OR 97060-9372 Home Phone: 503-665-9459; Office Phone: 503-669-7286. Personal E-mail: rlugg@comcast.net.

UNITHAN, DOLLY, visual artist; b. Kelantan, Malaysia; arrived in US, 1976; Postgrad., Brit. Coun. Fine Arts Exch., 1974, Ecole Nationale des Beaux Arts de Nancy, France, 1974; BFA, Hornsey Coll. Art, 1975; MFA, Pratt Inst., 1978. Summer intern Guggenheim Mus, NYC, 1976; panelist, artist in residence Asian Am. Arts Ctr., 1993; lectr. in field. One-woman shows include Internat. Art Ctr., London, 1975, Am. Assn. State Colls., Univ., Orlando, Fla., 1977, Sloan Gallery, Lock Haven State Coll., Pa., 1978, Permanent Mission Malaysia, UN, NYC, 1987, Kerr Gallery, 1987, Lyman Allyn Art Mus., New London, Conn., 1990, UN Secretariat, NYC, 1991, Gracie Mansion, 1994, Angel Orensanz Found., 1995, Cathedral of St. John the Divine, St. Boniface Chapel Gallery, 1996, exhibited in group shows at Palace of Westminster, Hos. of Parliament, London, 1978, City Mus. Art Gallery, Gloucester, Eng., 1978, Contemporary Gallery, Warsaw, Poland, 1978, BWA Gallery, Wroclaw, Poland, 1978, Szczecin, Poland, 1978, Arts Coun. Gallery, Belfast, No. Ireland, 1978, Parrish Art Mus., Southampton, NY, 1979, Modern Art Ctr., Guadalajara, Mex., 1979, Alternative Mus., NYC, 1981, Nat. Mus. Fine Arts, Havana, Cuba, 1986, Hillwood Art Mus., Brookville, NY, 1988, PS 1 Mus., NYC, 1990, Nat. Art Gallery, Kuala Lumpur, 1991—92, League of Nations Archives, Palais des Nations, Geneva, 1993, Jewish Mus., Vienna, Austria, 1993, Peace Mus., Remagen, Germany, 1994, Westbeth Galleries, NYC, 1994, Tweed Courthouse Gallery, 1994, China Art Mus., Beijing, 1994—95, Raiffeisenkasse, Ulrich bei Steyr, Peace parish, Austria, 1996, Ctrl. Children's & Youth Arts Palace, Samarkand, Uzbekistan, 1997, Palais des Nations, UN Office, Geneva, 1998, Firehouse, NYC, 1999, Cathedral of St. John the Divine Synod Hall, 2002, Asian Am. Arts Ctr., 2002, Polish Culture Ctr., Budapest, 2007, Represented in permanent collections Lock Haven State Coll., Pa., Am. Assn. State Colls., Univ., Washington, Permanent Mission of Malaysia to UN, Wilfredo Lam Ctr., Havana, Malaysian Embassy, Washington, Spirit Found., NYC, Asian Am. Arts Ctr., World Bank, Washington, Lib. Congress, artwork included in jours., Multicultural Edn., 1994, Artspiral, 1994, books, Imagine Strawberry Fields, Sculpture, Technique, Form, Content, exhibited in group shows at Modern Art Ctr. Wloclawck Poland, 2009. Recipient Artist award, Rainbow Art Found., NYC, 1985, Art award ArtQuest '88, Internat. Art Competition, Calif., 1988; named grad. scholar, Mara, Malaysia, 1976—78, Archives of Contemporary Arts, Venice Biennale, 1990; grantee, Lee Found., Singapore, 1972, 1976, Pollock-Krasner Found., 1991—92. Avocation: collecting antiques. Home and Office: West Beth Artist Cmty 463 W St Apt 809A New York NY 10014

UNPINGCO, JOHN WALTER SABLAN, federal judge; b. 1950; BA, St. Louis U., 1972; MBA, JD, NYU, 1976; LLM, Georgetown U., 1983. Bar: Guam 1977, D.C. 1983, Calif. 1992. Atty. Ferenz, Bramhall, Williams & Gruskin, Guam, 1976-77; atty. Office Staff Judge Advocate USAF, 1977-85, civilian atty., Office Staff Judge Advocate, 1985-87; counsel US Naval Air Warfare Ctr., China Lake, Calif., 1987-92; judge US Dist. Ct. (Guam dist.), 1992—, now chief judge. Part-time instr. U. Md. Far East divsn., Yokota Air Base, Tokyo, 1983-87, European divsn., RAF Mildenhall, Suffolk, U.K., 1979-82, U. Guam, 1994-99. Pres. Guam Swim League, 2000; pres. parish coun. Our Lady of Hope Parish, 2000-. Mem. ABA, State Bar Calif., Guam Bar Assn., Internat. Legal Soc. Japan, D.C. Bar Assn., NWC Community Fed. Credit Union (bd. dirs. 1991-92). Office: US Dist Ct 4th Fl US Courthouse 520 W Soledad Ave Hagatna GU 96910

UNRUH, GARY LEE, retired music educator; b. Reedley, Calif., July 7, 1941; 1 child, Holly Elizabeth. MusD, U. Ill., 1973. Prof. emeritus Calif. State U., Fresno, Calif., 1999—. Dir. performance tours Kingsway Internat., Colo. Springs, Colo., 1997—2003; condr. internat. choral performance tours; v.p. Santa Barbara Vocal Jazz Fund., 2005. Recipient Educator of Yr., Fresno Arts Coun., 1979, 1984, 2001, award, Calif. State Senate Resolutions, 1998; named Educator of Yr., Fresno Arts Coun., 1976. Mem.: Am. Choral Dirs. Assn. (life; pres. wc. divsn. 1989—91).

UNRUH, JAMES ARLEN, bank executive; b. Goodrich, ND, Mar. 22, 1941; m. Candice Leigh Voight, Apr. 28, 1984. BSBA, Jamestown Coll., 1963; MBA, U. Denver, 1964. Dir. corp. planning and analysis Fairchild Camera & Instrument, Calif., 1974-76, v.p. treasury and corp. devel. Calif., 1976-79, v.p. fin. Calif., 1979-80, Memorex Corp., Santa Clara, Calif., 1980-82, Burroughs Corp. (now known as Unisys Corp.), Detroit, 1982-84, sr. v.p. fin., 1984-86, exec. v.p. fin., 1986, exec. v.p., 1986-89, pres., COO, 1989-90, pres., CEO, 1990-91, chmn. bd. dirs., CEO, 1991-97; founding prin. Alerion Capital Group L.L.C., Scottsdale, Ariz., 1998—. Bd. dirs. Prudential Fin. Corp., Qwest Comm. Internat. Inc., Tenet Healthcare Corp., CSG Sys. Internat., Inc., LumenIQ Corp., BioVigilant Corp., Steton Tech. Group, Inc., Worldlink, Inc., VTI Instruments Inc. Trustee Jamestown Coll., N.D. Home: 5426 E Morrison Ln Paradise Valley AZ 85253 Office Phone: 480-367-0900. E-mail: jimunruh@alerion.com.

UNRUH, SUSAN MARIE, psychologist, educator; b. Kans. City, Kans., Feb. 11, 1951; d. Waldo and Doris Dick; m. Terry Unruh, Aug. 16, 1971; children: Marie, David. PhD, U. Kans., Lawrence, 2007. Cert. in sch. psychology Kans. Dept. Edn., 1991, NASP, 2007. Sch. psychologist USD 259, Wichta, Kans., 1991—; adj. faculty Wichita State U., 2003—, mem. sch. psychology adv. coun., 2003—08. Mem.: APA (Student Reviewer of Yr. 2007), NASP, Kans. Assn. Sch. Psychologists (Sch. Psychologist of Yr. 2005). Democrat. Office: USD 259 201 N Water Wichita KS 67203 Business E-Mail: sunruh@usd259.net.

UNSON, CECILIA G., science educator, researcher; married. PhD, Fordham U., Bronx, NY, 1978. Rsch. assoc. prof. Rockefeller U., NYC, 1978—. Office: Rockefeller Univ 1230 York Ave New York NY 10065

UNSWORTH, RICHARD PRESTON, minister, educator, director; b. Vineland, NJ, Feb. 7, 1927; s. Joseph Lewis and Laura (MacMillan) U.; m. Joy Merritt, Aug. 20, 1949; children: Sarah, John, Mary, Lucy. BA, Princeton U., 1948; BD, Yale U., 1954; ThM, Harvard U., 1963; STD, Dickinson Coll., 1971; LHD, Washington and Jefferson Coll., 1971; LLD, Smith Coll., 1992. Ordained to ministry Presbyn. Ch., 1953. Tchr. Bible and English Mt. Hermon Sch., 1948-50; asst. chaplain Yale U., New Haven, 1950-54; chaplain, assoc. prof. Smith Coll., Northampton, Mass., 1954-64, chaplain, prof. religion, 1967-80; dean William Jewett Tucker Found. and prof. religion Dartmouth (N.H.) Coll., 1963-67; headmaster Northfield (Mass.) Mt. Hermon Sch., 1980-88, pres., 1989-91, headmaster emeritus, 1991—; headmaster Berkshire Sch., Sheffield, Mass., 1991-96; dean of the chapel Smith Coll., 1996-98, lectr. religion, 1996—99, sr. fellow Kahn Inst., 1998—. Pres. Critical Langs. and Area Studies Consortium, 1987-97; cons. Ednl. Assocs., Inc., 1967-69, U.S. Office Edn., 1969-77. Author: Sexuality and the Human Community, 1970, Dignity and Exploitation: Christian Reflections on Images of Sex in the 1970s, 1974, A Century of Religion at Smith College, 1975; (with Arnold Kenseth) Prayers for Worship Leaders, 1978; editor: Rethinking Childhood, 2004; contbg author: The Dispossessed, 2005; Author: Their War Against War, Biography of Andre and Wagda Trocme; contbr. chpts. to books. Leader Operation Crossroads Africa unit, Nigeria, 1961, mem. adv. bd., 1961-66; mem. adminstrv. com. Student Christian Movement New Eng., 1964; mem. Mass. unit So. Christian Leadership conf., 1968; trustee Conf. on Religion in Ind. Schs., 1961-63; pres. Am. Friends of Coll. Cevenol, France, 1957-63, 90-94, Am. rep., 1958-82; trustee Mt. Holyoke Coll., 1982-89, chair, 1984-89, chmn. emeritus, 1989—, Am. Sch. Tangier, Morocco, 1982-87, Eaglebrook Sch., 1992-98, Acad. Music, Northampton, 1998-99, Mus. Sci., Boston, 1993-95; bd. dirs. Family Planning Coun. Western Mass., 1972-81; bd. dirs. Ind. Schs. Assn. Mass., 1992-96. Mem. AAUP, Nat. Assn. Coll. and Univ. Chaplains, Am. Acad. Religion, Assn. Ind. Schs. New Eng. (pres. 1993-96), Headmasters Assn., Nat. Commn. on Asia in Schs., Asia Soc. N.Y.C., U. Club.

UNTAROIU, COSTIN DANIEL, engineering educator, researcher; s. Gheorghe and Victoria Untaroiu; m. Alexandrina Untaroiu; children: Razvan, Ana. MS in Applied Math., U. Bucharest, 1995; MS in Mech. Engring., Poly. U., Bucharest, 1990, PhD in Mech. Engring., 1999, U. Va., Charlottesville, 2005. Jr. asst. prof. Poly. U., 1991—93, asst. prof., 1993—97, sr. lectr., 1997—2001; rsch. asst. U. Va., 2001—06, rsch. scientist, 2006—08, rsch. asst. prof. Leader Ctr. Applied Biomechanics, UVA, 2005—. Contbr. articles to profl. jours. Mem.: ASME, Am. Soc. Biomechanics, Soc. Automotive Engrs. Achievements include patents pending for a system for real-time optimization of active occupant restraints. Office: Ctr Applied Biomechanics Univ VA 1011 Linden Ave Charlottesville VA 22902 Home: 610 Rainier Rd Charlottesville VA 22903 Office Fax: 434-296-3453. Business E-Mail: costin@virginia.edu.

UNTERBERG, CRAIG SCOTT, lawyer; b. NYC, July 24, 1972; s. Mark and Madeline Unterberg; m. Robin Golman, Mar. 29, 1998; children: Tatum, Riley. BA, Tulane U., New Orleans, 1991—95, JD cum laude, 1995—98. Bar: Tex. 1998. Ptnr. Haynes & Boone, LLP, Dallas, 1998—. V.p. Am. Jewish Com., Dallas, 2005—09; mem. Dallas Assembly. Recipient Tex. Rising Star award, Tex. Monthly, 2005—08; named one of Best Lawyers under 40 in Dallas, D Mag., 2006; grantee Comay fellowship, Am. Jewish Com., 2005—06. Office: Haynes & Boone LLP 2323 Victory Ave Dallas TX 75219 also: Haynes & Boone LLP 1221 Ave Americas 26th Fl New York NY 10020 Office Phone: 214-651-5057. Office Fax: 214-200-0591. Business E-Mail: craig.unterberg@haynesboone.com.

UNTERBERGER, BETTY MILLER, retired history professor; b. Glasgow, Scotland, Dec. 27, 1922; d. Joseph C. and Leah Miller; m. Robert Ruppe, July 29, 1944; children: Glen, Gail, Gregg. BA, Syracuse U., NYC, 1943; MA, Harvard U., 1946; PhD, Duke U., 1950. Asst. prof. E. Carolina U., Greenville, 1948-50; assoc. prof., dir. liberal arts ctr. Whittier Coll., Calif., 1954-61; assoc. prof. Calif. State U.-Fullerton,

1961-65, prof., chmn. grad. studies, 1965-68; prof. history Tex. A&M U., College Station, 1968—2004, ret. Regents prof. emerita, 2004. Vis. prof. U. Hawaii, Honolulu, 1967, Peking U., Beijing, 1988; vis. disting. prof. U. Calif., Irvine, 1987—, Patricia and Bookman Peters prof. history, 1991-2005; vis. prof. Charles U., Prague, Czechoslovakia, 1992, Regents prof., 2000—; adv. com. fgn. rels. U.S. Dept. State, 1977-81, chair, 1981; hist. adv. com. U.S. Dept. Army, 1980-82, USN, 1991—; mem. Nat. Hist. Publs. and Records Commn., 1980-84; history rev. panel to Dir. of CIA, 1999—. Author: America's Siberian Expedition 1918-1920: A Study of National Policy, 1956, 69 (Pacific Coast award Am. Hist. Assn. 1956); editor: American Intervention in the Russian Civil War, 1969, Intervention Against Communism: Did the U.S. Try to Overthrow the Soviet Government, 1918-20, 1986, The United States, Revolutionary Russia and the Rise of Czechoslovakia, 1989, paperback edit. with a 2000 yr. perspective, 2000; contbr.: Woodrow Wilson and Revolutionary World, 1982, The Liberal Persuasion, 1997, The United States and the Russian Civil War, microfilm edit., 25 reels, 2001; mem. editl. adv. bd. The Papers of Woodrow Wilson, Princeton U., 1982-92, Internt. History, 1999—; bd. editors: Diplomatic History, 1981-84, Red River Valley Hist. Rev., 1975-84. Trustee Am. Inst. Pakistan Studies, Villanova U., Pa., 1981—, sec., 1989-92; mem. League of Women Voters. Woodrow Wilson Found. fellow, 1979; recipient Disting. Univ. Tchr. award State of Calif. Legislature, 1966; Betty Miller Unterberger dissertation prize, Soc. Historians Am. Fgn. Rels., 2004. Mem. LWV, NOW, AAUW, Am. Hist. Assn. (chair 1982-83, nominating com. 1980-83), Orgn. Am. Historians (govt. relations com.), Soc. Historians of Am. Fgn. Relations (exec. council 1978-81, 86-89, govt. relations com. 1982-84, v.p. 1985, pres. 1986, co-winner Myrna F. Bernath prize 1991), Am. Soc. for Advancement Slavic Studies, Coordinating Com. on Women in Hist. Profession, Rocky Mountain Assn. Slavic Studies (program chair 1973, v.p. 1973-74), So. Hist. Assn., Asian Studies Assn., Assn. Third World Studies, Czechoslovak Soc. Arts and Scis., Czechoslovak History Conf., Women in Nat. Security, Women's Fgn. Policy Coun., Beyond War, Peace History Soc., Sierra Club, Phi Beta Kappa, Phi Beta Delta.

UNTERMEYER, CHARLES GRAVES (CHASE UNTERMEYER), real estate company executive; b. Long Branch, NJ, Mar. 7, 1946; s. Dewitt Edward and Marguerite Alonza (Graves) U.; m. Diana Cumming Kendrick, Oct. 6, 1990; 1 child, Ellyson Chase. AB, Harvard Coll., 1968. Polit. reporter Houston Chronicle, 1971-74; exec. asst. County Judge of Harris County, Houston, 1974-76; state rep. Tex. Ho. of Reps., Austin, 1977-81; exec. asst. V.P. George H.W. Bush, Washington, 1981-83; dep. asst. sec. installations & facilities Navy Dept., Washington, 1983—84, asst. sec. manpower & reserve affairs, 1984—88; asst. to the pres. White House, Washington, 1989-91; dir. Voice of Am., Washington, 1991-93; dir. govt. affairs Compaq Computer Corp., Houston, 1993—2002; v.p. prof. pub. policy U. Tex. Health Sci. Ctr., Houston, 2002—04; U.S. amb. to Qatar US Dept. State, 2004—07, vice chmn., strategic real estate advisors, 2007—, mem. def., health bd., 2008—, coun. foreign rels., 2009—. Bd. visitors U.S. Naval Acad., Annapolis, Md., 1993-96, chmn., 1995; mem. Tex. State Bd. Edn., 1999-2003, chmn., 1999-2001. Author: Houston Survival Handbook, 1980. Commnr. Port of Houston, 1995-98; bd. dirs. Nat. Pub. Radio, 1996-98. Lt. USNR, 1968-70. Inst. Politics fellow Harvard U., 1980; recipient George Washington Honor medal Freedoms Found., 1969. Republican. Episcopalian. Home and Office: 10000 Memorial Dr Ste 920 Houston TX 77024 Office Phone: 974-488-4101 ext. 6055, 713-683-9885. E-mail: chase@untermeyer.com.

UNTHANK, MICHAEL GEORGE, architectural firm executive; b. Lincoln, Nebr., June 5, 1951; s. George Ralph and Maxine Gertrude Unthank; m. Toni Laine Freeman, Oct. 27, 1973; 1 child, Andrew Michael. BArch, U. Nebr., Lincoln, 1974, DDS, 1984. Cert. architect, Nebr., 1978. Dir. architecture Pride Inst., San Francisco, 1984—89; founder Unthank Design Group, Lincoln, 1989—. Contbr. articles to profl. jour. Recipient Office Design of Yr., Dental Economics Mag. & Matsco, 2005, 2007; named, 2003. Mem.: ADA (Chgo.) (spkr. 1993—), Acad. Gen. Dentistry. Office: Unthank Design Group 5930 Van Dervoort Dr Lincoln NE 68516 Business E-Mail: mike@unthank.com.

UNVER, M. UTKU, economics professor; s. Izzet and Zeynep Suay Unver; m. Lori Ann Hall; children: Berk Noah, Baran River. PhD, U. Pitts., 2000. Asst. prof. Koc U., Istanbul, Turkey, 2000—05, U. Pitts., 2005—08; assoc. prof. Boston Coll., Chestnut Hill, Mass., 2008—. Recipient Encouragement award, Turkish Acad. Sciences, 2004, Promotion award, Prof. Dr. Mustafa Parlar Found., 2005, Outstanding Faculty award, U. Pitts., 2006; Disting. Young scholar, Turkish Acad. Sciences, 2005, fellowship, Market Culture and Timing Transactions, NSF, 2004—, Summer Rsch. grant, U. Pitts., 2006, grant, Collaborative Rsch., Kidney Exch., NSF, 2006—08. Mem.: Soc. Econ. Design (pres. 2008). Avocation: reading. Office: Boston Coll Dept Economics 140 Commonwealth Ave Chestnut Hill MA 02467 Office Fax: 617-552-2308. Business E-Mail: unver@bc.edu.

UNWIN, STEPHEN FORMAN, advertising executive, educator; b. Higham, Leicestershire, Eng., Aug. 7, 1927; s. Philip Henry and Decima (Forman) Unwin; m. Pamela Susan Brett, June 6, 1953; children: Philip, Tessa, Sam. BA with honors, Oxford U., 1952, MA, 1968. Account exec. London Press Exch., 1951-66; dir. London Press Exch. Orgn. Ltd., 1966-67; assoc. dir. LPE Ltd., London, 1967-69; vis. lectr. U. Ill., Urbana, 1969-70, asst. prof., 1970-74; assoc. prof. U. Ala., Tuscaloosa, 1974-79, Wash. State U., Pullman, 1979-81, U. Oreg., Eugene, 1981-85; pres. Bus. Dynamics, Kingwood, Tex., 1985—. Cons. advt. Ill. Bell, Chgo., 1974—75, J. Walter Thompson, San Francisco, 1983; dir. Forest Industries Comm. Inst., Atlanta, 1975—76; publicist Brit. Tourist Authority, London, 1978—81; vis. prof. Am. Assn. Advt. Agys., Chgo., 1971, Am. Ad Fedn., San Francisco, 1983; instr. Lifelong Learning, Kingwood, 2005—. Author: How Nations Grow Rich, 1992, The New American Dream - How to Make it Happen, 2009, Science Reveals God Letters to Ruby, 2009; co-author: The Future of Advertising, 2003; contbr. articles to profl. jours. Mem. Nat. Com. Advt. Edn., NYC, 1983—84; bicentennial judge Advt. Age mag., Chgo., 1976; mem. Future Journalism Edn., Eugene, Oreg., 1982—84, Internat. Advt. Edn. Com., Chgo., 1982, Wheelwright Mus., Santa Fe, 1998, Worcester Coll., Oxford U. 2d lt. Brit. Army, 1946—48. Libr. fellow, Mass. Hist. Soc., 1990—95. Mem.: Am. Acad. Advt., Brotherhood St. Andrew (HS decision com, mem. 2005—07). Episcopalian. Avocations: travel, genealogy. Office Phone: 281-360-0393. Personal E-mail: sjfunwin@aol.com.

UPADHIAYA, UMESH CHANDRA, engineer, consultant; b. Dabha, India, July 11, 1927; arrived in US, 1977; s. Bhagwati Prashad and Shri Devi Upadhiaya; m. Susila Devi, Nov. 7, 1954; children: Anita, Amit. Diploma in Elec. and Mech. Engring., Tech. Coll., Dayalbagh, India, 1948; MSME, Fla. Internat. U., 1991. Registered profl. engr., Fla. Asst. engr. Hindusthan Sugar, Gola, India, 1954—60; mech. engr. Bagpat Sugar, India, 1960—61; erection engr. Dhampur Sugar, India, 1961—62; cons. Mehta Group, Uganda, 1962—73; project mgr. KCP Ltd., Madras, India, 1973—74; design engr. Joint Sugar Project Unit, Surabaya, Indonesia, 1974—77; cons. engr. Tate & Lyle Enterprises Inc., Miami, Fla., 1977—85, ATV Projects, Bombay, 1990—93; ind. cons. Davie, Fla., 1993—. Contbr. articles to profl. jours. Home and Office: 6510 Sedgewyck Cir W Davie FL 33331-3455 Office Phone: 954-434-5265. Personal E-mail: ravay2k@bellsouth.net.

UPADHYA, GIRISH, thermal mechanical engineer; s. Prafulla Upadhya; m. Manjula Raghavendra, Aug. 10, 1990; children: Gautam R., Vijay K. BTech in Materials Eng., Indian Inst. Tech., Kanpur, 1977—82; MTech in Materials Eng., Indian Inst. Tech., Chennai, 1986; PhD in Materials Eng., U. Ala., Tuscaloosa, 1991. Sr. modeling engr. Concurrent Techs. Corp, Johnstown, Pa., 1991—95; mgr., modeling and simulation Johnson Matthey Electronics, Spokane, Wash., 1995—98; sr. engr., thermal mgmt. Apple Computer, Cupertino, Calif., 1998—2002; dir., applications engring. Emerson Electric, Austin, Tex., 2002—. Contbr. scientific papers. Mem.: ASME, TMS, IMAPS. Liberal. Achievements include patents for thermal design of cooling systems for computers; patents pending for thermal design of microchannel cooling. Home: 9509 Tobrina Ln Austin TX 78759 Office: Emerson Electric 1421 Wells Branch Pky Ste 105 Pflugerville TX 78660 Office Phone: 512-964-2478. Personal E-mail: girish.upadhya@gmail.com. Business E-Mail: girish.upadhya@emerson.com.

UPADHYA, HIRAN S., environmental engineer; d. Sureshchandra J. and Ansuya S. Upadhya. MS in Computer Sci, NJ. Inst. Tech., Newark; MS in Enviorn. Engring., Drexel U., Phila.; MCE, SVREC, Surat, India, 2002. Ops. rsch. analyst Compliance Innovations Inc., Lake Hopatcong, NJ, 2003—. Contbr. scientific papers. Vol. Helpage India, Surat, 1985—85. Felloeship, Dupont, 1999—2000. Mem.: AWWA, All India Assn. Civil Engrs., X Ray Absorption Internat. Soc. Avocations: tennis, painting, reading, stamp collecting/philately. Office: Compliance Innovations Inc 706 Route 15 S Lake Hopatcong NJ 07849 Personal E-mail: hiranupadhya@yahoo.com.

UPADHYA, YOGENDRA NATH, physician, educator; b. Gorakhpur, India, Dec. 21, 1938; arrived in U.S., 1963; s. Murlidhar and Vansraji (Pande) U.; m. Cecile R. Yonish; children: Asha, Sameer, Sanjay. MB, BS, All India Inst. Med. Scis., New Delhi, 1962. Diplomate Am. Bd. Psychiatry and Neurology, Am. Bd. Psychiatry and Child and Adolescent Psychiatry. Instr. in pediatrics Johns Hopkins U. Sch. Medicine, Balt., 1969-71; fellow in child psychiatry Johns Hopkins Hosp./Johns Hopkins U., Balt., 1971-72; resident, then sr. resident in psychiatry Albert Einstein Coll. Medicine/Bronx Mcpl. Hosp. Ctr., 1972-74, fellow in child psychiatry, 1974-75; chief, partial hosp. program for children, dept. psychiatry Brookdale Hosp., Bklyn., 1976-77; med. dir. West Nassau Mental Health Ctr., Franklin Sq., NY, 1977-80; asst. prof. clin. psychiatry SUNY, Stony Brook, 1978-92; dir. child and adolescent psychiatry Nassau County Med. Ctr., East Meadow, NY, 1980-92; sr. psychiatrist South Oaks Hosp., Amityville, NY, 1992—, pres. med. staff, 1995-97, svc. med. dir. child and adolescent psychiatry, 1995-97, med. dir., 1997—; sr. v.p., Medical Affairs South Oak Hosp. and Broadlawn Nursing Home, 2001—. Sr. v.p. med. affairs LI Home, Amityville, NY, 2001—. Fellow Am. Psychiat. Assn. (cons. task force treatments psychiat. disorders 1989—), Am. Acad. Child and Adolescent Psychiatry, Allmsonians of Am. (founding pres. 1982-86), Disting. Life, Am. Psychiat. Assn., Am. Acad. Child and Adolescent Psychiatry. Office: S Oaks Hosp 400 Sunrise Hwy Amityville NY 11701-2508 Office Phone: 631-608-5227. Business E-Mail: yupadhyay@south-oaks.org.

UPADHYAYA, PRASHANT KUDIGRAM, surgeon; b. Udipi, Karnataka, India, Jan. 27, 1978; s. Vadiraja Kudigram and Sukanya Upadhyaya; m. Abha Harish, Apr. 18, 2006; 1 child, Prashant. MBBS, Mysore Med. Coll., 2001; CM, India Inst. Med. Scis., New Delhi, 2004; MD, ECFMG, 2005. Resident, gen. surgery Creighton U., Omaha, 2005—. Contbr. scientific papers. Office: Creighton Univ 601 N 30th st Omaha NE 68131 Personal E-mail: kpupadhyaya@gmail.com.

UPATNIEKS, JURIS, retired optical engineer; b. Riga, Latvia, May 7, 1936; arrived in U.S., 1951; s. Karlis and Eleonora (Jegers) Upatnieks; m. Ilze Induss, July 13, 1968; children: Ivars, Ansis. BSEE, U. Akron, Ohio, 1960; MSEE, U. Mich., 1965. Rsch. asst., then rsch. assoc. Willow Run Labs. U. Mich., Ann Arbor, 1960-69; rsch. engr. Inst. Sci. and Tech., U. Mich., Ann Arbor, 1969-72, Environ. Rsch. Inst. Mich., Ann Arbor, 1973-93; sr. engr. Applied Optics, Ann Arbor, 1993—2001; ret., 2001. Lectr. elec. engring. dept. U. Mich., 1971—73, adj. assoc. prof. elec. engring. and computer sci. dept., 1974—2001, adj. rsch. scientist dept. mech. engring. and applied mechanics, 1996—2001. Contbr. articles to profl. jours. 2d lt. US Army, 1961—62. Recipient Holley medal, ASME, 1976, Inventor of the Yr. award, Assn. Advancement Invention and Innovation, 1976. Fellow: Latvian Acad. Sci. (Grand medal 1999, Walter Zapp prize 2007), Acad. Soc. Austrums, Soc. Photographic Instrumentation Engrs. (Robert Gordon award 1965), Optical Soc. Am. (R. W. Wood prize 1975), Am. Latvian Assn. Achievements include patents in field. Avocations: camping, gardening, hiking. Personal E-mail: upatnks@netrek.net, juris@upatnieks.com.

UPBIN, HAL J., consumer products company executive; b. Bronx, NY, Jan. 15, 1939; s. David and Evelyn (Sloan) U.; m. Shari Kiesler, May 29, 1960; children: Edward, Elyse, Danielle. BBA, Pace Coll., 1961. CPA, NY. Tax sr. Peat, Marwick, Mitchell & Co., NYC, 1961-65; tax mgr. Price Waterhouse & Co., NYC, 1965-71; dir. taxes Wheelabrator-Frye Inc., NYC, 1971-72, treas., 1972-74; pres. Wheelabrator Fin. Corp., NYC, 1974-75; v.p., chief fin. officer Chase Manhattan Mortgage and Realty Trust (became Triton Group Ltd. 1980), NYC, 1975-76, pres., 1976-78, pres., chmn., 1978-83, also dir.; chmn., pres., dir. Isomedics, 1983-85; chmn., pres. Fifth Ave. Cards, Inc., Fifth Retail Corp., Ashley's Stores, Ashley's Outlet Stores, 1984-88; bd. dirs. Stacy Industries, 1984-88; vice chmn. Am. Recreation Products, St. Louis, 1985-88, vice chmn., pres., 1988—, chmn., 1992—; v.p. corp. devel., chmn. acquistion com. Kellwood Co., Chesterfield, Mo., 1990—, exec. v.p. corp. devel., chmn. acquisition com., 1992—, pres., COO, 1994—, pres., COO, dir., 1995-97, pres., CEO, 1997—2005, chmn., 1999—2006, chmn. emeritus, 2006—, past mem. Bd. dirs. First Banks, Inc., Regional Bus. Coun., Coun. Nat. Trustees, Nat. Jewish Med. and Rsch. Ctr., Nat. Coun. Wash. U. Olin Sch. Bus.; bd. mem. Brown Shoe; trustee Pace U. Past pres. Jewish Temple. Mem. AICPA, NY State Soc. CPA's, Franklin Jaycees (v.p.). Home: 3740 S Ocean Blvd Apt 801 Highland Beach FL 33487-3403 Home Phone: 561-276-4101.

UPBIN, SHARI, theater producer, director; m. Hal J. Upbin; children: Edward, Elyse, Danielle. Master tap instr. Talent mgr. Goldstar Talent Mgmt., Inc., NYC, 1989-91; theatre prodr., dir. Faculty Nat. Shakespeare Conservatory, N.Y. Asst. dir.: (plays, 1st Black-Hispanic Shakespeare prodn.) Julius Caesar, 1979; dir.(choreographer): (plays) Matter of Opinion, 1980, Side by Side, 1981; prodr.(dir.): Vincent, The Passions of Van Gogh, 1981,: (Broadway plays) Bojangles, The Life of Bill Robinson, 1984; dir.: Captain America, 1996; dir., choreographer (plays) Fiddler of the Roof, Cabaret, Life with Father, Roar of the Grease Paint, 1979—82; dir.: (plays) Feminist Movements, 1997, Danny Kaye and Sylvia, 2005; co-prodr.: One Mo' Time; prodr., dir.: Flypaper, 1991—92; Women on Their Own, Things My Mother Never Told Me; How Could Cupid Be So Stupid!, 1999; Timeless Divas, 2003, 2005; prodr., dir. (plays) Divas in Divaland, 2007; prodr.: (plays) Vintage 2001, Timeless Divas! Salute to Women in Cabaret, Broadway Over 40, Timeless Divas! Musical Stars of The Silver Screen, 2004, Dames in Divaland, 2007, Timeless Divas, Broadway Divas at Crest Theatre, 2008. Founder Queens Playhouse, N.Y., Children's Theatre, Flushing, N.Y.; mem. Willy Mays' Found. Drug Abused Children. Recipient Jaycees Svc. award Jr. Miss Pageants Franklin Twp., N.J., 1976. Mem. League Profl. Theatre Women (past pres.), Soc. Stage Dirs. and Choreographers, Coalition of Women in Arts & Media (bd. dirs.), Actors Equity Assn., Villagers Barn Theatre (1st woman pres.), N.Y. Womens Agenda (bd. dirs.). Personal E-mail: shariupbin@aol.com.

UPCHURCH, LESLIE PURCELL, music educator; b. Pitts., Sept. 22, 1953; d. John (Jack) Edward and Jeanne Jolliffe Purcell; 1 child, Alicia Nicole. BFA, Carnegie Mellon U., 1976; MusM, U. Wis., Madison, 1980. Elem. cert. in Dalcroze Eurhythmics Carnegie-Mellon U./Jaques-Dalcroze Inst., 1976, cert. in Dalcroze Eurhythmics Ithaca Coll./Jaques-Dalcroze Inst., 1981, lic. Carnegie-Mellon U./Jaques-Dalcroze Inst., 1982. Tchr. Muskingum Coll., New Concord, Ohio, 1981—83, Horace Mann Sch. Nursery Years, NYC, 1989—92, Sonatina Sch. Music and Sonatina Internat. Piano Camp, Bennington, Vt., 1992—97, Maple St. Sch., 1998—2005, music dept. dir., 1998—2005; tchr. Carnegie Mellon U., Pittsburgh, Pa., 2003—, Marta Sanchez Dalcroze Tng. Ctr., Mustard Seed Sch., Hoboken, NJ, 2005—06, dir. chorus, 2005—06; vocal accompanist Muskingum Coll., Ohio; tchr. trainer Westchester Conservatory Music, White Plains, NY, 1987—89; organist and choir dir. St. James Episcopal Ch., Arlington, Vt., 1994—99; dir. dalcroze eurhythmics program Thurnauer Sch. Music, Tenafly, NJ, 2004—; dalcroze specialist Lucy Moses Sch. Music, NYC, 2005—, Mini Masters, NYC, 2006—08; dalcroze eurhythmics tchr. Greater Hartford Arts Acad., 2008—09. Adv. bd. mem. Manchester Music Festival, Manchester, Vt., 1998—2001; bd. dirs. Vt. MIDI Project, Essex Junction, 2003—08, sec., 2003—05. Prodr., host (TV series) Music and The Young Child, 1994—96, asst. music dir., musician Arlington Lions Variety Shows, 1999—2005; musician, choir master children's chorus: opera Hansel and Gretel with Opera Theater of Weston, 2001, Help! Help! The Globolinks!, 2003; musician, music dir. Dorset Players holiday prodns., 2002, 2004; composer: Dance Recital, Lucy Moses Sch., Merken Concert Hall, 2008. Vol. Manchester Sch. Fund, 1999—2000; bd. dirs. GNAT-TV, Manchester, Vt., 1994—96. Grantee, Mockingbird Found., 2005. Mem.: FCW Soc., Dalcroze Soc. Am. (treas. tri-state chpt. 1983—85, treas. nat. assn. 1984—88, bd. dirs., treas. 2006—08, tri-state Chpt., Elsa Findlay scholar 1991). Achievements include invention of double adjusting piano seat that adjusts for seat and feet, In the Mode, circle of fifths with a twist music theory tool; founder, Music in the Moment, music improvisation ensemble, 2008. Avocations: cross country skiing, hiking, gardening, travel, yoga. Office Phone: 802-558-6469. Personal E-mail: upchurch_leslie@yahoo.com.

UPDEGRAFF, DAVID, music educator; b. Louisville, July 25, 1950; s. Norman and Patricia Updegraff; children: Paul, Christiana. MusB, U. Louisville, 1972; MusM, U. Mich., Ann Arbor, 1978. Assoc. prof. violin Western Mich. U., Kalamazoo, 1983—87; chmn., violin dept. Cleve. Inst. Music, 1988—. Petty officer 2nd class USN, 1968—70, Washington. Recipient Tchr. Recognition award, US Dept. Edn., 0200. Avocations: golf, tennis, travel, winemaking. Office: Cleve Inst Music 11021 East Blvd Cleveland OH 44106 Business E-Mail: duamati@sbcglobal.net.

UPDIKE, HELEN HILL, wealth manager; b. NYC, Mar. 27, 1941; d. Benjamin Harvey and Helen (Gray) Hill; m. Charles Bruce Updike, Sept. 7, 1963 (div. 1989); m. Asa Rountree, Oct. 10, 1998. BA, Hood Coll., 1962; PhD, SUNY, Stony Brook, 1978; postgrad., Harvard U., 1986. Lectr. SUNY, Stony Brook, 1969-75; asst. prof. U. Mass., Boston, 1975-77, Hofstra U., Hempstead, NY, 1978-85, assoc. prof., 1985-90, chmn. dept. econs. and geography, 1981-84, assoc. dean Hofstra Coll., 1984-87; pres. Interfid Capital Corp., 1987—2001; prin. Bridgewater Advisors, NYC, 2001—. Cons. econ. policy, 1973—; vis. asst. prof. SUNY, Stony Brook, 1977—78; commentator WNYC Radio, 1997—; bd. dirs. Faberge, McCrory Corp. Author: (book) The National Banks and American Economic Development, 1870-1900, 1985. Trustee Madeira Sch., Greenway, Va., 1984—88, Literacy, Inc., 1998—2001; mem. nat. adv. bd. Outward Bound, 1986—92; trustee, v.p. L.I. Forum Tech., 1979—85; trustee NY Outward Bound, 1988—97. Mem.: AAAS. Office: Bridgewater Advisors 489 Fifth Ave New York NY 10017

UPENIEKS, VALDA V., nursing educator; d. Kazimirs and Aina Upenieks; children: Laura Aina, Lasma Kristina. BSN, Seattle U., 1980; MPH, San Diego State U., 1989; PhD, U. Wash., Seattle, 2002. RN Wash., 1980. Asst. prof. UCLA Sch. Nursing, LA, 2003—. Cons. Upenieks Health Svcs. Consulting, Seattle, 2006—. Author: (novel) Percy; contbr. articles. Recipient UCLA Faculty Diversity award, 2006; Vitality Instrument grant, Robert Woods Johnson Found., 2006—08. Mem.: ANA, U. Wash. Alumni. Business E-Mail: vupeniek@ucla.edu.

UPHAM, STEADMAN, academic administrator, anthropologist, educator; b. Denver, Apr. 4, 1949; s. Albert Tyler and Jane Catherine (Steadman) U; m. Margaret Anne Cooper, Aug. 21, 1971; children: Erin Cooper, Nathan Steadman. BA in English Lit and Spanish, U. Redlands, Calif., 1971; MA in Anthropology, Ariz. State U., 1977, PhD in Anthropology, 1980. Dist. sales mgr. Ind. News Co. Inc., Los Angeles, 1971-72; regional sales mgr. Petersen Pub. Co, Los Angeles, 1972-74; archeologist, researcher Bur. Land Mgmt., Phoenix, 1979; research asst. Ariz. State U., Tempe, 1979-80; chief archeologist Soil Sytems Inc., Phoenix, 1980-81, N.Mex. State U., Las Cruces, N.Mex., 1981-85, asst. prof. to assoc. prof., 1982-87, assoc. dean, 1987-90; prof. anthropology, vice provost for rsch., grad. dean U. Oreg., Eugene, 1990—98; pres. Claremont Graduate Univ., Calif., 1998—2004, U. Tulsa, Okla., 2004—. Interim dir. Cultural Resources Mgmt. divsn. N.Mex. State U., Las Cruces, 1988; mem. exec. com. Assn. Grad. Schs., 1994—2004; bd. dirs. Coun. Grad. Schs., 1995—2004. Author: Polities and Power, 1982, A Hopi Social History, 1992; editor: Computer Graphics in Archaeology, 1979, Mogollon Variability, 1986, The Sociopolitical Structure of Prehistoric Southwest Societies, 1989, The Evolution of Political Systems, 1990; also articles. Advanced seminar grantee Sch. of Am. Rsch., 1987, research grantee NSF, 1979, 1984-85, Hist. Preservation grantee State of N.Mex., 1982-84, 1991, 92, Ford Found. 1991-92, U.S. Dept. Edn. 1991-93. Fellow Am. Anthropol. Assn.; mem. Nat. Phys. Sci. Consortium (pres. 1992-95), We. Assn. Grad. Schs (pres. 1994-95), Assn. Grad. Schs. (exec. com. 1995—), Coun. Grad. Schs. (bd. dirs. 1995—). Office: Off of Pres Univ of Tulsa 600 S College Ave Tulsa OK 74104 Office Phone: 918-631-2305. E-mail: steadman-upham@utulsa.edu.*

UPP, JANEANNE A., museum administrator; V.p. fin., CFO Mus. Sci. and Industry, Chgo.; assoc. dir., COO Mus. Contemporary Art Chgo.; exec. dir. Tacoma Art Mus., 1999—2004; pres. High Desert Mus, Bend, Oreg., 2008—. Office: High Desert Mus 59800 S Hwy 97 Bend OR 97702 Office Phone: 541-382-4754.

UPRIGHT, DIANE WARNER, art dealer; b. Cleve. d. Rodney Upright and Shirley (Warner) Lavine. Student, Wellesley Coll., 1965-67; BA, U. Pitts., 1969; MA, U. Mich., 1973, PhD, 1976. Asst. prof. U. Va., Charlottesville, 1976-78; assoc. prof. Harvard U., Cambridge, Mass., 1978-83; sr. curator Ft. Worth Art Mus., 1984-86; dir. Jan Krugier Gallery, NYC, 1986-90; sr. v.p., head contemporary art dept. Christie's, NYC, 1990-95; pres. Diane Upright Fine Arts, NYC, 1995—. Author: Morris Louis: The Complete Paintings, 1979, Ellsworth Kelly: Works on Paper, 1987, various exhbn. catalogues; contbr. articles to art jours. Mem.: Art Table, Inc. Office: Diane Upright Fine Arts 188 E 76th St New York NY 10021-2826

UPSHAW, ANTHONY N., lawyer; b. Washington, July 3, 1960; BS, US Coast Guard Acad., 1982; JD, Univ. Miami, 1990. Bar: Fla. 1990, US Dist. Ct. (so., mid. dists.) Fla. 1991, US Dist. Ct. (ea. dist.) Wis., US Ct. Appeals, 11th cir. Ptnr., admiralty, maritime law, products liability def., litig. Adorno & Yoss, Miami, Fla. Former bd. dirs. Univ. Miami Sch. Law Alumni Assn. Lt. USCG, 1982—87. Mem.: Fla. Bar Assn., Dade County Bar Assn. (pres., young lawyers sect. 1995—96), ABA (bd. govs. 2006—09). Office: Adorno & Yoss Ste 400 2525 Ponce de Leon Blvd Miami FL 33134 Office Phone: 305-460-1052. Office Fax: 305-460-1422. Business E-Mail: anu@adorno.com.

UPSHAW, DAWN, soprano; b. Nashville, Tenn., July 17, 1960; married; 2 children. BA, Ill. Wesleyan Univ., 1982; MA, Manhattan Sch. Music, 1984; studied with Jan DeGaetani at Aspen, Colo., Music Sch.; PhD (hon.), Yale U., Manhattan Sch. Music, Allegheny Coll., Ill. Wesleyan U. Artist Sony Classical, NYC; Kellogg prof. arts Bard Coll., Annandale-on-Hudson, NY, 2005—; artistic dir. vocal arts grad. program Bard Coll. Conservatory of Music; artistic ptnr. St. Paul Chamber Orch., Minn., 2007—. Mem. vocal studies faculty Tanglewood Music Ctr. Recitalist, opera singer; sang in 1983 premiere performance, Sancta Susanna (Hindemith); with Met. Opera, 1985—; other appearances include Salzburg Festival, 1987, Aix-en-Provence, 1988-89; recordings include Ariadne auf. Naxos, Shubert's Mass in G, Knoxville Summer of 1915 (Grammy award, Best Classical Vocal Soloist Performance, 1989), The Girl With Orange Lips, 1991 (Grammy award, Best Classical Vocal Soloist), Goethe Lieder, 1994, I Wish It So, 1995, Leonard Bernstein's New York, 1996, The World So Wide, 1998, Dawn Upshaw Sings Vernon Duke, 1999 (BBC Mag. Record of Yr., NY Times Top Adult Recording of Yr.), Angels Hide Their Faces, 2001, Berg: Lyric Suite (Grammy award, Best Chamber Music Performance, 2003), Voices of Light, 2004, Golijov: Ayre, Berio: Folksongs, 2005 (Grammy award, Best Opera Performance, 2007). Winner Young Concert Artist auditions; co-winner, Naumburg Competition, NYC, 1985; MacArthur fellow, 2007. Fellow: Am. Acad. Arts & Scis. Office: c/o Alec C Treuhaft IMG Artists Carnegie Hall Tower 152 W 57th St 5th Fl New York NY 10019 also: Bard Coll Conservatory Music 30 Campus Rd Annandale On Hudson NY 12504-5000 Office Phone: 212-994-3500. Office Fax: 212-994-3550. E-mail: atreuhaft@imgartists.com.

UPSHAW, HARRY STEPHAN, psychologist, educator; b. Birmingham, Ala., July 10, 1926; s. N.H. and Florence (Arnold) U.; m. Paula Binyon, June 18, 1950; children: Alan Binyon, Phyllis, David Arnold, Stephan Lipner. Student, U. Ala., 1946-47; AB, U. Chgo., 1949; MA, Northwestern U., 1951; PhD, U. N.C., 1956. Asst prof. psychology U. Ala., 1954-57; spl. instr. psychology Simmons Coll., Boston, 1957-58; research asso. Ednl. Research Corp., Cambridge, Mass., 1957-58; asst. prof., then assoc. prof. pub. health U. N.C., 1958-61, lectr., assoc. prof. psychology, 1958-64, rsch. prof. psychology, 1991-97; assoc. prof. Bryn Mawr (Pa.) Coll., 1964-65; assoc. prof., then prof. emeritus psychology U. Ill., Chgo., 1965-91, prof. emeritus, 1991—, dept. head, 1968-72; assoc. dir. Office of Social Sci. Rsch., 1981-87. Guest prof. U. Mannheim, Germany, 1975, Fulbright scholar Technische U., Berlin, 1978-79; vis. scholar Inst. for Rsch. in Social Sci., U. NC, 1991-92; del. to South Africa, People to People Amb. Program, 2004. Editorial cons., Jour. Exptl. Social Psychology, Research in Personality, Jour. Applied Social Psychology, Jour. Personality Social Psychology; Contbr. articles to profl. jours. Served with AUS, 1944-46. Fellow Am. Psychol. Assn., Soc. Exptl. Social Psychol. Office Phone: 312-819-0408.

UPSON, DONALD V., retired corporate financial executive; b. Hutchinson, Kans., Feb. 8, 1934; s. William Ernest and Luella Beatrice (Hutchison) U.; m. Janis Carol Anderson, Sept. 16, 1956; children: Mark Steven, Brent William. BS, Kans. State U., 1956. C.P.A. With Peat, Marwick, Mitchell & Co., 1956, 60-81, ptnr., 1974-81; exec. v.p., dir. internal audit Del E. Webb Corp., Phoenix, 1981-85; mgr. info. systems Tiernay Turbines Inc., Phoenix, 1986; chief fin. officer Schomac Corp., Tucson, 1986-88; adminstr. U. Ariz., Tucson, 1988-90; pres., chief exec. officer Ariz. Commerce Bank, Tucson, 1990-91; chief fin. officer O'Connor, Cavanagh, Anderson, Westover, Killingsworth & Beshears, P.A., Phoenix, 1991-94; fin. cons., 1995-97; ret., 1997. Pres. Community Orgn. for Drug Abuse, Alcohol and Mental Health Services, Inc., 1977-78; bd. dis. Phoenix council Boy Scouts Am., elder Presbyterian Ch. Served to lt. USAF, 1956-59. Mem. Am. Inst. C.P.A.s, Ariz. Soc. C.P.A.s, Beta Theta Pi (pres. 1955-56) Republican. Home and Office: 1313 E Sheena Dr Phoenix AZ 85022-4485 Personal E-mail: dupson2@cox.net.

UPSON, THOMAS FISHER, judge, retired state senator, lawyer; b. Waterbury, Conn., Sept. 30, 1941; s. J. Warren and Grace (Fisher) U.; m. Barbara Secor (div. Jan. 1979); children: Secor, Chauncey Julius; m. Katherine Wolff, June 1, 1996. BA in History, Washington and Jefferson Coll., 1963; LLB, U. Conn., 1968; postgrad., Trinity Coll., 1969—72, Georgetown U., 1971—72. Bar: Conn., 1969, U.S. Dist. Ct. (2d dist.) 1969, U.S. Supreme Ct. 1973. Lawyer Upson & Secor, Waterbury, 1969—70, 1974—76; lawyer, spl. asst. U.S. Dept. Commerce, Washington, 1970—72; lawyer, spl. asst. to adminstr. GSA, Washington, 1973—74; dir. admissions St. Margaret's McTernan Sch., Waterbury, 1977—78; with divsn. spl. revenue State of Conn., Hartford, 1978—82; assoc. Moynahan & Ruskin, Waterbury, 1979—81; ptnr. Upson & Daly, Waterbury, 1981—2001; mem. Conn. Senate, Hartford, 1985—2001, chmn. gen. law com., vice-chmn. jud. com., majority whip, 1985—86, asst. minority leader, 1987-88, 89-90, minority leader protempore, 1991-92, dep. minority leader, 1993-94, dep. majority leader, chmn. jud. com., 1995-96, dep., then asst. minority leader, ranking mem. jud. com., 1997-2000; judge Superior Ct. State of Conn., Hartford, 2001—. Moderator 1st Congl. Ch., Waterbury, 1986-91; bd. dirs. Easter Seals-United Way, Waterbury, 1984-88; Rep. candidate for Congress, 6th Dist. Conn., 1976; mem. Conn. Rep. Ctrl. com., 1983-91; mem. Waterbury Rep. Town Com., 1980-85; dir. Mattatuck Mus., 1993-2003; former dir. Waterbury Symphony Orch.; former sec. and dir. First Ch. Housing, Inc.; pres. Naugatuck Valley Devel. Corp., 1975-76. Mem. ABA, Conn. Bar Assn., Waterbury Bar Assn., SAR, Soc. Colonial Wars, Soc. of the Founders of the Hartford, Phi Gamma Delta, Univ. Club (Waterbury). Lodges: Kiwanis (former pres., lt. gov. SW New Eng. dist.), Elks. Republican. Congregationalist. Avocations: hiking, music, history. Home: 210 Southwest Rd Waterbury CT 06708-3214 Office: Waterbury Jud Dist 7 Kendrick Ave Waterbury CT 06702

UPTON, ARTHUR CANFIELD, experimental pathologist, educator; b. Ann Arbor, Mich., Feb. 27, 1923; s. Herbert Hawkes and Ellen (Canfield) Upton; m. Elizabeth Bache Perry, Mar. 1, 1946; children: Rebecca A., Melissa P., Bradley C. Grad., Phillips Acad., Andover, Mass., 1941; BA, U. Mich., 1944, MD, 1946. Intern Univ. Hosp., Ann Arbor, 1947, resident, 1948—49; instr. pathology U. Mich. Med. Sch., 1950—51; pathologist Oak Ridge (Tenn.) Nat. Lab., 1951—54, chief pathology-physiology sect., 1954—69; prof. pathology SUNY Med. Sch. at Stony Brook, 1969—77, chmn. dept. pathology, 1969—70, dean Sch. Basic Health Scis., 1970—75; dir. Nat. Cancer Inst., Bethesda, Md., 1977—79; prof., chmn. dept. environ. medicine NYU Med. Sch., NYC, 1980—92, prof. emeritus, 1993—; clin. prof. radiology U. N.Mex. Sch. Medicine, 1993—95, clin. prof., pathology, 1992—95; clin. prof. environ. and cmty. medicine U. Medicine and Dentistry N.J.-Robert Wood Johnson Med. Sch., 1995—. Attending pathologist Brookhaven Nat. Lab., 1969—77; dir. Inst. Environ. Medicine, Med. Sch., NYU, 1980—92; mem. various coms. nat. and internat. orgns.; lectr. in field; mem. adv. bd. GM Cancer Rsch. Found. Assoc. editor Cancer Rsch., mem. editl. bd. Internat. Union Against Cancer. With US Army, 1943—46. Recipient Ernest Orlando Lawrence award for atomic field, 1965, Claude M. Fuess award, 1980, Sarah L. Poilley award for pub. health, 1983, CHUMS Physician of Yr. award, 1985, Basic Cell Rsch. in Cytology Lectureship award, 1985, Fred W. Stewart award, 1986, Ramazzini award, 1986, Lovelace Med. Found. award, 1993; named nat. lectr., Sigma Xi, 1989—91. Fellow: N.Y. Acad. Sci., Soc. Risk Analysis (Outstanding Achievement award 1997); mem.: AAAS, Ramazzini Inst. (pres. 1992—2003), Assn. Univ. Environ. Health Sci. Ctrs. (pres. 1982—90), Internat. Assn. Radiation Rsch., N.Y. State Health Rsch. Coun. (chmn. 1982—90), Soc. Exptl. Biology and Medicine, Sci. Rsch. Soc. Am., Gerontol. Soc., Peruvian Oncology Soc. (hon.), Japan Cancer Assn. (hon.), Am. Soc. Exptl. Pathology (pres. 1967—68), Am. Assn. Cancer Rsch. (pres. 1963—64), Internat. Assn. Radiation Rsch. (pres. 1983—87), Radiation Rsch. Soc. (councilor 1963—64, pres. 1965—66), Inst. Medicine of NAS (Comfort-Crookshank award 1979), Internat. Acad. Pathology, Am. Assn. Pathologists and Bacteriologists, Sigma Xi, Nu Sigma Nu, Alpha Omega Alpha, Phi Gamma Delta, Phi Beta Kappa. Achievements include research in on pathology of radiation injury and endocrine glands, on cancer, on carcinogenesis, on experimental leukemia on aging. Home: 250 E Alameda Apt 636 Santa Fe NM 87501 Office: 303 George St Ste 110 New Brunswick NJ 08901 Office Phone: 732-579-1092. Business E-Mail: acupton@cresp.org.

UPTON, BECKY J., secondary school educator; b. Rome, NY, Feb. 21, 1976; d. Raymond C. and Elizabeth R. Williams; m. Pat W. Upton, June 12, 1994; children: Braxton Blake, Paige McKenzie, Melody Grace. Paraprofl. Friona ISD, Tex., 2001—.

UPTON, B.J. (MELVIN EMANUEL UPTON), professional baseball player; b. Norfolk, Va., Aug. 21, 1984; d. Manny and Yvonne Upton. Shortstop Tampa Bay Rays (formerly Devil Rays), 2004—05, third baseman, 2006—07, second baseman, ctr. fielder, 2007—. Named #1 Prospect, Baseball Am., 2004. Achievements include being the youngest player in Major League Baseball in 2004. Mailing: c/o Tampa Bay Rays Tropicana Field One Tropicana Dr Saint Petersburg FL 33705

UPTON, CINDY MCDONOUGH, economics professor; d. James A. and Marjory Lee McDonough; m. John W. Upton, Mar. 7, 1998; children: Derry H. Cannon, Erin Cannon Osner. Assoc. Arts, North Harris County Coll., Houston, 1982; BS in Economics, Sam Houston State U., Huntsville, Tex., 1985; MBA, Sam Houston State U., 1987. Benefits specialist & adminstr. intern Fed. Res. Bank Dallas, Houston Br., 1988—90; prof. economics Lone Star Coll., Houston, 1990—. Grants coord. North Harris Coll., 2000—02. Contbr. articles to profl. pubs. Vol. United Way Tex. Gulf Coast, 1998—2002; active Victory Christian Ctr., Houston, 1994—2008, co-founder, 1995—97, originator and instr., 2000. Recipient Excellence award, NISOD, 1997, Award Excellence in Economics, Sam Houston State U. & The Wall St. Jour., 1985. Mem.: Golden Key Nat. Honor Soc., Alpha Chi Nat. Scholastic Soc., Phi Theta Kappa Nat. CC Honor Soc, Tex. CC Tchrs. Assn. Avocations: swimming, sewing. Home: 5714 Glen Allen Ln Houston TX 77069 Office: Lone Star Coll Willow Chase 9449 Grant Rd Houston TX 00070 Business E-Mail: cupton@lonestar.edu.

UPTON, FREDERICK STEPHEN, United States Representative from Michigan; b. St. Joseph, Mich., Apr. 23, 1953; s. Stephen E. and Elizabeth Brooks (Vial) Upton; m. Amey Richmond Rulon-Miller, Nov. 5, 1983; 2 children. BA in Journalism, U. Mich., 1975. Staff asst. to Congressman David A. Stockman, Washington, 1976-81; legis. asst. Office Mgmt. and Budget, Washington, 1981-83, dep. dir. legis. affairs, 1983-84, dir. legis. affairs, 1984-85; mem. US Congress from 6th Mich. dist., Washington, 1987—; mem. energy and commerce com. Field mgr. Stockman for Congress, St. Joseph, 1975; campaign mgr. Globensky for Congress, 1981. Recipient Spirit Enterprise award, US C. of C., 1988—93; named Legislator of Yr., Am. Ambulance Assn., 2000. Mem.: Emil Verban Soc. Republican. Congregationalist. Office: US House of Reps 2183 Rayburn House Office Bldg Washington DC 20515-2206 also: District Office 157 S Kalamazoo Mall Ste 180 Kalamazoo MI 49006 also: District Office Ste 106 800 Ship Street Saint Joseph MI 49085-2182 Office Phone: 202-225-3761, 269-385-0039, 269-982-1986. Office Fax: 269-982-0237, 202-225-4986.*

URABE, TOHSUKE, mathematics professor, researcher; b. Tokyo, Aug. 3, 1953; s. Syun-ichi and Mariko (Namikawa) U.; 1 child, Mika. BA, Kyoto U., Japan, 1978, MA, 1980, PhD in Math., 1984. Sci. worker Max-Planck Inst. for Math., Bonn, Germany, 1987-89, 98-99; assoc. prof. math. Tokyo Met. U., 1981-87, 89-98; prof. math. Ibaraki (Japan) U., 1999—. Author: (with Heisuke Hironaka) Introduction to Analytic Spaces, 1981; Dynkin Graphs and Quadrilateral Singularities, 1993. Avocations: mountain climbing, personal computers. Office: Ibaraki U Dept Math Scis Mito Ibaraki 310-8512 Japan

URAIZEE, JOYA, literature and language professor; d. Kalyan Saha and Elaine Shaw, Madhusri Saha (Stepmother); m. Farooq Uraizee; children: Aisha, Omar. PhD, Purdue U., West Lafayette, Ind., 1994. Asst. prof. St. Louis U., 1994—2001, assoc. prof., 2001—. Vis. fulbright prof. Nelson Mandela Met. U., Port Elizabeth, Eastern Cape, South Africa, 2008; fulbright prof. US Dept. State, 2008. Contbr. articles to profl. jours. Mem.: African Lit. Assn. Office: Saint Louis Univ Dept English 3800 Lindell Blvd Saint Louis MO 63108

URAM, GERALD ROBERT, lawyer; b. Newark, July 11, 1941; s. Arthur George and Mildred (Stein) U.; m. Melissa Gordon, May 27, 1995; children: Michael, Alison, Carolyn Gordon Lewis. BA, Dartmouth Coll., 1963; LLB, Yale U., 1967. Bar: NY 1967. Assoc. Paul, Weiss, Rifkind, Wharton & Garrison, NYC, 1967-74; v.p., corp. counsel Prudential Bldg. Maintenance Corp., NYC, 1974; ptnr. Davis & Gilbert, NYC, 1974—. Lectr. NY Law Sch. Contbr. to profl. publs. Bd. dirs. St. Francis Friends of Poor, Inc. Mem. ABA, NY State Bar Assn., Assn. Bar City of NY. Office: 1740 Broadway Fl 3 New York NY 10019-4315 Office Phone: 212-468-4815. Business E-Mail: guram@dglaw.com.

URAYAMA, SHIRO, internist; b. Tottori, Japan, Dec. 23, 1963; s. Takashi and Reiko (Fujiwara) U.; m. Mikako Mori, June 17, 1995. MD, Med. Coll. Wis., 1992; BS with hons., U. Wash., 1988. Diplomate Am. Bd. Internal Medicine. Intern Virginia Mason Med. Ctr., Seattle, 1992-93, resident in internal medicine, 1993-95; fellow in gastrointestinal medicine U. Chgo., 1995—. Contbr. articles to profl. jours. Mem. AAAS, ACP, AMA, Am. Gastroent. Assn., Am. Soc. Gastronintestinal Endoscopy. Office: U Chgo 5841 S Maryland Ave Chicago IL 60637-1463

URAZGHILDIEV, ILDAR R., mathematician; b. Belushye, Arkhangelsk Reg., Russia, Sept. 22, 1967; s. Ravil I. Urazgildiyev and Iraida F. Urazgildiyeva; m. Tetiana V. Bruenko, Aug. 21, 2002; 1 child, Renat I. Urazgildiev. MS (hon.), Inst. Radioelectronics, Zhitomir, Ukraine, 1989; PhD, 1996. Rsch. assoc. Gen. Staff Rsch. Ctr. Armed Forces, Ukraine, 1989—94; scientist Gen. Stat. Rsch. Ctr. Armed Forces, Ukraine, 1994—97; leading scientist Nat. Rsch. Ctr. Def. Tech. and Mil. Security, Ukraine, 1997—2001; asst. prof. Nat. Tech. U. Ukraine, Kiev, 1999—2003; rsch. assoc. Cornell Lab Ornithology, Ithaca, NY, 2004—. Contbr. scientific papers to profl. jours. Recipient Young Scientist award Best Conf. Paper, MMET2000 Conf., 2000, Young Scientist award, URSI, 2002; fellow, Sensys Traffic AB, Sweden., 2001—02, Carl Trygger Found., Sweden, 2003—04, Uppsala U., Signals and Systems Group, Sweden, 2003—04. Mem.: IEEE. Home: 606 Winston CT apt 2 Ithaca NY 14850 Office: Cornell Lab of Ornithology BRP 159 Sapsucker Woods Rd Ithaca NY 14850 E-mail: iru2@cornell.edu.

URBACH, ADAM ROBERT, chemistry professor; s. Michael Urbach and Rose Marie Mauzy; m. Dana Michelle Norwood, June 11, 2000; 1 child, Sebastian River. BS in Chemistry, U. Tex., Austin, 1996; PhD in Chemistry, Calif. Inst. Tech., Pasadena, 2002. Postdoctoral rsch. fellow Harvard U., Cambridge, Mass., 2002—04. Faculty adviser Am. Chem. Soc. Student Affiliates, Trinity U., San Antonio, 2004—; asst. prof. chemistry Trinity U., San Antonio, San Antonio, 2004—. Contbr. articles to sci. jours. Recipient Dean's Honored Grad. award, Coll. Natural Sci., U. Tex., Austin, 1996, Nat. Rsch. Svc. award, NIH, 2003—04, Cottrell Coll. Sci. award, Rsch. Corp., 2006—08, Disting. Jr. Faculty award, Trinity U., 2007, NSF Career award, 2008; grad. fellowship, NSF, 1996—99. Mem.: Project Kaleidoscope, Coun. on Undergrad. Rsch., Am. Chem. Soc. (Outstanding Sr. award cen. Tex. divsn. 1996, student affiliate scholarship 1995), Phi Beta Kappa. Achievements include research in bioorganic chemistry and molecular recognition; artificial receptors and sensors for proteins. Avocations: snowboarding, skiing, rock climbing. Office: Trinity Univ Dept Chemistry One Trinity Pl San Antonio TX 78212 Business E-Mail: adam.urbach@trinity.edu.

URBAN, AMANDA (BINKY URBAN), literary agent; m. Ken Auletta, 1977; 1 child. BA in English, Wheaton Coll., Mass. Gen. mgr. N.Y. mag.; editl. mgr. Esquire mag.; literary agent Internat. Creative Mgmt., NYC, v.p., co-dir. lit. dept., 1988—2007, co-head, 1999—2008, exec. v.p., 2008—. Named one of The 100 Most Powerful Women in Entertainment, Hollywood Reporter, 2006, 2007. Office: Internat Creative Mgmt 825 8th Ave New York NY 10019 E-mail: aurban@icmtalent.com.

URBAN, GLEN L., management educator; b. Wausau, Wis., Apr. 15, 1940; BSME, U. Wis., 1963, MBA, 1964; PhD, Northwestern U., 1966. Asst. prof. MIT, Cambridge, Mass., 1966-70, assoc. prof., 1970-77, prof. mktg. and mgmt. sci., 1977—, Dai-Ichi Kangyo Bank prof. mgmt., 1987-93, dep. dean Sloan Sch. Mgmt., 1987-91, co-dir. Internat. Ctr. for Rsch. on Mgmt. of Tech., 1992-93, dean Sloan Sch. Mgmt., 1993-98, David Austin prof. mgmt., 1998—; co-dir. Ctr. for eBusiness@MIT. Co-founder Mgmt. Decision Systems, Inc., 1970, Mgmt. Sci. for Health, Inc., 1972, Mktg. Tech. Interface, Inc., 1991, InSite Mktg., 1997. Author: (with D.B. Montgomery) Management Science in Marketing, 1969, (with D.B. Montgomery) Applications of Management Science in Marketing, 1970, (with J.R. Hauser and N. Dholakia) Essentials of New Product Development, 1987, (with Steven H. Star) Advanced Marketing Stragety: Phenomena, Analysis and Decisions, 1991, Design and Marketing of New Products, 2d edit., 1993; mem. editl. bd. Mktg. Sci.; reviewer for Mgmt. Sci. (Best Paper award 1986), Jour. Mktg. Rsch. (O'Dell award 1983, 88), Ops. Rsch., Jour. Mktg. (Best Paper award 1996); contbr. over 30 articles to profl. jours. Recipient Best Paper award Jour. of Mktg., 1996. Mem. Inst. Mgmt. Sci., Ops. Rsch. Soc. Am., Am. Mktg. Assn. (Converse award for Lifetime Achievements in Mktg. 1996). Office: Sloan Sch Mgmt E56-332 50 Memorial Dr Cambridge MA 02142 E-mail: glurban@mit.edu.

URBAN, HENRY ZELLER, publishing executive; b. Buffalo, July 11, 1920; s. George Pennock and Florence Lenhard (Zeller) U.; m. Ruth deMoss Wickwire, Apr. 28, 1948; children: Ruth Robinson Urban Smith, Florence de Moss Urban Hunn, Henry Zeller, Ward Wickwire. Grad., Hotchkiss Sch., 1939; BS, Yale U., 1943. Treas. George Urban Milling Co., 1946-53; with Buffalo Eve. News, 1953—, asst. bus. mgr., 1957-62, bus. mgr., 1962-71, treas., dir., 1971-74, pres., pub., 1974-83. Bd. dirs. Travelers Aid Soc., 1953-59, Buffalo Fine Arts Acad., 1960-63, 73-76, 82-89, YMCA, 1955-68; trustee Elmwood-Franklin Sch., 1967-70; trustee Canisius Coll., 1977-83, bd. regents, 1972-78; adv. bd. Medaille Coll., 1968-83; chmn. parents council Hamilton Coll., 1977. Lt. USNR, 1942-46. Mem. Buffalo C. of C., N.Y. State Pubs. Assn. (dir. 1970-73, 76-79) Clubs: Mid-day (Buffalo), Tennis and Squash (Buffalo), Buffalo (Buffalo), Buffalo Country (Buffalo), Saturn (Buffalo), Pack (Buffalo); Sankaty Head (Nantucket); Nantucket Yacht. Home: 57 Tudor Pl Buffalo NY 14222-1615 Office: 1 News Plz Buffalo NY 14203-2930

URBAN, JEFF, food products executive; b. NJ; m. Kim Urban; children: Samantha, Nicole, Jeffrey, Kiley. B, James Madison U., 1985. Mktg. internship Chgo. White Sox, 1986; promotion mgr. Balt. Orioles, 1987; with Cato Johnson Sports Mktg., Chgo., 1988—91; dir., sports mktg. USA Today, 1991—98; v.p., sports and entertainment mktg. Frankel Promotion Agy., 1998; joined Gatorade/PepsiCo., Inc., 1999, dir., sports mktg., 2002—07, sr. v.p., sports mktg., 2007—. Named one of Most Influential People in the World of Sports, Bus. Week, 2008. Office: Gatorade PO Box 049003 Chicago IL 60604-9003

URBAN, KEITH, country singer, songwriter; b. New Zealand, Oct. 26, 1967; m. Nicole Kidman, June 25, 2006; 1 child, Sunday Rose. Former band mem. (with Peter Clarke) The Ranch, Nashville, 1997; signed record deal with Capital Nashville, 1997; signed mgmt. contract with I.R.S., Tenn., 1997. Singer: (albums) Keith Urban "1991", 1997, Ranch, 1997, Keith Urban, 1999, Golden Road, 2002, In the Ranch, 2004, Be Here, 2004 (Album of Yr., Acad. Country Music, 2005), Days Go By, 2005, Love, Pain & the Whole Crazy Thing, 2006, Defying Gravity, 2009, (songs) Raining on Sunday, 2003; singer, prodr.: songs Somebody Like You, 2003; singer Days Go By (Video of Yr., Country Music TV, 2005), You'll Think of Me (Grammy award for Best Male Country Vocal Performance, 2006), Stupid Boy (Grammy award for Best Male Country Vocal Performance, 2008), (with Brad Paisley) Start a Band (Vocal Event of Yr., Acad. Country Music, 2009). Recipient Grammy award nomination for best country instrumental performance for "Rollercoaster", ARIA award for outstanding achievement, Australian Record

Industry Assn., 2001, Horizon award, Country Music Assn., 2001, Video of Yr for Better Life, CMT award (Country Music TV), 2006; named Top New Male Vocalist, Acad. Country Music, 2001, 2005, Top Male Vocalist, 2006, Male Vocalist of Yr., Country Music Assn., 2004—06, Entertainer of Yr., 2005, Country Artist Yr., Radio Music Awards, 2005, Best-Selling Australian Artist, World Music Awards, 2007. Mailing: Capital Records 3322 W End Ave Nashville TN 37203 Office Phone: 615-269-2000.

URBAN, NICOLE D., biostatistician; b. Trenton, NJ, Aug. 16, 1946; d. James Ross Stewart and Patricia Bryant Urban; m. Lee Emery Edlefsen (div.); children: Kerstin Lara Edlefsen, Paul Thatcher Edlefsen. BA in English lit., Simmons Coll., 1970; MS in biostatistics, Harvard Sch. of Pub. Health, 1973, DSc, 1978. Prin. investigator, Specialized Program of Rsch. Excellence grant in ovarian cancer NIH/Nat. Cancer Inst., Seattle, 1999—; sci. dir. Marsha Rivkin Ctr. for Ovarian Cancer Rsch., Seattle, 1996—2005; mem., cancer prevention rsch. program, divsn. of pub. health sciences Fred Hutchinson Cancer Rsch. Ctr., Seattle, 1998—2005; rsch. prof., dept. of health services, sch. of pub. health and cmty. medicine U. of Wash., Seattle, 2000—; program head, gynecologic cancer rsch. program Fred Hutchinson Cancer Rsch. Ctr., Seattle, 2001—. Mem., p30/p50 working group Nat. Cancer Adv. Bd., 2002—; participant, strategic planning project meeting, applied cancer screening rsch. br. Nat. Cancer Inst., 2001—; mem., external adv. com., specialized program of rsch. excellence in breast cancer Vanderbilt U., 2001—; mem., med. adv. bd. Nat. Ovarian Cancer Coalition, 2001—; chair, external adv. com., specialized program of rsch. excellence in ovarian cancer U. of Tex., 2000—; co-chair, gynecologic cancers progress rev. group Nat. Cancer Inst., 2000—; mem., wash. state cancer registry adv. coun. Wash. State Dept. of Health, 1996—, mem., breast and cervical early detection exec. com., 1994—; mem. molecular diagnostic program, divsn pub. health scis. Fred Huthinson CRC, Seattle, 2006—. Contbr. articles to profl. jours. Grant, Nat. Institutes of Health/Nat. Cancer Inst., 1999—, US Dept. of Def., 2002—, Nat. Institutes of Health/Nat. Cancer Inst., 1997—2002, 1997—2002, US Dept. of Def./United States Army Med. Rsch. and Materiel Command (Ovarian Cancer Rsch. Program), 1998—2001. Mem.: Am. Assn. for Cancer Rsch., South West Oncology Group, Assn. for Health Services Rsch., Am. Soc. of Preventive Oncology, Soc. for Clin. Trials. Office: Fred Hutchinson Cancer Rsch Ctr PO Box 19024 Seattle WA 98109-1024*

URBAN, NINA B.L., psychiatrist, psychotherapist, researcher; b. Offenbach, Hessen, Germany, Oct. 10, 1975; arrived in U.S., 2003; d. Richard and Siegrun Urban. Attended, Free U. Berlin; MD, Humboldt U., Berlin, 2001; MS, U. Oxford, Eng., 2003. Cert. Ednl. Commn. Fgn. Med. Grads. Internship U. Rochester, NY, 2003—04; resident Mt. Sinai-Cabrini Med. Ctr., NYC, 2004—07, chief resident dept. psychiatry, 2006—07; rsch. fellow psychiatry Columbia U. Med. Ctr., NYC, 2007—. Fundraiser Leukemia and Lymphoma Soc., Frankfurt; local activist Worldwide Fund for Nature, Berlin, 1993—2002; healthcare vol. Missionaries Charity/Mother Teresa, Calcutta, India, 1994; fundraiser Leukemia and Lymphoma Soc., NYC, 2005. Recipient Young Investigation award, NARSAD, 2009—; fellow, McDonnell Inst. Neurosci., Oxford, Eng., 2002—03; grant, European Cmty. Action Scheme for Mobility U. Student Program, 1998. Mem.: Assn. Women Psychiatrists, Soc. Neurosci., Med. Soc. NY State, Am. Psychiat. Assn. (vice chair NY county dist. br. com. 2005—07, co-chair 2007—09), Oxford Alumni Soc. NY. Avocations: opera, equestrian, art, travel, participatory culture. Office: NY State Psychiat Inst 1051 Riverside Dr Unit 31 New York NY 10032 Office Phone: 212-543-6030. Business E-Mail: nu2118@columbia.edu.

URBANCIC, FRANK CHARLES, JR., United States Ambassador to Cyprus; b. Indpls. married; 2 children. BA in French Lit., NYU, NYC, 1974; MA in Byzantine History, City Coll. NY, 1978; MS in Nat. Security Strategy, Nat. Def. U., Washington, 1993. Joined US Fgn. Svc., 1983; with consular, polit. affairs sects. US Dept. State, Quebec City, Canada, Amman, Jordan, Tunis, Tunisia, Riyadh, Saudi Arabia, dep. chief of mission Abu Dhabi, United Arab Emirates, Freetown, Sierra Leone, Doha, Qatar, Ea. European, Mid. Ea. and African affairs, US Mission to the UN, 1990—91, 2004—05, dep. dir. office Egyptian affairs, 1995, consul gen. Istanbul, Turkey, 1999, dep. chief of mission Kuwait, 2002—04, prin. dep. asst. sec. and dep. to the coordinator, Office the Coordinator for Counterterrorism, 2005—08, US amb. to Cyprus, 2008—. Recipient Meritorious and Superior Honor awards, US Dept. State, Baker-Wilkins award, 2003, Presdl. Disting. Svc. award, The White House, 2006. Office: DOS Amb 5450 Nicosia Pl Washington DC 20521-5450

URBANELLI, LORA, museum director; b. Phila., 1956; married. BA magna cum laude, Rutgers U., 1980; MFA, Syracuse U., 1982. With dept. prints, drawings & photographs Yale U. Art Gallery; curator prints, drawings & photographs RI Sch. Design Mus., Providence, 1985—99, asst. dir., 1999—2005; dir. Farnsworth Art Mus. & Wyeth Ctr., Rockland, Maine, 2005—. Author: Lucien Pissarro: A Brief Account of the Work of Lucien Pissarro and the Eragny Press. Office: Farnsworth Art Mus & Wyeth Ctr 16 Museum St Rockland ME 04841 Office Phone: 207-596-6457. Office Fax: 207-596-0509. E-mail: lurbanelli@farnsworthmuseum.org.

URBANETTI, JOHN SUTHERLAND, internist, consultant; b. Mineola, NY, Aug. 14, 1943; s. Anthony Joseph and Mildred S. U.; children: Andrew, Alexis. AB, Johns Hopkins U., 1964, MD, 1967. Diplomate Am. Bd. Internal Medicine and Pulmonary Diseases. Internal medicine intern Johns Hopkins Hosp., Balt., 1967-68, internal medicine resident, 1968-69; fellow in pulmonary cardiology McGill U., Montreal, Can., 1971-74; asst. prof. medicine and dir. pulmonary lab. Tufts New Eng. Med. Ctr. Hosp., Boston, 1974-80; asst. prof. clin. medicine and pulmonary diseases Yale U., New Haven, Conn., 1980—. Cons. toxic inhalation US Surgeon Gen., U.S. Army, USN, USAF, 1974—; cons. biochem. terrorism Dept. of Def., Dept. Justice, 1974—, Dept. State, 1999—. Author: Carbon Monoxide Poisoning, 1980, Pulmonary Management of Surgical Patients, 1982, Battlefield Chemical Inhalation, 1988, Chemical and Biological Warfare, 1997; contbr. articles to profl. jours. Capt. USAF, 1969-71. Recipient Commdr's award for pub. svc. U.S. Army, 1990. Fellow Royal Coll. Physicians and Surgeons (Can.), Am. Coll. Physicians, Am. Coll. Chest Physicians; mem. Am. Thoracic Soc., Aerospace Medicine Soc.; gov. Soc of the Descendants and the Founders of the Hartford 2005-. Avocation: swimming. Office: Southeastern Pulmonary Assocs 155 Montauk Ave New London CT 06320-4842 Office Phone: 860-444-2223. Business E-Mail: jsu@jhu.edu.

URBANO, ARTHUR PETER, historian, theologian; s. Arthur and Phyllis (Cucca) Urbano. MDiv, Harvard Div. Sch., Cambridge, Mass., 1999; BA, Brown U., Providence, 1995, PhD, 2005. Asst. prof. Providence Coll., Providence, 2005—. Grant, Fulbright, 2003—04. Mem.: Soc. Bibl. Lit., N.Am. Patristics Soc. (1st Article prize 2005). Business E-Mail: aurbano@providence.edu.

URBANOWSKI, FRANK, publishing company executive; b. Balt., Mar. 5, 1936; s. Frank and Tofilla (Jakubik) U.; m. Julia Blocksma; children: Alexandra, Tasha. BS in Ceramic Enginng., Va. Poly. Inst.; postgrad., Columbia U. Rep. Ronald Press, 1960-61; editor coll. dept. Macmillan Co., 1961-66; editorial dir. Glencoe Press, 1966-68, v.p., 1968-72, pub., 1972-73; dir. market devel. Ednl. Testing Service, 1973-75; dir. Mass. Inst. Tech. Press, Cambridge, 1975—2003. Chmn. exec. coun. Profl. Scholarly Publs. divsn., 1979-81; bd. dirs. Cambridge Insight Meditation Ctr., 1985—; bd. dirs. Wisdom Press, U. Calif. Press., Transaction Press, U. Press NE; trustee MCLE. Mem. Am. Assn. Pubs. (dir. 1979-81), Assn. Am. Univ. Press (dir. 1979-81, pres. 1990-91), Cambridge Boat Club. Office: The Mit Press 55 Hayward St Cambridge MA 02142-1315 Home: 200 Lake St Apt 6 Burlington VT 05401-5236 E-mail: furb@mit.edu.

URBANSKI, JANE F., retired microbiologist; b. Buffalo, Aug. 21, 1943; d. Francis C. and Jane J. Urbanski. BS in Med. Tech. cum laude, Rosary Hill Coll., 1965. Registered med. tech. Am. Soc. Clin. Pathology. Med. tech. Millard Fillmore Hosp., Buffalo, 1965—68, microbiology supr., 1968—72; lab. supr. Physician's Diagnostic Lab., Buffalo, 1972—73; microbiology supr. Sister's of Charity Hosp., Buffalo, 1973—74; chief bacteriologist Erie County Pub. Health Lab. Health Dept., Buffalo, 1974—2002; ret., 2002. Clin. instr. SUNY, Buffalo, 1975—2002. Vol. Haven House, Buffalo, 1985, City Mission, Buffalo, 2004. Mem.: English First, Second Amendment Found., Am. Immigration Control, Mensa. Conservative. Roman Catholic. Avocations: travel, growing orchids, reading, logic puzzles. Home: 185 Bridle Path Orchard Park NY 14127

URBINA, RICARDO MANUEL, judge; b. 1946; BA, Georgetown U., 1967, JD, 1970. Bar: DC 1970. Trial atty. Pub. Defender Svc. DC, 1970-72; prin. Urbina & Libby, Washington, 1972-73, Law Office Ricardo M. Urbina, Washington, 1973-74; prof. law, dir. criminal justice prog. Howard U., Washington, 1974-81; assoc. judge DC Superior Ct., 1981-94; judge US Dist. Ct. DC, 1994—. Adj. prof. Antioch Sch. Law, Washington, 1976, Georgetown U. Law Ctr., 1982, George Washington U. Nat. Law Ctr., 1993—; instr. Nat. Inst. Trial Advocacy, 1976, 78; vis. instr. trial advocacy Howard Law Sch., 1996—. Named an All-Am. track and field NCAA 880 Champion, 1966; named one of Athletic Hall of Fame, Georgetown U. Mem.: ABA, Nat. Coun. La Raza, Coun. Ct. Excellence, Counsellors of Washington DC, Fahy Inns of Ct., DC Bar Assn., Hispanic Nat. Bar Assn., Nat. Bar Assn., DC Hispanic Bar Assn., Phi Delta Phi. Office: US Dist Ct DC US Courthouse Rm 4311 333 Constitution Ave NW Washington DC 20001-2802*

URBOM, WARREN KEITH, federal judge; b. Atlanta, Nebr., Dec. 17, 1925; s. Clarence Andrew and Anna Myrl (Irelan) U.; m. Joyce Marie Crawford, Aug. 19, 1951; children: Kim Marie, Randall Crawford, Allison Lee, Joy Renee. AB with highest distinction, Nebr. Wesleyan U., 1950, LLD (hon.), 1984; JD with distinction, U. Mich., 1953. Bar: Nebr. 1953. Mem. firm Baylor, Evnen, Baylor, Urbom, & Curtiss, Lincoln, Nebr., 1953—70; judge U.S. Dist. Ct. Nebr., 1970—; chief judge U.S. Dist. Ct. Dist. Nebr., 1972—86, sr. judge, 1991—. Mem. com. on practice and procedure Nebr. Supreme Ct., 1965-95; mem. subcom. on fed. jurisdiction Jud. Conf. U.S., 1975-83; adj. instr. trial advocacy U. Nebr. Coll. Law, 1979-90; bd. dirs. Fed. Jud. Ctr., 1982-86; chmn. com. on orientation newly apptd. dist. judges Fed. Jud. Ctr., 1986-89; mem. 8th Cir. Com. on Model Criminal and Civil Jury Instrns., 1983—; mem. adv. com. on alternative sentences U.S. Sentencing Com., 1989-91. Contbr. articles to profl. jours. Trustee St. Paul Sch. Theology, Kansas City, Mo., 1986-89; active United Methodist Ch. (bd. mgrs., bd. global ministries 1972-76, gen. com. on status and role of women, 1988-96, gen. conf. 1972, 76, 80, 88, 92, 96, 2000); pres. Lincoln YMCA, 1965-67; bd. govs. Nebr. Wesleyan U., chmn. 1975-80. With AUS, 1944-46. Recipient Medal of Honor, Nebr. Wesleyan U. Alumni Assn., 1983. Fellow Am. Coll. Trial Lawyers; mem. ABA, Nebr. Bar Assn. (ho. of dels. 1966-70, Outstanding Legal Educator award 1990, Pres.'s award for Professionalism 2006), Lincoln Bar Assn. (Liberty Bell award 1993, pres. 1968-69), Kiwanis (Disting. Svc. award 1993), Masons (33 deg., Grand Master's Humanitarian award 2003), Am. Inns of Ct. (Lewis F. Powell Jr. award for Professionalism and Ethics 1995), Robert Van Pelt Am. Inn of Ct. (Lifetime Mentor award, 2002). Methodist. Office: US Dist Ct 586 Fed Bldg 100 Centennial Mall N Lincoln NE 68508-3859 Office Phone: 402-437-5231. Personal E-mail: urbom1@neb.rr.com. Business E-Mail: warren_urbom@ned.uscourts.gov.

URCIOLO, JOHN RAPHAEL, II, finance and real estate educator, developer; b. Washington, June 29, 1947; s. Joseph John and Phillie Marie (Petrone) U.; m. Jean Marie Manning, Jan. 2, 1972 (dec. Jan. 1990); m. Andrea Zedalis, Mar. 9, 2002. BBA, Am. U., 1969, MS in real estate, 1971. Cert. real estate broker, appraiser. Rschr. Homer Hoyt Inst., Washington, 1967-69; econ. Nat. Assn. Home Builders, Washington, 1971-75; lectr., assoc. prof. Montgomery Coll., Rockville, Md., 1971-72; assoc. prof. U. Md., College Park, 1972-79; property mgr. Urciolo Realty Co., Washington, 1976-79; comml. broker Urciolo & Urciolo, Washington, 1980-82; real estate developer Urciolo Properties, LLC, Takoma Park, Md., 1982—. Cons. Nat. Ski Area Assn., Hartford, 1978-79, Montgomery County Govt., Rockville, 1980-81; adj. prof. Am. U., Washington, 1980-91; court expert Superior Ct. for D.C., Civil and Criminal divsns.; lectr. to various orgns. Author: Real Estate Manual, 1976; co-author: The White Book of Ski Areas (U.S. and Can.), 1977-79, Industry Edition-The White Book, 1978, The Housing Fact Book, 1976, Housing Component Costs, 1975, 2d edit., 1976, Material Usage in Housing, 1970; co-editor: Labor Wage Rate Bulletin, 1976. Co-chair bd. dirs. Liz Lerman Dance Exch., Takoma Park, Md., 1997—; chmn. facade adv. bd. and Econ. Devel. Com., City of Takoma Park; bd. mem. Lido Civic Club of Washington, editor Lido Star. Fellow Urban Mass Transp. Assn., 1969, Am. U., 1970; Soc. Real Estate Appraisers scholar, 1968. Mem. Cert. Real Estate Appraisers, Am. Planning Assn., Am. Univ. Real Estate Assn. (charter, v.p. edn., v.p. award 1983), Rho Epsilon (editor newsletter 1969). Republican. Roman Catholic. Avocations: skiing, golf. Office: Urciolo Properties LLC 6535 Laurel Ave Ste 100 Takoma Park MD 20912-4413 Office Phone: 301-270-4442. Personal E-mail: jurciolo@comcast.net.

UREMOVICH, MICHAEL ELLIOT, transportation company executive; b. Phila., Apr. 23, 1943; s. A. M. and Edythe (Fidcca) U.; m. Carrea S. Cotlow, Aug. 27, 1966. BA, U. Ariz., 1966; MBA, CCNY, 1972; MA, St. Johns Coll. Sr. v.p. mktg. Lee Way Motor Freight, Oklahoma City, 1976-79; prin. Booz, Allen & Hamilton, NYC, 1972-76, 1979-82; v.p. through sr. v.p. mktg. Am. Pres. Lines, Oakland, Calif.; v.p. mktg. So. Pacific Transp.; pres. TSSI; prin. Manalytics Internat., San Francisco; vice-chmn. Pacer Internat., Concord, Calif., 2003—06, chmn., CEO, 2006—. Served with USN, 1961-66. Office: Pacer Internat Ste 1200 2300 Clayton Rd Concord CA 94520

URENA-ALEXIADES, JOSE LUIS, electrical engineer; b. Madrid, Sept. 5, 1949; s. Jose L. and Maria (Alexiades Christodulakis) Urena y Pon. MS in EE, U. Madrid, Spain, 1976; MS in Computer Sci., UCLA, 1978. Rsch. asst. UCLA, 1978; sys. analyst Honeywell Info. Systems, LA, 1978-80; mem. tech. staff Jet Propulsion Lab., Pasadena, Calif., 1980-91; exec. dir. Empresa Nacional de Innovacion S.A., LA, 1991-96; sr. technologist Boeing Satellite Devel. Ctr., LA, 1996—. Contbr. various articles to profl. jours. Two times recipient NASA Group Achievement award. Mem. IEEE, IEEE Computer Soc., IEEE Communications Soc., Assn. for Computer Machinery, World Federalist Assn., Spanish Profl. Am. Inc. Roman Catholic. Avocations: photography, swimming. Office: Boeing Satellite Devel Ctr Mail Stop S50 x366 1700 E Imperial Hwy Los Angeles CA 90245 Home: PO BOX 3522 Idyllwild CA 92549-3522

URETZ, ROBERT BENJAMIN, biophysics educator, university dean; b. Chgo., June 27, 1924; s. Sol A. and Lottie (Kaplan) U.; m. Vi Fogle, June 30, 1955; children: Jane Elizabeth Uretz Miller, Alan Daniel. BS, U. Chgo., 1947, PhD, 1954. Mem. faculty U. Chgo., 1954—, prof. biophysics, 1964—, Ralph W. Gerard prof., 1972—, chmn. dept., 1966-69, assoc. dean div. biol. sci. Sch. Medicine, 1969-70, dep. dean Sch. Medicine, 1970-77, assoc. v.p. for Med. Center, 1976-77, dean div. biol. sci. and sch. medicine, v.p. for Med. Center, 1977-83, interim dean of students, 1987-88. Served to 1st lt. USAAF, 1943-46. Mem. Biophys. Soc., Radiation Research Soc., Am. Soc. Cell Biology, AAAS, Sigma Xi. Home: 5550 S Shore Dr Apt 1412 Chicago IL 60637-5061

UREY, RICHARD, legislative staff member; Radio and TV reporter, Las Vegas, 1983—93; news dir. KTNV-TV, Las Vegas; press sec. for Gov. Bob Miller, Carson City, Nev.; chief of staff for Rep. Shelley Berkley, US House of Reps., Washington, 2000—. Office: Office of Congresswoman Shelley Berkley 405 Cannon House Office Bldg Washington DC 20515-4708 Office Phone: 202-225-5965. Office Fax: 202-225-3119. E-mail: richard.urey@mail.house.gov.*

URI, GEORGE WOLFSOHN, accountant; b. San Francisco, Dec. 8, 1920; s. George Washington and Ruby Uri; m. Pamela O'Keefe, May 15, 1961. AB, Stanford U., 1941, IA, 1943, MBA, 1946; postgrad., U. Leeds, Eng., 1945. CPA, Calif.; CMA, ChFC; Accredited Estate Planner. Mem. acctg., econs. and stats. depts. Shell Oil Co., Inc., San Francisco, 1946—48; ptnr., ret. Irelan, Uri, Mayer & Sheppie; pres. F. Uri & Co., Inc. Instr. acctg. and econs. Golden Gate U., 1949-50. Contbr. articles to profl. jours. Chmn. San Rafael Redevel. Adv. Com., 1977-78, mem., 1978-91, mem. emeritus, 1991—; bd. dirs. San Francisco Planning and Urban Renewal Assn., 1958-60. Served with AUS, 1942-46, to col. Aus. (ret.). Recipient Meritorious Service medal, Sec. of Army, 1978. Mem. AICPA (hon., personal fin. specialist), Calif. Soc. CPA (hon.; sec.-treas. San Francisco chpt. 1956-57, dir. 1961-63, state dir. 1964-66, Forbes medal com. 1968-69, chmn. 1969-71), San Francisco Estate Planning Coun. (dir. 1965-68, Am. Soc. Mil. Comptr., Execs. Assn. San Francisco (pres. 1965-66), Soc. Fin. Profls., Fin. Planning Assn., Commonwealth Club (quar. chmn. 1971), Stanford Alumni Assn. (San Francisco; dir. 1990-99), Army and Navy Club Washington. Office: 1209 Tennessee St San Francisco CA 94107 Personal E-mail: georgeuri@aol.com.

URIBE, FERNANDO, JR., law educator; b. Weehawken, NJ, May 17, 1975; s. Fernando and Sira Uribe. BA in Sociology, Rutgers U., New Brunswick, 1998, BS in Adminstrn. Justice, 1998; MA in Criminal Justice, Rutgers U., Newark, NJ, 2002, MS in Global Affairs, 2006, attending, 2004—. Adj. prof. Seton Hall U. Dept. Criminal Justice, South Orange, NJ, 2006—, Montclair State U. Dept. Polit. Sci. & Law, NJ, 2008—. Chmn. Hudson County Young Republicans, Union City, NJ, 2004; parliamentarian Young Rep. Fedn., NJ, 2008. Mem.: NJ. Young Profls. Liberal. Roman Catholic. Avocations: travel, politics. Personal E-mail: professorfuj@yahoo.com. Business E-Mail: uribef@mail.montclair.edu.

URIBE, JENNIE ANN, elementary school educator; b. National City, Calif., Apr. 17, 1958; d. Robert and Alice (Packard) U. BA, San Diego State U., 1981, cert. teacher, 1982; MB, Nat. Univ., 2000. Tchr. Langdon Ave. Sch., L.A. Unified Sch. Dist., Sepulveda, Calif., 1984-94, tchr. potentally gifted students class, 1987-94; tchr. Spreckels Elem. Sch., San Diego City Schs., 1994—97, Rosa Elem., 1997—. Tchr./advisor for student govt., 1987-93; guide tchr., 1997—; prof. deve. advisor, 1997—. Mem. adv. coun. Sch. Site, 1992-1997. Avocations: tennis, music, movies, reading. Home: 2259 Peach Tree Ln Spring Valley CA 91977-7046 Office: Rosa Parks Elem Sch 4510 Landis St San Diego CA 92103

URIBE, MARTIN, economics professor; b. Cordoba, Argentina, Feb. 18, 1964; came to the U.S., 1989; s. Agustin Uribe and Delia Neuman; m. Stephanie Schmitt-Grohe, July 11, 1998; 1 child, Cristobal. PhD, U. Chgo., Ill., 1994. Economist Bd. Govs. FRS, Washington, 1994—98; asst. prof. U. Pa., Phila., 1998—2003; Prof. economics Duke U., Durham, NC, 2003—, Columbia U., NYC, 2008—. Cons. World Bank, Washington, 1993. Assoc. editor Internat. Econ. Rev., 1999—. Office: Columbia Univ 420 W 118th St New York NY 10027

URICK, JAMES R., dentist; DDS, UCLA Sch. Dentistry, 1996. Resident, chief resident, clin. instr. U. Calif. San Francisco Gen. Dentistry Residency, 1997—98; co-founder Calif. Ctr. Aesthetic Dentistry, DDS & Associates, San Francisco, 2002—. Named Best of the Bay, San Francisco Mag., Top Doc. Mem.: San Francisco Dental Soc., Calif. Dental Assn., Am. Dental Assn., Am. Acad. Cosmetic Dentistry. Office: DDS & Associates 230 California St Ste 200 San Francisco CA 94111*

URIE, ALAN T., bank executive; b. Ogden, Utah, Sept. 25, 1957; s. Hurschell G. and E. Mary (Petersen) Urie; m. M. Mae Christensen, July 26, 1980; children: Marcus Timothy, Kristi Mae Harvey, Scott Alan, Catherine Elizabeth, Teresa Janette, Mary Elizabeth. BS, Brigham Young U., 1982; MBA, U. Utah, 1984. National Compliance School Graduate Am. Bankers Assn., 1991. Officer First Security Bank of Utah, N.A., Salt Lake City, 1983—91, asst. v.p., 1991—94, v.p., sr. compliance officer, 1994—2000; v.p. First Security Corp., Salt Lake City, 1996—2000; sr. v.p. Wells Fargo Bank NW, N.A., 2000—, Wells Fargo Bank, N.A., 2004—, Wells Fargo Cmty. Devel. Corp., 2007—. Unit com. mem., leader Boys Scouts Am., South Salt Lake, 1985—; budget adv. bd. Ogden City, Utah, 1986—88; commr., chair South Salt Lake Planning Commn., 1985—86, 1988—95; chmn. Cmty. Affairs Com., South Salt Lake, 1988—90, Gen. Plan Com., South Salt Lake, 1992—96, City Housing Rehab. Loan Com., South Salt Lake, Utah, 2002—; bishop Ch. of Jesus Christ of Latter-day Saints, South Salt Lake, 2003—04, stake presidency mem., 2004—; bd. mem., exec. com. Utah Microenterprise Loan Fund, 2000—, vice chair, 2008—; bd. & exec. com., governance com. Girl Scouts Utah, 2002—08; bd. mem., incorporator South Salt Lake Works, Inc., 2004—; com. mem. Utah Bankers Assn., 1990—2009. Lds Ch. Office: Wells Fargo 299 South Main St Salt Lake City UT 84111-2263

URIE, JOHN JAMES, retired lawyer, former Canadian federal judge; b. Guelph, Ont., Can., Jan. 2, 1920; s. G. Norman and Jane A. U.; m. Dorothy Elizabeth James.; children: David, Janet, Alison. B.Commerce, Queen's U.; LL.B., Osgoode Hall Law Sch. Bar: Ont. 1948. Ptnr. firm Burke-Robertson, Urie, Weller & Chadwick, Ottawa, Ont., 1948-73;

judge Fed. Ct. Can., Ottawa, 1973-90; counsel Scott and Aylen, Ottawa, 1991-2000, Borden, Ladner, Gervais, Ottawa, 2000—. Gen. counsel to Joint Com. of Senate and House of Commons on Consumer Credit; chmn. planning com. First Nat. Conf. on Law, Ottawa, 1972; judge Ct. Martial Appeal Ct., 1973-90. Past pres. County of Carleton Law Assn.; past v.p. Children's Aid Soc.; past pres. Eastern Profl. Hockey League. Served with Cameron Highlanders of Ottawa Can. Army, 1942-45. Mem. Royal Can. Mil. Inst., Redears Club(past pres.), Phi Delta Phi. Mem. United Ch. of Canada. Clubs: Cameron Highlanders of Ottawa Assoc. (Ottawa), Ottawa Hunt and Golf (Ottawa), Rideau (Ottawa). Office: Borden Ladner Gervais 100 Queen St Ottawa ON Canada K1P1J9 Home Phone: 613-733-1977; Office Phone: 613-237-5160.

URKOWITZ, MICHAEL, banker; b. Bronx, NY, June 18, 1943; s. David and Esther (Levy) U.; m. Eleanor Naomi Dreazen, July 2, 1966; children— Brian, Denise. B.Engring., CCNY, 1965, M.M.E., 1967. Project engr. Lunar Module program Grumman Corp., Bethpage, NY, 1964-72; asst. to dep. commr. for housing code compliance, project mgr. City of N.Y., 1972-74; 2d v.p. Chase Manhattan Bank, NYC, 1974-77, v.p. group exec. ops. dept., 1977-80, sr. v.p., 1980-85, exec. v.p., corp. ops. and sys. exec., 1985-87; sector exec. Chase InfoServ Internat., NYC, 1987-95, exec. consumer products integration and tech., 1995-96, Chase credit card bus. exec., 1996-2000, ret., 2000; prin. Michael Urkowitz, LLC, 2005—. Bd. dirs. Bank Leumi, U.S.; lectr. CCNY, 1967—68. Contbg. author: Thermal Control and Radiation, 1972. Mem. adv. bd. NYC chpt. Salvation Army, 1989—2001. Mem. Tau Beta Pi, Pi Tau Sigma. Home Phone: 212-879-6123. Personal E-mail: murkowitz@aol.com. *Working against my own standards as opposed to the standards set by others, provides the greater challenge but yields greater satisfaction.*

URLACHER, BRIAN KEITH, professional football player; b. Pasco, Wash., May 25, 1978; s. Brad and Lavoyda Urlacher; m. Laure Urlacher (div.); 1 child, Pamela; 1 child, Riley. BA, U. N.Mex., Albuquerque, 2000. Linebacker Chgo. Bears, 2000—. Vol. United Way. Vol. Spl. Olympics, Ill., N.Mex. Named First Team All-Pro, NFL, 2001—02, 2005—06, NFL Defensive Rookie of Yr., AP, 2000, NFL Defensive Player of Yr., 2005; named to Nat. Football Conf. Pro Bowl Team, NFL, 2000—03, 2005—06. Achievements include leading the NFL in: fumble return yards, 2001. Office: Chgo Bears Halas Hall 1000 Football Dr Lake Forest IL 60045*

UROFSKY, MELVIN IRVING, historian, educator, director; b. NYC, Feb. 7, 1939; s. Philip and Sylvia (Passow) U.; m. Susan Linda Miller, Aug. 27, 1961; children: Philip Eric, Robert Ian. AB, Columbia U., 1961, MA, 1962, PhD, 1968; JD, U. Va., 1983. Instr. history Ohio State U., 1964-67; asst. prof. history and edn., then asst. dean SUNY, Albany, 1967-74; prof. history Va. Commonwealth U., Richmond, 1974—2003, dir. doctoral program pub. policy, 1996—, prof. emeritus, 2003—. Harrison vis. prof. Coll. William and Mary, 1990-91; adj. prof. law U. Richmond, 1989-2000. Author: Big Steel and Wilson Adminstration, 1969, Why Teachers Strike, 1970, A Mindo of One Piece, 1971, American Zionizm from Herzl to The Holocaust, 1976, We Are One!, 1978, Louis D. Brandeis and the Progressive Tradition, 1980, A Voice that Spoke for Justice: The Life and Times of Stephen S. Wise, 1981, The Supreme Court, the Bill of Rights and the Law, 1986, A March of Liberty, 1987, The Douglas Letters, 1987; Continuity of Change, 1990, A Conflict of Rights, 1991, Felix Frankfurter, 1991, Letting Go, 1993, Division and Discord, 1997, Commonwealth and Community, 1997, Lethal Judgments, 2000; co-editor: Brandeis Letters, 5 vols., 1971-78, Half Brother, Half Son, 1991, Money and Free Speech, 2005, Louis D. Brandeis:A Life, 2009; editor: Jour. of Supreme Court History, 1995-. Chmn. exec. com. Zionist Academic Council, 1976-79; mem. nat. bd. Am. Zionist Fedn., 1976-79; co-chmn. Am. Zionist Ideological Commn., 1976-78; nat. bd. Assn. Reform Zionists Am., 1978-84. Mershon Found. fellow, 1965, Sr. Rsch. fellow NEH, 1976-77, Sr. fellow NEH, 2005, Resident fellow Rockefeller Found, 2007; recipient Kaplun award Jewish Book Coun., 1976; grantee NEH, Am. Coun. Learned Socs.; NEH scholar-in-residence, 1994-95, univ. award for excellence, 1995. Mem. Am. Jewish Hist. Soc. (chmn. acad. coun. 1979-83), Am. Legal History Soc. (bd. dirs., exec. com. 1991-94), Orgn. Am. Historians, Va. Hist. Soc. (trustee 1992-98). Office Phone: 301-740-9145.

UROWSKY, RICHARD J., lawyer; b. NYC, June 28, 1946; s. Jacob and Anne (Granick) Urowsky. BA, Yale U., 1967, JD, 1972; BPhil, Oxford U., Eng., 1970. Bar: N.Y. 1973, U.S. Dist. Ct. (so. dist.) N.Y. 1973, U.S. Ct. Appeals (2d cir.) 1973, U.S. Supreme Ct. 1977. Law clk. to Justice Reed U.S. Supreme Ct., Washington, 1972—73; assoc. Sullivan & Cromwell LLP, NYC, 1973—80, ptnr., 1980—. Mem. ABA, NYC Bar Assn., Fed. Bar Coun., N.Y. County Lawyers Assn., Yale Club, Links Club, India House Club, Lyford Cay Club. Office: Sullivan & Cromwell LLP 125 Broad St New York NY 10004-2498 Business E-Mail: urowskyr@sullcrom.com.

URQUHART, BRUCE, government agency administrator, engineering educator; b. Montreal, Quebec, Can., Mar. 31, 1955; s. John Morrison and Vivian Elizabeth Urquhart; m. Jacqueline S. Clayton, Mar. 3, 2004. BA in Geography, San Diego State U., Calif., 1978. Cert. land surveyor, Calif., 1988. Dep. dist. dir. Calif. Dept. Transp., San Diego, 1978—; lectr. civil engring. San Diego State U., 1991—. Mem.: ASCE. Home: 2603 Grandview St San Diego CA 92110 Office: Calif Dept Transp 4050 Taylor St San Diego CA 92110 Business E-Mail: bruce_urquhart@dot.ca.gov.

URQUHART, JOHN, medical researcher, educator; b. Pitts., Apr. 24, 1934; s. John and Wilma Nelda (Martin) U.; m. Joan Cooley, Dec. 28, 1957; children: Elizabeth Urquhart Vdovjak, John Christopher (dec. 1965), Robert Malcolm, Thomas Jubal. BA with honors, Rice U., 1955; MD with honors, Harvard U., 1959; D honoris causa, U. Utrecht, 1997. Lic. physician, Calif. Walter B. Cannon fellow in physiology Harvard Med. Sch., Boston, 1956, Josiah Macy, Jr. fellow, 1956-58, 59-61; intern in surgery Mass. Gen. Hosp., 1959-60, asst. resident, 1960-61; investigator Nat. Heart Inst., NIH, Bethesda, Md., 1961-63; asst. prof. physiology U. Pitts. Sch. Medicine, 1963-66, assoc. prof., 1966-68, prof., 1968-70; prof. biomed. engring. U. So. Calif., LA, 1970-71; prin. scientist ALZA Corp., Palo Alto, Calif., 1970-86, dir. biol. scis., 1971-74, pres. rsch. divsn., 1974-78, dir., 1976-78, chief scientist, 1978-82, sr. v.p., 1978-85. Co-founder APREX Corp., Fremont, Calif., pres., 1986-88, dir., 1986-95, chmn., 1988-91, chief scientist, 1988-95; co-founder, chief scientist AARDEX Ltd., Zug, Switzerland, 1995-; vis. prof. pharmacology U. Limburg Sch. Medicine (now Maastricht U.), Maastricht, Netherlands, 1984-85, vis. prof. pharmacoepidemiology, 1986-91, extra ordinary prof. pharmacoepidemiology, 1991-2004, prof. emeritus, 2004-; adj. prof. biopharm. scis. U. Calif., San Francisco, 1984-; dir.'s adv. com. NIH, 1986-88; Boerhaave lectr. U. Leiden, Netherlands, 1991, 94-95, 97; bd. dirs. HBM BioVentures Ltd., Cayman Islands. Co-author: Risk Watch, 1984; contbr. articles to profl. jours.; patentee therapeutic systems for controlled drug delivery and regimen compliance monitoring. Trustee Kettering U. (formerly GMI Engring. and Mgmt. Inst.), Flint, Mich., 1983—. Served with USPHS, 1961-63. Recipient Disting. Alumni award, Rice U., 2002; NIH grantee, 1963-70. Fellow AAAS, Royal Coll. Physicians Edinburgh, Royal Soc. Edinburgh (corr.), Am. Assn. Pharmaceutical Scientists, Internat Soc. Pharmacoepidemiology, Biomed. Engring. Soc. (pres. 1976, Disting. Svc. award 2005); mem. Boylston Med. Soc., Am. Soc. Clin. Pharmacology and Therapeutics, Endocrine Soc., Saturday Morning Club Palo Alto, Am. Physiol. Soc. (Bowditch Lectr. award 1969), Calif. Acad. Medicine, Illuminati Edinburgh. Home and Office: 975 Hamilton Ave Palo Alto CA 94301-2213 Office Phone: 650-321-3961. E-mail: urquhart@ix.netcom.com.

URQUHART, TONY, artist, educator; b. Niagara Falls, Ont., Can., Apr. 9, 1934; s. Archer Marsh and Maryon Louise (Morse) U.; m. Madeline Mary Jennings, July 1958 (div. 1976); children: Allyson, Robin, Marsh, Aidan; m. Mary Jane Carter Keele, May 1976; 1 dau., Emily. At, Yale U., Summer Sch., Norfolk, Conn., 1955; diploma, Albright Art Sch. Buffalo Fine Arts Acad., 1956; BFA, U. Buffalo, 1958. Artist-in-residence U. Western Ont., London, 1960-63, 64-65, asst. prof. fine arts, 1967-70, assoc. prof., 1970-72; lectr. McMaster U., Hamilton, Ont., 1966—67; prof. fine art U. Waterloo, Ont., 1972—99, chmn. dept., 1977-79, 82-85, 94-96, ret., 1999. One-man shows Winnipeg Art Gallery, 1959, Walker Art Gallery, Mpls., 1960, Richard Demarco Gallery, Edinburgh, Scotland, 1975, Power of Invention: Drawings from seven decades, Nat. Gallery Can., 2003; group shows, Pitts. Biennial, 1958, Guggenheim Internat., N.Y.C., 1958, Art of the Ams. and Spain, Madrid, Barcelona, Rome, Paris, 1964, Nat. Gallery Can., Toronto, 1972, Mus. Modern Art, Paris, 1976, Mus. Modern Art, N.Y.C., 2006; represented permanent collections, Nat. Gallery Can., Art Gallery, Ont., Fed. Art Bank of Ottawa, Montreal Mus., Vancouver Art Gallery, Mus. Modern Art, NYC, Victoria and Albert Mus., London, Museo Civico, Lugano, Switzerland, Hirshhorn Mus., Washington, Bibliotec Nat., Paris; chmn., Jack Chambers Meml. Found., 1978-85, 2004—; artist in residence Kitchener-Waterloo Art Gallery, Kitchener, Ont., 1981-83, City of Kitchener, 2005; illustrator: (by Michael Ondaatje) The Broken Ark: A Book of Beasts, 1969, I Am Walking in the Garden of His Imaginary Palace by Jane Urquhart, 1982, False Shuffles by Jane Urquhart, 1982, (50 drawings) Cells of Ourselves (text G.M. Dault), 1989, Memories of a Governor General's Daughter, 1990, Warbrain: poems by Stuart MacKinnon, 1994, (by Anne McPherson) Walking to the Saints, 2000 (by Rohinton Mistry) The Scream, 2006, (paintings for sculptures) Off The Wall, 2008. Decorated Order of Can., 1995; recipient Edits, I Arts Coun., Ont., 1974, Kilchener Waterloo Visual Arts award, 1994, Gov. Gens. award, 2009, Kilchener Waterloo Lifetime Achievement award, 2009; winner Nat. Outdoor Sculpture Competition MacDonald Stewart Art Ctr., 1987, Outdoor Sculpture competition, Rim Park, Waterloo, 2002; grantee Can. Coun. award, 1963, 79, travel grantee, 1967, 69, 70, 74, 75, 76, 88, 91, project cost grantee, 1981, 82, short-term grantee, 1991, All Can. Coun. Mem. Can. Artists Representation (1 of 3 founding mem.'s, sec. 1968-71, life 1999), Nat. Gallery of Can. (life), Art Gallery of Ont. (life), London Reginal Art Gallery (life), MacDonald Stewart Art Centre Gallery Stratford (life). Office: Dept Fine Arts U Waterloo Waterloo ON Canada N2L 3G1 Home: PO Box 310 Colborne ON Kokiso Canada Office Phone: 519-885-1211. Personal E-mail: urk.art@hotmail.com.

URROZ-RAPOLD, PATRICIA JULIA S., retired diplomat, writer; b. Key West, Fla., Feb. 16, 1949; children: Jean Sebastien Bodin Rapold, Nicolas Richard Rapold. BA in Polit. Sci., Boston U., 1971. Consul ad-honorem Nicaragua Boston Ministerio de Relaciones Exteriores, Managua, Nicaragua, 1969—74, consul ad-honorem zurich Switzerland, 1974—78; pres. Banting Ltd., Nassau, Bahamas, 1978—83, Offshore Intarnat. Co., 1978—83; social security disability examimer Mass. Rehab. Commn., Boston, 1971—72. Author, pub., poet: Seasonal Living In The Catskills Windham High Peak And Trails, 1994 (Internat. Poet Of Merit award, 1996). Hospitality coord. for fgn. visitors Internat. Ctr., NYC, 1991—93. Recipient Appreciation award for vols., Internat. Ctr., N.Y.C., 1993. Mem.: AAUW (member). Roman Catholic. Achievements include development of mathmaticald models development for investment in the stock market. Avocations: hiking, swimming, reading, collecting. Office: Worldstar Corp 245 E 93d St Apt 29 C New York NY Office Phone: 212-410-5412, 646-315-5496. Personal E-mail: Rapold@aol.com. Business E-Mail: LordSeb@aol.com, patriciarapold@yahoo.com.

URRY, MEG (C. MEGAN URRY), physics professor; m. Andrew Szymkowiak; children: Amelia, Sophia. BS in Physics and Math. summa cum laude, Tufts U., 1977, DSc (hon.), 2009; MS in Physics, Johns Hopkins U., 1979, PhD in Physics, 1984. Postdoctoral rschr., Ctr. for Space Rsch. MIT, 1984—87; postdoctoral fellow, acad. affairs divsn. Space Telescope Sci. Inst., 1987—90, asst. astronomer, chief, rsch. and support br., 1990—95, assoc. astronomer, 1995—99, astronomer, head, Sci. Program Selection Office, 1996—2001; Israel Munson prof. physics and astronomy Yale U., 2001—, dir., Yale Ctr. Astronomy and Astrophysics, 2001—, chair, dept. physics, 2007—. Leader to US Delegation to 1st Internat. Conf. on Women in Physics, Paris, 2002. Mem. publ. bd. Astron. Soc. of the Pacific, 1997—99; editor: STATUS, 1998—2005; contbg. editor STATUS, 2005—07; contbr. chapters to books, articles to profl. jours. Recipient Annie Jump Cannon award in Astronomy, 1990, NASA Goddard Space Flight Ctr. Productivity Group award to PRESTO, 1996; NASA Grad. Fellowship award, 1980—83. Fellow: Am. Acad. Arts & Scis., Am. Women in Sci., Am. Phys. Soc. (com. on the status of women in physics 2000—02, mem. divsn. astrophysics); mem.: Conn. Acad. Sci. and Engring., Internat. Astron. Union, Am. Astron. Soc. (mem. nominating com. 1996—98, chair, nominating com. 1997—98, mem. nominating com. 2001—04, HEAD divsn. mem., com. status of women in astronomy 2000—03, chair, com. status of women in astronomy 1998—2000, 1994—96), Phi Beta Kappa. Office: Yale U Dept Physics Office JWGibbs 460 PO Box 208121 New Haven CT 06520-8121 Office Phone: 203-432-5997. Office Fax: 203-432-3824. Business E-Mail: meg.urry@yale.edu.*

URSANO, ROBERT JOSEPH, psychiatrist; b. Heidelberg, Ger., May 26, 1947; s. James Joseph and Neoma Faye (Summers) U.; m. Diane T. Ursano; children: Amy, Anna. BS magna cum laude, U. Notre Dame, 1969; MD, Yale U., 1973; grad., Washington Psychoanalytic Ins, 1986. Diplomate Nat. Bd. Med. Examiners, Am. Bd. Psychiatry and Neurology; lic. physician N.Y., Tex., Md. Resident in psychiatry Wilford Hall USAF Med. Ctr., 1973-75; postdoctoral fellow in psychiatry Yale U./Yale Psychiat. Inst., 1975-77; staff psychiatrist USAF Sch. Aerospace Medicine, Brooks AFB, Tex., 1977-79; clin. asst. prof. U. Tex. Health Sci. Ctr., San Antonio, 1977-79; asst. prof. and dir. third yr. clerkships dept. psychiatry Uniformed Svcs. U. Health Scis., Bethesda, Md., 1979-81, assoc prof. and dir. 3rd yr. clerkships, 1981-83, assoc. prof. and assoc. chmn. dept. psychiatry, 1983-86, prof. and assoc. chmn. dept. psychiatry, 1987-92, prof., chair dept. psychiatry, dir.Ctr. for the Study of Traumatic Stress Bethesda, Md., 1987—. Examiner Am. Bd. Psychiatry and Neurology, 1995; prof. Nat. Naval Med. Ctr Dept. Psychiatry, Georgetown U. Sch. Medicine, Washington, 1980-84, assoc. prof., 1984-88, prof., 1988—; mem. grant rev. study sect. for trauma and disaster, NIMH, 1990—, chmn. various study sects. Author: Concise Guide to Psychodynamic Psychotherapy, 1990, Concise Guide to Principles and Practice of Psychodynamic Psychotherapy in the Era of Managed Care, 1998; editor: Individual and Community Responses to Trauma and Disaster: The Structure of Human Chaos, 1994, Emotional Aftermath of The Persian Gulf War: Veterans, Families, Communities and Nations, 1996, Acute and Chronic PTSD, 1997, Trauma and Disaster: Responses and Management, 2003, Terrorism and Disaster: Individual and Community Mental Health Interventions, 2004, Bioterrorism: Indivduals and the Public's Health, 2004, Principles of Psychodynamics Psychotherapy: Brief, Intermittent and Long-Term, 2004, Textbook of Disaster Psychiatry, 2007, Intervention and Resilience after Mass Trauma, 2008; reviewer JAMA, NEJIN, Bitish Jour. Psycol., Am. Jour. Psychiatry, Jour. Nervous and Mental Disease, Psychosomatics, Psychiatry, Jour. Applied Social Psychology, Archives of Gen. Psychiatry, Hosp. and Community Psychiatry, all 1986—, Jour. Neuropsychiatry and Clin. Neurosci., 1988—, Jour. Traumatic Stress, 1989—; editor-in-chief Psychiatry, 1999—; mem. editl. bd. Mil. Medicine, 1999-2007; contbr. articles to profl. jours., chpts. to books. Decorated Air Force Commendation medal; recipient Dept. Def. Humanitarian Svc. medal, Dept. Def. Superior Svc. award, William C. Porter award Assn. Mil. Surgeons of U.S.; recipient Disting. Tchg. award Am. Soc. Psychoanalyst Physicians, Life Time Achievement award Internat. Soc. Traumatic Stress Studies. Fellow Am. Psychiat. Assn. (disting.), Am. Coll. Psychiatrists, Am. Coll. Psychoanalysts; mem. Am. Psychoanalytic Assn., Psychosomatic Soc., Washington Psychiat. Soc., Washington Psychoanalytic Soc., Acad. Medicine Washington DC, Soc. USAF Psychiatrists (v.p. 1981-82), Assn. for Acad. Psychiatry, Washington DC Academy Medicine, Alpha Epsilon Delta, Phi Beta Kappa. Office: Uniformed Svcs U Health Sci 4301 Jones Bridge Rd Bethesda MD 20814-4712 Office Phone: 301-295-3293.

URSCHEL, JOE, museum director, former news executive; m. Donna Urschel; 2 children. Grad., U. Ill., 1974. Reporter, features editor Star-Tribune, Ill.; reporter, critic, assoc. mag. editor, asst. Sunday editor Detroit Free Press; with USA Today, 1983—97; exec. dir., sr. v.p. Newseum, 1997—. Bd. dirs. InTune Found. Office: Newseum 555 Pennsylvania Ave NW Washington DC 20001 E-mail: info@newseum.org.

URSERY, FREDERICK STANLEY, lawyer; b. Pine Bluff, Ark., Mar. 5, 1942; s. William Stanley and Mary Charles (Lee) U.; m. Sharon Lee Davidson, Jan. 30, 1971; children: Stephen, Catherine. BA, Vanderbilt U., 1964; LLB, Columbia U., 1967. Bar: Ark. 1967, US Dist. Ct. (ea. and we. dists.) Ark. 1970, US Ct. Appeals (8th cir.) 1970. Atty. Friday, Eldredge & Clark, Little Rock, 1969—. Chmn. Pulaski County Red Cross, Little Rock, 1989-90; bd. dirs. Ouachita Girl Scout Coun., Little Rock, 1987-93. With U.S. Army, 1967-69, Vietnam. Fellow Am. Coll. Trial Lawyers, Am. Bar Found.; mem. State Bd. Law Examiners 1979-82, Am. Bd. Trial Advocates, Ark. Bar Assn. (exec. coun. chmn. 1989-90, pres. 2004, Outstanding Lawyer award 1996), Pulaski County Bar Assn. (pres. 1987-88), Downtown Kiwanis Club (pres. 1991-92), William R. Overton Inn of Ct. (pres. 1990-91). Democrat. Methodist. Home: 2804 N Taylor St Little Rock AR 72207-2837 Office: Friday Eldredge & Clark 2000 Regions Ctr 400 W Capitol Ave Little Rock AR 72201-3436 Office Phone: 501-370-1555. Business E-Mail: ursery@fec.net.

URTHALER, YETZIRAH YKSYA, Subsea Engineer; b. Caracas, Venezuela, Sept. 10, 1973; d. Kurt Joseph Urthaler and Delia Josefina Lapeira. BSME, U. Simon Bolivar, 1995, MSME, 2000, PhD in Mech. Engring., 2007. Lectr. U. Simon Bolivar, Venezuela, 1995—2000, asst. prof., 2000—. Rschr. stress analysis group U. Simon Bolivar, 1997—2001. Contbr. articles to profl. jours. Scholar, CEPET, Venezuela, 1991—95. Mem.: ASME (sec. 2000—01), Soc. Petroleum Engrs., Soc. Women Engrs. (co-chair 2003—), Phi Kappa Phi. Avocations: hiking, photography, dance. Home: 501 Westlake Park Blvd Office # 22 134 Houston TX 77079 Office: BP America Inc Houston TX 77079 Business E-Mail: urthaler@tamu.edu.

URY, FREDERIC STEPHEN, lawyer; b. Zanesville, Ohio, Sept. 11, 1952; s. Perry S. and Lorraine (Greenstein) U.; m. Debby Hagopian, June 6, 1976; children: Jennifer, Robert. BS, Babson Coll., 1974; JD, Suffolk U., 1977. Bar: Conn. 1977, U.S. Dist. Ct. Conn. 1978, U.S. Supreme Ct. 1982. Assoc., ptnr. Sherwood, Garlick & Cowell, Westport, Conn., 1977-84; ptnr. Rubenstein & Ury, Westport, Conn., 1984; mng. ptnr. Ury & Moskow LLC, Fairfield, Conn. Instr. Fairfield (Conn.) U., 1979-86; mem. exec. coun. Nat. Conf. Bar Pres., 2005. Pres. Cmty. Coun., Westport, 1983-85; bd. dirs. Westport-Weston United Way, 1985—, exec. v.p., 1988—; corp. mem., trustee Babson Coll., Wellesley, Mass., 1974-84, pres. Congregation For Humanistic Judaism 1997-2000; founder Charity Treks, Inc. Mem. ABA, Conn. Bar Assn. (exec. com. civil justice, pres. 2005), Assn. Trial Lawyers Am., Westport Bar Assn., Kiwanis. Democrat. Jewish. Avocations: hiking, skiing, long distance cycling. Office: Ury & Moskow LLC 883 Black Rock Tpk Fairfield CT 06825 Office Phone: 203-610-6393. Office Fax: 203-610-6399. Business E-Mail: fred@urymoskow.com.

URYASEV, STAN, science educator; PhD, Inst. Cybernetics, Kiev, Ukraine, 1982. Prof. U. Fla., Gainesville, 1997—. Office: Univ Fla PO Box 116595 303 Weil Hall Gainesville FL 32611-6595 Business E-Mail: uryasev@ufl.edu.

URZHUMOV, YAROSLAV ALEKSANDROVICH, application developer, researcher; s. Aleksandr Urzhumov and Tamara Urzhumova. BS in Applied Math. and Physics, Moscow Inst. Physics and Tech., 2000, MS in Applied Math. and Physics, 2002; PhD in Nanotechnology, U. Tex., Austin, 2007. Rsch. asst. Inst. Theoretical and Exptl. Physics, Moscow, 1999—2002; grad. rsch. tchg. asst. Ill. Inst. Tech., Chgo., 2002—03; rsch. asst. Inst. Fusion Studies, U. Tex., 2004—07; applications engr., customer svc. rep. COMSOL Inc., LA, 2008—. Jour. referee Optical Soc. Am., Washington, 2006—. Contbr. articles to profl. sci. jours. Mem.: Optical Soc. Am., SPIE (award 2006). Achievements include patents pending for wide-angle wavelength-selective infrared absorber (WAWS-AIR) and Wide-angle wavelength-selective emitter of thermal infrared radiation (WAWS-ETIR) based on a negative index impedance matched plasmonic; first to near-field microscopy through a SiC superlens; discovery of extreme anisotropy and a new kind of van Hove singularities in two-dimensional photonic crystals. Office: COMSOL Inc 10850 Wilshire Blvd Ste 800 Los Angeles CA 90024 Business E-Mail: yar@physics.utexas.edu.

USAMI, MASAHISA, physician, director; b. Tokyo, Sept. 6, 1931; s. Tomohisa Ishiyama and Terui Usami; m. Kohko Tomihira, Nov. 3, 1968; children: Atsuko, Masaya. B, U. Chiba, Japan, 1956. Med. dr. Chief dr. internal medicine Sumitomo Hosp., Osaka, Japan, 1971-89, vice dir., 1989-96, Sumitomo Life Ins. Co., Osaka, 1997—2004; head med. dir. Higashitemma Clinic, Osaka, 2004—. Mem. Japan Soc. Physical Fitness and Sports Medicine. Mem. Japan Soc. Internal Medicine (specialist), Japan Soc. Circulation (specialist), Japanese Soc. Avocations: fishing, gardening. Home: 5-6 Koyoenhigashiyamacho Nishinomiyashi Hyogo-ken 662-0012 Japan Office: Higashitemma Clinic 1-15 Higashitemma 1 Osaka 530-0044 Japan Home Phone: 0798-73-7256; Office Phone: 06-6352-7465. Personal E-mail: usami@e-temma.jp.

USCINSKI, RONALD HENRY, medical educator; b. NYC, Apr. 3, 1943; s. Henry John and Marie Antionette Uscinski; m. Donna Lyn Cutsail, May 25, 1975; children: Benjamin Joseph, David Michael, Daniel Eric, Jessica Lyn. BS, Fordham U., NYC, 1964; MD, Georgetown U., Washington, 1968. Clin. prof. neurol. surgery & pediat. Georgetown U., Washington, 1980—; clin. prof. neurol. surgery George Wash. U., 1995—. Lt. USN, 1969—71. Scholar, Potomac Inst. Policy Studies, Arlington, Va., 2004—. Fellow: ACS (life); mem.: Congress Neurosurgeons (licentiate), Am. Assn. Neurol. Surgeons (licentiate), Polish Acad. Neurosurg. (corr.), Potomac Boat Club. Roman Catholic. Avocations: rowing, music, writing. Business E-Mail: ruscinski@potomacinstitute.org.

USERY, WILLIE J., JR., former United States Secretary of Labor; b. Hardwick, Ga., Dec. 21, 1923; s. Willie J. and Effie Mae (Williamson) U.; m. Gussie Mae Smith, June 14, 1942; 1 child, Melvin J. Student, Mercer U., 1951-52; degree (hon.), U. Louisville, U. N. Ala., Southeastern U. Machinist various firms, 1946-56; grand lodge rep. Assn. Machinists and Aero. Workers AFL-CIO, Washington, 1956-69; chmn. Cape Kennedy Mgmt. Rels. Coun., Washington, 1968; asst. sec for labor-mgmt. rels. US Dept. Labor, Washington, 1969-73, spl. asst. to Pres. for labor mgmt. relations, 1973-77, sec., 1976-77; pres. Bill Usery Assoc., Washington, 1977. Indsl. union rep Pres.'s Missile Site Labor Com., Washington, 1961-67. Dir. Fed. Mediation and Conciliation Svc., 1973-76; bd. dirs. Brevard County United Fund, Brevard County Alcoholism Com.; bd. adv. Brevard Jr. Coll. Served with USNR, 1943-46. Mem.: Labor and Employment Relations Assn. (Lifetime Achievement Award 1999), Elks, Masons (Shriners). Baptist.

USHAKOV, SERGEY V., research scientist; PhD, St. Petersburg State U., Russia, 1994. Engr. Khlopin Radium Inst., St. Petersburg, 1993—99; postdoc. rsch. assoc. U. Calif., Davis, 1999—2003, staff rsch. assoc., thermochemistry facility and NEAT ORU, 2003—. Achievements include research in characterization of Zr-U-containing melts formed during Chernobyl Accident; water absorption calorimetry; patents for la-doped HfO2 as thermally stable high-k gate dielectric; invention of application of scanning calorimetry for in-situ characterization of fire effects on soil; research in thermochemistry of refractory ternary oxide systems with rare earths.

USHAKOV, YURY VIKTOROVICH, Russian government official, former ambassador; b. Moscow, Mar. 13, 1947; married; 1 daughter. Grad., Moscow State Inst. Internat. Rels., 1970; PhD in Hist., Diplomatic Acad. With Soviet Embassy in Denmark Ministry Fgn. Affairs of the USSR, 1970-75, with, 1975-86; dep. chief mission, min.-counsellor Embassy of the USSR/Russian Fedn., Denmark, 1986-92; dir. Dept. of All-European Coop. Ministry Fgn. Affairs Russian Fedn., 1992—96; amb., permanent rep. Russian Fedn. to the Orgn. Security and Coop. Europe, Vienna, 1996-98; dep. min. fgn. affairs Govt. Russian Fedn., 1998-99, amb. to the US Washington, 1999—2008, dep. cabinet chief of staff Moscow, 2008—. Office: Office of Prime Min 2 Krasnopresnenskaya Emb 103274 Moscow Russia

USHER, THOMAS JAMES, metal products executive; b. Reading, Pa., Sept. 11, 1942; s. Paul T. and Mary (Leonard) Usher; m. Sandra L. Mort, Aug. 14, 1965; children: Leanne, Jimmy, Lauren. BS in Indsl. Engring., U. Pitts., 1964, MS in Ops. and Rsch., 1965, PhD in Systems Engring., 1971. Indsl. engr. U. S. Steel Corp., Pitts., 1966—76, asst. gen. supt., 1975—78, asst. div. supt. Gary, Ind., 1978—81, asst. to pres., mng. dir. facility planning and engring. Pitts., 1982—83, v.p. engring., 1982—83, pres., 1991, U.S. Steel Mining Co., Inc., Pitts., 1983—84, v.p. engring. steel, 1984—, sr. v.p. steel ops., 1984—, exec. v.p. heavy products steel divsn., 1986—89, pres. steel divsn., 1990; pres., COO USX Corp., Pitts., 1994—95, chmn., CEO, 1995—2001; chmn. US Steel Corp., Pitts., 2001—06. Bd. dir. PNC Fin. Svcs.; bd. dirs. PPG Industries, H.J. Heinz Co.; bd. dir., non-exec. chmn. Marathon Oil Corp., 2007—. Mem. Leadership Pitts., 1984; trustee Multiple Sclerosis, Pitts., 1985; chmn. Allegheny Trails coun. Boy Scouts Am., Pitts, 1985, United Way, Pitts., 1985, U.S.-Korea Bus. Coun., 1993—; U.S.-Japan Bus. Coun.; trustee U. Pitts., 1994—, The Bus. Roundtable Nat. Found., 1995; vice chmn. Internat. Iron and Steel Inst. Bus. Coun., 1997. Mem.: Am. Iron and Steel Engrs. (bd. dirs. 1984—85), Dinamo/Ovia (bd. dirs. 1985), Am. Iron and Steel Inst., The Club at Nevillewood, Augusta Nat. Golf Club, Burning Tree Club, Oakmont Club, Dougle Eagle Club, Laurel Valley Club, Duquesne Club, Rolling Rock Club. Avocations: golf, tennis, racquetball, scuba diving, swimming. Mailing: Marathon Oil Corp Bd Directors 5555 San Felipe Rd Houston TX 77056-2723

USHER, TIMOTHY DWIGHT, physics professor; b. Rose Hill, NC, Aug. 8, 1958; s. Marvin Corner and Emma Catherine Usher; m. Carolyn Rolleri, May 15, 1988; children: Virginia Hope, Christian Dwight. PhD, U. SC., 1989. Rschr. Univ. SC, Columbia, 1981—89. Contbr. scientific papers. Grantee, NSF, NASA, DOD, Dept. Transp., Rsch. Corp. Mem.: Internat. Soc. Optical Engring., Coun. Undergraduate Rsch., Am. Phys. Soc. Achievements include invention of NI-ELVIS.

USHER, See RAYMOND, USHER IV

USHIJIMA, JEAN M., retired city official; b. San Francisco, Feb. 14, 1933; d. Toyoharu George and Frances Fujiko (Misumi) Miwa; m. Tad E. Ushijima; 1 child, Carol M. BS, U. San Francisco, 1981. City clk. City of Beverly Hills, Calif., 1973—94; ret., 1994. Chair Leadership Edn. for Asian Pacifics, 1997—; bd. dirs. West L.A. Japanese Am. Citizens League, 1979—, pres., 1988—91, 1994—2008. Mem.: Internat. Inst. Mcpl. Clks. (bd. dirs. 1988—91), League Calif. Cities (adminstrv. svcs. com. 1982—86, 1993—), Calif. Women in Govt. (program chmn. 1978—79), City Clks. Assn. Calif. (pres. 1986, City Clk. of Yr. award 1989), Acad. Advanced Edn., Beverly Hills C. of C. (Employee of Yr. award 1990). Avocations: reading, Japanese dancing.

USISKIN, ZALMAN PHILIP, mathematics educator; b. Chgo., Jan. 1, 1943; s. Nathan and Esther (Chukerman) U.; m. Karen Hesse, Sept. 2, 1979; children: Robert, Laura. BS in Math., U. Ill., 1963, BS in Edn., 1963; MA in Teaching of Math., Harvard U., 1964; PhD in Edn., U. Mich., 1969. Tchr. math. Niles Twp. High Sch.-West, Skokie, Ill., 1964-66; asst. prof. U. Chgo., 1969-74, assoc. prof., 1974-82, prof. edn., 1982—2007, prof. emeritus, 2008—. Vis. prof. U. Ga., Athens, 1980; mem. nat. adv. bd. Children's TV Workshop, Square One TV, N.Y.C., 1986-92; dir. U. Chgo. Sch. Math. Project, 1987—; mem. math. scis. edn. bd. NRC, Washington, 1988-91; mem. U.S. Nat. Commn. on Math. Instrn., 1995-97, chmn., 1998—2001; mem. com. on Mathematical Edn. of Tchrs., Math. Assn. Am., 2005-08. Co-author: Geometry-A Transformation Approach, 1971, UCSMP Geometry, 1990, 2nd edit., 1996; author: Advanced Algebra with Transformations and Applications, 1975, Algebra Through Applications, 1976, UCSMP Transition Mathematics, 1989, 2nd edit., 1995, Mathematics for High School Teachers, 2003; mem. editl. bd. Am. Jour. Edn., 1983—2003; contbr. articles to profl. jours. Recipient Max Beberman award Ill. Coun. Tchrs. Math., 1981, Glenn Gilbert award Nat. Coun. Suprs. Math., 1994; named Disting. speaker ASCD, 1991; grantee. Mem. Nat. Assessment Ednl. Progress (mem. math. adv. com. 1995—2005), Nat. Coun. Tchrs. Math. (bd. dirs. 1995-98, Lifetime Achievement award 2001), Math. Assn. Am., Nat. Coun. Suprs. Math. (1st v.p. 1982-83), Met. Math. Club Chgo. (bd. dirs. 1970-73), Phi Beta Kappa, Phi Delta Kappa. Office: U Chgo 6030 S Ellis Chicago IL 60637

USKOKOVIC, VUK, research scientist; b. Belgrade, Serbia, Sept. 2, 1976; s. Dragan and Jasmina Uskokovic. BSc in Phys. Chemistry, U. Belgrade, 2001; MSc in Elec. Engring., U. Kragujevac, Cacak, Serbia, 2003; PhD in Nanosci. and Nanotechs., Jozef Stefan Internat. Postgrad. Sch., Ljubljana, Slovenia, 2006. Rsch. assoc. Jozef Stefan Inst., 2002—06; rsch. fellow Clarkson U., Potsdam, NY, 2006—07, U. Calif., San Francisco, 2007—. Contbr. articles to profl. jours. Fellow: Postdoc. Scientists Assn., U. Calif. (San Francisco) (practice sci. chair 2008). Serbian Orthodox. Achievements include invention of production of first stable dispersions of cholesterol particles; development of biocompatible magnetic particles for hyperthermia treatment. Avocations: writing, music. Home: 2479 28th Ave San Francisco CA 94116 Office: 707 Parnassus Ave San Francisco CA 94143 Personal E-mail: vuk21@yahoo.com. Business E-Mail: vuk.uskokovic@ucsf.edu.

USPENSKIY, VLADIMIR VLADIMIROVICH, mathematics professor; b. Moscow, Jan. 30, 1959; s. Vladimir Andreevich Uspenskiy and Svetlana Markovna Uspenskaya; m. Vera Mikhaylovna Belousova; 1 child, Andrey Vladimirovich. PhD, Moscow State U., 1983. Prof. Ohio U., Athens, 1999—. Office: Dept Maths Ohio Univ Athens OH 45701 Business E-Mail: uspensk@math.ohiou.edu.

USSERY, TERDEMA L., II, professional sports team executive; b. Watts, Calif. B in Pub. and Internat. Affairs, Princeton U., 1981; M in Govt., Harvard U., 1984; degree in law, U. Calif., Berkeley, 1987. Bus. and entertainment atty. Morrison & Foerster, LA; dep. commr., gen. counsel Continental Basketball Assn., 1990—91, commr., 1991—93; pres. Nike Sports Mgmt., 1993—97; pres., CEO Dallas Mavericks, 1997—; CEO HDNet, 2001—. Bd. dirs. Timberland Co., 2005—, TreeHouse Food, Inc., 2005—; alt. gov. NBA. Bd. trustees Princeton U., 2004—, Presbyn. Healthcare Found. Named Corp. Exec. of Yr., Black Enterprise mag., 2003; named one of Top 100 Most Powerful People in Sports, Sporting News, Top 101 Most Influential Minorities in Sports, Sports Illus. Office: Dallas Mavericks The Pavilion 2909 Taylor St Dallas TX 75226-1909 E-mail: terdema.ussery@dallasmavs.com.*

USTIAN, DANIEL C., trucking executive; With Navistar Internat. Corp., 1973—, group v.p., gen. mgr. engine group, 1990—99, pres., 1999—, COO, 2002—03, CEO, 2003—, chmn., 2004—. Bd. dir. Monaco Coach Corp. Mem.: Am. Foundry Assn., Soc. Automotive Engineers, Bus. Rundtable. Office: Navistar International Corp PO Box 1488 4201 Winfield Rd Warrenville IL 60555 Office Phone: 630-753-5000.*

USTUN, CELALETTIN, hematologist, educator, bone marrow transplant specialist; b. Ankara, Turkey, Apr. 30, 1967; s. Zekiye Doganay; m. Christine Henly, June 12, 2004; 1 child, Joshua A. MD, Ankara U. Med. Sch., Ankara, Turkey, 1984—90. Diplomate Ankara U. Med. Sch., 1990, cert. in internal medicine 2005, in hematology 2006. Residency Ankara U. Med. Sch., dept. internal med., Ankara, Turkey, 1990—95; fellowship hematology Ankara U. Med. Sch., Med. Coll. of Ga., 1997—99; fellowship hematology / oncology Med. Sch. Georgia, dept. med., 2000—02; internship and residency in internal medicine The Brody Sch. Med., East Carolina U., 2002—05; asst. prof. medicine Med. Coll. Ga., 2006—. Contbr. articles to profl. jours. Recipient Nat. Med. Rschr. awards, Roche Co., 1997—2003, Turkish Soc. Hematology, 1997, Ankara U., 1997, Pfizer Pain Mgmt. award, 2004; fellow, Ankara U. Med. Sch., Dept. Internal Medicine, Sect. Hematology, 1997—99, Med. Coll. Ga., Augusta, 2000—02. Mem.: Infectious Disease Soc. Am., Am. Soc. Bonr Marrow Transplantation, Turkish Febrile Neutropenia Group (assoc.), Turkish Soc. Hematology (assoc.), Am. Soc. Hematology (assoc.), Alpha Omega Alpha (hon.). Office: Med Coll Ga Sect Hematology, Oncology 1120 15th St BAA-5407 Augusta GA 30912-2125 Office Fax: 706-721-5566. Business E-Mail: custon@mcg.edu.

UTELL, MARK JEFFREY, medical educator; b. NYC, July 25, 1946; m. Lois Brooks; 1 child, Michael Jon. BA cum laude, Dartmouth Coll., 1968; MD, Tufts U., 1972. Diplomate Am. Bd. Internal Medicine. Intern St. Elizabeth's Hosp., Boston, 1972-73, resident in internal medicine, 1973-75; from instr. to prof. sch. medicine U. Rochester, N.Y., 1975-92, prof. Sch. Medicine, 1992—, prof. medicine and environ. medicine Sch. Medicine. Dir. respiratory and med. ICUs Strong Meml. Hosp., Rochester, 1977-89, mem. intensive care com., 1977-87; co-dir. pulmonary and critical care sch. medicine U. Rochester, 1984-91, dir. pulmonary and critical care, 1991—; occupl. medicine program, 1988—, assoc. chmn. clin. affairs dept. environ. medicine, 1992—, dir. occupl. and environ. medicine divsn., 1992—, acting chair dept. medicine, 1998-99; cons. VA, 1977—, EPA, 1980—, mem. clean air sci. adv. com., 1988-94; chmn. Environ. health Com., 1998—; mem. exec. com. EPA Sci. adv. bd.; reviewer site visit com. NIH, 1982, outside reviewer respiratory and applied physiology sect. NHLBI, 1982; mem. rev. study sect. Nat. Inst. Environ. Health Scis., 1990-94, mem. task force for rsch. planning; mem. health rsch. com. Health Effects Inst., 1985-94, chair, 2000—; mem. N.Y. State Commr.'s Panel on Tuberculosis, Syracuse, 1988; mem. commn. life scis. NRC, NAS, 1989; mem. panel airborne particulate matter in spacecraft NASA, 1987, mem. environ. health scis. working group, 1993-94. Co-author: Inhalation Toxicology of Air Pollution: Clinical Research Considerations, 1985, Susceptibility to Inhaled Pollutants, 1989; co-editor: Advances in Controlled Clinical Inhalation Studies, 1993; mem. editl. bd. Jour. Aerosol Medicine, Annals of Internal Medicine, 1997-99, Inhalation Tech., Environ. Health Perspectives, Inhalation Toxicology, 1989-2001; guest reviewer various jours.; contbr. over 100 articles to profl. jours. Bd. dirs. Am. Lung Assn. N.Y. State, 1986-88. Grantee Nat. Inst. Environ. Health Scis., Nat. Heart Lung and Blood Inst., EPA, Elec. Power Rsch. Inst., Dow Corning Corp. Fellow AAAS, ACP, Am. Coll. Chest Physicians (mem. steering com. sect. environ. occupl. health 1983-87, assessment asthma in workplace com. 1994); mem. Am. Physiol. Soc., Am. Thoracic Soc. (chmn. scientific assembly on environ. and occupl. health 1987, mem. planning com., 1992-94, respiratory protective guidelines com., 1993-95, other coms.), Am. Coll. Occupl. Environ. Medicine, N.Y. Trudeau Soc. (pres. 1986). Home: 16 Framingham Ln Pittsford NY 14534-1048 Office: U Rochester Sch Medicine Dept Medicine Pulmonary 601 Elmwood Ave Dept Medicine Rochester NY 14642-0001

UTGOFF, KATHLEEN PLATT, former federal agency administrator; b. Trenton, NJ, Feb. 5, 1948; d. Francis J. and Helen Platt; m. Victor Utgoff; children: Anna, Margaret. Student, Rutgers U., 1966-68; BA in Econs., Calif. State U., Northridge, 1971; PhD in Econs., UCLA, 1978. Employment counselor Dept. Human Resources, Van Nuys, Calif., 1971-72; economist Ctr. for Naval Analysis, Alexandria, Va., 1974-83; sr. staff economist Coun. Econ. Advisors, Exec. Office of the Pres., Washington, 1983-85; exec. dir. Pension Benefit Guaranty Corp., US Dept. Labor, Washington, 1985—89; ptnr., chief economist Groom & Nordberg, Washington, 1989—95; v.p., dir. Ctr. for Naval Analysis, Alexandria, Va., 1995—99; commr. Bur. Labor Statistics, US Dept. Labor, Washington, 2002—06. Mem. Women in Govt. Relations, Am. Econ. Assn., Women in Employee Benefits. Republican.

UTHMANN, RICHARD W., retired music educator; b. Chanute, Kans., Mar. 18, 1938; s. Walter Henry and Susie Elizabeth Uthmann; m. Edith L. Uthmann, June 29, 1963; 1 child, James Richard. BA in Music Edn., Wash. State U., 1960; MA in Music Edn., Wash. Music Edn., 1971. Tchr. band Garfield Pub. Schs., Wash., 1961—63, Mukilteo Pub. Schs., 1963—67; tchr. music Granger Pub. Schs., 1967—68, Billings Pub. Schs., 1971—73; tchr. band Kelso Pub. Schs., Wash., 1973—88, Wahkiakum Pub. Schs., Cathlamet, 1988—97, Cornerstone Christian Sch., Kelso, 1997—2006; with Principally Winds Woodwind Quintet, 2004—. Dir. theatre orch. Performing Arts Ctr., Longview, Wash., 1976—; bd. dirs. Mt. Solo Homeowners Assn., 1997—. Capt. US Army, 1968—69, Vietnam. Mem.: Wash. Music Educators Assn. (Hall of Fame 2002), Southwest Wash. Symphony (bd. dirs. 1980—, Pres. Vol. Svc. award 2007), Southwest Wash. Youth Symphony (bd. dirs. 2006—07). Methodist. Avocations: gardening, woodworking, music. Home: 120 Ridgecrest Ln Longview WA 98632 Office Phone: 360-430-7283. Personal E-mail: duthmann@peoplepc.com.

UTIAN, WULF HESSEL, gynecologist, endocrinologist; b. Johannesburg, Sept. 28, 1939; came to U.S., 1976; s. Harry and Ethel Utian; m. Moira Mervis, Oct. 4, 1964; children: Brett David, Lara Peta. MBBCh, Witwatersrand U., Johannesburg, S.Africa, 1962; PhD, U. Cape Town, South Africa, 1970, DSc in Medicine, 2007. Lic. 1976, cert. ECFMG 1963, Clinical Densitometrist Internat. Soc. Clinical Densitometry, 2001, menopause practitioner NAMS, 2005. Cons. ob-gyn Groote Schuur Hosp., Cape Town, 1967-76; dir. reprodn. endocrinology Univ. Hosps., Cleve., 1976-80; dir. ob-gyn Mt. Sinai Med. Ctr., Cleve., 1980-89; pres. U. Ob-Gyn. Specialties, Inc., 1980-99; dir. Cleve. Menopause Clinic, 1986-2000; prof., chmn. dept. reproductive biology Case Western Reserve U., Cleve., 1989-99; dir. ob-gyn. U. Hosps. of Cleve., 1989-99. Cons. Internat. Health Found., Geneva, 1976-92; cons. women's health Cleve. Clinic Found., 2000—; cons. women's midlife health to nat. media, pharm. industry and health providers; assoc. prof. Case Western Res. U., Cleve., 1976-89, prof. reproductive biology, 1989-99, prof. emeritus reproductive biology and ob-gyn., 2000—; pres. Rapid Med. Rsch., 1996—. Author: Menopause in Modern Perspective, 1980, Your Middle Years, 1980, The Menopause and Hormonal Rplacement Therapy--Facts and Controversies, 1991, Managing Your Menopause, 1992; editor: Maturitas, 1980-93, Premenstrual Syndrome, 1981, Menopause Management, 1988—, Menopause, 1993—. Pres. North Am. Menopause Soc. Found., 2007—; bd. mem. Helen Moss Breast Cancer Found., 1996—2008. Named one of Top Ten Rschrs. in Women's Health, Ladies Home Jour., 1999. Fellow ACOG, Royal Coll. Ob-Gyn. (Am. rep. to com. 1994-2000, honored for menopause rsch. and tchg. 2000), Internat. Coll. Surgeons (v.p. 1983-89); mem. Internat. Menopause Soc. (exec. com. 1981-96, pres. 1993-96, sec. Coun. Affiliated Menopause Socs. 1996-99, chmn. 1999-2005), N.Am. Menopause Soc. (exec. dir., hon. founding pres. 1989—). Avocations: sailing, hiking. Home: Point East P-7 27500 Cedar Rd Beachwood OH 44122-8105 Office: NAMS 5900 Landerbrook Dr Ste 390 Cleveland OH 44124 Home Phone: 216-378-1840; Office Phone: 440-442-7680. Business E-Mail: utian@menopause.org.

UTKU, SENOL, civil engineer, computer science educator, mathematics professor; b. Suruc, Turkey, Nov. 23, 1931; arrived in USA, 1965, naturalized, 1987; s. Sukru and Sukufe (Gumus) U.; m. Bisulay Bereket, May 9, 1964; children: Ayda, Sinan. Diploma in structural engring., Istanbul Tech. U., 1954; MCE, MIT, Cambridge, 1959, DSc in Civil Engring., 1960. Cert. profl. engr., Turkish Chamber Civil Engrs., 1954. Field engr. Necmi Sahin Constrn. Co., 1949—54; site engr. Anadolu Ltd., 1955; rsch. asst., railroads chair, civil engring. Istanbul Tech. U., 1955—57; rsch, asst. dept. civil engring. MIT, 1957—59, asst. prof. structural engring, 1960-62; rsch. engr. math. and applications department IBM, NYC, 1959-60; assoc. prof. civil engring., head of founding com. Computation Ctr. Middle East Tech U., Ankara, Turkey, 1962-63; exec. dir. Computation Ctr. Istanbul Tech. U., 1963-65, prof. emeritus faculty arts and scis., 2002—; tech. staff Jet Propulsion Lab., Pasadena, Calif., 1965-70, tech. cons., 1975—91; assoc. prof. civil engring Duke U., Durham, N.C., 1970-72, prof., 1972-79, prof. civil engring., prof. computer sci., 1979—2001, dir. undergrad. studies, 1980-87, dir. grad. studies, 1987-89, prof. emeritus civil engring. and computer sci., 2002—. Tech. cons. Lincoln Lab., MIT, 1960—61, MITRE Corp., Bedford, Mass., 1961—62, IBM, NY, 1960—61, IBM Istanbul, Turkey, 1963—64, Westinghouse R&D Ctr., Pitts., 1970, NASA Langley Rsch. Ctr., Hampton, Va., 1971, DBA Sys., Melbourne, Fla., 1971, ITT Comm., Mackay Marine Divsn., Raleigh, NC, 1974—77; lectr. U. Southern Calif., LA, 1966—70, NSF, Osaka, Kyoto, Nagoya, Tokyo, Japan, 1991, U. Bucharest, Romania, 1993, 94; vis. lectr. U. Wash., Seattle, 1968; vis. prof. Istanbul Tech. U., 1977, Bogazici U., Turkey, 1977, 78, 79, Mid. East Tech. U., 1980, King Saud U., Riyadh, Saudi Arabia, 1985. Author: ELAS Software, 1968, Elementary Structural Analysis, 4th edit., 1991, Linear Analysis of Discrete Structures, 1991, Theory of Adaptive Structures, 1998; co-author: Dynamics of Offshore Structures, 1984, Finite Element Handbook, 1987, Parallel Processing in Computational Mechanics, 1992, Intelligent Structural Systems, 1992; contbr. articles to profl. jours. Tech. translator Turkish Army Corps of Engrs., 1955—57. Fulbright scholar, Turkey, 1957, Fulbright lectr., Turkey, 1998; recipient Pres.'s Fund award Calif. Inst. Tech., 1981, NASA award, 1969, 71, 77, 84, 86-87, Internat. Joint Rsch. award NSF, 1991. Fellow ASCE; mem. AAUP, Am. Acad. Mechanics, Fulbright Assn., Am. Soc. for Engring. Edn., Structural Engring. Inst. (charter), Sigma Xi, Chi Epsilon, Sierra Club. Democrat. Muslim. Avocations: jogging, hiking, classical music, reading. Home and Office: Dr Utku and Assocs M1 Blok 4/8 Atakoy 2 Kisim Bakirkoy Istanbul 34158 Turkey Office Fax: 90 266 714 1911. Business E-Mail: bsutku@ttmail.com, senolutku@ttmail.com.

UTLEY, CHASE, professional baseball player; b. Pasadena, Calif., Dec. 17, 1978; s. David and Terrell Utley; m. Jennifer Cooper, Jan. 20, 2007. Grad. in Sociology, UCLA, 2000. Second baseman Phila. Phillies, 2003—. Mem. US Team World Baseball Classic, 2006. Recipient Mike Schmidt MVP award, Baseball Writers' Assn. of Am., Phila. chpt., 2005, Silver Slugger award, 2006—08; named Phillies Player of Yr., 2005; named to Nat. League All-Star Team, 2006—09. Achievements include leading the National League in: runs scored (131), 2006; being a member of the World Series Championship winning Philadelphia Phillies, 2008. Avocations: golf, fishing. Mailing: c/o Phila Phillies Citizens Bank Pk One Citizens Bank Way Philadelphia PA 19148*

UTLEY, JON BASIL, think-tank executive, journalist; b. Moscow, Mar. 10, 1934; came to U.S., 1939, naturalized, 1952; s. Arcadi and Freda (Utley) Berdichevsky; m. Ana Maria Hijar, 1968. Student, U. Munich, 1952, Alliance Française, Paris, 1956; BS, Georgetown U., 1956. Mgr. Am. Internat. Underwriters, Cali, Colombia, 1959-60; editor, pub. Bogotá Bull., 1960-61; v.p. Universal Investors Svcs., Nassau, 1962-67; real estate developer Washington, 1968—; mng. gen. ptnr. Kimwill Oil Assocs., Warren, Pa., 1978-86; pres. Ocean McLean Corp.,

1989-97, Needle in a Haystack, Washington, 1990-98, Needle Express, 1993-98; fgn. corr. Jour. Commerce, Internat. Reports, S. Am., 1969-74; columnist Times of the Ams., 1974-92, assoc. editor, 1981-92; columnist Washington Inquirer, 1981-90, Washington Times, 1981-82; contbg. editor Conservative Digest, 1984-89; mem. editl. adv. bd. Internat. Reports, 1981-91. Lectr. Accuracy in Media, treas., Ukraine, 1997, Cyprus, 99, Freedoms Found. Valley Forge; commentator Voice of Am., 1985—2003; Jamestown Found. observer Russian elections, 2000. Assoc. pub. Lima Times, The Am. Conservative, 2005—; contbr. articles to Washington Post, Harvard Bus. Rev., Nat. Rev., Human Events, Miami Herald, Lincoln Rev., NYC Tribune, Am. Legion mag., El Salvador Gazette, The World and I, Reason.com, Fgn. Policy in Focus, Instapundit, Alternet, RealClearPolitics.com, Freerepublic.com, Anti-war.com, Instapunoti, others. Observer Guatemalan elections Georgetown U. Ctr. Strategic Studies, 1985, Romanian elections, 1990; trustee Ctr. Internat. Rels., adv. com. Solidarity Endowment; co-founder Com. to Avert a Mideast Holocaust, 1990-94; pres. Freda Utley Found., 2002—. Assoc. scholar Competitive Enterprise Inst., 1995-98; Robert A. Taft fellow Ludwig Von Mises Inst., 1998—. Fellow: Atlas Econ. Rsch. Found. (sr.; dir. Russian projects 2000—05); mem.: Coun. Nat. Policy, Ams. Against Bombing/Ams. Against World Empire (chmn. 1998—), Hispanic Am. Ctr. Econ. Rsch. (bd. dirs. 1997—), World English Lang. Newspaper Assn. (pres. 1996), United Srs. Assn. (bd. dirs. 1993—2001, v.p. Amcham Cuba 2003—), Coun. Inter-Am. Security (bd. dirs. 1988—93), Phila. Soc., Nat. Press Club. Office: 910 17th St NW Ste 422 Washington DC 20006-2605

UTLEY, NANCY, film company executive; MA in Journalism, Northwestern U., Ill. Asst. media dir. to v.p., assoc. media dir. Grey Advt., NYC; sr. v.p. new bus. BBDO Worldwide; v.p. media rsch. 20th Century Fox, Calif., 1985, sr. v.p. media rsch., exec. v.p. mktg., media, and rsch.; pres. mktg. Fox Searchlight Pictures, 1999—2006, COO, 2006—. Named an Entertainment Marketer of the Yr., Advt. Age mag., 2008; named one of The 100 Most Powerful Women in Entertainment, Hollywood Reporter, 2006, 2007. Office: Fox Searchlight Pictures 10201 W Pico Blvd Los Angeles CA 90035-0900 Office Phone: 310-369-4402. Office Fax: 310-369-2359.

UTT, GLENN S., JR., retired medical products executive; b. Neodesha, Kans., Aug. 7, 1926; s. Glenn S. and Reba Pauline (White) Utt; m. Mary Lou Ford, Aug. 8, 1948; 1 child, Jan A. BSEE, BSBA, Kans. State U., 1949; MBA, Harvard U., 1951. Salesman Drexel Furniture Co., NC, 1951-55; v.p. Booz Allen & Hamilton, Chgo. and Zurich, Switzerland, 1955-62; exec. v.p. Abbott Labs., North Chicago, Ill., 1962-83, also dir., ret., 1983. Chmn. bd. U.P. Hotel Group Inc., Houghton, Mich.; ret. dir. Synergen, Selectide and Sugen biotech cos. Co-author: Lalique Perfume Bottles, 1990. Alderman City of Lake Forest, Ill., 1972-76, chmn. recreational bd., 1975-78, Nitrate Elimination Co. Inc., Lake Linidon, Miss.; mem. exec. com. Lake County Republican Fedn., Waukegan, Ill., 1974-83. With USN, 1944-46, USAF (res.), 1948-53. Mem.: Beta Theta Pi. Avocations: antiques, art, golf. Home: PO Box 810 Houghton MI 49931 Home Phone: 906-482-7128. Personal E-mail: mlgu2@webtv.net.

UTT, WILLIAM P. (BILL UTT), construction executive; B in Mech. Engring., U. Va., 1979, M in Mech. Engring., 1980, MBA, 1984. With CRS Sirrine Engrs., Inc., 1984; various sr. mgmt. and exec. positions CRSS, Inc.; pres., CEO North Am. Energy businesses Tractebel, 1995—2000; pres., CEO SUEZ Energy N.Am., 2000—06, KBR, 2006—, chmn., 2007—. Chmn. Electric Power Supply Assn.; mem. Nat. Petroleum Coun. Trustee Sch. Engring. and Applied Sci. U. Va.; trustee Episcopal HS, Houston. Office: KBR 601 Jefferson St Houston TX 77002 Office Phone: 713-753-2000.

UTTAL, WILLIAM R(EICHENSTEIN), psychology and engineering educator, research scientist; b. Mineola, NY, Mar. 24, 1931; s. Joseph and Claire (Reichenstein) U.; m. Michiye Nishimura, Dec. 20, 1954; children: Taneil, Lynet, Lisa. Student, Miami U. Oxford, Ohio, 1947-48; BS in Physics, U. Cin., 1951; PhD in Exptl. Psychology and Biophysics, Ohio State U., 1957. Staff Psychologist, mgr. behavioral sci. group IBM Rsch. Ctr., Yorktown Heights, NY, 1957-63; assoc. prof. U. Mich., Ann Arbor, 1963-68, prof. psychology, 1968-86, rsch. scientist, 1963-86, prof. emeritus, 1986—; grad. affiliate faculty dept. psychology U. Hawaii, 1986-88; rsch. scientist Naval Ocean Systems Ctr.-Hawaii Lab., Kailua, 1985-88; prof., chmn. dept. psychology Ariz. State U., Tempe, 1988—90, prof. dept. indsl. engring., 1992—99, affiliated prof., Dept. of Computer Sci. and Engring., 1993-98, prof. emeritus, 1999—. Vis. prof. Kyoto (Japan) Prefectural Med. U., 1965-66, Sensory Sci. Lab., U. Hawaii, 1968, 73, 2003-09, U. Western Australia, 1970-71, U. Hawaii, 1978-79, 80-81, U. Auckland, 1996, U. Freiburg, 1997, U. Sydney, 1999; pres. Nat. Conf. on On-Line Uses Computers in Psychology, 1974. Author: Real Time Computers: Techniques and Applications in the Psychological Sciences, 1968, Generative Computer Assisted Instruction in Analytic Geometry, 1972, The Psychobiology of Sensory Coding, 1973, Cellular Neurophysiology and Integration: An Interpretive Introduction, 1975, An Autocorrelation Theory of Visual Form Detection, 1975, The Psychobiology of Mind, 1978, A Taxonomy of Visual Processes, 1981, Visual Form Detection in Three Dimensional Space, 1983, Principles of Psychobiology, 1983, The Detection of Nonplanar Surfaces in Visual Space, 1985, The Perception of Dotted Forms, 1987, On Seeing Forms, 1988, The Swimmer: A Computational Model of a Perceptual Motor System, 1992, Toward a New Behaviorism: The Case Against Perceptual Reductionism, 1998, A Computational Model of Vision: The Role of Combination, 1999, The War Between Mentalism and Behaviorism, 2000, The New Phrenology: Limits on the Localization of Cognitive Processes in the Brain, 2001, A Behaviorist Looks at Form Recognition, 2002, Psychomythics, 2003, Dualism, 2004, Neural Theories of Mind, 2005, Human Factors in the Courtroom, 2006, The Immeasurable Mind, 2007, Time, Space and Number in Physics and Psychology, 2008; editor: Readings in Sensory Coding, 1972, Neuroscience in the Courtroom, 2008, Distributed Neurol Systems, 2009; assoc. editor Behavioral Rsch. Method and Instrn., 1968—90, Computing: Archives for Electronic Computing, 1963—75, Jour. Exptl. Psychology, Perception and Performance, 1974—79, cons. editor Jour. Exptl. Psychology: Applied, 1994—97; contbr. articles to profl. jours. Served to 2d lt. USAF, 1951-53. USPHS spl. postdoctoral fellow, 1965-66; NIMH research scientist award, 1971-76 Fellow AAAS, APA, Am. Psychol. Soc. (charter), Soc. Exptl. Psychologists (chmn. 1994-95), Ariz. Acad. Sci., Arts & Tech. (founding fellow). Achievements include patents in field. Office: Ariz State U Dept Indsl Engring Tempe AZ 85287-1104 Business E-Mail: aowru@asu.edu.

UTTS, JESSICA MARIE, statistician, educator; b. Niagara Falls, NY, Oct. 13, 1951; d. Richard C. and Patricia (Highberger) U. BA, SUNY, Binghamton, 1973; MA, Pa. State U., 1975, PhD, 1978. Asst. prof. stats. U. Calif., Davis, 1978-84, assoc. prof., 1984-93, prof., 1993—2008, Irvine, 2008—. Author: Mind on Statistics 3rd edit., 2007, Seeing Through Statistics 3d edit., 2005, Statistical Ideas and Methods, 2006. Recipient Disting. Teaching award U. Calif., Davis, 1985, Carver medal, Inst. Meth. Stats, 2005, Founders award, Am. Stat. Assn., 2009, fellow, Assoc. Psychol. Sci., 2007. Fellow AAAS, Inst. Math. Stats. (treas. 1988-94, Carver medal 2008), Am. Statis. Assn. (Fopunder's award 2009), Assn. Psychol. Sci. Office: Univ Calif Dept Stats Irvine CA 92697 Business E-Mail: jutts@uci.edu.

UVA, JOE, broadcast executive; b. 1956; BA, SUNY Albany. Account exec. for CNN Turner Broadcasting Sales, Inc., 1984, v.p. & sales mgr., 1985—90, exec. v.p. sales for CNN/Headline News, 1990—95, pres., Turner Entertainment Group Sales & Mktg., 1996—2001; pres. & CEO OMD Worldwide, NYC, 2002—07; CEO Univision Comm. Inc., 2007—. Bd. dirs. TiVo, Inc., 2004—. Office: Univision Communications Inc Ste 3050 1999 Ave of the Stars Los Angeles CA 90067 Office Phone: 310-556-7665.

UYEDA, STEVEN, biology professor; s. Henry Fujiki and Sadako Joyce Uyeda; m. Kathryn Hansen-Uyeda, June 6, 1984 (div. May 7, 1994); 1 child, Jonathan; m. JodyLee Estrada Duek, Oct. 7, 1995. MA in Sci. Edn., U. Ariz., Tucson, 2002. Cert. tchr. Ariz. State Bd. Edn., 2000, tchr. biology endorsement 1996. Biology adj. instr. Pima C.C., Tucson, 2000—; biology instr. Sunnyside Unified Sch. Dist., Tucson, 2003—. Mem.: Phi Theta Kappa (Tucson) (advisor 2008—).

UYEHARA, CATHERINE FAY TAKAKO (YAMAUCHI), physiologist, educator, pharmacologist; b. Honolulu, Dec. 20, 1959; d. Thomas Takashi and Eiko Uyehara; m. Alan Hisao Yamauchi, Feb. 17, 1990. BS, Yale U., 1981; PhD in Physiology, U. Hawaii, Honolulu, 1987. Postdoctoral fellow SmithKline Beecham Pharms., King of Prussia, Pa., 1987-89; rsch. pharmacologist Kapiolani Med. Ctr. for Women and Children, Honolulu, 1990-91, dep. chief rechr., 2004—07; chief, dept. clin. investigation, 2007—. Statis. cons. Tripler Army Med. Ctr., Honolulu, 1984-87, 89—, chief rsch. pharmacology, 1991—, dir. collaborative rsch. program, 1995—, dep. chief rsch., 2004-07, mem. grad. faculty in pharmacology, pediatrics, physiology, U. Hawaii John A. Burns Sch. Medicine, 1991—; grad. faculty Interdisciplinary Biomed. Sci. program, 1991—. Contbr. articles to profl. jours. Decorated Med. Merit Order Mil. Mem. Am. Fedn. for Med. Rsch., Am. Physiol. Soc., Am. Heart Assn., Soc. Uniformed Endocrinologists, Endocrine Soc., We. Soc. Pediatric Rsch., N.Y. Acad. Scis., Hawaii Acad. Sci., Sigma Xi. Democrat. Avocations: swimming, diving, crafts, horticulture, music. Office: Dept Clin Investigation 1 Jarrett White Rd Bldg 40 Tamc HI 96859 Office Phone: 808-433-6709.

UYS, JURGEN PETER BRINKER, securities analyst; came to U.S., 1955; s. Johannes Marthinus and Reinette McKay (Weidemann) U. BS, U. Pa., 1974; MBA, Columbia U., 1978. CFA. Securities analyst Equibank, N.A., Pitts., 1974-76; fin. analyst Amax Inc., Greenwich, Conn., 1978-80; v.p. Equitable Investment Mgmt., NYC, 1980-85; securities analyst Swiss Am. Securities, NYC, 1986-91; gen. ptnr. PBU Ptnrs. L.P. Ltd., Atlanta, 1991—; mng. mem. J.P. Brinker Uys & Co. LLC, Atlanta, 2004—. Mem.: CFA Inst., Huguenot Soc. Am. (treas. 1991—92), Commerce Club. Episcopalian. E-mail: jpbu@msn.com.

UYSAL, ISMAIL, research scientist; s. Mehmet and Zehra Fatma Uysal; m. Dilek Dagdelen Uysal, Jan. 3, 2004. BS, Orta Dogu Teknik U., Ankara, Turkey, 2003; MS, U. Fla., Gainesville, 2006, PhD, 2008. Engring. intern Sci. and Tech. Rsch. Inst., Ankara, 2001, Info. Techs. and Electronics Rsch. Inst., Ankara, 2002, Motorola, Plantation, Fla., 2007; rsch. asst. U. Fla., 2004—08, postdoc., 2008—. Contbr. articles to engring. jours. Mem.: IEEE, Acoustical Soc. America, Eta Kappa Nu. Achievements include patents for method and system for bandwidth expansion for voice communications. Business E-Mail: uysal@ufl.edu.

UYSAL, MUZAFFER SHAMIL, management educator; s. Samil and Ifakat Uysal; m. Nese Kirimker, July 28, 1970; 1 child, Deylin Shamil. BS, Anakara Acad. Econs. and Comml. Scis., 1976; MBA, U. New Haven, 1980; PhD, Tex. A&M U., 1983. Asst. prof. Dokuz Eylul U., Izmir, Turkey, 1984—85, Clemson U., SC, 1985—88, assoc. prof., 1988—91, Va. Tech, Blacksburg, 1992—, prof. Contbr. articles to profl. jours.; co-editor: Tourism Analysis an Interdisciplinary Jour., 1996—. Fellow: Internat. Acad. Study Tourism, Phi Beta Delta (hon.; treas. 2000—02); mem.: Acad. Leisure Scis., Internat. Soc. Quality-of-Life Studies (bd. mem. 1999—2002), Internat. Travel and Tourism Rsch. Assn. (conf. program reviewer 1988—93). Home: 303 Seminole Dr Blacksburg VA 24060 Office: Virginia Tech HTM 355 Wallace Hall Blacksburg VA 24061-04 Business E-Mail: samil@vt.edu.

UZGOREN, ERAY, science educator; s. Ibrahim and Hurriyet Uzgoren. BS, Orta Dogu Teknik U., Ankara, 1999; MS, U. Fla., Gainesville, 2003; PhD, 2006. Postdoc. rsch. fellow U. Mich., Ann Arbor, 2006—07; vis. asst. prof. Va. Tech, Blacksburg, 2007—. Contbr. articles to profl. jours. Mem. Grad. Student Coun., U. Fla., 2003—04. Mem.: AIAA.

UZMAN, BETTY BEN GEREN, retired pathologist; b. Ft. Smith, Ark., Nov. 17, 1922; d. Benton Asbury and Myra Estelle (Petty) Geren; m. L. Lahut Uzman, Dec. 17, 1955 (dec.); 1 dau., Betty Tuba. Student, Ft. Smith Jr. Coll., 1939—40; BS, U. Ark., 1942; MD, Washington U., 1945; postgrad., MIT, 1948—50; MA (hon.), Harvard U., 1968. Intern Childrens Hosp., Boston, 1945—46; resident pathology Barnes Hosp., St. Louis, 1946—48; Am. Cancer Soc. rsrch. fellow MIT, Cambridge, 1948—50; chief biol. ultra structure and exptl. pathology Children's Cancer Rsch. Found., Boston, 1950—71; instr. Harvard Med. Sch., Boston, 1949—53, assoc., 1953—56, rsch. assoc., 1956—67, assoc. prof., 1967—71, prof., 1971-72; head rsch. dept. Sparks Regional Med. Ctr., Ft. Smith, 1972—74; prof. pathology La. State U., Shreveport, 1974—77, U. Tenn., Memphis, 1978—89, ret., 1989. Assoc. chief staff rsch. VA, Shreveport, 1974-77; staff pathologist VA, Memphis, 1978-89, chief lab. svc., 1986-87; chief field ops., spl. asst. to dir. VA Ctrl. Office, Washington, 1978-79, dir. med. rsch. svcs., 1979-80; chmn. pathology A Study sect. NIH, 1973-76; cons. to sci. dir. Children's Cancer Rsch. Found., Boston, 1971-73; mem. adv. com. on prevention, diagnosis and treatment Am. Cancer Soc., 1970-73, 77-80; mem. adv. bd. Office Regeneration Rsch., VA, 1985-89; disting. vis. investigator Inst. Venezolano Investigation Cientificas, Caracas, 1972-74 Decorated Order Andres Bello 1st class Venezuela; recipient Weinstein award United Cerebral Palsy, 1964 Mem. AAAS, Am. Soc. Cell Biology (emerita), Microscopy Soc. Am. (emerita, Diatome poster award 1985), Internat. Acad. Pathology (emerita), Am. Assn. Neuropathology (emerita, assoc.), Soc. Neurosci. (emerita), Am. Assn. Cancer Rsch. (emerita). Home and Office: Geren Farm 16048 E State Hwy 197 Scranton AR 72863-0048 Personal E-mail: bettyguzman@wildblue.net, bguzman@aol.com.

UZMAN, JAMES AKIF, biology professor; b. Ann Arbor, Mich., Feb. 24, 1953; s. Zeyn Nasut and Ayten Bikem Uzman; m. Amy Katherine Sater, Aug. 8, 1987; children: Jacob Mazhar, Seth Sater. BS in Zoology, U. Mich., Ann Arbor, 1975, MS in Environ. Scis., 1976; PhD in Zoology, U. Calif., Berkeley, 1983. Rsch. assoc. and lectr. U. Houston, 1993—97; dept. chair and assoc. prof. biology and biochemistry U. Houston-Downtown, 1997—. Staff scientist i Lawrence Berkeley Lab., Calif., 1991—93; editl. bd. mem. Biochemical and Molecular Biology Edn., 1999—. Author: (book) Student Companion to Fundamentals of Biochemistry. Mem.: Am. Soc. Biochemistry and Molecular Biology. Home: 3614 Cloverdale St Houston TX 77025 Office: Univ Houston-Downtown One Main St Houston TX 77002 Office Fax: 713-221-8528. Business E-Mail: uzmana@uhd.edu.

UZODINMA, MINTA LAVERNE SMITH, retired nursing administrator, nurse midwife; b. Des Moines, Mar. 29, 1935; d. Gerald Stanley and Dorothy LaVerne (Miles) Smith; m. John E. Uzodinma, Aug. 8, 1957 (dec. June 1994); children: Chinwe Uzodinma Thomas, Chika Uzodinma Hunter, Eze A., Amechi J. BSN, U. Iowa, 1957; cert nurse-midwifery, U. Miss., Jackson, 1970, MSN, 1975. Staff-head nurse pediatrics unit, supr. insvc. edn. Univ. Hosp., Iowa City, 1957-58, 61-64; clin. instr. med.-surg. nursing Iowa Meth. Sch. Nursing, Des Moines, 1958-59, 60; staff nurse, instr., assoc. dept. ob-gyn-dir. midwifery svc. U. Miss. Med. Ctr., Jackson, 1966-74, instr. nurse-midwifery edn., 1974-77, asst. prof., 1979-85, module coord. nurse-midwifery edn., 1977-81; staff nurse VA Med. Ctr., Jackson, 1985-87; nurse-midwife Coastal Family Health Ctr., Gulfport, Miss., 1987-89; asst. dir. nursing Miss. Dept. Health, Jackson, 1989-95, chief nurse cons., 1995—2001; clin. instr. nursing U. Miss. Med. Ctr., Jackson, 1992—2001, ret., 2001. Acting dir. nursing area Rust Coll., Holly Springs, Miss., 1975; mem. Miss. Bd. Nursing, 1979-84, treas., 1980-82, pres., 1983-84. Asst. editor region 3 Jour. Nurse-Midwifery, 1986-94; contbr. article to nursing jour. Bd. dirs. Hinds County unit Am. Cancer Soc., 1976-83; v.p. Poindexter Elem. Sch. PTA, 1966, pres., 1974-75. Recipient Alton B. Cobb Lifetime Achievement award Miss. Pub. Health Assn., 1996, Thelma Workman award LWV Miss., 1998, Nursing Alumni of Decade award U. Miss., 1998; U. Iowa scholar, 1953-56; named Maternal-Child Health Cmty. Nurse of Yr., Miss. March of Dimes, 1995,98. Fellow Am. Coll. Nurse-Midwives (chpt. sec.-treas. 1985-86, treas. 1978-80, proctor divsn. examiners 1975-85, nat. chmn. nominating com. 1978-79, mem. task force on refresher programs 1984-88, chpt. chair 1991-94, bd. rev. 1987-90, sec. region III chpt. 4 1984-86, bd. govs. regional gov. 1997—, award for excellence 1997); mem. ANA, Miss. Nurses Assn. (chmn. affirmative action com. 1977-78, continuing edn. approval unit 1990-95, nurse practitioner spl. interest group 1984—, dir. edn. 1995-97, Pub./Cmty. Health Nurse of Yr. 1998, named Nurse of Yr. 2001, Hall of Fame 2009), Eliza Pillars RN Assn., AAUW, U. Miss. Alumni Assn. (Nursing Alumni of Decade award 1971-80, 1998), Sigma Theta Tau. Home: 2832 Gretna Green St Jackson MS 39209-6907 Home Phone: 601-354-1908. Personal E-mail: muzocnm@aol.com.

UZZELL-BAGGETT, KARON LYNETTE, career officer; b. Goldsboro, NC, Apr. 28, 1964; d. Jesse Lee and Ernestine Smith Uzzell; m. Ronald Walter Baggett, July 26, 1990; 1 child, Kathleen; stepchildren: Christina, Brian, Adam. BS, U. N.C., Chapel Hill, 1986; postgrad., U. Md., College Park, 1993—96. Commd. 2nd lt. USAF, 1986, advanced through grades to lt. col., 1990, exec. officer 6ACCS Langley AFB, Va., 1986—88, ops. tng. officer 7393MUNSS Murted AFD, Turkey, 1988—89, command and control officer 52FW Spangdahlem AB, Germany, 1989—92, SENEX mission dir. 89AW Andrews AFB, Md., 1995—95, dep. chief classified control Office Sec. Def., 1995—97, chief classified control Office Sec. Def., 1998—99, flight comdr., dir. ops. 82TRSS Sheppard AFB, Tex., 1999—2001; detachment comdr. USAFE MSS, Vicenza, Italy, 2001—02; comdr. 78MSS, Robins AFB, Ga., 2002—04, 416EMSS, Karshi-Khanabad, Uzbekistan, 2003—04; dir. pers. OSC-A, Kabul, Afghanistan, 2005, plans officer, 2005; dir. pers. Air U., Maxwell AFB, Ala., 2004—08; comdr. Afrotc Det 790 TSU, Nashville, 2008—. Emergency med. technician Orange County Rescue Squad, Hillsborough, N.C., 1985-86; treas. Melwood PTA, Upper Marlboro, Md., 1994-97; meml. vol. Women in Mil. Svc., Washington, 1993—; entitlements vol. Whitman Walker Clinic, Washington, 1993-98. Mem. So. Poverty Law Ctr. Democrat. Baptist. Avocations: running, weightlifting, sewing, cross stitching, gardening. Home: 1212 Rockeford Dr Nashville TN 37221-4151 Office Phone: 615-963-5975.

UZZO, ROBERT G., physician, consultant; b. NYC, Feb. 4, 1967; s. Robert A Uzzo, Mary Ann Uzzo; m. Cheryl D. Uzzo. MD, Cornell U. Med. Coll., 1991. Diplomate Am. Bd. Urology, 2001. Staff surgeon Fox Chase Cancer Ctr., Phila., 2000—. Office: Fox Chase Cancer Ctr 7701 Burholme Ave Philadelphia PA 19111 Office Phone: 215-728-3501. Office Fax: 215-728-2773.

VAAMONDE-MARTIN, DIANA MARIA, biologist, embryologist, researcher, educator; b. Las Palmas, Spain, Oct. 28, 1976; d. Ricardo Vaamonde-Lemos and Maria Inmaculada Martin-Alvarez; m. Marzo Edir Da Silva-Grigoletto, Mar. 18, 2005; children: Daniel Alvaro Oquendo-Vaamonde, Diana Kym Da Silva-Vaamonde. BS cum laude, Wash. and Lee U., Lexington, Va., 1998; MS, Old Dominion U./ The Jones Inst. for Reproductive Medicine, Norfolk, Va., 2004; PhD cum laude, U. Cordoba, Spain, 2006. Cert. Colegio Oficial de Biologos de Andalucia, 2000. Dir. Andrology and Embryology Lab. Ctr. Embriologia and Reproduccion Asistida, Cordoba, 2000—04; asst. prof. Anatomy and Embryology Sch. Medicine U. Cordoba, 2004—; postdoc. rschr. Hosp. Clin. Parlo Alegre, Brazil, 2009—. Rschr. Sport Scis. Sch. Medicine U. Cordoba, 2002—; consulting biologist and rschr. Ctr. Iberoamericano Reproduccion Asistida, Punta del Este, Uruguay, 2005—, Insemine Ctr. Reproduçao Humana, Porto Alegre, Brazil, 2007—; invited lectr. in field. Ad hoc referee to numerous sci. jours.:; contbr. chapters to books, articles to profl. jours. Mem.: Spanish Fertility Soc., Spanish Soc. Histology and Tissue Engring. (mem. orgnl. com. XIV Nat. Congress and II Internat. 2007—), Assn. Study Biology and Reproduction, Alpha Epsilon Delta. Roman Catholic. Achievements include research in the existing relationship between male infertility and physical activity; the effect of novel training method for muscle and strength improvement; the effect of reactive oxygen species on sperm endometriosis; embryo metabolism, embryo implantation events, confocal microscopy and physiology of pregnancy special media insert in work in her 2009 GSHRE congress. Avocations: travel, Brazilian capoeira and dance, music, horseback riding, skiing. Home: C/Damasco 22 6-1 Cordoba 14004 Spain Office: Sch Medicine Univ Cordoba Avda Menendez Pidal s/n Cordoba 14071 Spain Office Phone: 01134957218262. Home Fax: 011-34-957452166. Personal E-mail: fivresearch@yahoo.com.

VACANTI, JOSEPH PHILIP, pediatric and transplant surgeon; b. Omaha, Oct. 31, 1948; BS summa cum laude, Creighton U., 1970; MD with high distinction, U. Nebr., 1974. Diplomate in gen. surgery and pediatric surgery Am. Bd. Surgery. Clin. fellow in surgery Harvard Med. Sch., Boston, 1979-83; asst. in surgery Children's Hosp., Boston, 1983-90, sr. assoc. in surgery, 1990-98, dir. organ transplant, 1990-98, dir. lab. for transplant and tissue engring., 1990—; asst. prof. surgery Harvard Med. Sch., Boston, 1983-90, assoc. prof., 1990-97, prof., 1997—; John Homans prof. surgery Harvard Med. Sch./Mass. Gen. Hosp., 1998—; dir. Lab. Tissue Engring. and Organ Fabrication Mass. Gen. Hosp., 1998—, dir. Pediat. Transplant, 1998—, chief Dept. Pediat. Surgery, 2003—; surgeon-in-chief Mass. Gen. Hosp. Children, 2003—. Rsch. affiliate MIT, Cambridge, 1988—. Author some 30 book chpts. and more than 150 sci. articles; co-founder, sr. editor Tissue Engring.; mem. editl. bd. Cell Transplantation; mem. editl. adv. bd. Tissue Engring. Intelligence Unit, R.G. Landes. Recipient Sidney Farber award

Children's Hosp., 1983, Spl. Recognition award Am. Liver Found., 1987. Fellow ACS; mem. Tissue Engring. Soc. (co-founder, pres.), Am. Soc. Transplant Surgeons, Transplantation Soc., Am. Pediat. Surg. Assn., Soc. Univ. Surgeons, Inst. Medicine. Office: Mass Gen Hosp 55 Fruit St Boston MA 02114-2696 Office Phone: 617-724-1725. Business E-Mail: jvacanti@parthners.org.

VACCA, JAMES, city councilman; b. Bronx, NY, 1955; m. Shirley Vacca; 1 child, Elizabeth. BA, SUNY; MA in urban studies, Queens Coll. CUNY. Pres. NE Bronx Sr. Ctr., 1975—2005; dist. mgr. NYC Cmty. Bd. 10, 1985—2002; city councilman Dist. 13 NY City Coun., 2002—. Chmn. Sr. Centers com. NY City Coun.; adj. prof. Queens Coll., Monroe Coll. Mem. adv. coun. Middletown Plz. Sr. Ctr.; v.p. Pelham Bay Taxpayers & Civic Assn.; sec. 45th Precinct Cmty. Coun. Mem.: KC. Democrat. Office: 3040 East Tremont Ave Room 104 Bronx NY 10461 Office Phone: 718-931-1721. Office Fax: 718-931-1605. Business E-Mail: vacca@council.nyc.ny.us.*

VACCARELLO, JANINE, museum administrator; BA, U. Ctrl. Fla.; MA, Rollins Coll. With Discovery Zone Inc., Fla., Wonderworks, Orlando, Fla., Orange County Govt., Fla., Lockheed Martin; cons. TissueNet; COO Nat. Mus. Crime & Punishment, Washington, 2007—. Bd. mem. Cystic Fibrosis Found., Buoniconti Fund to Cure Paralysis. Named an All-Star, Abbot Labs., Outstanding Young Professional, Cystic Fibrosis Found. Office: Nat Mus Crime & Punishment 575 7th St NW Washington DC 20004 Office Phone: 202-621-5556, 202-393-1099. E-mail: janine@crimemuseum.org.

VACCARIELLO, PATRICK, conductor; Musical dir., condr.: (Broadway plays) Joseph and the Amazing Technicolor Dreamcoat, 1993; Cabaret, 1998; Jesus Christ Superstar, 2000; Dance of the Vampires, 2002; Gypsy, 2003, 2008; The Boy from Oz, 2003; La Cage aux Folles, 2004; A Chorus Line, 2006; West Side Story, 2009. Mailing: 500 W 43rd St Apt 22F New York NY 10036*

VACCARINO, VIOLA, professor medicine; d. Carmelo Vaccarino and Francesca Galluppi; m. James Douglas Bremner, Aug. 1, 1990; children: Sabina Francesca Vaccarino Bremner, Dylan Vittorio Bremner. MD, Milan U., 1984, PhD, 1992, Yale U., New Haven, 1994. Asst. prof. Yale U. Sch. Medicine, 1995—2000; assoc. prof. tenure Emory U., Atlanta, 2000—06, prof. tenure, 2006—. Contbr. articles to profl. jours. Assoc. editor Psychosomatic Medicine, 2007, Circulation Cardiovasc. Quality and Outcomes, 2008; vice chair Nat. Forum Heart Disease and Stroke Prevention, Policy Rsch. Implementation Group, 2008. Recipient Mid-Career Devel. award, NIH, 2004—; R01grant, 2001—06, 2004—. Mem.: Am. Soc. Preventive Medicine, Am. Epidemiol. Soc., Am. Psychosomatic Soc., Am. Heart Assn. (steering com. mem. 2008, Established Investigator award 2002—06). Office: Emory Univ 1256 Briarcliff Rd NE Ste 1 N Atlanta GA 30306 Office Phone: 404-727-4849.

VACCARO, ANNETTE ANDRÉA, music educator; b. Port Chester, NY, June 12, 1957; BS in Music Edn., Mercy Coll., 1980; cert. in Tchg., Manhattanville Coll., 1980; MS in Music Edn., We. Conn. State U., 1984; PhD in Adminstrn. and Supervision, Fordham U., 1990. Music tchr. Lakeland Ctrl. Schs., Shrub Oak, NY, 1980—, theatre dir., 1980—2002, with adminstrn. support Lakeland H.S., 2005—06, interim asst. prin. Lakeland H.S., 2006; dist. coord. music dept. Lakeland Schs., 2007—08. Adj. prof. Mercy Coll., Yorktown Heights, NY, 1993—95; advisor Wig 'n' Whiskers Drama Club Lakeland HS, Shrub Oak, 1986—, mem. AIDS Awareness Com., 1990—93, adminstrv. support, 2005—06; guest condr. Dutchess County (N.Y.) Music Festival, 1991, Westchester Broadway Theatre, Elmsford, NY, 2006; adminstrn. mentoring com. Lakeland Sch. Dist., Shrub Oak, 2002—03. Recipient Nat. Theatre award, BRAVO Channel, 1999, Am. Tchr. award, The Walt Disney Corp., 2001, Cab Calloway Lifetime Achievement award, 2005; named Alumni of Yr., Lakeland (N.Y.) Edn. Found., 1999, Tchr. of Yr., Walmart Corp., 2001. Home: 129 Fields Lane Peekskill NY 10566 Office: Lakeland High School 1349E Main St Shrub Oak NY 10588

VACCHELLI, ROBERT FRANCIS, judge; b. Hartford, Conn., Jan. 29, 1951; s. Frank P. and Helen (DeRobertis) V.; m. Cathy Kinnane; 1 child. AB, Coll. of the Holy Cross, Worcester, Mass., 1973; JD, Suffolk U., 1977. Bar: Conn. 1977, U.S. Dist. Ct. Conn. 1978, U.S. Ct. Appeals 1979, U.S. Supreme Ct. 1981, Calif. 1983. Assoc. Stoner, Gross & Chorches, Hartford, 1977-78; asst. atty. gen. Conn. Atty. Gen.'s Office, Hartford, 1978—2007; judge Conn. Superior Ct., 2007—. Contbr. seminar U.S. Bur. Alcohol, Tobacco & Firearms, 1984; spkr. various seminars, 1986—; argued before U.S. Supreme Ct., 1989; advisor Conn. Gen. Assembly Law Revision Commn., 1992; state coord. Internat. Extraditions, 1998—2007. Author: Liquor Licensing in Connecticut, 1987. Mem. Glastonbury, Conn. Pub. Bldg. Commn., 1986, Glastonbury Wetlands Authority, 1987; mem. Dem. Town Com., Glastonbury, 1986-91; vice chmn. bd. dirs. Glastonbury ABC, 1989-94; elected mem. Glastonbury Conn. Bd. Assessment Appeals, 2003-07. Recipient Am. Jurisprudence Book prize Lawyer's Co-op. Publ. Co., 1976, proclamation Glastonbury Conservation Commn., 1988, Merit award State of Conn., 1986, 91, 92, 95, 97, 98, 2004, 06. Mem. ABA (mem. adv. panel 2006-07), Conn. Bar Assn. (chmn. adminstrv. law exec. com., specialization cert. subcom. 1982-89, mcpl. law com. 1982-87), Wadsworth Atheneum, Am. Judicature Soc., Am. Judges Assn., Conn. Judges Assn.

VACCHIO, RENE, language educator; d. Bruce Ronkette and Maria Vacchio. MA in Spanish Linguistics, U. Tex., Austin. Adj. assoc. prof. Spanish Austin CC, 1999—. Spanish faculty Concordia U., 2001—09. Office: Austin CC 1212 Rio Grande Austin TX 78701 Business E-Mail: rvacchio@austincc.edu.

VACCO, DENNIS C., lawyer, former state attorney general; b. Buffalo, Aug. 16, 1952; s. Carmen A. and Mildred V.; m. Kelly McIlroy; children: Alex, Connor. BA, Colgate U., 1974; JD, SUNY, Buffalo, 1978. Bar: N.Y. 1978, Fed. Ct. 1978, 82. Asst. dist. atty. Office of Erie County Dist. Atty., Buffalo, 1978-82, chief G.J. bureau, 1982-88; U.S. Atty. We. Dist. N.Y. Buffalo, 1988-93; atty. gen. State of New York, Albany, 1993-98; v.p. for govtl. affairs Waste Mgmt. Inc., 1998-99; pres. Waste Mgmt. N.Y. LLC, 1999—2003; pvt. practice atty. Boston, 2003—; ptnr. Carne & Vacco LLC, 2004—. Chmn. Atty. Gen.'s Environ. Subcom., Atty. Gen.'s Subcom. on Organized Crime and Violent Crime; mem. Nat. Environ. Enforcement Coun. Co-chair Erie County Community Commn. on Alcohol and Substance Abuse; bd. dirs. United Way of Erie County. Recipient Environ. Enforcement Leadership award Atty. Gen. Dept. of Justice, Washington, 1991. Mem. N.Y. State Bar Assn., Erie County Bar Assn., Nat. Dist. Attys. Assn., N.Y. State Dist. Attys. Assn., NCCJ, Hamburg Devel. Corp., 100 Club of Buffalo, U. Buffalo Law Alumni Assn. (bd. dirs.). Republican. Roman Catholic. Avocations: travel, sports.

VACEK, JAROSLAV, chemist, researcher; b. Prague, Czech Rep., Mar. 7, 1969; s. Jaroslav Vacek and Gabriela Vacková; m. Ivana Rulfova, 1991 (div. 2007); children: Jaroslav Gerard, Martin Josef; life ptnr. Jana Chocholousova. MS, Charles U., Prague, 1992; PhD, Charles U., 1996. Rsch. scientist U. Colo., Boulder, 1995—; postdoc. rschr. U. Calif., San Francisco, 1997—98; staff scientist Inst. Phys. Chemistry, Acad. Scis. Czech Rep., 1998—2004, scientist, 2004—. Contbr. scientific papers to profl. pubs. Grantee Rsch. award, EOARD, 1999, ARL-ERO, 2001—04. Mem.: Lifeboat Found. (sci. adv. bd. mem. 2008), Am. Chem. Soc. Achievements include design of molecular rotors and motors; research in nanomachine behavior, friction at molecular level; development of molecular dynamics code TINK. Office: Univ Colo Dept Chemistry and Biochemistry Boulder CO 80309-0215 Office Phone: 303-492-0998. Business E-Mail: vacek@eepus.colorado.edu.

VACHHARAJANI, TUSHAR JITENDRA, nephrologist, researcher; s. Jitendra Manilal and Jyoti Jitendra Vachharajani; m. Vidula Tushar Vidula Limaye, June 29, 1990; 1 child, Vipul Tushar. MBBS, Grant Med. Coll., Mumbai, India, 1985, MD, 1989; DNB in Nephrology, Bombay Hosp. Inst. Med. Scis., Mumbai, India, 1991. Diplomate Am. Bd. Internal Medicine. Asst. prof. nephrology La. State U. Health Scis. Ctr., Shreveport, 2001—05, assoc. prof., 2005—; dir. interventional nephrology and acute dialysis unit Overton Brooks VA Med. Ctr., Shreveport, 2001—, chief nephrology sect., 2002—. Contbr. articles to profl. jours. Fellow, La. State U. Health Scis. Ctr., Shreveport, 1999, 2001. Fellow: ACP, Internat. Soc. Nephrology, Am. Soc. Nephrology. Achievements include research in clincial nephrology. Office: Overton Brooks VA Med Ctr 510 E Stoner Ave Shreveport LA 71101 Office Fax: 318-424-6179. E-mail: tushar.vachharajani@med.va.gov.

VACHHARAJANI, VIDULA T., emergency physician; d. Shivram M. and Kumudini S. Limaye; m. Tushar J. Vachharajani, June 29, 1990; 1 child, Vipul T. MBBS, Grant Med. Coll., Mumbai, 1987; MD, Bombay U., 1990. Diplomate Am. Bd. Internal Medicine, 2000, in critical care medicine 2003. Asst. prof. La. State U. Health Scis. Ctr., Shreveport, 2001—06, dir. telemetry, 2001—03; asst. prof. Wake Forest U. Med. Sch., Winston-Salem, NC, 2006—. Contbr. articles to profl. jour. Grant, Fiest Weiler Found., 2004. Fellow: Am. Coll. Chest Physicians; mem.: Critical Care Soc., Microcirculation Soc. Achievements include research in obesity and sepsis. Office: Wake Forest Univ Sch Medicine Medical Center Blvd Winston Salem NC 27157

VACHON, CHRISTINE, film producer; b. NYC, Nov. 21, 1962; 1 child, Guthrie. Co-head Killer Films, NYC, 1995—. Jury mem. Sundance Film Festival, 1993, 2005, Venice Film Festival, 2005. Prodr.: (films) Tommy's, 1985, La Divina, 1989, He Was Once, 1989, Poison, 1991, Oreos with Attitude, 1991, Swoon, 1992, Geoffrey Beene 30, 1993, Post Cards from America, 1994, Safe, 1995, Stonewall, 1995, Plain Pleasures, 1996, I Shot Andy Warhol, 1996, Kiss Me, Guido, 1997, Office Killer, 1997, Happiness, 1998, Velvet Goldmine, 1998, I'm Losing You, 1998, Boys Don't Cry, 1999, Crime and Punishment in Suburbia, 2000, Fire and Mellow, 2001, Hedwig and the Angry Inch, 2001, Series 7: The Contenders, 2001, Women in Film, 2001, The Safety of Objects, 2001, Storytelling, 2001, The Gray Zone, 2001, Chelsea Walls, 2001, One Hour Photo, 2002, Far from Heaven, 2002, Party Monster, 2003, Camp, 2003, The Company, 2003, A Home at the End of the World, 2004, A Dirty Shame, 2004, The Notorious Bettie Page, 2005, Infamous, 2006, An American Crime, 2007, Savage Grace, 2007, I'm Not There, 2007, Then She Found Me, 2007; exec. prodr.: Nation, 1992, Wildflowers, 1999; co-prodr.: Kids, 1995; prodr.: (TV films) Dottie Gets Spanked, 1993; exec. prodr.: (films) Mrs. Harris, 2005; (TV series) This American Life, 2007—08. Recipient Frameline Award for Outstanding Achievement in Lesbian and Gay Media, 1994, Muse Award for Outstanding Vision and Achievement, NY Women in Film and TV, 1996, Prodrs. Award, Nat. Bd. Review, 2003; named one of The Most Powerful Women in NYC, NY Post, 2008, The 100 Most Powerful Women in Entertainment, Hollywood Reporter, 2007. Office: Killer Films 526 W 26th St Rm 715 New York NY 10001-5524 Office Phone: 212-473-3950. Office Fax: 212-473-6152.

VACHON, JACQUES P., lawyer, paper company executive; Grad. in Law, Sherbrooke U.; exec. program diploma in Human Resources & Orgnl. Devel., Stanford U., Calif. Sr. v.p., corp. affairs, sec. Abitibi-Consol. Inc., 1997—2007; sr. v.p., corp. affairs, chief legal officer AbitibiBowater Inc., 2007—. Office: AbitibiBowater Inc Ste 800 1155 Metcalfe St Montreal QC H3B 5H2 Canada Office Phone: 5148752160.*

VACHON, MARK L., manufacturing executive; Grad., Northeastern U., Boston. Joined GE, 1982, with Global Rsch. Ctr., with appliances, with plastics, with ABC, with investor rels., corp. officer, 1999, pres., CEO global diagnostic imaging, GE Healthcare. Mem. Ctr. Corp. Innovation; mem. overseers bd. Northwestern U. Mem.: Advanced Med. Tech. Assn. (vice chair imaging sector), Met. Milw. Assn. Commerce. Office: GE 3135 Easton Turnpike Fairfield CT 06828*

VACHON, REGINALD IRENEE, mechanical engineer; b. Norfolk, Va., Jan. 29, 1937; s. Rene Albert Vachon and Regina (Galvin) Radcliffe; m. Mary Eleanor Grigg, Jan. 16, 1960; children: Reginald Irenee, Eleanor Marie. Student, U.S. Naval Acad., 1954-55; BME, Auburn U., 1958, MS, 1960; PhD, Okla. State U., 1963; LLB, Jones Law Sch., 1969. Registered profl. engr., Ala., Ga., Miss., La., Wis., Tex., chartered engr., U.K., cert. d'Iugenieur Mecanicien, France, lic. engr., European Fedn. Nat. Engring. Assns.; bar: Ala. 1971. Engr. Hayes Internat., 1958; instr., rsch. asst. Auburn U., 1958-60, rsch. assoc., 1961, assoc., prof., 1963-78; R&D engr. E.I. DuPont, 1960; aerospace engr., technologist NASA Marshall Space Flight Ctr., summers, 1964, 65; pres. Vachon Nix & Assoc., 1977—, VNA Sys. Inc., 1982—. COO Thacker Constrn. Co., Thacker Orgn., Inc., 1981—90, United Info. Techs., Inc., Global Interated Techs. Inc.; pres., CEO Compris Tech., Inc., 1991—92; chmn. Global Risk Mgr., Inc., 1992—, Direct Measurements, Inc., 2002—; prin. Gipco Holdings Internat., Ltd., 1994—2008; mem. sci. tech. adv. com. U.S. Dept. Homeland Security. Contbr. articles to profl. jours. With US Army, 1960—61. Fellow: ASCE, AIAA (assoc.), Singapore Instn. Engrs., Hong Kong Instn. Engrs., Instn. Mech. Engrs. U.K.; mem.: NSPE, ABA, ASME (hon.; pres. 2003—04), Soc. Frances des Mecaniciens, Ala. Bar Assn., Pan Am. Acad. Engring., Phoenix Soc. Atlanta, Peachtree Racket Club, N.Y. Yacht Club, Cosmos Club. Roman Catholic. Achievements include patents in field. Home: 1414 Epping Forest Dr NE Atlanta GA 30319-2539 Office: PO Box 190093 Atlanta GA 31119-0093 Office Phone: 404-388-6588. Business E-Mail: vachonr@asme.org.

VACHRIS, MICHELLE ALBERT, economist, educator; b. Norfolk, Va., June 1, 1962; d. Walter John and Irene Jeanette (Piché) Albert; m. Scott Charles Vachris, Oct. 3, 1987. BA in Econs., Coll. William and Mary, 1984; MA in Econs., George Mason U., 1988, PhD in Econs., 1992. Economist divsn. internat. prices Bur. Labor Stats., Washington, 1984-91, chief sect. info. and analysis, 1991—94; asst. prof. econs. Christopher Newport U., Newport News, Va., 1994—99, assoc. prof. econs., 1999—. Cons. Orgn. Econ. Cooperation and Devel., Paris, 1986; adj. asst. prof. dept. econs., Loyola Coll. Md., 1993—. Contbr. articles to profl. jours. Mem. Am. Econs. Assn., Soc. Govt. Economists. Roman Catholic. Home: 4312 Lookout Rd Virginia Beach VA 23455-1521 Office: Christopher Newport U Newport News VA

VACHSS, ANDREW HENRY, lawyer, writer, juvenile justice and child abuse consultant; b. NYC, Oct. 19, 1942; s. Bernard and Geraldine (Mattus) V. BA, Case Western Res. U., 1965; JD magna cum laude, New Engl. Sch. Law, 1975; LLD (hon.), Case Western Res. U., 2004. Bar: N.Y. 1976, U.S. Dist. Ct. (so. and ea. dists.) N.Y. 1976. Program rep. USPHS, Ohio, 1965-66; unit supr N.Y.C. Dept. Social Svcs., 1966-69; urban coord. Community Devel. Found., Norwalk, Conn., 1969-70; dir. Uptown Community Orgn., Chgo., 1970-71; dep. dir. Medfield (Mass.)-Norfolk Prison Project, 1971-72; dir. intensive treatment unit ANDROS II, Roslindale, Mass., 1972-73; project dir. Mass. Dept. Youth Svcs., Boston, 1972-73; dir. Juvenile Justice Planning Project, NYC, 1975-85; pvt. practice NYC, 1976—. Organizer, coord. Calumet (Ind.) Cmty. Congress, 1970; bd. dirs. Libra Inc., Cambridge, Mass., Advocacy Assocs., N.Y. and N.J.; adj. prof. Coll. New Resources, N.Y.C., 1980-81; lectr. trainer, spkr. to numerous orgns.; cons. on juvenile justice and child abuse to numerous orgns., 1971—. Author: The Life-Style Violent Juvenile: The Secure Treatment Approach, 1979, (novels) Flood, 1985, Strega, 1987, Blue Belle, 1988, Hard Candy, 1989, Blossom, 1990, Sacrifice, 1991, Shella, 1993, Down in the Zero, 1994, Another Chance to Get it Right, 1995, 2003, Footsteps of the Hawk, 1995, Batman: The Ultimate Evil, 1995, False Allegations, 1996, Safe House, 1998, Choice of Evil, 1999, Dead and Gone, 2000, Pain Management, 2001, Only Child, 2002, The Getaway Man, 2003, Down Here, 2004, Two Trains Running, 2005, Mask Market, 2006, Terminal, 2007, Another Life, 2008, Haiku, 2009, (graphic novels) Predator: Race War, 1995, Hard Looks, 2002, (audiobook) Proving It, 2001, (short stories) Born Bad, 1994, Everybody Pays, 1999; editor-in-chief: New Eng. Law Rev., 1974—75; contbg. editor: Parade; contbr. articles. Mem. bd. counselors Childtrauma Acad., Baylor Coll. Medicine; mem. bd. advisors Protect PAC; mem. expert adv. panel on catastrophic child abuse N.Y. State Office of Mental Health. Recipient Grand Prix de Lit. Policiére, 1988, Falcon award Maltese Falcon Soc. Japan, 1988, Deutschen Krimi Preis, Die Jury des Bochumer Krimi Archivs, 1989, Raymond Chandler award Giuria a Noir Festival, 2000, 1st Annual Harvey R. Houck award Justice for Children, 2003, 1st Annual Illuminations award St. Vincent's Ctrs. Nat. Child Sexual Abuse Prevention Program, 2003; Indsl. Area Found. Tng. Inst. fellow, 1970-71, John Hay Whitney Found. fellow, 1976-77. Mem. PEN, Writers Guild Am. Office: 16 E 34th St Fl 16 New York NY 10016-4359 Office Phone: 917-806-2170.

VACKETTA, CARL LEE, lawyer, educator; b. Danville, Ill., Aug. 3, 1941; s. Peter G. and Julia M. (Columbus) V. BS with honors, U. Ill., Urbana-Champaign, 1963, JD, 1965. Bar: Ill. 1965, DC 1968, US Dist. Ct. DC 1968, US Ct. Fed. Claims 1968, US Supreme Ct. 1970. Tax lawyer GM, Detroit, 1965; ptnr. Sellers, Conner & Cuneo, Washington, 1968—74, Pettit & Martin, 1974—95, Piper & Marbury, 1995—99, Piper Rudnick LLP, 1999—2004; ptnr., former chmn. Govt. Contracts practice group DLA Piper Rudnick Gray Cary, Washington, 2005—06, DLA Piper US LLP, 2006—. Adj. prof. law Georgetown U., 1973—. Co-author: Government Contract Default Termination, 1991, 93, 95, 97, 99; co-editor Extraordinary Contractual Relief Reporter, 1974-2002; editor-in-chief, pub. contract law sect., Pub. Contract Law Jour., 1994-2006; mem. adv. bd. The Government Contractor. Past pres. bd. vis., U. Ill. Coll. Law; bd. mem. Capital Area Food Bank, U. Ill. Found. Capt. Judge Advocate Corps US Army, 1966—68. Fellow ABA (sec. pub. contract law sect. 1978-79, coun. 1979-82, Nat. Contract Mgmt. Assn.; mem. Fed. Bar Assn., DC Bar Assn., Ill. State Bar Assn., Nat. Assn. Purchasing Mgrs., Univ. Club Wash. Roman Catholic. Office: DLA Piper US LLP 500 8th St NW Washington DC 20004 Office Phone: 202-799-4402. Office Fax: 202-799-5000. Business E-Mail: carl.vacketta@dlapiper.com.

VADAKKUMPADAN, FIJOY, research scientist; b. Thrissur, Kerala, India, Feb. 20, 1981; s. George Thoman and Merina Vadakkumpadan. BS, Indian Inst. Tech. Madras, 2002; PhD, Purdue U., West Lafayette, Ind., 2007. Grad. asst. Purdue U., 2002—07; postdoc. fellow Johns Hopkins U., Balt., 2007—. Vp Johns Hopkins Homewood Postdoc. Assn., Balt., 2007—. Contbr. scientific papers to profl. jours. Vol. tutor Lafayette Adult Resource Acad., Ind., 2004—07, Incentive Mentoring Program, Johns Hopkins U., Balt. Travel grant, Purdue U. Dept. Computer Scis. Grad. Student Bd., 2006, 2007, IEEE Internat. Symposium Biomed. Imaging, 2007. Mem.: BMES, IS&T, ACM, IEEE. Office: Johns Hopkins Univ 3400 N Charles St Baltimore MD 21218

VADEN, WILLIAM R., oil industry executive, councilman; b. Grapeland, Tex., Apr. 7, 1948; Attended, Del Mar Coll., 1973. Asst. warehouse mgr. Texaco Inc., 1969—74; sr. field supr. SGS Control Svcs., 1978—87; CEO, pres. VIP Cargo Surveys, Inc., 1987—; councilman City of Ingleside, 1999—2000, 2006—, mayor, 2000—04. Voting mem. Am. Petroleum Inst., 1988—2006. Cpl. USMC, 1965—69. Mem.: Disabled Am. Veterans, Veterans Fgn. Wars, Am. Soc. Testing and Measurement, Navy League, Am. Legion. Republican. Office: 2043 La Quinta Ingleside TX 78362*

VADHANAM, MANICKA V., science educator; PhD, U. Madras. Asst. prof. U. Louisville, 2003—. Achievements include patents pending for delivery mechanism for phytochemicals. Office: Univ Louisville 580 S Preston St Louisville KY 40202 Office Fax: 502-852-3842.

VADIGEPALLI, RAJANIKANTH, engineering educator; b. India; married. BS in Tech., Indian Inst. Tech., Chennai, 1996; PhD, U. Del., Newark, 2001. Rsch. assoc. Thomas Jefferson U., Phila., 2001—04, asst. prof., 2004—. Mem.: AIChE, Rsch. Soc. Alcoholism, Am. Physiol. Soc., Sigma Xi (bd. mem., Thomas Jefferson U. chpt. 2008—). Achievements include development of bioinformatics tool named PAINT. Office: Thomas Jefferson Univ 1020 Locust St Rm 381 Philadelphia PA 19107 Office Fax: 215-503-2636. Business E-Mail: raj@mail.dbi.tju.edu.

VADIVEL, NIDYANANDH, nephrologist; s. C. Vadivel and Shanmuga Vadivoo; m. Subbulaxmi Trikudanathan, Sept. 3, 2000. MBBS, Tirunelveli Med. Coll., India, 1997. Instr. medicine Harvard Med. Sch., Boston, 2009—; assoc. physician nephrology Brigham & Women's Hosp., Boston, 2009—, cons. nephrologist & renal transplant physician, 2009—. Fellowship, Renal Medicine Brigham & Women's Hosp, Harvard Med. Sch., 2008. Mem.: RCP (specialist tng. nephrology 2008), Indian Med. Coun., Gen. Med. Coun., Am. Soc. Transplantation, Am. Soc. Nephrology. Achievements include research in renal transplant imunobiology. Office: Brigham & Women's Hosp Harvard Med Schl 75 Francis st Boston MA 02115

VADLAMUDI, RATNA K., healthcare educator; s. Venkateswara Rao and Koteswaramma Vadlamudi; m. Kumari Vadlamudi; 1 child, Chaitanya. PhD, U. Wyo., 1994. Postdoctoral rschr. Harvard Med. Sch., Boston, 1995—97; asst. prof. UT MD Anderson Cancer Ctr., Houston, 1998—2004; assoc. prof. LSU Health Scis. Ctr., New Orleans, 2004—05, UT Health Scis. Ctr., San Antonio, 2006—. Mem.: AACR.

Achievements include patents for estrogen receptor modulators and uses. Office: UT Health Scis Ctr 7703 Floyd Curl Dr San Antonio TX 78229 Business E-Mail: vadlamudi@uthscsa.edu.

VADUS, GLORIA A., scientific document examiner; b. Forrestville, Pa. Diploma, Cole Sch. Graphology, Calif., 1978; BA in Psychology Counseling, Columbia Pacific U., 1981, MA in Psychology, 1982; diploma handwriting expert, Edith Eisenberg, Bethesda, Md., 1991. Diplomate Am. Bd. Forensic Examiners (founding mem.); cert. Am. Acad. Graphology, Washington, 1978, ct. qualified sci. document examiner 1989, registered graphologist 1978, cert. behavioral profiling and cert. questioned documents Am. Bd. Forensic Examiners, 1993, CHS I Am. Bd. Homeland Security, 2004, cert. Am. Handwriting Analysis Found. Pres., owner Graphinc, Inc., 1985—. Accredited instr. graphology Montgomery County Schs., Md., 1978—79; cert. instr. Psychogram Centre, 1978—85, Coun. Graphol. Socs., 1980; developed Trilogy base for rsch. Am. Handwriting Analysis Found.; author, lectr, cons. rschr. studies in field; founding mem. Am. Bd. Forensic Examiners. Contbr. articles to profl. jours. Chmn. Letter of Hope for POWs; vol. Montgomery County, 1985—87; bd. dirs. East Gate I Civic Assn., Potomac, Md., 1985—87, cmty. affairs chair, 1985—87; founding mem., appointment Internat. Women's Review Bd., 2008—; sovereign amb. Order Am. Ambs. USA, 2006. Recipient Spl. award, US, Japan Marine Facilities Panel Valuable Contbr. Japanese Panel UJNR, MFP, 1978—94, Gold Nib Analyst of Yr. award, Am. Handwriting Analysis Found., 1982, Dancing Fan award, Marine Tech. Soc., Tokyo chpt., 1991, Profound Contbr. to Soc. to the Yr., 2000, Am. Bronze Medal of Hon., 2001, Internat. Peace prize, United Cultural Conv. of USA, 2003, Legion of Honor Gold medal, United Cultural Conf., 2005, Lifetime Achievement award, World Congress of Arts, Scis. and Comm., 2005, World Freedom medal, United Cultural Ctr., 2006, Excellence medal, World Congress Arts, Scis., and Comm., 2006, Svcs. and Achievement Gold medal, ABI, 2006, Internat. Comm. cert., World Forum, 2007, Spl. Artistic Exhibit Evolution Handwriting award, 2007; named Global fellow, World Forum Fedn., 2007, Disting. Symposium Lectr., 2007; named to Amb. USA, 2007, Great Minds of 21st Century, 2008, World Laureate, ABI, 2009—. Fellow: Am. Coll. Forensic Examiners Internat. (life; awards chair 1993—94, Meritorious award 1994, Outstanding Contbn. cert.); mem.: Coun. Graphical Socs. (bd. dirs. 1982—84), Soc. Francaise de Graphologie for Am. Handwriting Analysis Found., Nat. Assn Document Examiners (bd. dirs. 1985—92, ethics hearing bd. 1986, chmn. nominations com. 1987—88, elections chmn. 1988, parliamentarian 1988—92), Nat. Forensic Ctr., Am. Handwriting Analysis Found. (life; chmn. rsch. com., chmn. adv. bd. 1981—87, bd. dirs. 1981—91, pres. 1982—84, chmn. nominations com. 1985—86, officiator 1986, policy planning and ethics com. 1986—91, ethics chmn. 1989—91, chmn., past pres. adv. bd. 1989—91, hon. profl. women's adv. bd. 1999, cert.), Nature Conservancy, Charles F. Menninger Soc., IEEE-Distaff (internat. chmn. bd. dirs. 1969—72, fashion show chair 1969—72), Internat. Platform Assn., Nat. Wildlife Fedn., Nat. Capitol Jaguar Owners Club (judge 1975—78), Sierra Club, Henry Hicks Garden Club of the Westburys, NY (v.p., pres. elect, judge 1967—71, flower arranging, horticulture chair flower shows, bd. dirs. 1967—71), Soroptomist Internat. (internat. chair, regional del., v.p. chpt., bd. dirs. 1987—92, regional dir. 1987—92), Nat. Writers Club. Avocations: voice piano, music, reading, ornithology. Home: 8500 Timber Hill Ln Potomac MD 20854-4237 Office Phone: 301-299-5477. Personal E-mail: j.vadus@ieee.org.

VAFAI, KAMBIZ, mechanical engineering educator; b. Tehran, Iran, July 16, 1953; s. Abbas and Mansoureh (Emami) V.; m. Parisa Vafai, Aug. 12, 1980; children: Kiumars, Keyian. BSME, U. Minn., 1975; MSME, U. Calif., Berkeley, 1977, PhD in Mech. Engring., 1980. Rsch. assoc. in mech. engring. U. Calif., Berkeley, 1975-80; post-doctoral fellow in mech. engring. Harvard U., 1980-81; asst. prof. Ohio State U., Columbus, 1981-86, assoc. prof., 1986-91, prof., 1991—. Cons. Batelle Meml. Inst., 1982-86; vis. prof. Tech. U. Munich, Fed. Republic Germany, 1989, U. Bordeaux, Talence, France, 1990, U. Paul Sabatier, 1995, 98, Tech. U. Naples, 1997. Contbr. chpts. to books and numerous articles to profl. jours. Mary Ann Wheeler Acad. scholar U. Calif., Berkeley, 1975-76; Earle C. Anthony acad. fellow U. Calif., Berkeley, 1975-76, Du Pont Summer Faculty fellow, 1982, Owens/Corning faculty fellow, 1985; recipient Outstanding Rsch. awards Coll. Engring. Ohio State U., 1986, 91, 96. Fellow ASME, AIAA (assoc.); Pi Tau Sigma, Tau Beta Pi. Home: 4 Savannah Irvine CA 92620-2553 Office: Ohio State U Mech Engring 206 W 18th Ave Columbus OH 43210-1189 E-mail: vafai@engr.ucr.edu.

VAGET, HANS RUDOLF, language professional, educator; b. Marienbad, Czechoslovakia, Feb. 2, 1938; came to U.S., 1964; s. Hans Ernst and Berta (Isop) V.; m. Ann Leone; children: Melanie Claudine, Erec Alexander. MA, U. Tübingen, Fed. Republic Germany, 1964; PhD, Columbia U., 1969. Instr. Columbia U., NYC, 1964-67; from instr. to prof. Smith Coll., Northampton, Mass., 1967—. Vis. prof. U. Calif., Irvine, 1979, Columbia U., 1985, Princeton U., 1986-87, Yale U., 1991, U. Hamburg, 1992. Author: Dilettantismus bei Goethe, 1971, Goethe. Der Mann von 60 Jahren, 1982, Thomas-Mann Kommentar, 1984;Seelenzauber. T. Mauu and die Musik, 2006; author, editor: Briefwechsel T. Mann-Agnes Meyer, 1992, J.W. Goethe: Erotic Poems, 1996, Im Schatten Wagners, 1999; Getauft aut Musik. Festschrift for D. Borchmeyer, 2006; contbr. articles to profl. and ednl. publs. Recipient Thomas Mann-Medaille, 1994, Rsch. prize Alexander von Humboldt Found., 2002; grantee NEH, 1985, Am. Coun. Learned Socs., 1986. Mem. MLA, German Studies Assn., Deutsche Schillergesellschaft, Thomas-Mann-Gesellschaft, Goethe Soc. N.Am. (co-founder), Wagner Soc. Office: Smith Coll Dept German Northampton MA 01063-0001 Business E-Mail: hvaget@smith.edu.

VAGT, ROBERT F., foundation administrator, former academic administrator; b. 1947; m. Ruth Anne Vagt, 1968; children: Ashley, Lindsey. BA in Psychology, Davidson Coll., 1969; MDiv, Duke U., 1972. Ordained to ministry Presbyn. Ch. Dir. clin. programs N.W. Ala. Mental Health Ctr.; exec. dir. Mcpl. Assistance Corp., NYC, 1979—80; pres., COO Adobe Resources Corp., 1989—92; chmn., pres., CEO Global Nat. Resources, 1992—96; pres., COO Seagull Energy Corp., 1996—97; pres. Davidson Coll., 1997—2007, The Heinz Endowments, Pitts., 2008—. Bd. dirs. Cornell Cos., Inc., El Paso Corp., Houston, 2005—. Bd. vis. Davidson Coll., 1992—, mem. Ultra Soc., nat. leader Ann. Fund, 1993—95. Recipient Alumni Svc. award, Davidson Coll., 1996. Office: The Heinz Endowments 30 Dominion Tower 625 Liberty Ave Pittsburgh PA 15222 E-mail: info@heinz.com.

VAGTS, DETLEV FREDERICK, law educator; b. Washington, Feb. 13, 1929; s. Alfred and Miriam (Beard) Vagts; m. Dorothy Larkin, Dec. 11, 1954; children: Karen, Lydia. Grad., Taft Sch., 1945; AB, Harvard U., 1948, LLB, 1951. Bar: Mass. 1961. Assoc. Cahill, Gordon, Reindel & Ohl, NYC, 1951-53, 56-59; asst. prof. law Harvard U. Law Sch., Cambridge, Mass., 1959-62, prof., 1962—, Eli Goldston prof., 1981-84, Bemis prof. internat. law, 1984—2005, prof. emeritus, 2005—, dir. internat. tax program, 1998-2000. Counselor internat. law Dept. of State, 1976—77. Author (with others): Transnational Legal Problems, 1968, 4th edit., 1994, Basic Corporation Law, 1973, 3d edit., 1989; co-author: Transnational Business Problems, 2008; editor: Secured Transactions Under the Uniform Commercial Code, 1963—64; assoc. reporter (with others): Restatement of Foreign Relations Law, book rev. editor: Am. Jour. Internat. Law, 1986—93, co-editor-in-chief:, 1993—98. 1st lt. USAF, 1953—56. Recipient Max Planck Rsch. award, 1991. Mem.: ABA, Coun. Fgn. Rels., Am. Soc. Internat. Law, Phi Beta Kappa. Home: 29 Follen St Cambridge MA 02138-3502 Office: Sch Law Harvard U Cambridge MA 02138 Business E-Mail: vagts@law.harvard.edu.

VAHAVIOLOS, SOTIRIOS JOHN, electrical engineer, researcher, engineering executive; b. Mistra, Greece, Apr. 16, 1946; s. John Apostolos and Athanasia (Pavlakos) Vahaviolos; m. Aspasia Felice Nessas, June 1, 1969; children: Athanasia, Athena, Kristy. BSEE, Fairleigh Dickinson U., 1970; MSEE, Columbia U., 1972, M in Philosophy, 1975, PhDEE, 1976. Mem. tech. staff Bell Tel. Labs., Princeton, NJ, 1970-75, supr., 1975-76, dept. head, 1976-78; founder, pres., CEO Phys. Acoustics Corp., Princeton, 1978—, MISTRAS Group Inc., Princeton, 1984—94, chmn. quality svcs. labs., 2000—. Adviser Greece Ministry Def., Athens, 1986—88; bd. dirs. Orthosonics, Inc., NYC; chmn. policy com., life fellow Internat. Com. Nondestructive Testing, life mem. bd. dirs., 2004—. Contbr. scientific papers to profl. publs. Chmn. Princeton sect. United Fund, 1976—78; adv. bd. Trenton State Coll., 1983—; chmn. Greek Independence Parade, NYC, 2002—03; v.p. Fedn. Greek Soc. in Greater N.Y.; bd. dirs. Holy Cross Greek Orthodox Sch. Theology, Boston, 1989—; pres. bd. trustees St. George Greek Orthodox Cmty., Trenton, NJ; elector archon Order of St. Andrew the Apostle of the Holy Ecumenical Patriarchate of Constantinople, 2004. Recipient Spartan Merit award, Spartan World Soc., 1987, Entrepreneur of the Yr. award, Arthur Young/Inc. Mag., 1989. Fellow: IEEE (Centennial Medal award 1984, Mittleman Achievement award 1993), Acoustic Emission Working Group (Gold medal 2005), Am. Soc. Nondestructive Testing (bus. and fin. com. 1984—87, 1988—, bd. dirs. 1985, sec. 1989, treas. 1990, v.p. 1991, pres. 1992, chmn. bd. 1993, chmn. internat. com. nondestructive testing 1994—, editor handbook on acoustic emission 1988, Lester Honor award 1998, Gold medal 2001); mem.: ASTM, Acad. NDT Internat., Fairleigh Dickinson U., Coll. of Sci. and Math. Adv. Coun., Montclair State U., Internat. Fund Advancement Nondestructive Testing (v.p.), N.Y. Acad. Scis., IEEE Indsl. Electronics Soc. (sr. mem. adminstv. com. 1988, founder, v.p. conf. 1974—78, editor Trans. on Indsl. Electronics 1976—82, 2d prize Student Paper Constest 1970, Outstanding Young Engr. award 1984). Greek Orthodox. Achievements include patents in field. Avocations: bird hunting, soccer, technical writing, gardening. Home: 7 Ridgeview Rd Princeton NJ 08540-7601 Office: Mistras Holdings Group 195 Clarksville Rd Princeton Junction NJ 08550 Personal E-mail: sotirios@mistrasgroup.com.

VAIDA, FLORIN, statistician, educator; b. Bucuresti, Romania, Oct. 12, 1967; s. Cantemir Octavian Vaida and Monica Alexandra Ionescu. PhD, U. Chgo., Ill., 1998. Asst. prof. biostatistics Harvard Sch. Pub. Health, Boston, 1998—2004, U. Calif. San Diego, 2004—. Contbr. scientific papers to profl. jours. Mem.: Am. Statis. Assn. Home: 4780 35th St #4 San Diego CA 92116 Office: Univ CA San Diego 9500 Gilman Dr MC 0847 San Diego CA 92116 Business E-Mail: vaida@ucsd.edu.

VAIDYA, VISHAL S., biologist, educator; b. Mumbai, Maharashtra, India, Sept. 28, 1976; s. Sudhakar S. and Suhasini S. Vaidya; m. Alka V. Chauhan, May 20, 2002; 1 child, Ariv V. PhD, U. La., Monroe, 2003. Instr. medicine Harvard Med. Sch., Boston, 2005—; assoc. biologist Brigham and Women's Hosp., Boston, 2006—. Editor: (book) Biomarkers in Medicine: Drug Discovery of Environmental Health; contbr. articles to profl. jours. Recipient Arthur Furst award, 1999; Scientist Devel. grant, Am. Heart Assn., 2005—08, Pathway to Independence grant, Nat. Inst. Environ. Health Scis., 2007—, Postdoc. fellowship, Nat. Kidney Found., 2003—05. Mem.: Soc. Toxicologic Pathology, Am. Soc. Nephrology, Soc. Toxicology (Best Abstract award 2005). Home: 157 Pleasant St Cambridge MA 02139 Office: Harvard Inst Medicine Rm 550 77 Ave Louis Pasteur Boston MA 02115 Business E-Mail: vvaidya@partners.org.

VAIDYANATHAN, VIJAY V., engineering educator; arrived in US, 1988; s. P.B. and Radha Vaidyanathan; m. Sheela Vijay; children: Rohan, Rohit. BSc, U. Bombay, India, 1985, BSc in Tech., 1988; MS, Tex. A&M U., Coll. Sta., Tex., 1991, PhD, 1998. Registered profl. engr., Tex., 1992. R&D engr. Perkins Electronics Co., 1998—2000; cons. edn. svcs. i2 Techs., Irving, Tex., 2000—02; asst. prof. dept. engring. tech. U. North Tex., Denton, Tex., 2002—, dir. electronics engring. tech. program, 2002—. Contbr. articles to profl. jours. Grantee, NSF, 2002, 2006, Industry, 2003—07. Mem.: IEEE, Internat. Soc. for Optical Engring., Am. Soc. Elec. Engring., Soc. Photo-Optical Instrumentation Engrs., Tau Alpha Pi (advisor 2007). Achievements include research in biomedical optics and non-invasive detection of oral cancer. Office Fax: 940-565-2666. Business E-Mail: vvaidyan@unt.edu.

VAIL, CHARLES DANIEL, veterinarian, consultant; b. Denver, June 11, 1936; s. Allan Paden and Katherine Marie (Phillips) V.; m. Jean Williams Ebsen, June 15, 1963; children: Ellen Marie, David Elston. BS, Colorado A&M, 1958; DVM, Colo. State. U., 1960. Asst. veterinarian Colo. Racing Commn., Littleton, 1958-60; equine practitioner Littleton Large Animal Clinic, 1960—; track veterinarian Centennial Race Track, Littleton, 1962-63. Commr. Colo. Racing Commn., 2007—. Editor-in-chief: Equine Practice, 1986—2000; contbr. articles to profl. jours. Mem. selection com. Outstanding Biology Tchr. award Colo., 1978-80, 88—, Arapahoe Fair Assn., Littleton, 1965-84, gallery disting. grads. Colo. State U. Coll. Vet. Medicine, 1989; chmn. Littleton Rotary Western Heritage Art Fair; bd. dirs. Animal Assistance Found. Denver, 1991-2004, v.p., 1995-96, pres., 1996-97, Western Vet. Conf., 1997-2000, v.p., 2001, pres. elect, 2002, pres., 2003, Friends Littleton Pub. Libr./Mus., 2000-04, Rocky Mountain Stroke Assn., Araphoe C.C. Found., 2004—; mem. devel. coun. Colo. State U., 2002-06; examiner, Clin. Practitionary, 2007- Recipient Honor Alumni award, Coll. Vet. Medicine, Colo. State U., 1991, Meritorious Svc. award, Western Vet. Conf., 2008. Mem. AVMA (publs. com. 1981-87, clin. proficiency examination faculty 2005—), Am. Assn. Equine Practitioners (pres. 1985, dist. life mem.), Colo. Vet. Medicine Assn. (pres. 1980, Veterinarian of Yr. award 1987), Denver Area Vet. Medicine Soc. (pres. 1975), Arapahoe Town and Gown Soc. (v.p. 1999, pres. 2000), Colo. State U. Alumni Assn. (pres. 2001-02), Nottingham Club, Rotary (pres. Littleton 1992-93), Sigma Alpha Epsilon, Omicron Delta Kappa. Home: 5921 S Cherrywood Cir Littleton CO 80121-2465 Office: Littleton Large Animal Clinic 8025 S Santa Fe Dr Littleton CO 80120-4305 Office Phone: 303-794-6359. Office Fax: 303-794-9466. Personal E-mail: cdvm1@yahoo.com.

VAIL, IRIS JENNINGS, civic worker; b. NYC, July 2, 1928; d. Lawrence K. and Beatrice (Black) Jennings; grad. Miss Porters Sch., Farmington, Conn.; m. Thomas V.H. Vail, Sept. 15, 1951; children: Siri J., Thomas V.H. Jr., Lawrence J.W. Mem. exec. com. Garden Club Cleve., 1962—83; mem. women's coun. Western Res. Hist. Soc., 1960—, Cleve. Mus. Art, 1953—. Chmn. Childrens Garden Fair, 1966-75, Public Square Dinner, 1975; bd. dirs. Garden Center Greater Cleve., 1963-77; trustee Cleve. Zool. Soc., 1971-98, life trustee 1998—; mem. Ohio Arts Coun., 1974-76, pub. sq. com. Greater Cleve. Growth Assn., 1976-93, pub. sq. preservation and maintenance com. Cleve. Found., 1989-93, chmn. pub. sq. planting com., 1993. Hon. trustee Cleve. Bot. Garden, 2001. Recipient Amy Angell Collier Montague medal Garden Club Am., 1976, Ohio Gov.'s award, 1977. Mem. Chagrin Valley Hunt Club, Cypress Point Club, Kirtland Country Club, Colony Club, Women's City of Cleve. Club (Margaret A. Ireland award). Home: 14950 County Line Rd Chagrin Falls OH 44022-6800 Office Phone: 216-360-0505.

VAIL, NANCY L. SCOTT, retired elementary school educator, artist; d. Mitchell Clark and Mollie Lee (Turner) Savage; m. Jackie C. Scott (dec. 1999); 1 child, Jeff Michael Scott; m. Joseph L. Vail, Sr., Nov. 4, 2000; stepchildren: Joseph L. Vail, Jr., Chris, Jennifer Allison. BE with summa cum laude, Abilene Christian Coll., Tex., 1962, MEd with summa cum laude, 1965. Cert. in Tchg. Tex., 1962, Tex., 1985. Tchr. Jane Long Elem., Abilene, Tex., 1962—65, Canyon Creek Elem., Richardson, Tex., 1965—71, Prestonwood Elem., Richardson, 1971—78, Rountree Elem., Allen, Tex., 1978—89, Vaughan Elem., Allen, 1989—98; ret., 1998. Nominee Tchr. of Yr., Allen Ind. Sch. Dist., 1988, 1989. Mem.: Rountree Retirees Assn., Scarlet O'Hatters, Richardson Civic Art (Ribbon award 2000, 2001), Allen Ret. Educators Assn. (officer, com. chmn. 2001—, Outstanding Vol. of Yr. 2003, 2004), Alpha Delta Kappa (pres., v.p., historian, corresponding sec., Silver Sister award 2003). Republican. Ch. Of Christ. Achievements include starting the Epsilon Lambda Chpt. of Alpha Delta Kappa in Allen, Texas. Avocations: piano, reading, exercise, travel, painting.

VAIL, THOMAS LEIGHTON, military officer; b. Millinocket, Maine, Apr. 23, 1970; s. William Jackson and Sue Louise Vail; m. Melissa Ruth Williams, July 3, 1998; children: Audrey Elise, Thomas William. BS in Criminal Justice, St. Joseph's, Standish, Maine, 2006. 2d class petty officer US Navy, Charleston, SC, 1988—96; police officer Richland County Sheriff's Dept., Columbia, SC, 1996—2002, Biddeford Police Dept., Maine, 2002—04; army officer US Army, Ft. Walton Beach, Fla., 2006—. Instr. Naval Res. Security unit Naval Res. Ctr., Columbia, 1999—2002. Mem. SAR, Augusta, Maine, 1992—2007. Lt. US Army, 2006—07, Ft. Walton Beach. Decorated Surface Warfare Specialist US Navy, Meritorious Svc. medal, Navy Achievement medal, Vol. Svc. medal, Res. Forces Moblzn. medal US Dept. Def.; recipient Commendation letter, US Dept. Justice, 1999, Dep. of Yr. award, Richland County Sheriff's Dept., 2000, Age Grp. award, Various road racing bodies, 2000—07, Exemplary Pub. Svc. award, SC Dept. Pub. Safety, 2001, Citizenship medal, SAR, 2002, Disting. Mil. Grad. award, US Army ROTC Command, 2004—06, Leadership Excellence award, George C. Marshall Found., 2005—06, Disting. Honor Grad. award, US Army Ordnance Ctr., 2006, Ky. Col. award, Govt. Ky., 2006, Decius Wadsworth award, Army Ordinance Ctr. Schs., 2006, Exemplary Leadership award, Nat. Def. Indsl. Assn., 2006, Nebr. Adm. award, Govt. Nebr., 2007, Gold award, Pres. Coun. Phys. Fitness, 2005. Mem.: Assn. US Army (assoc.), Am. Legion (assoc.), Mensa (corr.). Conservative. Achievements include development of and implementation of a uniformed police drug unit model still in use. Avocation: running. Office: Naval Sch Explosive Ordnance Disposal Officer Detachment 304 N McCarthy Ave Eglin AFB FL 32542-5649 Business E-Mail: thomas.l.vail@us.army.mil.

VAIL, THOMAS PARKER, orthopaedic surgeon; m. Lisa Ann Giannetto. MD, Loyola U., 1985. Diplomate Am. Bd. Orthopaedic Surgery. Prof. orthop. surgery Duke U. Med. Ctr., Durham, NC, 1992—2007; prof. and dept. chmn. orthop. surgery U. Calif., San Francisco, 2007—. Dir. adult reconstructive surgery Duke U. Med. Ctr., Durham. Office: Univ Calif San Francisco MU 320W 500 Parnassus Ave San Francisco CA 94143-0728

VAIL, THOMAS VAN HUSEN, retired publishing executive; b. Cleve., June 23, 1926; s. Herman Lansing and Delia (White) V.; m. Iris W. Jennings, Sept. 15, 1951; children: Siri Jennings Burki, Thomas Van Husen, Jr. AB in Politics cum laude, Princeton U., 1948; HHD (hon.), Wilberforce U., 1964; LHD, Kenyon Coll., 1969, Cleve. State U., 1973. Reporter Cleve. News, 1949-53, polit. editor, 1953-57; with Cleve. Plain Dealer, 1957-91, v.p., 1961-63, pub., editor, 1963-91, pres., 1970-91; dir. AP, 1968-74; ret., 1991. Bd. dirs. Greater Cleve. Growth Assn.; bd. dirs., past pres. Cleve. Conv. and Visitors Bur.; mem. Nat. Adv. Commn. on Health Manpower; presdl. apptd. to U.S. Adv. Commn. on Info., Pres.'s Commn. for Observance 25th Anniversary UN; trustee No. Ohio region NCCJ, Nat. Brotherhood Week chmn., 1969; trustee Cleve. Coun. World Affairs; fellow Cleve. Clinic Found.; former mem. Downtown Cleve. Corp.; former mem. distbn. com. Cleve. Found.; chmn., founder New Cleve. Campaign; trustee, founder Cleve. Tomorrow; former trustee Com. Econ. Devel.; former mem. Pres.'s Adv. Coun. on Pvt. Sector Initiatives. With USNR, 1944-46, lt. (j.g.), 1950. Recipient Nat. Human Rels. award, 1970, Cleve. Man of Year award Sales and Mktg. Execs. Cleve., 1976, Ohio Gov.'s award, 1982, Downtown Bus. Coun. recognition award Greater Cleve. Growth Assn., 1983, award NCCJ, 1970, award Mt. Vernon Adv. Com., 1994. Mem. Nat. Assn. Profl. Journalists (Lifetime Hall of Fame), Am. Newspaper Pubs. Assn., Am. Soc. Newspaper Editors, Soc. Profl. Journalists, Kirtland Country Club (Willoughby, Ohio), Sand Ridge Golf Club (Chardon, Ohio), Cypress Point Club (Pebble Beach, Calif.), Bohemian Club (San Francisco), Chagrin Valley Hunt Club (Gates Mills, Ohio), Links Club (NYC). Episcopalian. Home: L'Ecurie 14950 County Line Rd Hunting Valley Chagrin Falls OH 44022 Office: 29225 Chagrin Blvd Ste 200 Pepper Pike OH 44122-4632

VAIL, VAN HORN, German language educator; b. Buffalo, Dec. 23, 1934; s. Curtis Churchill and Faith Newbrook (Ely) V.; m. Michele Juliette Edelstein, May 5, 1969; 1 son, Mark Curtis. BA, U. Wash., 1956; MA, Princeton U., 1961, PhD, 1964. Instr. Princeton U., 1962-65, asst. prof., 1965-66; asst. prof. German Middlebury (Vt.) Coll., 1966-69, assoc. prof., 1969-75, prof., 1975—; chmn. dept. Middlebury Coll., Vt., 1970-73, 87-88, dir. studies Middlebury Sch. in Germany, 1967-68, 70-71, 74-75, 85-86, 88-89, 92-93, 95-96. Mem. nat. screening com. Fulbright Scholarships, 1979-81. Author: German in Review, 1967, 4th edit., 2004, Der Weg zum Lesen, 1967, 3d edit., 1986, Modern German, 1971, 3d edit., 1992, Tonio Kröger als Weg zur Literatur, 1974, Workbook for Modern German, 1992, Student Manual for 3d edit. of German in Review, 2000, Classroom Manual for 4th Edit. of German in Review, 2004. Served to 1st lt. M.I., U.S. Army, 1956-58. Fulbright scholar U. Heidelberg, 1958-59 Mem. MLA Home: 352 Cider Mill Rd Middlebury VT 05753-9407 Office: Middlebury Coll Middlebury VT 05753 E-mail: vail@middlebury.edu.

VAILAKIS, IVONNE G., literature educator; married. PhD, U. of Calif., Irvine, 1989. Cert. translator ALTA, 1976. Prof. U. Redlands, Calif., 1991—. Author: (poetry books) Hummingbirds in Exile. Leader. Fellow, Fulbright Commn., 1999. Personal E-mail: ivonne_vailakis@redlands.edu.

VAILLANCOURT, JEAN-GUY, sociology educator, researcher; b. Chelmsford, Ont., Can., May 24, 1937; s. Royal A. and Marie (Lavallée) V.; m. Pauline Hansen, June 6, 1966 (div. 1983); 1 child, Véronique. BA magna cum laude, Laurentian U., Sudbury, Ont., 1957; licenciate in Philosophy, Faculté des Jésuites, Montreal, Que., Can., 1961; licentiate in Sociology, Gregorian U., Rome, 1964; PhD in Sociology, U. Calif., Berkeley, 1975. Lectr. St. Boniface (Man.) Coll., Canada, 1964-65; asst. prof. U. Montréal, Que., Canada, 1969-76, assoc. prof., 1976-83, prof. sociology, 1983—2007, adj. prof., 2007—, chmn. dept., 1984-87. Adminstr., 1998; mem. consultative com. Can. amb. for disarmament, Ottawa, Ont., 1984-91, consultative com. on environ. Hydro-Que., 1984-90. Author: Papal Power, 1980, Essais d'écosociologie, 1982; co-editor: Le processus électoral au Québec, 1976, Roots of Peace, 1986, Environnement et développement Problèmes socio-politiques, 1991, Gestion de l'environnement, éthique et société, 1992, Instituer le développement durable, 1994, Aspects sociaux des précipitations acides au Québec, 1994, La recherche sociale en environnement, Nouveaux paradigmes, 1996, L'énergie au Québec, Quels sont nos choix? Montréal, Ecosocieté, 1998, Les sciences sociales de l'environnement, 1999, La gestion écologique des déchets, 2000, Développement durable et participation publique, 2003, Mouvements Sociaux et Changements Institutionnels, 2005; La Mondialisation de La Religion, 2007, editor-in-chief Sociologie et Sociétés, 1978-87.Environnement et Sciences Sociales, 2007; La Religion alextrime 2009, Development Double et Solidanite Sociale 2009. Mem. coun. City of Dunham, Que., 1976-80; bd. dirs. Oxfam-Que., 1976-79, Can. Inst. Internat. Peace and Security, Ottawa, Ont., 1986-89, European Univ. Ctr. for Peace Studies, Burg Schlaining, Burgenland, Austria, 1989-93; pres. of exec. com., bd. dirs., Groupement forestier du Haut-Yamaska, 2007—, Club 2/3, 1995-2005. Grantee Conseil de Recherche en sci. sociale du Canada, 1982, FCAR, 1989-95, 96—, Social Sci. Rsch. Coun., 1983-86, 90—, Can. Inst. Internat. Peace and Security, 1985, 91; fellow Can. Coun., 1965-68. Mem. Internat. Sociol. Assn., Assn. Can. des sociologues et anthropologues de langue française, Sci. for Peace, Pugwash, Group 78, ACFAS (Michel Jurdant prize for Environment, 2009). Roman Catholic. Avocations: tree farming, travel. Office: U Montréal Dept Sociology Montreal PQ Canada H3C 3J7 Business E-Mail: jean.guy.vaillancourt@umontreal.ca.

VAILLANT, JEAN-LUC, Internet company executive; Grad., Ecole Nationale Superieure des Telecommunications. Rsch. project leader CNET - France Telecom Rsch., 1992—95; dir. server develop. Sophis, 1995—96; engring. mgr. Fujitsu, 1996—98; dir. tech. Socialnet.com, 1998—2001; dir. software develop. Spotlife Inc., 2001—02; dir. engring. video services Logitech, 2002—03; co-founder LinkedIn Corp., Mountain View, Calif., 2003, v.p. engring., 2003—07, CTO, 2007—. Office: LinkedIn Corp 2029 Stierlin Ct Mountain View CA 94043

VAIRA, PETER FRANCIS, lawyer; b. McKeesport, Pa., Mar. 5, 1937; s. Peter Francis and Mary Louise (Bedogne) V.; m. Mary Hohler, 1981. BA, Duquesne U., 1959, JD, 1962. Bar: Pa. 1963, D.C. 1968, Ill. 1984, U.S. Dist. Ct. (no. dist.) Ill., U.S. Dist. Ct. (ea. dist.) Pa., Ill. Supreme Ct. 1984. Atty. Chgo. Strike Force, Justice Dept., 1968-72; atty. in charge Phila. Strike Force, 1972-73, Chgo. Strike Force on Organized Crime, 1973-78; U.S. atty. Ea. Dist. Pa., Phila., 1978—83; ptnr. Lord Bissel & Brook, Chgo., 1983-86, Fox, Rothschild, O'Brien & Frankel, Phila., 1986-90, Buchanan Ingersoll, Phila., 1990-92, Vaira & Assocs., Phila., 1992-93, Vaira & Riley, Phila., 1993—. Exec. dir. Pres.'s Commn. on Organized Crime, 1983; ind. hearing officer Laborers Internat. Union N.Am., 1995—; panelist, seminar, controlling internat. organized crime, Rome, Sorrento, Italy, June 1994; panelist, Internat. Conf. on Trial by Jury, Buenos Aires, Oct. 1996. Author: Eastern District Practice Rules Annotated, 2009, Corporate Responses to Grand Jury Investigations, 2008; contbr. articles to profl. jours. Mem. Mayor's Search Com. Police Commr., Phila., 1992, Mayor Michael Nutter's Police Transition Team, 2007; corruption task force Phila. Police, 1997; press officer women's amateur championship U.S. Golf Assn., 2003. Lt. USNR, 1963-68. Recipient Spl. Commendation award Justice Dept., 1976, Disting. Alumni award Duquesne U. Law Sch., 2005; named a Pa. Super Lawyer, Phila. Mag., 2007-09. Fellow Am. Coll. Trial Lawyers (chmn. criminal procedure com. 1995-98, comms. com., mem. internat. com.), Chartered Inst. Arbitrators (criminal justice coun. 1986); mem. ABA (internat. com. mem. 2009), Am. Law Inst. (mem. editl. bd. Legal Intelligencer, Phila. Lawyer, editor, 2008-09), Union League (Chgo.), Phila. Country Club Office: Vaira & Riley 1600 Market St Ste 2650 Philadelphia PA 19103-7226 Home Phone: 610-353-7488; Office Phone: 215-751-2700. Personal E-mail: p.vaira@vairariley.com.

VAIRAVAN, KASIVISVANATHAN, electrical engineering and computer science educator; b. Kandanur, India, July 9, 1939; BE, U. Madras, India, 1962; MS, George Washington U., 1965; PhD, U. Notre Dame, 1968. Asst. prof. to prof. U. Wis., Milw., 1968—, chmn. computer sci. dept., 1987—2002. Cons. in field. Named one of Educator of Yr., U. Wis.-Milw., 2008—09. Mem.: IEEE Computer Soc. (pres. Milw. chpt. 1970, Milw. sect. Meml. award 1984). Avocation: photography, reading, biography and history, travel. Office: Univ Wisc - Milw Engring Sch Milwaukee WI 53201 Business E-Mail: kv@uwm.edu.

VAIRO, GIAMPIETRO LUCIANO, professional athletic trainer; b. Cosenza, Calabria, Italy, Feb. 12, 1977; s. Tommaso and Janice Lorraine Vairo. PhD, Pa. State U., U. Pk., 2007—. Cert. athletic trainer Bd. Certification for Athletic Trainer, 2000. Athletic trainer Princeton U., NJ, 2005—06; asst. athletic trainer U. Pitts., 2000—05, Pa. State U., 2006—07. Contbr. articles to peer-reviewed publ. (NATA Rsch. & Edn. Found. Osternig Master's Grant, 2001). Active Penn State Kinesiology Affiliate Program Group, U. Pk., 2006—. Recipient Doc. Scholarship award, NATA Rsch. & Edn. Found. Sayers Bud Miller Meml., 2008, Postgrad. Doc. Scholarship award, EATA Francis J George, 2009; Pa. Athletics Trainers Loyalty, Rsch. grant, 2009. Mem.: Nat. Athletic Trainers' Assn. Office: The PA State Univ 146 Recreation Bldg University Park PA 16802 Office Fax: 814-865-7936. Business E-Mail: glv103@psu.edu.

VAIRO, ROBERT JOHN, insurance company executive; b. Bklyn., Sept. 27, 1930; s. John and Antonietta (DeRose) V.; m. Carol P. Andross, Apr. 8, 1951 (div. Feb. 1979); children: Robert J., Gregory J.; m. Inge R. Buhlbecker, Feb. 20, 1979. Student, Coll. Ins., NYC, 1953-62; Exec. Program in Bus. Adminstrn., Columbia U., 1973. CPCU. Under asst. mgr. Atlantic Cos., NYC, 1952-62; underwriter mgr., v.p. Fireman's Fund Ins. Co., NYC, 1962-75; v.p., sr. v.p. underwriting C & F Ins. Cos., Morristown, NJ, 1975-79; exec. v.p., pres. U.S. Ins. Group, Morristown, NJ, 1979-82; chmn., chief exec. officer C & F Underwriters Group and The North River Ins. Co., Morristown, NJ, 1982-86; pres., chief oper. officer Crum and Forster, Inc., Morristown, 1987-88, pres., chief exec. officer, 1988-90, chmn., pres., chief exec. officer, 1990-92, also bd. dirs. Chmn. Ins. Services Office, N.Y.C., 1983, Am. Ins. Assn., Washington, 1990. Pres. Lincoln Park City Council, N.J., 1971-76. Served with USMC, 1951-53. Mem. Soc. CPCUs, Am. Inst. for Chartered Property Casualty Underwriters (dir., chmn. 1991-92), Desert Highlands Golf Club (pres. 1997-99), Coalition Pinnacle Peak, Inc. (pres. 1998—). Roman Catholic. Home: # 451 10040 E Happy Valley Rd Scottsdale AZ 85255-2388

VAISEY, DAVID GEORGE, librarian, archivist; b. Tetbury, Eng., Mar. 15, 1935; s. William Thomas and Minnie (Payne) V.; m. Maureen Anne Mansell, Aug. 7, 1965; children: Katharine, Elizabeth. BA, Oxford U., Eng., 1959, MA, 1962. Archivist Staffordshire County Council, Stafford, Eng., 1960-63; from asst. librarian to sr. asst. librarian Bodleian Library, Oxford, Eng., 1963-75, keeper of western manuscripts, 1975-86, Bodley's librarian, 1986-96, Bodley's librarian emeritus, 1997—. Dep. keeper Oxford U. Archives, 1966-75, keeper, 1995-2000; vis. prof. dept. library studies UCLA, 1985; commr. Royal Commn. Hist. Manuscripts, 1987-98; founding chmn. Nat. Coun. Archives, 1988-91. Served to 2d lt. Brit. Army, 1954-56. Decorated encomienda Order of Isabel la Catolica (Spain), comdr. Order Brit. Empire; fellow Exeter Coll., Oxford, 1975, emeritus fellow, 2000; hon. rsch. fellow, Univ. Coll., London, 1987, hon. fellow Kellogg Coll., Oxford, 1996. Fellow: Soc. Antiquaries, Royal Hist. Soc.; mem.: Soc. Archivists (pres. 1999—2002), Brit. Records Assn. (v.p. 1998—2006). Office: Bodleian Libr Broad St Oxford OX1 3BW England Business E-Mail: david.vaisey@bodley.ox.ac.uk.

VAJDA, EDWARD J., literature and language professor; b. Camp Lejeune, NC, Sept. 10, 1958; s. Richard Fuller and Elizabeth V. Johnson; children: Michael Edward, Derek Richard. PhD in Slavic Linguistics, U. Wash., Seattle, 1986. Prof. Western Wash. U., Bellingham, 1987—. Contbr. articles to profl. jours. Recipient Excellence Tchg. award, 1992. Office: Western Wash Univ 516 High St Modern Lang 9057 Bellingham WA 98225

VAJTAY, STEPHEN MICHAEL, JR., lawyer; b. New Brunswick, NJ, Mar. 18, 1958; s. Stephen Michael and Veronica Gizella (Fehèr) V.; m. Gabriella Katherine Soltèsz, Aug. 5, 1989; children: Stephen, Andrew, Gregory, Daniel. BA, Rutgers U., 1980; JD, Georgetown U., 1983; LLM, NYU, 1989. Bar: N.J. 1984, U.S. Tax Ct. 1985. Assoc. McCarter and English LLP, Newark, N.J., 1983-91, ptnr., 1991—. Dir., George St. Playhouse, NB, NJ; trustee Hungarian Scout Assn. in Exteris, Garfield, N.J., 1985—; trustee Partnership for a Drug-Free N.J., Inc., Montclair, 1993—; adj. prof. law Seton Hall U. Sch. Law, Newark, 1995—; spkr. at lectrs. and seminars, 1992—. Contbr. articles to profl. jours. Mem. Bd. of Adjustment, New Brunswick, N.J., 1993-98. Mem. ABA, N.J. Bar Assn. (chmn. tax sect. 2001-02), Essex County Bar Assn., Phi Beta Kappa. Roman Catholic. Office: McCarter and English LLP Four Gateway Ctr 100 Mulberry St Newark NJ 07102 Office Phone: 973-639-2004. Business E-Mail: SVAJTAY@mccarter.com.

VAKERICS, THOMAS VINCENT, lawyer; b. Lorain, Ohio, Mar. 26, 1944; s. Paul Peter and Margaret Theresa (Dobos) V.; m. Kathryn Ida Rogers, Aug. 7,1965; children: Meredith Vakerics Ehler, Mitchell Thomas. BA, Bowling Green State U., 1965; JD with honors, George Washington U., 1968. Bar: U.S. Dist. Ct. D.C. 1968, U.S. Ct. Appeals (D.C. cir.) 1969, U.S. Supreme Ct. 1974, U.S. Ct. Internat. Trade 1982, U.S. Ct. Appeals (Fed. cir.) 1982. Antitrust trial atty. FTC, Washington, 1969—73; assoc. Gore, Cladouhos & Brashares, Washington, 1973—75; ptnr. O'Connor & Hannan, Washington, 1975—84, Bayh, Tabbert & Capehart, Washington, 1984—86, Morgan, Lewis & Bockius, Washington, 1986—88, Winthrop, Stimson, Putnam & Roberts, Washington, 1988—94, Perkins Coie, 1994—2004, Sandler, Travis & Rosenberg, P.A., Washington, 2004—. Vis. prof. Nihon U., Tokyo, 1981-88. Author: Antitrust Basics, 1985, Antidumping, Countervailing Duty and Other Trade Actions, 1987; contbr. articles to profl. jours. Mem. ABA (vice chmn. internat. antitrust law com. sect. internat. law and practice 1992-95), Internat. Bar Assn., D.C. Bar Assn., Solar Energy Rsch. Inst. (editl. adv. bd. Solar Energy Law Reporter 1979-82), Order of Coif, Phi Delta Phi, Pi Sigma Alpha, Phi Alpha Delta, Sigma Chi. Democrat. Roman Catholic. Office: Sandler Travis & Rosenberg PA 1300 Pennsylvania Ave NW Ste 400 Washington DC 20004 Home Phone: 703-620-9163; Office Phone: 202-216-9307. Office Fax: 202-842-2247. Business E-Mail: tvakerics@strtade.com.

VAKILI, BAHMAN FAKHIMI, urologist; b. Soossangard, Khoozes, Iran, Jan. 22, 1936; arrived in U.S., 1962; s. Mehdi Fakhimi Vakili and Noah Jalali; m. Sarah Ann Lovejoy, June 4, 1967 (div. 2002); children: Susan Elizabeth Vakili Ballenwag, David Andrew, Daniel Edward. MD, Tehran U., Iran, 1962. Diplomate Am. Bd. Urology, 1974. Intern Worcester City Hosp., Mass., 1962—63; resident gen. surgery Beth Israel Hosp., NYC, 1963—64; resident Urology Boston U. Med. Ctr., 1964—67; fellow Urology and Nuc. Medicine Roger Williams Gen. Hosp., Providence, 1967—68; urologist VA, Newington, Conn., 1968—69; fellow Pediat. Urology Babies Hosp. Columbia-Presbyn. Med. Ctr., NYC, 1971—72; urologist A.O. Fox Meml. Hosp., Oneonta, NY, 1972—86, VA Hosp., Beckly, W.Va., 1986—87, Bath, NY, 1987—89, Lebanon, Pa., 1990—2000; ret., 2000. Assoc. clin. prof. Urology Pa. State Med. Sch., Hershey, 1990—98; cons. Urology Margarettvill Meml. Hosp., NY, 1972—86, Stamford Cmty. Hosp., NY, 1974—86. Contbr. articles to profl. jours. Maj. Med. Corps US Army, 1969—71. Fellow: ACS; mem.: AMA, Am. Urol. Assn. Republican. Unitarian Universalists. Avocations: carpentry, gardening, bicycling, writing, poetry.

VAKSER, ILYA, biophysicist, educator; b. Minsk, Belarus, July 8, 1955; came to U.S., 1993; s. Ari and Ida (Gruntfest) V.; m. Natalie Mnevetz, Oct. 3, 1986; children: Dina, Daniel. MSc, Belorussian U., Minsk, Belarus, 1981; PhD, Moscow U., 1989. Jr. scientist Genetics Inst., Minsk, 1982-89; rsch. fellow Weizmann Inst., Rehovot, Israel, 1990-93; rsch. assoc. Washington U., St. Louis, 1993-95; postdoctoral assoc. Rockefeller U., NYC, 1995-97; asst. prof. Med. U. S.C., Charleston, 1997—. Vis. scientist Hebrew U., Jerusalem, 1991-93; adv. bd. mem. Internat. Bus. Comms. USA Confs., Southboro, Mass., 1995-96; adv. panel mem. NSF, 1999, Dept. of Energy, 2000. Contbr. articles to Procs. NAS, Proteins, Protein Engring. Feinberg fellow Weizmann Inst., Israel, 1991; rsch. grantee Ministry of Sci., Israel, 1991, NSF, 1997, 98, NIH, 2000. Mem. Am. Chem. Soc., Protein Soc., N.Y. Acad. Scis., Sigma Xi. Jewish. Achievements include development of computational molecular recognition approach; author of hydrophobic and low resolution protein docking and structure prediction technique. Office: Med Univ SC Dept Pharmacology 171 Ashley Ave Charleston SC 29425-0001 E-mail: vakseri@musc.edu.

VALACHOVIC, RICHARD WILLIAM, medical association administrator; Former assoc. prof. oral medicine Harvard U., former chief dentistry, Health Svcs.; exec. dir. Am. Assn. Dental Schs., Washington, 1997; now exec. dir. Am. Dental Edn. Assn., Washington. Fellow: Am. Coll. Dentists, Am. Acad. Pediat. Dentistry. Office: Am Dental Edn Assn Ste 1100 1400 K St NW Washington DC 20005 Office Phone: 202-289-7201. Business E-Mail: ValachovicR@adea.org.*

VALADE, ALAN MICHAEL, lawyer; b. Berwyn, Ill., Jan. 26, 1952; s. Merle F. and Vera M. Valade; m. June 17, 1978. Attended, Oakland C.C., 1970—72; BA, U. Mich., 1974; JD, Wayne State U., 1977; LLM in Taxation, NYU, 1978. Bar: Mich. 1978, Fla. 1987. Assoc. Kemp, Klein, Endelman & Beer, Southfield, Mich., 1978-79; shareholder Valade, MacKinnon & Higgins, P.C., Detroit, 1979-84, Schwendener & Valade, P.C., Mason, Mich., 1985-91; ptnr. Honigman Miller Schwartz and Cohn LLP, Detroit, 1991—, chmn. tax. dept., 2002—06. Co-author: The Michigan Single Business Tax, 1991; contbr. articles to profl. jours. Fellow Mich. State Bar Found.; mem. ABA, State Bar Mich. (chmn. state and local tax com. 1991, tax. coun. 1989-92), State Bar Fla. Office: Honigman Miller Schwartz and Cohn LLP 2290 First National Bldg 660 Woodward Ave Detroit MI 48226-3506 Office Phone: 313-465-7636. Business E-Mail: avalade@honigman.com.

VALANTINE, HANNAH A., cardiologist, educator; b. Gambia, May 5, 1951; m. Denis Von Kaeppler; children: Ericka Von Kaeppler, Natasha Von Kaeppler. Cert. MD London U., 1988, MBBS St. George's Hosp., London U., 1978. Clin. asst. prof. Stanford U. Sch. Medicine, cardiology, Calif., 1986—88, asst. prof., 1988—96, assoc. prof., 1996—2000, sr. assoc. dean, 2004—08, prof, 2000—. Recipient Clin. Investigator award, Nat. Inst. Health, 1991—96; grantee Rsch. grant, 2001—06, Award, Am. Heart Assn., 1993—96. Mem.: Am. Heart Assn. (pres. 2004—06). Achievements include research in transplant arteriosclerosis: viral and host mechanisms program. Office: Stanford Univ 300 Pasteur Dr Stanford CA 94305-5119 Office Fax: 650-725-7368.

VALASQUEZ, JOSEPH LOUIS, industrial engineer; b. Balt., Apr. 15, 1955; s. Jose Louis and Edith Rosabel (Saunders) V.; m. Nicole Diane Feldser, Sept. 4, 1983; children: Alexandra Nicole, Joseph Jr. AA, Essex Coll., 1977; BS in Indsl. Engring., U. Ariz., 1982; MBA in Fin., So. Ill. U., 1985. Registered profl. engr., Fla.; cert. quality engr.; cert. quality auditor; cert. quality mgr.; cert. project mgmt. profl.; cert. integrated resource mgmt.; pvt. pilots license. Machinist Bausch & Lomb, Balt., 1974-77; indsl. engr. IBM Corp., Tucson, 1980-81; sr. indsl. engr. Gen. Dynamics, San Diego, 1981-83; supr. engring. Avco Corp., Nashville, 1983-84; mgr. engring. Burroughs Corp., Coral Springs, Fla., 1984-85; dir. total quality mgmt. Lambda Novatronics, Inc., Pompano Beach, Fla., 1984-94; champoint of continuous improvement Allied Signal, 1994-97, Sensormatic Corp., 1997-98; v.p. corp. quality Sunbeam Corp., Delray Beach, Fla., 1998-2001; quality/productivity exec. Bank Am., Charlotte, NC, 2001—. Computer cons., Margate, Fla., 1987; founder, owner E.P.I. Cos., Pompano Beach. Mem. Am. Inst. Indsl. Engrs., Fla. Engring. Soc. Republican. Roman Catholic. Avocations: real estate management, computer programming, mountain climbing, canoeing, private pilot. Home: PO Box 49616 Charlotte NC 28277 Personal E-mail: jlvalasquez@yahoo.com. Business E-Mail: joe.l.valasquez@bankofamerica.com.

VALBUENA-BRIONES, ANGEL JULIAN, retired language educator, author; b. Madrid, Jan. 11, 1928; naturalized, 1963; s. Angel Valbuena-Prat and Francisca Briones; m. Barbara Northrup Hobart, Nov. 9, 1957; children: Teresa, Vivian. Licenciado summa cum laude, Murcia U., Spain, 1949; PhD with honors, Madrid U., 1952. Prof. Ayudante Murcia U., 1949-51; lectr. Oxford (Eng.) U., 1953-55; prof. Ayudante Madrid U., 1955-56; vis. lectr. U. Wis., 1956-58; asst. prof. Yale U., 1958-60; Elias Ahuja prof. Spanish lit. U. Del., 1960-2000, Elias Ahuja prof. emeritus, 1999—. Lecture tour, S.Am., 1957; vis. prof. NYU, 1960, 61, U. Madrid, 1970-71, 1965, 77, U. Mex. at Aragon, 1979, Inst. Caro y Cuervo, Bogota, Colombia, 1980; mem. Fulbright-Hays nat. screening com., 1981-83, 89-90; mem. editl. com. for CD-ROM edit. Spanish Golden Age Theatre, Chadwyck-Healey/Spain, 1995-98; bd. dirs. publs. U. Barcelona, Spain, Bull. Comediantes, U. Calif., Riverside, Hispanic Jour., Pa., Juan de la Cuesta Edits., Del.; profl. cons. NEH. Author: Nueva Poesia de Puerto Rico, 1952, Comedias de Capa y Espada de Calderon, 1954, Dramas de Honor de Calderon, 2 vols., 1956, Obras Completas de Calderon, vol. I, 1959, 3d reprinting, 1991, vol. II, 1956, 6th edit. 2 vols., 1988, Literatura Hispanoamericana, 1962, revised and enlarged, 1969, Perspectiva critica de los dramas de Calderon, 1965, Ideas y Palabras, 1968, El alcalde de Zalamea de Calderon, 1971, rev. 13th edit., 1995, Primera Parte de Comedias de Pedro Calderon de la Barca, Vol. 1, 1974, Vol. 2, 1981, La Dama Duende de Calderon, 1976, 8th printing, 1986, Calderon y la comedia nueva, 1977, La vida es sueno. Antes que todo es mi dama. Pedro Calderon de la Barca, 1988, El mayor monstruo del mundo. de Calderon, 1995; author (cd-rom) Teatro Espanol de Siglo de oro, 1998, Historia y Creación Literaria en Don Pedro Calderón de la Barca, 2002. Founder, pres. Valbuena Inst. Spanish Lit., Inc., 1986-99. Consejo Superior de Investigaciones Cientificas fellw, 1951, 70-71, Instituto de Cultura Hispánica fellow, 1951-52; recipient Excellence in Teaching award U. Del., 1988, Outstanding Scholar award U. Del. Coll. Arts and Sci., 1996. Mem. MLA, AAUP, Am. Assn. Tchrs. Spanish and Portuguese, Inst. Iberoam. Lit., Internat. Fedn. Modern Langs. and Lits., Assn. Lit. Scholars and Critics, Internat. Assn. Hispanists, Am. Comparative Lit. Assn., Assn. for Hispanic Classic Theatre, Old Bohemia Hist. Soc., Sigma Delta Pi (hon., Order of Don Quijote, 1999), Phi Kappa Phi. Home: 726 Loveville Rd Cottage 6 Hockessin DE 19707-1504

VALCÁRCEL, MARTA IRIS, pediatric educator; b. Santurce, P.R., Mar. 26, 1931; d. Jose and Solveida (Teruel) V. BS, U. P.R., 1951, MD, 1955. Diplomate Am. Bd. Pediatrics. Intern, then resident Kings County Hosp., NYC, 1955-58; fellow in neonatology Columbia Presbyn. Med. Ctr., 1968; chief perinatalneonatal sects. and neonatal ICU U. P.R. Sch. Medicine, San Juan, 1967-78, 91, prof., chmn. dept. pediatrics, 1977—, assoc. dean for clin. affairs, 1976-77; exec. dir. Univ. Children's Hosp., San Juan, 1980-86; dir. newborn svcs. U. Dist. Hosp., San Juan, 1967-78, 91, pres. med. staff, 1975-76. Mem. Am. Pediatric Soc., Am. Acad. Pediatrics, P.R. Mked. Assn., So. Soc. Pediatric Rsch., Assn. Med. Sch. Pediatric Dept. Chmn. Roman Catholic. Office: U PR Med Scis Campus PO Box 5067 # U San Juan PR 00902-5067

VALCARENGHI, IVAN, dentist; m. Kathryn Valcarenghi; 2 children. Pvt. practice, Elmhurst, Ill. Contbr. articles to profl. jours. Spkr. Am. Cancer Soc.; active Am. Lung Assn. Fellow: World Congress of Microdentistry (founding mem.); mem.: Acad. Gen. Dentistry, Am. Acad. Cosmetic Dentistry (participant Give Back a Smile program), Advanced Dental Study Group (co-founder). Office: 127 West Vallette Elmhurst IL 60126 Office Phone: 630-834-8088. Office Fax: 630-834-8091. E-mail: ivan@toothbiz.com.

VALCIC, BRANKA, finance educator; b. Zagreb, Croatia, June 7, 1976; married. PhD, Oreg. State U., Corvallis, 2007. Asst. prof. U. Alaska, Fairbanks, 2005—. Recipient Bill Wick Marine Fisheries award, Hatfield Marine Sci. Ctr., 2004; Austin Cooley Talent grant, U. Alaska Fairbanks, 2000.

VALDEZ, KRISTINA LOUISE, secondary school educator; b. Corpus Christi, Tex., Oct. 7, 1978; d. Dale Weldon and Jonette Louise Antonell; m. Alvar David Valdez, Dec. 22, 2005; children: Joli Jonette Emory, Hallie Josette. BA in English, Tex. A&M U., Corpus Christi, 2001. Cert. secondary tchr. Tex., 2001. English and drama tchr. Pt. Aransas HS, Tex.,

2001—03; drama tchr., cheerleading coach West Oso HS, Corpus Christi, 2003—04; drama and journalism tchr. Calallen Mid. Sch., Corpus Christi, 2004—. Home: 2718 Wind Rock Dr Corpus Christi TX 78410 Business E-Mail: kemory@calallen.k12.tx.us.

VALDEZ, PATRICIA, language educator; Asst. prof. english CC, Phila, 2001—, spanish instr., 1993—. Med. spanish instr. U. Pa. Med. Sch. Translator fiction argentinean writers. Recipient, Tchg. Ctr. CC Phila, 2000. Mem.: TESOL, ACTFL. Business E-Mail: pvaldez@ccp.edu.

VALDIVIA, ANNARELLA, psychologist; d. Hugo Misael and Sofia Aleida Valdivia. MS, F.D.U, Teaneck, NJ, 1998; attending, Yeshiva U., NYC, 2009. Cert. sch. psychologist NJ., 1998, supr. 2009. Sch. psychologist Newark Pub. Schs., 2007—. Mem.: Psi Chi Psychology, Phi Omega Epsilon, Phi Theta Kappa.

VALDIVIESO, ANGELICA, physical therapist; b. LA, Calif., USA, Nov. 19, 1974; d. Jorge Valdivieso. Ceo therapist, 2002—. Administr. nurse Caremore Medica Group., 1993—97; nurse, cons Columbia Healthcare, 1997—2001; cofounder Kingdom Catering, Scottsdale, 2004—. Avocation: travel. Office: Doctor for Life 3301 N Miller Rd #4 Scottsdale AZ 85234 Office Phone: 480-949-6570.

VALDMAN, ALBERT, language and linguistics educator; b. Paris, Feb. 15, 1931; came to U.S., 1944, naturalized, 1953; s. Jacques and Rose (Standman) V.; m. Hilde Wieners, Aug. 19, 1960; 1 child, Bertrand André. AB, U. Pa., 1953; AM, Cornell U., 1955, PhD, 1960; PhD honoris causa (hon.), U. Neuschâtel, 1991. Linguistic scientist Fgn. Service Inst., 1957-59; asst. prof. Romance langs. Pa. State U., 1959-60; mem. faculty Ind. U., Bloomington, 1960—, prof. French, Italian and linguistics, 1966—, chmn. dept. linguistics, 1963-68, Rudy prof., 1986—; vis. prof. Harvard, summer 1965; with. Vis. lectr. U. West Indies, 1965-66; Fulbright lectr. U. Nice, France, 1971-72, 75-76, 83-87, 89; cons. in field. Author: Applied Linguistics-French, 1960, Drillbook of French Pronunciation, 1964, 70, Trends in Language Teaching, 1966, College French in the New Key, 1965, Saint-Lucian Creole Basic Course, 1969, Basic Course in Haitian Creole, 1970, First and Second Level High School French, 1972, 2d edit., 1977, Langue et Culture, 1975, Introduction to French Phonology and Morphology, 1976, Le Creole: Structure, Statut et Origine, 1978, Haitian Creole-French English Dictionary, 1982; co-author: En Route—Introduction au français et au monde francophone, 1986; editor: Pidgin and Creole Linguistics, 1977, Le Francais hors de France, 1979; co-editor: Theoretical Orientations in Creole Studies, 1980, Historicity and Variation in Creole Studies, 1981, Issues in International Bilingual Education, 1982, Haiti Today and Tomorrow: An Interdisciplinary Study, 1984, The Evaluation of Foreign Language Proficiency, 1987, Ann pale Kreyol: Learning Haitian Creole, 1987, Dis-Moi!, Viens Voir!, C'est Ça!, 1989, Bien Entendu! Introduction á la prononciation française, 1993, Learners' Dictionary of Haitian Creole, 1996, French and Creole in Louisiana, 1997, Chez Nous, 1997, 4th edot, 2009, Dictionary of Louisiana Creole, 1998, 3rd edit., 2006, Etude sur les variétés du francais 2003, Le Français en Amérique du Nord, 2005, Haitian Creole-English Bilingual Dictionary, 2007, Essays in Applied French Linguestics, 2005, Dictionary of Lousiana French, 2009. Decorated comdr. dans l'Ordre dans Palmes Académiques; recipient Florence Steiner prize, Am. Coun. Tchg. Fgn. Langs., 1998; Guggenheim fellow, 1968, Fulbright fellow, 1985. Mem. Internat. Assn. Applied Linguistics (sec.-gen. 1984-87, pres. 1987-94), Am. Assn. Tchrs. of French (v.p. 1990-94, pres. 1995-98), Comité Internat. des Créolistes (v.p. 1996-2004),Ordre Cles Francophones d' Amerique(Quebec) Phi Beta Kappa. Office: Ind U CREDLI BH 604 Bloomington IN 47405 Office Phone: 812-855-4988. Business E-Mail: valdman@indiana.edu.

VALE, FERNANDO LUIS, medical educator; b. San Juan, Dec. 8, 1965; s. Jose Luis Vale and Carmen Dalila Díaz; m. Lynda M. Vale, June 8, 1991; children: Gabriela, Fernando. BS, U. P.R., 1987, MD, 1991. Cert. bd. cert. neurosurgery. Intern U. Ala. Hosps., Birmingham, 1991—92, resident in neurosurgery, 1992—97; asst. prof. U. South Fla., Tampa, 1997—2004, assoc. prof., 2004—. Contbr. articles to profl. jours. Mem.: Alpha Omega Alpha. Office: USF Health 7th Fl 2 Tampa Gen Cir Tampa FL 33606 Home Phone: 813-920-9277; Office Phone: 813-259-0605. Business E-Mail: fvale@health.usf.edu.

VALE, PATRICE J., musician, consultant; d. Maurice Bob and June Gwendolyn (Olsen) Mizzell; m. L. Kenneth Vale, June 29, 1968; 1 child, Michelle Patrice Baggett. BS, Tex. Woman's U., 1962; MA in Sociology, U. Mo., 1998. Cert. cons. in workplace mediation Mediation Tng. Inst. Internat., Mo., 2003, ABE tchr. ABE State of Mo., 2000, paralegal diploma Paralegal Studies, Mo., 1983. Music therapist State Hosp., Fulton, Mo., 1962—64; music and dance therapist DePaul Hosp., New Orleans, 1964—66; exec. dir. lions eye tissue bank U. Mo., Columbia, 1967—73; harpist self-employed, Columbia, Mo., 1982—; paralegal and legal sec. Petri, Shurtleff, Froeschner & Smith Law Firm, Columbia, 1982—84; tchg. asst. U. oMo., Columbia, 1996—98; staff devel. trainer Mo. AEL Resource Ctr., Moberly and Fulton, 1998—2000; libr. cons. for continuing edn. Mo. State Libr., Jefferson City, 2000—04. Contbr. textbook. Recipient Nat. Honor, Nat. Music Fedn. Festivals, Tex., 1952, gold certificate for yrs. of superior rating in piano, Nat. Fedn. Music Clubs, 1952, winner piano contest judged by Liberace, Las Vegas, Nev. Mem.: TOPS, INTERTEL, Mensa, Alpha Kappa Delta. Home and Office: 908 Lynnwood Court Columbia MO 65203 Personal E-mail: patrice.vale@mchsi.com.

VALENCIA, MARGARITA, Spanish language educator; b. Bogotá, Colombia, Nov. 28, 1952; arrived in U.S., 1973; BA, U. Calif., Santa Barbara, MA in Polit. Sci. Profl. clear single subject tchg. credential in Spanish; cert. eligibility for Calif. prelim. adminstrv. svcs. credential. Tchr. Spanish Manual Arts H.S. L.A. Unified Sch. Dist., 1994—. Mem.: Acad. Polit. Sci. N.Y., L.A. World Affairs Coun., Sierra Club. Office Phone: 562-692-3778. Personal E-mail: mvalenciab@aol.com.

VALENCIA, MELANIE LAINE, music educator, performer; b. Oneonta, NY, Dec. 5, 1962; d. Jose Lardizabal and Marcell Jewell (Wiseman) V.; children: Laine Valencia, Kelly, Frederick Alexander. Student, Ithaca Coll., NY, 1981—85; BS in Music, Wells Coll., Aurora, NY, 1985; MFA, Carnegie Mellon U., Pitts., 1988. Tchr. flute, staff mem. various music stores, Johnson City & NYC, 1981—99; conc. bookings and adminstrv. various non-profit agys., NYC, 1988—94; flutist, founder Keeping Co. Ensemble, NYC, 1989—2002; flutist, dir. Valencia Duo, NYC & Binghamton, 1993—; flutist, founder, dir. Contemporary Collaborative Ensemble, NYC, 1993—; instr. toddler music class Vestal Recreation Dept., NY, 1995—2000; flutist Quintessence Woodwind Quintet, Binghamton, 1995—2000; piccoloist So. Tier Concert Band, Binghamton, 1995—2001; dir. elem. band Windsor Sch. Dist., NY, 1996—98; dir. small ensembles Binghamton H.S., 1998—2002; dir. West Mid. Sch., 6th grade concert band, 7th and 8th grade symphonic band, stage band, clarinet choirs, flute choirs, sax quartets, trios, duos 6th through 8 th Chorus Pride of Binghamton Marching Band, Binghamton City Sch. Dist., 1998—; dir. West Mid. Sch., 6-8th Grade Chorus. Cd with met. philomanic orchestra, Ulysseskoy, Kevin, Scott, 2007. Mem. NEA, Nat. Flute Assn., NY State United Tchrs., Broome County Music Educators Assn., NY State Sch. Music Assn., Music Educators Nat. Conf., Phi Beta Kappa. Avocations: cooking, travel, music collaborations, cross country skiing, gardening, movies. Home: 45 Lincoln Ave Binghamton NY 13905-4242 Office: West Mid Sch West Middle Ave Binghamton NY 13905-4242 Office Phone: 607-763-8400.

VALENCIA LAVAO, JESUS M., electrical engineer, consultant; b. Bogota, Distrito Capital, Colombia, Sept. 19, 1965; s. Jesus Maria Valencia Tapiero and Maria Elena Lavao de Valencia; m. Zoraya Ines Contecha Carrillo, Jan. 6, 1996 (div. May 15, 2002); m. Isabel Cristina Patino Devia, Feb. 20, 2005; children: Angel Gabriel Valencia Patino children: Nicolas Andres Valencia Contecha, Daniela Valencia Contecha. Degree in mgmt., Servicio Nacional De Aprendizaje, Bogota, 1988; degree in electrical engring., Distrital U., Bogota, 1994; MSEE, Los Andes U., Bogota, 2004. Lic. Consejo Nacional de Ingenierias, 1998. Radiofrequency engr. SKYTEL, Bogota, 1994—97; sr. engr. Avantel Motorola, Bogota, 1997—2001, Galaxy Engring. Svcs., Alpharetta, Ga., 2001—03, Incode Wireless, St. Louis, 2003—06, Verisign, Milw., 2006—07, Telnet, Columbia, Md., 2007—. Math and physics tchr. Grancolombiano H.S., Bogota, 1992—93; info. tech. and computer engr. cons. Microlink, Bogota, 1993—94; internat. telecom. cons. Skytel Mobile Telecomm. Techs. Corp., Bogota, 1995—97; assoc. prof. San Buenaventura U., Bogota, 1998—2001. Author: (drama) Once in the heavens; composer: (song) While the Sun Rises. Mem.: Profl. Assn. Diving Instrs. Diving Soc. (assoc.), IEEE (assoc.), Consejo Profesional Nacional de Ingenieria (life; electronic engr. 1998—). Achievements include invention of electronic circuit to generate chaotic signals for use in broadband telecommunications. Avocations: scuba diving, snowboarding, mountain biking, travel. Home: 18210 Northeast 112th Way Apt E2096 Redmond WA 98052 Office Phone: 425-216-4727. Business E-Mail: jesus.valencia@sprint.com.

VALENTA, JANET ANNE, substance abuse professional; b. Cleve., Sept. 22, 1948; d. Frank A. and Ann (Kogoy) Shenk; m. Mario Valenta, May 22, 1971. BA, Cleve. State U., 1970; postgrad., Rutgers U., 1973, U. Cin., 1976-84. Cert. prevention cons. Ohio, nat. trauma and loss school specialist 2002, nat. trauma loss in children cons. 2003. Purchasing clk./typist Restaurant div. Stouffer Foods Corp., Cleve., 1967-71; cmty. info. specialist Trumbull Warren Office of Econ. Opportunity, Warren, Ohio, 1972; edn. dir. Trumbull County Coun. on Alcoholism, Warren, 1973-78; rehab. counselor Trumbull County Bur. Vocat. Rehab., Niles, Ohio, 1979-80; owner, operator Ironsmith, Niles, 1978-79; cons., trainer Ohio Network Tng. and Assistance to Schs. and Cmty., Youngstown, Ohio, 1987—; prevention edn. coord. Cmty. Recovery Resource Ctr., Youngstown, 1979-94; prevention coord. Neil Kennedy Recovery Clinic, Youngstown, 1994—. Ohio tng. coord. Babesworld Home, Inc., Detroit, 1986-99; nat. chair pub. health caucus Nat. Assn. Prevention Profls., Chgo., 1976-77. Publicity chair Trumbull Art Guild, Warren, 1974—76; policy coun. Youngstown Cmty. Action, Headstart, 1988—90; active Summer Arts Butler Art Mus., 1997—2002, Ohio Violence Prevention Process, 2002; mem. Tri County Family Violence Prevention Coalition Speaker's Bureau, 2005, MYCAP Headstart Policy Coun., 2009—; bd. dirs. All Children Learn Differently, 2008, ACLD-Mollie Kessler Sch. Fiscal Office, 2009—, Ebony Life Support Group, Inc., Youngstown, 1992; bd. dirs.fiscal officer Mollie Kessler Sch. Named Woman of Yr., Warren Bus. and Profl. Women's Assn., 1978. Mem. Alcohol and Drug Abuse Prevention Assn. Ohio. Office: Neil Kennedy Recovery Clinic 2151 Rush Blvd Youngstown OH 44507-1535 Office Phone: 330-743-6671 ext 112.

VALENTE, ANA LUISA SCHIFINO, animal scientist, educator; b. Rio Grande, Brazil, July 31, 1970; d. Nestor S. and Elci Schifino Valente. D in Vet. Medicine, Fed. U. Pelotas, Brazil, 1993; MS in Biol. Oceanography, Fed. U. Rio Grande, Brazil, 1996; Specialist Degree in Wildlife Mgmt., Fed. Rural U. Amazonia, Brazil, 2000; PhD in Vet. Medicine, Autonomous U. Barcelona, 2007. Vet. surgeon and internal medicine Pvt. Clinic, Porto Alegre, Brazil, 1993—95; vet. cons. Tamandare Pk. Zoo, Rio Grande, 1995—97; asst. prof. Fed. U. Pelotas, 1997—2003, adj. prof., 2003—. Dir. Wildlife Rehab. Ctr., Pelotas, 1998—2003; cons. Brazilian Jour. Zoology, 1999, Jour. Rural Sci., 2002, Brazilian Jour. Biology, 2008. Contbr. various logos. Recipient Robin Best award, Marine Mammology Soc., 1996; grant, Nat. Counsel of Technol., 1990—92, 1994—96, Congress Participation grant, Internat. Sea Turtle Soc., 2006. Avocation: photography. Office: Univ Fed Pelotas Inst Biology Dept Morfology 96010 900 Pelotas Brazil Office Phone: 00 55 53 3275 7339. Business E-Mail: schifinoval@hotmail.com.

VALENTE, LOUIS PATRICK (DAN VALENTE), financial planner, director; b. Somerville, Mass., July 26, 1930; s. Luigi and Mary Constance (Fedele) Valente; m. Jeanne Barbara Peters, Oct. 3, 1992; children: Louis, Marianne, Steven, Diane, Richard, Carol, Susan. CPA, Bentley Coll., Boston, 1955. Cost acct. Cambridge Corp., Lowell, Mass., 1953-55; sr. acct. Flaherty, Bliss & Co., CPAs, Boston, 1956-61; fin. analyst Sanders Assocs., Nashua, NH, 1961-62; contract audit adminstr. Dept. Def. Audit Agy., Boston, 1962-66, DOE, Las Vegas, 1966-68; asst. controller EG&G, Inc., Wellesley, Mass., 1968-71, asst. v.p., treas., 1971-74, dir. fin., 1974-79, officer, corp. treas., 1979-83, v.p. bus. devel., 1985-91, sr. v.p. mergers, acquisitons and investments, 1991-95; bus. and fin. cons., 1995-97; chmn., CEO Palomar Med. Tech., Inc., Burlington, Mass., 1997—. Bd. dirs. Meditech, Inc., Westwood, Mass., MKS Instruments, Inc., Andover, Mass., Palomar Med. Tech. Inc., Burlington. Selectman Town of Burlington, 1970—73, 1976—79, chmn., 1972—79; trustee, mem. fin. com. Choate-Symmes Hosp., Woburn, Mass., 1972—80; mem. pres.'s adv. coun. Bentley Coll. With USAF, 1951—53. Mem.: AICPA, New Eng. Coun., Mass. Soc. CPAs, Fin. Execs. Inst., Bentley Coll. Alumni Assn., KC. Roman Catholic. Home: 44 Concord Rd Weston MA 02493-1223 Business E-Mail: dvalente@palmed.com.

VALENTE, PETER CHARLES, lawyer; b. NYC, July 3, 1940; s. Francis Louis and Aurelia Emily (Cella) V.; m. Judith Kay Nemeroff, Feb. 19, 1966; children: Susan Lynn, David Marc. BA, Bowdoin Coll., 1962; LLB, Columbia U., 1966; LLM, NYU, 1971. Bar: N.Y. 1967. Assoc. Blank Rome LLP (formerly Tenzer Greenblatt LLP), NYC, 1967-73, ptnr., 1973—, practice group leader pvt. client practice group, 2002—06. Co-author column on wills, estates and surrogates's practice N.Y. Law Jour. Fellow Am. Coll. Trust and Estate Counsel; mem. ABA, N.Y. State Bar Assn. (lectr. on wills, trusts and estates), Assn. of Bar of City of N.Y., N.Y. County Lawyers' Assn. (former bd. dirs. and chmn. com. on surrogates' ct., lectr. on wills, trusts and estates), Phi Beta Kappa. Office: Blank Rome 405 Lexington Ave New York NY 10174-0002 Office Phone: 212-885-5320. Office Fax: 917-332-3717. Business E-Mail: pvalente@blankrome.com.

VALENTI, LAURIE M., elementary school educator; b. Buffalo, Nov. 18, 1959; d. George A. Jr. and Doris P. Knab; m. Stephen Valenti, July 7, 1984; 1 child, Joseph Michael. BS in Music Edn., Nazareth Coll., Rochester, NY, 1981; MA in Elem. Edn., Adelphi U., Garden City, NY, 1990. Cert. tchr. N.Y., Tex., Nat. Bd. Profl. Tchg. Stds., 2004. Substitute tchr. Aldine Ind. Sch. Dist., Houston, 1981—83; jr. acct. exec. Johnson & Higgins of Tex. (now Marsh & McLennan), Houston, 1983—86; elem. music tchr. Aldine Ind. Sch. Dist., Houston; elem. music tchr./choral dir. Hicksville (NY) Unified Sch. Dist., 1988—89; elem. music tchr., choral dir. Port Wash. Unified Sch. Dist., Port Washington, NY, 1989—91, Shenendehowa Cen. Sch. Dist., Clfton Park, NY, 1993—. Sponsor tchr. for student tchr. Crane Sch. Music, Pottsdam, NY, 2005. Recipient Supt. Recognition award, Shenendehowa Cen. Sch. Dist., 2002, 2005. Mem.: Music Educators Nat. Conf. (assoc.). Home: 68 Algonquin Rd Clifton Park NY 12065 Office: Arongen Elem Sch 489 Clifton Park Ctr Rd Clifton Park NY 12065 Business E-Mail: valelaur@shenet.org.

VALENTINE, ALAN DARRELL, performing company executive, conductor; b. San Antonio, July 18, 1958; s. Lonnie Darrell Jr. and Marjorie (Childs) V.; m. Jari Ann Ruhl, Aug. 10, 1979 (div. 1987); children: Brandon Darrell, Chelsea Michelle; m. Karen Kay Bingham, Oct. 21, 1989 (div. 2001); 1 child, Nathan Lee; m. Connie Linsler, July 21, 2002. MusB, U. Houston, 1981. Orch. mgr. U. Houston Symphony, 1977-81; gen. mgr. Mid-Columbia Symphony Soc., Richland, Wash., 1981-83, Greensboro (N.C.) Symphony Soc., 1983-85; orch. mgr. Symphony Soc. San Antonio, 1985-87; mng. dir. Chattanooga Symphony and Opera, 1987-88; exec. dir. Okla. Philharm. Soc., Oklahoma City, 1988-98, Nashville Symphony, 1998—. Mem. adj. faculty Arts Administrn., Oklahoma City U., 1992— Recs. include Best of Greensboro Symphony Orchestra Silver Season, 1983, A Christmas Festival-San Antonio Symphony, 1986, A Time of Healing-Oklahoma City Philharmonic, 1995; (CD) Howard Hanson The Nashville Symphony, 2000, Charles Ives The Nashville Symphony, 2000, George Whitefield Chadwick-Nashville Symphony, 2002, Berntein's West Side Story, Nashville Symphonyh, 2002, Amy Beach Gaelic Symphony, Nashville Symphony, 2003, Beethoven's Missa Solemnis, 2004, Elliott Carter: Piano Concerto, 2004; TV prodns. include Music of the Americas-Placido Domingo with San Antonio Symphony, 1986, Perry Como Christmas Special-San Antonio Symphony, 1986, Sagebrush Symphony-Oklahoma City Philharmonic with Michael Martin Murphey, 1996, Kathie Lee: Just In Time for Christmas-Okla. City Philharmonic & Guests, 1996, Martina McBride Christmas Special Nashville, Symphony and Guests, 1998. Bd. dirs. Classen Sch. for Artistically and Academically Gifted, 1995-98, Arts Festival Okla., 1991-. Mem. NARAS (bd. dirs. 2002-), Am. Symphony Orch. League (bd. dirs. Cmty. and Urban Symphony Orch. divsn. 1981-83, policy com. A 1995-98, chmn. group III mgrs. 1996-98, vice chmn. group III mgr. 2003), Rotary, Phi Mu Alpha. Presbyterian. Avocations: computers, racquetball, reading. Office: Nashville Symphony 1 Symphony Pl Nashville TN 37201-2031 Personal E-mail: alandv@aol.com. Business E-Mail: alandv@nashvillesymphony.org.

VALENTINE, APRIL SUE, elementary school educator, department chairman; d. Frederick E. Krenz; m. Mark S. Valentine, June 29, 1985; 1 child, Rebecca M. B, U. Md. Balt. County, Catonsville, 1978—82; M, Loyola Coll., Balt., 1982—84. Gen. educator Anne Arundel County Pub. Sch., Annapolis, 1983—. Dept. chairperson (sci.) Anne Arundel Co Pub. Sch., 2000—; interdiscplinary leader Anne Arundel Co Pub. Schools, 1987—. Mem.: Nat. Sci. Assn. Office: Brooklyn Park Mid Sch 200 Hammonds Ln Baltimore MD 21225 Office Fax: 410-636-1774. Personal E-mail: avalentine@aacps.org.

VALENTINE, BOBBY (ROBERT JOHN VALENTINE), professional baseball manager; b. Stamford, CT, May 13, 1950; m. Mary Branca, Jan. 8, 1977; 1 child, Robert John Jr. Student, U. Southern California, Arizona State U. Player Pioneer League, Ogdon, 1968, Pacific Coast League, Spokane, Wash., 1969-71, Los Angeles Dodgers, Los Angeles, Calif., 1971-72, California Angels, Calif., 1973-75, International League, Charleston, W.Va., 1975, Pacific Coast League, Salt Lake City, 1975, Hawaii, Hawaii, 1976, San Diego Padres, San Diego, 1975-77, New York Mets, NY, 1977-78, Seattle Mariners, Seattle, W.Va., 1979; scout, infield instr. San Diego Padres, San Diego, 1981; minor league infield instr. New York Mets, 1982, third base coach, 1983-85; mgr. Texas Rangers, Arlington, Tex., 1985-96, N.Y. Mets, 1996—2002, Chiba Lotte Marines, Japan, 2004—; commentator, Baseball Tonight ESPN, 2003. Owner Bobby Valentine's Sports Gallery Cafe, Conn., Tex., and R.I. Named Am. League Mgr. of Yr. UPI, 1986; recipient William A. Shea Disting. Little League Grad. award, 1987; inductee Italian Am. Sports Hall Fame, 1990. mgr., Japan Series Champions, 2005. Office: Chiba Lotte Marines Chiba Marine Stadium 1 Mihama Mihama-ku Chiba-shi Chiba Japan also: Bobby Valentine's Sports Gallery Cafe 225 Main St Stamford CT 06903*

VALENTINE, CHARLES FRANCIS, retired educational administrator; b. Vineland, NJ, May 17, 1934; s. Quinton and Mary V.; m. Anne Marie Williams. BS, Glassboro State Coll., 1956, MA, 1965; EdD, Nova U., 1980. Cert. sch. adminstr., N.J. Tchr. Vineland Bd. Edn., 1956-65, prin., supr., 1965-77, dir. thorough and efficient edn. and supplementary programs, 1977-84, asst. supt. mandated, aux. and fed. programs, 1984-93, supt., 1993—97; ret., 1997. Adj. instr. Glassboro (N.J.) State Coll., 1974, Jersey City State Coll., 1981; audio-visual commr. Cumberland County, 1993—97; bd. dirs. Vineland Libr., 1993—97. Scoutmaster Vineland area Boy Scouts Am., 1956-62, committeeman, 1962—, mem. exec. com. So. NJ couns., 1978—, co-chmn. Atlantic So. NJ com., 1990; past pres., exec. com., bd. dir. Greater Vineland United Fund; chmn. Combined Health and Human Campaign Cumberland County, 1987-97; past pres. So. NJ chpt. Exceptional Children, 1984-85; mem. Cumberland County Pvt. Industry Coun., 1979-82, Vineland Edn. Found., 1985-97, South Jersey Employer Edn. Consortium, 1985-97; mem. Cumberland County Coll. Student Devel. Adv. Bd., 1981-2002; mem. Cumberland County Coll. Retirement Coll., 2001—; commentator St. Isidore Ch., Vineland, 1966—, mem. pastoral planning com., 1973-76, parish coun., 1982-85, 2001-; bd. dir. Vineland YMCA, 1975-99, devel. chmn., 1977-78; adv. bd. NJ Hist. Soc.; bd. dir. Cumberland unit Am. Cancer Soc., 1985-97, chmn. bd. dir., 1984-85; commr. Vineland Environmental, 1978-99, 2003—; bd. mem. Vineland Svc. Club Coun., 1991—, pres., 2005—; bd. trustees Vineland Devel. Ctr., 1991—; chmn. Vineland Teen Adv. Partnership, 2002—, Vineland Youth Ctr.; edn. chmn. Cumberland County Human Rels. Commn., 2002—; dir. Cumberland County PTA Dist., 1993—, legis. chmn., 2001—; citizen mem. Sch. Mgmt. Teams Johnston and Landis Schs., 1998—; v.p. Alzheimer's Support Group of Cumberland County, 2002—; vice chmn. Cumberland County Profl. Devel. Bd., 2000—; mem. Rowan U. Tchrs. Edn. Adv. Coun., 1993—; mem. adv. coun. Cumberland County Office on Aging, 2004—. Recipient Vineland Jaycees Outstanding Young Educator award, 1968—69, Citizen of the Year award, Greater Vineland C. of C., 1983, Patricia R. Kane Lifetime Achievement award, Alliance NJ Environ. Edn., 2005, Friend Edn. award, Vineland Edn Assn., 2005, I Have a Dream award, 2007, Boy Scouts Am. awards, NJ Coun. Lifetime Achievement Award, Hero award, Greater Cumberland County United Way Cmty., Liberty Bell award, Cumberland County Bar Assn., Outstanding Contbns. Economic Edn. award, NJ Coun. Economic Edn. Mem. NEA (life), Nat. Assn. Elem. Sch. Prins. (Life), N.J. Edn. Assn. (life), Glassboro State Coll.

Alumni Assn. (life), Vineland Hist. and Antiquarian Soc. (life), N.J. Folklore Soc. (life), Alliance N.J. Environ. Edn., N.J. Assn. Sch. Adminstrs. (life, diplomate 1988), Urban Tech. Alliance, South Jersey Schoolmen's Assn. (pres.), Friends of Vineland Pub. Libr. (life), N.J. Congress Parents and Tchrs. (life), Atlantic City Art Ctr. (life), Phi Delta Kappa (life), Kappa Delta Pi (life), Phi Gamma Sigma.

VALENTINE, DEAN, film producer; AB, U. Chicago, 1976. Pres. Walt Disney TV/Touchstone TV; pres., CEO United Paramount Network, Los Angeles, 1997—2002; with Europlay Capital Advisors, LLC, 2002—03; pres. First Family Entertainment, Beverly Hills, 2004. Named one of Top 200 Collectors, ARTnews Mag., 2004—08. Avocation: Collector of Comtemporary Art. Office: Dean Valentine 3212 Nebraska Ave Santa Monica CA 90404-4214

VALENTINE, GENE C., securities dealer; b. Washington, Pa., June 19, 1950; s. John N. and Jane S. Valentine. BS in Psychology, Bethany Coll., 1972; student, U. Vienna, Austria, 1971-72. Commd. ensign USN, 1972, advanced through grades to lt., 1987, hon. discharged, 1978; owner Horizon Realty, San Francisco, 1978-82; dir. land acquisitions Windfarms Ltd. subs. Chevron, U.S.A., San Francisco, 1980-82; v.p. mktg. Christopher Weil & Co., Sherman Oaks, Calif., 1982-85; chmn., CEO Pacific Asset Group Inc. (name now Fin. West Group, Inc.), Westlake Village, Calif., 1985—. Bd. dirs. Fin. West Group, Inc., Paradox Holdings; founder, chmn., dir. Second Byte Found.; founder, chmn. Peace Point Farms Equestrian Facility, LLC and Found., Bethany, W.Va. Mem. Rep. Party, L.A. Mem. NASD, Internat. Assn. Fin. Planning (bd. dirs. L.A. chpt. 1982-87). Episcopalian. Avocations: equestrian, sailing, tennis, golf, running. Home Phone: 304-829-9099; Office Phone: 304-829-4800. Personal E-mail: qcvalentine@yahoo.com.

VALENTINE, H. JEFFREY, legal association executive; b. Phila., Sept. 28, 1945; s. Joshua Morton and Olga W. (Wilson) V.; 1 child, Karyn. BS, St. Louis U., 1964, postgrad., 1966-68. Programmer, systems analyst Honeywell Electronic Data Processing, Wellesley Hills, Mass., 1964-66; account exec. Semiconductor div. Tex. Instruments, New Eng., 1966-68; New Eng. sales exec., Mid-Atlantic regional mgr. Electronic Instrumentation Co., 1968-70; pres. Nat. Free Lance Photographers Assn., Doylestown, Pa., 1970-89; pres., dir. Towne Print & Copy Ctrs. Inc.; v.p., exec. dir. Nat. Paralegal Assn., 1982—; pres. Paralegal Assocs., Inc., 1982—; chief operating officer Doylestown Parking Corp., 1977-88. Bd. dirs. Law Enforcement Supply Co., Solebury, Valtronics Supply Co., Towne Print & Copy Centers Inc., Solebury, Doylestown Stationery and Office Supply, Energy Mktg. Assocs., Inc., Solebury, Paralegal Placement Network; pres. Paralegal Pub. Corp., 1983-90; pub. Paralegal Jour.; pres. Valco Enterprises Inc., 1986—, Paralegal Employment Sys., Inc., 1988, Solebury Press, Inc., 1989—; ptnr. J&S Gen. Contractors, 1993—, J&S Landscaping Tree Svc., 1993—, J&S Estate and Property Mgmt., 2001--; owner Specialized Computer Consulting, 1992—. Author: Photographers Bookkeeping System, 1973, rev. edit., 1978, Photographers Pricing Guides, 1971, 72, 74, 75, Available Markets Director's - 4 Vols., 1973-77, National Model Sources Directory, Nat. Paralegal Salary and Employment Survey, 1985-86, 88, 90-92, 93-94; also articles, bulls. and pamphlets. Exec. sec. Doylestown Bus. Assn., 1972-78, pres., 1979, 83, v.p., 1981. Recipient Internat. Men of Achievement award, 1988; named Personalities of the Am., 1988. Mem. London Coll. Applied Scis., Nat. Fedn. Paralegal Assns., Photog. Industry Coun., Nat. Assn. Legal Assts., Am. Soc Assn. Execs., Soc. Assn. Mgrs., Nat. Fedn. Ind. Business (mem. action coun. com.), Nat. Parking Assn., Nat. Office Products Assn., Graphic Arts Assn. Delaware Valley, Nat. Assn. Federally Licensed Firearms Dealers, Nat. Compostition Assn., Internat. Platform Assn. Office: PO Box 406 Solebury PA 18963-0406

VALENTINE, JAMES WILLIAM, paleontologist, educator, writer; b. LA, Nov. 10, 1926; s. Adelbert Cuthbert and Isabel (Davis) V.; m. Grace Evelyn Whysner, Dec. 21, 1957 (div. 1972); children: Anita, Ian; m. Cathryn Alice Campbell, Sept. 10, 1978 (div. 1986); 1 child, Geoffrey; m. Diane Mondragon, Mar. 16, 1987. BA, Phillips U., 1951; MA, UCLA, 1954, PhD, 1958. From asst. prof. to assoc. prof. U. Mo., Columbia, 1958-64; from assoc. prof. to prof. U. Calif., Davis, 1964-77, prof. geol. scis. Santa Barbara, 1977-90, prof. integrative biology Berkeley, 1990-93, prof. emeritus, 1993—. Author: Evolutionary Paleoecology of the Marine Biosphere, 1973, On the Origin of Phyla, 2004; editor: Phanerozoic Diversity, 1985; co-author: Evolution, 1977, Evolving, 1979; contbr. articles to profl. jours. Served with USNR, 1944-46, PTO. Recipient Lapworth medal Palaeontological Assn., 2004; Fulbright rsch. scholar, Australia, 1962-63; Guggenheim fellow Yale U., Oxford U., Eng., 1968-69; Rockefeller Found. scholar in residence, Bellagio, Italy, summer 1974; grantee NSF, NASA. Fellow: AAAS, Paleontol. Soc. (medal 1996), Geol. Soc. Am., Am. Acad. Arts and Scis.; mem.: NAS, Am. Philosophy Soc. Avocation: collecting works of Charles Darwin. Home: 1351 Glendale Ave Berkeley CA 94708-2025 Office: U Calif Dept Integrative Biology Berkeley CA 94720-0001 Office Phone: 510-643-5791. Business E-Mail: jwvsossi@socrates.berkeley.edu.

VALENTINE, JOHN LESTER, state legislator, lawyer; b. Fullerton, Calif., Apr. 26, 1949; s. Robert and Pauline; m. Karen Valentine; 6 children. BS in Acctg. and Econs., Brigham Young U., 1973, JD, 1976. CPA; bar: Utah 1976, US Dist. Ct. Utah, US Ct. Appeals (10th cir.), US Tax Ct., US Supreme Ct. 2002. Atty. Howard, Lewis & Petersen, Provo, Utah, 1976—; mem. Dist. 14 Utah House of Reps., 1988—99, asst. majority whip, 1997—98; mem. Dist. 14 Utah State Senate, 1998—, pres., 2004—08. Instr. probate and estates Utah Valley State Coll.; instr. fin. planning., adj. prof. law Brigham Young U.; chmn. revenue and taxation com. Utah Senate, 1999-2000, vice chmn. exec. appropriations com., judiciary com., pub. edn. subcom., majority whip 2001—; mem. exec offices, cts., corrections and legis. appropriations subcom., Utah House of Reps., 1988-90, capital facilities subcom., 1988-90, retirement com., 1988-90, judiciary com., 1988-92, strategic planning steering com., 1988-90, interim appropriations com., 1988-94, tax. review commn., 1989-98, ethics com., 1990-92, human svcs. and health appropriations subcom., 1990-92, revenue and taxation com., 1988-98, vice chmn. 1990-92; vice chmn. exec. appropriations., 1990-92; chmn. exec. appropriations com., 1992-94, chmn. rules com., 1994-96, higher edn. appropriations com. 1994-96. Mem. adv. bd. Internat. Sr. Games, 1988—; active Blue Ribbon Task Force on Local Govt. Funding, Utah League Cities and Towns, 1990-94, Criminal Sentencing Guidelines Task Force, Utah Judicial Coun., 1990-92, Access to Health Care Task Force, 1990-92, Utah County Sheriff Search and Rescue, Orem Met. Water Bd., Alpine Sch. Dist. Boundary Line Com., 1986-90, Boy Scouts Am.; bd. regents Legis. Adv. Com. UVCC.; mem. exec. bd. Utah Nat. Parks Coun.; mem. adv. coun. Orchard Elem. Sch., Mountainlands Com. an Aging; bd. trustees Utah Opera Co.; judge nat. and local competitions Moot Ct.; voting dist. chmn.; state, county del.; lt. incident command sys. Utah County Sheriff. Recipient Silver Beaver award Boy Scouts Am., Taxpayer Advocate award Utah Taxpayer Assn. Mem. ABA (tax sect.), Utah State Bar, CPA Com., Tax Sect. Specialization Com., Bicentennial Com. Republican. Mem. Lds Ch. Avocation: mountain climbing. Office: Howard Lewis & Petersen 120 E 300 N Provo UT 84606-2907 also: W115 Capitol Complex Salt Lake City UT 84114 Office Phone: 801-373-6345, 801-538-1035. Office Fax: 301-326-1475. Business E-Mail: jvalentine@utahsenate.org.

VALENTINE, MARK CONRAD, dermatologist; b. Parkersburg, W.Va., Sept. 26, 1948; s. Sestel and Margaret Elaine (Sabolo) V.; m. Elizabeth Michelle Monezis, Apr. 21, 1975; children: Perry Martin, Owen Mark. BA, W.Va. U., 1970; MD, Johns Hopkins U., 1974. Intern, resident U. Hosps. Cleve., 1974-76, resident, 1976-79; dermatologist pvt. practice, Everett, Wash., 1979—. Clin. prof. U. Wash., Seattle, 1979—; active med. staff Providence Everett Gen. Med. Ctr., 1979—. Editl. bd. Jour. of Am. Acad. Dermatology, 1998—2005. Bd. dirs., sec. City Libr. Bd., Mukilteo, Wash., 1994-99; bd. dirs., v.p. Everett Symphony Bd., 1982-85, 2001—2006; bd. dirs. Book Arts Guild, Seattle, 1988-90. Nat. Merit scholar, 1966. Mem. AMA, Am. Acad. Dermatology (adv. coun. 1983-86), Wash. State Dermatol. Assn. (pres.-elect 1996, pres. 1996-97), Seattle Dermatology Soc. (pres. 1985-86), Snohomish County Med. Soc. (bd. dirs. 2001—, pres. 2006), Rotary (Everett), Phi Beta Kappa. Avocations: book collecting, book binding, guitar, piano. Office: 3327 Colby Ave Everett WA 98201-6403 Home Phone: 425-348-6256; Office Phone: 425-258-6767. Personal E-mail: mark1105@aol.com.

VALENTINE, PHYLLIS LOUISE, counseling administrator; d. Harold Gray and Velma Eura Long; m. Samuel L. Valentine, Dec. 30, 1995. BA, St. Augustine's Coll., 1970; MEd, Bowie State U., 1992; student, Trinity Coll., 1974—77, Georgetown U., 1989, U. D.C., 1974—88. Cert. sch. counselor K-12, reading tchr. K-12. Evening reading teacher Loton Reformatory Youth Ctr. II PSI Assocs., Washington, 1984—86; chpt. 1 reading/math. lab tchr. D.C. Pub. Schs., 1986—92, chpt. 1 resource asst., 1992—93; chpt. 1 CAI lab tchr./team coord. C.W. Harris Elem. Sch., Washington, 1992—95; sch. counselor J.C. Nalle Elem. Sch., Washington, 1995—. Mem. tchr. adv. bd. Ctr. for Artistry in Tchg., Washington, 1999—; dir., presenter J.C. Nalle Sch. Extended Day, 1998. V.p. Brandywine Sta. Townhouse Assn., Upper Marlboro, Md., 1990—97. Recipient Letter of Commendation, Exec. Dir. Chpt. 1 program, 1987, AIMs Pilot, Bryan Elem. Sch., 1984, HOST Corp., 1994, DCPS Parent Ctr. Incentive, 1997. Mem.: D.C. Sch. Counseling Assn. (newsletter editor 2004—05, corr. sec.), Am. Sch. Counseling Assn., Am. Counseling Assn., Tots & Teens Inc. (pres. 1985—93, corr. sec. 1985—93, youth leader 1987—91, D.C. chpt., award 1990—91), D.C. Counseling Assn. (pres.-elect 2001—02, pres. 2002, dedicated svc. plaque 1993), Phi Delta Kappa (mem. Beta chpt., grammateus 2003—), Nat. Sorority Phi Delta Kappa (Beta chpt.), Sigma Gamma Rho (recording sec., anti-basilus 1971—78). Avocations: gardening, listening to jazz music, dance. Business E-Mail: phyllis.valentine@k12.us.

VALENTINE, RALPH SCHUYLER, chemical engineer, director; b. Seattle, Nov. 3, 1932; s. John Campbell and Elizabeth Florence (Patterson) V.; m. Jeanne Marie Belanger, June 15, 1957; children: Susan Diana, Jacqueline Leigh, John Campbell. BSChemE, U. Wash., 1955, PhDChemE, 1963; MSChemE, U. Ill., 1956. Registered profl. engr., Calif., Va., Wash. Rsch. engr. Chevron Rsch. Corp., Richmond, Calif., 1956-61; instr. U. Wash., Seattle, 1961-63; mgr. fluid dynamics Aerojet-Gen., Sacramento, 1963-69; mgr. chem. tech. Atlantic Rsch. Corp., Alexandria, Va., 1969-79; mgr. rsch. United Techs. Chem. Systems, San Jose, Calif., 1979-91; gen. mgr. Greater Pocatello Sr. Citizens, Inc., 2001—08; dir. Sylvan Learning Ctr., 2008—. Lectr. U.S. Naval Postgrad. Sch., Monterrey, Calif., 1968, UCLA Modern Devels. in Propulsion, L.A., 1967-68, USAF Astronautics Labs., Lancaster, Calif., 1967, U.S. Army R & D Unit, Sacramento, 1966. Contbr. 23 tech. articles to profl. jours.; patentee in field. Recipient NASA commendation for Apollo work, Houston, 1969, 1st prize Ceramographic Exhbn. Am. Ceramics Soc., 1974, Andrus award AARP, 2005. Mem. AIChE (life). Republican. Personal E-mail: ralph_s_valentine@yahoo.com.

VALENTINE, STEVEN RICHARDS, lawyer; b. Memphis, Jan. 30, 1956; s. William Robert and Lenita Joanne (Nelms) V.; m. Susan Marie Burke, Jan. 14, 1984; children: Christina Michele, William Robert II, Steven Richards Jr., Thomas Burke, Diana Elizabeth. Grad., Capitol Page Sch., Washington, 1974; student, Earlham Coll., 1974-77; B of Gen. Studies with distinction, Ind. U., 1979, JD, 1982. Bar: Ill. 1983, D.C. 1985, U.S. Ct. Appeals (D.C. cir.) 1986, U.S. Supreme Ct. 1986, U.S. Ct. Appeals (9th cir.) 1989. Chief investigator consumer protection divsn. Office Atty. Gen., State of Ind., 1980-82; exec. dir. Ams. United for Life Legal Def. Fund, Chgo., 1982-83; chief counsel subcom. on separation of powers U.S. Senate, Washington, 1983-85, chief counsel subcom. on cts., 1985; adminstrv. asst. U.S. Senator John P. East, Washington, 1985-86; dir. Office of Policy Devel. and Comm. Legal Svcs. Corp., Washington, 1986-87; counselor to asst. atty. gen. civil divsn. U.S. Dept. Justice, Washington, 1987-88; dep. asst. atty. gen. civil divsn. U.S. Justice Dept., Washington, 1988-93, gen. counsel to U.S. Senator Robert C. Smith, 1993-99; legis. dir. to U.S. Senator Robert C. Smith, 1996-99; of counsel Preston Gates Ellis & Rouvelas Meeds LLP, Washington, 1999—2002; ptnr. K & L, Gates LLP, Washington, 2002—. Mem. exec. com., bd. dirs. Deluxe West, Inc.; sr. fellow John C. Stennis Ctr. for Pub. Svc.; vice chmn., bd. visitors Ind. U. Sch. Law, Indpls.; presdl. rank review bd. US Office Personnel Mgmt., 2006. Author: Each Time A Man, 1978, All Shall Live, 1980; co-author: Abortion and the Constitution, 1987, Principle Over Politics, 2004; contbr. articles to profl. jours. Recipient spl. commendation U.S. Atty. Gen., 1993; John C. Stennis Congl. staff fellow, 1995-96. Mem.: SAR, Federalist Soc., Capitol Hill Club. Republican. Roman Catholic. Avocations: history, baseball. Home: 6487 Warwick Cir Alexandria VA 22315-5045 Office: K & L Gates LLP 1601 K St NW Washington DC 20006 Home Phone: 703-924-3554; Office Phone: 202-661-3802. Personal E-mail: rick.valentine@cox.net.

VALENTINE, WILLIAM NEWTON, retired physician, educator; b. Kansas City, Mo., Sept. 29, 1917; s. Herbert S. and Mabel W. Valentine; m. Martha Hickman Winfree; children: William, James, Edward. Student, U. Mich., 1934—36, U. Mo., Columbia, 1936—37; MD, Tulane U., 1942. Diplomate Am. Bd. Internal Medicine. Intern Strong Meml. Hosp., Rochester, NY, 1942—43, asst. resident in medicine, 1943, chief resident in medicine, 1943—44; specialist, attending physician in internal medicine Wadsworth Hosp., LA, 1949—88, VA Ctr., LA, 1949—88; specialist, attending physician in internal medicine Ctr. Health Scis. UCLA, 1949—, prof. medicine, 1957—88, chmn. dept., 1963—71, prof. emeritus medicine, 1988—. Contbr. articles to profl. jours. Capt. MC AUS, 1944—47. Recipient Mayo Soley award for excellence in rsch., Western Soc. Clin. Rsch., 1978, 53d Annual UCLA faculty rsch. lectr., 1978. Master: ACP (John Phillips Meml. award for disting. achievements in internal medicine 1979); fellow: Am. Soc. Hematology (Henry Stratton lectr. 1978), Internat. Soc. Hematology (v.p. U.S. 1976—80); mem.: NAS, Am. Acad. Arts and Scis., We. Soc. Clin. Rsch., We. Assn. Physicians (pres. 1969—70), Assn. Am. Physicians, Am. Soc. Clin. Investigation (v.p. 1962), Am. Bd. Internal Medicine. Republican.

VALENTINO, (VALENTINO GARAVANI), retired fashion designer; b. Voghera, Italy, May 11, 1932; Student, Academia Dell'Arte, Paris, Ecole des Beaux-Arts. Asst. designer Fashion Ho. of Jean Dessès, 1950-55, Fashion Ho. of Guy Laroche, 1956-58; founder House of Valentino, Rome, 1959—2008, began partnership with Giancarlo Giammetti, 1960; internat. debut Florence, Italy, 1962; launched women's & men's ready-to-wear collections, 1972; opened boutiques in Rome and Milan, 1972; developer Valentino Più, 1973; launched Valentino perfume in Paris, 1978; established boutiques in US & Japan, 1980. Designer Italian athletes' uniforms Olympic Games, Los Angeles, Calif., 1984. Exhibited at Victoria and Albert Mus., London, 1971, La Jolla Mus. Art, Calif., 1982; costume designer (films) Wild and Wonderful, 1964, Hello-Goodbye, 1970; designer and prodr. exhibition: Atelier of Illusion, 1985, Accademia, 1991. Founder (with Giancarlo Giamcarlo) L.I.F.E., 1990—. Recipient Neiman-Marcus award, 1967, Grand'Ufficiale dell'Ordine al Merito, Italian Ministry of Industry, 1985, Lifetime Achievement award, American Designer awards, NY, 2000, Légion d'Honneur, France, 2005, Accessories Coun. of Excellence, 2007, Médaille de la Ville de Paris, Mayor of Paris, 2008; named Cavaliere di gran Croce, Italy, 1986, Cavaliere del Lavoro, 1996.

VALENZUELA, ARTURO ARMS, political science professor, writer, consultant; b. Concepcion, Chile, Jan. 23, 1944; s. Raimundo Arms and Dorothy Dewel (Bowie) V.; m. Kathryn Mudge; children: Jennifer, Mark. BA summa cum laude, Drew U., 1965; MA, Columbia U., 1967, PhD, 1971. Prof. polit. sci. Duke U., Durham, NC, 1970—87; prof. govt., dir. Ctr. for Latin Am. studies Georgetown U., Washington, 1987—; dep. asst. Sec. of State for Inter-Am. affairs US Dept. of State, Washington, 1994—96; spl. asst. to the pres., sr. dir. for intern-Am. affairs Nat. Security Coun., The White House, Washington, 1999—2001. Mem. Coun. on Fgn. Rels., NYC, 1989—; vis. scholar U. Sussex, 1977-78, Oxford U., 1985, U. Florence, 1992. Author: The Breakdown of Democratic Regimes: Chile, 1978; co-author: A Nation of Enemies: Chile Under Pinochet, 1992; co-author, co-editor The Failure of Presidential Democracy, 1994, Politics, Society and Democracy, 1997. Bd. dirs. Nat. Dem. Inst. for Internat. Affairs, 1996-97, 2001—, Santiago Coll., Chile, 1998—, Nat. Coun. of La Raza, 2002—, America's Watch, 2003-, Drew U., 2003-, Corpbanca, Chile, 2007—; mem. internat. adv. bd. Repsol YDF, Spain, 2007—. Decorated Order of the So. Cross (Brazil), Order of Boyaca (Colombia); Danforth fellow Danforth Found., 1965, fellow Woodrow Wilson Internat. Ctr. for Scholars, 1992-93. Mem. Am. Polit. Sci. Assn., Latin Am. Studies Assn. Democrat. Methodist. Office: Ctr for Latin Am Studies Georgetown Univ Washington DC 20057-1026 Office Phone: 202-687-0140. Business E-Mail: valenzue@georgetown.edu. E-mail: valenzuela.arturo@gmail.com.

VALENZUELA, JULIO SAMUEL, sociologist, educator; b. Concepción, Chile, Mar. 30, 1948; came to U.S., 1970; s. Raimundo Arms and Dorothy Dueul (Bowie) V.; m. Erika Fresia Maza, Mar. 22, 1969. Licenciatura, U. Concepción, Chile, 1970; PhD, Columbia U., NYC, 1979. Asst. prof. Yale U., New Haven, 1977-80, Harvard U., Cambridge, Mass., 1980-85, assoc. prof., 1985, U. Notre Dame, Ind., 1986—89, prof. Ind., 1989—, dept. chairperson Ind., 1989—92, fellow Kellogg Inst. Ind., 1986—. Sr. assoc. fellow St. Antony's Coll., Oxford U., 1992-93, 96—; campaign adv. presidl. election, Chile, 1999; cons. labor policy Chilean Govt., 2000, 01; advisor, Chilean Govt. Pension Reform Commn., 2006. Author: Democratización vía Reforma, 1986; co-author: Vinculos, Creencias e Ilusiones, 2008, Chile, A Country Study, 1994; co-editor: Chile: Politics And Society, 1976, Military Rule In Chile, 1986, Issues In Democratic Consolidation, 1992, El Eslabón Perdido: Familia, Modernización y Bienestar en Chile, 2006; contbr. chpts. to books, articles to profl. jours. Pres. New Eng. Coun. of Latin Am. Studies, 1984—85. Fellow NEH ind. scholarship rsch. 1983-84, conf. grant 1987; John Simon Guggenheim fellow, 1996. Mem. Am. Sociol. Assn., Internat. Sociol. Assn. (v.p. rsch. com. #44 1990-94), Latin Am. Studies Assn. (nominating com. 1987-88), Am. Polit. Sci. Assn., Soc. for the Advancement of Socio-econs., Chilean Polit. Sci. Assn. Methodist. Office: U Notre Dame Kellogg Inst Notre Dame IN 46556 Office Phone: 574-631-6410.

VALERI, TONY, Canadian government official, small business owner; m. Terri Boswell; 2 children. Degree in econs., McMaster U. M.P. for Hamilton East-Stoney Creek House of Commons, 1993—, parliamentary sec. to Min. Fin. Paul Martin, 1997—99, mem. standing com. on fin., vice chair standing com. on industry, chair standing com. on govt. ops., leader govt. Parliament Hill, 2004—06; min. transport Govt. of Canada, Ottawa, 2003—04; exec. in residence DeGroote Sch. Bus., McMaster U., 2006—; cons. for profit and not for profit orgns. in area of strategic advocacy programs, 2006—. Chair Nat. Liberal Caucus Task Force on Jobs and Small Bus.

VALERIN, MARCUS PAUL, school system administrator, director; s. Michael Antonio and Nancy Lynn Valerin. BS, Southern Meth. U., Dallas, 1998, MA in Liberal Arts, 1992, grad. in Dispute Resolution, 1999. Asst. dir. grad. admissions Southern Meth. U., 1994—96, asst. dir. grad. admissions & pre-coll. enrollment, 1996—97, assoc. dir. grad. admissions & pre coll. enrollment, 1997—2000, assoc. dir. grad. admissions & academic svcs., 2000—02, dir. grad., exec. admissions, 2002—, pres., Faculty Club, 1997—2008, dir. grad. coop. edn. & profl. experience, 2006—. Pres. Briarwood Neighborhood Assn., Dallas, 2004—. Recipient Outstanding award, Assn. Grad. Students Higher Edn., 2007—08, Outstanding Doctoral award, U. North Tex., 2008. Mem.: Kappa Delta Pi Internat. Honor Soc. Edn. Conservative. Roman Catholic. Avocations: movies, skeet shooting, reading. Home: 3728 Casa Del Sol Ln Dallas TX 75228-1818 Office: Southern Meth Univ 6251 Airline Rd Dallas TX 75275-0338 Office Fax: 214-768-3778. Business E-Mail: marc@smu.edu.

VALERIO, JOSEPH MASTRO, architectural firm executive, educator; b. Dec. 26, 1947; m. Linda A. Searl; children: Joseph Jr., Anthony. BArch, U. Mich., 1970; MArch, UCLA, 1972. Registered architect, Wis., Ill., Ind., Mo., Calif., Tex., Ariz., Minn., Ala., Iowa, Ind., Md., Mich., Okla., Ga., Mass., N.J., N.Y., N.C., Va., Utah, D.C., Wash., Oreg.; cert. Nat. Coun. Archtl. Registration Bds. Pres. Chrysalis Corp. Architects, 1970-85; assoc. prof. U. Wis., 1973-86; design dir. Swanke Hayden Connell Architects, 1985-86; v.p. architecture A. Epstein and Sons, Inc., 1986-88; pres. Valerio-Assocs. Inc., 1988-94; prin. Valerio Dewalt Train Assocs., Inc., Chgo., 1994—. Mem. nat. bd. peer reviewers GSA; spkr. Ariz. State U., UCLA, U. Ariz., U. Cin., others; cons. USG Interiors, Formica Corp., AAAS, NAS, NEA: vis. critic and lectr. in field. Prin. works include corp., high-tech. indsl., retail, instl. and residential bldgs.; author: Movie Palaces, 1983; (monograph) Joe Valerio, 1999; editor: Architectural Fabric Structures, 1985; featured in Inside Architecture, Domestic Interiors, 1997, New Am. Apt., 1997, Internat. Interiors, 1997, Lofts/Living and Working Spaces, 1999, Greater Chicagoan C. of C. (bd. dirs.). Mem. exec. bd. men's coun. Mus. Contemporary Art, 1989-91; mem. exec. bd. Contemporary Arts Coun., 1994-96 (pres. 1999). Recipient Honor awards Wis. Soc. Architects, 1975, 81, 84, 85, Gov.'s Award for Design Excellence, State of Mich., 1979, Gold medal Inst. Bus. Designers, 1988, Design award Progressive

Architecture, 1991, Architectural Record Interiors award 1993, 95, 96, Disting. Interior award Inst. Bus. Designers, Chgo., 1993; honored by Emerging Voices series Archtl. League N.Y., 1984, Met. Home mag., Interiors mag. Fellow AIA (programs chmn. design com. Chgo. chpt. 1990, long range planning com. 1992, chair nat. com. on design 1997, Nat. Honor award 1981, 93, Interiors award Chgo. chpt. 1988, 90, 92, 95-97, 99-2002, 04, Disting. Bldg. award 1991, 93, 2004, Nat. Interior Honor award 1993, 96, 2003, Divine Detail award 1999, 2001), Chgo. Architecture Club (pres. 1994), Lambda Alpha. Office: Valerio Dewalt Train Assocs 500 N Dearborn St Fl 9 Chicago IL 60610-4900 Office Phone: 312-332-0363. Business E-Mail: jvalerio@buildordie.com.

VALERIO, MICHAEL ANTHONY, diversified financial services company executive; b. Detroit, Sept. 20, 1953; s. Anthony Rudolph and Victoria (Popoff) V.; m. Barbara Ann Nabozny, Oct. 8, 1983. BA, U. Mich., Dearborn, 1975. CPA, Mich. Jr. acct. Carabell, Bocknek CPA's, Southfield, Mich., 1975-76; sr. acct. Purdy, Donovan & Beal, CPA's, Detroit, 1976-77; mgr. Buctynck & Co., CPA's, Southfield, 1978-79; contr. Transcontinental Travel, Harper Woods, Mich., 1979—80; exec. v.p. Holland Cons., Inc., Detroit, 1980-85; contr., CFO SLC Recycling Industries, Inc., Warren, Mich., 1985—98; owner Pinnacle Fin. Consulting, PLLC, Livonia, Mich., 1994—. Fin. cons. Am. Group Retirement Strategy Ctrs.; owner Michael Valerio, CPA/PFS, LLC, 2006—. Mem. AICPA, Mich. Soc. CPAs. Roman Catholic. Office: CPA/ PFS LLC Ste A 37771 Seven Mile Rd Livonia MI 48152-1003

VALERO, HENRI-PIERRE, research scientist; m. Anita Valero. PhD, Institut de Physique du Globe de Paris, 1997. Cert. in Geoscis., Institut de Physique du Globe de Paris, 1997. Project engr. CNES, Toulouse, France, 1993—94; rsch. scientist Institut de Physique du Globe de Paris, 1994—97; engr. project Schlumberger K K, Tokyo, 1998—2001, program mgr., 2001—04, Schlumberger Doll Rsch., Cambridge, Mass., 2004—, prin. rsch. scientist, 2004—. Assoc. editor Geophys. Prospecting, 2005—. Contbr. scientific papers to profl. jours. Lt. Engring., 1993—94, France. Achievements include 8 US patents award; patents pending for 10 US Patents under examination. Office: Schlumberger Doll Research 1 Hamspshire St MD B213 Cambridge MA 02139-1578 Office Fax: 617-768-2380. Business E-Mail: hvalero@slb.com.

VALERO, MARIA TERESA, photographer, art educator; b. Venezuela; BFA in Graphic Design, Art History, U. Kans., M in Art History. Dir. Sch. Art, U. Tulsa, prof., Gallery Dir., Alexandre Hogue Gallery; founder & dir. Third Floor Designs (a student run design studio). Exhibitions include, Kans., Mo., Okla., Ariz., Tex., Ark., Venezuela, Beauty of the Levant (Images of Lebanon & Syria Through Western Eyes), Syria. Recipient Graphex Award, Tulsa Addy, Creativity Today Award. Office: University of Tulsa Phillips Hall 104 600 South College Ave Tulsa OK 74104 Office Phone: 918-631-2740. Office Fax: 918-631-3423. E-mail: maria-valero@utulsa.com.

VALERO, RENÉ ARNOLD, retired bishop; b. NYC, Aug. 15, 1930; s. Caesar J. Valera and Maria Luisa (Cordova) Valero. BA, Immaculate Conception-Cathedral Coll., 1952; MSW, Fordham U., 1962. Ordained priest Diocese of Bklyn., NY, 1956; assoc. pastor St. Michael-St. Edward, Fort Greene, 1956—57, St. Agatha, Bay Ridge, 1957—60; with family svc. office, Kings County dir. Cath. Charities, 1960—69, dir. Office for Aging, 1969—74; coord. Spanish Apostolate Diocese of Bklyn., 1974—80; chmn. bd. Northeast Hispanic Pastoral Ctr., 1974—80; pastor Blessed Sacrament, Jackson Heights, NY, 1979—82; ordained bishop, 1980; aux. bishop Diocese of Bklyn., NY, 1980—2005, chmn. Com. on Racial Harmony NY, 1990; dir. Cath. Migration & Refugee Office, 1983—91; aux. bishop emeritus Diocese of Bklyn., 2005—. Roman Catholic.

VALETTE, JEAN PAUL, writer; b. Paris, Oct. 21, 1937; s. Jean and Monique (Lavie) V.; m. Rebecca M. Valette, Aug. 6, 1959; children: Jean-Michel, Nathalie, Pierre. Baccalaureat, U. Poitiers, France, 1954; Diplome, Hautes Etudes Commls. de Paris, 1959; PhD, U. Colo., 1962. Acct. Arthur Andersen, 1964-66; rsch. economist Charles River Assocs., 1966-69. Author: Lisons, 1968, The Role of Transportation in Regional Economic Development, 1971, France, A Cultural Review Grammar, 1973, C'est comme ça, 1978, 1986, Spanish for Mastery, 1980, 1984, 1988, 1996, French for Mastery, 1975, 1981, 1986, 1989, 1990, Contacts: langue et culture françaises, 1976, 1982, 1985, 1989, 1994, 1997, 2001, 2008, French for Fluency, 1985, Rencontres, 1985, Situaciones, 1988, 1994, Discovering French Nouveau, 1993, 5th edit., 2000, Discover French, 2004, 2007, Discovering French Interactive, 1994, A votre tour, 1995, Ventanas, 1998, Europak, 2000, Weaving the Dance, Navajo Yeibichai Textiles (1910-1950), 2000. Decorated officer Palmes Académiques (France). Mem. Am. Assn. Tchrs. French, Am. Coun. on Tchg. of Langs. Address: 16 Mount Alvernia Rd Chestnut Hill MA 02467-1019 Personal E-mail: jpvalette@comcast.net.

VALETTE, REBECCA MARIANNE, Romance languages educator; b. NYC, Dec. 21, 1938; d. Gerhard and Ruth Adelgunde (Bischoff) Loose; m. Jean-Paul Valette, Aug. 6, 1959; children: Jean-Michel, Nathalie, Pierre. BA, Mt. Holyoke Coll., 1959, LHD (hon.), 1974; PhD, U. Colo., 1963. Instr., examiner in French and German U. So. Fla., 1961-63; instr. NATO Def. Coll., Paris, 1963-64, Wellesley Coll., 1964-65; asst. prof. Romance Langs. Boston Coll., 1965-68, assoc., 1968-73, prof., 1973—2003, prof. emeritus, 2003—. Lectr., cons. fgn. lang. pedagogy; Fulbright sr. lectr., Germany, 1974; Am. Coun. on Edn. fellow in acad. adminstrn., 1976-77. Author: Modern Language Testing, 1967, rev. edit., 1977, French for Mastery, 1975, rev. edit., 1988, Contacts, 1976, rev. edit., 1993, 97, 2001, 08, C'est Comme Ça, 1978, rev. edit., 1986, Spanish for Mastery, 1980, rev. edit., 1989, 94, Album: Cuentos del Mundo Hispanico, 1984, 3d edit., 2005, French for Fluency, 1985, Situaciones, 1988, rev. edit., 1994, Discovering French, 1994, 97, 2001, A votre tour, 1995, 2nd edit., 2007, Ventanas Uno, 1998, Images 1, 2, 3, 1999, Reflections on the Connolly Book of Hours, 1999, Weaving the Dance, 2000, Discovering French Nouveau, 2004, 2d edit., 2007, Federation of Alliances Francaises USA Edn. Handbook, 2005; contbr. articles to fgn. lang. pedagogy and Native Am. art publs. Decorated comdr. Palmes Académiques, chevalier Ordre Nat. du Mérite (France). Mem. MLA (chmn. divsn. on tchg. of lang. 1980-81), Am. Coun. on Tchg. Fgn. Langs., Am. Assn. Tchrs. French (v.p. 1980-86, pres. 1992-94), Alliance Francaise of Boston and Cambridge (pres. 2002—08), Fedn. Alliances Francaises USA (v.p. 2003—06), Phi Beta Kappa, Alpha Sigma Nu, Pi Delta Phi. Home: 16 Mount Alvernia Rd Chestnut Hill MA 02467-1019 Office: Boston Coll Lyons 304 Chestnut Hill MA 02467-3804

VALEV, VENTZESLAV VASSILEV, computer scientist, educator, researcher; b. Pavlikeni, Bulgaria, July 6, 1944; s. Vassil Mintchev Valev and Maria Gentcheva Valeva; m. Lubomira Kraleva, Jan. 22, 1984; children: Ventzeslav Ventzeslavov, Krassimir Ventzeslavov, Hristo Ventzeslavov. D in Math. Informatics, Inst. Math. Informatics, Bulgarian Acad. Sci., Sofia, 1996; Magister in Computer Sci., Wroclaw U. Tech., Poland, 1970; Magister in Math., Wroclaw U., 1974; PhD in Math. Cybernetics, Computing Ctr., Russian Acad. Sci., Moscow, 1979. Asst. prof. Inst. Math. Informatics, Bulgarian Acad. Sci., 1971—89, assoc. prof., 1989—97, prof., 2002—; assoc. prof. U. Iowa, Iowa City, 1997—98, U. Medicine Dentistry, Newark, 1998—99, St. Louis U., 1999—2006, Mid. East Tech. U., Cyprus, 2006—07; prof. Wroclaw U. Tech., 2008—09; assoc. prof. Prince Mohammad U., Alkhoba, Saudi Arabia, 2009—. Home: Tcherni vrah blvd # 74 entr B ap 2B Sofia 1407 Bulgaria Office: Inst Math and Informatics Acad G Bontchev str Bl 8 Sofia 1113 Bulgaria Home Phone: 35929620012; Office Phone: 35929792830. Office Fax: 35929713649. Business E-Mail: valev@math.bas.bg.

VALIANTI, DEBORAH L., playwright; b. Marlboro, Mass., May 10, 1952; d. Frank J. and Kathlyn V. Valianti; m. Henry J. Klim; children: Genevieve Marie Klim, Delia Goodness Klim. MAET, Lesley Coll., Cambridge, Mass., 1992; MA, Boston U., 1987; BA, Goddard Coll., Plainfield, Vt., 1977. Dir. Mission-in-Action Players, Mission Hill, Mass., 2000—04, All-bad Teen Theater Co., Brighton, Mass., 1993—98; educator expressive therapies Lesley Coll., Cambridge, Mass., 1992—98; dir. City Hall Smoking Cessation Project, Boston Against Drugs, Boston, 1995; dir. and co-founder Uppity Productions, Boston Playwright Theater, Boston, 1985—90; tchg. fellow Creative Writing Program, Boston U., Boston, 1985—87; Celtic cantor All Saints Parish, Brookline, Mass., 2003—; instr. Northeastern U., 2004—. Lectr. in field. Author: (plays) 39 Witherbees St., 1977, Starcrossed, 1987, The Friendship of Her Thighs, 1992, Too Many Willies, 2002, Thou Shalt Break Them, 2005, Choir Stalls, 2007, (screenplays) Europe, 1988, Build to Suit, 2002, (book) First and Foremost A Playwright: the Dramatist's Tools as Applied to the Practice of Expressive Therapy, 1991. Recipient Late Blooms Poetry Postcard award, 2008. Mem.: Internat. Ctr. Women Playwright Platform. Democrat. Roman Catholic. Avocations: singing, tap dance, liturgical dance, travel, skiing. Home: 8 Oak Square Avenue Brighton MA 02135-2517 Office Phone: 617-669-0551.

VALIATHAN, MARTHANDA VARMA SANKARAN, cardiac surgeon; b. Mavelikara, Kerala, India, May 24, 1934; s. Marthanda Varma and Janaki Amma Valiathan; m. Ashima Sethi, Nov. 15, 1964; children: Manna, Manish. MB, BS, Med. Coll. Trivandrum, 1956; M in surgery, U. Liverpool, 1960. Resident in gen. surgery Greenwich Dist. Hosp., London, 1958, United Liverpool Hosp., 1959, Jefferson Med. Coll. Hosp., Phila., 1961; sr. lectr. surgery Postgrad. Inst., Chandigarth, India, 1963; resident in cardiovascular surgery Johns Hopkins Hosp., 1965, George Washington U. Hosp., 1966, Georgetown U. Hosp., 1967, instr. surgery, 1969; cons. cardiac surgery Safdarjung Hosp., New Dehli, 1972; prof. cardiac surgery, dir. Sree Chitra Tirunal Inst. Med. Scis. and Tech., Trivandrum, India, 1974—94; pres. Indian Nat. Sci. Acad., 2001—04. Examiner cardiothoracic surgery U. Madras, Bombay, Calcutta, India; mem. panel experts WHO; Homi Bhabha senior fellow Manipal Acad. of Higher Ed. Recipient Sci. and Tech. prize, Govt. of Kerala, India, 1980, Padma Bhushan, Pres. of India, Om Prakash Bhasin Nat. award, Govt. of India, Pres. India Birla Nat. award, PADMA award, 2005. Fellow: Nat. Acad. Med. Scis., Indian Acad. Scis., Royal Coll. Phys. and Surg. Can., Royal Coll. Surgeons Edinburgh, Am. Coll. Cardiology, Royal Coll. Surgeons Eng.; mem.: Soc. Thoracic Surgeons U.S.A., Inst. Med. Sci. (governing coun.), Cardiol. Soc. India, Assn. Thoracic and Cardiovascular Surgeons U.K. (corr.), Assn. Cardiovascular Surgeons India. Hindu. Office: Sree Chitra Tirunal Inst Med Scis and Tech Trivandrum 695 011 India

VALK, HENRY S(NOWDEN), physicist, researcher; b. Washington, Jan. 26, 1929; s. Henry Snowden and Dorothy (Blencowe) V.; m. Gillian Wedderburn; children: Alison, Diana, Robert, Richard. BS, George Washington U., 1953, MS (Agnes and Eugene Meyer scholar), 1954; postgrad., Johns Hopkins, 1953-54; PhD (Shell fellow), Washington U., St. Louis, 1957. Profl. asst. NSF, 1957, asst. program dir. physics, 1959-60; asst. prof. physics U. Oreg., 1957-59; mem. faculty U. Nebr., 1960-70, prof. physics, 1964-70, chmn. dept., 1966-70; prof. physics Coll. Scis. and Liberal Studies, Ga. Inst. Tech., Atlanta, 1970—, acting dir. physics, 1991-96, dean, 1970-82. Cons. physics sect. NSF, 1961-62, program dir. theoretical physics, 1965-66; chmn. Gordon Rsch. Conf. Photonuclear Reactions, 1969; vis. prof. U. Frankfurt/Main, Germany, 1970, Rensselaer Poly. Inst., 1982, 88, Cath. U. Am., 1982-83, 88-89; chmn. SE regional Marshall scholarship com., 1974-92. Author: (with M. Alonso) Quantum Mechanics: Principles and Applications, 1973; contbr. articles to profl. jours. Decorated Most Excellent Order Brit. Empire. Fellow Am. Phys. Soc.; mem. Am. Math. Soc., Am. Assn. Physics Tchrs., Math. Assn. Am., Cosmos Club (Washington), Phi Beta Kappa, Sigma Xi. Office: Sch Physics Ga Inst Tech Atlanta GA 30332-0430 Business E-Mail: henry.valk@physics.gatech.edu.

VALLABHAN, GIRISH C., urologist; b. Bombay, Sept. 25, 1963; arrived in US, 1965; s. C.V.G. and Shakuntala Vallabhan; m. Monique Vallabhan (div.); children: Tara, Sonia. BA in Chemistry, Tex. Tech. U., San Antonio, 1984; MD, U. Tex., San Antonio, 1988. Cert. Am. Bd. Urology, 1996. Intern then resident U. N.Mex., Albuquerque, 1988—93; pvt. practice Lubbock, Tex., 1994—2006. Fellow then staff robotics program Henry Ford Hosp., Detroit, 2006. Contbr. articles to profl. jours. Bd. mem. Internat. Cultural Ctr., Lubbock, Tex., 2006. Fellow: ACS; mem.: AMA, Am. Urological Assn. Avocations: racquetball, reading, music.

VALLADARES, MARIA ELENA, language educator; b. Havana, Cuba, Feb. 26, 1953; arrived in US, 1960; d. Joaquin Erviti and Angelina Garcia; m. Rodolfo Valladares, Aug. 29, 1974; children: Angelina, Rodolfo, David, Gloria, Carolina, Ariel, Miguel. AA, Miami Dade CC, 1973; BA, U. Fla., Gainesville, 1975, M in Spl. Edn., 1978. Elem. and HS Spanish tchr. Living Faith Fellowship Sch., Gainesville, 1990—98, Westwood Hills Christian Sch., 1999—. County coun. Green Cover 4-H Club, Gainesville, 1995—. Republican. Avocations: scrapbooks, travel. Home: 3848 SW 6th Pl Gainesville FL 32607

VALLAS, PAUL G., school system administrator; b. June 10, 1953; m. Sharon Vallas; children: Paul, Gus, Mark. BA in Polit. Sci. & History, We. Ill. U., 1976, MA in Polit. Sci., 1980. Policy adv. to Elementary & Secondary Edn. & Appropriations Com. Ill. State Senate; exec. dir. Ill. Econ. Fiscal Com., 1985—90; revenue dir. City of Chgo., 1990—93, budget dir., 1993—95; CEO Chgo. Pub. Schools Sys., 1995—2001, Phila. Pub. Schools Sys., 2002—07; supt. Recovery Sch. Dist., New Orleans, 2007—. Office: La Dept Edn Recovery Sch Dist PO Box 94064 Baton Rouge LA 70804*

VALLBONA, CARLOS, physician; b. Granollers, Barcelona, Spain, July 29, 1927; came to U.S., 1953, naturalized, 1967; s. José and Dolores (Calbó) V.; m. Rima Gretel Rothe, Dec. 26, 1956; children: Rima Nuria, Carlos Fernando, María Teresa, Marisa. BA, BS, U. de Barcelona, 1944, MD, 1950. Diplomate Am. Bd. Pediatrics. Child health physician Escuela de Puericultura, Barcelona, 1952, Stagier Etranger Hôpital des Enfants Malades, Paris, 1952-53; intern, resident U. Louisville, 1953-55; resident Baylor Coll. Medicine, Houston, 1955-56, prof. rehab. medicine, 1967—, assoc. prof. physiology and pediatrics, 1962-69, prof., chmn. dept. community medicine, 1969-95, prof. family medicine, 1980-95, Disting. Svc. prof. family and cmty. medicine, 1995—. Adj. prof. U. Tex. Sch. Pub. Health, U. Tex. Health Sci. Ctr., Houston; chief community medicine service Harris County Hosp. Dist.; staff gen. med. service Tex. Children's Hosp.; staff The Inst. Rehab. and Research; staff St. Luke's Episcopal Hosp., con. staff VA Med. Ctr., Houston; Fulbright vis. prof., 1967; cons. WHO, NIH, Nat. Center Health Stats. Pan Am. Health Orgn., Nat. Center Health Service Research; advisor Conseller Sanitat, Catalunya. Author numerous articles in field; editorial bd. several Sci. jours. French Ministry of Edn. fellow, 1952; Children's Internat. Center fellow, 1953; co-recipient Gold medal 6th Internat. Congress Phys. Medicine, 1972; Public Citizen of Yr. San Jacinto chpt. Nat. Assn. Social Workers, 1974; Outstanding Tchr. award Baylor Coll. Medicine Class of 1980, 83, 85, 87, 88; decorated officer Order of Civil Merit (Spain), Medalla Narcis Monturiol (Catalunya). Mem. Am. Acad. Family Physicians, Am. Coll. Med. Informatics (founding mem. 1984), Nat. Acad. Practice (disting. practitioner 1984), Soc. Pediatric Research (emeritus), AMA, Tex. Med. Assn., Am. Coll. Chest Physicians, Am. Pub. Health Assn. (chmn. elect med. care sect. 1989-90), Am. Coll. Preventive Medicine, U.S.-Mex. Border Health Assn., AAAS, Am. Congress Rehab. Medicine, Catalan Soc. Pediatrics (hon.), Argentinian Soc. Internal Medicine (hon. 1986), Argentinian Med. Soc. (hon. 1986), Spanish Acad. Pediatrics (ambulatory pediatrics sect. hon. 1987), Assn. Tchrs. Preventive Medicine, Spanish Profls. Am. (pres. 1988), Soc. Catalana Hipertensio (hon. pres.), Sigma Xi, Alpha Omega Alpha. Roman Catholic. Home: 2001 Holcombe Blvd #2903 Houston TX 77030-4222 Office: Baylor Coll Medicine One Baylor Plz Rm 650E Houston TX 77030-3404

VALLBONA, MARISA, public relations counselor; b. Houston, Jan. 2, 1964; d. Carlos and Rima (Rothe) Vallbona; m. Don R. Rayner Jr., July 12, 1986 (div.); children: Donald R. Rayner III, Timothy Carlos Rayner; m. Roger A. Freeman, July 29, 2000 (div. 2006). Student, U. Colo., U. de Dijon, France; BS in Journalism, U. Tex. Account exec. Jae Stefan & Assocs., Austin, Tex., 1987-88; media rels. asst. America's Cup XXVII, 1988; sr. account exec. pub. rels. Berkman & Daniels, 1988-90; prin. Rayner & Vallbona Inc. Advt. & Pub. Rels., San Diego, 1990-97; pres. CIM, Inc., San Diego, 1997—; dir., CFO PR Cons. Group, Inc. Editor: Flowering Inferno, 1994, Soldiers Cry By Night, 1994, Assumed Name, 1994, People on the Prowl, 1995; contbr. articles to profl. jours. Mem. pub. affairs disaster task force ARC, 1993—97; pub. rels. chair Sunkist Am. Cancer Soc. Cup Regatta, 1989; mem. elections mktg. task force City of San Diego, 1989; bd. dirs. Coggan Family Aquatic Complex, 2008—; pub. rels. chair, bd. dirs. Women of St. James Episc. Ch., 1994, 1st v.p. Mem.: Health Care Communicators San Diego (sec. 1993, bd. dirs. 1994, v.p., numerous awards), Am. Soc. Health Care Mktg. and Pub. Rels., Pub. Rels. Soc. Am. (San Diego chpt. chair accreditation com. 1994, dir.-at-large 1995, bd. dirs. 1996—2000, sec. 1997, assembly del. 1999—2000, 2005—07, San Diego chpt. ethics officer 2005—, chair 2007, internat. assembly del. 2007—08, past chair, universal accreditation bd. 2008, accredited, co-chair, PRSA, internat. conf., San Diego), United Cerebral Palsy Assn., Jr. League San Diego (sustainer mem.), Pub. Rels. Club San Diego (exec. bd. dirs. 1991—92, various awards). Avocations: skiing, tennis, marathon running. Office: CIM Inc 8677 Villa LaJolla Dr PMB 1105 La Jolla CA 92037 Office Phone: 858-467-7990, 858-550-2293. Business E-Mail: cim@cimincorporated.com.

VALLBONA, RIMA-GRETEL ROTHE, retired foreign language educator, writer; b. San Jose, Costa Rica, Mar. 15, 1931; arrived in U.S., 1956, naturalized, 1997; d. Ferdinand Hermann and Emilia (Strassburger) Rothe; m. Carlos Vallbona, Dec. 26, 1956; children: Rima-Nuri, Carlos-Fernando, Maria-Teresa, Maria-Luisa. BA/BS, Colegio Superior de Senoritas, San Jose, Costa Rica, 1948; diploma, U. Paris, 1953; diploma in Spanish Philology, U. Salamanca, Spain, 1954; MA, U. Costa Rica, 1962; D in Modern Langs., Middlebury Coll., 1981. Tchr. Liceo J.J. Vargas Calvo, Costa Rica, 1955—56; faculty U. St. Thomas, Houston, 1964—95, prof. Spanish, 1978—95, Cullen Found. prof. Spanish, 1989, head Spanish dept., 1966—71, chmn. dept. modern fgn. lang., 1978—80, prof. emeritus, 1995—. Vis. prof. U. Houston, 1975—76, Rice U., 1974, 1980—83, 1995, U. St. Thomas, Argentina, 1972, U. St. Thomas, Merida program, 1987—95. Author: Noche en Vela, 1968, Yolanda Oreamuno, 1972, La Obra en Prosa de Eunice Odio, 1981, Baraja de Soledades, Las Sombras que Perseguimos, 1983, Polvo del Camino, 1972, La Salamandra Rosada, 1979, Mujeres y Agonias, 1982, Cosecha de Pecadores, 1988, El arcangel del perdon, 1990, Mundo, demonio y mujer, 1991, Los infiernos de la mujer y algo mas, 1992, (crit. edit.) Vida i sucesos de la Monja Alferez, 1992, Flowering Inferno-Tales of Sinking Hearts, 1994, La narrativa de Yolanda Oreamuno, 1996, Tormy, la Prodigiosa Gata de Donaldito, 1997, Tejedoras de sueños versus realidad, 2003, A La deriva del tiempo y de la historia, 2007; mem. (editl. bd.) Letras Femeninas, 1984—98, Alba de America, U.S., sec. (culture) Inst. Literario y Cultural Hispanico; co-dir.: Foro Literario, 1987—89; contbg. editor: The Americas Rev., 1989—95; contbr. numerous articles and short stories to lit. mags. Mem. scholarship com. Inst. Hispanic Culture, 1978, 1979, 1988, 1991, chmn., 1979, bd. dirs., 1974—76, 1988—89, 1991—92, chmn. cultural activities, 1979, 1980, 1985, 1988—89; bd. dirs. Houston Pub. Libr., 1984—86, Cultural Arts Coun. Houston, 1991—92. Recipient Aquileo J. Echeverria Novel prize, 1968, Jorge Luis Borges Short Story prize, Argentina, 1977, Agripina Montes del Valle Novel prize, 1978, Constantin Found. grant for rsch., U. St. Thomas, 1981, Lit. award, S.W. Conf. Latin Am. Studies, 1982, Ancora Lit. award, Costa Rica, 1984, Civil Merit award, King Juan Carlos I of Spain, 1989, Children's Book award, Bay Area Writers League, 2003. Mem.: Soc. Children's Book Writers and Illustrators, Nat. Writers Assn., Inst. Lit. y Cultural Hispanico, Casa Argentina de Houston, Inst. Hispanic Culture Houston, Latin Am. Writers Assn. Costa Rica, Inst. Internat. de Lit. Iberoam., Latin Am. Studies Assn., Academia Norteamericana de la Lengua Espanola (elected), S.W. Conf. Orgn. Latin Am Studies, South Ctrl. MLA, Houston Area Tchrs. Fgn. Lang., Houston Area Tchrs. Spanish and Portuguese, Am. Assn. Tchrs. Spanish and Portuguese, Sigma Delta Pi, Phi Sigma Iota. Roman Catholic. Home: 3706 Lake St Houston TX 77098-5522 Personal E-mail: rvallbona@aol.com.

VALLE, RAFAEL F., obstetrician, gynecologist, educator; b. Mendoza, Veracruz, Mex., Sept. 6, 1935; came to US, 1966; MD, Madrid U., 1965. Diplomate Am. Bd. Ob-Gyn. Intern Mt. Sinai Hosp., Mpls., 1966-67, resident in surgery, 1967-69; resident in ob-gyn. U. Minn., Mpls., 1969-72; attending physician Hennepin County Med. Ctr. and U. Minn. Hosps., 1972—75, Northwestern U. Meml. Hosp., Chgo., 1975—; practice in ob-gyn. Northwestern U. Hosp., Chgo., 1975—. Prof. ob-gyn. Northwestern U. Med. Sch., 1994—. Mem. Am. Coll. Obstetricians and Gynecologist, Am. Coll. Surgeons, Am. Soc. for Reproductive Medicine, Assn. Prof. Obs. Gynecol., Am. Assn. Gynecol. Laparoscopists, Chgo. Gynecol. Soc., Internat. Soc. Gynecol. Endoscopy, European Soc. Human Reproduction and Embryology. Office: Northwestern U Med Sch 880 N Lake Shore Dr Ste 20-C Chicago IL 60611 Business E-Mail: r-valle@northwestern.edu.

VALLEE, MICHELLE LINDA, pre-school educator; b. Passaic, NJ, Dec. 18, 1973; d. Rudolph Herman Vallee Jr. and Linda Marguerite Lombardi. Cert. in Child-Related Careers, Morris County Sch. of Tech., Denville, NJ, 1991—93; AS, County Coll. of Morris, Randolph, NJ,

2002. Cert. child devel. assoc. Washington, 1999. Presch. tchr. Page Sch., Morris Plains, NJ, 1999—2003, PACE Presch., Lake Hiawatha, NJ, 2003—05; dance tchr. Mary Lou Hale's Sch. of Dance, Lake Hiawatha, NJ, 1998—; presch. tchr. Sunnyfields, Whippany, NJ, 2005—. 3rd grade ccd tchr. St. Peter the Apostle Ch., Parsippany, NJ, 1999—. (dance solo) Dinner Party Tap Solo. Mem.: MCSSA (assoc.). Republican. Roman Catholic. Avocations: bowling, soccer, volleyball, softball, travel. Home: 4 Oak Ln Lake Hiawatha NJ 07034 Office: Sunnyfields Learning Center 494 Rte 10 W Whippany NJ 07981 Personal E-mail: wrightgrl05@aol.com.

VALLEE, ROY A., electronics executive; b. Southbridge, Mass. married; 2 children. AS in Electronics Tech., Don Bosco Tech. Inst., 1971. Electronics tech. radio products Don Bosco Tech. Inst., 1971—77; field sales rep. Avnet, Inc., Great Neck, NY, 1977, systems bus. mgr. to gen. sales mgr. to gen. mgr. to regional dir. to v.p., pres. Hamilton/Avnet Computer, 1989—90, sr. v.p., dir. worldwide electronics ops., 1990—92, bd. dirs. Phoenix, 1991—, pres., COO, 1992—98, chmn., CEO Phoenix, 1998—. Bd. dirs. Teradyne, Synopsys, Inc.; mem. exec. com. Global Tech. Distbn. Coun. Mem. Govs. Coun. of Innovation and Tech. Named one of Hot 25 Execs., Electronic Buyer's News, 1997, 1999, 2000; named to CRN Industry Hall of Fame, 2007. Office: Avnet Inc 2211 S 47th St Phoenix AZ 85034-6403 Office Phone: 480-643-2000.

VALLE-GARCIA, ESTEBAN, social worker; b. David, Chiriqui, Panama, July 26, 1980; s. Leonel Valle and Arabella Garcia. BS, U. Mobile, 2001. Advisor to pres. Project H.O.P, E. Inc., Springfield, Mo., 1999—; cons. and vol. Christian Relief Fund, 1999—, coord. projects, 2005—. Photography, Sabor Hispano (2nd & 3rd Pl., 2007). Mem.: Sigma Delta Pi. Achievements include sustainable development. Home: 3306 22nd St Lubbock TX 79410 E-mail: esteban.valle@ttu.edu.

VALLEJO, FRANCES M., oil industry executive; b. Pueblo, Colo. BS in Mineral Engring. Math., Colo. Sch. Mines, 1987; MBA in Fin. and Internat. Mgmt., Rice U., Houston, 1996. Geophysicist Exploration & Prodn. Phillips Petroleum Co., Bartlesville, Okla., 1987—91, with seismic interpretation Bellaire, Tex., 1991—93, with gas supply reporting, 1993—94, fin. assoc. treasury Bartlesville, 1996—99, mgr. strategic transactions, 1999—2001; asst. treas. ConocoPhillips, 2001—04, v.p. upstream planning & portfolio mgmt., 2004—07, gen. mgr. corp. planning and budgets, 2007—08, v.p., treas., 2008—. Chmn. bd. dirs. 66 Fed. Credit Union, mem. bd. dirs.; grad. Ctr. for Houston's Future Leadership Forum, 2007. Office: ConocoPhillips 600 North Dairy Ashford Rd PO Box 2197 Houston TX 77079*

VALLEJO, JESUS G., medical educator; s. Jesus and Oralia Vallejo; m. Karen R. Baker, May 16, 1992; children: Cristian Daniel, Eric David. MD, Baylor Coll. Medicine, Houston, Tex., 1989. Diplomate Am. Bd. Pediat., 1998. Asst. prof. Baylor Coll. Medicine, 1996—2005, assoc. prof., 2005—. Fellow, ABP-Pediat. Infectious Diseases, 1997, Infectious Diseases Soc. America, 2008. Mem.: Soc. Pediatric Rsch., Am. Acad. Pediat., Pediat. Infectious Diseases Soc. (Young Investigator award 2003). Office: Baylor Coll Medicine One Baylor Plaza Houston TX 77030

VALLES, JUDITH, president, former mayor, retired academic administrator; b. San Bernardino, Calif., Dec. 14, 1933; d. Gonzalo and Jovita (Lopez-Torices) V.; m. Chad Bradbury, Sept. 30, 1956 (dec. Sept. 1969); children: Edith Renella, Nohemi Renella, Chad; m. Harry Carl Smith, Oct. 13, 1985. BA in English, Redlands U., Calif., 1956; MA in Spanish Lit., U. Calif., Riverside, 1966; doctorate (hon.), U. Redlands, 2000. Instr. Spanish San Bernardino Valley Coll., Calif., 1963-84, head dept. fgn. lang., 1971-76, chair div. humanities, 1976-81, dean extended day, 1981-83, adminstrv. dean acad. affairs, 1983-87, exec. v.p. acad. and student affairs, 1987-88; pres. Golden West CC, Huntington Beach, Calif., 1988—95; mayor City of San Bernardino, 1998—2006; pres. LA Mission Coll. Mem. adv. com. Police Officers Standards and Tng. Commn., Sacramento, 1991—. Author fgn. lang. annals and sociol. abstracts. Speaker statewide edn. and community orgns., 1988—; bd. dirs. exec. coun. and chief exec. officers Calif. Community Colls., 1990—. Recipient Bishops award for diocese, Outstanding Pub. Svc. award NALEO, 2001; named One of Outstanding Women Orange County YWCA, 1990, Citizen of Achievement LWV, 1989, Woman of Distinction Bus. Press, 1998, Influential Latina of the Yr. Hispanic Lifestyle, 1998, State of Calif. Woman of the Yr., 1999, Humanitarian Yr. Cath. charities, 1999, Citizen Yr. Boy Scouts Am., 1999, Empire Woman Yr. State Assembly, 1999, Outstanding Cmty. Leader, Cmty. Found., 2002, Woman of Yr., State Senate, 2003; inducted into Hall of Fame, San Bernardino Valley Coll. Mem. Women's Roundtable Orange County, Conf. and Visitors Bur., C. of C. (Vanguard), Kiwanis, Charter 100. Avocations: opera, theater, reading, running.

VALLET, SONIA, hematologist, researcher; b. Aosta, Italy, Sept. 18, 1976; d. Franco Vallet and Consolata Strati. MD, U. Torino, Italy, 2001. Lic. Ordine Dei Medici Della Valle d'Aosta, 2002. Clin. fellow hematology U. degli Studi, Torino, 2002—05; rsch. fellow, Harvard med. sch. Dana Farber Cancer Inst., Boston, 2005—07, Mass. Gen. Hosp., Boston, 2007—. Recipient Club Optime award, Unione Indsl. Torino, 2001, Best Grad. award, U. Torino, 2001, Brian D. Novis Rsch. award, Internat. Myeloma Found., 2008. Mem.: Am. Assn. Cancer Rsch., Club Optime. Achievements include patents pending for role of CCR1 inhibition in impairing osteoclast-myeloma interactions. Office: Mass Gen Hosp 185 Cambridge St Boston MA 02114 Office Fax: 617-724-2662. E-mail: svallet@partners.org.

VALLI, FRANKIE (FRANCIS CASTELLUCCIO), singer; b. Newark, May 3, 1937; Student pub. schs., Newark. With vocal group Four Lovers, 1956—61, The Four Seasons, 1962—77, albums (with The Four Seasons) Sherry, Greetings, Big Girls Don't Cry, Ain't That A Shame, 1963, Stay, Golden Hits, We Love Girls, Live On Stage, Dawn, Born To Wander, Rag Doll, 1964, Sing Big Hits, Entertain You, Gold Vault Hits, Working My Way Back To You, 1965, Christmas Album, Genuine Imitation, Life Gazette, Seasoned Hits, 1968, Edizione D'oro, 1969, Big Ones, 1971, Chameleon, 1972, Gold, Our Day Will Come, Close To You, Fallen Angel, Who Loves You, Helicon, 1975, The Four Seasons Story, 1976, Reunited, 1981, Hope and Glory, 1992, (as solo artist) Solo, 1967, Timeless, 1968, Inside You, Closeup, Our Day Will Come, 1975, Valli, 1977, Frankie Valli Is The Word, 1978, Grease (original soundtrack), 1978, The Very Best of Frankie Valli, 1979, Heaven Above Me, 1980, Frankie Valli: Hits from the 60's, 1983, Romancing the '60s, 2007; actor: (films) Beach Ball, 1965, All This and World War II, Ebony, Ivory and Jade, 1976, Grease, Sergeant Pepper's Lonely Hearts Club Band, 1978, Dirty Laundry, 1987, Eternity, 1989, Modern Love, 1990, Opposite Corners, 1995; (TV films) Witness to the Mob, 1998; (TV series) The Sopranos, 2004—. Named to Rock 'n' Roll Hall of Fame (with The Four Seasons), 1990. Office: c/o Michael Eisenstadt Amsel Eisenstadt & Frazier Inc 5505 Wilshire Blvd Ste 865 Los Angeles CA 90036

VALLIER, NANETTE, psychologist; b. Flint, Mich., Aug. 10, 1950; d. Bertilla Vallier; 1 child, Heather Hunter. Attended, Wayne State U., Detroit, 1978. Cert. sch. psychologist Mich., NJ., 1976. Ltd. lic. psychologist Psychiat. Clinics & Hosp., Dearborn, Mich., 1980—2007; sch. psychologist Cherry Hill Sch., Mich., 1976—86, Wayne-Westland Sch., Mich., 1986—96, Walled Lk. Sch., Mich., 1996—2007, Irvington Bd. Edn., NJ, 2007—08, Union Twp. Sch., NJ, 2008—. Pvt. practice, Mich., 1976—2007. Sponsor Med. Missionaries Mary, Chgo., 2005—09.

VALLONE, PETER F., city councilman, lawyer; b. Astoria, NY; 2 children. BA magna cum laude, Fordham Univ., 1983, JD, 1986. Bar: NY 1986. Asst. Dist. Atty. Office of Manhattan Dist. Atty.; mem. Vallone & Vallone; city councilman Dist. 22 NY City Coun., 2002—. Chmn. Pub. Safety com. NY City Coun.; vol. atty. Roman Catholic Diocese of Bklyn.; legal counsel Astoria Civic Assn., United Cmty. Civic Assn., Sponsors for Edn. Opportunity. Bd. trustees St. Johns Prep. Sch., Variety Boys & Girls Club of Queens; pro bono counsel Coalition Helping Org. a Kleaner Environ. (CHOKE). Mem.: Phi Beta Kappa. Democrat. Mailing: Dist Off 22-45 31st St Queens NY 11105 Office Phone: 718-274-4500, 212-788-6963. Office Fax: 718-726-0357. Business E-Mail: vallonejr@council.nyc.ny.us.*

VALLURI, CHANDRASEKHAR (CHANDU VALLURI), marketing and international business educator; b. Rajahmundry, Andhra Pradesh, India, Jan. 7, 1979; s. Sree Ram and Rajyalakshmi Valluri. Asst. prof. mktg. and internat. bus. St. Mary's U. Minn., Winona, 2006—. Avocations: singing, music, movies. Office: St Mary's Univ Minn 700 Terrace Heights # 1517 Sports Winona MN 55987

VALOIS, ROBERT ARTHUR, lawyer; b. NYC, May 13, 1938; s. Frank Jacob and Harriet Frances (LaCroix) V.; m. Ruth Emilie Skacil, Dec. 23, 1961; children: Marguerite Jeannette, Robert Arthur Jr. BBA, U. Miami, 1962; JD, Wake Forest U., 1972. Bar: N.C. 1972, Fla. 1972, U.S. Ct. Appeals (4th cir.) 1973, U.S. Dist. Ct. (ea. and mid. dists.) 1974, U.S. Supreme Ct. 1975, U.S. Ct. Appeals (6th cir.) 1986. Field examiner NLRB, Winston-Salem, NC, 1962-70; from assoc. to ptnr. Maupin, Taylor & Ellis, P.A., Raleigh, NC, 1972—, chmn. labor and employment sect., 1972-97, chmn. bd. dirs., pres., 1997—2002. Vice chmn. Legal Svcs. Corp., Washington, 1984-90, bd. dirs. Served with USN, 1956-59. Mem. Greater Raleigh C. of C. (chmn. fed. govt. com. 1991—). Democrat. Presbyterian. Home: 3952 Bentley Bridge Rd Raleigh NC 27612 Office Phone: 919-981-4000. E-mail: rvalois@maupintaylor.com.

VALONE, DAVID ANDREW, history professor; s. James Samuel and Geraldine Valone; m. Kathy Jane Cooke, Sept. 7, 1991; 1 child, Alexander Cooke. PhD, U. Chgo., Ill, 1992. Assoc. prof. history Quinnipiac U., Hamden, Conn., 2006—. Office: Quinnipiac Univ CL-AC3 275 Mt Carmel Ave Hamden CT 06518

VALSARAJ, KALLIAT THAZHATHUVEETIL, chemical engineering educator; b. Tellichery, Kerala, India, Oct. 2, 1957; came to U.S., 1980; s. Mundayat B. Nambiar and Kalliat T. Bhanumathy; m. Nisha Valsaraj, Dec. 24, 1990; children: Viveca, Vinay. MS, Indian Inst. Tech., Madras, India, 1980; PhD, Vanderbilt U., 1983. Affiliate faculty U. Ark., Fayetteville, 1983-86; sr. rsch. assoc. Hazardous Waste Rsch. Ctr. La. State U., Baton Rouge, 1986-90, asst. prof., 1990-93, assoc. prof., 1994-99, Ike East prof. chem. engring., 1999—2004, Charles and Hilda Roddey disting. prof., 2005—06, interim dept. chair, 2005—06, dept. chair, 2006—. Mem. panel directions in separations NSF, 1989-90; cons. Balsam Engr. Cons., Salem, N.H., 1990-91, Vicksburg (Miss.) Chems., Borden Chems. and Plastics, La.; presenter in field. Author: Elements of Environmental Engineering: Thermodynamics and Kinetics, 1995, 2nd edit., 2000; contbr. numerous articles to profl. jours. Grantee Dept. Def., 1986-89, 95-2004, NSF, 1989, 92-95, 2001-04, 2004—, EPA, 1989-92, 93-97, 97-98, 2000-07, U.S. Army, 1998-2007. Fellow. AIChE, mem. Am. Chem. Soc., Nat. Geographic Soc., Air and Waste Mgmt. Assn. Achievements include patent for innovative groundwater treatment; patent for subsurface NAPL treatment. Home: 6348 Hope Estates Dr Baton Rouge LA 70820 Office: La State U Dept Chem Engring Baton Rouge LA 70803-0001 Home Phone: 225-819-2118. Business E-Mail: valsaraj@lsu.edu.

VALTIER, SANDRA, toxicologist; d. Eduardo L. and Josefina C. Valtier; m. Donald Jay Klefforth, May 3, 1991. PhD, U. Tex. San Antonio, 2006. Cert. med. technologist Am. Soc. Clin. Pathology, Tex., 1983. Analytical toxicologist Clin. Rsch., Lackland Airforce Base, Tex., 1990—. Cons. SW Clin. Lab Consulting, San Antonio, 2008—. Contbr. chapters to books. Recipient Sci. Rsch. award, Air Force, 2001, 2004. Mem.: Soc. Forensic Toxicologist. Achievements include research in LC MS systems for the trace analysis and quantitative identification of drugs, metabolites; development of protocol involve method for analysis of drugs of abuse, alcohol biomarkers, ADHD and weight loss medications and other chemistry related methods.

VALUKAS, ANTON RONALD, lawyer, former prosecutor; b. Chgo., June 21, 1943; s. Anton J. and Mary Ann (Giusto) Valukas; m. Janice C. Valukas (div.); children: Amy Paige, Beth Catherine; m. Maria Finitzo; children: Catherine Sara, Paul Alexander. BA in Polit. Sci., Art History, Lawrence U., 1965; JD, Northwestern U., 1968. Bar: Ill. 1968, U.S. Dist. Ct. (no. dist.) Ill. 1968, U.S. Ct. Appeals (7th cir.) 1969, U.S. Ct. Appeals (10th cir.) 1977, U.S. Ct. Appeals (3d cir.) 1982. Asst. dir. Nat. Defender Project, Chgo., 1968-70; asst. US atty. (No. dist.) Ill. US Dept. Justice, Chgo., 1970—74, chief spl. prosecutions divsn., 1974, first asst. US atty, 1975—76, US atty., 1985-89; ptnr. Jenner & Block LLP, Chgo., 1976—85, 1989—, chmn., 2007—. Instr. John Marshal Law Sch., 1972—76; adj. prof. law Northwestern U. Sch. Law, 1980—82; dir., treas. Met. Fair and Exposition Authority, Chgo., 1985; spl. counsel to investigate report health care sys. City of Chgo., 1991. Bd. dirs. Boys Scouts Am., Bus. and Profl. People for Pub. Interest, 1998—, Smithsonian Inst. Librs., 2004—08, mem. judicial conf. adv. com. on civil rules, 2006—; chmn. Ill. Task Force Crime and Corrections, 1992—93; with Jewish Coun. Urban Affairs, 2009; mem. vis. com. Northwestern U. Sch. Law, 1992—95, with student funded pub. interest fellowship program, 2009. Recipient Spl. Commendation award, U.S. Dept. Justice, Chgo., 1975, Disting. Grad. award, Palatine HS, Ill., 1984, Freedom award, John Marshall Sch. Law, 1985, Citizen of the Yr. award, Constn. Rights Found., 1987, Civillian of the Yr. award, Armed Forces Coun. Chgo., 1988, Man of the Yr. award, WBBM Radio, 1988, Disting. Pub. Svc. award, Anti-Defamation League B'nai B'rith, 1990, Disting. Achievement award, Lawrence U., 1990, Disting. Svc. award, Chgo. C. of C. and Industry, 1990, Alumni Merit award, Northwestern U. Alumni Assn., 1995, Richard N. Rovner award, Epilepsy Found. Greater Chgo., 2004, Judge Learned Hand award, 2005, Arthur Goldberg award, 2009, Disting Alumni award, Northwestern Sch. Law, 2009; named one of Ten Outstanding Young Citizens of Chgo., Jr. C. of C., 1976. Fellow: Am. Coll. Trial Lawyers; mem.: ABA, Comml. Club Chgo., Chgo. Inn Ct. (pres. 2000—01), Ill. State Bar Assn., Chgo. Bar Assn., Chicagoland C. of C. (bd. dirs. 1999—), Law of Chgo. Club, Exec. Club Chgo., Econ. Club. Chgo. Office: Jenner & Block LLP 330 N Wabash Ave Chicago IL 60611-7603 Office Phone: 312-923-2903. Business E-Mail: avalukas@jenner.com.

VALVERDE, JOSÉ (RAFAEL), professional baseball player; b. San Pedro de Macoris, Dominican Republic, July 24, 1979; m. Luisa Valverde; 1 child, Montserrat. Pitcher Ariz. Diamondbacks, 2003—07, Houston Astros, 2008—. Recipient Hilton Smith Legacy award, Negro Leagues Baseball Mus., 2007, Nat. League Rolaids Relief award, 2007; named to Nat. League All-Star Team, 2007. Achievements include leading the National League in: saves, 2007, 2008; games finished, 2008. Mailing: c/o Houston Astros Minute Maid Pk 501 Crawford St Houston TX 77002

VALVERDE, PALOMA, biochemist, educator; b. Murcia, Murcia, Spain, Jan. 15, 1968; d. Gregorio Valverde and Paz de los Angeles Hernandez; m. David Irwin Sherris, Nov. 2, 1997; children: Gregory Alexander Sherris children: Michael Gregory Sherris. BSc, U. Murcia, Spain, 1990, MSc, 1991, PhD, 1994. Scientist Human Nutrition Rsch. Ctr. of Aging, Tufts U., Boston, 2002—04; asst. prof. Sch. Dental Medicine, Tufts U., Boston, 2004—. Vis. scientist Boston Biomed. Rsch. Inst., 2007—; biology lectr. Simmons Coll.; biology instr. Wenworth Inst. Tech., 2009—; rsch. scientist Boston Biomedicl Rsch. Inst. Contbr. articles to profl. jours. John W. Hein Rsch. fellow, Forsyth Inst., Boston, 1999—2002. Mem.: Am. Physiol. Soc., Internat. Assn. for Biomed. Rsch. (v.p. 2004—). Achievements include discovery of first mutations in human melanocortin receptor 1; gene called WW45 or Salvador; first to use of scorpion venom to treat periodontal disease; development of first antibody to recognize WW45/Salvador gene; discovery of axl receptor tyrosine kinase is ubiquitinated by its ligand Gas6; RANKL and BSP induce bone loss synergistically. Avocations: painting, writing. Home: 37 Neillian Crescent Jamaica Plain MA 02130 Personal E-mail: pvalverde@aol.com. Business E-Mail: paloma.valverde@tufts.edu.

VALVO, BARBARA-ANN, lawyer, surgeon; b. Elizabeth, NJ, June 7, 1949; d. Robert Richad and Vera (Kovach) V. BA in Biology, Hofsta U., 1971; MD, Pa. State U., 1975; JD, Loyola Sch. Law, 1993. Bar: La. 1993; diplomate Am. Bd. Surgery. Surg. intern Nassau County Med. Ctr., East Meadow, NY, 1975-76; resident gen. surgery Allentown-Sacred Heart Med. Ctr., Pa., 1976-80; asst. chief surgery USPHS, New Orleans, 1980-81; pvt. practice gen. surgery New Orleans, 1981-89; pvt. practice med. malpractice law, 1995—. Upjohn scholar, 1975. Fellow ACS; mem. ABA, Fed. Bar Assn., La. Bar Assn., La. Trial Lawyers Assn. Republican. Avocations: computers, raising animals. Office: 41 Harley Pl Willow Spring NC 27592 Personal E-mail: bavalvo@nc.rr.com.

VANAGAS, RIMANTAS ANDRIUS (RAY VANAGAS), entrepreneur, real estate developer, real estate company executive; b. Chgo., Jan. 10, 1958; s. Liudas and Birute A. (Bielskis) Vanagas. Student, Northwestern U., 1980-81; BA in Physics, Econs. and Polit. Sci., Lake Forest Coll., Ill., 1982. Prof. basketball player European divsn., Munich, 1982; ski instr., capt. race team Breckenridge (Colo.) Ski Sch., 1979-80; chmn. bd. dirs. Vancher Corp., Wheeling, Ill., 1980-84; sales exec. Chgo. HMO, 1984-85; exec. dir. Physique, Inc., Highland Park, Ill., 1985; pres., CEO Sports Life, Inc., Highland Park, 1985-88; sr. v.p. JPC Consulting, Chgo., 1988-91; pres., CEO Printing Advisors, Inc., Naperville, Ill., 1990-94, Cafe Alexander, Naperville, 1995—2002; sr. exec. George S. May Internat. Consulting Co., Park Ridge, Ill., 1994-95; pres. Movie Magic Workshops, 2002—; founder, real estate investor and devel. RBML Real Estate Inc., 2002—; pres. and CEO Pinemeadow Corp. DBA Park Shore Marina, 2004—, Vanagas Investment Group, LLC, 2005—. Cons. Nautilus Exercise Ctrs., Inc., Wheeling, 1979—83, G. Ross Comm., Lake Bluff, Ill., 1986; mng. dir. Ford Model Mgmt., Chgo., 2000—; pres., CEO Alexander Talent Mgmt., 2001—. Actor:, 1981—; (films) Shut-Eye, 2001; prodr.:, 1981—, numerous music videos, commls., inds. and corp. films. Leader Lithuanian Air Scouts, 1976—80; campaign asst. Ronald Reagan Re-Election Campaign, Ill., 1983; active Baltic Nations Athletic Olympiad; vol. coach basketball, baseball, 1984—87. Mem.: Mensa. Roman Catholic. Avocations: collecting coins and stamps, travel, skiing, golf, tennis. Home: 1684 Greene Ridge Dr Naperville IL 60565-6753 Office Phone: 269-445-3100. E-mail: rayvanagas@aol.com.

VAN AKEN, JOHN HENRY, retired marine engineer; b. Haarlem, Netherlands, Sept. 26, 1922; arrived in U.S., 1952; s. Antony and Maria Petronella (Renzen) van Aken; m. Hendrika A. Bonneur, Sept. 25, 1947 (div. Feb. 1960); 1 child, Antony Laurens; m. Helen Jemison Waterman, July 17, 1962 (dec. Feb. 1978); m. Marilyn McDaniel, July 13, 1980 (dec. Sept. 2001). Marine Engr., Acad. Tech. Sci. and Arts of Design, 1940. Asst. mgr. repair dept. Wilton-Feyenoord Dockyards, Schiedam, Netherlands, 1945—52; supt. machinery Ala. Dry Dock & Shipbldg. Co.; Mobile, 1958—60; mgr. project Kerr-McGee Oil Industries, Oklahoma City, 1954—58, 1960—63; insp. George Sharp Co., Naval Architects, Newport News, Va., 1960; pres. John H. van Aken Co. Inc., Marine Surveyors and Cons. Inc., Mobile, 1963—99; ret., 2002. Non-exclusive surveyor Panama Bur. Shipping, Internat. Cargo Gear Bur., Registr. Italiano Navale, Lloyd's Register of Shipping, Westminister Village Found., Inc., dir. Decorated comdr. Order Good Hope, South Africa; Paul Harris fellow Rotary. Mem. Soc. Naval Architects and Marine Engrs., Nat. Assn. Marine Surveyors, Netherlands Soc. Marine Technologists, Rotary Home: 500 Spanish Ft Blvd #52 Spanish Fort AL 36527-5004 Personal E-mail: jhvanaken@wvsf.org.

VAN ALLEN, WILLIAM KENT, lawyer; b. Albion, NY, July 30, 1914; s. Everett Kent and Georgia (Roberts) Van A.; m. Sally Schall, Nov. 11, 1944; children: William Kent, Jr., George Humphrey, Peter Cushing. AB, Hamilton Coll., 1935; LL.B., Harvard U., 1938. Bar: N.Y. 1938, D.C. 1939, N.C. 1951, U.S. Dist. Ct. (we. dist.) N.C. 1951, U.S. Dist. Ct. (mid. dist.) N.C. 1953, U.S. Ct. Appeals (4th cir.) 1951, U.S. Ct. Claims 1946, U.S. Tax Ct. 1940, FCC 1939, ICC 1940, U.S. Supreme Ct. 1946. With Hanson, Lovett & Dale, Washington, 1938-41, 46-50; ptnr. Lassiter, Moore and Van Allen and Moore and Van Allen, Charlotte, NC, 1951-87; of counsel Moore & Van Allen, Charlotte, 1988—. Permanent mem. Jud. Conf. 4th Jud. Circuit. Vestryman Episc. Ch., 1957-60, 66-69; mem. Mecklenburg County Bd. Public Welfare, 1954-59, chmn. 1957-59; bd. dirs. N.C. Found. Commerce and Industry, 1965-73, Found. U. N.C. at Charlotte, 1979-89, Charlotte Symphony Orch., 1981-82, Mercy Health Svcs., 1983-88; chmn. Charlotte Area adv. coun. Am. Arbitration Assn., 1967-76; bd. dirs. United Community Svcs., 1972-77, v.p., 1972; bd. mgrs. Charlotte Country Day Sch., 1956-61, chmn., 1959-61, bd. visitors, 1978-2004, chmn., 1987-88; bd. advisers U. N.C.-Charlotte, 1983-84; trustee Spastics Hosp., 1951-60, Mint Mus. Art, 1976-79, Surtman Found., 1955-90, Mercy Hosp. Found., 1979-84; bd. visitors Johnson C. Smith U., 1978-89; pres. Charlotte Symphony League, 1980-81, Friends of U. N.C. at Charlotte, 1990-91. Served with USNR, 1941-45, commdg. officer destroyer escort ATO and PTO; released to inactive duty as lt. comdr. Mem. ABA, Charlotte C. of C. (bd. dirs. 1971-75, v.p. 1972-75). Mil. Order of Carabao, Holland Soc. N.Y., Charlotte Country Club (past pres.),

Charlotte City Club, Chevy Chase Club (Md.), Mullett Lake Country Club (Mich.), Mill Reef Club, Phi Beta Kappa, Chi Psi. Office: Moore & Van Allen Ste 4700 100 N Tryon St Charlotte NC 28202-4003 Office Phone: 704-331-1021.

VAN ALSTINE, SHARRI KAY, music educator; b. Mpls., Sept. 25, 1967; d. Robert Duane and Kay Maxine Van Alstine. B.Music Edn., Bethel Coll., St. Paul, 1991; M.Choral Conducting, St. Cloud State U., Minn., 1999; attending, U. Minn., 2007—. Choir dir. First Bapt. Ch., Cambridge, Minn., 1990—2005, 2008—09; choir tchr. Cambridge H.S., 1991—92, Princeton H.S., Minn., 1992—98, St. Francis H.S., Minn., 1998—2005; tchr. choirs, music appreciation & dept. chair Black Forest Acad., Kandern, Germany, 2005—07, Anoka-Ramsey CC, 2008—. Mem.: Internat. Soc. Music Edn., Coll. Music Soc., Music Educators Nat. Conf., Minn. Music Educators Assn., Am. Choral Dirs. Assn. Baptist. Avocations: gardening, reading, travel. Office: Anoka Ramsey Community College CC F244A 300 Spirit River Dr Cambridge MN 55008

VAN ALSTYNE, VANCE BROWNELL, management consultant; b. Rochester, NY, Feb. 3, 1924; s. Guy and Jessie Van Alstyne; m. Jane Van Alstyne, Aug. 12, 1950; children: Cary B., Stacey E. Eptina. BA, U. Rochester, 1948; LLB, Blackstone Coll. Law, 1964. Rsch. asst. indsl. rels. Gilbert Assoc, Inc., NYC, 1950-56; corp. sec., v.p., dir. R.C. Simpson & Staff Inc., Newark and Ridgewood, NJ, 1956-74; pres., dir. R.C. Simpson, Inc., Ridgewood, NJ, 1975—91, Charlotte, NC, 1991—. 2d lt., Navigator 12th Air Force USAF, 1942—45, 30 missions Italy. Mem.: Indsl. Rels. Rsch. Assn., Am. Arbitration Assn., Atlantic Salmon Fedn. Republican. Office: RC Simpson Inc 5950 Fairview Rd Ste 604 Charlotte NC 28210-3178 Office Phone: 704-553-0716.

VAN ALSTYNE, W. SCOTT, JR., lawyer, educator; b. East Syracuse, NY, Sept. 21, 1922; s. Walter Scott and Cecil Edna (Folmsbee) Van A.; m. Margaret Reed Hudson, June 23, 1949 (div.); children: Gretchen Anne, Hunter Scott; m. Marion Graham Walker, May 3, 1980. BA, U. Buffalo, 1948; MA, U. Wis., 1950, LL.B., 1953, S.JD, 1954. Bar: Wis. 1953. Assoc. Shea & Hoyt, Milw., 1954-56; asst. prof. law U. Nebr., 1956-58; pvt. practice Madison, Wis., 1958-72; prof. law U. Fla., 1973-90, prof. emeritus, 1990—; lectr. law U. Wis., 1958-72; lectr. Cambridge-Warsaw Trade Program Cambridge U., England, 1976. Vis. prof. law Cornell U., 1977, U. Leiden, The Netherlands, 1988, 91; spl. lectr. U. Utrecht, The Netherlands, 1991; vis. prof. Wake Forest U., 1997; spl. counsel Gov. of Wis., 1966-70; bd. dirs. non-resident divsn. State Bar Wis., 1981-96, pres., 1988-90, bd. govs. 1988-90. Prin. author: Goals and Missions of Law Schools, 1990; contbr. articles to profl. jours. Mem. Gov.'s Commn. on Edn., Wis., 1969-71; cons. Wis. Commn. on Legal Edn., 1995-96. Served with AUS, 1942-45, 61-62; col. Res., ret. Decorated Legion of Merit. Fellow: Wis. Bar Found. (life); mem.: Holland Soc., S.R. (NY), Netherland Club (NYC), Madison Club (Wis.), Ft. Rensselaer Club (NY), Phi Beta Kappa, Order of Coif, Phi Delta Phi, Omicron Delta Kappa. Republican. Presbyterian. Office: U Fla Holland Law Ctr Gainesville FL 32611

VAN AMSTEL, LOUIS, dancer; b. Amsterdam, June 23, 1972; Grad., U. Arts, Amsterdam. Competitive & profl. dancer; winner European Amateur Latin Championship, 1995, World Amateur Latin Championship, 1994, 1995, Grand Slam Profl. Latin Championship, 1995, World Profl. Showdance Championship, 1996, US Nat. Latin Championship, 2000; founder & CEO VanDance, LLC, Visionworx Dance, 2007. Dir., choreographer, dancer (dance prodns.) Latin Fusion, Latin Revolution, 2004; dancer (TV series) Dancing with the Stars, 2005—. Office: Dance Notes PO Box 0001 New York NY 10028-0001 Office Phone: 877-336-6837.

VAN ANTWERP, ROBERT L., JR., career military officer; m. Paula Eberly; children: Jeff, Luke, Rob, Julia, Kathryn. BS, US Mil. Acad., 1972; MME, U. Mich.; MBA, LI U. Registered Profl. Engr., Va. Commd. 2d. lt. US Army, 1972, advanced through grades to lt. gen., 2007, platoon leader, 76th Engr. Battalion Fort Meade, Md., 1973—74; exec. officer 65th Engr. Battalion, 25th Infantry Div. Schofield Barracks, Hawaii, 1975—76, asst. div. engr. Hawaii, 1976—79, exec. officer 84th Engr. Battalion, 45th Gen. Support Group Hawaii, 1985—87; chief mil. construction US Army Western Command, Fort Shafter, Hawaii, 1987—88; exec. officer Office of Chief of Engrs. US Army, Washington, 1988—89; comdr. 326th Engr. Battalion, 101st Airborne Div., Fort Campbell, Ky., 1989—91; dist. comdr. LA Dist. US Army CE, LA, 1992—94, chief of staff Washington, 1994—95, comdr. South Atlantic Div. Atlanta, 1996—98; exec. asst. to vice chmn. Joint Chiefs of Staff US Dept. Def., Washington, 1995—96; dir. Office of Competitive Sourcing, Office of Asst. Sec. of Army US Army, Washington, 1998—99, asst. chief staff installation mgmt., 1999—2002; comdr. US Army Maneuver Support Ctr., 2002—04; chief US Army Accessions Command, Fort Knox, Ky., 2004—07; chief engrs., commdg. gen. US Army CE, Washington, 2007—. Instr., mech. engring. US Mil. Acad., West Point, NY, 1981—82, asst. prof., exec. officer, 1982—84; commdg. gen. US Army Engr. Sch., Fort Leonard Wood, Mo. Pres. Officers' Christian Fellowship. Decorated Defense Superior Svc. Medal, Legion of Merit, Bronze Star Medal, Meritorious Svc. Medal. Office: US Army Corps of Engineers 441 G St, NW Washington DC 20314-1000 Office Phone: 703-428-6572.

VAN ANTWERPEN, FRANKLIN STUART, federal judge; s. Franklin John and Dorothy Van Antwerpen; m. Kathleen Veronica O'Brien, Sept. 12, 1970; children: Joy, Franklin W., Virginia. BS in Engring. Physics, U. Maine, 1964; JD, Temple U., 1967; postgrad., Nat. Jud. Coll., 1980. Bar: Pa. 1969, US Dist. Ct. (ea. dist.) Pa. 1971, US Ct. Appeals (3d cir.) 1971, US Supreme Ct. 1972. Corp. counsel Hazeltine, Corp., NYC, 1967-70; chief counsel Northampton County Legal Aid Soc., Easton, Pa., 1970-71; assoc. Hemstreet & Smith, Easton, 1971-73; ptnr. Hemstreet & VanAntwerpen, Easton, 1973-79; judge Ct. Common Pleas of Northampton County, Pa., 1979-87, US Dist. Ct. (ea. dist.) Pa., Phila., 1987—2004, US Ct. Appeals (3rd. cir.), 2004—06, sr. judge, 2006—. Apptd. to US Sentencing Commn. Jud. Working Group, 1992-93; apptd. to US Jud. Conf. Com. on Defender Svcs., 1997, chmn. subcom. on fed. defender funding, 2000-01; trial judge US vs. Scarfo, 1988-89; adj. prof. Northampton County Area CC, 1976-81; solicitor Palmer Twp., 1971-79; gen. counsel Fairview Savs. and Loan Assn., Easton, 1973-79; lectr. on law of evidence Pa. Bar Inst., 1985-92. Contbr. articles to Cardozo Law Rev., 1967. Recipient Booster award Bus. Indsl. and Profl. Assn., 1979, George Palmer award Palmer Twp., 1980, Citizen of Yr. award, 1981, Law Enforcement Commendation medal Nat. Soc. SAR, 1990, Disting. Alumni Achievement award Newark Acad., 2001, Law Day award Temple Law Sch. Alumni Assn., 2004, Alumni Career award U. Maine, 2009; named an Alumnus Who Has Made a Difference in the World, U. Maine, 1991. Mem. ABA (com. on jud. edn.), Fed. Bar Assn. (hon.), Fed. Cir. Bar Assn., Pa. Bar Assn., Northampton County Bar Assn., Am. Judicature Soc., Fed. Judges Assn., Pomfret Club, Union League Club, Pa. Soc. Club, Sigma Pi Sigma. Office: 4th Fl Holmes Bldg 101 Larry HOlmes Dr Easton PA 18042-7722*

VAN ARENDONK, SUSAN CAROLE, special education educator; b. Marshalltown, Iowa, Feb. 16, 1954; d. Ernest Jerome and Alice Marjorie (Harmon) Groff; m. Wayne Alan Van Arendonk, Aug. 14, 1994. BS, Iowa State U., Ames, 1976; MS in Edn., U. Kans., Lawrence, 1981; EdS, U. Iowa, Iowa City, 2001. Professionally recognized spl. educator Coun. for Exception Children, 1999; nat. bd. cert. tchr. exceptional needs. Resource rm. aide Pinckney Elem., Lawrence, Kans., 1976-77; tchr. spl. edn. Booth Elem. Sch., Wichita, Kans., 1977-78; tchr. resource rm. Clinton Cmty. Schs., Iowa, 1978—80; tchr. spl. edn. Henry Sabin Elem. Sch., Clinton, 1980-83; edn. specialist U. Iowa, 1984; cons. No. Trails Area Edn. Agy., Clear Lake, Iowa, 1984-86; tchr. resource rm. Tomiyasu Elem. Sch., Las Vegas, 1986-88, 90-92, tchr. 3d grade, 1988-90, 92-94; tchr. lang. arts, spl. edn. Haysville (Kans.) Mid. Sch., 1996-97; tchr. behavior disorders Heartspring, Wichita, Kans., 1997-98; tchr. spl. edn. Gammon Elem., Wichita, 1998-2000, Curtis Mid. Sch., Wichita, 2000—04, Maize HS, Kans., 2004—06; cons. Grant Wood Area Edn. Agy., Cedar Rapids, Iowa, 2006—. Edn. specialist, student tchr. supr. U. Iowa, 1983, grad. asst. 1984; cons. Heartland Area Edn. Agy., Johnston, Iowa, 1994-96. Treas. State Rep. Campaign, Iowa, 1974, publicity chmn., 1974. Mem. Coun. Exceptional Children, Iowa State Alumni Assn. (life), U. Iowa Alumni Assn. (life), Humane Soc. Am., U. Kans. Alumni Assn., Phi Lambda Theta. Democrat. Jewish. Home: 1708 Lynncrest Dr Coralville IA 52241 Office: Grant Wood Area Edn Agy 200 Holiday Rd Coralville IA 52241 Office Phone: 319-351-2510, 319-358-6278. Personal E-mail: wvanarendonk@msn.com. Business E-Mail: sgroff-vanarendonk@aea10.k12.ia.us.

VAN ARK, BART (HUBERTUS HERMAN VAN ARK), economist; b. Heerde, Netherlands, June 20, 1960; married; 2 children. BA in Econs., U. Groningen, Netherlands, 1981, MA in Agrl. Devel. Econs. cum laude, 1985, MA in Econs., 1986, PhD in Econs., 1993. Rsch. assoc. Nat. Inst. Econ. Social Rsch., England, 1988—90; asst. prof. U. Groningen, 1990—96, assoc. prof., 1997—99, assoc. dean, internat. affairs, 2006—07, prof., 2000—04, 2004—; consulting dir., internat. econ. rsch. The Conf. Bd., Inc., NYC, 1997—2006, exec. dir., econ. rsch. for NY, Beijing, Brussels, 2007—08, chief economist, v.p., 2008—. Dir. Groningen Growth Devel. Ctr., 1991—; coord. European Union Capital Labor Energy Material Svc. Inputs (EUKLEMS); mem. numerous adv. coms.; mem. editl. bds. numerous profl. jours. Mng. editor Rev. Income and Wealth, 2004; contbr. articles to profl. jours. Mem.: NSF, Netherlands Sci. Coun. Office: The Conf Bd Inc 845 3rd Ave New York NY 10022-6679 also: Univ Groningen PO Box 300 9700 AV Groningen Netherlands Office Phone: 31 50 363 3674. Office Fax: 212-980-7014. Business E-Mail: h.h.van.ark@rug.nl.*

VAN ARSDALE, DENNIS G., librarian; MALS, U. Mo., Columbia, 1976. Regional libr. North Ark. Regional Libr., Harrison, 1986—90; tech. svcs. libr. U. Ark., Ft. Smith, 1990—. Chair Ark. Innovative Users Group, 2008—. Mem.: ALA, Ark. Libr. Assn. Office: Univ Ark Ft Smith PO Box 3649 Fort Smith AR 72913-3649 Business E-Mail: dvanarsd@uafortsmith.edu.

VAN ARSDALE, SHARON A., nurse; d. Victor E. and Eilena J. Laubhan; m. Robert W. Van Arsdale, Dec. 11, 1982; children: Katharine F., Robert W., Philip A. BSN, U. Okla., Norman, 1979; MSN, U. Mo., Columbia, 1999. Cert. family nurse practitioner, ANCC, 1999, gerontologic nurse practitioner, 1999. Charge nurse St. Mary's Hosp., Okla. city, 1979—81, Hurley Med. Ctr., Flint, Mich., 1982—89; evening float nurse St. Anthony Hosp., Enid, Okla., 1981—82; advance practice nurse Randolph County Health Dept., Moberly, Mo., 2002—05, U. Mo. Health Care, Columbia, 2005—; mem. Ethics Com. - U. Mo. Health Care, Mo., 2008—, Pain Task Force - U. Mo. Health Care, 2008—, Pharmacy & Therapeutics Com. - U. Mo. Health Care, 2008—. Contbr. articles to profl jours. Mem.: Oncology Nursing Soc., Sigma Theta Tau (Alpha Iota Chpt.).

VANARSDALL, ROBERT LEE, JR., orthodontist, educator; b. Crewe, Va., Feb. 7, 1940; s. Robert Lee Sr. and Margie Mae (Jenkins) V.; m. Sandra E. Hoffman, Aug. 11, 1962; children: Robert Lee III, Lesley, Ashley. BA in Econs., Coll. William and Mary, 1962; DDS, Med. Coll. Va., 1970; cert. Orthodontics and Periodontics, U. Pa., 1973. Diplomate Am. Acad. Periodontology, Am. Bd. Orthodontics. Staff Children's Hosp., Phila., 1973—; prof. orthodontics, chmn. dept. orthodontics U. Pa., Phila., 1981—; prof. dentistry, chmn. Med. Coll. Pa., Phila., 1989—99. K.G. prof. orthodontics U. Sydney, Australia, 2001; bd. dir. Nat. Dental Ins. Co., Denver. Editor: Internat. Jour. Adult Orthodontics and Orthognathic Surgery, 1986-2003, Orthodontoics: Current Principles and Techniques, 2d edit., 1994, 4th edit., 2005, Applications of Orthodontic Mini-Implants, 2007; editl. bd. profl. jours.; contbr. articles to profl. jours. Bd. dirs. Phila. Soc. William and Mary Alumni Assn. Lt. USNR, 1962-65. Fellow Coll. Physicians of Phila. 1978, Am. Coll. Dentistry 1980. Mem. ADA, Am. Assn. Orthodontists, Stomatological Club Phila., Angle Soc. Orthodontists (v.p. ea. component, pres. 2004-2005), Phila. Soc. Orthodontists (pres. 1989, chmn. sci. affairs coun. 1990—), Internat. Coll. of Dentists. Roman Catholic. Avocations: antiques, architecture. Home: 208 Ashwood Rd Villanova PA 19085-1504 Office: Penn Dental 34th and Market St Philadelphia PA 19104 Office Phone: 215-898-5910. Office Fax: 215-898-0998. Business E-Mail: rlv@pobox.upenn.edu.

VANATTA, BOB, athletic administrator; b. Columbia, Mo., July 7, 1918; s. Claude W. and Viola (Toler) V.; m. Lois A. Williams; children: Robert, Thomas, Timothy. BA, Ctrl. Meth. Coll., 1942; MEd, U. Mo., 1949. Tchr., coach Boonville (Mo.) High Sch., 1942-43, Kemper Mil. Sch., Boonville, 1943-44, Springfield (Mo.) High Sch., 1944-47; tchr., dir. athletics, coach Ctrl. Meth. Coll., Fayette, Mo., 1947-50, S.W. Mo. State U., Springfield, 1950-53, coach two NAIA champions, 1950—53; coach U.S. Mil. Acad., West Point, NY, 1953-54; dir. athletics, coach Bardley U., Peoria, Ill., 1954-56; tchr., coach Memphis State U., 1956-62, U. Mo., Columbia, 1962-68; bank mktg. officer Empire Bank, Springfield, 1968-71; prof. basketball exec. dir. Memphis Pros, 1971-72; tchr., coach Delta State U., Cleve., 1972-73; dir. athletics Oral Roberts U., Tulsa, 1973-77; commr. Ohio Valley Athletic Conf., Nashville, 1977-80, Trans Am. Athletic Conf., Shreveport, La., 1980-83; dir. athletics La. Tech. U., Rustin, 1983-86; commr. Sunshine State Athletic Conf., Jupiter, Fla., 1986-94. Assoc. dir athletics Fla. Atlantic U., coach basketball Ctrl. Meth. Coll., 1942 Author: Coaching Pattern Play Basketball, 1959; contbr. articles to profl. jours. Mem. Nat. Football Found. Hall of Fame Chpt., bd. mem., 2008 Named to Ctrl. Meth. Coll. Hall of Fame, S.W. Mo. State U. Hall of Fame, Nat. Athletic Intercollegiate Assn. Hall of Fame, Greater Springfield Hall of Fame, John Q. Hammons Mo. Sports Hall of Fame, U. Memphis Hall of Fame, Nat. Assn. Collegiate Dir. of Athletics, Nat. Assn. Collegiate Dir. of Athletics Hall of Fame, 1997, Helms Hall of Fame, Palm Beach Athletes Hall of Fame, 2007; recipient Lifetime Achievement award in football All-Am. Football Found., 1997, NCAA Divsn. II Commrs. award Merit, 1999, Champions of Character award NAIA, 2002, Coach of Yr., 1952, 53, Italian Am. Coach of Yr. 1953, numerous others. Mem. Nat. Assn. Basketball Coaches, Am. Football Coaches Assn., Nat. Assn. Collegiate Dirs. Athletics, All Am. Football Found. (Bud Dudley Outstanding Exec. award in Football, 2000, Asa Bushnell Commr. award 2001), Palm Beach County Sports Commn., Lou Groza, PBCS (mem. Hall of Fame Com.). Office: 300 N Highway A/A Bldg #F Unit #403 Jupiter FL 33477 Office Phone: 561-743-9763.

VANATTA, CHESTER B., management consultant, educator; b. Bartlesville, Okla., Sept. 3, 1935; s. Benjamin Franklin and Iona Ruth (Hayes) V.; m. Patsy Lou (Straub), May 29, 1958; children: Tracy Ann, Christopher B., John Scott BS in Mktg., U. Kans., Lawrence, 1959, MS in Acctg., 1962; Advanced Mgmt. Program, Harvard U., Cambridge, Mass., 1972; MA in Theology, Fuller Theol. Sem., Pasadena, Calif., 2006. Mem. staff Arthur Young and Co., Kansas City, Mo., 1962—69, regional dir, Dallas, 1969—72, ptnr., 1969—85, mng. ptnr. Chgo., 1972—76, dir., 1973—85, mng. ptnr., vice chmn. ops. NYC, 1976—81, mng. ptnr., vice chmn. S.W. Region Dallas, 1981—85; exec. in residence, Paul J. Adam Disting. lectr. U. Kans. Sch. Bus., Lawrence, 1985—90; pres. Exec. Cons. Group, Lawrence, 1985—96. Trustee Kans. U. Endowment Fund, 1983-2005; bd. dir. Kans. Alumni Assn., 1984-91, pres., 1986-87. Mem. AICPA, Leawood South Country Club. Avocations: golf, travel, auctioneering, photography. Home: 12614 Cedar St Leawood KS 66209-3148 Personal E-mail: chet@aboutvanatta.com.

VANAUSDALL, JOHN, museum director; BS, Indiana Univ., 1978, MBA, 1996. Curator physical sci. Children's Mus. Indpls., 1978—84, info. systems mgr., 1984—87, dir. exhibits, 1987—93, v.p., dir. rsch. & planning, 1993—96; pres., CEO Eiteljorg Mus. of Am. Indians & Western Art, Indpls., 1996—. Cons., SC State Mus., 1982; mem. Ind. Consortium for Computer & High Tech. Edn., 1983-89; cons. Ohio Hist. Soc., 1984-87; cons. St. Louis Sci. Ctr., 1988; mem. enterprise council, Ind. Dept. Edn., 1990-92; cons. NY Bot. Garden, 1992; reviewer, Fla Dept. State, 1993; bd. dir. Edyvean Repertory Theatre, 1998-2002; mem. adv. bd. Spirit & Place Festival, 2001-2004; mem. bd. vis. Kelly Sch. Bus., 1999-2003; mem. bd. adv. Indpls. Convention & Visitors Assn., 1997-; co-chmn. Assn. Midwest Museums, 1999; pres. Indpls Consortium of Arts Administrators, 1996-; bd. dir. Museums West, 1996-; mem. arts. com. Indiana Univ. Purdue Univ, 1998-; bd. mem. Hoosier Salon Patrons Assn.; chmn. host city com. Am. Assn. Museums, 2004-2005; pres. Museums West Collaborative, 2006-; reviewer Inst. of Museum & Libr. Sciences, 2006. Contbr. articles to profl. jours. & presentations at museums; mem. editl. bd. MuseuMedia, 1990—92, Native Peoples Mag., 1996—. Recipient Sagamore of the Wabash, Gov. of Indiana. Mem.: Beta Gamma Sigma. Office: Eiteljorg Mus White River State Park 500 W Washington St Indianapolis IN 46204 Office Phone: 317-636-9378.

VAN BEBBER, DAVID L., food products executive, lawyer; b. Hiawatha, Kans., May 10, 1956; m. Sue Van Bebber; 4 children. BA, U. Ark., 1978, JD, 1981. Bar: Ark. 1982. Sr. v.p., dir. legal svcs., dep. gen. counsel Tyson Foods Inc., Springdale, Ark., 1998—2008, exec. v.p., gen. counsel, 2008—. Pres. Ark. Bd. Edn., Springdale; active St. Thomas Episcopal Ch., Springdale. Mem.: ABA, Ark. Bar Assn. Office: Tyson Foods Inc 2210 W Oakland Dr Springdale AR 72762-6999*

VAN BEEK, EDWIN JACQUES RUDOLPH, radiologist, researcher; b. Rotterdam, The Netherlands, June 10, 1960; arrived in U.S., 2004; s. Adriaan and Helena Wilhelmina (Van Bree) Van Beek; m. Miriam Dorothy Sneddon, Aug. 22, 1988; children: Andrew, Steven. MD, Erasmus U., Rotterdam, 1987; PhD, U. Amsterdam, The Netherlands, 1994; MEd, U. Sheffield, Eng., 2004. Sr. house officer Black Notley Hosp., Braintree, England, 1987, Colchester Dist. Gen. Hosp., England, 1987-89; resident surgery Acad. Med. Ctr., Amsterdam, 1989-90, rsch. fellow, 1990-94, registrar radiology, 1994-98; sr. clin. lectr., hon. cons. radiology U. Sheffield, Sheffield, 1999—2004; prof. radiology Carver Coll. Medicine U. Iowa, Iowa City, 2004—09. Hon. lectr. U. Amsterdam, 1999—2004; vis. prof. U. Sheffield, 2004—. Author: Epidemiology and Diagnosis of Pulmonary Embolism, 1994; co-author: Diagnosistic Imaging in Suspected Scaphold Fractures, 1992; editor: Deep Vein Thrombosis and Pulmonary Embolism, 2009; co-editor: Pulmonary Embolism, 1994, Functional Lung Imaging, 2005; contbr. articles to profl. jours., chapters to books. Fellow: Royal Coll. Radiologists; mem.: Radiol. Soc. N.Am., Phi Kappa Epsilon. Avocations: sports, museums, travel. Office: Carver College of Medicine Univ of Iowa C-751 GH 200 Hawkins Dr Iowa City IA 52242-1077 Office Phone: 319-384-6133. Personal E-mail: ejrvanbeek@gmail.com, edwin-vanbeek@qi2inc.com. Business E-Mail: edwin-vanbeek@uiowa.edu.

VAN BENTHEM, JOHAN FRANCISCUS ABRAHAM KAREL, philosophy, mathematics and computer science educator; b. Rijswijk, The Netherlands, June 12, 1949; came to US, 1991; s. Abraham K. and Janna M.G. (Eggermont) van B.; m. Alida T. Blom, July 22, 1977; children: Arthur A., Lucas L. B Physics, U. Amsterdam, The Netherlands, 1969, MPhil, 1972, MMath., 1973, PhD in Math., 1977; PhD (hon.), U. Liège, 1998. Asst. prof. dept. philosophy U. Amsterdam, 1972-77, prof. dept. math. and computer sci., 1986—2003, univ. prof., 2003—; assoc. prof. U. Groningen, The Netherlands, 1977-86; prof. dept. philosophy Stanford (Calif.) U., 1991—, Bonsall prof. for disting. visitors in humanities, 1994—2005. Vis. prof. Zhongshan U., Guangzhou, China. Author: The Logic of Time, 1983, Modal Logic and Classical Logic, 1985, Essays in Logical Semantics, 1986, Language in Action, 1991, Exploring Logical Dynamics, 1996, Logic in Games, 2001, Logic and Information Dynamics, 2008; editor: Handbook of Logic and Language, 1997, Handbook of Modal Logic, 2006, Handbook of Spatial Logics, 2007, Handbook of Philosophy of Information, 2008; coord. editor Jour. Symbolic Logic, 1991-93; mng. editor Synthese, Logic and Computation. Recipient Spinoza award Dutch Rsch. Coun., 1997-2001. Mem.: Hollandsche Maatschappij van Wetenschappen, Institut Internat. de Philosophie, Internat. Fedn. for Computational Logic (v.p. 2000—), European Acad. Scis., Royal Dutch Acad. Scis., European Assn. for Logic, Lang. and Info. (hon.; life, chmn. exec. bd. 1991—95, 1st Hon. life mem. 2004). Office: Stanford U Dept Philosophy Stanford CA 94305 also: U Amsterdam Inst Logic Lan & Comp Plantage Muidergracht 24 NL-1018 TV Amsterdam Netherlands Fax: 31 20 525 5206. Business E-Mail: johan.vanbenthem@uva.nl.

VANBIESBROUCK, JOHN ROBERT, hockey analyst, retired professional hockey player; b. Detroit, Sept. 4, 1963; s. Robert C. Sara; m. Rosalinde V. Dap, June 21, 1986. Goaltender NY Rangers, 1981—83, Vancouver Canucks, Canada, 1993, Florida Panthers, 1993—97, Phila. Flyers, 1998—2000, NY Islanders, 2000—01, NJ Devils, 2001—02; head coach Sault Ste. Marie Greyhounds, 2002—03; analyst NHL on Versus. Mem. NHL All-Star Team, 1985—86; player NHL All-Star Game, 1994. Recipient Vezina Trophy, 1986, Terry Sawchuk Trophy, 1983—89, Tommy Ivan Trophy, 1983—84; named NHL All-Star, 1985—86, Sporting News NHL All-Star, 1985—86, 1993—94. Achievements include holding the all time record for most wins by American born goaltender with 374; being inducted into the US Hockey Hall of Fame, 2007. E-mail: vbkgolf@aol.com.

VAN BOKKELEN, JOSEPH SCOTT, federal judge, former prosecutor; b. Chgo., June 7, 1943; s. Robert W. and W. Louise (Reynolds) Van Bokkelen; m. Sally Wardall Huey, Aug. 14, 1971; children: Brian, Kate. BA, U. ind., 1966; JD, U. Ind., 1969. Bar: Ind. 1969, US Dist. Ct. (so. dist.) Ind. 1969, US Dist. Ct. (no. dist.) Ind. 1973, US Ct. Appeals (7th cir.) 1973, US Supreme Ct. 1973. Dep. atty. gen. State of Ind., Indpls., 1969—71, asst. atty. gen., 1971—72; asst. US atty. No. Dist. Ind., Hammond, 1972—75, US atty., 2001—07; ptnr. Goldsmith, Goodman, Ball & Van Bokkelen, Highland, 1975—78, Goodman, Ball, Van Bokkelen & Leonard, 1978—2001. Recipient Outstanding Asst. US Atty. award, US Dept. Justice, 1974. Mem.: ABA, Criminal Def. Lawyers Assn., Ind. Bar Assn., Fed. Bar Assn. Office: US Dist Ct 5400 Fed Plz Ste 4200 Hammond IN 46320

VAN BOSSE, HAROLD J.P., orthopedic surgeon; MD, U. Ill., 1984—89. Cert. Orthopedic Surgery, 1997. Residence orthopedics U. Ill., Chgo.; fellow Hosp. for Sick Children, Toronto, 1994—95; surgeon Schneider Children's Hosp. Long Island Jewish Med. Ctr.; pediatric orthopedic surgeon NYU Hosp. for Joint Diseases, 1998—; asst. prof. orthopaedic surgery NYU Med. Ctr. Founder A Leg to Stand On, India, 2003; vol. surgeon Silver Service Children's program, Colombia. Named one of Medical Marvels, New York Mag., 2006. Mailing: NYU Hosp for Joint Diseases 301 East 17 St New York NY 10003 Office: 4 Weber Ave Malverne NY 11565 also: 240 E 18th S 1st Fl New York NY 10003 Office Phone: 212-598-2310, 516-596-2514. Office Fax: 212-598-2311.

VAN BRUNT, WILLIAM A., lawyer; m. Gail Van Brunt; 3 children. BS with honors, Pa. State U.; MS, MIT; JD, Boston U. Sch. Law; LLM, Harvard Sch. Law. Rschr. AVCO Rsch. and Develop.; with Kenway and Jenny, Boston, McNee, Wallace, and Nurick, Harrisburg, Pa., Hershey Foods Corp., General Mills; sr. v.p., gen. counsel Carlson Companies, Inc, Minnetonka, Minn., 2000—. Office: Carlson Companies Inc PO Box 59159 Minneapolis MN 55459 E-mail: bvanbrunt@carlson.com.

VAN BUITEN, ROBERT D., management consultant, career planner; b. Paterson, NJ, Feb. 18, 1927; s. Jerrien and Nellie Ruhling (Bogert) Van Buiten; m. Phyllis Nerine Stoutenburgh, Oct. 14, 1950; children: Lauren, Gregory, Suzanne, Christopher. Degree in mech. engring., Stevens Inst. Tech., 1949. Rocket test engr. Curtiss-Wright Corp., Caldwell, NJ, 1949—51; subcontract engr. Goodyear Aircraft Corp., Glenn L. Martin Co., Hamilton Std. UTC, Engring. Rsch. Corp., 1951—57; advanced engring. mgr. Martin Marietta Corp., Balt., 1957—65; spacecraft program mgr. IBM Corp., Bethesda, Md., 1965—68, divsn. planner Gaithersburg, Md., 1968—70; owner, cons. Van Buiten & Assocs., Columbia, Md., 1971—. Editor: NAS, 1961, (report) Nat. Acad. Scis.; contbr. rsch. pubs. optimizing individual careers. With USN, 1943—46, PTO. Mem.: AIAA, Am. Mgmt. Assn., Johnson O'Connor Rsch. Found., Am. Rocket Soc. Achievements include design of USAF X24-A manned research aircraft, precursor to current NASA space shuttle; design with high temperature brittle materials; advanced engineering managment of GEMINI 2 man spacecraft rocket launcher, precursor to history's first manned moon landings; research in individual midlife optimization or change in careers (50+ clients) in technology and associated industries; specialize in college graduates with previous successes, needing to enrich future careers; 12 successful GEMINI launches achieved histories 1st rendevous and docking of 2 manned spacecraft in earth orbit, critical building blocks to Apollo 1969 and currently planned manned lunar landings. Avocations: architecture, sailing, music, history. Home: 10752 Faulkner Ridge Columbia MD 21044

VAN BUREN, ABIGAIL (JEANNE PHILLIPS), columnist, educator; b. Mpls., Apr. 10, 1942; d. Morton and Pauline (Friedman) Phillips, (the founder of the Dear Abby advice column in 1956). Student, U. Colo., 1960—62. Writer Dear Abby Radio Show, CBS, 1965—71; columnist Dear Abby, 1987—. Bd. mem. Planned Parenthood of Los Angeles, 1989—90; life-time cons. Group for Advancement of Psychiatry, 1995—; bd. adv. Alzheimers Assn. of Los Angeles, 1996—; bd. mem. Rose and Jay Phillips Found., 1991—, ACLU of So. Calif. Found., 1998—; adv. bd. L.A. Internat. Women's Media Found. Courage in Journalism, 2000—; bd. adv. UCLA Med. Ctr., Ctr. for Rsch. and Training in Humane and Ethical Med. Care (CHEC), 2000—. Bd. advs. Planned Parenthood Fedn. Am., 2004; bd. judges Talbot's Charitable Found. Women's Scholarship Fund, 2006—; mem. White House Commn. Rememberance; bd. dirs. Planned Parenthood of LA, 1989—90, MADD, 2003—, Children's Rights Coun., 2003—; mem. Leadership Coun. Aids Project, LA, 2004; bd. dirs. Nat. Kidney Found., 2004. Recipient Generations of Choice award, Planned Parenthood of L.A., 1999, Minority Organ/Tissue Transplant Edn. Program (MOTTEP) Key of Life award, Howard U., Wash. DC, 2000, award of appreciation, US Gen. Svcs. Adminstrn. Fed. Consumer Info. Ctr., 2000, Star on Hollywood Walk of Fame for Dear Abby Radio Show, 2001, Recognition by the Office of Nat. Drug Control Policy (ONDCP), award from the White House and Substance Abuse and Mental Health Svcs. Adminstrn. for help in launching Nat. Inhalants and Poisons Awareness Week, 2001, Erasing the Stigma Leadership award, Didi Hirsch Mental Health Ctr., 2001, MOTTEP Award of Excellence, 2001, Commendation for Operation Dear Abby and OperationDearAbby.net, Dept. Navy and USMC, 2002, Appreciation for support of the military svc. mems. of the U.S. for Operation Dear Abby and OperationDearAbby.net, Space and Naval Warfare Sys. Ctr. (SPAWAR), 2002, Alzheimer's Assn. Maureen Reagan Advocacy Award, 2003, Appreciation award, Overeaters Anonymous, 2003, Advocacy award, Alzheimer's Assn. L.A., 2003, award of appreciation, US GSA Fed. Citizen Info. Ctr., 2004, Woman of the Yr., Muses, 2007, Straight for Equality award, Parents, Families, Friends of Lesbians Gays, 2007, Media award, Southern Calif. Psychiatric Soc., 2009. Mem.: Nat. Adv. Coun. of Alzheimers Assn. Syndicated in the US, Brazil, Mex., Japan, Philippines, Fed. Republic Germany, India, Holland, Denmark, Can., Korea, Thailand, Italy, Hong Kong, Taiwan, Ireland, Saudi Arabia, Greece, France, Dominican Republic, P.R., Costa Rica, US Virgin Islands, Bermuda, China, Kuwait and Guam; published on the Internet at DearAbby.com and OperationDearAbby.net for messages to the military. Office: Phillips-Van Buren Inc 1880 Century Park E Ste 1400 Los Angeles CA 90067

VANBUREN, DENISE DORING, corporate communications executive; b. Troy, NY, May 15, 1961; d. James L. and Eunice A. (Myers) Doring; m. Steven Paul VanBuren, Apr. 1, 1989; children: Schuyler Paul, Troy James Doring, Brett Steven VanBuren. BA in Mass Comm. magna cum laude, St. Bonaventure U., 1983; MBA, Mount St. Mary Coll., 1997. Reporter, news anchor Sta. WGNY-AM-FM, Newburgh, NY, 1984; news dir., anchor NewsCtr. 6, Dutchess County, NY, 1985-90; dir. media rels. Ctrl. Hudson Gas & Electric, Poughkeepsie, NY, 1993—, mgr. corp. comms., 1998-99, asst. v.p. corp. comm., 1999-2000, v.p. corp. comm. and cmty. rels., 2000—07; v.p., Pub. Affairs and Energy Efficiency. Adj. prof. Marist Coll., Poughkeepsie, NY. Co-author: Historic Beacon, 1998, Beacon Revisited, 2003. Councilwoman City of Beacon, 1992-93, chmn. 85th anniversary celebration; pres. Beacon Hist. Soc., 1989-94; bd. dirs. Locust Grove Hist. Site, Stony Kill Found., Inc.; chmn. Dutchess County United Way Campaign, 2005. Recipient Salute to Women in Bus. & Industry award D.C. YWCA, 1990, 97, Outstanding Chpt. Regent award N.Y. State orgn. DAR, 1999, Dutchess award, Dutchess County Hist. Soc., 2005; named Vol. of Yr. award, City of Beacon, 1999. Mem.: DAR (vice regent Melzingah chpt. 1990—98, regent 1998—2001, chmn. state historian com. NY state 1998—2001, nat. chmn. PR 1999—2004, NY State vice regent 2007—, editor-in-chief, Am. Spirit mag.), Greater So. Dutchess C. of C. (bd. dirs., chmn. 2007), Nat. Soc. Daus. of Union Vets. of the Civil War, Exch. Club of So. Dutchess (bd. dirs.). Republican. Roman Catholic. Avocations: genealogy, needlecrafts. Office: CH Energy Group Inc 284 South Ave Poughkeepsie NY 12601-4838

VAN BUREN, WILLIAM RALPH, III, lawyer; b. Newport News, Va., May 28, 1956; s. William Ralph Jr. and Anna Lee (Hite) Van B.; m. Kathryn Ann Moore, Dec. 31, 1983; children: Kathryn Meagan, Kaitlin Marie, William R. IV. BBA, Coll. William and Mary, 1978; JD, U. Va., 1981. Bar: Va. 1981. Ptnr. Kaufman & Canoles, Norfolk, Va., 1981—. Newport News, 1983-86; mem. Peninsula adv. bd. Investors Savs. Bank, 1988-91, asst. sec., bd. dirs. Daily Press, Inc., chmn., pres., Kanfroms Ctr. 2008-. Vice chmn. United Way Campaign, Norfolk, 1990; bd. dirs., Va. Opera, Norfolk, 1986-95, mem. exec. com., 1986-95; pres. Norfolk Planning Coun., 1987-98, mem. exec. com., 1987-98; trustee Chrysler Mus., Norfolk, 1995-2003, trustee Shenandoah U., 1992-98; trustee, Capital Campaign chair Norfolk Acad., 1998-; chmn. bd. Va. Coll. Fund, Richmond, 1987-91; pres. Norfolk Forum, 1999-2000, bd. dirs., 1989-2000; bd. dirs. Peninsula Fine Arts Ctr., 1990-93; bd. visitors Ea. Va. Med. Sch., 1996-2002, bd. dirs. Va. Fair Trial project, Cancer Care Found., Future of Hampton Roads, chmn. Ft. Norfolk Retirement Cmty, 2009-, Ameri Comm., LLC, Centrie Data LLC, founder and mem. Va. Bar Assn. Commn. Mem. ABA (comml. bus. and banking sect.), Va. Bar Assn. (chmn. young lawyers sect. 1991, pres. 2006), Va. Law Found. (pres. 2000), Am. Health Lawyers Assn., Norfolk-Portsmouth Bar Assn. (chmn. young lawyers sect. 1988-89, Norfolk Yacht and Country Club, James River Country Club. Episcopalian. Avocations: golf, skiing, sailing. Home: 1552 Blanford Cir Norfolk VA 23505-1707 Office: Kaufman & Canoles PO Box 3037 150 W Main St Norfolk VA 23514-3037 Office Phone: 757-624-3220. Business E-Mail: wrvanburen@kaufcan.com.

VANBUTSEL, MICHAEL R., real estate broker, construction executive; b. Alma, Nebr., Dec. 7, 1952; s. Julius and Margaret (McCorkle) VanB.; m. Susan Parsons; children: Jamie, Krysta, Alexis. BArch, U. Nebr., 1975. Lic. real estate broker Fla. V.p. devel. J.C. Nichols Co. Real Estate, St. Petersburg, Fla., 1987-96; pres. North Star Devel., St. Petersburg, 1996—; real estate mgr., designated broker Danka Office Imaging, 1998-99; v.p., project exec. Beers Skanska USA Bldg. Co., Tampa, Fla., 1999—2004; project mgr. Tower divsn. Taylor Woodrow Cmtys., 2004—06; v.p. The Beach Residences Condominiums The Ritz Carlton Beach Club, 2004—06; sr. project mgr. tower divsn. WCI Cmtys. Inc., Palm Beach Gardens, Fla., 2006—, sr. project mgr., resort singer island one bal harbour resort Rybovich Marina; project dir. BELK Bldg. Group, Ft. Lauderdale. Chair Environ. Devel. Commn., St. Petersburg, 2003-04; chair cmty. advancement coun. U. So. Fla., St. Petersburg, 1998—2004. Housing commr. City of Phoenix; mem. Paradise Valley Planning Com.; bd. dirs. Cmty. Water Leadership Program; chmn. facilities and strategic planning com. U. South Fla., St. Petersburg, 1999—2002, chmn. acad. planning com.; bd. dirs. Pinellas Econ. Devel. Coun.; vice-chair environ. adv. com. S.W. Fla. Water Mgmt. Dist., 2002—; Pinellas adv. bd. ARC; allocations com. United Way, 1998—2000; mem. Real Estate Investment Coun., St. Petersburg USA and Russia Birthday Commemoration, 2002—03, Pinellas County Transp. Task Force, Pinellas Redevel. Task Force; mem. CEO search com. U. South Fla., St. Petersburg; chair legis. affairs com. devel. coun. All Children's Hosp.; pres. Mariners for Sen. John McCain, Ariz.; surrogate spkr. for Congressman Eldon Rudd; mem. Senate roundtable Sen. Connie Mack, Fla.; Westside campaign chair Rick Baker for Mayor, 2001; mem. Ivory Club Pinellas County Rep. Party, 2001—05, Pinellas County Assembly, 2002; bd. dirs. Gran Prix St. Petersburg 2003 Found. Mem. Fla. Gulfcoast Comml. Assn. Realtors, Pinellas Leadership (mem. selection com. 2003), Leadership Tampa Bay, St. Petersburg C. of C. (chair environ. com., chair transp. com.), Valley Leadership (Phoenix), Precinct Com., Martin County, Fla., 2007, Martin Crossings (pres. 2007-), Hoa, Stuart, Fla. Republican. Avocations: geo-political books, tai chi. Home Phone: 941-776-9648; Office Phone: 407-834-2300. Personal E-mail: michaelvb4@yahoo.com.

VAN CALKER, DIETRICH O., psychiatrist, educator; s. Jan H. Van Calker and Anneliese Arndt; m. Heide Hecht Van Calker; 1 child, Carola. Diploma in Chemistry, U. Freiburg, Germany, 1973; PhD, Ludwig-Max U. Munich, 1977, MD, 1983. Cert. in approbation 1983, in psychotherapy Bd., 1992, in psychiatry 1993. Rsch. assoc. Max Planck Inst. Biochemistry, Munich, 1977—79; resident physician, dept. psychiatry Ludwig Max U. Munich, 1984—91, U. Freiburg, 1991—92, head physician, psychiatry, 1993—, asst. prof., psychiatry, 1998—2000, prof., psychiatry, 2000—, head, divsn. psychopharmacotherapy dept. psychiatry, 2007—. Rsch. grant, Deutsche Forschugsgemeinschaft, 1985—90, 1994—2008, Sander Found., 1994—97, Ministry Edn. & Rsch. Fed. Rep. Germany, 1996—97, Stanley Rsch. Found., 1999—2001. Mem.: Deutsche Gesellschaft Psychiatry, Psychotherapy and Nervenheilkunde, Collegium Internat. Neuropsychopharmacol, Deutsche Gesellschaft Biologische Psychiatry, German Soc. Bipolar Disorders, Internat. Soc. Bipolar Disorders, Internat. Group Study Lithium Treated Patients. Office: Univ Freiburg Dept Psychiatry Hauptstr 5 Freiberg D-79104 Germany Business E-Mail: dietrich.calker@uniklinik-freiburg.de.

VAN CAMP, BRIAN RALPH, judge; b. Halstead, Kans., Aug. 23, 1940; s. Ralph A. and Mary Margaret (Bragg) Van C.; m. Diane D. Miller, 1992; children: M. Megan, Laurie E. AB, U. Calif., Berkeley, 1962, LLB, 1965. Bar: Calif. 1966. Dep. atty. gen., Calif., 1965-67; agy. atty. Redevel. Agy., City of Sacramento, 1967-70; asst./acting sec. Bus. and Trans. Agy., State of Calif., 1970-71; commr. of corps. State of Calif., Sacramento, 1971-74; partner firm Diepenbrock, Wulff, Plant & Hannegan, Sacramento, 1975-77, Van Camp & Johnson, Sacramento, 1978-90; sr. ptnr. Downey, Brand, Seymour & Rohwer, 1990-97; judge Superior Ct. Calif., Sacramento County, 1997—. Lectr. Calif. Continuing Edn. Bar, Practicing Law Inst., Calif. CPA Soc., Calif. Ctr. for Jud. Edn. and Rsch.; mem. jud. adv. bd. Am. Enterprise Inst./Brookings Jud. Edn. Program, 2007—. Contbr. articles to profl. jours. Mem. Rep. State Ctrl. Com. Calif., 1974-78; mem. electoral coll. Presdl. Elector for State of Calif., 1976; mem. Calif. Health Facilities Fin. Authority, 1985-89; mem. Capital Area Devel. Authority, 1989-97, chmn., 1990-97; mem. Calif. Jud. Coun. Task Force on Quality of Justice, 1998-99, Jud. Coun. Adv. Com. on Civil and Small Claims Law, 2002—, chair subcom. uniform rules, 2004-08, chair Subcom. on Complex Litig., 2008-; bd. dirs. Sacramento Symphony Assn., 1973-85, Sacramento Symphony Found., 1993-2003, Sacramento Area Commerce and Trade Orgn., pres. 1986-87, Sacramento Valley Venture Capital Forum, 1986-90, League to Save Lake Tahoe, 1988-95, Valley Vision, Inc., 1993-97; elder Fremont Presbyn. Ch., 1967-. Recipient Sumner-Mering Meml. award Sacramento U. Calif. Alumni Assn., 1962, Thos. Jefferson award Am. Inst. Pub. Svc., 1994, Excellence in Achievement award Calif. Alumni Assn., 1997; named Outstanding Young Man of Yr., Sacramento Jaycees, 1970, Internat. Young Man of Yr., Active 20-30 Club Internat., 1973, Judge of Yr., Capitol City Trial Lawyers Assn., 2003. Mem. Am. Coll. Bus. Ct. Judges (charter), Boalt Hall Alumni Assn. (bd. dirs. 1991-94), Lincoln Club Sacramento Valley (bd. dirs. 1975-90, pres. 1984-86), U. Calif Men's Club (pres. 1968), Sutter Club, Kanadhar Ski Club, Rotary Club Sacramento (pres. 1993-94, Paul Harris Fellow award 1995), Comstock Club (pres. 1976-77). Republican. Presbyterian. Office: 720 9th St Sacramento CA 95814-1302 Office Phone: 916-874-8030. Business E-Mail: vancamp@saccourt.com.

VAN CAMPEN, STEPHEN BERNARD, executive recruiter, consultant; b. East Stroudsburg, Pa., Oct. 1, 1941; s. Bernard Allen and Marion (Van Whye) Van C.; m. Ellen Baars, July 22, 1989; children: Brendon, Regan, Meghan, Taylor, Hannah. BS in Sci. and Pre-Veterinary Med., Pa. State U., 1959-64; postgrad. in indsl. rels., George Washington U. Grad. Sch, 1965-68; law student, U. Balt., 1966-68. Lic. pvt. detective, pvt. investigator NJ, soria cert. NY State Police, cert. Homeland Security Worldwide Intelligence Svcs. With FDA, Balt., Washington, 1964-66; indsl. rels. officer Joseph E. Seagrams & Sons, Balt., NYC, San Francisco, 1966-72; worldwide dir. exec. staffing RCA/Hertz Corp., NYC, 1972-74; dir. internat. indsl. rels. Revlon Internat., NYC, 1974; pres., owner, cons. Gilbert & Van Campen Exec. Search, Internat. (subs.: J.B. Gilbert Assocs., Inc., Amtrade Assocs., Internat., GVC Fin. Svcs.), NYC, 1974—; past owner, pres. Lillagaard Hotel Corp., Ocean Grove, NJ, 1992—; owner N.J. Profl. Meeting Planners Group; chmn. No. Shore Region Convention and Vis. Bur., Encore Svcs., Hackettstown, NJ, 1999—; pres. spl. investigations and verificatiuons divsn. Van Campen Assoc. Internat., 2003—; pres. Van Campen Investigations and Armed Security Svcs., 2006—. Appointed to N.J. Gov.'s Commn. on Internat. Trade, 1992; Bush White House nominee to Nat. Parks Adv. Commn., Dept. Interior; chmn. internat. trade subcom. ad hoc N.J. Assembly Small Bus. Adv. Coun.; bd. dirs. N.J. SBDC, N.J. Shore Region Tourism Coun.; named to Commerce and Econ. Devel. Transition Team for Gov.-elect Christine Todd Whitman; chmn. Econ. Devel. Task Force, Warren County, N.J., 1994; participant in meetings. with Pres. Castro 1st U.S.-Cuba Bus. Summit, Havanna, 1998. Rep. fundraiser; active N.J. Rep. Gov.'s Club, N.J. State Fin. Com.; appointed to Congressman Zimmer's Warren County N.J. Fed. Adv. Com., Warren County Econ. Adv. Coun., N.J. Gov.'s appointee 1988— and chmn. fed. enacted Del. Water Gap Nat. Recreation Area citizens adv. com., Gov.-elect Christie Todd Whitman Transition Team-Commerce and Econ. Devel. and Tourism; elected to Warren County Rep. Com.; chmn. adv. bd. Warren Presdl. Correctional Facility; chmn. Calno Cemetery Assn.; chmn. Warner County Econ. Devel. Blue Ribbon Task Force; vice chmn. bd. trustees Warren County C.C., 1983—, chmn. found. bd., presdl. search com. 2003, ops. com. 2003, ambassador N.Y. Coun. Cmty. Colls.; exec. bd. Tri-County Washington coun. and George Washington coun. Boy Scouts Am.; bd. dirs. N.J. Shore Regional Tourism Coun., N.Y. dir. SBDC, N.J. Juvenile Justice Adv. Bd.; mem. 1st N.J. Trade Del. Soviet Union; mem. commerce and econ. devel. transition team Gov.-elect Christie Whitman, N.J., 1994; chmn. N.J. assembly bus. retention Com. of Task Force for Bus. Rentention, Attraction, Expansion and Internat. Trade; chmn. N.J. Gov.'s Conf. Travel and Tourism, Atlantic City, 1994; chmn. N.J. No. Shore Region CUB Allaire Airport Conv. Ctr.; pres.-elect Warren County Econ. Partnership. Recipient Medal of Honor, Ellis Island, 1994, Disting. Citizen award Boy Scouts Am., 1992. Mem. ASTD, Am. Mgmt. Assns., Am. Coun. on Germany, U.S. C. of C., Nat. Fgn. Trade Coun., World Trade Inst., U.S.-USSR Trade and Econ. Coun., N.Y. C. of C. and Industry, N.J. C. of C., Commerce and Industry Assn. N.J., Am. C. of C.s and U.S. Bus. Couns. Abroad, Soc. Human Resource Mgmt., Nat. Assn. Corp. and Profl. Recruiters, Employment Mgmt. Assn., N.J. Hotel/Motel Assn. (bd. dirs., mem. exec. bd.), N.J. Travel Industry Assn. (bd. dirs., v.p. exec. bd.), N.Y. Pers. Mgmt. Assn., Soc. Plastics Engrs., Soc. Cosmetic Chemists, Small Bus. Adv. Coun., Ocean Grove C. of C. (vice chmn.). Republican. Methodist. Home: 39 Petersburg Rd Hackettstown NJ 07840-4903 Office: Lynch Profl Bldg 108 High St Ste 213 Hackettstown NJ 07840 Office Phone: 908-852-4945. Personal E-mail: stevevancampen@goes.com.

VANCASTLE, ROBIN, bank executive; b. Dec. 18, 1953; BS in Acctg., Northern Ill. U., 1977. CPA. Pub. acct., 1979—90; dir. internal audit Cole Taylor Bank, 1990—93; grp. sr. v.p. fin. mgmt. Taylor Capital Group, Inc., 1993—2006, chief acctg. officer, 2006—07, CFO, 2007—. Office Phone: 847-653-7978.

VANCE, CYRUS ROBERTS, JR., lawyer; b. NYC, June 14, 1954; s. Cyrus Roberts and Grace Elsie (Sloane) Vance; m. Peggy Vance; 2 children. BA, Yale U., 1977; JD, Georgetown U., 1982. Bar: NY 1983, DC 1988, Wash. 1989. Asst. dist. atty. NY County Dist. Atty.'s Office, 1982—88; adj. prof. law Seattle U. Law Sch., 1990—2004; cons. Office of Family and Children Ombudsman; founding ptnr. McNaul Ebel Nawrot Helgren & Vance, PLLC, Seattle, 1995—2004; spl. asst. atty. gen. Wash. State; prin. Morvillo, Abramowitz, Grand, Iason, Anello & Bohrer, P.C., NYC, 2004—. Mem. Wash. State Sentencing Guidelines Commn., 1994—2002, Criminal Justice Act Oversight Com., Western Dist. Wash., 1995—, Jud. Screening Panel, First Dept., NY State Appellate Divsn., NY State Commn. on Sentencing Reform; bd. dirs. Fund for Modern Cts., Sargent Shriver Nat. Ctr. on Poverty Law; com. mem. Cyrus R. Vance Ctr. for Internat. Justice. Bd. dirs. Alzheimer's Drug Discovery Found.; co-chair bd. dirs. Seattle Symphony. Named one of NY Area's Best Lawyers, NY Mag., NY Super Lawyers, 2006, 2007, Best Lawyers in America, 2007. Mem.: NYC Coun. Def. Lawyers, Fed. Bar Coun., NYC Bar Assn. (mem. criminal justice coun.). Office: Morvillo Abramowitz Grand Iason Anello & Bohrer PC 565 Fifth Ave New York NY 10017 Office Phone: 212-880-9490. Business E-Mail: cvance@maglaw.com.*

VANCE, DAVID A., information systems educator; b. Anchorage, 1948; s. Alvin V. and Mary Vance; m. Nancy; children: John, Emily, Ryan. AA, Grossmont Coll., 1976; BBA, Nat. U., 1982, MBA, 1984, postgrad., 1985; PhD, So. Ill. U., 2000; postgrad., Trinity Sem., Ind., 2004—. Ordained to ministry United Christian Faith Ministries, 2002. Tech. supr. USN, San Diego, 1970-74; engr., project mgr. Wavetek Data Communications, San Diego, 1975-79; v.p. ops. Specialized Systems, Inc., San Diego, 1979-81; prin. Sunhill R&D, San Diego, 1981-84; exec. dir. Brunswick Inst. Tech., San Diego, 1985; tech. staff mem. Veda, Inc., Orlando, Fla. and San Diego, 1985-88; tng. analyst Eagle Tech., Inc., Winter Park, Fla., 1988-89; prof. mgmt. Fla. So. Coll., Orlando, 1988-94; tchr., student mgmt. doctoral program So. Ill. U., Carbondale, 1994-99; asst. prof. Miss. State U., 1999—2006; prof. info systems Olivet Nazarene U., 2007—; prin. DKD Property Mgmt., LLC, 2008—. Prin. DA Vance & Assocs., Winter Park, 1986-94; adj. prof. mgmt. Webster U., 1991-94, Fla. So. Coll., 1988-91; vis. asst. prof. So. Ill. U., 1991-94; lectr. in field. Rep. precinct committeeman, Orange County, Fla., 1988, del. state conv., 1988; chmn. svc. com. CSO, Inc., 1991. Recipient Achievement award ACCESS, San Diego, 1980; Worthy scholar Woodrow Wilson Found., 1966, Leadership scholar Nat. U., San

Diego, 1984. Mem.: Info. Resources Mgmt. Assn., Computer Profls. for Social Responsibility, Am. MENSA, Ltd. Avocations: outdoor sports, music. Office: Olivet Nazarene Univ Dept Bus Box 6041 Bourbonnais IL 60914

VANCE, DIANNE SANCHEZ, mathematician, educator; d. Thomas Clarence and Jean Rose Sanchez; 1 child, Jeney Michelle Sanchez. BA, Calif. State U., Fullerton, 1977; MEd, U. Utah, Salt Lake City, 1993. Tchr. Tahoe Truckee Sch. Dist., Calif., 1971—76, Wasatch Sch. Dist., Heber City, Utah, 1980—90; tennis coach Park City High Sch., 1993—98, tchr., 1990—2002; tchr., coord. English as 2d lang. Phillips Acad., Andover, Mass., 1991—2003; tchr. math. TED Kolej, Ankara, Turkey, 2002—03, Fulbright Exch. Park City Sch. Dist., 2003—. Vol. Sundance, Park City, 1995—2006; gate judge Olympics, 2002. Mem.: ASCD, Park City Edn. Assn. Avocations: travel, skiing, tennis, golf. Office: Park City Sch Dist 2700 Kearns Blvd Park City UT 84060 Business E-Mail: dvance@pcshools.us.

VANCE, JOYCE WHITE, prosecutor; b. 1960; m. Bob Vance; children: Robert Smith III, Edward Rodman, Eleanor Rainey, William Oliver. BA in Polit. Sci., Bates Coll., 1982; JD, U. Va. Sch. Law, 1985. Assoc. Bradley Arant Rose & White, Birmingham, Ala., 1988—91; asst. US atty. criminal divsn. US Dept. Justice, Birmingham, Ala., 1991—2002, asst. US atty. appellate divsn., 2002—09, US atty. (no. dist.) Ala., 2009—. Office: US Attorneys Office 1801 Fourth Ave Birmingham AL 35203 Office Phone: 205-244-2001. Office Fax: 205-244-2171.*

VANCE, RALPH BROOKS, SR., oncologist, educator; b. Jackson, Miss., Dec. 4, 1945; s. Brooks C. and Chrystine G. (Gober) V.; m. Mary Douglas Allen, June 18, 1979; children: Brooks, Barrett. BA in Biology and German, U. Miss., 1968, MD, 1972. Asst. prof. medicine U. Miss., Jackson, 1978—86, assoc. prof. medicine, 1986—93, prof. medicine, 1993—. Chief of staff U. Miss. Hosp. and Clinics, Jackson, 1989-90; pres. faculty senate Univ. Med. Ctr., Jackson, 1986-87, univ. clin. assoc., pres., 1987-89. Author (with others) Development in Molecular Virology: Herpes Virus DNA, 1982; contbr. numerous articles and abstracts to profl. jours. Nat. pres. Am. Cancer Soc., 2003—04, bd. dirs. Atlanta, nat. pres., exec. com.; bd. dirs. ARC, Jackson; bd. Blue Cross/Blue Shield Miss., Jackson, 1989—92. Named to Hall of Fame, U. Miss., 1968. Fellow ACP; mem. Am. Assn. for Cancer Edn., Am. Fedn. for Clin. Rsch., Am. Soc. Clin. Oncology, Am. Assn. for Cancer Rsch., Miss. Acad. Scis., S.W. Oncology Group, U. Miss. Alumni Assn.(bd-.dirs. 2009-), Sigma Xi. Office: U Miss Sch Medicine 2500 N State St Jackson MS 39216-4505 Office Phone: 601-984-5590. Business E-Mail: rvance@medicine.umsmed.edu.

VANCE, RODNEY, film producer, writer; s. Clifford and Bonnie Vance; 1 child, Chelsea. MA, Andrews U., Berrien Springs, Mich., 1981; MFA, Cath. U. Am., Washington, 1988. Pres. Singular Entertainment, Angwin, Calif., 2007—. Head writer: (TV series) The Evidence (Best New Religion/Ethics Show and Best New Pilot, 2001); Lifestyle Magazine (Telly award, 2001); prodr.: (screenplays) Operation Babylift, Conspiracy Cafe; prodr.: (TV series) Discovery; author: (films) Angel in Chains (Best in Category Sonscreen Film and Video Festival, 2004), In the Shadow of Bin Laden, (plays) Token (Judge's Choice award Edward Albee Internat. Playwrighting Competition, 1999), The Man, the Woman, the Indian. Mem.: Acad. TV Arts and Sciences, Writer's Guild of Am. West, Dramatist's Guild (assoc.), Mensa. Office: Singular Entertainment PO Box 338 Angwin CA 94508 Office Fax: 310-492-5563. Business E-Mail: rod@singularent.com.

VANCE, SUE ANN, musician, educator; b. Medicine Lodge, Kans., Aug. 16, 1937; d. Trice Hubert and Catherine O. (Stone) Newsom; m. Jerry Wayne Vance, Aug. 15, 1962 (dec.); children: Todd, Kayla Vance Ginnings. B in Music Edn., Wichita State U., Kans., 1959, M in Music Edn., 1962. Piano instr. Labette County Cmty. HS, Altamont, Kans., 1959—61; accompanist U. La., 1967—88; K-12 music instr. Deer Pub. Sch. Dist., Ark., 1991—2002; adj. piano instr., accompanist Ark. Tech. U., Russellville, 2002—07. Part-time instr. piano U. La., Monroe, 1978—86; organist various chs., Monroe, 1976—88; organist 1st Presbyn. Ch., Harrison, Ark., 1993—2003; asst. organist 1st Methodist and 1st Christian Chs., Harrison, 2007—; piano adjudicator Federated Music Clubs, Monroe, 1970—88; mem. Vance-White Duo piano team, Monroe, 1978—90. Pres. NW Ark. Concert Assn., Harrison, 1995—99. Recipient Naftzager Judges award, Wichita Symphony, 1958. Mem.: Alpha Phi & Mu Phi Epsilon Alum, Music Educators Nat. Conf., Nat. Guild Piano Tchrs. (piano adjudicator 1999—). Avocations: knitting, reading, sewing, crossword puzzles. Home: HC31 Box 393 Deer AR 72628

VANCE, VERNE WIDNEY, JR., retired lawyer; b. Omaha, Mar. 10, 1932; s. Verne Widney and June Caroline (Henckler) V.; m. Anita Paine, June 27, 1970; children: Lisa J. Castleton, Charles Hebard Paine, Virginia Caroline. AB, Harvard U., 1954, JD, 1957. Bar: D.C. 1957, Mass. 1964. Law clk. U.S. Dist. Judge, Mass., 1957-58; assoc. Covington & Burling, Washington, 1958-60; atty. adv. Devel. Loan Fund, Washington, 1960-61; legal counsel US AID, Washington, 1961-63; assoc. Foley, Hoag & Eliot LLP, Boston, 1963-67, ptnr., 1967-2000; ret., 2001. Lectr. law Boston U., 1964-66; corp. clk. S.S. Pierce Co., 1971-72. Pres. UN Assn. Greater Boston, 1966-66, 77-78, treas., 1974-77; mem. Mass. Adv. Council on Edn., 1969-75, chmn., 1975; mem. Dem. City Com., Newton, Mass., 1972—, Gov.'s Local Govt. Adv. Commn., 1986-90; alderman City of Newton, 1982-91, 2004—09; pres. Newton Bd. of Aldermen, 1988-91; pres., emeritus Newton Bd. Aldermen, 2004-09; mem. Newton Sch. Com., 1994-2001, chair 2000-01; trustee Judge Baker Children's Ctr., 1994—, clk., 2002--; trustee Mass. Bay C.C., 1987-98, vice chmn., 1989-91, chmn. 1991-97; pres. Mass. C.C. Assn., 1996-97. Contbr. articles to profl. jours. Bd. dirs. Newton-Needham C. of C., Boston Archtl. Ctr. Recipient Disting. Cmty. Svc. award, Mass. Bay CC, 1997. Democrat. Unitarian Universalist. Avocations: politics, art, reading, cooking, travel. Home: 101 Old Orchard Rd Chestnut Hill MA 02467-1202 Home (Summer): 185 Colony Rd Arkville NY 12406 Personal E-mail: vvance@rcn.com.

VANCO, JOHN L., art museum director; b. Erie, Pa., Aug. 21, 1945; s. John Jr. and Alice (Crozier) V.; m. Kathleen Merski, 1971; children: John H., Jesse L. BA, Allegheny Coll., 1967. Dir. Erie (Pa.) Art Mus., 1968—. Mem. adv. panels Pa. Coun. on the Arts, Harrisburg, 1974—, Mid Atlantic Arts Found., Balt., 1992, 2002, Nat. Endowment for Arts, 2000; curator Contemporary Music Series, 1982—, Erie Art Mus. Blues and Jazz Festival, 1992—. Photographer miscellaneous exhbns.; curator miscellaneous exhbns. including A Peculiar Vision: The Work of George Ohr, Eva Zeisel: The Shape of Life, The Mad Potter of Biloxi, From Mickey to the Grinch: Art of the Animated Film, Poems in Clay: Arthur Osborne's Plastic Sketches for the Low Art Tile Works, Teco: Art Pottery of the Prairie Sch., In Harmony with the Earth, Kanga & Kitenge: Cloth and Culture in East Africa, 2008; author: A Roycroft Desktop: Musings on Elbert Hubbard and the Roycroft Shops, 1994, Loud & Clear: Resonator Guitars and the Dopyera Brothers' Legacy to American Music, 1998, Structured Color: Kiyokatsu Matsumiya, 2003. Chief adminstrv. officer Discovery Square, Erie, 1991-92; bd. dirs. Pa. Humanities Coun., 2001—07, Pa. Fedn. Mus. and Hist. Orgns. Office: Erie Art Mus 411 State St Erie PA 16501-1106 Office Phone: 814-459-5477. Business E-Mail: jvanco@erieartmuseum.org.

VAN CURA, JOYCE BENNETT, librarian; b. Madison, Wis., Mar. 25, 1944; d. Ralph Eugene and Florence Marie (Cramer) Bennett; m. E. Jay Van Cura, July 5, 1986. BA in Liberal Arts (scholar), Bradley U., Peoria, Ill., 1966; MLS, U. Ill., Champaign-Urbana, 1971. Libr. asst. Rsch. Libr. Caterpillar Tractor Co., Peoria, Ill., 1966-67; ref. libr., instr. libr. tech. Ill. Ctrl. Coll., East Peoria, Ill., 1967-73; asst. prof. Sangamon State U. (U. Ill.-Springfield), Springfield, Ill., 1973-80, assoc. prof., 1980-86; head libr. ref. and info. svcs. dept. Ill. Inst. Tech., 1987-90; dir. Learning Resources Ctr. Morton Coll., 1990—2003. Reviewer Libr. Jour., Am. Ref. Books Ann.; convenor Coun. II, Ill. Clearinghouse for Acad. Libr. Instrn., 1978; presentor 7th Ann. Conf. Acad. Libr. Instrn., 1977, Nat. Women's Studies Assn., 1983, others; participant Gt. Lakes Women's Studies Summer Inst., 1981, Nat. Inst. Leadership Devel. seminar, 1995. Contbr. articles to profl. jours. Pres. Springfield chpt. NOW, 1978—79; invited Susan B. Anthony luncheon, 1978, 1979; mem. adv. bd. Suburban Libr. Sys., 1992—94, Nat. Commn. Learning Resources; v.p. membership Riverside chpt. Lyric Opera Chgo., 1994—96, 1999—, mem. chpts. exec. bd., 2006—; active Riverside Arts Ctr.; Dem. precinct Committeewoman, 1982—85; vice-moderator Fourth Presbyn. Women, 1989—90; elder Riverside (Ill.) Presbyn. Ch., 1992—, mem. session, 1993—96, 2000—01, mem. adminstrn. com., 1993—2003, chmn. adminstrn. com., 1993—96, 1999, 2000—01, mem. endowment com., 1996—98, bd. trustees, 2005—, sec. bd. trustees, 2005—; bd. dirs. Berwyn-Cicero Coun. on Aging, 2000—03. Ill. state scholar, 1962-66; recipient Citizenship award Am. Legion, 1962, Cert. of Recognition Ill. Bicentennial Commn., 1974. Mem.: AAUW (bd. dirs. Riverside br. 1992—94, 1997—99, chmn. standing com. on women Springfield br., com. on women Ill. state divsn.), ALA, Ill. Libr. Assn. (presenter 1984), Nat. Assn. Women in C.C., Springfield Art Assn., No. Ill. Learning Resources Consortium (del. 1990—2003, steering com. West Suburban postsecondary consortium 1996—2000), Nat. Women's Studies Assn. (presenter 1983, 1984, 1995), Women in Mgmt., Am. Mgmt. Assn., No. Ill. Learning Resources Consortium Bd. (del. 2006—), Spl. Librs. Assn., Ill. Assn. Coll. and Rsch. Librs. (bibliog. instrn. com.), Libr. Info. and Tech. Assn., Libr. Adminstr. and Mgmt. Assn. (ref. and adult svcs. divsn.), Assn. Coll. and Rsch. Librs., Opera Vols. America, Riverside Presbyn. Ch. Women (bd. trustees session, chair adult edn. com.), Nat. Trust Hist. Preservation, Am. Opera Soc., Lyric Opera of Chgo. (chpts. exec. bd. 2006—, sec. 2008—), Riverside Dancing Club, Riverside Garden Club, Musicians Club of Women Chgo., Beta Phi Mu. Home: 181 Scottswood Rd Riverside IL 60546-2221

VAN DAALEN, ALBERT A., religious minister, CEO; b. Middelburg, Zeeland, The Netherlands, Apr. 4, 1955; s. Albertus J. van Daalen and Catharina J. Dourlein; m. Jarmila Fernanda Thodé, May 12, 2006; children: Amadeus J., Talitha M. BRS, Belgian Bible Inst., Brussels, 1979; Lic.Min., Mennonite Theol. Sem., Amsterdam, 1994; Cand. PhD, U. Liverpool, 1997; Cand.DD, Am. Inst. Holistic Theol., 2007. Chmn. Albert A. van Daalen Ministries (Alvadam), Kruiningen, Netherlands, 1974—2007; master Chr Scholengemeenschap De Oudenoord, Utrecht, 1978—90, Chr. Vocational Sch. Vredeborch, Utrecht, 1990—92; pastor Mennonite Ch., Hilversum, 1992; adminstrn. exec. Nat. Coun. Chs. and Bible Orgns., Kortenhoef, 1993—2007; EDM & CEO Alvadam Assn., Found. & Co. For a Sustainable Soc., Huizen, 2008. Pub.: Dutch Mennonite Mag. Mem.: Dutch Pastors Union, Christian Dem. Appeal, Rotary Club Hilversum (hon.; past pres.). Mennonite. Office Phone: 31 35 656 1378. Business E-Mail: albertavandaalen@alvadam.com.

VANDAELE, BART, chef; Chef de cuisine Piet Huyentruyt, 1990—96; sous chef de cuisine Restaurant Scholteshof, 1996—97; exec. chef residence of Head Del. European Comm. to US, 1997—2000, Dutch Amb. to US, 2000—03, Belga Café, Washington. Contbr. The new generation: young chefs from Belgium, Original restaurants: Jan Maesen, Piet Huysentruyt: Eigentijds & Eigenzinng. Named one of Washington DC's Rising Stars, StarChefs.com, 2006. Office: Belga Cafe 514 8th St SE Washington DC 20003 Office Phone: 202-544-0100. Office Fax: 202-522-0204.

VAN DAM, HEIMAN, psychoanalyst; b. Leiden, Netherlands; s. Machiel and Rika van D.; m. Barbara C. Strona, Oct. 6, 1945; children: Machiel, Claire Ilena, Rika Rosemary. AB, U. So. Calif., 1942, MD, 1945. Fellow in child psychiatry Pasadena (Calif.) Child Guidance Clinic, 1950; gen. practice psychiatry and psychoanalysis LA, 1951—2006; instr. L.A. Psychoanalytic Inst., LA, 1959—2000, co-chmn. com. on child psychoanalysis, 1960-67, tng. and supervising psychoanalyst, 1972—; supr. child and adolescent psychoanalysis So. Calif. Psychoanalytic Inst., 1986—. Cons. Reiss Davis Child Study Center, 1955-76, Neighborhood Youth Assn., LA, 1964-69; assoc. clin. prof. psychiatry and pediats. UCLA Sch. Medicine, 1960-96, clin. prof. psychiatry and pediats., 1996—; vis. supr. child psychoanalysis San Francisco Psychoanalytic Inst., 1969-79, 2002—, Denver Psychoanalytic Inst., 1972-74; adv. bd. Western State U. Coll. Law, Fullerton, Calif., 1965-83. Corr. editor Arbeits Hefte Kinderanalyse, 1985—2005; contbr. articles to profl. jours. Trustee, edn. com. Center for Early Edn., 1964-92, v.p., 1978-79; bd. dirs. Child Devel. and Psychotherapy Tng. Program, LA, 1975-80, pres., 1975-77; bd. dirs. LA Child Devel. Center, 1977-86, treas., 1978-80; mem. cult clinic Jewish Family Service, L.A., 1978-86; bd. dirs. Lake Arrowhead Crest Estates, 1990-99. Capt. M.C. AUS, 1946-48. Mem. Am. Psychoanalytic Assn. (com. on ethics 1977-80), Assn. Child Psychoanalysis (councillor 1966-69, sec. 1972-74, nominating com. 1978-84, membership com. 1988—2005, Marianne Kris lectr. 1995), Internat. Assn. Infant Psychiatry (co-chmn. program com. 1980-83), Internat. Soc. Adolescent Psychiatry (sci. adv. com. 1988-2004), Phi Beta Kappa. Office: 2864 McConnell Dr Los Angeles CA 90064-4658 Office Phone: 310-839-3232. Business E-Mail: opa5x@ucla.edu.

VAN DAM, ROBERT M., epidemiologist, educator; MSc in Nutrition & Epidemiology, Wageningen U., 1998; PhD, Vrije U. Amsterdam Med. Sch., 2003. Researcher Nat. Inst. for Pub. Health & Environ., 1998—2002; asst. prof. nutrition & health Inst. for Health Sciences, 2002—; rsch. scientist Harvard Sch. Pub. Health, 2005—07; co-dir. epidemiology & genetics core Boston Obesity & Nutrition Rsch. Ctr., 2006—; assoc. epidemiologist Brigham & Women's Hosp., 2006—; asst. prof. Harvard Med. Sch., 2007—. Office: Harvard School Of Public Health 665 Huntington Ave Boston MA 02115 E-mail: rvandam@hsph.harvard.edu.*

VANDAME, JEAN-MARIE RICHARD, financial professional services firm executive; b. Gien, France, Oct. 30, 1960; s. Marc and Antoinette (Dumouchel de Premare) V.; m. Chantal Marie de Blocquel de Croix de Wismes, Sept. 3, 1983; children: Thomas, Camille, Clemence, Alix. MS, Inst. Super. Electronique, Paris, 1982; MBA, Inst. Adminstrn. Entreprises, Paris, 1984. Product mktg. engr. Tex Instruments, Paris, 1983-84, field sales engr. Rennes, France, 1984-86; sr. mgr. Ernst & Young, Paris, 1986—92, assoc. ptnr., 1995—96, internat. ptnr., 1996—2000; pres. KnowledgeWare, Brussels, 1992—95; v.p. CG Ernst & Young, Chgo., 2000—03; ptnr. Ernst & Young, Paris, 2004—. Home: 24 Avenue Theophile Gautier 75016 Paris France Home Phone: +33 145 24 23 93; Office Phone: +33 146 93 44 03. E-mail: jean-marie.vandame@fr.ey.com.

VANDAMENT, WILLIAM EUGENE, retired academic administrator; b. Hannibal, Mo., Sept. 6, 1931; s. Alva E. and Ruth Alice (Mahood) V.; m. Margery Vandament, Feb. 2, 1952; children: Jane Louise, Lisa Ann. BA, Quincy Coll., 1952; MS, So. Ill. U., 1953; MS in Psychology, U. Mass., 1963, PhD, 1964; LittD, No. Mich. U., 1997. Psychologist Bacon Clinic, Racine, Wis., 1954-61; NDEA fellow U. Mass., Amherst, 1961-64; asst. prof. SUNY, Binghamton, 1964-69, univ. examiner and dir. instl. research, 1969-73, asst. v.p. planning, instl. research, 1972-76; exec. asst. to pres., dir. budget and resources Ohio State U., Columbus, 1976-79, v.p. fin. and planning, 1979-81; sr. v.p. adminstrn. NYU, NYC, 1981-83; provost, vice chancellor acad. affairs Calif. State U. System, Long Beach, 1983-87; Trustees prof. Calif. State U., Fullerton, 1987-92; pres. No. Mich. U., 1991-97, ret., 1997. Contbr. articles to psychol. jours. and books on higher edn. Office: 2662 E 20th St Apt 310 Signal Hill CA 90755 E-mail: vandament@aol.com.

VAN DE BOGART, DEBRA SCHERWERTS, medical/surgical nurse, researcher; b. Claremont, NH, Aug. 6, 1954; d. William Earl and Barbara Louise (Hadley White) Scherwerts. RN, Sacred Heart Sch. Nursing, Manchester, NH, 1975; student, Cypress Coll., Calif., 1976, U. Calif., Riverside, 1978. RN Calif., 1975, cert. home health nurse, Calif., 1997. Charge nurse, med.-surg. pediat. West Anaheim Cmty. Hosp., Anaheim, Calif., 1975—84; charge nurse, med.-surg. geriat. Humana West Anaheim, Anaheim, Calif., 1984—87; home health nurse, obstet. Physician's Care, Brea, Calif., 1988—90, Am. Home Health, Santa Ana, Calif., 1988—92; staff nurse, rsch. clin. studies ctr. Harbor-UCLA Med. Ctr., Torrance, Calif., 1993—94; nurse rschr. various profit and non-profit orgns., Anaheim, Calif., 1994—, RN coord., cons., 1994—. Contbr. workshop Focus on Health, 1982; mem. citizens adv. com., health Calif. State Assembly, 1982—; cons., home care for MD's Am. Home Health We. Med. Ctr., Santa Ana, 1991—; RN clin. advisor, staff devel. Cmty. Svcs. Projects, Orange and LA Counties, 2000—. Recipient cert. of recognition, Calif. State Legis., 1982. Mem.: ANA, Assn. Am. Acad. Bereavement, Sigma Theta Tau. Democrat. Roman Catholic. Avocations: violin, travel.

VANDEBROEK, SOPHIE VERDONCKT, printing company executive; b. Leuven, Belgium, Feb. 17, 1962; came to U.S., 1986; d. Norbert and Jeanine (Ringoir) V.; m. Bart Vandebroek, Aug. 2, 1986 (dec. Aug. 1996); children: Elena, Arno, Jonas. B in Engring. magna cum laude, Katholieke U., 1982, MS in Electro-Mech. Engring. magna cum laude, 1985; PhDEE in Microelectronics, Cornell U., 1990. Devel. staff mem. IBM T.J. Watson Rsch. Ctr., Yorktown Heights, NY, 1990-92; competency leader J.C. Wilson Ctr. for Rsch. and Tech., Xerox, Webster, NY, 1992-95, lab. mgr., 1995-96; platform mgr. Ink-Jet Supplies Bus. Unit Xerox Corp., Webster, 1996-97, mgr. document systems coherence program, 1997-98, tech. advisor Office of the Chmn., 1998-99, chief engineer Stamford, Conn., 2002—06, corp. v.p., 2006—, chief tech. officer, 2006—; v.p. Xerox Rsch. Ctr. Can., 1999—2000, Xerox Engring. Ctr., 2002—06; pres. Xerox Innovation Group, 2006—; chief tech. officer Carrier Corp., 2000—02. Bd. dirs. Analogic Corp., 2008—. Contbr. articles to profl. jours. Fulbright fellow, 1986; hon. grad. fellowship Belgian-Am. Ednl. Found., 1986; internat. travel grant Belgium Nat. Sci. Found., 1986-87; recipient Monsanto award 1986, Kieckhefer Adirondack award 1986; named one of Most Influential Women in Technology, Fast Company, 2009. Fellow IEEE; mem. IEEE Electron Devices Soc. (adminstrv. com. 1995-97, internat. electron device meeting 1994-98, tech. program com. 1994-95, chair solid state devices com. 1996, publicity chair 1998, chair Rochester chpt. IEEE/EDS 1994, disting. lectr. 1994). Avocations: reading, skiing, kayaking, rollerblading. Office: Xerox Corp 800 Long Ridge Rd Stamford CT 06904

VAN DECKER, WILLIAM ARTHUR, cardiologist; b. Passaic, NJ, May 27, 1957; s. William and Louise Adelaide (Meli) Van D.; m. Generosa Grana; children: Stephanie, William, Christopher. BS in Biology summa cum laude, Fairfield U., Conn., 1979; MD, Georgetown U., 1983. Diplomate Am. Bd. Internal Medicine, Cert. Bd. Nuclear Cardiology, Am. Bd. Cardiovascular Diseases; Am. Soc. Echocardiography spl. competency testing, Bd. Cardiovascular CT. Intern Temple U. Hosp., Phila., 1983—84, resident internal medicine, 1984—86, cardiology fellow, 1986—88, non-invasive cardiology imaging tng./rsch. fellow, 1988—89; assoc. dir. Non-Invasive Imaging, dir. Cardiology Clinic Med. Coll. Pa. Hosp.-Drexel U. Coll. Medicine, Phila., 1989—2004, asst. prof. medicine and cardiology, 1989—2004, dir. Heart Sta., 1990—2004; assoc. prof. medicine Temple U., Phila., 2004—. Mem. com. on radiation safety, 1990-2004, chmn. 1993-2004, mem. pharmacy and therapeutics com., 1992-2004, chmn. pharmacy and therapeutics com. 1993-2004, mem. continuing med. edn. com., 1992-96, vice-chmn. quality assurance com., 1993-2004, group leader freshman bioethics, 1992-95, med. student advisor, 1992-2004; presenter in field, bd. dirS. Cert. Bd. Nuclear Cardiology, 2003-08 Manuscript Peer reviewer Annals of Internal Medicine, 1993—; contbr. articles to profl. jours. Fellow Am. Heart Assn., Am. Coll. Cardiology, Am. Coll. Chest Physicians; mem. AMA, ACP, Am. Soc. Echocardiography, Am. Fedn. Med. Rsch.(ea. sect. chair 2001-2002), Pa. Med. Soc., Soc. Nuc. Medicine, Am. Assn. Nuc. Cardiology (founder), Am. Soc. Nuc. Cardiology (founder, bd. dirs., chmn. membership com. 2000—, bd. dirs. cert. bd. 2002—, nat. v.p. 2003-, pres. 2008), Soc. Cardiovasc. Magnetic Resonance (founding mem.), Philadelphia County Med. Soc. (ho. of dels. 1996—, bd. dirs. 2002—), Alpha Epsilon Delta, Alpha Omega Alpha, Phil County Med. Soc.(pres., 2008) Office: Temple Univ Hosp 3401 North Broad St Philadelphia PA 19140 Office Phone: 215-707-3347. Business E-Mail: vandecwa@tuhs.temple.edu.

VANDEGRIFF, KIM DENISE, biochemist; b. Roswell, N.Mex., Apr. 24, 1955; d. Howe Lee and Bette Jane (O'Bryant) V. BS in Biology, U. Houston, 1978; PhD in Biochemistry, Rice U., 1984. NIH fellow Rice U., Houston, 1980-84, instr., 1984-86; rsch. biochemist, prin. investigator Letterman Army Inst. Rsch., Presidio of San Francisco, Calif., 1986-93; rsch. assoc. dept. medicine U. Calif., San Diego, 1993—. Editor: Methods in Enzymology; contbr. articles to profl. jours. Recipient rsch. assoc. award NRC, 1986. Mem. AAAS (assoc. editor Science 1987), Internat. Soc. Oxygen Transport to Tissues, Biophys. Soc., Phi Kappa Phi (disting. grad. sr.), Iota Sigma Phi, Phi Lambda Upsilon, Sigma Xi (grad. merit award 1985). Achievements include derivation of 3-dimensional math. models that describe oxygen transport by red blood cells; description of mechanism of oxygen binding to product being examined as blood substitute. Office: Sangart Inc 6175 Lusk Blvd San Diego CA 92121 Office Fax: 858-450-2499. Business E-Mail: kvandegriff@sangart.com.

VANDE HEY, JAMES MICHAEL, retired air force officer; b. Maribel, Wis., Mar. 15, 1916; s. William Henry and Anna (Zimmerman) VandeH.; m. Jean Margretta Schilleman, June 23, 1944; children: James

Todd, Dale Michael, Dean Clark. Student, U. Wis., 1947-49; BA, U. Philippines, 1955; postgrad., Air War Coll., Maxwell AFB, Montgomery, Ala., 1956-57. Commd. 2d lt. USAAF, 1941; advanced through grades to brig. gen. USAF, 1967; fighter pilot PTO, 1941-45; including Hawaii, Dec. 7, 1941; duty in command and USAF level including duty in Europe (NATO) and Philippines, 1945-69; dep. chief of staff Hdqrs. USMACV, Saigon, Vietnam, 1969-71; assigned Hdqrs. Tactical Air Command, 1971—; mem. faculty Air War Coll., 1957-59, dep. for acads., dean of faculty, 1959-61; ret., 1971; pres. Vanson Inc., 1971—, Vande Hey Inc., 1976—. Decorated D.S.M., Legion of Merit with two oak leaf clusters, D.F.C. with two oak leaf clusters, Bronze Star, Air medal with 7 oak leaf clusters, decorations from Philippine, Vietnamese and Korean govts. Mem. USAF Hist. Found., Air Force Assn., Pearl Harbor Survivors Assn., Iwo Jima Survivors Assn. Roman Catholic. Home: 495 Covered Brg Schertz TX 78154-3642

VAN DE KAMP, JOHN KALAR, lawyer; b. Pasadena, Calif., Feb. 7, 1936; s. Harry and Georgie (Kalar) Van de K.; m. Andrea Fisher, Mar. 11, 1978; 1 child, Diana. BA, Dartmouth Coll., 1956; JD, Stanford U., 1959. Bar: Calif. 1960. Asst. US atty., LA, 1960—66; US atty., 1966—67; dep. dir. Exec. Office for US Attys., Washington, 1967—68, dir., 1968—69; spl. asst. Pres.'s Commn. on Campus Unrest, 1970; fed. pub. defender LA, 1971—75; dist. atty. LA County, 1975—83; atty. gen. State of Calif., 1983—91; ptnr. Dewey Ballantine, LA, 1991—96, of counsel, 1996—; pres. Thoroughbred Owners, Calif., 1996—2004. Mem. Calif. Dist. Attys. Assn. (pres. 1982), Nat. Dist. Attys. Assn. (v.p. 1975-83), Peace Officers Assn. LA County (past pres.), Nat. Assn. Attys. Gen. (exec. com. 1983-91), Conf. Western Attys. Gen. (pres. 1986), State Bar Calif. (bd. govs. 2001-04, pres. 2004-05), Calif. Commn. Fair Adminstrn. of Justice (chair 2006-08). Office: Dewey & LeBoeuf LLP 333 So Grand Ave Ste 2600 Los Angeles CA 90071-1530 Office Phone: 213-621-6511. Business E-Mail: jvandekamp@dl.com.

VANDE KOPPLE, WILLIAM JOHN, literature and language professor; b. Grand Rapids, Mich., Dec. 16, 1949; s. Roger James and Wilma Jane Vande Kopple; m. Wanda Beth Vande Kopple, July 25, 1980; children: Jonathan, Joel, Jason. BA, Calvin Coll., Grand Rapids, 1972; MA, U. Chgo., 1973, PhD, 1980. English tchr. Illiana Christian H.S., Lansing, Ill., 1973—80; English prof. Calvin Coll., Grand Rapids, Mich., 1980—. Author: Clear and Coherent Prose, 1986, The Catch, 2004; co-author (with Gary Schmidt): Communities of Discourse, 1993. Mem.: Conf. on Coll. Composition and Comm., Nat. Coun. Tchrs. English. Avocations: fishing, hiking, photography. Office: Calvin College English Dept 3201 Burton St SE Grand Rapids MI 49507

VANDELL, KERRY DEAN, real estate consultant, educator, director, finance educator; b. Biloxi, Miss., Jan. 8, 1947; s. Benedict Sandy and Eleanor Ruby (Lenhart) V.; m. Deborah Ann Lowe, May 16, 1970; children: Colin Buckner, Ashley Elizabeth. BA, MME, Rice U., 1970; M City Planning, Harvard U., 1973; PhD, MIT, 1977. Assoc. engr. Exxon Co., USA, Houston, 1970-71; asst. prof. So. Meth. U., Dallas, 1976-80, assoc. prof., 1980-86, prof., chmn. dept., 1986-89; prof. real estate and urban land econs., chm. dept. U. Wis., Madison, 1989-93, dir. Ctr. for Urban Land Econs. Rsch., 1991—2004, Tiefenthaler chair holder, 1996—2006; exec. dir. Bolz Ctr. Arts Adminstrn., Madison, 2000—05; deans prof. fin., dir. Ctr. Real Estate Paul Merage Sch. Bus. U. Calif.-Irvine, 2006—, prof. law, prof. planning policy design. Vis. assoc. prof. Harvard U., Cambridge, Mass., 1985-86; vis. prof. U. Calif., Berkeley, 1988-89, U. Hong Kong, 1997. Mem. editl. bd. Jour. Real Estate Fin. and Econs., 1989—, Land Econs., 1989—, Jour. Property Rsch., 1989-94, Real Estate Econs., 1980—, Internat. Real Estate Rev., 2002—; contbr. numerous articles on mortgage default risk, real estate liquidity, housing market behavior, econs. of architecture, and appraisal theory to profl. jours. Fellow Homer Hoyt Advanced Studies Inst. (faculty 1989—); mem. Urban Land Inst., Am. Real Estate and Urban Econs. Assn. (2nd v.p. 1989, 1st v.p. 1990, pres. 1991, co-editor jour. 1991-96), Asian Real Estate Soc. (bd. dirs. 2002—), Am. Real Estate Soc. Episcopalian. Office: U Calif Irvine Paul Merage Sch Bus Irvine CA 92697 Home: 2658 Victoria Dr Laguna Beach CA 92651 Office Phone: 949-824-1985. Business E-Mail: kvandell@uci.edu.

VAN DEMAN, BARRY ALAN, museum administrator; b. Chgo., May 5, 1950; s. Frank B. and Arlene Van Deman. BA, Lewis Coll., 1972; MS in Edn., No. Ill. U., 1978. Tchr. St. John Sch., Winfield, Ill., 1972-79; instr. No. Ill. U., DeKalb, 1979-81; coord. instrn. Summit Hill Pub. Schs., Frankfort, Ill., 1981-83; dir. sci. and edn. Mus. Sci. and Industry, Chgo., 1983—90; dir. Internat. Mus. Surg. Sci., Chgo., 1990—96; v.p. programs and sci. Orlando Sci. Ctr., Fla.; pres., CEO Mus. of Life and Sci., Durham, NC, 2004—. Cons. Harcourt Brace and Co., Orlando, Fla., Chgo. Botanic Garden, Jour. Films, Chgo. Author: Science Any-time, 1995, Nuts & Bolts, 1980; contbr. articles to profl. jours. Mem. Am. Assn. Mus., Nat. Sci. Tchrs. Assn. (Exemplary Elem. Teaching award 1976), Coun. for Elem. Sci. Internat. (pres. 1985-86, Outstanding Svc. award 1981). Avocations: writing, photography. Office: Mus Life and Sci 433 Murray Ave PO Box 15190 Durham NC 27704

VAN DEN BERG, BERT, biology professor, researcher; b. Nijmegen, Gelderland, Netherlands, Apr. 11, 1967; s. Chris van den Berg and Corrie Roza; m. Ildiko Barthos, Feb. 6, 1999. MS, Utrecht U., Netherlands, 1990, PhD, 1994. Postdoc. rschr. U. Oxford, Oxfordshire, England, 1995—2000, Harvard Med. Sch., Boston, 2000—04; asst. prof. U. Mass. Med. Sch., Worcester, 2004—. Contbr. scientific papers to rsch. publs. Achievements include discovery of structure of the protein translocation channel; structure of an outer membrane fatty acid transporter. Office: Univ Mass Med Sch 373 Plantation St Ste 115 Worcester MA 01605 Office Fax: 508-856-4289. Business E-Mail: bert.vandenberg@umassmed.edu.

VANDENBERG, BYRON F., cardiologist; b. Sacramento, Aug. 15, 1953; s. John Byron and Jeannette Vandenberg; m. Anne Carroll. BA, Occidental Coll., 1975; MD, Georgetown U., 1980. Diplomate cert. Bd. of Nuc. Cardiology, cert. in internal medicine, in cardiology, in echocardiography, in lipidology. Intern, resident Parkland Hosp., Dallas, 1980-83; fellow Med. Coll. Va., 1983—85, U. Iowa, 1985—86; mem. faculty U. Iowa Coll. Medicine, Iowa City, 1986—97, 2008—; cardiologist Prairie Cardiovascular Cons., Springfield, Ill., 1997—2003, Northern Calif. Cardiology Assoc., Sacramento, 2003—08. Med. dir. adult echocardiography lab. Prairie Heart Inst., Springfield, 1997-2003; mem. editl. bd. Am. Jour. Cardiology, Dallas, 1997-2006. Contbr. articles to profl. jours. Named Best Drs. in Am., Woodward/White, 2001-02, 05-06, 07-08, 09-. Fellow ACP, Am. Coll. Cardiology, Am. Heart Assn., Am. Soc. Echocardiography. Office: Univ Iowa Coll Medicine Divsn Cardiovasc Medicine 200 Hawkins Dr Iowa City IA 52242

VANDENBERG, EDWARD V., geriatrician, educator; b. David City, Nebr., Nov. 29, 1950; s. Ben and Betty Vandenberg; m. Marie Vandenberg, Dec. 27, 1973; children: Katherine Twenter, Quinn. MD, U. Nebr. Med. Ctr., 1976. Cert. med. dir. Am. Med. Dirs. Assn., 1987. Assoc. prof. U. Nebr. Med. Ctr., Omaha, 1998—. Med. dir. Amazing Angels hospice, Omaha, 2008—09. Contbr. articles to profl. jours. Recipient Shining Star award, Nebr. hospice & palliative care, 2005. Achievements include improving end-of-life care in nursing homes. Office: Univ Nebraska Med Ctr 981320 Nhc Omaha NE 68198-1320

VAN DEN BERG, SARA JANE, language educator; b. St. Paul, May 19, 1942; d. Henry John and Edith Ann (Hutchins) Streich; m. Kent Talbot van den Berg, June 11, 1976; 1 child, David Talbot. BA summa cum laude, U. Minn., 1964; MA, Yale U., 1965, PhD, 1969. Instr. Fordham U., NYC, 1968-70; asst. prof. Fairfield (Conn.) U., 1970-73, Occidental Coll., LA, 1973-76, Ohio State U., Columbus, 1976-80, U. Wash., Seattle, 1980-87, assoc. prof. English, 1987—2000, chmn. curricular policy bd., 1996-98; prof. English St. Louis U., 2000—, chmn. English dept., 2000—, Dorothy McBride Orthwein prof., 2004—05; dir. Walter J. Ong. S Ctr. Lang. and Culture, St. Louis, 2007—. Mem. editl. bd. Modern Lang. Quar., 1995-2000, Ben Jonson Jour., 1995—, (Discoveries award, 2009), Psyart: Jour. Psychology and the Arts, 1997—, Conversations, 2004-07, Explorations in Media Ecology, 2005-, Appositions, 2008-; author: The Action of Ben Jonson's Poetry, 1987. Huntington Libr. fellow, 1987, NEH fellow, 1987, 2003. Mem. MLA (divsn. lit. and psychology 1990-94, chmn. 1992-93), Renaissance Soc. Am., Milton Soc. Am., Pacific Ancient and Modern Lang. Assn. (exec. com. 1997-99), Phi Beta Kappa. Office: St Louis U Dept English 3800 Lindell Blvd Saint Louis MO 63108 Office Phone: 314-977-3010.

VAN DEN BERGH, SIDNEY, astronomer; b. Wassenaar, Netherlands, May 20, 1929; emigrated to U.S., 1948; s. Sidney J. and Mieke (van den Berg) vandenB.; m. Paulette Brown; children by previous marriage: Peter, Mieke, Sabine. Student, Leiden U., The Netherlands, 1947-48; AB, Princeton U., 1950; M.Sc., Ohio State U., 1952; Dr. rer. nat., Goettingen U., 1956, DSc (honoris causa), 1995, DSc (honoris causa), 2001. Asst. prof. Perkins Obs., Ohio State U., Columbus, 1956-58; research assoc. Mt. Wilson Obs., Palomar Obs., Pasadena, Calif., 1968-69; prof. astronomy David Dunlap Obs., U. Toronto, Ont., Canada, 1958-77; dir. Dominion Astrophys. Obs., Victoria, B.C., 1977-86; prin. rsch. officer NRC Can., 1977-98, rschr. emeritus, 1998—. Adj. prof. U. Victoria, 1977—2009. Decorated officer Order of Can. Fellow Royal Soc. London; mem. am., Royal Astron. Soc. (assoc.), Canadian Astronomy Soc. (sr. v.p. 1988-90, pres. 1990-92). Home: 418 Lands End Rd Sidney BC Canada V8L 5L9 Office Phone: 250-363-0006. Business E-Mail: sidney.vandenbergh@nrl.com, sidney.vandenbergh@nrc.ca.

VANDENBERGHE, JAMES H., manufacturing executive; BBA, Western Mich. U., Kalamazoo; MBA, Wayne State U., Detroit. Fin. analyst Lear Siegler, Inc., 1973, v.p. fin. plastics divsn., v.p. ops. gen. seating divsn.; sr. v.p. fin., CFO, sec. Lear Corp., Southfield, Mich., 1988-93, exec. v.p. fin., CFO, 1993-97, pres., COO N.Am. ops., 1997-98, vice-chmn., CFO, 1998—2007, vice-chmn., 2007—. Bd. dirs. DTE Energy. Bd. trustees Coll. Creative Studies; bd. visitors Wayne State U. Sch. Bus.; bd. dirs. United Way Southeastern Mich. Office: Lear Corp 21557 Telegraph Rd Southfield MI 48034-4248

VAN DEN BERGHE, PIERRE LOUIS, sociologist; b. Lubumbashi, Congo, Jan. 30, 1933; s. Louis and Denise (Caullery) van den B.; m. Irmgard C. Niehuis, Jan. 21, 1956; children: Eric, Oliver, Marc. BA, Stanford U., 1952, MA, 1953; PhD, Harvard U., 1960. Asst. prof. sociology Wesleyan U., Middletown, Conn., 1962-63; asso. prof. sociology SUNY, Buffalo, 1963-65; prof. sociology and anthropology U. Wash., Seattle, 1965-98, prof. emeritus, 1998—. Vis. prof. U. Natal, South Africa, 1960-61, Sorbonne, Paris, 1962, U. Nairobi, Kenya, 1967-68, U. Ibadan, Nigeria, 1968-69, U. Haifa, Israel, 1976, U. New South Wales, Australia, 1982, U. Strasbourg, France, 1985, U. Tuebingen, Germany, 1986, Tel Aviv U., 1988, U. Cape Town, South Africa, 1989, U. Ljubljana, Slovenia, 2005; fellow Advanced Study in Behavioral Scis., Stanford, Calif., 1984-85. Author: 22 books including South Africa, A Study in Conflict, 1965, Race and Racism, 1967, Academic Gamesmanship, 1970, Man in Society, 1978, Human Family Systems, 1979, The Ethnic Phenomenon, 1981, Stranger in Their Midst, 1989, State Violence and Ethnicity, 1990, The Quest for the Other, 1994. Served with M.C. U.S. Army, 1954-56. Mem. Am. Sociol. Assn., Am. Anthrop. Assn., Sociol. Rsch. Assn., Human Behavior and Evolution Soc. Home: 2006 19th Ave E Seattle WA 98112-2902 Office: U Wash Dept Sociology 353340 Seattle WA 98195-3340 Office Phone: 206-543-2051. Business E-Mail: plvdb@u.washington.edu.

VAN DEN BOSCH, MARGARETA, apparel company executive; Grad., Beckman's Sch. Design; educated as a profl. tailor, St. Göran's Sch., Stockholm. Designer, Italy, 1976—88; head of design H&M Hennes & Mauritz AB, 1988—. Head of design complete off-stage wardrobe for Team Madonna on Confessions World Tour, 2006. Named one of 25 Masters of Innovation, BusinessWeek. Office: H&M Hennes & Mauritz AB Regeringsgatan 48 SE-106 38 Stockholm Sweden

VANDEN BOUT, PAUL ADRIAN, astronomer, physicist, educator; b. Grand Rapids, Mich., June 16, 1939; s. Adrian and Cornelia (Peterson) Vanden B.; m. Rachel Ann Eggebeen, Sept. 1, 1961; children: Thomas Adrian, David Anton AB, Calvin Coll., 1961; PhD, U. Calif.-Berkeley, 1966. Postdoctoral fellow U. Calif., Berkeley, 1966-67, Columbia U., NYC, 1967-68, instr., 1968-69, asst. prof., 1969-70, U. Tex., Austin, 1970-74, assoc. prof., 1974-79, prof., 1979-84; dir. Nat. Radio Astronomy Obs., Charlottesville, Va., 1985—2002, sr. sci., 2003—; dir. Atacama Large Millimeter Array, Charlottesville, Va., 2002—03. Cons. NSF, NASA, NRC. Fellow Fulbright Found., Heidelberg, Fed. Republic Germany, 1961-62, Leiden, Netherlands, 1977 Fellow AAAS, Am. Phys. Soc.; mem. Am. Astron. Soc., Internat. Astron. Union, Internat. Radio Sci. Union. Office: Nat Radio Astronomy Obs 520 Edgemont Rd Charlottesville VA 22903-2454 Office Phone: 434-296-0231. Business E-Mail: pvandenb@nrao.edu.

VAN DEN HENDE, FRED J(OSEPH), human resources executive; b. Chgo., Sept. 28, 1953; s. Maurice Everett and Alice Helen (Davey) Van Den H.; m. Sharon Joyce Kucharski, Oct. 4, 1975; children: John Michael, Karen Michelle. BA in Secondary Edn. and Social Sci., DePaul U., Chgo., 1975; grad., U. Wash. Sch. Exec. Dev., Seattle, 1981; MS in Human Resource Mgmt. and Devel., Nat. Louis U., Evanston, Ill., 1998. Cert. sr. profl. human resources. Asst. v.p. human resources Land of Lincoln Savs. and Loan, Berwyn, Ill., 1977-84; v.p. human resources Uptown Fed. Bank FSB, Niles, Ill., 1984-88; dir. human resources Archdiocese of Chgo., 1988—. Mem. Savs. Assn. Pers. Adminstrn., Berwyn, 1977-84; part-time instr. Inst. Fin. Edn., Chgo., 1984-90, Moraine Valley C.C., Palos Hills, Ill., 1984-90; adj. prof. Coll. Mgmt. and Bus., nat. Louis U., 1998-, Coll. Commerce, Dept. Mgmt., Kellstadt Graduate Sch. Bus., De Paul U., 2006-, Sch. of Leadership, Duquesne U., Pitts., Pa., 2007-; cons. in field 1990- Sch. bd. treas. St. Rene Sch., Chgo., 1981; sch. bd. mem. St. Daniel the Prophet Sch., Chgo., 1986-88, 93-95, sch. bd. chmn., 1988-89; boy scout leader St. Daniel Parish, Chgo., 1987-94; coach, track, St. Rene Sch., 1979-81, Vittum Park boys' baseball, 1989-92, boys' basketball, St. Daniel the Prophet Sch., 1991-95, basketball coord., 1995-96; meet official Conf. USA Indor Track and Field Championships, 2000, Conf. USA Cross-Country Championship, 2004. Recipient Oustanding Achievement in the Field of Athletics award St. Rita H.S. Alumni Assn., Chgo., 1991; Athletic scholar DePaul U., Chgo., 1971-75. Mem. Nat. Assn. Ch. Pers. Adminstrs., Soc. for Human Resource Mgmt. (mem. sch.-to-work com. 1998-2000), Ill. State C. of C. (human resources com. 1979-2003, healthcare com. 1998-2003), Inst. Internat. Human Resources, Am. Mgmt. Assn. (Chicago Area Tng. Coun. 2001—), Soc. for Human Resource Profls. (edn. adv. com. 2002—), KC (4th degree). Roman Catholic. Avocations: camping, fishing, coaching youth sports teams, horseback riding. Home: 5130 S Mulligan Ave Chicago IL 60638-1316 Office: Archdiocese Chgo 835 N Rush St Chicago IL 60611 Office Phone: 312-534-5352. Business E-Mail: fvandenhende@archchicago.org.

VANDEN HEUVEL, KATRINA, publishing executive, editor; b. NYC, Oct. 7, 1959; d. William Jacobus and Jean Babette (Stein) Vanden H.; m. Stephen F. Cohen, Dec. 4, 1988; 1 child, Nicola Anna. BA summa cum laude in Politics, Princeton U., 1982. Prodn. assoc. ABC Closeup Documentaries, 1982-83; asst. editor The Nation, NYC, 1984-89, editor-at-large, 1989-93, acting editor-in-chief, 1994-95, editor-in-chief, 1995—, and pub., gen. ptnr., 2005—. Vis. journalist Moscow News, 1989; Moscow coord. Conf. Investigative Journalism After the Cold War, 1992; co-founder, co-editor Vyi i Myi, 1990—. Editor: The Nation, 1865-1990; The Best of the Nation, 1990-2000: Selections from the Independent Magazine of Politics and Culture, 2001, A Just Response: The Nation on Terrorism, Democracy and September 11, 2001, 2002, The Dictionary of Republicanisms, 2005, Meltdown: How Greed & Corruption Shattered Our Financial System and How We Can Recover, 2009; co-editor: Voices of Glasnost: Interviews with Gorbachev's Reformers, 1989, Taking Back America-And Taking Down the Radical Right, 2004; mem. nat. adv. bd. Facing South mag.; mem. editl. bd. The Progressive Book Club; contbr. articles to newspapers. Recipient Maggie award Planned Parenthood Fedn. Am., 1994, Nat. Mag. award for Reviews & Criticism, Am. Soc. Mag. Editors, 2007. Mem. Correctional Assn. N.Y. (dir.), Inst. for Women's Policy Rsch. (bd. dirs.), Coun. Fgn. Rels., Inst. Policy Studies (trustee), Network of East-West Women (bd. advisors), Franklin and Eleanor Roosevelt Inst. (trustee), Moscow Ctr. for Gender Studies (mem. adv. com.), Century Assn. Office: The Nation 33 Irving Pl Fl 8 New York NY 10003-2332 Office Phone: 212-209-5412.

VANDEN HEUVEL, MICHAEL JOHN, literature educator; b. Madison, Wis., Feb. 18, 1956; s. Norbert Anthony and Joan Marie (Sandman) V.; m. Tracy Lee Wolenec, July 11, 1992. BA in English, U. Wis., 1979; MA, U. Chgo., 1981; PhD, U. Wis., 1988. With Ariz. State U., Tempe. Author: Performing Drama/Dramatizing Performance, 1991, ELmer Rice: A Research and Production Sourcebook, 1995; contbr. articles to profl. jours. Am. Coun. Learned Soc. fellow, 1993. Avocations: softball, camping, theater. Office: Ariz State U Dept English PO Box 870302 Tempe AZ 85287-0302

VAN DEN HOOGEN, INGRID, information technology executive; BA in Math. and Computer Sci., San Jose State U., Calif. Various software devel. positions GTE Govt. Systems, United Techs., Megatek; with Sun Microsystems, Inc., Santa Clara, Calif., 1987—, head software strategic mktg., sr. v.p. brand, global comm. & integrated mktg., sr. v.p. corp. mktg. Office: Sun Microsystems Inc 4150 Network Cir Santa Clara CA 95054 Home: PO Box 145 Girdwood AK 99587-0145 Office Phone: 650-960-1300.*

VANDEPUTTE, DIXIE DIANNE, retired psychologist, educator; b. Little River, Kans., Oct. 16, 1942; d. William Dean and Charlotte Juanita Wright; m. Gregory Charles Vandeputte, Aug. 21, 1959; children: Holly Ann Bell, Gregory Jr., Kerry Lynn Doll. BA summa cum laude in English and Psychology, U. Colo., 1990, MA in Psychology, 1992; PhD in Clin. Psychology, U. Kans., 1997. Lic. clin. psychologist Colo. Program mgr., lead clinician Pikes Peak Mental Health, Colo. Springs, Colo., 1997—2002; dir. Rocky Mountain Brain Injury Rehabilitation Day Clinic, Colo. Springs, 2002—03; dir. Counseling and Testing Ctr. U. Colo., Colo. Springs, 2003—08. Mem. first del. to Vietnam and Cambodia APA, 2006; instr. U. Colo., 2003—08; presenter in field. Contbr. articles to profl. jours. Sec. bd. dirs. Suicide Prevention Partnership, Colo. Springs, 2001—08; sec. bd. Nat. Alliance for the Mentally Ill-CS, Colo. Springs, 2002—08; mem. steering com. KP Women's Endowment, Colo. Springs, 2003—08; bd. dirs. Suicide Prevention Edn. and Advocacy Coalition, Colo. Springs, 2004—08. Recipient Outstanding Undergrad. Social Sci. award, U. Colo., 1990. Republican. Avocations: reading, hunting, crafts.

VANDER AARDE, STANLEY BERNARD, retired otolaryngologist; b. Orange City, Iowa, Sept. 26, 1931; s. Bernard John and Christina (Luchtenberg) Vander A.; m. Agnes Darlene De Beer, June 19, 1956; children: Paul, David, Debra, Mary. BA, Hope Coll., 1953; MD, Northwestern U., 1957. Diplomate Am. Bd. Otolaryngology. Intern Cook County Hosp., Chgo., 1957-59; resident in otolaryngology Northwestern U. Hosp., Chgo., 1966-70; mem. staff Mary Lott Lyles Hosp., Madanapalle, India, 1961-66, 71-87, Affiliated Med. Clinic, Willmar, Minn., 1987-95; ret., 1995. Served to capt., USAF, 1959-60. Fellow ACS, Am. Bd. Otolaryngology, Am. Acad. Otolaryngology. Republican. Mem. Reformed Church in America. Home: 708 2nd St SE Apt 112 Orange City IA 51041-2165

VANDERBEEK, JEFFREY, professional sports team executive; b. July 19, 1957; m. Deborah Vanderbeek; children: Rem, McKenna, Rhiannon. BS, Bloomfield Coll. With Donaldson Lufkin & Jenrette; mng. dir., COO fixed income ctrl. funding dept. Lehman Brothers Holdings Inc., 1984—93, COO fixed income govt. dept., 1993—96, COO fixed income derivative dept., 1993—96, head global fixed income divsn., 1996—2000, head capital markets divsn., 2000—02, head global risk mgmt., pvt. equity and strategy, 2002—04; prin. owner, chmn., mng. ptnr. NJ Devils, 2004—. Pres. Devils Renaissance Devel., LLC. Vice chmn., bd. mem. Dorothy Rodbell Cohen Found. for Cancer Rsch.; chmn. Greater Newark Holiday Fund, 2006—; bd. mem. Newark Alliance, Boys & Girls Clubs of Greater Newark; mem. exec. com. Boston Coll. Wall St. Coun. Named Sportsman of Yr., NJ Sports Writers' Assn., 2008. Office: NJ Devils 165 Mulberry St Newark NJ 07102

VANDERBILT, ARTHUR T., II, lawyer; b. Summit, NJ, Feb. 20, 1950; s. William Runyon and Jean (White) V. BA, Wesleyan U., Middletown, Conn., 1972; JD, U. Va., 1975. Bar: N.J. 1975, U.S. Dist. Ct. N.J. 1975, U.S. Supreme Ct. 1978. Jud. clk. to presiding justice N.J. Superior Ct., 1975-76, dep. atty. gen., 1976-78, asst. counsel to gov., 1978-79; ptnr. Carella, Byrne, Bain & Gilfillan, Roseland, NJ, 1979—. Chmn. Supreme Ct. Ethics Com.; mem. Supreme Ct. Adv. Com. Profl. Ethics. Author: Changing Law, 1976, Jersey Justice, 1978, Law School, 1981, Treasure Wreck, 1986, Fortune's Children, 1989 (Book of the Month Club, Readers Digest and fgn. edits.), New Jersey's Judicial Revolution, 1997, Golden Days, 1998 (fgn. edits.), Jersey Jurists, 1998, The Making of a Bestseller, 1999, Gardening in Eden, 2003. Trustee Elizabeth Presbytery, Summit Free Pub. Libr., Manley-Winser Found., Land of PureGold Found., Greenwood Gardens, Friends Florham.

Named to N.J. Literary Hall of Fame. Fellow: ABA Found.; mem.: ABA (Scribes award 1976), Nat. Writers Union, The Authors Guild, Inc., Nat. Assn. Bond Lawyers, Am. Judicature Soc., N.J. Bar Assn., Eastward Ho Country Club, Baltusrol Golf Club, Capitol Hill Club, Hyannis Yacht Club. Republican. Presbyterian. Avocation: writing. Office: Carella Byrne Bain & Gilfillan 5 Becker Farm Rd Roseland NJ 07068-1735 Office Phone: 973-994-1700. Business E-Mail: avanderbilt@carellabyrne.com.

VANDERBURG, PAUL STACEY, insurance executive, consultant; b. Detroit, Apr. 13, 1941; s. Harold Stacey and Alice Bertha (Lyle) V. Cert. in plastics tech., Oakland U., 1966; AS in Bus., C.S. Mott C.C., 1971; Casualty Claims Law Assoc., Am. Ednl. Inst., 1986; BA in Bus. Adminstrn. and Mgmt., Columbia Pacific U., 1990; cert. in human resource devel., U. South Fla., 1992; fraud claims law assoc., Am. Ednl. Inst., 1995; grad., FBI Citizens Acad., Tampa, 2003. Lic. ins. adjuster Mich., Fla.; cert. cir. civil mediator U. South Fla. Mediation Inst., 2001, cert. county court mediator State Fla. Supreme Ct., 2002. Ins. field claims adjuster Underwriters Adjusting Co., Pontiac, Mich., 1972-76; pres., CEO Sun Cycle, Inc., Drayton Plains, Mich., 1975-77; sr. ins. claims adjuster Kemper Ins. Group, Tampa, Fla., 1979-80; ins. field claims adjuster Auto-Owners Ins. Co., Lakeland, Fla., 1981-82; sr. recovery specialist CIGNA Corp., Tampa, 1984-85; ins. field claims adjuster Seaboard Adjustment Bur., Lakeland, 1985-87; sr. field claims ins. adjuster Hallmark Ins. Adjusters, Clearwater, Fla., 1987-88; pvt. practice Tampa, 1988—. Author: Insurance Subrogation Management, 1991. Apptd. law enforcement rep. Hillsborough County (Fla.) Human Rels. Bd., 1999-2007. Staff sgt. U.S. Army, 1963-69. Mem.: Assn. Property and Casualty Claims Profls., Soc. of Claims Law Assocs., Assn. of Workers' Compensation Claims Profls., Fla. Acad. Profl. Mediators, Ctr. for Internat. Security Studies, Fla. Sheriffs Assn., Am. Security Coun. (nat. adv. bd.), FBI Citizens Acad. Alumni Assn. (v.p.), Am. Legion. Republican. Avocations: boating, fishing, photography. Home and Office: 5448 Circle Dr (WWG) Spring Hill FL 34607-1407 Office Phone: 813-886-9669. Office Fax: 352-592-2191. Personal E-mail: A_Van0123@comcast.net. Business E-Mail: A_0123@comcast.net.

VANDERBURG, TIMOTHY WARREN, history professor; b. Concord, NC, Aug. 10, 1959; s. Warren Howard and Elizabeth Henley Vanderburg; m. Marsha Shyrl Turner, Aug. 28, 1981; 1 child, Zachary Howard. BA, Gardner-Webb Coll., Boiling Springs, NC, 1977—81; MA, U. NC, Charlotte, 1991—94; PhD, Miss. State U., Starkville, 1995—2000. History tchr. First Assembly Christian Sch., Concord, NC, 1981—89, asst. prin., athletic dir., 1989—93; history instr. U. NC, Charlotte, 1994—95; grad. tchg. asst. Miss. State U., Starkville, 1996—2000, instr. coll. ind. study courses, 1998—2000; asst. prof. history Gardner-Webb U., 2000—. Adv. com. mem. NC Hwy. Hist. Marker Adv. Com., Raleigh, 2005—. Contbr. articles to profl. jours. Mem.: So. Hist. Assn. (assoc.), Alpha Theta Chi, Phi Alpha Theta. Home: 1810 Clary Rd Shelby NC 28152 Office: Gardner-Webb Univ PO Box 7343 Boiling Springs NC 28017 Business E-Mail: tvanderburg@gardner-webb.edu.

VAN DER GEER, PETER, biochemist, educator; b. Voorhout, Zuid Holland, Netherlands, May 8, 1961; s. Arie van der Geer and Dora de Boer; m. Sandra Eileen Wiley; children: Anneke, Marijke. MS in Biology; PhD in Biochemistry, U. Amsterdam, Netherlands. Postdoc. fellow Salk Inst., La Jolla, Calif., 1993—94, Samuel Lunenfeld Rsch. Inst., Toronto, Ontario, Canada, 1994—97; asst. prof. biochemistry U. Calif., San Diego, 1997—2006; assoc. prof. biochemistry San Diego State U., 2008—. Office: San Diego State Univ 5500 Campanile Dr San Diego CA 92182-1030 Office Phone: 619-594-5582. Business E-Mail: pvandergeer@sciences.sdsu.edu.

VAN DER HARST, JOHN JAY, environmentalist; b. Detroit, May 15, 1955; s. Juan and Marylyn Wilda van der Harst. Student in Landscape Architecture, Mich. State U., East Lansing, 1973—75, Calif. State Poly. U., Pomona, 1976; BA in Humanities (History of Art and English), Mich. State U., East Lansing, 1977; AS in Sci. and Engring., Schoolcraft Coll., Livonia, Mich., 1979; postgrad. in Civil Engring., U. Mich., Ann Arbor, 1979—81. Draftsman, delineator Grables, Mills and Young Inc., Lansing, Mich., 1975; designer, draftsman Leisure and Recreation Concepts, Inc., Dallas, 1976; project asst. Wehrman Chapman Assocs., Inc., Mpls., 1978; draftsman Cook Wandrey Peterman Design Group, John R. Cook Assocs., Ltd., Bartlett, Ill., 1980; designer, illustrator Ronald Sias and Assocs., Nashville, 1982; designer Cumberland Tectonics, Inc., Nashville, 1982—83; designer, draftsman Barge, Waggoner, Sumner and Cannon, Inc., Nashville, 1983—84; designer, technician Wamble and Assocs., Nashville, 1985; draftsman, delineator, designer Hastings Architecture Assocs., Nashville, 1986; contract draftsman IDI Corp., Milw.; assigned to Kroger Co., Nashville, 1988—89, Marquette U., Milw., 1990; contract draftsman, cons., illustrator various orgns., 1975—. Cons. in field; presenter in field. Contbr. articles to profl. jours.; radio and television guest (to various stations in Tenn. and Nebr.). Vol. Navajo Gospel Mission, Oraibi, Ariz., 1978, Recycle! Nashville, Methodology Com., 1988—89, Bring Urban Recycling to Nashville Today, 1989—92; rev. team mem. EPA, 1991—92. Mem.: Green Party Mid. Tenn., Cumberland Green Bioregional Coun., Recycling Advocates Mid. Tenn., Tenn. Environ. Coun. (life). Avocations: gardening, cartooning, triathlons. Home: 1407 Roberts Ave Nashville TN 37206 Home Phone: 615-227-3499. Personal E-mail: johnvanderharst@gmail.com.

VANDER HEIDE, RICHARD STUART, pathologist, educator, research scientist; b. Grand Rapids, Mich., Apr. 30, 1959; s. John Switch and Patricia Jane (King) Vander Heide; children: Benjamin Richard, Samuel Sjoerd. BS, Calvin Coll., 1981; PhD, Northwestern U., 1986, MD, 1989. Diplomate Am. Bd. Pathology. Intern, resident Duke U. Med. Ctr., Durham, N.C., 1989-93; asst. prof. Wayne State U., Detroit, 1994-2000, assoc. prof., 2000—06, prof. pathology, 2007—09; chmn. pathology Lo. State U. Med. Sch., New Orleans, 2009; prof. pathology LSU Med. Sch., 2009—. Chief of pathology John D. Dingell VA Med. Ctr., Detroit, 1999—2009; mem. cardiovasc. study sect. A, NIH, 2002—03, charter mem. myocardial ischema and metabolism study sect., 2003—05, 2009—; chmn. pathology Lo. State. Contbr. articles to profl. jours. Grantee NIH, 1999—2004, 2007—. Mem. Internat. Soc. Heart Rsch., Am. Heart Assn. (grant in aid 1994-99). Avocations: amateur radio, history, golf, travel, classic cars. Office: John D Dingell VAMC 4646 John Rd Detroit MI 48201-2018 E-mail: rvanderh@med.wayne.edu.

VANDERHEYDEN, JENNIFER SUE, language educator; d. Richard Elmer and Lottie Belle Vulgamore; m. Jean-Luc Vanderheyden, Aug. 23, 1986. PhD, U. Wash., Seattle, 1999. Asst. prof. Lindenwood U., St. Charles, Mo., 1995—2001; vis. asst. prof. Simmons Coll., Boston, 2001—03, Suffolk U., Boston, 2005—06, Bentley Coll., Boston, 2005—06, Marquette U., Milw., 2007—. Author: (book) The Function of the Dream and the Body in Diderot's Works. Cmty. vol. GE, Milw. Mem.: Am. Soc. Eighteenth Century Studies. Office: Marquette Univ Lalumiere Lang Hall Milwaukee WI 53201 Business E-Mail: jennifer.vanderheyden@marquette.edu.

VANDERHOEF, LARRY NEIL, biology professor, former academic administrator; b. Perham, Minn., Mar. 20, 1941; s. Wilmar James and Ida Lucille (Wothe) Vanderhoef; m. Rosalie Suzanne Slifka, Aug. 31, 1963; children: Susan Marie, Jonathan Lee. BS, U. Wis., Milw., 1964, MS, 1965; PhD, Purdue U., 1969, Doctorate (hon.), 2000, Inje U. Korea, 2002. Postdoctorate U. Wis., Madison, 1969—70; asst. prof. biology U. Ill., Urbana, 1970-74, assoc. prof., 1974—77, prof., 1977—80, head dept. plant biology, 1977—80; provost Agrl. and Life Scis., U. Md., College Park, 1980—84; exec. vice chancellor U. Calif., Davis, 1984—91, exec. vice chancellor, provost, 1991—94, chancellor, 1994—2009, prof. plant biology, 2009—. Rsch. assoc. U. Wis., 1970—72; vis. investigator Carnegie Inst., 1976—77, Edinburgh (Scotland) U., 1978; cons. in field. Grantee Dimond Travel grantee, 1975, NSF, 1972, 1974, 1976—79, NATO, 1980; fellow, NRC, 1969—70, Eisenhower fellow, 1987. Mem.: AAAS, Nat. Assn. State Univ. and Land Grant Colls. (exec. com. 2000—), Am. Soc. Plant Physiology (bd. editors 1977—82, trustee, exec. com., treas. 1982—88, chmn. bd. trustees 1994—97). Home: 16 College Park Davis CA 95616-3607 Office: U Calif Davis Fifth Fl, Mrak Hall Davis CA 95616*

VAN DER HORST, BRIAN CHRISTOPHER, communications consultant, author, educator; b. NYC, Sept. 11, 1944; s. Louis Ferdinand von Pritzelwitz Van der Horst and Emilia (Jennewein) Triggs; children: Nicholas Christopher, Lorelei Eloise. Student, Duke U., 1960-62, New Sch. for Social Rsch., 1962-64, NLP Ctr. for Advanced Studies, Larkspur, Calif., 1981-83. Promotion mgr. Loew's Theatres, NYC, 1965-66; publicist Metro-Goldwyn-Mayer, NYC, 1966-67; publicity mgr. 20th Century-Fox, NYC, 1967-70; v.p. Cannon Group, NYC, 1970-71; dir. publicity and advt. Atlantic Recording Corp., NYC, 1971-73; dir. Neuro-Linguistic Programming Ctr. for Advanced Studies, 1986—90, Repere: Centre Internat. des Etudes Advancees NLP, Paris, 1985—2003, Dirigeants et Partenaires, Paris. Chief facilitator Integral Inst. Europe, Paris, 2000—; columnist, staff writer Village Voice, N.Y.C., 1973-77; columnist Playboy mag., N.Y.C., 1975-77; editor J.P. Tarcher, Inc., San Francisco, 1979-82; cons. SRI Internat., Menlo Park, Calif., 1980-81. Author: Folk Music in America, 1970, Rock Music, 1971, The Outcome Strategy, 2006; author more than 1000 articles on sci., music, and psychology; contbr. articles to Playboy, Omni, Practical Psychology, Penthouse, Cosmopolitan, others. Recipient 5 Motion Picture Advertising of Yr. awards, 1970; named Toastmaster of Yr., Paris Toastmasters, 1989. Fellow Nat. Assn. NLP, Internat. Coaching Confederation (founder), Internat. Coaching Fedn.; mem. Assn. for Humanistic Psychology, Toastmasters Am., French Assn. NLP (founding fellow). Avocations: guitar, skin diving, painting, skiing, gardening, cooking. Personal E-mail: brianvdh@gmail.com.

VAN DER KLAAUW, WILBERT H., economics professor; b. Noordwijkerhout, Netherlands, Sept. 4, 1963; married. PhD in Economics, Brown U., Providence, 1991. Asst. prof. economics NYU, NYC, 1991—99; prof. economics U. NC, Chapel Hill, 1999—2006; asst. v.p. Fed. Res. Bank NY, NYC, 2006—. Office: Fed Reserve Bank NY 33 Liberty St 3rd Fl New York NY 10045 Business E-Mail: wilbert.vanderklaauw@ny.frb.org.

VAN DER KOOI, RIK, computer software company executive; married; 3 children. BBA, Nyenrode U., The Netherlands; MBA, Instituto de Estudios Superiores de la Empresa, Barcelona. Various fin. and bus. positions Gen. Motors Corp. Europe, Spain, UK; CFO IBC Vehicles Ltd., Luton, UK; fin. dir. Benelux (Belgium, the Netherlands, Luxembourg) Microsoft Corp., 1999—2001, contr. ctrl. & southern Europe, 2001—03, gen. mgr. fin. & adminstrn., sales, mktg. and services group Paris, 2003—06, CFO online services bus., 2006—09, corp. v.p. online services divsn., 2009—. Office: Microsoft Corp One Microsoft Way Redmond WA 98052-6399*

VANDER LAAN, MARK ALAN, lawyer; b. Akron, Ohio, Sept. 14, 1948; s. Robert H. and Isabel R. (Bishop) Vander L.; m. Barbara Ann Ryzenga, Aug. 25, 1970; children: Aaron, Matthew. AB, Hope Coll., Holland, Mich., 1970; JD, U. Mich., Ann Arbor, 1972. Bar: Ohio 1973, U.S. Dist. Ct. (so. dist.) Ohio 1973, U.S. Ct. Appeals (6th cir.) 1978, U.S. Supreme Ct. 1981. Assoc. Dinsmore, Shohl, Coates & Deupree, Cin., 1972-79; ptnr. Dinsmore & Shohl, Cin., 1979—. Chair litig. dept., 2001—, gen. counsel to the firms, 1999-; spl. counsel Ohio Atty. Gen.'s Office, 1983-2006; spl. prosecutor State of Ohio, 1985-94; city solicitor City of Blue Ash, Ohio, 1987—, City of Silverton, Ohio, 1999-2005; trustee Cin. So. Railway, 1994—, pres., 1999—. Mem. Cin. Human Rels. Commn., 1980-86; mem. Leadership Cin. Class XIII, 1989-90; trustee Legal Aid Soc. of Cin., 1981-94, pres., 1988-90; trustee Volunteer Lawyers for the Poor Found., 2003—, pres., 2003-06; dir. Ohio Justice and Policy Ctr., 2007-; sec. dir. Ctr. Closing The Health Gap Greater Cin., 2007-. Mem. ABA, Ohio Bar Assn., Cin. Bar Assn. (ethics com. 1983—), Sixth Cir. Jud. Conf. (life), Potter Stewart Am. Inn of Ct. (master), Am. Bds. Trial Advs., Queen City Club. Office: Dinsmore & Shohl 1900 Chemed Ct 255 E 5th St Cincinnati OH 45202-4700 Home Phone: 513-861-8818; Office Phone: 513-977-8200. Business E-Mail: mark.vanderlaan@dinslaw.com.

VAN DER LAAN, MIKELL F., landscape artist; s. Mikell F. Van der Laan, Sr and Mary-Jo van der Laan; m. Cynthia L. Smith. BA, U. Tex., Austin, 1987. Landscape, Nacotish Parish La. (Best Show: Richaland Coll., 1981). Home: 6520 Lickton Pike Goodlettsville TN 37072

VAN DER LEEUW, SANDER ERNST, archaeologist, educator; s. Piet Jacob van der Leeuw and Christine Moltzer; m. Anick Gabrielle Coudart, June 23, 2005. PhD, U. Amsterdam, 1976. Rschr. Netherlands Orgn. Pure Rsch., Leiden, 1972—76; lectr. U. Amsterdam, 1976—85, Cambridge U., England, 1985—95; prof. U. Paris I Panthéon-Sorbonne, 1995—2003, Ariz. State U. Sch. Human Evolution & Social Change, Tempe, 2003—, dir., 2003—. Sec.-gen. Coun. for Coordination Humanities and Social Scis., Paris, 2000—02; external prof. Santa Fe Inst., 2000—; dep. dir. Inst. Nat. Scis. of Universe, Paris, 2003—04. Mem. Fyssen Found., Paris, 2000—08, Ariz. Acad. Sci., Tech. and Arts, Phoenix, 2005—08. Fulbright Postdoctoral fellowship, US Govt., 1976—77, Disting. Rsch. fellowship, Ministry Edn., France, 1988, fellowship, Fitzwilliam Coll., Cambridge, 1986—95. Mem.: Inst. U. France (chair, archaeology 2002—07), Royal Netherlands Acad. Arts and Scis. Office: Ariz State Univ PO Box 872402 Tempe AZ 85287-2402

VANDERLINDE, DAISY, consumer products company executive; BA, Ohio State U., Columbus. Head human resources Broadway Stores, Marshalls Inc., Tractor Supply Co.; sr. v.p. human resources and loss prevention, mem. exec. com. AutoZone; exec. v.p. human resources Office Depot, Inc., 2005—. Office: Office Depot Inc 6600 N Military Trl Boca Raton FL 33496-2434*

VANDERLINDE, ROGER, social sciences educator; b. Sioux Falls, SD, Sept. 15, 1954; s. Carl and Iona Vanderlinde; m. Deborah Howard, Mar. 27, 1976; children: Christopher, Jaime Mitchell, Stephanie. BS in Social Scis., Upper Iowa U., Ft. Riley, Kans., 1994; BS in Comprehensive Social Studies, Kans. State U., Manhattan, 1998; MLS in Social Sci., Ft. Hays State U., Kans., 2002. First sgt. 1st Fin. Bn, Ft. Riley, Kans., 1974—94; ops. sgt. 7th Fin. Group, Stuttgart, Germany, 1988—91; instr. Barton County C.C., Ft. Riley, 1998—; bus. owner D & R Retail Liquor, Manhattan, 1994—2002. Decorated Meritorius Svc. medal VII Corps, Bronze Star medal, Meritorius Svc. medal 1st Inf. Divsn. Mem.: V.F.W. Independent. Avocations: hunting, fishing, golf, bowling.

VANDERLINDEN, CAMILLA DENICE DUNN, telecommunications industry executive; b. Dayton, July 21, 1950; d. Joseph Stanley and Virginia Danley (Martin) Dunn; m. David Henry VanderLinden; Oct. 10, 1980; 1 child, Michael Christopher. Student, U. de Valencia, Spain, 1969; BA in Spanish and Secondary Edn. cum laude, U. Utah, 1972, MS in Human Resource Econs., 1985. Asst. dir. Davis County Community Action Program, Farmington, Utah, 1973-76; dir. South County Community Action, Midvale, Utah, 1976-79; supr. customer service Ideal Nat. Life Ins. Co., Salt Lake City, 1979-80; mgr. customer service Utah Farm Bur. Mutual Ins., Salt Lake City, 1980-82; quality assurance analyst Am. Express Co., Salt Lake City, 1983-86, quality assurance and human resource specialist, 1986-88, mgr. quality assurance and engring. Denver, 1988-91; mgr. customer svc. Tel. Express Co., Colorado Springs, Colo., 1991-97; dir. Call Ctr. United Membership Mktg. Group, Lakewood, Colo., 1997-98; telesvcs. industry mgr. Piton Found., Denver, 1998—; customer care and tng. dir. SafeRent, 2000—; dir. quality assurance Tele-Servicing Innovations, 2000—02; ops. mgr. Bayaud Industries, 2002—05; enterpreneur, bus. owner, 2008—. Adj. faculty Westminster Coll., Salt Lake City, 1987-88. adj. faculty, quality adv. bd. Red Rocks C.C., 1990-91; cons. in field. Vol. translator Latin Am. community; vol. naturalist Roxborough State Park; internat. exch. coord. EF Fgn. Exch. Program. Mem. Internat. Customer Svc. Orgn. (officer call ctr. chpt.), Colo. Springs Customer Svc. Assn. (officer). Christian. Avocation: swimming. Home: 44 Lake Lea Rd Rochester NY 14617 Personal E-mail: camillavan@usa.net.

VAN DER LINDEN, FRANK MORRIS, historian; b. Hendersonville, NC, Mar. 8, 1919; s. William Harrison and Floride Bowden (Morris) van der L.; m. Georgia Kathlyn Huddle, Feb. 11, 1951; children: Frank Robert, Margaret Lyn, Anne Morris. AB, Lenoir-Rhyne Coll., 1939. Reporter, editl. writer Hickory N.C. Daily Record, 1939-42; mng. editor Hickory Daily Record, 1942-45; reporter Cottrell News Bur., Washington, 1945-52; Washington bur. chief Nashville Tenn. Banner, 1952-86; White House corr. Sacramento Calif. Union, 1979-89; columnist United Feature Syndicate, N.Y., 1971-76. Guest panelist NBC-TV Meet the Press, 1956-75. Author: Dark Horse, 1944, The Turning Point: Jefferson's Battle for the Presidency, 1962, Nixon's Quest for Peace, 1972, The Real Reagan, 1981, Lincoln: The Road to War, 1998, The Dark Intrigue: The True Story of a Civil War Conspiracy, 2007. Mem. The Lincoln Commn., Washington, 1989-98. Mem. U.S. Capitol Hist. Soc. (oral history program dir. 1976-94), The Cosmos Club (editl. bd. 1988—), The White House Correspondents Assn. Presbyterian. Avocation: historical research. Home and Office: 5301 Westbard Cir Apt 247 Bethesda MD 20816-1430 Office Phone: 301-654-1872.

VAN DER MARCK, JAN, art historian; b. Roermond, The Netherlands, Aug. 19, 1929; arrived in U.S., 1957; s. Everard and Anny (Finken) van der Marck; m. Ingeborg Lachmann, Apr. 27, 1961 (dec. 1988); m. Sheila Stamell, May 24, 1990. BA, U. Nijmegen, The Netherlands, 1952, MA, 1954, PhD in Art History, 1956; postgrad., U. Utrecht, The Netherlands, 1956-57, Columbia U., NYC, 1957-59. Curator Gemeentemuseum, Arnhem, Netherlands, 1959-61; asst. dir. fine arts Seattle World's Fair, 1961-62; curator Walker Art Ctr., Mpls., 1963-67; dir. Mus. Contemporary Art, Chgo., 1967-70; assoc. prof. art history U. Wash., Seattle, 1972-74; dir. Dartmouth Coll. Mus. and Galleries, 1974-80, Ctr. for Fine Arts, Miami, 1980-85; curator 20th century art, chief curator Detroit Inst. Arts, 1986-95. Author: (book) Romantische Boekillustratie in Belgie, 1956, Enrico Baj, 1969, Lucio Fontana, 1974, George Segal, 1975, Arman, 1984, Bernar Venet, 1988, The Art of Contemporary Bookbinding, 1997, Art and the American Experience, 1998, Lucio Pozzi, 2001, Jef Bourgeau: A User's Manual, 2007; contbr. articles to art jours., essays to catalogues. Decorated officer Order Arts and Letters, knight Order of Orange Nassau; fellow Netherlands Orgn. Pure Rsch., 1954—55, Rockefeller Found., 1957—59, Aspen Inst., 1974, 1994, Ctr. Advanced Study in Visual Arts, Nat. Gallery, Washington, 1986. Mem.: Les Amis de la Reliure Originale (Paris) (bd. mem.), Bibliotheca Wittockiana (Brussels).

VANDER MATEN, MARY ANN, biology professor, dean; b. Iowa; d. William and Ann Vander Maten; m. John Peterson; children: William Vanderson, Anne Vanderson, David Vanderson, John Vanderson. BA, Northwestern Coll., Orange City, Iowa, 1971; PhD, U. Kans., Lawrence, 1975. Asst. rsch. prof. George Wash. U., Washington, 1975—81; assoc. prof. biology & chemistry Northwestern Coll., 1983—87; prof. & asst. dean biology Northern Va. CC, Annandale, 1992—. Sec. Middleridge Civic Assn., Fairfax, Va., 2006—; handbell dir. Burke Presbyn. Ch., Va., 1998—. Recipient Golden Apple Tchg. award, Student Govt., Northern Va. CC, 2005. Mem.: Am. Sci. Affiliation, Am. Soc. Microbiology, Sigma Xi Sci. Rsch. Soc. Home: 10913 Spurlock Ct Fairfax VA 22032 Office: Northern Va CC 8333 Little River Turnpike Annandale VA 22003 Office Fax: 703-323-4250. Business E-Mail: mvandermate@nvcc.edu.

VANDERMEER, PHILIP R., history professor; m. Mary Ann Vander-Meer. PhD, U. Ill., Champaign-Urbana, 1976. Assoc. prof. Ariz. State U., Tempe, 1985—. Mem. exec. bd. Jour. Gilded Age and Prog. Era, 2003—. Contbr. articles to profl. jour.; author: (book) Phoenix Rising Belief & Behavior, The Hooser Pohtcun. Mem.: Soc. Historians Gilded Age and Prog. Era (Ohio) (treas. 2005—), Social Sci. History Assn. (treas. 2008—, exec. com. mem. 2005—08, editor SSHA news 1990—96), Ariz. Hist. Soc., Orgn. Am. Historians (membership com. mem. 2003—08). Office: History Dept Ariz State Univ Tempe AZ 85287-4302

VAN DER MERWE, NIKOLAAS JOHANNES, archaeologist; b. Riviersonderend, Republic of South Africa, Aug. 11, 1940; came to U.S., 1958; s. Johannes Abraham and Rachel Maria (Burger) van der M.; m. Julia Ann Feeny, Nov. 11, 1962 (div. 1969); 1 child, Kerstin; m. Karen Elaine Bardou, Feb. 19, 1973; 1 child, Nicolina Thandiwe. BA cum laude, Yale U., 1962, MA, 1965, PhD, 1966; MA (hon.), Harvard U., 1988; DSc (hon.), U. Port Elizabeth, 1995. Curatorial asst. Yale Peabody Mus., New Haven, 1962-64; rsch. asst. Yale Radiocarbon Lab., New Haven, 1963-66; asst. prof. anthropology SUNY, Binghamton, 1966-69, assoc. prof., 1969-74; prof. archaeology U. Cape Town, Republic of South Africa, 1974-88; Landon Clay prof. sci. archaeology, earth and planetary scis. Harvard U., Cambridge, Mass., 1988-2001; prof. natural history U. Cape Town, Rondebosch, 2000—06, prof. emeritus natural history, 2007—. Dir. Ctr. African Studies, U. Cape Town, 1976-80. Author: The Carbon 14 Dating of Iron, 1969; co-editor: (collection of essays) Perspectives on South Africa's Future, 1979, Iron Age in Southern Africa, 1979; contbr. articles to profl. jours. Fellow U. Cape Town, 1986; Ford Found. Fgn. Area fellow, 1964-66; recipient Pomerance Sci. medal Am. Inst. Archaeology, 1998; listed in 2000 Outstanding Scientists of 20th Century, 2d edit., Cambridge, Eng., 2000 Outstanding

Scientists of the 21st Century, Cambridge, Eng., 2003. Fellow AAAS, Royal Soc. South Africa (John F.W. Herschel medal 1994), Am. Anthrop. Assn., Explorers Club, Soc. Antiquaries (London); mem. South African Archaeol. Soc. (life), Soc. Am. Archaeology, Hist. Metallurgy Group, South African Assn. Archaeologists (founder), West African Assn. Archaeology (founder), Soc. Archaeol. Sci. (life), Wildlife Ranching South Africa We. Cape sect. (chmn.), Owl Club (Cape Town), Sigma Xi. Avocations: flying, diving, shooting, hiking, cooking. Home: 35 Duignam Rd Kalk Bay 7975 South Africa Office: U Cape Town Dept Archaeology Rondebosch 7700 South Africa Personal E-mail: kalkbaai@mweb.co.za. Business E-Mail: nikolaas.vandermerwe@uct.ac.za.

VAN DER MEULEN, JOSEPH PIERRE, neurologist; b. Boston, Aug. 22, 1929; s. Edward Lawrence and Sarah Jane (Robertson) Van Der Meulen; m. Ann Irene Yadeno, June 18, 1960; children: Elisabeth, Suzanne, Janet. AB, Boston Coll., 1950; MD, Boston U., 1954. Diplomate Am. Bd. Psychiatry and Neurology. Intern Cornell Med. div. Bellevue Hosp., NYC, 1954-55, resident, 1955-56, Harvard U., Boston City Hosp., 1958-60, instr., fellow, 1962-66; assoc. Case Western Res. U., Cleve., 1966-67, asst. prof., 1967-69, assoc. prof. neurology and biomed. engring., 1969-71; prof. neurology U. So. Calif., LA, 1971—2006, prof. emeritus, 2006—, chmn. dept., 1971—78, v.p. health affairs, 1977—2005, v.p. health affairs emeritus, 2006—, dean Sch. Medicine, 1985—86, 1995—97, vice dean med. affairs, 1995—97; dir. Ind. Health Professions, LA, 1991—2005. Dir. dept. neurology LA County/U. So. Calif. Med. Ctr., 1971—78; vis. prof. Autonomous U., Guadalajara, Mexico, 1974; pres. Norris Cancer Hosp. and Rsch. Inst., 1983—98, chmn., 2004; pres. Scott Newman Ctr., 1987—89. Contbr. articles to profl. jours. Mem. med. adv. bd. Calif. chpt. Myasthenia Gravis Found., 1971—75, chmn., 1974—75, 1977—78; mem. adv. bd. Amyotrophic Lateral Sclerosis Found., Calif., 1973—75, chmn. Calif., 1974—75; mem. Com. to Combat Huntington's Disease, 1973—; bd. dirs. Calif. Hosp. Med. Ctr., Good Hope Med. Found., LA Hosp. Good Samaritan, Barlow Respiratory Hosp., U. So. Calif. Univ. Hosp., chmn., 1991—2004; bd. dirs. Assn. Acad. Health Ctrs., chmn.; bd. dirs. Children's Hosp. LA, Eisenhower Med. Ctr. Served to lt. M.C. USN, 1956—58. Nobel Inst. fellow, Karolinska Inst., Stockholm, 1960—62, NIH grantee, 1968—71. Mem.: AMA, LA Acad. Medicine, Calif. Med. Soc., LA Med. Assn., LA Soc. Neurology and Psychiatry (pres. 1977—78), Am. Acad. Neurology, Am. Neurol. Assn., Phi Kappa Phi, Alpha Omega Alpha (councillor 1992—). Roman Catholic. Home: 39 Club View Ln Palos Verdes Peninsula CA 90274-4208 Personal E-mail: annvander@aol.com.

VAN DER PAARDT, TAMARA ANN, music educator; d. Glenn Elmer and Darlene Margaret Schultz; m. Peter van der Paardt, June 27, 1987; children: Nicole Marie, Melissa Krystine, Andrew Scott. BA in Music Edn., Calif. State U., Fresno, 1985. Cert. clear credential music edn. Calif., 1987. Profl. musician Fresno Philharm. Orch., Calif., 1979—; music tchr. Clovis Unified Sch. Dist., 1987—. Dir. Winter Drumline Ensemble, Jazz Ensemble. Named Outstanding Jazz Ensemble, Downbeat Internat. Music Awards, 1995, Class A World Champions, WGI Drumline Competition, 2003. Mem.: CBDA (assoc.), FMCMEA (assoc.), IAJE (assoc.), Internat. Assn. Jazz Educators, Calif. Band Dirs. Assn., Fresno-Madera (Calif.) County Music Educators Assn., Music Educators Nat. Conf. (assoc.), Calif. Music Edn. Assn. (assoc.; pres. ctrl. Calif. sect. 2003—), Winter Guard Internat. Avocations: travel, gardening, softball. Home: 1692 Richert Ave Clovis CA 93611 Office: Reyburn Intermediate Sch 4300 N DeWolf Clovis CA 93611

VANDERPAN, NORMA, retired elementary school educator; b. Starkweather, ND; m. Leslie Vanderpan; 7 children. BA, Concordia Coll.; MA, U. S.D. Mem. negotiation team West Lyon Tchr. Assn., Inwood, Iowa, 1967—69, Brookings Edn. Assn., 1973—74; organizer, rep. Ea. S.D. Uniserv, Sioux Falls, SD, 1974—75. Author: Book of Litanies, 2008; editor: Centennial History of Sons of Norway - District 1 1895-1995, 2008. Named Brookings Tchr. of Yr., Brookings Pub. Schs., 1976; Nat. Def. Edn. grant, U. S.D., 1965. Mem.: PEO (chaplain Chpt. P 2004—05), BARTA, Saturday Literary Club (pres. 2005—), Phi Delta Kappa, Alpha Delta Kappa (Eta chpt. sec., Eta chpt. treas., state treas. 1976—78, state chaplain 1990—92, Fidelis Gamma chpt. pres. 1992—94, Fidelis Gamma chpt. chaplain 1995—2005). Republican. Lutheran. Avocations: reading, writing, quilting, antiques, needlepoint. Home: 2009 Derdall Dr Brookings SD 57006

VANDER PLAATS, GARY PAUL, accounting educator; b. Holland, Mich., Oct. 2, 1959; s. Gerrit and Frieda (De Vries) V. P.; m. Jean Elinor Sybesma, Dec. 19, 1979; children: Jennifer, Kayla, Melissa, Jonathan, Lisa, Jacob, Caleb, Isaiah, Jiana, Shiyan. BA in Acctg., Dordt Coll., 1982; MBA in Fin., U. Iowa, 1984; DBA in Fin., Anderson U. CPA, Iowa; cert. mgmt. acct.; cert. sch. mgmt. Staff acct. McGladrey and Pullen, Iowa City, 1984-87, consulting mgr. Cedar Rapids, Iowa, 1987-90; v.p. fin. McGrath Automotive Group, Cedar Rapids, 1990-92; asst. prof. Roberts Wesleyan Coll., Rochester, N.Y., 1992-95, Geneva Coll., Beaver Falls, Pa., 1995—99; assoc. prof. Dordt. Coll., Sioux Ctr., Iowa. Mem. AICPA, Iowa Soc. CPAs, Inst. for Mgmt. Accts. Republican. Presbyterian. Avocations: fishing, camping, coin collecting/numismatics, stamp collecting/philately. Office: Dordt College 498 4th Ave NE Sioux Center IA 51250 Home: 2520 460th St Ireton IA 51027 Business E-Mail: gvanderp@dordt.edu.

VANDERPOOL, GUY CLIFTON, museum director; BA, Lipscomb Coll.; MA in History, Middle Tenn. State U. Grant adminstr. U. Alabamaas Ctr. for So. History and Culture, 1991—92; curator Dallas Hist. Soc., 1993—94; exec. dir. Texarkana Mus. Sys., 1994—2004, Panhandle-Plains Hist. Mus., Canyon, Tex., 2004—. Tchr. Am. history and world civilization Texarkana Coll. Office: Panhandle-Plains Hist Mus 2503 4th Ave Canyon TX 79015 Office Phone: 806-651-2245. E-mail: gcvanderpool@pphm.wtamu.edu.

VANDERRYN, JACK, environmental services administrator; b. Groningen, The Netherlands, Apr. 14, 1930; came to U.S., 1939; s. Herman Gabriel and Henrietta S.E. (Hartog) V.; m. Margrit Wolfes, Mar. 18, 1956; children: David, Judith, Amy, Daniel. BA, Lehigh U., 1951, MS, 1952, PhD, 1955. Rsch. and grad. teaching asst. Lehigh U., Bethlehem, Pa., 1952-55; asst. prof. chemistry Va. Poly. Inst., Blacksburg, 1955-58; rsch. participant Oak Ridge (Tenn.) Nat. Lab., 1957; chemist AEC, Oak Ridge, 1958-62, tech. adviser to asst. gen. mgr. R & D, Washington, 1962-67, asst. to gen. mgr., 1971-72, tech. asst. to dir. div. applied tech., 1972-73, chief energy tech. br., div. applied tech., 1973-75; acting dir. div. energy storage Energy Rsch. and Devel. Adminstrn., Washington, 1975, dir. Office Internat. R & D Programs, 1975-77; dir. Office Internat. Programs Dept. Energy, Washington, 1977-82; dir. energy and natural resources AID, Washington, 1982-91; program dir. environment Moriah Fund, Washington, 1991—2003; sr. fellow, environ. and devel. Moriah Fund, 2003—06. Sr. sci. adviser U.S. Mission to Internat. Atomic Energy Agy., Dept. State, Vienna, Austria, 1967-71; lectr. Brookings Instn., 1965-66. Mem., dep. pres., exec. bd. Am. Internat. Sch., Vienna, 1968-71; v.p. Oak Ridge Civic Music Assn., 1959-60; pres. Washington Print Club, 1986-91; pres. Consultative Group on Biodiversity, 1997-2000; bd. dirs. Ctr. for Internat. Environ. Law, 2004—, Forest Stewardship Coun. U.S., 2004-07, Inst. for Conservation Leadership, 2003—, Endangered Species Coalition, 2003—. Home: 1825 Cedar St San Carlos CA 94070 Personal E-mail: jackvanderryn@msn.com.

VANDERSLICE, ELLEN, architect, composer; b. Ann Arbor, Mich., 1953; d. Ralph L. Vanderslice, Carolyn G. Vanderslice; married. BS, U. Mich., Ann Arbor, 1981, MArch, 1983. Lic. Architect, Oreg., 1996. Project mgr. Office of Transp., City of Portland, 1994—99, 2003—; project designer David Giulietti and Assocs., Portland, 1990—94; pres. America Walks, Portland, Oreg., 1996—2003. Pres. Willamette Pedestrian Coalition, Portland, 2001—03; mem. com. on pedestrians Transp. Rsch. Bd., Washington, 2001—04; mem. adv. com. Pub. Rights-of-Way Access, Washington, 1999—2004; co-treas. Portland chpt. Women's Transp. Seminar, 1997—98; prin. Ellen Vanderslice AIA, Portland, 1999—2003; bd. dirs. Internat. Fedn. Pedestrians, 2007—. Composer (CD): Once in a Blue Moon, 2000, The Standard Vanderslice, 2001, Don't Look Before You Sing, 2003. Sec. Northwest Dist. Assn., Portland, 1986—88. Recipient Pl. Planning award for Portland Pedestrian Master Plan and Pedestrian Design Guide, Environ. Design and Rsch. Assn., 2000, Exemplary Svc. to Pedestrian Transp. Program and Unwavering Commitment to Advocacy of Walking award, Portland Office of Transp. Engring. and Devel., 1999, Outstanding Project award for Portland Pedestrian Design Guide, Inst. Transp. Engrs. Oreg. Sect., 1999, Reclaiming Our Streets All-Star award, City Commr. Earl Blumenauer, 1991, Northwest Traffic Circulation Project Leadership award, Neighbor Newspaper, 1987, 1st prize jazz, USA Songwriting Competition, 2002, Golden Sole award, Willamette Pedestrian Coalition, 2005, dir.'s team group award, Portland Office Transp., 2007. Mem.: AIA (sec. Portland chpt. 1998—99, Nehemiah Housing Project award of excellence Portland chpt. 1993), Assn. Pedestrian and Bicycle Profls., Women's Transp. Seminar (co-treas. Portland chpt. 1997, Woman of Yr. Portland chpt. 2000), Nat. Assn. Watch and Clock Collectors, Jazz Soc. Oreg., Portland Songwriters Assn. (1st pl. Blues/Jazz/R&B Category 1999, 2000, 2001, 2003). Office: 1120 SW 5th Ave Rm 800 Portland OR 97204 Office Phone: 503-823-4638. Business E-Mail: trans.ci@portland.or.us.

VANDERSLICE, STEPHEN J., literature and language professor; b. Dallas, Oct. 21, 1946; s. Marie Vanderslice Jones; m. Ann Gravel, Mar. 25, 1972; children: Chris Burleigh, Eric, Caroline Wagenhauser Demers, Sarah Luckett. PhD, U. Dallas, 1979. Prof., philosophy and english LSU, Alexandria, 1978—. Contbr. articles. Lay mem., instl. rev. bd. Christus St. Frances Cabrini Hosp., Alexandria, 1998—2009. Mem.: Claremont Inst. Study Polit. Philosophy and Statesmanship. Roman Catholic. Avocations: tennis, travel, classical music. Office: LSU Alexandria 8100 Hwy 71 S Alexandria LA 71302-9121

VANDERVEEN, JOHN E., nutritionist, federal agency administrator; b. Prospect Park, NJ, May 13, 1934; m. Ernestine Neuhardt, June 3, 1967; children: Keith Bradley, Kimetha Leigh. BS, Rutgers U., 1956; PhD, U. N.H., 1961. Nutritionist USAF, 1961-75; dir. divsn. nutrition FDA, Washington, 1975-92, dir. office plant & dairy foods and beverages, 1992-98, scientist emeritus, 1998—. Served to 1st lt. USAF, 1961-64. Office: FDA Ctr Food Safety and Applied Nutrition 5100 Paint Branch Parkway College Park MD 20740-3335 Office Phone: 301-436-2006. Business E-Mail: jvanderv@cfsan.fda.gov, john.vanderveen@fda.hhs.gov.

VANDERVEEN, R. PETE (RANDALL L. VANDERVEEN), dean, pharmacist, educator; b. Lafayette, Ind., Nov. 6, 1950; BS in Pharmacy, Purdue U., West Lafayette, Ind., 1974, MS in Clin. Pharmacy, 1976; PhD in Univ. Adminstrn., Mich. State U., 1987; grad. leadership devel. prog., Duke U. Fuqua Sch. Bus., 1998. Cert. psychiatric pharmacist. Instr. Ferris State U., Big Rapids, Mich., 1976-77, asst. prof., 1977-79, assoc. prof., chair clin. pharmacy dept., 1979-88; asst. dean pharmacy practice Oreg. State U., Corvallis, 1988—98; assoc. prof. Oreg. Health & Sci. U., Portland, 1988—98, dir. pharmacy prog., 1994—98; prof. Duquesne U. Grad. Sch. Pharm. Scis., Pits., dean Mylan Sch. Pharmacy, 1998—2005; dean U. So. Calif. Sch. Pharmacy, LA, 2005—, John Stauffer Dean's Chair in pharm. scis., 2005—. Bd. dirs. Nat. Inst. Pharm. Tech. & Edn. (NIPTE); mem. edn. adv. com. Nat. Assn. Chain Drug Stores; former cons. Oreg. Med. Assistance Prog., Mich. Dept. Mental Health, Providence Med. Ctr., Oreg. Health Sci. Hosp., Portland. Contbr. articles to profl. jours. Fellow: Am. Soc. Health-Sys. Pharmacists, Am. Pharmacists Assn.; mem.: Nat. Cmty. Pharmacists Assn., Coll. Psychiat. & Neurologic Pharmacists, Acad. Managed Care Pharmacists, Am. Coll. Clin. Pharmacy, Am. Soc. Cons. Pharmacists, Am. Assn. Pharm. Scientists, Am. Assn. Colleges of Pharmacy (past bd. dirs.). Office: USC Sch Pharmacy Office of Dean PSC 700 HSC Los Angeles CA 90003 Office Fax: 323-442-1369. Business E-Mail: phardean@usc.edu.*

VANDERVEER, TARA, women's college basketball coach; b. Niagara Falls, NY, June 26, 1953; Grad., Ind. U., 1975. Head coach U. Idaho Vandals, 1978—80, Ohio State U. Buckeyes, 1980—85, Stanford U. Cardinal, 1985—. Head coach US Olympic Women's Basketball Team (gold medal), 1996. Author: Shooting From The Outside, 1997. Named Big Ten Coach of Yr., 1984, 1985, Nat. Coach of Yr., 1988, 1989, 1990, Dist. Coach of Yr., 1988, 1989, 1990, Coach of Yr., Pacific-10 Conf., 1989, 1990, 1995, 1997, 2002, 2003, 2004, 2005, 2006, No. Calif. Women's Intercollegiate Coach of Yr., 1988, 1989, 1990, 1992, 1993, USA Basketball Nat. Coach of Yr., 1996, US Olympic Com. Elite Basketball Coach of Yr., 1996; named to Ind. U. Hall of Fame, 1995, Women's Basketball Hall of Fame, 2002, Women's Sports Found. Hall of Fame, Greater Buffalo Hall of Fame. Achievements include coaching the NCAA Women's Basketball Championship winning Stanford University Cardinal, 1990, 92. Avocation: piano. Office: Stanford U Womens Basketball Dept Athletics Arrillaga Family Sports Ctr Stanford CA 94305-6150 Office Phone: 650-723-0284. E-mail: tarahoop@stanford.edu.*

VANDERVELD, JOHN, JR., diversified financial services company executive; b. Chgo., Oct. 24, 1926; s. John J. and Rose (Renkema) V. Pres. Nat. Disposal Contractors, Barrington, Ill., 1952-71; sr. v.p., dir. Browning Ferris Industries, Houston, 1971-78; pres. Pioneer Equities, Inc., 1975-90, C.J.V. Corp., Dallas, 1990-92; sr. corp. advisor Vector Environmental Techs., Inc., 1993-96. Dir. Am. Far East, Inc., Dallas and Tokyo; adv. bd. Southwestern Legal Found., 1975-1998. Bd. dirs. Internat. Bible Soc., mem. exec.com., 1982-98; bd. dirs. Global Action; chmn. Brookshire Capital Corp., 2000—. Mem. Nat. Solid Waste Mgmt. Assn. (former chmn. govt. industry coordinating council, mem. environ. research com.) Home: 7031 Brookshire Dr Dallas TX 75230-4248 Office Phone: 214-692-8995. E-mail: jv-brookshire@sbcglobal.net.

VANDER VELDE, WALLACE EARL, aeronautical and astronautical engineering educator; b. Jamestown, Mich., June 4, 1929; s. Peter Nelson and Janet (Keizer) Vander V.; m. Winifred Helen Bunai, Aug. 29, 1954; children: Susan Jane, Peter Russell. BS in Aero Engring, Purdue U., 1951; Sc.D., Mass. Inst. Tech., 1956. Dir. applications engring. GPS Instrument Co., Inc., Newton, Mass., 1956-57; faculty MIT, Cambridge, 1957—2004, prof. aero. and astronautics, 1965—2004, prof. emeritus, 2004—. Cons. to industry, 1958— Author: Flight Vehicle Control Systems, Part VII of Space Navigation, Guidance and Control, 1966, (with Arthur Gelb) Multiple-Input Describing Functions, 1968; also papers. Served to 1st lt. USAF, 1951-53. Recipient Edn. award Am. Automatic Control Coun., 1988. Fellow AIAA; mem. IEEE. Home: 50 High St Winchester MA 01890-3314 Office: MIT Rm 9-335 Dept Aero and Astronautics Cambridge MA 02139

VANDERVER, TIMOTHY ARTHUR, JR., lawyer; b. Birmingham, Ala., Jan. 25, 1944; s. Timothy Arthur and Jeanette (Grimes) V.; m. Virginia Cassandra Nye, Oct. 1, 1966 (dec. July 2001); m. Susan Elliotte McVay, Mar. 20, 2003; children: Timothy A. III, Glenn Bruce, Benjamin Richard. BA, Washington and Lee U., 1965; BA in Law, Oxford U., Eng., 1967, MA, 1983; JD, Harvard U., 1969. Bar: D.C., U.S. Ct. Appeals (D.C. cir.) 1969, U.S. Ct. Appeals (5th cir.) 1984, U.S. Ct. Appeals (3d and 11th cirs.) 1989, U.S. Supreme Ct. 1978. Assoc. Covington & Burling, Washington, 1969—72, Dept. of Interior, Washington, 1972—73, Dept. Housing and Urban Devel., Washington, 1973—76; ptnr. Patton Boggs L.L.P., Washington, 1976—. Editor: Clean Air Law and Regulation, 1992, Environmental Law Handbook, 1994. Capt. U.S. Army, 1970-71. Presbyterian. Home: 9000 Congressional Ct Potomac MD 20854-4608 Office: Patton Boggs LLP 2550 M St NW Ste 500 Washington DC 20037-1350 Office Phone: 202-457-6074. Business E-Mail: tvanderver@pattonboggs.com.

VAN DER VEUR, PAUL W., humanities educator; b. Medan, Indonesia, Aug. 28, 1921; came to U.S., 1947; s. Wilhelmus Marius and Johanna (Guldemond) van der Veur; m. Karol Anne Kaiser, July 21, 1951 (div. Aug. 1971); children: Julia, Paul Roscoe; m. Barbara Walker, Sept., 1973; children: Anne, Mark. BA, Swarthmore Coll., Pa., 1949; MA, U. Minn., Mpls., 1950; PhD, Cornell U., Ithaca, NY, 1955. Instr. Yale U., New Haven, 1954-56; asst. prof. U. Hawaii, Honolulu, 1956-59, assoc. prof., 1959-61; sr. rsch. fellow Australian Nat. U., Canberra, 1961-66; prof. No. Ill. U., DeKalb, 1966-67, Ohio U., Athens, 1967-91, prof. emeritus, 1991—, dir. S.E. Asia studies, 1967-73, 77, 1981-85, 88-90. Cons. Veriation Films, Menlo Park, Calif., 1984-85. Co-editor and author: Papua-New Guinea Elections, 1965, Toward a Glorious Indonesia, 1987; author: New Guinea Boundaries 2 vols., 1966, The Lion and the Gadfly, 2006. Mem. Athens County Soil and Conservation Agy., 1967-91. With Royal Netherlands Indies Army, 1941-47 (POW, Japan, 1942-45). Fulbright fellow U.S. Fulbright Assn., 1980-81. Democrat. Avocation: tree planting and management. Home: 74 Crosslands Dr Kennett Square PA 19348 Home Phone: 630-388-1697.

VAN DER VOO, ROB, geophysicist; b. Zeist, The Netherlands, Aug. 4, 1940; arrived in U.S., 1970; s. Maximiliaan and Johanna Hendrika (Baggerman) Van der V.; m. Tatiana M. C. Graafland, Mar. 26, 1966; children: Serge Nicolas, Bjorn Alexander. BS, U. Utrecht, Netherlands, 1961, MS, 1965, PhD, 1969. Rsch. asst. U. Utrecht, 1964-65, rsch. assoc., 1965-69, sr. rsch. assoc., 1969-70; vis. asst. prof. U. Mich., Ann Arbor, 1970-72, asst. prof., 1972-75, assoc. prof., 1975-79, prof. geophysics, 1979—, chmn., 1981-88, 91-95, Arthur F. Thurnau prof., 1994-97, dir. honors program Coll. Lit., Sci. and the Arts, 1998—2003. Guest prof. ETH, Zurich, Switzerland, 1978, Kuwait U., 1979, Utrecht U. and Delft U. Tech., 1997-98. Author: Paleomagnetism of the Atlantic, Tethys and Iapetus Oceans, 1993; contbr. articles to profl. jours. Recipient Russell award, U. Mich., 1976, Disting. Faculty Achievement award, 1990, Benjamin Franklin medal in Earth Scis., 2001. Mem. Geol. Soc. Am. (pres. 2004), Am. Geophys. Union, Geologische Vereinigung (Germany), Royal Acad. Scis. (Netherlands), Royal Norwegian Soc. Scis. and Letters, Sigma Xi, Phi Kappa Phi. Home: 2305 Devonshire Rd Ann Arbor MI 48104-2703 Office: U Mich 4534 CC Little Bldg Ann Arbor MI 48109-1005 Office Phone: 734-764-8322. Business E-Mail: voo@umich.edu.

VANDERWAGEN, W. CRAIG (WILLIAM CRAIG VANDERWAGEN), physician, former federal agency administrator; b. Grand Rapids, Mich., 1949; m. Suzanne M. Vanderwagen; 3 children. BA, Calvin Coll. & Seminary; MD, Mich. State U., 1978. Advanced through ranks to rear adm. upper half US Pub. Health Svc. Corps., 2006; chief pub. health Coalition Provisional Authority, Iraqi Ministry of Health; dir., Office Clin. & Preventative Services, acting chief med. officer, Zuni Indian Hosp. Indian Health Svc., Albuquerque; spl. asst. to the dep. sec. for preparedness US Dept. Health & Human Services (HHS), Washington, asst. sec. for pub. health emergency preparedness, 2006, dep. asst. sec. for preparedness & response, chief preparedness officer, 2006—07, asst. sec. for preparedness & response, 2007—09. Decorated Meritorious Svc. medal; recipient Disting. Svc. award for leading fed. disaster response to Hurricanes Katrina and Rita, AMA, 2006; named Alumni of Yr., Mich. State U. Coll. Human Medicine, 2005.*

VANDER WEG, JOHN D., music educator; s. Sam D. and Trena Vander Weg; m. Judith C. Baker, June 17, 1972. BMus, U. Mich., Sch. Music, Ann Arbor, 1972, MMus, 1974; PhD in Music, U. Mich., Ann Arbor, 1984. Instr., music Douglass Coll., Rutgers U., New Brunswick, NJ, 1974—78; asst. dean, sch. music U. Mich., 1984—87; dir., sch. music DePauw U., Greencastle, Ind., 1987—89; assoc. editor U. Mich. Press, Ann Arbor, 1989—92; assoc. chair, music U. Tex., San Antonio, 1992—94, assoc. dean, fine arts, 1994—2001, Wayne State U., Detroit, 2001—07, chair, music, 2005—. Office: Dept Music Wayne State University Detroit MI 48202 Office Fax: 313-577-5420. Business E-Mail: jdvw@wayne.edu.

VANDER WEIDE, BOB, professional sports team executive; m. Cheri Vander Weide; 5 children. V.p. basketball ops. Orlando Magic, Fla., 1992—94, pres., CEO, 1994—; CEO RDV Sports, 1994—; pres., CEO Internat. Hockey League Orlando Solar Bears, 1995—2001; chmn. investment com. RDV Corp., bd. dirs. Mem. bd. govs. NBA, mem. planning com.; mem. Fla. Olympics and Pan Am. Games Task Force. Chmn. Orlando Magic Youth Found. Named Orlandoan of Yr., Orlando Mag., 1997. Office: Orlando Magic 8701 Maitland Summit Blvd Orlando FL 32810-5915*

VANDERWEIGHE, KIKI (ERNEST MAURICE VANDERWEIGHE III), professional sports team executive, retired professional basketball player; b. Wiesbaden, Fed. Republic Germany, Aug. 1, 1958; came to U.S., 1959; s. Ernest M., Jr. and Colleen Kay (Hutchins) V.; m. Peggy Vanderweighe; 1 child, Ernest Maurice IV BA in Economics, UCLA, 1980. Profl. basketball player Denver Nuggets, 1980-84, Portland Trailblazers, Oreg., 1985—87, NY Knicks, 1988—91, L.A. Clippers, 1992—93; gen. mgr Denver Nuggets, 2001—06; NBA analyst ESPN, 2006—07; spl. asst. to pres. NJ Nets, 2007—08, gen. mgr., 2008—. Ptnr. Summa Stables, Beverly Hills, Calif., 1980—; pres. Inner Winner, Newport Beach, Calif., 1984—; cons. Brooks Shoes, Kalamazoo, Gt. Am. Health and Nutrition, Orange, Calif. Named Acad. All Am., NCAA, 1978, 79, 80, NBA All-Star, 1983, 84 Republican. Mem. Lds Ch. Avocations: sports; golf; tennis; race horses. Office: NJ Nets 390 Murray Hill Pky East Rutherford NJ 07073

VAN DE VEN, MICHAEL G., air transporation company executive; BBA, U. Tex. Sr. dir., fin. planning & analysis Southwest Airlines Co., dir., internal audit, v.p., fin. planning & analysis, 2001—04, sr. v.p., planning, 2004—05, exec. v.p., aircraft ops., 2005—06, chief, ops., 2006—08, exec. v.p., 2006—, COO, 2008—. Office: Southwest Airlines Co 2702 Love Field Dr Dallas TX 75235 Office Phone: 214-792-5015. Office Fax: 214-792-4000.*

VANDEWALLE, GERALD WAYNE, state supreme court chief justice; b. Noonan, ND, Aug. 15, 1933; s. Jules C. and Blanche Marie (Gits) VandeWalle. BSc, U. ND, 1955, JD, 1958. Bar: ND, US Dist. Ct. ND 1959. Spl. asst. atty. gen. State of ND, Bismarck, 1958-75, 1st asst. atty. gen., 1975-78; justice ND Supreme Ct., Bismarck, 1978-92, chief justice, 1993—. Mem. faculty Bismarck Jr. Coll., 1972-76; mem. Nat. Ctr. State Cts. Rsch. adv. coun.; mem. fed.-state jurisdiction com. Jud. Conf. of US Editor-in-chief ND Law Rev., 1957—58. Active Bismarck Meals on Wheels. Recipient Sioux award, U. ND, 1992, Ednl. Law award, ND Coun. Sch. Attys., 1987, Love Without Fear award, Abused Adult Resource Ctr., 1995, ND State Bar Assoc. Dist. Svc. award, 1998. Mem. ABA (co-chmn. bar admissions com. 1991-99, mem. coun. sect. legal edn. and admissions, chmn. coun. sect. legal edn. and admissions), State Bar Assn. ND, Burleigh County Bar Assn., Conf. of Chief Justices (past pres., bd. dirs. 1996-98, chmn. fed.-state tribal rels. com.), Am. Contract Bridge League, Order of Coif, ND Jud. Conf. (exec. com.), Elks, KC, Phi Eta Sigma, Beta Alpha Psi (Outstanding Alumnus award Zeta chpt. 1995), Beta Gamma Sigma, Phi Alpha Delta. Roman Catholic. Office: ND Supreme Ct State Capitol 600 E Boulevard Ave Bismarck ND 58505-0530 Office Phone: 701-328-2221. Office Fax: 701-328-4480. Business E-Mail: GVandeWalle@ndcourts.gov.*

VAN DE WATER, THOMAS ROGER, neuroscientist, educator; b. Oceanside, NY, Dec. 6, 1939; s. Lynn and Lenora (Winterson) Van De W.; m. Jeanette Adele Vilece, July 11, 1964; children: Ann Marie, Thomas Scott, Christopher Lynlee, Elizabeth Adele. AAS in Forestry, Paul Smith Coll., 1959; BS in Biology, Western Carolina U., 1961; MA in Biology, Hofstra U., 1965; PhD in Biology, NYU, 1976. Rsch. assoc. Med. Sch. Yale U., 1964-65; rsch. scientist Med. Sch. NYU, 1967-68; dir. devel. otobiology Albert Einstein Coll. Medicine, Bronx, N.Y., 1981—, prof. otolaryngology, 1987—, prof. neurosci., 1991—, dir. rsch., 1990—. Lectr., author Nobel Symposium, 1985; acad. dir. N.Y. Acad. Medicine Otolaryngology basic sci. course, 1988—; organizer, lectr. Ciba Symposium #196, 1995. Editor: Biology & Change in Otobiology, 1986, Genetics of Hearing Impairment, 1990, Handbook of Auditory Research, Clinical Aspects; contbr. over 100 sci. publs. Eucharistic min. Holy Redeemer Ch., Freeport, N.Y. With U.S. Army Med. Corps, 1962. Fellow Am. Acad. Otolaryngology and Head and Neck Surgery; mem. Assn. for Rsch. in Otolaryngology (sec./treas. 1990-93), N.Y. Acad. Sci., Am. Otological Soc. (assoc.), Soc. Neurosci., Oto-Rhinolaryngologica Collegium Amitae Sacrum. Achievements include establishment of organotypic culture of mammalian inner ear; definition of neuron-sensory cell interactions during inner ear development, role of epithelial-mesenchymal tissue interactions in the developing inner ear, role of growth factors during inner ear embryogenesis in both sensory and non-sensory systems, growth factor stimulation of the regeneration-repair of mammalian hair cells in vivo; neurotrophin therapy to auditory neurons after loss of hair cells in vivo; gene therapy in the inner ear. Home: 262 Pennsylvania Ave Freeport NY 11520-1329 Office: Albert Einstein Coll Medicine 1410 Pelham Pky S Bronx NY 10461-1101

VANDEWEGHE, ERNEST MAURICE, III, (KIKI VANDEWEGHE), professional sports team executive, retired professional basketball player; b. Weisbaden, Germany, Aug. 1, 1958; s. Ernest and Colleen Vandeweghe; m. Peggy Vandeweghe; 1 child, Ernest Maurice. B in Econs., UCLA, 1980. Forward Denver Nuggets, 1980—84, Portland Trailblazers, 1984—89, NY Knicks, 1989—92, LA Clippers, 1992—93; ret., 1993; founder fin. planning bus.; coach basketball clinic; asst. coach, dir. player develop. Dallas Mavericks, 1999—2000; gen. mgr. Denver Nuggets, 2001—06; columnist ESPN, 2006—07; spl. asst. to the team pres. NJ Nets, 2007—08, gen. mgr., 2008—. Named to NBA All-Star Team, 1983, 1984; finalist Rhodes Scholar. Office: NJ Nets 390 Murray Hill Pky East Rutherford NJ 07073*

VAN DINE, ALAN CHARLES, advertising agency executive, writer; b. Ford City, Pa., Jan. 12, 1933; s. Albert and Helen (Remaley) Van D.; m. Joan Anne Hodges, Jan. 29, 1955 (div. Jan. 1971); children: Lynn, Mark, Barbara, Michael; m. Holly Long Shefler, Apr. 23, 1977. BA, Duquesne U., 1955; postgrad., U. Pitts., 1968—71. Editor Mt. Lebanon News, Pa., 1956-58; editorial dir. Pitts. Suburban Newspapers, 1958-61; writer and assoc. creative dir. Batten, Barton, Durstine & Osborne, Pitts., 1961-70; pres., creative dir. Van Dine, Horton, McNamara, Manges, Inc., Pitts., 1970-89; chmn. Van Dine, Humphrey, Inc., Pitts., 1989-95; cons. in field, 1996—. Mem. adv. coun. Internat. Poetry Forum, Pitts., 1969-80. Author: Can You Imagine?, 1967, Unconventional Builders, 1977, revised edit., 2001, 2007, (humor) The Encyclopedia of Advertising, 1987, Clyde Hare's Pittsburgh, 1994, Light Verse for a Heavy Universe, 2005; columnist Pitts. mag., 1977-78, Pa. Illustrated, 1979-81; contbr. articles, essays, short stories, and poems to mags. 1st lt. USAF, 1956. Recipient numerous awards Art Dirs. Club NY, 1964—, Bus. and Profl. Advt. Assn., 1964—, Am. Advt. Fedn., 1999. Mem.: Kittanning Country Club. Avocations: golf, tennis, darkroom photography, cartooning, computer programming. E-mail: AVDZZZ@bellatlantic.net.

VAN DINE, HAROLD FORSTER, JR., architect, artist; b. New Haven, Aug. 28, 1930; s. Harold Forster and Marguerite Anna (Eichstedt) Van D.; m. Maureen Kallick, Mar. 1, 1983; children by previous marriage: Rebecca Van Dine, Stephanie Van Dine Natale, Gretchen Van Dine Natale. BA, Yale Coll., 1952; MArch, Yale Sch. Arch., 1958. Registered architect. Designer Minoru Yamasaki & Assocs., Detroit, 1958-60; chief designer Gunnar Birkerts & Assocs., Detroit, 1960-67; prin. Straub, Van Dine & Assocs., Troy, Mich., 1967-80; chief architecture and design officer Harley Ellis, Southfield, Mich., 1980-95; archtl. cons. Birmingham, Mich., 1995—, San Miguel de Allende, Mexico, 1995—. V.p. Fields, Devereaux, HEPY, L.A., 1984-95. Prin. works include Mcpl. Libr., Troy, Mich., campuses for Oakland CC, Mich., North Hills Ch., Troy, First Ctr. Office Plaza, chemistry bldgs at. U. Mich. and Ind. U., G.M.F. Robotics Hdqrs., Flint Ink Rsch. and Devel. Ctr., Comerica Bank Ops. Ctr., Christ the King Mausoleum, Chgo., Resurrection Mausoleum, Staten Island, Mich. Biotech Inst., Ford Sci. Rsch. Labs, Fetzer Inst. Hdqrs. and Retreat Ctr., Cen. Mich. U. Music Sch., Oakland U. Sci. Techs. Bldg., Corning Credit Union, NY. Bd. dirs. Cultural Coun. Birmingham/Bloomfield, 1990-99. Served to lt. (j.g.) USN, 1952-55 Recipient Book award AIA, 1958, Excellence in Architecture Silver medal AIA, 1958, Gold medal Detroit chpt. AIA, 1987, Mich. Soc. of Architects gold medal, 1991, over 50 major design awards; William Wirt Winchester travelling fellowship Yale U. Sch. Architecture, 1958; elect. to AIA Coll. Fellows, 1979. Mem.: Pewabic Soc. (bd. dirs. 1983—2002). Home Phone: 248-246-5814; Office Phone: 248-246-5814. Personal E-mail: mvandhv@aol.com. E-mail: artwork@harryvandine.com.

VAN DINE, VANCE, investment banker; b. San Francisco, July 2, 1925; s. Melvin Everett and Grace Winifred (Harris) Van D.; m. Isabel Erskine Brewster, Sept. 8, 1956 (dec.); 1 dau., Rose M. (dec.). BA, Yale U., 1949; LLB, NYU, 1955. Assoc. Morgan Stanley & Co., NYC, 1953-59, 61-63, ptnr., 1963-75; mng. dir. Morgan Stanley & Co., Inc., NYC, 1970-83; adv. dir. Morgan Stanley & Co., NYC, 1983—. Cons. Internat. Bank for Reconstn. and Devel., 1959-61. Author: The Role of the Investment Banker in International Transactions, 1970, The US Market After Controls, 1974. Bd. dirs. Yale U. Alumni Fund, Rec. for Blind, Inc., NYC, 1979-89; trustee Cancer Rsch. Inst., NYC, Nassau County Art Mus., LI U., 1979-91; gov. dir. Fgn. Policy Assn., 1980-89. With USN, 1943-46. Recipient Yale Class of 1949 Disting. Service award, 1983. Mem. The Pilgrims of the US, Union Club, NY Yacht Club, Church Club, Yale Club (NYC), Met. Opera Club. Republican. Episcopalian. Home: Casa de Manara 849 Coast Blvd La Jolla CA 92037 Personal E-mail: vanvan515@aol.com, vancevandine@earthlink.net.

VANDIVER, SARA ELIZABETH SHARP RANKIN, retired postmaster; d. James Earl and Celeste Heskett Sharp; m. William Doyle Vandiver, Aug. 18, 1978 (dec. Feb. 27, 1997); m. James Dorothy Rankin, Sr., Aug. 25, 1934 (dec. Aug. 3, 1971); children: James Dorothy Rankin Jr., William Earl Rankin, Carolyn Vandiver Pollan. Postmaster US Postal Svc., Driver, Ark., 1954—80; ret. Sec. St. Louis Region Postmaster Tng. Conf., 1962—73; v.p. Ark. Chpt., Nat. Assn. Postmasters, 1976—78; columnist Ark. Postmaster. Charter mem. Nat. Mus. Women in the Arts, Washington, 1990—2006; contbg. mem. Smithsonian Instn., Washington, 2000—06; pres. Wilson PTA, Ark., 1950—52, Wilson Co-Operative Club, 1952—54, Gen. Fedn. of Women's Clubs Prog. Club, Osceola, 1985—90; organizer Adopt-a-Teacher Program, Osceola Pub. Schs., 1985, Kids and Kindness Program, Osceola Pub. Schs., 1985, Gt. Am. Family Recognition and Awards Program, Osceola, Ark., 1987; pres., state advisor Gen. Fedn. Women's Clubs, Dist. II, Ark., 1990—92, state chmn. cmty. improvement program, 1994—96; mem. Miss. County Geneal. and Hist. Soc., 1993—2006; bd. mem. Interfaith Neighbors, Osceola, 1996—2006; leader Miss. County Explorers Bible Study, Ark., 1983—96; pres. Wilson Women's Missionary Union, 1953—55; Sunday sch. tchr., 1963—. Mem.: Riverlawn Country Club.

VAN DOKKUM, JAN, electric power industry executive; m. Lynn van Dokkum; 3 children, B of Elec. Engring., M of Elec. Engring., Inst. Tech. Albertus Magnus, Netherlands. Regional v.p. sales Seimens Transmission and Distbn.; pres., COO Seimans Power Transmission & Distbn., Inc., 1997—2002; pres. UTC Power United Technologies, South Windsor, Conn., 2002—. Office: United Techs Corp UTC Power 195 Govs Hwy South Windsor CT 06074

VAN DOVER, JAMES KENNETH, education educator; b. St. Louis, Mo., Jan. 1, 1950; s. James Kenneth and Virginia Van Dover; m. Sarala Abreu, June 9, 1979; children: Lara Kiran, Andrew Siddharth. BA, Lafayette Coll., Easton, Pa., 1968—72; MA, Bryn Mawr Coll., Pa., 1972—74, PhD, 1974—78. Prof. Lincoln U., Pa., 1978—. Author: (literary criticism) Defoe's World Mapp'd, Murder in the Millions, You Know My Method, We Must Have Certainty, At Wolfe's Door, Polemical Pulps; editor: Critical Responses to Raymond Chandler; author: Isn't Justice Always Unfair, Centurions, Knights, and Other Cops, Understanding William Kennedy. Recipient Fulbright Prof., Fulbright Commn., Germany 80, 88; China 00; Austria 07, Lindback award for Tchg. Excellence, Lincoln U., 1986; fellow Whiting Dissertation, Whiting Found., 1976—77. Independent. Protestant. Office: English Dept Lincoln Univ Lincoln University PA 19352 Office Fax: 610-932-1256. Business E-Mail: vandover@lincoln.edu.

VAN DRESER, MERTON LAWRENCE, ceramics engineer; b. Des Moines, June 5, 1929; s. Joseph Jerome and Victoria (Love) Van D.; m. Evelyn Lenore Manny, July 12, 1952; children: Peter, Jennifer Sue. BS in Ceramic Engring., Iowa State U., 1951. Tech. supt. Owens-Corning Fiberglas Corp., Kansas City, Mo., 1954-57; rsch. engr. Kaiser Aluminum & Chem. Corp., Milpitas, Calif., 1957-60, rsch. sect. head, 1960-63, lab. mgr., 1963-65, assoc. dir. rsch., 1965-69, dir. refractories rsch. Pleasanton, Calif., 1969-72, dir. non-metallic materials rsch., 1972-83, v.p., dir. rsch. Indsl. Chem. div. and Harshaw/Filtrol Partnership Cleve., 1983-85, dir. bus. devel. Pleasanton, 1985-88, cons., 1988—2003. Mem. adv. bd. dept. ceramic engring. U. Ill., 1974-78; chmn. tech. adv. com. Refractories Inst., 1980-84; mem. nat. materials adv. bd. Nat. Acad. Sci.; mem. Indsl. Rsch. Inst. Contbr. articles to sci. jours.; patentee in field. Sustaining membership chmn. local dist. Boy Scouts Am., 1980; pres. PTA, 1967-68; vol. exec. Pakistan Internat. Exec. Svc. Corps, 1990-91. Aviator C.E., U.S. Army, 1951-54. Recipient Profl. Achievement citation Iowa State U., 1978; named to Lambda Chi Alpha hall of fame, 1996. Fellow: Am. Ceramic Soc. (v.p. 1973—74); mem.: AIME, ASTM (hon.), Metall. Soc., Nat. Inst. Ceramic Engrs., Brit. Ceramic Soc., Masons, Rotary (pres. Pleasanton Club 2002—03, pres. Club Found. 2003—04, Paul Harris fellow), Alpha Tau Zeta (Alumni of Yr. 2006), Keramos (pres. 1976—78, herald 1980—84, Greaves Walker Roll of Honor award). Avocation: flying. Home and Office: 40 Castledown Rd Pleasanton CA 94566-9749

VAN DRIEL, EDWIN CHRISTIAAN, theology studies educator; b. Rotterdam, Netherlands, Dec. 14, 1969; m. Kimberly Miller Van Driel, June 14, 2003; 1 child, Christiaan Edwin. M.Div., Utrecht U., Netherlands, 1999, M.Phil. in Philosophy, 2000; MA in Religious Studies, Yale U., New Haven, 2002, M.Phil. in Religious Studies, 2004, PhD in Religious Studies, 2006; diploma in Anglican Studies, Berkeley Divinity Sch. Yale, New Haven, 2006. Lectr. theology Fordham U., Bronx, 2006—08; asst. prof. theology Pitts. Theol. Sem., 2009. Contbr. articles to profl. publs. Mem. Presbyn. Hymnal Com., Louisville. Fellowship, Episcopal Ch. Found., 2003—05. Office: Pitts Theol Seminary 616 N Highland Ave Pittsburgh PA 15206 Office Phone: 412-362-5610 ext. 2172. Business E-Mail: evandriel@pls.edu.

VAN DYCK, PETER CUYLER, federal agency administrator; b. Dec. 9, 1939; married; 3 children. BA in Physiology, U. Ill., 1962; MS in Physiology, U. Ill., Chgo., 1966, MD, 1966; MPH in Maternal and Child Health, U. Calif., Berkeley, 1973. Diplomate Nat. Bd. Med. Examiners. Intern then resident in pediatrics Children's Meml. Hosp., Chgo., 1966-68, chief resident, 1968-89; instr. Med. Sch. Northwestern U., Chgo., 1968-89; chief pediatrics Health Clinic U.S. Army, Frankfurt, Germany, 1969-71, primary nursery physician 97th Gen. Hosp., 1971-72; pediatric cons. Internat. Red Cross, Amman, Jordan, 1973; dir. maternal and child health Utah State Divsn. Health, Salt Lake City, 1973-74, dir. divsn. family health services, 1974-92, acting exec. dir., 1984-85, acting dir. divsn. health care financing (Medicaid), 1986-87; asst. prof. Med. Ctr. U. Utah, Salt Lake City, 1976-82, prof. Med. Ctr.; sr. med. advisor to the directors of Maternal and Child Health Bur. and Health Resources and Services Adminstrn., HHS, 1992—95; dir. Office of State and Cmty. Health Maternal and Child Health Bur., Health Resources and Services Adminstrn., US HHS, 1995—98, acting assoc. adminstr., 1998—99, assoc. adminstr., 1999—. Adj. assoc. prof. health Univ. Utah, Salt Lake City, 1975—, adj. asst. prof. Coll. Nursing, 1976—; mem. adv. com. U. Utah Coll. Nursing, 1976-80, Albert Einstein Coll. Medicine, Ctr. for Disease Control, 1983-86, John F. Kennedy Child Devel. Ctr., Denver, 1979-82; faculty coord. Crippled Children's Svcs. Advanced Inst., Children's Hosp., Columbus, Ohio, 1983—; mem. maternal and child health/Medicaid tech. assistance group Health Care Financing Adminstrn., 1987-93; mem. planning com., faculty Surgeon Gens. Conf., 1987; mem. various coms. and task forces; presenter, cons., reviewer in field; cons. Interagy. Efforts Children Spl. Health Needs Federated States Micronesia, 1991, Third Pacific Basin Interagy Conf. Individuals Spl. Health Care Needs No. Marianas Islands, 1992; faculty mem. Med. Ctr. Georgetown U., Washington, 1993; chief party U.S. Del. Third Regional Follow-up Meeting World Summit Children, Antigua, Guatemala, 1995. Contbr. articles to profl. jours. Co-chmn. sch. health com. Utah State Bd. Edn., Utah Dept. Health, 1974-92, statewide immunization action com. Awareness Com., 1977-78; project dir. Sudden Infant Death Syndrome Regional Ctr., Utah, 1975-80; chmn. Govs. Adv. Coun. for Developmentally Disabled Children, 1976-78; mem. task force on svcs. to presch. handicapped children Utah State Legis., 1984, tech. adv. coun. Utah Children, 1985-88, adv. bd. Jr. League, 1985-88; bd. dirs. Exceptional Child Ctr., Utah, 1975-80. Recipient Nat. Leadership award Dept. Health and Human Svcs., 1989, Nat. Achievement award Healthy Mothers, Healthy Babies, 1991; named one of 500 Most Influential Healty Policymakers Health Care 500, 1992; grantee U.S. Dept. Health and Human Svcs., Ctrs. for Disease Control., Devel. Diabetes Coun., Bur. Edn. for the Handicapped, Bur. Community Health Svcs.; WHO fellow, 1995. Mem. APHA (mem. various coms., chmn. maternal and child health sect. 1988—, Ross award 1977), Nat. Acad. for State Health Policy (mem. steering com. 1987-95), Nat. Found. March of Dimes (chmn. med. adv. bd. 1975-93, Plaque for Outstanding Svc. 1977-78), Nat. Early Childhood Tech. Assistance System (mem. nat. adv. com. 1988-90), Am. Acad. Pediatrics (mem. various coms.), Nat. Assn. of State Bds. Edn. (mem. task force on adolescent pregnancy 1979-80), Nat. Assn. State and Territorial Maternal and Child Health and Crippled Children Dirs. (pres. 1978-80), March of Dimes Birth Defect Found. (mem. nat. chpt. grants rev. com. 1988-92), Intermountain Pediatrics Soc. (mem. legis. and child abuse coms. 1974-76), Utah Pub. Health Assn. (mem. various coms., pres. 1984-86, mem. editorial bd. 1976-77, Beaty award 1985). Office: Maternal & Child Health Bur Parklawn Bldg Rm 18-05 5600 Fishers Ln Rockville MD 20857 Office Phone: 301-443-2170.*

VAN DYK, FREDERICK THEODORE, political scientist, writer; b. Bellingham, Wash., Oct. 6, 1934; s. Ted and June Ellen (Williams) Van Dyk; m. Julia Jean Covacevich, Nov. 22, 1957 (dec. 1996); children: Theodore, Robert, Terry Jean, Sue Ellen. BA, U. Wash., Seattle, 1955; MS, Columbia U., NYC, 1956. Reporter, editor Seattle Times, 1956-57; advt. public relations exec. Boston and NYC, 1958-62; acting dir. European Community Info. Service, Washington, 1962-64; asst. to Hubert Humphrey, Vice Pres. of U.S., 1964-68; v.p. Columbia U., NYC, 1968-69; pres. Van Dyk Assocs., Washington, 1969-76; asst. adminstr. AID, Washington, 1977; v.p. Weyerhaeuser Co., Tacoma, 1978—80; pres. Center for Nat. Policy, Washington, 1981-85, Van Dyk Assocs., 1985-98; exec. v.p. Milken Inst., Santa Monica, Calif., 1998-99; vis. scholar Claremont (Calif.) Grad. U., 1999-2000; sr. fellow UCLA Sch. Pub. Policy and Social Rsch., 1999-2000; columnist Seattle Post-Intelligencer, 2001—07, Crosscut.com, 2008—. Author: Heroes, Hacks and Fools, U. Wash. Press, Memoirs, 2007; contbr. articles to newspapers incl. the Wall St. Jour., NY Times, Wash. Post, L.A. Times. Mem. Coun. Fgn. Rels., Presdl. Commn. Fgn. Assistance, Pacific Coun. Internat. Policy, Am. Democratic Action; bd. dirs. Com. Study Am. Electorate, Franklin and Eleanor Roosevelt Inst., Jean Monnet Coun., Humphrey Inst. With M.I. US Army, 1957, with Am. Dem. Action US Army, 1961—62. Mem.: Columbia Princeton Club, NY, Rainier Club (Seattle), Delta Upsilon.

VAN DYKE, DEBBIE K., special education services professional; d. Charles A. and Helen M. Wallace; m. Mike H. Van Dyke, Aug. 9; 1 child, Jason Michael. BS, Henderson State U., 1976, MS in Edn., 1976. Spl. edn. tchr. Pulaski County Sch. Dist., Little Rock, 1975; spl. edn. tchr. supr. Gosnell Sch. Dist., Ark., 1975—82; spl. edn. tchr. Greene County Tech, Paragould, Ark., 1982—85; spl. edn. supr. Arch Ford Ednl. Svc. Coop., Plumerville, Ark., 1986—92; dir. spl. svcs. Russellville (Ark.) Sch. Dist., 1992—96; area spl. edn. supr. Ark. Dept. Edn., Little Rock, 1996—2003; spl. svcs. supr. Benton County Sch. of the Arts, Rogers, Ark., 2004—. Ednl. cons. Spl. Solutions Ark., Pea Ridge, 2003—. Mem. chair Ark. Assn. Spl. Edn. Adminstrn., Little Rock, 1988—93, Ark. Coun. for Exceptional Children, Little Rock, 1988—96. Recipient Ark. Spl. Edn. Adminstr. of Yr. award, Ark. Assn. Spl. Edn. Adminstrn., 1994, Area I Beverly Benham Spl. Edn. Adminstr. of Yr. award, Area I Ark. Assn. Spl. Edn. Adminstrn., 2000. Mem.: Coun. Exceptional Children.

VAN DYKE, GENE, oil industry executive; b. Normal, Ill, Nov. 5, 1926; BS in Geol. Engring., U. Okla., 1950. Geologist Kerr-McGee, Oklahoma City, 1950; chief geologist S.D. Johnson Co., Wichita Falls, Tex., 1950-51; ind. geologist, oil operator, 1951-58; ptnr. Van Dyke and Mejlaender, Houston, 1958-62; founder, owner, chmn. Van Dyke Oil Co. (now Vanco Energy Co.), Houston, 1962—, also bd. dir. Bd. dirs. Van Dyke Netherlands, Inc. Compiler index of geol. articles to South La. With AC US Army, 1945. Named Living Legend in Wildcatting, Houston Geol. Soc., 2000; named to Hall of Fame, Dutch Am. Heritage Soc., 2001. Mem.: Am. Assn. Petroleum Geologists, Ind. Petroleum Assn., Houstonian Club, Houston Petroleum Club, Houston Club (pres.). Republican. Episcopalian. Vanco Energy Company is active in deepwater west Africa and is currently one of the largest license holder with over 5 million acres in depths between 1,000 and 10,000 feet; Vanco has been awarded the Prykerchenska Block in southeast Ukraine Black Sea, being 3.2 million acres and its water depth ranges from 150 meters to 2,200 meters. Office: Vanco Energy Co 3 Greenway Plz 12th Fl Houston TX 77046 Office Phone: 713-877-8544. Office Fax: 713-877-8476. Business E-Mail: info@vancoenergy.com, gvandyke@vancoenergy.com.

VAN DYKE, MICHELLE, bank executive; 4 children. BA in Bus. Econ., Calvin Coll., 1985. Joined Old Kent Bank, 1985, exec. v.p., mgr. retail distbn., Mich., Ind. and Ill., 1998—2004, pres., Ill. div., 2000—04; former sr. v.p., regional mgr., Ill. mortgage region Old Kent Mortgage Co., pres., ctrl. region, 1997—98; pres., CEO, western Mich. Fifth Third Bank, Grand Rapids, 2004—. Active YMCA; bd. dirs. ICCF, Porter Hills Retirement Village. Named one of 25 Women to Watch, US Banker mag., 2005, 25 Most Powerful Women in Banking, 2007. Office: Fifth Third Bank 3785 Plainfield Ave NE Grand Rapids MI 49525

VAN DYKE, RUSSELL BARRETT, medical educator; b. Pasadena, Calif., Mar. 14, 1950; s. Milton Denman Van Dyke and Barbara Anne (Barrett) Lock; m. Nadiene Lynn Horst, Dec. 18, 1971; children: Daryl Kloss, Elizabeth Grace. BA, Stanford U., 1971; MD, Med. Coll. Wis., 1975. Asst. clin. prof. U. Calif., San Diego, 1979; asst. prof. Tulane U., New Orleans, 1983-88, assoc. prof., 1988-95, prof., 1995—. Prin. invistigator Tulane/La. State U. Pediatric ACTV, 1990—. Mem. edit. bd. Pediatric AIDS and HIV Infection jour., 1994—. Mem. Gov.'s Task Force on HIV, La., 1994—. Fellow Am. Acad. Pediat., Pediatric

Infectious Diseases Soc.; mem. Infectious Diseases Soc. Am., Sierra Club. Democrat. Avocations: banjo, backpacking. Home: 235 Lavergne St New Orleans LA 70114-1009 Office: Tulane Sch Medicine 1430 Tulane Ave New Orleans LA 70112-2699

VAN DYKE, TERRY ANN, geneticist, researcher; b. Wake Island, Hawaii, May 2, 1955; d. Harold Quinton and Betty Irene (Wolf) Van D.; m. Richard Jude Samulski, Aug. 14, 1982; children: Danielle, Richard. BS, U. Fla., 1977, PhD, 1981. Postdoctoral fellow U. Fla., Gainesville, 1981-82, SUNY, Stonybrook, NY, 1982-84; rsch. assoc. Princeton U., NJ, 1984-86; asst. prof. U. Pitts., Pa., 1986, animal facilities chair, 1989-91, grad. student curriculum, 1990-91; faculty mem. U. NC, Chapel Hill, 1993—, faculty dir. Animal Models Core Faculty, 1998, founder Carolina Mutant Mouse Regional Resource Ctr. (MMRRC), 1999, now Sarah Graham Kenan disting. prof. genetics; dir. Mouse Cancer Genetics Program (MCGP) Ctr. Cancer Rsch., Nat. Cancer Inst., NIH, 2007—. Named Predoctoral trainee Nat. Inst. Health, 1978-81; postdoctoral fellow Am. Cancer Soc., 1982-84. Mem. AAAS, Am. Soc. for Microbiology, N.Y. Acad. Sci., Pitts. Cancer Inst. Avocations: swimming, dance, hiking. Office: Nat Cancer Inst at Frederick Bldg 560, Rm 22-63 Bethesda MD 20892 Office Phone: 304-846-1988. Office Fax: 304-846-1290. E-mail: vandyket@mail.nih.gov.*

VAN DYKE, THOMAS WESLEY, lawyer; b. Kansas City, Mo., May 12, 1938; s. Harold Thomas and Elizabeth Louise (Barritt) Van Dyke; m. Sharon Edgar, Jan. 30, 1960; children: Jennifer Van Dyke Winters, Jeffrey. BA, U. Kans., 1960; JD, U. Mich., 1963. Bar: Mo. 1963, Kans. 1983. Atty. SEC, Washington, 1963-64; legal asst. to commr. Hamer E. Budge, Washington, 1964-65; from assoc. to ptnr. Linde Thomson Langworthy Kohn & Van Dyke, P.C., Overland Park, Kans., 1965-91. Co-chmn. ALI-ABA Tax and Bus. Planning Seminar, 1987-96, 2005-08; securities adv. panel Sec. of State of Mo., 1984-89. Mem. ABA (fed. regulation securities com. bus. law sect. 1982-2009, mergers & acquisitions com. 1989-2009), Kans. Bar Assn., Mo. Bar Assn. (corp. banking and bus. law com., chmn. full com. 1983-84, past chmn. securities law subcom.), Carriage Club (bd. dirs. 1986-89). Republican. Avocations: tennis, golf, reading. Office: Bryan Cave LLP 3500 One Kansas City Pl 1200 Main St Kansas City MO 64105 Home Phone: 913-469-8638; Office Phone: 816-374-3201. Business E-Mail: twvandyke@bryancave.com.

VANE, SYLVIA BRAKKE, anthropologist, writer; b. Fillmore County, Minn., Feb. 28, 1918; d. John T. and Hulda Christina Brakke.; m. Arthur Bayard Vane, May 17, 1942; children: Ronald Arthur, Linda, Laura Vane Ames. AA, Rochester Jr. Coll., 1937; BS with distinction, U. Minn., Mpls., 1939; postgrad, Radcliffe Coll., Cambridge, Mass., 1944; MA, Calif. State U., Hayward, 1975. Med. technologist Dr. Frost and Hodapp, Willmar, Minn., 1939-41; head labs. Corvallis Gen. Hosp., Oreg., 1941-42; dir. lab. Cambridge Gen. Hosp., 1942-43; staff Peninsula Clinic, Redwood City, Calif., 1947-49; v.p. Cultural Systems Rsch. Inc., Menlo Park, Calif., 1978—; pres. Ballena Press, 1981—2005. Cons. cultural resource mgmt. So. Calif. Edison Co., Rosemead, 1978-81, San Diego Gas and Elec. Co., 1980-83, Pacific Gas and Elec. Co., San Francisco, 1982-83, Wender, Murase & White, Washington, 1983-87, Yosemite Indians, Mariposa, Calif., 1982-91, San Luis Rey Band of Mission Indians, Escondido, Calif., 1986-89, US Ecology, Newport Beach, Calif., 1986-89, Riverside County Flood Control and Water Conservation Dist., 1985-95, Infotec, Inc., 1989-91, Alexander & Karshmer, Berkeley, Calif., 1989-92, Desert Water Agy., Palm Springs, Calif., 1989-90, Met. Water Dist., 1992-2001, Nat. Park Svc., 1992-2001, Applied Earthworks, Inc., 1997-2001, NW Econ. Assocs., 2002-2004, County of Riverside, 2002-03, Aqua Caliente Cultural Mus., 2005—; bd. dirs. XEl Scientific. Author: (with L.J. Bean), California Indians, Primary Resources, 1977, rev. edit., 1990, The Cahuilla and the Santa Rosa Mountains, 1981, The Cahuilla Landscape, 1991, Ethnology of the Alta California Indians, vol. I Pre Contact, vol. II Post Contact, 1992, Spanish Borderlands Sourcebooks, vols. 3, 4; contbr. chpts. to books. Bd. dir. Sequoia Area coun. Girl Scouts US, 1954-61; bd. dirs., v.p., pres. LWV, South San Mateo County, Calif., 1960-65. Recipient Lifetime Achievement award, Calif. Indian Conf., 2005. Fellow Soc. Applied Anthropology, Am. Anthropology Assn.; mem. Southwestern Anthropology Assn. (prog. chmn. 1976-78, newsletter editor 1976-79), Soc. for Am. Archaeology, Soc. Calif. Archaeology (Martin A. Baumhoff Spl. Achievement award 1998). Mem. United Ch. of Christ. Office: 823 Valparaiso Ave Menlo Park CA 94025-4206 Office Phone: 650-323-9261.

VANE, TERENCE G., JR., finance company executive, lawyer; b. Elgin, Ill., Jan. 17, 1942; s. Terence Gregory and Velma Mary (Mersman) V.; m. Patricia Bryant, Aug. 29, 1964; children: Terence Gregory III, Lourdene DeLynne, Christopher Theodore. BA, Ind. U., 1964, JD, 1967. Bar: Ind. 1967, Tex. 1977, N.C. 1992, Fla. 2002. Staff atty. Assocs. Discount Corp., South Bend, Ind., 1967-69; asst. gen. counsel Assocs. Mgmt. Corp., South Bend, 1969-74, Assocs. Comml. Corp., South Bend, 1974-76, Assocs. Ins. Group, Inc., Dallas, 1976-77; gen. counsel, v.p. ins. ops. Assocs. Corp. N.Am., Dallas, 1977-80, gen. counsel, sr. v.p. ins. ops., 1981-82, gen. counsel, sr. v.p. consumer fin. and ins. ops., 1982-86, gen. counsel, sr. v.p. diversified consumer fin. svcs. and credit card ops., 1986-88; exec. v.p., gen. counsel, sec., dir. Barclays Am. Corp., Charlotte, NC, 1988-91; pres. Vector Fin. Svcs., Inc., Charlotte, 1991-95, bd. dirs.; sr. v.p., assoc. gen. counsel EquiCredit Corp., Jacksonville, Fla., 1996-97; sr. v.p., gen. counsel, sec. First Street Mortgage Corp., Jacksonville, 1997-98, Home Alliance Mortgage Co., Jacksonville, 1998-2000, Alliance Capital Ptnrs. Group, Jacksonville, 2000—02, Slott & Barker, Jacksonville, 2002—04; pvt. practice Jacksonville, 2005—. Chmn. bd. dirs., sec. Youth Concert Found. for Promotion Creative Arts, 1981—; bd. dirs. N.C. Bus. Com. Edn., 1988-91. Mem. ABA (com. on consumer fin. svcs. law), Fla. Bar Assn., Ind. Bar Assn., Tex. Bar Assn., N.C. Bar Assn., Nat. Assn. Ind. Insurers (laws com. 1978-86), Consumer Credit Ins. Assn. (chmn. property ins. legis. com. 1979-85), Am. Fin. Svcs. Assn. (law com., chmn. environ. law subcom.), Conf. Consumer Fin. Law (governing com.), Nat. Home Equity Mortgage Assn., Lawyers Round Table, Safari Club Internat. (pres., dir. North Fla. chpt.). Conservative. Episcopalian. Office: Terence G Vane Jr PA 233 E Bay St Ste 620 Jacksonville FL 32202-3447 Office Phone: 904-353-8285. Business E-Mail: tvane@tvanelaw.com.

VANEK, FRANCIS MICHAEL, engineering educator, researcher; b. Ithaca, NY, Feb. 12, 1967; s. Jaroslav and Wilda Marie Vanek; m. Catherine Lee Johnson, Oct. 30, 1992; children: Raymond Aaron Vanek-Johnson, Mira Marguerite Vanek-Johnson. BS in Mech. Engring., Cornell U., Ithaca, 1991, BA in Asian Studies, 1991; PhD in Sys. Engring., U. Pa., Phila., 1998. Lectr. logistics mgmt. Heriot-Watt U., Edinburgh, 1998—2000; sr. lectr. Cornell U., Sch. Civil & Environ. Engring., 2001—, rsch. assoc., 2001—. Author: (textbook) Energy Systems Engineering: Evaluation and Implementation. Fin. bd. mem. Ecovillage Ithaca 2nd Neighborhood, 2002—08; coord. Engrs. Sustainable World Cornell U., 2005—08. Avocations: bicycling, travel, camping, piano, yoga.

VANEK, JAROSLAV, economist, educator; b. Prague, Czechoslovakia, Apr. 20, 1930; came to U.S., 1955, naturalized, 1960; s. Josef and Jaroslava (Tucek) V.; m. Wilda M. Marraffino, Dec. 26, 1959; children: Joseph, Francis, Rosemarie, Steven, Teresa. Degree in stats., Sorbonne, Paris, 1951; license in econ., U. Geneva, 1954; PhD, MIT, 1957. Instr., then asst. prof. Harvard U., 1957-63; adviser AID, 1964; mem. faculty Cornell U., 1964-96, prof. econs., 1966-96, Carl Marks prof. internat. studies, 1969-96, dir. program comparative econ. devel., 1968-73, dir. program participation and labor-managed systems, 1969-96, prof. emeritus, 1996—. Mem. nat. adv. bd. econs. NSF, 1969-70; founder, pres. S.T.E.V.E.N. Found. (Sustainable Tech. and Energy for Vital Econ. Needs), 1985—. Author: International Trade: Theory and Economic Policy, 1962, The Balance of Payments, Level of Economic Activity and the Value of Currency, 1962, The Natural Resource Content of United States Foreign Trade, 1870-1955, 1963, General Equilibrium of International Discrimination, 1965, Estimating Foreign Resource Needs for Economic Development, 1966, Maximal Economic Growth, 1968, The General Theory of Labor-Managed Market Economies, 1970, The Participatory Economy, 1971, Self-Management: Economic Liberation of Man, 1975, The Labor-Managed Economy, 1977, Crisis and Reform: East and West: Essays in Social Economy, 1989, Toward Full Democracy, Political and Economic, In Russia, 1993, Destructive International Trade: from Justice for Labour to Global Strategy, 1998, Unified Theory of Social Systems: A Radical Christian Analysis, 2000; also manuscripts on solar tech., contbr. to Advances in the Economic Analysis of Participatory and Labor-Managed Firms, Vol. 2, 1987, Vol. 7, 2003, inventor several solar tech. designs, including solar steam engines, pumps, refrigerators, cookers, holder 1 patent. Roman Catholic. Home: 414 Triphammer Rd Ithaca NY 14850-2521 Business E-Mail: jv19@cornell.edu.

VANEK, THOMAS, professional hockey player; b. Vienna, Jan. 19, 1984; s. Zdenek and Jarmila Vanek; m. Ashley Vanek; 1 child, Blake Thomas. Attended, U. Minn., 2002—04. Left wing Buffalo Sabres, 2005—. Recipient NHL Plus/Minus Award, 2007; named to Second All-Star Team, NHL, 2007, NHL YoungStars Game, 2007, NHL All-Star Game, 2009. Achievements include being a member of NCAA National Championship Team, University of Minnesota, 2003. Avocations: golf, tennis, fishing, soccer. Office: Buffalo Sabres HSBC Arena One Seymour H Knox III Plaza Buffalo NY 14203-3096*

VANETTEN, HANS D., plant pathologist, educator; b. Peoria, Ill., Sept. 16, 1941; s. Cecil Herman and Freeda VanEtten; m. Martha Canter Hawes, Aug. 11, 1990; children: Erica Lynn, Laura Nadine. PhD, Cornell U., Ithaca, NY, 1970. Asst. prof. Cornell U., 1970—76, assoc. prof., 1976—84, full prof., 1984—89, U. Ariz., Tucson, 1989, dept. head, 2001. Grantee, Alexander von Humboldt Found., 1978, Fulbright Hays Found., 1978. Fellow: Am. Phytopathological Soc.; mem.: AAAS. Office: Plant Sci Dept Univ Ariz Tucson AZ 85721 Business E-Mail: vanetten@ag.arizona.edu.

VAN ETTEN, PETER WALBRIDGE, foundation executive; b. Boston, May 10, 1946; s. Royal Cornelius Van Etten and Peggy June (Walbridge) Hutchins; m. Mary Peters French, Sept. 5, 1968; children: Molly, Clarissa, Ellen. BA, Columbia U., 1968; MBA, Harvard U., 1973. Br. mgr. BayBanks, Brookline, Mass., 1968-71; loan officer Bank of Boston, 1973-76; CFO Univ. Hosp., Boston, 1976-79; exec. v.p., CFO New Eng. Med. Ctr., Boston, 1979-89; pres., CEO Transition Systems, Boston, 1986-89; dep. chancellor U. Mass. Med. Ctr., Worcester, 1989-91; CFO Stanford U., Calif., 1991-94; pres., CEO Stanford Univ. Hosp., 1994-97; CEO UCSF Stanford Health Care, 1997-99; exec. com. U. Healthsystem Consortium, 1997-99, vice chmn., 1998-99; dir. Calif. Healthcare Assn., 1998-99, IDX Sys., Inc., 1999-2001; pres., CEO Juvenile Diabetes Found. Internat., NYC, 2000—06. Dir. Transition Sys., Inc., 1996—98, Duke U. Health Sys., 2003—, vice chmn., 2007—; dir. Rsch. Am., 2005—06. Chair campaign United Way San Francisco, 1998. Business E-Mail: pvanetten1@yahoo.com.

VAN ETTEN, RICHARD A., hematologist, researcher; s. Chester L. and Marie O. Van Etten; 1 child, Christopher A. MD, Stanford U., Calif., PhD, 1984. Cert. hematologist Am. Bd. Internal Medicine, 1990. Assoc. prof. genetics Harvard Med. Sch., Boston, 1995—2003; investigator CBR Inst. Biomed. Rsch., Boston, 1991—2003. Investigator, molecular oncology rsch. inst. Tufts Med. Ctr., Boston, 2003—, chief, divsn. hematology-oncology, 2006—. Mem.: Blood Jour. Am. Soc. Hematology (assoc. editor 2007—08), Am. Soc. Hematology. Office: Tufts Med Ctr 800 Washington St PO Box 5609 Boston MA 02111 Business E-Mail: rvanetten@tuftsmedicalcenter.org.

VAN EXEL, NICKEY MAXWELL, retired professional basketball player; b. Kenosha, Wis., Nov. 27, 1971; s. Nickey Maxwell and Joyce Van Exel; 1 child, Nickey Maxwell III. Attended, Trinity Valley C.C., 1989-91; BA in Sociology, U. Cin., 1993. Guard L.A. Lakers, 1993-98, Denver Nuggets, 1998—2002, Dallas Mavericks, 2002—03, Golden State Warriors, 2003—04, Portland Trailblazers, 2004—05, San Antonio Spurs, 2005—06; ret., 2006. With Nat. Benevolent Assn., Christian Ch. Recipient Victor Award for Comeback Player of the Yr., 1998, Chopper Travaglini award; named to NBA All-Rookie Team, 1994, NBA All-Star Game, 1998. Avocation: collecting baseball cards, hats, books.

VAN FLEET, CONNIE JEAN, library and information scientist, educator; b. New Orleans, La., Oct. 3, 1950; d. Cornelius and Elizabeth Fisher Van Fleet; m. Danny Paul Wallace; children: Robyn Solomon, Elizabeth Wallace. BA, U. of Okla., 1972; M of Libr. Info. Sci., La. State U., 1987; PhD, Ind. U., 1990. Libr. assoc. New Orleans Pub. Libr., 1982—85; instr. La. State U., Baton Rouge, 1989—90, asst. prof., 1990—94, assoc. prof., 1994—96; adj. assoc. prof. Kent (Ohio) State U., 1996—98, assoc. prof., 1998—2000, U. of Okla., Norman, 2000—03, prof., 2003—. Panelist, proposal evaluator NEH, Washington, 1999; participant forum on libr. and info. svcs. policy Nat. Ctr. for Edn. Stats. and U.S. Nat. Commn. on Librs. and Info. Sci., Washington, 1996; panelist White House conf. on aging mini-conf. on the arts, the humanities, and older adults NEH/ Nat. Coun. on the Aging, Washington, 1995; co-investigator on grant project Okla. Dept. of Librs./U. of Okla., Oklahoma City, 2001—02, Inst. for Mus. and Libr. Svcs., USDE, Washington, 1999—2001; project cons. Ohio Libr. Coun. and State Libr. of Ohio, Columbus, 1998—99; co-investigator on grant Libr. Edn. and Human Resource Devel. Program, USDE, Washington, 1997—98; project cons. Ohio Libr. Coun., Columbus, 1996—98; inst. co-organizer Libr. Career Tng. and Devel. Program Inst. Awards, USDE, Washington, 1995—96, Libr. Career Tng. Program, USDE, Washington, 1994—95; project supr., grant adminstr. Libr. Career Tng. Program Fellowship Awards, USDE, Washington, 1992—94; project cons. Nat. Coun. on the Aging, Inc., Washington, 1990—91; guest instr. Mo. State Libr., Jefferson City, 1999. Editor: (jour.) Reference & User Svcs. Quar., 2000; co-editor: RQ, 1997, (book) Library Evaluation: A Casebook for Managers, 2001; co-author: Preparing Staff to Serve People with Disabilities, 1995; co-editor: A Service Profession, a Service Commitment: A Festschrift in Honor of Charles D. Patterson, 1992; co-author: (book chpt.) The Readers' Advisor's Companion, 2001, Research Issues in Public Librarianship: Trends for the Future, 1994; author: Adult Services: An Enduring Focus for Public Libraries, 1990, (procs.) Public Libraries and Community-Based Education for Lifelong Learning, 1995; co-author: Proceedings of Philosophical, Ethical and Practical Aspects of Refereed Science Journals; contbr. articles to profl. jours. Pres. Patrons of the Pub. Libr., East Baton Rouge Parish, Baton Rouge, 1994—96. Recipient John Edwards fellowship, Ind. U., 1988—89, grant Seminar: Ohio Libr. Evaluation, Libr. Edn. & Human Resource Devel. Program, U.S. Dept of Edn., 1997—98, grant for Rural Econ. Devel. Inst., Libr. Career Tng. and Devel. Program, U.S. Dept. of Edn., 1995—96, grant La. Pub. Librs. Electronic Access Seminar, 1994—95, scholarship support for interest in svcs. to people with disabilities, Libr. Career Tng. Program, U.S. Dept of Edn., 1993—94, 1992—93. Mem.: ALA (steering com., conf. on profl. edn. 1988—99, chair rsch. com. 1989—91, editl. adv. bd. co-chair Reference and Adult Svcs. Divsn. 1991—96, mem. (ex officio) bd. dirs. Reference and Adult Svcs. Divsn. 1991—97, Resolution of Appreciation Reference & User Services Assn. 1997, mem. task force on fgn. credentialing 1997—2000, chair, com. on edn. 1998—99, steering com. Congress on Profl. Edn. 1998—99, councilor at large 1998—2002, mem. (ex officio) bd. dirs. Reference and Users Svcs. Assn. 2000—06, reference & user svcs. quar. editl. adv. bd. co-chair 2000—06, planning and budget assembly 2001—02, nominating com. 2006, Pub. Libr. Assn., Assn. Specialized and Coop. Libr. Agys., Intellectual Freedom Round Table, Margaret E. Monroe Libr. Adult Svcs. award Reference and Adult Services Divsn. 1996), White House Conf. on the Aging Task Force, Assn. Libr. & Info. Sci. Edn. (pres.), La. Libr. Assn. (mem. com. on paraprofl. continuing edn. 1989—91, co-founder/mem. minority recruitment and profl. concerns group 1989—92, mem. scholarship com. 1989—92, mem. pub. libr. stds.com. 1993—95), Okla. Libr. Assn. (intellectual freedom com. 2001—04), Beta Phi Mu (chpt. advisor 1992—94, Rho chpt. advisor 1998—2000). Democrat. Avocations: reading, watercolor, needlecrafts. Office: U Oklahoma SLIS Rm 120 401 W Brooks Norman OK 73019-6032 Business E-Mail: cvanfleet@ou.edu.

VAN FLEET, DAVID DOMINIC, management educator; b. Binghamton, NY, Nov. 27, 1940; s. Walter Anthony Van Fleet, Sr. and Katherine Elizabeth Van Fleet; m. Ella Webb, Aug. 27, 1966; children: Marijke, Dirk. BS, U. Tenn., 1962, PhD, 1969. Instr. U. Tenn., Knoxville, 1963—67, Kingsport Grad. Study Program, Kingsport, Tenn., 1967—70; asst. prof. U. Akron, Akron, 1970—73; from asst. prof. to prof. Tex. A&M U., College Station, 1973—89; prof. Ariz. State U., Phoenix, 1989—, MBA dir., 1999—2004. Prin. lectr. A. Frank Smith Jr. Lectureship series Southwestern U., 2000. Author: (books) Military Leadership: An Organizational Behavior Perspective, 1986, Organizational Behavior: A Managerial Viewpoint, 1983, Contemporary Management, 1991, 2d edit., 1991, 3d edit., 1994, Behavior in Organizations, 1991, Workplace Survival: Dealing with bad Bosses, Bad Workes and Bad Jobs, 2007; contbr. numerous articles to profl. jours., chpts. to books; editor: N-File Newsletter, 1976—78, Acad. of Mgmt. Newsletter, 1979—82, Jour. of Mgmt., 1987—89, Jour. Behavioral and Applied Mgmt., 2006—. Recipient Faculty Achievement award in Rsch., Scholarship, and Creative Activity, Ariz. State U. West Campus, 2001, Faculty Achievement award in Svc., 2005, Outstanding Svc. award, Coll. Bus. Adminstrn., Tex. A&M U., 1985. Fellow: Acad. Mgmt. (chmn. mgmt. history divsn. 1980—81, dep. dean 1996—99, Cancer Svc. award 2008), So. Mgmt. Assn. (pres. 1995, dean 2008, Sustained Outstanding Svc. award 2005); mem.: Southwestern Fedn. of Adminstrv. Disciplines (bd. dirs. 1985—87), Allied So. Bus. Assn. (pres. 1995), S.W. Acad. of Mgmt. (pres. 1986—87). Home: 4849 E Altadena Ave Scottsdale AZ 85254 Office: Arizona State University PO Box 37100 Phoenix AZ 85069-7100 Office Phone: 602-543-6104. Personal E-mail: ddvf@asu.edu.

VAN FLEET, GEORGE ALLAN, lawyer; b. Monterey, Calif., Jan. 20, 1953; s. George Lawson and Wilma Ruth (Williams) Van F.; m. Laurie Elise Koch, July 20, 1975; children: Katia Elaine, Alexander Lawson. BA summa cum laude, Rice U., 1976; JD summa cum laude, Columbia U., 1977. Bar: Tex. 1978, US Dist. Ct. (so. dist.) Tex. 1978, US Dist. Ct. (we. dist.) Tex. 1987, US Dist. Ct. (no. dist.) Tex, 1988, US Dist. Ct. (ea. dist.) Tex. 1991, US Tax Ct., 1984, US Ct. Appeals (5th cir.) 1978, US Ct. Appeals (11th cir.) 1981, US Ct. Appeals (DC cir.) 1982, US Ct. Appeals (fed. cir.) 1993, US Supreme Ct. 1981. Law clk. U.S. Ct. Appeals (2d cir.), NYC, 1977; assoc. Vinson & Elkins, Houston, 1977-84, ptnr., 1984—2006; shareholder Greenberg Traurig, LLP, 2006—. Co-author: Federal Civil Procedure Before Trial--Firth Circuit, 1997, The Competition Laws of NAFTA, Canada, Mexico and the United States, 1997, Business and Commercial Litigation in Federal Courts, 1998, supplement, 2005; editor: Annual Review of Antitrust Law Developments, 2000; co-author: Am. Legal Ethics Libr., 2002, Doing Business in Texas, 2003, Spanish edit., 2007, State Antitrust Practice and Statutes, 2004, Inside the Minds: Leading Lawyers on Unfair Competition, Trade Regulation and Litig., 2003; contbr. articles to profl. jour. Mem. bd. visitors Columbia U., 1992—; mem. City of Houston Ethics Com., 1992—98, chmn., 1995—98; bd. dirs. Nat. Appleseed Found., 2002—08, Tex. Appleseed Ctr., 1998—, vice chmn., 1999—2002, chmn., 2002—04. Recipient Ordroneaux prize Columbia U., 1977, W. Frank Newton award for outstanding contbns. in provision of access to legal svcs. to the poor State Bar Tex., 2002; James Kent scholar Columbia U., 1974-77. Fellow: Am. Bar Found., Tex. Bar Found.; mem.: ABA (com. chmn. 1987—95, coun. 1996—99, com. chmn. 2000—02, ho. dels. 2002—05, sect. officer 2002—, nominating com. 2003—05), Latin Am. Law Initiative (coun. 2005—), Tex.-Mex. Bar Assn. (pres. 1998—2000), Houston Bar Assn. (sect. chair 1991—93), Tex. Commn. on Access to Justice (commr. 2005), State Bar Tex. (coun. 2000—04, dir. 2005—, 2005—08), Phi Beta Kappa. Democrat. Jewish. Home: 3430 S Parkwood Dr Houston TX 77021-1238 Office: Greenberg Traurig LLP 1000 Louisiana Ste 1800 Houston TX 77002 Home Phone: 713-748-6344; Office Phone: 713-374-3555. Business E-Mail: vanfleetg@gtlaw.com.

VAN FLEET, LISA A., lawyer; BSW, Valparaiso U., 1982, JD, 1985. Bar: Ind. 1985, US Tax Ct. 1987, US Claims Ct. 1988, Mo. 1989, Ill. 1990. Ptnr., practice leader Employee Benefits and Exec. Compensation Bryan Cave LLP, St. Louis. Office: Bryan Cave LLP One Metropolitan Square 211 N Broadway, Ste 3600 Saint Louis MO 63102 Office Phone: 314-259-2326. Business E-Mail: lavanfleet@bryancave.com.

VANG, CHIA YOUYEE, history professor; b. Xieng Khouang, Laos, June 5, 1971; d. You Yee Vang and Pang Thao; m. Tong Mabyias Yang, Dec. 30, 1994; children: Simone Maydeu Yang, Tujntsuj Laujxeeb Yang, Flasche Nrig Yang. BA, Gustavus Adolphus Coll., St. Peter, Minn., 1994; MA in Pub. Affairs, Humphrey Inst. Pub. Affairs-U. Minn., Mpls., 1996; PhD, U. Minn., Mpls., 2006. Asst. prof. history U. Wis-Milw, 2006—; pres. and ceo CHIA Consulting, Inc., St. Paul, 1999—2006; hunger and poverty program officer The Urban Coalition, St. Paul. Bd. mem. Hmong Cultural Ctr. Wis., Madison, 2008—08; bd. trustees Gustavus Adolphus Coll., St. Peter, Minn., 2006—08; bd. mem. Minn. League Women Voters, St. Paul, 2001—04, Women's Assn. Hmong and Lao, St. Paul, 1998—2002. Recipient Faculty Diversity Rsch. award, U.

Wis. Inst. Race and Ethnicity, 2008; scholar, U. Minn., 1994—96; Kaplan Fellowship, 2003—06. Office: Univ WIs-Milw PO Box 413 Milwaukee WI 53201 Office Fax: 414-229-2435. Business E-Mail: vangcy@uwm.edu.

VANG, TIMOTHY TENG, religious organization administrator; b. Xieng Khouang, Laos, May 10, 1956; came to U.S., 1976; s. Nao Chai and Mai (Yang) V.; m. Chee Yang, Jan. 1, 1974 (dec. June 1975); m. Lydia Joua Xiong, July 7, 1979; children: Jennifer P., Nathan K., Victor C., Richard M., Tiffany P., Jasmine M. BS in Missions, Cin. Bible Coll., 1984; MDiv in Ch. Ministries, Can. Theol. Sem., Regina, Sask., 1991; DMin in Ch. Leadership, Fuller Theol. Sem., Pasadena, Calif., 1999. Ordained to ministry Ch. of Christ, 1984, Christian and Missionary Alliance, 1986. Machine operator Pellet Co., Green Bay, Wis., 1977-78; mental health worker Inst. Human Design, Oshkosh, Wis., 1978-80; ch. planter Ch. of Christ, Eau Claire, Wis., 1984-86; pastor Boulder (Colo.) Hmong Alliance Ch., 1986-87; dir. Christian edn. Hmong dist. Christian and Missionary Alliance, Brighton, Colo., 1986-87, dist. supt., 1991-96; sr. pastor Sacramento Hmong Alliance, 1997—. Mem. bd. mgrs. Christian and Missionary Alliance, 1994-97; trustee Crown Coll., 1992-96. Organizer Fox Valley Lao/Hmong Assn., Appleton, Wis., 1979. Lt. U.S./Hmong Allied Army, 1971-75. Mem. Christian And Missionary Alliance Ch. Avocations: reading, writing, walking. Office: Sacramento Hmong Alliance Ch 9131 Locust St Elk Grove CA 95624-2017 E-mail: tmtvang@aol.com.

VAN GALDER, VALERIE, marketing executive; b. Chgo. Grad., UCLA. Asst. Rogers & Cowen, 1985—90; v.p. mktg. & publicity Hard Rock Am., 1990—94; head mktg. Fox Searchlight Pictures, 1994—99; exec. v.p. mktg. Sony Screen Gems, 1999—2004; pres. TriStar Pictures, 2004—05; pres. domestic mktg. Columbia TriStar Motion Picture Group, 2005—. Internat. adv. bd. Bermuda Internat. Film Festival, 2005—. Named one of The 100 Most Powerful Women in Entertainment, Hollywood Reporter, 2006, 2007. Mailing: Sony Pres TriStar Pictures 9050 West Washington Blvd Culver City CA 90232

VANGELDER, KIM E., information technology executive; BS, Rochester Inst. Tech. With Eastman Kodak Co., Rochester, NY, 1984—, dir. global ERP competency ctr., 1996—2000, dir. info. tech. for R&D org., 2000—03, dir. info. tech. digital & film imaging systems, 2003, v.p. chief info. officer, 2004—. Mem. dean's council Golisano Coll. Computing & Info. Office: Eastman Kodak Co 343 State St Rochester NY 14650

VANGER, MILTON ISADORE, historian, educator; b. NYC, Apr. 11, 1925; s. Max Manuel and Rose (Rothstein) V.; m. Elsa M. Oribe, Sept. 10, 1956; children: John, Mark, Rachel. AB, Princeton U., 1948; MA, Harvard U., 1950, PhD, 1958. Teaching fellow history Harvard U., 1952-56; instr. Okla. State U., 1956-58; asst. prof. history Sacramento State Coll., 1958-62; mem. faculty Brandeis U., Waltham, Mass., 1962—, prof. history, 1973-84, prof. emeritus, 1984—. Chmn. com. Latin Am. studies, 1971-81; invited lectr. 50th anniversary conf. commemorating death of Batlle y Ordoñez of Uruguay, 1979; invitee to inauguration of pres. Sanguinetti, Uruguay, 1985; Barnette Miller vis. prof. history, Wellesley Coll., 1990. Author: José Batlle y Ordoñez of Uruguay: The Creator of His Times, 1902-1907, 1963, 2d edit., 1980, Spanish transl., 1968, 2d edit., 1992, The Model Country: José Batlle y Ordoñez of Uruguay, 1907-1915, 1980, Spanish transl., 1983, 2d edit., 1991, Reforma o Revolución La Polémica Batlle-Mibelli, 1917, 1989; outside reviewer NEH, Radcliffe Inst.; contbr. articles to profl. jours. Juror for Lindahl Prize, Inst. Latin Am. Studies, Stockholm. With AUS, 1943-45. Doherty Found. fellow, 1950-52; grantee Am. Philos. Soc., 1966; recipient Hermes prize for best history pub. in Uruguay, 1983. Mem. New Eng. Council Latin Am. Studies (sec.-treas. 1970-72), Am. Hist. Assn., Conf. on Latin Am. History, Amnesty Internat., Phi Beta Kappa. Democrat. Jewish. Address: 931 Massachusetts Ave Ste 503 Cambridge MA 02139

VAN GESTEL, ALLAN, mediator, arbitrator; b. Boston, Dec. 3, 1935; BA, Colby Coll., 1957; LLB, Boston U., 1961; MA (hon.), Colby Coll., 1999. Bar: Mass. 1961, U.S. Dist. Ct. Mass. 1963, U.S. Ct. Appeals (1st cir.) 1969, U.S. Supreme Ct. 1972, U.S. Ct. Claims 1979, U.S. Ct. Appeals (2d cir.) 1980, U.S. Dist. Ct. (no. dist.) N.Y. 1980, U.S. Dist. Ct. (we. dist.) N.Y. 1993, U.S. Ct. Appeals (3d cir.) 1993, U.S. Ct. Appeals (5th cir.) 1995. Assoc. firm Goodwin, Procter & Hoar, Boston, 1961-70, ptnr., 1970-96; assoc. justice Superior Ct. Mass., 1996—2005, recalled, 2006—08; presiding justice Superior Ct. Bus. Litigation Session, 2000—08; mediator JAMS, 2008—, arbitrator, 2008—. Spl. counsel Boston Fin. Commn., 1974; spl. counsel to Mass. Commn. on Jud. Conduct, 1986; mem. Scituate (Mass.) Bd. Zoning Appeals, 1970, Scituate Planning Bd., 1972; spl. counsel Gov. of N.Y. on Indian Land Claims, 1985-96; spl. counsel to Gov. and Atty. Gen. of Vt. on Indian Claims, 1987-90; chmn. standing adv. com. Mass. Rules Civil Procedure, 1986-93; overseer Colby Coll., 1990-99, trustee, 1999—2005. Contbr. numerous articles on Eastern Indian land claims, ct. administrn., capital punishment to profl. jours. Recipient Haskell Cohn Disting. Jud. Svc. award, 2006. Fellow Am. Coll. Bus. Ct. Judges, Am. Coll. Trial Lawyers; mem. ABA, Mass. Bar Assn., Boston Bar Assn. (chmn., task force on drugs and the cts.), Supreme Jud. Ct. Hist. Soc. (chmn. bd. overseers 1993-96), Mass. Hist. Soc. Office Phone: 617-228-0200.

VAN GINKEL, BLANCHE LEMCO, architect, educator; b. London, 1923; d. Myer and Claire Lemco; m. H. P. Daniel van Ginkel, 1956; children: Brenda, Marc. B.Arch., McGill U., 1945; M.C.P., Harvard U., 1950; Doctorate (hon.), U. Aix-Marseille, France, 2005. Tech. asst. Nat. Film Bd. Can., 1943-44; mgr. City Planning Office, Regina, Sask., Canada, 1946; architect Atelier Le Corbusier, Paris, 1948; asst. prof. architecture U. Pa., 1951-57; ptnr. van Ginkel Assocs., Montreal, Que., Canada, also Toronto, Ont., Canada, 1957—; prof. architecture U. Toronto, 1977—92, dir. Sch. Architecture, 1977-80, dean faculty architecture and landscape architecture, 1980-82. Vis. critic Harvard U., 1958, 70; adj. prof. U. Montreal, McGill U., others; curator exhbns. RCA, U. Toronto, others. Contbr. articles to profl. jours. Mem. Nat. Capital Planning Com., Ottawa, Art Adv. Com., Ottawa; mem. adv. com. Nat. Mus.'s Corp.; mem. Que. Provincial Planning Commn.; founder, v.p. Corp. of Urbanists of Que., 1963-65; bd. dirs. Montreal Internat. Film Festival, 1961-66. Decorated Order of Can., 2000; recipient Internat. Fedn. Housing and Planning Grand Prix award, 1956, Massey medal for arch., 1962, Mademoiselle Mag. award, 1957, Queen's Silver Jubilee medal, 1977, Citizenship citation Can. Govt., 1991, Queen's Golden Jubilee medal, 2002, award Order of Urbanists of Que., 2003. Fellow AIA (hon.), Royal Archtl. Inst. Can. (exec. com. 1971-74), Toronto Soc. Arch.; mem. Can. Inst. Planners (bd. dirs. 1961-64), Assn. Collegiate Schs. Architecture (bd. dirs. 1981-84, v.p. 1985-86, pres. 1986-87, Disting. Prof. award 1989), Royal Can. Acad. Art (bd. dirs. 1992—2000), Internat. Archive of Women Architects (bd. dirs. 1985-2001), Ont. Assn. Arch. (life), Order of Can. Office: 38 Summerhill Gardens Toronto ON Canada M4T 1B4

VAN GINKEL, JOHANNES AUGUSTE, geographer, educator; b. Kota-Radjah, Indonesia, June 22, 1940; arrived in the Netherlands, 1950; s. Gysbert and Anna Sipkje W. (Westra) van G.; m. Anna Maria E. Teepen, Aug. 25, 1965; children: Auke Gysbert Heino, Mapje Ank Marit. MS in Geography and History cum laude, Utrecht U., Netherlands, 1966, PhD in Social Scis. cum laude, 1979; Doctorate (hon.), Babes-Bolyai U., Cluj-Napoca, 1996, State U. Calif., Sacramento, 2003, U. Ghana, Accra, 2005, Tech. U. Zvolen, Slowakia, 2006, McMaster U., Hamilton, Ont., Can., 2007. Prof. geography and history Thomas à Kempis Coll., Arnhem, Netherlands, 1965-68; assoc. prof. geography Utrecht U., 1968-80, prof. human geography & planning, 1980—2001, dean of faculty, 1980—85, mem. bd. govs., 1985-97, rector magnificus, 1986-97, hon. prof., faculty geo-scis., 2008—; rector UN U., Tokyo, 1997—2007. Chmn. Netherlands Trilateral Adv. Coun. Sci. Policy, 1991-97; bd. dirs. European Assn. Univs., 1989-98, v.p. 1994-98; mem. coun. UN U., 1992-97, v.p., 1995-97; bd. dirs. Internat. Assn. Univs., 1990-95, v.p., 1995-2000, pres., 2000-04; mem. European Sci. and Tech. Assembly, 1994-97; mem. adv. group higher edn. UNESCO, 1995—98; steering group World Conf. on Higher Edn., Paris, 1996-98, follow-up com., 1998-2007; vice chair bd. trustees Asian Inst. Tech., 1997—2006; chair Inst. Social Studies, The Hague, 2007-, chair Ctr. for Devel. Studies, Bonn, 2006-; chmn. organizing com. 28th Internat. Geog. Congress: Land, Sea and the Human Effort, The Hague, The Netherlands, 1996. Author: a.o. Zicht op de Stad, 1977, Die Randstad Holland, 1979, Suburbanisatie en Recente Woonmilieus, 1979, Algemene Sociale Geografie, 1984, Nederland in Delen, 1989, University 2050: the Organization of Creativity and Innovation, 1994, Networks and Strategic Alliances within and between Universities and with the Private Sector, 1999, In Quest of Human Security, 2000, Citizens Participation and Informed Consent in Urban Environmental Management, 2000, Variety and Impact: Differences that Matter. Some Thoughts on the Variety of University Governance Systems and their impact on University Policies and Strategies, 2001, Reflections on Human Development and the Environment, 2002, What Does Globalization Mean for Higher Education?, 2003, Asian Urbanization and Local and Global Environmental Challenges, 2005, Responsibilities, Challenges, Opportunities and Governance - Rethinking the University for the 21st Century, 2006, Institutional and Political Challenges of Accreditation at the International Level, 2007; editor: Geografisch Tijdschrift, 1970-79. Bd. govs. Netherlands Interdisciplinary Demographic Inst., chmn., 1995—2000. Decorated knight Netherlands Lion, Order of the Rising Sun, Grand Cordon. Fellow Acad. Scis. Developing World (assoc.), Internat. Tng. Ctr. Geo-Info. Scis. and Remote Sensing. (hon., bd. dirs. 1986-94, chmn. 1994-98); mem. Royal Netherlands Acad. Arts and Scis. (social scis. coun. 1993-2001), Academia Europea, Found. for Fundamental Rsch. in Geog. and Environ. Scis. (chmn. 1982-91), Netherlands Interdisciplinary Demographic Inst. (chmn. sci. com. 1986-95, bd. govs. 1996-2008, chmn. 1996-2000), Internat. Geog. Union (chmn. Netherlands br. 1988-92), Royal Netherlands Geog. Soc., Netherlands' Inst. Urban and Regional Planning and Pub. Housing, Rotary, Sports Coun. Hoevelaken Municipality (chmn., 1969-73), Hockey Club Amersfoort (mem. tech. com. 1970-75), Sports Club Kampong, Utrecht (chmn. youth divsn. 1976-82). Avocations: sports, travel. Home: Park Arenberg 63 De Bilt NL3731EP Netherlands Personal E-mail: h.vanginkel@geo.uu.nl.

VAN GOOR, ANTHONY JAY, retired military officer, medical executive; b. Yankton, SD, Feb. 16, 1953; s. Marjorie L Van Goor; m. Marilyn Judy Staehli, Oct. 27, 1990; children: Brittany Marie, Michael Joseph. MD, U. of SD, 1978—82; M in med. mgmt., Tulane U., 2004—05. Board Certification in Internal Medicine Am. Bd. of Internal Medicine, 1990, Board Certification in Medical Management Certifying Commn. in Med. Mgmt., 2004. Advanced through grades to col. USAF, commd. officer, 1978; chief med. staff 21st Med. Group, Peterson Air Force Base, Colo., 1994—97; comdr. 77th Med. Ops. Squadron, McClellan/Mather Air Force Base, Calif., 1997—2000, 347th Med. Group, Moody Air Force Base, Ga., 2000—02, 42nd Med. Group, Maxwell Air Force Base, Ala., 2002—04; assoc. chief, med. staff Keesler Med. Ctr., Keesler Air Force Base, Miss., 2004—06; exec. v.p., med. dir. Sutter Delta Med. Group, Antioch, Calif., 2006—07; med. dir. Pharm. Svcs. Health Net Inc., 2007—; ret. USAF, 2006. Pres. parish coun. Maxwell/Gunter Cath. Parish, Maxwell Air Force Base, Ala., 2002—03. Decorated Legion of Merit USAF, 5 Meritorious Svc. medals, Air Force Commendation Medal. Fellow: ACP; mem.: AMA, Am. Coll. Physician Execs. Catholic. Avocations: vocal performance, travel, physical conditioning, skiing.

VAN GORDER, JOHN FREDERIC, lawyer; b. Jacksonville, Fla., Mar. 22, 1943; s. Harold Burton and Charlotte Louise Van G.; m. Sandra Joan Hagen, June 4, 1977 (div. June 1995); children: Alyssa Jane, Kathryn Ann; m. Ann Michele Brancato, Oct. 7, 1995. Grad., Dover Coll., Eng., 1961; AB, Dartmouth Coll., 1965; postgrad., Air Force Inst. Tech., 1967-68; MS in Adminstrn., George Washington U., 1973; postgrad., U. Va., Coll. William and Mary, Cath. U. Am., Northeastern U., Babson Coll., U. South; JD, Fordham U., 1981. Bar: N.J. 1981, U.S. Dist. Ct. N.J. 1981, N.Y. 1983, U.S. Supreme Ct. 1989. Commd. 2d lt. USAF, 1965, advanced through grades to capt., 1968; weapons contr. Aerospace Def. Commd., Ft. Lee, Va., 1965-67; buyer electronics sys. divsn. Air Force Sys. Commd., Bedford, Mass., 1968-69; project mgr. rsch. and devel. Hdqrs. USAF, Washington, 1969-73, br. chief pers., 1973-74; presdl. social aide The White House, Washington, 1971-74; assoc. Louis C. Kramp & Assocs., Washington, 1975; program officer J.M. Found., NYC, 1975-81; assoc. Winne, Banta & Rizzi Esqs., Hackensack, N.J., 1981-83; asst. sec., program adminstr. Glenmede Trust Co., Phila., 1983—86; exec. dir., asst. sec. Leon Lowenstein Found., 1986—. Atty. Rent Leveling Bd., Borough of Bergenfield, N.J., 1983; pres. Vanguard Corp., Massapequa, N.Y., 1996-2001; adj. prof. Grad. Sch. Edn., Fordham U., N.Y.C., 1997—, mem. adv. com. N.Y.C. Pub. Schs. Supts.' Network, 1998—2007, judge Nat. Sch. Change awards, 2001—, mem. program devel. adv. com. Grad. Sch. Edn., 2000—07. Chmn. NYC steering com. Nat. Congress on Volunteerism and Citizenship, 1976; mem. exec. com. Mayor's Vol. Action Coun., 1977-78; bd. govs. NY Jaycees Found., 1978-79; bd. govs., 4th v.p. First Assembly Dist. Rep. Club, 1977-82; vestryman All Saints Episc. Ch., Bergenfeld, 1982-83; mem. Tabernacle Twp. Planning Bd., 1985-88, Tabernacle Bd. Edn., 1988-91, Tabernacle Rep. Club, 1983-93; jr. warden, 1987-88, sr. warden, 1989-90, vestryman, lay reader St. Peter's Episc. Ch., Medford, N.J., 1985-93; program adv. com. Toshiba Am. Found., 1993-99; trustee, dir. Support Ctr. of NY, 1995-97, Robert A. Taft Inst. Govt., NYC, 1994-97; bd. dirs. NYC Pub./Pvt. Initiatives, Inc., 1996-2000, NY Regional Assn. Grantmakers, 1998-2006; bd. trustees Calvin K. Kazanjian Econs. Found., 2002—; mem. adv. com. Ctr. for Advancement of Children's Mental Health, Columbia U., NYC, 2003-05; serving officer Priory in USA, Order of St. John, 2003-; bd. dirs. USO Met. NY, 2005-06. Col. USAFR, ret. Named Outstanding Young Man of VA., 1975, USAF Res. Officer of Yr., 1985. Mem. Internat. (senator; v.p. 1975; rep. to UN 1976), U.S. (nat. v.p. 1973-74), D.C. (pres. 1972-73), N.Y.C. (bd. govs. 1978-79) Jaycees, SAR, Soc. Mayflower Descs., ABA, N.Y. Bar Assn., Student Bar Assn. (class pres. 1978-81), Toastmasters (local pres. 1969-70, area gov. 1970-71), Lions (pres. Medford Twp. club 1985-86, co-chmn. Charity Ball 1987), Masons, Alpha Delta Phi. Republican. Episcopalian. Office Phone: 212-319-0670.

VAN GORP, JON D., lawyer; b. Denver, Colo., June 12, 1969; BA, Calvin Coll., 1991; JD cum laude, So. Methodist Univ., 1994. Bar: Tex. 1994, Ill. 1998, NY 2004. Assoc. Thompson & Knight, Dallas, 1994—97; atty. Mayer Brown, Chgo., 1997—2003, ptnr., fin. & securitization, 2003—. Spkr. in field on fin. and securitization topics. Editor (staff): The Internat. Lawyer; contbr. articles to profl. jours. Recipient Crain's Chgo. Bus. 40 under 40; named Chgo. Mag. Rising Star; Greater Chgo. fellow, Chambers USA, Leadership fellow, Chambers Global and Legal 500. Office: Mayer Brown Rowe Maw Llp 71 S Wacker Dr Chicago IL 60606-4637 Office Phone: 312-701-7091. Office Fax: 312-706-8362. Business E-Mail: jvangorp@mayerbrown.com.

VAN GUILDER, GARY PRESTON, medical researcher; b. Springfield, Vt. s. Herbert B. and Sandra M. Van Guilder. BS (hon.), Castleton State Coll., VT, 1999; MS, Colo. State U., Fort Collins, 2001; PhD, U. Colo., Boulder, 2006. Clin. pharmacology post-doc. rsch. fellow Vanderbilt U. Med. Ctr., Nashville, 2006—07; Colo. HIV-1 rsch. tng. program post-doc. fellow U. Colo., Boulder, 2007—. Contbr. scientific papers (Young Investigator Award, 2009). Vol. Nashville Rescue Mission, 2006—07, Sierra Club, Nashville, 2006—07, Boulder County AIDS Project, 2007—. Nat. Rsch. Svc. Fellowship, NIH, 2006, 2007, Loan Repayment Program Clincial Rsch. Fellowship, 2007. Mem.: Internat. AIDS Soc., Am. Heart Assn. Democrat. Agnostic. Office: Univ of Colo 354 Ucb Boulder CO 80309 Business E-Mail: gary.vanguilder@colorado.edu.

VAN GUNDY, GREGORY FRANK, retired lawyer; b. Columbus, Ohio, Oct. 24, 1945; s. Paul Arden and Edna Marie (Sanders) Van G.; m. Lisa Tamara Langer. BA, Ohio State U., Columbus, 1966, JD, 1969. Bar: N.Y. 1971. Assoc. atty. firm Willkie Farr & Gallagher, NYC, 1970-74; v.p. legal, sec. Marsh & McLennan Cos., Inc., NYC, 1974-79, v.p., sec., gen. counsel, 1979-2000, sec., 2000—03, retired, 2003. Mem. Phi Beta Kappa. Roman Catholic. Home: 232 Fox Meadow Rd Scarsdale NY 10583-1640 Personal E-mail: vgfam@aol.com.

VAN GUNDY, JEFF, sportscaster, former professional basketball coach; b. Hemet, Calif., Jan. 19, 1962; married. Grad. cum laude, Nazareth Coll., Rochester, NY. Head coach McQuaid Jesuit HS, Rochester, 1985-86; grad. asst. Providence Coll., 1986—87, 1987—88; asst. coach Rutgers U., NJ, 1988-89, NY Knicks, NYC, 1989-96, head coach, 1996—2001; NBA analyst Turner Sports, 2002—03; head coach Houston Rockets, 2003—07; NBA analyst ESPN, ABC Sports, 2007—. Head coach NBA Ea. Conf. All-Star Team, 2000. Named to Nazareth Coll. Sports Hall of Fame, 1996. Office: c/o ESPN ESPN Plz Bristol CT 06010

VAN GUNDY, SEYMOUR DEAN, plant pathologist, educator; b. Feb. 24, 1931; s. Robert C. and Margaret (Holloway) Van G.; m. Wilma C. Fanning, June 12, 1954; children: Sue Ann, Richard L. BA, Bowling Green State U., 1953; PhD, U. Wis., 1957. Asst. nematologist U. Calif., Riverside, 1957-63, assoc. prof., 1963-68, prof. nematology and plant pathology, 1968-73, assoc. dean rsch., 1968-70, vice chancellor rsch., 1970-72, chmn. dept. nematology, 1972-84; prof. nematology and plant pathology, assoc. dean rsch. Coll. Natural and Agrl. Scis., 1985-88, acting dean, 1986, interim dean, 1988-90, dean, 1990-93, emeritus dean, prof., 1993—. Former mem. editl. bd. Rev. de Nematologie, Jour. Nematology and Plant Disease; contbr. numerous articles to profl. jours. Grantee, Rockefeller Found., Cancer Rsch., NSF, USDA; NSF fellow, Australia, 1965—66. Fellow AAAS, Am. Phytopathol. Soc., Soc. Nematologists (editor-in-chief 1968-72, v.p. 1972-73, pres. 1973-74, hon. mem. 1997); mem. (hon.) Acad. Scis. Moldova. Home: 1188 Pastern Rd Riverside CA 92506-5619 Office: U Calif Dept Nematology Riverside CA 92521-0001 Personal E-mail: vangundy@hotmail.com.

VAN GUNDY, STAN, professional basketball coach; b. Indio, Calif., Aug. 26, 1959; s. Bill Van Gundy; m. Kim Van Gundy; children: Shannon, Michael, Alison, Kelly. BA in English, SUNY, Brockport, 1981, BS in Phys. Edn., 1981. Asst. coach U. Vt., 1981—83, Canisius Coll., 1987, Fordham U., 1988; head coach Castleton State Coll., Vt., U. Mass., Lowell, 1988—92; asst. coach to head coach U. Wis.; asst. coach Miami Heat, 1995—97, asst. head coach, 1997—2003, head coach, 2003—05, cons.; head coach Orlando Magic, Fla., 2007—. Office: Orlando Magic 8701 Maitland Summit Blvd Orlando FL 32810*

VAN HA, THUONG G., radiologist, educator; MD, U. Mass., Worcester, 1993. Diplomate Am. Bd. Radiology, 1998. Assoc. prof. radiology U. Chgo., 2000—.

VAN HANDEL, MICHAEL J., employment services executive; BS magna cum laude in Acctg., Marquette U., Milw.; MBA in Fin., U. Wis. Audit mgr. Arthur Andersen & Co.; dir. internal audit Manpower, Inc., Milw., 1989—93, v.p. internat. acctg., 1993—95, chief acctg. officer, treas., 1995—98, sr. v.p., 1998—2002, CFO, 1998—, exec. v.p., 2002—. Bd. dirs., mem. audit and risk oversight coms. Harris Bank. Bd. dirs., chmn. audit com. Milw. Pub. Mus. Named one of Best CFOs in Am., Instl. Investor, 2006.

VAN HANDLE, DONNA, language educator; d. Kathryne Van Handle. AB, Mt. Holyoke Coll., South Hadley, Mass., 1974; MA, U. Mass., Amherst, Mass., PhD, 1984. Lectr. German studies Mt. Holyoke Coll., 1983—2000, sr. lectr. German studies, 2000—, dean internat. students, 2003—. Recipient award, Fulbright Assn., 1990, ACTFL-FDP-Houghton Mifflin award, Am. Coun. Tchg. Fgn. Langs., 2005, Bundesverdienstkreuz, German Govt., 2007; named German Tchr. of Yr., Mass. Fgn. Lang. Assn., 2001; named one of Outstanding German Educator, Am. Assn. Tchrs. German, 2007. Mem.: Am. Assn. Tchrs. German (life; v.p. 2000—03, pres. 2000—03, Outstanding German Educator 2007). Independent. Avocations: travel, reading, computers. Office: Mt Holyoke Coll 50 College St South Hadley MA 01075 Business E-Mail: dvanhand@mtholyoke.edu.

VAN HEECKEREN, ANNA M., biomedical researcher, veterinarian; b. New Haven, Aug. 9, 1964; d. Daniel W. and Doris M. van Heeckeren; m. Edward B. Baker, Oct. 15, 1994; children: Marta L. Baker, K. Elise Baker. BS, U. Mich., Ann Arbor, 1987; MS, Ohio State U., Columbus, 1989, DVM, 1993. Lic. in medicine Ohio Vet. Med. Licensing Bd., 1993. Rsch. assoc. Case We. Res. U., Cleve., 1993—94, postdoc., 1994—97, sr. rsch. assoc., 1997—, CF animal core dir., co-dir., 1997—2008. Cons. Genzyme, Framingham, Mass.; sr. rsch. assoc. CF Animal Core Dir., 2008; exec. dir. and chair The Van Bakern Found., 2008—. Contbr. articles to profl. jours. Dir. Am. Vet. Med. Found., Schaumburg, Ill., 2002—, sec., chair grants-awards com.; advisor Safety Animals and Families in Emergencies, Cleve., 2007—. Mem.: AVMA, Am. Coll. Lab. Animal Medicine Found., Am. Soc. Microbiology, Am. Thoracic Soc., Am. Assn. Lab. Animal Sci. Office: Van Bakeren Found PO Box 214 Gates Mills OH 44040 Office Phone: 216-246-0255. Office Fax: 216-368-4223. Business E-Mail: dr.anna@vanbakerenfoundation.org.

VAN HEERTUM, RONALD LANNY, physician; b. Englewood, NJ, Nov. 23, 1940; s. Arnold and Irene Gladys (Ostheimer) V.; children: Richard Jonathan, Beth Jennifer, Jonathan Jason, Kristin Ashley; m. Elyse Ann Murphy, Apr. 3, 2004. BA, Gettysburg Coll., 1962; MD, N.J. Med. Sch., 1966. Diplomate Nat. Bd. Med. Examiners, 1967, Am. Bd. Radiology, 1971, Am. Bd. Nuclear Medicine, 1973. Intern Hackensack Hosp., NJ, 1966-67; resident in radiology St. Vincent's Hosp. & Med. Ctr. NY, 1967—70, fellow in radiology and nuclear medicine, 1970-71, clin. asst. dept radiology, 1971, asst. chief nuclear medicine sect., asst. attending radiologist, 1975-76, chief nuclear medicine sect., 1977-91, assoc. attending physician depts. radiology and medicine, 1977-78, attending physician depts. radiology and medicine, 1978-91, dir. Nuclear Radiology Residency Tng. Program, 1980-88, 80-91, asst. dir. dept. radiology, 1981-91, med. dir. Sch. Nuclear Medicine Tech., 1982-91; asst. chief nuclear medicine svc. Tripler Army Med. Ctr., Honolulu, 1972, chief nuclear medicine svc., 1972-74; adj. prof. Sch. Pharmacy U. Pacific, Stockton, Calif., 1973-74; fellow in nuclear medicine SUNY, 1974-75; clin. asst. prof. of radiology Sch. Medicine NYU, 1977-83; assoc. prof. clin. radiology NY Med. Coll., Valhalla, 1983-88, prof. clin. radiology, 1988-91; dir. mini-fellowship program St. Vincent's Hosp. Cerebral SPECT Learning Ctr., 1991—2001; prof. clin. radiology Coll. Physicians & Surgeons of Columbia U., NY, 1991—2001; attending physician dept. radiology Columbia-Prsbyn. Med. Ctr., 1991—, dir. nuclear medicine residency tng. program, 1980—88, 1991—; attending physician dept brain imaging NY Psychiatric Inst., 1993—, attending physician Dept. Neurosci., 1996—; vice chmn. dept. radiology Coll. Physicians and Surgeons Columbia U., 1993—, prof. radiology, 2002—; intern chair radiology Coll. Physicians & Surgeons, 2008—. Cons. nuclear medicine Catholic Med. Ctr. of Bklyn. and Queens, 1979-88, The Long Island Coll. Hosp., 1980-88, dept. radiology St. Vincent's Hosp. and Med. Ctr. of NY, 1991-92, biol. studies unit NY Psychiat. Inst., 1993—, The Oxford Project to Investigate Memory and Aging, The John Radcliffe Infirmary and Dept. of Clin. Pharmacology Oxford U., 1993—; alt. del. Am. Coll. Nuclear Physics, 1980-82; core mem. DOE Sponsored Consensus Panel Brain SPECT Perfusion Imaging: Optimizing Image Aquisition and Processing, 1991; vis. prof. Brooke Army Med. Ctr., San Antonio, 1978, Howard U. Med. Coll., Washington, 1980, South Hills Health Systems, Pitts., 1981, St. Barnabas Med. Ctr., Livingston, NJ, 1989, Eastern Va. Med. Sch. Norfolk Gen. Hosp., 1990, U. PR Med. Ctr., VA Med. Ctr., 1993, U. Wash. Med. Ctr., Seattle, 1994, Washington U., St. Louis, 1998, Robert Wood Johnson Med. Sch., 1999, Stonybrook Health Sci. Ctr., 2005, U. Puerto Rico, 2005; mem. Am. Bd. Nuc. Medicine, 1995-, vice chair, 1999-2000, chair, 2000-02; dir. Columbia Kreitchman PET Ctr., 1993-. Contbr. articles to profl. jours. Major USAR, 1971-74. Recipient Physician Recognition award AMA, 1974-93; numerous rsch. grants in field. Fellow Am. Coll. Radiology (commn. on nuc. medicine 1994-2000, chmn. nuc. medicine accreditation com. 2000-06, chair accreditation program chiefs com., 2002-06, vice chmn., 2002-06), NY Acad. Medicine (sec. nuclear medicine sect. 1993—); mem. Am. Roentgen Ray Soc., Radiological Soc. N. Am., NY Roentgen Soc., Soc. Nuclear Medicine (mem. bd. govs. greater NY chpt. 1982-84, 86-89, mem. acad. coun. 1988, mem. brain imaging coun. 1988—, sub-chmn. gastroenterology sci. program com. 1989-90, pres. elect brain imaging coun. 1990-92, pres. 1992-94, sub.-chmn. psychiatry-clin. sci. program com. 1993-94), Soc. Thoracic Radiology (sr. mem.). Presbyterian. Business E-Mail: rvhs@columbia.edu.

VAN HELDEN, PETER J., grocery company executive; Sr. v.p. of oper., Jewel-Osco (subs. of Albertson's Inc.), Melrose Park, Ill.; pres., Midwest Div. Albertson's Inc., Melrose Park, Ill., 1999—, pres. & CEO, Calif. Food Div., 2004—06; sr. v.p., pres. Retail We. Supervalu Inc., Eden Prairie, Minn., 2006—07, exec. v.p., pres. Retail We., 2007—09, exec. v.p. retail ops., 2009—. Mailing: Supervalu Inc PO Box 990 Minneapolis MN 55440 Office: Supervalu Inc 11840 Valley View Rd Eden Prairie MN 55344*

VAN HEMMEN, J. LEO, physics professor, researcher; b. Groningen, Netherlands, May 9, 1947; s. Jan and Lina (Boersma) Van H.; m. Paulina N.D. Broek, June 28, 1972; children: Paul, Saskelina. PhD in Physics, U. Groningen, 1976; Habil, U. Heidelberg, 1983. Rschr., pvt-docent U. Heidelberg, Germany, 1983—89; prof. TU Muenchen, Germany, 1989—. Editor/author: Models of Neural Networks, 1991—; editor-in-chief Biological Cybernetics, 2006-; contbr. articles to profl. jours. Netherlands Orgn. for Advancement of Pure Rsch. stipend, 1976. Fellow Am. Phys. Soc.; mem. Am. Math. Soc., European Phys. Soc. Avocation: photography. Office: Physics Dept T35 TU Muenchen James Franck Strasse Garching bei Muenchen 85748 Germany

VAN HISE, YVONNE, librarian; d. Emilio and Olga Tirado; m. Wayne L. Van Hise, June 11, 1977; children: Leslie Elaine, Dana Lynn Schleider, Lauren Marie, Jeffrey Wayne. BS, Trenton State Coll., Ewing, NJ, 1978. Cert. profl. libr. State NJ., 1978, ednl. media specialist, assoc. ednl. media specialist, elem. sch. tchr. Libr. media specialist bd. edn. Wash. Twp., Robbinsville, NJ, 1978—82, Pemberton Twp., Pemberton, 1991—98, Upper Freehold Twp., Allentown, 1998—. Mem.: NJASL. Conservative. Presbyterian. Avocation: reading. Office: Upper Freehold Bd Edn 27 High St Allentown NJ 08501

VAN HOENE, WILLIAM, JR., lawyer, utilities executive; BA, Yale Univ.; JD, Univ. Chgo., 1980. Sr. ptnr. Jenner & Block, Chgo.; dep. gen. counsel Exelon Corp., Chgo., 2002—04, sr. v.p. dep. gen. counsel, 2004—05, sr. v.p., acting gen. counsel, 2005—06, sr. v.p., gen. counsel, 2006—07, exec. v.p., gen. counsel, 2007—. Mem. Univ. Chgo. Law Rev. Past pres. Chgo. Lawyers Com. for Civil Rights Under Law; past gen. counsel Leadership Council for Metro. Open Communities; bd. dir. Joffrey Ballet, Legal Assistance Found. of Chgo. Mem.: Assn. Corp. Counsel (Pro Bono award 2007), Chgo. Bar Assn. (Vanguard award 2008), Order of the Coif. Office: Exelon Corp 10 S Dearborn St Chicago IL 60680*

VAN HOEY, NICOLE, pharmacist, writer; d. Anthony and Kathleen Russo; m. Gregory Van Hoey, Aug. 10, 2002; children: Olivia, Josephine. PharmD, U. Toledo, 2002. Cert. pharmacist Va., 2002. Pvt. practice, Arlington, Va., 2005—; tech. writer, drug info. cons. Lockheed Martin Healthcare Svcs. and Solutions, Rockville, Md., 2004—08. Contbr. articles to med. jours. Editor FCA All-Fairlington Bull., Arlington, 2007; mem. WETA Pub. Broadcasting, Arlington, 2007—09, Friends Nat. Zoo, Washington, 2006—09.

VAN HOLDE, KENSAL EDWARD, biochemistry educator; b. Eau Claire, Wis., May 14, 1928; s. Leonard John and Nettie (Hart) Van Holde; m. Barbara Jean Watson, Apr. 11, 1950; children: Patricia, Mary, Stephen, David. BS, U. Wis., 1949, PhD, 1952. Rsch. chemist E.I. du Pont de Nemours & Co., 1952-55; rsch. assoc. U. Wis., 1955-56, asst. prof. Milw., 1956-57; mem. faculty U. Ill., Urbana, 1957-67; prof. dept. biochemistry and biophysics Oreg. State U., Corvallis, 1967, Am. Cancer Soc. rsch. prof., 1977-93, disting. prof., 1988-93, disting. prof. emeritus, 1993—; instr.-in-charge physiology course Marine Biol. Lab., Woods Hole, Mass., 1977-80; mem. research staff Centre des Recherches sur les Macromolecules, Strasbourg, France, 1964-65; mem. study sect. USPHS, 1966-69, 91—; staff Weizmann Inst., Israel, 1981, Lab. Léon Brillouin, Saclay, France, 1989-90. Author: Physical Biochemistry, 1971, Chromatin, 1988; author: (with C. Mathews) Biochemistry, 1989, 3d edit., 2000; author: Principles of Physical Biochemistry, 1998, 2d edit., 2006; editor: Biochmica Biophysica Acta, 1966—68; mem. editl. bd. jours. Biol. Chemistry, 1968—75, 1981—87, 1991—92, assoc. editor, 1992—; assoc. editor: Biochemistry, 1973—76, 1982—89; contbr. articles to profl. jours. Trustee Marine Biol. Lab., Woods Hole, 1979—82, 1984—92. NSF sr. postdoctoral fellow, 1964—65, Guggenheim fellow, 1973—74, European Molecular Biology Orgn. fellow, 1975, Humboldt fellow, 2000—01. Fellow: AAAS; mem.: NAS, Am. Acad. Arts and Scis., Biophys. Soc., Am. Soc. Biochemistry and Molecular Biology. Home: 229 NW 32nd St Corvallis OR 97330-5020 Office: Oreg State U Dept Biochemistry Corvallis OR 97331 Office Phone: 541-737-4155.

VAN HOLLEN, CHRISTOPHER, JR., United States Representative from Maryland; b. Karachi, Pakistan, Jan. 10, 1959; s. Christopher and Eliza (Farnsworth) Van Hollen; m. Katherine A. Wilkens; children: Anna, Nicholas, Alexander. BA in Philos., Swarthmore Coll., Pa., 1982; MPP, Harvard U., 1985; JD cum laude, Georgetown U., 1990. Bar: Md. 1990. Legis. asst. for def. & fgn. policy to Senator Charles McC. Mathias US Senate, Md., 1985-87, profl. staff mem. Fgn. Rels. Com. Washington, 1987-89; sr. legis. adv. to Gov. William Donald Schaefer State of Md., Washington, 1989-91; assoc. Arent, Fox, Kintner, Plotkin & Kahn, Washington, 1991—2002; mem. Md. House Delegates, Annapolis, 1991—95, Md. State Senate from Dist. 18, Annapolis, 1995—2002, US Congress from 7th Md. dist. (formerly 8th dist.), Washington, 2003—, US House Ways & Means Com., 2007—, US House Govt. Reform & Oversight Com.; chmn. Dem. Congl. Campaign Com. (DCCC), 2007—. Recipient Environ. Leadership award, Md. League Conservation Voters, 1992, 1994, 1996, 1998, 2000, Outstanding Legislator award, Advocates Children, Youth & Family, 2000, Outstanding Advocacy award, Md. AIDS Legis. Com., 2001, Outstanding Legislator award, Md. Ctr. Community Devel., 2001, Conservation Legacy award, 2002, Legis. Legacy award, Arc of Md., 2002, Legislator Sponsor award, Md. Children's Action Network, 2002, Leadership award, Am. Cancer Soc., 2002, Disting. Superhero award, Nat. Assn. Cmty. Health Ctrs., 2005, Oustanding Leadership award, Am. Lung Assn., Outstanding Svc. award, Blinded Am. Vets. Found.; named Oustanding New Mem. of Yr., Com. Edn. Funding, 2003. Mem.: ABA, Md. Citizens Assn., Kensington Citizens Assn., Atlantic Coun., Montgomery Bar Assn., Md. Bar Assn. Democrat. Episcopalian. Office: US Congress 1707 Longworth Ho Office Bldg Washington DC 20515 also: 51 Monroe St Ste 507 Rockville MD 20850 Office Phone: 202-225-5341.*

VAN HOLLEN, J(OHN) B(YRON), state attorney general, former prosecutor; b. Rice Lake, Wis., Feb. 19, 1966; s. John C. and Rosella Van Hollen; m. Lynne Pliner; children: Byron, Madelyn. BA in Polit. Sci. and Econs., St. Olaf Coll., Northfield, Minn., 1988; JD, U. Wis., Madison, 1990. Bar: Wis. 1990, US Dist. Ct. (we. dist. Wis.) 1990. Asst. state pub. defender, Spooner, Wis., 1990—91; dist. atty. Ashland County, Wis., 1993—99, Bayfield County, Wis., 1999—2002; asst. US atty. (we. dist.) Wis. US Dept. Justice, 1991—93, US atty., 2002—05; atty. Dewitt, Ross & Stevens, S.C., Madison, Wis., 2005—07; atty. gen. State of Wis., Madison, 2007—. Mem.: ABA, Dane County Bar Assn. Republican. Office: Office of Atty Gen State Capitol Ste 114E PO Box 7857 Madison WI 53707-7857 Office Phone: 608-266-1221.*

VANHOOK, TRACIE LYNNETTE, small business owner; b. Oakland, Calif., May 17, 1965; d. Herman Curtis Gray and Ritchie Lee Ross; children: Titus Alexander, Lawrence Emanuel. Assoc. in Sci., Merritt Coll., 1999; BS, San Francisco State U., 2002; MS, Calif. U. Pa., 2005. Cert. health and fitness instr. Am. Coll. Sports Medicine, performance enhancement specialist, personal trainer Nat. Acad. Sports Medicine, in enhanced sports nutrition HK Academic Online Edn. Ctr. Cons., presenter E.C. Reems Women's Internat. Ministries Nat. Conf., Oakland, 1997—2000; fitness supr. Sports Club LA-San Francisco, 2002—05; therapy and rehab asst. Body Focus Health Ctr., San Francisco, 2003—04; fitness mgr./master trainer Axis Performance Ctr., Menlo Park, Calif., 2005—06; owner Fit to the Core Personal Tng., Menlo Park, 2006—. Dancer/actor (play) Navigators. Avocations: youth dance choreography, hiking. Office: Axis Performance Ctr 550 Ravenswood Ave Menlo Park CA 94025 Office Fax: 650-463-1926. Business E-Mail: tracie@fittothecorept.com.

VAN HOOMISSEN, GEORGE ALBERT, state supreme court justice; b. Portland, Oreg., Mar. 7, 1930; s. Fred J. and Helen F. (Flanagan) Van H.; m. Ruth Madeleine Niedermeyer, June 4, 1960; children: Geroge T., Ruth Anne, Madeleine, Matthew. BBA, U. Portland, 1951; JD, Georgetown U., 1955, LLM in Labor Law, 1957; LLM in Jud. Adminstrn., U. Va., 1986. Bar: D.C. 1955, Oreg. 1956, Tex. 1971, U.S. Dist. Ct. Oreg. 1956, U.S. Ct. Mil. Appeals 1955, U.S. Ct. Customs and Patent Appeals 1955, U.S. Ct. Claims 1955, U.S. Ct. Appeals (9th cir.) 1956, U.S. Ct. Appeals (D.C. cir.) 1955, U.S. Supreme Ct. 1960. Law clk. for Chief Justice Harold J. Warner Oreg. Supreme Ct., 1955-56; Keigwin teaching fellow Georgetown Law Sch., 1956-57; dep. dist. atty. Multnomah County, Portland, 1957-59; pvt. practice Portland, 1959-62; dist. atty. Multnomah County, 1962-71; dean nat. coll. dist. attys., prof. law U. Houston, 1971-73; judge Cir. Ct., Portland, 1973-81, Oreg. Ct. Appeals, Salem, 1981-88; justice Oreg. Supreme Ct., Salem, 1988—2001. Adj. prof. Northwestern Sch. Law, Portland, Willamette U. Sch. Law, Portland State U.; mem. faculty Am. Acad. Judicial Edn., Nat. Judicial Coll.; Keigwin Teaching fellow Georgetown U. Law Sch. Mem. Oreg. Ho. of Reps., Salem, 1959-62, chmn. house jud. com. Ret. col. USMCR. Recipient Disting. Alumnus award U. Portland, 1972. Master Owen M. Panner Am. Inn of Ct.; mem. ABA, Oreg. State Bar, Tex. Bar Assn., Oreg. Law Inst. (bd. dirs.), Arlington Club, Multnomah Athletic Club, Univ. Club. Roman Catholic. Office: Oreg Supreme Ct 2105 SW Elm St Portland OR 97201 Office Phone: 503-228-2202. Personal E-mail: gavanhoomissen@msn.com.

VAN HORN, HUGH M., physicist, astronomer, educator; b. Williamsport, Pa., Mar. 5, 1938; s. Robert Dix and Virginia Elizabeth (Moody) Van H.; m. Mary Susan Boon, Sept. 17, 1960; children: Kathleen Susan, Mary Margaret, Michael Hugh George. BSc, Case Inst. Tech., 1960; PhD, Cornell U., 1965. NASA predoctoral trainee Cornell U., Ithaca, 1963-65; rsch. assoc. U. Rochester, 1965-67, asst. prof., 1967-73, assoc. prof., 1973-77, prof., 1977-96, chmn. dept. physics and astronomy, 1980-86, acting assoc. dean Coll. Arts and Scis., 1987-89, acting chmn. dept. physics and astronomy, 1992-93, adj. prof., 1996—2005, prof. emeritus, 2005—; Shapley lectr. Am. Astron. Soc., 1981-95; dir. divsn. astron. sci. NSF, Arlington, Va., 1993-2000, sr. sci. advisor Directorate Math. Phys. Sci., 2000—02, dir. nat. facilities divsn. materials rsch., 2002—04; ret., 2004. Vis. fellow Joint Inst. Lab. Astrophysics, 1973—74; sr. scientist Lab. Laser Energetics, 1985—96; vis. prof. U. Tex., 1987; vis. investigator dept. terr. magnetism Carnegie Inst. Washington, 2000—02; prin. investigator NASA and NSF grants. Editor: (with V. Weidemann) White Dwarfs and Variable Degenerate Stars, 1979, (with S. Ichimaru) Strongly Coupled Plasma Physics, 1993; contbr. articles on white dwarfs, neutron stars and dense matter to profl. jours. Fellow AAAS; mem. Internat. Astron. Union. E-mail: vanhorns1@verizon.net.

VANHORN, KATE RAUDENBUSH, retired school psychologist; b. Pennsburg, Pa., Nov. 15, 1921; d. William John and Mabel Katie (Raudenbush) Buck; children: Vicki, Eric. AB magna cum laude, Immaculata Coll., 1981; MA, West Chester U., 1982; nat. cert., 1988. Cert. sch. psychologist, Del. Program coord., sch. psychologist Del. Autistic Program, Newark, 1983—99; ret. Active ACLU. Mem. NOW, Nat. Assn. Sch. Psychologists (cert.), Del. Assn. Sch. Psychologists (cert.), Sex Info and Edn. Coun. U.S., Autism Assn. Del., Phi Delta Kappa, Psi Chi. Democrat. Avocations: piano, organ, photography, writing. Personal E-mail: kvanhorn5000@yahoo.com.

VAN HORN, KEITH, retired professional basketball player; b. Oct. 23, 1975; m. Amy Van Horn; children: Sabrina, Nicholas. Grad., U. Utah, 1997. Basketball player NJ Nets, East Rutherford, NJ, 1997—2001, 2008—, Phila. 76ers, 2002—03, New York Knicks, 2003—04, Milwaukee Bucks, 2004—05, Dallas Mavericks, 2005—06. Named first team All-Am., U. Utah, 1997. Achievements include being the top scorer U. Utah and Western Athletic conf. hist; 3 time Western Athletic Conf. Player of Yr. 1995-97.

VAN HORN, O. FRANK, retired counselor, consultant; b. Grand Junction, Colo., Apr. 16, 1926; s. Oertel F. and Alta Maude (Lynch) Van H.; m. Dixie Jeanne MacGregor, Feb. 1, 1947 (dec. Nov. 1994); m. Evelyn Anne Carroll, Mar. 22,1998; children: Evelyn (dec.), Oertel (dec.), Dorothy. AA, Mesa Coll., 1961; BA, Western State Colo., 1963; MEd, Oreg. State U., 1969. Counselor, mgr. State of Oreg.-Employment, Portland and St. Helens, 1964-88; pvt. practice counselor and cons. St. Helens, 1988-96. Chair Task Force on Aging, Columbia County, 1977-79; advisor Western Interstate Commn. on Higher Edn., Portland, 1971, Concentrated Employment and Tng., St. Helens, 1977, County Planning Bd., Columbia County, Oreg., 1977-80, City Planning Bd., St. Helens, 1978, Youth Employment Coun., St. Helens, 1978, Task Force on Disadvantaged Youth, St. Helens, 1980; counselor Career Mgmt. Specialists Internat.; instr. Portland C.C. Mem. ACA, Oreg. Counseling Assn., Internat. Assn. Pers. in Employment Svc. (Outstanding Achievement award 1975), Nat. Employment Counselors Assn. Democrat. Avocation: singing. Home: 464 Leelo Ct Florence OR 97439-8909

VAN HORN, RICHARD LINLEY, academic administrator; b. Chgo., Nov. 2, 1932; s. Richard Linley and Mildred Dorothy (Wright) Van H.; m. Susan Householder, May 29, 1954 (dec.); children: Susan Elizabeth, Patricia Suzanne, Lynda Sue; m. Betty Pfefferbaum, May 29, 1988. BS with highest honors, Yale U., 1954; MS, MIT, 1956; PhD, Carnegie-Mellon U., 1976; D of Bus. (hon.), Reitsumeikan U., Kyoto, Japan, 1991. Asst. dir. Army EDP Project, MIT, Cambridge, 1956-57; rsch. staff Rand Corp., Santa Monica, Calif., 1957-60, head mgmt. sys. grp., 1960-67; dir., prof. mgmt. sys. European Inst. Advanced Studies in Mgmt., Brussels, 1971-73; asso. dean Grad. Sch. Indsl. Adminstrn., Carnegie-Mellon U., Pitts., 1967-71, dir. budget and planning, 1973-74, v.p. for bus. affairs, 1974-77, v.p. for mgmt., 1977-80, provost and prof. mgmt., 1980-83; chancellor U. Houston, 1983-86, pres., 1986-89; U. Okla., 1989-94; pres. emeritus and regent's prof. Coll. of Bus. U. Okla., Norman, 1994—; Clarence E. Page prof. aviation U. Okla., Norman, 1995—; dir. mgmt. info. sys. divsn. Coll. Bus. U Okla., 1997—2000. Author: (with Robert H. Gregory) Automatic Data Processing Systems, 1960, 2nd edit. 1963, (with R.H. Gregory) Business Data Processing and Programming, 1963, (with C.H. Kriebel and J.T. Heames) Management Information Systems: Progress and Perspectives, 1971, (with A. Schwarzkopf and R. Leou Price) Information System Solutions: a Project Approach, 2006; contbr. articles to profl. jours.; assoc. editor: Jour. Inst. Mgmt. Scis., 1964-78 Mem. Inst. Mgmt. Sci. (nat. coun. mem. 1963-65, sec.-treas. 1964), Assn. for Computing Machinery (nat. lectr. 1969-70), Coun. on Govt. Rels. (bd. dirs 1981-83) Avocation: commercial pilot. Office: U Okla Coll Of Bus Norman OK 73019-0001 Home: 2517 Stratlon DR Edmond OK 73013 Office Phone: 405-325-0900. E-mail: rvanhorn@ou.edu.

VAN HORNE, JAMES CARTER, economist, educator; b. South Bend, Ind., Aug. 6, 1935; s. Ralph and Helen (McCarter) Van H.; m. Mary A. Roth, Aug. 27, 1960; children: Drew, Stuart, Stephen. AB, De Pauw U., 1957, DSc (hon.), 1986; MBA, Northwestern U., 1961, PhD, 1964. Comml. lending rep. Continental Ill. Nat. Bank, Chgo., 1958-62; prof. fin. Stanford U. Grad. Sch. Bus., 1965-75, A.P. Giannini prof. fin., 1976—2007, assoc. dean, 1973-75, 76-80; dep. asst. sec. Dept. Treasury, 1975-76. Bd. dirs. Montgomery St. Income Securities, 2d Synnex Corp.; commr. workers compensation Rate Making Study Commn., State of Calif., 1990-92. Author: Function and Analysis of Capital Market Rates, 1970, Financial Market Rates and Flows, 2001, Financial Management and Policy, 2002; co-author: Fundamentals of Financial Management; assoc. editor Jour. Fin. and Quantitative Analysis, Jour. Fin., 1971—73, Jour. Fixed Income, 1990—. Mem. bd. trustees DePauw U., 1989-96. With AUS, 1957. Mem. Am. Fin. Assn. (past pres., dir.), Western Fin. Assn. (past pres., dir.), Fin. Mgmt. Assn. Home: 2000 Webster St Palo Alto CA 94301-4049 Office: Stanford U Grad Sch Bus Stanford CA 94305

VAN HOUTEN, G. DAVID, JR., beverage company executive; b. Waco, Tex. m. Carol Van Houten; children: Tara, Brant, Blaine. Mgmt. degree, Tex. A&M U. Various positions Coca-Cola Bottling Bus., 1972—86; pres., gen. mgr. Coca-Cola Bottling Co. of N. Tex., 1986—96; sr. v.p., pres., Ctrl. N.Am. Group Coca-Cola Enterprises Inc., Atlanta, 1996—2000, sr. v.p., pres., Western N.Am. Group, 2000—01, pres. N.Am. Group, 2001—05, exec. v.p., 2001—05, COO, 2004—05.

VAN HOUTEN, LEONARD ERSKINE, consulting engineer; b. Jersey City, Dec. 20, 1924; s. Leonard and Margaret Agnes (Molumby) Van H.; m. Marie K. Regan, Dec. 27, 1947; children: Elizabeth M., Peter J. B.C.E., Rensselaer Poly. Inst., 1945, M.C.E., 1947. Engr. to sr. v.p. Frederic R. Harris, Inc., NYC, 1947-65; pres., chmn. bd. Van Houten Assocs., Inc. and VHA Services, Inc., NYC, 1965-76; with Dravo Corp. Pitts., 1976-82; v.p. Dravo Engrs. and Constructors; chmn. Dravo Van Houten, Inc., 1982-86; sr. v.p., dir. Parsons Brinckerhoff Internat., Inc.; also sr. v.p. Parsons, Brinckerhoff, Quade & Douglas, Inc., NYC; now prin. Leonard E. Van Houten P.E. Consulting Engr., Greenwich, Conn., 2007. Contbr. articles to tech. jours., Ency. Americana. Bd. dirs. Nat. Waterways Found., 1983-92. With USNR, 1942-46. Fellow ASCE (hon.); mem. Soc. Naval Architects and Marine Engrs., The Moles. Clubs: N.Y. Yacht. Co-inventor devices for mooring large ships and offshore structures. Home and Office: 314 N Maple Ave Greenwich CT 06830-4754 Office Phone: 203-661-2753. E-mail: lenvh@aol.com.

VAN HOUTEN, RONALD, psychology professor; b. Bklyn., Aug. 3, 1944; s. Jack and Marion Theresa Van Houten; m. Joy Van Houten, Sept. 21, 1986; children: Lisa, Jason, Courtney, Jonathan, Ashleigh, Andrew, Xanthe. BA, SUNY, Stony Brook, 1968; MA, Dalhousie U., Halifax,

NS, 1969, PhD, 1972. Prof. Mt. St. Vincent U., Halifax, 1971—2005, Western Mich. U., Kalamazoo, 2005—. Chair, task force Assn. Behavior Analysis Internat., Kalamazoo, fellow, 2007; chair, pedestrian com. Transportation Rsch. Bd., Washington, 2005—08. Recipient Solicitation Gen. Crime Prevention award, Govt. Canada, 1984, Rsch. Excellence award, Mt. St. Vincent U., 2003. Avocation: flying.

VAN HOY, PHILIP MARSHALL, lawyer; b. Washington, Nov. 8, 1947; s. Joe Milton and Helen Virginia (Spangler) V.; m. Sylvia Kathryn Smith, Dec. 30, 1972; children: Marshall, Travis. AB, Duke U., Durham, NC, 1970; JD, U. NC, 1973. Bar: NC 1973, US Dist. Ct. (ea., we. and mid. dists.) NC 1974, US Ct. Appeals (4th cir.) 1974, US Supreme Ct. 1978. Labor counsel Duke Power Co., Charlotte, NC, 1973—80; assoc. Siegel, O'Connor & Kainen, Charlotte, 1980—83; ptnr. Mullins & Van Hoy, Charlotte, 1983—89, Van Hoy, Rentlinger, Adams & Dunn, Charlotte, 1989—. Mem. NC OSHA Rev. Bd., 1985—92, Mecklenburg County, NC Personnel Commn., 1985—92, NC Leadership Coun. Co-state chmn. Gardner for Lt. Gov., 1988, alt. del. Rep. Nat. Conv., Detroit, 1980; chmn. Mecklenburg County Young Rep. Com., 1979, vice chmn., 1980-83; Duke U. Athletics Coun., 1999-02. 1st lt. US Army, 1973-81. Recipient Salute to Am.'s Best Lawyers, Forbes mag. and Am. Airlines Sky Radio, 2005; named Top Employment Lawyer NC, Bus. NC mag., 2002—; named to Best Lawyers in Am., 2001—, Outstanding Lawyers of Am., 2003. Mem. NC Bar Assn. (councillor labor and employment law sect. 1985-88, chmn. EEOC com. 1983-92), NC State Bar, 4th Cir. Jud. Conf., Rotary, Charlotte Cotillion Club (pres. 1979-80), City Club, Myers Park Country Club (dir. 1994-96, 2000-03). Republican. Methodist. Office: Van Hoy Reutlinger Adams & Dunn 737 East Blvd Charlotte NC 28203-5113 Home: 16631 Harbor View Rd Charlotte NC 28278

VANIER, JACQUES, physicist; s. Henri and Emma Vanier; m. Lucie Beaudet, 1961; children: Lyne, Pierre. BA, U. Montreal, 1955, BSc, 1958; MSc, McGill U., 1960, PhD, 1963. Lectr. U. Montreal, 1961-63, McGill U., 1960-63; physicist Varian Assocs., Beverly, Mass., 1963-67, Hewlett Packard Co., Beverly, 1967; prof. elec. engring. U. Laval, Que., 1967-83; physicist Nat. Rsch. Coun., Ottawa, 1983-94, head elec. and time standards, 1984-86, dir. Lab. Basic Standards, 1986-90, dir. gen. Inst. for Nat. Measurement Standards, 1990-93; prof. physics U. de Montreal, 1995—. Gov.'s Bd. Symposium on Frequency Standards and Metrology, 1971-; cons. Comm. Components Corp., Costa Mesa, Calif., 1974-76, EGG Co., Salem, Mass., 1979-82, Kernco, Danvers, Mass., 1995-2007; chmn. com. A URSI, 1990-93; chmn. exec. com. CPEM, 1990-94; mem. Internat. Com. Weights and Measures, 1992-96; guest worker IEN, Torino, Italy, 1996-97; adv. bd. Precision Time and Time Interval Com., 2006—. Author: Basic Theory of Lasers and Masers, 1971, (with C. Audoin) The Quantum Physics of Atomic Frequency Standards, 1989; contbr. articles to profl. jours.; patentee (4) in field. Recipient Disting. Precision Time & Time Interval Svc. award PTTI Organizing Com., 1998. Fellow IEEE (Centennial medal 1984, I.I. Rabi award 1994, Instrument & Measurement Soc. award 1999), Royal Soc. Can., Am. Phys. Soc. Business E-Mail: jac.vanier@sympatico.ca.

VANINI, J. TIM, environmental educator, coach, consultant; b. Buffalo, May 31, 1969; s. Joseph James and Christina Ann Vanini. PhD, Mich. State U., East Lansing, 2005. Pres. New Dimensions Turfness; dir. big green initiative environ. Nichols Sch., Buffalo, 2005—09, dir. ice hockey, 2005—09. Head ice hockey coach Cortland State U., NY, 1997—2001; asst. ice hockey coach Hamilton Coll., Clinton, 1996—97. Recipient Dr. James R. Watson award, 2004; named Ice Hockey Coach of Yr., SUNY Athletic Conf., 2001. Mem.: Crop Sci. Soc. Am., Sports Turf Mgrs. Assn., Sphinx Head Soc., Chi Psi. Achievements include method for reducing abrasion to turfgrass. Avocations: golf, reading, travel, fitness. Home and Office: 9 Colvin Ave Buffalo NY 14216 Business E-Mail: tim@noturf.com. E-mail: lavanooche@mac.com.

VANINSKY, ALEXANDER YAN, mathematician, educator, researcher, financial analyst, systems analyst; b. Moscow, Oct. 14, 1943; arrived in Israel, 1991, US, 1998. s. Yan Boris and Yulia Yakov (Vaninskaya) Kheifets; 1 child, Marina. MEE, Moscow Power Engring. Inst., 1967; MS in Math. Edn., Moscow State U., 1971; PhD in Math. Econs., Moscow State Acad. Fin., 1979; DSc, Moscow Acad. Fin., 1990; MA in Maths., Bkln. Coll. Sr. rsch. fellow Ctrl. Inst. for Communications, Moscow, 1983-88; lead mathematician, rsch. fellow R&D Assn. Kvant, Moscow, 1988-89; prof. Moscow State U., 1990-91; rsch. fellow Technion, Haifa, Israel, 1992-97; prof. Moscow State Acad. Instrument-making & Info., 1995-98, Netanya Acad. Coll., Israel, 1997—99; adj. lectr. U. Conn., 2000—; prof. Hostos CC, CUNY, 2004—. Expert Bank Incombank, Moscow, 1991, Ministry of Fin., Moscow, 1991. Author: Computer Analysis of Economic Situations, 1991, Factor Analysis of Business Activity, 1987, Computer Forecast of Profit and Sales, 1982; co-author: Accounting and Audit of Effectiveness of Manufacturing, 1986. Recipient Stephen J. Shaw award for most outstanding paper So. Mktg. Assn., 1994, Channels Retail and Svcs. Mktg. Track, 1994. Mem. Am. Math. Soc., Global Assn. Risk Profls., Fin. Mgmt. Assn. Internat., Israeli Fgn. Trade Risk Insurance Co.(bd. dir., 1997-98), Math. Assn. Am., Am. Assn. U. Profs. Avocations: tennis, mountain skiing. Office: Hostos CC Math Dept 500 Grand Concourse Rm B409 Bronx NY 10451 Office Phone: 718-319-7930.

VAN INWAGEN, PETER JAN, philosophy educator; b. Rochester, NY, Sept. 21, 1942; s. George Butler and Mildred Gloria (Knudson) van I; m. Margery Bedford Naylor, Mar. 31, 1967 (div. Apr. 1988); 1 child, Elizabeth Core; m. Elisabeth Marie Bolduc, June 3, 1989. BS, Rensselaer Poly. Inst., 1965; PhD, U. Rochester, 1969. Vis. asst. prof. U. Rochester, NY, 1971-72; asst. prof. Syracuse U., NY, 1972-74, assoc. prof. NY, 1974-80, prof. philosophy NY, 1980-95; John Cardinal O'Hara prof. of philosophy U. Notre Dame, South Bend, Ind., 1995—. Vis. prof. U. Ariz., Tucson, 1981, Princeton U., 2002; lectr. U. of St. Andrews, 2003, Oxford U., 2000, U. London, 1998, U. Lublin, 2008, U. Tel Aviv, 2008, U. Leeds, 2009. Author: An Essay on Free Will, 1983, Material Beings, 1990, Metaphysics, 1993, God, Knowledge and Mystery, 1995, The Possibility of Resurrection, 1997, Ontology, Identity, and Modality, 2001, The Problem of Evil, 2006; editor: Time and Cause, 1980, Alvin Plantinga, 1985, Metaphysics: The Big Questions, 1998, Christian Faith and The Problem of Evil, 2004, Persons: Human and Divine, 2007; mem. editl. bd. Jour. Faith and Philosophy, Philos. Perspectives, Nous, Philos. Studies, Jour. of Ethics, Philosophy and Phenomenological Rsch.; contbr. articles to profl. jours. Served to capt. U.S. Army, 1969-71 NEH grantee, 1983-84, 89-90. Mem. Am. Acad. Arts and Scis., Am. Philos. Assn., Soc. Christian Philosophers. Democrat. Episcopalian. Home: 52145 Farmington Square Rd Granger IN 46530-6403 Office: U Notre Dame Dept Philosophy South Bend IN 46556-4619 Office Phone: 574-631-5910. E-mail: peter.vaninwagen.1@nd.edu.

VAN INWEGEN, PATRICK F., political science professor; b. Boise, Idaho; married. PhD, Loyola U., Chgo., 2004. Assoc. prof. Whitworth U., Spokane, Wash., 2005—. Achievements include research in understanding revolutions textbook.

VANITALLIE, THEODORE BERTUS, physician; b. Hackensack, NJ, Nov. 8, 1919; s. Dorus Christian and Lucy M. (Pohle) VanI.; m. Barbara Cox, Sept. 25, 1948 (div. Mar. 1992); children: Lucy M., Theodore Bertus, Christina M., Elizabeth B., Katharine R.; m. Sallie Newton Calhoun, Mar. 11, 1992. BS, Harvard U., 1941; MD, Columbia U., 1945. Diplomate: Am. Bd. Internal Medicine. Intern in medicine St. Luke's Hosp., NYC, 1945-46, asst. resident in internal medicine, 1948-49, resident, 1949-50, dir. nutrition and metabolism rsch. lab., 1952-55; assoc. Peter Bent Brigham Hosp., Boston, 1955-57; dir. medicine St. Luke's Hosp. Center, NYC, 1957-75. Dir. Obesity Rsch. Ctr., 1974-85, co-dir., 1986-88; asst. prof. Sch. Pub. Health, Harvard U., 1955-57; assoc. clin. prof. medicine Columbia, N.Y.C., 1957-65, clin. prof., 1965-71, prof., 1971-88, prof. emeritus, 1988—; vis. prof. internal medicine Am. U. Beirut, 1968-69, trustee, 1976-93; spl. advisor on human nutrition Surgeon Gen., 1980-81; mem. sci. adv. bd. Nutrition Found., 1967-71; pres. Am. Bd. Nutrition, 1968-71; mem. food and nutrition bd. NRC, 1970-76; med. adv. com. on cyclamates HEW, 1969-70; mem. gastrointestinal and nutrition tng. com. NIH, 1969-73, mem. adv. coun. Nat. Arthritis, Diabetes, Digestive and Kidney Diseases, NIH, 1978-81; mem. joint nutrition monitoring evaluation com. USDA and HHS, 1982-86; dir. Miles Labs., 1976-84; vis. physician Rockefeller U. Hosp., 1986-89; adj. prof. Rockefeller U., 1986-89; vis. prof. medicine in psychiatry, U. Pa., 1990-94. Mem. editorial bd.: Diabetes, 1960-71; editor-in-chief: Am. Jour. Clin. Nutrition, 1979-81. Mem. Englewood (N.J.) Bd. Edn., 1960-65, v.p., 1964-65; trustee St. Luke's-Roosevelt Hosp. Ctr., 1988-94. Lt. (j.g.) USNR, 1946-68. Recipient citation FDA, 1983. Fellow ACP (disting. physicians award 1987), AAAS, Am. Inst. Nutrition; mem. AMA (mem. coun. on foods and nutrition 1967-74, vice chmn. 1974, Joseph B. Goldberger award 1985), Am. Soc. Clin. Investigation, Soc. Exptl. Biology and Medicine, Am. Clin. and Climatol. Assn., Am. Soc. Clin. Nutrition (coun. 1970-73, pres. 1976-77, Elmer V. McCollum award 1985), Soc. Study of Ingestive Behavior (disting. sci. award 1994), Order of Malta (knight comdr. Quebec priory 1990—), Century Assn., Fla. Hist. Soc. (bd. dirs. 1995—). Research and contbr. numerous publs. on obesity, body composition, pancreatic hormone, glucagon, mechanism of energy balance regulation, treatment of pruritus and hypercholesteremia in biliary cirrhosis, physiology and clin. use of medium chain triglyceride.

VAN KAMPEN, DORIS J., librarian, educator; EdD Curriculum & Instrn., U. Ctrl. Fla., Orlando, 2003. Media specialist, K-12 Fla., 2008, lic. State of Fla. Media specialist Pasco County Schs., Hudson, Fla., 1991—2000; systems libr. St. Leo U., 2000—. Interim dir., FCIT U. South Fla., Tampa, 1994, Fla. Ctr. for Instrnl. Tech, Tampa, 1998. Contbr. chapters to books, articles to profl. jours. (Best Practices, ISTE, 1995). Legis. adv. Assn. Coll. and Rsch. Librs., Ill., 2007—; sec. Sunrise Pasco, Dade City, Fla., 2005—, Coll. Rsch. Librs., 2004; dir. Pasco-Hernando Early Childhood Coalition, New Port Richey, Fla., 2002—03. Mem.: FLA, ACRL, ALA. Conservative. Avocations: reading, hiking. Office: SainT Leo Univ 33741 Sr 52 Mc 2128 Saint Leo FL 33574 Business E-Mail: doris.vankampen@saintleo.edu.

VAN KIRK, CRAIG WILLIAM, petroleum engineer, educator; b. Downey, Calif., Aug. 4, 1945; m. Denice Diane Bryant, Jan. 29, 1967; children: Samuel David, Connie Diane Campbell. BS in Petroleum Engring., U. Southern Calif., LA, 1968, MS in Petroleum Engring., 1969; PhD in Petroleum Engring., Colo. Sch. Mines, Golden, 1972. Registered profl. engr., Colo., 1979. Prodn., reservoir engr. Humble Oil Co., Exxon, Long Beach, Calif., 1967—69; reservoir engr. Shell Oil Co., Denver, 1969—74; mgr. reservoir studies Sci. Software Corp., Denver, 1974—78; prof. petroleum engring. Colo. Sch. Mines, Golden, 1978—, spl. advisor to pres. Cons., advisor pvt. practice, Parker, Colo., 1978—; rsch. and grad. student supporter Dept. Energy Edn., Govt. Nat. Oil Co. and Internat. Oil Co., 1978—. Tng. native Am. Colo. Sch. Mines, Golden, 1974—; vol. tchr., mentor HS and Indian Reservations, 1974—. Named Faculty Senate Disting. Lectr., Colo. Sch. Mines, 2005. Mem.: Nat. Assn. Profl. Engrs., Soc. Petroleum Engrs. (mem. dirs. 1991—93, named Disting. Mem. 1997, Rocky Mountain Svc. award 1998), Tau Beta Pi. Avocation: travel. Office: Colorado School of Mines 1600 Illinois Street Golden CO 80401 Office Fax: 303-273-3189. E-mail: cvankirk@mines.edu.

VAN KIRK, JOHN ELLSWORTH, retired cardiologist; b. Dayton, Ohio, Jan. 13, 1942; s. Herman Corwin and Dorothy Louise (Shafer) Van K.; m. Patricia L. Davis, June 19, 1966 (div. Dec. 1982); 1 child, Linnea Gray. BA cum laude, DePauw U., Greencastle, Ind., 1963; BS, Northwestern U., Chgo., 1964, MD with distinction, 1967. Diplomate Am. Bd. Internal Medicine, Am. Bd. Internal Medicine subspecialty in cardiovasc. disease; cert. Nat. Bd. Med. Examiners. Intern Evanston (Ill.) Hosp., 1967-68; staff assoc. Nat. Inst. of Allergy & Infectious Diseases., Bethesda, Md., 1968-70; resident internal medicine U. Mich. Med. Ctr., Ann Arbor, 1970-72, fellow in cardiology, 1972-74, instr. internal medicine, 1973-74; staff cardiologist Mills Meml. Hosp., San Mateo, Calif., 1974—2001, vice-chief medicine, 1977-78, dir. critical care, 1978-96, critical care utilizaton rev., 1988-99, dir. pacemaker clinic, 1976-99; staff cardiologist Mills-Peninsula Hosp., Burlingame, Calif., 1996-99; ret., 1999. Dir. transitional care, 1996—99; mem. courtesy staff Sequoia Hosp., 1984—2001, ret., 1999. Contbr. rsch. articles to profl. jours. Recipient 1st prize in landscaping Residential Estates, State of Calif., 1977. Fellow Am. Coll. Cardiology; mem. AMA (Physician's Recognition award 1968, 72, 75, 77, 80, 82, 85, 87, 89, 93, 97, 2000), Calif. Med. Assn., San Mateo County Med. Soc., Am. Heart Assn., San Mateo County Heart Assn. (bd. dirs. 1975-78, mem. Bay area rsch. com. 1975-76, mem. edn. com. 1975-77, pres.-elect 1976-77, pres. 1977-79), Alpha Omega Alpha. Republican. Mem. United Brethren Ch. Avocations: gardening, computer science, tennis, woodworking, electronics, amateur radio. Home: 235 Amherst Ave San Mateo CA 94402-2201 Personal E-mail: John_VanKirk@msn.com.

VAN KIRK, ROBERT JOHN, nursing clinical manager, educator; b. Jersey City, Sept. 18, 1944; s. Robert and Doris Van Kirk; m. Marjorie Ann Carroll, Mar. 23, 1968 (div. Nov. 1993); children: Walter, Michael, Robert Jr., Peggy; m. Nancy A. Fix, Aug. 31, 1996. BA cum laude, U. Conn., Storrs, 1974; MEd, Kent State U., Ohio, 1983; D of Nursing, Case Western Res. U., Cleve., 1986. RN Ohio, cert. diabetes educator (CDE). Sales mgr. Nutmeg Home Protection, Middlebury, Conn., 1972-74; theater mgr. SBC Mgmt. Corp., Boston, 1974; dist. supr. Selected Theatres Mgmt. Corp., Lyndhurst, Ohio, 1974-86; nat. sales mgr. ZBS Video, Inc., Lyndhurst, 1981-82; staff nurse Cleve. Clinic Found., 1986-87, clin. instr., 1987-88, head nurse, 1988-93, case mgr., 1993—2002, diabetes educator, 2002—07, clin. mgr., 2007—; asst. clin. prof. Case Western Res. U., Frances Payne Bolton Sch. Nursing, Cleve., 1990—; case mgr. Cleve. Clin. Home Care, 1993—2002; CEO Lifelong Learning, Inc., Chagrin Falls, Ohio, 2002—. Health officer Lake County (Ohio) Bd. Alcohol, Drug Addiction and Mental Health Svcs., 1991—; co-chmn. United Way, Cleve., 1991-93. Staff sgt. US Army, 1964—71, Vietnam. Recipient Achievement award, Greater Cleve. Nurses Assn., 1986, Carol Udycz Nursing Excellence award, Cleve. Clinic, 2007. Mem. AACN, Am. Assn. Tchrs. German, Am. Assn. Tchrs. Portuguese and Spanish, Assn. Specialists in Aging, Frances Payne Bolton Sch. Nursing Alumni Assn. (pres. 1992-93), Kappa Delta Pi, Sigma Theta Tau, Ohio Coun. Home Care (mem. edn. oversight com.). Avocations: pocket billards, furniture making. Home: 495 Bell Rd Chagrin Falls OH 44022-4160 Office: Cleve Clinic Found 6801 Brecksville Rd Ste 10 Independence OH 44131 also: Lifelong Learning Inc 495 Bell Rd Chagrin Falls OH 44022 Home Phone: 440-247-0953.

VAN KIRK, THOMAS L., lawyer; b. Pa., June 25, 1945; s. Theodore and Mary Jane (Young) Van K.; children: Thomas Jr., Christopher. BA, Bucknell U., 1967; JD cum laude, Dickinson U., 1970. Bar: Pa., U.S. Dist. Ct. (we. and ea. dists.) Pa. 1971, U.S. Ct. Appeals (3d cir.) 1972, U.S. Supreme Ct. 1976. Clk. Pa. Superior Ct., 1970-71; assoc. Buchanan Ingersoll PC, Pitts., 1971-77, ptnr., 1978—, COO, 1985—2003; chmn., CEO Buchanan Ingersoll & Rooney PC, Pitts., 2006—. Bd. dirs. Buchanan Ingersoll P.C.; exec. com., sec. State Pa. Economy League; past bd. chair Western Pa. Economy League. Chmn. emeritus Pitts. Downtown Partnership; bd. dirs., exec. com. mem. Pitts. Cultural Trust; coun. mem. U. Pitts. Cancer Inst.; exec. com., bd. mem. DSN Innovations, Allegheny Conf.; past chair, bd. exec. com. mem. Pa. Bus. Coun. Mem.: ABA, August Wilson Ctr. African Am. Cultures (co-head, capital fundraising com.), Women & Girls Found. (bd. mem.), Allegheny County Bar Assn., The Club at Nevillewood, Rivers Club, Duquesne Club. Democrat. Lutheran. Home: 1010 Osage Rd Pittsburgh PA 15243-1014 Office: Buchanan Ingersoll Rooney One Oxford Ctr 301 Grant St Fl 20 Pittsburgh PA 15219-1410 Office Phone: 412-562-8875. Business E-Mail: vankirktl@bipc.com.

VANLANDINGHAM, MARK REED, materials engineer; b. Radford, Va., Oct. 16, 1968; s. Hugh Foch and Patricia Maureen VanLandingham; m. Jennifer Sorensen; 1 child, Luke George. PhD, U. Del., Newark, 1993—97. Nrc postdoctoral fellow Nat. Inst. Standards & Tech., Gaithersburg, Md., 1997—99, materials rsch. engr., 1999—2002; materials engr. US Army Rsch. Lab., Aberdeen Proving Ground, Md., 2002—05, chief multi-functional materials br., 2005—. Contbr. tech. papers in field. Mem.: Am. Chem. Soc., Materials Rsch. Soc. Achievements include patents for humidity chamber for scanning stylus atomic force microscope with cantilever tracking. Office: US Army Rsch Lab 4600 Deer Creek Loop Aberdeen Proving Ground MD 21005-5069 Office Fax: 410-306-0676. Business E-Mail: mark.vanlandingham@us.army.mil.

VAN LARE, WENDELL JOHN, lawyer, director; b. Newark, NY, Mar. 1, 1945; s. Julian J. and Doris Elizabeth (Lacknor) Van L.; m. Sheila Gilbert, Aug. 20, 1967 (div. Apr. 1987); children: Jonathan S., Allison R.; m. L. Karen Stack, May 7, 1987. BS, SUNY, New Paltz, 1967; JD, Union U., 1972. Bar: N.Y. 1973, U.S. Supreme Ct., 1980; cert. corp. counsel VA, 2004. Assoc. Harter, Secrest & Emery, Rochester, NY, 1972-77; asst. dir. labor rels. Gannett Co., Inc., Rochester, 1977-80, dir. labor rels. Rochester and Arlington, NY, 1980-93, v.p., labor counsel Arlington, 1993-94, v.p., sr. labor counsel, 1994—2006, sr. v.p. labor rels., 2006—. Comments editor Albany Law Rev., 1971-72. Pres. Opera Theatre of Rochester, N.Y., 1983-85; trustee SUNY New Paltz Found. Lt. (j.g.) USNR, 1968-70. Mem. ABA, N.Y. Bar Assn., Va. Bar Assn., River Bend Golf and Country Club. Avocation: genealogy. Office: Gannett Co Inc 7950 Jones Branch Dr Mc Lean VA 22102

VAN LEEUWEN, JEAN See GAVRIL, JEAN

VAN LEUVEN, ROBERT JOSEPH, lawyer; b. Detroit, Apr. 17, 1931; s. Joseph Francis and Olive (Stowell) Van Leuven; m. Merri Lee Van Leuven; children: Joseph Michael, Douglas Robert, Julie Margaret. Attended, Albion Coll., 1949-51; BA, Wayne State U., 1953; JD, U. Mich., 1957. Bar: Mich. 1957. Practice in law, Muskegon, Mich.; ptnr. Hathaway, Latimer, Clink,and Robb, Mich., 1957-68, McCroskey, Libner, and Van Leuven, Mich., 1968-81, Libner and Van Leuven, Mich., 1982—99; ret. Mich., 1999. Mem. coun. negligence law sect. State Bar Mich. Bd. dir., Muskegon Children's Home, 1965—75. With Aus., 1953—55. Fellow: Am. Coll. Trial Lawyers, Mich. Bar Found.; mem.: Delta Sigma Phi. Home: 8545 Gatewood Ct Englewood FL 34224 Home Phone: 231-247-8252.

VAN LINT, VICTOR ANTON JACOBUS, physicist; b. Samarinda, Indonesia, May 10, 1928; came to U.S., 1937; s. Victor J. and Margaret (DeJager) Van L.; m. M. June Woolhouse, June 10, 1950; children: Lawrence, Kenneth, Linda, Karen. BS, Calif. Inst. Tech., Pasadena, 1950, PhD, 1954. Instr. Princeton (N.J.) U., 1954-55; staff mem. Gen. Atomic, San Diego, 1957-74; physics cons. San Diego, 1974-75; staff mem. Mission Research Corp., San Diego, 1975-82, 83-91; cons., 1991—; spl. asst. to dep. dir. sci. and tech. Def. Nuclear Agy., Washington, 1982-83. Author, editor: Radiation Effects in Electronic Materials, 1976; contbr. articles to profl. jours. Served with U.S. Army, 1955-57. Recipient Pub. Service award NASA, 1981. Fellow IEEE. Republican. Mem. United Ch. of Christ. Home and Office: 1032 Skylark Dr La Jolla CA 92037-7733 Home Phone: 858-454-5978. Business E-Mail: vicvanlint@sbcglobal.net.

VAN LOPIK, JACK RICHARD, geologist, educator; b. Holland, Mich., Feb. 25, 1929; s. Guy M. and Minnie (Grunst) Van L.; 1 son, Charles Robert (dec.). BS, Mich. State U., 1950; MS, La. State U., 1953, PhD, 1955. Geologist, sect. chief, asst. chief, chief geology br. U.S. Army C.E., Waterways Expt. Sta., Vicksburg, Miss., 1954-61; chief engrs. environ. adv. bd. U.S. Army C.E., 1988-92; chief area evaluation sect., tech. dir., mgr. Space and Environ. Sci. Programs, tech. requirements dir. geosciences ops. Tex. Instruments, Inc., Dallas, 1961-68; chmn. dept. marine sci. La. State U., Baton Rouge, 1968-74; prof. dept. marine sci., dir. sea grant devel., dean Center for Wetland Resources, La. State U., Baton Rouge, 1968-91; prof. dept. oceanography and coastal scis. La. State U., Baton Rouge, 1991—; exec. dir. sea grant devel., La. State U., 1991—2005; chmn. Coastal Resources Directorate of U.S. Nat. Com. for Man and Biosphere, U.S. Nat. Commn. for UNESCO, 1975-82. Dir. Gulf South Rsch. Inst., 1974-89; mem. Nat. Adv. Com. Oceans and Atmosphere, 1978-84; mem. Lower Miss. River Waterway Safety Com. USCG 8th dist., 1983-94; mem. adv. coun. Nat. Coastal Resources Rsch. and Devel. Inst., 1985-98; ofcl. del. XX Congreso Internacional, Mexico City, 1956, XII Gen. Assembly Internat. Union Geodesy and Geophysics, Helsinki, 1960; chmn. panel on geography and land use Nat. Acad. Scis.-NRC, com. on remote sensing programs for earth resources surveys, 1969-77. Fellow Geol. Soc. Am., AAAS; mem. Am. Astronautical Soc. (dir. S.W. sect. 1967-68), Am. Soc. Photogrammetry (dir. 1969-72, chmn. photo interpretation com. 1960, 65, rep. earth scis. divsn. NRC 1968-71), Am. Geophys. Union, Am. Assn. Petroleum Geologists (acad. adv. com. 1973-78), Assn. Am. Geographers, Soc. Econ. Paleontologists and Mineralogists (rsch. com. 1962-65), Am. Mgmt. Assn., Soc. Rsch. Adminstrs., Marine Tech. Soc., Am. Water Resources Assn., Soc. Am. Mil. Engrs., Sea Grant Assn. (exec. bd. dirs. 1972-74, 80-82, 88-91, pres.-elect 1988-89, pres. 1989-90), Nat. Ocean Industries Assn. (adv. coun. 1973-83), Nat. Conf. Advancement Rsch. (exec. com. 1988-92), La. Partnership for Tech. and Innovation (bd. dirs. 1989—), Sigma Xi. Home: 333 Lee Dr G23 Baton Rouge LA 70808-4682 Office: La State U Office Sea Grant Devel Baton Rouge LA 70803-0001 Home Phone: 225-766-3585; Office Phone: 225-578-6710. Business E-Mail: jvl@lsu.edu.

VAN LOUCKS, MARK LOUIS, venture capitalist, financial planner; b. Tampa, Fla., June 19, 1946; s. Charles Perry and Lenn (Bragg) Van L.; children: Brandon, Charlie; m. Lee Ann Strubel, Oct. 1, 1998. BA in Comm. and Pub. Policy, U. Calif., Berkeley, 1969. Sr. v.p. mktg., programming and corp. devel. United Cable TV Corp., Denver, 1970-81, advisor, 1983-89; sr. v.p., office of chmn. Rockefeller Ctr. TV Corp., NYC, 1981-83; advisor United Artists Commun. Corp., Englewood, 1989-91; investor, business advisor in pvt. practice Englewood, 1983—; founder, prin. owner Glory Hole Saloon & Gaming Hall, Central City, Colo., 1990—, The Canyon Casino, Black Hawk, Colo., 1990—; chmn., CEO Bask Internat., Englewood, 1990—. Bd. dirs. Wild West Devel. Corp., Denver; sr. v.p., bd. dirs. GSI Cable TV Assocs., Inc., San Francisco, 1984-90; guest lectr. on cable TV bus., 1985-91; cons. Telecommunications, Inc., Denver, 1989-93. Producer HBO spl. Green Chili Showdown, 1985; producer TV spl. 3 Days for Earth, 1987; producer, commd. artist nuclear war armament pieces; contbr. articles to profl. jours. Chmn. Cops in Crisis, Denver, 1990—; bd. dirs. The NOAH Found., Denver, 1976—; founding dir. Project for Responsible Advt., Denver, 1991-92; chmn. mayor's mktg. adv. bd., Central City, Colo. Named hon. capt. Denver Police Dept., 1991—, fin. advisor L. Rose Co., 1995—. Mem. Casino Owners Assn. (founding dir. 1989—), Colo. Gaming Assn. (dir. 1990—), recipient S'nnaeel Evol award, 1995), Glenmoor Country Club, The Village Club. Republican. Jewish. Avocations: music, woodworking, philanthropy, classic cars. Office: MLVL Inc 1515 E Tufts Ave Cherry Hills Village CO 80113 Office Phone: 303-781-0827. E-mail: mvanloucks@msn.com.

VANMARCKE, ERIK HECTOR, civil engineer, educator; b. Menen, Belgium, Aug. 6, 1941; arrived in U.S., 1965, naturalized, 1976; s. Louis Eugene and Rachel Louisa (van Hollebeke) Vanmarcke; m. Margaret Marie Delesie, May 25, 1965 (div. Feb. 22, 1999); children: Lieven Vanmarcke, Ann Vanmarcke Forzani, Kristien Vanmarcke Webber; m. Marilyn Durkee, July 14, 2001. BS, U. Leuven, Belgium, 1965; MS, U. Del., 1967; PhD in Civil Engring, MIT, 1970. From instr. to prof. civil engring. MIT, Cambridge, 1969—85, Gilbert W. Winslow Career Devel. prof., 1974—77, dir. civil engring. sys. group, 1976—80; prof. civil engring. and ops. rsch. Princeton U., 1985—, affiliated faculty mem. Bendheim Ctr. Fin., 1998—, dir. grad. studies civil engring. and ops. rsch., 1990—94. Cons. Office Sci. and Tech. Policy, 1978—80, Nat. Inst. Stds. and Tech., 2003, Internat. Atomic Energy Agy., 2004, NASA, 2008, various govt. agys. and engring. firms; vis. scholar in engring. Harvard U., 1984—85; Shimizu Corp. vis. prof. Stanford U., 1991; mem. exec. com. Princeton Materials Inst., 1991—93; mem. Princeton Environ. Inst., 1996—; mem. com. vulnerability critical infrastructure Nat. Res. Coun., 1999—2001; mem. com. program on robotics and intelligent sys. Princeton U., 1999—. Author: Random Fields: Analysis and Synthesis, 1983, revised and expanded edit., 2009, Quantum Origins of Cosmic Structure, 1997; editor: Internat. Jour. Structural Safety, 1981—91. Recipient Sr. Scientist award, Japan Soc. Promotion Sci., 1991, Disting. Engring. Alumnus award, U. Del., 1994; named Disting. Probabilistic Methods Educator, Soc. Automotive Engrs., 2002. Mem.: ASME (mem. earthquake engring. rsch. inst.), ASCE (chair com. risk assessment and mgmt. Geo-Inst. 1996—2000, chair com. risk and vulnerability Coun. Natural Disaster Reduction 1998—2003, chair exec. com. coun. disaster risk mgmt. 2003—06, chair internat. roundtable disaster risk mgmt. 2005, Raymond C. Reese Rsch. award 1975, Walter L. Huber Rsch. prize 1984), Royal Acad. Arts and Scis. Belgium (fgn.), Internat. Soc. Soil Mechanics and Geotech. Engring. (chair com. TC32 risk assessment and mgmt. 1998—2001), Am. Geophys. Union. Home: 148 Springdale Rd Princeton NJ 08544 Office Phone: 609-258-5896. Business E-Mail: evm@princeton.edu.

VANMEER, MARY ANN, publishing executive, writer, webmaster; b. Mt. Clemens, Mich., Nov. 22, 1947; d. Leo Harold and Rose Emma (Gulden) VanM. Student, Micha. State U., 1965-66, 67-68, U. Sorbonne, Paris, summer 1968; BA in Edn., U. Fla., 1968-70. Pres. VanMeer Tutoring and Translating, NYC, 1970-72; freelance writer, 1973-79; pres. VanMeer Publs., Inc., Clearwater, Fla., 1980-88, VanMeer Media Advt., Inc., Clearwater, 1987-88; exec. dir., founder Nat. Ctrs. for Health and Med. Info., Inc., Palm Beach, Fla., 1990-93; pres., CEO ThriftyTraveling.com, Inc. (formerly Traveling Free Pubs.,), 1993—. Author: Traveling with Your Dog, U.S.A., 1976, How to Set Up a Home Typing Business, 1978, Freelance Photographer's Handbook, 1979, See America Free, 1981, Free Campgrounds, U.S.A., 1982, Free Attractions, U.S.A., 1982, VanMeer's Guide to Free Attractions U.S.A., 1984, VanMeer's Guide to Free Campgrounds, 1984, The How to Get Publicity for Your Business Handbook, 1987, Asthma: The Ultimate Treatment Guide, 1991, Allergies: The Ultimate Treatment Guide, 1992, Thrifty Traveling, 1995, 2d edit., 1996; pub. Nat. Health and Med. Trends Mag., 1986-88, ThriftyTraveling.com Newsletter and website, 1993—, online and hard-copy edits., 1999—, Over 50 Thrifty Traveler Newsletter, 1997-98, Free & Really Cheap Travel Newsletter, 2009-, Net News for the Thrifty Traveler Newsletter, 1997-98, LuxuryTraveling-.com newsletter and website, 2001—; webmaster ThriftyTraveling.com, Over 50 Travelling.com, Books-And-Cool-Stuff.com, LuxuryTraveling-.com and VanMeer.com websites. Pub. info. chairperson, bd. dirs. Pinellas County chpt. Am. Cancer Soc., Clearwater, 1983-84, 86-88; mem. fin. devel. com. ARC, Palm Beach County, 1990-92. Mem. Am. Booksellers Assn., Soc. Am. Travel Writers. Home: PO Box 1249 Port Richey FL 34673-1249 Office Phone: 800-532-5731. Personal E-mail: thriftytravel@aol.com.

VAN METER, ABRAM DEBOIS, lawyer, retired banker; b. Springfield, Ill., May 16, 1922; s. A.D. and Edith (Graham) Van M.; m. Margaret Schlipf, Dec. 1, 1956; children: Andy, Alice, Ann. BS, Kings Point Coll., 1946; JD, Northwestern U., 1948. Bar: Ill. 1949. Ptnr. Van Meter, Oxtoby & Funk, Springfield, 1949—2001; adminstrv. asst. to treas. State of Ill., Springfield, 1963; v.p. Ill. Nat. Bank, Springfield, 1964-65, pres., 1965-88, chmn. bd. dirs., 1988-90, also bd. dirs.; chmn. bd. dirs. Nat. City, Springfield, 1990-93, dir. emeritus, 1993—. Chmn. bd. dirs. Ill. Housing Devel. Authority, 1977-2003; chmn. bd. trustees So. Ill. U., 1989-2001; past bd. dirs., exec. com. Meml. Med. Ctr. Mem. ABA, Ill. Bar Assn., Sangamon Bar Assn., Chgo. Club, Chgo. Athletic Club, Sangamo Club, Island Bay Yacht Club, Cariton Club. Home: 6 Fair Oaks St Springfield IL 62704-3222 Office: Nat City 1 N Old State Capitol Plz Springfield IL 62701-1323

VANMETER, VANDELIA L., retired library director; b. Seibert, Colo., July 17, 1934; d. G.W. and A. Pearl Klockenteger; m. Victor M. VanMeter, Jan. 21, 1954; children: Allison C., Kristopher C. BA, Kansas Wesleyan U., 1957; MLS, Emporia State U., 1970; PhD, Tex. Woman's U., 1986. Cert. libr. media specialist. Tchr. Ottawa County Rural Sch., Kans., 1954-55; social scis. tchr. McClave (Colo.) High Sch., 1957-58, Ellsworth (Kans.) Jr. High Sch., 1959-68; libr., media specialist Ellsworth (Kans.) High Sch., 1968-84; asst. prof. libr. sci. U. So. Miss., Hattiesburg, 1986-90; chair dept. libr./info. sci. Spalding U., Louisville, 1990-96, libr. dir., 1991-99, prof., 1991—99. Cons. to sch., pub. and spl. librs., Kans., Miss., Ky., 1970-99; mem. Ky. NCATE Bd. Examiners. Author: American History for Children and Young Adults, 1990, World History for Children and Young Adults, 1992, America in Historical Fiction, 1997; editor: Mississippi Library Media Specialist Staff Development Modules, 1988, Library Lane Newsletter, 1991-99; contbr. chpts. to books; contbr. articles to profl. jours. Active City Coun., Ellsworth, Kans., 1975-79, Park Bd., Ellsworth, 1975-79; bd. dirs. Robbins Meml. Libr., 1977-79. Grantee Kans. Demonstration Sch. Libr., 1970-72, Miss. Power Found., 1989, Project Technology Enhances Curriculur Instrn., 1996-97; named Women of Yr. Bus. and Profl. Women of Ellsworth, Kans., 1976. Mem. ALA, Assn. Coll. and Rsch. Librs., Ky. Libr. Assn., Assn. for Libr. and Info. Sci. Educators.

VAN METRE, MARGARET CHERYL, performing company executive, dancer, educator; b. Maryville, Tenn., Nov. 24, 1938; d. Robert Fillers and Margaret Elizabeth (Goddard) Raulston; m. Mitchell Robert Van Metre II, Aug. 25, 1956; 1 child, Mitchell Robert. Elem., intermediate and advanced tchg. certs. Dir. Van Metre Sch. of Dance, Maryville, 1958-96; artistic dir. Appalachian Ballet Co., Maryville Coll., 1972-96; founding dir. Appalachian Ballet Co., 1972; dir. Van Metre Arts Mgmt., SC, 1996—. Chmn. dance panel Tenn. Arts Commn., 1973-74; chmn. Bicentennial Ballet Project, Tenn., 1975-76; mem. Nat. Bd. Regional Dance Am., 1997-2000; owner Van Metre Arts Mgmt., Edisto Island, S.C., 1996—. Choreographer ballets: Delusion, 1965, Hill Heritage Suite, 1972, Dancing Princesses, 1983. Mem. Tenn. Assn. of Dance (pres. 1972), Southeast Regional Ballet Assn. (pres. 1996, 97, 98, 99, 2003-2007). Democrat. Episcopalian. Home: 2103 Myrtle St Edisto Island SC 29438-3437

VAN MIDDLESWORTH, LESTER, physiology, biophysics and medicine educator, internist; b. Washington, Jan. 13, 1919; s. Lester and Hazel Lucile (Brandt) VanM.; m. Nellie Rue Franklin, June 29, 1948; children: Linda V. Anderson, Jane V. Norman, Frank L., Paul E. BS in Chemistry, U. Va., 1940, MS in Chemistry, 1942, MS in Physiology, 1944; PhD in Physiology, U. Calif., Berkeley, 1946; MD, U. Tenn., 1951, DSc (hon.), 2008. Teaching asst. dept. physiology U. Va., 1944, U. Calif., Berkeley, 1944—45; instr. U. Tenn. Med. Units, Memphis, 1946—52, instr. in medicine, 1953—57, asst. prof. physiology, 1952—54, assoc. prof., 1954—59, prof., 1959—89, prof. emeritus physiology and biophysics, 1989—, asst. prof. medicine, 1957—61, assoc. prof., 1961—72, prof. medicine, 1972—89, prof. medicine emeritus, 1989, Disting. prof. physiology and medicine, 1986—; U. disting. prof., 2007. Rotating intern City of Memphis Hosps., 1951-52; cons. chief chemist Piedmont Apple Products Corp., Charlottesville, Va., 1940-46, Crocker Radiation Lab., U. Calif., Berkeley, 1946-47, Oak Ridge Inst. Nuclear Studies, 1950-54; guest co-investigator Endocrine Labs. Tufts Med. Coll., Boston, summers 1954, 55, 56, 59, 61, 64, 66, 69, Scripps Clinic and Rsch. Found., La Jolla, Calif., 1957; guest investigator in endocrinology Harbor Gen. Hosp., UCLA, 1971, Frederick Joliot Hosp., Orsay, France, 1972, Lawrence Livermore Radiation Lab. U. Calif., 1970; staff mem. clinic for med. thyroid disease patients, City of Memphis and U., Tenn., 1951—; mem. internat. com., 1990-2002. Author 145 publs. in profl. jours., 186 abstracts and oral presentations; work on permanent display Smithsonian Nat. Mus. Am. History, Washington, D.C. Recipient Disting. Svc. award, 1985, Disting. Alumnus award, U. Tenn. Coll. Medicine, 1989, USPHS career rsch. grantee, 1962-89; nominee Prestigious Mahidol award. Mem. Am. Chem. Soc., Am. Physiol. Soc., AAAS, Soc. Exptl. Biology and Medicine, Am. Soc. Clin. Investigation, So. Soc. Clin. Investigation, Health Physics Soc., Endocrine Soc., Am. Thyroid Assn. (Disting. Svc. award 1988), Sigma Xi (rsch. award 1944, 86, nat. lectr. 1989-91), Alpha Chi Sigma. Achievements include research in audiogenic siezures and worldwide radioiodine fallout, and radium in normal human thyroid glands. Home: 1950 Lyndale Ave Memphis TN 38107-5109 Office: U Tenn Health Sci Ctr 894 Union Ave Memphis TN 38163-3514 Office Phone: 901-448-5837. Business E-Mail: lvanmid@physio1.utmem.edu.

VAN MOL, LOUIS JOHN, JR., public relations executive; b. Knoxville, Tenn., Oct. 7, 1943; s. Louis John and Evelyn (Ramsay) Van M.; m. Deborah Ruth Boyd, Nov. 1, 1969; children: Derek, Millicent. BS, U. Tenn., 1966. Staff writer, editor AP, Knoxville and Nashville, 1963-66, 69; account exec. to exec. v.p. Holder, Kennedy & Co., Nashville, 1970-74, exec. v.p., 1978-79; dir. info. TVA, Knoxville, 1974-78; co-founder, ptnr. Dye, Van Mol & Lawrence, Nashville, 1980—, CEO, 2003—; leader, 1992—93. Bd. dirs. East Tenn. Children's Hosp., Knoxville, 1977-78, Martha O'Bryan Ctr., Nashville, 1985-87, Crime Stoppers Nashville, 1986-92, Alcohol and Drug Coun. Mid. Tenn., Nashville, 1991-93, Martha O'Bryan Found., 1998-2000, Pencil Found., 2003—, Nashville Songwriters Found., 2004—, vice chmn., 2006-09, Tenn. C. of C. and Industry, 2005-, chmn. bd. dirs., 2008; bd. trustees Cumberland U., 2008-; chmn. bd. dirs. Nashville Downtown Partnership, 1999-2000, bd. dirs., 2006—; bd. govs., exec. com. Nashville C. of C., 1999-2000; chmn. Goodwill Industries Mid. Tenn., 1996-97, mem. exec. com., 1996-. Lt. U.S. Army, 1966-68. Lt. US Army, 1966—68, Ft. Eustis, Va.; Bien Hoa & Long Binh, Vietnam. Decorated Army Commendation medal, Bronze Star. Mem. Richland Country Club (bd. dirs. 1997-99, pres. 1999), Soc. Profl. Journalists. Presbyterian. Home: 2836 Wellesley Trace Nashville TN 37215-1049 Office: DVL Pub Rels & Advertising 209 7th Ave N Nashville TN 37219-1802

VAN MOLS, BRIAN, publishing executive; b. LA, July 1, 1931; s. Pierre Matthias and Frieda Carthyll (MacArthur) M.; m. Barbara Jane Rose, Oct. 1, 1953 (dec. 1968); children— Cynthia Lee, Matthew Howard, Brian; m. Nancy Joan Martell, June 11, 1977; children— Thomas Bentley, Cynthia Bentley, Kristi AB in English, Miami U., Oxford, Ohio, 1953. Media supr. McCann-Erickson Inc., 1955-58; salesman Kelly Smith Co., 1959; with sales Million Market Newspaper Inc., 1959-63; sales mgr. Autoproducts Mag., 1964; sr. salesman True Mag., 1965-68, Look Mag., 1969-70; regional advt. dir. Petersen Pub. Co., Los Angeles, 1971-74; pub. Motor Trend, 1982-84; nat. automotive mktg. mgr. Playboy Enterprises, Inc., NYC, 1984-85, nat. sales mgr., 1985—; western advt. dir. Playboy mag., 1985-86; assoc. pub., advt. dir. Cycle World CBS, Inc., Newport Beach, Calif., 1974-81, pub., 1981; v.p., advt. dir. Four Wheeler Mag., Canoga Pk., Calif., 1986-88; v.p., dir. advt. western div. Gen. Media, Inc., 1988-91; v.p., dir. new bus. devel. Paisano Pub., Inc., Agoura Hills, Calif., 1991-92; dir. mktg. Crown Publs., 1993-94; exec. v.p. Voice Mktg. Inc., Thousand Oaks, Calif., 1994, DMR The Reis Co., Tustin, Calif., 1995-96; COO Mesa Exhaust Products, Inc., Costa Mesa, Calif., 1996-97. Mktg. dir. McMullen Argus Pub., Inc., Anaheim, Calif., 1998-2001. Served with U.S. Army, 1953-55 Mem. Los Angeles Advt. Club, Adcraft Club Detroit, Advt. Sportsmen of N.Y. Home: 57 St Andrews Cir Durango CO 81301 E-mail: bvanmols@frontier.net.

VANN, ALBERT, city councilman, former state legislator; b. Bklyn., Nov. 19, 1934; m. Mildred; four children, eight grandchildren. BBA, Toledo Univ., 1959; MS, Yeshiva Univ., Long Island Univ. Adminstr. & tchr. PS 256, JHS 35, JHS 271, Bklyn.; assemblyman Dist. 56 N.Y. State Assembly, 1975—2001; city councilman Dist. 36 NY City Coun., 2002—. Chmn. Cmty. Develop. com. NY City Coun.; instr. Urban Ctr. for Black Studies, Vassar Coll. Del. Dem. Nat. Conv., 1980; N.Y. chmn. Jesse Jackson Presdl. Campaign, 1984; chmn. Randy Evans Meml. Scholar Fund; co-founder, chmn. Coalition for Cmty. Empowerment, 1982—; bd. dirs. N.Y.C. Black Leadership Commn. on AIDS; chmn. N.Y. State Black & Puerto Rican Legis. Caucus, 1977-78, 81-82, 89-92. Served to sgt. USMC. Mem. African-Am. Tchrs. Assn. (founder, past pres.), Vanguard Ind. Dem. Assn. (founder, exec. bd.). Democrat. Baptist. Office: 613-619 Throop Ave Brooklyn NY 11216 Office Phone: 718-919-0740, 212-788-7354. Office Fax: 718-919-0744. Business E-Mail: vann@council.nyc.ny.us.*

VANN, DAVID JAMES, author, professor; s. James E. and Lorraine I. Vann; m. Nancy A. Flores, July 21, 2001. BA, Stanford U., Calif., 1990; MFA, Cornell U., Ithaca, NY, 1994. Jones lectr. Stanford U.; lectr. Cornell U.; prof. Fla. State U., Tallahassee, 2006—, U. San Francisco, 2009—. Author: Caribou Island, Legends of a Suicide, Annte Union; contbr. articles to profl. jours. (Grace Paley prize, Wallace Stegner fellowship, Calif. Book award). Personal E-mail: david@davidvann.com.

VANN, ESTHER MARTINEZ, science educator; d. Gabriel Narvaez and Cecilia Wolfe Martinez; m. Raymundo Vann, June 10, 1973; children: Raymundo Jr., Joseph Noel, Michael Steven, Daniel Christopher. BA, St. Mary's U., San Antonio, Tex., 1975; MA, U. Tex., San Antonio, 1990. Sci. dept. head Wrenn Jr. H.S.-Edgewood Ind. Sch. Dist., San Antonio, 1978—83, Jordan Mid. Sch.-Northside Ind. Sch. Dist., San Antonio, 1992—93, Somerset Jr. H.S.-Somerset Ind. Sch. Dist., Tex., 1998—2004, Terrell Wells Mid. Sch.-Harlandale Ind. Sch. Dist., San Antonio, 2004—. Adminstrv. asst. Nurses At Home - Home Health Agy., San Antonio, 1993—98. Recipient Trinity Prize for Tchg. Excellence award, Trinity U., 2002, Tchr. of the Month award, Somerset Jr. H.S.-Somerset Ind. Sch. Dist., 2003, 2004; named one of Outstanding Young Women of Am., 1987; Tex. Aerospace scholar, NASA Johnson Space Ctr., 2002.

VANN, KEVIN WILLIAM, bishop; b. Springfield, Ill., May 10, 1951; s. William M. Vann, Jr. and Theresa (Jones) Vann. BS, Millikin Univ.; Licentiate in Canon Law, Pontifical U. St. Thomas Aquinas, Rome, D in Canon Law, 1985. Ordained priest Diocese of Springfield, 1981, parochial vicar, Blessed Sacrament Parish, Springfield, 1985—90; pastor St. Benedict Ch., Auburn, Ind., 1990—92, Our Lady of Lourdes Ch., Decatur, Ill., 1992—2001, Blessed Sacrament Parish, Springfield, 2001—05; ordained bishop, 2005; coadjutor bishop Diocese of Fort Worth, 2005, bishop, 2005—. Instr. canon law Kenrick Sem., St. Louis. Roman Catholic. Office: Diocese of Fort Worth 800 West Loop 820 S Fort Worth TX 76108 Office Phone: 817-560-3300. Office Fax: 817-244-8839.

VAN NAGELL, JOHN RENSSELAER, oncologist, gynecologist; b. NYC, Sept. 16, 1939; s. John Rensselaer and Rosamond Musgrave Van Nagell; m. Elizabeth Gay, June 10, 1977; children: John R Van Nagell III, Elizabeth Knox Pfister, Lucy Tepper. MD, U. Pa., 1967. Diplomate Am. Bd. Ob/Gyn. Prof., dir. divsn. gynecol. oncology U. Ky. Med. Ctr., Lexington, 1973—, Am. Cancer Soc prof. clin. oncology. Cons. NCI - PLCO Trial, Bethesda, Md., 1992—. Author: Modern Concepts of Gynecologic Oncology. Lt. USN, 1971—77. Named one of Top Doctors for Women, Ladies Home Jour., 2001—08, Ams. Top Doctors, Castle Connolly, 2002—08. Mem.: Masters of Foxhounds Assn. (bd.dirs. 2005, v.p. 2008), Soc. Gynecol. Oncologists (pres. 1994—95). Avocations: horseback riding, fox hunting. Business E-Mail: jrvann2@email.uky.edu.

VAN NATTA, OWEN THOMAS, Internet company executive; b. 1969; m. Jennifer Van Natta. B, U. Calif., Santa Cruz. V.p., worldwide bus. and corp. develop. Amazon.com, 1998—2005; part of the founding team A9.com; COO to chief revenue officer Facebook, 2005—08; CEO Playlist.com, Palo Alto, Calif., 2008—09, MySpace.com, Calif., 2009—. Office: MySpace.com 1223 Wilshire Blvd Ste 402 Santa Monica CA 90403-5400*

VANNELA, RAVEENDER, biotechnologist, environmental scientist; s. Lalitha and Hanmandlu Vannela; m. Archana Puliroju, Aug. 14, 2002; children: Aditi, Amogha. BS, Osmania U., Hyderabad, India, 1995; MS, Kakatiya U., Warangal, Andhra Pradesh, India, 1997; MPhil, Pondicherry U., India, 1999; PhD, Birla Inst. Tech. and Sci., Pilani, India, 2003. Cert. biotech. techniques Birla Inst. Tech. Sci., 2002. Rsch. assoc. Iowa State U., Ames, 2003—04; rsch. fellow scientist U. Mich., Ann Arbor, Mich., 2004—. Contbr. articles to profl. jours., chapters to books. Pres. Nat. Student Union India, Nizamabad, Andhra Pradesh, 1995—98; active Swadyaya, Nizamabad, 1987—91. Recipient Young Scientist Travel award, Fedn. European Microbiological Soc., 2002. Mem.: Assn. Environ. Engrs. and Sci. Profs., Am. Soc. for Microbiology, Am. Chem. Soc. (Best Paper Excellence award 2005), Indian Nuc. Chem. and Allied Scientists (life). Achievements include patents for photobioreactor SCALE-Up and DNAzyme-based nanosensor for Hg2+ and As5+; development of SpiSORB for Hg (II) removal; discovery of SpiSORB materials; development of Sun Greens nutraceuticals. Office: Ariz State U Biodesign Inst 1001 S McAllister Ave Tempe AZ 85287 Home: 1118 E Euclid Ave Gilbert AZ 85297 Office Fax: 480-727-0889. Personal E-mail: rvannela@gmail.edu. Business E-Mail: rvannela@asu.edu.

VAN NESS, JAMES EDWARD, electrical engineering educator; b. Omaha, June 24, 1926; s. Hubert James and Jean (Woodruff) Van N.; m. Mary Ellen Dolvin, Dec. 28, 1948; children: Rebecca Ellen, Barbara Jean, Margaret Ann, Julie Lynn. BS, Iowa State U., 1949; MS, Northwestern U., 1951, PhD, 1954. Faculty elec. engring. dept. Northwestern U., 1952—, prof. emeritus, chmn. dept., 1969-72; dir. Computer Center, 1962-65; vis. assoc. prof. U. Calif., Berkeley, 1958-59. Vis. prof. MIT, 1973-74, Ariz. State U., winter 1984 Contbr. articles to profl. jours. Served with USNR, 1944-46. Fellow: IEEE; mem.: NAE (elected). Home: 17 Calvin Cir Evanston IL 60201 Personal E-mail: vanness@northwestern.edu.

VAN NESS, MARY BETH, literature and language professor; m. Richard C. Van Ness, July 25, 1981; children: Brandon G., Ashleigh H. EdB magna cum laude, U. Toledo, Ohio, 1974, MA summa cum laude, 1984. Adj. instr. U. Toledo Cmty. & Tech. Coll., 1974, 1984—88, U. Toledo, 1984—88, sr. lectr. English, 1989—; adj. instr. Terra CC, Fremont, Ohio, 1989—. Office: Univ Toledo Dept English 2801 W Bancroft St Mail Stop 126 Toledo OH 43606-3390

VAN NESS, ROSS HOWARD, education educator; b. Constantine, Mich., Oct. 12, 1932; s. George Phillip and Dorris Gwen (Miller) Van N.; m. Harlean Gwen Bond, July 23, 1955; children: Connie, Lynne, Paul. MusB magna cum laude, Western Mich. U., Kalamazoo, 1955; MusM, U. Mich., Ann Arbor, 1960, EdD, 1970. Cert. tchr., Mich. Tchr. Mendon Schs., Mich., 1956-58, Quincy Schs., Mich., 1958-61; dir. music Marshall Schs., Mich., 1961-68; asst. prin. Marshall H.S., 1968-69; fellow C.S. Mott Found., U. Mich., Flint, 1969-70; asst. prof. community edn. Ball State U., Muncie, Ind., 1970-72, assoc. dir. Inst. for Community Edn. Devel., 1973-81, program dir., 1981-86, dir. program devel., prof. continuing edn., 1986-92, prof. emeritus, 1992—. Bd. dirs. Rehab. Plus, Inc., Muncie, 1990-92; pres. Growth and Effective Mgmt. Assocs., Muncie, 1985—; spkr. in field; presenter over 1,200 presentations on mgmt. and edn. in 42 states and 13 countries, 1970-2006. Author: I Win You Win, 1981, Eliminating Procrastination Without Putting It Off, 1988, Raising Self-Esteem of Learners, 1995, Words To Live By: 101 Key Words That Shape Our Lives, 2009; editor mgmt. div. Home Health Executive Report, 1986-88; contbr. articles to profl. jours. Choir dir. St. Andrew Presbyn. Ch., Muncie, 1971-88, bd. dirs., 1973-75, 85-87, 2000-04; chmn. bd. dirs. United Ministries of Ball State, 1989-91; chmn. Acad. Cmty. Leadership Del. County, 1998-2007, bd. dirs. 1998-, chmn. 1998-2007, Muncie Civic Theatre, 1993-95, United Way Delaware County, 1993-95, Christian Ministries Del. County, 1995—, pres. 2005, Masterworks Chorale, 1992-99, 2002-06, pres., 1997-99, East Ctrl. Ind. Cmty. Orch., 2004—. Lt. US Army, 1956. Mem. Mich. Sch. Band and Orch. Assn. (v.p. 1968, Orch. Dir. of Yr. 1967), Very Important Vol. award Del. County 2003), Ind. Cmty. Edn. Assn. (pres. 1982-83, bd. dirs. 1978-84), Ind. Assn. Adult and Continuing Edn. (bd. dirs. 1982-88, pres. 1986-87). Avocations: music, fishing, reading, cooking.

VAN NESTE, KAREN LANE, librarian, editor; b. Washington, Oct. 18, 1951; d. Wilbur Lane and Phyllis Worthington Van Neste; m. Howard Wayne Owen, Aug. 18, 1973. BA, U. Va., Charlottesville, 1973; MS in Libr. Sci., U. NC, Chapel Hill, 1976. Libr. divsn. disorders devel. and learning U. N.C., Chapel Hill, 1976—77; libr. Fla. State U., Tallahassee, 1977—78; libr., rschr. Media Gen., Inc., Richmond, Va., 1979—88; libr. Richmond Times-Dispatch, Va., 1988—98, restaurant critic, 2003—04, libr., 2004—07; pub. Van Neste Books, Midlothian, Va., 1996—2001; viewpoints editor & columnist Free Lance-Star, Fredericksburg, Va., 2007—. Copy editor Richmond Times-Dispatch, 1999—2002; freelance editor, Richmond, 2001—07. Author: The Question Finder, 1986; editor: Littlejohn, 1992, Fat Lightning, 1994, Answers to Lucky, 1996, The Measured Man, 1997, Styll in Love, 1998, One August Day, 1998, The Edge of Things, 1999, Floating in a Most Peculiar Way, 1999, Lumen, 1999, Survivors, 2000, A Better Man, 2000, Steal My Heart, 2000 (Peace Corps Fiction award, 2001), Harry and Ruth, 2000, Divisible by One, 2001, Liar Moon, 2001, The Rail, 2002, Turn Signal, 2004, Rock of Ages, 2006. Mem. Edgehill Condominium Assn., Richmond, Va., 1981—83; contbr. James River Writers Festival, Richmond, 2002—06; editor, writer newsletter The Prestwould Condominium Assn., Richmond, 2001—07. Mem.: Am. Biographical Inst., Va. Mus. Fine Arts, Spl. Libraries Assn., Profl. Women's Adv. Bd., U. Va. Alumni Assn. (life), 2300 Club (house rules com. 2006, mem. house rules com.). D-Liberal. Avocations: travel, interior decorating, cooking. Home: 900 Cadmus Dr Fredericksburg VA 22401 Office: Free Lance-Star 616 Amelia St Fredericksburg VA 22401 Office Phone: 540-374-5412. Personal E-mail: kvnowen@verizon.net.

VAN NESTE, RAY, religious studies educator, director; b. Memphis, Mar. 10, 1970; s. Larry and Barbara Van Neste; m. Tammie Van Neste. PhD, U. Aberdeen, Scotland, 2002. Assoc. prof. Christian studies Union U., Jackson, Tenn., 2001—, dir., ryan ctr. bibl. studies, 2001—. Author: (book) Cohesion and Structure in the Pastoral Epistles. Mem.: Evang. Theol. Soc. Office: Union Univ 1050 Union Univ Dr Jackson TN 38305

VANNICE, M. ALBERT, chemical engineering professor, researcher; b. Broken Bow, Nebr., Jan. 11, 1943; s. Duane M. and Eugenia R. (Farmer) Vannice; m. Bette Ann Clark, Jan. 2, 1971. BSChemE, Mich. State Univ., 1964; MS, Stanford Univ., 1966, PhD, 1970. Engr. Dow Chem. Co., Midland, Mich., 1966, Sun Oil Co., Marcus Hook, Pa., 1970; sr. rsch. engr. Esso Rsch. & Engr. Co., Linden, NJ, 1971—76; assoc. prof. Pa. State Univ., State College, 1976—80, prof., 1980—, disting. prof., 1991—2002, M.R. Fenske prof. chem. engring., 1996—2002, W.H. Joyce chair in chem. engring., 2002—05, emeritus, 2005—. Cons. Eastman Chem. Co., Kingsport, Tenn., 1980—2000; mem. adv. bd. Absorption Sci. and Tech., 1982—95. Mem. editl. bd. Jour. of Catalysis, 1988—94, assoc. editor, 1994—2001; contbr. articles to profl. jours. Recipient award, N.Y. Catalysis Soc., 1985, P.H. Emmett award, 1987, award, Pa.-Cleve. Catalysis Soc., 1988, Humboldt Rsch. award, 1990, Fulbright award, 1996. Mem.: AIChE (profl. Progress award 1986), N.Am. Catalysis Soc. (pres. 1997—2001), Am. Chem. Soc. Achievements include patents in field; research in effects of strong metal-support interactions on catalytic behavior; studies of CO hydrogenation; studies NOx reduction; catalyst characterization. Office: Pa State Univ 107 Fenske Lab University Park PA 16802-4400 Home Phone: 814-466-6115; Office Phone: 814-863-4803. Business E-Mail: mavche@engr.psu.edu.

VAN NORMAN, WILLIS ROGER, retired computer systems researcher, consultant; b. Windom, Minn., June 17, 1938; s. Ralph Peter and Thelma Pearl (Bare) Van N.; m. Irene Anna Penner, Sept. 7, 1959; children: Eric Jon, Brian Mathew, Karin Ruth. AA, Worthington Jr. Coll., 1958; BS, Mankato State Coll., 1960; MS, St. Thomas U., 1991. Tchr. chemistry, St. Peter, Minn., 1961, Byron, Minn., 1962; tchr. spl. edn. Rochester, Minn., 1963-65; instr. Pilots Ground Sch., Rochester Jr. Coll., 1968-69; with Mayo Clin., Rochester, 1962-88; developer biomed. computer sys., 1974—; staff analyst Analyst Internat., 1988—2002. Instr. Gopher Aviation, 1968-71; founder, mgr. Van Norman's Flying V Ranch, 1972—, Van Norman Airport, St. Charles, 1977—. Woodland advisor, 1995—; founding mem. Zumbro Valley Woodland Coun., 1996; treas. United Meth. Ch. Named Olmstead County Conservation Farmer of Yr., 1992; recipient River Friendly Farmer award, 1997. Mem. NEA, Minn. Edn. Assn., Mankato State Alumni Assn. (dir.), Minn. Flying Farmers (v.p., pres.), Internat. Flying Farmers (dir.), Am. Radio Relay League (mgr. Minn. sec. traffic net), Rochester Amateur Radio Club (pres.). Home: 19230 26th St NE Saint Charles MN 55972-2016 Personal E-mail: wrvn@aol.com.

VAN NORT, SYDNEY C., school librarian, archivist; d. Sturges F. and Sara S. Cary; m. Richard M. Van Nort, Jan. 10, 1981. AB, Vassar Coll., Poughkeepsie, NY, 1979; MLS, Columbia U. Sch. Libr. Svc., NYC, 1992; MA, CCNY, NYC, 2005. Cert. archivist Acad. Cert. Archivists, NY, 2008. Reference libr. Am. Bible Soc. Libr., NYC, 1996—98, Rockland CC Libr., Suffern, NY, 1998—99; libr. Internat. Nickel Corp., NYC, 1998; archivist and spl. collections libr. CCNY Libr., 1999—; project archivist Jr. League, NYC, 2000. Hist. demonstrator Olive Day, NY, 1999—2008, Scandinavian Mus. - Viking Day, Bklyn., 2003—08, St. James Ch. Fair, Bovina, NY, 2007—08. Mem.: Mus., Libr. and Cultural Properties Facility Group, Greater NYC, Archivists Roundtable of Met. NY, Inc., Libr. Assn. CUNY (sec. 2003—05). Office: City Coll NY Libr 160 Convent Ave New York NY 10031 Office Phone: 212-650-7609. Office Fax: 212-650-7604.

VAN NOSTRAND, RICHARD CHARLES, lawyer; b. Johnstown, NY, Sept. 20, 1955; s. Charles F. and Delores M. (Trajlinek) Van N.; m. Deborah A. Genovese, Aug. 6, 1977; children: Emily Kate, Kelsey Lynn. BA in History, Binghamton U., Binghamton, 1977; JD, Duke U., 1980. Bar: Mass. 1980, U.S. Dist. Ct. Mass. 1981, U.S. Ct. Appeals (1st cir.) 1983, U.S. Ct. Claims 1983, U.S. Supreme Ct. 2003. Assoc. Bloom and Schwartz, Westborough, Mass., 1980-83, Bloom and Van Nostrand, Westborough, 1983-84; pvt. practice Westborough, 1984; assoc. Mirick, O'Connell, DeMallie and Lougee, Worcester, Mass., 1984-87, ptnr., 1988—. Legal counsel Mass. Jaycees, 1985—86; bd. dirs. Legal Assistance Corp. of Cen. Mass., treas., 1996—99; chmn. Northborough Pers. Bd., 1994—97; trustee Mass. Legal Assistance Corp., 2001—; mem. Joint Bar on Judicial Appointments, 2001—04, chair, 2001—02. Bd. dirs. United Way of Cen. Mass., 1991—99, chmn. allocations divsn., 1991—93. Named Outstanding Young Leader of Worcester, 1995. Mem.: ABA (nat. conf. bar pres. 1995—96, del. 2003—), Judicial Nominating Commn. (commrs. 2007—), New Eng. Bar Assn. (v.p. 2003—04, pres. 2004—05), Mass. CLE, Inc. (trustee 1997—2004, 2006—), Worcester County Bar Assn. (chmn. trial practice sect. 1988—90, chmn. Superior Ct. com. 1990—91, exec. com. 1991—97, pres. 1995—96, Pres. award 1990, 1995, 1997), Mass. Bar Assn. (bd. dels. 1995—96, budget and fin. com. 1997—2004, bd. dels. 2000—06, v.p. 2001—02, pres.-elect 2002—03, pres. 2003—04), Worcester County Bar Found. (life; pres. 1996—97), Worcester Jaycees (pres. 1984—85). Democrat. Lutheran. Home: 109 Madison Rd Northborough MA 01532-2280 Office: Mirick OConnell 100 Front St Worcester MA 01608-1477 Home Phone: 508-393-5563; Office Phone: 508-791-8500. Business E-Mail: rvannostrand@modl.com.

VAN NOY, TERRY WILLARD, health care executive; b. Alhambra, Calif., Aug. 31, 1947; s. Barney Willard and Cora Ellen (Simms) V.; m. Betsy Helen Pothen, Dec. 27, 1968; children: Bryan, Mark. BS in Bus. Mgmt., Calif. State Poly. U., 1970; MBA, Pepperdine U., 1991. CLU. Group sales rep. Mutual of Omaha, Atlanta, 1970-74, dist. mgr., 1974-77, regional mgr. Dallas, 1977-82, nat. sales mgr. Omaha, Neb., 1982-83, v.p. group mktg., 1983-87, div. dir. Orange, Calif., 1987-95; pres., CEO, Amil Internat., Las Vegas, 1995-98; prin. Van Noy Consulting Group, Henderson, Nev., 1998—. Vice-chmn. State Nev. Reinsurance Bd., mem. divsn. ins. health adv. com.; presenter in field. Vice-chmn. Morning Star Luth. Ch., Omaha, 1987; adv. bd. Chapman U. Sch. Bus.; exc. com. ABL Orgn.; chmn. bd. trustees Desert Rsch. Inst. Found. Mem. Am. Soc. CLU, Orange County Employee Benefit Coun., We. Pension and Benefits Conf., Las Vegas Valley Soaring Assn. (v.p.), Great Basin Soaring Inc. (pres.), Internat. Found. Employee Benefit Plans. Republican. Avocations: skiing, scuba diving, soaring. Home and Office: 2312 Prometheus Ct Henderson NV 89074-5324 Office Phone: 702-433-9677. Personal E-mail: tvannoy@earthlink.net.

VANORA, JEROME PATRICK, lawyer; b. Dec. 18, 1941; s. Jerome Anthony and Mary (Fitzpatrick) V.; m. Marianne Elizabeth Hartmann, Oct. 12, 1968; children: Judith, Kimberly. BA, Queens Coll., 1963; JD, St. John's U., 1966. Bar: N.Y. 1967. Atty. N.Y. Dept. of State Corp. Bur., Albany, 1967-70; sr. atty. divsn. human rights NYC, 1970-81; assoc. atty. divsn. housing cmty. renewal, 1981—2002. Dir. hearings unit (chief adminstrv. law judge) office of rent adminstrn., divsn. housing and cmty. renewal, NYC, 1984—99; asst. counsel Nassau County Rent Guidelines Bd., 1982—86; lectr. (twice yearly) L.I. U., Greenvale, NY, 1984—85; per diem adminstrv. law judge N.Y. State Divsn. Human Rights, 2002—07. Author: John's Song of Life, 2008; contbr. articles to profl. jours. Mem.: N.Y. State Bar Assn., Nat. Assn. Adminstrv. Law Judges, Phi Beta Kappa. Republican. Roman Catholic. Home: 1100 Delmar Ave Franklin Square NY 11010-2703

VAN ORDEN, PHYLLIS JEANNE, librarian, educator; b. Adrian, Mich., July 7, 1932; d. Warren Philip and Mabel A. Nancy (Russell) Van O. BS, Ea. Mich. U., 1954; AMLS, U. Mich., 1958; EdD, Wayne State U., 1970. Sch. librarian East Detroit (Mich.) Pub. Schs., 1954-57; librarian San Diego Pub. Library, 1958-60; media specialist Royal Oak (Mich.) Pub. Schs., 1960-64; librarian Oakland U., Rochester, Mich., 1964-66; instr. Wayne State U., Detroit, 1966-70; asst. prof. Rutgers U., New Brunswick, NJ, 1970-76; prof. library science Fla. State U., Tallahassee, 1977-91, assoc. dean for instrn., 1988-91; prof. libr. sci. program Wayne State U., Detroit, 1991-93; dir. Grad. Sch. of Libr. and Info. Sci. U. Wash., Seattle, 1993-96; cons. in field, 1996—. Author: Collection Program in Schools, 2001, Library Service to Children, 2005, Selecting Books for the Elementary School Library Media Center, 2000, Children's Books: A Practical Guide to Selection, 2007; editor: Elementary School Library Collection, 1974—77. Fla. State Libr. grantee, 1984, 86, 88; Lillian Bradshaw scholar Tex. Woman's U., 1993. Mem.: ALA (libr. resources and tech. svcs. divsn., Blackwell/N.Am. scholarship award 1983), Assn. for Libr. and Info. Sci. Edn. (pres. 1990, Svc. award 1997), Assn. Libr. Svc. to Children (past pres., Dist. Svc. award 2002), Pi Lambda Theta. Avocations: music, knitting, physical fitness, cooking, travel. Personal E-mail: vanordp@u.washington.edu.

VAN OSS, HENDRIK G., geologist; MS in Geology, Dartmouth Coll., Hanover, NH, 1978. Country specialist, divsn. internat. minerals US Bur. Mines, Washington, 1988—95; mineral commodity specialist, minerals info. team US Geol. Survey, Reston, Va., 1996—. Minerals exploration geologist various mining cos., Tucson, 1979—84, Reno, 1984—88. Contbr. articles to profl. jour. Bd. mem. Am. Friends Waterford Kamhlaba, Washington, 1994—2008. Recipient Superior Svc. award, US Dept. Interior, 2002. Mem.: Geol. Soc. Wash., Geol. Soc. Nev., Am. Geophys. Union, Geol. Soc. South Africa, Soc. Mining Engrs., Am. Assoc. Petroleum Geologists, Soc. Econ. Geologists, NRA, Am. Canoe Assn. Achievements include contributing to the IPCC work on GHG emissions that led to the IPCC being awarded Nobel Peace Prize, 2007. Avocations: canoeing, hiking, hunting. Office: US Geol Survey 989 Nat Ctr Reston VA 20192 Office Fax: 703-648-7757.

VAN OSS, STEPHEN A., electronics executive; CPA. Auditor Price Waterhouse; with acctg., investor rels., ops. Reliance Electric; CAO, CFO Paper Back Recycling of America, 1995—96; dir. info. sys. Wesco Internat., Pitts., 1997—2000, v.p., CFO, 2000—04, sr. v.p., CFO, CAO, 2004—. Trustee Robert Morris Univ. Office: Wesco Internat 225 W Station Sq Dr Pittsburgh PA 15219

VAN OTTEREN, JULIET, photographer; d. Wilbur van Otteren. Student, Santa Monica City Coll., Calif., 1968—69, UCLA, 1968, student, 1970. Photography book, Heart of the Horse, Represented in permanent collections Bibliothèque Nat., Paris, Mus. City of NY, NYC, Nat. Portrait Gallery, London, Santa Barbara Mus. Art, Calif., Nat. Arts Club, N.Y.C., Nat. Portrait Gallery, Canberra, Australia, Nat. Mus. Women in Arts, Wash., Bklyn. Mus. Art, High Mus. Art, Atlanta, Internat. Ctr. Photography, N.Y.C., Musée d'Art Moderne et d'Art Contemporain, Nice, France, Internat. Mus. Horse, Lexington, Ky., Internat. Mus. the Horse, harry ransom Ctr. Mus., Austin. Mailing: PO Box 29282 Austin TX 78755 Personal E-mail: juliet@jvop.com. Business E-Mail: mail@jvop.com.

VAN PAASSCHEN, FRITS, hotel executive; married; 3 children. BA, Amherst Coll.; MBA, Harvard U. Mgmt. cons. Boston Consulting Group, McKinsey & Co.; v.p. fin. and planning Disney Consumer Products; head bus. Europe, the Middle East and Africa Nike, Inc.; pres., CEO Coors Brewing Co., 2005—07, Starwood Hotels & Resorts Worldwide, Inc., 2007—. Bd. dirs. Jones Apparel Group Inc., Oakley Inc. Office: Starwood Hotels & Resorts Worldwide, Inc 1111 Westchester Ave White Plains NY 10604 Office Phone: 914-640-8100. Office Fax: 914-640-8310.

VAN PATTEN, JAMES JEFFERS, education educator; b. North Rose, NY, Sept. 8, 1925; s. Earl F. and Dorothy (Jeffers) Van P.; married. BA, Syracuse U., 1949; ME, Tex. Western Coll., 1959; PhD, U. Tex., Austin, 1962. Asst. prof. philosophy and edn. Central Mo. State U., Warrensburg, 1962-64, assoc. prof., 1964-69; assoc. prof. fis. overseas U. Okla., Norman, 1969-71; prof. edn. U. Ark., Fayetteville, 1971-99, prof. emeritus, 1999—. Visiting scholar, U. Mich., 1981, UCLA, 1987, U. Tex., Austin, 1987; vis. prof./scholar U. Fla., Gainesville, 1994; adj. Fla. Atlantic U., 2000-07. Editor: Conflict, Permanency and Change in Education, 1976, Philosophy, Social Science and Education, 1989, College Teaching and Higher Education Leadership, 1990, Social-Cultural Foundations of Educational Policy in the U.S., 1991, Watersheds in Higher Education, 1997, Challenges and Opportunities For a New Millennium, 1998, Challenges and Opportunities for Education in the 21st Century, 1999, Higher Education Culture, Case Studies For A New Century, 2000, A New Century In Retrospect and Prospect, 2000; Author: Academic Profiles in Higher Education, 1992, The Many Faces of the Culture of Higher Education, 1993, The Culture of Higher Education: A Case Study Approach, 1996, What's Really Happening in Education: A Case Study Approach, 1997; Co-author: (with G. Chen and George C. Stone) Individual and Collective Contributions to Humaneness In Our Time, 1997, (with John Pulliam) History of Education in America, 9th edit., 2007, (with Timothy J. Bergen) A Case Study Approach to a Multi-Cultural Mosaic for Education, 2003; contbr. articles to profl. jours. including Futures Rsch. Quar.; founder Jour. of Thought, Educational Systems for the 21st Century, Futures Rsch. Quarterly, summer 2000. Served with inf. U.S. Army, 1944-45. Decorated Purple Heart, Bronze Star. Mem. Am. Ednl. Studies Assn., Southern Future Soc., World Future Soc., Am. Philosophy Assn., Southwestern Philosophy of Edn. Soc. (pres. 1970), Am. Ednl. Rsch. Assn., Edn. Law Assn., Nat. Assn. Legal Assts., Kiwanis, Phi Delta Kappa (pres. chpt. U. Ark. 1976-77). E-mail: jvanpatt@aol.com.

VAN PILSUM, JOHN FRANKLIN, biochemist, educator; b. Prairie City, Iowa, Jan. 28, 1922; s. John Peter and Vera Elisabeth (Moore) Van Pilsum; m. Shirley Elaine Newsom, Oct. 14, 1958; children: John Robert, Patricia Mona, Barbara Joyce, Mary Ann, Elizabeth Joan, William Franklin. BS, U. Iowa, 1943, PhD, 1949. Instr. L.I. Coll. Medicine, Bklyn., 1949-51; asst. prof. coll. medicine U. Utah, Salt Lake City, 1951-54; asst. prof. biochemistry U. Minn., Mpls., 1954-63, assoc. prof. biochemistry, 1963-71, prof. biochemistry, 1971—92, prof. biochemistry emeritus, 1992—. Contbr. articles to profl. jours. Lt. USN, 1944-46. Recipient numerous grants NIH. Mem. Am. Soc. Biochemistry and Molecular Biology, Am. Inst. Nutrition, Histochem. Soc. Achievements include work with Guanidinium compound metabolism. Home: 4356 Leander Ln Columbia Heights MN 55421-3067 Office: U Minn Dept Biochem Molecular Biolog & Biophysics 1395 Gortner Ave Saint Paul MN 55108 Office Phone: 612-624-1542.

VAN PRAAG, HERMAN MEIR, psychiatrist, educator, researcher; b. Schiedam, The Netherlands, Oct. 17, 1929; s. Marinus Maurits and Charlotte Frederique (Leverpoll) V.P.; m. Cornelia Eikens; children: Marinus, Gido, Charlotte, Bart. MD, Leiden U., The Netherlands, 1956; PhD in Neurobiology, U. Utrecht, The Netherlands, 1962. Chief of staff dept. psychiatry Dijkzigt Hosp., Rotterdam, The Netherlands, 1963-66; founder, prof., head dept. biol. psychiatry Psychiat. Univ. Clinic State U., Groningen, Netherlands, 1966-77; prof., head dept. psychiatry Acad. Hosp. State U., Utrecht, 1977-82, prof. head dept. psychiatry; prof., head dept. psychiatry Albert Einstein Coll. Medicine, Bronx, NY, 1982—92; prof., head dept. psychiatry and neuropsychology Acad. Hosp. U. Maastricht, Netherlands, 1992—99, sci. advisor dept. psychiarty and neuropsychology, 1999—. Emeritus prof. Albert Einstein Coll. Medicine, 1992—; psychiatrist-in-chief Montefiore Med. Ctr., Bronx, 1982—92; Lady Davis vis. prof. Hebrew U. Hadassah U. Hosp., Jerusalem, 1976—77; head WHO Nat. Ref. Ctr. for Study of Psychotropic Drugs, 1969, WHO Collaborating Ctr. for Rsch. and Tng. in Biol. Psychiatry, 1974; founder Interdisciplinary Soc. Biol. Psychiatry, 1966, Found. for Psychiatry and Religion, 1998; guest lectr. numerous univs. around the world. Editor: Psychiatria Neurologia Neurochirurgia, 1968-70, Advances in Biological Psychiatry, 1978—; editor-in-chief Psychiatria Neurologia Neurochirurgia, 1971-74, Biology of Behavior, 1975-82, Handbook of Biological Psychiatry, 1975-81, Einstein Monograph Series in Experimental and Clinical Psychiatry, 1988—; European chief-editor Progress in Neuro-Psychopharmacology, 1993—; mem. editl. bd. numerous publs. in field; reviewer Am. Jour. Psychiatry, Archives of Gen. Psychiatry, Jour. Nervous and Mental Disease; mem. internat. scientific commn. Jour. Brazilian Psychiat. Assn. Decorated knight Order of the Dutch Lion, Queen Beatrix of The Netherlands; recipient numerous awards and honors. Fellow Am. Coll. Neuropsychopharmacology, Am. Psychiat. Assn.; mem. Royal Acad. Scis. of The Netherlands, Soc. Biol. Psychiatry, Collegium Internationale Neuro-Psychopharmacologicum, Assn. for Advancement of Psychotherapy, Internat. Group for Study of Affective Disorders, Internat. Soc. Psychoneuroendocrinology, European Brain and Behavior Soc., Internat. Assn. for Suicide Prevention, Brit. Pharmacol. Soc., European Soc. for Clin. Investigation, Bataafsch Genootschap der Proefondervindelijke Wijsbegeerte, Am. Coll. Neuropharmacology, Deutsche Gesellschaft fur Psychiatrie und Nervenheilkunde, Israel Med. Assn., Psychiat. Rsch. Soc., NY Acad. Medicine, Am. Psychopathol. Assn., Internat. Coll. Neurobiology, Biol. Psychiatry and Psychopharmacology, Serotonin Club, Internat. Soc. for Rsch. on Emotion, Internat. Soc. Psychoneuroendocrinology, Arbeitsgemeinschaft fur Neuropsychpharmakologie und Pharmakopsychiatrie, World Psychiat. Assn. (chmn. religion, spirituality and psychiatry sect.). Office: Acad Hosp Maastricht PO Box 5800 6202 AZ Maastricht Netherlands Office Phone: 31-55-5760795. Personal E-mail: h.m.van.praag@vanpraag.com.

VAN PRAAGH, JAMES, spiritual medium; b. Bayside, NY, Aug. 23, 1958; married. Degree in Broadcasting and Comm., San Francisco State U. Author: Talking to Heaven: A Medium's Message of Life After Death, 1999, Reaching to Heaven: A Spiritual Journey Through Life & Death, 1999, Looking Beyond: A Teen's Guide to the Spiritual World, 2003, Meditation with James Van Praagh, 2004, Heaven & Earth: Making the Psychic Connection, 2006, Healing Grief: Reclaiming Life After Any Loss, Ghosts Among Us, 2008; host (daytime talk show TV series) Beyond with Van Praagh, 2002; prodr.: (TV series) Living With The Dead, The Dead Will Tell, Ghost Whisperer.*

VAN REES, CORNELIUS S., lawyer; b. NYC, May 29, 1929; s. Cornelius Richard and Beatrice Martin (Shreve) Van R.; m. Virginia Vandewater, Mar. 15, 1953 (div. 1984); children: Pamela Millet Van Rees Lundquist, Claire Katherine; m. Alix McIvor, Jan. 2, 1985. BA, Denison U., 1951; JD, Columbia U., 1954. Bar: N.Y. 1956, U.S. Dist. Ct. (so. dist.) N.Y. 1956. Con. 1994. Assoc. Thacher Proffitt & Wood, NYC, 1956-62, ptnr., 1963-93, of counsel, 1994—; corp. sec. Graham Corp. Writer in field. Trustee, sec. Williston Northhampton Sch.; mem. senate, honors and prizes com. Columbia U. Harlem Fisk Stone scholar Columbia U., 1954. Mem. ABA, Alumni Fedn. Columbia U., Inc. (Alumni medal 1984, pres. 1979-81). Avocations: sailing, skiing. Office: Graham Corp 20 Florence Ave Batavia NY 14020 Office Phone: 585-343-2216. Office Fax: 585-343-1097.*

VAN REGENMORTEL, MARC HUBERT VICTOR, virologist, educator, director; b. Brussels, Dec. 6, 1934; s. Joseph and Catherine (Stinkens) van R.; m. Johanna Alida Boltman, Aug. 1958 (div. 1972); children: Sonia, Loubie; m. Petra Jeanne Schonborn, June 24, 1972. BSc, Stellenbosch, South Africa, 1957, MSc, 1959; PhD, Cape Town U., S. Africa, 1961; DHC (hon.), Liege U., Belgium, 2003. Lectr. U. Stellenbosch, 1960-61, sr. lectr., 1961-65; rsch. fellow U. Calif., Berkeley, 1965-66; prof. U. Stellenbosch, 1967-70; vis. prof. U. Strasbourg, France, 1970-72; prof. U. Capetown, 1972-77; rsch. dir. Inst. of Molecular and Cellular Biology, Strasbourg, 1978—. Bd. dirs. Biacore Corp., Sweden, 1995-05. Author: Serology and Immunochemistry of Plant Viruses, 1982, Synthetic Peptides as Antigens, 1999; editor: Synthetic Polypeptides as Antigens, 1988, Structures of Antigens, Vol. I, 1992, Vol. II, 1993, Vol. III, 1996, Immunochemistry of Viruses, Vol. I, 1985, Vol. II, 1990, Immunochemistry, 1994, 7th ICTV Report, 2000, Promises and Limits of Reductionism in the Biomedical Sciences, 2002; editor Advances in Virus Rsch., 1985—, Archives of Virology, 1987—, Rsch. in Virology, 1987-97, Jour. Molecular Recognition, 1988—, Methods, 1992-, J. Immunological Methods, 1994—, Biologicals, 1993-, Analytical Biochemistry, 1995—, Exptl. Rev. Proteomics, 2004-. Mem.: Internat. Union Microbiol. Scis. (vice chmn. virology divsn. 1984—87, chmn. 1987—90, sec.-gen. 1990—99, pres. internat. com. on taxonomy viruses 1996—2002). Office: Ctr Nat Rsch Sci School of Biotechnology -U of Strasbourg Blv Sebastian Brandt 67400 Strasbourg France E-mail: vanregen@esbs.u-strasbg.fr.

VAN RIPER, PAUL PRITCHARD, retired political science professor; b. Laporte, Ind., July 29, 1916; s. Paul and Margaret (Pritchard) Van R.; m. Dorothy Ann Dodd Samuelson, May 11, 1964; 1 child, Michael Scott Samuelson. AB, DePauw U., 1938; PhD, U. Chgo., 1947. Instr. Northwestern U., 1947-49, asst. prof. polit. sci., 1949-51; mgmt. analyst Office Comptroller Dept. Army, 1951-52; mem. faculty Cornell U., 1952-70, prof., 1957-70; chmn. gov. bd., exec. com. Cornell Social Sci. Research Center, 1956-58; prof., head dept. polit. sci. Tex. A&M U., 1970-77, prof., 1977-81, prof. emeritus, 1981—, coordinator M.P.A. program, 1979-81, named prof. Bush Sch. Govt. and Pub. Svc., 1997—2008; ret., 2008. Vis. prof. U. Chgo., 1958, Ind. U., 1961, U. Strathclyde, Scotland, 1964, U. Mich., 1965, U. Okla., 1969-97, U. Utah, 1979. Author: History of the United States Civil Service, 1958, Some Educational and Social Aspects of Fraternity Life, 1961, (with others) The American Federal Executive, 1963, Handbook of Practical Politics, 3d edit., 1967; editor and co-author: the Wilson Influence on Public Administration, 1990. Exec. com. Civil Svc. Reform Assn., NY, 1960-64, hist. adv. com. NASA, 1964-66; bd. dir. Brazos Valley Cmty. Action Agy., 1975-79, Brazos County Hist. Commn., 1976-2006; charter mem. Brazos Heritage Soc., pres. 1977-79. Maj. AUS, 1942-46; lt. col. USAR ret. Decorated Croix de Guerre (France). Mem. Am. Polit. Sci. Assn., Am. Soc. Pub. Adminstrn. (nat adv. com. 1957-60, Dimock award 1984, Waldo award 1990, Van Riper award created in his honor 2002), Rotary (pres. Bryan club 1991-92, Rotary Dist., Roll of Fame award 2008), Phi Beta Kappa, Beta Theta Pi (v.p. 1962, gen. sec. 1963-65), Pi Alpha Alpha, Pi Sigma Alpha, Phi Kappa Phi, Sigma Delta Chi. Republican. Baptist. Home: 713 E 30th St Bryan TX 77803-4789 Home Phone: 979-822-2082.

VANRYCKEGHEM, MARTINE, speech language professional, educator; b. Gent, East Flanders, Belgium, Aug. 14, 1955; arrived in U.S., 1989; d. Roger Vanryckeghem and Juliette Vleeshouwers; m. Gene J. Brutten, Oct. 8, 1993. Grad. in Logopedics, Higher Inst. of Paramed. Professions, Gent, 1977; MS, So. Ill. U., Carbondale, 1991, PhD, 1994. Speech-lang. pathologist Clin. Ctr., Gent, 1977—89; prof. U. Cen. Fla., Orlando, 1994—, U. Utrecht, 2006—, U. Gent. Cons. U. Zagreb, Croatia, 1998—, Artevelde Hogeschool, Gent, 1994—, U. Gent, 1994—; fellow Am. Speech Language & Hearing Assoc. Author: Behavior Assessment Battery: A Multi-dimensional and Evidence-based Approach to Diagnostic and Therapeutic Decision Making for Children and Adults who Stutter, 2003, Behavior Assessment Battery for School-Age Children who Stutter, 2007, Kiddy Cat: Communication Attitude Test for Preschool and Kindergarten Children Who Stutter, 2007; managing editor: Jour. Fluency Disorders, 1990—2000; contbr. articles to profl. jours. Recipient award. Mem.: Orgn. for Integration of Handicapped People (sci. bd. mem. 1995—), Internat. Fluency Assn., Am. Speech-Lang.-Hearing Assn. (clin. competence in speech-lang. pathology, fluency specialist, fluency mentor). Achievements include research in Behavior Assessment Battery for Adults; Behavior Assessment Battery for Children; The KiddyCAT: A test investigating speech-associated attitude in preschoolers. Avocations: travel, cooking, hiking. Office: U Ctrl Fla HPA-2 Ste 101 4000 Central Blvd Orlando FL 32816-2215 Business E-Mail: martinev@mail.ucf.edu.

VAN SANT, GUS (GUS GREENE VAN SANT JR.), film director; b. Louisville, July 24, 1952; s. Gus Greene and Betty (Seay) Van Sant. BA in Filmmaking, RISD, 1975. Dir., screenwriter William Morris Agy., Inc., Beverly Hills, Calif. Dir., prodr., writer: (films) Even Cowgirls Get the Blues, 1993; dir., writer: (films) Mala Noche, 1985 (L.A. Film Critics award 1987), Drugstore Cowboy, 1989 (with Daniel Yost: Nat. Soc. Film Critics Best Dir. award 1990, Best Screenplay award 1990, N.Y. Film Critics Best Screenplay award 1990, L.A. Film Critics Best Screenplay award 1989), Internat. PEN Literary award for Screenplay Adaptation (with Daniel Yost 1989), My Own Private Idaho, 1991 (Best Screenplay 1992, Best Film 1992), Gerry, 2002, Elephant, 2003, Last Days, 2005, Paranoid Park, 2007; dir.: (films), To Die For, 1995, Good Will Hunting, 1997, Psycho, 1998, Finding Forrester, 2000, Milk, 2008 (Best Dir. Boston Soc. Film Critics, 2008; (TV films) Understanding, 1996; prodr. (films) Kids, 1995, Speedway Junky, 1999, Tarnation, 2003, Wild Tigers I Have Known, 2006; appeared in: (films) Jay and Silent Bob Strike Back, 2001; (TV series) Entourage, 2008; author: Pink, 1997; singer: (albums) Gus Van Sant, 1997, 18 Songs About Golf, 1997 Recipient Oreg. Freedom of Expression award, ACLU, 1992, Sonny Bono Visionary award, Palm Springs Internat. Film Soc., 2009. Office: William Morris Agency Inc 151 S El Camino Dr Beverly Hills CA 90212-2775*

VAN SCHENKHOF, CAROL DOUGHERTY (CAROL DOVAN), soprano, educator; b. Reading, Pa., Apr. 20, 1942; d. Harry Hammond Dougherty and Magdalen Mary Doviak; m. Mark Anton van Schenkhof, Feb. 18, 1995; m. John William Heierman, Sept. 4, 1965 (div. July 6, 1986). BA, Chatham Coll., 1964; student, Julliard Sch., NYC, 1964—65, student, 1970; MA Ethno-musicology, Hunter Coll., 1970, student, 1971, Mannes Coll., 1980, Westminster Choir Coll., Princeton, NJ, 1992, student, 1996, Oberlin Conservatory, 2000, student, 2002, Westminster Choir Coll. Conservatory, 2004. Tchr. voice Sch. Music Lab. Chatham Coll., Pitts., 1964; resource profl. Lincoln Ctr., NYC, 1972; vis. artist, lectr. Ewha U., Seoul, 1975, Emissora Nacional de Radioifusao, Lisbon, Portugal, 1976, Conservatorio Nacional, Lisbon, 1976; lectr. opera C.W. Post Coll., LI U., Greenvale, NY, 1982—83; profl. coord. Port Washington Libr.-Music Adv. Coun., NY, 1985—87; tchr. voice Stony Brook U., NY, 1988—99, Carol Dovan-van Schenkhof Studios, Port Washington, 1980—. Singer: Rhodesia TV Ltd., 1974, Rhodesia Orgn., 1974, South African Broadcasting, 1974, Emissora Nacional de Radiodifušao, 1976, (soloist) Met. Opera Studio, 1971—72, Alice Tully Hall, 1983, recitals with composer Jeanne Singer, 1983—87, Nat. Grand Opera, 1983, (Operas) Best of Opera, Carnegie Hall, 1982, La Boheme, 1981, Ninth Symphony of Beethoven- Reading Sympony Orch., 1983, others. Recipient 1st Pl. award, Competition Pitts. Musicians Club, 1962, Pitts. Concert Soc. Youth Auditions, 1962, Pitts. Concert Soc. Major Auditions, 1963; scholar, Chautauqua Inst. Music, NY, 1962—63, Aspen Music Festival, 1964. Mem.: N.Y. Singing Tchrs., Am. Guild Musical Artists, Nat. Assn. for Music Edn., Nat. Assn. Tchrs. Singing (adjudicator, Ea. Region auditions), Associated Music Tchrs. League (exec. bd. 1994—). Episcopalian. Avocations: gardening, sailing. Home and Studio: 6 Hillview Ave Port Washington NY 11050 Office Phone: 516-944-5140. Personal E-mail: caroldov@optonline.net.

VAN SCHOONENBERG, ROBERT G., lawyer, consumer products company executive; b. Madison, Wis., Aug. 18, 1946; s. John W. and Ione (Henning) Schoonenberg. BA, Marquette U., 1968; MBA, U. Wis., 1972; JD, U. Mich., 1974. Bar: Calif. 1975, Fla. 1976. Atty. Gulf Oil Corp., Pitts., 1974-81; v.p., gen. counsel to sr. v.p., gen. counsel, sec. Avery Dennison Corp., Pasadena, Calif., 1981—2004, exec. v.p., chief legal officer, sec., 2007—, exec. v.p., gen. counsel, sec., 2004—07; chmn., CEO BayPoint Capital Ptnrs. LLC, Newport Beach, Calif. Judge pro tem Pasadena Mcpl. Ct., 1987-89. bd. dirs. Premiere Entertainment LLC, bd. dirs. Altair Nanotechnologies Inc., bd. dirs. Guidance Software Inc., bd. dirs. The Ryland Group Inc., 2009- Dir., v.p. fin. adminstrn. Am. Cancer Soc., San Gabriel Vally Unit, 1987—; v.p., treas., dir., v.p. investments Pasadena Symphony Assn.; bd. dirs. Pasadena Recreation and Parks Found., 1983-84; mem. Pasadena Citizens Task Force on Crime Control, 1983-84; dir. Boy Scouts, San Gabriel Valley Coun., dir. pub. coun.; bd. dirs. Verugo Hills Hosp. Found.; trustee Southwestern U. Sch. Law. Mem.: Am. Soc. Corp. Secs. (pres., so. Calif. chpt.), Am. Corp. Counsel Assn. (dir.), L.A. County Bar Assn. (past chmn., corp. law dept. sect.). Office: The Ryland Group Inc Ste 400 24025 Park Sorrento Calabasas CA 91302 Office Phone: 818-223-7500. Office Fax: 818-223-7667. E-mail: rgvs@averydennison.com.*

VAN SCOTER, JOHN C., electronics executive; BS in Engring., U. Vt., 1983. Tech. sales engr. Tex. Instruments, Inc., Boston, 1983, dep. fab mgr. Miho5 wafer fabrication facility Japan, mgr. worldwide ASIC product devel. & engring., v.p., sr. v.p., gen. mgr. DLP Products, 2000—. Mem.: IEEE, Soc. Motion Pictures and TV Engrs., Consumer Electronics Assn. Office: Tex Instruments Inc PO Box 660199 Dallas TX 75266-0199 Office Phone: 972-995-2011. Office Fax: 972-995-4360.

VANSCOY, HOLLY CAROLE, social and educational researcher; b. Houston, Sept. 17, 1944; d. York Parrish and Erlene Ann (Whitehead) Pope; m. Pat Van Dyke, Aug. 15, 1990; children: Thomas, David, Ted, Kayte, Alex, Ginny. BA, Baylor U., 1965; MSW, U. Louisville, 1969; PhD, U. Tex., 1986. Pres. Acad. Rsch. Assocs., Austin, Tex., 1984-87; asst. prof. Am. Technol. U., Killeen, Tex., 1986-87; assoc. prof. Grand Valley State U., Grand Rapids, Mich., 1987-89; dir. rsch. Kent Cmty. Mental Health, Grand Rapids, 1989-92; prss. Acad. Rsch. Assocs., Grand Rapids, 1992—. Chmn. bd. dirs. environ. action City of Grand Rapids, 1994-97. Bd. dirs. West Mich. Environ. Action, Grand Rapids, 1996-97; adv. bd. Women's Resource Ctr., Grand Rapids, 1995-97, N.Am. Indian Ctr., Grand Rapids, 1994—; chair Bear Creek Watershed Com., 1992-94; mem. cmty. learning exch. Jackson (Mich.) C.C., 1995-96; commr. City Grand Rapids Hist. Preservation Bd. Mem. Lesbian & Gay Cmty. Network (pres. 1990-93). Democrat. Baptist. Office: Acad Rsch Assocs Inc 910 Cherry St SE Grand Rapids MI 49506-1472 Office Phone: 512-689-5677. Personal E-mail: academres@aol.com.

VAN SCOYOC, STU (H. STEWART VAN SCOYOC), lobbyist, lawyer; b. 1947; BS in Chem. Engring., Lehigh U., 1969; JD, U. Md. Bar: Del., DC, US Supreme Ct. 1974. Engr. DuPont Co.; founding ptnr. Winburn, Van Scoyoc & Hooper; v.p. Charles Walker Assocs.; founder, pres., CEO Van Scoyoc Assocs. Inc. (VSA), 1990—; founder The Implementation Group, 1994, Capitol Decisions, Inc., 2000, Van Scoyoc Kelly PLLC, 2002. Named one of 50 Top Lobbyists, Washingtonian mag., 2007. Office: Van Scoyoc Assocs 101 Constitution Ave, NW, Ste 600 W Washington DC 20001 Office Phone: 202-638-1950. Office Fax: 202-638-7714.

VANSELOW, NEAL ARTHUR, retired academic administrator, internist; b. Milw., Mar. 18, 1932; s. Arthur Frederick and Mildred (Hoffmann) Vanselow; m. Mary Ellen McKenzie, June 20, 1958; children: Julie Ann, Richard Arthur. AB, U. Mich., 1954, MD, 1958, MS, 1963. Diplomate Am. Bd. Internal Medicine, Am. Bd. Allergy and Immunology. Intern Mpls. Gen. Hosp., 1958—59; resident Univ. Hosp., Ann Arbor, Mich., 1959—63; instr. medicine U. Mich., 1963—64, asst. prof., 1964—68, assoc. prof., 1968—72, prof., chmn. dept. postgrad. medicine and health professions edn., 1972—74; dean Coll. Medicine U. Ariz., Tucson, 1974—77; chancellor med. ctr. U. Nebr., Omaha, 1977—82, v.p., 1977—82; v.p. health scis. U. Minn., 1982—89, prof. internal medicine, 1982—89; chancellor Tulane U. Med. Ctr., New Orleans, 1989—94, chancellor emeritus, 1997—; prof. internal medicine Tulane U., New Orleans, 1989—97, prof. internal medicine emeritus, 1997—. Adj. prof. health sys. mgmt. Tulane U., New Orleans, 1993—99, prof. emeritus, 1999—; chmn. Joint Bd. Osteo. and Med. Examiners Ariz., 1974—77; chmn. coun. on Grad. Med. Edn. Dept. Health and Human Svcs., 1986—91; mem. com. on educating dentists for future Inst. Medicine NAS, 1993—95, chairperson com. on future of primary care, 1994—96, co-chairperson com. on U.S. physician supply, 1995—96, scholar in residence, 1994—95, mem. com. to assess occupl. health and safety tng. needs, 1999—2000, chmn. com. on introducing social and behavioral sci. into med. sch. curriculum, 2002—04; chairperson continuing eval. panel Am. Internat. Health Alliance, 2000—01; mem. adv. com. Medschool.com, 2000—01; adj. prof. Sch. Health Adminstrn. and Policy Ariz. State U., 2000—05; mem. spl. emphasis panel NIH, 2005; mem. Health Sci. Adv. Com. U. Ariz., 2009—. Panel on interdisciplinary health profl. edn. Nat. League Nursing, 1996—97; exec. com. United Way Midlands, 1980—82, vice-chmn. 1981 campaign; mem. Commn. on Health Professions Pew Charitable Trusts, 1990—92, 1997—99, Commn. on the Future of Med. Edn. U. Calif, 1996—97; mktg. mgmt. governing coun. U. Hosp. Consortium, 1993—95; trustee Meharry Med. Coll., 1996—, chair presdl. search com., 2006; pres., chmn. bd. Am. Friends London Sch. Hygiene and Tropical Medicine, 1998—2002; com. on relationships between medicine and nursing Josiah Macy Jr. Found., 1999—2000; mem. Gov.'s Pan Am. Commn., La., 1991—92; bd. dirs. Devel. Authority for Tucson's Economy, 1975—77, Minn. High Tech. Coun., 1983—86, Minn. Coalition for Health Care Costs, 1983—87, La. Health Care Authority, 1989—90, United Way Greater New Orleans Area, 1992—97; bd. dirs., exec. com. Health Planning Coun. Midlands, Omaha, 1978—82, v.p., 1981—82. Recipient Disting. Alumnus award, U. Mich. Med. Ctr. Alumni Soc., 2007. Fellow: ACP (workgroup on physician workforce and financing med. edn. 1996), Ariz. Acad. Arts, Sci. and Tech. (bd. govs. 2005—, 2005—, founding mem.), Am. Coll. Physician Execs., Am. Acad. Allergy; mem.: Inst. Med. NAS, Soc. Med. Adminstrs., Assn. Acad. Health Ctrs. (bd. dirs. 1983—89, chmn. bd. dirs. 1988), Rio Verde (Ariz.) Cmty. Assn. (bd. dirs. 2000—04), Phi Beta Kappa, Nu Sigma Nu, Beta Theta Pi, Alpha Omega Alpha, Sigma Xi. Home: 18942 E Mountainaire Dr Rio Verde AZ 85263-7093

VAN SETERS, JOHN, retired biblical literature educator; b. Hamilton, Ont., Can., May 2, 1935; s. Hugo and Anne (Hubert) Van S.; m. Elizabeth Marie Malmberg, June 11, 1960; children: Peter John, Deborah Elizabeth. BA, U. Toronto, 1958; MA, Yale U., 1959, PhD, 1965; BD, Princeton Theol. Sem., 1962; ThD (hon.), U. Lausanne, Switzerland, 1999. Asst. prof. dept. Near Eastern studies Waterloo Luth. U., 1965-67; assoc. prof. Old Testament Andover Newton Theol. Sch., 1967-70; assoc. prof. dept. Near Eastern studies U. Toronto, 1970-76, prof., 1976-77; James A. Gray prof. Bibl. lit., dept. religion U. N.C., Chapel Hill, 1977-2000, chmn. dept. religious studies, 1980-88, 93-95, prof. emeritus, 2000—. Adj. prof. dept. religion and culture Wilfrid Laurier U., 2000—. Author: The Hyksos: A New Investigation, 1966, Abraham in History and Tradition, 1975, In Search of History, 1983, Der Jahwist als Historiker, 1987, Prologue to History, 1992, The Life of Moses, 1994, The Pentateuch, 1999, A Law Book for the Diaspora, 2003, The Edited Bible, 2006, The Biblical Saga of King David, 2009. Recipient James Henry Breasted prize Am. Hist. Assn., 1985, Book award Am. Acad. Religion, 1986, R.B.Y. Scott Book award Can. Soc. Bibl. Studies, 2004; Woodrow Wilson fellow, 1958; J.J. Obermann fellow, 1962-64; Guggenheim fellow, 1979-80; NEH fellow, 1985-86, Am. Coun. Learned Socs. fellow, 1991-92, sr. rsch. fellow Cath. U. Leuven, Belgium, 1998, Fgn. Rsch. fellow Nat. Rsch. Fund S.Africa, 2002. Mem. Soc. Bibl. Lit., Cath. Bibl. Assn., Can. Soc. Bibl. Studies (pres. 1999-2000), Old Testament Soc. South Africa (hon.). Home: 70-139 Father David Bauer Dr Waterloo ON Canada N2L 6L1 E-mail: john.vanseters@sympatico.ca.

VÄNSKÄ, OSMO, conductor, music director; b. Finland, Feb. 28, 1953; m. Pirkko Vänskä; 3 children. Studied conducting with Jorma Panula, Sibelius Acad., Finland; D (hon.), U. Glasgow, Scotland. Orchestral clarinetist Turku Philharm., 1971—76; prin. clarinet Helsinki Philharm., 1977—82; prin. guest condr. Lahti Symphony Orch., 1985—88, chief condr., 1988—2008, condr. laureate, 2009—; chief condr. Iceland Symphony Orch., 1993—96, BBC Scottish Symphony Orch., Glasgow, 1996—2002; music dir. Minn. Orch., 2003—. Guest condr. Boston Symphony Orch., 2002. Condr. numerous recordings with the Lahti Symphony Orch. (Gramophone award, 1996, Cannes Classical award, 2002), (recording) The Tempest (1993 Prix Academie Charles Cros.). Recipient First prize, Besancon Internat. Young Conductor's Competition, 1982, Royal Philharm. Soc. award, 2002; named Conductor of Yr., Musical Am. Internat. Dir. Performing Arts, 2005; nominee Grammy award for Best Orchestral Performance for a recording with the BBC Scottish Symphony. Avocations: sports, motorcycling. Office: Minn Orch Orchestra Hall 1111 Nicollet mall Minneapolis MN 55403*

VAN SLAMBROUCK, JOHN G., lawyer; b. Toledo, Sept. 27, 1955; BA summa cum laude in Polit. Sci., Western Mich. U., 1977; JD cum laude, Thomas M. Cooley Law Sch., 1981. Bar: Mich. 1981, US Dist. Ct. (we. dist. Mich.) 1981, US Dist. Ct. (ea. dist. Mich.) 1983. Legis. aide Mich. Ho. Reps., 1978—79; law clk. State of Mich., 1979—81, asst. atty. gen., 1981—85; pvt. practice atty. The Navigators, Inc., 1985—93; shareholder Ford, Krikard, Domeny & Byrne, P.C., 1994; sr. atty. Miller, Canfield, Paddock & Stone, PLC, Kalamazoo, 1994—97, prin., 1998—, dep. leader personal svcs. grp., 2004—. Bd. dirs. Western Mich. U., 2002—. Named one of Top 100 Attys., Worth mag., 2005. Mem.: West Mich. Estate Planning Coun., Western Mich. Planned Giving Grp., Nat. Acad. Elder Law Attys., State Bar Mich. (mem. probate and estate planning sect. 1991—), ABA (real property, probate and trust law sect.), Kalamazoo County Bar Assn. (chmn. probate practice com., chmn. profl. responsibility com.). Office: Miller Canfield 277 S Rose St Ste 5000 Kalamazoo MI 49007-4730 Office Phone: 269-383-5829. Office Fax: 269-382-0244. E-mail: vanslambrouck@millercanfield.com.

VAN SLYKE, ANDREW JAMES, professional baseball coach, retired professional baseball player; b. Utica, NY, Dec. 21, 1960; m. Lauri Van Slyke; children: A.J., Scott, Jared. Outfielder St. Louis Cardinals, 1983—86, Pitts. Pirates, 1987—94, Balt. Orioles, 1995, Phila. Phillies, 1995; game analyst ESPN; guest host, Best Damn Sports Show Period FOX Sports Net; broadcast analyst St. Louis Cardinals; co-host, weekly radio show Sta. KFNS, St. Louis; first base coach Detroit Tigers, 2005—. Golfer Celebrity Players Tour. Recipient Gold Glove award, 1988—92, Silver Slugger award, 1988, 1992; named to Nat. League All-Star Team, Maj. League Baseball, 1988, 1992, 1993. Office: Detroit Tigers Comerica Pk 2100 Woodward Ave Detroit MI 48201*

VAN SLYKE, ROSEMARY, retired tax specialist; b. Albany, NY, June 23, 1939; d. William and Edna Elizabeth (Lawler) Van Slyke; children: Rosemary Van Vorse, Christopher Van Vorse, Elizabeth Hudson. Assoc. Bus. Adminstrn., Albany Bus. Coll., NY, 1969; cert. med. asst., Mildred Elley Coll., Colonie, NY, 1993. With NY Staet Dept. Labor, Albany, 1969—96, Albany County Mental Health, Albany, 1997—2001, NY State Tax Dept., Albany, 2002—04, GE Corp. Tax, Albany, 2005—. Mem.: ACLU, NOW, CSEA (sec. 1981—88). Democrat. Roman Catholic. Avocations: exercise, reading, internet. Home: 115 Krumkill Rd Apt 413 Albany NY 12208 Home Phone: 518-459-1834. E-mail: vanslyker@aol.com.

VAN STEENWYK, JOHN JOSEPH, healthcare plan consultant; b. Mpls., July 25, 1931; s. Elmer Arnold and Marion Ione (Thompson) van S.; m. Janice Kevin Sharp, July 11, 1959; children: Jennifer Lee, Edward Arnold, Julie Anne AB, Oberlin Coll., 1953; MBA, U. Pa., 1955. V.p., cons. The Segal Co., NYC, 1957—81; pres. Health Econs., Inc., Spring House, Pa., 1982—. Clin. asst. prof. cmty. and preventive medicine N.Y. Med. Coll., Valhalla, NY, 1980—2002; population health assoc. Sch. Population Health, Jefferson U., 2009—. With USN, 1955-57. Sr. scholar, Dept. Health Policy, Jefferson U., 2005—09. Mem.: APHA, Am. Health Ins. Plans, Acad. Health. Episcopalian. Avocation: gardening. Home: 921 Tennis Ave Ambler PA 19002-2312 Office: Health Economics Inc 768 N Bethlehem Pike PO Box 710 Spring House PA 19477 Office Phone: 215-628-3838.

VAN SUSTEREN, GRETA CONWAY, newscaster, lawyer; b. Appleton, Wis., June 11, 1954; d. Urban Peter and Margery (Conway) Van Susteren; m. John Purcell Coale, Oct. 12, 1987. BA in Econs., with distinction, U. Wis., 1976; JD, Georgetown U., 1979, LLM, 1982; LLD (hon.), Stetson Law Sch. Bar: DC 1979, US Supreme Ct. 1982, Md. 1985, Wis. 1987, US Ct. Appeals (DC, 2d and 4th cirs.). Ptnr. Milliken, VanSusteren & Canan, Washington, 1982—; with CNN, 1991—2002, host The Point with Greta Van Susteren, legal cons. The World Today, co-host Burden of Proof, 1994—2002; host On the Record With Greta Van Susteren Fox News Channel, 2002—. Adj. prof. Georgetown Law Ctr., Washington, 1984—99; lectr., panelist Jud. Conf., Washington, 1986. Co-author: My Turn at the Bully Pulpit: Straight Talk About the Things That Drive Me Nuts, 2003. Bd. dirs. Stuart Stiller Found., Washington, 1982—. Recipient Sandra Day O'Conner Medal of Honor,

Seton Hall U., 2001; co-recipient Nat. Headliners award, 2002; named one of 100 Most Powerful Women, Forbes mag.; Stiller fellow, Georgetown Law Ctr., 1980. Mem.: ATLA (lectr. conf. 1986—), ABA (Presdl. award for Excellence in Journalism 2001), DC Bar Assn. Office: FOX News Channel 1211 Ave Americas New York NY 10036*

VAN TASSEL, LOWELL THOMAS, mathematics professor; b. Mpls., Jan. 31, 1932; s. Evan Thomas Van Tassel and Sophia Anna Huebner; m. Diane Laura Diedrich, June 14, 1953; children: Thomas, Laurie, Karin. BS, U. Minn., 1952, MA, 1962. Cert. secondary tchr. Calif. Rsch. asst. U. Minn., Mpls., 1954-56; math. tchr. San Diego Unified Sch. Dist., 1956-65; prof. math. San Diego C.C. Dist., 1965-92, prof. emeritus of math., 1992—. Dept. chmn. math. dept. San Diego City Coll., 1971-72, 74-75; math/physics instr. Naval Tgn. Ctr., San Diego, 1962-66; proctor profl. engring. exams State of Calif. License Bd., Sacramento, 1957-65. Contbr. articles to profl. jours. V.p. Am. Fedn. of Tchrs., San Diego, 1971-72; faculty advisor Ind. Dems. for Action San Diego City Coll., 1967-71; mem. Clairemont Dem. Club, San Diego, 1966-76; juror, criminal trial Superior Ct., San Diego, 1990; elder Holy Cross Luth. Ch., San Diego, 1972-74, 92-94. With USMC, 1951-54; USMCR, 1954-71, maj., 1966-71. Mem. Math. Assn. Am., Calif. Retired Tchrs. Assn., Marine Corps Mus., U. Minn. Alumni Assn. (life.), Nat. Coun. of Tchrs. of Math., Am. Fedn. of Tchrs. (retiree mem.), Phi Delta Kappa, Psi Chi. Lutheran. Avocations: travel, reading, word puzzles, games, bridge. Home: 5550 Lodi St San Diego CA 92117-1138

VAN TIENHOVEN, ARI, education educator, educator; b. The Hague, The Netherlands, Apr. 22, 1922; came to U.S., 1949; s. Adrianus Baltus and Willemina Hendrika (Mulder) van T.; m. Annie van Haselen, Mar. 14, 1950; children: Richard Ari, Arianne Jeanette, Andrew Wijnand. Landbouwkundig Ingenieur, U. Wageningen, The Netherlands, 1949; MS, U. Ill., 1951, PhD, 1953. Asst. prof. Miss. State Coll., Starkville, 1953-55; from asst. prof. to prof. emeritus Cornell U., Ithaca, N.Y., 1955—. Assoc. editor Poultry Sci., Urbana, Ill., 1964-67, 80-83, Biology of Reproduction, Urbana, 1975-77, Gen. and Comparative Endocrinology, N.Y.C., 1968-74, Veterinary Quarterly, Utrecht, Netherlands, 1980-87. Author: Physiology of Reproduction of Vertebrates, 1968, 83; co-author: Asdell's Patterns of Mammalian Reproduction, 1993. Bd. dirs. Ithaca City Sch. Dist., 1968-71, pres., 1970-71; bd. dirs. Economic Opportunity Corp., Ithaca, 1969-70, 82-84, 86-89, v.p., 1988-89. Recipient Tchr. of Merit award, Marjorie Penalver Edn. award, Edgerton Career Tchg. award Tompkins County Human Rights Commn., 1992. Fellow AAAS, Poultry Sci. Assn., NSF. Democrat.

VAN TINE, KIRK KELSO, lawyer, former federal agency administrator; b. Syracuse, NY, Aug. 30, 1948; s. George Kelso and Hariot (Van Alst) V.; m. Barbara Ann Byers, Aug. 14, 1971; children: Lindsay, Meredith. BS in Fgn. Affairs, U.S. Naval Acad., 1970; JD, U. Va., 1978. Bar: D.C. 1978, U.S. Ct. Appeals (D.C. crct.) 1979, U.S. Ct. Appeals (5th crct.) 1980, U.S. Ct. Appeals (8th crct.) 1992, U.S. Ct. Appeals (9th crct.) 1992, U.S. Ct. Appeals (10th crct.) 1993, U.S. Supreme Ct., 1982, U.S. Dist. Ct. D.C. 1979. Commd. ensign USN, 1970, advanced through grades to lt., 1974, resigned, 1975; assoc. Baker & Botts LLP, Washington, 1978-86, ptnr., 1986—2001, sr. ptnr., 2005—; gen. counsel U.S. Dept. Transp., Washington, 2001—03, acting dep. sec., 2003—04, dep. sec., 2004. Mem.: Order of the Coif, DC Bar Assn. (former co-chair litig. and law practice mgmt. sect., chair election bd.). Office: Baker Botts LLP 1299 Pennsylvania Ave NW Washington DC 20004 Office Phone: 202-639-7741.

VANTSEVICH, VLADIMIR V., engineering educator, director; s. Vladimir A. and Antonina G. Vantsevich; m. Svetlana I. Demyantseva, June 23, 1984; children: Michael V., Anna V., Ivan V. DSc, DSc, Belarusian Nat. Tech. U., Minsk, PhD, 1981. Diploma engr., sr. engr. Belarusian Nat. Tech. U., Collaborative Vehicle Rsch. & Design Lab., 1977—78, sr. rschr., 1981—83; assoc. prof. and group leader, r&d group on multi-wheel dr. vehicle engring. Belarusian Nat. Tech. U., Tractor Engring. Dept., 1983—92, prof., 1993—98; head of r&d group on multi-wheel dr. vehicle engring. Belarusian Nat. Tech. U., NAS, 1993—2003; head dept. internat. r & d collaboration Ministry of Fgn. Affairs, Minsk, 1994—97; counselor and dept. permanent rep. Permanent Mission Belarus to UN, NYC, 1997—2001; assoc. prof. Mech. Engring. Dept., Lawrence Tech U., Southfield, 2001—04, prof., 2005—; assoc. dir. Automotive Engring. Inst. Lawrence Tech U., 2003—, dir. mechatronic sys. engring., 2006—. Editl. bd. mem. Int. Jour. Vehicle Autonomous Sys. Contbr. articles to profl. jours. Decorated Rsch. Achievement medal Govt. USSR; recipient Inventor award, USSR Govtl. Body; named Best Tech. Book, NAS, Belarus, 1999. Fellow: ASME, Belarusan Inst. Arts and Scis., BINIM, NJ; mem.: Assn. Unmanned Vehicle Sys. Internat., Internat. Assn. Vehicle Sys. Dynamics, Internat. Soc. Terrain-Vehicle Sys., SAE. Office: Lawrence Technol Univ 21000 W Ten Mile Rd Southfield MI 48075 Personal E-mail: awdrive@comcast.net. Business E-Mail: vantsevich@ltu.edu.

VANTYLE, JEANNE HAWKINS, pharmacy educator, consultant; b. Indpls., Jan. 3, 1951; m. W. Kent Van Tyle, July 24, 1982; children: Rachel Elizabeth, Emily Kathleen. BS in Pharmacy, Butler U., 1974, MS in Pharmacy, 1980; PharmD, Mercer U., 1976. Reg. pharmacist. From asst. to assoc. prof. pharmacy Butler U., Indpls., 1976-97, prof., 1997—; clin. pharmacy coord. St. Vincent Hosp., Indpls., 1976-81; dir. learning resource ctr. Butler U., Indpls., 1996-99; vol. pharmacist Gennesaret Free Med. Clinic, 2001—, mem. bd. dir., 2008—; vol. pharmacist Shepherd Cmty. Ctr. Mem. bd. dirs. Lupus Found. of Ind., Indpls., 1976—; H.S. rschr. Am. Lung Assn.-Ind., Indpls., 1989-98, Science Edn. Found., Indpls., 1976—; mem. bd. dirs., profl. educator Am. Cancer Soc.-Ind., Indpls., 1976-82. Contbr. chpts. to textbooks and articles to profl. jours. Mem. Caroline Scott Harrison DAR, Indpls., 1982—; adult leader Girl Scouts U.S., 1992—. Mem. Am. Assn. Colls. Pharmacy, Am. Soc. Hosp. Pharmacists, Ind. Soc. Hosp. Pharmacists. Roman Catholic. Avocations: antiques, genealogy. Home: 502 Buckingham Dr Indianapolis IN 46208-3614 Office: Butler University 4600 Sunset Ave Indianapolis IN 46208-3487

VAN VALER, JOE NED, lawyer, real estate developer; b. Gas City, Ind., Mar. 13, 1935; s. Richard Carl and Wilma Amy (Kelly) Van V.; m. Constance Joy Richardson, June 25, 1960; children: Kimberly Joy, Kelli June, Lynn Louise, Joseph Jeffrey. AB, Franklin Coll., 1959; LLB, Ind. U., 1963. Bar: Ind. 1963, U.S. Dist. Ct. (so. dist.) Ind. 1963. Assoc. Van Valer Law Firm and predecessor firms, 1963-65, ptnr., 1965-75, sr. ptnr., 1975—. Pres. Home Owners Warranty Corp. of Central Ind., Indpls., 1984-91, chmn. bd. dirs. 1991-95; cons. bd. Nat. City Bank Greenwood; chmn. adv. group Home Owners Warranty Corp., Washington, 1988-90, 92-94 also bd. dirs.; pros. atty. 8th Jud. Dist., Franklin, Ind., 1967-74; chmn. Johnson County, Ind., Contractors' Listing Bd.; chmn. bd. Bldg. Industry Svc. Corp., 1995-2000. With AUS, 1957-58. Recipient Alumnus Citation award Franklin Coll., 1996, Franklin Coll. Williams Chair in Law and Pub. Svc. award, 2008. Mem. ABA, Indpls. Bar Assn., 8th Jud. Cir. Bar Assn., Nat. Assn. Home Builders (bd. dirs.), Ind. Builders Assn. (bd. dirs), Builders Assn. Greater Indpls. (dir., pres. 1981, parliamentarian emeritus 2007), Indpls. Soc. Republican. Methodist. Office: 299 W Main St Greenwood IN 46142-3129 Office Phone: 317-881-7575. Business E-Mail: joe@vanvalerlaw.com.

VAN VALEY, THOMAS LEE, sociologist, educator; b. Cin., Aug. 31, 1942; s. Leland Hudson and Elizabeth Jane (Skinner) Van V.; m. Janet Lynn Whisler, June 13, 1965; children: Jennifer Lynn, Christine Anne. BA, Hanover Coll., 1964; MA, U. Wash., 1969; PhD, U. N.C., 1971. Asst. prof. Colo. State U., Ft. Collins, 1970-74; vis. rsch. assoc. U. Mass., Amherst, 1974-75; vis. lectr. U. Va., Charlottesville, 1975-77; asst. prof. Western Mich. U., Kalamazoo, 1977-78, assoc. prof., 1978-84, full prof., 1984—, prof. emeritus, 2007. Dir. Ctr. for Social Rsch., Kalamazoo, 1985-89, 91-94, chair, 1999-2005; ptnr. Advanced Data Svcs., Portage, Mich., 1987—. Co-editor Jour. Applied Sociology, 1998-2000, 02; co-author: Census '80, 1980; contbr. articles to profl. jours. Mem. Am. Sociol. Assn., North Ctrl. Sociol. Assn., Assn. Applied & Clin. Sociology Avocations: english handbells, science fiction, golf. Home: 29462 Heritage Ln Paw Paw MI 49079-9493 Office: Dept Sociology 2208 Sangren Hall Kalamazoo MI 49008

VAN VALKENBURG, EDGAR WALTER, lawyer; b. Seattle, Jan. 8, 1953; s. Edgar Walter and Margaret Catherine (McKenna) Van V.; m. Turid L. Owren, Sept. 29, 1990; children: Ingrid Catherine, Andrew Owren. BA, U. Wash., 1975; JD summa cum laude, Willamette Coll. of Law, 1978; LLM, Columbia U., 1984. Bar: Oreg. 1978, U.S. Dist. Ct. Oreg. 1979, U.S. Ct. Appeals (9th cir.) 1980. Law clk. to assoc. justice Oreg. Supreme Ct., Salem, 1978-79; assoc. Stoel, Rives, Boley, Fraser & Wyse, Portland, Oreg., 1979-82, 84-86; ptnr. Stoel Rives LLP, Portland, Oreg., 1986—; instr. Columbia U., NYC, 1982-84. Bd. dirs. Oreg. Sports Authority; chair Oreg. Econ. and Cmty. Devel. Commn., 2003—. Editor-in-chief: Williamette Law Jour. 1977-78. Bd. dirs., chmn. Multnomah County Legal Aid, 1997-98; bd. dirs. Portland Ctr. Stage, 2004—. Mem. ACLU (pres. Oreg. chpt. 1991-93), Oreg. State Bar (chmn. antitrust sect. 1989-90, mem. Ho. of Dels. 1996-98). Office: Stoel Rives LLP 900 SW 5th Ave Ste 2600 Portland OR 97204-1229

VAN VALKENBURGH, HOLLY VIOLA, librarian, consultant; b. NYC, Nov. 22, 1936; d. Horace Bulle III and Viola Van V.; children: Leland V. Lammert, Jeni L. Muniz, Gary F. Ohm. BA, U. Colo., 1957; MA, U. Denver, 1965; MEd, Lesley Coll., Cambridge, Mass., 1988. Elem. sch. tchr., Tenn., 1958-60, Colo., 1961-62; sch. librarian Colo., 1962-66, Wyo., 1984-88; coll. librarian Sheridan (Wyo.) Coll., 1966-74, Morrison Coll., Reno, Nev., 1989-92; owner, operator Nanny Placement Agy., Reno, 1991-96, Word Pro, Carson City, Nev., 1996—. Cons. Nev. State Libr., Carson City, 1993—; adminstr. weatherization assistance project Dept. of Energy, Sheridan, 1975-84. Bd. dirs. Grassroots Lobby, Carson City, 1995-99; chmn. Nev. Women's History Project, Reno, 2000-02, treas., 2004—, Letters from Nev. Daughters., 2000—; treas., mem. Sheridan County Recreation Bd., 1972-78. Josephine Halverson Morris scholar U. Denver, 1965. Mem.: AAUW (pres. local chpts. 1972—73, 1996—98, newsletter editor), Nev. Libr. Assn. (newsletter editor 1997—2002, pres. 2003), Red Hat Soc., Nat. Assn. Van Valkenburgh Family (newsletter editor 1991—, bd. dirs. 1998—2004). Avocations: white water rafting, reading.

VAN VLECK, FRED SCOTT, mathematician, educator, researcher; b. Clearwater, Nebr., Dec. 12, 1934; s. Harold F. Van Vleck and Patricia A. Scott; m. Charlotte T. Allen, June 18, 1960; children: Erik S., Paul F., Karl J., Kristina M., Teresa A. BS, U. Nebr., Lincoln, 1956; MA, U. Nebr., 1957; PhD, U. Minn., 1960. Instr. math. MIT, Cambridge, Mass., 1960—62; asst. prof. math. U. Kans., Lawrence, 1962—65, assoc. prof. math., 1965—68, prof. math., 1968—2004, prof. emeritus, 2004—. Chancellors Club tchg. prof. math. U. Kans., Lawrence, 1985—2004. Co-author: (rsch. monograph) Linear Systems over Communicative Rings, 1986; contbr. articles to profl. jours. Mem.: Math. Assn. Am., Soc. for Indsl. and Applied Math., Am. Math. Soc. Avocations: genealogy, running. Office: Univ Kans Dept Math Jayhawk Blvd Lawrence KS 66045

VAN VLEET, WILLIAM BENJAMIN, lawyer, retired insurance company executive; b. Milw., Dec. 4, 1924; s. William Benjamin and Irene (Peppey) Van V.; m. Marilyn Nilles, Dec. 26, 1946; children: Terese Van Vleet Svetich, Susan Van Vleet Waldo, William Benjamin III, Monica Van Vleet McCarthy, Mark. Student, Marquette U., 1942-43, Lawrence Coll., Appleton, Wis., 1943-44; LLB, JD, Marquette U., 1948. Bar: Wis. 1948, Ill. 1950. Gen. counsel George Rogers Clark Mut. Casualty Co., Rockford, Ill., 1948-59, Pioneer Life Ins. Co. Ill., Rockford, 1950-68, 81-94, v.p., 1959-91, gen. counsel, 1968-91, exec. v.p., 1981-95, also bd. dirs.; exec. v.p., gen. counsel Pioneer Fin. Svcs., Inc., Rockford, 1985-95, gen. counsel emeritus, dir., 1995-97; pres. Nat. Group Life Ins. Co., Rockford, 1992-93, exec. v.p., gen. counsel, 1993-94, also bd. dirs. Pres. Western Life Ins. Co. Am., Rockford, 1981-82, Health & Life Ins. Co. Am., Rockford, 1984-92, exec. v.p., gen. counsel, 1993-94; pres. Manhattan Nat. Life Ins. Co., Cin., 1990-92, exec. v.p., gen. counsel, 1993-94, also bd. dirs.; exec. v.p., gen. counsel Continental Life and Accident Co., Boise, Idano, 1993-94, also bd. dirs.; bd. dirs. Nat. Health Svcs. Milw. Mem. adminstrn. Boylan Ctrl. Cath. H.S., Rockford, 1965-72; pres. Diocesan Bd. Edn., Rockford, 1970-78; v.p., pres. Nat. Assn. Bds. Edn., 1972-78; mem. bd. advisors Marion Coll., 1976-79; mem. adv. bd. St. Anthony's Hosp., Rockford, 1978-91; bd. dirs. Crimestoppers, Rockford, 1982-90; co-chmn. United Cerebral Palsy Telethon, Rockford, 1985-95. Mem. Ill. Bar Assn., Winnebago County Bar Assn.

VAN VLIET, CAROLYNE MARINA, physicist, researcher; b. Dordrecht, Netherlands, Dec. 27, 1929; arrived in U.S., 1960, naturalized, 1967; d. Marinus and Jacoba (de Lange) Van V.; m. A.J. Cappon, Dec. 29, 1953 (div. 1983); children: Elsa Marianne, Mark Edward, Cynthia Joyce, Renata Annette Carolina. BS, Free U. Amsterdam, Netherlands, 1949, MA, 1953, PhD in Physics, 1956. Rsch. fellow Free U. Amsterdam, 1950-54, rsch. assoc., 1954-56, conservator, 1958-60; fullbright fellow U. Minn., Mpls., 1956-57, faculty, 1957-58, 60-70, prof. elec. engring. and physics, 1965-70; prof. theoretical physics U. Montreal, Que., Can., 1969-95, sr. rschr. math. rsch. ctr. Que., 1969-2000, prof. emerita, 1998—. Vis. prof. U. Fla., 1974, 78-88; prof. elec. and computer engring. Fla. Internat. U., 1992-2000; adj. prof. physics U. Miami, 2001—. Contbg. author: Fluctuation Phenomena in Solids, 1965; author Equilibrium and Non-Equilibrium Statistical Mechanics, 2008; contbr. articles to profl. jours. Rsch. grantee, NSF, Air Force OSR, Wright Patterson AFB, Nat. Sci. and Engring. Rsch. Coun., Ottawa. Fellow IEEE (life); mem. Am. Phys. Soc., Am. Math. Soc., NY Acad. Scis. Office: U Miami James L Knight Physics Bldg 1320 Campo Sano Dr Coral Gables FL 33146 Business E-Mail: vanvliet@physics.miami.edu. *The purpose of life is to honor God and to serve mankind.*

VAN VLIET, CLAIRE, artist; b. Ottawa, Ont., Can., Aug. 9, 1933; d. Wilbur Dennison and Audrey Ilene (Wallace) Van Vliet. AB, San Diego State Coll., 1952; MFA, Claremont Grad. Sch., 1954; DFA (hon.), U. of the Arts, Phila., 1993, San Diego State U., 2002. Instr. printmaking Phila. Coll. Art, 1959-65; owner The Janus Press, 1954—; vis. lectr. printmaking U. Wis.-Madison, 1965-66. Mem. bd. advisors Hand Papermaking. One-man exhbns. include Print Club Phila., 1963, 66, 73, 77, Wiggin Gallery, Boston Pub. Libr., 1977, Rutgers U. Art Gallery, 1978, AAA Gallery, Phila., 1980, Dolan/Maxwell Gallery, Phila., 1984, 91, Mary Ryan Gallery, NYC, 1986, Mills Coll., 1986, U. of the Arts, Phila., 1989, Victoria and Albert Mus., London, 1994, Ottawa Sch. of Art Gallery, Can., 1994, Bates Coll. Mus. of Art, Lewiston, Maine, 1994, 99, ND Mus. Art, 1999, Rosenwald Wolf Gallery U. Arts. Phila, 2001, La. State U. Libr., 2005, Grolier Club, NY, 2006, Nat. Gallery Art Libr., 2006, Humanities Gallery, Scripps Coll., 2006, Boston Pub. Libr., 2006, Wellesley Coll. Libr., 2006, U. Va. Libr., 2007, Smith Coll. Libr., 2007; group exhbns. include Bklyn. Nat., Phila. Arts Festival, Kunst zu Kafka, Germany, Paper as Medium, Smithsonian Instn., Washington, Paper Now, Cleve. Mus. Art, 1986, Boyle Arts Festival, Ireland, 1993, Libr. Congress, 1997—, ND Mus. Art, 1999; represented in permanent collections Nat. Gallery Art, Phila. Mus. Art, Boston Pub. Libr., Libr. of Congress, Cleve. Mus. Art, Montreal Mus. Fine Arts, Victoria and Albert Mus. London, Tate Gallery, London, US Dept. State, Nat. Libr. Can., British Libr. Grantee, Ingram-Merrill Found., 1989; NEA grantee, 1976—80, MacArthur fellow, 1989—94. Mem.: Nat. Acad., Soc. Printers Boston, Vt. Arts and Scis. Home and Office: 101 Schoolhouse Rd West Burke VT 05871-9773 Office Phone: 802-467-3335.

VANVOORHIS, REBECCA JANE, social sciences educator, consultant; b. Canton, Ohio, Mar. 8, 1945; d. Clancy Ellsworth and Forest Rose Morrison; children: Troy Andrew children: Katrina Marie Getts. BA, Baldwin Wallace Coll., Berea, Ohio, 1966; MS in Social Work, Ohio State U., Columbus, 1970, PhD, 1974. Lic. Ind. Health Professions Bur., 1999. Faculty Ohio State U., coll. Social Work, Columbus, 1977—80; faculty mem. Ind. U., Sch. Social Work, Indpls., 1980—. Comm. cons. Anderson Consulting, Chgo., 1983—2002. Contbr. jours. on social work edn., chapters to books. Bd. mem. Women's Fund Ctrl. Ind., Indpls., 1996—2008. Hoosier Assurance Plan Provider Profile Grant, Ind. Consortium for Mental Health Services Rsch., 2000-2001, U. Coll. Faculty Fellow, Ind. U. Purdue U. Indpls., 2007-2008, 2000-2001. Home: 3738 Bay Road South Dr Indianapolis IN 46240 Office: Indiana Univ Sch of Social Work 902 West New York St Indianapolis IN 46202-5154 Business E-Mail: rvanvoor@iupui.edu.

VAN VOORST, CAROL, United States Ambassador to Iceland; BA, Hope Coll.; MA, Nat. War Coll., 1998; MA, PhD, Princeton U. Tchr. City U. NY; spl. asst. to dep. sec. US Dept. State, 1984—85, Norway/Denmark desk officer, 1989—91, spl. asst. to under sec. polit. affairs, 1991—92, assigned to Panama, 1992—95, dir. Office Nordic & Baltic Affairs, 1995—97, chief polit. dept. to dep. high rep. office of high rep. Sarajevo, 1998—99; dep. chief of mission Am. Embassy, Helsinki, 1999—2002; dir. Austrian, German, Swiss affairs. Bur. European and Eurasian Affairs US Dept. State, 2002—04, US. amb. to Iceland Reykjavik, 2005—. Office: DOS Amb 5640 Reykjavik Pl Washington DC 20521*

VAN VORHIS, ANDREA CHRISTINE, literature and language professor; b. Wiener Neustadt, Austria, Apr. 19, 1961; d. Friedrich Karl and Helga Christine Riedl; m. James Richard Van Vorhis; 1 child, Nicholas. MA in English & Am. Studies, Spanish, U. Salzburg, Austria, 1986; MA in English, TESL, Bowling Green State U., Ohio, 1988. Instr. Bowling Green State U., 1988—; prof. Owens CC, Findlay, Ohio, 1999—. Desktop pub. Root Pub., Perrysburg, Ohio, 1995—97. Recipient Outstanding Tchr. award, non-traditional Student Assn., BGSU, 1995; Fulbright Travel grant, Fulbright Commn., 1992—93. Office: Owens CC 3200 Bright Rd Findlay OH 45840 Business E-Mail: andrea_vanvorhis@owens.edu.

VAN VUGT, WILLIAM E., history professor; s. Van Vugt-Bratt; m. Lynn Heemstra, Sept. 30, 1958. PhD, London Sch. Economics, England, 1986. Prof. history Calvin Coll., Grand Rapids, 1986—2008. Achievements include research in British Immigration to North America. Home and Office: Calvin Coll 1845 Knollcrest Cir Grand Rapids MI 49546

VAN WACHEM, LODEWIJK CHRISTIAAN, petroleum company executive; b. Pangkalan Brandan, Indonesia, July 31, 1931; m. Elisabeth G. Cristofoli, June 10, 1958; 3 children. Degree Mech. Engring., Delft U., Delft, The Netherlands., 1953. With Bataafsche Petroleum Maatschappij, The Hague, Netherlands, 1953; pres. Royal Dutch Petroleum Co., The Hague, The Netherlands, 1982-92; chmn. com., mng. dir. Royal Dutch/Shell Group, The Hague, Netherlands, 1985—92; chmn. supr. bd. Royal Dutch Petroleum Co., The Hague, Netherlands, 1992—2002; with Maersk Holding B.U., Rotterdam, Netherlands, 2002—. Chmn. bd. dirs. Zurich Fin. Svcs., 2002—05, Global Crossing Ltd.; supervisory bd. De Nederlandsche Bank N.V., 1987—92, AKZO Nobel n.v., Arnhem, 1992—2002, BMW A.G., Munich, 1994—2002, Bayer A.G., Leverkusen, 1997—2002; non. exec. dir. IBM Corp., Armonk, 1992—2002, AAB Area Brown Boveri Ltd, Zurich, 1996—99; chmn. supervisory bd. Philips Electronics n.v., Amsterdam, 1993—2005; bd. dirs. Atco Ltd., Calgary. Decorated comdr. Brit. Empire, knight Brit. Empire (Eng.), comdr. Order of Oranje Nassau, knight Order Netherlands Lion (Netherlands). Office: Maersk Holding BU PO Box 487 NL-3000 AL Rotterdam Netherlands

VAN WINGERDEN, DANIEL J., retired physics professor; s. Arie J. and Roslyn Van Wingerden; m. Caryl S. Blankenship; children: Sarah Elisabeth Gilbert, Michelle Marie Rossi, Mark Daniel Van Wingerden. BS, Eastern Mich. U., Ypsilanti, 1972, MS, 1973; MS in Engring., Rensselaer Poly. Inst., Troy, NY, 1997. Instr., dept. head physics math electronics Wayne-Westland Cmty. Sch., Mich., 1973—84; physics guest lectr. Eastern Mich. U., 1978—. Project scientist Gen. Motors Rsch. Labs., Warren, Mich., 1984—92; sr. mfg. engr. Gen. Motors Mfg., Warren, 1992—98; sr. contact engr. ops. rsch. Gen. Motors Engring., Warren, 1998—2004; project mgr. Gen. Motors Global Engring. Processes, Warren, 2004—05; adj. faculty Henry Ford CC, Dearborn, Mich., 2005—. Contbr. scientific papers (Gen. Motors Chmn.'s Honors award, 2004). Commodore, flag officer, bd. dirs. Doublehanded Sailing Assn., Mich., 1994. Mem.: Am. Assn. Physics Tchrs., Am. Phys. Soc., Crescent Sail Yatch Club (chair hoists 1997). Achievements include patents for Fred Pinkerton for Sm Fe V magnetic materials and the making of same. Avocation: sports. Office: Eastern Mich Univ 327 Strong Ypsilanti MI 48197 Business E-Mail: dvanwinge@emich.edu.

VAN WINKLE, WILLIAM, financial planner; b. Englewood, NJ, July 3, 1934; s. Marshall Jr. and Helen (Wescott) V.; m. Beverly Elsie Peterson, Sept. 9, 1956; children: Stuart Wilson, Ainsley Van Winkle Hilfiker, Carrie Van Winkle White. BS in Mech. Engring. and Bus. Adminstrn., Lehigh U., 1957; MS in Fin. Svcs., The Am. Coll., Bryn Mawr, Pa., 1996. Cert. fin. planner. With Procter and Gamble, 1957-67, Sheffield Chem. div. Kraftco, Union, NJ, 1967-71, C.R. Bard, Inc., Murray Hill, NJ, 1971-74; v.p. mfg. Estey Corp., Eatontown, NJ, 1974-79; pres. Van Winkle Assocs., Tinton Falls, NJ, 1979—. Host, prodr. (cable TV program) Financial Matters, 1980. Past pres., trustee Brookdale C.C. Found., Lincroft, N.J. Mem. Million Dollar Round Table (v.p. 1994-95), Past Commodore Shrewsbury Sailing and Yacht Club, NJ Yacht Racing Assn., Navesink Country Club (Middletown, NJ),

Seabright (NJ) Beach Club, Holland Soc. NY (pres. 2002-06), Useppa Island Club, Root Beer and Checkers Club. Republican. Episcopalian. Avocations: sailing, walking, reading. Home: 41 Breezy Pt Little Silver NJ 07739-1703 Office: Van Winkle Assocs 776 Shrewsbury Ave Tinton Falls NJ 07724-3006 Office Phone: 732-741-4046.

VANWOERKOM, JACK A., lawyer, consumer products company executive; b. 1953; m. Barbara L. Moore; 1 child, Carolyn. BS, MIT, 1975; JD cum laude, Boston U., 1978. Atty. Hale & Door, LLP, Boston, 1978—85; with Winthrop Fin. Assocs., Boston, 1985—94, gen. counsel, COO, vice chmn., mng. dir. Asian ops., 1993—94; chief legal counsel, v.p. devel., mng. dir. Europe A.W. Chesterton Co., 1994—97; gen. counsel Teradyne, Inc., 1998—99; sr. v.p., gen. counsel, sec. Staples, Inc., Framingham, Mass., 1999—2003, exec. v.p., gen. counsel, sec., 2003—07; exec. v.p., gen. counsel, corp. sec. The Home Depot, Inc., Atlanta, 2007—. Office: The Home Depot Inc 2455 Paces Ferry Rd Atlanta GA 30339*

VAN WORMER, KATHERINE STUART, social work educator; b. New Orleans, July 24, 1944; m. Robert Van Wormer; children: Flora, Rupert. BA, U. N.C., 1966; grad. diploma in edn., Queen's U., Belfast, Northern Ireland, 1967; PhD in Sociology, U. Ga., 1976; MSSW, U. Tenn., Nashville, 1984. Instr. Livingstone Coll., Salisbury, N.C., 1976-77; asst. prof. Kent (Ohio) State U., 1978-83, Winona (Minn.) State U., 1985-86; alcoholism counselor Community Alcohol Ctr., Longview, Wash., 1983-85; program dir. Vangseter Treatment, Hamar, Norway, 1988-90; asst. prof. U. No. Iowa, Cedar Falls, 1990-92, assoc. prof., 1992—97, prof., 1997—. Author: Social Welfare: A World View, 1997, Social Work with Lesbians, Gays and Bisexuals, 2000, Addiction Treatment: A Strength Perspective, 2008, Confronting Oppresion, Restoring Justice, 2004, Introduction to Social Welfare and Social Work The U.S. in Global Perspective, 2006, Women and the Criminal Justice System, 2007, Human Behavior and the Social Environment, 2007, Death by Domestic Violence: Preventing the Murders and the Murder-Suicides, 2009; contbr. articles on harm reduction and restorative justice to profl. jours. Mem.: NASW, Parents Families and Friends of Lesbians and Gays. Socialist. Mem. Soc. Of Friends. Home: 610 Tremont St Cedar Falls IA 50613-2927 Office: U No Iowa Dept Social Work 36 Sabin Hl Cedar Falls IA 50614-0001 Home Phone: 319-266-4447; Office Phone: 319-273-6379. Business E-Mail: vanworme@uni.edu.

VAN WYCK, GEORGE RICHARD, insurance company executive; b. Wilmington, Vt., Feb. 6, 1928; s. Harold Wait Van Wyck and Ruth Anna Learnard; m. Jeanne Mildred Anderson, Apr. 17, 1948; children: Diana Lee Van Wyck Jenkins, Beryl Jeanne. BS in Math. cum laude, St. Lawrence U., 1953. Actuarial clk. Aetna Life Ins. Co., Hartford, Conn., 1953-55; with Am. Bankers Ins. Group, Miami, Fla., 1955-91, sec., bd. dirs., 1983-89, ret., 1991. Bd. dirs. Jr. Achievement of Greater Miami, 1966-83, pres., 1975-76; bd. dirs. Epworth Village Retirement Complex, Miami, 1966-2000, v.p., 1998-99, chmn. investment com. 1995-99; founding dir., pres. Brickel Children's Ctr., Miami, 1980-82; mem. pers. adv. bd., vice chmn. Dade County, Miami, 1987-89. With USAF, 1946-49. Fellow Life Office Mgmt. Inst.; mem. 1st United Meth. Ch. So. Miami, Phi Beta Kappa. Democrat. Methodist. Avocations: photography, golf, bridge, writing. Home: 8455 SW 44th St Miami FL 33155-4126 Personal E-mail: gvanwyck@cs.com.

VAN WYLEN, GORDON JOHN, former college president; b. Grant, Mich., Feb. 6, 1920; s. John and Effa (Bierema) Van W.; m. Margaret E. DeWitt, Dec. 29, 1951; children: Elizabeth Ann Van Wylen Rudenga, Stephen John, Ruth Margaret Van Wylen Jasperse, David Gordon, Emily Jane Van Wylen Overway. AB, Calvin Coll., 1942; BSE., U. Mich., 1942, MS, 1947; Sc.D., MIT, 1951. Indsl. engr. duPont Co., 1942-43; instr. mech. engring. Pa. State U., 1946-48; asst. prof. mech. engring. U. Mich., 1951-55, assoc. prof., 1955-57, prof., 1957-72, chmn. dept., 1958-65, dean Coll. Engring., 1965-72; pres. Hope Coll., Holland, Mich., 1972-87, pres. emeritus, 1987—. Author: Thermodynamics, 1959; author: (with R.E. Sonntag) Fundamentals of Classical Thermodynamics, 1965; author: 6th edit., 2003, Fundamentals of Statistical Thermodynamics, 1966, Introduction to Thermodynamics, 1971, 3d edit., 1991, Encounter at Sea, 1994; contbr. articles to profl. jours. Trustee Van Andel Edn. Inst. Lt. USNR, 1943-46. Fellow ASME, AAAS; mem. Phi Beta Kappa (hon.), Sigma Xi, Tau Beta Pi, Phi Kappa Phi. Mem. Reform Ch. Am. Home: Apt 600 145 Columbia Ave Holland MI 49423-2980

VAN ZANDT, DAVID E., dean, law educator; b. Princeton, NJ, Feb. 17, 1953; m. Lisa A. Huestis; children: Caroline, Nicholas. AB summa cum laude, Princeton U., 1975; JD, Yale U., 1981; PhD in Sociology, U. London, 1985. Bar: Ill. Lectr. New England Coll., Arundel, England, 1977, U. London, England, 1977—78; clk. to Hon. Pierre N. Leval U.S. Dist. Ct. (so. dist.) N.Y., 1981-82; clk. to Hon. Harry A. Blackmun U.S. Supreme Ct., Washington, 1982-83; atty. Davis, Polk & Wardwell, 1984-85; spl. U.S. legal counsel Artal Grp. S.A., 1985—; asst. prof Northwestern U. Law Sch., Chgo., 1985—88, assoc. prof, 1988—91, prof., 1991—95, dean, 1995—. Mem. planning com. Northwestern U. Corporate Counsel Inst., Northwestern U. Corp. Counsel Ctr. Author: Living in the Children of God, 1991; mng. editor Yale Law Jour., 1980-81; contbr. articles to profl. jours. Recipient Isidore Brown Thesis Prize, Princeton U., 1975. Mem.: Am. Law Dean's Assn. (dir. 1998—), AMR Rsch., Inc. (dir. 1998, audit com. 2000—, compensation com. 2000—), Am. Bar Assn. (dir. 1995—, exec. com. 1998—, treas. 2000—), Phi Beta Kappa. Office: Northwestern U Sch Law Office of Dean 357 E Chicago Ave Chicago IL 60611-3059 Office Phone: 312-503-8460. Office Fax: 801-650-6873. Business E-Mail: d-van2@law.northwestern.edu.

VAN ZANDT, STEVEN, actor, musician, radio personality; b. Winthrop, Mass., Nov. 22, 1950; m. Maureen Santoro. Guitarist E-Street Band, 1975—84, 1999—; host/D.J. Little Steven's Underground Garage, Syndicated Radio, 2002—. Actor: (TV series) The Sopranos, 1999—2007 (Outstanding Performance by an Ensemble in a Drama Series, SAG, 2008); musician: (albums) Men Without Women, 1982, Voices of America, 1984, Sun City, 1985, Freedom - No Compromise, 1987, Revolution, 1989, Born Again Savage, 1999. Office: c/o The Endeavor Agy 10th Fl 9601 Wilshire Blvd Beverly Hills CA 90212

VAN ZANTEN, FRANK VELDHUYZEN, library director; b. Heemstede, The Netherlands, Oct. 21, 1932; came to U.S., 1946, naturalized, 1953; s. Adrian V. and Cornelia (Van Eesteren) Van Z.; m. Lois Ruth Holkeboer, June 17, 1961; children: Kiki Maria, Lili Roxanne, Amy Suzanne. AB, Calvin Coll., Mich., 1959; postgrad., U. Wash., 1960; MA in L.S, U. Mich., 1961. Cataloger, extension project asst. Mich. State Library, Lansing, 1961-62; dir. Dickinson County (Mich.) Library, 1962-65, Mid-Peninsula Library Fedn., Iron Mountain, Mich., 1963-65, St. Clair County (Mich.) Library, 1965-68, Tucson Pub. Library, 1968-73; library cons. Ill. State Library, Springfield, 1973-75, asso. dir. for library devel., 1975-78; dir. Mid-Hudson Library System, Poughkeepsie, NY, 1978-95; ret., 1996. Served with AUS, 1953-55. Mem. ALA, N.Y. Libr. Assn. Home: 138 Wilbur Blvd Poughkeepsie NY 12603-4635 Personal E-mail: fvzcolors@aol.com.

VAN ZELST, THEODORE WILLIAM, civil engineer, engineering company executive; b. Chgo., May 11, 1923; s. Theodore Walter and Wilhelmina (Oomens) Van Z.; m. Louann Hurter, Dec. 29, 1951; children: Anne, Jean, David. BS, U. Calif., Berkeley, 1944; BS in Naval Sci., Northwestern U., 1944, BAS., 1945, MS in Civil Engring., 1948. Registered profl. engr., Ill. Pres., Soil Testing Services, Inc., Chgo., 1948-52; pres. Soiltest, Inc., Chgo., 1948-78, chmn. bd., 1978-80; sec., dir. Exploration Data Cons., Inc., 1980-82; exec. v.p. Cenco Inc., Chgo., 1962-77, vice chmn., 1975-77, also dir., 1962-77. Bd. dirs. Minann, Inc., Testing Sci., Inc., Van Zelst, Inc.; chmn. bd. dirs. Envirotech Svcs., Inc., 1983-85; sec., bd. dirs. Van Zelst, Inc. Wadsworth, Ill., 1983—; pres. Geneva-Pacific Corp., 1969-83, Geneva Resources, Inc., 1983-91. Treas. Internat. Road Fedn., 1961-64, sec., 1964-79, dir., 1973-88, vice chmn., 1980-87; pres. Internat. Road Edn. Found., 1978-80, 87-88, hon. life bd. dirs., 1988—; bd. dirs. Chgo. Acad. Scis., 1983-86, v.p., 1985-86, hon. dir., 1986-2007; bd. dirs. Pres.'s Assn., Chgo., 1985-86, Friends of Mitchell Mus., 2003-2004; Asian art coun. Art Inst. Chgo., 2004—. Lt. j.g. USNR, 1944—46. Recipient Service award Northwestern U., 1970, Merit award, 1974, Alumni medal, 1989, Svc. award U. Wis., 1971, La Sallian award, 1975; named Disting. Engring. Alumnus, U. Calif., Berkeley, 2002. Mem. ASCE (Chgo. Civil Engr. of Yr., 1988), Nat. Soc. Profl. Engrs., Western Soc. Engrs., Evanston C. of C. (v.p. 1969-73), Ovid Esbach Soc. (pres. 1968-80), Northwestern U. Alumni Assn., Tau Beta Pi, Sigma Xi. Clubs: Economic, North Shore. Achievements include invention of engring. testing equipment for soil, rock, concrete and asphalt; co-invention of Swing-wing for supersonic aircraft. Home: 1213 Wagner Rd Glenview IL 60025-3297 Office: PO Box 582 Glenview IL 60025-0582

VANZURA, LIZ (ELIZABETH K. VANZURA), automotive executive; b. May 1964; m. Rick Vanzura; children: Danielle, Jacqueline. BS, GMI Engring. and Mgmt. Inst.; MBA, Harvard U. With GM Corp., 1984—96; dir. mktg. Volkswagen of Am., 1996—2000; global dir. mktg. Hummer GM Corp., 2001—06, mktg. dir. Cadillac, 2006—08. Exec. bd. mem. Internat. Automotive Advt. Awards. Recipient Top Women to Watch Award, Advertising Age, 2001, All Star award, Automotive News, 1999, 2000; named Marketer of Yr., Advertising Age, 1998; named one of Top 100 Mktg. Profls., 1999, 50 Women to Watch, Wall St. Jour., 2006.

VAN ZWEDEN, JAAP, conductor, music director; b. Amsterdam, Dec. 12, 1960; m. Aaltje van Buuren, 1983; children: Anna-Sophie, Daniel, Benjamin, Alexander. Student, Julliard Sch., NYC. Violinist, concertmaster Royal Concertgebouw Orch., 1979—95; chief condr. Netherlands Symphony Orch., Enschede, 1996—2000, Residentie Orch., The Hague, Netherlands, 2000—05; chief condr., artistic dir. Netherlands Radio Philharm., Hilversum, 2005—; music dir. designate Dallas Symphony Orch., 2007—08, music dir., 2008—; chief condr. Royal Flemish Philharm., Antwerp, Belgium, 2008—. Guest condr. St. Louis Symphony Orch., Orchestre National de France, Munich Philharm., Rotterdam Philharm., Oslo Philharm., St. Petersburg Philharm., Tokyo Philharm., Hong Kong Philharm., London Philharm., City of Birmingham Symphony Orch., West German Radio Symphony Orch. Cologne, Danish Radio Orch. Co-founder found. for autistic children Papageno Found., Netherlands. Office: Dallas Symphony Orch 2301 Flora St Dallas TX 75201 Office Phone: 214-871-4000.*

VARADARAJ, KULANDAIAPPAN, medical researcher, educator; s. Nanjappan Kulandaiappan and Palanisamy Subbulakshmi; m. Sindhu Kumari; children: Murali, Sangeeth. BS, Madras U., India, 1980, MSc, 1982; MPhil, Bharathiar U., Coimbatore, India, 1983; PhD, Sch. Biol. Scis., Madurai Kamaraj U., Tamil Nadu, India, 1991. Educator SUNY Rsch. Found., Stony Brook, 1994—2008, radiation safety officer, physiology and biophysics, 1994—, rsch. asst. prof., 1995—, mgr., confocal microscopy facility, 2003—, co-investigator, 2005—, prin. investigator, 2006—, sr. rsch. scientist, 2007—. Nominee Young Scientist award, Coun. Sci. and Indsl. Rsch., New Delhi, 1989; Internat. Sci. award, Asian Molecular Biologist Assn., 1987, Rsch. grant, NIH, Bethesda, Md., 2005—, Indsl. grant, Alcon Rsch. Ltd., Ft. Worth, 2006—08. Mem.: Internat. Soc. Eye Rsch. (San Francisco), Assn. Rsch. Vision and Ophthalmology (Rockville, Md.). Achievements include discovery of severity of lens cataract depend on the quantity of mutant AQP0 protein in the lens fiber cells; denaturants or cosolvents can improve amplification of GC-rich satellite DNA by PCR; sodium-dependent glucose co-transporter expression in mammalian lens; sodium-dependent Vitamin C co-transporter expression in mammalian lens fiber cells; aquaporin 1 begins to express in lens epithelial cells as pupillary membrane; lens epithelial cells as papillary membrane vasculature begins to regress; development of transgenic mouse model which expresses human AQP1 tagged with green fluorescent protein in the lens fiber cells; discovery of adhesion function of aquaporin 0 protein. Office: SUNY Physiology & Biophysics Dept BST-6 Rm#165 Stony Brook NY 11794-8661

VARADARAJAN, SRINIDHI, computer scientist; PhD in Computer Sci., SUNY, Stony Brook, 2000. Dir. Terascale Computing Facility Va. Polytechnic Inst. and State U., asst. prof. computer sci. Named one of Top 100 Young Innovators, MIT Tech. Review, 2004. Achievements include architect of System X, the third fastest supercomputer in the world. Office: Terascale Computing Facility Va Polytechnic Inst and State U Blacksburg VA 24061 Business E-Mail: srinidhi@cd.vt.edu.

VARAKIN, DONALD ALEXANDER, psychology professor; married. PhD, Vanderbilt U., Nashville, Tenn., 2006. Asst. prof. Knox Coll., Galesburg, Ill., 2006—.

VARANASI, KRIPA KIRAN, research scientist; b. Bhimavaram, Andhra Pradesh, India, Jan. 2, 1977; s. Jagan Mohan Rao Varanasi and Suryakantham Kompella; m. Manasa Kambhampati, Dec. 13, 2004. B in Tech., Indian Inst. Tech., Madras, Chennai, India, 1998; MS in Mech. Engring., MIT, Cambridge, 2002, MS in Elec. Engring. and Computer Sci., 2002, PhD in Mech. Engring., 2004. Grad. rschr. MIT, Cambridge, 1998—2004; rsch. scientist Gen. Electric Global Rsch. Ctr., Nanotechnology Advanced Tech. Program, Energy and Propulsion Technologies, Niskayuna, NY, 2004—. Summer intern Bajaj Auto Ltd., Pune, Maharastra, India, 1996—96; student rschr. Machine Dynamics Lab, Indian Inst. Tech., Madras, Chennai, 1997—98, Thermodynamics Lab, Indian Inst. Tech., Madras, Chennai, 1997—98, Machine Elements Lab, Indian Inst. Tech., Madras, Chennai, 1997—98; cons. Indian Space Rsch. Orgn., 1997; cons. Precision Engring. Rsch. Group MIT, Cambridge, 1998—2004; cons. Rapid Autonomous Machining Lab, 2002; cons. New Way Air Bearings, Aston, Pa., 1999, Optikos Inc., Cambridge, 2000, Laser Interferometer Gravity Wave Obs. (LIGO), MIT/Caltech, Cambridge, 2003—04; vis. rschr., cons. Silicon Valley Group Inc., Ridgefield, Conn., 2000—01. Contbr. articles to profl. jours. Vol., blood donor Red Cross, 1994—98. Recipient Best Sci. Project award, Dept. Edn., A.P., India, 1988—92, Math. Olympiad award, Assn. Math. Tchrs., India, 1993, Inventor award, GE, 2005, GE Mgmt. award for rsch. in nanotechnology, GE Rsch. Ctr., 2005; named Best Tech. Project of Yr., 2005; scholar, Eveready Welfare Svcs., 1994—98, H.E.H. Nizam Trust, India, 1998; Merit scholar, Dept. Telecom., India, 1989—94, Govt. Andhra Pradesh, India, 1989—94, Nat. Merit scholar, Govt. India, 1994—98, Excel scholar, Excel Industries India, Ltd., 1998. Mem.: ASME (mem. nanomanufacturing com. Nanotechnology Inst.), Internat. Soc. for Optical Engring., Am. Soc. Precision Engring., Materials Rsch. Soc., Sigma Xi. Achievements include patents pending for method and apparatus for damping vibrations using low-wave-speed media; area of nanotechnology; area of energy at GE Research; research in Low-Wave-Speed Materials at MIT; nanotextured superhydrophobic and superhydrophilic surfaces at GE Research. Avocations: music, reading, sports, documentaries, movies, cooking. Office: General Electric Global Research Center One Research Circle Niskayuna NY 12309 Home: 100 Memorial Dr Apt 223B Cambridge MA 02142-1327 Office Fax: 518-387-7292. Personal E-mail: kripa@alum.mit.edu. Business E-Mail: varanasi@research.ge.com.

VARANASI, VENU GOPAL, biomedical researcher; s. Murali and Padma Varanasi. BS in chemistry, U. South Fla., Tampa, 1998; MS, U. Fla., Gainesville, 2003, PhD, 2004. Postdoc. fellow U. Calif., San Francisco, 2004—. Acad. advisor U. Calif., 2006—. Contbr. articles to profl. jours. (NIH Career Devel. award, 2007). Vol. Hand & Feet Bapt. Ch., Knoxville, Tenn., 2001—04. Recipient First Pl., UCSF Sch. Dentistry, 2006; Hawkins fellowship, U. Fla., 1998, Rsch. fellowship, Oak Ridge Nat. Lab., 2000—04. Mem.: AIChE, Internat. Assn. Dental Rsch., Phi Kappa Phi. Hindu. Achievements include research in si ions on production of bone. Office: Univ CA San Francisco 707 Parnassus Ave D2244 MS 0758 San Francisco CA 94143-0758 Office Fax: 415-476-0858. Personal E-mail: vvaranasi2002@yahoo.com. Business E-Mail: venu.varanasi@ucsf.edu.

VARAT, JONATHAN D., law educator, dean; b. 1945; BA, U. Pa., Phila., 1967, JD, 1972. Law clk. to judge Walter Mansfield U.S. Ct. Appeals (2d cir.), NYC, 1972-73; law clk. to justice Byron White U.S. Supreme Ct., Washington, 1973-74; assoc. O'Melveny & Myers, Los Angeles, 1974-76; acting prof. UCLA Sch. Law, 1976-81, prof., 1981—, assoc. dean, 1982-83, 91-92, dean, 1998—2003. Co-author: Constitutional Law: Cases and Materials, 2005. Office: UCLA Sch Law PO Box 951476 Los Angeles CA 90095-1476

VARCOE, JEFFREY JOHN, food service executive; PhD, U. Minn., Mpls., 2002. Dir. R & D Schwan Food Co., Marshall, Minn., 2005—07, v.p. food safety & quality, 2007—. Pres. Canby Econ. Devel. Authority, Minn., 2004—08. Office: Schwan Food Co Marshall MN 56258

VARDA, AGNES, scriptwriter, film director; b. Brussels, May 30, 1928; d. Eugene Jean and Christiane (Pasquet) Varda; m. Jacques Demy, Jan. 8, 1962; children: Rosalie Demy, Mathieu Demy. Student, Coll. de Sète, U. Paris, Ecole du Louvre. Ofcl. photographer Théâtre Nat. Populaire, 1951-61; filmmaker, dir., 1954—. Dir.(film): La Pointe Courte, 1954, Cléo de 5 a 7, 1961, Le Bonheur, 1964, Les Créatures, 1966, Lions Love, 1969, Nausicaa, 1970, Daguerréotypes, 1975, L'Une Chante l'Autre Pas, 1976, Mur Murs, 1980, Documenteur, 1981, Sans Toit ni Loi (Vagabond), 1985, Kung-Fu-Master, 1987, Jane B. par Agnès V, 1987, Jacquot de Nantes, 1990, Les Demoiselles ont eu 25 ans, 1998, L'univers de Jacques Demy, 1993, Les Cent et une Nuits, 1994, The Gleaners and I, 2000, Two Years Later, 2002, The Beaches Of Agnes, 2008, (short films): O Saisons, O Chateaux, 1957, L'Opéra-Mouffe, 1958, Du côté de la côte, 1958, Salut les Cubains, 1963, Elsa la Rose, 1966, Uncle Yanco, 1967, Black Panthers, 1968, Réponse de Femmes, 1975, Plaisir d'Amour en Iran, 1976, Ulysse, 1982, Les Dites Cariatides, 1984, 7P. cuis., s de b., 1985, T'as de beaux escaliers. tu sais, 1986, Le Lion Volatil, 2003, Ydessa, the bears and etc..., 2004, (video installations) Venise Biennale, 2003; exhibitions include video installations Galerie Martine Aboucaya Paris, 2005, Found. Cartier Paris ILLE ET EVE, 2006, Pantheon "LESJUSTES" THE RIGHTEOUS, 2007. Decorated comdr. des Arts et des Lettres, comdr. de l'Ordre du Mérite, comdr. de la Légion d'Honneur; recipient Prix Méliès, 1962, 2000, Prix Louis Delluc, 1965, David Selznick award, 1965, Bronze Lion, Venice Festival, 1964, Golden Lion, 1985, Silver Bear, Berlin Festival, 1965, 1st prize Oberhausen, Popular Univs. Jury, 1970, Grand Prix Taormina, Sicily, 1977, Golden Plaque award, Chgo., 1993, French Cesar award, 1986, Best European Documentary, 2000, Cesar of honor, 2001, Best Non-fiction Film award, N.Y.C. Film Critics, 2001, Documentary award, L.A. Film Critics, 2002, Pioneer award, Assn. des Critiques de Cinema, L.A., 2002, Best Documentary award, U.S. Nat. Assn. Film Critics, Washington, 2002, Pioneer award, L.A. IDA, Cesar Best Documentary award, 2008. Office Phone: 33 0 143 22 66 00.

VARDALOS, NIA, actress, screenwriter; b. Winnipeg, Can., Sept. 24, 1962; d. Constantine and Doreen Vardalos; m. Ian Gomez, 1993. Attended, Ryerson U. Actor: (films) No Experience Necessary, 1996, Men Seeking Women, 1997, Short Cinema, 1998, Meet Prince Charming, 1999, My Life in Ruins, 2009, (actor, writer) My Big Fat Greek Wedding, 2002, (actor, writer, exec. prodr.) Connie and Carla, 2004, (actor, dir., writer) I Hate Valentine's Day, 2009, (voice): (TV series) Team Knight Rider, 1997, (guest appearance): High Incident, 1996, Common Law, 1996, The Drew Carey Show, 1997, Boy Meets World, 1998, It's Like, You Know, 1999, Two Guys, a Girl, and a Pizza Place, 1999, Curb Your Enthusiasm, 2000. Office: c/o Brillstein Grey Mgmt 9150 Wilshire Blvd Ste 350 Beverly Hills CA 90212*

VARDAMAN, JOHN WESLEY, lawyer; b. Montgomery, Ala., Apr. 22, 1940; s. John Wesley and Elizabeth (Merrill) V.; m. Marianne Fay, June 14, 1969; children: Thomas, Shannon, John Wesley III, Davis. BA, Washington & Lee U., 1962; JD, Harvard U., 1965. Bar: D.C. 1966, U.S. Dist. Ct. (D.C.) 1967, U.S. Supreme Ct Justice. 1970. Law clk. to justice Hugo Black U.S. Supreme Ct., 1965-66; assoc. Wilmer, Cutler & Pickering, Washington, 1966-70; ptnr. Williams & Connolly, Washington, 1970—; gen. counsel U.S. Golf Assn., Washington, 1999—2003, mem. exec. com., 2003—04. Bd. trustees Washington and Lee U., 2005—. Contbr. articles to profl. jours. Mem. ABA, Am. Coll. Trial Lawyers, U.S. Golf Assn., Congl. Country Club (Bethesda, Md.). Baptist. Avocation: golf. Office: Williams & Connolly 725 12th St NW Washington DC 20005-5901

VARDIN, PATRICIA ANNE, education educator; b. Chgo. d. William and Catherine Vardin; m. Thomas W. Vris; 1 child, Elizabeth Vardin Newman. BS, U. Wis.; Doctorate, M, Columbia U. Tchr's. Coll., 1984. Adj. assoc. prof. Columbia U. Tchr's Coll., NYC, 1983—84; assoc. prof. St Francis Coll., Dept Edn., Bklyn. Heights, NY, 1992—99, Manhattanville Coll., Purchase, NY, 2002—, chmn. early childhood edn., 2002—. Editor: Children's Rights: Contemporary Perspectives, 1979; author: Internat. Encyclopedia of Education, 1984, Montessori Life, 2003. Founder, bd chair New Amsterdam Sympony Orchestra, NYC, 1976—80; bd. chair New Amsterdam Symphony Orchestra, NYC, 2004—; mem. Norwalk Hosp., Norwalk, Conn., 2001—; ednl. coord. Armstrong Chamber Concerts Music Enrichment Program; co-chair MEP Gala. Mem.: Westchester Assn. for the Edn. of Young Children (bd. dirs.), Nat. Assn. Edn. of Young Children. Episcopalian. Avocations: swimming, sailing, violin, cmty. vol. Office: Manhattanville Coll 2900 Purchase St Purchase NY 10577 E-mail: vardinvrisp@mville.edu.

VAREJAO, ANDERSON FRANCA, professional basketball player; b. Santa Teresa, Brazil, Sept. 28, 1982; Profl. basketball player F.C. Barcelona, 2001—04, Euroleague, 2001—04; draft pick Orlando Magic, Fla., 2004; forward-ctr. Cleve. Cavaliers, 2004—. Mem. Brazil Jr. Nat. Team; mem. Brazilian Nat. Team Goodwill Games, 2001, World Championships, 2002. Named MVP, Brazilian League, 2001. Office: Cleve Cavaliers Quicken Loans Arena One Center Court Cleveland OH 44115-4001*

VARELA, ALAN MARK, state agency administrator, lawyer; b. Santa Fe, NMex., 1962; BA in Philosophy and Psychology, Univ. NMex., JD, 1987; graduate Leadership for 21st Century, Harvard JFK Sch. Govt. Prin. Varela Law Office, Albuquerque; engring. dept. Qwest Comm.; policy, law dept. US West Comm.; now exec. dir. State Workers' Compensation Adminstrn., Albuquerque, 2004—. Mem.: NMex Hispanic Bar Assn. (past pres.), Hispanic Nat. Bar Assn. (pres. 2004—05, regional pres., NMex, Utah, v.p., pres.-elect). Office: Workers' Compensation Adminstrn 2410 Centre Ave SE PO Box 27198 Albuquerque NM 87106 Office Phone: 505-841-6007. Office Fax: 505-841-6009. Business E-Mail: a.varela@state.nm.us.

VARELA, MANUEL FRANCISCO, molecular biologist, microbiologist, biochemist; b. Santa Fe, Dec. 3, 1962; s. Phil and Josephine (Flores) V.; m. Ann Frances Higgins, Apr. 6, 1990. BA in Biochemistry, U. N.Mex., 1987, MS in Biochemistry, 1989, PhD in Biomed. Scis., 1994. Rsch. analyst U. N.Mex. Sch. Medicine, Albuqueque, 1983-89; postdoctoral fellow Harvard U. Med. Sch., Boston, 1994-97; asst. prof. biology Eastern N.Mex. U., Portales, 1997—2003, assoc. prof. biology, 2003—08, prof. biology, 2008—. NSF grantee, 1999-2001, NIH, 2001—; rsch. fellow Am. Soc. for Cell Biology, 1991, NIH postdoctoral fellow, 1994-97. Mem. AAAS, Am. Soc. for Microbiology, Am. Soc. Biochemistry and Molecular Biology, Phi Kappa Phi, Sigma Xi. Avocations: photography, golf. Office: Eastern NMex U Dept Biology Sta #33 Roosevelt Hall Rm 101 1500 S Ave K Portales NM 88130 Office Phone: 575-562-2464. Business E-Mail: Manuel.Varela@enmu.edu.

VARELLA, HAZEL L., historian, educator; b. Beverly, Mass., Dec. 17, 1932; d. John Luke and Olivia McDonald Luke; m. M David Varella, June 24, 1961; children: John David, James Robert. BS, Bridgewater State Coll., 1954, MEd, 1956; MA, Boston U., 1962. Chmn. social studies Easton (Mass.) Sch. Sys., 1956—97; adj. faculty Bridgewater State Coll., Mass., 1998—; sr. lectr. Curry Coll., Milton, Mass., 1988—. Adv. placement cons. Coll. Bd., Princeton, 1988—. Author: (book) History of Easton V II, 1972, (pamphlets) Growing Up at Sheep Pasture, 1976. Trustee North Easton Savings Bank, 1996—; dir. Ames Free Libr., Easton, 1989—. Recipient Hon. Grand Marshall, Town of Easton, Mass., 2000, Ind. Study Scholar, NEH, Washington, DC, 1984, Outstanding Svc. award, Easton Lions Club, 1997, Disting. Svc. award, Curry Coll., 2004. Mem.: Easton Hist. Soc. (sec., pres. 1969—71, 1990—94), Delta Kappa Gamma. Episcopalian. Avocations: reading, travel. Home: 121 Center St North Easton MA 02356 Home Phone: 508-238-3614. Personal E-mail: mdhvarella@comcast.net.

VARELLAS, SANDRA MOTTE, judge; b. Anderson, SC, Oct. 17, 1946; d. James E. and Helen Lucille (Gilliam) Motte; m. James John Varellas, July 3, 1971; children: James John III, David Todd. BA, Winthrop U., 1968; MA, U. Ky., 1970, JD, 1975. Bar: Ky. 1975, Fla. 1976, U.S. Dist. Ct. (ea. dist.) Ky. 1975, U.S. Ct. Appeals (6th cir.) 1976, U.S. Supreme Ct. 1978. Instr. Midway Coll., Ky., 1970-72; adj. prof. U. Ky. Coll. Law, Lexington, 1976-78; instr. dept. bus. adminstrn. U. Ky., Lexington, 1976-78; ptnr. Varellas, Pratt & Cooley, Lexington, 1975-93, Varellas & Pratt, Lexington, 1993-97, Varellas & Varellas, Lexington, 1998—. Fayette County judge exec., Ky., 1980—; hearing officer Ky. Natural Resources and Environ. Protection Cabinet, Frankfort, 1984-88; bd. trustees Lexington Network 1994-98, 2002-2004, sec., 1994-98. Committeewoman Ky. Young Dems., Frankfort, 1977-80; pres. Fayette County Young Dems., Lexington, 1977; bd. dirs. Ky. Dem. Women's Club, Frankfort, 1980-84, bd. dirs., Bluegrass Estate Planning Coun., 1995-98; grad. Leadership Lexington, 1981; chairwoman Profl. Women's Forum, Lexington, Ky., 1985-86, bd. dirs., 1984-87, Aequum award com., 1989-92; mem. devel. coun. Midway Coll., 1990-92; co-chair Gift Club Com., 1992; mem. pub. svc. sector com. United Way of Bluegrass, 2004. Named Outstanding Young Dem. Woman, Ky. Young Dems., Frankfort, 1977, Outstanding Former Young Dem., Ky. Young Dems., 1983. Mem. Ky. Bar Assn. (treas. young lawyers divsn. 1978-79, long range planning com. 1988-89), Fla. Bar, Fayette County Bar Assn. (treas. 1977-78, bd. govs. 1978-80), LWV (nominating com. 1984-85), Greater Lexington C. of C. (legis. affairs com. 1994-95, bd.d irs. coun. smaller enterprises 1992-95), The Lexington Forum (bd. dirs. 1996-99), Lexington Philharm. Guild (bd. dirs. 1979-81, 86-2006), Nat. Assn. Women Bus. Owners (chmn. cmty. liaison/govt. affairs com. 1992-93); Clubs: Creative Camera Club (bd. dirs. 2008-). Office: Varellas & Varellas 167 W Main St Ste 1310 Lexington KY 40507-1398 Office Phone: 859-252-4473. Business E-Mail: sandra@varellaslaw.com.

VARESE, FEDERICO, sociology professor; b. Italy, Nov. 12, 1965; m. Galia Kravtchenko. Laurea, Bologna U., Italy, 1990; PhM, Cambridge U., Eng., 1991; PhD, Oxford U., Eng., 1997. Rsch. fellow Oxford U., 1996-2000; William H. Orrick asst. vis. prof. Yale U., New Haven, 2000—02; asst. prof. Williams Coll., Williamstown, 2002—03; sr. lectr. in criminology Ctr. for Criminological Rsch. U. Oxford, England, 2003—06, prof. criminology Law Faculty, 2006—; dir. Extra-legal Governance Inst. Oxford U., 2007—. Author: The Russian Mafia, 2001; editor-in-chief, Global Crime, 2007-. Cpl. maj. paratrooper Italian armed forces, 1992-93. Grantee Internat. Consortium for Polit. and Social Rsch., 1997; Nuffield Coll. studentship, 1991; Lester B. Pearson scholar Ministry of Fgn. Affairs, 1982; receipient Ed. A. Hewett Book Prize, Am. Assoc. for the Advancement of Slavic Studies, in conj. with Nat. Coun. for Eurasian and East European Rsch., 2002. Mem. Am. Polit. Sci. Assn., Am. Sociol. Assn. Office: Linacre Coll Univ Oxford St Cross Rd Oxford OX1 3JA England Office Phone: 44-1865-281150. Business E-Mail: federico.varese@linacre.ox.ac.uk.

VARET, MICHAEL A., lawyer; b. NYC, Mar. 9, 1942; s. Guster V. and Frances B. (Goldberg) V.; m. Elizabeth R. Varet, June 3, 1973; 3 children. BS in Econs., U. Pa., 1962; LLB, Yale U., 1965. Bar: N.Y. 1966, U.S. Supreme Ct. 1975, U.S. Dist. Ct. (ea. and so. dists.) N.Y. 1975, U.S. Tax Ct. 1975, U.S. Claims Ct. 1975, U.S. Ct. Appeals (2d cir.) 1975. Mem., chmn. Varet & Fink PC (formerly Milgrim Thomajan & Lee PC), NYC, 1982—95; mem. DLP Piper LLP (US), NYC, 1995—2009, sr. counsel, 2009—. Bd. dir., presiding dir. and chmn. exec. com., audit com., compensation com., Salisbury Bank and Trust Co., Lakeville, Conn., Salisbury Bancorp, Inc., Lakeville. Trustee Montefiore Med. Ctr., Bronx, NY, 1980-92, mem. exec. com., 1985-92; bd. dirs. Sem. Libr. Corp. Jewish Theol. Sem., NYC, 1983-87, United Jewish Appeal-Fedn. Jewish Philanthropies of Greater NY, Inc., 1979-86, coun. of overseers, 1986-95, bd. overseers, 2005—; bd. dirs. Mosholu Preservation Corp., Bronx, 1982-88, Yale Law Sch. Fund, 2000—; bd. overseers Jewish Theol. Sem., 1982-90, Jewish Publ. Soc. Am., 1986-96, exec. com., 1989-96; exec. com. Yale Law Sch. Assn., 1990-93; bd. dirs. B. de Rothschild Found. for Advancement Sci. in Israel, 1986—, Piatigorsky Found., 1990—, Scenic Hudson, Inc., 2003-06; v.p., sec., bd. dirs. Am. Found. for Basic Rsch. in Israel, 1990—; dir. Plz. Jewish Cmty. Chapel, 2001—; bd. dirs. Am. and Internat. Friends of Victoria and Albert Mus., Inc., 1997-99, treas., 1997-99. Mem. ABA, N.Y. State Bar Assn., Assn. of Bar of City of N.Y. (bd. dirs., exec. com. 1971-75), Internat. Fiscal Assn., Internat. Tax Planning Assn., Yale Club of N.Y.C., Lotos Club. Democrat. Office: DLP Piper LLP (US) 1251 Ave of Americas New York NY 10020-1104 Office Phone: 212-335-4650. Business E-Mail: mavaret@varet.com, michael.varet@dlapiper.com.

VARGA, PAUL C., beverage products executive; b. Louisville, 1964; m. Melissa Varga; 2 children. BA business administration, finance, U Ky.; MBA, Purdue U. Various marketing positions Brown-Forman Corp., 1987—96, sr. v.p., 1996—2003, global chief mktg. officer, Brown-Forman Spirits, 2000—03, pres., CEO, Brown-Forman Beverages, 2003—05, pres., CEO, 2005—07, CEO, 2005—, chmn., 2007—. Office: Brown-Forman Corp 850 Dixie Hwy Louisville KY 40210 Office Phone: 502-585-1100. Office Fax: 502-774-6633.*

VARGA, RICHARD STEVEN, retired mathematics professor; b. Cleve., Oct. 9, 1928; s. Steven and Ella (Krejcs) V.; m. Esther Marie Pfister, Sept. 22, 1951; 1 dau., Gretchen Marie. BS, Case Inst. Tech., Cleve., 1950; AM, Harvard U., Cambridge, Mass., 1951, PhD, 1954; doctorate (hon.), U. Karlsruhe, Germany, 1991, U. Lille, France, 1993. With Bettis Atomic Power Lab., Westinghouse Electric Co., 1954-60, adv. mathematician, 1959-60; prof. math. Case Inst. Tech. (now Case We. Res. U.), Cleve., 1960—69; univ. prof. math. Kent State U., Ohio, 1969—2006, dir. rsch. Inst. for Computational Math., 1980—; ret., 2006. Cons. to govt. and industry. Author: Matrix Iterative Analysis, 1962, Functional Analysis and Approximation Theory in Numerical Analysis, 1971, Topics in Polynomial and Rational Interpolation and Approximation, 1982, Zeros of Sections of Power Series, 1983, Scientific Computation on Mathematical Problems and Conjectures, 1990, Matrix Iterative Analysis, 2d revised and expanded edit., 2000, Gersgorin and his Circles, 2004; editor: Numerical Solution of Field Problems in Continuum Physics, 1970, Padé and Rational Approximations: Theory and Applications, 1977, Rational Approximations and Interpolation, 1984, Computational Methods and Function Theory, 1990, Numerical Linear Algebra, 1993; editor-in-chief. Numerische Math., 1988-2002, Electronic Transactions Numerical Analysis; mem. editl. bd. Linear Algebra and Applications, Constructive Approximation, Computational Mathematics (China), Numerical Algorithms, Analysis, Electronic Jour. Linear Algebra, Comms. in Applied Analysis. Recipient Rsch. award Sigma Xi, 1965, von Humboldt prize, 1982, Pres.' medal Kent State U., 1981, Hans Schneider prize, 2005; Guggenheim fellow, 1963; Fairchild scholar, 1974. Home: 7065 Arcadia Dr Cleveland OH 44129-6065 Office: Kent State U Inst Computational Mat Kent OH 44242-0001 Business E-Mail: varga@math.kent.edu.

VARGAS, ELIZABETH, newscaster; b. Paterson, NJ, Sept. 6, 1962; m. Marc Cohn, July 20, 2002; children: Zachary Raphael, Samuel Wyatt; 2 stepchildren. BA in Journalism, U. Mo., Columbia. Reporter/anchor KOMU-TV, Columbia, Mo.; reporter KTVN-TV, Reno; lead reporter KTVK-TV, Phoenix, 1986—89; reporter/anchor WBBM-TV, Chgo., 1989—93; corr./anchor NBC News, NYC, 1993—97; corr. Dateline, NBC, NYC, 1993—96; news anchor, substitute co-host Good Morning Am., NBC, NYC, 1996—97; corr. ABC News, NYC, 1997—2005, co-anchor, 20/20 newsmagazine, 2004—; interim anchor ABC World News Tonight, NYC, 2005, co-anchor, 2006. Recipient Emmy award for Outstanding Instant Coverage of News Story (Elian Gonzales case), 2000. Office: ABC News Press Rels Fl 2 47 W 66th St New York NY 10023-6201

VARGAS, JULIE S., behaviorologist, educator; b. Mpls., Apr. 28, 1938; d. Burrhus Frederic and Eve (Blue) Skinner; m. Ernest A. Vargas, June 30, 1962; children: Lisa Kristina Tillman, Justine Unger. AB in Music, Harvard U., Cambridge, Mass., 1960; MA in Music Edn., Columbia U., NYC, 1962; PhD in Ednl. Rsch., U. Pitts., 1969. Tchr. third grade Spense Sch., NYC, 1960-61; tchr. fourth grade Monroeville (Pa.) Area Schs., 1961-62; prof. ednl. psychology W.Va. U., Morgantown, 1966—2003. Pres. B.F. Skinner Found., Cambridge, Mass., 1988—; cons. New Century Edn. Corp., Piscataway, N.J., 1975-88. Author: Writing Worthwhile Behavioral Objectives, 1973, Behavioral Psychology for Teachers, 1977; co-author: Teaching Behavior to Infants, 1990, Behaviour Analysis for Effective for Teaching, 2009; author: (software tutorial) Something to Think About (Reading), 1986; chief editor: The Behavioral Analyst jour., 1979-81. Vis. scholar Harvard U., 1994. Mem. Assn. for Behavior Analysis (pres. 1989-90), Internat. Soc. for Behaviorology (sec. 1992-95, chmn. bd. publs. 1995—). Democrat. Avocations: classical guitar playing, amateur violoist, orchestra, sailing. Home: 11 Old Dee Rd Cambridge MA 02138-4633 Office Phone: 617-661-9209. Personal E-mail: julie.vargas@bfskinner.org.

VARGAS, LOUIS F., marketing executive, author, speaker; s. Rafael A. and Ligia M. Vargas; 3 children. MSc in Program Internat. Adminstrn., U. Southern Calif., BA, 1985. Pres. Nat. Mkg. Comm. Cons., Calabasas, 2002—. Cons. Latin Bus. Assn., LA, 2006, Nat. Mktg. & Comm. Corp., LA, 2002—; bd. dirs. US Capital Group, Rancho Cucamonga, Calif., 2000—; bd. dirs. cons. Nat. Coolar Sys., Las Vegas, Nev., 2003—; cons. & trainer Westcoast Ins., Rancho Cucamonga. Contbr. articles to profl. jours. Mem. WorldVision Internat., Spokane, 1998—2008; bus. adv. coun. mem. Nat. Rep. Congl. Com., Washington, 2006—08; vol. Prison Fellowship Ministries, Northridge, Calif., 2001—05; adv. bd. USC Mex.-Am. Alumni Found., LA, 2006—08; mem. Hispanic Adv. Coun., LA, 2007—08. Recipient Presdl. Comm. award, Exec. Coun. Nat. Rep. Com., 2008. Mem.: Inc. Mag., Latin Bus. Assn. Independent. Avocations: travel, photography, reading, writing. Office: PO Box 8961 Brea CA 92822-5961 Business E-Mail: nationalgroupofcompanies@yahoo.com.

VARGAS, ROGER IRVIN, entomologist, ecologist; b. Long Beach, Calif., Jan. 10, 1947; s. Roger E. and Olga (Irvin) V.; m. Kathylyn Richardson, July 28, 1990; children: Noelani, Kela. BA in Zoology, U. Calif., Riverside, 1969; MS in Biology, San Diego State U., 1974; PhD in Entomology, U. Hawaii, 1979. Rsch. assoc. U. Hawaii, Honolulu, 1979-80; rsch. entomologist USDA Agr. Rsch. Svc., Honolulu, 1980—. USDA cons. on fruit flies, Mex., Cen. Am., Calif., 1980—. Contbr. articles on ecology, biol. control, behavior, pest mgmt. and mass-rearing of fruit flies to Jour. Econ. Entomology, Environ. Entomology, other profl. publs. Mem. AAAS, Entomol. Soc. Am., Hawaiian Entomol. Soc. Achievements include patent for Mediterranean fruit fly egg collection system, devel. of demographic and ecological data for Hawaiian fruit flies, devel. of mass-rearing techniques for sterile insect technique control of fruit flies. Office: USDA Tropical Fruit and Vegetables Rsch Lab PO Box 2280 Honolulu HI 96804-2280

VARGAS, TRACI JUNELLE, special education educator; b. Wichita, Kans., Mar. 30, 1964; d. Judith Ann and James Dwayne Hilliard (Stepfather); children: Steven Dwayne, Christopher Jordan. BS, Northeastern State U., Tahlequah, Okla., 1997; attending, Northeastern State U. Cert. tchr. Nat. Bd., 2007. Spl. educator Claremore Pub. Schs., Okla., 1997—2009, Broken Arrow Pub. Schs., 2009—. Trainer Crisis Prevention and Intervention, Claremore, 2000—06; presenter Diffusing Volatile Situations in Classrooms Okla. Edn. Assn. Conv. Named Tchr. of Yr., 1998, 2004. Mem.: NEA (corr.), Okla. Edn. Assn. (corr.), Coun. Exceptional Children (corr.). Democrat. Avocations: gardening, reading, interior decorating. Office: Broken Arrow Pub Schs Country Ln 4th 5th Grade Ctr 301 East Omaha Broken Arrow Broken Arrow OK 74012 Home Phone: 918-355-8006; Office Phone: 918-449-5600. Personal E-mail: nanatraci@cox.net. Business E-Mail: tvargas@claremore.k12.ok.us, tvargas@baschools.org.

VARGAS LEGASPI, JUAN, manufacturing executive; b. Aguascalientes, Mex., Feb. 25, 1953; s. Juan Medina and Maria Legaspi De La Luz; m. Martha Perez Carreño; children: Juan, Abraham, Christopher. Bookkeeper, UNAM, Mexico City, 1974-78; diploma in taxes and fin., Inst. of Specialization, Mexico City, 1987; diploma human resources, U. Iberoam., Mexico City, 1979; diploma in fin. analysis, Dun & Bradstreet Inc., 1980; diploma in Econs., Inst. Integration Ibero Am., Mexico City; MBA in Mgmt., Grad. Coll., Mexico City, 1992. Dir. Guantes Vargas, S.Am., 1977—. Chmn. bd. Colegio de Graduados en Alta Direccion, 1995-2000, Centro de Investigaciones sobre la Libre Empresa, A.C., 1990-2000; CEO Grupo Banacci, 1996-2000; fin. cons. in field. Contbr. articles to profl. publs. Cesar Gaviria's bus. assessor Am. States Orgn., 1994-98. Roman Catholic. Avocations: writing, speaking, Karate, soccer. Home: Col Indsl Calz de Guadalupe 392 07800 Mexico City Mexico Office: Guantes Vargas SAm Calzada de Guadalupe 392 Col Industrial 07800 Mexico City Mexico Personal E-mail: juanvargaslegaspi@yahoo.com.

VARGHA, REBECCA BROGDEN, librarian, library association executive; BA, U. NC, Chapel Hill, 1979; MLS, NC Ctrl. U., 1980. Libr. asst. Nat. Humanities Ctr., Rsch. Triangle Park, NC, 1979—80, asst. libr., 1980—87, assoc. libr., 1987—94; info. analyst SAS Inst. Inc., Cary, NC, 1994; sr. rsch. specialist Nortel Networks; adj. faculty U. NC, Chapel Hill, 1996—98; libr. U. NC Sch. Info. & Libr. Sci., Chapel Hill, 2001—. Mem.: ALA, Spl. Librs. Assn. (chair conf. com. 1993, chair elect & chair divsn. cabinet 1996—98, pres. 2006—07, NC ch. archivist, chair networking com., chair scholarships com., chair student & academic rels. com., NC ch. Meritorious Achievement award 1994), Beta Phi Mu. Office: U NC Manning Hall CB #3360 Chapel Hill NC 27599-3360 Office Phone: 919-962-8361. Office Fax: 919-962-8071. Business E-Mail: vargha@ils.unc.edu.

VARGHESE, GEORGE, systems engineer; arrived in UK, 2008; s. Varghese Chengadakary and Mariyakutty Varghese; m. Susy George, Aug. 25, 1991; children: Riana George, Milan George, John George. B Engring. in Elec. Engring., Maulana Azad Nat. Inst. Tech., Bhopal, India, 1984; M Engring., Inst. Armament Tech., Pune, India, 1986. Cert. chartered engr., Instn. Indian Engrs.; spl. weapons course diploma Inst. Armament Tech., 1986. Scientist Inst. Armament Tech., Def. Rsch. and Devel. Orgn., Pune, India, 1986—87; lectr. RAIT CBD, Navi Mumbai, India, 1987—88, Def. Rsch. and Devel. Lab., Hyderabad, India, 1988—90; scientist engr. Vikram Sarabhai Space Ctr., Trivandrum, India, 1990—98, Aero. Devel. Agy., Bangalore, India, 1998—2003; lead engr. GETS, GE-Rail, JFWTC, Bangalore, 2003—05; project mgr. Satyam Computer Services Ltd., Bangalore, Karnataka, India, 2005—08, KPIT Infosys. Ltd. UK, 2008; dir. Rimajohns Ltd. UK, 2008. Contbr. scientific papers to profl. pubs. Child sponsor World Vision India, 1998—. Integrated Guided Missiles Devel. Program fellowship, Def. Rsch. and Devel. Orgn., Inst. Armament Tech., India. Fellow: Sys. Soc. India (life), Inst. Electronics Telecom. Engrs. (life), Instn. Engrs. India (life); mem.: Project Mgmt. Inst. (assoc.), Aero. Soc. India (life), Computer Soc. India (life). Roman Catholic. Achievements include development of flight control actuation systems for military aircrafts; flight control actuator checkout systems for satellite launch vehicles; dSPACE-based hardware in loop simulator for automotive chassis control system development projects; design of flight control systems for missiles; design and development of engine control systems for locomotive diesel engines; management of automotive embedded system modeling and simulation projects with various OEM and tier-1 companies in Europe and US; expert in model-based software engineering for embedded control systems; HILS Simulator for Automotive embedded System controller development. Engine Control system development for Heavy Duty diesel engine systems. Avocations: travel, swimming, music. Home and Office: RIMAJOHNS LTD 178 Rotherham Rd Coventry CV6 4FN England Personal E-mail: georgevarghese_chenga@yahoo.com, george.chengadakary@gmail.com.

VARGHESE, SAKOORIKAL LONAPPAN, physicist, researcher; b. Narakal, Kerala, India, Mar. 13, 1943; came to U.S., 1966; s. Lonappan Cheriathu and Anna Kanjooparampil S.; m. Leela Philip Thayil, Jan. 21, 1971; children: Teena-Ann, Emma-Betty, Geena-Mary, Binu-John. BSc, Kerala U., Trivandrum, India, 1963, MSc, 1965; MS, U. Louisville, 1967; PhD, Yale U., 1974. Lectr. Fatima Coll., Quilon, Kerala, India, 1965-66; rsch. staff physicist Yale U., New Haven, 1974; rsch. assoc. Kans. State U., Manhattan, 1974-76; vis. asst. prof. U. Okla., Norman, 1976-77, E Carolina U., Greenville, N.C., 1977-80; from asst. prof. to prof. U. South Ala., Mobile, 1980-85, prof., 1985—, chmn. physics dept., 1994—. Cons. Burroughs Wellcome Co., Greenville, N.C., 1981-85; vis. researcher Oak Ridge Nat. Lab., 1981— Contbr. articles to profl. jours. including Adventures in Exptl. Physics, Jour. Physics B., Physical Review, Nuclear Instruments & Methods. Grantee Rsch. Corp., 1985; named Outstanding scholar, U. South Ala. Alumni Assn., 1986. Mem. Am. Physical Soc., Sigma Xi, Sigma Pi Sigma, Phi Kappa Phi. Achievements include patent for high pressure liquid chromatographic system; invention of universal solvent and column selector; baseline attenuation and wavelength automation system; first observation of first excited state of positronium; pico second lifetime measurements. Home: 804 Brighton Pl Mobile AL 36693-2931

VARGO, LOUISE, landscape artist, music educator; d. Charles and Loretta Vargo. BA, Benedictine U., Lisle, Ill., 1997. Irrigation designer Century Rain Aid, Downers Grove, Ill., 1996—99, John Deere Landscapes, Downers Grove, 2002—05, irrigation design mgr., 2006—08. Piano tchr. Louise Vargo Studio, Plainfield, Ill., 1997—; sales cons. Mary Kay Cosmetics, Plainfield, 2003—. Mem.: Music Educators Nat. Conf. Avocations: gardening, cooking.

VARGO, ROBYN, orthopedist, surgeon; DO, Ohio Univ. Coll. Osteopathic Medicine, Athens. Cert. Bd. Orthopaedic Surgery Examiners. Intern, resident Brentwood Hosp., Cleve.; fellow in adult reconstructive foot and ankle surgery Centennial Med. Ctr., Nashville; staff physician Hinsdale Hosp., Ill., Good Samaritan Hosp., Hinsdale Surg. Ctr., Ill., Salt Creek Surgery Ctr.; ptnr. Hinsdale Orthopaedic Assoc., Ill., 1995—. Contbr. articles to numerous profl. jours. Mem.: DuPage County Med. Soc., Am. Osteopathic Assn., Am. Osteopathic Acad. Orthopaedics, Am. Orthopaedic Foot and Ankle Soc. Office: Hinsdale Orthopaedic Assoc 550 W Ogden Ave Hinsdale IL 60521*

VARGO, RONALD PAUL, information technology executive; b. Painesville, Ohio, Mar. 26, 1954; s. Anton M. and Ingrid E. (Olson) V.; m. Kathleen M. Martell, Nov. 20, 1976; children: Mary Christine, Kevin Matthew. BA in Econs., Dartmouth Coll., 1976; MBA, Stanford U., 1981. Various fin. positions GE, Stamford, Conn., 1976-79, Standard Oil Co., Cleve., 1981-87, dir. corp. fin., 1986-87; comml. mgr. BP Exploration, Houston, 1987-89; gen. mgr. crude oil trading BP Oil Supply Co., 1989—91; joined TRW, 1991, v.p. bus. devel. automotive electronics, v.p., treas., corp. treas., v.p. investor relations, 2001—04; v.p., treas. Electronic Data Systems Corp., 2004, co-interim CFO, 2006, exec. v.p., CFO, 2006—. Office: EDS Corp 5400 Legacy Dr Plano TX 75024

VARGO, STEPHEN LOUIS, travel company executive; b. Shawnee, Okla., July 26, 1945; s. Louis George Vargo and Wanda (Lewis) Hilditch. BA, U. Okla., 1967, MS, 1969, postgrad., 1969-73. V.p. Antec Corp., Okla. City, 1970-75; pres. Leisurex Corp., Okla. City, 1974—, chmn. bd., 1978—. Bd. dirs. Community Bank, Okla. City, Security Bank, Midwest City (Okla.) Trustee Ballet Okla., Okla. City, 1986— (v.p. long range planning 1987—, v.p. devel. 1988-89, v.p. trustees 1989-90, 90-91). Mem. Inst. Cert. Travel Agts. (life), Am. Soc. Travel Agts. (state chmn. 1982-83, southwest chpt. bd. dirs. 1982-83), Assn. Retail Travel Agts. (state bd. dirs. 1981-82), Okla. C. of C. & Industry (bd. dirs. 1981—, vice chmn. bd. adminstrn. 1988—, vice chmn. bd. pub. rels. 1989), Midwest City C. of C. (pres. 1986, pres.' award 1988), Mid-Del 100 Club (bd. dirs. 1986-89, treas. 1987, 88). Avocations: bicycling, reading, travel, art. Home: 11300 N Pennsylvania Ave Oklahoma City OK 73120-7781 Office: Leisurex Corp 331 N Air Depot 2913 NW 122nd St Oklahoma City OK 73120-1933

VARIAN, HAL RONALD, economics professor; b. Wooster, Ohio, Mar. 18, 1947; s. Max Ronald and Elaine Catherine (Shultzman) V.; m. Carol Johnston, Nov. 1986. S.B., MIT, 1969; MA, U. Calif.-Berkeley, 1973, PhD (NSF fellow), 1973. Asst. prof. econs. MIT, 1973-77; prof. U. Mich., 1977-95, prof. fin., 1983-95, Reuben Kempf prof. econs., 1984-95; prof. sch. bus., dean sch. info. mgmt. and sys. U. Calif., Berkeley, 1995—, Class of 1944 prof., 1996—. Siena chair in econs., U. Siena, Italy, 1990. Author: Microeconomic Analysis, 1978, Intermediate Microeconomics, 1987, Information Rules, 1998; co-editor Am. Econ. Rev., 1987-90. Guggenheim fellow, 1979-80; Fulbright scholar, 1990 Fellow AAAS, Econometric Soc.; mem. Am. Econ. Soc. Office: U Calif Sims 102 South Hl Berkeley CA 94720-0001 Home: 576 Del Amigo Rd Danville CA 94526-3215

VARILEK, JULIE, music educator; b. Fort Dodge, Iowa, Mar. 14, 1956; d. Earl and Mavis Freeman; m. Charles Varilek, Aug. 5, 1978; children: Jennifer Marie, Audra Ann. BFA, U. SD, Vermillion, 1974—78. Music tchr. Bon Homme Sch. Dist., Tyndall, SD, 1980—85, Centerville Pub. Sch. Dist., SD, 1985—89, Thompson Sch. Dist., Loveland, Colo., 1990—95, Pk. Sch. Dist., Estes Park, Colo., 1995—. Ch. choir dir. Our Lady Mountains Cath. Ch., Estes Park, 1995—2006; mem. Fine Arts Guild Rockies, Estes Park, 2003—06. Recipient Outstanding Women Educator of Yr., AAUW, 2000. Mem.: Delta Kappa Gamma (mem. tchrs. orgn. 1993—2003, v.p. 1995—97), Rotary (hon.). Home: 1010 Acacia Dr Estes Park CO 80517 Office: Estes Park Intermediate Sch 1505 Brodie Ave Estes Park CO 80517

VARITEK, JASON, professional baseball player; b. Apr. 11, 1972; Attended, Ga. Inst. Tech., Atlanta. Catcher Boston Red Sox, 1997—. Mem. US nat. team World Baseball Classic, 2006. Recipient Golden Spikes award, USA Baseball, 1994, Silver Slugger award, Maj. League Baseball, 2005, Am. League Gold Glove award, 2005; named to Am. league All-Star Team, 2005. Achievements include being a member of World Series Champion Boston Red Sox, 2004, 2007. Office: Boston Red Sox Fenway Park 4 Yawkey Way Boston MA 02215*

VARIYAM, JAYACHANDRAN N., economist; b. India; married. PhD, U. Ga., Athens, 1990. Br. chief Econ. Rsch. Svc., USDA, Washington, 2006—. Office: Econ Rsch Svc USDA 1800 M St NW Washington DC 20036-5831 Business E-Mail: jvariyam@ers.usda.gov.

VARJAVAND, REZA, finance educator; b. Qum, Iran, Mar. 10, 1949; s. Hassan Gholami and Zahra Tabatabaee; m. Mayam Almohammad; children: Melody, Nader, Nathan. BS, Tehran U., Iran, 1971; MBA, U. Ctrl. Okla., Edmond, 1976; PhD, Okla. U., Norman, 1983. Assoc. prof. St. Xavier U., Chgo., 1986—2008. Named Outstanding Tchr. of Yr., St. Xavier U., GSM, 2003—04. Office Fax: 773-298-3610. Business E-Mail: varjavand@sxu.edu.

VARLEY, HERBERT PAUL, Japanese language and cultural history educator; b. Paterson, NJ, Feb. 8, 1931; s. Herbert Paul and Katharine L. (Norcross) V.; m. Betty Jane Geiskopf, Dec. 24, 1960 BS, Lehigh U., 1952; MA, Columbia U., 1961, PhD, 1964; DHL (hon.), Lehigh U., 1988. Asst. prof. U. Hawaii, Honolulu, 1964-65; asst. prof. dept. East Asian Langs. and Cultures Columbia U., NYC, 1965-69, assoc. prof., 1969-75, prof., 1975-94, prof. emeritus Japanese history, 1994—, chmn. dept. East Asian Langs. and Cultures, 1983-89. Sen Soshitsu XV prof. Japanese cultural history U. Hawaii, spring 1991-93, 94—2004, prof. emeritus, 2004—. Author: The Onin War, 1967, The Samurai, 1970, Imperial Restoration in Medieval Japan, 1971, Japanese Culture, 1973, 4th edit., 2000, A Chronicle of Gods and Sovereigns, 1980, Tea in Japan: Essays on the History of Chanoyu, 1989, Warriors of Japan, As Portrayed in the War Tales, 1994; co-editor Sources of Japanese Tradition, Vol. 1, 2d edit., 2001. Bd. govs. Japanese Cultural Ctr. of Hawaii. Served with U.S. Army, 1952-54, Japan. Recipient Imperial Decoration Govt. Japan, Order of Rising Sun, Gold Rays With Rosette. Mem. Assn. Asian Studies, Japan Soc., Soc. Am. Magicians (pres. local chpt. 1983-84). Avocations: magic, piano. Home: 28 Coppa Rd West Paterson NJ 07424 Business E-Mail: pvarley@hawaii.edu.

VARMA, ARVIND, chemical engineering educator, researcher; b. Ferozabad, India, Oct. 13, 1947; s. Hans Raj and Vijay L. (Jhanjhee) V.; m. Karen K. Guse, Aug. 7, 1971; children: Anita, Sophia. BS ChemE, Panjab U., 1966; MS ChemE, U. N.B., Fredericton, Can., 1968; PhD ChemE, U. Minn., 1972. Asst. prof. U. Minn., Mpls., 1972-73; sr. research engr. Union Carbide Corp., Tarrytown, NY, 1973-75; asst. prof. chem. engring. U. Notre Dame, Ind., 1975-77, assoc. prof., 1977-80, prof., 1980-88, Arthur J. Schmitt prof., 1988—2003, chmn. dept., 1983-88; dir. Ctr. for Molecularly Engineered Materials, 2000—03; R. Games Slayter Disting. prof., head Purdue U. Sch. Chem. Engring., 2004—. Vis. prof. U. Wis., Madison, 1981; Chevron vis. prof. Calif. Inst. Tech., Pasadena, 1982; vis. prof. Ind. Inst. Tech.-Kanpur, 1989, U. Cagliari, Italy, 1989, 92; vis. fellow Princeton U., 1996; Piercy vis. prof. U. Minn., 2001; Kane vis. prof. U. Mumbai, 2007. Co-author: Mathematical Methods in Chemical Engineering, 1997, Parametric Sensitivity in Chemical Systems, 1999, Catalyst Design, 2001; editor: (with others) The Mathematical Understanding of Chemical Engineering Systems, 1980, Chemical Reaction and Reactor Engineering, 1987; series editor: Cambridge Series in Chemical Engineering, 1996—; contbr. numerous articles to profl. jours. Recipient Tchr. of Yr. award Coll. Engrng. U. Notre Dame, 1991, Spl. Presdl. award 1992, R.H. Wilhelm award AIChE, 1993, Burns Grad. Sch. award 1997, E.W. Thiele award AIChE, 1998, Chem. Engring. Lectureship award, ASEE, 2000, Rsch. Achievement award U. Notre Dame, 2001, Techs. of Yr. award Industry Week, 2005; Fulbright scholar; Indo-Am. fellow, 1988-89. Office: Purdue U Sch Chem Engring West Lafayette IN 47907 Office Phone: 765-494-4075. Business E-Mail: avarma@purdue.edu.

VARMA, DATLA G.K., radiologist, researcher; b. Bobbili, Andhra, India, June 2, 1951; came to U.S., 1976; now naturalized; s. Datla V. Raju and Datla Satyavathi; m. Siva Kumari, Dec. 20, 1980; children: Datla Kirti, Datla Vivek. MBBS, Andhra Med. Coll., 1975. Diplomate Am. Bd. Radiology, Am. Bd. Nuclear Medicine. Intern King George Hosp., Visakha Patnam, India, 1974-75; resident in anat. pathology Good Samaritan Hosp., Cin., 1977-78; resident in nuclear medicine Univ. Hosp., Cin., 1978-80, resident in radiology, 1980-83; asst. prof. radiology Tulane U., New Orleans, 1983-88, med. dir. diagnostic svcs./radiology dept., 1987-89, assoc. prof. radiology, 1988-89, sect. chief body CT, 1983-89, sect. chief body MRI, 1988-89; assoc. prof. radiology U. Tex./M.D. Anderson Cancer Ctr., Houston, 1989-99, acting sect. chief MRI, 1991-99, prof. radiology, 1999—. Contbr. articles to profl. jours., chpts. to books. Avocations: sports, travel, reading. Home: 3915 Marlowe St Houston TX 77005-2045 Office: Md Anderson Cancer Ctr PO Box 57 Houston TX 77001-0057 E-mail: dvarma@di.mdacc.tmc.edu.

VARMA, MADHULIKA G., colon and rectal surgeon; BA, Brown U., Providence, 1987, MD, 1991. Chief, colon and rectal surgery U. Calif., San Francisco, 2000—. Office: Univ Calif San Francisco 2330 Post St San Francisco CA 94115

VARMA, NIRAJ, cardiologist, physiologist, researcher; s. Alakh Niranjan Varma and Shashi Bala Prasad. BA, Oxford U., 1978—81; MB, Edinburgh U., 1984. Registrar Cambridge U., England, 1987—90; rsch. fellow Boston and Harvard Univs., 1992—94; fellow in cardiac electrophysiology Beth Israel Hosp., Harvard Med. Sch., Boston, 1994—96; dir. Cardiac EP Labs., dir. Cardiac EP Fellowship Program, Loyola U. Med. Sch., Maywood, Ill., 2005—. Electrophysiologist and test prof. U. Hosp. and Case Western Reserve U., Cleve., 1998—2005; dir. cardiac electrophysiology labs. and assoc. prof. Loyola U., Chg., 2005—. Author books and sci. articles. Mem.: Royal Coll. Physicians, London and Edinburgh, N.Am. Soc. Pacing and Electrophysiology. Office: Cardiology Divsn Loyola U Med Sch 2160 S First Ave Maywood IL 60153 Personal E-mail: nivarma@lumc.edu.

VARMUS, HAROLD ELIOT, health science administrator, educator, science researcher; b. Oceanside, NY, Dec. 18, 1939; s. Frank and Beatrice (Barasch) V.; m. Constance Louise Casey, Oct. 25, 1969; children: Jacob Carey, Christopher Isaac. BA in English, Amherst Coll., 1961; MA in Lit., Harvard U., 1962; MD, Columbia U. Med. Sch., 1966. Intern, resident Presbyn. Hosp., NYC, 1966-68; lectr. dept. microbiology U. Calif., San Francisco, 1970-72, asst. prof., 1972-74, assoc. prof., 1974-79, prof. departments microbiology & immunology, biochemistry & biophysics, 1979—93, Am. Cancer Soc. research prof., 1984—93; clin. assoc. Nat. Inst. Arthritis & Metabolic Disease, Bethesda, Md., 1968-70; dir. NIH, Bethesda, Md., 1993—99; pres., CEO Meml. Sloan-Kettering Cancer Ctr., NYC, 2000—. Chmn. bd. on biology NRC, 1991—93; served on WHO Commn on Macroeconomics and Health; co-founder, chmn. bd. dirs. Pub. Libr. Sci. (PLoS), 2003—; sci. bd. Grand Challenges in Global Health; co-chair sci. adv. group Presdl. Coun. of Advisers on Sci. and Tech., 2008—. Recipient Nat. Medal of Sci., 2002, Vannevar Bush award, NSF, 2001; co-recipient Scientist of Yr. award, Calif. Acad. Sci., 1982, Lasker Found. award, 1982, Passano Found. award, 1983, Armand Hammer Cancer prize, GM Alfred Sloan award, Shubitz Cancer prize, 1984, Internat. award, Gardner Found., 1984, Nobel Prize in Physiology or Medicine, 1989; named one of America's Best Leaders, US News & World Report, 2007. Fellow World Tech. Network (World Tech. Network award Media and Journalism, 2005); mem. NAS, Inst. Medicine, Am. Soc. Virology, Am. Soc. Microbiology, Am. Soc. Cell Biology, Am. Acad. Arts and Scis., Am. Soc. for Biochemistry and Molecular Biology. Democrat. Achievements include rsch. (with J. Michael Bishop) on the the cellular origin of retroviral oncogenes. Office: Meml Sloan-Kettering Cancer Ctr 1275 York Ave New York NY 10021-6094 also: PLoS 185 Berry St St 3100 San Francisco CA 94107 Business E-Mail: varmus@mskcc.org.*

VARNER, CHARLEEN LAVERNE MCCLANAHAN, nutritionist, educator, administrator, dietitian; b. Alba, Mo., Aug. 28, 1931; d. Roy Calvin and Lela Ruhama (Smith) McClanahan; student Joplin (Mo.) Jr. Coll., 1949-51; BS in Edn., Kans. State Coll. Pittsburg, 1953; MS, U. Ark., 1958; PhD, Tex. Woman's U. 1966; postgrad. Mich. State U., 1955, U. Mo., 1962; m. Robert Bernard Varner, July 4, 1953. Apprentice county home agt. U. Mo., 1952; tchr. Ferry Pass Sch., Escambia County, Fla., 1953-54; tchr. biology, home econs. Joplin Sr. H.S., 1954-59; instr. home econs. Kans. State Coll., Pittsburg, 1959-63; lectr. foods, nutrition Coll. Household Arts and Scis., Tex. Woman's U., 1963-64, rsch. asst. NASA grant, 1964-66; assoc. prof. home econs. Central Mo. State U., Warrensburg, 1966-70, adviser to Colhecon, 1966-70, adviser to Alpha Sigma Alpha, 1967-70, 72, bd. adv. Honors Group, 1967-70; prof., head dept. home econs. Kans. State Tchrs. Coll., Emporia, 1970-73; prof., chmn. dept. home econs. Benedictine Coll., Atchison, Kans., 1973-74; prof., chmn. dept. home econs. Baker U., Baldwin City, Kans., 1974-75; owner, operator Diet-Con Dietary Cons. Enterprises, cons. dietitian, 1973—, Home-Con Cons. Enterprises; adj. prof. Highland (Kans.) CC, 2004—. Active Joplin Little Theater, 1956-60. Mem. NEA, AAUW, AAUP, Mo. State Tchr. Assn., Kans. State Tchr. Assn., Am. Dietetic Assn., Mo. Dietetic Assn., Kans. Dietetic Assn., Am. Home Econs. Assn., Mo. Home Econs. Assn., Kans. Home Econs. Assn., Mo. Acad. Scis., U. Ark. Alumni Assn., Alumni Assn. Kans. State Coll. of Pittsburg, Am. Vocat. Assn., Assn. Edn. Young Children, Sigma Xi, Beta Sigma Phi, Beta Beta Beta, Alpha Sigma Alpha, Delta Kappa Gamma, Kappa Kappa Iota, Phi Upsilon Omicron, Theta Alpha Pi, Kappa Phi. Methodist (organist). Home: PO Box 1009 Topeka KS 66601-1009

VARNER, CHILTON DAVIS, lawyer; b. Opelika, Ala., Mar. 12, 1943; d. William Cole and Frances (Thornton) Davis; m. K. Morgan Varner, III, June 19, 1965; 1 child, Ashley Elizabeth. AB with distinction, Smith Coll., 1965; JD with distinction, Emory U., 1976. Assoc. King & Spalding, Atlanta, 1976-83, ptnr., 1983—, mem. mgmt. com., 1996—98. Bd. dirs. Wesley Woods Healthcare, 1997—2007, 11th Cir. Ct. Appeals Hist. Soc.; trustee Emory U., Atlanta, 1995—, Product Liability Adv. Coun., 1987—; mem. Adv. Com. Fed. Civil Rules, 2004—. Author: Appellate Handbook for Georgia Lawyers, 1995. Mem. Leadership Atlanta, 1984—85; mem. exec. com. Atlanta Arts Alliance, 1981—85; mem. Atlanta Symphony Chorus, 1970—74; asst. clk., elder, bd. elders Trinity Presbyn. Ch., Atlanta, 1975—78. Recipient Disting. Alumna award, Emory U. Law Sch., 1998; named one of Top 10 Women Litigators, Nat. Law Jour., 2001. Fellow: Am. Coll. Trial Lawyers; mem.: ABA, Atlanta Bar Assn., Ga. Bar Assn., Phi Beta Kappa, Order of Coif. Office: King & Spalding 1180 Peachtree St NE 37th Fl Atlanta GA 30309-3521 Office Phone: 404-572-4789, 404-572-4789. Office Fax: 404-572-5100. E-mail: cvarner@kslaw.com.

VARNER, DAVID EUGENE, lawyer; b. Dallas, Oct. 9, 1937; s. E.C. and D. Evelyn (Bauguss) V.; m. Joan Paula Oransky, Aug. 13, 1962; children: Michael A., Kevin E., Cheryl L. BA, So. Meth. U., Dallas, 1958, JD, 1961. Bar: Tex. 1961, Fla. 1974, Okla., 1977, U.S. Supreme Ct. 1978. Assoc. Eldridge, Goggans, Davidson & Silverberg, Dallas, 1962-65; atty., asst. sec. Redman Industries, Inc., Dallas, 1965-66; assoc. gen. atty. Tex. Instruments, Inc., Dallas, 1966-73; sr. atty., asst. sec. Fla. Gas Co., Winter Park, 1973-76; v.p., gen. counsel, sec. Facet Enterprises, Inc., Tulsa, 1976-78, Summa Corp., Las Vegas, Nev., 1978-82; sr. v.p., gen. counsel, sec. Transco Energy Co., Houston, 1982-95; pres. The MKC Group, Houston, 1995—. Mem. royalty mgmt. adv. com. U.S. Minerals Mgmt. Svc., 1985—87. Mng. editor Southwestern Law Jour., 1960-61 Mem.: Fla. Bar Assn., Tex. Bar Assn. Office: PO Box 79571 Houston TX 77279-9571

VARNER, JOYCE EHRHARDT, retired librarian; b. Quincy, Ill., Sept. 13, 1938; d. Wilbur John and Florence Elizabeth (Mast) Ehrhardt; m. Donald Giles Varner, Sept. 12, 1959; children: Amy, Janice, Christian, Matthew, Nadine. BA, Northeastern Okla. State U., 1980; MLS, U. Okla., 1984. Lab. analyst Gardner Denver Co., Quincy, 1956-60; sales rep. Morrisonville, Ill., 1963-69; libr. clk. U. Ill., Urbana, 1973-75; libr. tech. asst. Northeastern Okla. State U., Tahlequah, 1976-86; asst. reference libr. Muskogee (Okla.) Pub. Libr., 1986-90; libr. Jess Dunn Correctional Ctr., Taft, Okla., 1990-98; ret., 1998; field office supr. Census 2000 Dept. of Commerce, Welling, Okla., 1998. Editor Indian Nations Audubon Nature Notes, 1977-81, 96-2007; contbr. articles to newspaper. Vol. Lake-Wood coun. Girl Scouts U.S.A., 1975-98, bd. dirs. 1992-98, pres., 1995-96; sec.-treas. Cherokee County Rural Water Dist. 7, 1987—; edn. chmn. Indian Nations chpt. Nat. Audubon Soc., 1989-2000, pres., 2000-04, v.p. 2008-; project dir. Tahlequah Friends of the Libr., 2002-04, pres., 2004-08, program dir., 2008-. Recipient Thanks Badge, Lake-Wood coun. Girl Scouts U.S.A., 1990. Mem. AAUW (chair diversity com. 2000), Okla. Libr. Assn. (nominating com. 1989), Okla. Acad. Sci., Okla. Ornithol. Soc. (chmn. libr. com. 1978-88, Award of Merit 1990, pres.-elect 1994, pres. 1995-96, chair spl. projects com., 2009-), Alpha Chi, Beta Beta Beta, Phi Delta Kappa (Found. rep. 1984-86, historian 1992-2006). Avocations: nature study, needlecrafts, square dancing, genealogy.

VARNER, JOYCE MCCULLERS, geriatric nurse practitioner, educator; d. Clayton McCullers and Joyce Kelly; m. Rick Varner, June 5, 1988. PhD in Nursing Practice, U. South Ala., Mobile, 2000. Cert. geriat. nurse practitioner, ANCC, 2001. Clin. coord. Rocky Ridge Family Health Ctr., Birmingham, Ala., 1995—99; clin. assoc. prof. U. South Ala., 2001—. Geriat. cons. pvt. practice, Foley, Ala., 2008—. Contbr. articles to profl. jours. Bd. mem. State Ala. Bd. Examiners Nursing Home Administrs., Montgomery, 2007—. Recipient Excellence Svc. award, U. South Ala., 2008. Mem.: Ala. State Nurses Assn. (pres. elect 2008—). Conservative. Presbyterian. Achievements include development of toolkit for retention of nursing personnel in long term care settings. Avocations: travel, reading, gardening.

VARNER, MARLEEN ALLEN, retired academic administrator; b. West Chester, Pa., May 6, 1932; d. Lester Rueben and Florence Winegar Bengel; m. William Theodore Allen (dec. June 1965); children: David Avery Allen, Paul Charlton Allen; m. James Edward Ingle (div. Oct. 1980); 1 child, Jay Edward Ingle; m. Carroll H. Varner, Apr. 8, 1998 (dec. Apr. 2006); stepchildren: Carolyn R. Stone, Katherine M., Corinne, Carroll H. III. Student, U. Buffalo, 1949—51; AB, Coll. Wooster, Ohio, 1953; MA, Syracuse U., NY, 1956. Sec. World U. Svc., NYC, 1953—54; asst. instr. edn. Syracuse U., 1956—57; conselor, history tchr. Elizabethtown Area HS, Elizabethtown, Pa., 1957—58; dir. reading and study skills lab. Franklin & Marshall Coll., Lancaster, Pa., 1958—59; dir. fin. aid and placement U. South, Sewanee, Tenn., 1967—69; dir. state grant programs Ky. Higher Edn., Frankfort, 1974—80; dir. fin. aid U. NC, Greensboro, 1980—93; ret., 1998; pres. Sewanee Nursery & Kindergarden Sch., Tenn., 1965—66. Cons. Fin. Aid Svcs., 1996—98; sec. U. NC System Faculty Assembly. Contbr. articles to profl. jours. Tax aide instr., vol. Am. Assn. Ret. Persons, 2002—07; mem. Friends of the Libr. U. NC, 1993—, U. South, Sewanee, Tenn., 1994—; pres. Sewanee Civic Assn., Tenn., 1996—97; bd. dirs. Sewanee Cmty. Chest, 1995—98; sec. Carpenter's Home Estates Resident Assn., 2002—06; life mem., v.p., editor Nat. Continuing Care Residents Assn., 2006—, lifetime editor, 2009—; supporter Land Trust Tenn., 2008; at large rep. house del. Assn. Homes, Svc. Aging, 2009—; house of del. Am. Assn. Homes and Svcs. Aging, 2009—; leadership Meth. Ch., Lexington, Ky., Greensboro, NC, Lakeland, Fla.; bd. chmn. Wesley Luther House, Greensboro, NC, 1990—92. Recipient Leadership award, U.S. Dept. Edn. Quality Control Project, 1991; fellow, Soc. Advancement Fin. Aid Mgmt. in Higher Edn., 1991. Mem.: Southern Assn. Student Fin. Adminstrs. (pres. 1991—92), Fla. Life Care Residents Assn. (chpt. sec. 2002—05), Sewanee Trust Hist. Preservation (life), Junaluska Assocs. (v.p. 2000—02, life mem.), Emerald Hodgson Hosp. Auxiliary (life), Lake Junaluska (NC) Woman's Club (pres. 1999—2008), EQB Club Sewanee (pres. 1997—99, 2007—09, dr. 2009—), Woman's Club, Sewanee (pres. 1964—65, TN diocesan creation care task force sec. 2009—), Pi Sigma Alpha, Phi Delta Kappa, Pi Lambda Theta, Delta Kappa Gamma. Democrat. Episcopalian. Avocations: travel, music, reading, bridge. Home: 257 Wiggins Creek Dr Sewanee TN 37375-3032 Personal E-mail: travelgal2342@aol.com.

VARNER, WILLIAM, religious studies educator; b. Spartanburg, SC, May 26, 1947; s. William and Eloise Varner; m. Helen Vivian, Aug. 28, 1971; children: Jonathan, Amy Haskell. EdD, Temple U., Phila., 1995. Prof. Phila. Coll. Bible, 1984—, Master's Coll., Santa Clarita, Calif., 1996—. Pastor Ind. Bible Ch., Willow Grove, Pa., 1972—. Author: (bibl. works) Messiah, Didache, James. Named Tchr. of Yr.; Sabbatical fellowship, Fund., 2004. Mem.: Evang. Theol. Soc. Conservative. Home: 19429 San Marino Ct Santa Clarita CA 91321 Office: Master's Coll Santa Clarita CA 91321 Personal E-mail: ibexdr@yahoo.com.

VARNEY, CARLETON BATES, JR., interior designer, columnist, educator; b. Lynn, Mass., Jan. 23, 1937; s. Carleton Bates and Julia (Raczkowskos) V.; divorced; children: Nicholas, Seamus, Sebastian. BA, Oberlin Coll., 1958; student, U. Madrid, 1957; MA, NYU, 1969; LHD (hon.), U. Charleston, 1987. Sch. tchr., 1958-59; asst. to pres. Dorothy Draper & Co., Inc., 1959-63, exec. v.p., 1963-66, pres., 1966—; dean Carleton Varney Sch. of Art & Design, U. Charleston, W.Va. Designer: Varney and Sons Furniture Collection Kindel Furniture Co., Carleton Varney by-the-yard decorative fabrics, dinnerware and china, crystal glassware, table and bed linen, lamps and light fixtures, ready to wear resort collection Cruzanwear, 1987, mens' wear furnishings for Rawlinson & Marking, London, 1987; Ready to wear resort coll., "A Perfect Day in Paradise", 1998, Colours Resort Collection, 2000; interior designer: Dromoland Castle, Ireland, 1963, 88, Westbury Hotel, Belgium, 1964, NY World's Fair, 1965, Clare Inn, Ireland, 1968, Greenbrier Hotel, White Sulphur Springs, W.Va., 1968-, Westbury Hotel, San Francisco, 1973, Copley Plaza Hotel, Boston, 1976, 96, Amway Grand Plaza Hotel, Grand Rapids, Mich., 1980, The Grand Hotel, Mackinac Island, Mich., 1978-, Equinox House, Manchester, Vt., 1984, Brazilian Ct. Hotel, Palm Beach, Fla., 1985, Waldorf Towers, NYC, 1985, Dawn

Beach Hotel, St. Maarten, 1985, Christian Broadcasting Conv. Ctr., 1986, Met. Opera House boutique, NYC, 1985, (cruise ship) World Discoverer, 1984, Arrowwood Conv. Ctr., Purchase, NY, 1987, Boca Raton Hotel and Club, Fla., 1987, Speedway Club, Charlotte, NC, 1987, Coccoloba Plantation, Anguilla, Brit. Virgin Islands, 1987, Villa Madeleine, St. Croix, VI, 1987, Ashford Castle, Ireland, 1988, Adare Manor, Ireland, 1988, The Breakers, Palm Beach, Fla., 1989, Jackson Lake Lodge, Wyo., 1989, V.P.'s Residence, Washington, 1989, Cormorant Cove, St. Croix, VI, 1990, The Buccaneer Hotel, St. Croix, 1991, Dromoland Castle, Internat. Ctr., Ireland, 1991, West Village Golf Resort, Tokyo, 1993, Half Moon Bay Club, Jamaica, The Plaza, NY, 1997, The Hibiscus Restaurant, Palm Beach, Fla., 1999, North Shore Country Club, LI, NY, 2002, Mount Wash. Hotel and Resort, N.H., 2003, Lago Mar Resort and Club, Ft. Lauderdale, Fla., 2003-04, McJukin Corp., W.Va., 2005, Harder Hall Resort and Spa, Sebring, Fla., 2005, Stoneleigh Hotel Penthouse Suites, Dallas, 2007, Archtl. Digest Green Room 80th Ann. Acad. awards, LA, 2008; numerous pvt. residences; designer: White House party for celebration Israel-Egypt Peace Treaty, 1979; Palm Beach Cares fashion benefit for Am. Found. for AIDS Research, 1988, log home for Pres. and Mrs. Carter, Ellijay, Ga., 1983; color cons. Carter Presdl. Library, 1986; trustee and curator: former presdl. yacht U.S.S. Sequoia, 1982; author: numerous books including You and Your Apartment, 1960, The Family Decorates a Home, 1962 Carleton Varney Decorates Windows, 1975, Be Your Own Decorator, 1979, There's No Place Like Home, 1980, Down Home, 1981, Carleton Varney's ABC's of Decorating, 1983, Staying in Shape: An Insider's Guide to the Great Spas, 1983, Room by Room Decorating, 1984, Color Magic, 1985, The Draper Touch, 1988, Kiss the Hibiscus Goodnight, 1992, The Decorator, 1999, In the Pink--Dorothy Draper, America's Most Fabulous Decorator, 2006, Houses in my Heart, 2008;syndicated columnist: Your Family Decorator, 1968—; decorating column Family-click.com, 2000, Inside Design column N.Y. Post, 2001; contbg. editor Good Housekeeping Mag., 1993-95; contbg. design editor Social and Personal Mag. (Ireland) 1996-; style editor Men's Style mag.; editor-at-large Hamptons Mag., 2000—; Live Vivioly TV Show, HSN, 2009. Recipient Shelby Williams award for design achievement, 1967, Tommy design award for Covington's Heraldry collection, 1989, Interior Design Hall of Fame award, 1990; named as one of 30 Deans of Am. Design, Archtl. Digest, 2005. Mem. Indsl. Designers Soc. Am., NY State Bd. for Interior Design, NY Athletic Club, Shannon Rowing Club (Ireland), Millbrook Golf and Tennis Club (NY). Office: Dorothy Draper & Co Inc 60 E 56th St New York NY 10022-3204 Office Phone: 212-758-2810. Business E-Mail: cvarney@dorothydraper.com. *My success, I believe, is due to an ability to understand and use vibrant color appropriately, and to strive for perfection of detail in all my designs as details separate the excellent from the ordinary.*

VARNEY, CHRISTINE ANNE, federal agency administrator, lawyer; b. Dec. 17, 1955; m. Thomas J. Graham; children: John Walsh, Michael. Degree in Politics, Philosophy and Econs. (hon.), Trinity Coll., Dublin, Ireland, 1975; BA in Polit. Sci. and History magna cum laude, SUNY, Albany, 1977; MPA in Policy Analysis, Legislation and Rsch. magna cum laude, Syracuse U., 1978; JD cum laude, Georgetown U., 1986. Legis. asst. NY State Senate, Albany, 1977; econ. analyst Govt. Accountability Office, Washington, 1978; econ. devel. dir. El Centro, Calif., 1979; dir. Neighborhood Outreach Program, San Diego, 1980-82; assoc. Surry & Morse, Washington, 1984-86, Pierson, Semmes & Finley, Washington, 1986-88; counsel Hogan & Hartson LLP, Washington, 1990-92; chief counsel Bill Clinton for Pres. Primary Campaign, 1992, Clinton-Gore Campaign, 1992; gen. counsel Dem. Nat. Com., 1992, Presdl. Inauguration Com., 1993; dep. asst. to Pres. The White House, Washington, 1993-94; commr. FTC, Washington, 1994—97; ptnr. Hogan & Hartson LLP, Washington, 1997—2009; asst. atty. gen. antitrust divsn. US Dept. Justice, Washington, 2009—. Active Women's Legal Def. Fund. Mem. D.C. Bar Assn., N.Y. State Bar Assn., Nat. Lawyer's Coun. Democrat. Office: US Dept Justice 950 Pennsylvania Ave NW Washington DC 20530*

VARNEY, GLENN HERBERT, finance educator; b. Jefferson, Ohio, Dec. 1, 1926; s. Herbert Henry and Edna (Schwartz) V.; m. Ruth Constance Park, June 30, 1951; children: Janice McKnight, Kenneth. BSc in Bus. Adminstrn., Ohio State U., 1949, MBA, 1951; PhD, Case Western Res. U., 1971. Cert. sr.profl. in human rels. Pers. mgr. Glidden Co., Cleve., 1951-55; mgr. recruitment and mgmt. devel. Diamond Shamrock, Dallas, 1955-65; dir. human resources Harshaw Chems., Cleve., 1965-68; asst. to dean Case Western Res. U., Cleve., 1968-70; dir. Mgmt. Ctr. Bowling Green (Ohio) State U., 1970-83; pres. Mgmt. Adv. Assocs., Bowling Green, 1968—; prof. mgmt. Bowling Green (Ohio) State U., 1970—96, prof. mgmt. emeritus, 1970—. Bd. dirs. Self-Directed Resource Ctr., Bowling Green, 1992—, Inst. for Orgnl. Effectiveness, 1979-96; cons., ptnr., founder MAA Change Mgmt. Ctr. Author: Building Productive Teams, 1990, Management by Objectives, 1969, 3 other books; co-author (with Robert Golembiewski) Cases in Organizational Development, 1999 edition, 2003, edition, Bibliography of Organization Devel. and Change Literature pub. by Bowling Green State U.; contbr. over 100 articles to profl. jours. Vol. work with non-profit orgns.; mem. various ch. and cmty. related coms. and projects. Recipient Disting. Svc. award, Acad. Mgmt. Orgn., 2001. Mem. ASTD (nat. v.p. 1980-81, award for leadership 1992, award for excellence 1993, Disting. Svc. award 2001); Soc. for Human Resources (life accreditation), Acad. Mgmt. (Disting. Svc. award 2001), Beta Gamma Sigma, Omicron Delta Kappa. Republican. Avocations: farm management, jogging. Home: 546 Hillcrest Dr Bowling Green OH 43402-3616 Fax: 419-354-8781. Business E-Mail: gvarney@bgsu.edu.

VARNEY, JOLENE, corporate financial executive; Gen. mgr., Ctrl. and Eastern European ops. and European adult care divsn. Kimberly-Clark Corp., global treas.; sr. v.p., corp. fin., prin. acctg. officer Dr Pepper Snapple Group Inc., 2009; CFO, exec. v.p. Mylan Inc., 2009—. Office: Mylan Inc 1500 Corp Dr Canonsburg PA 15317 Office Phone: 724-514-1800. Office Fax: 724-514-1870.*

VARNEY, NILS ROBERTS, neuropsychologist, researcher; b. St. Louis, Aug. 25, 1949; s. Robert Nathan and Astrid (Riffolt) V.; m. Emily Jean Martin, June 2, 1980; children: Colleen M., Tess M. BA, Occidental Coll., 1971; MA, U. Iowa, 1974, PhD, 1977. Diplomate Am. Bd. Psychology, Am. Bd. Clin. Neuropsychology. Staff neuropsychologist VA Med. Ctr., Iowa City, Iowa, 1977—, dir. psychol. tng., 1990—. Examiner Am. Bd. Clin. Neuropsychology, 1988—. Co-author (book and tests): Contributions to Clinical Neuropsychology, 1983, 2d edit., 1994; mem. editl. bd. Developmental Neuropsychology, 1984-93, Neuropsychology, 1987-92, Applied Neuropsychology, 1994—, Evaluation and Treatment of Mild Traumatic Brain Injury; contbr. articles to profl. publs., chpt. to book. Bd. govs. Iowa Head Injury Assn., 1984-88, bd. advisors, 1988-95. Fellow APA, Nat. Acad. Neuropsychology; mem. Internat. Neuropsychology Soc., Internat. Soc. for History of Neuroscis., Acad. of Aphasia, Am. Speech, Lang. and Hearing Assn. (hon.). Avocations: reading history, Tae Kwon Do, opera. Home: 403 Holland St Le Claire IA 52753-9547

VARNEY, RICHARD ALAN, health facility administrator; b. Concord, NH, July 8, 1950; s. John Berry and Hattie Elizabeth (Harrington) V.; m. Suzanne Glaab, Dec. 31, 1983; stepchildren: Alysen Suzanne Bidle, Craig Judson Bidle. BS in Phys. Edn., U. N.H., 1972; MHA in Healthcare Adminstrn., Baylor U., 1984; diploma, Command and Gen. Staff Coll., 1986. Commd. 2d lt. U.S. Army, 1973, advanced through grades to lt. col., 1991; dep. asst. CEO Cutler Army Hosp., Ft. Devens, Mass., 1973—76; field med. asst. 38th ADA Bde., Osan Air Base, Republic of Korea, 1977—78; dep. asst. CEO 15th Med. Battalion, Ft. Hood, Tex., 1979—81; adminstrv. resident Ireland Army Hosp., Ft. Knox, Ky., 1982—83; COO, exec. officer U.S. Army Dental Activity, Ft. Knox, 1983—86; grad. instr. Army-Baylor Healthcare Program, San Antonio, 1986—90; project mgr. Office of the Army Surgeon Gen., Washington, 1990—93; ret. U.S. Army, 1993; office mgr. Aebi, Ginty, Romaker & Sprouse MD's, Inc., Lancaster, Ohio, 1993—2000; dir. gen. internal medicine program The Ohio State U. Med. Ctr., Columbus, 2000—04; dir. ops. Fairfield Dept. Health, Lancaster, 2005—. Mem. Source Selection Evaluation Bd.-Champus Reform, Arlington, Va., 1987; mem. adv. com. for assoc. degree program in med. assisting Ohio U., Lancaster, 1998-2000. Adult leader Boy Scouts Am., Tex., Va. and Ohio, 1988-97, 2003—; mem. Lancaster City Bd. of Health, 1996-2001, pres. pro tem, 1999-2001; mem. Fairfield County Combined Gen. Health Dist. Bd., 2002-04. Officer US Army Med. Svc. Corps, 1973—93. Decorated Legion of Merit, Order of Mil. Med. Merit award, Expert Field Med. badge; named to Hon. Order Ky. Cols., 1989, Outstanding Young Man of Am., 1982. Fellow Am. Coll. Healthcare Execs.; mem. Ctrl. Ohio Health Adminstrs. Assn., Ohio Med. Group Mgmt. Assn., Mid-Ohio Med. Mgmt. Assn., Profl. Assn. Med. Mgrs., Am. Assn. Procedural Coders, Lancaster Area Soc. for Human Resource Mrmt. (legis. rep. 1998-99, membership chair 1999—), Am. Hosp. Assn., Nat. Eagle Scout Assn., The Ret. Officers Assn., Am. Legion, Fraternal Order of Eagles, Alpha Phi Omega. Avocations: home improvement, music. Home: 1025 E 5th Ave Lancaster OH 43130-3276 Home Phone: 740-681-5665; Office Phone: 740-653-4489 x155. Personal E-mail: richvarneyosu@yahoo.com. Business E-Mail: rvarney@co.fairfield.oh.us.

VARRICCHIO-DI VITO, ANDREA, language educator; d. Louis and Serafina Bigatel Varricchio; m. Robert A. Di Vito, Nov. 21, 1981; 1 child, Alexandra Varricchio Di Vito. AB, Chestnut Hill Coll., Phila., 1972; MA, Middlebury Coll., V., 1973; PhD, Temple U., Phila., 1984. Spanish educator Allentown Ctrl. Cath. HS, Pa., 1973—78, Wilmington Friends Sch., Del., 1982—87; prof. Spanish West Chester U., Pa., 1987—. Spanish music reviewer Nat. Capital Lang. Resourse Ctr., Washington. Contbr. articles to profl. jours. Vol. Spanish interpreter AAUW, Wilmington, Del., 1998—2008. Grantee, New Eng. Resource Ctr. Higher Edn., 2001, Pa. Campus Compact, 2002—03, Pa. State Sys. Higher Edn., 1997. Mem.: Am. Coun. Tchg. Fgn. Langs., Am. Assn. Tchrs. Spanish and Portuguese. Avocations: travel, photography. Office: Dept Langs & Cultures West Chester Univ West Chester PA 19383

VARRO, BARBARA JOAN, retired editor; b. East Chicago, Ind., Jan. 25, 1938; d. Alexander R. and Lottie R. (Bess) V. BA, Duquesne U., 1959. Feature reporter, asst. fashion editor Chgo. Sun-Times, 1959-64, fashion editor, 1964-76, feature writer, 1976-84; v.p. pub. rels. Daniel J. Edelman Inc., Chgo., 1984-85; v.p. PRB/Needham Porter Novelli, Chgo., 1985-86; editor Am. Hosp. Assn. News, Chgo., 1987-94; editor spl. sects. Chgo. Tribune, 1995-2000; ret. Recipient awards for feature writing Ill. AP, 1978, 79, 80 Mem.: PEO. Home: 219 Autumn Trail N Michigan City IN 46360

VARS, JOHN, Internet company executive; b. St. Paul; Grad., U. Wis. Dir. software devel. Preview Travel, Travelocity.com, mgr., lead software engr. internat. partnerships & joint ventures Sydney, 2002—04; co-founder, chief product officer Dogster.com, San Francisco, 2004—, Catster.com, 2004—. Office: Dogster Inc Ste 350 555 DeHaro St San Francisco CA 94107 Office Phone: 415-934-0400. Office Fax: 415-864-6261. E-mail: john@dogster.com.

VARSHAVSKY, ALEXANDER JACOB, molecular biologist, educator; b. Moscow, Nov. 8, 1946; arrived in US, 1977; s. Jacob M. and Mary B. (Zeitlin) Varshavsky; m. Vera Bingham, Aug. 30, 1990; children: Roman, Anna, Victoria. BS in Chemistry, Moscow State U., 1970; PhD in Biochemistry, Moscow Inst. Molecular Biology, 1973. Rsch. fellow Moscow Inst. Molecular Biology, 1973—76; asst. prof. dept. biology MIT, Cambridge, 1977-80, assoc. prof., 1980-86, prof., 1986-92; Howard & Gwen Laurie Smits prof. cell biology Calif. Inst. Tech., Pasadena, 1992—. Mem. molecular cytology study sect. NIH, 1983—87; vis. fellow Internat. Inst. for Advanced Studies, Kyoto, 2001; bd. dirs. Encyclopedia Molecular Cell Biology & Molecular Medicine, 2002—05; mem. med. adv. bd. Gairdner Found., Canada, 2002—06. Contbr. articles to profl. jours. Recipient Novartis-Drew award in biomed. sci., Novartis, Inc./Drew U., 1998, Merit award, NIH, 1998, Gairdner Found. Internat. award, 1999, Alfred P. Sloan Jr. prize, GM Cancer Rsch. Found., 2000, Lasker award for basic med. rsch., 2000, Hoppe-Seyler award, German Soc. Biochemistry & Molecular Biology, 2000, Merck award, Am. Soc. Biochemistry & Molecular Biology, 2001, Pasarow award in cancer rsch., Pasarow Found., 2001, Wolf Found. prize in medicine, Israel, 2001, Massry Found. prize, 2001, Max Planck Rsch. prize, Germany, 2001, Louisa Gross Horwitz prize, Columbia U., 2001, Wilson medal, Am. Soc. Cell Biology, 2002, Stein & Moore award, Protein Soc., 2005, March of Dimes prize in devel. biology, 2006, Gagna & Van Heck prize, Belgium, 2006, Griffuel Cancer Rsch. prize, France, 2006, Schleiden medal, Germany, 2007, Gotham prize for cancer rsch., 2008. Fellow: AAAS, Am. Acad. Arts & Scis., Am. Acad. Microbiology; mem.: NAS, Acad. Europaea, European Molecular Biology Orgn., Am. Philos. Soc. Achievements include patents in field. Office: CalTech Divsn Biology 147 75 1200 East California Blvd Pasadena CA 91125-0001 Office Phone: 626-395-3785. Office Fax: 626-440-9821. Business E-Mail: avarsh@caltech.edu.

VARTANIAN, A. JOHN, otolaryngologist, researcher; b. Joliet, Ill., May 28, 1971; MD, Chgo. Med. Sch., 1998. Dept. otolaryngology-head and neck surgery U. Ill., Chgo., 1998—. Pres. med. student's sect. AMA, North Chicago, 1995—96. Contbr. articles to profl. jours. Mem.: Am. Acad. Otolaryngology - Head and Neck Surgery. Office: Univ Ill Chgo 1855 W Taylor St Chicago IL 60611 Home: 1078 Trafalgar Dr Glendale CA 91207

VARVAK, MARK, mathematician, researcher; b. Kiev, Russia, Feb. 13, 1939; came to U.S., 1987; s. Shlyoma and Anna (Berimskaya) V.; m. Nellie Albert, Feb. 1, 1973 (div. Oct. 1983); 1 child, Alexander; m. Lidiya Zolotarenko, Aug. 30, 2002. MS in Applied Math., Ukraine U., 1969; candidate of sci., Rsch. Inst. of Structures, Kiev, 1970. Sr. rschr. Rsch. Inst. of Structures, Kiev, 1963-79; sr. engr. Constrn. Authority, Kiev, 1979-86; programmer Consulting Engring. Co., NYC, 1988-91; scientist Sci. Application Internat. Corp., 1997—99, Navair Tng. Sys. Divsn., Orlando, Fla., 2002—. Contbr. more than 40 articles to profl. jours. Mem. Am. Math. Soc. Office: Training Sys Divsn 12350 Rsch Park Orlando FL 32826

VASA, ROBERT FRANCIS, bishop; b. Lincoln, Nebr., May 7, 1951; MDiv, Dallas Univ., 1976; JCL, Pontifical Gregorian Univ., Rome, 1981. Ordained priest Diocese of Lincoln, 1976, asst. chancellor, vicar gen.; ordained bishop, 2000; bishop Diocese of Baker, Oreg., 2000—. Roman Catholic. Office: Diocese of Baker Chancery Office 911 SE Armour St Bend OR 97708 Office Phone: 541-388-4004. Office Fax: 541-388-2566.

VASANA, SUSAN (CHUN-YE), engineering educator; d. De-Jun and Yi-Hua Ye; m. William Vasana, Feb. 14, 2001; children: Danica Hill Chang, Anna Ye Vasana. BS, Shanghai Jiaotong U., 1983; MS, Tongji U., 1986; PhD, Queen's U., Can., 1994. Lectr. Tongji U., Shanghai, 1986—89; scientist Nat. Inst. Sci. Rsch., Montreal, Que., Canada, 1994; sr. staff engr. Motorola Inc., Boynton Beach, Fla., 1994—2002; adj. prof. Fla. Atlantic U., Boca Raton, Fla., 2000—01; assoc. prof. U. North Fla., Jacksonville, 2002—. Actor:. Recipient Silver Quills award, Motorola Inc., 2000. Mem.: IEEE, Internat. Assn. Sci. and Tech. Devel. Achievements include patents for communication device having antenna switch diversity and method therefor; method and apparatus for demodulating a frequency shift keyed signal; method and apparatus for decoding a 2-level radio signal; method in a selective call receiver for synchronizing to a multi-level radio signal; method and apparatus for baud detection in a communication device; method and apparatus for accurate synchronization using symbol decision feedback; method and apparatus for correlation detection of multi-level signals with non-standard deviations; method and apparatus for automatic simulcast correlation for a correlation detector; method and apparatus for gain normalization of a correlation demodulator; Manchester code delta detection. Office: Engineering Univ N FL 1 UNF Rd Jacksonville FL 32224

VASCONCELOS, MARCO, psychologist; s. Antonio Vasconcelos and Isabel Barbosa. BSc, U. Minho, Portugal, 1999, MSc, 2004; PhD in Psychology, Purdue U., West Lafayette, Ind., 2008. Rsch. asst. U. Porto, Portugal, 2000—01, U. Minho, Braga, Portugal, 2003—04, Purdue U., 2004—08, tchg. asst., 2005—; asst. prof. Lusiada U., 2001—03. Recipient C. Eugene Walker award, António Almeida Engr. prize; Grindley grant, Exptl. Psychology Soc., Eng., 2007, Postdoc. grant, Sci. and Tech., Portugal, 2008. Mem.: Nat. Scholars Honor Soc.

VASERSTEIN, LUDMILA, music educator; b. Odessa, Ukraine, Sept. 21, 1949; arrived in USA, 1987; d. Peter and Rozalia Ruvinsky; m. Vladimir Vassershteyn, July 8, 1972; 1 child, Gabriel. MusB, Nicolaev Coll. Music, Ukraine, 1969; MusM, Odessa State Conservatory, Ukraine, 1974. Piano tchr. Sch. of Music, Odessa, Ukraine, 1974—87, MDCC, Miami, Fla., 1987—96; music and piano tchr. Montessoir Sch. of Miami Beach, No. Bay Village, Fla., 1988—2003, Gulfstream Montessoir Sch., Inc., Hallandale, Fla., 2003—. Mem.: Nat. Guild of Piano Tchr. (Nat. Honor Roll 2001—03), Music Tchr. Nat. Assoc., Suzuki Assoc. of Am. Republican. Judaism. Avocations: jogging, reading. Home: 251 174th St #1202 Miami Beach FL 33160 Office: Gulfstream Montessori Sch 750 Hallandale Beach Blvd Hallandale FL 33009

VASHOLZ, LOTHAR ALFRED, retired insurance company executive; b. Milw., Feb. 20, 1930; s. Alfred and Charlotte Vasholz; m. Marji Cartwright, Dec. 26, 1954; children: Julie, Ann, Eric. BS, U. Colo., 1952; M of Pub. Svc. (hon.), U. Rio Grande. ChFC. Sr. cons. Life Ins. Mktg. & Rsch., Hartford, Conn., 1966—70; v.p. N.Am. Life, Chgo., 1970—73; sr. v.p. Bankers Mut., Freeport, Ill., 1973—75; dir. sales Security Life Denver, 1975—81; v.p. Union Ctrl. Life Ins. Co., Cin., 1981—85, sr. v.p., 1985—86, mgr. Columbus, Ohio, 1986—87, sr. v.p., chief mktg. officer Cin., 1987—91, exec. v.p., corp. mktg. officer, 1991—95; chmn. Carillon Investments, 1991—95; cons. mktg. and sales to life ins. industry, 1995—. Emeritus trustee U. Rio Grande, Ohio; chair adv. bd. Salvation Army, Coachella Valley, Calif., 2006—; chair reach out ministries St. John's Cathedral Ch., Palm Desert, Calif., 2009. Fellow Life Mgmt. Inst.; mem. Phi Delta Theta (past internat. pres., past pres. ednl. found.) Republican. Office Phone: 760-345-5052.

VASILAKI, LINDA BOOZER, music educator; b. Grand Rapids, Mich., Jan. 2, 1949; d. Gordon and Dianne (Demmon) Boozer; m. Yuri G. Vasilaki, Sept. 29, 1979; children: Camilla Dianne, Andrew Alten, Maria Demmon. BMus in Edn., Mich. State U., 1971; MFA, U. Iowa, 1973; EdD in Curriculum and Instrn., Argosy U., Sarasota, Fla., 2003. Cert. kindergarten-12 music tchr., 7-8 all subjects tchr., Mich., Fla.; cert. Orff, Level 1. Kindergarten-6 music cons. Grand Rapids (Mich.) Pub. Schs., 1973-75; tchr., founder Suzuki violin program Grand Rapids Bd. Edn., 1976-80; tchr. violin Nat. Music Camp, Interlochen, Mich., 1981, 82; chair music dept., orch. dir. Out of Door Acad., Sarasota, Fla., 1983—; founder, dir. Encore Fine Arts Program, Sarasota, Fla., 1988—. Tchr. viola Blue Lake Fine Arts Camp, Muskegon, 1973; violist Fla. West Coast Symphony, Sarasota, 1982—; mem. Grand Rapids Symphony, 1973-80; tchr. Suzuki Assn. Am., Sarasota, 1976—; adj. music/viola faculty Hope Coll., Grand Valley State Coll. Author: Music Lovers' Cookbook, 1983, Symbol of Liberty, 1985; editor: Out of Door Academy Cuisine, 1983; contbr. articles to profl. jours. Counselor, music therapist Indian Trails Camp for the Phys. Handicapped, Grand Rapids, 1968-69; violist Venice (Fla.) Symphony, 1991-92; former mem. faculty New Eng. Music Camp. Scholar New Coll. Music Festival, 1971, Lenox String Quartet Seminar, 1971, Banff (Can.) Centre-Fine Arts String Quartet Seminar, 1972, U. Iowa, 1972-73; Fla. Humanities grantee, summer 1995. Mem. Phi Kappa Lambda, Kappa Alpha Theta, Delta Omicron (pres. 1971), Delta Kappa Gamma. Avocations: music, reading, writing. Home: 3341 Bougainvillea St Sarasota FL 34239-5704 Business E-Mail: lvasilaki@oda.edu.

VASILAROS, STEVEN THOMAS, lawyer; b. Pitts., Jan. 10, 1951; s. Thomas and Katerine Vasilaros; m. Jerilyn K. Vasilaros, Dec. 7, 1991; 1 child, Nicole. JD, Ohio No. U., Ada, 1978. Bar: Ohio 1978, Fla. 1985, U.S. Dist. Ct. (mid. dist.) Fla. 1988. Atty. Mascio, Blake, Hershey, & Vasilaros, Steubenville, Ohio, 1978—85; police prosecutor City of Steubenville, 1980—84; atty. Becks, Becks, & Wickersham, Daytona Beach, Fla., 1985—88; pres. Vasilaros and Politis, P.A., 1988—. Circuit ct. mediator Fla. Supreme Ct., Daytona Beach, 2004—. Participant Fla. Patient Protection Assoc., Tallahassee, 2004—06; fund raiser Dem. Party, Daytona Beach, 2000—06. Recipient Tiger in the Bush award, Fla. Patient Protection Assoc., 2005. Mem.: Acad. Fla. Trial Lawyers (assoc.; dir. 2005—06, Silver Eagle award 2005), Am. Trial Lawyers Assoc. (assoc.), Fla. State Bar Assoc. (assoc.), Ohio State Bar Assoc. (assoc.). Democrat. Greek Orthodox. Avocation: fishing. Office: Vasilaros & Politis PA 730 Dunlawton Ave Daytona Beach FL 32127 Office Fax: 386-767-1994. Business E-Mail: info@hereforyou.net.

VASILESKA, DRAGICA, electrical engineer, educator; b. Gostivar, Macedonia, Oct. 12, 1961; arrived in US, 1990, naturalized, 2002; d. Zdravko Vasileski and Antigona Vasileska; life ptnr. Moma Petrovich. PhD in Elec. Engring., Ariz. State U., Tempe, 1995. Faculty Sch. Elec. Engring., Skopje, Macedonia, 1985—91; grad. rsch. assoc. Ariz. State U., 1991—95, postdoc, 1995—97, prof., 1997—. Contbr. proposal (NSF Carreer award, 1998), chapters to books, articles to profl. jours. Recipient Career award, NSF, 1998. Mem.: APS, IEEE (sr.). Democrat.

Achievements include research in quantum transport in nanostructures, discrete impurity effects, unintentional dopants, Green's functions formalism. Avocations: skiing, swimming, movies, hiking. Home: 8270 N Hayden Rd 2050 Scottsdale AZ 85258 Office: Arizona State U PO Box 875706 Tempe AZ 85287-5706 Business E-Mail: vasileska@asu.edu.

VASILYEV, VLADISLAV YURIEVICH, chemist, researcher, engineer; b. Saratov, Russia, Oct. 8, 1953; s. Yuri Vyacheslavovich and Margarita Nikolaevna Vasilyev; m. Lidia Ivanovna Tretyakova; children: Olga Vladislavovna Shklovchik, Yuri Vladislavovich, Ioulia Vladislavovna Vasilyeva. M in Chemistry, Novosibirsk State U., Russia, 1976; PhD in Phys. Chemistry, Inst. Solid State Chemistry and Mechanochemistry, USSR Acad. Scis., Russia, 1990, DSc in Solid State Chemistry, 2002. Prin. engr., project mgr., chief tech. engr. Novosibirsk Semiconductor Devices Plant, 1976—; prof. Novosibirsk State Tech. U., 2003—. Leading rsch. scientist Inst. Semiconductor Physics, Russian Acad. Scis., Novosibirsk, 2001—05; prof. Korea Polytech. U., Republic of Korea, 2006—. Contbr. articles to profl. jours. Recipient 1st, 2nd and 3rd prize, Novosibirsk Semiconductor Devices Plant, 1980, 1982, 1984, 1987, 1990, 3rd prize, Bronze medal, Ann. USSR State Industry Achievements Exhbn., 1987, 3rd, 2nd prize, Inst. Semiconductor Physics, Russian Acad. Scis., 2002, 2004. Mem.: Electrochem. Soc. Achievements include 15 patents in field. Avocations: travel, tourism. Home: Apt 153 Deputatskaya St 60 630099 Novosibirsk Russia Office: Siberian Integrated Systems LLC Office Rm 300 Bldg 2 Krasnii Prospect 220 630049 Novosibirsk Russia Home Fax: 7-383-2100533. Personal E-mail: vladislav_v_2000@yahoo.com.

VASILYEVA, ANNA, artist, writer; b. Kiev, Ukraine, Nov. 24, 1977; d. Tamara Balenko and Vladimir Vasylyev. Fine Art Degree, T.G. Shevchenko State Art Sch., 1997; BA in Art, Calif. State U., Northridge, 2005. Tchr. asst. KidsArt, Tarzana, Calif., 1999; designer, illustrator Pub. House KM Academia, Kiev, 1996, All Electronics Corp., Van Nuys, Calif., 2002—07; tchr. art Marina's Sch. Music and Art, Northridge, Calif., 2001; tchg. assoc. Calif. State U., Northridge, 2004—; graphic designer Big Screen Network Prodns., Westlake Village, Calif., 2005—06; web master, project mgr. Dinair Airbrush Makeup Inst., Van Nuys, Calif., 2006—; art dir., owner Digital Saddle Prodns., Tarzana, Calif., 2006—. Exhibitions include State Fall Exhbn. Art, 1993, First Internat. Exhbn. -Presentation of Periodical Publs. about Pets, 1995, Art Gallery of U. Kiev-Mogila Acad., 1996, Art Acad. LA, 1999, Svitozor Gallery, 1999—2001, LA Valley Coll., 2000, LA Mission Coll., 2002, Limner Gallery, 2003, Pacific Design Ctr., LA, 2004, 2006, Art Assn. Harrisburg's 76th Ann. Juried Exhbn., 2004, Venturous Vanguard Video Festival, 2007, Palos Verde Art Ctr., Calif., 2007; film editor, designer: Streetlight Cinema, 2004—; contbr. articles to mags. Recipient Biography Pub., The Nat. Dean's List, 2002—03; State U. Fee grant, Calif. State U., Northridge, 2003—, Campus Fee grant, 2003—. Avocations: reading, travel, horseback riding. Office: Dinair Airbrush Makeup Inst 5315 Laurel Canyon Blvd North Hollywood CA 91607 Personal E-mail: anya@artistanya.com.

VASKEVITCH, DAVID, computer software company executive; 3 children. BS in Math., Computer Sci., Philosophy, U. Toronto, M in Computer Sci. With Standard Software; owner PlanDesign, Toronto, Canada; with 3Com Corp., Microsoft Corp., Redmond, Wash., 1986—, dir. U.S. mktg., 1986, gen. mgr. enterprise computing, 1993, v.p., distributed applications platform, chief architect, 1998—99, sr. v.p., developer, 1999—2000, sr. v.p. bus. applications divsn., 2000—01, sr. v.p., chief tech. officer bus. platform, 2001—09, sr. v.p., chief tech. officer server & tools, 2009—. Mem. adv. bd., Live Labs (Rsch. partnership between MSN and Microsoft Rsch.) Microsoft Corp., 2006—. Author: Client/Server Strategies: A Survival Guide for Corporate Re-engineers, 1993. While at the U. Toronto in the 1970's, he invented a typewriter-terminal-based communications messaging network that predated PC-based e-mail systems. Office: Microsoft Corp One Microsoft Way Redmond WA 98052-6399*

VASKO, FRANCIS JOSEPH, mathematics professor; b. Bethlehem, Pa., Mar. 23, 1952; s. Frank and Ann Vasko; m. Nancy Louise Rosenberger, July 1, 1978; 1 child, Lisa Elizabeth. MS in Math., Lehigh U., Bethlehem, Pa., 1976; MS in Indsl. Engring., Lehigh U., 1978, PhD, 1983. Math. prof. Kutztown U., Pa., 1986—. Applied math. cons. Dr.Francis Vasko, Cons., Hellertown, Pa., 1986—. Contbr. over 50 articles to profl. jours. Bd. of trustees Hellertown Libr., Pa., 1995—98. Recipient Big Brother of the yr., Big Bros./Big Sisters of the Lehigh Valley, 1994. Mem.: Sigma XI (full mem.). Achievements include research in new mathematical solution procedures for steel industry production planning and scheduling problems. Home: 510 Ellen St Hellertown PA 18055 Office: Kutztown Univ 230 A Lytle Hall Kutztown PA 19530 Business E-Mail: vasko@kutztown.edu.

VASKO, PETER THEODORE FREDERICK, priest; b. Bklyn., Nov. 28, 1943; s. Theodore Frederick and Catherine (Buday) V. BA in Philosophy, Cath. U. Am., 1966, BD in Theology, 1969; postgrad., Duke U., 1972-73, Franciscan Studium Biblicum, Jerusalem, 1985-86. Ordained priest Roman Cath. Ch., 1987. Pub. rels. asst. Holiday Inn/Oak Grove, Durham, N.C., 1972-74; dir. devel. NAA, Charlotte, N.C., 1974-76; dir. CETA, New Orleans, 1976-78; v.p. sales Peachtree Corners Corp. Travel, Atlanta, 1978-81; bd. dirs. Franciscan Custody, Jerusalem, 1992—2001; pres. Franciscan Found. for The Holy Land, Jerusalem, 1994—. Editor photo essay See the Holy Land, 1993, Our Visit to The Holy Land, 2004; editor The Holy Land Mag., 1993-95; writer, narrator video On the Road of Christ, 1994; narrator video The Life of Jesus: Scriptural Journey, 1997; guest Mother Angelica Live, 1996-98, 02-03, Pat Robertson 700 Club, 1996, EWTN's World Over Show, 2004-06, others; co-prodr.: (documentary) Crisis in the Holy Land, 1994; (TV series) The Holy Land with Fr. Peter Vasko, 2006. Bd. dirs. St. Ives Soc., Jerusalem, 1992-94; guide White House Via U.S. Embassy, Jerusalem, 1992—; chaplain U.S. Marines/U.S. Consulate, Jerusalem, 1988—. Decorated mem. Equestrial Order of the Holy Sepulchre, 1992, order of merit Sovereign Mil. Order of The Knights Templar, 2005, order of the Holy Spirit Knights Templar, 2007, Hon. Marine Comdt. Conway USMC, 2008; recipient Achievement in Pub. Rels. award Pub. Rels. Soc., Raleigh, 1975, Marine Security Guard Bn. Co. B Cert. of Appreciation, 1995, 99, U.S. Marine Security Detachment Comdr. Commendation award, 1999, State of Tex. Commn.: Theodore Peter F. Vasko commd. as Hon. Texan by Gov. R. Perry, 2002, Cert. of Flag Presentation of USS Ariz. by Rear Adm. Robert T. Conway, Jr., USN, Comdr., Navy Region, Hawaii, 2002, Cert. of Appreciation for Good Conduct, 2002-03, UNMC-MSG Detachment of Jerusalem, Cert. of Appreciation, MSG Det. for Outstanding Svc. as Det. Chaplain, 2003; named Jaycee of Yr., NC chpt., 1973, Top Ten People in Cath. Ch. Inside the Vatican mag., 2006. Mem.: Marine Embassy Guard Assn. (mem. 2003).

VASLEF, STEVEN NICHOLAS, surgeon; b. Colorado Springs, Colo., Aug. 16, 1958; s. Nicholas P. and Irene I. (Koncz) V.; m. Maria E. Vaslef, July 11, 1988. BS, MIT, 1980; MD, U. Va., 1984; PhD, Northwestern U., 1990. Diplomate Am. Bd. Surgery with subspecialty in surg. critical care. Intern U. Ill., Chgo., 1984-85, resident in gen. surgery, 1985-92; mem. staff Evanston/Glenbrook Hosps., 1992-94; asst. prof. surgery, asst. pro. bio-med. engring. Northwestern U. Med. Sch., Chgo., 1992-94; asst. prof. surgery Duke U. Med. Ctr., Durham, N.C., 1994-2000, assoc. prof., 2000—, asst. prof. bio-med. engring., 1994—97, asst. prof. anesthesiology, 1996—. Mem. ACS; mem. Soc. Critical Care Medicine, Am. Soc. Artificial Internal Organs, Soc. for Surgery of Alimentary Tract, Am. Assn. Surgery of Trauma, Ea. Assn. for Surgery of Trauma. Office: Duke Univ Med Ctr Dept Surgery Box 2837 Durham NC 27715-2601 Home Phone: 919-382-8208. E-mail: vasle001@mc.duke.edu.

VASQUEZ, GADDI H., United States Ambassador to the United Nations, Rome; b. Carrizo Springs, Tex., Jan. 22, 1955; m. Elaine Vasquez; 1 child, Jason. AA in Criminal Justice, Rancho Santiago C.C., 1972; BA in Pub. Svc. Mgmt., U. Redlands, 1980; DHL (hon.), U. LaVerne, 2003. Police officer City of Orange, Calif., 1975-79; coord. community rels., mgr.'s office City of Riverside, Calif., 1979-81; exec. asst. Orange County Bd. Suprs., 3d Dist., Calif., 1981-85, mem. Calif., 1987—95; area mgr. So. Calif. Edison Co., 1985; hispanic liaison Office of Gov. George Deukmejian, Calif., 1985, from dep. appointments sec. to chief dep. appointments sec. Calif., 1985-87; dir. Peace Corps, Washington, 2002—06; US rep. to UN agencies US Dept. State, Rome, 2006—. Mem. Transp. Corridor Agys. Bd., 1987-93, local agy. formation commn., 1988-93, chmn. 1990-91; mem. Calif. Film Commn., 1988-91, Calif. Coun. Criminal Justice, 1989—; founder, co-chair, Orange County Health Care Task Force, 1990—; with White House Fellowships Commn., 1990-91; co-chmn. Orange County Congestion Mgmt. Policy Task Force, 1990—; bd. dirs. Orange County Transp. Authority, 1991-95, exec. com. 1992-95, vice chmn. 1993-95; regional advisory and planning coun., 1991-95, vice chmn. 1992, chmn. 1993; official observer Armenian Independence elections, 1991. Bd. dirs. Future Leaders Am., Southwest Voter Rsch. Inst., calif. First Amendment Coalition, Orange County Boy Scout Coun., So. Area Foster Care Effort, Orange County Performing Arts Ctr., Opera Pacific; trustee Am. Coun. Young Polit. Leaders; adv. bd. Pediatric Cancer Rsch. Found, Orange County Juvenile Connection Project, Calif. Office Traffic Safety, The Salvation Army Orange County, Project AERO, Constitutional Rights Found. Orange County; community coun. Prentice Day Sch.; hon. adv. bd. Adam Walsh Ctr.; hon. bd. govs. Bower Mus.; leadership coun. Orange County Points Light. Named Officer of Yr., Am. Legion, 1977. Outstanding Young Man of Am. U.S. C.of C., 1985, One of 100 Most Influential Hispanics in U.S. Hispanic Bus. Mag., 1986-87, 88-89, 91-92, 92-93, 2002-03, Govt. Hispanic Bus. Advocate of Yr. U.S. Hispanic Champer Region I, 1991; recipient Alumni Achievement award Santa Ana Coll., 1988, Alumni of Yr.award U. Redlands, 1989, Humanitarian award NCCJ, 1989, award State Child Devel. Adv. Com., 1990, Tree of Life award Jewish Nat. Fund, 1991, Ralph E. Hudson Open Space award Landscape Architects Found., 1992, Disting. Alumni award Coun. Young Polit. Leaders, 2002, Outstanding Alumni award Am. Assn. C.C.s, 2003. Office: US Mission to the UN Agencies in Rome Piazza del Popolo 18 4th Fl Via Sallustiana 49 00187 Rome Italy*

VASQUEZ, JENNIFER, marketing and public relations executive, researcher; d. Rene and Dinora Vasquez. BA in Govt., George Mason U., Fairfax, Va., 2001; BA in Internat. Politics, George Mason U., 2000; degree in Mgmt. in Non-Profit, U. Miami, 2006; M in Latin Am. and Caribbean Studies, Fla. Internat. U., Miami, 2006, MS in Internat. Studies, 2007. Cert. in project. mgmt. Fla. Internat. U., 2006. Exec. dir. UN Assn. Miami, Miami, 2003—06; dir. dowtown ctr., mktg. and outreach Fla. Internat. U., 2006—; regional mktg. exec. Holland and Knight, 2007. Mem. Greater Miami C. of C.; appointed commr. Regalado cmty. relations bd. City of Miami; mem. appointed summer team leader Svc. for Peace, Summer, 2006; grants panelist Miami Dade Cult. Affairs; active Nat. Latino AIDS Commn., US Global Leadership Campaign, United Way Young Leaders, Miami Coalition Gang Task Force; lobbyst US Global Leadership Campaign, Miami, 2006—07. Recipient Global Young Adv. of Yr. award, UN Assn., 2006, Bronze and Silver Vol. Presdl. award, Healthy Cmty. LEADERSHIP Miami, Greater Miami C. of C., 2006—07; finalist Essie Silva Cmty. award, United Way, 2006. Mem.: Women's Bus. Coun. Dade Chpt., Human Svcs. Coalition, League United Latin Am. Citizens, Am. Red Cross Young Profls., Miami Internat. Film Festival, Emerging Arts Leader, Nat. Soc. Hispanic Profls., Grad. Student Network, Hands On Miami. Baptist. Avocations: travel, languages, politics, sports, reading. Office: Fla Internat Univ 22 E Flagler St Miami FL 33131 Personal E-mail: jvasquez.miami@gmail.com.

VÁSQUEZ, JOSÉ STEPHEN, bishop; b. Stamford, Tex., July 9, 1957; s. Juan and Elvira Vásquez. B in Theology, U. St. Thomas, 1980. Ordained priest Diocese of San Angelo, Tex., 1984; parochial vicar St. Joseph Ch., Odessa, Tex., 1985—97, pastor, 1997—2002, St. Joseph's Ch., Ft. Stockton, Tex., 1987—97; ordained bishop, 2002; aux. bishop Archdiocese of Galveston-Houston, Tex., 2002—. Roman Catholic. Office: Chancery Office PO Box 907 1700 San Jacinto Houston TX 77001-0907 Office Phone: 713-659-5461. Office Fax: 713-759-9151.

VASQUEZ, JUAN FLORES, federal judge; b. San Antonio, June 24, 1948; s. Jose and Amelia (Flores) V.; m. Mary Theresa Schultz, Aug. 22, 1970; children: Juan Jr., Jaime. BA, U. Tex., 1972; JD, U. Houston, 1977; LLM in Taxation, NYU, 1978. Bar: Tex. 1977, US Dist. Ct. (southern dist. Tex.) 1982, US Dist. Ct. (western dist.) Tex. 1985, US Ct. Appeals (5th circuit) 1982, US Supreme Ct. 1996, US Tax Ct. 1978. Acct. Coopers & Lybrand, LA, 1972-74; tax atty. Office of Chief Coun. IRS, Houston, 1978-82, Leighton, Hood & Vasquez, San Antonio, 1987; pvt. practice San Antonio, 1987-95; judge US Tax Ct., Washington, 1995—. Mem. ABA, Mex.-American Bar Assn. Tex. and San Antonio, Nat. Hispanic Bar Assn., Nat. Jud. Coll., Hispanic Bar Assn. DC, Coll. State Coll. Tex., Tex. State Bar Assn., San Antonio Bar Assn. Office: US Tax Ct 400 2nd St NW Washington DC 20217-0002 Office Phone: 202-521-0778.*

VASQUEZ, MARGARITA M., pediatrician, educator; d. Luis E. and Ofelia H. Londono; m. Paul E. Vasquez, May 26, 2001; 1 child, Brianna C. MD, U. Mo., Kans. City, 2000. Neonatal fellow U. Health Sys., San Antonio, 2003—06; asst. prof. pediat. U. Tex. Health Sci. Ctr., San Antonio, 2006—, fellowship dir., 2009—. Recipient Young Investigator award, So. Soc. Pediat. Rsch., 2006, Marshall Klaus Rsch. award, Am. Acad. Pediat., 2003; Rsch. grant, 2003, Discovery Labs., 2006—07. Mem.: Bexar County Med. Soc., Tex. Med. Assn.

VASQUEZ, SABRINA CLAUDINE, choreographer, educator; b. Tucson, Ariz., Apr. 16, 1971; d. Nestor and Georgia Ellen Vasquez; m. Constantine Nicholas Johnson, Dec. 19, 1998; 1 child, Zoe Domnika Johnson. Dancer Hubbard St. Dance Chgo., 1994—95; instr. dance Wichita State U., Kans., 1997—; co artistic dir. Alithea Mime Theatre, Wichita, Kans., 1997—. Choreography fellowship, Kans. Arts Commn., 2007. Liberal. Business E-Mail: sabrina.vasquez@wichita.edu.

VASQUEZ, VIVIAN, education educator; d. Reggie and Lilly Vasquez; m. Andy Bilodeau, Dec. 17, 1994; 1 child, T. J. Bilodeau. BS, U. Toronto, Ont., Can., 1985; EdB, Lakehead U., Thunder Bay, Ont., 1986, York U., Toronto, 1990; MA, Mt. St. Vincent U., Halifax, Nova Scotia, Can., 1994; EdD, Ind. U., Bloomington, 1999. Cert. elem. sch. tchr. Can., 1985, primary edn. specialist York U., 1988, reading specialist 1990, spl. edn. specialist 1990. Elem. sch. tchr. Dufferin Peel, Mississauga, Ont., 1986—97; adj. prof. York U., 1991—92; instr. Mt. St. Vincent U., 1994—97, Ind. U., 1997—99; asst. prof. Am. U., Washington, 1999—2005, assoc. prof., 2005—. Author: (book) Negotiating Critical Literacies with Young Children (Rsch. SIG award, 2004, James N. Britton award, 2005, AERA Outstanding Book of Yr. award, 2006); contbr. chapters to books. Bd. dirs. Whole Lang. Umbrella, 1996; commr., primary edn. reform DC: Kevin Chavous Office, 2001. Recipient Recognition award, Whole Lang. Umbrella, 1999, Senate Curriculum Devel. award, Am. U., 2000; finalist Podcast Peer awards, 2007; grantee, Am. U. Mem.: NCTE (com. mem. 2008—, Chair Elem. Sect. Steering Com. 2000—02, Nat. Co-Learn Sr. Rsch. Team 2002, Presdl. Team Nominating com. 2007, Recognition award 2000, Whole Lang. Umbrella Recognition award 2000), Am. Ednl. Rsch. Assn. LSP SIG (program chair 2007—), Early Childhood Edn. Assembly (chair 2008—), Ctr. Expansion Lang. and Thinking (sec. 2008—). Avocations: travel, music. Office: Am Univ SETH 4400 Mass Ave NW Washington DC 20016 Business E-Mail: vvasque@american.edu.

VASQUEZ, WILLIAM LEROY, business educator, consultant; b. Austin, Tex., Mar. 9, 1944; s. Eliseo M. and Janie (Garcia) V. BS with distinction, Nova Southeastern U., 1983, MBA, 1985, DBA, 1992. Cert. Inst. Cert. Profl. Mgrs., 1990, Inst. Cert. Computing Profls., 1993. Svc. mgr. Data Gen. Corp., various, Latin Am., 1972-80; product mgr. Gould, Inc., Ft. Lauderdale, Fla., 1980—84, Tektronix Inc., Portland, Oreg., 1984—86, Racal-Milgo, Ft. Lauderdale, 1988—90, Citibank Internat., Ft. Lauderdale, 1991—2001; ret., 2001. Instr. City U., Portland campus, 1987-88; Maryhurst Coll., 1985-88, Nova Southeastern U. (domestic and internat.), 1988—, pres. internat. alumni assn.; instr. St. Thomas U., 1989—, Fla. Atlantic U., 1993—. Mem. VFW, Nat. Bus. Edn. Assn., U.S. Submarine Vets., Inc., Mensa. Republican. Avocations: guitar, model trains, fine arts. Home: 9788 NW 18th St Coral Springs FL 33071-5824 Office Phone: 954-309-3507. E-mail: vasquezw@bellsouth.net.

VASSALLO, BRETT JOSEPH, gynecologist, surgeon; b. Stamford, Conn., Oct. 16, 1969; s. Charles Anthony and Elizabeth Joan Vassallo; m. Carol Frances Ellman, May 1, 1999; children: Charles Joseph, John Michael. BA, Georgetown U., 1991; MD, U. Chgo., 1995. Resident ob-gyn U. Chgo. Hosp., 1995—99; clin. assoc. urogynecology and reconstructive pelvic surgery Good Samaritan Hosp./U. of Cin., 1999—2002; asst. prof. U. Chgo., 2002—. Contbr. chapters to books, articles to profl. jours. Mem.: ACOG, Am. Urogynecologic Soc. Office: U Chgo 5841 S Maryland Ave MC 2050 Chicago IL 60637 E-mail: bvjmd@iultd.org.

VASSALLO, JOHN A., lawyer; b. NYC, Aug. 19, 1937; s. John and Gilda (Di Desidero) Vassallo; children: John C., Elena L., Edward F. AB, Columbia U., 1959, JD, 1962. Bar: N.Y. 1963, U.S. Dist. Ct. (so. and ea. dists.) N.Y. 1964, U.S. Ct. Appeals (2d cir.) 1965. Assoc. Saxe, Bacon & O'Shea, NYC, 1962-68; ptnr. Barovick & Konecky, NYC, 1968-70, Kurtz & Vassallo, NYC, 1970-78, Franklin, Weinrib, Rudell & Vassallo, NYC, 1978—. Fellow: Am. Coll. Family Trail Lawyers (diplomate), Am. Acad. Matrimonial Attys.; mem.: Friars Club. Office: Franklin Weinrib Rudell & Vassallo 488 Madison Ave New York NY 10022-5702 Office Phone: 212-935-5500. Business E-Mail: jvassallo@fwrv.com.

VASSELL, GREGORY S., electric utility consultant; b. Moscow, Dec. 24, 1921; came to U.S., 1951, naturalized, 1957; s. Gregory M. and Eugenia M. Wasiljeff; m. Martha Elizabeth Williams, Apr. 26, 1957; children: Laura Kay, Thomas Gregory. Dipl. Ing. in Elec. Engring, Tech. U. Berlin, 1951; MBA in Corp. Fin., NYU, 1954. With Am. Electric Power Svc. Corp., Columbus, Ohio, 1951-88, v.p. system planning, 1973-76, dir., 1973-88, sr. v.p. system planning, 1976-88; electric utility cons. Upper Arlington, Ohio, 1988—. Bd. dirs. Columbus & Southern Ohio Electric Co., 1981-88, Cardinal Operating Co.; mem. tech. adv. com. transmission FPC, 1968-70, FERC Task Force on Power Pooling, 1980-81 Contbr. articles to profl. jours. Fellow IEEE (life); mem. NAE, Athletic Club Columbus Home and Office: 6000 Riverside Dr Dublin OH 43017

VASSEUR, ALEXIS FREDERIC, mathematics professor; married. PhD in Math., U. Jussieu, Paris. Rschr. U. Nice, France, 1999—2003; asst. prof. U. Tex., Austin, 2003—07, assoc. prof., 2007—. Mem.: NSF.

VASSILEV, PETER MIHAILOV, biomedical researcher; b. Sofia, Bulgaria, Mar. 26, 1947; s. Michael Antonov and Margarita Penkova (Aladjova) V.; m. Marie Petrova Kanazirska, Oct. 27, 1971; children: Michael, Peter Jr. MD, Med. Acad., Sofia, 1972; PhD, Bulgarian Acad. of Scis., 1983. Rsch. assoc. Ctrl. Lab. of Biophysics, Sofia, 1976-83, Dept. of Physiology, Mich. State U., East Lansing, 1983-84, asst. prof., 1986-87; rsch. assoc. Dept. Pharmacology, Mich. State U., 1984-86; sr. fellow Dept. Pharmacology, U. Wash., Seattle, 1987-89; asst. prof. Dept. Medicine, Harvard Med. Sch., Boston, 1989—. Dept. Medicine, Brigham & Women's Hosp., Boston, 1989—. Dir. electrophysiology lab., endocrinology hypertension divsn. Brigham & Women's Hosp., Boston, 1989—. Contbr. articles to profl. jours; author: (with others) Structure and Properties of Cell Membranes, 1985. Rsch. grantee NIH, 1991-94, 92—. Mem. AAAS, N.Y. Acad. Sci. Avocations: mountain hiking, running marathons. Office: Harvard Med Sch Brigham & Women's Hosp 221 Longwood Ave Boston MA 02115-5804

VASSILYADI, MICHAEL, pediatric neurosurgeon; b. Istanbul, Turkey, Nov. 25, 1961; s. Irakli and Cristal Vassilyadi; m. Anastasia Lyras, Aug. 23, 1986; children: Frank Photios, Christal, Anthony Irakli. BSc, McGill U., 1980—83, MSc, 1984—86, MD, CM, 1986—90. Diplomate Am. Bd. Pediat. Neurol. Surgery, Am. Bd. Neurol. Surgery. Med. staff Children's Hosp. of Ea. Ont., Ottawa, Canada, 1996—. Asst. prof. surgery U. of Ottawa, 1996—2003; assoc. prof. surgery and pediat. U. Ottawa, 2003—; investigator Children's Hosp. Ea. Ont. Rsch. Inst., Canada; mentor faculty medicine U. Ottawa, Spina Bifida & Hydrocephalus Assn. Ontario Med. Adv. Contbr. articles to profl. jours.; mem. editl. bd. Pediat. Neurosurgery. Ottawa chpt. dir. Think First Can. Recipient Matching Travel award, Children's Hosp. of Ea. Ont. Rsch. Inst., 1998, 2003—05, Best sci. posters, Neurol. Sciences of Que., 1995, Tchg. Skills Attainment award, Faculty of Medicine, U. Ottawa, 2007; Farquharson Rsch. scholarship, Med. Rsch. of Can., 1987, Dr. James Douglas Rsch. fellowship in Pathology, McGill U., 1985. Fellow: ACS, Am. Acad. Pediat., Royal Coll. Physicians and Surgeons Can.; mem.: Can. Neurol. Scis. Fedn., Can. Pediat. Neurosurgery Group, Am. Bd. Neurol. Surgery, Am. Bd. of Pediat. Neurol. Surgery, Can. Neurosurg. Soc., Am. Soc. Pediatric Neurosurgeons, Coll. Physicians and Surgeons Ont., Coll. des Medecins du Que., Can. Med. Assn., Am. Epilepsy Soc., Am. Assn. Neurol. Surgeons (pediat. neurol. surgery sect.), Ont. Med. Assn., Internat. Soc. Pediatric Neurosurgery, Congress Neurol. Surgeons (pediat. neurol. surgery sect.). Greek Orthodox. Achievements include research in pediatric neurosurgery. Office: Children's Hosp of Eastern Ontario 401 Smyth Rd Ottawa ON Canada K1H 8L1 Business E-Mail: vassilyadi@cheo.on.ca.

VASTI, THOMAS FRANCIS, III, lawyer; b. Poughkeepsie, NY, Sept. 22, 1966; s. Thomas F., Jr. and Faith Vasti; m. Suzanne Hammond, Aug. 17, 1991; children: Annelise Nicole, Matthew Thomas. BA, U. Notre Dame, 1988; JD, U. St. John's, 1991. Bar: N.Y. 1992, Conn. 1992, U.S. Dist. Ct. (ea. & so. dists.) N.Y. 1995, U.S. Supreme Ct. 2001. Law clk. Vasti & Rutberg Esq., Pleasant Valley, NY, 1988—91; assoc. Vasti & Sears, Pleasant Valley, NY, 1991—96; ptnr. sr. atty. Spigel Brown Fischer Acad. & Vasti, LLC, Pleasant Valley, 2003; pres., sr. atty. Vasti & Farley, P.C., Pleasant Valley, NY, 2004—05; pres. sr. atty. Vasti & Vasti, PC, Pleasant Valley, NY, 2000—02, v.p., sr. atty., 2005—, Vasti & Sears, P.C., Pleasant Valley, 1996—2000. Mem. Pleasant Valley C. of C., NY, 1992—, v.p., 1995—96, trustee, 1995—98; asst. coach No. Dutchess Raiders Pop Warner Football Assn., 1992, 1993, 1995, head coach, 1994, 1996—2001, treas., 1996—99, v.p., 1999—2000; head coach Hudson Valley Knights A. Y. F. and Pop Warner, 2003—; incorporator, legal counsel Mid-Hudson Conf. Pop Warner Little Scholars, Inc., 2000—04; coach Pleasant Valley Little League, NY, 1992—96, sponsor, 2002—; councilman Town of Pleasant Valley, NY, 2003—07; mem. Pleasant Valley Rep. Com., NY, 1998—, Dutchess County Rep. Com., NY, 1998—, treas., 2006—; vice chmn. Pleasant Valley Rep. Com., NY, 2001—03, chmn., 2003—08. Mem.: ABA, Dutchess County Bar Assn., N.Y. State Trial Lawyers Assn., N.Y. State Bar Assn., Am. Trial Lawyers Assn., Notre Dame Alumni Club of the Mid-Hudson Valley (sec. 1997—2002, pres. 2003), KC. Republican. Roman Catholic. Avocations: youth sports coaching, golf, hunting, fishing. Office: Vasti & Vasti PC PO Box 656 1733 Main St Rte 44 Pleasant Valley NY 12569-0656 Office Phone: 845-635-8866.

VASU, SUBITH, research scientist; s. Vasu and Valiyaparambath. BTech Summa Cum Laude, Indian Inst. Tech. Madras, Chennai, 1999—2004; PhD student, Stanford U., Calif., 2004—. Orgnl. Prathamusa, Silicon Valley, Calif. Personal E-mail: subith@stanford.edu.

VASUDEV, BRAHM SARUP, nephrologist; b. New Delhi, Apr. 12, 1971; MBBS, U. Pune, India, 1994. Resident Brookdale Hosp. Med. Ctr., Bklyn., 2001, chief resident in internal medicine, 2001; fellow critical care medicine Albert Einstein Coll. Medicine, NYC, 2002—03; fellow nephrology Med. Coll. of Wis. Affiliated Hosps., Milw., 2004, fellow transplant nephrology, 2004—. Evaluator kidney transplantation Froedtert Meml. Luth. Hosp., Milw., 2004—; clin. rschr. Med. Coll. Wis., 2002—, investigator clin. trials, 2004—; instr. Med. Coll. of Wis. Affiliated Hosps., 2002—; cons. Shire Pharmaceuticals, Milw., 2003—04. Recipient Excellence award, American Transplant Congress, 2004, Young Investigator award, 2005. Mem.: Am. Soc. Nephrology (assoc.), Renal Physician Assn. (assoc.), Delhi Med. Assn. (assoc.), Indian Med. Assn. (assoc.), Am. Soc. Transplantation (assoc.).

VASUDEVAN, GOPALA, finance educator; s. Gopala Krisha Pillai and Sarojini Amma; m. Sreekala Gopinathan, Aug. 8, 1994; children: Mahesh, Gauri. PhD, NYU, NYC, 1994. Asst. prof. Northeastern U., Boston, 2001—04; assoc. prof. U. Mass., North Dartmouth, 2004—. Contbr. scientific papers to fin. publs. Mem. New Eng. Malayalee Assn., Boston. Mem.: Fin. Mgmt. Assn. Achievements include research in corporate finance, mergers and acquisitions, security offerings. Home and Office: Univ Mass Dartmouth 285 Old Westport Rd North Dartmouth MA 02747 Office Phone: 509-999-8426. Business E-Mail: gvasudevan@umassd.edu.

VATANNIA, SHAHLA, mechanical engineer; b. Bijar, Kurdestan, Iran; d. Mahmood Vatannia and Rafat (Jaferpor); m. Mehdi Yahyavi, May 1, 1986; 1 child, Hooman Mani. MS, SJSU, 2004. Cert. in peng, PEO, 2001. Sr. mech. engr. PSI, Concord, Calif., 2006—, Brinderson, Costa Mesa, Calif., 2008—. Project mgr. Namvaran, Tehran, Iran, 1993—98. V.p. Fourieridea, San Ramon, Calif., 2004—. Achievements include research in electronic cooling. Office: Fourieridea 7572 Northland Pl San Ramon CA 94583 Business E-Mail: svatanni@comcast.net.

VATER, CHARLES J., lawyer; b. Pitts., Feb. 8, 1950; s. Joseph A. and Helen M. (Genellie) V.; m. Diane E. Vater, June 10, 1972; children: Allison D., Elizabeth A. BA, U. Notre Dame, 1971; JD, U. Pitts., 1975. Bar: Pa. 1975, U.S. Dist. Ct. (we. dist.) Pa. 1975, U.S. Ct. Appeals (3d cir.) 1979. Assoc. Tucker Arensberg, P.C., Pitts., 1975-80, ptnr., shareholder, 1980—. Contbr. articles to profl. jours. Mem.: Estate Planning Coun. Pitts. (bd. dirs. 1988—90, 1995—97, past pres.), Allegheny County Bar Assn. (probate coun. 1988—98, 1999—2000, past chair), Phi Beta Kappa, Order of Coif. Home: 1615 Trolist Dr Pittsburgh PA 15241-2650 Office: Tucker Arensberg 1 Ppg Pl Ste 1500 Pittsburgh PA 15222-5413 Office Phone: 412-594-5556. Business E-Mail: cvater@tuckerlaw.com.

VATER, YOURI L., medical educator; b. Riga, Latvia, Apr. 14, 1954; s. Eva Lazar Vater; m. Hanna Vater; 1 child, Maxim; 1 child, Roman. MD, Riga Univ. Sch. of Medicine, Riga Latvia, 1977; PhD, U. Tartu, Estonia, 1988. Cert. sr. bd. anesthesia Israel, 1997. Rsch. fellow Riga Med. Sch., 1980—87, sr. rsch. fellow, 1987—90; dir. cardioanesthesiology dept. Heart Surgery Ctr. Sch. of Medicine Republic of Latvia, Riga, Latvia, 1980—90; residency anesthesia U. Tel Aviv Sackler Med. Ctr., Ichilov, 1990—97; assoc. prof., attending anesthesiologist U. Wash. Sch. of Medicine, Seattle, 1999—. Contbr. articles various profl. jours. Active participant Doctors for Democracy, Tel Aviv, Israel, 1995. Lt. Israeli Mil. Forces., 1995—2004, Israel. Mem.: Am. Soc. Transplantaion Anesthesiologists, Latvian Soc. Anesthesiologists, Am. Soc. Anesthesiologists, Israeli Soc. Anesthesiologists. Achievements include Art Show Promotions. Avocations: travel, journalism, research in anesthesiology, art show promotion. Home: 11323- 24 th Ave NE Seattle WA 98125 Office: U Wash 1959 Pacific St POB 356540 Seattle WA 98105-6540 Home Phone: 206-367-3356; Office Phone: 206-598-4260. Personal E-mail: yvater@yahoo.com.

VATSA, MAYANK, computer scientist, researcher; married. BTech, Purvanchal U., Jaunput, 2002; MS, W.Va. U., Morgantown, 2005, PhD, 2008. Sr. rsch. assoc. Indian Inst. Tech. Kanpur, Uttar Pradesh, 2002—04; grad. rsch. asst. W.Va. U., 2004—08. Recipient Two Outstanding Paper awards, Summer Sch. Biometric Authentication: Multimodality and Sys. Integration, Italy, 2005, Third prize, Sigma Xi, 2007; IAPR Travel grant, Internat. Assn. Pattern Recognition, 2008. Mem.: IEEE (Best Student Paper award 2007). Office: Ln Dept CSEE West Va Univ Morgantown WV 26506

VAUDRY, J. WILLIAM, JR., lawyer; b. Jacksonville, Fla., Jan. 18, 1941; BBA, Tulane U., 1962, LLB, 1967. Bar: La. 1967. Of cousel Lemle & Kelleher, LLP, New Orleans. Bd. editors Tulane Law Rev., 1965-67. Lt. (j.g.) USN, 1962-64. Mem. ABA, La. State Bar Assn., Order of Coif, Phi Delta Phi. Address: Lemle & Kelleher LLP Pan Am Life Ctr 21st flr 601 Poydras St New Orleans LA 70130-6029 Office Phone: 504-584-9408.

VAUGHAN, ALDEN TRUE, history professor; b. Providence, Jan. 23, 1929; s. Dana Prescott and Muriel Louise (True) V.; m. Lauraine A. Freethy, June 1, 1956 (div. 1981); children: Jeffrey Alden, Lynn Elizabeth; m. Virginia Mason Carr, July 16, 1983. BA, Amherst Coll., 1950; MEd, Columbia U., 1956, MA in History, 1958, PhD, 1964. Tchr. Hackley Sch., Tarrytown, NY, 1950-51, A.B. Davis High Sch., Mt. Vernon, NY, 1956-60; From history instr. to prof. Columbia U., NYC, 1961—, prof. emeritus, 1994. Editor Polit. Sci. Quar., NY, 1970-71; vis. adj. prof. CUNY, Lehman Coll., NYC, 1971; vis. prof. Clark U., Worcester, Mass., 1987. Author: New England Frontier, 1965, 3d edit., 1995, American Genesis, 1975, Shakespeare's Caliban, 1991, Roots of American Racism, 1995, Transatlantic Encounters, 2006, others; co-editor: Arden Shakespeare's The Tempest, 1999; gen. editor Early Am. Indian Documents, 20 vols., 1977-2004; mem. editl. bd. Ency. of the N.Am. Colonies, 1993; contbr. articles to profl. jours. including Am. Heritage, Am. Hist. Rev., New Eng. Quar. Lt. (j.g.) USNR, 1951-55. Guggenheim Found. fellow, 1973, Sr. fellow Folger Shakespeare Libr., 1977, 89, Sr. fellow Am. Antiquarian Soc., 1983. Mem. Am. Antiquarian Soc., Am. Soc. for Ethnohistory, Shakespeare Assn. Am., Soc. Am. Historians (exec. sec., treas. 1965-70), Orgn. Am. Historians (program chmn. 1976), Inst. Early Am. History and Culture (coun. mem. 1985-87), Colonial Soc. Mass., Mass. Hist. Soc. Home: 50 Howland Ter Worcester MA 01602-2631

VAUGHAN, CATHY ANN, pharmacist; b. Ahoskie, NC, Feb. 7, 1977; D in Pharmacy, U. NC, Chapel Hill, 2002. Drug info. splty. resident Thomas Jefferson U. Hosp., Phila., 2002—03; clin. pharmacist, medication safety Duke U. Med. Ctr., Durham, NC, 2003—06, drug info. specialist, 2006—, investigational rev. bd. mem., 2007—. Contbr. articles to profl. jours. Mem.: NC Assn. Pharmacists, Am. Soc. Health-Sys. Pharmacists. Office: Duke Univ Med Ctr Erwin Rd Durham NC 27710 Office Fax: 919-684-5249. Personal E-mail: cathyvaughan@msn.com. Business E-Mail: vaugh033@mc.duke.edu.

VAUGHAN, DIANA, political organization administrator; Vice chmn. Wyo. Rep. Party, chmn., 2008—. Mem. Teton County Rep. Party. Republican. Office: PO Box 9405 Jackson WY 83002 also: Wyo Rep Party PO Box 241 Casper WY 82602-0241 Office Phone: 307-234-9166. Office Fax: 307-473-8640.*

VAUGHAN, DOUGLAS EUGENE, medical association administrator, department chairman; b. Oklahoma City, Mar. 19, 1954; s. Clifford Clay and Barbara Frances Vaughan; m. Susannah Hitchings Hawks, May 7, 1988; children: Emily Allerton, James Clifford. BA, U. Okla., Norman, 1976; MD, U. Tex. Southwestern, Dallas, 1980. Cert. Am. Bd. Internal Medicine, 1984, cardiovas. disease 1987. Asst. prof. medicine Harvard Med. Sch., Boston, 1987—93; assoc. prof. medicine Vanderbilt U., Nashville, 1993—98, chief, divsn. cardiovasc. medicine, 1999—2008, dir., 1995—99; chair, medicine Northwestern U., Chgo., 2008—. Contbr. scientific papers. Mem.: Assn. Am. Physicians, Am. Soc. Clin. Investigation. Achievements include patents for role of angiotensin IV in regulating fibrinolytic balance; PAI-1 antagonists for treatment of human disease. Office: Northwestern Univ 251 E Huron St Galter 3-150 Chicago IL 60611 Office Fax: 312-926-7260. Business E-Mail: d-vaughan@northwestern.edu.

VAUGHAN, EDWIN DARRACOTT, JR., urologist, surgeon; b. Richmond, Va., May 13, 1939; s. Edwin Darracott and Blanche V. (Bashaw) V.; m. Virginia Anne Lloyd, June 30, 1962; children: Edwin Darracott III, Barbara Anderson. BS, Washington and Lee U., 1961, DSc, 1982; MD, U. Va., 1965, MS, 1969. Diplomate Am. Bd. Urology (trustee, v.p. 1988, pres. 1989). Intern Vanderbilt U., 1965—66, asst. resident, 1966—67; chief resident in urology U. Va., 1970—71, asst. prof. urology, 1973—75, assoc. prof., 1975—78, prof., 1978; clin. rsch. fellow Columbia U., 1971—72, rsch. assoc. dept. medicine, 1972—73; James J. Colt prof. urology, chmn. dept. urology Cornell U. Med. Coll., NYC; attending urologist-in-chief NY Hosp., NYC, 1978—2001; sr. assoc. dean clin. affairs Cornell U. Med. Coll., NYC, 1993—2001, chmn. dept. urology, 1993—2001, exec. vice dean sr. assoc. dean clin affairs, 2005. Chief med. officer Cornell Physician Orgn., 1997-2005; sci. adv. bd. Nat. Kidney Found., 1977-81; sec.-treas. Urology Coun., 1977-80, chmn., 1980-81; med. adv. bd. Coun. High Blood Pressure, 1977; acting co-chief exec. officer Columbia-Cornell Care, L.L.C., 1997; adv. coun. Nat. Diabetes and Digestive and Kidney Diseases, 2002-06; bd. visitors U. Va. Editor: Seminars in Urology, 1983-95, Timely Topics in Urology, 2007; assoc. editor Investigative Urology, 1977-78, mem. editl. bd., 1978-94, assoc. editor, 2004; mem. editl. bd. Brit. Jour. Urology, 2004; editor Campbell's Urology; assoc. editor Brit. Jour. Urology, 2004, asst. editor, 2004—; editor-in-chief Timely Topics in Urology, 2007; contbr. articles to profl. jours. Mem. adv. coun. Nat. Diabetes and Digestive and Kidney Diseases, 2002—; bd. visitors, chair med. ctr. oper. bd. U. Va., 2002—. Recipient Rsch. Career Devel. award NIH, 1976-78, Russell and Mary Hugh Scott award Am. Found. Urol. Disease, 1998, J.K. Latimer award NY-NJ Kidney Found., 1999, Valentine medal NY Acad. Medicine, 2000, Maurice R. Greenberg Disting. Svc. award, 2002, Good Scout award, BSA, 2002, Presdl. award Soc. Basic Sci. Rsch., 2004, Walter Reed award U. Va. Med. Sch., John Latimer award, NY nat. Found., 2005, John C. Coleman Tchg. award, Dept. Urology, Weill-Cornell Med. Sch., 2008, Australian Cross, Australian Govt., 2008; NIH tng. grantee, 1967-68; USPHS grantee, 1971-77; Am. Heart Assn. grantee, 1976-79, Mem. ACS, AAAS, Internat. Soc. Urology, NY Acad. Scis., Soc. Univ. Urologists, Am. Urol. Assn. (hon., chmn. rsch. com. 1980-91, treas. NY sect. 1985, v.p. NY sect. 1986, pres. NY sect. 1987, bd. dirs. 1992-97, pres.-elect 2000, pres. 2001, immediate past pres. 2002, Golden Cystoscope award 1981, Disting. Contbn. award 1992, Hugh Hampton Young award 2000, Russell Lavengood award, NY sect., 2008), Urol. Soc. Australasia (hon.), Soc. Exptl. Biology and Medicine, Soc. Univ. Surgeons, Soc. Internat. Urology (chmn. bd. 1997—), Am. Found. Urol. Disease (pres. 1987-92, Presdl. Founder award 2004), NY Med. Surgical Soc. (pres. 2005), Soc. Basic Urol. Rsch. (Pres. award 2004), Nat. Kidney and Urol. Disease Adv. Bd. (dep. chmn.), Intersoc. for Kidney and Urol. Disease Rsch. (chmn. 1987), Am. Assn. Genito-Urinary Surgeons Coun.(pres. elect 2009; Barringer medal 1993), Am. Surg. Assn., Brit. Assn. Urol. Surgeons (hon., St. Paul's medal), Japanese Urol. Soc. (hon.), Clin. Soc. Genitourinary Surgeons (pres. 2006), Sigma Chi (Significant Sig award 2000), Alpha Omega Alpha (award 1976), Omicron Delta Kappa (award 1981). Home: 1165 Park Ave Apt 6A New York NY 10128-1210 Office: 525 E 68th St New York NY 10065 Office Phone: 212-746-5480. Business E-Mail: evaughan@med.cornell.edu.

VAUGHAN, ELIZABETH JEAN, education educator; d. Richard Curtis and Ida Martell Vaughan. BSEd, Stephen F. Austin State U., 1974, MEd, 1977; PhD, U. South Fla., 1984. Assoc. prof. Stephen F. Austin State U., Nacogdoches, Tex., 1983—92; prof. Shippensburg (Pa.) U., 1992—2008, Stephen F. Austin State U., 2008—. Author: (book) Learning Centers for Child-Centered Classrooms, 1992, Teaching Numeracy, Language and Literacy with Blocks, 2006. Mem. Success by 6 Leadership Coun., Carlisle, Pa., 2001—06; bd. dirs. Montessori Acad. of Chambersburg, Pa., 2006—08. Mem.: Am. Ednl. Rsch. Assn., Pa. Assn. for Edn. of Young Children (pres. 2005—07), Mid-Atlantic Assn. for Edn. of Young Children (pres. 2001—03), Assn. Childhood Edn. Internat., Nat. Assn. for Edn. of Young Children. Home: 149 Sandstone Ln Nacogdoches TX 75965-6985 Office: Stephen F Austin State Univ PO Box 13017 SFA Sta Nacogdoches TX 75962 Office Phone: 936-468-1759. Business E-Mail: vaughanej@sfasu.edu.

VAUGHAN, EUGENE H., investment company executive; b. Brownsville, Tenn., Oct. 5, 1933; s. Eugene H. Sr. and Margaret (Musgrave) V.; m. Susan Bolinger Westbrook, May 11, 1963; children: Margaret Corbin, Richard Bolinger. BA, Vanderbilt U., 1955; MBA, Harvard U., 1961. CFA, 1967. Security analyst Putnam Mgmt. Co., Boston, 1961-64; dir., dir. rsch. Underwood, Neuhaus & Co., Inc., Houston, 1964-70; pres., chief exec. officer Vaughan, Nelson & Boston, Inc., Houston, 1970-77, Vaughan, Nelson, Scarborough & McCullough, L.P., Houston, 1970—. Chmn. bd. dirs. Dreyfus Founders Asset Mgmt. Co., Denver, 1970—. Chair Fin. Analyst Fedn., N.Y.C., 1973-74, bd. dirs., 1969-76; dir. U. Tex. Health Sci. Ctr., Houston, 2002—; pres. Houston Soc. Fin. Analysts, 1967-68; trustee exec. com. Vanderbilt U., Nashville, 1972—, St. John's Sch., Houston, 1980-85, Goodwill Industries, Houston, 1978—, United Way of Tex. Gulf Coast, 1994—; elder First Presbyn. Ch., 1976—; founding chmn., trustee Presbyn. Sch., Houston, 1986-90. Lt. USN, 1955-58. Recipient Disting. Svc. award Fin. Analyst Fedn., 1978, Humanitarian award Am. Jewish Com., 1993, Bus. Leader of Yr. award U. St. Thomas, 1996. Mem. Inst. Chartered Fin. Analysts (trustee 1986-93, chmn. 1989), Assn. for Investment Mgmt. and Rsch. (founding chmn. 1990-91, gov. 1990-93), Greater Houston Partnership (bd. dirs. 1990—, exec. com. 1993—; chair Ctr. Houston's Future 1999—), Houston Club (pres. 1983-84, bd. dirs. 1979-85, chair centennial celebration, 1992-94), Houston Country Club, Coronado Club (Houston), Houston Forum (pres. 1991-92, chmn. 1992-93), Harvard U. Bus. Sch. Club Houston (pres. 1968-69, bd. dirs. 1966-71, 86-90), Vanderbilt Club Houston (chmn. 1984—, pres. 1966-68, Disting. Svc. award 1994), Conferie des Chevaliers du Tastevin, Belle Meade Country Club (Nashville). Republican. Avocations: travel, sailing. Home: 3465 Inwood Dr Houston TX 77019-3129 also: 4400 Post Oak Pkwy Ste 1270 Houston TX 77027-3455

VAUGHAN, HERBERT WILEY, retired lawyer; b. Brookline, Mass., June 1, 1920; s. David D. and Elzie G. (Wiley) Vaughan; m. Ann Graustein, June 28, 1941 (dec. June 2002). BS cum laude, Harvard U., 1941, LLB, 1948. Bar: Mass. 1948. Assoc. Hale and Dorr, Boston, 1948-54, jr. ptnr., 1954-56, sr. ptnr., 1956-89, co-mng. ptnr., 1976-80, ret. ptnr., 1990—2004, Wilmer Cutler Pickering Hale and Dorr LLP, 2004—. Bd. dirs. fin. com. Boston and Maine RR, 1961—64; vis. fellow New Coll., Oxford U., 1985. Mem. standing com. Trustees of Reservations, 1986—98, chmn., 1988—92, sec., 1992—98, asst. sec., mem. adv. coun., 1998—2006, life trustee, 2004—; mem. adv. coun. James Madison Program in Am. Ideals and Instns., Princeton U. Fellow: Mass. Hist. Soc., Am. Bar Found. (life); mem.: ABA, Am. Coun. Trustees and Alumni (mem. alumni leadership coun.), Am. Coll. Real Estate Lawyers (charter mem.), Am. Law Inst., Boston Bar Assn., Mass. Bar Assn., Boston Econ. Club, Union Club (Boston), Badminton and Tennis Club. Office: Wilmer Cutler Pickering Hale and Dorr LLP 60 State St Boston MA 02109-1816 Office Phone: 617-526-6718. Business E-Mail: herbert.vaughan@wilmerhale.com.

VAUGHAN, JOSEPH LEE, JR., entrepreneur, realtor, educational consultant; s. Joseph Lee and Ann (Doner) Vaughan; m. Mary Linda De Silva; children: Leigh Ann, Kelley, Stephen, Kathleen. BA, U. Va., 1964, MEd, 1968, EdD, 1974. Real estate lic. Tex. Assn. Realtors, 1999, cert. entrepreneur bus. Southern Meth. U., Dallas, 2007. Tchr. Madison HS, Va., 1965-67, Darlington Sch., Rome, Ga., 1967-69, Woodberry Forest Sch., Va., 1969-74; asst. prof. edn. U. Ariz., Tucson, 1974-80; prof. Tex. A&M U.-Commerce, Mesquite, 1980—2006, dir. grad. programs in reading edn., 1980—86, 1991—92, 2000—06; real estate agent Adleta & Poston, Dallas, 1999—2000, RE/MAXLandmark, 2007—08, Network Realtors, Royse City, 2008—. Dir. Tex. Ctr. Learning Styles, 1989—95; exec. dir. Children's Inst. Literacy Devel., Inc., 1995—2004, The Ctr. Acad. Progress, Inc., 2004—05; cons. faculty in humanities St. Alban's Episcopal Sch., 2000—07; CEO Learning and Literary Sys., 2006—. Co-author: Reading and Learning in Content Classrooms, 1978, 2d rev. edit., 1985, Reading and Reasoning Beyond The Primary Grades, 1986. Bd. govs. Sancta Sophia Sem., 1991—98, Royse City Rotary Club, 2007—, Royse City C. of C., 2007—. Mem. Internat. Reading Assn., MetroTex Realtors Assn. Methodist. Avocations: golf, travel, reading, antiques. Home: 447 Ridgemont Dr Heathridge TX 75126

VAUGHAN, KEITH W., lawyer; b. Bluefield, W.Va., Oct. 1, 1950; BA cum laude, Wake Forest U., 1972; JD cum laude, U. Ga., 1975. Bar: Ga. 1975, NC 1975, US Dist. Ct. (Eastern, Middle & Western Dists. NC), NC Supreme Ct., US Ct. Appeals (4th Cir.), US Supreme Ct. Ptnr. litigation practice group leader, mem. firm mgmt. com. Womble Carlyle Sandridge & Rice PLLC, Winston-Salem, NC, chmn. mgmt. com., mng. mem. Bd. dir. NC Assn. Def. Attys., 1985—88. Editor-in-chief Ga. Law Rev., 1974-75. Named to Bus. North Carolina's Legal Elite (Litigation). Mem. ABA, NC Bar Assn., Forsyth County Bar Assn., Ga. Bar Assn., Forsyth County Young Lawyers Assn. (pres., 1981), Am. Inns of Ct. (Master of the Bench), Omicron Delta Kappa, Delta Sigma Rho, Tau Kappa Alpha; Fellow, Am. Coll. of Trial Lawyers Office: Womble Carlyle Sandridge & Rice PLLC One W 4th St Winston Salem NC 27101 Office Phone: 336-721-3600. Office Fax: 336-733-8417. Business E-Mail: kvaughan@wcsr.com.

VAUGHAN, MARTHA, biochemist, educator; b. Dodgeville, Wis., Aug. 4, 1926; d. John Anthony and Luciel (Ellingen) V.; m. Jack Orloff, Aug. 4, 1951 (dec. Dec. 1988); children: Jonathan Michael, David Geoffrey, Gregory Joshua. Ph.B., U. Chgo., Ill., 1944; MD, Yale U., New Haven, Conn., 1949. Intern New Haven Hosp., Conn., 1950-51; research fellow U. Pa., Phila., 1951-52, Nat. Heart Inst., Bethesda, Md., 1952-54, mem. research staff, 1954-68; head metabolism sect. Nat. Heart and Lung Inst., Bethesda, 1968-74; acting chief molecular disease br. Nat. Heart, Lung and Blood Inst., Bethesda, 1974-76, chief cell metabolism lab., 1974-94, dep. chief pulmonary and critical care medicine br., 1994—2007, head, metabolic regulation sect., translational medicine br., 2007—. Mem. metabolism study sect. NIH, 1965-68; mem. bd. sci. counselors Nat. Inst. Alcohol Abuse and Alcoholism, 1988-91. Mem. editl. bd. Jour. Biol. Chemistry, 1971-76, 80-83, 88-90, assoc. editor, 1992—; editl. adv. bd. Molecular Pharmacology, 1972-80, Biochemistry, 1989-94; editor: Biochemistry and Biophysics Rsch. Comms., 1990-91; contbr. articles to profl. jours., chpts. to books. Bd. dirs. Found. Advanced Edn. in Scis., Inc., Bethesda, 1979-92, exec. com., 1980-92, treas., 1984-86, v.p., 1986-88, pres., 1988-90; mem. Yale U. Coun. com. med. affairs, New Haven, 1974-80. Recipient Meritorious Svc. medal HEW, 1974, Disting. Svc. medal HEW, 1979, Commd. Officer award USPHS, 1982, Superior Svc. award USPHS, 1993. Mem. NAS, Am. Acad. Arts and Scis., Am. Soc. Biol. Chemists (chmn. pub. com.

1984-86), Assn. Am. Physicians, Am. Soc. Clin. Investigation. Home: 11608 W Hill Dr Rockville MD 20852-3751 Office: Nat Heart Lung & Blood Inst Nih Bldg 10 Rm 5N 307 Bethesda MD 20892-0001 Business E-Mail: vaughanm@nih.gov.

VAUGHAN, MICHAEL RICHARD, lawyer; b. Chgo., Aug. 27, 1936; s. Michael Ambrose and Loretta M. (Parks) Vaughan; m. Therese Marie Perri, Aug. 6, 1960; children: Charles Thomas, Susan Enger. Student, U. Ill., 1954-59; LLB, U. Wis., 1962. Bar: Wis. 1962. Chief atty. bill drafting sect. Wis. Legislature, Madison, 1962-68, dir. legis. attys., 1968-72; assoc. Murphy Desmond, and predecessor, Madison, 1972-73, ptnr., 1974—. Mem. Commn. Uniform State Laws, 1966—72; cons. Nat. Commn. Marijuana and Drug Abuse, 1971—73; lectr. CLE seminars. Contbr. articles to profl. jours. Warden, vestryman St. Dunstan's Episcopal Ch., 1973—78, 1980—87; mem. Wis. Episcopal Conf., 1972—76. Mem.: ABA, Dane County Bar Assn., State Bar Wis. (dir. govtl. and adminstrv. law sect. 1971—78, mem. interprofl. and bus. rels. com. 1976—89), The Club at Olde Cypress (Naples, Fla.), Nakoma Golf Club, Madison Club, U. Wis. Law Sch. Bencher Soc., Delta Kappa Epsilon. Office: 33 E Main St Ste 500 Madison WI 53703-2287 Office Phone: 608-257-7181.

VAUGHAN, ROBERT OREN, lawyer; b. Elko, Nev., Mar. 19, 1925; m. Barbara Schreiner, 1950 (dec. June 1996); children: Meg, Brad; m. Betty Kelly Pearson, 1997. BA, U. Nev., Reno, 1950; JD cum laude, U. Denver, 1952; Assoc. degree (hon.), Gt. Basin Coll., 1996. Bar: Nev. 1952, U.S. Dist. Nev. 1955, U.S. Supreme Ct. 1961, U.S. Ct. Appeals (9th cir.) 1973. Ptnr. Vaughan & Hull, Ltd. and predecessor firms, Elko, 1953—; mem. Nev. State Assembly, 1955-58, minority floor leader, 1958. City atty. City of Wells, Nev., 1957-75; dep. city atty. City of Elko, 1962-82; gen. counsel Wells Rural Electric Co., 1958—, Mt. Wheeler Power, Inc., 1963-92, Nev. Rural Electric Assn., 1974; mem. Nev. Jud. Selection Commn., 1960-66; ptnr. AAA Self Storage, Western Enterprises; owner Vaughan Ranch, Ruby Valley, Nev., 1958-95. Bd. editors U. Denver Law Rev., 1952. Trustee Elko County Libr. Bd., 1959-63; bd. dirs. Elko Knife and Fork Club, 1962; dir. Heart Fund, 1957-85; active youth sports; trustee Gt. Basin Coll. Found., 1983-2002, mem. exec. com., planned giving com., 1991—, chmn. spkrs. bur., 1989-90, chmn. major gifts com., 1991-98; deacon, ruling elder 1st Presbyn. Ch. of Elko. 1st lt. USAF, 1943-47; with Nev. N.A.G., 1948-50. Mem. Nev. Jud. Selection Commn., 1960-66; ptnr. AAA Self Storage, Western Enterprises; owner Vaughan Ranch, Ruby Valley, Nev., 1958-95; Bd. editors U. Denver Law Rev., 1952. Trustee Elko County Libr. Bd., 1959-63; bd. dirs. Elko Knife and Fork Club, 1962; dir. Heart Fund, 1957-85; active youth sports; trustee Gt. Basin Coll. Found., 1983-2002, mem. exec. com., planned giving com., 1991-, chmn. spkrs. bur., 1989-90, chmn. major gifts com., 1991-98; deacon, ruling elder Ist Presbyn Ch. of Elko. 1st lt. USAF 1943-47; with Nev. N.A.G., 1948-50; Mem. ABA, Nev. State Bar Assn. (adminstrv. com. 1956-66, probate and property practice com., unauthorized practice of law com., fee dispute com.), Elko County Bar Assn. (pres. 1963-64), Elko C. of C. (past bd. dirs., treas.), Rotary (pres. 1964-65), Masons, Royal and Select Masters, Royal Arch, K.T., Shriners, Ea. Star. Republican. Home: PO Box 281859 Lamoille NV 89828-1859 Business E-Mail: rvaughan@frontiernet.net.

VAUGHAN, SAMUEL SNELL, editor, writer, publishing executive; b. Phila., Aug. 3, 1928; s. Joseph and Anna Catherine (Alexander) Vaughan; m. Jo LoBiondo Vaughan, Oct. 22, 1949; children: Jeffrey Marc, Leslie Jane, Dana Alexander, David Samuel. BA, Pa. State U., 1951. Deskman, King Features Syndicate, NYC, 1951; asst. mgr. Doubleday Syndicate, 1952—54; advt. mgr. Doubleday, NYC, 1954—56; sales mgr., 1956—58; sr. editor, 1958—68; exec. editor Doubleday, 1969—70; pub., pres. pub. div. Doubleday & Co., Inc., 1970—82, v.p. parent co., 1970—86, editor in chief, 1982—86; sr. v.p. and editor Random House, Inc., 1986—90, editor-at-large, 1990—2009. Mem. faculty, Columbia U., 1978-88, The New Sch., 2005; bd. dirs. Ch. Pub. Co.-Seabury Press; lectr. in field. Author: (juveniles) Whoever Heard of Kangaroo Eggs? 1957, New Shoes, 1961, The Two-Thirty Bird, 1965, (history) The Little Church, 1969, Medium Rare: A Look at the Book and Its People, 1977, (humor) Little Red Hood, 1979, The Accidental Profession, 1979, The Community of the Book, 1983, The State of the Heart, 1985; editor: Buckley: The Right Word, 1996; contbr. to N.Y. Times, Sunday Times of London, Daedalus, Am. Heritage, others. Served with USMC, 1946-48. Named Disting. Alumnus, Pa. State U., 1977, Alumni fellow, 1979. Mem. Tenafly Tennis Club, Quantuck Beach Club (Westhampton, N.Y.), Century Assn. Episcopalian. Office Phone: 201-568-6986. Personal E-mail: samuelsvaughan@aol.com.

VAUGHAN, THERESE MICHELE, insurance educator; b. Blair, Nebr., June 12, 1956; d. Emmett John and Lonne Kay (Smith) V.; m. Robert Allen Carber, Aug. 15, 1993; children: Kevin Leo Vaughan-Carber, Thomas S. Vaughan-Carber. BBA, U. Iowa, 1979; PhD, U. Pa., 1985. CPCU. Asst. prof. Baruch Coll., CUNY, 1986-87; cons. Tillinghast, NYC, 1987-88; dir. ins. ctr. Drake U., Des Moines, 1988-94; ins. commr. State of Iowa, Des Moines, 1994—2004; Robb B. Kelley Disting. prof. ins. and actuarial sci. Drake U., 2005—. Bd. dirs. Endurance Splty. Holdings, Prin. Fin. Group, Nat. Coun Comp. Ins. Editor Jour. Ins. Regulation, 2005—; co-author: Fundamentals of Risk and Insurance, 1996, 99, 2003, 08, Essentials of Insurance: A Risk Management Approach, 1995, 2001; contbr. articles to profl. jours. S.S. Huebner fellow U. Pa., 1979-82; recipient Outstanding Young Alumnus award U. Iowa, 1996; named to Iowa Ins. Hall of Fame, 2003. Mem. Nat. Assn. Ins. Commrs. (pres. 2002), Ins. Marketplace Stds. Assn. (bd. dirs. 2004—), Am. Risk and Ins. Assn. (pres. 2008), Beta Gamma Sigma, Omicron Delta Epsilon. Avocations: hiking, biking, reading. Home: 4632 Elm St West Des Moines IA 50265-2993 Office: Drake Univ 2507 University Ave Des Moines IA 50311 Office Phone: 515-271-2830. Business E-Mail: terri.vaughan@drake.edu.

VAUGHAN, THOMAS JAMES GREGORY, historian, writer; b. Seattle, Oct. 13, 1924; s. Daniel George and Kathryn Genevieve (Browne) V.; m. Elizabeth Ann Perpetua Crownhart, June 16, 1951; children: Meagan, Margot, Stephen, Cameron. BA, Yale U., 1948; MS, U. Wis., 1950, doctoral residence, 1951-53; LittD, Pacific U., 1969; LLD, Reed Coll., 1975. Exec. dir. Oreg. Hist. Soc., Portland, 1954-90; editor in chief Oreg. Hist. Quar., 1954-89; adj. prof. Portland State U., 1968—. Chmn. bd. Salar Enterprises, Ltd.; bd. dir. Am. Heritage Pub. Co., 1976-85; film producer, 1958-99; historian laureate State of Oreg., 1989—. Author: A Century of Portland Architecture, 1967, Captain Cook, R.N, The Resolute Mariner: An International Record of Oceanic Discovery, 1974, Portland, A Historical Sketch and Guide, 1976, 2d edit., 1983, Voyage of Enlightenment: Malaspina on the Northwest Coast, 1977; editor: Space, Style and Structure: Building in Northwest America, 2 vols., 1974, The Western Shore, 1975, Ascent of the Athabasca Pass, 1978, Wheels of Fortune, High and Mighty, 1981, Soft Gold, 1982, 2d edit., 1990, To Siberia and Russian America, Vols. I, II and III, Frances Fuller Victor, 2002, others; co-editor: Siberica, 1989; mem. adv. bd. Am. Heritage Mag., 1977-90; prodr. film The Crimean War, 1994, Wellington's Last Parade, 1997, George Dewey: A Monarch of the Seas, 2003, George Catlin: the American Indians' Painter, 2006, The Russo-Japanese War 1904-05 A Study in Extremes, 2007, Incredible Lies: Stories of Old Fashioned Golf, 2007. 1st chmn. Oreg. State Com. for Humanities, NEH, 1969—; 1st chmn. Gov.'s Adv. Com. on Historic Preservation Oreg., 1970-77; sec. Oreg. Geog. Names Bd., 1958-89; adviser 1000 Friends of Oreg., 1972—; lay mem. Oreg. State Bar Disciplinary Rev. Bd., 1975-82; vice chmn. adv. panel Nat. Endowment Arts, 1975—; mem. Nat. Hist. Publs. and Records Commn. Matrix, 1975-76; historian laureate State of Oreg., 1989. With USMC, 1942-45. Decorated comdr. Order Brit. Empire; recipient Aubrey Watzek award Lewis and Clark Coll., 1975;, Edith Knight Hill award, 1977, Disting. Svc. award U. Oreg.; grantee English Speaking Union, 1961; Columbia Maritime Mus. 1st rsch. fellow, 1992, Thomas Jefferson medal, 2002. Fellow Royal Geog. Soc.; mem. Am. Assn. State and Local History (bd. dir. 1955-74, pres. 1976-78), Am. Assn. Mus. (coun., exec. com.), Nat. Trust Hist. Preservation (adv. coun.), Ctr. for Study Russian Am., Russian Acad. Scis., City Club (Portland, bd. govs.), Univ. Club (Portland, bd. govs.), The Arts Club (London). Home: 620 SW Caruthers St Ste 481 Portland OR 97201-5054 Personal E-mail: goldengrove@spiretech.net.

VAUGHAN, WILLIAM WALTON, atmospheric scientist; b. Clearwater, Fla., Sept. 7, 1930; s. William Walton and Ella Vermelle (Warr) Vaughan; m. Wilma Geraldine Stapleton, Dec. 23, 1951; children: Stephen W., David A., William D., Robert T. BS with honors, U. Fla., 1951; grad. cert., USAF Inst. Tech./Fla. State U., 1952; PhD, U. Tenn., 1976. Cert. AMS cons. meteorologist. Sci. asst. Air Force Armament Ctr., Eglin AFB, Fla., 1955-58, Army Ballistic Missile Agy., Huntsville, Ala., 1958-60; chief aerospace environ. div. Marshall Space Flight Center, NASA, Huntsville, 1960-76, chief atmospheric scis. div., 1976-86; rsch. prof. atmospheric sci. U. Ala., Huntsville, 1986—, dir. Rsch. Inst., 1986-94; ret., 1994. Cons. atmospheric sci. and tech. stds.; mem. adv. com. NASA. Contbr. articles to profl. jours. Served to capt. USAF, 1951—55. Recipient Exceptional Svc. medal, NASA, 1971. Fellow: AIAA (standard exec. coun., Losey Atmospheric Scis. award 1980, Excellence in Aerospace Stds. award 2003, disting. Svc. award 2007), Am. Meteorol. Soc.; mem.: AAAS, Am. Geophys. Union, Stds. Engring. Soc., Sigma Xi. Office: Univ Ala Atmospheric Sci Dept Huntsville AL 35899-0001 Office Phone: 256-961-7759. Personal E-mail: Williamwvaughan@aol.com. Business E-Mail: vaughan@nsstc.uah.edu.

VAUGHAN, WORTH EDWARD, retired chemistry professor; b. NYC, Feb. 1, 1936; s. Royal Worth and Sylvia Marie (Fernholz) V.; m. Diane Marilyn Mayer, Aug. 9, 1969; 1 child, Wayne John BA, Oberlin Coll., 1957; MA, Princeton U., 1959, PhD, 1960. Asst. prof. chemistry U. Wis.-Madison, 1961-66, assoc. prof., 1967-76, prof., 1977—2002, prof. emeritus, 2002—. Mem. bd. advisors Am. Exchange Bank West Br., Madison, 1983-87. Author: Dielectric Properties and Molecular Behavior, 1969; editor: Digest of Literature on Dielectrics, 1974; translation editor: Dipole Moments of Organic Compounds, 1970; contbr. articles to profl. jours. Mem. Am. Chem. Soc. (pres. Wis. sect. 1968, 1998), Phi Beta Kappa Avocations: canoeing, contract bridge. Home: 501 Ozark Trl Madison WI 53705-2538 Office: Univ Wis 1101 University Ave Madison WI 53706-1322 Office Phone: 608-262-7924. Business E-Mail: vaughan@chem.wisc.edu.

VAUGHN, CARY EDWARD, minister, director; b. Memphis, May 16, 1971; s. Brenda Jane Vaughn; m. Lalania Star Goodman, June 26, 1992; children: Logan Star, Colton Edward. BA, Lambuth U., 1993; MSc in Orgnl. Leadership, Breyer State U., 2004. Cert. in Christian Leadership Belmont U., Tenn., 2004, in Advanced Skilltrack Christian Leadership Belmont U., Tenn., 2004, in Bivocational Ministry Leadership Belmont U., Tenn., 2005; Payroll Adminstr. HRCertification.com., Ga., 2005, ROI bd. devel. cert. YMCA. Min. lay leadership Bellevue Bapt. Ch., Cordova, Tenn., 2002—, dir. lay ministry, 2002—, dir. men's ministry, 2003—, dir. new mems., 2004—, dir. career svcs., 2004—, program adminstr. spl. events, 2005—, dir. guest svcs., 2005—; pres. Convenant Staffing Solutions LLC, 2006—. Co-chmn. capital campaign Tipton-Rosemark Acad., 2007. Mem. Rotary Internat., Millington, Tenn., 2005—06; bd. dirs. Am. Families Assn. Discipleship Ministry, 2006; chmn. Tipton-Rosemark Acad., Millington, 2000—; ex-officio mem. Lambuth U., Jackson, Tenn., 2003—04; chmn. fundraising com. YMCA, Millington, Tenn., 2005—; chmn. bd. dirs. Millington Family YMCA, 2007; bd. dirs. Metro YMCA, 2007—, Chrosscheck Athletic Assn., 2006; chmn. bd. dir. Millington Family YMCA, 2007. Recipient John G. Tower Disting. Alumni award, Kappa Sigma Nat. Frat., 1999, First Yr. Outstanding Vol. award, Kappa Sigma Nat. Fraternity, Leadership award, Comforce, Inc., 1998, Alumnus of Yr., Lambuth U., 2000; grantee Leadership scholarship, Kappa Sigma Nat. Frat., 1992. Mem.: Christian Educators Assn. Internat. (dir. pub. rels. Lower Miss. Valley region 2006), Assn. Christian Schs. Internat., Christian Mgmt. Assn., Harvard U. Prin. Ctr., Rotary Internat. (chmn. Taste of Millington 2007). R-Conservative. Baptist. Avocations: reading, exercise, hunting. Home: 8880 Gragg Rd Millington TN 38053-4945 Office: Covenant Staffing Solution LLC 6465 Quail Hollow Ste 102 Memphis TN 38120 Home Fax: 901-829-2994. Personal E-mail: caryvaughn@peoplepc.com. Business E-Mail: cary@covenantstaffingsolutions.net.

VAUGHN, JOHN ROLLAND, retired auditor; b. Iola, Kans., Aug. 4, 1938; s. Ralph H. and Alice (Dille) V.; m. Doris K. Black, Sept. 4, 1960; children: Lisa Ann, Brian Douglas. BS in Bus., Emporia State U., 1960. Sr. auditor Arthur Andersen & Co., Kansas City, Mo., 1961-66; gen. auditor First Nat. Bank Kansas City, 1966-69, Commerce Bancshares, Inc., 1969-73; sr. v.p. adminstrv. svcs. divsn. Peoples Trust Bank, Ft. Wayne, Ind., 1973-77; dep. gen. auditor, v.p. Crocker Nat. Bank, San Francisco, 1978-79; v.p., gen. auditor S.W. Bancshares, Houston, 1980-83; sr. v.p., gen. auditor MCorp., Houston, 1984-87, mng. dir., 1988-89; audit dir. Banc One Corp., Dallas, 1990-92; v.p., gen. auditor St. Paul Cos., St. Paul, 1992-97; dir. internal audit Conseco Fin., St. Paul, 1998—2001; v.p., chief audit officer Calif. State Automobile Assn., 2001—02, v.p., chief risk officer (ret.), 2002—07. Treas. Overland Park (Kans.) Jr. C. of C., 1965—66; outside dir. Overland Park Credit Union; contr. Ft. Wayne Bicentennial Commn., 1974—77; mem. chmns. cabinet Indianhead coun. Boy Scouts Am., 2000—01. Mem. Inst. Internal Auditors (1st v.p. Kansas City 1969-70, pres. 1970-71, midwest regional v.p. 1971-72, Twin Cities chpt. gov. 1993-97, pres. 1994-95, internat. profl. conf. com. 1995-98, internat. ednl. products com. 1999-2002, San Francisco chpt. gov. 2004—07), Fin. Execs. Inst. (dir. Ft. Wayne 1976-77), Risk and Ins. Mgmt. Soc., Hartsmen, Voices in Harmony Chorus, Vocal Majority Chorus, Barbershop Harmony Soc., Gt. No. Union Chorus, Sigma Tau Gamma.

VAUGHN, LINDA F., musician, educator; b. Morrison, Ill., Feb. 3, 1952; d. Edwin J. and Nora E. Bush; m. Charles W. Vaughn, Apr. 23, 1999; children: Timothy M. Deal, Andrew E. Deal, Peter G. Deal. MusB, BA, Hope Coll., 1974; MusM, U. Ill., 1975, MA, 1979. Cert. tchr. Ill. Vocal music tchr. Urbana (Ill.) Sch. Dist., 1990—; tchr. Danville (Ill.) Area C.C., 1996—99. Organist, choir dir. First Bapt. Ch., Urbana, 1984—93; organist Cmty. United Ch. of Christ, Champaign, Ill., 1993—; accompanist The Chorale, Champaign, 1994—2001; mem., performer Evening Etude Mozart Music Club, Champaign-Urbana. Mem.: Music Educator's Assn., Am. Choral Dir.'s Assn. (life), Delta Phi Alpha (life), Delta Omicron (life). Avocations: sewing, crocheting, cooking, baking, genealogy. Home: 2606 Wadsworth Ln Urbana IL 61802 Personal E-mail: lfvaughn@yahoo.com.

VAUGHN, LINDA MARIE, municipal official; b. Moline, Ill., Aug. 6, 1947; d. Merwin Perry and Margaret Anne Baker; m. Jeffery M. Vaughn, Aug. 16, 1969; children: Jason P., Eric M. Student, Moline Inst. Commerce, 1965. Clk. data entry Eagle Warehouse, Milan, Ill., 1966—69, Lennox Heating/AC, Marshalltown, Iowa, 1970—73, Farmall (Internat. Harvester), Rock Island, Ill., 1973—75, Ingersoll, Rockford, 1975—87; trustee Village of Machesney Park, Ill., 1987—89, clk., 1989—2001, mayor, village pres., 2001—. Guest columnist Parks Jour., 1997—; charter mem. Parks Chamber Women's Network, Loves Park, Ill., 1995; 8 gal. mem. Rock River Valley Blood Ctr. Mem. Northwestern Ill. Mcpl. Clks. Assn. (sec. 1990-92, treas. 1997-99), C. of C. (ambassador 1987—). Democrat. Roman Catholic. Avocations: writing, fishing, reading, walking. Home: 9519 Shore Dr Machesney Park IL 61115-2058 Office: Village Machesney Park 300 Machesney Rd Machesney Park IL 61115-2495

VAUGHN, LISA DAWN, physician, educator; b. Ashland, Ky., May 10, 1961; d. Charles Clinton and Mildred Darlene (Cantrell) V. AS in Biology, U. Ky., 1981, BS in Zoology, 1983; DO, W.Va. Sch. Osteo. Medicine, 1988. Diplomate Nat. Osteo. Med. Bd., cert. Am. Assn. Med. Rev. officer, 1996. Gen. intern Doctors Hosp. Inc., Massillon, Ohio, 1988-89, family practice resident, 1989-91; emergency room physician Coastal Emergency Svcs., Snowpark, Ohio, 1989-90; urgent care physician Acute Care Specialists, Akron, Ohio, 1991; physician Portage Family Practice Clinic, North Canton, Ohio, 1991-95, First Care Family Health & Immediate Care Ctr., Canton, Ohio, 1995-95; dir. occupl. medicine First Care, Canton, 1996, med. dir. urgent care sys., 1996-97; physician Mercy Health Ctr. Jackson, Ohio, 1997—. Clin. asst. faculty Ohio U. Coll. Medicine, Athens, 1990-91, adj. clin. faculty, 1992—; asst. dir. family practice residency Ohio U. Coll. Medicine-Doctors Hosp. Inc., Massillon, 1992-95; urgent CARE physician First Care, Canton, Ohio, 1995—; med. dir. family home health svc. Doctors Hosp., 1992-94, chmn. dept. family medicine, 1994-95; med. dir. Riczo and Co. Managed Care Orgn., 1997—;med. adv. to Canton City Schools, Med. Assisting Program; med. advisor Boy Scouts Med. Explorers, Massillon, 1989-90; med. career advisor Girl Scouts Career Day, Canton, 1990; affiliate physician Cleve. Clinic, 1991—; med. advisor Canton City Sch. Med. Assisting Program, 2002—. Contbr. poems. Col. Ky. Cols. Assn., Ashland, 1989—; vol. United Way of Stark County, 1990-91. Mem. Cleve. Clinic Found. (affiliate physician), AMA, Am. Coll. Osteo. Family Physicians, Am. Osteo. Assn. (cert.), Ohio State Med. Assn., W.Va. Soc. Osteo. Medicine, Stark County Med. Soc., Sigma Sigma Phi (sec. 1985-86). Democrat. Avocations: writing, reading, history. Office: Statcare Jackson 7452 Fulton Dr NW Massillon OH 44646-9393

VAUGHN, MICHAEL OSCAR, history professor; b. Forest, Miss., July 19, 1954; s. Ray Daniel Vaughn and Christine Cornelius Chambers; m. Donna M. Harris, Mar. 12, 1994; children: T'a Michelle, Jacob Tyler Harris. MA in History, U. Southern Miss., Hattiesburg, MS in Psychology, 1993. Instr. U. Southern Miss., 1996—2000; asst. prof. history Ala. A&M U., Normal, 2000—. Dir. Partnership Drug-Free Lamar County, Hattiesburg, 1994—96. Com. drug-free Lamar County Sch., Purvis, Miss., 1994—96. Tchr. Tng. grant, Dept. Alcohol & Drug Awareness Prevention, 1993, Aubrey K. Lucas fellowship, Pvt., 1996—2000. Mem.: Southern Hist. Assn. Liberal. Avocation: reading. Office: Ala A&M Univ Meridian St Normal AL 35762 Office Fax: 256-372-5226. Business E-Mail: michael.vaughn@aamu.edu.

VAUGHN, MICHAEL S., law educator; s. Harley (Bud) Dewitt and Judith Ann Vaughn; m. Tzu-Hsiu Nancy Vaughn, Dec. 2, 1989; 1 child, Rachel. PhD in Criminal Justice, Sam Houston State U., Huntsville, Tex., 1990—93. Prof. Ga. State U., Atlanta, 1993—2006, chmn. dept. criminal justice, 2002—05; prof. Sam Houston State U., Huntsville, Tex., 2006—; co-dir. Inst. Legal Studies Criminal Justice, 2006—, asst. dean grad. studies, dir. criminal justice doctoral program, 2009—; asst. dean grad studies & dir. criminal justice doctoral program SHGU, 2009—. Editor: Internat. Criminal Justice Rev., Criminal Justice Rev., Ga. State U., 2001-05;book rev. editor Jour. Criminal Justice Edn. Acad. Criminal Justice Scis., Greenbelt, Md., 1993—1996, editor, police forum police sect., Md., 1996—2001; contbr. correctional health care report Civic Rsch. Inst., NYC, 1999—2006, articles to profl. jours. and publs. Recipient Outstanding Service award, Police Section, Acad. of Criminal Justice Sciences, 1998, Outstanding Paper, Acad. of Criminal Justice Scis., 1996, Outstanding Faculty Achievement award, Ga. State U., 2004; named Outstanding Alumnus, Coll. of Criminal Justice, Sam Houston State U., 2002. Mem.: Am. Assn. Univ. Profs., Am. Judicature Soc., Am. Psychology-Law Soc., Am. Soc. Criminology, Acad. Criminal Justice Scis. Democrat. Methodist. Avocation: reading. Office: Sam Houston State Univ Criminal Justice PO Box 2296 Huntsville TX 77341-2296 Office Phone: 936-294-1349. Business E-Mail: mvaughn@shsu.edu.

VAUGHN, NOEL WYANDT, lawyer; b. Chgo., Dec. 15, 1937; d. Owen Heaton and Harriet Christy (Smith) Wyandt; m. David Victor Koch, July 18, 1959 (div.); 1 child, John David; m. Charles George Vaughn, July 9, 1971. BA, DePauw U., 1959; MA, So. Ill. U., 1963; JD, U. Dayton, 1979. Bar: Ohio 1979, U.S. Dist. Ct. (so. dist.) Ohio 1979, U.S. Cir. Ct. (6th cir.) 1987. Lectr. Wright State U., Dayton, 1965-67; communications specialist Charles F. Kettering Found., Dayton, 1968-71; tchr. English Miami Valley Sch., Dayton, 1971-76; law clk. to judge Dayton Mcpl. Ct., 1978-79; coordinator Montgomery County Fair Housing Ctr., Dayton, 1979-81, 85-89; atty. Henley Vaughn Becker & Wald, Dayton, 1981-90; pvt. practice Noel W. Vaughn Law Offices, Dayton, 1990—. Chmn. Dayton Playhouse, Inc., 1981—92; pres. Freedom of Choice Miami Valley, 1980—83, 1986—87; com. mem. Battered Woman Project-YWCA, 1983—84; pres. Legal Aid Soc., 1983—84; chmn. Artemis Ctr. Alternatives Domestic Violence, 1985—88; bd. dirs. Artemis House, Inc., 1988—97, ACLU, 1982—86, Miami Valley Arts Coun., 1985—86, AIDS Found., 1988—90, Miami Valley Fair Housing Ctr., Inc., 1992—94, Human Race Theatre Co., Inc., 1995—2000, Housing Justice Fund, 1979—, Dayton Sister City Comn., 2001—02, Muse Machine, 2004—. Recipient Order of Barristers award U. Dayton, 1979, Peace Keeper award, Artemis Ctr., 2008. Mem.: ABA, Ohio State Bar Assn., Ohio Fair Plan Underwriting Assn. (bd. govs. 1986—92), Dayton Bar Assn. (chmn. delivery legal svcs. com. 1983—84, family law com. 1991—, chmn. juvenile law com. 2001—03). Office: 1205 Talbott Tower 131 N Ludlow St Dayton OH 45402-1110 Office Phone: 937-222-6635.

VAUGHN, ROBERT CANDLER, JR., lawyer; b. Winston Salem, NC, Sept. 6, 1931; s. Robert Candler and Douglas Arthur V.; m. Carolyn (Hartford), May 2, 1959; children: Patricia Anne, Robert Candler III. BS in Bus. Adminstrn., U. N.C., 1953, JD, 1955. Bar: N.C., 1955, U.S. Dist. Ct. (mid. dist.), 1959, U.S. Tax Ct., 1981. Assoc. Petree, Stockton, Robinson, and predecessor firms, Winston Salem, 1959-65, ptnr., 1965-2000. Bd. dirs. Forsyth Bank & Trust Co., Winston-Salem. Pres. United

Way Forsyth County, Winston Salem, 1970-71, Forsyth County Bar Assn.; chmn. Winston Salem Coliseum and Conv. Ctr. Commn., 1974-78; bd. adv.U. NC Tax Inst., Chapel Hill; bd. dirs. Leadership Winston Salem; chmn. Winston Salem Found., 2003,chmn, Forsyth Med. Ctr. Found., 1999-01; chmn. Forsyth Tech. Coll. Found., 2006-. Lt. USN, 1955-58. Fellow Am. Bar Found., Am. Coll. Trusts and Estates Counsel (N.C.chmn. 1990-1995); mem. N.C. Bar Assn. (pres. 1985-86, bd. dirs.), U. N.C. Law Alumni Assn. (pres. 1974-75), Am. Coll. Tax Counsel, Old Town Club, Piedmont Club, Rotary. Republican. Methodist. Home: 2575 Club Park Rd Winston Salem NC 27104-2009 Office: Vaughn Perkinson Ehlinger & Moxley PO Box 25715 Winston Salem NC 27114 Home Phone: 336-722-8068; Office Phone: 336-794-6001. E-mail: bob.vaughn@vpems.com.

VAUGHN, ROSALYN MAE, academic administrator; d. Emmet and Rosie Mae Smith; children: Sherolyn Yvonne Spencer, Sonja Annette King, Rosa Leoma. BS in Elem. Edn., So. Ill. U., Carbondale, 1968, PhD in Workforce Edn. Devel. and Adminstrn., 1996; MA in Ednl. Leadership, Western Mich. U., Kalamazoo, 1974. Cert. CITI, employment law cert., ednl. leadership Fla., Ga. Educator St. Clair County Pub. Schs., Caseyville, Ill., 1968—69, University City (Mo.) Pub. Schs., 1970—71, Calhoun County Pub. Schs., Battle Creek, Mich., 1971—72; pers. rep., trainer Ralston-Purina Co., Battle Creek, Mich., 1972—74; pub. affairs specialist Kellogg Co., Battle Creek, Mich., 1974—76; MIOSHA dir. Mich. Dept. Labor, Lansing, 1976—80; educator Escambia County Pub. Schools, Pensacola, 1980—83; mgr. Combined Ins. Co. Am., New Orleans, 1983—87; instr., rschr. Pensacola (Fla.) Jr. Coll., 1990—91; grad. internist La. Dept. Labor, Metarie, La., 1993—93; assoc. dean Jones Coll., Jacksonville, Fla., 1996—97; human resources mgr. Dynamic Ednl. Sys., Inc., Jacksonville, Fla., 1997—99; asst. prof. Barry U., Miami Shores, Fla., 1999—, adminstr. human resources devel. and adminstrn. Orlando, Fla., 2000—03; site adminstr. higher edn. leadership doctoral program Nova Southeastern U., Orlando, 2004—; prof. U. Phoenix, 1999—. Author: The Art of Raising a Successful Child, 2004. Rev. panelist Family Transition Program, Fla. Dept. Health and Rehab. Svcs., Jacksonville, 1997—99; adminstrv. vol. Polk County Adult Edn. Program, Davenport, Fla., 2002—03; chairperson Mich. Commn. Employment Handicap Persons, Lansing, Mich., 1976—80; steering com., exec. bd. Ctrl. Fla. Higher Edn. Alliance, Orlando, 1999—; mem. Fla. Hosp. Diabetes Ctr., Orlando, 2000—. Recipient Diana award, Mich. Safety Conf., 1978; fellow Ill. Consortium Ednl. Opportunity Program fellow, State Ill. Dept. Edn., 1994—96; scholar State Tchrs.' scholar, 1964—68. Mem.: Ctrl. Fla. Higher Edn. Alliance (mem.-at-large 2001—), Paul S. Morton Scholarship Found. (bd. mem.-at-large 2008—), Assn. Career Tech. Educators (exec. bd. 2001—), Fla. Exec. Women (assoc.). Democrat. Achievements include development of Employment Law Certification Program. Home: Nova Southeastern Univ 155 Amicalola Way Jonesboro GA 30236 Personal E-mail: rvmshrda@aol.com.

VAUGHN, RYAN, councilman; b. Indpls. B cum laude, Wabash Coll., Crawfordsville, Ind.; JD, Ind. U. Sch. Law, Indpls. Atty. Tabbert, Hahn, Earnest & Weddle, LLP; dep. prosecutor Marion County, Ind.; atty. Barnes & Thornburg, LLP; councillor, dist. 3 Indpls.-Marion County City-County Coun., 2007—, v.p. Former polit. dir. Marion County Rep. Party. Republican. Office: 8212 N College Ave Indianapolis IN 46240 also: Indpls Marion County City County Coun 241 City County Bldg 200 E Washington St Indianapolis IN 46204 Office Phone: 317-437-7701, 317-327-4242. Business E-Mail: vaughnforcouncil@gmail.com.*

VAUGHN, VINCE, actor; b. Mpls., Mar. 28, 1970; s. Vernon and Sharon Vaughn. Actor: (films) For the Boys, 1991, Rudy, 1993, At Risk, 1994, Swingers, 1996, Just Your Luck, 1996, The Lost World: Jurassic Park, 1997, The Locusts, 1997, A Cool, Dry Place, 1998, Return to Paradise, 1998, Clay Pigeons, 1998, Psycho, 1998, South of Heaven, West of Hell, 2000, The Cell, 2000, The Prime Gig, 2000, Zoolander, 2001, Domestic Disturbance, 2001, Dust: An Extraordinary Correspondence, 2002, Old School, 2003, I Love Your Work, 2003, Blackball, 2003, Starsky & Hutch, 2004, Dodgeball: A True Underdog Story, 2004, Anchorman: The Legend of Ron Burgundy, 2004, The Sky Is Green, 2004, Thumbsuckers, 2005, Be Cool, 2005, Mr. & Mrs. Smith, 2005, Wedding Crashers, 2005, The Break-Up, 2006 (with Jennifer Aniston Movies-Choice Chemistry, Teen Choice Awards, 2006), Other Side of Simple, 2006, Into the Wild, 2007, Fred Claus, 2007, Four Christmases, 2008; prodr.: Made, 2001, Wild West Comedy Show: 30 Days & 30 Nights - Hollywood to the Heartland, 2008; actor: (TV films) Lies of the Heart, 1991, Sex and the Matrix, 2000, (guest appearance): (TV series) China Beach, 1989, 21 Jump Street, 1989, Hercules, 1998, Mr. Show with Bob and David, 1998, Sex and the City, 2000, Dinner for Five, 2001; guest appearance (TV series) Getaway, 2005. Recipient Best On-Screen Team (with Owen Wilson), MTV Movie awards, 2006; named Favorite On-Screen Match-Up (with Owen Wilson), People's Choice Awards, 2006, Favorite Leading Man, 2007; named one of 50 Most Powerful People in Hollywood, Premiere mag., 2006, 100 Most Powerful Celebrities, Forbes.com, 2007. Address: United Talent Agy Ste 500 9560 Wilshire Blvd Beverly Hills CA 90212*

VAUGHN, WILLIAM PRESTON, retired historian, educator; b. East Chgo., Ind., May 28, 1933; s. James Carl and Georgiana (Preston) V.; m. Virginia Lee Meyer, June 10, 1961 (dec. 2007); 1 child, Rhonda Louise Horton. AB, U. Mo., Columbia, 1955; MA, Ohio State U., 1956, PhD, 1961. Instr. in history U. So. Calif., 1961-62; asst. prof. history U. N. Tex., Denton, 1962-65, assoc. prof., 1965-69, prof., 1969-91; ret., 1991. Instr. Tex. Project, Malaysia, 1986, 88. Author: Schools for All: The Blacks and Public Education in the South, 1865-77, 1974, The Antimasonic Party in the United States, 1826-43, 1983, Masonic Home and School of Texas, 2002; editor Transactions Tex. Lodge of Rsch., 1988—; contbr. articles to profl. jours. With arty. U.S. Army, 1956-57 Mem. SAR, SCV, So. Hist. Assn. (life), Historians Early Am. Republic, Blue Friars, Masons, Phi Beta Kappa, Phi Alpha Theta (manuscript competition winner 1972). Republican. Disciples Of Christ. Home: 2009 N Edwards Apt 15 Mount Pleasant TX 75455-8450

VAUGHN-DANIELS, KYMBERLY LOUISE, healthcare educator, consultant; d. Richard H. and Lynda R. Vaughn; children: Micheaux D. Daniels, Mari D. Daniels, MiAusha K. Daniels, Malyk K. Daniels, Mykai D. Daniels. AA, Tulsa CC, Okla., 1999; BA in Family Rels. and Child Devel., Northeastern State U., Tahlequah, Okla., 2002; MA in Early Childhood Edn., Northeastern State U., Broken Arrow, Okla., 2006. Tchr. asst. Tulsa Pub. Schls., 1991—95; lead tchr. Cmty. Action Agy., Tulsa, 1995—99; health edn. specialist Tulsa Health Dept., 2002—06; asst. prof. Tulsa CC, 2006—. Cons. T.O.O.L.S. Tulsa, 2008—. Organizer leader Local affiliate NBCDI, Tulsa, Okla., 2008—09. Mem.: Nat. Black Child Devel. Inst. Democrat.

VAUGHT, KARIN HAMPTON, music educator; b. Ft. Worth, June 15, 1960; d. Mary Jane Oliveto and John George Hampton; m. James Alan Vaught, Mar. 26, 1994; children: Tracy Vaught McKinney, Leslie Calhoun. BS, Tex. Wesleyan Coll., Fort Worth, 1981; MA, Tex. Woman's U., Denton, 2005. Owner Vaught Music Studio, Bedford, Tex., 2002—; adj. instr. Tarrant County Coll., Ft. Worth, 2006—. Treas. Regal Opera Co., Bedford, 2003—05. Mem.: Nat. Assn. Tchrs. Singing. Avocations: gardening, travel, cooking. Home: 3912 Candlewick Ct Bedford TX 76021 Personal E-mail: karinsings@gmail.com.

VAUGHT, LAURA E., legislative staff member; BS cum laude, Wake Forest U., 1993; MPA, Va. Polytechnic Inst. and State U., 1995. With staff of Rep. Rick Boucher, US House of Reps., 1997—, casework specialist, legis. dir., legis. asst., press. sec., dep. chief of staff, 2001—07, chief of staff, 2007—. Office: Office of Congressman Rick Boucher 2187 Rayburn House Office Bldg Washington DC 20515*

VAUPEL, JAMES W., demographer; b. NYC, May 2, 1945; m. Bodil Larsen; children: Anna Bodil, Sofie Gøbel. BA highest honors in Math. Statistics, Harvard U., 1967; MPP in Demographics, Harvard U., Kennedy Sch. Govt., 1971, PhD in Demographics, 1978. Rsch. assoc. Harvard Multinational Enterprise Project, Harvard Bus. Sch., Boston, 1967—75; lectr. to tenured assoc. prof., Inst. Policy Scis. and Policy Affairs Duke U., Durham, NC, 1972—85, rsch. prof. Sanford Inst.; cons. US EPA, Washington, 1979—82; rsch. scholar Internat. Inst. for Applied Systems Analysis, Laxenburg, Austria, 1984—85; prof. ancient studies, adj. prof. epidemiology U. Minn., 1988—91, prof. public affairs and planning, Humphrey Inst. Pub. Affairs, 1985—91; prof. demography & epidemiology, Inst. Pub. Health U. So. Denmark, Odense, Denmark, 1991—2002; sr. rsch. scientist, Sanford Inst. Duke U., Durham, NC, 1992—2005; sr. rsch. scientist Terry Sanford Inst. Public Policy, 1992—2005; founding dir. Max Planck Inst. for Demographic Rsch., Rostock, 1996—; hon. prof. U. Rostock, Germany, 2003—; dir. Rostocker Zentrum zur Erforshung des Demografischen Wandels, Germany, 2004—, Max Panck Internat. Rsch. Network on Aging, 2007—. Mem. adv. com. U. Minn. China Ctr., 1986—91; dir., Ctr. for Population Analysis and Policy U. Minn., 1986—91, examining mem. grad. faculty in Gerontology, 1987—91; mem., gerontology review com. Nat. Inst. Aging, NIH, U.S.A., 1986—90; head Aging Rsch. Ctr., Odense U. Med. Sch., Denmark, 1992—96; mem., social sci. and population review com. NIH, 1992—97, mem., Nat. Adv. Coun. on Aging, 1998—2002; chair, sci. adv. bd. Danish Ctr. for Demographic Rsch., Denmark, 1998—2000; mem. sci. adv. bd. Chinese Nat. Rsch. Ctr. on Aging, 1998—2002, German Socio-Economic Panel, Germany, 1999—2001; mem. Commn. on Global Aging. Global Aging Initiative, 1999—2002; honorarprofessor U. Rostock, Germany, 2003—; sr. fellow Ctr. for the Study of Aging and Human Develop., Duke U. Med. Ctr., 2003—; scientific adv. coun. of the Netherlands Interdisciplinary Demography Inst., Netherlands, 2004—; vis. prof. London Sch. Economics and Polit. Sci., 2004—06; rector Internat. Max Planck Rsch. Sch. for Demography, 2000—, European Doctoral Sch. Demography, 2005—; adv. bd. mem. Population and Development Review, Population Coun., U.S.A., 2008—. Assoc. editor Journal Policy Analysis and Management, 1980—85, founding editor Insights, Journal Policy Analysis and Management, 1980—85, founding pub., mem. sci. review bd. (online jour.) Demographic Research, 1999—, dep. editor Demography, U.S.A., 2007—; contbr. several articles to profl. jours. Recipient Irene B. Tauber prize, Population Assn. Am., 2001, Mindel C. Sheps award for Math. Demography, 2008, Ipsen Found. Longevity prize, 2003. Fellow: Am. Acad. Arts & Scis.; mem.: European Assn. for Population Studies (co-chair, com. on the use biol. indicators in social sci. surveys, NRC 1999—2000, com. on tng. in population studies in Europe 2003—, chair of the coun. 2003—), Max Planck Soc. for the Advancement of Sci. (scientific mem.), NAS (study dir., com. on risk and decision making 1979—81, mem. standing com. on population, NRC 1999—2005, com. on population forecasting, NRC 1998—2000). Office: Max Planck Inst für Demografische Forschung Konrad Zuse Strasse 1 18057 Rostock Germany also: Sanford Inst Pub Policy Rubenstein Hall Rm 186 302 Towerview Rd Durham NC 27708-0309 Office Phone: 49 0381-2081-102. Office Fax: 49 0381-2081-202. Business E-Mail: jwv@demogr.mpg.de.

VAUX, HENRY JAMES, JR., economics professor; b. Portland, Oreg., Feb. 2, 1940; s. Henry James and Jean (Macduff) V.; m. Prindle Anders, June 19, 1964; children: Robert, Katherine. BA, U. Calif., Davis, 1962; MA, U. Mich., 1964, MS, 1968, PhD, 1973. Examiner U.S. Office Mgmt. and Budget, Washington, 1964-67; economist U.S. Nat. Water Commn., Arlington, Va., 1969-70; prof. econs. U. Calif., Riverside, 1970—, dir. water resources, 1986-93, assoc. v.p., 1992—. Pres. Nat. Inst. Water Resources, Washington, 1986-93; pres. bd. dirs. Water Edn. Found., Sacramento, 1990—; mem., chair water sci. and tech. bd. Nat. Rsch. Coun., 1994-2001; co-chair adv. bd. Rosenberg Internat. Forum, Oakland, 1996—. Recipient Nat. Leadership award Univ. Coun. Water Resource Rsch., 1994. Mem. Cosmos Club.

VAVALA, DOMENIC ANTHONY, medical research scientist, educator, retired military officer; b. Providence, Feb. 1, 1925; s. Salvatore and Maria (Grenci) V BA, Brown U., Providence, 1947; MS, U. RI, Kingston, 1950; MA, Trinity U., San Antonio, 1954; PhD Physiology, Accademia di Studi Superiori "Minerva", Italy, 1957; MEd, U. Houston, 1958; LittD, Univ. Internazionale Sveva "Frederick II", Bergamo, Italy, 1979; DSc (hon.), Nobile Accademia di Santa Teodora Imperatrice, Rome, 1966, DMS (hon.), 1970; DPH (hon.), Nobile Accademia di Santa Teodora Imperatrice, 1983; D Pedagogy (hon.), Studiorum Universitas Constantiniana of Sovrano Ordine Constantiniano di San Giorgio, Rome, 1966; EdD (hon.), Imperiale Accademia di San Cirillo, Pomezia, Italy, 1977; D Health Scis. (hon.), Johnson & Wales U., 1993; LLD (hon.), Fridericus II U., Capua, Italy, 1997; MD (hon.), Frederick II U., Providence, 1999. Cert. Yale U. Army Specialized Tng. Program, 1944. Asst. tumor rsch. U. R.I., also asst. entomol. rsch., 1950; rsch. asst. pharmacology Boston U. Sch. Medicine, 1950—51; commd. 2d lt. med. svc. USAF, 1951, advanced through grades to lt. col., 1968; rsch. team physiologist cold injury Army Med. Rsch. Lab., Osaka Army Hosp., Osaka, Japan, 1951—52; rschr. aviation physiologist USAF Sch. Aviation Medicine, Randolph AFB, Tex., 1952—54, 3605th USAF Hosp., Ellington AFB, Tex., 1955—57, chief physiol. tng., 1957; cons. aviation physiology, film prodn. dept. U. Houston, 1956; rschr. aviation physiologist, head acad. sect. dept. physiol. tng. Wilford Hall USAF Hosp., Lackland AFB, Tex., 1957—58; vis. prof. physiology Incarnate Word Coll., San Antonio, 1958; rschr. aviation physiologist, chief physiol. tng. comdr. 832d Physiol. Tng. Flight, 832d Tactical Hosp., Cannon AFB, N.Mex., 1958—64; adjunct prof. Ea. N.Mex. U., Portales, 1959—64; instr. adult edn. divsn. Clovis Mcpl. Schs., N.Mex., 1960; rschr. aviation physiologist, comdr. 15th Physiol. Tng. Flight, 824th USAF Dispensary, Kadena Air Base, Okinawa, 1965—66; rsch. scientist, directorate fgn. tech., aerospace med. divsn. Brooks AFB, Tex., 1966—68; chief R & D support and interface divsn., dep. dir. for fgn. tech., 1969—70; adj. instr. Johnson & Wales U., Providence, 1973—74; instr. humanities Johnson and Wales U., Providence, 1974—75, asst. prof. humanities, 1975—77, prof. health scis. and nutrition, 1977—93, prof. emeritus, 1993—, coord. biomed. and behavioral scis. Day Coll. divsn., 1973—75, psychology coord. vets. divsn. Coll. Continuing Edn., 1974—76, assoc. dean adj. faculty, 1975, dean faculty, 1975—77, coord. acad. devel., 1977—78, dir. mus. series, 1990—, curator Chapel Empress St. Theodora, 1992—; with Vet. Adminstrn. Med. Ctr., Providence. Pres. corp., chmn. bd. dir. Sovereign Constantinian Order of St. George, Inc., R.I., 1986—; pres. corp., chmn. bd. dir. The Noble Acad. of Empress St. Theodora of R.I., Inc., 1988—2008; instr. anatomy, physiology and med. terminology R.I. Hosp., Providence, 1987-90 Writer, prodr.: (TV Series) Your Body in Flight, Sta. KUHT, Houston, 1956; (TV series) Highway to Health, Okinawa, 1965; compiled and edited: Fifty Years of Progress of Soviet Medicine, 1917-67; abstractor, translator in medicine Chem. Abstracts Svc., Am. Chem. Soc., Ohio State U., 1963-74; editor: (Cath. parish newspaper) The Logos, Kadena Air Base, Okinawa, 1965-66 (1st pl. 5th Air Force chapel printed news contest); contbr. articles to profl. jours Pres. Holy Name Soc., Kadena Air Base, Okinawa, 1965-66; trustee, Gov. Ctr. Sch., Providence, 1979-85; mem. scholarship com. St. Sahag and, St. Mesrob Armenian Apostolic Ch., Providence; choir master, music dir. Cannon AFB, Cath. Parish, 1958-65; received in pvt. audience Pope John Paul II, 1997. Served with AUS, 1943-44 Recipient Disting. Svc. award Clovis Jaycees, 1959, Acad. Palms Gold medal Accademia Studi Superiori "Minerva", 1960, citation, chief chaplains USAF, 1970, commendation medal USAF, 1970, chief biomed. scientist insignia, biomed. scis. corps USAF Med. Svc., 1970, spl. faculty citation Johnson and Wales U., 1981, contbn. awd. doctoral program ednl. leadership Alan Feinstein Grad. Sch., Johnson and Wales U., Providence, 1999, academician divsn. scis. Accademia di Studi Superiori "Minerva", 1960; Min. Plenipotentiary for U.S. of Nobile Accademia di Santa Teodora Imperatrice, Rome, 1967, rector pro tempore, France, 1980, Achievement cert. Dept. Army Headquarters, US Army Ryukyu Islands, APO San Francisco, 1966; decorated knight grand officer Merit Class, Sovereign Constantinian Order St. George, Rome, 1969, Knight of Grand Cross with Constantinian neckchain, Justice Class, Sovereign Constantinian Order St. George, 1969, Knight of Grand Cross Justice Class, Order St. John of Jerusalem, Knights of Malta, Bari, Italy, 1984, Knight of Grand Cross Justice Class, Order St. John of Jerusalem, Knights of Cyprus, Rhodes and Malta, Bari, 1984, Knight of Grand Cordon Justice Class, Order Teutonic Knights, Sao Paulo, 1986, Knight of Grand Cross Justice Class, Mil. Order St. Gereon, Sao Paulo, 1986, Knight of Grand Cross Justice Class, Mil. and Hospitalier Order St Jean d'Acre and St. Thomas, Capua, Italy, 1987, Knight of Grand Cross Justice Class, Mil. and Hospitalier Order St. Mary of Bethlehem, Capua, 1987, Knight of Grand Cross Disting. Assoc. of Am. Soc., Italian Legions of Merit, Class of 2007; recipient Ednl. Professionalism award Domei Toastmasters Internat., 1965; named Magnificent Rector and Pres., The Constantinian U. (Studiorum Universitas Constantiniana), Italy, 1970, Marquis of Royal Throne of Swabia of Hohenstaufen Dynasty, Prince Jean von Schwaben, Bergamo, Italy, 1984, Duke of the New Rome, Constantinople, of Imperial Dynasty of Amorium by His Imperial Highness Prince Don Francesco Amoroso d'Aragona, Capua, 2000, Citizens Citation, Hon. Vincent A. Cianci Jr., Mayor City Providence, 1995, Spl. Citation, Johnson & Wales U., Alan Shawn Feinstein Grad. Sch., Sch. Edn., 2007. Fellow AAAS (emeritus, life), RSPH (emeritus), Tex. Acad. Sci.(life), Royal Soc. Health (London; emeritus), Royal Soc. Pub. Health (emeritus, 2009), Am. Inst. Chemists (emeritus); mem. Assn. Mil. Surgeons US (life), Nat. Assn. Doctors US (founder 1958, sec.-treas. 1958-85, editor-in-chief The NADUS Jour. 1963-68), Accademia di San Cirillo Italy (hon.), NY Acad. Scis., Phi Sigma, Kappa Delta Pi, Phi Kappa Phi, Alpha Beta Kappa (charter, pres. RI Alpha chpt. Johnson and Wales U. 1984-92, Vavala Nutrition award, Noble Acad. of Empress Saint Theodora award, Outstanding Culinary Fellow award), Acad. Europea for Econ. Cultural Rels. (acad. senate, medallion 2004), 1916 Soc. RI Found., Providence; Dir., Singing Chapel Prog., The Bridge at Cherry Hill Assisted Living Cmty., One Cherry Hill Rd., Johnston Rhode Island, Am. Legion, Disabled Am. Vets., Mil. Officers Assn. America.

VAVRINA, CHARLES LAUREL, art director; s. Charles and Theresa Baker Laurel; m. Mary M. Laurel, June 22, 1957; children: Charles A. Laurel, Ardas Kaur Khalsa, Carol L. Griffith, Christopher B. Laurel. Degree, Fond du Lac Coll., Wis., 1950. Pres. Charles Laurel Co., Inc., Fort Myers, Fla., 1958—88; dir. Laurel Fine Arts Found., Fort Myers, 2003—. Office: Laurel Fine Arts Fund 12577 New Brittany Blvd Fort Myers FL 33907 Personal E-mail: claurel@comcast.net.

VAYALAKKARA, JYOTHI, neuropsychologist, director, educator; b. Kannur, Kerala, India, July 20, 1968; d. Gangadharan Nambiar and Jayalakshmi Vayalakkara; m. Karamdas Velluva Puthiya, Apr. 23, 1990; 1 child, Jyotsna Vayalakkara Karamdas. BS in Chemistry, Calicut U., India, 1989, MA in English Lit., 1991; MS in Clin. Psychology, Nova Southeastern U., Ft. Lauderdale, Fla., 1996, PsyD, 2000; diploma in journalism, Bharatiya Vidya Bhavan, India, 1991. Cert. clin. psychologist Conn., 2004. Postdoctoral fellowship in neuropsychology New Eng. Med. Ctr., Boston, 2001—03; clin. neuropsychology fellow Tufts Med. Sch., New Eng. Med. Ctr., Boston, 2001—03; program dir., neuropsychologist Conn. Valley Hosp., Middletown, Conn., 2004—. Program dir. Conn. Valley Hosp., Middletown, 2004—; adj. psychology faculty U. Hartford, Conn., 2005—. Contbr. articles to profl. jours., chapters to books. Mem. Psychologists for Peace (PsySR), Washington, 2006—; com. mem. South Asian Womens' Network (SNEHA), Hartford, 2006—. Ann. Scholarship award, Broward Internat. Womens' Club, Fla., 1994—99. Mem.: APA (assoc.), Conn. Psychol. Assn. (assoc.), Bharatiya Vidya Bhavan (life), Asia-Pacific Coalition, Phi Theta Kappa (hon.). Avocations: writing, volunteering. Personal E-mail: kjjy@earthlink.net.

VAYANIAN, SOLARA ZAKELI, artist, educator, researcher; b. Chgo., June 14, 1947; d. Ralph William Forst, Marion Elizabeth Engel; children: Michael Paul Catlett, Noel Thomas Catlett. BA in Phys. Edn. and Dance, San Diego State U., 1975. Founder, dir. Winged Fire Prodns., Sedona, Ariz., 1978—; founder, facilitator Kinesio-Emotional Release System, Sedona, 1978—. Author: (novels) Time Dancer, 1972, The Stars Gave Passion, 1977, Octangle Blue, 1989, Time Out of Mind, 2000; co-author: (stage prodns.) Journey thru the Mask, The Doorway of the Heart. Founder, dir., project renaissance: Move IT! & other workshops for releasing trauma, abuse & old issues, and healing the human heart & spirit; founder, dir. compassionate care teams pilot program Kachina Point Rehab. and Healthcare Ctr., Sedona. Recipient Barbara Marx Hubbard Women of Vision award, 1996. Achievements include development of workable systems for healing, wholeness and human potential development through the arts, education, interactive community programs, performances and events. Personal E-mail: solaravayanian@yahoo.com, projectren@gmail.com.

VAYGHAN, JAMSHID ABDOLLAHI, architectural engineer; PhD, U. Minn., Mpls., 2000. Dir. engring.; chief engr.; adj. faculty; chief enterprise info. arch. IBM Corp., Mpls., 1990—2008. Adv. bd. mem. Minn. High Tech. Assn. Master: IEEE.

VAYMAN, ANNA, music educator; d. Mikhail Vayman and Alla Zhokhova; m. Leonid Sirotkin; 1 child, Mikhail. MusM (hon.), St. Petersburg State Conservatory, 1993; diploma, Coll. Conservatory Music, U. Cin. Asst. concertmaster Kirov Orch., Mariinski Theatre, St. Petersburg, 1995—2000; violin instr. Coll. Conservatory Music, U. Cin., 2001—06; assoc. prof. music performance, violin Ball State U., Muncie, 2006—, violinist, Am. Piano Trio, 2006—. Musician performing solo and chamber music. Mem.: St. Petersburg Conservatory Grads. Assn.,

Am. Fedn. Musicians. Home: 1325 W University Ave Muncie IN 47303 Office: Ball State Univ Sch Music 2000 W University Ave Muncie IN 47306 Business E-Mail: avayman@bsu.edu.

VAYO, DAVID JOSEPH, composer, music educator; b. New Haven, Mar. 28, 1957; s. Harold Edward and Joan Virginia (Cassidy) V.; m. Marie-Susanne Langille, 2002; children; Rebecca Lynn, Gordon Francis. MusB, Ind. U., 1980, MusM, 1982; D of Musical Arts, U. Mich., 1990. Prof. Nat. U., Heredia, Costa Rica, 1982-84, Nat. Symphony Youth Sch., San Jose, Costa Rica, 1982-84; asst. prof. music Conn. Coll., New London, 1988-91, Ill. Wesleyan U. Sch. Music, Bloomington, 1991-95, assoc. prof., 1995-2000, prof., 2000—. Resident artist Banff Ctr. for Arts, 1992, 94, Centrum, Port Townsend, Wash., 1996, Lillian E. Smith Ctr. Creative Arts, Clay Ga., 2009; participating composer Internat. Soc. Contemporary Music-World Music Days, Hong Kong, 2007, Yokohama, 2001, Mexico City, 1993, Internat. Double Reed Festival, Rotterdam, The Netherlands, 1995, Grand Teton Music Festival, 2006, Thailand Composition Festival, 2007, 08. Composer chamber composition Signals, 1997 (commd. by Koussevitzky Music Found. and Orkest de Volharding), Symphony: Blossoms and Awakenings, 1990 (performer St. Louis Symphony, Leonard Slatkin condr. 1993), Musical Festival Ground, 2006(commd. Prairic Fire Theatre), Eight Poems of William Carlos Williams for solo trombonist, 1994 (commd. by St. Louis Symphony), piano trio Awakening of the Heart (commd. Barlow Endowment for Music Composition), 1998; works pub. by Internat. Trombone Assn. Press, Berben/Italia Guitar Soc. Series and A.M. Percussion Publs. John Simon Guggenheim Meml. Found. fellow, 2001; Ill. Arts Coun. fellow, 2000. Mem. ASCAP (awards 1988—), Am. Music Ctr. (copying assistance grantee 1992, 2008), Coll. Music Soc. (presenter nat. confs.), Soc. for Electro-Acoustic Music in U.S. (presenter nat. conf.), Soc. Composers (membership chmn. 1990-2000, presenter at nat. confs.), Am. Composers Forum. Avocations: athletics, free improvisation, travel, reading, cooking. Office: Ill Wesleyan U Sch Music PO Box 2900 Bloomington IL 61702-2900 Home Phone: 309-828-3192; Office Phone: 309-556-3068. E-mail: dvayo@iwu.edu.

VAZACOPOULOS, ALKIS, application developer, educator; b. Athens, Greece, Mar. 18, 1965; arrived in US, 1986; s. Panagiotis and Dominique Vazacopoulos; m. Lora Pilalis; children: Andonis children: Dominique, Theodora, Anastasia. BBA, U. Piraeus, Greece, 1986; MSc, Fla. Internat. U., Miami, Fla., 1988; MSc in Ops. Rsch., Carnegie Mellon U., Pitts., Pa., 1990, PhD in Indsl. Adminstrn., 1994. Asst. prof. Fairleigh Dickinson U., Hackensack, NJ, 1994—99, assoc. prof., 2000—02; dir. Dash Optimization, Inc., Englewood Cliffs, NJ, 1998—2006, mng. dir., 2007—08; v.p. Fair Isaac, Inc., 2008—. Vis. scientist Faw U., Ulm, Germany, 1997; adj. assoc. prof. Fairleigh Dickinson U., 2002—; panelist, reviewer NSF, Washington, 2004—07; faculty ctr. applied optimization U. Fla., Gainesville, 2005—09. Author: (book) Data mining in Biomedicine; contbr. articles to profl. jours. Recipient Rsch. award, Fairleigh Dickinson U., 2000; fellow, Nat. Found. Fellowships, Greece, 1986; William Larimer fellow, Carnegie Mellon U., 1988—91. Business E-Mail: alkisvazacopoulos@fairisaac.com.

VAZE, SHILPA ARUN, software, firmware, modeling engineer; d. Arun Ramchandra and Mrudul Arun Vaze; m. Anand Arun Karnik, Feb. 17, 2009. BE in Instrumentation, U. Pune, Maharashtra, India, 1996; MS in Mech. Engring., Kans. State U., Manhattan, 2002, PhD in Elec. Engring., 2007. Grad. rsch. & tchg. asst. Kans. State U., Manhattan, 1999—2007; software engr. Schlumberger Tech. Ctr., Sugar Land, Tex., 2007—. Co-instructor, intro. computer engring., freshman level course Kans. State U. - Elec. Engring. Dept., Manhattan, 2004—07, grad. rep. engring. recruitment, 2006—07, treas., grad. student coun., 2006—07, lead tchg. asst., 2004—06. Contbr. scientific papers to numerous profl. jours. Recipient Outstanding award, 12 th Ann. Grad. Rsch. Forum, Kans. State U., 2007, Badminton Intramural Champion, Kans. State U. Recreation Svcs., 2004, Co-Rec Racquette Ball Intramural Championship, 2007, Badminton Intramural Champion, 2006, 2007. Mem.: ASME (edtl. bd), IEEE (edtl. bd.), MENSA, Eta Kappa Nu.

VAZIRANI, KAVITA, broadcast company executive; b. 1967; BA in Radio Broadcasting, Columbia Coll., Chgo.; MA in Profl. Comm., La Salle U., Phila. With Comcast Cable Comm., Inc., 1997—, nat. dir. media svcs., nat. sr. dir. media svcs., 2002—, v.p. mktg. media svcs., 2004—. Grad. Comcast Exec. Leadership Forum. Recipient Dale Carnegie Human Rels. award, Dale Carnegie Special Achievement award; named a Woman to Watch, Advt. Age, 2008. Mem.: Women in Cable & Telecomm., Cable TV Assn. for Mktg. (Mktg. Coop Team Effort award, Rainmaker award). Office: Comcast Cable Comm Inc Hdqs 1500 Market St Philadelphia PA 19102 Office Phone: 215-665-1700. Office Fax: 215-981-7790.*

VAZIRANI, VIJAY V., science educator; b. Mumbai, Maharashtra, India, Apr. 20, 1957; s. Virkumar and Kamla Vazirani; m. Milena Mihail; 1 child, Michel. PhD, U. Calif., Berkeley, 1983. Prof. Ga. Tech, Atlanta, 1995—. Author: (book) Approximation Algorithms. Fellow, ACM, 2005. Office: Georgia Tech 266 Ferst Ave Atlanta GA 30332 Business E-Mail: vazirani@cc.gatech.edu.

VAZIRI, NOSRATOLA DABIR, internist, nephrologist, educator; came to U.S., 1969, naturalized, 1977; s. Abbas and Tahera Vaziri. MD, Tehran U., Iran, 1966. Diplomate Am. Bd. Internal Medicine, Am. Bd. Nephrology; cert. hypertension specialist Am. Soc. Hypertension. Intern Cook County Hosp., Chgo., 1969-70; resident Berkshire Med. Ctr., Pittsfield, Mass., 1970-71, Wadsworth VA Med. Ctr., LA, 1971-72, UCLA Med. Ctr., 1972-74; prof. medicine U. Calif.-Irvine, 1979—, prof. physiology and biophysics, 2001—, prof. biol. scis., 2006—, chief nephrology and hypertension divsn., 1977—, dir. hemodialysis unit, 1977-94, vice chmn. dept. medicine, 1982-94, chmn. dept. medicine, 1994-98, chair faculty Coll. Medicine, 2000—02. Sr. assoc. editor: Jour. Spinal Cord Medicine, 1991-2005; mem. editl. bd. Kidney Internat., 2003—, Am. Jour. Nephrology, 1999-02, Nephron, 1999-02, Advancements in Renal Replacement Therapies, 1999-04, Internat. Jour. Artificial Organs, 1990—, Spinal Cord Medicine, 1991-2005, Jour. Renal Nutrition, 2006—; contbr. articles to profl. jours. Mem. sci. adv. coun. Nat. Kidney Found., 1977—. Recipient Golden Apple award, U. Calif. Irvine Coll. Medicine, 1977, Lauds and Laurels award, U. Calif. Irvine Alumni Assn., 1999, Spirit Nephrology award, Nat. Kidney Found., 2002, Athalie Clarke's Outstanding Health Sci. Rschr. award, 2003, Presdl. Lectureship award, Can. Hypertension Soc., Disting. Svc. award, Western Assn. Physicians, 2007. Master: ACP; fellow: Am. Heart Assn. (fellow coun. high blood pressure rsch.); mem.: Am. Soc. Hypertension, Internat. Soc. Nephrology, Assn. Profs. Medicine, Western Assn. Physicians (councilor 2003—05, pres. 2006—07), Am. Paraplegia Soc. (pres. 1992—94, Donald Munro award 2002), Am. Physiol. Soc., Am. Soc. Nephrology, Alpha Omega Alpha. Avocation: gardening. Home: 66 Balboa Cv Newport Beach CA 92663-3226 Office: U Calif Irvine Med Ctr Div Nephrology Dept Medicine 101 The City Dr Orange CA 92868-3201 Office Phone: 714-456-5142. Business E-Mail: ndvaziri@uci.edu.

VAZQUEZ, AMERICA, language educator; b. Caguas, PR, Oct. 28, 1948; d. Jose V. Vazquez and America Martinez; 1 child, Romualdo Palacios. Med, Temple U., Phila., Pa., 1973. ESL prof. Miami Dade Coll. InterAm. Campus, Fla., 1981—2008; ESL instr. U. PR, Carolina. Composer: (poem) Pensamientos (Nat. Winner O. T. I. Festival US, 1988, Finalist Internat. Poetry Contest, Rincon Poetico, Madrid, Spain, 2006). Vol. work St. Rose Lima Parish, Miami. Mem.: Fla. T.E.S.O.L. Office: Miami Dade Coll InterAm Campus 627 SW 27th Ave Miami FL 33135 Business E-Mail: avazquez@mdc.edu.

VAZQUEZ, DELIA M., psychology professor, director; married, June 25, 1983; children: MariaEsperanza Lopez, MariaCristina Lopez. MD, U. PR, San Juan, 1982. Clin. fellow U. Iowa, Iowa City, 1984—85; postdoc. rsch. fellow U. Mich., Ann Arbor, 1986—88, lectr., 1988—93, asst. prof., dept. pediat., 1994—2000, dir. pediat. endocrine fellowship, dept. pediat, 1999—, assoc. prof., dept. pediat. and psychiatry dept., 2000—07, assoc. dir., brain behavior program Ctr. Human Growth and Devel., 2001—06, assoc. chair rsch., dept. pediat., 2002—, prof., dept. pediat. and psychiatry dept., 2007—, co-dir., pediat. program clin. and translational sci. awards, 2007—. Co-dir. migrant ministry St. Thomas Apostle Ch., Ann Arbor, Mich., 1992; coun. mem. Soc. Pediat. Rsch., 2003—06. Recipient Curt P. Richter award, Internat. Soc. Psychoneuroendocrinology, 1997, Kenneth J. Povish Cmty. Svc. award, Dioceses of Lansing, Mich., 2004, Cmty. Svc. Recognition award, KC, Ann Arbor, 2005. Mem.: Lawson-Wilkins Pediat. Endocrine Soc. (coun. mem. 2003—06), Soc. Neurosci. (com. mem. elected 2002—06, rep. minority affairs 2002—06). Achievements include development of stress systems. Office: Univ Mich 1500 E Medical Center Dr MPB Rm 1121 Ann Arbor MI 48109

VAZQUEZ, JAVIER CARLOS, professional baseball player; b. Ponce, PR, July 25, 1976; m. Kamille Vazquez; children: Kamila, Javier Josue. Attended, Colegio Ponceno, PR. Pitcher Montreal Expos, 1998—2003, NY Yankees, 2004, Ariz. Diamondbacks, 2005, Chgo. White Sox, 2006—08, Atlanta Braves, 2008—. Mem. Maj. League Baseball All-Star Team, Japan, 2000; mem. Puerto Rican nat. team World Baseball Classic, 2006, 09. Founder Save The Kids Found. Named to Am. League All-Star Team, Maj. League Baseball, 2004. Office: Atlanta Braves Turner Field 755 Hank Aaron Dr Atlanta GA 30315*

VÁZQUEZ, MARTHA ALICIA, federal judge; b. Santa Barbara, Calif., Feb. 21, 1953; d. Remigio and Consuelo Medina Vazquez. BA in Govt., U. Notre Dame, 1975, JD, 1978. Bar: N.Mex. 1979, admitted to practice: US Dist. Ct. (Dist. N.Mex.) 1979. Atty. Pub. Defender's Office, Santa Fe, 1979-81; ptnr. Jones, Snead, Wertheim, Rodriguez & Wentworth, Santa Fe, 1981-93; chief judge U.S. Dist. Ct. N.Mex., Santa Fe, 1993—. Democrat. Roman Catholic. Office: US Courthouse PO Box 2710 Santa Fe NM 87504-2710 Home Phone: 505-231-3810; Office Phone: 505-988-6330. Business E-Mail: vazquezchambers@nmcourt.fed.us.

VAZQUEZ, MIGUEL ANGEL, literature and language professor; b. San Juan, Jan. 16, 1968; s. Heriberto and Luz C. Vazquez. BA, U. de PR, Rio Piedras, 1991; MA; PhD in Spanish Lit. Golden Age, Ind. U., Bloomington, 2001. Asst. prof. Harriet L. Wilkes Honors Coll., Jupiter, Fla., 2001—07, assoc. prof., 2007. Author: (book) Desde la penumbra de la fosa; contbr. articles to profl. jour. Mem.: Am. Assn. Tchrs. Spanish & Portuguese, MLA. Liberal. Avocations: horses, travel. Office: Harriet L Wilkes Honors Coll 5353 Parkside Dr Jupiter FL 33458 Office Fax: 561-799-8602. Personal E-mail: mavazquezvazquez@gmail.com. Business E-Mail: mvazquez@fau.edu.

VAZQUEZ-AZPIRI, A. JAMES, lawyer; b. Madrid, May 3, 1962; s. Hector Tomas and Iris Belinda Mary Vazquez-Azpiri; m. Yanira E. Molina, July 22, 2002; 1 child, Virginia M. MA, U. St. Andrews, Scotland, 1985, Princeton U., 1987; JD, NYU, 1992; LLM, Harvard U., 1995. Bar: Calif. 1992. Adj. atty. U.S. Commn. on Immigration Reform, Washington, 1996—97; atty. Morrison & Foerster, San Francisco, 1992—97; ptnr. Cooley Godward LLP, San Francisco, 1997—2004, Morgan, Lewis & Bockius, San Francisco, 2005—. Co-author: (book) Immigration Practice Under AC21; contbr. articles to profl. jours. Recipient C. Arthur Friedrich award, Internat. Human Rights Law Group, 1993, Wiley M. Manuel award, State Bar of Calif., 1998, Armstrong prize, Princeton U., 1997. Mem.: MLA, Royal Overseas League, Hispanic Bar Assn., Bar Assn. San Francisco, Am. Immigration Lawyers Assn., Princeton Alumni Assn., Princeton Club of No. Calif., Harvard Club, Sigma Delta Pi, Phi Eta Sigma, Phi Delta Theta. Avocations: hiking, scuba diving, travel, literature. Home: 672 Sky Hy Cir Lafayette CA 94549 Office: Morgan Lewis & Bockius Spear St Tower One Market San Francisco CA 94105 E-mail: ajvazquez@morganlewis.com.

VAZZANO, FRANK PAUL, historian, educator; b. Lorain, Ohio, July 31, 1941; s. Anthony Joseph and Dorothy Marie Vazzano; m. Charlotte Louise Schmidt, Aug. 17, 1963; children: Frank Jr., Kristen, Ann-Marie. BS, Bowling Green State U., Ohio, 1964, MA, 1965; PhD, Kent State U., Ohio, 1972. Prof. Walsh U., North Canton, Ohio, 1971—. Adj. prof. Kent State U., Stark Campus, Canton, Ohio, 1990—2001. Author: Politician Extraordinaire: The Tempestuous Life and Times of Martin L. Davey, 2008 (Best Non-fiction, Best Ohio Biography award, 2009); contbr. articles to profl. jours. Recipient Tchg. Excellence award, Ohio Coun. Higher Edn., Scholarship award, Walsh U.; scholar. Mem.: Am. Italian Hist. Assn., Ohio Acad. History, Orgn. Am. Historians. Roman Catholic. Avocations: writing, gardening, sports. Home: 1906 Hollythorne Rd Ne Canton OH 44721-3851 Business E-Mail: fvazzano@walsh.edu.

VEACH, ROBERT RAYMOND, JR., lawyer; b. Charleston, SC, Nov. 28, 1950; s. Robert Raymond and Evelyn; m. Lori Sue Erickson, May 27, 1989. Student, St. Olaf Coll., 1968-70; BS in Acctg., Ariz. State U., 1972; JD, So. Meth. U., 1975. Bar: Tex. 1975, Nebr. 1975, US Dist. Ct. Nebr. 1975, US Dist. Ct. (no. dist.) Tex. 1975, Temporary Emergency Ct. Appeals 1975. Acctg. instr. Sch. Bus. So. Meth. U., Dallas, 1973-74; law clk. to Hon. Joe E. Estes US Dist. Ct. No. Dist. Tex.-Temp. Emergency Ct. Appeals, Dallas, 1975-76; assoc. Locke Purnell Boren Laney & Neely, Dallas, 1976-80; v.p. The Lomas & Nettleton Co., Dallas, 1980-83, Rauscher Pierce Refsnes, Inc., Dallas, 1983-87; pres. RPR Mortgage Fin. Corp., Dallas, 1985-87; sr. shareholder Locke Purnell Rain Harrell, Dallas, 1987-97; exec. v.p. Precision Imaging Solutions, Inc., Dallas, 1998—; pvt. practice Dallas, 1998—. Allied mem. NY Stock Exch., 1985-87; lectr. securities and banking confs.; bd. dirs. pvt. corps.; trustee CentraCore Properties Trust (NYSE-CPV), chmn. audit and fin. com., 1998-2002, 05-07, chmn. bd., 2002-07, chmn. corp. gov. and nominating com., 2003-07. Author legal articles. Dir. North Tex. affiliate Am. Diabetes Assn., Dallas, 1978-81; mem. Gov.'s Task Force Wash. State Housing Commn., 1982-83. Fellow Nebr. State Bar Found.; mem. ABA, State Bar of Tex., Nebr. State Bar Assn., Fed. Bar Assn., Dallas Bar Assn. Republican. Methodist. Avocation: golf. Home: 4223 Brookview Dr Dallas TX 75220-3801 Office: 2911 Turtle Creek Blvd Ste 1240 Dallas TX 75219-6277 Office Phone: 214-520-7544. Business E-Mail: bob@veachlaw.com.

VEACO, KRISTINA, lawyer; b. Sacramento, Mar. 4, 1948; d. Robert Glenn and Lelia (McCain) V.; 1 child, Nina Katherine. BA, U. Calif., Davis, 1978; JD, Hastings Coll. Law, 1981. Legal adv. to commr. William T. Bagley Calif. Pub. Utilities Commn., San Francisco, 1981-86; sr. counsel Pacific Telesis Group, San Francisco, 1986-94; sr. counsel corp. and securities and pol. law AirTouch Comms., San Francisco, 1994-98; asst. gen. counsel, asst. sec. McKesson Corp., San Francisco, 1999—2006; corp. governance advisor Veaco Group, 2006—. Mem.: NACD, ABA, Soc. Corp. Secs. and Governance Profls. (pres. San Francisco chpt. 2001—02, nat. bd. dirs. 2002—07, pres. Northern Calif. 2008—09, mem. adv. com. chpt.), Phi Beta Kappa. Office: 2470 16th Ave San Francisco CA 94116 Office Phone: 415-731-3111. Personal E-mail: kveaco@veacogroup.com.

VEALE, TINKHAM, II, retired chemicals executive, engineer; b. Topeka, Dec. 26, 1914; s. George W. and Grace Elizabeth (Walworth) V.; m. Harriett Alice Ernst, Sept. 6, 1941; children: Harriett Elizabeth Veale Leedy, Tinkham III, Helen Ernst Veale Gelbach. BS in Mech. Engring., Case Inst. Tech., 1937; LLD, Kenyon Coll., 1981. Registered profl. engr. With Gen. Motors Corp., 1937-38, Avery Engring. Co., 1939, Reliance Electric Co., 1940-41; asst. to pres. Ohio Crankshaft Co., 1942-46; gen. mgr. Tocco Co., 1947-51; pres. Ric Wil Corp., 1952-53, Alco Chem. Corp., 1954-56, dir., 1954-86. Spl. ptnr. Ball Burge & Kraus, investment bankers, 1957-60; chmn. bd. V. and V. Cos., Inc. and subs., Cleve., 1960-65, Alco Standard Corp. and subs., Valley Forge, Pa., 1965-86, Horsehead Industries, Inc. and subs., N.Y.C., 1981—2001, HTV Industries Inc. and subs., Cleve., 1978—; ptnr. Fair Elm Farm, 1948-2000, Kennedy Veale Stable, 1954-2000. Trustee Veale Charitable Found., 1966—. Recipient Silver Bowl award Case Inst. Tech., 1980; recipient Gold Medal Case Inst. Tech., 1982, Univ. medal Case We. Res. U., 2003. Mem. Cleve. Engring. Soc., Nat. Soc. Registered Profl. Engrs., Newcomen Soc., Phi Kappa Psi. Home: PO Box 39 Gates Mills OH 44040-0039 Office Phone: 440-423-4144, 440-423-4473.

VEASEY, PAMELA RENEA, television producer; b. May 25, 1962; BA in Polit. Sci. and Journalism, U. So. Calif. Career start as receptionist NBC TV. Writer (TV series) Gimme a Break, 1981, In Living Color, 1990, Nash Bridges, 1996, Between Brothers, 1997, Martial Law, 1998—99, The District, 2003—04, CSI: NY, 2004—; dir.: (TV series) The District, 2002—03; prodr.: (TV series) Matt Waters, 1996, The Gregory Hines Show, 1997, Martial Law, 1998, Get Real, 1999; exec. prodr.: (TV series) Between Brothers, 1996, The District, 2001—03, CSI: NY, 2005—. Named to Power 150, Ebony mag., 2008. Office: CBS Studios 7800 Beverly Blvd Los Angeles CA 90036 Office Phone: 323-575-2345.

VEATCH, ROBERT MARLIN, philosopher, researcher; b. Utica, NY, Jan. 22, 1939; s. Cecil Ross and Regina V.; m. Laurelyn Kay Lovett, June 17, 1961 (div. Oct. 1986); children: Paul Martin, Carlton Elliot; m. Ann Bender Pastore, May 23, 1987. BS, Purdue U., 1961; MS, U. Calif. at San Francisco, 1962; BD, Harvard U., 1964, MA, 1970, PhD, 1971; DHL (hon.), Creighton U., 1999, Union U., 2004. Teaching fellow Harvard U., 1968-70; research assoc. in medicine Coll. Physicians and Surgeons, Columbia U., 1971-72; assoc. for med. ethics Inst. of Society, Ethics and Life Scis., Hastings-on-Hudson, NY, 1970-75, sr. assoc., 1975-79; prof. med. ethics Kennedy Inst. Ethics Georgetown U., 1979—, prof. philosophy, 1981—, dir., 1989-96; adj. prof. depts. community and family medicine and ob/gyn, 1984—. Mem. vis. faculty various colls. and univs.; mem. gov. bd. Washington Regional Transplant Consortium, 1988—; bd. dirs. Hospice Care D.C., 1989-96, 97-99, pres., 1993-95; active United Network Organ Sharing Ethics Com., 1989-95. Author: Value-Freedom in Science and Technology, 1976, Death, Dying and the Biological Revolution, 1976, rev. edit., 1989, Case Studies in Medical Ethics, 1977, A Theory of Medical Ethics, 1981, The Foundations of Justice, 1987, The Patient as Partner, 1987; (with Sara T. Fry) Case Studies in Nursing Ethics, 1987, 3d edit., 2006, The Patient-Physician Relationship: The Patient as Partner, Part 2, 1991; (with James T. Rule) Ethical Questions in Dentistry, 1993, 2nd edit., 2004, (with Harley Flack) Case Studies in Allied Health Ethics, 1997, (with Paul DeVries and Lisa Newton) Ethics Applied, 2d. edit., 1999, (with Amy Haddad) Case Studies in Pharmacy Ethics, 1999, 2nd edit., 2008, The Basics of Bioethics, 2000, 2d edit., 2003, Transplantation Ethics, 2000, Disrupted Dialogue, 2005, Patient Heal Thyself, 2009; editor or co-editor: Bibliography of Society, Ethics and the Life Sciences, 1973, rev. edit., 1978, The Teaching of Medical Ethics, 1973, Death Inside Out, 1975, Ethics and Health Policy, 1976, Teaching of Bioethics, 1976, Population Policy and Ethics, 1977, Life Span: Values and Life Extending Technologies, 1979, Cases in Bioethics From the Hastings Center Report, 1982, Medical Ethics, 1989, 2d edit., 1997, Cross Cultural Perspectives in Medical Ethics, 1989, rev. edit., 2000; (with Edmund D. Pellegrino and John P. Langan) Ethics, Trust, and the Professions, 1991; (with Tom L. Beauchamp) Ethical Issues in Death and Dying, 1996, (with Hans-Martin Sass and Rihito Kimura) Advance Directives and Surrogate Decision Making in Health Care: United States, Germany, and Japan, 1998, (with Albert R. Jonsen and LeRoy Walters) Source Book in Bioethics: A Documentary History, 1998; assoc. editor Encyclopedia of Bioethics, 1998; editl. bd. Jour. AMA, 1976-86, Jour. Medicine and Philosophy, 1980—, Harvard Theol. Rev., 1975—, Jour. Religious Ethics, 1981—; editl. adv. bd. Forum on Medicine, 1977-81; contbg. editor Hosp. Physician, 1975-85, Am. Jour. Hosp. Pharmacy, 1989-99; sr. editor Kennedy Inst. Ethics Jour., 1991—; contbr. articles to profl. jours. Bd. dir. Washington Reg. Transplant Consortium, 1988-, Hospice Care of DC, 1989-1998, pres. bd., 1993-96; mem. United Network for Organ Sharing Ethics Com., 1989-95, Ad Hoc Living Donor Com., 2002-06. Recipient Disting. Svc. award, United Meth. Assn., Career Achievement award, Georgetown U., 2005. Mem.: Am. Soc. Bioethics and Humanities, Luckett's Bluegrass Found. (pres. 2008—, bd. dirs. 2008—). Office: Georgetown U Kennedy Inst Of Ethics Washington DC 20057-0001 Office Phone: 202-687-8099. Business E-Mail: veatchr@georgetown.edu.

VEAZEY, DORIS ANNE, retired state agency administrator; b. Dawson Spring, Ky., Feb. 16, 1935; d. Bradley Basil and Lucy Mable (Hamby) Sisk; m. Herman Veazey Jr., Aug. 15, 1964 (dec. Sept. 1987); 1 child, Vickie Dianne Veazey Kicinski., Murray State U., 1952-54. Unemployment ins. examiner Dept. for Employment Svcs., Madisonville, Ky., 1954-73, unemployment ins. supr., 1973-85, field office mgr., 1985-96; ret., 1996. Bd. dirs., adv. bd. region II Vocat. Tech. Schs., Madisonville, 1988-92. Mem. Mayor's Work Force Devel. Com., 1993-96, Ky. Indsl. Devel. Com., 1992-96; dept. dir. Adult III Sunday Sch., 1994-96, tchr., 2005-, ch. choir, 1990—; mem. staff devel. com. Madisonville First Bapt. Ch., 1997-99 Mem. Internat. Assn. of Pers. in Employment Svcs., Tenure, Order of Ky. Cols., Greater Madisonville C. of C. (dir. leadership 1988-93). Baptist. Avocations: reading, travel, photography. Home: 697 Brown Rd Madisonville KY 42431-2258

VEAZEY, RICHARD EDWARD, accounting educator; b. Highland Park, Mich., June 20, 1941; s. Earl Leroy Veazey and Laura Louise (Madsen) Gruettner; m. Jeanne Ann Bayak, Aug. 9, 1969 (dec. Dec. 1969). BS, Ferris State U., 1964; MBA, Cen. Mich. U., 1966; PhD, St. Louis U., 1981. Staff acct. Ternstedt div. GM, Warren, Mich.; adminstrv. asst. Homelite div. Textron Corp., Madison Heights, Mich.; instr. acctg. Oakland Community Coll., Bloomfield Hills, Mich., 1966-70, asst. prof., 1970-71; assoc. prof. Walsh Coll., Troy, Mich., 1971-73; grad. fellow St. Louis U., 1973-75, instr., 1975-79; assoc. prof. acctg. Grand Valley State U., Allendale, Mich., 1979-85, 86—; lectr. European div. U. Md., Spain, Fed. Republic Germany, 1985-86. Founder, exec. dir. West Mich. PDI, 1987-2007. Contbr. articles to profl. jours. Mich. Accountancy Found. grantee, 1973-76; Price Waterhouse scholar, 1975-76. Mem. Inst. Mgmt. Accts. (nat. dir. 1997—), Am. Acctg. Assn., Midwest Acctg. Soc. (pres. 1990-91), Stuart Cameron McLeod Soc., Masons, Shriners, Beta Alpha Psi, Sigma Phi Epsilon. Avocations: sailing, travel, photography. Home: 2651 Westbrook Dr NW Grand Rapids MI 49504-2346 Office: Grand Valley State U De Vos Ctr 401 Fulton St W Grand Rapids MI 49504-6431 Office Phone: 616-331-7408. Business E-Mail: veazeyr@gvsu.edu.

VEBER, DANIEL FRANK, research chemist; pharmaceutical company executive; b. New Brunswick, Sept. 9, 1939; s. Frank B. and Agnes Olam Veber; m. Marilyn Jane Franck, Sept. 12, 1959; children: Paul Daniel, David Frank. BA, Yale U., New Haven, 1961, MS, 1962, PhD 1964. sr. dir. Merck & Co. Inc., West Point, Pa., 1964—93, dir. med. chemistry SmithKline, King of Prussia, Pa., 1993-2002; cons. med. chemistry, Ambler, Pa., 2002-. contbr. articles to profl. jours. Mem. NIH, 1981-87. Mem. editl. bd. Jour. Medicinal Chemistry, 1989-93, Jour. Peptide Sci., 1994-2005, Jour. Peptide Rsch., 1997—2005, Molecular Pharmaceutics, 2003—08. Recipient Phila. Sect. award Am. Chem. Soc., 1988. Fellow N.Y. Acad. Scis. (hon.), AAAS; mem. Am. Chem. Soc. (Ralph F. Hirschmann award 2001), Am. Soc. Biol. Chemists, Am. Peptide Soc. (coun. mem. 1991-97; Merrifield award 2001), Sigma Xi. Lutheran. Patentee in field. Home: 290 Batleson Rd Ambler PA 19002-4116 Personal E-mail: verberdf@comcast.net.

VEBLEN, THOMAS CLAYTON, management consultant; b. Hallock, Minn., Dec. 17, 1929; s. Edgar R. and Hattie (Lundgren) V.; m. Susan Alma Beaver, Sept. 1, 1950 (div. 1971); children: Kari Kristen, Erik Rodli, Mark Andrew, Sara Catherine; m. Linda Joyce Eaton, Aug. 30, 1975; 1 child, Kristen Kirby. Student, U. Calif., Santa Barbara, 1950—51; BS, Calif. Poly. U., 1953; MS, Oreg. State U., 1955. Corp. v.p. Cargill, Inc., Wayzata, Minn., 1955-75; spl. asst. Sec. Interior, Washington, 1965; dir. food and agr. SRI Internat., Menlo Park, Calif., 1975-80; pres. Food Sys. Assocs., Inc., Washington, 1980-94; also bd. dirs. Food System Assocs., Inc., Washington; chmn. Enterprise Cons. and Devel., Inc., Mpls., 1990—; dir. Georgetown Cons., Inc., 1993-95; convener The Superior Bus. Firm Roundtable, 1993—; chmn. Kirby Ventures LLC, Mpls., 1997—, Wyatt Ventures, LLC, Mpls., 1999—, Northshore, LLC, Mpls., 2000—. Mem. CMC Inst. Mgmt. Cons., 1988—97, pres. Washington chpt., 1991—93. Co-author: (with M. Nichols) The U.S. Food System, 1978; (with M. Abel) Creating a Superior National Food System, 1992; author: The Way of Business: An Inquiry Into Meaning and Superiority, 2006, Going Viking, 2008; editor Food System Update, 1986-95. Treas., bd. dirs. White House Fellows Assn., Washington, 1985; trustee Freedom from Hunger Found., Davis, Calif., 1980-99, chmn., 1986-89; bd. dirs. Patterson Sch., U. Ky., Lexington, 1976-99, Am. Near East Refugee Aid, 1994-. Recipient Presdl. Appointment White House Fellows Program, Washington, 1965. Mem.: Coun. on Fgn. Rels., Cato Inst., Cosmos Club. Episcopalian. Avocations: canoeing, gardening, writing. Office: Enterprise Cons and Devel Inc 1806 LaSalle Ave S Ste 10 Minneapolis MN 55403 Office Phone: 202-342-7640. Personal E-mail: superbizrt@aol.com.

VECCHIO, MARIA THERESA, history professor; d. Joseph and Augustina Eufemia; 1 child, Renee. PhD, Fordham U., Bronx, NY, 1976. Lic. tchg. NY, 1970. Adj. asst. prof. Pace U., NYC, 1975—90; assoc. prof. history Felician Coll., Lodi, NJ, 1985—. Named Faculty Tchg. Excellence, Felician Coll., 2008. Mem.: Harvard Nat. Model UN, NE Regional Honors Coun., Nat. Collegiate Honors Coun. Conservative. Roman Catholic. Avocations: travel, reading. Office: Felician Coll 262 S Main St Lodi NJ 07644

VECCHIOTTI, ROBERT ANTHONY, management and organizational consultant; b. NYC, May 21, 1941; s. R. Lucien and Louise Victoria V.; m. Dorothea Irene Hoban, Oct. 12, 1963; children: John Robert, Rachel Irene, Sara Christine. BS, St. Peter's Coll., 1962; MA, Fordham U., 1964; PhD, St. Louis U., 1973. Lic. psychologist, Mo. Psychologist Testing and Advisement Ctr., NYU, Washington Sq. campus, 1964-65; group psychologist McDonnell Douglas, St. Louis, 1967-76, sr. bus. analyst, 1976-77, mgr. bus. planning, 1977-79; pres. Orgnl. Cons. Svcs., Inc., St. Louis, 1980—. Adj. assoc. prof. mgmt. Maryville Coll., St. Louis, 1975-81. Bd. dirs. Cath. Charities St. Louis, 1981-86, Cath. Family Svc., 1986-00, Mental Health Assn. St. Louis, 1989-05, Sta. KWMU-FM, 1989-94; trustee St. Patrick;s Ctr., 2001-. With US Army, 1965-67. Fellow Soc. Indsl. and Orgnl. Psychologists; mem. APA, Rotary (past pres.). Home and Office: 27 Forbush Rd Dublin NH 03444-8606 Office Phone: 314-706-1721.

VECCHIOTTI, TONY V., insurance agent; b. Rochester, NY, Mar. 16, 1960; s. Anthony V. and Julia D. Vecchiotti; m. Leslie A. Elliott, Feb. 16, 1985; children: Julianna C., Anthony E., Carly S. B of Mgmt. Sci., Nazareth Coll. Rochester, NY, 1981. Lic. agt. NY, 1982. Sales mgr. Prudential Fin. Svcs., Fairport, NY, 1982—92; comml. account exec. Barker, Heslip, Bradshaw Agy., Rochester, 1992—97; personal lines mgr. Riedman Ins./Brown and Brown of NY, Rochester, 1997—2003; pres. Northcoast NY, Geneva, 2004—; v.p. The Northwoods Corp, Avon, Sodus, Geneva and Williamsville, NY, 2006—. Cont. edn. instr. ins. Ctr. Profl. Advancement, Rochester, 1992—98, Ind. Ins. Agents Assn. NY, 1997—2005. Pres. Honeoye Lake Park Assn., 2003—; chmn. Genesee Valley/FingerLakes chpt. March of Dimes, Rochester, 1995—99, chmn. pub. affairs com. NY state chpt. NYC, 2003—. Named Vol. of Yr. Genesee Valley FingerLakes chpt., March of Dimes, 1996, 2006, Citizen of Yr., Monroe County Fire Chiefs Assn., 2002, Rochester Ins. Profl. of Yr., Ind Ins Agents and Rochester CPCU Soc., 2006. Mem.: Ind. Ins. Agents Monroe (dir. 1996—2007), Ind. Ins. Agents NY (pres. 1999—2000, dir. 2000—01), Am. MENSA. Democrat. Roman Catholic. Avocations: bicycling, boating, golf. Office: The Northwoods Corp Geneva Ins Agency 742 A Pre Emption Rd Geneva NY 14456 also: Sodus Ins Agency 13 W Main St Sodus NY 14551 also: Avon Ins Agency 49 Park Pl Avon NY 14414 Office Fax: 315-789-0474. Personal E-mail: tonyvinsurance@aol.com. Business E-Mail: tvecchiotti@thenorthwoodscorp.com.

VECENTI, GENE ORTIZIO JUANAJILLO ALITIZAR, educator; s. Willetto C and Marie R Vecenti. M, Northern Ariz. U., Flagstaff, 2001. Faculty Diné Coll., Tsaile, Ariz., 1991—. Office: Ctr Diné Studies One Cir Dr - NHC 5th Fl Rm 501E Tsaile AZ 86507 Business E-Mail: gvecenti@dinecollege.edu.

VEDDER, DEBRA SCOTT, language educator; d. Charles Clifford and Ruth Phillips Scott; m. Charles Lord Vedder, June 15, 1974; 1 child, Rodger Scott. BA, Otterbein Coll., Westerville, Ohio, 1973; MA, Ashland U., Ohio, 1997. Spanish tchr. Westerville City Sch., 1973—2003; instr. Spanish Ohio Wesleyan U., Delaware, 2003—. Recipient Educator of Yr. award, Westerville Edn. Assn., 2003. Mem.: Sigma Alpha Tau Sorority (advisor 2004—). Conservative. Methodist. Avocations: travel, reading, music, art. Office: Ohio Wesleyan Univ 61 S Sandusky St Delaware OH 43015 Personal E-mail: dvedder@aol.com.

VEDDER, EDDIE, singer; b. Evanston, Ill., Dec. 23, 1965; m. Beth Liebling, June 3, 1994 (div. Sept. 2000); m. Jill McCormick, 2004; 1 child. Lead singer (band) Pearl Jam, 1991—, albums Ten, 1991—, Vs., 1993—, Vitalogy, 1994—, No Code, 1996—, Binaural, 2000, Save You, 2002, Riot Act, 2002, Pearl Jam, 2006, contbr. vocals album Temple of the Dog, 1991, Mother Love Bone, 1992, Bob Dylan Thirtieth-Anniversary Tribute, Sweet Relief: A Tribute to Victoria Williams, Shame, Judgement Night Soundtrack, 1993, Yield, 1998, Pearl Jam Live, 1999, appearances (films) Singles, 1992, Dead Man Walking, 1995; singer: (songs) Guaranteed, 2007 (Best Original Song-Motion Picture, Golden Globe award, Hollywood Fgn. Press Assn., 2008).

VEDDER, NICHOLAS BLAIR, plastic surgeon, educator; b. Chgo., Mar. 27, 1955; s. Beverly Blair and Geraldine (Bovbjerg) V.; m. susan Russell Heckbert, June 26, 1978; children: Katherine Anne, Nicholas Russell. BS with distinction in Biology, Stanford U., 1977; MD, Case Western Res. U., 1981. Diplomate Am. Bd. Surgery with added qualification in hand surgery, Am. Bd. Plastic Surgery, Nat. Bd. Med. Examiners; lic. physician, Wash., Mass. Resident in surgery U. Wash., Seattle, 1981-86, NIH rsch. fellow, 1986-88, hand surgery fellow, 1990-91, asst. prof. plastic surgery and orthop., 1991-95, assoc. prof. plastic surgery and orthop., 1995—, head divsn. plastic surgery Harborview Med. Ctr.; resident in plastic surgery Mass. Gen. Hosp., Boston, 1988-90. Attending surgeon U. Wash. Hosps., 1990—, Children's Hosp. and Med. Ctr., VA Med. Ctr.; lectr. in field; vis. prof. Johns Hopkins U., Balt., 1991, Nat. Heart and Lung Inst., London, 1991, So. Ill. U., 1991 Contbr. numerous articles to profl. jours., chpts. to books; referee Jour. Clin. Investigation, Am. rev. of Respiratory Diseases, Jour. Surg. Rsch., Jour. Pharmacology and Exptl. Therapeutics, Jour. of trauma, Plastic and Reconstructive Surgery, Annals of Plastic Surgery. Recipient Peter Gingrass award Plastic Surgery Rsch. Coun., 1995; ACS First Prize Nat. scholar, 1987; grantee NIH, 1988-89, 89-94, 91-92, 95—, Genentech, Inc., 1991-93, Biomembrante Inst., 1993-94, Cell Therapeutics, Inc., 1995-96, CDC, G.D. Searle, Inc., 1995-96. Fellow ACS; mem. AAAS, Henry N. Harkins Surg. Soc., N.W. Soc. Plastic Surgeons, Wash. Soc. Plastic Surgeons, seattle Surg. Soc., King County Med. Soc., Wash. Med. Soc., Assn. Acad. Chmn. Plastic Surgery, Am. assn. Hand Surgery, Assn. Acad. Surgery, Am. Soc. Plastic and Reconstructive Surgeons (Robert H. Ivy award 1994), Am. Soc. Surgery or the Hand, Plastic Surgery Ednl. Found., Sigma Xi. Office: Divsn Plastic Surgery Harborview Med Ctr Univ Wash Box 359796 325 Ninth Ave Seattle WA 98104-2499 Office Phone: 206-731-3209. Office Fax: 206-731-3656.

VEDDER, RICHARD KENT, economics professor; b. Urbana, Ill., Nov. 5, 1940; s. Byron C. and Kathleen (Fry) V.; m. Karen Pirosko, June 18, 1968; children: Virin, Vanette. BA, Northwestern U., Evanston, Ill., 1962; MA, U. Ill., 1963, PhD, 1965. Asst. prof. econs. Ohio U., Athens, 1965-69, assoc. prof. econs., 1969-74, prof. econs., 1974-85; economist Joint Econ. Com. of Congress, Washington, 1981-82; Dist. Prof. of econs. Ohio U., Athens, 1985—. Vis. prof. Claremont McKenna Coll., Calif., 1979-80, Econs. Inst. U. Colo., Boulder, 1979, 80, Washington U., St. Louis, 1995, 96; adj. scholar Am. Enterprise Inst., 2003-; dir. Ctr. for Coll. Affordability and Productivitiy, 2006; mem. Sec. of Edn.'s Commn. on Future of Edn., 2005. Author: American Economy in Historical Perspective, 1976, Can Teachers Own Their Own Schools?, 2000, Going Broke by Degree: Why College Costs Too Much, 2005; co-author: Out of Work: Unemployment and Government in Twentieth-Century America, 1993, rev. edit., 1997, The Wal-Mart Revolution. 2006. Mem. Athens Bd. Edn., 1987-91; bd. dirs. Athens Cmty. Music Sch., 1987-92, Ohio Valley Summer Theater, 2002—. Recipient rsch. grants Earhart Found., 1970, 90, Rockefeller Found., 1974, Nat. Chamber Found., 1990, fellowship Inst. for Humane Studies, Palo Alto, Calif., 1983. Mem. Am. Econ. Assn., Econ. History Assn., Rotary, U. Club. Republican. Presbyterian. Home: 7464 Ridgeview Cir Athens OH 45701-9005 Office: Ohio Univ Dept Econs Bentley Hall Annex 316 Athens OH 45701 Home Phone: 740-593-0813. Business E-Mail: vedder@ohio.edu.

VEDROS, NEYLAN ANTHONY, microbiologist, educator; b. New Orleans, Oct. 6, 1929; s. Phillip John and Solange Agnes (Melancon) V.; m. Elizabeth Corbett, Apr. 9, 1955; children: Sally Ann, Philippa Jane. BS in Chemistry, La. State U., 1951, MS in Microbiology, 1957; PhD, U. Colo., 1960. Postdoctoral fellow Nat. Inst. Allergy and Infectious Diseases, U. Oreg., Portland, 1960-62; microbiologist Naval Med. Research Inst., Bethesda, Md., 1962-66; research microbiologist Naval Biosci. Lab., Oakland, Calif., 1966-67; assoc. prof. med. microbiology and immunology U. Calif., Berkeley, 1967-72, prof., 1972-91, prof. emeritus, 1991—. Dir. Naval Biosci. Lab., 1968-81; mem. expert panel on bacteriology WHO, 1972-91. Bd. trustees Alameda (Calif.) Library, 1973-78. Served to comdr. M.S.C. USNR, 1952-55, 62-67. Mem.: Internat. Assn. Aquatic Animal Medicine, Internat. Assn. Microbiol. Sci., Am. Soc. Microbiology. Home: 209 Almond Way Healdsburg CA 95448 E-mail: nvedros@earthlink.net.

VEEDER, PETER GREIG, lawyer; b. Pitts., Aug. 13, 1941; AB, Princeton U., 1963; JD, U. Pitts., 1966. Bar: Pa. 1966, D.C. 1976. Lawyer Thorp Reed & Armstrong, Pitts., 1970-99; of counsel Thorp, Reed & Armstrong LLP, Pitts., 1999—. Office: Thorp Reed & Armstrong LLP 1 Oxford Ctr 301 Grant St Fl 14 Pittsburgh PA 15219-1425 Office Phone: 412-394-7793.

VEERAMALAI, MALLIKA, research scientist; MSc in Math., Madurai Kamaraj U., Tamilnadu, India, 1997; PhD, U. Glasgow, Scotland, 2005. Jr. rsch. fellow Nat. Ctr. Biol. Scis., Bangalore, India, 1999—2001; postdoc. rsch. asst. U. Dundee, Scotland, 2005—06, bioinformatics cons., 2006; postdoct. rsch. assoc. Burnham Inst. Med. Rsch., San Diego. Contbr. scientific papers. Travel fellowship, ISMB/ISCB, 2002—03, 2008, ECCB, 2003, Jr. Rsch. fellowship, TATA Inst. Fundamental Rsch. (NCBS-TIFR), 1999—2002, DBT fellowship, Dept. Bio-Tech., Govt. of India, 1998—99, Rsch. Asst. fellowship, Wellcome Trust Grant, 2000—01. Fellow: Internat. Soc. Computational Biology — Student Coun. (student coun. sec. 2005—06); mem.: Asia-Pacific Bioinformatics Networks, UK Bioinformatics Forum. Achievements include development of a novel method for comparing topological models of protein structures enhanced with ligand interaction information; semi-automated database of protein alignments organized as structural super families; splicing factors database.

VEGA, CAROLYN JANE, elementary educator, consultant, writer; b. Loma Linda, Calif., June 29, 1949; d. Ora Harrison Miller and Magil Muriel Rhodes; children: Matthew Harrison, Sarah Christine. AA, Orange Coast Coll., Costa Mesa, Calf., 1970; BA in Fine Arts and Humanities, San Diego State U., 1972; MA in Ednl. Tech., US Internat. U., San Diego, 1987. Std. elem. tchg. credential Calif., specially designed academic instrn. in English and lang. devel. Calif., cert. gifted and talented edn. Calif. Classroom tchr. San Diego Unified Sch. Dist., 1973—, edn. tech. resource tchr., 1988—95. Lectr. U. Calif. San Diego, La Jolla, 1989—95; cons. AAAS, Washington, 1994—2000; project 2061 team contb. Benchmarks for Sci. Literacy, 1993. Author: (textbooks) SRA Real Science, SRA Science Math and You. Del. NEA, Washington, 2000—; bd. dirs. San Diego Educators Assn., San Diego, 2004—. Mem.: NEA (del. 2000—), San Diego Educators Assn. (elem. seat 2004—), San Diego Edn. Assn. (bd. dirs. 2004—), Calif. Tchrs. Assn. (svc. ctr. coun. 2001—08, We Honor Ours award 2005), Delta Kappa Gamma. Democrat. Achievements include research in implementing technology in the curriculum. Home: 6218 Winona Ave San Diego CA 92120 Office: San Diego Unified Sch Dist 4100 Normal St San Diego CA 92103 Personal E-mail: cjvega@cox.net.

VEGA, EDWIN SALVADOR, media specialist, educator; s. Luis Salvador Vega and Nellie Pabon; m. Heidi Lee Schnackenberg, Aug. 5, 2006. AAS, Borough Manhattan CC, NYC, 1990; BA, BS, SUNY, Plattsburgh, 2005; student, SUNY, Potsdam. Digital media specialist VISIONES, Plattsburgh, 2001—; instr. profl. devel. North Country Tchr. Resource Ctr., Plattsburgh, 2002—; digital media specialist Amikorika, Plattsburgh, 2006—07. Cons. VISIONES, Plattsburgh, 2001—; adj. prof. dept. edn. SUNY, 2002—, adj. prof. dept. comm., 2006—. Mem.: Assn. Ednl. Comm. and Tech., Lambda Pi Eta. Avocations: comic book collecting, drawing, travel, movies, video games. E-mail: eddie.vega@plattsburgh.edu.

VEGA, FRANK J., publishing executive; b. Tampa, Fla., 1948; With Gannett Co. Inc., 1978—; asst. to pub., circulation dir. Oakland Tribune; mem. task force to launch USA Today, 1980—82, v.p. circulation, 1982—83; asst. to pres. Mid-Atlantic Regional Newspaper Group, 1983—84; gen. mgr. El Diario-La Prensa, NYC, 1983—84; pub., CEO Cape Publications, Brevard County, Fla., 1984—91; pres. South Regional Newspaper Group, 1985—91; pres., CEO Detroit Newspaper Agy., 1991—2004; pres., pub. San Francisco Chronicle, 2005—08, chmn., pub., 2008—. Office: San Francisco Chronicle 901 Mission St San Francisco CA 94103 Office Phone: 415-777-1111.*

VEGA, VANESSA LEIGH, English educator; BA, Tex. Tech U., Lubbock, 1992; MS, U. Tex., Galveston, 1996. Secondary edn. cert. Tex. English tchr. Galveston Ind. Sch. Dist., 1993—94, Irving Ind. Sch. Dist., Tex., 1999—; exploring exec. Boy Scouts Am., Dallas, 1997—99. Author: Comes the Darkness, Comes the Light: A Memoir of Cutting, Hope and Healing; contbg. author (anthology) Taste Berries for Teens Vol. IV. Fellow, NEH, 2003. Mem.: Assn. Tex. Profl. Educators. Avocations: travel, writing, reading, running. Office: Irving HS 900 N O'Connor Blvd Irving TX 75061 Office Fax: 972-273-8319. Personal E-mail: vanessa747@msn.com. E-mail: vvega@irvingisd.net.

VEGA, WILLIAM A., psychiatrist, educator; b. LA; BA in sociology, U. Calif., Berkeley, MA, PhD in criminology, 1971. Prof. U. Calif. Berkeley Sch. Pub. Health, 1990—99; prof. psychiatry, Robert Wood Johnson Med. Sch. U. Medicine and Dentistry of NJ, rsch. dir. behavioral healthcare; prof. family medicine, David Geffen Med. Sch. UCLA, 2007—, co-founder, dir. Multicultural Rsch. Network on Health and Healthcare, founding dir., assoc. vice provost Luskin Ctr. Innovation, 2008—. Founding mem. WHO Internat. Consortium Psychiat. Epidemiology. Mem.: Inst. Medicine. Office: Luskin Ctr Innovation 2333 Murphy Hall Box 951405 Los Angeles CA 90095-1405*

VEGHTE, BILL, computer software company executive; married; 2 children. BA with hon. in East Asian Studies, Harvard U. Joined Microsoft Corp., Redmond, Wash., 1990, product mgr., corp. v.p. windows server group, corp. v.p. North America, corp. v.p. Windows bus. group, 2007—08, sr. v.p. online services & Windows bus. group, 2008—09, sr. v.p. the Windows bus., 2009—. Bd. dir. nPower. Avocations: backcountry skiing, climbing, fishing. Office: One Microsoft Way Redmond WA 98052-6399*

VEHSE, CHARLES THEODORE, humanities educator; s. William Everett and Edith Louise (Starr) Vehse; m. Elizabeth Angel Stoloff, July 29, 1984; 1 child, Nathan Everett. PhD, U. Chgo., 1998. Lectr. theology Loyola U. Chgo., 1988—93; lectr. humanities & religious studies W.Va. U., Morgantown, 1996—. Pres. to bd. dirs. Bartlett Ho., Inc., Morgantown, 2004—06. Mem. Bartlett Ho., Inc., 2002—08. Office: W Virginia Univ PO Box 6430 Morgantown WV 26506-6430 Office Fax: 304-293-6169. Business E-Mail: ted.vehse@mail.wvu.edu.

VEIGA JARDIM, OSWALDO, conductor, composer, researcher; b. Rio de Janeiro, Apr. 6, 1959; s. Gontran Veiga Jardim and Avahy (Riccio) Xavier. MusB in Conducting magna cum laude, Fed. U. Rio de Janeiro, 1981, MusB in Composition, 1983; diploma with honors, Câmara Mcpl. Rio de Janeiro, 1983; studied with Creusa Rebello, Myrian Dauelsberg, Murillo Santos, Virginia Fiuza, David Machado and Gennady Rozhdestvensky, Accademia Musicale Chigiana, Italy, 1988; MPhil in Musicology, U. Hong Kong, 2002. Choir condr. Radio MEC FM, Rio de Janeiro, 1983-85, prodr., 1985-87; asst. condr. Rio de Janeiro Youth Symphony Orch., 1983-87; condr., opera coach Theatro Mcpl. Rio de Janeiro, 1986-88; prin. condr., artistic dir. Macau Chamber Orch., 1988-95; founder Macau Sinfonietta, 1989; assoc. prof. music Sch. Arts Macau Poly., 1997—; with PhonoArt Producoes Artisticas, Macau, China, 2005—. Guest lectr. Univ. Macau, 1996; guest condr. numerous orchs. and choirs including Orch. Sonfonica Paraiba, Orch. Sinfonica Brasileira, Orch. Sinfonica Minas Gerais, Orch. Sinfonica San Remo, Italy, Rousse State Philharm. Orch., Bulgaria, Gulbenkian Choir, Portugal, Hong Kong Oratorio Soc., Hong Kong Sinfonietta, Macao Orch., China Broadcasting Symphony Orch., Ctrl. Opera Symphony Orch. China, Canton Symphony Orch., People's Republic of China; mem. Consultative Coun. Cultural Affairs Macau SAR Govt.; adviser, guest condr., condr., hon. music dir. Macau Youth Symphony Orch., Ordem Músicos Brazil, Sindicato Músicos Profissionais Rio de Janeiro. Recorded: (albums) Macau Chamber Orch., Macau Sinfonietta play works by Mozart, Grieg and Tchaikovsky, 1993, (CD film music) The Bewitching Braid, 1996, (CD) Veiga Jardim Conducts, 2001, G. Verdi, Messa da Requiem, 1999; composer piano solos: Suite Barroca Opera 1, 1979, Suite Brasiliera Opera 2, 1980, Valsa Antiga Opera 6, 1986, rev., 1999; composer songs for voice and piano: (with Cecília Meirelles) Apresentação, 1980, (with Cecília Meirelles) Canção quase melancólica, 1981, (with Carlos Drummond de Andrade) Sem Título, 1983, (with Eugénio de Andrade) Os amantes sem dinheiro, 1991; contbr. music column Macau mag., 1992-04. Recipient 1st prize, Gold medal and Arnaldo Rebello award 1st Abrarte piano competition, 1976, 2nd and 3d prize composition competition Fed. U. Rio de Janeiro, Brazilian Nat. Found. Arts, 1981, Dell'Arte Nat. award, Rio de Janeiro, 1987, Spl. Prize VI Gino Marinuzzi Internat. Conducting Competition, 1987, Orch. Sinfonica di San Remo, Italy, 1988, Macau Poly. Jour. award, 1998, nominee Li Ka Shing award U. Hong Kong, 2003; Accademia Musicale Chigiana scholar Inst. Italian-Latin Am., 1988. Roman Catholic. Avocations: photography, sailing, computers, cooking. Office: PhonoArt Producoes Artisticas PO Box 1569 Macau China Personal E-mail: phonoart@yahoo.com.

VEIHMEYER, JOHN BRADY, public accounting firm executive; b. 1955; m. Beth Veihmeyer; children: Bridget, Patrick, Eileen. BBA cum laude, U. Notre Dame, Ind., 1977. CPA NYC, DC, Md., Va. Joined KPMG LLP, Washington, 1977, numerous positions including mng. ptnr. Mid-Atlantic area, mng. ptnr. Washington DC, ptnr.-in-charge audit practice Washington/Balt., lead SEC ptnr. & profl. practice ptnr. Mid-Atlantic area, global head risk mgmt. & regulatory, mem. Internat. Exec. Team, elected ptnr., 1987—, dep. chmn., 2005—, CEO, 2009—; chmn. Americas region KPMG Internat., 2007—. Bd. dirs. KPMG LLP, 2003—; chmn. KPMG Found., 2003—; mem. gov. bd. Ctr. for Audit Quality, Washington; spkr. ethics/integrity in leadership U. Notre Dame, Brigham Young U., U. Ill., Howard U.; former mem. SEC Adv. Com. on Smaller Pub. Co.'s. Mem. Kennedy Ctr. Corp. Fund Bd., Washington, 2008—09; active Partnership for NYC; mem. bd. trustees St. Mary's Coll., South Bend, Ind.; past chmn. Cultural Alliance of Washington, DC; past mem. exec. com. Greater Washington Bd. Trade, Fed. City Coun., Washington. Named one of Top 100 Most Influential People in Acctg., Acctg. Today mag., 2008. Mem.: Am. Inst. CPA's, Md. Assn. CPA's. Office: KPMG LLP Corp Hdqs 345 Park Ave New York NY 10154 Business E-Mail: jveihmeyer@kpmg.com.*

VEILLE, JEAN-CLAUDE, obstetrician, educator; b. France; came to U.S., 1982; m. Ann Veille; children: Olivier, Xavier, Patrique, Robert. BS, McGill U., 1971; MD, U. Montpellier, France, 1977. Fellow in maternal-fetal medicine Oreg. Health Scis., Portland, 1982-84; from asst. prof. to assoc. prof. Case Western Res. U., Cleve., 1984-90; chief maternal, fetal medicine Case Western Reserve U., Cleve., 1989-90; assoc. prof., dir. maternal-fetal med. fellowship program Wake Forest U. Sch. Medicine, Winston-Salem, NC, 1990-95, prof., 1995—, chief maternal-fetal medicine sect., 1997—2002; chmn. dept. ob-gyn. Albany (N.Y.) Med. Ctr., 2002—. Contbr. articles to profl. jours. Grantee NIH, 1991-2002. Office: 47 New Scotland Ave Albany NY Office Phone: 518-262-5013. E-mail: veillej@mail.amc.edu.

VEILLEUX, SYLVAIN, astrophysicist, educator; b. Montreal, Quebec, Canada, July 7, 1962; s. Paul-Emile Veilleux and Lucille Cyr; m. Panida Tong-On, Aug. 12, 1998. BS, Universite de Montreal, Canada, 1984; PhD, U. Calif., Santa Cruz, 1989. Natural sci. and engring. rsch. coun. fellow Inst. Astronomy, U. Hawaii, Honolulu, 1989—92; Hubble fellow Kitt Peak Nat. Obs., Tucson, 1992—95; asst. prof. U. Md., Coll. Pk., 1995—2000, assoc. prof., 2000—05, prof., 2005—; vis. faculty Calif. Inst. Tech., Pasadena, 2003—03; vis. rsch. fellow Carnegie Observatories, Pasadena, 2003—03. Dir., Md. nat. optical astronomy observation collaboration U. Md., College Park, 2003—. Recipient Career award, NSF, 1999, Rsch. award, Alexander von Humboldt Found., 2008, LTSA award, NASA, 1997; grant, 1995, NSF, 1995, Postdoc. Fellowship, NSERC, 1989—91, Hubble Fellowship, Space Telescope Sci. Inst., 1992—95. Mem.: Can. Astron. Soc., Am. Astron. Soc. Office: Univ of Md Dept of Astronomy College Park MD 20742

VEITCH, JONATHAN, academic administrator; m. Sarah Veitch; 3 children. BA, Stanford U., 1981; PhD in History of Am. Civilization, Harvard U. Tchr. English dept. U. Wis., Madison; joined faculty New Sch. U., 1997, assoc. provost, chair of humanities; dean Eugene Lang Coll.: The New Sch. for Liberal Arts, NYC, 2003—08, assoc. prof. lit. and history; pres. Occidental Coll., 2009—. Vis. prof. Steinhardt Sch. Edn., NYU, Doshisha U., Doshisha University, Japan. Author: American Superrealism: Nathanael West and the Politics of Representation in the 1930s, 1997. Office: Occidental Coll / Office of Pres 3rd Fl, Coons Adminstrn Bldg 1600 Campus Rd Los Angeles CA 90041-3314 Office Phone: 323-259-2691. Office Fax: 323-259-2907.*

VEITH, FRANK J., vascular surgeon, researcher, educator; Cert. in gen. sugery 1961, in thoracic surgery 1968, in vascular surgery 1983. William J. von Liebig chmn. for vascular surgery Montefiore Med. Ctr., Bronx, NY, vice-chmn., prof. surgery, Albert Einstein Coll. Medicine, Bronx, NY. Ann. host VEITHsymposium. Contbr. more than 1,000 articles and chapters in profl. med. jours. and books.; serves on editl. bds. for four major vascular jours., editor-in-chief Vascular. Recipient Julius H. Jacobson, II, MD award for Physician Excellence, Vascular Disease Found., 2004. Mem.: Internat. Soc. for Vascular Surgery (founding sec.), Eastern Vascular Soc. (past pres.), Soc. for Vascular Surgery (past pres.). Considered role model in the field of vascular surgery; heading effort to have vascular surgery as a specialty board under the umbrella of the American Board of Specialties. Office: Montefiore Medical Ctr Med Arts Pavilion 3400 Bainbridge Ave 4th Fl Bronx NY 10467 Office Phone: 718-920-4108. Office Fax: 718-231-9811.

VEITZ, SISTER MARY FRANCES, director; b. Phila., Jan. 10, 1941; d. Samuel Louis and Edith Geraldine (Laquintano) V. BA in French, Holy Family Coll., Phila., 1965; MA in French, Pa. State U., 1972; EdD in Curriculum Devel., Nova U., 1983. Joined Sisters of the Holy Family of Nazareth, 1960; permanent cert. tchr., translator, interpretor, Pa. Tchr. St. Katherine's Elem. Sch., Phila., 1963-65; tchr. French, Nativity BVM High Sch., Pottsville, Pa., 1965-72; prof. French, Holy Family Coll., 1972-86, dir. Translation Ctr., 1976-86, coord. internat. bus. French program, 1978-88, head div. bus. adminstrn., 1986-91, coord. coop. edn. bus. adminstrn., 1991-92; dir. coop. edn., 1992—. Mem. instl. scholarship selection com. Holy Family U., 1999—; co-chair, sub com. Middle States, 2009—. Project dir. Title VIII fed. grant for coop. edn. Mem. adv. bd. Swenson Skill Ctr., Phila., 1988-91. Recipient Disting. Svc. award Holy Family Coll., 1980, diplome superieur français des affaires Paris C. of C., NYC, 1986, Tchg. Excellence and Campus Leadership award Sears Roebuck Found., 1991; Am. Assn. Tchrs. French scholar U. Grenoble, 1975; alumni grantee Pa. State U., 1979, Rsch. grantee Que. Govt. for Exch. Coop. Edn. Program, 1992, US Dept. Edn., 1992-1997, Title VIII for coop. edn. grantee, 1992-95. Mem.: Kappa Theta Eplison (Mu chpt. mem. 1997—), Nat. Assn. Coll. & Employers, Mid-Atlantic Coop. Assn., Coop Edn. and Internships Assn., Nat. Soc. for Exptl. Edn., Kappa Theta Epsilon (hon.), Nat. Coop. & Intern. Home and Office: Holy Family Univ 9801 Frankford Ave Philadelphia PA 19114-2009 Office Phone: 267-341-3406. Business E-Mail: mfveitz@holyfamily.edu.

VEIZER, JÁN, geology educator; b. Pobedim, Slovakia, June 22, 1941; arrived in Can., 1973; s. Viktor and Brigita (Brandstetter) Veizer; m. Elena Ondrus, July 30, 1966; children: Robert, Andrew Douglas. Prom. Geol., Comenius U., Bratislava, Slovakia, 1964; RNDr, Comenius U., Bratislava, Slovak Republic, 1968; CSc, Slovak Acad. Sci., Bratislava, Slovakia, 1968; PhD, Australian Nat. U., Canberra, 1971. Asst. lectr. Comenius U., 1963-66; research scientist Slovak Acad. Sci., 1966-71; vis. asst. prof. UCLA, 1972; vis. rsch. scientist U. Göttingen, Fed. Republic Germany, 1972-73; rsch. scientist U. Tübingen, Fed. Republic Germany, 1973; from asst. prof. to full prof. U. Ottawa, Ont., Canada, 1973—2004, rsch. chair NSERC/Noranda/Can. Inst. Advanced Rsch. Ont., 1997—2006; prof. Ruhr U., Bochum, Germany, 1988—2004; Disting. Univ. prof. U. Ottawa, 2001—, prof. emeritus, 2004—. Cons. NASA, Houston, 1983—86; vis. prof., scholar Northwestern U., Evanston, Ill., 1983—87; vis. fellow Australian Nat. U., 1979; vis. prof. U. Tübingen, 1974; Lady Davis professorship Hebrew U., Jerusalem, 1987; Fullbright fellow Caltech, 2007—08. Contbr. articles to profl. jours., chapters to books. Served to jr. lt. Med., 1965—66. Recipient W. Leibniz prize, German Rsch. Found., 1992, gold medal, Slovak Geol. Survey, 2000; named Rsch. Prof. of Yr., 1987; fellow Humboldt, 1980, 2006, 2009, Killam Rsch., Can. Coun., 1986—88. Fellow: US Geochemical Soc., European Assn. Geochemistry (elected geochemistry fellow 1998), Geol. Soc. Am., Geol. Assn. Can. (Logan medal 1995, past pres. medal 1987), Royal Soc. Can. (W.G. Miller medal 1991, Bancroft medal 2000), Slovak Geol. Soc. (hon.); mem.: Ski Club. Roman Catholic. Avocations: reading, hiking, skiing, history. Office: Dept Earth Scis U Ottawa Ottawa ON Canada K1N 6N5 Home Phone: 613-747-9801; Office Phone: 613-562-5800 6461. Business E-Mail: jveizer@uottawa.ca.

VEKLEROV, EUGENE, mathematician, computer scientist, educator; b. Kamen, Altay Territory, Russia, Nov. 17, 1942; arrived in US, 1976; s. Benish Veksler and Serafima Fridland; children: Mark Wexler, Jessica, Kimberly. BS, Moscow U., Russia, 1965; PhD, Inst. for Info. Transmission Problems, Moscow, 1972. Rsch. scientist Inst. for Control Problems, Moscow, 1969—75, Lawrence Berkeley Nat. Lab., Berkeley, Calif., 1977—. Editor, translator: 2 books on human rights in post-Soviet Russia; author: 2 computer science textbooks; editor: Computer Science, Electrical Engineering Dictionaries; contbr. articles to profl. jours. Home: 555 Pierce St Apt 628 Albany CA 94706 Office: Lawrence Berkeley Lab 1 Cyclotron Rd Berkeley CA 94720 Personal E-mail: eveklerov@yahoo.com.

VELA, DIANA, educational association administrator; b. Lima, Peru, July 9, 1980; BA & Licenciatura in Comm., U. de Lima, Lima, 2003; MA in Latin Am. Lit., U. Buffalo, NY, 2007. Tchg. asst. U. Buffalo, 2004—, v.p.,co-founder latin am. grad. student assn., 2005—, senator Romance Languages & Literatures Grad. Student Assn., 2004—05. Recipient Profl. Devel. award, State New York,Grad. Students Employees Union, 2006; Tchg. fellowship and Tuition scholarship, U. Buffalo, 2004—09, Nonresident Alien fellowship, 2004—08. Mem.: MLA, North East MLA, Nat. Collegiate Hispanic Honor Soc., Sigma Delta Pi (social coord. 2005—06, Grad. Rsch. grant 2008). Office: Univ Buffalo 910 Clemens Hall Buffalo NY 14260-4620 Business E-Mail: dvela@buffalo.edu.

VELA, MOE (MOISES VICENTE VELA JR.), federal official, communications executive; s. Moises and Mary Jo Vela. BA in Govt., U. Tex., Austin, 1984; JD, St. Mary's Law Sch., 1990. Bar: Tex. CFO, sr. advisor on Hispanic affairs to v.p. The White House, Washington, 1996—2000; Lieberman family coord. Gore/Lieberman 2000; founder Diverse Directions LLC; exec. dir. Nat. Assn. Hispanic Real Estate Profls. (NAHREP), San Diego; sr. v.p. multicultural strategy United Dominion Realty Trust, Inc. (UDR), 2005—06; founder, ptnr. The Comunidades Group, Denver; dir. adminstrn. for V.P. Joseph Biden The White House, Washington, 2009—. COO Soloella.com. Democrat. Office: The White House 1600 Pennsylvania Ave NW Washington DC 20500*

VELA CÓRDOVA, ROBERTO J., literature and language professor; b. San Juan, Mar. 19, 1971; s. María Isabel Córdova, Tomás Céspedes (Stepfather); m. Michelle R. Johnson; children: Vela Johnson Julian Dylan, Brody Vela Johnson, Liam Vela Johnson. PhD, Ind. U., Bloomington, 2005. Vol. tchr. Juan Domingo Pub. Sch., Guaynabo, PR, 1994—95; grad. tchg. asst. Ind. U., 1995—2003; vis. asst. prof. Tex. A & M Kingsville, 2003—05, asst. prof., 2005—08, assoc. prof. Cons. NEH, Washington, 2006. Author: (poetry) Exégesis. Parent leader Cub Scouts of America, Kingsville, 2008—; coach Kingsville Youth Soccer Orgn., 2004—08; basketball coach Boys and Girls Club, Kingsville, 2006; cmty. organizer ACORN, NYC, 1992—92. Recipient Outstanding Hispanic Heritage Faculty award, Tex. A & M U., 2007; named Disting. Tchr. of Yr., Tex. A & M U. & Alumni Assn., 2007; grantee GAANN, Fed. Govt., 1995—96. Mem.: Tex. Faculty Assn., South Ctrl. MLA, Popular Culture Assn., Moder Langs. Assn., Sigma Delta Pi Hispanic Honor Soc. Office: Tex A & M Kingsville 700 University Blvd Kingsville TX 78363 Office Fax: 361-593-2116.

VELAMAKANNI, GOPALA KRISHNA, geophysicist, seismologist, researcher; b. Eluru, Andhra Pradesh, India, Jan. 1, 1945; s. Venkatalakshmi Narasimham and Rajyalakshmi Velamakanni; m. Rajarajeswari Kapilavayi, Oct. 3, 1968; children: Vijaya Nirmala, VenkataSatya Ravindrakumar, Swapna. BSc, Andhra U., Vijayawada, India, 1962; MSc in Geophysics, Andhra U., Waltair, India, 1965; PhD in Seismology (hon.), Indian Sch. Mines, Dhanbad, 1980. Rsch. fellow, sr. sci. asst. Nat. Geophys. Rsch. Inst., Hyderabad, Andhra Pradesh, 1967—74, scientist, 1974—2004, dep. dir. grade scientist, 1993—2004. Presenter in field. Contbr. articles to profl. publs. Recipient Commemoration medal, USSR Acad. Scis., 1985; fellow postdoctoral fellow, European Cmty., 1992; scholar CDG German Govt. scholar, Carl Duisberg Gesselschaft e.v., 1980. Fellow: Indian Geophys. Union (hon.), Assn. Exploration Geophysicists, India (hon.). Achievements include development of novel approaches for seismic data processing; appropriate software for seismic data processing; patents for computerised method for effective velocity determination from reversed reflection data; discovery of deep crustal structure from short-offset seismic refraction sections, VSP gathers of local earthquake seismograms, delineation of upper mantle reflectors from coincident reflection and refraction data; upper mantle transition zone seismic velocity discontinuities. Home: 10-2-267/2 West Marredpally Andhra Pradesh Secunderabad 500026 India also: Ravi Velamakanni 15377 Eastwood Dr Monroe MI 48161 Personal E-mail: v_gopalak@yahoo.com.

VELASCO, MARTHA, literature and language professor; US, 1979, NY; d. Ricardo N. and Natty (Bacarreza) Velasco; divorced; children: Martha Karen Valdez, Diana Laura Valdez. BA in Liberal Studies, Spanish, Calif. State U., San Marcos, 1995; MA in Spanish, Latin Am. Lit., San Diego State U., 1999. Cert. in tchg. Calif. State U., 2005. Tchr., instl. bilingual aide San Marcos Unified Sch. Dist., 1987—93; Spanish instr., Fgn. lang. dept. San Diego State U., 1995—97; Spanish prof., Fgn. lang. dept. Calif. State U., 1999—2003, Palomar Coll., San Marcos, 1997—, Spanish, ESL prof., Workforce & Cmty. Devel., 2003—, Mira Costa Coll., 2005—. Vol. Domestic Violence, 2001—, Nat. Inst. Adult Edn., 2001—02; bd. dirs. Edn. Med. Assn., 2002—03; exec. dir., bd. dirs. EDMED Inc., 2003—07; exec. dir. Luz Betania, 2004—07; mem. Binational Health Fair, 2005—. Recipient Tchr. Corp. award, Palomar Coll., 1986—92, Excellence Tchg. award, 2001—02, 0204—2005, 2008—. Mem.: Ctr. Study Books Spanish Children & Adolescents Amigos, Latino Assn. Faculty & Staff (San Marcos), World Latin Club (advisor 2002). Roman Catholic. Home: PO Box 2197 San Marcos CA 92079-2197 Office Phone: 760-477-1180 ext. 2694. Business E-Mail: mvelasco@palomar.edu.

VELÁSQUEZ, LUCÍA E., language educator, researcher; b. Medellín, Antioquia, Colombia, Dec. 4, 1964; d. Francisco and Lucia Velásquez. BS in Bus. and Fin., EAFIT U., 1988; MS, Ga. State U., Atlanta, 2003; cert., N. Ga. Coll. State, Atlanta; postgrad., Nova Southeastern Edn., 2007—. Cert. tchr. Spanish, ESOL and early childhood edn. Dir. EF Learn Lang., Medellín, 1997—99; tchr. Wall St. U., Medellín, 1999—2000, English Internats., Atlanta, 2001—02, Cobb County Sch. Dist., Atlanta, 2003—; grad. asst. Ga. State U., Atlanta, 2000—03; instr. Ga. Tech. U., Atlanta, 2003—04. Mem.: NEA, TESOL, Ga. Edn. Assn., Phi Beta Delta. Roman Catholic. Avocations: travel, swimming, reading, exercise, movies. Home: 3301 Henderson Hill Rd D1 Atlanta GA 30341 Office Phone: 678-471-1631. Personal E-mail: lucia1204@netzero.net.

VELÁZQUEZ, NYDIA MARGARITA, United States Representative from New York; b. Yabucoa, PR, Mar. 28, 1953; BA in Polit. Sci., magna cum laude, U. PR, Rio Piedras, 1974; MA in Polit. Sci., NYU, 1976. Mem. faculty U. PR, Humacao, 1976—81; adj. prof. Puerto Rican studies CUNY Hunter Coll., 1981—83; spl. asst. to Rep. Edolphus Towns US Congress, 1983; city councilwoman Dist. 12 NYC, 1984—86; dir. Migration Divsn. Office Puerto Rico Dept. Labor and Human Resources, 1986—89; dir. Dept. Puerto Rican Cmty. Affairs in the US for the Commonwealth of PR, 1989—92; mem. US Congress from 12th NY dist., 1993—, US House Financial Services Com.; chair US House Small Bus. Com., 2007—. Chair Congressional Hispanic Caucus, 2009—. Recipient Small Bus. Beacon award, Nat. Small Bus. United, 2000, HerMANA award, MANA, 2002, Champion of Small Bus. Devel. award, Assn. Small Bus. Devel. Ctr., 2005; named Woman of Yr., Hispanic Bus. Mag., 2003. Democrat. Achievements include being the first Puerto Rican woman elected to the US Congress. Office: US Congress 2466 Rayburn House Office Bldg Washington DC 20515 also: 266 Broadway Ste 201 Brooklyn NY 11211 Office Phone: 202-225-2361, 718-599-3658. Office Fax: 202-226-0327, 718-599-4537.*

VELAZQUEZ, OMAIDA CARIDAD, vascular surgeon, researcher; b. Pinar del Rio, Cuba, Oct. 25, 1966; d. Telesforo and Andrea Velazquez; m. Romulo Cuy, 1991; 1 child, Peter James Cuy. MD, U. Medicine and Dentistry N.J., 1991. Lic. physician N.J. Instr. gen. surgery U. Pa. Med. Sch., Phila., asst. instr. gen. surgery, 1992—96; attending surgeon Hosp. U. Pa., Phila., 1999—. Clin. faculty gen. and vascular surgery U. Pa. Med. Sch., Phila., 1999—; adj. asst. prof. Wistar Inst., Phila., 2001—, vis. scientist, 1999—2001; attending surgeon Presbyn. Med. Ctr., Phila., 1999—, Phila. VA Med. Ctr., 2001—03, Children's Hosp. Phila., 2001—; asst. prof. surgery U. Pa. Med. Sch., 1999—, ednl. coord. vascular divsn., 2002—. Contbr. articles to sci. rsch. jours. (Joel J. Roslyn award Assn.for Acad. Surgery, 2003); external reviewer: med. jours. Recipient Scholarship for the Advancement of Med. Edn., William F. Grupe Found., Inc., 1988, 1990, Krans-Henle Meml. Fund Scholarship, Krans-Henle Meml. Fund, 1989, von Liebig Found. Award for Excellence in Vascular Surg. Rsch., von Liebig Found., 2001, Residents Rsch. award, Phila. Acad. of Surgery, 1996, Young Careerist award, N.J. Bus. and Profl. Women, 1995, Surg. Student Rsch. award, Assn. for Academic Surgery, 1991, Dr. Gertrude Ash Meml. award, N.J. Med. Women's Assn., 1991, Merck Manual award for highest grade in internal medicine, 1990; grantee, NIH, 2003—. Fellow: ACS; mem.: AMA, AAAS, John Morgan Soc., Internat. Acad. Clin. and Applied Thrombosis/Hemostasis, Pa. Med. Soc., Am. Soc. Angiology, Soc. U. Surgeons, Phila. Acad. Surgery, Internat. Soc. Vascular Surgery, Bus. and Profl. Women, Assn. Women Surgeons, Assn. for Acad. Surgery, Am. Surg. Assn. Found., Am. Assn. Vascular Surgery, Soc. Clin. Vascular Surgery, N.Y. Acad. Sci., N.J. Med. Sch. Alumni Assn., Sigma Xi, Alpha Omega Alpha.

VELDERS, DEBORAH, museum director; Attended, U. Md., 1969—71; BA in Art History summa cum laude, U. Houston, MA in English and Am. Lit. Registrar Nat. Collection Fine Arts, Smithsonian Instn., Washington, 1976—78; dir. Arlington Arts Ctr., Va., 1979—80, Cameron Art Mus., Wilmington, NC, 2005—; conservation rsch. assoc., Dept. Conservation Menil Collection, Houston, 1985—89, head, exhbns. and pub. programs, 1989—2005. Exhbns./performance dir. Mus. Temporary Art, Washington, 1977—79; mus. specialist Nat. Collection Fine Arts, Smithsonian Instn., 1978—80; mem. adv. bd. DiverseWorks Alternative Artspace, Houston, 1986—89; mem. strategic planning com. Cultural Arts Coun. Houston and Harris Counties, 1998—99; mem. curriculum adv. bd., English dept. U. Houston, 2000—05; bd. dirs. Creative Wilmington, 2007—. Mem. cmty. adv. bd. Fotofest, Houston, 1999—2005; mem. adv. com. bd. Wilmington Symphony, 2006. Office: Cameron Art Mus 3201 S 17th St Wilmington NC 28412 Office Phone: 910-395-5999 ext. 1001. Office Fax: 910-395-5030. Business E-Mail: dvelders@cameronartmuseum.com.

VELEV, MIROSLAV N., electrical and computer engineer, educator, entrepreneur, inventor; arrived in US, 1991; BSEE, Yale U., New Haven, Conn., 1994, BS in Econs., 1994, MSEE, 1994; PhD in Elec. and Computer Engring., Carnegie Mellon U., Pitts., 2004. Tech. assoc. info. svcs. Credit Suisse First Boston Corp., NYC, 1994—95; rsch. asst. Carnegie Mellon U., 1995—2001; vis. asst. prof. Sch. elec. and computer engring. Ga. Inst. Tech., Atlanta; pvt. practice rschr. and cons., 2003—05; founder, pres., CEO Aries Design Automation, LLC, 2005—. Asst. prof., dept. elec. and computer engring. U. Ill., Chgo., 2006—; mem. program coms. over 135 internat. computer sci. and computer engring. confs.; co-chair 3rd Internat. Workshop Constraints in Formal Verification, Talin, Estonia, 2005; chair 6th Internat. Workshop Constraints in Formal Verification, Grenoble, France, 2005, 4th Internat. Workshop Constraints in Formal Verification, Bremen, Germany, 2007, 5th Internat. Workshop Constraints in Formal Verification, Sydney, 2008; editl. bd. mem. Jour. Universal Computer Sci., 2001—08, Jour. Satisfiability, Boolean Modeling and Computation, 2003—08, Internat. Jour. Design Analysis & Tools Integrated Circuits & Sys., 2008—, Jour. Microprocessors & Microsys., 2008—. Contbr. over 50 refereed publs. to confs. and jours. Recipient Franz Tuteur Meml. prize, Yale U., 1994, EDAA Outstanding Dissertation award, 2005. Mem.: IEEE (sr.), Am. Assn. for Artificial Intelligence, Am. Soc. for Engring. Edn., Assn. for Computing Machinery. Achievements include development of over 1,100 formulas used in research in the computer science field of Boolean satisfiability (SAT).

VELEZ, CARLOS, minister; b. Long Island City, NY, Oct. 1, 1954; m. Miriam R. Velez, Dec. 24, 1977; children: Carlos Manuel, Diana Yvette. M, Alliance Theol. Sem., NYC, 2005; PhD, Pastoral Ministry. Ordained minister Assemblies of God, 1986. Asst. pastor Evangel Ch., Long Island City, 1982—2001; instr. pastoral ministries Nyack Coll., NYC, 2003—. Home: 2224 Center St Bethlehem PA 18017 Office: Nyack Coll 361 Broadway New York NY 10013 Business E-Mail: carlos.velez@nyack.edu.

VELEZ, INES, oral pathologist, educator; b. Bogota, Colombia, Apr. 15, 1946; arrived in US, 1999; d. José and Emilia (Marulanda) Velez; m. Eduardo Tamara (div.); children: Luis Tamara, Clara Lucia Tamara; m. Guillermo Torres, Mar. 30, 1992. DDS, Colombian Coll. Odontology, 1979; postgrad., U. Fla., 1982—84; MEd, U. Los Andes, 1989; M in

Laser Dentistry, Acad. Laser Dentistry, 1997. Cert. tchr. Fla. Chair., prof. pathology Colombian Coll. Odontology, 1984—92, pres. asst., 1989—92, dir. biopsy svc., 1984—95; chair, prof., dir. biopsy svc. Columbian Sch. Medicine, 1991—98, dir. bioclinical area, 1997—98; asst. prof. to assoc. prof., dir. oral and maxillofacial pathology, dir. biopsy svc. Nova Southeastern U., Ft. Lauderdale, Fla., 2000—. Lectr. in field. Contbr. articles to profl. jours. Recipient Best Student award, Coll. Sans Facon, 1963, Colombian Coll. Odontology, 1979, Educator award, Fla. Dental Assn., 2003, Golden Apple award, Nova Southeastern U., 2003, Ctr. of Excellence award, 2004. Mem.: ADA, Broward County Dental Assn., Fla. Dental Assn., Pierre Fouchard Acad., Acad. Laser Dentistry, Columbian Acad. Oral Pathology (founder), Am. Acad. Oral and Maxillofacial Pathology, Omicron Kappa Upsilon. Home: 3524 Parkside Dr Davie FL 33328 Office: Nova Southeastern U 3200 S University Dr Fort Lauderdale FL 33328 Home Phone: 954-262-7382; Office Phone: 954-472-7810. Business E-Mail: ivelez@nova.edu.

VÉLEZ-CARDONA, WALDEMIRO, education educator, consultant; b. San Juan, Sept. 26, 1960; s. Waldemiro Vélez-Ríos and Amparo M. Cardona-Vélez; life ptnr. Myra M. Torres-Alamo; 1 child, Waldemiro Vélez-Soto. MA in Econ., U. PR, 1985, U. Autonoma, Barcelona, Spain, 1993, PhD, 1998. Prof. U. PR, 1987—. Rsch. cons. PR Coun. on Higher Edn., San Juan, 2002—. V.p. PR Assn. U. Profs., San Juan, 1997—99. Mem.: Assn. for the Study Higher Edn. (assoc.). Home: Cond Puerta del Sol Apt 807 San Juan PR 00926 Office: Univ PR Ponce de Leon Ave Río Piedras San Juan PR 00931 Personal E-mail: waldemirov@hotmail.com.

VELICER, JANET SCHAFBUCH, retired elementary school educator; b. Cedar Rapids, Iowa, Aug. 27, 1941; d. Allan J. and Geraldine Frances (Stuart) Schafbuch; m. James J. Geiger, Oct. 27, 2007; m. Leland Frank Velicer, Aug. 17, 1963 (dec. Dec. 2000); children: Mark Allan, Gregory Jon, Daniel James. BS, Iowa State U., 1963, MS, 1966; cert. Elem. Edn., Mich. State U., 1976. Tchr. chemistry Prendergast High Sch., Upper Darby, Pa., 1964-65; tchr. home econs. Cardinal O'Hara High Sch., Springfield, Pa., 1965-66; substitute tchr. Pa., Mich., 1967-76; elem. tchr. Winans Elem. Sch., Waverly, Mich., 1976-78, Wardcliff Elem. Sch., Okemos, Mich., 1978-94; tchr. gifted and talented alternative program grades 4 and 5 Hiawatha Elem. Sch., Okemos, 1994-95; tchr. grade 4 Wardcliff Elem. Sch., 1995-2001; ret., 2001. Computer coord., Great Books coord.; dist. com. mem. math, computer, substance abuse, cable TV, evaluation revision Okemos Pub. Schs., Instrnl. Coun.; del. Mich. Edn. Exch. Opportunity Program, Germany, 1999. Author: (video) Wardcliff School Documentary, 1982, The Integrated Arts Program of the Okemos Elementary Schools, 1983. Citizens adv. com. to develop a five-yr. plan, 1982-83, bldg. utilization adv. com., 1983-84, cmty. use of schs. adv. com., 1984-85, strategic planning steering com., 1989-90, taking our schs. into tomorrow com., 1990-91, bonding election steering com., 1991; chmn. wellness com. Okemos Pub. Schs., 1993-95; bd. dirs. Okemos Music Patrons, 1981-86, pres., 1984-86; faculty rep. PTO; leadership coun. Nat. Inst. Clin. Application Behavioral Medicine, 1998-; chaperone Okemos HS German Club Exch., 1987, 90, Benton Cmty. HS Spanish Club Exch., Mex., 1995, Costa Rica, 1999, Spain, 2001, 03; mem. Shawnee Mission Unitarian Universalist Ch. Recipient Classrooms of Tomorrow Tchr. award, Mich. Dept. Edn., 1990; fellowship, Gen. Food Fund, 1963—64. Mem. NEA, AARP, Nat. Ret. Tchrs. Assn., Mich. Assn. Retired Sch. Pers., Mich. Edn. Assn., Okemos Edn. Assn. (exec. coun.), fellow: Gen. Foods Fund, Mich. Coun. Tchrs. Math., Lansing Woman's Club (social com. 2003-04, program com. 2005-06), Lifetime Fitness Athletic Club, Phi Kappa Phi, Omicron Nu, Iota Sigma Pi. Democrat. Unitarian Universalist. Avocations: swimming, reading, hiking, travel, cultural events. Home: 12880 Bradshaw St Overland Park KS 66213 Business E-Mail: jvelicer@msu.edu.

VELIKANOVA, OLGA, historian, educator; married. PhD in Russian history, St. Petersburg State U., Russia. Asst. prof. Dalhousie U., Halifax, Nova Scotia, Canada, 2005—07, U. North Tex., Denton, 2007—. Vis. scholar Tuebingen U., 1992—93, Germany, 1995—96, Maison des Sciences de l'Homme, Paris, 1994—95; resident scholar U. Toronto, Ontario, Canada, 2000—05. Author: (book) The Public Perception of the Cult of Lenin, Making of an Idol:On Uses of Lenin; contbr. consultant (One World Award from US Internat. Film and Video festival, 2004), to numerous profl. jours.;. Gen. Rsch. Grant, Social Sciences and Humanities Rsch. Coun. Can., 2002—05, Fellowship, Internat. Rsch. Exch. Program, 1998, Alexander von Humboldt Stiftung, Germany, 1995—96, Grant, Maison des Sciences de l'Homme, Paris, France, 1994—95, Fellowship, Volkswagen Stiftung, Germany, 1993, Friedrich Ebert Stiftung, Germany, 1992—93, Rsch. Grant, Open Soc. Found., 1998—2000, Ctrl. European U. Found., 1992—94.

VELISEK, LIBOR, medical educator; s. Frantisek Velisek and Marie Veliskova; m. Jana Veliskova; children: Ivana Veliskova, Jana. MD in Gen. Medicine, Charles U., Prague, Czech Republic, 1984; PhD, Czechoslovak Acad. Sci., Prague, 1989. Adj. faculty Charles U., 1989—94, assoc. prof., chmn., 1995—97; rschr. Inst. Physiology, Czech. Acad. Sci., Prague, 1994—95; asst. prof. neurology and neurosci. Albert Einstein Coll. Medicine, Bronx, NY, 1997—2002, assoc. prof. neurology and neurosci., 2002—. Cons. Allergan, Irvine, Calif., 2004, CHC, Inc., Chadds Ford, Pa., 2008—; med. writer Progenics, Eastview, NY, 2006—07. Rsch. grant, CURE, 2000—01, NIH, NINDS, 2005, 2008, March of Dimes, 2008—. Mem.: Am. Epilepsy Soc. (com. mem. 2005), Soc. Neurosci. Achievements include development of infantile spasm model.

VELLA, RUTH ANN, real estate executive; b. West Chester, Pa., Aug. 18, 1942; d. Eric and Carmella Tanberg; children: Michele Francette Vella, Nicole Renae Vella. Grad., Realtor's Inst. Real estate sales assoc. Reeve Realty, Wilmington, Del., 1966-72; owner Realtor Heritage Realty, Wilmington, 1972—92; instr. sales Wilmington Coll., 1978-85; mem. faculty Del. State Coll., 1979—; prin., owner Omega Real Estate Sch., Newark, Del., 1989—; mgr. Weichert Realtors, 1996—; profl. devel. coord. Prudential Fox & Roach Realtors, 2002—. Instr. Realtor's Inst., dean, 1983, asst. dean, 1983—; owner, pres. Corporate Fitness of Del., 1991—; mem. edn. com. Del. Real Estate Commn., 2003-07; spkr. in field. Edn. com. Real Estate Commn., 2002—06, Del. Real Estate Commn.; dir. Del. Assn. Realtors, 2006—. Named Educator of Yr., New Castle County, 1996, New Castle County Bd. Tchrs. Mem. Del. Assn. Realtors (dir. 2005-), New Castle County Bd. Realtors (dir. 1983-86, edn. com.), Womens Coun. Realtors (past state pres., gov.), Nat. Assn. Realtors (nat. speaker, energy conservation instr., Cert. Real Estate Broker instr.), Leading Edge Soc. Roman Catholic. Avocation: aerobics instr. and personal trainer. Office Phone: 302-235-0400. Personal E-mail: ruthvella@peoplepc.com. Business E-Mail: omega@realestateschool.com.

VELLANKI, GANGADHAR B., information scientist, consultant; b. Andhra Pradesh, India; m. Praveena Gudapati; 1 child, Chandana. BS, Andhra Loyola Coll., Vijayawada, India, 1976; MBA, Indian Inst. Social Welfare & Bus. Mgmt., Calcutta, 1979; MS, Birla Inst. Tech. & Sci., India, 1997. Regional systems engring. mgr. HCL Hewlett-Packard Ltd., New Delhi, 1979—94; gen. mgr. Satyam Computer Svcs., Hyderabad, Andhra Pradesh, India, 1994—97, v.p. Ill., 1997—2005, Farmington Hills, Mich., 2005—06; bus. devel. exec. IBM, Farmington Hills, 2007—08, Dallas, 2008—. Mem.: Am. Mgmt. Assn., Project Mgmt. Inst., Telugu Assn. N.Am. (life). Personal E-mail: vbg@sysorg.com.

VELLELLA, CHRISTOPHER A., science educator; b. Menominee, Mich., July 25, 1966; s. George J. and Ann E. Vellella; m. Gail Vellella, Feb. 9, 2008; 1 child, Joseph. BS in Civil Engring., U. Wis., Platteville, 1989; MS in Math., Southern Ill. U., Carbondale, 2000. Civil engr. Crawford, Murphy & Tilly, Springfield, Ill., 1989—99; instr. Shawnee CC, Ullin, Ill., 2000—. Office: Shawnee CC 8364 Shawnee CC Tamms IL 62988

VELLENGA, KATHLEEN OSBORNE, state legislator; b. Alliance, Nebr., Aug. 5, 1938; d. Howard Benson and Marjorie (Menke) Osborne; m. James Alan Vellenga, Aug. 9, 1959; children: Thomas, Charlotte Vellenga Landreau, Carolyn Vellenga Berman. BA, Macalester Coll., 1959. Tchr. St. Paul Pub. Schs., 1959-60, Children's Ctr. Montessori, St. Paul, 1973-74, Children's Ho. Montessori, St. Paul, 1974-79; mem. Minn. Ho. of Reps., St. Paul, 1980-94, mem. tax. com. and rules com., 1991—94, chmn. St. Paul del., 1987—90, chmn. criminal justice div., 1987—90, mem. Dem. steering com., 1981—94, chmn. judiciary, 1991, 92, chmn. edn. fin., 1993—94. Mem. St. Paul Family Svcs. Bd., 1994-95; exec. dir. St. Paul/Ramsey County Children's Initiative, 1994-2000. Chmn. Healthstart, St. Paul, 1987-91; mem. Children, Youth and Families Consortium, 1995-99, Macalester Coll. Bd. Alumni, 1995-2001; chair Minn. Higher Edn. Svcs. Coun., 2000—05, mem. 1995—; mem. Citizens League Bd., Minn., 1999-2002, State Commn. Cmty. Svc., 2000-04; bd. dirs. Sexual Violence Ctr., 2004-06; mem. U. Minn. Out of School Time Commn., 2004; mem. H.B. Fuller Found. Bd., 2005—. Mem. LWV (v.p. St. Paul chpt. 1979), Minn. Women Elected Ofcls. (vice chair 1994). Democrat. Presbyterian.

VELOSO, FRANCISCO, science educator; s. Francisco Veloso and Maria Helena Rogado. PhD in Tech., Mgmt., and Policy, MIT, 2001. R&D mgr. ITEC, Lisbon, 1993—96; asst. prof. Carnegie Mellon U., Pitts., 2002—. Editor: (book) Knowledge for Inclusive Development, Investing in the future: University Industry Collaborations in Portugal and USA; contbr. scientific papers to profl. jours. Grantee, Portuguese Govt., 2001, NSF, 2004, 2005, Internat. Motor Vehicle Program, 2004; fellow, Portuguese Sci. Found., 1996—2001, Portuguese Govt., 2002—04. Mem.: Acad. Mgmt., Inst. Ops. Rsch. and Mgmt. Scis. (vice chair membership and comm., tech. mgmt. sect. 2004—). Avocation: squash. Personal E-mail: fveloso@cmu.edu.

VELTMAN, MARTINUS J.G., retired physics educator; b. Waalwijk, The Netherlands, June 27, 1931; m. Anneke Veltman; children: Helene, Hugo, Martijn. BS in math and physics, U. Utrecht, The Netherlands, 1953, MS in theoretical physics, 1956, PhD in theoretical physics, 1963. Mem. FOM, Utrecht, Netherlands, 1959—61; fellow CERN, Geneva, 1961—63, staff mem., 1963—66, cons., 1966—72, sci. assoc., 1972—73, mem. sci. policy com., 1976—81, sci. assoc., 1996—97; prof. U. Utrecht, Netherlands, 1966—81; vis. prof. U. Mich., Ann Arbor, 1980, John D. McArthur prof. of physics, 1981—97, emeritus John D. McArthur prof. of physics, 1997—; prof. U. Autonoma de Madrid, 1988—96; Lorentz prof. of physics U. Leiden, Netherlands, 1989; Humboldt scientist Max Planck Inst., Munich, 1989—90, DESY, Hamburg, Germany, 1989—90. Postdoctoral SLAC, Stanford, Calif., 1963—64, Brookhaven Nat. Lab., LI, NY, 1966; vis. prof. U. Paris, Orsay, France, 1968—69. Author: Facts and Mysteries in Elementary Particle Physics, 2003. Recipient High Energy and Particle Physics prize, European Physics Soc., 1993, P.A.M. Dirac Medal and Prize, Internat. Ctr. for Theoretical Physics, 1996, Nobel prize in Physics, 1999. Office: U Mich Dept Physics Randall Lab 500 E University Ave Ann Arbor MI 48109-1120

VELU, SADANANDAN E., science educator; s. Velu E. and Karthiayani K. K.; m. Anitha C. Balakrishnan, Apr. 25, 1995; children: Karthik E. Sadanand, Midhun S. Sadanand. PhD, U. Madras, 1992. Res. asst prof. U. Ala., Birmingham, 2002—04, asst. prof., 2004—. Mem.: Am. Heart Assn., Am. Assn. Cancer Rsch., Am. Chem. Soc. Office: Univ Alabama Birmingham 901 14th St South Birmingham AL 35294

VELZY, CHARLES O., mechanical engineer; b. Oak Park, Ill., Mar. 17, 1930; s. Charles R and Ethel B. V.; m. Marilyn A. Gilman, Aug. 17, 1957; children: Charles Mark, Barbara Helen, Patricia Ethel. BSME, U. Ill., 1953, MS in San. Engring., 1959, BS in Civil Engring., 1960. Registered profl. engr., Pa., 8 other states. Design engr. Nussbaumer, Clarke & Velzy, NYC, 1957—59, sr. design engr., 1959—62, project engr., 1962—66; sec.-treas. Charles R. Velzy Assocs., Inc., Armonk, NY, 1966—76, pres., 1976-92; v.p. Roy F. Weston Inc., 1987-92; pres. Charles O. Velzy, P.E., White Haven, Pa., 1992—. Contbr. over 32 articles to profl. publs. Mem. White Plains (N.Y.) Bldg. Code Appeals Bd., 1970-92; mem. Kidder Township Planning Bd., 2006—. With U.S. Army, 1954-56. Recipient Disting. Alumnus award U. Ill., 1989. Fellow ASME (hon. mem., chmn. solid waste processing divsn 1973-74, mem. bd. rsch. and tech. dev. 1974-78, 2000—, bd. govs. 1983-84, pres. 1989-90, Centennial medal 1980, medal of achievement 1981, Dedicated Svc. award 1986), mem. ASCE (life), NYPE (Engr. of the Yr. 1980), Am. Acad. Environ. Engrs. (trustee 1984-87, treas. 1993-97, Stanley E. Kappe award 1998), Am. Water Works Assn. (life), Water Environ. Fedn., Air Waste Mgmt. Assn. Methodist. *After deciding on what is needed in a specific situation, based on the facts, establish your objectives and goals and persist to a successful conclusion.*

VENABLE, CHARLES L., museum director; life ptnr. Martin Webb; 1 child, Alexandra. BA in Am. Hist. and Art Hist., Rice U.; MA in Fine Arts and Decorative Art, U. Del.; PhD in Am. Studies, Boston U. With Dallas Mus. Art, 1986—2002, asst. cur., dep. dir.; dep. dir. collections and programs Cleve. Art Mus.; dir., CEO Speed Art Mus., Louisville, 2007—. Author: American Furniture in the Bybee Collection, 1989 (Charles F. Montgomery award), Silver in America, 1840-1940: A Century of Splendor, 1994 (Montgomery prize), China and Glass in America, 1880-1980, 2000. Office: Speed Art Mus 2035 S Third St Louisville KY 40208

VENAYAGAMOORTHY, GANESH KUMAR, electrical engineer, educator; b. Jaffna, Sri Lanka, Feb. 25, 1972; s. Sinnathamby Nagalingam Venayagamoorthy and Neelambigai Kathiravetpillai. B of Engring. with honors, Abubakar Tafawa Balewa U., Bauchi, Nigeria, 1994; MS of Engring., U. Natal, Durban, South Africa, 1999, PhD, 2002. Grad. asst. Abubakar Tafawa Balewa U., Bauchi, Nigeria, 1994—94; computer engr. Sq. One Comnet, Maseru, Lesotho, 1994—95; sr. lectr. Durban Inst. Tech., Durban, Kwazulu Natal, South Africa, 1996—2002; asst. prof. Mo. U. Sci. and Tech., Rolla, 2002—06, assoc. prof., 2006—. Dir. real-time power and intelligent sys. lab. Mo. U. Sci. and Tech., Rolla, 2004—. Contbr. articles to profl. jours. Recipient Young Investigator award, Office Naval Rsch., 2002, Internat. Neural Network Soc., 2003, Outstanding Young Engr. award, IEEE St. Louis Sect., 2004, Outstanding Mem. award, 2006, Faculty Excellence award, U. Mo., Rolla, 2005, 2007, 2008, Tchg. Excellence award, 2006, Outstanding Young Mem. award, IEEE Industry Applications Soc., 2005, Young Achievers award, South Inst. Elec. Engrs., 2005, Walter Fee Outstanding Young Engr. award, IEEE Power Engring. Soc., 2006; grantee, NSF, 2004, NSF Career award, 2004. Fellow: Inst. Engring. and Tech. UK, South African Inst. Elec. Engrs. (sr.); mem.: IEEE (sr.; chair St. Louis CIS & IAS chpt. 2004—, Outstanding Sect. Mem. 2006, Outstanding Educator award St. Louis sect. 2008), Inst. Elec. Engrs., Am. Soc. Engring. Edn., Internat. Neural Network Soc. (bd. govs. 2009). Office: Mo Univ Sci and Tech 132 Emerson Electric Co Hall Rolla MO 65409 Office Fax: 573-341-4532.

VENAYAGAMOORTHY, SUBHAS KARAN, civil engineer, educator; m. Lumina S. Albert, Dec. 15, 2003; 1 child, Ruth Nadiya Karan. BSc in Civil Engring. summa cum laude, U. Natal, Durban, South Africa, 2000, MSc in Civil Engring. cum laude, 2002; PhD in Civil and Environ. Engring., Stanford U., Calif., 2006. Cert. engr., Calif., 2005. Lectr. U. Natal, 2001—02; rsch. asst. Stanford U., Calif., 2003—06, postdoc. rsch. fellow, 2006—07; asst. prof. Colo. State U., Fort Collins, 2008—. Recipient JR Daymond prize, Dept. Civil Engring., U. Natal, 2000, K Knight prize, 2000, HA Smith prize, 2000, Best Final Yr. Student prize, 2000, Best Student prize, South Instn. Civil Engring. and Instn. Structural Engring. UK, 2000, Water Inst. South Africa, 2000, S2A3 medal, South African Assn. Advancement Sci., 2002, Best Spkr. award, SIAM, Stanford Student Chpt., 2005, NSF, ONR, NASA and NOAA, 2006; Harvey fellow, Mustard Seed Found., 2005. Mem.: Am. Geophys. Union, Am. Phys. Soc., Am. Soc. Civil Engrs. Office: Colo State Univ Campus Delivery 1372 Fort Collins CO 80523 Office Fax: 970-491-7727. Business E-Mail: vskaran@colostate.edu.

VENDÉ, SANDRA, lab administrator; b. Agen, Lot-et-Garonne, France, Jan. 2, 1978; Maîtrise d'anglais, U. Avignon, France, 2004. Tchg. asst. French Inst. Vienna, Graz, Styria, Austria, 2003—06, Macalester Coll., St. Paul, 2006—. Personal E-mail: sandravende@gmail.com.

VENDETTA, CONSTANCE JOAN, language educator; b. Rome, NY, Nov. 15, 1945; d. John Joseph Damon and Jennie Alexandra Butkiewicz; m. Richard Anthony Vewndetta, Oct. 30, 1976. BA in Edn., SUNY, Potsdam, 1967; MA in Edn., SUNY, Cortland, 1975. Cert. secondary French tchr. NY, 1972. French tchr. Utica Free Acad., NY, 1967—2004, John F. Kennedy HS, Utica, 2005—; chmn. second lang. dept. Donovan Jr. HS, Utica, 1990—94, Proctor Sr. HS, Utica, 1994—2004; cons. Vol. Ctr., Mahawk Valley, 2008—. Adj. edn. prof. Utica Coll., 2005—. Cons. Mohawk Valley Vol. Ctr., 2008—. Mem.: Fgn. Lang. Assn. Ctrl. NY, Am. Coun. on Tchg. Fgn. Langs., NY State Fgn. Lang. Tchrs., Pi Delta Kappa, Delta Kappa Gamma (pres. 2002—04). Home: 2 Forest Rd Utica NY 13501 Personal E-mail: cvendetta@aol.com.

VENDITTI, CLELIA ROSE See PALMER, CHRISTINE

VENDITUOLI, ELIZABETH ANN, special education educator; d. Joseph Furtado and Virginia Borges Brum; m. Thomas Vendituoli, May 25, 1973; children: Michael Thomas, Bethany Ann Romoser, Karen Elizabeth. BA, Salve Regina U., Newport, RI, 1973, MA, 1977. Cert. spl. edn. tchr. mild & moderate disabilities State RI, 1973. Spl. edn. tchr. Bristol Warren Regional Sch. Dist., RI, 1973—2006; adj. spl. edn. prof. Salve Regina U., 2005—. Chairperson Our Lady Mt. Carmel Sch. Bd., Bristol, 1997—2009. Recipient Chief Marshal award, Our Lady Mt. Carmel Ch., 2004, Italian Heritage award, LaBella Sicilia, 2005; named Tchr. of Yr., Bristol Warren Regional Sch. Dist., 2004. Mem.: Coun. Exceptional Children.

VENDLER, HELEN HENNESSY, literature educator, poetry critic; b. Boston, Apr. 30, 1933; d. George and Helen (Conway) Hennessy; 1 son, David. AB, Emmanuel Coll., 1954; PhD, Harvard U., 1960; PhD (hon.), U. Oslo, 1981; DLitt (hon.), Smith Coll., 1980, Kenyon Coll., 1982, U. Hartford, 1985, Union Coll., 1986, Columbia U., 1987, Washington U., 1991, Marlboro Coll., 1989, Yale U., 2000; DHL (hon.), Fitchburg State U., 1990, Dartmouth Coll., 1992, U. Mass., 1992, Bates Coll., 1992, U. Toronto, Ont., Can., 1992, Trinity Coll., Dublin, Ireland, 1993, U. Cambridge, 1997, Nat. U., Ireland, 1998, Wabash Coll., 1998, U. Mass, Dartmouth, 2000, Yale U., 2000, U. Aberdeen, 2000, Tufts U., 2001, Amherst Coll., 2002, Colby Coll., 2003; DHL, Bard Coll., 2005, Willamette U., 2008. Instr. Cornell U., Ithaca, NY, 1960-63; lectr. Swarthmore (Pa.) Coll. and Haverford (Pa.) Coll., 1963-64; asst. prof. Smith Coll., Northampton, Mass., 1964-66; assoc. prof. Boston U., 1966-68, prof., 1968-85. Fulbright lectr. U. Bordeaux, France, 1968-69; vis. prof. Harvard U., 1981-85, Kenan prof., 1985—, Porter U. prof., 1990—, assoc. acad. dean, 1987-92, sr. fellow Harvard Soc. Fellows, 1981-93; poetry critic New Yorker, 1978-99; mem. ednl. adv. bd. Guggenheim Found., 1991-01, Pulitzer Prize Bd., 1991-99; Mellon lectr. Nat. Gallery, 2006. Author: Yeats's Vision and the Later Plays, 1963, On Extended Wings: Wallace Stevens' Longer Poems, 1969, The Poetry of George Herbert, 1975, Part of Nature, Part of Us, 1980, The Odes of John Keats, 1983, Wallace Stevens: Words Chosen Out of Desire, 1984; editor: Harvard Book of Contemporary American Poetry, 1985, Voices and Visions: The Poet in America, 1987, The Music of What Happens, 1988, Soul Says, 1995, The Given and the Made, 1995, The Breaking of Style, 1995, Poems, Poets, Poetry, 1995, The Art of Shakespeare's Sonnets, 1997, Seamus Heaney, 1998, Coming of Age as a Poet, 2003, Poets Thinking, 2004, Invisible Listeners, 2005, Our Secret Discipline, 2007. Bd. dirs. Nat. Humanities Ctr., 1989—93. Recipient Lowell prize, 1969, Explicator prize, 1969, award Nat. Inst. Arts and Letters, 1975, Radcliffe Grad. Soc. medal, 1978, Nat. Book Critics award, 1980, Keats-Shelley Assn. award, 1994, Truman Capote award, 1996; Fulbright fellow, 1954, Guggenheim fellow, 1971-72, Am. Coun. Learned Socs. fellow, 1971-72, NEH fellow, 1980, 85, 94, 04, 05, fellow Churchill Coll., Cambridge, 1980, Charles Stewart Parnell fellow Magdalene Coll., Cambridge, 1996, hon. fellow, 1996—, fellow Siemens, Munich, 2009; NEH Jefferson Lectr. scholar US Fed. Govt., 2004-05, Mellon Lectr. Nat. Gallery Art Mem. MLA (exec. coun. 1972-75, pres. 1980), AAAL (bd. mem. 2007-), English Inst. (trustee 1977-85), Am. Acad. Arts and Scis. (v.p. 1992-95), Norwegian Acad. Letters and Sci., Am. Philos. Soc. (Jefferson medal 2000), Phi Beta Kappa. Home: 54 Trowbridge St 2 Cambridge MA 02138-4113 Office: Harvard U Dept English Barker Center Cambridge MA 02138-3929 Office Phone: 617-496-6028.

VENEGAS-PONT, MARCIA, physiologist, educator; d. Antonio Benegas and Graciela Pont; m. Julio Sartori-Valinotti, Apr. 4, 2009. MD magna cum laude, U. Nat. de Asuncion, Asuncion-Paraguay, 2000. Intern Hosp. de Clinicas, Asuncion, 2001—02, internal medicine resident, 2002—05, chief clinician, 2005—07; postdoc. fellow U. Miss. Med. Ctr., Jackson, 2007—09, instr. physiology, 2009—. Contbr. scientific papers (recognition award, 2008). Postdoc. fellowship, Am. Heart Assn., 2009—. Mem.: AHA, Am. Physiol. Soc. Roman Catholic. Avocations: travel, reading. Office: Univ Miss Med Ctr 2500 N State St Jackson MS 39216

VENEMA, JEREMY, literature and language professor; PhD, Ariz. State U., Tempe, 2006. Faculty Mesa CC, Ariz., 2002—.

VENEMAN, ANN MARGARET, international organization official, former United States Secretary of Agriculture; b. Modesto, Calif., June 29, 1949; d. John G. and Nita D. (Bomberger) V.; div. BA in polit. sci., U. Calif., Davis, 1970; MA in pub. policy, U. Calif., Berkeley, 1971; JD, Hastings Coll. Law, 1976. Bar: Calif. 1976, US Supreme Ct. 1981. Atty. San Francisco Bay Area Rapid Transit Dist., 1976-78; dep. pub. defender Stanislaus County., Calif., 1978-80; ptnr. Damrell, Damrell & Nelson, Modesto, 1980-86; asst. to adminstr., Fgn. Agrl. Svc. USDA, Washington, 1986-87, assoc. adminstr., Fgn. Agrl. Svc., 1987-89, dep. under sec. Internat. Affairs and Commodity Programs, 1989-91, dep. sec., 1991-93, sec. of agr., 2001—05; atty. Patton, Boggs & Blow LLP, Washington, 1993—95; sec. Calif. Dept. Food and Agr., 1995—99; ptnr. Nossaman, Guthner, Knox & Elliott LLP, Sacramento, 1999—2000; exec. dir. UNICEF, 2005—. Bd. dir. Close Up Found. Named one of 100 Most Powerful Women, Forbes mag., 2009. Office: UNICEF 3 United Nations Plz New York NY 10017*

VENERABLE, GRANT DELBERT, II, chemist, educator, systems scientist; b. LA, Aug. 31, 1942; s. Grant Delbert and Thelma L. (Scott) Venerable. BS Chemistry, UCLA, 1965; MS Chemistry, U. Chgo., 1967, PhD Physical Chemistry, 1970; postdoctoral studies, UCLA Lab. Nuclear Medicine, 1971. Assoc. prof. chemistry Calif. Polytech. State U., San Luis Obispo, 1972—78; Sloan lectr. chemistry U. Calif., Santa Cruz, 1978—80; cons. software Motorola and other Cos., Cupertino, 1981—89; lectr. Coll. Ethnic Studies San Francisco State U., 1989—96; assoc. provost, assoc. v.p., prof. chemistry Chgo. (Ill.) State U., 1996—98; provo and v.p. acad. affairs Morris Brown Coll., Atlanta, 1998—2002; v.p. acad. affairs Lincoln U., Pa., 2002. Sec. State Bd. Calif. Alliance for Arts Edn., 1985—91. Author: (Book) The Discovery of Calculus of Transformations in Chemistry, 1974, The Paradox of the Silicon Savior, 1988, Managing in a Five Dimension Economy, 1999. Bd. dirs. City Quest, Chgo., 1998—2000. Recipient Achievement award, Calif. Alliance for Art Edn., 1990, Urban Edn. Achievement award, JGT Found., San Francisco, 1996. Mem.: AAAS, Am. Chem Soc., Nat. Orgn. for Profl. Advancement of Black Chemists and Chem. Engrs., Alpha Chi Sigma. Avocations: organist, painting, swimming. Office: Office Acad Affairs Lincoln U Box 179 Lincoln University PA 19352 Home: PO Box 103 Lincoln University PA 19352-0103 Office Phone: 484-365-7436. Office Fax: 484-365-8108. Personal E-mail: ventwo@aol.com.

VENERABLE, SHIRLEY MARIE, retired gifted and talented educator; b. Washington, Nov. 12, 1931; d. John Henry and Jessie Josephine (Young) Washington; m. Wendell Grant Venerable, Feb. 15, 1958; children: Angela Elizabeth Maria Venerable-Joyner, Wendell Mark. PhB, Northwestern U., 1963; MA, Roosevelt U., 1976, postgrad., 1985; student in Life Long Studies, Triton C.C., River Grove, Ill., 2002. Cert. in diagnostic and prescriptive reading, gifted edn., finger math., fine arts, Ill. Tchr. Lewis Champlin Sch., 1963-74, John Hay Acad., Chgo., 1975-87, Leslie Lewis Elem. Sch., Chgo., 1988-99, Robert Emmet Sch., Chgo., 1999—; self employed tutorial programs, 1999—2003; ret., 2003. Sponsor Reading Marathon Club, Chgo., 1991—; co-creator Project SMART-Stimulating Math. and Reading Techniques John Hay Acad., Chgo., 1987-90, curriculum coord., 1985-87; creative dance student, tchr. Kathryn Duham Sch., NYC, 1955-56; creative dance tchr. Doris Patterson Dance Sch., Washington, 1953-55; recorder evening divsn. Northwestern U., Chgo., 1956-62; exch. student tchr. Conservatory Dance Movements, Chgo., 1958-59; art cons. Chgo. Pub. Sch., 1967. Author primary activities Let's Act and Chat, 1991-94, Teaching Black History Through Classroom Tours, 1989-90. Solicitor, vol. United Negro Coll. Fund, Chgo., 1994; sponsor 37th Ward Reading Assn. Marathon, Chgo., 1991-94, 99; active St. Giles Coun. Cath. Women, 1985-96; vol. REAC Ctr. Programs Books, Info., Literacy and Learning, 1997-98. Recipient Meritorious award United Negro Coll. Fund, 1990, 94, Recognition award Alderman Percy Giles, Chgo., 1993, Hall of Fame award Nat. Women in Achievement, Inc., 2005. Mem.: ASCD (assoc. Recognition of Svcs. award 1989), Internat. Reading Assn., Nat. Women of Achievement Assn. (Chgo. chpt.), Nat. Women's History Mus., Phi Delta Kappa (charter), Sigma Gamma Rho (Delta Sigma grad. chpt. 1963—93, Sigma chpt. 1992, Eta Xi Sigma chpt.), Eta Xi Sigma (Pearl award for excellence in edn. 1997). Roman Catholic. Home: 1108 N Euclid Ave Oak Park IL 60302-1219

VENETSANOPOULOS, ANASTASIOS NICOLAOS, electrical engineer, educator; b. Athens, Greece, June 19, 1941; arrived in Can., 1968; s. Nicolaos Anastasios and Elli (Papacondilis) Venetsanopoulos. Diploma, Athens Coll., 1960; B in Elec. and Mech. Engring., Nat. Tech. U., Athens, 1965; MS, Yale U., 1966, MPhil, 1968, PhD, 1969; doctorate (hon.), Nat. Tech. U., Athens, 1994. Registered profl. engr., Greece, Ont. Asst. in instrn. engring. and applied sci. Yale U., 1966-68, research asst., 1968-69; lectr. U. Toronto, Ont., Can., 1968-69, asst. prof. elec. engring., 1970-73, assoc. prof., 1973-81, prof., 1981—, chmn. communications group dept. elec. engring., 1974-78, 81-86, assoc. chmn. elec. and computer engring., 1978—79, 1997—, acting chmn. elec. and computer engring., 1998—99, dean applied sci. and engring., 2001—06; v.p. rsch.-innovation Ryerson U., Toronto, 2006—. Acad. visitor Imperial Coll. Arts and Tech. U. London, 1979—80; vis. prof. Nat. Tech. U. Athens, 1979—80, Fed. U. Tech. Lausanne, Switzerland, 1986—87, Switzerland, 1993—94, U. Florence, Italy, 1987; cons. elec. engring. Consociates Ltd.; chmn. multimedia Bell-Can., 1999—. Editor: Can. Elec. Engring. Jour., 1981—83; contbr. articles to profl. jours., chapters to books. Mem. allocations and agy. rels. com. United Cmty. Fund, Toronto, 1971—74; pres. Hellenic-Can. Cultural Soc., 1972—75; sec. gen. Greek Cmty. Met. Toronto, 1973—75. Recipient Excellence in Innovation award, Info. Tech. Rsch. Ctr., 1996; grantee Fulbright Travel, US, 1965, Def. Rsch. Bd. Can., 1972—75, UN, NSF, J. P. Bickell Found., Natural Scis. and Engring. Rsch. Coun. Can. Fellow: IEEE (fin. chmn. internat. symposium on circuit theroy 1973, tech. program chmn. internat. conf. comm. 1978, 1986, vice-chmn. Toronto sect. 1976—77, chmn. 1977—79, assoc. editor Transactions on circuits and sys. 1985—87, guest editor spl. 1987, tech. prgram chmn. internat. conf. on acoustics speech and signal proc 1991, Millenium medal 2001—), Can. Acad. Engring., Engring. Inst. Can.; mem.: Intercultural Coun. (chmn. ednl. com. 1971—80, sr. v.p. 1977—80), Am.-Hellenic Ednl. Progress Assn. (v.p. Toronto sect. 1973—75, pres. 1975—77), N.Y. Acad. Scis., Yale Sci. and Engring. Assn., Can. Soc. Elec. Engring. (chmn. Toronto sect. 1975—77, nat. dir. 1976—88, pres. 1983—86), Assn. Profl. Mech. Engrs. Greece, Assn. Profl. Elec. Engrs. Greece, Assn. Profl. Engrs. Ont., Tech. Chamber Greece, Sigma Xi. Office: Ryerson U 350 Victoria St Toronto ON Canada M5B 2K3 Office Phone: 416-979-5283. Business E-Mail: tasvenet@ryerson.ca.

VENEZIA, ANTHONY D., multimedia designer; b. New York, Oct. 6, 1952; s. Eugene Michael and Patricia Dawn Venezia, Barbara Venezia (Stepmother); m. Rebecca F. Fuller; children: Samuel Anthony, Naomi Rebecca. MFA, UCLA, Los Angeles, 1982. Spl. effects dir. pres. Electric Filmworks, Glendale, Calif., 1985—98; animator graphic designer Harpo Productions, Chicago, Ill., 2000—04; assoc. prof. Coll. DuPage, Glen Ellyn, 2005—; animator designer Total Living Network, Aurora, 2000—. Dir.(animator creator): (animated film) Ghost Dance (Am. Film Inst. Grant, 1987), (animator) Revelation (Student Acad. award, 1982); supervisor (opening titles) Total Recall, special effects director (motion picture) Cold Heaven. Video maker Ray Graham Assn., Downers Grove, Ill., 2008—. Independent. Methodist. Achievements include development of advanced techniques in slit scan, a method of painting & animating with light directly to motion picture film; first to early techniques of motion control animation. Avocations: drawing, researching animation history, travel, jogging. Office: Coll DuPage 425 Fawell Blvd Glen Ellyn IL 60137 Business E-Mail: venezia@cod.edu.

VENEZIA, WILLIAM THOMAS, school system administrator, counseling consultant; b. Jersey City, Mar. 20, 1952; s. Thomas Michael and Carmela (Crocamo) Venezia; m. Josephine DePaul. BA in History, St. Peter's Coll., 1974, postgrad., 1978-79, MA in Adminstrn./Supervision, 1984; postgrad., Jersey City State Coll., 1988-90. Cert. tchr., prin., supt., N.J.; cert. in student personnel svcs., N.J. Tchr. various schs. Jersey City Bd. Edn., 1976-92; guidance counselor P.S. # 27/Dickinson High Sch., Jersey City, 1990-92; counselor Montclair (N.J.) State Coll., 1991-92; asst. prin. Frelinghuysen Sch., Morristown, NJ, 1992-97; prin. Alexander Hamilton Sch., Morristown, 1997—2001; dir. guidance Morris Sch. Dist., 2001—02; interim prin. Frelinghuysen Mid. Sch., 2003; prin. Thomas Jefferson Sch., Morristown, 2002—08, Sch. St. Elizabeth, Bernardsville, NJ. Asst. football coach various schs., 1975-89; instr., adminstr. G.E.D. and A.B.E. programs Jersey City Bd. Edn., 1977-82; interim bd. sec., bus. adminstr. Weehawken Bd. Edn., 1984; mem. adv. bd. Cornerstone Sch., Jersey City, 1988-91; pre-coll. counselor UPWARD Bound project Montclair State Coll., 1991; cons. N.J. Devils hockey team, East Rutherford, 1992, D.A.R.E. program Hudson County Prosecutor, Jersey City, 1992.h Vol. counselor Giant Steps adolescent substance abuse treatment facility; active Jersey City, 1993, Jersey City Parents' Coun. Mem. ASCD, NEA, Am. Football Coaches Assn., N.J. Edn. Assn., Assn. Adult Edn. in N.J., N.J. Assn. Sch. Bus. Officials, Hudson County Personnel and Guidance Assn., Morris Sch. Dist.Adminstrv. Assn. (pres. 2004—), Iron Bound Execs. Assn., Hoboken Elks. Avocations: basketball, travel, antiques. Home: 1 Hickory St Clark NJ 07066-1924 Office: Sch St Elizabeth 30 Seney Dr Bernardsville NJ 07924 Office Phone: 973-292-2089. Business E-Mail: vendpl@comcast.net.

VENINGA, JAMES FRANK, humanities educator, editor, writer; b. Milw., Aug. 26, 1944; s. Frank and Otila Ann (Mauch) V.; m. Catherine M. Williams, Apr. 5, 1969; 1 child, Jennifer Elisa. BA, Baylor U., 1966; MTheol Studies, Harvard U., 1968; MA, Rice U., 1973, PhD, 1974. Instr. U. St. Thomas, Houston, 1971-73, asst. prof., 1974; asst. dir. Tex. Coun. for Humanities, Austin, 1975, exec. dir., 1976-97; pres., dir. Inst. for the Humanities at Salado, 1997—2000; CEO, campus dean U. Wis.-Marathon County, Wausau, 2000—07, assoc. prof. religious studies, 2000—. Dir. Nat. Fedn. State Humanities Couns., Washington, 1980-83; trustee Inst. for Humanities at Salado, Tex., 1980-85; vis. prof. Am. studies U. Tex., Austin, 1984, sr. lectr. Am. studies, 1986; vis. prof. Am. studies Baylor U., 1999; bd. dirs. Wisc. Humanities Coun., 2007-; chair Wisc. Inst. Pub. Policy and Svc., 2007-. Author: The Humanities and Civic Imagination, 1999; editor: The Biographer's Gift, 1983, Vietnam in Remission, 1985, Standing with the Public, 1997; editor-in-chief Tex. Jour. Ideas, History and Culture, 1982-97. Recipient Baylor Man of Merit award, Baylor U., 1985. Office: U Wis 518 S 7th Ave Wausau WI 54401-5362 Home: 11074 N Loon Bay Ln Hayward WI 54843 Office Phone: 715-261-6289. Business E-Mail: james.veninga@uwc.edu.

VENIT, WILLIAM BENNETT, electrical products company executive, consultant; b. Chgo., May 28, 1931; s. George Bernard and Ida (Schaffel) V.; m. Nancy Jean Carlson, Jan. 28, 1956; children: Steven Louis, Aprilann. Student, U. Ill., Champaign, 1949. Sales mgr. Coronet, Inc., Chgo., 1952-63, pres., chmn. bd. dirs., 1963-74, Roma Wire Inc., Chgo., 1971-74; chmn. bd. dirs. Swing Time #2, Chgo., 1988-89; pres. Wm. Allen Inc., Chgo., 1972-74; pres., chmn. bd. dirs. Wraprama Inc., 1988-95, Swag Lite, Inc., 1989—92. Pres. William Lamp Co., Inc., 1993, 97, William Wire Co., Inc., 1974-76; chmn. bd. dirs. MSWV, Inc., 1978—, pres. bd. dirs. 1985—; pres. Trio Steel Inc., Chgo., 1987-90; chmn. bd. Chgo. Lamp Works LLB, 1995, 98, chair 1996, 98; CEO Chgo. Chair Works, 1998, 2000, 2001; pres. MSWV Inc. Mobile Home Divsn., 2001, spl. cons. Roto Products, 1998-2002, DMSI Inc., 2002-2008; cons. Nu Style Lamp Shade, 2002-08. Patentee Printed-Cir., 1964. With QMC AUS, 1949-52, dir. Timber Oaks, 2000-08. Avocations: bicycling, golf. Home and Office: 323 Suwanee Ave Sarasota FL 34243-1930 Home Phone: 941-351-5265; Office Phone: 847-477-9997. Personal E-mail: lampbill@aol.com.

VENKATA, SUBRAHMANYAM SARASWATI, engineering educator, researcher; b. Nellore, Andhra Pradesh, India, June 28, 1942; came to U.S., 1968; s. Ramiah Saraswati and Lakshmi (Alladi) V.; m. Padma Subrahmanyam Mahadevan, Sept. 3, 1971; children: Sridevi Ramakumar, Harish Saraswati. BSEE, Andhra U., Waltair, India, 1963; MSEE, Indian Inst. Tech., Madras, 1965; PhD, U. S.C., 1971. Registered profl. engr., W.Va., Wash. Lectr. in elec. engring. Coimbatore (India) Inst. Tech., 1965-66; planning engr. S.C. Elec. & Gas Co., Columbia, 1969-70; postdoctoral fellow U. S.C., Columbia, 1971; instr. elec. engring. U. Mass., Lowell, 1971-72; asst. prof. W.Va. U., Morgantown, 1972-75, assoc. prof., 1975-79; prof. U. Wash., Seattle, 1979-96; prof., chmn. dept. elec. and computer engring. Iowa State U., Ames, 1996—2002, Palmer chair prof. dept. elec. and computer engring., 2003—04, prof. and chair emeritus, 2004—; dean, disting. univ. prof. Wallace H. Coulter Sch. Engring., Clarkson U., Potsdam, NY, 2004—05; v.p., exec. cons. KEMA, 2005—07; pres. Venkata Cons. Inc., 2007—; prof. U. Wash, Seattle, 2008—. Cons. Puget Sound Energy Co., Bellevue, Wash., 1980-93, GEC/Alsthom, NYC, 1991-92; series editor, bd. dirs. PWS Pub. Co., 1991-98; affiliate prof. U. Wash., Seattle, 1997-07. Author: Introduction of Electrical Energy Devices, 1987; editor, IEEE Transactions on Power Systems, 1998-00, IEEE/PES Rev. Letters, 1999-03, Internat. Jour. Sys.; mem. editl. bd. IEEE/PES/Power and Energy Mag., 2003-; patentee adaptive var compensators, adaptive power quality conditioner, distribution reliability based design software. Advisor Explorers Club, Morgantown, 1976-78; sec. Hindu Temple and Cultural Ctr. Pacific N.W., Seattle, 1990, chmn., 1991, 95; founding chmn. Hindu Temple and Cultural Ctr., Ames, Iowa, 1999—. Recipient W.Va. U. Assocs. award W.Va. U. Found., 1974, 78. Fellow IEEE (editor IEEE Trans. Power Sys. 1998-00, IEEE/PES Rev. Letters 1999-03, Internat. Jour. Sys., mem. editl. bd. IEEE/PES/Power and Energy Mag., 2003-, v.p. publs., 2004-07, Best Paper award 1985, 88, 91, 2005, mem. Conf. Internat. des Grands Reseaux Electriques, IEEE Press for Power Series, 1998—, Outstanding Power Engring. Educator award 1996, chmn. power engring. edn. com. 2000—, Millenneum medal 2000, Power Edn.Com. Disting. Svc. award 2005), Power Engring. Soc. IEEE (v.p. 2004—), Sigma Xi, Tau Beta Pi, Eta Kappa Nu, Rotary. Democrat. Avocations: photography, tennis, ping pong/table tennis. Home and Office: 13224 N Risky Dr Tucson AZ 85755 Office Phone: 520-797-1161, 206-543-2386. Personal E-mail: psvenkata@comcast.net. Business E-Mail: ss.venkata@kema.com, venkata@ee.washington.edu.

VENKATACHALAM, KALLIDAIKURICHI, biochemist, educator, researcher; b. Kalakad, Tamilnadu, India, July 3, 1960; s. Kallidaikurichi Venkatraman and Vasanthalakshmi Venkatachalam; m. Usha Shankaranarayanan, June 16, 1988. BSc, MSc, Madurai Kamraj U.; BS, MS, Wash. State U.; PhD, Tex. A&M U., 1990. Postdoctoral fellow Baylor Coll. Medicine, Houston, 1990—93; rsch. fellow, scientist NIH, Bethesda, Md., 1993—99, mem. faculty in biochemistry FAES, 1996—99; assoc. prof. biochemistry Nova Southeastern U., Ft. Lauderdale, Fla., 1999—2005, prof. biochemistry, 2005—. Contbr. articles to profl. jours. Sec., v.p, pres., Indian Cultural Orgn., Houston. Rsch. grantee Great Lakes Ecology, 2000. Mem. AAAS, Am. Soc. Biochemistry and Molecular Biology, Am. Chem. Soc. (chair South Fla. chpt. 2006). Avocation: music. Office: Nova Southwestern U 3200 S University Dr Fort Lauderdale FL 33328-2018 Fax: (954) 262-1802.

VENKATARAMAN, SATCHI, engineering educator; married. PhD, U. Fla., Gainesville, 1999. Postdoc. rsch. assoc. U. Fla., Gainesville, 2000—01, vis. asst. prof., 2001—02; rsch. engr. Aerochem Inc., Gainesville, Fla., 2001—02; asst. prof. Dept. Aerospace Engring. and Mechanics, San Diego State U., 2002—07, assoc. prof., 2007—. Contbr. articles to profl. sci. jours. Named one of Most Influential Faculty, Coll. Engring., San Diego State U., 2005. Mem.: AIAA. Achievements include research in structural optimigation, reliability based design and design for robustness and predictatility. Office: San Diego State Univ 5500 Campanile Dr Mail Code 1308 San Diego CA 92182-1308 Office Fax: 619-594-0933. Business E-Mail: satchi@mail.sdsu.edu.

VENKATESH, MURALI, engineering educator; s. Abhinavam Venkatesan and Vimala Subramanian; m. Laila M. Thomas; children: Rahul T., Ranjana M. PhD, Ind. U., Bloomington, 1991. Assoc. prof. Sch. Info. Studies, Syracuse U., NY, 1990—. At-large mem. Syracuse MetroNet, 2008.

VENKATESH, VISWANATH, information systems professional, educator, consultant; s. Viswanath Hariharan and Subhalakshmi Viswanath. BE, Bharathiar U., Coimbatore, India, 1991; post grad., Temple U., Phila., 1993; PhD, U. Minn., Mpls., 1997. Cert. bus. process mgr. and practitioner del. Bus. Process Mgmt. Group, 2006. Asst. prof. and Tyser fellow U. Md., College Park, 1997—2002, assoc. prof. and Tyser fellow, 2002—04; prof. and George and Boyce Billingsley chair info. sys. Walton Coll. Bus. U. Ark., Fayetteville, 2004—. Dir. MBA consulting U. of Md., College Park, 2002—04; doctoral program dir. info. sys. U. Ark., Fayetteville, 2004—; assoc. editor Mgmt. Sci., Jour. Assn. of Info. Sys., Info. Sys. Rsch., MIS Quar.; invited spkr. at univs. Contbr. scientific papers to refereed profl. jours., articles. Vol. tax preparation for underprivileged, College Park, Md., 1997—2003, Fayetteville, Ark., 2004—05; donor and social supporter Lions Orgn., Chennai, Tamil Nadu, India, 1995—2006. Recipient Tchg. Innovation award, U. Md., 1998, 2001, Gen. Tchg. Excellence award, 2000, 2003, Celebrating Teachers award, 2002; named Reviewer of the Yr., MIS Quar., 1999, 4th most cited article 1970-2005, Decision Scis. Jour., 2005; grantee, NSF, Microsoft, U.S. Dept. Transportation, Veterans Health Admnstrn. Mem.: Assn. Info. Sys., Inst. Ops. Rsch. and the Mgmnt. Scis. Achievements include research in technology acceptance; design of 10 different courses at the PhD, MBA, and undergraduate levels. Avocations: travel, badminton, racquetball, swimming, stamp collecting/philately. Office: Univ Ark Walton Coll of Bus Fayetteville AR 72701 Business E-Mail: vvenkatesh@vvenkatesh.us.

VENKATESHAN, PRAHALAD, Senior Financial Analyst; b. Chennai, TamilNadu, India, July 23, 1979; s. Maharajapuram Subramanian and Vijaya Venkateshan; m. Nanditha Sankararaman, Dec. 13, 2007. PhD, Case Western Res. U., Cleve., 2006. Mortgage banking fin. analyst AMTRUST Bank, Cleve., 2006—08. Contbr. articles to profl. jours. Office: AMTRUST Bank 1801 E 9th St Cleveland OH 44114 Business E-Mail: pvenkateshan@amtrust.com.

VENKATESWARLU, DIVI, chemistry professor; m. Sumana Choudhury; 1 child, Divi Varun. PhD, North Eastern Hill U., India, 1996. Rsch. assoc. U. NC, Chapel Hill, 1999—2004; asst. prof. NC A&T State U., Greensboro, NC, 2004—. AREA Rsch. grant, NIH, 2007—. Home: 125 Picardy Ct Kernersville NC 27284 Office: NC A&T State Univ 1600 E Market St Greensboro NC 27411 Home Phone: 336-653-6212. Business E-Mail: divi@ncat.edu.

VENKETARAMAN, VISHWANATH, microbiologist, immunologist, educator; s. Thangamani Raman; m. Lakshmi Krishnaswamy. Asst. prof. rsch. track UMDNJ, Newark, 2003—07; asst. prof. Coll. Osteo. Medicine Pacific, Western U. Health Scis., Pomona, Calif., 2008—. Scientist Devel. grant, Am. Heart Assn., 2003—07. Office: Western Univ Health Scis 309 E Second St Pomona CA 91766

VENNING, ROBERT STANLEY, lawyer; b. Boise, Idaho, July 24, 1943; s. William Lucas and Corey Elizabeth (Brown) V.; m. Sandra Macdonald, May 9, 1966 (div. 1976); 1 child, Rachel Elizabeth; m. Laura Siegel, Mar. 24, 1979; 1 child, Daniel Rockhill Siegel. AB, Harvard U., 1965; MA, U. Chgo., 1966; LLB, Yale U., 1970. Bar: Calif., U.S. Dist. Ct. (no. dist.) Calif., 1971, U.S. Dist. Ct. (cen. dist.) Calif. 1973, U.S. Ct. Appeals (9th cir.) 1977, U.S. Supreme Ct. 1977, U.S. Ct. Appeals (fed. cir.) 1986, U.S. Ct. Appeals (D.C. cir.) 1987, U.S. Ct. Fed. Claims 1996. Assoc. Heller Ehrman White & McAuliffe (now known as Heller Ehrman LLP), San Francisco, 1970-73, 73-76, ptnr., 1977—, mem. exec. com., 1991-94. Vis. lectr. U. Wash., Seattle, 1973, Boalt Hall Sch. Law, U. Calif., Berkeley, 1982-85, 89, Sch. Bus., Stanford U., 1986-87. Editor Yale Law Jour., 1969-70. Early neutral evaluator U.S. Dist. Ct. (no. dist.) Calif. Alternative Dispute Resolution Program, 1987—, mediator, 2000-. Fellow Am. Bar Found. (life); mem. ABA, San Francisco Bar Assn. (past chair judiciary com.), CPR Inst. for Dispute Resolution, Olympic Club. Office: Heller Ehrman LLP 333 Bush St San Francisco CA 94104-2878 Office Phone: 415-772-6158. Business E-Mail: robert.venning@hellerehrman.com.

VENTANTONIO, JAMES BARTHOLOMEW, lawyer; b. Orange, NJ, Jan. 5, 1940; s. Benjamin B. and Grace (D'Onofrio) V.; m. Anita L. Winkler, July 7, 1962; children: Peter, Lisa. BS, Seton Hall U., 1961, JD, 1964. Bar: NJ 1965, US Dist. Ct. NJ 1965, US Ct. Mil. Appeals 1965, US Supreme Ct. 1969, NY 1981. Dir. Somerset Sussex Legal Services Corp., NJ, 1969-74; assoc. prof. law Seton Hall U., Newark, 1974-78; atty. Bell Labs., Murray Hill, NJ, 1978-83; gen. atty. NJ Bell Co., Newark, 1983-91; counsel Bell Atlantic, 1991-93; mcpl. prosecutor Bridgewater, NJ, 1996—2000, Manville, 2004—08; mcpl. judge Bridgewater, 2000—03; city solicitor Plainfield, NJ, 2005—; prosecutor South Bound Brook, NJ, 2007—08. Pres. Somerset-Sussex Legal Services Corp., 1978-85. Chmn. govs. adv. com. Legal Services, Trenton, NJ, 1979-83; pres. Community Health Law Project, East Orange, NJ, 1980-81; vice chmn. Somerset Alliance For The Future, 1991-94, mem. bd. visitors, Seton Hall Law Sch., 2004-, vice chair bd. trustees, Raritan Valley C.C., counsel Coun. State Pub. Affairs, 2008-. Served to maj. US Army, 1965-69. Mem. ABA, NJ Bar Assn. (chmn. standing com. on legal services 1979-80), Somerset County C. of C. (chair 1995),

Somerset County Bus. Partnership (founding chair). Home: 747 Foothill Rd W Bridgewater NJ 08807-1804 Office: Ventantonio & Wildenhain 95 Mount Bethel Rd Warren NJ 07059-5126 Home Phone: 908-725-7816; Office Phone: 908-757-3900. Business E-Mail: jventantonio@vwlaw.com.

VENTER, J. CRAIG (JOHN CRAIG VENTER, CRAIG VENTER), science foundation director, geneticist; b. Salt Lake City, Oct. 14, 1946; m. Claire Fraser. BS in Biochemistry, U. Calif., San Diego, 1972, PhD in Physiology and Pharmacology, 1975; D (hon.), Ariz. State U., 2007. Prof. SUNY, Buffalo; with Roswell Pk. Meml. Inst.; sect. and lab chief Nat. Inst. Neurol. Disorders and Stroke NIH, Bethesda, Md., 1984—92; co-founder, chair, chief scientist The Inst. for Genomic Rsch., 1992—98; co-founder, CEO, pres., chief sci. officer Celera Genomics Corp., Rockville, Md., 1998—2002; chmn. sci. adv. bd. Applera Corp., Norwalk, Conn.; chmn., co-founder, pres. The J. Craig Venter Sci. Found. Joint Tech. Ctr., 2003—, J. Craig Vetner Inst.; co-founder, pres. Ctr. for the Advancement Genomics, 2003—, Inst. for Biol. Energy Alternatives, 2003—. Bd. dirs. High Tech. Coun. Md.; mem. sci. adv. bd. ValiGene; chmn., bd. trustees The Inst. for Genomic Rsch. Contbr. several articles to profl. jours.; author: A Life Decoded, My Genome: My Life, 2007. Served in USN, 1967—68, South Vietnam. Recipient Beckman award, 1999, Chiron Corp. Biotech. Rsch. award, 1999, King Faisal Internat. award for sci., 2000, Taylor Internat. prize in medicine, Robarts Rsch. Inst., 2001, Gairdner Found. Internat. award, 2002, Indsl. Application of Sci. award, NAS, 2002, Eni award for rsch. & environment, 2008; named one of The 100 Most Influential People in the World, TIME mag., 2007, 2008, 10 People Who Mattered, Newsweek, 2008. Fellow: AAAS, Am. Soc. Microbiology; mem.: NAS. Achievements include research in functional and comparative analysis of genome and gene products in viruses, eubacteria, pathogenic bacteria, archea and eukaryotes, both in plants and animals including humans; first to use automated gene sequencers; development of expressed sequence tags (ESTs); discovery of more than half of all human genes. Office: J Craig Venter Inst 9712 Medical Ctr Dr Rockville MD 20850 also: J Craig Venter Sci Found 5 Research Pl Rockville MD 20850*

VENTERS, DANIEL JOSEPH, state supreme court justice; b. Charleston, W.Va., Apr. 13, 1950; s. Joseph Coleman and Mary Delores (Brand) Venters; married; 3 children; 2 stepchildren. BS, Ohio State U., 1972; JD, U. Ky., 1975. Bar: Ky. 1975, U.S. Dist. Ct. (ea. dist.) Ky. 1977. Ptnr. Rogers & Venters, Somerset, Ky., 1975-79; pros. atty. Office of Commonwealth's Atty., Somerset, 1975-79; dist. ct. judge 28th Jud. Dist. Ky., Somerset, 1979-84; cir. ct. judge 28th Jud. Cir. Ct. Ky., Somerset; pvt. practice; assoc. justice Ky. State Supreme Ct., 2008—. Mem. Ky. Bd. Bar Examiners. Recipient Outstanding Trial Judge award Ky. Acad. Trial Lawyers, 1986. Mem. ABA, Nat. Conf. State Trial Judges, Ky. Bar Assn., Pulaski County Bar Assn. (sec.-treas. 1975-76). Republican. Methodist. Office: Ky State Supreme Ct Adminstrv Office the Courts 100 Millcreek Pk Frankfort KY 40601 Office Phone: 502-573-2350.*

VENTERS, HARLEY EUGENE, lawyer; b. Okla., Nov. 12, 1922; s. Albert Harley Venters and Margaret Emily Tate; m. Anne Matilda Liccione, Oct. 4, 1946; children: Anne Eleanor, Christopher William, Harley Eugene Jr., Wanda Jean, Shelly Laura. BS, US Mil. Acad., West Point, 1946; LLB, Okla. U. Law Coll., Norman, 1953. Bar: US Supreme Ct. 1971; cert. in advancced single engine tng. course Tex. Air cadet US Army Air Corps, San Antonio, 1942—43; cadet West Point Corps Cadets, NY, 1943—46; lt. US Army, 1946—50; county judge Carter County, Ardmore, Okla., 1953—54, state counsel, 1957—58; state rep. Okla. State Legis., Oklahoma City, 1955—56; presiding judge Okla. State Indsl. Ct., Oklahoma City, 1960—61; sr. ptnr. Venters & Venters, Oklahoma City, 1961—. Bd. dirs. UN Assn.-USA, Oklahoma City. Founder Okla. Interfaith Alliance, Oklahoma City. Decorated Wingsard 2nd Lt. Comdr. Mem.: ACLU, Sierra Club, Phi Alpha Delta. Democrat. Congregationalist. Office Phone: 405-478-1177. Personal E-mail: anneventers@yahoo.com.

VENTERS, TERESA ANNE, elementary school educator; d. William Edward and Rosalie Scott Venters; 1 child, Kelly Nicole McMullen. BS, Ea. Ky. U., 1974; edn. cert., Pikeville Coll., 1988; MA, Morehead State U., 1991. Interior designer Continental Interiors, Pikeville, 1974—76; ins. clk. Pikeville Nat. Bank, 1979—85; dep. clk. County Clk. Ky., Pikeville, 1985—87; reading recovery tchr. Pikeville Ind. Schs., 1988—. Mem. piloted-Ky. edn. learning profile State of Ky., Frankfort, 1991—92, mem. primary adv. com. for continued assessment, 1992—93. Contbr. poetry to anthologies. Mem. Pike County Humane Soc., Pikeville, 1987—; sponsor 4-H, Pikeville, 2000. Mem.: NEA, Pikeville Edn. Assn., Ky. Edn. Assn. Baptist. Avocations: painting, reading. Office: Pikeville Elem 105 Bailey Blvd Pikeville KY 41501

VENTIMIGLIA, MILO ANTHONY, actor; b. Anaheim, Calif., July 8, 1977; s. Peter and Carol Ventimiglia. Attended, UCLA. Actor: (films) Must Be the Junky, 1996, Boys Life 2, 1997, She's All That, 1999, Speedway Junky, 1999, Massholes, 2000, Nice Guys Finish Last, 2001, Winter Break, 2003, Cursed, 2005, Dirty Deeds, 2005, Intelligence, 2006, Stay Alive, 2006, Rocky Balboa, 2006, Pathology, 2008; (TV series) Rewind, 1997, Opposite Sex, 2000, Gilmore Girls, 2001—06, Boston Public, 2003, American Dreams, 2004—05, The Bedford Diaries, 2006, Heroes, 2006—08; (TV films) Gramercy Park, 2004; prodr.: (TV miniseries) Winter Tales, 2007; prodr., dir. (TV miniseries) It's a Mall World, 2007. Avocations: snowboarding, skateboarding, wake boarding. Office: c/o Creative Mgmt Group 9465 Wilshire Blvd Ste 335 Beverly Hills CA 90212

VENTIMIGLIA, VINCENT J., JR., consulting firm executive, former federal agency administrator; b. 1962; married; 5 children. BA magna cum laude, Yale U., 1984; JD, Georgetown U., 1990. Legis. asst. to Senator Gordon Humphrey US Senate Com. on Health Issues, Washington, 1985—88; dir. Capitol Hill Housing Improvement Partnership, 1988—90; staff atty. US Sentencing Commn., 1990—94; counsel to Senator Dan Coats US Senate Labor & Human Resources Com., 1995—98; dir. Govt. Affairs Office Medtronic, Inc., 1998—2001; health policy dir. Health Policy Team US Senate Health Edn. Labor & Pensions Com., 2001—05; policy dir. US Senate Budget Com., 2005; asst. sec. for legis. US Dept. Health & Human Services (HHS), 2005—09; sr. v.p. health & life sciences practice B&D Consulting, Washington, 2009—. Mem.: Md. State Bar Assn. Office: B&D Consulting 1050 K St NW Ste 400 Washington DC 20001 Office Phone: 202-312-7463. Office Fax: 202-312-7460. E-mail: vincent.ventimiglia@bakerd.com.*

VENTO, M. THÉRÈSE, lawyer; b. NYC, June 30, 1951; d. Anthony Joseph and Margaret (Stechert) V.; m. Peter Michael MacNamara, Dec. 23, 1977; children: David Miles, Elyse Anne. BS, U. Fla., 1974, JD, 1976. Bar: Fla. 1977, U.S. Dist. Ct. (so. and mid. dists.) Fla. 1982, U.S. Ct. Appeals (5th and 11th cirs.) 1981, U.S. Supreme Ct. 1985. Clk. to presiding justice U.S. Dist. Ct. (so. dist.) Fla., Miami, 1976-78; assoc. Mahoney, Hadlow & Adams, 1978-79, Shutts & Bowen LLP, 1979-84, ptnr., 1985-95; founding ptnr. Gallwey Gillman Curtis & Vento, P.A., 1995—2004; ptnr. Shutts & Bowen, LLP, 2004—. Trustee Miami Art Mus., 1988—, v.p., 1999—; trustee The Beacon Coun., 1995-97, Law Sch. Alumni Coun., U. Fla., 1994-2004. Fellow Am. Bar Found.; mem. Dade County Bar Assn. (dir. young lawyers sect. 1978-83, editor newsletter 1981-83), Fla. Assn. for Women Lawyers, Fla. Bar Assn. (bd. govs.; young lawyers div. 1983-85, civil procedure rules com. 1983-90, exec. coun. trial lawyers sect. 1996-2004), The Miami Forum (v.p. 1987-88, bd. dirs. 1989-91, co-pres. 2001-2002). Home: 3908 Main Hwy Miami FL 33133-6513 Office: Shutts & Bowen LLP 201 S Biscayne Blvd Ste1500 Miami FL 33131 Office Phone: 305-347-7318. Business E-Mail: TVento@shutts.com.

VENTO, SERGIO, former ambassador; b. May 30, 1938; m. Maria Magdalena Zelent; 2 children. M Polit. Sci., U. Rome. Cabinet sec. State Fgn. Affairs, Italy, 1963—67; 2nd sec. then 1st sec. Italian Embassy, The Hague, Netherlands, 1967—70; Italian consul Buenos Aires, 1970—72; counsellor Italian Embassy, Ankara, 1972—75; with Italian Fgn. Min., 1975—79; 1st counsellor permanent Italian del. Orgn. Cooperation and Devel. Europe, 1979—85; min. plenipoteniary 2nd class, 1985—87; min., fin. min., 1987—89; diplomatic counsel Italy's Prime Min., 1988; chief of mission Italian Embassy, Serbia and Montenegro, 1989—92; diplomatic counsellor Prime Min. Italy, 1992—95; amb. to France, 1995—99; permanent rep. UN, NYC, 1999—2003; Italian amb. to US, 2003; sr. advisor McDermott Will & Emery Studio Legale Associato, Rome. Italian rep. Halifax and Lyon Summits Grp. of Seven. Office: McDermott Will & Emery Via Parigi 11 00185 Rome Italy

VENTOLA, FRANCES ANN, mathematics professor; d. Joseph Robert Kenny and Katherine Julia Franek; m. Ralph Frank Ventola, July 6, 1975; 1 child, Lauren Katherine. BA, Montclair State Coll., Upper Montclair, NJ, 1971; MEd, Rutgers U., New Brunswick, NJ, 1974. Cert. math. tchr. NJ, 1971. Math. tchr. Hazlet Bd. Edn., NJ, 1971—82; prof. math. Brookdale CC, Lincroft, NJ, 1982—. Coord. summer inst. for new precalculus tchrs. & leadership inst. Rutgers U., 1991—91; site coord. for sci. edn. grant NSF. Recipient Outstanding Colleague award, Brookdale C.C., 2000; Rsch. grant, Steven's Inst. Tech., 1994—95. Mem.: NEA, NJ Edn. Assn. Office: Brookdale CC Newman Springs Rd Lincroft NJ 07738

VENTURA, JESSE (JAMES JANOS, "THE BODY"), former Governor of Minnesota, retired professional wrestler; b. Mpls., July 15, 1951; s. George and Bernice Janos; m. Theresa Larson Masters, July 18, 1975; children: Tyrel, Jade. Student, North Hennepin C.C., 1974—75. Profl. wrestler, 1973-84; co-host Saturday Night's Main Event, 1985—90; commentator World Champioship Wrestling, 1992—94; mayor City of Brooklyn Park, Minn., 1991—95; gov. State of Minn., St. Paul, 1999—2003; host The Jesse Ventura Show, 2003—. Actor: (films) Predator, 1987, The Running Man, 1989, No Holds Barred, 1989, Thunderground, 1989, Abraxas, Guardian of the Universe, 1991, Ricochet, 1991, Living and Working in Space: The Countdown Has Begun, 1993, Demolition Man, 1993, Batman and Robin, 1997, 20/20 Vision, 1999, Stuck On You, 2003, (voice only) The Ringer, 2005, Borders, 2008, Woodshop, 2009, (TV appearances) Hunter, 1985, 1990, Zorro, 1991, The X-Files, 1996, Arli$$, 1996; appeared in (documentaries) Beyond the Mat, 1999; author: The Wit and Wisdom of Jesse 'The Body--The Mind' Ventura, 1999, I Ain't Got Time to Bleed: Reworking the Body Politic from the Bottom Up, 1999; co-author (with Julie Mooney): Do I Stand Alone?: Going to the Mat Against Political Pawns and Media Jackals, 2000; (with Heron Marquez) Jesse Ventura Tells It Likes It Is: America's Most Outspoken Governor Speaks Out About Government, 2002, (with Dick Russell) Don't Start the Revolution Without Me!, 2008. Bd. advisors Make a Wish of Minn.; mem. Izaak Walton League America; vol. football coach Champlin Park H.S. Served with Underwater Demolition Team 12 USN, 1969—75, South Vietnam. Decorated Nat. Def. Svc. medal, Vietnam Svc. medal; recipient Iron Mike Mazurki award, Calif. Alley Club, 1999, Frank Gotch award, Internat. Wrestling Inst. & Mus., 2003; named to The World Wrestling Entertainment (WWE) Hall of Fame, 2004. Mem. Am. Fedn. TV & Radio Announcers, Screen Actors Guild. Independent.*

VENTURI, MARGHERITA, chemistry professor, researcher; b. Forlì, Italy, Feb. 6, 1947; d. Boris Venturi and Elisabetta Quercia; m. Sergio Flamigni, Mar. 2, 1972; 1 child, Simona Flamigni. Laurea, U. Bologna, Italy, 1971. Cert. prof. U. Bologna, 2005. Rschr. U. Bologna, 1981—92, assoc. prof., 1992—2005. Office: Dept Chemistry G Ciamician Selmi N 2 Bologna 40126 Italy Business E-Mail: margherita.venturi@unibo.it.

VENTURI, ROBERT, architect; b. Phila., June 25, 1925; s. Robert C. and Vanna (Lanzetta) Venturi; m. Denise Lakofski, July 23, 1967; 1 child, James Charles. Grad., Episcopal Acad., 1944; AB summa cum laude, Princeton U., 1947, MFA, 1950, DFA (hon.), 1983, Oberlin Coll., 1977, Yale U., 1979, U. Pa., 1980; Laurea Honoris Causa in Architecture, U. Rome "La Sapienza", 1994. Designer firms of Oskar Stonorov, Eero Saarinen and Assos., Louis I. Kahn, 1950—58; ptnr. firm Venturi, Cope & Lippincott, Phila., 1958—61, Venturi and Short, Phila., 1961—64, Venturi and Rauch, Phila., 1964—80, Venturi, Rauch & Scott Brown, Phila., 1980—89, Venturi, Scott Brown and Assocs., Inc., 1989—; from asst. to assoc. prof. architecture U. Pa., 1957—65; Charlotte Shepherd Davenport prof. architecture Yale, 1966—70. Author: Complexity and Contradiction in Architecture, 1966, Iconography and Electronics upon a Generic Architecture, 1996; co-author (with Denise Scott Brown and Steven Izenour): Learning from Las Vegas, 1972; 2d edit., 1977; co-author: (with Denise Scott Brown) A View from the Campidoglio, Selected Essays, 1953-84, Architecture as Signs and Systems for a Mannerist Time, 2004; contbr. articles to profl. jours.; prin. works include Vanna Venturi House, Phila., 1961, Guild House, 1961, Humanities Bldg., SUNY, 1972, Franklin Ct., Phila., 1972, addition to Allen Meml. Art Mus., Oberlin Coll., 1973, Inst. for Sci. Info. Corp. Hdqs., Phila., 1978, Gordon Wu Hall, Princeton U., 1980, Seattle Art Mus., 1984, The Nat. Gallery, Sainsbury Wing, London, 1986, Fisher and Bendheim Halls, Princeton U., 1986, Gordon and Virginia MacDonald Med. Rsch. Labs. (with Payette Assocs.), UCLA, 1986, Charles P. Stevenson Jr. Libr., Bard Coll., 1989, Roy and Diana Vagelos Labs. IAST (with Payette Assocs.), U. Pa., 1990, Regional Govt. Bldg., Toulouse, France, 1992, Kirifuri Resort Facilities, Nikko, Japan, 1992, Trabant U. Ctr., U. Del., Newark, 1992, Meml. Hall Restoration and Addition, Harvard U., 1992, The Barnes Found. Restoration and Renovation, Merion, Pa., 1993, Disney Celebration (Fla.) Bank, 1993, Gonda (Goldschmied) Neuroscience and Genetics Rsch. Ctr. (with Lee, Burkhart, Liu Inc.), UCLA, 1993, Princeton Campus Ctr., Princeton U., 1996, Anlyan Ctr. for Med. Rsch. and Edn., Yale U. Sch. Medicine, 1998, (with Payette Assocs.) Master Plan and Buildings for U. Mich., 1997—, Baker/Berry Libr., Dartmouth Coll., 1996, Woodmere Art Mus. addition, 2000, Biomed. Rsch. Bldg., U. Ky., 2000, Dumbarton Oaks Libr. Expansion, Washington, D.C., 2001, Stuart Country Day School Theater/Auditorium/Sanctuary, Princeton, N.J., 2001, Nano Sys. Inst., NC, Santa Barbara, 2001, Lehigh Valley Hosp.-Muhlenberg, Allentown, Pa., 2002, LVH-Cedar Crest, 2003, Episcopal Acad. Chapel, Newtown Sq., Pa., 2004, Congregation Beth El, Sunbury, Pa., 2004, Lenfest Hall, Curtis Inst. Music, Phila., 2006. Trustee Am. Acad. Rome, 1966—71. Decorated comdr. Order Arts and Letters (France); recipient Nat. Medal of Arts, 1992, Pritzker Architecture prize, 1991, Benjamin Franklin medal, The Royal Soc. for Encouragement of Arts, Mfrs. and Commerce, 1993, Vincent J. Scully prize, 2002; fellow Rome Prize Am. Acad., Rome, 1954—56. Fellow: AIA (award 1974, 1977, 1978), Accademia Nazionale di San Luca, Am. Acad. Arts and Scis., Am. Acad. of Arts and Letters, Royal Inc. Architects of Scotland (hon.), Royal Inst. Brit. Architects (hon.), Am. Acad. in Rome; mem.: European Acad. Scis. and Arts, Phi Beta Kappa. Office: Venturi Scott Brown & Assocs Inc 4236 Main St Philadelphia PA 19127-1603 Office Phone: 215-487-0400. Business E-Mail: venturi@vsba.com.

VENTURINI, JUDITH ANNE, education educator; b. Oakland, Calif. d. Arthur Francis Venturini and Germaine Junet. BS, Calif. State U., Hayward, 1969, MS in Phys. Edn., 1985, MS in Edn. Leadership, 1991; MS in Edn., Nat. U., San Jose, Calif., 1999. Practitioner of science of mind RScP. Tchr., adminstrv. intern Redwood City (Calif.) Elem. Sch. Dist., 1970—91; edn1. cons., exec. dir. Kids-at-Heart, Fremint, Calif., 1991—94; D.A.T.E. coord. Hayward Unified Sch. Dist., 1994; regional dir. Sonoma County Office of Edn., Santa Rosa, Calif., 1994—95; prin. tchr. San Jose Unified Sch. Dist., 1995—2000; spl. edn. tchr. for autistic students Santa Clara County Office of Edn., San Jose, 2001—02; adj. prof. Calif. State U., Hayward, 2000—, Nat. U., San Jose, 2000—, Nat. Hispanic U., San Jose, 2000—. Facilities chair Bay Area Career Women, San Francisco, 1987—90; chair Sonoma County Phys. Edn. Com., Santa Rosa, Calif., 1994—95; dir. Sonoma County Office of Edn. Gang Prevention Network Task Force, Santa Rosa, 1994—95. Contbr. poetry to anthologies. Bd. dirs. Ardenwood Homeowners, Fremont, Calif., 1987—88; practitioner, divinity student Ctr. of Positive Living, 2000—. Recipient multiple honors in athletics, Playmates award, Calif. Dept. Edn., 1994, Healthy Start award, 1994, 1996, award for inspirational programs for children, Housing Authority of Santa Clara County, 2000. Mem.: NEA, Calif. Tchrs. Assn. Avocations: dancesport, poetry, art, golf, writing songs. Home: 5206 Tacoma Ln Fremont CA 94555 Office: Kids-at-Heart 5206 Tacoma Ln Fremont CA 94555 Personal E-mail: junu@earthlink.net, jav123@earthlink.net.

VENUTI, ELAINE M., biology professor; d. John and Florence Venuti. BSc, Thomas Jefferson U., Phila., 1988, MSc, 1994. Cert. med. technologist Am. Soc. Clin. Pathology. Microbiology technologist Methodist Hosp., Phila., 2002—; asst. prof. Montgomery County CC, Bluebell, 2004—. Mem.: Am. Soc. Clin. Pathology, Am. Soc. Microbiology. Office: Montgomery County CC 340 Dekalb Pike Blue Bell PA 19422

VENZAGO, MARIO, conductor, former music director; b. Zurich, Switzerland, 1948; m. Marianne Venzago; children: Mario, Gabriel. Studied with Hans Swarowsky, Vienna; studied with Leonard Bernstein, LA Philharm. Inst. Music dir. Stadtorchester Winterthur, Switzerland, 1978—86, Heidelberg Opera, Germany, 1986—89, Deutsche Kammerphilharmonie, Frankfurt/Bremen, Germany, 1989—92, Graz Opera Ho., Austria, 1990—95, Basel Symphony Orch., 1997—2003, Basque Euskadi Nat. Orch., Spain, 1998—2001, Indpls. Symphony Orch., 2002—09, Swedish Nat. Orch., 2003—; prin. condr. Gothenburg Symphony Orch., Sweden, 2004—07. Artistic dir. Balt. Symphony Orch. Summer Music Fest, 2000—03. Guest condr. Berlin Philharm., BBC, London, Leipzig Gewandhaus Orch., London Philharm., City of Birmingham Symphony, Orchestre de la Suisse Romande, Phila. Orch., Tonhalle Orch. Zurich, Tokyo's NHK Symphony, Berlin's Komische Opera, Salzburg Festival; guest condr.: Boston Symphony, Helsinki Philharm., Helsinki Radio; guest condr. Lucerne Opera Ho., Am. debut Hollywood Bowl, 1988, appeared with NJ Symphony, Indpls. Symphony Orch., Fla. Philharm., 1988. Mailing: c/o Jessica Ford Intermusica Artists Mgmt Ltd 16 Duncan Terrace London N1 8BZ England also: c/o Bill Capone Arts Mgmt Group 37 W 26th St Ste 403 New York NY 10010*

VEPRASKAS, MICHAEL J., soil scientist, educator; b. Beloit, Wis., Nov. 17, 1951; s. Michael D. and Olga Vepraskas; m. Claudia J. Nuedling, June 2, 1973; children: Matthew J., Laura A. BS, U. Wis., Madison, 1973, MS, 1975; PhD, Tex. A&M U., Coll. Sta., 1980. Lic. NC Bd. Lic. Soil Scientists, 1996. Asst. prof. NC State U., Raleigh, 1980—86, assoc. prof., 1986—93, prof., 1993—2008, William Neal Reynolds disting. prof., 2008—. Author: (textbook) Wetland Soils. Fullbright fellow, Agrl. U., Wageningen, Netherlands, 1988—89. Fellow: Soil Sci. Soc. America (tech. editor 1999—2005, award 2000, Rsch. award 2004, Edn. award 2006); mem.: AAAS, Soc. Wetland Scientists (assoc. editor 1999—2001), Am. Soc. Agronomy. Office: NC State Univ PO Box 7619 Raleigh NC 27695-7619

VÉR, ISTVÁN LÁSZLÓ, acoustical engineer, consultant; b. Tápiószecsö, Hungary, Dec. 22, 1934; came to U.S., 1965; s. István and Erzsebet G. V.; 1 child, Kristina M. BSEE, Tech. U., Budapest, 1956; MSEE, Tech. U., Aachen, Germany, 1960; PhD in Acoustics, Tech. U., Munich, 1963. R&D engr. Rohde and Schwarz, Munich, 1960-65; prin. cons. BBN Techs., Cambridge, Mass., 1965—2000; ind. cons. acoustics, noise and vibration control, 2000—. Vis. scientist Indian Inst. Sci., Bangalore, India, 2005. Author, editor: Noise & Vibration Control Engineering, 1992, 2005; holder patents. Recipient U.S. Sr. Scientist award Alexander von Humboldt Found., Germany, 1978, Best Paper award Am. Soc. Heating and Refrigeration Engring., 1979. Fellow Acoustical Soc. Am.; mem. Inst. Noise Control Engring. USA (dir. 1976-77), European Acoustics Assn. Avocations: literature, philosophy, travel, tennis. Office Phone: 978-568-0556. Business E-Mail: iver@onemain.com.

VERANT, WILLIAM J., state banking agency administrator; b. Washington, Dec. 19, 1941; m. Donna M. Verant; children: Bill Jr., Sharon. BSBA, Am. U., Washington, DC. V.p. Fed. Home Mortgage Corp., Calif.; dept. head comml. and multi-family real estate loans/assets Resolution Trust Corp., Newport Beach, Calif.; dir. fin. instns. divsn. N.Mex. Regulation and Licensing Dept., Santa Fe, 1995—, acting dir. securities divsn. Avocation: restoring old cars. Office: NMex Fin Instns Divsn PO Box 25101 Santa Fe NM 87504 Office Phone: 505-476-4885. Office Fax: 505-476-4670. E-mail: william.verant@state.nm.us.*

VERBA, LINDA, bank executive; m. Bob Hofman; 1 child, Mackenzie. BS in Edn., Pa. State U. With Filene's, Boston, Strawbridge & Clothier; head, human resources PHH Mortgage, head, call ctr.; sr. v.p. retail banking Commerce Bancorp, Inc., exec. v.p. retail ops., 2006—. Bd. mem. Am. Heart Assn., South Jersey C. of C., Arts & Bus. Coun./Greater Phila. C. of C. Recipient Shatter the Glass Ceiling award, Nat. Assn. Women Bus. Owners, 2005; named one of 25 Women to Watch, US Banker, 2007, Best 50 Women in Bus., NJBIZ mag., 2007. Office: Commerce Bancorp Inc 17000 Horizon Way Mount Laurel NJ 08054-5105 Office Phone: 856-533-1170.

VERBA, SIDNEY, political science professor, retired library director; b. Bklyn., May 26, 1932; s. Morris Harold and Recci (Salman) Verba; m. E. Cynthia Winston, June 17, 1955; children: Margaret Lynn, Ericka Kim, Martina Claire. BA, Harvard U., 1953; MA, Princeton U., 1955, PhD, 1959. Asst. prof. polit. sci. Princeton U., 1960-63, assoc. prof.,

1963-64; prof. Stanford U., 1964-68, U. Chgo., 1968-72; prof. govt. Harvard U., 1972—, chmn. dept. govt., 1976-80, Carl H. Pforzheimer U. Prof., assoc. dean Faculty Arts and Sciences, 1981—84; dir. Harvard U. Libr., 1984—2007. Chmn. bd. dirs. Harvard U. Press, 1991-2005; chmn. policy com. Social Sci. Rsch. Coun., 1980-86; mem. Commn. on Behavioral and Social Sciences, NRC, 1986-91; Commn. on Preservation and Access, chair com. on internat. conflict and cooperation, NRC, 1991-93; vis. com. MIT Polit. Sci. Dept.; bd. dirs. Social Sci. Rsch. Coun.; Tanner Lectr., Oxford, 1998. Author: Small Groups and Political Behavior, 1961, The Civic Culture, 1963, Caste, Race and Politics, 1969, Participation in America, 1972 (Gladys Kammerer Award, Am. Polit. Sci. Assn., 1972), Vietnam and the Silent Majority, 1972, The Changing American Voter, 1976 (Woodrow Wilson Found. Award, Am. Polit. Sci. Found., 1976), Participation and Political Equality, 1978, Injury to Insult, 1979, Introduction to American Government, 1983, Equality in America, 1985, Elites and the Idea of Equality, 1987, Designing Social Inquiry, 1994, Voice and Equality, 1995, The Private Roots of Public Action, 2001. Recipient Johan Skytte Prize in Polit. Sci., Skytte Found., 2002; Guggenheim Fellow, 1980-81. Fellow: Am. Acad. Arts and Sciences; mem.: NAS (chair social and polit. sci. sect. 2002-), Am. Philos. Soc., Am. Polit. Sci. Assn. (exec. coun. 1971-74, v.p. 1979-81, pres.-elect 1993-94, pres. 1994-95, James Madison Award 1993, Warren Miller Award 2000), Internat. Studies Assn. (v.p. 1971-72, John Skytte prize 2002). Jewish. Office: Harvard Univ Govt Dept 1737 Cambridge St Cambridge MA 02138 Office Phone: 617-495-4421. Business E-Mail: sverba@harvard.edu.

VERBECK, ALISON, librarian; b. St. Louis, Jan. 9, 1961; d. Robert and Nancy Van Patten; m. Mark Verbeck, June 7, 1980; children: Megan, Ryan. BS in Physics, U. Mo., Columbia, 1983, MLS, 1984. Libr. Union Electric Co., St. Louis, 1985—98; physics libr. Wash. U., St. Louis, 1998—. Mem.: Spl. Librs. Assn. (treas. 2002—04). Office: Wash Univ Physics Libr 1 Brookings Dr Saint Louis MO 63130

VERBEKE, JOHAN C., ambassador; b. 1951; married; 3 children. MA, LLD, Ghent U., Belgium, 1974; diploma, U. de Nancy, France, 1975; LLM, Yale U., New Haven, 1978. Asst. prof. European law U. Ghent, 1975—77; jr. assoc. lawyer Cleary, Gottlieb, Steen & Hamilton, NYC, 1978—81; diplomat Govt. Belgium, Beirut, 1982, Amman, Jordan, 1984, Bujumbura, Burundi, 1985, Santiago, Chile, 1988, spokesman Ministry Fgn. Affairs, 1990, diplomat Mission to European Union, 1993, dep. chief of mission Washington DC, 1994, dep. dir. gen. polit. affairs Ministry Fgn. Affairs, 1998, chef de cabinet of min. fgn. affairs, 2000, permanent rep. to UN NYC, 2004—08; spl. coord. for Lebanon UN, 2008—, sec.-general's spl. rep. in Georgia, head, UN Observer Mission in Georgia, 2008—. Office: c/o UN Hdqs First Ave at 46th St New York NY 10017

VERBITSKY, VLADIMIR, conductor; b. Leningrad, USSR; Grad., Leningrad Conservatoire; studied with Yevgeny Mravinsky. Conducting debut, Moscow; condr. Moscow Orch., St. Petersburg (Russia) Orch., Russia; chief condr., music dir. Voronezh Philharm., 1972—; condr., condr. laureate West Australian Symphony Orch., Perth, Australia, 1997—; music dir. Slovak Philharmonic Orchestra, Bratislava, Czech Republic, 1982—84, State Orchestra of Victoria, Melbourne, Australia, 1987—88; U.S. engagements with Fla. Orch., Tucson Symphony; U.S. engagement with Naples Philharmonic Orch., Fla. Guest condr. in Russia State Orch. of the USSR, Moscow Philharmonic Orch., St. Petersburg Philharmonic Orch., St. Petersburg Academic Symphony Orch., Saratov Philharmonic, Novosibirsk Philharmonic, Lipetzk Philharmonic, Omsk Philharmonic Orch.; guest condr. in Australia Adelaide Symphony Orch., Queensland Symphony Orch., Sydney Symphony Orch., Melbourne Symphony Orch., Canberra Philharmonic Orch., State Orch. of Victoria, West Australian Symphony Orch., Tasmanian Symphony Orch., Australia; guest condr. in New Zealand Auckland Philharmonic Orch., Christchurch Symphony Orch., Southern Sinfonia; guest condr. Azerbaijan Philharmonic Orch., Bratislava Philharmonic Orch., Budapest Radio and Television Orch., Trondheim Symphony Orch., Saarbrucken Radio Orch., Baden-Baden Philharmonic Orch., Lucerne Symphony Orch., Nice Philharmonic Orchestra, France, Cape Town Philharmonic Orchestra, South Africa, Prague Radio Symphony Orch., Nat. Symphony Orchestra, Taipei, Kaohsiung Symphony Orch., Mex. Philharmonic Orch.; guest condr., opera/ballet Eugene Onegin, Madama Butterfly, Carmina Burana, Storm, Aleko; guest condr., festivals Tchaikovsky Festival, Izhevsk, Votkinsk, Rachmaninov Festival, Tambov, Taneev Festival, Vladimir, Glinka Festival, Smolensk, White Nights Festival, St. Petersburg, Russia, Bratislavske Slavnosti Festival, Prague Autumn Festival, Pragske Jaro Festival, Prague, Castlemaine Festival, Victoria, Australia; guest condr., youth orchs., competitions Australian Nat. Acad. Music, Western Australia Youth Music Assn., Voronezh Acad. Music, Symphony Australia Young Performer of Yr. Award, Cello Competition, Starts of XXI Century - Young Talents of Russia, Goldsmiths U. London. Condr. recordings: ABC Classics, Melodia, Olympia, Opus, Prestige Classics, Musicline London Ltd., Classic Visions, Internat. Music Co. AG, Sontel AG, Vista Vera CD. Decorated Order Badge of Hon. Moscow, Order for Svcs. to Fatherland; recipient diploma, Herbert von Karajan Internat. Conductors Competition, Berlin, 1973, Laureate, Villa Lobos Internat. Conductors' Competition, Rio de Janiero, 1975, Hungarian Radio and TV Conductors' Competition, Budapest, 1976; named People's Artist, Russian Fedn. Office: West Australian Symphony Orchestra PO Box Y3041 East St Georges Tce Perth 6832 Australia Home Phone: 7 812 3552411; Office Phone: 7 812 3552411. Personal E-mail: vnverbitsky@aol.com. Business E-Mail: vnvertitsky@yandex.ru.

VERBURG, EDWIN ARNOLD, management consultant; b. Lakehurst, NJ, Oct. 6, 1945; s. Edwin Donald Verburg and Dorothy (Orrell) Hoodless; m. Joyce Elaine Majack, Sept. 14, 1968; children: Adelle Kristine, Wendi Elizabeth. BS, Calif. Poly. U., 1968; M in City Planning, U. Calif., Berkeley, 1970; D in Pub. Adminstrn., George Washington U., 1975. Asst. planner City of Inglewood, Calif., 1970-71; planner City of Glendale, Calif., 1971-72; grad. assoc. U.S. Army Corps Engrs., Washington, 1974-75; mgr. fiscal analysis Met. Washington Coun. Govt., 1975-77; sr. program analyst U.S. Fish and Wildlife Svc., Washington, 1977-79, asst. divsn. chief, 1979-80, divsn. chief, 1980-82, asst. dir. planning and budget, 1982-86, dep. asst. dir. policy budget and adminstrn., 1986-87; dir. office of fin. U.S. Dept. Treas., Washington, 1987-88, dir. fin. svc. directorate, 1988-91, dir. fin. svc. directorate, dep. CFO, 1991-95; assoc. adminstr. adminstrn. FAA, 1995-98; prin. ptnr. Avant Mgmt. Group, Inc., 1998-99; prin., fedn. govt. svc. Kelly, Anderson & Assocs., 1999—2002, v.p., 2003—08, trustee, bd. dirs., 2005—07, sr. assoc., 2008—. Author: Local State and Federal Fiscal Flows, 5 Vols., 1976; contbr. articles to profl. jours. Recipient Disting. Pub. Svc. award George Washington U., Sch. Bus. and Pub. Mgmt., 1994, Sec. of Treasury Disting Svc. award, 1995, Fin. Mgmt. Svc. Commr. award, 1996. Mem. Am. Inst. Cert. Planners, Am. Planning Assn. (Merit award Calif. chpt. 1973, First award Nat. Capital area chpt. 1980, Peer award for pub. svc. Dept. of Treasury 1990, sec. of treas. cert. appreciation 1991, Pres.'s Meritorious Svc. award 1991, Commr. Citation Fin. Mgmt. Svc. 1996, Pres. award Combined Fed. Campaign 1997), Kiwanis (Arlington chpt. bd. dirs. 1999-2001, v.p. 2001-02, pres.-elect 2002-03, disting. pres. 2003-04, Capitol dist. disting. lt. gov. 20th divsn. capitol dist. Kiwanis Internat. 2005-06, Tucson-de Amigos chpt. bd. dirs. 2009-, Hixson award 2004), Assn. Govt. Accountants (cert. govt. fin. mgr.). Office: Kelly Andersen & Assocs Inc 424 N Washington St Alexandria VA 22314-2312 Home: 5555 W Lazy C Dr Tucson AZ 85745-9055 Personal E-mail: eaverburg@yahoo.com.

VERCAMMEN, KENNETH ALBERT, lawyer, prosecutor; b. Edison, NJ, Aug. 7, 1959; BS, U. Scranton, 1981; JD, Univ. Del. Law Sch., 1985. Bar: N.J., Pa. 1985, N.Y. 1986, D.C. 1987; cert. mediator N.J. Superior Ct., 1997-. Mng. atty., Cranbury, NJ, 1990—; prosecutor Township of Cranbury, Middlesex County, NJ, 1991—99; spl. acting prosecutor Delaware County, Pa. District Office, Middlesex County Probation Dept., Scranton Dist. Magistrate Office, Woodbridge, East Brunswick, Metuchen, South Brunswick, Clark, Berkeley; acting assoc. prosecutor Carteret Mcpl. Ct., Middlesex County, NJ, 2000. Adj. prof. Middlesex County Coll., Edison, 1990-91, 2001; instr. criminal law and procedure and bus. law; mem. com. mcpl. ct. edn. N.J. Supreme Ct., 1990-97; spkr. litig. engagements, wills, elder law and probate. Author 132 separate law rev. and legal periodicals articles to profl. jours. including N.J. Law Jour., ABA Barrister, N.J. Lawyer, ABA Law Practice Mgmt., Dictum; editor N.J. Municipal Ct. Law Review, 1993-; author, DWI & Drug Cases, 2005. Winner of NJ State Bar Gen. Practitioner of Yr. award, 2002, Atty. of Yr. award NJ Bar Assn. Mcpl. Ct., 2006. Mem.: N.J. State Bar Assn. (chair mcpl. ct. sect.), Middlesex Mcpl. Prosecutor's Assn. (co-chmn. mcpl. ct. practice com. 1997—, mem. bd. trustees 2000—). Avocations: cross-country running, soccer. Office: 2053 Woodbridge Ave Edison NJ 08817

VERCELLOTTI, JOHN RAYMOND, chemist, researcher; b. Joliet, Ill., May 2, 1933; s. Joseph Francis and Mary Teresa (Walowski) V.; m. Sharon Cecile Vergez, Sept. 3, 1966; children: Ellen Theresa, Paul Auguste. BA, St. Bonaventure U., 1955; MS, Marquette U., 1960; PhD, Ohio State U., 1963. Lectr., rsch. assoc. Ohio State U., Columbus, 1963-64; asst. prof. Marquette U., Milw., 1964-67; assoc. prof. U. Tenn., Knoxville, 1967-70; prof. Va. Poly. Inst. & State U., Blacksburg, 1970-79; vis. prof. Inst. G. Ronzoni, Milan, 1977-78; sr. scientist Gulf South Res. Inst., New Orleans, 1980-85; rsch. chemist, rsch. leader So. Regional Rsch. Ctr. USDA, New Orleans, 1985-96, collaborator, 1999—. V.p. and sr. chemist V-Labs Inc., Covington, La., 1980-85, 96—; sr. rsch. advisor Sugar Processing Rsch. Inst., Inc., New Orleans, 1996-99, 2001--; adj. prof. chemistry and physics S.E. La. U., Hammond, 1986—. Contbr. articles to profl. jours., chapters to books. U. Tenn. minority colls. grantee, 1968-70, NSF grantee, 1964—. Fellow Sigma Xi; mem. Am. Chem. Soc. (sec. 1968-90, Melville L. Wolfrom award 1994), Inst. Food Technologists. Democrat. Roman Catholic. Achievements include research on food flavor quality and agricultural commodity utilization, origin of flavor from carbohydrates, lipid oxidation products, and peptides. Home: 113 E 25th Ave Covington LA 70433-2819 Office: V-Labs Inc 423 N Theard St Covington LA 70433-2837 Office Phone: 985-893-0533. Business E-Mail: v-labs@v-labs.com.

VERDIER, DAVID D'OOGE, ophthalmologist, educator; b. Grand Rapids, Mich., Jan. 22, 1949; s. Leonard D'Ooge and Anita Beatrice (Carvalho) V.; m. Beverly Deane Johnson; children: Renée Leigh, Travis D'Ooge, Eric Leonard, Nora Claire. BA in Polit. Sci., U. Mich., 1971; MD, U. Mich. Med. Sch., 1977. Resident in family practice Med. U. S.C., Charleston, 1977-80; resident in ophthalmology Pitts. Eye and Ear, U. Pitts., 1980-83; corneal and external eye fellowship U. Iowa, Iowa City, 1983-84; pvt. practice med. and surg. ophthalmology Verdier Eye Ctr. P.L.C., Grand Rapids, Mich., 1984—; clin. prof. Mich. State U. Coll. Medicine, East Lansing, 1986—. Med. dir. Mich. Tissue Bank, Lansing, Mich., 1995-98; mem. med. adv. bd. Eye Bank Assn. Am. 2003-, Cape Elethra Found., 2004—. Contbr. articles to profl. jours. and textbook chpts. Bd. dirs. East Grand Rapids (Mich.) Sch. Found., 1992-2000, Macatawa Bay Yacht Club, Holland, Mich., 1988-90, 94-95, Grand Rapids Art Mus., 1995-2001; bd. dirs. Macatawa Park Cottagers Assn., Holland, 1993-99, pres., 1993-98. Named to Galens Hon. Med. Soc., 1975-77. Mem. Mich. Ophthalmologic Soc. (bd. dirs. 1994-2000), Mich. State Med. Soc. (del. 1993-2000, Eye Bank Assn. Am. (med adv bd. 2003—). Home: 3043 Mary St SE Grand Rapids MI 49506-3150 Office: Verdier Eye Center PLC 1000 E Paris Ave SE Ste 130 Grand Rapids MI 49546-3680 Office Phone: 616-949-2001.

VERDILE, VINCENT PAUL, dean, emergency physician; b. Troy, NY, Aug. 13, 1955; s. Raphael Mario and Frances (Marinucci) V.; m. Louise Ann Wickware, Aug. 30, 1985. BS, Union U., 1977, MS, 1980; MD, Albany Med. Coll., 1984. Intern U. Pitts., 1984-85, resident in emergency medicine, 1985-87; assoc. med. dir. dept. pub. safety City of Pitts., 1985—93; flight physician Ctr. for Emergency Medicine, Pitts., 1988—93; chair. dept. of emergency med. Albany Med. Coll., 1993—2000, interim dean, 2000, dean, 2001—. Mem. adj. staff dept. emergency medicine Mercy Hosp., Pitts, 1987—93; med. dir., emergency med. technician Community Coll. Allegheny Coll., 1987—93; attending physician emergency dept. Presbyn.-Univ. Hosp., 1987—93; assoc. program dir. residency in emergency medicine Univ. of Pitts., 1987—93, asst. prof. medicine, 1987—93. Contbr. numerous articles to profl. jours. Mem. Soc. Acad. Emergency Medicine, Nat. Assn. Emergency Med. Svcs. Physicians (chmn. membership com. 1988—), Am. Coll. Emergency Physicians, Pa. chpt. Am. Coll. Emergency Physicians, Pa. State Med. Soc., Allegheny County Med. Soc., Am. Assn. Poison Control Ctrs. Roman Catholic. Office: Albany Med Coll Office of Dean 43 New Scotland Ave Albany NY 12208*

VER DUIN, D'ARLENE K., sociologist, researcher; m. O. Lynn Sims, Mar. 15, 1996. BA in Sociology, U. North Tex., Denton, 1995, MPA, 1998. Rsch. scientist U. North Tex., 1999—. Author: (plays) Not Even a Goodbye, 1983. Mem. Ft. Worth Civic Orch. (pres. 1985-87), Pi Alpha Alpha. Democrat. Christian. Avocations: genealogy, needle arts, viola. Office: Univ North Tex Survey Rsch Ctr PO Box 310637 Denton TX 76203 Office Phone: 940-565-4939. Business E-Mail: dverduin@unt.edu.

VEREB, TERESA B., psychiatrist; b. Poland; d. Joseph and Henryka Biskup; m. Bartholomew Vereb, Aug. 3, 1968; children: Bartholomew Jr., Teresa Tilden. MD, Acad. Medicine, Warsaw, 1966. Cert. stress mgmt. Am. Acad. Experts in Traumatic Stress, 2005. Resident psychiatry Hosp. Wolsky, Warsaw, 1966—68, Med. Sch. Safarik U., Kosice, Czech Republic, 1968—70, staff psychiatry, 1971—72; resident psychiatry SUNY, Buffalo, 1977—78; clin. instr. psychiatry Meyer Meml. Hosp., Buffalo, 1977—78; resident psychiatry U. Fla., Gainesville, 1978—80; pvt. practice gen. psychiatry Bradenton, Fla., 1980—; staff psychiatrist Blake Hosp., Bradenton, 1980—, Manatee Meml. Hosp., Bradenton, 1980—, chief psychiatry, sectional chief psychiatry, 1981—85, 1987—91, chairperson psychiat. sect., 2000. Active Sacred Heart Cath. Ch., Bradenton, 1980—. Recipient Disting. Physician award, Fla. Med. Assn., 2005; named Profl. of Yr., 2008; named to Am. Top Psychiatrists, Consumer's Rsch. Coun. Am., 2006, 2007. Mem.: AMA (Physician Recognition award 1995—2002, 2005—06), Am. Acad. Experts in Traumatic Stress, Manatee County Med. Soc., Fla. Psychiat. Assn., Fla. Med. Assn. (Physician Recognition award 1995—2005, Rogeriem Pfizer Re-Commn. 1999, Am. Top Rate Physician 1999, Top Psychiatrist 2004—08, Boar Cert. for stress mgmt. 2005, Am. Top Rate Physician 2008), Am. Psychiat. Assn. Achievements include successfully climbed Mount Kilimanjaro, 1997. Avocations: water-skiing, skiing, swimming, hiking, mountain climbing. Office: Vereb and Vereb MDs PA 5015 Manatee Ave West Bradenton FL 34209

VEREBEY, KARL GEZA, toxicologist, pharmacologist, educator; b. Budapest, Hungary, Mar. 12, 1938; came to U.S., 1956; s. Karoly and Etelka (Szabo) V.; m. Debra Adler, Feb. 22, 1962; children: Rita, Todd, Marc. AA, Eotvos J. Gimnazium, Budapest, Hungary, 1956; BA, Hunter Coll., 1965; MA, CUNY, 1968; PhD, Cornell U. Med. Coll., 1972. Diplomate Am. Bd. Forensic Toxicology; cert. clin. lab. dir. Am. Bd. Bioanalysis; lic. clin. lab. dir., N.Y., N.J., Ill., Md., Vt. Dir. clin. pharmacology State of N.Y., NYC, 1973-88; dir. clin. lab. Psychiat. Diagnostic Lab. Am., South Plainfield, N.J., 1982-89; chief toxicologist City of N.Y., 1989-92; dir. toxicology N.Y. State Inst. Basic Rsch., SI, 1992-95; pres., dir. Leadtech Corp., North Bergen, NJ, 1992—2001; dir. Ammon Analytical Lab., 1999—. Assoc. prof. SUNY Health Sci. Ctr., 1978-2000; mem. exec. com. Drug Abuse Adv. Bd., N.Y. State Dept. Health, 1985; advisor subcom. on trace metals analysis to Nat. Com. Clin. Lab. Stds., 1992; insp. Nat. Lab. Cert. Program dept. Health and Human Svcs., 1989. Mem. editl. bd. Jour. Addictive Diseases, 1981; contbr. over 100 articles to sci. jours., chpts. to books. With U.S. Army, 1961-63. Rsch. fellow USPHS, 1968-73; grantee Cornell U. Med. Coll., 1974-77, Narcotic and Drug Rsch., Inc., 1974-76, 79-81, DuPont Pharm., 1985; inductee Hunter Coll. Hall of Fame, 1989; named Water Polo Nat. Champion, NY Athletic Club, 1959, 60, 61. Fellow Am. Acad. Forensic Sci.; mem. Am. Soc. Pharmacology and Exptl. Therapeutics, Soc. Forensic Toxicologists. Internat. Assoc. Forensic Toxicologists. Avocations: water polo, kayaking, tennis, photography. Home: 638 Debchar Ct River Vale NJ 07675-6409 Home Phone: 201-391-0015; Office Phone: 908-862-4404. Personal E-mail: k.verebey@att.net.

VEREEN, ROBERT CHARLES, retired trade association administrator; b. Stillwater, Minn., Sept. 8, 1924; s. George and Leona Lucille (Made) Wihren; m. Rose Catherine Blair, Nov. 5, 1945; children: Robin, Stacy, Kim. Grad. high sch. Mng. editor Comml. West Mag., Mpls., 1946-50, Bruce Pub. Co., St. Paul, 1950-53, Nat. Retail Hardware Assn., Indpls., 1953-59; mng. dir. Liberty Distbrs., Phila., 1959-63; editor Hardware Retailing, Indpls., 1963-80; assoc. pub., dir. communications Nat. Retail Hardware Assn., 1980-84, sr. v.p., 1984-87; Vereen & Assocs., Mgmt., Mktg. Cons., 1987—. Lectr. mgmt. insts.; guest lectr. on distbn. pub.; co-founder U.S.A. Direct; co-founder, ptnr. Eurotrade Mktg., 1988-2005; ptnr. Hardlines Pers. Finders, 1987-2006. Author: (with Paul M. Doane) Hunting for Profit, 1965, The Computer Age in Merchandising, 1968, Perpetuating the Family-Owned Business, 1970, The How-To of Merchandising, 1975, The How-To of Store Operations, 1976, A Guide to Financial Management, 1976, Productivity: A Crisis for Management, 1978, Hardlines Rep Report Newsletter, 1984-94, Guidelines to Improve the Rep/Factory Relationships, 1992; contbr. articles to profl. jours. and mags. Served with AUS, 1943-46. Mem. Am. Soc. Bus. Press Editors (dir., v.p. 1966-70), Soc. Nat. Assn. Publs. (dir., pres. 1970-75, chmn. journalism edn. liaison com. 1976-79), Toastmasters (v.p., treas., sec. 1955-59), Am. Hardware Mfrs. Assn. (co-founder, sec.-treas. Young Execs. Club 1958-.59, 63-65), Hardware-Housewares Packaging Expn. (founder 1960, chmn. com. packaging 1960-62, chmn. judging com. Hardware-Packaging Expn. 1975-78), Packaging Inst., Household Consumer Products Export Coun. (chmn. 1981-83), World-Wide DIY Coun. (exec. sec. 1981-99, dir. emeritus 1999-2007, newsletter editor, 2008-). Home and Office: 10769 Oriole Ct Indianapolis IN 46231-1006

VERGE, PIERRE, legal educator; b. Quebec City, Can., Jan. 9, 1936; s. Francis and Regina (Roy) V.; m. Colette Habel, June 29, 1963; children— Marc, Caroline, Louis. BA, Laval U., 1956, LL.L., 1959, LL.D., 1971; MA, McGill U., 1962, Cambridge U., 1977; LL.M., U. Toronto, 1968; 1971. Bar: Que. 1961, Queen's Counsel 1976. Pvt. practice law, Quebec City, Can., 1961-66; mem. faculty Laval U. Faculty of Law, 1966—, dean, 1973-77, prof. emeritus, 2003—. Commonwealth fellow St. John's Coll., Cambridge U., 1977-78 Mem. Assn. Can. Law Tchrs. (pres. 1972-73, chmn. conf. law deans 1975-76), Que. Bar, Canadian Bar, Royal Soc. Can. Home: 2542 avenue de Parc-Falaise Sillery PQ Canada G1T 1W3 Office: Cite Universitaire Universite Laval Quebec City PQ Canada

VERGNAUD, JEAN-MAURICE, science educator, researcher; b. Audincourt, Doubs, France, Dec. 3, 1932; s. Joseph and Marie-Louise (Buthod-Ruffier) V.; m. Michele Trouin, Dec. 20, 1979. MS, U. Lyon, France, 1956, PhD in Chromatography, 1965; PhD in Catalysis, U. Dijon, France, 1960. Engr. CEA, Paris, 1959, Progil, Lyon, 1960-68; prof. U. Algiers, Algeria, 1968-71, U. St. Etienne, France, 1972—. Spkr. in field. Author: Drying of Polymeric and Solid Materials, 1992, Cure of Thermosetting Resins, 1992, Dosage Forms for Controlled Release with Polymers, 1993, Liquid Transport Processes in Polymeric Materials, 1994, Assessing Bioavailability of Drug Delivery Systems, 2005, Assessing Food Safety with Polymer Packaging, 2006, In the Light of Gabe, Birth of an Engineer, 2006; Cure of Rubbers: Process and Applications, 2008; mem. editl. adv. bd. Polymer Testing, Rubber Plastics and Composites, Polymer and Polymer Composites, Jour. Polymer Engring., Jour. Drying Tech.; referee Am. Assn. Pharm. Sci., 7 jours. on polymers and 2 jours. on pharmacy; contbr. over 500 articles to internat. jours., chapter to books. Pres. French Chem. Soc. Lyon, 1963-68; v.p. U. St. Etienne, 1972-75. Recipient French Indsl. Soc. award, Paris, 1965, French Acad. Scis. award, Paris, 1977. Mem. Am. Chem. Soc. (George S. Whitby award 1998), Soc. Encouraging Progress, French (Gold medal 2007). Avocations: skiing, tennis, piano. Home: Rte de Chavanne Chemin de Grange Bruyas 42400 Saint Chamond France Office: Univ St Etienne 23 Dr P Michelon 42023 Saint Etienne France Personal E-mail: vergnaud.jean-maurice@wanadoo.fr.

VERGNE, PHILIPPE, art foundation administrator; b. Troyes, France, 1966; Doctorate in art history, Sorbonne, Paris. Dir. Mus. d'Art Contemporain, Marseille, France, 1994—97; curator visual arts Walker Art Ctr., Mpls., 1997—2003, sr. curator, 2003—04, dep. dir. and chief curator, 2005—08; dir. François Pinault Found. Contemporary Art, Paris, 2004—05, Dia Art Found., NYC, 2008—. Co-curator Whitney Biennial, 2006; vis. critic Cranbrook Art Acad., U. Ill., Sch. Art Inst. Chgo. Recipient Chevalier, Order Arts and Letters, France, 2004, award for Best Monographic Mus. Show, AICA, 2008. Office: Dia Art Found 535 W 22nd St New York NY 10011 Office Phone: 212-989-4055. Office Fax: 212-989-5566. E-mail: info@diaart.org.*

VERHEIJEN, JEROEN CUNERA, research scientist; b. Ede, Netherlands, Apr. 26, 1973; s. Cees and Conny Verheijen; m. Laura Lenox Fitch, July 31, 1999; children: Liesbeth, Ben, Max. MSc, Leiden U., Netherlands, 1996, PhD, 2000. Program dir., medicinal chemistry Sention, Providence, 2001—05; prin. rsch. scientist Wyeth Rsch., Pearl River, NY, 2005—. Young chemists com. mem. Am. Assn. Cancer Rsch., 2007—. Recipient Young Investigator award, Sixth Internat.

Solid Phase Synthesis Symposium, 1999. Mem.: Am. Chem. Soc. Achievements include research in design and synthesis of artificial ribonucleases. Office: Wyeth Rsch 401 N Middletown Rd Pearl River NY 10965

VERHEYEN, PETER DAVID, librarian, conservator; b. Princeton, NJ, Jan. 14, 1963; s. Egon Verheyen and Hanne Schulten; m. Hope Elizabeth Kuniholm, June 4, 1994; 1 child, Sofia Klara. BA in German Lit., Johns Hopkins U., 1985; MLS, Syracuse U. Sch. Info. Studies, 1997. Hand bookbinding apprentice Chamber of Trades, Munster, Germany, 1987; asst. conservator William Minter Bookbinding and Conservation, Chgo., 1988—91, Yale U. Libr., New Haven, 1991—92; rare book conservator Cornell U. Libr., Ithaca, NY, 1993—95; conservation libr. Syracuse U. Libr., NY, 1995—98; archival product mgr. Gaylord Bros., 1998—99; preservation and digital access libr. Syracuse U. Libr. Spl. Collections Rsch. Ctr., NY, 1999—2008, head of preservation, 2008—. Exhbns. chair Guild Book Workers, NYC, 1990—96, 2004—06, publicity chair, 1998—2002. Exhibitions include Reliures du Monde: Les Amis de la Reliure d'Art, 2nd Nat. Book and Paper Arts Biennial, Guild Book Workers, Columbia Coll. Ctr. for Book and Paper Arts, Chgo., 2000, Soc. Bookbinders Bookbinding Competition, 2003 (Harmatan Leather award, 2003); author: Springback Ledger Bindings in German Tradition, 2003; contbr. articles to profl. jours. Recipient Laura Young Outstanding Svc. award, Guild of Book Workers, 2009. Mem.: ALA, Can. Bookbinders and Book Artists Guild, Designer Bookbinders, Soc. Am. Archivists, Am. Inst. Conservation (cipp web, list mgr. 2002—04). Achievements include design of Tube storage unit for architectural and other oversized archival materials; development of and coordination of special collections digitization projects; Bonefolder: an e-journal for the bookbinder and book artist, 2004-; Book Arts Web, 1994-. Office: Peter Verheyen Preservation Dept Syracuse Univ Libr Syracuse NY 13244 Office Fax: 315-443-2671. Personal E-mail: verheyen@philobiblon.com. Business E-Mail: pdverhey@syr.edu.

VERHOEK, SUSAN ELIZABETH, botany educator; b. Columbus, Ohio, 1942; m. S.E. Williams; 1 child. Student, Carleton Coll., 1960-62; BA, Ohio Wesleyan U., 1964; MA, Ind. U., 1966; PhD, Cornell U., 1975. Herbarium supr. Mo. Bot. Garden, St. Louis, 1966-70; asst. prof. Lebanon Valley Coll., Annville, Pa., 1974-82, assoc. prof., 1982-85, prof., 1985—2008, prof. emeritus, 2008—. Vis. researcher Cornell U., Ithaca, N.Y., 1982-83; content cons. Merrill Pub. Co., 1987-89; vis. profl. Chgo. Bot. Garden, 1991. Author: How to Know the Spring Flowers, 1982; contbr. articles to profl. jours., newspapers, and bulls. Trustee Lebanon Valley Coll., Annville, 1979-82, 84-90, 92-98; dir. Lebanon Valley Coll. Arboretum, 1996-2008. Mem. Soc. for Econ. Botany (pres. 1985-86), Bot. Soc. Am., Am. Pub. Gardens Assn. Office: Lebanon Valley Coll Dept Biology Annville PA 17003-0501 Office Phone: 717-867-6178. Business E-Mail: verhoek@lvc.edu.

VERHOEVEN, LINDA STRANSKY, librarian, educator; children: Jace, Nicolaas A. MEd, Heritage U., Toppenish, Wash., 1991. Cert. in tchg. Wash., 1989. Tchr. Denver Pub. Schs., 1967—68, 1971—82, Garden Grove, Calif., 1968—70, Brussels Am. Sch., 1970—71, Grandview Pub. Schs., Wash., 1989—, libr., 1989—. Sec. Ch. Christ Scientist, Sunnyside, Wash., 1998—. Mem.: Wash. Edn. Assn., Grandview Edn. Assn., Wash. Libr. Media Assn., Delta Kappa Gamma. Office: McClure Elem 811 W 2nd St Grandview WA 98930

VERHOVEN, VICTORIA, voice educator; d. George Martin Verhoven and Phyllis Adelaide Heinz; m. Drew Arthur Lecher, May 3, 1980. MusB, Ind. U., Bloomington, 1976, MusM, 1979. Applied voice instr. Lewis U., Romeoville, Ill., 1987—91; prep sch. voice instr. Benedictine U., Lisle, Ill., 1987—, applied voice instr., 1995—, North Ctrl. Coll., Naperville, Ill., 1995—. Mem. Nat. Assoc. Tchrs. Singing, Jacksonville, Fla., 2007—. Singer: (M&W prodns.) Children's Music Theatre, (soprano soloist) Light Opera Works of Chicago, Chamber Opera Chicago, Lincoln Opera, Naperville Chorus & Orchestra, (chorus) Lyric Opera of Chicago. Hist. home Hist. Soc. Oshkosh, Wis.; mem. echo Naperville, 1986—2008; chmn. cir. mem. Christian Broadcasting Network, Va. Beach, 1991—2008. Recipient Matinee Musicale award, Indpls., 1975, Model Integrity award, Benedictine U., Lisle, 2006; named to Dean's List, Ind. U., Bloomington, 1973—79. Mem.: AGMA, Actors Equity Assn., NATS. Office: North Ctrl Coll 30 N Brainard St Naperville IL 60540 Business E-Mail: vverhoven@noctrl.edu.

VERING, JOHN ALBERT, lawyer; b. Marysville, Kans., Feb. 6, 1951; s. John Albert and Bernadine E. (Kieffer) V.; m. Ann E. Arman, June 28, 1980; children: Julia Ann, Catherine Ann, Mary Ann. BA summa cum laude, Harvard U., 1973; JD, U. Va., 1976. Bar: Mo. 1976, U.S. Dist. Ct. (we. dist.) Mo. 1976, U.S. Ct. Appeals (8th cir.), 1977, U.S. Ct. Appeals (10th cir.), 1980, U.S. Ct. Appeals (4th cir.) 1987, Kans. 1990, U.S. Dist. Ct. Kans. 1990; arbitrator, mediator. Assoc. Dietrich, Davis, Dicus, Rowlands, Schmitt & Gorman, Kansas City, Mo., 1976-81, ptnr., 1982—88, Armstrong Teasdale LLP, Kansas City, 1989—. Editor: U. Va. Law Rev., 1974—76. Bd. dirs. Greater Kansas City YMCA Southwest Dist., 1987. Recipient Career Rsch. Excellence award, U. Coop. Soc., 2009; named 9th US Congress on Computational Mechanics, 2007, Best Lawyers in Am., 2008; named one of Am.'s Leading Lawyers for Bus., Chambers USA, 2008, Super Lawyers, Mo., 2008, Kans., 2008; named to Hall of Fame, La. State U. Civil and Environ. Engring., 2008. Fellow: AAAS; mem.: Soc. Indsl. and Applied Math., Kansas City Metro Bar Assn. (chmn. labor and employment law com. 2003, chmn. fed. cts. com. 2007), Harvard Club (adv. bd. schs. com. Kansas City 1977—2009, v.p. 1981—82, 1992—93, pres. 1994—96). Home: 1210 W 68th Ter Kansas City MO 64113-1904 Office: Armstrong Teasdale LLP 2345 Grand Blvd Ste 2000 Kansas City MO 64108-2617 Office Phone: 816-221-3420. Business E-Mail: jvering@armstrongteasdale.com.

VERKHOVSKY, BORIS, computer scientist, educator; PhD, USSR Acad. Scis. Wallace J. Eckert scientist IBM TJW Rsch. Ctr.; assoc. prof. Princeton U.; mem. tech. staff Bell Labs; Charles A. Dana Endowed chair professorship; prof. computer sci. NJIT, Newark. Recipient USSR Ministry of Radio-Electronics award, USSR award, Acad. Scis., Alvin Johnson award, Millennium award and Medal of Excellence. Fellow: European Acad. Scis. (v.p., bd. govs. 2004—, gov. 2002, v.p. 2003, mem. nominating com. for Nobel Prize, Blaise Pascal medal in Computer Sci. 2003). Office: NJIT Computer Sci Dept GITC 4407 University Heights Newark NJ 07102 Office Fax: 973-596-5777. Personal E-mail: verb73@gmail.com. Business E-Mail: verkhovsky@homer.njit.edu, verb@cs.njit.edu.

VERKUIL, PAUL ROBERT, law educator, lawyer, former dean; b. S.I., NY, Dec. 4, 1939; s. Marinus and Elsie Dorothy (Pohlmann) V.; m. Frances H. Gibson, Aug. 31, 1963; children: Tara Aldridge, John Gibson. BA, Coll. William and Mary, 1961; LLB, U. Va., 1967; LLM, NYU, 1969, JSD, 1972; MA, New Sch. Social Rsch., 1971. Bar: NY 1968, Va. 1988, DC 1990. Assoc. Cravath, Swaine & Moore, NYC, 1967-69, Paul, Weiss, Rifkind, Wharton & Garrison, NYC, 1969-71; asst. prof. U. NC Law Sch., Chapel Hill, 1971-74, assoc. prof., 1974-76, prof., 1976-78; dean and Jospeh Jones prof. Tulane Law Sch., New Orleans, 1978-85; pres., prof. law and govt. Coll. William and Mary, Williamsburg, Va., 1985-92; pres. CEO Am. Automobile Assn., 1992—95; dean Benjamin N. Cardozo Sch. Law, Yeshiva U., 1997—2001, prof. law, 1997—; sr. counsel Boies, Schiller & Flexner LLP; acting dean U. Miami Sch. Law, 2008—09. Vis. prof. Duke U., 1973—74; cons. US Dept. Energy, 1977—79; Kenan rsch. prof., vis. scholar Columbia U., 1978; mem. Adminstrv. Conf. US, 1982; spl. master US v LA, 1989, NJ v NY; vis. prof. U. Pa. Co-author: Public Control of Business, 1977, Social Security Hearings and Appeals, 1978, Economic Regulation of Business, 1985, Administrative Law and Process, 1985, 1992, 2004, Regulation and Deregulation, 2004; contbr. articles to law jours. Served with US Army, 1962-64. Fellow: Am. Law Inst. (life), Am. Bar Found. (life); mem.: ABA, Maritime Law Assn., Am. Law Inst., Raven Soc., Order of Coif. Office: Benjamin N Cardozo Sch Law 55 Fifth Ave, Ste 515 New York NY 10003 also: Boies, Schiller & Flexner LLP 575 Lexington Ave, 7th Fl New York NY 10022 Office Phone: 212-790-0496, 212-446-2365. Office Fax: 212-446-2350. E-mail: verkuil@yu.edu, pverkuil@bsfllp.com.*

VER KUILEN, MARION JANE, retired instructional aide; b. Junction City, Wis., July 22, 1928; d. Fred A. and Mary Swanson; m. Theodore William Ver Kuilen, Feb. 8, 1947 (dec. Oct. 24, 1990); children: Victor Vernon, Van Vardon, Valerie Victoria, Venetta Venise Parrish(dec.), Vincent Vaughn. Student, Mt. San Antonio Coll., Walnut, Calif., 1977—78. Asst. mgr. Plz. Stationers and Book Store, West Covina, Calif., 1971—77; instrnl. aid elem. and ESL adult edn. Hacienda La Puente Unified Sch. Dist., La Puente, Calif., 1985—2005; ret., 2005. Photographer Reflections from the Past: Desert Twilight, America at the Millennium- The Best Photos of the 20th Century. Sec. Sunset Wesleyan Ch., La Puente, 1985—86; pres. Am Vets Auxillary, La Puente, 1958—61; den mother Cub Scouts, Rockford, Ill., 1954—57, San Pedro, Calif., 1958—59, La Puente, 1969—71. Recipient In Svc. of Our Youth award, Mayor of Rockford, 1956, Best Photos of 2003 award, Editors Choice award, Internat. Libr. Photography, 1998—99; named Outstanding Salesperson of Yr., West Covina C. of C., 1977, Outstanding Classified Employee of the Yr., Hacienda-La Puente Unified Sch. Dist., 1997. Mem.: DAV (assoc.), Nat. Geog. Soc. (corr.), Mt. Vernon Assn. (corr.), Colonial Williamsburg Assoc. (assoc.), WWII Veterans Meml. (life Charter Mem.), History (assoc.), WWII Mus. (assoc.), Sierra Club (corr.). Achievements include being a lung cancer survivor since October 2004. Avocations: photography, reading, gardening. Home: 16105 Harvest Moon St La Puente CA 91744-1337

VERLANDER, JUSTIN BROOKS, professional baseball player; b. Manakin Sabot, Va., Feb. 20, 1983; s. Richard Verlander. Student, Vanderbilt U., Nashville. Pitcher Detroit Tigers, 2006—. Named Am. League Outstanding Rookie, Players Choice Awards, 2006, Am. League Rookie of Yr., Maj. League Baseball Writers Assn., 2006; named to Am. League All-Star Team, Maj. League Baseball, 2007, 2009. Achievements include pitching in World Series during rookie season, 2006; pitched a no-hitter against the Milwaukee Brewers, June 12, 2007. Office: Detroit Tigers Comerica Park 2100 Woodward Ave Detroit MI 48201*

VERLICH, JEAN ELAINE, writer, public relations executive, consultant; b. McKeesport, Pa., July 5, 1950; d. Matthew Louis and Irene (Tomko) Verlich; m. S(tanley) Wayne Wright, Sept. 29, 1979 (div. June 1988). Student, Bucknell U., 1968-69; BA, U. Pitts., 1971. Pres. sec. Com. to Re-elect Pres., S.W. Pa., 1972; adminstrv. asst. Pa. Rep. James B. Kelly III, 1972-73; reporter Beaver (Pa.) County Times, 1973-74; proofreader Ketchum, MacLeod & Grove, Pitts., 1975-76; cmty. rels. specialist PPG Industries, Pitts., 1976-77; editor PPG News, 1977-79, sr. staff writer, 1979-84, comm. coord., 1984-85; pub. rels. assoc. Glass Group, 1986-87; mgr. pub. rels. Glass Group PPG Industries, 1987-92; account mgr. Maddigan Comm., Pitts., 1992-93; owner JV Comm., Pitts., 1993—2006, Clovis, N.Mex., 2006—08, Braintree, Mass., 2008—; news editor Clovis News Jour., 2006—07. Bd. dirs. Travelers Aid Soc. Pitts., 1992—95, v.p., 1994—95. Mem.: Automotive Pub. Rels. Coun., Internat. Assn. Bus. Communicators (bd. dirs. Pitts. chpt. 1981, v.p. pub. rels. Pitts. chpt. 1982, v.p. programs Pitts. chpt. 1985, pres. Pitts. chpt. 1986), Phi Beta Kappa, Delta Zeta. Business E-Mail: jverlich@jvcommunications.com.

VERLIN, JONATHAN R., secondary school educator; b. Phila., Jan. 3, 1966; s. Jerome Robert and Eileen Lois Verlin. BA, Ursinus Coll., Collegeville, Pa., 1988; MA, Duquesne U., Pitts., 1990; MEd, Arcadia U., Glenside, Pa., 1992; MSIS, MS, Drexel U., Phila., 1999. Cert. instrnl. tchr. I Pa., 1988, instrnl. tchr. II Pa., 2007. Specialist microcomputer support W.B. Saunders Co., Phila., 1996—2000; programmer Jerome Software, Inc., Elkins Pk., Pa., 2000—02; tchr. Hope Charter Sch., Phila., 2002—03, career edn. dept. head, 2003—04, info. tech. dir., 2003—04; tchr. Sch. Dist. Phila., 2004—. Co-author: Sanctity of Reason: Science, Religion and the State in Samuel Clarke Boyle's Lectures: 1704-1705, 1996; co-author: (with Goldstein J.) By No Means Run in Debt: Richard Price's Life Expectancy Analysis and England's National Debt, 1997; co-author: The Consortium on Revolutionary Europe, 1750-1850: Selected Papers, 1997; contbr. chapters to books. Treas. Ogontz Vol. Fire Co., Elkins Park, 2002—03; sec. Ogontz Vol. Fire Co. Relief Assoc., Elkins Park, 2007—. Recipient Citation Valor award, Cheltenham Twp., Elkins Park, Pa., 1998. Avocations: amateur radio, bicycling, computers. Office: South Phila HS 2101 Broad St Philadelphia PA 19148

VERMA, ARUN K., mathematician, educator; b. Dibrugarh, India, June 1955; 3 children. MSc, Dibrugarh U., India, 1977; Diploma, PhD, Indian Inst. of Tech., Kharagpur, 1984. Lectr. in math. Regional Engring. Coll., Silchar, Assam, India, 1984—89; rsch. assoc. Hampton U., Hampton, Va., 1989—89, vis. lectr. in math., 1989—92, asst. prof. of math., 1992—93, assoc. prof. of math., 1993—2001, prof. of math., 2001—. Reader for AP calculus Ednl. Testing Svcs., Princeton, NJ, 1998—2004; ASEE summer faculty fellow NASA Langley Rsch. Ctr., Hampton, Va., 2000; US EdD project cons. Ala. State U., Montgomery, Ala., 2002—03; Schev project cons. Norfolk State U., Norfolk, Va., 2002—03; faculty summer rsch. participant Oak Ridge Inst. for Sci. and Rsch., Oak Ridge, Tenn., 1993—93; lead tchr. Thompson Learning Brooks Coll., Inc., 2004—; coord. Math. Counts Peninsula Chpt., Va., 2005—; project dir. various grants. Treas. Yorktown 4th July Committe, Yorktown, Va., 2003—; elected com. mem. Internat. Baccalaureate Adv. Coun., Yorktown, Va., 2000—04; nominated com. mem. New Horizon Governors Sci. & Tech. Adv. Com., Hampton, Va., 2000—07; sec. exec. com. Hindu Temple of Hampton Roads, Chesapeake, Va., 2006—. Recipient William C. Lowry Outstanding Math. Tchr. award, coll. level, Va. Coun. of Teachers of Math., 2001, 2002 QEM (Quality Edn. for Minorities) Excellence in Math. and/or Sci. Tchg. award, 2002; named Leader in Edn., Hewlett-Packard Inc., 2000. Mem.: Va. Acad. Sci. (pres. elect. 2009), Nat. Tech. Assn., Va. Coun. of Teachers of Math., Math. Assn. of Am., Sigma Xi (regional coord. nationwide mathcounts competition 2006—). Office: Hampton U E Queen St Hampton VA 23668 Business E-Mail: arun.verma@hamptonu.edu.

VERMA, INDER M., biochemist; b. Sangrur, Punjab, India, Nov. 28, 1947; MSc in Biochemistry, Lucknow U., India, 1966; PhD in Biochemistry, Weizmann Inst. Sci., Rehovot, Israel, 1971. From asst. prof. to assoc. prof. Salk Inst., 1974-83; sr. mem. Molecular Biology & Virology Lab, 1983-85; prof. Molecular Biology, 1985-95; prof. Lab. Genetics Salk Inst. for Biol. Sciences, 1995—, Am. Cancer Soc. prof. Molecular Biology. Fellow Jane Coffin Childs Meml. Fund, 1970-73; Reverend Soloman B. Caulker Meml. fellow, 1967-70; adj. assoc. prof. U. Calif. San Diego, 1979-83, adj. prof. Biology, 1983—; March of Dimes Birth Defects Found. Franklin D. Roosevelt Investigator, 1997; mem. Virology Study Sec., 1981-85, elected mem., Inst. of Medicine, 1999. Recipient medal Outstanding Scientist N. Am. Scientists of Indian Origin, 1985-86; merit award NIH, 1987, outstanding investigator award, 1988; bd. trustees Salk Inst., 1989-91 & 94—; mem. acad. coun., 1989—; vchmn. Fac. and Acad. coun., 1989-90 & 94-95; chmn., 1991-92 & 96-97; prof. Molecular Biology, Am. Cancer Soc., 1990; lectr. Purdue U., 1991, Sch. Med. Vanderbilt U., 1992, TATA Meml. Hosp., Bombay, India, 1992, U. Chgo., 1992, Queenstown, New Zealand, 1993, N.Y.U., 1993, Bar-Ilan U., Ramat Gan, Israel, and others. Mem. NAS (councilor, 2006-), Am. Cancer Soc., Third World Acad. Sciences, IOM, Am. Soc. for Gene Therapy (pres. 2000-2001). Office: Salk Inst Biol Studies PO Box 85800 10010 N Torrey Pines Rd San Diego CA 92186-5800 Office Phone: 619-453-4100. Business E-Mail: verma@salk.edu.

VERMA, NIKHIL, orthopedist; b. Feb. 8, 1973; BS with highest distinction in Cellular and Microbiology, Univ. Mich., 1994; MD, Univ. Penn. Sch. Med., 1998. Cert. orthopaedic surgery ABOS, 2003. Orthopaedic resident Rush-Presbyterian St. Luke's Med. Ctr., Chgo., 1998—; fell., sports med. Hosp. Spl. Surgery, 2003—04. Recipient James B. Angell Scholar, Univ. Mich., 1994, Gallo award Young Rschrs., The Cancer Inst. NJ, 1995, Jorge O. Galante MD Excellence in Rsch. award, Rush-Presbyterian St. Lukes Med. Ctr., 2001—02. Mem.: Asian Pacific Am. Med. Students Assn. Office: Midwest Orthopedics at Rush 1725 W Harrison, Ste 1063 Chicago IL 60612 Office Fax: 312-243-8925. Business E-Mail: nverma@rushortho.com.

VERMA, RICHARD R. (RAHUL VERMA), federal agency administrator, lawyer; BS, Lehigh U., 1990; JD cum laude, Am. U., 1993; LLM with distinction, Georgetown U., 1998. Bar: Pa. 1993, DC 1996. Staff asst. to Rep. Jack Murtha, US House of Reps., Washington; officer USAF JAGC; mem. Internat. and Tech. Practices Steptoe & Johnson LLP, 1998—2002, ptnr. Govt. Rels. and Pub. Policy Group, 2007—09; sr. nat. security advisor to Senator Harry Reid, US Senate, 2002—07; asst. sec. for legis. affairs US Dept. State, 2009—. Bd. mem. Marsh Inst. Govt. and Pub. Policy, Shenandoah U.; mem. Com. on Critical Infrastructure Protection and the Law, NAS, Coun. of Fgn. Rels., Congl. Com. on Prevention of Weapons of Mass Destruction Proliferation and Terrorism, 2008. Trustee Lehigh U., 1999—2002; adv. bd. mem. U. Pitts. at Johnstown. Decorated Nat. Defense Svc. Medal, Air Force Commendation Medal, Meritorious Svc. Medal; named one of Tthe 50 Most Influential Indian-Americans in the US, India Abroad, 2007; Internat. Affairs Fellow, Coun. of Fgn. Rels., 2002. Mem.: South Asian Bar Assn. (pres., bd. mem. 1999—2001). Office: US Dept State 2201 C St NW Washington DC 20520*

VERMA, SURJIT KUMAR, retired school system administrator; b. India, May 17, 1940; arrived in Canada 1966; s. Sohara Lal and Gian Devi V.; m. Raj Verma; 1 child, Soania. MEd, St. Francis Xavier U., NS, 1975; postgrad., Dalhousie U., NS, U. Ottawa, Ont., Can, 1979. Cert. tchr. Nova Scotia. Sci. dept. head Halifax County Bedford Dist. Sch. Bd., N.S., Canada, 1968-88, curriculum supr. N.S., 1988-94; ret., 1995. Served on C.T.F. Project Overseas Can. Teams, W.I., Nigeria, 1976, 77; mem. provincial sci. task force, biology rev. com., elem. sci. Nova Scotia Dept. Edn.; mem. Internat. Sci. Symposium, 1979; mem. selection panel PromoSci. Program. Natural Scis. and Engring. Rsch. Coun. of Can.; mem. exec. coun. N.S. Inst. Sci.; worksop presenter numerous sci. workshops. Contbr. to profl. jours. Chmn. First Metro Halifax Dartmouth Reg Sci. Fair, 1975; co-chmn. Canada Wide Sci Fair, 1984. Recipient Sci. Tchg. Achievement Recognition award, U.S. Nat. Sci. Tchrs. Assn. and Am. Gas Assn., 1993, Profl. Devel. award, N.S. Tchrs. Union, Tchg. Excellence in Sci., Tech. and Math. award, Prime Min. Can., 1993, 1994, Sci. on Display award, NASCO, 1993—94, Outstanding Achievement in Sci. Edn. award, Halifax County Sch. Bd., 1993, Surjit Verma award for tchg. excellence created in his honor, Halifax County Bedrod Dist. Sch. Bd., 1994, Michael Smith award, Industry Can., 1996, Maritimer of the Week award, Atlantic TV and Can. TV Network, 2003, Maritimer of Week award, Atlantic T.V. and Can. T.V. Network, 2003; fellow, U. Ottawa, 1979; scholar, N.S. Tchrs. Union, 1979; grad. fellow, Dalhousie U., 1980, Math. Sci. Tech. Edn. fellow, Royal Bank Queen's U., 1994, rsch. devel. grantee, Dalhousie U., 1979, Can./N.S. Tech. Devel. grantee, 1995. Mem. Nova Scotia Inst. Sci. (coun. mem.), Natural Sci. and Engring. Rsch. Coun. (mem. selection panel promosci. project). Avocations: jogging, yoga. Personal E-mail: rsverma49@yahoo.ca.

VERMEIL, DICK (RICHARD ALBERT VERMEIL), retired professional football coach; b. Calistoga, Calif., Oct. 30, 1936; m. Carolyn Drake; 3 children. Head coach UCLA, 1974—75, Phila. Eagles, 1976—82, St. Louis Rams, 1997-2000, Kans. City Chiefs, 2001—05; pub. spkr. Nationwide Spkrs. Bur., Beverly Hills, Calif., 2000—01. Tv analyst with CBS, ABC. Named NFL Coach of the Yr. 1980, 1999; Sportsman of Yr., The Sporting News, 2003, Man of the Yr., Walter Camp Football Found., 2006 Career highlights include:first fulltime spl. teams coach in NFL history, L.A. Rams, 1969; head coach Super Bowl XXXIV champion St. Louis Rams, 2000, becoming the oldest coach in NFL history to win a Super Bowl; only coach in history to win both the Super Bowl and the Rose bowl; only 4th coach in history to lead two different teams to Super Bowl (Phil., St. Louis).

VERMEIRE, JON J., research scientist; b. Moline, Ill., Feb. 9, 1979; m. Margaret M. Carney. PhD, U. Wis.-Madison, 2006. Rsch. asst. Ill. State U., Normal, 1997—2001; postdoc. fellow Yale U. Sch. Medicine, New Haven, 2006—. Home: 464 Congress Ave Rm 230 New Haven CT 06510 Office: Yale Univ Sch Medicine 464 Congress Ave Rm 230 New Haven CT 06510 Business E-Mail: jon.vermeire@yale.edu.

VERMILYE, PETER HOAGLAND, banker; b. NYC, Jan. 17, 1920; s. Herbert Noble and Elise Tace (Hillyer) V.; m. Lucy Shaw Mitchell, Oct. 14, 1950; children: Peter H., Dana R., Andrew R., Mary S. AB, Princeton U., 1940. V.p. pension investments J.P. Morgan & Co. and Morgan Guaranty Trust, 1940-64; ptnr. State St. Research & Mgmt., Boston, 1965-69; pres. Alliance Capital Mgmt., NYC, 1970-77; sr. v.p., chief investment officer Citibank, NYC, 1977-84; chmn. Baring Am. Asset Mgmt., Boston, 1984-89; sr. advisor Baring Asset Mgmt., 1990-95, Harbor Capital Mgmt., Boston, 1996—2003, Fortis Investments, 2004—. Chmn. Huntington Theatre, 1989—96; bd. dirs. Engelhard Hanovia, Breadstreet Holdings Corp., 1970—2008. Trustee Boston U., 1970—. Mem.: Brook, Somerset, Myopia. Home: 157 School St Manchester MA 01944-1236 Office: Fortis Investments 75 State St Ste 2700 Boston MA 02109

VERMUND, STEN HALVOR, epidemiologist, educator; b. Mpls., Jan. 31, 1954; s. Halvor and Karen (Bergfjord) V.; m. Pilar Vargas, Apr. 8, 1978; children: Julian, Gabriel. BA, Stanford U., 1974; MD, Albert Einstein Coll. Medicine, 1977; MSc, London Sch. Hygiene and Tropical Medicine, 1981; PhD, Columbia U., 1990. Diplomate Am. Bd. Pediatrics, Am. Bd. Preventive Medicine. Intern Presbyn. Hosp., NYC, 1977-78, resident in pediat., 1978-80; asst. prof. Columbia U., NYC, 1982-85, Albert Einstein Coll. Medicine, Bronx, NY, 1985-88; chief epidemiology br. divsn. AIDS Nat. Inst. Allergy and Infectious Diseases, Bethesda, Md., 1988-92, chief vaccine trials and epidemiology br. divsn. AIDS, 1992-94; prof. epidemiology, internat. health, medicine & pediat. U. Ala., Birmingham, 1994—2005, chmn. dept. epidemiology, 1994-98, dir. divsn. geog. medicine, 1994—2005, sr. scientist Comprehensive Cancer Ctr., 1994—2005, assoc. dir. Ctr. for AIDS Rsch., 1994—2003, pres. Gorgas Meml. Inst., 1995—2005, dir. John J. Sparkman Ctr. for Internat. Pub. Health Edn., 1999—2005; prof. pediat., medicine, preventive medicine and ob/gyn Vanderbilt U., Nashville, 2005—, dir., inst. for global health, 2005—, Amos Christie chair in global health, 2005—. Cons. NYC Dept. Environ. Protection, 1986-88, Med. Bd. Nat. Coun. Chs., NYC, 1984-85, CDC, Atlanta, 1989—, FDA, Rockville, Md., 1991-94, NIH, 1994—; mem. Inst. Medicine Panel on Perinatal Transmission of HIV, 1997-98, mem. Inst. Medicine Panel on HIV Prevention, 1999-2000. Contbg. author: AIDS Epidemiology, 1993, Until the Cure: Caregiving for Women with HIV, 1993, Parasitic Protozoa, 2d edit., vol. 6, 1993, HIV in Women, 1995, AIDS, 4th edit., 1997; co-editor, contbg. author: Preventing HIV Infection in Developing Countries, 1999; contbr. articles to profl. jours. Mem. adv. bd. health rsch. tng. program N.Y.C. Dept. Health, 1986—88; mem. sci. adv. bd. World AIDS Found., 1994—95; mem. adv. com. Office AIDS Rsch., NIH, 2000—. Recipient Curnan award Babies Hosp., NYC, 1980, Lalcaca medal U. London, 1981, Commrs. Spl. Svc. award NYC Dept. Health, 1988, Merit award USPHS, Bethesda, 1989, Cert. of Appreciation, U.S. Surgeon Gen., 1993, Superior Svc. award USPHS, 1994; med. rsch. grantee Ctrs. for Disease Control, Nat. Cancer Inst., Nat. Inst. Allergy Infectious Diseases, Nat. Inst. Child Health and Devel., others, 1986-88, 94—. Fellow Am. Acad. Pediatrics (sec., founding mem. regional com. on homeless children 1986-88), Am. Coll. Epidemiology, Soc. Adolescent Medicine, Royal Soc. Tropical Medicine and Hygiene, Infectious Disease Soc. Am.; mem. APHA, Internat. AIDS Soc., Internat. Epidemiologic Assn., Am. Soc. Tropical Medicine and Hygiene. Avocations: hiking, tennis, violin, ping pong/table tennis. Office: Vanderbilt U Inst Global Health Light Hall 319 0242 Nashville TN 37232 E-mail: sten.vermund@vanderbilt.edu.*

VERMYLEN, PAUL ANTHONY, JR., oil industry executive; b. NYC, Dec. 5, 1946; s. Paul Anthony and Nancy Primrose (Barr) Vermylen; m. Robin S. Collins, Jan. 24, 1970; children: Robert T.C., Nancy Barr Vermylen Thornton, Sarah Morgan Vermylen Trust, Paul Anthony III. AB, Georgetown U., 1968; MBA, Columbia U., 1971. V.p. Citibank N.A., NYC, 1971-78; treas. Commonwealth Oil Refining Co., San Antonio, 1978-81, v.p. fin., CFO, 1981—82; v.p., CFO, dir. Meenan Oil Co., Inc., Syosset, NY, 1982—91, pres., 1992—2001, Meenan Oil Co., L.P., 1992—2001; chmn. Kestrel Energy Co., Inc., Huntington, NY, 2002—05; pres., bd. dirs. Kestrel Energy Ptnrs. LLC, 2005—; chmn. Stargas Partners (NYSE: SGU), 2006—. Bd. dirs. Petroleum Industry Rsch. Found., 1992—2002, Downeast LNG, Inc., 2005—. Bd. dirs. Huntington Arts Coun., NYC, 1983—89, v.p., 1986—87, pres., 1987—89; bd. dirs. Cold Spring Harbor Whaling Mus., 1995—2000; bd. advisors Cold Spring Harbor Lab. DNA Learning Ctr., 1991—2000; bd. regents Georgetown U., Washington, 1997—2003; trustee Girls Prep. Charter Sch., NYC, 2004—, bd. dirs., 2004—, Soc. for Preservation of Long Island Antiquities, 2006—, treas., 2007—, pres., 2009—. Mem.: Causeway Club Southwest Harbor, Maine, NY Yacht Club, Cold Spring Harbor Beach Club.

VERNA, ANNA CIBOTTI, councilwoman; b. Phila., Apr. 15, 1931; d. William and Pauline (Fusco) Cibotti; m. Severino Verna. LLD (hon.), Chestnut Hill Coll., Phila. Exec. sec. Dist. Atty. of Phila., 1952-67, City of Phila., 1967-68; adminstrv. asst. Phila. City Coun., 1968-75, councilwoman, dist. 2, 1976—, city coun. pres., 1999—. Bd. dirs. Penn's Landing Corp., Phila.; chmn. ethics com., rules com., whole coun. com. Phila. City Coun. Bd. mem. Franklin Inst., Phila. Art Mus., Phila. Orch., Phila. Hist. Commn., Bd. of City Trusts, Phila. Decorated Commendatore Republic of Italy; named Pub. Official of Yr., Pa. Assn. Non-Profit Homes for the Aging. Mem.: Grand Lodge Pa., Order Sons Italy in America. Democrat. Roman Catholic. Office: Phila City Coun City Hall Rm 405 Philadelphia PA 19107-3290 Office Phone: 215-686-3412. Office Fax: 215-686-1932.*

VERNACOTOLA, JOSEPH N., librarian; s. George Ray and Mary Ann Vernacotola. BS in Edn., Kent State U., Ohio, 1993, MS in Libr. and Info. Sci., 2002. Cert. in technol. skills competence Fresno Pacific U. Calif., 2005; profl. lic. Dept. Edn., Ohio, 2007. Jr. high tchr. St. Pius X Sch., Bedford, Ohio, 1998—99; tchr. Barberton City Sch.-Highland Mid. Sch., Barberton, Ohio, 1999—2009; libr. Barberton City Schs., U.L. Light Mid. Sch., Ohio, 2009—. Mem. PPG-HMS Ptnrs. Edn., Barberton, 1999, Highland Mid. Sch. Faculty Adv. Com., Barberton, 2002; profl. rights and responsibilities v.p. Barberton Edn. Assn., 2005—08. Recipient Young Alumni award, Kent State U., 1996; named Highland Mid. Sch. Educator of Yr., Barberton City Sch. PTA, 2006; named to, Nat. Dean's List, 1990—93. Mem.: Ohio Mid. Sch. Assn., Ohio Ednl. Libr. Media Assn., Akron East HS Alumni Assn., Kent State U. Alumni Assn., Beta Phi Mu. Avocations: travel, photography, reading. Office: U L Light Mid Sch 292 E Robinson Ave Barberton OH 44203 Office Fax: 330-848-1272. Personal E-mail: joenv@aol.com. Business E-Mail: jvernacotola@barbertonschools.org.

VERNARELLI, MICHAEL JOSEPH, economics professor, consultant, academic administrator; b. Rochester, NY, Nov. 24, 1948; s. S. John and Angelica Dolores (Morabito) V.; m. Joan Ann Taylor, Oct. 4, 1975; children: Jacqueline Andrea, Laurel Aileen. BA in Econs., U. Mich., 1970; MA in Econs., SUNY, Binghamton, 1974, PhD in Econs., 1978; MA in Pastoral Studies, St. Bernard's Sch. Theology & Ministry, 2009. Account analyst Travelers Ins. Co., Rochester, 1970-71; rsch. assoc. Ctrl. Adminstrn. SUNY, 1975-76; prof. econs. Rochester Inst. Tech., 1976—, chmn. dept., 1987—. Cons. econs. Rochester Downtown Devel. Corp., 1980; rsch. economist divsn. housing rsch. HUD, Washington, 1980-81, vis. scholar, 1980; pres., forensic economist Rochester Econ. Cons., 1983—; vis. prof. U.S. Bus. Sch. in Prague, 1992-96. Contbg. author: Federal Housing Policy and Desegregation, 1986. Mem. Brighton (N.Y.) Bd. Archtl. Rev., 1990-91, mem. planning bd., 1991-98. Recipient Eisenhart award Rochester Inst. Tech., 1987; grantee SUNY, Binghamton, 1974. Mem. Am. Econ. Assn., Nat. Assn. Forensic Economists, Ea. Econ. Assn., Greater Rochester C. of C. (panel mem. bus. trends com. 1987—), Omicron Delta Epsilon. Roman Catholic. Avocation: golf. Home: 133 Esplanade Dr Rochester NY 14610-3325 Office: Rochester Inst Tech Rochester NY 14623-0887 Office Phone: 585-475-2455. Personal E-mail: mjvern11@aol.com. Business E-Mail: mjvgss@rit.edu.

VERNAZZA, TRISH BROWN (TRISH EILEEN BROWN), visual artist, art therapist, sculptor, psychotherapist; b. Tampa, Fla., Mar. 22, 1958; d. Burrell Joseph and Katharine Stowell (Weekly) B. BFA in Art History, U. South Fla., 1993; MA in Clin. Feminist Psychology, New Coll. Calif., 1997; postgrad., U. Calif., Berkeley, 1997. Lic. marriage and family therapist, art therapist; bd. cert. older adult tchr. Flight attendant Pan Am. World Airways, NYC, 1989—91; art therapist jail psychiat. svcs. Haight Ashbury Free Clinics, San Francisco, 1997—99; art instr. to older and disabled adults, 1999—; pvt. practice psychotherapy Carlsbad, Calif., 2003—; co-propr. Venus Bloom Online Boutique & Art Gallery. Judge John's Seafood Festival, Madeira Beach, Fla., program mgr., Mental Health Sys., 2002—04; expert Starting Over, NBC Warner Bros., 2006; chair Vagina Day, 2006-07; chmn. Vagina Monologues, Carlsbad, 2007; presenter in field.; guest expert, Fox6 News Kusi Holiday Tips Blended Familys, 2007; guest spkr. Girls Empowerment, Oceanside, Calif., 2008-; spkr. expert Calif. Marriage Therapists, 09-; guest spkr. NBC, Kusi, CW San Diego, 09-; lectr. Nat. U. Curlsbad, Calif. Art Therapy and Couples, 2009-; guest expert Calif. Assn. Marriage Family Therapist, 2009. Artist: worked with HIV Women/AIDS Artreach phase 3, sculpture, 1994; group shows include Centre Gallery, U. So. Fla., 1994, U. Mobile Ala., 1994, Ctr. for Contemporary Art, Tampa, 1994, Fla. State U. Gallery and Mus., Tallahassee, 1994, Valencia C.C., Orlando, Fla., 1993, Tandemn Art Ctr., Venice, Fla., 1993, Richmond Art Ctr., Calif., 1996, calendar Richmond Art Ctr., 1997, Sonoma Art Festival, 1997, Napa Valley Mustard Festival, 1998, Sebastopol Art Ctr., 1999, Vista Utility Box, Calif., 2003, 2004, co-proprietor Art Boutique Gallery, Ctr. Arts, Escondido Mus. Gifstore, 2009, (trunk show jewelry) Fashion Week Escondido, 2009, 9th Ann. Women's Conf., Prooram Cauer Art, North County African Am. Women's Assn., 2008, 10th Ann. Women's Conf., 2009; author: Women Art & Mental Illness; works included in pvt. collections, Ctr. Arts Escondido, Gift Store, 2009, Fashion Weekin Escondido, 2009, Trunk Show Jewelry Mus. Escondido, 2009; co-chair Vagina Monologues, Carlsbad, Calif., 2006, chair, 2007; guest lectr. Nat. U. Carlsbad, Calif. Art Therapy and Couples, 2009-; guest expert, art therapist TV reality NBC Show Starting Over, 2006—; guest spkr. Girls Empowerment Ceanside, Calif., 2008, CAMFT, NBC-KUSI, Cowsan Diego-May Mental Health Month, 2009; contbr. articles to profl. jours. Vol. art/crafts instr. Substance Abused Mothers Against Drugs, Tampa, 1993; vol. docent Salvador Dali Mus., St. Petersburg, Fla., 1986-88; mem. Women's Caucus for Art; active multicultural workshops arts & crafts for children, Clearwater, Fla., 1995; intersession instrs. arts & crafts for children, Alameda, Calif., 1995-98; vol. art therapist chronic mentally ill adults Berkeley Creative Living Ctr., 1996-97. Recipient Hillsborough County Emerging Artist award; named to Wall of Tolerance So. Poverty Law, Ala.; named Woman of Merit, North County San Diego; grantee Serpent Source Found. women, San Francisco. Mem. Women in Psychology, Calif. Assn. Marriage and Family Therapists, San Diego North County Assn. Marriage Family Therapists, North County African-Am. Women's Assn., Oceanside Mus. Art, Calif. Ctr. Arts (Escondido). Independent. Avocations: art therapist and visual artist with a feminist, female and feminine voice addressing social, political and gender issues. Office Phone: 760-439-8874. Personal E-mail: info@trishv.com.

VERNER, JAMES MELTON, lawyer; b. Selma, Ala., Sept. 19, 1915; s. Singleton Foster and Jennie (Harris) V.; m. Gretchen Gores, Aug. 12, 1939; children: Ann Verner Picardo, James Singleton, William Melton. Student, Biltmore Coll., 1932—34; AB, U. N.C., 1936, JD, 1938. Bar: NC 1938, Tenn. 1947, D.C. 1950, Va. 1986. Assoc. firm Gover & Covington, Charlotte, NC, 1938; law clk. atty. gen. NC, 1938-40; atty. CAB, Washington, 1940-43; asst. gen. counsel Chgo. & So. Airlines, Memphis, 1946-47; atty. Air Transport Assn. Am., Washington, 1947-49; hearing examiner CAB, 1949-50, exec. asst. to chmn., 1950, exec. dir., 1950-53; from atty. to ptnr. Turney & Turney, 1953—60; ptnr. firm Verner, Liipfert, Bernhard, McPherson & Hand, Chartered (and predecessor firms), 1960-88; hon. mem. bd. dirs., spl. coun. Piper Rudnick Gray Cary (merged with Verner, Liipfert, Bernhard, McPherson & Hand, Chartered), Washington. Assoc. editor N.C. Law Rev., 1937—38. Former mem., chmn. policy bd. Legal Counsel for Elderly, Washington. Lt. (j.g.) USNR, 1943-46; legal officer Naval Air Transport Svc., 1945-46. Mem.: ABA, Cosmos Club (Washington), Order of Golden Fleece. Home: 900 N Taylor St # 2104-2106 Arlington VA 22203-1858 Office: Piper Rudnick Gray Cary 500 8th St NW Washington DC 20004 Office Phone: 202-861-6247. *My belief is that if you treat other people fairly and trust them, you will seldom be disappointed and will be the better for it.*

VERNER, MARY, Mayor, Spokane, Washington; 2 children. BA, Davidson Coll.; MS in Environ. Studies, Yale U.; JD, Gonzaga U., 1999. Former Environ. Programs Mgr. Territorial Govt., US VI; former exec. dir. Upper Columbia United Tribes; councilwoman City of Spokane from Dist. 2, 2004—08; mayor City of Spokane, 2008—. Served on City Coun. Fin. Com., City Coun. Pub. Safety Com., City Coun. Pub. Works Com. Bd. mem. Firefighters Pension Bd., Lodging Tax Adv. Bd., Spokane Regional Health Dist. Bd., Spokane County Air Pollution Control Authority, Native Am. Alliance for Policy & Action, Human Rights Commn.; liaison Chase Youth Commn. Teen Adv. Coun. Mem.: Wash. State Bar Assn., Native American Bar Assn., Kiwanis Internat., Experimental Aircraft Assn. Democrat. Office: Spokane City Hall 808 W Spokane Falls Blvd Spokane WA 99201 Office Phone: 509-625-6250. Business E-Mail: mayor@spokanecity.org.*

VERNEUILLE, KIM R., dean, educator; BS in Comm., Mid. Tenn. State U., Murfreesboro, 1990; A in Graphic Design, Antonelli Coll., Jackson, Miss., 2000; MEd, U. Phoenix, 2004. Graphic designer WLBT-TV 3, Jackson, Miss., 1999—2003; acad. dean distance learning Antonelli Coll. Office: Antonelli College 2323 Lakeland Dr Flowood MS 39232 Office Fax: 601-362-2333. E-mail: kim.verneuille@antonellicollege.edu.

VERNEY, RICHARD GREVILLE, paper company executive; b. Providence, Aug. 24, 1946; s. Gilbert and Virginia Ruth (Piggott) Verney; m. Dorothy Howard, Aug. 26, 1967; children: Virginia F., Elizabeth I., Heather B., Eric B. AB, Brown U., 1968. Mgmt. trainee Monadnock Paper Mills, Bennington, NH, 1969-70, asst. gen. mgr., 1970—, exec. v.p., 1970-76, pres., 1977-85, chmn., CEO, 1978—, Monadnock Non-Wovens, LLC, 1998—, Monadnock Specialty Coatings, LLC, 2000—07. Mem. exec. com. Crotched Mt. Found., Greenfield, NH, 1974—87, trustee, 1974—, St. George's Sch., Newport, RI, 1978—93, chmn., 1985—89, hon. trustee, 1993—, Monadnock Cmty. Hosp., 1993—2000, v.p., 1997—99; trustee Nantucket Conservation Found., Inc., 1994—, pres., 1998—2008. Mem.: Bus. Industry Assn. NH (bd. dir. 1991—, mem. exec. com. 1998—2004), Boston Paper Trade Assn. (pres. 1985—86), Sales Assn. Paper Industry, Am. Forest and Papers Assn. (chmn. exec. bd. pulp consumers divsn. 1980—82, chmn. splty. packaging and indsl. divsn. 1984—85, chmn. cover and text exec. com. 1989—91, bd. dir. 1991—98, chmn. printing, writing exec. com. 2002—03, co-chmn. printing, writing exec. com. 2005—07, bd. dirs. 2007—), NY Yacht Club (NYC), Nantucket Yacht Club (Mass.), Algonquin Club (Boston). Republican. Episcopalian. Home: PO Box 145 Verney Farm Bennington NH 03442-0145 Office: Monadnock Paper Mills Inc 117 Antrim Rd Bennington NH 03442-4205 Business E-Mail: rverney@mpm.com.

VERNILLET, LAURENT, pharmacologist, researcher; b. La Garenne-Colombes, Hauts de Seine, France, Oct. 27, 1959; s. Serge Raymond and Raymonde Marguerite Vernillet; m. Maryse Renee Muller, Sept. 7, 1985; children: Cathelyne Sylvie, Emeline Josiane, Johann Remi, Chloe Valerie. BTech in Biochemistry, Nat. Sch. Chemistry, Biology and Physics, Paris, 1977; Diploma in Applied Biology, U. Tech. Inst., Caen, France, 1979; PharmD, Rene Descartes U., Paris, 1983; Diploma in Pharmacokinetics and Drug Metabolism, U. Paris-South, Chatenay-Malabry, France, 1984; PhD in Exptl. and Clin. Pharmacology, Rene Descartes U., Paris, 1992. Asst. chemist Thibault's Pharmacy, Saint-Mande, Val de Marne, France, 1983—86; sr. rsch. scientist Novartis (formely Sandoz), Rueil-Malmaison, Hauts de Seine, France, 1987—95; rsch. fellow, drug metabolism and pharmacokinetics dept. Sanofi-Aventis (formely Rhone-Poulenc Rorer), Antony, Hauts de Seine, France, 1995—2000; sr. pharmacokineticist, pharmacokinetics, pharmacodynamics and trial simulations dept. Eli Lilly and Co Ltd., Windlesham, England, 2000—02; asst. dir. drug metabolism and pharmacokinetics dept. TAP Pharm. Products Inc., Lake Forest, Ill., 2002—06; sr. scientist and group leader, pharmocokinetics, pharmacodymamics and bioanalytical sci. Genentech Inc., South San Francisco, Calif., 2006—08; dir. Clin. Pharmacology, Vertex Pharm. Inc., Cambridge, Mass., 2008—. Presenter at profl. meetings and confs.; peer reviewer clin. pharmacology chptrs. in scientific books. Contbr. scientific papers, articles to profl. jours. Recipient Laroze Found. prize, 1992. Mem.: Am. Coll. Clin. Pharmacology, Am. Soc. Clin. Pharmacology and Therapeutics. Achievements include significant involvement in the development of some key drugs such as ciclosporin (immunosuppresant), docetaxel and irinotecan (oncology) and febuxostat (metabolic disorder). Avocations: skiing, volleyball, tennis, genealogy, stamp collecting/philately. Office: 130 Waverley St Cambridge MA 02139 Personal E-mail: golden2003@astound.net.

VERNON, ALEX, literature and language professor; BS, US Mil. Acad., West Point, NY, 1989; MA, U. NC, Chapel Hill, 1994, PhD, 2001. Assoc. prof. Hendrix Coll., Conway, Ark., 2001—. Author: (memoir) The Eyes of Orion: Five Tank Lieutenants in the Persian Gulf War (Army Hist. Found. Disting. Book award, 1999), Most Succinctly Bred; co-author (James Salters, Tim O'Brien): Soldier Once and Still: Ernest Hemingway. 1st lt. US Army, 1989—92. Decorated Army Commendation medal with V-device for valor US Army.

VERNON, CARL ATLEE, JR., retired wholesale food distributor executive; b. Topeka, Aug. 15, 1926; s. Carl Atlee and Capitola May (Jarboe) V.; m. Marion Leila Colton, May 7, 1950; children: Mary Catherine, Matthew Fowler, Susan Elizabeth. BS, Yale U., 1947. Merchandising mgr. Fleming Cos., Topeka, 1957-61, dir. merchandising, 1961-66, dir. info. services, 1966-72, v.p. info. services, 1972-74, v.p. regional systems, 1974-79, sr. v.p. mktg. services Oklahoma City, 1979-88. Chmn. Shawnee County chpt. ARC, Topeka, Kans., 1957-58. Served to ensign USNR, 1944—46. Republican. Episcopalian. Avocations: golf, travel. Personal E-mail: cavernonjr@aol.com.

VERNON, DEAN MATTHEW, psychology educator; b. Milw., Mar. 30, 1964; s. Kenneth Leo and Pauline Marie Vernon; m. Lori Lundell Vernon, June 28, 1986; children: Amanda Joy, Deanna Rae, Adam Xavier, Kenny Joseph, Simon Lawrence, Veronica Rita, Leah Marie. BS in Psychology, Carroll Coll., Waukesha, Wis., 1986; BS in Communication, Carroll Coll., 1986; MS in Edn., U. Wis.-LaCrosse, 1988. Cert. sch. psychologist Mich., 1988. Sch. psychologist Grand Rapids Pub. Sch., Mich., 1988—; pres. North Grand Rapids Grizzlies, 2006—08, basketball coach, 2008. Author: (book) Deception. Deacon candidate Cath. Ch., Grand Rapids, 2005—08. Roman Catholic. Avocation: basketball.

VERNON, GARY WAYNE See LEVOX, GARY

VERNON, LAWRENCE GORDON, librarian; b. May 19, 1937; s. Angus Vernon and Anna Drucilla (Elliott) Vernon gabourel; m. Crystal Yvonne Gibson, July 18, 1959; children: Marlon, Dylan, Karen. A, Brit. Libr. Assn. Corr. Course, London, 1959-63. Libr. asst. Nat. Libr. Svc., Belize, 1956-58, jr. asst. libr., 1958-66, asst. libr., 1966-76, sr. libr., 1976-78, chief libr., 1978-92; asst. libr. Univ. Coll. Belize, 1992, libr. dir., 1993-96, assoc. libr., 1996—2003; prin. libr. Nat. Libr. Svc., 2003—. C0-author: Among My Souvenirs, 1966. Sec. bd. govs. Excelsior Cmty. H.S., Belize City, 1979; vice-chmn. Coun. of Vol. Social Svcs., 1986, rec. sec., 1989; chmn. Belize Scholarship Com., 1983. Mem. Belize Libr. Assn. (treas. 1978). Methodist. Office Phone: (501) 2234248.

VERNON, MARGARET KATHERINE, psychologist; b. Evanston, Ill., Feb. 4, 1978; d. Laird Earl and Margaret Lee Vernon; m. James Sampson Kurtz, June 17, 2004. PhD, Pa. State U., Univ. Pk., 2004. Rsch. psychologist Bur. Labor Stats., Washington, 2004—06; sr. rsch. assoc. United BioSource Corp., Bethesda, Md., 2006—08, rsch. scientist, 2008—, rsch. assoc. III supr., 2008—. Contbr. articles to profl. publs., chapters to books. Personal E-mail: mkvernon@gmail.com. Business E-Mail: margaret.vernon@unitedbiosource.com.

VERNON, WESTON, III, (WES VERNON), broadcaster, writer, actor; b. NYC, Aug. 23, 1931; s. Weston, Jr. and Adelaide (Neilson) V.; m. Alida Steinvoort, Oct. 5, 1951; children: Rosanne, Weston IV, Diane, John Randall. Student, Utah State U., Logan, 1949-50, Brigham Young U., Provo, Utah, 1953-54. Early broadcasting career on staff of radio stas., in Utah and Wyo., 1950-54; news and announcer KBMY, Billings, Mont., 1954-63; news dir., polit. specialist KSL Radio-TV, Salt Lake City, Utah, 1963-68; bur. chief Bonneville Internat. Corp., Washington, 1968-72; corr. CBS Radio Stas. News Svc. CBS Radio, Washington, 1972-97; host CBS Crosstalk, 1975-97. Columnist RenewAmerica.us, US AIM Report, The High Green, The Timetable, The Accuracy In Media Report, Washington columnist Railfan & Railroad Mag., guest host Dateline: Washington Radio Am. Network, 1998—; actor:. Bd. dirs. Winding-Orchard Citizens Assn., Wheaton-Glenmont, Md., 1974—77, 1986—, pres., 1975—76. Served with AUS, 1951—52. Recipient Journalism awards, Mont. A.P. Press Stas., 1960, Utah Bar Assn., 1965, Utah Broadcasters Assn., 1965—66, Nat. Press Club. Mem. SAG, AFTRA (exec. bd. Balt.-Wash. local 1997—), Am. Legion (comdr. Yellowstone Post 4 1962-63), Chesapeake Rlwy. Assn. (pres. 1992-94, bd. dirs. 1984-2006). Office: 1605 Billman Ln Silver Spring MD 20902-1417

VERONEAU, JOHN K., lawyer, former ambassador; b. 1960; m. Carol Svoboda; 2 children. BA magna cum laude, U. Maine, 1983, JD, 1989. Legis. dir. to Senator William S. Cohen US Senate, Washington, legis. dir. to Senator Bill Frist, chief of staff to Senator M. Susan Collins, 1989—97; prin. dep. asst. sec. for legis. affairs US Dept. Def.,

Washington, 1997—99, asst. sec. for legis. affairs, 1999—2001; asst. US Trade Rep. congressional affairs Office US Trade Rep., Exec. Office of the Pres., Washington, 2001—03, gen. counsel, 2003—05, dep. US Trade Rep., 2006—09; ptnr. DLA Piper Rudnick Gray Cary, Washington, 2005—06, Covington & Burling LLP, Washington, 2009—. Recipient Disting. Pub. Svc. award, Office US Trade Rep., US Dept. Def., US Dept. Navy, Exceptional Pub. Svc. award, US Dept. Army, Disting. Pub. Svc. award, US Dept. Air Force, Disting. Alumni award, U. Maine Sch. Law, 2005. Mem.: DC Bar Assn., Md. Bar Assn. Office: Covington & Burling LLP 1201 Pennsylvania Ave NW Washington DC 20004 Office Phone: 202-662-5034. E-mail: jveroneau@cov.com.*

VERONIS, GEORGE, educator; b. New Brunswick, NJ, June 6, 1926; s. Nicholas Emmanuel and Angeliki (Efthimakis) V.; m. Anna Margareta Olsson, Nov. 8, 1963; m. Catherine Elizabeth, Jan. 29, 1949 (div. Nov. 1962); children: Melissa, Benjamin. AB, Lafayette Coll., 1950; PhD, Brown U., 1954; MA (hon.), Yale U., 1966; DSc (hon.) Lafayette Coll. 1997. Staff meteorologist Inst. Advanced Study, Princeton, 1953-56; staff mathematician Woods Hole Oceanographic Inst., Mass., 1956-64, mem. staff, dir. geophys. fluid dynamics summer program, 1959—, assoc. prof. MIT, Cambridge, 1961-64, research oceanographer, 1964-66; prof. geophysics and applied sci. Yale U., New Haven, 1966—, Henry Barnard Davis prof., 1985—, chmn. geology and geophysics, 1976-79, dir. applied math, 1979-93. Editor Jour. Marine Rsch., 1973—; contbr. articles to profl. jours. Recipient AGU Excellence award Woods Hole Oceanog. Inst., 2008. Served with USN, 1943-46. Fellow Am. Acad. Arts and Scis., Am. Geophys. Union; mem. NAS, Norwegian Acad. Scis. (Robert L. and Bettie P. Cody award 1989, Henry Stommel Rsch. award 1997). Greek Orthodox. Office Phone: 203-432-3148. Business E-Mail: george.veronis@yale.edu.

VÉRONNEAU-TROUTMAN, SUZANNE, retired ophthalmologist; b. Coaticook, Que., Can., Oct. 30, 1928; d. Sarto Veronneau and Victorine Marcoux; m. Richard C. Troutman, July 12, 1967; stepchildren: David Troutman, Anne Troutman, Richard Troutman. BA, Coll. St. Maurice, St. Hyacinthe, Que., 1951; BSc II, U. Montreal, Que., 1952, MD, 1957; postgrad. in ophthalmology/pathology, Inst. Ophthalmology, London, 1960—61. Diplomate ophthalmology Royal Coll. Physicians of London, Royal Coll. Surgeons of Eng., lic. Med. Coun. Can., physician N.Y. State, diplomate ophthalmology Coll. of Physicians and Surgeons Province of Que., Royal Coll. of Physicians and Surgeons of Can., Am. Bd. of Ophthalmology. Sr. plastic surgery, neurosurgery resident Notre Dame Hosp., Montreal, 1957—58; resident in ophthalmology Hosp. Maisonneuve, Montreal, 1958—59; asst. in ophthalmology Hosp. Edouard Herriot, Lyon, France, 1959—60; clin. asst., OPD officer Royal Eye and Moorfields Eye Hosps., London, 1961; ophthalmic surgeon Ghandi Eye Hosp., Aligarh, India, 1962; instr. basic scis., asst. ophthalmologist Maisoneuve Hosp., Montreal, 1963—67; clin. assoc. prof. ophthalmology SUNY Downstate Med. Ctr., Bklyn., 1971—82; clin. instr. dept. ophthalmology Cornell U. Med. Coll., NYC, 1971—74, clin. asst. prof. ophthalmology, 1974—77, clin. assoc. prof. ophthalmology, 1977—98, clin. prof. ophthalmology, 1998—2000; clin. prof. emeritus Weill Med. Coll. of Cornell U., NYC, 2000—. Dir. strabismus clinic and orthoptics Maisoneuve Hosp., Que., 1963—67; chief ocular motility clinic Manhattan Eye Ear and Throat Hosp., NYC, 1970—2000; asst. attending physician dept. surgery, divsn. ophthalmology Hosp. of the Holy Family, 1973—77, assoc. attending physician, 1977—80; asst. dir. dept. motor anomalies N.Y. Eye and Ear Infirmary, 1970—74, assoc. attending surgeon, 1971—82, assoc. dir., 1974—82; adj. attending ophthalmologist Bronx Lebanon Hosp. Ctr., 1975—77, assoc. attending ophthalmologist, 1977—79; cons. dept. ophthalmology Beth Israel Med. Ctr., 1979—87; lectr. in field. Editor, transl.: Hugonniers' textbook Strabismus, Heterophoria, Oculomotor Paralysis; author: (textbook translated in French, Japanese and Portuguese) Prisms in the Medical and Surgical Management of Strabismus; contbr. 32 chpts. to books, articles more than 35 articles to sci. jours. Established endowment of biennial internat. prize Pan Am. Assn. Ophthalmology, 1991; established ann. prize Women in Ophthalmology, San Francisco, 1999; established perpetual endowment ann. scholarships and prize dept. edn. U. Que., Montreal, 1999; established perpetual endowment ann. scholarships dept. ophthalmology U. Montreal, 2006. Recipient Residents award for outstanding tchg., N.Y. Eye and Ear Infirmary, 1970, Spl. Achievement medal, U. Montreal, 1993. Fellow: ACS (life), Royal Coll. Surgeons Can.; mem.: AMA (life), Am. Ophthalmol. Soc., Am. Acad. Ophthalmology (life Honor award 1981), Pan Am. Assn. Ophthalmology (life; bd. dirs. 1993—2003), Med. Soc. of the State of N.Y. (life), Am. Assn. Pediat. Ophthalmology and Strabismus (life; charter mem.). Home: Apt 30 A 860 United Nations Plz New York NY 10017 Personal E-mail: sveronneau@msn.com.

VERPLANK, SCOTT RACHAL, professional golfer; b. Dallas, July 9, 1964; m. Kim Verplank; children: Scottie, Hannah, Emma, Heidi. BS in Bus., Okla. State U., 1986. Profl. golfer PGA Tour, 1986—; US Amateur champion, 1984; NCAA champion, 1986; winner Western Open, 1985, Buick Open, 1988, World Cup of Golf (individual), 1998, Reno-Tahoe Open, 2000, Bell Can. Open, 2001, EDS Byron Nelson Championship, 2007. Mem. Walker Cup team, 1985, World Cup team, 1998, 2004, Ryder Cup team, 2002, 06, Presidents Cup team, 2005. Recipient Ben Hogan award, 2002. Avocations: reading, kids, sports, quail hunting. Office: PGA 100 Ave of Champions Palm Beach Gardens FL 33418*

VERRECCHIA, ALFRED JOSEPH, toy company executive; b. Providence, Feb. 19, 1943; s. Alfred Augustus and Elda Lucy (Tortolani) V.; m. Geraldine Macari, June 11, 1964; children: Michael, Michele, Melisa, Lisa. BS, U. R.I., 1967, MBA in Fin., 1971; Doctorate (hon.), Johnson & Wales U., 1991. Joined as jr. accountant Hasbro, Inc., Pawtucket, RI, 1965, v.p. fin., 1980-82, sr. v.p. fin., CFO, 1982-86, exec. v.p. fin., CFO, 1986-89, exec. v.p., 1989, pres. Hasbro mfg. svcs., 1989, co-COO, 1989, COO, domestic toys, exec. v.p. global ops., CFO, 1990—96, exec. v.p., pres., global ops., 1996—99, exec. v.p., pres., global ops and develop., 1999; exec. v.p., global ops., CFO Hasbro Inc., Pawtucket, 1999—2000; pres., COO, CFO Hasbro, Inc., Pawtucket, 2000—01, pres., COO, 2001—03, pres., CEO, 2003—08, chmn., 2008—. Bd. dirs. Old Stone Corp., 1987—, Hasbro, Inc., 1992—. Chmn. Bradley Hosp., East Providence, R.I.; pres. R.I. Pub. Expenditure Coun., Providence; bd. mem. Bd. of Govs. for Higher Edn., Providence, U. R.I. Coll. Bus., Kingston, R.I. Mem. Toy Mfrs. Am. (bd. mem.). Office: Hasbro Inc 1027 Newport Ave Pawtucket RI 02862

VERRETT, SHIRLEY, soprano; b. New Orleans, May 31, 1931; d. Leon Solomon and Elvira Augustine (Harris) V.; m. Louis Frank LoMonaco, Dec. 10, 1963; 1 dau., Francesca. AA, Ventura Coll., Calif., 1951; diploma in voice (scholarship 1956-61), Juilliard Sch. Music, 1961; MusD (hon.), Coll. Holy Cross, Mass., 1978. CPA, Cert. real estate broker. Faculty U. Mich. Sch. Music, 1996—, James Earl Jones disting. univ. prof. voice, 1999—. Mem. adv. bd. Opera Ebony. Recital debut Town Hall, N.Y.C., 1958; appeared as Irina in Lost in the Stars, 1958; orchestral debut Phila. Orch., 1960; operatic debut in Carmen, Festival of Two Worlds, Spoleto, Italy, 1962; debuts with Bolshoi Opera, Moscow, 1963, N.Y.C. Opera, 1964, Royal Opera, Covent Garden, 1966, Maggio Fiorentino, Florence, 1967, Met. Opera, 1968, Teatro San Carlos, Naples, 1968, Dallas Civic Opera, 1969, La Scala, 1970, Vienna State Opera, 1970, San Francisco Opera, 1972, Paris Opera, 1973, Opera Co. Boston, 1976, Opera Bastille, Paris, 1990; guest appearances with all major U.S. symphony orchs.; toured Eastern Europe and Greece with La Scala chorus and orch., 1981; TV debut on Ed Sullivan Show, 1963; TV performances include: Great Performances series, live performance of Macbeth at La Scala, Santuzza in Cavalleria Rusticana; film debut Maggio Musicale, 1989, Macbeth, 1986; rec. artist, RCA, Columbia, ABC (Westminster), Angel Everest, Kapp, Philips Records and Deutsche Grammophon. Recipient Marian Anderson award, 1955, Nat. Fedn. Music Clubs award, 1961, Walter Naumberg award, 1958, Blanche Thebom award, 1960; named Chevalier Arts and Letters (France), 1970, Commandeur, 1984; John Hay Whitney fellow, 1959; Ford Found. fellow, 1962-63; Martha Baird Rockefeller Aid to Music Fund fellow, 1959-61; grantee William Matteus Sullivan Fund, 1959; grantee Berkshire Music Opera, 1956; recipient Achievement award Ventura Coll., 1963, Achievement award N.Y. chpt. Albert Einstein Coll. Medicine, 1975; 2 plaques Los Angeles Sentinel Newspaper, 1960; plaque Peninsula Music Festival, 1963; Los Angeles Times Woman of Yr. award, 1969 Mem. Mu Phi Epsilon. Office: U Mich Sch Music 1100 Baits Dr Ann Arbor MI 48109-2085 E-mail: verrett@umich.edu.

VERRILL, CHARLES OWEN, JR., lawyer; b. Biddeford, Maine, Sept. 30, 1937; s. Charles Owen and Elizabeth (Handy) V.; m. Mary Ann Blanchard, Aug. 13, 1960 (dec.); children: Martha Anne, Edward Blanchard, Ethan Christopher, Elizabeth Handy, Matthew Lawton, Peter Goldthwait; m. Diana Baber, Dec. 11, 1993. AB, Tufts U., 1959; LLB, Duke U., 1962. Bar: D.C. 1962. Assoc. Weaver & Glassie, 1962-64, Barco, Cook, Patton & Blow, 1964-66, ptnr., 1967, Patton, Boggs & Blow, 1967-84, Wiley, Rein LLP (and predecessor firm), Washington, 1984—. Adj. prof. internat. trade law/internat. bus. transaction Georgetown U. Law Ctr., Washington, 1978—, Charles Fahy Disting. adj. prof., 1993; vis. sr. lectr. internat. trade law Duke U. Law Sch., 1998—; nat. adv. bd. Natural Resources Coun. of Maine, 2002—; panel mem. CPR Washington, 2003—. Local dir. Tufts U. Ann. Fund, 1965-69; mem. Duke Law Alumni Coun., 1972-75; trustee Internat. Law Inst., 1981—, chmn. bd. trustees, 1983-87, pres., 2002—; pres. Friends Law Libr. Congress, 2008-; apptd. to roster of dispute settlement panelists World Trade Orgn., 1995, 97; bd. visitors Duke U. Law Sch., 2000—. Recipient Charles B. Rhyne Disting. Alumni award, Duke U. Law Sch., 2007. Mem. ABA, Internat. Bar Assn., D.C. Bar Assn., Am. Soc. Internat. Law (editl. adv. com. Internat. Legal Materials, 2007-), Internat. Law Assn. (Am. br.), Order of Coif, Theta Delta Chi, Phi Delta Phi, Met. Club (Washington), Chevy Chase Club (Md.), Tarratine Club (Dark Harbor, Maine). Office: Wiley Rein LLP 1776 K St NW Washington DC 20006-2304 Office Phone: 202-719-7323. Business E-Mail: cverrill@wileyrein.com.

VERRILL, F. GLENN, advertising executive; b. NYC, Dec. 17, 1923; s. Ralph Francis and Rose (Cuva) V.; m. Jean Demar, Aug. 25, 1946; children: Gary, Joan. AB, Adelphi Coll., 1949; A.M., Harvard U., 1950. With Batten, Barton, Durstine & Osborn, Inc., 1952—98, v.p., 1964; pres. Batten, Barton, Durstine & Osborn, Inc. (Burke Dowling Adams div.), Atlanta, 1971-88, chmn., 1988—98, also dir. parent co. Bd. dirs. High Mus. Art, Atlanta, 2005—. Author: Advertising Procedure, 1983, rev. edit., 1986, 88. Mem. adv. bd. U. Ga.; vice chmn. bd. overseers Coll. Bus. Adminstrn., Ga. State U.; bd. dirs. Atlanta Humane Soc., pres., 1980-81; chmn. Advanced Advt. Inst. Atlanta, 1981; mem. Peabody award com., 1984—90; bd. dirs. Atlanta Coll. of Art, 1990. With USAAF, 1943-46. Mem. Am. Assn. Advt. Agys. (nat. dir. 1973—), Atlanta Athletic Club, Cherokee Club, Harvard Club (Atlanta). Episcopalian. Home: 1730 Winterthur Close Atlanta GA 30328 Office Phone: 678-428-6600.

VERRILLI, DONALD B., JR., federal agency administrator, lawyer; b. New Rochelle, NY, June 29, 1957; BA cum laude, Yale U., 1979; JD, Columbia U., 1983. Bar: NY 1987, Washington, DC 1989. Law clk. Hon. J. Skelly Wright, US Ct. Appeals, DC Cir., 1983—84, Justice William J. Brennan, Jr., US Supreme Ct., 1984—85; rsch. fellow Columbia U., 1985—86; adj. prof. law Georgetown U. Law Ctr., 1991—2007; lectr. Washington Coll. Law, Am. U., 1995; ptnr. Jenner & Block LLP, Washington, chair telecom. practice, co-chair appellate and supreme ct. practice, mem. policy com., chair diversity com.; assoc. dep. atty. gen. US Dept. Justice, Washington, 2009—. Mem. bd. visitors Columbia Law Sch., 2000—, chair reunion com. Recipient Arthur von Briesen award, Nat. Legal Aid and Defender Assn., 2004, Equal Justice award, Southern Ctr. for Human Rights, 2006; named one of 500 Leading Lawyers in America, Lawdragon Mag., 2006, Entertainment Top 100 Power Lawyers - Litig., Hollywood Reporter, ESQ, 2007; named to Litig. list, Chambers USA, 2003—07, Telecom., Broadcast & Satellite list, 2005—07, Best Lawyers in America, 2006, 2007, 2008. Office: US Dept Justice 950 Pennsylvania Ave NW Rm 4111 Washington DC 20530*

VERSACE, DONATELLA, fashion designer; b. Reggio di Calabria, Italy, May 2, 1955; d. Antonio and Francesca V.; m. Paul Beck (div.); children: Allegra, Daniel. Degree in lit., U. Florence, Italy. Head designer Versus label Gianni Versace Group, 1978—97, vice chmn., style and image dir. NYC, 1997—. Released fragrance Versace Woman, 2001. Achievements include created children's line, 1993; launched fragrance Versace Woman, 2001. Office: Gianni Versace SpA Via Ges 12 20121 Milan Italy Address: Instante Vesa srl Via Spiga 25 20121 Milan Italy Office Phone: 02 7610931. Office Fax: 02 798572.

VERSCH, ESTHER MARIE, artist; b. Santa Monica, Calif., May 27, 1927; d. Claro Contreras Santellanes and Juana Hernandez; m. Chester Ray Fraelich, Nov. 14, 1943 (div. Nov. 1964); children: Joe Fraelich, Diane Fraelich Foster Viramontes; m. Terry Lee Versch, June 21, 1969; stepchildren: Fred, Roman, Joseph, Terry Jr., Michael. Student, East L.A. Coll., Pasadena City Coll. Lic. vocat. nurse. Nurse pvt. dr.'s office, LA, 1968-69, U. So. Calif. Med. Ctr., LA, 1963-68; artist Altadena, Calif., 1972—. Artist: (front cover) Library Services L.A., 1983, Christmas card for Western Greeting Inc., (back cover) Moccasin Tracks, 1984-85; one woman shows include Republic Fed. Savings, Altadena, Calif., Pasadena Pub. Libr., Whites Art Store and Gallery, La Canada, Calif., 1979, Windmill Gallery, 1985; group exhbns.: Women Artists of the West Internat. Exhbn. and Sale, Cody Western and Wildlife Classyc, 1979, Nat. Cowgirl Hall of Fame, Hereford, Tex., 1978, Beauty for the Best Benefit, 1980, Ducks Unltd. Invitational Art Show, Taylor, Mich., 1986-87, Lawrence (Kans.) Indian Art Show, Mus. Anthropology, 1989-90, Snake River Showcase, Lewiston, Idaho, 1992, Women Artists of the West, 1992, 98, 99, Death Valley 49's Invitational Art Show, 1994-2000, 2001, George Ohr Cultural Arts and Cultural Ctr., Biloxi, Miss., 1998, Western and Wildlife Invitational Art Show, Estes Park, Colo., 2000, WAOW Art Show Pinedale, Wyo, 2002, Art and Music Festival, Dublin, Ohio, 2002, West Wind Gallery, Casper, Wyo., 2003-04, Pomerene Ctr. for the Arts, 2004, Zanesville Ctr. for the Arts, 2004, 05, Red River Valley Mus., Vernon, Tex., 2004, Ronald Reagan Mus., Simi Valley, Calif., 2004, Johnsonhumrick House Mus., 2004-05, Dogwood Festival Artists Tour Studio, 2006, Juliet Art Exhibit Nat. Arts Found., Skokie, Ill., 2006, Past Present Perfect, Johnson Humrick House Mus., 2006, West Wind Gallery, Casper, Wyo., 2006, others; collections: Johnson Humrickhouse Mus., Coshocton, Ohio, East to West Meeting in the Middle, Hilligoss Gallery, Chgo., Renaissance Gallery, Huntington, W.Va, 2008, Living With Crows, Pomevene Ctr. Arts CoShocton Ohio, Red River Valley Mus. Vernon Tex, 2009; illustrator back cover Moccasin Tracks, 1984-85. Vol. nurses aide City View Hosp., L.A., 1960-63; vol. Arroyo Rep., Pasadena, Calif., St. Luke Hosp., Pasadena, 1990-94, flu immunization ARC, 1977-78; vol. Journeys End Food and Clothing Bank, 2008-09. Recipient Gold medal for watercolor San Gabriel Fine Arts, 1979, Best of Show award for watercolor Am. Indian and Western, 1990, Hon. mention San Gabriel Fine Arts, 1990, 3rd Place Watercolor Women Artists of the West Saddle Back Art Gallery, 1982. Mem. Women Artists of the West (emeritus mem., treas., asst. sec., editor West Wind, membership chmn.), Ohio Art League, Coshocton Art Guild (v.p. Juried Art Show 2004-05). Republican. Roman Catholic. Avocations: walking, gardening, sewing. E-mail: everschart@newsguy.com.

VERSCHOOR, CURTIS CARL, author, consultant; b. Grand Rapids, Mich., June 7, 1931; s. Peter and Leonene (Dahlstrom) V.; m. Marie Emilie Kritschgau, June 18, 1952; children: Katherine Anne, Carolyn Marie, John Peter, Carla Michelle. BBA with distinction, U. Mich., 1951; MBA, U. Mich., Ann Arbor, 1952; EdD, No. Ill. U., DeKalb, 1977. CPA; cert. mgmt. acctg., cert. fin. planner, cert. fraud examiner, cert. internal auditor; chartered fin. cons. Pub. accountant Touche, Ross, Bailey & Smart (C.P.A.'s), 1955-63; with Singer Co., 1963-68, asst. controller, 1965-68; controller Colgate-Palmolive Co., 1968-69; asst. controller bus. products group Xerox Corp., 1969-72; controller Baxter Internat., 1972-73; CFO, v.p. fin. Altair Corp., Chgo., 1973-74; prof. DePaul U., Chgo., 1974-94, ledger and quill alumni rsch. prof., 1994—; pres. C.C. Verschoor & Assocs., Inc., 1981—. Part-time instr. Wayne State U., 1955-60. Author: Audit Committee Essentials, 2008, Understanding the 21st Century Audit Committee Governance Roles, 2000, Audit Committee Briefing: Facilitating New Audit Committee Responsibilites, 2001, Ethics and Compliance: Challenges for Internal Auditing, 2007, Governance Update: Impact of the New Initiatives, 2003, contbg. editor: Jour. Accountancy, 1961-62, Jour. Strategic Fin., 1999-; editl. adv. bd. Acctg. Today, 1991-2004, Internal Auditor, 1993—. Trustee Hektoen Inst. for Medicine, Chgo., 1996—, chair audit com., 1998-, mem. Audit Com. Bd. Pension & Health Benefits United Methodist Ch., 2008-. Served with AUS, 1953-55. Recipient Elijah Watts Sells award Am. Inst. C.P.A.'s, 1953; rsch. scholar Ctr. for Bus. Ethics, Bentley U. Mem. AICPA, Fin. Execs. Inst., Am. Acctg. Assn., Inst. Mgmt. Accts., Inst. Internal Auditors, Nat. Assn. Corp. Dirs., Assn. Cert. Fraud Examiners, Soc. for Bus. Ethics, Beta Gamma Sigma, Beta Alpha Psi, Delta Pi Epsilon, Phi Kappa Phi, Phi Eta Sigma. Home and Office: 231 Wyngate Dr Barrington IL 60010-4840 Personal E-mail: curtisverschoor@sbcglobal.net.

VERSFELD, LEON, lawyer; s. Johannes Hendrik and Lorraine Versfeld; m. Heather Lea Hunter, Sept. 27, 2003; children: Annike Grace, Johannes Aletander. BLC, U. Pretoria, South Africa, 1996, LLB, 1998; tng. diploma (hon.), Law Soc. South Africa, 1999; grad., Greater Kans. City Bar Leadership Acad., 2006. Bar: The High Ct. South Africa 1999, Mo. 2003, U.S Dist. Ct. Kans. 2003, U.S Dist. Ct. (we. dist.) Mo. 2003, Solicitor Eng. & Wales. Law clk. to Hon. NG Manitz Dept. Justice, Pretoria, 1997, law clk. to Hon. Dep. Judge Pres. P.J. Van Der Walt, 1998—99; pvt. practice, advocate of Higher Ct. Pretoria, 1999—2003; assoc. Wirken Law Group, P.C., 2003—06; mng. mem. Versfeld & Hugo, LLC, 2006—. Grad. Greater Kansas City Bar Leadership Acad., 2005—06; mem. congress Fellows of Ctr. for Internat. Legal Studies; presenter and spkr. in field. Contbr. articles to profl. pubs. and confs. Bd. mem. Ctrl. Youth Rugby, Kansas City, 2004—05; bd. dirs. Tru-Friends, Truman Med. Ctr., 2006; barrister Kans. City Met. Bar. Assn. Inn of Ct., Kansas City, 2004—05. Recipient Outstanding CLE Contbr. award, KCMBA; named one of Super Lawyer, 2008, Upcoming Lawyer, 2008; nominee Best of the Bar, Kans. City Bus. Jour., 2007—08; scholar, Delta Motor Corp., South Africa, 1994-1998. Mem.: Am. Immigration Lawyer Assn., Kans. City Met. Bar Assn. (chmn. internat. law com., barrister inns of ct. 2004—05). Avocations: rugby, tennis, golf. Office: Versfeld Hugo LLC 4740 Grand Blvd Ste 200 Kansas City MO 64112 Business E-Mail: lv@versfeldlaw.com.

VERSFELT, DAVID SCOTT, lawyer; b. Mineola, NY, Feb. 17, 1951; s. William H. and Ruth (Gerland) V.; m. Mary Deborah Garber, Aug. 31, 1974; children: Christopher L., William S., Kathryn H. AB, Princeton U., 1973; JD, Columbia U., 1976. Bar: N.Y. 1977, U.S. Dist. Ct. (so. and ea. dists.) N.Y. 1977, U.S. Ct. Appeals (D.C. cir.) 1979, U.S. Ct. Appeals (2d and 7th cirs.) 1980, U.S. Supreme Ct. 1980, U.S. Ct. Appeals (9th cir.) 1981, U.S. Ct. Appeals (3d cir.) 1982, Ct. Internat. Trade 1990, U.S. Ct. Appeals (fed. cir.) 1994, U.S. Ct. Appeals (6th cir.) 1996. With Kirkpatrick & Lockhart LLP, NYC, 1998—2005, Kirkpatrick & Lockhart Nicholson Graham LLP, NYC, 2005—06, Kirkpatrick Lockhart Preston Gates Ellis LLP, NYC, 2007—08, K&L Gates LLP, NYC, 2008—. Mem. vol. divsn. Legal Aid Soc., N.Y.C., 1985-88, Partnership for a Drug-Free Am., 1989—. Mem. ABA, Fed. Bar Coun., Phi Beta Kappa. Office: K&L Gates LLP 599 Lexington Ave New York NY 10022-6030

VERSHBOW, ALEXANDER RUSSELL (SANDY VERSHBOW), federal agency administrator, former ambassador; b. Boston, July 3, 1952; m. Lisa (Kaufman) Vershbow; two children. BA in Russian and East European Studies, Yale Coll., 1974; MS in Internat. Rels., Columbia U., 1976. Various fgn. svc. positions, 1977—; dir. Office Soviet Union Affairs US Dept. State, Washington, 1988-91, prin. dep. asst. sec. for European & Can. Affairs, 1993-94; spl. asst. to Pres., sr. dir. European Affairs NSC, Washington, 1995-97; US amb. to NATO and permanent rep. to North Atlantic Coun. US Dept. State, Brussels, 1998—2001, US amb. to Russian Fedn. Moscow, 2001—05, US amb. to Republic of Korea (South Korea) Seoul, 2005—08; asst. sec. for internat. security affairs US Dept. Def., Washington, 2009—. Contbr. articles to profl. jours. Recipient Anatoly Sharansky Freedom award Union of Couns. of Soviet Jews, 1990, 1st ann. Joseph J. Kruzel award, Sec. of Def. William Cohen, 1997, Disting. Honor award US Dept. State, 2001. Office: US Dept Defense 2400 Def Pentagon Rm 3C889 Washington DC 20301 Office Phone: 703-697-2788. Business E-Mail: alexander.vershbow@usd.mil.

VER STEEG, DONNA LORRAINE FRANK, nurse, sociologist, educator; b. Minot, ND, Sept. 23, 1929; d. John Jonas and Pearl H. (Denlinger) Frank; m. Richard W. Ver Steeg, Nov. 22, 1950; children: Juliana, Anne, Richard B. BSN, Stanford, 1951; MSN, U. Calif., San Francisco, 1967; MA in Sociology, UCLA, 1969, PhD in Sociology, 1973. Clin. instr. U. ND Sch. Nursing, 1962-63; USPHS nurse rsch. fellow UCLA, 1969-72, asst. prof. Sch. Nursing, 1973-79, assoc. prof. Sch. Nursing, 1979-94, asst. dean Sch. Nursing, 1979-81, chmn. primary ambulatory care Sch. Nursing, 1976-87, assoc. dean Sch. Nursing, 1983-86, prof. emeritus chair primary care Sch. Nursing, 1994-96, prof. emeritus Sch. Nursing, 1996—; spl. cons., mem. adv. com. on physicians' assts. and nurse practitioner progs. Calif. State Bd. Med. Examiners, 1972-73. Co-prin. investigator PRIMEX Project Family Nurse Practitioners, UCLA Ext., 1974—76; assoc. cons. Calif. Postsecondary Edn. Commn., 1975—76; spl. cons. Calif. Dept. Consumer Affairs, 1978; chair nurse practioner/physician's asst. statewide program planning com. Calif. Area Health Edn. Ctr., 1978—89; mem. Calif. State Legis. Health Policy Forum, 1980—81; accredited visitor Western Assn. Sch. and Coll., 1985; mem. nurse practitioner adv. com. Calif. Bd. RN, 1995—97; mem. Edn. Industry Interface, Info. Devel. Mktg. Sub Com., 1995—99, recruitment, 1999—2001; archivist Calif. Strategic Planning Com. Nursing/Colleagues in Caring Project, 1995—. Contbr. chpts. to profl. books, articles to profl. jours. Recipient Leadership award Calif. Area Health Edn. Ctr. Sys., 1989, Commendation award Calif. State Assembly, 1994; named Outstanding Faculty Mem., UCLA Sch. Nursing, 1982. Fellow Am. Acad. Nursing; mem. AAAS, AAUW, ANA (Calif.) (pres. 1979-81, interim chair 1995-96), Nat. League Nursing, Calif. League Nursing, N.Am. Nursing Diagnosis Assn., Am. Assn. History Nursing, Stanford Nurses Club, Sigma Theta Tau (Alpha Eta chpt. Leadership award Gamma Tau chpt. 1994), Sigma Xi. Home: 708 Swarthmore Ave Pacific Palisades CA 90272-4353 Office: UCLA Sch Nursing Box 956917 Los Angeles CA 90095-6917 Personal E-mail: dversteeg@aol.com. Business E-Mail: dverstee@sonnet.ucla.edu.

VERSTEEG, ROBERT JOHN, minister, actor, writer; b. Oradell, NJ, July 7, 1930; s. John Marinus and Edna Elizabeth (Ames) Versteeg; m. Sally Maude Youngblood Creel, Feb. 17, 1951 (div. Apr. 1976); children: Cassandra Lee, John Richard, Jay Russell; m. Donna Marie Stevens, June 22, 1977; 1 child, Rick. BA, Ohio Wesleyan U., 1952; MDiv, Garrett Theol. Sem., Evanston, Ill., 1955; student, Baldwin-Wallace Coll., Berea, Ohio, 1962; MA, U. N.C., 1971. Ordained to ministry Meth. Ch., 1955. Pastor Ohio Meth. Ch., 1955-62; prof., dir. drama Louisburg (N.C.) Coll., 1962-75; assoc. prof., dir. Conservatory Acting Program, Va. Commonwealth U., Richmond, 1975-76; pastor Peebles (Ohio) United Meth. Ch., 1977-79, Point Place United Meth. Ch., Toledo, 1979-82, First United Meth. Ch., Ada, Ohio, 1982-86, Oak Hills United Meth. Ch., Cin., 1986-94, Trinity United Meth. Ch., Bowling Green, Ohio, 1994-99; writer LectionAid, 1997—99, Lectionary Homiletics, 1999—. Author: The Gracious Calling of the Lord, 1960, The Secret Life of the Good Samaritan, 1963, Whose Church is This Anyway?, 1985, Tales of Tittivillus, 1992, LectionAid, 1998, The Star Thrower, 2003; contbr. articles to profl. jours.; author, performer: (TV series) The Browning Show, 1974; Men of Faith, 1990—; (TV films) Paul A Prisoner, 1993—95; founder, dir.: Playback Theatre N.W. Ohio; Life Stage Theatrical Troupe, Inc. Recipient Best Sermons award, HarperCollins, 1991; named Seminarian Preacher of the Yr., Pulpit mag., 1955; named an Outstanding Educator, 1972; named to Outstanding Young Men of Am., 1965; NEH fellow, 1972. Mem.: Nat. Assn. Drama Therapy, Fellowship United Meths. in Worship, Music and Other Arts. Democrat. Avocations: reading, piano, conditioning. Home and Office: 616 Flanders Ave Bowling Green OH 43402-1519 Office Phone: 419-601-0499. Business E-Mail: bojov@wcnet.org.

VERSTEGEN, JOHN P.L., theriogenologist, educator; b. Duren, Germany, May 16, 1956; Degree in Vet. Medicine, U. Liege, Belgium, 1980, PhD, 1986; M in Biostats., U. Paris, 1983; M in Informatics, U. Brussels, 1984. Asst. U. Liege, 1980-86, agregg, 1980-91; prof. small animal theriogenology Diplomate ECAR. Cons. pharm. co., Belgium, France, Germany, U.K. and Italy; bd. dirs. Sperm Bank in Canine, Belgium; bd. dirs. Belgium Coun. for Lab. Animal Sci., FELASA, ECAR, EVSSAR. Author: Adrenergic Agents, 1993; editor: Fertility and Infertility, 1993-97. Mem. Soc. Study Reprodn., Soc. for Theriogenology, Assn. for the Study of Animal Reprodn. (v.p.), Assn. Vet. Anesthesiologist, European Soc. Cellular Biology, European Soc. for Study of Small Animal Reprodn. (founding mem.). Avocations: climbing, squash, swimming. Office: Univ of Florida 2016 SW 16th Ave Gainesville FL 32610-0136

VERTEFEUILLE, CHRISTINE SIEGRIST, state supreme court justice; b. New Britain, Conn., Dec. 10, 1950; BA in Polit. Sci., Trinity Coll., 1972; JD, U. Conn., 1975. Pvt. practice, 1975-89; judge Conn. Superior Ct., 1989—99; adminstrv. judge Waterbury Jud. Dist., 1994-99, complex litig. judge, 1999; judge Appellate Ct., 1999-2000; assoc. justice Conn. Supreme Ct., 2000—. Alternate mem. Waterbury and New Haven (Conn.) Grievance Panels, 1985-89; faculty Conn. Judges Inst., 1989-94. Recipient Jud. award Conn. Trial Lawyers Assn., 1995. Mem. Conn. Bar Assn. (mem. exec. com. real property 1988-89). Office: Conn Supreme Ct 231 Capitol Ave Hartford CT 06106 Office Phone: 860-757-2117.*

VERTS, LITA JEANNE, academic administrator; b. Jonesboro, Ark., Apr. 13, 1935; d. William Gus and Lolita Josephine (Peeler) Nash; m. B. J. Verts, Aug. 29, 1954 (div. 1975); 1 child, William Trigg. BA, Oreg. State U., 1973; MA in Lingustics, U. Oreg., 1974; postgrad., U. Hawaii, 1977. Librarian Forest Research Lab., Corvallis, Oreg., 1966-69; instr. English Lang. Inst., Corvallis, 1974-80; dir. spl. svcs. Oreg. State U., Corvallis, 1980-96, faculty senator, 1988-96; ret., 1996. Editor Trio Achievers, 1986, 3rd edit., 1988; contbr. articles to profl. jours. Precinct com. Rep. Party, Corvallis, 1977-80; adminstrv. bd. 1st United Meth. Ch., Corvallis, 1987-89, fin. com., 1987-93, tchr. Bible, 1978—; bd. dirs. Westminster Ho., United Campus Ministries, 1994-95; adv. coun. Disabilities Svc., Linn, Benton, Lincoln Counties, 1990-99, vice-chmn., 1992-93, chmn. 1993-94; citizen adv. bd. on Transit, 1999—2008, intercity steering com., 1999—2008, Corvallis Downtown Parking Commn., 1999—2008; Oreg. Longterm Care Ombudsman, 1999—2009. Mem. N.W. Assn. Spl. Programs (pres. 1985-86), Nat. Coun. Ednl. Opportunities Assn. (bd. dirs. 1984-87), Nat. Gardening Assn., Alpha Phi (mem. corp. bd. Beta Upsilon chpt. 1990-96). Republican. Methodist. Avocations: gardening, photography, golf. Home: 530 SE Mayberry Ave Corvallis OR 97333-1866 Personal E-mail: l.verts@comcast.net.

VERTULLO, CHRISTINA A., mathematics professor, director; d. John Theofil and Mary Veronica Cheyer; children: Kristie Marie, Collette Anne. BA, Coll. St. Rose, Albany, NY, 1965; MS, SUNY, New Paltz, NY, 1968, Marist Coll., Poughkeepsie, NY, 1994. High sch. math tchr. Hyde Pk. Ctrl. Sch. Dist., NY, 1965—69, substitute tchr., 1969—74; adj. instr. Dutchess CC, Poughkeepsie, 1974—75, instr., 1983—85; adj. instr. Marist Coll., Poughkeepsie, 1976—77, instr., 1977—80, 1985—, dir. math., 1999—. Contbr. to numerous manuscript. Moderator ocd-l, internet discussion forum ocd Marist Coll., 1994—2000, founder, 1994—2000; spkr. new comers orientation ann. confs. Obsessive Compulsive Found., Boston, 2003—08; mem. bd. assessment rev. Town Clinton, Clinton Corners, NY, 1978—86; analyzed flow info. Rehabil. Programs Inc., Poughkeepsie, 1991; develop. decision support sys. Dutchess County Office Aging, Poughkeepsie, 1993; organizer, OCD ann. confs. Marist Coll., 1996—2001, spkr., 1996—2001; founder Hudson Valley OCD Support Group, Poughkeepsie, 1996—2008, co-facilitator, 1996—2008; vol. Hudson Valley Coalition Homeless, Poughkeepsie, 2000—08, web designer, 2000—08; mem. Leave A Legacy, Poughkeepsie, 2000—01; develop. info. standards Office Cult Awareness, Poughkeepsie, 1994; organizer devotion and healing mass st. dymphna, patron st. mental illness Mt. Alvernia Friary, Wappingers Falls, NY, 2000—08; organizer devotion and healing mass st. colette, patron st. couples desiring children Poor Clares, Wappingers Falls, 2008. Just-inTime Pub. grant, Marist Coll., 1994, Presvc. Tchrs. grant, 1998. Mem.: Assn. Women Math., Nat. Coun. Tchrs. Math., Assn. Math. Tchrs. (NY), Math. Assn. Am. Office: Marist Coll 3399 North Rd Poughkeepsie NY 12601 Business E-Mail: christina.vertullo@marist.edu.

VERVEER, MELANNE S., ambassador; b. Ukraine, June 24, 1944; m. Philip Verveer; 3 children. BSc cum laude, Georgetown U., 1966, MSc, 1969. Spl. asst. to Senator George McGovern US Senate, Washington, 1973-75; field dir. Common Cause, 1976-80; dir. coop. devel. for voluntary assns. Nat. Consumer Coop. Bank, 1980; coord. civil rights and urban policy US Cath. Conf., 1981-82; legis. dir. to Rep. Marcy Kaptur US House of Reps., Washington, 1983-84; pub. policy dir., exec. v.p. People for the Am. Way & PFAW Action Fund, 1985-92; dep. asst. to Pres., dep. chief staff to First Lady The White House, Washington, 1993-97, asst. to Pres., chief of staff to First Lady, 1997—2001; co-founder, chair, co-CEO Vital Voices Global Partnership, Washington, 2000—09; amb.-at-Large for Women's Global Issues US Dept. State, Washington, 2009—. Mem. Pres.'s Interagy. Coun. on Women. Contbr. chpts. to books; cons. editor: Jour. Arts Mgmt. and Law. Bd. dirs. Leadership Conf. on Civil Rights, 1987-93, Coalition on Human Needs, founding mem., 1981, legis. chair, 1981-82, dir., 1987-92; bd. dirs. Advocacy Inst., 1990-93, Pub. Allies, Nat. Ctr. for Careers in Pub. Life, 1991-93, NETWORK Nat. Cath. Social Justice Lobby; active Interreligious Campaign on Econ. Justice, founding mem., 1981; bd. advisers Ctr. for Policy Alternatives, 1990-93; active D.C. Adv. Coun. on Cmty. Svcs., 1992-93. Recipient Basilian Humanitarian award, Pub. Svc. award Ukrainian Nat. Women's League, 1997, Woman of Distinction award, Am. Assn. University Women Mem.: Women in Internat. Security, The Washington Inst. on Fgn. Affairs, Women's Fgn. Policy Group, Coun. Fgn. Rels. Democrat. Office: US Dept State 2201 C St NW Washington DC 20520*

VERVEER, PHILIP L., lawyer; b. Corvallis, Oreg., 1944; m. Melanne Verveer; 3 children. BSFS, Georgetown U., 1966; JD, U. Chgo., 1969. Bar: DC 1969, US Dist. Ct., DC 1969, US Ct. Appeals, DC Cir. 1971, US Ct. Appeals, 10th Cir. 1982, US Supreme Ct. 1986. Trial atty. antitrust divsn. US Dept. Justice, 1969—77; supervisory atty. Bur. Competition FTC, 1977—78; chief Cable Television Bur., Broadcast Bur. and Common Carrier Bur. FCC, 1978—81; ptnr. telecom. dept. Willkie Farr & Gallagher LLP, Washington, DC; of counsel Jenner & Block LLP, Washington, 2009—. Chair Fed. Pub. Safety Wireless Advisory Com., 1995—96. Recipient Disting. Presdl Rank award, 1980, Telecommunication Industry Association's President's award, 1996; named one of The 500 Leading Lawyers in America, Lawdragon mag., 2006. Mem.: ABA, Fed. Comm. Bar Assn. Office: Jenner & Block LLP 1099 New York Ave NW Ste 900 Washington DC 20001 Office Phone: 202-639-6070. Office Fax: 202-661-4944.*

VERVILLE, ELIZABETH GIAVANI, federal official; b. NYC, July 13, 1940; d. Joseph and Gertrude (Levy) Giavani. BA, Duke U., 1961; LLB, Columbia U., 1964. Bar: Mass. 1965, U.S. Supreme Ct. 1970, D.C. 1980. Assoc. Snow Motley & Holt, successor Gaston Snow & Ely Bartlett, Boston, 1965-67; asst. atty. gen. Commonwealth of Mass., Boston, 1967-69; atty. advisor for African affairs U.S. Dept. State, Washington, 1979-72, asst. legal adviser for East Asian and Pacific affairs, 1972-80, dep. legal adviser, 1980-89; dep. asst. sec. state Bur. Politico-Mil. Affairs Bur. Politico-Mil. Affairs, Washington, 1989-92, sr. coord., 1992-95; dir. for global and multilateral affairs Nat. Security Coun., Washington, 1995-98; dep. dir. Critical Infrastructure Assurance Office, Washington, 2000—01; spl. rep. Bur. Narcotics and Law Enforcement, Washington, 2000—02, 2005—; acting dep. asst. sec. Bur. Internat. Narcotics and Law Enforcement, Dept. State, Washington, 2001—02, sr. advisor, 2002—05, acting dep., asst. sec., 2005—07, dep., asst. sec., 2007—. Recipient presdl. rank of meritorious exec., 1985, 90, 2003, presdl. rank disting. exec., 1988. Mem. Am. Soc. Internat. Law, Coun. on Fgn. Rels. Home: 3012 Dumbarton Ave NW Washington DC 20007-3305 Office: Bur Internat Narcotics & Law Enforcement State Dept Washington DC 20520-0001 Home Phone: 202-337-6079; Office Phone: 202-647-9822.

VERYSER, HARRY CORNELIUS, manufacturing executive, educator; b. Mt. Clemens, Mich., July 8, 1943; s. Harry Cornelius and Loraine Delphine (Steckley) V. AB, U. Detroit, 1966, MA, 1983-84. Cert. tchr., Mich. Tchr. St. Mary's High Sch., Mt. Clemens, 1967-68, Clintondale Pub. Schs., Mt. Clemens, 1968-870, Star of the Sea High Schs., Grosse Pointe Shores, Mich., 1970-72; instr. Northwood Inst., Midland, Mich., 1972-73; asst. to pres. Hillsdale (Mich.) Coll., 1974-78; chmn. Stampings, Inc., Fraser, Mich., 1978—; assoc. prof., chmn. dept. Walsh Coll., Troy, Mich., 1982—. Chmn. Americans for Robertson, Mich., 1987-88; chmn. 12th Congl. Dist. Rep. Com., Mt. Clemens, 1986—. Mem. Am. Coun. Econs. and Soc. (chmn. 1984—), Phila. Soc., Soc. Mfg. Engrs. Roman Catholic. Office: Stampings Inc 34152 Doreka Dr Fraser MI 48026-3434 Home: 44523 Patricia Dr Sterling Heights MI 48314-1586

VESELINOVIČ, DRAŠKO, stock exchange executive; b. Ljubljana, Slovenia, Feb. 26, 1959; s. Branko and Breda (Pokorn) V.; children: Eva, Gal, Rea. M of Internat. Fin., U. Ljubljana, 1986, DSc in Econs., 1996. Fgn. exch. dealer Ljubljanska Bank, fgn. exch. and internat. treasury mgr.; assoc. prof. Faculty of Econs.; fin. adviser Slovene Govt.; CEO Ljubljana Stock Exch., gen. mgr., 1993—2004; CEO Dezelna Banka Slovenije DD, 2005—. Founder The Yugoslav Stock Exch., 1989. Author: Foreign Exchange in Developed World & in Yugoslavia, 1988, Foreign Exchange Trading, 1991, Stock Exchange Handbook, 1991, 95, Options and Other Derivative Financial Instruments, 1998, Aphorisms, 1996, 2002, Foreign Exchange Act with a Commentary and By-laws, 1999; contbr.more than 200 articles to profl. jours. Avocations: tennis, music. Office Phone: 386 1 4727 111. Personal E-mail: draskoveselinovic@yahoo.com.

VESELL, ELLIOT SAUL, pharmacologist, educator; b. NYC, Dec. 24, 1933; s. Harry and Evelyn (Jaffe) Vesell; m. Kristen Paige Peery, Mar. 24, 1968; children: Liane Clark, Hilary Peery. AB magna cum laude, Harvard U., 1955, MD magna cum laude, 1959; DSc (hon.), Phila. Coll. Pharmacy & Sci., 1988; PhD (hon.), Philipps U., Marburg, Germany, 1991. Intern, children's med. svc. Mass. Gen. Hosp., Boston, 1959-60; rsch. assoc. Rockefeller U., NYC, 1960-62; asst. resident medicine Peter Bent Brigham Hosp., Boston, 1962-63; clin. assoc. Nat. Inst. Arthritis Metabolic Diseases, NIH, Bethesda, Md., 1963-65; head sect. pharmacogenetics Nat. Heart Inst., NIH, Bethesda, 1965-68; Evan Pugh prof. pharmacology Pa. State U., Hershey, 1968—, asst. dean grad. edn., 1973-96, chmn. dept. pharmacology Coll. Medicine, 1968—2000, Bernard B. Brodie prof., 1991—. Pfizer vis. prof.; Burroughs Wellcome vis. prof. Editor: The Life and Works of Thomas Cole, 1964, Progress in Basic and Clin. Pharmacology, 1990, others; contbr. articles to profl. jours. Recipient Von Humboldt award, 1988. Fellow: AAAS, Royal Soc. Medicine (Frohlich vis. prof. 1985); mem.: Am. Soc. Clin. Pharmacology Therapeutics (Oscar B. Hunter Meml. award 1991), Am. Coll. Clin. Pharmacology (pres. 1980—82, Disting. Investigator award 1999), Am. Soc. Pharmacology Exptl. Therapeutics (sec.-treas. 1995—98, Exptl. Therapeutics award 1971, Harry Gold award clin. pharmacology 1985), Am. Soc. Clin. Investigation, Assn. Am. Physicians, Phi Beta Kappa, Alpha Omega Alpha. Office: Pa State U Coll Medicine Dept Pharmacology PO Box 850 Hershey PA 17033-0850 Office Phone: 717-531-8285. Business E-Mail: esv1@psu.edu.

VESELY, DAVID LYNN, medical educator, research scientist; b. Omaha, Mar. 6, 1943; s. Raymond James and Cecila Jane (O'Keefe) V.; m. Clo M. Farrell (dec. 2002); children: Susanna, Catherine, Matthew, Brian, Jonathan. BS in biology, Creighton U., 1967; MD, PhD, U. Ariz., 1972. Asst. prof. medicine U. Miami Med. Sch., 1974-78; asst. prof., chief endocrinology U. Ark. Med. Sci., Little Rock, 1978-79, assoc. prof., 1979-83, prof., 1983-89; prof. medicine, molecular pharmacology and physiology Univ. S. Fla. Med. Sch., Tampa, 1989—; chief endocrinology and metabolism J.A. Haley Vets. Med. Ctr., Tampa, 1993—; dir. Cardiac Hormone Ctr. U. South Fla., Tampa, 1999—. Disting. vis. prof. Christchurch, New Zealand, 1995. Author: Atrial Natriuretic Hormones, 1992, 97, 2007; contbr. 305 articles to profl. jours. Rsch. advisor Am. Heart Assn. Fla. Affiliate, 1993—; chmn. profl. com. Am. Diabetes Assn. Ark. chpt. 1982-85. Recipient Alumni Medal U. Ariz, 1992, Native Son award C. of C., Scribner, Nebr., 1990; finalist Tampa Bay Health Care Heroes Lifetime Achievement award, 2006, Am. Career Achievement medal, 2007, Disting. Scientist award, 2008, Richard A. Kern award, 2008; grantee NIH, Dept. Vets. Affairs, Am. Heart Assn.; Sr. Fogarty Internat. fellow, Nice, France, 1984-85. Fellow ACP, Am. Coll. Endocrinology; mem. Endocrine Soc. (chmn. membership 1983-86), So. Soc. Clin. Investigation (coun. 2001—), N.Y. Acad. Sci. Achievements include discovery of three new peptide hormones, made by the heart, which lower blood pressure and increase sodium and water excretion useful in the treatment of congestive heart failure, renal failure, and cancer. Office: Univ S Fla Health Scis Ctr 13000 Bruce B Downs Blvd Tampa FL 33612-4745 Office Phone: 813-972-7624. Business E-Mail: david.vesely@va.gov.

VESELY, PAMELA J., social studies educator; b. Erie, Pa. PhD in Edn., Tenn. State U., Nashville, 2002. Ministerial ordination Fellowships of Spirit, 2005, christian spiritualism ordination Fellowships of Spirit, Lily Dale, 2005; lic. tchr. NC Licensure. Asst. prof. Western Carolina U., Cullowhee, NC, 2000—; ednl. cons. & exec. dir. RAE Ednl. Svcs., Bakersville, NC, 1999—. Contbr. articles to profl. jours. With Mountain Med., Burnsville, NC, 2008—09. Grant, Wachovia Found., 2008. Mem.: Coun. Exceptional Children. Avocations: horseback riding, travel, hiking, reading. Office: RAE Ednl Svcs PO Box 47 Bakersville NC 28705

VESPA, NED ANGELO, photographer; b. Streator, Ill., May 31, 1942; s. Ned James and Evelyn Blanche (Flanigan) V.; m. Carol DeMasters, Sept. 11, 1976; 1 child, Nicole Marie; 1 son by previous marriage, James Paul. BS, So. Ill. U., 1965. Photographer Milw. Jour. Co., 1965-95, Milw. Sentinel, 1965-95; ret., 1995. Freelance, 1995—. Mem. Nat. Press Photographers Assn., Wis. News Photographers Assn. (past pres.), Milw. Press Photographers. Personal E-mail: nedvespa@yahoo.com.

VESPER, KARL HAMPTON, business and mechanical engineering educator; b. San Marino, Calif., Aug. 12, 1932; s. Karl Conrad and Roxie (Armstrong) V.; m. Joan Frantz, June, 1964; children— Karen, Linda, Holly, Nancy. BS in Mech. Engring, Stanford U., 1955; MS in Mech. Engring, 1965, PhD, 1969; MBA, Harvard U., 1960. Casewriter Harvard Bus. Sch., 1960-61; bus. mgr., mech. engr. Marine Advisers, 1961-62; cons. Dept. State, summer, 1963; dir. Hosmer Machine Co., Contoock, N.H., 1966-67; dir. summer insts. Stanford U., 1966, 67, dir. case devel., research asso., lectr. mech. engring., 1963-69, research asso., NASA faculty fellow in air pollution research design project, summer 1970; editor mech. engring. series McGraw Hill Book Co., NYC, 1966-74; prof. bus. adminstrn., mech. engring. and marine studies U. Wash., Seattle, 1969—, prof. emeritus; Paul T. Babson prof. Babson Coll., 1980-81. Author: How To Write Engineering Cases, 1966, 73, Engineers at Work, 1975, The Entrepreneurial Function, 1977, Entrepreneurship Education, 1985, New Venture Strategies, 1980, rev. edit., 1990, Frontiers of Entrepreneurship Research, 1981-91, Entrepreneurship and National Policy, 1983, New Venture Mechanics, 1993, (with Paul Larson) Washington Entrepreneur's Guide, 1993, New Venture Experience, 1993, rev. edit., 1996; contbr. chpts. to books and articles to profl. jours. Served with USAF, 1955-57. Mem. Am. Inst. for Decision Scis., Acad. Mgmt., Sigma Xi. Home: 3721 47th Pl NE Seattle WA 98105-5224 Office: Hawaii-Hilo Sch Bus and Econs Hilo HI 96720 E-mail: vesper@hawaii.edu.

VESPOLI, LEILA L., lawyer, energy executive; b. Akron, Ohio, 1959; BS, Miami U., Ohio, 1981; JD, Case Western Res. U., 1984. Bar: Ohio 1984. Atty. to sr. atty. Ohio Edison, Akron, 1985—97; assoc. gen. counsel FirstEnergy Corp., Akron, 1997—2000, v.p., gen. counsel, 2000—01, sr. v.p, gen. counsel, 2001—08, exec. v.p. & gen. counsel, 2008—. Exec. v.p., gen. counsel, bd. dirs. Summa Health Sys., 2008—. Bd. trustees The NEOUCOM Found. Named a Women of Profl. Excellence, YWCA. Mem.: Greater Cleve. Gen. Counsel Assn., Ohio C. of C., Energy Assn. Pa. (bd. dirs.), NJ Utilities Assn. (bd. dirs.). Office: FirstEnergy Corp 76 S Main St Akron OH 44308-1890

VESS, DEBORAH LYNN, history professor; b. Amarillo, Tex., Apr. 6, 1957; d. Omer Ray and Charlotte Halley Vess; children: Christina Lynn White, Nicholas Robert White, Joseph Robert Halley White, Brandon Michael White. BA in Philosophy, Ind. U., Bloomington, 1979; MA in Philosophy, U. Pitts., 1981; MusB, Pa. State U., Univ. Pk., 1985; PhD, U. North Tex., Denton, 1991. Assoc. prof. history and philosophy Ga. Perimeter Coll., Atlanta, 1992—97, coord. interdisicplinary studies, 1995—97; dir. interdisciplinary studies Ga. Coll. & State U., Milledgeville, 1997—2001, prof. history and interdisciplinary studies, 1997—, coord., Ctr. Excellence Tchg. and Learning, 2004—, coord. instl. effectiveness academic affairs, 2008—. Editor Magistra, Atchison, Kans., 1992—98, bd. editors, 1997—, Internat. Jour. Scholarship Tchg. and Learning, Statesboro, Ga., 2007—; editor, H-cath. HNET, 2006—. Author: (book) Best Prep for the SAT II World History Exam., Best Prep for the AP World History Exam.; contbr. articles to numerous profl. jours., chapters to books. Oblate, St. Benedict Mt. St. Scholastic Monastery, Atchison, Ga., 1993—2008; adult edn. tchr. Sacred Heart Cath. Ch., Milledgeville, Ga., 2005—08; tchr., commentator Coun. Cath. Women, Milledgeville, 2008. Recipient Academic Affairs award, U. North Tex., 1992, Arts and Scis. Dean's award for Rsch. Excellence, 1992, New Faculty award, Ga. Perimeter Coll. (formerly DeKalb Coll.), 1993, Gen. Edn. Outcome award, 1995, Instrnl. Enhancement award, 1996, Excellence in Tchg. award, Nat. Inst. Staff and Orgnl. Devel., 1994—97, Powell-Whipple award, Ga. Coll. & State U., 1999, Excellence Tchg. award, 2007, Ernest L. Boyer Internat. award, Internat. Conf. Coll. Tchg. and Learning, 2008, Innovative award in Excellence Tchg., 2008; named Disting. Prof. Tchg. and Learning, U. Sys. Ga. Bd. Regents, 1996; named to Hall of Fame, 2007; Outstanding Tchg. fellow, U. North Tex., 1992, Monastic Rsch. fellowship, Mt. Angel Abbey, 1993, Pew Nat. fellowship, Carnegie Found. Pew Found., 1999—2000. Mem.: Tchg. and Learning Consortium Ga. (chair elect 2008—),

Southern Regional Faculty Devel. Consortium, Medieval Acad. America, Am. Hist. Orgn., Phi Kappa Phi, Pi Kappa Lambda, Golden Key Nat. Honor Soc., Phi Alpha Theta, Phi Beta Kappa. Democrat. Roman Catholic. Avocations: weightlifting, piano, boating. Office: GA Coll & State Univ 424 W Hancock St Milledgeville GA 31061

VESSEY, JOHN WILLIAM, JR., former Chairman of the Joint Chiefs of Staff; b. Mpls., June 29, 1922; s. John William and Emily (Roche) V.; m. Avis Claire Funk, July 18, 1945; children: John William, David, Sarah. BS, U. Md., 1963; MS, George Washington U., 1967; LLD, Concordia Coll., St. Paul, 1978, U. Md., 1983, Concordia Sem., St. Louis, 1983; DMS (hon.), Norwich U., Northfield, Vt., 1985; grad., Command and Gen. Staff Coll., 1958, Indsl. Coll. Armed Forces, 1966. Commd. 2nd lt. U.S. Army, 1944, advanced through grades to gen., 1976; comdr. U.S. Army Support Command Thailand, 1970-71; chief Mil. Assistance Adv. Group Laos, 1972-73; dir. ops. Dept. Army Washington, 1973-74; comdr. 4th Inf. Div. Ft. Carson, Colo., 1974-75; dep. chief of staff-ops. Dept. Army Washington, 1975-76; comdr.-in-chief UN Command/U.S. Forces in Korea Seoul, 1976-79; comdr.-in-chief Republic of Korea/U.S. Combined Forces Command, 1978-79; vice chief of staff US Army, Washington, 1979-82; chmn. Joint Chiefs of Staff US Dept. Def., Washington, 1982-85; ret. US Army, 1985; presdl. emissary to Hanoi for POW/MIA matters, 1987-93. Bd. dirs. Nat. Flag Day Com.; mem. bd. vistors UMUC; chmn. bd. Ctr. Preventive Action, Def. Sci. Bd. Decorated D.S.C., Def. D.S.M., D.S.M., AF D.S.M., Navy D.S.M., Legion of Merit, Bronze Star, Air medal, Joint Svcs. Commendation medal, Army Commendation medal, Purple Heart (U.S.), Presdl. Medal of Freedom, decorated by govts. of Austria, Belgium, Chile, Colombia, Germany, France, Greece, Honduras, Korea, Luxembourg, Norway, Pakistan, Saudi Arabia, Spain, Thailand, Uruguay; recipient State of Minn. Disting. Svc. medal, Excellence in Diplomacy award Am. Acad. of Diplomacy, Sylvanus Thayer award USMA, Alumni Achievement award and Disting. Pub. Svc. award George Washington U., Disting. Alumnus award U. Md., Golden Plate award Am. Acad. Achievement, Adm. John M. Will award N.Y. Coun. Navy League, hon. award Nat. League Families. Mem. VFW (Eisenhower medal), Assn. U.S. Army (George Marshall medal), Army Aviation Assn., U.S. Armor Assn., Coun. Fgn. Rels. (chair bd. dirs. ctr. for prevention action), Phi Kappa Phi. Lutheran.*

VESSOT, ROBERT FREDERICK CHARLES, physicist, researcher; b. Montreal, Que., Can., Apr. 16, 1930; s. Robert Charles Ulysses and Marguerite Yvonne (Giauque) V.; m. Norma Newman Wight, Apr. 18, 1959; children: Judith Norma, Margaret Anne, Nancy Elizabeth. BA, McGill U., 1951, MSc, 1954, PhD, 1956. Mem. research staff MIT, 1956-60; mgr. Maser Research and Devel., Varian Assos., Hewlett Packard, Beverly, Mass., 1960-69; sr. physicist Harvard-Smithsonian Center for Astrophysics, Cambridge, Mass., 1969-2001, rsch. assoc., 2002—. Contbr. articles to profl. jours.; patentee in field. Served with RCAF, 1951-53. Recipient medal for outstanding sci. achievement NASA, 1978, I.I. Rabi award IEEE, 1993. Fellow Am. Phys. Soc.; mem. Eastern Yacht Club. Office: 60 Garden St Cambridge MA 02138-1516

VEST, CHARLES MARSTILLER, engineering educator, former academic administrator; b. Morgantown, W.Va., Sept. 9, 1941; s. Marvin Lewis and Winifred Louise (Buzzard) V.; m. Rebecca Ann McCue, June 8, 1963; children: Ann Kemper, John Andrew. BS in Mech. Engring., W.Va. U., 1963; MS in Mech. Engring., U. Mich., 1964, PhD, 1967; degree (hon.), Mich. Tech. U., 1992, W.Va. U., 1994, Ill. Inst. Tech., 1998, U. Notre Dame, 1998, Musashi Inst. Tech., 1999, NC State U., 2002, Colo. Sch. Mines, 2005, Harvard U., 2005, Ohio U., 2006; LLD (hon.), Cambridge U., Eng., 2006. Asst. prof., then assoc. prof. U. Mich., Ann Arbor, 1968—77, prof. mech. engring., 1977—90, assoc. dean acad. affairs Coll. Engring., 1981—86, dean Coll. Engring., 1986—89, provost, v.p. acad. affairs, 1989—90; pres. MIT, Cambridge, 1990—2004, pres. emeritus, prof. mech. engring., 2004—. Bd. dirs. E.I. du Pont de Nemours and Co., IBM, Math. for Am., Ithaka Harbors, Inc., Blanchette Rockefeller Neurosci. Inst., Kavli Found., In-Q-Tel; vis. assoc. prof. Stanford (Calif.) U., 1974-75; mem. Commn. on the Intelligence Capabilities of the U.S. Regarding Weapons of Mass Destruction, 2004-05; mem. Ctr. for Strategic and Internat. Studies Commn. on Sci. Comm. and Nat. Security; mem. Mass. Gov.s Coun. on Econ. Growth and Techn. 1990-99; chmn. Presdl. Adv. Com on Redesign of Space Stat., 1993-94; chmn. U.S. Dept. Energy Task Force on Future of Sci. Programs, 1992-93; vice-chmn. Coun. on Competitiveness, 1996-04; mem. Commn. Future Higher Edn., 2005-, President's Com. Advisors on Sci. and Tech., Iraq Intelligence Commn., 2004; mem. adv. com. On Transformational Diplomacy for the U.S. Sect. State; mem. adv. bd. subcommittee Rice-Chertoff Secure Borders and Open Doors, U.S. Dept. Homeland Security.; life mem. MIT Corp., bd. trustee. Author: Holographic Interferometry, 1979, Pursuing the Endless Frontier: Essays on MIT and the Role of Research Universities, 2005; assoc. editor Jour. Optical Soc. Am., 1982-83; contbr. articles to profl. jours. Trustee Woods Hole Oceanographic Inst., 1991-2004, New England Aquarium; Univ. Corp. for Advanced Internet Devel., 2002-04; WGBH Ednl. Found., 2002-04; adv. trustee TIAX adv. bd., Environ. Rsch. Inst. Mich. Recipient Excellence in Rsch. award, U. Mich., 1980, Disting. Svc. award, 1972, Disting. Visitor award, U. La Plata, Argentina, 1979, Centennial medal, Am. Soc. Engring. Edn., 1993, Nat. Leadership award, Phi Kappa Psi, 1999, Arthur M. Bueche award, Nat. Acad. Engring., 2000, Pres.' award Accrediation Bd. for Engring. and Tech., 2002, U. Mich. Engring. Alumni award, 2004; named 2006 Nat. Medal Tech. Laureate. Fellow: ASME, Optical Soc. Am., Am. Acad. Arts and Scis., AAAS (2006 Philip Hauge Abelson prize 2007); mem.: Assn. Am. Univs. (past chmn.), NAE (councillor 2005—, pres.-elect 2007, mem. governing bd., pres. 2007—, Arthur M. Bueche Award 2000), Pi Tau Sigma, Tau Beta Pi, Sigma Xi. Presbyterian. Office: NAE 500 Fifth St NW Washington DC 20001 Office Phone: 202-334-3201. E-mail: cvest@nae.edu.

VEST, CHRISTINA WEAVER, private equity firm executive; b. 1971; BA, Harvard U., 1993; MBA, Harvard Bus. Sch., 1999. Former policy dir. for US Senate candidate Richard Fisher; prin. analyst Hicks, Muse, Tate & Furst Inc., 1995—2005; sr. v.p. Hicks Holdings, LLC, 2005—07; mng. dir., ptnr. Hicks Equity Partners LLC, 2007—. Bd. dirs. Ocular LCD, Inc., Greatwide Logistics Svcs., Sturm Foods, Inc., iParty Corp., Fox Pan Am. Sports, Claxson Interactive Group, Inc., Digital Latin America LLC. Office: Hicks Equity Ptnrs LLC Hdqs 100 Crescent Ct Ste 1200 Dallas TX 75201*

VEST, GAYLE SOUTHWORTH, obstetrician, gynecologist; b. Duluth, Minn., Apr. 7, 1948; d. Russell Eugene and Brandon (Young) Southworth; m. Steven Lee Vest, Nov. 27, 1971; 1 child, Matthew Steven. BS, U. Mich., 1970. Diplomate Am. Bd. Ob-Gyn. Intern in ob-gyn. Milw. County Gen. Hosp., 1974-75, So. Ill. U. Sch. Medicine, 1975-78; pvt. practice Chapel Hill (N.C.) Ob-Gyn., 1978-80; asst. attending physician dept. ob-gyn. U. N.C. Sch. Medicine, Chapel Hill, 1978-80; clin. assoc. dept. ob-gyn. Duke U. Med. Ctr., Durham, NC, 1978-80; pvt. practice Big Stone Gap (Va.) Clinic, 1980-88, Norwise Ob-Gyn. Assocs., Norton, Va., 1988—. Fellow: ACOG; mem.: Med. Soc. Va., Christian Med. and Dental Assn. Avocations: skiing, kayaking, travel.

VEST, GEORGE SOUTHALL, retired diplomat; b. Columbia, Va., Dec. 25, 1918; s. George Southall and Nancy Margaret (Robertson) V.; m. Emily Barber Clemons, June 21, 1947; children: Jeannie, George, Henry BA, U. Va., 1941, MA, 1947. Fgn. service duty SHAPE and NATO, Quito, Ottawa, Paris; dir. bur. polit. mil. affairs Dept. State, asst. sec. of state for European affairs Washington, 1977-81; ambassador to European Communities Brussels, 1981-85; dir. gen. Fgn. Svc. Dept. State, Washington, 1985-89, career amb., 1987-89, ret., 1989. Served to capt. U.S. Army, 1941-46, ETO Mem. Phi Beta Kappa Episcopalian. Avocations: bicycling, gardening. Home: 5307 Iroquois Rd Bethesda MD 20816-3104 Home Phone: 301-229-7021.

VEST, HYRUM GRANT, JR., retired horticultural sciences educator; b. Salt Lake City, Sept. 23, 1935; s. Hyrum and Josephine Gwendolyn (Lund) V.; m. Gayle Pixton, Sept. 18, 1958; children: Kelly, Lani, Kari, Kamille, Kyle. BS, Utah State U., 1960, MS, 1964; PhD, U. Minn., 1967. Pathologist, agronomist U.S. Dept. Agr., Beltsville, Md., 1967-70; vegetable breeder Mich. State U., East Lansing, 1970-76; dept. head dept. hort. and landscape architecture Okla. State U., Stillwater, 1976-83; head dept. hort. scis. Tex A & M U., College Station, 1983-89; head dept. plants, soils and biometeorology Utah State U., Logan, 1989-95, assoc. dir. Utah Agrl. Experiment Sta., 1995-2000; mem. Nat. Plant Genetics Resource Bd., Washington, 1982-88; ret., 2000. Served to 1st lt. U.S. Army, 1960-63. Univ. research fellow Utah State U., 1963-64 Fellow: Am. Soc. Hort. Sci. Republican. Mem. Lds Ch. Home: 368 Spring Creek Rd Providence UT 84332-9432 Personal E-mail: grantvest@comcast.net.

VESTAL, ALLAN W., dean, law educator; BA, Yale U., 1976, JD, 1979. Assoc. Foley & Lardner, Milw., 1979—82; assoc., ptnr. Shuttleworth & Ingersoll, Cedar Rapids, Iowa, 1982—89; asst. prof. law Wash. and Lee U. Sch. Law, 1989—94, assoc. prof. law, 1994—97, prof. law, 1997—2000; dean U. Ky. Coll. Law, Lexington, 2000—09, Drake U. Law Sch., Des Moines, 2009—, Pub. (treatise with Prof. Hillman and Dean Weidner) The Revised Uniform Partnership Act; contbr. chapters to books, articles to law revs. Mem.: Am. Law Inst. Office: Drake Univ Sch Law Cartwright Hall 2507 University Ave Des Moines IA 50311-4505 Office Phone: 515-271-3985. Business E-Mail: allan.vestal@drake.edu.*

VESTAL, RICHARD D., biology professor; b. Winston-Salem, NC, June 16, 1964; s. Richard D. and Geraldine R. Vestal; m. Elizabeth Ann Vestal, Aug. 13, 2001. BA in Biology & Hist., Duke U., Durham, NC, 2007. Cert. instl. review board Office Rsch. Compliance UNCG, 2008; in biotech. lab. techniques Alamance C.C., 2003. Facility mgr. Empire Rm., Greensboro, NC, 2000—03; grad. asst., biology dept. UNCG, 2007—. Recipient Pres. award, Alamance C.C., 2003—04; Rsch. fellowship, Duke U., Dept. Brain Sci., 2006. Mem.: Phi Theta Kappa. Independent. Home: 5008 US Hwy 220 N Summerfield NC 27358 Office: UNCG Biology Dept 232 Eberhart Bldg Greensboro NC 27402

VETERE, MICHAEL J., III, theater educator; MFA, Va. Commonwealth U., Richmond. Asst. prof. Ill. State U., Normal, 2005—. Office: Ill State Univ 5700 Sch Theatre Normal IL 61790

VETRANO, ANTHONY JOSEPH, foreign language and literature professor; b. Endicott, NY, Feb. 3, 1931; s. Joseph and Stella Maria Vetrano; m. Kathleen Mary McEvoy, Aug. 26, 1964; children: Mark Christopher, Kathryn Ann. BA with honours, Harpur Coll., SUNY, Binghamton, 1955; MA, U. Rochester, NY, 1956; PhD, Syracuse U., NY, 1966. Full prof., fgn. langs. & lits. Le Moyne Coll., Syracuse, 1959—2007, prof. emeritus fgn. langs. & lit.; chair, dept. fgn. langs. and lits., 1962—86. Author: A Critical Study on Jorge Icaza, Outstanding 20th Century Ecuadorian Novelist, 1974; contbr. articles to profl. jours. Recipient Loyola award, Adminstrn. Le Moyne Coll., 1999. Mem.: MLA, Assn. Ecuatorianistas (treas. 1987—2006), Am. Assn. Tchrs. Spanish and Portuguese. Democrat. Roman Catholic. Avocations: sports, travel. Home: 3527 Hillside Dr Skaneateles NY 13152 Home Phone: 315-685-3329. Business E-Mail: vetrano@lemoyne.edu.

VETRI, MARC, chef; Cook Wolfgang Puck's Granita; chef Coco Pazzo, NYC; exec. chef Bella Blu, NYC; owner, chef Vetri Ristorante, 1998—. Recipient Best Mid-Atlantic Chef, The James Beard Found., 2005; named one of America's Best New Chefs, Food & Wine mag., 1999. Office: Vetri Ristorante 1312 Spruce St Philadelphia PA 19107

VETROVEC, GEORGE WAYNE, cardiologist, medical researcher, educator; b. Akron, Ohio, Aug. 12, 1943; MD, U. Va., 1970. Diplomate Am. Bd. Internal Medicine, Am. Bd. Cardiovascular Medicine. Intern, medicine Med. Coll. Va., Richmond, 1970-71, resident, cardiology, 1971-74, fellow in cardiology, 1974-76; faculty mem. Va. Commonwealth U., Richmond, 1976—, chmn., prof. med. cardiology, 1986—, chmn. divsn. cardiology, Pauley Heart Ctr., dir. Adult Cardiac Catheterization Lab., assoc. chmn. of medicine for clin. affairs, Dept. Internal Medicine, Martha M. and Harold W. Kimmerling, M.D. chair cardiology. Mem. staff Med. Coll. Va.; mem. VCUHS Authority Bd. Dirs. Contbr. several articles to journals, chapters to books; mem. of several editl. bds. Recipient W. Robert Irby Philanthropic Leadership Award, MCV Found.; named Clinician of Yr., 1997; named one of Best Doctors in Am., Best Doctors Inc.; named to AOA Med. Honor Soc. Fellow: ACP, European Soc. Cardiology, Royal Coll. Physicians of Thailand, Soc. Cardiac Angiography and Interventions (past pres.), Am. Coll. Cardiology, Am. Coll. Chest Physicians; mem.: Irish Cardiac Soc., Assn. Univ. Cardiologists (past pres.), Assn. Profs. Cardiology (past pres.), Physician Workforce Adv. Com. (former chmn. bd. trustees), Am. Heart Assn. (former pres. Richmond Coun. and Va. Affiliate, chmn. Mid Atlantic Regi, chmn. Catheterization Com, Coun. Clin. Cardiology, Nat. Award of Merit 1991, Richmond Golden Heart Award 1997). Office: Divsn Cardiology Virginia Commonwealth U Health Sys PO Box 980036 Richmond VA 23298-0036 Office Phone: 804-828-8885. Business E-Mail: gvetrovec@mcvh-vcu.edu.

VETTER, DAVID R., lawyer; b. Balt., Apr. 3, 1959; BA in English and Econs., Bucknell U., 1981; JD, U. Fla., 1984. Bar: Fla. 1984, US Dist. Ct. (mid. dist. Fla.) 1985. Atty. Robbins, Gaynor and Bronstein, Tampa, Fla., 1984—93, ptnr., 1991—93; v.p., gen. counsel Tech Data Corp., Clearwater, Fla., 1993—2000, corp. v.p., gen. counsel, 2000—03, sr. v.p., gen. counsel, sec., 2003—. Mem.: ABA, Assn. Corp. Counsel, Fla. Bar Assn. Office: Tech Data Corp 5350 Tech Data Dr Clearwater FL 33760-3122*

VETTER, LAWRENCE ANTHONY, art educator, consultant; s. Anthony Lawrence and Lilly Vetter; m. Andrea Kay Oppelt, Jan. 12, 1968; 1 child, Rachel Tomeo. BA, Calif. State U., Fullerton, 1968, MA, 1970; postgrad., U.S. Internat. U., 1972, U. Calif., Irvine, 1974—75. Cert. coll. tchr. Calif., 1970, secondary tchr. Calif., 1975. Instr. and counselor Calif. State U., Fullerton, 1970—73, adj. lectr., 2000—; art educator Hacienda-LaPuente Unified Sch. Dist., City of Industry, 1973—; adj. lectr. Calif. Poly. U., Pomona, 2000—01. Ceramic chemistry cons. Laguna Clay Co., City of Industry, Calif., 1989—; ceramicist stoneware and porcelain vessels; adj. lectr. Calif. State U., Fullerton, 2000—, studio art cons., 2008—; lead tchr. Performing Arts Acad., 2006—, advanced placement coord., 1995—2000, 2007—, Puente HS, 2007—; art edn. cons. Whihier Sch. Dist. Calif., 2008—; spkr. in field. Vol. Calif. State Parks Sys., Dana Point, 1996—. Recipient Outstanding Secondary Educator, LA County Supervisors, 1999—2000, Outstanding Advanced Placement Tchr., City of La Puente, 1996, Outstanding Secondary Tchr., U. Calif. San Diego, 2000—01, 2001—02; named Nat. Outstanding Pub. Secondary Educator in the Ceramic Arts, Studio Potter Mag. N.H., 1990—91; grantee Instrn. of Advanced Placement Art History, Hacienda-LaPuente Unified Sch. Dist., 1997, Coll. Bd./ Mellon Found., 1998. Master: Dave Hebler's Original Am. Kenpo Karate Assn. (life seventh degree black belt); mem.: NEA, Hacienda-LaPuente Unified Tchrs. Assn., Calif. Tchrs. Assn. Achievements include research in 35 stoneware glazes and 21 Raku glazes developed for international sales for Laguna Clay Company. Avocations: art, martial arts, volleyball. Home: 33472 Intera Way Dana Point CA 92629 Office: LaPuente HS 15615 East Nelson Ave La Puente CA 91744 Home Phone: 949-496-6447; Office Phone: 626-934-6841.

VETTER, VICTORIA L., pediatric cardiologist, educator; b. Louisville, Aug. 15, 1946; d. Albert Elmo and Mildred Irene Vetter; m. Anthony S. Jennings, June 8, 1974; children: Jennifer, Jonathan, Jason. BA in Chemistry, U. Ky., 1968, MD, 1972. Bd. cert. Am. Bd. Pediat. in Pediat. and Pediat. Cardiology. Intern pediat. Johns Hopkins Hosp., Balt., 1972—73, resident pediat., 1973—74; sr. resident pediat. Vanderbilt U. Hosp., Nashville, 1974—75; fellow pediat. cardiology The Children's Hosp. Phila., 1975—78, asst. cardiologist, 1978—82, assoc. cardiologist, 1982—89, sr. cardiologist, 1989—, dir. pediat. electrophysiology lab., 1978—95, dir. pediat. electrocardiography lab., 1978—, chief divsn. cardiology, 1993—; sr. physician dept. pediat. U. Pa. Sch. Medicine, 1989—. Instr. pediat. U. Pa. Sch. Medicine, 1978, asst. prof. pediat., 1978—81, prof. pediat., 1999—; asst. prof. pediat. The Children's Hosp. Phila., U. Pa. Sch. Medicine, 1981—87, assoc. prof. pediat., 1987—99, Evelyn R. Tabas chair in pediatric cardiology, 2005—; lectr. in field. Sci. reviewer: jours. Circulation, Am. Jour. Cardiology, Jour. Am. Coll. Cardiology, Pediat. Cardiology, Pacing and Clin. Electrophysiology, Pediat. Rsch., Clin. Pediat., Annals of Internal Medicine, New Eng. Jour. Medicine, Jour. Cardiovasc. Electrophysiology, Jour. Pediat., Am. Jour. Diseases of Children, Pediat. Emergency Care; contbr. chapters to books, articles and abtracts to jours. Grantee in field. Fellow: Am. Coll. Cardiology (mem. emergency cardiac care com. 1992—98, mem. pediat. cardiology com. 1994—96, mem. 1996 annual sci. session program com. 1995—96, mem. credentials com. 1997—2000), Am. Acad. Pediat. (mem. exec. com. pediat. cardiology subsect. 1989—92, Young Investigator award sect. on cardiology 1978); mem.: AMA, NHLBI Pediatric Network (prin. investigator 2001—), John Morgan Soc., Phila. Arrhythmia Group, Pediat. Arrhythmia Group (mem. steering com.), Phila. County Med. Soc., Internat. Registry for Drug-Induced Arrhythmias (mem. sci. adv. com.), Sudden Arrhythmia Death Syndromes Found. (mem. sci. adv. bd.), Cardiac Arrhythmias Rsch. and Edn. Found., Inc. (mem. sci. adv. bd., Heart of the Child award 1996), N.Am. Soc. Pacing and Electrophysiology (mem. annual sci. sessions program com. 1998—2001, mem. pediat. com. 1998—2001), Pediat. Electrophysiology Soc., Am. Heart Assn. Coun. on Cardiovasc. Disease in the Young (mem. exec. com. 1993—98, mem. com. on tng. in pediat. cardiology 1994—96, mem. com. on electrocardiography and arrhythmias 1995—97, mem. membership com. 1996—97, chair Rashkind lecture selection com.), Am. Heart Assn. (med. spokesperson), Am. Heart Assn. Southeastern Pa. Affiliate (mem. rsch. peer rev. com. 1987—92, program chairperson 1988—90, mem. exec. com. 1988—93, v.p. 1989—90, pres.-elect 1990—91, pres. 1991—92, past-pres. 1992—93, mem. bd. dirs. 1993—96, mem. bd. govs. 1994—96, mem. pediat. sub-com. cardiac support coalition 1997—, post-doctoral fellow 1976—77, 1978—79), Alpha Omega Alpha, Phi Beta Kappa. Home: 110 Willow Way Cherry Hill NJ 08034-3049 Office: The Childrens Hosp Phila 34th St & Civic Center Blvd Philadelphia PA 19104 Home Phone: 856-429-5745; Office Phone: 215-590-3529.

VEURINK, GARY R., chemicals executive; m. Ruth Veurink; 3 children. BSChemE, SD Sch. Mines and Tech.; graduate student in Chem. Engring., U. Mich.; grad. Advanced Mgmt. Prog., INSEAD, Fontainebleau, France; D (hon.), SD Sch. Mines and Tech., 2002. Rschr. Electro Mech. Rsch. Lab. Mich. divsn. Dow Chem. Co., 1972, global mfg. dir. engring. plastics, 1995, v.p. global purchasing, 1998, site dir. Mich. ops., bus. ops. dir. performance chems., 2000, bus. ops. leader, v.p. mfg. and engring. Chems. and Intermediates Portfolio, 2004, corp. v.p. mfg. and engring., 2004—, mem. Office of the Chief Exec., 2004—. Bd. dirs. Dow Corning Corp., 2005—08, adv., 2008—; bd. dirs. Dorinco Reinsurance Co., NAM. Pres., mem. exec. coun. Lake Huron Area Coun. Boy Scouts Am.; bd. trustees Mich. chpt. Nature Conservancy. Mem.: AIChE. Office: Dow Chem Co 2030 Dow Ctr Midland MI 48674

VEVERKA, DONALD JOHN, lawyer; b. Chgo., July 20, 1935; s. John Edward and Irene Cecelia (Wasil) V.; m. Mary Almjeld, May 27, 1967 (dec.); children: Tanya, Holly, Marc. BS, Loyola U., Chgo., 1957; JD, DePaul U., 1963. Bar: Ill. 1963, U.S. Dist. Ct. (no. dist.) Ill. 1963, U.S. Ct. Appeals (7th cir.) 1963, U.S. Supreme Ct. 1968. Asst. state's atty. civil appeals sect. Cook County State's Attys. Office, 1963-67; asst. atty. gen. appeals sect. Ill. Atty. Gen. Office, 1967-68; house counsel Kenilworth Ins. Co., 1968-69; ptnr. Bradshaw, Speranza, Veverka & Brumlik, 1969-72; spl. asst. atty. gen., 1970-72; ptnr. Speranza & Veverka, Chgo., 1972-73, 74-90, Veverka Rosen & Haugh, 1990—. Officer Henehan Donovan Isaacson Speranza & Veverka, Ltd., Chgo., 1973-74; bd. dirs., officer DePaul Law Coun., 1972-83; mem. Ill. Supreme Ct. Com. on Pattern Jury Instrns. Assoc., 1973-96, chmn., 1993-96. Author: How To Buy or Sell Your Home Without a Lawyer, 1982; also articles. Bd. dirs. LaGrange Cmty. Meml. Hosp., 1979-89, officer, 1982-85, pres., 1986-87; bd. dirs. Rich Port YMCA, 1981—, chmn., 1997-99; trustee Village of LaGrange Park, Ill., 1981-95; police bd. Village of LaGrange Park, 1979-80, chmn. 2000—. 1st lt. U.S. Army, 1967-69; capt. Res. Mem. ABA (faculty mem. Nat. Inst. Appellate Advocacy 1980, Ill. chmn. young lawyers com. on jud. selection 1971-72), Ill. State Bar Assn. (mem. com. on corrections reform 1973, also past mem. spkrs. bur., young mems. conf.), Bar Assn. Seventh Fed. Cir. (Ill. chmn. meetings com. 1976), DePaul Alumni Assn. (governing bd. 1975-82), Phi Alpha Delta, Blue Key, Rich Port YMCA Men's Club, Oak Brook Park Dist. Racquet Club, U. Club Chgo. Roman Catholic. Home: 709 N Park Rd La Grange Park IL 60526-1428 Office: 180 N Michigan Ave Chicago IL 60601-7401 Office Phone: 312-372-3665. *Notable cases include: Witherspoon vs. Ill., U.S. Supreme Ct. Case involved the qualification of jurors in death penalty cases.*

VEVERKA, KAREN ELIZABETH, music educator; b. San Diego, Jan. 20, 1961; d. Rudolph Edward and Ruth Tonry Veverka. BA, St. Olaf Coll., Northfield, Minn., 1983; MA in English, U. Nebr., Lincoln, 1984; MusM, Syracuse U., NY, 1989, PhD student, 2005—. Cert. in k-12 tchr.in music NY, 1990, major orgn. adjudicator NY State Sch. Music Assn., NYC, 2001. Music educator Skaneateles HS & MS, NY, 1990—; adj. instr. Syracuse U., 2005—08. Violinist Joffrey Ballet, Omaha, 1985, Syracuse Symphony Orch., 1986—, selection com. mem. music educator award; violinist Tri-Cities Opera Orch., Binghamton, NY, 1990—92, Vt. Symphony Orch., Burlington, 1993—97; mem. bd. dirs. Skaneateles Festival, 1998—, v.p., 2000—04; mem. NY State Sch. Music Assn. Mem. dist. planning team Skaneateles Ctrl. Schs., 1998—2001; mem. sch. improvement team Skaneateles HS, 2007—. Mem.: Onondaga County Music Educators Assn., Am. String Tchrs. Assn., Am. Fedn. Musicians. Democrat. Lutheran. Avocations: kickboxing, reading, tennis, golf. Office: Skaneateles Central Schools 49 E Elizabeth St Skaneateles NY 13152

VEYERA, JEFFREY ALAN, bank executive; b. Providence, Jan. 12, 1971; s. George Webster and Barbara Joan Veyera; m. Anita Veyera. BS in History, US Air Force Acad., Colorado Springs, Colo., 1993. Commd. 1st lt. USAF, 1993; ret., 1998; strategic sourcing leader GE Med. Sys., Milw., 1998—2001; six sigma master black belt Rhythms Net Connections, Denver, 2001; supplier quality mgr. Black & Decker, Lake Forest, Calif., 2001—03; sr. v.p. quality & productivity Bank of Am., Charlotte, NC, 2003—. Mem.: Am. Soc. Quality (cert.). Republican. Roman Catholic. Avocations: photography, writing, music. Home: 717 Meadow Lake Dr Matthews NC 28105 Office: NCI 023 06 04 525 N Tryon St Charlotte NC 28203

VEYLANSWAMI, SATGURU BODHINATHA, head of religious order; b. Berkeley, Calif., Oct. 15, 1942; Spiritual studies, Self Realization Fellowship, Vedanta Soc.; studies with Gurudeva. Mgr. Gurudeva's Master Course Corr. Study; v.p. Gurudeva's several nonprofit corps., 1970—; tchr., counsellor younger monks NH; pujari Murugan Temple; sr. adminstrv. positions, tchr. Innersearch Travel-Study progs.; lectr. tours Mauritius, Malaysia, Singapore; lectr. Innersearch Travel Study Progs.; sr. monk Kadavul Hindu Temple; Guru Mahasannidhanam, preceptor of Nandinatha Sampradaya's Kailasa Parampara Kauai's Hindu monastery, 2001—. Devel., arch. Hindu Heritage Endowment, 1993—; creator Kauai Aloha Endowment. Named to 1st Acharya, Gurudeva's Order. Office: Kauai Aadheenam Ashram 107 Kaholalele Rd Kapaa HI 96746-9304

VEZEAU, TIMOTHY J., lawyer; BSEE cum laude, St. Louis U., 1966; JD, Georgetown U., 1971. Bar: Ill. 1972. Patent examiner US Patent Office, 1968—70; patent advisor US Office of Navel Rsch., 1971; founding ptnr. patent practice Katten Muchin Rosenman LLP, Chgo. Mem.: ABA, Intellectual Property Law Assn. of Chgo., Ill. Bar Assn., Chgo. Bar Assn., Eta Kappa Nu, Pi Mu Epsilon. Office: Katten Muchin Rosenman LLP 525 W Monroe St Ste 1900 Chicago IL 60661-3693 Office Phone: 312-902-5516. Office Fax: 312-577-4513. Business E-Mail: timothy.vezeau@kattenlaw.com.

VEZERIDIS, MICHAEL PANAGIOTIS, surgeon, educator; b. Thessaloniki, Greece, Dec. 16, 1943; came to U.S., 1974; s. Panagiotis and Sofia (Avramidis) V.; m. Therese Mary Statz; children: Peter Statz, Alexander Michael. MD, U. Athens, 1967; MA ad eundem (hon.), Brown U., 1989. Diplomate Am. Bd. Surgery. Fellow surg. rsch. Harvard Med. Sch./Mass. Gen. Hosp., Boston, 1974-77; resident U. Mass., Worcester, 1977-80; fellow in surg. oncology Roswell Park Meml. Inst., Buffalo, 1980-81, attending surgeon, 1981-82; staff surgeon VA Med. Ctr., Providence, 1982-84; asst. prof. surgery Brown U., Providence, 1982-88; chief surg. oncology VA Med. Ctr., Providence, 1984—, assoc. chief surgery, 1986-98, chief surgery, 1998—; cons. in surgery R.I. Hosp., Providence, 1987—; surg. oncologist Roger Williams Med. Ctr., Providence, 1989—; assoc. dir. divsn. surg. oncology Brown U., Providence, 1989—98, assoc. prof. surgery, 1988-94, prof., 1994—; prof. surgery Boston U. Sch. Medicine, 1999—. Chmn. profl. edn. com. R.I. divsn. Am. Cancer Soc., Providence, 1987-89, pres.-elect 1989-91, pres. 1991-93, del. dir. to nat. bd. dirs., 1993-96, mem. Nat. Assembly of the Am. Cancer Soc., 1997-2003, mem. internat. activities adv. com., 2003-07, bd. dirs. New Eng. divsn., 1997-2005, chief med. officer New Eng. divsn., 1999-2001; chmn. R.I. State Cancer Liaison Program Am. Coll. Surgeons, 1999-2008, mem. commn. on cancer, 2003-, bd. dirs. Rhode Island Cancer Coun., 2004-; vis. prof. U. Patras (Greece) Med. Sch., 1988; mem. sci. adv. com. Clin. Rsch. Ctr., Brown U., Providence, 1989-91. Contbr. articles to profl. jours. and chpts. in med. books. Mem. parish coun. Ch. of Annunciation, Cranston, R.I., 1985-91; v.p. Hellenic Cultural Soc. Southeastern New Eng., Providence, 1987-89. Decorated Navy Commendation medal; named Profl. Fed. Employee of Yr., R.I. Fed. Exec. Coun., 1987; recipient St. George medal Am. Cancer Soc.; Merit Rev. Cancer Rsch. grantee VA, 1983-89. Fellow ACS (treas. R.I. chpt. 1996-2000, pres.-elect 2000-2002, pres. 2002-2004); mem. Soc. Surg. Oncology, Assn. for Acad. Surgery, Am. Soc. Clin. Oncology, N.Y. Acad. Scis. (life), Soc. for Surgery Alimentary Tract, Am. Assn. for Cancer Rsch., Collegium Internat. Chirurgiae Digestivae, Assn. Mil. Surgeons U.S., Soc. for Metastasis Rsch., New Eng. Cancer Soc., New Eng. Surg. Soc., Quidnessett Country Club. Greek Orthodox. Avocations: classical music, reading, fencing, tennis, squash, cross country skiing. Home: 50 Limerock Dr East Greenwich RI 02818-1643 Office: Univ Surg Assocs Ste 470 Two Dudley St Providence RI 02905 Office Phone: 401-331-1036. Business E-Mail: michael_vezeridis@brown.edu.

VEZIROGLU, TURHAN NEJAT, mechanical engineering educator, researcher; b. Istanbul, Turkey, Jan. 24, 1924; came to U.S., 1962; s. Abdul Kadir and Ferruh (Bürün) V.; m. Bengi Isikli, Mar. 17, 1961; children: Emre Alp, Oya Sureyya. A.C.G.I., City and Guilds Coll., London, 1946; B.Sc. with honors, U. London, 1947; D.I.C., Imperial Coll., London, 1948; PhD, U. London, 1951. Engring. apprentice Alfred Herbert Ltd., Coventry, U.K., 1945; project engr. Office of Soil Products, Ankara, Turkey, 1953-56; tech. dir. M.K.V. Constrn. Co, Istanbul, 1957-61; assoc. prof. mech. engring. U. Miami, Coral Gables, Fla., 1962-65, prof. Coral Fables, Fla., 1966—, dir. grad. studies mech. engring. Coral Gables, Fla., 1965-71, chmn. dept. mech. engring., 1971-75, assoc. dean research Coll. Engring., 1975-79, dir. Clean Energy Research Inst., 1974—. UNESCO cons., Paris; vis. prof. Middle East Tech. U., Ankara, 1969 Editor-in-chief: Internat. Jour. Hydrogen Energy, 1976—. Pres. Learning Disabilities Found., Miami, 1972-73, advisor, 1974-80. Recipient Turkish Presdl. sci. award Turkish Sci. and Tech. Research Found., 1975; named hon. prof. Xian Jiaotong U., China, 1982 Fellow AAAS, ASME, Instn. Mech. Engrs.; mem. Internat. Assn. Hydrogen Energy (pres. 1975), AIAA, Assn. Energy Engrs., Am. Nuclear Soc., Am. Soc. Engring. Edn., AAUP, Internat. Soc. Solar Energy, Systems Engring. Soc., Sigma Xi Home: 5783 SW 40th St # 303 Miami FL 33155 Home Phone: 305-442-4540; Office Phone: 305-284-4666. Business E-Mail: veziroglu@iahe.org. *Hydrogen energy system will provide the world with clean and abundant energy, while doing away with pollution, acid rains and the greenhouse effect. It is a noble and worthwhile goal to strive for.*

VIAMONTE ROS, ANA M., state agency administrator, public health service officer; 2 children. MD, U. Miami Sch. Medicine, Fla., 1983; MPH, Harvard U. Sch. Pub. Health, Mass., 2005; D (hon.), Nova Southeastern U., Ft. Lauderdale, Fla., Lake Erie Coll. Osteopathic Medicine. Resident, dept. radiology Mount Sinai Med. Ctr., Miami Beach, Fla., 1983—85; post grad. resident Armed Forces Inst. Pathology, Washington, Shands Hosp., Gainesville, Fla.; dir. clin. ops. support Armor Correctional Health Services, Coconut Creek, Fla.; state surgeon gen., dir. Fla. Dept. Health, Tallahassee, 2007—. Adv. group mem. Gov. Coun. on Phys. Fitness, Fla., Gov. Task Force on Autism Spectrum Disorders, Fla., Children and Youth Cabinet, Fla. Contbr. articles to profl. jours. Vol. Camillus House Homeless Initiative, Health through Walls Orgn., Caribbean, Brookside Cmty. Health Ctr., Mass. Office: Fla Dept Health State Surgeon General 4052 Bald Cypress Way Bin A00 Tallahassee FL 32399-1701 Office Phone: 850-245-4321. Office Fax: 850-922-9453. Business E-Mail: statesurgeongeneral@doh.state.fl.us.

VIANI, JAMES LAURENCE, retired lawyer; b. Kincaid, Ill., Dec. 24, 1932; s. Frank Jerome and Alfonsina V.; m. Virginia Lee Wilson, Dec. 27, 1958; children: Theresa, Diana, Deborah. BS, Millikin U., 1954; LLB, Wash. U., St. Louis, 1957. Bar: Ill. 1957, Mo. 1957. Assoc. Blackmar, Swanson, Midgley, Jones & Eager, Kansas City, Mo., 1958-59, Stinson, Mag & Fizzell, Kansas City, 1960-62, ptnr., 1962-87; chmn. corp. dept. Stinson, Mag & Fizzel, Kansas City, 1979-87, cons. ptnr., 1988-92; ret., 1988. Br. bd. chmn. YMCA, Kansas City, 1979-81. With U.S. Army, 1957-63. Mem. ABA, Phi Kappa Phi, Order of the Coif. Republican. Avocations: hiking, reading, farming. Home: 11106 Belleview Ave Kansas City MO 64114-5115

VIBE, KJELD, ambassador; b. Stavanger, Norway, Oct. 5, 1927; came to U.S., 1989; s. Christopher Andreas and Thordis (Amundsen) V., July 1, 1953; m. Beate Meyer; children: Annette, Margery, Johan Christopher, Ingeborg. LLD, U. Oslo, 1954; grad., Fgn. Svc. Sch., Oslo, 1955. Sec. of Norwegian Embassy, del. to NATO and OEEC, Paris, 1956-59; prin. pvt. sec. to fgn. min. Norwegian Ministry of Fgn. Affairs, Oslo, 1962-65; counsellor Norwegian Embassy, Washington, 1965-69; dep. dir. gen. polit. affairs Ministry of Fgn. Affairs, Oslo, 1969-72, dir. gen. for polit. affairs, 1972-77, sec. gen., 1984-89; amb. to NATO Brussels, 1977-84; amb. to U.S. Washington, 1989-96. Mem. Norwegian Govt. Commn. on the Freedom of Expression, 1996-99. Home: Holmenkollv 35 Oslo 0376 Norway

VICARI, ANDREW, artist; b. Port Talbot, Wales, Apr. 20, 1938; s. Cavaliere Vittorio Vicari and Italia Bertani. Student, Slade Sch. of Fine Art, London, 1951-53. Pres. Carwyn James Rugby Sch., Wales. Exhibitions include New Burlington Galleries, London, 1955, Redfern Gallery, 1956, Obelisk Gallery, 1956, Exhibitions Grand Palais des Champs Elyseés Soc. des Artists Français, Paris, 1957, RBA Galleries, London, 1957, United Soc. Artists, 1957, Grand Palais des Champs Elyseés Paris, 1959, Faces in Wales, Temple of Peace Civic Ctr. Cardiff, 1960, The Last Supper, Foyle's Art Gallery, London, 1960, Thomson House Cardiff, 1960, Vicari Exhibition of Paintings and Drawings, Leicester Sq., London, 1961, Kalamazzo Mus. of Art., 1962, Columbus Mus. of Art, 1963, Harrison Libr., NY, 1963, Contemporary Art Soc. of Great Britain Vicari Retrospective, UC Wales, 1963, Bath Festival, 1964, Circolo Della Stampa Rome, 1965, The Virgin and the Gypsy (London Screenplays), 1970, Archer Gallery, London, 1972, Madden Galleries, London, 1973, Galerie Vendome Beirut, 1974, The Triumph of the Bedouin (King Faisal Conf. Ctr. Riyadh), 1974-78, Romantic Realism of Vicari (8th Internat. Art Fair Basle), 1977, Chevy Chase Art Ctr., Washington, 1978, Salle Empire Hotel de Paris Monte Carlo, 1981, Galerie du Carlton Cannes, 1981, The Majesty of King Faisal (King Faisal Fndn Riyadh), 1984, Petit Palais MOMA Geneeva, 1984, Les Vigonades de la Concorde (Hotel de Crillon Paris), 1988, Interpl World HQ Lyons, 1989, Siege Credit Lyonnais Bank Lyons, 1989, The Majesty of King Fahd (Rashid Engrg Mus. Riyadh), 1989, Palais Amerique-Latin Monaco, 1991, La Guerre du Golfe (Les Invalides Paris), 1991, Hotel Meurice Paris, 1991, CRS Versailles, 1994, Palais des Beaux Arts Beijing, 1995, Govenor's Palace, St. Petersburg, 1995, La Vigonade des Motards de la Police Nationale (Min. of the Interior Paris), 2000, The Vicari Collection of Paintings and Drawings Produced in the Kingdom of Saudi Ara bia 1998-2001 (Royal Suite Riyadh Intercontinental Hotel) 2001, An Essex Celebration of Constable and Gainsborough (10 landscapes), 2003, Parable of Majesty and Reconciliation (retrospective, Abu Dhabi and The Palace One and Only Royal Mirage Dubai), 2005, 4 Carvaggios and 1 Vicari (Sardinia, Malta and Minorca), 2006, portraits of iconic figures of the 20th Century (Dubai Cmty. Theatre and Arts Ctr.), 2006, The Enigma: A Retrospective Exhibition of Paintings and Drawings 1956-2006 (Grosvenor House Dubai), 2006; Commissions include: The Children of Tymorfafour panels for Glamorgan Educn Authy, 1956, Cyclorama: Harlequins, Colombines & CHildren for Nat. Eisteddfod Llandudno, 1964, Bath Festival Exhibition, 1964, The Vifonade of the Millennium Stadium Mural, 2002, Triptych of Sir Alex Ferguson 2003 for Manchester United Carrington Training Ground, 2003; contbr. work to collections, including: Dallas Mus. of Fine Arts, Nat. Libr. of Wales, Mus. of Tel Aviv, Contemporary Arts Soc. of Great Britain, Tate Gallery, Columbus Mus. of Fine Arts, Pezzo Pozzoli Mus. Mulan, Petit Palais MOMA Geneva, David Lloyd Kreeger Collection, Washington, IBM Collection, Armonk, Palais Princier Monaco, Mus. Timbres et Monnaie Monaco, Hermitage Mus. St. Petersburg, King Faisal Cong. Ctr. Riyadh, Chinese Min. of Culture Beijing, King Faisal Found. Mus. Riyadh, Rashid Engrg Mus. Riyadh, Collection Nat. Libr. Riyadh, Credit Lyonnais Bank Lyons and Paris; publications include Triumph of the Bedouin, 1978, Ghazi A Al Ghosaibi: From the Orient to the Desert (illustrations 1984), The Mystery of Memory: The Truth is Not Enough, vol.1, 2008. World patron Beacon Millenium Trust; official painter: King and Govt. of Saudi Arabia, Interpol, Compagnie Republicaine de Securite, European Parl and Coun. of Europe Beaux Arts Prize, 1995; hon. v.p. Neath Male Voice Choir; Freeman, City of London, 2002; mem. The Guild of Freeman of the City of London, Liveryman of Wales, Worshipful Co. Firefighters. Decorated Chevalier Order of Merit (Monaco); brigadier d'honneur Compagnie Republicaine de Securite (France); recipient European Beaux Arts prize, 1995; named Official Artist for 2010 Ryder Cup Venue. Fellow London Zool. Soc.; mem. European Hotel Mgrs. Assn. (hon.), East India and Pub. Schs. Club (London), Cardiff (Wales) and County Club, Bristol Channel Yacht Club, Lords Cricket Ground London, Marylebone Cricket Club, Rotary Internat. (hon.). Avocations: films, squash, food and wine. Home: Le Shakespeare 12 Bd Princesse Charlotte 98000 Monaco Business E-Mail: a.vicari@andrew-vicari.com, p.oag@andrew-vicari.com.

VICAS, ASTRID, philosopher, educator; BA, MBA, U. Ottawa, Ontario, Can.; MA, PhD, McGill U., Montreal, Can. Vis. asst. prof., philosophy U. Ottawa, Erindale Coll., U. Toronto, Ontario, Canada; lectr., philosophy U. BC, Vancouver, Canada; assoc. prof., philosophy St. Leo U., Fla., 1994—. Contbr. articles to profl. jours. Office: St Leo Univ PO Box 6665 Saint Leo FL 33574-6665 Personal E-mail: avicas@verizon.net. Business E-Mail: astrid.vicas@saintleo.edu.

VICE, CHARLES A., state banking agency administrator; BS in Fin., U. Southern Miss., Hattiesburg; grad. from Grad. Sch. Banking program, La. State U., Baton Rouge. Bank examiner FDIC, Lexington, Ky.; commr. Ky. Dept. Fin. Instns., Frankfort, 2008—. Vice chmn. Dist. II region Conf. State Bank Suprs., mem. Fed. Fin. Instn. Exam. Coun. State Liaison Com., 2009—, mem. bd. trustees Ednl. Found. State Banking Suprs., 2009. Office: Ky Dept Fin Instns 1025 Capital Center Dr Ste 200 Frankfort KY 40601 Office Phone: 502-573-3390. Office Fax: 502-573-8787. E-mail: charles.vice@ky.gov.

VICE, ROY LEE, history professor; b. Lynchburg, Va., Oct. 12, 1950; s. Cline Lowell and Ruth Burchell (Newman) V.; m. Sara Pearsaul, June 2005. BA in History, BS in Physics, Carson-Newman Coll., 1972; MA in History, U. Chgo., 1976, PhD in History, 1984. Lectr. Continuing Edn. program U. Chgo., 1985-86, 87-88, rare books asst. univ. librs., 1986; asst. prof. Pacific Luth. U., Tacoma, 1986-87, Clemson (S.C.) U., 1988-90, Wright State U., Dayton, Ohio, 1990-95, assoc. prof., 1995—. Contbr. articles to profl. jours. Vol. tutor CYCLE Cabrini-Green Projects, Chgo., 1981—86; vol. lectr. LaSalle St. Ch., Chgo., 1989—98, 2000—08. With US Army, 1972—74. Mem. Soc. Reformation Rsch., 16th Century Studies Conf. Democrat. Baptist. Home: 111 Brown St Dayton OH 45402 Office: Wright State Univ Dept History 3640 Colonel Glenn Hwy Dayton OH 45435-0001 Business E-Mail: roy.vice@wright.edu.

VICE, SUSAN F., medicinal chemist; b. Oshawa, Ont., Can., Apr. 19, 1956; m. Andrew S. Thompson, Nov. 27, 1987. BS in Chemistry, U. We. Ont., London, Can., 1980; PhD, U. Waterloo, Ont., 1984. Postdoc. fellow U. Calif., Irvine, 1984—86; rsch. scientist Polysar Ltd., Sarnia, Canada, 1986—88; sr. prin. scientist Schering Plough Rsch. Inst., Kenilworth, NJ, 1988—2000; freelance tech. writer, 2001—05; sr. devel. editor John Wiley & Sons, Inc., Hoboken, 2005—. Recipient Thomas Alva Edison Patent award, Rsch. and Devel. Coun. N.J., 2004; fellow Charles S. Humphrey grad. fellow, Guelph-Waterloo Ctr. Grad. Work in Chemistry, 1983, postdoc. fellow, Natural Scis. and Engring. Rsch. Coun., 1984—86, inds. postdoc. fellow, 1986; scholar, 1981—84. Mem.: Am. Soc. Microbiology, Editl. Freelancers Assn., Chem. Inst. Can. and Soc. Chemistry, Am. Chem. Soc. Home: 1144 Sawmill Rd Mountainside NJ 07092-2213 Personal E-mail: vicesf@yahoo.com.

VICENCIO, ALFIN GEMIL, pediatrician; s. Alfin S. and Miguela Vicencio; life ptnr. Rose Anne Mallon. MD, Med. Coll. Ohio, Toledo, 1996. Cert. in medicine NY. Pediatric resident, babies and childrens hosp. Columbia U., NYC, 1996—99; fellow, pediatric pulmonology Yale U., New Haven, 1999—2002; attending physician Children's Hosp. Montefiore, Bronx, NY, 2002—.

VICHINSKY, ELLIOTT P., pediatrician, director; Med. dir. Children's Hosp., Oakland, Calif., 1988—. Office: Children's Hospital Oakland 747 52nd St Oakland CA 94609 Office Fax: 510-450-5647.

VICHIOLA, CHRISTOPHER MICHAEL, writer, educator; b. Bridgeport, Conn., Apr. 27, 1959; s. Michael Richard and Delores (Distaci) Vichiola; m. Tracey Vichiola, Nov. 12, 1997; children: Michael, Christopher, Anthony. AS, Western Conn. State U., 1981, BA, 1983; grad., Colonel James "Bo" Gritz's Spec. Forces Green Beret On-Field Med. Surg. Sch. Cert. nursing asst, in hort., forklift, power equipment Home Depot Co. Martial arts tchr. Am. Bujinkan Dojo, Danbury, Conn., 1993—; tchr. Ctr. for Action, Kamiah, Idaho, 1997—; sales rep., safety capt. fertilizer toxic fertilizer program, power equipment specialist Home Depot, 1998—, power equipment specialist; clk. A&P Foodmart, 1999—2003; safety capt. Hazardous Waste Fertilizer Program; power equipment specialist, customer svc. program specialist Home Depot, 2006—, coord. extended warranty program, 2007—; sales assoc. toys Walmart, 2007. Educator, cons. Primerica Fin. Svcs., Danbury, 1997—; educator Christic Inst. Law Firm, Washington, 1995—. *Christopher Michael Vichiola served as a key supporter and educator of the Christic Institute Law Firm's Iran-Contra LA Penca Lawsuit. As a martial arts expert, Mr. Vichiola performed exceptional and successful displays of strength such as walking over burning hot coals. During Colonel Gritz's special Forces Training, Mr. Vichiola performed major surgery by extracting bullets from injured animals. During Navy Seal Training, he mapped out underwater locations for demolition. Mr. Vichiola received a black belt in the martial art of Ninjutsu from Masaaki Hatsumi, Japan.* Author: Above the Law - The Real Story's Files, 1995, Above the Law Part II, 1995, The Real Story of Christopher Vichiola and Colonel Gritz, 1997, The Real Story of Christopher Vichiola's and Colonel Gritz's Training, 1997. Educator Rev. Jesse L. Jackson's Rainbow Coalition, Washington, 1992—, Mayor Eugene Eriquez Dem. Party, Danbury, 1987-93; key dem. leader Pres. Barack Obama and V.P. Joe Biden. Recipient Commendation award for work with mentally-ill and developmentally disabled Gov. Michael Dukakis, 1989, Commendation for work with Christic Inst. Law Firm, Rep. Jack Brooks, 1991, Eagle award Col. James "Bo" Gritz, 1997, Spike Navy Seal Scuba badge Col. James "Bo" Gritz, 1997, Nat. Outstanding Safety award, Home Depot, 2006; named one of 2000 of the Most Influential People of 21st Century, 2004. Mem.: Amnesty Internat. Orgn., H.A.L.T. Attys. Orgn., Drug Policy Alliance Orgn., Nat. Dem. Com. (Commendation award), Southern Poverty Law Ctr., Martin Luther King Jr. Ednl. Found. Avocations: camping, scuba diving, basketball, football, martial arts. Home Phone: 860-489-5752; Office Phone: 203-730-9600, 860-496-8620, 860-409-0404.

VICK, COLUMBUS EDWIN, JR., retired civil engineering design firm executive; b. Jacksonville, Fla., Nov. 8, 1934; s. Columbus Edwin Sr. and Lucretia (Dean) V.; m. Laura Anne McGowan, Mar. 28, 1964; children: Jennifer, Carolyn, Elizabeth. BSCE, N.C. State U., 1956, MSCE, 1960. Registered profl. engr., 15 states. Rsch. asst. N.C. State Civil Engring. Dept., Raleigh, 1958-60; transp. planning engr. Harland Bartholomew & Assocs., Memphis, 1960-64, office and project mgr. Raleigh, 1964-67; prin., co-founder Kimley-Horn and Assocs. Inc., Raleigh, 1967-72, pres., 1972-92; chmn., 1992-2000. Bd. dirs. Wachovia Bank, Design Profls. Coalition Am. Cons. Engrs. Coun. Co-author: North Carolina Atlas; contbr. articles to profl. jours. Past pres., bd. dirs. NC State U. Engring. Found.; past pres. bd. assocs. Meredith Coll.; past dir. NC State U. Alumni Assn.; bd. visitors NC State U.; past 2d v.p. Bapt. State Conv. of NC; bd. dirs. Assoc. Bapt. Press, past chmn.; bd. dirs. Bibl. Recorder; trustee Kenan Inst. for Engring. Tech. and Sci., Gardner Webb U., Meredith Coll.; bd. advisors Wake Forest U. Sch. Divinity; bd. trustees Cooperative Bapt. Fellowship Found., past chmn. Recipient Meritorious Svc. award, NC State U., 2006; named Disting. Engring. alumnus, 1991. Fellow ASCE (Outstanding Young Engr. award ea. br. NC sect. 1966), Inst. Transp. Engrs. (Outstanding Individual Activity award so. sect. 1978, Disting. Svc. award so. sect. 1981, Lifetime Svc. award N.C. sect. 1995); mem. NSPE (Disting. Svc. award), Am. Con. Engrs. Coun., Am. Inst. Cert. Planners, Profl. Svcs. Mgmt. Assn. (Coll. of Fellow, Leonardo da Vinci award 2005), NC Soc. Engrs. (Outstanding Engring Achievement award 1992, NC Transp. Hall of Fame 2007). Baptist. Home: 2205 Nancy Ann Dr Raleigh NC

27607-3318 Office: Kimley-Horn and Assocs Inc 3001 Weston Pky Cary NC 27513-2301 Home Phone: 919-787-8859; Office Phone: 919-677-2002. E-mail: ed.vick@kimley-horn.com.

VICK, DANA JAMES, physician; b. Rochester, Minn., June 21, 1962; s. Alan George and Patricia Ann (Korum) V.; m. Anne Marie Troisi, Oct. 30, 1993. BA, U. Va., 1984; postgrad., Piedmont Va. C.C., Charlottesville, 1985-89; MD, Va. Commonwealth U., 1994; MBA in Healthcare Mgmt., Regis U., 2008. Cert. grad. with honors Inducted to Alpha Sigma Nu, 2008. Summer rsch. student The Mayo Clinic, Rochester, Minn., 1982, 83; telemktg. rep. Comdial Corp., Charlottesville, Va., 1984-86; lab. specialist U. Va. Sch. of Medicine, Charlottesville, 1986-89, summer rsch. student, 1990; commd. 2d lt. USAR, 1989, advanced through grades to maj., 2000, resigned, 2003; transitional intern Walter Reed Army Med. Ctr., Washington, 1994-95, Nat. Capital Consortium pathology resident, 1995-99; chief anat. pathology DeWitt Army Cmty. Hosp., Ft. Belvoir, Va., 1999—2002; chief anat. pathology, med. dir. microbiology Eisenhower Army Med. Ctr., Ft. Gordon, Ga., 2002—03; assoc. pathologist St. Josph's Pathology, P.C., Syracuse, NY, 2003—; med. advisor microbiology Lab. Alliance Ctrl. N.Y., 2003—. Adj. asst. prof. dept. pathology USUHS, Bethesda, Md., 1996-2003; lectr. specialist in blood banking program Walter Reed Army Med. Ctr., Washington, 1996-99; guest lectr. specialist in blood banking NIH, Bethesda, 1997-99; guest lectr. immunohematology rev. course, 1996—99. Contbr. articles to profl. jours. Chair U.S. Army delegation AMA-RFS, 1996-99, reference com., 1997, Md. state coord. Smoking is Not for Me Nat. Essay Contest, 1998; others. Decorated Meritorious Svc. medal (2), Army Commendation medal; recipient Excellence in Medicine Leadership award, AMA Found., 2006, NY State Conspicuous Svc. Cross. award, 2006. Fellow Coll. Am. Pathologists (chmn. NY delegator, 2005-); mem. AMA (mem.-at-large AMA-RFS governing coun. 1998-99, US Army del. young physicians sect. 1999-2001, mem.-at-large AMA-YPS governing coun. 2001—03), Wash. Soc. Pathologists (exec. coun.), Am. Soc. Clin. Pathologists, Am. Soc. Cytopathology, Assn. Mil. Surgeons of US, Nat. Med. Vets. Soc.(bd. dirs., 2004-05), Res. Officers Assn., U.S. and Can. Acad. of Pathology, Med. Soc. State NY, NY State Soc. Pathologists (chmn. profl. affairs com., sec. & treas. 2007-), Onondaga County Med. Soc., Soc. Med. Cons. to the Armed Forces, Syracuse Symphony Orch. (bd. dirs. 2008-), Alpha Sigma Nu, Med. Soc. State NY Task Force Bioterrorism & Emergency Preparedness (mem. budget fin. com. 2008-, mem. benifits com. 2006-). Avocations: instrumental and choral music, photography, collecting antique fountain pens, golf. Home: 4443 Treetop Cir Manlius NY 13104 Office Phone: 315-448-5416. E-mail: djvick615@pol.net.

VICK, DWIGHT HAROLD, educator; b. Water Valley, Miss., Oct. 19, 1963; AA, N.W. Miss. C.C., Senatobia, 1984; BBA, Delta State U., 1987; MPA, U. Memphis, 1992. Programming instr. United Cerebral Palsy, Memphis, 1991-92; rsch. assoc. Ariz. State U., Tempe, 1992-95; cons. City of Winslow, Ariz., 1993; govs. intern Dept. Corrections, Phoenix, 1994; intern Hispanic Assn. Coll. and Univ., Washington, 1995; intern 104th Congress U.S. Ho. of Reps., Washington, 1995; intern White House, Washington, 1996. Ariz. bd. mem. ASPA, Phoenix, 1996. Rschr.: Citistates, 1994. Vol. EVAC, Mesa, Ariz., 1992-96, Pastor for Congress, Phoenix, 1994-96, Clinton-Gore '96, Washington, 1996. Pvt. USAF, 1988. Democrat. Roman Catholic.

VICK, JEFFREY HARRISON, musician, educator; b. Denver, Nov. 5, 1965; s. Donald James and Sharlene Marie (Savage) Vick; m. Jacquelyn Campeau, Nov. 20, 1999; 1 child, Teresa Irene. BS in Music, U. Ariz., 1989; MEd in Music, Mont. State U., 1991. Cert. music tchr. grades K-12 Mont., secondary tchr. grades 5-12, secondary tchr. music, Office of Pub. Instrn., State Mont. Music educator Bozeman (Mont.) Pub. Schs., 1990—91, Willow Creek (Mont.) Sch., 1991—92, Anderson Sch. Dist. #41, Bozeman, 1993—. Pvt. percussion tchr., Bozeman, 1989—; prin. timpanist and percussionist Bozeman Symphony Orch., 1989—, Intermountain Opera Assn., Bozeman, 1990—, Mont. Ballet Co., Bozeman, 1993—; prin. timpanist Mont. Summer Symphony, Helena, 1998—2002, Billings Symphony Orch., Billings, 2007—; libr., coach Mont. chamber music workshop Mont. State U., Bozeman, 1990—2008, adj. instr. music, 1992—96, adv. bd. Mont. chamber music workshop, 1998—2003; dist. and state music festival adjudicator, 1994—; clinician Internat. Conf. on Percussion Music, Tucson, 1995; founding dir. PercOrchestra, Bozeman, 2000—; mem. Flutes and Friends, 2000—. Editor (newsletter): Montana Percussion News, 1998—, composer numerous compositions for band, percussion, Balinese gamelan; numerous concerto and chamber music recitals. Recipient Individual Artist Fellowship award, Mont. Arts Coun., 1992—93. Mem.: NEA, Mont. Music Educators Assn., Music Educators Nat. Conf., Percussive Arts Soc. (sec. Ariz. chpt. 1986—87, v.p. Ariz. chpt. 1987—88, sec. Mont. chpt. 1998—2007, v.p. Mont. chpt. 2007—), Am. Fedn. Musicians (exec. bd. local 709 1996—99, pres. local 709 1999—2002), Phi Delta Kappa (profl. rsch. grant 1999). Avocations: collecting instruments and masks, photography, world music. Home: 529 South Black Ave Bozeman MT 59715-5301 Office: Anderson Sch Dist #41 10040 Cottonwood Rd Bozeman MT 59718 Office Phone: 406-587-1305 ext. 110. Business E-Mail: jeffreyhvick@gmail.com, jvick@andersonmt.org.

VICK, LINDA H., biology professor; b. RI, Dec. 21, 1945; d. Arthur Alfred and Elna Linnea Helgerson; m. Maurice Robert Vick; children: Robert Alfred, Kimberly Sharma. PhD, U. Ill., Chgo., 1971. Instr. William Rainey Harper Coll., Palatine, Ill., 1973—76; prof. North Pk. U., Chgo., 1976—. Office: North Pk Univ 3225 W Foster Ave Chicago IL 60625

VICK, MARSHA COOK, writer, humanities educator; b. Charlotte, NC; d. Conley and Elizabeth (Voltz) Cook; m. Paul Allen Vick, Apr. 6, 1968 (div. 2005); children: Paul Allen Jr., Brian Conley. BA, U. N.C., 1963, MEd, 1965, PhD, 1996; MA, Duke U., 1985. Spanish translator Transl. Svc. Duke U., Durham, NC, 1974—76, speech writer for v.p., 1976—77, speech writer for pres., 1977—85; rsch. and editl. asst. U.S. Senate, Durham, 1986—92; lectr. Afro-Am. studies U. N.C., Chapel Hill, 1990—97; writer Durham, 1996—. Contbr. essays to various publs Mem. MLA, Coll. Lang. Assn., Sigma Delta Pi, Alpha Chi Omega. Home: 105 Harkness Cir Durham NC 27705

VICK, MICHAEL (MICHAEL DWAYNE VICK), professional football player; b. Newport News, Va., June 26, 1980; s. Brenda Vick and Michael Boddie; 2 children. Grad., Warwick High Sch., Newport News, VA, 1998; attended, Va. Tech., 2001. Quarterback Atlanta Falcons, 2001—09, Phila. Eagles, 2009—. Indicted by a federal grand jury, July 17, 2007 on charges of sponsoring a dog fighting operation, called Bad Newz Kennels; pleaded guilty to felony conspiracy charges for his role in a dogfighting ring on August 20, 2007; indicted by Grand Jury, September 25, 2007 on state charges for beating or killing or causing dogs to fight other dogs & engaging in or promoting dogfighting; sentenced to 23 months in prison on dogfighting charges on December 10, 2007; released from federal prison on May 20, 2009; released from federal custody on July 20, 2009; conditionally reinstated to play in the NFL by commissioner Roger Goodell on July 27, 2009. Spokesperson Boys & Girls Club of Metro Atlanta, Empty Stocking Fund; co-founder Vick Found., 2006—. Recipient Excellence in Sports Performance Yearly (ESPY), 1999, Archie Griffin award, 1999, Toyota Gator Bowl MVP, 2001; named Big East Conf. Rookie of Yr., 1999, Big East Conf. Offensive Player of Yr., 1999; named one of 101 Most Influential Minorities in Sports, Sports Illustrated, 2003; named to NFC Pro-Bowl, 2002, 2004—05. Achievements include leading the NFL in: yards per rushing attempt, 2002, 04-06; setting the NFL record for most rushing yards by a quarterback, 2006. Office: Phila Eagles 3501 S Broad St Philadelphia PA 19101*

VICKERS, LEE LOUISE, minister; b. Suffern, NY, Dec. 20, 1954; d. Chester E. and Dorothy Jean (Allen) Vickers; 1 child, Seth. Diploma summa cum laude, We. Bapt. Coll., 1977; A in Forestry, Flathead Valley Cmty. Coll., 1979, A, 1980; BA in Liberal Arts, Regents Coll., 1988. Sec.-clk. Glacier Ch., Kalispell, Mont., 1988—91; pastor Hearing The Distant Drummer Ministry, Mont., 1991—. Poem, E Duo Unum, 1993; author: Earth and Sky, 2002, A Path Less Traveled, 2009. Firefighter, dept. sec. Marion Vol. Fire Dept., Mont., 1996—98. With US Army, 1982—84. Avocations: reading, poetry. Home: PO Box 9155 Kalispell MT 59904

VICKERS, MICHAEL G., federal agency administrator; b. 1953; m. Melana Zyla; 5 children. BA, U. Ala.; MA Strategic Studies and Internat. Econ., Johns Hopkins U.; MBA, Wharton Sch., U. Pa. Spl. forces officer US Army; ops. officer CIA; dir. strategic studies Ctr. for Strategic & Budgetary Assessment, sr. v.p.; asst. sec. for spl. ops. & low intensity conflict & ind. capabilities US Dept. Def., 2007—. Author: The Revolution in War, 2004. Office: US Dept Def 1000 Def Pentagon Rm 3C683 Washington DC 20301-1000 Office Phone: 703-695-9667. Office Fax: 202-331-8019.

VICKERS, NANCY J., retired academic administrator; BA, Mt. Holyoke Coll., 1967, LHD (hon.), 1999; MA, Yale U., 1971, PhD, 1976. Prof. French and Italian Dartmouth Coll., 1973—87; prof. French, Italian, and comparative literature U. Southern Calif., 1987—97, dean curriculum and instrn. Coll. Letters, Arts and Scis., 1994—97; pres. Bryn Mawr Coll., 1997—2008. Vis. prof. Harvard U., U. Pa., UCLA; bd. dirs. Bryn Mawr Bank Corp.; bd. govs. Coun. Dante Soc. Am. Recipient Presdl. medal Outstanding Leadership and Achievement, Dartmouth Coll., 1991; fellow vis. fellow, Princeton U. Office: Bryn Mawr Coll 101 N Merion Ave Bryn Mawr PA 19010-2899 Office Phone: 610-526-5156.

VICKERY, JON LIVINGSTONE, neurologist; b. Freeport, Ill., May 30, 1955; s. Eugene Livingstone and Millie Margaret (Cox) V.; m. Diane Antoinetti; children: Daniel Scott, John Michael. BA, Northwestern U., 1976; MD, U. Ill., Chgo., 1980. Diplomate Nat. Bd. Med. Examiners. Resident in neurology U. Va., Charlottesville, 1980-84; staff neurologist Pinnacle Health Sys., Harrisburg, Pa., 1984—2004; v.p. Pa. Neurol. Assocs., Lemoyne, Pa., 1984—2004, pres., 2004—06; assoc. prof. of medicine Hershey Med. Ctr., Pa. State U., 1984-99; chief of medicine Holy Spirit Hosp., Camp Hill, Pa., 1992-95; with Vickery Neurodiagnostics Group Ltd., Carlisle, Pa., 2006—; clin. assoc. prof. neurosurgery Pa. State U., 2008—. Asst. coach Dickinson Coll. Fencing Team. Named to Am.'s Top Physicians Consumer Rsch. Coun., 2005. Fellow Am. Acad. Neurology; mem. AMA, Dauphin County Med. soc. (del. 1985-98), U.S. Fencing Coaches Assn., U.S. Fencing Assn. (life), U.S. Fencing Coaches Assn. (cert. moniteur de armes), Am. Orchid Soc. (cert. judge, mem. conservation com, 1989-91), Beaufort Hunt Club (bd. dirs. 1990-2000), Masons, Shriners. Avocations: fencing, photography, theater, breeding Hanoverian horses. Office: Vickery Neurodiagnostics Group Ltd 3 Jennifer Ct Ste B Carlisle PA 17013 Office Phone: 717-245-2226. Personal E-mail: jvickeryvng@gmail.com.

VICKERY, KAREN S., education educator, director; d. Herman Lee and Sarah Ludean Clark; m. James L. Vickery. AA, Southern Bapt. Coll., Walnut Ridge, Ark., 1964; BS in Edn., Ark. State U., Jonesboro, 1964—66, MS in Edn., 1972; D in Edn., East Tex. State U., Commerce, 1978. Cert. in edn. Tex. Edn. Agy., 1975, academic Lang therapist Dean Learning Ctr., 1982, qualified instr. EDMAR Ednl. Assocs., 1985. Tchr. Arcadia Valley Pub. Schs., Ironton, Mo., 1966—67, Hazelwood Sch. Dist., Mo., 1967—68, Cape Girardeau Pub. Schs., Mo., 1968—70, Hoxie Pub. Schs., Ark., 1971—75, reading tchr., 1971—75; upward bound program Southern Bapt. Coll., Walnut Ridge, Ark., 1974—74; reading tchr. Royse City Ind. Sch. Dist., Tex., 1975—82; intermediate sch. reading tchr. Greenville Ind. Sch. Dist., Tex., 1982—95, dist. dyslexia coord., 1995—2001, coord., 1995—; dir. Multisensory Learning Ctr., Greenville, 1986—2002; learning therapy program introductory coord. Southern Meth. U., Dallas, 1999—2001, dir. learning therapy ctr., 2001—; dir. academic enhancement workshops Southrn Meth. U., 2001—. Treas. Internat. Multisensory Structured Lang. Edn. Coun., Dallas, 2006—09; founding mem., adv. bd. Legacy Sch. Rockwall, Tex., 2009. Recipient Key Communicator award, Greenville Ind. Sch. Dist.; named Outstanding Educator, Internat. Multisensory Structured Lang. Edn. Coun., 2008; named one of Alumni of Yr., Williams Bapt. Coll., 2001—02. Mem.: Dallas Br. Internat. Dyslexia Assn., Academic Lang. Therapy Assn. Found., Internat. Dyslexia Assn. (Edn. award 2002), Academic Lang. Therapy Assn. (bd. mem. & chmn. 1985—). Avocations: golf, travel, reading. Office: Southern Meth Univ 5236 Tennyson Parkway 4-108 Plano TX 75024 Office Fax: 972-473-3442. Business E-Mail: kvickery@smu.edu.

VICKERY, RAYMOND EZEKIEL, JR., international business consultant, lawyer; b. Brookhaven, Miss., Apr. 30, 1942; s. Raymond Ezekiel and Clarene Helen (Dickens) V.; m. Raymond Clair Brown, Dec. 23, 1967 (div. June 1976); m. Ann Morgan, June 23, 1979; children: Raymond Morgan, Philip Dickens. AB, Duke U., 1964; postgrad., U. Sri Lanka, 1964-65; LLB, Harvard U., 1968. Assoc. Hogan & Hartson, Washington, 1968-77, ptnr. McLean, Va., 1985-93, Johnson & Vickery, Vienna, Va., 1977-81, Reed Smith Shaw & McClay, McLean, Va., 1981-85; asst. sec. for trade devel. U.S. Dept. Commerce, Washington, 1993-97; prin. Vickery Internat., 1977—; pvt. practice Washington, 1997—; of counsel Williams Aron & Assocs., Washington, 2002—06; sr. dir. Stonebridge Internat. LLC, 2006—; pub. policy scholar Woodrow Wilson Internat. Ctr. Scholars, 2008—09. Adj. prof. internat. transactions George Mason U., Fairfax, Va., 1997-99; pub. policy scholar Woodrow Wilson Internat. Ctr. Scholars, 2008-09. Contbr. articles to profl. jours. Del. Va. Gen. Assembly, Richmond, 1974-80; mem. Dem. Com., Farifax County, Va., 1971-93; Dem. nominee for Congress, Va., 1992; mem. State Ctrl. Com., Va., 1993; mem. Libr. Bd., Fairfax County, 1972-74. Fulbright scholar, 1964. Mem. ABA, Va. Bar Assn., D.C. Bar Assn., City Club, Phi Beta Kappa, Omicron Delta Kappa. Baptist. Avocations: fishing, horseback riding. Home: 2733 Willow Dr Vienna VA 22181-5310 Office: 555 13th St NW Washington DC 20004-2514

VICKREY, ROBERT REMSEN, artist; b. NYC, Aug. 20, 1926; s. Claude Claire and Caroline (McKim) V.; m. Marjorie Elizabeth Alexander, Sept. 18, 1950 (dec. 1997); children: Remsen Scott, Elizabeth Nicole, Wendy Caroline, Alexander Sean (dec. 2007); m. Beverly B. Rumage, July, 1999. Studied with Victoria Huntley; BA, Yale U., 1947, B.F.A., 1950; student, Art Students League. Art dealer Harmon-Meek Galleries, Naples, Fla. Co-author: New Techniques in Egg Tempera, 1973; author: Robert Vickrey-Artist at Work, The Affable Curmudgeon, 1979; one-man shows, Midtown Galleries, NYC, 1954-58, 62, 65, 69-70, 72, Columbia Mus. Art, SC, 1959, Davison Art Ctr., Wesleyan U., 1966, Va. Mus. Fine Arts, 1965, retrospective, U. Ariz. Mus. Art, 1973, San Diego Fine Arts Gallery, 1973, (27 shows) Harmon-Meek Gallery, Naples, Fla., 1982-2009, retrospective The Von Liebig Art Ctr., Naples, 2006; exhibited in group shows; represented in permanent collections, Whitney Mus., Corcoran Gallery of Art, Washington, Lakeland (Fla.) Mus., Sara Roby Found., Parrish Art Mus., Southampton, Isaac Delgado Mus., Dallas Mus., Munson-Williams-Proctor Inst., Utica, NY, Met. Mus. Art, NAD, Butler Inst. Am. Art, New Britain Mus. Am. Art, Gallery Modern Art, Birmingham Mus., Spelman Coll., Newark Mus., others; illustrator mag. covers, books; author: Cape Cod's Cockiest Crook, 1996. Recipient award Edward Austin Abbey mural competition, 1949, top prize Fla. Internat. Art Exhbn., 1952, 2d prize Internat. Hallmark competition, 1955, Am. Artist mag. citation, 1956, Winsor and Newton award Am. Water Color Soc., 1956, S.J. Wallace Truman prize Nat. Acad. ann., 1958, Salmagundi Club award Audubon Artists, 1971, spl. prize Internat. Biennial of Sport in Fine Arts, Mus. Contemporary Art, Madrid, 1973, Gold Medal NAD, Gerard Manley Hopkins award, 2009, numerous others. Mem. Audubon Artists, Am. Water Color Soc., Nat. Acad. Achievements include two books, Robert Vickrey's Nun Paintings by Donald Miller (2002), Robert Vickrey's Magic of Realism by Philip Elisoph (2009). Home: 8231 Bay Colony Dr #1202 Naples FL 34108

VICTOR, A. PAUL, lawyer; b. NYC, Nov. 6, 1938; s. Samuel L. and Sophie (Ostrow) V.; m. Ellen Grabois, Aug. 30, 1959; children: Stephanie, Rebecca, Diana. BBA, U. Mich., 1960, JD with distinction, 1963. Bar: N.Y. 1964, D.C. 1964. Atty. antitrust divsn. US Dept. Justice, Washington, 1963-66; assoc. Kirkland, Ellis & Rowe, Washington, 1966-68, Weil, Gotshal & Manges, NYC, 1968-72, ptnr., 1972—2006, Dewey & Le Boeuf LLP, NYC, 2006—. Adj. prof. law Fordham U. Sch. of Law, NYC, 1983—; mem. adv. bd. Ctr. Am. and Internat. Law, Dallas, 1984-07; bd. dirs. Toray Industries (Am.) Inc., NYC, 1987—, vis. lectr. U. Mich. Law Sch., Columbia U. Law Sch., NYU Sch. of Law; presenter in field. Contbr. numerous articles to law revs., other legal publs. regarding U.S. internat. antitrust and trade law. Antitrust Class Actions, International Cartel Enforcements Non-govtl. advisor US Del. Internat. Competition Network, 2002-04, 06-09; mem. visitors com. U. Mich. Law Sch., 1980-06, mem. dean's adv. com., 2006-; trustee Mass. Sch. Law, Andover, 1989—, chmn., 1998—; sec. Japan Soc., NYC, 1999-00; bd. dirs. NY chpt. Juvenile Diabetes Rsch. Found., 1994-99, 04—. Mem. ABA (vice-chair sect. antitrust law 1994-95, mem. coun. 1983-86, 91-94, chmn. internat. antitrust com. 1982-85, 87-90, mem. internat. task force, 2005-09, co-chair, Internat. Task Force, 2009-), Internat. Bar Assn., N.Y. State Bar Assn., Order of Coif Jewish. Avocations: golf, travel, swimming. Office: Dewey & Le Boeuf LLP 1301 Ave of the Americas New York NY 10019 Office Phone: 212-259-6930. Business E-Mail: pvictor@dl.com.

VICTOR, JOHN C., epidemiologist; PhD, U. Mich., Ann Arbor, MPH, 2004. Clin. trials advisor PATH, Seattle, 2006—.

VICTOR, MICHAEL GARY, lawyer, physician; b. Detroit, Sept. 20, 1945; s. Simon H. and Helen (Litsky) V.; children: Elise Nicole, Sara Lisabeth. Degree in Sci., Wayne State U., Detroit, 1967. Bar: Ill. 1980, U.S. Dist. Ct. (no. dist.) Ill. 1980, U.S. Ct. Appeals (7th cir.) 1981; diplomate Am. Bd. Legal Medicine, Am. Bd. Emergency Medicine, 2003. Of counsel Bollinger, Ruberry & Garvey, Chgo., 1980—99; pres. Advocate Adv. Assocs., Chgo., 1982-95; asst. prof. medicine Northwestern U. Med. Sch., Chgo., 1982—2006; lectr. U. Ill., Chgo., 1999—, asst. clin. prof., 2008. Dir. emergency medicine Loretto Hosp., Chgo., 1980-85, chief. sect. of emergency medicine St. Josephs Hosp., Chgo., 1985-87; pvt. practice med. law Barrington, Ill, 1982-; v.p. Med. Emergency Svcs. Assocs., Buffalo Grove, Ill., 1989; v.p. MESA Mgmt. Corp.; exec. leadership coach Lee Hecht Harrison, Chgo. Author: Informed Consent, 1980; Brain Death, 1980; (with others) Due Process for Physicians, 1984, A Physicians Guide to the Illinios Living Will Act, The Choice is Ours!, 1989. Recipient Svc. awards Am. Coll. Emergency Medicine, 1973-83. Fellow Am. Coll. Legal Medicine (bd. govs. 1996-97, alt. del. to AMA House of Dels. 1996-97), Chgo. Acad. Legal Medicine; mem. Am. Coll. Emergency Physicians (pres. Ill. chpt. 1980, med.-legal-ins. coun. 1980-81, 83-84), ABA, Ill. State Bar Assn., Am. Soc. Law and Medicine, Chgo. Bar Assn. (med.-legal coun. 1981-83), AMA, Ill. State Med. Soc. (med.-legal coun. 1980-86, 88), Chgo. Med. Soc. Jewish. Home and Office: 153 Aberdour Ln Palatine IL 60067-8001 Office Phone: 847-934-8404. Personal E-mail: mgv@comcast.net.

VICTORINO, SHANE PATRICK, professional baseball player; b. Wailuku, Hawaii, Nov. 30, 1980; m. Melissa Smith; 1 child, Kali'a Makenna. Outfielder San Diego Padres, 2003, Phila. Phillies, 2005—. Mem., vol. Phila. Action Team. Recipient Gold Glove award, 2009; named to Nat. League All-Star Team, Maj. League Baseball, 2009. Achievements include member of World Series championship winning Philadelphia Phillies, 2008. Office: Phila Phillies One Citizens Bank Way Philadelphia PA 19148*

VICTORY, JEFFREY PAUL, state supreme court justice; b. Shreveport, La., Jan. 29, 1946; s. Thomas Edward and Esther (Horton) V.; m. Nancy Clark Victory, Jan. 20, 1973; children: Paul Bradford, William Peter, Christopher Thomas, Mary Katherine. BA in History and Govt., Centenary Coll., 1967; JD, Tulane U., 1971. Bar: La. 1971. Ptnr. Tucker, Jeter, Jackson & Victory, Shreveport, 1971-82; dist. ct. judge 1st Jud. Dist. Ct., Shreveport, 1982-90; appellate judge 2d Circuit Ct. of Appeal, Shreveport, 1991-95; assoc. justice Supreme Ct. La., 1995—. Bd. dirs. La. Judicial Coll. Bd. dirs. CODAC Drug Abuse, Shreveport; mem. La. Sentencing Commn. La. NG, 1969-75. Mem. ABA, Shreveport Bar Assn., La. Bar Assn. Republican. Baptist. Avocations: tennis, motorcycles, classic cars. Office: Supreme Ct 400 Royal St New Orleans LA 70130*

VICUÑA, MAXIMO QUINTILIANO, retired language educator; b. Aquia, Ancash, Peru, Apr. 13, 1936; s. Calixto Carlos Vicuña Calderon and Rosa Maria Arrieta-Barreto; m. Elcira Balvina Plansencia, Sept. 9, 1964; children: Luis Benjamin, Isabel Ruth Poikkimaki, Cecilia Maria Vicuna-Keady, Sophia Irene Milano. BE with honors, U. Nat. Mayor San Marcos, Lima, Peru, 1965, EdD, 1966; MA in Bibl. Langs., Andrews U., Berrien Springs, Mich., 1971; ThD, Inst. Superior Evangelico Estudios Teologicos, Buenos Aires, 1982; HHD (hon.), U. Apurimac, Abancay, Peru, 1994. Pres., prof. Peruvian Union U., Nana, Lima, 1983—94; prof. Spanish Worcester State Coll., Mass., 1995—96, Coll. Holy Cross, Worcester, 1996—98; Spanish prof. Quinsigamond CC, Worcester, 1996—; Quechua prof. Harvard U., Cambridge, Mass., 2002—06. Author: (book) Studies of the Book of Daniel, (textbook) Greek Grammar of the New Testament, American Religions Compared. Mem.: Nat. Assembly Pres.'s (rectors 1989—94). Democrat. Adventist. Avocations: walking, writing, reading, gardening. Home: 37 Ledgecrest Dr Worcester MA 01603 Personal E-mail: maxelsie@charter.net, maxelsie@gmail.com.

VIDAL, ALEJANDRO LEGASPI (ANDY VIDAL), architect; b. Kawit, Cavite, The Philippines, May 3, 1934; came to U.S. 1954; s. Antonio and Patrocinia Santonil (Legaspi) V.; m. Fe Del Rosario, Aug. 16, 1962; 1 child, Alex Anthony. BS in Architecture, Mapua Inst. Tech., 1962. Registered arch., The Philippines. Prin. A.L. Vidal Arch., Manila, 1962-63; staff arch. Vinnell Wall & Green, Agana, Guam, 1963-64; project engr. Dillingham Corp. of Nevada, Hawaii and Guam, 1964-74; sr. project mgr., preconstrn. svc. mgr., constrn. disputes resolutions negotiator Fletcher-Pacific Constrn. Co. Ltd., Honolulu, 1974—96; prin. A.L. Vidal Constrn. Cons., Honolulu, 1996—, A.L. Vidal Arch., Cavite, The Philippines, 1996-2000. Designer, builder first application of integrated aluminum forming sys. for high rise concrete construction; contbr. articles to profl. jours. Active Rep. Presdl. Task Force, Washington, 1980-88, Rep. Senatorial Com., Washington, 1980-88. With USN, 1954-58, Korea. Mem. VFW (life, sr. vice comdr. post 2004-05), Am. Mgmt. Assn., Soc. Am. Mil. Engrs., U. Hawaii Found., Chancellor's Club, Disabled Am. Vets., Comdrs. Club. Roman Catholic. Avocations: golf, swimming, volunteer work. Home: 1051 Kaluanui Rd Honolulu HI 96825-1321 E-mail: avidal96825@yahoo.com.

VIDAL, DAVID JONATHAN, insurance company executive, journalist; b. Bayamón, PR, Oct. 11, 1946; s. Jesus Maria and Ercira Audacia (Mejia) V.; m. Watuza Leal, Jan. 25, 1975; 1 child, Katalyn. AB cum laude, Princeton U., 1968; student, Sch. Advanced Internat. Studies, Washington, 1982-83; MBA, Columbia U., 1991. Reporter The Caracas (Venezuela) Daily Jour., 1969-70; reporter, news editor AP, Caracas, NY and Sao Paulo, 1970-73, corr. Brasilia, Brazil, 1973-75; reporter, bur. chief N.Y. Times, NYC and Rio de Janeiro, 1975-80; spl. asst., White House fellow Dept. State, Washington, 1980-81; cons. U.S. AID, Washington, 1981-82; dept. mgr. task force Pres.'s Pvt. Sector Survey on Cost Control, Washington, 1982-83; exec. dir. Nat. Commn. Secondary Schooling for Hispanics, Washington, 1983-84; dir. pub. affairs N.Y.C. Partnership, 1984-85; asst. v.p. Continental Ins., NYC, 1985-95; v.p. Coun. on Fgn. Rels., NYC, 1995-97; dir. rsch. global corp. citizenship The Conf. Bd., NYC, 1997—; pub. Across the Board, 2001—. Adj. prof. journalism Columbia U. Grad. Sch. Journalism, N.Y.C., 1985-86; bd. dirs. Pub. Affairs Coun., Washington, 1988-95; trustee Found. for Pub. Affairs, Washington, 1989-95; mem. Contbns. Adv. Group, 1988-95, chmn., 1994-95; mem. corp. adv. group Schomburg Ctr. for Rsch. in Black Culture, 1988-95, Ad Hoc Com. on Charter Revision, 1988, Nat. Hispanic Agenda, 1988; mem. adv. group Latino Leadership Fund, 1991-95; vice-chmn. Nat. Civic League, 1999—. Author: (newspaper series) NY Times, 1980; pub. Across the Board, 2001—; contbr. articles and reports in field. Trustee N.Y. Theol. Sem., NYC, 1990—; mem. Coun. Fgn. Rels.; prin. Coun. for Excellence in Govt., Washington, 1992—; dir. Coun. on Internat. Ednl. Exch., NYC, 1997—2003; elder, trustee West End Presbyn. Ch., NYC, 1986—. Recipient Hispanic Achievement award Wall Street chpt. IMAGE, N.Y.C., 1989; Fulbright scholar, Washington and Venezuela, 1968. Fellow Royal Soc. for encouragement of Arts, Manufacturers and Commerce; mem. N.Y. Regional Assn. Grantmakers (dir., sec. 1988-95), Nat. Inst. Industry Assn. (corp. adv. group 1990-95), Nat. Civic League, Coun. on Fgn. Rels. Democrat. Office: The Conf Bd 845 3rd Ave New York NY 10022-6601 E-mail: david.vidal@conference-board.org.

VIDAL, GORE (EUGENE LUTHER VIDAL JR.), writer; b. West Point, NY, Oct. 3, 1925; s. Eugene L. and Nina (Gore) V. Grad., Phillips Exeter Acad., 1943; DLitt (hon.), Brown U., 1988. Author: (novels) Williwaw, 1946, In a Yellow Wood, 1947, The City and the Pillar, 1948, The Season of Comfort, 1949, A Star's Progress, 1950, A Search for the King, 1950, Dark Green, Bright Red, 1950, Death in the Fifth Position, 1952, Death Before Bedtime, 1953, Thieves Fall Out, 1953, Death Likes It Hot, 1954 The Judgment of Paris, 1952, Messiah, 1954, Julian, 1964, Washington, D.C, 1967, Myra Breckinridge, 1968, Two Sisters, 1970, Burr: A Novel, 1973, Myron, 1974, Eighteen Seventy-Six, 1976, Kalki, 1978, Creation, 1981 (Prix Deauville 1983), Duluth, 1983, Lincoln, 1984, Empire, 1987, Hollywood: A Novel of America in the 1920's, 1990, Live From Golgotha: The Gospel According to Gore Vidal, 1992, The Smithsonian Institution, 1998, The Essential Vidal, 1998, The Golden Age, 2000; (non-fiction) Perpetual War for Perpetual Peace: How We Got So Hated, 2002, Dreaming War: Blood for Oil and the Cheney-Bush Junta, 2002, Inventing A Nation: Washington, Adams, Jefferson, 2003, Imperial America: Reflection on the United States of Amnesia, 2004; (memoirs) Screening History, 1992, Palimpsest, 1995, Point to Point Navigation: A Memoir, 2006; (short stories) A Thirsty Evil, 1956, Clouds and Eclipses: Collected Short Stories, 2006; (essays) Rocking the Boat, 1962, Sex, Death, and Money, 1968, Reflections upon a Sinking Ship, 1969, Homage to Daniel Shays, 1973, Matters of Fact and of Fiction, 1977, The Second American Revolution, 1982 (Nat. Book Critics Circle award for criticism 1982), Armageddon?, 1987 (London), United States: Essays 1952-1992, 1993 (Nat. Book award for nonfiction 1993), The Last Empire: Essays 1992—2000, 2001; (plays) Visit to a Small Planet, 1957, The Best Man, 1960, (Broadway revived 2000) Romulus, 1962, Weekend, 1968, An Evening with Richard Nixon, 1972, On the March to the Sea, 2005; (screenplays) The Catered Affair, 1956, I Accuse, 1958, The Left-Handed Gun, 1958, The Scapegoat, 1959, Suddenly Last Summer, 1959, The Best Man, 1964 (Cannes Critics prize 1964), Is Paris Burning?, 1966, The Last of the Mobile Hotshots, 1970; (teleplays) Barn Burning, 1954, Dark Possession, 1954, Smoke, 1954, Visit to a Small Planet, 1955, Dr. Jekyll and Mr. Hyde, 1955, A Sense of Justice, 1955, Summer Pavilion, 1955, The Turn of the Screw, 1955, Stage Door, 1955, A Farewell to Arms, 1955, The Death of Billy the Kid, 1955, Honor, 1956, The Indestructible Mr. Gore, 1959, Dress Gray, 1986, Billy the Kid, 1989; actor (films) Ritual in Transfigured Time, 1946, Suddenly, Last Summer, 1959,The Best Man, 1964, Bob Roberts, 1992, With Honors, 1994, Shadow Conspiracy, 1997, Gattaca, 1997, Igby Goes Down, 2002 Mem. Pres.'s Adv. Com. on Arts, 1961-63; Dem.-Liberal candidate for U.S. Congress, 1960, candidate for Dem. nomination from Calif., 1982; co-chmn. The New Party, 1970-71. Served with AUS, 1943-46. Named hon. citizen Ravello, Italy, 1983, Chevalier de l'Ordre des Arts et des Lettres, France, 1995; recipient Golden Plate award, Acad. Achievement, 2006.

VIDAL, MANOLO (MANNY), marketing communications agency executive; Degree in Mktg., Fairleigh Dickinson U., Teaneck, NJ. Various mktg. positions Grey/FOVA Advt., Revlon Inc., Dannon Co., Inc.; pres. The Nat. Hispanic Merchandising Group (divsn. Castor Internat. Advt.); founder, pres., CEO Vidal Partnership, NYC, 1991—. Named one of 40 Under 40 Rising Stars, Crain's NY Bus., 2002. Office: Vidal Partnership 228 E 45th St 11th Fl New York NY 10017 Office Phone: 212-867-5185. Office Fax: 212-661-7650. Business E-Mail: mvidal@vidalpartnership.com.*

VIDAL, MAUREEN ERIS, theater educator, actress; b. Bklyn., Mar. 18, 1956; d. Louis and Lillian (Kaplan) Hendelman; m. Juan Vidal, June 25, 1974 (div. Sept. 1981); m. Guillermo Eduardo Uriarte, Dec. 22, 1986. BA, Bklyn. Coll., 1976, MS, 1981. From English tchr. to drama tchr. N.Y.C. Bd. Edn., 1976—, chair women's history dept., 1984—, dean, 1997—, drama tchr., 2002—. Mem PETA Humane Soc. Mem.: AFTRA, Gorilla Soc., Nat. Anti-Vivisection Soc. (mem. physicians' com. responsible medicine), Heights Players Theater Co. (arranger theatrical performance for residents of homeless shelters 1986—2003, exec. bd., sec. 1993—, actress), Doris Day Animal League, Delta Psi Omega. Avocations: travel, white-water rafting, scuba diving, skydiving, theater. Office: I S 318 101 Walton St Brooklyn NY 11206-4311 also: Heights Players 26 Willow Pl Brooklyn NY 11201-4513 Office Phone: 718-782-0589. E-mail: MVidal4942@aol.com.

VIDAVER, ANNE MARIE, plant pathology educator; b. Vienna, Mar. 29, 1938; came to U.S., 1941; d. Franz and Klara (Winter) Kopecky; children: Gordon W.F., Regina M. BA, Russell Sage Coll., 1960; MA, Ind. U., 1962, PhD, 1965. Lectr. U. Nebr., Lincoln, 1965-66, rsch. assoc., 1966-72, asst. prof., 1972-74, assoc. prof., 1974-79, prof. plant pathology, 1979—, interim dir. Ctr. Biotech., 1988-89, 97-00, head dept. plant pathology, 1984-2000, 2003—06; chief scientist USDA's NRICGP, 2000—02. Contbr. articles to profl. jours. and books; patentee in field. Recipient Pub. Svc. award Nebr. Agri-Bus., 1977, Sci. award for excellence NAMA, New Orleans, 1991. Fellow AAAS, Am. Phytopath. Soc., Am. Soc. Microbiology; mem. Intersoc. Consortium for Plant Protection, Internat. Soc. Plant Pathology, Alliance for Prudent Use of Antibiotics. Avocations: indoor gardening, reading. Office: U Nebr Dept Plant Pathology Lincoln NE 68583-0722 Office Phone: 402-472-2858. E-mail: avidaver1@unl.edu.

VIDAVER, ROBERT MAXWELL, medical educator; b. Mpls., June 17, 1932; s. Robert William and Helen Mary (Ford) Vidaver; m. Virginia Moore Sewell, May 27, 1960. AB, Columbia U., 1953; MD, SUNY, 1956; MA (hon.), Dartmouth Coll., 1993. Diplomate Am. Bd. Psychiatry and Neurology, 1963. Intern in medicine U. Md., Balt., 1956—57; resident in psychiatry Yale U. Sch. Medicine, New Haven, 1957—60; asst. prof., coord. undergrad. edn. U. Md., Balt., 1962—65; state dir. psychiat. edn. Md. Dept. Health & Mental Hygiene, Balt., 1965—71; instr., asst. prof. Johns Hopkins Sch. Medicine, Balt., 1965—72; pres. First Md. Health Care Corp., Balt., 1971—72; assoc. prof. medicine and psychiatry N.J. Med. Sch., Newark, 1973—81, assoc. dean for hosp. affairs, 1979; med. dir. Martland Hosp., N.J. Med. Sch., Newark, 1974—78; prof., chmn. dept. psychiatry and behavioral sci. Ea. Va. Med. Sch., Norfolk, 1981—88; med. dir. N.H. Hosp., Concord, 1988—2008; prof., vice chmn. dept. psychiatry Dartmouth Med. Sch., Hanover, NH, 1988—2008, prof. emeritus, 2008—. Bd. dirs. NH Hosp., Concord, 1988—2004. Author: Developments in Human Services' Education and Manpower, 1973; contbr. articles to profl. jours. Capt. US Army, 1960—62. NY State Regents scholar, NY State Dept. Edn., Columbia U., 1949—53, NY State Profl. scholar, SUNY Coll. Medicine, 1952—56. Fellow: Am. Psychiat. Assn. (life; Disting.); mem.: NH Psychiat. Assn. (councillor), Alpha Omega Alpha (Leonard Tow Humanism in Medicine award, NH bd. medicine 2008). Episcopalian. Office: NH Hosp 36 Clinton St Concord NH 03301-2359 Personal E-mail: vvidaver@hotmail.com.

VIDELL, JARED STEVEN, cardiologist; b. Phila., Apr. 9, 1947; s. Harry and Rose (Malken) V.; m. Cyla Trocki, Dec. 27, 1969; children: Haviv Elana, Mikhael Alon, Samara Pilar. BEd, U. Miami, 1969; DO, Phila. Coll. Osteo. Medicine, 1976. Resident and chief resident in internal medicine Atlantic City (N.J.) Med. Ctr., 1976-79; fellow in cardiovascular diseases Albert Einstein Med. Ctr., Phila., 1979-81; rsch. fellow in nuclear cardiology Deborah Heart and Lung Ctr., Browns Mills, NJ, 1981-82, dir. employee health svcs., 1982-84; asst. dir. cardiology Pritikin Longevity Ctr., Downington, Pa., 1984-87; cardiologist, dir. clin. lab. Physician Care, P.C., Towanda, Pa., 1987-90; from co-chmn. intensive care to dir. cardiac stress lab. Meml. Hosp., Towanda, 1987-90; dir. house staff, intensive/cardiac care Lower Bucks Hosp., Bristol, Pa., 1992-94; dir. house staff ICU-CCU North Phila. Health Systems, 1994-97; med. dir. North Phila. Health Sys. Girard Med. Ctr., 1997—, chmn. clin. medicine, 1997—. Med. dir. Am. Cancer Soc. chpt., 1989-90; state peer rev. KEPRO, 1989-90. Contbr. rsch. articles to profl. jours. With M.C. USAR. Fellow: Am. Soc. Angiology; mem.: AOA, Alumni Assn. Phila. Coll. Osteo. Medicine, Phila. County Med. Soc., Pa. Med. Soc., Am. Soc. Law, Medicine and Ethics, Internat. Platform Assn., Am. Coll. Physician Execs., Internat. Soc. Endovascular Surgery, Internat. Soc. Internal Medicine, Am. Soc. Internal Medicine, Am. Coll. Chest Physicians. Avocations: travel, fishing. Office: 408 N Exeter Ave Margate City NJ 08402-1868 Office Phone: 609-823-1989. Office Fax: 609-823-1989.

VIDENIEKS, BARBARA J., legislative staff member; m. Peter Videnieks. Chief of staff to Senator Robert Byrd US Senate, Washington. Democrat. Office: 311 Hart Senate Office Bldg Washington DC 20510 Office Phone: 202-224-3954. Business E-Mail: barbara_videnieks@byrd.senate.gov.*

VIDENOVIC, ALEKSANDAR, medical educator; m. Nancy Gracin; 1 child, Stefan. MD, Belgrade U. Sch. Medicine, Serbia, 1994; MS, Rush Grad. Coll., Chgo., 2007. Diplomate Am. Acad. Psychiatry and Neurology, 2006. Instr. Belgrade U. Sch. Medicine, Serbia, 1995—98; postdoc. rsch. assoc. U. Ill., Chgo., 1999—2000; instr. Rush U. Med. Ctr., Chgo., 2000—01, 2005—07; med. intern Hahnemann U., Phila., 2001—02; med. resident Northwestern U., Chgo., 2002—05, asst. prof. neurology, Feinberg Sch. Medicine, 2007—. Recipient Sigma Xi award, Rush Grad. Coll., 2006, Clinician Scientist Devel. award, Am. Acad. Neurology and Parkinson Disease Found., 2008. Mem.: Am. Acad. Sleep Medicine, Parkinson Study Group, Am. Acad. Neurology. Office: Northwestern Univ 710 N Lake Shore Dr Ste 1106 Chicago IL 60611 Office Fax: 312-908-5073. Business E-Mail: a-videnovic@northwestern.edu.

VIDETIC, GREGORY, physician; b. Schefferville, Quebec, Can., Feb. 23, 1961; s. Martin and Thelm A. (Edith) Videtic. BSc, McGill U., Montreal, Can., 1981; MD CM, McGill U., Can., 1986. Pvt. practice, Halifax, NS, Canada, 1988—91; clin. rsch. fellow, geriat. U. Western Ont., London, Canada, 1991—92, radiation oncology resident, 1994—97; hospitalist Nova Scotia Cancer Ctr., 1992—94; clin. fellow Wayne State U., Detroit, 1997—98; staff physician London Regional Cancer Ctr., 1998—2000, Dana-Farber Cancer Inst., Harvard U., Boston, 2000—03, Cleve. Clinic, 2003—. Office: Cleveland Clinic 9500 Euclid Ave Cleveland OH 44195

VIDIC, RADISAV, engineering educator; b. Kraljevo, Serbia-Monteneg, July 13, 1963; s. Dusan and Zdravka Vidic; m. Natasa Vukadinovic, Feb. 27, 1993; children: Nikola, Sofia, Dana. BS, U. Belgrade, Serbia, 1987; MS, U. Ill., Urbana-Champaign, 1990; PhD, U. Cin., 1992. Cert. profl. engr., Tex., 2005. Asst. prof. U. Pitts., 1992—98, assoc. prof., 1998—2003, prof., 2003—, dept. chair, 2007—. Contbr. articles to profl. jour. Recipient Profl. Svc. award, Pa. Water Environment Assn., 2000; Fulbright scholar, U. Belgrade, 2003—04. Mem.: Am. Chem. Soc., ASCE (Prof. of Yr. 2008), AWWA, AEESP. Office: Univ Pitts 3700 O'Hara St Pittsburgh PA 15261 Office Fax: 412-624-0135. Business E-Mail: vidic@pitt.edu.

VIDO, KAREN PHINNEY, education educator; d. Waldo Adams and Lottie Phinney; m. Joseph Allen Vido, Mar. 25, 2000; 1 child, Joseph Allen II. BA in Mass Communication, Winthrop U., Rock Hill, SC, 1993, BA in History, 1993; MA in Tchg., U. SC., Columbia, 1997. Cert. in elementary edn. SC, 1997, in early childhood edn. SC, 1998. Multi age tchr. Port Royal Elem., SC, 1999—2000; dept. head early care & edn. Tech. Coll. Lowcountry, Beufort, SC, 2000—. Trainer SC First Steps, Greenville, 2002—. Bd. mem. TEAM Lowcountry, Beaufort, 2007. Recipient Achievement award, Champions Children, 2007. Mem.: ACCESS, Beaufort County First Steps (bd. mem. 2000—06), NAEYC. Home: 15 Quail Ridge Cir N Beaufort SC 29906

VIDRINE, MALCOLM FRANCIS, biology educator; b. Eunice, La., June 23, 1949; s. Numa Lee and Marie Odile (Hidalgo) V.; m. Connie Lucille Fontenot, Aug. 8, 1970 (div. July 4, 1983); 1 child, Malcolm Francis II; m. Gail Jeanne Quillman, Sept. 23, 1983; children: Daniel Joseph, Caroline Elizabeth. BS in Zoology, La. State U., 1970, MS in Zoology, 1974; PhD in Biology, U. Southwestern La., 1980. Tchr. math. and chemistry Evangeline Acad. High Sch., Ville Platte, La., 1970-71; biologist, mgr. Gulf South Rsch. Inst., New Iberia, La., 1973-76; rsch. dir. Jefferson Davis Parish Mosquito Abatement Dist., Jennings, La., 1980-84; prof, La. State U., Eunice, La., 1984—. Cons. in field; v.p., co-founder Cajun Prairie Habitat Preservation Soc., Eunice, 1989—. Contbr. articles to profl. jours., 100 profl. sci. papers; achievements include co-discovery leprosy naturally occurring in armadillos, 1976; co-developed mosquito larvicidal technique with bacteriotoxin, 1984; co-producer video including Wildflowers of the Cajun Prairie; author: The Historical Distributions of Freshwater Mussels in Louisiana, 1993, A Cajun Prairie Restoration Journal: 1988-1995, 1995. Sec. Cajun Prairie Habitat Preservation Soc., Eunice, 1989—. Recipient Jessup fellowship Acad. Natural Scis. of Phila., 1979, Nat. Merit scholarship, Regional Semi-finalist 1967. Mem. Cajun Prairie Habitat Preservation Soc. (v.p. 1989—). Avocations: gardening for butterflies, plant propagation of native prairie species. Office: La State U PO Box 1129 Eunice LA 70535-1129 Office Phone: 337-550-1245. Business E-Mail: mvidrine@isue.edu.

VIDWANS, SMRUTI JAYANT, microbiologist; b. India; BS in Biology, MIT; PhD in Microbiology, U. Calif., San Francisco, 2001. Amgen rsch. fellow Irvington Inst. Immunological Rsch., 2003; postdoctoral fellow in microbiology and immunology U. Calif., San Francisco, 2004; co-founder Phenotypica. Contbr. articles to profl. jour. Named one of Top 100 Young Innovators, MIT Tech. Review, 2004. Office: U Calif Ctr Bioentrepeneurship 185 Berry St Ste 4603 San Francisco CA 94143-1016

VIE, RICHARD CARL, insurance company executive; Student, St. Louis U., U. Mo. With Reliable Life Ins. Co., St. Louis, 1962-79; pres. Commonwealth Life Ins. Co., St. Louis, 1979-82; pres., chmn. bd. dirs. United Ins. Co. Am., Chgo., 1983—90; sr. v.p., bd. dirs. Unitrin, Inc., Chgo., 1990-92, pres., CEO, 1992—99, chmn., pres., CEO, 1999—2006, chmn., 2006—. Chmn. Life Insurers Conf., 1994; trustee Life Underwriters Tng. Coun. Bd. dirs. Concordia U. Found., 1985-94, Valparaiso U., 1995—. Lt. USN, 1958-62. Mem. The Racquet Club St. Louis, Execs. Club Chgo. Office: Unitrin Inc 1 E Wacker Dr Chicago IL 60601-1802

VIEGAS, JENNIFER, journalist, writer; b. Calif. BA, Wellesley Coll., Mass., 1987. Columnist Knight Ridder, McClatchy Newspapers, Sacramento, 1995—2004, Carmel Comm., Inc., Calif., 1996—98; reporter Discovery Channel News, Silver Spring, Md., 1998—, ABCNews.com, NYC, 1998—2001; journalist San Jose Mag., Calif., 1997—99; tech. writer Physicians for Social Responsibility, Washington, 1999—2001; mng. editor Studio One Networks, NYC, 2006—. Author: (book series) The 3-D Library of the Human Body, 2001, The Library of Future Medicine, 2002, Scientific American: Forces of Nature, 2007, The Declaration of Independence: A Primary Source Investigation into the Actions of the Second Continental Congress, 2003, Physics Anthology, 2004, Cell Functions, 2004, The Fort Laramie Treaty, 2005, Pierre Omidyar: The Founder of eBay, 2006, Beethoven, 2007. Mem.: Nat. Assn. Sci. Writers. Personal E-mail: reporterofnews@aol.com.

VIEIRA, CARLOS JOSE, construction equipment company president; b. Aveiro, Portugal, Apr. 3, 1937; s. Ernesto Rodrigues and Ana (Coluna) V.; m. Maria Elisa Barroso, July 25, 1964. Student in bus. adminstrn. and acctg., Instituto Comercial do Porto, 1960. Ptnr., mgr. Ernesto Vieira & Filhos, Lda., Aveiro, 1964—; ptnr., mng. dir. Auto-Sueco (Coimbra), Lda., Leiria, Portugal, 1968—; ptnr. Soc. Construções Arnado, Coimbra, Portugal. Mem. Santa Casa da Misericordia, Leiria, Portuguese Red Cross, Leiria. Recipient Thankfulness medal Portuguese Red Cross, 1987, Merit medal Portuguese Red Cross, 1988. Mem. Mgmt. Protuguese Assn., Nucleo Indsl. Regiao Leiria (bd. dirs. 1980—), Lions (pres., award 1985-90). Home: R Coronel Pinheiro Correira 2400 Leiria Portugal Office: Auto-Sueco Coimbra Lda Apartado 120 2402 Leiria Portugal Office Phone: 351 21 994 6500, 351 244 849910. Business E-Mail: carlos.vieira@ascoimbra.pt.

VIEIRA, MEREDITH, television personality; b. Providence, Dec. 30, 1953; d. Edwin and Mary Elsie Vieira; m. Richard Cohen, June 14, 1986; children: Benjamin, Gabriel, Lily, Max. BA in English, magna cum laude, Tufts U., Mass., 1975. News announcer WORC-Radio, Worcester, Mass., 1975; reporter, anchor WJAR-TV, Providence; reporter WCBS-TV, NYC, 1979-82; from reporter, Chgo. bur. to news correspondent CBS News, NYC, 1982—84; Chgo. bur. chief, contbg. nat. corr. CBS Evening News with Dan Rather, NYC, 1982—84; substitute co-anchor Morning, 1984—85; prin. corr. West 57th, 1985—89; corr., co-editor 60 Minutes, 1989—91; contbg. corr., CBS Primetime series Verdict, 1991; co-anchor CBS Morning News, 1992—93; host, chief corr. Turning Point, 1993—97; chief correspondent ABC News, NYC, 1993; co-host, moderator The View, NYC, 1997—2006; co-host Today Show, NYC, 2006—. Narrator ABC TV special Open Sesame: The Making of Arabian Nights, 2000; host 78th Ann. Miss America Pageant, 1998, Lifetime's Intimate Portrait, 1999—, ABC special The Beatles Revolution, 2000, ABC TV Network's Countdown to Oscar, 2000, Who Wants to Be a Millionaire, 2002—, co-exec. prodr., 2005—; host ABC News Spl. Fat Like Me: How to Win the Weight War, 2003. Broadway debut Thoroughly Modern Millie, 2003, cameo appearance The Stepford Wives, 2004, guest host Larry King Live, 2005, host (spl. featurette) Desperate Housewives Season 1 DVD Set, 2005, guest appearances Sports Night, 1998, Walt Disney World Christmas Day Parade, 2002, Party Planner with David Tutera, 2005, Hi-Jinks, 2005, Celebrity Jeopardy, Between the Lions (PBS), (TV series) Healthy Kids, 1998, Spin City, 2000, All My Children, 2001, General Hospital, 2003, The Practice, 2003, (talk shows) The Tonight Show with Jay Leno, Late Show with David Letterman, Late Night with Conan O' Brien, Charlie Rose and Live with Regis and Kelly, appeared in (nat. TV commercials) Bayer Aspirin, Got Milk?, featured on the cover of numerous magazines including TV Guide, Ladies Home Journal and others. Frequent contbr. several charitable foundations; co-founder, mem. sr. adv. bd. Club Mom's, 2004—. Recipient Front Page award, Newswomen's Club NY, Five Emmy awards for work with 60 Minutes, Four Emmy awards for stories on West 57th, 1987—88, Emmy award for report Inside the Hate Conspiracy: America's Terrorists, 1995, Robert F. Kennedy journalism award, 1995, Safe Horizon

Champion award, 2001, Woman of Yr. award, City of Hope, 2001, Mother of Yr. award, Pajama Program, 2004; named Best Game Show Host for "Who Wants to Be a Millionaire", Daytime Emmy award, Acad. TV Arts & Scis., 2005; named one of 100 Most Powerful Women, Forbes Mag., 2006—08; honored by Anti-Defamation League, Found. Am. Women in Radio and TV, 1997. Achievements include hosting more episodes as a game show host than any women in TV history. Office: ABC 320 W 66th St New York NY 10023-6304

VIELE, PATRICIA THOMPSON, physics and astronomy librarian; b. Massena, NY, Aug. 25, 1941; d. Edith Thompson Cuglar and Bruce Webster Thompson; m. Howard S. Viele, Jan. 27, 1962; children: David D., Sarah Viele McLean, Joy A. BS, St. Lawrence U., Canton, NY, 1963; MLS, Syracuse U., NY, 1992. Registered med. technologists Am. Soc. Clin. Pathologists, 1963. Rsch. assoc. Bristol Labs., Syracuse, 1964—67; libr. clk. Syracuse U., 1988—92; physics & astronomy libr. Cornell U., Ithaca, NY, 1994—2008. Author: (book) Physics Info. Fluency Blog.; contbr. articles to profl. jours. Mem.: Am. Assn. Physics Tchrs. (chair, Com. Profl. Concerns 2008—), Am. Phys. Soc., Spl. Librs. Assn. Achievements include first to build a bridge between physics faculty and librarians. Home: 8 Dove Dr Ithaca NY 14850 Office: Cornell Univ East Ave Ithaca NY 14850 Office Fax: 607-255-5288. Business E-Mail: ptv1@cornell.edu.

VIELMETTI, EDWARD MARSHALL, webmaster; b. 1964; BA in Econ., U. Mich., 1988. With Cisco Systems, Inc., 1998—2001; tech. mktg. mgr. Arbor Networks, 2002—; founder The Vacume Group LLC, 2001—. Founder MSEN Inc., 1991—, Cisco Alumni Assn., 2001—, wireless.mi.org, 2002—; bd. dirs. Jewbilation, Ann Arbor, Mich., 2002—. Author: The Revolution of Useful Web Services, 1999; contbr. PC World mag., 1994. Mem.: Internet Engring. Task Force, Internat. Network Social Network Analysis. Home: 317 S Division St PMB 218 Ann Arbor MI 48104 Personal E-mail: emv@monkey.org.

VIEN, PATRICK, music company executive; b. 1967; B. Econ., McGill U., 1989; M. Bus. Comm., U. So. Calif. Annenberg Sch. Comm., 1992. With Power Corp., 1992—2000; pres. & COO N.Am. TV, 2000—02; pres. Universal TV Networks, Calif., 2002—04; pres. Global Networks div. NBC Universal, Calif., 2004—06; chmn. & CEO Warner Music Internat., NYC, 2006—. Mem.: Young Presidents' Orgn. Office: Warner Music Group 75 Rockefeller Plaza New York NY 10019

VIENNEAU, LAURENCE EDWARD, JR., art educator; b. Boston, June 1, 1954; married. MFA, Southern Ill. U., Carbondale, 1981. Assoc. prof. U. Alaska Fairbanks, 1989—2001; adj. faculty Century Coll., White Bear Lake, Minn., 2001—06; prof. Seminole CC, Sanford, Fla., 2006—. Author: (children's book) The Boy who was once a Caribou; exhibitions include Halbert Biennial (award, 1995, Best Painting award, 1995). Recipient UAF Honoring Tchg. Excellence award, U. Alaska, 1996, Reader's Choice award, ORBIS Internat., 1998; Travel grant, U. Alaska, 1992—99, Curriculum Devel. grant, Century Coll., 2003—04. Mem.: Coll. Art Assoc., Soc. Children Book Writers and Illustrators. Home: 452 Via tuscany Loop Lake Mary FL 32746 Office: Seminole CC 100 Weldon Blvd Sanford FL 32773 Business E-Mail: vienneaul@scc.fl.edu.

VIERA, LORRAINE, psychologist; d. M. and L. Ortiz; m. Ariel Viera, May 22, 1987; 1 child, Ariel. PhD, Caribbean Ctr. Postgrad. Studies, San Juan, 1987. Cert. psychologist Dept. Health, PR, 1983. Psychologist Dept. Mental Health, San Juan, 1981—87; bilingual sch. psychologist NYC DOE, 1988—2008, NYC DOE Bryant HS, Long Island City, 2003—. Contbr. scientific papers. Recipient Dissertation award, Caribbean Ctr. Postgrad. Studies, 1995. Roman Catholic. Avocations: travel, art, history. Home: 35 Audrey Ave Elmont NY 11003 Office: NYC DOE Bryant HS 48-10 31st Ave Long Island City NY 11103 Business E-Mail: lviera@schools.nyc.gov.

VIERI, CHRISTIAN, professional soccer player; b. Bologna, Italy, July 12, 1973; s. Roberto and Nathalie V. Player Prato FC, Italy, 1989-90, Torino FC, Italy, 1990-93, Pisa FC, Italy, 1992—93, Ravenna FC, Italy, 1993—94, Venezia FC, Italy, 1994-95, Atalanta, Italy, 1995—96, Juventus Torino, Italy, 1996—97, Atletico Madrid, Spain, 1997—98, Lazio Roma, Italy, 1998—99, Inter Milan, Italy, 1999—2005, AC Milan, Italy, 2005—06, Monaco, France, 2005, Sampdoria, Italy, 2006—07, Atalanta, Italy, 2006—07, ACF Fiorentina, Italy, 2007—08, Atalanta, Italy, 2008—. Mem. Italy Nat. team, 1998—, European Super Cup Champion, Juventus Torino, 1996, European Cup Winners Cup Champion, Lazio Roma, 1999. Named Spanish La Liga Top Scorer, 1998, Italian Serie A Footballer of the Yr., 1999, 2002, Italian Serie A Top Scorer, 2003; named to FIFA 100, 2004. Mailing: Atalanta BC Corso Europa snc Ciserano 24040 Ciserano di Zingonia Italy

VIERLING, JOHN MOORE, physician; b. Bellflower, Calif., Nov. 20, 1945; s. Lester Howard and Ruth Ann (Moore) V.; m. Gayle Aileen Vandermast, June 30, 1968 (div. 1984); children: Jeffrey M., Janet A; m. Donna Marie Sheps, May 4, 1985; children: Matthew R., Mark L. (dec.). AB in Biology with great distinction, Stanford U., 1967, MD, 1972. Intern then resident Strong Meml. Hosp. U. Rochester, N.Y., 1972-74; clin. assoc. liver unit NIH, Bethesda, Md., 1974-77; gastroenterology fellow U. Calif., San Francisco, 1977-78, instr. medicine, 1978-79; from asst. to assoc. U. Colo. Sch. Medicine, Denver, 1979-90; dir. hepatology, med dir. liver transplantation Cedars-Sinai Med. Ctr., LA, 1990—. Assoc. prof. medicine UCLA, 1990-96, prof. medicine & surgery, 1996—2005; chief hepatology, Baylor Coll. Med., Houston, 2005-. Assoc. editor: Prinicples and Practice of Gastroenterology and Hepatology, 1992; editorial bd. Hepatology, 1985-90, Gastroenterology, 1993-98, Liver Transplantation, 2004-; co-editor Liver Immunology, 2002, 2007; co-patentee in hybridization assay for hepatitis virus, 1992; mouse model for hepatitis C, 1997. Fellow ACP; mem. Am. Assn. Study Liver Diseases (pres. 2006), Am. Gastroenterolog. Assn., Internat. Assn. for Study Liver, European Assn. for Study Liver, Am. Liver Found. (chmn. bd. dirs. 1994—2000, sec. treas., Digestive Disease Week 2008-). Avocations: photography, tennis, hiking. Home: 1709 Dryden Suite 1500 Houston TX 77030

VIERS, HILLARY WICAI, legislative staff member; m. Steven Viers. Comm. dir. to Rep. Charlie Wilson US House of Reps., Washington, 2007—. Democrat. Office: 226 Cannon House Office Bldg Washington DC 20515 Office Fax: 202-225-5705, 202-225-5907.*

VIERTHALER, BONNIE LOUISE, artist, educator; b. Milw., Sept. 11, 1941; d. Charles Adam Orth, Jr. and Ruth Louise Orth; children: Heidi Johanna, Hans Andrew. BS in Art Edn., U. Wis., Madison, 1963; MFA in Fiber Arts, U. Ga., Athens, 1972. Cert. in Chinese lang. Cornell U., 1998. Self-employed artist, 1963—; prof. English, aesthetics Xiamen U., Fujian, China, 2000—. Artist in residence Seattle Arts Commn., 1977—78, Wash. State Arts Commn., 1977—78; owner Four Valley Books, Deer Isle, Maine, 1981—88; founder, dir. Maybe Someday, Portland, Maine, 1988—92; founder, advisor, educator Green Breathing Assn., Xiamen, 2006—. Traveling exhibition, The Joy of Smoking, 1986. Grantee Artist/Industry Collaborations, Nat. Endowment for Arts, 1977-1978, NJ Group Against Smoking Pollution, 1986-92; Craftsman's fellowship, Nat. Endowment for Arts, 1976. Mem.: Globalink (assoc.). Achievements include Xiamen University in China going smoke free as a result of The Green Breathing Association's efforts. Avocation: gardening. Office: 14380 W Capital Dr #3 Brookfield WI 53005 Personal E-mail: bv@badvertising.org, salzklmblaz@sbcglobal.net.

VIESSMAN, WARREN, JR., professor emeritus; b. Balt., Nov. 9, 1930; s. Warren and Helen Adair (Berlincke) V.; m. Gloria Marie Scheiner, May 11, 1953 (div. Apr. 1975); children: Wendy, Stephen, Suzanne, Michael, Thomas, Sandra; m. Elizabeth Gertrude Rothe, Aug. 8, 1980; children: Heather, Joshua B in Engring., Johns Hopkins U., 1952, MS in Engring., 1958, DEng, 1961. Registered profl. engr., Md. Engr. W. H. Primrose & Assocs., Towson, Md., 1955-57; project engr. Johns Hopkins U., Balt., 1957-61; from asst. to assoc. prof. N.Mex. State U., Las Cruces, 1961-66; prof. U. Maine, Orono, 1966-68, U. Nebr., Lincoln, 1968-75; sr. specialist Libr. Congress, Washington, 1975-83; prof., chmn. U. Fla., Gainesville, 1983-90, assoc. dean for rsch. and grad. study, 1990-91, assoc. dean for acad. programs, 1991—2003, prof. emeritus environ. engring., 2003—. Vis. scientist Am. Geophys. Union, 1970-71; Maurice Kremer lectr. U. Nebr., 1985, 2001; lectr. Harvard U. Water Policy Seminar, 1988; Wayne S. Nichols Meml. Fund lectr. Ohio State U., 1990; mem. steering com. on groundwater and energy U.S. Dept. Energy, 1979-80; mem. task group on fed. water rsch. U.S. Geol. Survey, 1985-87; mem. com. of water sci. and tech. bd. NAS, 1986-90; mem. water resources working group Nat. Coun. on Pub. Works Improvement, 1987; chmn., chief of engrs. Environ. Adv. Bd., Washington, 1991-93; chmn. solid and hazardous waste mgmt. adv. bd. State U. Sys. Fla. Co-author: Water Management: Technology and Institutions, 1984, Introduction to Hydrology, 2003, Water Supply and Pollution Control, 2005; contbr. over 167 articles to profl. jours. Mem. Water Mgmt. Com., Gainesville, 1983-88, Fla. Environ. Efficiency Study Commn., 1986-88. 1st lt. U.S. Army C.E., 1952-54, Korea. Recipient Comdr.'s award for pub. svc., U.S. Dept. Army, 1993. Diplomate Am. Acad. Water Resources Engrs. (hon. diplomate); fellow ASCE (hon. mem., Julian Hinds award 1989), Am. Water Resources Assn. (nat. pres. 1990, Icko Iben award 1983, Henry P. Caulfield Jr. medal 1996), Univs. Coun. on Water Resources (pres. 1987, Warren A. Hall medal 1994), Sigma Xi, Tau Beta Pi. Democrat. Lutheran. Avocations: scuba diving, woodworking. Office: U Fla Coll Engring PO Box 116450 Gainesville FL 32611-6450 Office Phone: 352-392-2312, 352-392-2317. Business E-Mail: wvies@eng.ufl.edu.

VIEST, IVAN MIROSLAV, structural engineer, consultant; b. Bratislava, Slovakia, Oct. 10, 1922; came to U.S., 1947, naturalized, 1955; s. Ivan and Maria (Zacharova) V.; m. Barbara K. Stevenson, May 23, 1953. Ing., Slovak Tech. U., Bratislava, 1946; MS, Ga. Inst. Tech., 1948; PhD, U. Ill., 1951; doctorate (hon.), Tech. U. Kosice, 2002. Registered profl. engr., Pa. Research asst. U. Ill., Urbana, 1948-50, research assoc., 1950-51, research asst. prof., 1951-55, research assoc. prof., 1955-57; bridge research engr. Am. Assn. State Hwy. Ofcls., Nat. Acad. Scis., Ottawa, Ill., 1957-61; structural engr. Bethlehem Steel Corp., Pa., 1961-67, sr. structural cons., 1967-70, asst. mgr. sales engring. div., 1970-82; pvt. cons. structural engr. IMV Cons., 1983—. Cons. in field. Author: Composite Construction, 1958, History of Engineering Foundation, 1991, Composite Construction--Design for Buildings, 1997, Seventy-Five Years of the Lehigh Valley Section, 1997, An Immigrant's Story, 2006; translator, commentaries: Call to Arms Came in 1938, Gen. Viests Notebooks, 2009; contbr. over 130 articles to profl. jours. Recipient Constrn. award Engring. News Record, 1972, Special Achievement award, Am. Inst. Steel Constrn., 2004; named to Hall of Fame, Ga. Inst. of Tech., 1998. Fellow AAAS, Am. Concrete Inst. (Wason Rsch. medal 1956); mem. NAE, ASCE (hon., v.p. 1973-75, Rsch. prize 1958, Ernest E. Howard award 1991), Internat. Assn. Bridge and Structural Engring., Transp. Rsch. Bd. (emeritus 1999—), Czechoslovak Soc. Arts and Scis. (exec. v.p. 1992-93), Earthquake Engring. Rsch. Inst., Saucon Valley Country Club (Bethlehem). Achievements include research in steel and concrete structures, the development and promotion of composite construction for bridges and bldgs, and the development of load and resistance factor design. Office Phone: 610-865-1041.

VIETH, CHRISTOPHER W., former publishing executive; BS in Acctg., St. Francis U. Various fin. positions Amerada Hess Corp., 1987—95; dir. fin. Barnes and Noble, 1995—98, dir. fin. and ops., 1998—99, v.p., corp. controller, 1998—99; comptroller Dow Jones & Co., NYC, 2000—01, v.p. fin., 2001—02, v.p., treasurer, CFO, 2002—06. Mem. adv. coun. Villanova U. Ctr. for Responsible Leadership & Governance; mem. NJ Certified Pub. Accountants.

VIETH, RONJA, literature and language professor; b. Johannesburg, Oct. 8, 1973; d. Udo Vieth and Renate Eberle. MA in Am. Lit., Psychology, Linguistics, Tech. U. Carolo Wilhelmina, Braunschweig, Germany, 2002, diploma in Tchg. German as a Second Lang., 2001; MA, U. La., Lafayette, 2007. Tutor German U. RI, Kingston, 1996—97; tour guide Italy, France, Switzerland Rainbow Tours, Hamburg, Germany, 2000—03; pvt. practice Frankfurt, Germany, 2000—; instr. bus. English Foerderverein BBS 22 Hoefestrasse e.V., Hannover, Germany, 2002—03; on-site coord. Horizonte Reisen, Montfrin, France, 2003; tchg. asst. U. La., 2004—07, chair hospitality com., 2005—07, panel chair, 2006; grad. part time instr. Tex. Tech U., Lubbock, 2007—. Panel chair Symbiosis Biennial Conf., London, 2007, Lit. London Conf., London, 2008; chair profl. devel. Grad. English Soc., Lubbock, 2008—. Contbr. articles to profl. jours. Mem.: Sigma Tau Delta/Psi Delta, Phi Beta Delta (mem. hospitality com. 2006—07), Phi Kappa Phi, Sigma Tau Delta/Lambda Zeta (treas. 2006—07). Avocations: dance, horseback riding, snowboarding, travel. Office: Tex Tech Univ English Dept PO Box 43091 Lubbock TX 79409-3091 Business E-Mail: ronja.vieth@ttu.edu.

VIETH, WILLIAM CHAPMAN, secondary school educator; b. Mauston, Wis., Feb. 12, 1954; s. Roland W. and Joan F. (Chapman) V.; m. Mara P. O'Neill, Dec. 29, 1979; children: Aaron Thoreau, Alexander O'Neill, Miles Darwin. BA, U. Wis., 1976, JD, 1979; BS, U. Minn., 1984, MEd, 1993. Cert. secondary English tchr., Minn. Tchr. English, St. Michael (Minn.)-Albertville Sch. Dist., 1984-85, Ind. Sch. Dist. 284, Wayzata, Minn., 1985—. Mem. academic standards com., Minn., 2003. Author: Hands Linking Hands to God, 2007; contbr. short stories and poetry to various publs. Recipient Whole Tchr. award Minn. Learning Disabilities, 1997, Golden Apple award (9). Home: 1740 Laurel Ave Saint Paul MN 55104-6128 Office: Wayzata HS 4955 Peony Ln N Plymouth MN 55446-1606 Office Phone: 763-745-6891. Personal E-mail: bill_vieth@wayzata.k12.mn.us.

VIETH, WOLF RANDOLPH, chemical engineering educator; b. St. Louis, May 5, 1934; s. Hans W. and Hedy (Fahrig) V.; m. Peggy Schira, July 6, 1957; children: Jane, Linda, Christopher, Mark. S.B. in Chem. Engring, Mass. Inst. Tech., 1956, Sc.D., 1961; M. Sc., Ohio State U., 1958. Registered profl. engr., N.J. From asst. prof. to assoc. prof. chem. engring. MIT, Cambridge, 1961-68, dir. Sch. Chem. Engring. Practice, 1965-68; prof. chem. and biochem. engring. Rutgers U., New Brunswick, N.J., 1968—, chmn. dept., 1968-78, now prof. emeritus. Cons. to govt. and industry; chmn. Gordon Research Conf. on Separation and Purification, 1975, Engring. Conf. on Biochem. Engring., 1978 Author: Membrane Systems, 1988, Diffusion in Polymers, 1991, Bioreactor Engineering, 1993. Mem. econ. study subcom., planning bd. Montgomery (N.J.) Twp., 1970-. Served to 1st lt. AUS, 1961. Recipient DuPont Co. Invention award, 1960, St. Albert the Great medal for sci. Aquinas Coll., 1952, Vis. Fgn. Scientist award Japan Soc. for Promotion Sci., 1975, Leadership award Biochem. Engring. Conf., 1993; Ford postdoctoral fellow, 1961. Fellow Am. Inst. Chemists, N.Y. Acad. Scis.; mem. Am. Inst. Chem. Engrs., Am. Chem. Soc., Am. Soc. Engring. Edn., Sigma Xi, Phi Lambda Upsilon. Research on applied molecular biology, semipermeable membranes, polymers. Office: Rutgers Sch Engring Dept Chem and Biochem Engring 98 Brett Rd Piscataway NJ 08854-8058

VIG, JOHN, electronics engineer, consultant; b. Budapest, Hungary; m. Arianna Vig. BS in Physics, City Coll. NY, 1964; PhD in Physics, Rutgers U., 1969. Head R&D programs US Dept. Def.'s, 1980—97; lead electronics engr. R&D programs US Army Comm. and Electronics Rsch., Develop. and Engring. Ctr., Ft. Monmouth, NJ; ret., 2006; tech. cons. Sys. Planning Corp., Arlington, Va. Mem. tech. adv. bd. SiTime Corp., Silicon Valley; tech. adv. to program mgrs. US Def. Advanced Rsch. Projects Agy., 1997—. Contbr. chapters to books, articles to profl. publs. Fellow: IEEE (bd. dirs. 2002—03, mem. investment com. 2002—03, mem. trust and comm. working group 2003, mem. investment adhoc com. 2003, v.p. tech. activities 2005, bd. dirs. 2005, mem. mktg. and sales com. 2005—07, pres.-elect 2008, pres. 2009—, disting. lectr. Ultrasonics, Ferroelectrics and Frequency Control Soc., past pres. Ultrasonics, Ferroelectrics and Frequency Control Soc., founding pres. Sensors Coun. 2000—01, Sawyer award 2006, Cady award 1990, Ultrasonics, Ferroelectrics, and Frequency Control Soc. Disting. Svc. award, Ultrasonics, Ferroelectrics, and Frequency Control Soc. Achievement award). Achievements include being awarded 55 patents in field. Avocation: ballroom dancing. Office: SiTime Corp 990 Almanor Ave Sunnyvale CA 94085 Office Phone: 408-328-4400. Office Fax: 408-328-4439.

VIG, PRADEEP KUMAR, geophysics educator; b. Kanpur, India, July 6, 1954; came to U.S., 1985; s. Girdhari Lal and Usha Rani (Raghubir Lamba) V.; m. Neelu Kumar Mahindru, June 24, 1981; children: Sanjana, Dhruv. BS, Meerut U., India, 1972; MTech, U. Roorkee, India, 1975; M. in Profl., St. Louis U., 1988, PhD, 1989. Sr. geophysicist Oil India Ltd., Duliajan, Assam, 1976-82; geophysicist Seiscom Delta United, Inc., Singapore, 1982-83, Oceaneering Internat., Inc., Singapore, 1983, Geomex Surveys Ltd., Hong Kong, 1983-85; rsch. asst. St. Louis U., 1986-89; assoc. prof. sci. and math. Louisburg (N.C.) Coll., 1989-94; earth sci. instr. Central Lakes Coll., 1994—. Contbr. articles to profl. jours. Merit scholar Univ. Grants Commn., U. Roorkee, 1972-75, Soc. Exploration Geophysicists, 1986-89. Mem. Alpha Sigma Nu. Avocations: swimming, reading, bridge. Home: 516 W College Dr Apt 101 Brainerd MN 56401-5903

VIG, VERNON EDWARD, lawyer; b. St. Cloud, Minn., June 19, 1937; s. Edward Enoch and Salley Johanna (Johnson) V.; m. Susan Jane Rosenow, June 10, 1961; 1 child, Elizabeth Karen. BA, Carleton Coll., 1959; LLB, NYU, 1962, LLM, 1963; postdoctoral studies, Univ. Paris, Fac. de Droit, 1964. Bar: N.Y. 1962; avocat, Paris, 1992. Assoc. Cleary, Gottlieb, Steen & Hamilton, Paris, 1964, Donovan, Leisure, Newton & Irvine, NYC and Paris, 1965-72, ptnr., 1972-86, LeBoeuf, Lamb, Greene & MacRae, LLP, NYC, Brussels, 1986—2001, of counsel, 2002—07; spl. counsel Dewey & LeBoeuf LLP, 2007—. Editor: NYU Law Rev. Sr. warden Grace Ch., Bklyn., 1986-2001. George F. Baker scholar, Fulbright scholar, 1963-64, Ford Found. scholar, 1963-64. Mem. ABA (internat. and antitrust sects.), N.Y. State Bar Assn. (chmn. antitrust sect. 1987-88), Assn. of Bar of City of N.Y., Internat. Bar Assn., Union Internat. des Avocats, Heights Casino (bklyn.), Merriewold Club (Forestburgh, N.Y., bd. dirs. 1985-91), Phi Beta Kappa. Episcopalian. Office: Dewey & LeBoeuf LLP 125 W 55th St New York NY 10019-5369 Office Phone: 212-424-8007. Business E-Mail: vvig@dl.com.

VIGDOR, JUSTIN LEONARD, lawyer; b. NYC, July 13, 1929; s. Irving Barton and Ida (Devins) V.; m. Louise Martin, Mar. 8, 1952; children: Robert, Jill Vigdor-Feldman, Lisa Vigdor-Peck, Wendy Vigdor-Hess. LLB magna cum laude, St. John's U., 1951; LLM, N.Y.U., 1952. Bar: N.Y. 1951, U.S. Supreme Ct 1951, Fla. 1975. Sr. counsel Boylan, Brown, Code, Vigdor & Wilson LLP, Rochester, NY, 1958—. Bd. dirs. IEC Electronics Corp.; mem. N.Y. Uniform Law Commn., Nat. Conf. Uniform Law Commrs. Contbr. articles to profl. jours. Bd. dirs. Found. for Jewish Cmty., Ames Amzalak Meml. Trust; pres. AAA N.Y. State, Inc., Al Sigl Ptnrs. Found.; chmn. N.Y. State IOLA Fund. Served with JAGC, AUS, 1952-54. Recipient Community Svc. award, 1960, award for Svc. to Community and Legal Profession, 1983, Disting. Svc. award N.Y. State Assn. County Clks., 1985. Fellow Am. Bar Found., N.Y. Bar Found. (Nathaniel award for cmty. svc. and profl. accomplishment); mem. Fla. Bar Assn., N.Y. State Bar Assn. (past pres. Ho. of Dels.), Monroe County Bar Assn. (past pres.), Estate Planning Coun., Am. Arbitration Assn. (nat. panel 1962—), N.Y. State C. of C. (Disting. Svc. award 1964), Irondequoit Country Club. Democrat. Jewish. Office: Boylan Brown Code Vigdor & Wilson LLP 2400 Chase Sq Rochester NY 14604 Home Phone: 585-381-6696; Office Phone: 585-232-5300. Business E-Mail: jvigdor@boylanbrown.com.

VIGIL, ALFREDO, state agency administrator; MD, U. N.Mex. Sch. Medicine, Albuquerque, 1977. Diplomate Am. Bd. Family Practice. Resident in family practice U. N.Mex., prof. family medicine; pvt. practice family physician Taos, N.Mex.; adminstr. Questa Health Ctr., N.Mex.; v.p. clin. affairs Presbyn. Med. Services, Santa Fe; CEO El Centro Family Health, Espanola, N.Mex., 2002—07; sec. N.Mex. Dept. Health, Santa Fe, 2007—. Former mem. N.Mex. Med. Bd., N.Mex. EMS Lic. Commn. Vol. Cmty. Wellness Ctr., Taos, Voices for Children, Albuquerque. Fellow: U. NC Nat. Pub. Health Leadership Inst., Am. Acad. Family Physicians. Office: NMex Dept Health 1190 S St Francis Dr Santa Fe NM 87502 Office Phone: 505-827-2613. Office Fax: 505-827-2530.*

VIGIL, CHARLES J., lawyer; b. Los Alamos, N.Mex, Aug. 24, 1964; s. John Carlos and Catherine Elizabeth (Salazar) V. BBA, U. N.Mex., 1986; JD, U. Mich., 1989. Bar: N.Mex 1989, US Dist. Ct. (Dist. N.Mex) 1989, US Ct. Appeals (10th Cir.) 1989. Atty. Rodey, Dickason, Sloan, Akin & Robb, PA, Albuquerque, 1989—, pres., mng. dir. Articles editor Michigan Jour. of International Law, 1988-89. Co-chmn. N.Mex Commn. on Professionalism, 2005; mem. adv. com. N.Mex Compilation Com.; mem. H. Vearle Payne Am. Inn of Ct., 1999—2002. Mem. ABA (labor law sect., standing com. lawyers' professional liability), Albuquerque Bar Assn., N.Mex State Bar Assn. (pres.-elect 2004, pres. 2005), Nat. Conf. Bar Presidents (exec. coun.) Democrat. Roman Catholic.

Office: Rodey Dickason Sloan Akin & Robb PA Ste 2200 201 3rd St NW Albuquerque NM 87103-1888 Office Phone: 505-768-7377. Office Fax: 505-768-7395. Business E-Mail: cvigil@rodey.com.

VIGIL, HENRY P., computer software company executive; BA in Philosophy, Stanford U., MBA. Dir. mktg. desktop applications Microsoft Corp., Redmond, Wash., 1990—95, gen. mgr. interactive TV bus. unit, gen. mgr. internet commerce bus. unit, corp. v.p. consumer strategy & partnerships, sr. v.p. consumer strategy & partnerships, 2006—. Bd. dir. Thomson SA. Founder City Yr. Seattle; mem. bd. adv. Stanford Bus. Sch.; mem. bd. ambassadors Mercy Corps. Office: One Microsoft Way Redmond WA 98052-6399*

VIGILANCE, PIERRE, state agency administrator, public health service officer; b. London; B in Biology, George Wash. U., Washington, 1990; MD, Johns Hopkins U. Sch. Medicine, Balt., 1996; MPH, Johns Hopkins U. Bloomberg Sch. Pub. Health, Balt., 1997. Residency in emergency medicine Howard U. Hosp., Washington, 1997—2000; assoc. Johns Hopkins U. Bloomberg Sch. Pub. Health; asst. commr. health promotion and disease prevention Balt. County Dept. Health, 2002—05, dir., health officer, 2005—08; dir. DC Dept. Health, 2008—. Mem.: APHA, Washington, DC Young Profls., George Wash. Alumni Assn., Johns Hopkins Med. Instns. Alumni Network, Alpha Phi Alpha. Office: DC Dept Health 825 N Capitol St NE Washington DC 20002 Office Phone: 202-442-5955. Office Fax: 202-442-4795.*

VIGLIOTTA, MARGARET D., retired secondary school educator, art educator, artist; BEd in Art cum laude, Long Island U., C.W. Post, Brookville, NY, 1979; MALS, Weslyn Univ., Middletown. Conn., 1984. Permanent cert. tchr. N.Y. State, 1989. Art tchr. profoundly deaf students Mercy HS 75, Riverhead, NY, 1979—85; art tchr. Sachem Ctrl. Sch. Dist., Holbrook, NY, 1985—2007; ret., 2007. Rep., art edn. del. Russian Joint Edn. Conf., St. Petersburg, 2006; art edn. delegate U.S. Russia Joint Edn. Conf., St. Petersburg, Russia, 2006—08. Meml., sculptural Acolyte Candle Stands, St. Marks, prin. works include ceramic advent wreath on pedstal 3ft. high, ceramic chalices. Vol. Wading River Sch. Dist., 1968—92; fund raiser Boy Scouts; parent liaison com. Mid. Sch.; religiuos educator St. Mark's Parish, 1968—88, parish coun., liturgy com., 1975—2000. Mem.: Nat. Art Edn. Assn. (assoc.). Independent. Avocations: travel, crafts, reading, architecture, opera. Home: PO Box 853 Sayville NY 11782 Home Phone: 631-750-5040. Personal E-mail: pegal4@aol.com.

VIGNEAULT, ALAIN, professional hockey coach; b. Quebec City, Can., May 14, 1961; m. Josée Doucet; children: Andréanne, Janie. Player St. Louis Blues, 1981—83; head coach Can. Nat. Jr. Team, 1989-91, Trois-Rivières Draveurs, 1986—87, Hull Olympiques, 1988—92, Beauport Harfangs, 1995—97, Montreal Canadiens, 1997—2000, PEI Rocket, Charlottetown, 2003—05, Manitoba Moose (AHL), 2005—06, Vancouver Canucks, 2006—; asst. coach Ottawa Senators, 1992—95. Recipient Jack Adams Award, 2007. Office: Vancouver Canucks 800 Griffiths Way Vancouver BC Canada V6B 6G1

VIGNERON, ALLEN HENRY, archbishop; b. Mt. Clemens, Mich., Oct. 21, 1948; s. Elwin and Bernardine (Kott) Vigneron. AB in Philosophy, Sacred Heart Sem., Detroit, 1970; STL in Fundamental Theology, Pontifical Gregorian U., 1977; PhD in Philosophy, Cath. U. Am., 1987. Ordained priest Archdiocese of Detroit, 1975; assoc. pastor Our Lady Queen of Peace Ch., Harper Woods, Mich., 1975-79; addetto of the secretariat of his Holiness the Pope The Holy See, Vatican City, 1991-94; aux. bishop Archdiocese of Detroit, 1996—2003; ordained bishop, 1996; coadjutor bishop Diocese of Oakland, Calif., 2003, bishop Calif., 2003—09; archbishop Archdiocese of Detroit, Mich., 2009—. Asst. prof. philos. & theology Sacred Heart Coll. Sem., Detroit, 1985—88, dean, 1988—91; adj. prof. theology Pontifical Gregorian U., Rome, 1992—94; rector, pres. Sacred Heart Major Sem., Detroit, 1994—2003. Trustee Nat. Cath. Bioethics Ctr., St. Patrick Sem., Menlo Park, Calif., Cath. U. Am., Washington. Mem.: US Conf. Cath. Bishops (Doctrine com., Catechism com.). Roman Catholic. Office: Archdiocese of Detroit 1234 Washington Blvd Detroit MI 48226 Office Phone: 313-237-5816. Office Fax: 313-237-4642.*

VIGNESWARAN, WICKII THAMBIAH, cardiothoracic surgeon, educator; b. Jaffna, Sri Lanka, Jan. 25, 1955; arrived in USA, 1991, naturalized, 1994; s. Murugesu and Rajapoopathy (Nagalingam) Thambiah; m. Jnanarupy Thillainayagam, Dec. 3, 1984; children: Yalini, Hari, Janani. MB BChir, U. Sri Lanka, Peradeniya, 1978. Cert. in cardiothoracic surgery. Advanced cardiothoracic surg. fellow Mayo Clinic, Rochester, Minn., 1991-93; dir. gen. thoracic surgery U. Ill.-Chgo. Med. Ctr., 1994-98; dir. thoracic organ, dir. cardiothoracic transplant U. Ill.-Chgo., 1994-98; chief cardiothoracic surgery Westside VA Med. Ctr., Chgo., 1994-98; staff mem. Hines VA Med. Ctr., Chgo., 1998—2005; chief thoracic surgery Loyola U. Med. Ctr., Maywood, Ill., 1998—2005, dir. lung transplantation, 1998—2005; prof. surgery U. Chgo., 2006—; assoc. chief cardiac and thoracic surgery, dir. lung and heart-lung transplant U. Chgo. Hosps., 2006—. Contbr. numerous articles to med. jours. including Thorax, Jour. Cardiovasc. Surgery, Jour. Clin. Transplantation. Sen. U. Ill.-Chgo., Champaign and Rockford, Ill., 1996-98; chmn. cardiothoracic subcom. Regional Organ Bank of Ill., Chgo., 1996-97. Recipient Trainee Investigator award Midwestern Award Cen. Soc. for Clin. Investigation and Am. Fedn. for Clin. Rsch., 1993, Young Investigator award DuPont Pharm./ACP, 1993; named to Top Surgeons List Consumer Rsch. Coun. Am. Fellow: ACS, Royal Coll. Physicians and Surgeons Can., Royal Coll. Surgeons Edinburgh; mem.: AMA, AAAS, European Soc. Cardiothoracic Surgery, Internat. Coll. Surgeons (v.p. 2003—06, pres. 2009, chair coun. surg. spltys., v.p. U.S. sect., pres.-elect US sect.), Am. Coll. Chest Physicians (bd. regents 2005—09, trustee Chest Found. 2009—), Chgo. Surg. Soc., Gen. Thoracic Surgery Club, Ill. Thoracic Surg. Soc. (pres. 2001, 2003), Soc. Thoracic Surgeons, Royal Coll. Surgeons Eng., Internat. Soc. Heart and Lung Transplantation. Hindu. Avocations: travel, nature, medical missions. Office: U Chgo 5841 S Maryland Ave MC5040 Chicago IL 60637-1470 Office Phone: 773-795-1267, 773-834-7812. Business E-Mail: wvignesw@surgery.bsd.uchicago.edu.

VIGODA, PAUL EVAN, secondary school educator; b. Fresh Meadows, NY, July 5, 1981; s. Scott N. and Bonnie W. Vigoda. BA, postgrad., CUNY, Flushing, NY, 2003—. Social studies tchr. Mid. Sch. 216, NYC Dept. Edn., Fresh Meadows, NY, 2003—06, head basketball coach, 2003—, acad. coord., dean, 2006—. Head basketball coach Kew-Forest Sch., Forest Hills, NY, 2001—03. Author: A Class of Heroes, 2005. Dir. Jr. Knicks Cross Island YMCA, Bellerosa, NY, 2000—02; aux. police officer NY Police Dept., Flushing, 2006—. Recipient Citation of Honor, Queen's Borough Pres., 2001, Citation, NYC Coun., 2001. Mem.: Golden Key Internat. Honor Soc., Pi Sigma Alpha. Avocations: sports, politics, movies, memorabilia. Office: Mid Sch 216 64-20 175 St Fresh Meadows NY 11365

VIGTEL, GUDMUND, retired museum director; b. July 9, 1925; came to U.S., 1948, naturalized, 1966; s. Arne Jonsen and Elisabeth (Petri) V.; m. Solveig Lund, 1951 (div. 1964); 1 child, Elisabeth; m. Carolyn Gates Smith, July 18, 1964; 1 child, Catherine Higdon. BFA, U. Ga., 1952, MFA, 1953; DFA (hon.), Atlanta Coll. Art, 1991. Adminstrv. asst. Corcoran Gallery Art, Washington, 1954-61, asst. dir., 1961-63; dir. High Mus. Art, Atlanta, 1963-91, dir. emeritus, 1991—. Contbr. articles to profl. jours. With Royal Norwegian Air Force, 1944-45. Decorated Chevalier des Arts et Lettres, Min. of Culture, France, 1985; recipient Order of Merit 1st Class, Fed. Republic Germany, 1989, The James R. Short Lifetime Achievement award, 2003. Home: 2082 Golfview Dr NW Atlanta GA 30309-1210

VIGUERA, ADELE CASALS, psychiatrist, researcher; MD, Dartmouth Med. Sch.; MPH, Harvard Sch. Pub. Health. Intern & resident Mass. Gen. Hosp., assoc. dir. Perinatal & Reproductive Psychiatry Program, 1996—, Cleveland Clinic; asst. prof. psychiatry Harvard Med. Sch., 1996—. Mem.: North Am. Menopause Soc., Am. Teratology Soc., Am. Psychiatric Assn. Office: Womens Health Center Simches Research Bldg 185 Cambridge St Ste 2200 Boston MA 02114*

VIJH, UMA PARVATHY, astrophysicist, researcher; d. Ganesan Anantharaman Valliyoor and Vishalam Ganesan; m. Aarohi Vijh, July 2, 2001. PhD in Physics, U. Toledo, 2005. Post-doctoral fellow Space Telescope Sci. Inst., Balt, 2005—07; rsch. asst. prof. U. Toledo, 2007—. Grantee, NSF, 2006—. Mem.: Americal Astron. Soc., Sigma Pi Sigma, Sigma Xi (Most Outstanding Presentation in Doctorate Category award 2004). Achievements include discovery of blue luminescence by interstellar nanoparticles. Office: Ritter Astrophys Rsch Ctr MS 113 U Toledo 2801 W Bancroft St Toledo OH 43606

VIJVERBERG, WIM PETRUS MARIA, economics educator; b. The Hague, The Netherlands, Sept. 30, 1955; came to U.S., 1977; m. Chu-Ping Chen, May 26, 1981; children: Michelle, Andrea, William. BA, Erasmus U. of Rotterdam, The Netherlands, 1975; MA, U. Pitts., 1979, PhD, 1981. Postdoctoral fellow Yale U., New Haven, 1981-84; vis. asst. prof. econs. U. Hawaii at Manoa, Honolulu, 1984-85; asst. prof. Ill. State U., Normal, 1985-86; asst. prof. econs. and polit. economy U. Tex. at Dallas, Richardson, 1986-91, assoc. prof., 1991-97, prof., 1997—. Cons. The World Bank, Washington, 1985-91, 94-96, 2002—, Axiometrics, Dallas, 1999—. Contbr. articles to profl. jours., 1980—. Deacon, Calvary Chapel Assembly of God, Richardson, 1991-2000. Andrew Mellon Found. predoctoral fellow, Pitts., 1979-81. Mem. Am. Econ. Assn., Econometric Soc. Office: Univ Tex Dallas Sch Social Sci 2601 N Floyd Rd Richardson TX 75080-1407

VIKCERS, TOM M., secondary school educator; b. Eufaula, Ala., Oct. 6, 1942; s. J. C. and Catherine Virginia Vickers; m. Penny Jo Bowden, Aug. 8, 1981; children: Thomas M. Vickers Jr., Kimberly Hope Cochran, Vickers Jr., Thomas Marion Vickers Jr., Kimberly Hope Cochran, Hayley Joy Chestnut. AA, Marion Mil. Inst., Al, 1963; BS in Physical Edn., Social Sci., U. Martin, Tenn., 1965; M, Troy U., Al, 1974. Cert. tchr. Fla., 2004. Head coach, tchr. Graceville HS, Fla., 2000—02; tchr. coach Chipley HS, Fla., 2002—. Councilman Malvern City Coun. Named to Wiregrass Hall of Fame. Home: 270 West Reeves St Slocomb AL 36375

VIKE-FREIBERGA, VAIRA, former President of Latvia; b. Riga, Latvia, Dec. 1, 1937; d. Karlis and Annemarie (Rankis) V.; m. Imants F. Freibergs, July 16, 1960; children: Karlis Roberts, Indra Karoline. BA, MA, U. Toronto; PhD, McGill U. Clin. psychologist Toronto Psychiat. Hosp., 1960—61; prof. psych. U. Montreal, 1965—98, prof. emerita, 1998—; dir. Latvian Inst., Riga, 1998—99; pres. Republic of Latvia, 1999—2007. Pres., com. mem. Can. Profl. and Scholarly Assns., 1975—98; mem., chair Human Factors Panel NATO Sci. Prog., 1978—81; mem. Sci. Coun. Can., 1980—89, vice-chmn., 1984—89; pres. Acad. 1 Royal Soc. Can., 1998—99; invited spkr. numerous internat. events. Author 10 books. Recipient Gold Plate award, Am. Acad. Achievement, 2000, Hannah Arendt prize polit. thinking, 2005, 34 Highest Orders of Merit; named one of 100 Most Powerful Women, Forbes mag., 2006. Lutheran. Achievements include received 16 honorary doctorate; leading role in achieving Latvia's membership in NATO and European Union in 2004.

VIKEN, LINDA LEA MARGARET, lawyer; b. Sioux Falls, SD, Oct. 27, 1945; d. Carl Thomas and Eleanor Bertha (Zehnpfennig) Crampton; m. Jerry Lee Miller, June 10, 1967 (div. 1975); m. Jeffrey Lynn Viken, Feb. 2, 1980. BS in Bus. Edn., U. S.D., 1967, JD in Law, 1977. Bar: S.D. 1978, U.S. Dist. Ct. S.D. 1978, U.S. Ct. Appeals (8th cir.) 1981, US Supreme Ct., 2005; cert. in family law trial adv. Nat. Bd. Trial Advocacy, matrimonial law arbitrator Am. Acad. Matrimonial Lawyers; diplomate Am. Coll. Family Trial Lawyers. Tchr. Yankton (S.D.) High Sch., 1967-69, Edison Jr. High Sch., Sioux Falls, 1969-75; pvt. practice law Sioux Falls, 1978; ptnr. Finch, Viken, Viken, & Pechota, Rapid City, SD, 1978-92, Viken, Viken, Pechota, Leach & Dewell, Rapid City, SD, 1992—2003; prin. Viken Law Firm, Rapid City, SD, 2003—. Part-time instr. Nat. Coll., Rapid City, 1978-80; magistrate judge Seventh Jud. Cir., Rapid City, 1983-84; chair S.D. Commn. on Child Support, 1985, 88, mem. 96, vice chair 2000, mem. 2004, 08, mem. S.D. Bd. of Bar Examiners, 1987-88. Contbr. articles to profl. jours. State rep. S.D. Legislature Minnehaha County, 1973-76, Pennington County, 1988-92; state party vice chair S.D. Dem. party, 1978-80, 92-94; chair Pennington County Dem. Party, Rapid City, 1985-87. Recipient award-Failure is Impossible, Women's Equality Day, 1998, named Woman Atty. of Yr. Law Sch. Women, 1987, Girl Scout Woman of Distinction, 1998. Fellow Am. Acad. Matrimonial Lawyers (1st v.p.); mem. ABA, S.D. Bar, S.D. Trial Lawyers Assn., Pennington County Bar Assn. (pres., Best Lawyers in America, 2007-09, Super Lawyer, 2007-09). Democrat. Roman Catholic. Avocations: poetry, skiing. Office: Viken Law Firm 4200 Beach Dr Ste 4 Rapid City SD 57702 Office Fax: 605-721-7233. E-mail: llmv@vikenlaw.com.

VILA, ADIS MARIA, lawyer, educator, business government executive; b. Guines Habana, Cuba, Aug. 1, 1953; d. Calixto Vila and Adis C. Fernandez. BA with distinction, Rollins Coll., Winter Park, Fla., 1974; JD with honors, U. Fla., Gainesville, 1978; LLM with high honors, Institut Universitaire de Hautes Estudes Internationales, Geneva, 1981; MBA, U Chgo., 1997. Bar: Fla. 1979, DC 1984. Assoc. Paul & Thomson, 1979-82; White House fellow Office Pub. Liaison, Washington, 1982-83; spl. asst. to sec. state for inter-Am. affairs Dept. State, Washington, 1983-86; dir. Office of Mex. and Caribbean Basin, Dept. Commerce, Washington, 1986-87; sec. Dept. Adminstrn., State of Fla., 1987-89; asst. sec. for adminstrn. USDA, Washington, 1989-91; vis. fellow Nat. Def. U., Washington, 1992-93; v.p. internat. devel. Vigoro Corp., Chgo., 1994-95; v.p. govt. affairs regulatory policy, Carribean & Latin Am. Nortel Networks, 1997-2000; pres., CEO Vila & Assocs., 2001—. Vis. asst. prof. Fla. Internat. U., 1993—94; mem. adv. bd. Ams. Global Asset Mgmt. Fund, 1999—; v.p. external affairs Miami Dade C.C., 2002—03; adj. faculty bus. law various not-for-profit, for profit instns., 2002—; vis. prof. Internat. Bus. and Mgmt. Dickinson Coll., 2007—09; prof., scholar in residence Winter Park Inst., Rollins Coll. Trustee So. Ctr. Internat. Studies, 1987—. Named one of 100 Most Influential Hispanics, 1988; Paul Harris fellow, Rotary Internat., 1983, US-Japan Leadership fellow, 1991—92, Eisenhower Exch. fellow, Beca Fiore, Argentina, 1992. Mem.: Women Execs. in State Govt. (bd. dirs. 1987—89), Am. Coun. Young Polit. Leaders (bd. dirs. 1984—), Internat. Women's Forum, Coun. Fgn. Rels. (term mem. 1987—92), Dade County Bar Assn. (bd. dirs. young and lawyers sect. 1979—87). Republican. Roman Catholic. Avocations: tennis, skiing, golf, theater, art. Home: 1340 Orchid Ave Winter Park FL 32789 Personal E-mail: adisvila@bellsouth.net.

VILARDELL, FRANCISCO, gastroenterologist, educator; b. Barcelona, Apr. 1, 1926; s. Jacinto Vilardell and Mercedes Viñas; m. Leonor March; children: Mercedes, Carmen, Xavier. MD, U. Barcelona, 1949, DSc, 1961; DSc in Medicine, U. Pa., Phila., 1962; PhD (hon.), U. Toulouse, France, 1974, U. Zaragoza, Spain, 1990. Resident medicine Hosp. del Mar, Barcelona, 1949-52; fellow gastroenterology Hosp. de la Santa Cruz & San Pablo, 1952-55, chief gastroenterology svc., 1963—; fellow gastroenterology Grad. Hosp., Phila., 1959-62; prof., dir. Postgrad. Sch. Gastroenterology U. Barcelona, 1970—; hon. prof. U. Valparaiso, Chile, 1996. Pres. European Assn. Study Liver, 1975-76, Coun. Internat. Orgns. Med. Scis. coms., 1987-91; sec.-gen. World Orgn. Gastroenterology, 1974-82, pres., 1982-90. Editor: Enfermedades Difusas del Estomago, 1962, others; assoc. editor Bockus Gastroenterology, 3rd edit., 1972, editl. cons., 4th edit., 1986; contbr. articles to profl. jours. Asst. dir. gen. med. edn. Spanish Ministry Health, 1978-80, dir. gen. health planning, 1980-82, mem. med. rsch. coun., 1982-91. Fellow ACP, Royal Coll. Physicians, Royal Coll. Physicians Edinburgh, Am. Coll. Gastroenterology; mem. Catalan Soc. Bioethics (pres. 1994-96); hon. mem. French Gastroenterology Soc., Brit. Gastroenterology Soc., German Gastroenterology Soc., Japanese Gastroenterology Soc., Spanish Gastroenterology Soc., Polish Gastroenterology Soc., Hungarian Gastroenterology Soc., Portuguese Gastroenterology Soc., Argentinian Gastroenterology Soc., Colombian Gastroenterology Soc., Nat. Health Coun. Avocations: music, philology, medical history. Home: Reina Victoria 26 08021 Barcelona Spain Office: Hosp Santa Cruz & San Pablo 08025 Barcelona Spain

VILARDI, CHARLES RONALD, principal; b. Patterson, NJ, Oct. 30, 1970; s. Richard Joseph and JoAnn Barbara (Anthony) Vilardi; m. Tracy LYnn Blatchford, July 31, 1993; children: Carly Marie, Nicholas Anthony. AA, Edison CC, Ft. Myers, Fla., 1991; BS in Elem. Edn., U. S. Fla., 1993, MEd in Ednl. Leadership, 1997. Cert. prin. Fla., 2001. Aide City of Cape Coral, Fla., 1986-88, counselor, 1988-93, dir. summer programs, 1993-99, asst. prin., 1999—2003, prin., 2003—; tchr. emotionally handicapped Lee County Sch. Bd., Ft. Myers, Fla., 1993-94, tchr. 1st grade, 1994-97, tchr. 4th grade, 1997-99. Sch. adv. chairperson Gulf Elem., Cape Coral, 1995—98, grade level chairperson, 1995—97, mem. tech. com., 1995, Cape Coral, 97, mem. sch. improvement com., 1996—99, chairperson 5 star award com., 1997—99; mem. Lee County Quality Improvement Com. Mem.: ASCD, Nat. Coun. Tchrs. English. Avocations: cooking, swimming, vacationing. Office: Skyline Elem 620 SW 19th St Cape Coral FL 33991 Office Phone: 239-772-3223. Business E-Mail: chuckv@leeschools.net.

VILASECA, ARMANDO, state official, school system administrator; BS in Edn., U. Vt.; MS in Edn., Lesley Coll. Tchr. Georgia Middle Sch., Vt.; tchg. prin. Reading Elem. Sch., Vt.; prin. Westford Elem. and Middle Sch., Vt.; asst. prin. then prin. Essex HS, Vt.; supt. Colchester Sch. Dist., Vt., Franklin West Supervisory Union, Vt.; edn. commr. Vt. Dept. Edn., Montpelier, 2009—. Office: Vt Dept Edn Office of Commr Edn 120 State St Montpelier VT 05620-2501 Office Phone: 802-828-3135. E-mail: armando.vilaseca@state.vt.us.*

VILCEK, JAN TOMAS, immunologist, medical educator; b. Bratislava, Czechoslovakia, June 17, 1933; came to U.S., 1965, naturalized, 1970. s. Julius and Friderika (Fischer) V.; m. Marica F. Gerhath, July 28, 1962 MD, Comenius U., Bratislava, 1957; CSc (PhD), Czechoslovak Acad. Sci., Bratislava, 1962. Fellow Inst. Virology, Bratislava, 1957-62, head of lab., 1962-64; asst. prof. microbiology NYU Med. Ctr., NYC, 1965-68, assoc. prof., 1968-73, prof., 1973—. Chmn. nomenclature com. WHO, 1981—86; mem. adv. com. Am. Cancer Soc., 1981—87, chmn., 1983; mem. sci. adv. bd. Max Planck Inst., Munich, 1987—95; pres. Vilcek Found., 2003—. Author: Interferon, 1969; editor in chief Archives of Virology, 1975-86, Cytokine and Growth Factor Revs., 1995-2005; editor: Interferons and the Immune System, 1984, Tumor Necrosis Factor: Structure, Function and Mechanism of Action, 1991, Cytokine Reference, 2000; mem. editl. bd. Virology, 1979-81, Archives of Virology, 1986-92, Infection and Immunity, 1983-85, Antiviral Rsch., 1984-88, Jour. Interferon and Cytokine Rsch., 1988—, Jour. Immunological Methods, 1986—, Natural Immunity and Cell Growth Regulation, 1986-92, Jour. Immunology, 1987-89, Lymphokine Rsch., 1987-94, Jour. Biol. Chemistry, 1988-90, ISI Atlas Sci., Immunology, 1988-89, Jour. Cellular Physiology, 1988-2008, Cytokine, 1989—, Biologicals, 1989-95, Acta Virologica, 1991—, Internat. Archives of Allergy and Immunology, 1992-98, Folia Biologica, 1993-96, Cellular Immunology, 1993-96, Jour. of Inflammation, 1994-97, Cytokines, Cellular & Molecular Therapy, 1998-2005; contbr. articles to profl. jours.; co-inventor of anti-inflammatory drug infliximab used in rheumatoid arthritis and Crohn's disease, other inflammatory disorders. Mem. rev. panel Israel Cancer Rsch. Fund, 1993-96; mem. fellowship rev. com. Am. Heart Assn., 1992-94. Recipient Rsch. Career Devel. award, USPHS, 1968—73, Recognition award, Japanese Inflammation Soc., 1989, Outstanding Investigator award, Nat. Cancer Inst., NIH, 1991—98, Elliott Osserman Disting. Svc. Cancer Rsch. award, Israel Cancer Rsch. Fund, 1996, Disting. Alumnus award and medal, Comenius U., Bratislava, 2001, Albert Gallatin medal, NYU, 2005, Jan E. Purkyne medal, Czech Acad. Scis., 2008; grantee, USPHS, others. Fellow AAAS; mem. Am. Soc. Microbiology, Am. Assn. Immunologists, Internat. Soc. Interferon and Cytokine Rsch. (hon. life), Czech Immunology Soc., Internat. Cytokine Soc. (hon. life, pres. 1997-98), Czechoslovak Soc. Microbiology. Office: NYU Med Ctr 550 1st Ave New York NY 10016-6402 Business E-Mail: jan.vilcek@nyumc.org.

VILCHEZ, RICARDO S., library director; b. Masaya, Nicaragua, Jan. 20, 1953; s. Adrian Zamora and Maria M. Vilchez; children: Ricardol E., Nidia E. BA, Fordham U., 1990; MBA, CES, Managua, Nicaragua, 1978; diploma, Inst. of Christian Econs., 1982; MLS, Pratt Inst., Bklyn., 1995. With Nat. Police Nicaragua, Managua, 1968-72; presdl. asst. Govt. Nicaragua, 1972-74; libr. asst. Ctrl. Bank Libr., Managua, 1974-75; asst. presdl. office Ctrl. Bank Managua, 1975-79; libr. supervisor Fordham U., NYC, 1989—. Editor (CD) Los Motivos Del Lobo, 2000. V.p. Nicaraguan Children's Found., N.Y.C., 1999—; cultural dir. Nicaraguan Support Group, N.Y.C., 1999—; pres. Comision Hispana Pro Obra Rubén Dario N.Y., 1998—. Mem. Am. Libr. Assn., Am. Soc. Info. Sci., Libr. Congress. Republican. Roman Catholic. Avocations: cultural activities, travel, walking, rare books, community activities. Home: 13 Van Pelt Ave Staten Island NY 10303-2478 Office: Fordham U 113 W 60th St New York NY 10023-7484 E-mail: rsvilchez@yahoo.com.

VILCHEZ, VICTORIA ANNE, lawyer; d. Angel and Mary Ida Vilchez; m. Louis J. Deutsch; children from previous marriage: Matthew Stephen Williams, Michael Paul Williams, Heather Margaret Williams. BA, Fla. State U., Tallahassee, 1977; JD, Mercer U., Macon, Ga., 1980. Bar: Fla. 1980. Trial atty. Office Pub. Defender, Miami, Fla., 1980-83; pvt. practice, 1983—. Traffic magistrate Palm Beach County Ct., 1991—95; mem. Class 1994 Leadership Palm Beach County; bd. dirs. Girl Scouts coun., Palm Glades, Fla., 1995—2004, 2006—08, 1st v.p., 2003—04, 2d v.p., 2006—08; mem. Rep. Nat. Conf. Women and Law, Atlanta, 1978; vol. Coun. Cath. Women. Recipient cert. of achievement, 8th Nat. Conf. Juvenile Justice, 1981, Livingstone Hall award, Juvenile Justice ABA, 1998; grantee, Mercer U., 1977. Mem.: Legal Aid Soc. Palm Beach (bd. dirs. 1992—, v.p. 1999—2001, pres. 2001—03), Guild Cath. Lawyers (pres.-elect 2004—06, pres. 2006—09), Palm Beach County Hispanic Bar Assn. (pres.-elect 1990—91, pres. 1991—92), Hispanic Bar Assn. (bd. dirs. 1990—97, treas. 1993—94, 1994—97), Fla. Assn. Women Lawyers (sec., newsletter editor Palm Beach County chpt. 1985—86, mentor chair 2003, pres.-elect 2004—05, pres. 2005—06), Fla. Bar, Leadership Palm Beach County (bd. govs. 1999—2001, grad. 1994, 2004), Fla. State U. Alumni Assn. Roman Catholic. Address: PO Box 221922 West Palm Beach FL 33422-1922 Office Phone: 561-471-0001. Business E-Mail: vilchezlaw@gmail.com.

VILIM, NANCY CATHERINE, advertising executive; b. Quincy, Mass., Jan. 15, 1952; d. John Robert and Rosemary (Malpede) V.; m. Geoffrey S. Horner, Feb. 16, 1992; children: Matthew Edward Cajda, Megan Catherine Cajda, Margaret Horner. Student, Miami U., Oxford, Ohio, 1970-72. Media asst. Draper Daniels, Inc., Chgo., 1972—74; asst. buyer Campbell Mithun, Chgo., 1974—75; buyer Tatham, Laird & Kudner, Chgo., 1975—77; media buyer Adcom, Inc. div. Quaker Oats Corp., Chgo., 1977—79; media supr. G.M. Feldman, Chgo., 1979—81; v.p. media dir. Media Mgmt., 1981—83; v.p. broadcast dir. Bozell, Jacobs, Kenyon & Eckhardt, Chgo., 1983—88; v.p., media mgr. McCann-Erickson, Inc., 1989—2002; broadcast supr. OMD USA, Chgo., 2002—04; sr. media buyer GSD&M, Chgo., 2004—05; media dir. Jordan, Ross & Rose, Northfield, Ill., 2005—. Judge 27th Internat. Broadcast Awards, Chgo., 1987. Co-pres. Immaculate Conception Religious Edn. Parents Club, 1995-96. Recipient Media All Star awards Sound Mgmt. Mag., N.Y.C., 1987. Mem. Broadcast Advt. Club Chgo., Mus. Broadcast Communications, NAFE. Office: JRR Advt 790 Frontage Rd Northfield IL 60093

VILLABLANCA, JAIME ROLANDO, neuroscientist, medical educator; b. Chillan, Chile, Feb. 1929; arrived in U.S., 1971, naturalized, 1985; s. Ernesto and Teresa (Hernàndez) V.; m. Guillermina Nieto, Dec. 3, 1955; children: Amparo C., Jaime G., Pablo J., Francis X., Claudio I. Bachelor in Biology, Nat. Inst. Chile, 1946; licentiate medicine, U. Chile, 1953, MD, 1954. Cert. neurophysiologist. Rockefeller Found. postdoctoral fellow in physiology John Hopkins and Harvard Med. Schs., 1959-61; Fogarty internat. rsch. fellow in anatomy UCLA, 1966-68, assoc. research anatomist and psychiatrist, 1971-72; assoc. prof. psychiatry and biobehavioral scis. UCLA Sch. Medicine, 1972-76; prof. psychiatry and biobehavioral scis. UCLA, 1976—2004, prof. neurobiology, 1977—2004, disting. prof. psychiatry and biobehavioral scis., neurobiology, 2004—07, disting. emeritus prof., 2007—. Mem. faculty U. Chile Sch. Medicine, 1954-71, prof. exptl. medicine, 1970-71; vis. prof. neurobiology Cath. U. Chile Sch. Medicine, 1974; cons. in field. Author numerous rsch. papers, book chpts., abstracts; chief regional editor Developmental Brain Dysfunction, 1988-99; editor Intermalional Journal of Developments Neuroscience, 2007-. Decorated Order Francisco de Miranda (Venezuela), 1987; recipient Premio Reina Sofia, Madrid, 1990, Lifetime Achievement award UCLA Sch. Medicine, 2001, Emeritus award Colegio Medico de Chile, 2004; fellow Rockefeller Found., 1959-61, Fogarty Internat. Rsch. fellow NIH, 1966-68; grantee USAF Office Sci. Rsch., 1962-65, Found. Fund Rsch. Psychiatry, 1969-72, USPHS-Nat. Inst. Child Human Devel., 1972-96, USPHS-Nat. Inst. Drug Abuse, 1981-85, USPHS-Nat. Inst. Neurol. Disorders and Stroke, 1988-92, Fgn. Scientist Traveling grant Tokyo Met. Govt., 1995. Mem. AAAS, AAUP, Sleep Rsch. Soc. (Significant Early Contbr. award 2003), Intellectual & Developmental Disabilities Rsch. Ctr., Brain Rsch. Inst., Internat. Brain Rsch. Orgn., Am. Physiol. Soc., Soc. for Neurosci., Assn. Venezolana Padres de Niños Excepcionales, Soc. Child and Adolescent Psychiatry and Neurology (Chile, hon.), Johns Hopkins Med. and Surg. Assn., Sigma Xi. Home: 200 Surfview Dr Pacific Palisades CA 90272-2911 Office: UCLA Dept Psychiatry & Biobehavioral Scis Los Angeles CA 90024-1759 Home Phone: 310-459-2452. Business E-Mail: jvillablanca@mednet.ucla.edu.

VILLA-FLORES, JAVIER, history professor; b. Guadalajara, Jalisco, Mex., Oct. 13, 1966; s. Rodolfo Villa Medina and Carmen Lucia Flores Arufe; m. Maria Eugenia De la Torre, May 21, 1993; 1 child, Olivia Villa. PhD, U. Calif. San Diego, La Jolla, 2001. Asst. prof. U. Ill., Chgo., 2001—06, assoc. prof., 2007—. Contbr. monographs. Recipient Rsch. award, U. Ill., 2002; grantee, 2002, Tchg. Recognition Program, 2007, Harvard Atlantic Seminar, Harvard U., 2003, Ministry Culture, Spain, 2006, Mellon Found. grant, Soc. Values Higher Edn.; fellow Mrs. Francis J. Weber Rsch. fellow, Huntington Libr., 1998, Everett Helm Vis. fellowship, Lilly Libr., 2005; Short-term Rsch. fellowship, Newberry Libr., 2000, Grant-in-aid, U. Ill., 2003, Jr. Faculty Rsch. grant, 2005, Faculty fellow, Inst. Humanities, U. Ill., 2002. Office: Univ Ill Chgo MC219 601 South Morgan St Chicago IL 60607-7115 Business E-Mail: javier@uic.edu.

VILLAGOMEZ, JOSEPH K., state agency administrator, public health service officer; MA. Addiction services mgr. Cmty. Guidance Ctr., Saipan, Northern Mariana Islands; dir. mental health & social services Dept. Pub. Health, Saipan, sec. health, 2006—. Sec. Pacific Islands Health Officers Assn., bd. dirs., pres. Mem.: APA. Office: Dept Pub Health PO Box 500409 CK Saipan MP 96950 Office Phone: 670-236-8201. Office Fax: 670-234-8930. Business E-Mail: jkvsaipan@saipan.com.*

VILLA-KOMAROFF, LYDIA, molecular biologist, educator, health product executive, academic administrator; b. Las Vegas, N.Mex., Aug. 7, 1947; d. John Dias and Drucilla (Jaramillo) V.; m. Anthony Leader Komaroff, June 18, 1970. BA, Goucher Coll., 1970; PhD, MIT, 1975; DSc (hon.), St. Thomas U., 1996, Pine Manor Coll., 1997; PhD (hon.), Goucher Coll., 1997. Rsch. fellow Harvard U., Cambridge, 1975-78; asst. prof. dept. microbiology U. Mass. Med. Ctr., Worcester, 1978-81, assoc. prof. dept. molecular genetics micro, 1982-85; assoc. prof. dept. neurology Harvard Med. Sch., Boston, 1986-95; sr. rsch. assoc. neurology Children's Hosp., Boston, 1985-95, assoc. dir. mental retardation rsch. ctr., 1987-94; prof. dept. neurology Northwestern U., Evanston, Ill., 1995—2002, assoc. v.p. rsch., 1995-97, v.p. rsch., 1998—2002; v.p. for rsch., COO, Whitehead Inst. for Biomed. Rsch., Cambridge, Mass., 2003—05; chief sci. officer Cytonome, Inc., 2005—; CEO Ctyonome Inc., 2006—; chief sci. officer Cytonome ST LLC, 2009—. Mem. mammalian genetics study sect. NIH, 1982-84, mem. reviewers rsch., 1989, mem. neurol. disorders program project rev. com., 1989-94; mem. adv. bd. Biol. Sci. Directorate, NSF, 1994-99; bd. dirs. Nat. Ctr. Genome Rsch., 1995-00, TransKaryotic Therapies, 2003-05, chair 2005, bd. dirs. Mass. Life Sci. Ctr., 2008-; mem. adv. coun. Nat. Inst. Neurol. Disorders and Stroke, NIH, 2000-04; bd. trustees Pine Manor Coll., 2004—, chair, 2007-; sr. lectr. Sloan Sch. Mgmt. MIT, 2003--05; bd. chair Pine Manor Coll., 2007-. Contbr. articles and abstracts to profl. jour.; patentee in field. Recipient Hispanic Engr. Nat. Achievement award, 1992, Nat. Achievement award Hispanic Mag., 1996, Lifetime Achievement award, Hispanic Bus. Mag., 2008; inducted Hispanic Engr. Nat. Achievement Hall of Fame, 1999; selected 50 most important Hispanics by "business & Tech., Hispanic Engr. & Info. Tech." mag. 2003; named Hispanic Scientist of Yr. Mus. Sci. and Industry, Tampa, 2008; Helen Hay Whitney Found. fellow, 1975-78; NIH grantee, 1978-85, 89-96. Mem. AAAS (bd. dirs. 2000-05), Am. Soc. Microbiology, Assn. for Women in Sci., Soc. for Neurosci., Am. Soc. Cell Biology, Soc. for Advancement Chicanos and Native Ams. in Sci. (founding, bd. dir. 1987-93, v.p. 1990-93), Internat. Soc. for Cellular Therapy, Am. Soc. for Blood and Marrow Transplantation. Office Phone: 617-330-5030 ext. 354. Business E-Mail: lvk@cytonomest.com.

VILLALOBOS, LIGIAH, former international programming manager, film producer, scriptwriter; b. Chihuahua, Mexico, Nov. 5, 1963; came to U.S., 1975; d. Efraïn Villalobos and Olivia Rojas. BA in Geography, Brigham Young U., 1985. Advt. asst. Action in Advt., LA, 1985; traffic coord. Sta. KSKQ Radio, LA, 1985-87; polit. sales Sta. KCBS-TV, LA, 1987-89, office mgr., 1989-90; programming supr. Buena Vista Prodns. of The Walt Disney Co., Burbank, Calif., 1990-91, mgr. programming, 1991—; dir. current programming WB Network; v.p. creative affairs Esparza/Katz Prodns.; dir., writer, prodr. Jalapeno Films, 2007—. Co-prodr.: (films) Dancing in September, 2000; prodr., writer, dir. (films) One World, 2001, exec. prodr., writer La misma luna, 2007; prodr.: (TV films) Walkout, 2006; writer (TV series) Ed, 2000, Go, Diego! Go!, 2005—07. Recipient Outstanding Achievement award, Nat. Assn. Latino Ind. Producers, 2008; named one of 25 Most Powerful and Talented Hispanic Women in the Entertainment Industry, Hollywood Reporter and Billboard Mag., 2007. Avocations: reading, writing, music, dance.

VILLALONGA, BELEN, finance educator, director; b. Madrid, July 4, 1968; MA in Economics, U. Calif., LA, 1998, PhD in Mgmt., 2001; PhD in Economics and Mgmt., U. Complutense, Madrid, 1996. Asst. prof. Harvard Bus. Sch., Boston, 2001—05, assoc. prof., 2005—. Dir. Acciona, Madrid, 2006—. Contbr. articles to profl. jours. Recipient Brattle prize, 2004, Addison-Wesley prize, 2004. Office: Harvard Bus Sch Soldiers Field Boston MA 02163

VILLARAIGOSA, ANTONIO RAMON, Mayor, Los Angeles; b. East LA, Jan. 23, 1953; m. Corina Raigosa, 1987 (separated 2007); children: Marisela, Prisila, Antonio Jr., Natilia Fe. BA in History, UCLA, 1977; JD, People's Coll. of Law, 1985. Mem. Calif. State Assembly, 1995—2001, Dem. whip and mem. appropriations and budget coms., majority leader, 1997, speaker, 1998—2001; city councilman, dist. 14 LA City Coun., 2003—05; mayor City of LA, 2005—. Mem. LA Met. Transp. Bd., 1990—94; nat. co-chair Kerry Presdl. Campaign, 2003—04; chair LA City Coun. Transp. Com.; bd. dirs. Met. Transit Authority. Mem. Greater Eastside Voter Registration and Edn. Project, Jobs with Peace, LAUSD Mex. Am. Edn. Commn., L.A. Ctr. for Law and Justice. Recipient Golden Plate award, Acad. Achievement, 2006; named one of 25 Most Influential Hispanics, Time Mag., 2005; disting. fellow at UCLA and U. So. Calif. Achievements include first Latino mayor for LA since Cristobal Aguilar left office in 1872. also: Ste 3200 725 S Figueroa St Los Angeles CA 90017-5432 Office: Office of Mayor City Hall 200 North Spring St Los Angeles CA 90012

VILLARINI, GABRIELE, geophysicist; b. Rome, July 30, 1978; married. PhD, U. Iowa, Iowa City, 2008. Grad. rsch. asst. U. Iowa, 2003—08; rsch. assoc. Princeton U., NJ, 2008—. Contbr. articles to profl. jours. Mem.: Am. Geophys. Union (Outstanding Student Paper award 2007). Office: Princeton Univ E-Quad Princeton NJ 08544 Business E-Mail: gvillari@princeton.edu.

VILLAROSA, SHARI, former ambassador; BA in Internat. Studies, U. NC, Chapel Hill; JD, Coll. William and Mary. Diplomat in residence East-West Ctr., Honolulu; desk officer Office Investment Affairs US Dept. State, Washington, Singapore and Indonesia desk officer, dep. dir. Office Burma, Cambodia, Laos, Thailand and Vietnam Affairs, spl. asst. to undersecretary econ. affairs, dir. Philippines, Malaysia, Brunei, Singapore Affairs, East Asia and Pacific Bur., US Chargé d'Affaires to Burma Rangoon, 2005—08.

VILLARREAL, CARLOS CASTAÑEDA, engineering executive; b. Brownsville, Tex., Nov. 9, 1924; s. Jesus Jose and Elisa L. (Castañeda) Villarreal; m. Doris Ann Akers, Sept. 10, 1948 (dec. 1995); children: Timothy Hill, David Akers; m. June Ricchezza McElroy, Oct. 3, 2002. BS, US Naval Acad., 1948; MS, US Navy Postgrad. Sch., 1950; LLD (hon.), St. Mary's U., 1972. Registered profl. engr. Commd. ensign US Navy, 1949, advanced through grades to lt., 1956; comdg. officer U.S.S. Rhea, 1951, U.S.S. Osprey, 1952; comdr. Mine Divsn. 31, 1953; instr. elec. engring. US Naval Acad., 1954—56; resigned, 1956; mgr. marine and indsl. operation Gen. Electric Co., 1956—66; v.p. mktg. and adminstrn. Marquardt Corp., 1966—69; adminstr. Urban Mass Transit Adminstrn., Dept. Transp., Washington, 1969—73; commr. Postal Rate Commn., 1973—79, vice chmn., 1975—79; v.p. Washington ops. Wilbur Smith and Assocs., Fairfax, Va., 1979—84, sr. v.p., 1984—86, exec. v.p., 1987—, also bd. dirs. Lectr. in field; mem. industry sector adv. com. Dept. Commerce; mem. sect. 13 adv. com. Dept. Transp., 1983—86. Contbr. articles to profl. jours. Mem. devel. com. Wolftrap Farm Pk. Performing Arts, 1973—78; bd. edn. St. Elizabeth Sch.; bd. dirs. Assoc. Cath. Charities, 1983—86; chmn. fin. com. Cath. Charities, USA; coun. mem. St. Elizabeth Ch., 1982—86, chmn. fin. com.; active John Carrol Soc. Decorated Knight Sovereign Mil. Hospitaller Order St. John of Jerusalem of Rhodes and Malta, Equestrian Order of Holy Sepulchre of Jerusalem, Knight Comdr.; recipient Outstanding Achievement award, Dept. Transp., 1974. Fellow: ASCE, Am. Cons. Engrs. Coun. (vice chmn. interna. com.); mem.: NSPE (pres. DC soc. 1986—87, bd. dirs. 1988—91), IEEE, Intelligent Transp. Soc. Am. (chmn. fin. com., bd. dirs.), Inst. Traffic Engrs., Inst. World Politics, Internat. Bridge, Tunnel and Turnpike Assn., Washington Soc. Engrs., Transp. Rsch. Bd., Am. Rds. and Transp. Builders Assn. (chmn. pub. transp. adv. coun.), Soc. Am. Mil. Engrs., Soc. Naval Archs. and Marine Engrs., Am. Pub. Transit Assn., Army-Navy Club (pres. 1999—2004), Univ. Club. Republican. Roman Catholic. Office: Wilbur Smith Assocs 300 Williams Dr Ste 300 Fairfax VA 22031 Office Phone: 703-698-9780. Personal E-mail: cvillarreal-1@comcast.net. Business E-Mail: cvillarreal@wilbursmith.com.

VILLARREAL, JUNE PATRICIA, retired sales executive; b. Atlantic City, Sept. 26, 1929; d. Edmund N. and Dorothy R. (McDowell) Ricchezza; m. Ottavio Gelmi, Dec. 16, 1954 (div. 1964); 1 child, Alessandra; m. Robert Joseph McElroy, Oct. 16, 1970 (dec. May 1974); m. Carlos Castañeda Villarreal, Oct. 3, 2002. Student, Temple U., 1947-48, Georgetown U., 1951-53. Staff mem. Am. Consulate Gen., Milan, 1954; legis. asst. U.S. Senate, Washington, 1956; social sec. Amb. of Finland, Washington, 1958; adminstrv. asst., translator Roosevelt and Clark Lobbyists, 1958—59; legis. asst. to congressman Washington, 1960-65; sr. assoc. Gillmore M. Perry Co., Washington, 1965-76; sales exec., cons., 1980-87; ptnr. Mfrs. Representatives Internat., Washington, 1987-97; ret., 1997. Pres. Spanish-Portugese Study Group, 1994—95. Mem.: Alianza Ibero-Americana, D.C. League Rep. Women, Equestrian Order Holy Sepulchre of Jerusalem (Lady Comdr. 2003—), Georgetown U. Alumni Assn., John Carroll Soc., Army Navy Club (Washington). Republican. Roman Catholic. Home: 4000 Cathedral Ave NW Apt 208B Washington DC 20016-5254

VILLARREAL, ROBERTO ESCAMILLA, retired political science researcher, educator, administrator; b. Karnes City, Tex., Oct. 20, 1936; s. Epifanio Sr. and Antonia (Escamilla) V.; m. Norma Pedraza, June 12, 1965; children: Marco Dante, Carlo Renato, Ethel Minerva. BS, Tex. A&I U., 1962, MS, 1966; MA, U. Okla., 1972, PhD, 1975. Tchr. Pawnee Ind. Sch. Dist., Tex., 1962-63, Pharr-San Juan-Alamo Ind. Sch. Dist., Tex., 1963-66; instr. Bee County Coll., Beeville, Tex., 1967-70, U. Okla., Norman, 1970-72; chmn. Bee County Coll., Dept. Social Scis., 1972-73; dir. Bee County Coll., Fed. Programs, 1973-76; prof. U. Tex. Polit Sci. Dept., El Paso, 1976—2003, chmn., 1987—, prof. emeritus, 2003—. Advisor U. Tex. System, Austin, 1990-91; assoc. v.p. acad. affairs U. Tex., El Paso, 1991-96; exec. dir. Internat. Consortium for Health and Environ. Security, 2003— Author: Chicano Elites and Non-Elites, 1979; author/editor: Latino Empowerment, 1988, Latinos and Political Coalitions, 1991. Mem. exec. com. Hispanic Leadership Inst., El Paso, 1989— Recipient Ford Found. fellowship, 1979-71, Disting. Svc. award U. Tex., El Paso, 1985, Outstanding Achievement award in edn. Mex. Am. Bar Assn., 1991; Fulbright scholar, Mex., 1998-99; named one of 100 Most Influential Hispanics in U.S., Hispanic Bus., Mag., 1997 Mem. Nat. Assn. Chicano Studies (exec. officer 1985-86), Am. Assn. for Higher Edn. (chair Hispanic Caucus 1991), Tex. Assn. Coll. Tchrs. (v.p. 1979-80, pres. 1980-82) Democrat. Roman Catholic. Home: 172 Oak Fields Dr Floresville TX 78114 Office: AFIOH/RSRH 2513 Kennedy Cir Brooks City-Base TX 78235-5226 Office Phone: 210-710-8698. Personal E-mail: revilla@tgti.net.

VILLARRUBIA, GLENDA BOONE, reading specialist and coordinator, educator, consultant; d. Albert Jewel and Tommie Lee Boone; m. David Daniel Villarrubia, Apr. 2, 1977; children: David Daniel Jr., Steven Joseph, John Albert. BA, Southeastern La. U., 1976, MBA, 1978. La. Teaching Certificate 1976, Reading Specialist Certification 1978, Behavior Specialist Certification 2000. Tchr. Wash. Parish Schools, Franklinton, La., 1976—79; tchr./coord. Jefferson Parish Schools, New Orleans, 1979; tchr. Ouachita Parish, Monroe, La., 1980; tchr. edn. Bogalusa City Schools, La., 1981—82, tchr., 1982—96, individualized edn. program cons., 1999—2005, individualized edn. program facilitator, resource teachers spl. edn., 1998—2000, dir./supr. spl. edn., 2000—01, individualized edn. program facilitator, 2001—04, compliance monitoring facilitator, 2005—. Spl. edn. cons., 2000; owner The Tchrs. Desk, 1989—99. Mem. Crisis Prevention Inst.; troop supporter Bogalusa, La, 2002—05; tiger cub leader Boy Scouts Am., Bogalusa, 1985; 4-H leader sponsor Bogalusa City Schools, 1985; beta club leader Wash. Parish Schools, 1977. Recipient Tchr. of Yr., Bogalusa City Schools, 1983, 1993, La. Dept. Edn., 1992. Mem.: Associated Profl. Educators of La., La. Pub. Sch. Rels. Assn., La. Ednl. Rsch. Assn., La. Assn. Supervision and Curriculum Devel., La. Assn. Educators, Learning Disability Assn., La. Assn. Sch. Execs., Nat. Edn. Assn., Coun. Exceptional Children, Southeastern La. Alumni Assn., Alpha Signa Tau. Avocations: travel, gardening, church, reading.

VILLARUEL, ANTONIA M., nursing educator; BSN, Nazareth Coll., Kalamazoo, Mich., 1978; MSN, U. Pa., Phila., 1982; PhD, Wayne State U., Detroit, 1993. RN. Fellow U. Mich., Ann Arbor, 1995; prof. risk reduction and health promotion U. Mich. Sch. Nursing, Ann Arbor, dir. Ctr. Health Promotion. Named to Mich. Nurses Hall of Fame, 2004. Fellow: Am. Acad. Nursing; mem.: Inst. Medicine, Nat. Assn. Hispanic Nurses, Nat. Coalition Ethnic Minority Nursing Associations (founding mem., v.p.). Office: U Mich Sch Nursing Rm 4320 400 N Ingalls Bldg Ann Arbor MI 48109-0482 Office Phone: 734-615-9696. Office Fax: 734-647-0351. E-mail: avillarr@umich.edu.*

VILLAVECES, JAMES WALTER, allergist, immunologist, consultant; b. San Luis Obispo, Calif., Nov. 4, 1933; s. Robert and Solita (Combariza) V. BA, UCLA, 1955; MD (hon.), U. Calif. Med. Sch., 1960. Diplomate Am. Bd. Allergy and Immunology. Intern Sawtelle VA Hosp., LA, 1960-61; preceptorship in adult allergy L.A. County Hosp., LA, 1964-66; fellow in allergy White Meml. CCM, LA, 1966-67; co-chief allergy divsn. Ventura (Calif.) Med. Ctr., 1969—87; practice medicine specializing in allergy-immunology Ventura, 1984—; lectr. wellpoint Calif. RAST, IVIG. Founder botanical weed allergy walks, 1970; cons. in allergy/immunology, Blue Cross, 1991-96; medical invention cons., Inventor Internat., Inc.; inventor, cons. Sprixx: Alcohol-gel Clip on Dispensers, 2001, 3M; mem. Pharmacy and Therapeutics Com., Wellpoint (Blue Cross Calif.) Inc., 1991-96; prodr. Ventura County cities street-tree guide for asthma patients; peer reviewer Blue Cross So. Calif. Wellpoint, 1980, 1994-95; cons., lectr., peer reviewer in field. Writer, prodr., editor films; contbr. articles on biology of pollens and molds of Ventura County to profl. jours.; patentee in field. Bd. dir. Am. Lung Assn., Ventura, 1969-85, pres., 1974, advisor air pollution control com., 1971-74; judge Ventura Sci. Fair, 1970-85; lectr. in field. Recipient commendation County Bd. Suprs., Ventura, 1974; named one of Am.'s Top Physicians Consumers Rsch. Coun. Am., 2003-05. Fellow Am. Acad. Allergy(emeritus mem.), Asthma, Immunology, Am. Coll. Allergy, Asthma, Immunology; mem. Calif. Soc. Allergy-Immunology, Calif. Med. Assn., Ventura County Med. Assn., Gold Coast Tri-County Allergy Soc. (pres. 1987), CAL Club (hon.), Ventura County Sports Hall of Fame (mem. founding bd.), Mensa. Republican. Achievements include development of infection protection device for hospital and food service establishments; research in sprixx invention has cut infection rate & death rate; set standard for RAST use for wellpoint to governing standard for and use of IVIG. Avocations: writing, photography, lecturing, pistol target shooting, fishing. Home: 928 High Point Dr Ventura CA 93003-1415 Office: Dudley Profl Ctr 4080 Loma Vista Rd Ste M Ventura CA 93003-1811 Office Phone: 805-656-0433. Personal E-mail: allergycare2006@yahoo.com.

VILLAVICENCIO, JOSÉ ANTONIO, secondary school educator; b. Guatemala City, Guatemala, June 19, 1942; came to U.S., 1956; s. José G. and Josefa (Aguilar) V.; m. Joanna Helen Silva, Oct. 25, 1969; children: Antonio, John Joseph. BA, San Francisco State U., 1965; EdD, U. So. Calif., 1992. Cert. tchr. gen. edn., Spanish, French, Italian. Tchr. Crestmoor H.S., San Bruno, Calif., 1972-80, Mercy H.S., San Francisco, 1980-81; Burlingame (Calif.) H.S. Burlingame (Calif.) High Sch., 1981—; coord. fgn. lang. edn. Coll. Edn. Columbus State U., 2009—. Coach Crestmoor, Burlingame, 1974-88; mem. Bay Area Fgn. Lang. Project, Stanford, Calif., 1985—, team leader, 1994—, reader cons. AP Spanish Lit. Exam. Coach, referee, bd. dirs. Am. Youth Soccer Orgn. Region 145, Millbrae, Calif., 1977—. With U.S. Army, 1967-69, Korea. Recipient Svc. award, Coll. Edn., 2007. Mem. ASCD, NEA, Nat. Staff Devel. Coun., Calif. Tchrs. Assn., U. S.C. Alumni Assn., San Francisco

State Alumni Assn., Phi Delta Kappa. Avocations: reading, writing, computers, soccer. Home: 3 Villa Ln Millbrae CA 94030-2917 Office: Burlingame H S 400 Carolan Ave Burlingame CA 94010-2708 Home Phone: 650-697-6525. Business E-Mail: villavicencio_iose@colstate.edu.

VILLEGAS, CAMILO, professional golfer; b. Medellin, Colombia, Jan. 7, 1982; Grad. in bus., U. Fla., Gainesville, 2004. Profl. golfer, 2004—, PGA Tour, 2006—. 1st Pl. Colombian Open, 2001, Coca-Cola Tokai Classic, 2007, BMW Championship, 2008, Tour Championship, 2008. Named First Team All-Am., NCAA, 2001, 2002, 2004, First Team All Conf., Southeast Conf., 2001, 2002, 2004, Player of Yr., 2002, 2004, Most Improved Player, PGA Tour, Golf Digest, 2008. Office: PGA Tour 100 PGA Tour Blvd Ponte Vedra Beach FL 32082*

VILLELLA, EDWARD JOSEPH, dancer, choreographer, performing arts association administrator; b. Long Island, NY, Oct. 1, 1936; s. Joseph and Mildred (DeGiovanni) Villella; m. Janet Greschler (div.); 1 child, Roddy; m. Linda Carbonetta; children: Crista Francesca, Lauren. BS in Marine Transp., NY State Maritime Coll., 1957; LHD (hon.), Boston Conservatory, 1985, degree (hon.), Union Coll., Schenectady, NY, 1991; DHL (hon.), St. Thomas U., Miami, Fla., 1994, U. SC, 1997; DFA (hon.), SUNY Maritime Coll., Bronx, 1998; Doctor (hon.), Fla. Atlantic U., 2000, U. NC, Asheville, 2002, Coll. Charleston, 2002; degree (hon.), LI U., 2005. Mem. N.Y.C. Ballet, 1957, soloist, 1958—60, prin. soloist, 1960—83; artistic dir. Ballet Okla., Oklahoma City, 1983—86; founding artistic dir., CEO Miami (Fla.) City Ballet, 1985—. Vis. artist U.S. Mil. Acad., West Point, 1981—82; vis. artist Salute to Balanchine residency Harvard U., 1999—2000; vis. prof. dance U. Iowa, 1981; resident Heritage chair arts and cultural criticism George Mason U.; Dorthy F. Schmidt artist-in-residence Coll. of Arts and Letters, 2000—01. Dancer Symphony C., Scotch Symphony, We. Symphony, Donizetti Variations, Swan Lake, La Source, The Nutcracker, Agon, Stars and Stripes, The Prodigal Son, The Figure in the Carpet, 1960, Electronics, 1961, A Midsummer Night's Dream, 1962, Bugaku, 1963, Tarantella, 1964, Harlequinade, 1965, The Brahms-Schoenberg Quartet, 1966, Jewels, 1967, Symphony in Three Movements, 1972, Schéhérazade, 1975, choreographer Narkissas, 1966, Shostakovitch Ballet Suite, 1972, Shenandoah, 1975, Gayane Pas de Deux, 1972, Salute to Cole, 1973, Sea Chanties, 1974, Prelude, Riffs and Fugues, 1980, dancer TV The Ed Sullivan Show, Bell Telephone Hour, Mike Douglas Show, TV spl. Harlequin, 1975 (Emmy award); co-author (autobiography): Prodigal Son, 1991. Mem. Nat. Coun. Arts, 1968—74; chmn. Commn. for Cultural Affairs, NYC, 1978; bd. visitors N.C. Sch. for Arts; mem. adv. panel Nat. Endowment for Arts; trustee Wolf Trap Found. for Arts. Recipient Dance Mag. award, 1964, Lions of Performing Arts award, N.Y. Pub. Libr., 1987, Capezio Dance award, 1989, Gold medal, Nat. Soc. Arts and Letters, 1990, William G. Anderson Merit award, AAHPERD, 1991, Nat. Medal of Arts award, 1997, Kennedy Ctr. Honors, 1997, Cultural Soc. award, Bklyn. Ctr. for Performing Arts at Bklyn. Coll., 1998, Am. Irreplaceable Dance Treasures: The First 100, Disting. Achievement award, U. Fla., 2005, U. Fla. Coll. Fine Arts, 2005; named Miamian of Yr., UNICO Nat., 1993, Miracle Maker, Big Bros. Big Sisters of Greater Miami, 2003; named to Fla. Artists Hall of Fame, 1997, Dance Hall of Fame, 2004; Robert J.H. Kiphuth fellow, Yale U., 2001, Hon. Theater Arts Br. fellow, U.S. Imperial Soc. Tchrs. Dancing, 2003. Fellow: Am. Acad. Arts & Scis.*

VILLERE, ROGER F., JR., political organization administrator; Pres. Villere Corp., 1978—; chmn. Rep. Party East Jefferson, 1989—92, Rep. Party Jefferson Parish, La., 1993, La. Rep. Party, 2004—. Vol. Rep. Nat. Com. Conv., New Orleans, 1988, del., Phila., 2000; mem. rules com. Rep. Nat. Com., 1997—2000; fellow La. State U. Acad. Politics, 1989, Loyola Inst. Politics, 1990, bd. mem., 2004—; fellow U. New Orleans Govt. Leadership Inst., 1991; charter mem., parliamentarian Jefferson Parish Young Republicans, 1991; mem. Rep. Parish Exec. Com., 1992—96, Rep. State Ctrl. Com., 1992—2000; bd. mem. East Jefferson Hosp. Found., 1995—, chmn., 1997; founder, charter mem. Jefferson Chamber, 1998; bd. mem. Woman's New Life Ctr., 2003—, v.p., 2004. Mem.: Alliance for Good Govt. (pres. 2002—04), Am. Acad. Florist, NRA, Metairie Jaycees (pres.), La. Jaycees (v.p.), La. State Florist Assn. (pres.), Pelican State Pachyderms (founder, charter mem., bd. mem. 2002—), Lafreniere Kiwanis (pres.). Republican. Office: La Rep Party 11440 N Lake Sherwood Ste A Baton Rouge LA 70816*

VILLERS, LYNNE M., curator; BS, Butler U., Indpls., 1981. Animal keeper Indpls. Zoo, 1981—87, head keeper forests, deserts, 1988—99, curator forests, deserts, 2000—. N.Am. regional studbook keeper, ring-tailed lemur Assn. Zoos and Aquariums, Silver Spring, Md., 1993—, species coord., ring-tailed lemur species survival plan, 1995—, N.Am. regional studbook keeper, Guinea baboon, 2001—07, chair, prosimian taxon adv. group, 2004—. Contbr. articles to zoological publs. Office: Indpls Zoo 1200 W Washington St Indianapolis IN 46222 Business E-Mail: lvillers@indyzoo.com.

VILLERS, PHILIPPE, mechanical engineer; b. Paris, June 20, 1935; arrived in U.S., 1940, naturalized, 1946; s. Raymond and Garda (Schmidt) Villers; m. Annie Louise Young, July 13, 1957 (div. 1973); children: Jocelyn Anne(dec.), Renata Jane; m. Katherine Stephan, 1973; children: Noel Stephan, Carolyn Grace. AB in Applied Scis. cum laude, Harvard U., 1955; SM in Mech. Engring, MIT, 1960. Mem. mfg. tng. program GE, 1955-58; project engr. Perkin-Elmer Corp., Wilton, Conn., 1959-62; project engr. Apollo Antenna pointings sensor Barnes Engring. Co., Stamford, Conn., 1962-65; project mgr. Advanced Products Ctr., Link Group, Gen. Precision, Inc., Binghamton, NY, 1965-67; mgr. advanced products Concord Control, Inc., Boston, 1967-69; co-founder, sr. v.p., dir. Computervision Corp., Bedford, Mass., 1969-80; founder, pres., dir. Automatix, Inc., Billerica, Mass., 1980-84; chmn. bd. Automatix Inc., Billerica, Mass., 1984-86; founder, pres., dir. Cognition Inc., 1985-88. Bd. dir. Xyvision, Inc., Wakefield, Mass., chmn., 1992—94; bd. dir. Grainpro Inc., Concord, Mass., pres., 1996—; bd. dir. Voxiva Inc., 2001—07, Mercy Corps, United Villages, Herndon Alliance, 2006—. Del. Dem. Nat. Conv., 1988, 1992; mem. Dem. Town Com., Wilton, 1963, Concord, Mass., 1978—, chmn., 1984—96; mem. Harvard Com. Univ. Resources, 1981—92; mem. various vis. coms. MIT, 1981—91; mem. vis. com. Nat. Bur. Stds., 1981—84; trustee U. Lowell, 1985—91; mem. adv. bd. Inst. Global Leadership Tufts U., Medford, Mass., 2005—; founder and pres. Families U.S.A. Founds. (formerly Villers Found.), Washington, 1981—, Bay State Retiree Vol. Coun., Concord, 1989—92. Grad. fellow, NSF, 1959—60. Mem.: ACLU (pres. com. 1981—, bd. dirs. Physicians Human Rights 1991—94), ASME, Unitarian-Universalist Assn. (pres. coun. 1982—86), Amnesty Internat. (bd. dirs. 1990—96, ombudsman 1992—96, mem. exec. com. 1994—96, mem. leadership coun. 1995—, coord. Concord group 15 1998—), Sigma Xi. Achievements include patents for process welding aluminum liners to steel surfaces; a horizon sensor for visible wavelength; infrared roughness testing instrument; improved thermopile construction thermal die marker; method for long term storage of a bulk biologically active commodity; solar sail applications for interplanetary probe propulsion and stabilization; method and apparatus for targetless wafer alignment; method and system for transporting and storing commodities. Home: 20 Whits End Rd Concord MA 01742-5411 Office: 200 Baker Ave Ste 309 Concord MA 01742-2170 Home Phone: 978-369-1053; Office Phone: 978-371-7400. Business E-Mail: pvillers@grainpro.com.

VILLFORTH, JOHN CARL, engineer, health physicist; b. Reading, Pa., Dec. 28, 1930; s. Carl and Grace L. (Fichthorn) Villforth; m. Joanne E. Heine, Sept. 12, 1953; children: Mary Jane Villforth Smith, Elaine, Jennifer Villforth Veazy. BS in San. Engring., Pa. State U., 1952, MS, 1954; MS in Physics, Vanderbilt U., 1958. Cert. Am. Bd. Health Physics. With USPHS, 1961-90; dir. Ctr. Devices and Radiol. Health, 1969-90, asst. surgeon gen., 1972-90, chief engr., 1985-89; pres. Food and Drug Law Inst., Washington, 1990—2001. Bd. dirs. Vasogen Inc., EduNeering Inc. Served to capt. USAF, 1954—61, served to rear adm. USPHS, 1961—90. Decorated DSM, Outstanding Svc. medal; recipient Outstanding Engring. Alumnus award, Pa. State U., 1987, Recognition award, HHS, 1987, Disting. Alumni award, FDA, 2000, Pa. State U., 2005; Univ. Alumni fellow, 2002. Mem.: USPHS Commd. Officers Assn. (chmn. bd. dirs. 1999—2000), Regulatory Affairs Profl. Soc., Internat. Radiation Protection Assn., Health Physics Soc. (pres. 1976—77, Elda Anderson award 1970), FDA Alumni Assn. (chmn. 2001—). Home Phone: 240-361-3187. Personal E-mail: jcvillforth@comcast.net. *Understand the problem! Too much energy is wasted and too many relationships are strained because we fail to understand the underlying problem before we embark on a solution.*

VILLINSKI, JENNIFER C., geochemist; b. Austin, Tex., Dec. 31, 1969; d. Terry and Pamela Rogers; m. Jeffrey T. Villinski; children: Julia R., Emma G., Benjamin Jacob. PhD, Ind. U., Bloomington, 2000. Petroleum sys. analyst BP America, Houston, 2000—04, BP Egypt, Cairo, 2004—. Mem.: Am. Geophys. Union. Democrat. Achievements include research in organic components of antarctic sediment. Home: PO BOX 4381-Cairo Houston TX 77210 Personal E-mail: villinjc@bp.com.

VILLOCH, KELLY CARNEY, art director; b. Kyoto, July 22, 1950; d. William Riley and stepdaughter Hazel Fowler Carney; m. Joe D. Villoch, Aug. 9, 1969; children: Jonathan, Christopher, Jennifer. A in Fine Arts, Dade C.C., Miami, Fla., 1971; student, Metro Fine Arts, 1973-74, Fla. Internat. U., 1985-88. Design asst. Lanvin, Miami, 1971—74, Fieldcrest, Miami, 1974-77; art dir. Advercolor, Miami, 1977-78; art dir. copywriter ABC, Miami, 1978-89; writer Armed Forces Radio & TV Network; multimedia dir. ADVITEC, 1989-91; art dir. writer Miami Write, 1979—89; owner Beach Point Prodns., 1992—; editor-in-chief L'Avenue Mag., 1998—. Lectr. Miami Dade C.C., cons. Studio Masters, North Miami, 1979-89; writer Lucent Techs., Telephonetics, Algorhythm, Inter-tel, 1997—; creative mktg. dir. Raintree Media, 2000. Prin. works include mixed media, 1974 (Best of Show 1974), pen and ink drawing, 1988 (Best Poster 1988); writer, dir., editor, prodr. (video film) Bif, 1988, Drink + Drive = Die, 1994; scriptwriter (film) The Raft, 1994, (charity video) Rosie O'Donnell, 2002; writer, dir., prodr. (pub. svc. announcement) Reading is the Real Adventure, 1990; film editor Talent Times Mag.; author: Winds of Freedom, 1994; art dir., exec. com. Miami Hispanic Media Conf., 1992, 93, 94; editor-in-chief, film editor: In Grove Miami Mag., 1994-96; webmaster, web content provider, website design cons., writer, graphic artist Guru Comms., 1996; editor-in-chief L'Avenue Mag., Miami Mag., Fla. Journey and Miami Guide, 1998-99, Paladar mag., 2002, Decasa mag., 2002, Flash Animation: Passionate Nomad-A Journey Through Cairo, 2002, Collins Ave. Mag., Markee Mag., 2006; web content provider WEBCOM; webmaster Miami Metro Mag., 2000; sr. editor Channels Intl. Mag., 2001; web site designer, multimedia dir.; creative mktg. dir. Light Sculptor Jim Morrison, 2005. State of Fla. grantee LimeLite Studios, Inc., 1990, William Douglas Pawley Found. grantee, Frances Wolfson scholar, Cultural Consortium grantee, 1993. Mem. Am. Film Inst., Phi Beta Kappa. Avocations: animation, printmaking, skin diving, boating, painting. Personal E-mail: villochk@bellsouth.net.

VILMA, JONATHAN POLYNICE, professional football player; b. Coral Gables, Fla., Apr. 16, 1982; BS in Fin., U. Miami, 2004. Linebacker NY Jets, 2004—07, New Orleans Saints, 2008—. Recipient Ed Block Courage award, 2008; named NFL Defensive Rookie of Yr., 2004; named to Am. Football Conf. Pro Bowl Team, 2005. Office: New Orleans Saints 5800 Airline Dr Metairie LA 70003*

VILSACK, TOM (THOMAS JAMES VILSACK), Secretary of Agriculture, former Governor of Iowa; b. Pitts., Dec. 31, 1950; adopted s. Bud and Dolly Vilsack; m. Ann Christine Bell, Aug. 1973; children: Jess, Doug. BA in History, Hamilton Coll., Clinton, NY, 1972; JD, Albany Law Sch., 1975. Pvt. practice, Mt. Pleasant, Iowa, 1975—87; mayor City of Mt. Pleasant, Iowa, 1987—92; mem. Iowa State Senate from Dist. 49, Des Moines, 1992-98; gov. State of Iowa, Des Moines, 1999—2007; sec. USDA, Washington, 2009—. Chmn. Midwest Gov. Conf., Dem. Gov. Assn.; mem. Nat. Gov. Assn. (exec. com.); vis. prof. Drake U., 2007—; bd. dir. Carnegie Learning Inc., 2007—. Founding mem. & former chmn. Governors Biotechnology Partnership; former chmn. Ethanol Coalition; bd. dir. United Way, Mt. Pleasant; former chmn. Midwest Governor's Conference. Mem. Mt. Pleasant C. of C. (pres.), Rotary (pres.). Democrat. Office: USDA James L Witten Fed Bldg 1400 Independence Ave SW Rm 200-A Washington DC 20250*

VINA, FERNANDO, sportscaster, retired professional baseball player; b. Sacramento, Calif., Apr. 16, 1969; 1 child, Fernando Jr. Attened, Ariz. State Univ., Sacramento City Coll. 2nd baseman Seattle Mariners, 1993—94, N.Y. Mets, 1994—95, Milw. Brewers, 1995—99, St. Louis Cardinals, 2000—03, Detroit Tigers, 2004—05; ret.; analyst, Baseball Tonight ESPN, 2007—, contbr., SportsCenter, ESPNEWS and ESPN Radio. Mem. US Nat. Team, 1989. Active Spl. Olympics Programs. Recipient Gold Glove award, 2001, 2002; named to Nat. League All-Star Team, Maj. League Baseball, 1998. Office: ESPN ESPN Plz Bristol CT 06010*

VINATIERI, ADAM MATTHEW, professional football player; b. Yanktown, SD, Dec. 28, 1972; s. Paul and Judy; m. Valerie Vinatieri. BS in Fitness and Wellness, SD State U. Kicker New Eng. Patriots, 1996—2006, Indpls. Colts, 2006—. Named 1st Team All-Pro, NFL, 2002, 2004; named to Am. Football Conf. Pro-Bowl Team, 2002, 2004. Achievements include being a member of Super Bowl Championship winning: New England Patriots, 2002, 2004, 2005, Indianapolis Colts, 2007; kicking the game winning field goal in Super Bowls XXXVI and XXXVIII, 2002, 2004; leading the NFL in: points scored (141), 2004, field goals made (31), 2004. Office: Indpls Colts 7001 W 56th St Indianapolis IN 46254

VINCENT, ANGELIA ANNETTE, librarian; d. Noley and Helen Vincent. BS in Computer Sci. with emphasis in Bus., U. Ark., Monticello, 1988. Customer svc. rep. Burlington Inc., Monticello, 1984—99; circulation and spl. collections asst. U. Ark. Monticello Fred J. Taylor Libr., 1999—2004, circulation mgr. and libr. supr., 2004—. Youth program dir. Morning Star Missionary Bapt. Ch., Monticello, 2003—. Contbr. articles to profl. jour. Participant Susan B. Komen Race, Little Rock, 1996—2008. Mem.: Ark. Libr. Paraprofls., U. Ark. Monticello African Am. Alumni (African Am. Achievement award 2006). Office: U Ark Monticello Fred J Taylor Libr PO Box 3599 Monticello AR 71656

VINCENT, DAVID RIDGELY, financial consultant; b. Detroit, Aug. 9, 1941; s. Charles Ridgely and Charlotte Jane (McCarroll) Vincent; m. Margaret Helen Anderson, Aug. 25, 1962 (div. 1973); children: Sandra Lee, Cheryl Ann; m. Judith Ann Gomez, July 2, 1978; children: Amber, Jesse Joseph Flores(dec.) 1 stepchild, Micheal Flores Jr. BSBA, Calif. State U., Sacramento, 1964; MBA, Calif. State U., Hayward, 1971; PhD, Somerset U., 1991. Cert. mgmt. cons., chartered retirement planning counselor 2008. Sr. ops. analyst Aerojet Gen. Corp., Sacramento, 1960-66; contr. Hexcel Corp., Dublin, Calif., 1966-70; mng. dir. Memorex, Vienna, 1970-74; sales mgr. Ampex World Ops., Friebourg, Switzerland, 1974-76; dir. product mgmt. NCR, Sunnyvale, Calif., 1976-79; v.p. Boole & Babbage Inc., Sunnyvale, 1979-85; gen. mgr. Inst. Info. Mgmt., Sunnyvale Calif., Calif., 1979-85; pres., CEO The Info. Group, Inc., Santa Clara, Calif., 1985—2005; fin. advisor, dist. mgr. Ameriprise Fin. Svcs., Campbell, Calif., 2005—. Author: Perspectives in Information Management, Information Economics, 1983, Handbook of Information Resource Management, 1987, The Information-Based Corporation: Stakeholder Economics and the Technology Investment, 1990, Reengineering Fundamentals: Business Processes and the Global Economy, 1994—96; contbr. articles to profl. jours. Referee emeritus U.S. Soccer Fedn. Mem.: Inst. for Mgmt. Cons., Product Devel. and Mgmt. Assn., Am. Mktg. Assn., Nat. Investor Rels. Inst., Assn. Fin. Profl., World Future Soc., Soc. Competitive Intelligence Profl., Am. Electronics Assn., Nat. Alliance Bus. Econ., Silicon Valley Roundtable, Soc. Info. Mgmt. (treas.), Knights of Columbus (4th degree). Home: 2803 Kalliam Dr Santa Clara CA 95051-6838 Office: Ameriprise Fin Svcs Inc 1919 S Bascom Ave Campbell CA 95008 Office Phone: 408-963-2372. Business E-Mail: david.r.vincent@ampf.com.

VINCENT, DEBORAH, nursing educator; b. Ny; m. James Maluta. PhD, U. Mich., Ann Arbor. Adult nurse practitioner, ANCC. Assoc. prof. U. Ariz., Tucson, 2004—. Fellow, Amercian Acad. of Nurse Practitioners, 2004. Office: Univ of Ariz 1305 N Martin Tucson AZ 85721 Business E-Mail: dvincent@nursing.arizona.edu.

VINCENT, FRANCIS THOMAS, JR., (FAY VINCENT), former baseball commissioner; b. Waterbury, Conn., May 29, 1938; s. Francis Thomas and Alice (Lynch) V.; m. Valerie McMahon, July 3, 1965; children: Anne, William, Edward. BA cum laude, Williams Coll., 1960; LLB, Yale U., 1963. Bar: Conn. 1963, N.Y. 1964, D.C. 1969. Assoc. Whitman & Ransom, NYC, 1963-68; ptnr. Caplin & Drysdale, Washington, 1968-78; assoc. dir. div. corp. fin. SEC, Washington, 1978; pres., chief exec. officer Columbia Pictures Industries, Inc., NYC, 1978-83, chmn., chief exec. officer, 1983-87; pres., chief exec. officer entertainment bus. sect. The Coca-Cola Co., NYC, 1987; dep. commr., chief oper. officer Major League Baseball, NYC, 1989, commr., 1989-92; pres. New England Collegiate Baseball League, 1998—2003. Non-exec. dir. Westfield Am. Mgmt. Ltd., 2002—; bd. dir. Time Warner, Inc, 1993—2008. Author: The Last Commissioner, 2002, The Only Game in Town: Baseball Stars of the 1930s and 1940s Talk About the Game They Loved, 2006, We Would Have Played for Nothing, 2008. Trustee Williams Coll., 1970-88, Hotchkiss Sch., 1975—, Carleton Coll., 1988—. Mem. NY Athletic Club, Belle Haven Club, Phi Beta Kappa. Clubs: University, Belle Haven. Roman Catholic.

VINCENT, HAL WELLMAN, retired military officer, investor; b. Pontiac, Mich., Sept. 27, 1927; s. Harold and Glenda (Wellman) V.; m. Virginia Bayler, June 9, 1951; children: David B., Dale W., Deborah K. Vincent. Student, Navy V-5 program Western Mich. Coll./Colgate U., 1945; BS in Engring., U.S. Naval Acad., 1950; postgrad., Marine Officers Basic Sch., 1950, Flight Sch., 1952, Test Pilot Sch., 1955, Navy Fleet Air Gunnery Sch., 1958, Air Force Fighter Weapons Sch., 1959, Marine Corps Command and Staff Coll., 1964, Indsl. Coll., 1969, Marine Air Weapons Tng. Unit, 1972. Commd. 2d lt. U.S. Marine Corps, 1950, advanced through grades to maj. gen., 1974; rifle and machinegun platoon comdr. Camp Lejeune, NC, 1951; fighter pilot El Toro, Calif., 1953-54, Republic of Korea, 1953—54; test pilot Flight Test Div., Patuxent River, Md., 1955-57; ops. officer, squadron asst. and fighter pilot El Toro, 1958-59; conventional weapons project test pilot Naval Air Weapons Test Ctr., China Lake, Calif., 1960-62; squadron ops. and exec. officer El Toro and Japan, 1962-64; aviation specialist Marine Corps amphibious warfare presentation team and staff officer Quantico, Va., 1965-66; comdg. officer 2d Marine Aircraft Wing fighter-attack squadron, Beaufort, SC, 1967-68; exec. officer Marine Aircraft Group, Vietnam, 1969; logistics staff officer Fleet Marine Force Pacific, Hawaii, 1970-72; comdg. officer Marine Aircraft Group, Yuma, Ariz., 1972-73; chief of staff 3d Marine Aircraft Wing, El Toro, 1973-76; dep. chief of staff plans and policy to Comdr. in Chief Atlantic, Norfolk, Va., 1976-78; comdg. gen. 2d Marine Aircraft Wing, Cherry Point, NC, 1978-80; dep. comdg. gen. Fleet Marine Force Atlantic, Norfolk, 1980-81; ret., 1981; pvt. investor, 1981—. Weapons test pilot; preliminary pilot, evaluator new mil. aircraft. Contbr. numerous articles on tactics and conventional weapons delivery, flight test stability and control to various mil. publs. Decorated Legion of Merit with 2 gold stars, D.F.C., Bronze Star with combat V, Air medal with star and numeral 14, Honor medal 1st class, Cross of Gallantry with gold star (Republic of Vietnam); recipient Wright Bros. Master Pilot award, 2005. Mem. SAR, Soc. Exptl. Test Pilots, Early Pioneer Naval Aviators, Marine Corps Aviation Assn., Mach 2 Club, Marbella Country Club. Achievements include invention of triple ejector rack for delivery of conventional bombs, 1961; devel. of fighter tactics in F8 and F4 aircraft, 1958-69; flew 165 models of fgn. and U.S. mil. aircraft; flew 8 models of fixed wing and helicopters on 242 combat missions; first Marine to fly MACH-2; pilot for 62 years recruted to join the early pioneer naval aviation (Golden Eagles) in 1980, while on duty as CG2MAW. Home Phone: 949-240-8073. Personal E-mail: hwvincent@webtv.net. *In all 36 years in the service I am convinced that war is bad, and little is accomplished in the long term by warfare. However when National policy dictates a war, then we must not limit what can be done. We must win! My thought "Winning isn't everything, it's the only thing!" When I must go to battle I want to be allowed to "fight to win".*

VINCENT, HEATHER KETELAAR, physiologist, educator; married. MS, U. Mass., Amherst, 1995; PhD, U. Fla., Gainesville, 1999; Postdoctorate, U. Va., Charlottesville, 2005. Faculty Stetson U., Deland, Fla., 1999—2003, U. Va., 2006—07, U. Fla., 2006—. Grantee, Internal Grant Stetson U., 2001—02, NIH GCRC, NCCAM, 2003—06, AMRPA, 2006—08. Mem.: Am. Heart Assn., Sigma XI, Am. Acad. Phys. Medicine & Rehab., Am. Coll. Sports Medicine. Achievements include research in physiological & psychosocial effects of exercise and physical rehabilitation in clinical populations such as obesity, heart disease & cancer. Office: Univ FL PO Box 112727 Gainesville FL 32611-2727 Office Fax: 352-273-7388. Business E-Mail: vincehk@ortho.ufl.edu.

VINCENT, JAMES LOUIS, biotechnology company executive; b. Johnstown, Pa., Dec. 15, 1939; s. Robert Clyde and Marietta Lucille (Kennedy) V.; m. Elizabeth M. Matthews, Aug. 19, 1961 (div. 1998); children: Aimee Archelle, Christopher James; m. Joyce Anne Fitzgibbons, Dec. 30, 1999 (div. 2002). BSME, Duke U., 1961; MBA in Indsl. Mgmt., U. Pa., 1963; DBA (hon.), U. New Haven, 1998. Mgr. Far East divsn. Tex. Instruments, Inc., Tokyo, 1970—72; pres. Tex. Instrument Asia, Ltd., Tokyo, 1970—72; v.p. diagnostic ops., pres. diagnostics div. Abbott Labs., North Chgo., Ill., 1972—74, group v.p., bd. dirs., 1974—81, exec. v.p., COO, bd. dirs., 1979—81; corp. group v.p., pres. Allied Health and Sci. Products Co. Allied Corp., Morristown, NJ, 1982—85; CEO Biogen, Inc., Cambridge, Mass., 1985—97, 1999—2000, chmn. bd., 1997—2002; ret., 2002. Trustee Duke U., Com. for Econ. Devel.; bd. dirs. Alnylam Pharms. Recipient Young Exec. Achievement Young Execs. Club, Chgo., 1976, Disting. Alumni award Duke U., 1988, Biotech. award Wall St. Transcript, 1997. Mem. Mass. Bus. Roundtable, The Comml. Club Boston, Algonquin Club Boston, The Links (N.Y.C.). Republican. Presbyterian.

VINCENT, JENNIFER A., economics professor, consultant; b. Poughkeepsie, NY, Aug. 8, 1970; d. Francis P. and Marjorie A. Hetling; m. Jeffrey M. Vincent, Oct. 10, 1998; children: Grace Mae, Sadie Anne, Elijah Thomas children: Claire Eleanor. BS in Indsl. and Labor Rels., Cornell U., Ithaca, NY, 1992; MA in Economics, PhD in Economics, U. Colo., Boulder, 1998. Adj. prof. economics St. Michael's Coll., Colchester, Vt., 1998—2001, Vt. Tech. Coll., Burlington, 2001—03, U. Vt., Burlington, 2003—05; asst. prof. economics Champlain Coll., Burlington, 2005—, core devel. team mem., 2005—. Contbr. articles. V.p. Overlake Day Sch., Southern Burlington, 2002—08. Achievements include first to Interdisciplinary Curriculum Design. Avocations: reading, travel. Office: Champlain Coll 163 Southern Willard St Burlington VT 05401 Business E-Mail: jvincent@champlain.edu.

VINCENT, JIM, performing company executive; b. NJ; m. France Nguyen; children: Lena, Claire, June. Studied at, Wash. Sch. of Ballet, Harkness House of Ballet, N.C. Sch. of the Arts. Profl. dancer Nacho Duato's Compania Nacional de Danza in Spain; asst. artistic dir. Compania Nacional de Danza, 1990—94; ballet master, repetitor Lyon Opera Ballet, 1994—97; concept designer, show dir. Disneyland Paris, 1997—2000; artistic dir. Hubbard St. Dance Chgo., 2000—09; profl. dancer Nederlands Dans Theater, 1978—90, artistic dir., 2009—. Ballet master Nederlands Dans Theater II, Compa a Nacional de Danza, Opera National de Lyon. Office: Netherlands Dance Theater Postbus 333 2501 CH The Hague Netherlands*

VINCENT, KEVIN ROBERT, physician, educator; MD, U. Fla., Gainesville, PhD, 2003. Lic. in med. Fla., 2007. Asst. prof. U. Fla., 2007—, med. dir.; asst. prof. divsn. physical medicine & rehab. Coll. Medicine Applied Physiology & Kinesiology; dir. running medicine clinic Dept. Orthop. Rehab. Office: Univ Fla PO Box 112727 Gainesville FL 32611 Office Phone: 352-273-7461. E-mail: kvincent@ufl.edu.

VINCENT, MARK See DIESEL, VIN

VINCENT, NORMAN FULLER, broadcast executive; b. Boston, Oct. 5, 1930; s. Norman Harrison and Marian Bernice (Fuller) V.; m. Karen Ann Walter, June 21, 1969. BA, Denison U., 1953. Sales mgr. Sta. WMBR, Jacksonville, Fla., 1956-62; gen. mgr. Sta. WZOK, Jacksonville, 1962-66; owner, pres. Norm Vincent Sound Recording Studios, Inc., Jacksonville, 1966-75; dir. radio ops. Sta. WJCT, Jacksonville, 1975-91; announcer, narrator radio, TV film and video, talking books, 1976—. Producer, host (radio): Swing Time with Norm Vincent, 1992—. Served with USN, 1953-56; to comdr. USNR, 1958-80. Mem.: Navy League, Exch. Club, Sigma Alpha Epsilon. Republican. Episcopalian. Home: 2110 The Woods Dr Jacksonville FL 32246-1016 Office Phone: 904-221-5218. Personal E-mail: vincentswing@aol.com.

VINCENT, NORMAN L., retired insurance company executive; b. Milw., July 21, 1933; s. Victor V. Vincent and Hilda I. (Boedecker) Vincent Patlow; m. Arlene Page, Jan. 31, 1953 (div. 1978); children: J. Todd, Meg; m. Donna Jean Doll, Aug. 8, 1980. BS, U. Wis., 1957; MS, Purdue U., 1958, PhD, 1960. Diplomate Am. Bd. Profl. Psychology; registered psychologist., Ill., C.P.C.U., C.L.U. Supr. agy. research State Farm Ins. Cos., Bloomington, Ill., 1960-63, dir. agy. research., 1963-66, asst. v.p. agy., 1966-69, asst. v.p. exec., 1969-70, v.p. data processing, 1970-94; systems v.p., 1994-95. Pres. Bloomington Bd. Edn., 1974-77; bd. dirs. YMCA, Bloomington, 1971-85. Served with M.I. U.S. Army, 1953-55. Mem. AAAS Home: W332 N 5861 Meadowlark Ct Nashotah WI 53058-9528

VINCENT, RICHARD C., communications educator, researcher; b. Allentown, Pa., Mar. 1, 1949; s. Charles L. and Elizabeth A. Vincent; m. Christine LaCaruba, Jan. 29, 1971; children: Marisa Claire, Marielle Bryce. BA, Mansfield U., 1972; MA, Temple U., 1977; PhD, U. Mass., Amherst, 1983. Instr. Slippery Rock U., Pa., 1979—81; asst. prof. Western Ill. U., Macomb, 1981—83, So. Ill. U., Carbondale, 1983—86; assoc. prof. U. Hawaii-Manoa, Honolulu, 1986—2001; chairperson dept. comm. Ind. State U., Terre Haute, 2001—04, prof., 2005—. Author: Financial Characteristics of Selected B Film Productions of Albert J. Cohen, 1980, Global Glasnost: Toward a New International Information/Communication Order?, 1992, U.S. Glasnost: Missing Political Themes in U.S. Media Discourse, 2004; editor: Towards Equity in Global Communication: MacBride Report Update, 1999; supervisory editor: International Communication Book Series, 1994—; contbr. chapters to books, articles to profl. jours. Chartered mem. Honolulu Cmty. Media Coun., 1999—2001; del. UN & ITU's World Summit on Info. Soc., Geneva, Tunis, 2003—05. Fulbright scholar, U.S. State Dept., USIA, Dublin (Ireland) City U., 1994—95. Mem.: HCMC Freedom of Info. Day (assoc.; co-chair 2000—01), MacBride Round Table (assoc.; pres. and past pres. 1994—2000), Broadcast Edn. Assn. (assoc.; internat. divsn. rsch. chair 2006—), Am. Edn. in Journalism and Mass Comm. (assoc.; internat. divsn. sec. 2001—02, internat. divsn. rsch. chair 2002—03), Internat. Comm. Assn. (assoc.), Nat. Comm. Assn. (assoc.), Internat. Assn. Mass Comm. Rschrs. (assoc.), Union for Dem. Comm. (assoc.). Achievements include research in mass media, information and communication technologies, and international communication. Avocations: photography, travel. Office: Indiana State U Comm Dept 217 N 6th St Terre Haute IN 47809 Office Fax: 812-237-3217. Business E-Mail: rvincent@indstate.edu.

VINCENT, SAM (JAMES SAMUEL VINCENT), former professional basketball coach, former professional basketball player; b. Lansing, Mich., May 18, 1963; Grad., Mich. State U., East Lansing, 1985. Guard Boston Celtics, 1985—87, Seattle SuperSonics, 1987—88, Chgo. Bulls, 1988—89, Orlando Magic, 1989—92; spl. advisor to v.p. Reggie Williams Disney Wide World of Sports, 1992—93; head coach Cape Town Kings, South Africa, 1996—99, Greek A-2 Men's Basketball League, Larissa, Greece, 1999—2000, A1 Dutch League Canoe Jeans, Den Bosch, Netherlands, NBA Devel. League Ft. Worth Flyers, 2005—06; asst. coach Dallas Mavericks, 2006—07; head coach Charlotte Bobcats, 2007—08. Head coach Men's and Women's South African Sr. Nat. Teams, 1999, Nigerian Women's Nat. Team; head coach Nigerian Nat. Team FIBA (Internat. Basketball Fedn.) World Championship, 2006. Achievements include winning a FIBA (International Basketball Federation) Championship as head coach of the Nigerian Women's National Team, 2003.

VINCENT, SHARON ELAINE, nursing educator; m. David Vincent; children: Daniel, Hannah. MS in Nursing, U. So. Miss, Hattiesburg, 0200. Cert. CNOR, Am. Assoc. Oper. Rm. Nurses. Nurse instr. U. Southern. Ms; RN Forrest Gen. Hosp. Contbr. chapters to books. Office: Univ Southern Miss 118 College Dr #5095 Hattiesburg MS 39406-0001 Office Fax: 601-266-6643. Business E-Mail: sharon.vincent@usm.edu.

VINCENT, THOMAS JAMES, retired manufacturing executive; b. Balt., Mar. 17, 1934; s. Thomas Alonzo and Helen Geraldine (Cloman) V.; divorced; children: Wayne S. MS, MIT, 1968. Div. gen. mgr. Fairchild Industries, St. Augustine, Fla., 1969-72; pres. T.J. Vincent Properties Ltd., St. Augustine, 1972-75, Pacific Concrete & Rock Co., Honolulu, 1975-77, Ramsey Engring. Co., St. Paul, 1977-80, Kobe Inc., LA, 1980-84, Milchem Inc., Houston, 1984-85, York (Pa.) Internat. Corp., 1985-88, also bd. dirs., cons.; chmn., CEO Hawaii Seafood Growers, Inc., Kahuku, 1990-92. Author: Fairplan, 1962; publ.: In the Name of the Boss Upstairs, The Father Ray Brennan Story, 2004; prodr. (film) Legacy of Father Ray, 2009. Founder, pres. Thomas J. Vincent Found. Inc., Kaneohe, Hawaii, 1990—; founder, v.p., treas. Winter Park (Fla.) Family Health Ctr., Inc., 1995—. Named one of Outstanding Young Men in Am., Jaycees, 1965; Alfred P. Sloan fellow MIT, 1967; recipient Rsch. for Progress Achievement award, 1972. Avocations: deep sea fishing, orchid growing. Home and Office: 44-447 Kanoehe Bay Dr Kaneohe HI 96744

VINCENTI, GENE A., director, consultant; b. Elizabeth, NJ, Oct. 2, 1949; s. Charles and Lucy (Diange) Vincenti; m. Regina Abrantes, July 10, 1971; children: Michael James, Jason Luis. BA, Rutgers U., Newark, 1971, MBA, 1973; Cert., Harvard Grad. Sch. Edn., Cambridge, Mass., 1990. Student asst. Kean U., Union, NJ, 1968—71, offsite program mgr. Boonton, NJ, 1971; budget resource officer Rutgers U., New Brunswick, NJ, 1973—76, asst. provost, 1973—76, Newark, 1976—80, assoc. provost, 1980—2003, exec. v.p. adminstrn., 2003—08, exec. vice chancellor, 2008—. Interfunctional and team cons. Rutgers U., 1972; mem. Newark Regional Bus. Partnership, Evaluator Mid. States, 1980—; mem. gov.'s mgmt. improvement agy. State of N.J., Trenton, 1982; evaluator Middle States Assn., Phila., 1985. Many other church, state and county roles; lector, Eucharistic minister, pres. parish coun. St. Thomas More Ch., Manalapan, 1989—2003; trustee Univ. Heights Sci. Park, Newark, 1990—; mem. Recreation Commn., Manalapan, NJ, 1994—2001, chmn.., 1996—2001. Recipient Bus. Ptnrship award, N.J. Transit, 1987; grantee, N.J. Commn. on Higher Edn., 1995. Mem.: Am. Planning Assn., Nat. Assn. Coll. and Univ. Bus. Officers, Internat. Econ. Devel. Coun. Roman Catholic. Avocations: baseball, basketball, travel. Home: 15 Mt Stream Ct Barnegat NJ 08005 Office: Rutgers Univ Ste 590 123 Washington St Newark NJ 07102 Office Phone: 973-353-5541. Business E-Mail: gav@newark.rutgers.edu.

VINCENTI, WALTER GUIDO, aeronautical engineer, emeritus educator; b. Balt., Apr. 20, 1917; s. Guido A. and Agnes (Nicolini) V.; m. Joyce H. Weaver, Sept. 6, 1947; children— Margaret Anna, Marc Guido. AB, Stanford U., 1938, Aero. Engr., 1940. Aero. research scientist NACA, 1940-57; prof. aero. and astronautics and history of tech. Stanford U., 1957-83, prof. emeritus, 1983—. Cons. to industry, 1957—; mem. adv. panel engring. sec. NSF, 1960-63. Author: (with Charles H. Kruger, Jr.) Introduction to Physical Gas Dynamics, 1965, (with Nathan Rosenberg) The Britannia Bridge, 1978, What Engineers Know and How They Know It, 1990; also papers.; co-editor (with Milton Van Dyke) Annual Review of Fluid Mechanics, 1970-76. Served with USN, 1945-46. Recipient Gold medal Pi Tau Sigma, 1948, Engr.-Historian award ASME, 1997; Rockefeller Pub. Service award, 1956; Guggenheim fellow, 1963 Fellow AIAA; mem. Internat. Acad. Astronautics (corr.), Soc. History Tech. (Usher prize 1984, Leonardo da Vinci medal 1998), Nat. Acad. Engring., Phi Beta Kappa, Sigma Xi, Tau Beta Pi. Home: 555 Byron St #306 Palo Alto CA 94301 Office: Stanford U Stanford CA 94305 Home Phone: 650-328-1815. Business E-Mail: sts@stanford.edu.

VINE, BARBARA See RENDELL, RUTH

VINE, HOWARD A., lobbyist, lawyer; BA, American U., 1975; JD, George Mason U., 1978. Bar: DC, Va. Asst. v.p. Nat. Assn. Mfrs.; sr. assoc. Vorys, Sater, Seymour and Pease LLP; sr. v.p., dir. internat. trade, head bus. devel. The Jefferson Group; founder, former mng. shareholder DC office Greenberg Traurig, LLP; ptnr. Pub. Policy & Law Practice Dickstein Shapiro LLP, Washington, 2003—. Chair Clinton/Gore transition team; mem. exec. coun. Policy Roundtable, Dem. Leadership Council. Bd. dirs. Nat. Jewish Dem. Coun., Faith in Am., Nat. Music Ctr. Mus. and Found. Named one of 50 Top Lobbyists, Washingtonian mag., 2007. Mem.: ABA. Office: Dickstein Shapiro LLP 1825 Eye St NW Washington DC 20006-5403 E-mail: vineh@dicksteinshapiro.com.

VINE, KIMBERLY ANN, public relations executive; d. Henry Bynum and Linda Suggs; m. John Edward Vine, Mar. 17, 1996; children: Jordan, Sydney. BS, Tex. A&M U., College Station, 1993. Lic. recreation & parks, tourism sciences Tex., 1993. Dist. mgr. ADP, Houston, 1994—97, San Deigo, Calif., 1997—98, Parsippany, NJ, 1998; v.p. Dermatology and Skin Surgery Ctr., Princeton, NJ, 2000—06; pub. rels., fundraising U. Princeton Hosp., 2000—06. Com. mem. Nat. Jr. Tennis League Trenton, NJ, 1998—2007; chair, ann. tennis fundraiser Princeton HealthCare Systems, 2004—06. Recipient Cryan award, USTA, 2006. Mem.: Pretty Brook Tennis Club (life; bd. dirs. 2007, sports dir. 2007). Avocations: tennis, travel, art. Personal E-mail: kimberlyvine@earthlink.net.

VINEGRAD, ALAN, prosecutor; Grad. magna cum laude, U. Pa, 1980; JD, NYU, 1984. Bar: NY, practice before: US Ct. Appeals (2nd and 3rd Cirs.), US Dist. Cts. (Eastern and So. Dist., NY). Staff acct. Price Waterhouse & Co.; clerk for Hon. Leonard B. Sand US Dist. Ct. (So. Dist.), NY, student law clerk for the Hon. Naomi Reice Buchwald; private practice Meister Leventhal & Slade, 1985—90; chief of general crimes US Atty. Office, Brooklyn, NY, 1990—94, chief of civil rights litig., 1994—97, dep. chief of the criminal divsn., 1999, chief of the criminal divsn., chief asst. US atty.; interim US Atty. US Atty. Office, Eastern Dist., New York, 2001; ptnr., white collar def. and trial practice groups Covington & Burling, NY. Adj. prof. New York Law Sch., 1996—; guest lectr. Brooklyn Law Sch., Cardoza Sch. Law, Fordham Law Sch., Hofstra Law Sch., New York U. Law Sch., Yale Law Sch., Dept. Justice's Office of Legal Edn. Sr. editor NYU Law Review, bd. editor NY Law Journal; contbr. articles to profl. jours. and reviews. Bd. dir. Legal Aid Soc. Recipient Atty. Gen. award for Distinguished Service, Stimson Medal for Outstanding Prosecutor, US Atty. Office for Eastern Dist. of NY, Henry L. Stimson medal, Assn. Bar of City NY, 1993, Atty. General's award for Disting. Svc., 1997. Mem.: Fed. Bar Coun. (bd. trustee, chmn., com. on 2nd cir. cts.). Office: Covington & Burling 620 8th Ave Fl 42 New York NY 10018-1572 Office Phone: 212-841-1000. Business E-Mail: avinegrad@cov.com.

VINENT-CANTORAL, AIDA R., mediator; b. Havana, Cuba, Nov. 8, 1948; arrived in U.S., 1959; d. Roberto M. Vinent and Carmen; m. Ennio Cantoral, Dec. 26, 1979 (div. 1981); 1 child, Alfredo Cantoral. BA, Alverno Coll., Milw., 1969; MA, Marquette U., Milw., 1971, cert. dispute resolution, 1998; cert. negotiating labor agreements, Harvard U., Cambridge, Mass., 2000, U. Mich., 2002, Northwestern U., Evanston, Ill.; cert. mediation sys. design, U. Tex.; postgrad., U. So. Tex. Coll. Law, 2004, Fed. Mediation and Conciliation Inst., 2004. Family health asst. Milwaukee County Dept. Human Svcs. & Hosp., 1975—; human svcs. case coord. Milwaukee County Dept. Human Svcs. and Hosp., 1998—; mediator pvt. practice Milw., 1979—; mediator Milwaukee County Family Ct., 1998—, USPS, 1998—, Bus. to Bus., 1998—, CHIPS, 1997, Wis. Spl. Edn. Mediation Sys., 2001—; case mgr. Milw. Co. Disability Svs., 1996—. Cons. in field. Active ACR, 1998—, Wis. Assn. Homicide Investigators, 2000—; parent educator Centro Legal, Milw., 1998—. Named Human Svcs. Worker of Yr., Wis. Foster Parents, 1980. Mem.: Wis. Coun. Problem Gambling, Wis. Assn. Mediators. Republican. Address: PO Box 462 Greendale WI 53129-0462 Office Phone: 414-550-8772. E-mail: avinent@aol.com.

VINER-BROWN, SAMARA I., public health administrator; b. Providence, Dec. 14, 1958; d. Robert J. and Doris S. McGarry; m. Peter C. Viner-Brown, Apr. 25, 1982; 1 child, Tristan C. BA, Smith Coll., Northampton, Mass., 1980; MS, Harvard Sch. Pub. Health, Boston, 1985. Chief, data & evaluation RI Dept. Health, Providence, 1991—2008, chief, ctr. health data, analysis, 2008—. Bd. mem. RI Chpt. Mar. Dimes, Providence, 1995—; exec. com. mem. Nat. Birth Defects Prevention Network, Tex., 2004—, pres., 2008—. Recipient Vol. Action award, All Children's Theater, 2003. Avocations: running, swimming, travel, theater. Office: RI Dept Health 3 Capitol Hill Rm 407 Providence RI 02908 Business E-Mail: samara.viner-brown@health.ri.gov.

VINES, JIM (JAMES K.), lawyer, former prosecutor; b. Dec. 1959; BS in Acctg., Washington & Lee U., 1981, JD, 1988. Law clk. to Hon. Robert R. Merhige, US Dist. Ct.; law clk. to Chief Justice William H. Rehnquist, US Supreme Ct., 1989—90; assoc. King & Spalding LLP, Atlanta, 1990—93; exec. dir., gen. counsel for environ. affairs Bridgestone/Firestone, Nashville, 1993—2000; ptnr. Baker, Donelson, Bearman & Caldwell, Nashville, 2000—02; US atty. (mid. dist.) Tenn. US Dept. Justice, Nashville, 2002—06; ptnr. King & Spaulding LLP, Washington, 2006—. Adj. prof. environ. law Vanderbilt U. Mem.: Tenn. Bar Assn., Ga. Bar Assn. Office: King & Spalding LLP 1700 Pennsylvania Ave NW Ste 200 Washington DC 20006 E-mail: jvines@kslaw.com.

VINES, JOHN R., career military officer; BS, U. Ala.; MA, Naval War Coll. Advanced through grades to lt. gen. US Army, 2003; with 3rd Infantry Divsn., US Army Europe & Seventh Army, Ranger Dept. US Army Infantry Ctr., Ft. Benning, Ga.; comdr., specialist 1st Ranger Batallion, Hunter Army Airfield, Ga.; exec. officer 3rd Ranger Battalion, Ft. Benning, Ga., 1984—87; numerous command and staff positions Ft. Bragg, 1987—2000; comdr. 82nd Airborne Divsn., 2000—02, Coalition Task Force 82, 2002—03, Combined/Joint Task Force-180, Bagram, Afghanistan, 2003, XVIII Airborne Corps, Ft. Bragg, NC, 2003—, Multi-Nat. Corps-Operation Iraqi Freedom, Iraq, 2005—06. Decorated Def. Disting. Svc. medal, DSM, Def. Superior Svc. medal, Bronze Star (with Oak Leaf cluster), Combat Infantry Badge, Master Parachutist Badge (with Bronze Svc. Star), Pathfinder Badge, Ranger Tab.

VINGOE, D. GRANT, lawyer; b. 1957; BA, U. Toronto, Can., 1979; LLB, Osgoode Hall, Toronto, 1981; LLM, NYU, 1984. Bar: Ontario, Canada 1983, NY 1985. Counsel Toronto Stock Exchange, 1984—85; assoc. Kramer, Levin, Naftalis & Frankel, 1986—93, ptnr., 1994—96; ptnr., corp. dept. Dorsey & Whitney LLP, NYC, 1996—2004; ptnr., cross-border securities, fin. services regulation Arnold & Porter, NYC, 2004. Securities adv. com. Ontario Securities Commn., 1999—2001; bd. dir. Mkt. Regulation Services, Inc., Toronto, ON, Canada, 2004—. Mem.: ABA, Securities Industry Assn., Canadian Bar Assn., Canadian Soc. of NY, Americas Soc. Office: Arnold & Porter LLP 399 Park Ave New York NY 10022-4690 Office Phone: 212-715-1130. Office Fax: 212-715-1399. Business E-Mail: Grant_Vingoe@aporter.com.

VINIAR, DAVID ALAN, diversified financial services company executive; b. July 19, 1955; BS summa cum laude in Econs., Union Coll., 1976; MBA, Harvard U., 1980. Joined The Goldman Sachs Group, Inc., 1980, ptnr., 1992-96, mng. dir., 1992—94, dep. CFO, 1994—98, exec. v.p., CFO, 1999—, head, fin. divsn. and co-head credit risk mgmt. and adv. and firm wide risk, 2001—02; head ops., tech. & fin. divsn. The Goldman Sachs Group, Inc., 2002—. Bd. trustees Union Coll. Mem. bd. trustees Union Coll. Recipient CFO Excellence Award for Risk Management, CFO mag., 2001. Office: The Goldman Sachs Group Inc 85 Broad St New York NY 10004*

VINIKAS, VINCENT, historian, educator; b. Erie, Pa., Mar. 29, 1951; s. Matthias Vytautas Vinikas and Eva Aldona Damarodas. BA magna cum laude, Pa. State U., 1972; MA, Columbia U., 1974, PhD, 1983. Asst. prof. U. Ark., Little Rock, 1983—89, assoc. prof., 1989—98, prof., 1998—. Inst. fellow NEH, Ariz. State U., Tempe, 1984; conferee Newberry Libr., Smithsonian Instn., Washington, 1985; inst. fellow NEH, U. N.C., 1993; vis. prof. Karl Franzens U., Graz, Styria, Austria, 1994; inst. fellow NEH, Columbia U., NY, 1998; referee/cons. St. Martin's Press, Prentice-Hall, McGraw-Hill, Houghton-Mifflin, Wadsworth. Author: (monograph) Soft Soap Hard Sell: American Hygiene in an Age of Advertisement; reviewer: Am. Hist. Rev., Jour. So. History, Jour. Social History, Jour. Econ. History, The Historian, Tech. and Culture, Ark. Hist. Quar., Jour. Am. History; contbr. articles to profl. jours.; conferee Sandage Symposium, U. Ill, 2000. Mem. ACLU, Gurdjieff Found. of Ark., Little Rock. Recipient Rsch. award, U. Ark., 1984, 1996; Pres.'s fellow, Columbia U., 1974-1975. Mem.: Am. Hist. Assn., Ark. Assn. of Coll. History Tchrs. (Biennial Essay Award 1993), Phi Alpha Theta (advisor Iota Zeta chpt.), Phi Kappa Phi (exec. bd. chpt. 134 1989—92), Phi Beta Kappa. Avocations: duplicate bridge, wilderness camping, boating. Home: 3312 W Capitol Ave Little Rock AR 72205 Office: Univ Ark History Dept Little Rock AR 72204 Office Fax: 501-569-3059. Business E-Mail: vxvinikas@ualr.edu.

VINING, (GEORGE) JOSEPH, law educator; b. Fulton, Mo., Mar. 3, 1938; s. D. Rutledge and Margaret (McClanahan) V.; m. Alice Marshall Williams, Sept. 18, 1965; children: George Joseph IV, Spencer Carter. BA, Yale U., 1959, Cambridge U., 1961, MA, 1970; JD, Harvard U., 1964. Bar: DC 1965. Atty. Office Dep. Atty. Gen., Dept. Justice, Washington, 1965; asst. to exec. dir. Nat. Crime Commn., 1966; assoc. Covington and Burling, Washington, 1966-69; asst. prof. law U. Mich., 1969-72, assoc. prof., 1972-74, prof., 1974-85, Hutchins prof., 1985—.

Sir Edward Youde prof., Hong Kong, 2002. Author: Legal Identity, 1978, The Authoritative and the Authoritarian, 1986, From Newton's Sleep, 1995, The Song Sparrow and the Child, 2004. NEH sr. fellow, 1982-83, Bellagio fellow Rockfeller Found., 1997. Fellow Am. Acad. Arts and Scis.; mem. ABA, D.C. Bar Assn., Am. Law Inst. (life), Century Assn., Clare Hall Cambridge U. (life). Office: U Mich 964 Legal Rsch Ann Arbor MI 48109-1215

VINJE, THOMAS C., lawyer; b. Seattle, 1954; BA summa cum laude, U. Wash., 1977; JD, Columbia U., 1982. Bar: Hawaii 1983, Calif. 1996, Brussels (fgn. mem.) 1996, Eng. and Wales 2006. Law clk. to Hon. Martin Pence US Dist. Ct., Dist. Hawaii; law clk. to Hon. Edmund Palmieri US Dist. Ct., (So. Dist.) NY; assoc. Morrison & Foerster LLP, San Francisco, 1983—89, mng. ptnr. Brussels, 1989; ptnr. Clifford Chance LLP, Brussels, 2004—. Co-founder European Com. on Interoperable Sys. (ECIS), 1989; mem. faculty of law U. Namur, Belgium; lectr. internat. bus. law U. Zurich. Chair US bd. editors Droit de l'Informatique et des Télécoms, bd. editors Computer und Recht, Computer Law and Security Report; editor: Computer und Recht Internat.; contbr. articles to profl. jours. Mem.: Licensing Exec. Soc. Internat. Office: Clifford Chance LLP Ave Louise 65 1050 Brussels Belgium E-mail: thomas.vinje@cliffordchance.com.

VINKEY, RACHEL BURDICK, psychiatrist; b. Rochester, NY, Aug. 13, 1965; d. Victor Fowler and Karen Farney Vinkey; m. Shriram Krishnan, July 5, 1996; 1 child, Anya Vinkey Kirshnan. BA, U. Chgo., 1988; MD, SUNY, 1997. Resident Harvard/Cambridge Hosp., Mass., 2001; clin. instr. U. Calif., San Francisco, 2001—03, asst. clin. prof., 2003—; pvt. practice psychiatrist Oakland, 2004—; assoc. psychiatrist U. Calif. Student Health, Berkeley, 2004—05. Contbr. chapters to books. Scholar, U. Chgo., 1983, Bklyn. Psych. Soc. award, 1997. Mem.: APA, No. Calif. Psychol. Soc. Avocations: running, painting, poetry. Office Phone: 510-368-1884.

VINNAKOTA, BAPESWARA-RAO VENKATA, engineering educator; b. Dowleswaram, Rajahmundry, Andhra Pradesh, India, Aug. 3, 1940; s. Bapiraju and Sundaramma Vinnakota; m. Devi Subhadra Palagummi, Feb. 19, 1965; children: Bapiraju, Neeraja Venkata. PhD, Indian Inst. Tech., Madras, 1970. Faculty Indian Inst. Tech., Chennai, Tamil Nadu, 1963—86, ND State U., Fargo, 1986—. Contbr. articles to profl. jours. Home: 81 32 Ave NE Fargo ND 58102 Office: ND State Univ Fargo ND 58105 Business E-Mail: bapeswara.rao@ndsu.edu.

VINOGRADOV, SERGUEI V., medical educator; b. Moscow City, Sept. 7, 1951; s. Vladimir N. Vinogradov and Kaleria S. Sokolova; m. Irina A. Kozlova, Apr. 5, 1985 (div. July 20, 1998); m. Irina I. Murogina, Jan. 19, 1974 (div. Nov. 15, 1984); children: Samuel S., Elena S. Vinogradova, Denis S.; m. Elena V. Batrakova, Jan. 11, 2001 (div. Oct. 29, 2008). MS in Chemistry, Moscow State U., 1973; PhD, Russian Acad. Sci., Moscow, 1978. Rschr. Inst. Bio Organic Chemistry, Moscow, 1978—88; prin. rschr. Ctr. Molecular Diagnostic and Therapy, Moscow, 1988—94; vis. scientist Ctr. Biophysique Moleculaire, Orleans, France, 1994—96; vis. prof. U. Nebr. Med. Ctr., Omaha, 1996—98, rsch. prof., 1998—. Postdoc. fellow Mus. Nat. D'Histoire Naturelle, Paris, 2002. Named Disting. Scientist, U. Nebr. Med. Ctr., 2008; grant, NIH, 2004—, 2005—, 2008—. Conservative. Greek Orthodox. Achievements include patents for drug delivery and gene therapy. Avocations: travel, bicycling, swimming. Home: 7567 Bondesson St Omaha NE 68122-9704 Office: Univ Nebr Med Ctr 986025 Nebr Med Ctr Omaha NE 68198-6025 Office Fax: 1-402-559-9543. Personal E-mail: sergevv@yahoo.com. Business E-Mail: vinograd@unmc.edu.

VINOGRADOVA, NATALYA, mathematician, educator; b. Russia, Aug. 10, 1969; MS in Math., St. Petersburg State U., Russia, 1991; PhD in Math. Edn., SUNY, Buffalo, 2005. Cert. tchr. N.Y. Instr. math. Pedagogical U., Russia, 1991—99, Phillips Exeter Acad., NH, 2000—01; prof. dept. math. Plymouth State U., NH, 2005—. Spkr. in field. Author: (book) The First Steps in the Theory of Probability, 1996. Mem.: Math. Assn. of Am., Nat. Coun. Tchrs. of Math. Home: PO Box 433 Plymouth NH 03264 Personal E-mail: nvinogradova@hotmail.com.

VINROOT, RICHARD ALLEN, lawyer, mayor; b. Charlotte, NC, Apr. 14, 1941; s. Gustav Edgar and Vera Frances (Pickett) V.; m. Judith Lee Allen, Dec. 29, 1964; children: Richard A., Laura Tabor, Kathryn Pickett. BS in Bus. Adminstrn., U. N.C., 1963, JD, 1966. Bar: N.C. 1966, U.S. Dist. Ct. (ea., mid. and we. dists.) N.C. 1969, U.S. Ct. Appeals (4th cir.) 1969. Ptnr. Robinson, Bradshaw & Hinson, P.A., Charlotte, 1969—. Mayor City of Charlotte, 1991-95; bd. dirs. Martin-Marietta Materials Inc. Tchr. sr. h.s. sunday sch. Myers Park Presbyn. Ch., 1970—, ruling elder, 1970-76, 1978-84, 1996-2000, chmn. of session, 1984; mem. Charlotte City Coun., 1983-91. With U.S. Army, 1967-68, Vietnam. Recipient Bronze Star, 1968; named Mcpl. Leader of the Yr. Am. City & County Mag., 1995. Mem. ABA, VFW, N.C. Bar Assn., Mecklenburg County Bar Assn. (sec. 1976, bd. dir. 1970-76), Mecklenburg County Vietnam Vets. Assn., Mecklenburg County Eagle Scouts Assn., Am. Legion, Phalanx Lodge Mason. Republican. Presbyterian. Office: Robinson Bradshaw & Hinson PA 1900 Independence Ctr 101 N Tryon St Ste 1900 Charlotte NC 28246-0103

VINSON, AUDREY LAWSON, retired literature and language professor; b. Temple, Tex., July 4, 1928; d. John McGregor and Jemima Belle (Hamilton) Lawson; m. James Vinson, Dec. 23, 1948 (dec.); 1 child, Paul Everett. BA, St. Augustine Coll., Raleigh, NC, 1948; MA, Fisk U., Nashville, 1962; CAS, Wesleyan U., Middletown, Conn., 1970. Tchr. Nashville City Schs., 1958—62; prof. Ala. A&M U., Huntsville, 1962—93, prof. emeritus, 1993—. Dept. chair Ala. A&M U., 1980—84. Co-author: The World of Toni Morrison, 1985. Bd. chair Huntsville Sickle Cell Ctr., 1968—72. Fellow, Rockefeller Found., 1968. Mem.: Modern Lang. Assn. Episcopalian. Avocations: poetry, writing. Home: 19950 Hueber Rd #1501 San Antonio TX 78258 Personal E-mail: audreyvinson@msn.com.

VINSON, CLYDE ROGER (ROGER VINSON), federal judge; b. Cadiz, Ky., Feb. 19, 1940; BS, U.S. Naval Acad., 1962; JD, Vanderbilt U., 1971. Bar: Fla. 1971. Commd. ensign USN, 1962, advanced through grades to lt., 1963, naval aviator, until 1968, resigned, 1968; assoc. to ptnr. Beggs & Lane, Pensacola, Fla., 1971-83; judge US Dist. Ct. (no. dist.) Fla., Pensacola, 1983—, chief judge, 1997—2004, sr. judge, 2004—; judge Fgn. Intelligence Surveillance Ct. (FISC), 2006—. Mem. Jud. Conf. Adv. Com. on Civil Rules, 1993-99; mem. 11th Cir. Pattern Instrn. Com. Contbr. articles to profl. jours. Divsn. chair, area chair United Way of Escambia County; bd. dirs. Pensacola Arts Coun., also treas.; mem. corp. bd. Bapt. Hosp. of Pensacola, 1977-82; co-founder, v.p., charter bd. dirs. Escambia County Epilepsy Soc.; trustee, sec., chair Fellows Meml. Fund Found.; trustee Fla. Bapt. Found., 1979-83; Sunday sch. tchr., bd. dires. First Bapt. Ch. Pensacola. Recipient J. Nixon Daniel Leadership award, 1976, Rinehardt Holm Disting. Svc. award, 1976, Pensacola Action '76 Achievement award, 1976; Wilson Merit scholar, 1968-71. Mem. Am. Judicature Soc., Fla. Bar, Escambia-Santa Rosa Bar Assn., Soc. Bar of 1st Jud. Cir., N.W. Fla. Fed. Bar Assn. (co-founder), Rotary Club of Pensacola (bd. dirs. 1997—, pres. 1998-99), Panhandle Tiger Bay Club (co-founder, pres. 2002-03). Office: US Courthouse 5th fl 1 N Palafox St # 32501 Pensacola FL 32501-5665*

VINSON, JACK ROGER, mechanical engineer, educator; b. Kansas City, Nov. 10, 1929; s. Harry Roger and Myrtle (Kiple) V.; m. Gertrude (Trudy) Hovey, June 11, 1955 (dec. Sept. 1977); children: Jack R. Jr., Stephen Scott, Jeffrey Alan, Christopher Lee; m. Mildred (Midge) Cohen, June 25, 1983. BME, Cornell U., 1952; PhD, U. Pa., 1961. Engr. student Black & Veatch Consulting Engrs., Kansas City, 1947-52; functional engr. GE, Phila., 1956-61; v.p. Dyna/Structures, Inc., Drexel Hill, Pa., 1961-65; ptnr. Structural Mechanics Assocs., Penn Valley, Pa., 1965—; from assoc. prof. to H. Fletcher Brown prof. U. Del., Newark, 1964—. Author: The Behavior of Thin Walled Structures, 1989, Structural Mechanics: The Behavior of Plates and Shells, 1974, The Behavior of Shells Composed of Isotropic and Composite Materials, 1993, The Behavior of Sandwich Structures of Isotropic and Composite Materials, 1999, Plate and Panel Structures of Isotropic, Composite, and Piezoelectric Materials, Including Sandwich Construction, 2005; co-author: Composite Materials and Their Use in Structures, 1975, 2d edit., 2002, The Behavior of Structures Composed of Composite Materials, 1985; editor-in-chief Jour. of Sandwich Structures and Materials. 1st Lt. USAF, 1954-56. Fellow AIAA (Award in Structural Mechanics 1977), ASME (life, chmn. aerospace divsn. 1980-81, Centennial medal 1981), Am. Soc. for Composites (v.p. 1996-97, pres. 1998-99, Techmonic award 1998, Rsch. award 2007, mem. internat. conf. on composite materials exec. com., region 3 v.p. 1999-2001). Episcopalian. Home: 1433 Sandy Cir Narberth PA 19072-1121 Office: U Del Dept Mech Engring Newark DE 19716 Office Phone: 302-831-2338. Personal E-mail: vinsonsma@aol.com. Business E-Mail: vinson@me.udel.edu.

VINSON, LAURENCE DUNCAN, JR., lawyer; b. Gadsden, Ala., Mar. 17, 1947; BS with hons., U. Ala., Tuscaloosa, 1969; JD, U. Ala., 1973. Bar: Ala., U.S. Dist. Ct. (no., mid. and so. dists.) Ala., U.S. Ct. Appeals (11th cir.), U.S. Supreme Ct. Assoc. Bradley Arant Boult Cummings, LLP, Birmingham, Ala., 1973—79, ptnr., 1979—. Bar: Ala. 1973, U.S. Dist. Ct. (no. dist.) Ala. 1973, U.S. Supreme Ct. 1977, U.S. Ct. Appeals (11th cir.) 1981, U.S. Dist. Ct. (so. dist.) Ala. 1989, U.S. Dist. Ct. (mid. dist.) Ala. 1991. Chmn. Ala. Uniform Comml. Code Revisions Coms., 1991-2004. Mem. ABA, Birmingham Bar Assn., Ala. State Bar, Ala. Law Inst., Order of Coif, Phi Beta Kappa, Omicron Delta Kappa. Office: Bradley Arant Boult Cummings LLP One Federal Pl 1819 5th Ave N Birmingham AL 35203-2104 Office Phone: 205-521-8000. Business E-Mail: lvinson@babc.com.

VINSON, WILLIAM THEODORE, lawyer; BS, USAF Acad., 1965; JD, UCLA, 1969. Bar: Calif. 1970. Judge advocate USAF, 1970-74; trial counsel Phillips Petroleum, San Mateo, Calif., 1974-75; atty. Lockheed Corp., Westlake Village, Calif., 1975-90, v.p., sec., 1990-92, v.p., gen. couns., 92-95; v.p., chief counsel Lockheed Martin Corp., Westlake Village, 1995-98; cons. Lockheed Corp., Westlake Village, 1998; chmn. Siemens Govt. Svcs., Inc., 2001—. Chmn. SAP Govt. Support and Svcs. Inc., 2006—. Bd. dirs. Westminster Free Clinic, 2001—. Office: 5560 E Napoleon Ave Oak Park CA 91377-4746

VIOLA, MARY JO, art history educator; b. Yonkers, NY, July 25, 1941; d. William F. and May (Cleary) O'Connor; m. Jerome Joseph Viola, June 21, 1967 (dec. Feb. 1990). BA in Fine Arts, Coll. of Mt. St. Vincent, Riverdale, NY, 1963; MA in Art History, NYU, 1966; MPhil in Art History, CUNY, 1983, PhD in Art History, 1992. Art history tchr. Georgian Ct. Coll., NJ, 1965-66, Hollins Coll., Roanoke, Va., 1966-67, Marymount Coll., Tarrytown, NY, 1967-71, Baruch Coll., CUNY, NYC, 1974-97, Bklyn. Coll., 1990-97, Parsons Sch. of Design, NYC, 1991-93, Rutgers U., 1993-95, Bronx C.C. CUNY, 1997—. Curator exhbns. Baruch Coll. Gallery, N.Y.C., 1987-88. Editor: A World View of Art History, 1985; art exhibited at Tribes Gallery, N.Y.C., 1996; creater ednl. videos. Rschr. for ethnic festivals, N.Y.C., 1993—. Fellow Nat. Trust for Hist. Preservation, 1964, Marymount Coll., 1970, Boston Mus. Fine Arts/CUNY, 1978, Luce Found., 1988. Mem. Coll. Art Assn., Historians of Am. Art, City Lore. Avocations: tai chi, dance. Home and Office: 37 Roosevelt St Yonkers NY 10701-5823

VIOLANTE, PATRICIA, translator, language expert, writer, interpreter; b. Pescara, Italy, Dec. 13, 1950; came to U.S., 1956; d. Renato Osvaldo and Agata (Vento) V.; m. Guido Marco Cassetta, May 22, 1986. BA, U. Md., 1972; MS, Georgetown U., 1976. Lectr. in translation Georgetown U., Washington, 1976—2001; dir. grad. admissions Southeastern U., Washington, 1980-82; ofcl. translator, interpreter Embassy of Italy, Washington, 1991—. CEO, Comalux, Inc., doing bus. as Trappings, Washington, 1981-86; voice talent; scriptwriter, cons. Cassetta/Hunt & Co., Washington, 1980—. Translator: The Goddess of Kisses, 2001, Italian Botanical Art Today, Women's Law Project, 2000, Italy in the Balkans, 1998, Happy Birthday, 1989, Dolce Susanna, 1992, Attidunal Survey: Sacred Heart of Jesus, 1977. Mem. Leadership Greater Washington. Mem. Nat. Assn. Jud. Interpreters and Translators, European Soc. for Translation Studies. Avocations: poetry, gardening, pasta cookery and menu planning. Home: 1409 Foxhall Rd NW Washington DC 20007-2006 Office: Embassy of Italy 3000 Whitehaven St NW Washington DC 20008-3612 Office Phone: 202-612-4408. Business E-Mail: patricia.volante@esteri.it.

VIORST, JUDITH STAHL, writer; b. Newark, Feb. 2, 1931; d. Martin Leonard and Ruth June (Ehrenkranz) Stahl; m. Milton Viorst, Jan. 30, 1960; children: Anthony Jacob, Nicholas Nathan, Alexander Noah. BA, Rutgers U., 1952; grad., Washington Psychoanalytic Inst., 1981. Author: (children's books) Sunday Morning, 1968, I'll Fix Anthony, 1969, Try It Again Sam, 1970, The Tenth Good Thing About Barney, 1971 (Silver Pencil award 1973), Alexander and the Terrible, Horrible, No Good, Very Bad Day, 1972, My Mama Says There Aren't Any Zombies, Ghosts, Vampires, Creatures, Demons, Monsters, Fiends, Goblins or Things, 1973, Rosie and Michael, 1974, Alexander, Who Used to Be Rich Last Sunday, 1978, The Good-Bye Book, 1988, Earrings!, 1990, The Alphabet from Z to A (with Much Confusion on the Way), 1994, Alexander, Who's Not (Do You Hear Me? I Mean It!) Going to Move, 1995, Super-Completely and Totally the Messiest, 2001, Just in Case, 2006, No Body Here But Me, 2008; (poetry) The Village Square, 1965-66, It's Hard to Be Hip Over Thirty and Other Tragedies of Married Life, 1968, People and Other Aggravations, 1971, How Did I Get to Be Forty and Other Atrocities, 1976, If I Were in Charge of the World and Other Worries, 1981, When Did I Stop Being Twenty and Other Injustices, 1987, Forever Fifty and Other Negotiations, 1989, Sad Underwear and Other Complications, 1995, Suddenly Sixty and Other Shocks of Later Life, 2000, I'm Too Young to be Seventy and Other Delusions, 2005; (with Milton Viorst) The Washington Underground Gourmet, 1970, Yes Married, 1972, A Visit From St. Nicholas (To a Liberated Household), 1977, Love and Guilt and the Meaning of Life, Etc., 1979, Necessary Losses, 1986, Murdering Mr. Monti, 1994, Imperfect Control, 1998, You're Officially a Grown-Up, 1999, Grown-up Marriage, 2003, Alexander and The Wonderful, Marvelous, Excellent, Terrific Ninety Days, 2007; (musical) Love and Shrimp (book and lyrics), 1990; (HBO children's movie) Alexander and the Terrible, Horrible, No Good, Very Bad Day (book and lyrics), 1990, (children's stage musical) Alexander and the Terrible, Horrible, No Good, Very Bad Day, 1998, Alexander, Who's Not Not Not Not Not Not Going to Move (book and lyrics), 2003. Recipient Emmy award for poems used in Anne Bancroft Spl., 1970. Jewish.

VIORST, MILTON, writer; b. Paterson, NJ, Feb. 18, 1930; s. Louis and Betty (LeVine) Viorst; m. Judith Stahl, Jan. 30, 1960; children: Anthony, Nicholas, Alexander. BA summa cum laude, Rutgers U., 1951; student (Fulbright scholar), U. Lyon, France, 1952; MA, Harvard U., Cambridge, Mass., 1955; MS, Columbia U., NYC, 1956. Reporter Bergen Record, NJ, 1955-56, Newark StarLedger, 1956-57, Washington Post, 1957-61; Washington corr. NY Post, 1961-64; syndicated columnist Washington Evening Star, 1971-75; staff writer New Yorker, NYC, 1987-93; Ferris prof. journalism Princeton U., NJ, 1995-96. Lectr. in field. Author: (book) Hostile Allies: FDR and deGaulle, 1965, Great Documents of Western Civilization, 1965, Fall from Grace: The Republican Party and the Puritan Ethic, 1968, Hustlers and Heroes, 1971, Fire in the Streets: America in the 1960's, 1980, Making a Difference: The Peace Corps at Twenty-Five, 1986, Sands of Sorrow: Israel's Journey from Independence, 1987, Reaching for the Olive Branch: UNRWA and Peace in the Middle East, 1990, Sandcastles: The Arabs in Search of the Modern World, 1994, In The Shadow of the Prophet: The Struggle for the Soul of Islam, 1998, What Shall I Do With This People? Jews and the Fractious Politics of Judaism, 2002, Storm from the East: The Struggle Between the Arab World and the Christian West, 2006; contbr. articles to profl. jours.; contbg. corr.: Washington Quar. Mem. nat. adv. com. Mid. East Policy Coun.; chmn. Fund Investigative Journalism, 1969—78; bd. dirs. Georgetown Day Sch., 1977—80, Inst. World Affairs. Officer USAF, 1952—54. Recipient Columbia Journalism Alumni award, 1992, Human Rights award, UN Assn. DC, 2002, chevalier, Legion d'Honneur, France, 2005; named to Hall of Fame, Eastside HS, Paterson, NJ, 2007; scholar, Mid. East Inst.; Woodrow Wilson Sr. fellow, 1973—79, Alicia Patterson fellow, 1979. Mem.: Coun. Fgn. Rels., Author's Guild, Soc. Profl. Journalists, PEN, Am. Peace Now, Phi Beta Kappa. Office Phone: 202-966-8676. Personal E-mail: mviorst@aol.com.

VIRDEN, FRANK STANLEY, naval officer; b. Long Beach, Calif., Sept. 21, 1933; s. Frank and Katherine Stanley Virden; m. Jacquelin Ann Moseley, 1954 (div. 1979); children: Yvette Virden Parsons, Geoffrey Alexander; m. Elisabeth Burns Virden, 1991; stepchildren: Wesley Delwin Bonds III, Charles Cary Bonds. BA in Polit. Sci., Duke U., Durham, NC, 1955; MBA in Transp. Adminstrn., Mich. State U., East Lansing, 1966. Commdg. officer Navy Cargo Handling Bn. One, Williamsburg, Va., 1969—72; grp. supply officer Svc. Grp. Three, US Seventh Fleet, 1972—74; dir. storage & transp. Def. Constrn. Supply Ctr., Columbus, Ohio, 1974—77; commdg. officer Naval Sch., Transp. Mgmt., Oakland, Calif., 1977—79; dep. comdr. Mil. Traffic Mgmt. Command, DC, 1979—81; cons. in field, 1981—93; exec. dir. Episcopal Cmty. Svcs. Found., Cin., 1993—96; ret., 1996. Pres. US Navy League Coun., Cin., 1989—92. Dir., pres. Baldwin County Pub. Transit Coalition, Robertsdale, Ala., 1999—2007; bd mem., chair Nat. Network Lay Profls., NYC, 1994—2000; standing com. mem. Episcopal Diocese Ctrl. Gulf Coast, Pensacola, Fla., 2001—04; exec. mem. Episc. Cmty. Svcs., 1993—96; infrastructure com. co-chair Charter Party, Cin., 1983—87. Capt. USN, 1955—81. Decorated Meritorious Svc. Medal Sec. Navy, Commendation medal, Legion of Merit award; recipient Unsung Hero award, ACT II Cmty. Organizing Fedn., 2003, 2005. Mem.: SAR (pres. Gen. Galvez chpt.), Am. Legion, Navy League US, Mensa, Am. Assn. Woodturners. Independent. Episcopalian. Achievements include being the driving force in the development of Baldwin County Public Transit Coalition; development of church organization being responsible for successfully curtailing drug trafficking in county public schools. Avocations: woodworking, travel. Home: PO Box 475 Gulf Shores AL 36547-0475 Personal E-mail: vivahaus@gulftel.com.

VIRELLI, LOUIS JAMES, JR., lawyer; b. Phila., Nov. 4, 1948; s. Louis James and Elsie Antoinette (Colombo) V.; m. Barbara Ann Rotella, Aug. 22, 1970; children: Louis J. III, Christopher F. BE in Mech. Engring., Villanova U., 1970; JD, U. Tenn., 1972. Bar: Pa. 1973, U.S. Patent and Trademark Office, 1973, U.S. Ct. Customs and Patent Appeals 1974, U.S. Dist. Ct. (we. dist.) Pa. 1976, U.S. Dist. Ct. (ea. dist.) Pa. 1977, U.S. Ct. Appeals (9th cir.) 1980, U.S. Ct. Appeals (D.C. cir.) 1982, U.S. Supreme Ct. 1982. Patent atty. Sperry New Holland Co., Pa., 1973—74; assoc. counsel Westinghouse Co., Pitts., 1974—76; assoc. Paul & Paul, Phila., 1976—80, ptnr., 1980—84; patent counsel Nat. Starch and Chem. Co., Bridgewater, NJ, 1984—88, asst. gen. counsel, intellectual property, 1988—92, gen. counsel, intellectual property, 1992—95; asst. gen. counsel Patents Unilever US, Inc., Edgewater, NJ, 1988—95; v.p. gen. patent counsel Unilever N.V., P.L.C., Englewood Cliffs, 1995—96, sr. v.p., gen. patent counsel, 1997—2003, sr. v.p., gen. counsel intellectual property, 2003—06; sr. counsel Morgan Lewis, NYC, 2007—. Arbitrator U.S. Dist. Ct. (ea. dist.) Pa., Phila., 1982-84. Mem.: ABA, Assn. Corp. Patent Counsel (treas., v.p., pres.), Phila. Patent Law Assn., NJ Patent Law Assn., Intellectual Property Owners Assn. (bd. dirs.). Office: Morgan Lewis 1701 Market St Philadelphia PA 19103-2921 also: Morgan Lewis & Bockius LLP 101 Park Ave New York NY 10178-0060 Office Phone: 215-963-5125. Business E-Mail: lvirelli@morganlewis.com.

VIRK, SUBHDEEP, psychiatrist; b. Jalandhar, Punjab, India, Nov. 03; d. Devinder Singh and Manjeet Virk; m. Arvinder S. Bhinder, Nov. 30, 2000; 1 child, Panya Gurbax Bhinder. MBBS, Amritsar Med. Coll., India, 1993; MD, SUNY, Syracuse, 2005. Intern Gen. Hospita, Chandigarh, India; med. officer Lamba Nursing Hosp., Chandigarh, 1995—95; ho. officer Gen. Hosp., Chandigarh, 1995; jr. resident psychiatry Govt. Med. Coll., Chandigarh, 1996; clin. observer oncology Alameda County Med. Ctr., Oakland, Calif., 1998—99; clin. intern VA Med. Ctr., Syracuse, NY, 1999—2000; clin. rsch. assoc. SUNY, Upstate Med. U., Syracuse, 2000—01, resident psychiatry and behavioral sci., 2001—. Vol. Helpage India, Chandigarh, 1994, Govt. Rural Health Ctr., Dadumajra, Punjab, India, 1994, Highland Gen. Hosp., Oakland, 1998; student adv. Kaplan Ednl. Ctr., Berkeley, Calif., 1998—99, med. adv, med. coll. admissions test instr., Syracuse, 1999—2000, med. adv., Hackensack, NJ. Contbr. articles to profl. jours. Scholar, Am. Psychosomatic Soc., 2005; All India Army scholar, ESSA, India. Mem.: AMA, Am. Psychosomatic Soc., Assn. Psychiat. Medicine, Am. Assn. Physicians, Am. Psychiatry Assn., Med. Coun. India (licentiate). Achievements include research in psychiatry and behavioral health. Office: Ohio State Med Ctr 1670 Upham Dr Columbus OH 43210 Office Phone: 614-293-8283. Home Fax: 315-293-4200. Business E-Mail: virk.1@osu.edu.

VIRKHAUS, TAAVO, symphony orchestra conductor; b. Tartu, Estonia, June 29, 1934; came to U.S., 1949; s. Adalbert August and Helene Marie (Sild) V.; m. Nancy Ellen Herman, Mar. 29, 1969. MusB U. Miami, 1955; MusM Eastman Sch. of Music, Rochester, 1957, DMA, 1967. Dir. music U. Rochester (N.Y.), also assoc. prof. Eastman Sch., Rochester, 1967-77; music dir., condr. Duluth (Minn.) Superior Symphony Orch., 1977-94; guest condr. Rochester Philharm., Minn. Orch.,

Balt. Symphony, Vancouver Symphony and others, 1972—; music dir., condr. Hunstville (Ala.) Symphony Orch., 1989-2003, condr. emertius, 2003—; guest condr. at Tallinn, Estonia, 1978, 88, 90, 92, 93, 94, 99, 2004; lectr. U. Minn.-Duluth, U. of Wis.-Superior. With U.S. Army, 1957-58, USAR, 1957-61. Recipient Howard Hanson Composition award, 1966, Am. Heritage award JFK Libr. for Minorities, 1974; Fulbright scholar, Musikhochschule, Cologne, 1963. Mem. Am. Symphony Orch. League, Am. Fedn. of Musicians. Composer: Violin Concerto, 1966, Symphony No. 1, 1976, Symphony No. 2, 1979, Symphony No. 3, 1984, Symphony No. 4, 1989, Symphony No. 5, 1994, Symphony No. 6, 2008, Violin Concerto No. 2, 1995. Lutheran. Personal E-mail: taavo@knology.net.

VIRTUE, TED, investment company executive; BA in econ. & psychology, Middlebury Coll. Fin. positions in spl. loan group & US banking group Bankers Trust, NYC; sr. v.p. high yield capital markets & loan syndication Drexel Burnham Lambert, NYC; sr. mng. dir. to exec. v.p., head global fin. & mem. mgmt. com. Bankers Trust, NYC, 1990—97; pres. BT Alex. Brown Inc. (merged with Deutsche Bank), 1997—99, Deutsche Bank Alex. Brown, 1999; CEO DB Capital Ptnrs., 1999—2003; mem. exec. com. Deutsche Bank; founder, CEO MidOcean Ptnrs., NYC, 2003—. Bd. dirs. Noveon, Inc., Celerity Group, Inc., Ctr. Parcs UK, Kinetics Group. Chmn. Youth I.N.C.; trustee Middlebury Coll. Named one of 40 Under 40 Rising Stars, Crain's NY Bus., 1994, Top 50 Under 40 Rising Stars, Euromoney mag., 1998. Office: MidOcean Ptnrs 320 Park Ave Ste 1700 New York NY 10022 Office Phone: 212-497-1401. Business E-Mail: tvirtue@midoceanpartners.com.*

VISCHER, HAROLD HARRY, manufacturing executive; b. Toledo, Oct. 17, 1914; s. Harry Philip and Hazel May (Patterson) V.; m. DeNell Meyers, Feb. 18, 1938; children: Harold Harry, Robert P., Michael L. BBA, U. Toledo, 1937. With Ohio Bell Telephone Co., 1937-38; with Firestone Tire & Rubber Co., Toledo, 1948-61, nat. passenger tire sales mgr., 1953-57, dist. mgr., 1957-61; with Bandag Inc., Muscatine, Iowa, 1961-80; exec. v.p., pres. Bandag Inc. (Rubber and Equipment Sales group), 1975-80; also dir.; pres., gen. mgr. Hardline Internat., Inc., Jackson, Mich., 1980-82; chmn. Tred-X Corp., 1982—. Mem. City Council, Muscatine, 1964-76; chmn., mem. Dist. Export Council Iowa, 1964-81; chmn. Muscatine United Way, 1969-70; mem. adv. bd. Engring. Coll. Iowa State U., 1970-81; mem. Muscatine Light & Water Bd., 1979-80. Elected to Nat. Tire Dealers and Retreaders Assn. Hall of Fame, 1988, to Internat. Tire Retreading and Repairing Hall of Fame, 1990. Mem. Nat. Tire and Retreaders Suppliers Group Assn. (chmn. 1979-80, exec. com. 1977-80), Tire Retread Info. Bur. (exec. com. 1974-81), Am. Retreading Assn. (adv. bd. 1970-72), Retreading Industry Assn., Industry Man of Yr. 1979), Christian Business men's Com., Gideons. Republican. Home: 13500 Vischer Rd Brooklyn MI 49230-9022 Home Phone: 517-467-4117.

VISCLOSKY, PETER JOHN, United States Representative from Indiana, lawyer; b. Gary, Ind., Aug. 13, 1949; s. John and Helen (Kauzlaric) Visclosky; m. Anne Marie O'Keefe; children: John, Timothy. BS in Acctg., Ind. U., Indpls., 1970; JD, U. Notre Dame, 1973; LLM in Internat./Comparative Law, Georgetown U., 1983. Bar: Ind., DC, US Supreme Ct. Legal asst. Dist. Atty.'s Office, NYC, 1972; assoc. Benjamin, Greco & Gouveia, Merrillville, Ind., 1973-76, Greco, Gouveia, Miller, Pera & Bishop, Merrillville, Ind., 1982-84; assoc. staff appropriations com. US Ho. Reps., Washington, 1976-80, assoc. staff budget com., 1980-82; mem. US Congress from 1st Ind. dist., 1985—; mem. appropriations com., subcoms. treasury, postal svc., gen. govt. and military constrn. Democrat. Roman Catholic. Office: US Ho Reps 2256 Rayburn Ho Office Bldg Washington DC 20515-1401 also: Dist Office Ste 9 701 E 83d Ave Merrillville IN 46410 Office Phone: 202-225-2461.*

VISCOMI, FRANK JOSEPH, pharmaceutical executive; b. Easton, Pa., Dec. 18, 1951; s. John Dominic and Catherine Viscomi; m. Janet Lynn Wilson, Sept. 29, 1979; children: Lauren Michelle, Rebecca Elizabeth. BS in Biology, Alderson Broaddus Coll., Phillipi, W.Va., 1973; MAT in Edn., Coll. NJ, Trenton, 1988, MA in Math. Physics, 1988. Biologist Colgate Palmolive Co., Piscataway, NJ, 1977—88; mgr. Johnson & Johnson Pharm. R&D, Raritan, NJ, 1988—. Tchr. Hun Sch. of Princeton, NJ, 1998—2000. Contbr. scientific papers to profl. jours.; author: 47, 2006, The Pinhole: A Theory in n-Dimensions, 2007. Mem.: Math. Assn. of Am., Mensa (life). Achievements include patents pending for Mathematical Algorythm to Calculate the Area of and Object in n-Dimensional Space; Anti-Inflammatory Agent Extracted from Milkweed Plants; Development of Laser System to Detect Tissue Degradation. Home: 82 Knapp Ave Trenton NJ 08610 Personal E-mail: fviscomi@aol.com.

VISCONTI, JOSEPH B., contractor, small business owner; b. Hartford, Conn., Dec. 9, 1956; children: Joey, Gabriella, Michael. A in Telecomm., U. Hartford, 1978. Former crew worker Internat. Alliance Theatrical Stage Employees; founder, pres. Joseph Visconti, LLC. Mem. West Hartford Rep. Town Com., West Hartford Taxpayer's Assn. Prodr.: (PBS ednl. programming) Disabilities & Possibilities (Emmy award, 1997, Gov. Lawton Chiles Media award). Founding mem., chmn. Disabilities & Possibilities Found.; vol. Safe Neighborhood Parks, Dade County, Fla., 1995—99; mentor Hartford Children's Theater; mem. St. Peter Claver Ch., West Hartford; bd. dirs. West Hartford Vision. Mem.: Patriot Guard Riders. Republican. Mailing: PO Box 270043 West Hartford CT 06127 Office Phone: 860-521-6939. Office Fax: 860-989-0471.*

VISCUGLIA, JENNY LOU, music educator; b. Englewood, Colo., Sept. 12, 1967; d. Dwight B and Lynda Lee Eames; m. Felix Alfred Viscuglia, Apr. 5, 1997; m. Andrew Norvelle, Nov. 19, 1989 (div. Sept. 27, 1996). BS in Music Edn., U. Nev., Las Vegas, 2003. Cert. nursing asst., Colo., 1986; music tchr. K-12 Nev., 2003. Cert. nursing asst. Cherry Creek Nursing Ctr., Aurora, Colo., 1986—87; class a alarm operator Regent Security, Englewood, Colo., 1987—88; waitress, asst. mgr. McCoy's Family Restaurant, Littleton, Colo., 1988—89; clerical Kelly Services, Las Vegas, Nev., 1989—90; adminstrv. asst. Nathan Adelson Hospice Found., Las Vegas, Nev., 1990—95; sec. Rio Suites Hotel and Casino, Wine Cellar, Las Vegas, Nev., 1996—97; libr. Nev. Symphony, Las Vegas, Nev., 1994—98; pers. mgr., libr., clarinet sub The Las Vegas Philharm., Las Vegas, Nev., 1998—2004; k-8 music tchr. Clark County Sch. Dist., Las Vegas, Nev., 2003—. Mem. Goodsprings Citizens Adv. Coun., Goodsprings, Nev., 1998—2004; treas., mem. Goodsprings Hist. Soc., Goodsprings, 2001—04. Mem.: NEA, Music Educators Nat. Conf., Am. Orff-Schulwerk Assn., Nat. Assn. Music Educators. Avocations: travel, music. Office: Sandy Valley Elem Mid Sch Sandy Valley NV 89019 Home: HC 31 Box 116 Sandy Valley NV 89019 Personal E-mail: viscuglia@aol.com.

VISCUSI, W(ILLIAM) GREGORY KIP, law and economics educator; b. Trenton, NJ, Oct. 3, 1949; s. William Edward and Evelyn (Martin) V.; m. Catherine Makdisi, Sep. 26, 1972 (div.); children: Kira Margaret, Michael Kip; m. Joni Hersch, Jan. 18, 1998. AB summa cum laude, Harvard U., Cambridge, Mass., 1971, MPP, 1973, AM, 1974, PhD, 1976. Prof. econs. Northwestern U., Evanston, Ill., 1976-80, 85-88; dep. dir. White House Council on Wage and Price Stability, Washington, 1979-81; prof. econs. Duke U., Durham, NC, 1981-85; John M. Olin prof. econs. U. Chgo., 1985-86; George G. Allen prof. econs. Duke U., Durham, NC, 1988-96; John M. Olin vis. prof. law and econs. Harvard Law Sch., Cambridge, Mass., 1995, John F. Cogan Jr. prof. law and econs., 1996—2006; univ. disting. prof. law, econs., mgmt. Law Sch. Vanderbilt U., Nashville, 2006—. Rsch. assoc. Nat. Bur. Econ. Rsch., 1978—, Nat. Commn. for Employment Policy, 1981; mem. EPA Sci. Adv. Bd., 1986—, econs. bd., 1992—, Clean Air Act, 1992—. Nat. Acad. Sci. Panel, 1978-79; cons. US Gen. Acctg. Office, 1981-85, Dept. Justice, 1986-87, 89-91, U.S. Office Mgmt. and Budget, 1983; assoc. reporter Am. Law Inst., 1986-91; adj. fellow in civil justice Manhattan Inst., 1987—; inaugural spkr. Geneva Risk Econ. Lectrs., Geneva Assn. Risk and Ins., 1989; John R. Commons lectr. U. Wis., 1990; Ayne Ryde lectr. Lund U., Sweden. Author: Employment Hazards, 1979 (Wells prize 1977), Risk by Choice, 1983, Reforming Products Liability, 1991, Fatal Tradeoffs, 1992, Smoking, 1992, Rational Risk Policy, 1998, Smoke-filled Rooms: A Post-mortem on the Tobacco Deal, 2002; founding editor Jour. Risk and Uncertainty; contbg. editor Regulation mag.; assoc. editor Internat. Rev. of Law Econs., Geneva Papers on Risk and Ins. Theory, Jour. Regulatory Econs., Jour. Environ. Econs. and Mgmt., J Risk and Ins., Rev. Econs. and Stats., Am. Econ. Rev., Managerial and Decision Econs., Contemporary Econ. Policy. Recipient Article of the Yr. award Econ. Inquiry, 1988, Royal Econ. Soc., 1999; Book of the Yr. awards Am. Risk and Ins. Assn., 1992, 93, 94, 2000, Article award Am. Risk and Ins. Assn., 1999. Mem. Am. Econs. Assn., Econometric Soc., Assn. Environ. and Resource Economists, Assn. for Pub. Policy Analysis and Mgmt., So. Econs. Assn. We. Econs. Assn., Managerial and Decision Econs. Roman Catholic. Office: Vanderbilt Univ Law Sch 131 21st Ave South Nashville TN 37203-1181

VISH, DONALD H., lawyer, writer, photographer; b. Ft. Benning, Ga., Jan. 18, 1945; s. D. H., Jr. and Dorris (Parrish) Vish; m. Catherine Pence Hamilton, Aug. 20, 1966 (div. 1986); children: Donald Hamilton, Daphne Mershon Sullivan. BA in English, Bellarmine Coll., 1968; JD cum laude, U. Louisville, 1971. Bar: Ky. 1971, Fla. 1972. Sec., gen. counsel Gen. Energy Corp., Lexington, Ky., 1978-83; ptnr. Wyatt, Tarrant & Combs, Lexington, 1980-88, Frost Brown Todd, Lexington, 1988-89, 1991-98; gen. counsel Ky. Coal Producers' Self-Ins. Fund, 1992-98; sec., gen. counsel AIK Workers Compensation Fund, 1998—2004, exec. v.p., 2002—04, Middleton, Reutlinger, 2004—; exec. dir. The J & L Found., 2008—; dir. advocacy ky. Coalition Against The Death Penalty. Apptd. assoc. solicitor U.S. Dept. Interior, 1989—91; adj. assoc. prof. mineral law U. Ky., Lexington, 1979—85. Author: Poems and Musings, 2001; contbr.; contbg. author: American Law of Mining, 2d edit., 1984, bd. editors and contbg. author: Coal Law and Regulation, 1983—93, Kentucky Election Law, 1995. Trustee Syre Sch., Lexington, 1980—88, chmn. bd. dir., 1986—88; mem. Blue Grass coun. Boy Scouts Am., 1988—93; apptd. gov. Ky. Registry Election Fin., 1991—93; bd. dir. Highlands Cmty. Ministries, 2001—04; bd. dirs. Ky. Shakespeare Festival, 2005—, Interfaith Paths to Peace, 2006—, pres., 2007—; bd. dirs. Louisville Bar Assn. Named to Gallery of Disting. Grads., Bellarmine Coll., 2008. Fellow: Am. Bar Found. (life); mem.: ABA (chmn. coal com., natural resources sect. 1987), Louisville Bar Assn. Com. Judicial Integrity & Independence, Ky. Bar Assn. (mem. ethics com. 1983—85, chair residency com. 1998—2002), Fla. Bar, Energy and Mineral Law Found. (mem. exec. com. 1979—82, trustee 1979—91, trustee emeritus 1998), Louisville Bar Found. (life), Am. Law Inst. (life), Ky. Bar Found. (life). Office: Middleton Reutlinger 2500 Brown and Williamson Tower Louisville KY 40202 Home: 2403 Top Hill Rd Louisville KY 40206 Home Phone: 502-896-1906; Office Phone: 502-584-1135. Personal E-mail: donaldvish@att.net.

VISHNIVETSKAYA, TATIANA ALEKSANDROVNA, microbiologist, researcher; b. Izyum, Kharkiv Oblast, Ukraine, Nov. 14, 1964; d. Aleksandr Nikolaevich Ilyukhin and Svetlana Pavlovna (Sapronova) Ilyukhina; m. Sergey Aleksandrovich Vishnivetskiy, Nov. 10, 1987; children: Yelena Sergeevna, Natalie Sergeevna. BS, MS, Moscow State U., 1990; PhD, Russian Acad. Scis., Pushchino, 2003. Rsch. scientist Russian Acad. Scis., 1990—97; rsch. scholar Ctr. Microbial Ecology, East-Lansing, Mich., 1997—98; rsch. technician Sun Health Rsch. Inst., Sun City, Ariz., 2000—01; rsch. asst. Vanderbilt U. Med. Ctr., Nashville, 2001—03; rsch. assoc. NC State U., Raleigh, 2003—05, Oak Ridge Nat. Lab., Tenn., 2006—. Mem.: Am. Soc. Microbiology. Achievements include discovery of viable cyanobacteria and green algae in the deep subsurface permafrost sediments. Office: Oak Ridge Nat Lab 1 Bethel Valley Rd Oak Ridge TN 37831

VISITANTE, EL (EDUARDO CABRA), singer, musician; b. Santurce, PR, Sept. 10, 1978; Co-founder, pianist & singer Calle 13; signed to White Lion Records Inc., Santurce, PR. Musician: (albums) Calle 13, 2005 (Latin Grammy award for Best Urban Music Album, 2006), Residante O Visitante, 2007 (Best Urban Music album, Latin Grammy Awards, 2007, Grammy award, Best Latin Urban Album, 2008), Los de Atrás Vienen Conmigo, 2008, (songs) Atrévete Te, Te!, 2005 (Latin Grammy award for Best Short Form Music Video, 2006), Pal Norte, 2007 (Best Urban song, Latin Grammy Awards, 2007). Recipient Best New Artist award, also Best Urban Music Album & Best Short Music Video awards, Latin Grammy Awards, 2006. Office: White Lion Records Inc Urb Ocean Park 2072 Calle Cacique Santurce PR 00911-1514

VISKANTA, RAYMOND, mechanical engineering educator; b. Lithuania, July 16, 1931; came to U.S., 1949, naturalized, 1955; s. Vincas and Genovaite (Vinickas) V.; m. Birute Barbara Barpsys, Oct. 13, 1956; children: Renata, Vitas, Tadas. BSME, U. Ill., Champaign, 1955; DEng (hon.), Tech. U. Munich, 1994; MSME, Purdue U., West Lafayette, Ind., 1956, PhD, 1960, DEng (hon.), 2007. Registered profl. engr., Ill. Asst. mech. engr. Argonne (Ill.) Nat. Lab., 1956-59, student rsch. assoc., 1959-60, assoc. mech. engr., 1960-62; assoc. prof. mech. engring. Purdue U., West Lafayette, Ind., 1962-66, prof. mech. engring., 1966-86, Goss disting. prof. engring., 1986—. Guest prof. Tech. U. Munich, Germany, 1976-77, U. Karlsruhe, Germany, 1987; vis. prof. Tokyo Inst. Tech., 1983. Contbr. over 500 tech. articles to profl. jours. Recipient Sr. U.S. Scientist award Alexander von Humboldt Found., 1975, Sr. Rsch. award Am. Soc. Engring. Edn., 1984, Nusselt-Reynolds prize, 1991, Thermal Engring. award for Internat. Activity, Japan Soc. Mech. Engrs., 1994, Alumni award for Disting. Svc. U. Ill.-Urbana-Champaign, 2000, Stodola medal ETH, Zurich, 2007; Japan Soc. for Promotion of Sci. fellow, 1983. Fellow ASME (Heat Transfer Meml. award 1976, Max Jakob Meml. award 1986, Melville medal 1988), AIAA (Thermophysics award 1979); mem. AAAS, NAE, Acad. Engring. Scis. Russian Fedn. (fgn.), Lithuanian Acad. Scis. (fgn.), Sigma Xi, Pi Tau Sigma, Tau Beta Pi. Home: 3631 Chancellor Way West Lafayette IN 47906-8809 Office: Purdue Univ 585 Purdue Mall West Lafayette IN 47907-2088 Office Phone: 765-494-5632. Personal E-mail: rviskanta@comcast.net. Business E-Mail: viskanta@ecn.purdue.edu.

VISO, OLGA, museum director; b. Fla. MA in Art History, Emory U., 1992. Positions in dept. modern & contemporary art, office of registrar and office of dir. High Mus. Art, Atlanta, 1989—93; asst. cur. Norton Mus. Art, West Palm Beach, Fla., 1993, Hirshhorn Mus. and Sculpture Garden, Washington, 1995, assoc. cur., 1998, cur. contemporary art, 2000—03, dep. dir., 2003—06, dir., 2006—07, Walker Art Ctr., Mpls., 2008—. Mem. Fed. Adv. Com. Internat. Exhibitions; co-commr., US Pavilion Venice Biennial, 2001. Arranged (exhibitions) Distemper: Dissonant Themes in the Art of the 1990s, 1996, Regarding Beauty: A View of the Late Twentieth Century, 1999—2000. Office: Walker Art Ctr 1750 Hennepin Ave Minneapolis MN 55403 Office Phone: 612-375-7600. E-mail: info@walkerart.org.

VISOCKI, NANCY GAYLE, information services consultant; b. Dumont, NJ, May 13, 1952; d. Thomas and Gloria Visocki. BA in Math., Manhattanville Coll., 1974; MS in Ops. Rsch. and Stats., Rensselaer Poly. Inst., 1977. Rsch. asst. Coll. Physicians and Surgeons Columbia U., NYC, 1974-75; programmer analyst R. Shriver Assocs., Parsippany, NJ, 1977-79; sr. tech. rep. GE Info. Svcs. Co., East Orange, NJ, 1979-81, mgr. project office Morristown, NJ, 1981-83, tech. dir., 1983-87, tech. mgr., 1988-89, area mgr. sys. devel. and consulting Parsippany, 1989-92, area tech. mgr. sys. devel. and cons., Fin. Info. Sys., 1992-93, sr. cons. info. svcs., 1993-98, project mgr. e-commerce sys. integration, 1998-2000; mgr. Major e-commerce Applications Practice, 2000—03. Active Western Hills Christian Ch., Tranquility, N.J., 1986—; vol. Women's Ctr., Hackettstown, N.J., 1989-93; class fundraising and gift chmn. Rensselaer Poly. Inst., Troy, N.Y., 1991-95; vol. Elfun Soc., 1981—; vol. bd. dirs., treas. NJCFS Assn., 2004— Manhattanville Coll. grantee, Purchase, N.Y., 1970-71; tuition fellow Rensselaer Poly. Inst., 1975-77. Mem. Elfun, Women of Accomplishment. Avocations: tai chi, hiking, bicycling, reading, puzzles.

VISSCHER, MARTY ORRICO, biomedical researcher; d. Frank Paul and Elizabeth Brinkley Orrico; m. Ronald Bosman Visscher, June 10, 1972; children: Paul David, Robert Christopher. PhD, Ind. U., Bloomington, Ind., 1973; student, Xavier U., Cin., Ohio, 2005—. Postdoctoral fellow chemistry Ind. U., Bloomington, 1973—74, vis. prof. chemistry, 1974—76; asst. prof. chemistry U. Cin., 1976—78; sr. scientist R&D The Procter & Gamble Co., Cin., 1978—95; co-founder, dir. The Skin Sciences Inst. Cin. Children's Hosp. Med. Ctr., 1995—, rschr. The Skin Scis. Inst., 1995—. Mem. ADHD collaborative and task force Cin. Children's Hosp. Med. Ctr., 2002—; spkr. in field. Author: The Ideas of Chemistry, Harcourt Brace Jovanovich Inc., Laboratory Manual for The Ideas of Chemistry, Harcourt, Brace, Jovanovich, Inc., New York; contbr. chapters to books, articles to profl. jours. Mem. troop com. troop 417 Boy Scouts of Am., Cin., 1992—2006, merit badge counselor troop 417, 1996—2006; pres. Glendale Youth Sports, Cin., 1994—96, coach soccer, 1990—94; pres. Princeton Aquatics Parent Bd. Princeton City Schs., Cin., 1998—2000. Mem.: WGUC Pub. Radio, Glendale Lyceum. Achievements include patents in field. Avocations: running, fashion design, sewing, art, embroidery. Office: Cincinnati Children's Hospital Medical C 3333 Burnet Avenue Cincinnati OH 45229 Business E-Mail: visschmo@email.uc.edu.

VISSER, ROBIN, humanities educator; b. Dearborn, Mich. d. Henry Gordon and Rita Jean Visser; m. Qingguo Ren; children: Takoda Lei Ren, Jordan Shan Ren, Zoe Ahn Ren. BS, U. Mich., Ann Arbor; MA, U. Colo., Boulder; PhD, Columbia U., NYC, 2000. Faculty Valparaiso U., Ind., 2000—03, U. NC, Chapel Hill, 2003—. Contbr. chapters to books, articles to profl. jours.; author: (book) Cities Surround the Countryside: Urban Aesthetics in Postsocialist China. Humanities in China grant, Am. Coun. Learned Socs., 2003—04, Grier-Woods Presbyn. Initiative fellowship, U. NC, Chapel Hill, 2007. Fellow: Ctr. Urban and Regional Studies; mem.: MLA, Assn. Asian Studies. Office: Univ NC Dept Asian Studies CB 3267 Chapel Hill NC 27599-3267 Office Phone: 919-962-1027.

VISSERS, MICHELLE, psychologist; b. Wausau, Wis. d. Steven and Renata Vissers. BA in Psychology, U. Wis., Stevens Point, 2002; MEd, U. Wis., La Crosse, 2005. Group home facilitator Choices Change Inc., Stevens Point, 2001—04; psychologist Marathon County Spl. Edn., Abbotsford, Wis., 2005—06, New Berlin Pub. Sch., Wis., 2006—, reach co-project coord., 2008—. On-site coord. Big Bros.Big Sisters, Abbotsford, 2005—06, New Berlin, 2007—08. Reach grant, WI Dept. Instrn. Mem.: NASP, WI Sch. Psychologists Assn., Phi Kappa Phi, Phi Eta Sigma. Office: New Berlin Pub Sch 5900 S Sunny Slope Rd New Berlin WI 53151 Business E-Mail: michelle.vissers@nbexcellence.org.

VISTE, ARLEN ELLARD, chemistry professor; b. Austin, Minn., Aug. 13, 1936; s. Arthur E. and Edith L. (Kehret) V.; m. Elizabeth Ann Lindbeck, June 14, 1959; children: Solveig, David, Mark. BA, St. Olaf Coll., 1958; PhD, U. Chgo., 1962. Asst. prof. chemistry St. Olaf Coll., Northfield, Minn., 1962-63; NSF fellow Columbia U., NYC, 1963-64; asst. prof. Augustana Coll., Sioux Falls, SD, 1964-68, assoc. prof., 1968-73, prof., 1973—, prof. emeritus, 2002—. Contbr. articles to profl. jours. Mem. Am. Chem. Soc., Royal Soc. Chemistry (London), S.D. Acad. Sci., Midwest Assn. Chemistry Tchrs. in Liberal Arts Colls., Phi Beta Kappa, Sigma Xi. Home: 1500 W 30th St Sioux Falls SD 57105-3622 Office: Augustana Coll Chemistry Dept Sioux Falls SD 57197-0001 Business E-Mail: arlen.viste@augie.edu.

VISWANATHAN, AKILA, oncologist; BA, Harvard U., Cambridge, Mass., 1991; MD, U. Pitts., 1997; MPH, Harvard U., Boston, 2001. Internship in internal medicine Beth Israel Deaconess Med. Ctr., Boston, 1997—98, attending physician, 2002—05; resident Joint Ctr. for Radiation Therapy, Boston, 1998—2001, chief resident, 2001—02; attending physician Children's Hosp., Boston, 2002—05, Dana-Farber/Brigham and Women's Cancer Ctr., Boston, 2002—, dir. mr-guided gynecologic brachytherapy program, 2002, dir. gynecologic radiation oncology program, 2002—. Dir. longwood radiation oncology program, med. student elective Harvard Med. Sch., Boston, 2002—. Contbr. articles to profl. jours. Recipient Shield award for Svc. to Dunster Ho. Cmty., Harvard Coll., 1991, Friends award for Brachytherapy, Brigham and Women's Hosp., 2005, Ptnrs. in Excellence Team award, Dana-Farber/Brigham and Women's Hosp. Gynecologic Oncology Disease Ctr., 2005; grantee, Ford Found., 1990—91, U. Pitts. Sch. Medicine, 1993, 1995, NIH, 1995—96; fellow, Howard Hughes Med. Inst., 1995—96, Am. Coll. Radiation Oncology, 2001, Carl and Lily Pforzheimer Found., Inc., 2001; John Harvard and Elizabeth Carey Agassiz scholar, Harvard Coll., 1987—91. Mem.: Mass. Med. Soc., Am. Soc. Clin. Oncology, Radiol. Soc. N.Am., Gynecologic Oncology Group, Soc. of Epidemiology Rsch., Am. Brachytherapy Soc. (Judith Stitt Best Oral Presentation award 2005), Am. Soc. Therapeutic Radiology and Oncology, Am. Assn. Cancer Rsch. (assoc.). Achievements include research in analysis of risk factors for endometrial cancer; pathological predictors in cervical cancer; vaginal cancer; magnetic resonance image-guided gynecologic brachytherapy; efect of dosimetric variation of vaginal cuff brachytherapy; vulvar carcinoma; CT simulation in brachytherapy. Office: Brigham and Women's Hosp 75 Francis St ASB1 L2 Boston MA 02115 Office Fax: 617-278-6988.

VITA, STEVEN, poet; b. Chgo., July 16, 1960; s. John and Rosemarie V. BA in Art and English, Denison U., Granville, Ohio, 1982; MFA in English, CUNY, 1985. Founder, editor Veery, Chgo., 1991—. Author: The Heart of Tents, 1991.

VITALE, DICK, sportscaster, commentator; b. Garfield, NJ; m. Lorraine Vitale; children: Terri, Sherri. Basketball coach East Rutherford HS, NJ, 1965-71; asst. basketball coach Rutgers U., New Brunswick, NJ, 1972; basketball coach U. Detroit, 1973-77, athletic dir., 1978; basketball coach Detroit Pistons, Auburn Hills, Mich., 1978-79; TV commentator, sports analyst ESPN Sports, 1979—; sports columnist Basketball Times, 1979—, Ea. Basketball, 1979—; TV commentator ABC Sports, 1987—; sports radio commentator ABC Radio Network, 1987—. Radio commentator The J. P. McCarthy Show, Detroit; guest spkr., lectr. Co-author: (with Curay Kirk Patrick) Vitale: Just Your Average, Bald, One-Eyed Basketball Wacko Who Beat the Ziggy and Became a PTP'er, 1989, (with Dick Weiss) Time Out, Baby!, 1992, Living a Dream, 2003, (with Mike Douchant) Tourney Time, It's Awesome Baby, 1994; co-author various computer games; appeared in TV comms. for Adidas, Taco Bell. Named Sports Personality of Yr., Am. Sportscasters Assn., 1989; named to Basketball Hall of Fame, 2008, Nat. Collegiate Basketball Hall of Fame, 2008; named one of Top 50 Sportscasters Am. Sportscasters Assn., 2009. Roman Catholic. Achievements include earning 5 sectional and 2 consecutive state championships as a high school basketball coach. Office: ESPN ESPN Plz Bristol CT 06010*

VITALE, JOSEPH F., state legislator; b. Elizabeth, NJ, Nov. 10, 1954; Pres. Vitale Sign Corp., Woodbridge, NJ, 1986—; mem. Dist. 19 NJ State Senate, Trenton, 1998—, dep. majority leader, 2004—07; interim mayor City of Woodbridge, 2006—. Mem. environ. com. N.J. State Senate, health com., women's issues, children and family svcs. com. Vice chair Habitat for Humanity; Middlesex County chair Walk for Health, Am. Heart Assn.; mem. mayor's adv. com. Middlesex County Paraiso Assistance Project; mem. Woodbridge Twp.; chmn. Woodbridge Twp. Dem. Party, 1992-97. Named one of 2007 People to Watch, Sunday Star Ledger. Mem. Woodbridge Twp. C. of C. Democrat. Presbyterian. Office: NJ State Senate PO Box 098 Trenton NJ 08625-0099 also: 569 Rahway Ave Woodbridge NJ 07095 Office Phone: 732-855-7441. Business E-Mail: SenVitale@njleg.state.nj.us.*

VITALE, RUTH ANN, former film company executive; b. Boston, Oct. 20, 1952; d. Joseph J. and Gilda J. (Camuso) V. BA in English, Tufts U., 1974; MS in Journalism, Boston U., 1975. Account exec. Sta. WNAC-TV, Boston, 1976-78, Top Market TV/Post-Newsweek, NYC, 1978-79; v.p., media account exec. McCann Erickson, NYC, 1979-81; mgr. sales ops. Hearst/ABC Video Services, NYC, 1981-82; dir. film acquisition The Movie Channel, NYC, 1982-83; sr. v.p. prodn. Vestron Pictures, Stamford, Conn., 1983-87, ind. producer, 1987-88; sr. v.p. prodn. United Artists/Metro-Goldwyn-Mayer, Inc., Beverly Hills, Calif., 1988—95, Fine Line Features/New Line Cinema Corp., Los Angeles, Calif., 1995—97; co-pres. Paramount Classics, Los Angeles, Calif., 1997—2005; pres. First Look Studios, Inc., Los Angeles, Calif., 2005—07.

VITALIANO, ERIC NICHOLAS, federal judge; b. SI, NY, Feb. 27, 1948; m. Helen M. Fleming, Sept. 9, 1983; children: Michael, Emma, Abigail, Halle. AB, Fordham Coll., 1968; JD cum laude Order of Coif, NYU, 1971; postgrad, Nat. Inst. Trial Advocacy U. Colo., 1977. Bar: NY 1971. Law clk. to Mark A Costantino, US Dist. Ct. (Ea. dist.) NY, NYC, 1971-72; assoc. Simpson Thacher & Bartlett, NYC, 1972-79; chief staff to Congressman John M. Murphy US Ho. Reps., NYC, 1979-80; ptnr. Russo, Silverman & Vitaliano, NYC, 1982-86; mem. NY Assembly, Albany, 1982—2002; counsel Behrins & Behrins, 1999—2001; judge NY State Unified Ct. Sys., 2002—06, US Dist. Ct. (Ea. dist.) NY, 2006—. Rsch. editor NYU Law Rev., 1970-71. Co-founder Citizens Against Bus Exhaust; co-founder Bodine Creek Civic Assn.; former parish chmn. Cardinal's Archdiocesan Appeal; former mem. Dem. Com. Richmond County, NY; past pres. NY Conf. Italian-Am. State Legislators; past adv. Assumption Coun., KC. Recipient Stella Falletta Meml. award Clifton Homeowners and Tenants Assn., SI, 1986, Aldo R. Benedetto Outstanding Citizen award Am. Legion, 1994, Pub. Policy award NY State Cath. Conf., 1998; named Dem. of Yr., Young Dems. Richmond County, 1980, Friend of Edn., Susan E. Wagner HS, SI, 1983, Legislator of Yr., NY State Clks. Assn., 1987, Friend of Italian-Am. Inst. Inst., CUNY, 1990, Man of Yr., Italian Club SI, 1991, Man of the Yr., Met. Police Conf. of NY State, 1995, Legislator of the Yr. Supreme Ct. Officers, 2000, Detective Investigators Assn., 2000. Mem.: Richmond County Bar Assn. (NY) (Person of Yr. 2009). Office: US Dist Ct 225 Cadman Plaza E Brooklyn NY 11201 Office Phone: 718-613-2135.

VITE, FRANK ANTHONY, realtor; b. Aurora, Ill., Feb. 9, 1930; s. Frank A. and Rose (Cosentino) V.; grad. Marmion Mil. Acad., 1948; student Sch. Mgmt., U. Notre Dame, 1958; D.B.A. (hon.), Hillsdale Coll., 1972; m. Barbara Ann Decio, Oct. 23, 1954; children: Bradley Scott, Mark Steven, Michael Lee, Leslie Ann, Lisa Ann. Plant engr. Lyon Metal Products, Aurora, 1951-52, purchasing agt., 1953-54; became sales mgr., exec. v.p., owner, dir. Skyline Homes, Inc., Elkhart, Ind., 1954; pres., owner B&F Realty, Inc., No. Ind. Appraisal Co., Golden Falcon Homes, Inc.; real estate broker; dir. 1st Nat. Bank, Elkhart, Ind. Trustee Hillsdale (Mich.) Coll., Holy Cross Coll., South Bend, Ind.; bd. dirs. Ind. Commn. Higher Edn. With AUS, 1952-53, Korea. Mem. Elkhart Bd. Realtors, Nat. Sales Execs. Assn., Ind. Real Estate Assn., Nat. Inst. Real Estate Brokers, Holy Name Soc., K.C. (4 deg.), Knight of Malta, Elks. Republican Home: 9 Colonia Miramonte Paradise Valley AZ 85253 Office: 2851 E Bristol St Elkhart IN 46514 Office Phone: 574-264-0651.

VITEK, REG(INALD) A., lawyer; b. Bakersfield, Calif., Apr. 23, 1942; BA, San Diego State Coll., 1964; JD, UCLA, 1967. Bar: Calif. 1967, US Ct. Appeals (2d, 9th cir.), US Supreme Ct. 1976. Ptnr., bus. litigation Seltzer Caplan McMahon Vitek, San Diego. Lectr. Nat. Inst. Trial Advocacy. Mem.: ABA, State Bar Calif., San Diego County Bar Assn., Fed. Bar Assn., Assn. Trial Lawyers Am., San Diego County Trial Lawyers Assn., Assn. Bus. Trial Lawyers (founding mem. San Diego chpt.), Am. Inns of Ct., Louis M. Welsh San Diego chpt. (Master, mem. exec. com.). Office: Seltzer Caplan McMahon Vitek Symphony Towers 750 B St San Diego CA 92101 Office Phone: 858-685-3075. Office Fax: 858-702-6804. Business E-Mail: vitek@scmv.com.

VITEK, VACLAV, materials scientist; b. Olomouc, Czechoslovakia, Sept. 10, 1940; came to U.S., 1978; s. Josef and Ruzena V.; m. Ludovita Stankovicova, Aug. 5, 1972; children: Adrian Joseph, Clementine Mary. BSc in Physics, Charles U., Prague, 1962; PhD in Physics, Czechoslovakian Acad. Scis., Prague, 1966; doctorate (hon.), Tech. U. Brno, 1999. Research assoc. dept. metall. materials sci. and research fellow Wolfson Coll., Oxford U., England, 1967-75; research officer Central Elec. Research Labs., Central Elec. Generating Bd., Leatherhead, England, 1975-78; prof. materials sci. and engring. U. Pa., 1978—. Vis. prof. U. Groningen, Netherlands, 1985-86. Recipient Humboldt award for sr. scientists, Germany, 1992-93, Acta metallurgica Gold medal, 1996, Mach medal Czech Acad. Scis., 1999. Fellow Inst. Physics (London), Am. Soc. Metals Internat., Metals, Minerals Materials Soc.; mem. NAE (elected 2006), Am. Phys. Soc., Materials Rsch. Soc. Office: U Pa Dept Materials Sci and Engring 3231 Walnut St Philadelphia PA 19104-6202 Business E-Mail: vitek@seas.upenn.edu.

VITETTA, ELLEN S., microbiologist, immunologist, educator; BA, Conn. Coll.; MS, NYU, 1966, PhD, MD, 1968. Prof. microbiology Southwestern Med. Sch., U. Tex., Dallas, 1976—; dir. Cancer Immunobiology Ctr., U. Tex., Dallas, 1988—; Sheryle Simmons Patigian Disting. chair in cancer immunobiology Southwestern Med. Sch., U. Tex., Dallas, 1989—. Bd. sci. coun. NCI Cancer Treatment Bd., 1993; sci. adv. bd. Howard Hughes Med. Inst., 1992—; Kettering selection com. GM Cancer Rsch. Foun., 1987-88; task force NIAID in Immunology, 1989-90; mem. sci. bd. Ludwig Inst., 1983—. Mem. editl. bd.: Advances in Host Defense Mechanisms, 1983—, Annual Review of Immunology, 1991—, Bioconjugate Chemistry, 1989-93, Cellular Immunology, 1984-93, Current Opinions in Immunology, 1992—, FASEB Journal, 1987—, Internat. Jour. of Oncology, 1992—, Internat. Soc. Immunopharmacology, 1989—, Jour. of Immunology, 1975-78, Molecular Immunology, 1978-93; assoc. editor Cancer Research, 1986—; Immunochemistry sect. editor: Jour. of Immunology, 1978-82; co-editor in chief: Therapeutic Immunology, 1992—. Recipient Women's Excellence in Sci. award Fedn. Am. Soc. Exptl. Biology, 1991, Taittinger Breast Cancer Rsch. award Komen Found., 1983, Pierce Immunotoxin award, 1988, NIH Merit award, 1987—, U. Tex. Southwestern Med. Sch. Faculty Teaching awards 1989, 91, 92, 93, 94, FASED Excellence in Sci. award, 1991, Abbot Clinical Immunology award Am. Soc. Microbiologists, 1992, Past State Pres. award Tex. Fed. Bus. Profl. Women's Club, 1993, Richard and Hinda Rosenthal Found. award Am. Assn. Cancer Rsch 1995, Charlotte Friend award Am. Assn. Cancer Rsch., 1995, AAAS Mentreny award, 2002. Mem. Am. Assn. Immunologists (pres. 1994), Nat. Acad. Scis., Am. Acad. Microbiology (hon.). Achievements include co-discovery of IL-4, development of immunotoxins and identification of IgD on murine B cells. Office: Univ Texas Cancer Immunobiol Ctr 6000 Harry Hines Blvd Dallas TX 75235-5303 Address: 6914 Pemberton Dr Dallas TX 75230-4260 E-mail: ellen.vitetta@utsoutheastern.edu.

VITHAYATHIL, VARKEY CARDINAL, cardinal, archbishop; b. Paur, Ernakulam, India, May 29, 1927; s. Joseph and Thresiamma Vithayathil. M in Philosophy, U. Karnataka, India; D in Canon Law, Pontifical U. St. Thomas Aquinas, Rome. Professed Congregation of Most Holy Redeemer, 1947, ordained priest, 1954; prof. canon law Redemptorist Houses of Study, Bangalore, India; Redemptorist provincial for India & Sri Lanka, 1978—84; apostolic adminstr. Benedictine Monastery, Asirvanam, India, 1990—96, Archdiocese of Ernakulum-Angamaly (Syro-Malabarese), 1996—99; ordained bishop, 1997; major archbishop Archdiocese of Ernakulum-Angamaly (Syro-Malabarese), 1999—; elevated to cardinal, 2001; cardinal-priest S. Bernardo alle Terme, 2001—. Pres. Conf. of Religious of India, India, 1984—85, Synod of the Syro-Malabarese Church. Roman Catholic. Office: Archdiocesan Curia PO Box 2580 Kochi 682031 Kerala India Home: Archbishop's Home Ernakulam PO Box 2580 Kochi 682031 Kerala India Home Phone: 0091-0484-2355010; Office Phone: (0484) 2352629, (0484) 2352906, (0484) 2363664. Office Fax: (0484) 2366028. Business E-Mail: abperang@asianetindia.com.

VITKOWSKY, VINCENT JOSEPH, lawyer; b. Newark, Oct. 3, 1955; s. Boniface and Rosemary (Ofack) Vitkowsky; m. Mary Gunzburg, May 16, 1981 (div. 1997); children: Vincent Jr., Victoria, Pierce; m. Pandora Strasler, Sept. 18, 1999. BA, Northwestern U., 1977; JD, Cornell U., 1980. Bar: NY 1981. Assoc. Hart and Hume, NYC, 1980-84, Kroll & Tract, NYC, 1984-87; of counsel Nixon, Hargrave, Devans & Doyle, NYC, 1988-89; ptnr. Buchalter, Nemer, Fields & Younger, NYC, 1990-95, Edwards Angell Palmer & Dodge LLP, NYC, 1996—. Mem. London Ct. Internat. Arbitration; lectr. in field. Contbr. articles to profl. jours. Mem. Am. Arbitration Assn. (internat. panel arbitrators), Internat. Bar Assn. (former com. officer), Internat. Law Assn. (Am. br. com. on formation customary internat. law), Assn. Bar City NY, Cornell Club, Federalist Soc. Law and Pub. Policy (chair exec. com. internat. and nat. security practice group, mem. nat. practioners adv. coun.), IBA Human Rights Inst. (former officer, com. interventions and trial observations 2000-04). Home: 422 E 72d St Apt 15E New York NY 10021 Office: Edwards Angell Palmer & Dodge LLP 750 Lexington Ave Fl 12 New York NY 10022-1253 Office Phone: 212-912-2828. Business E-Mail: vvitkowsky@eapdlaw.com.

VITRANO, FRANK G., retail executive; b. 1955; With Pathmark Stores Inc., Carteret, NJ, 1972—2008, v.p., treas., exec. v.p., treas., CFO, 1998—2002, pres., CFO, 2002—05, co-pres., CFO, 2005—08; sr. exec. v.p., CFO, chief adminstrv. officer Rite Aid Corp., Camp Hill, Pa., 2008—. Office: Rite Aid Corp 30 Hunter Ln Camp Hill PA 17011

VITT, DAVID AARON, health products executive; b. Phila., Aug. 3, 1938; s. Nathan and Flora B.; m. Renee Lee Salkever, Oct. 20, 1963; children: Nadine Lori Einiger, Jeffrey Richard. BS, Temple U., 1961. Sales engr. X-Ray Corp., Phila., 1961-65, Midwest Am., Chgo., 1965-67, product mgr., 1967-68, product mgr. regional sales, 1968-70; dir. mktg. Valtronic & Living Wills, Bronx, NY, 1970-74; v.p., gen. mgr. dental divsn. Siemens Med. Sys. Inc., Iselin, NJ, 1974—86, past corp. v.p., gen. mgr. dental divsn.; CEO, pres. Pelton & Crane, Charlotte, NC, 1986-89; v.p. govt. sales, ret. Siemens Med. Sys., 1994; founder, pres., CEO D.A.V., Inc., 1995—; founder, co-owner RealDental.com. Pres. Denx Am. Inc., 1998; industry rep. to Am. Nat. Stds. Inst.; co. rep. U.S.-USSR Trade and Econ. Coun.; co-founder Enter Am. Group Exec. Consultants. Bd. dirs. Am. Fund for Dental Health; apptd. mem. Charlotte Mecklenburg Cmty. Rels. Com.; mem. bd. visitors U. N.C., Charlotte; officer, mem. exec. com. Jr. Achievement. Served in USAR, 1961-68. Mem. Am. Mgmt. Assn. (bd. dirs. N.J. chpt.), Am. Mktg. Assn., Am. Dental Trade Assn. (bd. dirs.), Dental Mfrs. Am. (past pres.), Am. Acad. Dental Radiology, Charlotte C. of C. (bd. advisors), Acad. Gen. Dentists (bd. mem. found.), Masons (32d deg.), Shriners. Republican.

VITTAL, VIJAY, electrical engineer, educator; b. Bangalore, India, Dec. 25, 1955; arrived in U.S., 1979; s. H.S. Padmanabha and K. Shakuntala V.; m. Sunanda Vittal, June 8, 1980; children: Eknath, Vinayak. B in Engring., B.M.S. Coll. Engring., Bangalore, India, 1977; M, Indian Inst. of Tech., Kanpur, India, 1979; PhD, Iowa State Univ., 1982. Asst. prof. Iowa State Univ., Ames, 1982-86, assoc. prof., 1986-90; program dir. NSF, Washington, 1993-94; prof. Iowa State U., Ames, 1990—2004, Murray and Ruth Harpole prof., 2000—04, Anson Marston Disting. prof., 2004; Ira A. Fulton Chair prof. Ariz. State U., Tempe, 2005—. Cons. Siemens Energy Automation, Plymouth, Minn., 1992-93, G.E. Power Systems, Schenectady, N.Y., 1999. Author: Power System Analysis, 2000, Power System Transient Stability, 1992; contbr. articles to profl. jours. Recipient Presdl. Young Investigator award NSF, 1985. Fellow IEEE (chair power sys. dynamic performance com.); mem. US Nat. Acad. Engring. Office: Ariz State U Ira A Fulton Sch Engring PO Box 875706 Tempe AZ 85287-5706 Office Phone: 480-965-1879. Office Fax: 480-965-0745. E-mail: vijay.vittal@asu.edu.

VITTECOQ, GERARD R., manufacturing executive; Grad., Ecole Superieure Commerce, Rouen, France; MBA, Laval Univ., Canada. Fin. mgmt. positions Caterpillar Inc., 1975—82; fin. rep., asst. mgr. Caterpillar Overseas S.A., 1982—85, comptroller, 1985—87; strategy mgr. Caterpillar Inc., 1987—89, dir., strategy & planning, 1990—95; mng. dir. Caterpillar France S.A., 1995—98, Caterpillar Belgium S.A., 1998—2001; v.p. EAME prod. develop. & ops. Caterpillar Inc., 2001—03, group pres., 2003—. Mem. European Am. Indsl. Council; mem. mgmt. bd. Fedn. des Syndicats Patronaux, Geneva; mem. exec. com. Internat. Inst. Mgmt. Develop.; exec. mem. World Bus. Council for Sustainable Develop.; bd. dir. Best Buy Co., 2008—. Office: Caterpillar Inc 100 NE Adams St Peoria IL 61629*

VITTER, DAVID BRUCE, United States Senator from Louisiana, former congressman; b. New Orleans, May 3, 1961; s. Al and Audrey Vitter; m. Wendy Baldwin, 1991; children: Sophie, Lise, Airey, Jack BA magna cum laude, Harvard U., 1983; BA/MA in History/Econs. with highest honors, Oxford U., 1985; JD with honors, Tulane U. Sch. Law, 1988. Bar: La. 1988. Bus. atty., La., 1988—99; assoc. Golden, Kingsmill and Riess, New Orleans, Duplass, Witman, Zwain and Williams, Metairie, La., Duplass, Zwain and Bourgeois, Metairie, La.; mem. La. Ho. of Reps., 1991—99, U.S. Congress from 1st. dist. La., 1999—2005, mem. transp. and judiciary com., govt. reform com., appropriations. com. Washington, 1999—2005; US Senator from La., 2005—. Adj. prof. law Tulane U., 1993—99, Loyola U., 1993—99; mem. com. security and coop. in Europe US Senate, com. commerce, sci. and transp., com. environment and public works, com. small bus. and entrepreneurship. Articles editor Tulane Law Rev., 1987-88. Lector, St. Francis Xavier Cath. Ch., Metairie, La.; Mem. Coastal Conservation Assn., Ducks Unlimited. Rhodes scholar; Recipient Legis. of Yr., Alliance for Good Govt., Lifetime Achievement award Victims & Citizens Against Crime, Republican of Yr. award Northshore Republican Men's Club, 2005. Mem. ABA, New Orleans Bar Assn., Phi Beta Kappa, Nat. Rifle Assn.; former mem. La. Bar Assn. Republican. Roman Catholic. Office: US Senate 516 Hart Senate Office Bldg Washington DC 20510 also: District Office Ste 201 2800 Veterans Blvd Metairie LA 70002 Office Phone: 504-589-2753, 202-224-4623. Office Fax: 504-589-2607, 202-228-5061.*

VITTER, JEFFREY SCOTT, academic administrator, computer science educator, researcher; b. New Orleans, Nov. 13, 1955; s. Albert Leopold Jr. and Audrey Malvina (St. Raymond) V.; m. Sharon Louise Weaver, Aug. 14, 1982; children: Jillian St. Raymond, J. Scott Jr., Audrey Louise. BS in Math. with highest honors, U. Notre Dame, 1977; PhD in Computer Sci., Stanford U., 1980; AM (hon.), Brown U., 1986; MBA, Duke U., 2002. Asst. computer performance analyst Standard Oil Co. Calif., San Francisco, 1976—77; rsch. and tchg. asst. Stanford (Calif.) U., 1977—80, tchg. fellow, 1979; asst. prof. computer sci. Brown U., Providence, 1980—85, assoc. prof. computer sci., 1985—88, prof. computer sci., 1988—93; Gilbert, Louis and Edward Lehrman prof. computer sci. Duke U., Durham, NC, 1993—2002, chmn. dept., 1993—2001, co-dir. Ctr. for Geometric and Biol. Computing, 1997—2002; prof. computer sci. Purdue U., 2002—08, Frederick L. Hovde dean Coll. of Science, 2002—08; provost and exec. v.p. acads. Tex. A&M U., College Station, 2008—, prof. computer sci. and engring., 2008—. Cons. IBM, 1981-86, Inst. for Def. Analyses, 1986, Ctr. for Computing Scis., 1992-94, Lucent Technologies, Bell Labs., 1997; mem. rsch. staff Math. Scis. Rsch. Inst., Berkeley, 1986, Inst. Recherche en Informatique et en Automatique, Roquencourt, France, 1986-87, Inst. Recherche en Informatique et en Automatique, Sophia Antipolis, France, 1998-1999; vis. prof. Ecole Normale Superieure, Paris, 1986-89; vis. and adj. prof. Tulane U., 1990-2006, mem. bd. advisors Sch. Sci. and Engring., 2006—; lectr. Asian Sch. on Computer Sci., Bangkok, 1987; assoc. mem. Ctr. Excellence in Space Data and Info. Scis. Author: The Design and Analysis of Coalesced Hashing, 1987, Efficient Algorithms for MPEG Video Compression, 2002, Algorithms and Data Structers for External Memory, 2008; editor Algorithmica, 1994—, guest editor, 1988, 94; editor Math. Sys. Theory: Internat. Jour. on Math. Computing Theory, 1991—, Soc. for Indsl. and Applied Math. Jour. on Computing, 1989-1997, Algorithm Engineering, 1999, External Memory Algorithms, 1999; contbr. articles to profl. jours.; patentee in field. Recipient Faculty Devel. award IBM, 1984, NSF Presdl. Young Investigator award, 1985, Test of Time award ACM Sigmod, 2009; NSF grad. fellow, 1977-80; Guggenheim fellow, N.Y.C., 1986-87. Fellow IEEE (editor Trans. on Computers 1985, 87-91), Assn. for Computing Machinery (editor Comms. 1988-95, Jour. Exptl. Algorithmics, 2000; mem.-at-large spl. interest group on automata and computability theory 1987-91, vice chair spl. interest group on algorithms and computation theory 1991-1997, chair 1997-2001, exec. com. 2001-05, Recognition of Svc. award 1997, 2001); mem. Computing Rsch. Assn. (bd. dirs. 2000-, co-chair govt. affairs com. 2001-), Phi Beta Kappa, Sigma Xi. Avocations: reading, golf, basketball, football, genealogy. Office: Office Provost and Exec VP Acads Tex A&M Univ 1248 Tamu College Station TX 77843-1248 Office Phone: 979-845-4016. Business E-Mail: jsv@tamu.edu.

VITTETOE, MARIE CLARE, retired clinical laboratory science educator; b. Keota, Iowa, May 19, 1927; d. Edward Daniel and Marcella Matilda Vittetoe. BS, Marycrest Coll., 1950; MS, W.Va. U., 1971, EdD, 1973. Staff technologist St. Joseph Hosp., Ottumwa, Iowa, 1950-70; instr. Ottumwa Hosp. Sch. Med. Tech., 1957-70, St. Joseph Hosp. Sch. Nursing, Ottumwa, 1950-70; asst. prof. U. Ill., Champaign-Urbana, 1973-78; prof. clin. lab. scis. U. Ky., Lexington, 1978-94. Mem. Sisters of Humility of Mary, 1946—; chair Congregation of Humility of Mary; clin. lab. asst., lab. cons. 6 clinics in Haiti, 2000—; cons. Nat. Pub. Health Lab., Port au Prince, Haiti, 2007—, Internet Tng. Edn. Ctr. AIDS/HIV, Haiti, 2007—. Author: Vittetoe Family Tree and Scrapbook, 2000, Peiffer-Berg Family Tree and Scrapbook, 2000, Lutz/Peiffer Family Tree Update, 2002, Vittetoe Family Tree Update, 2002; contbr. articles to profl. jours. Vol. hosp. labs., Haiti, 1999—; apptd. to advisory bd. CRUDEM Found., 2005—. Recipient Kingston award for Creative Tchg., Recognition award for svc. to edn., Commonwealth of Ky. Coun. on Higher Edn., disting. grad. award, Nat. Cath. Ednl. Assn., 1995, devel. of youth award, Iowa 4-H Found., 1996, award for devel. Best Little Lab. in Haiti, 2002, award, CRUD Em Found., 2009; named Ky. Col., Marie Vittetoe award for excellence in svc. named for her, U. Ky., 1999. Mem. Am. Soc. for Med. Tech. (chmn. 1986-89, Profl. Achievement award 1991, Ky. Mem. of Yr. award 1994), Am. Soc. Clin. Lab. Scis., Am. Soc. Clin. Pathologists (assoc.), Alpha Mu Tau, Phi Delta Kappa, Alpha Eta. Avocations: walking, genealogy.

VITTONE, JOHN MICHAEL, federal judge; b. Masontown, Pa., Apr. 29, 1942; s. August and Sarah (Rao) Vittone; m. Karen Talbott, May 2, 1964; children: John Michael, Anthony Fauster. BA in English, U. Richmond, Va., 1964; JD, U. Ky., 1967. Bar: Ky. 1967, DC 1973, US Supreme Ct. 1978. Atty. FTC, Washington, 1967-68, 70-72; trade regulation counsel G.A. Saxton & Co., Washington, 1972-74; atty.

antitrust divsn. US Dept. Justice, Washington, 1974-80; adminstrv. law judge Civil Aeronautics Bd., Washington, 1980-84, US Dept. Transp., Washington, 1985-87; dep. chief judge US Dept. Labor, Washington, 1987-96, chief judge, 1996—. Capt. US Army, 1968—70. Mem.: ABA (chmn. nat. com. adminstrv. law judges). Roman Catholic. Office: Office Adminstrv Law Judges 800 K St NW Ste 400 N Washington DC 20210*

VITTOR, KENNETH MARK, lawyer; BS with honors, Cornell U., 1971; JD, U. Chgo., 1974. Assoc. Cahill, Gordon & Reindel, NYC, 1974-80; sr. v.p., assoc. gen. counsel McGraw-Hill Cos., NYC, 1980-95, sr. v.p., gen. counsel, 1995—99, exec. v.p., gen. counsel, 1999—. Chmn. Libel Def. Resource Ctr., 1999-2000. Mem. Copyright, Patent and Trademark Commn., Freedom to Read Commn., Assn. Am. Pubs., Mag. Pubs. Am. (chmn. legal affairs com.), Lawyers Commn. (chmn. libel, privacy and first admendment subcommittee 1983-86). Office: McGraw-Hill Cos 48th Fl 1221 Avenue Of The Americas New York NY 10020-1095

VITTY, RODERIC BEMIS, retired financial planner, publishing executive; b. St. Johnsbury, Vt., July 28, 1933; s. Clarence Lucian and Leota (Cobleigh) V.; m. Virginia Gable, March, 1960 (div. 1983); chilldren: Roderic G., Virginia A., David P., Suzanne L.; m. Patricia Lyster, June 21, 1986. BS, U.S. Mil. Acad., 1955; MS in Fin. Svcs., Am. Coll., Bryn Mawr, Pa., 1977, MS in Mgmt., 1987; postgrad. exec. mgmt. program, Columbia U., 1985. CLU; chartered fin. cons.; cert. fin. planner. With Conn. Gen. Life Ins. Co. (CIGNA-Lincoln Fin. Advisor), 1960, mgr. br. office Cherry Hill, NJ, 1968—, mgr. Greater Phila. office, 1981—, mktg. gen. mgr., 1983—85, gen. mgr., regional v.p., 1985—94. Pub., owner Vt. Heritage press, Caber Pub. Ltd. Trustee St. Johnsbury Acad., Vt., 1993—, co-chair capital campaign, 1999; mem assembly of overseers Dartmouth-Hitchcock Med. Ctr.; civilian aide Sec. Army State of Vt., 2005-. Served with inf. U.S. Army, 1955-59, Pa. N.G., 1961-68. Recipient GAMA Master Agy. Builder award, 1982-92, Nat. Mgmt. awards (20), 1972-92, Outstanding Agy. awards (9), CIGNA; named to CIGNA Hall of Fame, 1998. Mem. West Point Soc. Phila. (pres. 1969-71, 89-94, emeritus, 1994), Nat. Assn. Ins. and Fin. Advisors, South Jersey Fin. Planning Coun., Internat. Assn. Fin. Planners, Soc. of Fin. Svc. Profls., So. N.J. Gen. Agts. and Mgrs. Assn. (pres. 1979-80), Nat. GAMA (regional v.p. 1986-89, treas., exec. com. 1991-94), Assn. Grads U.S. Mil. Acad. (trustee 1992—2005, emeritus 2005-, pres. Class of 1955, 1995-2000), Soc. Colonial Wars, Soc. Mayflower Descendants, Army Athletic Assn., Sunnybrook Swim Club, Cherry Hill Raquet Club, Riverton Country Club, Quechee Club Vt., St. Johnsbury Country Club, Safari Club Internat., Chevaliers du Tastevin, Union League Phila., St. Andrews Soc. Vt., Masons (32 deg.), Shriners, K.T. Presbyterian. Address: Twildoon Lodge-Angell Trail PO Box 151 Quechee VT 05059-0151

VITULLI, WILLIAM FRANCIS, retired psychology educator; b. Bklyn., July 17, 1936; s. William S. and Sadie Rosaria (Stallone) V.; m. Betty Jean Sheubrooks, June 15, 1961; children: Paige Vitulli Baggett, Quinn Anthony, Sherik Vitulli Butler. BA, U. Miami, 1961, MS, 1963, PhD, 1966. Lic. psychologist, Ala. Grad. asst. U. Miami, Coral Gables, Fla., 1961-65; asst. prof. psychology U. South Ala., Mobile, 1965-69, assoc. prof., 1969-75, prof., 1975-2001, chair sr. faculty caucus, 1999—2001, emeritus prof., 2001—. V.p. Ala. Bd. Examiners in Psychology, Montgomery, 1982-84; rsch. cons. Drug Edn. Coun., Mobile, 1988-94. Mem. editl. bd. Jour. Sport Behavior, 1978—; cons. editor Jour. Genetic Psychology, 1999—; contbr. articles to profl. jours. Mem. adv. bd. Contact Mobile, 1987-92. Named Prof. of Quar., Alpha Lambda Delta, Faculty Mem. of Yr., 1993-94; recipient Outstanding Prof. award Alumni Assn., 1994; named to Golden Key Nat. Honor Soc., 200. Mem. APA, Southeastern Psychol. Assn., Ala. Psychol. Assn. (pres. 1975), Italian-Am. Cultural Soc. South Ala. (chair hist.-cultural com. 1982), Sigma Xi (pres.-elect U. South Ala. chpt. 1996-97), Psi Chi (faculty adviser U. South Ala. chpt. 1972-80, chair sr. faculty caucus U. South Ala. 1999-00). Avocations: sports research and analysis, fishing. Home: 2025 Maryknoll Ct Mobile AL 36695-3829 E-mail: wvitulli@usouthal.edu.

VITULLO, DOLORES, cardiologist, director; b. Chgo., Apr. 18, 1947; MD, Chgo. Med. Sch., 1972. Diplomate Am. Bd. Pediat. Cardiology, 1977. Dir., cardiology outreach Children's Meml. Hosp., Chgo., 2001—. Bd. mem. Ill. Divsn. Specialized Care Children, Chgo., 2003—. Office: Childrens Meml Hosp 2300 Childrens Plz Chicago IL 60614 Office Fax: 773-880-3286. Business E-Mail: dvitullo@childrensmemorial.org.

VITZ, PAUL CLAYTON, psychologist, educator; b. Toledo, Aug. 27, 1935; m. Evelyn Birge; 6 children. BA high honors in Psychology, U. Mich., 1953; PhD, Stanford U., 1962. Instr. psychology Pomona (Calif.) Coll., 1962-64; asst. prof. NYU, 1965-70, assoc. prof., 1970-85, dir. psychology dept. undergrad. program, 1973-79, prof., 1985—2004, prof. emeritus, 2004—. Adj. prof. John Paul II Inst. on Marriage and Family, Washington, 1990-2003, Internat. Acad. Philosophy, 1994-98; prof./sr. scholar Inst. for Psychol. Scis., 2000—; lectr. in field. Author: Psychology as Religion: The Cult of Self-Worship, 1977, 2d edit., 1994, (with A.B. Glimcher) Modern Art and Modern Science: The Parallel Analysis of Vision, 1984, Censorship: Evidence of Bias in Our Children's Textbooks, 1986, Sigmund Freud's Christian Unconscious, 1988, Faith of the Fatherless: The Psychology of Atheism, 1999; editor: (with S. Krason) Defending the Family: A Sourcebook, 1998, (with S. Felch) The Self: Beyond the Postmodern Crisis, 2006; contbr. articles to profl. jours., chpts. to books. Grantee Nat. Inst. Mental Health, 1963-64, 64-66, 66-67, Nat. Inst. Neurol. Diseases and Blindness grantee, 1970-73, 73-74, Nat. Inst. Edn., 1983, 84-85, Dept. Edn., 1986-87. Office: Inst for the Psychol Scis Ste 511 2001 Jefferson Davis Hwy Arlington VA 22202

VIVACQUA, RITAMARIE LILLIAN, psychology educator; b. Ilion, NY, Dec. 26, 1980; d. Fred James and Ann Elizabeth Vivacqua. MS, Coll. St. Rose, Albany, NY, 2005. Cert. sch. psychologist U. State NY Edn. Dept., 2006. Sch. psychologist West Can. Valley Ctrl. Schs., Newport, NY, 2006—. Home: 40 W River Dr Ilion NY 13357 Office: W Can Valley Ctrl Schs 5447 State Route 28 PO Box 360 Ilion NY 13357 Business E-Mail: rvivacqua@westcanada.org.

VIVIAN, KIM, language educator; b. Austin, Tex., July 28, 1951; PhD, U. Calif., Santa Barbara, 1979. Asst. prof. German Guilford Coll., Greensboro, NC, 1982—89; prof. German Augustana Coll., Rock Island, Ill., 1989—. Author: (novel) In the Company of Angels; editor: (textbook) An Anthology of German Literature. Vol. 1: Vom frühen Mittelalter bis zum Sturm und Drang. Vol. 2: Von der deutschen Klassik bis zum Naturalismus., Mosaik: Deutsche Literatur; translator: (medieval literature) Arthurian Romances, Tales, and Lyric Poetry. The Complete Works of Hartmann von Aue., (saint's life) The Lives of the Jura Fathers., The Life of Saint Servatius. Liberal. Office: German Dept Augustana Coll 639 38th St Rock Island IL 61201-2296 Office Fax: 309-794-7443. Business E-Mail: kimvivian@augustana.edu.

VIVIANI, FABIO, chef; b. Florence, Italy; Pvt. chef for William Shatner; owner, exec. chef Café Firenze Italian Restaurant and Martini Lounge. Contestant (TV series) Bravo's Top Chef, 2009. Office: Cafe Firenze 563 W Los Angeles Ave Moorpark CA 93021 Office Phone: 805-532-0048. Office Fax: 805-530-0930.*

VIZCAINO, JOSE LUIS PIMENTAL, professional baseball coach, retired professional baseball player; b. San Cristobal, Dominican Rep., Mar. 26, 1965; Grad. high sch., Dominican Rep. Infielder LA Dodgers, 1989-90, 1998—2000, spl. asst., 2008—; infielder Chgo. Cubs, 1991-93, NY Mets, 1994-96, Cleve. Indians, 1996, San Francisco Giants, 1997, 2006, NY Yankees, 2000, Houston Astros, 2001—05, St. Louis Cardinals, 2006. Achievements include being a member of the World Series Championship winning New York Yankees, 2000. Office: c/o LA Dodgers Dodger Stadium 1000 Elysian Pk Ave Los Angeles CA 90012-1500

VLACH, JIRI, electrical engineering educator, researcher; b. Prague, Czechoslovakia, Oct. 5, 1922; arrived in Can., 1969; s. Frantisek and Bozena (Papouskova) V.; m. Dagmar Gutova, Oct. 22, 1949; 1 son, Martin. Dipl.eng., Tech. U. Prague, 1947, C.Sc., 1957. With Research Inst. for Radio Communications, Prague, 1948-67, head math. dept., until 1967; vis. prof. U. Ill., Urbana, 1967-69; prof. elec. engring. U. Waterloo (Ont., Can.), 1969—. Author: Computerized Approximation and Synthesis of Linear Networks, 1969, (with others) Computer Methods for Circuit Analysis and Design, 1983, 2nd edit., 1994, Basic Network Theory with Computer Applications, 1992; assoc. editor IEEE Trans. on Circuits and Systems, 1979-80, 87-88, 98—. Fellow: IEEE (life); mem.: Eta Kappa Nu. Home: 355 Craigleith Dr Waterloo ON Canada N2L 5B5 Office: U Waterloo 200 University Ave West Waterloo ON Canada N2L 3G1 Office Phone: 519-888-4567 ext 33671. Personal E-mail: jvlach@uwaterloo.ca.

VLADECK, BRUCE CHARNEY, healthcare consultant, former academic administrator; b. NYC, Sept. 13, 1949; s. Stephen Charney and Judith (Pomarlen) V.; m. Fredda Wellin, Aug. 5, 1973; children—Elizabeth Charney, Stephen Isaiah, Abigail Sarah. BA, Harvard U., Cambridge, Mass., 1970; MA, U. Mich, 1972, PhD in Polit. Sci., 1973. Assoc. social scientist NYC-Rand Inst., 1973-74; asst. prof. Columbia U., NYC, 1974-78, assoc. prof., 1978-79; asst. commr. health planning and resources devel. NJ Dept. Health, Trenton, 1979-82; asst. v.p. Robert Wood Johnson Found., Princeton, NJ, 1982-83; pres. United Hosp. Fund, NYC, 1983-93; adminstr. HCFA, Washington, 1993-97; prof. health policy and geriatrics Mt. Sinai Med. Ctr., NYC, 1997—2004; prin. Health Scis. Adv. Svcs. Ernst & Young LLP, 2004—06, 2007—09; interim pres. U. Medicine and Dentistry NJ, Newark, 2006—07; sr. advisor Neycera Inc., 2009—. Mem. NY State Coun. on Health Care Financing, Albany, 1978-92; mem. com. on nursing home regulation Inst. Medicine, Washington, 1983-85, chmn. com. on health care for homeless people, 1986-88, mem. prospective payment assessment com., 1986-93; mem. Nat. Bipartisan Commn. on Future of Medicare, 1997-98. Author: Unloving Care: The Nursing Home Tragedy, 1981. Contbr. numerous articles to profl. publs. Fellow N.Y. Acad. Medicine; mem. Inst. Medicine, Nat. Acad. Scis., Phi Beta Kappa. Office Phone: 212-773-0111, 212-506-5453. Personal E-mail: bvladeck@earthlink.net. Business E-Mail: bruce.vladeck@ey.com, bvladeck@nexevaconsultancy.com.

VLADEM, STEVEN ALLEN, writer, film producer, motivational speaker; b. Chgo., July 24, 1949; s. Arthur and Elaine Edythe (Ascher) Vladem. BA with honors and distinction, U. Ill., Chgo., 1970; MEd in Math., Northeastern Ill. U., Chgo., 1973; MA in Ednl. Adminstrn./Supervision, Roosevelt U., Chgo., 1975; ScD, London Sch. Applied Rsch., 1993. Tchr. math. Chgo. Bd. Edn., 1971-81, statistician and evaluator dept. rsch. and evaluation, 1979; supr. program svcs. Dept. Planning, Chgo. City Hall, 1981; coord. alt. sch. without walls program Chgo. Met. HS, 1982-87, coord. computer assisted instrn., 1987-91; developer ednl. software Chgo., 1987-92; freelance computer cons., 1987-92; writer/lectr., 1994—; prodr. Image Lost Film, 2003—. Lectr. in field; mktg. cons. Enoch Searle Prodns., 2001—, Cosmic Films, 2001—; motivational spkr. Profl. Spkrs. Bur. Internat., 2001—. Author: (poetry) The Jigsaw People, 1997; exhibitions include Gallery Art, Internat. Congress Arts and Commn., Keble Coll., Oxford U., Eng.; prodr.: Image Last Films, 2003—; exec. prodr.: (films) Gein, 2003. Mem. Internat. Parliament Safety and Peace, Palermo, Italy, 1993—95; bd. dirs. Nat. Coalition health Care Reform, 1998—; founder coun. London Diplomatic Acad., Internat. Diplomatic Acad., Albert Schweitzer Inst., Chgo. Coun. Fgn. Rels., Internat. Fellowship Christians and Jews; sec.-gen. United Cultural Conv.; hon. amb. laureates Jr. Achievement and Chgo. Assn. Bus. and Industry, 1990; support group leader, outreach vol. Nat. Keratoconus Found., LA, 1995—; docent Tour of Old Town Old Town C. of C., Chgo., 1993; patron various arts orgns.; vol. Sight Savers Internat., Karen Or Ctr. Multi-Handicapped Blind Children, State of Ill. Transplant Program, 2003, Am. Transplant Assn., Cinema for Deaf Film Festival, 2003; judge Daniel Webster Acad. Poets Competition, 1998; nominator Col.'s Way Award. Recipient Congress Star of Distinction, Internat. Congress Arts and Comm./St. John's Coll., Cambridge U., 1992, medal of Merit, Republic of Peru, 1992, Alzheimers Rsch. award, Alzheimers Assn. Am., 2000, Internat. Peace prize, 2002, Congl. medal of Excellence, 2002, Am. medal of Honor, 2002; named John W. Rogers Educator of the Yr., Jr. Achievement, Chgo., 1990; named to Wall of Tolerance, Civil Rights Meml. Ctr., 2003; finalist, U.S. Nat. Memory Championship, N.Y.C., 1997. Mem. NATAS, Ill. Prodn. Alliance, Internat. Platform Assn. (bd. govs. internet team, red carpet com., Gold Ribbon Most Popular Artist 1995), United Writers Assn. (life fellow), World Univ. Roundtable, Toastmasters Internat., Internat. Order of Merit (Cambridge, Eng.), Daniel Webster Acad. Poets (Cert. of Merit 1995), Chrysopoets, Order of Templars of Jerusalem (knight), Lofsensic Ursinius Order (knight comdr.), World Order of Sci. Edn. Culture. (knight-cavalier), Am. Order Excellence, Order of San Ciriaco (count), Internat. Diplomatic Acad., Am. Legion (gold medal, sch. leadership award 1967), Rotary Club, Lions Club. Avocations: cinema, musical theatre, backgammon, architecture, world travel. Address: Profl Spkrs Bur Internat 1112 5th Ave Ste 101 Worthington OH 43085 Home: 1720 Maple Ave Apt 302 Evanston IL 60201-3103 E-mail: stevevladem@yahoo.com.

VLADIMIROV, KATYA, history professor; d. Natalia Tikhomirova and Vladimir Tikhomirov. MA, George Mason U., Fiarfax, Va., 1994; PhD, Georgetown U., Wash., 1999. Assoc. prof. history Kennesaw State U., Ga., 2000—. Author: (book) Russian, Soviet and World History; contbr. articles to profl. jours. Grantee, ACLS, Nat. Endowment Humanities, IREX, 1995, 2000, 2004, 2006. Office: Kennesaw State Univ 1000 Chastain Rd Kennesaw GA 30144 Business E-Mail: kvladimi@kennesaw.edu.

VLADIMIROV, VASILIY SERGEYEVICH, mathematician; b. Diaglevo, Leningrad, USSR, Jan. 9, 1923; s. Sergei and Maria (Sokolova) V.; m. Nina Ovsjannikova; children: Sergei, Michail. D of Math., Steklov Inst., Moscow, 1960; prof., Phys.-Tech. Inst., Moscow, 1965; academician, Acad. Sc. of USSR, 1970. Jr. rsch. worker Steklov Inst. Math. Acad. Sci. USSR, Leningrad, 1948-50; head math. dept. All-Russian Rsch. Inst. Exptl. Physics, Arsamas-16, 1950-55; sr. rsch. worker Steklov Inst. Math. Acad. Sci. USSR, Moscow, 1956-69, head dept. math. physics, 1969—2003, vice-dir., 1986-88, dir., 1988-93. Prof. Moscow Phys. Tech. Inst., 1964—87. Author: Mathematical Problems in One-Speed Theory of Transfer, 1961 (Liapount gold medal 1971), Methods of Several Complex Variables, 1964, Equations of Mathematical Physics, 1967, Generalized Functions in Mathematical Physics, 1976, Tauberian Theorems for Generalized Functions, 1986, p-Adic Numbers and Mathematical Physics, 1994, Methods of the Theory of Generalized Functions, 2002. Soldier Air-Forces, 1941—45. Recipient Gold Star Sickle and Hammer, Russian Govt., 1983, Lenin Orders, 1975, 1983, Labour Red Banner Orders, 1967, 1973, Gold medal, Bernardo Bolzano Chescoslovenska Acad. Sci., 1982, Order of the Great Pathriotic War II Degree, 1985, State Prises, 1953, 1987, Bogoliubov prize, Nat. Acad. Sci. Ukraine, 1997, Bogoliubov Gold medal, Acad. Scis. Russia, 1999, prize, Russian Govt., 2003. Mem. Acad. Scis. of Russia, Saxsonian Acad. Sci. (fgn.), Serbian Acad. Sci. and Arts (fgn.), Voievoding Acad. Sci. and Arts (fgn.), Soc. Math. and Physics of Czechoslovakia (hon.), Moscow Math. Soc., Internat. Assn. Math. and Physics, Am. Math. Soc. Office: Steklov Inst Math Gubkin Str 8 Moscow 119991 GSP Russia Office Phone: 4951351449. E-mail: vladim@mi.ras.ru.

VLADUTIU, ADRIAN O., physician, educator; b. Bucharest, Romania, Aug. 5, 1940; came to U.S., 1969, naturalized 1974; s. Octavian and Veturia (Chirescu) Vladutiu; m. Georgirene V. Dietrich; children: Christina Lynn, Catherine Joy. MD, Sch. Medicine, Bucharest, 1962; PhD in Immunopathology, Sch. Medicine, Jassy, Romania, 1968. Diplomate Am. Bd. Pathology. Asst. prof. physiopathology Sch. Medicine, Bucharest, 1968-71; assoc. prof. pathology SUNY Sch. Medicine, Buffalo, 1978-81, prof. pathology, 1981—, pathologist, 1974—2006; dir. clin. labs. Buffalo Gen. Hosp., 1982—2001, prof. microbiology, 1982—, prof. medicine, 1985—. Cons. Niagara Falls (N.Y.) Meml. Hosp., 1976—82, Tri-County Hosp., Gowanda, NY, 1991—93; acting head dept. pathology Buffalo Gen. Hosp, 1985—86; dir. lab. Deaconess Hosp. Buffalo, 1982—91, Columbus Meml., Buffalo, 1996—98. Author: Pleural Effusion, 1986; contbr. chapters to books, articles to profl. jours. Med. Rsch. Coun. Can. fellow, 1968, Buswell fellow, 1969; recipient rsch. prize Ministry Edn. Romania, 1965, rsch. award NIH, 1985. Fellow: ACP, Nat. Acad. Clin. Biochemistry, Coll. Am. Pathologists; mem.: Am. Soc. Investigative Pathology, Am. Assn. Immunologists. Achievements include first demonstration of the association of autoimmunity with major histocompability antigens; discovery of Buffalo thyroxine binding globulin gene. Home: 80 Oakview Dr Buffalo NY 14221-1420 Business E-Mail: vladutiu@buffalo.edu. E-mail: guthormones@yahoo.com.

VLAHOV, DAVID, epidemiologist; b. Washington, Aug. 31, 1952; s. William John and Helga Rose Vlahov; m. Robyn Randice Mione; children: Alexander, Alexandra Gershon. BA, Earlham Coll., 1974; BSN, MS, U. Md., 1980; PhD, Johns Hopkins U., 1988. RN 1977. Prof. epidemiology Sch. Pub. Health Johns Hopkins U., Balt., 1988—2001; dir. Ctr. for Urban Epidemiologic Studies, v.p. for rsch. NY Acad. Medicine, NYC, 1999—; prof. clin. epidemiology Sch. Pub. Health Columbia U., NYC, 1999—. Mem. nat. adv. coun. on drug abuse Dept. HHS. Contbr. more than 550 sci. papers to profl. jours.; editor: Jour. Urban Health, 2000—. Recipient Merit award, NIH, 1995—2005; grantee, 1990—, CDC, 1990—, Robert Wood Johnson Found., 1990—, NY Cmty. Trust, 1990—. Fellow: NY Acad. Medicine, Infectious Disease Soc. of Am.; mem.: Am. Pub. Health Assn., Am. Epidemiol. Soc., Soc. for Epidemiol. Rsch. Home: 401 E 86th St Apt 12 E New York NY 10028 Office: NY Acad Medicine 1216 Fifth Ave New York NY 10029 Office Phone: 212-822-7382. Business E-Mail: dvlahov@nyam.org.

VLAZNY, JOHN GEORGE, archbishop; b. Chgo., Feb. 22, 1937; s. John George and Marie Hattie (Brezina) Vlazny. BA, St. Mary of the Lake Coll., Mundelein, Ill., 1958; STL, Pontifical Gregorian U., Rome, 1962; MA in Classics, U. Mich., 1967; MEd, Loyola U., 1972; LLD (hon.), U. Portland, 1999. Ordained priest Archdiocese of Chgo., 1961, aux. bishop, 1983—87; assoc. pastor St. Paul of the Cross Ch., Park Ridge, Ill., 1962—63, St. Clement Ch., Chgo., 1963—68, St. Aloysius Ch., Chgo., 1968—72, pastor, 1979—81; assoc. pastor St. Sylvester Ch., Chgo., 1972—74, Precious Blood Ch., Chgo., 1974—79; faculty Quigley Prep., North Chgo., Ill., 1963—79, dean of studies, 1969—79; rector Niles Coll., Chgo., 1981—83; ordained bishop, 1983; bishop Diocese of Winona, Minn., 1987—97; archbishop Archdiocese of Portland, 1997—. Pres. Presbyteral Senate, Chgo., 1976—77; mem. Diocesan Clergy Personnel Bd., Chgo., 1981—84, chmn., 1983—84. Bd. dirs. NED, Latino Tng. Ctr., Chgo., 1980—81, Sacred Heart Sch. Theology, Hales Corners, Wis., 1986—, St. Mary's Coll., Winona, 1987—. Mem.: Nat. Conf. Cath. Bishops (various coms. 1983—), Nat. Comms. Found. (bd. dirs. 1990—). Roman Catholic. Avocations: music, running.

VLCEK, BRIAN L., engineering educator; PhD in Mech. Engring., Rensselaer Poly. Inst., Troy, NY. Prof. Ga. Southern U., Statesboro, 1997—. Faculty advisor ASME and Eagle Motorsports, Statesborto, 1997. Office: Ga Southern Univ 2121 Sci and Tech Bldg Statesboro GA 30460-8045

VLCEK, DONALD JOSEPH, JR., food products executive, wholesale distribution executive, writer; b. Chgo., Oct. 30, 1949; s. Donald Joseph and Rosemarie (Krizek) V.; m. Claudia Germain Meyer, July 22, 1978 (div. 1983); 1 child, Suzanne Mae; m. Valeria Olive Russell, Nov. 11, 1989 (div. Mar. 2006); children: James Donald, Victoria Rose. BBA, U. Mich., 1971. Cert. facilitator Adizes Inst. Gen. mgr. Popps, Inc., Hamtramck, Mich., 1969-76; sr. v.p. Domino's Pizza Inc., 1978—93; pres. Domino's Pizza Distbn. Corp., Ann Arbor, Mich., 1978-93, chmn., 1993-94, also bd. dirs.; pres. Don Vlcek & Assocs., Ltd., Plymouth, Mich., 1994—; CEO Beaver Buddies, LLC, Plymouth, Mich., 2001—04; master franchisee Beaver Tails Can., Inc., Mich., Ind., Ill., Ohio, Wis.; pres. WonderPizzaUSA, 2005—07, bd. mgrs., 2005—07, COO, 2005—07; v.p. Marco's Franchising LLC, Toledo, 2007—. Profl. speaker, personal coach, seminar leader, bus. cons., workshop facilitator; trustee Domino's Pizza Ptnrs. Found.; bd. dirs. RPM Pizza Inc., Gulfport, Miss., Dimango Corp., South Lyon, Mich.; sr. v.p. distbn. and tech. Domino's Ohio Commissary, Zanesville; pres. Morel Mountain Corp.; judge 1994 Duck Stamp contest U.S. Dept. Interior, Jr. Fed. Duck Stamp Contest, 1995; bd. dirs. Beaver Tails Can. Author: The Domino Effect, 1992 (Best of Bus. award ALA 1992, Soundview's Top 30 Business books of 1993), SuperVision, 1997, Job Planning and Review System Manual, 1997, 2001; (audio cassette tape series Super Vision; contbr. articles to profl. jours. Bd. dirs. Men's Hockey League of Oak Park, Mich., 1973-78; asst. coach Redford Scorpions Jr. Travel Hockey Team. Named Person of Yr. Bd. Franchises, Boston, 1981; recipient Teal award Ducks Unltd., 1992, State Major Gifts Chmn. award, 1992, 93, State Chmn.'s award, 1992, State Major Gifts award, 1994, Russ Bengal award, 2003, Mr. Producer award, 1997, 98, 2000, others. Mem. Am. Soc. Industry Leaders, Soc. of Tng. Dirs., Mich. Steelheaders Assn. (life), Ducks Unltd. (life, Domino's Pizza chpt. treas., sponsor, chmn. 1988—, Mich. state bd. dirs., life sponsor, chmn. 1989, 91-92, state trustee 1992-98, hon. trustee 2001—, chmn. exec. com. 1992-94, major gifts chmn. 1993-98, chmn. strategic devel. com. 1994, sponsor in perpetuity Grand Slam Life, Heritage sponsor, recipient Russ Bengal award, 2003), Mich. United Conservation Club (life), Whitetails Unltd. (life), Pheasants Forever (life), Midstates Masters Bowling Assn. (bd. dirs. 1976-85), Barton Hills Country Club (golf com., capt. dist. team), U. Mich. Alumni Assn. (life), Domino's Lodge/Drummond Island Wildlife Habitat Found. (pres., chmn. bd.), Vlcek Family Wildlife Found. (pres., chmn. bd.), Elks (life), Die Hard Cubs Fan Club, Greater Detroit C. of C., Profl. Spkrs. Assn. of Mich. (bd. dirs. 1997-99), Mich. Soc. Assn. Execs., Sm. Bus. Assn. Mich., Nat. Spkrs. Assn., Profl. Spkrs. Ill. (profl.), Internat. Coaching Fedn. (cert. master), Am. Soc. Tng. Dirs., Bus. Network Profls. Republican. Roman Catholic. Avocations: hunting, fishing, hockey, art, coin collecting/numismatics. Office: Don Vlcek & Assoc Ltd PO Box 701353 Plymouth MI 48170-0963 Home: 9045 Rawsonville Rd Belleville MI 48111-9318 Office Phone: 734-266-2260, 419-885-7000 ext 2209. Personal E-mail: dvlcek@marcos.com.

VLIET, MARNI, health policy and health program consultant; d. James and Mary Louise Tasheff; m. Richard Wayne Vliet, Jan. 26, 1944; children: Whitney Aletia, Sasha Marie. BEd, Wichita State U., 1970, MEd, 1977. Lectr. Wichita State U., 1977—85; program cons. Kans. Health Found., Wichita, 1985—86, program officer, 1986—88, v.p. programs, 1988—92, sr. v.p., 1992—96, exec. v.p. and COO, 1996, pres. and CEO, 1996—2007. Bd. dir. Ctrs. Disease Control Found., 1999—; spkr. in field; bd. chair Cerantmahers Health, Washington, 1999—2001; bd. dirs. Drug Strategies, Washington, 2002—; bd. chair Wichita Art Mus., Kans., 2009—, mem., 2000—. Co-author: Public Health Reports, Community Grantmaking: A Strategic Approach; contbr. articles to jour. Founding chair Funders Concerned Against Substance Abuse, Washington, 1989—94; chair health com. Wichita Commn. on Status of Women, 1975—80, co-chair legis. com.; vice chair bd. Women's Studies Cmty. Coun., Wichita; co-founder Old Town Assn. Wichita, mem. bd.; founding chair Wichita Farm & Art Market Com., mem.; founding dir. Parent Awareness Group and Teen Awareness Day, Robinson Jr. HS, Wichita; founder, dir. Women Alive & Well I & II, Wichita; mem. exec. bd. Women's Alcohol Treatment Services, Wichita; mem. Wichita Children's Mus., Women in the Arts, Wichita; vice chair bd. Wichita Commn. on Status of Women; mem. health promotion adv. bd. Kaiser Family Found., Menlo Park, Calif., 1988—90; bd. dir. Drug Strategies, Washington, 2002—; mem. Grantmakers in Health, 1995—2001, chair bd. dirs., 1999—2001; mem. Cmty. Anti-Drug Coalitions Am., Washington, 1992—98, chair bd. dirs., 1996—98; mem. State of World Forum, San Francisco, 1998; bd. dir. Wichita Symphony Soc., 2000—, Wichita Art Mus., 2000—; mem. bd. Clearinghouse Midcontinent Founds., Kansas City, 1993—97. Recipient President's Drug Adv. Coun. Leadership award, Exec. Office Pres. U.S., 1992, Cmty. Coun. Adv. Bd. award, Wichita State U. Ctr. Women's Studies, 1996, Bd. Trustees' award, Wichita State U., 1996, Exec. of Yr. award, Clarus, 1997—98, Nat. Leadership award, Cmty. Anti-Drug Coalitions Ams., Washington, DC, 1998, Pub. Policy award, Kans. State U. Coll. Human Ecology, 2004, Women Bus. Honoree, Wichita Bus. Jour., 2004, Brotherhood/Sisterhood award, Nat. Conf. Cmty. and Justice, 55th Annual Humanitarian award, Wichita, 2005. Mem.: Coun. Founds. (assoc.), Sigma Theta Tau Internat. (adv. coun.). Avocations: reading, gardening, travel. Office Phone: 316-618-1081. Office Fax: 316-618-1054.

VO, ASHLEY, medical association administrator; married. PharmD, U. Southern Calif., LA, 1992. Dir. transplant immunotherapy Cedars-Sinai Med. Ctr., LA, 1992—. Contbr. articles to profl. jour. Mem.: Am. Transplant Congress. Office: Cedars-Sinai Med Ctr 8635 W 3rd St Ste 590W Los Angeles CA 90048

VO, HIEU N., architect; b. Cantho City, Cantho, Vietnam, June 2, 1963; s. Tan T. Vo, Tiet L. Lam; m. Hanh T. none. AA, L.A. Pierce Coll., 1994; BArch (hon.), Calif. State Poly. U., 1998. Project mgr. Underwood Assocs. Architects, Decatur, Ala., 1998—99, L. Hughes Assoc. Architects, Huntsville, Ala., 2000—05, Goodrum Knowles, Inc., Huntsville, 2005—. Recipient Concour d'Elegance, Calif. State Poly. U. Coll. of Environ. Design, 1998, Internat. Biog. Centre's 21st award for Achievement; named to The Talent Roster for Disting. Acad. Performance, The Coll. Bd.s Coll. Scholarship Svc., 1993. Mem.: AIA (assoc.), Golden Key (life; California State Polytechic University, Pomona, Outstanding Achievement Scholastic and Excellent 1997). Home: 429 Barrington Hills Dr Madison AL 35758 Office Phone: 256-539-3431. Personal E-mail: HVO24@aol.com. Business E-Mail: hieu.vo@gmcnetwork.com.

VOEGELI, VICTOR JACQUE, historian, educator, dean; b. Jackson, Tenn., Dec. 21, 1934; s. Victor Jacque Voegeli and Winnie Lassiter; m. Anna Jean King, Oct. 14, 1956; children: Victor Jacque, Charles Lassiter. BS, Murray State Coll., Murray, Kentucky, 1956; MA, Tulane U., New Orleans, 1961, PhD, 1965. Instr. history Tulane U., 1963-65, asst. prof., 1965-67; asst. prof. history Vanderbilt U., 1967-69, assoc. prof., 1969-73, prof. history, 1973-98, chmn. history dept., 1973-76, dean Coll. Arts and Sci., 1976-92, acting dean Coll. Arts and Sci., 1996-97, prof. emeritus, dean emeritus, 1998—. Author: Free But Not Equal: The Midwest and the Negro During the Civil War, 1967. Served with US Army, 1956-58. Nat. Endowment Humanities grantee, 1969-70, 72. Mem. So. Hist. Assn. Address: 2110 Golf Club Ln Nashville TN 37215-1224

VOEGTLIN-ANDERSON, MARY MARGARET, music educator, small business owner; b. Seattle; d. Joseph Walter and Veronica Margaret (Conroy) Voegtlin; m. Terry Lee Anderson, Mar. 19, 1977 (div. July 20, 1982). BA cum laude, Marylhurst U., 1963; postgrad., U. Wash., 1963—65, Oakland U., 1968, Seattle Pacific U., 1982—84. Cert. std. tchg. grades K-12 Wash. Profl. cellist Oreg. Symphony, Portland, 1962—63; tchr. music and humanities Chinook Mid. Sch., Seattle, 1963—89, gifted edn. specialist, 1983—89; tchr. music, music dept. chair Highline H.S., Seattle, 1989—2004, tchr. honors English, 1989—2004; owner, tchr. Anderson Music Studio, Seattle, 2004—. Contralto soloist Mt. Baker Pk. Presbyn. Ch., 1966—68, U. Congl. Ch., Seattle, 1968—73; profl. singer Seattle Opera Co., 1968—70, Seattle Chambers Singers, 1975—76; vocal coach, advisor Highline Jazz Ensemble, Seattle, 1990—2004; pvt. piano, cello and voice tchr., Seattle, 1991—; astronomy club advisor Highline H.S., Seattle, 1998—2004; dir. Highline Dist. Youth Orch., 2003—04, Burien Sr. Choir, 2003; trustee Sunlight Waters Corp., 2002—; pres., owner Anderson Music Studio. Contbr. articles to profl. jours.; Seattle Chambers Singers, 1975—76. Officer, sec. 46th Legis. Dist. Dem. Party, Seattle, 1974—78, chairperson Initiative 314 Campaign, 1975; Wash. state conv. del. Dem. Party, Olympia, 1976, Dem. precinct chairperson Seattle, 1976—77, legis. dist. alternate del., presdl. campaign worker, 2008. Fulbright Scholarship grantee, Nat. Tchrs. Performance Inst., Oberlin Coll., Ohio, 1970. Mem.: NEA, Planetary Soc., Nat. Coun. Tchrs. English, Seattle Astron. Soc., Music Educators' Nat. Conf. Roman Catholic. Avocations: astronomy, reading, bicycling, writing, hiking. Personal E-mail: mvanderson03@aol.com.

VOELL, RICHARD ALLEN, retired private investor; b. Chgo., Dec. 29, 1933; s. John Herman and Esther Frances (Anderson) V.; m. Virginia Charlotte Broderick, Dec. 20, 1958; children: David Broderick, Gregory Jon, Jeffrey Scott. BA, U. Ill., 1956; MBA, U. Hawaii, 1960. With Beatrice Foods Co., Chgo., 1958-79, group mgr. recreational products group, 1971-73, corp. v.p., 1973-75, vice chmn., 1975-79; pres., chief operating officer Penn Central Corp., Greenwich, Conn., 1979-81, chief exec. officer, 1981; pres., chief exec. officer The Rockefeller Group, NYC, 1982-95. Chmn. Harbor Rock Corp.; mem. adv. bds. Fiat and Club Med; mem. bds. SPA Exor and Con Edison; vice chmn. N.Y.C. Partnerships. Chair nominating com. Wildlife Conservation Soc.; chmn. Bus. Coun. for UN, 1982-97; mem. adv. bd. Ctr. for Sustainable Fisheries—Rosentiel Sch. Marine and Atmospheric Sci. 1st lt. AUS, 1956-58. Mem. UN Assn. (vice chmn.), Chief Execs. Orgn., Coun. on Fgn. Rels., Econ. Club N.Y. (past chmn.), Rockefeller Ctr. Club, Greenwich (Conn.) Country Club, Riverside (Conn.) Yacht Club, Chgo. Club, U. Ill. Founders Club. E-mail: pigoose@aol.com.

VOETEN, ERIK, political scientist, educator; b. Nijmegen, Netherlands, Jan. 11, 1972; m. Kimberly Morgan; 1 child, Anniek. MPA, MCE, U. Twente, Netherlands, 1996; PhD in Politics, Princeton U., NJ, 2001. Postdoc. scholar CISAC, Stanford U., Calif., 2001; asst. prof. George Washington U., Washington, 2002—06; Peter F. Krogh asst. prof. geopolitics and global justice Georgetown U. Contbr. articles to profl. jours. (Robert O. Keohane award, 2008). Office: Georgetown Univ SFS ICC 301 39th and O Sts Washington DC 20052 Business E-Mail: ev42@georgetown.edu.

VOEVODSKY, VLADIMIR, mathematician; b. Russia, June 4, 1966; BS in Math., Moscow State U., 1989; PhD in Math., Harvard U., 1992. Assoc. prof. Northwestern U., 1996—99; prof. Inst. for Advanced Study, Princeton, NJ, 2002—. Mem. Inst. for Advanced Study, Harvard U., 1992—93, 1998—2001; visiting prof. Max Planck Inst. for Math., 1996—97, Harvard U., 1996—97. Co-author: Cycles, Transfers and Motivic Homology Theories, 2000. Recipient Fields medal, 2002, rsch. grants, NSF, Clay Prize fellowship, 1999, 2000. Office: Inst for Advanced Study Sch Math Fuld 116 Einstein Dr Princeton NJ 08540 Office Phone: 609-734-8117. E-mail: vladimir@math.ias.edu.

VOGEL, ALEX N., lobbyist, lawyer; BA, U. Calif., San Diego; JD, George Washington U. Atty. Wiley, Rein & Fielding; dep. counsel RNC; gen. counsel Nat. Rep. Senatorial Com. (NRSC); chief counsel to Senate Majority Leader Bill Frist US Senate; ptnr. HoltzmanVogel PLLC, Mehlman Vogel Castagnetti, Inc., Washington, 2004—. Gen. counsel to v.p. Dan Quayle Quayle 2000 presdl. campaign; bd. mem. Va. Bd. Juvenile Justice, 2001—03; counsel Presdl. Recount in Fla. and Oreg., 2002. Polit. commentator Fox News, CNN, NPR. Named one of Most Powerful Men Under 39, Details mag., Fabulous 50, Roll Call, Sharpest Shooters on K St., The Hill, 2006. Mem.: ABA (mem. Adv. Commn. to the Standing Com. on Election Law). Office: Mehlman Vogel Castagnetti Inc 1341 G St, NW Ste 1100 Washington DC 20005 also: HoltzmanVogel PLLC 98 Alexandria Pike, Ste 53 Warrenton VA 20186 Office Phone: 202-585-0258. Office Fax: 202-393-3031. E-mail: alex@mvc-dc.com.

VOGEL, ARTHUR ANTON, clergyman; b. Milw., Feb. 24, 1924; s. Arthur Louis and Gladys Eirene (Larson) V.; m. Katharine Louise Nunn, Dec. 29, 1947; children: John Nunn, Arthur Anton, Katharine Ann. Student, U. of South, 1942-43, Carroll Coll., 1943-44; B.D., Nashotah House Theol. Sem., 1946; MA, U. Chgo., 1948; PhD, Harvard, 1952; S.T.D., Gen. Theol. Sem., 1969; D.C.L., Nashotah House, 1969; D.D., U. of South, 1971. Ordained deacon Episcopal Ch., 1946, priest, 1948; teaching asst. philosophy Harvard, Cambridge, Mass., 1949-50; instr. Trinity Coll., Hartford, Conn., 1950-52; mem. faculty Nashotah House Theol. Sem., Nashotah, Wis., 1952-71, asso. prof., 1954-56, William Adams prof. philosophical and systematic theology, 1956-71, sub-dean Sem., 1964-71; bishop coadjutor Diocese of West Mo., Kansas City, 1971-72, bishop, 1972-89; rector Ch. St. John Chrysostom, Delafield, Wis., 1952-56; dir. Anglican Theol. Rev., Evanston, Ill., 1964-69; mem. Internat. Anglican-Roman Cath. Consultation, 1970-90, Nat. Anglican-Roman Catholic Consultation, 1965-84, Anglican chmn., 1973-84; mem. Standing Commn. on Ecumenical Relations of Episcopal Ch., 1957-79; mem. gen. bd. examining chaplains Episcopal Ch., 1971-72. Del. Episcopal Ch., 4th Assembly World Council Chruches, Uppsala, Sweden, 1968, and others. Author: Reality, Reason and Religion, 1957, The Gift of Grace, 1958, The Christian Person, 1963, The Next Christian Epoch, 1966, Is the Last Supper Finished?, 1968, Body Theology, 1973, The Power of His Resurrection, 1976, Proclamation 2: Easter, 1980, The Jesus Prayer for Today, 1982, I Know God Better Than I Know Myself, 1989, Christ in His Time and Ours, 1982, God, Prayer and Healing, 1995, Radical Christianity and the Flesh of Jesus, 1995; editor: Theology in Anglicanism, 1985; contbr. articles to profl. jours. Vice chmn. bd. dirs. St. Luke's Hosp., Kansas City, Mo., 1971, chmn., 1973-89. Research fellow Harvard, 1950 Mem. Am. Philos. Assn., Metaphys. Soc. Am., Soc. Existential and Phenomenological Philosophy, Catholic Theol. Soc. Am. Episcopalian. Home: 720 W 44th St Apt 2005 Kansas City MO 64111-3413 E-mail: akvogel@swbell.net.

VOGEL, CEDRIC WAKELEE, lawyer; b. Cin., June 4, 1946; s. Cedric and Patricia (Woodruff) V. BA, Yale U., 1968; JD, Harvard U., 1971. Bar: Ohio 1972, Fla. 1973, U.S. Tax Ct. 1972, U.S. Supreme Ct. 1975. Ptnr. Vogel, Heis, Wenstrup & Cameron, Cin., 1972-96; sole practice, 1997—. Chmn. mem.'s com. Cin. Art Mus., 1987-88; chmn. auction Cin. Hist. Soc., 1985; local pres. English Speaking Union, 1979-81, nat. bd. dirs., 1981; chmn. Keep Cin. Beautiful, Inc., 1994-96; active Bravo! Cin. Ballet, 1989; chmn. Act II Nutcracker Ball, 1987-88; bd. dirs. Merc Libr., 1991-98, Cin. Preservation Assn., 1990-93, Cin. Opera Guild, 1997-99, Pro Srs., 1996-2005; vice chmn. Children's Heart Assn. Reds Rally, 1989; bd. dirs. Cin. Country Day Sch., 1983, pres. Alumni Coun. and Ann. Fund, 1983. Mem.: Fla. Bar Assn., Cin. Bar Assn., Harvard Alumni Assoc. (regional dir. ohio valley 2007—), Harvard Law Sch. Assn. Cin. (pres. 1997—99, 2003—), Heimlich Inst. (trustee 1987—2001), Yale Alumni Assn. (del. 1984—87), Travel Club Cin. (pres. 2009—), Pro Srs. (bd. dirs. 1996—2005), Harvard Club of Cin. (bd. dirs. 1996—98, pres. 1999—2000), The Lawyers Club Cin. (pres. 1995), Cincinnatus, Cin. Yale Club (pres. 1980—81, 1996—97). Republican. Home: 3473 Forest Oak Ct Cincinnati OH 45208-1842 Office: 817 Main St Ste 800 Cincinnati OH 45202-2183 Home Phone: 513-871-7953; Office Phone: 513-421-4225. Personal E-mail: rvogel@iac.net.

VOGEL, EZRA F., sociology educator; b. Delaware, Ohio, July 11, 1930; s. Joseph H. and Edith (Nachman) V.; m. Suzanne Hall, July 5, 1953 (div.); children: David, Steven, Eva; m. Charlotte Ikels, Nov. 3, 1979. BA, Ohio Wesleyan U., 1950; MA, Bowling Green State U., 1951; PhD, Harvard U., 1958; LittD (hon.), Kwansai Gakuin, 1980, Wittenberg Coll., 1981, Bowling Green State U., 1982, U. Md., 1983, Albion Coll., 1988, Chinese U., Hong Kong, 1992, Ohio Wesleyan, 1996; LittD (hon.), U. Mass., Lowell, 1996, Yamaguchi U., 1998, Monterrey Inst., 2002. Rsch. fellow Harvard (for work in Japan), 1958-60; asst. prof. Yale U., 1960-61; rsch. assoc., lectr. Harvard U., 1961-67, prof., 1967—2000, Henry Ford II prof. social scis., 1990—2005, emeritus, 2005—, assoc. dir. East Asian Rsch. Ctr., 1967-73, dir., 1973-77, chmn. council East Asian studies, 1977-80, dir. program on U.S.-Japan relations, 1980-87, hon. chmn. program on U.S.-Japan rels., 1988—, mem. faculty council, 1981-84, dir. Asia Ctr., 1997-99, rsch. prof., 2000—; nat. intelligence officer for East Asia Nat. Intelligence Coun., 1993-95, dir. Fairbank Ctr. East Asian Studies, 1995-99. Mem. Joint Com. on Contemporary China, 1968-75, Com. on Scholarly Communication with Peoples Republic China, 1973-75, Joint Com. Japanese Studies, 1977-79 Author: Japan's New Middle Class, 1963, Canton Under Communism, 1969, Japan As Number One, 1979, Comeback, 1985, The Impact of Japan on a Changing World, 1987, One Step Ahead in China, 1989, The Four Little Dragons, 1991, Is Japan Still Number One?, 2000; co-editor: (with Norman W. Bell) A Modern Introduction to the Family, 1960, (with George Lodge) Ideology and National Competitiveness, Living With China, 1997, (with Ming Yuan and Akihiko Tanaka) The Golden Age of the U.S.-China Japan Triangle, 2002, (with Stephen Mackinnon and Diama Lary) China At War, 2007; editor: Modern Japanese Organization and Decision-Making, 1975. Trustee Ohio Wesleyan U., 1970-75, 80-94. Served with AUS, 1951-53. Recipient Harvard faculty prize for book of year, 1970, Japan Found. prize, 1996, Japan Soc. prize 1998, Howard Graduate Sch. Centennial medal, 2008; Guggenheim fellow, 1972 Mem. Assn. Asian Studies (bd. dirs. 1970-72), Am. Acad. Arts and Scis. Home: 14 Sumner Rd Cambridge MA 02138-3018

VOGEL, H. VICTORIA, psychotherapist, educator, writer, stress disorder and addiction recovery counselor; BA, U. Md., 1968; MA, NYU, 1970, MA, 1975; MEd, postgrad., Columbia U., 1982—; cert., Am. Projective Drawing Inst., 1983; CASAC, New Sch. U. for Social Rsch., 2000. Diplomate Am. Acad. Experts in Traumatic Stress; cert. addiction recovery counselor, expert in traumatic stress, alcohol and substance abuse counselor, addictions treatment, addiction counseling alcohol and substance abuse. Art therapist Childville, Bklyn., 1962-64; tchr. Montgomery County (Md.) Jr. H.S., 1968-69; with H.S. divsn. N.Y.C. Bd. Edn., 1970—; guidance counselor, instr., psychotherapist in pvt. practice. Guidance counselor, instr., psychotherapist in pvt. practice; clin. counseling cons. psychodiagnosis and devel. studies, art/play therapy The Modern Sch., 1984—; art/play therapist Hosp. Ctr. for Neuromuscular Disease and Devel. Disorders, 1986—; employment counselor-adminstr. N.Y. State Dept. Labor Concentrated Employment Program, 1971-72; intern psychotherapy and psychoanalysis psychiat. divsn. Ctrl. Islip Hosp., 1973-75, Calif. Grad. Inst., L.A.; intern psychol. counseling and rehab. N.J. Coll. Medicine, Newark, 1979. Author: The Never Ending Story of Alcohol, Drugs and Other Substance Abuse, 1992, Variant Sexual Behavior and the Aesthetic Modern Nudes, 1992, Psychological Science of School Behavior Intervention, 1993, Joycean Conceptual Modernism: Relationships and Deviant Sexuality, 1995, Electronic Evil Eyes, 1995 (U.S. Cert. of Recognition, 1996), Psychological Paradigms of Alcohol Violence Suicide Trauma Addiction Variant Pathologies PTSD and Schizophrenia, 1999. Mem. com. for spl. events NYU, 1989; participant clin. and artistic perspectives Am. Acad. Psychoanalysis Conf., 1990, participant clin. postmodernism and psychoanalysis, 1996; aux. police officer N.Y. Police Dept., 1994—; chair bylaws com. Columbia U., 1995—. Mem.: ACA, AAAS, APA, NY Acad. Sci., Tchrs. Coll. Adminstrv. Women in Edn., Assn. Humanistic Psychology (exec. sec. 1981), Art/Play Therapy, N.Y. Art Tchrs. Assn., Am. Acad. Experts Traumatic Stress (diplomate in expert traumatic stress), Am. Soc. Group Psychotherapy and Psychodrama (publs. com. 1984—), Am. Orthopsychiat. Assn., Am. Psychol. Soc., Phi Delta Kappa (editor chpt. newsletter 1981—84, exec. sec. Columbia U. chpt. 1984—, chmn. nominating com. for chpt. officers 1986—, rsch. rep. 1986—, pub. rels. exec. bd. dirs. 1991, NYU chpt. v.p. programs 1994—).

VOGEL, HOWARD H., lawyer; b. Paris, Tenn., Sept. 4, 1949; s. Herman Lentz and Caroline Powell (Carothers) V.; m. Kathryn Lynn Massey, Sept. 14, 1974; children: Caroline Carothers, Patrick Alexander, Anna Kathryn. BA, Vanderbilt U., 1971; JD, U. Tenn., 1974. Assoc. atty. O'Neil, Parker & Williamson, Knoxville, Tenn., 1976-77, ptnr., 1977—. Pres. Dogwood Arts festival Inc., Knoxville, 1990-92. Fellow Tenn. Bar Found., Am. Bar Found.; mem. ABA (house dels. 1983-89, bd. govs. 1985-88, 2008-, chmn. standing com. on meetings and travel 1990-92, chair 1993-94, Tenn. state del. 2001-06), Tenn. Young Lawyers Conf. (pres. 1980-81), Knoxville Bar Assn. (pres.-elect 1990-92, pres. 1993), Tenn. Bar Assn. (v.p. 1993-94, pres.-elect 1994). Office: O'Neil Parker & Williamson 416 Cumberland Ave SW PO Box 217 Knoxville TN 37902 Office Phone: 865-546-7190.*

VOGEL, JAMES M., hematologist, oncologist; b. NYC; s. Peter Vogel and Helen M. Mandlebaum; m. Judith Anne Resnick; 1 child, Jennifer. BA, Wesleyan U., 1958, MA, 1959; MD, Columbia U., 1962. Diplomate Am. Bd. Internal Medicine, Am. Bd. Hematology, Am. Bd. Med. Oncology. Intern Mt. Sinai Hosp., NYC, attending physician - medicine, 1968—, resident in hematology and internal medicine; chief hematology/med. oncology medicine divsn. Beth Israel Hosp., NYC, 1968; assoc. prof. medicine Mt. Sinai Sch. Medicine, NYC, 1986—; fellow in med. oncology Nat. Cancer Inst., Bethesda, Md. Author: How to Live with Hemophilia, 1972. Lt. comdr. USPHS, USCG, 1964—66. Named Best Doctor in N.Y., Met. Area Connally Rehab., 1995—, N.Y. Mag., 1998—. Avocations: skiing, stamps, military history. Office: 1125 Park Ave New York NY 10128 Office Phone: 212-369-4250.

VOGEL, JEFFREY C., state banking agency administrator; m. Kathy Vogel; children: Sam, Chase. BS in Acctg., U. Wy., 1983. Acting commr. Wyo. Divsn. Banking, 1996, 2002, dep. banking commr., commr., 2002—. Vice chmn. Mo. Conf. State Bank Suprs., 2005. Office: Wyo Divsn Banking Herschler Bldg 3rd Fl E 122 W 25th St Cheyenne WY 82002 Office Phone: 307-777-7797. Office Fax: 307-777-3555. E-mail: jvogel@wyaudit.state.wy.us.*

VOGEL, JENNIFER L., lawyer, air transportation executive; BBA, U. Iowa, Iowa City; JD, U. Tex. Sch. Law, Austin, 1987. Atty. Vinson & Elkins, LLP; v.p., gen. counsel Enron Global Power & Pipelines; v.p. legal, asst. sec. Continental Airlines, Inc., Houston, 1995—2001, gen. counsel, 2001—, sr. v.p., chief compliance officer, corp. sec., 2003—. Mailing: Continental Airlines Inc PO Box 4607 Houston TX 77210-4607 Office Phone: 713-324-2950. Office Fax: 713-324-2637.*

VOGEL, JON, political organization executive; b. 1975; m. Kate Kumpuris. B in Internat. Rels., Conn. Coll., 1997. Fin. dir. to NY rep. Mike Forbes, campaign mgr. to Va. del. Robert Hull, 1997—2000; fin. dir. Congl. campaign Steve Israel for Congress, 2000, dep. chief of staff to congressman Israel Washington, 2001—03; Midwest fin. dir. Gephardt for Pres. Campaign, 2004; v.p. Winning Directions, Inc., 2004—05; joined as fin. asst. Dem. Congl. Campaign Com. (DCCC), Washington, 2005, NE/Fla. regional dir., 2006, polit. dir., 2007—08, dir. Ind. Expenditure Program, 2008, exec. dir., 2009—; ptnr. Global Strategy Group, LLC, Washington, 2009. Democrat. Office: DCCC 430 S Capitol St SE Washington DC 20003 Office Phone: 202-863-1500. Business E-Mail: vogel@dccc.org.

VOGEL, NELSON J., JR., lawyer; b. South Bend, Ind., Oct. 13, 1946; s. Nelson J. and Carolyn B. (Drzewiecki) V.; m. Sandra L. Cudney, May 17, 1969; children: Ryan C., Justin M., Nathan J., Lindsey M. BS cum laude, Miami U., Oxford, Ohio, 1968; JD cum laude, U. Notre Dame, 1971. Bar: Ind. 1971, Mich. 1971, U.S. Dist. Ct. (no. dist.) Ind. 1971, U.S. Tax Ct. 1972, U.S. Ct. Appeals (5th cir.) 1975, U.S. Ct. Claims 1980. Acct. Coopers & Lybrand, South Bend, 1969-71; assoc. Barnes & Thornburg, South Bend, 1971-76, ptnr., 1977—. Lectr. U. Notre Dame, South Bend, 1971, 74-80; instr. Ind. U., South Bend, 1971-74; vice-chair Barnes & Thornburg, 2001—, mng. ptnr. South Bend office, 2001—. Trustee Project Future, St. Joseph Co., 2002-; pres. Big Bros./Big Sisters, South Bend, 1978-79; bd. pres. South Bend Regional Mus. Art, 1984-86; ethics com. Meml. Hosp., South Bend, 1986-94; bd. adv. Goshen Coll. Family Bus. program, 1993-99; bd. dirs. Madison Ctr., 2003-06. Fellow: Am. Coll. Tax. Coun.; mem. Nat. Employee Stock Ownership Plan Assn. (sec.-treas. Ind. chpt. 1993-95), Nat. Assn. State Bar Tax Sec. (exec. com. 1982-84), Ind. State Bar Assn. (chmn. taxation sect. 1981-82, Citation of Merit 1979), Mich. Bar Assn. (tax sect.), Ind. State HS Hockey Assn., Inc. (bd. dirs. 1998-01, treas. 1998-01), Michiana World Affairs Coun. (bd. dirs. 1992-96), Michiana World Trade Club (bd. dirs. 1992-96), Mental Health Assn. St. Joseph County (bd. dirs. 1997-01), St. Joseph County C. of C. (bd. dirs. 2005—). Home: 1146 Dunrobbin Ln South Bend IN 46614-2150 Office: Barnes & Thornburg 600 1st Source Bank 100 N Michigan St Ste 600 South Bend IN 46601-1632 Office Phone: 574-233-1171. Business E-Mail: nvogel@btlaw.com.

VOGEL, PHYLLIS JEAN, music educator; b. Hamilton, Ohio, Oct. 1, 1940; d. Orville Fred Hays and Marian Elizabeth Maus; m. Chester Allen Hays, Apr. 10, 1971. DMA, Peabody Conservatory Johns Hopkins U., Balt., 1973. Tchr. Peabody Conservatory, Balt., 1965—66; assoc. prof. West Chester U., Pa., 1966—71; adj. prof. U. SC, Columbia, 1971—72; prof., music NC State U., Raleigh, 1975—. Artistic dir. NC Bach Festival, Raleigh. Home: 308 Lake Boone Trail Raleigh NC 27608 Office: NC State Univ Price Music Ctr Raleigh NC 27607 Personal E-mail: chetvogel@aol.com. Business E-Mail: phyllis_vogel@ncsu.edu.

VOGEL, SCOTT CHARLES, music educator; b. Mpls., Minn., Apr. 14, 1963; s. Wayne Kent Vogel and Karen Marie Vogel-Pearsal; m. Kari Ann Laine, July 25, 1992; children: Tristan, Carli, Collin. AA, No. Hennepin Cmty. Coll., 1984; BSc, Bemidji State U., 1988. Dir. bands, tchr. Princeton Pub. Schs., Minn., 1988—92, Mahnomen Pub. Schs., Minn., 1992—98, Coon Rapids HS, Minn., 1998—. Mem.: Minn. Band Dirs. Assn., Internat. Assn.of Jazz Educators (treas. 1992—95), Minn. Music Educators Assn., Music Educators Nat. Conf., Sons of the Am. Legion. Avocations: archery, fishing, camping, hunting. Home: 31512 104th St Princeton MN 55371 Office: Coon Rapids HS 2340 Northdale Blvd Coon Rapids MN 55433 Office Phone: 763-506-7175. Business E-Mail: scott.vogel@anoka.k12.mn.us.

VOGEL, STEVEN, biologist, educator; b. Beacon, NY, Apr. 7, 1940; s. Max and Jeanette Rachel (Zucker) V.; m. Mariette Seeley Booth, June 3, 1963 (div. Jan. 1974); 1 child, Roger Booth; m. Jane Gregory, Dec. 13, 1974. BS, Tufts U., 1961; AM, Harvard U., 1963, PhD, 1966. 01. Instr. Tufts U., Medford, Mass., 1962; from asst. prof. to prof. Duke U., Durham, NC, 1966-93, James B. Duke prof., 1993—2006, prof. emeritus, 2006—. Instr. U. Wash., Friday Harbor, summer, 1979, 81, 83; cons. in field. Author: Life in Moving Fluids, 1981, Life's Devices, 1988, Vital Circuits, 1991, Cats' Paws and Catapults, 1998, Comparative Biomechanics, 2003; contbr. articles to profl. jours. Jr. fellow Harvard U., 1964; recipient Stone prize for sci. writing L.A. County Museum, 1990. Fellow AAAS. Achievements include findings concerning the interrelationships between the shapes of organisms (from algae to mammals) and the fluid mech. phenomena around and within them. Home: 1212 Woodburn Rd Durham NC 27705-5757 Office: Duke Univ Dept Biology PO Box 90338 Durham NC 27708-0338 Business E-Mail: svogel@duke.edu.

VOGEL, THOMAS TIMOTHY, surgeon, educator, lay worker; b. Columbus, Ohio, Feb. 1, 1934; s. Thomas A. and Charlotte A. (Hogan) V.; m. M.M. Darina Kelleher, May 29, 1965; children: Thomas T., Catherine D., Mark P., Nicola M. AB, Coll. of Holy Cross, 1955; MS, Ohio State U., 1960, PhD, 1962; MD, Georgetown U., 1965. Pvt. practice surgery, Columbus, 1971-2001; chmn. liturgy com., pres. parish coun. St. Catharine Parish, Columbus, 1971-73; chmn. diocesan adminstrn. com. Diocesan Pastoral Coun., Columbus, 1972-73, chmn., 1973-75; vice prefect Sodality of Holy Cross, 1953-55; mem. Ohio Bishop's Adv. Coun., Columbus, 1976-79. Clin. asst. prof. surgery Ohio State U., Columbus, 1974—; past trustee Peer Rev. Sys., Inc.; assoc. med. dir. United Health Care, Columbus, 1997-2000; cons. Rehabilitation Svcs.; commr., surveillance utilization rev. mem. Medicaid, State of Ohio, 1998-2000; assoc. med. dir. Palmetto GBA, 1999—. Contbr. articles to profl. jours. Chmn. coun. grad. students Ohio State U., 1961; bd. dirs. St. Vincent's Children's Ctr., 1975-83, chmn., 1981-82; past chmn. bd. trustees St. Joseph Montessori Sch. Recipient Layman's award, Columbus Ea. Kiwanis, 1972; named Knight of the Holy Sepulchre, Equestrian Order of the Holy Sepulchre of Jerusalem, 2001. Mem. ACS, Am. Physiol. Soc., Assn. for Acad. Surgery, Ohio State Med. Assn. (del. 1993—), Sigma Xi, Delta Epsilon Sigma. Roman Catholic. Home: 247 S Ardmore Rd Columbus OH 43209-1701 Office: 621 S Cassingham Rd Columbus OH 43209-2403 E-mail: vogel.3@osu.edu.

VOGEL, VICTOR GERALD, medical educator, researcher; b. Bethlehem, Pa., Mar. 14, 1952; s. Victor Gerald Jr. and Margaret Moser (Smith) V.; m. Saralyn Sue Schaffner, June 25, 1977; children: Heather Marie, Christiaan Keith. Diplomate Am. Bd. Internal Medicine, Am. Bd. Preventive Medicine, Nat. Bd. Med. Examiners. Resident in internal medicine Balt. City Hosps., 1978-81; fellow in med. oncology Johns Hopkins Oncology Ctr., Balt., 1983-86; Andrew W. Mellon fellow Johns Hopkins Sch. Hygiene Pub. Health, Balt., 1984-86; asst. prof. medicine and epidemiology U. Tex./M.D. Anderson Cancer Ctr., Houston, 1986-93, assoc. prof. clin. cancer prevention, 1993-95; asst. prof. epidemiology U. Tex. Sch. Pub. Health, Houston, 1987-95; prof. medicine and epidemiology U. Pitts. Cancer Inst./Magee-Womens Hosp., 1996—2008, dir. MAGEE/UPCI breast cancer program, 1996—2002, dir. MAGEE/UPCI breast cancer prevention program, 2003—08; v.p. Rsch. Am. Cancer Soc., Atlanta, 2009—. Epidemiologist Tex. breast screening project Am. Cancer Soc., 1986-93; mem. data and safety monitoring bd. Women's Health Initiative, NIH, 1994—2004; bd. dirs. Nat. Surg. Adjuvant Breast and Bowel Project Found., Inc., 1997—, AMC Cancer Ctr., Denver, 1996-99; protocol chmn. Nat. Cancer Inst. Study of Tamoxifen and Raloxifene. Contbr. articles to profl. jours. Founding mem. Nat. Surg. adjuvant Breast and Bowel Project Found., Inc.; founding pres. Internat. Soc. Cancer Risk Assessment and Mgmt., 2003. Served with USPHS, 1981-83. Recipient award, Am. Cancer Soc., 1987, career devel. award, 1990—93, Impact award, Nat. Consortium Breast Ctrs., 2008; named Med. Vol. of Yr., Am. Cancer Soc., 1983; fellow, Susan G. Komen Breast Cancer Found., 1990—93. Fellow Am. Coll. Preventive Medicine, ACP; mem. Am. Soc. Clin. Oncology, Am. Soc. Preventive Oncology, Christian Med. and Dental Assn., Am. Assn. Cancer Rsch. Republican. Presbyterian. Avocation: flying. Office: Am Cancer Soc 250 Williams St Atlanta GA 30303 Office Phone: 404-929-6850. Personal E-mail: vvogel@aol.com. Business E-Mail: victor.vogel@cancer.org.

VOGEL, WARREN, lawyer; b. Phila., Oct. 2, 1948; BA, Temple U., 1970; JD cum laude, Temple U. Sch. Law, 1973. Bar: Pa. 1973, US Fed. Ct. 1973. Mem. Eckert Seamans Cherin & Mellott, LLC, Phila. Panelist Pa. Bar Inst. seminar; lectr. Nat. Bus. Inst., Bnai Brith Internat. Planned Giving. Editor, contbr. Temple U. Law Quar., 1972—73. Bd. dirs. JCCs of Greater Phila. With Pa. Air Nat. Guard, 1970—73. Recipient Corpus Juris Secundum award, 1973; named to Pa. Super Lawyers, Phila. Mag., 2004, 2005—06; Sr. scholar Sch. Health Policy & Population Health, Thomas Jefferson U. Med. Sch. Mem.: B'nai B'rith Internat. Planned Gring (lectr.), Nat. Bus. Inst. Programs LLC (lectr.), Phila. Estate Planning Coun., Pa. Bar Assn. (mem. task force ltd. liability co. documents), Phila. Bar Assn. (mem. sect. on corp., bus. and banking law 1973—), ABA (subcom. on tax matters 1979—, mem. sect. bus. law). Office: Eckert Seamans Cherin & Mellott LLC 2 Liberty Pl 22nd Fl 50S 16th St Philadelphia PA 19102 Office Phone: 215-851-8400, 215-851-8448. Office Fax: 215-851-8383. Business E-Mail: wvogel@eckertseamans.com.

VOGELGESANG, SANDRA LOUISE, writer, consultant, former ambassador; b. Canton, Ohio, July 27, 1942; d. Glenn Wesley and Louise (Forry) Vogelgesang; m. Geoffrey Ernest Wolfe, July 4, 1982. BA, Cornell U., 1964; MA, Tufts U., 1965, MA in Law and Diplomacy, 1966, PhD, 1971. With Dept. State, Washington, 1975-97, policy planner for sec. state and European Bur., 1975-80, dir. Econ Policy Office, Orgn. Econ. Coop. and Devel., 1981-82, econ. minister U.S. Embassy, Ottawa, Can., 1982-86, dep. asst. sec. Internat. Orgn. Affairs Bur., 1986-89; dep. asst. adminstr. Office Internat. Activities Environ. Protection Agy., Washington, 1989-92; with Dept. State, Washington, 1992; sr. policy advisor Agy. for Internat. Devel., 1993; US amb. to Nepal Dept. State, Washington, 1994-97; pres. Everest Assocs. and Himalaya, 1997—2004. Bd. dirs. Ctr. for Econ. Devel. and Population Activities; mem. women and conservation com. World Wildlife Fund, 1997—2004, mem. Nat. Coun., 1999—2004; bd. advisors Am.'s Soc., NYC, 1986—89; mem. Pres.'s Coun. of Cornell Women Cornell U., 1998—; adv. com. Dept. of Treasury com. on Internat. Child Labor Enforcement, 1999—; mem. global coun. Internat. Mus. Women, 2004—07; writer, cons. internat. devel. issues. Author: Long Dark Night of the Soul, The American Intellectual Left and the Vietnam War, 1974, American Dream-Global Nightmare: The Dilemma of U.S. Human Rights Policy, 1980. Bd. dirs. Crafts Ctr., 1999-2000. Recipient Meritorious Service awards, 1973, 74, 82, 83, 86, Disting. Honor award, 1976 Dept. State, Pres.' Disting. Service award, 1985. Mem. Council on Fgn. Relations. Office: 9009 Charred Oak Dr West Bethesda MD 20817-1923 Business E-Mail: everest.associates@erols.com.

VOGELMAN, JOSEPH HERBERT, scientific engineering company executive; b. NYC, Aug. 18, 1920; s. Jacob and Sabina (Weingarten) V.; m. Norma Schneider, Dec. 8, 1946; children: Jeffrey Allan, Leslie Sue, Linda Leigh. BS, CCNY, 1940; M.E.E., Poly. Inst. Bklyn., 1948, D.Elec. Engring., 1957. Registered profl. engr., N.Y., N.J. Project engr. Signal Corps Engr. Labs., Belmar, NJ, 1943-45; chief devel. br. Watson Labs., Eatontown, NJ, 1945-50; chief scientist Rome Air Devel. Center, Griffiss AFB, NY, 1951-52, chief electronic warfare lab., 1953-56, dir. communications, 1956-59; v.p., dir. Capehart Corp., NYC, 1959-64; dir. electronics Chromalloy Am. Corp., NYC, 1964-67, gen. mgr. pocket fone div., 1966-67, v.p., 1967-73; v.p., dir. Cro-Med Bionics Corp., 1968-73; vice chmn. bd., dir. Laser Link Corp., 1968-73; chief scientist, dir. Orentreich Found. for Advancement Sci., 1973—; pres. Vogelman Devel. Corp., 1973—. Chmn. tech. adv. com. Compupix, Inc., 1984-86. Contbr. articles to profl. jours. and encys.; patentee in field. Served with AUS, 1942-43. Recipient Outstanding Performance award USAF, 1957 Fellow AAAS, IEEE; mem. Titulaire, Societe Francaise de Electroniciens et des Radio Electriciens, N.Y. Acad. Scis., Sigma Xi, Eta Kappa Nu. Home: 48 Green Dr Roslyn NY 11576-3221 Office: 910 5th Ave New York NY 10021-4155 Personal E-mail: dr.jhv@juno.com.

VOGELSANG, ERIC R., language educator, basketball and soccer coach; b. Latrobe, Pa., Sept. 29, 1978; s. Keith R. Vogelsang and Shirley J. LaMantia. B in Elem. Edn., Ind. U. of Pa., 2002. Cert. elem. tchr. Pa., 2002, mid. level English tchr. Pa., 2003. 8th grade English tchr. Ligonier Valley Sch. Dist., Pa., 2002—, H.S. girls soccer coach, 2002—, H.S. girls basketball coach, 2003—; tchg. cons. Southcentral Pa. Writing Project, Indiana, Pa., 2004—. Youth soccer coach Loyalhanna United Soccer Club, Latrobe, Pa., 2000—, youth soccer camp assoc. dir., 2002—, youth soccer referee, 2003—; youth soccer camp dir. Ligonier Valley YMCA, Pa., 2004—; literacy coach Ligonier Valley Sch. Dist., Pa., 2004—; bd. mem. Southcentral Pa. Writing Project, Indiana, Pa., 2005—, young writers camp dir., 2005—. Presenter (PSSA writing assessment workshop) Changes in PSSA Writing Test. Bd. mem. Loyalhanna United Soccer Club, Latrobe, Pa., 2001—05. Nominee Young Educator of Yr., PASCD, 2006; grantee, Thoburn Found., 2004. Mem.: NEA, ACSD, Pa. State Edn. Assn., Pa. Mid. Sch. Assn., Nat. Coun. of Tchrs. of English. Democrat. Methodist. Office: Ligonie Valley Mid Sch Bell Street Extension Ligonier PA 15658 Home: 110 W Vincent St Ligonier PA 15658-1219 Personal E-mail: erv3@hotmail.com. Business E-Mail: vogelsang@iu7.wiu.k12.pa.us.

VOGELSTEIN, BERT, oncology educator; b. Balt., June 2, 1949; BS in Math., U. Pa., 1970; MD, Johns Hopkins U. Sch. Medicine, 1974. Rsch. assoc. Nat. Cancer Inst., 1976—78; pediatric intern and resident Johns Hopkins U. Sch. Medicine, Balt., 1974—76, asst. prof., 1978—83, assoc. prof., 1983—89, Clayton prof. oncology and pathology, 1989—, Howard Hughes Med. Inst. investigator, 1995—. Advisor NIH Sci. Rev. Groups, Nat. Cancer Inst.; bd. reviewing editors Science; assoc. editor Molecular Cell and Cancer Cell; sci. adv. bd. U, Calif., San Francisco, Cancer Ctr., GMP Genetics, Morphotek; sci. review bd. Pediatric Brain Tumor Found., US. Assoc. editor: Genes, Chromosomes and Cancer, mem. bd. reviewing editors: Sci. mag.; contbr. articles to profl. jours., 99 US patents in the field. Recipient Alfred G. Knudson award, Nat. Cancer Inst., Anne & Jason Farber Lecture award, Am. Acad. Neurology, 1991, Internat. award, Gairdner Found., 1992, Medal of Honor, Am. Cancer Soc., 1992, Richard Lounsbery award, NAS, 1993, Baxter Rsch. award, Assn. Am. Med. Coll., 1994, laureates Passano Found., 1994, G.H.A. Clowes Meml. award, Am. Assn. Cancer Rsch., 1995, Paul Erlich and Ludwig Darmstaedter prize, Paul Erlich Found., 1997, William Beaumont prize, Am. Gastroenterological Assn., 1997, Sartstedt Rsch. prize, Inst. Clin. Chemistry, 1997, Louisa Gross Horwitz prize, Columbia U. Med. Ctr., 1998, William Allan award, Am. Soc. Human Genetics, 1998, Charles S. Mott prize, GM Cancer Rsch. Found., 2000, Prince of Asturias award in Sci., 2004. Mem.: NAS, European Molecular Biology Orgn., Am. Philosophical Soc., Inst. Medicine, Am. Acad. Arts and Scis. Achievements include revolutionizing our understanding of complex genetic mutations that occur when an normal bowel epithelial cell is transformed into a malignant cell. Office: Johns Hopkins Sch Medicine 589 Cancer Rsch Bldg 1650 Orleans St Baltimore MD 21231*

VOGELSTEIN, JOHN L., venture capitalist; b. NYC, Dec. 9, 1934; s. Hans A. and Ruth E. (Krieger) V.; m. Jacqueline C. Wolf, Sept. 5, 1957 (div. Sept. 1983); children: Hans A. II, Andrew W.; m. Lee Gibouleau, Dec. 29, 1983. Grad., The Taft Sch., 1952; student, Harvard U., 1954. Assoc. Lazard Freres & Co., NYC, 1954-64, ptnr., 1964-66; v.p. E.M. Warburg, Pincus & Co., Inc., NYC, 1967-70, exec. v.p., 1970-82, vice chmn., 1982—. Bd. dirs. Mattel, Inc., Hawthorne, Calif., Ingersoll Newspapers, Inc., Princeton, N.J., Community Newspapers, Inc., Princeton, JPT Holdings, Inc., N.Y.C., Adv0-System, Inc., Windsor, Conn., Magma Copper Co., San Manuel, Ariz, NH Acquisition Corp., Princeton; vice-chmn., bd. of overseers, Leonard N. Sch. of Bus., NYU; trustee, NYU, Temple Emanu-El; mem. bd. govs., RAND Grad. Sch. Trustee The Taft Sch., Watertown, Conn., 1982—, Prep for Prep, N.Y.C., 1983—; bd. dirs. N.Y. City Ballet, 1989—. Mem.: Jewish Mus. (pres.). Office: EM Warburg Pincus & Co Inc 466 Lexington Ave Fl 10 New York NY 10017-3147*

VOGELZANG, JEANNE MARIE, professional society administrator, lawyer; b. Hammond, Ind., Apr. 15, 1950; d. Richard and Laura Ann (Vanderaa) Jabaay; m. Marc Steven Barter, 2007; children: Nicholas J., Adam R., Timothy P. BA, Trinity Christian Coll., Palos Heights, Ill., 1972; MBA, U. Minn., 1981; JD, U. Chgo., 1987. Bar: Ill. 1987; CPA, Ill.; CAE. Tchr. Timothy Christian HS., Elmhurst, Ill., 1972-74; tchg. assoc. fin. U. Minn., Mpls., 1980-81; fin. analyst Quaker Oats Co., Chgo., 1982-84; assoc. Baker & McKenzie, Chgo., 1987-89, Jenner & Block, Chgo., 1989-91; pres., owner J.M. Vogelzang & Assocs., Western Springs, Ill., 1991-99; exec. dir. Structural Engrs. Assn. Ill., Chgo., 1992—2005, Nat. Coun. Structural Engrs. Assn., Chgo., 1996—, Structural Engring. Cert. Bd., 2004—; pub., editor Structure mag., 1996—; v.p. ops. NCSEA Media, 2009—. Com. mem. Western Springs Planning Commn., 1991—95; village trustee Village of Western Springs, 1995—99, chmn. fin., chmn. gen. govt. com.; adv. bd. Coll. DuPage Internat. Trade Ctr., Glen Ellyn, Ill., 1992—94; bd. dirs., acad. affairs com., planning com., exec. com. sec. Trinity Christian Coll., 1992—98; trustees' evaluation com. Christian Ref. Ch. N.Am., 1998; treas. The Tower Party of Western Springs, 1999—2001; jud. code com. Christian Reformed Ch. N.Am., Grand Rapids, Mich., 1991—97; bd. dirs. Austin Christian Law Ctr., Chgo., 1989—92, Barnabas Found., Palos Heights, Ill., 1989—95; treas. Ctrl. Park Chapel, Holland, Mich., 2001—07. Fellow Ill. Lincoln Excellence in Pub. Svc., 1999. Mem. ABA, Am. Soc. Assn. Execs., Ill. Bar Assn., Chgo. Bar Assn., Elim Work Svcs. Bus. Roundtable. Presbyterian. Office: 645 N Michigan Ave Ste 540 Chicago IL 60611 Office Phone: 312-649-4600. Business E-Mail: execdir@ncsea.com.

VOGES, LINDA KAY, mathematics professor, communications engineer, educational coordinator; b. Oklahoma City, Oct. 23, 1946; d. James W. and Betty J. (Palmer) Bolt; m. Erich Nolan Voges, Jan. 26, 1991; 1 child, Virginia Lynn Simon. BS in Edn., East Ctrl. U., Ada, Okla., 1968; MS, U. North Tex., Denton, 1972; EdD, Baylor U., Waco, Tex., 1998. Cert. planning engr., Southwestern Bell Tel. Co.; secondary math. tchr. Tex. Math. tchr. Arlington Ind. Sch. Dist., Tex., 1970-71; tel. engr. Bell Tel. Co., Dallas, 1973-81; planning engr. Southwestern Bell Tel. Co., Dallas, 1982-89, mgr., course developer, 1990; dept. chair Ctr. Applied Learning Tex. State Tech. Coll., Waco, 1991-94; tech.-prep. curriculum coord. McLennan CC, Waco, 1994-95; workforce edn. coord. Tex. Higher Edn. Coordinating Bd., Austin, 1995-96; asst. prof. Concordia U., Austin, 1996-99, edn. prof., 2000—, dir. sect. edn., 2000—02; program specialist Tex. Coun. Work Force Econs., Office of Gov., Austin, 1999-2000; ednl. designer Viviance New Edn., Austin, 2000—; lectr., cohort N coord. Dept. Curriculum and Instrn. Coll. Edn. U. Tex., Austin, 2002—. Adj. faculty LeTourneau U., Austin, 2004—. Planning and zoning bd. dirs. City of Woodway, Tex., 1992—95; rschr. Tex. Senate Edn. Com., Austin, 1995—98; compaign coord. YMCA-YWCA, Waco, 1991; vol. Jr. Achievement, Dallas, 1988; pub. sch. vol. Dallas Ind. Sch. Dist., 1987—89. Recipient Key Contrb. awards, Southwestern Bell Tel. Co., Dallas, 1987—89, Project Amigos, 1999—2002; grantee, Project Passage, 1994. Mem.: AAUP (campus rep. 1997—98), Assn. Tex. Profl. Educators, Nat. Coun. Tchrs. Math., Phi Delta Kappa, Kappa Delta Pi (rec. for blind and dyslectic com.). Achievements include successfully implementing laptop initiative with cohorts in EC-4 education. Avocations: writing, research, politics, theater. Office: UTex Austin Coll Edn Dept Curriculum and Instrn Mail Code D5700 Sanchez Rm 406 Austin TX 78712 Home: 2204 Twin Peaks Cir Leander TX 78641 Office Phone: 512-232-4146. Personal E-mail: voges@swbell.net. Business E-Mail: lvoges@mail.utexas.edu.

VOGRIN, JOSEPH EDWARD, III, lawyer; BA magna cum laude, Duquesne U., Pitts, 1969, JD, 1972. Bar: Pa. 1972, U.S. Ct. Appeals (3rd cir.) 1972, US Supreme Ct. 1984. Dep. dist. atty. Dist. Atty's Office Allegheny County, Pitts., 1972—79; ptnr. Scott, Vogrin & Riester, Pitts., 1980—96, Vogrin & Riester, P.C., Pitts., 1996—2000, Meyer Darragh Buckler Bebenek & Eck, Pitts., 2000—07; of counsel Meyer Darragh, Pitts., 2007—. Mem. curriculum rev. commn. Pa. Mcpl. Police Officer's Tng. Commn., Harrisburg, 2000—. Solicitor Ohio Twp. San. Authority, Pitts., 1983—2007, Shaler Twp., Pitts., 1986—, Quaker Valley Coun. Govts., Pitts., 1987—2007, North Hills Coun. Govts., Pitts., 1988—, Boroughs Assn. Allegheny County, Pitts., 1991, 1994, 2003, Ross Twp. CSC, Pitts., 1993—2007, Borough Avalon, Pitts., 1992—2005, Twp. Res., Pitts., 1998—; co-counsel Allegheny County and Western Pa. Assn. Twp. Commrs., Pitts., 1997—2008. Mem.: Allegheny County Bar Assn. (chmn. assn. mcpl. and sch. solicitors Allegheny County 1998—99, Listed in Pa. Super Lawyers 2006—09). Office: Shaler Twp 300 Wetzel Rd Glenshaw PA 15116 Home Phone: 412-553-7130; Office Phone: 412-486-9700. Personal E-mail: jvogrin@shaler.org.

VOGT, ERIK MICHAEL, philosophy professor; m. Olga Adriana Timofeyeva-Vogt. MPhil, U. Vienna, PhD, 1992. Asst. prof. Loyola U., New Orleans, 1995—2000; tutor Wadham Coll., Oxford, England, 2001—02; assoc. prof. Trinity Coll., Hartford, Conn., 2002—07, prof., 2007—; dozent U. Vienna, 2003—. Translator: (book) Der Nie Aufgehende Rest, Denn Sie Wissen Nicht Was Sie Tun, Sehr Innig und Nicht Zu Rasch, Lacan aus Hollywood, Der Mut, den Ersten Stein zu Werfen, Existenzialismus, De Kesel, Hoens; Wieder Religion?, Simon Critchley, Über Humor, Drew Hyland, Die Frage des Platonismus, Amerikanische PhilosophInnen in Selbstdarstellungen, James Watson, Die Auschwitz Galaxy, Textualitäten, Anson Rabinbach, Motor Mensch; author: Zugänge Zur Politischen Ästhetik, Sartres Wieder-Holung, contbg. editor chpt. to books. Mem.: SPSGH (v.p. 1998). Office: Trinity Coll 300 Summit St Hartford CT 06106 Business E-Mail: erik.vogt@trincoll.edu.

VOGT, KIMBERLY ANN, sociologist, educator; b. Kittery, Maine; d. Richard Lee and Judith Ann Vogt. BA, Alfred U., NY, 1981; MA, U. NH, Durham, PhD, 1989. Exec. asst. to dean, liberal arts U. NH, 1986—93, lectr., 1989—93; prof., sociology U. Wis. La Crosse, 1994—, interim asst. dean, 2000—01, chair, dept. sociology & archaeology, 2001—. Contbr. chapters to books & articles to profl. jours. Mem. Gay Alliance La Crosse Area Youth, YWCA, 1998—2005, ATTIC Correctional Svcs. Cmty. Adv. Bd., La Crosse, 2006, La Crosse County Criminal Justice Mgmt. Coun., 2000—07, chairperson, 2006—07; mem., steering com. Youth Violence Prevention Project, La Crosse, 2003—05. Recipient

Faculty Recognition Excellence Svc. award, U. Wis. La Crosse Coll. Liberal Studies, 2009; named Most Accessible Prof., U. Wis. La Crosse SAPA, 2007. Mem.: Homicide Rsch. Working Group (membership coord. 2007), Soc. Study Social Problems, Am. Sociol. Assn., Am. Soc. Criminology, Pi Gamma Mu Social Sci. Honor Soc., Alpha Kappa Omicron (treas. 1979—80). Liberal. Avocations: walking, swimming, travel. Office: Univ Wis La Crosse 1725 State St 435 Wimberly Hall La Crosse WI 54601 Business E-Mail: vogt.kimb@uwlax.edu.

VOGT, LORNA CORRINE, retired librarian, small business owner; b. Rochelle, Ill., Feb. 18, 1936; d. Chester Floyd and Vera Mae (Worthington) Patton; m. Norman E. Vogt, Aug. 18, 1957; 1 child, Cindy Jean Vogt Welch. BE, No. Ill. U., DeKalb, 1957, MA, 1972; postgrad., Western Ill. U., Macomb, 1989-90. Tchr. speech and English Harlem H.S., Loves Park, Ill., 1957-58; tchr. English, libr. Alden-Hebron Jr.-Sr. H.S., Ill., 1958-59; traffic mgr. Sta. WLBK Radio, DeKalb, Ill., 1964-65; libr. No. Ill. U., DeKalb, 1967, Malta Schs., Ill., 1968-71, Sycamore H.S., Ill., 1971-94; ret., 1994; owner Sesquicentennial Farm. Mem. Ogle County (Ill.) Farm Bur.; presenter in field. Author: The Heritage of the Lafayette Township Schools, 1990; compiler (book) James Reed Family, 1991, William Patton Family, 1987, Lafayette Township Officers, 1993; photographer (exhibits) Freeport Area Camera Club, 2004, 05; compiler: Mayflower Descendan Edward Fuller to Cindy Welch, 2008. Chmn. Books South Africa Commn., DeKalb, 1991-92; co-chmn. Literary Festival Little 7 Conf., 1991-93; mem. Stephenson County Hist. Soc., 2002-; former mem. Assn. Gravestone Studies; chmn. bd. deacons Conglist. Ch., 1993-94, vice moderator, 1994-95, moderator, 1995-96; mem. Ill. Conf. United Ch. of Christ Bd., 1996-98, exec. bd., 1996-98; vice moderator Prairie Assn., 1996-97, moderator, 1997-98, Congl. United Ch. of Christ, Dekalb, 1995-96, Ill. Conf. del. United Ch. of Christ Gen. Synod, Providence, 1999, Kansas City, Mo., 2001. Mem. NEA, Popular Culture Assn. (presenter 1989), John & Mable Ringling Mus. Art, Ill. Assn. Tchrs. English (presenter 1988-90), Nat. Coun. Tchrs. English (presenter 1991, 93), Ill. Edn. Assn., Ill. Assn. Media Edn., Midwest Gilbert and Sullivan Soc., Somerset County Pa. Hist. and Geneal. Soc., Ill. Ret. Tchrs. Assn., Ret. Tchrs. Assn. Stephenson County (sec. 2004-06), Ret. Educators Assn. Sarasota, Freeport Area Camera Club, Stephenson County Hist. Soc., Ill. State Geneal. Soc. (cert. descendant civlil war svc. men), Alpha Sigma Alpha (life), Nat. Coun. Tchrs. English Ctr. of Excellence (co-dir., 1989-1991). Congregationalist. Avocations: writing, genealogy. Home: 3167 Sandy Pointe Dr Freeport IL 61032-2824 Personal E-mail: lornapat218@aol.com.

VOGT, ROCHUS EUGEN, physicist, researcher; b. Neckarelz, Germany, Dec. 21, 1929; came to U.S., 1953; s. Heinrich and Paula (Schaefer) V.; m. Micheline Alice Yvonne Bauduin, Sept. 6, 1958; children: Michele, Nicole. Student, U. Karlsruhe, Germany, 1950-52, U. Heidelberg, 1952-53; SM, U. Chgo., 1957, PhD, 1961. Asst. prof. physics Calif. Inst. Tech., Pasadena, 1962-65, assoc. prof., 1965-70, prof., 1970—2002, R. Stanton Avery disting. svc. prof., 1982—2002, R. Stanton Avery disting. svc. prof. and prof. physics emeritus, 2002—, chmn. faculty, 1975-77, chief scientist Jet Propulsion Lab., 1977-78, chmn. div. physics, math. and astronomy, 1978-83, acting dir. Owens Valley Radio Obs., 1980-81, v.p. and provost, 1983-87. Vis. prof. physics MIT, 1988-94; dir. Caltech/MIT Laser Interferometer Gravitational Wave Observatory Project, 1987-94. Author: Cosmic Rays (in World Book Ency.), 1978, (with R.B. Leighton) Exercises in Introductory Physics, 1969; contbr. articles to profl. jours. Fulbright fellow, 1953-54; recipient Exceptional Sci. Achievement medal NASA, 1981, Profl. Achievement award U. Chgo. Alumni Assn., 1981. Fellow AAAS, A. Phys. Soc. Achievements include research in astrophysics and gravitation. Office: Calif Inst Tech 103-33 1200 E California Blvd Pasadena CA 91125-0001 Home Phone: 626-398-5066; Office Phone: 626-395-3800. Business E-Mail: vogt@caltech.edu.

VOGT, THOMAS, physics professor, director; m. Sonia Michelle Jacobsen; 1 child, Veronica Lea. PhD, U. Tuebingen, Germany, 1987. Scientist Inst. Laue-Langevin, Grenoble, France, 1988—92; assoc. physicist Brookhaven Nat. Lab., Upton, NY, 1992—95, physicist & group leader, 1995—2005; Adj. prof. philosophy U. SC, SC, 2004—, dir. nanoctr., 2005—, rsch. prof., 2006—. Internat. rsch. fellow U. Sydney, 2009—; faculty African U. Sci. & Tech., Abuja, Nigeria, 2009—. Recipient award, R & D Magazine, 1996, Design & Engring. award, 2002. Fellow: AAAS, Am. Phys. Soc. Office: Univ SC 1212 Greene St Columbia SC 29208 Business E-Mail: tvogt@mailbox.sc.edu.

VOGT-LOWELL, ROBERT W., pediatric cardiologist; b. Havana, Cuba, Aug. 28, 1959; B, Univ. Miami; MD, Univ. Puerto Rico, 1986. Diplomate Am. Bd. Pediatrics, 1989, in pediatric cardiology Am. Bd. Pediatrics, 1996. Intern in pediatrics, resident in pediatric cardiology Miami Children's Hosp., 1986—89; fellow in pediatric cardiology LI Jewish Med. Ctr., Albert Einstein Med. Ctr., NY, 1989—92, asst. prof., 1992—94; pediatric cardiologist Single Source Pediatric Heart Ctr., Miami, Fla., 1994, Miami Children's Hosp., 1998—. Office: Miami Children's Hosp Ste 110 7765 SW 87th Ave Miami FL 33173 Office Phone: 305-595-1833, 866-756-9355. Office Fax: 305-595-2024.

VOGUIT, STEVE GEORGE, humanities educator; b. Reading, Pa., June 8, 1947; s. George Steve and Elizabeth Voguit; m. Ellen Marie Stewart, Aug. 16, 1969; children: Tracey Lynn Pollackov, Melinda Anne Clark, Steven Robert. MEd, Millersville U., Pa., 1975. Tchr. Wilson Sch. Dist., West Lawn, Pa., 1969—99; prof. Flagler Coll., Saint Augustine, 2000—. Cons. Fla. Veterans, Saint Augustine, 2007—. Mem. Meml. Presbyn. Ch., Saint Augustine, 2008. Named Faculty Mem. of Yr., 2005—08. Mem.: Am. Assn. Geographers, Orgn. Am. Historians. Avocations: golf, fishing, camping, travel, reading. Home: 27 Madeira Dr Saint Augustine FL 32080 Office: Flagler Coll 74 King St Saint Augustine FL 32085 Office Fax: 904-819-6430. Business E-Mail: svoguit@flagler.edu.

VOHRA, AMIT, mechanical engineer; PhD, U. Fla., Gainesville, 2005. Sr. rsch. assoc. Am. Air Liquide, Newark, Del., 2006—08; scientist & sr. mech. engr. Eigen, Grass Valley, Calif., 2008—, engring. mgr., 2009—. Contbr. scientific papers to profl. jours. With Gainesville Chpt. Nat. Solar Home Tour, 2004. Recipient Achievement award, U. Fla., 2002—04, Gold medal, Maharshi Dayanand U., India, 2001. Mem.: ASME, ASES, Sigma Xi, Phi Kappa Phi. Achievements include patents pending for tracking assembly and mounted transrectal ultrasound probe; 3-D kidney imaging device; development of silver doped titanium dioxide photocatalyst for destruction of hazardous microorganisms.

VOHS, JAMES ARTHUR, health plan administrator; b. Idaho Falls, Idaho, Sept. 26, 1928; s. John Dale and Cliff Lucille (Packer) Vohs; m. Janice Hughes, Sept. 19, 1953 (dec. Oct. 1999); children: Lorraine, Carol, Nancy, Sharla; m. Eileen Galloway, Oct. 8, 2005. BA, U. Calif., Berkeley, 1952; postgrad., Harvard Sch. Bus., 1966. Employed by various Kaiser affiliated orgns., 1952—92; chmn., pres., CEO Kaiser Found. Hosps. and Kaiser Found. Health Plan, INc., Oakland, Calif., 1975—92, chmn. emeritus; chmn. bd. dirs. Holy Names Coll., 1981—92; chmn. Marcus Foster Inst., 1981—. Chmn. Fed. Res. Bank San Francisco, 1991—94. Mem. Oakland Bd. Port Commrs., 1993—96; bd. dirs. Oakland-Alameda County Coliseum Complex, 1986—96, Bay Area Coun., 1985—94, chmn., 1991—92. With US Army, 1946—48. Mem.: Inst. Medicine NAS. Personal E-mail: javohs@sbcglobal.net.

VOIGHT, JON, actor; b. Yonkers, NY, Dec. 29, 1938; s. Elmer and Barbara (Camp) Voight; m. Lauri Peters, 1962 (div. 1967); m. Marcheline Bertrand, Dec. 12, 1971 (div. 1978); children: James Haven, Angelina Jolie. BFA, Cath. U., 1960; studied with, Sanford Meisner and Samantha Harper, NYC. Stage appearances include O Oysters Revue, 1961, The Sound of Music, 1961, A View from the Bridge, 1965, Romeo and Juliet, 1966, The Tempest, 1966, Two Gentlemen of Verona, 1966, That Summer-That Fall, 1967 (Theatre World award 1967), A Streetcar Named Desire, 1973, The Hashish Club, 1975, Hamlet, 1976, The Seagull, 1992; TV appearances include Cimarron Strip, Gunsmoke; films include Fearless Frank, 1967, Hour of the Gun, 1967, Out of It, 1969, Midnight Cowboy, 1969 (Acad. award nom. best actor 1969, NY Critics Circle award 1969, L.A. Film Critics award best actor 1969, BAFTA award most promising newcomer 1969, Golden Globe award most promising newcomer 1969), Catch-22, 1970, The Revolutionary, 1970, Deliverance, 1972, The All American Boy, 1973, Conrack, 1974, The Odessa File, 1974, End of the Game, 1976, Coming Home, 1978 (Acad. Award for Best Actor 1978, Golden Globe award 1978, Cannes Internat. Film festival award 1978, NY Film Critics best actor award 1978, L.A. Film Critics award best actor 1978), The Champ, 1979 (Golden Globe award 1979), Runaway Train, 1985 (Acad. award nominee best actor 1986, London Film Critics award nominee 1986, Golden Globe best actor 1986), Desert Bloom, 1986, Eternity, 1990, The Rainbow Warrior, 1992, Heat, 1995, Mission Impossible, 1996, Rosewood, 1997, Anaconda, 1997, Most Wanted, 1997, The Rainmaker, 1997, U Turn, 1997, I Once Had a Life, 1998, Enemy of the State, 1998, Varsity Blues, 1999, A Dog of Flanders, 1999, Pearl Harbor, 2001, Lara Croft: Tomb Raider, 2001, Zoolander, 2001, Ali, 2001, Holes, 2003, Karate Dog, 2004, The Manchurian Candidate, 2004, Superbabies: Baby Geniuses 2, 2004, National Treasure, 2004, September Dawn, 2006, Transformers, 2007, National Treasure: Book of Secrets, 2007, Pride and Glory, 2008, Four Christmases, 2008; (TV films) Chernobyl: The Final Warning, 1991, The Last of His Tribe, 1992, Convict Cowboys, 1995, Boys Will Be Boys, 1997, Noah's Ark, 1999, Second string, 2002, Jasper, Texas, 2003, The Five People You Meet in Heaven, 2004, Pope John Paul II, 2005; (mini-series) Return to Lonesome Dove, 1993; actor, prodr., co-writer (films) Lookin' To Get Out, 1982, The Fixer, 1998; actor, prodr. (films) Table for Five, 1983, A Tribute to Dustin Hoffman, 1999, Noah's Ark, 1999, Second String, 2000.*

VOIGT, BARTON R., state supreme court chief justice; b. Scotland, SD; BA in History, MA in History, U. Wyo., Laramie, JD. Atty., Thermopolis, Wyo.; former Hot Springs County atty.; former county ct. judge Gillette; judge Wyo. Eigth Jud. Dist., Douglas, 1993—2001; justice Wyo. Supreme Ct., 2001—, chief justice, 2006—. Mem. Bd. of Jud. Policy and Adminstrn. Mem.: Wyo. Bar Assn. Office: Wyo Supreme Ct 2301 Capitol Ave Cheyenne WY 82001 Office Phone: 307-777-7573.*

VOIGT, DAVID WILLIAM, surgeon, director; s. Leonard LeRoy and Minerva Verona Voigt; m. Eileen McKittrick, Jan. 2, 1982; children: Christia Nichole, Nicholas Christian, Charles David. BSc in Chemistry, Mont. State U., Bozeman, 1981; MD, Med. Coll. Ohio, 1989. Diplomate Nat. Bd. Med. Examiners, 1990, Am. Bd. Surgery, 2005. State tax appraiser, land classifier State Mont., Circle, 1977, rabies control agt., dept. agr., 1977; change control mgr. USAF B-1B Sys. Program Office, Dayton, Ohio, 1981—85; gen. surgeon US Army Surg. Rsch., Fort Sam Houston, Tex., 1994—96, Lincoln Surg. Group, PC, Nebr., 1996—. Clin. instr. gen. surgery U. Tex. Health Sci. Ctr., San Antonio, 1994—95, clin. asst. prof. gen. surgery, 1995—97, Creighton U. Med. Ctr., Omaha, 1996—, U. Nebr. Med. Ctr., Omaha, 1996—; dir. burn rsch. St. Elizabeth's Regional Burn and Wound Care Ctr., Lincoln, 1996—; faculty Lincoln Family Practice Program, 1999—; editl. adv. bd. Wounds, Malvern, Pa., 2001—, sect. editor burns, 2001—; med. dir. St. Elizabeth's Regional Burn and Wound Care Ctr., Lincoln, 2004—. Contbr. articles to numerous profl. jours., chapters to books. 1st lt. USAF, 1981—85, maj. US Army, 1981—96. Decorated First Oak Leaf Cluster USAF, Tng. Ribbon, Expert Marksman Ribbon, Commendation medal, Nat. Def. Ribbon US Army, Army Svc. Ribbon, Humanitarian Svc. medal, Commendation medal, Achievement medal; recipient Admirl Gt. Navy award, Gov. State Nebr., 1998, Recognition award, 2003. Mem.: AMA, Ohio Med. Assn., Assn. Advancement Wound Care, Wound Healing Soc. (com. mem. web devel.), Soc. Critical Care Medicine, Lancaster County Med. Assn., Nebr. Medial Assn., Lancaster County Med. Assn., Am. Burn Assn. (rsch. com. mem. 1997—99). Conservative. Avocations: woodcarving, travel, hunting, fishing. Office: Lincoln Surg Group PC 4740 A St Lincoln NE 68510

VOIGT, RICHARD, lawyer; b. Oskaloosa, Iowa, Jan. 20, 1946; s. Franz Otto Wilhelm and Minni (Heilbrunn) V.; m. Annemarie H. Riemer, Oct. 2, 1976; children: Samuel, Nicholas. BA, Conn. Wesleyan U., 1968; JD, U. Va., 1974. Bar: Va. 1974, U.S. Dist. Ct. (ea. dist.) Va. 1979, Conn. 1981, U.S. Dist. Ct. Conn. 1982, U.S. Ct. Claims 1982, U.S. Ct. Appeals (4th cir.) 1982. Assoc. counsel regional litigation Solicitor's Office Osha Div., 1978-80; staff atty. U.S. Dept. Labor, Washington, 1974-78; prin. Siegel, O'Connor, Schiff, Zangari & Kainen, P.C., 1981-88, 87-88; ptnr. Cummings & Lockwood, Hartford, 1988—2003, McCarter & English, Hartford, 2003—. Contbg. author: ABA Treatise on Occupational Safety and Health Law, 1988; contbr. articles to profl. jours. Bd. dirs. Urban League Greater Hartford, 1984-88, Isnt. for Non-Profit Tng. and Devel., 1991-95, Hartford Proud and Beautiful, 1995-2007, Greater Hartford Arts Coun., 2001—, Knox parks Foundation 2007-. Mem. ABA (labor and employment law sect., OSHA com., litigation sect.), Conn. Bar Assn. (labor employment law sect., employment discrimination com., com. on alternative dispute resolution). Avocations: acrylic design, history, sports. Office: McCarter & English LLP 36th Floor Cityplace I Hartford CT 06103 Office Phone: 860-275-6776.

VOINOVICH, GEORGE VICTOR, United States Senator from Ohio; b. Cleve., July 15, 1936; m. Janet (Allen) Voinovich; 3 children. BA in Govt., Ohio U., 1958; JD, Ohio State U., 1961; LLD (hon.), Ohio U., 1981. Bar: Ohio 1961, US Supreme Ct. 1968. Asst. atty. gen. State of Ohio, 1963-64; mem. Ohio Ho. of Reps., 1967-71; auditor Cuyahoga County, Ohio, 1971-76; commr., 1977-78; lt. gov. State of Ohio, Columbus, 1979, gov., 1991-98; mayor City of Cleve., 1979-89; US Senator from Ohio, 1999—; mem. US Senate Appropriations Com., 2009—. Pres. Nat. League Cities, 1984-85; trustee US Conf. Mayors; chmn. Midwestern Govs. Conf., 1991-92, Coun. Gt. Lakes Govs., 1992-94; chmn. Jobs for America's Graduates Program, 1995- (Nat. Leadership award 1993); mem. State and Local Govt. Coalition, 1994- Recipient Tree of Life award, Jewish Nat. Found., 1981, Cert. of Merit award Ohio U., Humanitarian award NCCJ, 1986, Disting. Urban Mayor award Nat. Urban Coalition, 1987, Nat. Public Svc. award SADD, 1991, Edn. Reform Pioneer award Nat. Bus. Roundtable, 1994, George Falcon Golden Spike award, Nat. Assn. Railroad Passengers, 2000; named one of Outstanding Young Men in Ohio Ohio Jaycees, 1970; one of Outstanding Young Men in Greater Cleve. Cleve. Jaycees; named to All-Pro City Mgmt. team City & State Mag., 1987. Mem. Rep. Govs. Assn. (vice chmn. 1991-92, chmn. 1992-93), Nat. Govs. Assn. (chmn. edn. action team on sch. readiness 1991, chmn. child support enforcement work group 1991-92, mem. strategic planning task force 1991-92, mem. human resources com., co-chmn. task force on edn. 1992-93, mem. exec. com. 1993-98, co-lead gov. on fed. mandates, chmn. 1997-98), Omicron Delta Kappa, Phi Alpha Theta, Phi Delta Phi. Republican. Roman Catholic. Office: US Senate 524 Hart Sentate Office Bldg Washington DC 20510-0001 also: Central Ohio Office Rm 310 37 West Broad St Columbus OH 43215 Office Phone: 202-224-3353, 614-469-6697. Office Fax: 202-228-1382, 614-469-7733. E-mail: columbus_voinovich@voinovich.senate.gov.*

VOJCANIN, SAVA ALEXANDER, lawyer; b. Oak Lawn, Ill., Oct. 15, 1964; s. Jovan and Lili (Yovanovich) V.; m. Valerie S. Rupich, Oct. 12, 2002; 2 children: John William, Elizabeth Sophia, George Anderson. Diploma, Culver Mil. Acad., 1981; BA with distinction, DePauw U., 1985; JD, Washington U., 1988. Bar: Ill. 1988, US Dist. Ct. (no. dist.) Ill. 1989, US Dist. Ct. (no. dist.) Tex. 1996, US Supreme Ct. 2006, registered: Eng. and Wales (in fng. lang.) 2008. Assoc. Schaffenegger, Watson & Peterson Ltd., Chgo., 1988-91, Clausen Miller P.C., Chgo., 1991-98, ptnr., 1999—, shareholder, 2002—. Editor: Law, Culture and Values, 1989. Mem. Mayor's Adv. Coun. on Immigrant and Refugee Affairs, Chgo., 1992-97; trustee St. Basil Orthodox Ch. of Lake Forest, 1997-2006, sec. bd. trustees, 1999-2002, nominating com., 2002-2005. Mem.: ABA, Chgo. Bar Assn., Serbian Bar Assn. Am. (treas. 1999—2000, sec. 2000—01, v.p. 2001—02, pres. 2002—03, bd. dirs.). Orthodox. Office: Clausen Miller PC 10 S LaSalle St Chicago IL 60603-1098 Business E-Mail: svojcanin@clausen.com.

VOJCIC, BRANIMIR R., engineering educator, consultant; b. Belgrade, Serbia-Monteneg, Dec. 27, 1955; s. Radovan S. and Vera A. Vojcic; m. Jasminka P. Kuis, Oct. 19, 1983; 1 child, Daria B. Diploma in Engring., U. Belgrade, 1980, MS, 1986, DSc, 1989. Prof. George Washington U., Washington, 1991—. Author: (book) The cdma2000 System for Mobile Communications; editor: Multiaccess, Mobility and Teletraffic in Wireless Communications. Recipient Career award, NSF, 1995, Best Paper award, ACM MSWiM, 1999. Mem.: IEEE. Office: George Washington Univ ECE Dept 801 22nd St NW Washington DC 20052 Office Fax: 202-994-0227. Business E-Mail: vojcic@gwu.edu.

VOJDANI, ARISTO, medical association administrator, researcher; s. Mordechani and Mahboubah Rahimian Vojdani; m. Georgette Ghassab, Sept. 13, 1976; children: Elroy, Rubina, Charlene. BS in Microbiology, Biochemistry, Bar Ilan U., Israel, MSc in Microbiology, Immunology, 1972, PhD in Microbiology, Immunology, 1976. Cert. in postdoc. tng. for cellular immunology Tel Aviv U. Med. Ctr., Assaf Harofe Hosp., 1978, in postdoc. tng. for comparative immunology UCLA, 1981, clin. lab. scientist Calif. DHHS, 2008. Adj. asst. prof. dept. surgery Surgery Dept. Harbor, UCLA Med. Ctr., Torrance, 1981—82, rschr., prof. microbiology, 1981—82; rschr., prof. immunology workshops for MARC and MBRS students Pathology Dept., Charles Drew Postgrad. Med. Sch., Compton, Calif., 1982—84; asst. prof. dept. pathology Charles R. Drew U. Medicine and Sci., 1982—92, assoc. prof. dept. internal medicine, 1993; dir. rsch. & devel. Advanced Allergy Rsch. Ctr., LA, 1984—86; v.p. rsch. & devel. Allergy Immunotechs., Newport Beach, Calif., 1986—88; founder, CEO, v.p. rsch. & devel. Immunoscis. Lab., Inc., LA, 1988—. Contbr. articles to profl. jours. Recipient Herbert J. Rinkle award, Am. Acad. Environ. Medicine, 2006, Sci. Presentation award, Am. Acad. Otolaryngologic Allergy, 1984; grant, EPA, 1981—83, NIH MBRS, 1982—85, NIH Nat. Inst. Allergy and Infectious Diseases, 1990—91, Dept. Vets. Affairs, Vet. Health Adminstrn.'s Office R & D, 1999. Mem.: Am. Assn. Immunologists. Conservative. Achievements include patents for various immunological tests for blood and saliva. Avocations: travel, scientific lectures. Office: Immunoscis Lab Inc 822 S Robertson Blvd Ste 312 Los Angeles CA 90035 Office Fax: 310-657-1053. Personal E-mail: drari@msn.com. Business E-Mail: immunsci@ix.netcom.com.

VOJNOVIC, IGOR ZORAN, geographer, urban planner, educator; b. Belgrade, Yugoslavia, Jan. 26, 1966; arrived in U.S., 1997; s. Zoran and Branislava Vojnovic; m. Ghada Georgis, June 10, 1999. BA, York U., Toronto, Can., 1990; MSc, U. Toronto, 1992, PhD, 1997. Instr. urban design U. Toronto, 1994—97; rsch. assoc. Intergovernmental Com. on Urban and Regional Rsch., Toronto, 1996—97; instr. urban-environmental policy Syracuse U., 1997—98; sr. urban planning and design cons. Pub. Sector Innovations, Halifax, NS, Canada, 1998—99; asst. prof., urban-environmental design Dalhousie U., Halifax, 1998—99; asst. prof. urban-environ. policy Tex. A&M U., College Station, 1999—2002; prin. urban planning and design cons. Paul Raff Studio, Toronto, 2001—; assoc. prof., met. environments Mich. State U., East Lansing, 2002—. Adj. prof. govt. U. Alta., Edmonton, Canada, 2004—. Author: (monograph (in english & french) Municipal Consolidation in the 1990s, 1997; contbr. articles to profl. jours. Outreach planning and design svc. staff Dalhousie U., 1998—99, Tex. A&M U., 1999—2002, Mich. State U., 2002—06. Recipient Founders Coll. Book award, York U., 1990, Griffith Taylor Meml. award in Recognition of Acad. Excellence, U. Toronto, 1996—97, The Corps of Cadets Tchg. award, Tex. A&M U., 2002; grantee, Can. Donner Found., 1998—99, Tex. A&M U., 2001, Inst. Pub. Policy and Social Rsch., 2003, Land Policy Program, 2004—, Com. Vitality Program Grant, 2005—; fellow, Social Sci. and Humanities Rsch. Coun. of Can., 1993—96, Syracuse U., 1997—98; scholar, Province of Ont., 1990—92; Human-Social Dynamics grant, NSF, 2006—. Achievements include research in local policy framework for regional restructuring used as a guide in the amalgamation of Halifax Regional Municipality; framework for municipal tax structure used for the Provincial-Municipal Service Exchange Amendments/General Work Plan and Guide to Principles. Avocations: music, saxophone. Business E-Mail: vojnovic@msu.edu.

VOJTA, PAUL ALAN, mathematics professor; b. Mpls., Sept. 30, 1957; s. Francis J. and Margaret L. V. B in Math., U. Minn., 1978; MA, Harvard U., 1980, PhD, 1983. Instr. Yale U., New Haven, 1983-86; fellow Math. Scis. Rsch. Inst., Berkeley, Calif., 1986-87, Miller Inst. for Basic Rsch., Berkeley, 1987-89; assoc. prof. U. Calif., Berkeley, 1989-92, prof., 1992—. Mem. Inst. for Advanced Study, Princeton, 1989-90, 96-97. Author: Diophantine Approximations and Value Distribution Theory, 1987; editor: Jour. Reine Angew Math., 2004—. Recipient perfect score Internat. Math. Olympiad, 1975. Mem. Am. Math. Soc. (Frank Nelson Cole Number Theory prize 1992), Math. Assn. Am., Phi Beta Kappa, Tau Beta Pi. Avocations: dance, computers. Office: Univ Calif Dept Math 970 Evans Hall 3840 Berkeley CA 94720-3840

VOKETAITIS, ARNOLD MATTHEW, bass-baritone, educator; b. East Haven, Conn., May 11, 1930; s. Mathew Joseph and Agnes Mary (Pilvelis) V.; m. Marion Lee Dever, June 1959 (div. 1967); children: Arnold Mathew Jr., Paul Stanley; m. Nijole Lipciute, Sept. 6, 1968. BS in Bus. Adminstrn, Quinnipiac Coll., 1954. Dir. opera program De Paul U., Chgo., 1987-89. Lectr. techniques for mus. stage, author singing technique Northwestern U., Evanston, Ill., 1986; mem. adv. panels in music and ethnic affairs Ill. Arts Coun.; mem. panel for opera and mus. theatre NEA; faculty mem. Brevard (N.C.) Summer Music Ctr., 1987, 88; artist-in-residence for opera and voice Auburn U., Ala., 1990-93; artist/mgr. for pianists, formed Keyboard Artists Internat., 1998. Condr. master classes in singing; author on voice technique; operatic debut with N.Y.C. Opera, 1958, European debut at Liceo, Barcelona, Spain, 1968; mem. Met. Opera Nat. Co., appeared with maj. operatic and symphonic orgns. in U.S., Can., Mex., Cen. Am., S.Am., Lyric Opera of Chgo., 1966-84, 89, rec. artist for Desto, Vox, Columbia, RCA; recitalist appearances on Pay-TV; classical soloist U.S. Army Band, Washington. Served as sgt. U.S. Army, 1954-56. Recipient 1st place award, Conn. Opera Assn. auditions, 1957, Rockefeller Found. award, 1964, Lithuanian Man of Yr. award, 1990, Disting. Alumni award, Quinnipiac U., 1991. Mem. AFTRA, Am. Guild Mus. Artists (life), Actors Equity. Avocations: golf, fishing, theater. Personal E-mail: avkey@juno.com. *I have felt very strongly over the years that opera was written to be enjoyed, not revered, and that it cried out to be acted as well as sung. With television's influence on the viewer, necessity became reality and my hopes are being realized.*

VOLANAKIS, JOHN EMMANUEL, immunologist, rheumatologist; b. Thessaloniki, Greece, Mar. 17, 1938; arrived in US, 1968, naturalized, 1978; s. Emmanuel (Manolis) John and Cleo (Agathonos) Volanakis; children: Emmanuel (Manolis) John, Marina Cleo. MD, Aristotle U., Thessaloniki, 1962; DMed, Nat. U. Athens, Greece, 1968, PhD (hon.), 2003. Cert. Bd. Internal Medicine Ministry Health, Greece, 1967. Fellow rheumatology Cleve. Met. Gen. Hosp., 1968—71; instr. dept. medicine U. Ala., Birmingham, 1971—73, asst. prof. dept. medicine, 1973—77, assoc. prof. dept. medicine, 1977—83, prof. dept. medicine, 1983—2003; pres., sci. dir. Biomedical Sciences Rsch. Ctr. Alexander Fleming, Vari, Greece, 1997—2003. Dir., rsch. component Multipurpose Arthritis Ctr., Birmingham, Ala., 1984—97. Editor: The Human Complement System in Health and Disease; contbr. articles to profl. jours. Cadet Mil. Med. Sch., 1956—61, Thessaloniki, Greece. Recipient Alexander von Humbolt, Rsch. award for Sr. U.S. Scientists, Alexander von Humbolt Stiftung, 1996—97; named Anna Lois Waters Chair of Medicine in Rheumatology, U. Ala., 1989—97; Robert M. Stecher fellow, Arthritis Found. Ohio, 1969—71, Fogarty Sr. Internat. Rsch. fellow, NIH, 1978—79. Mem.: Assn. Am. Physicians. Achievements include patents for crystals of human factor D. Avocation: literature. Home: 2900 Redmont Park C 302W Birmingham AL 35205 Office: Univ Alabama at Birmingham 1530 3rd Ave South BDB 479 Birmingham AL 35294-0012 Office Fax: 205-934-1477. Business E-Mail: volanaki@uab.edu.

VOLANAKIS, PETER F., manufacturing executive; B in Economics, Dartmouth Coll., 1977; M in Finance, Tuck Sch. Bus. Dartmouth Coll., 1982. Market devel. specialist optical products Corning Inc., 1982, product mgr. tech. ceramics then various comml. positions environmental products, 1985—91, dir. corp. mktg., 1991, gen. mgr. environmental products Wiesbaden, Germany, 1992—95, exec. v.p. Siecor Corp. Hickory, NC, 1995—97, sr. v.p. advanced display products, 1997—99, exec. v.p. display sector and life sciences divsn., 1999—2001, pres. Corning Technologies with responsibility info. display and advanced materials groups internat. operations and central engring., 2001—05, COO, 2005—07, pres., COO, 2007—, bd. dir., 2000—, Dow Corning, 2001—. Bd. trustees Corning Inc. Found., Corning Mus. Glass; bd. overseers Amos Tuck Sch. Bus. Adminstrn. Dartmouth Coll. Office: Corning Inc 1 Riverfront Plaza Corning NY 14831-0001

VOLBERDING, PAUL ARTHUR, academic physician; b. Rochester, Minn., Sept. 26, 1949; s. Walter A. and Eldora M. (Prescher) V.; m. Juline Christofferson, June 15, 1971 (div. June 1976); m. Mary M. Cooke, June 6, 1980; children: Alexander, Benjamin, Emily. AB, U. Chgo., 1971; MD, U. Minn., 1975. Resident in internal medicine U. Utah, Salt Lake City, 1975-78; fellow in oncology U. Calif., San Francisco, 1978-81; dir. med. oncology San Francisco Gen. Hosp., 1981—, dir. AIDS program, 1983—; dir. Ctr. for AIDS Rsch. U. Calif., San Francisco, 1988—, prof. medicine, 1990—. Bd. dirs. Dignity Ptnrs. Inc., 1996—; elected mem., Inst. of Medicine, 1999. Editor: Medical Management in AIDS, 1986; editor Jour. of AIDS, 1990—. Fellow ACP, AAAS; mem. Internat. AIDS Soc. (founder, chmn. bd.). Office: U Calif San Francisco San Francisco AIDS Program 995 Potrero Ave San Francisco CA 94110-2859

VOLCKER, PAUL ADOLPH, economist, former Chairman of the Board of Governors of the Federal Reserve System; b. Cape May, NJ, Sept. 5, 1927; s. Paul A. and Alma Louise (Klippel) V.; m. Barbara Marie Bahnson, Sept. 11, 1954 (dec. June 1998); children: Janice, James. AB summa cum laude, Princeton U., 1949; MA, Harvard U., 1951; LLD (hon.), Princeton U., 1982, Harvard U., 1985, London U., 1994. Economist Fed. Res. Bank N.Y., 1952-57, pres., 1975-79; fin. economist Chase Manhattan Bank, NYC, 1957-61, v.p., dir. forward planning, 1965-68; dir., Office Fin. Analysis US Dept. Treasury, Washington, 1961—63, dep. under sec. monetary affairs, 1963-65, under sec., 1969-74; chmn. bd. govs. Fed. Res. Sys., Washington, 1979-87; chmn. James D. Wolfensohn, Inc., 1988—96, President's Econ. Recovery Advisory Bd., 2009—. Prof. internat. econ. policy Princeton U., 1988-95, prof. emeritus, 1995-; chmn. Nat. Commn. Pub. Svc., 1987-90, 2002-03, Trilateral Commn., 1990-2001, Internat. House 1998—, Fin. Svcs. Vol. Corps., 1998-2005, Ind. Inquiry into the UN Oil for Food Programme, 2004-05; bd. trustees Internat. Acctg. Stds. Com., 2000-06; dir. Inst. Internat. Econs. Recipient Arthur S. Fleming award, US Treasury Dept. Exceptional Svc. award, 1965, Alexander Hamilton award, 1973; Sr. fellow Woodrow Wilson Sch. Pub. and Internat. Affairs, 1974-75. Office: The White House 1600 Pennsylvania Ave NW Washington DC 20500*

VOLD, ROBERT LAWRENCE, science educator; b. LA, Sept. 20, 1942; s. Robert Donald and Marjorie Jean Vold; 1 child, Tanya Nicole Vold Hoatson. BSc, U. Calif., Berkeley, 1963; PhD, U. Ill., Urbana, 1967. Prof. chemistry U. Calif., San Diego, 1969—90; prof. applied sci. Coll. William and Mary, Williamsburg, Va., 1990—. Office: Coll William and Mary Dept Applied Sci Williamsburg VA 23187-8795

VOLEK, EMIL, educator; s. Jan Volek and Anna Volkova. PhD, Charles U., Prague, Czech Republic, 1970. Prof. Czechoslovak Acad. Scis., Prague, 1969—74; vis. prof. U. Cologne, Germany, 1974—76; asst. prof. Ariz. State U., Tempe, 1976—78, assoc. prof., 1978—83, prof., 1984—. Contbr. articles to profl. jours. Recipient Disting. Rsch. and Creative Activity award, Grad. Coll. Ariz. State U., 1989—90, Outstanding Mentor award, Ariz. State U., 1993, Commemorative medal, Inst. Cultura Puertorriqueña, San Juan, 1999; fellowship, NEH, 1978. Home: 8237 E Montecito Scottsdale AZ 85251 Office: Ariz SU Silc Tempe AZ 85287-0202

VOLENTINE, RICHARD J., JR., lawyer; b. Tampa, Fla., Apr. 2, 1955; s. Richard J. Sr. and Mary Francis (Shaw) V.; children: Rachel Elizabeth, Scott Thomas, Melissa Mary. BS, Spring Hill Coll., 1977; JD, U. Ala., 1980. Bar: Ala. 1980, Mo. 1982, Fla. 1984, Ga. 2005. Staff atty. Ala. Jud. Coll., Tuscaloosa, 1980-81; staff counsel Citicorp Person-to-Person, Inc., St. Louis, 1982; regional counsel Citicorp Person-to-Person Corp., Tampa, 1982-84; asst. gen. counsel Citicorp Savs. Fla., Miami, 1984-85; assoc. counsel Home Fed./Capital Corp., Atlanta, 1985-86; regional atty. FDIC, Atlanta, 1986-88; gen. counsel, v.p. Altus Bank, Mobile, Ala., 1988-90; v.p., assoc. gen. counsel Chase Home Mortgage Corp., Tampa, Fla., 1990-91; sr. v.p., chief legal officer Prudential Bank, Atlanta, 1991—2000; assoc. gen. counsel Fannie Mae, Atlanta, 2000—. Mem. ABA, Assn. Corp. Counsel, Ala. Jud. Coll. Faculty Assn. (hon.). Republican. Roman Catholic. Avocations: playing golf, basketball, and other sports, photography, writing. Home: Unit 201 3920 Riverlook Pky Marietta GA 30067 Office: 950 E Paces Ferry Rd Ste 1900 Atlanta GA 30326 Home Phone: 770-953-3157; Office Phone: 404-398-6022. Business E-Mail: richard_volentine@fanniemae.com.

VOLFSON-DOUBOVA, ELENA, psychiatrist, researcher; b. St. Petersburg, Russia, Oct. 27, 1971; d. Valeriy Dmitrievich Dubov and Larisa Alexandrovna Dubova; m. Ilya Alexander Volfson, Aug. 18, 2000; children: Veronique Anna Volfson, Erik Robert Volfson. BS, St. Petersburg State Pavlov Med. U., Russia, 1992, MD, 1996; MPH, SUNY, Albany, 2000. Lic. Med. NJ, St. Petersburg Acad. Postgraduate Edn., Russia. Internal medicine resident St. Petersburg State Med. Acad. Postgraduate Edn., 1996—98; psychiatry resident U. Med. Dental NJ, Robert Wood Johnson Med. Sch. Psychiatry Residency Program, Piscataway, 2001—06; fellowship addiction psychiatry U. Med. Dental NJ, 2006—. Rschr. addiction psychiatry U. Med. Dental NJ, 2004—05; rschr. mental illness, health policy Health Policy Rsch. Ctr., New Sch. U., NYC, 2000; rschr. infectious diseases epidemiology Pub. Health Rsch. Inst., NYC, 2000; med. interpreter St. Petersburg City Health Dept., 1995—98. Contbr. articles various profl. jours. Grantee, Fogarty Internat. Ctr., 1999-2000; Prof. Eichvald scolarship, St. Petersburg Med. Acad. Postgraduate Edn., 1997. Edmund S. Muskie, FREEDOM Support Act Grad. Fellowship Program, US Dept. State, Bur. Cultural, Ednl. Affairs, 1998-2000. Mem.: APHA (assoc.), NJ Psychiat. Assn. (assoc.), Am. Psychiat. Assn. (assoc.). Office: U Med Dental NJ Robert Wood Johnson Med Sch 671 Hoes Ln C 205 Piscataway NJ 08854 Office Fax: 732-235-4277; Home Fax: 732-235-4649. Business E-Mail: volfsoel@umdnj.edu.

VOLICER, LADISLAV, physician, educator; b. Prague, Czechoslovakia, May 21, 1935; came to U.S., 1969, naturalized, 1977; s. Ladislav and Vilma (Molnarova) V.; m. Olga Holeckova, July 14, 1959 (div. 1970); children: Irena, Katerina; m. Beverly J. Beers, May 20, 1972 (div. 1998); children: Zuzka, Marika, Nadine, m. Joyce Simard, Jan. 1, 2009. MD, Charles U., 1959; PhD of Pharmacology, Czechoslovak Acad. Scis., 1964. Rsch. assoc. Czechoslovak Acad. Sci., Prague, 1966—68; rsch. asst. prof. U. Munich, 1968—69; from asst. prof. to assoc. prof. pharmacology Boston U. Sch. Medicine, 1969—77, asst. prof. medicine, 1975—2004, prof. pharmacology, 1977—2004, prof. psychiatry, 1985—2004, mem. inst. rev. bd., 1975—78; courtesy prof. Sch. Aging Studies U. South Fla., Tampa, 2004—; external prof., head 3d med. faculty Charles U., Prague, Czech Republic, 1995—. Clin. pharmacologist E.N. Rogers Meml. Vets. Hosp., Bedford, Mass., 1980-87, dep. dir. Geriatric Research Edn. Clin. Ctr., 1987-92, clin. dir., 1992-2004; mem. drug formulary com. State Mass., Boston, 1977-83; mem. inst. rev. bd. McLean Hosp., Belmont, Mass., 1980-2000, rsch. psychiatrist, 1997-2004 Editor: Clinical Aspects of Cyclic Nucleotides, 1977, Clinical Management of Alzheimer's Disease, 1988, Hospice Care for Patients with Advanced Progressive Dementia, 1998; Enhancing Quality of Life in Advanced Dementia, 1999, Management of Challenging Behaviors in Dementia, 2000; contbr. papers to profl. publs. Grantee Nat. Inst. Aging, 1986-2004, Nat. Inst. Alcoholism and Alcohol Abuse, 1972-79, Nat. Inst. Drug Abuse, 1973-78, Merck, Sharp & Dohme, 1971; recipient Alcoholism Research award VA, 1979-85. Fellow Gerontol. Soc. Am., Am. Acad. Nursing Democrat. Unitarian Universalist. Office: U South Fla Sch Aging Studies 4202 E Fowler Ave MHC 1342 Tampa FL 33620 Home: 2337 Dekan Ln Land O Lakes FL 34639 Office Phone: 813-909-0539. E-mail: lvolicer@cas.usf.edu.

VOLK, AUSTIN N., retired insurance company executive; b. NYC, Dec. 28, 1918; s. Nicholas and Helen Volk; m. Rae Petigrue, Aug. 17, 1979; children: Deborah Saliba, John Glidden, James L.P. Glidden, Gordon G. Glidden. BA in Econ., Brown U., Providence, 1941. V.p. Nicholas Volk & Co. Inc., NYC, 1946—55, pres., 1955—75, ret., 1975. Pres. Nat. Naval Res. Surface Policy Bd., Omaha, 1964—66; mem. Nat. Naval Res. Policy Bd., Washington, 1967—69. Pres. Englewood Cemetery Assn., NJ, 1988—2006; trustee, chmn. Naval War Coll. Found., 1997—99; councilman, coun. pres. City of Englewood, 1955—60, mayor, 1960—64, 1966—68; assemblyman State of N.J., Trenton, 1968—72. Capt. USNR, 1941—73, PTO, WWII, ATO, Korean War. Mem.: Navy League (pres. N.Y. coun. 1982—84, Teddy Roosevelt Leadership award 1982), Naval Order U.S. (pres. 1990—92, mem. N.Y. coun.).

VOLK, DAVID PAUL, music educator; b. Atlanta, Nov. 12, 1968; s. Douglas Bodine and Janet May Volk; m. Heather Lynn Scull; children: Reese David, Julian Alden. MusB, Fla. State U., Tallahassee, 1992, MusM, 1994; MusD, U. Ga., Athens, 2004. Asst. prof., adj. instr. Piedmont Coll., Demorest, Ga., 1995—2005; asst. prof. music U. Va. Coll., Wise, 2005—. Composer: (opera) A Good Man is Hard to Find, (choral) a capella Mass. Amb. family Mar. Dimes, Richmond, 2007. Home: 208 Clinton Ave E Big Stone Gap VA 24219 Office: Univ Va Coll One College Ave Wise VA 24293 Business E-Mail: dpv4a@uvawise.edu.

VOLK, KENNETH HOHNE, lawyer; b. Hackensack, NJ, Nov. 8, 1922; s. Henry L. and Constance (Brady) V.; m. Joyce Geary, May 11, 1954; children: Christopher H., Cynthia. BS, U.S. Naval Acad., 1946; LLB, Yale U., 1953. Ptnr. Burlingham, Underwood, NYC, 1955-92; of counsel McLane, Graf, Raulerson & Middleton, Portsmouth, N.H., 1992—. Speaker various symposia and confs. on maritime law. Assoc. editor Am. Maritime Cases; contbr. articles to profl. jours. Pres. Maritime Assocs., N.Y.C., 1967-68; chmn. bd. dirs. Seamen's House YMCA, N.Y.C., 1971-76; sec., bd. dirs. Seamen's Ch. Inst., N.Y.C., 1977-92; bd. dirs. Strawbery Banke Mus., Portsmouth, N.H.; mem. adv. bd. Tulane Admiralty Law Inst. Fellow Am. Bar Found., Am. Coll. Trial Lawyers; mem. ABA, Assn. Bar of City of N.Y., Maritime Law Assn. U.S. (exec. com. 1977-80, pres. 1990-92), Comite Maritime Internat. (titulary mem.), Quaker Hill Country Club (pres. 1976-78). Republican. Espicopalian. Avocations: reading, hiking, fishing. Office: McLane Graf Raulerson & Middleton 100 Market St Portsmouth NH 03801 Office Phone: 603-436-2818. E-mail: kenneth-volk@mclane.com.

VOLK, KRISTIN, advertising agency executive; b. Phila., Feb. 26, 1953; d. Richard H. and Doris (Colasanti) V. BS in Biology, Tufts U., 1976; MPH, Boston U. Sch. Med., 1981. Rsch. technician Beth Israel Hosp., Boston, 1976; rsch. asst. Dana-Farber Cancer Inst., Boston, 1976-78; sr. rsch. asst. Beth Israel Hosp., Boston, 1978-81; rsch. supr. Schneider Parker Jakuc Advt., Boston, 1981-86; v.p., assoc. rsch. dir. HBM/Creamer, Boston, 1986-88, Della Femina McNamee, Boston, 1988-90; v.p., dir. rsch. Lawner Reingold Britton & Ptnrs., Boston, 1990-93; sr. v.p., dir. consumer insight group Arnold Fortuna Lawner & Cabot, Boston, 1993-95; exec. v.p., dir. consumer insight group Arnold Comm., Inc., Boston, 1995-99; exec. v.p., dir. strategic planning Deutsch Boston, 1999—2001; exec. v.p., chief mktg. officer Arnold Worldwide, NYC, 2001—06; exec. v.p., dir. strategic planning Saatchi & Saatchi, NYC, 2007. Guest lectr. colls. and univs., Boston. Contbr. articles to profl. jours. Mem. Am. Assn. Advt. Agencies (account planning group com., chmn. conf. 1998), Ad Club N.Y. Home: 252 7th Ave Apt 15k New York NY 10001-7349

VOLK, NORMAN HANS, financial executive; b. NYC, Jan. 10, 1935; s. Hans and Mary (Zurl) V.; m. Karlyn Schram, Aug. 17, 1959; children: Kari, Heidi, Jenny. BA, Valparaiso U., Ind., 1957; MA, Marquette U., Milw., 1959. Dir. pub. rels. Wagner Coll., NYC, 1961-62; asst. to owner Alan M. Wood, NYC, 1962-72; sr. v.p. Bessemer Trust Co., NYC, 1972-85; pres. Chamberlain & Steward, NYC, 1985—. Trustee John Hartford Found., N.Y.C., 1979—. With U.S. Army, 1959-61. Mem. Univ. Club, Univ. Glee Club of N.Y.C., Doubles Club. Lutheran. Home: 445 Walton Rd Maplewood NJ 07040-1119 Office: 400 Park Ave New York NY 10022-4406

VOLK, PATRICIA GAY, novelist, essayist; b. NYC, July 16, 1943; d. Cecil Sussman and Audrey Elaine (Morgen) Volk; m. Andrew Blitzer, Dec. 21, 1969; children: Peter Morgen, Polly Volk BFA cum laude, Syracuse U., 1964; student, Sch. Visual Arts, NYC, 1968, New Sch., 1975, Columbia U., 1977-88. Art dir. Appelbaum & Curtis, NYC, 1964-65, Seventeen Mag., Triangle Publs., NYC, 1966-68; copywriter Doyle, Dane, Bernbach, Inc., NYC, 1969-88, also sr. v.p., creative mgr., 1969-87, sr. v.p.- assoc. creative dir., 1987-88; columnist N.Y. Newsday, 1995-96; fiction instr. Yeshiva Coll. Fiction instr. Playwrights Horizon Theater Sch., Marymount Coll., MFA Instr. Bennington Coll. Author: The Yellow Banana, 1985 (Word Beat Press Fiction Book award 1984), White Light, 1987, All it Takes, 1990, Stuffed: Adventures of a Restaurant Family, 2001, To My Dearest Friends, Knopf, 2007; contbr. articles to N.Y. Times mag., Redbook, Allure, Mirabella, Family Circle, The New Yorker, The Atlantic, Playboy, others; contbr. short stories to popular and small press publs. and anthologies. Recipient Stephen E. Kelly award, 1983, Various Andy, Clio, Effie and One Show awards, 1970—88, Yaddo fellow, 1983, 1999, 2001—08, MacDowell fellow, 1984, 2000. Mem.: PEN, Century Assn., Author's Guild, Juliana Berner's Anglers.

VOLK, STEPHEN RICHARD, diversified financial services company executive, investment banker, lawyer; b. Boston, Apr. 22, 1936; s. Ralph and Miriam (Rose) V.; m. Veronica J. Brown, June 19, 1959 (dec. Feb. 1989); children: Jeffrey A., Andrew M., Michael J.; m. Diane Kemelman, Apr. 22, 1990; 1 child, Anne. Grad. cum laude, Dartmouth Coll., 1957; JD cum laude, Harvard Law Sch., 1960. Bar: NY 1961. Assoc. Shearman & Sterling, NYC, 1960-68, ptnr., 1968—88, dep. sr. ptnr., 1988-91, sr. ptnr., 1991—2001. Bd. dirs. Consol. Edison, Inc., 1996-2007, Trizec Prop., 2002-05, Continental Grain Co., 2005-; trustee Consol. Edison Co. NYC, Inc., 1998-2007; vice chmn. Credit Suisse First Boston, 2001-02, chmn., 2002-04; vice chmn. Citigroup Inc., 2004-. Fellow Am. Bar Found.; mem. Assn. Bar City NY, Harvard Law Sch. Assn. (NYC), Coun. Fgn. Rels., Univ. Club, Phi Beta Kappa. Office: Citigroup Inc 399 Park Ave New York NY 10022

VOLK, STEVEN S., history professor; s. Nathan N. Volk and Esther Segal; m. Dinah Hirschfeld, July 6, 1969; children: Jonah C., Anna N. BA, Brandeis U., Waltham, Mass., 1968; MA, Columbia U., NY, 1971, PhD, 1983. Rsch. dir. North Am. Congress L.Am., NYC, 1973—84, dir., 1984—2008; vis. asst. prof. NY U., 1985—86; prof. Oberlin Coll., Ohio, 1986—. Dir., tchg. innovation & excellence Oberlin Coll., 2006—. Dir. Bill Rights Found., NYC, 1990—2008, Oberlin Choristers, 1992—2008. Recipient award, Govt. Chile, 2001, Tchg. Excellence award, Oberlin Coll., 2003, Disting. Tchg. award, NE Ohio Coun. Higher Edn., 2002—03. Mem.: Latin Am. Studies Assn., Am. Hist. Assn. (Nancy Lyman Roelker Mentorship award 2002). Office: Dept History Oberlin Coll Rice 309 Oberlin OH 44074 Business E-Mail: steven.volk@oberlin.edu.

VOLK, WILLIAM R., lawyer; b. Corpus Christi, Tex., Aug. 11, 1950; BA, Vanderbilt U., 1972; JD with honors, U. Tex., 1975. Bar: Tex. 1975. Ptnr., co-head Corp. Fin. & Securities Sect. Vinson & Elkins LLP, Austin, Tex. Fellow: Texas Bar Found. (life); mem.: ABA, Austin Bar Assn. Office: Vinson & Elkins LLP 2801 Via Fortuna, Ste 100 Austin TX 78746 Business E-Mail: wvolk@velaw.com.

VOLKAMER, RAINER MARTIN, physicist, researcher, aerospace scientist; b. Freiburg, Breisgau, Germany, June 18, 1970; s. Klaus Volkamer and Helga Ingrid Volkamer-Gutwill; life ptnr. Carmen Eugenia Pastor Gradolí. Dr. rer. nat., Ruperto Carola U., Heidelberg, Germany, 2001. Rsch. asst. Inst. Environ. Physics, Heidelberg, 1995—97; Dreyfus fellow MIT, Cambridge, Mass., 2002—. Contbr. articles to profl. jours. Scholar, Faculty of Física Aplicada, 1993—94; Marie Curie fellow, European Commn., 1998—2002. Mem.: Am. Geophys. Union, German Physikalische Assn. (assoc.). Avocations: outdoor recreation, backpacking. Office: Univ of Colorado at Boulder UCB 215 Boulder CO 80309-0215 Business E-Mail: rainer@mit.edu.

VOLKAY, CHRIS JOHN, investment company executive; b. Hollywood, Calif., Nov. 14, 1954; s. Robert and Yvonne Pearl Volkay. Lic. real estate agt. Calif. V.p. Rubicon Corp. Am., Van Nuys, Calif., 1986—. Mentor investment counselors and brokers Paladin Mortgage, Van Nuys, 1995—. Author: Laughing Gas, 2000; contbr. articles to profl. jours., poems, short stories to lit. publs. Mem.: Brights, Ctr. for Inquiry West, Coun. Secular Humanism. Libertarian. Secular Humanist. Office Phone: 818-765-8800. E-mail: cvolkay@aol.com.

VOLKER, DALE MARTIN, state legislator, lawyer; b. Lancaster, NY, Aug. 2, 1940; s. Julius J. and Loretta (O'Neill) Volker; m. Carol A. Suchyna, Nov. 28, 1970; children: Martin Andrew, Mark Dale, Meredith Ann. BA, Canisius Coll., 1963; JD, SUNY, Buffalo, 1966. Bar: NY 1967. Police officer Village of Depew, NY, 1966—72; mem. NY State Assembly, Albany, 1972—74; atty. Fowler and Volker, Lancaster, NY, 1978—; mem. Dist. 59 NY State Senate, Albany, 1975—, asst. majority leader Dist. 59. Mem.: Erie County Bar Assn., Eagles, Moose, Elks. Republican. Roman Cath. Home: 92 Center Dr Depew NY 14043-1706 Office: Capitol Office 808 Legislative Office Bldg Albany NY 12247 also: Dist Office 4729 Transit Rd Ste 5 Depew NY 14043 also: Dist Office 143 N Main St Rm 103 Warsaw NY 14569 Office Phone: 518-455-3471, 716-656-8544, 585-786-5048. Business E-Mail: volker@senate.state.ny.us.

VOLKER, KURT DOUGLAS, former United States permanent representative to NATO; b. 1964; married; 2 children. BA, Temple U., Phila.; MA in Internat. Rels., George Washington U., Washington. Analyst CIA, 1986—88; joined US Fgn. Svc., 1988, on assignment Budapest, Hungary, London; various positions including spl. asst. to the counselor and spl. asst. to the US spl. envoy for Bosnia negotiations US State Dept., dep. polit. counselor, polit.-mil. officer, US Embassy

Budapest, Hungary, 1994—97, first sec., the US Mission to NATO, 1998—99, prin. dep. asst. sec. European and Eurasian affairs, 2005—08; fgn. policy staff mem., Senator John McCain US Senate, Washington, 1997—98; dep. dir., pvt. office of sec. gen. Lord Robertson NATO, 1999—2001; US permanent rep. to NATO US Dept. State, Brussels, 2008—09; acting sr. dir. European and Eurasian affairs and dir. NATO and West Europe NSC, 2001—05. Senate Legis. fellow, US Dept. State, 1997—98.*

VOLKHARDT, JOHN MALCOLM, retired food products executive; b. Chester, Pa., Apr. 13, 1917; s. George Thomas and Evelyn (Mitchell) V.; m. Linda J. Volkhardt; children: Michael, Jacqueline, Janet, Dana. AB cum laude, Brown U., 1939. Product mgr. Vick Chem. Co., NYC, 1939-48; gen. mgr. Northam Warren Co., Stamford, Conn., 1948-56, Rit div. Best Foods Co., NYC, 1956-58; with Best Foods div. CPC Internat. Inc., Englewood Cliffs, N.J., 1958-78, exec. v.p., 1968-71, pres., 1971-78; pres. North Am. div. CPC Internat. and exec. v.p. CPC Internat., 1978-82, group v.p., 1979; v.p. CPC, 1971-78, dir., 1977-82; pres., chmn. Full Circle Corp., Moss Creek, 1985-91; pres. Water Oak Utility, 1985-91. Dir. Storm Eye Inst., 2002—05. Chmn. bd. Keep Am. Beautiful, Inc., 1979-82, chmn. bd. trustees, 1982. Recipient Herbert Hoover award Nat. Assn. Wholesale Grocers Am.; honoree Nat. Jewish Hosp., 1976. Mem. Phi Beta Kappa.

VOLKMAR, FRED ROBERT, psychiatrist, educator, director; b. Highland, Ill., Mar. 26, 1950; s. Fred Harwood and Ella Josephine (Smith) Volkmar; m. Elizabeth Anne Wiesner, Sept. 2, 1984; children: Lucy Amelia, Emily Louisa. BS, U. Ill., Urbana-Champaign, 1972; MA, MD, Stanford U., Calif., 1976. Diplomate Am. Bd. Psychiatry and Neurology. Resident psychiatry Stanford U., Calif., 1976—80; fellow child psychiatry Yale U., New Haven, 1980—82; asst. prof. Child Study Ctr., 1982—88, assoc. prof., 1988—98, prof., 1998—, Irving B. Harris chair, 2003—, chmn., dir., chief child psychiatry Yale New Haven Hosp., 2006—. Cons. psychiatrist Benhaven Sch., New Haven, 1984—, med. dir., 1982—85; mem. sci. com. Nat. Ctr. for Clin. Infant Programs, Washington, 1985. Recipient Sandoz award, 1980, Ittelson award, Am. Psychiat. Assn., Faculty Scholar award, William T. Grant Found., 1982, Rsch. Career award, NIMH, 1983, Tarjan award, Am. Acad. Child Adolescent Psychiatry, 2007; James scholar, Laughlin fellow, 1982. Mem.: Am. Acad. Child Psychiatry, Soc. for Rsch. in Child Devel., Phi Beta Kappa. Democrat. Avocations: astronomy, photography, sailing. Office: Yale U Child Study Ctr 230 S Frontage Rd PO Box 207900 New Haven CT 06519-1124 Home Phone: 203-481-0743; Office Phone: 203-785-5759. Business E-Mail: fred.volkmar@yale.edu.

VOLKOW, NORA DOLORES, federal agency administrator, medical researcher; b. Mexico City, Mar. 27, 1956; m. Steven Adler. BA, Modern Am. Sch., Mexico City, 1974; MD, Nat. U. Mex., 1980. Diplomate Am. Bd. Psychiatry & Neurology. Rsch. asst. Registro Nacional de Anatomia Patologica, Mexico City, 1975-76, Miles Lab. Exptl. Therapeutics, Mexico City, 1977-78; intern St. Anne Psychiat. Hosp., Paris, 1979-80; resident dept. psychiatry NYU, 1981—84; asst. prof. U. Tex. Med. Sch., Houston, 1984-87; attending physician psychiat. unit Herman Hosp., Houston, 1985-87; assoc. scientist dept. medicine Brookhaven Nat. Lab., Upton, NY, 1987-89, assoc. chief of staff, Clin. Rsch. Ctr., 1990, dir. nuclear medicine divsn., 1994—2003, dir. NIDA/DOE Imaging Ctr., 1997—2003, assoc. dir. life scis., 1999—2003; assoc. prof. dept. psychiatry SUNY, Stony Brook, 1991—2003, assoc. dean, Sch. Med., 1997—2003; dir. Nat. Inst. Drug Abuse (NIDA), NIH, Washington, 2003—. Elected mem. Inst. Medicine, 2000; mem. adv. com. minority tng. in psychiatry, Washington, 1991—; mem. study sect. clin. neuroscis. NIH, Washington, 1992—. Co-editor: Positron Emission Tomography in Schizophrenia Research, 1991. Recipient Premio Robins award, U. Mex., 1978, Premio Gabino Barrera award, 1981, Laughlin fellowship, Am. Coll. Psychiatry, 1984, Scanditronix scholarship, 1985, Paul C. Aebersold award, Soc. Nuclear Medicine, 2003; named Innovator of Yr., US News & World Report, 2000; named one of The World's Most Influential People, TIME mag., 2007; named to Who's Next in 2007, Newsweek. Office: NIDA 6001 Exec Blvd Rm 5213 Bethesda MD 20892-9581 Business E-Mail: nvolkow@nida.nih.gov.*

VOLL, JOHN OBERT, history professor; b. Hudson, Wis., Apr. 20, 1936; s. Obert Frank and Ruth Olivia (Seaberg) V.; m. Sarah Lynne Potts, June 12, 1965; children: Sarah Layla, Michael Obert. AB summa cum laude, Dartmouth Coll., 1958, PhD (Ford Found. fellow), 1969; AM (Danforth fellow), Harvard U., 1960. Instr. history U. N.H., Durham, 1965-69, asst. prof., 1969-74, assoc. prof., 1974-82, prof., 1982-95, chair dept., 1988-91; prof. Georgetown U., Washington, 1995—, dep. dir. Ctr. for Muslim-Christian Understanding, 1996—2004, 2006—, dir. Ctr. for Muslim-Christian Understanding, 2004—06, interim chair Arabic & Islamic studies, 2009—. Mem. history and social scis. adv. com. Coll. Bd. 1983-86, chmn. European history and world cultures achievement test com., 1985-88; tchg. fellow Harvard U., 1969. Harvard Ctr. for Middle Eastern, Studies Vist. Com., 2003-05 Author: Historical Dictionary of the Sudan, 1978, 2nd edit., 1992, Islam Continuity and Change in the Modern World, 2nd edit., 1994; (with others) The Sudan: Unity and Diversity, 1985, Eighteenth Century Renewal and Reform in Islam, 1987, Sudan: State and Society in Crisis, 1991, Islam and Democracy, 1996, Makers of Contemporary Islam, 2001, Asian Islam in the 21st Century, 2008; contbr. articles to profl. jours. Mem. bd. Ecumenical Ministry U. N.H., 1974-78, pres., 1975-77; chmn. social action Durham Cmty. Ch., 1974-75, mem. ch. coun., 1977-78, deacon, 1986—. Sheldon traveling fellow, 1960-61, U. N.H. summer fellow, 1969, 89, NEH fellow, 1971-72, Fulbright faculty rsch. abroad fellow, 1978-79, Inst. Advanced Studies fellow Hebrew U., 1984-85; recipient Egyptian Presdl. medal, 1991. Mem. Am. Coun. Learned Socs. (del. 1989-96, del. exec. com. 1989-92, bd. dirs. 1990-92), New England Hist. Assn. (sec. 1975-78, v.p. 1981, pres. 1982), Sudan Studies Assn. (bd. dirs. 1981-82, co-exec. dir. 1990-94), N.H. Coun. on World Affairs (bd. dirs. 1978-95), World History Assn. (bd. dirs. 2005-08), Am. Hist. Assn. (chmn. program com. 1999), Mid. East Studies Assn. (bd. dirs. 1987-89, pres. 1992-93), Am. Coun. for Study of Islamic Socs. (bd. dirs. 1989—, v.p. 1989-91), N.H. Humanities Coun. (bd. dirs. 1991-95). Mem. United Ch. of Christ. Home: 4000 Cathedral Ave NW Apt 652B Washington DC 20016-5205 Office: Ctr Muslim Christian Understanding Georgetown U Washington DC 20057-0001 Office Phone: 202-687-8375. E-mail: vollj@georgetown.edu.

VOLLACK, LIA, broadcast executive; Joined Sony Pictures Entertainment, 1997, sr. v.p., 1999—2000, exec. v.p., 2000, pres. worldwide music Columbia Pictures, 2002—. Named one of the top women in music, Billboard, 2005, The100 Most Powerful Women in Entertainment, Hollywood Reporter, 2006, 2007. Achievements include becoming first female theatrical sound designer on Broadway. Office: Columbia Pictures 10202 West Washington Blvd Culver City CA 90232 Office Phone: 310-244-4000. Office Fax: 310-244-2626. E-mail: lia_vollack@spe.sony.com.

VOLLEN, ROBERT JAY, lawyer; b. Chgo., Jan. 23, 1940; s. Ben N. and Rose (Belonsky) V.; m. Judith Paula Spector, Aug. 12, 1961; children: Steven, Neil, Jennifer. AB, U. Mich., 1961; JD, U. Chgo., 1964. Bar: Ill. 1964, D.C. 1965, U.S. Supreme Ct. 1975. Atty. appellate sect. Civil Div., U.S. Dept. Justice, Washington, 1964-65; asso. firm Schiff Hardin & Waite, Chgo., 1965-70, partner firm, 1971-72; gen. counsel BPI (Bus. and Profl. People for Pub. Interest), Chgo., 1972-83; ptnr. Schwartz & Freeman, Chgo., 1983-87. Mem. vis. com. U. Chgo. Law Sch., 1978—81. Mem. ABA (ho. of dels. 1974-76), Chgo. Coun. Lawyers (gov. 1972-76, 79-81). Home: 2 Kingswood Ct Riverwoods IL 60015-1912 E-mail: rvollen@ameritech.net.

VOLLMER, DAVID L., museum director; Dir. Janice Mason Art Mus., Cadiz, Ky., Swope Art Mus., Terre Haute, Ind., 2001—. Office: Swope Art Mus 25 S 7th St Terre Haute IN 47807 Office Phone: 812-238-1676. E-mail: vollmer@swope.org.

VOLNER, IAN D., lawyer; b. NYC, June 2, 1940; BA, Colgate Univ., 1962; JD (LLB), Columbia Univ., 1965. Bar: NY 1967, DC 1970. Staff atty. FCC Rev. Bd., 1968—70; ptnr. Venable LLP, Washington. Adj. prof. NY Law Sch., 1981—88, Catholic Univ. Am., Univ. Md. Mem.: ABA, Fed. Comm. Bar Assn., NY State Bar Assn., DC Bar Assn., Phi Beta Kappa. Office: Venable LLP 575 7th St NW Washington DC 20004 Office Phone: 202-344-4814. Office Fax: 202-344-8300. Business E-Mail: idvolner@venable.com.

VOLONTS, MARGUERITE LOUISE, music educator, singer; b. Jamaica, NY, July 21, 1954; d. Louis John Rub and Marquerite Signe Gustafson; children: Alex, Julia. BFA in Music, magna cum laude, Ithaca Coll., NY, 1976; MA, SUNY, Stony Brook, 1979. Cert. in tchg. NY. Tchr. Dalton Sch., NYC, 1976, Rocky Point Schs., 1977—82, William Floyd Schs., 1982—87, Riverhead Schs., 1987—. Staff mem., camp dir. Frost Valley YMCA, 1969—95, trip leader, 1974—79; musical dir., condr., treas., pres. Riverhead Faculty Cmty. Theatre, 1982—; condr. Three Village Festival, 1990, 1995; vocalist Gordon Hurley Big Band, 1994—, Sound Symphony, North Shore Chamber Orch.; youth choir dir. Wading River Congregational Ch., 1989—2002. Mem.: LI String Festival Assn. (chairperson 1985—95, condr. 1997), Suffolk County Music Edn. Assn. (chairperson 1985—95, condr., 1984, 2001), NY State Sch. Music Assn., Music Educator's Nat. Conf. Home: 51 Northside Rd Wading River NY 11792 Personal E-mail: mrub2@aol.com.

VOLOSHIN, ARKADY, mechanical engineering and mechanics educator; b. Kishinev, USSR; came to U.S., 1979; s. Saul and Ita V.; m. Ilana Gitelman, Nov. 26, 1972; children: Ronen, Dan. MS, Leningrad Poly. Inst., Russia, 1969; PhD, Tel-Aviv U., 1978. Rsch. engr. Inst. for Non-destructive Evaluation, Kishinev, USSR, 1969-70; rsch. asst. Tel-Aviv U., 1973-78, post-doctoral fellow, 1978-79; asst. prof. Iowa State U., Ames, 1979-89; assoc. prof. Lehigh U., Bethlehem, Pa., 1987-91, prof., 1991—. Assoc. editor: Experimental Mechanics, 1992—; contbr. articles to profl. jours.; presenter in field. Recipient M. Hetenyi award, 1983, Brewer award Exptl. Mechanics Soc. Jewish. Avocations: skiing, scuba, music, reading. Office: Lehigh U 369 Packard Lab # 19 Bethlehem PA 18015

VOLOSHIN, BEVERLY R., literature and language professor; b. New Haven, Dec. 19, 1949; d. Milton L. and Edna Pogrotsky Voloshin; m. Alan F. Sandy; children: Joseph Voloshin Sandy children: Rachel Voloshin Sandy. BA, UCLA, 1971; PhD in English and Am. Lit., U. Calif., Berkeley, 1979. Instr. English U. Rochester, NY, 1977—79, founding mem., program women's studies, 1979—81, asst. prof. English, 1979—87, San Francisco State U., 1987—90, assoc. prof. English, 1990—96, prof. English, 1996—, chair, dept. English lang. & lit., 2007—. Scholar Beatrice Bain Rsch. Group, U. Calif., 2001; editor spl. issues Pacific Coast Philology, 2004—. Exhibitions include Paintings and Works on Paper. Mem. Faculty Israeli-Palestinian Peace, 2004—, Bay Area Grandmothers Against War, Berkeley, Calif., 2003—. Recipient Vice-Presdl. award, San Francisco State U., 1979; scholarship, Nat. Merit Found., 1967—71, US Presdl. scholarship, Pres. Lyndon Johnson, 1967, fellowship, Woodrow Wilson Found., 1971—72, Dean's fellowship, U. Calif., Berkeley, 1973—75, Mellon Faculty fellowship, U. Rochester, 1984. Mem.: AAUP, MLA, Pacific Ancient & MLA (2nd v.p. to v.p., pres. 2008—), Women & Work, Phi Beta Kappa (pres. 2007—).

VOLPE, ANGELO ANTHONY, retired academic administrator, chemist, educator; b. Nov. 8, 1938; s. Bernard Charles and Serafina (Martorana) V.; m. Jennette Murray, May 15, 1965. BS, Bklyn. Coll., 1959; MS, U. Md., 1962, PhD, 1966; M in Engring. (hons.), Stevens Inst. Tech., 1975. Rsch. chemist USN Ordnance Lab., Silver Spring, Md., 1961-66; from asst. prof. to prof. chemistry Stevens Inst. Tech., Hoboken, NJ, 1966-77; chmn. dept. chemistry East Carolina U., Greenville, NC, 1977-80, dean Coll. Arts and Scis., 1980-83, vice chancellor for acad. affairs, 1983-87; pres. Tenn. Technol. U., Cookeville, 1987-2000, ret., 2000, pres. emeritus, 2000—; mem. bd. of trustee Tusculum Coll., 2005—, acting pres., 2007. Adj. prof. textile chem. N.C. State U., Raleigh, 1978-82; guest lect. Plastics Inst. Am., Hoboken, 1967-82. Contbr. articles to profl. jours. Recipient Ednl. Svc. award Plastics Inst. Am., 1973; named Freygang Outstanding Tchr., Stevens Inst. Tech., 1975. Mem. Am. Chem. Soc., Tenn. Acad. Scis., Sigma Xi, Phi Kappa Phi. Democrat. Roman Catholic. Avocations: golf, reading. Home: 734 Loweland Rd Cookeville TN 38501-2888 Home Phone: 931-526-9543; Office Phone: 931-372-3220. Personal E-mail: avolpe@tntech.edu.

VOLPE, CHRISTOPHER THOMAS, history educator; b. Glen Cove, NY, Dec. 21, 1965; s. Thomas Henry Volpe and Carol Anne Strath; m. Anna Volpe, June 18, 2005; 1 child, Max Tyler. MA, U. NH, Durham, 1996. Comm. and info. coord. interoperability lab U. NH, 2003—; instr. art history, lit., mythology Chester Coll. New Eng., NH, 2006—. Asst. curator and cons. Banks Gallery, Portsmouth, NH, 2006—. Painting, Contemporary Fine Art Landscape Paintings Oils. Calderwood fellowship, Franklin Pierce U., 2006. Mem.: NH Plein Air Painters. Achievements include first to history of nineteenth-century American art. Avocations: travel, painting, music. Office: Chester Coll New Eng 40 Chester St Chester NH 03036

VOLPE, DORIS, artist; b. Rockford, Ill., Dec. 22, 1930; d. August and Grace Adelaide Meenen; m. Samuel Volpe, Dec. 26, 1950 (dec. July 1994); children: Michael, Margaret. Group exhbns. include Art Inst. Chgo., Deer Path Gallery, Lake Forest, Ill., Gregoire Galleries, N.Y.C., Rhoda Sande Gallery, N.Y.C., Yolanda Kelly Gallery, Chgo., Peoria (Ill.) Regional Gallery, Old Orchard Shopping Ctr., Skokie, Ill., New Horizons, Chgo., Lake County Mus., Wauconda, Ill., Open Spectrum, Libertyville, Ill., Coll. Lake County, Grayslake, Ill., Neville-Sargent Gallery, Chgo., Sonnenschein Gallery, Lake Forest, Chgo. Botanic Gardens, Galleria Renata, Chgo., Clementi House Gallery, London, Millburn (Ill.) Gallery, Art in the Barn, Barrington, Ill., Art Expo, Lake Forest, Plaza del Lago, Wilmette, Ill., The Artists' Den, Valparaiso, Ind., Heirloom Gallery, Wilmette, North Shore Art League Fall Festival, Later Impressions, Chgo., Gallery 203, Chgo. Fountain Square, Evanston IL, Arts in Northbrook, Northbrook, Cantigny Fine Art Festival, Wheaton IL, Artcetera Gallery Grays Lake, Ill, Art Fair on The Sq. lake Forest, Ill.; solo exhbns. include Covenant Club, Chgo., 1st Fed. Savs. and Loan, Chgo., Lake County Court House, Waukegan, Ill., Kemper Group, Long Grove, Ill., The Stanley Gallery, Norfolk, Va., Univ. Club, Chgo., Chgo. Cultural Ctr. Avocations: gardening, art league activities.

VOLPE, EILEEN RAE, retired special education educator; b. Fort Morgan, Colo., Aug. 23, 1942; d. Earl Lester and Ellen Ada (Hearting) Moore; m. David P. Volpe, July 28, 1965 (div. 1980); children: David P. Jr., Christina Marie. BA, U. No. Colo., Greeley, 1964, MA, 1978. Cert. fine art tchr., learning handicapped specialist, resource specialist. 5th grade tchr. Meml. Elem. Sch., Milford, Mass., 1967-68; fine arts jr./sr. high tchr. Nipmuc Regional Jr. Sr. H.S., Mendon, Mass., 1968-69; substitute tchr. K-12 Greeley (Colo.) Dist. 6 Schs., 1976—79; spl. edn. tchr. Saugus (Calif.) H.S., 1979—98, Valencia (Calif.) H.S., 1998—2003; ret., 2003; substitute tchr. grades K-12 Dist. 6, 2005—. Publicity dir. Sacred Heart Ch. Sch., Milford, Mass., 1974-75, float coord. bicentennial parade, 1975; substitute tchr. K-12 Dist. 6 Sch., Greeley, Colo., 2005-. Author: (poetry) Seasons to Come, 1994, Best Poems of 1997, 04, The Other Side of Midnight, 1997, Best of 2001 Poems, Best Poems and Poets of 2003, Best of 2005 Poems; contbr. to Best of Millennium Poetry, 1999-00, Best of 2002 Poems, Best Poems of 2004, Labours of Love, 2006, Songs of Honor, 2006, Best of 2006 Poems; artist over 300 oil and watercolor painting, Impressionist and Modern Art, Favourite Memories, 2009. Mem. Calif. Tchr. Assn., Coun. for Exceptional Children, DAR, Phi Delta Kappa, Kappa Delta Pi. Republican. Avocations: arts and crafts, photography, travel, doll collecting and creation.

VOLPE, JOSEPH JOHN, pediatrician, neurologist, educator; b. Salem, Mass., Dec. 17, 1938; s. John Rosario and Anne Eleanor (Femino) V.; m. Sara Lee Solov, June 2, 1980; children from previous marriage: Joanna Marie, Joseph Anthony, John Matthew. BA, Bowdoin Coll., 1960; MD, Harvard U., 1964. Diplomate Am. Bd. Pediatrics, Am. Bd. Neurology and Psychiatry with spl. competence in child neurology. Pediatric intern Mass. Gen. Hosp., Boston, 1964-65, pediatric resident, 1965-66, neurology and pediatric resident, 1968-71; rsch. assoc. Nat. Inst. Child Health and Human Devel., Bethesda, Md., 1966-68; asst. prof. pediatrics and neurology Washington U. Med. Sch., St. Louis, 1971-76, assoc. prof. pediatrics and neurology, 1976-79, prof. pediatrics and neurology, 1979—, prof. biol. chemistry, 1980-90, dir. div. pediatric neurology, 1984-90; Bronson Crothers prof. neurology Harvard Med. Sch., Boston, 1990—; neurologist in chief Children's Hosp., Boston, 1990—. Author: Neurology of the Newborn, 1981, 4th edit., 2000; contbr. over 300 articles to profl. jours. Capt. USPHS, 1966-68. Recipient Weinstein-Goldensohn award United Cerebral Palsy Assn., 1985; rsch. grantee NIH, 1973—, March of Dimes Nat. Found., 1985-87. Mem. Nat. Acad. Scis. Inst. Medicine. Office: Children's Hosp 300 Longwood Ave Boston MA 02115-5737

VOLPE, MARYANN VITORIA, pediatrician; married. MD, Dartmouth Med. Sch., Hanover, NH, 1988. Neonatologist Tufts Med. Ctr., Boston, 1995—. Rsch. grant, Am. Lung Assn., 1997, NIH, 2001, 2005. Fellow: Am. Acad. Pediat. Office: Tufts Med Ctr 750 Washington St Box 44 Boston MA 02111 Office Fax: 617-636-4233.

VOLPE, PETER ANTHONY, surgeon; b. Columbus, Ohio, Dec. 17, 1936; s. Peter Anthony and Jeanette Katherine (Volz) V.; m. Suzanne Stephens, Sept. 5, 1959; children: John David, Michael Charles; m. Kathleen Ann Townsend, Mar. 28, 1978; 1 child, Mark Christopher; m. Theresa Ann Morse, Aug. 27, 2000. BA cum laude, Ohio State U., 1958, MD summa cum laude, 1961. Diplomate Am. Bd. Surgery, Am. Bd. Colon and Rectal Surgery (pres. 1988). Pvt. practice, San Francisco, 1969—; sr. ptnr. Volpe, Chui, Abel, Yee, Sternberg, San Francisco, 1987—; clin. prof. surgery U. Calif., San Francisco, 1995—. Asst. clin. prof. surgery U. Calif., San Francisco, 1972-95; chmn. dept. surgery St. Mary's Hosp. and Med. Ctr., San Francisco, 1978-90. Contbr. articles to profl. jours. Lt. USN, 1962—64. Fellow ACS (bd. govs. 1988-94), Am. Soc. Colon and Rectal Surgeons (treas. 1985-89, pres. 1990); mem. San Francisco Surg. Soc., San Francisco Med. Soc. Office: Volpe Chiu Abel and Yee Sternberg 3838 California St San Francisco CA 94118-1522 Office Phone: 415-668-0411.

VOLPE, RALPH PASQUALE, retired insurance company executive; b. Souderton, Pa., Sept. 20, 1936; s. Pasquale S. and Katie M. (Hartzell) Volpe; m. Marie F. Romano, Feb. 6, 1962; children: William, Anthony, Lynda. BA in Polit. Sci., Pa. State U., 1963. Claim cons. Aetna Life & Casualty Co., King of Prussia, Pa., 1964-97; litig. cons. Hartford Ins., King of Prussia, 1998—2003; ret., 2003. Bd. suprs. Upper Merion Twp., 1974—79, 1982—87, 1994—2005, chmn. bd. suprs., 1984, 1986—87, 1996—97, 2003—05, vice chmn. bd. suprs., 1985, 1995; 2d v.p. Montgomery County Assn. Twp. Ofcls., 1995—97, pres., 1997—99; exec. bd. Greater Valley Forge Transp. Mgmt. Assn., 1994—2003; study commn. Upper Merion Govt., 1974; exec. com. Rt. 202, 1994—2003; chmn. blue ribbon panel Montgomery County Waste Sys. Authority, 1997—98; sec. Montgomery County Assn. Twp. Ofcls., 2007—; chmn. Montgomery County Dem. Campaign, 1975, Upper Merion Dems., 1980—81, Upper Merion Twp. Vacancy Bd., 2009—. With US Army, 1959—61. Recipient Good Govt. award, Upper Merion Jaycees, 1977, Excellence in Govt. Svc. award, King of Prussia C. of C., 1997, Earth Day award, Upper Merion Twp., 2004, Friend of Libr. award, Upper Merion Twp. Libr., 2005, Pub. Sector award, Greater Valley Forge Transp. Mgmt. Assn., 2005. Mem.: Southeastern Assn. Twp. Ofcls., Pa. State Assn. Twp. Suprs. (chmn. rules com. 1997—2000, chmn. resolution-legislation com. 2002—05, 17th Ann. Pres.'s Leadership award 2006), Montgomery County Assn. Twp. Ofcls. (life), Chapel Four Chaplains (Legion of Honor), Valley Forge Hist. Soc., Valley Forge Order Sons of Italy Am., Optimists. Republican. Roman Catholic. Home: 240 Strawberry Ln King Of Prussia PA 19406 Personal E-mail: ralphvolpe@comcast.net.

VOLQUEZ, EDINSON, professional baseball player; b. Barahona, Dominican Republic, July 3, 1983; Pitcher Tex. Rangers, 2005—07, Cin. Reds, 2008—. Mem. Dominican Republic nat. team World Baseball Classic, 2009. Recipient Nolan Ryan Pitcher of Yr. award, Tex. Rangers Orgn., 2007; named to Nat. League All-Star Team, Maj. League Baseball, 2008. Office: Cin Reds Great Am Ball Pk 100 Main St Cincinnati OH 45202*

VOLTZ, STERLING ERNEST, physical chemist, researcher; b. Phila., Apr. 17, 1921; s. Harry John and Gertrude Irene (Derr) V.; m. Betty Morgan, Nov. 6, 1943; children: Sandra Elizabeth, Karen Lee. BA, Temple U., 1943, MA, 1947, PhD, 1952. Rsch. chemist Houdry Process Corp., Linwood, Pa., 1951-58; group leader Sun Oil Co., Marcus Hook, Pa., 1958-60; supervising engr. GE, Phila., 1960-62, cons. liaison scientist Valley Forge, Pa., 1962-68; rsch. assoc. Mobil Rsch. & Devel. Corp., Paulsboro, NJ, 1968-80, adminstrv., 1980-86; pvt. practice Media, Pa., 1986—. Contbr. articles to profl. jours. including Jour. Phys. Chem., Jour. Am. Chem. Soc., Jour. Organic Chemistry, Analytical Chemistry, Jour. Soc. Automotive Engrs., Jour. Chem. and Engring. Data, Jour. Am. Inst. Chem. Engrs. and others. Lt. (j.g.) USN, 1943-46, ETO. Mem. AAAS, Am. Chem. Soc. (Phila. sect.), Catalysis Soc., Catalysis Club. Phila. (sec.-treas., chmn., dir. 1957-60), Am. Legion,

Disabled Am. Vets., Sigma Xi. Achievements include 23 patents for Simulation of Catalytic Cracking Process, for Compatible Mixtures of Coal Liquids and Petroleum Based Fuels, for Reactivation of Automotive Exhaust Oxidation Catalyst, for Increasing Antiknock Value of Olefinic Gasoline, for Preparation of Aromatic Hydrocarbons, for Process for Dehydrocyclizing Heterocyclic Organic Compounds, for Alumina Stabilized by Thoria to Resist Alpha Alumina Formation, for Method of Treating Chromium Oxide, others; invention of plastic dry bag; co-development of commercial methanol-to-gasoline process, of fuel cell for space power applications, including first successful operation in space flight; development of catalysts and processes for petroleum and petrochemical conversions, of electronic apparatus to measure dielectric properties during oxidation reactions and establish reaction kinetics; establishment of relationship between catalytic properties, surface chemistry, and semiconductivity properties of metal oxide catalysts; research on catalytic systems for automotive emissions control including kinetic model of oxidation of carbon monoxide and hydrocarbons. Home: 6 E Glen Cir Media PA 19063-4712

VOLUSE, CHARLES RODGER, III, retired education educator; b. Balt., Oct. 14, 1943; s. Charles Rodger Jr. and Beulah (Gisriel) V.; children: Steven Michael, Andrew Craig. BS in Edn., Southwestern U., Georgetown, Tex., 1965; MEd, Boston U., 1968; EdD, U. Va., 1973. Prof. grad. reading edn. SUNY, Potsdam, 1973-77; assoc. dir. grad. reading program Xavier U., Cin., 1976-83, prof., 1977-80; cons. Hamilton County Office Edn., Cin., 1980—2000, activegifted and talented programs, 1985—2000. Dir. Curriculum Devel. Assocs., Cin., 1982—; cons. Hamilton County Bd. of Mental Retardation, Cin., 1983-85; prof. Coll. Mt. Joseph. Author: Adult Subvocalization Behaviors, 1973, Experiences in Language for the Learning Handicapped, 1985; creator ednl. programs. Mem. Internat. Reading Assn., Nat. Council Tchrs. of English, Nat. Council Tchrs. of Math, Ohio Valley Assn for the Talented and Gifted. Home: 594 Laurel Oaks Dr Loveland OH 45140-9119 E-mail: drcvoluse@fuse.net.

VOLZ, WILLIAM HARRY, lawyer, educator; b. Sandusky, Mich., Dec. 28, 1946; s. Harry Bender and Belva Geneva (Riehl) V. BA, Mich. State U., 1968; MA, U. Mich., 1972; MBA, Harvard U., 1978; JD, Wayne State U., 1975. Bar: mich. 1975. Atty. pvt. practice, Detroit, 1975-77; mgmt. analyst Office of Gen. Counsel, HEW, Woodlawn, Md., 1977; from asst. prof. to prof. Wayne State U., Detroit, 1978—86, prof., 1986, dean, 1986—96; dir. Ctr. for Legal Studies Wayne State U. Law Sch., 1996-97; instr. Pa. State U., Coll. Sta., 1997—; vice chair Academic Senate. Cons. Merrill Lynch, Pierce, Fenner & Smith, N.Y.C., 1980-83, City of Detroit Law Dept., 1982, Mich. Supreme Ct., Detroit, 1981; ptnr. Mich. CPA Rev., Southfield, 1983-85; expert witness in product liability, comml. law and bus. ethics; pres. Wedgewood Group. Author: Managing a Trial, 1982; contbr. articles to legal jours.; mem. editl. bds. bus. and law jours. Internat. adv. bd. Inst. Mgmt., L'viv, Ukraine, Legal counsel Free Legal Aid Clinic, Inc., Detroit 1976-96, Shared Ministries, Detroit, 1981, Sino-Am. Tech. Exch. coun., China, 1982; chair advt. rev. panel BBB, Detroit, 1988-90; pres. Mich. Acad. Sci., Arts and Letters, 1995-96, 98-2000, bd. dirs. Common Ground, Greater Detroit Alliance Bus., Olde Custodian Fund. Mem.: ABA, Players (bd. dirs.), Amateur Medicant Soc. (commissionaire 1981—85), Harvard Bus. Sch. Club Detroit, Econ. Club Detroit, Detroit Athletic Club, Beta Alpha Psi, Alpha Kappa Psi, Golden Key. Home: 3846 Wedgewood Dr Bloomfield Hills MI 48301-3949 Office: Wayne State U Sch Bus Adminstrn Cass Ave Detroit MI 48202 Home Phone: 248-644-1035; Office Phone: 313-577-4694. Business E-Mail: ab9241@wayne.edu.

VOM BAUR, DAPHNE DE BLOIS, artist; d. Francis Trowbridge vom Baur and Carolyn Bartlett Laskey; m. David Verner Hamilton, Sept. 3, 1973; children: Zoe Hamilton-vom Baur, Nerissa Alexandra Hamilton-vom Baur. BFA, Boston U., 1968. Fellow Atlantic Ctr. for Arts, New Smyrna Beach, Fla., 1986; mem. acquisitions com. S.C. Arts Commn., Columbia, SC, 1989—91. Vis. artist Susquehanna Studio, Union Dale, Pa., 1985—86. Exhbn., The Frye Mus., Seattle, 2002. Recipient Purchase award, S.C. State Art Collection, 1986. Mem.: Cosmos Club (mem. arts coun. 2001—05). Avocations: cross country skiing, opera, horses, painting. Office: Verner Gallery LLC 1 West Washington St PO Box2270 Middleburg VA 20118 Business E-Mail: vombaur@earthlink.net.

VON AH, DIANE MARIE, nursing researcher, educator; d. Alvin Peter and Joanne Julia Winter; m. Lance William Von Ah, July 1, 1989; children: Lance William Jr., Nicole Marie, Halle Elizabeth. BSN, U. Iowa, 1987, MSN, 1996; PhD, U. Ala., Birmingham, 2003. RN Iowa, 1987, cert. nurse adminstr., AACN, Iowa, 1996. Grad. rsch. asst. U. Ala. Sch. Nursing, 1999—2003, nat. cancer inst., predoc. fellow, 2004—05; asst. prof. U. Louisville, 2003—05; postdoc. fellow, behavior oncology Ind. U., Indpls., 2005—08, asst. prof., 2008. Pres. Sigma Theta Tau, Iota Zeta Chpt., Louisville, 2004—06. Mem. Behavioral Cognitive Oncology Group, Indpls., 2008; mem. clin. trial rev. bd. Ind. U. Melvin and Bren Cancer Ctr., 2008. Recipient grant, Sigma Theta Tau, Nu Chpt., 2000—01, 2001—02, Susan G. Komen, Birmingham Affiliate, 2002—03; Postdoc. fellowship, Nat. Inst. Health, 2005—08, Nat. Inst. Nursing Rsch., 2005—08, Oncology Nursing Found., 2005—06. Mem.: Oncology Nursing Soc. (new investigator 2008), Psychoneuroimmunology Rsch. Soc. (Trainee award 2003), Midwest Nursing Rsch. Soc. (mem. com. 2007, women's health sect. new investigator 2008), Internat. Soc. Nurses Genetics, Coun. Advancement Nursing Sci. Office: Ind Univ Sch Nursing 1111 Middle Dr NU430 Indianapolis IN 46202 Office Fax: 317-278-2856. Business E-Mail: dvonah@iupui.edu.

VON AHN, LUIS, computer science educator, computer scientist; b. Guatemala City, Guatemala, 1978; BS in Math. (summa cum laude), Duke U., Durham, NC, 2000; MS in Computer Sci., Carnegie Mellon U., Pitts., Pa., 2003, PhD in Computer Sci., 2005. Summer intern U. Calif., Berkeley, 2001, IBM T.J. Watson Rsch. Lab, Hawthorne, NY, 2002, Microsoft Rsch., Redmond, Wash., 2004; post-doctoral fellow, computer sci. dept., Ctr. for Algorithm Adaptation Dissemination and Integration (ALADDIN) Carnegie Mellon U., Pitts., 2005—06, asst. prof., computer sci. dept., 2006—. Tchg. asst., Abstract Algebra Duke U., 1999, tchg. asst., Software Design and Implementation, 99, tchg. asst., Algorithms, 2000; tchg. asst., Great Theoretical Ideas in Computer Sci. Carnegie Mellon U., 2001, instr., Formal Languages, Automata and Computability, 05, 05, instr., Great Theoretical Ideas in Computer Sci., 06; program com. mem. Workshop on Human Interactive Proofs, 2005; invited spkr. in field. Contbr. articles to profl. jours.; invited reviewer for conferences and jours., work has been featured in news articles, TV and Radio The Discovery Channel, AP, NY Times, BBC Worldwide, CNN, USA Today, PC Mag., Slashdot, New Scientist and several others. Recipient Best Doctoral Dissertation Award, Carnegie Mellon University School of Computer Science, Carnegie Mellon U. Sch. of Computer Science., 2006, Alan J. Perlis Student Teaching Award, 2006; named one of Brilliant 10, Popular Sci. mag., 2006, TR35: Young Innovators Under 35, Tech. Review, 2007; Microsoft Grad. Rsch. fellowship, 2004, MacArthur Fellow, John D. and Catherine T. MacArthur Found., 2006, Microsoft New Faculty Fellowship, 2007. Achievements include patents pending in field; research includes CAPTCHAs and novel techniques for utlizing the computational abilities of humans; credited with inventing the ESP Game. Office: Computer Sci Dept Wean Hall 4121 Carnegie Mellon U 5000 Forbes Ave Pittsburgh PA 15213 Business E-Mail: biglou@cs.cmu.edu.

VON ALLMEN, DANIEL, pediatric surgeon; b. Boston, June 4, 1958; BA, Williams Coll., Mass., 1980; MD, U. Vt. Coll. Medicine, 1986. Diplomate Am. Bd. Surgery, cert. in pediatric surgery. Intern U. Cin., 1986—87, resident, 1987—93; fellow Children's Hosp. Med. Ctr., Cin., 1993—95; asst. prof. surgery & pediat. U. NC Sch. Med., Chapel Hill, 1995—96, assoc. prof. then prof. surgery, divsn. chief pediatric surgery, 2003—; surgeon in chief NC Children's Hosp.; asst. prof. surgery U. Pa. Sch. Med., Phila., 1996—2003. Contbr. articles to profl. jours. Named a Top Doc. for Kids, Phila. Mag., 2001. Office: UNC Dept Surgery Divsn Pediatric Surgery 170 Manning Dr CB 7223 Chapel Hill NC 27599 Office Phone: 919-966-4643. Office Fax: 919-843-2497.*

VON ARX, DOLPH WILLIAM, food products executive; b. St. Louis, Aug. 30, 1934; s. Adolph William and Margaret Louise (Linderer) von A.; m. Sharon Joy Landolt, Dec. 21, 1957; children: Vanessa von Arx Gilvarg, Eric S., Valerie L. BSBA, Washington U., St. Louis, 1961; LHD, St. Augustine Coll., 1988. Account exec. Compton Advt., NYC, 1961-64; v.p. mktg. Ralston Purina Co., St. Louis, 1964-69; exec. v.p. mktg. Gillette Personal Care Div., Chgo., 1969-72; exec. v.p. gen. mgmt. group T.J. Lipton Inc., Englewood Cliffs, NJ, 1973-87; pres., chief exec. officer R.J. Reynold Tobacco Co., Winston-Salem, NC, 1987-88; chmn., chief exec. officer Planters LifeSavers Co., Winston-Salem, 1988-91. Bd. dirs. Internat. Multi Food, Mpls., Hosp. Ptnrs. Am., Charlotte, N.C., No. Trust Fla. Corp., Miami, Cree Rsch. Inc., Durham, N.C., Ruby Tuesday Inc., BMC Fund Inc., Hosp. Ptnrs. Am., Charlotte, NC, Aquascent, Inc.; chmn. Morrison's Restaurant Atlanta, 1996-98, Juice Techs., Columbus, Ohio, Sanibel Captiva Trust Co., Fla. Bd. visitors U. NC, 1988-92; chmn. bd. trustees Wake Forest U. Grad. Sch. Mgmt., 1988-96; pres. bd. trustees NC Dance Theater, Winston-Salem, 1989-90; bd. dirs. Forsyth Meml. Hosp., 1988-92, Naples Conservancy, Naples Philharm. Ctr. for Arts, 1994-2009, Fla. Arts Coun., Reynolds Mus. Am. Art, Naples Cmty. Hosp., chmn., 1994-99, Health Care Sys., chmn., 1995-2005; chmn. Regional Bus. Alliance SW Fla., Naples, Fla., 2004—; Conservancy SW Fla.; mem. bd. Fla. Gulf Coast U. Found. Mem. Belle Haven Club (Greenwich) (bd. dirs. 1983-87), Naples Yacht Club, Univ. Club (N.Y.C.), Linville Ridge Country Club (Linville, N.C.), Royal Poinciana Club (Naples, Fla.), Port Royal Club (Naples). Avocation: tennis. Home: 3663 Rum Row Naples FL 34102 Personal E-mail: dvonarx@comcast.net.

VON BAILLOU, ASTRID, executive search consultant; b. Neutitschein, Czech Republic, Mar. 2, 1944; d. Karl von Baillou and Angela Stillfried; m. Dennis Hallam Bigelow, Oct. 21, 1967 (div. Oct. 1994). BA in English, Sweet Briar Coll., 1965. Creative dir. Freeman Advt., Washington, 1969-72; on-air reporter, prodr. PBS, BBC, London Weekend TV, NYC, 1972-80; v.p. Sci. Program Group TV, Washington, 1980-82; pres. Cullen & Casey, NYC, 1982-86; sr. v.p. Ruder Finn, NYC, 1986-87; pres. Baillou Internat., NYC, 1988-94; prin., mgmt. dir. Kinser & Assocs., NYC, 1994-2000; prin. Kinser & Baillou, NYC, 2000—. Home: 1245 Park Ave Apt 19F New York NY 10128-1740 Office Phone: 212-534-2161, 212-588-8801. Business E-Mail: search@kinserbaillou.com.

VON BOTHMER, BERNARD NICHOLAS, history professor; b. NYC, Jan. 1967; s. Dietrich Felix and Joyce Campbell von Bothmer; m. Jane Cowley, July 7, 2001; children: Athena Joyce, Tatiana Sierra. BA, Brown U., Providence, RI, 1989; MA, Stanford U., Calif., 1993; PhD, Ind. U., Bloomington, 2006. History prof. U. San Francisco, 2005—, Dominican U., San Rafael, Calif., 2006—. Author: (history book) Framing The Sixties: The Use and Abuse of a Decade from Ronald Reagan to George W. Bush.

VON BRAUN, PETER CARL MOORE STEWART, finance company executive; b. Greenwich, Conn., June 24, 1940; s. Carl Conrad and Martha Irwin (Moore) von B.; m. Elisabeth Esser, July 1, 1967 (div. Dec. 1980); m. Denene Jensen, Sept. 26, 1987; children: Christina Stewart, Alexander Stewart. BA with high honors, Yale U., 1964; PhD summa cum laude, U. Cologne, 1966. Assoc. McKinsey & Co., Inc., NYC, 1966-72, prin., 1972-77; chief internat. program devel. Order of St. John, London, 1977-80; exec. dir. Sight Programme, London and Sultanate of Oman, 1977-84; mng. ptnr. Leyton Assocs., Greenwich, 1980—; chmn., CEO Am. Microtrace Corp., Virginia Beach, Va., 1987-95, RusPetrol (USA), LLC, Greenwich, Conn., 1989-99. Mng. dir. LabelADD, LLC, Greenwich, Conn., 1987—99; chmn. Leix LLC, Riverside, Conn., 2000—. Author: Die Verteidigung Indiens, 1968, How to Save a Life, 1977, How to Save An Eye, 1981; contbr. articles to profl. jours.; producer (film) How to Save a Life, 1977. Chmn. Battle Harbour Found., Greenwich, 1972—; vestryman Trinity Parish, N.Y.C., 1977-84; chmn. Anglican Svc. Tng. & Relief Orgn., London, 1986—; bd. dirs. Presiding Bishop's Fund, N.Y.C., 1977-81; mem. exec. bd. Greenwich Coun. Boy Scouts Am. With USN, 1956-58, U.S. Army, 1958-64. Decorated knight of grace and knight of justice Order of St. John, companion with star Order of Merit (Cyprus), other fgn. and U.S. decorations; Fulbright scholar, 1964-66. Mem.: Cavalry, Guards Polo (London); N.Y. Yacht (N.Y.C.), Yale Club, Indian Harbor Yacht Field Club (Greenwich, Conn.), Battle Harbour Yacht (Newfoundland, Can.), Commodore, Stewart Soc. (Edinburgh). Republican. Episcopalian. Avocations: sailing, military history, cooking. Home: 36 Zaccheus Mead Ln Greenwich CT 06831-3753 Office Phone: 203-661-5442. E-mail: vonbraun@optonline.net.

VON DASSANOWSKY, ROBERT, literature and film professor, writer, producer; b. NYC, Jan. 28, 1960; s. Elfi von Dassanowsky. Grad., Am. Acad. Dramatic Arts, Pasadena; BA with honors, UCLA, 1985, MA, 1988, PhD, 1992. Actor, 1975—; asst. prof. German, UCLA, 1992-93; asst. prof. German U. Colo., Colorado Springs, 1993-99, assoc. prof. German and film, 1999—2006, head German studies, 1999—2006, dir. film studies, 1999—, interim chair dept. visual and performing arts, 2000-01, chair dept. langs. and cultures, 2001—06, prof. German and film, 2006—. CEO, prodr. Belvedere Film, LLC, 1999; vis. prof. German UCLA, 2007—08; interim chair dept. langs. & cultures, 2009; bd. dirs. Internat. Devel.; v.p. IIBSC: Intern. Inst. Bus. & Social Comm. Author: (plays) The Birthday of Margot Beck, 1980, Briefly Noted, 1981, Vespers, 1982 (Beverly Hills Theatre Guild award 1984), Tristan in Winter, 1986, Songs of a Wayfarer, 1986, Coda, 1991, (criticism) Phantom Empires: The Novels of A. Lernet-Holenia and the Question of Postimperial Austrian Identity, 1996, Verses of a Marriage, Translation of Poetry Collection by Hans Raimund, 1996, Telegrams from the Metropole: Selected Poetry, 1999, Gale Encyclopedia of Multicultural America, 2nd edit., 2000; contbg. editl. advisor: International Dictionary of Films and Filmmakers, 4th edit., 2001, Mars in Aries, trans. of novel by A. Lernet-Holenia, 2003, Austrian Cinema: A History, 2005; co-editor New Austrian Film, 2009, Hugo Von Hofmannsthal's Der Schwierige: New Approaches, 2009; founding editor Rohwedder: Internat. Jour. Lit. and Art, 1986-93; editor Pen Center mag., 1992-98; contbg. editor Osiris, Rampike, Poetry Salzburg Rev.; mem. editl. bd. Modern Austrian Lit., 1997-01; exec. prodr. The Nightmare Stumbles Past, 2002, Semmelweis, 2001, Wilson Chance, 2005; co-prodr. Epicure, 2002, Believe, 2003; assoc. prodr. The Last Bogatyr, 2009; co-prodr. The Archduke and Herbert Hinkel, 2009; columnist Celluloid Mag., Austria; editl. adv. bd. Ariadne Press, 1999—; editor U. Press. of South, 2004-; contbr. (European cinema) Greenwood Encyclopedia of World Popular Culture, 2007, dir. Elfi Von Dassanowsky Found., geust editor Modern Austrian Lit. Michael Haneke Spel Issue, 2009 Mem. bd. advisors The Internt. Exptl. Cinema Exposition, program com. mem. Intersect. Film Festival, Colo, Rockefeller Found. Media Arts Fellowship Recipient Decoration of Honor in Silver, Austria, 2005, Order of the Vitez (Hungary); Cultural grantee City of L.A., 1990, 91, 92; Pres.'s Fund for Humanities grantee U. Colo., 1996, 2001; named Colo. Prof. of Yr., Carnegie Found./Coun. for Advancement and Support of Edn., 2004; recipient Residency award Karolyi Found., France, 1979, Letters, Arts and Scis. Rsch. and Creative Work award U. Colo., 2002, Chancellor's award, 2006 Mem. MLA, PEN USA (bd. dirs. L.A. 1992-99, founder and pres. Colo. chpt. 1994-99 2002-03), PEN Austria, Internat. Lernet-Holenia Soc. (v.p. 1998-2006), Austrian Am. Film Assn. (v.p. 1997—2009), Austria Mundi (US rep. 2002—), Soc. Cinema and Media Studies, Poets and Writers, Modern Austrian Lit. and Culture Assn. (mem. exec. coun. 2006—09), L.A. Poetry Festival, SAG, Concordia Assn. Journalists and Writers (Austria), Am. Coll. Heraldry (bd. govs. 2000-08), Fencing Assn., Constantinian Order St. George, Mensa; fellow Royal Hist. Soc, Europa Nostra, European Acad. Scis. & Arts(US Delegate), US ctrl. states delegate 2009-, dir. Vienna Hollywood Project, 2009-), Blue Shield Cultural Heritage Protection Office: U Colo Dept Langs and Cultures Colorado Springs CO 80933-7150 Home: 2859 Country Club Colorado Springs CO 80909 E-mail: belvederefilm@yahoo.com.

VONDERHAAR, BARBARA K., medical researcher; Grad., Clarke Coll., Dubuque, Iowa, 1965; PhD, U. Wis., Madison. Postdoctoral training in mammary gland biology NIH; now chief Mammary Biology and Tumorigenesis Lab. Ctr. Cancer Rsch., Nat. Cancer Inst., head Molecular and Cellular Endocrinology Sect., Mammary Biology and Tumorigenesis Lab.; chair Breast and Gynecologic Malignancies Faculty Nat. Cancer Inst.; co-chair Intramural Program for Rsch. on Women's Health NIH. Recipient Award for Excellence in Mentoring, Bethesda Assn. for Women in Sci., 2000, Helen F. Cserr Award for outstanding woman scientist, Mt. Desert Island Biol. Laboratories, 2004. Office: Mammary Biology and Tumorigenesis Lab Ctr Cancer Rsch 37 Convent Dr Bldg 37 Rm 1106A1 Bethesda MD 20892-4254 Office Phone: 301-435-7587. Office Fax: 301-402-0711. E-mail: bv10w@nih.gov, vonderhb@exchange.nih.gov.*

VONDER HAAR, THOMAS H., meteorology educator; b. Quincy, Ill., Dec. 28, 1942; m. Dee M. Clark, 1980; children: Kim, Kurt, Nicholas, Krista, Matthew. BS, St. Louis U., 1963; MS, U. Wis., 1964, PhD in Meteorology, 1968. Assoc. scientist meteorology Space Sci. & Engring. Ctr. U. Wis., Madison, 1968-70; assoc. prof. meteorology Colo. State U., Ft. Collins, 1970-77, prof. atmospheric sci., 1977—, univ. disting. prof., 1994, head dept. atmospheric sci., 1974-84, acting dean Coll. Engring., 1981-82. Cons. U.S. Army, ITT Aerospace, Sci. and Tech. Corp., World Meteor Orgn. UN, Ball Aerospace Corp., 1969—. Mem. Am. Meteorol. Soc., Sigma Xi. Office: Coop Inst Rsch in Atmosphere Colo State U Fort Collins CO 80523-1375

VON DER HEYDEN, KARL MUELLER, retired manufacturing executive; b. Berlin, July 18, 1936; arrived in U.S., 1957, naturalized, 1967; s. Werner and Erika (Mueller) von der Heyden; m. Mary Ellen Terrell, Aug. 17, 1963; children: Ellen, Eric. Student, Free U., Berlin, 1959—61; BA, Duke, 1962; MBA, U. Pa., 1964. CPA Pa., 1965. Mgmt. trainee Berliner Bank, Berlin, 1955-57; sr. staff acct. Coopers & Lybrand, Phila., 1963-66; asst. comptr., corporate comptr. Pitney-Bowes, Inc., Stamford, Conn., 1966-74; v.p., contr. PepsiCo., Inc., Purchase, 1974-77; v.p. fin. Pepsi-Cola Co., 1977-79, v.p. mfg., 1979-80; v.p. fin., treas. H.J. Heinz Co., Pitts., 1980-83, sr. v.p. fin., CFO, 1983-89; exec. v.p., CFO RJR Nabisco Inc., NYC, 1989-93, co-chmn., CEO, 1993; pres., CEO Metallgesellschaft Corp., NYC, 1993-94; vice chmn. PepsiCo, Inc., Purchase, NY, 1996—2001; sr. advisor Clipper Group, 1994-97. Chmn. Fin. Acctg. Stds. Adv. Coun., 1995—96; bd. dirs. H.J. Heinz Co., 1983—89, Macy's. Co-chmn. Am. Acad. in Berlin; trustee NY Global Ptnrs., Inc. Mem.: Univ. Club N.Y.C. Office: 14 E 60th Ste# 604 New York NY 10022

VON DER HEYDT, JAMES ARNOLD, federal judge; b. Miles City, Mont., July 15, 1919; s. Harry Karl and Alice S. (Arnold) von der H.; m. Verna E. Johnson, May 21, 1952. BA, Albion Coll., 1942; JD, Northwestern U., 1951. Bar: Alaska 1951. Pvt. practice, Nome, Alaska, 1953—59; judge superior ct. Juneau, Alaska, 1959—66; from judge to sr. judge U.S. Dist. Ct. Alaska, 1966—; U.S. commr. Nome, 1951—; U.S. atty. divsn. 2 Dist. Alaska, 1951—53; mem. Alaska Ho. of Reps., 1957—59. Author: Mother Sawtooth's Nome, 1990, Alaska, The Short and Long of It, 2000. Pres. Anchorage Fine Arts Mus. Assn. Recipient Disting. Alumni award Albion Coll., 1995, Professionalism and Ethics award Inn of Ct., 2005. Mem. Alaska Bar Assn. (bd. govs. 1955-59, pres. 1959-60), Am. Judicature Soc., Masons (32d degree), Shriners, Phi Delta Phi, Sigma Nu. Avocations: researching arctic bird life, creative writing, painting. Office: US Dist Ct 222 W 7th Ave Box 40 Anchorage AK 99513-7564 Home Phone: 907-279-4298; Office Phone: 907-677-6254.

VON DER MEHDEN, FRED R., political science professor; b. San Francisco, Dec. 1, 1927; s. Fred G. and Margaret (de Valasco) von der M.; m. Audrey Eleanor Whitehead, Dec. 27, 1954; children: Laura Davis, Victoria Margaret Fredrickson. BA, U. of Pacific, 1948; MA, Claremont Grad. Sch., 1950; PhD, U. Calif., Berkeley, 1957. Mem. faculty U. Wis. Madison, 1957-68; chmn. East Asian studies U. Wis.-Madison, 1963-65, 67-68; Albert Thomas prof. polit. sci. Rice U., 1968—2000, dir. Center for Research, 1969-70, chmn. dept., 1975-78, dir. program devel. studies, 1978-83; editor Rice U. Press, 1982-95; Albert Thomas prof. emeritus Rice U., 2000—. Cons. AID, 1967-78 Author: Politics of the Developing Nations, 1964, 2d edit., 1969, Religion and Nationalism in Southeast Asia, 1963, Comparative Political Violence, 1973; co-author: Issues of Political Development, 1967, The Military and Politics of Five Developing Nations, 1970, Southeast Asia 1930-1970, 1974, Religion and Modernization in Southeast Asia, 1986, Two Worlds of Islam, 1993; editor: (with R. Soligo) Issues on Income Distribution, 1975, Ethnic Groups of Houston, 1984, Radical Islam in Southeast Asia, 2006. Mem. Mid-West Conf. Asian Affairs (pres. 1968-69), Assn. Asian Studies, Am. Polit. Sci. Assn., SW Conf. Asian Affairs (pres. 1976-77) Home: 12530 Mossycup Dr Houston TX 77024-4937

VON DER SCHMIDT, EDWARD, III, neurosurgeon, veterinarian; b. Jan. 13, 1953; BS in Animal Sci., Rutgers U., 1975; DVM, Cornell U., 1979; MD, U. Medicine and Dentistry N.J., Newark, 1984. Diplomate Nat. Bd. Med. Examiners, Am. Bd. Neurol. Surgery. Veterinarian Secaucus (N.J.) Animal Hosp., 1979-82; pvt. practice vet. medicine NJ, 1980-85; gen. surg. intern Washington Hosp. Ctr., Washington, 1984-85;

resident in neurosurgery George Washington U. Med. Ctr., Washington, 1985-90; pvt. practice neurosurgery Princeton (N.J.) Healthcare Ctr., 1990—. Neurosurgeon Robert Wood Johnson U. Hosp., New Brunswick, NJ, St. Peter's Med. Ctr., New Brunswick, Somerset Med. Ctr., Somerville, NJ; chief neurosurgery sect. Med. Ctr. Princeton; mem. search com. for chief divsn. neurosurgery U. Medicine and Dentistry N.J./Robert Wood Johnson Med. Sch. Mem.: AAAS, AMA, N.J. Soc. Med. Specialty (pres. 2000—02), Coun. State Neurosurgical Safety (mem. reform commn. 2001, vice chmn. N.E. quadrant 2003—), Am. Assn. Med. Transcription (bd. dirs. Ctrl. N.J. chpt.), Am. Coll. Physician Execs., Soc. Exec. Physicians, Soc. Critical Care Medicine, N.J. Neurosurgical Soc. (trustee at large 2000—, sec. treas. 1998—2000), N.Y. Acad. Sci., Middlesex Med. Soc. (sec. 2003, del.), Middlesex County Med. Soc., Med. Soc. N.J., Congress Neurol. Surgeons (mem. joint sect. disorders spine and peripheral nerves), Am. Assn. Neurol. Surgeons, Alpha Zeta (Best Freshman award). Home: 140 Hodge Rd Princeton NJ 08540-3014 Office: Princeton Healthcare Ctr 419 N Harrison St Ste 204 Princeton NJ 08540-3521

VON DREHLE, RAMON ARNOLD, lawyer; b. St. Louis, Mar. 12, 1930; s. Arnold Henry and Sylvia E. (Ahrens) Von D.; m. Gillian Margaret Turner, Sept. 13, 1980; children by previous marriage: Carin L., Lisa A., Courtney A. BS, Washington U., St. Louis, 1952; JD, U. Tex., Austin, 1957; postgrad, Parker Sch. Internat. Law, Columbia U., 1965. Bar: Tex. 1956, Mich. 1957, U.S. Supreme Ct. 1981. Sr. atty. Ford Motor Co., Dearborn, Mich., 1957-67; assoc., asst. gen. counsel Ford of Europe, Inc., Brentwood, Essex, Eng., 1967-75, v.p., gen. counsel, 1975-79; v.p. legal Ford Motor Credit Co., Dearborn, 1979-87; v.p., gen. counsel Am. Road Ins. Co., Dearborn, 1979-87; exec. dir. legal affairs Ford Fin. Services Group, Dearborn, 1987-91; leader in residence Walsh Coll., Mich., 1992. Panelist large complex case program Am. Arbitration Assn., 1993—; advisor to Czech Republic Ministry of Privatization, Prague, 1993-94; leader Russian Def. Conversion Project, 1995-96; lectr. in Ea. Europe, 1995; pres. Focus Internat. LLC, 1995—. Article editor: Tex. Law Rev, 1956-57. Trustee Birmingham Unitarian Ch., 1966-67. Served to 1st lt. AUS, 1952-54, Korea. Mem. ABA, Mich. Bar Assn., Tex. Bar Assn., Internat. Bar Assn., Am. Fin. Svcs. Assn. (chmn. 1990-91, bd. dirs. 1981-91), Fin. Svcs. Coun. (bd. dirs. 1987-91), Washington U. Alumni Club Detroit (past pres.), Order of Coif, Tower Club (Tysons, Va.), Confrèrie des Chevaliers du Tastevin (France, Washington), Royal Automobile Club (London), Cosmos Club (Washington). Mem. Christ Ch. Home and Office: 519 Princess St Alexandria VA 22314-2332 E-mail: rvond2@aol.com.

VON ESCHEN, ROBERT LEROY, electrical engineer, consultant; b. Glasgow, Mont., Oct. 3, 1936; s. Leroy and Lillian Victoria (Eliason) Von E.; m. Carolyn Kay Frampton, Dec. 14, 1965 (dec. Feb. 1999); children: Eric Leroy, Marc Alfred. BSEE, Mont. State U., 1961; postgrad., U. Liberia, Lakeland C.C., Glendale C.C. Registered profl. engr., Pa. Hydro constrn. engr. U.S. Army Corps of Engrs., Mont., 1961-62, SD, 1961—62; hdqrs. chief engr. Eagle Constrn. Co., Colo., 1962; resident transp./distbn. elec. engr. Stanley Cons., Inc., West Africa, 1962-63, hydro cons., startup engr. Manila, West Africa, 1965-66; with Stanley Cons., 1962-68, Gilbert Assoc./United Energy Svc., 1968-92; performance based assessment program sect. engr., maintenance planning engr., condition assessment survey sec. mgr. Gilbert Assocs., Inc., Tex., 1992—. Cons. engr. fossil power plant, Ky., Colo., Mo., Korea; site project mgr., Ariz., Aruba; nuclear constrn. startup engr., Pa., Ala., Ohio; safety sys. functional inspector, Calif., Wis., Oreg.; performance based assessment program project mgr., Tex.; tech. cons. World Bank, Liberia; engrng. cons. USN, Manila, 1967; founding dr. Madison Comptr. Soc., Ohio, 1983-85; v.p., dir. Boy Scouts Am., 1981-84. Founder, dir. Madison (Ohio) Computer Soc., 1983—85; v.p., bd. dirs. N.E. coun. Boy Scouts Am., Painesville, 1983—85; bd. dirs. Let's Shoot Gun Club, LLC, 2003—, Kids World Multimedia. Recipient Silver Beaver award Boy Scouts Am., 19 other awards. Mem.: AFIO, NARP, NPSE, IEEE, NRA, Tex. State Engrng. Soc., Ohio State Engrng. Soc., Nat. Def. Indsl. Orgn., Soc. Am. Mil. Engrs., Shriners, Masons (life). Avocations: target and skeet shooting, construction design, computers, electronics. Home: 1001 S Girl Scout Rd Amarillo TX 79124-2135 Office: BWXT Pantex LLC PO Box 30020 Amarillo TX 79120-0020

VON ESCHENBACH, ANDREW C., oncologist, former federal agency administrator; b. Phila., Oct. 30, 1941; BS, St. Joseph's U., Phila., 1963; MD, Georgetown U., 1967. Diplomate Am. Bd. Urology. Intern U. Pa./Phila. Gen. Hosp., 1967—68; resident gen. surgery Pa. Hosp., Phila., 1971—72, resident urology, 1972—75; instructor, urology U. Pa. Sch. Medicine; fellow urol. oncology U. Tex. MD Anderson Cancer Ctr., Houston, 1976—77, prof. urology, 1980—2002, chmn. dept. urology, 1983—96, cons. prof., cell biology, prof. urology, exec. v.p., chief acad. officer, dir. program ctr. Genitourinary Cancer Ctr. Houston, 1997—2002, founding dir., Prostate Cancer Research Prog., 1996, v.p. for academic affairs, Roy M. and Phyllis Gough Huffington Clin. Rsch. Disting. Chair in Urologic Oncology; dir. Nat. Cancer Inst., NIH, Bethesda, Md., 2002—06; acting commr. FDA, Rockville, Md., 2005—06, commr., 2006—09; sr. adv. to sec. US Dept. Health & Human Services, Washington, 2006—09. Founding mem. C-Change. Contbr. articles to profl. jours., chapters to books. Lt. comdr. US Navy Med. Corps, 1968—71. Recipient Carpe Diem award, Lance Armstrong Found., 2007, Julie Rogers "Spirit of Love" award; named one of 100 Most Influential People in the World, TIME Mag., 2006, Best Doctors in Am., Am. Radium Soc., 2007. Mem.: AMA, Am. Med. Writers Assn., Soc. Surg. Oncology, Am. Urological Assn., Am. Cancer Soc. (pres.-elect 2002), Uniformed Svcs. Univ. of Health Sciences (Cert. Meritorious Svc. for outstanding contbn. to prostate disease rsch.).*

VON FRIEDERICHS-FITZWATER, MARLENE MARIE, researcher; b. Beatrice, Nebr., July 14, 1939; d. Paul M. and Velma B. (von Friederichs) Fitzwater; children: Richard Nielson, Kevin T. Young, James L. Nielson, Paul M. Nielson. BS, Westminster Coll., 1981; MA, U. Nebr., Omaha, 1981; PhD, U. Utah, 1987; cert. in death edn., Temple U., 1982; MPH, Waden U., 2008. Various pub. rels., writing and editing positions, 1957-78; teaching fellow in comm. U. Nebr., Omaha, 1978-83, U. Utah, Salt Lake City, 1978-83; asst. prof. mass comm. U. So. Colo., Pueblo, 1983-85; prof. comm. studies Calif. State U., Sacramento, 1985—, chair comm. studies, 1996-2000; assoc. clin. prof. family practice Sch. Medicine U. Calif., Davis, 1987—, asst. adj. prof. internal medicine, 2003—, adj. asst. prof. hematology and oncology, 2005—; dir., outreach rsch. and edn. US Davis Cancer Ctr., 2005—. Condr. workshops on communication skills for health care profls. Bergan Mercy Hosp., Omaha, 1980-81, Mercy Care Ctr., Omaha, 1980-81, Am. Cancer Soc., 1981-82, Hospice of Salt Lake, Utah, 1981-82; condr. seminars, workshops and courses on health communication, death and dying, patient edn. and compliance, other related topics, 1983—; presenter in health communication various profl. orgn. meetings and confs., 1981—; dir., co-founder The Health Communication Rsch. Inst., Sacramento, 1988—. Contbr. articles to profl. jours. Trainer United Way, Sacramento, project mgr., 1986—; pres. bd. dirs. Hospice Care Sacramento, Inc., 1986-87; instr. vol. tng. program Hospice Consortium Sacramento; hospice vol. 1980—. Recipient Lifetime Achievement award Sacramento Pub. Rels. Assn., also numerous state, regional and nat. awards for writing, editing, publ. design and photography. Fellow Am. Acad. on Physician & Patient; mem. Internat. Communication Assn. (health communication div., newsletter editor 1987-89, sec. 1989-91), AAUP, Assn. Behavioral Scis. and Med. Edn., Assn. Women in Sci., Pub. Rels. Soc. Am. (bd. dirs. Calif. Capital chpt. 1987-91), Soc. Tchrs. Family Medicine, Soc. Health Care Pub. Rels. and Mktg. No. Calif. Office: Calif State U Communication Studies Dept 6000 J St Sacramento CA 95819-2605 Office Phone: 916-734-8810. E-mail: marlene.vonfriederichs-fitzwater@ucdmc.ucdavis.edu.

VON FURSTENBERG, BETSY, actress, writer; b. Neiheim Heusen, Germany, Aug. 16, 1931; d. Count Franz-Egon and Elizabeth (Johnson) von F.; m. Guy Vincent de la Maisoneuve (div.); 2 children.; m. John J. Reynolds, Mar. 26, 1984. Attended Miss Hewitt's Classes, N.Y. Tutoring Sch.; prepared for stage with Sanford Meisner at Neighborhood Playhouse. Made Broadway stage debut in Second Threshold, N.Y., 1951; appeared in Dear Barbarians, 1952, Oh Men Oh Women, 1954, The Chalk Garden, 1955, Child of Fortune, 1956, Nature's Way, 1957, Much Ado About Nothing, 1959, Mary Mary, 1965, Paisley Convertible, 1967, Avanti, 1968, The Gingerbread Lady, 1970 (toured 1971), Absurd Person Singular, 1976; off Broadway appearances include For Love or Money, 1951; toured in Petrified Forest, Jason and Second Man, 1952; appeared in Josephine, 1953; subsequently toured, 1955; What Every Woman Knows, 1955, The Making of Moo, 1958 (toured 1958), Say Darling, 1959, Wonderful Town, 1959, Season of Choice, 1959, Beyond Desire, 1967, Private Lives, 1968, Does Anyone Here Do the Peabody, 1976; appeared in Along Came a Spider, Theatre in the Park, N.Y.C., 1985; appeared in film Women Without Names, 1950; TV appearances include Robert Montgomery Show, Ed Sullivan Show, Alfred Hitchcock Presents, One Step Beyond, The Mike Wallace Show, Johnny Carson Show, Omnibus, Theatre of the Week, The Secret Storm, As the World Turns, Movie of the Week, Your Money or Your Wife, Another World; writer syndicated column More Than Beauty; contbr. articles to newspapers and mags. including N.Y. Times Sunday Arts and Leisure, Saturday Rev. of Literature, People, Good Housekeeping, Art News, Pan Am Travel; co-author: (novel) Mirror, Mirror, 1988; author, illustrator Grandmothers Surprise, 2004. Avocations: tennis, painting, photography.

VON FURSTENBERG, DIANE, fashion designer, writer, entrepreneur; b. Brussels, Dec. 31, 1946; arrived in US, 1969, naturalized, 2002; d. Leon L. and Liliane L. (Nahmias) Halfin; m. Eduard Egon von Furstenberg, July 16, 1969 (div. 1983); children: Alexandre, Tatiana; m. Barry Diller, Feb. 2, 2001. Student, U. Madrid, 1965-66, U. Geneva, 1966-68. Founder, pres. Diane von Furstenberg Studio, L.P., NYC, 1970—; pres. Diane von Furstenberg Ltd., NYC; founder Salvy, Paris, 1985. Bd. dir. InterActiveCorp. Author: Diane Von Furstenberg's Book of Beauty, 1977; Beds, 1991, The Bath, 1993, The Table, 1996, DIANE: A Signature Life, 1998; contbg. editor Vanity Fair mag., 1993; prodr.: (films) Forty Shades of Blue, 2005, Andy Warhol: A Documentary Film, 2006. Recipient Ellis Island Medal of Honor, 1986; named one of The 100 Most Influential Women in NYC Bus., Crain's NY Bus., 2007, The 50 Most Powerful Women in NYC, NY Post, 2007; named to Fashion Walk of Fame, 2008. Mem.: Coun. of Fashion Designers of Am. (pres. 2006—, Lifetime Achievement award 2005). Achievements include development of creative and live on-air selling of Silk Assets collection; design of DIANE line including signature dresses and the wrap. *Honesty in all ways: honest products, honest and straight approach to needs.*

VON FURSTENBERG, GEORGE MICHAEL, economics professor, researcher; b. Germany, Dec. 3, 1941; arrived in U.S., 1961; m. Gabrielle M. Koblitz von Willmburg, June 9, 1967; 1 child, Philip G. PhD, Princeton U., 1967. Asst. prof. Cornell U., Ithaca, NY, 1966-70; assoc. prof. Ind. U., Bloomington, 1970-73, prof., 1976-78, Rudy prof. econs., 1983—2006, emeritus; sr. staff economist Coun. Econ. Advisors, Washington, 1973-76; div. chief rsch. dept. IMF, Washington, 1978-83; Robert Bendheim prof. econ. and fin. policy Fordham U., NYC, 2000—03; econ. program dir. NSF, Arlington, Va., 2006—08. Project dir. Am. Coun. Life Ins., Washington, 1976—78; sr. advisor Brookings Instn., Washington, 1978—90; vis. sr. economist planning and analysis staff Dept. State, Washington, 1989—90; Bissell-Fulbright vis. prof. Can.-Am. rels. U. Toronto, 1994—95. Contbg. author, editor: The Government and Capital Formation, 1980, Capital, Efficiency and Growth, 1980, Acting Under Uncertainty: Multidisciplinary Conceptions, 1990, Regulation and Supervision of Financial Institutions in the NAFTA Countries and Beyond, 1997; editor: Internat. Money and Credit: The Policy Roles, 1983; co-author: Learning from the World's Best Central Bankers, 1998; co-editor: Monetary Unions and Hard Pegs: Effects on Trade, Financial Development, and Stability, 2004; assoc. editor: Rev. Econs. and Stats., 1987—92, Open Econs. Rev., 1997—2007, Jour. Econ. Asymmetries, 2004—; contbr. articles to profl. jours. Fulbright grantee, Poland, 1991—92. Mem.: Am. Econ. Assn., N.Am. Econs. and Fin. Assn. (pres. 2000). Roman Catholic. Avocation: tennis. Office: Dept Economics Wylie Hal Indiana Univ Bloomington IN 47405 Office Phone: 812-856-1382. Business E-Mail: vonfurst@indiana.edu.

VON GELDERN, JAMES ROBERT, law educator; b. Morristown, NJ, Nov. 8, 1958; s. Robert Hasso and Louise Anne von Geldern; children: Thomas Theodoroe, William James, Olga Marie. PhD, Brown U., Providence, 1987; JD, U. Minn. Law Sch., Mpls., 2005. Prof. Russian and internat. studies Macalester Coll., St. Paul, 1988—. Vol. lawyer Advs. Human Rights, Mpls., 2005—08. Mem.: Minn. Bar Assn. Office: Macalester Coll 1600 Grand Ave Saint Paul MN 55105

VONGERICHTEN, JEAN-GEORGES, food service executive, chef; b. Alsace, France, Mar. 16, 1957; arrived in US, 1985; m. Marja Allen; 1 child, Chloe;children from previous marriage: Louise, Cedric. Studied with chef Paul Hueberlin, Auberge de l'Ill. Worked with Paul Bocuse L'Oasis Market, Paris; worked with master chef Louis Outhier L'Oasis, France; chef Oriental Hotel, Bangkok; owner Meridian Hotel, Singapore, Mandarin Hotel, Hong Kong, Lafayette, Boston, 1985, exec. chef NYC, 1986; owner Jo Jo, NYC, 1991—, Vong, NYC, London, 1995—, Hong Kong, 1997—, Vong's Thai Kitchen, Chgo., 1999—, Jean-Georges, NYC, 1997—, Shanghai, Nougatine, NYC, 1997—, Mercer Kitchen, NYC, 1998—, The Lipstick Cafe, Prime Steakhouse, Las Vegas, Nev., 1998—, Dune, Bahamas, 2000—, V Steakhouse, NYC, 2004—, 66, 2003, Spice Market, NYC, 2005—, Perry St., 2005, Cafe Martinique, Bahamas, Chambers Kitchen, Mpls., Lagoon, French Polynesia, Rama, London; ptnr. Culinary Concepts by Jean-Georges, 2007—. Author: Simple Cuisine, 1990, Jean-Georges: Cooking at Home with a Four-Star Chef, 1998 (Best Cookbook award, James Beard Found., 1999), Simple to Speculate, 2000, Asian Flavors of Jean-Georges, 2007; appeared Martha Stewart Show, Live! with Regis and Kathie Lee, Today Show, Good Morning Am., Food Network, (TV series) Julia's Kitchen with Master Chefs with Julia Child, 1995. Recipient four stars for Lafayette, NY Times, three stars for Jo Jo, three stars for Vong, four stars for Jean Georges, 1997, Best New Restaurant award for Jean Georges, James Beard Found., 1998, Outstanding Restaurant award, 2009, America's Top Restaurant award for Jean Georges, Zagat Survey, 2008; named Jo Jo Best New Restaurant of Yr., Esquire Mag., Chef of Yr., Outstanding Chef, James Beard Found., 1998. Office: Jean Georges Mgmt LLC 111 Prince St New York NY 10012 Office Phone: 212-358-0688. Office Fax: 212-358-0685.*

VONGRUENIGEN, CHRISTINE MICHELLE, microbiologist, educator; d. Richard John and Barbara Ann Pull. BS in Applied Biology, Ga. Tech, Atlanta, 1992; MS in Microbiology, U. South Fla., Tampa, 1994. Cert. jr. coll. instructor State Fla., 1995. Microbiology instr. St. Petersburg Jr. Coll., Tarpan Springs, Fla., 1994—96; postgrad. rschr. Inst. Molecular Medicine & Genetics, Augusta, Ga., 1998—99; prof. anatomy & physiology St. Johns River C.C., Orange Pk, Fla., 2003—. Principle investigator NSF Grant, Tampa, 1995—96. Contbr. articles to profl. jours. (Outstanding Tchg. Asst. award, 1993). Vol. spkr. HS sci. students SERVE Spkr. Bur. Program, Tampa, 1993—94. Mem.: Am. Soc. Microbiology (Pres. award 1994). Home: 4504 Comanche Trail Blvd Jacksonville FL 32259 Office: St Johns River CC 283 Coll Dr Orange Park FL 32065

VON HAGEN, MARK LOUIS, history professor, director; b. Cin., July 21, 1954; s. Daniel William and Martha Berta Von Hagen, Martha Berta Von Hagen; life ptnr. Johnny Roldan-Chacon. BS in Fgn. Svc., Georgetown U., 1976; MA in Slavic Lang. & Lit., Ind. U., 1978; PhD in History & Humanities, Stanford U., 1984. Dir. Harriman inst. Columbia U., NYC, 1985—2001, prof. history, 1985—. Cons. Primary Source Microfilms, Woodbridge, NY, 1986—; mem. editl. bd. Ab Imperio, Kazan, Russia, 2000—. Author: (book) Soldiers in the Proletarian Dictatorship, 1990; editor: After Empire, 1997. Fulbright fellowship, IREX, 1982—83, fellowship, Social Sci. Rsch. Coun., 1986, Alexander-von-Humboldt Stiftung, 1991, Russian-Ukrainian Encounter grant, Nat. Endowment Humanities, Alexander-von-Humboldt Found., 1994—96, History Human Rights Movement Era Sakharov grant, Ford Found., Russian Case grant, 1997—2002. Mem.: Shevchenko Sci. Soc., Am. Assn. Advancement Slavic Studies (bd. dir. 2000—), Coun. Fgn. Rels., Internat. Assn. Ukrainists (v.p. 1999—2002). Office: Dept History Columbia Univ Fayerweather 611 New York NY 10027 Business E-Mail: mark.vonhagen@asu.edu.

VON HAKE, MARGARET JOAN, librarian; b. Santa Monica, Calif., Oct. 27, 1933; d. Carl August and Inez Garnet (Johnson) von Hake. BA, La Sierra Coll., 1955; MS in Library Sci., U. So. Calif., 1963. Tchr. Newbury Park Acad., Calif., 1955—60, librarian, 1957—60; circulation libr. Wash. Adventist U. (formely Columbia Union Coll.), Takoma Park, Md., 1962—67, lib. dir., 1967—2007, prof. emerita, 2007—. Chair Md. Ind. Coll. and Univ. Assn. Libr. Dirs. Round Table, 1996—98, Adventist Libr. Info. Cooperative Coun., 2005—07; pres. Congress Acad. Libr. Dirs., Md., 1999—2000. Mem. ALA, Md. Libr. Assn., Assn. Coll. & Rsch. Librs., Assn. Seventh Day Adventist Librs. (newsletter editor 1981-83, pres. 1989-90), Sligo Federated Music Club (pres. 1988-89, yearbook co-editor 2000—).

VON HIPPEL, ERIC ARTHUR, innovation educator; b. Boston, Aug. 27, 1941; s. Arthur Robert and Dagmar von Hippel; m. Jessie Roberta Janjigian; children: Christiana Dagmar Jessie, Eric James. BA, Harvard U., Cambridge, Mass., 1964; MS, MIT, 1966; PhD, Carnegie-Mellon U., Pitts., 1973; PhD in econ. (hon.), Ludwig Maximilans Univ., 2004; PhD in Mgmt. (hon.), Copenhagen Bus. Sch., 2007. Engrng. mgr. Graphic Sciences, Inc, Danbury, Conn., 1966—69; cons. McKinsey and Co., NYC, 1970—72; prof. Sloan School of Management, MIT, Cambridge, 1973—; head Innovation and Entrepreneurship Group. Pres. Lead User Concepts Inc, Cambridge, 1996—. Author: The Sources of Innovation, 1988, Democratizing Innovation, 2005; contbr. articles to scholarly jours. Named Sir Walter Scott Disting. Prof., Australian Grad. Sch. Mgmt., 1997—98; grantee, NSF, Alfred P. Sloan Found., 3M; Nortel Networks; NYNEX; Xerox; Bush,Boake,Allen,Bell-Atlantic; fellow, Canadian Inst. for Advanced Rsch., 1995—97. Achievements include patents for facsimile technology. Avocation: industrial archaeology. Office: MIT Rm E52-566 50 Memorial Dr Cambridge MA 02141 Business E-Mail: evhippel@mit.edu.

VON HIPPEL, PETER HANS, chemistry professor, researcher; b. Goettingen, Germany, Mar. 13, 1931; came to U.S., 1937, naturalized, 1942; s. Arthur Robert and Dagmar (Franck) von H.; m. Josephine Baron Raskind, June 20, 1954; children: David F., James A., Benjamin J. BS, MIT, Cambridge, Mass., 1952; MS, MIT, 1953, PhD, 1955. Phys. biochemist Naval Med. Research Inst., Bethesda, Md., 1956-59; from asst. prof. to assoc. prof. biochemistry Med. Sch. Dartmouth Coll., 1959-67; prof. chemistry, mem. Inst. Molecular Biology U. Oreg., 1967-79, dir. Inst. Molecular Biology, 1969-80, chmn. dept. chemistry, 1980-87; rsch. prof. chemistry Am. Cancer Soc., 1989—. Chmn. biopolymers Gordon Conf., 1968; mem. trustees vis. com. biology dept. MIT, 1973—76; mem. bd. sci. counsellors Nat. Inst. Arthritis, Metabolic and Digestive Diseases NIH, 1974—78, mem. coun. Nat. Inst. Gen. Med. Scis., 1982—86, mem. dir.'s adv. com., 1987—92; bd. dirs. Fedn. Am. Socs. for Exptl. Biology, 1994—98; mem. NIH-CSR panel on boundaries for sci. rev., 1998—2003, mem. joint steering com. for pub. policy, 1998—2005. Mem. editl. bd. Jour. Biol. Chemistry, 1967-73, 76-82, Biochem. Biophys. Acta, 1965-70, Physiol. Revs., 1972-77, Biochemistry, 1977-80, Trends in Biochem. Soc., 1987—, Protein Sci., 1990-95; editor Jour. Molecular Biology, 1986-94; contbr. articles to profl. jours., chpts. to books. Lt. M.S.C. USNR, 1956-59. Recipient Merck award Am. Soc. Biochem. and Molecular Biology, 2000; NSF predoctoral fellow, 1953-55; NIH postdoctoral fellow, 1955-56; NIH sr. fellow, 1959-67; Guggenheim fellow, 1973-74 Fellow: Biophys. Soc., Am. Acad. Arts and Scis.; mem.: AAAS, Am. Philosophic Soc., Fedn. Am. Scientists, Nat. Acad. Scis., Biophys. Soc. (coun. 1970—73, pres. 1973—74), Am. Soc. Biochem. and Molecular Biology, Am. Chem. Soc., Sigma Xi. Home: 1900 Crest Dr Eugene OR 97405-1753 Business E-Mail: petevh@molbio.uoregon.edu.

VON HOFF, DANIEL DOUGLAS, oncologist, researcher; b. Oshkosh, Wis., Apr. 29, 1947; BS, Carroll Coll., 1969; MD, Columbia U. Coll. Physicians & Surgeons, 1973. Diplomate Am. Bd. Internal Medicine, Am. Bd. Oncology. Intern internal medicine U. Calif., San Francisco, 1973-74, resident internal medicine, 1974-75; med. oncology fellow Nat. Cancer Inst.; faculty, prof. dept. medicine, dept. cellular & structural biology U. Tex. Health Sci. Ctr., San Antonio, 1975—99; founding dir. Inst. Drug Devel., Cancer Therapy & Rsch. Ctr., San Antonio, 1989; prof. medicine, dir. Cancer Ctr. U. Ariz., 1999—; exec. v.p., dir. translational drug devel. divsn., head pancreatic cancer rsch. program Translational Genomics Rsch. Inst. (TGen), Phoenix, 2003—. Mem. Nat. Cancer Adv. Bd., 2004—, acting chair, 2005—06. Recipient Block Award, Ohio State U., 2003, Frances E. Bull Award, U. Mich. Comprehensive Cancer Ctr., 2003, Weinberg Award, Harvard Med. Sch. Dana Farber Cancer Ctr.; grantee Frederick S. Philips Lectureship, Meml. Sloan-Kettering Cancer Ctr., Michel Clavel Lectureship, European Orgn. Rsch. & Treatment of Cancer, Bagshawe Lectureship, Brit. Assn. Cancer Rsch. Fellow: Am. Coll. Physicians; mem.: AMA, Am. Soc. Clin. Oncology, Am. Assn. Cancer Rsch. (pres. 1999—2000, Richard and Hinda Rosenthal Found. award 1997). Office: Translational Genomics Rsch Inst Ste 660 445 N 5th St Phoenix AZ 85004

VON HOFFMAN, NICHOLAS, writer, retired reporter; b. NYC, Oct. 16, 1929; s. Carl and Anna (Bruenn) von H.; m. Ann Byrne, 1950 (div.); children: Alexander, Aristodemos, Constantine; m. Patricia Bennett, 1979 (div.). Grad., Fordham Prep. Sch., 1948. Assoc. dir. Indsl. Area Found., Chgo., 1954-63; mem. staff Chgo. Daily News, 1963-66, Washington Post, 1966—76; columnist N.Y. Observer, 1993—2008; contbg. writer Archtl. Digest, 1996—2007. Author: Mississippi Notebook, 1964, Multiversity, 1966, We Are The People Our Parents Warned Us Against, 1968, Two, Three, Many More, 1969, Left at The Post, 1970, (with Garry Trudeau) Fireside Watergate, 1973, Tales From the Margaret Mead Taproom, 1976, Make-Believe Presidents: Illusions of Power from McKinley to Carter, 1978, Organized Crimes, 1984, Citizen Cohn, 1988, Capitalist Fools, 1992, Hoax, 2004, Devil's Dictionary of Business, 2005; also articles.

VON HOLDEN, MARTIN HARVEY, psychologist; b. Bronx, NY, May 29, 1942; s. Leon and Gertrude (Fishbein) Von H.; m. Virginia T. Brown, Dec. 17, 1971; 1 child, Mark Walter; children by previous marriage: Sandi Gwen Bitton, David Lawrence; 1 stepchild, Theresa Ann Brilli-Rogers. BA, NYU, 1964; MA, U. Toledo, 1965; D Pub. Adminstrn., NYU, 1981. Sr. psychologist N.Y. State Dept. Mental Hygiene, Rockland State Hosp., Orangeberg, 1966-67, team leader, 1970-71, dir. interdisciplinary tng. team, 1971-73; chief of service Metro Unit Harlem Valley Psychiat. Ctr., Wingdale, NY, 1973-74, dep. dir. programs, 1974-75; dep. dir. treatment svcs. Pilgrim Psychiat. Ctr., West Brentwood, NY, 1975-76; dir. Matteawan State Hosp., Beacon, NY, 1977, Ctrl. N.Y. Psychiat. Ctr., Marcy, NY, 1977-82; exec. dir. Rochester (N.Y.) Psychiat. Ctr., 1982-97; privatization project mgr. Fla. Dept. Children & Families, Tallahassee, 1997-98; from svc. team coord. to adminstr. G. Pierce Wood Meml. Hosp., Arcadia, Fla., 1998-2000; adminstr. G. Pierce Wood Meml., Arcadia, Fla., 2000—02; ops. mgmt. cons. mgr. DeSoto Juvenile Correctional Facility, 2002—06; cons. mental health Fla. Dept. Juvenile Justice, 2006—, sr. psychologist, Detention North Region, 2008—. Assoc. dir. Inst. Motivation Rsch., Croton-on-Hudson, N.Y., 1965-73; dir. Martin H. Von Holden Assocs., motivation rsch., Fairlawn, N.J., 1970-74; cons. psychologist, group therapist Green Haven Correctional Facility, Stormville, N.Y., 1970-77; cons. psychologist, group therapist Auburn (N.Y.) Correctional Facility, 1977-94, Butler Correctional Facility, 1994-96, Willard Drug Treatment Ctr., 1997; clin. assoc. prof. dept. psychiatry Sch. Medicine, U. Rochester, 1983-97; cons. in field; spkr. in field. Contbr. articles to profl. jours. Mem. adv. coun. N.Y. State Commn. Quality Care to Mentally Disabled, 1989-97. Capt. MSC, U.S. Army, 1967-70. Recipient James Gordon Bennett prize NYU, 1964, Outstanding Achievement award United Way of N.Y. State, 1994. Fellow Am. Assn. Mental Health Adminstrs. (cert. mental health adminstr.); mem. Am. Psychol. Assn., Am. Correctional Assn., Am. Assn. Correctional Psychologists, Assn. Facility Dirs. N.Y. State Office Mental Health (pres. 1984-85), Order of Arrow, Psi Chi, Fla. Suicide Prevention Coun. Jewish. Home: 1250 Peppertree Ln Port Charlotte FL 33952-1357 Office Phone: 863-990-0739. Personal E-mail: vonholden@comcast.net.

VON HOLT, LAEL POWERS, retired psychotherapist, psychiatric social worker; b. Boston, Apr. 9, 1927; d. Merritt Adams and Rea Francisca (Hunt) Powers; m. Henry William Von Holt, Jr., Sept. 18, 1954; children: Gardner, Dudley, Edward. BA, U. Mass., 1950; MSW, U. Mo., 1972, postgrad., 1978; postgrad. Menninger Found., Topeka, 1977-85. Diplomate Bd. Clin. Social Work, Internat. Acad. of Behavioral Medicine Counseling and Psychotherapy; lic. clin. social worker, Mo. Psychiat. social worker N.Y. Dept. Mental Hygiene, Wingdale, 1950-51, Mass. Dept. Mental Health, Worcester, 1951-54; instr., social worker U. Oreg., Eugene, 1954-59; psychiat. social worker Mo. Dept. Mental Health, Fulton State Hosp., 1973-81, Columbia (Mo.) Regional Hosp. Psychiat. Svcs., Inc., 1977-82, Family Mental Health Ctr., Jefferson City, Mo., 1982-91, 99-2001; ret., 2001; mental health cons. Midland Counseling Ctrs./Focus, Inc., Hermann, Mo., 1991-99; field instr. U. Mo., Columbia, 1988. Bd. dirs. PTA, 1970-74, 77-78; mem. health com. Boone County Cmty. Svcs. Coun., 1975-76; vol. Meals on Wheels, 1972-73, 76-79; den mother Boy Scouts Am., 1968-69, 71-72; mem. by-laws com. Springdale Neighborhood Assn., 1977. Named Social Worker of Yr. Cen. Mo., 1986. Mem. Nat. Assn. Social Workers, Acad. Cert. Social Workers, LWV (state bd. dirs. 1995—, city coun. observor 1976-82, chmn. local action com. 1979-80, sec. 1974-77, chmn. Observer Corps 1981-83, chmn. com. mental health 1988-89, chair health com. 1991-94, co-pres. 1992-94, state v.p. 1997-99), Stephens Coll. Faculty Wives (pres. 1979-80, 89-90, 1997-98), Kappa Kappa Gamma. Republican. Methodist. Home: 378 Crown Pt Columbia MO 65203-2242

VON KALINOWSKI, JULIAN ONESIME, lawyer; b. St. Louis, May 19, 1916; s. Walter E. and Maybelle (Michaud) von K.; m. Penelope Jayne Dyer, June 29, 1980; children by previous marriage: Julian Onesime, Wendy Jean von Kalinowski. BA, Miss. Coll., 1937; JD with honors, U. Va., 1940. Bar: Va. 1940, Calif. 1946. Assoc. Gibson, Dunn and Crutcher, LA, 1946-52, ptnr., 1953-85, mem., chmn. exec. com., 1962—, adv. ptnr., 1985—; CEO, chmn. Litigation Scis., Inc., Culver City, Calif., 1991-94, chmn. emeritus Torrance, Calif., 1994-96, Dispute Dyamics, Inc., Torrance, Calif., 1996-2000. Instr. antitrust law So. Meth. Sch. of Law, 1982-84, bd. visitors, 1982-85; bd. dirs. W.M. Keck Found.; faculty Practising Law Inst., 1971, 76, 78-80; spkr. spl. program on antitrust litigation Columbia U. Law Sch., NYC, 1981; lawyers dels. com. to 9th Cir. Jud. Conf., 1953-67; UN expert Mission to People's Republic China, 1982. Contbr. articles to legal jours.; author: Antitrust Laws and Trade Regulation, 1969, desk edit., 1981; gen. editor: World Law of Competition, 1978, Antitrust Counseling and Litigation Techniques, 1984; gen. editor emeritus Antitrust Report. Mem. adv. bd. Salvation Army, LA. With USN, 1941-46, capt. Res. ret. Fellow Am. Bar Found., Am. Coll. Trial Lawyers (chmn. complex litigation com. 1984-87); mem. ABA (ho. of dels. 1970, chmn. antitrust law sect. 1972-73), State Bar Calif. (Anti-Trust Lawyer of Yr. award 2002), L.A. Bar Assn., U. Va. Law Sch. Alumni Assn. (mem. deans adv. coun.), Calif. Club, L.A. Country Club, La Jolla Beach and Tennis Club, Phi Kappa Psi, Phi Alpha Delta. Republican. Episcopalian. Home and Office: 12320 Ridge Cir Los Angeles CA 90049-1151 Office Phone: 310-472-1977.

VON KAPPELHOFF, DORIS See DAY, DORIS

VON KLAN, LAURENE, museum administrator; b. NY; BA in Econ., Williams Coll.; MA in Internat. Rels., U. Chgo. Tchr. Northeastern Ill. U.; dir. devel. Nature Conservancy, Ill. chpt., 1986—92; exec. dir. Friends of Chgo. River, 1992—2005; pres., CEO Peggy Notebaert Nature Mus., Chgo., 2005—. Founding mem. Coalition to Restore Urban Waters (nat. steering com.); bd. dir. River Network; steering com. Chgo. Wilderness. Founding mem., nat. steering com Coalition to Restore Urban Waters (CRUW); citizen mem. Ill. River Coordinating Coun., 1998—; bd. dir. Nat. River Network, 2002—. Recipient Protector of Environment award, Chgo. Audubon, 2003; named one of 100 Most Influential Women, Crain's Chgo. Bus., 2004. Office: Notebaert Nature Mus 2430 N Cannon Dr Chicago IL 60614 Office Phone: 773-755-5100.

VON KLEMPERER, KLEMENS, historian, educator; b. Berlin, Nov. 2, 1916; came to U.S., 1938; s. Herbert O. and Frieda (Kuffner) Von K.; m. Elizabeth Lee Gallaher, Dec. 19, 1953; children: Catharine Lee, James Alfred Abitur, Französisches Gymnasium, Berlin, 1934; MA, Harvard U., 1940, PhD, 1949; MA, Cambridge U., 1974. Vis. prof. Stanford U., Palo Alto, Calif., 1960; prof. history Bonn U., Fed. Republic Germany, 1963-64; L. Clark Seelye prof. history Smith Coll., Northampton, Mass., 1960-87, prof. emeritus, 1987—. Vis. prof. Amherst (Mass.) Coll., 1989, 91, 96; vis. fellow Trinity Coll., Oxford, Eng., 1982. Author: Germany's New Conservatism, 1957, Mandate for Resistance, 1969, Ignaz Seipel: Christian Statesman, 1972, German Resistance Against Hitler: The Search for Allies Abroad 1938-1945, 1992, The German Incertitudes, 1914-1945, 2000; editor: A Noble Combat. The Letters of Shiela Grant Duff and Adam von Trott, 1988, "Für Deutschland" Die Männer des 20 Juli, 1994; contbr. articles to profl. jours. Served with AUS, 1943-46, ETO Recipient Austrian Cross of Honor for Sci. and Art 1st class, 1997; Guggenheim Found. fellow, 1957-58; Fulbright fellow, 1957-58, 63-64; Overseas fellow Churchill Coll., Cambridge, Eng., 1973-74; Inst. for Advanced Study fellow, Berlin, 1986; Am. Philos. Soc. grantee, 1977-78, Am. Council of Learned Socs. grantee, 1978-79 Mem. Am. Hist. Soc. (chmn. conf. group for central European history 1982-83) Clubs: Century (N.Y.C.). Avocations: mountain climbing, hiking. Home: 23 Washington Ave Northampton MA 01060-2822 Office: Smith Coll Northampton MA 01063-0001 Office Phone: 413-585-3705. Business E-Mail: kvonklem@smith.edu.

VON KUSTER, LEE NORMAN, retired mathematics professor; b. Scobey, Mont., Mar. 28, 1932; s. Roger Norman and Ragnild Matilda von Kuster; m. Cleo Lorraine Forbes; children: Jeffrey Lee, Gregory Hal, Lowell Eron. BA, U. Mont., Missoula, 1954, MEd, 1967, EdD, 1971. Math. and sci. tchr. Turner Pub. Schs., Mont., 1955—56, Frazer Pub. Schs., Mont., 1958—61, Wolf Point Pub. Schs., Mont., 1961—63, Glendive Pub. Schs. and Dawson CC, Mont., 1964—67; state supr. math. Dept. Pub. Instrn., Helena, Mont., 1967—69; instr. math. U. Mont., 1969—71, prof. math. edn., 1971—94, U. Tex. Pan Am., Edinburg, 1994—2007; ret., 2007. Cons. U. Mont., 1980—88; cons. math. in 10 foreign countries; tchr. conf., Amman, Jordan, New Delhi, 1980, Milan, Island of Rhodes, Greece, 83, 31st Internat. Coun. Edn. Tchg., Bangkok, 1984. Named Most Inspirational Prof., U. Mont., 1986; scholar NSF scholar, Boston Coll., 1963—64;, Wayne State U., Detroit, 1962. Mem.: Nat. Coun. Suprs. Math., Assn. Math. Tchrs. Eng., Nat. Coun. Tchrs. Math., Phi Delta Kappa. Republican. Home: 2808 Umbrella Bird Ave Mcallen TX 78504 Personal E-mail: lvonkuster@rgv.rr.com.

VON MAYRHAUSER, JENNIFER, costume designer; d. Thomas G. Bergin. BS, Northwestern U., 1970. Head costume design Brandeis U. Costume designer (to numerous TV shows, films & plays). Recipient award, OBIE, 1995; nominee Hewes Design award, 2007, Emmy, 1999. Mem.: NY Women in Film and Television. Personal E-mail: r2j22@aol.com.

VON MEHREN, GEORGE M., lawyer; b. Boston, Nov. 2, 1950; m. Barbara A. von Mehren, Dec. 20, 2003; children: Paige E., Reed C. AB, Harvard U., 1972, JD, 1977; BA, Cambridge U., Eng., 1974, MA, 1985. Bar: Ohio 1977, registered: US Supreme Ct., US Ct. Appeals (6th cir.), US Dist. Ct. (No. Dist.) Ohio. Assoc. Squire, Sanders & Dempsey LLP, Cleve., 1977-86, ptnr., 1986—, chair Internat. Dispute Resolution Practice Group, 1998—. Contbr. articles to profl. jours.; spkr. in field. Office: Squire Sanders & Dempsey 127 Public Sq Ste 4900 Cleveland OH 44114-1304 Office Phone: 216-479-8614. Office Fax: 216-479-8777. Business E-Mail: gvonmehren@ssd.com.

VON MEHREN, ROBERT BRANDT, retired lawyer; b. Albert Lea, Minn., Aug. 10, 1922; s. Sigurd Anders and Eulalia Marion (Anderson) von M.; m. Mary Katharine Kelly, June 26, 1948 (dec. Mar. 1985); children: Carl S., John M. (dec.), Katharine, Jane, Margaret; m. Susan Heller Anderson, Apr. 2, 1988. BA summa cum laude with philosophical oration, Yale U., 1943; LLB magna cum laude, Harvard U., 1946. Bar: N.Y. 1946, U.S. Supreme Ct. 1954. Law clk. to Judge Learned Hand U.S. Ct. Appeals (2d cir.), 1946-47; law clk. to Assoc. Justice Stanley Reed U.S. Supreme Ct., 1947-48; assoc. Debevoise & Plimpton, NYC, 1946, 48-57, ptnr., 1957-93, of counsel, 1994-95, ret., 1995. Arbitrator in internat. and other matters; sr. lectr. in law Wharton Sch. U. Pa., Phila., 1985-86; legal counsel Prep. Commn. for Internat. Atomic Energy Agy., N.Y.C., 1956-57; trustee Practising Law Inst., N.Y.C., 1972-96, emeritus, 1996, pres., 1979-86, chmn. bd., 1986-96. Bd. editors Harvard Law Rev., 1944-46, Am. Jour. Internat. Law, 1981-89, hon. editor, 1990-2000; contbr. articles to profl. jours. Trustee Axe Houghton Found., N.Y.C., 1965—; bd. dirs. Legal Aid Soc., N.Y.C., 1966-70; pres. Harvard Law Sch. Assn. N.Y., 1982-83. Mem. Assn. Bar City N.Y., Internat. Law Assn. (vice chmn. 1989-2009, pres. Am. br. 1978-86, chmn. exec. com. 1986-92), Coll. of Comml. Arbitrators, Coun. on Fgn. Rels., Univ. Club, Century Assn. N.Y.C., The Comml. Bar Assn. (hon. mem.). Home: 925 Park Ave New York NY 10028-0210 Office: 919 3rd Ave 46th Fl New York NY 10022 Office Phone: 212-909-6588. Business E-Mail: rbvonmeh@debevoise.com.

VON MERING, OTTO OSWALD, anthropology educator; b. Berlin, Oct. 21, 1922; came to Switzerland, 1933, to U.S., 1939, naturalized, 1954; s. Otto O. and Henriette (Troeger) von M.; m. Shirley Ruth Brook, Sept. 11, 1954; children: Gretchen, Karin, Gregory, Hilary, Celia. Grad., Belmont Hill Sch., 1940; BA in History, Williams Coll., 1944; PhD in Social Anthropology, Harvard U., 1956. Instr. Belmont Hill Sch., Belmont, Mass., 1945-47, Boston U., 1947-48, Cambridge Jr. Coll., 1948-49; rsch. asst. lab. social rels. Harvard U., 1950-51, Boston Psychopathic Hosp., 1951-53; Russell Sage Found. fellow NYC, 1953-55; asst. prof. social anthropology U. Pitts. Coll. Medicine, 1955-60, assoc. prof., 1960-65, prof. social anthropology, 1965-71; prof. child devel. and child care U. Pitts. Coll. Allied Health Professions, 1969-71; prof. anthropology and family medicine U. Fla., 1971-76, prof. anthropology in ob-gyn, 1979-84, prof. anthropology and gerontology, 1986-96, prof. anthropology and gerontology emeritus, 1998, joint prof. dept. medicine, coll. medicine, 1994-96. Lectr. Sigmund Freud Inst., Frankfurt, Germany, 1962-64, Pitts. Psychoanalytical Inst., 1960-71, Interuniv. Forum, 1967-71; tech. adviser Maurice Falk Med. Fund, 1964-75; Fulbright vis. lectr. 1962-63; Richard-Merton guest prof. Heidelberg U., Germany, 1962-63; vis. prof. Dartmouth, 1970-71; vis. lectr. continuing edn. Med. Coll. Pa., 1990-92; vis. lectr. U. Sheffield, Eng., 1995, U. Liverpool, 1995, U. Augsburg, 1997, U. Heidelberg, 1997; hon. vis. prof. U. Coll. London Med. Sch., 1997; supr. grad. study program Ctr. Gerontologic Studies, U. Fla., 1983-85, assoc. dir. 1985-86, dir. 1986-96, prof. emeritus 1998; coord. com. Geriat. Edn. Ctr., Coll. Medicine, U. Fla., 1986-96; med. selection com. Coll. Medicine U. Fla., 2000-07; adv. bd. nursing programs Santa Fe CC, 2001-07; nat. tech. expert panel long-term care Health Care Financing Adminstrn., Washington; adv. bd. Internat. Exch. Ctr. Gerontology State U. System Fla., 1987-92, Second Season Broadcasting Network, Palm Beach, Fla., 1989-92, Fla. Policy Exch. Ctr. Aging, State U. System Fla., 1991-95, Assoc. Health Industries Fla., Inc., Nat. Shared Housing Resource Ctr., Balt., 1994-95; cons. in field. Author: Remotivating the Mental Patient, 1957, A Grammar of Human Values, 1961, (with Mitscherlich and Brocher) Der Kranke in der Modernen Gesellschaft, 1967, (with Kasdan) Anthropology in the Behavioral and Health Sciences, 1970, (with Maria Alvarez) Aging, Demography and Well-Being in Latin America, 1989; (with R. Binstock and L. Cluff) The Future of Long Term Care, 1996; contbr. book chpt. Anthropology The margin, 2008; also articles; commentary editor: Human Organization, 1974-76; corr. editor Jour. Geriatric Psychiatry, 1990-98; mem. editl. bd. Med. Anthropology, 1976-84, Ednl. Gerontology, 1990-2005, Australasian Leisure for Pleasure Jour., 1995-2000, Jour. Cross-Cultural Gerontology, 1996-2002; contbr. essays to books. Pres. Dedicated Alt. Resources for the Elderly, 1996-98; bd. dirs. No. Ctrl. Fla. chpt. Alzheimer's Assn., 1996—2002; bd. dirs. Shepherd's Ctrs. Am., Gainesville, 1998-2000. Recipient Fulbright-Hayes Travel award, 1962-63; grantee Wenner-Gren Found., N.Y., 1962-63, Am. Philos. Soc., 1962-63, Maurice Falk Med. Fund, 1970-71, US-DHHS, 1979-83, Walter Reed Army Inst. Rsch., 1987-91, US-ADA/Fla. Dept. Elder Affairs, 1993-94, Rockefeller Bros. Fund, 1950-51; spl. fellow NIMH, 1971-72. Fellow AAAS, Am. Anthrop. Assn. (mem. James Mooney award com. 1978-81, vis. lectr. 1961,-62, 71-74, 91-92), Am. Gerontol. Soc., Royal Soc. Health, Acad. Psychosomatic Medicine, Am. Ethnological Soc., Soc. Applied Anthropology, Royal Anthrop. Inst.; mem. Assn. Am. Med. Colls., Assn. Anthrop. Gerontol. (pres.-elect 1991-92, pres. 1992-93), Am. Fedn. Clin. Research, Am. Public Health Assn. (capacity proposal evaluator-reviewer, 2007), Canadian Assn. Gerontology, British Soc. Gerontology, So. Gerontol. Soc. (Gerontol. Pioneer honor 2005), Med. Group Mgmt. Assn., World Fedn. Mental Health, Internat. Assn. Social Psychiatry (regional counselor 1973-81), Internat. Hosp. Fedn., Help Age Internat. (London), Am. Assn. Integrated Medicine (diplomate Coll. Behavioral Health, 2009) Home and Office: 818 NW 21st St Gainesville FL 32603-1027 Office Phone: 352-376-9512. *Three guides to conduct I value most: always search for the best fit of fact, argument, and experience. Every first remedy must be amended quickly. When the past disturbs the present, more work on the future is needed.*

VON MOLTKE, GEBHARDT, retired diplomat; b. Wernersdorf, Silesia, Germany, June 28, 1938; married; 2 children. Student, U. Heidelberg, U. Grenoble, U. Berlin, U. Freiburg, 1958-63; Dr. h.c. in Law (hon.), U. Birmingham, Eng., 1999. Legal tng., 1963-67; with Fed. Fgn. Office, Bonn, 1968-71, German Embassy, Moscow, 1971-75, Yaunde, 1975-77; with personnel adminstrn. office Fed. Fgn. Office, Bonn, 1977-82; with German Embassy, Washington, 1982-86; head U.S. dept., with Fed. Fgn. Office, Bonn, 1986-91; asst. sec.-gen. for polit. affairs NATO, 1991-97; amb. Fed. Republic of Germany to Ct. of St. James London, 1997-99; per. rep. of Fed. Republic of Germany, North Atlantic Coun. NATO, Brussels, 1999—2003; ret., 2003. Mem.: German British Soc. (pres.).

VON MOSCH, WANDA GAIL, principal; b. Richmond, Va., Jan. 21, 1952; d. Jesse James, Sr. and Thelma Arleen (Bruce) Perdue; m. Carl Allan Von Mosch, June 24, 1978; children: Carl Allan Jr., Sarah Ashley, Katie Danielle. BS, Longwood Coll., 1974; MS in Ednl. Leadership, Old Dominion U., 2005. Tchr. pub. schs. City of Hampton, Va., 1974-77, City of Virginia Beach, Va., 1977—. Mem., planning coun., mem. faculty coun. Gt. Neck Mid. Sch., coord. ptnrs. edn., comm. liaison; coord., forensics coach Odyssey of Mind, Gt. Neck, 1997—98; adj. instr. career switcher program Old Dominion U. Sunday sch. tchr. Va. Marine Sci. Mus., Virginia Beach, 1983—, Bethel Bible grad., tchr., 1990—; participant Malcolm Baldridge TQM procedure U.S. Congress for Ind. Learning; mem. PTA; active Virginia Beach Prins. Futures Acad., 2007; mem. adminstrv. bd. Francis Asbury United Meth. Ch., Virginia Beach, 1986—, supt., 1991. Recipient PTA award for Disting. Svc., 1990; named Tchr. of the Yr., Walmart, 2002, Gt. Neck, 2002. Mem.: NEA, Virginia Beach Tchr. Forum, Virginia Beach Reading Coun., Va. Math. League, Va. Reading Coun., Virginia Beach Edn. Assn., Va. Edn. Assn. Republican. Avocations: reading, cooking, music, board games, golf. Office: Arrowhead Elem Sch Susquehana Dr Virginia Beach VA 23464 Personal E-mail: stargazer2116@cs.com.

VON OHLEN, ROBERT CHARLES, lawyer; m. Colleen McCloskey von Ohlen, Nov. 30, 1991; children: Maximilian, Grace, Blaise. BA, U. Notre Dame, Ind., 1981; JD, Notre Dame Law Sch., Ind., 1984. Bar: Ill. 1984, US Dist. Ct. (no. dist.) Ill. 1984, US Dist. Ct. (no. dist.) Ind. 1990, US Dist. Ct. (no. dist.) Calif. 1990, US Dist. Ct. (ea. dist.) Wis. 1994, US Dist. Ct. Ariz. 1997, US Dist. Ct. (ea. dist.) Ark. 1999, US Dist. Ct. (we. dist.) Ark. 1999, US Dist. Ct. (we. dist.) Tex. 2001, US Ct. Appeals (7th cir.) 1984, US Ct. Appeals (4th cir.) 1994, US Ct. Appeals (5th cir.) 1997, US Ct. Appeals (3d cir.) 1997, US Ct. Appeals (9th cir.) 1998, US Ct. Appeals (8th cir.) 2004, US Supreme Ct. 1991. Atty. Lord Bissell & Brook, Chgo., 1984—89; mem. Kaplan, von Ohlen & Massamillo, LLC, Chgo., 1990—. Named Ill. Superlawyer, Law & Politics, 2005; named one of Leading Lawyers Ill., Leading Lawyers Network, 2005—08. Mem.: ABA, Juvenile Diabetes Rsch. Found., Arias Reinsurance Soc., Aircraft Owners and Pilot Assn., Regional Airline Assn., Aviation Ins. Assn. Office: Kaplan von Ohlen & Massamillo LLC 120 N LaSalle St Chicago IL 60602

VON PRINCE, KILULU MAGDALENE, retired occupational therapist, sculptor; b. Bumbuli, Lushoto, Tanzania, Jan. 9, 1929; arrived in U.S., 1949; d. Tom Adalbert and Juliane (Martini). BA in Occupl. Therapy, San Jose State U., 1958, MS in Occupl. Therapy, 1972; EdD, U. So. Calif., 1980; doctorate in Higher Edn., 1978. Registered occupl. therapist; cert. work evaluator, work adjustment specialist. With US Army, 1952—55, commd. 2d lt., 1959, advanced through grades to lt. col., staff asst. Denver, 1959-62, sr. occupl. therapist Inst. Surg. Rsch. Ft. Sam Houston, Tex., 1967-70, occupl. therapy clinic, cons. LAMC Presido, Calif., 1975; ret., 1975; hand rehab. asst., hand therapy Walter Reed Army Med. Ctr., 1962-65; hand rehab. asst. occupl. therapist 97th Gen. Hosp., U.S. Army, Frankfurt, Germany, 1965-68; dir. occupl. therapy clinics Tripler Army Med. Ctr., Honolulu, 1972-75; asst. evening coll. program San Jose CC, Calif., 1976-77; fellow allied health adminstrn. SUNY, Buffalo, 1978, Commonwealth U., Richmond, Va., 1978-79; staff project devel. pre-retirement program older adults De Anza Coll., Cupertino, Calif., 1980—81; project dir. Ctr. of Design, Palo Alto, 1980; part-time instr. Stroke Activity Ctr. Cabrillo Coll., Santa Cruz, Calif., 1981; dir. occupl. therapy clinics Presbyn. Med. Ctr., 1981-86; ptnr., mgr. retail store, 1986-89; dir. rehab. clinics Merrithew Meml. Hosp. Contra Costa Med. Ctr., Martinez, Calif., 1990-93; sculptor, 1993—; activity program coord. Calif. Womens Detention Facility, Chowchilla, 1994-97; ret., 1997. Co-author: Splinting of Burned Patients, 1974; producer videos: Elbow Splinting of the Burned Patient, 1970, Self-Instruction Unit: Principles of Elbow Splinting, 1971; contbr. articles to profl. jours. Decorated Legion of Merit; recipient Disting. Alumni Honors award San Jose State U., 1982, Best of Show award Nat. Veteran's Creative Arts Competition, Fresno Local Vet Art Show, 2004; honored by having Ballon painting to be first mosaic mural on Hwy. 168, Rotary Club, Fresno., 2006; scholar U.S. Surgeon Gen., 1972; fellow Kellogg Found., 1979. Mem.: Occupl. Therapy Assn. Calif. (v.p. 1981—84, state chair pers. 1981—84, state chair continuing edn. 1984—86, award of excellence 1986, Lifetime Achievement award

1994), Am. Occupl. Therapy Assn., Am. Soc. Hand Therapists (life), Alliance Calif. Artist. Avocations: stone sculpture, painting, kayaking, travel, fossil hunting. Home: 172 N Karen Ave Clovis CA 93612-0112 Personal E-mail: kiluluv@aol.com.

VON RHEIN, JOHN RICHARD, music critic, journalist, writer; b. Pasadena, Calif., Sept. 10, 1945; s. Hans Walter and Elsa Maryon (Brossmann) von R. AA, Pasadena City Coll., 1965; BA in Eng., UCLA, 1967; BA in Music, Calif. State U., Los Angeles, 1970. Music reviewer Hollywood (Calif.) Citizen-News, 1968-70; music editor and critic, dance critic Akron (Ohio) Beacon Jour., 1971-77; music critic Chgo. Tribune, 1977—; prof. music appreciation Rio Hondo Jr. Coll., Calif., 1970-71. Lectr., TV host, rec. annotator. Co-author (with Andrew Porter): Bravi; contbr. articles to World Book Ency., New Grove Dictionary of Music, mags. and papers. Music Critics Assn.-Kennedy Center for Performing Arts fellow, 1972, 75; recipient Peter Lisagor award Soc. Profl. Journalists, 1999. Mem. Music Critics Assn. N.Am. (edn. com., dir. 1988), Ravinia Critics Inst. (dir. 1988). Office: Chgo Tribune Co 435 N Michigan Ave Chicago IL 60611-4066 Home Phone: 773-561-2620; Office Phone: 312-222-3570. Business E-Mail: jvonrhein@tribune.com.

VON ROEDERN, BOLKO GRAF, energy executive, researcher; b. Johannesburg, Dec. 20, 1950; arrived in US, 1979; s. Conrad Graf and Dagmar Grafin (Lubbert) von Roedern; m. Susan Kathryn Bateman, July 6, 1982; children: Gabriele Kathryn, Meredith Margret, Christina Barbara. Diploma in physics, Tech. U. Clausthal, Germany, 1976; PhD, U. Stuttgart, 1979. Postdoctoral fellow Harvard U., Cambridge, Mass., 1979—83; sr. scientist Solar Energy Rsch. Inst., Golden, Colo., 1983—85; mgr. Glasstech Solar, Inc., Wheat Ridge, Colo., 1985—89; ptnr., co-owner MV Systems, Inc., Golden, 1989—90; sr. project mgr. Nat. Renewable Energy Lab., Golden, 1990—. Contbg. author Ency. of Energy, 2004, inventor in field. Bd. mem. Col. Renewable Energy Soc., 2008—. Recipient R&D 100 award, 2003; co-finalist, World Tech. Network and The Economist, 1999. Mem.: Materials Rsch. Soc., Am. Phys. Soc., German Phys. Soc. Avocations: horseback riding, skiing, flying. Office: Nat Renewable Energy Lab 1617 Cole Blvd Golden CO 80401-3393 Office Phone: 303-384-6480. Office Fax: 303-384-6430. Business E-Mail: bolko_von_roedern@nrel.gov.

VON RYDINGSVARD, URSULA KAROLISZYN, sculptor; b. Deensen, Germany, July 26, 1942; came to US, 1950; d. Ignacy and Konegunda (Sternal) Karoliszyn; m. Paul Greengard. BA, MA, U. Miami, Coral Gables, Fla., 1965; postgrad., U. Calif., Berkeley, 1969-70; MFA, Columbia U., 1975; PhD (hon.), Md. Inst. Art, 1991. Instr. Sch. Visual Arts, NYC, 1981-82; asst. prof. Pratt Inst., Bklyn., 1978-82, Fordham U., Bronx, NY, 1980-82; assoc. prof. Yale U., New Haven, 1982-86; prof. grad. divsn. Sch. Visual Arts, NYC, 1986—. One-woman shows include Laumeier Sculpture Gallery, St. Louis, 1988, Capp St. Project San Francisco, 1990, Lorence-Monk Gallery, NYC, 1990-91, Zamek Ujazdowski Contemporary Art Ctr., Warsaw, Poland, 1992, Storm King Art Ctr., Mountainville, NY, 1992-94, Galerie Lelong, NYC, 1994, Weatherspoon Art Gallery, Grensboro, NC, 1994, Univ. Gallery, Amherst, 1995, Mus. Art, Providence, 1996, Mus. Art RI Sch. Design, Providence, 1996, Yorkshire Sculpture Pk., Wakefield, England, 1997, Nelson-Atkins Mus., Kansas City, Mo., 1998, Madison (Wis.) Art Ctr., 1998, Chgo. Cultural Ctr., 1998, Indpls. Mus. Art, 1999, The Contemporaty Mus., Honolulu, 1999, Barbara Krakow Gallery, Boston, 1999, Galerie Lelong, Zurich, 2000, NYC, 2000, Doris C. Freedman Plz., Ctrl. Pk., NYC, 2000, Neuberger Mus. Art, SUNY, Purchase, 2002, Herbert F. Johnson Mus. Art, Cornell U., 2007; exhibited in group shows at Contemporary Arts Ctr., Cin., 1987, Damon Brandt Gallery, NYC, 1989, Met. Mus. Art, NYC, 1989-93, Whitney Mus. Contemporary Art, 1990, Cultural Ctr., Chgo., 1991, Ctrl. Bur. Art Exhbns., Warsaw and Krakow, Poland, 1991, The Cultural Space/Exit Art, NYC, 1992, Galerie Lelong, NYC, 1993, Denver Art Mus. and Columbus Art Mus., 1994, others; outdoor exhbns include Pelham Bay Park, Bronx, NY, 1978, Neuberger Mus., Purchase, NY, 1979, Artpark, Lewiston, NY, 1979, Laumeier Sculpture Park, St. Louis, 1989-94, Walker Art Ctr., Mpls., 1990-93, Oliver Ranch, Geyserville, Calif., Storm King Art Ctr., Mountainville, NY, 1992-93; contbr. articles to profl. jours. Recipient Best Small Mus. Exhbn. award Ursula von Rydingsvard Strom King Art Ctr., Am. Sect. Internat. Assn. Art Critics, 1992, 2nd prize Best Show, Comml. Gallery, Internat. Assn. art Critics, 2000; named Mary Miss Resident Visual Arts Am. Acad. Rome, 2007; Fulbright Hays travel grantee, 1975; grantee NY State Coun. Arts, Am. the Beautiful Fund, Nat. Endowment for Arts, Creative Artists Program Svc.; Griswald traveling grantee Yale U., 1985; Guggenheim fellow, 1983-84; Nat. Endowment for Arts individual artists grantee, 1986-87; Alfred Jurzykowski Found. Fine Arts award, 1996, Joan Mitchell fellowship, 1997. Mem.: AAAL (elected mem. 2008, Acad. award in Art 1994). Studio: 78 Ingraham St Brooklyn NY 11237-1406 E-mail: art@galerielong.com.

VON SCHACK, WESLEY W., utilities executive; b. NY, 1944; married. AB, Fordham U., 1965; MBA, St. John's U., Jamaica, NY, 1971; doctorate, Pace U., 1990. Chmn., CEO, pres. DQE, Pitts., 1986-96, ret., 1996; chmn., pres., CEO N.Y. State Electric and Gas Corp., Binghamton, 1996-99, chmn. bd. dirs., 1999—; chmn., pres., CEO Energy East Corp., New Gloucester, Maine, 1998—. Bd. dirs. Bank of NY Mellon Corp., Energy East Corp., Teledyne Techs., Inc.; chmn., dir. AEGIS Ins. Co., Inc. Trustee Gettysburg Found. Mem.: Am. Gas Assn. Found. (trustee). Office: Energy East Corp 217 Commercial St Portland ME 04101 Business E-Mail: wwvonschack@energyeast.com.

VON SPEYER, JACQUES, financier; b. Munich, June 12, 1950; s. Naftalie and Leah von Speyer; m. Alexa Andrea Petschek; children: Dahlia Petschek-von Speyer, Sarah Petschek-von Speyer. Degree in Internat. Fin., London Sch. Econs., 1970. Vice-chmn. Zentral Bank, Zurich, Switzerland, 1974—85; sr. adv. FDIC Mfr. Hanover Bank, Continental Ill. Bank, 1985—86; founder Seychelles Cinnamon Industry, 1986—90; chmn. Palm Beach Milk Co., 1990—94, Global Interact, 1994—99, Deerfalls Internat., Issaquah, Wash., 1999—. Amb. EEC, Brussels, 1971—73. Recipient Order Merit award, Italian Govt., 1975, Quuen's medal, Hong Kong, 1977. Republican. Jewish. Achievements include invention of micro heat technology; 747 airport catering system; 1000 meter sniper scope spotting rig. Home and Office: Deerfalls Interantional 4580 Klahanie Drive South East Issaquah WA 98029 Office Fax: 425-222-0054; Home Fax: 425-222-0054. Personal E-mail: deerfalls@comcast.net.

VON SPIEGEL, JANICE KRIEGER, mathematics educator; d. Donald and Frances Krieger; m. Charles F. von Spiegel, Mar. 20, 1971; children: Heidi Robinson, Jacqueline. BA in Edn., U. Akron, 1971, MA in Edn., 2003. Tchg. cert. OH Dept. Edn., 2005. Math tchr. Akron Pub. Schs., Ohio, 1972—76; math instr. U. Akron, 1982—85; math tchr. St. Vincent-St. Mary H.S., Akron, 1985—88, Archbishop Hoban HS, Akron, 1988—. Spkr. in field. Adviser Academic Challenge Team, Akron, 1992—2004, Future Tchrs. Club, Akron, 2004—05. Mem.: Greater Akron Math. Educators Soc. (pres. 1996—2003), Math. Assn. Am., Nat. Coun. Tchrs. Math., OH Coun. Tchrs. Math. (east dist. dir. 2000—03, spkr., gen. co chair statewide conf. 1998, 2004, Outstanding Math. Classroom Tchr. East Dist. OH 1999), Pi Mu Epsilon. Home: 202 Mineola Ave Akron OH 44313 Office: Archbishop Hoban HS 1 Holy Cross Blvd Akron OH 44306 Personal E-mail: jvonspiegel@neo.rr.com. Business E-Mail: vonspiegelj@hoban.org.

VON STACKELBERG, KATHERINE ELLEN, environmental scientist, consultant; d. John Roderick von Stackelberg and Steffi Heuss; m. Garth Wayne Jonson, July 14, 1995; children: Sigurgeir Temple Jonson, Bryndis LeRoy Jonson. AB, Harvard U., 1988, MS, 1998, ScD, 2006. Sr. scientist Menzie-Cura and Assoc. Inc., Winchester, Mass., 1993—2006; rsch. mgr. Harvard Ctr. for Risk Analysis, Boston, 2003—; mng. scientist Exponent Inc., Winchester, 2006—. Grantee NSF and EPA, 2003—. Mem.: Assn. Environ. and Rsch. Economists, Soc. Environ. Toxicology and Chemistry (assoc.; del. Pellston Workshop 2003, tech. com.), Soc. Risk Analysis (assoc.; program com.). Achievements include research in evaluation of alternative air pollution control strategies for Slovak Republic through the Harvard Institute for International Development; design of contingent valuation survey to value noncancer and ecological effects of exposure to PCBs in the environment; development of probabilistic modeling tools to support risk-based decision making involving environmental contaminants; providing technical leadership in developing software to support risk-based decisionmaking. Avocations: travel, Muay Thai. Office: Harvard Ctr for Risk Analysis Harvard Sch for Pub Health 401 Park Dr Landmark 404C Boston MA 02215 Home Fax: 617-783-4827. Personal E-mail: kvon@igc.org. Business E-Mail: kvon@hsph.harvard.edu.

VON STEIN, NICHOLAS, political organization worker; b. Hamilton, Ohio; m. Summer Von Stein; children: Payton, Jonas. BA in Polit. Sci. cum laude, U. Cin., 2005; grad. student in polit. sci., Miami U., Oxford, Ohio. Field intern David Pepper for Mayor Campaign; field organizer America Votes Ohio. Structural mechanic USAF, Yokota AFB, Japan. Democrat. Home: 42 Loomis St Apt 323 Malden MA 02148-2005 Office Phone: 513-607-6861.

VON VOLBORTH, ALEX (ALEXIS), geochemist, geological engineering educator; b. Viipuri, Finland, July 11, 1924; came to U.S. 1955, naturalized; m. Nadia Hasso, 1947; children: Tatyana, Swetlana, Maria, Gregory, Anna, Nicholaus H.W., Elisabeth. PhC, U. Helsinki, 1950, PhLic and PhD in Geology-Mineralogy, 1954. Mineralogist, rsch. assoc., assoc. prof., prof. U. Nev., Reno, 1956—68; Killam vis. prof. geology, Killam rsch. prof. Dalhousie U., Canada, 1968—72; vis. prof. NASA Lunar Sci. Inst., U. Houston, 1972—73; vis. rsch. chemist U. Calif., Irvine, 1973—76; prof. geology and chemistry N.D. State U., 1975—78; prof. geology, scientist Nuc. Radiation Ctr., Wash. State U., Pullman, 1978—79; prof. geochemistry and chemistry Mont. Coll. Mineral Sci. and Tech., Butte, 1979—94, prof. geol. engring., 1987—92, dir. accelerator lab., 1983—86, sr. radiation safety officer, 1983—86; prof. emeritus Mont. Tech./U. Mont., Butte, 1995—. Prin. investigator Stoichiometry Study Lunar Rocks, NASA, 1972-73; cons. AEC, 1961-63, NASA, 1965-73, Anaconda Co., 1968, Atomic Energy Orgn. Iran, 1975, King Abdul Aziz U., Jeddah, Saudi Arabia, 1975-76, Johns Manville Corp., Chevron, 1980-83, Pegasus Gold Inc., 1987, Placer Dome Inc., Echo Bay, Inc., 1990; U.S. rep., del. 2d Conf. on Natural Reactors, IAEC, Paris, 1977; U.S. rep. Internat. Geol. Correlation Program, 1990-96; interpreter, Russian translator in Soviet Siberia for U.S. and Can. mining cos., 1990-96. One-man photo exhibits include, All-Russian Geol. Rsch. Inst. and Mus. of A.P. Karpinsky, St. Petersburg, 2006 (Photograph of Yr., Art Index, 2007), Gallery P, Las Vegas, Nev., 2006, State Geol. Mus. of V.I. Vernadsky, Moscow, 2006, Ctrl. Exhbn. Hall, St. Petersburg, 2006, Stroganov Palace - Russian Mus., 2007, Nature is a Great Artist, Stroganov Palace Russian Mus., St. Petersburg, 2007, Central Exhbn. Hall Manesh, St. Petersburg, 2007, Represented in permanent collections Smithsonian Nat. Mus. of Natural History, Washington, DC, Mineralogical Mus., Harvard Univ., Am. Mus. Natural History; contbr. articles to profl. jours. Traveling rsch. fellow Outokumpu Found., U. Vienna, U. Heidelberg, 1954-55, Hoover fellow Calif. Inst. Tech., 1955-56, sr. fellow Australian Acad. Sci., 1965, fellow Guggenheim Found., 1965-66; fossil Elkoceras Volborthi named in his honor. Fellow Mineral. Soc. Am., Am. Inst. Chemists; mem. Am. Chem. Soc., Am. Nuclear Soc., Soc. Econ. Geologists, Internat. Precious Metals Inst. Achievements include discovery of two new minerals, Vayrynenite and Tarkianite. Home and Office: PO Box 80 Dayton MT 59914-0080 Office Phone: 406-849-5830. Personal E-mail: aalex000@centurytel.net.

VON WACHTER, TILL MARCO, economics professor; b. Bonn, Germany, July 26, 1973; PhD in Economics, U. Calif., Berkeley. Asst. prof. Columbia U., NYC, 2003—08.

VON WEIZSÄCKER, ERNST ULRICH, environmental scientist, dean; b. Zürich, Switzerland, June 25, 1939; s. Carl Friedrich and Gundalena (Wille) Von W.; m. Christine Radtke; children: Jakob, Paula, Adam, Franz, Maria. Diploma in Physics, U. Hamburg, Germany, 1965; PhD in Biology, U. Freiburg, Germany, 1969; degree (hon.), Soka U., Tokyo. Fellow Protestant Interdisc Rsch. Inst., Heidelberg, Germany, 1969-72; prof. Biology U. Essen, Germany, 1972-75; pres. U. Kassel, Germany, 1975-80; dir. UN Ctr. for Sci. and Tech., NYC, 1981-84, Inst. for European Environ. Policy, Bonn, 1984-91; pres. Wuppertal Inst. for Climate, Environment and Energy, Germany, 1991-2000; mem. Parliament (Bundestag), 1998—2005, chmn. environment com., 2002—05; dean Donald Bren Sch. Environ. Sci. and Mgmt. U. Calif., Santa Barbara, 2006—. Co-chair internat. panel for sustainable resource use UN Environ. Program. Author, editor: Offene Systeme I, 1974, New Frontiers in Technology Application, 1983, Ecological Tax Reform, 1992, Earth Politics, 1992, Factor Four (translated in 12 langs.), 1997, Limits to Privatization, 2005. Recipient Pfaff prize, Pfaff Found., 1977, Premio de la Natura award, 1989, Duke of Edinburgh medal, 1996, Takeda award of techo-entrepreneurial achievement, 2001. Mem. German Zool. Soc., Club of Rome. Mem. Social Dem. Party. Lutheran. Avocation: chess. Office: U Calif Santa Barbara Bren Hall Santa Barbara CA 93106-5131 Home: 3767 Greggory Way Santa Barbara CA 93105 Office Phone: 805-893-7577. Business E-Mail: ernst@bren.ucsb.edu.

VOOK, FREDERICK LUDWIG, physicist, consultant; b. Milw., Jan. 17, 1931; s. Fred Ludwig and Hedwig Anna (Werner) V.; m. Frederica Jean Sandin, Aug. 16, 1958; children: Eric Robert, Dietrich Werner. BA with honors, U. Chgo., 1951, BS, 1952; MS, U. Ill., 1954, PhD in Physics, 1958. With Sandia Labs., Kirtland AFB East, N.Mex., 1958-94; div. supr., 1962-71; mgr. dept. research, 1971-78; dir. research, 1978-94; pvt. cons. Albuquerque, 1994—. Editor: Radiation Effects in Semiconductors, 1968; co-editor: Applications of Ion Beams to Metals, 1974. Mem. coll. engring. adv. bd. U. Ill.; mem. policy bd. Nat. Nanofabrication Facility Cornell U.; mem. basic energy sci. adv. com. Panel on Value of Basic Rsch; mem. Okla. State Univ. Ctr. for Laser and Photonics Rsch. adv. bd. U. Chgo. and U. Ill. scholar and fellow. Fellow Am. Phys. Soc.; mem. IEEE (sr. mem.), Böhmische Physikalische Gesellschaft, Phi Beta Kappa, Sigma Xi. Office Phone: 505-884-4754. Personal E-mail: fandfvook@msn.com.

VOORAKARANAM, RAM, optics scientist; b. Hyderabad, India; PhD, Ga. Inst. Techs., Atlanta, 2002. Prin. engr. Ardext Techs., Atlanta, 2000—03, co-founder, 2000—03; RF test engr. Amkor Techs., Chandler, Ariz., 2003—04; test engr. Tex. Instruments High Performance Analog Divsn., Tucson, 2004—06; adj. prof. U. Ariz., Tucson, 2005, rsch. assoc., coll. optical sci., 2006—; adj. prof. Pima CC, Tucson, 2008. Mem.: IEEE. Office: Univ Ariz Optical Sci 1630 E University Blvd Tucson AZ 85721 Business E-Mail: ram@optics.arizona.edu.

VOORHEES, JAMES DAYTON, JR., lawyer; b. Haverford, Pa., Nov. 14, 1917; s. James Dayton Voorhees and Elsa Denison Jameson; m. Mary Margaret Fuller, Sept. 5, 1942 (dec. Apr. 1991); m. Rosemarie Stewart, Jan. 7, 2004; children: J. Dayton III, Susan F. Voorhees-Maxfield, Jane Voorhees Kiss. BA, Yale U., 1940; JD, Harvard U., 1943. Bar: N.H. 1947, Colo. 1948, U.S. Dist. Ct. Colo. 1948, U.S. Ct. Appeals (10th cir.) 1949, U.S. Ct. Appeals (5th cir.) 1956, U.S. Supreme Ct. 1960. Assoc. Johnson & Robertson, Denver, 1947-50; atty. Conoco Inc., Denver, 1950-56; ptnr. Moran, Reidy & Voorhees, Denver, 1956-78, Kutak, Rock & Huie, Denver, 1978-80; ptnr., counsel Davis, Graham & Stubbs, Denver, 1980—. Mem. Denver Bd. Edn., 1965-71, pres. 1967-69. Lt. comdr. USNR, 1941-46, ATO, PTO. Mem.: ABA, Denver Bar Assn., Colo. Bar Assn., University Club, Denver Country Club.

VOORHEES, KENT JAY, chemist; b. Provo, Utah, Sept. 7, 1943; s. Melrose and Beulah Madge (Hansen) V.; m. Tamara Lee Lasson, June 9, 1966; children: Christian Ward, Danielle Kay. BS, Utah State U., 1965, MS, 1968, PhD, 1970. Fellow Mich. State U., East Lansing, 1970—71; instr. U. Utah, Salt Lake City, 1971-73, asst. rsch. prof., 1973-76, assoc. rsch. prof., 1976-79; asst. prof. Colo. Sch. Mines, Golden, 1979-83, assoc. prof., 1983-86, prof., 1986—. Cons. 1979—; scientific adv. bd. Colo. Health Care, Denver, 1997-2003; bd. dirs. Petrex, Golden, 1982-86; founder, chief sci. officer MicroPhage, Inc., 2002-2004; editorial bd. Analytical Pyrolysis, Amsterdam, The Netherlands, 1988-2000, editor, Analytical Pyrolysis, 2001—. Author: Analytical pyrolysis, 1982; contbr. articles to profl. jours. Recipient Rsch. award, Am. Chem. Soc., 1995, Orise Faculty fellow, FDA, 1995, 100 award, R&D Mag., 2000, Disting. Alumni award, Utah State U. Dept. Chemistry, 2001, Dean's Excellence award, Colo. Sch. Mines, 2003, Colo. Svc. award, Am. Chem. Soc., 2005. Mem.: ACS (nominations and elections com. 1988—92, com. on coms. 1993—98, coun. policy com. 1999—2004, bd. dirs. 2004—, CS mem. 2006—08, chair, realtions com. mem.), Green Chemistry Inst. (governance bd. 2007—), Am. Soc. Mass Spectrometry, Colo. Am. Chem. Soc. (councilor 1981—). Avocations: golf, fishing, boating. Office Phone: 303-273-3616. Personal E-mail: kvoorhee@mines.edu.

VOORHEES, THEODORE, JR., lawyer; b. May 24, 1949; AB, Harvard U., 1971; JD, Catholic U., 1974. Bar: DC 1975. Ptnr. Covington & Burling, Washington, chmn. Product Liability and Toxic Tort Practice Group, co-chmn. Antitrust and Consumer Law Practice Group. Office: Covington & Burling 1201 Pennsylvania Ave NW Washington DC 20004-2401 Office Phone: 202-662-5236. Office Fax: 202-778-5236. Business E-Mail: tvoorhees@cov.com.

VOORHESS, MARY LOUISE, pediatric endocrinologist; b. Livingston Manor, NY, June 2, 1926; d. Harry William and Helen Grace (Schwartz) V. RN, City Hosp. Sch. Nursing, Binghamton, NY, 1946; BA in Zoology, U. Tex., 1952; MD, Baylor Coll., Houston, 1956. Diplomate Am. Bd. Pediatrics and Pediatric Endocrinology. Rotating intern Albany (N.Y.) Med. Ctr., 1956-57, asst. resident pediatrics, 1957-58, chief resident pediatrics, 1958-59; rsch. fellow pediatric endocrinology and genetics SUNY Health Sci. Ctr., Syracuse, 1959-61, asst. prof. pediatrics, 1961-65, assoc. prof. pediatrics, 1965-70, prof. pediatrics, 1970-76, SUNY Sch. Medicine and Biomed. Scis., Buffalo, 1976-91, prof. pediatrics emeritus, 1991—; co-chief div. endocrinology Children's Hosp. Buffalo, 1976-91; retired, 1997. Mem. nat. adv. environ. health scis. coun. NIH, 1980-83. Ad hoc reviewer Jour. Pediat., Pediat., Am. Jour. Diseases Children, others, 1960-97; contbr. sci. articles to profl. jours., chpts. to books. Mem. adv. bd. Interim Healthcare inc., 1991-97; mem. devel. coun. Children's Hosp. Buffalo Found., 1991-97; med. dir. Children's Growth Found., Buffalo, 1976-97; cmty. advisor Assn. for Rsch. Childhood Cancer, Buffalo, 1990-97. Recipient rsch. career devel. award Nat. Cancer Inst., 1961-71, Dean's award SUNY Sch. Medicine and Biomed. Scis., 1991. Fellow Am. Acad. Pediatrics, AAAS; mem. Soc. Pediatric Rsch. (emeritus), Am. Pediatric Soc. (emeritus), Endocrine Soc. (emeritus), Lawson Wilkins Pediatric Endocrine Soc. (emeritus), Phi Beta Kappa, Alpha Omega Alpha. Presbyterian. Home: Apt 33 5707 Williamsburg Landing Dr Williamsburg VA 23185-8008 E-mail: mvoorhess@cox.net.

VOORHIS, BRENDA HEATH JACOBSEN, retired psychiatrist; b. Buffalo, Feb. 22, 1930; d. Alfred Wilmot and Evelyn (Heath) Jacobsen; BA, Wellesley Coll., 1951; MD, Johns Hopkins U., 1955; children: Catherine, Mary Jo, Brenda, Ann, Edward, Karin. Intern in pediatrics Johns Hopkins Hosp., Balt., 1955-56, fellow in pediatric cardiology, 1957, resident in psychiatry Erie County Med. Ctr. and Gowanda Psychiat. Ctr., Helmuth, NY, 1967-69, 82-83, mem. staff, 1969—, unit chief, 1979, dep. program dir., 1980, with cmty. svcs., 1983-84; practice medicine specializing in psychiatry, Gowanda, NY. Bd. dirs. Cattaraugus County Coun. on Alcoholism and Substance Abuse, 1979—. Mem. Cattaraugus County Mental Health Assn. Democrat.

VOORSANGER, BARTHOLOMEW, architect; b. Detroit, Mar. 23, 1937; s. Jacob H. and Ethel A. (Arnstein) V.; m. Lisa Livingston, 1964; m. Catherine Hoover, Sept. 10, 1983 (dec. Dec. 2001); children: Roxanna Virginia (dec.), Matthew Ansley; m. Peggy Loar, June 5, 2004. AB cum laude, Princeton U., 1960; diplome, Fontainebleau, 1960; MArch, Harvard U., 1964; D (hon.), U. Architecture and Urbanism, Romania. Assoc. Vincent Ponte, Montreal, Que., Canada, 1964-67, I.M. Pei & Ptnrs., 1968-78, dir. Iran, 1975-78; co-chmn. Voorsanger & Mills (Architects), NYC, 1978-90; founder, prin. Voorsanger & Assocs., Architects, NYC, 1990—; founder Taylor/Voorsanger Urban Designers, 1991. Lectr. Bennington (Vt.) Coll., U. Pa., Columbia U., Harvard U.; guest critic, lectr. Yale U., Pratt Inst., CUNY, R.I. Sch. Design, U. Cin., Syracuse U., U. Tex., Arlington; mem. adv. bd. Parson Sch. Architecture; mem. archtl. rev. panel Port Authority of NY & NJ; advisor to Samsung Corp., Korea. Exhbns. include: NYU, Archtl. Assn., London, Harvard Grad. Sch. Design, Vacant Lots Housing Study, NY, Deutsches Architeckur Mus., Frankfurt, Mus. Finnish Architecture, Avery Lib. Centennial Exhbn. Columbia Univ., Helsinki, Bklyn. Mus.; major projects include: Le Cygne Restaurant, Neiman houseboat, NYU Midtown Ctr., NYU Bus. Sch. Library, La Grandeur housing, NYU dormitories, Hostos Cmty. Coll., NY; finalist Bklyn. Mus. masterplan internat. competition, expansion and master plan Pierpont Morgan Libr., Wethersfield Carriage Mus., Amenia, NY; Montana and Wyoming Residences; Advanced Tng. Ctr., NYU, New York Apt., NYC, Riverdale (NY) Jewish Ctr.; fellow J. Pierpont Morgan Libr., NY, Asia Soc., NY, Brody Residence, VA, Daniels/Falks Residence, Ariz., Wildcat Ridge Residence, Snowmass, Calif., Nemerever Residence, Napa, Calif., Port Authority NY/NJ Air Traffic Control Towers, Univ. Art Mus., U. Va., Asia Soc. and Mus., NYC, Olana Mus., Hudson, NY, Elie Tahari Offices, NJ; winner Nat.

World War II Mus., New Orleans Competition, UAE Nat. Mil. Mus. Mem. vis. com. RI Sch. Design, U. Tex., Arlington; mem. Pt. Authority NY/NJ Ground Zero Archive, NY Hist. Soc., also mem. archtl. cir. steering com.; chmn. bd. advisors Temple Hoyne Buell Ctr., Study Am. Architecture, Columbia U., NYC, 1989—; mem. adv. bd. Parsons Sch. Architecture; chair archtl. rev. panel Port Authority NY, NJ; bd. dirs. Worldesign Found.; mem. Regent's Panel NY State U., NY State Regents' Com. on Schs; pres. NY Found. for Architecture 2000-01. 1st lt. US Army, 1960-61. Recipient Cannon prize NAD, state and nat. awards NYC chpt. AIA, AIA/Better Homes, Bard City Club, Interiors mag., Stone Inst., AIA/Libr., Lumen, Pratt Inst., NYU, NYC Art Commn.; competition winner Nat. WWII Mus., New Orleans, UAE nat. Military Mus. Competition. Fellow: NAD, AIA (numerous offices, including pres. N.Y.C. chpt. 1987, Nat. Honor awards, N.Y. State and NYC awards); mem.: Alumni Coun. Grad. Sch. Design Harvard (editl. bd. Harvard Design mag.), Wadawanuck Club, Century Assn., Sir John Soane Mus. Found., Archtl. League NYC (bd. dirs.), Ellis Island Yacht Club (commodore 2001—). Office: 246 W 38th St Fl 14 New York NY 10018-5805 Home Phone: 212-832-1668; Office Phone: 212-302-6464. Business E-Mail: bvoorsanger@voorsanger.com.

VORA, MANU KISHANDAS, chemical engineer, consultant; b. Bombay, Oct. 31, 1945; s. Kishandas Narandas and Shantaben K. (Valia) V., m. Nila Narotamdas Kothari, June 16, 1974; children: Ashish, Anand. BSChemE, Banaras U., India, 1968; MSChemE, Ill. Inst. Tech., Chgo., 1970, PhD in ChemE, 1975; MBA, Keller Grad. Sch. Mgmt., Chgo., 1985. Grad. asst. Ill. Inst. Tech., 1969-74; rsch. assoc. Inst. Gas Tech., Chgo., 1976-77, chem. engr., 1977-79, engring. supr., 1979-82; mem. tech. staff AT&T Bell Labs. (now Lucent Techs.), Holmdel, NJ, 1983-84, Naperville, Ill., 1984—, mgr. customer satisfaction, 1990-96, voice of the customer mgr., 1997-2000; pres., CEO Bus. Excellence, Inc., 2000—. Adj. prof. Ill. Inst. Tech., Chgo., 1993—; spkr. in field. Editor: Internat. Petroleum Encyclopedia, 1980. Chmn. Save the Children Holiday Fund Drive, 1986-99; trustee Avery Coonley Sch., Downers Grove, Ill., 1987-91; pres., dir. Blind Found. for India, Naperville, 1989—. Recipient Non-Supervisory AA award Affirmative Actions Adv. Com., 1987, 92, 97, Outstanding Contbn. award Asian Am. for Affirmative Actions, 1989, Disting. Svc. award Save the Children, 1990, Ann. Merit award Chgo. Assn. Tech. Socs., 1992. Fellow Am. Soc. for Quality (standing rev. bd. 1988—, editl. rev. bd. 1989, tech. media com. 1989, mixed media rev. bd. 1994, nat. quality month regional planning com. 1989-94, nat. cert. com. 1989-94, chmn. cert. process improvements subcom. 1990-94, testimonial awards 1995, 96, 2001, 02, exec. bd. Chgo. sect., vice chmn. sect. affairs 1993-94, sect. chmn. 1994-95, nat. dir. at large, 1996-98, nat. dir. 1998-2000, v.p. 2000-2002, vice chmn. investing in quality capital campaign, spl. award 1991, Century Club award 1992, Founders' award 1993, Joe Lisy Quality award 1994, Grant medal 2001, Lancaster medal 2005); mem. Ill. Team Excellence award (chief judge 1993-99, steering com. 1993-99, award). Hindu. Avocations: reading, photography, travel, philanthropic activities. Home: 1256 Hamilton Ln Naperville IL 60540-8373 Office: Bus Excellence Inc PO Box 5585 Naperville IL 60567-5585 Office Phone: 630-548-5531. Personal E-mail: manuvora@yahoo.com.

VORCE-TISH, HELENE R., writer; d. Palmer Lemuel Vorce and Adelaide Catherine Miller; m. Charles Ronald VanBuren, Dec. 23, 1950 (div. Aug. 1967); children: Gail Rae, Karen Helene; m. William David Tish, Oct. 20, 1978 (dec.). BA in Psychology, Mich. State U., 1950, tchrs. cert. in English, 1961; M in English, U. N.Mex., 1968. Secondary tchr. English and creative writing Grant Unified Tchrs. Dist., Sacramento. Spkr. in field; instr. workshops in field. Author: (novels) The Wounds of Hate, 2001, Challenging the Forces of Hate, 2002, (nonfiction) Fencing With Danger, 2006, Bobby The Miracle Dog, 2008; regular contbr.: Foothill Times; contbr. articles to profl. jours., popular mags. and newspapers. Fellow: Am. Soc. Journalists and Authors, Calif. Writers Club (bd. mem. 1999—2000). Avocations: tennis, swimming, jogging. Office Phone: 530-677-3327. Personal E-mail: tish@directcon.net.

VORHES, ANNA KIRSTINE, music educator; b. St Louis, June 23, 1952; d. Carl Edwin Vorhes and Harriet Eleanor Christensen; m. Dwayne Harold Sandberg (dec. Mar. 2, 2008); 1 child, Nathan Thomas Sandberg. BA in music, Macalester Coll., St Paul, 1974; BA in psychology; MusM, U. Ariz, Tucson, 1984. Cert. tchr. music Music Tchrs Nat. Assn., 1985. Harp tchr. U. SD, Vermillion; touring artist SD Arts Coun., Pierre; assoc. prin. harpist SD Symphony, Sioux Falls, 1986—; harp tchr.,faculty mem. Augustana Coll., 1989—; harp tchr. U. Sioux Falls, 1997—; prin. harpist Black Hills Symphony, Rapid City, Fargo-Moorhead Symphony, Fargo, ND, Sioux City Symphony, Iowa, 1985—; harpist NW Iowa Symphony Orch., Sioux Ctr.; harp tchr. Dordt Coll., Northwestern Coll., Orange City. Program annotator SD Symphony, Sioux Falls. Constn. rev. com. Music Tchrs Nat. Assn., Cin.; pres. Sioux Falls Music Tchrs. Assns., SD; state second v.p., first v.p. & pres. SD Music Tchr's Assn.; exec. chair Siouxland Renaissance Assn., 2001—08. Mem.: Music Tchrs. Nat. Assn., World Harp Congress, Am. Harp Soc. Lutheran. Avocations: travel, needlecrafts. Home: 1124 S Spring Ave Sioux Falls SD 57105 Office: Augustana Coll 2001 South Summit Ave Sioux Falls SD 57105

VORIS, HAROLD K, curator; b. Chgo., Oct. 5, 1940; s. Harold C. and Ila K. Voris; m. Helen H. Hahn, Sept. 1, 1967. PhD, U. Chgo., Ill, 1969. Curator Field Mus. Natural History, Chgo., 1984—2008. Home: 229 Stone Dr Brevard NC 28712 Office: Field Mus Natural History 1400 S Lake Shore Dr Chicago IL 60605 Business E-Mail: hvoris@fieldmuseum.org.

VORNBERG, JAMES ALVIN, education educator; b. Corpus Christi, Tex., Nov. 23, 1943; s. Hadley F. and Gladys O. (Smith) V.; children: Scott, Mark. BS in Edn., S.E. Mo. State U., 1965; MEd, U. Ariz., 1969, PhD, 1973. Cert. tchr., prin., supt., Mo., Tex., Ariz. Tchr. Pattonville Schs., St. Ann, Mo., 1965-66; asst. to supt. Am. Sch., São Paulo, Brazil, 1971-73; asst. prof. U. Ariz., Tucson, 1973-74; from. asst. prof. to assoc. prof. Tex. A&M U., Commerce, 1974-81, prof., 1981—, head dept., 2001—06, interim dean coll. edn. and human svcs., 2006—07. Co-author: The New School Leader for 21st Century: The Principal, 2002; co-author, editor: Texas Public School Organization and Administration, 11th edit., 2008. Lt. col. USAFR, 1967-94. Office: Tex A&M U-Commerce Edn Leadership Commerce TX 75429 Office Phone: 903-886-5520.

VORNDRAN-JONES, MACHARRI, lawyer, chemist; d. James R. and Dorothy M. Vorndran; m. Tony R. Jones, May 25, 1985; children: James R. Jones, Mary E. Jones, Chelsea R. Jones. BS, Manchester Coll., North Manchester, Ind., 1982; MS, St. Louis U., 1985; JD, Ind. U., 1992. Bar: Ind. 1993, US Patent Office 1993, US Dist. Ct. (so. dist.) Ind. 1993, US Ct. Appeals (fed. cir.) 2005. Chemist FDA, St. Louis, 1984—85; biochemist Ind. U. Med. Ctr., Indpls., 1985—86; chemist Eli Lilly and Co., 1986—89, patent assoc., 1990—93, patent atty., 1993—97, patent counsel, 1997—. Mem. internat. patent laws com. Intellectual Property Owners, 2004—09. Leader Girl Scouts Am., Brownsburg, Ind., 1998—2009; tchr. religious edn. St. Malachy Ch., 1997—2009. Scholar, Manchester Coll., 1978—82. Mem.: AIPLA (assoc.), ABA (assoc.; chair com. internat. patent laws and treaties 2006—09, chair patent legislation), Ind. Bar Assn. (assoc.; mem. pro bono acitivities 1993—2009), Intellectual Property Owner's (assoc.; com. mem. 2002—09), Chartered Inst. Patent Attorneys (assoc.; fgn. assoc.), Am. Chem. Soc. (assoc.), Girl Scouts of Am. (life), Nat. Honor Soc. Avocations: running, travel. Home: 6620 E CR 350 N Brownsburg IN 46112 Office: Eli Lilly and Co Lilly Corporate Center DC 1104 Indianapolis IN 46285 Office Phone: 317-276-1665. Business E-Mail: m.vorndran@lilly.com.

VOROBIEFF, PETER VLADIMIROVICH, mechanical engineer, researcher; b. Moscow, Oct. 28, 1967; came to the U.S., 1992; MSME and Applied Math., M.V. Lomonosov Moscow State U., 1989; PhDME, Lehigh U., 1996. Rsch. asst. Inst. for High Temperatures, Moscow, 1989-91; interpreter, programmer Assn. Space Explorers, Moscow, 1991-92; tchg. and rsch. asst. Lehigh U., Bethlehem, Pa., 1992-96; rsch. assoc. Los Alamos (N.Mex.) Nat. Lab., 1996-99; asst. prof. mech. engring. U. N.Mex., 1999—2001, assoc. prof., 2001—. Author: Del Squared, 1992 (Galactic Empire award 1992). Grantee Soros Found., 1992. Mem. Am. Phys. Soc. (Gallery of Fluid Motion award 1996, 98). Achievements include development of first particle-image velocimetry (PIV) systems for study of shock-tube flows and two-dimensional turbulence in soap films; co-discoverer of mixing transition in shock-accelerated flows. Office: U New Mexico Dept Mech Engring MSC01 1150 Albuquerque NM 87131-0001 E-mail: kalmoth@unm.edu.

VOROBYEV, ANATOLIY Y., research scientist; m. Zoya F. Vorobyeva, June 25, 1983. PhD in Physics, Kharkov State U., Ukraine, 1985. Sr. scientist Kharkov State U., 1987—97; rsch. assoc. U. Rochester, NY, 2009. Contbr. scientific papers to sci. jours. Achievements include research in laser physics. Office: Univ Rochester 275 Hutchison Rd Inst Optics Rochester NY 14627 Office Phone: 585-275-5561. Business E-Mail: vorobyev@optics.rochester.edu.

VORONINA, VALERIYA, language educator, consultant; d. Vladimir Neiman and Galina Voronina; children: Igor Koznov, Stanislav Pivovarov. Diploma in Fgn. Lang. Tchg., Pyatigorsk State Linguistic U., Russia, 1984; AS in Computer Applications, Flathead Valley CC, Kalispell, Montana, 1999. Cert. LAN 1999, MIS FVCC, 1999. Russian lang. instr. Flathead Valley CC, Kalispell, Mont., 1997—; workforce cons. State Mont. Workforce Ctr., Kalispell, 2004—. Interpreter VVV Transl. Svc., Kalispell, 2007—. Vol. Orphanact Project, Rotary Club. Office: Flathead Valley CC 777 Grandview Dr Kalispell MT 59901 Business E-Mail: vvoronin@fvcc.edu.

VORT, ROBERT A., lawyer; b. Newark, Sept. 24, 1943; s. Saul S. and Ruth J. (Jacobson) Vort; m. Elizabeth Hornstein, June 25, 1968 (div. Nov. 1979); m. Marcelle Greenstein, Nov. 18, 1979 (div. Jan. 1991); children: Joel, Abigail, Rebecca; m. Tina Kruh, Feb. 4, 1996; 1 child, Hannah. BS in Econs., U. Pa., 1965; JD, Columbia U., 1968. Bar: NJ 1968, NY 1970, US Ct. Appeals (2d and 3d cirs. 1975), US Ct. Appeals (9th cir.) 1980, US Ct. Appeals (5th cir.) 1981, US Ct. Appeals (fed. cir.) 1984, US Dist. Ct. NJ 1968, US Dist. Ct. (so. and ea. dists.) NY 1984, US Supreme Ct. 1977. Law clk. to Hon. Theodore I. Botter Superior Ct. of NJ, 1968-69; assoc. Davis & Cox, 1969-71, Israel B. Greene, 1971-73; sole practitioner, 1973-82; ptnr. Balk, Goldberger, Seligsohn, O'Connor & Rhatican, 1982-84, Kirsten, Friedman & Cherin, 1986, Goldberg, Mufson & Spar, West Orange, NJ, 1988-91, Pearce, Vort & Fleisig LLC, Hackensack, 2001—04; ptnr., mem. Vort & Horgen LLC, 2008—; pvt. practice, 1984-85, 87-88; counsel Donald Friedman, West Orange, 1991-92; pvt. practice Tenafly, NJ, 1997—; atty. pvt. practice, 2005—, Vort & Morgen LLC, 2008—. Mem.: ABA (litigation sect., family law sect., legal econs. sect.), Bergen County Bar Assn., NJ State Bar Assn. (appellate practice subcom.). Office: 2 Univ Plz Ste 101 Hackensack NJ 07601 Office Phone: 201-342-9501. Business E-Mail: rvort@vortlaw.com.

VOS, HUBERT DANIEL, investor; b. Paris, Aug. 2, 1933; s. Marius and Aline (Porge) V.; m. Susan Hill, Apr. 18, 1958; children: Wendy, James. BA, Institut d'Etudes Politiques, U. Paris, 1954; M in Pub. Adminstrn., Princeton U., 1956. Internal auditor Internat. Packers Ltd., 1957-61, dir. fin., 1962-64; asst. to contr. Monsanto Co., 1964-66, contr. internat. div., 1966-69; v.p. planning and fin. Smith Kline Corp., 1969-72; sr. v.p. fin. Comml. Credit Co., Balt., 1972-74; sr. v.p. fin. and adminstrn., dir. Norton Simon Inc., NYC, 1974-79; sr. v.p. fin., dir. Becton Dickinson and Co., Paramus, NJ, 1979—2004; pres. Stonington Capital Corp., Santa Barbara, Calif., 1984—. Mem. Santa Barbara Mus. Art, Scholarship Found. of Santa Barbara, La Cumbre Golf and Country Club. Home: 800 Via Hierba Santa Barbara CA 93110-2222 Personal E-mail: hubertvos@aol.com.

VOSBECK, ELIZABETH JUST, retired geneticist; b. Mankato, Minn., May 24, 1925; d. Frederick William and Frances Beneta (Johnson) Just; m. William Frederick Vosbeck, Aug. 2, 1947; children: Lee, William Frederick III, Lynn, Jon Scot, James Stephen. BBA, U. Minn., 1947; MS in Anatomy, George Washington U., Washington, 1965; PhD in Human Genetics, George Washington U., 1975. Mktg. rsch. dir. Mpls. C. of C., 1947—48; embryology lab. instr., lectr., human genetics rschr. George Washington U., Washington, 1965—75; lab. dir. cell chromosome analysis Reprodn. Genetics Ctr., McLean, Va., 1976—87; ret., 1987. Grantee, NIH grantee, 1968—70. Mem.: DAR, Sigma Xi, Beta Gamma Sigma. Republican. Avocations: golf, bridge, genealogy, astrology, ice skating. Home: 7512 Fort Hunt Rd Alexandria VA 22307 E-mail: vosbeck01@aol.com.

VOSBECK, ROBERT RANDALL, architect; b. Mankato, Minn., May 18, 1930; s. William Frederick and Gladys (Anderson) V.; m. Phoebe Macklin, June 21, 1953; children: Gretchen, Randy, Heidi, Macklin. BArch, U. Minn., Mpls., 1954. Various archtl. positions, 1956-62; ptnr. Vosbeck-Vosbeck & Assocs., Alexandria, Va., 1962-66, VVKR Partnership, Alexandria, 1966-79; exec. v.p. VVKR Inc., 1979-82, pres., 1982-88; prin. Vosbeck/DMJM, Washington and Alexandria, Va., 1989-94; v.p. DMJM Arch. and Engring., 1990-94; pvt. practice archtl. cons., 1994—. Mem. Nat. Capital Planning Commn., 1976-81, U.S./USSR Joint Group on Bldg. Design and Constrn., 1974-79; mem. Nat. Park System Adv. Bd., 1984-88. Archtl. works include Pub. Safety Ctr., Alexandria, Va., 1987, Yorktown Visitors Ctr, Va., 1976, Frank Reeves Mcpl. Office Bldg., Washington, 1986, Fed. Bldg., Norfolk, Va., 1979, Jeff Davis Assocs. Office Complex, Arlington, Va., 1991, Westminster Continued Care Retirment Community, Lake Ridge, Va., 1993; author: Design Matters: The Story of VVKR, 2003, A Legacy of Leadership-The Presidents of the American Institute of Architect, 2007. Pres. Alexandria Jaycees, 1960-61; v.p. Va. Jaycees, 1962-63; pres. Alexandria Ch. of Com., 1974-75; bd. dirs. Vail Religious Found., 1995-2008. Engring. officer USMC, 1954-56. Recipient Plaque of Honor, Fedn. Colegios Architects, Republic of Mexico, Alumni Achievement award U. Minn. Coll. Arch., 2001, hon. fellowship Colegios Architects of Spain, Royal Archtl. Inst. Can., Soc. Architects of Mex., AIA Kemper award, 2007, Outstanding Achievement award, U. Minn., 2008; named Outstanding Young Man in Va., 1963, Acadamecian, Internt. Acad. Arch. Fellow AIA (bd. dirs. 1976-78, v.p. 1979-80, pres. 1981), Internat. Union Architects (coun. 1981-87), Nat. Trust Hist. Preservation. Presbyterian. Home and Office: 9064 Ranch River Cir Highlands Ranch CO 80126

VOSBECK, WILLIAM FREDERICK, JR., architect; b. Mankato, Minn., May 13, 1924; s. William Frederick and Gladys (Anderson) V.; m. Elizabeth Just, Aug. 2, 1947; children: Lee, William Frederick III, Lynn, James Stephen. Student, U. Notre Dame, 1943, Cornell U., 1945; BArch, U. Minn., 1947. Ptnr. Vosbeck & Ward, Alexandria, Va., 1957-62, Vosbeck Vosbeck & Assos. (changed to Vosbeck Vosbeck Kendrick Redinger, Architects, Engrs., Planners), Alexandria, 1962-68; chmn. bd. dirs. VVKR, Inc., merged with Suter & Suter, Basel, Switzerland. Bd. dirs. Dominion Resources Va. Power, Crestar Fin. Corp. Prin. works include Nat. Automobile Dealers Assn. Hdqs., Am. Trucking Assn. Hdqs., Woodrow Wilson Rehab. Bldgs. and campus planning. Mem. Gov.'s Com. Employment Handicapped, 1973; trustee Va. Found. Ind. Colls., Va. Mus. Fine Arts, Va. C. of C.; vis. design critique, U. Va. Architecture; mem. Alexandra Hosp. Bd., pres., 1970, Mt. Vernon Presbyn. Ch. With USMCR, 1943—50. Recipient Wash. Acad. Sci. Nat. Capital award for achievement in arch., Nat. Rehab. Assn. citation tech. svcs., Gargoyle award, T. David Fitz-Gibbon Archt. Firm awrd, numerous honor and merit awards Va. Soc. AIA, Va. Mus. Fine Arts, Outstanding Achievement award Engring. News Record, 1977. Fellow AIA (pres. Va. chpt. 1971), Sigma Alpha Epsilon Found., Belle Haven Country Club, Cosmos Club, Rotary. Home: 7512 Fort Hunt Rd Alexandria VA 22307-1924 Office: Vosbeck Assocs 211 N Union St Alexandria VA 22314-2643 Home Phone: 703-765-6117; Office Phone: 703-765-5526. Fax: 703 683-4707.

VOSBURG, BRUCE DAVID, lawyer; b. Omaha, June 17, 1943; s. Noble Perrin and Dena V. (Ferrari) V.; m. Susan Simpson, May 27, 1972; children: Margaret Amy, Wendy Christine, Bruce David. BA, U. Notre Dame, 1965; BSME, 1966; JD, Harvard U., 1969. Bar: Nebr. 1969, Ill. 1970, U.S. Supreme Ct. 1974. Law clk. U.S. Dist. Ct. Nebr., 1969-70; assoc. Kirkland & Ellis, Chgo., 1970-72; ptnr. Fitzgerald & Schorr, Omaha, 1972—, pres. Author: Financing Small Businesses, 1981, Securities Law Practice, 1987, Securities Law-Going Public, 1989, Trade Secret Protection, 1994, Protecting Intellectual Property, 1998, Intellectual Property Law, 2000. Pres. Children's Crisis Ctr., 1984-85, bd. dirs., 1973-84, Childrens Savinds Inst. 1985-86, bd. dirs. 1984-90; pres. Nebr. Tennis Assn., 1976-77, Nebr. Corp. Law Sect., BNA Corp. Br. Svcs., 2006; mem. Leadership Omaha, 1979; chmn. bd. dirs. City of Omaha Parks and Recreation, 1985-92; founding dir. Friends of the Parks, 1988; bd. dirs. Omaha Pub. Libr. Found., 1997—, pres., 1999; bd. dirs. Western Heritage Mus., 1998-2005; exec. com. U.S. Tennis Assn., 2004—06, Rules Com., 2008-, v.p., bd. dirs. Nebr. Appleseed Ctr. Pub. Interest Law, 2007-. Named to, Nebr. Tennis Hall of Fame. Fellow Nebr. Bar Found.; mem. ABA, Nat. Assn. Bond Attys., Nebr. Bar Assn. (chmn. securities com.), Omaha Bar Assn. (exec. coun. 1983-86), Rotary (dir. 1993-98), USTA/Mo. Valley Tennis Assn. (chmn. grievance com. 1978—), Am. Intellectual Property Lawyers Assn., Tau Beta Pi. Republican. Roman Catholic. Office: Ste 400 13220 California St Omaha NE 68154-5228 Office Phone: 402-342-1000.

VOSEVICH, KATHI ANN, writer, editor; b. St. Louis, Oct. 12, 1957; d. William and Catherine V.; m. James Hughes Meredith, Sept. 6, 1986. AB with honors, St. Louis U., 1980, MA, 1983; PhD, U. Denver, 1988. Tchg. fellow St. Louis U., 1980-83, acad. advising fellow, 1983-84; tchg. fellow U. Denver, 1985-87; prof. ESL BNM Talensch., Uden, Netherlands, 1988-91; instr. English, mentor U. Ga., Athens, 1992-94; vis. asst. prof. Colo. Coll., Colorado Springs, 1994; sr. tech. writer and editor Titan Client/Server Techs., Colorado Springs, 1994-96, head documentation, libr., 1996-97; documentation mgr. Beechwood, Colorado Springs, 1997-98, tech. mgr., 1998-99; tech. writer Microsoft, Redmond, Wash., 1999-2000; documentation and process mgr. Sprint, Denver, 2000; practice and group mgr. e-bus. Sprint Corp., Denver, 2000—02, svc. launch mgr. Mobile Computing Svcs., 2002—03, strategic market mgr., 2003—05, strategic alliances mgr., 2005, lead bus. strategist, 2005—06, sr. comm. mgr., 2006—07; pres. The Dufallu Group, Denver, 2007—, CEO, 2007—; asst. prof. & asst. dir. honors program Shorter Coll., 2008—; sr. telecom analyst Faulkner Info., 2008—. Forensic judge USAF Acad., Colo., 1987-88; edn. officer Volkel (The Netherlands) Air Base, 1988-91; instr. English European divsn. U. Md., The Netherlands and Belgium, 1989-91. Author: Customer Care User's Guide, 1996, Interview with Joseph Heller, 1999, Conversations with Joseph Heller in Understanding the Literature of World War II, 1999, Office Update, 1999-2000, Tutoring the Tudors, 2000, Sprint Takes Messaging into the Future, 2003; editor: Subscription Services System Documentation, 1996, Titan Process Documentation, 1994-96; copy editor: Language, Ideas, and American Culture; War, Literature and the Arts; contbr. over 100 electronic texts and articles to profl. jours. Colo. scholar U. Denver, 1985-86, grad. dean scholar, 1988; NEH fellow U. Md., 1994 Mem. MLA, Phi Beta Kappa, Alpha Sigma Nu. Roman Catholic. Avocations: writing, drawing, raising Bernese mountain dogs.

VOSIK, WAYNE GILBERT, lawyer; b. Phila., July 22, 1945; s. Alexander Frank and Dorothy Marie (Yarnell) V.; m. Helga Maria Kuepper, Oct. 31, 1970 (div. Nov. 1995); m. Mary Helen Welch, Mar. 21, 1997; children: Melissa Marie Vosik Osborne, Douglas Wayne, Dorothy Marie Zhen. BA, Temple U., 1967, JD, 1970. Bar: Pa. Asst. dist. atty. Phila. Dist. Atty.'s Office, 1970-72; sec., gen. counsel Ins. Fedn. Pa., Phila., 1972-74; gen. counsel, asst. sec. Acad. Ins. Group, Valley Forge, Pa., 1974-78; pvt. practice Feasterville, Pa., 1979-92; v.p. legal and govt. affairs, asst. sec., dir. human rels. Am. Travellers Corp., Bensalem, Pa., 1992-97; pvt. practice Warrington, Pa., 1997—. Cons. ins. dept. US VI, St. Thomas, 1993; bd. dirs. Greater Delaware Valley Health Underwriters Assn., Phila.; instr. Am. Coll., Brwyn Mawr, Pa., 1998. Mem. ABA, Pa. Bar Assn., Pa. Health Underwriters Assn. (mem. legis. com. 1997-2001), Life and Health Compliance Assn. (edn. com. 1996-, exec. com. 2003-06), Phi Alpha Delta. Republican. Methodist. Avocation: coaching youth soccer. Office: 1800 Street Rd 300 Warrington PA 18976-2566 Home: 55 Great Oak Dr Southampton PA 18966-1209 Office Phone: 215-491-3790. Personal E-mail: wgvosik@aol.com.

VOSK, TED W., lawyer; b. Detroit, Mich., Sept. 6, 1967; s. Stuart Allan Vosk and Susan Helen Stevens; m. Kristine Erin Kelly. BS in Physics and Math., Ea. Mich. U., 1995; Juris Doctorate, Harvard Law Sch., Cambridge, MA, 1996—99. Bar: Mass. 1999, Wash. 2000, US Dist. Ct. (we. dist.) Wash. 2003, US Supreme Ct. 2007. Acting mng. dir. NSF Sci. and Tech. Ctr. on Materials and Devices for Info. Tech. Rsch., Seattle, 2002—03; assoc. Magnuson Lowell, Redmond, Wash., 2003—04; pvt. practice, cons. Bothell, Wash., 2004—; of counsel PJC Law Group, Oreg., 2006—, Callahan Law, Wash., 2007—, Padula & Assoc., Wash., 2007—. V.p. Celestial North, Bothell, 2004—; presenter, spkr. in field. On air performer (radio broadcast) Its Over Your Head; contbr. articles to profl. pubs., chapters to books. Active voter protection program Wash. State Dem. Party, Seattle, 2004, 2006; moderator Ea. Mich. U., Ypsilanti, 2005—05. Recipient Pro Bono Pub. Svc. commendation, Wash. State Bas Assn., 2006, cert. Distinction, Wash. Found. Criminal Justice, 2007; named Wash. Rising Star in Criminal Law, Wash. Law and Politics

Mag., 2005; Leib scholar, Ea. Mich. U. Dept. of Physics, 1992—94, Recognition of Excellence scholar, Ea. Mich. U., 1992—94, Goldwater scholar in math., sci. and engring., Barry Goldwater Excellence in Edn. Found., 1993—95, Sandra J. Lobbestael scholar, Ea. Mich. U. Dept. of Math., 1993—94, Campus Leader scholar, Ea. Mich. U., 1994. Mem.: AAAS, ACLU, Am. Phys. Soc., Nat. Criminal Civil Defense Lawyers, Assn. for Symbolic Logic, Wash. Alliance DUI Trial Lawyers, NW Acad. DUI Def., Wash. Assn. of Criminal Def. Lawyers (mem. legis. com. 2006—), Math. Assn. of Am., Mensa, Sigma Pi Sigma, Phi Kappa Phi. Democrat. Avocations: astronomy, mathematics, scuba diving, skydiving, motorcycling. Office Fax: 425-820-7532. Business E-Mail: tvosk@comcast.net.

VOSS, DAVID ALBERT, mathematics professor; b. Lismore, Minn., Dec. 10, 1943; s. Edward John Voss and Coletta Margaret Loebig; m. Mary Kathleen Walker, June 3, 1967; children: David Edward, Melissa Voss Lapsa, Suzanne Voss U'Ren. PhD, Iowa State U., Ames, 1971. Coord., pre-engring. & architecture studies Western Ill. U., Macomb, 1976—2001, prof. emeritus, math., 2007—. NASA-ASEE summer faculty Langley Rsch. Ctr., Hampton, Va., 1975—77; consulting analyst Boeing Computer Svcs., Tukwila, Wash., 1980—81; NORCUS summer faculty Battelle Pacific NW Labs., Richland, Wash., cons., 1980; vis. prof., math. Rose Hulman Inst. Tech., Terre Haute, Ind., 1999—2000. Contbr. numerous sci. papers to profl. jours. Chmn., mentally retarded Knights Columbus Drive, Macomb, 1974—78. Recipient Faculty Excellence award, Western Ill. U., 1989, 1991, 1994, Summer Stipend award, 1990, Outstanding Tchg. award, 1997, U. Profl. Achievement award, 1998, 2002, Outstanding Rsch. award, 2003; Rsch. Coun. grant, 1976, 1979, 1983—84, 1988. Mem.: Soc. Indsl. and Applied Math. Roman Catholic. Avocations: fishing, jogging. Home: 6505 US Hwy 67 Macomb IL 61455 Business E-Mail: d-voss1@wiu.edu.

VOSS, LINDA L, finance company executive; b. Pigeon, Mich., Dec. 4, 1959; d. Edward and Pearl (Riffel) Ulrich; m. Timothy Voss, Aug. 9, 1980; 1 child, Jason Adam. BS in Mgmt., Oakland U., Rochester, Mich., 1982; MBA in Fin., U. Mich., 1986. Student asst. Oakland U., Rochester, 1981; acct. GMAC, Detroit, 1982-84, fin. analyst, 1985-87, asst. mgr., 1988-89, mgr., 1989-90, credit analysis mgr., 1992-93, fin. planning mgr., 1993-94, asst. treas., 1995-96, fin. dir., 1996-97; mem. fin. staff GM, Detroit, 1990-91; CFO, exec. v.p. Nuvell Fin. Svcs./Credit Corp., Little Rock, 1997—2004; mng. dir., exec. v.p. Nat. Auto Fin., Jacksonville, Fla., 2004—06; CFO, COO GMAC Comml. Fin., NYC, 2006—. Bd. dir. GMAC Comml. Fin., NYC. Author fin. software, 1988. Coach Rochester YMCA, 1988-91; bd. dirs. Luth. HS, Little Rock, 2003; tchr. St. John Sunday Sch., Rochester, 1987-91; mem. Ark. Sales Tax Adv. Com., 2000. GM fellow, 1984. Mem. Fin. Mgmt. Assn., Golden Key, Beta Gamma Sigma. Lutheran. Avocations: antiques, golf, piano. Office: GMAC Comml Fin 1290 Ave of Americas New York NY 10104 Business E-Mail: lvoss@swbell.net.

VOSS, OMER GERALD, farm equipment executive; b. Downs, Kans., Sept. 14, 1916; s. John and Grace (Bohlen) V.; m. Annabelle Katherine Lutz, June 30, 1940; 2 children. AB, Ft. Hays State Coll., Kans., 1937; JD, U. Kans., 1939. Bar: Kans. bar 1939. With Internat. Harvester Co., 1936-79, v.p. farm equipment div., 1962-66, exec. v.p., dir., 1966—, vice chmn., 1977-79. Served with USAAF, 1943-46 Mem.: Comml. Club.

VOSS, REGIS DALE, agronomist, educator; b. Cedar Rapids, Iowa, Jan. 4, 1931; s. Francis Joseph and Mary Valeria (Womichil) V.; m. Margaret Anne Mitchell, Nov. 24, 1956; children: Lori Anne, John Patrick, David James. BS, Iowa State U., 1952, PhD, 1962. cert. profl. agronomist. Agriculturist Tenn. Valley Authority, Muscle Shoals, Ala., 1962-64; prof. Iowa State U., Ames, 1964-99, prof. emeritus, 1999—. Co-contbr. chpt. to: Fertilizer Technology and Use, 1985, Soil Testing and Plant Analysis, 1990; assoc. editor Jour. Prodn. Agr., 1988-92. Pres. FarmHouse Frat. Alumni Assn. Bd., Ames, 1990. 1st lt. USAF, 1952-56, Korea., sec. treas. Iowa State U. Retirees Assn., 2003-2004 Recipient Burlington No. Found. award Iowa State U., 1990, disting. svc. award Iowa State U. Ext., 1996, Iowa Master Farmer Exceptional Svc. award, 1998. Fellow AAAS, Am. Soc. Agronomy (bd. dirs. 1976-78, Agronomic Extension Edn. award 1984, Agronomic Achievement award 1989, Werner L. Nelson award 1992), Soil Sci. Soc. Am. (bd. dirs. 1980-83). Republican. Roman Catholic. Achievements include development of field laboratory for training of crop advisors on diagnosis of crop problems; research on effects of soil amendments on chemical indices and crop yields and economic analysis of crop yield. Business E-Mail: rvoss@iastate.edu.

VOSS, THOMAS R., electric power industry executive; B in Elec. Engring., U. Mo., Rolla, 1969. Registered profl. engr., Mo., Ill. Student engr. Union Electric (now AmerenUE), 1969, asst. engr., engr. to staff engr., supt. and dist. mgr., 1975—87, mgr. distbn. operating, 1988; v.p. region ops. AmerenCIPS Ameren Corp., 1998, sr. v.p. energy delivery/customer svcs., sr. v.p. generation, pres. AmerenEnergy and AmerenEnergy Resources, exec. v.p., COO, 2004—09, pres., CEO AmerenUE, 2006—09, pres., CEO, 2009—. Served in USAF. Office: Ameren Corp One Ameren Plz 1901 Chouteau Ave Saint Louis MO 63103*

VOSSLER, DEBORAH J., mathematics and science educator; b. Portland, Oreg., May 15, 1954; d. Louis Paul and Ruth Ella Varga; m. V. Vic Vossler, June 30, 1972; children: Christopher Isaac, Erin Renee, Sierra Amira. BA in Bus. Adminstrn., U. Wash., 1977; M in Tchg., Wash. State U., 1995. CPA Wash., 1980; profl. educator Wash., 1998. Acct. Rainier Nat. Bank, Seattle, 1977—79; bus. adminstr. Luth. Family Svcs., Portland, Oreg., 1979—81; tchr., adminstr. Maasae Girls Luth. Secondary Sch., Monduli, Tanzania, 1995—98; math, sci. tchr. Frontier Mid. Sch., Vancouver, Wash., 1998—. Math dept. chair Frontier Mid. Sch., Vancouver, Wash., 2003—; leadership tchr. Ptnr. for Reform in Secondary Sci. and Math., Vancouver, 2004—. Vol. libr. Moringe Secondary Sch., Monduli, Tanzania, 1994; chair youth and family ministry Family of Christ Luth. Ch., Vancouver, 2000—06; bd. mem. Interracial Family Assn., Portland; bd. dirs. Orgn. Developmentally Accelerated Youth, Vancouver, 1981—85; leader Camp Fire, Vancouver, 1987—90; asst.leader Boys Scouts of Am., Vancouver, 1990—95; referee Evergreen Soccer League, Vancouver, 1992—94. Mem.: Nat. Sci. Tchrs. Am., Nat. Coun. Tchrs. Math. Lutheran. Avocation: travel. Home: 3106 NE 146 Pl Vancouver WA 98682 Office: Frontier Mid Sch 7600 NE 166 Ave Vancouver WA 98682 Personal E-mail: uwdog@comcast.net. Business E-Mail: dvossler@egreen.wednet.edu.

VOSSOUGHIAN, NADER, architecture educator, curator; b. Newburgh, NY, Mar. 13, 1973; s. Shamsi Raissi and Ahad Vossoughian; m. Saskia Karin Rifkin, June 6, 2008; 1 child, Amalia Rifkin. BA, Swarthmore Coll., Pa., 1995; PhD, Columbia U., NYC, 2004. Lectr. Mus. Modern Art, NYC, 2004—; asst. prof. of architecture NYIT Sch. Architecture and Design, 2005—. Author: (book) Otto Neurath: The Language of the Global Polis; curator (exhbn.) After Neurath: The Global Polis. Office: NYIT Sch Architecture and Design 1855 Broadway 11th Fl New York NY 10023 E-mail: nv1@hotmail.com.

VOTAW, JOHN FREDERICK, SR., educational association administrator, educator; b. Richmond, Va., May 9, 1939; s. Frederick Lee and Katherine (B.) V.; m. Joyce Marie Miller, June 8, 1961; children: Laura, Cynthia, Mary, John Jr. BS, U.S. Mil. Acad., 1961; MA in History, U. Calif., Davis, 1969; grad., U.S. Army Command and Gen Staff Coll., 1970, U.S. Army War Coll., 1985; PhD in History, Temple U., 1991. Commd. 2d lt. U.S. Army, 1961, advanced through grades to lt. col., 1976; comdr. Company C 1st bn. 69th Armor U.S. Army, Hawaii, 1964-65; comdr. Troop A 1st Squadron 11th ACR U.S. Army, South Vietnam, 1966-67, comdr. C&C Squadron 11th ACR Fulda, Germany, 1975-77; asst. prof. history U.S. Mil. Acad., West Point, N.Y., 1970-73, asst. dean for plans and programs, 1980-81, asst. prof., 1981-82; dep. dir. U.S. Army Mil. History Inst., Carlisle Barracks, Pa., 1983-86; ret. U.S. Army, 1986; dir. First Divsn. Mus., Wheaton, 1986—2005; exec. dir. Cantigny First Divsn. Found., Wheaton, 1991—2005, exec. dir. emeritus, 2005—. Adj. asst. prof. history Dominican U. (formerly Rosary Coll.), River Forest, Ill., 1991-98, adj. assoc. prof. history, 1998—; dir. Col. Robt. R. McCormick Rsch. Ctr., Wheaton, 1991-2002; series editor Cantigny Mil. History Series, 1993-2005. Contbg. author: The D-Day Encyclopedia, 1993, The Encyclopedia of American Wars - The First World War, 1994, The European Powers in the First World War: An Encyclopedia, 1996, Encyclopedia of the Vietnam War, 3 vols., 1998, A Guide to the Study and Use of Military History, 1979, History in Dispute, vol. 5, Encyclopedia of American Military History, 3 vols., 2003, The American Expeditionary Forces in WWI, 2005; contbr. articles to profl. jours. Mem. adv. com. Ctr. for the Study of Force and Diplomacy, Temple U., 1996—. Decorated Legion of Merit, Bronze Star with "V" device, Purple Heart (3 awards) and others. Mem. Am. Hist. Assn., Orgn. Am. Historians, Soc. for Mil. History (trustee 2001—), U.S. Naval Inst. (life), U.S. Army War Coll. Alumni Assn. (life), Ret. Officers Assn. (life), Disabled Am. Vets., Assn. Grads. U.S. Mil. Acad., U. Calif. Davis Alumni Assn. (life), Am. Vets. (life), Am. Legion (life), Kiwanis (Wheaton club 1986—, pres. 1991-92), Phi Alpha Theta, Phi Kappa Phi (life). Avocations: reading, writing, classical music, golf. Personal E-mail: allons667@bigfoot.com.

VOTO-BERNALES, JORGE, ambassador; b. Lima, Peru, Jan. 19, 1944; married; 3 children. B in Econs., M in Internat. Rels. 3rd sec. gen. divsn. planning Peruvian Ministry Fgn. Affairs, 1971, chief of cabinet to Sec. Gen. Fgn. Affairs, 1980, positions in Ecuador, Soviet Union, Germany, Spain, Austria and Argentina, dir. Ams. gen. divsn. polit. affairs, 1987—90, dir.-gen. planning, 1993, dir.-gen. bilateral polit. affairs, 1994—95, vice-min., sec. gen. fgn. affairs, 1995—97, permanent rep. to European Office of UN Geneva, 1997—2004, amb., permanent rep. to UN NYC, 2006—; non-resident permanent rep. UN Environment Programme and UN Human Settlements Programme, Nairobi, Kenya, 1998—2004; v.p. Human Rights Commn., Geneva; chmn. agr. com. World Trade Orgn., Geneva; exec. sec. Fund for Peace and Devel. Peru-Ecuador, 2004—06. Office: Permanent Mission of Peru to UN 820 2nd Ave Fl 16 New York NY 10017 Office Phone: 212-687-3336. Office Fax: 212-972-6975. E-mail: misionperu@aol.com.

VOWLES, RICHARD BECKMAN, literature educator; b. Fargo, ND, Oct. 5, 1917; s. Guy Richard and Ella (Beckman) V.; m. Ellen Noah Hudson, Aug. 1, 1942 (div. 1969); children: Elizabeth Ellen, Richard Hudson. BS, Davidson Coll., 1938; postgrad., U. N.C., 1938—39, U. Stockholm, 1939—40; MA, Yale U., 1942, PhD, 1950. Engr. Hercules Powder Co., Wilmington, Chattanooga, 1941—43; chemist Rohm & Haas, Knoxville, Tenn., 1943—44; econ. cons. War Dept., 1944; Am. vice consul Gothenburg, Sweden, 1945—46; asst. prof. English Southwestern U., Memphis, 1948—50, Queens U., NYC, 1950—51; assoc. prof. English U. Fla., 1951—60; prof. Scandinavian and comparative lit. U. Wis., Madison, 1960—85, prof. emeritus, 1985—, chmn. comparative lit., 1962—63, 1964—67, 1971—72, chmn. Scandinavian studies, 1977—80. Am. specialist in Scandinavia Dept. State, 1963; vis. prof. NYU, 1964, U. Helsinki, Finland, 1968, Stockholm, 1969; lectr., Sydney, Australia, 1975, Paris, 1975; master ceremonies Santa Fe Scandinavian Film Festival, 1984 Editor: Eternal Smile, 1954, Dramatic Theory, 1956, Comparatists at Work, 1968; Adv. editor: Nordic Council Series, 1965-70, Herder Ency. of World Lit; contbr. articles to profl. jours. Am.-Scandinavian Found. fellow, Stockholm, 1939-40, Lassen fellow Am. Scandinavian Found., 1986, Fulbright fellow Copenhagen, 1955-56, Strindberg fellow Stockholm, 1973, Norwegian Govt. fellow, 1978; recipient Rsch. award Swedish govt., 1978. Mem. Modern Lang. Assn., Soc. Advancement Scandinavian Study (mem. exec. com.), Internat. Comparative Lit. Assn., Am. Comparative Lit. Assn. (adv. bd.), Strindberg Soc., Phi Beta Kappa. Home: 345 W Main St #8 Madison WI 53703

VOYLES, C. ROBERT, electronics executive; BSEE, post grad., S.D. Sch. Mines and Tech. Accredited sr. exec. cons. Inst. Ind. Bus., 2005. Mgr. Magnetic Peripherals, Inc.; gen. mgr. Dakota Mountain Dragway, 1978—98; mgr. engring. svcs. SCI Sys., Inc., 1987—94; v.p and founder Electronics Assembly Resource Network, Inc., 1994—. Address: 5607 Pioneer Cir Rapid City SD 57702

VOYLES, KYLE, research scientist; b. Dinuba, Calif., Dec. 8, 1972; s. Darrell Leland and Jean N. Voyles; m. Marai Carmen Jordan, Mar. 18, 2002; 1 child, Kendra. BS in Electronics, North East Tex. State U., 1993. Electrician Ty Water Cons., Mt. Pieasant, 1991—93; Karate instr. NETCC, Mt. Pieasant, 1993—94; compaction Inspector Swtesting, 1996—97; floor person WAI-MART, 1997—2001; rschr. CAUESP NPS-Blm, 2001—, rschr., 1996—. CAUE cons. NPS, Elmal Pais, 2008; CAUE coord. Blm, 2001—, CAUE dir., 2001—. Contbr. articles to profl. jours. Mem.: Color Country Grotto, NSS (Conservatin 2007). Avocations: scuba diving, martial arts, hiking.

VOYLES, ROBB LAWRENCE, lawyer; b. Toledo, May 26, 1957; s. Lawrence E. and Marilyn L. (McQuade) V.; m. Loretta F. Herbert, July 19, 1980; children: Lindsay Ann, Erin Lynn. BBA in Acctg. summa cum laude, U. Dayton, 1979; JD magna cum laude, U. Mich., 1982. Bar: Tex. 1982, US Dist. Ct. (no. dist.) Tex. 1982, US Ct. Appeals (5th cir.) 1983, US Dist. Ct. (we. dist.) Tex. 1986, US Dist. Ct. (no. dist.) Calif. 1989. Assoc. Rain, Harrell, Emery, Young & Doke, Dallas, 1982-87, Baker Botts LLP, Dallas, 1987-88, ptnr., litigation dept. Austin, Tex., 1989—, ptnr. in charge Austin office, 1994—2005, mem. exec. com., 2000—, chair firm-wide litig. dept., 2005—. Editor U. Mich. Law Rev., 1981-82. Bd. dir. & legal counsel Greater Austin C. of C. Named Best Lawyer in Am., 2004—07; named a Texas Super Lawyer, Texas Monthly mag. & Law & Politics mag., 2003—04, 2006—07; named one of Best of Bus. & Corp. Law, Austin Bus. Jour., 2004. Fellow Tex. Bar Found., Dallas Bar Found., Travis County Bar Found.; mem. ABA (profl. liability com. litig. sect.), State Bar of Tex., Dallas Bar Assn., Dallas Young Lawyers Assn., Travis County Bar Assn., Order of Coif, Alpha Sigma Tau. Roman Catholic. Office: Baker Botts LLP Ste 600 2001 Ross Ave Dallas TX 75201 Home: 3831 Turtle Creek Blvd #19E Dallas TX 75219 Office Phone: 512-322-2626. Office Fax: 512-322-8326. Business E-Mail: robb.voyles@bakerbotts.com.

VOYNICK, JOHN S., JR., lawyer; BA in English, Rutgers U., 1975. Bar: NJ 1980, US Dist. Ct. NJ 1980, US Dist. Ct. (ea. and so. dists.) NY 1981, cert.: Supreme Ct. NJ (civil trial atty.) 1987. Assoc. law clk. Podvey & Sachs, Newark, 1978—83; assoc. Carpenter, Bennett & Morrissey, Newark, 1983—86; ptnr. Renda & Voynick, Cedar Grove, NJ, 1986—. Arbitrator Superior Ct. Essex County, 1987—. Officer, trustee Wynona's House. Named Superlawyer, NJ Monthly Mag., 2005—09; scholar, Essex County Bar Fund. Mem.: ABA, Trial Attys. NJ, Assn. Trial Lawyers Am. (bd. govs. 1997—), Trial Attys. NY, NJ State Bar Assn., Essex County Bar Assn. (arbitrator 1987—, mem. pres.' coun. 1999—2000, jud. and prosecutorial appointments com. 2000—09, chmn. best practices com. 2001, civil practices com. 2001—02, bd. trustees 2001—07, chair lawyer referral svc. 2001—), ATLA, Am. Bd. Trial Advocates (bd. govs. 1997—). Office: Renda & Voynick 912 Pompton Ave Ste B2 Cedar Grove NJ 07009 Business E-Mail: jsvesq@aol.com.

VOYTEK, MARY SULLIVAN, sculptor; b. Memphis, July 26, 1957; d. Herbert Dean and Mary Josphine Sullivan; m. Lawrence Voytek, June 30, 1986; children: Alexa, Zachary. BFA, Calif. Coll. of the Arts, Oakland, Calif., 1980; MFA, R.I. Sch. of Design, Providence, RI, 1982. Vis. prof. R.I. Sch. of Design, Providence, 1980—81, Brown Univ., Providence, 1981—82; adj. prof. Fla. Gulf Coast Univ., Ft. Myers, Fla., 2000—04, asst. prof., 2004—. Pvt. cons. Fla. Gulf Coast Univ., Ft. Myers, Fla., 2000—01. Pub. commns., Dream to Connect, 2004 (Fla. Arts in Pub. Pl. award), exhibitions include TVS Internat., Atlanta, Ga., 2000, Atla. Internat. Mus. Art and Design, 2000, Gallery Camino Real, Gallery Ctr., Boca Raton, Fla., 2004, Zenith Gallery, Washington, 2007, H.W. Gallery, Naples, Fla., 2007, Union Sq. Gallery, San Francisco, 2007, numerous others, Represented in permanent collections Hsinchu Mus. Art, Taiwan, Sherman Gallery, Chgo., R.I. Sch. Design Mus., numerous others. Art in pub. places bd. City of Ft. Myers, Fla., 2004—; bd. mem. Fla. Arts, Ft. Myers, Fla., 2002—07. Mem.: DAR, Internat. Sculptors Ctr. Avocations: hiking, travel. Office Phone: 239-590-7241.

VOZNESENSKY, NIKOLAY BORIS, mechanical engineering educator; b. St. Petersburg, Russia, Aug. 21, 1952; s. Boris Pavel and Margarita Voznesensky; m. Tatiana Dobrovidova, June 30, 1978; children: Natalya, Elena, Maria. Degree in mech. engring., St. Petersburg State Inst. Fine Mechanics and Optics, 1975; PhD, St. Petersburg Inst. Fine Mechanics and Optics, 1983; DSc, St. Petersburg State Inst. Fine Mechanics and Optics, 2000. Engr. St. Petersburg State Inst. Fine Mechanics and Optics, 1975—83, sr. scientist, 1983—88, asst. prof., 1988—2000, prof., 2000—07; CEO VTT Optik Ltd., Vaerska, Poelvamaa, Estonia, 2002—. Cons. Carl Zeiss, Oberkochen, Baden-Wuertemberg, Germany, 2000—02, LG Electronics Inc., Pyungtaek, 2000—06; cons. Inst. Physics Microstructures Russian Acad. Scis., Nizhny Novgorod, 2004—06; cons. SYNOPSYS GmbH, Munich, 2006—. Editor: Principles of Optics; contbr. articles to profl. jours. Mem. Estonian Cultural Soc., St. Petersburg, 2003, Estonian Flag Soc., Tartu, 2004. Mem.: Internat. Soc. Optical Engrs. (assoc.). Lutheran. Achievements include patents for point diffraction interferometer; design, analysis and testing of optics for EUV lithography; research in method of far-field evaluation of subwavelength optical scanning probes; development of theory and fast algorithms for light diffraction modelling; first to created laboratory and industrial sample of point diffraction interferomer for testing reference elements of traditional interferometers and EUV mirrors; design of computer-aided techniques for analyzing and adjusting projection optical systems for photolithography; development of method and alogrithm of aberration measurements and processing for optical systems for photolithography. Avocations: painting, bicycling, medieval history, languages, music. Office: VTT Optik Ltd Riia 185A 51014 Tartu Estonia Office Fax: 372-7993340. Personal E-mail: vttoptikvnb@hot.ee. Business E-Mail: nikolayv@synopsys.com.

VOZZELLA, THOMAS R., musician, conductor, composer, organist; b. Boston, July 5, 1963; m. Cathy L Knight, July 1, 1989; 1 child, Ashley Nicole. BS, Ea. Nazarene Coll., 1986; MusM, U. La., 1996; D of Musical Arts, U. SC., 2003. Cert. in choral conducting Royal Sch. Ch. Music, Croydon, Eng., 1985. Music dir., organist various churches in the Boston and Kansas City areas, 1978—92; dir. music, organist First United Meth. Ch., El Dorado, Ark., 1993—97, Trinity United Meth. Ch., Sumter, SC, 2000—03, First Meth. Ch., Midland, Tex., 2006—; asst. prof. music Free Will Bapt. Coll., Nashville, 1997—2000, U. West Ala., Livingston, 2003—04; asst. prof. music, dept. chair Sterling Coll., Kans., 2004—05. Musician: (songs) Augsburg Fortress, Selah, Abingdon, Alliance and Canticanova. Grantee Bulgarian Sacred Music Rsch. Grant, U. West Ala., 2004. Mem.: Conductors Guild, Am. Choral Directors Assn., Am. Guild Organists. Personal E-mail: vozzella.music@hotmail.com.

VRABEL, JOSEPH P., lawyer; b. Adams, Mass., Feb. 8, 1948; BA, Lake Forest Coll., Ill., 1970; JD, Boston Coll., 1977; Mediator Cert., Harvard U., 1997. Bar: Mass., N.Y. Shareholder atty. Cope & Wilson, PC, 1979—84; sr. ptnr. Bowditch & Dewey, 1984—2001; v.p., gen. counsel Capital Risk Mgmt., Framingham, Mass., 2001—. Adj. prof. bus. law grad.-MBA program Babson Coll. Founder Crossroads Cmty. Found.; trustee Framingham State Coll.; treas., trustee Longfellow's Wayside Inn; former chmn. United Way MetroWest; trustee MCLE; dir. John J. Tobin Found., Maynard Food Pantry, Inc.; steering com. Equal Justice Coalition; former regional dir. Am. Cancer Soc.; mem. Maynard Town Counsel. Mem.: ABA, Worcester County Bar Assn., South Middlesex County Bar Assn., Boston Bar Assn., N.Y. Bar Assn., New Eng. Bar Assn. (bd. dirs.), Mass. Bar Assn. (chmn. bldg. and ops. com. 1988—, budget and fin. com. 1992—, exec. com. 1995—, governance task force 1996—98, sec. 1998—99, dues restructuring task force 1999—2000, v.p. 1999—2000, treas. 2000—01, by-law com. 2001—02, pres.-elect 2001—02, pres. 2002—03). Office: Capital Risk Mgmt 1661 Worcester Rd Ste 303 Framingham MA 01701

VRABLIK, EDWARD ROBERT, import/export company executive; b. Chgo., June 8, 1932; s. Steven Martin and Meri (Korbel) V.; m. Bernice G. Germer, Jan. 25, 1958; children: Edward Robert, II, Scott S. BS in Chem. Engring, Northwestern U., 1956; MBA, U. Chgo., 1961; postgrad., MIT, 1970. Registered profl. engr., Ill. Dir. indsl. mktg. Eimco Corp., 1956-61; dir. indsl. mktg. and planning Swift & Co., Chgo., 1961-68; v.p., gen. mgr. Swift Chem. Co., Chgo., 1968-73; pres., chief exec. officer Estech Gen. Chems. Corp., Chgo., 1973-86; pres. Kare Internat. Inc., Chgo., 1986—. Pres. Julius and Assocs., Inc., Kare Internat., Inc.; bd dirs. Potash Phosphate Inst., Consol. Fertilizers, Ltd.; mem. mgmt. com. Esmark Inc., Korbel, Inc., Mister Lawn Care, Inc. Author; patentee in field. Bd. dirs., v.p. Northwestern U. Tech. Inst.; trustee Future Farmers Am. Mem. Internat. Superphosphate Mfrs. Assn. (dir.), Am. Inst. Chem. Engrs., Fertilizer Inst. (dir.) Clubs: Butler Nat. (Oak Brook, Ill.). Lutheran. Home: 631 Thompsons Way Palatine IL 60067-4653 Office: 141 W Jackson Blvd Chicago IL 60604-2992 Home Phone: 847-358-2265; Office Phone: 847-358-4948. Personal E-mail: vrabliker@aol.com.

VRAJITORU, DANA, engineering educator; b. Iasi, Romania, Feb. 1, 1969; d. Dan Alexandru and Ana Vrajitoru. DSc, U. Neuchatel, Switzerland, 1997. Postdoc Ecole Poly. Federale Lausanne, Lausanne, Switzerland, 1998—2000; assoc. prof. computer sci. Ind. U. South Bend, 2001—. Contbr. articles. Mem. program com. World Congress Computer Sci. Info. Engring., LA, 2008—. Faculty Rsch. grant, Ind. U. South Bend, 2004. Mem.: Assn. for Computer Machinery. Office: Ind Univ South Bend 1700 Mishawaka Ave South Bend IN 46634

VRANISH, JOHN MICHAEL, electrical engineer, researcher; b. Brainerd, Minn., May 20, 1939; s. John Paul and Louise Ann (Jenkins) V.; m. Dorothy Jean Ward, June 27, 1980; children: John Christopher, Anthony Brian. BS, U.S. Mil. Acad., 1962; MSEE, George Washington U., 1973. Staff engr. robotics rsch. Naval Surface Weapons Ctr., White Oak, Silver Spring, Md., 1971-82, Nat. Bur. Standards, Gaithersburg, Md., 1982-86; staff engr. space mechanisms and space robotics Goddard Space Flight Ctr., Greenbelt, Md., 1986—2006, emeritus, 2006—; pres. Vranish Innovative Techs., 2006—. Mem. tech. task force Office of Sec. Def., 1981-82, fact finding com., 1981; cons. U.S. Congress, 1983, 87, 96; spkr. in field. Contbr. articles to profl. pubs. Capt. US Army, 1962—70. Recipient Bose award, Design News Mag., 1997, 100 award, R&D Mag., 1997, 2006, Exceptional Engring. Achievement medal, NASA, Exceptional Achievement Tech. medal, Exceptional Svc. medal; grantee, Productivity Enhancement Program, Dept. of Defense, 1979. Mem. Robotics Internat. of Soc. Mfg. Engrs. (charter, award 1981). Achievements include development of actuator upgrade designee, F-35 joint strike fighter; invention of capaciflector, driven ground, virtual feel 3-D sprags, carrier-less anti-backlash transmission, robotic deriveter, magnetostrictive direct drive rotary motor, spin bearings, continuously variable planetary transmission, gear bearings, flexure wedges, stepping flexures; 3-D interactive display, screw locking clickless wrench, conformal robot gripper; world record holder in single stage gear reduction and for precision non-contact robotic assembly in space; patents pending in field. Avocations: sports, physical fitness, military history. Home and Office: Vranish Innovative Techs 900 Truro Ln Crofton MD 21114-1207 Office Phone: 410-721-2650. Personal E-mail: jmvranish@comcast.net.

VRATIL, JOHN LOGAN, state legislator; b. Great Bend, Kans., Oct. 28, 1945; s. Frank and Althea; m. Teresa Vratil; 4 children. BS in Edn., U. Kans., 1967; postgrad., U. Southampton, Eng., 1967-68; JD, Kans. U. Sch. law, 1971; postgrad., U. Exeter, Eng., 1972. Bar: Kans. 1971, US Dist. Ct. Kans. 1971, US Ct. Appeals (10th and 8th cirs.) 1975, US Supreme Ct. 2005. Atty. Lathrop & Gage, Overland Park, Kans., 1983—; mem. Dist. 11 Kans. State Senate, Kans., 1998—, v.p. Kans., 2003—; atty. Contbr. articles to profl. jours. Mem. recreation commn. Prairie Village, 1982-83, mem. planning commn., 1983-84; v.p. Usher Mansion Hist. Found., Lawrence, Kans., 1990—. Fellow ABA Found.; mem. ABA, Kans. Bar Assn. (pres. 1995-96, gov. 1988-97), Kans. Bar Found. (trustee 1996-2002), Johnson County Bar Assn. (pres. 1979), Kans. Sch. Attys. Assn. (pres. 1985), Overland Park C. of C. (bd. dirs. 1985-94, pres. 1988). Republican. Protestant. Avocations: sports, hunting, reading. Home: 9534 Lee Blvd Leawood KS 66206-2261 Office: Lathrop & Gage 10851 Mastin Blvd Ste 1000 Overland Park KS 66210-2007 also: Capitol Office 300 SW 10th St Rm 281-E Topeka KS 66612 Office Phone: 913-451-5100. Business E-Mail: jvratil@lathropgage.com, John.Vratil@senate.ks.gov.

VRATIL, KATHRYN HOEFER, federal judge; b. Manhattan, Kans., 1949; BA, U. Kans., 1971, JD, 1975; postgrad., Exeter U., 1971-72. Bar: Kans. 1975, Mo. 1978, U.S. Supreme Ct., 1995. Law clk. U.S. Dist. Ct., Kansas City, Kans., 1975-78; assoc. Lathrop Koontz & Norquist, Kansas City, Mo., 1978-83; ptnr. Lathrop & Norquist, Kansas City, 1984-92; judge City of Prairie Village, Kans., 1990-92, US Dist. Ct. Kans, 1992—. Bd. dirs. Kans. Legal Bd. Svcs., 1991-92; mem. com.on admistrv. office Jud. Conf. of the U.S., 2000-06; mem. jud. coun. U.S. Ct. Appeals for the Tenth Cir., 2002-04; mem. dist. judge adv. com. Fed. Jud. Ctr., 2003—, chair, 2006—; mem. U.S. Jud. Panel on Multi Dist. Litigation, 2004—. Bd. editors Kans. Law Rev., 1974-75, Jour. Kans. Bar Assn., 1992-94. Mem. nat. adv. bd. U. Kans. Ctr. for Environ. Edn. and Tng., 1993-95. Fellow Kans. Bar Found., Am. Bar Found.; mem. ABA (editl. bd. Judges Jour. 1996-98), Am. Judicature Soc., Nat. Assn. Judges, Fed. Judges Assn., Kans. Bar Assn. (mem. bench bar com., 2000—), Mo. Bar Assn., Kansas City Met. Area Bar Assn., Johnson County Bar Assn., Assn. Women Judges, Lawyers Assn. Kansas City, Kans. State Hist. Soc., U. Kans. Law Soc. (bd. govs. 1978-81, 2005—), Kans. U. Alumni Assn. (mem. Kansas City chpt. alumni bd. 1990-92, nat. bd. dirs. 1991-96, bd. govs. Adams Alumni Ctr. 1992-95), Native Sons and Daus of Kans. (life), Jr. League Wyandotte and Johnson Counties, Order of Coif, Kans. Inn of Ct. (master 1993—, pres. 1999-2000), Phi Kappa Phi. Republican. Presbyterian. Office: Robert J Dole US Courthouse Ste 511 500 State Ave Kansas City KS 66101-2403 Office Phone: 913-551-6550.

VREDENBURGH, JAMES JOSEPH, medical educator; b. Mt. Kisco, NY, Feb. 17, 1957; BA in Psychology, U. Va., Charlottesville, 1979; MD, U. Vt., 1983. Lic. Conn., NH, Vt., NC, cert. Med. Oncology, Hematology. Resident St. Francis Hosp. and Med. Ctr., Hartford, Conn., 1983—86; fellow Dartmouth-Hitchcock Med. Ctr., Hanover, NH, 1986—90; instr., medicine Dartmouth Med. Sch., Hanover, NH, 1986—90, assoc. medicine, 1990; asst. prof. Duke U. Med. Ctr., Durham, NC, 1990—96, assoc. prof. medicine, dept. medicine, dept. surgery, divsn. neurosurgery, 1996—2003, prof. medicine, 2003—, med. dir., adult clin. services. Med. dir. stem cell cryopreservation lab., 1990—2002; med. dir. Hillandale Clin. Lab., 1992—2002; interim dir. bone marrow transplant program, 1995; mem. cancer protocol review com., 1991—2001, 2004—; med. dir., pharmacology lab., 1995—; mem. clin. microbiology users com., 1998—; mem. cancer ctr. users exec. com., 2000—; med. dir. clin. ops., 2005—. Contbr. several articles to profl. jours.; refereed journals. Mem.: Soc. Neuro-Oncology, Internat. Soc. for Hematotherapy and Graft Engring., Am. Soc. Blood & Marrow Transplantation, Am. Soc. Hematology, Am. Soc. Clin. Oncology, Phi Beta Kappa, Sigma Xi, Alpha Omega Alpha. Office: Duke U Med Ctr DUMC Box 3624 Durham NC 27710 Office Phone: 919-668-2993. Office Fax: 919-684-6674. Business E-Mail: vrede001@mc.duke.edu.*

VREDEVOE, DONNA LOU, academic administrator, microbiologist, educator, biomedical researcher; BA in Bacteriology, UCLA, 1959, PhD in Microbiology, 1963. USPHS postdoctoral fellow Stanford (Calif.) U., 1963—64; instr. bacteriology UCLA, 1963, postgrad. rsch. immunologist dept. surgery Ctr. Health Scis., 1964-65, asst. rsch. immunologist dept. surgery Ctr. Health Scis., 1964-67, asst. prof. Sch. Nursing, Ctr. Health Scis., 1967-70, assoc. prof., 1970-76; prof. Sch. Nursing, Ctr. Health Scis., 1976—, assoc. dean Sch. Nursing, 1976-78, acting assoc. dean Sch. Nursing, 1985-86, asst. dir. space planning Cancer Ctr., 1976-78, dir. space planning, 1978-90, cons. to lab. nuc. medicine and radiation biology, 1967-80, acting dean Sch. Nursing, 1995-96. Chair acad. senate UCLA, 1999—2000, vice chancellor acad. pers., 2001—06, spl. asst. to chancellor, 2006—07, prof., vice chancellor emerita, 2006—. Contbr. articles to profl. pubs. Postdoctoral fellow USPHS, 1963-64; Mabel Wilson Richards scholar UCLA, 1960-61; rsch. grantee Am. Cancer Soc., Calif. Inst. Cancer Rsch., Calif. divsn. Am. Cancer Soc., NIH, USPHS, Am. Nurses Found., Cancer Rsch. Coordinating Com. U. Calif., Dept. Energy, UCLA. Mem Am. Soc. Microbiology, Am. Assn. Immunologists, Am. Assn. Cancer Rsch., Nat. League Nursing (2d v.p. 1979-81), Sigma Xi, Alpha Gamma Sigma, Sigma Theta Tau (nat. hon. mem.). Office: UCLA Sch Nursing 700 Tiverton Ave 3-232 Factor Bldg Box 951702 Los Angeles CA 90095-1702

VREELAND, RUSSELL GLENN, senior tax manager, accountant, consultant; b. Princeton, NJ, Apr. 27, 1960; s. Glenn Earl and Barbara Ann (Jungels) Vreeland; m. Traci Ann Harbold, Dec. 17, 1988 (div. 2006); children: Hans Russell, Anna Patricia. BSBA, Bloomsburg U., Pa., 1982. CPA Pa., Md. Sr. acct. Louis H. Linowitz & Co., Trenton, N.J., 1982-85; tax supr. Horty & Horty, P.A., Wilmington, Del., 1985-87; tax mgr. Stewart Waddell & Co. P.A., Columbia, Md., 1988-92; assoc. in charge of tax Hillman & Glorioso, P.L.L.C., Vienna, Va., 1993-98; ptnr. Vreeland & Assocs., LLC, 1998—2006, Vreeland & Co., Ltd., 2001—06; sr. tax mgr. Clifton Gunderson, LLP, 2006—. Spkr. in field. Author: Foreign Sales Corporations - A Primer, 1992, Exporting - Are You Ready?, 1993; contbr. articles to profl. jours. Mem. Sykesville Econ. Devel. Commn., Md., 1998—2001; chair Sykesville Budget Com., 2000—07, Sykesville Capital Improvement Com., 2000—07; chmn. fin. com. Woodland Village Condominium Assn., 1989—90; mem. Sykesville Town Coun., 2000—07, pres., 2002—05; mem. Sykesville Hist. Dist. Commn., 2002—07; com. chair Sykesville Centennial, 2003—04; co-chair fin. com. Messiah Luth. Ch., 2000—06. Mem.: AICPA (adv. group mem. partnership taxation com. 1997—98, apptd. mem.partnership taxation com. 1998—99, tax divsn. mem., S. Corp. Tech. Resource Panel 2007—, accredited bus. valuations), Md. Assn. CPAs (mem. fed. taxation com. 1990—91). Republican. Lutheran. Office Phone: 301-931-2050.

VRENTAS, JAMES SPIRO, chemical engineering professor; b. Danville, Ill., Apr. 14, 1936; s. Spiro and Evanthia (Guintonis) V.; m. Christine Mary Jarzebski, June 8, 1975; children: Catherine Eva, Jennifer Marie. BS, U. Ill., 1958; MSChE, U. Del., 1961, PhD, 1963. Rsch. engr. Dow Chem. Co., Midland, Mich., 1963-69, sr. rsch. engr., 1969-72; asst. prof. Ill. Inst. Tech., Chgo., 1972-73, assoc. prof., 1973-76, prof., 1976-80, Pa. State U., University Park, 1980-85, Dow prof., 1985—. Contbr. articles to profl. jours. Recipient William H. Walker Nat. Rsch. award AIChE, 1981, Charles Stein Materials Rsch. award, 1989. Mem. AIChE. Greek Orthodox. Achievements include development of theories for diffusion, rheology, and sorption in polymers. Home: 1705 Princeton Dr State College PA 16803-3260 Office: Pa State U 119 Fenske Lab University Park PA 16802-4400 Office Phone: 814-863-4808. Business E-Mail: jsv1@psu.edu.

VRONTIS, DEMETRIS, dean, marketing professor; b. Nicosia, Cyprus, Nov. 27, 1972; s. Andreas Vrontis and Theotimi Vronti; m. Peri Vronti; children: Angelos D., Andreas D. BSc in Bus. with honors, Manchester Met. U., Eng., 1997, degree in Edn., 2002, PhD, 2003; MBA with distinction, U. Hull, Eng., 2000. Cert. virtual mgmt. Henley Mgmt. Coll., Eng., 2004, mktg. cons. Chartered Assn. Bus. Adminstrs., Can., 2006, bus. cons. Chartered Assn. Bus. Adminstrs., Can., 2007, chartered marketer Chartered Inst. Marketing, Eng., 2008. Sr. lectr. Sch. Bus. Manchester Met. U., 1997—2003; head mktg. dept. Sch. Bus. Intercollege, Nicosia, 2004—05, assoc. dean Sch. Bus., 2005—06, dean Sch. Bus., 2006—. Vis. faculty Bus. Sch., U. Reading, 2004—; external examiner Nottingham Trent U., England, 2000—; rsch. fellow Leeds Met. U., 2003—; vis. prof. Voralberg U. Applied Scis., Austria, 2000—; vis. rsch. fellow Manchester Met. U., 2006—; external examiner Cape Peninsula U. Tech., Cape Town, South Africa; presenter in field; founder, exec. pres. EuroMed Rsch. Bus. Inst.; mkg. prof. Sch. Bus., U. Nicosia; founder & chmn. EuroMed Acad. Bus.; founder EuroMed Rsch. Ctr. Co-author: Cases for the International Marketing Reader, 1999, An International Marketing Reader, 1999, STRATICS: Strategy and Tactics in Marketing, 2002, Marketing Planning: Analysis, Tactics and Strategy, 2003, Basic Selling Skills, 2006, Global Marketing and Export Management, 2006, Retail Fashion Marketing, The Complete Strategic Guide, 2006, Marketing and Retailing Strategy, 2006; founder, editor EuroMed Jour. Bus., 2004—, country editor Jour. Global Bus. Advancement, Cyprus, 2006—, cons. editor Jour. Internat. Bus. and Entrepreneurship Devel., 2006—, mem. editl bd. various acad. and sci. jours., guest editor various jours.; contbr. articles to profl. and acad. jours., chapters to books; author: (book) Stratgic Marketing and Retail Thought, 2008, Wine Worship, 2009, Wine Knowledge and Wine Testing Technique. Recipient 1st World Best Paper award, Internat. Fedn. Wine & Spirits Journalists & Writken, Universal award, ABI, 2008, Gt. Minds of 1st Century award, 2008; named European dean, Acad. Global Bus. Advancement, 2007, Outstanding Intellectual, Internat. Biol. Ctr., 2000, Scientist of Yr., Internat. Biog. Ctr., 2008, Outstanding Scientists, 2008, Leading Scientist Of World, Internat. Biol. Ctr., 2008, Gt. Leader, ABI, 2009; grantee, Rsch. Promotional Found., 2000—06. Fellow: Chartered Inst. Mktg.; mem.: Greek Acad. Mktg., Acad. Mktg. Greek Orthodox. Avocations: reading, sports. Office: Univ Nicosia POBox 24005 46 Makedonitissas Ave Nicosia 1700 Cyprus Home: PO Box 24530 1300 Nicosia Cyprus Office Phone: 357 228 41615. Business E-Mail: vrontis.d@unic.ac.cy.

VROOM, VICTOR HAROLD, management consultant, educator; b. Montreal, Que., Can., Aug. 9, 1932; s. Harold Heard and Avice May (Brown) V.; m. Ann Louise Workman, June 12, 1956 (div. Jan. 1989); children: Derek Alan, Jeffrey James; m. Julia Ann Francis, Dec. 27, 1989; children: Tristan Alexander, Trevor Huston. B.Sc., McGill U., Montreal, 1953, M.Sc., 1955; PhD, U. Mich., 1958; MA (hon.), Yale, 1972. Lectr., study dir. U. Mich., Ann Arbor, 1958-60; asst. prof. psychology U. Pa., Phila., 1960-63; assoc. prof. psychology and indsl. adminstrn. Carnegie-Mellon U., Pitts., 1963-66, prof., 1966-72; John G. Searle prof. orgn. and mgmt. Yale U., 1972—2007, Bearing Point prof. mgmt., 2007—. Author: Work and Motivation, 1964, rev. edit. 1995, Leadership and Decision Making, 1973, The New Leadership, 1988. Recipient Ford Found. Doctoral Dissertation award, 1958-59; McKinsey Found. research design award, 1967; Fulbright lectr. U.K., 1967-68; Disting. Sci. Contbn. award, Soc. Indsl. and Orgnl. Psychology, 1998; Disting. Scholarly Cont. award, Acad. Mgmt., 2004. Fellow APA (James McKeen Cattell award 1970), APS Acad. Mgmt. Business E-Mail: victor.vroom@yale.edu.

VRUGT, JASPER ALEXANDER, research scientist; b. Amsterdam, North Holland, Netherlands, Feb. 28, 1976; s. Robert Vrugt and Berendina de Groot; m. Roya Adeli, July 29, 1981. PhD cum laude, U. Amsterdam, 2004. Dirs. postdoctoral fellow Los Alamos Nat. Lab., N.Mex., 2004—06, J. Robert Oppenheimer fellow, 2007—. Contbr. articles to profl. jours. Mem.: Dutch Hydrologic Soc., Soil Sci. Soc. Am. (Early Career award 2007), European Geophys. Union, Am. Geophys. Union. Office: Los Alamos Nat Lab Ctr for Nonlinear Studies Mail Stop T003 Los Alamos NM 87545 Office Fax: 505-665-8737.

VU, BRUCE THANH, aerospace engineer, educator; b. Vungtau, Vietnam, Sept. 26, 1962; s. Toai Minh Vu and Thao Thi Dao; m. Diane Luong Dao Luong, Aug. 26, 1995; children: Jennifer MyTruc, Jessica VietTrinh, Jordyn NgocTran. PhD, Miss. State U., Starkville, 1999. Aerospace engr. NASA Marshall Space Flight Ctr., Huntsville, Ala., 1989—2002, NASA Kennedy Space Ctr., Cape Canaveral, Fla., 2002—. Adj. prof. Fla. Inst. Tech., Melbourne, 2004—08, adv. bd. mem., 2006—08; NASA chair prof. Naval Postgrad. Sch., Monterey, Calif., 2008—. NASA Adminstr. fellowship, NRC, 2000—02, Michael Smith and Willie McCool Chair Professorship fellow, NASA HQ, 2008—. Mem.: AIAA. Conservative. Achievements include research in NASA technology transfer. Avocations: tennis, swimming. Home: 3543 Siderwheel Dr Rockledge FL 32955 Office: Naval Postgrad Sch Mail Code SP Monterey CA 93943 Business E-Mail: btvu@fit.edu, btvu@nps.edu.

VU, JOSEPH DUONG, financial educator; b. Hanoi, Vietnam, Mar. 13, 1952; s. Phuong and Nhan (Trinh) V.; m. Huyen Tran T. Do, July 1, 1978; children: Christine, Daniel. BBA, Ohio U., 1973; MBA, U. Chgo., 1975, PhD in Fin., 1984. Chartered fin. analyst. Asst. prof. Loyola U., Chgo., 1981-85, U. Ill., Chgo., 1985-88; assoc. prof. fin. DePaul U., Chgo., 1988—. Fin. advisor, arbitrator Nat. Assn. Securities Dealers. Author: Investment Management, 1993. Hospice vol. Midwest Palliative & Hospice Care Ctr., Mediator Ctr. Conflict Resolution. Mem. Am. Fin. Assn., Vietnamese Assn. Ill. (pres. 1993-98), Fin. Mgmt. Assn., Midwest Fin. Assn., Chartered Fin. Analyst Inst. Avocation: tennis. Office Phone: 312-362-5121. Business E-Mail: jvu@depaul.edu.

VU, NHAT TAN, composer; b. Hanoi, Vietnam, Aug. 8, 1970; Cert., Nat. Conservatory Music, Hanoi, 1987, degree in composition edn. & musicology, 1991, BMus, 1995; student, Staatliche Hochschule für Musik, Cologne, 2000—01; guest student, U. Calif., San Diego, 2002. Composition & musicology lectr. Nat. Conservatory Music, Hanoi, Vietnam, 1995—. Composer: Doan Trang, 1989—96, Ky Uc, 1993—94 (1st prize, Saint-German-en-Laye competition, 1995), 1995—96, Hat Tho, 1995, Phac Thao, 1995, Trang, 1996, Ngu Doi Dang Dan, 1998 (Vietnamese Composers Assn. award, 1998), Thanh Thuy, 1998, Vong Co, 1998, Tranh Khac Da, 1998, Dong Ai, 1998, Ao Don Ao Kep, 1998—99 (Vietnamese Composers Assn. award, 2003), My Xuan, 1999, Sao Mo, 1999—2000, Phac Thao 2000, 1999—2000 (Vietnamese Composers Assn. award, 2001), Khong Gian, 2000—01, Hallo, 2000, Cologne 2000, 2001, My Improvisation, 2001, Graphic Notation, 2001, Moment, 2001, Cong, 2001, Nhip Don Nhip Kep, 2001—02 (Vietnamese Composers Assn. award, 2002), Hoa Mua, 2002, Meditation and-...ABC, 2002, Tre, 2002—03, Di Vao Di Ra, 2003, Nhi, 2003, The Ten Courts of the Kings of Hell, 2003, Com, 2004, Body Frame/Video Frame, 2004; dir.: (performance projects) Sleepless Night, 2001, Chao HoiAn, 2002, KhaT, 2003, Space of Traditional & Contemporary Music, 2003. Grantee Arts Network Asia, 2001, 2003, Asian Cultural Coun., 2002, Brit. Coun. Hanoi, 2002, Ford Found., 2004. Home: So 7 Ngo 39 Haonam Ochodua-Dongda Hanoi Vietnam Personal E-mail: vunhattan@yahoo.com.

VU, QUAT THUONG, electrical engineer; b. Vietnam, Aug. 5, 1944; came to U.S., 1988; s. Quy-Mao and Thi-Phung Vu; children: Thuong-Hien, Thuong-Duc. BSEE, U. Ky., 1965; MSEE, Calif. Inst. Tech., 1967, PhDEE, 1970. Dean MINH-DUC U. Coll. Engring., Saigon, Vietnam, 1971-75; rschr. Hochiminh City, Vietnam, 1977-87, CNRS-CRN, Strasbourg, France, 1987-88, Calif. Inst. of Tech., Pasadena, 1989-90, Intel Corp., Santa Clara, Calif., 1990—. Achievements include two dozen patents in field. Office: Intel Corp M/S SC1-05 2200 Mission College Blvd Santa Clara CA 95052 Home Phone: 405-531-8418; Office Phone: 408-765-2410. Business E-Mail: quat.t.vu@intel.com.

VUCHETICH, JOHN PATRICK, psychiatrist; b. Park Falls, Wis., Nov. 20, 1961; s. John Richard and Nancy Ann (Johnson) V. BS, U. Wis., 1984; MD, U. Pa., Phila., 1993, PhD, 1998. Intern internal medicine Mass. Gen. Hosp., Boston, 1993-94; resident psychiatry McLean Hosp., Belmont, Mass., 1994-97, staff psychiatrist, 1997—2000. Instr. psychiatry Harvard Med. Sch., 1997-2000, asst. prof. psychiatry U. Minn., 2000-. Contbr. articles to profl. jours. William Penn fellow U. Pa., 1985-86, deans fellow U. Pa., 1986-87, med. scientist tng. program fellow NIH, U. Pa., 1986-93; behavior neurobiology trainee NIMH/Measey Found., U. Pa., 1991-92. Mem. Internat. Genetic Epidemiology Soc., Assn. Psychol. Sci., Am. Psychiat. Assn. Home: 600 N 2nd St Apt 106 Minneapolis MN 55401-3336 Office: F 282/2A West Bldg 2450 Riverside Ave Minneapolis MN 55454-1495 Office Phone: 612-273-9781. Business E-Mail: vuche002@umn.edu.

VUJANOVIĆ, FILIP, President of Republic of Montenegro; b. Belgrade, Sept. 1, 1954; married; 3 children. Trainee, collaborator Regional Orrice Pub. Min., Belgrade, 1978—80; sec. Regional Ct., Podgorica, 1980—81; atty., 1982—93; min. justice Govt. of Montenegro, 1993—95, min. interior, 1993—98, prime min., 1998—2002, pres., 2003—, Montenegrin Parliament, 2002—03. Office: Blvd Sv Petra Cetinjskog 3 Podgorica Montenegro Office Fax: +381 81 246 608. E-mail: predsjednik@nm.su.

VUKELICH, SHARON IRENE, aerospace engineer, consultant; b. 1952; d. Donald B. and Dorothy Violet Williams; m. Thomas Harvey Havens; children: Christopher Michael, Charles Edward Havens, Flora Irene Havens. BSAE, U. of Mich., 1974; MSAE, U. of Cin., 1980. Design engr. GE Aircraft Engines, Cin., 1974—82; propulsion engr. USAF/ASC/YZ, Dayton, 1982—95; propulsion structures tech. expert USAF/ASC/ENFP, Dayton, 1995—2000; chief engr. USAF/ASC/LPJ, Dayton, 2000—03; sr. rsch. engr. U. of Dayton Rsch. Inst., Ohio, 2003—. Contbr. reference book; assoc. editor (jour.) Materials Evaluation; contbr. articles to profl. jours. Decorated Outstanding Civilian Career Svc. award USAF, Exceptional Civilian Svc. award DOD, Exemplary Civilian Svc. award USAF; recipient Outstanding Profl. Achievement award, Affiliates Societies Coun., 2002, Value Engring. Suggestion award, DOD, 1987, Value Engr. of the Yr., 1985—86, ASC Value Engr. of the Yr., USAF, 1985—86. Mem.: ASM Internat., Am. Helicopter Soc., Am. Soc. Nondestructive Testing (sec.-treas. 2003—04, v.p. 2004—05, pres. 2005—, dir. 2001—03). Office: University of Dayton Research Institute 300 College Pk Dayton OH 45469-0120 Office Fax: 937-229-2650. E-mail: sharon.vukelich@udri.udayton.edu.

VUKSTA, MICHAEL JOSEPH, surgeon; b. Pitts., Apr. 25, 1926; s. Michael and Mary Sarah (Hanulya) V.; m. Dorothy Ann Bosak, Sept. 12, 1953; children: Patricia, Michael, Carol, Janet. BA, Youngstown State U., 1949; MD, Ohio State U., 1957. Diplomate Am. Bd. Surgery. Enlisted USN, advanced through grades to capt., 1974; intern St. Elizabeth Hosp., Youngstown, Ohio, resident in gen. surgery, 1958-62; pvt. practice gen. surgery Youngstown, 1962-89; head blue team surgery Oak Knoll U.S. Naval Hosp., Oakland, Calif., 1989-93; assoc. prof. surgery NEOUCOM. Capt. USN retired. Fellow ACS, Am. Coll. Sports Medicine, Southwestern Surg. Congress; mem. Nat. Athletic Trainers Assn. (advisor). Byzantine Catholic. Home: 131 Lovett Pl Pensacola FL 32506-5265 E-mail: mvukie@aol.com.

VULGAMORE, ALLISON BETH, performing arts association administrator; b. 1958; m. Peter Marshall. BMus, Oberlin Coll., 1980. Gen. mgr., artistic adminstr., mgr. ops. Nat. Symphony Orch., Washington; orch. mgr. NY Philharm. Orch., 1987—91, acting mng. dir., 1990—91, gen. mgr., 1991—93; pres. Atlanta Symphony Orch., 1993—2002, pres., mng. dir., 2002—08, pres., CEO, 2008—. Hon. dir. Oberlin Coll.; mem. arts challenge panel in music NEA. Bd. dirs. Midtown Alliance; mem. Vision 2000 Econ. Devel. Collaborative; Cultural Olympiad and opening ceremonies coord. Centennial Olympic Games, Atlanta, 1996. Am. Symphony Orch. League fellow, 1980. Mem. Atlanta Rotary.

VUOLA, OLLI, engineering company executive; b. Turku, Finland, Apr. 17, 1969; s. Pauli Mikael and Seija Sinikka Vuola; m. Anu Pohjonen, May 23, 1992; children: Aleksi Eemeli, Saara Laura, Anna Elena. MSEE, Helsinki U. of Tech., Espoo, Finland, 1996; PhD, U. Lausanne, Switzerland, 2006. Trainee KONE Corp., Hyvinkää, Finland, 1994—94; rsch. scientist and project mgr. Helsinki U. Tech., Espoo, Finland, 1995—96, sr. lectr., 2007—; dir. Cerntech, Geneva, 1996—2001; dir. new projects TeliaSonera Finland, Helsinki, 2002—03; pres., CEO Networked Bus. Solutions Sàrl, Rolle, Switzerland, 2003—07. Head Nordic Del. to the European Synchrotron Radiation Facility Purchasing Com., Grenoble, 1996—2002; mem. of del. European Lab. for Particle Physics Fin. Com., Geneva, 1997—2002; rep. European Indsl. Rsch. Mgmt. Assn., Paris, 2002—04; pres. Finnish Guild of Commerce, Geneva, 2005—. Reviewer Jour. Techn. Transfer, Internat. Jour. Tech. Mgmt. Rsch. Policy, Jour. Product Innovation Mgmt. Mem. Conseil de l'Église Evangélique de St.Genis-Pouilly, St.Genis-Pouilly, 2000—02; mem. bd. Coast Arty. Sch. Student Del., Helsinki, Finland, 1989—90; mem. student parliament Helsinki U. of Tech., Espoo, Finland, 1992—93. Officer Finnish Mil., 1989—90. Rsch. grant, Outokumpu Found., 2002-2004, Finnish Found. for Econ. Edn., 2005, European Lab. for Particle Physics, 2004-2005, Vis. Scholar, Ga. Tech Sch. of Pub. Policy, 2005-. Mem.: European Indsl. Rsch. Mgmt. Assn., Tech. Transfer Soc., IEEE Engring. Mgmt. Soc., Acad. of Mgmt. Avocations: running, reading, sailing. Office: Ga Tech Sch of Public Policy DM Smith Bldg Atlanta GA 30332-0345 Office Fax: 404-385-0504. E-mail: olli.vuola@pubpolicy.gatech.edu.

VUONG, JOSEPH TRUNG, humanities educator; came to U.S., 1975; s. Chanh Huu and Manh Thi (Do) V.; married, Chot Trang Vuong Dec. 27, 1966; children: Tam Huu, Trang Kieu, Theresa Kieu, Jude Thien H. BS, Loyola U., New Orleans, 1980; MEd, Loyla U., 1983; PhD, Walden U., St. Paul, 1992. Lic. counselor, La. Guidence counselor Jefferson Parish, Harvey, 1983—2003; coll. prof. U. New Orleans, La., 1996; adj. prof. Tulane U., New Orleans, 1993—. Vocat. coord. Bilingual Voclep Program, Harvey, 1984-85; Vietnamese counseling Bilingual Program, Harvey, 1984-85; Calif. testing basic skills coord. John Ehret High Sch., Marrero, 1986-89. Author: Vietnamese Cross-Cultural Adjustment, 1980, Vietnamese History, 1983, Vietnamese New Year, 1984, The Origin of the Vietnamese People, 1987. V.p. Vietnamese Community, Harvey, 1986. Capt. Polit. Warfare, 1972—75, Vietnam. Named Outstanding Counselor Loyola U., 1987. Mem. Am. Assn. Counseling and Devel., Multicultural Counseling, Internat. Counseling, La. Assn. Counseling Devel., Jefferson Tchr. Fedn., Delasalle Alumni Assn. (pres. 1985). Republican. Roman Catholic. Avocations: basketball, tennis, ping pong. Home Phone: 504-347-7050; Office Phone: 504-865-5555. Business E-Mail: jvuong@tulane.edu.

VUONG, LYNETTE DYER, literature and language professor; b. Owosso, Mich., June 20, 1938; d. Wilbur La Vergne Dyer and Brandon Richardson; m. Ti Quang Vuong, Jan. 9, 1962 (div. Nov. 2002); children: Timothy Tuan Quang, Ted Tan Quang, Tamara Linh Sembritzky, Tania Lan. BA in Classical Studies summa cum laude, U. Houston, 1997, MA in English Literature, 2001. RN Milw. County Hosp. Sch. Nursing, 1959. Neonatal nurse St. Joseph Hosp. & Mt. Sinai Hosp., Milw., 1959—61; tchr. ESL Vietnamese Am. Assn., Saigon, Vietnam, 1962—69; tchr. SL Pvt. Classes, Saigon, 1969—74; prin. Internat. Sch., Saigon, 1974—75; neonatal nurse Spartanburg Gen. Hosp., SC, 1977—79; Vietnamese lang. translator & cons. Span Tran Ednl. Svcs, Houston, 1983—96; lectr. Latin U. Houston, 1999, 2001, 2002—; instr. ESL North Harris CC, Houston, 2002—. Author: (book) The Brocaded Slipper and Other Vietnamese Tales, Sky Legends of Vietnam, The Golden Carp and Other Tales from Vietnam, A Friend for Carlita. Recipient Ann Martin Book award, Cath. Libr. Assn., 1991, Classical Greek award, U. Houston, Dept. Modern & Classical Langs., 1996; named Outstanding Woman of Year, Greenville Jr. Woman's Club, SC, 1976. Mem.: Romance Writers America, Soc. Children's Book Writers & Illustrators.

VUONO, CARL E., communications systems company executive, retired military officer; b. Monongahela, Pa., Oct. 18, 1934; BS in Engring., US Mil. Acad., West Point, NY, 1957; grad., Field Artillary Sch., USMC Command and Staff Coll., US Army War Coll.; MS in Pub. Adminstrn., Shippensburg State Coll., Pa., 1973; D in Pub. Adminstrn. (hon.), Shippensburg U. Commd. 2nd lt. US Army, 1957, advanced through grades to gen., 1986, dep. chief. of staff Ops. and Plans Washington, chief of staff, 1987-91; with MPRI, Alexandria, Va., 1993, pres., 1999; sr. v.p., pres. L-3 Svcs. Group L-3 Comm. Holdings, Inc. Roman Catholic. Office: L-3 Comm Holdings Inc 1215 S Clark St Ste 1205 Arlington VA 22202

VUOTO, ANTHONY (TONY) F., bank executive; BA, Princeton U., NJ; MBA, U. Pa. Wharton Sch. Bus. Pres. consumer lending divsn. Bank One Corp., pres., COO First USA Bank; vice chmn., CFO Providian Fin. Corp., San Francisco, 2002—05; sr. v.p., CFO Card Services Washington Mutual Inc., Seattle, 2005—07, exec. v.p., pres. Card Svcs., 2007—08.*

VUURSTEEN, KAREL, beverage industry executive; b. Arnhem, The Netherlands, July 25, 1941; s. Cornelis Willem and Hendrika Eliza (Weddepohl) V.; m. Juliette H.J. Pronk, Apr. 4, 1964; 3 children. M in Agrl. Engring., U. Wageningen, Holland, 1968. With Philips, The Netherlands, 1968-79, consumer goods dir. Sweden, 1979-81, CEO Norway, 1982-83, consumer goods dir. Germany, 1984-87, CEO Austria, 1987-90; pres., CEO Philips Lighting Co., 1990-91; mem. exec. bd. Heineken N.V., Amsterdam, Netherlands, 1991-92, dep. chmn. exec. bd., 1992-93, chmn. exec. bd., 1993—2002; mem. supervisory bd. Royal Ahold NV, 2002—, chmn. supervisory bd., 2003—04. Bd. dirs. Whitbread PLC, London, Gucci Group N.V., The Netherlands, Nyenrode U., The Netherlands, AB Electrolux, Sweden; mem. adv. coun. ING Group N.V., The Netherlands; mem. adv. bd. CVC Capital Ptnrs., B.V., The Netherlands. Office: Royal Ahold NV Albert Heijnweg 1 NL-1507 EH Zaandam Netherlands

VYAS, DEEPTI, pharmacist; d. Yashwant and Savita Vyas; m. Abhirjun Dutta, Feb. 25, 2008. PharmD, Purdue U., West Lafayette, Ind., 2006. Cert. in pharmacy Mo., 2007. Resident Moses Cone Health Sys., Greensboro, NC, 2006—07; clin. asst. prof. U. Mo.-Kans. City, Columbia, 2007—.

VYAZOVKIN, SERGEY, chemistry professor; b. Kazan, Russia, Feb. 20, 1960; came to U.S., 1995; s. Valentin and Irma Vyazovkin; m. Sasha Vyazovkin, Oct. 1, 1983; 1 child, Polina. BS, Belorussian U., Minsk, 1982, PhD in Chemistry, 1989. Rsch. prof. U. Utah, Salt Lake City, 1998—2001; prof. U. Ala., Birmingham, 2001—. Editor: Thermochim. Acta; mem. editl. bd.: Macromol, RAP Commn. Macromolchem Phys. Lise Meitner Rsch. fellow Austrian Rsch. Fund, 1992-93, Rsch. fellow NATO, 1994 Mem.: ACS, N.Am. Thermal Analysis Soc. (elected fellow 2006, Mettler award 2004). Office: U Ala Dept Chemistry 901 S 14th St Birmingham AL 35294 E-mail: vyazovkin@uab.edu.

VYDELINGUM, NADARAJEN AMEERDANADEN, cell biologist, educator, researcher, health administrator; b. Curepipe, Mauritius, June 1, 1945; came to U.S., 1977, U.S. citizen, 1985; s. Vythilingum Francis Vydelingum and Mareeaya Paratian; m. Rosemary Dowland, Nov. 6, 1971 (div.); children: Natalie, Eric; m. Nancy Yurman, 2005. BS in Cell Biology with honors, Birkbeck London U., Eng., 1972, MS in Biochemistry, 1974; PhD in Clin. Biochemistry, St. Mary's Med. Sch., London, 1979; postgrad., Inst. Biology London U., 1990. Adj. asst. prof. cell biology U. Wis., Milw., 1979; asst. prof. medicine and pharmacology Med. Coll. Wis., Milw., 1979-86; dir. rsch. and surg. metabolism lab. Sloan-Kettering Cancer Ctr., NYC, 1986-91; health sci. adminstr. bioengring. and physiology NIH, Bethesda, Md., 1991—; core lab. dir. Gen. Clin. Rsch. Ctr. Med. Coll. Milw.; dep. dir. Nat. Cancer Inst., 2001—08, biologist, health scientist admin., 2008—. Reviewer Health Sci. Consortium Peer Rev. Bd., Carrboro, N.C., 1984—, for Sci. Book, Boston U.; peer reviewer Am. Diabetic Assn., 1989-96; faculty mem. Found. for the Advancement of Edn. in the Scis., NIH, 1993—; lectr. cell biology Johns Hopkins U., Balt., 1994-98. Contbr. articles to profl. jours. Am. heart Assn. fellow, 1979-81; NIH grantee, 1985—. Mem. AAAS, Inst. Biology London, Am. Assn. Cancer Rsch., Am. Diabetes Assn. (grantee 1982-84), N.Y. Acad. Scis., Am. Inst. Nutrition, Am. Soc. Biol. Chemists and Molecular Biology, Biochem. Soc. London, Couns. on Edn. Nutrition, Coun. Biology Editors, Am. Med. Writers Assn., Soc. Math. Biology, Union Concerned Scientists, Am. Assoc. Advancement Sci. Democrat. Unitarian Universalist. Avocations: arabic, african and indian drum. Home: 17629 Prince Edward Dr Olney MD 20832-2140 Office: NIH 6130 Executive Blvd MSC 7315 Bethesda MD 20892-7315 Office Phone: 301-402-6837. Personal E-mail: drums12@verizon.net. Business E-Mail: vydelinn@mail.nih.gov.

VYHMEISTER, NANCY JEAN, retired religious studies educator; b. Portland, Oreg., Aug. 31, 1937; d. Charles Joseph and Hazel Marion (Ausherman) Weber; m. Werner Konrad Vyhmeister, July 12, 1959; children: Heidi Annette, Ronald Elmar. BA in French, Pacific Union Coll., 1958; MA in Biblical Langs., Andrews U., 1967, EdD in Religious Edn., 1978. Instr. River Plate Coll., Villa Libertador, Entre Rios, Argentina, 1961-71; prof. biblical studies Adventist Internat. Inst., Silang, Cavite, The Philippines, 1985-90; asst. prof. world mission Andrews U., Berrien Springs, Mich., 1979-81, assoc. prof. world mission, 1982-84, sem. libr., 1982-84, prof. world mission, 1991—2000; ret., 2000; tchg. Spicer Coll., 2000, Montemorelos U., Mexico, 2001, Adventist U. Africa, Zimbabwe, 2006, Nigeria, Kenya. Editl. asst. Bibl. Rsch. Inst., Silver Spring, Md. 1992-96. Author: (books) Gramatica Griega, 1968, 2nd rev. edit. 1981, Handbook for Rsch., 1989, 2nd rev. edit. 1997; editor (jour.) Andrews Univ. Sem. Studies, 1994-2000, Quality Research Papers, 2001, 2nd edit. 2007; editor: (book) Comentario Biblico Andventista, 1972-89, Women in Ministry: Biblical and Historical Perspectives, 1998. Mem. Soc. Biblical Lit., Avocations: travel, reading, writing. Personal E-mail: vyhmeist@andrews.edu.

VYN, ELEANOR MEARS, physical therapist; d. David A. and Mary A. Mears; divorced; children: Michael, Katherine, Mary. AA, Colby Jr. Coll., 1968; BS, Columbia U., 1970. Phys. therapist VNA Care Network, Gloucester, Mass., 1997—. Avocations: dance, music, art, swimming, reading. Office Phone: 978-325-1755. Personal E-mail: elievyn@comcast.net.

WAAGE, FREDERICK OSWIN, English educator; b. Ithaca, NY, Dec. 1, 1943; s. Frederick O. and Dorothy (Boylan) W.; m. Margaret McGregor Best, July 2, 1965 (div. 1973); m. Virginia Rose Renner, June 18, 1977; children: Melissa Rose, Erick Renner Waage. AB, Princeton U., NJ, 1965, PhD, 1971. Instr. in English Northwestern U., Evanston, Ill., 1968-71; jr. rsch. assoc. Huntington Libr., San Marino, Calif., 1971-73; lectr. in English Calif. State U., LA, 1971-73; asst. prof. English Douglass Coll., New Brunswick, N.J., 1974-77; asst. prof. lit. Coll. Misericordia, Dallas, Pa., 1977-78; asst. prof. English East Tenn. State U., Johnson City, 1978-83, assoc. prof. English, 1983-88, prof. English, 1988—. Editl. bd. mem. Interdisciplinary Studies Lit. and Environment, 2000—. Author poetry and short stories, Environment in the Writings of George R. Stewart, 2006; editor: Teaching Environmental Literature, 1985; co-editor: Teaching North American Environmental Literature, 2008. Huntington Libr. fellow, 1979; NEA grantee, 1987. Mem. Modern Lang. Assn., Assn. Study Lit. and Environment, Phi Beta Kappa. Democrat. Avocations: cooking, running. Home: 2127 Sinking Creek Rd Johnson City TN 37604-7708 Personal E-mail: renwag@charter.net.

WAAGEN, LINDA LOUISE, elementary school educator; b. Ft. Collins, Colo., Apr. 9, 1956; d. William Albert Vanderlaan and Vera Louise (Curtis) Wilson; m. Jack A. Waagen (div.); m. James Eugene Scholz, Feb. 20, 2000. BS, Southern Adventist U., Collegedale, Tenn., 1976; MSEd, Old Dominion U., Norfolk, Va., 1994. Profl. tchg. cert. Tchr. Greene Valley SDA Sch., Rochester, Minn., 1979—86, Ft. Smith SDA Sch., Ark., 1986—90, Tidewater Adventist Acad., Chesapeake, Va., 1990—97, Tualatin Valley Jr. Acad., Hillsboro, Oreg., 1997—2000, Portland Adventist Elem. Sch., Gresham, Oreg., 2000—. Author: Roll the Presses, 2001 (Intel's Top 50, 2001). Recipient Don Keele Acad. Excellence, N. Pacific Union SDA, 1999, 2004, 2008. Mem.: Nat. Coun. History Edn., Orgn. Am. Historians, Nat. Coun. Social Studies. Adventist. Avocations: raising and showing Arabian horses, photography. Home: PO Box 2415 Gresham OR 97030 Office: Portland Adventist Elem 3990 NW 1st St Gresham OR 97030

WAAK, PATRICIA ANN, political organization administrator; b. Muskogee, Okla., Feb. 1, 1943; d. Boxly William and Anne Nell (Smith) Waak; children: Cinira Anne Baldi, Rachel Nell Carter. Student, Tulane U., 1961—62, U. Houston, 1964—65, George Mason U., 1976—77. RN Va. Vol. nurse Peace Corps, Maceio, Brazil, 1966—68; staff nurse U. Wis. Children's Hosp., Madison, 1968—70; dir. counseling Planned Parenthood, Washington, 1973—75; spl. asst. Devel. Support Bur. US Agency for Internat. Devel. (USAID), Washington, 1977—78, assoc. dir. Office of Population, 1978—82, project design team Zimbabwe, 1985, evaluation team Kenya, Uganda, Nigeria, 1987; asst. dir. Columbia U. Ctr. Population and Family Health, NYC, 1982—85; dir. population Nat. Audubon Soc., 1985—2002; chairwoman Colo. Dem. Party, Denver, 2005—. US del. UN Population Commn., 1981—82; cons. Family Planning Internat., 1973, Global Com. of Parliamentarians on Population and Devel., 1984—85; project design team US AID, Zimbabwe, 1985; NGO participant UN Mid-Decade Conf. of Women, Copenhagen, 1981; moderator global population anniversary Peace Corps Conf., 1981; mem. environ. strategy and planning commn. World Conservation Union; lectr. in field. Exec. prodr.: (population videotape) What is the Limit, Sharing the Earth, Finding the Balance, Population and Wildlife; author: Planet Awakening, My Bones are Red. Mem. McGovern-Shriver Presdl. Campaign Staff, 1972; vice chmn. Arlington Dem. Com., 1974; chmn. Arlington Com. on Status of Women, 1975; dep. campaign mgr. Shriver for Pres. Com., 1976; del. Va. Dem. Conv., 1976, 1982. Recipient Population Fellows award, Population Ref. Bur., 1993. Mem.: Women in Def. of Environment, Soc. Internat. Devel., Nat. Women's Polit. Caucus, Assn. for Women in Devel., Nat. Council for Internat. Health (pub. policy com.), Am. Pub. Health Assn. (population sect. coun., com. on women's rights). Democrat. Office: Colorado Dem Party 777 Santa Fe Ave Denver CO 80204 Office Phone: 303-623-4762. Business E-Mail: pwaak@coloradodems.org.*

WAALAND, IRVING T., retired aerospace engineer; b. Bklyn., July 2, 1927; s. Trygve and Marie Waaland; m. Helen Rita Katz, Apr. 7, 1961; children: Theodore, Neil, Elizabeth, Scott, Diane; m. Kay Williams Oct. 22, 2005 B of Aero. Engring. magna cum laude, NYU, 1953. Project engr. Grumman Corp., Bethpage, NY, 1953—74; v.p., B-2 Chief Designer Northrop Corp., Pico Rivera, Calif., 1974—93. Patentee in field. With USAF, 1946-48. Recipient Leslie E. Simon award, Am. Def. Preparedness Assn., 1990, Aerospace Engring. Leadership award, SAE, 1993. Fellow AIAA (Aircraft Design award 1989, Aircraft Design cert. merit 1989, Wright Bros. lectr. in aeronautics 1991); mem. NAE. Office Phone: 714-721-4944.

WAAS, GEORGE LEE, lawyer; b. NYC, July 12, 1943; s. George and Anne Waas; m. Harriet I. Waas, July 18, 1971; children: Elaine Beth Hudgins, Amy Michelle Kinsey. BS in Journalism, U. Fla., 1965; JD, Fla. State U., 1970. Bar: Fla. 1970; cert. in state and fed. govt. law and administrv. practice, Fla., US Supreme Ct., 1973. Asst. atty. gen. State of Fla., 1970-71; staff atty. Fla. League of Cities, 1971; asst. to sec. and dir. labor Fla. Dept. Commerce, 1971-73; assoc. dir. continuing legal edn. Fla. Bar, 1973-74; asst. dean, instr. coll. law Fla. State U., 1974-75; atty. Fla. Dept. Health and Rehab. Services, 1977-80; ptnr. Slepin, Slepin, Lambert & Waas, 1981-86; counsel state elections Fla. Dept. of State, 1986-87; asst. atty. gen. State of Fla., Tallahassee, 1987—2003, sr. asst. atty. gen., 2003—04, special counsel to Fla. atty. gen., 2004—. Contbr. articles to profl. jours. including Fla. Bar Jour. and Law Revs.; extra: (TV films) Recount. Bd. dir. Big Bend Muscular Dystrophy Assn., 1980-83 (pres. 1983); mem. Leon County Cultural Resources Comn., 1985-87; mem. Gov.'s Coun. on the Voter Registration Act, 1993-96. Recipient Claude Pepper Outstanding Govt. Lawyer award, Fla. Bar, 2000; named one of Legal Elite, Fla. Trend Mag., 2008—09. Mem. Fla. Govt. Bar Assn. (pres. 1976-77), Fla. Bar (exec. council administrv. law sect. 1981-86, chmn. 1985-86, Fla. Govt. Lawyer Sec.), Masons, Capital Tiger Bay Tallahassee (dir. 1974-80), Fla. Bar Profl. Com. Democrat. Jewish. Home: 3797 Sally Ln Tallahassee FL 32312-1018 Office: Collins Bldg Tallahassee FL 32399-1050 Office Phone: 850-414-3662. Personal E-mail: waas01@comcast.net.

WAAS, HARRIET ISSNER, elementary school educator; b. Miami, Fla., July 6, 1949; d. Martin and Hildegard (Wimpfheimer) Issner; m. George L. Waas, July 18, 1971; children: Elaine Beth, Amy Michelle. BS, Fla. State U., 1971, MS, 1978. Cert. elem., reading, lang. arts, gifted-talented tchr., ESL Fla. Elem. tchr. Leon County Schs., Tallahassee; mem. Fla. Title I Statewide Team Dist. Educators, 1997—2002, ETS/Region XIV Comprehensive Ctr. Leadership Team, Pineview. Profl. reading developer Just Read Fla., 2002—09; mem. Fla. Elem. Reading Adv. Bd., 2006—07. Contbr. articles to profl. jours. Recipient Extra Mile award, 1986, 1987, 1988. Mem.: SACS. Home: 3797 Sally Ln Tallahassee FL 32312-1018

WABBY, JAMES PATRICK, quality assurance professional, educator; b. Pitts., Apr. 20, 1976; s. James and Patricia Wabby. BSc in Biol. Scis., Duquesne U., 2000, MSc in Health Mgmt. Systems, 2002. HIPAA cons. C.C. Allegheny County, Pitts., 2002—03, adj. prof., 2003—04; clin. regulatory affairs and quality assurance Abbott Labs., Chgo., 2004—, sr. global compliance, 2008; auditor Abbott Vascular. Mem. bioethics oversight com. Abbott Labs., Chgo., 2004—, mem. human factors coun., 2004—; adj. prof. Robert Morris Coll. Ill., Chgo., 2005—. Mem. philanthropy team Abbott Labs., Pitts., 2004—; polit. campaign mgr. Dist. Justice, Pitts., 1998. Recipient Health Sci. award, Duquesne U., 2000. Mem.: Regulatory Affairs Profl. Soc., Am. Soc. Law, Medicine, and Ethics, Am. Health Lawyers Assn. Avocations: fishing, running, exercise, reading, travel. Home: 4783 Willow Dr Pittsburgh PA 15236

WABUDA, SUSAN, historian, educator; b. Derby, Conn., Jan. 22, 1957; d. Nicholas and Ruth Wabuda. BA, Southern Conn. State U., New Haven, 1979; MA, Wesleyan U., Middletown, Conn., 1980; PhD, U. Cambridge, England, 1992. Assoc. prof. history Fordham U., Bronx, NY, 1993—. Author: (edited vol.) Belief and Practice in Reformation England, Preaching During The English Reformation. Fellow: Royal Hist. Soc. Office: Fordham Univ 441 E Fordham Rd Bronx NY 10458-5159

WACHENHEIM, EDGAR, III, investment company executive; b. NYC, Oct. 14, 1937; s. Edgar Jr. and Elizabeth (Lewis) W.; m. Sue Wallach, June 6, 1963; children: Lance, Kim, Chris, Amy. BA, Williams Coll., 1959; MBA, Harvard U., 1966. Securities analyst Goldman, Sachs & Co., NYC, 1966-69; mng. dir. Cen. Nat. Gottesman Inc., NYC, 1969-88; chmn., chief exec. officer Greenhaven Assocs., Inc., NYC, 1988—. Bd. dirs. Sejak, N.Y.C.; vice chmn. Ctrl. Nat. Gottesman, Inc., N.Y.C.; pres. trustees Rye Country Day Sch., 1985-93; bd. dirs. Miriam and Ira D. Wallach Found.; trustee, treas. N.Y. Found., 1993—99; trustee Skidmore Coll. 1993-2001, trustee emeritus 2001-; trustee Mus. Modern Art N.Y.C.; trustee, chair exec. com. NY Pub. Libr., 1988-; chmn. Sue and Edgar Wachenheim Found. Trustee Arthur Ross Found., N.Y.C., 1978—; chmn. investment com., trustee UJA Fedn. Jewish Philanthropies, N.Y.C., 1985-97; mem. fin. com., trustee Rye Country Day Sch., N.Y., 1985-97; bd. dirs. Miriam and Ira D. Wallach Found. Mem. N.Y. Soc. Security Analysts, Harvard Club, Century Country Club. Avocations: skiing, tennis. Office: Greenhaven Assocs Inc 3 Manhattanville Rd Purchase NY 10577-2116

WACHHOLTZ, AMY B., psychologist, educator; MDiv, Boston U., 2000; PhD, Bowling Green State U., Ohio, 2006. Lic. psychologist NC, 2007, Ma., 2008. Med. psychology fellow Duke U. Med. Ctr., Durham, NC, 2005—08; asst prof. psychiatry U. Mass. Med. Ctr., Dept. Psychiatry, 2008—. Office: Univ Mass Med Ctr 55 Lake Ave N Worcester MA 01655 Business E-Mail: amy.wachholtz@umassmemorial.org.

WACHMAN, MURRAY, retired mathematics professor; b. Tel Aviv, Feb. 1, 1931; arrived in U.S., 1941; s. Samuel David and Jean (Kuselewitz) Wachman; m. Helene Leibowitz; children: Elliot S., Ronald M., Adina R. BS, Bklyn. Coll., 1953; MS, NYU, 1956, PhD, 1961. Analyst Republic Aviation, Farmington, NY, 1955-59; group leader G.E. Space Sci. Labs., Valley Forge, Pa., 1959-67; prof. U. Conn., Storrs, 1967-97; ret., 1997. Cons. Naval Underwater Sys. Ctr., 1981—92. Recipient Founders Day award, NYU, 1961. Mem.: Soc. Indsl. and Applied Math., Am. Math. Soc. Home: 34 Timber Dr Storrs Mansfield CT 06268-1227

WACHOWSKI, ANDY, film director; b. Chgo., Dec. 29, 1967; s. Ron and Lynne Wachowski; m. Alisa Blasingame, 1991. Attended, Emerson Coll., Boston. Motion picture dir., writer, prodr. Co-writer (with brother Andy): Assassins, 1995 (story, hon. mention Stockholm Film Festival); exec. prodr., writer, dir. (films): Bound, 1996 (Internat. Fantasy Film award 1997), The Matrix, 1999 (Saturn award for best dir., Las Vegas Film Critics Soc. for best original screenplay), The Matrix Reloaded, 2003, The Matrix Revolutions, 2003, V for Vendetta, 2006, Speed Racer, 2008. Office: William Morris Agy One William Morris Pl Beverly Hills CA 90212

WACHOWSKI, LARRY, film director; b. Chgo., June 21, 1965; s. Ron and Lynne Wachowski; m. Thea Bloom, Oct. 30, 1993 (div. Dec. 2002). Attended, Bard Coll. Motion picture dir., writer, prodr. Co-writer (with brother Andy): Assassins, 1995 (story, hon. mention Stockholm Film Festival); exec. prodr., writer, dir. (films): Bound, 1996 (Internat. Fantasy Film award 1997), The Matrix, 1999 (Saturn award for best dir., Las Vegas Film Critics Soc. for best original screenplay), The Matrix Reloaded, 2003, The Matrix Revolutions, 2003, V for Vendetta, 2006, Speed Racer, 2008. Address: William Morris Agy care Dave Wirtschafter One William Morris Pl Beverly Hills CA 90212

WACHS, MARTIN, urban planning educator, author, consultant; b. NYC, June 8, 1941; s. Robert and Doris (Margolis) Wachs; m. Helen Poliner, Aug. 18, 1963; children: Faye Linda, Steven Brett. BCE, CUNY, 1963; MS, Northwestern U., 1965, PhD, 1967. Asst. prof. U. Ill., Chgo., 1967-69, Northwestern U., Evanston, Ill., 1969-71; assoc. prof. urban planning UCLA, 1971-76, prof., 1976-96; dir. U. Calif. Transp. Ctr., 1996-99; prof. civil and environ. engring. and city/regional planning U. Calif., Berkeley, 1996—2005, dir. Inst. Transp. Studies, 1999—2005; dir. transp. space and tech. group RAND Corp., Santa Monica, Calif., 2006—. Vis. disting. prof. Rutgers U., New Brunswick, NJ, 1983—84; mem. exec. com. Transp. Rsch. Bd., 1995—2004, chmn., 2000; vis. fellow Oxford U., England, 1976—77. Author: Transportation for the Elderly: Changing Lifestyles, Changing Needs, 1979, Transportation Planning on Trial, 1996; contbr. articles to profl. jours.; editor: Ethics in Planning, 1984, The Car and the City, 1992. Mem. steering com. LA Parking Mgmt. Study, 1976—78; bd. dirs. LA Commuter Computer, 1978—94; mem. Calif. Commn. Transp. Investment, 1995. Served to capt. Ordnance Corps. US Army, 1967—69. Recipient Pike Johnson award, Transp. Rsch. Bd., 1976, W. N. Carey Disting. Svc. award, 2002, Disting. Tchg. award, UCLA Alumni Assn., 1986, Disting. Planning Educator award, Calif. Planners Found., 1986, Disting. Educator award, Coun. U. Transp. Ctrs., 2003, Disting. Planning Educator award, Assn. Collegiate Schs. Planning, 2006; named Mem. of the Yr., San Francisco chpt. Women's Transp. Seminar, 2006; Guggenheim fellow, 1977, Humanities fellow, Rockefeller Found., 1980, Rsch. lectr., Soc. Sigma Xi, 2004—. Fellow: Am. Inst. Cert. Planners, Am. Coun. Edn.; mem.: ASCE, Inst. Transp. Engrs., Cosmos Club. Jewish. Home: 670 Harbor St #3 Venice CA 90291-5519 Office: RAND Corp Santa Monica CA 90401-3208 Home Phone: 310-306-2080. Business E-Mail: wachs@rand.org.

WACHSBERGER, CHAIM, lawyer; b. Tel Aviv, Sept. 15, 1951; BA, Queens Coll. CUNY, 1973; JD, Columbia U., 1976. Bar: NJ 1976, NY 1977. Ptnr. Chadbourne & Parke LLP, NYC, head, Project Fin. Practice Group, mem. mgmt. com. Contbr. articles to profl. jour. Mem.: ABA (Corp., Banking & Bus. Law Sect., Am. Bar Assn.), NJ State Bar Assn., NY State Bar Assn. Office: Chadbourne & Parke LLP 30 Rockefeller Plaza New York NY 10112 Office Phone: 212-408-5232. Office Fax: 212-541-5369. Business E-Mail: cwachsberger@chadbourne.com.

WACHSMAN, ERIC D., engineering educator; PhD, Stanford U., 1990. Sr. scientist SRI Internat., Menlo Park, Calif., 1990—97; prof. U. Fla., Gainesville, 1997—; dir. Fla. Inst. Sustainable Energy, Gainesville, 2006—. Fellow: Electrochem. Soc. Achievements include patents in fields. Office: Univ Fla 100 Rhines Hall Gainesville FL 32611 Business E-Mail: ewach@mse.ufl.edu.

WACHTEL, ALBERT, writer, educator; b. NYC, Dec. 20, 1939; s. Jacob and Sarah Rose (Kaplansky) W.; m. Sydelle Farber, Mar. 9, 1958; children: Sally Rose, Seth Laurence, Stephanie Allyson, Synthia Laura, Jonathan Benjamin, Jessica Eden, Jacob Ethan. BA, CUNY, 1960; PhD, SUNY, Buffalo, 1968. Instr. SUNY, Buffalo, 1963—66, asst. to dean, 1966—68; asst. prof. U. Calif., Santa Barbara, 1968—74; prof. English, creative writing Pitzer Coll., Claremont (Calif.) Colls., 1974—. Playwright: Paying the Piper, 1968, Prince Hal, 1995; co-editor Modernism: Challenges and Perspectives, 1986; author: The Cracked Looking Glass: James Joyce and the Nightmare of History, 1992; contbr. stories, creative essays to lit. jours., newspapers, and mags. NDEA fellow, 1960-63, fellow Creative Arts Inst., U. Calif., Berkeley, 1970, NEH Summer Inst., Dartmouth Coll., 1987; Danforth Found. assoc., 1978, NEH Seminar, Cornell U., 1998. Jewish. Office: Pitzer Coll Claremont Colls Claremont CA 91711-6101 Office Phone: 909-607-3641. Business E-Mail: awachtel@pitzer.edu.

WACHTEL, LEE ELIZABETH, psychiatrist, educator; b. Atlanta, July 15, 1971; m. Yoel Wachtel, July 1995; children: Naava Bracha, Shaya Kfir. AB, Princeton U., NJ, 1993; MD, Johns Hopkins Sch. Medicine, Balt., 1998. Diplomate in psychiatry Am. Bd. Psychiatry and Neurology, 2004, in child and adolescent psychiatry 2005. Child and adolescent psychiatrist Kennedy Krieger Inst., Balt., 2003—, med. dir., neurobehavioral unit, 2004—; clin. instr. Johns Hopkins U. Sch. Medicine, Dept. Psychiatry, Balt., 2003—06, asst. prof., 2006—. Contbr. articles to numerous sci. jours., chapters to books. Office: Kennedy Krieger Inst 707 N Broadway St Baltimore MD 21205 Office Phone: 443-923-7732. Business E-Mail: wachtel@kennedykrieger.org.

WACHTEL, MITCHELL STEVEN, pathologist; b. NYC, May 22, 1959; s. Herbert Leonard and Lenore Esther Wachtel; m. June Grace Wagner, July 20, 1984. BA in Chemistry, Columbia Coll., 1981; MD, U. Miami, 1985. Cert. anatomic and clin. pathology Am. Bd. Pathology, 1991. Resident New England Deaconess Hosp., 1985—89; fellowship Meml. Sloan Kettering Cancer Ctr., 1989—92; assoc. prof. Tex. Tech. health Scis. Ctr., Lubbock, 2004—, dir. cytology, 2004—05; asst. prof. Oregon Health Svcs. Ctr., UAML, 1992—94; pathologist Associated Pathologists Chartered, Las Vegas, 1994—97, Fair Fox Pathology Assocs., 1997—2000, Austin Pathology Assocs., 2000—04. Contbr. articles to profl. jours. Alt. del. Coll. Am. Pathologists, Chgo., 2003—05. Mem.: Alpha Omega Alpha. Achievements include research that proved Bayes' thoerem does not apply in certain situations. Office: TTUHSC-School of Medicine Dept Pathology STOP 8115 Lubbock TX 79430-8115 Office Fax: 806-743-2117. Personal E-mail: mitchellwachtel@msn.com. E-mail: mitchell.wachtel@ttuhsc.edu.

WACHTEL, PAUL, economist; b. NYC, Nov. 18, 1945; s. Mitchell and Dora Wachtel; m. Claire Reich, Feb. 20, 1983; children: Chaim, Rachel. BA, Queens Coll. CUNY, Flushing, 1966; PhD, U. Rochester, 1971. Prof. NY U., 1972—. Home: 771 West End Ave New York NY 10025 Office: NYU Stern Sch 44 West 4th St 7-87 New York NY 10012 Business E-Mail: pwachtel@stern.nyu.edu.

WACHTER, SUSAN MELINDA, finance educator; b. June 22, 1943; d. Nathaniel and Edith (Dubow) Jaffe; m. Michael Lawrence Wachter, June 23, 1968; children: Jessica, Jonathan. BA, Radcliffe Coll., 1965; PhD, Boston Coll., 1974; MA (hon.), U. Pa., 1978. Lectr. Bryn Mawr Coll., Pa., 1969-72; lectr. Wharton Sch. U. Pa., Phila., 1972-74, asst. prof. fin., 1974-78, assoc. prof., 1978-95, prof. real estate and fin., 1995—, chmn. real estate dept., 1997—99; asst. sec., policy devel. and rsch. HUD, 1999—2001; Richard B. Warley prof. fin. mgmt., 2003—. Bd. dirs. Beneficial Corp., Beneficial Mortgage Corp. Author: Latin American Inflation: The Structuralist-Monetarist Debat, 1976, Inflation and Pensions, 1987; co-author: Redlining and Public Policy, 1980; co-editor: Towards a New U.S. Industrial Policy?, 1981, Removing Obstacles to Economic Growth, 1984, Real Estate Economics, 1997, Savings and Capital Formation: The Policy Options; editor: Social Security and Private Pensions: Planning for the 21st Century, 1988; bd. editors Jour. Real Estate Rsch., Jour. Am. Real Estate and Urban Econs., Jour. Housing Econs., Jour. Real Estate Fin. and Econs. Recipient Lindbach award Lindbach Soc., 1974-75; Rsch. fellow Harvard U., 1966. Mem. Am. Econ. Assn., Am. Fin. Assn., Econometric Soc., Am. Real Estate and Urban Econs. Assn. (bd. dirs. 1984-91, pres. 1988), Lambda Alpha. Home: 355 Margo Ln Berwyn PA 19312-1453 Office: U Pa Finance Dept Philadelphia PA 19104 Home Phone: 610-294-9714; Office Phone: 215-898-6355. Business E-Mail: wachter@wharton.upenn.edu.

WACHTLER, SOL, lawyer, educator; b. NYC, Apr. 29, 1930; s. Philip Henry and Fay (Sobel) W.; m. Joan Wolosoff, Feb. 23, 1952; children: Lauren Jane, Marjorie Dru, Alison Toni, Philip Henry. BA, Washington and Lee U., 1951, LLB, 1952, postgrad., 1980, LLD (hon.), 1981, New Eng. Sch. Law, 1978, Bklyn. Law Sch., 1978, Hofstra U., 1980, SUNY, 1981, Syracuse U., Dowling Coll., 1990, Thomas M. Cooley Law Sch., 1990, New. Eng. Law Sch.; LHD (hon.), LIU, Coll. of St. Rose. Bar: N.Y. 1956. Justice NY State Supreme Ct., 1968-72; judge NY State Ct. Appeals, Albany, 1972-84, chief judge, 1985-93; prof. law Touro Law Sch., 1997—. Guest lectr. Bklyn. Law Sch., Hofstra Law Sch., Yale U. Sch. Law, Albany Law Sch., St. John's Law Sch., 1968-77, USIA, Munich, Germany, 1973, Stuttgart, Germany, 1977, U. Leyden, Amsterdam, Stockholm, 1988, Madrid, 1989; chmn. NY State Fair Trial/Free Press Conf., NY State Commn. on Bicentennial of US Constitution.; bd. dirs. Confs. Chief Justices; trustee Nat Jud. Coll. Author: After the Madness, 1997, Blood Brothers, 2003; critic-at-large New Yorker mag., 1996; contbr. articles to legal jours. Councilman Town of North Hempstead, N.Y., 1963-65, chief exec., 1965-67; mem. Nassau County Bd. Suprs., 1965-67, chmn. com. pub. safety, 1965-67; trustee L.I. Jewish-Hillside Med. Ctr., 1970-98, L.I. U.; exec. com. North Shore L.I. Jewish Health Sys., 1998—; bd. overseers Nelson A. Rockefeller Inst. Govt., Touro Law Sch., 2002-; dist. chmn. Boy Scouts Am., 1968-69; trustee Cerebral Palsy Assn., Assn. for Help of Retarded Children, 1966-67. Mem. Am. Law Inst., Assn. N.Y. State Supreme Ct. Justices, ABA, N.Y. State Bar Assn., Nassau County Bar Assn., Order of Coif, Phi Delta Phi. Jewish. Home: 10 Stonehill Dr N Manhasset NY 11030-4438 Personal E-mail: SWCADRE@aol.com. *As a people, we are fond of the observation that ours is a nation of laws and not of men. It too, like the words of our great laws, seems to lend security, a sense of certainty, and a predictability to the paths we travel. In the law particularly, the thought that past generations have separated right from wrong and good from evil can be comforting. Yet, here again, if we will just scratch the surface, we will find that the greatest responsibility for our national welfare does not rest with statutes carved in stone but with the principles, conscience, and morality of the individuals who constitute this generation.*

WACHTMAN, JEANETTE MARIE, art educator, artist, writer; d. John and Margaret Wachtman. BS in Art Edn., State U. Coll., Buffalo, 1971, MS in Art Edn., 1972. Cert. permanent tchg. State U. Coll. -Buffalo, 1972, tchr. 1-5 Ga., 1991. Tchr. art Phoenix Sch. Dist., 1973—83, Suzuki Internat. Learning Ctr., Atlanta, 1984—85, Clayton State Coll., Ga., 1984—85, Chastain Art Ctr., Atlanta, 1984—86, Atlanta Coll. Art, 1988—92, Steeple Art Ctr., Marietta, Ga., 1990—92, Kennesaw State U., Ga., 1988—, Cobb County Schs., Marietta, 1991—. Mem. bd. Ga. Art Edn. Assn., 1995—2001, chair state capitol art exhibit, 1995—2000, co-chair office of govt. art exhibit, Ga., 1996—2000, chair elem. divsn., 1999—2001, art advocacy rep., 2000; mem. elem. divsn. devel. com. Nat. Art Edn. Assn., 1999—2000; presenter, lectr. in field. Author: (book) The How of It - A Cultural Program Resource Guide, 1995, Artists, Elements, and Principles of Art, 2001; co-author: Rhythmongs - The History of Art, 2000; one-woman shows include The Octagon House, Camillus, NY, 1977, Seneca Wall Gallery, Liverpool, NY, 1979, Woman in the Arts Festival, Syracuse, NY, 1980, Penfield Libr., SUNY, Oswego, 1981, Liverpool Art Gallery, NY, 1982, Trail of Tears Art Gallery, Atlanta, 1984, Inner Space Gallery, 1993, Istanbul Ctr. for Culture and Dialogue, Norcross, Ga., 2006, The Art Station, Big Shanty, Kennsaw, Ga., 2007. Organizer and presenter cmty. based arts edn. program Blackwell Elem. Sch., Cobb County, Marietta. Recipient Youth Art Month award of Excellence, Ga. Art Edn. Assn., 1999, Outstanding Continuing Educator award, Kennesaw State U., 1993, Target, 2002; named Tchr. of Yr., Bryant Elem. Sch., 1996—97, Ga.'s Elem. Art Educator of Yr., Ga. Art Edn. Assn., 1997—98, Elem. Art Educator of Yr., Nat. Art Edn. Assn., 1999; grantee, CVS, 2001, So. Bell, 1992—93, N.Y. State Edn. Dept., 1979, Ga. Coun. Arts, 2007. Mem.: Ga. Art Edn. Assn., Nat. Art Edn. Assn. Avocations: travel, art, writing. Home Fax: 770-894-3934. Personal E-mail: rajean@tds.net.

WACHTMANN, LYNN R., state legislator; b. Napoleon, Ohio, Dec. 24, 1954; m. Trudy Blue; children: Cory, Aaron. Grad., Four County Joint Vocat. Sch. Owner, pres. Maumee Valley Bottlers, Inc., Napoleon, Ohio; Owner/Pres. Culligan Water Conditioning; former councilman City of Napoleon; mem. Ohio House of Reps., Ohio, 1985—98, Ohio Senate from 1st dist., Columbus, 1999—2007, chmn. health, human svcs. and aging com., mem. energy, natural resources, environment, highways and transp., ins., commerce and labor coms.; mem. Dist 75 Ohio House of Reps., 2007—. Vol. fundraiser Crisis Pregnancy Ctrs. of N.W. Ohio, Bryan; vol. Orphan Grain Train; mem. Rep. Ctrl. Com.; Sunday sch. tchr., usher St. Paul Luth. Ch.; bd. dirs. Ohio Water Quality Assn. Recipient Bobcat Legis. award, 1993, Watchdog of the Treasury award, United Conservatives of Ohio, Oustanding Freshman Legislator of Yr. award, 2000, Grad. Wall of Fame award, Four County Joint Vocat. Sch., 1997, Legislator of Yr. Defender of Life award, Ohio Right to Life, 1997, Conservation Legis. award, League of Ohio Sportsmen Nat. Wildlife Fedn., 1997, Guardian of Small Bus. award, Nat. Fedn. Ind. Bus., 1998; named Nat. Legislator of Yr., Am. Legis. Exch. Coun., 1994, State Legislator of Yr., Nat. Retail Fedn., 1996, Legislator of Yr., Am. Legion, 2000. Mem.: NRA, Ohio Twp. Assn., Nat. Assn. Sportsman Legislators, Am. Legis. Exch. Coun. (state chmn.), Ohio Right to Life Soc., Gideon's Internat., Ohio Farm Bur., Pheasants Forever, Ducks Unlimited. Republican. Lutheran. Office: 550 Euclid Ave Napoleon OH 43545-2028 also: 10th Fl 77 S High St Columbus OH 43215 Office Phone: 614-466-8150, 614-466-3760. E-mail: district75@ohr.state.oh.us.*

WACHTMEISTER, COUNT WILHELM H.F., retired diplomat; b. Vanas, Sweden, Apr. 29, 1923; s. Gustaf and Margaretha (Trolle) W.; m. Ulla Leuhusen, 1947; children: Anna, Erik. LLD, U. Stockholm, Sweden, 1946. Attache Swedish Ministry for Fgn. Affairs, 1946-47; attache Swedish Embassy, Vienna, Madrid and Lisbon, 1947-50; 2d sec. Swedish Ministry Fgn. Affairs, Stockholm, Sweden, 1950-55; 1st sec. Swedish Embassy, Moscow, 1955-58; personal asst. to UN Sec. Gen., 1958-61; head UN sect. Fgn. Ministry, Stockholm, 1962-65, dep. under-sec. polit. affairs, 1965-66; ambassador to Algeria Swedish Embassy, 1966-67; under-sec. for polit. affairs Swedish Ministry Fgn. Affairs, Stockholm, 1968-74; Swedish ambassador to U.S. Swedish Embassy, Washington, 1974-89; dean diplomatic corps in Washington, 1986-89. Sr. advisor to chmn. AB Volvo, 1989-94. Mem. Soc. Cincinnati (France), Nya Sällskapet, Swedish-Am. C. of C. (chmn. 1993-95), Sällskapet, Stockholm. Avocation: tennis. Address: Karlavagen 59A SE 11449 Stockholm Sweden

WACKER, KELLY LYNN, audiologist, educator; BE in Communication Disorders, U. Nebr., Kearney, 2000; MS in Audiology, U. Nebr., Lincoln, 2002; PhD in Audiology, Pa. Coll. Optometry, Sch. Audiology, Elkins Pk., 2007. Audiologist Bloomington-Normal Audiology, Ill., 2005—07; audiology clin. coord., asst. prof. practice U. Nebr., Lincoln, 2007—.

WACKER, WARREN ERNEST CLYDE, internist, educator; b. Bklyn., Feb. 29, 1924; s. John Frederick and Kitty Dora (Morrissey) W.; m. Ann Romeyn MacMillan, May 22, 1948; children: Margaret Morrissey, John Frederick. Student, Georgetown U., 1946—47; MD, George Washington U., 1951; MA (hon.), Harvard U., 1968. Intern George Washington U. Hosp., 1951-52, resident in internal medicine, 1952-53; resident Peter Bent Brigham Hosp., Boston, 1953-55; Nat. Found. Infantile Paralysis fellow, 1955-57; investigator Howard Hughes Med. Inst., Boston, 1957-68; from faculty to prof. hygiene Harvard U., Cambridge, Mass., 1955-71, assoc. prof. medicine, 1968—71, 1971—89, acting master Mather House, 1974-75, acting master Kirkland House, 1975-76, master Cabot House, 1978-84; sr. med. cons. Risk Mgmt. Found., Cambridge, 1992—; Henry K. Oliver prof. hygiene emeritus Harvard U., Cambridge, 1995—. Dir. health svcs. Harvard U., Cambridge, 1971-89; vis. scholar St. Mary's Hosp. Med. Sch., 1964; vis. prof. U. Tel Aviv, 1987; chmn. bd. Applied Mgmt. Sys., Burlington, Mass., 1982-97, Millipore Corp., Bedford, Mass., 1971-94. Author: Magnesium and Man, 1981; sec., editl. adv. bd. Biochemistry, 1962-76; assoc. editor Magnesium; mem. editl. bd. Toxiogical and Environ. Chemistry, 1989-2006; contbr. articles to profl. jours. Vestryman St. Paul's Episc. Ch., Brookline, Mass., 1965-68, 76-79, 91-94; bd. dirs. Harvard Cmty. Health Plan, Boston, 1973-84, mem. fin. com., 1984-86, mem. corp., 1986-96; bd. dirs. Bishop Rhinelander Found., Cambridge, 1973-76, 78-84, Controlled Risk Ins. Co., 1976-78; pres. bd. overseers Peter Bent Brigham Hosp., Boston, 1979-84; trustee Brigham and Women's Hosp., Boston, 1984-89, Risk Mgmt. Found., 1979-92; mem. mgmt. bd. MIT, 1985-95; mem. corp. Mt. Auburn Hosp., Cambridge, 1986—2006; mem. adv. bd. hospitality program Episc. Diocese Mass., 1989-95. 1st lt. USAAF, 1942-45. Decorated Air medal, D.F.C., Liberation medal, Greece; named Disting. Alumnus, George Washington U., 1963; recipient Cert. of Merit, Soc. Magnesium Rsch., 1985. Mem. AMA, Am. Chem. Soc., Am. Soc. Biol. Chemistry, Am. Soc. Clin. Investigation, Mass. Med. Soc., ACP, Am. Coll. Health Assn. (pres. 1981, Boynton award 1986), Biochemistry Soc. (London), Am. Coll. Nutrition, Harvard Club (Boston), Sigma Xi, Alpha Omega Alpha. Office: Crico/Risk Mgmt Found 101 Main St Cambridge MA 02142-1519 Home: 77 Pond Ave Apt 401 Brookline MA 02445 Office Phone: 617-679-1216. Business E-Mail: wwacker@rmf.harvard.edu.

WACKERMANN, WILLIAM J., publishing executive; m. Regina Wackermann; 3 children. Grad., Villanova U., Pa., 1989. Mktg. mgr. Bus. Week, NY Times; various positions Vanity Fair; assoc. pub. House & Garden, 1998—99; NY advt. mgr. Condé Nast Traveler Condé Nast Publs., 1996—97, advt. mgr., 1997—98, assoc. pub., 1999—2000, v.p., pub. Details mag., 2000—04, v.p., pub. Glamour mag., 2004—08, sr. v.p., pub. dir., 2008—, sr. v.p., pub. dir. Condé Nast Bridal Media, 2008—. Recipient Media Mavens award, Advt. Age, 2003; named Mag. Pub. of Yr., Delaney Report, 2002; named one of Top 40 Under 40, Crain's NY Bus., 2004. Office: Glamour Mag 4 Times Sq New York NY 10036-6522*

WADA, YUMIKO, pharmacologist; PhD, Hokkaido U., Japan. Rsch. scientist Fuji Immunopharmaceuticals Corp., Lexington, Mass., 1993—97; sr. scientist Shionogi BioRsch. Corp., Lexington, 1997—2002; dir. pharmacology Synta Pharms. Corp, Lexington, 2002—07, sr. dir. pharmacology, 2007—. Mem.: Am. Assn. Immunologists. Office: Synta Pharms Corp 45 Hartwell Ave Lexington MA 02421 Office Fax: 781-274-8228. Business E-Mail: ywada@syntapharma.com.

WADDELL, DON, professional sports team executive; b. Detroit, Aug. 19, 1958; m. Cheryl Waddell; 1 child, Chelsea. Defenseman No. Mich. U. (Divsn. I Hockey), 1976—80; defenseman, coach Toledo Goaldiggers, 1985—86, Flint Spirits, 1986—88, head coach, gen. mgr., 1988—90; v.p., exec. com. San Diego Gulls, 1990—95, head coach, 1991—92; v.p., exec. com. Orlando Solar Bears, 1995—97; asst. gen. mgr. Detroit Red Wings, 1997—98; v.p., gen. mgr. Atlanta Thrashers, Atlanta, 1998—, interim head coach, 2007—. Mem. US Nat. Team, 1983; asst. gen. mgr. Team USA World Championships, 1999—2000, gen. mgr., 2001—02. Named First Team Internat. Hockey League All-Star, 1982, 1986, Second Team Internat. Hockey League All-Star, 1988; named to CCHA All-Decade Team, No. Mich. U., 1970. Achievements include inducted into the Northern Michigan University Sports Hall of Fame, 1992; being the assistant general manager of Stanley Cup Champion Detroit Red Wings, 1997, 1998. Office: c/o Atlanta Thrashers 101 Marietta St NW Atlanta GA 30303

WADDELL, DOUGLAS HOWARD, family physician; b. Bluff City, TN, May 6, 1943; s. Cecil Howard and France Daisy (Boling) W.; m. Luz Isabel Garza, Jan 2, 1971; children: Amy, Christopher, Brandon. BS in Biology, Chemistry, Carson-Newman Coll., Jefferson City, Tenn., 1965; MD, U. Tenn., 1969. Diplomate Am. Bd. Family Practice. Intern Baylor U. Med. Ctr., Dallas, 1970; physician, owner Launey Med. Clinic, Dallas, 1971-82, Beltline North Med. Clinic, Dallas, 1983-85, Atrium Med. Clinic, Dallas, 1985—. Fellow Am. Acad. Family Physicians; mem. Tex. Med. Assn., Dallas County Med. Soc., Tex. Acad. Family Physicians (bd. dirs. state assn., past sec., treas., v.p., pres. Dallas chpt.), Am. Coll. Occupational and Environ. Medicine. Republican. Baptist. Avocations: gardening, cooking. Home: 10473 Epping Ln Dallas TX 75229-6310 Office: PO Box 670589 Dallas TX 75367-0589 Home Phone: 214-350-2370; Office Phone: 972-247-6900. Personal E-mail: dhwaddell@yahoo.com.

WADDELL, ELIZABETH NEEDHAM, research scientist, educator; b. Murfreesboro, Tenn., Feb. 12, 1973; d. Merrill Arthur Needham, Jr. and Donna Dorr Needham; m. Perry Waddell, Aug. 16, 2003. BA in English and Urban Studies, U. Pa., Phila., 1995; MA in Sociology, Columbia U., NYC, 1998; PhD in Sociomed. Scis., Columbia U., 2003. Postdoctoral fellow Med. Health & Rsch. Assn. NYC, Inc., 2003—05; lectr. Mailman Sch. Pub. Health, Columbia U., 2004—; rsch. scientist NYC Dept. Health & Mental Hygiene, NYC, 2005—, dir. health & nutrition exam. survey, 2007—. Contbr. articles to profl. jours. Fellow Health Disparities Rsch. LRP, NIH, 2004—09; U. Profs. fellowship, Columbia U., 1998—2003, Grad. fellowship, Inst. Social & Econ. Rsch. & Policy, Columbia U., 2001—03. Mem.: Am. Soicological Assn., Pub. Health Assn. NYC, APHA. Office: NYC Dept Health & Mental Hygiene 125 Worth St Rm 315 CN-6 New York NY 10013 Business E-Mail: ewaddell@health.nyc.gov.

WADDELL, FREDERICK H. (RICK WADDELL), finance company executive; b. June 14, 1953; BA, Dartmouth Coll., 1975; MBA, Northwestern U., 1979. Various positions Northern Trust Corp., Chgo., 1975—83, v.p., 1983—89, exec. v.p., Northern Trust Bank Calif., 1991—94, exec. v.p., wealth mgmt. group, 1994—2003, pres., corp. & instl. svc., 2003—06, pres., COO, 2006—08, pres., CEO, 2008—. Bd. dirs. Fed. Res. Bank Chgo., 2008—. Chmn. bd. trustees Kohl Children's Mus.; trustee Art Inst. Chgo., treas., mem. exec. com. Mem.: Comml. Club Chgo., Fin. Svcs. Roundtable, Exec. Club Chgo. (bd. dirs.). Avocations: reading, travel, golf. Office: Northern Trust Corp 50 S LaSalle St Chicago IL 60603 Office Phone: 312-444-3939. Office Fax: 312-444-7843.

WADDELL, JOHN COMER, electronics executive; b. Bridgeport, Conn., Sept. 10, 1937; s. John and Dorothy Margot (Comer) W. BA, Yale U., New Haven, 1959; MBA, Harvard U., 1965. Assoc. R.W. Pressprich & Co., NYC, 1965-68; ptnr. Glenn, Green & Waddell, NYC, 1968-80; exec. v.p. Arrow Electronics, Inc., Melville, NY, 1969-80, chmn., CEO, 1980—86, chmn., 1986—94, vice chmn., 1994—. Mem. com. arch. & design Mus. Modern Art, NYC; mem. com. photographs Met. Mus. Art, NYC; co-chmn. Joffrey Ballet; past pres. Found. for Joffrey Ballet; dir. 55th St. Dance Theater Found., Nat. Corp. Fund for Dance, Am. Arts Alliance. Officer Office of Naval Intelligence USN. Office: Arrow Electronics Inc 50 Marcus Dr Melville NY 11747-4210 Office Phone: 631-847-2000.*

WADDELL, M. KEITH, consulting company executive; From v.p. to vice chmn., CFO, treas. Robert Half Internat. Inc., Menlo Pk., Calif., 1986—93, treas., 1987—2004, vice chmn., CFO, 1999—2004, vice-chmn., pres., CFO, 2004—. Office: Robert Half International Inc 2884 SandHill Rd Menlo Park CA 94025

WADDELL, MARK E., lawyer; b. Dec. 3, 1957; BSChemE, NJ Inst. Tech., 1979; JD, Seton Hall U., 1984. Bar: NJ 1985, NY 1985, US Ct. Appeals (Fed. Cir.), registered: US Patent & Trademark Office. Process develop. engr., 1979—83; patent atty. Hubbell Cohen, NYC, 1983—86; atty., patent law dept. Hoffmann-La Roche Inc., NYC, 1986—87; patent atty. Cohen, Pontani & Lieberman, NYC; ptnr. Bryan Cave LLP, NYC, 1991—2001, mem. exec. com & strategic planning com., chmn., Intellectual Property Practice Group; ptnr., intellectual property dept., litig. dept. Chadbourne & Parke LLP, NYC, 2001—07; ptnr. Loeb & Loeb LLP, NYC, 2007—. Spkr. in field; contbr. articles to profl. jour. Mem.: Intellectual Property Owners Assn., Fed. Cir. Bar Assn., NY Intellectual Property Law Assn. Office: Loeb & Loeb LLP 345 Park Ave New York NY 10154 E-mail: mwaddell@loeb.com.

WADDELL, WILLIAM JOSEPH, pharmacologist, toxicologist; b. Commerce, Ga., Mar. 16, 1929; s. Daniel and Lillian Marie (Vollrath) Waddell; m. Grace Carolyn Marlowe, Oct. 19, 1974; children: William Joseph, James Glenn, Martin Christie, Amy Allison. AB in Chemistry, U. N.C., 1951, MD, 1955. Postdoctoral rsch. fellow U. N.C. Sch. Medicine, 1955-58, asst. prof. pharmacology, 1958-62, asso. prof., 1962-72, assoc. prof. oral biology Dental Rsch. Ctr., 1967-69, prof., 1969-72, assoc. dir., 1968-72; prof. pharmacology U. Ky. Coll. Medicine, Lexington, 1972-77; prof., chmn. dept. pharmacology and toxicology U. Louisville, 1977-97, emeritus chmn., 1997—, prof. emeritus, 1998—. Centennial Alumni Disting. vis. prof. U. N.C. Sch. Medicine, 1979. Contbr. articles to profl. jours. Fellow: Acad. Toxicological Scis.; mem.: Soc. Toxicology, Soc. Exptl. Biology and Medicine, Internat. Soc. Study Xenobiotics, Am. Teratology Soc., Am. Physiol. Soc., Am. Soc. Pharmacology and Exptl. Therapeutics, Sigma Xi. Home: 14300 Rose Wycombe Rd Prospect KY 40059-9024 Office: U Louisville Dept Pharmacology Louisville KY 40292-0001 Office Phone: 502-228-4220. Business E-Mail: bwaddell@louisville.edu.

WADDELL, WILLIAM ROBERT, lawyer; b. Ft. Thomas, Ky., Nov. 24, 1940; s. Ewell Edward and Sara Isabel (Dean) W.; m. Linda Kay Waddle, Aug. 25, 1962; children: Robert William, Keith Edward, Alex Watson. AB, Williams Coll., 1962; JD, U. Va., 1965. Bar: Va. 1965, U.S. Dist. Ct. (ea. dist.) Va. 1966, U.S. Ct. Appeals (4th cir.) 1966, U.S. Supreme Ct. 1966, N.C. 1991. Assoc. McGuire, Woods, Battle & Boothe, Richmond, Va., 1965—69, ptnr., 1969—. Adj. faculty Sch. Law, U. Va., 1995-; bd. dirs. Cmty. Bank Virginia Beach, Va., The George Found., Alex Lee, Inc., Hickory, N.C., Downtown Rep. Club, Norfolk, Va., Greater Norfolk Corp. Author: Virginia Corporations, 2009, Dispute Resolution: A Survey, 2008; contbr. articles to profl. jours Pres. Bon Air Cmty. Assn., Richmond, 1979-80; bd. dirs., sec. Va. Advanced Tech. Assn., Richmond, 1986-96; chmn. The Steward Sch., 1985-88, Jr. Achievement of Richmond, Inc., 1989-90. Mem. ABA (comml. code com., sales subcom. 1982—, chmn. telecomm. com. 1986-90, 94-96, vice-chmn. com. on law of commerce in cyberspace 1996-98, dispute resolution com. 1990—), Order of Coif. Avocations: tennis, history, woodworking. Office: McGuireWoods LLP 1 James Ctr 901 E Cary St Richmond VA 23219 also: McGuireWoods LLP World Trade Ctr 101 W Main St Ste 9000 Norfolk VA 23510-1655 Business E-Mail: wwaddell@mcguirewoods.com.

WADDEN, RICHARD ALBERT, environmental engineer, educator, science administrator, consultant; b. Sioux City, Iowa, Oct. 3, 1936; s. Sylvester Francis and Hermina Lillian (Costello) Wadden; m. Angela Louise Trabert, Aug. 9, 1975; children: Angela Terese, Noah Albert, Nuiko Clare. Student, St. John's U., Collegeville, Minn., 1954-56; BSChemE, Iowa State U., 1959; MSChemE, N.C. State U., 1962; PhD in Chem. and Environ. Engring., Northwestern U., 1972. Registered profl. engr., Ill., cert. indsl. hygienist. Engr. Linde Co., Tonnawanda, NY, 1959-60, Humble Oil Co., Houston, 1962-65; instr. engring. Pahlavi U. Peace Corps, Shiraz, Iran, 1965-67; tech. adviser Ill. Pollution Control Bd., Chgo., 1971-72; asst. dir. Environ. Health Resource Ctr. Ill., Chgo., 1972-74; from asst. prof. to assoc. prof. environ. and occupational health scis. Sch. Pub. Health U. Ill., Chgo., 1972—79, prof., 1979—2003, dir., 1984-86, 88-92, dir. Office Tech. Transfer Ctr. Solid Waste Mgmt. and Rsch., 1987-92, dir. indsl. hygiene and hazardous waste tng. programs Occupl. Safety and Health Ctr., 1987—2002, prof. emeritus, 2003—. Vis. scientist Nat. Inst. Environ. Studies, Japan, 1978—79, invited scientist, Japan, 1983, Japan, 84, Japan, 88; cons. air pollution control, health implications energy devel., indoor air pollution. Author: (book) Energy Utilization and Environmental Health, 1978; author: (with P. A. Scheff) Indoor Air Pollution, 1983; author: Engineering Design for Control of Workplace Hazards, 1987; contbr. articles to profl. publs. Vis. scholar, Northwestern U., Evanston, Ill., 1997; Sr. Internat. fellow, Fogarty Internat. Ctr.-NIH, 1978—79, 1983, WHO fellow, 1984. Mem.: AIChE, Am. Conf. Govtl. Indsl. Hygienists, Am. Indsl. Hygiene Assn., Air and Waste Mgmt. Assn., Am. Acad. Indsl. Hygiene (diplomate), Am. Acad. Environ. Engrs. (diplomate), Am. Chem. Soc. Address: 816 16th St Wilmette IL 60091

WADDEN, THOMAS ANTONY, psychologist, educator; b. Richmond, Va., Sept. 3, 1952; s. Thomas Antony Jr. and Mary Lloyd (Cradock) W.; m. Jan Robin Linowitz, Nov. 11, 1984; children: David Joseph, Michael James, Steven Zachary. AB magna cum laude, Brown U., 1975; PhD, U. NC, 1981; MA (hon.), U. Pa., 1994. Psychology intern Boston VA Med. Ctr., 1980-81; instr. in psychology U. Pa. Sch. Medicine, Phila., 1981-82, asst. prof. psychology, 1982-87, assoc. prof. psychology, 1987-91, prof. psychology, 1994—; prof. psychology, dir. clin. tng. Syracuse U., NY, 1992-93. Clin. dir. Obesity Rsch. Group, U. Pa., Phila., 1983-91, dir. Ctr. for Weight and Eating Disorders, 1994—; dir. Ctr. for Health and Behavior, Syracuse U., 1992-93. Author (with K.D. Brownell): LEARN Program for Weight Control, 1998; assoc. editor: Annals of Behavioral Medicine, 1990—93, Obesity, 2007—, mem. editl. bd.: Internat. Jour. Eating Disorders, Internat. Jour. Obesity, Jour. Cons. and Clin. Psychology, Obesity Rsch.; editor (with T.B. VanItallie): Treatment of the Seriously Obese Patient, 1992; editor: (with A.J. Stunkard) Obesity: Theory and Therapy, 1993, Handbook of Obesity Treatment, 2002; editor: (with A.J. Stunkard & R.I. Berkowitz) Obesity: A Guide for Mental Health Professionals, 2005; contbr. chapters to books; writer: numerous sci. papers. Recipient Nat. Rsch. Svc. award NIMH, 1983-85, Rsch. Scientist Devel. award, 1987-91, 94-2000, Midcareer Investigator award in patient oriented rsch., 2003—. Mem. APA, Soc. Behavioral Medicine (bd. dir. 1987-90), Assn. for Advancement of Behavior Therapy (New Rschr. award 1986), Acad. Behavioral Medicine, Obesity Soc. (v.p. 2003-04, pres. 2005-06), Germantown Cricket Club, Cosmos Club, Phi Beta Kappa, Sigma Xi. Democrat. Avocations: squash, music. Office Phone: 215-746-5046. Business E-Mail: wadden@mail.med.upenn.edu.

WADDILL, CYNTHIA KAY, orthopaedic nurse practitioner; d. Owen Lee and Epsie Adrias Sugg; m. Dale Alin Waddill, July 16, 1993; children: Stacy Kay Emfinger, Christopher Ryan Emfinger, Jamison Matthew Emfinger. ADN, U. Ark., Little Rock, 1984; BSN, U. Phoenix, 2000, MSN, 2001, Graceland U., 2003. RN, cert. orthop. nurse, oper. rm. nurse. Orthop. trauma charge nurse U. Ark. Med Sci. Campus, Little Rock, 1991—96, Shands Hosp., Jacksonville, Fla., 1996—2001; nurse Shands U. Fla. Hosp., Jacksonville, 2004—05, Mcleod Regional Med. Ctr., 2005—08, Ctrl. Vets. Hosp., 2008—. Sr. nurse cons. Orthop. Trauma Practice Cons., Jacksonville, 2001—. Mem.: ANA, Fla. Nurses Assn., Am. Acad. Nurse Practitioners, Nat. Assn. Orthop. Nurses, Sigma Theta Tau. Baptist. Avocations: scuba diving, golf, fishing. Personal E-mail: cbones100k@aol.com.

WADDINGTON, RAYMOND BRUCE, JR., language educator; b. Santa Barbara, Calif., Sept. 27, 1935; s. Raymond Bruce and Marjorie Gladys (Waddell) W.; m. Linda Gayle Jones, Sept. 7, 1957 (div.); children: Raymond Bruce, Edward Jackson; m. Kathleen Martha Ward, Oct. 11, 1985. BA, Stanford U., 1957; PhD, Rice U., 1963; postdoctoral (Univ. fellow in Humanities), Johns Hopkins U., 1965-66. Instr. English U. Houston, 1961-62; instr. U. Kans., 1962-63, asst. prof., 1963-65; asst. prof. English lit. U. Wis., Madison, 1966-68, assoc. prof., 1968-74, prof., 1974-82; prof. English lit. U. Calif., Davis, 1982—2005. Author: The Mind's Empire, 1974, Aretino's Satyr, 2004, (Italian transl.), 2009; co-editor: The Rhetoric of Renaissance Poetry, 1974, The Age of Milton, 1980, The Expulsion of the Jews, 1994; mem. editl. bd. The Medal, 1991; sr. editor: Sixteenth Century Jour.; editor: Praeger Series on the Early Modern World. Recipient Scaglione prize for Italian Studies, 2005; Huntington Libr. fellow, 1967, 75; Inst. Rsch. in Humanities fellow, 1971-72; Guggenheim fellow, 1972-73; NEH fellow, 1977, 83; Newberry Libr. fellow, 1978; Am. Philos. Soc. grantee, 1965, Gladys Krieble Delmas Found. grantee, 2007. Mem. Renaissance Soc. Am., Milton Soc. Am., Am. Numismatic Soc., 16th Century Soc. and Conf. (pres. 1985), Brit. Art Medal Soc., Logos Club. Home: 39 Pershing Ave Woodland CA 95695-2845 Office: U Calif Dept English Davis CA 95616 E-mail: rbwaddington@ucdavis.edu.

WADDOUPS, CLARK, federal judge; b. Arco, Idaho, Apr. 21, 1946; s. Royal and Veta Lorene (Jones) W.; m. Vickie Lee Tibbitts, Dec. 16, 1967; children: Douglas Clark, Lorene, James Clark, Mary, Amy. Student, Ricks Coll., 1964-65; BA, Brigham Young U., 1970; JD, U. Utah, 1973. Bar: Calif. 1973, Utah 1982. Law clk. to Hon. J. Clifford Wallace US Ct. Appeals (9th cir.), San Diego, 1973-74; assoc. O'Melveny & Myers LLP, LA, 1974-81; ptnr. Kimball, Parr, Waddoups, Brown & Gee, Salt Lake City, 1981—2008; judge US Dist. Ct. Utah, Salt Lake City, 2008—. Office: US District Court District of Utah 350 S Main St Rm 150 Salt Lake City UT 84101 E-mail: utdecf_waddoups@utd.uscourts.gov.*

WADDY, LAWRENCE HEBER, writer; b. Sydney, Oct. 5, 1914; came to U.S., 1963; s. Percival Stacy and Etheldred (Spittal) W.; m. Laurie Hancock, July 10, 1972. BA, Oxford U., 1937, MA, 1945. Asst. master Winchester Coll. Eng., 1938—42; headmaster Tonbridge Sch., England, 1949—62; edn. officer BBC, 1962—63; chaplain The Bishop's Sch., La Jolla, Calif., 1963—67; lectr. in Greek and Latin lit. U. Calif., San Diego, 1969—80; vicar Ch. of Good Samaritan, University City, Calif., 1970—74; hon. asst. St. James By The Sea Episcopal Ch., La Jolla, 1975—. Author: Pax Romana & World Peace, 1950, Symphony, 1976, A Parish By the Sea, 1988, Shakespeare Remembers, 1994, First Bible Stories, 1994, Florence Nightingale, 1996, Bible Drama, 2004. Chaplain, British Navy, 1942-46. Recipient Drama 1st prize BBC, 1964. Republican. Episcopalian. Home: 5910 Camino De La Costa La Jolla CA 92037-6550

WADDY, PATRICIA A., art historian, retired architecture educator; b. Cannelton, Ind., July 29, 1941; d. Luther and Gertrude Viola (Brandyberry) W. BA, Rice U., 1963; MA, Tulane U., 1965; PhD, NYU, 1973. Vis. lectr. Carnegie-Mellon U., Pitts., 1970-71, asst. prof., 1971-77; assoc. prof. archtl. history Syracuse U., NY, 1977-91, prof., 1991—2002, disting. prof. architecture, 2002—; prof. emeritus, 2006. Vis. lectr. Cornell U., Ithaca, N.Y., 1977, vis. assoc. prof., 1980; Frederic Lindley Morgan prof. archtl. design U. Louisville, 2006. Author: Seventeenth-Century Roman Palaces: Use and The Art of the Plan, 1990 (Alice Davis Hitchcock award 1992); co-author: (with D. DiCastro and A.M. Pedrocchi) Il Palazzo Pallavicini Rospigliosi e la Galleria Pallavicini, 2000; editor Nicodemus Tessin the Younger, Traicté dela decoration interieure (1717), 2002. Fulbright grantee, Rome, 1968-69; fellow Am. Acad. in Rome, 1970, Nat. Humanities Ctr., 1984-85, Samuel H. Kress sr. fellow Nat. Gallery Art, 1994-95, NEH fellow, 1998-99, Guggenheim fellow, 1999-00, Am. Coun. Learned Soc. fellow, 1978. Mem. Soc. Archtl. Historians (book rev. editor Jour. 1985-88, editor 1990-93, 2d v.p. 1993-94, 1st v.p. 1994-96, pres. 1996-98), Coll. Art Assn., Renaissance Soc. Am. Office: Syracuse U Sch Architecture Syracuse NY 13244-1250 Business E-Mail: pwaddy@syr.edu.

WADE, ABDOULAYE, President of Senegal; b. Saint-Louis, Senegal, May 29, 1926; s. Momar Tolla and Aissatou Dabo Wade; children: Karim, Syndiely. Degree in math., U. Paris, 1951, U. Besancon, France, 1952; Licencié es Lettres, U. Besancon et Grenoble, 1958; DS, U. Grenoble, France, 1959; Agrégation Sci. Econs., U. Sorbonne, Paris, 1970. Avocat Senegalese Bar, Dakar, 1959-90; prof. U. Dakar, 1959, dean faculty law and econs., 1970; sec. of state Coalition with Socialists, Govt. of Senegal, 1991-92; sec. of state, mem. pres.' cabinet Govt. of Senegal, Dakar, 1995—2000, pres., 2000—. Author: L'Economie de L'Ouest Africain, 1959. Sec. gen., founder Parti Démocratuqie Sénégalais, Dakar, 1974; v.p. Literal Internat., London, 1970. Recipient Commandeur de l'Ordre du Mérite, Republic of Senegal, 1962, Grand Officier de la Légion d'Honneur, France, 1992, Golden Plate award, Acad. Achievement, 2005. Mem. Internat. Acad. Trial Lawyers, Internat. Acad. Comparative Law. Liberal. Home: Parti démocratique sénégalais Rue A X 7 Point E Dakar Senegal Office: Presidence de la Republique Ave Roume Dakar Senegal

WADE, DAVID ECKELS, legislative staff member; b. Conn. BA in Polit. Sci., Brown U., Providence. Speechwriter, Senator John Kerry US Senate, Washington, comm. dir., Senator John Kerry, press sec., small bus. and entrepreneurship com., 2001, dep. chief of staff, Senator John Kerry, 2006—08, profl. staff, small bus. and entrepreneurship com., 2007, chief of staff to Senator John Kerry, 2009—. Nat. press sec. Senator John Kerry's Presdl. Campaign, 2004; nat. press sec., vice-presdl. nominee Senator Joe Biden Senator Barack Obama's Presdl. Campaign, 2008. Nat. pres. Coll. Democrats America; mem. exec. com. Dem. Nat. Com.; spkr. Dem. Nat. Convention, 1996. Harry S. Truman scholar, 1996. Democrat. Office: 304 Russell Senate Office Bldg Washington DC 20510-2102 Office Phone: 202-224-2742. Business E-Mail: david_wade@kerry.senate.gov.*

WADE, DWYANE (DWYANE TYRONE WADE JR.), professional basketball player; b. Chgo., Jan. 17, 1982; s. Dwyane and Jolinda Wade; m. Siohvaughn Funches, 2002; children: Zaire Blessing, Zion Malachi Airamis. Student, Marquette U., 2000—03. Guard Miami Heat, 2003—. Mem. US Men's Sr. Nat. Basketball Team, Athens, Greece, 2004, Beijing, 08. Recipient Bronze medal, men's basketball, Athens Olympic Games, 2004, Gold medal, men's basketball, Beijing Olympic Games, 2008, Best Breakthrough Athlete, ESPY awards, 2005, Best NBA Player, 2006; named Sportsman of Yr., Sports Illus., 2006, NBA Finals MVP, 2006; named to NBA All-Rookie 1st Team, 2004, All-NBA 2nd Team, 2005, 2006, Ea. Conf. All-Star Team, NBA, 2005—09, All-NBA 1st Team, 2009. Achievements include being a member of the NBA Championship winning Miami Heat, 2006; leading the NBA in: scoring, 2009. Office: c/o Miami Heat American Airlines Arena 601 Biscayne Blvd Miami FL 33132*

WADE, EDWIN LEE, lawyer, writer; b. Yonkers, NY, Jan. 26, 1932; s. James and Helen Pierce (Kinne) W.; m. Nancy Lou Sells, Mar. 23, 1957; children: James Lee, Jeffrey K. BS, Columbia U., 1954; MA, U. Chgo., 1956; JD, Georgetown U., 1965. Bar: Ill. 1965. Fgn. svc. officer U.S. Dept. State, 1956-57; mktg. analyst Chrysler Internat., S.A., Switzerland, 1957-61; intelligence officer CIA, 1961-63; industry analyst U.S. Internat. Trade Commn., 1963-65; gen. atty. Universal Oil Products Co., Des Plaines, Ill., 1965-72; atty. Amsted Industries, Inc., Chgo., 1972-73; chief counsel dept. gen. svcs. State of Ill., Springfield, 1973-75; sr. atty. U.S. Gypsum Co., Chgo., 1975-84; gen. atty. USG Corp., 1985, corp. counsel, 1986, asst. gen. counsel, 1987, corp. sec., 1987-90, corp. sec., asst. gen. counsel, 1990-93; prin. Edwin L. Wade, 1993-95; instr. Roosevelt U., Chgo., 1995-96. Author: (books) Constitution 2000: A Federalist Proposal for the New Century, 2000, Talking Sense at Century's End: A Barbarous Time...Now What?, 2000; editor: Let's Talk Sense, A Pub. Affairs Newsletter, 1994-98. Fellow Chgo. Bar Assn. (life); mem. ABA, Ill. Bar Assn., Am. Philatelic Soc. Home: 434 Mary Ln Crystal Lake IL 60014-7257 Office: Let's Talk Sense Pub Co PO Box 2195 Crystal Lake IL 60039-2195

WADE, ESTELLE B., psychologist, psychoanalyst; b. Bklyn., July 20, 1938; d. David and Selma Jobyna Schwartz; m. Donald E. Wade (div.); m. Alan L. Cantor. BA magna cum laude, Clark U., 1959; MA, Brandeis U., 1961; PhD, Columbia U., 1971. Lic. psychologist NY, 1972, cert. profl. qualification psychology Assn. State Provincial Bds., 2001; bd. cert. found. fellow Am. Coll. Advanced Practice Psychologists, 1999. Postdoctoral fellowship in psychoanalysis Post-grad. Ctr. Mental Health, NYC, 1980—83; counselor Inst. Crippled & Disabled, NYC, 1961—62, N.Y.C. Dept. Hosps., Bklyn., Queens, 1962—65; psychology intern VA, NYC, 1966—68; tchg. asst. Columbia U., NYC, 1968—69; lectr. psychology CUNY, 1969—70; staff psychologist Queens County Neuropsychiatric Inst., Jackson Heights, 1969—71, chief psychologist, 1971—81; supervising psychologist Fifth Ave. Ctr. Psychotherapy, NYC, 1981—84; pvt. practice psychoanalysis & psychotherapy NYC, 1977—. Host several radio programs, 1971—75. Singer: Amato Opera Chorus, 1976—77. Mem. Pinewoods Folk Music Soc., 1966—75, program chair, 1971—75; mem. Queens Ind. Democrats, Jackson Heights, 1967—69, Sloop Clearwater-NYC Chapter, 1969—75, program chair, 1973—75. Mem.: APA (life; program chair divsn. independent practice 1980—81, psychologist psychoanalyst practitioner, divsn. psychoanalysis 1984—), NY State Psychological Assn. (emeritus), Nat. Register Health Svc. Providers Psychology (platinum registrant 1994), Phi Beta Kappa. Democrat. Jewish. Avocations: classical music, opera, reading, walking. Office: 141 E 55th St Ste 9B New York NY 10022

WADE, GARY R., state supreme court justice; b. Tenn., May 31, 1948; married; 3 children. BS, U. Tenn., 1970; JD, U Tenn. Coll. Law, 1973. Pvt. practice, 1973—87; judge Tenn. Ct. Criminal Appeals, 1987—2006; assoc. justice Tenn. Supreme Ct., 2006—. Mem. Chancellor's Assocs. U. Tenn., 1988—91, bd. visitors Coll. Arts & Sciences, mem. Coll. Law Dean's Cir., mem. devel. coun.; bd. trustees Walters State Cmty. Coll. Found.; pres. assoc. Pellissippi State Tech. Cmty. Coll.; mem. Tenn. Sentencing Commn., 1990—94. Mayor City of Sevierville, Tenn., 1977—87; pres. Friends of the Great Smoky Mountains Nat. Park; bd. dirs. East Tenn. Found.; hon. chmn. Boys & Girls Club of the Smoky Mountains; bd. dirs. AAA East Tenn., Tenn.'s Resource Valley. Recipient Presdl. award, Am. Heart Assn., 1987, Key to the City of Sevierville, 1987, Sevierville C. of C. award, 1987; named Mover & Shaker of Yr., Mountain Press, 1983—85, 1997. Fellow: Tenn. Bar Found.; mem.: Tenn. Jud. Conf. (exec. com. 1990—97, pres. 1995—96), Am. Inns of Ct., Tenn. Assn. Criminal Def. Lawyers, Tenn. Trial Lawyers Assn., Tenn. Bar Assn., Sevier County Heart Assn., Sevierville Lions, Phi Delta Theta (pres. Eta S. Province 1990—97). Methodist. Office: 505 Main St Ste 200 Knoxville TN 37902 Office Phone: 865-549-6121.*

WADE, GAYLIA SUZANNE, secondary school educator; d. Paul Hamilton Garrett and Sylvia Maurice Smith; m. Lorrin Louis Dreier (div.); children: Lorri Anne Dreier(dec.), Christopher Eric Dreier; m.

Richard Merrill Wade, Dec. 20, 1997; 1 stepchild, Staci Lanell Wade Watkins. BA cum laude, So. Nazarene U., Bethany, Okla., 1967; postgrad., U. N.Mex., Albuquerque, 1985—97. Cert. English, social studies secondary tchr. N.Mex., Tex. Tchr. Burges HS, El Paso, Tex., 1967—68, Albuquerque Pub. Schs., 1968—70, 1985—, Socorro (Tex.) Ind. Sch. Dist., 1980—84. Newspaper sponsor Roosevelt Mid. Sch., 1968—70; lit. mag. sponsor Socorro Jr. HS, 1981—83; mentor tchr. for students tchrs. U. N. Mex., Coll. Santa Fe, 1992—2007; coord. mid. sch. initiative at-risk students City of Albuquerque/Albuquerque Pub. Schs., 1995—97; literacy com. Grant Mid. Sch., 2003, reading intervention program advisor, 2005—; mentor gateway to tchg. program Golden Apple Found., U. N.Mex., Albuquerque Pub. Schs., 2005—; tutor Advantage Tutoring, Albuquerque, 2005—06. Sponsor World Vision, 1992—94, Lamplighters Club, 1995—2008, Voice of Martyrs, Bartlesville, Okla., 2005—08, Homework Club, 2006, 2007, 2008; contbr., supporter Albuquerque Rescue Mission, Storehouse, Joy Junction, Roadrunner Food Bank, The Salvation Army, Am. Bible Soc., Paralyzed Vets. Am.; small groups leader Crown Fin., 2006—08; mem. Sagebrush Cmty. Ch., Albuquerque. Recipient Excellence in Tchg. award, N.Mex. Golden Apple Found., 1997, Grant Middle Sch., 2006, 2007; named Best All-Around Tchr., Truman Mid. Sch., 1988. Fellow: Golden Apple Found. (life); mem.: Phi Delta Lambda. Republican. Baptist. Achievements include being asked to serve on the New Mexico governor's task force on education. Avocations: quilting, gardening, reading, piano, writing. Office: Grant Mid Sch 1111 Easterday Dr NE Albuquerque NM 87112 Office Phone: 505-299-2113.

WADE, HEATHER A., archivist, educator; d. Carroll Van and Carrie Sue Wade; BA, Seton Hill U., Greensburg, Pa., 1996; MA, George Mason U., Fairfax, Va., 2002. Cert. Acad. Cert. Archivists, 2005. Archives asst. to historian gen. Nat. Soc. DAR, Washington, 1999—2001; archivist Chemung County Hist. Soc., Elmira, 2001—05; asst. prof., archivist Emporia State U., Kans., 2005—. Dir. Chemung Valley Vets. History Project, Elmira, NY, 2002—05; item writer Measurement, Inc., Durham, NC, 2003—07. Contbr. articles to profl. jours. Mem., collection devel. com. Lyon County Hist. Soc., Emporia, Kans., 2007; v.p. Jasper Hist. Soc., NY, 1996—2000; mem. steering com. Emporia State U., Ctr. Innovation, 2006, Kans. Digital Libr., Manhattan, 2005—07, Emporia State U., Archives Cert. Program, 2005. Mem.: Kans. City Area Archivists, Midwest Archives Conf., NY State Amphibious Vets. Assn. (life; hon. mem. 2003). Office Phone: 620-341-5034. Business E-Mail: hwade@emporia.edu.

WADE, JAMES O'SHEA, editor, writer; b. Atlanta, June 17, 1940; s. Richard J. and Mary Clare (O'Shea) W.; m. Linda Norman, June 19, 1971; 1 child, Christopher Scott. AB magna cum laude, Harvard U., 1962. Editor Blaisdell Pub. Co., NYC, 1963-65; asst. to pres., sr. editor Macmillan Co., 1966-69; editor-in-chief World Pub. Co., 1969-71; v.p., editorial dir. David McKay Co., 1971-74; founder, pres. Wade Pub. Co., Inc., NYC, 1975-78; exec. v.p. Rawson, Wade Pubs., Inc., NYC, 1978-82; sr. editor Crown Pubs., Inc., NYC, 1982-85, exec. editor, 1985-95, v.p., 1988-95; with Ind. Editors Group, 1996—. Mem. Century Club (N.Y.C.), Iroquois/D.U. Club (Harvard), Hasty-Pudding Inst. 1770 (Harvard U.). Democrat. Home and Office: 1565 Baptist Church Rd Yorktown Heights NY 10598-5812 Personal E-mail: jedit@optonline.net.

WADE, JIM L. (JIMMIE L. WADE), automotive executive; m. Ellen E. Wade. B in Acctg., Va. Tech. CPA. V.p. fin. Am. Motor Inns, 1979—87; v.p. fin. and ops. S.H. Heironimus, 1987—93; joined Advance Auto Parts, Inc., Roanoke, Va., 1994, pres., 1999—, sec., 2000—01, CFO, 2000—03, exec. v.p. bus. devel., 2005—08, exec. v.p. customer devel. officer, 2008. Bd. dirs. Advance Auto Parts, Inc., 1999—. Established Jimmie L. Wade Acctg. Fellowship Va. Tech. Office: Advance Auto Parts Inc 5008 Airport Rd Roanoke VA 24012 Office Phone: 877-238-2623.*

WADE, JUNE BOOTH, secondary school educator; b. St. Petersburg, Fla., Dec. 24, 1934; d. Monroe Phillippi and Julia Lenoir (Burdett) Booth; m. Charles Wade, Feb. 18, 1956; children: Susan Wade Infanzon, John Eric. BSJM, U. Fla., 1956. Tchr. English and journalism Hillsborough County Schs., Tampa, Fla. Mem. Nat. Coun. Tchrs. English, Fla. Coun. Tchrs. English, Hillsborough Coun. Tchrs. English, Ret. Educators Fla. (West Hillboraigh chpt.), Delta Kappa Gamma

WADE, LEROY GROVER, JR., chemistry educator; b. Jacksonville, Fla., Oct. 8, 1947; s. Leroy Grover and Margaret Lena (Stevens) W.; m. Sandra Martinez Kooreny; children: Christine Elizabeth, Jennifer Diane. BA summa cum laude, Rice U., 1969; AM, Harvard U., 1970, PhD, 1974. Resident rsch. fellow Du Pont Corp., Wilmington, Del., 1969; tchg. fellow in chemistry Harvard U., Cambridge, Mass., 1969-74, sr. adviser to freshmen, 1971-74; resident sci. tutor Radcliffe Coll., Cambridge, 1970-74; asst. prof. chemistry Colo. State U., Ft. Collins, 1974-80, assoc. prof., 1980-89; prof. chemistry Whitman Coll., Walla Walla, Wash., 1989—. Author: Annual Reports in Organic Synthesis, 1975-82, 8 vols., Compendium of Organic Synthetic Methods, Vols. III, IV, V, 1977, 80, 84, Organic Chemistry, 1987, 6th edit., 2005; contbr. articles to sci. jours.; reviewer profl. jours., textbooks. Mem. AAAS, Am. Chem. Soc., Am. Acad. Forensic Scis., Phi Beta Kappa (pres. chpt. 1983-84), Sigma Xi. Office: Whitman Coll Chemistry Dept Walla Walla WA 99362 E-mail: wadelg@whitman.edu.

WADE, MICHAEL ROBERT ALEXANDER, import/export company executive; b. NYC, June 29, 1945; s. Burton and Celia W.; m. Carole Kay West, Aug. 25, 1974. AB, U. Chgo., 1967; postgrad. in pub. adminstrn., Am. U., 1967—71; MBA in Fin., NYU, 1975. Program analyst, mgmt. intern HUD, 1967—71; dep. dir. Mgmt. Comm. and Briefing Ctr. U.S. Price Commn., 1972; asst. exec. sec. policy coordination U.S. Cost of Living Coun., 1973—74; assoc. dir. U.S. Indochina Refugee Program, 1975—76; pres. China Trade Devel. Corp. Chgo., 1979—. Participant in Okla. oil and gas prodn. Recipient Meritorious Svc. award Exec. Office of Pres., 1972, Disting. Svc. award U.S. Cost of Living Coun., 1974. Mem. Soc. Contemporary Art, Internat. Bus. Coun. MidAm. (bd. dirs.). Office: China Trade Devel Corp 1110 Granville Dr 1st Fl Newport Beach CA 92660-6227 Office Phone: 949-759-6950. Business E-Mail: china-trade@worldnet.att.net.

WADE, NICHOLAS MICHAEL LANDON, journalist; b. Aylesbury, Buckinghamshire, U.K., May 17, 1942; came to U.S., 1971; s. Michael Rubens and Laurien (Beesley) W.; m. Mary Veronica Scallan; children: Jessica, Alexander. Student, Eton Coll., Eng., 1955-59; BA, Cambridge U., Eng., 1960, MA, 1963. Journalist Nature mag., London, 1967-71, Science mag., Washington, 1972-82; editorial writer New York Times, 1982-90, editor sci. sect., 1990—97. Author: The Ultimate Experiment, 1977, The Nobel Duel, 1981, A World Beyond Healing, 1987; co-author: Betrayers of the Truth, 1983, Lifescript, 2001, Before the Dawn, 2006, The Faith Instinct, 2009. Office: New York Times 620 8th Ave New York NY 10018 Office Phone: 212-556-4302. Business E-Mail: nwade@nytimes.com.

WADGAONKAR, RAJ, biologist, director; m. Kaumudi Somnay, May 11, 1990; children: Priyanka, Rishi. PhD, SUNY Downstate Med. Ctr., Bklyn., 1993. Rsch. fellow Harvard Med. Sch., Boston, 1995—99; rsch. faculty Johns Hopkins U., Balt., 1999—2004; dir., vascular biology lab. VA Med. Ctr., Bklyn., 2006—. Libr. Sai Temple USA, Baldwin, NY. Office: SUNY Downstate Med Ctr 450 Clarkson Ave PO Box 50 Brooklyn NY 11203 Personal E-mail: dr.wadgaonkar@gmail.com. Business E-Mail: raj.wadgaonkar@downstate.edu.

WADHAMS, RICHARD IVORY (DICK WADHAMS), policitcal organization administrator; b. La Junta, Colo., Aug. 26, 1955; s. Victor Frederick and Anna Bell (Goodman) Wadhams; m. Susan Farrell, 1982 (dec.); 2 stepchildren. AA, Otero Jr. Coll., 1975; BA, U. Southern Colo., 1982. Chmn. Bent County Rep. Com., Colo.; staff asst. to US Senator William L. Armstrong, Colo., 1980—83, press sec. re-election com., 1984, press contact, 1985; campaign mgr. US Senator Wayne Allard, Colo., 1996, 2002, Gov. Bill Owens, Colo., 1998, Senator John Thume, SD, 2004; press sec. Senator Conrad Burns, Mont., Gov. Bill Owens, 1999—2001, Senator Wayne Allard; chief of staff US Senator George Allen, 2005—06; chmn. Colo. Rep. Party, 2007—. Mem. YMCA. Mem.: Kiwanis. Republican. Office: Colo Rep Party 5950 S Willow Dr Ste 220 Greenwood Village CO 80111 Business E-Mail: dickwadhams@cologop.org.*

WADHAMS, TIMOTHY, consumer products company executive; BA in Economics, U. Mich., MBA. CPA Coopers & Lybrand, 1972; joined Masco Corp., Taylor, Mich., 1976, various positions MasocTech, 1984—2000, v.p. fin., CFO, 2001—04, sr. v.p., CFO, 2004—07, pres., CEO, 2007—. Bd. trustees Ann Arbor Area Cmty. Found., Arbor Hospice Found.; bd. dir., M Club U. Mich.; cmty. adv. bd. Kellogg Eye Inst. Campaign. Office: Masco Corp 21001 Van Born Rd Taylor MI 48180

WADKINS, LANNY LANSTON, professional golfer; b. Richmond, Va., Dec. 5, 1949; s. Jerry Lanston and Francis Ann (Burnett) W.; m. Rachel Irene Strong, Jan. 2, 1971; 1 child, Jessica; m. Penelope Elizabeth Atwood, Nov. 11, 1978; 2 children Travis and Tucker. Student, Wake Forest U. Profl. golfer PGA, 1971—. Mem. numerous nat. teams including Walker Cup (2), 1969, 71, World Amateur Cup, 1970, Ryder Cup (8), 1977, 79, 83, 85, 87, 89, 91, 93, Ryder Cup Capt., 1995, World Cup (3), 1977, 84, 85, U.S. vs. Japan (2), 1982, 83, Nissan Cup, 1985, Dunhill Cup, 1986, Kirin Cup, 1987, Asahi Glass Four Tours, 1991; golf analyst, CBS Sports, 2003-06. Winner 1968, 70 So. Amateur champion, Sahara Invitational, 1972, PGA, 1977, World Series of Golf, 1978, Can. PGA, 1978, Tournament Players' Championship, 1979, 82, 83, (4) 1978 Victoria PGA Championship (Australia), Can. PGA Championship, 1979 Bridgestone Open (Japan), L.A. Open, 1979, 85, Phoenix Open, 1982, Greater Greensboro, 1983, Bob Hope Desert Classic, 1985, Doral Ryder, 1987, 1984 World Nissan Championship (Japan), Hawaiian Open, 1988, 91, Colonial Open, 1988, Anheuser Busch Classic, 1990, 1990 Fred Meyer Challenge, PGA of AmericaPlayer of Yr., 1985, Greater Hartford Open, 1992, 2000 ACE Group Classic, among others. Address: PGA America/Senior Tour 100 Ave of the Champions PO Box 109601 Palm Beach Gardens FL 33410-9601

WADKINS, THERESA A., psychology professor, researcher; m. Douglas R. Wadkins, Apr. 10, 1982. BS, Kearney State Coll., Nebr., 1987; MS, Ft. Hays State U., Kans., 1991; PhD, U. Nebr., Lincoln, 1999. Assoc. prof. psychology U. Nebr., Kearney, 1990—. Contbr. articles to profl. jour. Trainer, vol. Nebr. Critical Incident Stress Mgmt., 1995—2008. Recipient Outstanding Tchg. and Instrnl. Creativity award, U. Nebr., 2008. Mem.: Nebr. Psychol. Soc. (past pres. 2005—07).

WADLEY, M. RICHARD, consumer products executive; b. Lehi, Utah; s. Merlyn R. and Verla Ann (Ball) W.; children: Lisa Kathleen, Staci Lin, Eric Richard, Nicole Marie. BS, Brigham Young U., 1967; MBA, Northwestern U., 1968. Brand asst. packaged soap and detergent divsn. Procter & Gamble Co., Cin., 1968-69, asst. brand mgr. packaged soap and detergent divsn., 1970-71, brand mgr. Dawn detergent, 1972-73, copy supr. packaged soap and detergent divsn., 1974-75, brand mgr. Tide detergent, 1975-77, assoc. advt. mgr. packaged soap and detergent divsn., 1977-81; corp. product dir. Hallmark Cards, Inc., Kansas City, Mo., 1982-83, corp. product dir. Ambassador Cards divsn., 1983-85; v.p., gen. mgr. feminine protection divsn. Tambrands Inc., Lake Success, NY, 1986-88; sr. v.p. Bongrain, Inc., NYC, 1988-89, pres., CEO AltaDena Inc. divsn. City of Industry, Calif., 1989-91; pres. The Summit Group, 1991-93; chmn., CEO, bd. dirs. T-Chem Products Inc., Santa Fe Springs, Calif., 1993-99; CEO The Bayshore Group, 1999—; sr. cons. Ironwood Adv., 1999—. Bd. dirs. Legacy Interactive, Mellano & Co.; adj. prof. MBA program Pepperdine U., 1998—99. Bd. dirs. Long Beach Opera, 1991-95, L.I. Friends of the Arts, 1986-88; mem. adv. bd. Bus. Sch. Calif. State U., Long Beach, 1991-93. Avocations: civil war history, tennis, travel. Personal E-mail: rwbayshore@aol.com.

WADLINGTON, WALTER JAMES, law educator; b. Biloxi, Miss., Jan. 17, 1931; s. Walter and Bernice (Taylor) Wadlington; m. Ruth Miller Hardie, Aug. 20, 1955; children: Claire, Charlotte, Ian(dec.), Susan, Derek Alan. AB, Duke U., 1951; LLB, Tulane U., 1954. Bar: La. 1954, Va. 1965. Pvt. practice, New Orleans, 1954—55, 1958—59; asst. prof. Tulane U., 1960—62; mem. faculty U. Va., 1962—, prof law, 1964—, James Madison prof., 1970—2002, James Madison prof. emeritus, 2002—, prof. legal medicine Med. Sch., 1979—2002, Harrison Found. rsch. prof., 1990—92. Tutor civil law U. Edinburgh, Scotland, 1959—60; vis. Tazewell Taylor prof. law Coll. William and Mary, 1986; dir. med. malpractice program Robert Wood Johnson, 1985—91, mem. adv. com. clin. scholars program, 1989—97; chmn. nat. adv. bd. Improving Malpractice Prevention and Compensation Sys., 1994—98; disting. health law tchr. Am. Soc. Law, Medicine and Ethics, 1988; trustee-at-large Edn. Commn. Fgn. Med. Grads., 1995—2003. Author (with O. Brien): Cases and Materials on Domestic Relations, 1970, 6th edit., 2007, Family Law in Perspective, 2001; author: 2d edit., 2007; author: (with Waltz and Dworkin) Cases and Materials on Law and Medicine, 1980; editor-in-chief: Tulane U. Law Rev., 1953—54; author (with Davis, Scott, and Whitebread): Children in the Legal System, 3rd edit., 2004; author: 4th edit., 2009. Fulbright scholar, U. Edinburgh, 1959—60. Mem.: Am. Law Inst., Inst. of Medicine of NAS, Found. Advancement Internat. Med. Edn. and Rsch. (bd. dirs., sec. 2001—03). Home: 1620 Keith Valley Rd Charlottesville VA 22901-3018 Office: U Va Sch Law 580 Massie Rd Charlottesville VA 22903-1738 Home Phone: 434-293-5261; Office Phone: 434-293-5261. Personal E-mail: wjwadlington@gmail.com. Business E-Mail: wjw@virginia.edu.

WADLOW, JOAN KRUEGER, retired academic administrator, construction executive; b. LeMars, Iowa, Aug. 21, 1932; d. R. John and Norma I. (Ihle) Krueger; m. Richard R. Wadlow, July 27, 1958; children: Dawn, Kit. BA, U. Nebr., 1953, PhD, 1963; MA, Fletcher Sch. Law and Diplomacy, 1956; cert., Grad. Inst. Internat. Studies, Geneva, 1957. Mem. faculty U. Nebr., Lincoln, 1966-79, prof. polit. scis., 1964-79, assoc. dean Coll. Arts and Scis., 1972-79; prof. polit. scis., dean Coll. Arts and Scis., U. Wyo., Laramie, 1979-84, v.p. acad. affairs, 1984-86; prof. polit. sci., provost U. Okla., Norman, 1986-91; chancellor U. Alaska, Fairbanks, 1991-99. Cons. on fed. grants; bd. dirs. Alaska Sea Life Ctr., Key Bank Alaska; mem. Commn. Colls. N.W. Assn.; pres. Lan Constrn., Inc., 1999-2004. Contbr. articles to profl. jours. Bd. dirs. Nat. Merit Scholarship Corp., 1988-97, Lincoln United Way, 1976-77, Bryan Hosp., Lincoln, 1978-79, Washington Ctr., 1986-99, Key Bank of Alaska, Alaska SeaLife Ctr.; v.p., exec. commr. North Ctrl. Assn., pres., 1991; pres. adv. bd. Lincoln YWCA, 1970-71; mem. def. adv. com. Women in the Svcs., 1987-89; mem. cmty. adv. bd. Alaska Airlines; mem. Univ. Pres.'s Mission to Israel, 1998; mem. bd. dirs. Netarts Oceanside Sanitary Dist., 2002-04. Recipient Mortar Board Tchg. award, 1976, Alumni Scholar Achievement award Rotary Internat., 1998, Alumni Achievement award U. Nebr., 2003; Seacrest Journalism fellow 1953-54, Rotary fellow, 1956-57, fellow Conf. Coop. Man, Lund, Sweden, 1956. Mem. NCAA (divsn. II pres. coun. 1997-99), Internat. Studies Assn. (co-editor Internat. Studies Notes 1978-91), Nat. Assn. State Univs. and Land-Grant Colls. (exec. com. coun. acad. affairs 1989-91, chair internat. affairs counsel 1996-97), Western Assn. Africanists (pres. 1980-82), Assn. Western Univs. (pres. 1993), Coun. Colls. Arts and Scis. (pres. 1983-84), Greater Fairbanks C. of C., Gamma Phi Beta. Republican. Congregationalist. Address: Chancellor Emerita PO Box 246 Oceanside OR 97134-0246 Personal E-mail: wadlow@hughes.net.

WADSWORTH, DYER SEYMOUR, minerals executive; b. NYC, June 16, 1936; s. Seymour and Phoebe Armistead (Helmer) Wadsworth; m. Beverley Allen Dunn Barringer, Feb. 2, 1963; children: Sophia, Jennifer. BA, Yale U., 1959; JD, Harvard U., 1962. Bar: N.Y. 1963, Pa. 1979. Assoc. Humes, Andrews & Botzow, NYC, 1962-64; with Inco Ltd. and subs., NYC, 1964-96; asst. gen. counsel Inco Ltd., NYC, 1982-96; pres. Inco US, Inc., NYC, 1993-96; chmn., CEO, treas., dir. Cass County Iron Co., Linden, Tex., 1992—; chmn. Barringer Crater Co., Flagstaff, Ariz., 1996—. Gen. counsel Sailors Snug Harbor, Sea Level, NC, 1987—2000, Baseline Fin. Svcs., Inc., NYC, 1997—2000. Trustee Isaac Tuttle Fund for Aged, NYC, 1968—96; bd. dirs. Frenchman Bay Conservancy, Hancock, Maine, 1997—, Amsterdam Nursing Home Corp., NYC, 1982—, chmn. bd. dirs., 1986—2000. Named Trustee of the Yr., N.Y. Assn. Homes and Svcs. for Aging, 1995. Mem.: Meteoritical Soc., Yale Club Suncoast (bd. dirs. 2001—, pres. 2002—04), Union Club (N.Y.C.), Ivy League Club (Sarasota, Fla.) (bd. dirs. 2005—07), Pilgrims Soc. (N.Y.C.). Home: 8466 Lockwood Ridge Rd PMB 304 Sarasota FL 34243-2951

WADSWORTH, JEFFREY, research and development institute executive, metallurgist; b. Hamburg, Germany, May 12, 1950; s. Frank William and Irene Wadsworth; m. Geraldine McCulley, Oct. 11, 2006; children: Emma Claire, Thomas Frank. BMet, Sheffield U., Eng., 1972, PhD, 1975, DMet, 1990, Deng (hon.), 2004. Rsch. assoc. Stanford U., Calif., 1976-80, cons. prof. Calif., 1996—2002; staff scientist, then mgr. metallurgy Lockheed R&D Div., Palo Alto, Calif., 1980-92; assoc. dir. chemistry and materials science Lawrence Livermore Nat. Lab., Livermore, Calif., 1992-96, dep. dir. sci. & tech., 1996—2002; sr. exec. Battelle Meml. Inst., Columbus, Ohio, 2002—07, exec. v.p. lab. ops., 2007—09, pres., CEO, 2009—; dir. Oak Ridge Nat. Lab. US Dept. Energy, Oak Ridge, Tenn., 2003—07; distinguished rsch. prof. U. Tenn., 2005—. Contbr. numerous articles to profl. jours.; co-inventor, patentee novel steels and aluminum alloys; discoverer process to reinvent ancient discovery Damascus Steels. Recipient Brunton medal Sheffield U., 1975, Metallurgica/Aparecida, 1976. Fellow ASM Internat., AAAS, TMS; mem. NAE, Am. Inst. Mining, Metall. and Petroleum Enging., Am. Ceramic Soc., Materials Rsch. Soc. Office: Battelle Meml Inst 505 King Ave Columbus OH 43201*

WADSWORTH, JOHN (JACK) SPENCER, JR., investment banker; b. Ft. Thomas, Ky., Sept. 12, 1939; s. John Spencer and Mary Claire (Walker) W.; m. Bette Sue Pendery, June 17, 1961; children: Elizabeth J., John S. III, Christopher W. BA in Economics, Williams Coll., 1961; MBA in Fin., U. Chgo., 1963. Exec. v.p., bd. dirs. First Boston Corp., NYC, 1963-78; joined Morgan Stanley, NYC, 1978, mng. dir., various positions US investment banking divsn., 1978—87; pres. Morgan Stanley Japan, Tokyo, 1988—93; chmn. Morgan Stanley Asia Ltd., 1993—2000, hon. chmn.; now adv. dir. Morgan Stanley; ptnr. Manitou Ventures. Bd. dirs. Pixar Inc., 2002—; chmn. bd. Littleford Bros. Inc., Florence, Ky. Trustee Asia Soc., Williams Coll.; bd. trustees Solomon R. Guggenheim Mus., NYC. Mem.: Asia Am. MultiTechnology Assn. (charter mem.). Office: Morgan Stanley 1585 Broadway New York NY 10036

WADSWORTH, ROBERT DAVID, advertising executive; b. Prestbury, Cheshire, Eng., May 20, 1942; came to U.S., 1978; s. Eric and Irene (Thorpe) W.; m. Kathleen O'Meara, Dec. 13, 1968; children: Tracey, Charles Robert. BA, U. Natal, S. Africa, 1963. With Lever Bros. S. Africa, 1960-66, sr. brand mgr., 1964-66, Gen. Foods S. Africa, 1967; account exec. London Press Exch., S. Africa, 1968, Grant Advt., S. Africa, 1969; dir., then mng. dir. Cen. Advt., Johannesburg, S. Africa, 1970-73; dir. new bus. coord. McCann-Erickson, South Africa, 1973-78; sr. v.p., mng. rep., new bus. coord. McCann-Erickson, Inc., NYC, 1978-82; client dir., exec. v.p. Lintas, NYC, 1983-90; dir. corp. strategy, regional dir. So. Africa Lintas Worldwide, NYC, 1991-97; cons. Midlothian, Va., 1998—. Home and Office: 14018 Bayport Landing Ter Midlothian VA 23112-2038

WADSWORTH, STEVE, Internet company executive; BS in Engring., U. Va.; MBA, UCLA. Prin. Windsor Pk. Group, LA, Calif.; sr. v.p., CFO Walt Disney Co., North Hollywood, Calif., 1993—95, with Disney Online, 1995—99; pres. Walt Disney Internet Group, Walt Disney Co., North Hollywood, Calif., 1999—. Spkr. in field. Mem.: Internet Advt. Bur. (vice-chmn. 2001—02, pres. 2004—06, chmn. emeritus 2006). Office: Walt Disney Co 5161 Lankershim Blvd North Hollywood CA 91601

WADSWORTH, WILLIAM GRAHAM, biology professor, researcher; b. Phila., Dec. 25, 1959; s. William Steele and Nancy Hegan Wadsworth; m. Vassiliki Karantza, July 6, 1996; children: George William, Alexander Graham. BA, St. Olaf Coll., Northfield, Minn., 1982; MA, U. Mo., Columbia, 1985, PhD, 1989. Postdoc. fellow Johns Hopkins U., Balt., 1989—93; asst. prof. UMDNJ-Robert Wood Johnson Med. Sch., Piscataway, NJ, 1993—2001, assoc. prof., 2001—06, prof., 2006—. Contbr. articles numerous rsch. publ. Grants, NIH, 1994—. Achievements include research in molecular genetics of nervous system development. Home: 100 Chestnut Ave Bernardsville NJ 07924-1700 Office: UMDNJ-Robert Wood Johnson Medical Sch 675 Hoes Ln W Piscataway NJ 08854-5635 Business E-Mail: william.wadsworth@umdnj.edu.

WADSWORTH WALKER, CHERILEE, music educator; b. Port Clinton, Ohio, Mar. 15, 1961; d. Richard Vernon Wadsworth and Joyce Marie Meter Wadsworth; m. James Edward Walker, May 2, 1996. MusB in Music Theory, Baldwin Wallace Coll., 1991; MusM in Jazz Studies, Ind. U., 1993; PhD in Music Edn., U. Okla., 2005. Musician 3d class 6th fleet USN, Naples, Italy, 1994—96, musician 2d class NATO, 1996—98; asst. prof. East Ctrl. U., Ada, Okla., 1998—2001; tchg. chmn. performing arts Ill. Ctrl. Coll., East Peoria, 2001—. Adjudicator, clinician Performing Arts Cons., Keyport, NJ, 2003—; res. musician 85th Divsn. Band, US Army, Arlington Heights, Ill., 2005—07; presenter in field; spkr. in field. Contbr. articles to profl. publs.; performer: Montreux Jazz Festival, 2003, Ill. Gubernatorial Inauguration, 2003, Ft. Des Moines Meml. Pk. Dedication, 2004, Nat. Boy Scout Jamboree, 2005, WCBU 35th ann. broadcast concert, 2005. Recipient Ednl. award, Harmony Found., Inc., Minn., 2001, Commn. award, Heartland Music Found., Oklahoma City, 2001, Presentation award, Peoria World Affairs Coun., 2005. Mem.: Am. Choral Dirs. Assn., Nat. Assn. Tchrs. Singing. Office: Ill Ctrl Coll 1 College Dr East Peoria IL 61635 Office Phone: 309-694-5548. Business E-Mail: cwadsworthwalker@icc.edu.

WADYKO, MICHAEL ANTHONY, historian, educator; s. Mitchell Anthony and Ann Phyllis Wadyko; m. Judith Ann Daniel, Jan. 13, 1990. PhD, W.Va. U., Morgantown, 2000. Instr. Colo. Mountain Coll., Glenwood Springs, 1996, Norwich U., Northfield, Vt., 2006—. Instr. Northwestern State U., Natchitoches, La., Fla. C.C., Jacksonville, Miss. Gulf Coast C.C., Perkinson, Southeastern C.C., Whiteville, NC, C.C. Northwestern Colo., Rangely. Lector St. Mary's Crown, Carbondale, Colo. E4 USNR, 1978—83, Pitts. Roman Catholic. Avocations: travel, music, writing. Home: 2560 Hwy 82 Glenwood Springs CO 81601 Personal E-mail: mikewadyko@yahoo.com.

WADZINSKI, MARY BETH, administrative assistant; b. Wausau, Wis., Apr. 26, 1953; d. Erwin Fredrick Hackbart and Selma Ruth Margaret Krueger; m. William R. Wadzinski, June 20, 1987 (div. June 1997); children: Bethany Dawn, Andrew William. AS, Northcentral Tech. Coll., 1973. Typist Wausau (Wis.) Abstract and Title Co., 1973-76; adminstrv. asst. Marathon County Dept. Social Svcs., Wausau, 1977—. Author poems, songs. Recipient Poet Merit award, Am. Poetry Assn., 1989, Editors Choice awards, Nat. Libr. Poetry, 1996—98, 2001, Honorable Mention award, Iliad Press, 1996—98. Mem.: America's Registry, Famous Poets Soc. (Shakespeare Trophy of Excellence 2002, Poet of Yr. medallion 2002, Diamond Homer trophy 1996, Recognition award 1998, Poet of Yr. medallion 1999, Diamond Homer trophy 1999, Recognition award 2001), Internat. Poetry Hall of Fame, Internat. Soc. Poets. Democrat. Lutheran. Avocations: shopping, garage sales, writing, singing. Home: 1113 N 6th Ave Wausau WI 54401-2747 Home Phone: 715-675-3517; Office Phone: 715-261-7595.

WAFAPOOR, FARZAD, information technology executive, educator; m. Afroz Afroz, Nov. 9, 1997; 2 children. Masters, Webster U., Saint Louis, 1997. Interpretor Internat. Inst., 2006. Sr. adj. lectr. U. Missouri, St. Louis, 1995—; mgr., media svcs Graphic World, Saint Louis, 2000—06; adj. lectr. Webster U., Saint Louis, 2006—; directing mgr.-founder AdvanTech Media, Saint Louis, 2006—. Ind. media prodr. Ind., Saint Louis, 1994—; interpretor-translator Internat. Inst., Saint Louis, 2006—. Dir.: (documentary video) Plight of the Refugees (Emmy Award - Mid Am. Chpt., 1996); editor: (documentary video) Virtual Objectivity; contbr. articles. Selection com. St. Louis Internat. Film Festival - Interfaith Sidebar, Saint Louis, 2002—06; interfaith activities Ind., St. Louis, 1994—2008; founder and bd. dir. AZI - helping refugees, St. Louis, 2008; vol.-soc. svces. Internat. Inst., St. Louis, 2003—08. Recipient Best Spkr., U. Mo. - Debate Club, 1995, Most accomodating faculty yr., 2004. Achievements include development of courses in new media at the university of missouri - St. Louis; research in on the role of new media in educational publishing. Avocations: reading, poetry, swimming. Office: AdvanTech Media 1033 Corp Sq Dr Saint Louis MO 63132 Office Phone: 314-485-5200.

WAGAR, ELIZABETH ANN, microbiologist, director; d. Kenneth H. and Annabel Wagar; m. Michael Lee Gerson, Feb. 2, 1985. MD, Mich. State U., East Lansing, 1981. Diplomate Am. Bd. Pathology, 1985. Assoc. chief microbiology clin. labs. UCLA, 1989—, dir. clin. labs., 1999—. Fellow, NIH, 1985—88. Mem.: Coll. Am. Pathologists (mem. quality practices com. 2004). Office: UCLA Dept Pathology 10833 Le Conte Ave Los Angeles CA 90095-1732 Business E-Mail: ewagar@mednet.ucla.edu.

WAGENER, CHRISTINE ELIZABETH, psychotherapist, educator; b. Alexandria, Va., Sept. 1, 1948; d. Harry F. and Elizabeth Whitmore Wagener; m. Lawrence L. Foust, Aug. 20, 1977. BA, Jacksonville U., 1970; MSW, Va. Commonwealth U., Richmond, 1976. LCSW Tex. Clin. asst. prof. psychiatry U. Va. Med. Sch., Charlottesville, 1976—80; asst. clin. prof. psychiatry U. Tex. Med. Sch., Houston, 1980—88; pvt. practice psychotherapist Houston, 1988—. Adj. asst. prof. U. Houston Grad. Sch. Social Work, 1980—88; field instr. Va. Commonwealth U. Sch. Social Work, Richmond, 1977—80. Mem. exec. bd. Mental Health Assn., Houston, 1991—97. Mem.: NASW, Acad. Cert. Social Workers. Avocations: sailing, travel, cooking. Office: 2 Chelsea Blvd Houston TX 77006 Office Phone: 713-521-9222.

WAGENER, THORSTEN, hydrologist, educator; b. Siegen, Germany, Jan. 24, 1971; Diploma in Engring., U. Siegen, 1995; IR, Delft U. Tech., Netherlands, 1998; PhD, Imperial Coll., London, 2002. Rsch. assoc. U. Ariz., Tucson; asst. prof. Pa. State U., University Pk., 2004—. Contbr. to monograph. Recipient Unwin prize, Imperial Coll. London, 2002, Early Career Rsch. Excellence prize, Internat. Environ. Modeling and Software Soc., 2006. Office: Pa State Univ 226B Sackett Bldg University Park PA 16802 Office Fax: 814-863-7304. Business E-Mail: thorsten@engr.psu.edu.

WAGGETT, REBECCA JANE, research scientist; m. Matthew Palmtag. BS, Providence Coll., RI, 1999; PhD, U. Tex., Austin, 2005. Postdoc. fellow U. RI Grad. Sch. Oceanography, Narragansett, RI, 2005—06; NRC postdoc. rsch. assoc. NOAA/NOS, Beaufort, NC, 2006—. Mem. PEO Sisterhood, Jacksonville, NC, 2005; sci. judge score keeper Nat. Ocean Sciences Bowl, 2006—07. Recipient Rachael Dougherty Endowed Excellence Fund in Marine Studies, U. Tex. Marine Sci. Inst., 2001; E.J. Lund fellowship, 2001—04. Mem.: AGU, ERF, ASLO. Office: NOAA/NOS 101 Pivers Island Rd Beaufort NC 28516

WAGGONER, ANDREW, composer; b. New Orleans, 1960; m. Caroline Stinson. Student, New Orleans Ctr. for Creative Arts, Eastman Sch. Music; DMA, Cornell U., 1986. Founding dir. Seal Bay Festival of Am. Chamber Music, Vinalhaven, Maine; composer-in-residence Setnor Sch. Music, Syracuse U., chair composition and theory; assoc. dean visual and performing arts Syracuse U.; founder Open End chamber ensemble, 2004—. Recipient Lee Ettelson Composer's award, Composers Inc., Roger Sessions prize, Liguria Study Ctr., Bogliasco, Italy, 2008, Acad. award in Music, AAAL, 2009; fellow John S. Guggenheim Meml. Found., 2005. Office: Crouse Coll Rm 119B Coll Visual and Perfoming Arts Syracuse U Syracuse NY 13244-1010 Office Phone: 315-443-5892. E-mail: andywaggoner@mac.com, waggoner@nyc.rr.com, abwaggon@syr.edu.*

WAGGONER, CHERI, psychologist; d. Billy Jack and Anita Rodgers; m. Edward Wayne Waggoner; children: Amanda Lehde, Andrew. MA, Tex. Woman's U., Denton, 2000, PhD, 2005. Cert. Nat. Cert. Sch. Psychologist, 2006. Grad. tchg. asst. Tex. Woman's U., 1999—2002; LSSP Van Zandt SSA, Edgewood, Tex., 2003—08. Mem.: Tex. Assn. Sch. Psychologist, Nat. Assn. Sch. Psychologist.

WAGGONER, ERIC, literature and language professor; b. Charleston, W.Va., Sept. 24, 1970; s. James Waggoner and Nancy Lyons. MA, Old Dominion U., Norfolk, Va., 1995; PhD, Ariz. State U., Phoenix, 2001. Assoc. prof., Am. lit. W.Va. Wesleyan Coll., Buckhannon, 2001—. Editor: (book) Approaches to Teaching First-Year Composition; contbr. articles to profl. jours. Office: W Va Wesleyan Coll 59 College Ave Buckhannon WV 26201 Business E-Mail: waggoner@wvwc.edu.

WAGGONER, HEATHER E., theater educator; b. Vancouver, British Columbia, Canada, Sept. 25, 1947; m. Leland Waggoner. MFA, Ill. State U., Normal, 1995. Costume shop supr. Ill. State U., 1995; prof theatre arts Mesa State Coll., Grand Junction, Colo., 1995—. Judge 4-H clothing, Delta, Colo., 2007. Recipient Excellence Tchg., City Grand Junction and Coll. students, 2005. Mem.: USITT. Office: Mesa State Coll 1100 N Ave Grand Junction CO 81501 Office Fax: 970-248-1159. Business E-Mail: hwaggone@mesastate.edu.

WAGGONER, JAMES CLYDE, lawyer; b. Nashville, May 7, 1946; s. Charles Franklin and Alpha (Noah) W.; m. Diane Dusenbery, Aug. 17, 1968; children: Benjamin, Elizabeth. BA, Reed Coll., 1968; JD, U. Oreg., 1974. Bar: Oreg. 1974, U.S. Dist. Ct. Oreg. 1975, U.S. Ct. Appeals (9th cir.) 1980, U.S. Tax Ct. 1979, U.S. Supreme Ct. 1979. Clk. to presiding justice Oreg. Supreme Ct., Salem, 1974-75; assoc. Martin, Bischoff & Templeton, Portland, Oreg., 1975-78, ptnr., 1978-82, Waggoner, Farleigh, Wada, Georgeff & Witt, Portland, 1982-89, Davis Wright Tremaine, Portland, 1990—. Contbr. articles to profl. jours. Fulbright scholar U. London, 1968-69. Mem. ABA, Oreg. Bar Assn., Multnomah Bar Assn., Reed Coll. Alumni Assn. (v.p. 1988, pres. 1989, bd. mgmt.) Alzheimers Assn. of Columbia-Willamette (v.p. 1992, pres. 1993), Order of Coif, Phi Beta Kappa. Democrat. Avocations: woodworking, calligraphy. Office: Davis Wright Tremaine 1300 SW 5th Ave Ste 2300 Portland OR 97201-5682 Home Phone: 503-284-6685; Office Phone: 503-778-5326. Business E-Mail: jimwaggoner@dwt.com.

WAGGONER, LAWRENCE WILLIAM, law educator; b. Sidney, Ohio, July 2, 1937; s. William J. and Gladys L. Waggoner; m. Lynne S. Applebaum, Aug. 27, 1963; children: Ellen, Diane. BBA, U. Cin., 1960; JD, U. Mich., 1963; PhD, Oxford U., Eng., 1966. Assoc. Cravath, Swaine & Moore, NYC, 1963; prof. law U. Ill., Champaign, 1968-72, U. Va., Charlottesville, 1972—74, U. Mich., Ann Arbor, 1974-84, Lewis M. Simes prof. law, 1987—. Dir. rsch., chief reporter joint editorial bd. for Uniform Trust and Estate Acts, 1986-94, dir. rsch., 1994—, mem. joint editl. bd. uniform trust and estate acts; reporter restatement (3d) of property, 1990—; adviser restatement (3d) of trusts, 1993—. Author: Family Property Law: Wills, Trusts, and Future Interests, 4th edit., 2006, Uniform Trust and Estate Statutes, 2009—. Served to capt., U.S. Army, 1966-68. Fulbright scholar Oxford U., 1963-65; named to Sidney City Schs. Hall of Honor, Ohio, 2007. Mem. Am. Law Inst., Am. Coll. Trust and Estates Counsel, Internat. Acad. Estate and Trust Law. Office: U Mich Law Sch 625 S State St Ann Arbor MI 48109-1215 Office Phone: 734-763-2586. Business E-Mail: waggoner@umich.edu.

WAGGONER, PAUL EDWARD, agricultural scientist; b. Appanoose County, Iowa, Mar. 29, 1923; s. Walter Loyal and Kathryn (Maring) W.; m. Barbara Ann Lockerbie, Nov. 3, 1945; children: Von Lockerbie, Daniel Maring S.B., U. Chgo., 1946; MS, Iowa State Coll., 1949, PhD, 1951. From asst. to chief scientist Conn. Agrl. Expt. Sta., New Haven, 1951-71, vice dir., 1969-71, dir., 1972-87, disting. scientist, 1987—. Mem. panels on policy implications of global warming NAS, 1989-91; chmn. sci. adv. bd. Giant Sequoia Nat. Monument, 2001-02. Contbr. articles to profl. jours. Served to capt. USAAF, 1943-46 Guggenheim fellow, 1963 Fellow AAAS (chmn. climate changes and water resources com. 1986-89), Am. Phytopath. Soc.; mem. NAS, Am. Meteorol. Soc. (Outstanding Achievement in Biometerology award 1967), Conn. Acad. Sci. and Engring. (Anton-de-Bary medal 1996). Achievements include rsch. in hydrologic role of foliar pores, climate change on agriculture and water resources, how much ten billion can spare for nature, returning forests. Home: 314 Vineyard Point Rd Guilford CT 06437-3255 Office: Conn Agrl Expt Sta PO Box 1106 New Haven CT 06504-1106 Office Phone: 203-453-2816. Personal E-mail: agwagg@comcast.net.

WAGGONNER, JOSEPH DAVID, III, architect; b. Shreveport, La., Feb. 27, 1949; s. Joseph David Waggonner, Jr. and Mary Ruth (Carter) Waggonner. BA, Duke U., Durham, NC, 1971; MArch, Yale U., New Haven, 1975. Draftsman Arch. of the Capitol, Washington, 1974; archtl. designer Bechtel Corp., San Francisco, 1976—78; staff arch. DMJM/Curtis and Davis, New Orleans, 1978—80; assoc. Labouisse, Graeber Ltd., New Orleans, 1980—82; prin. Labouisse & Waggonner, New Orleans, 1982—89, Waggonner & Ball Archs., New Orleans, 1989—. Vis. critic Tulane U., New Orleans, 1980, design prof., 1983—84. Prin. works include 400 Lafayette St. (Gambit Best Comml. Renovation award, 1984), 430 Notre Dame St. (LAA Honor award, 1984), Mignon Faget Canal Pl. (New Orleans chpt. AIA Honor award, 1987), Dominican HS (Gulf State region AIA Honor award, 1995), Dog Trot Weekend Home (AIA La. Honor award, 2005), Isidore Newman Lower Sch. Expanion (AIA La. Honor award, 2005), A.B. Freeman Sch. Bus. (AIA La. Honor award, 2005). Mem.: AIA (Honor award 1987), Assn. Preservation Tech., Soc. Archtl. Historians. Democrat. Methodist. Office: Waggonner & Ball Archs 2200 Prytania St New Orleans LA 70130-5804 Office Phone: 504-524-5308. Office Fax: 504-524-5314. E-mail: d_waggonner@wbarchitects.com.

WAGLE, A. TINA, education educator, researcher; d. Datta and Sue Wagle. BA, Colgate U., Hamilton, NY, 1996; MA, Middlebury Coll., Vt., 1999; PhD, SUNY, Buffalo, 2003. Cert. in secondary Spanish tchg. NY, 2000. Tchr. Portsmouth Abbey Sch., RI, 1996—99; instr. Canisius Coll., Buffalo, 2000—03; asst. prof. Daemen Coll., Amherst, 2002—03; prof. SUNY Empire State Coll., 2003—. Bilingual edn. adv. com. mem. Buffalo Pub. Schools, 2004—; redesign team mem. Grover Cleve. HS, Buffalo, 2005—. Bd. trustees Cath. Charities of Western NY, Buffalo, 2005—. Mem.: Am. Ednl. Rsch. Assn. Office: 2875 Union Rd Cheektowaga NY 14227 Home Fax: 716-853-7713. Business E-Mail: tina.wagle@esc.edu.

WAGMAN, ROBERT JOHN, journalist, writer; b. Chgo., Nov. 11, 1942; s. Albert Alan and Rosamond (Horner) Wagman; m. Carol Ann Mueller, Jan. 30, 1965; children: Jennifer, Patricia, Marilyn. AB, St. Louis U., 1966, MA, 1968, JD, 1971. Analyst Dun & Bradstreet, 1965-67; with CBS News, 1967-71, 74-77; asst. to dean St. Louis U. Sch. Law, 1971-74; Washington bur. chief N.Am. Newspaper Alliance, 1977-80, Ind. News Alliance, 1980-82; columnist Newspaper Enterprise Assn., 1980-95. Sr. corr. Soccertimes, VP, Washington, SMA Global. Author, co-author: Hubert Humphrey, The Man and His Dream, 1978, Citizens Guide to the Tax Revolt, 1979, Asbestos: The Silent Killer, 1982, Lord's Justice, 1985, Instant Millionaires, 1986, The Nazi Hunters, 1988, The First Amendment Book, 1991, 2d edit., 1996, World Almanac Guide to the Supreme Court, 1993, Blood Oath, 1994, Hong Kong, 1997, And Beyond, 1997, The Engine of America, 2007; editor: World Almanac of U.S. Politics, 1994—2000. Recipient Thomas Stokes award in Journalism. Personal E-mail: mobilewag@aol.com.

WAGNER, ALLAN RAY, psychology professor; b. Springfield, Ill., Jan. 6, 1934; s. Raymond August and Grace (Johnson) W.; m. Barbara Rae Meland, Nov. 21, 1959, (dec. Nov. 1994); children: Krystn Rae, Kathryn Rae. BA, U. Iowa, 1956, MA, 1958, PhD, 1959; MA hon., Yale U., 1970. Asst. prof. psychology Yale U., New Haven, 1959-64, assoc. prof., 1964-69, prof., 1970-89, chmn. psychology dept., 1983-89, James Rowland Angell prof. psychology, 1990—, chmn. philosophy dept., 1991-93, dir., divsn. of the soc. sci., 1992-98. Cons. NIMH, 1968-71; mem. Pres. Biomed. Research Panel, 1975-76; adv. bd. Cambridge Ctr. Behavioral Studies, 1982-2000; mem. psychobiology panel NSF, 1984-85, com. on basic research in behavioral and social scis. NRC, 1984-87. Author: Reward and Punishment, 1965; assoc. editor: Learning and Motivation, 1969-74, Animal Learning and Behavior, 1972-74; editor: Jour. Exptl. Psychology, 1974-81, Quantitative Analyses of Behavior, Vol. 3, 1982, Vol. 4, 1983, Vol. 7, 1988. Grantee, NSF, 1960—2004; fellow, 1958, NIMH, 1963. Fellow APA (Disting. Scientific Contbn. award 1998-99), AAAS (mem. coun. 1988-91), Soc. Exptl. Psychologists (Howard Crosby Warren medal 1991), Am. Psychol. Soc.; mem. NAS, Psychonomic Soc., So. Quantitative Analysis of Behavior (sec. 1983-92), Ea. Psychol. Assn. (bd. dirs. 1985-88), Sigma Xi, New Haven Lawn Club. Home: 1405 Ridge Rd North Haven CT 06473-3051 Office: Yale U Dept Psychology PO Box 208205 New Haven CT 06520-8205 Office Phone: 203-432-4691. Business E-Mail: allan.wagner@yale.edu.

WAGNER, ANDREW JAMES, retired meteorologist, elder, educator; b. Greenwich, Conn., Apr. 12, 1934; s. Andrew and Ruth (Machette) Wagner; m. Betty Christina Ritenour, Aug. 9, 1969; children: Jonathan, Nathaniel, Carmen, Manuel. BA, Wesleyan U., 1956; MS, MIT, 1958. Meteorologist Nat. Weather Svc., NOAA, 1965—2007, sr. forecaster, 1990—2007; ret., 2007; elder, tchr. Sunday sch. Garden Meml. Presbyn. Ch., Washington, 1966-68; elder Ch. No. Va., Oakton, 1969—2004, elder emeritus, 2004—, treas., 1969-75, tchr. adult Sunday sch., 1990—2002. Adj prof N T Greek Whole Word Sem, Oakton, 1981—82. Pres Beverly Forest Civic Asn, Springfield, Va., 1976—77, vpres, 1977—78. Mem.: Nat Weather Asn, Am Sci Affiliation, Am Geophysical Union, Am Meteorol Soc. Republican. Avocations: photography, music. Home: 7568 Cloud Ct Springfield VA 22153-1804 Personal E-mail: wagjames@gmail.com. *As a scientist and Christian layman, I see increasing evidence that scientific advances alone can better life in only a limited way. Only when we individually and as a nation return to the "faith of our fathers" and put Jesus Christ in His rightful position as Lord of all, will we find true meaning and purpose in life.*

WAGNER, ANN LOUISE, United States Ambassador to Luxembourg, former political organization executive; m. Ray Wagner; children: Raymond III, Stephen, Mary Ruth. BSBA, U. Mo., 1984. Mem. com. Lafayette Twp.; chmn. com. St. Louis County Republican Ctrl. Com.; mem. Mo. Fedn. Republican Women; dir. ho. and senate redistricting commn. Mo. Rep. Party, 1991, chmn. Jefferson City, 1999—2001; Mo. state exec. dir. Bush/Quayle Campaign, 1992; advisor Ashcroft for Senate Campaign, 1994; 2nd congl. dist. chair Dole for Pres. Campaign, 1996; co-chmn. Rep. Nat. Com., Wash., 2001—05; US amb. to Luxembourg US Dept. State, 2005—. Mem.: Republican Nat. Conv. Midwestern State Chmn.'s Assn. (com. on arrangements 2000, del. 2000, del. chmn. 2000). Office: 5380 Luxembourg Pl Washington DC 20521 also: Am Embassy Luxembourg Unit 1410 APO APO AE 09126*

WAGNER, ANNETTE M., dermatologist, surgeon; b. Halifax, Nova Scotia, Can., Sept. 14, 1960; d. Ronald Clarence and Thelma May Dillman; children: Hadley Ann, Kirstin Laurel, Michela Jean, Charles Norman, Madison Leah, Gavin Lewis. BSc, U. Calgary, Alberta, Can., 1984; MDCM, McGill U., Montreal, Quebec, Can., 1988. Cert. in pediat. Tucson, 1997, in dermatology 1995, in pedait. dermatology 2006. Dir. pediats. dermatol. surgery Children's Meml. Hosp., Chgo., 1994—, attending physician, 1994—; intern. pediat. U. Ariz., 1988—89, resident pedait., 1989—91, resident dermatalogy, 1991—94. Clin. practice dir. Childrens Meml. Hosp., Chgo., 1996—98. Office: Childrens Meml Hosp 2300 Children's Plz Box 107 Chicago IL 60524 Office Fax: 708-836-4805; Home Fax: 773-327-3448.

WAGNER, ANNICE MCBRYDE, Senior Judge, DC Court of Appeals; b. DC; BA, JD, Wayne State U. Administrative aide to pres. Barnstable County Mental Health Assn.; with Houston and Gardner; gen. counsel Nat. Capital Housing Authority; people's counsel D.C.; assoc. judge Superior Court DC, 1977-90, DC Ct. Appeals, 1990—94, 2005—, chief judge, 1994—2005, sr. judge, 2005—. Mem. bd. directors Conf. Chief Justices; mem. bd. trustees United Planning Org., 1979—, v.p. bd. trustees, 1988—; chair Task Force On Gender Bias In The Courts, DC Judicial Conf. Arrangements Com., Com. on Selection & Tenure of Hearing Commrs.; mem. teaching team, trial advocacy workshop Harvard U. Office: DC Ct of Appeals 500 Indiana Ave NW Ste 6000 Washington DC 20001-2131*

WAGNER, ANTHONY E., academic administrator, former state official; b. Chambersburg, Pa. m. Lisa Wagner; 2 children. BA, Pa. State Univ. Fiscal policy specialist Pa. Gov. Budget Office, 1989—91; exec. asst. Sec. of Budget, 1991—93; dep. sec. for adminstrn. Pa. Dept. Agriculture, 1993—95; dir., govt. rels. Pa. State Univ., 1995—2001, spl. asst. to sr. v.p., fin., bus., 2001—02, asst. corp. controller, 2004—05; dep. sec. budget to Pa. budget sec., 2001—03; dep. state treas. investments and programs Pa. State Treas. Dept., 2005—06; exec. dep. state treas. State of Pa., 2006—07; v.p., CFO Temple Univ., 2007—. Deep-sea diver USN. Cath.

WAGNER, ANTONIN, economics professor; s. Anton and Cécile Wagner; m. Miriam Victory Spiegel, Mar. 3, 1984; 1 child, Ruth. ThM, U. Fribourg, Switzerland, 1965; PhD, U. Zurich, Switzerland, 1972. Prof. U. Zurich, 1975—2000, New Sch., NYC, 2000—. Contbr. articles to profl. jours. Mem. OneMarketing, Zurich, 1999. Scholar, Swiss Nat. Sci. Fund, 1988—98. Mem.: Verein fur Socialpolitik, Internat. Soc. Third Sector Rsch. (chair 1997—2001), Assn. Rsch. Nonprofit Orgs. and Voluntary Action.

WAGNER, ARTHUR WARD, JR., lawyer; b. Birmingham, Ala., Aug. 13, 1930; s. Arthur Ward and Lucille (Lockheart) W.; m. Ruth Shingler, May 11, 1957; children: Celia Wagner Minter, Julia Wagner Dolce, Helen Wagner McAfee. BSBA, U. Fla., 1954, JD, 1957. Bar: Fla. 1957, U.S. Dist. Ct. (so. dist.) Fla. 1957, U.S. Dist. Ct. (mid. dist.) Fla. 1975. Ptnr. Wagner & McAfee, P.A., West Palm Beach, Fla., 1959-2000; ret., 2000—. Lectr. in field. Author: Art of Advocacy: Jury Selection, 1981; co-author: Anatomy of Personal Injury Lawsuit I & II, 1968 and 1981. Mem. 15th Jud. Nominating Com., Palm Beach City, 1979—82, 4th

Dist. Nominating Commn., Palm Beach City, 1982—86; mem. pres.'s coun. U. Fla.; vestry Holy Trinity Parish, v.p., 2002—; bd. dirs., chmn. U. Fla. Found., 2004—, chmn, 2005—06. Fellow Internat. Acad. Trial Lawyers, Am. Coll. Trial Lawyers, Internat. Soc. Barristers, Am. Bd. Trial Advs.; mem. Assn. Trial Lawyers Am. (pres. 1975-76, hon. life trustee Roscoe Pound Found.), So. Trial Lawyers Assn. (pres. 1991), U. Fla. Law Coll. Alumni (mem. bd. govs.). Democrat. Episcopalian. Personal E-mail: wag8553@aol.com.

WAGNER, AUREEN PINTO, psychologist, educator; d. Baptist and Winifred Pinto; m. Scott C. Wagner, June 25, 1994; 2 children. BA, St. Agnes Coll., Mangalore, India, 1981; MA, Mysore U., India, 1983; PhD, U. Iowa, 1989. Lic. psychologist NY. Clin. intern Yale U. Child Study Ctr., New Haven, 1988—89; postdoctoral fellow Brown U., Providence, 1989—91; asst. prof. psychiatry/psychology U. Rochester (NY) Sch. Medicine and Dentistry, 1991—98; founder, dir. Lighthouse Press, Inc., Rochester, 1998—2006, The Anxiety Wellness Ctr., Rochester, 2006—; clin. assoc. prof. neurology U. Rochester (NY) Sch. Medicine and Dentistry, 2003—. Mem. profl. adv. bd. Tourette Syndrome Assn. Rochester, 1997—; dir. The Anxiety Wellness Ctr., Rochester, 2006—; mem. sci. adv. bd. Obsessive Compulsive Found., Boston, 2005—; internat. spkr. in field. Author: Up and Down the Worry Hill: A Children's Book about Obsessive-Compulsive Disorder and its Treatment, 2000 (Reader's Preference Editors' Choice Award, 2003), What to Do When Your Child Has Obsessive-Compulsive Disorder: Strategies and Solutions, 2002, (manual) Treatment of OCD in Children and Adolescents, 2003, Worried No More: Help and Hope for Anxious Children, 2002, 2d edit., 2005. Grantee J.N. Tata scholar, Tata Found., Bombay, India, 1984—88; Lady Meherbai Tata scholar, Lady Meherbai Tata Edn. Trust, Bombay, India, 1984—88, Robert J. Haggerty Rsch. scholar, U. Rochester Sch. of Medicine, 1995, Nat. Merit scholar, Govt. of the State of Karnataka, India, 1981—83. Mem.: APA, Genesee Valley Psychol. Assn. (chmn. newsletter com. 2005—), Anxiety Disorders Assn. Am., Obsessive Compulsive Found. Roman Catholic. Achievements include development of conceptual framework to explain treatment of OCD to children. Avocations: travel, gardening, choral music, walking. Office: 2300 Buffalo Road #100B Rochester NY 14624 Personal E-mail: aureen@rochester.rr.com.

WAGNER, BILLY (WILLIAM EDWARD WAGNER), professional baseball player; b. Tannersville, Va., July 25, 1971; m. Sarah Wagner. Student, Ferrum Coll., Va. Pitcher Houston Astros, 1995—2003, Phila. Phillies, 2003—05, NY Mets, 2006—09, Boston Red Sox, 2009—. Mem. US nat. team World Baseball Classic, 2006. Recipient Rolaids Relief award, 1999; named to Nat. League All-Star Team, 1999, 2001, 2003, 2005, 2007—08. Achievements include holding the NCAA single-season record for most strikeouts per nine innings (19.1), 1992; setting the NCAA Division III record for career strikeouts (327 in 182.1 innings). Office: Boston Red Sox 4 Yawkey Way Boston MA 02215*

WAGNER, BRADLEY JEREMIAH, agricultural engineer; b. Hershey, Pa., Dec. 19, 1981; s. George and Sonja Wagner; m. Julie LeAnn Stone, May 22, 2004. BS in Agrl. and Biol. Engring., Pa. State U., 2004. EIT Pa., registered hydraulic specialist, Pa. Engr. CNH Am. LLC, New Holland, Pa., 2004—. Mem. crop harvesting com. Agrl. Equipment Tech. Conf., 2003—. Mem.: Fluid Power Soc., Am. Soc. Agrl. Engrs., Coaly Honor Soc., Golden Key Internat. Honor Soc., Alpha Epsilon. Mem. Ch. Of Brethren. Avocations: woodworking, mechanics, outdoor activities. Office: CNH Hydraulic Lab Engr 200 George Delp Rd New Holland PA 17557 Business E-Mail: bradley.wagner@cnh.com.

WAGNER, BRUCE HERMAN, school librarian, educator; s. Herman Heinley Wagner and Elizabeth Landis Landes; m. Margaret Ann Kippycash, Dec. 26, 1975; children: Sherry Ann Toonder, Rebekah Edith Hoskins, Leah Lily, Margaret Elizabeth Wright, Sarah Katharina. BA, Pa. State U., State College, 1971; MDiv, Luther Rice Sem., Jacksonville, Fla., 1980; MS in Libr. and Info. Studies, Fla. State U., Tallahassee, 2003. Cert. in libr. Fla. Educators Certification. Bible tchr. Westgate Christian Sch., Tampa, Fla., 1975—76; tchr. Bible, math., sci. Mueller Christian Sch., Miami, 1977—78; Bible tchr. NW Christian Acad., North Miami, Fla., 1978—80; coord. Miami Beach Ext. Ctr. Guided Study Luther Rice Bible Coll. and Sem., Jacksonville, 1980—85; tchr. Hebrew club Word of Life Bible Inst., Pottersville, NY, 1989—90; tchr. English Westwood Christian Day Schs., Miami, 2001, head libr., 2001—. Pres. student coun. and Nat. Honor Soc. Schwenksville HS, Pa., 1966—67; counselor Word of Life Island Word of Life Fellowship, Schroon Lake, NY, 1967—68; mem. undergrad. student affairs com. Pa. State U. Senate, University Park, 1969—70; chmn. steering com. Miami Beach 1st Bapt. Ch., 1980—81; prin. Calvary Bapt. Sch., Hanson, Mass., 1996; mem. Dade Reading Coun., Miami, 2006—09. Presenter: cassette/CD Study to Show Thyself Approved Unto God..., 2004; author: Letters from Mt. Zion, 1979; composer: (cassette tape) Psalm 1, 2, 3, 4, 1981. Friend of libr. Miami Dade Pub. Libr. Sys., Miami Beach, 2006. Recipient SAR Good Citizenship award, Babe Ruth Sportsmanship award, Schwenksville HS, 1967, Newspaper Boy of Yr. award, Norristown Times Herald, 1960. Mem.: Am. Assn. Christian Schs., Fla. Assn. Christian Colls. and Schs. (secondary tchr.), Assn. Christian Librs. (assoc.; secondary tchr.), Phi Eta Sigma. Avocations: reading, singing, Bible study.

WAGNER, BRUCE STANLEY, marketing professional; b. San Diego, Aug. 1, 1943; s. Robert Sheldon and Janet (Lowther) Wagner; m. Elizabeth Pearsall Winslow, Oct. 4, 1975; children: Sage Elizabeth, Alexander Winslow. BA, Dartmouth Coll., 1965; MBA, U. Pa., 1984. Sr. v.p. Grey Advt., Inc., NYC, 1967-81; exec. v.p., chief oper. officer Campaign '76 Media Comm., Inc., Washington, 1975-76; exec. v.p., bd. dirs. Ross Roy, Inc., Bloomfield Hills, Mich., 1981-91, Ross Roy Group, Inc., Bloomfield Hills, 1991—94; v.p. mktg. and comms. ITT Automotive Inc., Auburn Hills, Mich., 1995-99; pres. Wagner & Co., Ltd., Birmingham, Mich., 1999—2000, Glen Arbor, Mich., 2004—; v.p. mktg. and corp. comms. MSX Internat. Inc., Southfield, Mich., 2001—03. Mem. parents bd. Bucknell U., pres. parents bd., 1999—2000, mem. bus. adv. bd., chmn., 2003—. Mem.: Am. Assn. Advt. Agys. (chmn., bd. govs. Mich. coun. 1985—86, bd. govs. ctrl. region 1988—94), U. Club Chgo., Wharton Alumni Assn. (chmn. 1983—85), Birmingham Athletic Club, Orchard Lake Country Club, Detroit Athletic Club, Wharton Club Mich. (bd. dirs. 1985—90). Office: PO Box 194 Glen Arbor MI 49636

WAGNER, CAROLINE S., research and development company executive; b. Newport, RI, June 5, 1955; m. Dennis J. McIntosh; children: Julia L. McIntosh, Gregory B. McIntosh, Eleanor R. McIntosh. PhD, U. Amsterdam, 2004. Sr. analyst RAND Corp., Leiden, Netherlands, 1993—2004, SRI Internat., Arlington, Va., 2005—. Mem. US congress Com. Sci., Space, and Tech., Washington, 1990—93. Author: (book) The New Invisible College: Science for Development. Vis. scholar, Fulbright Found., 2005; Summer fellow, Hasting Ctr. Ethics Sci., 1984, fellow, AAAS, 2006—. Office: SRI Internat 1100 Wilson Blvd Arlington VA 22209

WAGNER, CHARLENE BROOK, retired secondary school educator; b. LA; d. Edward J. and Eva (Anderson) Brook; children: Gordon, Brook, John. BS, Tex. Christian U., 1952; MEd, Sam Houston U., 1973; postgrad., U. Tex., Austin, 1975, Tex. A&M U., 1977. Sci. educator Spring Branch Ind. Sch. Dist., Houston, 1970-98; ret., 2000; dir. CompuKidZ, Houston, 1998—2000; cons. Scott Foresman, Addison Wesley, Ginn, Houston. Cons. Scott Foresman Pub. Co., Houston, 2000-01; owner Sci. Instrnl. Sys. Co., 1988—; dir. Compukidz. Mem. Houston Symphony League, 1992, Mus. Fine Arts, Mus. of Art of Am. West, Houston, 1989, Mus. Natural Scis., Women's Christian Home, Houston, 1991; mem. Houston Grand Opera Guild, mem. exec. bd. 1999-2000, rec./corr. sec.; social chmn. Encore, 1988; mem. Magic Circle Rep. Women's Club. Mem.: AAUW, NAFE, NEA, Internat. Platform Assn., Spring Branch Edn. Assn., Tex. State Tchrs. Assn., Heather and Thistle Soc., Wellington Soc. for Arts (Houston chpt.), Clan Anderson Soc., Art League Houston, Shepherd Soc., Watercolor Arts Soc. (Houston), Houston Highland Games Assn., Space City Ski Club. Episcopalian. Avocations: painting, watercolor media. Home: 2670 Marilee Ln Apt B54 Houston TX 77057-4264 E-mail: wagner2670@aol.com.

WAGNER, CHRISTIAN NIKOLAUS JOHANN, materials engineering educator; b. Saarbrucken-Dudweiler, Germany, Mar. 6, 1927; arrived in U.S., 1959, naturalized, 1969; s. Christian Jakob and Regina (Bungert) W.; m. Rosemarie Anna Mayer, Apr. 5, 1952; children: Thomas Martin, Karla Regine, Petra Susanne. Student, U. Poitiers, France, 1948-49; Licence es Sci., U. Saar, Ger., 1951, Diplom-Ingenieur, 1954, Dr.rer.nat., 1957. Research asst. Inst. fur Metallforschung, Saarbrucken, 1953-54; vis. fellow M.I.T., 1955-56; research asso. Inst. fur Metallforschung, 1957-58; teaching, research asst. U. Saarbrucken, 1959; asst. prof. Yale U., New Haven, Conn., 1959-62, assoc. prof., 1962-70; prof. dept. materials engring. UCLA, 1970-91, prof. emeritus, 1991—, chmn. dept., 1974-79, asst. dean undergrad. studies Sch. Engring. and Applied Sci., 1982-85, acting chmn., 1990-91. Vis. prof. Tech. U., Berlin, 1969, U. Saarbrücken, 1979—80. Contbr. articles to profl. jours. Recipient U.S. Sci. Humboldt award, U. Saarbrucken, 1989—90, 1992. Fellow Am. Soc. Metals Internat.; mem. Am. Crystallographic Assn., Minerals, Metals and Materials Soc. Home: 37621 Golden Pebble Ave Palm Desert CA 92211-1430 Office: UCLA 6532 Boelter Hl Los Angeles CA 90095-0001 Personal E-mail: cnjwagner@verizon.net.

WAGNER, CURTIS LEE, JR., judge; b. Nov. 8, 1928; m. Jeanne E. Allen (dec.); children: Curtis L. III, Rex A. Student, Tenn. Poly. Inst., 1947-49; LLB, U. Tenn., 1951. Bar: Tenn. 1952. Assoc. Kramer, Dye, McNabb and Greenwood, Knoxville, Tenn., 1951-54; atty.-adv. gen. crimes and fraud sect. Criminal Divsn. Dept. Justice, Washington, 1954-56; trial atty. Dept. Justice, Washington, 1954-60; assigned to Ct. of Claims sect. Civil Divsn., Washington, 1956-60; spl. asst. to JAG comms., transp. and utilities Dept. Army, Washington, 1960-64; chief Regulatory Law Divsn., Washington, 1964-74; adminstrv. law judge FERC, Washington, 1974-79, chief adminstrv. law judge, 1979—. Mem. army civilian lawyer career com., 1960-74; chmn. JAG incentive awards com. 1960-74; mem. Army Staff Awards Bd., 1964-74, Army Environ. Policy Council, 1972-74. Dist. commr. Nat. Capital Area coun. Boy Scouts Am., 1967-69; mem. Bd. Govts. Watergate of Alexandria Condo, 1996-2007; commr. Alexandria Redevel. and Pub. Housing Commn., 1996-2000; mem. waterfront com. City of Alexandria, 2005-07. Decorated Meritorious Civilian Svc. award, Exceptional Civilian Svc. award; recipient citation for outstanding performance Dept. Army, 1961-74, Scouter's Tng. award Boy Scouts Am., 1965, Scoutmaster's Key, 1966, Commr.'s Key, 1968, Commr.'s Arrowhead Honor, 1966, Silver Beaver award 1969, Alumni award U. Tenn., 2008. Mem. Order of Arrow, Annapolis Yacht Club. Methodist. Office: Fed Energy Regulatory Comm 888 1st St NE Washington DC 20426-0002 Office Phone: 202-502-8500. Business E-Mail: curtis.wagner@ferc.gov.

WAGNER, CYNTHIA GAIL, editor, writer; b. Bethesda, Md., Oct. 3, 1956; d. Robert Cheney and Marjory Jane (Kletzing) W. BA in English, Grinnell Coll., 1978; MA in Comms., Syracuse U., 1981. Editl. asst. The Futurist/World Future Soc., Bethesda, Md., 1981—82, staff editor, 1982-85, asst. editor, 1985-91, sr. editor, 1991-92, mng. editor, 1992—. Editor: (newsletter) Futurist Update, 2000—, (book) Foresight, Innovation, and Strategy: Toward a Wiser Future, 2005, Seeing the Future Through New Eyes, 2008, Innovation and Creativity in a Complex World, 2009; columnist: 3-2-1 Contact, 1994; contbr. Encyclopedia of the Future, 1995, The 21st Century, 1999; contbg. writer/music reviewer BeaversonIdol.com., 2004—07. Mem. Theatre Comm. Group, Shakespeare Readers. Avocation: theater. Office: The Futurist World Future Soc 7910 Woodmont Ave Ste 450 Bethesda MD 20814-3066 Business E-Mail: cwagner@wfs.org.

WAGNER, DALE R., science educator; s. Roy and Mary Ellen Wagner. BEd., Slippery Rock U., Pa., 1988; MEd., Temple U., Phila., 1991; PhD., U. N.Mex, Albuquerque, 1997. Cert. health fitness specialist Am. Coll. Sports Medicine, 1993, Nat. Strength & Conditioning Assn., 1993, Am. Soc. Exercise Physiologists, 2000. Asst. prof. Vanguard U., Costa Mesa, Calif., 1998—2003, Utah State U., Logan, 2004—. Author: (text book) Applied Body Composition Assessment; contbr. articles to jours. Mem.: Internat. Soc. Mt. Medicine, Wilderness Med. Soc., Nat. Strength & Conditioning Soc., Am. Coll. Sports Medicine, Am. Soc. Exercise Physiologists (bd. dirs. 2008—09). Office: Utah State Univ HPER Dept 7000 Old Main Hill Logan UT 84322-7000 Business E-Mail: dale.wagner@usu.edu.

WAGNER, DARRYL WILLIAM, lawyer; b. Dixon, Ill., Jan. 14, 1943; s. Earl L. and Lois Mae W.; m. Susan A. Aldrich; children: Peter Alan, Nicholas William. BA, Northwestern U., 1965, JD, 1968. Bar: Ill. 1968, U.S. Dist. Ct. (no. dist.) Ill. 1969, U.S. Ct. Appeals (7th cir.) 1971, Calif. 1982. Sr. counsel Sidley Austin LLP, Chgo., 1969—. Dir. Housing Options for People to Excell, Inc., 1992-94, 96—. Co-author: Illinois Municipal Law: Subdivisions and Subdivisions in Controls, 1978, 81. Mem. ABA, Internat. Assn. Attys. and Execs. in Corp. Real Estate, Ill. State Bar Assn., Chgo. Bar Assn. Presbyterian. Home: 526 A San Ysdidro Rd Santa Barbara CA 93108 Office: Sidley Austin LLP 555 W 5th St Ste 4000 Los Angeles CA 90013-3000 E-mail: dwagner@sidley.com, dwwagnere@ix.netcom.com.

WAGNER, DONALD BERT, health facility administrator; b. York, Pa., July 27, 1930; s. Bert Daniel and Mary Elizabeth (Roelke) W.; m. Janet Louise Bankert, July 12, 1952; children: Kimberly, Susan, David, John. Student, Franklin & Marshall, 1948-50; BS in Phys. Therapy, Columbia U., 1952; MHA, Baylor U., 1960. Commd. 2d lt. USAF, 1952, advanced through grades to brig. gen., 1982; physical therapist Randolph AFB, San Antonio, 1952-55; asst. adminstr. USAF/RAF S. Ruislip, London; adminstr. USAF/RAF Bentwaters, Ipswich, England, 1955-58; various adminstrv. roles USAF Hosps. and Commands, Europe and U.S., 1958-73; dep. comdr. USAF Sch. Health Care Sci., Wichita Falls, Tex., 1973-75; adminstr. Wilford Hall Med. Ctr., San Antonio, 1975-79; chief med. svc. corps Office Surgeon Gen. USAF, San Antonio, 1979-82; dep. surgeon gen. USAF Med. Svc. Ctr., San Antonio, 1981-82, ret., 1982; adminstr., assoc. v.p. M. D. Anderson/U. Tex. Cancer Ctr., Houston, 1982-85; chief exec. officer Meml. Southwest Hosp., Houston, 1985-91; v.p. Meml. Hosp. System, Houston, 1985-91, internal cons., interim hosp. CEO, 1991—2005; mem. adv. bd. Grad. Program in Healthcare Adminstrn. Texas Women's U., Houston. Adj. prof. Baylor and Trinity U., San Antonio, 1975-82; assoc. prof. U. Houston, St. Louis U., 1982-88; CEO Woodlands Hosp., Angleton-Danbury Hosp., Prevention and Recovery Ctr., Bellville Hosp., MHHS Long Term Acute Care Hosp., MH S.E. Hosp.; chief operating officer St. Joseph Med. Ctr.; cons., El Salvador, Nicaragua, China, Saudi Arabia, Japan, Korea, 1991-02. Bd. dirs. Hospice at the Med. Ctr., 1982-2001, Child Advocates, Houston, 1985-89, Kidney Found., Houston, 1985-88, Westland YMCA, Houston, 1985-88, 90-94, Ft. Bend County YMCA, 1998-03, Greater Houston Hosp. Coun., 1983-87, Sam Houston area Alzheimer's Assn. 1990-94; mem.n. external adv. bd. Sch. Allied Health, U. Tex. Med. Br.; mem. adv. bd. gradrogram healthcare adminstrn. Tex. Women's U., Houston. Named Disting. Alumnus Baylor U. Program in Healthcare Adminstrn., 1993. Fellow Am. Coll. Healthcare Execs. (life fellow, edn. com., ethics com., comm. com.), Royal Soc. Health; mem. Am. Hosp. Assn. (bd. dirs. hosp. rsch. and edn. found. 1990—), Tex. Hosp. Assn., Assn. Mil. Surgeons U.S. (Am. coll. healthcare exec. Ray E. Brown award 1982, Lifetime Achievement award, 2009, Outstanding Sr. Level Healthcare Exec. Regents award 1991, Regents Lifetime Achievement award 2004), Am. Mgmt. Soc. Republican. Methodist. Avocation: music. Home and Office: 1746 Carriage Way Sugar Land TX 77478-4201 Home Phone: 281-980-5613.

WAGNER, EDWARD HARRIS, epidemiologist, educator; b. Buffalo, 1940; AB, Princeton U., 1961; MD, SUNY: Buffalo, 1965; MPH, U. NC, Chapel Hill, 1972. Cert. Internal Medicine, 1972. Intern Buffalo Gen. Hosp., 1965—66; asst. dir. VA outpatient dept. McDonald Army Hosp., Ft. Eustis, Va., 1967—68; resident SUNY Buffalo, 1968—70, chief tchg. fellow, 1970—71; instr. medicine and family medicine U. NC, Chapel Hill, 1971—72, asst. prof. epidemiology and medicine, 1972—78, assoc. prof. epidemiology and medicine, 1978—83, dep. dir. health services rsch. ctr., 1980—83, prof. epidemiology and medicine, 1983, clin. prof. epidemiology, 1984—, assoc. Cecil G. Sheps Ctr. Health Services Rsch., 1995—, adj. prof. epidemiology, 2000—; dir. Ctr. Health Studies Group Health Coop. of Puget Sound, Seattle, 1983—98, dir. W.A. MacColl Inst. Healthcare Innovation, 1992—; prof. health services U. Wash. Sch. Pub. Health and Cmty. Medicine, Seattle, 1984—. Bn. surgeon US Army, 1966—76, Vietnam. Recipient Gilbert S. Beck award, 1965, Cecil G. Sheps Disting. Investigator award, U. NC, 1988, John Atkinson Ferrell prize, 1999, Disting. Alumnus award, 1999, Tyroler Alumni award, 2008, Edward Henderson award, Am. Geriatrics Soc., 2004, Pres.'s award, NY Health and Hospitals Corp., 2006, Health Care Quality award, Nat. Com. Quality Assurance, 2007, Picker award, Picker Inst., 2007. Fellow: ACP, Soc. Behavioral Medicine; mem.: Inst. Medicine, Am. Heart Assn., Assn. Teachers of Preventive Medicine, Internat. Epidemiologic Assn., Soc. Gen. Internal Medicine, Assn. Health Services Rsch., HMO Rsch. Network, Delta Omega, Alpha Omega Alpha. Office: 1730 Minor Ave Ste 1290 Seattle WA 98101 Office Phone: 206-287-2877. E-mail: wagner.e@ghc.org.*

WAGNER, EDWARD KURT, publishing company executive; b. NYC, Sept. 29, 1936; s. Kurt Henry and Julia Marie (Selesky) W.; m. Ann Marie Philbin, Jan. 31, 1959; children: Denise, Steven, Kenneth, Jeanne. BBA, St. Francis Coll., 1961. With Pitman Pub. Corp., NYC, 1952-75, v.p., treas., 1968-71, exec. v.p., 1971-75; financial mgr. Dun-Donnelley Pub. Corp., NYC, 1975-76, contr. gen. book div., 1976-77; sr. mgr. contr.'s dept. Dun & Bradstreet, Inc., NYC, 1977-78, asst. contr., 1978-83, contr., 1983-88, v.p., contr., 1989-96; ret., 1996—. Home: 55 Shoal Rd Jackson NJ 08527

WAGNER, ELLYN SANTI, retired mathematics educator; BS, No. Ariz. U., 1971, MA, 1974; postgrad., George Mason U., 1980-82. Cert. tchr., Va. Tchr. math. Flagstaff (Ariz.) Pub. Schs., 1972-76, head math. dept., 1974-76; asst. prof. math. No. Va. C.C., Annandale, Va., 1976—2004. Participant Writing Across the Curriculum Workshops, Annandale, 1992-93. Recipient recognition for outstanding contbns. to edn. No. Va. C.C. Alumni Fedn., 1993. Mem. Am. Math. Assn. Two-Yr. Colls., Va. Math. Assn. Two-Yr. Colls. (regional v.p. 1989-91, coord. spring conf. 1992), Phi Kappa Phi. Avocations: classical piano, ballroom dancing.

WAGNER, FREDERICK REESE, retired language educator; b. Phila., Apr. 15, 1928; m. Barbara Alexander Brady, May 9, 1959 (div. 1968); 1 child, Christopher A. BA summa cum laude, Duke U., 1948, MA, 1949, PhD, 1971. Advt mgr. Prentice-Hall, Inc., NYC, 1955-57; promotion mgr. Harper & Row, NYC, 1957-65; instr. English Duke U., Durham, NC, 1967-69; asst. prof. Hamilton Coll, Clinton, NY, 1969-73, assoc. prof., 1973-78, prof. English, chmn. dept., 1978-90, prof. English, 1990-95, ret., 1995. Author: Famous Underwater Adventurers, 1962; Submarine Fighter of the American Revolution, 1963; Patriot's Choice: The Story of John Hancock, 1964; Robert Morris, Audacious Patriot, 1976. Mem. Thoreau Soc. (pres. 1984-86), Hawthorne Soc., Phi Beta Kappa. Home: 2160 Bleecker St Apt A-215 Utica NY 13501

WAGNER, FREDERICK WILLIAM (BILL WAGNER), lawyer; b. Daytona Beach, Fla., Apr. 13, 1933; s. Adam A. and Nella (Schroeder) W.; m. Ruth Whetstone; children: Alan Frederick, Darryl William, Thomas Adam. BA, U. Fla., 1955, LLB with honors, 1960. Bar: Fla. 1960, U.S. Supreme Ct. 1967, D.C. 1989; cert. civil trial lawyer, Fla. Bar; cert. aviation lawyer, Fla. Bar. Pvt. practice law, Miami, Fla., 1960-63, Orlando, Fla., 1963-65, Tampa, Fla., 1965—; ptnr. Nichols, Gaither, Beckham, Colson, Spence & Hicks, Tampa, 1965-67; ptnr., shareholder Wagner, Vaughan & McLaughlin, P.A., 1967—. Mem. Gov.'s Jud. Nominations Commn., 1971-72, Constnl. Jud. Nominations Commn., 1972-75; mem. Fla. Bd. Bar Examiners, 1974-77, emeritus mem., 1995—; chmn. Civil Procedure Rules Com. Fla. Bar, 1977-78; bd. govs. Fla. Bar, 1978-83; trustee Roscoe Pound Inst., 1984-92; mem. civil jury instrn. com. Fla. Supreme Ct., 1985-2003. Contbr. articles to profl. jours. 1st lt. USAF, 1955-57. Fellow Am. Bar Found., Am. Coll. Trial Lawyers, Internat. Acad. Trial Lawyers, Am. Bd. Trial Advs.; mem. Am. Assn. for Justice (formerly known as ATLA; bd. govs. 1973-80, 84-89, chmn. pub. affairs dept. 1984-89, treas. 1982-84, v.p. 1986-87, pres.-elect 1987-88, pres. 1988-89), Am. Inns of Ct. Found. (trustee 1996-2000), Fla. Justice Assn. (formerly known as Acad. Fla. Trial Lawyers; bd. dirs. 1965-84, pres. 1972-73), Bay Area Trial Lawyers Assn. (v.p. 1966-68), Am. Law Inst. (coun. 1993—), Lawyer-Pilots Bar Assn., Fla. Bar Found., U. Fla. Alumni Assn., Nat. Bd. Trial Advocacy (cert. civil), Assn. Personal Injury Lawyers, Australian Lawyers Alliance, Pan European Orgn. Personal Injury Lawyers, So. Trial Lawyers Assn., Tampa Bay Trial Lawyers Assn. Democrat. Methodist. Avocations: travel, boating. Home: 901 Mariner Way Tampa FL 33602-5759 Office: Wagner Vaughan & McLaughlin 601 Bayshore Blvd Ste 910 Tampa FL 33606-2786 Office Phone: 813-225-4000. Business E-Mail: billwagner@ragnerlaw.com.

WAGNER, GERALDINE MARIE, nursing educator, consultant; b. Renton, Wash., Apr. 12, 1948; d. Ernest F. and Vera P. (Temiraeff) W. AA, Pasadena City Coll., 1970; BA cum laude, Calif. State U., Northridge, 1977; BSN, Calif. State U., LA, 1982; MEd summa cum laude, Azusa Pacific U., 1993. Cert. pub. health nurse, Calif. Dept. Health Svcs. In utilization mgmt. Blue Cross, Woodland Hills, Calif., 1987-88, Healthmarc, Pasadena, Calif., 1988-90; nursing educator, asst. dir. vocat. nursing program Casa Loma Coll., LA, 1991-92, dir. program planning and devel., and coord. continuing edn. Lake View Terrace, 1992-93; dir. vocal. nursing program Glendale (Calif.) Career Coll., 1994-95; with patient care rev. svcs. U. So. Calif. U. Hosp., LA, 1996—; med.-legal nurse cons., 2000—. Docent Mission La Purisima Concepcion. Capt. Nurse Corp, U.S. Army, 1979-84. Mem.: ASPCA, VFW, G.K. Chesterton Soc., Calif. Mission Studies Assn., Assn. for Women in Math., Fellowship Cath. Scholars, Computer Using Educators, Nat. Coun. Tchrs. Math., Am. Math. Soc., Blue Army Our Lady Fatima, Soc. Cath. Social Scientists, Mil. Officer Assn. Am., Assn. Hebrew Catholics, Order of Preachers, Inst. Religious Life, AMVETS, Res. Officers Assn. U.S., Army Nurse Corps. Assn., Cath. War Vets, History Channel Club, Disabled Am. Vets., Am. Legion, Sigma Theta Tau, Pi Lambda Theta. Roman Catholic. Home: 924 Rock Rose Ln Lompoc CA 93436 Office Phone: 805-735-3575. Personal E-mail: sistergeraldinemarie@comcast.net.

WAGNER, GREG WILLIAM, computer scientist, educator; s. William Frederick and Margaret Mary Wagner; m. Cathy Lynn Wilczynski, Mar. 26, 1983; children: Gretchen Antonina Miller, Elyse Elizabeth. BA, Duquesne U., Pitts., 1965—69, MAT, 1972—79; BSIS, U. Pitts., Pitts., 1979—84, MSIS, 1984—86. Cert. instr. II Pa., 1979. Info. sci. instr. Chatham Coll., Pitts., 1989—91; cit prof. Boyce Campus CCAC, Monroeville, Pa., 1991—. Eucharistic min. Mother Sorrows Ch., Murrysville, Pa., 1994—2006, webmaster, 2001—06. Capt. US Army, 1969—72, Vietnam. Decorated Joint Svc. Commendation medal US Army; recipient Excellence award, CCAC, 1997; fellow Tchg. Assistantship, Duquesne U., 1973, Grad. Assistantship, U. Pitts., 1984—86. Mem.: Computer Sci. Tchrs. Assn. (assoc.), Spl. Interest Group Computer Sci. Edn. (assoc.), Assn. Computing Machinery (assoc.). Avocations: basketball, reading. Home: 4098 Benden Cir Murrysville PA 15668 Office: CCAC Boyce Campus 595 Beatty Rd Monroeville PA 15146 Personal E-mail: ccacman@yahoo.com. Business E-Mail: gwagner@ccac.edu.

WAGNER, HAROLD A., retired gas industry executive; b. Oakland, Calif., Nov. 12, 1935; s. Harold A. and Lurline Frances (Madsen) Wagner; m. Marcia Kenaston, July 17, 1956; children: Sandra Wagner Boyce, Kristi Wagner Schwiering, Tracey, Eric. BS in Mech. Engring., Stanford U., 1958, SEP, 1982; MBA, Harvard U., 1963. Regional sales mgr. ind. gases U.S. Air Products & Chems., Allentown, Pa., 1963—70; mgr. GM ind. gases U.K.Air Products & Chems., 1970—76; regional sales mgr. GM Ind. Gases Continental Europe, 1976—80, GM Ind. Gases U.S., 1980—81; v.p. sales ind. gases div. FM, 1981—82; v.p. corp. planning Air Products & Chems., 1982—87, v.p. bus. div. chems., 1987—88; pres. AP Europe, 1988—90, exec. v.p., 1990—91, pres., COO, 1991—92, past chmn. pres., CEO; chmn., pres., CEO, dir. Air Products and Chems., 1992—2001, chmn., CEO, dir., ret.; chmn. Agere Systems, 2001—. 1st lt. USAF, 1958—61. Avocations: squash, photography. Home: 4031 Savannah Trl Santa Rosa CA 95404-8897

WAGNER, HARVEY M., finance educator, consultant; b. San Francisco, Nov. 20, 1931; s. Max and Bernice Wagner. BS, Stanford U., Palo Alto, Calif., 1953, MS, 1954; PhD, MIT, Cambridge, 1957; degree (hon.), Kathololieke Universeit, Leuven Belgium, 1980. Instr. Sloan Sch. MIT, Cambridge, 1955—57; prof. Stanford Sch. Bus., Palo Alto, 1957—67, Yale Sch. Orgn. and Mgmt., New Haven, 1967—76; dean U. NC Bus. Sch., Chapel Hill, 1976—78; prof. Kenan-Flagler Bus. Sch., U. NC, Chapel Hill, 1978—. Rschr. RAND Corp., Santa Monica, Calif., 1957—60; cons. Electric Power Rsch. Inst., Palo Alto, McKinsey & Co., NYC, 1960—. Author: (text book) Principles of Operations Research, (book) Statistical Management of Inventory Systems, Simulated Economic Models; contbr. articles to profl. jours. (INFORMS Edelman award, 1984, INFORMS Writing award, 1996). Recipient Larnder award, Can. Oreg. Soc., 1988; named Book of the Yr., AIIE, 1970; Marshall fellowship, Brit. Govt., 1954—55, Rsch. grant, Office of Naval Rsch., 1973—84, NSF, 1960—69, 1985—87. Fellow: MSOM, Am. Statis. Assn. (assoc. editor 1963—69), INFORMS (pres. 1973—74).

WAGNER, HELEN ADEENE, elementary school educator; b. Burlington, Kans., Mar. 9, 1931; d. John Floyd and Clara Myrtle (Jasper) Stone; m. Kenneth Edward Wagner, Sept. 20, 1949; children: Karen, Kent, Kirk. BS, Kans. State Tchrs. Coll., 1964; MS, Emporia U., Kans., 1968, postgrad., 1983, 88-90, Fort Hayes State U., 1978, 1983-84, Kans. State U., 1979-80, Butler County Community Coll., 1983. Cert. master tchr., Kans. Tchr. Sunnyside Rural Sch., Gridley, Kans., 1948-50; tchr. spl. reading Haviland (Kans.) Grade Sch., 1958-60, tchr. grade 8, 1960-61; edn. sec. Skelly-Jefferson Elem. Sch., El Dorado, Kans., 1962-64; tchr. Skelly Elem. Sch., El Dorado, 1964-81, El Dorado Mid. Sch., 1981-91; ret., 1991. Chmn. social studies elem. schs. El Dorado Unified Sch. Dist. 490, 1978-82; chmn. lang. arts dept. El Dorado Mid. Sch., 1987-91; mem. profl. teaching practices commn. Kans. State Bd. Edn., 1976-82, mem. bd. dirs., 1975-80; tchr. edn. teams Nat. Coun. Accreditation, 1974-86; presenter seminars Brooks Jr. H.S., Wichita, 1990; supr. student tchrs.; tchr. mentor El Dorado Pub. Schs., 1991-97; mem. Kans. Found. for Excellence in Edn., 1992-95; mem. Kans. Tchr. of Yr. Steering Com., 1992-95. Instr. CPR ARC, 1977-86; vol. El Dorado Helpline, 1972; ruling elder, 1984-86; special gifts com. co-chair Presbyn. Ch., 2003-, fellowship com. 2002-08, personnel com. 2000-03. Named Kans. Tchr. of Yr. Dept. Edn., 1981, Outstanding History Tchr. DAR, 1983, Kans. Outstanding History Tchr. Daus. Colonial Wars, 1983; named to Kans. Tchr. Hall of Fame, 1991; recipient Kans. Master Tchr. award, 1991. Mem. AAUW (chair future astronaut tng. program com. 1991-93), NEA (life; rep. various confs.), Nat. Assn. Mid. Level Educators, Nat. State Tchr. of Yr. Assn. (del. state conf., steering com. 1989-90), Kans. Edn. Assn., Kans. Assn. Mid. Level Educators (presenter 1987, 91), Kans. Tchr. of the Yr. Assn. (v.p. 1989-91, pres. 1992-95, 2d v.p. 1995-97, organizer, presenter celebration of teaching 1989, 95), Kans. Tchr. of Yr. Congl. Dist. 4 (co-chair 1992-95, mem. steering com. 1992-95), El Dorado Edn. Assn. (pres. 1970-71, chmn., mem. various coms. 1964-91), Order Ea. Star (sec. 1960-62), Chelsea Swingin' Sq. Dance Club (bd. dirs., sec.-treas. 1972-94, v.p. 2004-09), El Dorado C. of C. (sr. ambs. 1988—, co-chmn. 2005—), Am. Legion Ladies Golf Assn. (sec. 1997-2000, 2002-04), Phi Delta Kappa (coop. learning presenter conf. 1989), Butler County Ret. Sch. Pers. Presbyterian. E-mail: hawagner@cox.net.

WAGNER, JAMES WARREN, academic administrator, engineering educator; b. Washington, July 12, 1953; s. Robert Earl and Bernice (Bittner) W.; m. Debbie Kelley, July 31, 1976; children: Kimberly Renee, Christine Kelley. BSEE, U. Del., 1975; MS, Johns Hopkins U., 1978, PhD, 1984. Electronics engr. U.S. FDA, Washington, 1975-84; asst. prof. Johns Hopkins U., Balt., 1984-88, assoc. prof., 1988-93, prof., 1993-97, chmn. dept. materials scis. and engring., 1993-97; prof. materials sci. and engring., dean Case Sch. Engring. Case Western Res. U., Cleve., 1998—2000, provost, 2000-01, interim pres., 2001—02; pres. Emory U., Atlanta, 2003—. Contbr. articles to profl. jours. Elder Presbyn. Ch. U.S.A.; bd. mem. Carter Ctr., Ga. Rsch. Alliance, SunTrust Banks, Metro Atlanta C. of C. Mem. IEEE, Optical Soc. Am., Laser & Electro-Optics Soc. Presbyterian. Achievements include scientific contributions to the field of optical metrology applied to materials characterization, especially advanced holographic and laser-based ultrasonic methods. Office: Emory U Office of Pres Atlanta GA 30322

WAGNER, JUDITH BUCK, investment firm executive; b. Altoona, Pa., Sept. 25, 1943; d. Harry Bud and Mary Elizabeth (Rhodes) B.; m. Joseph E. Wagner, Mar. 15, 1980; 1 child, Elizabeth. BA in History, U. Wash., 1965; grad., N.Y. Inst. Fin., 1968. Registered Am. Stock Exch., N.Y. Stock Exch., investment advisor. Security analyst Morgan, olmstead, Kennedy & Gardner, LA, 1968-71, Boettcher & Co., Denver, 1972-75; pres. Wagner Investment Mgmt., Denver, 1975—. Chmn. The Women's Bank, N.A., Denver, 1977-94, organizational group pres., 1975-77; chmn. Equitable Bankshares Colo., Inc., Denver, 1980-94; pres. Equitable Bank of Littleton, Colo., 1985; lectr. Denver U., Metro State, 1975-80. Author: Woman and Money series Colo. Woman Mag., 1976, moderator "Catch 2' Sta. KWGN-TV, 1978-79. Pres. Big Sisters Colo., Denver, 1977-82, bd. dirs., 1972-83; bd. fellows U. Denver, 1985-90; bd. dirs. Red Cross, 1980, Assn. Children's Hosp., 1985, Colo. Health Facilities Authority, 1978-84, Jr. League Cmty. ADv. Com., 1979-82, Bros. Redevel., Inc., 1979-80; mem. agy. rels. com. Mile High United Way, 1978-81, chmn. United Way Venture Way, 1978-81, chmn. United Way Venture Grant com., 1980-81; bd. dirs. Downtown Dener, Inc., 1988-95; bd. dirs., v.p., treas. The Women's Found. Colo., 1987-91; treas., trustee, v.p., Graland Country Day Sch., 1990-97, pres., 1994-97; trustee Denver Rotary Found., 1990-95, Hunt Alternatives Fund, 1992-97; trustee The Colo. Trust, 1998—, chmn., 2003-05; steering com. chair, Ctr. Women's Health Rsch., 2000-07; Major Gifts Com.; co-chair, Planned Parenthood Rocky Capital Campaign. Recipient Making It award Cosmopolitan Mag., 1977, Women on the Go award, Savvy Mag., 1983, Minouri Yasoui award, 1986, Salute Spl. Honoree award, Big Sisters, 1987; named one of the Outstanding Young Women Am., 1979, Woman Who Makes A Difference award Internat. Women's Forum, 1987, Maverick Thinker award Urban Park, 2003; named Disting. Citizen award U. Colo., 2005. Fellow Assn. Investment Mgmt. & Rsch.; mem. Women's Forum Colo. (pres. 1979), Women's Found. Colo., Inc. (bd. dirs. 1986-91), Denver Soc. Security Analysts (bd. dirs. 1976-83, v.p. 1980-81, pres. 1981-82), Colo. Investment Advisors assn., Rotary (treas. Denver chpt. found., pres. 1993-94), Leadership Denver (Outstanding Alumna award 1987), Pi Beta Phi (pres. U. Wash. chpt. 1964-65). Office: Wagner Investment Mgmt Inc Ste 240 3200 Cherry Creek South Dr Denver CO 80209-3245 Office Phone: 303-777-1800.

WAGNER, KAREL, retired nuclear engineer, educator; b. Prague, ČSR, Czech Republic, Feb. 15, 1931; s. Karel and Anna (Tittl) W.; m. Sonja Vavrova, Sept., 24, 1953; children: Karel, Antonin. MEE, Tech. U., Plzeň, ČSSR, 1950-54, PhD Reactor Engring., 1968; M Reactor Engring., Charles U., 1957; MBA, CEI U. Geneva, 1970. Testing engr. ŠKODA Elect. Machinery Plant, Plzeň, 1954-56; R & D officer ŠKODA Nuc. Machinery Plant, Plzeň, 1957-68, head R & D group, 1968-80, sci. officer, 1985-89, advisor to dir., 1993—99, head commissioning J. Bohunice, 1981-85; chmn. CS Atomic Energy Commn., Prague, 1990-92; ret., 2007. Lector Tech. U., Plzeň, 1964-95; chmn. Complex State Rsch. and Devel. Program for LWR, Prague, 1969-73, State Rsch. and Devel. Program for Instrumentation and Control. Light Water Reactor, 1965-80, cons. Instrumentation and Control Modern Nuc. Power Plant, 2000-07. Author: (textbook) Control of Nuclear Power Plant, 1964, (screenplay) A New Way of Reactor Control, 1963; translator Instrumentation of NPP, 1965, System Logistic, 1971. Recipient Tech. Project award CS Min. Heavy Industry, 1960, State Sci. Prize CS Govt., 1963, Commissioning Nuclear Power Plant award CS Min. Energy, 1985. Mem. CS Sci. and Tech. Soc., CS Nuclear Soc., CS Auto-Moto Club. Achievements include patents for device for measuring the thickness of austenitic weld deposits on carbon steel wells (reactor pressure vessels), device for position measurement of reactor control rod drives. Home Phone: 420 371131407. Personal E-mail: k.f.wagner@seznam.cz.

WAGNER, LESLIE, lawyer; b. Houston, July 18, 1953; d. Jacob and Geraldine (Harris) W. BA in Am. Studies, cum laude, U. Tex., Austin, 1975; JD, U. Houston, 1980. Bar: Tex. 1980, US Dist. Ct. (so. dist.) Tex. 1981; cert. employment lawyr., Cornell, 2000. Trial atty. civil rights EEOC, Houston, 1981—84; pvt. practice Houston, 1984—85, 1987—88, 2004—; dir. law placement U. Houston Law Ctr., 1985—87; employee rels. atty, sr. employee rels. analyst The Meth. Hosp. System, Houston, 1988—97; employee rels. cons. Prudential Fin., Houston, 1997—2003; equal employment affirmative action cons., 2004—. Cons. EEOC, Houston, 1984—; v.p., treas. Houston Soc. Healthcare Human Resources Adminstrns., 1995-97; dir., gen. counsel Hematology/Oncology Assistance Resource Coalition, 1995-2002. Editor: U. Houston Law Rev., 1979, assoc. editor, 1980. Mem. health and edn. com. Jewish Cmty. Ctr., Houston, 1983-85; polit. cons. Houston, 1984-85; vol. instr. Seven Acres Jewish Home for the Aged, 2006-. Named Honors Day Honoree U. Tex., 1971; Arts and Scis. scholar U. Tex., 1971-74. Mem. ABA (com. employee and labor rels. 1983-85, employment rights com. gen. practice sect. 1986), ATLA, Houston Bar Assn., Tex. Young Lawyers Assn. (job fair com.), Tex. Hosp. Assn., Soc. of Human Resources Mgmt., Nat. Assn. Law Placement (careers com. 1986-87, minority placement com. 1987), Am. Studies Assn., Soc. Human Resources Mgmt., HR Houston, Houston Festival Dancers (treas. 1976-77), Eta Phi Sigma. Democrat. Jewish. Avocations: creative writing, dance, reading, yoga, pilates. Home: 5407 Wigton Dr Houston TX 77096-4005 Personal E-mail: leslie.wagner@earthlink.net.

WAGNER, MARK A., retail executive; BS, No. Ky. Univ., 1985; MBA, We. New England Coll., 1993. Joined Walgreen Co., Deerfield, Ill., 1977, mgmt. positions from dist. mgr. to operational v.p., 1993—2000, treas., 2000—02, sr. v.p., 2002—06, exec. v.p. ops. & cmty. mgmt., 2006—. Office: Walgreen Co 200 Wilmot Rd Deerfield IL 60015*

WAGNER, MARSDEN GRIGG, medical educator, director; s. Clarence Ruebin and Cavie Adeline Wagner; m. Patricia Ann Stephenson, Dec. 10, 1990; children: Dana Howard, Peter Scott, Karen Joan, Karl Philip. BS, MD, UCLA, MS, 1961. Diplomate Med. Bd. Calif., 1955. Asst. prof. UCLA Sch. Pub. Health & Medicine, 1961—69; co-dir., maternal & child health Calif. State Health Dept., LA, 1969—71; dir. women, children's health WHO, Copenhagen, 1979—91. Capt. USAR, 1957—59, Hampton, Va. Named one of Alumnus of Yr., UCLA Sch. Medicine, 1996. Home: 123 Sherman Ave Takoma Park MD 20912 Personal E-mail: marsden.patricia@stapower.net.

WAGNER, MARTHA JO, lawyer; b. Chgo., Apr. 6, 1951; d. Joseph Richard and Mary Marjorie W. BA summa cum laude, U. Md., 1979; JD cum laude, Georgetown U., 1982. Bar: DC 1982, Pa. 1985, Ga. 1997, U.S. Dist. Ct. D.C. 1983, U.S. Dist. Ct. (we. dist.) Pa. 1985, U.S. Ct. Appeals (3d cir.) 1985. Motions clk. DC Ct. Appeals, Washington, 1982-83; atty. Pension Benefit Guaranty Corp., Washington, 1983-85; assoc. Reed, Smith, Shaw & McClay, Pitts., 1985-88, Kilpatrick & Cody, Washington, 1988—91, ptnr., 1991, Kilpatrick & Stockton, Atlanta and Washington, 1999; ptnr., employee benefits practice Venable LLP, Washington. Adj. prof. Georgetown U., Law Ctr. Editor (lead articles): The Tax Lawyer; contbr. articles to profl. jours. Fellow Am. Coll. Employee Benefits Counsel; mem. ABA (former co-chmn. Employee Benefits Com., Labor & Employment Law sect.), State Bar Ga., DC Bar Assn., Phi Beta Kappa, Phi Kappa Phi, Phi Alpha Theta. Democrat. Office: Venable LLP 575 7th St NW Washington DC 20004 Office Fax: 202-344-8300. Business E-Mail: mjwagner@venable.com.

WAGNER, MARY, medical educator; d. Richard Hipskind; m. Barry Wagner, June 20, 1980. BS, U. Fla., Gainesville, 1976; MD, U. Fla. Coll. Medicine, 1980. Diplomate Am. Bd. Sleep Medicine, 2003, in pulmonary medicine Am. Bd. Pediat. Assoc. prof. dept. pediat. U. Fla., Gainesville, 2005—, pediatric med. dir. shands sleep disorders ctr. Mem.: Am. Acad. Sleep Medicine. Office: Univ Fla Dept Pediat 1600 SW Archer Rd Gainesville FL 32610 Office Fax: 352-392-4450.

WAGNER, MARY MARGARET, library and information scientist, educator; b. Mpls., Feb. 4, 1946; d. Harvey F.J. and Yvonne M. (Brettner) W.; m. William Moore, June 16, 1978; children: Lebohang Y.C., Nora M. BA, Coll. St. Catherine, St. Paul, 1969; MLS, U. Wash., 1973; PhD, U. Minn., 2003. Asst. libr. St. Margarets Acad., Mpls., 1969-70; libr. Derham Hall High Sch., St. Paul, 1970-71; youth worker The Bridge for Runaways, Mpls., 1971-72; libr. Guthrie Theater Reference and Rsch. Libr., Mpls., 1973-75; asst. br. libr. St. Paul Pub. Libr., 1975; prof. dept. info. mgmt. Coll. St. Catherine, St. Paul, 1975—. Del. Minn. Gov.'s Pre-White House Conf. on Librs. and Info. Svcs., 1990; mem. Minn. Pre-White House Program Com., 1989-90, Continuing Libr. Info. and Media Edn. Com. Minn. Dept. Edn., Libr. Devel. and Svcs., 1980-83, 87-2002; mem. cmty. faculty Met. State U., St. Paul, 1980—; mem. core revision com. Coll. St. Catherine, 1992-93, faculty budget adv. com., 1992-95, faculty pers. com., 1989-92, 2001-04, acad. computing com. 1991-96, ednl. policies com., 1998-01; chair curriculum subcom. Minn. Vol. Cert. Com., 1993—. Contbr. articles to profl. jours. Bd. dirs. Christian Sharing Fund, 1976-80, chair, 1977-78. Recipient Bonnie Jean Keley and Jean Kelly award Faculty Excellence, 2006; grantee U.S. Embassy, Maseru, Lesotho, Africa, Brit. Consulate, Maseru, Fed. Inst. Mus. and Libr. Scis., various founds., Upper Midwest Assn. for Intercultural Edn. travel grantee Assoc. Colls. Twin Cities. Fellow: Higher Edn Consortia for Urban Affairs (bd. dirs. 1998—2007); mem.: ALISE (chair internat. rels. com. 2001—03), ALA (libr. book fellows program 1990—91), Minn. Ednl. Media Orgn., Minn. Libr. Assn. (pres. 1981—82, chair continuing edn. com. 1987—90, steering com. Readers Adv. Roundtable 1989—91), Spl. Libr. Assn., Am. Soc. Indexers, Am. Soc. Info. Sci. Office: Coll St Catherine Dept Info Mgmt 2004 Randolph Ave Saint Paul MN 55105-1750 Office Phone: 651-690-6843. Business E-Mail: mmwagner@stkate.edu.

WAGNER, MICHAEL, medical researcher, educator; s. John Joseph and Elsie Wagner; m. Kathryn Miles, May 15, 1992. BS, Georgetown U., Washington, 1976; PhD, U. Pa., Phila., 1984. Rsch. technician Frederick Cancer Rsch. Inst., Md., 1976; rsch. technician Coll. Physicians and Surgeons Columbia U., NYC, 1977—79, postdoc. fellow to assoc. rsch. scientist Howard Hughes Med. Inst., 1988—94; postdoc. fellow Rockefeller U., NYC, 1984—88; rsch. asst. prof. SUNY Downstate Med. Ctr., Bklyn., 1994—. Postdoc. fellowship, Muscular Dystrophy Assn., 1985—87, Howard Hughes Med. Inst., 1988—91.

WAGNER, PAUL ANTHONY, JR., education educator; b. Pitts., Aug. 28, 1947; s. Paul A. and Mary K. Wagner; m. Kerry Wagner; children: Nicole S., Eric P., Jason G., Emily Ryanne. BS, N.E. Mo. State U., 1969; MEd, U. Mo., 1972; MA in Philosophy, 1976, PhD in Philosophy of Edn., 1978. Internal expeditor electromotive div. GM, La Grange, Ill., 1970-71; instr. Moberly Jr. Coll., Mo., 1972-73, U. Mo., Columbia, 1973-78, acting dir. instl. rsch. and planning, 1990-92, dir. univ. self study, 1991-92; instr. Mo. Mil. Acad., 1978-79; prof. edn., philosophy U. Houston-Clear Lake, Atrium Cir. disting. rsch. prof., 1980, dir., Inst. Logical and Cognitive Studies, 1980—, chancellor's disting. svc. prof., 1985, dir., project in profl. ethics, 1989—, chmn., dept. edn. found., 2003—, founding doctoral faculty mem., 2006—; rsch. prof. Pres. U., 2009—. Judge Sears Intercollegiate Ethics Bowl, Dallas, 1998; pres. Wagner & Assoc. Ednl. Consulting, 1988-93; dir. Tex. Ctr. for Study Profl. Ethics in Tchg., 1988-95; rsch. assoc. Ctr. for Moral Devel., Harvard U., 1985-86; vis. scholar Stanford U., Palo Alto, Calif., 1981; cons. total quality mgmt. Golden Gate U., 1992-93, M.D. Anderson Cancer Ctr. and Hosp., 1992-93, U. Houston-Victoria, 1993; cons. strategic planning Houston Chronicle Newspaper, 1997; chair So. Accreditation of Coll. and Sch. steering com. U. Houston, Clear Lake, 1990-93, pres. faculty senate, 1999-2001; chair planning and budgeting com., 1996-98, Univ. Life com., 2003-2007, Houston Tenneco Marathon, 1992-94; dir. U. Gifted Acad.; steering com. Trilateral Conf. and Supershow Greater Human Partnership, 1994-95; cons., ethics trainer Am. Leadership Forum, 1995-98; chair Tchr. Cert. Coun. 2000-; planning com. Tex. Ethics in Govt. Ann. Conf., 1995-98; adj. prof. ethical theory U. Houston, 2000—; faculty exec. com. U. Houston Sys., 1999-2001, chair univ. life com., 2003—, faculty senate exec. comm., 1999— dept. chair Ednl. Found., 2003—, mem. doctoral faculty, 2005—, mem. grad. faculty, 1990—; adj. prof. bus. mgmt. U. Houston, Victoria, chmn. edn. dept., 2003—, chair economics day Fed. Res. Bank, pres. rsch. professor; cons. in field Author: (with F. Kierstead) The Ethical Legal and Multicultural Founds. of Teaching, 1992, Understanding Professional Ethics, 1996, Wagner-Kierstead Moral Self-Assessment Protocol, 2d edit., 2002; co-author: Educational Leadership as Moral Architecture, 2007; contbr. articles to profl. jours. on sci. edn., mgmt. theory and philosophy of edn.; mem. editl. bd. Jour. of Thought, 1981-85, Focus on Learning, 1982-85; editl. cons. Instrnl. Scis., 1981-83; editl. assoc. Brain and Behavioral Scis., 1985. Vice-chmn. Human Rights Com., Columbia, Mo., 1978-79; Sunday sch. tchr. Mary Queen Cath. Ch., Friendswood, Tex., 1979-85; founding bd. dir. Bay Area Symphony Soc., 1983-85; capital campaign com. Soc. Prevention Cruelty to Animals, 1989-91; publicity com. Am. Cancer Soc., Houston chpt., 1989-92; cons. in strategic planning M.D. Anderson Cancer Ctr. vol. divsn., 1992-93; steering com. City of Houston Emerging Bus. Conf., 1994-95, Trilateral Conf., Greater Houston Partnership, 1994-95; active Houston Bus. Promise; chair strategic planning com. Leadership Houston, 1996-98; bd. dirs. Houston Vol. Ctr., Leanna Spraianno Dance Co., 1999-2002, Baker Inst., 1998-2001, chair, 1999-2001; bd. dirs. Hope Village Friendswood, Tex.; ann. leadership briefing com. Rice U., 2001-03; mem. Linda Lorelle Scholarship Com., 1995—, Project Grad Coordinating Coun., 1994-96, pres., 1995-96; emcee, expert commentator for pub. TV, Channel 8, Houston, 1989-2002. Sgt. Mo. N.G., 1970-76; mem. choir Queen of Angels Cath. Ch., Dickinson, Tex., 2003—. Recipient Cert. of Appreciation, City of Columbia, 1978; K.E. Graessle scholar, 1968, Mo. Peace Studies Inst. grantee, 1971, U. Career Reward, 2009. Mem. AAUP, Assn. Applied and Profl. Ethics, Am. Assn. Pub. Adminstrs. (ethics com.), Am. Philos. Assn., Assn. Philosophers in Edn. (exec. bd., v.p.), Philosophy of Edn. Soc. (exec. sec.-treas., hospitality chair 1995-96), Am. Ednl. Studies Assn., Philosophy Sci.

Assn., S.W. Philosophy Edn. Soc., Tex. Network for Tchr. Tng. in Philosophy for Children (bd. dirs. 1983-90), Tex. Ctr. for Ethics in Edn. (bd. dirs. 1990-98), Tex. Ednl. Found. Soc. (pres. 1995-98), Tex. Assn. Coll. Tchrs., So. Assn. Colls. Coord., Houston Bar Assn. (steering com. NAFTA Conf. 1993-94), Informal Logic Assn., Leadership Houston, Friends Hermann Pk., Clearlake Cir. (chair 1979-85), Phi Delta Kappa, Kappa Delta Pi. Roman Catholic. Avocations: running, reading, opera, ballet. Home: RR 4 Box 217 Navasota TX 77868-9413 Office: U Houston 2700 Bay Area Blvd Rm 338 Houston TX 77058-1002 Office Phone: 281-283-3571. Business E-Mail: wagner@cl.uh.edu.

WAGNER, PAULA, film company executive; b. Youngstown, Ohio, 1948; m. Robin Wagner (div.); m. Rick Nicita, 1984. BFA in Drama, Carnegie-Mellon U. Agent Creative Artist Agy.; co-founder (with Tom Cruise) Cruise/Wagner Productions, 1993—2006; co-owner (with Tom Cruise) United Artists Entertainment, LLC, 2006—08, CEO, 2006—08. Pres. Dirs. Jury Venice Film Festival; co-chair Hollywood Film Festival. Actress on & off Broadway, (TV miniseries) Loose Change, 1978; co-author: Out of Our Father's House; prodr.: (films) Mission: Impossible, 1996, Without Limits, 1998, Mission: Impossible II, 2000, Vanilla Sky, 2001, The Last Samurai, 2003, Suspect Zero, 2004, Elizabethtown, 2005, Ask the Dust, 2006, Mission: Impossible III, 2006; exec. prodr.: The Others, 2001, Narc, 2002, Shattered Glass, 2003, War of the Worlds, 2005; prodr.: (TV miniseries) Nightmares and Dreamscapes: From the Stories of Stephen King, 2006. Bd. trustees Carnegie-Mellon U.; bd. dir. Nat. Film Preservation Found., Am. Cinematheque, Interlochen Ctr. for the Arts; mem. exec. com. UCLA Sch. Theater, Film and TV. Recipient Women in Hollywood Icon award, Premiere mag., 2001, Excellence in Producing award, Sarasota Film Festival, 2006; co-recipient Nova award for outstanding achievement by new or emerging prodr. in theatrical motion pictures, Producer's Guild, 1997; named a Billion-Dollar Prodr., Daily Variety, 2004; named one of The 100 Most Powerful Women in Entertainment, Hollywood Reporter, 2006, 2007.

WAGNER, RAYMOND THOMAS, JR., lawyer; b. St. Louis, June 8, 1959; s. Raymond T. and Loretto (Muenster) W.; m. Ann L. Trousdale, Feb. 20, 1987. BA, St. Louis U., 1981, MBA, 1984; JD, U. Mo., Kansas City, 1985; LLM in Taxation, Washington U., St. Louis, 1993. Bar: Mo. 1985, Ill. 1986, U.S. Supreme Ct. 1989, U.S. Tax Ct. 1989. Legal rsch. and writing instr. U. Mo., Kansas City, 1983-84; law clk. to chief justice Mo. Supreme Ct., Jefferson City, 1985-86; assoc. Gilmore & Bell, St. Louis, 1986-87, Suelthaus & Kaplan P.C., St. Louis, 1987-89; gen. counsel Mo. Dept Revenue, 1989-90; counsel to gov. State of Mo., Jefferson City, 1990-91; dir. revenue Mo. Dept. Revenue, 1991-93; counsel Armstrong Teasdale Schlafly & Davis, St. Louis, 1993; dir. revenue Ill. Dept Revenue, Springfield, 1993-95; legal and legis. v.p. Enterprise Rent-A-Car, St. Louis, 1995—; mcpl. judge City of Ballwin, Mo., 1999—2005. Adj. prof. law LLM taxation program sch. law Washington U., St. Louis, 1993—; adj. prof. tax law Fontbonne U., St. Louis, 2002-03; chmn. Gov.'s Ethics Com., 1991-92, Mo. Hwy. Reciprocity Commn., 1991-93; commr. Multistate Tax. Commn., 1991-93, Mo. Mil. Adv. Commn., 1991-93; IRS Oversight Bd., 2003-, chmn., 2004-06. Bd. dirs. Shelter the Children, St. Louis, 1988-95; bd. dirs. Foster Care Coalition St. Louis, 1995-2002, pres. 1998-2000; exec. bd. dirs. St. Louis U. Sch. Bus.; mem. chancellor's coun. U. Mo., St. Louis, 1998—, St. Louis County Bd. Police Commns., 2009. Mem. ABA, Ill. Bar Assn., Mo. Bar Assn., Bar Assn. Met. St. Louis (chmn. law student svcs. com. 1986-87, chmn. social com. 1987-88, mem. exec. com. young lawyers assn. 1988-89, co-chmn. administrv. law com., govt. liaison com. young lawyers sect. 1989-90, chmn. legis. com. 1991-2004, Regional Commerce and Growth Assn. (vice chair pub. policy coun. 1996, chair pub. policy coun. 1998-2000, vice chair govt. affairs exec. com. 2000-02), Associated Industries Mo. (bd. dirs. 1996-2003), Mo. C.of C. (bd. dirs. 1998-2004). Republican. Roman Catholic. Home: 313 Saint Andrews Ct Ballwin MO 63011-2504 Office: Enterprise Rent-A-Car 600 Corporate Park Dr Saint Louis MO 63105-4204 Office Phone: 314-512-5000, 314-512-2897. Business E-Mail: rwagner@erac.com.

WAGNER, RICHARD E., economist, educator; b. Jamestown, ND, Apr. 28, 1941; s. Herbert and Dorothy Mae King; m. Barbara Helen (Westgate) W., June 9, 1962; children: Stephanie Wagner Tice, Valerie Wagner Smith. AA, Fullerton CC, Calif., 1961; BS, U. So. Calif., 1963; PhD, U. Va., 1966. Asst. prof. econs. U. Calif., Irvine, 1966-68, Tulane U., New Orleans, 1968-73; prof. econs. Va. Poly. Inst. and State U., Blacksburg, 1973-79, Auburn (Ala.) U., 1979-81, Fla. State U., Tallahassee, 1981-88; Holbert L. Harris prof. econs. George Mason U., Fairfax, Va., 1988—. Sr. fellow, chmn. acad. adv. bd. Pub. Interest Inst., Mt. Pleasant, Iowa, 1995—. Author: Democracy in Deficit, 1977, To Promote the General Welfare, 1989, The Economics of Smoking, 1991, Trade Protection in the United States, 1995, Fiscal Sociology and the Theory of Public Finance, 2007; editor: Public Choice and Constitutional Economics, 1988, Charging for Government, 1991, Limiting Leviathan, 1999, Federalist Government in Principle and Practice, 2001, Politics, Taxation, and The Rule of Law, 2002, Fiscal Sociology and the Theory of Public Finance, 2007. Mem. Am. Econ. Assn., So. Econ. Assn. (exec. com. 1987-88), Internat. Inst. Pub. Fin., Internat. Soc. New Indtl. Econs., Pub. Choice Soc. Home: 11845 Clara Way Fairfax Station VA 22039 Office: George Mason U Dept Econs Fairfax VA 22030 Office Phone: 703-993-1132. Business E-Mail: rwagner@gmu.edu.

WAGNER, ROBERT EARL, retired agronomist; b. Garden City, Kans., Mar. 6, 1921; s. Fay Arthur and Margaret (Longbottom) W.; m. Bernice Bittner, Aug. 7, 1948; children— Robert Earl, James Warren, Douglas Alan. BS, Kans. State Coll., 1942; MS, U. Wis., 1943, PhD, 1950. Forage crops specialist Ft. Hays Expt. Sta., Hays, Kans., 1943—45; assoc. agronomist Plant Industry Sta., U.S. Dept. Agr., Beltsville, Md., 1945—48, rsch. agronomist, asst. project leader pasture and range project, 1951—54, rsch. agronomist, project leader we. pasture and range project, 1954—56; prof., head dept. agronomy U. Md., 1956—59; regional dir. Am. Potash Inst., 1959—66; v.p. Am. Potash Inst., Found. Internat. Potash Rsch., 1966—67; dir. Coop. Ext. Svc., U. Md., 1967—75; pres., bd. dirs. Potash Inst., 1975—77, Potash and Phosphate Inst., 1977—88, pres. emeritus, 1988—; chmn., bd. dirs. Potash & Phosphate Inst. Can., 1975—88; pres., bd. dirs. Found. for Agronomic Rsch., 1980—87; owner Wagner Performance Cattle, Stone Mountain, Ga., 1985—; mem.bd. trustee Pk. Springs Found., 2006—. Bd. dirs., mem. exec. com. Internat. Fertilizer Devel. Ctr., 1975-98; chmn. Nat. Ext. Com. on Orgn. and Policy; mem. U.S. del. 7th Internat. Grassland Congress, New Zealand. Author tech., popular publs.; Editor: Proc. Sixth Internat. Grassland Congress. Chmn. fin. com. Parks Springs Retirement Cmty., 2005—06; trustee Parks Springs Found. Recipient Medallion award Am. Forage and Grassland Coun., Disting. Grasslander award, 1994; award Md. Farm Bur.; Disting. Svc. award in agr. Kansas State U., 1985, Disting. Alumnus award, 1990; Cert. of Disting. Citizenship, State of Md.; Robert E. Wagner Efficient Agr. award established in his honor; Disting. Grasslander award Am. Forage and Grassland Coun., 1994; named to Am.'s Registry of Outstanding Profls., 2003. Fellow AAAS, Am. Soc. Agronomy (chmn. grassland com., exec. com., bd. dirs., pres. N.E. br.), Crops Sci. Soc. Am., Soil Sci. Soc. Am.; mem. Grassland Coun. (pres.), Am. Soc. Range Mgmt., Cosmos Club (Washington), Atlanta Athletic Club, Sigma Xi, Alpha Zeta, Gamma Sigma Delta, Phi Kappa Phi Presbyterian. Home: 1495 Parkview Blvd Stone Mountain GA 30087-1016 Office: 3500 Pky Ln Ste 550 Norcross GA 30092-2806 Office Phone: 678-684-3725.

WAGNER, ROBERT WALTER, photographer, communications educator, film producer, consultant; b. Newport News, Va., Nov. 16, 1918; s. Walter George and Barbara Anne Wagner; m. Betty Jane Wiles, Nov. 21, 1948; children: Jonathan R., Jeffrey A., Jennifer J. BSc, Ohio State U., 1940, MA, 1941, PhD, 1953. Motion picture writer-dir. Office War Info., NYC and Washington, 1942-43; writer-dir. Office Coord. Interam. Affairs for South and Ctrl. Am., 1943-44; chief info. Divsn. Mental Hygiene, Ohio Dept. Pub. Welfare, 1944-46; dir. divsn. motion pictures Ohio State U., Columbus, 1946-58, prof. comms., photography and cinema, 1960—, chmn. dept. photo-cinema, 1966-74. Pres. Univ. Film Found., 1979-85; writer, dir. James Thurber's Columbus Town, 1990, Images of the Depression, 1990; writer, prodr. TV series The Last of the Silents, 1975; internat. cons. comms.; bd. dirs. Am. Film Inst., 1974-81; mem. faculty U. So. Calif., 1958-59, U. P.R., 1961, 66, 68, San Jose State U., 1967, Ariz. State U., 1971, Concordia U., Montreal, 1980, 81, Danish Nat. Film Sch., 1983, 94, Emerson Coll., Boston, 1987. Author film series: Series of Motion Picture Documents on Communication Theory and New Educational Media, 1966; co-author: The American Tintype, 1999; editor: Education of Film Maker, 1975; co-producer: Cognizant Media, Studio City, Calif., 1997, The View from Malabar, 2000; curator: The Art of Humane Propaganda, Columbus Mus. of Art, 2001, Pioneers of The American Tintype, Columbus Mus. of Art, 2003, Photography in The Midwest, Encl. of The Midwest, 2007; author: Not On Your Tintype, 2005. Recipient Disting. Svc. award Columbus Cmty. Film Coun., 1986, Disting. Svc. award Ohio State U., 1988, Ohiana Pegasus award, 1985; Ency. Brit. fellow, 1953; Sr. Fulbright fellow, Peru, 1976; Lifetime Svc. award, 2008. Fellow Soc. Motion Picture and TV Engrs. (Eastman Gold Medal award 1981); mem. Acad. TV Arts and Scis. (Disting. Svc. award 1966), Univ. Film & Video Assn. (bd. dirs., bd. editors jour. 1975-85, editor jour. 1956-75) Univ. Film & Video Found. (bd. trustees, Lifetime Svc. award 2009), Internat. Congress Schs. Cinema and TV (v.p. 1964-82), Assn Ednl. Comm. and Tech. (bd. editors jour. 1976—), Torch Club (Columbus, pres. 1996). Home: 1353 Zollinger Rd Columbus OH 43221-2939 Personal E-mail: profwags@aol.com.

WAGNER, ROBERT WAYNE, management consultant; b. Kiowa, Okla., Aug. 30, 1926; s. Leroy E. and Elizabeth (Armstrong) W.; m. Barbara Jean Shirley, Jan. 29, 1949; children— Carol Elizabeth, Sharon Ann. BS in Bus. Adminstrn, Okla. U., 1949. With IBM Corp., 1949-65, sales trainee, br. mgr. at Joplin, Mo. office, computer sales mgr., br. mgr. Oklahoma City, Indpls., Kansas City, Mo. offices; asst. to pres., also v.p. systems and corporate Planning Waddell & Redd, Inc., Kansas City, Mo., 1965-67, exec. v.p. sales, 1967-68, pres., 1968-69; founder, pres. Adv. Assos., Inc., mgmt. cons. Kansas City, Mo., 1969-70; pres., chmn. bd. Tech. Resources Corp., Kansas City, Mo., 1969—; pres. Marlennan Mgmt. Systems, Inc., Kansas City, 1970-76; v.p. Marsh & McLennan, 1973-76; owner, pres. Adv. Assos. Systems, Oklahoma City, 1974—, Profl. Resource Ctr., Overland Park, Kans., 1984—. Mem. Kappa Alpha (chpt. pres. 1948) Home: 4417 W 111th Ter Shawnee Mission KS 66211-1703

WAGNER, ROBIN JUDY, interior designer, consultant; b. Morgantown, W.Va., July 6, 1961; d. Harris W. and Dorothea P. Judy; m. David H. Wagner, May 16, 1987; children: Justin David, Jason Harris. AA in Graphics Art, Art Inst. Atlanta, 1981; BA, Marymount U., Arlington, Va., 1991, MA, 1999. Cert. Nat. Coun. Interior Design Qualification, Qashington, DC, 1999. Assoc. prof. Marymount U., 2000—, dir. grad. interior design dept., 2007—; sr. interior design cons. Wagner - Somerset, Fairfax, Va., 2001—07. Chair, multiple choice com. Nat. Coun. Interior Design Qualification, 2004—07. Recipient Louise Tregre award, Nat. Coun. Interior Design Qualification, 2007, Arts & Sci. Svc. award, Marymount U. Arts and Sci., 2008. Mem.: IDEC, ASID. Office: Marymount Univ 2807 N Glebe Rd Arlington VA 22207 Business E-Mail: robin.wagner@marymount.edu.

WAGNER, ROBIN SAMUEL ANTON, stage and set designer; b. San Francisco, Aug. 31, 1933; s. Jens Otto and Phyllis Edna (Smith-Spurgeon) W.; children: Kurt, Leslie, Christie. Student, Calif. Sch. Fine Arts, 1953-54. Pres. Scarab Prodns., Inc., 1975—; prof. theatre arts Columbia U., 1988—; sr. v.p. The Design Edge, 1989—. Adv. com. Broadway Theatre Inst. Set designer (Broadway plays) The Condemned of Altona, 1966, Galileo, 1967, The Trial of Lee Harvey Oswald, 1967, Hair, 1968, Lovers and Other Strangers, 1968, The Cuban Thing, 1968, The Great White Hope, 1968, Promises Promises, 1968, The Watering Place, 1969, My Daughter, Your Son, 1969, Gantry, 1970, The Engagement Baby, 1970, Lenny, 1971 (Drama Desk award, outstanding set design, 1971), Jesus Christ Superstar, 1971, Inner City, 1971, Sugar, 1972, Lysistrata, 1972, Seesaw, 1973, Full Circle, 1973, Mack & Mabel, 1974, The Fifth Dimension with Jo Jo's Dance Factory, 1974, A Chorus Line, 1975, Hair, 1977, On the Twentieth Century, 1978 (Tony award, best scenic design, 1978, Drama Desk award, outstanding scenic design, 1978), Ballroom, 1978, Comin' Uptown, 1979, 42nd Street, 1980, Dreamgirls, 1981 (Drama Desk award, outstanding set design, 1982), Merlin, 1983, Song and Dance, 1985, Teddy & Alice, 1987, Chess, 1988, Jerome Robbins' Broadway, 1989, City of Angels, 1989 (Tony award, best scenic design, 1990, Drama Desk award, outstanding set design, 1990), Crazy for You, 1992, Jelly's Last Jam, 1992, Angels in America: Millennium Approaches, 1993, Angels in America: Perestroika, 1993, Victor/Victoria, 1995, Big, 1996, The Life, 1997, Side Show, 1997, Saturday Night Fever, 1999, Kiss Me, Kate, 1999 (Tony award, best scenic design, 2000, Drama Desk award, outstanding set design of a musical, 2000), The Wild Party, 2000, The Producers, 2001 (Tony award, best scenic design, 2001, Drama Desk award, outstanding set design of a musical, 2001), Flower Drum Song, 2002, The Boy From Oz, 2003, Never Gonna Dance, 2003, A Chorus Line, 2006, (plays) Resurrection Blues, 2006, Young Frankenstein, 2007, (off-Broadway) Putting It Together, Hamlet 90, In White America, View from the Bridge, Mahogany, The Prodigal, Between Two Theives, Cages. Mem. adv. bd. Nat. Corp. Theatre Fund, Theatre Adv. Coun. for City of N.Y.; mem. art adv. com. N.Y. Internat. Festival of the Arts; bd. trustees N.Y. Shakespeare Festival. Recipient Theatre World award, 1975, Outer Circle Critics award, 1978, 90, 92, 00, Maharam award, 1973, 75, 82, Lumen award, 1975, Dramalogue award, 1980, Boston Critics award, 1974, 92, award for excellence in theatre Ensemble Studio Theatre, 1990, Dora award, 1995, New Eng. Theatre Conf. 1996 Lifetime Achievement award, En Garde Arts honoree, N.Y.C., 1996. Mem. United Scenic Artists Elected to The Theatre Hall of Fame, 1999. Office: Robin Wagner Studio 890 Broadway New York NY 10003-1211

WAGNER, ROD, library director; b. Oakland, Nebr., Sept. 14, 1948; s. Francis Lynn and Doris Jean (Egbers) W.; m. M. Diane Kennedy, June 14, 1969; children: Jennifer, Brian, James. BA Social Sci. Edn., Wayne State Coll., Nebr., 1970; MA Polit. Sci., U. Nebr. Lincoln, 1971; MA Libr. Sci., U. Mo., 1981. Rsch. coord. Nebr. Libr. Commn., Lincoln, 1972, planning, evaluation, rsch. coord., 1972-73, adminstrv. asst., 1973-74, dep. dir., 1974-87, dir., 1988—. Bd. dirs. Nebr. Universal Svcs., 1998-2006. Mem. state govt. coun. Nebr. Info. Tech. Commn., 1999—. With U.S. Army N.G., 1970-77. Mem. ALA (contbr. yearbook 1981-84), Assn. Specialized and Cooperative Libr. Agys. (bd. dirs. 1998-2000), Nebr. Libr. Assn. (pres.-elect 1993-94, pres. 1994-95), Chief Officers State Libr. Agys. (dir. 2006-08), Western Coun. State Librs. (pres. 1992-93), Friends Librs. USA (bd. dirs. 2008-09), Assn. Libr. Trustees, Advs., Friends & Found. (bd. dirs. 2009), Nebr. Ctr. Book Bd. Dir. (ex-officio bd. mem. 1990-). Presbyterian. Office: NE Libr Commn 1200 N St Ste 120 Lincoln NE 68508-2023 Office Phone: 402-471-4001. Business E-Mail: rod.wagner@nebraska.gov.

WAGNER, RON, entrepreneur; BS in Math., US Naval Acad., Annapolis, Md., 1974; MS, Naval Postgrad. Sch., Monterey, Calif., 1979. Cert. in program mgmt. Def. Sys. Mgmt. Coll., Va., 1984, in acquisition profl. US Dept. Def., 1994. Innovation & growth initiative leader, mission capability support integration BAE Sys., Merrimack, NH, 2006—08, entrepreneur, innovation & growth initiative, telenostics Nashua, NH, 2008—. Aviation maintenance officer US Navy, various cities, Fla., 1970—96; sr. v.p. RJO Enterprises, Hunt Valley, Md., 1996—99; sr. assoc. Ga. Tech Rsch. Inst., Atlanta, 1999—2002; CEO Cobalt LLC, Savannah, Ga., 2002—06. Contbr. articles to profl. jours. Assisting min. St. Peter's Luth. Ch., Stafford, Va., 1992—97. Dir. ops. Aviation Depots USN, Washington, asst. program mgr. logistics USN, 1991—94, Fla., capt. USN, 1994—96, Washington. Recipient Capt. Virgil Lemmon award, US Navy, 1991, Gold award, 2001—02; named Sailor of Yr., US Navy, 1978. Mem.: Assn. Naval Aviation. Independent. Lutheran. Business E-Mail: ronald.wagner@baesystems.com.

WAGNER, ROY, anthropology educator, researcher; b. Cleve., Oct. 2, 1938; s. Richard Robert and Florence Helen (Mueller) W.; m. Brenda Sue Geilhausen, June 14, 1968 (div. Dec. 1994); children: Erika Susan, Jonathan Richard. AB, Harvard U., 1961; AM, U. Chgo., 1962, PhD, 1966. Asst. prof. anthropology So. Ill. U., Carbondale, 1966-68; assoc. prof. Northwestern U., Evanston, Ill., 1969-74; prof. U. Va., Charlottesville, 1974—, chmn. dept., 1974-79. Mem. cultural anthropology panel NSF, Washington, 1981-82. Author: (novels) Habu, 1972, The Invention fo Culture, 1975, Lethal Speech, 1978, Symbols That Stand for Themselves, 1986, An Anthropology of the Subject, 2001. Social Sci. Research Council faculty research grantee, 1968; NSF postdoctoral research grantee, 1979. Fellow Am. Anthropol. Assn. Avocation: flying hot air balloons. Home: 726 Cargil Ln Charlottesville VA 22902-4302

WAGNER, RUDOLPH STEVEN, ophthalmologist, educator; b. Passaic, NJ, Aug. 5, 1952; s. Rudolph Jospeh and Helen Loretta (Rzucidlo) W.; m. Jean Ann Wagner, June 6, 1981; children: Katherine, Elizabeth, Julie, Christine. BS, U. Notre Dame, 1974; MD, N.J. Med. Sch., Newark, 1978. Diplomate Am. Bd Ophthalmology. Attending physician St. Barnabas Med. Ctr., Livingston, N.J., 1983—, Univ. Hosp., Newark, 1983—; intern Thomas Jefferson U. Hosp. of Medicine, 1978-79; resident in ophthalmology N.J. Med. Sch., Newark, 1979-82; fellow pediatric ophthalmology Wills Eye Hosp., Phila., 1983; dir. pediatric ophthalmology Children's Hosp. N.J., Newark, 1983—. Assoc. prof. clin. ophthalmology and pediatrics N.J. Med. Sch., 1983—. Editor Jour. Pediatric Ophthalmology and Strabismus, 1997. Fellow Am. Acad. Ophthalmology; mem. N.Y. Soc. Pediatric Ophthalmology and Strabismus (pres. 1995—). Office: Children's Eye Care Ctr 1 Clara Maass Dr Belleville NJ 07109-3550 Office Phone: 973-751-1702.

WAGNER, SAMUEL ALBIN MAR, state agency administrator; b. Brighton, Colo., Feb. 23, 1942; s. Jacob Doer and Leota Garnet (Wilson) W.; m. Donna Dee Person, Mar. 20, 1987; children: Kurt, Andrea, Autumn, Jan, Arthur. BA in History, U. Colo., 1964, MA in History, 1965; STB (MTS) in History of World Religions, Harvard U., Cambridge, Mass., 1968; cert. in archival adminstrn., U. Denver, 1978. Cert. CC tchr. Calif., 1980, Colo. State Bd. CC Occupl. Edn. Credential, 1986, cert. archivist Acad. Cert. Archivists, 1994, Inst. Cert. Records Mgrs., 1983. Archival asst. Harvard U. & Harvard Bus. Sch., Cambridge, Mass., 1965—68; asst. curator we. hist. collections, u. archives U. Colo., Boulder, 1968-70; sr. asst. archivist regional history collection, u. archives Cornell U., Ithaca, NY, 1971-73; editor Brighton Blade, Market Pl., Ft. Lupton Press, Brighton Pub. Co., Colo., 1973—77; county historian Adams County, Colo., 1977—78; city archivist City of Providence, 1978-80; state records analyst Wyo. State Archives, Cheyenne, 1979-83; pres. Records Mgmt. Cons. Internat., Ft. Collins, Vancouver, BC, Trenton, 1983—; records mgr. Ft. Collins Police Dept., Colo., 1984-87; pub. records adminstr. State RI, Providence, 1987-90; asst. prof. master archival studies program U. BC, Vancouver, Canada, 1990-93; cataloging editor, electronic records analyst Mo. State Archives, Jefferson City, 1993—96; prodr. community access Sta. JCTV, Jefferson City, Mo., 1994—96; pres. Historic Rsch. Svcs., Jefferson City, Trenton, 1994—; chief NJ Bur. Records Mgmt., Trenton, 1996—; dep. dir. divsn. archives and records mgmt. State NJ, Trenton, 2007—. Instr., prof. Boston Archtl. Inst., 1967-68, LA Met. Coll., 1980-82, Chapman U., 1981-87, Laramie County CC, 1982-83, Colo. State U., 1985-87, Lincoln U., 1995-96, U. BC, 1990-93; speaker in field, nat. and internat. confs. Author: Brighton Reflections, 1976, Adams County: Crossroads of the West, 1977, Directory of Automated Records Management Systems, 1985-91, Crossroads of the West: A History of Brighton and the Platte Valley, 1977, The Fort Lupton Story, 1977, Adams County Colorado: A Centennial History, 2002, Moving Archives, 2002, Brighton Reflections, 2006, Images of America: Brighton, Colorado, 2009; editor: Brighton Blade, Ft. Lupton Press, Colo., 1973-77; editor, Mo. State Archives, Jefferson City, 1994-96; contbr. articles to profl. jours, stories to anthologies. Officer, bd. dirs. Adams County Hist. Soc., 1973-77; county historian Adams County, Colo., 1977-78; mem. Brighton Human Rels. Commn., 1977-78; bd. dirs. Brighton Bicentennial Com., 1975-76, Ft. Lupton Bicentennial Com., 1975-76, RI RSVP, 1978-80, mem. RI Pub. Records Adv. Coun., 1987-90, RI Hist. Records Adv. Bd., 1987-90; chmn. info. profls. legis. task force Freedom of Info. and Privacy Assn., 1991-93; chmn. oral history project Cole County Hist. Soc., 1996; judge Nat. History Day, Mo., 1993-96, NJ, 2005-, nat., 2008-. Recipient Hist. Preservation award, Adams County Hist. Soc., 1978, award, Freedom of Info. and Privacy Assn., 1993, Cert. of Spl. Congl. Recognition, 2006; grantee Ethnic Heritage Project, Colo. Humanities Coun., 1977, Humanities and Social Scis., U. BC, 1993, Nat. Historic Pub. and Records Commn., 1988—92; fellow, Ford Found., 1964—65. Mem. Assn. Records Mgrs. and Adminstrs. (pres. No. Colo. chpt. 1984-85, v.p. Ocean State chpt. 1987-90, bd. dirs., editor Vancouver chpt. 1991, bd. dirs. Ctrl. NJ chpt. 2000-, pres. 2002-04, bd. dirs. Ctrl. South Jersey chpt. 2004—), records mgmt. standards and glossary task forces, Mem. Yr. 1985, microcomputer/PC industry action com., chmn. 1984-86, editor Software Dir. 1985-91, co-chmn. tech. applications com. 1989-90, chmn. Archives ISG 1997-99, ISG mid-year seminar program com. 1998-2002, mgr. edn. sector 1999-2002), Inst. Cert. Records Mgrs. (regional coord., exam proctor, grader 1982-, cert. records mgr. 1983), Soc. Am. Archivists (com. automated records and techniques 1990-94, select com. task force on automated records and techniques 1994-98, chmn. MicroMARC users group 1994-96, rep. joint SAA-ARMA Com. 1995-97), Nat. Assn. Govt. Archivists an Records Adminstrs., Archives Assn. B.C. (freedom of info. and privacy legis. com. 1990-93), Assn. Can. Archivists (electronic records select com. 1991-93, Acad. Cert.

Archivists (outreach com. 1996-98, mem. commn. on future of archival enterprise 1999-2000), Sch. Libr. and Info. Sci.(master archives and records adminstrn., adv. com. San Jose U.), Pub. Sector Mgrs. Assn., ACLU, Am. Assn. for State and Local History, Nature Conservancy, Am. Hist. Soc. Germans from Russia (charter mem.), Mid-Atlantic Regional Archives Conf. (program com. 1999-2000, 2002-, local arrangements com. 2003—); mem. Lawrence Hist. Soc., Lawrence Arts Coun., NJ Studies Academic Alliance Com., Adams County Hist. Soc., South Plate Valley Hist. Soc. Democrat. Unitarian Universalist. Avocations: history, art, photography, filmmaking. Home: 387 N 6th Ave Brighton CO 80601 Office Phone: 609-530-3204. Business E-Mail: albin.wagner@sos.state.nj.us.

WAGNER, SANDRA M., lawyer; b. Utica, NY; BA, St. Lawrence U., Canton, NY, 1974; JD, U. San Diego, 1977. Bar: Calif. 1981, U.S. Dist. Ct. (no. dist.) Calif. 1981, U.S. Tax Ct. 1981. Assoc. Law Offices Timothy A. Tosta, San Francisco, 1981—83, Law Offices Jesse W. Jack, San Jose, Calif., 1983—87; ptnr. Froman and Wagner LLP, San Diego, 1999—2003; pvt. practice Cupertino, Calif., 1987—89, San Diego, 1990—98, 2003—. Author, editor: AILA's 12th Annual California Chapters Conference Handbooks, AILA's 15th, 19th...22nd Annual California Chapters Conference Handbooks. Cub Scout leader Boy Scouts Am., Solana Beach, Calif., 1991—97, Boy Scout leader, 1994—. Recipient Scout Leader Recognition award, Del Mar Solana Beach Optimist Club, 1993, 1994, 1998, Dist. award Merit, Boy Scouts Am., 1996, Silver Beaver award, 2002. Mem.: Am. Immigration Lawyers Assn. (chair San Diego chpt. 2002—03, vice chmn. San Diego chpt. 2006—07, chair San Diego chpt. 2007—08), Order of Arrow (mem. election com. 1999—), Rotary (mem. svc. com. 2000—), Sigma Delta Pi. Avocations: camping, backpacking, rock climbing, music. Office: 12770 High Bluff Dr Ste 370 San Diego CA 92130 Business E-Mail: swagner@wagnerimmigrationlaw.com.

WAGNER, STEPHEN C., biology professor; b. Tiffin, Ohio, Oct. 10, 1959; s. Charles Anthony and Charlotte Hedwig Wagner; m. Lynn Anne Wagner, Dec. 29, 1984; children: Michael Stephen, Melissa Lynn. BS, Heidelberg Coll., Tiffin, 1982; MS, NC. State U., Raleigh, 1984; PhD, Clemson U., SC., 1993. Agrl. rsch. assoc. Clemson U., 1985—94; postdoc. rsch. assoc. USDA-ARS, Stoneville, Miss., 1994—96; asst. prof. Stephen F. Austin State U., Nacogdoches, Tex., 1996—2002, assoc. prof., 2002—, prof., 2009—. Mem.: AAAS (BEN scholar 2006), Am. Soc. Microbiology. Independent. Christian Ch. Avocations: gardening, hiking, woodworking, travel. Office: Stephen F Austin State Univ 1201 Northwood Ctr Nacogdoches TX 75962 Business E-Mail: swagner@sfasu.edu.

WAGNER, SUSAN LAURENE, elementary gifted education educator; b. Evergreen Park, Ill., Oct. 3, 1964; d. Arthur Patrick and Carolyn (Ruzella) Moore; m. Jeffrey David Wagner, Oct. 13, 1984; children: Jeffrey Jr., Brent, Krystin. BA, St. Xavier U., 1992; EdM, U. Ill., 1998. Type 03 cert., Ill. Tchr. St. Hugh Sch., Lyons, Ill., 1993; math. and social studies tchr. grades 6 and 8 St. Cletus Sch., La Grange, Ill., 1993-95; tchr. grade 2 Roy De Shane Sch., Carol Stream, Ill., 1995-97; tchr. grade 5 gifted math. Jay Stream Sch., Carol Stream, 1997-99; tchr. grade 6 Jay Stream Middle Sch., Carol Stream, 1999—; 4-5 grade gifted math Cloverdale Elem., Carol Stream, Ill., 2000—02; 6th grade sci. tchr. Hadley Jr. High, Glen Ellyn, Ill., 2002—04, dist. sci. coord. k-8, 2000—02; exec. scholar Northwestern U. Kellogg Grad. Sch. Mgmt. Exec. Studies; edn. dir. Adler Planetarium Chgo., 2004—05, v.p., 2005—; with AAM Ctr. Future Mus. IPS. Tchr.-leader Near and Far Scis., Ill., 1997—; sci. cons. West 40 Regional Office Edn., Riverside and Wheaton, Ill., 1998—. Recipient Excellence in Sci. Tchg. award NSF, Chgo., 1998, Presdl. award for Excellence in Tchg., 1999, Sch. Bd. Recognition for Tchg. Excellence, NASA, 1999, Larry Stilgbauer award 2004. Mem. ASCD, NEA, Nat. Coun. Tchrs. Math., Nat. Sci. Tchr. Assn., Assn. for Sci. and Tech. Ctrs., Astronomical Soc. of the Pacific Office: Adler Planetarium and Astronomy Museum 1300 South Lake Shore Dr Chicago IL 60605 Office Phone: 312-377-0526. E-mail: swagner@adlerplanetarium.org.

WAGNER, THOMAS EDWARD, academic administrator, educator; b. Lexington, Ky., Dec. 6, 1937; s. Thomas Caney and Gaynell (Waggoner) W.; m. Susan Adell Brant, Sept. 3, 1960; children: Brant, Brian, Jennifer. BS, U. Cin., 1962; MA, Miami U., Oxford, Ohio, 1967; EdD, U. Cin, 1973. Tchr. Finneytown Sch. Dist., Cin., 1962—67; admissions officer U. Cin., 1967—70, summer sch. dean, 1970—73, asst. to pres., 1973—74, asst. v.p., 1974—77, vice provost faculty affairs, 1977—85, sr. vice provost, 1985—91, dean for undergrad. and student affairs, 1987—91, v.p. student affairs and svcs., 1991—94, prof. planning, 1983—2000, prof. emeritus, 2000—. Mem. adv. com. The Collegeboard, N.Y.C., 1989-91. Author 3 books; contbr. articles to profl. jours and chpts. to books. Bd. dirs. Charter Com., Cin., 1985-88, Inroads, Cin., 1990-96, Presbyn. Child Welfare Agy., 1992-98, Buckhorn Children's Ctr., 1992-98; mem. steering com. Cin. Youth Collaborative, 1988-91; active Fernald Citizens Adv. Bd., 1993—. With USAFR, 1955-63. Fulbright fellow, 1992, USIA rsch. fellow, 1997. Fellow Ctr. for Dispute Resolution, Soc. for Values in Higher Edn. Presbyterian. Avocations: reading, sports, photography. Home: 1086 W Galbraith Rd Cincinnati OH 45231-5612 Office: Univ Cin Sch of Planning PO Box 210016 Cincinnati OH 45221-0016

WAGNER, WILLIAM G., academic administrator; BA in Russian Studies, Haverford Coll., 1972; B.Phil in Russian and East European Studies, U. Oxford, 1974; D.Phil in Modern History, 1981. Faculty mem. Williams Coll., Williamstown, Mass., 1980—, chair History Dept., asst. dean, Dir. Williams-Exeter Program at Oxford U., dean faculty, Brown prof. history, interim pres., 2009—. Rsch. lectr. Christ Ch. Coll. Oxford U., sr. assoc. mem. St. Antony's Coll.; vis. scholar Harvard Divinity Sch. Author: Marriage, Property, and Law in Late Imperial Russia (Barbara Heldt Prize for Best Book in Women's Slavic Studies, 1995). Grantee Nat. Endowment for Humanities, Am. Coun. Learned Societies, Internat. Rsch. and Exchanges Bd. Office: Office of Pres Williams Coll PO Box 687 Williamstown MA 01267-0687 Office Phone: 413-597-4233. Office Fax: 413-597-4015. E-mail: William.G.Wagner@williams.edu.*

WAGNER, WILLIAM GERARD, dean, information scientist, consultant, physicist, investment manager; b. St. Cloud, Minn., Aug. 22, 1936; s. Gerard C. and Mary V. (Cloone) W.; m. Janet Agatha Rowe, Jan. 30, 1968 (div. 1978); children: Mary, Robert, David, Anne; m. Christiane LeGuen, Feb. 21, 1985 (div. 1989); m. Yvonne Naomi Moussette, Dec. 4, 1995. BS, Calif. Inst. Tech., 1958, PhD (NSF fellow, Howard Hughes fellow), 1962. Cons. Rand Corp., Santa Monica, Calif., 1960-65; sr. staff physicist Hughes Research Lab., Malibu, Calif., 1960-69; lectr. physics Calif. Inst. Tech., Pasadena, 1963-65; asst. prof. physics U. Calif. at Irvine, 1965-66; assoc. prof. physics and elec. engring. U. So. Calif., LA, 1966-69, prof. depts. physics and elec. engring., 1969—, dean div. natural scis. and math. Coll. Letters, Arts and Scis., 1973-87, dean interdisciplinary studies and developmental activities, 1987-89, spl. asst. automated record services, 1975-81; founder program in neural, informational & behavioral scis., 1982—. Chmn. bd. Malibu Securities Corp., L.A., 1971—; cons. Janus Mgmt. Corp., L.A., 1970-71, Croesus Capital Corp., L.A., 1971-74, Fin. Horizons Inc., Beverly Hills, Calif., 1971—; allied mem. Pacific Stock Exch., 1974-82; fin. and computer cons. Hollywood Reporter, 1979-81; mem. adv. coun. for emerging engring. techs. NSF, 1987-89; cons. Wagner Tech. Solutions, L.A., 2001—. Contbr. articles on physics to sci. publs. Richard Chase Tolman postdoctoral fellow, 1962—65. Mem.: Am. Phys. Soc., Nat. Assn. Security Dealers, Sigma Xi. Home: 183 Beloit Ave Los Angeles CA 90049-3007 Office: Univ So Calif Hedco Neurosci Bldg Los Angeles CA 90089-2520 Office Phone: 213-740-7839. Business E-Mail: wwagner@usc.edu.

WAGONER, ANNA MILLS S., prosecutor; b. 1949; BA, Agnes Scott Coll.; JD, Wake Forest U. Assoc. Woodson, Linn, Sayers, Lawther, Short and Wagoner, 1985—87, ptnr., 1987—90; chief dist. ct. judge Dist. 19-C, NC, 1994—2001; US atty. (mid. dist.) NC US Dept. Justice, 2001—. Office: US Attys Office PO Box 1858 Greensboro NC 27402*

WAGONER, DAVID EVERETT, lawyer, arbitrator; b. Pottstown, Pa., May 16, 1928; s. Claude Brower and Mary Kathryn (Groff) W.; children: Paul R., Colin H., Elon D., Peter B., Dana F.; m. Jean Morton Saunders; children: Constance A., Jennifer L., Melissa J. BA, Yale U., 1950; LLB, U. Pa., 1953. Bar: DC 1953, Pa. 1953, Wash. 1953. Law clk. US Ct. Appeals (3d cir.), Pa., 1955-56; law clk. US Supreme Ct., Washington, 1956-57; ptnr. Perkins & Coie, Seattle, 1957-96. Panel mem. of arbitration forum worldwide including People's Republic of China, B.C. Internat. Comml. Arbitration Ctr., Hong Kong Internat. Arbitration Ctr., London Ct. Internat. Arbitration, AAA's Internat. Ctr. Dispute Resolution. Mem. sch. com. Mcpl. League Seattle and King County, 1958—, chmn., 1962-65; mem. Seattle schs. citizens coms. on equal ednl. opportunity and adult vocat. edn., 1963-64; mem. Nat. Com. Support Pub. Schs.; mem. adv. com. on cmty. colls., to 1965, legislature interim com. on edn., 1964-65; mem. cmty. coll. adv. com. to state supt. pub. instrn., 1965; chmn. edn. com. Forward Thrust, 1968; mem. Univ. Congl. Ch. Coun. Seattle, 1968-70; bd. dirs. Met. YMCA Seattle, 1968; bd. dirs. Seattle Pub. Schs., 1965-73, v.p., 1966-67, 72-73, pres., 1968, 73; trustee Evergreen State Coll. Found., chmn. 1986-87, capitol campaign planning chmn.; trustee Pacific NW Ballet, v.p. 1986. Served to 1st lt. M.C., AUS, 1953-55 Fellow Coll. Comml. Arbitrators, Am. Coll. Trial Lawyers (mem. ethics com., legal ethics com.), Chartered Inst. Arbitrators, Singapore Inst. Arbitrators; mem. ABA (chmn. standing com. fed. jud. improvement, chmn. appellate advocacy com., mem. commn. on separation of powers and jud. independence), Wash. State Bar Assn., Seattle-King County Bar Assn., Acad. Experts, Swiss Arbitration Assn., Nat. Sch. Bds. Assn. (bd. dirs., chmn. coun. Big City bds. edn. 1971-72), English-Speaking Union (v.p. Seattle chpt. 1961-62), Chi Phi. Office: Internat Arbitration Chambers US BankCtr 1420 5th Ave Fl 22 Seattle WA 98101-4087 Home: 1633 Broadmoor Dr E Seattle WA 98112-3747 Office Phone: 206-224-2872. E-mail: email@davidwagoner.com.

WAGONER, GERALDINE VANDER POL, music educator; b. Kankakee, Ill., Sept. 16, 1931; d. Ralph and Josie (Mieras) VanderPol; children: Joel Timothy, Stephanie Anne. BA, Central U. Of Iowa, 1954; MA, Montclair U., 1968; postgrad., Juilliard Sch. Music, 1955-56, 66-67, NYU, Royal Conservatory, Toronto, 1971, Mozarteum, Salzburg, Austria, 1972. Music specialist Bd. Edn., Edison, NJ, 1954—56, Ridgewood, NJ, 1975—95; dir. Musical Spheres Co., 1995—. Mem. Amb. to Amb. program Russian Conservatories, 1998. Trustee, Hudson Symphony Orch., 1965-71; mem. Met. Mus. of Art, Teaching fellow NYU, 1990-91; adj. prof. music William Paterson Coll., Wayne, N.J. Mem. Profl. Music Tchrs. Guild (cert. for highest goals and achievements 1966), Nat. Music Tchrs. Nat. Assn., N.J. Music Tchrs. Assn., Am. Orff Schulwerk Assn., NEA, Music Educators Nat. Conf. (Recognition and Appreciation award 2005), Nat. Guild Piano Tchrs. (judge 2003—), Met. Opera Guild, Netherland-Am. Found., Collegiate Chorale N.Y.C. 1995—, Lyceum Soc. of N.Y. Acad. Scis., Netherland Club. Office Phone: 757-645-4840. E-mail: grazioso@cox.net.

WAGONER, MICHAEL D., ophthalmologist; b. Dallas, Tex., Aug. 7, 1953; s. Charles and Jo Ann Wagoner; life ptnr. Barbara Elias. BS, U. Tex., 1975; MD, Baylor Coll. Medicine, 1978. Cert. med. intern St. Elizabeth's Hosp. of Boston,Tufts Med. Sch., 1979, ophthalmic pathology Mass. Eye and Ear Infirmary, Harvard Med. Sch., 1980, ophthalmology residency Mass. Eye and Ear Infirmary, Harvard Med. Sch., 1983, ophthalmology cornea and external disease Masschusetts Eye and Ear Infirmary, Harvard Med. Sch., 1985, ophthalmology bd. Am. Bd. of Ophthalmology, 1985. Asst. prof. of ophthalmology Harvard Med. Sch., Boston, 1985—99; prof. of clin. ophthalmology U. of Iowa, Iowa City, 1999—2002, adj. prof. of ophthalmology, 2006—. Dir., cornea and external disease svc. Mass. Eye and Ear Infirmary, Harvard Med. Sch., Boston, 1991—94; med. dir. King Khaled Eye Specialist Hosp., Riyadh, Saudi Arabia, 1995—99, 2002—. Author: (textbook) Atlas of Cornea Disease, Excimer Laser Surgery; contbr. articles to sci. jours., chapters to books. Recipient Honor award, Am. Acad. of Ophthalmology, 1992, Secretariat award, 2003, Sr. Achievement award, 2004. Mem.: Am. Acad. Ophthalmology (licentiate). Unitarian. Avocations: running, travel, popular culture. Home: 1451 Grand Ave Iowa City IA 52246 Office: King Khaled Eye Specialist Hospital One Arruba Rd Riyadh 11462 Saudi Arabia Office Fax: 966-1-482-1234 x3645. Personal E-mail: michaelwagoner625@yahoo.com. Business E-Mail: mwagoner@kkesh.med.sa.

WAGONER, RICK (GEORGE RICHARD WAGONER JR.), former automotive executive; b. Wilmington, Del., Feb. 9, 1953; s. George Richard and Martha Wagoner; m. Kathleen Kaylor, 1979; children: W. Matthew, Scott Kaylor, George Richard III. BS in Economics, Duke U., 1975; MBA, Harvard U., 1977. Analyst in treas.'s office, mgr. Latin Am. financing, dir. Can. and overseas borrowing, dir. capital analysis and investment Gen. Motors Co., NYC, 1977-81, treas. Sao Paulo, Brazil, 1981-84, exec. dir. fin., 1984-87, v.p., fin. mgr., 1987-88, group dir. strategic bus. planning, 1988-89, v.p. fin. Zurich, Switzerland, 1989-91, pres. Brazil, 1992-93, head Worldwide Purchasing Group, 1993-94, exec. v.p., pres. N. Am. ops., 1994-98, pres., COO, 1998—2000, pres., CEO, 2000—03, chmn., CEO, 2003—09. Bd. dirs. Gen. Motors Co., 1998—2009. Chmn. bd. visitors Fuqua Sch. Bus. Duke U.; trustee Detroit County Day Sch. Mem. Soc. Automotive Engrs. (mem. VISION 2000 exec. com.).*

WAGONER, ROBERT VERNON, astrophysicist, educator; b. Teaneck, NJ, Aug. 6, 1938; s. Robert Vernon and Marie Theresa (Clifford) W.; m. Lynne Ray Moses, Sept. 2, 1963 (div. Feb. 1986); children: Alexa Frances, Shannon Stephanie; m. Stephanie Brewster, June 27, 1987. BME, Cornell U., 1961; MS, Stanford U., 1962, PhD, 1965. Rsch. fellow in physics Calif. Inst. Tech., 1965-68, Sherman Fairchild Disting. scholar, 1976; asst. prof. astronomy Cornell U., 1968-71, assoc. prof., 1971-73; assoc. prof. physics Stanford U., 1973-77, prof., 1977—2004, emeritus prof., 2005—. George Ellery Hale disting. vis. prof. U. Chgo., 1978; mem. Com. on Space Astronomy and Astrophysics, 1979-82, theory study panel Space Sci. Bd., 1980-82, physics survey com. NRC, 1983-84; grant selection com. NSERC (Can.), 1990-93; mem., Kavli Inst. Particle Astrophysics Cosmology, 2004-; mem. visitors com. divsn. astron. scis. NSF, 2005 Contbr. articles on theoretical astrophysics and gravitation to profl. jours., mags.; co-author Cosmic Horizons, 1982; patentee in field. Sloan Found. rsch. fellow, 1969-71; Guggenheim Meml. fellow, 1979; grantee NSF, 1973-90, 2000-03, NASA, 1982-99. Fellow Am. Phys. Soc.; mem. Am. Astron. Soc., Internat. Astron. Union, Tau Beta Pi, Phi Kappa Phi Office: Stanford U Dept Physics Stanford CA 94305-4060 Home Phone: 650-493-4241; Office Phone: 650-723-4561. Business E-Mail: wagoner@stanford.edu.

WAGONER, WALTER DRAY, JR., lawyer; b. New Haven, Dec. 25, 1942; s. Walter D. and Mariana (Parcells) Wagoner; m. Rosa Nilda Morales, Jan. 22, 1980; children: David, William Carlos, Brenda, Lisa. BA, Yale U., 1965, LLB, 1970. Bar: Conn. 71, U.S. Dist. Ct. Conn. 71. Staff atty. New Haven Legal Assistance Assn., 1970—74, mng. atty., 1974—76, dir. legal edn., 1976—78; sole practice New Haven, 1978—; chair Sta. WPKN-FM, Bridgeport, Conn., 2008—. Chmn. New Haven City Commn. Cultural Affairs, 1977—79; trustee Conn. Pub. TV, 1977—83, U.S. Bankruptcy Ct. for Dist. Conn., 1983—87. Mem.: Conn. Bar Assn., Loizenos Club (hon.). Democrat. Office: 840 Elm St New Haven CT 06511-4010 Office Phone: 203-624-7759. E-mail: wdwagoner@yahoo.com.

WAGSTER, JOHN DOUGLAS, finance educator; b. Union City, Tenn., June 9, 1951; s. John Lewis and Demetra Helen (Parker) W.; m. Phyllis Ann Goff, Mar. 17, 1974. BS, U. Tenn., 1974; MS in Fin., Tex. A&M U., 1986, PhD in Fin., 1992. Distbn. sys. co. exec. Ralston Purina Co., St. Louis, 1974-77, Roadway Sys., Nashville, 1977-81; owner, pres. Wagster, Wagster & Gypsy, Bryan and College Station, Tex., 1981-87; grad. instr. Tex. A&M U., College Station, 1988-92; asst. prof. Wayne State U., Detroit, 1992-97, assoc. prof. fin., 1997—. Contbr. articles to profl. jours. Grantee U.S. Dept. Edn. Ctr. for Internat. Bus. Edn. Rsch., 1991-92. Mem. Am. Fin. Assn., Fin. Mgmt. Assn. (program com. mem. 1996-97, 99-2001), Beta Gamma Sigma. Avocations: hiking, foreign travel, enjoying the arts. Home: 321 Aqua Ct Royal Oak MI 48073-4003 Office Phone: 313-577-4537. E-mail: j.d.wagster@wayne.edu.

WAGUESPACK, SCOTT, Alderman; BA in Polit. Sci., Colo State U., Fort Collins; JD, Chgo.-Kent Coll. Law Ill. Inst. Tech. US Peace Corps UNICEF, Kenya; atty. Kirkland & Ellis; former adv. to interim govt. & pres. Kosovo; campaign mgr. Ind. Voters of Berwyn, Ill., 2005; city adminstr. City of Berwyn; alderman, 32d Ward Chgo. City Coun., 2007—. Co-creator Global Chgo.; mem. Chgo. Coun. Global Affairs. Mem.: Chgo. Area Returned Peace Corps Assn., ABA. Democrat. Office: 2657 N Clybourn Chicago IL 60614 also: City Hall 121 N La Salle Rm 300 Chicago IL 60602 Office Phone: 773-248-1330, 312-744-6567. Office Fax: 312-744-4852. E-mail: ward32@cityofchicago.org.*

WAH, BENJAMIN WAN-SANG, electrical and computer engineering educator; b. Hong Kong, Sept. 7, 1952; s. Hsien-Feng and Chi-Ching (Wong) W.; m. Christine Hai-Ling Lee, Nov. 4, 1981; children: Catherine Lih-Lien, Elaine Yin-Lien. BSEE, Columbia U., 1974, MSEE, 1975; MS in Computer Sci., U. Calif., Berkeley, 1976, PhD, 1978. Asst. prof. elec. engring. Purdue U., West Lafayette, Ind., 1979-84, assoc. prof. elec. engring., 1984-85; assoc. prof. elec. and computer engring. U. Ill., Urbana-Champaign, 1985-89, prof. elec. and computer engring., 1989—, Robert T. Chien disting. prof. engring., 1998—2003, Franklin W. Woeltge endowed prof. elec. and computer engring., 2004—. Program dir. NSF, Washington, 1988-89; Fujitsu vis. chair prof. intelligence engring. U. Tokyo, 1992; McKay vis. prof. U. Calif., Berkeley, 1994; dir. Advanced Digital Scis. Ctr., 2008-. Editor: Computers for Artificial Intelligence Applications, 1986 (Best Seller, Computer Soc. Press 1987, 88); contbr. articles to profl. jours. Recipient Lifetime Achievement award, R.T. Yeh, 2004. Fellow ACM, AAAS, IEEE (co-founder jour. 1988, editor-in-chief IEEE Trans. on Knowledge and Data Engineering, 1993-96), Soc. for Design and Process Sci.; mem. IEEE Computer Soc. (bd. govs. 1989-93, 96-97, treas. 1997, 2d v.p. publs. 1998, 1st. v.p. publs. 1999, pres. 2001, Tech. Achievement award 1998, W. Wallace-McDowell medal 2006), Pan Wen Yuan Found. (Outstanding Rsch. award, 2006, R.E. Merwin award, 2007, Tsutomu Kana award, 2008). Avocations: bicycling, building computers, tennis. Office: Univ Ill Rm 456 CSRL 1308 W Main St Urbana IL 61801-2307 Home Phone: 217-398-1701; Office Phone: 217-333-3516. Office Fax: 217-244-7175. Business E-Mail: wah@uiuc.edu.

WAH, ROBERT M., reproductive endocrinologist, obstetrician, gynecologist; m. Debra Ann Wah; 1 child, Renee Megan. BA, U. Oreg.; MD, Oreg. Health Scis. U. Assoc. chief info. officer Military Health Sys., Office of Sec. of Defense; physician, tchr. Nat. Navel Med. Ctr., Bethesda, Walter Reed Army Med. Ctr., NIH; acting dep. nat. coord. Office of Nat. Coord. for Health Info. Tech., US Dept. Health and Human Svcs., 2005—06; chief med. officer, v.p. North Am. Pub. Sector Computer Scis. Corp. (CSC), Falls Church, Va., 2006—. Faculty mem. Harvard Med. Sch., U. Calif., San Diego, Uniformed Svcs. U. of Health Scis. Capt, USN Med. Corps. Named one of 50 Most Powerful Physician Execs. in US, Modern Physician and Modern Healthcare mag., 2008. Mem.: AMA (bd. trustees 2005—, mem. Ho. of Dels., past chair Coun. on Long Range Planning and Develop.), Assn. Mil. Surgeons of US (exec. adv. coun.), Oreg. Med. Assn., Med. Soc. Va. Office: CSC 3170 Fairview Park Dr Falls Church VA 22042*

WAHBE, ROBERT, computer software company executive; Grad., Univ. Calif., Berkeley. Co-founder Colusa Software Inc.; product develop. positions for enterprise develop. tools Microsoft Corp., Redmond, Wash., 1996—2007, corp. v.p. connected systems divsn., 2007—. Office: Microsoft Corp 1 Microsoft Way Redmond WA 98052-6399

WAHEED, KHURRAM, electrical and electronics engineer, educator; s. Abdul-Waheed Khawaja and Najma Waheed; m. Ayesha Khurram, Sept. 12, 1998; children: Rafay Khurram, Iqra Khurram. BSEE, U. Engring. and Tech., Lahore, Pakistan, 1994; MSEE, Mich. State U., 2000, PhD in Elec. Engring., 2003. Asst. prof. San Diego State U., 2003—04, adj. faculty, 2004—; lead radio frequency sys. engr. Tex. Instruments, Dallas, 2004—. Contbr. articles to profl. jours. Fellow, Semiconductor Rsch. Corp., 2000, U. Mich., 2001—02. Mem.: IEEE (mem. circuits and sys. conf. rev. coms. 2001, mem. vlsi sys. and applications tech. com. 2002, mem. neural networks tech. com. 2002, fellowship 2001, Student Paper award 2001, Vol. award 2000). Achievements include patents for self-programmable chip; patents pending for blind multi-user detection CDMA systems; adaptation on deep-submicron VLSI using the hybrid stochastic gradient. Office: Texas Instruments Inc 12500 TI Blvd MS 8723 Dallas TX 75243 E-mail: khurramwaheed@ieee.org.

WAHID, ABU N. M., economics professor; married; 3 children. BSc in Economics with honors, Jahangirnagar U., Dhaka, Bangladesh, 1976, MSc in Economics, 1978; MA in Economics, U. Manitoba, Winnipeg, Can., 1980, PhD in Economics, 1989. Lectr. dept. economics Jahangirnagar U., 1978—79; tchg. asst. dept. economics U. Manitoba, 1979—80, tchg. asst. lectr. dept. economics, 1983—88; asst. prof. dept.

economics Eastern Ill. U., Charleston, 1988—92; assoc. prof. dept. economics Tenn. State U. Dept. Economics and Fin., Nashville, 1992—99, prof., 1999—. Lectr. U. Coll. Northeastern U., Boston, 1981—83; adj. instr. dept. quantitative analysis Bentley Coll., Waltham, Mass., 1982; lectr. dept. economics U. Mass. Harbor Campus, Boston, 1983; editor Jour. Developing Areas, Tenn. State U., 2001—. Contbr. articles to profl. jours. Recipient Presdl. faculty Excellence award, Eastern Ill. U., 1992, Faculty Rsch. award, Tenn. State U. Coll. Bus., 1995, Disting. Faculty Rsch. award, Tenn. State U., 1998; Rsch. fellowship, Am. Inst. Bangladesh Studies, 1994, 1999, Fulbright Rsch. fellowship, 1997, Rsch. grant, Ctr. South and Southeast Asian Studies, U. Mich. Aim Arbor, 1992. Fellow: Asian Rsch. Svc. (Hong Kong); mem.: Bangladesh Assn. (Urbana-Champaign, Ill.) (treas.), Assn. Econ. and Devel. Studies of Bangladesh, Am. Econ. Assn., Ill. Econ. Assn., Midwest Econ. Assn. Chgo., Soc. Internat. Devel. (Rome). Office: Tenn State Univ Coll Bus 330 10th Ave N Nashville TN 37203-3401 Office Fax: 615-963-7139. Business E-Mail: awahid@tnstate.edu.

WAHL, FLOYD MICHAEL, geologist; b. Hebron, Ind., July 7, 1931; s. Floyd Milford and Ann Pearl (DeCook) W.; m. Dorothy W. Daniel, July 4, 1953; children: Timothy, David, Jeffrey, Kathryn. AB, DePauw U., 1953; MS, U. Ill., 1957, PhD, 1958. Cert. profl. geologist. Prof. geology U. Fla., Gainesville, 1969-82, assoc. dean Grad. Sch., 1974-80, acting dean, 1980-81; exec. dir. Geol Soc Am., Boulder, Colo., 1982-94; ret., 1994. Contbr. articles to profl. jours. Served to cpl. U.S. Army, 1953-55. Recipient Outstanding Tchr. award U. Ill., 1967 Fellow Geol. Soc. Am. (Outstanding Svc. award 1994); mem. Am. Inst. Profl. Geologists (chpt. pres.), Sigma Xi

WAHL, RICHARD LEO, radiologist, educator, nuclear medicine physician, researcher; b. Iowa, July 13, 1952; s. Max Henry and Josephine Elizabeth (Hogan) Wahl; m. Sandra K. Moeller, June 28, 1975; children: Daniel, Matthew, Peter, Katherine. BA in Chemistry, Wartburg Coll., 1974; MD, Washington U., St. Louis, 1978. Diplomate Am. Bd. Nuc. Medicine (pres. 1998-), Am. Bd. Radiology. Intern U. Calif., San Diego, 1978—79; resident in radiology Mallinckrodt Inst. Washington U., 1979—82, fellow in nuc. medicine and immunology, 1982—83; asst. prof. U. Mich. Med. Ctr., Ann Arbor, 1983—87, assoc. prof., 1987—90, prof., 1990—2000; dir. gen. nuc. imaging, dir. radiopharm. program U. Mich. Cancer Ctr., 1999—2003; prof., dir. nuc. medicine, vice chair tech. and new bus. devel. Johns Hopkins U., Balt., 2002—. Mem. exptl. immunology study sect. NIH, Bethesda, Md., 1990—94; sec. Am. Bd. Nuc. Medicine, 1997, chmn., 98. Editor: 2 textbooks; contbr. more than 240 articles to profl. jours., chapters to books. Recipient Disting. Scientist award, Acad. Molecular Imaging, 2001, Jerome W. Conn rsch. award, U. Mich., 1989; named Eugene Prendegreer New Horizon lectr., RSNA, 1999; grantee ACS, Dept. of Army; rsch. grantee, NIH. Fellow: Am. Coll. Radiology, Am. Coll. Nuc. Physicians; mem.: AMA, Inst. for Clin. Positron Emission Tomography (bd. dirs., pres. 1996), Am. Assn. for Cancer Rsch., Am. Soc. for Clin. Investigation, Radiol. Soc. N.Am., Soc. Nuc. Medicine (Marc Tetalman award 1986, Berson and Yalow rsch. award 1992, Hounsfield rsch. award 1992). Achievements include development of the drug Bexxar, approved by US Food and Drug Adminstrn. in 2003 to treat follicular non-Hodgkin's lymphoma; 10 patents in field. Avocations: reading, sports. Office: Johns Hopkins Outpatient Ctr Divsn Nuclear Medicine 601 N Caroline St Rm 3223 Baltimore MD 21287

WAHL, ROSEMARIE, biologist, educator; d. Arnold Spencer and Rosemary Doyle Wahl; m. Michael Leroy Tumlinson, May 31, 1992; m. Miroslav Synek (div.); children: Mary Rose Synek, Thomas Robert Synek. BS, MIT, 1956; MS, U. Chgo., 1961, PhD, 1967. Instr. U. Ill., Chgo., 1965—66; asst. prof. Tex. Christian U., Ft. Worth, 1967—72; assoc. prof. St. Mary's U., San Antonio, 1976—83, prof., 1983—, chair dept. biol. scis., 1979—2004. Vis. asst. prof. U. Tex., Austin, 1972—75; chief advisor health professions St. Mary's U., 1979—2004, chair premed./predental adv. com., 1979—2004. Mentor, advisor on biotechnology, mayor, city ofcl. City of San Antonio, 1984—95. Recipient Disting. Faculty award, St. Mary's U. Sch. Sci., Engring and Tech., 1986. Mem.: MIT Class 1956 (v.p. 2001—), Tex. Genetics Soc., Tex. Assn. Advisors for Health Professions (exec. com.), Am. Soc. Microbiology, Sigma Xi. Avocations: travel, culture, welfare of children, veterans and american indians. Office: St Marys U Dept Biol Scis 1 Camino Santa Maria San Antonio TX 78228 Office Phone: 210-431-8064. Business E-Mail: rwahl@stmarytx.edu.

WAHL, SHARON MARIE, immunologist; b. Mt. Vernon, Wash., Mar. 16, 1945; d. Leonard A. and Clara Marie (Soine) Knudson; m. Larry Marion Wahl, Dec. 26, 1971; children: Allison Marie, Christopher Loren. BS, Pacific Luth. U., 1967; PhD, U. Wash., 1971. Postdoctoral fellow dept. pathology U. Wash., Seattle, 1971-72; postdoctoral fellow lab. micro and immunology NIDR NIH, Bethesda, 1972-74, staff fellow, 1974-76, sr. staff fellow, 1974-76, rsch. microbiologist, humoral immunology divsn., 1976-83, chief cellular immunology divsn., 1983—. Chief, Oral Infection and Immunity Branch NICDR, NIH, 1997—, project officer George Washington U. NIH, Bethesda, 1991-2003, U. Minn. NIH, Bethesda, 1994-2002, ViroMed Labs., NIH, Bethesda, 1998-2000; adj. prof. dept. molecular microbiology & immunology, Johns Hopkins U., Balt., 2000-, adj. prof. dept periodontics U. Md., Balt., 2000-; mem. sci. & med. adv. com. Canadian Arthritis Network, 2000-07; chair NIH History Office Adv. Com., 2006-07, NIH Investigation Com., 2006-07, mentor. Mem. editl. bd. Jour. Immunology, 1983-87, Cellular Immunology, 1992-96, Wound Repair and Regeneration, 1992-96, Am. Jour. Pathology, 1992—2004, Cytokine and Growth Factor Reviews, 1999—; sect. editor Jour. Immunology, 1993-98, Jour. Leukocyte Biology, 1993-98, Jour. Exptl. Medicine, 1994-2007, Biology Direct, 2006-; contbr. chpts. to books, articles to profl. jours. Mem. NIH Adv. Coun. for Women, 1991-95, Pfizer Cytokine Rsch. Coun., 1994-97, Fogarty Scholars Adv. Panel, 1994-96; bd. dirs. Found. Advanced Edn. in the Scis., 1995-2003; Sec., Exec. Com., Found. for Advanced Edn. in the Scis. (FAES) 1995-2001, councilor Soc. of Leukocyte Biology, 1996-99, pres. Soc. Leukocyte Biol., 2000—, SLB Nominating Com., 2007-09, NIH Office of AIDS Rsch. Etiology and Pathogenesis Coordinating Com. 1995—, chair, NIH Cytokine Interest Group, 1999—; steering com. mem. NIH Cytokine Interest Group, 1999-; mem. Howard Hughes Program Com., 2000—; mem. Stetten Mus. Adv. Com., 2001—; v.p. FAES, 2003. Recipient Holley Rsch. prize in Rheumatology, 1990, Dirs. award NIH, 1985, Merit award NIH, 1994, USPHS Superior Svc. award, 1992; NIDR Director's Exemplary Svc. Awd., 1997, elected mem., Sr. Biomed. Rsch. Svc., 1997, grantee NIH, 1989-90, Seragen, Hopkinton, Mass., 1989-90, Upjohn, Kalamazoo, 1991, Pfizer, N.Y., 1995—, Amgen, Boulder, 1995. Fellow AAAS (NIDCR Emerging Sci. Opportunities awards, 1998-2002, Coop. Rsch. Devel. award, 1998-2000), Am. Acad. Microbiology (ISI highly cited immunology rschr., 2005-, NIH Dir.'s award, 2005), Am. Assn. Immunolgists, Wound Healing Soc., Soc. Leukocyte Biology (Marie T. Bonazinga award, 2007), Inflammation Rsch. Assn., Internat. Interferon Soc. Lutheran. Avocations: travel, skiing, boating. Office: 30 Convent Dr MSC 4352 Bldg 30 Rm 320 Bethesda MD 20892-4352 Business E-Mail: smwahl@mail.nih.gov.

WAHL, WILLIAM BRYAN, marketing professional, real estate company officer; b. Aurora, Colo., Dec. 17, 1963; s. Harold Edward Wahl and Dianne (Fowler) Armstrong. m. Tiffany Yao Wahl. BBA in Mgmt., St. Edward's U., 1987; MBA in Gen. Bus., Kent Coll., 1991; MBA in Management, La Salle U., 1993; PhD in Bus., U. San Moritz, 1999. Asst. store mgr. Handy Dan, Austin, Tex., 1981-88; real estate broker Powell/Armstrong Realty, Austin, 1985—88, S&W Realty, Austin, 1988—; nat. mktg. dir. Am. Home Products, Austin, 1988—; pres. Wahl Success Systems, Austin, 1989—, project mgr. applied materials, 1995—98; procurement mgr. Dell Computer Corp., 2000—08; pres. O.H.S. Prodns., 2000—, Brigadier Group LLC, 2003—, Am. Healthcare Options LLC, 2003—. Bd. dirs. Pahl Enterprises, Austin, 1988—. Named Outstanding Citizen, Berkeley Davis, Inc., Berkeley, Calif., 1988. Mem. Austin Assn. Life Underwriters, Austin Bd. Realtors, Tex. Assn. Realtors, Nat. Assn. Realtors, Nat. Assn. Life Underwiters, Mktg. and Distributive Edn. Roman Catholic. Avocations: black belt in taekwondoe, golf, weightlifting. Home: 10305 Button Quail Cove Austin TX 78758

WAHLBERG, MARK, actor; b. Dorchester, Mass., June 5, 1971; s. Donald and Alma Wahlberg; m. Rhea Durham, Aug. 1, 2009; children: Ella Rae, Michael, Brendan Joseph. Singer: (albums with Marky Mark and the Funky Bunch) Music for the People, 1991, You Gotta Believe, 1992; Actor: (films) Renaissance Man, 1994, The Basketball Diaries, 1995, Fear, 1995, Boogie Nights, 1997, Traveller, 1997, The Big Hit, 1998, Three Kings, 1999, The Corruptor, 1999, The Yards, 1999, The Perfect Storm, 2000, The Planet of the Apes, 2001, Rock Star, 2001, The Truth About Charlie, 2002, The Italian Job, 2003, I Heart Huckabees, 2004, Four Brothers, 2005, Invincible, 2006, The Departed, 2006 (Best Supporting Actor, Nat. Soc. Film Critics, 2007), Shooter, 2007, The Happening, 2008, Max Payne, 2008; (TV films) The Substitute, 1993; actor, prodr.: (films) We Own the Night, 2007; exec. prodr.: Juvvies, 2004; (TV series) Entourage, 2004-, In Treatment, 2008-. Office: c/o Cortina Bus Mgmt PO Box 610287 Newton MA 02461*

WAHLGREN, FRANCIS J., art appraiser; MA in Art History, Queens Coll., NY, 1985; attended, Parsons Sch. Design, NY, Am. Coll., Paris. With Christie's, NYC, 1987—, specialist in books and manuscripts, internat. dept. head. Catalogued and auctioned the Fox-Bute Set of Audubon's Birds of America (2000) for $8 million, a world auction record for any printed book. Office: Christie's/NY 20 Rockefeller Plz New York NY 10020 Office Phone: 212-636-2665. Office Fax: 212-636-4928. Business E-Mail: fwahlgren@christies.com.

WAHLQUIST, ANDREA K., lawyer; b. 1970; BA, U. Va., 1992; JD, Washington and Lee U., 1995. Bar: Va. 1995, NY 2000. Law clk. to Hon. Stephen J. Swift US Tax Ct., Washington, 1995—97; assoc. exec. compensation and employee benefits Simpson Thacher & Bartlett LLP, NYC, 1997, sr. counsel, ptnr., 2008—. Named a Dealmaker of Yr., The Am. Lawyer mag., 2008. Mem.: ABA. Office: Simpson Thacher & Bartlett LLP 425 Lexington Ave New York NY 10017-3954 Office Phone: 212-455-2622. Office Fax: 212-455-2502. E-mail: awahlquist@stblaw.com.

WAHLQUIST, ANDREW FOLKMAN, government affairs executive; b. Ogden, Utah, Jan. 29, 1940; s. Keith Campbell and Ruth (Folkman) W.; m. Myrna Helen Kasparek, July 13, 1962; children: Kristin Diane, Andrea Katherine. BS in Comm., U. Utah, 1963. Asst. news dir. KCPX-TV & Radio, Salt Lake City, 1959-67; pub. relations asst. U.S. Steel, Pitts., 1967-72; nat. coord., Let's Clean Up Am. Office Sec. Interior, Washington; spl. asst. The White House, Washington, 1973-74; deputy asst. adminstr. Am. Revolution Bicentennial Adminstrn., Washington, 1974—76; pres. Commemorative Mktg., Washington, 1976; chief of staff to Senator John Warner US Congress, Washington, 1979-86; v.p. govt. relations, v.p. corp. relations Greenwich Air Services, Miami; v.p. bus. devel. Kellstrom Industries; ptnr. Alcalde & Fay, Arlington, Va., 2002—. Dir. Wolf Trap Assocs., Vienna, Va., 1995; mem., Salt Lake City C. of C.; commr. Va. Port Authority, Norfolk, 1994-97; guest lectr. U. Va., George Mason U., Am. U. Producer, writer (documentary) Utah Hoover Commission, 1970 (Utah Broadcasters award 1970), Scrapbook of a Grand Old Lady, 1968 (1st pl. award Utah Broadcasting 1968). Dir. Claude Moore Colonial Farm, McLean, Va., 1980—; dir. emeritus Fairfax (Va.) Symphony, 1980—; adminstr. Am. Revolution Bicentennial. Recipient George Washington medal Freedoms Found., Valley Forge, Pa., 1972, Man of Yr. award Utah Jaycees, Salt Lake City, 1966. Mem. Pub. Rels. Soc. Am., Soc. Profl. Journalists, Army and Navy Club Washington, Am. League Lobbyists. Republican. Mem. Lds Ch. Office: Alcalde & Fay 2111 Wilson Blvd Ste 850 Arlington VA 22201-3058 Office Phone: 703-841-0626. Office Fax: 703-243-2874. Business E-Mail: wahlquist@alcalde-fay.com.

WAHLQUIST, BRENT T., federal agency administrator; b. Utah, Mar. 28, 1942; BS in Botany, MA in Botany, Brigham Young U.; PhD in Biology, N.Mex. State U. Prin. investigator, project mgr. on environ. studies for electric generating stations, transmission lines and coal mines Westinghouse Electric, 1971; prin. investigator, project mgr. Rocky Mountain Energy Corp., Carbon Fuel Corp., W.Va., 1978—82; dep. dir. W. Va. State Water Resources Divsn. and Reclamation Divsn., 1982—83; asst. dir. Office Surface Mining, US Dept. Interior, 1983—95, regional dir., Mid-Continent Region, 1995—99, regional dir. Denver, 1999—2002, regional dir., Appalachian Region, 2002—07, acting dir., 2005—07, dir., 2007—. Recipient Pres. Rank award for Meritorious Exec. Svc., 2005. Office: US Dept Interior Office Service Mining Reclamation 1849 C St NW Washington DC 20240 Office Phone: 202-208-3100.*

WAHLSTEN, DOUGLAS, psychology professor; b. Allegan, Mich., Oct. 13, 1943; s. Carl Evic and Ruth Elijabeth Wahlsten. BSc in Physics with magna cum laude, Alma Coll., Mich., 1965; grad. in Pshycholgy, Yale U., 1966; PhD in Psychology, U. Calif., Irvine, 1969. Postdoc. fellow Inst. Behavioral Genetics, U. Colo., Colo., 1968—69; asst. prof. psychology U. Waterloo, Waterloo, 1969—74, assoc. prof., 1974—80, prof. psychology, 1982—89, U. Alberta, Canada, 1989—99, prof. emeritus, 1999—; pres. Internat. Behavioral & Neural Genetics Soc., 2001; prof. biol. scis. U. Windsor, Canada, 2004—07, adj. prof. biol. sci., 2007; prof. psychology U. NC, Greensboro, 2008—. Vis. asst. prof. psychology U. Calif., 1971; dir. Mus Ware Tech. Inc., Edmonton, Canada, 2002—. Contbr. chapters to books. Grant, NIH, 1998—2009. Mem.: Soc. Neurosci., Am. Assoc. Advancement Sci., Internat. Behavioural & Neural. Soc. (pres. 2001, Distinguished Sci. 2006). Avocations: photography, fishing, running. Office: Univ NC 1000 Spring Garden St Greensboro NC 27403 Office Fax: 336-334-5066. Business E-Mail: dlwahist@uncg.edu.

WAHOME, JOSEPH MURIUKI, zoologist, educator; s. Wahome Muriuki and Elizabeth Wahome; m. Agnes Nganga, Mar. 15, 1988; children: Elizabeth Muriuki, Muriuki Wairimu, Wahome Muriuki. Phd, U. Calif., Berkeley, 1995. Instr. U. Calif., 1990—95; assoc. prof. & chair Miss. Valley State U., Itta Bena, 1995—. Home Phone: 662-254-3377. Home Fax: 662-254-3668. Personal E-mail: wahome@mvsu.edu.

WAHOSKE, MICHAEL JAMES, lawyer; b. Ripon, Wis., June 4, 1953; children: Jennifer, John. BA with highest honors, U. Notre Dame, 1975, JD summa cum laude, 1978. Bar: Minn. 1978, U.S. Dist. Ct. Minn. 1979, U.S. Ct. Appeals (7th cir.) 1979, U.S. Ct. Appeals (8th and 9th cirs.) 1980, U.S. Ct. Appeals (10th cir.) 1982, U.S. Supreme Ct. 1982, U.S. Ct. Appeals (6th cir.) 1988, U.S. Ct. Appeals (fed. cir.) 1989, U.S. Ct. Appeals (D.C. cir.) 1992, U.S. Ct. Appeals (4th cir.) 1994, U.S. Ct. Appeals (11th cir.) 1996, Supreme Ct. of Winnebago Tribe of Nebr., 1996. Law clk. to judge Luther M. Swygert U.S. Ct. Appeals (7th cir.), Chgo., 1978-79; law clk. to chief justice Warren E. Burger U.S. Supreme Ct., Washington, 1979-80; assoc. Dorsey & Whitney, Mpls., 1980-85, ptnr., chmn., appellate practice, 1986—2008, of counsel, 2009—. Adj. prof. law U. Minn., Mpls., 1981-83. Exec. editor U. Notre Dame Law Rev., 1977-78; co-editor: Freedom & Education: Pierce v. Society of Sisters Reconsidered, 1978. Recipient Vol. Recognition award Nat. Assn. Attys. Gen., 1993, Spl. Recognition award, 2003; Supreme Ct. Reception honors State and Local Legal Ctr., 1991, 92, 93, 95. Fellow: Am. Acad. Appellate Lawyers; mem.: FBA, ABA (standing com. on Amicus Briefs 1997—2002), Hennepin County Bar Assn., Minn. Bar Assn., U.S. Ct. Appeals (8th cir.) Bar Assn., Phi Beta Kappa. Office: Dorsey & Whitney LLP Ste 1500 50 S Sixth St Minneapolis MN 55402-1498 Office Phone: 612-340-8755. Office Fax: 952-516-5549. Business E-Mail: wahoske.michael@dorsey.com.

WAHWEAH, LINDA MCNEIL, insurance agent, writer; b. Albuquerque, Apr. 2, 1955; d. Ernest Neil and Elizabeth Ann (Murane) Lemke; m. Eugene Gerald Wahweah, Feb. 14, 1979 (div. June 2001). Bus., Cannon's Internat. Bus. Coll., 1976. Legal sec. Manpower Gen. Dynamic, San Bernardino, Calif., 1980—82; ins. c.s.r. p.l. and comml. Ctrl. City Ins. Agy., San Bernardino, 1982—84; ins. office mgr. Bankers Life Ins., Riverside, Calif., 1984—85; ind. ins. agt. Am. Family Life Ins., Redlands, Calif., 1985—88; civil rights adv. Walker River Palute Tribe, Schurz, Nev., 1989—95; freelance writer Native Am. Civil Rights, San Clemente, Calif., 1996—2003; chronical specialist Native Am. Civil Union, San Bernardino, West Cajon, Calif., 2000—03. Promotor specialist Karaoke of Inland Empire, San Bernardino, 2000—03; council mem. Native Am. Civil Rights Union, 1992—95, fellow founder, 1993; freelance writer, 1989—. Author: Poetry's "Guardian" Best Poems and Poets of 2003. Organizer cmty. workshop Strike This Cmty., 2007; lobbyist Walker River Piaute Tribe, Schurz, Nev., 1993—95, civil rights adv. San Clemente, 1995—. Recipient Editor's Choice award, Internat. Libr. Poetry, 2003, Outstanding Achievement in Poetry award, Internat. Soc. Poets, 2004, Poet of Merit award, Internat. Soc. Poetry, 2005, 2006, 2007; named World Champion Amateur Poet, Internat. Soc. Poets, 2002, No. Am. Poet of Merit, Internat. Libr. Poetry, 2002, New Country Female Vocalist, CCMA of Inland Empire, 1999. Mem.: ACLU, San Bernardino County Bar Assn., European Soc. Lit., Humane Soc., Am. Poetry Assn., Am. Lit. Guild, N.Am. Fishing Club. Democrat. Ch. Of Christ. Avocations: writing, karaoke, cooking, sewing. Office Phone: 909-379-5227. Personal E-mail: wllply9@aol.com. E-mail: lml9m@aol.com.

WAID, THOMAS HENRY, physician, researcher, educator; b. Ashtabula, Ohio, May 21, 1949; s. Carl Thomas and Ruth Agusta Waid; m. Nancee Ann Bartlett; children: Ashley Nicole, Andrew McClellan. BS in Pharm., U. Cin.; MS; MD, U. Ky., Lexington. Cert. internal medicine, nephrology Am. Bd. Internal Medicine, 1985. Med. dir. kidney transplantation U. Ky. Med. Ctr., 1985—; prof. medicine U. Ky., 2000—. Med. dir. heart transplantation U. Ky. Med. Ctr., 1992—, med. dir. lung transplantation, 1992—, med. dir. pancreas transplantation, 1994—, med. dir. dialysis, 1996—2007. Recipient Lifetime Achievement award, Harbor HS, Chief Residents Faculty award, 1991, 1994—95. Mem.: Rho Chi Soc., Lexington Med. Soc. (svc. coun. chair. elect 2005—). Republican. Methodist. Achievements include research in immunosuppression. Avocations: golf, fishing, travel, ballroom dancing, waterskiing, antiques. Office: Univ Ky Med Ctr 800 Rose St C-347 Lexington KY 40536

WAIDMANN, BRIAN K., former federal agency administrator; b. 1953; Grad., U. Colo., 1975. Legis. asst. to Rep. Bill Armstrong US Congress, Washington; legis. asst. to Senator Bill Armstrong US Senate Banking, Housing & Budget Com., legis. dir.; spl. asst. legis. affairs to Pres. The White House; adminstrv. asst. to Senator Dirk Kempthorne US Senate, 1993—2000, adminstrv. asst. to Senator John Ashcroft, 2000—01; chief of staff US Dept. Interior, 2001—09.*

WAILAND, GEORGE, lawyer; b. Munich, Mar. 14, 1947; came to US, 1951; s. Max and Bella (Grylak) W.; m. Adele M. Rosen, Aug. 20, 1972; children: J. Zachary, William J. BS, NYU, 1969, JD, 1972. Bar: NY 1973, US Supreme Ct. 1976, US Dist. Ct. (so., ea. dists.) NY 1973, US Dist. Ct. (no. dist.) NY 1981, US Claims Ct. 1979, US Tax Ct., 1979, US Ct. Appeals (2d cir.) 1973, US Ct. Appeals (fed. cir.) 1982, US Ct. Appeals (4th cir. and 9th cir.) 1986, (10th cir.) 2007, US Ct. Appeals (7th cir.) 1987. Assoc. Cahill Gordon & Reindel LLP, NYC, 1972-80, ptnr., 1980—. John Norton Pomeroy scholar NYU, 1970. Home: 1050 Park Ave New York NY 10028-1031 Office: Cahill Gordon & Reindel LLP 80 Pine St Fl 17 New York NY 10005-1790 Office Phone: 212-701-3212. Business E-Mail: gwailand@cahill.com.

WAILOO, KEITH ANDREW, historian, educator; BA in chem. engring., Yale U., 1984; MA, U. Pa., 1989, PhD in history and sociology of sci., 1992. From asst. prof. to prof. U. NC, Chapel Hill, 1992—2001; prof. history Rutgers U., New Brunswick, 2001—, prof. Inst. for Health, Health Care Policy, and Aging Rsch., 2001—, founding dir. Ctr. Race and Ethnicity, 2006—, Martin Luther King, Jr. prof. history, 2006—. Vis. prof. Harvard U., 1998—99. Author: Drawing Blood, 1997 (Arthur Viseltear award, Am. Pub. Health Assn., 1997), Dying in the City of the Blues, 2001 (Lillian Smith book award, Southern Regional Coun., 2002, NJ Coun. Humanities Honor book, 2002, Am. Polit Sci. Assn. award, 2002, Susanne Glasscock Humanities book award, 2003, William H. Welch medal, Am. Assn. History of Medicine, 2005); co-author (with Stephen Pemberton): The Troubled Dream of Genetic Medicine, 2006; co-editor: A Death Retold, 2006. Fellow Ctr. Advanced Study Behavioral Sciences, Stanford U., 2006—07; Investigator award, Robert Wood Johnson Found., 2002—05, Centennial fellow in the history of sci., James S. McDonnell Found., 1999—2008. Mem.: Inst. Medicine, Assn. for the History of Medicine, Am. Hist. Assn., Orgn. Am. Historians. Office: Inst Health Health Care Policy and Aging Rsch Rutgers U 30 Coll Ave New Brunswick NJ 08901 also: Dept History Rutgers U 16 Seminary Pl New Brunswick NJ 08901 Office Phone: 732-932-8419. Office Fax: 732-932-1358. E-mail: kwailoo@rci.rutgers.edu, kwailoo@ifh.rutgers.edu, kwailoo@history.rutgers.edu.*

WAINBERG, MARK ARNOLD, medical educator, director; b. Montreal, Quebec, Canada, Apr. 21, 1945; s. Abe Wainberg and Fay Haffner; children: Zev, Jonathan. PhD, Columbia U., NY, 1972. Cert. med. rschr. McGill U., 1972. Assoc. prof. McGill U. AIDS Ctr., Montreal, 1974—89, prof. & dir., 1989—. Pres. Internat. AIDS Soc., Geneva, 1998—2000. Contbr. scientific papers. Recipient honor, Officer Order of Canada, Govt. of Can., 2001, Officer Order of Que., Govt. of Que., 2005, Legion of honor, Govt. of France, 2008, Lifetime Achievement award,

AIDS Soc. India, 2009. Fellow: Royal Soc. Can., Coll. Physicians & Surgeons Can. (hon.). Home: 6506 Fern Rd Montreal PQ Canada H4V 1E4 Office: McGill Univ AIDS Ctr 3755 Cote Ste Catherine Montreal PQ Canada H3T 1E2 Office Phone: 514-340-8307. Business E-Mail: mark.wainberg@mcgill.ca.

WAINSCOTT, JAMES LAWRENCE, steel industry executive; b. LaPorte, Md., Mar. 31, 1957; s. James J. and Frances J. (Cunningham) Wainscott. BS magna cum laude, Ball State U., 1979; MBA, U. Notre Dame, 1987. CPA Ind., cert. mgmt. acct., internal auditor, info. sys. auditor, chartered fin. analyst. Sr. auditor Geo. S. Olive & Co., CPAs, Indpls., 1979—82; fin. mgr. Midwest Divsn. Nat. Steel Corp., Portage, Ind., 1982—88, mgr. pension investments Pitts., 1988—90, asst. treas., asst. sec., 1991—92, treas., asst. sec. Mishawaka, Ind., 1993—95; v.p. & treas. AK Steel Holding Corp., Middletown, Ohio, 1995—98, CFO, 1998—99, sr. v.p., CFO, 1999—2003, pres., CEO, 2003—06, chmn., pres., CEO, 2006—. Instr. acctg. Purdue U., Westville, 1980—82, Valparaiso U., 1980—84; cons. Edward J. Wainscott, CPA, LaPorte, Ind., 1982. Advisor Jr. Achievement, 1984; vol. Am. Cancer Soc., Calparaiso Income Tax Assistance Program, Calparaiso Cmty./U. Campaign; pres., treas. Midwest Steel Employees Fed. Credit Union; pres. Midwest Steel Employees Assn.; mem. Ball State U. Cardinal Connection, Northwest Ind. Open Housing Coun.; chmn. dean's adv. coun. Valparaiso U.; chmn. fin. com. Good Shepherd Parish, Cin., 1999—2001; bd. dirs. Youth Svc. Bur. St. Joseph County. Mem.: U. Notre Dame Exec. MBA Alumni Assn., Chgo. Soc. Fin. Analysts, Assn. for Investment Mgmt. and Rsch., Inst. Chartered Fin. Analysts, Inst. Internal Auditors, Inst. Mgmt. Acctg., Am. Inst. CPA's, Nat. Assn. Accts. (chpt. bd. dirs. 1982—86, chpt. pres. 1983—84, Past Pres. award 1984), Ind. CPA Soc. (chpt. bd. dirs. 1983—86, chpt. pres. 1984—85, chmn. chpt. activities com. 1985—86, state bd. dirs. 1987—90, chmn. chpt. task force, Pres. award 1994), Mensa, Delta Sigma Pi, Intertel, Golden Key, Blue Key. Roman Catholic. Avocations: music, chess, coin collecting/numismatics, sports, travel. Office: AK Steel Holding Corp 703 Curtis St Middletown OH 45043 Home: 7925 Graves Rd Cincinnati OH 45243-3626

WAINSTEIN, KENNETH L., lawyer, former prosecutor; b. Alexandria, Va., 1962; BA in Govt. & Internat. Rels., U. Va., 1984; JD, U. Calif., Berkeley, 1988. Corr., caseworker to Representative Carl D. Perkins US Congress, Washington, 1984; paralegal securities sect. Cleary, Gottlieb, Steen & Hamilton, Washington, 1984—85; summer assoc. for litigation, environ., tax and labor teams Hunton & Williams, Washington, 1986; summer assoc. for litigation, corp. and labor depts. Gibson, Dunn & Crutcher, Washington, 1987; law clk. to Hon. Thomas Penfield Jackson US Dist. Ct. DC, Washington, 1988—89; asst. US atty. (So. dist.) NY US Dept. Justice, 1989—92, line prosecutor, dep. chief homicide sect. Washington, 1994—99, prin. asst. US atty. DC, 1999—2000, interim US atty. DC, 2001, dir. Exec. Office US Attorneys, 2001—02; gen. counsel FBI, Washington, 2002—03, chief of staff, 2003—04; interim US atty. DC US Dept. Justice, 2004—05, US atty. Washington, 2005—06, asst. atty. gen. for nat. security, 2006—08; asst. to Pres for homeland security & counterterrorism The White House, Washington, 2008—09; ptnr. O'Melveny & Myers LLP, Washington, 2009—. Recipient Director's award for Superior Performance, US Dept. Justice, 1997, 2000, Edmund J. Randolph award for Outstanding Service, 2008. Mem.: Phi Beta Kappa. Office: O'Melveny & Myers LLP 1625 Eye St Washington DC 20006 Office Phone: 202-383-5300. Office Fax: 202-383-5414. E-mail: kwainstein@omm.com.*

WAINWRIGHT, CARROLL LIVINGSTON, JR., retired lawyer; b. NYC, Dec. 28, 1925; s. Carroll Livingston and Edith Katherine (Gould) W.; m. Nina Walker, July 2, 1948; children: Delos Walker, Mark Livingston. AB, Yale U., 1949; LL.B., Harvard U., 1952. Bar: N.Y. 1953. Atty. Milbank, Tweed, Hadley & McCloy (and predecessor), NYC, 1952-58, 60-62, ptnr., 1963—2005; ret., 2005. Asst. counsel Gov. N.Y., 1959-60; mem. State Commn. Jud. Conduct, 1974-83; hon. dir. U.S. Trust Corp.; hon. trustee U.S. Trust Co. N.Y.; adj. prof. law Washington and Lee U. Sch. Law, 1991-97; mem. governing bd. N.Y. Cmty. Trust, 1991—2004. Hon. trustee Am. Mus. Natural History, Boys' Club N.Y.,; trustee Edward John Noble Found.; trustee 1966—, pres., 1986-94, hon. trustee, 1999; vice-chmn. Cooper Union Advancement Sci. and Art, 1988-95, hon. trustee; trustee Ch. Pension Fund and Affiliates, 1974-91, treas. 1974-78; mem. univ. coun. Yale U., 1978-81; mem. vestry Trinity Ch., N.Y.C., 1983-90; dir. Greater Yellowstone, 1999-05. Served with USMCR, 1943-46. Mem. ABA, N.Y. State Bar Assn., Assn. Bar City N.Y. (treas. 1970-73, v.p. 1975-76), Union Club, Down Town Assn. (pres. 1985-92), Maidstone Club (pres. 1970-73). Home: 57 Dunemere Ln East Hampton NY 11937-2705

WAINWRIGHT, DALE V., state supreme court justice; b. Tenn. m. Debbie Wainwright; 3 children. Studied, London Sch. of Economics, 1981; BA, Howard U., 1983; JD, U. Chgo. Law Sch., 1988. With Andrews & Kurth, Houston, Haynes & Boone, Houston; dist. judge. Harris County, 1999—2002; justice Tex. Supreme Ct., Austin, 2002—. Mem. Am. Law Inst., Tex. Commn. on Jud. Efficiency. Co-founder Aspiring Youth Program; bd. mem. Houston Volunteer Lawyers Program, Texas Young Lawyers Assn.; former pres. Houston Young Lawyers Assn. Recipient Legal Excellence award, NAACP, 2000. Fellow: Houston Bar Found., Tex. Bar Found.; mem.: ABA, Houston Bar Assn., State Bar Tex. Office: Tex State Supreme Ct PO Box 12248 Austin TX 78711 Office Phone: 512-463-1332.*

WAINWRIGHT, DAVID STANLEY, patent agent; b. New Haven, May 23, 1955; s. Stanley Dunstan and Lillian (Karelitz) W.;m. Catherine Demetra Kefalas, Aug. 11, 1984; children: Maxwell Stanley Hector, Eric George Alexander. BSc in Physics with 1st class honors, Dalhousie U., Halifax, NS, 1976; MSc in Physics, U. BC, Vancouver, 1979. Registered patent agt., U.S., Can. Model plant supr., scientist, technician Moli Energy Ltd., Maple Ridge, BC, Canada, 1978-84, project leader cell devel., 1984-88, cell devel. mgr., 1988-90, 1990-92, mgr. intellectual property, 1992-98; patent agt. Ballard Power Sys., Burnaby, BC, 1998—2005; sr. patent agent Cardiome Pharma Corp., Vancouver, Canada, 2005—06; IP specialist Questair Techs. Inc., Burnaby, Canada, 2006—08; sr. IP analyst Anqstrom Power, North Vancouver; mgr. IP Liqnol Energy Corp., Bunasy, Canada, 2009—. Contbr. articles to profl. jours. Mem. Patent and Trademark Inst. Can. Home: 2585 W 1st Ave Vancouver BC Canada V6K 1G8 Office: Questair Technologies Inc 6961 Russell Ave Burnaby BC Canada V5J 4R8 also: Liqnol Energy Corp 4705 Wayburne Dr Burnaby BC Canada V5934 Office Phone: 604-453-6896. Business E-Mail: dwainwright@liqnol.ca.

WAINWRIGHT, GEOFFREY JOHN, archaeologist; b. Pembrokeshire, Wales, 1937; BA, U. Wales; PhD, U. London. Prof. archaeology U. Baroda, India, 1961—63; prin. inspector English Heritage, London, chief archaeologist, 1989—99; fellow U. Cardiff, Wales, 1985, U. Wales, Lampeter, 1996; chmn. Wessex Archaeology, 2004—. Mem. Royal Commn. Ancient and Hist. Monuments in Wales, 1987—2005, Stonehenge Steering Group; vis. prof. U. Southampton, U. Coll. London. Appears in (documentaries) Stonehenge Deciphered, 2008. Recipient Grahame Clark medal, Brit. Acad., 2006. Fellow: Soc. Antiquaries London (dir. 1982—90, v.p. 1997—2001, treas. 2001—07, pres. 2007—, sec. Stonehenge com.); mem.: Prehistoric Soc. (former pres.), Inst. Field Archaeology (hon.), Cambrian Archaeological Soc. (pres. 2006), Order Brit. Empire (mem. 1992). Office: Soc Antiquaries London Burlington House London W1J OBE England Office Phone: 01348 881423. E-mail: geoff@bluestone.eu.com.

WAINWRIGHT, PAUL EDWARD BLECH, construction company executive; b. Annapolis, Md., Jan. 28, 1917; s. Richard and Alice Sorrel (Blech) W.; m. Helen Mae Rogers, July 10, 1941; children: Richard, Paul Edward Blech, John. BS in Civil Enging, Va. Mil. Inst., 1938. Cost engr. Turner Constrn. Co., NYC, 1938-40, cost engr., asst. supt., 1945-46; cost. engr. for contractors Pacific Naval Air Bases, Honolulu, 1940-42; with Dillingham Corp., Honolulu, 1946-82, asst. v.p., then v.p., 1961-69, group v.p. constrn., 1969-82; cons. constrn. Honolulu, 1982—. Bd. dirs. Hawaii Visitors Bur., 1967, Goodwill Industries Hawaii, 1965-70; pres. Citizens Adminstrn. of Justice Found., 1968, Hawaii Epilepsy Soc., 1975. Served with AUS, 1942-45. Decorated Legion of Merit, Bronze Star, Air medal. Mem. Am. Soc. Mil. Engrs., Beavers, Gen. Contractors Assn. Hawaii (pres. 1966), Hawaii C. of C. (dir. 1964-65), Waikiki Yacht Club, Outrigger Canoe Club. Republican. Episcopalian. Home: Cheney Care Ctr 2229 N 5th St Apt 111 Cheney WA 99004

WAINWRIGHT, RUFUS, musician, singer; b. Rhinebeck, NY, July 22, 1973; s. Loudon Wainwright III and Kate McGarrigle. Singer: (albums) Rufus Wainwright, 1998 (Juno award for Best Alternative Album, 1999), Poses, 2001 (Juno award for Best Alternative Album, 2002), Want One, 2003, Want Two, 2004, Release the Stars, 2007, Rufus Does Judy at Carnegie Hall, 2007, (with Kate & Anna McGarrigle) Love Over & Over, 1983, Heartbeats Accelerating, 1990, McGarrigle Hour, 1998, McGarrigle Christmas Hour, 2005, (soundtracks) Myth of Fingerprints, 1997, Big Daddy, 1999, I Am Sam, 2001, Moulin Rouge, 2001, Shrek, 2001, Brokeback Mountain, 2005; composer: (films) Meet the Robinsons, 2007; actor: (films) Tommy Tricker & the Stamp Traveller, 1988, Heights, 2004, The Aviator, 2004, The Age of Ignorance, 2007. Recipient Stephen F. Kolzak award, Gay and Lesbian Alliance Against Defamation, 2008; named Best New Artist, Rolling Stone, 1998. Office: c/o Sam Kirby William Morris Agy 1325 Ave of the Americas New York NY 10019 also: c/o Carla Sacks/Krista Williams Sacks & Co 427 W 14th St New York NY 10014

WAISANEN, CHRISTINE M., lawyer, writer; b. Hancock, Mich., May 27, 1949; d. Frederick B. and Helen M. (Hill) W.; m. Apr. 21, 1979; children: Jeffrey Hunt, Erick Hill. BA with honors, U. Mich., 1971; JD, U. Denver, 1975. Bar: Colo. 1975, D.C. 1978. Labor rels. atty. U.S. C. of C., Washington, 1976-79; govt. rels. specialist ICI Americas, Inc., Wilmington, Del., 1979-87; dir. cultural affairs City of Wilmington, 1987; founder, chief writer Hill, Katzenstein & Waisanen, 1988—. Chmn. Delaware State Coastal Zone Indsl. Control Bd., 1993—. Mem. Fed. Bar Assn., Jr. League of Wilmington (v.p. 1985-86), Women's Rep. Club of Wilmington (bd. dirs. 1988-93), U. Mich. Club of Del. (pres. 1999—). Republican. Presbyterian. Home: 1609 Mt Salem Ln Wilmington DE 19806-1134 Personal E-mail: cwais23@aol.com.

WAISSMAN, NAOMI ASSADIAN, biology professor; b. Austin, Tex., Oct. 7, 1954; d. Joe Dukler Waissman and Estela Licon Vasquez; m. Hamid Assadian, May 1, 1986; children: Mariam Shahla Assadian, Darius Nathan Assadian, Zubin Aaron Assadian. PhD, N.Mex State U., Las Cruces, 2004. Assoc. rsch. scientist Tex. Agr. Expt. Sta., El Paso, 1984—2006; asst. prof. biology El Paso CC, Tex., 2006—. Prin. investigator US Bur. Reclamation, El Paso, El Paso Water Utilities, Tex., 2000—05, Tex. Dept. Agr. - Tex.-Israeli Exch., El Paso, 2002—05, Ctr. Border Health Rsch., El Paso, 2003—04; investigator USDA Rio Grande Basin Initiative, El Paso, 2004—05, Cotton Inc., El Paso, 2005, Minority Sci. & Engring. Improvement Program, US Dept. Edn., El Paso, 2008—. Vol. Civic Ctr. Engagement, Adult Day Care, El Paso, 2009. Achievements include research in beneficial use of lime stabilized biolsolids on alkaline soils. Office: El Paso CC El Paso TX 79998-0500 Office Fax: 915-831-5122. Business E-Mail: nwaissma@epcc.edu.

WAIT, CHARLES VALENTINE, banker; b. Albany, NY, May 28, 1951; s. Newman Edward Jr. and Jane Caroline (Adams) W.; m. Candace Ellin Hollar, May 27, 1978; children: Charles Valentine Jr., Christopher David, Alexandra Dallas Wait. BA, Cornell U., 1973; cert. in banking, Rutgers U., 1981; LHD (hon.), SUNY Empire State Coll., 2001. Asst. v.p. The Adirondack Trust Co., Saratoga Springs, NY, 1974, treas., 1978-81, sec., treas., 1981-84, pres., 1984—. Trustee NY Bus. Devel., 1997-2003; mem. Saratoga County Indsl. Devel. Agency, 1998-2006; mem. Yaddo Corp., Saratoga Springs, 1996-2004, sec., treas., 1997-2004; class A dir. Fed. Res. Bank NY, 2003-; chmn. Fed. Res. Bank NY Audit Com., 2006-, Cornell U. Coun., 2006-. Chmn. Saratoga Springs City Ctr. Authority, 1983—89; trustee Skidmore Coll., Saratoga Springs, NY, 1984—2002, Nat. Mus. Dance, Saratoga Springs, NY, 1987—2002, Charles R. Wood Found., 1991—98, NY Racing Assn., 1985—2008, Saratoga Hosp., 2003—04, Nat. Mus. Racing, 1988—91, v.p., 1989—91; with Saratoga Care, Inc., 2002—04; mem. Saratoga County Water Authority, 2007—; chmn. Face of the Future Capital Campaign. Recipient Pvt. Sector Initiative award, Pres. Ronald Reagan, Commitment to Cmty. award, NY State Bus. Coun., 1983, Liberty Bell award, Saratoga County Bar Assn. for cmty. svc., Good Scout award, Twin Rivers Coun., 1997, Sam Walton Bus. Leader award, 1997, Exec. of Yr. award, Capital Dist. Bus. Rev., 1999, Denis Kemball-Cook award, 2003, Lucy Skidmore Scribner award, Skidmore Coll., Saratoga Springs, 2003, J. Michael O'Connell Cmty. Svc. award, Saratoga Jaycees, 2004, Disting. Econ. Devel. Leadership award, SEDC, Saratoga Springs, 2007, Cmty. Recognition award, Saratoga County, EOC, 2008; named Outstanding New Yorker, NY State Jaycees, 1984, Disting. Citizen, Saratoga Springs Sr. Citizens, 2002; Paul Harris fellow Rotary Dist. 7190, 1997. Mem. Ind. Bankers Assn. of N.Y. State (bd. dirs., sec. 1986-87), N.Y. Bankers Assn. (bd. dirs. 1995—, chmn. 1997-99), N.Y. State Bankers Retirement System (trustee 1987-95, vice chmn., chmn. 1992-94), Am. Inst. Banking (Counsel of Yr. 1976), Greater Saratoga C. of C., Pillar Soc. Republican. Home: 658 N Broadway Saratoga Springs NY 12866-1624 Office: The Adirondack Trust Co 473 Broadway Saratoga Springs NY 12866-2262 Office Phone: 518-584-5844.

WAIT, SCOTT D., neurosurgeon; MD, East Carolina U. Resident in neurosurgery St. Joseph's Hosp. & Med. Ctr. Office: 350 West Thomas Rd Phoenix AZ 85013 Office Phone: 602-406-3000.*

WAITE, CHARLES MORRISON, food products executive; b. Chgo., Oct. 1, 1932; s. Norman and Lavinia M. (Fyke) W.; m. Barbara Chowning Wham, Aug. 21, 1954; children: Susan R., Charles M., John B., David T. BA, Yale, 1954; MBA, Harvard, 1958. Mgr. planning and analysis Standard Fruit & Steamship Co., New Orleans, 1958-62, v.p., exec. v.p., 1969-72, dir., 1972-76; div. mgr. Standard Fruit Co., La Ceiba, Honduras, 1962-69; dir. Standard Fruit Tropical Charities, Inc., 1970-76; sr. v.p. Castle & Cooke, Inc., Honolulu, 1972-76; exec. v.p. Castle & Cooke Foods, San Francisco, 1974-76; pres. United Fruit Co., Boston, 1976-77; sr. v.p. United Brands Co., Boston, 1976-77; pres. Genoa Packing Co., Boston, 1977-78, Catelli Foods, Inc., 1979-90, Howard Foods Inc., Danvers, Mass., 1990—, also bd. dirs. Bd. dirs. Rock of Ages Corp., Barre, Vt., Swenson Granite Co., Concord, N.H. Served to 1st lt. USAF, 1955-57. Mem. Zeta Psi. Clubs: Harvard (Boston). Republican. Episcopalian. Home: 520 Cherry Valley Rd Gilford NH 03249-7841 Office: Howard Foods Inc 5 Ray St Danvers MA 01923-3531

WAITE, LAWRENCE WESLEY, osteopathic physician, educator; b. Chgo., June 27, 1951; s. Paul J. and Margaret E. (Cresson) W.; m. Courtnay M. Snyder, Nov. 1, 1974; children: Colleen Alexis, Rebecca Maureen, Alexander Quin. BA, Drake U., 1972; DO, Coll. Osteo Medicine and Surgery, 1975; MPH, U. Mich., 1981. Diplomate Nat. Bd. Osteo. Med. Examiners; bd. cert. family practice, holistic medicine, neuromusculoskeletal medicine, Osteopathic Manipulative Medicine. Intern Garden City Osteo. Hosp., Mich., 1975—76; practice gen. osteo. medicine Garden City, 1979—82, Battle Creek, 1982—96, La Crosse, Wis., 1996—2004; emergency rm. physician, 2004—; sect. head Onalaska Family Practice, 1999—2002, coord. rsch., chmn. dept., 1996—99, chmn. integrative medicine edn./rsch. com., 2002—04, vice chair, dept. integrative medicine, 2004. Cons. Nat. Bd. Examiners Osteo. Physicians and Surgeons, 1981—88, 1998—; chief med. examiner Calhoun County, 1991—93; preceptor U. Wis. Med. Sch., 1997—2000, assoc. clin. prof., 2000—, Mich. State U. Coll. Osteo. Medicine, East Lansing, 1979—97, Lakeview Gen. Osteo. Hosp., Battle Creek, Mich., 1983—87; mem. profl. adv. coun. Good Samaritan Hosp., Battle Creek, 1982—83; exec. bd. Primary Care Network, 1994—96; assoc. clin. prof. Des Moines U. Coll. Osteo. Medicine, 2002—05; mem. evaluations registry Commn. on Osteo. Coll. Accreditation, 2006—; vol. radio announcer Wis. Pub. Radio, 2006—. Writer TV program Cross Currents Ecology, 1971; editor radio series Friendship Hour, 1971-72 Bd. dirs. La Crosse YMCA, 2000-03, Internat. Log Rolling Assn., 2000-04; cert. judge U.S. Log Rolling Assn., 2006—; bd. dirs., instr. Hospice Support Services, Inc., Westland, Mich., 1981-86; exec. bd. officer Battle Creek Area Urban League, 1987-91; bd. dirs., mem. exec. com. Clearwater Farm Found., Inc., 1999-04; vestryman St. Thomas Episcopal Ch., 1990-93; bd. mem. Eagle Bluff Environ. Learning Ctr., Lanesboro, 2003-; leader Boy Scouts Am.; bd. sec. Internal Soc. Complementary Medicine Rsch., 2004-05. Served to lt. comdr. USN, 1976-79. U. Wis. fellow, Madison, 2003-04; State of Iowa scholar, 1969. Mem.: US Log Rolling Charitable Found. (officer 2009—), Am. Coll. Osteo. Emergency Physicians (govtl. affairs com. 2007—), Am. Acad. Osteopathy, South Ctrl. Osteo. Assn. (officer, state del. 1983—96), Am. Osteo. Assn., Internat. Soc. Complementary Medicine Rsch. (sec. 2004—05), Population Inst. (population action coun. 1984—99), Upper Miss. River Osteopathic Study Group (sec. 2008—), Brotherhood St. Andrews (life), Bermuda Hist. Soc. (life), Nat. Eagle Scouts Assn. (life). Avocations: geography, medieval history, genealogy. Home and Office: 2110 Evenson Dr Onalaska WI 54650-8772 Office Phone: 608-397-6678. Business E-Mail: lwwaite@wisc.edu.

WAITE, STEPHEN HOLDEN, lawyer; b. Rochester, NY, Dec. 5, 1936; s. Richard Holden and Judith H. (Lapp) Waite; m. Sarah T. Caswell, Aug. 20, 1960 (dec. Mar. 1996); children: Sarah T., Richard H. BA, Amherst Coll., 1958; JD, Yale U., 1961. Bar: N.Y. 1961. Mem. firm Nixon, Hargrave, Devans & Doyle, Rochester, NY, 1961-69; v.p., counsel Lincoln First Banks Inc., Rochester, 1969-73, sr. v.p., 1973-77, exec. v.p., 1978-81, CFO, 1973-81; sr. v.p. Schlegel Corp., 1981-82; mem. firm Harris, Beach, Wilcox, Rubin & Levey, Rochester, 1982-88, Underberg & Kessler, Rochester, 1988—; mem. exec. commn. Friends U. Rochester Librs., 2008—. Past chmn. Rochester Area Hosp. Assn.; strategic planning commn. Monroe Cmty. Hosp.; past bd. dirs., treas. Hosp. Trustees N.Y. State; past bd. dirs., past chmn. Ctr. Govtl. Rsch.; past treas., bd. dirs. Planned Parenthood Rochester/Syracuse Region; past bd. dirs. Mercy Flight Ctrl., Inc., Highland Hosp., Monroe County Long Term Care, Inc., Rochester Regional Rsch. Libr. Coun., Hosp. Assn. N.Y. State, Health Futures for Rochester, Harley Sch., Hearing and Speech Ctr. Rochester. With US Army, 1962. Mem.: Monroe County Bar Assn., Country Club Rochester. Home: 68 N Main St Pittsford NY 14534 Office: 300 Bausch and Lomb Pl Rochester NY 14604 Office Phone: 585-258-2826.

WAITES, HOUSTON CHASE, theater educator; b. Ft. Worth, Tex., Feb. 9, 1969; s. William Gordon Waites and Virginia Lauricella Sams; m. Amanda Elizabeth Norman, July 26, 2003; children: Sawyer Joseph, Peyton Chase. BA in Theatre, Centenary Coll., Shreveport, La., 1991; MFA in Directing, U. New Orleans, La., 2003. Fine arts dept. chair and instr. theatre and speech JHS, New Orleans, 1998—2006; prof. theatre Lone Star Coll. Montgomery, Conroe, Tex., 2006—. Pres. and artistic dir. Chase Prodns. Ltd., New Orleans, 1998—2006. Mem.: Unites State Inst. Theatre Tech., Tex. Ednl. Theatre Assn., Soc. Am. Fight Directors, Assn. Theatre Higher Edn. (coll. program focus group rep. 2008). Methodist. Office: Lone Star Coll Montgomery 3200 Coll Pk Dr Conroe TX 77384 Office Fax: 936-271-6143. Business E-Mail: chase@lonestar.edu.

WAITKUS, JAY, writer; b. Grosse Pointe Farms, Mich., Oct. 7, 1968; s. Gerald C. Waitkus and Sara W. Kent. BS, Charter Oak State Coll., New Britain, Conn., 2003; MA, Fla. Atlantic U., 2005. Freelance journalist Sun-Sentinel, Palm Beach Post, South Fla. Bus. Jour., others, Fla., 1998—2001. Founder pub. Nat. Times Online News Publs., 2009. Author: (novels) In the Depths of Shadows, 2003, Dividing Line, 2006, short stories, (plays) The Fallen Angel's Redeemer, 2002. Founding sponsor Disabled Vets. LIFE Meml. Found., Washington; donor USO, VFW, Carter Ctr., UNICEF, hon. amb. US fund, 2009; mem. Habitat Partners Coun. Habitat for Humanity, 2006—, donor; Christian missionary, ch. planter Bapt. Ch. Palm Beach, Fla., 1997—98. Named Writer of Month, Gulf Coast Writers Assn., 2002. Mem.: Nat. Writers Assn., Nat. Geog. Soc., Golden Key Internat. Honor Soc. Conservative.

WAITZKIN, HOWARD BRUCE, internist, sociologist, educator; b. Akron, Ohio, Sept. 6, 1945; s. Edward and Dorothy (Lederman) W.; m. Jean Ellis-Sankari, Nov. 12, 2005; 1 stepchild, Daren; 1 child, Sofia. BA summa cum laude, Harvard U., 1966, MA, 1969, MD, PhD, 1972. Diplomate Am. Bd. Internal Medicine, Am. Bd. Geriatric Medicine. Resident in medicine Stanford U. Med. Ctr., Calif., 1972-75, Robert Wood Johnson clin. scholar depts. sociology-medicine Calif., 1973-75; sr. resident in medicine Mass. Gen. Hosp., Boston, 1977-78; assoc. prof. sociology, clin. asst. prof. medicine U. Vt., Burlington, Vt., 1975-77; vis. assoc. prof. health and med. scis. U. Calif., Berkeley, 1978-82, clin. asst. prof. medicine San Francisco, 1978-82; internist La Clínica de la Raza, Oakland, Calif., 1978-82; prof. medicine and social scis. U. Calif., Irvine, 1982-96, chief div. gen. internal medicine and primary care, 1982-90; med. dir. U. Calif.-Irvine-North Orange County Community Clinic, Anaheim, 1982-90; disting. prof. U. N.Mex., 2005—, prof. sociology, family and cmty. medicine, internal medicine and Latin Am. studies, 1997—, sr. fellow, Robert Wood Johnson Found. Ctr. Health Policy, 2008—; internist El Centro Family Health, N.Mex., 2007—. Regional rep., nat. sec. bd. dir. Physicians for Nat. Health Program, Cambridge, Mass., 1989-91; cons. documentary Health Care Across the Border, Nat. Pub. TV, NYC, 1989-90, documentary on US health care system Nat. TV Austria, 1991; cons. BBC, 1992, Pew Health Professions Commn., 1992-94, Assn. Am. Med. Colls., 1992-93, Robert Wood Johnson Found., 1992, Rsch. and Tng. Group in Social Medicine, Santiago, Chile, 1990—, Eisenhower Rural Health Ctr., Idyllwild, Calif., 1995-96, office of pres. breast cancer rsch. initiative U. Calif, 2001, John D. & Catherine T. MacArthur Found., 2004, 09; lectr. med. sociology U. Amsterdam, The Netherlands, 1977; vis. prof. Northwestern U., 1994, U. Ill., Chgo., 1994, U. Wash., 1996, U. N.Mex., 1996, U. Ky., 1996, U. Guadalajara, 1997, 2002, 03, Simon Fraser U., 1997, U. Campinas, Brazil, 1999, Cornell Med. Coll., 1999, U. Utah, 2002, Nat. Inst. Pub. Health, Cuernavaca, Mex., 2003, 06, Robert Wood Johnson Sch. Medicine and Dentistry, NJ, 2003-04, State U. Rio de Janerio, Brazil, 2008; expert panel on comm. with elderly patients Nat. Inst. Aging, 1997; prin. investigator US Agy. for Healthcare Rsch. and Quality, NIMH, 1991-, Robert Wood Johnson Found., 2003-05, 08-09. Co-author: The Exploitation of Illness in Capitalist Society, 1974; author: The Second Sickness: Contradictions of Capitalist Health Care, 1983, paperback edit., 1986, revised edit., 2000, The Politics of Medical Encounters: How Patients and Doctors Deal with Social Problems, 1991, paperback edit., 1993, At the Front Lines of Medicine: How the Health Care System Alienates Doctors and Mistreats Patients...and What We Can Do About It, 2001, paperback edit., 2004; mem. editl. bd. Internat. Jour. Health Svc., Social Problems, Western Jour. Medicine, Cambio y Salud (Chile), Investigacion en Salud (Mex.), Internat. Jour. Cuban Health and Medicine. Cons. on health policy Jesse Jackson Presdl. Campaign, 1988; bd. dirs., mem. com. on litigation Orange County Pub. Law Ctr., 1990-96. Fellow in ind. study and rsch. NEH, 1984-85, Fulbright fellow, 1983, 88-90, 93-94, sr. fellow NIA, 1989-91, Fogarty Internat. Ctr., NIH, 1994-98, Fulbright New Century Scholar, 2001-02, Guide to Am. Top Physicians, 2002-2008, John Simon Guggenheim Meml. Found. fellow, 2002-03, Jonathan Mann Award for Lifetime Commitment to Pub. Health and Social Justice Issues, N.Mex. Pub. Health Assn., 2003. Fellow ACP, Am. Acad. Physician and Patient, Soc. for Applied Anthropology; mem. APHA, Am. Sociol. Assn. (nat. coun.-at-large med. sociology sect. 1989-92, coord. resolution process concerning nat. health program 1990-91, Leo G. Reeder award for disting. career in medicine and social sci., 1997), Soc. Gen. Internal Medicine, Phi Beta Kappa, Salvador Allende Program Social Medicine (pres. 2006-09). Avocations: music, athletics, gardening, mountain hiking. Office: U NMex Sociology MSC05 3080 Rm 1103 1915 Roma NE Albuquerque NM 87131 Office Phone: 505-277-0860. Business E-Mail: waitzkin@unm.edu.

WAJENBERG, ARNOLD SHERMAN, retired librarian, educator; b. Indpls., Apr. 11, 1929; s. Henry and Hazel L. (Johnson) W.; m. Joyce E. Dunham, Sept. 6, 1952; 1 child, Earl S. BA, Butler U., Indpls., 1951, MA, 1953, U. Chgo., 1955. Cataloger U. Chgo. Library, 1953-69; catalog librarian U. Ill., Chgo., 1969-74, asst. catalog librarian Champaign-Urbana, 1974-78, prin. cataloguer, 1979-94; ret., 1994; prof. library adminstrn. U. Ill., Champaign-Urbana. Prin. educator, Ill. Tng. Program for Implementation of Anglo-Am. Cataloguing Rules, 2d edit., 1979-80; mem. editorial policy com. Dewey Decimal, 1981-92; Ill. rep. cataloging adv. com., Online Computer Libr. Ctr. 1979-82, cataloging and database svcs. adv. com., 1989-92. Author: FLC FEDLINK AACR 2 Cataloging Manual for Federal Libraries, 1981; contbr. articles to profl. jours. Mem. ALA (com. on cataloging: description and access 1981-86, mem.-at-large exec. com. cataloging and classification sect. 1982-86, Margaret Mann citation 1995) Avocations: walking, science fiction. Home: 240 Donald Dr Goffstown NH 03045-6214

WAJER, RONALD EDWARD, management consultant; b. Chgo., Aug. 31, 1943; s. Edward Joseph and Gertrude Catherine (Rytelny) W.; m. Mary Earlene Hagan, July 5, 1969; children: Catherine, Michael. BSIE, Northwestern U., 1966; MBA, Loyola U., Chgo., 1970. Project engring. mgr. Procter & Gamble, Chgo., 1966-67; indsl. engring. mgr. Johnson & Johnson, Bedford Park, Ill., 1967-71; project mgr. Jewel Cos., Franklin Park, Ill., 1971-73; divsn. engring. mgr. Abbott Labs., North Chicago, Ill., 1973-79; pres. bus. engring. divsn. R.E. Wajer & Assocs., Northbrook, Ill., 1979—. Contbr. articles to profl. jours. Sec. Downtown Redevel. Commn., Mt. Prospect, Ill., 1977-78; fundraising vol. Maryville Acad., Des Plaines, 1985—; bd. dirs. Lattof YMCA, Des Plaines, 1994-96; profl. advisor Sch. for New Learning, DePaul U., 1994—; mem. indsl. sector com. Lincoln Found. for Bus. Excellence, 1997-99. Recipient Cmty. Svc. award Chgo. Lighthouse for the Blind, 1989, Cert. of Merit, Village of Mt. Prospect, 1978. Mem. Inst. Indsl. Engrs. (cmty. svc. chmn. 1984), Inst. Mgmt. Cons. (cert., exec. v.p., bd. dirs. 1987-94), Assn. Mgmt. Cons. (ctrl. regional v.p. 1985-87), Midwest Soc. Profl. Cons., Assn. Indsl. Real Estate Brokers, Pres.'s Resource Group, Samurai Exec. Network Group, Northwestern Club Chgo. Roman Catholic. Office: Bus Engring 5 Revere Dr Ste 200 Northbrook IL 60062-8000 Office Phone: 847-824-0809. Business E-Mail: rewajer@busnengg.com.

WAJERT, SEAN PETER, lawyer; b. Chester, Pa., Feb. 2, 1960; s. John Max and Kathleen Francella (Gorand) W.; m. Lisa Marie. AB magna cum laude, Harvard U., 1981; JD cum laude, U. Pa., 1984. Bar: Pa. 1984, US Dist. Ct. Ea. Dist. Pa. 1986, US Ct. Appeals 3rd Cir. 1985, US Ct. Appeals 10th Cir. 1986. Law clk. to Hon. Arlin M. Adams US Ct. Appeals 3rd Cir., Phila., 1984-85; assoc. Pepper, Hamilton & Scheetz, Phila., 1985-87, Hoyle, Morris & Kerr, Phila., 1988-91, ptnr., 1992-95; of counsel Dechert Price & Rhoads (now Dechert LLP), Phila., 1995—97, ptnr., 1997—, chair firm mass torts & product liability practice group. Adj. prof. U. Pa. Law Sch., 1990-98, Thomas O'Boyle hon. lectr.-in-law, 1999-2000. Editor in chief: U. Pa. Law Rev., 1983-84. Vol. Congl. campaign., Phila., 1988, Bucks City, 1989. James Finnegan Fellow, 1979; recipient Am. Jurisprudence Award, 1982, Edwin R. Keedy Award, 1984, John H. Maurer Meml. Prize, 1984. Mem. ABA, Pa. Bar Assn., Phila. Bar Assn., Def. Rsch. Inst., Order of Coif. Republican. Roman Catholic. Office: Dechert LLP Cira Centre 2929 Arch St Philadelphia PA 19104-2808 Office Phone: 215-994-2387. Office Fax: 215-994-2222. Business E-Mail: sean.wajert@dechert.com.

WAJSGRAS, DAVID C., manufacturing executive; m. Teena Wajsgras; 3 children. BS in Acctg., U. Md., College Park; MBA in Fin., Am. U. CPA. CFO Maserati Automobile, Balt.; sr. auditor Coopers & Lybrand; contr. Contellation Investments, C.G.I.; from contr. to v.p. fin. UNC Inc., Annapolis, Md.; various sr. fin. positions AlliedSignal, Inc., Morristown, NJ, 1992—97; corp. contr. Engelhard Corp., Iselin, NJ, 1997—99; v.p. contr. Lear Corp., Southfield, Mich., 1999—2002, sr. v.p., CFO, 2002—05, exec. v.p., CFO, 2005—06; CFO, sr. v.p. Raytheon Corp., Waltham, Mass., 2006—. Mem.: Fin. Execs. Inst. Office: Raytheon Corp 870 Winter St Waltham MA 02451-1449

WAKABAYASHI, JUDY, translator, educator; b. Australia; PhD, U. Queensland, Brisbane, Australia. Advanced cert. Nat. Accreditation Authority Translators and Interpreters. Lectr. U. Queensland, 1992—2002; assoc. prof. Kent State U., Ohio, 2002—. Grant, Australian Rsch. Coun. Mem.: Japanese Studies Assn. Australia, Japan Studies Assn., Japan Assn. Translators, Internat. Assn. Transl. and Intercultural Studies, Asian Studies Assn. Australia, Am. Translators Assn., Am. Transl. Studies Assn., Can. Assn. Transl. Studies, Soc. Writers, Editors and Translators, Ohio Assn. Tchrs. Japanese, Northeast Ohio Translators Assn., Nat. Coun. Japanese Lang. Tchrs., Assn. Tchrs. Japanese. Office: Kent State Univ Main St Kent OH 44242

WAKAMATSU, DON (WILBUR DONALD WAKAMATSU), professional baseball coach; b. Hood River, Oreg., Feb. 22, 1963; m. Laura Wakamatsu; children: Jacob, Lucas, Jadyn. Attended, Ariz. State U., Tempe. Minor league catcher, 1985—96; catcher Chgo. White Sox, 1991; mgr. Peoria Rookie, Ariz. Summer League, 1997, Class-A High Desert Mavericks, 1997—99, Double-A El Paso, Double-A Erie, Eastern League, 2000; minor league catching coord., roving catching instr. LA Angels, 2001—02; bench coach Tex. Rangers, 2003—06, third base coach, 2007; bench coach Oakland Athletics, 2008; mgr. Seattle Mariners, 2008—. Named Mgr. of Yr., Calif. League, 1998. Achievements include becoming the first Asian-American manager in Major League Baseball history, 2008. Office: Seattle Mariners Safeco Field PO Box 4100 Seattle WA 98134-0100*

WAKATA, KOICHI, astronaut; b. Saitama, Japan, Aug. 1, 1963; s. Nobutaka and Takayo Wakata; m. Stefanie von Sachsen-Altenburg; 1 child. BS in Aero. Engring., Kyushu U., 1987, MS in Applied Mechanics, 1989, D in Aerospace Engring., 2004. Structural engr. Japan Airlines, Narita, Japan, 1989—91, with engring. dept. airframe group, systems engring. office, 1991—92; astronaut Nat. Space Devel. Agy. Japan, NASA Johnson Space Ctr., Houston, 1992—, payload sci. support staff Astronaut Office Mission Devel. Br., 1993—95, with Space Shuttle flight software verification testing, Shuttle Avionics Integration Lab (SAIL), 1994, with Space Shuttle and Space Sta. Robotics, Astronaut Office Robotics Br. Houston, 1996—2006, with Extravehicular Activities (EVA) develop., Astronaut Office EVA Br., 2001—06, mission specialist STS-72 Endeavor (first Japanese mission specialist) Houston, 1996, asst. payload ops. dir. for manipulator flight demonstration (STS-85 mission), 1997, mem. STS-92 Discovery flight (first Japanese to work on the Internat. Space Station assembly), 2000; NASA robotics instructor astronaut, 2000—; comdr. NASA Extreme Environment Mission Ops. (NEEMO) mission, 2006; crew mem., mission specialist STS-119 and become the first resident station crew mem. from Japanese Aerospace Exploration Agy. (JAXA), 2009; flight engr. to Internat. Space Station Expedition 18, 2007; crew mem. STS-127 Mission (Endeavour), 2009. NASA robotics instr. astronaut, 2000—; flight engring. tng. for Russian Soyuz spacecraft, 2006; flight engr. to Internat. Space Station Expedition 18, 07. Recipient commendation, Min. of State for Sci. and Tech., 1996, Spl. award, Saitama Prefecture, 1996, Omiya City, 1996, Outstanding Svc. award, Nat. Space Devel. Agy. Japan, 1996, Diplome pilote-cosmonaute, URSS V.M. Komarov, 1997, 2001, Exceptional Svc. medal, NASA, 2001, Fgn. Min.'s Cert. of Commendation, 2004. Mem.: AIAA, Japanese Soc. Biol. Scis. in Space (Disting. Svc. award 2001), Robotics Soc. Japan, Japan Soc. Aero. and Space Scis. Avocations: flying, hang-gliding, baseball, tennis, skiing. Office: NASA Johnson Space Ctr Astronaut Office/CB 1601 NASA Pky Houston TX 77058*

WAKE, MARVALEE HENDRICKS, biology professor; b. Orange, Calif., July 31, 1939; d. Marvin Carlton and Velvalee (Borter) H.; m. David B. Wake, June 23, 1962; 1 child, Thomas A. BA, U. So. Calif., 1961, MS, 1964, PhD, 1968. Tchg. asst., instr. U. Ill., Chgo., 1964, asst. prof., 1968—69; lectr. U. Calif., Berkeley, 1969—73, asst. prof., 1973—76, assoc. prof., 1976—80, prof. zoology, 1980—89, chmn. dept. zoology, 1985—89, chmn. dept. integrative biology, 1989—91, 1999—2002, assoc. dean Coll. Letters and Sci., 1975—78, prof. integrative biology, 1989—2003, Chancellor's prof., 1997—2000, prof. of the Grad. Sch., 2004—. Mem. NAS/NRC Bd. on Sustainable Devel., 1995-99, NSF Bio Adv. Commn., 1997-2002; Smithsonian Sci. Commn., 2001-02; dist. adv. bd. Eneye Life, 2007-.examiner FGGS, Am Mus. Nat. Hist., 2007 Editor, co-editor: Hyman's Comparative Vertebrate Anatomy, 1979, The Origin and Evolution of Larval Forms, 1999, Ecology and Evolution in the Tropics, 2005; co-author: Biology, 1978; contbr. articles to profl. jours. NSF grantee, 1978—; Guggenheim fellow, 1988-89. Fellow: AAAS (chair Biology Sect. G 1998), Calif. Acad. Sci. (trustee 1992—98, hon. trustee 1998—), Am. Acad. Arts and Scis.; mem.: Internat. Soc. Vertebrate Morphology (pres. 2007—), Am. Inst. Biol. Sci. (pres. 2005), World Congress of Herpetology (sec. gen. 1994—97), Internat. Union Biol. Scis. (U.S. nat. com. 1986—2007, chair 1992—95, sec. gen. 1994—2000, pres. 2000—04), Soc. Integrative Comparative Biology (pres. 2001—03), Am. Soc. Ichthyologists and Herpetologists (bd. govs. 1978—, pres. 1984). Office: U Calif Dept Integrative Biology 3060 VLSB Berkeley CA 94720-3140 E-mail: mhwake@socrates.berkeley.edu.

WAKEFIELD, MARIE A., counselor, educational association administrator; b. Elyria, Ohio, Aug. 9, 1947; stepd. Orville B. and and d. Ethel A. Thomas; m. Charles F. Wakefield, Nov. 13, 1975; children: Paul, Philip, Charlene, Conya. BS in Edn., Cen. State U., Wilberforce, Ohio, 1969; MS, U. Nev., Las Vegas, 1979, adminstrv. endorsement, 1989. Cert. profl. elem. tchr., K-8 counselor, Nev. Elem. tchr. Clark County Sch. Dist., Las Vegas, elem. counselor. Pres. Am. Counseling Assn., Alexandria, Va. Editor parents newsletters. Recipient Outstanding Counseling Edn. award, Dr. Kay P. Carl, John A. Bailey Disting. Profl. award, Profl. Black Women's Rose award. Mem.: ACA (pres.), Assn. Multicultural Counseling Devel., Assn. Adult Devel. Aging (Disting. Svc. award), Western Region Governing Coun., Nev. Counseling Assn., Am. Bus. Womens Assn., Southern Nev. Sch. Counselors Assn., Nat. Self-Esteem Coun. Avocations: piano, reading. Office: 8091 Petunia Flower Way Las Vegas NV 89147 Office Phone: 702-876-5926. Business E-Mail: mawakefield@cox.net.

WAKEFIELD, MARK RICHARD, urologist, educator; b. Sacramento, Calif., Jan. 18, 1968; s. James L. and Mary K. Wakefield; m. Lara Lynn Creech; children: Maria, James. BS in Zoology, U. Tex., Austin, 1990; MD, U. Mo., Columbia, 1994. Med. specialty bd. cert. Am. Bd. Urology, 2002. Asst. prof. surgery, urology U. Mo. Sch. Medicine, Columbia, 2004—. Dir. and primary surgeon, renal transplantation U. Mo. Health Care, 2004—. Bd. mem. Midwest Transplant Network, Kans. City, Kans., 2007—08. Maj. staff urologist USAF, 2000—04, Wright-Patterson AFB, Ohio. Recipient Tow Humanism in Medicine awards, Gold Found., 2008. Fellow: ACS (state chpt. v.p. 2008—). Office: Univ Mo Sch Medicine M562 One Hospital Dr Columbia MO 65212 Office Phone: 573-882-1151. Office Fax: 573-884-7453.

WAKEFIELD, MARY KATHERINE, medical association administrator, medical educator; b. Aug. 12, 1954; BSN, Mary Coll., Bismarck, ND, 1976; MSN, U. Tex., Austin, 1978, PhD, 1985; grad. program for sr. mgrs. in govt., Harvard U., 1991. RN. Staff nurse ICU St. Alexius Hosp., Bismarck, ND, 1975-76; nurse United Hosp., Grand Forks, ND, 1976-77; acad. asst. sch. nursing U. Tex., Austin, 1977-78; instr. Brackenridge Sch. Nursing Austin Community Coll., 1978-79; mem. faculty U. ND, Grand Forks, 1979-87, assoc. prof., chairperson, 1985-87; legis. asst. health and edn. issues Senator Q. Burdick, Washington, 1987-89; chief of staff Senator Kent Conrad, Washington, 1989—96; prof., dir. Ctr. Health Policy, Rsch. & Ethics George Mason U., Fairfax, Va., 1996—2001; prof., dir. Ctr. Rural Health U. ND Sch. Medicine & Health Sciences, Grand Forks, 2001—, assoc. dean, 2001—. Bd. dirs. AcademyHealth, ND Health Care Rev., Blue Cross Blue Shield ND; mem. VA spl. med. adv. group; bd. trustees Catholic Health Initiatives; part-time staff nurse The United Hosp., Grand Forks, 1979-86; mem. faculty assoc. U. Md. Sch. of Nursing, 1990—; mem. adj. faculty George Mason U. Sch. of Nursing, Va., 1990—; selected to participate in 1991 Cong. Bundestag Staff Exchange Program, Germany; presenter in field. Editorial bd. Nursing Econs., 1990—, Jour. Rural Health, Annals of Family Medicine; contbr. articles to profl. jours. Recipient Nurse Rsch. award, Am. Orgn. Nurse Execs., 2006. Fellow Am. Acad. Nursing; mem. AAUW, ANA (coun. nursing rsch.), Inst. Medicine, ND Acad. Sci., Nat. League for Nursing, Philippine Nurses Assn. of Met. Washington (hon. 1991), Sigma Theta Tau, Sigma Xi. Office: Ctr Rural Health PO Box 9037 Grand Forks ND 58202-9037 Office Phone: 701-777-3848. Office Fax: 701-777-6779.

WAKEFIELD, SARAH REBECCA, literature and language professor; b. NY; d. Terry and Virginia Wakefield. BA in Chemistry and English, Bryn Mawr Coll., Pa., 1997; MA in English, U. Tex., Austin, 1999, PhD in English, 2002. Assoc. prof. English Prairie View A&M U., Tex., 2002—. Author: (book) Folklore in British Literature: Naming and Narrating in Women's Fiction, 1750-1880. Business E-Mail: srwakefield@pvamu.edu.

WAKEFIELD, TIMOTHY STEPHEN (TIM WAKEFIELD), professional baseball player; b. Melbourne, Fla., Aug. 2, 1966; m. Stacy Wakefield. Student, Fla. Tech. Pitcher NY-Pa. League, Welland, 1989, Carolina League, Salem, 1990, So. League, South Carolina, 1991, 93, Am. Assn. League, Buffalo, 1991-92, 94, Pitts. Pirates, 1992-93, Internat. League, Pawtucket, 1995, Boston Red Sox, 1995—. Donates money to the Make-A-Wish Foundation for every strikeout and win. Named Nat. League Rookie of Yr. The Sporting News, 1992, Am. League Comeback Player of the Yr., 1995; named to Sunshine State Conf. Hall of Fame, 1998, Am. League All-Star Team Maj. League Baseball, 2009. Achievements include member of the World Series Championship winning Boston Red Sox, 2004, 2007. Office: c/o Boston Red Sox Fenway Pk 4 Yawkey Way Boston MA 02215-3409*

WAKEFIELD, WANDA ELLEN, historian, educator, sports association executive; b. Olney, Ill., Sept. 6, 1953; d. Melvin Dale and Eileen Louise Wakefield; life ptnr. Pamela Sue Bakst, Apr. 1, 1979. AB, Grinnell Coll., Iowa, 1975; JD, U. Ill., Urbana, 1978; MS, SUNY, Buffalo, PhD, 1995. Asst. prof. Mid. Tenn. State U., Murfreesboro, 1995—98; assoc. prof. SUNY Coll., Brockport, 1998—. Bd. mem. SW Ecumenical Ministries, Rochester, NY; ofcl., judge US Luge Assn., Lake Placid, NY, 1988—2009. Milton Plesur fellowship, SUNY, 1990—95. Avocation: sports. Office: SUNY Coll Brockport 350 New Campus Dr Brockport NY 14420 Business E-Mail: wwakefie@brockport.edu.

WAKELEE, DANIEL WILLIAM, academic administrator; s. Earl and Marcia Wakelee; m. Joanne Powell Wakelee, Aug. 16, 1987; 1 child, Andrew Arthur. AB, Occidental Coll., 1982; MPA, Calif. State U. Northridge, 1990; PhD, U. Calif. Santa Barbara, 1995. Coord. food and shelter Project Understanding, Ventura, Calif., 1983—84; exec. dir. FOOD Share, Oxnard, Calif., 1984—88; asst. dir. Calif. State U. Nortridge, Ventura, 1988—98; assoc. dir. Calif. State U. Channel Islands, Camarillo, 1999—2001, assoc. dean of faculty, 2001—, assoc. prof. pub. adminstrn., 2005—. Mem. Channel Islands Inter Disc Rsch. Group, 2006—. Patient vol. Camarillo Hospice, Calif., 2001—06; elder Eastminster Presbyn. Ch., Ventura, Calif., 1988—2000; bd. dirs. Project Understanding, Ventura, Calif., 1987—89. Ventura County Scholarship Project, Ventura County Cmty. Found., 1999—2001, Calif. History Social Sci. Project grant, U. Calif., 2000-2002. Mem.: Western Assn. of Br. Campus Adminstrs. (nat. conf. chair 2002—02), Calif. Intersegmental Articulation Coun. (instl. rep. 2001—03), Calif. Assn. for Bilingual Edn., Am. Assn. for Higher Edn., Coun. Colls. of Arts and Sci. (liberal arts com. 2003—05, assoc. deans commn.). Office: Calif State Univ Channel Islands One University Dr Camarillo CA 93012 Business E-Mail: dan.wakelee@csuci.edu.

WAKELING, WILLIAM MICHAEL, librarian, director; b. Southampton, United Kingdom, Sept. 26, 1951; s. George Dennis and Barbara Dyson Wakeling; m. October Ivins, 2001; children: Katharine, Simon. BA in English Lit., Leeds U., 1974; MA, 1975; MA in Librarianship, U. Sheffield, 1977. Sr. libr. asst. U. Bristol, 1977—80; asst. libr. U. York, 1980—90; sub-librarian, tech. svcs.,U. libr. U. Birmingham, 1991—92, head collection mgmt., U. libraries, 1992—95, asst. dir., info. svcs., 1995—98; collection devel. officer, U. libraries Northeastern U., Boston, 1998—2002, assoc. dean, U. libraries, 2002—08, dean libraries, 2008—; bd. dirs. Boston Libr. Consortium, 2007—. Bd. dirs. NELINET, Southboro, Mass., 2007—. Mem.: Soc. Scholarly Pub., History Sci. Soc., ALA. Office: Northeastern Univ Snell Libr 360 Huntington Ave Boston MA 02115 Business E-Mail: w.wakeling@neu.edu.

WAKEMAN, ROSEMARY, history professor; b. Rockville Ctr., NY, Sept. 3, 1948; d. Charles and Georgianna Mangiaracina; m. Thomas Wakeman, July 12, 1980; children: Gabrielle, Jessica. PhD, U. Calif., Davis, 1983. Author: (book) Modernizing the Provincial City: Toulouse, 1945-1973, The Heroic City: Paris, 1945-1958; editor: Themes in Modern European History Since 1945-2003. Home: 24 W 55th St Apt 2B New York NY 10019 Office: Fordham Univ 113 W 60th St New York NY 10024 Office Phone: 212-636-7359. Business E-Mail: rwakeman@fordham.edu.

WAKEMAN, THOMAS HERBERT, III, civil engineer, regional administrator; b. Apr. 20, 1946; BS, Calif. Polytech. U., 1970; MA, San Francisco State U., 1975; MS, U. Calif., Davis, 2002; Eng.Sc.D., Columbia U., 2006. Pres. Earth Doctors, Davis, Calif., 1982-85; dir. bay model US Army Engrs., Sausalito, Calif., 1985-89, spl. projects mgr. San Francisco, 1990-94; gen. mgr. waterways devel. Port Authority NY, 1994—2005, program mgr. regional port progs. (ret.), 2005—07; chmn. transp. rsch. bd. Marine Environ. Com., 2003—; exec. dir. DHS Ctr. Excellence Port Security, Stevens Inst. Tech., Hoboken, NJ. Mem.: PIANC Internat. (v.p. 2003—07), Marine Transp. Sys. Nat. Adv. Coun. Office: Dep Dir Ctr Maritime Systems Rsch Prof Civil Environ Ocean Eng Stevens Inst Tech Castle Point on Hudson Hoboken NJ 07030 Office Phone: 201-216-5669. Office Fax: 201-216-8214. Business E-Mail: thomas.wakeman@stevens.edu.

WAKIM, FAHD GEORGE, physicist, researcher; b. Mieh-Mieh, Lebanon, Aug. 6, 1933; s. George Hanna and Marriam (Semaan) W.; m. Bertha Villarreal. BSc in Physics, Am. U. Beirut, 1956; MA in Solid State Physics, U. Tex., Austin, 1960, PhD in Solid State Physics, 1964. Rsch. physicist Itek Corp., Lexington, Mass., 1965-70; investigator Tex. Christian U., Ft. Worth, 1970-71; assoc. prof. Am. U. Cairo, 1971-73; prof. physics Kuwait U., Kuwait, 1973-84; assoc. prof. dept. elec. engring U. Mass., Lowell, 1984—, coord. for EET program, 1996—. Presenter numerous seminars. Patentee process for producing images with photosensitive materials and their products; contbr. articles to profl.

jours. Grantee Kuwait Inst. for Sci. Rsch., 1978, 79, 91, Kuwait U., 1979. Mem. Am. Phys. Soc. Office: U Mass Lowell 1 University Ave Lowell MA 01854-5009 Office Phone: 978-934-3312.

WAKIMOTO, ROGER MASAO, meteorology educator, researcher; b. San Jose, Dec. 11, 1953; s. Tsutomu and Magarita rose (Kurokawa) Wakimoto; m. Jina Choi, Mar. 7, 1981; children: Paul, Sean. BS, San Jose State U., Calif., 1976; PhD, U. Chgo., 1981. Rsch. assoc. U. Chgo., 1981-83; asst. prof. meteorology UCLA, 1983-89, assoc. prof., 1989—. Recipient Nat. Weather Svc. award, 1984, Pub. award EPA, 1988. Mem. Am. Meteorol. Soc. (chmn. undergrad. awards com. 1987-88, severe local storms com. 1988-91, Meisinger award 1992), Univ. Corp. for Atmospheric Rsch. (chmn. univ. rels. com. 1991-92), Office: UCLA 405 Hilgard Ave Los Angeles CA 90095-9000

WAKOSKI, DIANE, poet, educator; b. Whittier, Calif., Aug. 3, 1937; d. John Joseph and Marie Elvira (Mengel) W. BA in English, U. Calif., Berkeley, 1960. Writer-in-residence Mich. State U., East Lansing, 1976—, Univ. disting. prof., 1990—. Vis. writer Calif. Inst. Tech., 1972, U. Va., 1972-73, Wilamette U., 1973, Lake Forest Coll., 1974, Colo. Coll., 1974, U. Calif., Irvine, 1974, Macalester Coll., 1975, U. Wis., 1975, Hollins Coll., 1974, U. Wash., 1977, Whitman Coll., 1976, Emory U., 1980-81, U. Hawaii, 1978. Author: Coins and Coffins, 1962, Discrepancies and Apparitions, 1966, Inside The Blood Factory, 1968, The George Washington Poems, 1967, The Magellanic Clouds, 1969, The Motorcycle Betrayal Poems, 1971, Smudging, 1972, Dancing On The Grave of A Son Of A Bitch, 1973, Trilogy, 1974, Virtuoso Literature For Two and Four Hands, 1976, Waiting For the King of Spain, 1977, The Man Who Shook Hands, 1978, Cap of Darkness, 1980, The Magician's Feastletters, 1982, The Collected Greed: Parts I-XIII, 1984, The Rings of Saturn, 1986, Emerald Ice: Selected Poems 1962-87, 1988 (William Carlos Williams prize 1989), Medea The Sorceress, 1991, Jason the Sailor, 1993, The Emerald City of Las Vegas, 1995, Argonaut Rose, 1998, The Butcher's Apron: New & Selected Poems, 2000. Recipient award, Mich. Arts Found., 1989, Disting. Faculty award, Mich. State U., 1989; named Univ. Disting. Prof., Mich. State U., 1990, Author of Yr., Mich. Libr. Assn., 2003; grantee Cassandra Found., 1970, N.Y. State Cultural Coun., 1971—72, Guggenheim Found., 1972—73, Fullbright, 1984, Mich. Arts Coun., 1988. Office: Mich State U 207 Morrill Hall East Lansing MI 48824-1036 Personal E-mail: dwakoski@aol.com.

WAKSCHLAG, MILTON SAMUEL, lawyer; b. Omaha, July 4, 1955; s. Fishel and Stefa (Kleiner) W.; m. Laurie S. Weinzweig, June 15, 1980; children: Tmima, Shira, Efraim. BA, Loyola U., 1977; JD, U. Chgo., 1980; LLM in Taxation, DePaul U., 1987. Bar: Ill. 1980. Assoc. Borge and Pitt, Chgo., 1980-85, ptnr., 1986, Katten Muchin Rosenman LLP, Chgo., 1987—, chair, pub. fin. dept., chair, fin. products group, mem. pro bono com. Adv. com. on svcs. to disabled, Ill. Atty. Gen's Office; prin. faculty mem. nat. tng. seminar, Govt. Fin. Officers Assn.; co-chair Bond Buyer's Ninth Ann. Midwest Pub. Fin. Conf.; nat. conf. chmn., Ctr. Bus. Intelligence; spkr. in field. Author: Important Developments During the Year: Tax Exempt Financing, 1989; contbr. papers in field, articles to profl. jours. Founder, v.p., bd. dirs., trustee Keshet: Jewish Parents of Children with Spl. Needs, 1984—2006; trustee Lincolnwood Dist. Pub. Libr., 1988-90; bd. dirs. Brisk Rabbinical Coll., 1990-2006. Recipient Pro Bono Svc. award, Katten Muchin Rosenman LLP, Guardian of Hope award, Keshet, 2006. Mem. ABA (chmn. com. on tax-exempt fin., 1999-2001), Nat. Assn. Bond Lawyers (mem. steering com. bond attys.' workshop). Office: Katten Muchin Rosenman LLP 525 W Monroe St Chicago IL 60661 Office Fax: 312-577-8897. Business E-Mail: milton.wakschlag@kattenlaw.com.

WAKSMAN, BYRON HALSTED, immunologist, educator, medical association administrator; b. NYC, Sept. 15, 1919; s. Selman A. and Bertha (Mitnik) W.; m. Joyce Ann Robertroy, Aug. 11, 1944; children: Nan, Peter. BS, Swarthmore Coll., 1940; MD, U. Pa., 1943. Intern Michael Reese Hosp., Chgo., 1944; fellow Mayo Found., 1946-48; NIH fellow Columbia U. Med. Sch., 1948-49; assoc., then asst. prof. bacteriology and immunology Harvard Med. Sch., 1949-63; rsch. fellow, then assoc. bacteriologist (immunology) Mass. Gen. Hosp., 1949-63; prof. microbiology Yale U., 1963-74, prof. pathology, 1974-78, chmn. dept., 1964-70, 72-74, prof. pathology and biology, 1979-89; v.p. rsch. programs Nat. Multiple Sclerosis Soc., NYC, 1979—87, v.p. rsch. and med. programs, 1987-89; adj. prof. pathology NYU, 1979—, rsch. prof. biomedicine and sci. edn., 2002—, dir. (ad interim) programs for prep. edn. sci. and medicine, 2002—03, sr. advisor collaborative edn. programs, 2003—; vis. scientist in neurology Harvard U., 1990—. Mem. expert panel immunology WHO, 1963—83; microbiology fellowships panel and study sect. mem. NIH, 1961—69; bd. trustees Found. for Microbiology, 1968—, pres., 1970—2000, chmn. bd. trustees, 2001—; bd. trustees Biosis, 1988—91; dir. sci. writing fellowships program Marine Biol. Lab., Woods Hole, Mass., 1990—95; Humboldt prof. Max Planck Inst., Martinsried, 1991—92; dir. European Initiative for Communicators Sci., 1992—95; chmn. bd. Sci. Counsellors Nat. Inst. Aging, 1977—79. Contbr. articles to profl. jours.; editor: Progress in Allergy/Chemical Immunology, 1962—; mem. editl. adv. bd.: Cellular Immunology, 1970—95, Immunol. Comms., 1970—95, Inflammation, 1975—90, assoc. editor: Bacteriol. Revs., 1963—67, Jour. Immunology, 1962—66, Internat. Archives Allergy and Applied Immunology, 1962—95. Served as psychiatrist AUS, 1944-46. Fellow Am. Acad Arts and Scis.; mem. Am. Assn. Immunologists (councillor 1965-70, pres. 1970-71), Brit. Soc. Immunology, Am. Soc. Microbiology (councillor 1967-71), Am. Acad. Microbiology, Am. Acad. Neurology, Am. Neurol. Assn. Home: Brookhaven at Lexington 1010 Waltham St Apt 462 Lexington MA 02421 Office Phone: 781-862-3839. Business E-Mail: bwaksman@partners.org.

WALBERG, HERBERT JOHN, psychologist, educator, consultant; b. Chgo., Dec. 27, 1937; s. Herbert J. and Helen (Bauer) W.; m. Madoka Bessho, Aug. 20, 1965; 1 child, Herbert J. III. BE in Edn. and Psychology, Chgo. State U., 1959; ME in Counseling, U. Ill., 1960; PhD in Ednl. Psychology, U. Chgo., 1964. Instr. psychology Chgo. State U., 1962—63, asst. prof., 1964—65; lectr. edn. Rutgers U., New Brunswick, NJ, 1965—66; asst. prof. edn. Harvard U., Cambridge, Mass., 1966—69; assoc. prof. edn. U. Ill., Chgo., 1970—71, prof., 1971—84, rsch. prof., 1984—, external examiner, 1981. External examiner, 1981; ednl. cons. numerous orgns.; external examiner Monash U., 1974, 76, Australian Nat. U., 1977; speaker in field; former coord. worldwide radio broadcasts on Am. Edn. Voice of Am., USIA, Office Pres. U.S., cons. Ctr. for Disease Control U.S. Pub. Health Svcs., 1985-90. Author, editor: 49 books, chmn. editl. bd.: Internat. Jour. Ednl. Rsch., 1985—; contbr. over 350 articles to profl. jours., chapters to books. Mem. Chgo. United Edn. Com., also other civic groups, 1971-86; bd. dirs. Family Study Inst., 1987; chmn. bd. dirs. Heartland Inst., 1995. Nat. Inst. Edn. rsch. grantee, 1973, NSF rsch. grantee, 1974, March of Dimes rsch. grantee, 1976, numerous others. Fellow AAAS, Am. Psychol. Assn., Royal Statis. Soc.; mem. Internat. Acad. Edn. (founding), Am. Ednl. Rsch. Assn., Assn. for Supervision and Curriculum Devel., Brit. Ednl. Rsch. Assn., Nat. Soc. for Study Edn., Evaluation Rsch. Soc., Internat. Acad. Scis., Phi Delta Kappa (Disting. Rsch. award U. Chgo. chpt. 1971, cert. of recognition 1985), Phi Kappa Phi (hon.). Lutheran. Avocation: travel. Office: U Ill 1040 W Harrison St Chicago IL 60607-7129 Office Phone: 312-505-0528.

WALBERG, TIM (TIMOTHY LEE WALBERG), former United States Representative from Michigan, former state legislator; b. Chgo., Apr. 12, 1951; s. John Andrew and Alice (Wilcox) Walberg; m. Susan Gail Polensky, 1973; children: Matthew Lee, Heidi Gail, Caleb Paul. Grad., Western Ill. U., 1970; Diploma, Summit Christian Coll., 1973; BS, Ft. Wayne Bible Coll., 1975; MA with honors, Wheaton Coll. Grad. Sch., 1978. Pastor New Haven (Ind.) Bapt. Ch., 1973-77, Union Gospel Ch., Tipton, Mich., 1978-83; mem. Mich. Ho. of Reps. from 57th dist., 1983—98; pres. Warren Reuther Ctr. for Edn. & Cmty. Impact, 1999—2001; divsn. mgr. Moody Bible Inst., Chgo., 2001—06; mem. US Congress from 7th Mich. dist, Mich., 2007—09, mem. agrl. com., edn. & labor com. Mem. Lenawee County Basic Human Needs Task Force; asst. minority whip Mich. Ho. of Reps., vice chmn. corrections com., mem. agr., forestry & minerals, edn. econ. devel. & energy coms., mem. Children at Risk Task Force, Prison Reform Task Force. Mem.: Lenawee County Riding for Handicapped, Tecumsoh Kiwanis Club. Republican. Protestant.*

WALBESSER, HENRY HERMAN, computer science educator; b. Buffalo, May 9, 1935; s. Henry Herman and Florence (Schoenl) W.; m. Diane L. Walker, Aug. 16, 1958; children: Henry, Kathleen, James. BS, SUNY, Buffalo, 1958; MA, U. Md., 1960, PhD, 1965; DSc, U. of the Republic, Uruguay, 1976. Asst. prof. U. Tex., Austin, 1961-63; assoc. dir. AAAS, Washington, 1963-68; assoc. prof. U. Md., College Park, 1968-76, assoc. dean/assoc. provost, 1971-76, prof., chair Catonsville, 1976-92, prof. emeritus, 1992—; prof. Baylor U., Waco, Tex., 1992—, dean, 1992—96; COO, provost Henry Cogswell Coll., Everett, Wash., 2005—06; dir. Human-Computer Interaction Rsch. Lab., Hewitt, Tex., 2006—. Author: Evaluation Model, 1965, Integrity and Higher Education, 2001, A Brief Primer on Teaching: For New University Personnel, 2002, Imagination, 2003, An Introduction to Data Analysis for Computer Scientists and Engineers, 2003; co-author: Descriptive Data Analysis, 1991, Inferential Data Analysis, 1994; contbr. articles to profl. jours. Active adv. bd. Gov.'s Econ. Devel. Office, Annapolis, Md., 1988-91, Strecker Mus., Waco, 1992-2006, Lyric Opera of Waco, 1997-2006; worker Habitat for Humanity, Waco, 1996—. Fulbright-Hays fellow, 1967, 68, SEAMEO fellow, 1981, 82, OECD fellow, 1988. Fellow: AAAS; mem.: Nat. Hist. Soc. Democrat. Baptist. Avocations: bioinformatics, history of university presidents, gardening. Office: PO Box 1428 Hewitt TX 76643 Home: 400 Shadow Mt Waco TX 76712 Office Phone: 254-644-0841. Personal E-mail: hhwalbesser@aol.com.

WALBURN, JOHN CLIFFORD, retired mental health services professional; b. Marion, Ind., Apr. 6, 1945; s. Rex Raymond and Norma Jane (Clifford) W.; m. Linda Sue Spall, Sept. 21, 1968 (div. Dec. 1987); 1 child, Geoffrey Jacob; m. Mitzi Lynn Johnson, June 20, 1992; 1 child, Abigail Rae. BS, Ball State U., 1969, MA, 1975; JD, I.U., Indpls., 1991. Bar: Ind. 1992. Planner Metro. Planning Commn., Muncie, Ind., 1970-72; dir. adult svcs. Del. County Assn. for Retarded, Muncie, Ind., 1972-76; exec. dir. Fayette-Union Assn. for Retarded, Connersville, Ind., 1976-83; cons. Ind. Protection and Advocacy, Indpls., 1984-86; case mgr. Ind. Dept. Mental Health, Indpls., 1986-87; exec. dir. Cardinal Svc. Mgmt., New Castle, Ind., 1987-2000; founding ptnr. Creative Human Resource Solutions, New Castle, Ind., 1998—2008; exec. dir. Cmty. Alternative, Southeast Divsn. of Rescare, Jeffersonville, Ind., 2000—08. Ofcl. Ind. Spl. Olympics, 1973—; chmn. Ind. Residential Mgmt. Com., 1991—; cons. DLG Cons. and Mktg. Svc., Ind., 1992; treas. Cmty. Action, So. Ind. Co-author: Feldman/Walburn Habilitation System, 1998; photo, drawing artist, 1978—. Treas. cmty. action, So. Ind., Madison Area C. of C.; bd. dirs. Arts Coun. of So. Ind., 2004-. With USN, 1965-67, chair Ohio River Valley Folk Festival, 2005-, music Com. mem., Ribberfest, 2001-. bd.dir. Pathways Youth Svcs.,2004-, pres., 2009. Named Ky. Col., Commonwealth of Ky., 1978. Mem. Am. Assn. Mental Retardation (bd. dirs. 1991-98), Ind. Assn. Rehab. Facilities (bd. dirs. 1996—, Pres.'s award 1998), Madison Area C. of C. Avocations: sports, playing/listening to music, movies, art, reading fiction. Home: 2559 So College Hill Dr Hanover IN 47243-9177 Office: RES-CARE Twenty-Five-O-One Pl 6200 E Hwy 62 Ste 675 Jeffersonville IN 47130 Business E-Mail: jwalburn@rescare.com.

WALCH, TIMOTHY GEORGE, library director; b. Detroit, Dec. 6, 1947; s. George Louis Walch and Margaret Mary (Shields) DeSchryver; m. Victoria Irons, June 24, 1978; children: Thomas Emmet, Brian Edward. BA, U. Notre Dame, 1970; PhD, Northwestern U., 1975. Lectr. history Northwestern U., 1974—75; assoc. dir. Soc. Am. Archivists, Chgo., 1975-79; program analyst Nat. Hist. Publ. and Records Commn., Washington, 1979-81; budget analyst Nat. Archives and Record Svc., Washington, 1981-82; chief, publs. devel. br. Nat. Archives and Records Adminstrn., Washington, 1982-88; asst. dir. Hoover Presdl. Libr. and Mus., West Branch, Iowa, 1988-93, dir., 1993—. Co-dir. Modern Archives Inst., Nat. Archives and Records Adminstrn., 1981—88; pres. Cath. Cmty. Found. of Iowa, 2002—03; chair Iowa Ctr. Book, 2005—07, Iowa Hist. Found., 2006—07. Author: Catholicism in America, 1989, Pope John Paul II, 1989, Parish School, 1996, reprinted, 2003 and others; editor: Prologue, 1982-88, The Heritage of American Catholicism, 1988, (with Edward R. Kantowicz) European Immigrants in American Society, 1990, Herbert Hoover & Harry S Truman, 1992, Immigrant America, 1994, At the President's Side, 1997, Herbert Hoover & Franklin D. Roosevelt, 1998, Uncommon Americans, 2003, and others; assoc. editor: U.S. Cath. Historian, 1983—; guest columnist: Cedar Rapids Gazette, 1996-2006; contbr. articles to profl. jours.; guest commentator: CNN, MSNBC, Fox News, C-SPAN and others. Named to Pres.'s Club St. Ambrose U., 2005; recipient Journalism award, U.S. Cath. Press Assn., 1986, 1st place publ. award, Nat. Assn. Govt. Communicators, 1988, U.S. Archivist's award, Nat. Archives, 1993, Iowa Gov.'s Vol. award, 1995, 97, 2006, Dominican Veritas Forum award, 1996, Rogus Lecture, U. Dayton, 1999, Williams Lecture, La. State U., Shreveport, 2000, Hatfield Lecture, Oreg. Hist. Soc., 2003. Mem. Orgn. Am. Historians, US Cath. Hist. Soc., State Hist. Soc. Iowa (trustee 2005—), Rotary Internat. (Harris fellow 2005-). Office: Hoover Presdl Libr and Mus 210 Parkside Dr West Branch IA 52358 Office Phone: 319-643-6029. Personal E-mail: twalch47@aol.com. Business E-Mail: timothy.walch@nara.gov.

WALCHAK, KAROL LYNN, literature and language professor, department chairman; d. Patricia Loucille Walchak; children: Alexander Brendon, Jacqueline Lucinda. PhD, U. Nev. Reno, 1991. Cert. Jr. Coll. Tchg. Credential, Calif., 1992, Tesol Calif., 1985. Instr. Alpena CC, 2000—, chair english, fine arts & humanities, 2007—. Moderator WBKB, Alpena, Mich., 2002—; advisor Phi Theta Kappa, Nu Omicron Chpt., Alpena, 2007—. Actor(costanza): (civic theatre) Enchanted April; editor: (spanish book) Impresiones. Judge Sci. Olympiad, Alpena, 2009; moderator Knowledge Bowl, 2001—. Grantee Faculty Rsch. & Creative Endeavors grant, Ctrl. Mich. U., 2000; Ednl. Opportunity grant, Alpena CC, 2007. Fellow: Books & Brown Bags (reviewer 2005—); mem.: Mich. Humanities (award 2008). Office: Alpena CC 665 Johnson St Alpena MI 49707 Office Phone: 989-358-7349. Business E-Mail: walchakk@alpenacc.edu.

WALCHER, ALAN ERNEST, lawyer; b. Chgo., Oct. 2, 1949; s. Chester R. and Dorothy E. (Kullgren) Walcher; children: Dustin Alan, Michael Alan, Christopher Ray. BS, U. Utah, 1971; JD, 1974. Bar: Utah 1974, US Dist. Ct. Utah 1974, US Ct. Appeals (10th cir.) 1977, Calif. 1979, US Dist. Ct. (cen. dist.) Calif. 1979, US Ct. Appeals (9th cir.) 1983, US Dist. Ct. (ea., no., and so. dists.) Calif. 1994; cert. in internat. rels. 1971. Sole practice, Salt Lake City, 1974—79, 2003—; ptnr. Costello & Walcher, LA, 1979—85, Walcher & Scheuer, 1985—88, Ford & Harrison, 1988—91, Epstein Becker & Green, 1991—2003; judge pro tem LA Mcpl. Ct., 1986—91; dir. Citronia, Inc., LA, 1979—81. Trial counsel Utah Cht. Common Cause, Salt Lake City, 1978—79. Robert Mukai scholar, U. Utah, 1971. Mem.: ABA, Owl & Key, Assn. Bus. Trial Lawyers, Century City Bar Assn., LA County Bar Assn., Fed. Bar Assn., Soc. Bar & Gavel (v.p. 1975—77), Phi Delta Phi. Home: 1050 S Flower St #605 Los Angeles CA 90015 Office Phone: 310-344-6570. Personal E-mail: alan1002@earthlink.net.

WALCHER, GREG E., small business owner; s. Wendell Barge and Adeline Delilah Walcher; m. Diana Schlauger, July 12, 1992; 1 child, Amber Duncan. BA in Polit. Sci. and History, Mesa State Coll., Grand Junction, Colo., 1979. Senate staff US Senator William Armstrong, Washington, 1979—89; pres., CEO Club 20, Grand Junction, 1989—99; exec. dir. Colo. Dept. Natural Resources, Denver, 1999—2004; owner, CEO Natural Resources Group LLC, Washington, 2005—. Owner Walcher Orchards, Palisade, Colo., 1992—; sr. assoc. Stillwell Group, Washington, 2006—; sr. advisor Dawson and Assocs., Washington, 2006—. Exec. com. mem. Aspinall Meml. Commn., Palisade, 1998—2007; commr. Colo. Wildlife Commn., Denver, 1999—2004; bd. mem. Colo. Water Conservation Bd., Denver, 1999—2004, Gt. Outdoors Colo. Trust Fund, Denver, 1999—2004, Colo. Commn. of Indian Affairs, Denver, 1999—2004; GOP nominee US Congress, Colo., 2004—04; bd. mem. Pinchot Inst. for Conservation, Millford, Pa., 2000—04. Recipient John Vanderhoof award, Club 20, 1999. Mem.: Grand Junction Rotary Club. Conservative. Methodist. Home: PO Box 1393 Palisade CO 81526 Office: Natural Resources Group 1501 Crystal Dr Ste 925 Arlington VA 22202 Personal E-mail: gregwalcher@aol.com.

WALCOTT, CHARLES, neurobiology and behavior educator; b. Boston, July 19, 1934; s. Charles Folsom and Susan (Cabot) W.; m. Jane Clayton Taylor, Aug. 14, 1976; children: Thomas Stewart, Samuel Cabot. AB, Harvard U., 1956; PhD, Cornell U., 1959. Asst. prof. div. engring. and applied physics Harvard U., Cambridge, Mass., 1961-65; asst. prof. biology Tufts U., Medford, Mass., 1965-67; assoc. prof. dept. biology SUNY, Stony Brook, 1967-74, prof. dept. biology, 1974-81; prof., exec. dir. Cornell Lab. of Ornithology, Ithaca, NY, 1981-93, Louis Agassiz Fuertes dir., 1992-95; prof. neurobiology and behavior Cornell U., 1981—2008, prof. emeritus, grad sch. prof., 2008—, dir. divsn. biol. scis., 1998-99, assoc. dean of the univ. faculty, 2000—03, dean of univ. faculty, 2003—08. Cons., dir. Elem. Sci. Study, Watertown, Mass., 1961-67; dir. 3-2-1- Contact, Children's TV Workshop, N.Y.C., 1978—80; dir. L.A. Fuertes. Contbr. many rsch. papers to sci. jours. Dir. sci. TV, Mass. Audubon, Lincoln, 1959—61. Avocations: gardening, sailing, photography. Home: 84 Besemer Hill Rd Ithaca NY 14850-9636 Office: Cornell U Dept Neurobiology Behavior W255 Seeley Mudd Hall Ithaca NY 14853 Office Phone: 607-254-4382. Business E-Mail: cw38@cornell.edu.

WALCOTT, DEREK ALTON, poet, playwright; b. Castries, St. Lucia, Jan. 23, 1930; s. Warwick and Alix W.; m. Fay Moston, 1954 (div. 1959); 1 son; m. Margaret Ruth Maillard, 1962 (div.); 2 daus.; m. Norline Metivier (div.). BA, U. West Indies, Kingston, Jamaica, 1953, DLitt, 1972. Former tchr., St. Lucia, Grenada, Jamaica; poet-in-residence Hollins Coll., Roanoke, VA, 1980; prof. English Boston U. Founding dir. Trinidad Theatre Workshop, 1959—; lectr. Rutgers U., Yale U.; vis. prof. Columbia U., 1981, Harvard U., 1982, Boston U., 1985. Author: (poetry) Twenty-Five Poems, 1948, Epitath for the Young: A Poem in XII Cantos, 1949, Poems, 1953, In A Green Night: Poems, 1948-1960, 1962, Selected Poems, 1964, The Castaway and Other Poems, 1965 (Heinemann award Royal Soc. Lit. 1966), The Gulf and Other Poems, 1969 (Cholmondeley award 1969), Another Life, 1973 (Jock Campbell/New Statesman prize 1974), Sea Grapes, 1976, Selected Verse, 1976, The Star-Apple Kingdom, 1979, The Fortunate Traveller, 1981 (Heinemann award Royal Soc. Lit. 1983), Selected Poetry, 1981, Midsummer, 1984, Collected Poems, 1948-1984, 1986 (L.A. Times Book Rev. prize 1986), The Arkansas Testament, 1987, Omeros, 1990 (W.H. Smith Literary award 1991), Selected Poetry, 1993, Antiles: Fragments of Epic Memory, 1993, The Bounty, 1997, What the Twilight Says, 1998, Tiepolo's Hound, 2000, The Prodigal, 2004, Selected Poems, 2007; (plays) Henry Christophe: A Chronicle in Seven Scenes, 1950, Henry Dernier, 1951, Wine of the Country, 1953, The Sea at Dauphin: A Play in One Act, 1953, Ione: A Play with Music, 1957, Drums and Colours: An Epic Drama, 1958 (Jamaica Drama Festival prize 1958), Ti-Jean and His Brothers, 1958, Malcochon; or, Six in the Rain, 1959, Dream on Monkey Mountain, 1967 (Obie award 1971), In a Fine Castle, 1970, The Joker of Seville, 1974, The Charlatan, 1974, O Babylon!, 1976, Remembrance, 1977, Pantomine, 1978, The Isle Is Full of Noises, 1982, The Last Carnival, 1986, Beef, No Chicken, 1986, A Branch of the Blue Nile, 1986, The Odyssey, 1992. Decorated Order of the Hummingbird Trinidad and Tobago, 1969; recipient Guinness award, 1961, Nat. Writer's Coun. prize Welsh Arts Coun., 1979, Queen Elizabeth II Gold medal for poetry, 1988, Nobel Prize for lit., 1992; Rockefeller Found. fellow, 1957, 58; Eugene O'Neill Found.-Wesleyan U. fellow, 1969; MacArthur Found. grantee, 1981. Achievements include being the founder of Trinidad Theater workshop. Office: 165 Duke of Edinburgh Ave Diego Martin Trinidad and Tobago also: Farrar Straus Giroux 18 W 18th St New York NY 10011-4607

WALCOTT, JOHN L., communications executive; b. Paterson, NJ, Aug. 29, 1949; s. Henry Richards Jr. and Katharine McCauley (Fearing) W.; m. Nancy Bittles, Aug. 11, 1973; children: Jennifer James, Allison Tierney, Elizabeth Bittles. BA, Williams Coll., 1971. With Ridgewood (NJ) News, 1972, The Record, Hackensack, NJ, 1972—77; econ. corr., nat. polit. corr., chief diplomatic corr. Newsweek, 1977—86; nat. security corr. Wall St. Jour., 1986—89; fgn. editor, nat. editor US News & World Report, 1989—96; fgn. editor, news editor Knight Ridder, Inc., 1997—2002, bur. chief, 2002—06; bur. chief Washington bur. The McClatchy Co., 2006—. U.S. rep. U.N. Conf. on Media, Igls, Austria, 1983; mem. Georgetown U. Sch. Fgn. Svc. Leadership Seminar, Washington, 1985; profl. lectr. Georgetown U. Sch. Fgn. Svc., 1996—; bd. advisors SmartBrief, Inc., 1997—. Co-author: (with David C. Martin) Best Laid Plans: The Inside Story of America's War Against Terrorism, 1988. Named Disting. Friend, Georgetown U. Sch. Fgn. Svc., 1985—; recipient Edward Weintal prize Georgetown U., 1988, Edwin M. Hood award Nat. Press Club, 1983, Freedom of the Press award, 1995, Overseas Press Club award, 1983, 84, Newspaper Guild of N.Y. award, 1985, Nat. Headline award, 2005, I.F. Stone medal for Journalistic Independence, Harvard U., 2008. Mem. Overseas Writers Club (pres. 1986-88), Am. Soc. Newspapers Editors, Nat. Press Found. (bd. dirs.), Gridiron Club, Sigma Delta Chi. Presbyterian. Office: McClatchy Newspapers One Metro Ctr Ste 1000 700 12th St NW Washington DC 20005-3994 Office Phone: 202-383-6000. Business E-Mail: jwalcott@mcclatchydc.com.

WALD, ARNOLD, gastroenterologist; b. NYC, June 10, 1942; s. Jack and Ruth (Fox) W.; m. Ellen Faith Rashkow, June 26, 1966; children: Elissa Karen, Eric Lawrence. BA, Colgate U., 1964; MD, SUNY, NYC, 1968. Diplomate Am. Bd. Internal Medicine, Am. Bd. Gastroenterology. Intern Kings County Hosp., Bklyn., 1968-69, resident, chief resident, 1969-71; fellow in medicine Johns Hopkins Hosp., Balt., 1973-75; asst. prof. medicine U. Pitts. Sch. Medicine, 1978-83, assoc. prof., 1983-91, prof., 1991—2006; chief gastroenterology divsn. Montefiore U. Hosp., Pitts., 1991-95; assoc. chief divsn. gastroenterology and hepatology U. Pitts. Med. Ctr., 1993—2000, dir. fellowship tng. and edn. divsn. gastroenterology, hepatology and nutrition, 1999—2006, prof. medicine, obstetrics, gynecology and reproductive scis., 2005—06; prof. medicine U. Wis. Sch. Medicine and Pub. Health, Madison, 2006—. Head gastroenterology unit Montefiore Hosp., Pitts., 1985-91; mem. adv. bd. Internat. Found. Bowel Dysfunction, 1992—; bd. dirs. Pitts. chpt. Nat. Found. Ileitis and Colitis, Inc., 1980-84. Contbr. articles to profl. jours and books. Maj. U.S. Army, 1971-73. Master Am. Coll. Gastroenterology (bd. trustees 1991-98, gov. western Pa. 1988-90, chmn. internat. rels. com. 1993); fellow ACP, Am. Gastroent. Assn.; mem. Ctrl. Soc. Clin. Rsch. (councillor 1985-90, chmn. gastroent. sect. 1989-90), Am. Motility Soc., Internat. Found. for Functional Gastrointestinal Disorders, Gastroenterology Rsch. Group. Democrat. Jewish. Avocations: tennis, reading, hiking. Office: Sect GI and Hepatology H61 516 CSC 600 Highland Ave Madison WI 53792 Home: 2510 Marshall Pkwy Madison WI 53713 Office Phone: 608-263-4033. Business E-Mail: axw@medicine.wisc.edu.

WALD, BERNARD JOSEPH, lawyer; b. Bklyn., Sept. 14, 1932; s. Max and Ruth (Mencher) W.; m. Francine Joy Weintraub, Feb. 2, 1964; children— David Evan, Kevin Mitchell. B.B.A. magna cum laude, CCNY; J.D. cum laude, NYU, 1955. Bar: N.Y. 1955, U.S. Dist. Ct. (so. dist.) N.Y. 1960, U.S. Dist. Ct. (ea. dist.) N.Y. 1960, U.S. Ct. Appeals (2d cir.) 1960, U.S. Supreme Ct. 1971. Mem. Herzfeld & Rubin, P.C. and predecessor firms, N.Y.C., 1955—. Mem. ABA, N.Y. State Bar Assn., Assn. Bar City N.Y., N.Y. County Lawyers Assn. Office: Herzfeld & Rubin PC 40 Wall St Ste 5400 New York NY 10005-2301 Office Phone: 212-471-8475. Business E-Mail: bwald@herzfeld-rubin.com.

WALD, DOUGLAS L., lawyer; b. Sept. 16, 1954; AB, Harvard Univ., 1975, JD, 1979. Bar: D.C. 1979. Law clk. Judge William H. Timbers, US Ct. Appeals, 2d Cir., 1979—80; ptnr., chmn. Assoc. Com. Arnold & Porter, Washington, 1980—. Contbr. articles to profl. jours. Office: Arnold & Porter 555 Twelfth St NW Washington DC 20004-1206 Office Phone: 202-942-5112. Office Fax: 202-942-5999. Business E-Mail: douglas_wald@aporter.com.

WALD, MICHAEL LEONARD, public relations executive; b. Balt., Jan. 5, 1951; s. Leonard Marvin and Frances (Kosinski) Wald; m. Marlena Malmstedt, June 10, 1972. BA, Am. U., 1972; MPA, U. Ga., Athens, 2006. Mgr. Woodward and Lothrop Dept. Store, Washington, 1972-75, Hecht Co., Washington, 1975-76; store mgr. W.J. Sloane & Co., Washington, 1976-77; economist U.S. Bur. Labor Stats., Balt., 1977-85, Washington, 1985-86, Atlanta, 1986-96, S.E. regional economist, 1996—2006; pub. rels. specialist U.S. Dept. Labor, Office Pub. Affairs, Atlanta, 2007—. Lectr. fed. compensation issues. Mem. editl. bd. HR Atlanta, 1993—95; contbr. articles to profl. jours.; reviewer Monthly Labor Rev., 1992—, peer reviewer ACA Jour., 1995—99. Bd. dirs. Athens (Ga.) Habitat for Humanity, 1990—93; venue mktg. liaison mgr. 1996 Centennial Olympic Games. Recipient Commr.'s award for Outstanding Mgmt. Performance, 2000, Sec.'s Exceptional Achievement award, 2001. Mem.: Nat. Assn. Govt. Comm., Nat. Assn. Bus. Econ., Pi Alpha Alpha, Phi Kappa Phi, Am. Soc. for Pub. Adminstrn., Pub. Rels. Soc. Am., Alpha Tau Omega. Avocations: reading, home improvement, travel, history. Home: 5015 Fawn Valley Dr Loganville GA 30052-3879 Office: US Dept Labor 61 Forsyth St SW Ste 6B75 Atlanta GA 30303-8817 Home Phone: 770-267-7641; Office Phone: 404-562-2078. Business E-Mail: wald.michael@dol.gov.

WALD, NIEL, public health educator; b. NYC, Oct. 1, 1925; s. Albert and Rose (Fischel) W.; m. Lucienne Hill, May 24, 1953; children: David, Phillip. AB, Columbia U., NYC, 1945; MD, NYU, 1948. Sr. hematologist Atomic Bomb Casualty Commn., Hiroshima, Japan, 1954-57; head biologist health physics divsn. Oak Ridge Nat. Lab., 1957-58; med. rsch. and tchg. specializing in radiation medicine and cytogenetics Pitts., 1958—; mem. faculty U. Pitts. Grad. Sch. Pub. Health and Med. Sch., 1958—2004, prof. radiation health, 1962-91, prof. environ. and occupl. health, 1991—2004, prof. radiology, 1965—2004; prof. human genetics U. Pitts., 1991—2004, prof. emeritus, 2004—; chmn. dept. radiation health U. Pitts. Grad. Sch. Pub. Health and Med. Sch., 1969-76, 77-89, chmn. dept. occupl. health, 1975-76, chmn. dept. indsl. environ. health scis., 1976-77. Dir. radiation medicine dept. Presbyn.-Univ. Hosp., 1966-2004; med. dir. Clin. Cytogenetics Lab., U. Pitts., 1982-99, chmn. Radiation Safety Com. 1960-2005, radiation cytogenetics cons., 1999-2004; dir. U.S. Dept. Energy postdoctoral fellowship program in radiation scis., 1997-2004; cons. U.S. NRC Office of Nuc. Materials Safety and Safeguards, mem. adv. panel for decontamination of Three Mile Island Nuc. Power Sta. Unit 2, 1981-93, cons. adv. com. on reactor safeguards, 1989-94; mem. U.S. working group on health effects, U.S.-USSR Joint Coordinating Com. for Civilian Nuc. Reactor Safety, 1989-92; cons. USN, nuc. industries and utilities; chmn. radiol. health study sect. USPHS, 1967-71; mem. Nat. Coun. Radiation Protection and Measurements, 1969-81, consociate mem., 1981—; mem. Gov. Pa. Adv. Com. Atomic Energy Devel. and Radiation Control, 1966-84, chmn., 1974-76; mem. Pa. Dept. Environ. Protection adv. com. on low level radioactive waste disposal, 1985-2009; mem. U.S. nuc. tech. adv. group Internat. Stds. Orgn., 2003-. Contbr. numerous articles to sci. and med. publs. Vol. U.S. Citizens Def. Corps Air Warden Svc., 1943—45, capt. USAF, 1952—54. Recipient Health Physics Faculty Rsch. award U.S. Dept. Energy, 1992-95. Mem. Health Physics Soc. (pres. 1973-74), Am. Pub. Health Assn. (governing coun. 1971-73, program devel. bd. 1973-74), Radiation Rsch. Soc. (assoc. editor jour. 1965-68), Soc. Nuc. Medicine (assoc. editor jour. 1959-69), Am. Soc. Human Genetics, Am. Coll. Occupl. & Environ. Medicine, AAAS, AMA, Internat. Soc. Hematology. Achievements include research in the diagnosis and treatment of accidental human radiation injury, in human radiation dosimetry by automatic image analysis of radiation-induced chromosome aberrations, in the cytogenetics of murine radiation-induced leukemia and in health studies of irradiated human populations in U.S., Japan and Russia. Office: U Pitts Grad Sch Pub Health 100 Technology Dr Rm 561 Pittsburgh PA 15219-3130 Office Phone: 412-624-2735. Business E-Mail: wald@pitt.edu.

WALD, PATRICIA MCGOWAN, retired federal judge; b. Torrington, Conn., Sept. 16, 1928; d. Joseph F. and Margaret (O'Keefe) McGowan; m. Robert L. Wald, June 22, 1952; children: Sarah, Douglas, Johanna, Frederica, Thomas. BA, Conn. Coll., 1948; LLB, Yale U., 1951; HHD (hon.), Mt. Vernon Jr. Coll., 1980; LLD (hon.), George Washington Law Sch., 1983, CUNY, 1984, Notre Dame U., John Jay Sch. Criminal Justice, Mt. Holyoke Coll., 1985, Georgetown U., 1987, Villanova U., Amherst Coll., NY Law Sch., 1988, Colgate U., 1989, Hofstra U., 1991, New Eng. Coll., 1991, Vermont Law Sch., 1995; LLD, Yale U., 2001, Duke U., 2008. Bar: DC 1952. Clk. to Hon. Jerome Frank US Ct. Appeals, 1951—52; assoc. Arnold, Fortas & Porter, Washington, 1952—53; mem. DC Crime Commn., 1964—65; atty. Office of Criminal Justice, 1967—68, Neighborhood Legal Svc., Washington, 1968—70; co-dir. Ford Found. Project on Drug Abuse, 1970, Ctr. for Law and Social Policy, 1971—72, Mental Health Law Project, 1972—77; asst. atty. gen. for legis. affairs US Dept. Justice, Washington, 1977—79; judge US Ct. Appeals (DC cir.), 1979—99, chief judge, 1986—91; judge Internat. Criminal Tribunal for Former Yugoslavia, The Hague, Netherlands, 1999—2001. Bd. dirs. Am. Constn. Soc., 2002—. Author: Law and Poverty, 1965; co-author: Bail in the United States, 1964, Dealing with Drug Abuse, 1973; bd. editors: ABA Jour., 1978—86; contbr. articles to profl. jours. Mem. Commn. on Intelligence Capabilities of the US Regarding Weapons of Mass Destruction, 2004—05; trustee Ford Found., 1972—77, Phillips Exeter Acad., 1975—77, Agnes Meyer Found., 1976—77, Conn. Coll., 1976—77; active Carnegie Coun. on Children, 1972—77; bd. dirs. Mental Disability Rights Internat., 2002—. Recipient Lifetime Achievement award, Am. Lawyer mag., 2004; named one of 100 Most Influential Lawyers in America, Nat. Law Jour., 2006, 50 Most Influential Women Lawyers in America, 2007. Mem.: ABA (exec. bd. 1994—99, ABA Medal 2008), Ctrl. and Ea. European Law Inst., Am. Constitution Soc. (bd. dirs. 2004—), Am. Philos. Assn., Inst. Justice Initiative (bd. dirs.), Am. Acad. Arts and Scis., Am. Law Inst. (coun. mem. 1979—, exec. com. 1985—99, 2d v.p. 1988—93, 1st v.p. 1993—98), Open Soc. Inst. (Justice Initiative chair 2002—04), Phi Beta Kappa. Office: 2101 Connecticut Ave NW Washington DC 20008 Personal E-mail: patwald2@cs.com.

WALD, PETER ALLEN, lawyer; b. 1953; AB magna cum laude, Brown U., 1974; JD magna cum laude, Harvard U., 1977. Bar: Calif. 1979. Law clk. to Hon. James R. Browning US Ct. Appeals (9th cir.), 1977—78; ptnr. Latham & Watkins LLP, San Francisco, 1996—, global dept. chair, litig. dept. and chair, Bay Area litig. dept. Notes editor Harvard Law Rev., 1977. Named one of The Nation's Top Litigators, The Nat. Law Jour., 2006. Mem.: Phi Beta Kappa. Office: Latham & Watkins LLP Ste 2000 505 Montgomery St San Francisco CA 94111-2562 Office Phone: 415-395-8006. Office Fax: 415-395-8095. E-mail: peter.wald@lw.com.

WALD, RICHARD CHARLES, media consultant, educator; b. NYC; s. Joseph S. and Lily (Forstate) W.; m. Edith May Leslie; children: Matthew Leslie, Elizabeth Tole, Jonathan Simon. BA, Columbia U., 1952, MA, 1953; AB, Clare Coll., Cambridge, 1955. From reporter to mng. editor NY Herald Tribune, 1951—66; asst. mng. editor Washington Post, 1967; exec. v.p. Whitney Comm. Corp., NYC, 1968; pres. NBC News, 1968-77; asst. to chmn. bd. Times-Mirror Co., LA; sr. v.p. ABC News, 1978—99, sr. v.p. editl. quality, 1993—99; Fred Friendly Prof. Journalism Columbia U., 1999—. Annotator: (with James Bellows) The World of Jimmy Breslin, 1967; bd. Columbia Daily Spectator. Bd. dir. Correspondents Fund. Mem.: Fedn. Am. Scientists. Office: Columbia Sch Journalism 2950 Broadway New York NY 10027 E-mail: rew25@columbia.edu.

WALD, ROBERT LEWIS, lawyer; b. Worcester, Mass., Sept. 9, 1926; s. Lewis and Freda Ann (Rosenfield) W.; m. Patricia Ann McGowan, June 22, 1952; children: Sarah Elizabeth, Douglas Robert, Johanna Margaret, Frederica Nora, Thomas Robert. AB, Harvard U., 1947; LLB, Yale U., 1951. Bar: Mass. 1951, D.C. 1959, U.S. Ct. Appeals (4th cir.) 1957, U.S. Supreme Ct. 1957, U.S. Ct. Appeals (D.C. cir.) 1959, U.S. Ct. Appeals (6th cir.) 1975. Clerk to Judge Irving R. Kaufman U.S. Dist. Ct. (so. dist.) N.Y., 1951-52; asst. to gen. counsel, chief div. export trade FTC, Washington, 1954—56; ptnr. Wald, Harkrader & Ross and predecessors, Washington, 1961—87, Nussbaum & Wald, Washington, 1989—96; sr. counsel Baach Robinson & Lewis, Washington, 1996—. Dir., trustee Washington Lawyers' Com. for Civil Rights, Urban Affairs and predecessor, 1969—, co-chmn., 1976—78; dir. Romanian-Am. Enterprise Fund, 1994—97, chmn., 1994—96; dir. Global Rights and predecessor, 1991—, Frederic B. Abramson Mem. Found., 1998—; hon. dir. Capital Area Immigrants' Rights Coalition, 1999—; dir. Internat. Sr. Lawyers Project, 2001—; bd. mgmt. trustees Internat. Assn. Women Judges, 1997—. Served to lt. USNR, 1944-46, 52-53. Mem. ABA, D.C. Bar Assn. Home: 2101 Connecticut Ave NW Washington DC 20008-1728 Office: Baach Robinson & Lewis 1201 F St NW Ste 500 Washington DC 20004 Office Phone: 202-833-8900. Business E-Mail: robert.wald@baachrobinson.com.

WALD, SYLVIA, artist; b. Phila., Oct. 30, 1915; Student, Moore Inst. Art, Sci. and Industry. One-woman shows include U. Louisville, 1945, 49, Kent State Coll., 1945, Nat. Serigraph Soc., 1946, Grand Central Moderns, N.Y.C., 1957, Devorah Sherman Gallery, Chgo., 1960, New Sch., 1967, Book Gallery, White Plains, N.Y., 1968, Benson Gallery, Bridgehampton, L.I., 1977, Knoll Internat., Munich, 1979, Amerika Havs, Munich, 1979, Aaron Berman Gallery, N.Y.C., 1981, Hirschlt and Adler Gallery, 1994, New Britain (Conn.) Mus., 1994, Dongah Art Gallery, Seoul, Korea, 1995, Hanlim Art Gallery, Daejūn, 1995-96, Kwangju City Art Mus, Pusan, Korea, Dong Shin U., Kwangju, 1996, Chosun U. Mus., Kwangju City, 2001, Chosun Univ. Mus. Art, Kwangju, Korea, 2002, 05, Tenri Gallery, N.Y.C., 2004, 05; exhibited in group shows at Nat. Sculpture Soc., 1940, Sculpture Internat., Phila., 1940, Chgo. Art Inst., 1941, Bklyn. Mus., 1975, Libr. of Congress, 1943, 52, 58, Smithsonian Instn., 1954, Internat. Print Exhbn., Salzburg and Vienna, 1952, 2d Sao Paulo Biennial, 1953, N.Y. Cultural Ctr., 1973, Mus. Modern Art, N.Y.C., 1975, Benson Gallery, Bridgehampton, L.I., 1982, Dumon-Landis Gallery, New Brunswick, N.J., 1982-83, Suzuki Gallery, N.Y.C., 1982, Sid Deutch Gallery, N.Y.C., 1983, Aaron Berman Gallery, N.Y.C., 1983, Full House Gallery, Kingston, N.J., 1984, Nabi Gallery, Sag Harbor, N.Y., 1989, Worcester Mus., 1991, Boston Mus. Fine Arts, 1991, Hirschl and Adler Gallery, N.Y.C., 1993, Celebrations of Women Artist, 2008, Parrish Mus., Southampton, 2002, Tenri Galleru, NYC, 2005, 2x13 Gallery, 2006, Korea Gallery, 2006, Hinschl and Adler Gallery, NYC, 2007-08, A Parallel Presence, Zimmerla Art Mus., NYC, UBC Art Gallery, NYC, 2009, Sylvia Wald & Pokim Gallery, NYC, 2009, others; represented in permanent collections Aetna Oil Co., AAUW, Ball State Tchrs. Coll., Bibliotheque Nat., Paris, Bklyn. Mus., Howard U., State U. Iowa, Libr. of Congress, U. Louisville, Nat. Gallery, Mus. Modern Art, Phila. Mus., N.C. Mus., Rose Mus. Art at Brandeis U., Whitney Mus., N.Y.C., Finch Coll. Mus., N.Y.C., U. Nebr., Ohio U., U. Okla., Princeton, Victoria and Albert Mus., Walker Gallery, Worcester (Mass.) Art Mus., Guggenheim Mus., N.Y.C., Grunewald Mus., UCLA, Rutgers Mus., N.J., Aschenbach Collection Mus., San Francisco, Grunewald Coll. Mus. UCLA, Wellesley Coll.; acquisitions Yale U. Art Gallery, 1998, Cleve. Mus., 1998; contbr. articles to profl. jours. Address: 417 Lafayette St New York NY 10003-7005 Home Phone: 212-673-0437. Personal E-mail: pokim417@yahoo.com.

WALDECK, DAVID H., chemistry professor; b. Cin. married. PhD, U. Chgo., 1983. Postdoc. fellow U. Calif., Berkeley, 1983—85; chemistry faculty U. Pitts., Pitts., 1985—. Author: (textboook) Principles of Physical Chemistry. Office: Univ Pitts 219 Parkman Ave Pittsburgh PA 15260

WALDECK, JOHN WALTER, JR., lawyer; b. Cleve., May 3, 1949; s. John Walter Sr. and Marjorie Ruth (Palenschat) W.; m. Cheryl Gene Cutter, Sept. 10, 1977; children: John III, Matthew, Rebecca. BS, John Carroll U., 1973; JD, Cleve. State U., 1977. Bar: Ohio 1977, cert.: Ohio State Bar Assn. (in bus., comml. and indsl. real property law) 2007. Product applications chemist Synthetic Products Co., Cleve., 1969—76; assoc. Arter & Hadden, Cleve., 1977—85, ptnr., 1986—88, Porter, Wright, Morris and Arthur, Cleve., 1988—90, ptnr. in charge, 1990—96; ptnr. Walter & Haverfield LLP, Cleve., 1996—, mem. exec. com., 2003—07. Bd. advisors Litigation Mgmt., Inc., 2000—04. Chmn. Bainbridge Twp. Bd. Zoning Appeals, Chagrin Falls, Ohio, 1984-94; trustee Greater Cleve. chpt. Lupus Found. Am., 1978-91, sec., 1979-86; trustee LeBlond Housing Corp., Cleve., 1990-96, sec., 1996, Univ. Circle, Inc., 1993-97, Fairmount Ctr. for Performing and Fine Arts, Novelty, Ohio, 1993-96, sect., 1994-95; bd. dirs. Geauga County Mental Health Recovery Svc. Bd., Chardon, Ohio, 1988-97, treas., 1991-93, vice-chmn., 1993-95, chmn., 1995-97; mem. bd. advisors Palliative Care Svcs., Cleve. Clinic Cancer Ctr., 1989-91; specialization bd. Real Property Law, 2007-, chmn., 2009-. Named an Ohio Super Lawyer, Law & Politics Mag., 2007—09. Mem. Ohio State Bar Assn. (real property sect. bd. govs. 1992, 2008-, real property specialty cert. bd. 2007—, cert. real property specialist, 2007—), Greater Cleve. Bar Assn. (real property, corp. banking sect, co-chair real estate law inst. 1990, 95, 96). Roman Catholic. Avocations: beekeeping, gardening, jogging. Home: 18814 Rivers Edge Dr W Chagrin Falls OH 44023-4968 Office: Walter & Haverfield LLP suite 3500 1301 E Ninth St Cleveland OH 44114 Office Phone: 216-781-1212. Business E-Mail: jwaldeck@walterhav.com.

WALDEN, DANA, broadcast executive; BA in Comm., U. So. Calif. Formerly with Bender, Goldman & Helper; former v.p. mktg. Arsenio Hall Comm., Paramount; former sr. v.p. media and corp. rels. 20th Century Fox TV, v.p. current programming, 1994—96, former v.p. drama, former sr. v.p. drama, former exec. v.p. drama devel., pres., 1999—, chmn., 2007—. Named one of The 100 Most Powerful Women in Entertainment, Hollywood Reporter, 1999—2007. Mem.: Hollywood Radio and TV Soc. (v.p. 2003—). Office: 20th Century Fox TV 10201 W Pico Blvd Bldg 88 Rm 29 Los Angeles CA 90035

WALDEN, GREG, United States Representative from Oregon; b. The Dalles, Oreg., Jan. 10, 1957; s. Paul Walden; m. Mylene Walden; 1 child. BS in Journalism, U. Oreg., Eugene, 1981. Press sec. Staff of US Rep. Denny Smith of Oreg., 1981—84, chief of staff, 1984—86; owner Columbia Gorge Broadcasters, Inc., The Dalles, 1986—; mem. Oreg. State Ho. Reps., 1989-95, majority leader, 1991-93; mem. Oreg. State Senate, 1995-97, asst. majority leader, 1995-97; mem. US Congress from 2nd Oreg. dist., 1999—, mem. energy and commerce com., vice chmn. oversight and investigations subcommittee, mem. energy independence and global warming com., dep. whip, 2002—. Owner MSW Comm. Bd. dirs., exec. com. Assn. Oreg. Industries; bd. dirs. Oreg. Health Scis. Found. Recipient Benjamin Franklin award, 60+ Assn., Pub. Svc. award, Am. Coll. Nurse-Midwives, Thomas Jefferson award, Food Distbrs. Internat., Disting. Svc. award, Forest Counties Schs. Coalition, Champion award, League Pvt. Property Owners, Congl. Champion award, Nat. Assn. Svc. Conservation Corps, Wheat Adv. award, Nat. Assn. Wheat Growers, Appreciation award, Oreg. Nat. Guard, Sr. Legis. Achievement award, Seniors Coalition, Spirit of Enterprise award, US C. of C., Golden Bulldog award, Watchdog of Treasury; named Outstanding Young Oregonian, Oreg. Jaycees, 1991, Legislator of Yr., Nat. Rep. Legislators Assn., 1993, Agr. Retailers Assn., Ctrl. Oreg. Visitors Assn., Nat. Assn. Home Care, Nat. Rural Health Assn., Oreg. Assn. Home Care, Oreg. Rural Electric Coop. Assn., Safari Club Internat., Oreg. Person of Yr., Dorchester Conf.; named a Hero of Taxpayer, Americans for Tax Reform, Friend of Shareholder, Am. Shareholders Assn., Friend of Pear Industry, N.W. Pear Industry, Friend of Farm Bur., Oreg. Farm Bur. Mem.: Nat. Fedn. Ind. Bus., Hood River C. of C., Elks Club, Rotary Club. Republican. Episcopalian. Office: US House Reps 1210 Longworth House Office Bldg Washington DC 20515 Office Phone: 202-225-6730. Office Fax: 202-225-5774. E-mail: greg.walden@mail.house.gov.*

WALDEN, JAMES WILLIAM, accountant, educator; b. Jellico, Tenn., Mar. 5, 1936; s. William Evert and Bertha L. (Faulkner) Walden; m. Eva June Selvia, Jan. 16, 1957 (dec. Aug. 1988); 1 child, James William; m. Hattie Nan Lamb, Jan. 6, 1990 (div. June 1992); m. Janet Faulkner, Aug. 12, 1993 (div. May 2001); m. Louise Davis, Apr. 28, 2004. BS, Miami U., Oxford, Ohio, 1963; MBA, Xavier U., Cin., 1966. CPA Ohio. Tchr. math. Middletown (Ohio) City Sch. Dist., 1963-67, Fairfield (Ohio) High Sch., 1967-69; instr. accounting Sinclair Community Coll., Dayton, Ohio, 1969-72, asst. prof., 1972-75, assoc. prof., 1975-78, prof., 1978-89, prof. emeritus, 1991—. Cons., public acct.; mem. adj. faculty in acctg. Capital U., 1980—. Group comdr., fin. officer and chief staff Ohio wing CAP; bd. dirs. Frankin Cmty. Svcs.; bd. dir. Franklin Food Pantry. With USAF, 1954—59. Mem.: Campbell County Libr. Bd., Ohio Soc. CPAs, Greater Hamilton Estate Planning Coun., Nat. Soc. Pub. Accts., Pub. Accts. Soc. Ohio (pres. S.W. chpt. 1985—86), Springboro C. of C. (bd. dirs., treas.), Kiwanis (pres. Springboro chpt.), Lions, Rotary, Butler County Torch Club, Am. Legion (life), Beta Alpha Psi. Office: Sinclair CC 251 Siler St Jellico TN 37762 Office Phone: 423-784-1502. Personal E-mail: jwalden@one.net.

WALDEN, JENNIFER LEE, plastic surgeon; b. Austin, Tex., Nov. 17, 1971; d. Richard M. and Shirley T. Walden. BA, U. Tex., Austin, 1994, MD, 1998. Intern U. Tex., Galveson, 1998—99, resident in plastic surgery, 1999—2003; aesthetic surgery fellow Manhattan Eye, Ear and Throat Hosp., NYC, 2003—04, asst. attending, 2004—, Lenox Hill Hosp., NYC, 2004—. Co-dir. Nat. Student Rsch. Forum. Contbr. articles to profl. jours. Med. mission vol. surgeon Austin Smiles, 2005—06; med. vol. NYC Dept. of Health Med. Res. Corps. Recipient Mavis P. Kelsey Excellence in Medicine award, Kelsey Seybold Found., Houston, 1998, Hermann Barnett Meml. award, U. Tex., 1998, Janet M. Glasgow Meml. award, Am. Med. Women's Assn., 1998, Merck Manual award, Merck and Co., 1998, Best Sci. Exhibit award, Am. Soc. for Aesthetic Plastic Surgery, 2004; Vaughn Found. scholar, U. Tex., 1995—97, Isabella H. Brackenridge scholar, 1996, 1998, Donald P. Duncan Meml. scholar, 1997. Mem.: ACS (assoc.; plastic and maxillofacial surgery adv. coun. 2002—03), NY Med. Soc., NY County Med. Soc., Northeastern Soc. Plastic Surgeons, Assn. Women Surgeons, Am. Soc. Plastic

Surgeons, Alpha Omega Alpha (Tex. alpha chpt. pres. 1997—98), Pi Beta Phi (ednl. enrichment chair 1993—94). Office: 50 E 71st St New York NY 10021 Office Fax: 212-737-8340. E-mail: drjenniferwalden@hotmail.com.

WALDEN, JOSEPH LAWRENCE, career officer; b. Paducah, Ky., Oct. 2, 1956; s. Thomas Lorenzo and Betty Jo (Miller) W.; m. Julia Kay Johnson, Oct. 9, 1982; children: Amber Marie, Bobbi Michelle. BS in Rural Sociology, N.C. State U., 1978; MBA, Fla. Inst. Tech., Melbourne, 1988; MS in Sys. Mgmt., Fla. Inst. Tech., 1989; grad., USAF Command and Staff Coll., 1990, U.S. Army/Command Gen. Staff, 1992, U.S. Air War Coll., 1997; MS in Strategic Planning, U.S. Army Command/Gen. Staff Coll., 2001. Commd. U.S. Army, 1978, advanced through grades col., to date, supply platoon leader 25th Inf. divsn. Schofield Barracks, Hawaii, 1979-81, supply control officer, 1981-82, installation supply officer Signal Sch. Ft. Gordon, Ga., 1983, brigade logistics officer 2d Signal Brigade, 1983-84; co. comdr. Co. B, 3rd Batallion, 2d Signal Brigade, Ft. Gordon, 1984-86; logistics plans officer Combat Devel., Quartermaster Sch., Ft. Lee, Va., 1988-89; chief gen. support U.S. Army Quartermaster Sch., Ft. Lee, 1989-91; assigned to U.S. Army Command and Gen. Staff Coll., Ft. Leavenworth, Kans., 1991-92; exec. officer 19th Corps Materiel Mgmt. Ctr., Wiesbaden, Germany, 1992-94; chief supply mgmt. 3D Corps Support Command, Wiesbaden, 1994-95; comdr. Materiel Mgmt. Ctr., Ft. Irwin, Calif., 1995-97; program mgr. Logistics Reengring., Ft. Lee, Va., 1997-99; sr. fellow adv. operational art Ft. Leavenworth, Kans., 1999-2000; mem. faculty U.S. Army Sch. Advanced Mil. Studies, 2000-2001; comdr. nat. tng. Ctr. Theater Support Command, Ft. Irwin, Calif., 2001—03; dir. Sch. of Command Preparation, Ft. Leavenworth, Kans., 2003—04; exec. dir. Supply Chain Rsch. Inst., 2004—; lectr., supply chain mgmt. U. Kans., 2009—. Mem. adj. faculty St. Leo Coll., Ft. Lee, 1988-91; mem. faculty City Coll. of Chgo., 1994-95, Webster Univ., 2004—; pres. Walden Fitness Systems, Ft. Leavenworth, 1984-92. Author: The Forklifts Have Nothing To Do!, 2003, Velocity Management, 2005, Modeling and Benchmark Supply Chain Leadership, 2009; contbr. articles to profl. jour. Mem. Bldg. Code Appeals Bd., City of Hopewell, 1988-91; vol. staff Negro Leagues Baseball Mus., Kansas City, Mo., 2001. Named Armed Forces Powerlifting Champion, 1983, Va. State Powerlifting Champion, 1983, Kans. State Powerlifting Champion, 1992, Nat. Powerlifting Champion, 1992, European Armed Forces Powerlifting Champion, 1993, 1994, Supply Chain Practitioner of Yr., Spply and Demand Chain Exec. Mag., 2004; named one of Top 10 Logistics Execs. in Am., Logistics and Supply Chain Forum, 2003. Mem. APICS (cert. fellow in prodn. and inventory mgmt.), Internat. Soc. of Logistics (demonstrated master logistician), Warehousing Edn. and Rsch. Coun. (mem. edn. com., dir. edn., bd. dirs. 2008-09), Material Handling Mgmt. Soc., Va. Assn. of U.S. Powerlifting Fedn. (pres. 1989-91), U.S. Golf Assn., Am. Sunbathing Assn., Fellowship Christian Athletes, Fla. Sheriffs Assn., San Diego Zool. Soc., Assn. Quartermasters, Mus. Tolerance, Save the Manatee Club. Republican. Methodist. Avocations: powerlifting, golf. Office Phone: 760-447-3651. E-mail: joewalden@supplychainresearch.com.

WALDEN, OLGA ASCHER, music educator; b. Hamburg, Germany, May 19, 1930; came to U.S., 1952; d. Viktor and Martha M. (Schuett) Ascher; married, Nov. 20, 1955 (dec. July 1979); m. Roy Walden, Oct. 2, 2004. MusB, U. So. Calif., 1954, MusM, 1957, PhD, 1970. Instr. music Stevenson Jr. H.S., LA, 1954-57, Fairfax H.S., LA, 1957-72; asst. prof. music Calif. State U., LA, 1972-76, assoc.prof. music, 1976-81, prof. music, 1981-96, part-time prof. music, 1996—2003, prof. emeritus, 1997—. Instr. voice classes LA City Coll., 1957-64; instr. music history and theory Pasadena City Coll., Calif., 1973-76; vis. prof. musicology Claremont Grad. Sch., Calif., 1986, 1995, 1998, 2002, Pomona Coll., 2003; diction coach, LA Opera, 2005. Contbr. articles to music revs. and profl. publs.; translator various German-English articles for profl. jours. Mem. edit. bd. Jour. of the Arnold Schoenberg Inst., 1974-81; bd. dirs. Glendale (Calif.) Chamber Orch., 1985-89, CSULA Friends of Music, pres., 1997—2007; vp. bd. dirs. Pacific Contemporary Music Ctr., 1987-96, newsletter editor, 1988-96; substitute soloist 1st Ch. Christian Scientist, Alhambra, Calif., 1990-2001; bd. dirs. Neighborhood Music Sch. Music scholar Ebell Club, 1953-54, Fulbright grantee, Venice, Italy, 1966-67, Calif. State U. Instnl. grantee, 1974-75, 75-76; recipient Trustees' Outstanding Prof. award Calif. State U. Sys., 1990. Mem. NEA, Am. Musicol. Soc. (Pacific S.W. chpt. sec. 1981-83, v.p. 1984-86, pres. 1986-88, elective counselor 1990-92), Coll. Music Soc. (life), Calif. Music Tchrs. Assn., Music Tchrs. Assn. Calif. (Glendale br.), Friends of Music Calif. State U. L.A., Phi Kappa Phi, Phi Kappa Lambda. Democrat. Avocations: concerts, operas, museums. Home: 4278 Sea View Ln Los Angeles CA 90065-3350 Home Phone: 323-225-8087. Personal E-mail: owalden@roadrunner.com.

WALDERA, WAYNE EUGENE, crisis management executive; b. Cayuga, ND, Mar. 23, 1930; s. Bernard Cyril and Eleanor Nee (Kugler) W.; m. Eva Jenzene Personius, Jan. 13, 1958; children: Anthony, Lori, Mia, Shauna. BSBA, N.D. State U., 1952. With Gamble-Skogmo, 1954-88; pres. Gamble div. Gamble-Skogmo, Mpls., 1972-88; pres., CEO Retail Resource Co., Mpls., 1988-89, Amdura Corp., Denver, 1989-92, also bd. dirs.; chmn. Sullivan Waldera, Inc., Mpls., 1992-93; prin., CEO Waldera & Co. Inc., Mpls., 1993—. 1st lt. USAF, 1952-54. Home: 12125 62nd St Waconia MN 55387-9411 Office: Waldera & Co Inc 700 Twelve Oaks Ctr Dr Ste 208 Wayzata MN 55391-1435 Business E-Mail: wwaldera@questoffice.net.

WALDHAUSEN, JOHN ANTON, retired surgeon, editor; b. NYC, May 22, 1929; s. Max. H. and Agnes H. (Stettner) W.; m. Marian Trescher, June 4, 1957; children: John H., Robert Rodney, Anthony Gordon Scarlett. BS magna cum laude, Coll. Great Falls, 1950; MD, St. Louis U., 1954. Diplomate Am. Bd. Surgery, Am. Bd. Thoracic Surgery. Intern Johns Hopkins Hosp., 1954-55, resident, 1955-57; clin. asst. Nat. Heart and Lung Inst., NIH, 1957-59; resident Hosp. U. Pa., 1959, Ind. U. Med. Ctr., 1960-62; practice medicine specializing in cardiothoracic surgery Indpls., 1962-66, Phila., 1966-70; mem. staff Milton S. Hershey Med. Ctr., Hershey, Pa., 1969-96. From instr. to asst. prof. Ind. U. Med. Ctr., 1962—66; assoc. prof. surgery U. Pa., Phila., 1966—70; prof. surgery Pa. State U. Coll. Medicine/Milton S. Hershey Med. Ctr, 1966—83, chmn. dept. surgery, 1969—94, sr. mem. grad. faculty, 1970—94, interim provost, dean, 1972—73, assoc. dean health care, 1973—75, assoc. dean and dir. Univ. Physicians, 1993—96, J.W. Oswald prof., 1983—99, J.W. Oswald prof. emeritus, 1999—; trustee U. Great Falls, Mont., 2001—04. Mem. editl. bd. Jour. Cardiovasc. Surgery, 1985-93, Jour. Pediatric Surgery, 1972-78, Jour. Thoracic and Cardiovasc. Surgery, 1982, editor, 1994-2000; cons. editor Archives of Surgery, 1972-74; contbr. chpts. to books and articles to med. jours. Recipient Career Devel. award USPHS, 1964. Fellow AAAS; mem. AMA, ACS (chpt. pres. 1974-75, gov. 1979-85, chmn. adv. coun. cardiothoracic surgery 1992-97), Am. Acad. Pediat., Am. Assn. Surgery of Trauma, Am. Coll. Cardiology (sec. 1981-82, trustee 1984-89, mem. editl. bd. jour. 1983, assoc. editor 1986-89), Am. Fedn. Clin. Rsch., Am. Heart Assn., Am. Physiol. Soc., Am. Soc. Artificial Internal Organs, Am. Assn. Thoracic Surgery (1st v.p. 1990-91, pres., 1991-92), Am. Surg. Assn. (1st v.p. 1984-85), Ctrl. Surg. Assn., Internat. Cardiovasc. Soc. (chpt. recorder 1969-74), Pa. Assn. Thoracic Surgery (pres. 1977-78), Thoracic Surgery Dirs. Assn. (pres. 1977-79), Societe International de Chirurgie (membership chmn. 1987-92, treas. 1992-94), Soc. Clin. Surgery (treas. 1971-80, v.p. 1981-82, Pres. 1982-83), Soc. Surg. Chairmen, Soc. Thoracic Surgeons, Soc. Univ. Surgeons, Soc. Vascular Surgery, So. Surg. Assn., Sigma Xi, Alpha Omega Alpha. Home: 515 Bridgeview Dr Lemoyne PA 17043 Office: Pa State U Coll Med MS Hershey Med Ctr PO Box 850 Hershey PA 17033-0850 Office Phone: 717-531-8329. Personal E-mail: jwaldhausen@aol.com.

WALDHORN, ARTHUR, literature educator, researcher, scriptwriter; b. NYC, Sept. 30, 1918; s. David Mark Waldhorn and Carolyn Barnett; m. Hilda Kurland, Dec. 24, 1942 (dec. 1999); children: Valerie M. Auerbach, Stephen Edward. B.A. with honors in English, NYU, 1938, PhD in English and Am. Lit., 1950. Instr. English CCNY, NYC, 1945—53, asst. prof. English, 1953—57, assoc. prof English, 1957—67, prof. English, 1967—76; vis. adj. prof. English NYU, 1978—81. Dir. Davis Ctr. for Performing Arts CCNY, 1972—73; Fulbright prof., Italy, 1958, England, 65, Japan, 73. Author: (television documentary) The Stations of Bach, Reader's Guide to Ernest Hemingway, Hemingway and Faulkner In Their Time; editor: Ernest Hemingway, Good Reading. Recipient 125th Anniversary Svc. award medal, CCNY, 1973. Mem.: MLA (life). Democrat. Home: 7 Stuyvesant Oval New York NY 10009 Office: The City College of New York 135 Street Convent Ave New York NY 10031 Personal E-mail: hawk22@nyc.rr.com.

WALDINGER, ROGER, social studies educator; b. NYC, Oct. 22, 1953; s. Hermann V. and Renee Waldinger; m. Hilary K. Kantrowitz; children: Max Ethan, Miriam Suzanna, Joseph Daniel. PhD, Harvard U., Cambridge, Mass., 1983. Asst. prof. Dept. Sociology City Coll. CUNY, NYC, 1983—87, assoc. prof., 1987—90; prof. Dept. Sociology, UCLA, LA, 1990—2007, disting. prof., 2007—. Fellowship, John Simon Guggenheim Meml. Found., 2008. Office: Dept Sociology UCLA 264 Haines Hall Los Angeles CA 90095 Office Fax: 310-206-9838. Business E-Mail: waldinge@soc.ucla.edu.

WALDKOETTER, RAYMOND OLIVER, psychologist, consultant; b. Indpls., Oct. 25, 1928; s. Raymond Oliver Waldkoetter, Sr. and Viola Simmons Waldkoetter; m. Mary Frances McBane, Sept. 25, 1953; children: Lisa K. Keenan, Greta A. Banner, Eric R., William H., Janet M. Turko, Olivia E. BS in Edn., Ind. U., 1951, MS in Edn., 1955, EdD in Psychol. Studies, 1963. Cert. psychologist Ind. Health Professions Bur. Dir. student activities U. Toledo, 1957—59; expatriate tutor Techiman Tng. Coll., Abetifi, Ghana, 1959—60; counselor Testing Bur. Depauw U., Greencastle, Ind., 1960—61; rsch. psychologist Enlisted Evaluation Ctr., Ft. Harrison, Ind., 1961—63, tech. advisor, 1965—73; dean of students Shepherd Coll., Shepherdstown, W.Va., 1963—64; sr. rsch. psychologist Army Rsch. Inst., Alexandria, Va., 1974—82; consulting psychologist U.S. Army Soldier Support Ctr., Ft. Harrison, 1982—93; pvt. practice Greenwood, Ind., 1993—. Mem. bd. advisors The Monroe Inst., Faber, Va., 1986—. Capt. USMC, 1951—59. Recipient Harry Greer award, Internat. Mil. Testing Assn., USN, 1983, Comdrs. award for Civil Svc., Dept. of the Army, 1993. Mem.: APA, Masons, Phi Delta Kappa, Theta Xi. Methodist. Achievements include personnel rating form design; sound-wave acoustic therapy; occupational analysis for performance enhancement. Avocations: reading, parapsychology, travel.

WALDMAN, MICHAEL, economist, educator; b. Paterson, NJ, May 12, 1955; s. Henry and Nettie Waldman; m. Karen Voris, July 9, 1982 (div. Jan. 1992); m. Lisa Berki, July 18, 1999; children: David Henry, Emma Nicole. BS in Econs., MIT, 1977; PhD in Econs., U. Pa., 1982. From asst. prof. to prof. econs. UCLA, 1983-93; prof. econs. Cornell U., Ithaca, NY, 1991-97, Charles H. Dyson prof. in mgmt., 1997—. Vis. prof. econs. Yale U. Sch. Orgn. and Mgmt., New Haven, 1989—90, U. Chgo. Grad. Sch. Bus., 1997—99. Co-editor: Jour. Econ. Perspectives, 2000—06; assoc. editor: Quar. Jour. Econs., 2000—; contbr. articles to profl. jours. Recipient Warren C. Scoville Disting. Tchg. award, Dept. Economics, UCLA, 1984—86, Faculty Rsch. award, Johnson Grad. Sch. Mgmt., Cornell U., 2003. Mem.: Indsl. Orgn. Soc. (mem. program com. 2009), Western Econ. Assn., Soc. Labor Economists, Royal Econ. Soc., Econometric Soc., Am. Econ. Assn. (program com. 2004). Office: Cornell U Johnson Grad Sch Mgmt Sage Hall Ithaca NY 14853 Business E-Mail: mw46@cornell.edu.

WALDMAN, MICHAEL, lawyer; b. 1960; BA, Columbia Coll., 1982; JD, NYU Sch. Law, 1987. Pvt. practice, NYC; dir. Pub. Citizen's Congress Watch; spl. asst. to Pres. for policy coordination The White House, 1993—95, dir. speechwriting, 1995—99; dir. Brennan Ctr. for Justice, 2005—. Lectr. pub. policy John F. Kennedy Sch. Govt., Harvard U., 2001—03. Author: Who Robbed America? A Citizens' Guide to the Savings and Loan Scandal, 1990, POTUS Speaks: Finding the Words that Defined the Clinton Presidency, 2000, My Fellow Americans: The Most Important Speeches of American Presidents, 2003. Office: Brennan Center for Justice NYU School of Law 161 6th Ave 12th Fl New York NY 10013 Office Phone: 212-887-6730. Office Fax: 212-995-4550. E-mail: brennancenter@nyu.edu.*

WALDMAN, STEVEN, editor; Former advisor to CEO Corp. Nat. Svcs.; editor Washington Monthly; nat. editor US News & World Report; CEO, co-founder, editor-in-chief Beliefnet.com, 1999—. Contbr. articles to numerous profl. jours.; TV Appearances CNN, Fox News, ABC News, Radio Appearances Nat. Pub. Radio; author: The Bill (a textbook used in college courses around the US); regular contbr. Slate & National Review; author: Founding Faith: Providence, Politics, and the Birth of Religious Freedom in America, 2008. Recipient Nat. Mag. award for General Excellence in Online Jour., Am. Soc. Mag. Editors, 2007; named one of Nation's top "spiritual innovators", Time Mag., 2000. Jewish. Office: BeliefNet Inc Box 1062 303 Park Ave S New York NY 10010 Fax: 212-533-1492.

WALDMANN, THOMAS ALEXANDER, medical researcher, physician; b. NYC, Sept. 21, 1930; s. Charles Elizabeth (Sipos) Waldmann; m. Katharine Emory Spreng, Mar. 29, 1958; children: Richard Allen, Robert James, Carol Ann. AB, U. Chgo., 1951; MD, Harvard U., 1955; PhD (hon.), U. Med. Sch., Debrecin, Hungary, 1991. Diplomate Am. Bd. Allergy and Immunology. Intern Mass. Gen. Hosp., Boston, 1955—56; clin. assoc. Nat. Cancer Inst., NIH, Bethesda, Md., 1956—58, sr. investigator, 1958—68, head Immunophysiology Sect., 1968—73, chief Metabolism Br., 1971—. Cons. WHO, 1975, 78; bd. dirs., v.p. Found. Advanced Edn. in Scis., Bethesda, 1980—2002, treas., 1988—90, v.p., 1990—92; William Dameshek vis. prof. U. Calif., Irvine, 1984; mem. med. adv. bd. Howard Hughes Med. Inst., 1987—93; vis. com. mem. Harvard Med. Sch., Boston, 1988—94; mem. sci. adv. com., chmn. Mass. Gen. Hosp., 1992—96; chmn. sci. adv. bd. HealthCare Investment Corp., Princeton, NJ, 1986—2003. Author: Plasma Protein Metabolism, 1970; contbr. articles to profl. jours. With USPHS, 1956—58, 1959—63, 1975—94. Recipient Henry M. Stratton medal, Am. Hematology Soc., 1977, G. Burroughs Mider award, NIH, 1980, DSM, Dept. Health and Human Svcs., 1983, Abbott Lab. award in Clin. and Diagnostic Immunology, Am. Soc. Microbiology, 2002, Debrecen prize, Debrecen Med. Sch., Hungary, 2005, Dana Found. prize, Am. Assn. Immunologists, 2007; named Man of Yr., Am. Leukemia Soc., 1980. Fellow: Am. Acad. Allergy (Bela Schick award 1974, John M. Shelton award 1984, Lila Gruber prize 1986, Simon Shubitz prize 1987, CIBA-GEIGY Drew award 1987, Milken Family Med. Found. Disting. Basic Scientist prize 1991, Artois Latour Internat. Rsch. prize 1991, Bristol-Myers Cancer prize 1992, Paul Ehrlich medal 1997), Acad. Med. Scis. (hon.); mem.: NAS (chmn. 1985—89), UK Acad. Med. Scis., Clin. Immunology Soc. (pres. 1988), Am. Soc. Clin. Investigation (mem. editl. bd. 1978—80, 1983—88), Hungarian Acad. Scis. (hon.), Assn. Am. Physicians, Inst. Medicine, Am. Acad. Arts and Scis. Achievements include research in defining structure multisubunit IL-2 receptor; identifying novel cytokine IL-15; forms of IL-2R-directed therapy using alpha and beta-emitting radionuclide chelate versions of humanized monoclonal antibodies (Zenapax daclizumab) for treatment cancer and Multiple Sclerosis; analysis immunoglobulin gene rearrangements define clonality and classifying human lymphoid neoplasia; discovery of intestinal lymphangeictasia and allergic gastroenteropathy. Office: Nat Inst Health Bldg 10, Rm 4N115 10 Center Dr Bethesda MD 20892-1374 Office Phone: 301-496-6656. Business E-Mail: tawald@helix.nih.gov.

WALDMEIR, PETER NIELSEN, retired journalist; b. Detroit, Jan. 16, 1931; s. Joseph John and Helen Sarah (Nielsen) W.; m. Marilyn C. Choma; children— Peter William, Patti Ann, Lindsey Marilyn, Christopher Norman. Student, Wayne State U., 1949-58. From mem. staff to sports columnist Detroit News, 1949—72, gen. columnist, 1972—2004; ret., 2004. Pres. Old Newsboys Goodfellow Fund, Detroit, 1988; mem. city coun. Grosse Pointe Woods, Mich., 2005. With USMC, 1951-53. Recipient Headliners award Nat. Headliners Club, 1971, SDX Lifetime Achievement award, 2000; named Mich. Sports Writer of Yr., Nat. Sportscasters and Sportswriters, 1967, 69, 71; Heart award Variety Club Internat., 1985; inducted Mich. Journalism Hall of Fame, 2000, named Good Fellow the Yr., 2007. Mem. Sigma Delta Chi. Roman Catholic. Personal E-mail: pwaldmeir@aol.com.

WALDO, ALBERT LEON, cardiologist, educator; b. NYC, Nov. 25, 1936; MD, SUNY Coll. Medicine, Bklyn., 1962. Cert. in internal medicine, specialty in clin. cardiac electrophysiology, specialty in cardiovasc. Intern Kings County Hosp., Bklyn., 1962-63, resident in medicine, 1965-66, Balt. City Hosps., 1963-65, chief resident medicine SUNY downstate med. ctr., 1965—66; fellow Coll. Physicians and Surgeons Columbia U., 1966—68, from assoc. to asst. prof. dept. pharmacology, Coll. Physicians and Surgeons, 1969—72; fellow cardiology Columbia-Presbyn. Med. Ctr., NYC, 1968-69; from assoc. prof. to prof. medicine U. Ala., 1972—86; with U. Hosps. Case Med. Ctr., Cleve., 1986—, dir., clin. cardiac electrophysiology program; prof. medicine Case Western Res. U., Cleve., 1986—, Walter H. Pritchard Prof. Cardiology, prof. medicine, and prof. Biomedical Engineering. Cons., Circulatory Sys. Devices Panel of the Medical Devices Advisory Com., FDA. Serves or has served on the editl. bds. of peer reviewed journals in the field, including Circulation, Journal American College Cardiology, American Journal Cardiology, Pacing and Clinical Electrophysiology, Journal Cardiovascular Electrophysiology, Journal Electrocardiology, Heart Rhythm, (audio journals) American College of Cardiology (ACCEL), North American Society of Pacing and Electrophysiology (NASPETapes) (also editor-in-chief); contbr. articles to profl. jours. Recipient award for Achievements in Clin. and Exptl. Cardiology, Found. Hartsvrienden RESCAR of The Netherlands, Master Tchr. award, SUNY-Downstate Coll. Medicine, 2002. Fellow Am. Coll. Cardiology (past pres. Ohio Chpt.), ACP, Am. Coll. Chest Physicians, Am. Heart Assn., Heart Rhythm Soc. (founding mem., past pres. formally called N.Am. Soc. Pacing and Electrophysiology, Disting. Scientist award, 1997, Founders award, 2007, Michael Mirowski Award of Excellence, 2007) mem. Am. Physiol. Soc., Am. Soc. Clin. Investigation, Assn. Am. Physicians, Assn. Univ. Cardiologists, Cardiac Electrophysiology Soc. (past pres.), Am. Coll. Cardiology (Disting. Scientist award, 2009). Office: U Hosps Case Med Ctr 11100 Euclid Ave Cleveland OH 44106-1736 Office Phone: 216-844-7690.

WALDO, KURT, lawyer, metal products executive; B in Polit. Sci., Pa. State U.; JD, Case Western Res. U., Cleve. Joined legal dept. Alcoa, Inc., Pitts., 1980, European regional counsel Lausanne, Switzerland, 1987—91, sr. counsel Pitts., 1991—99, asst. gen. counsel, 1999—2007, dep. gen. counsel, 2007—08, v.p., gen. counsel, 2008—. Office: Alcoa Corp Ctr 201 Isabella St Pittsburgh PA 15212-5858 Office Phone: 412-553-4545. Office Fax: 412-553-4498.*

WALDO, ROBERT LELAND, retired insurance company executive; b. Pittsville, Wis., Sept. 1, 1923; s. Elmer Harley and Edith Viola (Senter) W.; m. Elaine Anne Jossie, June 4, 1947; children: Daniel Robert, Thomas Parker, Susan Jeanne. BA, U. Wis., 1949, JD, 1951. Assoc. atty. Foley & Lardner, Milw., 1951-59; asst. sec., asst. gen. counsel Wis. Gas Co., Milw., 1959-69; v.p., gen. counsel Verex Corp. and Subss., Madison, Wis., 1969-72; exec. v.p., sec. Verex Corp. and subs., Madison, Wis., 1972-78, pres., chief operating officer, 1978-82, pres., chief exec. officer, 1982-85, chmn., chief exec. officer, 1985-86. Served as sgt. U.S. Army, 1943-46, ETO. Mem. Wis. Bar Assn., Dane County Bar Assn., Mortgage Ins. Co.'s Am. (pres. 1980-82), Maple Bluff Country Club. Republican. Methodist. Avocations: travel, golf. Home: 818 Charing Cross Rd Madison WI 53704-6010

WALDON, ALTON RONALD, JR., judge; b. Lakeland, Fla., Dec. 21, 1936; s. Alton Ronald and Rupert Juanita (Wallace) W.; m. Barbara De Costa, June 3, 1961; children: Alton II, Dana Olive, Ian Patrick. BS, John Jay Coll., NYC, 1968; JD, NY Law Sch., 1973. Capt. NYC Housing Authority Police Dept., 1962—75; dep. commr. NY State Divsn. Human Rights, 1975—82; assemblyman NY State Assembly, 1983—86; congressman US Ho. Reps., Washington, 1986—87; commr. NY State Commn. Investigation, 1987—90; senator NY State, 1991—2000; judge Ct. of Claims State of NY, 2000—06; commr. NY State Victims Bd., 2007—. Recipient Thurgood Marshall fellow, NY State Trial Lawyers Assn., 1970-73. Mem. Met. Black Bar Assn., Macon B. Allen Bar Assn., Comus Club NY, Alumni Assn. NY Law Sch., Alumni Assn. John Jay Coll., Masons (33 deg.), Sigma Pi Phi. Democrat. Roman Catholic. Avocation: sports. Office Phone: 212-946-4737. Business E-Mail: awaldon@waldonlaw.com.

WALDORF, GREGORY, Internet company executive, venture capitalist; s. Toby and Bob Waldorf. BA, UCLA; MBA, Stanford U. Co-founder, co-chair devel. com. Startup, East Palo Alto, Calif., 1994; dir. Internet group Pacific Edge Investment Mgmt., Palo Alto; ptnr. Fayaz Sarofim & Co.; gen. ptnr., mgr. W. Coast ops. Charles River Ventures, Palo Alto, 2000; founding investor eHarmony, Pasadena, 2000, CEO, 2006—; co-founder Destination-U, Menlo Park, 2004. Founding mem. Stanford Grad. Sch. Bus. Mgmt. Bd.; bd. overseers Stanford U. Hoover Inst. Mem. SV2, the Silicon Valley Social Venture Fund, 1999—. Office: eHarmony PO Box 60157 Pasadena CA 91116 Office Phone: 626-795-4814.

WALDRIP, KAREN MARIE, career planning administrator; b. Tacoma, Oct. 17, 1961; d. Mike and Ethel Gray; m. Edwin Thomas Waldrip, Aug. 25, 1990. BS in Psychology, U. Puget Sound, 1984, M in Edn. and Counseling, 1987. Lic. profl. counselor Alaska, 2000. Counselor, social worker Ryther Child Ctr., Seattle, 1985—87; edn. specialist Petersburg Coun. on Alcoholism, Alaska, 1987—88; adult treatment specialist Lakeside-Milam Recover Ctrs., Juneau, Alaska, 1988—90; employment career counselor State of Alaska Dept. Labor and Workforce Devel., Juneau, 1990—2006; pvt. practice DBA: Alaska's Renewable Resources and Workforce Consulting, Auke Bay, 2006—; job developer, career counselor, cmty. rehab. provider Dept. Vocat. Rehab. Supporter Big Bros., Big Sisters, Boy Scouts of Am., Girl Scouts of Am., Juneau, 2002; doner ARC Assn., Juneau, 1999—2006; cmty. workforce incentive coord. SSI/SSDI Benefits Planner, 2007; active Ptnr. in Hope donor registry St. Jude's Med. Ctr., Juneau, 2005; active Paralyzed Vets. Am., Juneau, 2000—06. Recipient 15 Yr. Svc. award, State of Alaska, 2000, E-Commerce 900+ Feedback award, 2005; grantee State Tng. and Employment Program, State of Alaska, 1993, 1994, 1995, 1995—2000. Mem.: Cmty. and Econ. Devel. (licentiate). Independent. Avocations: fishing, hunting. Home: 19935 Cohen Dr Juneau AK 99801 Office: DBA: Alaska's Renewable Resources PO Box 210555 Auke Bay AK 99821 Personal E-mail: etwaldrip75@msn.com. Business E-Mail: alaskarenewableresources@msn.com.

WALDRON, JENNIFER, science educator; b. St. Cloud, Minn., Mar. 4, 1974; d. John Waldron and JoAnn Thorson; life ptnr. Brenda Fite. MEd, Bowling Green State U., Ohio, 1999; PhD, Mich. State U., East Lansing, 2003. Asst. prof. U. Northern Iowa, Cedar Falls, 2003—. Bd. mem. Girl Scouts. Mem.: AAHPERD (Rsch. Consortium fellow), Assn. Applied Sport Psychology. Achievements include research in health-compromising behaviors in exercise and sport. Office: Univ Northern Iowa 203 WRC Cedar Falls IA 50614-0241

WALDRON, JILL GENEVIEVE, retired language educator; b. Evanston, Ill., Dec. 17, 1936; d. Frank Wesley Rorabach and Helen Montgomery (Davenport) Davee; m. Benny Lee Bohlander, June 10, 1958 (div. 1966); m. Raymond Wilson Keller, June 1, 1971 (div. 1983); 1 child, Eric Douglas Bohlander. BA, Ill. Wesleyan U., 1958; MA, U. Ill., 1959; postgrad., UCLA, 1965—68. English tchr. Danvers H.S., Ill., 1958—59; English instr. Ill. State U., Normal, 1959—63; instr. English U. Md., Hanau and Wurzberg, Germany, 1963—65; English instr. UCLA, 1965—68, Santa Monica City Coll., 1968; English prof. Pierce Coll., Woodland Hills, Calif., 1968—98, prof. emeritus, 1998—. Mem. instrnl. TV com. L.A.C.C. Dist.-ITV, 1969—. Author: The Scope of Recognition, 1971; contbr. poetry to profl. publs. Talk show host Sta. KCRW, Santa Monica, 1981-82; bd. dirs. Welsh Pony Futurity, Pacific Saddlebred Assn., 1979-1989; co-chair LA county adn. and comm. adhoc work group Topanga Disaster Survival Guide, 2004-06; mem. level 2 Equine Response Team LA County, 2000—. Named San Fernando Valley Tchr./Poet of Yr., 1995. Mem. Pacific Saddlebred Assn. (bd. dirs., sec., writer), DAR (Temescal chpt.). Democrat. Avocations: driving ponies and riding, oil and tempra painting. Home: PO Box 270 Topanga CA 90290-0270 Personal E-mail: horse.poet@verizon.net.

WALDRON, ROBERT LEROY, II, radiologist, educator; b. Carbondale, Ill., Feb. 6, 1936; s. Robert Leroy and Violet Mae (Thompson) W.; m. Sandra Sellers; children: Richard, Robert Leroy III, Ryan, Burton Johnson. AB, Princeton U., 1958; MD, Harvard U., 1962. Diplomate in radiology and neuroradiology Am. Bd. Radiology. Intern Mass. Gen. Hosp., Boston, 1962-63; resident radiology Columbia-Presbyn. Med. Ctr., NYC, 1965-68; instr. radiology Coll. Physicians and Surgeons Columbia U., NYC, 1968-69, assoc. prof. clin. radiology Coll. Physicians and Surgeons, 1971-73, spl. fellow neuroradiology Neurol. Inst., 1968-69; clin. asst. radiology Harvard Med. Sch., Cambridge, Mass., 1969-71; asst. radiologist Mt. Auburn Hosp., MIT, Cambridge, 1969-71; dir. radiology French Hosp., French Med. Clinic, San Luis Obispo, Calif., 1973-80, v.p., dir., 1976-77; assoc. clin. prof. radiology Loma Linda (Calif.) U. Sch. Medicine, 1977-80; dir. radiology Richland Meml. Hosp., Columbia, SC, 1980-90, trustee, 1990-98; clin. prof. radiology U. SC Sch. Medicine, Columbia, 1985—. Mng. ptnr. Richland Radiol. Assocs., Columbia, 1988-90; founder Chilean N.Am. Hosp. Corp., 1989; pres. MedBill, 1984-95. Contbr. articles to profl. jours. Bd. dirs. Am. Cancer Soc., San Luis Obispo. With USPHS, 1963-65. Recipient grants James Picker Found., Am. Cancer Soc., NRC, NAS, Nat. Cancer Inst. Fellow Am. Coll. Radiology, Soc. Internat. Med. Sci. Cooperation; mem. AMA, Am. Roentgen Ray Soc., Radiol. Soc. N.Am., Am. Soc. Neuroradiology, San Luis Obispo County Med. Soc. (pres. 1979), Columbia Med. Soc., Sierra-Cascade Trauma Soc. (pres. 1983-84), S.C. Radiol. Soc. (pres. 1992-93), Ivy Club of Princeton, Woodcreek & Wildewood Club, Govs. Club (Kiawah Island). Republican. Methodist. Home: 1420 Adger Rd Columbia SC 29205-1406 Office: Richland Meml Hosp 5 Medical Park Rd Columbia SC 29203-6873

WALDRON, THEODORE CHARLES, physician; b. West Hazleton, Pa., June 3, 1946; s. Leonard Raymond Waldron; m. Gloria Jean Koziel, June 24, 1978; children: Theodore Leonard, Darren Christopher. BS in Biology, Alliance Coll., 1968; D of Osteopathy, Phila. Coll. Osteopathic Medicine, 1978. Diplomate Am. Osteo. Coll. Gen. Practice; diplomate Nat. Bd. Examiners of Osteo. Medicine and Surgery; diplomate State Bd. Osteo. Examiners; cert. gen./family practice; lic. Pa., S.C. Gen. practice medicine, Conyngham, Pa., 1979-00; chief family practice dept. Hazleton St. Joseph Med. Ctr., 1989-90; physician specialist II White Haven (Pa.) Ctr., 1993-96; disability physician specialist Pa. Dept. Labor and Industry Bur. Disability Determination, Wilkes-Barre, 1996—; med. dir. Lattimer ICF-MR Facility, 1995—2000. Med. dir. Hazleton Nursing & Geriatric Ctr., Mountain City Convalescent Ctr., Hazleton, 1983-91; occupational health physician Workmed, Hazleton, 1991-93. Dir. vector control for Lycoming, Clinton, Snyder and Union counties, Pa. following Hurricane Agnes flooding, 1972. Served as sgt. USAR, N.G., 1969-76. Mem. Am. Osteopathic Assn., Pa. Osteopathic Med. Assn., Am. Osteopathic Coll. Family Practice, Pa. Osteopathic Gen. Practice Soc., S.C. Osteopathic Med. Assn. Republican. Roman Catholic. Avocations: fishing, photography, gardening, electronics, science. Home: 146 Hickory Rd Sugarloaf PA 18249-9556 Personal E-mail: twaldron@pa.metrocast.net.

WALDROP, FRANCIS NEIL, physician; b. Asheville, NC, Oct. 5, 1926; s. Troy Lester and Emma Louise (Ballard) W.; m. Eleanor Dorothy Wickes, June 10, 1950; children: Mark Lester, Barbara Louise. AB, U. Minn., 1946; MD, George Washington U., 1950. Intern George Washington U. Hosp., Washington, 1950-51; resident St. Elizabeth's Hosp., Washington, 1951-54, med. officer, 1951-71; dir. manpower and tng. programs NIMH, Rockville, Md., 1972-75; dep. adminstr. Alcohol, Drug Abuse and Mental Health Adminstrn., HEW, Rockville, 1975-79; ret., 1979. Clin. prof. psychiatry George Washington U. Recipient Superior Service award HEW, 1962, Disting. Service award, 1964. Fellow Am. Psychiat. Assn. (Distinguished life, Vestermark award 1980). Achievements include research, publs. in field. Home: 1775 Elton Rd Silver Spring MD 20903-1726

WALE, KEVIN E., automotive executive; b. Melbourne, Australia, 1954; Degree in Commerce (hon.), U. Melbourne. Fin. mgr. Holden, 1975—83, dir. fin., 1985—93, dir. sales, mktg., 1993—98; mem. fin. staff GM Corp., New York, 1983—85, exec.-in-charge ops. GM Asia Pacific Ltd. Singapore, 1998—2001, v.p. GM Europe, 2001—05, pres., mng. dir. GM China Group, 2005—; mng. dir. Vauxhall Motors, 2001—, chmn., mng. dir., 2002—05. Office: GM PO Box 33170 Detroit MI 48232-5170

WALECKI, WOJCIECH JAN, physicist, engineer; b. Warsaw, Jan. 10, 1964; came to U.S., 1988; s. Jan Andrzej and Stanislawa M. (Prusak) W.; m. Anna Maria Klosowska; 1 child, Katherine. MSc, Warsaw U., 1988, Brown U., 1992. Teaching asst. Purdue U., West Lafayette, Ind., 1988-89; rsch. asst. Brown U., Providence, 1989-92. Ind. cons. elec. engring., constrn., 1992; materials engr. MIM Corp., Providence, 1990-91. Mem. Am. Phys. Soc. Office: Brown Univ Dept Physics PO Box 1843 Providence RI 02912-1843

WALEK, DAVID B., lawyer; b. Ft. Monmouth, NJ, May 18, 1954; s. Walter J. and Charlotte H. (Haag) W.; m. Elizabeth R. Gibson; children: Christopher, Emily, Merritt. BA cum laude, Yale U., 1976; JD, Harvard U., 1980. Bar: Mass., 1980. Assoc. Ropes & Gray, Boston, 1980-89, ptnr. corp. dept., 1989—, co-head tech. co. practice group. Lectr. Sloane Sch. Mgmt., MIT. Chmn. Artists for Humanity, Boston. Mem.: ABA, Boston Bar Assn. Office: Ropes & Gray 1 International Pl Boston MA 02110-2624 Home: 279 South Ave Weston MA 02493 Office Phone: 617-951-7388. Office Fax: 617-951-7050. Business E-Mail: david.walek@ropesgray.com.

WALENDOWSKI, GEORGE JERRY, accounting and business educator; b. Han-Minden, Germany, Mar. 25, 1947; arrived in US, 1949; s. Stefan (dec.) and Eugenia (Lewandowska) W. AA, LA City Coll., 1968; BS, Calif. State U., LA, 1970, MBA, 1972; cert., Inst. Mgmt. Accts., 2004; cert. in leadership, Cornell U., 2006; master cert., Villanova U., 2006, cert. in fin. and acctg., orgnl. leadership and bus. analysis, 2007. Cert. community coll. instr. acctg. and mgmt., Calif., in new economic powers, U. Oxford, 2008. Acct. Unocal (formerly Union Oil Co. Calif.), LA, 1972-76, data control supr., 1976-78, acctg. analyst, 1978-79; sr. fin. analyst Hughes Aircraft Co., El Segundo, Calif., 1979-83, fin. planning specialist, 1983-84, program controls specialist, 1984-86, bus. mgmt. specialist, 1986-92, bus. analyst, 1993-95. Adj. assoc. prof. bus. math. L.A. City Coll., 1976-80, acctg., 1980-97, 99—, mem. acctg. adv. com., 1984, 87, 89, 99, acctg. and bus. Pasadena City Coll., 1996-2001, 2003-07; reviewer conf. papers. Contbr. articles to profl. jours. Mem. commn. Rep. Pres. Task Force, 1986; mem. Tchrs. Acctg. Two Yr. Colls. Scholarship Com., 2007 Recipient Medal of Merit, Rep. Presdl. Task Force, 1984, cert. of merit, named registered life mem. commn., 1986, named Honor Roll life mem., 1989, named to Hall of Fame IQ World Review Com.; recipient Vice-Presdl. Cert. of Commendation, Rep. Nat. Hall of Honor, 1992, Rep. Congl. cert. of Appreciation, 1993, Rep. Congl. Order of Freedom award Nat. Rep. Congl. Com., 1995, Recognition award LA chpt. Strategic Leadership Forum, 1983. Mem.: Top One Percent Soc., Internat. High IQ Soc., Tchrs. Acctg. at Two-Yr. Colls. (scholarship com. 2007), High Potentials Soc., Mysterium Soc., Midwest Fin. Assn. (program rev. com. 2002), Ea. Fin. Assn. (program rev. com. 2000), Soc. Advancement Mgmt. (editl. rev. bd. Advanced Mgmt. Jour. 1999—, selection com. mem. Internat. Conf. 2000, editl. rev. bd. mem. mgmt. in practice 2007—), Nat. Bus. Edn. Assn., Am. Acctg. Assn. (competitive manuscript com. 1997—98, reviewer tchg. curr. sect. 1998, tchg. and curriculum sect. two-yr. coll. issues com. 1998—99, Tchg. and Cirriculum Innovative Tchg. award com. 2004—05), Inst. Mgmt. Accts. (author's cir. L.A. chpt. 1980, mem. editl. adv. bd. Strategic Fin. and Mgmt. Acctg. Quarterly 2002—, Robert Half author's trophy 1980, cert. of appreciation 1980, 1983), Acad. Mgmt. (reviewer social issues in mgmt. divsn. 1991, mgmt. edn. and devel. divsn. program rev. com. 1998—99, reviewer bus. policy and strategy divsn. 2002—04, reviewer for acad. of mngmt. learning & ed. Jour. 2003, Bus. Policy and Strategy Divsn. Outstanding Reviewer award 2004), Mind Soc., High IQ Soc. for Gifted and Talented (hon.), Alpha Iota Delta, Pi Lambda Theta, Nat. Scholars Honor Soc., Kappa Delta Pi, Delta Pi Epsilon (proposal reviewer 2005, editl. bd. mem. 2008—), Beta Gamma Sigma. Republican. Roman Catholic. Home: 426 N Citrus Ave Los Angeles CA 90036-2632 Office: LA City Coll 855 N Vermont Ave Los Angeles CA 90029 Personal E-mail: geowalen@sbcglobal.net.

WALES, GWYNNE HUNTINGTON, retired lawyer; b. Evanston, Ill., Apr. 18, 1933; s. Robert Willett and Solace (Huntington) W.; m. Janet McCobb, Feb. 8, 1957; children— Thomas Gwynne, Catherine Anne, Louise Carrie. AB, Princeton U., 1954; JD, Harvard U., 1961. Bar: N.Y. 1962. Assoc. White & Case, NYC, 1961-69, ptnr., 1969-2000, resident ptnr. Brussels, 1969-75, Ankara, Turkey, 1998-2000, of counsel, 2008—. Author: (novel) The Valley of Death, 2007. Served with USN, 1954-58. Mem.: Am. Law Inst. (life). Home: 1406 Brookside Dr Fairfield CT 06824

WALES, JIMMY DONAL (JIMBO WALES), Internet company executive; b. Huntsville, Ala., Aug. 7, 1966; m. Christine Wales; 1 child, Kira. Attended, Auburn U.; attended PhD programs in finance, U. Ala., Ind. U. Faculty mem. U. Ala., Ind. U.; futures and options trader Chgo. Options Assocs., Chgo.; founder Nupedia.com, 1999—2000; CEO Bomis, Inc., San Diego, 2000—01; founder Wikipedia (Parent orgn.- Wikimedia Found., Inc.), 2001—, Wikimedia Found. Inc., St. Petersburg, Fla., 2003—, pres., dir., chmn. bd. trustee, 2005—; founder Wikia, Inc., 2004—. Recipient 100 Most Influential People, Time Mag., 2006; named one of 50 Who Matter Now, Business 2.0, 2007, Top 25 Web Celebs, Forbes mag., 2006, 50 Most Important People on the Web, PC World, 2007; nominee Rave award in Technology, WIRED, 2005.

WALES, LORENE M., film producer, educator; MA, Regent U., Va. Beach, 1996, PhD, 1999. Cert. Stanislavsky Acad. Dramatic Arts, LA, 1987. Prodn. cons. Various Ind. Films, 1999—2008. Prodr.: (film and video) First Landing (Telly award, 2008, Accolade award, 2008, Redemptive Storyteller award, 2008); prodr.: (film and video) On the Edge (Worldfest Houston Internat. Film Festival award, 2001), Smoke Rings (Acad. Motion Picture Arts and Scis.-Regional Student award, 2000). Co-founder Mei Ming Orphan and Adoption Missions, Va. Beach, 2004—08. Mem.: U. Film and Video Assn. (Judges award 2004). Office: Regent Univ 1000 Regent Univ Dr Virginia Beach VA 23456 Home Fax: 757 416-9598.

WALES, ROSS ELLIOT, lawyer; b. Youngstown, Ohio, Oct. 17, 1947; s. Craig C. and Beverly (Bromley) W.; m. Juliana Fraser, Sept. 16, 1972; children: Dod E., J. Craig. AB, Princeton U., 1969; JD, U. Va., 1974. Bar: Ohio 1974, U.S. Dist. Ct. (so. dist.) Ohio 1974, U.S. Ct. Appeals (5th cir.) 1979. Assoc. Taft, Stettinius & Hollister, Cin., 1974-81, ptnr., 1981—. Pres. US Swimming, Inc., Colorado Springs, 1979-84, US Aquatic Sports, Inc., Colorado Springs, 1984-88, 94-98, Cin. Active to Support Edn., 1987-88; chmn. sch. tax levy campaign, Cin., 1987; trustee The Childrens Home Cin., 1987—2008, v.p., 1995-98, pres., 1998-02; bd. dirs., sec., v.p. FINA Bur., 1988-2000; trustee Cin. State Tech. and CC, 1994—, sec. bd., 1995-98, vice-chmn., 1998-00, chair 2000-02; pres. Cin. Arts Sch., Inc., 2000-01; sec. Greater Cin. Arts and Edn. Ctr., 1996-05; mem. Anti-Doping Rev. Bd., US Anti-Doping Agy., Colo. Springs; dir. Child Welfare League Am., 2003-, treas., 2005-06, chair, 2007-09. Mem. ABA, Ohio Bar Assn., Cin. Bar Assn. Presbyterian. Office: 425 Walnut St Ste 1800 Cincinnati OH 45202-3957 Home Phone: 513-321-8637; Office Phone: 513-357-9351. Business E-Mail: wales@taftlaw.com.

WALES, WALTER D., physicist, researcher; b. Oneonta, NY, Aug. 2, 1933; s. Walter D. and Anna Laura (Brockway) W.; m. Margaret Irene Keiter, June 19, 1955; children: Stephen Dirk, Carolyn Sue. BA, Carleton Coll., 1954; MS, Calif. Inst. Tech., 1955, PhD, 1960. Instr. physics U. Pa., Phila., 1959-62, asst. prof., 1962-64, assoc. prof., 1964-72, prof., 1972—, chmn. dept. physics, 1973-82, assoc. dean, 1982-87, acting dean, 1987-88, assoc. dean, 1988-92, dep. provost, 1992-95, interim dean, 1996-98, ombudsman, 1999-2001, interim assoc. provost, 2002—04; assoc. dir. Princeton (N.J.)-Pa. Accelerator, 1968-71; staff physicist AEC, 1972-73. Fellow Am. Phys. Soc.; mem. Am. Assn. Physics Tchrs. Achievements include research in exptl. particle physics. Home: 404 Drew Ave Swarthmore PA 19081-2406 Office: 209 S 33rd St Philadelphia PA 19104-6317 Business E-Mail: wales@physics.upenn.edu.

WALHEIM, REX J., astronaut, military officer; b. Redwood City, Calif., Oct. 10, 1962; s. Lawrence M. Walheim, Jr. and Avis L. Walheim; m. Margie Dotson; 2 children. BS in Mech. Engring., U. Calif., Berkeley, 1984; MS in Indsl. Engring., U. Houston, 1989. Commd. 2nd lt. USAF, 1984, advanced through grades to lt. col.; missile warning ops. crew cmmdr. USAF Cavalier (N.D.) Air Force Sta., 1984—86; mech. systems flight engr., lead ops. engr. for Space Shuttle landing gear, brakes and emergency runway barrier. NASA, Houston, 1986—89; mgr. upgrading missile warning radar USAF Hdqtrs. Air Force Space Command, Colo. Springs, Colo., 1989—91; flight test engr. course USAF Test Pilot Sch., 1991; attended course Edwards AFB, Calif., 1992; project mgr. to comdr. avionics and armament flight F-16 Combined Test Force, Edwards AFB, Calif., 1993—96; astronaut NASA Johnson Space Ctr., Houston, 1996—. Served on EVA (extravehicular activity) crew STS-110 Atlantis Mission, 2002; astronaut office rep. for the Extra Vehicular Mobility Unit (EVA spacesuit) NASA; crew mem. STS-122 Atlantis Mission to deliver the European Space Agency's Columbus Lab. to the Internat. Space Station, 2008. Named Disting. grad and top flight engr., USAF Test Pilot Sch. 92A. Avocations: football, hiking, skiing, softball. Office: Astronaut Office/CB Johnson Space Ctr Houston TX 77058

WALHOUT, JUSTINE SIMON, chemistry professor; b. Aberdeen, SD, Dec. 11, 1930; d. Otto August and Mabel Ida (Tews) S.; m. Donald Walhout, Feb. 1, 1958; children: Mark, Timothy, Lynne, Peter. BS, Wheaton Coll., 1952; PhD, Northwestern U., 1956. Instr. Wright City Community Coll., Chgo., 1955-56; asst. prof. Rockford (Ill.) Coll., 1956-59, assoc. prof., 1959-66, 81-89, prof., 1989-96, prof. emeritus, 1996—, dept. chmn., 1987-95; cons. Pierce Chem. Co., Rockford, 1968-69; trustee Rockford (Ill.) Coll., 1987-91. Contbr. articles to profl. jours. Mem. Ill. Bd. Edn., 1974-81. Mem. AAUW (Ill. bd. dirs. 1985-87), Am. Chem. Soc. (councilor 1993-99), Rockford LWV (bd. dirs. 1983-85, 2002-04), Sigma Xi. Presbyterian. Home: 3204 Wesley Way Rockford IL 61101-8803 Office: Rockford Coll 5050 E State St Rockford IL 61108-2311

WALI, MOHAN KISHEN, environmental scientist, forester, educator; b. Kashmir, India, Mar. 1, 1937; came to U.S., 1969, naturalized, 1975; s. Jagan Nath and Somavati (Wattal) W.; m. Sarla Safaya, Sept. 25, 1960; children: Pamela, Promod. BS, U. Jammu and Kashmir, 1957; MS, U. Allahabad, India, 1960; PhD, U. B.C., Can., 1970. Lectr. S.P. Coll., Srinagar, Kashmir, 1963-65; rsch. fellow U. Copenhagen, 1965-66; grad. fellow U. B.C., 1967-69; asst. prof. biology U. N.D., Grand Forks, 1969-73, assoc. prof., 1973-79, prof., 1979-83, Hill rsch. prof., 1973; dir. Forest River Biology Area Field Sta., 1970-79, Project Reclamation, 1975-83; spl. asst. to univ. pres., 1977-82; staff ecologist Grand Forks Energy Rsch. Lab. U.S. Dept. Interior, 1974-75; prof. Coll. Environ. Sci. and Forestry SUNY, Syracuse, 1983-89, dir. grad. program environ. sci., 1983-85, prof. Sch. Natural Resources, 1990—, dir. Sch. Natural Resources, assoc. dean Coll. Agr., 1990-93; dir. Environ. Sci. Grad. program Ohio State U., Columbus, 2001—06. Vice chmn. N.D. Air Pollution Adv. Coun., 1981-83; co-chair IV Internat. Congress on Ecology, 1986. Editor: Some Environmental Aspects of Strip-Mining in North Dakota, 1973, Prairie: A Multiple View, 1975, Practices and Problems of Land Reclamation in Western North America, 1975, Ecology and Coal Resource Development, 1979, Ecosystem Rehabilitation-Preamble to Sustainable Development, 1992; co-editor Agriculture and the Environment, 1993; sr. editor Reclamation Rev., 1976-80, chief editor, 1980-81; chief editor Reclamation and Revegetation Rsch., 1982-87; contbr. articles to profl. jours. Recipient B.C. Gamble Disting. Tchg. and Svc. award, U. ND, 1977. Fellow AAAS, Nat. Acad. Scis. India; mem. Ecol. Soc. Am. (chmn. sect. internat. activities 1980-84), Bot. Ecol. Soc., Can. Bot. Assn. (dir. ecology sect. 1976-79, v.p. 1982-83), Am. Soc. Agronomy, Am. Inst. Biol. Sci. (gen. chmn. 34th ann. meeting), Internat. Assn. Ecolog (co-chmn. IV Internat. Congress Ecology), Internat. Soc. Soil Sci., N.D. Acad. Sci. (chmn. editl. com. 1979-81), Sigma Xi (nat. lectr. 1983-85, pres. Ohio State chpt. 1993-94, pres. Syracuse chpt. 1984-85, Outstanding Rsch. award U. N.D. chpt. 1975). Office: Ohio State U Sch Environ and Natural Resources 2021 Coffey Rd Columbus OH 43210-1044 Business E-Mail: wali.1@osu.edu.

WALJI, JABIR MOHAMED, strategist, futurist and systematic innovation consultant; b. Kampala, Uganda, Mar. 2, 1959; s. Razahusein Virji and Kubra (Mauji) W.; m. Ahlam Jaffer Ali, Nov. 8, 1989. BS with honors, John Moores U. Liverpool, Eng., 1982; DMS, U. North London, 1984; MBA, Manchester Bus. Sch., Eng., 1996. Mktg. mgr. Tara Arts Group, England, 1985—87; assoc. dir. Indus Textile Mills Ltd., Pakistan, 1987—94; dir. Indus Marines, Pakistan, 1988-92; strategy cons. Shell Oils, England, 1996-98, strategic advisor serviceteam/cleanaway, 1999—2002; sr. cons. IMES Cons. Ltd., 2003—05; lead strategist Global NGO, 2003; ind. cons., 2003—. Mem. Royal Soc. Arts, Chartered Inst. Mktg., Inst. Mgmt. Consultants, Strategy and Planning Soc., Dubai Soc., Inst. Leisure and Amenity Mgmt., Assn. MBA, Tourism Soc., Futurelogy Network & Systematic Innovation (TRIZ) Network. Avocations: jet skiing, watersports, squash. Home: 6 Penshurst Ct Penshurst Gardens Edgware HA8 9TL England Address: PO Box 75512 Flat 104 Al JAz 4B St No 3 Tire Greens Dubai United Arab Emirates Home Phone: 020-8958-7593, 00971 4-368 3881; Office Phone: 0044103779-61-8182. Home Fax: 020 8958-7593. E-mail: jabirwalji@yahoo.co.uk.

WALK, BARBRA DENISE, customer service administrator, tutor; b. Tacoma, Wash., Aug. 29, 1969; d. Robert Edward and Connie Lee Walk. A, Pierce Coll., Tacoma, 1993; BA, Wash. State U., Pullman, 1996. Office mgr. Comcast, Douglasville, Ga., 1999—2003; warranty adminstrn. coord. Rinnai, Peachtree City, Ga., 2004—; writer Gallopade Internat., Peachtree City, 2005—06; tutor Peachtree City, 2005—. Mem. edn. com. Japanese Am. Friendship Soc., Peachtree City, 2005—06.

Recipient Scholastic Achievement award, Miss TEEN pageant, 1983, 5 achievement awards, Dale Carnegie; named Miss Congeniality, Miss TEEN pageant, 1983. Mem.: Mensa, Phi Alpha Theta. Avocations: travel, tap dancing, music.

WALK, CHARLIE, music company executive; m. Lauren Walk; 4 children. BA in Bus. Adminstrn., Boston U., 1990. Coll. mktg. rep. Sony Music Distribution's New England branch, 1987—90, account service rep., 1990; promotion mgr. Columbia Records, N.E. Region, 1990—94; assoc. dir. Pop Promotion, Columbia Records, 1994, dir., 1994—95, v.p., 1997—98, sr. v.p., 1998—99; v.p. Promotion, Columbia Records, 1999—2000, exec. v.p., 2000—04, Creative Mktg. & Promotion, Coumbia Records, 2004—05; pres. Epic Records, 2005—. Named a Maverick, Details mag., 2007. Office: Epic Records 550 Madison Ave New York NY 10001 Office Phone: 212-833-8000. Office Fax: 212-833-4818.

WALKEN, CHRISTOPHER, actor; b. Astoria, NY, Mar. 31, 1943; s. Paul Walken; m. Georgianne Thon, Jan. 1969. Attended Hofstra U., studied with Wynn Handman, Actors Studio. Stage appearances include Broadway, off-Broadway and regional theatres throughout US and Can.; Broadway debut in J.B. 1959; other stage appearances include Best Foot Forward, West Side Story, Macbeth, The Lion in Winter (Clarence Derwent award 1966), Hamlet, The Rose Tatoo (Theatre World's Most Promising Personality 1966-67), Romeo and Juliet, The Seagull, 2001, The Night Thoreau Spent in Jail (Joseph Jefferson award 1970-71), Kid Champion (Obie award 1975), Miss Julie, Sweet Bird of Youth, Hurlyburly, 1984, Cinders, 1984, A Bill of Divorcement, 1985, Coriolanus, 1988, Othello, 1992, (also playwright) Him, 1995, Mother Courage, 2006; films include The Anderson Tapes, 1971, Next Stop Greenwich Village, The Sentinel, 1977, Roseland, 1977, Annie Hall, 1977, The Deer Hunter, 1978 (NY Film Critics Best Supporting Actor award 1978, Acad. award Best Supporting Actor 1979), Last Embrace, 1979, Dogs of War, 1981, Heavens Gate, 1980, Pennies From Heaven, 1981, The Happiness Cage, 1982, The Dead Zone, 1983, Brainstorm, 1983, A View to a Kill, 1984, At Close Range, 1986, Deadline, 1987, Puss in Boots, 1988, The Milagro Beanfield War, 1988, Biloxi Blues, 1988, Communion, 1989, King of New York, 1990, Homeboy, 1991, The Comfort of Strangers, 1991, McBain, 1991, All American Murder, 1992, Batman Returns, 1992, True Romance, 1993, A Business Affair, 1994, Wayne's World II, 1994, Pulp Fiction, 1994, Search and Destroy, 1995, Nick of Time, 1995, The Addiction, 1995, The Prophecy, 1995, The Funeral, 1996, Basquiat, 1996, The Wild Side, 1996, Things To Do in Denver When You're Dead, 1995, Last Man Standing, 1996, Touch, 1997, Mousehunt, 1997, Excess Baggage, 1997, Suicide Kings, 1997, Antz (voice), 1998, Illuminata, 1998, New Rose Hotel, 1998, The Prophecy II, 1998, Trance, 1998, Sleepy Hollow, 1999, Blast From the Past, 1999, Kiss Toledo Goodbye, 1999, Vendetta, 1999, Scotland PA, 2001, Joe Dirt, 2001, America's Sweethearts, 2001, Chelsea Walls, 2001, The Affair of the Necklace, 2001, Jungle Juice, 2001, Poolhall Junkies, 2002, The Country Bears, 2002, Plots with a View, 2002, Catch Me If You Can, 2002 (Best Actor in Supporting Role, British Acad. Film Award (BAFTA) 2003), Kangaroo Jack, 2003, Gigli, 2003, The Rundown, 2003, Man on Fire, 2004, Envy, 2004, The Stepford Wives, 2004, Around the Bend, 2004, Wedding Crashers, 2005, Domino, 2005, Click, 2006, Man of the Year, 2006, Hairspray, 2007, Balls of Fury, 2007; TV films include Sarah, Plain and Tall, 1991 (Emmy nominee), Skylark, 1993, Scam, 1993; The Opportunists, 1999, The Prophecy III: The Ascent, 1999, Sarah, Plain and Tall: 3, 1999, Julius Caesar, 2002; (TV series) Saturday Night Live (Am. Comedy award 2001), Naked City, 1958, Hawaii Five-O, 1968, Kojak, 1973; (TV mini-series) Julius Caesar, 2002. Recipient Best Supporting Male Performance (True Crime: NYC), Spike TV Video Game awards, 2005, Man of the Yr., Hasty Pudding Theatrical Soc., 2008. Office: c/o Toni Howard Internat Creative Mgmt 10250 Constellation Blvd Los Angeles CA 90067*

WALKER, ALICE MALSENIOR, writer; b. Eatonton, Ga., Feb. 9, 1944; d. Willie Lee and Minnie (Grant) Walker; m. Melvyn R. Leventhal, Mar. 17, 1967 (div. 1976); 1 child, Rebecca. Attended, Spelman Coll.; BA, Sarah Lawrence Coll., Bronxville, NY, 1966; PhD (hon.), Russell Sage U., 1972; DHL (hon.), U. Mass., 1983. Co-founder, pub. Wild Trees Pr., Navarro, Calif., 1984-88. Cons. Friends of the Children, Miss., 1967; tchr. black studies Jackson State Coll., Miss., 1968—69, Tougaloo Coll., Miss., 1970—71; lectr. lit. Wellesley Coll., Mass., 1972—73, U. Mass., Boston, 1972—73; disting. writer Afro-American studies dept. U. Calif., Berkeley, 1982; Fannie Hurst prof. lit. Brandeis U., Waltham, Mass., 1982. Author: (novels/short stories) The Third Life of Grange Copeland, 1970, Everyday Use, 1973, In Love and Trouble: Stories of Black Women, 1973, Roselily, 1973, Meridian, 1976, The Color Purple, 1982 (Nat. Book award, 1983, Pulitzer Prize for fiction, 1983), You Can't Keep a Good Woman Down: Stories, 1982, Beauty: When the Other Dancer Is the Self, 1983, Am I Blue?, 1986, To Hell With Dying, 1988, The Temple of My Familiar, 1989, Finding the Green Stone, 1991, Possessing the Secret of Joy, 1992, The Complete Stories, 1994, By The Light of My Father's Smile, 1998, The Way Forward Is with a Broken Heart, 2000, Now Is The Time to Open Your Heart, 2005, (poetry collections) Once, 1968, Revolutionary Petunias and Other Poems, 1973, Good Night, Willie Lee, I'll See You in the Morning, 1979, Horses Make a Landscape Look More Beautiful, 1985, Her Blue Body Everything We Know: Earthling Poems, 1991, Absolute Trust in the Goodness of the Earth, 2003, A Poem Traveled Down My Arm: Poems And Drawings, 2003, Collected Poems, 2005, (non-fiction) In Search of Our Mothers' Gardens: Womanist Prose, 1983, Living by the Word, 1988, Warrior Marks, 1993, The Same River Twice: Honoring the Difficult, 1996, Anything We Love Can Be Saved: A Writer's Activism, 1997, Go Girl!: The Black Woman's Book of Travel and Adventure, 1997, Pema Chodron and Alice Walker in Conversation, 1999, Sent By Earth: A Message from the Grandmother Spirit After the Bombing of the World Trade Center and Pentagon, 2001, We Are the Ones We Have Been Waiting For, 2006. Recipient O. Henry award, 1986, Nora Astorga Leadership award, 1989, Fred Cody award for lifetime achievement, Bay Area Book Reviewers Assn., 1990, Freedom to Write award, PEN Ctr. USA, 1990, Lillian Smith award, Nat. Endowment Arts, Rosenthal award, Nat. Inst. Arts & Letters, Front Page award for best mag. criticism, Newswoman's Club NY, Radcliffe Inst. fellowship, Merrill fellowship, Guggenheim fellowship; named to Hall of Fame, Calif. Mus. Hist., Women & Arts, 2006. Address: Random House Inc 1745 Broadway #B1 New York NY 10019-4305

WALKER, ANNETTE, retired counseling administrator; BS in Edn., Huntingdon Coll., 1974; MS in Adminstrn. and Supervision, Troy State U., 1977-78, MS in Sch. Counseling, 1990, AA in Sch. Adminstrn., 1992; diploma, World Travel Sch., 1990; diploma in Cosmetology, John Patterson Coll., 1992; MEd in higher Edn. Adminstrn., Auburn U., Ala., 1995. Cert. tchr., adminstr., Ala.; lic. cosmetologist, Ala.; lic. funeral dir., Ala. Tchr. Montgomery (Ala.) Pub. Sch. System, 1976-89, sch. counselor, 1989—2000, behavioral interventionist, 2008; lit. tchr. Fed. Bur. of Justice, 1997—2000; ret., 2000; acad. advisor Cmty. Coll. of Air Force; acad. counselor Maxwell Air Force Base, Ala., guidance counselor edn. office, 2001—; tchr. Evangelical Christian Acad.; master gardener, 2009. Tchr. Fed. Govt., 1997—, US Bur. Justice, 1997—; gymnastics tchr. Cleveland Ave. YMCA, 1971-76; girls coach Montgomery Parks and Recreation, 1973-76; summer sch. sci. tchr. grades 7-9, 1977-88; chmn. dept. sci. Bellingrath Sch., 1987-90, courtesy com., 1987-88, sch. discipline com., 1977-84; recreation asst. Gunter AFB, Ala., 1981-83; calligraphy tchr. Gunter Youth Ctr., 1982; program dir. Maxwell AFB, Ala., 1983-89; vol. tchr. Internat. Officer Sch., 1985—, Adult Laubach Reading Prog., Ala. Goodwill Amb., 1985—, day camp dir., 1987, calligraphy tchr., 1988; trainer internat. law for sec. students, Ala., 1995—; sales rep. Ala. World Travel, 1990—; behavior aid Brantwood Children's Home, 1996—; computer tchr. hs diploma program Montgomery County Sch., 1995—; hotel auditor, 1995—; Am. del. to China, People to People Internat., 1998; acad. advisor CC of Air Force, Maxwell AFB, Ala., 2002—; ESL tchr., counselor, Okinawa, Japan, 2000-02, Germany, 2005-06; behavior specialist Group Homes for Children, 2006; greeter FedEx Kinko's, 2006-; tchr. Independent Sch. Assn., 2007—, Evangel Christian Acad.; leader workshops in field. Mem. CAP; vol. zoo activities Tech. Scholarship Program for Ala. Tchrs. Computer Courses, Montgomery; bd. dirs. Cleveland Ave. YMCA, 1976—80; sponsor Belle-Howe chpt. Young Astronauts, 1986—90, Pate Howe chpt., 1991—92; judge Montgomery County Children Festival Elem. Sci. Fair, 1988—90; bd. dirs. Troy State U. Drug Free Schs., 1992—; chmn. Maxwell AFB Red Cross-Youth, 1986—88; goodwill amb. sponsor to various families (award 1989, 95); State of Ala. rep. P.A.T.C.H.-Internat. Law Inst., 1995; founder Okinawa, Japan chpt., bd. dirs. People to People Internat., 2000; tchr. Club Z, 2006—; officer Montgomery Police Dept., 2007—; behavior interventionist Montgomery County Pub. Sch., 2008—; tchr. Sunday sch. Beulah Bapt. Ch., Montgomery. Recipient Outstanding High Sch. Sci./Math. Tchr. award, Sigma Xi, 1989, Most Outstanding Youth Coun. Leader award, Maxwell AFB Youth Ctr., 1987, Outstanding Ala. Goodwill Amb. award, 1989, 1995, Tchr. of Yr. award, Paterson Sch., 1990, Career Infusion award (Most Appreciated Tchr. award), 1987, Montgomery Pub. Sch., 1982, 1984, Earthwatch Ednl. award, Israel, 1997, 20 Class award, Maxwell AFB Internat. Fgn. Officer Program, 25 Class award, 2003, 30 Class award, 2005, Ala. Goodwill Amb. award, Maxwell AFB Inernat. Officer Program 30 Class award, 2005; named Tchr. of the Week, WCOV-TV, 1992, Ala. Tchr. in Space Program, summer, 1989, Local Coord. Young Astronaut Program, 1988, Citizen Amb. to China, People to People Internat., 1999; Fulbright scholar, Japan, 1999. Mem. NEA, Internat. Platform Assn., People to People Internat. (founder, bd. trustees, organizer, pres. Ala. chpt. 1998), Nat. Sci. Tchrs. Assn., Ala. Sch. Counselors, Montgomery Sch. Counselors Assn., Montgomery County Ednl. Assn., Space Camp Amb., Huntingdon Alumni Assn. (sec.-treas.), Ala. Goodwill Amb., Montgomery Capital City Club, Young Astronauts, Ea. Star, Japan Friends of Fulbright Meml. Fund Tchr. Prog., Water Watch, Montgomery, AL, Zeta Phi Beta, Chi Delta Phi, Kappa Pi. Avocations: international travel, calligraphy, international food, cruising. Personal E-mail: awalker2001@yahoo.com.

WALKER, ANTOINE DEVON, professional basketball player; b. Chgo., Aug. 12, 1976; s. Diane Walker; children: Crystal, Alana. Attended, U. Ky. Forward Boston Celtics, 1996—2003, 2005, Dallas Mavericks, 2003—04, Atlanta Hawks, 2004—05, Miami Heat, 2005—07, Minn. Timberwolves, 2007—08, Memphis Grizzlies, 2008. Co-owner Walker Williams. Founder The 8 Found., Boston, Chgo., 1997—. Named to NBA All-Rookie Team, 1996—97, NBA All-Star Team, 1997—98, 2001—02, 2002—03. Avocations: golf, basketball, football, video games, music.*

WALKER, AUDREY THAYER, clinical social worker, psychotherapist; b. Quincy, Mass., June 29, 1935; d. Paul Clifton and Dorothy Ritchie Thayer; m. David A. Walker, Aug. 21, 1982; children: Elizabeth Penniman Billett Bilhartz, Matthew Thayer Billett. AB, Wheaton Coll., Ill., 1957; MSS/MSW, Smith Coll., Northampton, Mass., 1959. Acad. Cert. Social Workers, 63, LICSW DC, 1985, bd. cert. diplomate in clin. social work 1990. Caseworker Ch. Home Soc., Boston, 1959—61; caseworker, family therapist Family Svc. Agy. of Sacramento, 1961—63; chief psychiat. social worker, supr. dept. psychiatry George Washington U., 1969—90, adj. assoc. prof., 1971—, dir. social work tng., 1975—90; adj. assoc. prof. Smith Coll. Sch. for Social Work, Northampton, Mass., 1971—2003; pvt. practice clin. social worker, psychotherapist, 1990—; adj. faculty Counseling and Psychiat. Svcs., Georgetown U., 1993—2006; field faculty advisor Smith Coll. Sch. for Social Work, Northampton, Mass., 1996—2003, adj. assoc. prof., 2006—07. Co-chair Smith Coll Sch. Social Work/Washington Psychoanalytic Inst. Jour. Club, 1975—76; co-leader theoretical integrative seminar Smith Coll. Sch. for Social Work, 2003—07, Clin. Social Work Inst., Washington; lectr., presenter m-svc. tng. faculty Am. U., lectr. student counseling & psychiat. svc., 1990—2000, student counseling. Author: Psychoanalysis and Society: Can Psychoanalysis Help to Understand Modern Conflicts?, Freud at 150: Twenty-First Century Essays on a Man of Genius, 2008; contbr. articles to profl. jours. Administrv. collaboration Life Cycle Courses George Washington U. Dept. Psychiatry, Washington Psychoanalytic Inst., 1975—85; co-chair benefit ann. lectures Smith Coll. Sch. for Social Work Alumni Assn., Washington, 1978—88. Recipient Day-Garrett award for significant and maj. contbns. to social work, Smith Coll. Sch. Social Work, 2005; nominee Disting. Practitioner, Nat. Acads. of Practice, 2005—; Grad. Study scholar, Episcopal Ch. of Am., Youth Svcs. Divsn., 1957-1959, Sr. Class Grad. Study awardee and scholar, Wheaton Coll. Sr. Class, 1957, Freudian Scholar presenter, Austrian Embassy Symposium, 2006. Mem.: Am. Assn. Psychoanalysis (presenter clin. social work nat. conf., NYC 2009), Washington Psychoanalytic Ctr. (full elected mem. 2009—), Am. Psychoanalytic Assn. (psychotherapy assoc.), Psychoanalysis and Brain Study Group, Am. Assn. Psychoanalysis in Clin. Social Work (diversity com. 2007—), Am. Group Psychotherapy Assn. (clin. mem. 1982—2004), Smith Coll. Sch. for Social Work Alumni Assn. (Greater Washington chpt. steering com. 1974—93, co-chair Washington Psychoanalytic Jour. Club 1975—76, co-chair, annual benifit lectr. 1975—85), Greater Washington Soc. for Clin. Social Work (v.p. profl. affairs 1990—94, bd. mem.-at-large, advisor 1994—2005, continuing edn. com. 1995—2008, founding chair consultation svcs. com. 1997—98, ethics conf. com. 2004, 2006, ad hoc ethics com. 2006—07, ethics conf. com. 2008, Cert. of Appreciation 1991—97, 2002—04), Nat. Membership Com. Psychoanalysis Social Work (Washington-Balt. area chair 1997—2003), Smith Coll. Club (Washington) (bd. dirs. 1983—87), Social Sci. Honor Soc., Pi Gamma Mu. Avocations: travel, literature, theater, dance, art. Office: 3 Washington Cir NW Ste 406 Washington DC 20037 Business E-Mail: audrey.walker@msb.edu.

WALKER, BERNICE BAKER, artist; b. Carbondale, Pa., Dec. 25, 1928; d. William Robert and Bernice Mary (Parry) Baker; m. Joseph Henry Walker, Sept. 13, 1952. Student, Richmond Profl. Inst., 1946-47; BFA, RI Sch. Design, 1952. Artist Highlights for Children, 1952-55, Studio K, Lancaster, Pa., 1959-64; tchr. Heintzelman Art Assn., Manheim, Pa., 1975-86; owner The Design Corner, Lancaster, 1989—2003. Tchr. Lancaster County Art Assn. Mem. Pa. Watercolor Soc., Venice Art Ctr., Englewood Art Ctr., Longboat Key Ctr. of the Arts, Am. Soc. Portrait Artists, Sarasota Portrait Soc., SW Pastel Soc., Am. Portrait Soc., Manasota Weavers and Spinners. E-mail: bernspin1@aol.com.

WALKER, BEVERLY ANN, minister, health facility administrator; b. Baltimore, Md., Mar. 17, 1950; d. Morris Allen and Mary Estelle Johnson; children: Tyrone Anthony Jeffries, Towanda Tonette Fortune, Bernard Alexander Jeffries, Charlotte Shrae Young, Harold Lawrence. BA, Va. Sem. and Coll., 1998; M. Religious Edn., Andersonville Bapt. Sem., 2000, DRE, 2002; MDiv, Va. U.-Lynchburg, 2005. Supr. ins. processing Va. Health Svcs. Found., Charlottesville, 1982—95; pastor North River Bapt. Ch., Bridgewater, Va., 1983—2001; founder Va. Women in Ministry, Charlottesville, 1990—95; moderator Berean Bapt. Assn., Bridgewater, 1994—98; founder God Called and Chosen Vessels, Stuarts Draft, 2002—; pastor Rising Sun Bapt. Ch., North Garden, 2004—. Counselor Harrisonburg Jail, Va., 1998—2001; bd. dirs. Helping Hand Ministry, Harrisonburg, 2002—. Contbr.: ch. adminstrn. book and handbook Decently and In Order. Mem. NAACP, Harrisonburg, Va., 1985. Recipient Female Ministerial award, Shenandoah Valley Hit Newspaper, 1994, Outstanding Svc. award, Va. Women in Ministry, 1995. Mem.: Hampton's Min. Conf., Bapt. Gen. Conf., Va. Bapt. Conf., Berean Valley Bapt. Assn. (life). Liberal. Baptist. Avocations: travel, reading, singing, dance, exercise. Personal E-mail: beverlymrd3@aol.com.

WALKER, BRIAN C., manufacturing executive; Pres., N. Am. Herman Miller, Inc., 1999—2003, pres., COO, 2003—04, pres., CEO, 2004—. Bd. dirs. Herman Miller, Inc. Office: Herman Miller 855 E Main Ave Zeeland MI 49464-0302 Office Phone: 616-654-3000. Office Fax: 616-654-3632.

WALKER, CARLENE MARTIN, state legislator; b. Sept. 2, 1947; m. Gordon D. Walker; 4 children. BS, Brigham Young U., 1969. Supr. coding & data entry the Wirthlin Group, 1982-86; cons. D.K. Shifflet & Assocs., 1987-88; ptnr., mgr. Covecrest Properties, 1978-99; tech. recruiter Manpower Tech., 1999-2000; mem. Utah State Senate, Salt Lake City, 2001—. Chair, founder Women's Polit. Action Com., chair transp. appropriations. Active AGs Task Force on ID Theft, Capitol Preservation Bd.; bd. dirs. United Way, Salt Lake Convention and Vis. Bur., Hogle Zoo. Republican. Mormon. Office: 4085 E Prospector Dr Salt Lake City UT 84121 Office Phone: 801-773-4599.

WALKER, CAROLYN MAE, retired secondary school educator; b. Neptune, NJ, Apr. 29, 1941; d. Frank and Estella (Matutis) W; m. Philp A. Carr, Jan. 28, 2006. BA in Sci., Montclair State Coll., 1963; MA in Edn., Newark State Coll., 1970. Cert. tchr., N.J. Elem. tchr. Howell Twp. Bd. Edn., NJ, 1963-65, Englishtown-Manalapan Regional Schs., NJ, 1965-67, Freehold Borough Schs., NJ, 1967-70, Freehold Regional HS, 1970-73, North Brunswick Twp. Bd. Edn., NJ, 1975—2002; ret., 2002. Vol. St. Vincent de Paul. Mem. NSTA, NJ Sci. Tchrs. Assn., NJ Schoolwomen's Club, Alpha Delta Kappa (chair pres. 1972-74, state sec. 1974-76, state v.p. 1976-78), Deep Cut Bonsai Club. Roman Catholic. Avocations: cruising, dressmaking, needlecrafts, gardening, classical/popular music. Personal E-mail: caramw@verizon.net.

WALKER, CHARLES DODSLEY, conductor, organist; b. NYC, Mar. 16, 1920; s. Marshall Starr and Maude Graham (Marriott) Walker; m. Janet Elizabeth Hayes, May 30, 1949 (dec. Feb. 1997); children: Peter Hayes, Susan Starr; m. Elizabeth Ann Phillips, Jan. 14, 2001. BS, Trinity Coll., 1940; AM, Harvard U., 1947. Organist, choirmaster Am. Cathedral, Paris, 1948-50, Ch. of the Heavenly Rest, NYC, 1951-88; music dir. Blue Hill Troupe, Ltd., NYC, 1955-90, Chapin Sch., NYC, 1961-85; mem. organ faculty Union Theol. Sem., NYC, 1962-73, NYU, NYC, 1968-80; dean, music dir. Berkshire Choral Inst., Sheffield, Mass., 1982-91; organist, choirmaster Trinity Episcopal Ch., Southport, Conn., 1988—2007; artist-in-residence St. Luke's Parish, Darien, Conn., 2007—. Contbr. articles to profl. jours. Lt. comdr. USNR, 1942—46. Recipient Disting. Alumnus award, Cathedral Choir Sch., 1988; named Artist of Yr., Fairfield Arts Coun., 2004. Fellow: Am. Guild Organists (nat. pres. 1971—75); mem.: Canterbury Choral Soc. (founder, condr. 1952—), Am. Fedn. Musicians, St. Wilfrid Club, Bohemians. Avocations: travel, photography. Home: 160 W 96th St Apt 15N New York NY 10025-9212 Office: Ch Heavenly Rest 2 East 90th St New York NY 10128 Home Phone: 212-222-9458; Office Phone: 212-289-3400. Personal E-mail: dodsley@aol.com.

WALKER, CHARLES EUGENE, retired science educator; b. Winterset, Iowa, Dec. 17, 1936; s. Albert Cecil Walker and Bessie Irene Headley; m. Shannon Rose Philp, June 1, 1958; children: Alan Eugene, Tomas Charles, Bekianne Covalt. PhD, ND State U., Fargo, 1966. Rsch. engr. Gen. Mills Ctrl. Rsch., Mpls., 1959—62; prof. & chmn. Valley City State Coll., ND, 1965—74; assoc. dir. rsch. Fairmont Foods Co., Omaha, 1974—80; prof. U. Nebr., Lincoln, 1980—87, Kans. State U., Manhattan, 1987—; sr. rsch. scientist Bread Rsch. Inst., North Ryde, Australia, 1998—99. Recipient Fellow, Am. Assn. Cereal Chemists, 2002. Mem.: AACC Internat. Achievements include research in food and baking technonologies. Office: Kans State Univ Shellenberger 107 Manhattan KS 66506-2201 Office Fax: 1 785 532 7010. Business E-Mail: chuckw@ksu.edu.

WALKER, CHARLES URMSTON, retired university president; b. Bolivar, Pa., June 20, 1931; s. Charles William and Frances May (Urmston) W.; m. Cherie Hall Duckworth, Aug. 7, 1959; children: Douglas Leland, Christy Lynn. BA, U. Pitts., 1953; MA, Columbia U., 1958; PhD, Stanford U., 1964; LLD (hon.), Kanto Gakuin U., 1979; LHD (hon.), Linfield Coll., 1992. Asst. prof. English Rockford Coll., Ill., 1958-61; dept. head, residence dir. Menlo Coll., Menlo Park, Calif., 1961-64; v.p., dean Hamline U., St. Paul, 1964-70; pres. Russell Sage Coll., Troy, NY, 1970-75, Linfield Coll., McMinnville, Oreg., 1975-92, pres. emeritus, 1992—; ednl. cons., 1992—; vice chair, dir. Ford Family Found., Roseburg, Oreg., 1993, dir. managed programs, 1993-98. Mem. Univ. Pres. Initiative, IIE/USIA/NATO, Brussels, 1991. Bd. dirs. South Tillamook County Libr., 1994, pres., 2004; pres. Neskowin (Oreg.) Chamber Music; dir. Oreg. Cultural Trust, Found. Better Oreg.; trustee James & Marion Miller Found., Portland. Warg scholar U. Pitts., 1949-51; Univ. fellow Stanford U., 1963-64; Hill Found. grantee, St. Paul, 1970; Paul Harris fellow Rotary Internat., 1987; recipient Community Svc. award Troy, N.Y. Troy C. of C., 1975, First Citizen award McMinnville, Oreg., 1989, Govs. award Oreg. Vol. of Yr., 2006, Dean Men award Rockford, Disting. Svc. award U. Oreg., 2009; named Man of Yr., Troy C. of C., 1975. Mem. Univ. Club (Portland), Rotary (past pres. McMinnville). Home: 1324 SW Gilorr St Mcminnville OR 97128-6617 Personal E-mail: cwalkc@oregoncoast.com.

WALKER, CHARLS EDWARD, economist, consultant; b. Graham, Tex., Dec. 24, 1923; s. Pinkney Clay and Sammye D. (McCombs) W.; m. Harmolyn Hart, June 24, 1949; children: Carolyn, Charls Edward. BBA, U. Tex., 1947, MBA, 1948; PhD in Econs., U. Pa., 1955. Instr. fin. U. Tex., 1947-48, asst. prof., then assoc. prof., 1950-54; instr. fin. U. Pa. Wharton Sch., 1948-50; fin. economist Fed. Res. Bank Phila., 1953; with Fed. Res. Bank Dallas, 1954-61, v.p., econ. adviser, 1958-61; economist Republic Nat. Bank Dallas, 1955-56; asst. to sec. treasury, 1959-61; exec. v.p. Am. Bankers Assn., NYC, 1961-69; under sec. treasury, 1969-72; dep. sec., 1972-73; pilot instr. USAF, 1945. Adj. prof. U. Tex., Austin, 1986-96, Tex. A&M U., 2000-2003; bd. dirs. Nat. Coun. Econ.

Edn.; chmn., CEO Charls E. Walker Assocs., Inc., 1973-96; disting. vis. prof. Emory U., 2000-02. Co-editor: The Bankers Handbook, New Directions in Federal Tax Policy, The Consumption Tax: A Better Alternative, 1987, Intellectual Property Rights and Capital Formation, 1988, The U.S. Savings Challenge, 1990; contbr. articles to profl. jours. and newspapers, chpts. to books. Founder, chmn. emeritus Am. Coun. for Capital Formation; co-founder, chmn. exec. com. Com. on the Present Danger, 1976; chmn. Pres.'s adv. coun. on minority enterprise, 1973-75; co-chmn. Presdl. Debates, 1976; founder chmn. Bretton Woods Com.; chmn. Ronald Reagan's Task Force on Tax Policy, 1980; sr. advisor Ctr. for Deliberative Polling, U. Tex., 1996, Stanford U., 2003. 2d lt. USAAF, 1943—45. Recipient Alexander Hamilton award U.S. Dept. Treasury, Urban League award, Baker award for Exemplary Svc. to Econ. Edn., 1991, Disting. Svc. award, 2002, Pro Bono Meritas award Coll. Liberal Arts U. Tex., 2003; named Disting. Alumnus, U. Tex., 1994. Mem.: Coun. Fgn. Rels., Congl. Club (Bethesda, Md.), Burning Tree Club. Home: 9426 Thrush Ln Potomac MD 20854-4143 Personal E-mail: charlswalk@aol.com. *What's good for the public interest ultimately is good for every person, business, or other group in the nation. This, combined with modern application of the Golden Rule, about sums it up.*

WALKER, CLARENCE EUGENE, psychology professor; b. Monongahela, Pa., Jan. 8, 1939; s. Lewis G. Walker and Olga T. Brioli; div.; children: Chad Eugene, Kyle Lewis, Cass Emanuel. BS in Psychology summa cum laude, Geneva Coll., 1960; MS in Clin. Psychology, Purdue U., 1963, PhD in Clin. Psychology, 1965. Lic. psychologist, Okla. Psychology trainee West 10th St. VA Hosp., Indpls., 1962—63; intern in clin. psychology Riley Children's Hosp., West 10th St. VA Hosp., Indpls., 1963—64; asst. prof. Westmont Coll., 1964—68; pvt. practice clin. psychology Santa Barbara, Calif., 1965—68; from asst. prof. to assoc. prof. Baylor U., 1968—74; pvt. practice clin. psychology Waco, Tex., 1970—74; assoc. prof. med. sch. U. Okla., Oklahoma City, 1974—80, prof. med. sch., dir. pediatric psychology tng. program, 1980—95, prof. emeritus, 1995; chief pediatric psychology svc. Okla. Children's Meml. Hosp., 1974—80, dir. out-patient pediatric psychology clinic, 1974—80; assoc. chief mental health svcs. Children's Hosp. Okla., 1980—95; pres. Psychol. Cons., Inc., 1998—. Cons. Head Start Program, Waco, 1968-70, VA Hosp, Waco, 1969-74, VA Ctr., Temple, Tex., 1969-74, Region XII Ednl. Svc. Ctr., Waco, 1971-74, Rusk (Tex.) State Hosp., 1972-74, Bapt. Children's Home, Oklahoma City, 1975-79; rsch. cons. Los Alamos (N.Mex.) Pub. Schs., 1975-79; chmn. divsn. edn. and psychology Westmont Coll., 1966-68; consulting psychologist, 1995—. Author: Learn to Relax, 1975, 3d edit., 2001, (with P. Clement, A. Hedberg and L. Wright) Clinical Procedures for Behavior Therapy, 1981, (with B.L. Bonner and K. Kaufman) The Physically and Sexually Abused Child, 1988, others; editor: The History of Clinical Psychology in Autobiography, vol. I, 1992, vol. II, 1993, (with M.C. Roberts) Handbook of Clinical Child Psychology, 1983, 3d edit., 2001; contbr. articles to profl. jours. Fellow APA; mem. AAAS, Southwestern Psychol. Assn. (pres. 1977), Okla. Psychol. Assn. (pres. 1983), Soc. Pediatric Psychology (pres. 1986), Ctrl. Tex. Psychol. Assn. (pres. 1973), Sigma Xi. Avocations: reading, wine tasting, travel. Office Phone: 405-341-7399. Business E-Mail: genewalker@iname.com.

WALKER, CLINT B., Russian language and literature educator; b. Norway, Maine, Oct. 18, 1968; s. Clifford Lincoln and Pearl Christine Walker; m. Alice Anne Harris; children: Meredith, Owen. BA, Colby Coll., Waterville, Maine, 1991; MA, U. Wis., Madison, 1993, PhD, 2006. Tchg. asst. U. Wis., 1993—2001; vis. instr. Coll. William and Mary, Williamsburg, Va., 2001—02; grad. fellow Trinity Coll., Hartford, Conn., 2002—04, vis. instr., 2004—06; vis. asst. prof. U. Notre Dame, Ind., 2006—; asst. prof. Russian dept. modern & classical Langs. & Lit. U. Mont. Office: U Notre Dame 318 O'Shaughnessy Hall Notre Dame IN 46556

WALKER, DALE MAXWELL, city official; b. Big Rapids, Mich., Dec. 18, 1947; s. Lewis M. and Hilma I. (Windquist) W.; m. Joanne Kay Richmond, June 22, 1968; children: Christina Elizabeth, Heather Marie. BS, Ferris State U., 1970; MBA, Ctrl. Mich. U., 1981. Cert. govt. fin. mgr., credentialed city mgr. Dir. fin. City of Owosso, Mich., 1970-74; internal auditor John Wesley Coll., 1974—76; corp. treas. Mich. Bapt. Homes, Detroit, 1976-77; dir. fin. City of Cadillac, Mich., 1977—2007; CFO DC Retirement Bd., 2008—09; dir. Fin. City Suffolk, Va., 2009—. Pres. Gospel Bookstore, Inc., Cadillac, 1983-98; bd. dirs. Workplace Ministry, 2001-05. Bd. dirs. Wexford County United Way, 1980-82, Shiawassee County United Way, 1971-72; sec.-treas. Cadillac Police and Fire Retirement System, 1977-87, bd. dirs. 1987-2007; chmn. Mcpl. Employees Retirement System, Mich., 1997-2007. Fellow Govtl. Fin. Officers Assn. U.S. and Can. (Profl. Achievement award 1984-2008); mem. Mich. Mcpl. Fin. Officers Assn. (bd. dirs. 1983-2007, Va. Govt. Fin. Officer, 2009-), Internat. City Mgrs. Assn., Mcpl. Treas. Assn. U.S. and Can. (bd. dirs. 1982-84), Assn. Govt. Accts. Avocations: golf, swimming, reading. Home: 2062 Nick Laks Suffolk Suffolk VA 23435

WALKER, DAVID ALAN, finance educator; b. York, Pa., Jan. 5, 1941; s. Arthur Benjamin and Alva (Strasbougher) Walker; m. Audrey Thayer, Aug. 21, 1982; children: Matthew Billett, Elizabeth Penniman Bilhartz. BA, Pa. State U., 1962; MS, Iowa State U., 1964, PhD, 1968. Asst. prof. Pa. State U., 1968-70; economist FDIC, 1970-76, 78-80; vis. assoc. prof. Northwestern U., 1976-77; dir. rsch. Office Comptroller Currency, 1977-78; assoc. prof. fin. Georgetown U., 1980-82, prof., 1982-92, assoc. dean, 1985-87, John A. Largay prof., 1992—. Chair governing bd. Credit Rsch. Ctr., 1997-05; dir. Capital Mkts. Rsch. Ctr., 1989-2005; mem. quality assessment team Israel Coun. Higher Edn., 2005-07; cons. in field. Co-author textbooks; editor Jour. Fin. Rsch., 1981-87; co-editor Jour. Small Bus. Fin., 1992-95; mem. editl. bd. Jour. Applied Fin., Jour. Fin. Rsch., Fin. Mgmt., J.F.Q.A., Fin. Rev., Quar. Rev. Econ. and Fin., Jour. Small Bus. Fin.; contbr. articles to profl. jours. NDEA fellow, 1962-64. Mem. Am. Econ. Assn., So. Fin. Assn. (bd. dirs.), Ea. Fin. Assn. (bd. dirs.), Fin. Mgmt. Assn. (v.p. 1990-91, pres. 1994-95, trustee 1995-2005, chair bd. trustees 1999-2005), Beta Gamma Sigma. Republican. Home: 4416 Que St NW Washington DC 20007 Office: Georgetown U Sch Bus Washington DC 20057-0001 Home Phone: 202-363-0276; Office Phone: 202-687-4582. E-mail: walkerd@georgetown.edu.

WALKER, DAVID H., medical educator; b. Nashville, May 31, 1943; s. William and Sarah Huddleston Walker; m. Marjorie B. Walker, May 31, 1968. BA, Davidson Coll., 1965; MD, Vanderbilt U. Sch. Medicine, 1969; Docteur Honoris Causae (hon.), U. Mediterranee, Marseille, France, 1999. Asst. surgeon USPHS, 1973—75; rsch. med. officer CDC, Atlanta, 1973—75; clin. asst. prof. Emory U., 1974—75; asst. prof. U. NC, Chapel Hill, 1975—80, assoc. prof., 1980—86, prof., 1986—87; prof., chmn. U. Tex. Med. Br., Galveston, 1987—; com. mem. Armed Forces Epidemiol. Bd., 2006, Def. Health Bd., 2006—; with, nat. rsch. coun. standing com. US Dept. Def., 2007—. Com. mem. Nat. Biodefense Network, 2003—; mem. sci. adv. bd. Armed Forces Inst. Pathology, 1996—2004. Editor: (book) Tropical Infectious Diseases: Principles, Pathogens, and Practice, 8 books; contbr. articles to profl. jours., chapters to books. Grantee, NIH, 1980—, 1991—, 2003—. Mem.: Am. Soc. Rickettsiology, Am. Soc. Tropical Medicine and Hygiene, US-Can. Acad. Pathology. Achievements include patents for Homologous 28-kDa immunodominant protein genes of Ehrlichia canis and uses thereof; 28-kDa immunoreactive protein gene of Ehrlichia canis and uses thereof; P43 antigen for the immunodiagnosis of canine ehrlichiosis and uses thereof; Homologous 28-kilodalton immunodominant progein genes of Ehrlichia canis and uses thereof; Ehrlichia canis 120-kDa immunodominant antigenic protein and gene; Immunodominant 120k-Da surface-exposed adhesion protein genes of Ehrlichia chaffeensis. Office Phone: 409-772-3989.

WALKER, DAVID MICHAEL, foundation administrator; b. Birmingham, Ala., Oct. 2, 1951; s. David Sellers and Dorothy Ann (West) Walker; m. Mary Carmel Etheredge, June 12, 1971; children: Carol Marie, James Andrew. BS in Acctg., Jacksonville U., Fla., 1973, PhD (hon.), 2006; Sr. Mgmt. Govt. Cert., Harvard U. John F. Kennedy Sch. Govt., 1986; PhD (hon.), Bryant Coll., 2002, Lincoln Meml. U., 2004, Am. U., 2007. CPA Fla., Tex. Sr. auditor Price Waterhouse & Co./Coopers & Lybrand, Jacksonville, 1973-76; dir. pers. Coopers & Lybrand, Atlanta, Houston, 1976-79; Eastern regional mgr. Source Svcs. Corp., Washington, 1979-83; acting exec. dir., dep. exec. dir. Pension Benefit Guaranty Corp., Washington, 1983-85; dep. asst. sec. US Dept. Labor, Washington, 1985-87, asst. sec. for pension & welfare benefit programs, 1987-89; ptnr., global mng. dir. human capital svcs. practice Arthur Andersen LLP, Atlanta, 1989-98; US comptroller gen. US Govt. Accountability Office (GAO), Washington, 1998—2008; pres., CEO Peter G. Peterson Found., NYC, 2008—. Pub. trustee for social security & medicare US Dept. Labor, 1990—95; chmn. UN Ind. Audit Adv. Com.; bd. dirs. Com. for Responsible Fed. Budget, Partnership for Pub. Svc. Author: Retirement Security: Understanding and Planning Your Financial Future, 1996; co-author: Delivering on the Promise: How to Attract, Manage and Retain Human Capital, 1998; contbr. articles to profl. jours. Mem.: Trilateral Commn., PCAOB Adv. Coun., Nat. Acad. Pub. Adminstrn., Am. Soc. Pub. Adminstrn. (mem. adv.), Sons of Am. Revolution, Cosmos Club, City Tavern Club. Roman Catholic. Office: Peter G Peterson Found 712 Fifth Ave 48th Fl New York NY 10019 Business E-Mail: dwalker@pgpf.org.

WALKER, DENNIS KENDON, retired botany professor; b. Sacramento, Calif., Aug. 1, 1938; s. William Thomas and Jesse Vergene Walker; m. Harriet Rae Swensen, Sept. 4, 1960; children: Rebecca Rae Logsdon, Montgomery Brent, Juliet Jean, Gregory Owen. AA, Am. River Jr. Coll., Sacramento, 1958; BA, Humboldt State Coll., Arcata, Calif., 1960; MS, U. Calif., Davis, 1964, PhD, 1966. Rsch. asst. U. Calif., 1960—63, tchg. asst., 1963—65; asst. prof. botany Humboldt State Coll., Arcata, Calif., 1965—70, assoc. prof. botany, 1970—76, prof. botany, 1976—2005, emeritus prof. botany, 2005—. Home: 2010 Arthur Ln Mckinleyville CA 95519-9437 Office Fax: 707-826-3201. Business E-Mail: dkw1@humboldt.edu.

WALKER, DEWARD EDGAR, JR., anthropologist, educator; b. Johnson City, Tenn., Aug. 3, 1935; s. Deward Edgar and Matilda Jane (Clark) W.; m. Candace J. Arroyo; children: Alice, Deward Edgar III, Mary Jane, Sarah, Daniel, Joseph Benjamin. Student, Ea. Oreg. Coll., 1953-54, 56-58, Univ. of the Americas, 1958-59; BA in Anthropology with honors, U. Oreg., 1960-61, PhD in Anthropology, 1964; postgrad., Wash. State U., 1962. Asst. prof. anthropology George Washington U., Washington, 1964-65, Wash. State U., Pullman, 1965-67, research collaborator, 1967-69; assoc. prof., chmn. dept. Sociology/Anthropology, lab. dir. U. Idaho, Moscow, 1967-69; prof. U. Colo., Boulder, 1969—, research assoc. in population processes program of inst. behavioral sci., 1969-73, assoc. dean Grad. Sch., 1973-76. Founder, v.p. Walker Rsch. Group, Ltd., Boulder, Colo., 1995. Founder, co-editor Northwest Anthropol. Rsch. Notes, 1966—; editor, Plateau Vol.: Handbook of North American Indians, 1971-98; author of over 250 publs. Mem. tech. steering panel Hanford Environ. Dose Reconstrn. Project, 1988-95, Basalt Waste Isolation Project, Hanford, 1986-88; advisor Native Am. affairs. With U.S. Army, 1954-62. Fellow NSF, 1961, NDEA, 1961-64. Fellow Am. Anthropol. Assn. (assoc. editor Am. Anthropologist 1973-74), Soc. Applied Anthropology (hon. life, exec. com. 1970-79, treas. 1976-79, chmn. 1960-2000, cons., expert witness, editor Human Orgn. 1970-76, High Plains Applied Anthropologist); mem. AAAS, Am. Acad. Polit. and Social Scis., N.W. Anthropol. Conf. Achievements include research in Yakama, Colville Salish-Kootenai, Sioux, Cayuse, Washo, Shoshone, Paiute, Bannock, Umatilla, Tulalip, Blackfeet, Arapaho, Navajo, Mohawk, Sioux, Bannock and affiliated tribes of Northwest Indians. Avocations: geology, mining, ranching. Home: PO Box 4147 Boulder CO 80306-4147 Office: U Colo PO Box 233 Boulder CO 80309-0233 Office Phone: 303-492-6719. Business E-Mail: walkerde@colorado.edu. *I have been both lucky and happy to have had the opportunities to do so many wonderful things in my life as an anthropologist.*

WALKER, DIANNE, dancer, performing company executive; studied with Mildred Kennedy-Bradic, Leon Collins, Jimmy Mitchell and Jimmy Slyde, EdM. Performed with Collins & Co.; dir. Leon Collins Dance Studio, Inc., Brookline, Mass., 1982—95; artistic dir. TapDancin' Inc., Boston. Mem. Dance USA Task Force on Dance Edn.; bd. dirs. Mass. Cultural Coun., 1996—; US adjudicator World Tap Dance Championships, Dresden, Germany, 1997. Dancer (Broadway plays) Black and Blue, 1989, (films) Tap, 1989, (TV films) Black and Blue, 1993, (documentaries) Gregory Hines' Tap Dance in America, 1989, Songs Unwritten: A Tap Dancer Remembered, 1989. Recipient Living Treasure in Am. Dance award, Oklahoma City U., 1998, Savion Glover award, St. Louis, 2000, Flo-Bert award, NY Com. to Celebrate Nat. Tap Dance Day, 2003, Humanitarian award, Debbie Allen Dance Acad., Gregory Hines Meml. award, LA Tap Dance Festival, 2004, Hoofers award, Tap City NYC, 2004, Lifetime Achievement award, Vancouver Tap Dance Soc., 2005, Living Legend award, Tapology Festival, Flint, Mich., 2006; fellow US Artists, 2008. Office: TapDancin Inc 67 Blake St Mattapan MA 02126-1061*

WALKER, DONALD BURKE, retired music educator, archivist, composer; b. Ventura, Calif., Dec. 18, 1941; s. Marion Russell and Dorothy Burke Walker; m. Harrie Alley (div.); children: Nathaniel Burke, Anthony Cannon; m. Ellen Iris Amsterdam, Aug. 20, 1993. MA in Composition, U. Calif., Berkeley, 1966, MLS, 1974, PhD in Music, 1971; MA in History, Calif. State U., Sacramento, 1992. Vis. asst. prof. Sonoma State U., Rohnert Park, Calif., 1973—74, 1977—78, U. South Fla., Tampa, 1975—77, Oreg. State U., Corvallis, 1979; organist St. Paul's United Meth. Ch., Stockton, Calif., 1980—2000; univ. archivist U. of Pacific, Stockton, 1991—2003; ret., 2004. History columnist San Joaquin Farm Bur. News, Stockton, 1990—98. Composer: Symphony # 5, 2002, Seven Psalms, 2003, musician numerous compositions on VVM label. Archivist San Joaquin County Hist. Soc., Lodi, Calif., 1989—2003, editor quar. publ., 2000—03; historian exhbn. catalog and exhibit Italian Presence in San Joaquin Valley, 1994. Grantee, NEH, 1977, Composer in Cmty., Oakland, Calif., 1997. Mem.: Am. Music Ctr. Democrat.

WALKER, DORETTA ANITA, director; b. Memphis, Tenn., Feb. 21, 1942; d. Elgin and Mary Ella Walker. BS, So. Ill. U., 1970; cert. reading specialist, Harris Stowe Tchrs. U., 1978; MEd, Nat. Coll. Edn., 1989. Cert. officer African Meth. Episc. Ch., 2004. Mem. Divsn. Curriculum Com., St. Louis, Chpt. I Staff Devel. Planning Com., St. Louis; mem. curriculum com. SAT-MMA, St. Louis; coord. After Sch. Tutorial Program, St. Louis. Recipient Shining Star award, 2004, Tchr. Appreciation award, Urban League of Metro, St. Louis, 1990; named to Wall Tolerance, 2005. Mem.: NAACP, Nat. Bethou Edn. Alumni, So. Ill. U Alumni Assn., The Symner Alumni Assn. (life), Tu Gamma Delta. Democrat. Avocations: travel, photography, jazz. Home: 3026A N Taylor Ave Saint Louis MO 63115

WALKER, DORIS ISAAK, writer, historian, educator; b. Cleve. d. Alphonse Charles and Rose Emma (Gibbons) Isaak; children: Brent Evan Walker, Blair Dana Walker; m. Jack Pierson Smith, 2001. AB, Case Western Reserve U.; postgrad., Northwestern U., U. Calif., Irvine. Publs. editor Brunswick Corp., Chgo.; pub. rels. mgr. Dana Point (Calif.) Harbor, 1970-84; field rsch. writer Kessler Exch., LA, Calif., 1984-89. Instr. Calif. history South Orange County Coll. Dist.; lectr. in field. Author: A Guide Book of Philatelic-Numismatic Covers, 1970, Dana Point Harbor/Capistrano Bay: Home Port for Romance, 1981, 4th edit., 1995, The Whales of Capistrano Bay, 1982, Sections of Orange, 1989, Adventurer's Guide to Dana Point, 1992, Orange County Adventures with Children, 1997, The Heritage of San Clemente, 2000, Coastal Reflections, 2001, Mission Viejo: The Ageless Land, 2005, Orange County Then and Now, 2006, Images of America: Dana Point, 2007, Orange County: A Natural History, 2009; contbr., editor, photographer newspapers, mags. Commr. Orange County Hist. Commn., 1994—; co-founder, coord. Dana Point Festival of Whales, 1975-84; dir. South Coast YMCA. Recipient more than 100 awards including Am. History award DAR, Clarion award, Unique Coverage award, Women in Comm., Woman of Distinction award Capistrano Bay Area, Soroptimist Internat., Crisis Comm. Award Internat. Coun. Indsl. Editors, cert. of recognition Calif. State Senate, Calif. Assembly, US House Reps.; named Orange County Woman of Achievement in Comm. YWCA, First Woman Editor-in-Chief Res. Tribune, Case Western Reserve Univ., Dana Point Citizen of 2006, Dana Point C. of C. Mem. AAUW (pres. San Clemente-Capistrano Bay br.), Nat. Fedn. Press Women (5 Nat. First Place History Book awards), So. Calif. Media Profls. (pres. 2005-07), Calif. Press Women (pres. Orange County dist., state sec.), Dana Point Hist. Soc. (hon. life, co-founder, dir., 1988-, founders day, 2009), San Juan Capistrano Hist. Soc. (dir.), Orange County Hist. Soc. (dir.), Dana Point Lighthouse Soc. (hon. life), Friends of Libr. (hon. life). Avocations: travel, photography. Office: PO Box 546 Dana Point CA 92629-0546 Office Phone: 949-496-6677. E-mail: homeports@aol.com.

WALKER, DOROTHEA LEIGH (THEA WALKER), art therapist, educator; d. Allen L. and Kathryn Walker. BFA, Coll. Creative Studies, Detroit, 1990; MEd, Wayne State U., Detroit, 2002, Grand Valley State U., Traverse City, Mich., 2006. Art therapist, adj. tchr. Children's Home Detroit, 2000—04; art therapist, tchr. Luth. Child Family Svcs., Detroit, 2003—04; adj. prof. art Grand Valley State U., 2006—07. Asst. dir. Children's Home Detroit, 2003—04; guest lectr. Ctrl. Mich. U., Traverse City, 2006, Ferris State U., Traverse City, 2006. Fellow: Nat. Art Edn. Assn., Am. Art Therapy Assn., Nat. Art Therapy Assn., Mich. Art Edn. Assn.; mem.: NEA (life), Am. Soc. Women Educators (assoc.), Mich. Edn. Assn. (life), Kappa Delta Pi (assoc.). Avocations: reading, writing, walking, computers. Home: 6179 Red Fox Run Traverse City MI 49686 Office: Grand Valley State U Dendrinos Dr Traverse City MI 49684 Office Fax: 231-995-7961; Home Fax: 231-995-7961. Personal E-mail: d2psychat@yahoo.com. Business E-Mail: walkedor@student.gvsu.edu.

WALKER, EDWARD KEITH, JR., retired management consultant, military officer; b. Annapolis, Md., Jan. 23, 1933; s. Edward Keith and Miriam (Whitmore) W.; m. Carol Ann Turner, June 12, 1954 (dec. June 14, 2002); children: Lynn Walker Streett, Wendy Louise. BS, U.S. Naval Acad., Annapolis, Md., 1954; postgrad., Armed Forces Staff Coll., Norfolk, Va., 1966; MBA in Fin. Mgmt., George Washington U., Washington, 1970. Commd. ensign U.S. Navy, 1954, advanced through grades to rear admiral, 1981; force supply officer COMSUBLANT Norfolk, Va., 1975—78; exec. officer SPCC Mechanicsburg, Pa., 1978—80; comdr. Naval Supply Ctr., Puget Sound, Bremerton, Wash., 1980—81; Atlantic Fleet supply officer CINCLANTFLT Norfolk, 1981—83; asst. comptroller Navy Dept., Washington, 1983—84; comdr. Naval Supply Systems Command and 35th Chief Supply Corps Washington, 1984—88; v.p. adminstrn. and corp. strategy Resource Cons. Inc., Vienna, Va., 1989—2000, v.p. emeritus, 2000—. Vice chmn. bd. dirs. Herley Industries; bd. visitors Elon U. Decorated D.S.M., Legion of Merit (3 awards); recipient Def. Superior Service medal, 1983 Mem. Vinson Hall Corp. (bd. dirs., chmn. 2003), Naval Acad. Found. (trustee), U.S. Navy Meml. Found. (bd. dirs., treas.), Supply Corps Found. (past pres.), Supply Corps Assn. (past pres.), U.S. Naval Inst. (golden life), Naval Submarine League (life), Naval Order U.S. (life), Surface Navy Assn. (life), Navy League U.S. (life), Naval Acad. Alumni Assn. (life), Mil. Officers Assn. (life), N.Y. Yacht Club, Chesapeake Yacht Club. Republican. Episcopalian. Home: 3520 Saylor Pl Alexandria VA 22304-1831 Office Phone: 202-380-0739. *There is no greater satisfaction than to see your people succeed, and then to insure they get the credit.*

WALKER, EDWARD S., JR., political science professor, former ambassador; b. Abington, Pa., June 13, 1940; s. Edward Stanley and Rosabel Dunlop (Gould) W.; m. Wendy Jane Griffiths, Apr. 7, 1973; Kathryn Erica, Christopher James. BA, Hamilton Coll., 1963; MA, Boston U., 1965. Joined Fgn. Svc., US Dept. State, Washington, 1967; polit. officer US Embassy, Tel Aviv, 1969-73; staff asst. Nr. Ea. affairs US Dept. State, Washington, 1974-75; Arabic lang. trainee Fgn. Svc. Inst., Lebanon, Tunis, Egypt, 1975-77; polit. officer US Embassy, Damascus, Syria, 1977-79; spl. asst. to Pres. The White House, Washington, 1980-82; exec. dir. Office of Dep. Sec. US Dept. State, Washington, 1982-84; mem. Royal Coll. Def. Studies, London, 1984-85; dep. chief of mission US Embassy, Riyadh, Saudi Arabia, 1985-88; dep. asst. sec. Bur. Near East Affairs US Dept. State, 1988-89, US amb. to United Arab Emirates Abu Dhabi, 1989-92, dep. permanent rep. to UN NYC, 1993-94, US amb. to Egypt Cairo, 1994-97, US amb. to Israel Tel Aviv, 1997—99, asst. sec. for Near Ea. Affairs Washington, 2000—01; pres., CEO Mid. East Inst., Washington, 2001—06; Christian A. Johnson Disting. Professorship in Global Polit. Theory Hamilton Coll., 2006—. Adj. scholar Mid. East Inst., 2006—. With U.S. Army, 1962-65. Decorated Order of Independence (Abu Dhabi); recipient Superior Honor award Dept. State, 1975, Meritorious Honor award, 1976, Disting. Civilian Svc. award Dept. Def., 1997. Episcopalian. Office: Hamilton College Dept Government 198 College Hill Rd Clinton NY 13323 Office Phone: 315-859-4310, 315-859-4477. E-mail: ewalker1@hamilton.edu.*

WALKER, FRANCIS JOSEPH, lawyer; b. Aug. 5, 1922; s. John McSweeney and Sarah Veronica (Meechan) W.; m. Julia Corinne O'Brien, Jan. 27, 1951; children: Vincent Paul, Monica Irene Hylton, Jill Marie Nudell, John Michael, Michael Joseph, Thomas More. BA, St. Martin's Coll., 1947; JD, U. Wash., 1950. Bar: Wash. Asst. atty. gen.

State of Wash., 1950-51; pvt. practice Olympia, Wash., 1951—. Gen. counsel Wash. Cath. Conf., 1967-76. Lt. (j.g.) USNR, 1943-46; PTO. Home and Office: 2723 Hillside Dr SE Olympia WA 98501-3460 Office Phone: 360-352-2245.

WALKER, F(RANK) BORDEN, oil industry executive; b. 1953; m. Michele Walker. BS, U. NC, 1975; MBA, Dartmouth Coll., Hanover, NH, 1977. Sr. v.p. retail mktg. Hess Corp. (formerly Amerada Hess), 1996, exec. v.p., pres. mktg. and refining, 2002—, bd. dirs., 2004—. Office: Hess Corp 1185 Avenue of the Americas New York NY 10036 Office Phone: 212-997-8500.*

WALKER, FRED ELMER, broadcast executive; b. Trenton, NJ, May 31, 1931; s. Elmer and Adele F. (Decker) W.; m. Catharine Middleton Sullivan, Nov. 26, 1952; children: Catharine Walker Bergstrom, Elizabeth Walker Phillips, Frederick Christopher. Student, Coll. NJ, 1952, NYU, 1953. Dir. pub. relations Sta. WPTZ-TV, Phila., 1953; v.p., gen. mgr. Sta. WTTM-AM, Trenton, 1956-59; gen. sales mgr. Sta. KYW-AM, Cleve., 1959-62; v.p., gen. mgr. Sta. KDKA-AM, Pitts., 1962-65, Sta. KYW-TV, Phila., 1965-67, Sta. KPIX-TV, San Francisco, 1967-69, Sta. WLWT-TV, Cin., 1969-71; pres. Broad St. Communications Corp., New Haven, 1971-85, WELI, New Haven, WICSS, Hartford, WYOR, Miami, WVCG, Miami, KTOK, Oklahoma City, KYVE, Oklahoma City, WGSO, New Orleans, WQUE, New Orleans; exec. v.p. Broad St. Ventures, NYC, 1988—94; v.p. radio group Westinghouse Broadcasting, NYC, 1985-88; mng. ptnr. Broad St. Consulting, 1997—2005. Pres. Broad St. TV Corp., 1988-96, Broad St. Mgmt. Corp., 1988-96; bd. dirs. Broadcast Music, Inc., 1984-87, Call for Action, Washington, 1993-2000. Bd. dirs. Long Wharf Theatre, New Haven, WXEL-TV, 1998-2005; chmn. Long Wharf Theatre Future Fund campaign, 1983-85, chmn. devel., 1986-90, chmn. and pres., 1990-97; mem. Pres.'s Coun. Albertus Magnus Coll.; trustee Hamden Hall Country Day Sch., chmn. devel. com.; chmn. 250th fund dr. United Ch. Christ, 1987-89; chmn. Call For Action, Washington, 1994-2000; trustee Fla. Stage, 1998-2000; pres. Edn. TV Fund, 2006—. Recipient Alfred P. Sloan award, 1954, Ohio State Ednl. award, 1953; fellow Berkeley Coll. Yale U., 1976. Mem. Radio Advt. Bur. (dir.), TV Bur. Advt., Nat. Assn. Broadcasters, New Haven Lawn Club. Democrat. Personal E-mail: fredewalk1@aol.com.

WALKER, GEORGE H., investment company executive; BA/BS, MBA, U. Pa., Phila. Ptnr., head alternative investment strategies, mem. partnership com. Goldman Sachs Asset Mgmt.; global head investment mgmt. divsn., mem. exec. com. Lehman Bros. Holdings, NYC, 2006—. Vice chair bd. trustees The New Sch.; mem. bd. overseers U. Pa. Sch. Arts & Sci.; bd. dirs. Local Initiatives Support Cooperation. Office: Lehman Bros Holdings 745 Seventh Ave New York NY 10019 Office Phone: 212-526-7000.

WALKER, GEORGE HERBERT, III, former ambassador, retired investment banking company executive; b. St. Louis, Mar. 16, 1931; s. George H. and Mary (Carter) W.; m. Sandra E. Canning, Dec. 23, 1955 (div. Oct. 1962); children: Mary Elizabeth, Wendy, Isabelle; m. Kimberly Gedge, July 27, 1968 (div. Jan. 1977); children: George H. IV, Carter; m. Carol Banta, Feb. 21, 1987. BA, Yale U., 1953; LL.B., Harvard U., 1956. Bar: Conn. 1956. Gen. ptnr. G.H. Walker & Co. (later G.H. Walker, Laird Inc.), 1961-74; sr. v.p., also bd. dirs. White, Weld & Co. Inc., 1974-75; chmn. bd. dirs. G.H. Walker & Co., 1973-74; exec. v.p. Stifel Nicolaus & Co., 1976-78, pres., CEO, 1978-92, chmn., 1982—2001, chmn. emeritus, 2001—; US amb. to Hungary US Dept. State, Budapest, 2003—06. Civilian aide to sec. U.S. Army for Ea. Mo., 1973-80; bd. dirs. Laidlaw Corp., Laclede Steel Co., Eck-Adams Corp.; bd. govs. Midwest Stock Exch., 1982-88. Bd. dirs. Downtown St. Louis Inc., 1975-90, chmn., 1984-86; bd. dirs. Webster U., chmn. bd., 1987-92; trustee Mo. Hist. Soc., St. Louis Children's Hosp., 1972-92, Jefferson Nat. Expansion Meml. Assn., 1992; vestryman St. Ann's Ch., Kennebunkport, Maine; mem. Mo. Rep. Ctrl. Com., 1983—; adv. bd. St. Louis Area coun. Boy Scouts Am., 1989—; trustee investment trust Episcopal Diocese of Mo.; hon. bd. dirs. Anti-Drug Abuse Edn. Fund, Inc., 1990—; bd. dirs. St. Louis Zoo, 1992. With USAF, 1956-58. Mem. Rotary (St. Louis club). E-mail: walkergh@stifel.com.

WALKER, GEORGE KONTZ, law educator; b. Tuscaloosa, Ala., July 8, 1938; s. Joseph Henry and Catherine Louise (Indorf) W.; m. Phyllis Ann Sherman, July 30, 1966; children: Charles Edward, Mary Neel. BA, U. Ala., 1959; LLB, Vanderbilt U., 1966; AM, Duke U., 1968; LLM, U. Va., 1972; postgrad. (Sterling fellow), Law Sch. Yale U., 1975-76. Bar: Va. 1967, NC 1976. Law clk. US Dist. Ct., Richmond, Va., 1966—67; assoc. Hunton, Williams, Gay, Powell & Gibson, Richmond, 1967—70; pvt. practice Charlottesville, Va., 1970-71; asst. prof. Law Sch. Wake Forest U., Winston-Salem, NC, 1972-73, assoc. prof. Law Sch., 1974-77, prof. Law Sch., 1977—, mem. bd. advisors Divinity Sch., 1991-94; Charles H. Stockton prof. internat. law US Naval War Coll., 1992—93. Vis. prof. Marshall-Wythe Sch. Law, Coll. William and Mary, Williamsburg, Va., 1979-80, U. Ala. Law Sch., 1985; cons. Naval War Coll., 1976—, Nat. Def. Exec. Res., 1991—, Naval War Coll., Internat. Law Dept. Adv. Bd., 1993—. Author: The Tanker War, 1980-88, 2000; contbr. articles to profl. jours. With USN, 1959-62, capt. USNR, ret. Woodrow Wilson fellow, 1962-63; decorated Order of the long Leaf Pine; recipient Joseph Branch Alumni Svc. award, Wake Forest, 1988, Meritorious Unit Commendation, USN, 1992-93; named Hon. Atty. Gen. NC, 1986. Mem.: ABA, Internat. Inst. Humanitarian Law, Maritime Law Assn., Am. Law Inst., Am. Judicature Soc., Internat. Law Assn. (exec. com. Am. br. 2001—), Am. Soc. Internat. Law (exec. coun. 1988—91), N.C. Bar Assn. (v.p. 1997—98), Va. Bar Assn., Order of Barristers (hon.), Piedmont Club, Phi Delta Phi, Sigma Alpha Epsilon, Phi Beta Kappa, Order of the Coif (hon.). Democrat. Episcopalian. Home: 3321 Pennington Ln Winston Salem NC 27106-5439 Office: Wake Forest U Sch Law PO Box 7206 Winston Salem NC 27109-7206

WALKER, GEORGE THEOPHILUS, JR., composer, music educator, pianist; b. Washington, June 27, 1922; s. George Theophilus Sr. and Rosa (King) W.; children: Gregory, Ian. MusB, Oberlin Coll., 1941; student of, Rudolf Serkin, Rosario Scalero; Artist Diploma, Curtis Inst. music, 1945; D of Mus. Arts, U. Rochester, 1957; DFA (hon.), Lafayette Coll., 1982; MusD (hon.), Oberlin Coll., 1983; student of, Nadia Boulanger; MusD (hon.), Curtis Inst. Music, 1997; DHL (hon.), Montclair State U., 1997; MusD (hon.), Bloomfield Coll., 1997; DFA (hon.), Spelman Coll., 2001. Instr. Dillard U., New Orleans, 1953-54; instr. Dalcroze Sch. Music, NYC, 1960-61, New Sch. Social Research, NYC, 1961; instr. to assoc. prof. Smith Coll., Northampton, Mass., 1961-68; assoc. prof. U. Colo., Boulder, 1968-69; disting. prof. Rutgers U., Newark, 1976-92, prof. emeritus, 1992. Concert pianist Nat. Concert Artists, N.Y.C., 1950-53, Columbia Artists, N.Y.C., 1959-60; adj. prof. Peabody Inst. Johns Hopkins U., Balt., 1975-78; disting. prof. U. Del., Newark, 1975-76. Composer: Sonata for 2 Pianos (Harvey Gaul prize 1963), numerous sonatas, cantatas and concertos, Concerto for Cello and Orch., 1982, Sinfonias for Orch. Bd. dirs. Am. Bach Found., 1988; mem. Mary Flagler Cary Trust Commn., 1998. Recipient award Am. Acad. and Inst. Arts and Letter, 1982, Koussevitsky award, 1988, Pulitzer prize, 1996, L.J. Govs. award 1997, Koussevitsky award 1998, Mary Flagler Cary Charitable Trust award, 1998, Dorothy Maynor Arts Citizens award, 2000, A.I. duPont award Del. Symphony, 2001, Classical Roots Lifetime Achievement award Detroit Symphony, 2001, Foils for Orch. award, Eastman Commn., 2006, Legacy award, Nat. Opera Assn., 2007; grantee Smith Coll., U. Colo., Rutger U. Rsch. Coun., NEA, NJ State Coun. for Arts; Fulbright fellow, 1957, John Hay Whitney fellow, 1958, Guggenheim fellow, 1969, 88, Rockefeller fellow, 1971, 74; Disting. scholar U. Rochester, 1996; commd. NY Philharm., Kennedy Ctr., Cleve. Orch., Boston Symphony, NJ Symphony, Am. Guild of Organists; inducted Am. Classical Music Hall of Fame, 2000. Mem. ASCAP, Am. Acad. Arts and Letters (mem.-elect), Am. Bach Found. (bd. dirs. 1988), Am. Symphony League. Democrat. Avocations: tennis, photography, audio. Home: 323 Grove St Montclair NJ 07042-4223 Personal E-mail: gtwalker@verizon.net.

WALKER, GEORGE W. C., bishop; b. Oct. 11, 1940; m. Geraldine J. Walker; 4 children. AB, Benedict Coll., Columbia, SC, 1970; MDiv., Hood Theol. Sem., 1971. Bishop African Meth. Episcopal Zion Ch., Charlotte, NC, 1988—2004, sr. bishop, 2004—. Mem. Publishing House Bd., Harriet Tubman Found., Restructuring Com., Balm in Gilead. Named one of 100 Most Influential Black Americans, Ebony mag., 2006; named to Power 150, 2008. Office: AME Zion Hdqs 3225 Suqar Creek Rd Charlotte NC 28262

WALKER, GLORIA LEE, training services executive; b. Oklahoma City, Dec. 31, 1942; d. Russell Holland and Ethel Wanita (Kierig) Walker; m. Thomas William Rupprath, June 3, 1966 (div. Feb. 1995); children: Robert Rupprath, John Rupprath. BA in Sociology, U.S.C., 1965; MS in Elem. Edn., U. Nebr., 1971; EdD in Adminstrn., Fla. Atlantic U., 1986. Ops. rsch. analyst U.S. Bur. Mines, Washington, 1988-90; employment devel. specialist IRS, Dallas, 1991-92; pres. AMERITRAIN, Dallas/Lubbock, Tex., 1992—. Author: Training a Diversified Workforce, 1993, Developing Training Materials, 1995, Instructing Diversified Employee, 1995, Seminars in Training, 1995, The Educated Instructor, 2008. E-mail: walker@omega.net.

WALKER, GORDON DAVIES, government official, writer, lecturer, consultant; b. Logan, Utah, July 10, 1944; s. Rudger Harper and Fawn Lucile (Davies) W.; m. Carlene Martin, June 5, 1968; children—Kimberly Anne, Kelly Anne, Gordon Davies Jr., Bradford Martin AB, Brigham Young U., 1968; MBA, Harvard U., 1971. Project dir. Becker Research Co., Boston, 1969-71; dir. mktg. Am. Nat. Enterprises, Salt Lake City, 1971-72; v.p., dir. Sweetwater Properties, Salt Lake City, 1972-76; gen. ptnr. Covecrest Properties, Salt Lake City, 1976—; spl. asst. to sec. HUD, Washington, 1981-82, dep. under sec., 1983-86; cons. real estate, fin. Commerce Cons., Washington, 1986-87; pres., chief exec. officer Deseret Fed. Savs. and Loan, Salt Lake City, 1987-88; pres. U.S. Resources, Inc., Phoenix, 1988-92, also bd. dirs.; pres. Energy Lock Inc., Salt Lake City, 1992—2002; exec. dir. Utah chpt. Alzheimer's Assn., 2002—06; dir. housing cmty. devel. State of Utah, 2003—. Author: Finance Your Own Way to Success, 1980; Develop Your Way to Success, 1981; Hottest New Ideas of the 1980's, 1982. Rep. state del., Salt Lake City, 1974; del. Rep. Nat. Conv., 1988 Mem. Nat. Assn. Realtors Mem. Lds Ch.

WALKER, GRAHAM CHARLES, biology professor; b. Boston, Feb. 8, 1948; s. Charles Bertram and Margaret Elizabeth (Biehn) W.; m. Janet Elizabeth Haliburton, May 30, 1970; 1 child, Gordon Andrew. BSc with honors, Carleton U., Ottawa, Ont., Can., 1970; PhD, U. Ill., 1974. Asst. prof. biology MIT, Cambridge, Mass., 1976-80, assoc. prof. biology, 1980-86, prof. biology, 1986—. Rsch. prof. Howard Hughes Med. Inst., 2002—, Am. Cancer Soc., 2003—. Co-author: DNA Repair and Mutagenesis; editor-in-chief Jour. Bacteriology, 1991-2001, editor, 1985-91; editl. bd. Mutation Rsch., Amsterdam, Netherlands, 1982—; editl. bd. DNA Repair, 2002—, contbr. articles to Procs. NAS USA, Cell, Microbiology Rev., Jour. Bacteriology. Housemaster McCormick Hall, MIT, Cambridge, 1986-92, Margaret MacVicar Faculty fellow MIT, 1992-2002, John Simon Guggenheim Meml. fellow, 1984, Woodrow Wilson fellow, 1970; recipient Rita Allen Cancer Devel. award, 1978-83, Howard Hughes Med. Inst. grantee in biology, 2002. Fellow Am. Acad. Arts & Scis.; mem. Am. Acad. Microbiology, Am. Soc. for Microbiology, Genetics Soc. Am., Am. Chem. Soc., Environ. Mutagen Soc. Achievements include discovery of umuDC analogs on plasmid pKM101; demonstration of repetoire of SOS genes; demonstrated critical role of exopolysaccharide in nodule invasion by Rhizobium meliloti; cloning and analysis of roles of UmuDC in UV mutagenesis; demonstrated RecA-mediated cleavage activates UmuD, second symbiotically active exopolysaccharide in R. meliloti. Office: MIT Biology Dept 77 Massachusetts Ave Cambridge MA 02139-4307 Business E-Mail: gwalker@mit.edu.

WALKER, GWENDOLYN KAYE, guest teacher elementary education; b. Houston, Aug. 11, 1956; d. Willie Lee Sr. and Juanita W.; 1 child, Nika Ayanna Sewell. Student, U. Nev., 1973-74, Massey Bus. Coll., Houston, 1978-79; grad., So. Nev. Sch. Cosmetology, Las Vegas, 1988. Lic. manicurist. Mgr. snack shop St. Lukes Hosp., Houston, 1976-80; svc. rep. Centel Tel., Las Vegas, 1980-85; owner Nika's Gifts, Las Vegas, 1985-87; co-owner Genesis Nails and Gifts, 1987-89, Clark County Libr. Dist., Las Vegas, 1988—2000, Nika's Afrocentric Gifts, Las Vegas, 1992—. Author: (poetry) Feelings, 1996, Memories, Book II, 1997, Mommie and Me, 2003; co-author: From the Kitchen to the Boardroom, Nevada's Black Women, Courage, Strength and Faith, Nevada's Black Men; columnist Las Vegas Sentinel Newspaper, 1988-95, (cd) DaSpell Mem. bd. City North Las Vegas Crime Prevention Task Force, 1992-95; mem. North Las Vegas Police Area Command Children's Adv. Bd., 2005—; co-chmn. North Las Vegas Traffic and Parking Bd., 2005—; adv. bd. Kyle Ranch, 1982-84; capt. neighborhood watch Valley View Estates, 1984—; founder, pres. Walker African-Am. Mus. and Rsch. Ctr., Las Vegas, 1992—; sec., chmn. souvenir booklet and food basket com. Dr. Martin Luther King Jr. Com., 1985-88; mem. Mems. and Advs. for Minority Adoptions, 1982-84, Dem. Ctrl. Com., 1984-85, Nev. Black C. of C., various election coms.; leader 4-H, 1969-73; leader Swappett drill team, 1970-73. Recipient Cmty. Svc. award North Las Vegas City Coun., 1992, Clark County Commn., 1997, Outstanding Mem. and Sec. award Dr. Martin Luther King Jr. Com., 1987-88. Mem. NAACP, Nat. Assn. African-Am. History Preservation, Nev. Women in History, Tuskegee Airmen, Inc. (Nev. Chpt. sec. 1996—). Baptist. Avocations: sewing, poetry, singing, crafting, collecting. Office: Walker African-Am Mus 705 W Van Buren Ave Las Vegas NV 89106-3042 Office Phone: 702-649-2238.

WALKER, H. REED, lawyer; b. Kansas City, Mo., Dec. 3, 1952; s. Huffman Walker and Marjorie Hallier. BSBA, William Jewell Coll., Liberty, Mo., 1974; JD (hon.), Washburn U., Topeka, Kans., 1977. Bar: Kans. Supreme Ct. 1977, Mo. Supreme Ct. 1995, US Ct. Appeals (8th cir.) 1988, US Ct. Appeals (10th cir.) 2000, US Supreme Ct. 1984. Ptnr. Barnett, Walker & O'Connor, Chartered, Kansas City, 1986—96; pres. Law Offices H. Reed Walker, P.A., Overland Pk., Kans., 1997—. Presenter in field. Contbr. articles to profl. jours. Mem.: Johns County Kans. Dist. Ct. (pro tem judge), Kans. Bar Assn. (former pres. litig. section.), Kans. Trial Lawyers Assn., Wyandotte County Bar Found. (pres. 1987—88, mem. grievance and ethics Com 1987—, sec. 2000—). Republican. Presbyterian. Office: Law Offices H Reed Walker PA 5800 Foxridge Dr Ste 306 Overland Park KS 66202 Office Fax: 913-236-7115. Business E-Mail: reed@reed-walker.com.

WALKER, HOWARD ERNEST, lawyer; b. Mobile, Ala., Mar. 3, 1944; s. Ernest W. and Denise (Kearney) W.; m. Michelle Anne Pinsonneault, June 20, 1992. BA, U. Ill., 1966; JD, Boston U., 1974. Bar: R.I. 1974. Assoc. Hinckley, Allen & Snyder, Providence, 1974-80, ptnr., 1980—2004. Trustee Providence Pub. Libr., 1978-2000, pres., 2002—, vice chmn. programs; trustee R.I. Wild Plant Soc., 1995-97—; trustee R.I. Civic Chorale & Orchestra, 1988-95, Providence Pub. Libr. Found., 2008—, chmn, 2009-; dir. South Shore Mental Health Ctr., 1997—, v.p. 2000—; trustee and sec. Hopkinton Land Trust, 2000-04; mem. Hopkinton Planning Bd., 2002—, sec., 2003-04. Lt. USNR, 1967-71. Mem. ABA, R.I. Bar Assn. (mem. ad hoc com. on future of law practice, chmn. superior ct. bench/bar com. 1990-93, 94-95, Dorothy Lohmann Cmty. Svc. award 2003), Maritime Law Assn. of US, Phi Kappa Phi, Phi Beta Kappa. Avocations: western Americana, natural history. Home: 39A Berrie Ln PO Box 118 Rockville RI 02873-0118 Office Phone: 401-539-6767. Business E-Mail: hewlaw@hughes.net.

WALKER, IAN DAVID, engineering educator; BSc in Math., U. Hull, Eng., 1983; MS in Elec. and Computer Engring., U. Tex., Austin, 1985, PhD in Elec. and Computer Engring., 1989. Asst. prof., elec. and computer engring. Rice U., Houston, 1989-95, assoc. prof. dept. elec. and computer engring., 1995-97, Clemson U., SC, 1997—2001, prof., dept. elec. and computer engring. SC, 2001—. Contbr. articles to profl. jours.; assoc. editor Internat. Jour. Robotics and Automation, Internat. Jour. Environmentally Conscious Design and Mfg.; sr. editor IEEE Trans. on Robotics and Automation; mem. editl. bd. IEEE Transactions on Robotics, the IEEE Transactions on Robotics and Automation, the International Journal of Robotics and Automation, the IEEE Robotics and Automation Magazine, and the International Journal of Environmentally Conscious Design and Manufacturing. Fellow IEEE (program com., v.p. fin. activities Robotics and Automation Soc.), AIAA (chair, tech. com. on space automation and robotics)., Am. Nuclear Soc. Achievements include research in robotics, biologically inspired continuum robots, multifingered robot hands, cooperating manipulators, trunk and tentade robots, robot reliability and safety. Office: Clemson U 320 Flour Daniel Engring Innovation Bldg Dept Electrical & Computer Engring Clemson SC 29634 Home Phone: 864-656-7209. Office Fax: 864-656-7220. Business E-Mail: ianw@ces.clemson.edu.

WALKER, IRVING EDWARD, lawyer; b. Balt., Jan. 31, 1952; s. Bertram and Mildred (Shapiro) W.; m. Leslie A. Walker; children: Brandon Harris, Aaron Seth, Emily Celeste. BA, Duke U., 1973; JD, U. Md., 1978. Bar: Md. 1978, US Dist. Ct. Md. 1978, US Ct. Appeals (4th cir.) 1980, US Supreme Ct. 1995, US Ct. Appeals (3d cir.) 2001. Assoc. Frank, Bernstein, Conaway & Goldman, Balt., 1978-85, ptnr., 1986-91; prin. Miles & Stockbridge, Balt., 1991-2001; ptnr. Saul Ewing LLP, Balt., 2001—08; mem. Cole, Schotz, Meisel, Foreman & Leonard, P.A., 2008—. Chmn. Bankruptcy & Creditors Rights Group, 1991-2000. Contbg. author: Bankruptcy Deskbook, 1986. Bd. dirs. Jewish Cmty. Ctr. Greater Balt., 1986-88, Temple Emanuel of Balt., Inc., 1996-02, Homeless Persons Representation Project, 2005-, bd. pres. 2008- Mem. ABA, Md. Bar Assn., Bar Assn. Balt. City (chmn. bankruptcy and bus. law com. 1989-90), Am. Bankruptcy Inst. (co-chair Bankruptcy Lihgahn com., faculty advisor), Bankruptcy Assn. Dist. Md. (pres. 1992-93, chmn. Balt. chpt. 1989-91), Order of Coif. Avocation: weightlifting. Office: Cole Schotz Meisel Foreman & Leonard PA 300 E Lombart St Ste 2000 Baltimore MD 21202 Office Phone: 410-528-2970. Business E-Mail: iwalker@coleschotz.com.

WALKER, JAMES EDWARD, humanities educator; s. John Willard and Lola Margauriete Walker; m. Nancy Ann Chapman, Aug. 30, 1969; children: Susan Lee Sova, Jeffrey James. BA, Lake Superior State U., Sault Ste. Marie, 1970; MA, Western Mich. U., Kalamazoo, 1973; PhD, Fla. State U., Tallahassee, 1983. Prof. U. South Fla., Tampa, 1983—86, Ferris State U., Big Rapids. Contbr. articles to profl. jours. Recipient Beyond award, Ferris State U., 2005; named Disting. Tchr., 1999, Internat. Tchr. of Yr., 2002; nominee CASE Prof. of Yr. Competition, 2002. Methodist. Avocation: travel. Office Phone: 231-591-2776. Business E-Mail: walkerj@ferris.edu.

WALKER, JAMES WILLIAM, physics educator, freelance/self-employed writer; b. Akron, Ohio, Feb. 5, 1947; s. Arthur Hobart and Ella Mae (Slade) W.; 1 child, Michael James. BS, Kent State U., Ohio, 1973, MEd, 1979. Lic: educator in physics, English, ednl. media, Ohio. Journeyman pipefitter Goodyear Tire & Rubber Co., Akron, 1968-76; tchr. sci., media specialist Jackson Local Schs., Massillon, Ohio, 1976—99, curriculum specialist, 1999—2004; instr. physics, math. Stark State Coll., 2005—. Author: (autobiography) Before I Go, 2003; Guest columnist The Canton Repository, 1986—; contbr. articles to profl. jours. Pres. Friends of the North Canton (Ohio) Libr., 1981-82, Unitarian Universalist Congregation of Canton, 1992-94, 2000; bd. dirs. Hunger Task Force of Stark County, Ohio, 1991-95, Coming Together Stark County, 2008-; county organizer Ams. United for Separation of Ch. and State, 1997; chmn., bd. trustees Massillon Mus., 2002-2003. Cameras in the Curriculum grantee Eastman Kodak Corp., Rochester, N.Y., 1984, grantee Martha Holden Jennings Found., Cleve., 1984-85; recipient Acker award Ohio Acad. Sci., Columbus, 1986, Krecker award Battelle Rsch. Inst., Columbus, 1986. Mem. NEA, Jackson Profl. Edn. Assn. (bldg. rep. 1988-89, 98-99). Avocations: motorcycling, art collecting, photography, vintage baseball. Office: Stark State Coll Gen Studies Divsn 6200 Frank Ave NW Canton OH 44720 Office Phone: 330-830-1836, 330-966-5457. Business E-Mail: jwalker@starkstate.edu. E-mail: jww2jc@hotmail.com.

WALKER, JANE STEWART, small business owner, publishing executive, educator; b. Connersville, Ind., July 9, 1938; d. George Sinks and Cornelia Stewart Tatman; m. Frank Dilling Walker, Aug. 25, 1979; m. Guy Thomas Connelly (div.); children: Kevin Connelly, Katherine Connelly. BA, Sweet Briar College, Va., 1960. Asst. tchr. The Children's Corner, Indpls., 1971—75; historic interpreter Conner Prairie Pioneer Settlement, Noblesville, Ind., 1975; staff asst. Hist. Landmarks Found. Ind., Indpls., 1975—78; classified ads, credit and purchasing Topics Newspapers, 1978—80; staff edn. docent Children's Mus., 1981—88; part owner News Examiner Co., Connersville, 1991—93, Winchester (Ky.) Sun, 1991—2005, Comml. Printing Svc., Connersville, Ind., 1989—. Dir. and v.p. Tatman, Inc., Connersville, Ind., 1983—; sec. and pres. Found. Hand Rsch. and Edn., Indpls., 1988—94; dir. and v.p. Walker Family Found., 1993—. Author: The Encyclopedia of Indianapolis, 1994. State co-chair Phillips Acad. Nat. Centennial Fund Dr., Andover, Mass., 1977—79; dir. and pres. Coleman Adoption Svcs., 1982—88; chmn. fin. devel. Arthritis Found. Ind., Indpls., 1989—97; mem. alumni coun. Phillips Acad., Andover, Mass., 1984; bd. dir. Sweet Briar Coll., Va., 1999—2006, vice chair. bd. dir., 2003—06. Co-recipient

Humanitarian of Yr., Arthritis Found. Ind., 1998. Mem.: Sweet Briar Alumnas Club of Ind. (co-pres. 1990—), Univ. Park Country Club. Avocations: photography, golf, reading, travel. Office: 7361 Eaton Ct University Park FL 34201

WALKER, JAY SCOTT, media company executive; b. Queens, NY, Nov. 5, 1955; s. Arthur W. and Jeanette W.; m. Eileen mcManus, Apr. 18, 1982; children: Evan, Lindsey. BS in Indsl. Rels., Cornell U., 1977. Rsch. dir. Folio Pub. Corp., Stamford, Conn., 1977-84; pres. Visual Tech. Corp., Glenbrook, Conn., 1984-85; co-founder Catalog Media Corp., Ridgefield, Conn., 1985, Synapse, 1991, Target Comm.; founder Walker Digital LLC, Stamford, Conn., 1994, chmn., CEO, 2000—; founder Priceline.com, Norwalk, Conn., 1997, vice chmn., 1997—2000. Bd. dirs. World Info. Transfer; spkr. in field. Co-author (Jeffrey Lehman): (book) 1000 Ways to Win Monopoly Games, 1975. Named Direct Marketer of Yr., Target Mktg. Mag., 1998, Direct Mktg. Days NY, 1999; named one of 50 Most Influential Bus. Leaders in Digital Age, Time Mag., 25 Internet Pioneers, Bus. Week; named to 200 Industry Leaders, Target Mktg. Mag., 1989. Mem. Sigma Phi (chmn. bd. dirs. 1988-90). Achievements include patents in field. Avocations: book collecting, fine wines. Office: Walker Digital LLC 5 High Ridge Pk Ste 1B Stamford CT 06905 Office Phone: 203-321-1240.

WALKER, JEFFREY CLEMENS, venture capitalist; b. Knoxville, Tenn., Sept. 22, 1955; s. William Clemens and Joyce Hazel (Harkins) W.; m. Suzanne Marie Connelly, Apr. 27, 1984; children: Courtney, Ryan, Morgan, Hunter. BS, U. Va., 1977; MBA, Harvard U., 1981. CPA, Tex.; cert. mgmt. acct., Tex. Sr. auditor, cons. Arthur Young & Co., Houston, 1977-79; assoc. Chem. Bank, NYC, 1981-82, v.p., 1982-83; ptnr. Chase Capital Ptnrs., NYC, 1984-87, mng. ptnr., 1988—95; co-founder, gen. ptnr. JP Morgan Ptnrs. at JP Morgan Chase & Co., 1984—, vice-chmn., mng. ptnr., 1988—, dir., 1995—. Bd. dirs. Timothys, Inc., Toronto, Monet Corp., NYC, Guitar Ctr., LA, Metroplex Corp., NJ, Doaneroducts, Mo., Metakote, Lima, Ohio, Chase Asia Fund, NYC, Chase Equity Ptnrs, NYC, Thomas Jefferson Found. (Monticello), JP Morgan Chase Found.; dir. Domain, 1-800-Flowers, Metroplex, Doane Pet Care, House of Blues, Metkote, Axis Ins. and Guitar Center; chmn., NPower NY, Finance Com., U. Va.; serves on adv. bd., Solera Capital; mem.Investment Com., JPMorgan Partners Asia, JP Morgan Private Equity Partners Select, and JPM organ Horizon Funds Mem. Young Pres. Orgn.; chmn. Bd. Edn., Wilton, Conn.; bd. dirs. WPA Theatre, NYC; pres. of bd. of trustees, McIntire Sch., U. Va. Endowment, chmn., Finance Com.; dir., NYC Investment Fund, Lincoln Center Film Soc., The Big Apple Circus, The Internat. Center of Photography, Wilton Y; bd. trustees, Morgan Library and St. Luke's School Mem. AICPA, Nat. Venture Capital Assn., Nat. Assn. Small Bus. Investment Cos. (bd. govs., vice chmn.), Silver Spring Country Club, Golf Club of Purchase, Pawling Mountain Hunt Club, wilton Riding Club, Beta Gamma Sigma. Republican. Unitarian Universalist. Office: JP Morgan Ptnrs 1221 Ave of the Americas New York NY 10020 Home: 230 W 56TH ST # 58 New York NY 10019-4306 Office Phone: 212-899-3400. Office Fax: 212-899-3401.

WALKER, JERALD CARTER, academic administrator, minister; b. Bixby, Okla., May 22, 1938; s. Joseph Carter and Trula Tosh (Jackson) W.; m. Virginia Canfield, Apr. 14, 1963; children: Elisabeth Katherine, Anne Carter. BA in Sociology, Oklahoma City U., 1960; BD, U. Chgo., 1964; D of Religion, Sch. Theology at Claremont, 1966; LHD (hon.), Shiller U., 1994. Ordained to ministry Meth. Ch., 1964. Dir., campus minister Campus Christian Assn., Chgo., 1961-64; minister of outreach Temple Meth. Ch., San Francisco, 1965-66; chaplain, asst. prof. religion Nebr. Wesleyan U., Lincoln, 1966-69; pres. John J. Pershing Coll., Beatrice, Nebr., 1969-70; v.p. univ. rels., assoc. prof. Southwestern U., Georgetown, Tex., 1970-74; pres. Baker U., Baldwin, Kans., 1974-79, Oklahoma City U., 1979-97, chancellor Okla., 1997—. Ednl. adv. to bd. dirs. Tianjin U. Commerce, People's Republic of China; participant Okla. Ann. Conf. of United Meth. Ch. Co-author: The State of Sequoyah: An Impressionistic View of Eastern Oklahoma, 1985; contbr. chpt. book, articles to profl. jours. Bd. dirs., past chmn. Okla. Ind. Coll. Found. Recipient Alumni Recognition award Nebr. 4H Club, 1970, Okla. 4H Club, Disting. Alumnis award Oklahoma City U., 1974, Outstanding Citizen award Dist. 575 Rotary Internat., 1990, Award for Excellence Asia Soc. Okla., 1990, Humanitarian award for Okla/Ark. region NCCJ, 1992, Nat. Police Adminstrn. award for promotion or peace and order Rep. of China, 1992, Francis Asbury award for fostering United Meth. Ministries in Higher Edn., 1994, Excellent Leader award Mgmt. Devel. Inst. Singapore, 1996, Benjamin Franklin award Downtown Olka. City Sertoma Club, 1992, Excellent Leader award Mgmt. Devel. Inst. of Singapore, 1996, Nat. Medal of Honor Cherokee Nation, 2000; inducted to Okla. Higher Edn. Hall of Fame, 1999. Mem. Nat. Assn. Schs. and Colls. of United Meth. Ch. (past pres.), Nat. Assn. Colls. and Univs. (bd. dirs.). Office: Oklahoma City U 6826 E 112th St S Bixby OK 74008-2062

WALKER, JEWETT LYNIUS, clergyman, church official; b. Beaumont, Tex., Apr. 7, 1930; s. Elijah Harvey and Ella Jane (Wilson) W.; m. Dorothy Mae Croom, Apr. 11, 1965; children: Cassandra Lynn, Jewett L., Kevin, Michelle, Ella, Betty Renne, Kent, Elijah H. BA, Calif. Western U., 1957; MA, Kingdom Bible Inst., 1960; B Religious Edn., St. Stephens Coll., 1966, DD, 1968; LLD, Union Bapt. Sem., 1971; postgrad., St. Paul Sch. Theology, 1979, Southwestern Bapt. Theol. Sem., 1985-86; grad., Nat. Planned Giving Inst., 1981, Philanthropy Tax Inst., 1982; DD, Clinton Jr. Coll., 1992; PhD, Mcpl. Govt., Concord, 2006. Ordained to ministry African Methodist Episcopal Zion Ch., 1957. Pastor Shiloh A.M.E. Zion Ch., Monrovia, Calif., 1961-64, Martin Temple A.M.E. Zion Ch., LA, 1964-65, 1st A.M.E. Zion Ch., Compton, Calif., 1965-66, Met. A.M.E. Zion Ch., LA, 1966-73, Logan Temple A.M.E. Zion Ch., San Diego, 1973-74, Rock Hill A.M.E. Zion Ch., Indian Trail, NC, 1974-79, Bennettsville A.M.E. Zion Ch., Norwood, NC, 1979-86, Price Meml. A.M.E. Zion Ch., Concord, NC, 1986-89, Mt. Zion A.M.E. Zion Ch., Hickory Grove, SC, 1989-91, NewHope AME Zion, Lancaster, SC, 1991—92, Mt. Zion A.M.E. Zion Ch., Lancaster, SC, 1992—2001, Mt. Moriah A.M.E. Zion Ch., Richburg, SC, 2001—03, New Hope A.M.E. Zion Ch., Lancaster, SC, 2003—06, North Corner A.M.E. Zion, Lancaster, 2007—. Sec.-treas. dept. home missions, brotherhood pensions and relief African Methodist Episcopal Zion Ch., Charlotte, N.C., 1974-92; mem. exec. bd. Prophetic Justice Unit Com. Nat. Coun. Chs., co-chairperson pers. com.; mem. World Meth. Coun., del. 14th World Conf Author: Is There a Man in the House, 1975, Lets Get Serious about Missions, 1991, Issues Facing the Ministry, 1991, The Denominational Dollar, 1992, also articles. Chmn. Minority Affairs Adv. Com., Mecklenburg County; trustee Clinton Coll., dir. planned giving, 1992; trustee Rock Hill, Lomax-Hannon Coll., Greenville, Ala., Union Bapt. Theol. Sem., Birmingham, Ala.; bd. mgrs. McCrorey br. YMCA; pres. Am. Ch. Fin. Svc. Corp., Carolina Home Health Svc. Inc., Meth. Life Ins. Soc. Inc., bd. trustees State N.C. Coll. Found., Inc., 1987, del. Presbyn. Ptnrs. in Ecumenism Nat. Coun. Chs. Christ, 1986, pres., 1988—; pres. Walker Funeral Home Inc. (formerly The House of Irma Funeral Home), Concord, 1995, Am. Ch. Econ. Devel. Corp.; del. Presbyn. Ch. U.S. Gen. Assembly, 1985; mem. citizens parole accountability com. Mecklenburg County, Charlotte, 1993; mem. planned giving adv. bd. Livingston Coll., Salisbury, N.C.; pres. Jewett L. Walker & Assocs.; chmn. minority affairs adv. com. Mecklenburg County; com. mem. Charlotte Mecklenburg Citizen Parole Accountability Com., 1994, vice chmn., 1998; pres. Pardue St. Apts. Inc., Lancaster, S.C., 1997—, Am. Ch. Econ. Devel. Corp., 1999; elected to jud. coun. African Meth. Episcopal Zion Ch., 2000; mem. adv. bd. Mechanics and Farmers Bank, Charlotte, 2001 Fellow Nat. Assn. Ch. Bus. Adminstrs., Ch. Bus. Adminstrn., Presbyn. Ch. Bus. Adminstrn. Assn.; mem. NAACP (life), Nat. Soc. Fund Raising Execs., Am. Bible Soc. (state dir. vols., N.C. and S.C. dir. vol.), Nat. Spkrs. Bur., Christian Ministries Mgmt. Assn., Am. Soc. Assn. Execs., Funeral and Cremation Soc. South, Inc. (founding mem. 1998), Shriners, Masons (33 deg.), Prince Hall Affiliation. Republican. Home: 910 Bridlepath Ln Charlotte NC 28211-2022 Office: 4501 Walker Rd Charlotte NC 28211-2047

WALKER, JOAE BROOKS, retired psychiatrist; b. Boston, June 14, 1926; d. Collins and Hannah Slade (Benton) Graham; m. Bernard Charles Brooks, Jan. 11, 1976; children by previous marriage: Anne Benton Millman, Jane Graham Selzer. Nursing degree, Mass. Gen. Hosp. Sch. Nursing, 1947; AB with distinction, U. Rochester, 1950, MD, 1954. Diplomate Am. Bd. Psychiatry and Neurology. Intern in medicine Duke Hosp., Durham, N.C., 1954-55; resident in psychiatry Mass. Mental Health Ctr., Boston, 1955-57; resident in child psychiatry Beth Israel Hosp., Boston, 1957-59, mem. staff, 1959-97; pvt. practice Brookline, Mass., 1959-97. Cons. New Eng. Home for Little Wanderers, Boston, 1959-75, Kimberly Clark Corp., 1983-97; asst. clin. prof. psychiatry Harvard U. Med. Sch., Boston, 1978-97; vol. psychiatrist Sr. Friendship Ctr. Health Clinic, Naples, Fla., 1998-2007; mem. Bd. Registration in Medicine of Mass., 1991-95. Author: No More Diapers! A Guide to Toilet Training, 1971, 2d edit., 1991, When Children Ask About Sex-A Guide for Parents, 1975, I'm A Big Kid Now! A Guide to Toilet Training for Children and Parents, 1989. Distinguished fellow APA (life), Acad. Child and Adolescent Psychiatry (life); mem. Mass. Psychiat. Soc., New Eng. Coun. Child Psychiatry (bd. dirs. 1979-82, pres. 1987-89).

WALKER, JOAN H., insurance company executive; m. George Walker. BA, Rutgers U., New Brunswick, 1968, MA in Sociology, 1973. Sr. exec. mktg. and govt. N.J. State Govt., 1973-83; pres. Richmann & Ptnrs., 1983-88; exec. v.p. Saatchi & Saatchi, 1988-90; mng. dir. mktg. comm. NYNEX Corp., 1990-93; pres., CEO Bozell Pub. Rels., NYC, 1993-96; ptnr. Bozell Sawyer Miller Group, 1996; sr. v.p. corp. comm. Ameritech, Chgo., 1996-99; sr. v.p. global pub. affairs Monsanto (merged with Pharmacia & UpJohn, now Pharmacia), Skolie, Ill., 1999—2002; exec. v.p. corp. mktg. and comm. Qwest Comm. Internat., 2002—05; sr. v.p. corp. rels. Allstate Corp., Northbrook, Ill., 2005—, interim chief mktg. officer, 2007—. Bd. dir. Qwest Found.; mem. bd. trustees Colo. Symphony Orch. Office: Allstate Corp 2775 Sanders Rd Northbrook IL 60062 E-mail: Joan.H.Walker@am.pnu.com.*

WALKER, JOHN E. (NED WALKER), air transportation executive; married. B in Mass Comm., U. Colo., Boulder. News dir. KLMO Radio, Colo.; various positions including reporter, weekend anchor and asst. news dir. KWGN-TV, Denver; dir. corp. comm. Frontier Horizon Frontier Airlines; with Continental Airlines, Inc., Houston, 1987—, sr. dir. comm. dept., staff v.p. corp. comm., v.p. corp. comm., 1995—2000, sr. v.p. worldwide corp. comm., 2000—. Bd. dirs. Theater Under the Stars, Houston. Named an Employee Comm. All-Star, Inside PR, 1996. Office: Continental Airlines Inc PO Box 4607 Houston TX 77210 Office Phone: 713-324-5000. Office Fax: 713-324-2637. E-mail: ned.walker@coair.com.

WALKER, JOHN ERNEST, molecular biologist, researcher; b. Halifax, Yorkshire, Eng., Jan. 7, 1941; s. Thomas Ernest and Elsie (Lawton) W.; m. Christina Jane née Westcott, 1963; children: Esther, Miriam. BA in Chemistry, U. Oxford, Eng., 1964, MA, DPhil, U. Oxford, Eng., 1969, DSc (hon.), 1999, U. Buenos Aires, 1998, U. Huddersfield, 1998, U. Manchester Inst. Sci. & Tech., 1999, Groningen U., 1999, U. Leeds, 1999, U. London, 2002, U. Sussex, 2003, U. Liverpool, 2004, U. East Anglia, Norwich, 2006, Moscow State U., 2007. Postdoc. fellow U. Wis., Madison, 1969—71; NATO rsch. fellow CNRS, Gif-sur-Yvette, France, 1971—72; EMBO rsch. fellow Pasteur Inst., Paris, 1972—74; mem. scientific staff, Molecular Biology Lab. Med. Rsch. Coun., Cambridge, England, 1982—87, sr. scientist lab. molecular biology, 1987—98, dir. Dunn Human Nutrition Unit, 1998—. Smith-Kline Beecham vis. prof. Royal Soc. Medicine Found., 1995—; hon. prof. Peking Union Med. Coll., Beijing, 2001—, U. Cambridge, 2002, prof. molecular bioenergetics, 2002—. Contbr. articles to profl. jours. Recipient A. T. Clay Gold medal, 1959, Johnson Found. prize U. Pa., 1994, CIBA medal and prize Biochem. Soc., 1995, Peter Mitchell medal European Bioenergetic Congress, 1996, Gaetano Quagliariello prize U. Bari, 1997, Nobel prize in chemistry, 1997; named Nobel Laureate in Chemistry, 1997, hon. fellow Inst. Biology, 2002—. Fellow Royal Soc. (Chemistry award 2003), Sidney Sussex Coll., Acad. Med. Scis., London (founding fellow 1998-); mem. European Molecular Biology Orgn. (Knight Bachelor 1998), Soc. Chem. Industry (Messel medal 2000); L'Accademia Nazionale Dei Lincei; NAS (fgn. assoc. 2004), Brit. Biophysical Soc. (hon.), Acad. Europaea. Avocations: cricket, opera music, walking. Office: Mitochondrial Biology Unit Wellcome Trust MRC Bldg Hills Rd Cambridge CB2 0XY England Business E-Mail: walker@mrc-dunn.cam.ac.uk.

WALKER, JOHN MERCER, JR., federal judge; b. NYC, Dec. 26, 1940; s. John Mercer and Louise (Mead) W.; m. Cristy West, June 20, 1980 (div. Apr. 1983); m. Katharine Kirkland, Feb. 14, 1987. BA, Yale U., 1962; JD, U. Mich., 1966. Bar: NY 1969, US Dist. Ct. (so. dist.) NY 1971, US Ct. Appeals (2d cir.) 1972, US Supreme Ct. 1977, US Ct. Appeals (DC cir.) 1982. Maxwell Sch. Pub. Adminstrn. fellow, state counsel Republic of Botswana, Africa, 1966-68; assoc. Davis, Polk and Warwell, NYC, 1969-70; asst. US atty. criminal divsn. (So. dist.) NY US Dept. Justice, NYC, 1971-75; assoc. to ptnr. Carter, Ledyard and Milburn, NYC, 1975-81; asst. sec. enforcement ops. US Dept. Treasury, Washington, 1981-85; judge US Dist. Ct. (so. dist.) NY, 1985-89, US Ct. Appeals (2d cir.), New Haven, 1989—2006, chief judge, 2000—06, sr. judge, 2006—. Adj. prof. NYU Law Sch., 1995—; gen. counsel Nat. Coun. on Crime and Deliquency, NYC, 1977-81; chmn. Fed. Law Enforcement Tng. Ctr., Washington, 1981-85; spl. counsel Adminstrv. Conf. US, Washington, 1986-92; mem. budget com. jud. conf. Inst. Jud. Adminstrn., 1992—, dir., 1992—. Del. Rep. Nat. Conv., Detroit, 1980. With USMCR, 1963-67. Recipient Alexander Hamilton award Sec. of Treas., Washington, 1985, Secret Service Honor award, 1985. Mem. ABA, DC Bar Assn., Assn. Bar City of NY, Fed. Judges Assn. (pres. 1993-95). Republican. Episcopalian. Office: US Ct Appeals 157 Church St New Haven CT 06510-2100*

WALKER, JOHN STANLEY, legislative staff member; b. Jackson, Miss., Apr. 6, 1962; s. Emmett Hudson Jr. and Elizabeth Ann (Parsons) W.; m. Kristina Louise Smith, Jan. 5, 1991; children: Jordan Veronica, Shelby Elizabeth. BBA, James Madison U., 1984; MBA, George Washington U., 1987. Computer programmer Computer Science Corp., Arlington, Va., 1984-85; fin. counselor US House of Reps., Washington, 1985-88; exec. asst. for Rep. Larkin Smith, Washington, 1989; exec. dir. Conservative Opportunity Soc., Washington, 1989-90; dep. dir. govt. rels. Family Rsch. Coun., Washington, 1990-92; chief of staff Rep. Bill Baker, Washington, 1993—94, Rep. Charlie Norwood, Washington, 1995—2007; spl. project coord. US House Office of the Minority Whip, Washington, 2007—08; chief of staff Rep. John Carter, Washington, 2008—. Deacon McLean (Va.) Presbyn. Ch., 1995—. Republican. Office: Office of Congressman John Carter 408 Cannon House Office Bldg Washington DC 20515 Office Phone: 202-225-3864. E-mail: john.walker@mail.house.gov.*

WALKER, JONATHAN J., art educator; m. Cherie Walker; children: Shannon, Jon-Ryan. MFA, U. Conn., 1983. Pvt. practice Ind. Cons., 1981; assoc. prof. Keene State Coll., Keene, NH, 1985—89, U. Fla., Gainesville, 1981—89; art dir. Med. Edn. and Advt., Wilton, Conn., 1991—93; cons.-art dir. Philip Morris Mgmt., Rye Brook, NY, 1993—94; digital, print and multimedia designer Jon Walker Design, Fairfield, 1994—; design dir. Soccer Jr. Mag., Scholastic Inc., NYC, 1994—2001; theme Pk. designer, ind. cons. Mus. Svcs., Gainesville, Fla., 1991—91; multimedia design dir. Coerver Soccer, New Canaan, Conn., 2000; assoc. prof. and chmn. Dept. Art & Design, Sacred Heart U., Fairield, Conn., 2002—. Design dir. (mag. design) Soccer Jr. Magazine (APEX Award, Ozzie Award), art dir. (newspaper design) Philip Morris Globe (Golden Quill Award, 1994), designer (graphic design) Poster Design for Of Mice and Men (First Pl. Award, 1991), theater designer (scenic and lighting design) Career (Nat. Recognition, 1991, Featured Designer, 1991). Mem.: United Scenic Artists, AIGA. Avocations: bicycling, kayaking, snorkeling. Office: Sacred Heart Univ 5151 Park Ave Fairfield CT 06825 Business E-Mail: walkerj@sacredheart.edu.

WALKER, JOYCE L., music educator; b. Rochester, July 8, 1949; d. Albert Leroy and Doris Lucille Eshelman; m. David B. Walker, July 1, 1972; children: Julie L., Jacqueline L. BS, Ind. State U., Terre Haute, 1972; MA in Liberal Studies, Valparaiso U., Ind., 1976. Tchr. music Porter Twp. Sch. Corp., Valparaiso, Ind., 1972—; ch. organist, pianist Hebron United Meth. Ch., Hebron, Ind., 1972—. Home: 205 W Sigler St Hebron IN 46341 Office: Porter Lakes Elem Sch 208 S 725 W Hebron IN 46341 Office Phone: 219-988-2727. E-mail: djwalker@netnitco.net.

WALKER, KARA, artist; b. Stockton, Calif., Nov. 26, 1969; BA in Painting/Printmaking, Atlanta Coll. Art, 1991; MFA in Painting/Printmaking, RI Sch. Design, 1997. Prof. art Columbia U., NYC. US representative São Paolo Bienal, Brazil, 2002. One-woman shows include Gallery 100, Atlanta, 1991, Ctr. Curaltorial Studies, Bard Coll., Annandale-on-Hudson, NY, 1995, Nexus Contemporary Arts Ctr., Atlanta, 1995, Wooster Gardens/Brent Sikkema, NYC, 1995, 1998, Bernard Toale Gallery, Boston, 1996, Huntington Beach Arts Ctr., Calif., 1997, U. Chgo., 1997, Contemporary Arts Ctr., Cin., 1997, Henry Art Gallery, U. Wash., Seattle, 1997, The Carpenter Ctr., Harvard U., Cambridge, Mass., 1997, San Francisco Mus. Modern Art, 1997, The Forum, St. Louis, 1998, Vienna State Opera House, Austria, 1998, The Print Ctr., Phila., 1998, Galleri Index, Stockholm, 1998, Contemporary Arts Mus., Houston, 1999, Calif. Coll. Arts and Crafts, Oliver Art Ctr., Oakland, 1998, Brent Sikkema, NY, 1998, McKinney Ave. Contemporary, Dallas, 1999, Des Moines Art Ctr., 2000, The Emancipation Approximation, Tel Aviv Mus. Art, 2001, Disturbing Allegories, Vanderbilt U. Fine Arts Gallery, Tenn., 2001, American Primitive, Brent Sikkema Gallery, NYC, 2001, Nat Turner's Revelation (an Important Lesson from our Negro Past You Will Likely Forget to Remember), Galerie Max Hetzler, Berlin, 2002, For the Benefit of All the Races of Mankind (Mos' Specially the Master One, Boss), Germany, 2002, Mannheimer Kunstverein, Germany, 2002, Internat. Bienal of Sao Paolo, Brazil, 2002, An Abbreviated Emancipation, U. Mich. Mus. Art, 2002, Narratives of a Negress, Tang Tchg. Mus. and Art Gallery, Skidmore Coll., 2003, Drawings, Brent Sikkema, 2003, Excavated from the Black Heart of a Negress, Studio Mus., Harlem, 2003, Centro Nazionale per le Arti Contemporanee, Rome, 2003, Fibbergibbet and Mumbo Jumbo, Fabric Workshop and Mus., Phila., 2004, Grub for Sharks: A Concession to the Negro Populace, Tate Liverpool, 2004, Museo de Arte Carrillo Gil, Mexico City, 2005, Event Horizon, New Sch. U., 2005, Song of the South, REDCAT, LA, 2005, My Complement, My Enemy, My Oppressor, My Love, 2007, exhibited in group shows at New Visions Gallery, Atlanta, 1991, MU Gallery, Boston, 1993, Sol Koffler Gallery, Providence, 1994, Paul Morris Gallery, NYC, 1995, Mills Gallery, Boston, Inst. Contemporary Art, 1996, Greg Kucera Gallery, Seattle, 1997, Stephen Friedman Gallery, London, 1998, Looking Forward Looking Backward, Elaine L. Jacob Gallery, Wayne State U., 1999, Istanbul Biennial: The Passion and the Wave, 1999, This Is Not the Place, Ramapo Coll. NJ, 2000, Blurry Lines, John Michael Kholer Arts Ctr., Wis., 2000, The Print World, Ljubljana Biennial, Slovenia, 2001, The Americans, Barbican Art Galleries, London, 2001, Form Follow Fiction, Castello di Rivoli Museo d'Arte Contemporanea, 2001, Moving Pictures, Solomon R. Guggenheim Mus., NYC, 2002, Telling Tales: Narrative Impulses in Recent Art, 2002, Tempo, MoMAQNS, NYC, 2002, Black President: The Art and Legacy of Fela Anikulapo-Kuti, New Mus., NYC, 2003, Comic Release: Negotiating Identity for a New Generation, Carnegie Mellon U., 2003, Provocations, Bronx Mus. Art, 2004, Monument to Now, DESTE Found. Contemporary Art, Athens, Greece, 2004, Fairy Tales Forever: Internat. Homage to H.C. Andersen, Copenhagen, 2005, Kiss the Frog! The Art of Transformation, Nat. Mus. Art, 2005, Getting Emotional, Inst. Contemporary Art, Boston, 2005, The Shadow, Vestsjaellands Kunstmuseum, Denmark, 2005, The World is a Stage, Mori Art Mus., Tokyo, 2005, Trials and Terrors, Mus. Contemporary Art, 2005, Met. Mus. Art, NYC, 2006, Venice Biennale, 2007, numerous others; author: Freedom, A Fable, A Curious Interpretation of the Wit of a Negress in Troubled Times; contbr. articles to profl. jours. Recipient Lucelia Artist award, Smithsonian Am. Art Mus., 2004, Internat. Assn. Art Critics award, 2008; named Presdl. scholar, Atlanta Coll. Art, Ida Blank Ocko scholar, Individual Artist's fellow, Art Matters, Inc.; named one of The World's Most Influential People, TIME mag., 2007; fellow John D. and Catherine T. MacArthur Found. Office: c/o Sikkema Jenkins & Co 530 West 22d St New York NY 10011

WALKER, KAREN D., lawyer; b. Tampa, Feb. 24, 1968; BS in Comm. Studies, Fla. State U., 1990; JD with high honors, U. Fla., 1993. Bar: Fla. 1993, US Dist. Ct. (No. and So. Districts Fla.) 2000. Ptnr. Holland & Knight LLP, Tallahassee. Mng. editor U. Fla. Law Rev., 1991—92, title standards editor, 1992—93. Past chair bd. dirs. United Way of the Big Bend, Inc. Mem.: ABA (chair young lawyers divsn., com. on women in the profession 2000—02, mem. standing com. on pub. edn. 2000—02, state chair pub. contract law sect. state/local procurement divsn. 2002—, mem. sect. on pub. utilities, comm., and transp. law, chair IT procurement com.), Tallahassee Women Lawyers, Tallahassee Bar Assn., Fla. Bar (mem. adminstrv. law sect.), Order of Coif. Office: Holland & Knight LLP 315 S Calhoun St Ste 600 Tallahassee FL 32301 Office Phone: 850-425-5612. Business E-Mail: karen.walker@hklaw.com.

WALKER, KAREN LOUISE, music educator; d. Louis Edward and Kay Diane Walker; m. Robert Peter Larson; children: Rachel Cecelia Larson, Sarah Catherine Larson. DMA, Cath. U. America, Washington, 2000. Prof. music, adv. arts Shenandoah U., Winchester, Va., 1983—. Liberal. Roman Catholic. Avocation: music.

WALKER, KELLYE L., lawyer; b. Little Rock, Aug. 1966; BS, La. Tech. U., 1987; JD, Emory U., 1992. Atty. Boult, Cummings, Conners & Berry PLC, Nashville; assoc. Chaffe, McCall, Phillips, Toler & Sarpy LLP, New Orleans, 1995—98, ptnr., 1998—2000; mem., counsel Hill & Barlow LLP, Boston, 2000—03; sr. v.p., gen. counsel, sec. BJ's Wholesale Club Inc., Natick, Mass., 2003—07; gen counsel Diageo N. Am., 2007—. Bd. dirs. Assn. Corp. Counsel, New England Legal Found., Mus. Afro-Am. History. Office: Diageo 801 Main Ave Norwalk CT 06860

WALKER, KENNETH LYNN, lawyer; b. New Haven, Nov. 22, 1948; s. John Charles and Virginia Clare (Lovett) W.; m. Suzanne Kay Thompson, Jan. 27, 1979; children: Katherine Leslie, Caroline Leigh, Christine Lynn. BA, Coe Coll., 1969; MA, New Sch. Social Research, 1973; JD, U. Iowa, 1975. Bar: Ohio. Assoc. Baker & Hostetler, Cleve., 1975-79; atty. Cole Nat. Corp., Cleve., 1979-84; sr. group counsel TRW, Inc., Cleve., 1984-91; v.p., gen. coun. sec. Varity Corp., 1991-97; v.p. gen coun. sec. Sealy Corp., 1997-2000, sr. v.p., gen. counsel, sec. 2000-. Editor Jour. Corp. Law, 1974-75. Mem. ABA, Ohio Bar Assn., Cleve. Bar Assn. Office: Sealy One Office Parkway at Sealy Dr Trinity NC 27370 Business E-Mail: kwalker@sealy.com.

WALKER, KRISTIN, legislative staff member; Intern, Rep. Barbara Cubin US House of Reps., Washington, 2004, schedule coord., Rep. Barbara Cubin, 2005—08, press sec., Rep. Ed Whitfield, 2008—. Republican. Office: 2411 Rayburn House Office Bldg Washington DC 20515 Office Phone: 202-225-3115. Office Fax: 202-225-3547.*

WALKER, LELAND JASPER, civil engineer; b. Fallon, Nev., Apr. 18, 1923; s. Albert Willard and Grayce (Wilkinson) W.; m. Margaret Frances Noble, Jan. 21, 1946; children: Thomas, Margaret, Timothy. BS in Civil Engring, Iowa State U., 1944; D. Eng. (hon.), Mont. State U., 1983. Engr. with various govtl. depts., 1946-51, 53-55; v.p. Wenzel & Co. (cons. engrs.), Great Falls, Mont., 1955-58; pres., chmn. bd. No. Engring. and Testing, Inc., Great Falls, 1958-88. Pres. Ind. Labs. Assurance Co., 1977-79; bd. dirs. Applied Tech., Inc. Pres., trustee Endowment and Rsch. Found. Mont. State U., 1969-82, Mont. Deaconess Hosp., Great Falls, 1959-67. McLaughlin Rsch. Inst. Biol. Scis., 1989-92, Mont. Sch. Deaf and Blind Found., 1984—; trustee Rocky Mountain Coll., 1977-80, Dufresne Found., 1979-87; chmn., bd. dirs. Mont. Tech. Svcs. Adv. Coun. adv. coun. Engring. Coll. Mont. State U.; bd. dirs. Mont. State Fair, Engring. Socs. Commn. on Energy, 1977-79, Mont. Bd. Sci. and Tech., 1983-88, Great Falls Chamber Found., 1989-91, trustee Great Falls Public Libr. Found., 1995-2001. Named to Mont. Engrs. Hall Fame, 2003. Fellow ASCE (pres. 1976-77), AAAS, Cons. Engrs. Coun. (pres. Mont. 1971), Accrediting Bd. Engring. and Tech. (v.p. 1978-79, pres. 1980-83); mem. Nat. Acad. Engring., Am. Coun. Ind. Labs. (hon., sec. 1973-76), Meadowlark Country Club, Pachyderm Club (bd. dirs., v.p. 1992-94), Chi Epsilon (nat. hon.), Tau Beta Pi (hon.). Republican. Methodist. Home: 1200 32nd St S Apt 9 Great Falls MT 59405-5333

WALKER, LINDA ANN, financial planner; b. Denver, May 10, 1956; d. John Bruce Elmer and Ruth Evelyn (Rogers) Metsker; m. Sidney Carr Walker III, Feb. 9, 1992; 1 child. BA, U. Colo., 1978. CFP. Account exec. E.F. Hutton, Boulder, 1980-84; with Fin. Planning and Mgmt., Boulder, 1984-91, pres., 1989-91, Premier Planning Assocs., Boulder, 1991-95; pvt. practice, 1995—. Actress (play) Shadow of a Gunman, 1991, La Ronde, 1992 (dancer) Who's There, 1991. Bd. dirs. Nancy Spanier Dance Theatre, Boulder, 1986-91; mem. Win/Win, Boulder, 1989-91. Mem. Fin. Planners Assn., Phi Beta Kappa Soc. Democrat. Avocations: reading, writing, meditating, horseback riding. Office: 5150 E PCH Ste 520 Long Beach CA 90804-3326

WALKER, LINDA LEE, lawyer; b. Phila., Jan. 24, 1954; d. M. Lorenzo and Romaine Yvonne (Smith) W.; m. Steve Collins; children: Jessica Marie McIntyre, Nicole Yvonne McIntyre. BA, U. Penn., 1975; JD, Yale U., 1978. Bar: NY 1979, US Dist. Ct. (so. and ea. dists.) NY 1982, US Ct. Appeals (1st cir.) 1982; NASD. Asst. regional atty. HHS, NYC, 1978-82; assoc. Shea and Gould, NYC, 1982-85; v.p., sr. assoc. counsel Chase Manhattan Bank, N.A., NYC, 1985-89; v.p., assoc. gen. counsel Citicorp Credit Svc., NYC, 1989-97; asst. gen. counsel Prudential Ins. Co. Am., Iselin, 1997—2000, v.p., chief compliance officer for Prudential Retirement, 2000—04; dir. compliance UBS Fin. Svcs., Inc., Weehawken, NJ, 2004—. Mem., Phi Beta Kappa. Office Phone: 201-352-4959. Business E-Mail: linda.walker@ubs.com.

WALKER, LLOYD T., food scientist; b. Port Morant, Jamaica, Jan. 30, 1954; s. Leonard T. Walker and Remella Nesbith; m. Fay A. Almon; children: Carol O. Walker-Thompson, Kibwe D., Karlene D. BS in Animal Sci., Prairie View A&M U., Tex., 1983, MS in Animal Sci., 1986; PhD in Food Sci., Tex. A&M U., Coll. Station, 1991. Dept. chair Ala. A&M U., Normal, 1999—2008, assoc. provost, dean, 2008—. Recipient Outstanding Rschr. award, Ala. A&M U. Mem.: Inst. Food Technologists (regional chair 2007—08). Liberal. Episcopalian. Achievements include research in phyto-chemicals in peanuts and other foods. Avocations: reading, cricket. Office: Ala A&M Univ 4900 Meridian St PO Box 1212 Normal AL 35762 Home Phone: 256-882-2034; Office Phone: 256-372-4166. Business E-Mail: lloyd.walker@aamu.edu.

WALKER, MARILYN SUAREZ, educator; m. Gene Thomas Suarez, Dec. 1, 2001; children: Scott Andrew Suarez, Julie María Suarez, Terrance Michael Suarez. MS, U. Kans., Lawrence, 1970. Instr. Emory and Henry Coll., Va., 2004—. Supportive mem. tchg. First United Meth. Ch., Marion, Va., 1990—2008. Home: 356 W Main St Marion VA 24354 Office: Emory and Henry Coll PO Box 947 Emory VA 24327 Business E-Mail: mwalker@ehc.edu.

WALKER, MARK A., lawyer; b. NYC, June 24, 1941; s. Joseph and Eleanor (Junger) W.; m. Tania Khodjamirian; children: Marie, Andrew. BA, Stanford U., 1963; LLB, Yale U., 1966. Bar: N.Y. 1967, U.S. Dist. Ct. (so. dist.) N.Y. 1977. Assoc. Cleary, Gottlieb, Steen & Hamilton, Paris, Brussels and NY, 1966-75, ptnr. NYC, 1975—2005, mng. ptnr., 2005—. Mem. Assn. Bar City N.Y. Office Phone: 212-225-2240. E-mail: mwalker@cgsh.com.

WALKER, MARK ALAN, legislative staff member; b. Montpelier, Ohio, Aug. 10, 1965; BA, Wabash Coll., 1988; attended, Coll. Internat., Cannes, France, 1986, Sorbonne, Paris, 1987. With Bush-Quayle Campaign Com.; fin. dir. The Congl. Inst.; comm. dir. for Rep. Michael Forbes, US House of Reps.; press sec. for Rep. Dan Burton, now chief of staff. Profl. staff mem. Subcommittee on Western Hemisphere, Com. of Fgn. Affairs US House of Reps. Office: Office of Congressman Dan Burton 2308 Rayburn House Office Bldg Washington DC 20515-0001 Office Phone: 202-225-2276. Office Fax: 202-225-0016.*

WALKER, MARTHA YEAGER, state agency administrator, former state senator; b. May 15, 1940; m. H. Jarrett Walker; children: Meredyth, Brent, Melissa. BS, W.Va. U. Speech therapist Charleston Meml. Hosp., W.Va. Bureau Public Health, Kanawha Charleston Health Dept., Eye & Ear Clinic, Charleston, W.Va.; mem. W.Va. Ho. of Reps., Charleston, 1990-92, W.Va. Senate, Charleston, 1993—2001; sec. W.Va. Dept. Health & Human Resources, Charleston, 2005—. Mem. fin. com., govt. orgn. com., health and human resources com., pensions com., rules com., enrolled bills com.; with Byrd Inst. Studies, U. Charleston. Mem. W.Va. Dem. Exec. Com., Charleston Zoing Appeals Bd., Ctr. for Econ. Options, Byrd Inst. Govt. Studies, U. Charleston; former mem. Cabin Creek Health Ctr.; former treas. Kanawha County Pvt. Industry Coun.; active Literacy Vols. W.Va.; bd. dirs. Poison Control Ctr., Cabin Creek Health Ctr., Multiple Sclerosis Soc. W.Va., W.Va. Children's Health Policy Bd., Gov.'s Cabinet on Children and Families, Regional Contracting Assistance Ctr., Charleston Capitol Market, Literacy Vols. of Am.; sustaining mem. Jr. League Charleston; treas. PIC Kanawha County. Mem. Charleston C. of C., W.Va. U. Alumni Assn., Rotary. Democrat. Presbyterian. Office: Dept Health & Human Resources Bldg 3 Rm 206 State Capitol Complex Charleston WV 25305 Office Fax: 304-558-1130. Business E-Mail: dhhrsecretary@wv.gov.*

WALKER, MARY ALEXANDER, author; b. Beaumont, Tex., Sept. 24, 1927; d. James Cosper Alexander and Mary Helen (Johnson) Alexander Shelley; m. Tommy Ross Walker, Dec. 23, 1952; children: Timothy Ross, Mark Thomas, Miles Stephen. AA, Lamar Inst. Tech., 1945; BS, Tex. Women's U., 1950; MA, San Francisco State U., 1981; grad. studies in Playwriting, U. London, U. Alaska. Instr., Dominican U., San Rafael, Calif., 1972-80; lectr. U. San Francisco, 1983-84; reader Justice NYC, French Heels, Santa Cruz, Calif., The Borin, Ross, Calif. Author: Year of the Cafeteria (Breadloaf Writers' Conf. fellow for disting. book for young people 1972), 1971; To Catch a Zombi, 1979; Maggot, 1980, Scathach and Maeve's Daughters, 1990, Brad's Boys (Florida Sunshine prize); also short stories; (performances) Our Girl, Phoenix, NY, Dominican U. French Heels.

WALKER, MATTHEW VINCENT, legislative staff member; Legis. asst. for Rep. Robert Andrews, US House of Reps., Washington, 2000—02, adminstrv. asst., legis. dir., 2002—03, chief of staff, 2003, 2008—. Office: Office of Congressman Robert Andrews 2265 Rayburn House Bldg Washington DC 20515 Office Phone: 202-225-6501. Office Fax: 202-225-6583. E-mail: matt.walker@mail.house.gov.*

WALKER, MELVETA, librarian, director; b. Portales, New Mex., Jan. 29, 1940; d. Charles Melvin and Veda Joy Baker; m. Jerry Clayton Walker; children: Koetta Kay Carrell, Michala May Ruechel. BS, Eastern New Mex. U., Portales, 1965; MS in Ednl. Media, Nrthern Ariz. U., Flagstaff, 1972. Cert. adminstrn. Ariz., 1975, New Mex., 1988. Libr. dir. ENMU Golden Libr., Portales, 1999—, asst. dir., 1991—99. Libr. Bur. Indian Affairs, Tuba City, Ariz., 1965—82, TeecNosPos, Ariz., 1982—88. Pres. Friends Portales Pub. Libr., 1988—2003, Meals Wheels, Portales, 1988—2008, mem., 1988—2003, Eastern New Mex. U. Found., Portales, 2005—08; devel. officer Habitat Humanity, Roosevelt & Curry Counties, N.Mex., 2005—08; pres. New Mex. Consortium Academic Librs., 2005—07. Recipient Spirit award, Eastern New Mex. U., 2008. Mem.: New Mex. Libr. Assn. (Libr. Leadership award 2003). Home: 263 New Mex 88 Portales NM 88130 Office: Eastern New Mex Univ Golden Libr Portales NM 88130 Office Fax: 575-562-2647. Business E-Mail: melveta.walker@enmu.edu.

WALKER, MICHAEL ANGUS, economist, director; b. Corner Brook, Nfld., Can., Sept. 11, 1945; m. Janet Walker; children: Margot, Joel. BA, St. Francis Xavier U., 1966; MA, U. Western Ont., 1967, PhD, 1971. Instr. U. Western Ont., Canada, 1968—69; with Bank of Can., 1969—72; instr. Carleton U., Canada, 1971; with Fed. Dept. Fin., Canada, 1973—74; exec. dir. The Fraser Inst., Vancouver, B.C., Canada, 1974—2005, sr. fellow, 2005—; pres. The Fraser Inst. Found., 2005—. Bd. dirs. Mancal Corp., The Milton and Rose D. Friedman Found., Canaccord Capital Inc., dir., 2006—. Office: The Fraser Inst 4th Floor 1770 Burrard St Vancouver BC Canada V6J 3G7 Office Phone: 604-688-0221. Business E-Mail: michaelw@fraserinstitute.ca, michael_walker@fraserinstitute.org.

WALKER, MORGAN WAILES, art educator; b. Alexandria, La., June 21, 1957; s. Morgan Wailes Walker, Jr. and Susan Field Walker; m. Laura Ruth Smith, June 10, 1989; 1 child, Lucy Jane. BA in Philosophy, Wash. and Lee U., 1979; JD, Tulane U. Sch. Law, New Orleans, 1982; BFA, Pacific NW Coll. Art, Portland, 1993; MFA, U. Oreg., Eugene, 1995. Adj. asst. prof. Pacific NW Coll. Art, 2000—07, assoc. prof., 2007—, chair, curriculum, 2008—. Exhibitions include Louisiana Sweet, New Drawings and Paintings, Imaginary Dog. Vol. Barack Obama presdl. campaign, Portland, 2008—08. Fellowsip, Fulbright Assn., 1996—97. Liberal. Avocations: bicycling, gardening, ukelele. Office: Pacific NW Coll of Art 1241 NW Johnson Portland OR 97209

WALKER, MORT, cartoonist; b. El Dorado, Kans., Sept. 3, 1923; s. Robin A. and Carolyn (Richards) W.; m. Catherine Carty Prentice, Aug. 24, 1985; children: Greg, Brian, Polly, Morgan, Marjorie, Neal, Roger, Whitney, Cathy, Jr., Priscilla. Student, Kansas City Jr. Coll., 1941-42, Washington U., St. Louis, 1943-44; BA, U. Mo., 1948; LL.D., William Penn Coll., 1981. Designer Hallmark Greeting Cards, 1941; editor Dell Pub. Co., 1948-49; free lance cartoonist Saturday Evening Post, other popular mags., 1948-50. Scholar in residence Mo. U., 1992. Comic strip artist King Features, 1950—; creator Beetle Bailey, 1950, Hi and Lois, 1954, Sam's Strip, 1961, Boner's Ark, 1968, Sam and Silo, 1977, The Evermores, 1982, Betty Boop and Felix, 1984, (for United Features) Gamin and Patches, 1987; author: Most, 1971, Land of Lost Things, 1973, Backstage at the Strips, 1975, The Lexicon of Comicana, 1981, The Best of Beetle Bailey, 1984, The Coconut Crew, 1997, (autobiography) Mort Walker's Private Scrapbook, 2001, (novel) The World Tallest Man; contbr. 92 paperback collections. Mem. Pres.'s Com. to Hire Handicapped, People to People Com. Exhbn. touring group show Met. Mus. Art, N.Y.C., 1951; chmn. Internat. Mus. Cartton Art. Served to 1st lt. AUS, 1943-46, ETO, intelligence & investigating officer Decorated chevalier Order Arts and Letters (France); recipient Outstanding Cartoonist award The Banshees, 1955, Il Secolo XIX award (Italy), 1972, Adamson award (Sweden), 1975, 88, Segar award, 1977, 4th Estate award Am. Legion, The Jester, 1979, Power of Printing, 1977, NCS Golden T-Square award, 1999, Disting. Civilian Svc. award U.S. Army; named Man of Yr. NCCJ, 1988, Artist of Yr., Capuchin Order, 2006. Mem. Nat. Cartoonists Soc. (pres. 1959-60, Reuben award 1953, Best Humor Strip award 1966, 69, named to Hall Fame, Nat. Cartoon Mus. 1989, CT NCS Legend award, 2006, Gold Key award, 2007), Artists and Writers, Newspaper Features Coun. Authors Guild, Soc. Illustrators, Nat. Press Club, Silvermine Club (Norwalk, Conn.), Greenwich Country Club, Quechee Club, Kappa Sigma (named Man of Yr. 1988). Office: King Features 300 W 57Th St New York NY 10019-3741 *If I enjoy my own life that's one life enjoyed. But if I can help others enjoy their lives more, many lives are made more enjoyable.*

WALKER, OLENE S., former governor; b. Ogden, Utah, Nov. 15, 1930; d. Thomas Ole and Nina Hadley (Smith) W.; m. J. Myron Walker, 1957; children: Stephen Brett, David Walden, Bryan Jesse, Lori, Mylene, Nina, Thomas Myron. BA, Brigham Young U., 1954; MA, Stanford U., 1954; PhD, U. Utah, 1986; HHD (hon.), Weber State U., 1997. V.p. Country Crisp Foods, 1969-92; mem. Utah Ho. of Reps. Dist. 24; lt. gov. State of Utah, 1993—2003, gov., 2003—05. Mem. Salt Lake Edn. Found. bd. dirs. 1983-90; dir. community econ. devel.; mem. Ballet West, Sch. Vol., United Way, Commn. on Youth, Girls Village, Salt Lake Conv. and Tourism Bd.; mem. adv. coun. Weber State U. Mem. Nat. Assn. Secs. of State (Western chmn., nat. lt. gov.'s conf., pres. 1997-98). Republican. Mem. Lds Ch. Achievements include becoming first female elected to office of governor of Utah. Home: 3135 Jacob Hamblin Dr Saint George UT 84790-7807

WALKER, PAM, biology educator; BA, Ga. Coll.; MA, Ga. State Univ.; EdS, Ga. So. Univ. Sci. tchr. Telfair County, Ga., Fitzgerald City, Ga., Laurens County, Ga., Alexander H.S., Douglasville, Ga., 1990—. Named Douglas County Tchr. of Yr., 2005, Ga. Tchr. of Yr., 2007. Achievements include authoring 20 textbooks and tchr. resource books. Office: Alexander H S 6500 Alexander Pkwy Douglasville GA 30135 Business E-Mail: pam@sciencebookwriters.com.

WALKER, PAMELA, mathematics educator; BS, Utah State U., Logan, 1974. Cert. early childhood/elem. edn. and libr. media tchr. Utah. 4th grade tchr. A.W. Johnson Elem. Sch., Firth Sch. Dist., Idaho, 1974—83, Washington Ter. Elem. Sch., Weber Sch. Dist., Ogden, Utah, 1984—89; 3rd grade tchr. Mcpl. Elem. Sch., Weber Sch. Dist., Roy, Utah, 1989—91; math tchr. Sand Ridge Jr. HS, Weber Sch. Dist., Roy, 1991—92, Roy Jr. HS, Weber Sch. Dist., Roy, 1992—2006; tchr. libr. media ctr. Sand Ridge Jr. High, Weber Sch. Dist., 2006—. Recipient Apple for Tchr. award, Std. Examiner Newspaper, 1992—2008, Teacher's Recognition award, Remax Realtors, 1996, April award, 1992—2009; named Tchr. of Yr., Firth Sch. Dist., 1983. Mem.: Utah Edn. Assn. (assoc.). Avocations: sewing, needlecrafts.

WALKER, PATRICIA ANN, special education educator; b. Medford, Oreg., July 29, 1962; d. Oran C. Chastain and Sadimae J. Chastain-Jones, Benjamin Jones (Stepfather); m. John Walker; 1 child, Robert Owen. BS in Elem. Edn., So. Oreg. State Coll., 1985. Store mgr. 7-Eleven Store, Costa Mesa, Calif., 1986—90; sales rep. Mclanes So. Calif., San Bernardino, 1990—93, Sales Mark, Santa Fe Springs, Calif., 1993—98; substitute tchr. San Diego City Union Sch. Dist., 2000—02; spl. edn. pre-k tchr. Escondido Union Sch. Dist., Calif., 2002—. Recipient Nicolaysen Ctr. Employee of the Yr. award, Escondido Union Sch. Dist., 2004-05, Nicolaysen Ctr. Educator of the Yr. award, Escondido Elem. Educators Assn., 2004-05; grantee, Delta Kappa Gamma, 1981; scholarship, Ben Ziri Caravan of the Alhambra, 2001, Found. of Devel. Disabilities Peterson, 2001. Mem.: Nat. PTA, Coun. for Exeptional Children, Escondido Elem. Educators Assn., Autism Soc. of Am. (San Diego chpt.). Avocations: swimming, spending time with my son. Office: Escondido Union School District 1330 E Grand Ave Escondido CA 92027-3099 Home: 444 E 4TH Ave Apt 603 Escondido CA 92025-4372 Personal E-mail: pwalker714@yahoo.com.

WALKER, PHILIP CHAMBERLAIN, II, retired health facility administrator; b. Big Spring, Tex., July 7, 1944; s. Philip Chamberlain and Mary Catherine (St. John) W.; m. Linda Jane Holsclaw, Jan. 21, 1978; children: Shannon M., Meghan M. BA, Cen. Wash. State Coll., 1970; MS, U. Idaho, 1971. Exec. dir. Multnomah Found. for Med. Care, Portland, Oreg., 1972-81; chief exec. officer Peer Rev. Orgn. for Wash. State, Seattle, 1981-84; dir. Preferred Provider Orgn. devel. Provident Life and Accident, Chattanooga, 1984-88; v.p. Maxicare Health Plans, LA, 1988-91; v.p., gen. mgr. Maxicare Health Plans Midwest, Chgo., 1991-92; pres. Health Plus, Peoria, Ill., 1992—2007; CEO, chmn. bd. HCH Adminstrn., Peoria, Ill., 1992-98; sr. v.p. Health Care Horizons, Albuquerque, 1992-98; exec. v.p. Proctor Health Sys., 1998—2007. Bd. dirs. RMR Group, HCH Adminstrn., Health Care Horizons; cons. in field. Contbr. articles to profl. jours. Bd. dirs. Boys and Girls Club of Greater Peoria, 2003—06; v.p. Boys and Girls Club Peoria, 2004—06; Ctrl. Ill. regional adv. bd. Multiple Sclerosis Assn., 2002—04; chmn. Hult Health Edn. Ctr., 1999—2003; bd. dirs. Boys & Girls Club Olympic Peninsula, 2008, pres., 2009—; bd. dirs. Olympic Med. Ctr. Found., 2008—; mem. Olympic Area Agy. Aged Coun., 2008—; bd. dirs. Hult Health Edn. Ctr., Cancer Ctr. for Health Living, 2001—03, Heart of Ill. United Way, 2004—07. With USAF, 1961—66, Vietnam. Mem.: Creve Coeur Club (bd. govs., pres.). Business E-Mail: plwalkerii@yahoo.com.

WALKER, PHILIP DOOLITTLE, retired literature and language professor, composer; b. Newburyport, Mass., 1924; m. Corlette Rossiter, Mar. 23, 1952; children: Melissa Sokol, Laura Ragan, Barbara McMillan. BA, Yale U., New Haven, Conn., 1947, MA, 1951, PhD, 1956. Instr. Lawrence Coll., Appleton, Wis., 1954—57, U. Calif., Santa Barbara, 1957—60, asst. prof., 1960—64, assoc. prof., 1964—70, prof., 1970—90, prof. emeritus French lit., 1990—. Chair dept. French and Italian U. Calif., 1971—75. Author: (book) Germinal and Zola's Philosophical and Religious Thought, (biography) Zola; contbr. articles to profl. jours. Bd. mem. Yale Lit. Mag., New Haven, 1944—45. Lt. (j.g.) USNR, 1942—46. Grantee, Fulbright Found., 1951—52; fellow, John Simon Guggenheim Meml. Found., 1967—68, Fitzwilliam Coll., Cambridge, England, 1986. Mem.: Mil. Order Two World Wars, Yale Club Santa Barbara, Elizabethan Club Yale U. Democrat. Episcopalian. Avocation: composing.

WALKER, PHILLIP, finance company executive, insurance company executive; b. Jacksonville, Ark., Mar. 15, 1985; s. Michael and Patricia Walker; m. Amber Works; 1 child, Brayden. Cert. Assn. Fin. & Ins. Profls., 2007. Fin. & ins. mgr. M & J Motors, Boaz, Ala., 2003—05, Howard Bentley Buick Pontiac GMC, Albertville, Ala., 2005—. Mem. Civitans Internat., Boaz, Ala., 2000—08. Home: 191 Noblitt Cir Boaz AL 35956 Afghanistan Office: Howard Bentley Buick Pontiac GMC 4321 US Hwy 431 Albertville AL 35950

WALKER, R. A., oil industry executive; m. Stephanie Walker; 2 children. BS, MBA, U. Tulsa. Various mcht. banking positions up to sr. mng. dir, co-head Prudential Capital Group; pres., CEO 3TEC Energy Corp.; mng. dir. Global Energy Group UBS Investment Bank; sr. v.p. fin., CFO Anadarko Petroleum Corp., 2005—09, COO, 2009—. Bd. trustees United Way Greater Houston, Houston Mus. Natural Sci., treas., 2007. Office: Anadarko Petroleum Corp 1201 Lake Robbins Dr The Woodlands TX 77380-1046 Office Phone: 832-636-1000.*

WALKER, RACHEL BRADY, retired literature and language professor; d. Carl Dimette and Lola Mae Smith Brady; m. James Robert Walker, Dec. 16, 1961; children: Melanie Walker Tripp, James Robert Jr.

BS in English, Appalachian State U., Boone, NC, 1964, MA, 1965. Grad. tchg. fellow Appalachian State U., 1964—65; instr. English Coll. Albemarle, Elizabeth City, NC, 1965—67; assoc. prof. English Wingate U., NC, 1967—2008, English dept. coord., 1993—95, dir. freshman experience and academic advising, 1999—2003, coord. English and edn. program, Thayer sch. edn., 2003—08, dir. London, 1991. Patient vol. Hospice Union County, Monroe, 1999—2002; dir. vacation bible sch. spl. needs children Union Bapt. Assn., Monroe, 1978—83; dir. single adult ministry Mill Creek Bapt. Ch., Monroe, 1995—2000; care group ministry coord. First Bapt. Ch. Indian Trail, NC, 2005—08; exec. bd. Assn. Retarded Citizens, Monroe, NC, 1975—85; exec. bd. mem. Arthritis Patient Svcs., Monroe, 1988—90; adv. bd. mem. Unionville Elem. Sch., Monroe, 1977—79. Recipient Yearbook Dedication, Coll. Albemarle, 1965, Pres. award, Assn. Retarded Citizens, 1980, Outstanding Svc. award, Hospice Union County, 2001, Charles and Hazel Corts award, Wingate U., 2006; named one of Outstanding Educators America, John F. Kennedy Found., 1972; nominee Nine Who Care, Hospice Union County, 2001; Grad. Tchg. fellowship, Appalachian State U., 1964—65. Mem.: Unionville Lions Club (pres. 2007—08, adv. bd. mem. 1977—79, Lion of Yr. 2008), NC Lions Found. (life; summer camp vol. 2004—08, William L. Woolard Ptnr. Svc. award 2006, Jack Stickley fellowship 2001). Avocation: travel.

WALKER, RANDALL WAYNE, lawyer; b. Pampa, Tex., Mar. 13, 1956; s. Jimmy Wayne and Dorothy Evelyn (Mercer) W.; m. Patricia Gale Vernon Walker, Dec. 12, 1992; children: Alissa Gail Walker, Angie Marie Walker Grimsey, Cory Wayne, Nicholas Russell Rattan. AA, Clarendon Coll., Tex., 1980; BS, West Tex. State U., Canyon, 1984; JD, Tex. Tech. U., Lubbock, 1986. Bar: Tex., 1987. Pvt. practice, Clarendon, Tex., 1987-91; asst. atty. gen. Tex. Atty. Gen. Office, Wichita Falls, Tex., 1991—, mng. atty., 1992—. Cubmaster Boy Scouts Am., Clarendon, 1988-89. Mem. State Bar Tex., Wichita County Bar Assn., Lions (v.p. Clarendon 1989). Avocations: fishing, camping, woodworking. Office: Attorney General Office 813 8th St Wichita Falls TX 76301-3305

WALKER, RAYMOND JOHN, physicist; b. LA, Oct. 26, 1942; s. Raymond Osmund and Marie Dorothy (Peterman) W. BS, San Diego State U., 1964; MS, UCLA, 1969, PhD, 1973. Rsch. assoc. U. Minn., Mpls., 1973-77; rsch. geophysicist Inst. Geophysics and Planetary Physics UCLA, 1977—, prof. in residence Inst. Geophysics and Planetary Physics and Dept. Earth and Space Sci., 1999—. Mgr. planetary plasma interactions node NASA, 1990-, project scientist planetary data sys., 1992-96, prin. investigator virtual magnetospheric observatory, 2007—; mem. numerous coms. on space physics and the mgmt. of space physics data NRC and NASA. Contbr. articles to profl. jours. Mem. AAAS, Am. Geophys. Union (chair info. tech. com. 1990-92, Edward A. Flinn III award 1996), Am. Astron. Soc. (div. Planetary Sci.). Achievements include research in magnetospheric physics, in planetary magnetospheres, in global magnetohydrodynamic simulation of solar wind-magnetosphere interaction, in data management, in magnetic field modeling. Home: 11053 Tennessee Ave Los Angeles CA 90064-1936 Office: UCLA IGPP 405 Hilgard Ave Los Angeles CA 90095-1567 Home Phone: 310-477-3637; Office Phone: 310-825-7685. Business E-Mail: rwalker@igpp.ucla.edu.

WALKER, RICHARD BRIAN, chemistry professor; b. Quincy, Mass., May 14, 1948; s. George Edgar and Eva Mary (Taylor) W. BS in Biochemistry, U. So. Calif., 1970; PhD in Pharm. Chemistry, U. Calif., San Francisco, 1975. Rsch. assoc. Oreg. State U., Corvallis, 1975-76, U. Wash., Seattle, 1976-78; lectr. U.S. Internat. U., San Diego, 1978-81, Hamdard Sch. Pharmacy, New Delhi, 1981-82; rsch. scientist Biophysica Found., San Diego, 1982-83; assoc. prof. chemistry U. Ozarks, Clarksville, Ark., 1983-84; asst. to assoc. prof. chemistry U. Ark., Pine Bluff, 1984-96, prof. chemistry, 1996—, interim chair dept. chemistry and physics, 2007—. Prin. investigator minority biomed. rsch. support program NIH, Bethesda, Md., 1986—; project dir. Ark. Systemic Sci. Initiative; chair U. Ark. Pine Bluff Instl. Rev. Bd., 2003-, interim chair dept. chemistry and physics, 2007; rev. in field. Contbr. articles to profl. jours. Coord. home Bible fellowship The Way Internat., Pine Bluff, 1984-99, North Little Rock, 2007—; judge Ctrl. Ark. Sci. Fair, Little Rock, 1986—. NIH rsch. grantee, 1986, 89, 93, 2006. Mem. Am. Chem. Soc., Ark. Acad. Scis., Am. Assn. Pharm. Scientists, Sigma Xi (sec.-treas. ctrl. Ark. chpt. 2005-06, v.p. 2000-07). Avocations: fishing, golf, skiing. Office: 1200 University Dr Pine Bluff AR 71601-2799 Home: 2401 Lakeview Rd Apt K3 North Little Rock AR 72116-9410 Office Phone: 870-575-8894. Personal E-mail: walkerr2@swbell.net. Business E-Mail: walker_r@uapb.edu.

WALKER, RICHARD DAVID, retired civil engineer; b. Wash., Feb. 19, 1931; s. Stanton and Amelia (Ramseyer) W.; m. Alice Patricia Davis, June 6, 1953; children: Patricia Vawn, Jean Brianne, Sharyl Elise. BCE, U. Md., 1953; MCE, Purdue U., 1955, PhD, 1961. Registered profl. engr. Va., Ind. Instr., Purdue U., 1957-61; asst. prof. Va. Poly. Inst., 1961-62, asso. prof., 1962-68, prof., 1968-96, head dept. civil engring., 1970-83; prof. emeritus, 1996. Cons. in hwy. design & safety. Author: (with R.D. Krebs) Highway Materials, 1971. Mem. Montgomery County Rep. Com.; elder Presbyn. Ch., 1973—2007. Lt. USAF, 1955—57. Fellow ASCE; mem. ASTM (sec. com. C-9 on concrete and concrete aggregates 1970-76), NSPE (life), Transp. Rsch. Bd., Am. Soc. for Engring. Edn., Sigma Xi, Chi Epsilon. Presbyterian. Avocation: photography. Home: 701 Broce Dr Blacksburg VA 24060-2803 E-mail: walkerrd@vt.edu. *Have respect for others, their opinions and beliefs. At the same time, stand firm for what you believe. Remember, even a firmly rooted tree stands because it is flexible and can bend with the wind. Concerning goals, avoid rigidity; include service to others, then set goals sufficiently general to embrace the total purpose God has for you in this life.*

WALKER, RICHARD HAROLD, pathologist, educator; b. Cleve., Dec. 2, 1928; s. Harold Deford and Bernice Margaret (Wright) W.; m. Carolyn Franklin, Sept. 28, 1954; children: Bruce, Lynn, Cara, Leah. BS, Emory U., 1950, MD, 1953. Intern City of Memphis Hosps., 1953-54; resident in pathology Coll. Medicine U. Tenn., Memphis, 1954-55, 57-59, prof. pathology, 1966-70; Am. Cancer Soc. clin. fellow U. Tenn. Coll. Medicine, 1957-59; med. dir. blood bank and transfusion svc. City of Memphis Hosps., Memphis, 1961-70; chief of blood bank and transfusion service William Beaumont Hosp., Royal Oak, Mich., 1970-95, med. dir. Sch. Med. Tech., 1970-91. Clin. prof. pathology Sch. Medicine Wayne State U., Detroit, 1982-95. Contbr. articles on blood transfusion, blood group genetics and transfusion medicine to med. jours. Capt. USNR ret. Recipient Murray Thelin Humanitarian award Memphis chpt. Nat. Hemophilia Found., 1968. Mem. AMA, Coll. Am. Pathologists, Am. Soc. Clin. Pathologists (Disting. Svc. award 1977, Ward Burdick award 1992), Am. Assn. Blood Banks (pres. 1976-77, John Elliott Meml. award 1986), Tenn. Assn. Blood Banks (L.W. Diggs award 1986), Internat. Soc. Blood Transfusion, Am. Soc. for Histocompatibility and Immunogenetics. Republican. Presbyterian. Home: 4204 Fleet Landing Blvd Atlantic Beach FL 32233-4590

WALKER, RICHARD HENRY, lawyer; b. Wilmington, Del., Dec. 29, 1950; s. Henry H. and Mary L. (Meister) W. BA, Trinity Coll., 1972; JD cum laude, Temple U., 1975. Bar: Pa. 1976, U.S. Supreme Ct. 1977, N.Y. 1978, D.C. 1981. Law clk. to Hon. Collins J. Seitz U.S. Ct. Appeals (3rd cir.), Wilmington, Del., 1975-76; assoc., ptnr. Cadwalader, Wickersham & Taft, NYC, 1976-91; regional dir. N.E. office U.S. SEC, NYC, 1991-95, gen. counsel Washington, 1996-98, dir. enforcement, 1998—2001; global gen. counsel Deutsche Bank, 2001—. Mem. legal adv. com. NYSE. Trustee Am. Folk Art Mus. Recipient Presdl. Rank Disting. Svc. award, SEC, 1997, Disting. Svc. award. Fellow Am. Bar Found.; trustee SEC Historical Soc.; mem. Phi Beta Kappa

WALKER, RICHARD HUGH, orthopaedic surgeon; b. Elgin, Ill., Jan. 29, 1951; m. Wendy Allen; children: Ashley Elizabeth, Blake Allen, Emily Paige. AB cum laude, Occidental Coll., 1973; MD, U. Chgo., 1977. Diplomate Nat. Bd. Med. Examiners, Am. Bd. Orthopaedic Surgery. Jr. resident in surgery UCLA, 1977-79; jr. resident in orthopaedic surgery Stanford (Calif.) U., 1979-81, sr. resident, 1981-82, chief resident, 1982-83; clin. mem. divsn. orthop. surgery, sect. lower extremity reconstructive surgery Scripps Clinic, La Jolla, Calif., 1983—, co-dir. lower extremity reconstructive surgery fellowship, divsn. orthopaedic surgery, 1989—, assoc. head. divsn. orthopaedic surgery, 1990-97, chmn. dept. surgery, 1998—; v.p. surg. radiol. svcs. Golden Gate U., 2001—. Staff physician dept. surgery Scripps Green Hosp., La Jolla, 1983—; mem. exec. com. Green Hosp. of Scripps Clinic, La Jolla, 1994—2001, chief of staff, 1995—97; Team physician San Diego Padres, 1983—86, team physician, 1995—99; Clin. instr. dept. orthopaedics and rehab. U. Calif., San Diego, 1983—92, asst. clin. prof., 1992—; Mem. bd. dir. Scripps Clinic Med. Group, La Jolla, 1992—, mem. exec. com., 1998—, med. dir. surg. specialties, 1998—2001, mem. joint exec. bd., 1992—93. Cons. reviewer Clin. Orthopaedics and Related Rsch., 1989—, Jour. Bone and Joint Surgery, 1994—; contbr. articles to profl. jours. Mem. AMA, ACS, Am. Acad. Orthopaedic Surgeons, We. Orthopaedic Assn. (program chmn. San Diego chpt. 1994-95, treas. 1995-96, v.p. 1996-97, pres. 1997-98, Resident Paper award 1983), Calif. Orthopaedic Assn., Assn. Arthritic Hip and Knee Surgery (charter mem. 1991), Am. Assn. Hip and Knee Surgeons, Assn. Bone and Joint Surgeons (Nicholas Andry Rsch. award 1997). Office: Scripps Clinic Divsn Orthop Surgery 10666 N Torrey Pines Rd La Jolla CA 92037-1092 Office Phone: 858-554-9882. Business E-Mail: rwalker@scrippsclinic.com.

WALKER, RICHARD K., lawyer; b. Knoxville, Tenn., Oct. 21, 1948; BA with honors, U. Kans., 1970, JD, 1975; student, U. Bonn, Germany; grad. student, U Tübingen, Germany. Bar: Ariz. 1975, D.C. 1977, U.S. Supreme Ct. 1977. Asst. prof. law U. S.C., 1977-81, assoc. prof. law, 1981-82; ptnr. Bishop, Cook, Purcell & Reynolds, Washington, 1981-90, Winston & Strawn, Washington, 1990-93; dir. Streich Lang, Phoenix, 1993-2000; ptnr. Quarles & Brady, Phoenix, 2000—, Walken & Peskind, Scottsdale, 2008—. Bd. trustees Ariz. Theatre Co., 1995-2001, 2004-; bd. dirs. Phoenix Cmty. Alliance, 2001—04. Fulbright Direct Exch. scholar. Mem. ABA, Labor and Employment Law Sec. (mem. equal employment opportunity law com. and devel. of the law under the NLRA com., 1979—), Litigation Sec. (mem. class actions and derivitive suits com. and trial pratice com., 1998—, mem. employment rels. and labor law com., 1979—), Ariz. Assn. Def. Counsel (bd. dirs. 1997-2000). Office: SGA Corp Ctr 16100N 71st St Scottsdale AZ 85254 Office Phone: 480-483-6336. E-mail: rkw@azlewpartner.com.

WALKER, ROBERT F., social studies educator; b. Van Nuys, Calif., Sept. 9, 1977; s. Carol Walker. BA, U. Calif., Davis, 2000; MA in History, Stanford U., Calif., 2002; MA in Ednl. Tech., Calif. State U., Northridge, 2005. Cert. single subject tchg. credential in Social Studies Calif. State U., 2003. Social studies tchr. Bishop Alemany HS, Mission Hills, Calif., 2003—04, Acad. Canyons, WSHUHD, Santa Clarita, Calif., 2004—. Mem.: Internat. Soc. Tech. in Edn., Nat. Coun. Social Studies, Am. Hist. Assn. Green Party. Office: Acad Canyons 26455 Rockwell Canyon Rd Santa Clarita CA 91355

WALKER, ROBERT R., music educator; b. Electra, Tex., Oct. 23, 1963; s. Bobby Walker and Jan Kaspar; m. Elizabeth Pond, Aug. 23, 1986; children: Emily Hamilton, Bo Hamilton, Katherine, Hannah, Michael, Matthew, Bryan. MusB, Emporia State U., 1992, MusM, 1995. Cert. interactive TV instr. Kellogg C.C. Music instr. Kellogg C.C., Battle Creek, Mich., 1995—2001; dir. music Labette C.C., Parsons, Kans., 2001—. Recipient Disting. Faculty award, Labette C.C., 2005, Exemplory Online Course Design award, Kans. Blackboard Users Group, 2003. Mem.: Am. Choral Directors Assn. (assoc.). Office: Labette CC 200 South 14th St Parsons KS 67357 Home: 2305 Crawford Ave Parsons KS 67357-2524 Business E-Mail: robertw@labette.edu.

WALKER, ROBERT SMITH, lobbyist, former United States Representative from Pennsylvania; b. Bradford, Pa., Dec. 23, 1942; s. Joseph Erdman and Rachael Viola (Smith) W.; m. Sue Ellen Albertson, Apr. 13, 1968 (dec. May 9, 2007). Student William & Mary, 1960—61; BS in Edn., Millersville U., Pa., 1964; MA in Polit. Sci, U. Del., 1968; LLD (hon.), Franklin & Marshall Coll., 1998. Tchr. Penn Manor High Sch., Lancaster, Pa., 1964-67; legis. asst. to Congressman Edwin D. Eshleman, 1967-74, adminstrv. asst., 1974-76; mem. US Congress from 16th Pa. dist., Washington DC, 1977-96, chmn. House Com. Sci.; vice chmn. house budget com., chmn. house rep. leadership, 1995-97; chief dep. minority whip, 1989-95; spkr. pro tempore, 1996; exec. chmn. Wexler & Walker Pub. Policy Assocs., Washington DC, 1997—. Chmn. Commn. on the Future of the US Aerospace Industry, 2001—02; mem. Nat. Acads. Aeronautics and Space Engring. Bd., 2004—06, Pres.'s Commn. on the U.S. Postal Svc., 2003, Pres.'s Commn. on Space Exploration, 2004; polit. analyst Fox News, 2005—. Co-author: Congress-The Pennsylvania Dutch Representatives, 1774-1974, Can You Afford This House, 1978, House of Ill Repute, 1987, Space: The Free Market Frontier, 2003, Crossroads: The Future of American Politics, 2003; contbr. articles to profl. jours. Trustee Aerospace Corp., 1997—; vice chmn. Space Found. 2004-06, chmn. 2006-2008; mem. Susquehana Valley Ctr. Pub. Policy, 1998—. With Pa. NG, 1967-73, bd. dirs. Space Devel., 2001-08, Zero G, 2005-08, Space Adventures, 2008-, bd. dirs. Australian-Am. Leadership Dialogue, 2008-. Pa. Nat. Guard, 1967—73. Recipient NASA Disting. Svc. medal, 1996, NASA Disting. Pub. Svc. medal, 2004; fellow Millersville U., 1996-2001, Franklin & Marshall Coll., 1997-2001. Mem. Am. League of Lobbyists (bd. dirs. 2000-04). Republican. Presbyterian. Office: Wexler & Walker Pub Policy Assocs 1317 F St NW Ste 600 Washington DC 20004-1157 Home: 643 Northfield Rd Lititz PA 17543-8360 Office Phone: 202-638-2121. Business E-Mail: walker@wexlerwalker.com. *The revolution sweeping politics, economics, culture and technology will produce new opportunities but at the same time will demand a new way of thinking about our economy and our society.*

WALKER, RONALD EDWARD, psychologist, educator; b. East St. Louis, Ill., Jan. 23, 1935; s. George Edward and Marnella (Altmeyer) W.; m. Aldona M. Mogenis, Oct. 4, 1958; children: Regina, Mark, Paula, Alexis. BS, St. Louis U., 1957; MS, Northwestern U., 1959, PhD, 1961. Lectr. psychology Northwestern U., 1959-61; faculty dept. psychology Loyola U., Chgo., 1961—, asst., then asso. prof., 1961-68, prof., chmn. dept., 1965—73, prof. emeritus, 1999—, acting dean Coll. Arts and Scis., 1973-74; dean Loyola U. (Coll. Arts and Scis.), 1974-80, academic v.p., 1980-81, sr. v.p., dean faculties, 1981-89, exec. v.p., 1989-99. Cons. VA, Chgo., 1965-74; Am. Psychol. Assn.-NIMH; vis. cons., 1969; vis. scientist Am. Psychol. Assn. NSF, 1968; Cook County (Ill.) rep. from Ill. Psychol. Assn., 1969-72; cons.-evaluator North Cen. Assn., 1986-99. Contbr. articles to profl. jours. Bd. trustees St. Francis Hosp., Evanston, Ill., 1986—92, Chgo. Archdiocesan Sems., 1985—97, Loyola Acad., Wilmette, Ill., 1987—93, St. Louis U., 1988—97; bd. dirs. Holy Family Villa Nursing Home, Lemont, Ill., 2002—05. Recipient Disting. Psychologist of Yr. award Ill. Psychol. Assn., 1986. Business E-Mail: rwalker@luc.edu.

WALKER, RONALD HUGH, foundation administrator; b. Bryan, Tex., July 25, 1937; s. Walter Hugh and Maxine (Tarver) W.; m. Anne Lucille Collins, Aug. 8, 1959; children: Lisa, Marjorie, Lynne. BA, U. Ariz., 1960. With Allstate Ins. Co., Pasadena, Calif., 1964-67, Hudson Co., 1967-69; asst. to sec. interior, 1969-70; founder, 1st dir., staff asst. to Pres. U.S. White House Advance Office, 1970-72; spl. asst. to Pres., 1972-73; dir. Nat. Park Service, Washington, 1973-75; cons. Saudi Arabia, 1975; assoc. dir. World Championship Tennis, 1975-77; pres. Ron Walker & Assocs., Inc., Dallas, 1977-79; sr. ptnr., mng. dir. Korn/Ferry Internat., Washington, 1979—2001; ret., 2000; pres. Richard Nixon Found.; bd. dir. Green Hunter Energy Inc. Bd. dirs., chmn. Guest Svcs. Inc., Mullin Cons., Inc., Vinson & Co.; chmn. NOVAVAX, 1999-2005; bd. dir. Green Hunter Energy Inc., 2007-. Bd. dirs. U.S.S. Arizona Found. and Memorial; mem. Nat. Pk. Svc. Dirs. Coun.; founder, chmn. emeritus Order of Raft, 1972; spl. presdl. del. to Prime Min. Indira Gandhi's funeral New Delhi, 1984; spl. presdl. del. to Games of XXIV Olympiad Seoul, 1988; trustee Nat. Outdoor Leadership Sch., Nat. Fitness Found., Pres.'s Coun. on Phys. Fitness and Sports, 1981—85; bd. dirs. NCAA Found., mem. exec. com., mem. adv. bd.; bd. dirs. Meridian Internat.; mem. Ctr. for Study of Presidency, 1988—95; chmn. Freedom Found. at Valley Forge, 1989—2000; trustee Ford's Theater, Washington; men's chair Project Hope Ann. Ball, 1989, 1990, 1991; chmn. ann. dinner Boys and Girls Clubs Am., 1993; chmn. 50th Presdl. Inauguration, Dedication Richard Nixon Libr., Birthplace, 1990, bd. dirs., 1990; nat. chair Celebrities and Sports for Bush-Quayle; mem. over-site com. U.S. Rowing, 1993; mem. com. Preservation of White House, 1973—75; mem. Nat. Pk. Adv. Bd., 1973—75, Nat. Pk. Found., 1973—75, John F. Kennedy Ctr. for Performing Arts, 1973—75, Friends of Nancy Hanks Ctr.; bd. trustees Mridian House Internat., 1992—; mem. USA Gymnasium Found., 1993—99; trustee U. Ariz. Found.; chair Nat. Pk. Found. Alumni Assn.; bd. dirs Saguaro Nat. Park; mem. adv. bd. Nat. Park Sys., 2004—; vol. Nixon/Agnew Campaign, 1968, transition and inauguration team, 1969; vice chmn., mem. Pres.'s Commn. on Bicentennial U.S. Constn., 1985—88; mem. Coun. for Excellence in Govt., 1988—; mgr., CEO Rep. Nat. Conv., 1984, sr. advisor, 1988, 1992, 1996, 2000, 2004, Bush/Quayle Presdl. Campaign, 1988, Bush/Cheney Presdl. Campaign, 2000, 2004, Bush/Cheney Inauguration; hon. chmn. Cheney Inaugural Activities; coord. v.p. debate Cheney and Lieberman, 2000, Cheney and Edwards, 2004; mem. leadership adv. bd. NCAA; bd. dirs. Grand Teton Nat. Pk. Found., Saquaro Nat. Pk. Found.; vice chair Eastern Nat. Pk. Svc.; chair Hartgog Inst., Clemson U., 2007—; bd. trustee Sarver Heart Ctr., U. Arz., 2008—; mem. Nat. Soc. Scabbard & Blade, 2008. Capt. US Army, 1961—64. Recipient Disting. Citizen award U. Ariz., 1973, Outstanding Svc. award Dept. Interior, 1975, Centennial Medallion award U. Ariz., 1989, Ellis Island Congl. medal of honor, 1992, Lincoln medal Ford's Theater, 2002. Mem. NCAA (bd. dirs. 1992-2003, exec. com. 1992-2003, adv. bd.), Econs. Club of Washington, Met. Club of Washington, Congl. Country Club, Georgetown Club, City Club of Washington, Univ. Club. of N.Y., Burning Tree Club, Phi Delta Theta (named to Hall of Fame, 1991). Republican. Methodist. Home (Winter): 13535 Placita Montanas de Oro Tucson AZ 85755 E-mail: roadrunnerrhw@aol.com.

WALKER, RONALD R., editor, educator, writer; b. Newport News, Va., Sept. 2, 1934; s. William R. and Jean Marie (King) W.; m. O. Diane Mawson, Apr. 16, 1961; children: Mark Jonathan, Steven Christopher. BS, Pa. State U., 1956; postgrad., Harvard U., 1970-71. Reporter, news editor, sr. editor, editorial page editor, mng. editor San Juan Star, PR, 1962—73, Washington columnist, 1982—84, city editor, 1984—87, ind. profl. writer, columnist editl. page, 1993—; instr. journalism Pa. State U., State College, 1973—74; asst. prof. Columbia U. Grad. Sch. Journalism, NYC, 1974—76; editor The Daily News, 1976—77; press sec. Gov. VI, 1978—79; spl. asst., chief of staff Rep. James H. Scheuer, US Congress, 1980—82, Resident Commr. Jaime B. Fuster, US Congress, 1987—92; spl. asst., press sec. Resident Commr. Antonio J. Colorado, 1992—93; regular columnist St. John Times, 1997—2005. Contbr. articles to nat. mags. and jours. including The Nation, The NY Times, The Washington Post, and others. Served with US Army, 1957-59. Nieman fellow in journalism Harvard U., 1970-71. Mem. Soc. Nieman Fellows, Leica Hist. Soc. Am. Home: PO Box 1358 St John VI 00831-1358 Office Phone: 340-693-7001. Personal E-mail: rrwalker340@earthlink.net.

WALKER, ROSLYN ADELE, retired museum director; b. Memphis, July 26, 1944; Student Gen. Studies, U. Poitiers, France, 1965; BS in Art Edn. with high honors, Hampton U., 1966; MA in History of Art, Indiana U., 1969, PhD in History of Art, 1991. Registrar Mus. African Art, Washington, 1968-69; coord. Univ. Art Gallery U. Mass., Amherst, 1969-70; temporary registrar Fed. Dept Antiquities Nat. Mus., Lagos, Nigeria, 1970; curator of collections Inst. African Studies U. Idaban, Nigeria, 1973-75; curator ethnographic art collection Univ. Mus. Ill. State U., Normal, 1975-81, interim adminstr., 1975, adminstr., 1975-77, dir., 1977-81; curator Nat. Mus. African Art Smithsonian Instn., Washington, 1981-93, sr. curator, 1993-97, dir., 1997—2002; sr. curator The Arts of Africa, the Pacific and the Americas Dallas Mus. Art, Margaret McDermott curator African art. Rsch. asst. Mus. Modern Art, N.Y.C., 1971-72, guest curator African Women/African Art, The African-Am. Inst., N.Y.C., 1976, Lakeview Mus. Arts and Scis., Peoria, Ill., 1981; instr. in primitive art U. Mass., Amherst, 1969-70, in African decorative art USDA Grad. Sch., Washington, 1984. in Art in Africa, Dept. Art History, U. Md., College Park, 1990; vis. lectr. Afro-Am. Art, Ind. U., Bloomington, 1970-71, lectr. 1971-72, summer program, U. Idaban, Nigeria, 1974; asst. prof. Art Dept., Ill. State U., Normal, 1975-81. Author: (with Roy Sieber) African Art in the Cycle of Life, 1987, Olowe of Ise: A Yoruba Sculptor to Kings, 1998; contbr. catalogs for exhibitions of African Art to Royal Acad. of Arts, London, 1995, Guggenheim Mus. N.Y. and Afro-Am. Hist. and Cultural Mus., Phila., 1996; contbr., reviews, essays and articles to profl. jours. and mags. Mem. visual arts and crafts adv. panel Washington Commn. on the Arts. Recipient Ford Found. Fgn. Study grant, 1965, Faculty Rsch. grant, U. Mass., 1970, Fgn. Lang. fellowship Ind. U., Bloomington, 1971, Grant in Aid, Ind. U., 1972, Rsch. Fund grant (collections-based), Smithsonian Instn., Washington, 1994; named Twenty Yr. Student, Hampton U., 1986. Mem. Arts Coun. African Studies Assn. (past bd. dirs.), ArTable, Assn. Art Mus. Dirs.

WALKER, RUTH CHARLOTTA, language educator, real estate broker; b. Kirksville, Mo., Oct. 3, 1931; d. Marion S. and Fern Thomas Schott; m. Dennis O. Walker, Nov. 21, 1954 (dec.). BS in Edn., Ctrl. Mo. State Coll., Warrensburg, 1952. Lic. real estate broker Wis., 1982. Tchr.

English and speech, Warrensburg, Mo., 1951—53; pvt. tutor English and speech Mexico, 1956—57, Milw., 1968—95; profl. spkr., 1970—95; real esate broker, 1982—90; writer profl. book revs., 1990—. Author: (booklet) What Does P.E. Mean?, 1983. Pres. Woman's Club of Am. Fedn. Women, So. Milw., 1975—78, P.E.O. Sisterhood, So. Milw., 1979—81; sec. Woman's Courtroom Civic Conf., Milw., 1980. Mem.: Book Club So. Milw., Delta Zeta. Republican. Presbyterian. Achievements include raising funds for police department equipment, establishing camp Wil-o-Way in Grant Park, Milwaukee, creating drive for civic auditoriums. Avocations: travel, writing, reading. Personal E-mail: schott31@tds.net.

WALKER, RYAN P., legislative staff member; BA in Criminal Justice, Polit. Sci., Kent State U., Ohio, 2000; MPA in Govt. Rels. Mgmt. & Strategic Comm., George Wash. U., Washington, 2005. Staff asst., Rep. Paul Gillmor US House of Reps., Washington, 2002—03, legis. correspondent, Rep. Paul Gillmor, 2003—04, legis. asst., Rep. Paul Gillmor, 2004—05, sr. legis. asst., Rep. Paul Gillmor, 2005—06, legis. dir., Rep. Paul Gillmor, 2007, chief of staff to Rep. Robert Latta, 2008—. Republican. Office: 1531 Longworth House Office Bldg Washington DC 20515 Office Phone: 202-225-6405. Office Fax: 202-225-1985.*

WALKER, SAMUEL DAVID, lawyer; b. Madison, Wis., June 21, 1958; s. William Delaney and Suzanne Jamison (Porter) W.; m. Cynthia Fiora Elizabeth Nardini, Aug. 6, 1983; children: John Renato, Samuel Alexander. AB magna cum laude, Duke U., 1980; JD cum laude, Harvard U., 1984. Bar: NC 1984, DC 1992, Colo. 2003, US Supreme Ct., numerous US cts. of appeal and dist. cts. Law clk. to Hon. John D. Butzner Jr. US Ct. Appeals (4th cir.), Richmond, Va., 1984-85; assoc. Robinson, Bradshaw & Hinson, Charlotte, NC, 1985-89; spl. asst. to asst. sec. labor for employment stds. US Dept. Labor, Washington, 1989-90, dep. wage-hour adminstr. and acting wage-hour adminstr., 1990, acting asst. sec. labor for employment stds., 1990-91, dep. asst. sec. labor for employment stds., 1991; dep. asst. sec. edn. for intergovernmental and interagency affairs US Dept. Edn., Washington, 1991-92, acting asst. sec. edn. for intergovernmental and interagency affairs, 1992; of counsel Wiley, Rein & Fielding, Washington, 1992-93, ptnr., 1993—2002; v.p. Coors Brewing Co., Golden, Colo., 2002—05; sr. v.p., global chief legal officer, corp. sec. Molson Coors Brewing Co., Denver, 2005—. Asst. clearance coun. Pres.-elect George W. Bush, 2000—01. Fellow Am. Bar Found.; mem. ABA, Colo. Bar Assn., DC Bar Assn. Avocations: outdoor sports, tennis. Office: Molson Coors Brewing Co 1225 17th St Denver CO 80202 Home: 5330 S Marshall St Littleton CO 80123 Office Phone: 303-277-2164. Office Fax: 303-277-7848. Personal E-mail: samuel.walker@molsoncoors.com.

WALKER, STEPHEN D., history professor; s. Richard Walker and Cheryl Herring; m. Cindy Walker, June 10, 1989; children: Hannah, John, Eliza. MA in History, Va. Commonwealth U., Richmond, 1998. Tchr. Southside Va. CC, Alta., 2000—. Coord. Va. Tchrs.' Acad., Alta. Mayor Town Coun., Charlotte Ct. House, Va., 2002—08. Office: Southside Va CC 109 Campus Dr Alberta VA 23821

WALKER, STEVEN CHARLES, literature and language professor; b. Payson, Utah, Oct. 15, 1941; s. Jess R. Walker and Elaine DeGraff; m. Mary Carter; m. Ardith Walker (div.); children: Scott, Rebecca, Emily. BS, Brigham Young U., Provo, Utah, 1965, MA, 1966; AM, Harvard U., Cambridge, Mass., 1971, PhD, 1973. Instr. Brigham Young U., 1965—69, asst. prof., 1973—78, assoc. prof., 1978—87, 1988—2007. Grad. coord. English dept. Brigham Young U., 1983—90, chair Univ. Senate, 1988—89, chair univ. coun. on rank and status, 1988—94, assoc. chair English dept., 1993—98. Editor: Literature and Belief, 1979—98, BYU Studies, 1991—2007; author: (textbook) Christian Fantasy, 1983 (Nat I.S. Textbok the Yr., 1983), (cultural studies) A Book of Mormons, 1981 (Best Book award, 1982), (criticism book) Seven Ways of Seeing, 1987 (Best Criticism award, 1988), (cultural studies) Mourning with Those Who Mourn, 1999; contbr. articles to profl. jours. Spkrs. bur. Utah Humanities Coun., Salt Lake City, 1992—2002; dir. Ctr. for Values, Provo, 1994—95. Sgt. US Army, 1960—69, Fort Ord. Recipient Honors Prof. the Yr., Brigham Young U., 1980, Tchr. the Yr. Independence award, 1984, Maeser Disting. Tchr. Professorship, 1987, Disting. Alumni Professorship, 1992—95, Alcuin award, 1997—2000, Nan Osmond Professorship, 2001—04; grantee, Eyre Found., 1984, 1989; fellow, Harvard U., 1969—74. Mem. Lds Ch. Avocations: poetry, tennis, reading. Office Phone: 801-422-3203.

WALKER, TAMMIE LEIGH, music educator; d. Dennis Edwin Behr and Elaine Rita Creager; m. Chad Lynn Walker, July 29, 1995; children: Sophia Marian, Bennett Chad, Lucy Isabel, Grace Tammie. DMA in Piano Performance, U. Ill., 2001. Tchg. asst. U. Ill., Champaign-Urbana, 1995—98; prof. music Western Ill. U., Macomb, 1998—. Musician: performances in continental U.S., Hawaii, and Western Europe. Scholar, U. Wis., 1991—95. Fellow: Ill. State Music Tchrs. Assn. (coord. music competitions 2002—); mem.: Coll. Music Soc., Music Tchrs. Nat. Assn., Pi Kappa Lambda, Phi Kappa Phi. Democrat. Presbyterian. Avocations: travel, camping, cooking, running. Home: 426 W Jackson St Macomb IL 61455 Office: Western Illinois Univ Browne Hall 219 1 University Cir Macomb IL 61455 Office Fax: 309-298-1968. Business E-Mail: tl-walker4@wiu.edu.

WALKER, THOMAS SCOTT, actor; b. Torrington, Conn., May 12, 1947; s. Andrew Scott and Helen Cox Walker. BA, Yale U., New Haven, 1970. Actor Sony Living Theatre, 1971—, Mabou Mines, NYC, 1986, Dry Opera, 1985, 2004, Dar A Luz, 1994—95, Gale Gates, 1999, Teatro Alfieri, Asti, Italy, 1997—99. Editor: (book) Diaries of Julien Beck, 2008. Home: 215 E 10th St New York NY 10003

WALKER, VAUGHN R., federal judge; b. Watseka, Ill., Feb. 27, 1944; s. Vaughn Rosenworth and Catharine (Miles) W. AB, U. Mich., 1966; JD, Stanford U., 1970. Intern economist SEC, Washington, 1966, 68; law clk. to the Hon. Robert J. Kelleher US Dist. Ct. Calif., LA, 1971-72; assoc. atty. Pillsbury Madison & Sutro, San Francisco, 1972-77, ptnr., 1978-90; judge US Dist. Ct. (no. dist.) Calif., San Francisco, 1990—, chief judge, 2004—. Mem. Calif. Law Revision Commn., Palo Alto, 1986-89; bd. advisors Law and Econs. Ctr., George Mason U., 1999—; mem. civil rules adv. com. Jud. Conf. U.S., 2006—. Bd. dirs. Jr. Achievement of Bay Area, San Francisco, 1979-83; bd. dirs. St. Francis Found., San Francisco, 1991-97, 98—, vice chair, 2004-06, chair, 2007-08. Woodrow Wilson Found. fellow U. Calif., Berkeley, 1966-67. Fellow Am. Bar Found.; mem. ABA (jud. rep., antitrust sect. 1991-95), Lawyers' Club of San Francisco (pres. 1985-86), Assn. Bus. Trial Lawyers (dir. 1996-98), Am. Law Inst., Am. Saddlebred Horse Assn., San Francisco Mus. Modern Art, Bohemian Club, Olympic Club, Pacific-Union Club. Office: US Dist Ct 450 Golden Gate Ave San Francisco CA 94102-3482

WALKER, VICKIE ELAINE, nursing educator; m. Mikel Lee Walker, Nov. 22, 1990; 1 child, Crystal McCord. DNP in Nursing Practice, Case Western Res. U., Cleve., 2008. Supr. Cleve. Regional Hosp., Shelby, NC, 1993—2003; prof. Gardner-Webb U., Boiling Springs, NC, 2003—. Office: Gardner Webb Univ PO Box 997 Boiling Springs NC 28017 Business E-Mail: vwalker@gardner-webb.edu.

WALKER, WALDO SYLVESTER, retired biologist, retired academic administrator; b. Fayette, Iowa, June 12, 1931; s. Waldo S. and Mildred (Littelle) W.; m. Marie J. Olsen, July 27, 1952 (div.); children: Martha Lynn, Gayle Ann; m. Rita K. White, June 16, 1984. BS cum laude, Upper Iowa U., Fayette, 1953; MS, U. Iowa, 1957, PhD, 1959; D of Sci. (hon.), Upper Iowa U., 2004. Mem. faculty Grinnell (Iowa) Coll., 1958, assoc. dean coll., 1963-65, chmn. div. Natural Scis., 1968-69, dean of adminstrn., 1969-73, exec. v.p., 1973-77, dean coll., 1973-80, provost, 1977-80, exec. v.p., 1980-90, exec. v.p. and treas., 1988-90, v.p. for coll. svcs., 1990-95, prof. biology, 1968-2001, prof. emeritus, 2001—. Research assoc. U. B.C. Dept. of Botany, 1966-67. Author articles on plant physiology, ultrastructural cytology. Served with U.S. Army, 1953-55. Fellow NSF Sci. Faculty, 1966-67; recipient NSF research grants, 1960-63, 68. Mem. Am. Assn. Colls., Am. Conf. Acad. Deans (nat. chmn. 1977-78), Am. Assn. Higher Edn., Sigma Xi. Home: 1920 Country Club Dr Grinnell IA 50112-1130 Address: 1920 Country Club Dr Grinnell IA 50112 E-mail: walkerws@iowatelecom.net.

WALKER, WILLIAM BOND, painter, retired librarian; b. Brownsville, Tenn., Apr. 15, 1930; s. Marshall Francis and Mary Louise (Taylor) W. BA, State U. Iowa, 1953; M.L.S., Rutgers U., 1958. Librarian-trainee Donnell br. N.Y. Public Library, NYC, 1955-57; reference librarian/cataloger Met. Mus. Art, NYC, 1957-59; chief librarian Bklyn. Mus., 1959-64; supervisory librarian Library of Nat. Collection Fine Arts and Nat. Portrait Gallery, Smithsonian Instn., Washington, 1964-80; Arthur K. Watson chief librarian Thomas J. Watson Library, Met. Mus. Art, NYC, 1980-94; ret., 1994. Adj. lectr. Columbia U. Sch. Library Service, 1987-88. Author: annotated bibliography American Sculpture, 18th-20th Century, 1979; retrospective exhbn. paintings, 1954-96, Pittsfield, Mass., 1996-97; solo and group exhbns. Columbia County, NY, Berkshire County, Mass., Rochester, NY, 1997-2007. Mem. ALA, Art Librs. Soc. N.Am (charter; pres. 1975, Disting. Svc. award, 1992), Geneal. and Biog. Soc. (corr.), Phi Beta Kappa. Home: 54 Queechy Lake Dr PO Box 237 Canaan NY 12029-0237 Home Phone: 518-781-4153. Business E-Mail: lakequeechy@taconic.net.

WALKER, WILLIAM EASTON, surgeon, educator, lawyer; b. Glasgow, Scotland, Aug. 7, 1945; came to U.S., 1969; s. William Telfer and Josephine Blair (Easton) W.; m. Mary Fraley Cooley, June 23, 1973; children— Sarah Cooley, Blair Easton, Denton Arthur Cooley, William Easton, II MD, Glasgow U., Scotland, 1968; PhD, Johns Hopkins U., 1975; JD, South Tex. Coll Law, 1993. Diplomate Am. Bd. Surgery, Am. Bd. Thoracic Surgery, Am. Bd. Vascular Surgery. Intern, resident Johns Hopkins U., Balt., 1969-75; resident Vanderbilt U., Nashville, 1975-79; assoc. prof., dir. div. thoracic and cardiovascular surgery U. Tex. Med. Sch., Houston, 1979-94. Cons. M.D. Anderson Hosp., Houston, 1979—. Recipient Harwell Wilson award Vanderbilt U., Nashville, 1979 Fellow ACS, So. Surg. Assn., Royal Coll. Surgeons, Am. Coll. Cardiology; mem. Am. Assn. Thoracic Surgery, Coun. Fgn. Rels., Houston Country Club, Belle Meade Country Club, Cosmos Club (Washington), Krewe of Endymion (New Orleans), Phi Beta Kappa, Sigma Xi. Republican. Presbyterian. Avocations: law, bridge, Wagner, World War I history, cooking. Home and Office: 2831 Sackett St Houston TX 77098-1125 Home Phone: 713-520-0545; Office Phone: 713-520-0021. E-mail: ww19@comcast.net.

WALKER, WILLIAM F., medical educator; b. Williamsport, Pa., Jan. 16, 1968; s. Elizabeth Ann Walker; m. Anissa Yvonne Veshela, July 7, 2001; children: Willow Grace, Teagan Ann, Kallan Lewis. BSEE, Duke U., Durham, NC, 1990, PhD, 1995. Asst. prof. biomed. engrng. and elec. and computer engrng. U. Va., Charlottesville, 1997—2003, assoc. prof. biomed. engrng. and elec. and computer engrng., 2003—; founder and pres. NovaSon Corp., Durham, 1995—97; asst. rsch. prof. biomed. engrng. Duke U., Durham, 1996—97; founder PocketSonics, Inc., Charlottesville, 2003—, Leesburg, Va., 2003—; founder and pres. HemoSonics, LLC, Charlottesville, 2004—. Contbr. scientific papers to profl. jours. Achievements include invention of of the sonic window, an easy to use ultrasound imaging system; of sonorheometry, an ultrasound technique for measuring the properties of clotting blood to assess the risk of bleeding and inappropriate clotting; first to determine the fundamental limits on motion estimation using ultrasound. Office: Biomed Engring Univ VA 415 Ln Rd Charlottesville VA 22936

WALKER, WILLIAM OLIVER, JR., retired humanities educator, dean; b. Sweetwater, Tex., Dec. 6, 1930; s. William Oliver and Frances Baker (White) W.; m. Mary Scott Daugherty, Dec. 22, 1955 (div. Dec. 29, 1978); children: William Scott, Mary Evan, Michael Neal. BA, Austin Coll., 1953; MDiv, Austin Presbyn. Sem., 1957; MA, U. Tex., 1958; PhD, Duke U., 1962. Instr. greek religion Austin Coll., Sherman, Tex., 1954—55, Duke U., 1960—62; from asst. to prof. religion Trinity U., San Antonio, 1962—2000, Jennie Farris Railey King prof. religion, 2000—02; ret., 2002. Chair dept., 1980-88, acting dean divsn. Humanities and Arts, 1988-89, dean, 1989-1999. Author: Interpolations in the Pauline Letters, 2001; editor: The Relationships, 1978, The HarperCollins Bible Pronunciation Guide, 1994; assoc. editor HarperCollins Bible Dictionary, 1996. Mem. Studiorum Novi Testamenti Soc., Soc. Bibl. Lit. (regional sec.-treas. 1980-86, pres. 1999-2000), Cath. Bibl. Assn. Am. Democrat. Presbyterian. Avocations: tennis, travel, photography. Home: 315 Cloverleaf Ave San Antonio TX 78209-3822 Office Phone: 810-999-8325.

WALKER, WILLIAM TIDD, JR., investment banker; b. Detroit, Sept. 5, 1931; s. William Tidd and Irene (Rhode) W.; m. Patricia Louise Frazier, Sept. 10, 1953; children: Donna Louise, Carol Ann, Sally Lynn, Alyssa Jane. Student, Stanford, 1950. Stockbroker William R. Staats & Co., Los Angeles, 1952-57, sales mgr., 1957-58, syndicate partner, 1958-65; sr. v.p. Glore Forgan, William R. Staats Inc., NYC, 1965-68; partner, exec. com. Lester, Ryons & Co., Los Angeles, 1968; exec. v.p. Bateman Eichler, Hill Richards Inc., Los Angeles, 1969-85. Pres., CEO WTW Inc.; chmn., CEO Walker Assocs.; bd. dirs. Digid, Inc.; chmn. King-Thomason Group, Inc., Stone Mountain Data Ctrs. Inc.; adv. mem. Am. Stock Exch., 1981—; bd. trustee Columbia Coll. Hollywood. With USAF, 1949-52. Mem. Securities Industry Assn. (dir. nat. syndicate com., chmn. Calif. Dist. 10), Pacific Coast Stock Exch. (bd. govs. 1971-72), Investment Bankers Assn. (nat. pub. rels. com. 1966—), Bond Club L.A. (pres. 1973), Calif. Yacht Club, Columbia Coll. Hollywood (trustee). Office: Walker Assocs PO Box 10684 Beverly Hills CA 90213-3684

WALKER, WINNETTA DORREAN, social studies educator; b. Prescott, Ariz., May 12, 1947; d. Samuel George Graves and Elizabeth Ava Henderson; m. Marcus Rockford Walker, July 16, 1977; children: James Marcus, Marla Ruth Payne, Elizabeth Margaret Martz. BA Edn., U. Ariz., Tucson, 1969. Cert. Std. Secondary Tchr. with Gifted Endorsement Ariz. Dept. Edn., 1969, Trainer Project READS, 1989, ATLES Instr. Ariz. Bar Found., 1990. Substitute tchr. Tucson Unified Sch. Dist., 1969—70; classroom tchr. Ganado Pub. Schs., 1970—73, Red Mesa HS, 1974—75, Chinle Pub. Schs., 1975—89, Prescott Unified Sch. Dist., 1989—2007. Adj. faculty Prescott Coll., 1993—94; sponsor Mock Trial Team Prescott HS, 1989—2007, sponsor We the People Team, 2002—07, dist. coord., We the People Team, 2007—08; cooperating tchr. No. Ariz. U., Flagstaff, 1999—2002; coord. We the People Program, Ariz. Congl. Dist., 2007—08; vol., instr. Yavapai County HS-Mook Trial Team, 2008—. Vol. fund raiser Chino Valley Swimming Pool com., Ariz.; dir. toys for tots program Chinle Jr. High Student Coun., dir. coats for kids program; advisor adopt a family for Christmas Prescott H.S. Cmty. Works Class, 2004—05; advisor Prescott Teen Ct., 1996—2006; site coun. mem. Prescott H.S. Site Coun., Prescott, 1997—2003; mem. feeding displaced persons from the Indian fire com. Red Cross, Prescott; leader bill of rights issues book discussion group Humanities Coun., Chino Valley, 1992; mem. com. to create a libr. Gen. Dynamics, Chinle; served Christmas dinner to the elderly and homeless Chino Valley Ministerial Assn.; mem. Chino Valley Cmty. Ch., Yavapai Fed. Credit Union, Prescott, 2005—06; mem. interest based negotiations team Prescott Edn. Assn., 2002—06. Recipient John J. Ross Meml. Award, Ariz. Bar Found., 1995, Cmty. Svc. award, Alpha Delta Kappa, 1983, Hon. Jack Ogg award, Yavapai County Bar Assn., 2004, Women Educators honoree, Delta Kappa Gamma, Eta chpt., 2004, 2006; nominee Ariz. Tchr. of Yr., Ariz. Dept. Edn., 1985, Yavapai County Tchr. of Yr., Prescott H.S., 2002; Scholarship Tchr. for Nat. We The People Finals, Constl. Rights Found., 2006. Mem.: NEA (life), Hacienda De Los Milagros (vol., Lifetime Animal Shelter 2008—09), AEA Reservation Task Force (vol. 2008—09), AEA Ret., AEA Compliance Review Com., AFA (compliance review com. 2007—09), Ariz. Edn. Assn. (bd. dirs. 1985—89, legis. and govtl. task force 2002—05, small and rural sch. task force 2005—07, compliance review com. 2007—09, Region 10 Bill Hodge award 1990), Prescott Edn. Assn. (pres. 2002—06, retired del. 2008—09, AFA restoration task force mem. 2008—09), U. Ariz. Alumni Assn. (del. 2008—09, vol 2008—09). R-Conservative. Avocations: travel, yardwork, politics, china painting. Home: 1929 W Rd 4 North Chino Valley AZ 86323

WALKER, WOODROW WILSON, retired lawyer, real estate investor, farmer; b. Greenville, Mich., Feb. 19, 1919; s. Craig Walker and Mildred Chase; m. Janet K. Keiter, Oct. 7, 1950; children: Jonathan Woodrow, William Craig, Elaine Virginia. BA, U. Mich., 1943; LLB, Cath. U., 1950. Bar: D.C. 1950, U.S. Supreme Ct. 1958, Va. 1959. Operator family farm, 1937-39; dir. Libr. of Congress Fed. Credit Union, 1957-60; atty. Am. law div. legis. reference Libr. Congress, Washington, 1951-60; pvt. practice, Arlington, Va., 1960—2000. Counsel, bd. dirs. Calvary Found., Arlington, 1970-85, first pres., 1972; judge moot ct. George Mason Law Sch., 1986, Columbus Law Sch., 2007, Cath. U., 2007; owner-operator Walker Farm Front Royal, Va., 1972—. Author: (book) The Adventures of Woody Walker, Attorney, Farmer, World War II Soldier, 2009; co-author rsch. publs. for U.S. Govt.; featured in Washington Post. V.p. Jefferson Civic Assn., Arlington, 1955-61; pres. Nellie Custis PTA, Arlington, 1960-61; sec. Arlington County Bd. Equalization Real Estate Assessment, 1962, chmn. 1963; troop com. chmn. of honor Boy Scouts Am., 1964-69, life scout, sr. patrol leader troop 131; mem. Arlington County Pub. Utilities Commn., 1964-66, vice chmn., 1965-66; pres. Betschler Class Adult Sunday Sch., Calvary United Meth. Ch., Arlington, 1965. With U.S. Army, 1943-45, PTO. Cited for notable deed in conduct of his legal duties Washington Post, 1996. Mem. ABA, Arlington County Bar Assn., Va. Farm Bur., Va. Cattleman's Assn. Democrat. Methodist. Home and Office: 2822 Ft Scott Dr Arlington VA 22202-2307 Office Phone: 703-684-6578.

WALKER NEVE, DIANA, singer, voice educator; d. Ellis Roy Walker and Beth Swenson; m. Charles Montgomery, Jr. Neve; 1 child, Nicholas Pietro Joseph Neve stepchildren: Meisha E. Neve, Charles M. Neve, Robert B. Neve, Mariah A. Neve, Isaiah A. Neve. MusB Performance Highest Honors, U. Mo.-Kansas City Conservatory Music, 1977, MusM Performance High Honors, 1979. Coloratura soprano soloist St. Louis Opera, 1983—84, N.Y.C. Opera, 1983—90; soprano recitalist Carnegie Hall, Carnegie Recital Hall, NYC, 1983—94, Town Hall (Winners Cir. Series), NYC, 1984; soprano concert recitalist Internat. Art Song Festival, Petit Jean, Ark., 1985—86; coloratura soprano soloist Bklyn. Philharm., 1985—86, Balt. Renaissance Opera, 1985—86, Miami Chamber Symphony, Fla., 1986, Chattanooga Opera, 1986, Seattle Opera, 1985—87, Handel Festival Soc., Washington, 1987—88, Utah Opera, Salt Lake City, 1987—88, Chgo. Opera Theatre, 1989, Nat. Ballet Can., Toronto, 1985—89, Lyric Opera Kansas City, Mo., 1985—96, L'Opera de Nice, France, 1989; singing prin. role of Carlotta and Madame Firmin in Phantom of the Opera Live Entertainment Corp Can., Toronto, 1991—95; coloratura soprano soloist Roanoke Opera and Symphony, Va., 1994—96; guest artist The Vocal Majority (Award Winning Male Choir), Dallas, 1998—99; classical/musical theatre concert performer Utah Arts Coun., Salt Lake City, 1998—. Tchr. voice, Salt Lake City, 1997—; guest artist prof., lectr. Brigham Young U., Provo, Utah, 1995—2000; guest artist prof. U. Mass., Amherst, 1983, U. Hawaii, Honolulu and Hilo, 2002—03. Vocalist (with David Glen Hatch): CD Broadway Classics, vocalist (with Mormon Symphony & Youth Chorus): CD You'll Never Walk Alone, soprano soloist: CD A Mormon Tabernacle Choir Christmas; actor: (documentaries) The Earthquake Zone, (and singer): (films) Look at Me (Innovation in Film award, Kans. City Film Festival, 1997); soundtrack soloist: films The Ghost of Dickens Past, soundtrack artist: films Cold Mountain, guest artist: soap opera Another World, 1984. Guest artist performer The Nat. Assn. of Christians and Jews, Salt Lake City, Utah, 1993—94, Hugh O Brian Youth Found., Honolulu, 1994—95; vocal rec. guest artist Sweet Songs of Liberty CD Benefit for 9/11 Victims by MoV'N Pictures, Inc., NYC, Salt Lake City, 2001; artist Utah Arts Coun. Performing Arts Tour Broadway Classics in Concert, 1999—; guest artist performer Com. to Elect Mit Romney for Gov. of Mass.; soprano soloist Mormon Tabernacle Choir, Salt Lake City, 1988—90. Recipient 2d Pl., Naefger Competition, 1978, Met. Opera Young Artist Awards, 1979, Internat. Am. Music Competition at Carnegie Hall, 1983, Alumni Achievement award, U. Mo.-Kansas City Conservatory Music, 1985, Gov.' s Artist award, Gov. Michael Leavitt, Utah, 2000; grantee Monetary award for Career Devel., The Sullivan Found., N.Y.C, 1980—85, Monetary award for Film Project, Nat. Endowment for Arts, 1993; scholarship, Music Acad. West, Santa Barbara, Calif., 1977, fellowship, Tanglewood Music Festival, Mass., 1978, scholarship, Banff Sch. Music, Alta., Can., 1979, Aspen Summer Music Festival, 1979. Mem.: Can. Actors Equity, Nat. Assn. Tchrs. Singing (Kansas City Conservatory Music award 1977—79), Am. Guild Musical Artists, Actors Equity. Republican. Mem. Lds Ch. Avocations: travel, scuba diving, camping, horseback riding, violin. Home: 2763 Evergreen Ave Salt Lake City UT 84109 Home Phone: 801-485-7280. Personal E-mail: charles_diana@comcast.net.

WALKER TUCKER, DANA, lawyer; b. St. Louis, Oct. 23, 1963; d. Donald Edward and Mary Louis Walker; 1 child, Jackson Miles Tucker. BS, U. Mo., 1986; JD (scholar 1991-94), St. Louis U., 1994. Bar: Mo. 1995, Ill. 2003. With Husch and Eppenberger, St. Louis, 1994—96, Banks and Assocs., 1996—2000; atty. Gary, Williams, Parenti, et. al., Stuart, Fla., 2000—02; atty., ptnr. Fox Galvin LLC, St. Louis, 2002—08; chief counsel Eastern Region Mo. Atty. Gen. Office. Adj. prof. Washington U. Law Sch., 2004—. Mem.: Jack and Jill America, Bar Assn. Met. St. Louis, Mound City Bar Assn., Def. Resource Inst., Nat. Bar Assn., Delta Sigma Theta. Democrat. Baptist. Office: 815 Olive St Ste 200 Saint Louis MO 63101 Office Phone: 314-340-7653. Office Fax: 314-340-7891. Personal E-mail: dana.tucker@ymail.com.

WALKINSHAW, NICOLE M., performing arts educator; B in Com. Processes & Disorders, U. Fla., 1988—92, B, 1988—92; M in Social Foundations in Multicultural Edn., Fla. Atlantic U., 2004—05. Cert. in Adolescent Young Adulthood/English Lang. Arts U.S. Nat. Bd. Edn., Fla., 2003, Speech, English & English for Speakers of Other Lang. Fla. Dept. Edn., 1992. Educator Nova HS, Davie, Fla., 1992—. S.t.a.r. mentoring program dir. Nova HS, 1996—, broadway series interactive achievers program dir., 2001—, e.a.g.l.e. tolerance tng. initiative program dir., 2002—. Facilitator (seminar) Integrating Literary Circles Across the Curricular Disciplines, Honae vs Tatamya: Exploring the Multifaceted & Mystical World of Japan; editor: (pub.) SNAPSHOT Entertainment Newsletter. Fundraiser project dir. Until There's A Cure, Davie, 1997—98; youth vol. coord. Read Across Am., Davie, 2002—05; fundraiser project coord. Broadway Cares Equity Fights A.I.D.S., Davie, 2003—05; vol. supr. Kids In Distress, Davie, 2003—05. Recipient Broward's Best, Broward County Sch. Bd., 2003, Alumni Assn. Appreciation award, U. Fla., 2004; Team Mentor grant, Citibank, 2002—03, Fulbright Meml. Fund. scholar, 2002. Mem.: NEA, Fla. Edn. Assn., Nat. Assn. Multicultural Edn., Fla. Humanities Coun., So. Poverty Law Ctr. Avocations: writing, travel, cinematic & arts appreciation. Office: Nova HS 3600 College Ave Davie FL 33314

WALKLEY, MARY L., voice and music educator; b. Storm Lake, Iowa, Oct. 17, 1947; d. Leonard Leroy Gustafson and Betty Angelyne Barnes; m. Robert Wayne Gustafson, Feb. 10, 1965 (div. Feb. 11, 1983); children: Robert Scot, Andrea Lynn Jenkins. MusB in Performance, U. Tampa, Fla., 1983. Cert. level V speech level singing Instr. Seth Riggs Speech Level Singing Internat., 2000. Founder and dir., pre-coll. music program U. of Tampa, Fla., 1983—93; fine arts dir. Tampa Prep. Sch., 1983—96, 1983—97; founder and music dir. The Broadway Theatre Project, 1990—; founder and program dir. The Speech Level Singing Inst., LA, 1998—2002; guest artist and workshop presenter Internat. Thespian Assn., Tampa, 1998—. Vocal cons. Busch Gardens Entertainment, Tampa, Fla., 1998—. Musician, arranger: vocal arrangements, orchestrations Broadway Theatre Project. Grantee study with Seth Riggs, Benedict Found., 1997. Mem.: NARAS, Nat. Assn. Tchrs. of Singing, Inc. Avocations: travel, reading, singing, piano. Home: 775 NE 76th Street Miami FL 33138 Office: FloridaSings 775 NE 76th Street Miami FL 33138 E-mail: mary@floridasings.com.

WALKOWIAK, VINCENT STEVEN, lawyer; b. Apr. 22, 1946; s. Vincent Albert and Elizabeth (Modla) W.; m. Linda Kae Schweigert, Aug., 1968; children: Jenifer, Steven. BA, U. Ill., 1968, JD, 1971. Bar: Ill. 1971, Minn. 1971, Tex. 1981, U.S. Ct. Appeals (8th cir.) 1971, (5th cir.) 1982, U.S. Dist. Ct. (ea., we., so., and no. dists.) Tex. 1982. Assoc. Dorsey, Marquart, Windhorst, West & Halladay, Mpls., 1971-74; ptnr. Fulbright & Jaworski LLP, Dallas, 1982—. Prof. Fla. State U., Tallahassee, 1974-76, So. Meth. U., Dallas, 1976-84. Editor: Uniform Product Liability Act, 1980, Trial of a Product Liability Case, vol. 1, 1981, vol. 2, 1982, Preparation and Presentation of Product Liability, 1983, Attorney Client Privilege in Civil Litigation, 4th edit., 2008. Office: Fulbright & Jaworski LLP 2200 Ross Ave Ste 2800 Dallas TX 75201-2784 Home Phone: 214-692-6046; Office Phone: 214-855-8037. Business E-Mail: vwalkowiak@fulbright.com.

WALKUP, JOHN TIMOTHY, psychiatrist, educator; b. St. Paul, Oct. 11, 1951; s. John William and Lydia Sadie Ester (Natzke) W.; m. Jennifer Ann Haythorenthwaite. BA in Humanities, U. Minn., 1975, MD, 1982. Diplomate Am. Bd. Psychiatry and Neurology. Resident in adult psychiatry Yale U. Med. Sch., New Haven, 1982-85; resident in child psychiatry Yale Child Study Ctr., New Haven, 1985-88; asst. prof. psychiatry Johns Hopkins U., Balt., 1988, assoc. prof. psychiatry, dep. dir. child and adolescent psychiatry. Co-editor: Treating Tourette Syndrome and Tic Disorders, A Guide for Practitioners, 2007; co-author: Managing Tourette Syndrome, 2008. Laughlin fellow Am. Coll. Psychiatrists, 1987. Mem. AMA, Am. Psychiat. Assn., Am. Acad. Child and Adolescent Psychiatry (presdl. scholar 1987), Nat. Tourette Syndrome Assn. (chmn. med. adv. bd., sci. adv. bd.) Office: Johns Hopkins Hosp CMSC 314 600 N Wolfe St Baltimore MD 21287-5371 Office Phone: 410-955-5823. Office Fax: 410-955-8691. E-mail: jwalkup@jhmi.edu.*

WALKUP, ROBERT E., Mayor, Tucson; b. Ames, Iowa, Nov. 14, 1936; m. Beth Walkup; 3 children; 2 stepchildren. BS in Indsl. Engring., Iowa State U. Exec. Rockwell Internat., Fairchild Republic; sr. exec. Hughes Aircraft Co.; mayor City of Tuscon, Ariz., 1999—. Chmn. Greater Tucson Econ. Coun.; founder, first chmn. Ariz. Space Commn.; vol. Tucson Cmty. Food Bank; co-founder Pima-Santa Cruz County Sch.-to-Work Program; co-founder El Centro Cultural de las Americas. Capt. U.S. Army. Republican. Avocations: playing guitar, sketching, studying astronomy, restoring antique cars and motorcycles. Office: City Hall 255 W Alameda St Tucson AZ 85701-1362 Fax: 520-791-4213. Business E-Mail: mcweb@tucsonaz.gov.*

WALL, BRIAN RAYMOND, forest economist, business consultant, researcher; b. Jan. 26, 1940; s. Raymond Perry and Mildred Beryl (Pickert) W.; m. Joan Marie Nero, Sept. 1, 1962 (div. Aug. 1990); children: Torden Erik, Kirsten Noel. BS, U. Wash., 1962; MF, Yale U., 1964. Forestry asst. Weyerhaeuser Timber Co., Klamath Falls, Oreg., 1960; inventory forester West Tacoma Newsprint, Steilacom, Oreg., 1961-62; timber sale compliance forester Dept. Nat. Resources, Kelso, Wash., 1963; rsch. forest economist Pacific N.W. Rsch. Sta., USDA Forest Svc., Portland, Oreg., 1964-88; cons., 1989—. Co-founder, bd. dirs. Cordero Youth Care Ctr., 1970-81; owner Brian R. Wall Images and Communications; Nikken ind. distbr. Sage Mentor Lifestyles; owner Sage Mentors Bus. Consultancy; cons. to govt. agys., Congress univs., industry, small bus.; freelance photographer. Co-author: An Analysis of the Timber Situation in the United States, 1982; contbr. articles, reports to profl. publs., newspapers. Interviewed and cited by nat. and regional news media. Recipient Cert. of Merit U.S. Dept. Agr. Forest Svc., 1982. Mem. ACLU, Soc. Am. Foresters (chmn. Portland chpt. 1973, Forester of Yr. 1975), Conf. of Western Forest Economists Inc. (founder, bd. dirs. 1988-91, treas. 1982-87), Portland Photographic Forum, Common Cause, Oregon Economists Assn., Nat. Audubon Soc., Amnesty Internat., Zeta Psi. Home: 7310 SW Florence Ln Portland OR 97223-2217 Personal E-mail: brianr.wall@msn.com.

WALL, CHARLES R., tobacco company executive, lawyer; BA in History, Grinnell Coll., Iowa, 1967; JD, U. Mo. Law Sch., 1970. Assoc. and ptnr. Shook, Hardy & Bacon, Kans. City, Mo., 1970—90; v.p.,assoc. gen. coun. Philip Morris Co. Inc., NYC, 1990—94, sr. v.p. litig., 1994—95, dep. gen. coun., 1995—2000; sr. v.p., gen. coun. Altria Group, Inc., NYC, 2000—08; vice-chmn., gen. counsel Philip Morris Internat., 2008—. Mem.: bd. dirs. NY City Opera, Neurosciences Inst., La Jolla, Calif. Office: Philip Morris Internat Ave de Rhodanie 50 1007 Lausanne Switzerland Office Phone: 917-663-5000.*

WALL, CHRISTOPHER READ, lawyer; b. Norfolk, Va., Oct. 6, 1952; s. Maurice E. Wall and Marilyn (Murrah) Hardin; m. Barbara L. Wartelle, June 21, 1980; children: Read, Louisa BA summa cum laude, Yale U., 1974; BA, Oxford U., 1976; JD, U. Va., 1979. Bar: N.Y. 1980, U.S. Dist. Ct. (so. dist.) N.Y. 1980, U.S. Ct. Internat. Trade 1985, D.C. 1986, U.S. Dist. Ct. D.C. 1986, U.S. Ct. Appeals (fed. cir), 2002. Ptnr. Winthrop, Stimson, Putnam & Roberts and Pillsbury Winthrop LLP, NYC & Washington, 1979—2005; co-chmn., sr. ptnr. Internat. Trade practice Pillsbury Winthrop Shaw Pittman LLP, Washington, 2005—; asst. sec. for export adminstrn., Bur. Industry & Security US Dept. Commerce, Washington, 2008—09. Contbr. articles to profl. jours. Vice chmn & past chmn. Swedish-Am. C. of C.; chmn. trade & investment adv. com. British-Am. Bus. Assn. Mem. ABA (chmn. spl. adv. com. internat. activities, vice chmn. internat. law & practice sect., co-chmn. internat. litigation com.), Assn. of Bar of City of N.Y., DC Bar, Phi Beta Kappa. Office: US Dept Commerce 14th St and Constitution Ave NW Washington DC 20230

WALL, CLARENCE VINSON, state legislator; b. Athens, Ga., Oct. 17, 1947; s. Clarence Jacob and Fannie Lucile (Clark) W.; m. Linda Gail Mason, Dec. 6, 1969 (div. 1980); 1 child, Jeffrey Vinson. Grad. high sch., Lawrenceville, Ga., 1965. Rep. Ga. Ho. of Reps., Lawrenceville, 1973-82, 85-96. Staff sgt. Ga. Air N.G., 1967-73. Republican. Baptist. Home: 354N Chestnut St Lawrenceville GA 30046-4987

WALL, CONRAD, III, lab administrator, researcher; b. Boston, June 13, 1939; s. Conrad and Nell Kennedy Wall; m. Susan Ann Vieth; children: Conrad Carter, Richard Alison. BS in Physics, Tulane U., New Orleans, 1961, MS in Physics, 1968; PhD in Bioengineering, Carnegie Mellon U., Pitts., 1975. Engring. tech. staff Boeing Co., New Orleans, 1965—70; postdoc. fellow (NIH) U. Pitts. Med. Sch., 1975—76, rsch. asst. prof. otolaryngology, 1976—82; dir., Raymond Jordan human vestibular lab. Eye and Ear Hosp., Pitts., 1982—87; assoc. prof. otology and laryngology Harvard Med. Sch., Boston, 1987—; founding dir., jenks vestibular diagnostic lab. Mass. Eye and Ear Infirmary, Boston, 1987—; assoc. prof., affiliated faculty, HMS-MIT health scis. and tech. MIT, Cambridge, 1987—, rsch. affiliate, man-vehicle lab., dept. aero. engring., 1989—; affiliated rsch. assoc. prof., neuromuscular rsch. ctr. Boston U., 2003—. Mem., human studies com. Schepens Eye Rsch. Inst., Boston, 1991—; chair, working group on basic vestibular function test battery Am. Nat. Standards Inst., Washington, 1992—; assoc. team lead, nat. space biomedical rsch. inst. NASA, Houston, 2000—06. Mem. corp. Old North Ch., Boston, 2005—08. 1st lt. US Army, 1963, Fort Eustis, Va. Fellow: Am. Inst. Medicine and Biol. Engring. (elect 2008). Episcopalian. Achievements include first to electric stimulation of the human posterior ampullary nerve which demonstrate robust nystagmus eye movements -a crucial step in showing feasibility of balance prosthesis implants. Avocation: skeet shooting. Office: Massachusetts Eye & Ear Infirmary 243 Charles St Boston MA 02114 Office Fax: 617-573-4154. Business E-Mail: cwall@mit.edu.

WALL, DONALD ARTHUR, lawyer; b. Lafayette, Ind., Mar. 17, 1946; s. Dwight Arthur and Myra Virginia (Peavey) W.; m. Cheryn Lynn Heinen, Aug. 29, 1970; children: Sarah Lynn, Michael Donald. BA, Butler U., 1968; JD, Northwestern U., 1971. Bar: Ohio 1971, U.S. Dist. Ct. (no. dist.) Ohio 1973, U.S. Supreme Ct. 1980, Ariz. 1982, U.S. Dist. Ct. (no. dist.) W.Va. 1982, U.S. Ct. Appeals (6th cir.) 1982, U.S. Dist. Ct. Ariz. 1983, U.S. Ct. Appeals (9th and 10th cirs.) 1984, U.S. Ct. Appeals (5th cir.) 1988. Assoc. Squire, Sanders & Dempsey, Cleve., 1971-80, ptnr., 1980-82, Phoenix, 1983—. Spkr. at profl. meetings; program moderator. Contbr. articles to profl. jours. Trustee Ch. of the Saviour Day Ctr., Cleveland Heights, 1979-82; mem. adminstrv. bd. Ch. of Saviour, Cleveland Heights, 1980-83; fin. com. Paradise Valley (Ariz.) United Meth. Ch., 1986-87; bd. dirs., divsn. commr. North Scottsdale (Ariz.) Little League, 1983-92; bd. dirs. Epilepsy Found. N.E. Ohio, 1976-82, pres., 1981-82; bd. dirs. N.E. Cmty. Basketball Assn., 1993-99; bd. visitors U. Ariz. Law Sch., 1996—; bd. mgrs. Scottsdale-Paradise Valley YMCA, 1999—. Mem. ABA (torts and ins. practice and litigation sect., past chmn. r.r. law com., litigation sect.), Def. Rsch. Inst., Ariz. Bar Assn. (labor and trial practice sects.), Maricopa County Bar Assn., Ariz. Assn. Def. Counsel. Methodist. Office: Squire Sanders & Dempsey LLP 40 N Central Ave Ste 2700 Phoenix AZ 85004-4498 E-mail: dwall@ssd.com.

WALL, G. MICHAEL, medical chemist; PhD, U. Miss., Oxford, 1988. Pharm. developer Alcon Rsch., Ltd., Ft. Worth, 1988—. Achievements include development of CIPRODEX otic suspension; PATANASE nasal spray. Office: Alcon Rsch Ltd 6201 S Freeway Fort Worth TX 76134

WALL, HELENA M., historian, educator; b. NYC, Nov. 22, 1955; BA, Brandeis U., Waltham, Mass., 1977; MA, PhD, Harvard U., Cambridge, Mass., 1983. Warren finney day prof. history Pomona Coll., Claremont, Calif., 1998—, dir., hart inst. Am. history. Recipient Wig Disting. Prof. award, Pomona Coll., 2008; fellowships, NEH, 1985, 1988—89. Mem.: Phi Beta Kappa. Office: Pomona Coll Dept History Claremont CA 91711 Business E-Mail: hwall@pomona.edu.

WALL, JAMES S., bishop; b. Ganado, Ariz., Oct. 11, 1964; s. James A. and Joan L. Wall. BA, Univ. Ariz., 1993; MDiv, St. John's Sem., Camarillo, Calif., 1998. Ordained priest Diocese of Phoenix, Ariz., 1998; parochial vicar St. Theresa parish, Phoenix, 1998—2001, St. Timothy parish, Mesa, Ariz., 2001—02; pastor St. Thomas the Apostle parish, Phoenix, 2002—07; vicar for priest personnel Diocese of Phoenix, 2007—09; dir. Mt. Claret Retreat Ctr., 2008—09; ordained bishop, 2009; bishop Diocese of Gallup, N.Mex., 2009—. Roman Catholic. Mailing: Diocese of Gallup PO Box 1338 Gallup NM 87305-1338 Office: Diocese of Gallup 711 S Puerco Dr Gallup NM 87305 Office Phone: 505-863-4406. Office Fax: 505-722-9131.*

WALL, JEFF, photographer; b. Vancouver, 1946; MA in art history, U. BC, Vancouver, 1970; student, Courtland Inst., London, 1970—73. One-man shows include Inst. Contemporary Arts, London, 1984, Kunsthalle Basel, Switzerland, 1984, 1987, Marian Goodman Gallery, NYC, 1989, 1990, 1992, 1995, 1998, 2001, 2002, 2004, 2007, Carnegie Mus. Art, Pitts., 1990, Vancouver Art Gallery, 1990, San Diego Mus. Contemporary Art, 1991, Fondation Cartier, Paris, 1993, Reina Sofia Mus., Madrid, 1994, Jeu de Paume, Paris, 1995, Mus. Contemporary Art, Chgo., 1995, Mus. Contemporary Art, LA, 1997, Hirshhorn Mus. and Sculpture Garden, Washington, 1997, Hammer Mus., LA, 2003, Galerie Marian Goodman, Paris, 2006, Mus. Modern Art, NYC, 2007, Art Inst. Chgo., 2007, San Francisco Mus. Art, 2007, exhibited in group shows at About Place: Recent Art of the Americas, Art Inst. Chgo., 1996, Public Information: Desire, Disaster, Document, San Francisco Mus. Modern Art, 1995, Seeing Time, 1999, Whitney Biennial, Whitney Mus. Am. Art, NYC, 1995, Hall of Mirrors: Art & Film Since 1945, traveling, 1996, The Time of Our Lives, New Mus. Contemporary Art, NYC, 1999, The Museum as Muse: Artists Reflect, Mus. Modern Art, NYC, 1999, Carnegie Internat., Carnegie Mus. Art, Pitts., 1999, Around 1984: A Look at Art in the Eighties, P.S.1 Contemporary Art Ctr., 2000, Open City: Aspects of Street Photography, Hirshhorn Mus. and Sculpture Garden, Washington, 2002, The Last Picture Show: Artists Using Photography, 1960-1982, Walker Art Ctr., Mpls. and Hammer Mus., LA, 2003—04, Shadowland: An Exhibition as Film, Walker Art Ctr., Mpls., 2005, Super Vision, Inst. Contemporary Art, Boston, 2006, Moscow Biennial, 2007. Recipient Paul de Hueck and Norman Walford Career Achievement award for Art Photography, Ontario Arts Coun., 2001, Internat. award in Photography, Erna and Victor Hasselblad Found., 2002, Roswitha Haftmann prize in Visual Arts, 2003, Audain prize for Lifetime Achievement, Audain Found. Visual Arts, 2008. Fellow: Royal Soc. Can. Office: c/o Marian Goodman Gallery 24 W 57th St New York NY 10019*

WALL, JERRY LEON, dean, management educator, university administrator; b. Minot, ND, Sept. 30, 1942; s. Claude Leon and Beulah Dollie (Widney) W.; m. Katharine Hoffmann, Sept. 4, 1965; children: Christopher, Stephan, Alison. BA, Okla. State U., 1964; MBA, East Carolina U., 1968; PhD, U. Mo., 1974. Cert. sr. profl. human resources; accredited pers. diplomate. From asst. to full prof. mgmt. Western Ill. U., Macomb, 1972-81, prof. mgmt., 1982; prof. mgmt. scis. U. Iowa, Iowa City, 1981-82; dir. Ctr. Bus. and Econ. Rsch. N.E. La. U., Monroe, 1983—2005; dean Coll. Bus. Northwestern State U., Natchitoches, La., 2007—. Pres., prin. JKW Assocs., West Monroe, 1972—; adj. prof. law enforcement Western Ill. U., Macomb, 1979-81. Editor Jour. of Behavioral Economics, 1975-81, Northeast La. Bus. Rev., 1983-89, Delta Bus. Rev., 1989-91; contbr. over 100 articles to profl. jours., papers and books. Mem. joint legis. com. on alt. econ. strategy La., Baton Rouge, 1986-87; grad. Leadership La.; mem. La. Data Base Commn., 1996-04, La. Tax Commn., 1995-03. Ret. col. AUS. Mem. Assn. for U. Bus. and Econ. Rsch. (pres. 2001), Midwest Soc. for Human Resources/Indsl. Rels. (pres. 1986-87), S.W. Decision Scis. Inst. (adv. coun., area chmn. 1984-86), Am. Arbitration Assn. (panel mem. 1973-90), Am. Nat. Bus. Hall of Fame (bd. dirs. 1983—), Ill. Bus. Hall of Fame (bd. dirs. 1978-83), Small Bus. Inst. (dir. 1976-81), Rotary, Mil. Officers Assn. Am. (bd. dirs. 1999-2004), Beta Gamma Sigma. Republican. Presbyterian. Avocations: scuba diving, magic, racquet sports. Office: Northwestern State U Coll Bus Russell Hall 201D Natchitoches LA 71497 Office Phone: 318-357-5162. Business E-Mail: wall@nsula.edu.

WALL, JOHN C., manufacturing executive; Student, Ga. Inst. Tech., 1969—71; BS in Mech. Engring., MIT, 1975. Rsch. engr., engine lubricants Chevron Rsch. Co., 1978—82, sr. rsch. engr., emissions, 1982—85, unit leader, diesel & aviation fuels rsch., 1985—86; chief engr., heavy-duty projects Cummins, Columbus, Ind., 1986—87, dir., emissions rsch., 1987—88, dir., 94 heavy duty engines, 1988—89, exec. dir., adv. heavy duty engine devel., 1989—91, v.p., adv. heavy duty engine devel., 1991—92, v.p., adv. engring., tech. planning, 1992—95, v.p., rsch. & devel., 1995—2000, v.p., CTO Ind., 2000—. Office: Cummins Box 3005 Columbus IN 47202-3005

WALL, KENNETH E., JR., lawyer; b. Beaumont, Tex., Apr. 6, 1944; s. Kenneth E. and W. Geraldine (Peoples) W.; m. Marjorie Lee Hughes, Dec. 21, 1968; children— Barbara, Elizabeth, Kenneth. Grad. Lamar U., 1966, U. Tex.-Austin, 1969. Bar: Tex. 1969, U.S. Supreme Ct. 1979. Asst. city atty., Beaumont, 1969-73, city atty., 1973-84; with firm Olson & Olson, Houston, 1984—; dir. Tex. Mcpl. League Ins. Trust, 1979-84, vice chmn., 1983-84; counsel S.E. Tex. Regional Planning Commn., 1974, 76. Active Boy Scouts Am., Girl Scouts U.S.A. Mem. Nat. Inst. Mcpl. Law Officers (chmn. com. on local govt. pers. 1979-81, 82-84), State Bar Tex., Tex. City Attys. Assn. (pres. 1982-83), Jefferson County Bar Assn. (dir. 1975-77), Houston Bar Assn., Phi Delta Phi. Methodist. Office: 2727 Allen Pkwy Houston TX 77019 Home Phone: 281-359-6280; Office Phone: 713-533-3800. Business E-Mail: kwall@olsonolson.com.

WALL, M. DANNY, retired finance company executive; BArch, N.D. State U., 1963. Exec. dir. Urban Renewal Agy., Fargo, ND, 1964-71, Salt Lake City Redevel. Agy., 1971-75; dir. legis. Office US Senator Jake Garn, Washington, 1975-78; minority staff dir. Senate Com. Banking, Housing and Urban Affairs, Washington, 1979-80, staff dir., 1980-86, rep. staff dir., 1987; chmn. Fed. Home Loan Bank Bd./Fed. Home Loan Mortgage Corp., Washington, 1987-89; dir. Office Thrift Supervision (formerly Fed. Home Loan Bank Bd.), 1989-90; fin. svcs. cons., 1990—2002; sr. v.p. Dougherty Funding LLC, 1997—2002; chmn, pres. Capmark Bank (formerly GMAC Comml. Mortgage Bank), 2003—07; pres. Morgan Stanley Bank, 2007—09. Home Phone: 801-596-0650. Personal E-mail: alvinadan@aol.com.

WALL, PHIL, information technology executive; B in mech. engring., Imperial Coll., London Univ.; MBA, Brookes Univ., Oxford. Chartered Acct. Fin. mgmt. positions Schlumberger Inc., Equifax Inc.; v.p. fin. internat. fin. ops. First Data Corp., Greenwood Village, Colo., 2002—08, exec. v.p., CFO, 2008—. Office: First Data Corp 6200 S Quebec St Greenwood Village CO 80111

WALL, ROBERT ANTHONY, JR., lawyer; b. Hartford, Conn., Mar. 3, 1945; s. Robert Anthony and Eileen (Fitzgerald) W.; children: Andrea, Melanie, Victoria, Robert, Natalie. BA, Georgetown U., Washington, 1968; JD, Am. U., Washington, 1973. Bar: Conn. 1974, U.S. Ct. Appeals (D.C. cir.) 1974, U.S. Dist. Ct. Conn. 1974, U.S. Supreme Ct. 1977. Ptnr. Wall, Wall & Frauenhofer, Torrington, Conn., 1974-87; pvt. practice Torrington, 1987—. Mem. State of Conn. Rep. Ctrl. Com., 1976-79. Mem. Conn. Trial Lawyers Assn. (bd. govs. 1984-86), Ct. Washington #67 Foresters of Am. (trustee 1988—). Roman Catholic. Home: 55 Quail Run Torrington CT 06790-2550 Office: 8 Church St Torrington CT 06790-5247 Home Phone: 860-489-6485; Office Phone: 860-496-8383. Fax: 860-496-0128. E-mail: wallgawrych@yahoo.com.

WALL, SIMEON HENINGER, JR., plastic surgeon; b. Madison, Wis., Apr. 8, 1970; m. Holly Casey; children: Trace, Casey. Grad. with honors, U. Tex., Austin; MD, U. Tex., San Antonio, 1996. Cert. Am. Bd. Plastic Surgery, 2002, lic. La., Calif. Intern gen. surgery Stanford U. Med. Ctr., Calif., 1996—97, resident plastic surgery, 1997—99, resident, 1999—2001; active staff mem. Christus Schumpert, Shreveport, La., 2001, Doctors Hosp., Shreveport, 2001; assoc. staff mem. Willis Knighton Med. Ctr., Shreveport, 2001; clin. faculty mem. La. State U. Health Scis. Ctr., Shreveport; plastic surgeon Wall Ctr. Plastic Surgery, Shreveport, 2001—. Del. to La. State Med. Soc. Com. Med. Profl. Liability. Patients have been featured on internat. infomercials, The Discovery Channel, local news and nat. advertising campaigns. Plastic surgeon Interplast. Mem.: Shreveport Med. Soc. (bd. dir.), La. State Med. Soc. (mem. med. specialties com.), La. Soc. Plastic Surgeons (sec./treas.), Am. Soc. Plastic Surgeons, Zedplast (Stanford U. Plastic Surgery Alumni Assn.). Avocations: golf, tennis, guitar, singing, snowboarding, hunting, fishing, duck hunting. Office: Wall Ctr Plastic Surgery 1400 E Bert Kouns Ste 106 Shreveport LA 71105 Office Phone: 318-795-0801. Office Fax: 318-795-9492.

WALL, SONJA ELOISE, nursing administrator; b. Santa Cruz, Calif., Mar. 28, 1938; d. Ray Theothornton and Reva Mattie (Wingo) W.; m. Edward Gleason Holmes, Aug. 1959 (div. Jan. 1968); children: Deborah Lynn, Lance Edward; m. John Aspesi, Sept. 1969 (div. 1977); children:

Sabrina Jean, Daniel John; m. Kenneth Talbot LaBoube, Nov. 1, 1978 (div. 1989); 1 child, Tiffany Amber; m. Charles Borsic, July 2002. BA, San Jose Jr. Coll., 1959; BS, Madonna Coll., 1967; postgrad., Wayne State U., 1967—68; student, U. Mich., 1968—70. RN, Calif., Mich., Colo. Staff nurse Santa Clara Valley Med. Ctr., San Jose, Calif., 1959-67, U. Mich. Hosp., Ann Arbor, 1967-73, Porter and Swedish Med. Hosp., Denver, 1973-77, Laurel Grove Hosp., Castro Valley, Calif., 1977-79, Advent Hosp., Ukiah, Calif., 1984-86; motel owner LaBoube Enterprises, Fairfield, Point Arena, Willits, Calif., 1979—; staff nurse Northridge Hosp., LA, 1986-87, Folsom State Prison, Calif., 1987; co-owner, mgr. nursing registry Around the Clock Nursing Svc., Ukiah, 1985—; critical care staff nurse Kaiser Permanente Hosp., Sacramento, 1986-89; nurse Snowline Hospice, Placerville, Calif., 1989-92; carepoint home care and travel nurse Hosp. Staffing Svcs. Inc., Placerville, 1992-94, interim home health nurse, 1994-95; nurse Finders Home Health Care, 1996; owner Sunshine Manor Residential Care Home, Placerville, 1995—, Rainbow Manor Residential Care Home, 2000—02; psychol. and trauma RN Folsom State Prison, 2002—04, Calif. Dept. Mental Health, Placerville, Calif., 2004—. Owner Royal Plantation Petites Miniature Horse Farm. Contbr. articles to profl. jours. Leader Coloma 4-H, 1987-91; mem. mounted divsn. El Dorado County Search and Rescue, 1991-93; docent Calif. Marshall Gold Discovery State Hist. Park, Coloma, Calif. Mem. AACN, NAFE, Oncology Nurses Assn., Soc. Critical Care Medicine, Am. Heart Assn. (CPR trainer, recipient awards), Calif. Bd. RNs, Calif. Nursing Rev., Calif. Critical Care Nurses, Soc. Critical Care Nurses, Alzheimers Aid Soc. No. Calif., Am. Motel Assn. (beautification and remodeling award 1985), Nat. Hospice Nurses Assn., Cmty. Residential Care Assn. Calif., Soroptimist Internat. Calif., Am. Miniature Horse Assn. (winner nat. grand championship 1981-83, 85, 89), DAR (Jobs Daus. hon. mem.), C. of C. of El Dorado County, Kiwanis, Cameron Park Country Club. Republican. Episcopalian. Avocations: pinto, paint and miniature horses, real estate development, swimming. Office Phone: 530-622-3940. Fax: 530-622-2233. E-mail: sunshinemanor@directcon.net.

WALL, WENDY LYNN, history professor, writer; b. Charlotte, NC, Mar. 17, 1962; d. John Kliewer and Joyce Brickman Wall; m. Andrew Whitmore Robertson, Oct. 14, 2000; children: Laura Joyce Robertson, Thaddeus Daniel Wall Robertson. AB, Harvard U., Cambridge, Mass., 1983; MA, PhD, Stanford U., Palo Alto, Calif., 1998. Reporter Wall St. Jour., Chgo., 1983—88; vis. instr., asst. prof. Duke U., Durham, NC, 1996—2000; asst. prof. history Colgate U., Hamilton, NY, 2000—08, Queen's U., Kingston, Ont., Canada, 2008—. Author: (historical books) Inventing the "American Way": The Politics of Consensus from the New Deal to the Civil Rights Movement. Recipient Ellis W. Hawley prize, Orgn. Am. Historians, 2008; named Best First Book award, Phi Alpha Theta, 2008, Outstanding Academic Title, 2009. Liberal. Episcopalian. Avocations: hiking, photography, jazz, music. Office: History Dept Queens Univ 49 Bader Ln Watson Hall Rm 212 Kingston ON K7L 3N6 Canada Office Phone: 613-533-6000 ext. 78991. Business E-Mail: wendy.wall@queensu.ca.

WALL, WILLIAM HERBERT, state coordinator student loan programs; b. St. Augustine, Fla., June 9, 1943; s. Harold C. and Martha D. W.; m. Hallie Josephine Wynne, July 8, 1972; 1 child, Nancy Wynn Wall. BS in Journalism, U. Fla., 1964, MEd, 1965; PhD, U. Ala., 1978. Asst. to v.p. for student affairs U. Fla., Gainesville, 1965-69, fin. aid counselor, 1969-70; asst. dir. fin. aid U. Ala., Tuscaloosa, 1970-78; sr. staff assoc. Ala. Commn. on Higher Edn., Montgomery, 1978-80, asst. dir., 1980-91, dir. grants and scholarships, 1991—2000, assoc. exec. dir., 2000—03; dir. Ala. Coll. Loan Prgm Office, Montgomery, 2004—. Advisor Ala. Indian Affairs Commn., Montgomery, 1989-94. Sec. bd. and chmn. nominating com. Ala. Indian Community Loan Fund, 1989-90; pres. Our Lady Queen of Mercy PTO, 1991—92, Endowment Found., 1990-92. Recipient Cert. of Appreciation, Nat. Health Agys., 1987, Dist. IX State Employee of Yr. award Ala. State Employees Assn., 1999, 2000, 03. Mem. Ala. Assn. Student Fin. Aid Adminstrs. (pres. 1986-87, M. Cecil Padgett award 1981, Disting. Pres. award 1987, John H. Buchanan Jr. award, 2008), So. Assn. Student Fin. Aid Adminstrs. (conf. chmn. 1989, 90, exec. bd. 1981-87, recipient Disting. Svc. award 1990, Spl. Recognition plaque 1989, 80, citation 1984, 91, hon. life mem. 2004), Nat. Assn. Student Fin. Aid Adminstrs. (mem. editl. bd. jour. 1995—2008, Leadership award, 2002), Nat. Assn. State Scholarship and Grant Progs., Civitan (dist. tng. coord. 1985, lt. gov. 1987, edn. officer 1988, sec.-treas. 1989, 92, distinct dir., 2009-, Disting. Svc. award 1988, Govs. award 1989, club honor key 1994, dist. honor key 1996, internat. honor key 2000, internat. grants and scholarships com. 1999-2002, 05-08, chmn. 2002, 07), Montgomery Quarterback Club (treas. 1999-2004, mem. exec. bd. 1999-, mem. found. bd. 1999-, v.p., 2008-), Capital City Club(Inner Cir. 2007-08, pres. 2008, bd. govs. 2009-), Halycon Garden Homes South Neighborhood Assn. (pres., 2009-). Episcopalian. Avocation: classical music. Home: 1641 Prairie Ln Montgomery AL 36117-3427 Office: Student Loan Program 100 North Union St Ste 390 Montgomery AL 36104 Office Phone: 334-265-9720. Personal E-mail: wwall@kheslc.com.

WALLA, CHRIS, musician, music producer; b. Bothell, Wash., Nov. 2, 1975; Founding mem., guitarist, prodr. Death Cab for Cutie, 1997—; founder Hall of Justice Recording, Portland, Oreg., 1997. Musician, prodr. (solo albums) Field Manual, 2008, (Death Cab for Cutie albums) Something About Airplanes, 1999, We Have the Facts and We're Voting Yes, 2000, The Photo Album, 2001, Transatlanticism, 2003, Plans, 2005, Narrow Stairs, 2008, (Death Cab for Cutie songs) I Will Possess Your Heart, 2008 (MTV Video Music award for Best Editing, 2008); prodr.: albums for various artists, including Travis Morrison, The Decemberists, Nada Surf, Tegan and Sara, and Hot Hot Heat. Office: c/o Zeitgeist Artist Mgmt Ste 216 660 W York St San Francisco CA 94110 also: c/o Zeitgeist Artist Mgmt Ste 408 39 W 14th St New York NY 10011 E-mail: info@deathcabforcutie.com.

WALLACE, AMY ELIZABETH, psychiatrist; b. Lakewood, Calif., Aug. 9, 1958; d. Myron Marshall and Joan Marie Wallace; life ptnr. William Brinson Weeks; children: Tanner Adams, Atticus Collins, Savannah Boone, Scout Tecumseh, Harper Oklahome, Joplin Maycomb. BS, Willamette U., Salem, Oreg., BA, 1979; MD, U. Tex. Med. Br., Galveston, 1987; MPH, Dartmouth Med. Sch., Hanover, NH, 2005. Diplomate NH, Vt., 1991, in adult psychiatry Am. Bd. Psychiatry, Neurology, 1993, in child adolescent psychiatry Am. Bd. Psychiatry, Neurology, 1994, in addiction psychiatry Am. Bd. Psychiatry, Neurology, 1996. Assoc. prof. psychiatry Dartmouth Med. Sch., Lebanon, 2003—; sr. rschr. Vets. Rural Health Resource Ctr., Eg. Region, White River Junction, Vt., 2008—. Mem.: APHA (co-chair, vets. affairs sect.), Nat. Rural Health Assn., Am. Acad. Child Adolescent Psychiatry, Am. Psychiatric Assn. Office: Vets Administrn Med Ctr 215 N Main St White River Junction VT 05009 Business E-Mail: aew@dartmouth.edu.

WALLACE, ANDERSON, JR., lawyer, educator; b. Cleve., Sept. 24, 1939; s. Anderson and Agatha Lee (Culpepper) Wallace; m. Kristine Lee Gough; children: Anderson III, Whitney, Nicole Belcher. BA, George Washington U., 1962, JD, 1964, LLM, 1966. Bar: Tex. 68, U.S. Dist. Ct. (no. dist.) Tex. 68, U.S. Ct. Claims 68, U.S. Tax Ct. 68, U.S. Ct. Appeals (5th cir.) 68, U.S. Supreme Ct. 71, U.S. Ct. Appeals (11th cir.) 81. Program mgmt. asst. NASA, Washington, 1962—64; atty. U.S. Dept. Treasury, Washington, 1964—66; tax atty. Price Waterhouse & Co., Atlanta, 1966—67; tax ptnr. Jackson, Walker, Winstead, Cantwell & Miller, Dallas, 1967—84; dir. in charge tax dept. Baker, Mills & Glast, P.C., Dallas, 1984—93; pres. Anderson Wallace, Jr., P.C., Attys., Dallas, 1993—. Instr. Sch. Law So. Meth. U. Trustee S.W. Mus. Sci. and Tech., Dallas, 1974—, Girls Found. Dallas Inc.; chmn. Inst. on Employee Benefits, Southwestern Found., 1976. Mem.: ABA. Office: 3328 Purdue Ave Ste 100 Dallas TX 75225-7635 E-mail: awallacejr@sbcglobal.net.

WALLACE, ANTHONY FRANCIS CLARKE, anthropologist, educator; b. Toronto, Ont., Can., Apr. 15, 1923; s. Paul A.W. and Dorothy Eleanor (Clarke) W.; m. Betty Louise Shillott, Dec. 1, 1942; children: Anthony, Daniel, Sun Ai, Samuel, Cheryl, Joseph. BA, U. Pa., 1948, MA, 1949, PhD, 1950; L.H.D. (hon.), U. Chgo., 1983. Instr. anthropology Bryn Mawr Coll., 1948-50; asst. instr. anthropology U. Pa., research sec. Behavioral Research Council, 1951-55; research asst. prof. U. Pa., 1952-55, vis. assoc. prof., 1955-61, prof., 1961—, chmn. dept., 1961-71, Geraldine R. Segal prof. Am. social thought, 1980-83, Univ. prof. anthropology, 1983-88, prof. emeritus, 1988—. Sr. rsch. assoc. anthropology Eastern Pa. Psychiat. Inst., 1955-60, dir. clin. research, 1960-61, med. research scientist, III, 1961-80; mem. tech. adv. com. N.J. Psychiat. Inst., 1958; cons. disaster studies NRC, 1956-57; cons. Phila. Housing Authority, 1952; mem. rsch. adv. com. Commonwealth Mental Health Research Found., 1960-61, U.S. Office Edn., 1965-68; mem. behavioral scis. study sect. NIMH, 1964-68; mem. NRC, 1963-66; mem. various adv. coms. NIMH, 1962—; mem. social sci. adv. council NSF, 1969-72 Author: King of the Delawares: Teedyuscung, 1700-1763, 1949, Culture and Personality, 1961, rev. edit., 1970, Religion: An Anthropological View, 1966, Death and Rebirth of the Seneca, 1970, Rockdale: The Growth of an American Village in the Early Industrial Revolution, 1978, new. edit., 2004, Social Context of Innovation, 1983, new ed., 2003. St. Clair, 1987, The Long, Bitter Trail, 1993, Jefferson and the Indians, 1999, Revitalizations and Mazeways, 2003, Modernity and Mind, 2005 Bd. mgrs. Founds. Fund for Research in Psychiatry, 1969-71. Served AUS, 1942-45. Recipient Bancroft prize in Am. History, 1979, Dexter prize in History of Technology, 1989, Caroline Bancroft prize in history, 2000; Guggenheim fellow, 1978-79 Fellow Am. Anthrop. Assn. (pres. 1971-72),; mem. Nat. Acad. Scis., Am. Philos. Soc., Am. Acad. Arts and Scis. Office: Univ Pa Dept Anthropology 33rd and Spruce Sts Philadelphia PA 19104 Home: 1 Main St Unit 10 Youngstown NY 14174 Personal E-mail: blswallace@earthlink.net.

WALLACE, BARBARA BROOKS, writer; b. Soochow, China, Dec. 3, 1922; arrived in U.S., 1938; d. Otis Frank and Nicia Brooks; m. James Wallace, Jr., Feb. 27, 1954; 1 child, James V. BA, UCLA, 1945. Script sec. Foote, Cone & Belding, Hollywood, Calif., 1946-49; tchr. Wright MacMahon Secretarial Sch., Beverly Hills, Calif., 1949-50; head fund drive Commerce and Industry Divsn. ARC, San Francisco, 1950-52. Author: Claudia, 1969 (Nat. League Am. Pen Women Juvenile Book award, 1970), Andrew the Big Deal, 1970, The Trouble with Miss Switch, 1971, Victoria, 1973, Can Do, Missy Charlie, 1974, The Secret Summer of L.E.B. (Nat. League Am. Pen Women Juvenile Book award, 1974), Julia and the Third Bad Thing, 1975, Palmer Patch, 1976, Hawkins, 1977, Peppermints in the Parlor, 1980 (William Allen White award, 1983), The Contest Kid Strikes Again, 1980, Hawkins and the Soccer Solution, 1981, Miss Switch to the Rescue, 1981, Hello, Claudia, 1982, Claudia and Duffy, 1982, The Barrel in the Basement, 1985, Argyle, 1987, 1992, Perfect Acres, Inc., 1988, The Twin in the Tavern, 1993 (Edgar award Mystery Writers Am., 1994), Cousins in the Castle, 1996, Sparrows in the Scullery, 1997 (Edgar award, 1998), Ghosts in the Gallery, 2000, Secret in St. Something, 2001, Miss Switch Online, 2002, The Perils of Peppermints, 2003, Have Dragon, Will Travel, 2009, Anastasia Florence Nightingale and I, A Nurse's Story, 2009. Mem.: Authors Guild, Children's Book Guild of Washington, Alpha Phi. Episcopalian. Home: 6251 Old Dominion Dr Apt 436 Mc Lean VA 22101-4810 E-mail: bbwallace@cox.net.

WALLACE, BEN, professional basketball player; b. White Hall, Ala., Sept. 10, 1974; m. Chanda Wallace. Student, Va. Union U., Richmond, 1996. Forward-ctr. Washington Bullets, 1996—99, Orlando Magic, Fla., 1999—2000, Detroit Pistons, 2000—06, 2009—, Chgo. Bulls, 2006—08, Cleve. Cavaliers, 2008—09, Phoenix Suns, 2009. Mem. USA Team. Named NBA Defensive Player of Yr., 2002, 2003, 2005, 2006; named to NBA All-Defensive Team, 2002, 2003, 2004, 2005, 2006. Achievements include being a member of NBA Champion Detroit Pistons, 2004. Office: Detroit Pistons Palace of Auburn Hills 2 Championship Dr Auburn Hills MI 48326*

WALLACE, BONNIE ANN, biochemist, biophysicist, educator; b. Greenwich, Conn., Aug. 10, 1951; d. Arthur Victor and Maryjane Wallace. BS in Chemistry, Rensselaer Poly. Inst., 1973; PhD in Molecular Biophysics and Biochemistry, Yale U., 1977; DSc (hon.), U. London, 1995. Postdoctoral rsch. fellow Harvard U., Boston, 1977-78; asst. prof. dept. biochemistry and molecular biophysics Columbia U., NYC, 1979-86, assoc. prof., 1986; prof. dept. chemistry, dir. Ctr. for Biophysics Rensselaer Poly. Inst., 1987-92; reader in crystallography U. London, 1991—2001, prof. molecular biophysics, 2001—; dir. Ctr. for Protein and Membrane Structure and Dynamics, Daresbury Lab., 1999—2006. Vis. scientist MRC Lab. Molecular Biology, Cambridge, Eng., 1978; Fogarty sr. fellow Birkbeck Coll., U. London, 1990; Disting. vis. prof. Tzu-Chi U. and Academia Sinica, Taiwan, 2004. Assoc. editor Peptide and Protein Letters; mem. editl. adv. bd. Biochemistry; co editor (with Wallace B.A. & Jones R.W.)Modern Techniques for Circular Dichroism and Synchrotron Radiation Circular Dichroism Spectroscopy, 2009;contbr. articles to profl. jours., chpts. to books. Internat. adv. bd. Inst. Synchrotron, Rings, Denmark, Ctr. Coherent X-rays, Australia; Hisor Synchrotron Japan; chmn. sci. adv. bd. Brookhaven Nat. Lab., Upton, NY; chmn. SRCD sci. adv. bd. Diamond Synchrotron, England. Jane Coffin Childs fellow, 1977-79; recipient Irma T. Hirschl award, 1980-84, Sci Web award, 1998, Interdisciplinary prize, Royal Soc. Chemistry, 2009; Camille and Henry Dreyfus tchr.-scholar, 1986; named Hot Young Scientist Fortune Mag., 1990; Subject of Documentary Film: Hypertension Research for the Future, 1995. Fellow: AAAS, HFSP, Inst. Biology, Royal Soc. Chemistry (Interdisciplinary prize 2009); mem.: BBSRC, Brit. Crystallographic Assn. (BSG award 1994), Biophysics Soc. (nat. coun., mem. internat. rels. com., Dayhoff award 1985), Phi Lambda Upsilon, Sigma Xi. Office: U London Birkbeck Coll Dept Crystallography London WC1E 7HX England

WALLACE, CANDY, culinary association administrator; Exec. dir. Am. Personal & Pvt. Chef Inst. & Assn., San Diego. Co-author: The Professional Personal Chef: The Business of Doing Business as a Personal Chef, 2007. Mem.: Internat. Assn. Culinary Professionals (Businessperson/Entrepreneur of Yr., Award of Excellence 2003), Women Chefs & Restaurants, Am. Culinary Fedn. (bd. mem. San Diego chpt.), Les Dames d'Escoffier Internat. (bd. mem. San Diego chpt.). Office: Am Personal & Pvt Chef Assn 4572 Delaware St San Diego CA 92116 Business E-Mail: info@personalchef.com.

WALLACE, CHARLES ALAN, plastic surgeon; b. Ft. Worth, Tex., Feb. 13, 1957; MD, U. Tex. Southwestern Med. Sch., 1982. Cert. Am. Bd. Plastic Surgery. Intern, gen. surgery U. Hawaii, Honolulu, 1982—83; resident Baylor U. Med. Ctr., Dallas, 1984—87, resident, plastic surgery, 1986—87; resident St. Joseph-MD Anderson, Houston, 1987—89; private practice Dallas, 1989—. Fellow: ACS; mem.: Tex. Soc. Plastic and Reconstructive Surgeons, Dallas Soc. Plastic Surgeons, Cronin and Brauer Soc., AMA, Tex. Med. Assn., Dallas County Med. Assn., Am. Soc. Plastic Surgeons, Soc. Baylor Surgeons. Avocations: riding motorcycles, fixing cars, boats & airplanes. Office: 17110 Dallas Pky Ste 100 Dallas TX 75248 Office Phone: 972-380-7090. Office Fax: 972-380-7016.

WALLACE, CHRIS, professional sports team executive; m. Debby Wallace; 1 child, Truman. Founder Blue Ribbon Coll. Basketball Yearbook, 1981; draft cons. US Basketball League; with NY Knicks, LA Clippers, Denver Nuggets, Portland Trail Blazers; scout Miami Heat, dir. player pers.; gen. mgr. Boston Celtics, 1997—2007; v.p. basketball ops., gen. mgr. Memphis Grizzlies, 2007—. Mem. NBA Basketball Without Borders Africa Camp, Johannesburg. Named one of Most Influential Members of Coll. Basketball Media, Sports Illus., 1991. Office: Memphis Grizzlies 191 Beale St Memphis TN 38103*

WALLACE, CURTIS WILBERN, JR., music director, organist; b. Roanoke, Va., Apr. 30, 1962; s. Curtis Wilbern and Shirley Jean Wallace. BA in Sacred Music, Roanoke Coll., 1984. Organist Midland Bapt. Ch., Vinton, Va., 1977—80; music dir. Our Lady Perpetual Help Cath. Ch., Salem, Va., 1980—85; dir. music ministries Holy Redeemer Cath. Ch., Coll. Park, Md., 1985—87; organist, choir master St. Mark's Luth. Ch., Roanoke, 1988—90; dir. music St. Margaret Mary Cath. Ch., Winter Park, Fla., 1990—. Dir. music ministries divsn. Nat. Assn. Pastoral Musicians. Prodr.: (St. Margaret Mary Choir CD) Sounds of Christmas, 2002, Taizé Prayer, 2003, Jubilate Deo, 2005. Mem.: Am. Guild Organists. Republican. Roman Catholic. Achievements include leading St. Margaret Mary Catholic Church pilgrimage to Rome, Italy in November 2003. Avocations: aquarium fish, travel. Home: 648 Tuskawilla Point Lane Winter Springs FL 32708-4902 Office: St Margaret Mary Catholic Ch 526 Park Ave N Winter Park FL 32789-3208 Office Fax: 407-647-4492. Personal E-mail: curtiswallace@cfl.rr.com. Business E-Mail: curtis@stmargaretmary.org.

WALLACE, DEE, actress; b. Kansas City, Mo., Dec. 14, 1948; d. Robert Stanley and Maxine (Nichols) Bowers; m. Christopher Stone, June 28, 1980 (dec.); m. Skip Belyea; 1 child, Gabrielle. BA, U. Kans., 1971. Actress feature films The Christmas Visitor, Secret Admirer, Cujo, E.T., Jimmy the Kid, The Howling, 10; actress ABC movies of the week Eminent Domain, Hostage Flight, A Whale for a Killing; actress CBS movies of the week An Enemy Among Us, Sin of Innocence, The Sky is No Limit, Happy, Surprise, Surprise, The Five of Me, Young Love, First Love; actress NBC movies of the week Wait Til Your Mother Gets Home, Child Bride of Short Creek, Skeezer; actress CBS After School Special Dad's Out of a Job; actress ABC After School Special Run Don't Walk; actress CBS series Police Story, Together We Stand/Nothing is Easy, Lou Grant; actress stage prodns. including Annie Get Your Gun, Oklahoma, My Fair Lady, Applause, Butterflies are Free, Middle of the Night. Spkr. in field; mgr. DWS Acting Studio, Burbank, Calif. Appeared in films including Nevada, 1997, Mutual Needs, 1997, Black Circle Boys, 1997, Bad As I Wanna Be: The Dennis Rodman Story, 1998, Flamingo Dreams, 1998, To Love, Honor and Betray, 1999, Invisible Mom II, 1999, Pirates of the Plain, 1999, Out of the Black, A Month of Sundays, Dead Canaries, Spice of Life, Total Rex, Abominable, Expiration Date, Rob Zombie's Halloween, 2007, others; appeared on TV shows Cold Case, 2005, Crossing Jordan, 2005, Sons and Daughters, 2005, Without a Trace, Close to Home, Bones, Ghost Whisperer, My Name is Earl. Fundraiser Actors and Others for Animals, L.A., 1980—, Amanda Found., L.A., 1986, 87; co-host, fundraiser Children's Hospital Telethon, Sta. KCET, L.A., 1985—; spokesperson Nat. Assn. of Children of Alcoholics, 1987—. Mem. Screen Actors Guild, Actors Equity, AFTRA. Methodist. Avocations: dance, singing. Office Phone: 818-876-0386. Personal E-mail: consciouscreation101@yahoo.com.

WALLACE, DON, JR., law educator; b. Vienna, Apr. 23, 1932; s. Don and Julie (Baer) Wallace; m. Daphne Mary Wickham, 1963; children: Alexandra Creed, Sarah Deckey, Benjamin James. BA with high honors, Yale U., 1953; LL.B. cum laude, Harvard U., 1957. Bar: N.Y. 1957, D.C. 1978, U.S. Supreme Ct. Assoc. Fleischmann, Jaeckle, Stokes and Hitchcock, NYC, 1959-60, Paul, Weiss, Rifkind, Wharton and Garrison, NYC, 1957-58, 60-62; rsch. asst. to faculty mem. Harvard Law Sch., Cambridge, Mass., 1958-59; regional legal adv. Middle East AID, Dept. State, 1963-65, dep. asst. gen. counsel, 1965-66; assoc. prof. law Georgetown U. Law Ctr., Washington, 1966-71, prof., 1971—2002; chmn. Internat. Law Inst., Washington, 1969—; adj./emeritus prof. Georgetown U. Law Ctr., Washington, 2002—. Cons. AID, 1966-70, UN Centre on Transnat. Corps., 1977-78; counsel Wald, Harkrader & Ross, Washington, 1978-86, Arnold & Porter, 1986-89, Shearman & Sterling, 1989-98, Morgan, Lewis & Bockius, 1998—; legal advisor State of Qatar, 1979-82; chmn. adv. com. on tech. and world trade Office of Tech. Assessment, U.S. Congress, 1976-79; mem. Sec. of State's Adv. Com. on Pvt. Internat. Law, 1979—; mem. U.S. del. UN Conf. on State Succession in Respect of Treaties, Vienna, 1978; mem. U.S. del. UN Commn. Internat. Trade Law, Vienna, 1981—; vis. com. Harvard Law Sch., 1996-97; mem. panel of judges World Trade Orgn., 1996-2000. Co-author: Internat. Business and Economics: Law and Policy; Investor-State Arbitration; author: International Regulation of Multinational Corporations, 1976, Dear Mr. President: The Needed Turnaround in America's International Economic Affairs, 1984; editor: A Lawyer's Guide to International Business Transactions, 1977-87; contbr. numerous articles on internat. trade and law to profl. jours., books revs. on law and bus. to profl. jours. Coord. Anne Arundel County (Md.) Dem. Nat. Com., 1972-79; sec. Chesapeake Found., 1972-73; nat. chmn. Law Profs. for Bush and Quayle, 1988, 92, for Dole and Kemp, 1996; v.p., bd. govs. UNIDROIT Found., Rome, 1997—. Fulbright fellow, 1967, Eisenhower Exch. fellow, 1976. Mem. ABA (chmn. sect. internat. law 1978-79, ho of dels. 1982-84, mem. adv. bd. Ctrl. European and Eurasian Law - Mid. East and North Africa, Rule of Law (Initiative), Am. Law Inst., Repub. Nat. Lawyers Assn., Internat. Law Assn., Shaybani Soc. of Internat. Law (v.p.), Cosmos Club, Met. Club Acad. Coun. (v.p.), European Ctr. Peace and Devel. (Belgrade). Republican. Home: 2800 35th St NW Washington DC 20007-1411 Office: Georgetown U Law Ctr 600 New Jersey Ave NW Washington DC 20001-2022 E-mail: wallace@ili.org.

WALLACE, DONALD JOHN, III, rancher; b. Houston, May 17, 1941; s. D. J., Jr. and Doris Jill (Gano) Wallace; m. Patricia Anne McShane, Sept. 3, 1964 (div. 1984); children: Donald John IV, Megan; m. Nena Jo Isenhower, June 1, 1985 (div. 1989); 1 child, Andrew; m. Kay Fulkerson, May 31, 1997. BBA in Mktg., Texas A&M U., 1963. Regional sales dir. Orkin Exterminating Co., Inc., Dallas, 1977-79, br. mgr., 1979-80, dist. mgr., 1980-83, comml. region mgr., 1983-85, regional sales dir., 1985-86; owner Omega Telex, Dallas, 1986-88;

rancher Valley View, Tex., 1988—. Leader Big Mineral Trail Riders Club, Boy Scouts Am.; pres. Frank Buck Zool. Soc.; mem. Tex. Structural Pest Control Bd., Austin, 1983—84; bd. dirs. Frank Buck Zoo, Gainesville, Tex., 1997—98, North Tex. Med. Found., Gainesville Econ. Devel. Corp.; chmn., bd. dirs. North Tex. Med. Ctr. Republican. Methodist. Avocations: hiking, fishing, hunting, skiing, horseback riding. Home: 1034 Trails End Valley View TX 76272-6114 Personal E-mail: kay1711don@cooke.net.

WALLACE, ELIZABETH, medical/surgical nurse; b. Hartford, Conn., May 24, 1951; d. Anna Flannery Wallace; m. Joseph H. Taylor (div.); children: Lauren Taylor, Julia Taylor. Student, Seattle U., 1969—70; degree, Royal Acad. Music, London, 1974; diploma in nursing, Mass. Coll. Nursing, Framingham, 2004. RN Mass. Singing tchr. Cork Sch. Music, Ireland, 1973—75; singer Coro Nacional d'España, Teatro Zarzuela, Madrid, 1975—77, Hochschule fur Musik, Frankfurt, Germany, 1977—78, Teatro Margherita, Genova, Italy, 1978—80, Boston Concert Opera, 1981—89, Tanglewood Fesitval Chorus, 1987—97; prin., owner Allegro Piano Svc.; nurse H. William Fegley, MD, 2001—06; sales rep. M. Steinert & Sons, Natick, Mass., 2007—. Singer: Tanglewood Festival Chorus, Boston Concert Opera. Recipient 1st Pl. Close Up Magic Contest award, Soc. Am. Magician's, 1996; named Artist of the Month, Copley Soc. Boston, 1984. Mem.: Nat. Assn. Tchrs. Singing, Assn. Tchrs. Singing, Mass. Assn. Nurses. Avocations: writing, magic, painting, drawing. Home: 70 Harrington Rd Framingham MA 01701 Office: M Steinert & Sons 1298D Worcester Rd Natick MA 01760 Office Phone: 508-655-7373. Business E-Mail: beth@msteinert.com.

WALLACE, EMILY MITCHELL, writer, editor, educator; d. George Lafayette and Prewitt Carlisle (Evans) Mitchell; m. Gregory Merrill Harvey, June 14, 1969; m. Robert Arthur Wallace, June 8, 1954 (div. 1964). BA, Southwest Mo. State, 1958; MA, Bryn Mawr Coll., 1959, PhD, 1965. Tutor, history and lit. Curtis Inst. of Music, Phila., 1957—58, chair English dept., 1976—78, 1979—83; tchr. lit. Shipley Sch., Bryn Mawr, Pa., 1959—60; instr. to asst. prof. U. Pa., Phila., 1962—67; vis. asst. prof. Swarthmore Coll., Pa., 1967—68, 1969—70; leader interdisciplinary seminar Yale U., New Haven, 1979; rsch. assoc. Ctr. Visual Culture Bryn Mawr Coll., 2003—. Mem. sponsoring com. Marianne Moore Fund for Poetry, Bryn Mawr Coll., 1975—; mem. adv. com. Rosenbach Mus. and Libr., Phila., 1980—; curriculum cons. Cooper Union of Art, Sci. and Tech., NY, 1984—85; interdisciplinary rsch. scholar in poetry and visual arts; writer photographic essays and multimedia lectrs. scholarly and acad. audiences, double-screen lectrs. confs. and symposia univs. and mus. Author: (book) A Bibliography of William Carlos Williams, 1969; guest editor (periodical) W.C. Williams Review, Centennial Issue, 1983, PAIDEUMA (Spcl. James Laughlin Vol.), 2002; author: (photo essay) Youthful Days and Costly Hours: The Education of Ol' Ez and Billy Williams at Penn, U. Pa. Conf. Papers, 1983, Athena's Owls: The Education of Marianne Moore and Hilda Doolittle, Bryn Mawr '09 in Poesis, 1985, Some Friends of Ezra Pound in the Yale Rev., 1986, Saffron Honey: A Love Song by William Carlos Williams, in The Idea and The Thing in Modernist American Poetry, 2001, Why Not Spirits?-The Universe is Alive, in Ezra Pound and China, 2003. Mem. bd. dirs. Am. Found., Bok Tower, Fla., 1976—86; shareholder The Libr. Co., Phila., 1981—; lifetime mem. Friends of the Bryn Mawr Coll. Libr., Pa., 1996—; mem. Yale Libr. Assocs., Franklin Inn., Phila. Fellow, AAUW, 1968—69; Workman Traveling fellowship, Bryn Mawr Coll., Eng., France, Italy, 1961—62, Inaugural Beinecke fellow, Yale U., 1987, Everett Helm Vis. fellow, Lilly Libr., Ind. U., 2003. Mem.: Modern Lang. Assn., Harvard Humanities Ctr. Faculty Arts and Scis., Conn. Acad. Arts and Sci., Assn. Lit. Scholars and Critics, Emily Dickinson Soc., H.D. Soc., Ezra Pound Soc., William Carlos Williams Soc. (first pres.), Marianne Moore Soc., Wallace Stevens Soc., Henry James Soc., Ernest Hemingway Soc., Merion Cricket Club. Democrat. Avocations: chess, music, travel, gardening, tennis. Home: 1939 Panama St Philadelphia PA 19103-6609 Office Phone: 610-718-0503. Personal E-mail: emwallace@aol.com.

WALLACE, F. BLAKE, retired aerospace transportation executive, retired mechanical engineer; b. Phoenix, Jan. 10, 1933; BMechE, Calif. Inst. Tech., 1955; MS in Engring., Ariz. State U., 1963, PhD in Engring., 1967. Preliminary design engr. Pratt & Whitney, East Hartford, Conn., 1955-59; chief engr. advanced tech. Garrett Corp., Phoenix, 1959-80; mgr. advanced plans and programs Aircraft Engine Group GE, Evendale, Ohio, 1981-83; gen. mgr. Allison div. GM, Indpls., 1983-93, v.p., 1987-93; chmn. & CEO Allison Engine Co., Indpls., 1993-95; ret., 1995. Author numerous tech. papers. Fellow AIAA (chmn. air breathing propulsion tech. com. 1977-78, Air Breathing Propulsion award 1991), U.S. Advanced Ceramic Assn. (chmn. 1987-89).

WALLACE, FRANKLIN SHERWOOD, lawyer, director; b. Bklyn., Nov. 24, 1927; s. Abraham Charles and Jennie (Etkin) Wolowitz; m. Eleanor Ruth Pope, Aug. 23, 1953; children: Julia Diane, Charles Andrew. Student, U. Wis., 1943-45; BS cum laude, U.S. Mcht. Marine Acad., 1950; LLB, JD, U. Mich., 1953. Bar: Ill. 1954. Practice law, Rock Island, Ill.; ptnr. Winstein, Kavensky & Wallace. Asst. state's atty. Rock Island County, 1967-68; local counsel UAW at John Deere-J.I. Case Plants; boxing commr. State of Ill., 2005 Former bd. dirs. Tri City Jewish Ctr.; former trustee United Jewish Charities of Quad Cities; former bd. dirs. Blackhawk Coll. Found. Mem. ABA, Ill. Bar Assn. (chmn. jud. adv. polls com. 1979-84), Rock Island County Bar Assn., Am. Trial Lawyers Assn., Ill. Trial Lawyers Assn., Nat. Assn. Criminal Def. Lawyers, Ill. Appellate Lawyers Assn., Am. Judicature Soc., Blackhawk Coll. Found, Ill. State Boxing Bd. Commn. Democrat. Jewish. Home: 3409 20th St Rock Island IL 61201 Personal E-mail: fnewallace2000@yahoo.com.

WALLACE, GLADYS BALDWIN, retired librarian; b. Macon, Ga., June 5, 1923; d. Carter Shepherd and Dorothy (Richard) Baldwin; m. Hugh Loring Wallace Jr., Oct. 14, 1941 (div. Sept. 1968); children: Dorothy, Hugh Loring III. BS in Edn., Oglethorpe U., 1961; MLS, Emory U., 1966; EdS, Ga. State U., 1980. Libr. pub. elem. schs., Atlanta, 1956-66; libr. Northside HS, 1966-87, Episc. Cathedral St. Philip. Author: The Time of My Life, 1994, Just a Moment, a Book of Poetry, 2005, Glorious Grass, 1999. Mem. Madison-Morgan Cultural Ctr. Recipient Poet of Merit award, 1999; Ga. Dept. Edn. grantee, 1950, NDEA grantee, 1963, 65. Mem.: Am. Assn. Ret. Persons. Home: NC 6 136 Peachtree Memorial Dr NW Atlanta GA 30309-1096

WALLACE, HARRY LELAND, lawyer; b. San Francisco, June 26, 1927; s. Leon Harry and Anna Ruth (Haworth) W.; m. Ruth Goldman; 1 child, Mary Ann Wallace Frantz. AB in Govt.; BS in Bus, Ind. U., 1949; JD, Harvard U., 1952. Bar: Wis. 1953. Law clk. U.S. Supreme Ct. Justice Sherman Minton, Washington, 1952-53; assoc. firm Foley & Lardner, Milw., 1953-61, partner, 1961-96, retired, 1996; officer and/or dir. various corps. Treas. Mequon-Thiensville Sch. Bds., 1966-67, 71-73, pres., 1965-66, 67-71, 73-75; bd. dirs. Milw. County Assn. for Mental Health, 1970-76, Milw. Mental Health Found., 1983-94; chmn. financing policies com. Gov.'s Commn. on Edn., 1969-70; mem. Gov.'s Task Force on Sch. Financing and Property Tax Reform, 1972-73; chmn. Gov.'s Commn. on State-Local Rels. and Fin. Policies, 1975-76; trustee Pub. Policy Forum, 1976-92, sec., 1984-86, pres., 1986-88. With USN, 1945-46. Mem. Wis. Bar Assn., Am. Law Inst., Phi Beta Kappa, Beta Gamma Sigma, Delta Tau Delta. Clubs: Milwaukee. Methodist. Home: 2204 West Charter Mall Mequon WI 53092 Home Phone: 262-242-0127. Personal E-mail: harrylwallace@biul.com, harrylwallace@live.com.

WALLACE, HENRY JARED, JR., lawyer; b. Pitts., Oct. 26, 1943; s. Henry Jared and Jane (Bowman) Wallace. BA, Harvard U., 1965, JD, 1968. Bar: Pa. 1969, U.S. Supreme Ct. 1973. With Reed Smith, Pitts., 1968—94; pvt. practice Pitts., 1995—. Served with U.S. Army, 1968-70. Mem. Duquesne Club, Fox Chapel Golf Club, Harvard-Yale-Princeton Club (Pitts.). Home and Office: 149 Ridgeview Dr New Kensington PA 15068-9389

WALLACE, J. CLIFFORD, federal judge; b. San Diego, Dec. 11, 1928; s. John Franklin and Lillie Isabel (Overing) Wallace; m. Virginia Lee Schlosser, 1957 (dec.); m. Elaine J. Barnes, Apr. 8, 1996 (dec.); m. Dixie Jenee Robison Zenger, Apr. 2, 2001. BA, San Diego State U., 1952; LLB, U. Calif., Berkeley, 1955. Bar: Calif. 1955. With Gray, Cary, Ames & Frye, San Diego, 1955—70; judge US Dist. Ct. (so. dist.), Calif., 1970—72, US Ct. Appeals (9th cir.), San Diego, 1972—96, chief judge, 1991—96, sr. judge, 1996—. Contbr. articles to profl. jours. Stake pres. San Diego East LDS Ch., 1962—67, regional rep., 1967—74, 1977—79. With USN, 1946—49. Recipient Edward J. Devitt Disting. Svc. to Justice award, 2006. Mem.: Inst. Jud. Adminstrn., Am. Bd. Trial Advocates. Mem. Lds Ch. Office: US Ct Appeals 9th Cir 940 Front St Ste 4192 San Diego CA 92101-8918 *My principles, ideals and goals and my standard of conduct are embodied in the Gospel of Jesus Christ. They come to fruition in family life, service, industry and integrity and in an attempt, in some small way, to make my community a better place within which to live.**

WALLACE, JANE HOUSE, retired geologist; b. Ft. Worth, Aug. 12, 1926; d. Fred Leroy and Helen Gould (Kixmiller) Wallace. AB, Smith Coll., 1947, MA, 1949; postgrad., Bryn Mawr Coll., 1949—52. Geologist US Geol. Survey, 1952—97; chief Pub. Inquiries Offices, Washington, 1964—72, spl. asst. to dir., 1974—97, dep. bur. ethics counselor, 1975—97, Washington liaison Office of Dir., 1978—97; ret., 1997. Recipient Meritorious Service award Dept. Interior, 1971, Disting. Svc. award, 1976, Sec.'s Commendation, 1988, Smith Coll. medal, 1992. Fellow Geol. Socs. Am., Washington (treas. 1963-67); mem. Sigma Xi (assoc.)

WALLACE, JOHN E., state supreme court justice; b. Pitman, NJ, 1942; m. Barbara Wallace; 5 children. BA in Political sci., U. Del., 1964; JD, Harvard U. Sch. of Law, 1967. Atty. Trustees of Penn Central Transportation Co., Montgomery, McCracken, Walker & Rhoads, Phila.; partner Atkinson, Myers, Archie & Wallace; municipal judge Wash. Township, Gloucester County; judge NJ Superior Ct., 1984—92, judge appellate div., 1992—2003; justice NJ Supreme Ct., 2003—. Former mem. NJ Supreme Ct. Task Force for Minority Concern; mem. NJ Ethics Commn., Jud. Advisory Com. on Americans with Disabilities Act, Supreme Ct. Special Com. on Matrimonial Litigation, Appellate Div. Rules Com.; former chmn. Supreme Ct. Ad Hoc Com. on Admissions. Coach Washington Twp. H.S. Served to rank of captain US Army, 1968—70. Mem.: ABA, Garden State Bar Assn. (Van J. Clinton award 2002), NJ State Bar Assn., Nat. Bar Assn., Camden County Bar Assn., Gloucester Bar Assn. Office: Richard J Hughes Justice Complex 25 Market St PO Box 970 Trenton NJ 08625*

WALLACE, JOHN LOYS, retired aviation services executive; b. Decatur, Tex., July 31, 1941; s. John K. and Flora Viola (Lumsden) Montgomery W.; m. Linda M. Jackson, May 18, 1962; children— John, Amy Lynn, Katherine Lea, Elizabeth D'Ann Student, U. Tex.-Arlington, 1961-65, North Tex. State U., Denton, 1960-61. V.p. acctg. svcs. Cooper Airmotive, Dallas, 1975-77, v.p. fin., 1977-80, exec. v.p., gen. mgr. Gen. Aviation div., 1980-82; exec. v.p. fin., adminstrn. Aviall, Dallas, 1982-85; exec. v.p., chief oper. officer Aviall, Inc., Dallas, 1985-89, pres. Gen. Aviation Svcs. div., 1989-93; ret., 1993. Mem. Fin. Execs. Inst., North Dallas C. of C., U.S./Mex. C. of C. (bd. dirs.), Chif Exec.'s Round Table, Cotton Creek Club, Delta Sigma Phi. Republican. Presbyterian. Avocations: gardening, fishing, golf. Home: 3651 Pinehurst Cir Gulf Shores AL 36542-9052 Personal E-mail: wallaces@gulftel.com.

WALLACE, JOYCE IRENE MALAKOFF, internist; b. Phila., Nov. 25, 1940; d. Samuel Leonard and Henrietta (Hameroff) Malakoff; m. Lance Arthur Wallace, Aug. 30, 1964 (div. 1974); 1 dau. Julia Ruth; m. Arthur H. Kahn, Oct. 7, 1979 (div. 1986); 1 son, Aryeh N. Kahn. AB, Queens Coll., CUNY, 1961; postgrad., Columbia U., 1962-64; MD, SUNY, 1968. Diplomate Am. Bd. Internal Medicine. Intern St. Vincent's Hosp. Med. Ctr., NYC, 1968-70; practice medicine NYC, 1970-71; resident Manhattan VA Hosp., NYC, 1972, Nassau County Med. Ctr., East Meadow, N.Y., 1972-73; practice medicine North Conway, NH, 1973—74; practice medicine specializing in internal medicine NYC, 1976—; med. dir. FROST'D Primary Care, 1999—2003. Mem. attending staff Nassau County Med. Ctr., 1974, St. Vincent's Hosp. and Med. Ctr., N.Y.C., 1977—; asst. prof. medicine Mt. Sinai Med. Sch., N.Y.C.; pres. Found. for Rsch. on Sexually Transmitted Diseases, Inc., 1986-89, exec. and med. dir., 1989-2003. Fellow ACP, N.Y. Acad. Medicine; mem. Am. Med. Women's Assn., N.Y. County, N.Y. State Med. Socs.

WALLACE, JULIA DIANE, editor; b. Davenport, Iowa, Dec. 3, 1956; d. Franklin Sherwood and Eleanor Ruth (Pope) W.; m. Doniver Dean Campbell, Aug. 23, 1986; children: Emmaline Livingston Campbell, Eden Jennifer Campbell. BS in Journalism, Northwestern U., 1978. Reporter Norfolk Ledger-Star, Va., 1978-80, Dallas Times Herald, 1980-82; reporter, editor News sect. USA Today, Arlington, Va., 1982-89, mng. editor spl. projects, 1989-92; mng. editor Chgo. Sun-Times, 1992-1996; exec. editor Statesman Jour., Salem, Oreg., 1996—98; mng. editor Ariz. Republic, Phoenix, 1998—2000, Atlanta Jour.-Constitution, 2001—02, editor, 2002—. Mem. Am. Soc. Newspaper Editors (bd. dirs.). Mailing: Atlanta Journal-Constitution PO Box 4689 Atlanta GA 30302*

WALLACE, KIM N., federal agency administrator; b. 1958; m. Robin Vink; children: Ava, Harrison. BA in Govt., U. Tex., Austin; MS in Bus., Johns Hopkins U., Balt. Analyst under chmn. US Senate Budget Com., Washington; legis. aide to Senator George Mitchell US Senate, 1989—94; sr. analyst fin. svcs. Lehman Brothers Inc., Washington, 1994—2008; mng. dir., chief polit. startegist Barclays Capital, Washington, 2008; counselor to sec. US Dept. Treasury, Washington, 2009, asst. sec. for legis. affairs, 2009—. Office: US Dept Treasury 1500 Pennsylvania Ave NW Washington DC 20221 Office Phone: 202-622-1900. Office Fax: 202-622-0534.*

WALLACE, LINDA KAY, mathematics professor; d. John Edward and Marion Sue Wallace. BS, Radford U., 1989, MS, 1991. Educator Prince William County Pub. Sch., Manassas, Va., 1991—98, math. instrnl. specialist, 1998—2001, algebra readiness coord., 2001—06; math. coord. Roanoke City Pub. Schs., Va., 2006—07; ednl. cons. Neufeld Learning Sys. Inc., New London, Ont., Canada. Ednl. cons. Casio, Inc., Dover, NJ, 2004—, Neufeld Learning Sys., New London, Ontario, Canada, 2007—. Mem.: Nat. Coun. Tchrs. Math. (assoc.), Nat. Coun. Suprs. Math. (assoc.), Phi Delta Kappa (assoc.; pres. chpt. 1448 2004—05, Outstanding Student of Yr. 1991). Business E-Mail: iwallace@neufeld.com.

WALLACE, MARK ALEXANDER, social studies educator; b. Pitcairn, Pa., May 27, 1959; s. Algert Donald and Phyllis Wallace; m. Barbara Ann Wallace, July 16, 1983; children: Vincent Algert, Maria Margaret, Matthew Alexander. BS in Edn., Indiana U. Pa., 1981; MA in Edn., U. Pitts., 1987. Tchr. ICM Sch. Bus., Pitts., 1982—85; coord. Learning Ctr. Westmoreland County C.C., Youngwood, Pa., 1983—90; tchr., chair social studies dept. Gateway HS, Monroeville, Pa., 1990—. Bd. dirs. Autism Speak and Walk Cmty., Pitts., 2002—; mem. zoning bd. Pitcairn Zoning Bd., 1990—; bd. dirs. Gateway Sch., Monroeville, 1983—87. Named All-Star Educator, U. Pitts.-Pitts. Post Gazette, 1993; finalist Pa. Tchr. Yr., Pa. Dept. Edn., 2005. Mem.: Nat. Coun. for History Edn. (Pa. State Am. History Tchr. of Yr. 2008), Pa. Coun. for Social Studies. Democrat. Home: 605 12th St Pitcairn PA 15140 Office Phone: 412-373-5741. Business E-Mail: mwallace@gatewayk12.org.

WALLACE, MARK ALLEN, hospital administrator; b. Oklahoma City, Apr. 24, 1953; s. William Howell and Mollie Marie (Godsy) W.; children: Emily, Benjamin. BS, Okla. Bapt. U., 1975; MS, Washington U., St. Louis, 1978. Adminstrv. asst. Bapt. Med. Ctr., Oklahoma City, 1975-77; administrv. resident Meth. Hosp., Houston, 1977-78; asst. v.p. Tex. Meth. Hosp., Houston, 1978-80, v.p., 1980-83, sr. v.p., 1983-89; pres., CEO Tex. Children's Hosp., Houston, 1989—. Adj. instr. Washington U., 1984—; adj. asst. prof. Tex. Womans U., Houston, 1983—; bd. dirs., chmn. fin. com., treas. Greater Houston Hosp. Svc. Corp., 1986-90; bd. trustees, Nat. Assn of Children's Hospitals and Related Institutions Contbr. articles to profl. jours. Chmn. campaign drives United Way, Houston, 1984, 86, corporate walk for Juvenile Diabetes Found. Walk to Cure Diabetes, 2000; class chmn. alumni vision for excellence and growth for future campaigns Okla. Bapt. U., 1982; bd. dirs. Tex. Gulf Coast chpt. March of Dimes Birth Defects Found., 1985-91, Zoological Society of Houston, Sam Houston Area Coun. of the Boy Scouts, World Health & Golf Assn., Greater Houston Partnership (vice-chair Flood Control Task Force), Greater Houston Community Found.; bd. governors, Houston Forum; active mem. Second Baptist Ch., Houston, Young Presidents' Orgn., and Houston Country Club Recipient Emerging Leaders in Health Care award Healthcare Forum Mag. and Korn/Ferry Internat., 1987. Fellow Am. Coll. Healthcare Execs. (com. on membership, subcom. on recruitment 1990—, Robert S. Hudgens Meml. award, 1992, Young Healthcare Exec. of Yr., 1992); mem. Am. Heart Assn. (med. adv. com. 1990-91), Healthcare Forum (pres. emerging leaders alumni group 1988-91), Am. Hosp. Assn., Tex. Hosp. Assn. (bd. dirs., bd. dirs. polit. action com. 1988—, chmn. bd. trustees, 1998-1999), Greater Houston Hosp. Coun. (bd. dirs. 1991—, chmn. 1993-1994), Houston Area Health Care Coalition, Childrens Hosp. Assn. Tex. (pres. 1992—, chmn. 2002-2003), Tex. Gulf Coast Arthritis Found. (bd. dirs. 1990-91). Republican. Baptist. Office: Tex Children's Hosp 6621 Fannin St Houston TX 77030 also: PO Box 300630 Houston TX 77230-0630*

WALLACE, MARYJEAN ELIZABETH, science educator; b. Cedar Grove, NJ, July 19, 1963; d. Albert Joseph and Jean Wallace. BS summa cum laude, Adelphi U., Garden City, NY, 1985; MA summa cum laude, Ind. State U., Terre Haute, Ind., 1987. Cert. elem. tchr. NJ, secondary edn. earth sci. tchr. NJ, ednl. supr. NJ. Sci. tchr. Meml. Mid. Sch., Cedar Grove, NJ, 1987—91, Burnet Mid. Sch., Union Township, NJ, 1991—2000, Briarcliff Mid. Sch., Mountain Lakes, NJ, 2000—. Eucharistic min. Notre Dame of Mt. Carmel Ch., Cedar Knolls, NJ, 2002—. Named one of Outstanding Softball Players in NJ, Star Ledger, 2000; named to Athletic Hall of Fame, Adelphi U., 2000; Postgraduate scholar, NCAA, 1985. Mem.: NSTA, NJ Sci. Tchrs. Assn., Mountain Lakes Edn. Assn. (v.p. and membership chmn. 2005—), Phi Kappa Pi, Delta Tau Alpha, Kappa Delta Phi. Roman Catholic. Avocations: photography, travel, camping, hiking. Office: Briarcliff Mid Sch 93 Briarcliff Rd Mountain Lakes NJ 07046 Personal E-mail: mjwallace15@optonline.net. Business E-Mail: mwallace@mtlakes.org.

WALLACE, MATTHEW WALKER, retired entrepreneur; b. Salt Lake City, Jan. 7, 1924; s. John McChrystal and Glenn (Walker) W.; m. Constance Cone, June 22, 1954 (dec. May 1980); children: Matthew, Anne; m. Susan Struggles, July 11, 1981. BA, Stanford U., 1947; MCP, MIT, 1950. Prin. planner Boston City Planning Bd., 1950-53; v.p. Nat. Planning and Rsch., Inc., Boston, 1953-55; pres. Wallace-McConaughy Corp., Salt Lake City, 1955-69, Ariz. Ranch & Metals Co., Scottsdale, 1969-84, Idaho TV Corp., Channel 6, ABC, Boise, 1976-78; chmn. Wallace Assocs., Inc., Salt Lake City, 1969-98. Dir. 1st Interstate Bank, Salt Lake City, 1956—90, Wells Fargo Bank Cmty. Bd., 2000, Arnold Machinery Co., 1988—, Roosevelt Hot Springs Corp., 1978—; mem. adv. bd. Mountain Bell Tel. Co., Salt Lake City, 1975—85. Pres. Downtown Planning Assn., Salt Lake City, 1970; chmn. Utah State Arts Coun., Salt Lake City, 1977; chmn. hon. bd. Planned Parenthood; humanities and scis. coun. Stanford U., athletics bd., alumni assn. exec. bd., bd. vis. sch. law; nat. adv. bd. U. Utah Coll. Bus.; lifetime dir. Utah Symphony Orch.; chmn. arts, adv. coun. and Capital Campaign Westminster Coll. Lt. (j.g.) USN, 1944-46, PTO. Recipient Contbn. award Downtown Planning Assn,. 1977, Gov.'s award in the Arts, 1991, Utah Nat. Guard Minuteman award, 1994. Mem. Am. Inst. Cert. Planners (charter), Am. Arts Alliance (bd. dirs. 1991), Alta Club (dir.), Cottonwood Club (pres. 1959-63), Salt Lake Country Club (dir.), Desert Island Golf and Country Club (Rancho Mirage, Calif.), Flat Rock Club (Island Park., Idaho pres. 1994-98), Phi Kappa Phi (hon., life). Home: 2230 E Parleys Terr Salt Lake City UT 84109-1530 E-mail: mww@xmission.com.

WALLACE, MICHAEL J., energy executive; m. Victoria Lynn Wallace; 2 children. BSEE, Marquette U., Milw.; MBA, U. Chgo. Prin. engr. Unicom/ComEd, Chgo., 1974—79, plant mgr., 1979—82, exec., mgr., 1982—90, v.p., 1990—93, sr. v.p., chief nuc. officer, 1993—99; founder, mng. dir. Barrington Energy Partners, LLC, 1998—2002; pres. Constellation Generation Group, LLC, Annapolis, Md., 2002—08, CEO, 2005—08; exec. v.p. Constellation Energy Group, Inc., Balt., 2004—08, vice chmn., COO, 2008—; chmn. UniStar Nuc. Energy, 2007—. Mem. new plant oversight steering com. Nuc. Energy Inst., chmn. security working group; chmn. Dept. Homeland Security's Nat. Infrastructure Protection Plan Nuc. Sector Coord. Coun., Partnership Critical Infrastructure Security; dir. Nuc. Electric Ins. Ltd. Active Boy Scouts America, Big Shoulders Fund Chgo., Cath. Charities Md., Ocean Race Chesapeake. Officer nuc. submarine force USN. Decorated Navy Achievement Medal. Avocation: sailing. Office: Constellation Energy 750 E Pratt St Baltimore MD 21202 Office Phone: 410-783-2800.

WALLACE, MICHELE, writer, educator; b. NYC, Jan. 4, 1952; d. Robert Earl Wallace, Burdette (Stepfather) and Faith Ringgold; BA, CCNY, 1974, MA in English, 1990; PhD in Cinema Studies, NYU, 1998. Asst. prof. English CUNY, 1989—91; assoc. prof. English, women's studies and film CUNY and CUNY Grad. Ctr., 1991—97, prof., 1998—. Pres. Art Without Walls, 1974; vis. prof. African studies Conwell U., Ithaca, NY, 2004—06. Author: Black Macho and the Myth of the Superwoman, 1979, Invisibility Blues: Pop to Theory, 1990, 2008, Black Popular Culture, 1992, Dark Designs and Visual Culture, 2004 (CCNY Journalism Alumni Achievement award, 2008); columnist: The Village Voice, 1996; editor: Women in Art, 1971; mem. editl. bd.: Social Identities, Souls; contbr. to newspapers and popular mags. including Ms., The Village Voice, The Nation, The N.Y. Times, Art Forum, Art In America; editor-at-large: Essence Mag., 1983. Founding mem. Nat. Black Feminist Orgn., 1974; pres. Women Students and Artists for Black Art Liberation, 1970—76. Mem.: PEN, MLA, Oscar Micheaux Soc., Soc. Cinema Studies, Am. Studies Assn., Phi Beta Kappa. Office Phone: 212-650-6367. Personal E-mail: olympiax@aol.com. Business E-Mail: mwallace@ccny.cuny.edu.

WALLACE, MIKE (MYRON LEON WALLACE), newscaster, television personality; b. Brookline, Mass., May 9, 1918; s. Frank and Zina (Sharfman) Wallace; m. Lorraine Perigord, 1955 (div. 1983); children: Peter(dec.), Christopher, Pauline; m. Mary Yates, June 28, 1986. BA, U. Mich., 1939; LHD (hon.), U. Mass., 1978; LLD (hon.), U. Mich., 1987, U. Pa., 1989. Associated with radio, 1939—; TV, 1946—; commentator CBS-TV, 1951—55, TV interviewer, reporter, 1951—; CBS news corr., 1963—; corr., co-editor 60 Minutes, CBS, 1968—. Numerous TV appearances include Night Beat, 1956—57, The Mike Wallace Interview, 1957—60, anchor Biography, 1959—61 (George Foster Peabody award, 1962), CBS Reports: 1968, 1993, presenter Mike Wallace Then and Now, 1990, co-anchor Watergate: The Secret Story, 1992, In the Killing Field of America, 1995 (Robert F. Kennedy Journalism award grand prize and TV first prize, 1996, George Foster Peabody award, 1995); author: Mike Wallace Asks, 1958; co-author (with Gary Paul Gates): (memoir) Close Encounter, 1984, Between You and Me: A Memoir, 2005. Naval comm. officer USN, 1943—46. Recipient Robert Sherwood award, 19 ATVAS Emmy awards, Disting. Achievement award, U. So. Calif. Sch. Journalism, Robert F. Kennedy Journalism award in Internat. broadcast category, George Foster Peabody award for 60 Minutes: The CIA's Cocaine, 1993, Alfred I. DuPont Columbia U. Journalism award, 1972, 1983, 1999, Carr Van Anda award, 1977, Thomas Hart Benton award, 1978, Paul White award, Radio/TV News Directors Assn., 1991, Lifetime Achievement Emmy, 1993, Fred Friendly First Amendment award, Quinnipiac Coll., 2002, honored for lifetime contribution to radio and TV, Chgo. Mus. Broadcast Comm., 1989; named Broadcaster of Yr., Internat. Radio and TV Sco., 1993; named to TV Acad. Hall of Fame, 1991. Mem.: Soc. Profl. Jounalists, Century Assocs., Sigma Delta Chi.

WALLACE, NATHANIEL OWEN, English language educator; b. Charleston, SC, July 26, 1948; s. James Irvin Sr. and Bella Goldin W.; m. Janet Lynne Kozachek, May 26, 1979. AB in French, Classics, Coll. Charleston, 1969; MA in Comparative Lit., Rutgers U., 1975, PhD in Comparative Lit., 1979. Instr. Rutgers U., New Brunswick, N.J., 1974-77, Rider Coll., 1978-80; lectr. Brit. and Am. lit. Hebei U., Baoding, China, 1981-82, Jilin U., Changchun, China, 1982-83; lectr. English and comparative lit. Beijing (China) Normal U., 1983-85; lectr. English Univ. Coll.-European Divsn. U. Md., 1985-87; asst. prof. English Del. Valley Coll., 1988-91; from asst. prof. English to prof. SC State U., Orangeburg, 1991—2003, prof. English, 2003—. Grad. student rep. bd. trustees, Rutgers U., 1975-76; mem. faculty coun. Del. Valley Coll., 1990-91; rsch. com. S.C. State U., 1991-93; chmn. Internat. Programs comm., 1994-98; vis. lectr. U. Konstanz, Germany, 1994-95, session chair; papers presented at various confs. Contbr. articles to profl. jours.; exhibited photography in various exhbns. NEH fellow, 1994-95, Camargo fellow, Cassis, France, 1998; Walter C. Russell grad. scholar Rutgers U.; NEH summer programs, 1980, 87, 89, 90. Mem. Am. Comparative Lit. Assn., So. Comparative Lit. Assn., Renaissance Soc. Am., South Atlantic MLA, Book Prize Com., Soc. Am. Mosaic Artists (sec. 1999-2002). Democrat. Jewish. Avocations: photography, travel, gardening. Office: SC State U Dept English and Modern Langs Orangeburg SC 29117-0001

WALLACE, NICOLLE (NICOLLE DEVENISH), former federal official; b. Orinda, Calif., 1972; m. Mark Wallace. BA, U. Calif., Berkley; MA, Medill Sch. of Journalism, Northwestern U. With Calif. Assembly Rep. Caucus, 1997—98, Calif. Rep. Party, 1998; former press aide to CEO Grassroots.com; former press secretary to Gov. Jeb Bush State of Fla.; former communications dir. Fla. State Tech. Office; spl. asst. to Pres. & dir. of media affairs The White House, Washington, 2000—05, asst. to Pres. for comm., 2005—06; polit. cons. CBS News, 2006—; sr. adv. John McCain Presdl. Campaign, 2008—. Communications dir. Bush-Cheney '04 campaign.*

WALLACE, NORA ANN, lawyer; b. Phila., May 24, 1951; AB, Vassar Coll., 1973; JD cum laude, Harvard U., 1976. Bar: N.Y. 1977. Mem. Willkie Farr & Gallagher, NYC. Trustee Vassar Coll., Bklyn. Acad. Music, Bklyn. Acad. Music Endowment Trust; bd. dirs. Joseph Collins Found. Office: Willkie Farr & Gallagher 787 7th Ave New York NY 10019-6099

WALLACE, PAUL J., lawyer; s. Joe and M. Joyce Wallace; m. Brenda C. Baehl; 1 child, Kaitlin Rinehart. BA in Acctg., Ind. U., 1975, MBA in Fin. Econs., 1979, JD, 1979. Bar: United States Supreme Ct., United States Tax Ct., United States Ct. of Appeals, 7th Circuit, United States Dist. Ct., So. Dist. of Ind., Ind. Supreme Ct. Ptnr. Bowers, Harrison, Kent & Miller, Evansville, Ind., 1979—86, Jones & Wallace, Evansville, Ind., 1987—90; equity ptnr. Bowers Harrison LLP, Evansville, Ind., 1990—2008; founding ptnr. Jones Wallace LLC, 2009—. Mem. Ind. Corp. Law Survey Commn., Lawyer Pilots Bar Assn.; counsel Area Plan Commn. of Evansville and Vanderburgh County, Ind., 1982—87; lectr. U. Evansville Bus. Orgn., 1983—84; dir. Evansville Parks Found., 1994—95; VIP chmn. 1992 Arthritis Found. Telethon Leadership Evansville; dir. St. Mary's Hosp. Found. Recipient Sagamore of the Wabash, 1987, 1999. Master: Ind. State Bar Assn. (chair taxation sect. 1996—97, mem. aviation law com., mem. legal ethics com.); mem.: Evansville Bar Assn., ABA (mem. health car law sect.), United States Golf Assn., Evansville Country Club, Victoria Nat. Golf Club. Office: Bowers Harrison LLP 25 NW Riverside Dr 2d Fl Evansville IN 47708 also: Jones Wallace LLC 420 Main St Ste 1600 Evansville IN 47708 Office Phone: 812-426-1231, 812-402-1600. Office Fax: 812-464-3676. Business E-Mail: pjw@bowersharrison.com, pwallace@pajwallace.com.

WALLACE, PAULA S., academic administrator; married; 4 children. BA, Furman U.; MEd, EdS, Ga. State U.; LLD (hon.), Gonzaga U. Co-founder Savannah Coll. Art and Design, 1979, pres., 2000—. Author: (children's books) World of Birthdays, World of Food, World of Holidays, World of Sports, several others. Mem. Skidaway Island United Meth. Ch., Savannah, Ga. Film and Videotape Commn., Ga. C. of C.; bd. dirs. B. B. & T. Bank, Nat. Mus. Women in the Arts. Recipient Oglethorpe Bus. and Profl. Women award, James T. Deason Human Rels. award, Principled Leadership award southeast Ernst & Young, 2004; named Outstanding Young Woman of Am., Ky. Col., One of Most Influential Georgians Ga. Trend mag., 2005; named to Savannah Bus. Hall of Fame, Chevalier dan l'Ordre des Palmes Academique, 2005. Office: Savannah Coll Art and Design PO Box 3146 Savannah GA 31402-3146 Office Phone: 912-525-5200.

WALLACE, PETER MARSDEN, radio personality and producer, commentator, writer; b. Parkersburg, W.Va., Aug. 15, 1954; s. Aldred Pruden and Margaret Anne (Yoak) Wallace; m. Bonita Lucille Shock, Oct. 15, 1977 (div. 2005); children: Meredith Anne, Matthew Edward. AB in journalism/advt., Marshall U., 1976; ThM, Dallas Theol. Sem., 1984. Editor W.Va. Hillbilly, Richwood, W.Va., 1976-79; editl. asst. Dallas Theol. Sem., 1981-84; editl. mgr. Walk Thru the Bible Ministries, Atlanta, 1984-85, editl. dir., 1985-90; sr. copywriter & broadcast prodr. Larry Smith & Associates, Atlanta, 1990—2001; exec. prodr. Day 1 radio program (formerly The Protestant Hour), Atlanta, 2001—, host, 2005—; v.p. Alliance for Christian Media. Mem. Faith & Values Media Mem. Coun. Author: What Jesus Is Saying to You Today, 1994, What the Psalmist is Saying to You Today, 1994, What God Is Saying to You Today, 1995, Psalms for Today, 2001, TruthQuest Devotional Journal, 2002, Old Testament for Today, 2003, Out of the Quiet: Responding to God's Whispered Invitations, 2004, Living Loved: Knowing Jesus as the Lover of Your Soul, 2007; co-author: The West Virginia Picture Book, 1979; contbr. articles to religious magazines; editor: The Daily Walk Bible, 1987. Recipient Outstanding Young Men Am. Award, US Jaycees, 1984. Democrat. Avocations: reading, camping, travel. Office: Day 1 Ste 300 644 W Peachtree St Atlanta GA 30308-1925 Home: 3972 Briarcliff Rd NE Atlanta GA 30345-2648 Office Phone: 404-815-9110. Office Fax: 404-815-0495. E-mail: pwallace@day1.net.

WALLACE, R. H., JR., lawyer; b. Livingston, Tex., Oct. 9, 1943; BS, U.S. Naval Acad., 1966; JD, Baylor U., 1973. Bar: Tex. 1973, US Dist. Ct. (no., so., ea. we. dist. Tex.), US Ct. Appeals (5th cir.), US Supreme Ct.; cert. civil trial & criminal law Tex. Bd. Legal Specialization. Atty. criminal div., appellate sect. US Dept. Justice, 1973—76; asst. U.S. atty. US Dept. Justice, No. Dist. Tex., 1976-84, dep. chief criminal div., 1983-84; mem., comml. litig. practice Shannon Gracey Ratliff & Miller LLP, Fort Worth. Fellow Am. Coll. Trial Lawyers; life fellow Tex. Bar Found.; mem. ABA, State Bar Tex. Office: Shannon Gracey Ratliff & Miller Ste 3800 777 Main St Fort Worth TX 76102 Office Phone: 817-336-9333. Office Fax: 817-336-3735. Business E-Mail: rhwallace@shannongracey.com.

WALLACE, RASHEED, professional basketball player; b. Sept. 17, 1974; s. Jackie Wallace; m. Fatima Sanders, July 18; 3 children. Attended, U. N.C. Forward Washington Wizards, 1995—96, Portland Trailblazers, 1996—2004, Atlanta Hawks, 2004, Detroit Pistons, 2004—09, Boston Celtics, 2009—. Co-founder Urban Life Music; CEO Direct Hit Studios, Phila. Founder Rasheed A. Wallace Found., Phila., 1997. Named to We. Conf. All-Star Team, NBA, 2000, 2001, Ea. Conf. All-Star Team, 2006, 2008. Achievements include being a member of the NBA Championship winning Detroit Pistons, 2004. Office: Boston Celtics 226 Causeway St 4th Fl Boston MA 02114*

WALLACE, RICHARD EDWARD, JR., lawyer; b. Boston, Nov. 24, 1954; s. Richard E. and Irene Webster (Howard) W.; m. Anne Barnes Secor, Jan. 11, 1956; children: James K., Madeline S., Abbey P., Samuel B. BA magna cum laude, U. Mass., 1978; JD, Harvard U., 1982. Bar: DC 1982, Md. 1988, US Dist. Ct. DC 1982, US Dist. Ct. Md. 1987, US Dist. Ct. (so. dist.) Tex. 1996, US Ct. Appeals (DC cir.) 1988, US Ct. Appeals (4th cir.) 1990, US Ct. Appeals (2nd & 5th cir.), US Supreme Ct., 1997, US Tax Ct., DC Ct. Appeals, Md. Ct. Appeals. Assoc. White & Case, Washington, 1982-85, Kaye, Scholer, Fierman, Hays & Handler, Washington, 1985-90, ptnr., 1991-92, Howrey & Simon, Wash., 1992—, Wallace King Domike & Branson, PLLC, Wash., DC. Mem. faculty Internat. Law Inst., Washington, 1987—. Co-author: Legal Rights and Mental Health Care, 1983; contbr. articles to profl. jours. Bd. dirs. Homeless Persons Representation Project, Balt., 1989-91; co-counsel D. C. Prisoners Legal Assistance Project, Washington, 1994—; mem. Mental Patients Advocacy Project, Northampton, Mass., 1976-79. Recipient Am.'s Leading Lawyers for Bus., Chambers USA. Fellow Chartered Inst. Arbitrators; mem. ABA (internat. law sect. 1982—), Am. Arbitration Assn. (panel arbitrators 1987—), D.C. Bar Assn., Md. Bar Assn. Avocations: pilot, hockey, skiing, golf. Office: Wallace King Domike & Reiskin PLLC 2900 K St NW Washington DC 20007 Office Phone: 202-204-3710, 202-204-1000. Office Fax: 202-204-1001. Business E-Mail: rwallace@wallaceking.com.

WALLACE, RICHARD LE ROY WAYNE, language educator; b. Kan. City, Kans., Jan. 1, 1975; s. Pamela Ann Yeager-Walker and Robert Walker (Stepfather). ABD, Capella U., Minn., 2006—. Spanish instr. Crowder Coll., Neosho, Mo., 2003. Home: 434 N Moffet Joplin MO 64801 Office: Crowder Coll 601 Laclede Neosho MO 64850

WALLACE, RICHARD P., computer company executive; BSEE, Univ. Mich.; M engring. mgmt., Santa Clara Univ. Engring. positions Ultratech Stepper, Cypress Semiconductor; mgmt. positions KLA-Tencor Corp., 1988—95, v.p., gen. mgr. Wisard San Jose, Calif., 1995—98, v.p., gen. mgr. Mirage group, 1998—99, group v.p., 1999—2000, exec. v.p., 2000—05, CEO, 2006—, pres., COO, 2005, pres., 2008—. Bd. dirs. KLA-Tencor Corp., 2006—. Office: KLA-Tencor Corp 160 Rio Robles San Jose CA 95134 Office Phone: 408-875-3000. Office Fax: 408-434-4270.*

WALLACE, ROBERT BRUCE, retired surgeon; b. Washington, Apr. 12, 1931; s. William B. and Anne E. W.; m. Betty Jean Newel, Aug. 28, 1955; children: Robert B., Anne E., Barbara N. BA, Columbia U., 1953, MD, 1957. Diplomate Am. Bd. Surgery, Am. Bd. Thoracic Surgery. Chmn., prof. dept. surgery Mayo Clinic and Mayo Med. Sch., Rochester, Minn.; bd. govs. Mayo Clinic, 1968-79; prof. dept. surgery Georgetown U. Sch. Medicine, 1980—96, chmn. dept. surgery, 1980-95, surgeon and chief univ. hosp., 1980-95; retired, 1996. Trustee Mayo Found., 1970—78; chmn. sci. adv. com. LeDucq Found., 2000—05. Recipient Disting. Alumni award, Mayo Clinic, 2008. Mem. ACS (bd. govs. 1975-79), Am. Surg. Assn., Soc. Clin. Surgery, Am. Assn. Thoracic Surgery (pres. 1994-95), Internat. Cardiovascular Soc., Soc. Vascular Surgery, Thoracic Surgery Found. Rsch. & Edn. (bd. dirs. 1993-2001, pres. 1998-2001). Home: 1322 Darnall Dr Mc Lean VA 22101-3009 E-mail: rbwallace@cox.net.

WALLACE, ROBERT BRUCE, neuroscience educator; b. Stoneham, Mass., Jan. 16, 1937; s. William Sheperd Wallace and Dorothy (Constance) Gilbert. AB, Boston U., 1960, AM, 1961, PhD, 1966. Rsch. assoc. MIT, Cambridge, 1966-68; lectr. psychology Boston U., 1967-68; asst. prof. U. Hartford, West Hartford, Conn., 1968-72, assoc. prof., 1972-80, dir. neurosci. program, 1976-99, prof. psychology and biology, 1980-99, prof. psychology and biology emeritus, 2000—, chmn. dept. psychology, 1986-91, chmn. dept. biology, 1994-99; rsch. assoc. Inst. of Living, Hartford, Conn., 1971-99. Cons. Purdue Univ. Dept. Biological Scis., West Lafayette, Ind., 1968-70, State of Conn., Personnel Examining Com., Hartford, 1971, 74. Author: Neural Tissue Transplantation Research, 1983, Neural Transplantation and Regeneration, 1985; contbr. articles, chapters, abstracts to profl. jours. Site review group Nat. Cancer Inst., 1978. Mem. Soc. for Neuroscience, Am. Assn. Anatomists, N.Y. Acad. Sciences, Sigma Xi. Republican. Congregationalist. Avocations: reading, writing. Personal E-mail: rwall35618@aol.com.

WALLACE, ROBERT BRUCE, lawyer, educator; b. Washington, Apr. 23, 1944; s. Thomas Edward and Mary (Beeler) W.; m. Jane Susan Johnson, Sept. 13, 1969; children: Mead Alison, Jared Corwin. BA in Econs., George Washington U., 1966, JD, 1970. Bar: Va. 1970, US Ct. Appeals (6th cir.) 1970, DC 1971, US Dist. Ct. DC 1971, US Ct. Appeals (10th and DC cirs.) 1971, US Ct. Appeals (4th cir.) 1975, US Supreme Ct. 1975, US Dist. Ct. (ea. dist.) Va. 1974, US Dist. Ct. (we. dist.) Va. 1975, US Ct. Appeals (5th cir.) 1979, US Dist. Ct., Md., US Ct. Appeals (2nd, 3rd, 9th and fed. cir.), US Ct. Appeals (DC), Va. Supreme Ct. Atty. Office of Gen. Counsel, EEOC, Washington, 1970-71; atty., project dir. Washington Lawyers Com. for Civil Rights Under Law, 1971-74, atty., nat. coordinator, 1974-77, mem. exec. com., 1982—; assoc. Surrey & Morse, Washington, 1977-80, ptnr., 1980-86, Wilson, Elser, Moskowitz, Edelman & Dicker, Washington, 1986-89, regional mng. ptnr., 1990—. Adj. prof. law Cath. U., Washington, 1974-77, Howard U., 1975-76; guest lectr. George Washington U. Sch. Law, 1976, U. Va. Sch. Law, 1970. Author: (chpt.) Conflict of Law-Reinsurance IBA, 1988; contbr. articles to profl. jours. 1st lt. USAR, 1966-72. Fellow: Chartered Inst. Arbitrators; mem.: ABA (mem. internat. law, bus. law, labor and employment law, antitrust law, and tort and insurance practice sect, construction industry forum), Am. Arbitration Assn., Nat. and Internat. Panel of Arbitrators, Washington Bd. Trade, Am. Soc. Internat. Law, DC Bar Assn., Va. Bar Assn., Internat. Bar Assn., Belle Haven Country Club. Democrat. Roman Catholic. Avocations: tennis, golf, sailing. Home: 1113 Prince St Alexandria VA 22314-2934 Office: 700 11th St Suite 400 Washington DC 20001 Office Phone: 202-626-7660 7667. Office Fax: 202-628-3606. E-mail: wallacer@wemed.com.

WALLACE, ROBERT JAMES, mathematics and science educator; b. Chgo., Sept. 1, 1942; s. James H. and Maryella (Wilder) W.; m. Amy S. Briskin, Nov. 10, 1991; children: Lisa, Brenda. BS, No. Ill. U., 1964, MA, 1970, Princeton U., PhD, 1975. Geologist CUNY, Bklyn., 1972-80; v.p. Audio Vistas, Inc., NYC, 1980-85; computer cons. N.Y.C. Bd. Edn., 1984-86; computing chair St. Ann's Sch., Bklyn., 1985-93; cons. sci., math. The Harbor Acad. for Math./Sci., NYC, 1985—. Cons. Packer Collegiate Inst., Bklyn., 1987-93; cons. educator Metrotech, Bklyn., 1988-90. Author: Geology Lab Manual, 1980, New York City-Wide Test Results, 1986. Adventure facilitator Harbor for Girls and Boys, N.Y.C., 1990—. Mem. AAAS, Nat. Sci. Tchrs. Assn., Sigma Xi. Avocations: tennis, bicycling, roller-skating. Office: Harbor for Girls and Boys 1 E 104th St New York NY 10029-4402 Address: 340 E 80th St Apt 1-f New York NY 10021-0928

WALLACE, RUSTY, sportscaster, retired race car driver; b. St. Louis, Aug. 14, 1956; m. Patti Wallace; children: Greg, Katie, Stephen. Stock race car driver Miller Genuine Draft team, 1980—2005; analyst, IndyCar series ESPN, 2005—06, analyst, NASCAR series, 2006—. Named winner, NASCAR Winston Cup, 1989, Miller High Life, 1989, Champion Spark Plug 400, 1989, Bud at the Glen, 1989, Valleydale Meats 500, 1989, 1991, Goodwrench 500, 1989, 1993, 1994, Pontiac Excitement 400, 1989, 1997, Coca-Cola 600, 1990, Banquet Frozen Foods 300, 1990, Miller Genuine Draft 500, 1991, Miller Genuine Draft 400, 1992, 1993, 1st Union 400, 1993, Slick 50 300, 1993, Tyson/Holly Farms 400, 1993, AC Delco 500, 1993, Hooters 500, 1993, Split Fire 500, 1993, 1994, Hanes 500, 1993, 1994, 1995, Food City 500, 1993, 1999, 2000, UAW-GM 500, 1994, Bud 500, 1994, Miller 400, 1994, 1995, 1996, Goody's 500, Martinsville, 1994, 1996, Goody's 500, Bristol, 1994, 1996, Save Mark 300, 1996, Miller 500, 1996, Dura Lube/KMart 500, 1998, Pepsi 400, 2000, Penn. 500, 2000, Goracing.com 500, 2000, NAPA Auto Parts 500, 2001, Advanced Auto Parts 500, 2004; named one of Nascar's 50 greatest drivers, 1998. Office: ESPN ESPN Plz Bristol CT 06010

WALLACE, STEWART F., composer; b. Phila., Nov. 21, 1960; s. Sidney and Marsha Joan Wallace. BA, U. Tex., 1982. Composer: (operas) Where's Dick?, 1989, Kabbalah 1989, Harvey Milk, 1995, Hopper's Wife, 1997, Supermax, 2001, Yiddisher Teddy Bears, 2001, The Bonesetter's Daughter, 2008; (orchestral works) Gorilla in a Cage, 1997, Book of Five for Icebreaker and Orchestra, 2002, Skvera for Electric Guitar and Orchestra, 2004, (ballet) Peter Pan, 2000, (film scores) Afraid of Everything, 1999, Seven Days, 2004, Book of Love, 2004; also one-act operas, (opera 3 acts) Houston Grand Opera, San Francisco Opera, NYC Opera, Opera of City of Dortnmund, Germany, (chamberwork) The Cheese and the Worms for Bagpipes, Percussion and Piano, 1999, other pieces; premiered with Bochum (Germany) Symphony, 1997, Nat. Symphony Orch., 1999, Sundance Film Festival. Recipient Young Composer award ASCAP, 1987, 88, 89; Composer's fellow Nat. Endowment for the Arts, 1988-89, N.Y. Found. for the Arts, 1990, commissioning grantee Readers Digest, 1995, Inst. on the Arts and Civic Dialogue Harvard. U., 1998. Office: Apt 2 458 Broadway New York NY 10013-5804*

WALLACE, TERESA LYNN, art educator; b. Springfield, Mo., Dec. 8, 1962; d. Joe Mack and Lanora Nadine Sanders; m. Richard Everett Wallace, June 6, 1986; children: Hannah Kate, Allison Rae. BA in Elem Edn., Coll. Ozarks, 1986; art cert., Southwest Mo. State U., 2002. Art tchr. Couch Sch., Myrtle, Mo., 1999—2001, Alton Elem. Sch., Alton, Mo., 2002—. V.p. Parent Tchr. Orgn., Alton, 1999; co-creator art scholarships, Alton, 2001. Prin. works include (paintings) The Wailing Wall, Harlin Mus., 1997—, French City Sidewalks, 2001, Mexico, 2003, Mexico Moment, 2004, Open Air Market, Art Show, 1998—, Visions of China, West Plains, Mo., 2000—. Leader PTO, Youth Cmty. Betterment, Alton, 1999. Outstanding Achievement honoree, Internat. Reading Assn., 2005. Baptist. Avocations: flute, reading. Office Phone: 417-778-7217. Personal E-mail: twallace001@centurytel.net.

WALLACE, THOMAS C., editor, publishing executive; b. Vienna, Dec. 13, 1933; came to U.S., 1938; s. Don and Julia (Baer) W.; m. Lois Kahn, July 19, 1962 (div. May 2000); 1 son, George Baer; m. Barbara Shortt, Nov. 12, 2000. Grad., Peddie Sch., 1951; BA, Yale U., 1955, MA in History, 1957. Editor G.P. Putnam Sons, NYC, 1959-63; with Holt, Rinehart & Winston, NYC, 1963-81, editor-in-chief gen. books divsn., 1968-81; v.p., sr. editor Simon and Schuster, NYC, 1981; editor W.W. Norton, NYC, 1982-87; v.p. Wallace Lit. Agy., NYC, 1987-98; pres. T. C. Wallace Agy., NYC, 1998—. Bd. dirs. Roger Klein Found. Mem. PEN, Yale Club, Century Assn. (N.Y.C.). Home and Office: 2 S End Ave Apt 4M New York NY 10280 Office Phone: 212-678-4330. Personal E-mail: tcwallace2@aol.com.

WALLACE, TIMOTHY R., manufacturing executive; b. 1954; Grad., So. Meth. U., 1975. Joined Trinity Industries, 1975, v.p., 1984, sr. v.p., 1989, COO railcars and containers segment, chmn., pres., CEO, 1996—. Bd. dirs. VIAD Corp., Phoenix. Office: Trinity Industries 2525 Stemmon Freeway Dallas TX 75207

WALLACE, WALTER L., retired sociologist, educator; b. Washington, Aug. 21, 1927; s. Walter L. and Rosa Belle (Boisseau) W.; children: Jeffrey Richard, Robin Claire, Jennifer Rose. BA, Columbia U., 1954; MA, Atlanta U., 1955; PhD, U. Chgo., 1963. Instr. Spelman Coll., Atlanta U., 1955—57; from lectr. to prof. sociology Northwestern U., Evanston, Ill., 1963—71; prof. sociology Princeton U., 1971—2001, prof. emeritus, 2001—. Staff sociologist Russell Sage Found., N.Y.C., 1969-77, vis. scholar, 1968; fellow Ctr. for Advanced Study in Behavioral Scis., Stanford, Calif., 1974-75. Author: Student Culture, 1966, Logic of Science in Sociology, 1971, (with James E. Conyers) Black Elected Officials, 1975, Principles of Scientific Sociology, 1983, A Weberian Theory of Human Society, 1994, The Future of Ethnicity, Race, and Nationality, 1997, Malthus, Darwin, Durkheim, Marx, Weber, Ibn Khaldun: On Human Species Survival, 2009; editor, author: Sociological Theory, 1969; mem. social scis. adv. com. World Book, 1977-94; mem. editl. bd. Social Forces, 1984-87, Am. Sociologist, 1988-91, Sociol. Quar., 1989-92, Am. Sociol. Rev., 1997-2000, Sociol. Theory, 2000-03. Mem. exec. com. Assembly of Behavioral and Social Scis. Nat. Rsch. Coun., 1974-77. With AUS, 1950-52. Mem. Am. Sociol. Assn. (council 1971-74, theory sect. 1988—), Sociol. Rsch. Assn. Office: Princeton U Dept Sociology Princeton NJ 08544-0001 Office Phone: 609-258-4744. Business E-Mail: wwallace@princeton.edu.

WALLACE, WILLIAM S., bank executive; BS in Math., U. Vt., Burlington, 1984. Programmer/analyst GE Aerospace, Valley Forge, Pa., mgmt. positions; with GE Advanced Concepts Ctr.; head software devel. program Bank One, 1993—99; CIO card svcs. Bank One (merged with JP Morgan Chase), 1999—2004; head partnership mgmt. bus. JP Morgan Chase & Co., 2004, pres. mass affluent bus. divsn. Mem. bd. advisors Coll. Engring. and Math. Scis., U. Vt. Office: JP Morgan Chase & Co 270 Park Ave New York NY 10017*

WALLACH, ALAN, art historian, educator; b. Bklyn., June 8, 1942; s. Israel and Vivian (Esner) W.; m. Phyllis Rosenzweig, Jan. 3, 1988. BA in Math., Columbia U., 1963, MA, 1965, PhD, 1973. Assoc. prof. Kean Coll., Union, NJ, 1974-89; Ralph H. Wark prof. art and art history, prof. Am. studies Coll. William and Mary, Williamsburg, Va., 1989—. Vis. prof. UCLA, 1982-83, Stanford (Calif.) U., 1987, CUNY, 1988, U. Mich., 1989; disting. vis. prof. U. Del., 2006; disting vice prof., Clark Instn. and Williams Coll. FACC, 2008, co-curator Nat. Mus. Am. Art, Washington, 1991-94. Author: (with William Truettner) Thomas Cole: Landscape into History, 1994; Exhibiting Contradiction: Essays on the Art Museum in the United States, 1998; mem. editl. bd. Am. Quar., 2000-03; contbr. articles to profl. jours. Mem. Am. Studies Assn. (bd. mng. editors, 2000-03), Coll. Art Assn. (bd. dirs. 1996-2000, Disting. Tng. Art History award, 2007), Assn. Art Historians. Home: 2009 Belmont Rd NW Washington DC 20009-5449 Office: Coll William and Mary Dept Art and Art History Williamsburg VA 23187-8795 Office Phone: 757-221-2530. Business E-Mail: axwall@wm.edu.

WALLACH, ANNE JACKSON See JACKSON, ANNE

WALLACH, ELI, actor; b. Bklyn., Dec. 7, 1915; s. Abraham and Bertha (Schorr) W.; m. Anne Jackson, Mar. 5, 1948; children: Peter Douglas, Roberta Lee, Katherine Beatrice. AB, U. Tex., 1936; MS in Edn, CCNY, 1938; student, Neighborhood Playhouse Sch. of Theatre, 1940; doctorate (hon.), Emerson Coll., Boston, Sch. Visual Arts, 1991. Corp. mem., dir. Neighborhood Playhouse Sch. Theatre. Actor, 1945—; Broadway plays include Antony and Cleopatra, 1948, Mr. Roberts, 1949-50, Rose Tatoo, 1950-52, Camino Real, 1953, Mademoiselle Colombe, 1953, Teahouse of the August Moon, 1954-55, London prodn., 1954, Major Barbara, 1956, Rhinoceros, 1961, Luv, 1964, Promenade All, 1972, Twice Around the Park, 1983, Opera Comique, Kennedy Ctr. Performing Arts, 1987, The Flowering Peach, Fla., 1987, Broadway, 1994, Cafe Crown, 1989; appeared off-Broadway prodn. Typists and the Tiger, 1962-63, London prodn., 1964, Saturday, Sunday, Monday, 1974, (with wife and 2 daus.) Diary of Anne Frank, 1977-78, Visiting Mr. Green, 1997; off-Broadway in Tennessee Williams Remembered, 1999; on tour Down the Garden Paths, 1998-99; appeared in: nat. tour co. Waltz of the Toreadors, 1973-74; appeared in TV films Executioner's Song, 1982, Murder By Reason of Insanity, 1985, Monday Night Mayhem, 2000, Monday Night Mayhem, 2002; TV series Batman, 1966, Kojak, 1973, Highway to Heaven, 1984, Our Family Honor, 1985, L.A. Law, 1986, Law & Order, 1990, The Education of Max Bickford, 2001-02; TV miniseries Christopher Columbus, 1985, The Education of Max Bickford, 2002; motion pictures include Baby Doll, 1955, The Misfits, 1960, The Victors, 1962, Lord Jim, 1964, How To Steal a Million, The Good, the Bad and the Ugly, The Tiger Makes Out, Band of Gold, Zig-Zag, Cinderella Liberty, 1973, Crazy Joe, 1973, Movie, Movie, 1976, Sam's Son, 1985, Tough Guys, 1986, Rocket to the Moon,1986, Nuts, 1987, The Impossible Spy, 1987, Godfather III, 1990, The Two Jakes, 1990, Article 99, Mistress, 1991, Night and the City, 1991, Honey, Sweet Love, 1993, Two Much, 1995, The Associate, 1996, Keeping the Faith, 2000, Mystic River, 2003, King of the Corner, 2004, (voice) The Easter Egg Adventure, 2004, The Moon and the Son: An Imagined Conservation, 2005, A Taste of Jupiter, 2005, The Hoax, 2006, The Holiday, 2006, Mama's Boy, 2006; author: The Good, The Bad, And Me: In My Anecdotage, 2005, Tickling Leo, 2009, Nurse Jackie, 2009, The Ghost Roman Palanaly, 2009. Served to capt. Med. Adminstrn. Corps AUS, World War II. Recipient Donaldson, Theatre World, Variety, Antoinette Perry, Drama League awards, Brit. Film Acad. award, 1956, Disting. Alumnus award U. Tex., 1989, Career Achievement Award Nat. Bd. Review, 2006. Original mem. Actors Studio. Office: Talent Works 220 E 22nd Ste 400 New York NY 10010

WALLACH, ERIC JEAN, lawyer; b. NYC, June 11, 1947; s. Milton Harold and Jacqueline (Goldschmidt) W.; m. Miriam Grunberger, Mar. 21, 1976; children: Katherine, Emily, Peter. BA, Harvard U., 1968, JD, 1972. Bar: N.Y. 1973, U.S. Dist. Ct. (so. and ea. dists.) N.Y. 1973, U.S. Dist. Ct. (no. dist.) N.Y. 1989, U.S. Ct. Appeals (2nd cir.) 1973, (3d cir.) 1996, U.S. Tax Ct. 1976. Assoc. Webster & Sheffield, NYC, 1972-77, Rosenman & Colin, NYC, 1977-80, ptnr., 1981-96, mem. mgmt. com., 1993-96, chmn. employment practice group, 1985-96; ptnr., chmn. employment practice group Kasowitz, Benson, Torres & Friedman LLP, NYC, 1996—. Arbitrator Internat. Ct. Arbitration, Am. Arbitration Assn., others; presenter, chmn. CLE programs, Practising Law Inst., Cambridge Inst. Mem. editl. bd. You and the Law, 1992-96; contbr. articles to profl. jours. Sec.-treas. Art Dealers Assn. Am., Inc., N.Y.C., 1985-96; trustee C.G. Jung Found. for Analytical Psychology; trustee Am. Jewish World Svc., Inc., N.Y.C., 1989-97, chmn., 1995-97; dir. N.Y. Jr. Tennis League. Named to NY Super Lawyers. Mem. Harvard Club N.Y.C. (admissions com. 1992-94), Sunningdale Country Club, Poughkeepsie Tennis Club. Democrat. Avocations: sports, travel, reading. Home: 940 Park Ave New York NY 10028 also: 16 Buttonwood Ln Rhinebeck NY 12572-3510 Office: Kasowitz Benson Torres & Friedman LLP 1633 Broadway New York NY 10019 Office Phone: 212-506-1750. Business E-Mail: ewallach@kasowitz.com.

WALLACH, EVAN JONATHAN, federal judge, educator; b. Superior, Ariz., Nov. 11, 1949; s. Albert A. and Sara Florence (Rothaus) W. BA, U. Ariz., 1973; JD, U. Calif., Berkeley, 1976; LLB in Internat. Law, Cambridge U., Eng., 1981. Bar: Nev. 1977, US Dist. Ct. Nev. 1977, US Supreme Ct. 1984, DC 1987, US Ct. Appeals (9th circuit) 1989. Assoc. Lionel, Sawyer & Collins, Las Vegas, 1976-82, ptnr., 1983-95; judge US Ct. Internat. Trade, NYC, 1995—. Gen. counsel, public policy advisor to US Senator Harry M. Reid, Washington, 1987-88; gen. counsel Nev. State Press Assn. 1989-95; instr. internat. law U. Nev., Las Vegas, 1981-82; atty., advisor internat. affairs Office Judge Advocate Gen. The Pentagon, 1991; adj. prof. law of war NY Law Sch., 1997—, Bklyn. Law Sch., 2001—; vis. prof. U. Muenster, 2001—, George Mason Law Sch., 2004-. Sr. editor: Nevada Civil Practice Handbook, 1993, Legal Handbook for Nevada Reporters, 1994; contbr. articles to profl. jours. Gen. counsel Nev. Dem. Party, 1980-84, 88-90; coord. Nevadans for Mondale, 1983-84, Nevadans for Gore, 1987-88; delegate Democratic Nat. Conv., San Francisco, 1984, alt., Atlanta, 1988; state dir. campaign in Nev. and Ariz. Gore for Pres., 1988. With US Army, 1969-71, Vietnam; maj. US Army N.G., 1989—. Decorated Bronze Star, Air medal, Meritorious Svc. medal, Nev. Medal of Merit. Mem. ABA (Liberty Bell award 1992), Am. Law Inst., Phi Beta Kappa, Phi Kappa Phi. Democrat. Jewish. Office: US Ct Internat Trade One Federal Plaza New York NY 10278-0001*

WALLACH, HAROLD CHARLES, health policy and health services research administrator, educator; b. NYC, Oct. 25, 1935; s. Albert and Sarah Wallach; m. Anita Deanna Gambone, May 7, 1967; children: Jason, Noah. BA, U. Bridgeport, 1957; MS, U. Mich., 1958. Rsch. psychologist Human Factors Lab., Aberdeen, Md., 1960-62; statistician Bur. Census, Suitland, Md., 1962-64, chief social rsch. staff, 1975-80; supr. statistician HUD, Washington, 1964-66; sr. social scientist Booz Allen, Bethesda, Md., 1966-70; prin. statistician U.S. Gen. Acctg. Office, Washington, 1981—97. Cons., adj. prof. U. Md., College Park, 1970-75, adj. prof. Dept. Social/Med. Sci., 1995—; adj. prof. Georgetown Med. Sch., Washington.; advisor, Health and Aging Issues, Montgomery County Exec., 2008. Contbr. articles to profl. jours. Adj. minister Washington Ethical Soc., Washington, 1990-1998, v.p., bd. trustee, 1988-89; pres. Civic Assn., 1972-80, PTA, Montgomery County, Md., 1972-80; bd. dirs. United Way Metro Area, Washington, 1975-79; chair health com. Am. Ethical Union, 2000-04; mem. Aging Commn., Montgomery County, 2001-07; chmn. Md. State Coalition for Health Care Accountability, 2001-04; chmn. Aging Commn., Montgomery County, 2005-06. Named Ky. Col. Gov. Ky., Frankfurt, 1977. Mem. Am. Sociol. Assn. (com. mem. 1985-87, 96), Am. Stat. Assn. (com. chmn. 1984-85), Am. Pub. Health Assn. (com. sect. 1977), Nat. Coun. Family Relations (v.p. 1987-91, Svc. award 1987-91), Nat. Assn. Retired Fed. Employees (legis. v.p. 2000-05, 2009-), AFNYCOMM (chmn. 2005-07). Home: 32360 Townsend Rd Dagsboro DE 19939 Home Phone: 302-732-9187.

WALLACH, JACQUES BURTON, pathologist, educator; b. NYC, Jan. 25, 1926; s. Joseph Irving and Rose Gertrude (Bernstein) W.; m. Doris Foss, Sept. 5, 1953; children: Kim, Lisa, Tracy. Student, NYU, 1941-43; MD, L.I. Coll. Medicine, SUNY, 1947. Diplomate Am. Bd. Pathology. Instr. pathology Albert Einstein Coll. Medicine, Bronx, N.Y., 1954-55, asst. prof. pathology, 1955-59, vis. asst. prof. pathology, 1959-69; clin. assoc. prof. pathology Rutgers Med. Sch., Piscataway, N.J., 1971—; emeritus clin. prof. pathology SUNY, Bklyn., 1979—. Cons. in clin. pathology N.Y. Zool. Soc., Bronx (N.Y.) Zoo, 1954-84. Author: Rheumatic Heart Disease, 1962, Interpretation of Diagnostic Tests, 1970, 8th edit., 2007 (translated into Spanish, Italian, Portuguese, Greek, Russian, Polish, Turkish, Chinese and Japanese), Interpretation of Pediatric Tests, 1983, Timetables of American Presidents. A Concise Tabular Chronology of People and Events during Each Year of the Terms of American Presidents from 1789 to 2000, Giants, Giant Steps, and Gigantic Events in Medicine: A Timetable of Medical History, 2009. With USNR, 1944-45. Named Hon. Prof. of Pathology, Univ. Ica, Peru, 1981. Fellow Am. Coll. Physicians, Am. Soc. Clin. Pathologists, Coll. Am. Pathologists, N.Y. Acad. Medicine. Achievements include patents in apparatus and method for processing flexible medical slides. Home and Office: 10 Ashbourne Dr Monroe Township NJ 08831-4655

WALLACH, KENNETH L., paper company executive; b. NYC, 1946; m. Susan Wallach. BA, Harvard Coll., 1968, JD, 1972. Chmn., pres., CEO Ctrl. Nat.-Gottesman Inc., Purchase, NY, 1998—. Mem. regional adv. bd, J.P. Morgan Chase. Trustee Am. Mus. Natural History; dir. 92d St. Y, Syracuse Pulp and Paper Found., Nat. Book Found. Fellow: Am. Acad. Arts & Scis. Office: Ctrl Nat-Gottesman Inc 3 Manhattanville Rd Purchase NY 10577

WALLACH, LESLIE ROTHAUS, architect; b. Pitts., Feb. 4, 1944; s. Albert and Sara F. (Rothaus) W.; m. Susan Rose Berger, June 15, 1969; 1 child, Aaron. BS in Mining Engring., U. Ariz., 1967, BArch, 1974. Registered arch., Ariz.; registered contractor, Ariz. Prin. Line and Space LLC, Tucson, 1978—. Mem. awards jury Sunset mag., 1997, Ariz. Homes of Yr., 1997, LA AIA; keynote spkr. various confs; lectr. New Zealand, 2007, Calif., 2008, China, 2009. Rep. projects include Ariz. Sonora Desert Mus. Restaurant Complex, Tucson, Elgin Elem. Sch., Ariz., Hillel Student Ctr. U. Ariz., Tucson, Boyce Thompson Southwestern Arborteum Vis. Ctr., Superior, Ariz., San Pedro Riparian Ctr., Sierra Vista, Ariz., Nat. Hist. Trails Ctr., Casper, Wyo., 2002, Vis. Ctr. and Arborteum, Flagstaff, Ariz., 2001, Regional Libr., Phoenix, 2002, Poetry Ctr. for U. Ariz., 2003, New Regional Libr. U. Ariz., Phoenix, 2006; contbr. Sunset Mag., Architecture Mag. and Fine Homebuilding; pub.: Space and Society (Italy), Hinge (Hong Kong), Wallpaper (London); exhibited at U. Ariz., AIA Nat. Conv., Washington, The Dutch Jour., Objekt, 2003; interview and profile pub. in Architecture and Urbanism, 2006. Bd. dirs Tucson Regional Plan, Inc.; pres. Civitas Sonoran (The Environ. Design Coun. of the U. of Ariz. Coll. of Arch.). Recipient Roy P. Drachman Design award, 1982, 85, 93, 2001, Electric League Ariz. Design award, 1987, 88, Gov. Solar Energy award, 1989, Desert Living awards citation, 1991, Ariz. Architect's medal, 1989, Disting. Alumni award U. Ariz., 1998, also 60 additional design awards, including 8 received in 2007, winner $25,000 prize, nat. Endowment of the Arts, 2002, Coll. of Architecture Alumni of Yr., U. Az., 2001, Nat. AIA award, 2008, Top 10 UG Green Project award AIA, 2008 Fellow AIA (Ariz. Honor award 1989, 92, 96, AIA/ACSA Nat. Design award 1991, Western Mountain region Design award 1992, 96, CA AIA/Phoenix Homes and Gardens Home of the Yr. Honor award 1992, 96, Western Region Silver medal 1996, design award, 2004); mem. SAC AIA (past pres., Design award 1985, 88, 90, 2004-07), Western Mountain Region AIA (named Firm of Yr. 1999), Tex. AIA (jury mem. design awards, 2005—). Achievements include being selected as the architect to design the 300 acre Desert Learning Center Campus and new visitor center in Red Rock Canyon, Nevada. Office: Line and Space 627 E Speedway Blvd Tucson AZ 85705-7433 Office Phone: 520-623-1313. Business E-Mail: studio627@lineandspace.com.

WALLACH, MAGDALENA FALKENBERG (CARLA WALLACH), writer; b. Brussels; d. Carl Albert and Renee Antoinette (Meunier) Falkenberg; m. Philip Charles Wallach, Mar. 5, 1950. Student, Columbia U., NYC, Hunter Coll., New Sch. U. Ptnr. Williams-Falkenberg Advt. Assocs., Inc., NYC, 1951-55. Author: Reluctant Weekend Gardener, 1971, Interior Decorating with Plants, 1976, Gardening in the City, 1976, Garden in a Teacup, 1978; contbr. articles to NY Times, Glamour, Working Woman, columnist Greenwich Time, Stamford Adv., 1992-. Former bd. dirs. ARC, NYC; active Bruce Mus., 1987-2007, chmn. spl. events 75th anniversary gala, chmn. Renaissance Ball, bd. dirs., also other fundraising activities; bd. dirs., v.p., chair annual fund raiser Greenwich Adult Day Ctr. Mem. Nat. League Am. PEN Women (pres. Greenwich br. 1987-92, Owl award 1996), Authors Guild, Garden Writers Assn., English-Speaking Union (past bd. dirs. Greenwich br.). Roman Catholic. Avocations: gardening, reading, travel, music, theater. Home: 126 W Lyon Farm Dr Greenwich CT 06831-4352

WALLACH, MARK IRWIN, lawyer; b. Cleve., May 19, 1949; s. Ivan A. and Janice (Grossman) W.; m. Karla L. Wallach, 1996; children: Kerry Melissa, Philip Alexander; stepchildren: Daniel Kanter, Rachel Kanter, Adam Kanter. BA magna cum laude, Wesleyan U., 1971; JD cum laude, Harvard U., 1974. Bar: Ohio 1974, US Dist. Ct. (no. dist.) Ohio, 1974, US Ct. Appeals (6th cir.) 1985, US Supreme Ct. 1985. Law clk. U.S. Dist. Ct., Cleve., 1974-75; assoc. Baker & Hostetler, Cleve., 1975-79; chief trial counsel City of Cleve., 1979-81; assoc. Calfee, Halter & Griswold, Cleve., 1981-82, ptnr., 1982—, co-chmn. litigation dept., 2004—; adv. bd. mem. Space Energy Inc., 2009—. Mem. fed. ct. adv. com. US Dist. Ct. (no. dist.) Ohio, 1991-95; chmn. bd. trustees Ohio Group Against Smoking Pollution, 1986-90; trustee Cleve. chpt. Am. Jewish Com., 1986—, sec. 1989-91, v.p., 1991-95, pres., 1995-97; bd. trustees Citizens League of Greater Cleve., 1978-79, 87-92; trustee Democratic Lawyers Group of Northeastern Ohio, 2009-. Author: Christopher Morley, 1976. Pres. Wesleyan Alumni Club, Cleve., 1983—87, 1992—2006; trustee Lyric Opera, Cleve., 1995—2006, pres., 1996—98, Ratner Schs., 1994—96, Performing Arts Together, 1997—2001; trustee The Sculpture Ctr., 2001—; pres., 2001—; trustee Bellefaire Jewish Children's Bur., 2001—06; trustee, sec. Opera Cleve., 2006—07; pres. Space Solar Power Assn., 2006—; exec. bd. Cleve. chpt. Am. Constn. Soc., 2006—; trustee Western Reserve Chorale, 2008—. Mem.: Greater Cleve. Bar Assn., Cuyahoga County Law Dirs. Assn., Fed. Bar Assn., Ohio Bar Assn., The Club at Key Ctr., The Cleve. Racquet Club. Democrat. Jewish. Avocations: reading, bicycling, space exploration, politics. Home: 2758 Claythorne Rd Shaker Heights OH 44122-1938 Office: Calfee Halter & Griswold 1400 Key Bank Ctr 800 Superior Ave E Cleveland OH 44114-2688 Home Phone: 216-371-0287; Office Phone: 216-622-8344. Business E-Mail: mwallach@calfee.com.

WALLACH, MORTON L., scientist; s. Herman and Helen Wallach; children: Bonalynn, Richard, Hillary. BS in Chemistry, Wayne State U., 1951—55, PhD in Phys. Chemistry, 1955—59. Sci. advisor & tech. operation mgr. Polysar, Inc., Leominster, Mass., 1987—90; pres./ceo PEL Associates, Groton, Conn., 1975—. Expert Teltech Network of Experts, Mpls., 1990—; v.p. Ocean Tech. Found., 2000—; indsl. affiliate U. of Conn., Groton, Conn., United States, 2001—. Author: 5 books; contbr. 25 articles to sci. publs. Recipient Gold Innovation prize Sensors, CQIA, 2004, Silver Innovation prize for smart coating, Ronal Reagan award for leadership in bus. and entrepreneurship, 2005—06; Fulbright fellow, State Dept., USA, 1960. Mem.: Conn. Tech. Coun., Am. Chem. Soc., Licensing Execs. Soc., Soc. Plastics Engrs. Achievements include invention of novel sensors, coatings, plastics, polymer films; first to Polymer Films, Polymer Blends; patents for Novel Sensors; New Smart Coatings; development of light scattering theory and applications to polymers and colloids; patents for novel stents for angioplasty, port security, ship antifouling, and aircraft deicing. Avocations: swimming, travel. Home: 187 Ledgewood Rd Groton CT 06340 Office: PEL Associates 1084 Shennecossett Rd Groton CT 06340 E-mail: mlwallach@pelassociates.com.

WALLACH, NOLAN R., mathematician, consultant; b. Bklyn., Aug. 3, 1940; s. Morris and Pauline Wallach; m. Barbara Hawkins, Apr. 25, 1965; children: Dana, Pamela. BS, U. Maryland, 1962; MA, Wash. U., St. Louis, Mo., 1963, PhD, 1966. Instr. U. of Calif., Berkeley, 1966—69; asst. prof. math. Rutgers U., New Brunswick, NJ, 1969—70, assoc. prof. math., 1970—72, prof. math., 1972—86, Hermann Weyl prof. math., 1986—89; disting. prof. math. U. Calif.-San Diego, La Jolla, 1989—. Cons. Ctr. for Comm. Rsch., La Jolla, 1995—; mem. Mat. Math. Com., 1985—92. Author: (book) Real Reductive Groups I, II, 1988, Continuous Cohomology, 2d edit., 1999; editor: Mathematics: Theory and Applications, 2001—; co-editor: Annals of Math., 1997—2003. Recipient Sloan fellowship, Alfred Sloan Found., 1972—74, Linback award for rsch. excellence, 1977. Fellow: Am. Acad. Arts and Scis.; mem.: Am. Math. Soc. (mem. editl. com. 1991—93, editor bull. 1995—98, mem. coun. 1999—2002). Office: U Calif San Diego Dept Math La Jolla CA 92093 Business E-Mail: nwallach@ucsd.edu.

WALLACH, PATRICIA, councilman, retired mayor; b. Chgo. m. Ed Wallach; 3 children. Grad., Pasadena City Coll. Mem. city coun. City of El Monte, Calif., 1990-92, mayor, 1992-99, elected mem. of city coun., 2003—. Ret. tchr.'s aide Mountain View Sch. Dist. Past trustee El Monte Union High Sch. Dist., L.A. County High Sch. for the Arts; amb. of goodwill Zamora, Michoacan, Mex., Marcq-en-Baroeul, France, Yung Kang, Hsiang, Republic of China, Minhang, Peoples Republic of China; bd. dirs. Cmty. Redevel. Agy., El Monte Cmty. Access TV Corp.; del. Foothill Transit. Mem. League of Calif. Cities, San Gabriel Valley Coun. of Govts., Independent Cities Assn., U.S./Mex. Sister Cities Assn., Sister Cities Internat., Women of the Moose, El Monte Women's Club (Women of Yr., 2006, Citizen of Yr., 2008) Office Phone: 626-580-2001.

WALLACH, STANLEY, medical educator, consultant, administrator; b. Bklyn., Dec. 10, 1928; s. Abraham and Ida Helen Wallach; m. Pearl Small, 1973; children: Sara Lynn, Rhonda, Peter, Francine, Shellie, Allen, Corinne, Mara. AB, Cornell U., 1948; MA in Phys. Chemistry, Columbia U., 1949; MD, SUNY Downstate Med. Ctr., 1953. Diplomate Am. Bd. Internal Medicine, Am. Bd. Endocrinology and Metabolism. Intern Kings County Hosp., Bklyn., 1953-54; resident in internal medicine VA Hosp./Salt Lake Gen. Hosp., Salt Lake City, 1954-56; fellow in endocrinology and metabolism Mass. Gen. Hosp., Boston, 1956-57; attending physician Kings County Hosp., Bklyn., 1957-73, SUNY Hosp., Bklyn., 1966-73, Albany (N.Y.) Med. Ctr., 1973-83; chief of med. svc. VA Med. Ctr., Albany, 1973-83, Bay Pines, Fla., 1983-90, cons. Tampa, Fla., 1991-92; attending physician Tampa Gen. Hosp., 1991—92, Moffitt Cancer Ctr., 1991-92; dir. med. edn. Cath. Med. Ctr., Jamaica, N.Y., 1992-93; dir. endocrinology and co-dir. osteoporosis ctr. Hosp. for Joint Diseases, NYC, 1993—2001; instr. in medicine SUNY Downstate Med. Ctr., 1957-58, from asst. prof. to assoc. prof., 1960-71, prof., 1971-73; prof., asst. chmn. dept. medicine Albany Med. Coll., 1973-77, prof., assoc. chmn. dept. medicine, 1977-83; prof. internal medicine Coll. Medicine U. South Fla., 1983-92, assoc. chmn. dept. internal medicine, 1988-92; exec. dir. Am. Coll. Nutrition, 1993—2003; clin. prof. medicine NYU Sch. Medicine, NYC, 1995—. Pres. Certification Bd. for Nutrition Specialists, 1992-96; career scientist Health Rsch. Coun., City of N.Y., 1967-71; program dir. USPHS Clin. Rsch. Ctr., SUNY Downstate Med. Ctr., 1966-73; rsch. collaborator Brookhaven Nat. Lab., Upton, N.Y., 1970-82; vice-chmn. Gordon Rsch. Conf. on Magnesium in Biochem. Processes and Medicine, 1987, chmn., 1990; cons. NIH, NSF, USDA, Nat. Osteoporosis Found., Nat. Arthritis Found., U.S. Pharmacopeial Conf. Mem. editl. bd. Jour. Am. Coll. of

Nutrition, 1981—, Magnesium and Trace Elements, 1982—90, Jour. Trace Elements in Exptl. Medicine, 1987—90; reviewer Am. Jour. Medicine, Annals of Internal Medicine, Archives of Internal Medicine, Jour. Clin. Endocrinology and Metabolism, Endocrinology, Metabolism, Calcified Tissue Internat., Jour. Bone and Mineral Rsch., Osteoporosis Internat., Procs. of Soc. Exptl. Biology and Medicine, Jour. Nutritional Biochemistry; contbr. numerous articles to profl. jours. Capt. med. corps. USNR, 1968—99. Co-recipient Hektoen Silver award AMA Conv., 1959, John B. Johnson award Paget's Disease Found., 1989, honoree of 20th ann. gala, 1998. Fellow ACP (emeritus), Am. Coll. Clin. Pharmacology, Am. Coll. Endocrinology, Am. Coll. Nutrition (bd. dirs. 1982-93, v.p. 1983-85, pres.-elect 1985-87, pres. 1987-89, sec., treas. 1991-93, exec. dir. 1993-2003), Am. Soc. Nutrition (emeritus).; mem. Assn. Am. Physicians, Am. Soc. for Clin. Investigation (emeritus), Am. Fedn. Clin. Rsch. (emeritus), Am. Soc. Bone and Mineral Rsch. (emeritus), Am. Assn. Clin. Endocrinology (emeritus), Endocrine Soc. (emeritus), Paget's Disease Found. (pres., bd. dirs. med. adv. panel), Internat. Bone and Mineral Soc., Internat. Soc. Trace Element Rsch. in Humans. Office: 1200 80th St S Saint Petersburg FL 33707 Personal E-mail: stanthemensch@gmail.com.

WALLACK, RINA EVELYN, lawyer; b. Pitts.; d. Erwin Norman and Gloria A. (Schacher). AD in Nursing, Delta Coll., 1973; BS cum laude in Psychology, Eastern Mich. U., 1980; JD cum laude, Wayne State U., 1983. Registered nurse Mich.; bar: Calif. 1983. Psychiat. head nurse Ypsilanti (Mich.) State Hosp., 1973-77, instr., nursing educator, 1977-80; teaching asst. contracts Wayne State U., Detroit, 1981-83; legal asst. Wayne County Prosecutor's Office, 1982-83; atty. NLRB, L.A., 1983-86, dir. employee rels. legal svcs. Paramount Pictures Corp., L.A., 1986-89, v.p., 1989-98, v.p., sr. counsel, 1998-2002, sr. v.p., 2002-; Contbr. articles to profl. jours. Instr. ARC, Mich., 1978-80. Recipient Am. Jurisprudence Book award, 1983. Mem. ABA, L.A. County Bar Assn., Am. Trial Lawyers Assn., Mich. Bar Assn., Calif. Bar Assn., Order of Coif. Avocations: shooting, movies, dancing, reading, photography. Address: 11382 Cherrylawn Dr Brighton MI 48114

WALLENBERG, PETER, banker, investor; b. Stockholm, May 29, 1926; s. Marcus Wallenberg and Dorothy Mackay; divorced; 3 children. LLM, U. Stockholm; degree (hon.), Stockholm Sch. Econs., Augustana Coll., Upsala Coll., Stockholm, 1984, Georgetown U. Various positions Atlas Copco Group, 1953-67; dep. mng. dir. Atlas Copco AB, 1970-74, chmn., 1974; first vice chmn. Skandiaviska Enskilda Banken, 1974—96, hon. chmn. bd. dirs. Investor AB, Wallenberg Found.; hon. pres. ICC. Avocations: hunting, tennis, sailing. Office: Investor AB 10332 Stockholm Sweden Address: Arsenalsgatan 8c S-10332 Stockholm Sweden

WALLENBERGER, FREDERICK T., fiber scientist; BA in Chemistry, U. Graz, Austria, 1954; MS, Fordham U., NY, 1956; PhD, Fordham U., 1958. Lectr. in Chemistry Fordham U., NY, 1957—58; rsch. fellow Harvard U., Cambridge, Mass., 1958-59; rsch. scientist Du Pont Fibers, Wilmington, Del., 1959-63, rsch. supr., 1963-79, sr. rsch. assoc., 1979-92; rsch. prof. U. Ill., Urbana-Champaign, 1992-95; staff scientist advanced tech. PPG Industries, Inc., Pitts., 1995—2008. Cons. natural, organic and inorganic fibers, 1992-95, 2008—; vis. prof. U. Calif. Davis, 1995. Author: (book) Fiberglass & Glass Technology, Energy-Friendly Composition & Applications, 2009, Advanced Inorganic Fibers, 1999, Advanced Reinforcing Fibers, 2002, Natural Fibers, 2004; contbr. more than 150 articles to sci. and profl. jours. Recipient Environ. Respect award Du Pont, 1992, others. Fellow Am. Ceramic Soc.; mem. Am. Chem. Soc. (chmn. conf. Chem. and Environ., 1971, Nat. Lecture Tour award 1981), Materials Rsch. Soc. Achievements include patents in field. Home and Office: 708 Duncan Ave Apt 1108 Pittsburgh PA 15237-5051 Office Phone: 412-369-0437. Personal E-mail: wallenbergerf@aol.com.

WALLENDER, WESLEY WILLIAM, engineering professor; b. Bismarck, ND, Feb. 16, 1954; s. Frederick Jacob and Esther (Frey) W.; m. Karen Flanagan, Jan. 1, 1978; children: Erika Karen, Brett William. BS in Agrl. Engring. Tech., Oreg. State U., 1976; BS in Engring., Utah State U., 1981; MS in Water Sci., U. Calif., 1978; PhD in Engring., Utah State U., 1982. Registered profl. engr., Calif. Asst. prof. U. Calif., Davis, 1982-88, assoc. prof., 1988-92, prof., 1992—. Cons. Nat. Sci. Found., Washington, 1985, Sultanate of Oman, Muscat, 1989, Contadina Foods, L.A., 1989, Ray Chem Corp., Palo Alto, Calif., 1983. Contbr. articles to profl. jours. Mem. Am. Geophys. U., Am. Soc. Agrl. Engrs., Phi Kappa Phi, Alpha Zeta. Avocations: home building, photography. Office: U Calif Dept Land/Air/Water Davis CA 95616

WALLENMEYER, WILLIAM ANTON, retired physicist; b. Evansville, Ind., Feb. 3, 1926; s. William Anton and Mindie (Madden) W.; m. Diane May Hankins, June 1, 1952; children: Wendy Kauffman, Jon, Ann Ellis, Timothy. BS, Purdue U., 1950, MS, 1954, PhD, 1957, PhD (hon.), 1989. Jr. rsch. assoc. Brookhaven Nat. Lab., LI, NY, 1954—55; asst. prof. physics Wabash Coll., Crawfordsville, Ind., 1955-56; dir. accelerator divsn. Midwestern U. Rsch. Assn., Madison, Wis., 1957-62; dir. divsn. high energy physics U.S. Dept. Energy, Germantown, Md., 1962-87; pres. Southeastern Univ. Rsch. Assn., Washington, 1987-92; spl. asst. to pres. Univ. Rsch. Assn., Washington, 1993-94. With Air Corps US Army, 1944—46. Fellow: AAAS, Am. Phys. Soc. Home: 1204 Azalea Dr Rockville MD 20850-2024 E-mail: bantonw@verizon.net.

WALLER, EDWARD MARTIN, JR., lawyer; b. Memphis, July 2, 1942; s. Edward Martin and Freda (Lazarov) W.; m. Laura Jayne Rhodes, June 18, 1982; children: Lauren, Jonathan, Melissa. BA, Columbia U., 1964; JD, U. Chgo., 1967. Bar: Fla. 1967. Assoc. Fowler, White, Boggs, P.A., Tampa, Fla., 1967-72, ptnr., 1972—. Mem.: ABA (chmn. 1995—97, standing com. professionalism, lit. sec. budget officer 1996—2000), Bay Area Legal Svcs. (bd. dir. 2003—09, pres. 2006—07), Hillsborough County Bar Assn., Fla. Bar Assn., Fla. Supreme Ct. Commn. on Professionalism. Democrat. Jewish. Office: Fowler White Boggs PO Box 1438 Tampa FL 33601-1438 Office Phone: 813-222-1137.

WALLER, EUNICE MCLEAN, retired educator; b. Lillington, NC, June 29, 1921; d. Absolom and Mary W. (Tucker) McLean; m. William DeHomer Waller, Aug. 9, 1958; m. Henry W. Ferguson, June 29, 1942 (div. June 1954). BS summa cum laude, Fayetteville U., NC, 1942; MS in Edn., U. Pa., 1952; 6th yr. Cert., U. Vt., 1965. Tchr. Harnett H.S., Dunn, NC, 1942—46, Shawtown H.S., Lillington, NC, 1946—56; demonstration tchr. Fayetteville State U., NC, 1956—58; tchr. 2d and U. Elem. Sch., Washington, 1958—60; tchr., asst. to prin. Fitch Elem. Sch., Washington, 1960—62; 7th grade tchr. Sarah Nance Elem. Sch., Columbia, SC, 1963—64; tchr. 8th grade Clark Lane Mid. Sch., Waterford, Conn., 1969—93; ret., 1993. Instr. dept. edn. Conn. Coll., New London, 1970—2001. Corporator Lawrence Meml. Hosp., New London; commr. ethics City Coun. of New London, Conn., 1990—2001; mayor, dep. mayor New London, 1986—88; Civil Rights commr. City New London, 2006—; state convener State of Conn. Nat. Coun. Negro Women, Inc. sects., Washington, 2006—; v.p. NAACP, New London, 1990—2001; pres. Nat. Coun. Negro Women, New London, 1993—2000; trustee Mitchell Coll., New London, Waterford Country Sch., Conn. Recipient Lifetime Achievement award, W.E.B. DuBois, 1999, Cmty. Svc. award for outstanding achievement, Opportunities Industry Coun., 1983, Dr. E.E. Smith Highest Honors award, Fayetteville State U., 1942; named Woman of the Yr., Nat. Coun. Negro Women, 1993; grantee, NSF, 1965. Mem.: NEA (life; Conn. state dir. 1984—88), Conn. Edn. Assn. (Pub. Relations Achievement award 1988), New London Lions (v.p. 1989—99). Democrat. Baptist. Avocations: civic volunteer, civil rights activitst.

WALLER, GEORGE DARRYL, music educator; b. Elizabeth City, NC, May 19, 1961; s. George Alexander and Jean Faye Brickhouse Waller. MusB, Greensboro Coll., NC, 1983; MA, The George Wash. U., Washington, 1996; PhD in Ednl. Leadership and Policy Studies, Va. Ply. Inst., 2007. Cert. supr. and adminstr. Va. Dept. of Edn., 1996. Choral dir. Denbigh H.S., Newport News, Va., 1983—96; program adminstr. Ctr. for the Arts at Woodside H.S., Newport News, Va., 1996—2001; min. of music Hilton Bapt. Ch., Newport News, Va., 1983—86; music dir. Deer Pk. Bapt. Ch., Newport News, Va., 1988—94, Hilton Christian Ch., Newport News, Va., 1994—. Supr. of music Newport News Pub. Schs., Newport News, Va., 2001—. Singer: (professional singer) The Chamber Singers. Bd. dirs. Peninsula Youth Orch., Newport News, Va., 2000—04; arts commr. Newport News Arts Commn., Newport News, Va., 2003—05. Mem.: ASCD, Va. Assn. Music Edn. Adminstrs. (pres. 2002—), Va. Assn. of Phys. Edn., Recreation, and Dance, Southeastern Theatre Conf., Nat. Art Edn. Assn., Nat. Assn. of Tchrs. of Singers, Va. Music Educators Assn. (sect. pres. - vamea 2002—06). Christian. Avocations: travel, theater. Home: 108 Wendy Ct Newport News VA 23601 Office: Newport News Public Schools 12465 Warwick Blvd Newport News VA 23606 Office Fax: 757-595-7522. E-mail: darryl.waller@nn.k12.va.us.

WALLER, GEORGE ROZIER, JR., retired biochemistry educator; b. Clinton, NC, July 14, 1927; s. George Rozier Waller and Lola Jane Phillips; m. Hilda Marie Lominac, Sept. 6, 1946; children: Anne Marie Ramsby, Rebecca Jane Gillan, Catherine Irene Hoopert. BS in Chemistry, NC State U., Raleigh, 1950; MS in Chemistry, U. Del., Newark, 1952; PD in Biochemistry, Okla. State U., Stillwater, 1962. Rsch. asst., instr. U. Del., 1950—53; rsch. chemist Imperial Paper and Color Corp, Glens Falls, NY, 1953—56; asst. prof. Okla. State U., 1956—62, assoc. prof., 1962—66, prof., 1966—88. Pres., mng. dir. Midcontinent Environ. Ctr. Assn., Tulsa, Okla., 1969—77; ret. asst. dir. Okla. AG Expt. Sta., Stillwater, 1969—77; rschr. Swedish Food Rsch. Inst. Gothenburg, Inst. Botany U. Zurich, Sch. Pharmacy U. London, 1977—78; vis. rsch. prof. Inst. Botany Academia Sinica, Taipei, Taiwan, 1992—99; vis. rsch. prof. dept. soil sci. and chemistry Nat. Chung Hsing U., Taichung, 1994—95. Contbr. articles to profl. jours.; editor: Biochemical Applications of Mass Spectrometry, 1972; co-editor: Proceedings of the National Forum on Growth with Environmental Quality, 1974; co-author: Alkaloid Biology and Metabolism in Plants, 1978; co-editor: Topics in Biochemistry of Natural Products, 1979, Biochemical Applications of the Mass Spectrometry, First Supplemental Volume, 1980, The Maillard Reaction in Foods and Nutrition, 1983, Saponians used in Food and Agriculture, 1996, Saponins Used in Food and Agriculture, 1996, Biodiversity and Allelopathy: From Organisms to Ecosystems in the Pacific, 1999. Faculty advisor Delta Upsilon, Stillwater, Okla., 1957—63; ruling elder, chmn. edn. bd. Presbyn. Ch., Stillwater, Okla., 1962—69; chmn. of long range planning com. Unitarian-Universalist Ch., 2003, chmn. of environ. quality com., 2000—05. Seaman, 1st class USNR, 1945—46, Bainbridge, Md. and Argentia, Newfoundland. Recipient award, Nat. Acad. Scis., 1979; grantee, NSF, 1964—99, NIH, 1957—69; scholar, 1963—64. Mem.: Internat. Allelopathy Soc. (pres. 1994—99, founding pres. 1996—99), Payne County Geneal. Soc. (pres. 1988—2008), Phytochemical Soc. N.Am., Am. Soc. Mass Spectrometry (life), Okla. Acad. Sci. (life), Am. Chem. Soc. (life; pres., Okla. sect. 1949—2008, chmn., Okla. sect. 1968—69, Okla. Chemist award 2001), Payne County Hist. Soc. Unitarian Universalist. Avocations: gardening, bowling. Home: 220 South Stallard Stillwater OK 74074 Office: Dept Biochemistry Molecular Biology 246 Noble Rsch Ctr Stillwater OK 74078 Office Fax: 405-744-7799. Personal E-mail: george.waller@okstate.edu. Business E-Mail: gwaller@biochem.okstate.edu.

WALLER, HAROLD MYRON, political science professor; b. Detroit, Oct. 12, 1940; s. Allan L. and Lillian R. (LeVine) W.; m. Diane Carol Goodman, June 28, 1966; children: Sharon, Dahvi, Jeffrey. SB, MIT, 1962; MS, Northwestern U., 1966; PhD, Georgetown U., 1968. Asst. prof. McGill U., Montreal, 1967-71, assoc. prof., 1971-93, prof., 1993—, chmn. polit. sci. dept., 1969-74, 89-90, acting chmn., 1980-81, 86-87, assoc. dean (acad.) faculty arts, 1991-94, acting dean faculty arts, 1994-95, chair N.Am. studies program, 2003—04, 2007—. Pres. McGill Assn. Univ. Tchrs., Montreal, 1978-79; fellow Jerusalem Ctr. Pub. Affairs, 1980—, Canadian Inst. for Jewish Rsch., 1988—; dir. Can. Ctr. Jewish Cmty. Studies, Montreal, 1980—; vis. scholar Hudson Inst., Washington, 2004-05. Co-author: Maintaining Consensus: The Canadian Jewish Polity in the Postwar World, 1990; co-editor: Canadian Federalism: From Crisis to Constitution; contbg. editor: Middle East Focus; mem. editorial bd. Jewish Political Studies; chmn. editorial bd. Viewpoints; contbr. numerous articles to profl. jours. and books in field. Com. chmn. Can. Jewish Congress, Montreal, 1971-74; chair, nat. exec. Can. Profs. for Peace in Middle East, Toronto, 1975-85; pres. Akiva Sch., Montreal, 1984-85; com. chmn. Jewish Edn. Council, Montreal, 1986-88. Recipient Nat. Jewish Book award Jewish Book Coun., N.Y.C., 1991; Grad. fellow NSF, Washington, 1965-66, Leave fellow Social Sci. Humanities Rsch. Coun., Ottawa, 1981-82. Mem. Am. Polit. Sci. Assn., Can. Polit. Sci. Assn., Assn. Jewish Studies, Assn. Sociol. Study Jewry, Assn. Israel Studies, Faculty Club, Sigma Xi, Pi Sigma Alpha. Jewish. Avocations: travel, athletics, reading, politics. Office: McGill U Dept Polit Sci 855 Sherbrooke St W Montreal PQ Canada H3A 2T7 Office Phone: 514-398-4806. Business E-Mail: harold.waller@mcgill.ca.

WALLER, JOHN HENRY, JR., state supreme court justice; b. Mullins, SC, Oct. 31, 1937; s. John Henry and Elnita (Rabon) Waller; m. Jane McLaurin Cooper, Nov. 16, 1963 (div.); children: John Henry III, Melissa McLaurin; m. Debra Ann Meares, May 9, 1981; children: Ryan Meares, Rand Ellis. AB in Psychology, Wofford Coll., Spartanburg, SC, 1959; LLB, JD, U. SC, 1963. Mem. SC Ho. of Reps., 1967—77, asst. majority leader, 1973—74, majority leader, 1975—76; mem. SC Senate, 1977—80; judge SC Cir. Ct., 1980—94; assoc. justice SC Supreme Ct., 1994—. Capt. US Army, 1959—60. Recipient Disting. Svc. award, Municipal Assn. SC, 1968. Mem.: Millins Rotary Club (1st pres.), Shriners, Masons. Avocations: woodworking, golf, water sports, skiing. Office: SC Supreme Ct Supreme Court PO Box 11330 Columbia SC 29211-1330*

WALLER, JOHN LOUIS, anesthesiologist, educator; b. Loma Linda, Calif., Dec. 1, 1944; s. Louis Clinton and Sue (Bruce) W.; m. Jo Lynn Marie Haas, Aug. 4, 1968; children: Kristina, Karla, David. BA, So. Coll., Collegedale, Tenn., 1967; MD, Loma Linda U., 1971. Diplomate Am. Bd. Anesthesiology. Intern Hartford (Conn.) Hosp., 1971—72; resident in anesthesiology Harvard U. Med. Sch.-Mass. Gen. Hosp., Boston, 1972—74, fellow, 1974—75; asst. prof. anesthesiology Emory U. Sch. Medicine, Atlanta, 1977—80, assoc. prof., 1980—86, chmn. dept. anesthesiology, 1986—2000, prof., 1986—2001, prof. emeritus, 2001—; chief anesthesiology Emory U. Hosp., Atlanta, 1986-94, med. dir., 1993-95; assoc. v.p. info. svcs. Woodruff Health Scis. Ctr., 1995-97; chief info. officer Emory U. System Healthcare, Atlanta, 1995-97; prof. anesthesiology Med. U. S.C., Charleston, 2002—, chmn. dept. anesthesia and perioperative medicine, 2002—05, dir. med. informatics, 2005—. Cons. Arrow Internat., Inc., Reading, Pa., 1988—; mem. adv. com. on anesthetic and life support drugs FDA, Washington, 1986—92; numerous vis. professorships and lectures. Contbr. articles to med. jours. Bd. dir. Picis Inc., 2006—. Maj. MC USAF, 1975—77. Recipient cert. of appreciation Office Sec. Def., 1983. Fellow: Am. Coll. Chest Physicians, Am. Coll. Anesthesiologists; mem.: Assn. Cardiac Anesthesiologists, Soc. Acad. Anesthesia Chmn. (councillor 1989—), Assn. Univ. Anesthesiologists, Internat. Anesthesia Rsch. Soc. (trustee 1984—2002, sec. 1996—98, chair 1998—2000), Soc. Cardiovascular Anesthesiologists (pres. 1991—93), Am. Soc. Anesthesiologists. Avocations: fishing, sailing, swimming. Office: Med Univ SC Dept Anes and Perioperative Medicine 167 Ashley Ave Ste 301 Charleston SC 29425 Business E-Mail: wallerj@musc.edu.

WALLER, STEVEN R., engineer; b. Moline, Ill., June 17, 1957; m. Dawn M. Vroman, June 4, 1977. AAS, Hamilton Tech. Coll., Davenport, Iowa, 1985, student. Cert. interconnect designer, IPC, 2000. Engring. technician Rockwell Collins, Cedar Rapids, Iowa, 1985—2004; sr. pcb designer Crystal Group, Inc., Hiawatha, Iowa, 1999—2001; sr. deployment engr. Trapeze Group, Inc., Cedar Rapids, 2005—06; engr. Rockwell Collins, 2007—. Designer's coun. IPC, Hiawatha, Iowa, 2000—01. City councilman Hiawatha City Govt., 2001—03. Mem.: Mensa (life). Achievements include patents for LCD/keyboard system; PC to K/V/M/serial port extension. Personal E-mail: s.waller@mchsi.com.

WALLER, WILLIAM LOWE, JR., state supreme court chief justice; b. Miss., Feb. 9, 1952; s. Bill and Carroll (Overton) Waller; m. Charlotte Brawner, Aug. 4, 1979; children: William, Jeannie, Clayton. BA in Bus., Miss. State U., 1974; JD, U. Miss., 1977; grad., U.S. Army War Coll. Bar: Miss. 1977. Ptnr. Waller and Waller, 1977-97; judge City of Jackson, Miss., 1995-96; justice Miss. Supreme Ct., Jackson, 1998—, presiding justice, 2004—08, chief justice, 2009—. Chmn. Miss. Pub. Defenders Task Force, 2000-05; mem. Study Commn. on the Miss. Jud. Sys.; chmn. Supreme Ct. Rules Com., 2001-. Deacon First Bapt. Ch., Jackson, Miss. Recipient Chief Justice award, 2005. Mem. ABA, Miss. Bar Assn. (chmn. Lawyer Referral Service 1987-89), Miss. Trial Lawyers Assn. (bd. mem. 1979-82), Hinds County Bar Assn. (Jud. Innovation award 2003-04), Jackson Young Lawyers Assn., Christian Legal Soc., Am. Legion, Miss. Army Nat. Guard. Office: PO Box 117 Jackson MS 39205-0117*

WALLER-NIEWOLD, MARILYN J., podiatric surgeon; m. John W. Niewold; 5 children. Student, Bethel Coll., 1969-71; BS, U. Minn., 1975; postgrad., Calif. Poly., 1983-86; DPM, Calif. Coll Podiatric Medicine, 1990. Cert. foot and ankle surgeon Calif. Bd. Podiatric Medicine, Oreg. Bd. Med. Examiners. Resident in surgery VA Med. Ctr., San Francisco, 1990—93; rsch. fellow in HBO and wound healing VA Med. Ctr./Travis AFB, San Francisco, 1992-93; pvt. practice Hayward, Calif., 1993—2003; chief podiatry svcs. Warm Springs (Oreg.) Health and Wellness Ctr., 2003—. Fellow Am. Profl. Wound Care Assn., 2008; dir. Amputation Prevention Program. Mem. Am. Podiatric Med. Soc., Am. Diabetes Assn., Am. Assn. Women Podiatrists, Fed. Podiatric Med. Soc., Omicron Nu. Avocations: gardening, needlecrafts, photoscrapbooking. E-mail: marilyn.Waller@ihs.gov.

WALLERSTEIN, BETTY COOPER, clinical social worker, family therapist; b. Ohio, Mar. 24, 1936; d. Joseph and Adele (Haberfeld) Cooper; m. David D. Wallerstein, May 29, 1966; children: Andrew Jonathan, Susan Eva AB, Goucher Coll., 1958; MSW, Howard U., 1960; SSW Cert. in Social Agy. Supervision/Adminstrn., Hunter Coll., Sch. Social Work, 1980; ACSW. Cert. clin. social worker. Caseworker Mass. Soc. Prevention Cruelty Children, Boston, 1960—62; psychotherapist Jewish Bd. Guardians, Manhattan, 1962—65; caseworker Georgetown Adolescent Clinic, Washington, 1965; family therapist Family Mental Health Clinic Jewish Family Svcs., Manhattan, 1966—71, supr. casework, 1968; pvt. practice NYC, 1971—80. Guest lectr. various colls.; presenter Am. Ortho Psychiat. Assn., 1966. Co-chair, founder Coalition to Save City and Suburban Housing, Inc., NYC, 1985—94; founder, pres. 49 Blocks E. 79th St. Neighborhood Assn., NYC, 1984—2009; founder Neighbors R Us, 1996, Cmty. Coalition, 1998; co-founder CPR Zoning Coalition, 2001, Cmty. Planning Bd. 8M, NYC. Recipient Disting. Pub. Svc. award, Goucher Coll., Our Town Leadership awards, Mayor's award for Vol. Leadership Excellence, Boro Pres. award for Vol. Pub. Svc., FUESHD, 1995, Ralph Menapace award in Historic Preservation, Civitas August Heckscher award in Zoning Planning, 1996, Lenox Hill NH Brooke Russell Astor award, 2000, East Sider awards, 2001, 2005, NY State Senate Woman of Distinction awards, 2001, 2009, Jane Brown award for Housing Adv., 2005, Our Town East Sider award, 2001, 2005, Outstanding New Yorker award, Citizen Com. NY, 1987, Licia Albanese Puccini Found. award, 2003, Coun. Proclamation award, NY City, 2009. Mem. NASW, ACSW. Avocations: philanthropic work, arts groups, hospitals, Jewish/Israeli causes, travel, opera, classical music, theater.

WALLERSTEIN, IMMANUEL, sociologist; b. NYC, Sept. 28, 1930; a. Lazar and Sally (Guensberg) W.; m. Beatrice Friedman; children: Katharine Ellen; stepchildren: Susan E. Morgenstern, Robert S. Morgenstern. BA, Columbia U., 1951, MA, 1954, PhD, 1959; D (hon.), U. Paris Denis Diderot, 1976; DLitt, York U., Toronto, Can., 1995; D (hon.), Free U. Brussels, 1996, U. Nat. Autonoma Mex., Mexico City, 1998, Inst. Superior Ciencas o Trabalho e Empresa, Lisbon, 1999, U. Autonoma, Puebla, Mex., 1999, U. Bucharest, 2001, U. Alicante, 2002, U. San Marcos, 2004, U. Lund, 2005, Higher Sch. Econ., Moscow, Russia, 2005, Kharkov Nat. U., 2005, Coimbra U., 2006. With Columbia U., NYC, 1958-71; prof. McGill U., Montreal, Que., Can., 1971-76; disting. prof. Binghamton (N.Y.) U., 1976-99; dir. Fernand Braudel Ctr. Study of Econs., 1976—2005; sr. rsch. scholar Yale U., New Haven, 2000—. Dir. d'etudes associé Ecole des Hautes Etudes en Scis. Sociales, Paris, 1975-76, 80-95; chair Gulbenkian Com. on Restructuring of Social Scis., 1993-95; mem. sci. com. Ist. Internat. di Storia Econ. "F. Datini", Prato, 1977—; Leerstoel Immanuel Wallerstein U., Ghent, 2002-, Wei Lun vis. prof. Chinese U. of Hong Kong, 1991; Tripartite lectr. Royal Geog. Soc., Geog. Assn., Inst. Brit. Geographers, London, 1988. Author: The Modern World-System, I: Capitalist Agriculture and the Origins of the European World-Economy in the Sixteenth Century, 1974, The Capitalist World-Economy, 1979, The Modern World-System, II: Mercantilism and the Consolidation of the European World-Economy, 1600-1750, 1980, The Modern World-System III: The Second Great Expansion of the Capitalist World-Economy, 1730-1840's, 1989, Geopolitics and Geoculture: Essays on the Changing World-System, 1991, Unthinking Social Science: The Limits of Nineteenth Century Paradigms, 1991, Historical Capitalism, with Capitalist Civilization, 1995, Utopistics/or Historical Choices of the Twenty-First Century, 1998, The End of the World As We Know It: Social Science for the 21st

Century, 1999, The Essential Wallerstein, 2000, Decline of American Power: The U.S. in a Chaotic World, 2003, The Uncertainties of Knowledge, 2004, Alternatives: The U.S. Confronts the World, 2004, World Systems Analysis: An Introduction, 2004, Africa: The Politics of Independence and Unity, 2005, European Universalism: The Rhetoric of Power, 2006; co-author: (with others) Open the Social Sciences: Report of the Gulbenkian Commission on the Restructuring of the Social Sciences, 1996; (with T.K. Hopkins) The Age of Transition: Trajectory of the World-System, 1945-2025, 1996, (with R.E. Lee) Overcoming the Two Cultures, 2004. With U.S. Army, 1951-53. Recipient medal U. Helsinki, 1992, Career Disting. Scholarship award Am. Sociol. Assn., 2003; named Officer of Ordre des Arts et des Lettres, France, 1984. Fellow Am. Acad. of Arts and Scis.; mem. Internat. Sociol. Assn. (pres. 1994-98), African Studies Assn. (pres. 1973-74). Democrat. Jewish. Office: Yale U Dept Sociology PO Box 208625 New Haven CT 06520-8265 Office Phone: 203-432-3334. Office Fax: 203-432-6976. E-mail: immanuel.wallerstein@yale.edu.

WALLERSTEIN, MITCHEL BRUCE, dean, political science professor; b. NYC, Mar. 8, 1949; s. Melvin Julian and Rita Helen (Nomburg) W.; m. Susan Elyse Perlik, June 29, 1974; children: Matthew, Leah. AB, Dartmouth Coll., 1971; MPA, Syracuse U., 1972; MS, MIT, 1977, PhD, 1978. Assoc. dir. Internat. Food Policy Program MIT, Cambridge, Mass., 1978-83, lectr. dept. polit. sci., 1978-83; asst. prof. dept. polit. sci. Holy Cross Coll., Worcester, Mass., 1979-81; exec. dir. office internat. affairs NRC, NAS, Washington, 1983-89; dep. exec. officer NRC, Washington, 1989-93; dep. asst. sec. of def. US Dept. Def., Washington, 1993-97; disting. rsch. prof. Nat. Def. U., Washington, 1998; v.p. John D. and Catherine T. MacArthur Found., Chgo., 1998—2003; dean, prof polit. sci. and pub. adminstrn. Maxwell Sch. Citizenship and Pub. Affairs, Syracuse U., NY, 2003—. Adj. prof. Sch. Advanced Internat. Studies, Johns Hopkins U., Washington, 1992-98; adj. prof. Sch. Fgn. Svc., Georgetown U., Washington, 1989-93. Author: Combating Terrorism, Strategies and Approaches, 2008; author, dir. reports in field including multiple NAS reports on nat. security topics. Recipient Sec. Def. medal for Outstanding Pub. Svc., 1997, 98. Fellow Nat. Acad. Pub. Adminstrn.; mem. AAAS, Internat. Inst. Strategic Studies, Coun. on Fgn. Rels. Democrat. Office: Maxwell Sch Citizenship and Pub Affairs Syracuse Univ 200 Eggers Hall Syracuse NY 13244-1020 Office Phone: 315-443-3461. Office Fax: 315-443-3385. Business E-Mail: mwallers@maxwell.syr.edu.

WALLERSTEIN, ROBERT SOLOMON, retired psychiatrist; b. Berlin, Jan. 28, 1921; s. Lazar and Sarah (Guensberg) Wallerstein; m. Judith Hannah Saretsky, Jan. 26, 1947; children: Michael Jonathan, Nina Beth, Amy Lisa. BA, Columbia U., 1941, MD, 1944; postgrad., Topeka Inst. Psychoanalysis, 1951-58. Assoc. dir., then dir. rsch. Menninger Found., Topeka, 1954-66; chief psychiatry Mt. Zion Hosp., San Francisco, 1966-78; tng. and supervising analyst San Francisco Psychoanalytic Inst., 1966—; clin. prof. U. Calif. Sch. Medicine, Langley-Porter Neuropsychiat. Inst., 1967-75, prof., chmn. dept. psychiatry, also dir. inst., 1975-85, prof. dept. psychiatry, 1985-91, prof. emeritus, 1991—, ret. Vis. prof. psychiatry La. State U. Sch. Medicine, New Orleans Psychoanalytic Inst., Pahlavi U., Shiraz, Iran, 1977, Fed. U. Rio Grande do Sul, Portol Alegre, Brazil, 1980; mem., chmn. rsch. scientist career devel. com. NIMH, 1966—70; fellow Ctr. Advanced Study Behavioral Scis., Stanford, Calif., 1964—65, 1981—82, Rockefeller Found. Study Ctr., Bellagio, Italy, 1992. Author: 21 books; mem. editl. bd.: numerous profl. jours.; contbr. 380 articles to profl. jours. With US Army, 1946—48. Recipient Heinz Hartmann award, N.Y. Psychoanalytic Inst., 1968, Disting. Alumnus award, Menninger Sch. Psychiatry, 1972, J. Elliott Royer award, U. Calif., San Francisco, 1973, Outstanding Achievement award, No. Calif. Psychiat. Soc., 1987, Mt. Airy gold medal, 1990, Mary Singleton Sigourney award, 1991, Outstanding Contbn. to Psychoanalytic Edn. award, Internat. Fedn. Psychoanalytic Edn., 1999. Fellow: ACP, Am. Orthopsychiat. Assn., Am. Psychiat. Assn., Am. Coll. Psychoanalysts; mem.: Group Advancement Psychiatry, Brit. Psycho-Analytic Soc. (hon.), Mex. Psychoanalytic Assn. (hon.), Mex. Assn. Psychoanaltyic Practice, Tng. Rsch. (hon.), Internat. Psychoanalytic Assn. (v.p. 1977—85, pres. 1985—89, hon. v.p. 1999—), Am. Psychoanalytic Assn. (pres. 1971—72), Phi Beta Kappa, Alpha Omega Alpha. Office Phone: 415-435-3417.

WALLES, JACOB, Consul General in Jerusalem; b. Wilmington, Del. Grad., Wesleyan U., Middletown, Conn., Johns Hopkins U. Sch. Advanced Internat. Studies. Am. consulate gen. US Dept. State, Amsterdam, 1982—84, various positions involving Mid. Ea. affairs, including spl. asst. to the under sec. state for econ. affairs, spl. asst. the Mid. East Peace process, first sec., US Embassy Tel Aviv, dep. prin. officer Jerusalem, 1996—98, dir. office Israel and Palestinian affairs, 1998—2000, acting dep. asst. sec. state Near Ea. affairs, 2001, mem. sr. seminar, 2001—02, dep. chief of mission Athens, 2003—05, consul gen. and chief of mission Jerusalem, 2005—. Recipient Superior Honor award, US Dept. State, 1994, 2001. Office: DOS Amb 6350 Jerusalem Pl Washington DC 20521-6350*

WALLEVIK, JON ELVAR, engineer, researcher; b. Reykjavik, Iceland, Oct. 17, 1968; s. Harald Andersen Wallevik and Inga Sigurlaug Thorsteinsdóttir. BSc in Physics, U. Iceland, Reykjavik, 1990—94, MSc in Physics, 1996—97; PhD in Civil Engring., Norwegian U. Sci. & Tech., Norway, 1998—2003. Lic. civil engr., Assn. Chartered Engrs. Iceland, 2003. Rsch. scientist Icelandic Meteorol. Office, Reykjavik, Iceland, 1995—98; rsch. fellow Norwegian U. Sci. & Tech., 1998—2003, post doctoral fellowship, 2004—07; rsch. engr. SINTEF Tech. & Soc., Trondheim, 2003, Icelandic Bldg. Rsch. Inst., Reykjavik, 2003—04, Innovation Ctr., Reykjavik, 2007—. Award com. Nordic Rheology Soc., The Nordic Countries, 2003—. Contbr. articles to profl. jours. Mem.: Nordic Rheology Soc. (award com. mem. 2003—). Achievements include research in calculating sea ice flow in Icelandic waters; energy flux calculations in the ESOP-project; calculation of Koch-index for the North Atlantic Ocean; relate coagulation and dispersion of cement particles with fluid mechanical response of the cement based material; effect of the different lignosulfonate types on the rheological properties of the cement based material as a function of temperature and time. Office: Innovation Ctr Keldnaholt 112 Reykjavik Iceland Office Fax: 354-5229311. Business E-Mail: jon.wallevik@vvpf.net.

WALLFESH, HENRY MAURICE, communications executive, writer; b. NYC, June 15, 1937; s. David Shibe and Rose (Silk) W.; m. Suzanne Krakowitch, Dec. 26, 1960; children: Saundra Kay, Gerald Bruce. Grad. indsl. and labor rels., Cornell U., 1958. Editor, co-pub. Indsl. Rels. News, NYC and Stamford, Conn., 1960-67; pres., chief exec. officer RAI div. Hearst Bus. Communications, NYC, 1968-91, sr. v.p., editor at large, 1991; pres. Whale Communications, Inc., Stamford, Conn., 1992—. Pres. Indsl. Rels. Inst., Stamford, 1964-67; founder, bd. dirs. Internat. Soc. Pre-Retirement Planners, 1975-88; bd. dirs. VSOP Mktg., Boston. Author: Implications of the Age Discrimination in Employment, 1977, When a CEO Retires, 1978. Bd. dirs. Aging in Am., N.Y.C., 1985-90, N.Y.C. Anti-Defamation League, 1987-89; mem. alumni bd. dirs. Cornell Inst. Labor Rels., 1995—99. Capt. inf. USAR, 1958-67. Recipient Corp. Achievement award Nat. Assn. for Sr. Living Industries, 1990; inducted into Internat. Soc. Pre-Retirement Planners Hall of Fame, 1988. Mem. Roxbury Swim and Tennis Club (bd. dirs. 1975-78), Cornell Club. Jewish. Avocations: tennis, theater, writing. Home and Office: 341 Biltmore Ln Somerset NJ 08873-6004 Personal E-mail: hswhale@aol.com.

WALLIN, LELAND DEAN, artist, educator; b. Sioux Falls, SD, Oct. 14, 1942; s. Clarence Forrest and Leona Mae (McInnis) W.; m. Meredith Maria Hawkins, Mar. 26, 1977; 1 child, Jessica Hawkins. Student, Columbus Coll. Art and Design, 1961-62; BFA in Painting, Kans. City Art Inst., Mo., 1965; MFA in Painting, U. Cin. with Cin. Art Acad., 1967. Prof. drawing, painting, sculpture St. Cloud State U., Minn., 1967-86; prof. Queens Coll., CUNY, Flushing, NY, 1983-84; prof., coord. MFA painting Marywood U., Scranton, Pa., 1985-90; prof. painting and drawing East Carolina U., Greenville, 1992—2008, prof. emeritus, 2006. Lectr. Carnegie-Mellon U., Pitts., 1988; curator Philip Pearlstein Retrospective Exhibit, Scranton, 1988; juror Belin Arts Grant Com., Waverly, Pa., 1986-89; judge, juror No. Nat. Art Competition, 1993. One-man shows include Mpls. Coll. Art and Design, 1977—78, Harold Reed Gallery, NYC, 1983, Gallery Henoch, 1991, Greenville Mus. Art, NC, 2007, exhibited in group shows at Bklyn. Mus., 1983, Greenville County Mus. Art, SC, 1983, Huntsville Mus. Art, 1994, San Bernardino County Mus. Internat., Calif., 1995, Contemporary Realism, Phila., 1996, Ctr. Arts, Laredo, Tex., 1997 (Internat. First Pl. award, 1997), Downey Mus. Art, Calif., 1998, Ctr. Arts, Laredo, Tex., 1999 (Internat. First Pl. award, 1999), Palm Springs Desert Mus., 1999, Fine Arts Ctr., Sacramento, 1999, Bellevue Art Mus., Wash., 2001, Morris Mus. Art, Ga., 2001, Huntsville Mus. Art, Ala., 2002, Miss. Mus. Art, 2002, Barret Art Ctr., Poughkeepsie, NY, 2003, Myth, Magic & Metaphor, Chgo., 2004, Union St. Gallery, 2004, Fayetteville Mus. Art, NC, 2008; contbr. articles to profl. jours. Recipient Scholar-Tchr. award for Coll. Fine Arts and Comm., East Carolina U. Sch. Art and Design, 2005—, numerous rsch. awards, East Carolina U., 1994—; named Outstanding Tchr., 1994, 1995. Home: 218 York Rd Greenville NC 27858-5601

WALLING, DONOVAN ROBERT, editor, writer; b. Kansas City, Mo., Jan. 9, 1948; s. Donovan Ernest and Dorothy Jane (Goyette) W.; m. Diana Lynn Eveland, Oct. 19, 1968 (dec. 1991); children: Katherine Anne, Donovan David, Alexander James. BS in Edn., Kans. State Tchrs. Coll., 1970; MS, U. Wis., Milw., 1975. Cert. tchr., adminstr., Wis., Ind. Tchr. Sheboygan (Wis.) Area Sch. Dist., 1970-81, 83-86, coord. lang. arts and reading, 1986-91; tchr. Dept. Def. Dependents Schs., Zweibruecken, Germany, 1981-83; dir. instrnl. svcs. Carmel (Ind.)-Clay Schs., 1991-93; dir. publs. Phi Delta Kappa Internat., Bloomington, Ind., 1993—2006; sr. cons. Ctr. for Civic Edn., Calabasas, Calif., 2007—. Mem. adj. faculty U. Wis., Oshkosh, 1986-91, Silver Lake Coll., Manitowoc, Wis., 1987-91. Author: Complete Book of School Public Relations, 1982, How To Build Staff Involvement in School Management, 1984, Teachers as Leaders, 1994, Rethinking How Art Is Taught, 2000, Visual Knowing, 2005, Teaching Writing to Visual, Auditory, and Kinesthetic Learners, 2006, Writing for Understanding, 2009; also numerous articles.

WALLIS, CARLTON LAMAR, librarian; b. Blue Springs, Miss., Oct. 15, 1915; s. William Ralph and Tellie (Jones) W.; m. Mary Elizabeth Cooper, Feb. 22, 1944; 1 child, Carlton Lamar. BA with spl. distinction, Miss. Coll., 1936; MA, Tulane U., 1946; B.L.S., U. Chgo., 1947; L.H.D., Rhodes Coll., Memphis, 1980. English tchr., coach Miss. Pub. Schs., 1936-41; teaching fellow Miss. Coll. and Tulane U., 1941-42; chief librarian Rosenberg Library, Galveston, Tex., 1947-55; city librarian Richmond, Va., 1955-58; dir. Memphis Pub. Library, 1958-80, ret., 1980. Author: Libraries in the Golden Triangle, 1966; contbr. articles to library jours. Trustee Belhaven Coll., 1978-82, Nat. Ornamental Metal Mus., 1989—. Served as chief warrant officer AUS, 1942-46. Decorated Bronze Star. Mem. ALA (chmn. library mgmt. sect. 1969-71), Pub. Library Assn. (dir. 1973-77), Tex. Library Assn. (pres. 1952-53), Va. Library Assn., Southwestern Library Assn. (exec. bd. 1950-55), Southeastern Library Assn. (chmn. pub. library sect. 1960-62), Tenn. Library Assn. (pres. 1969-70, Distinguished Service award 1979, Intellectual Freedom award 1998). Presbyterian (elder). Club: Egyptian (pres. 1973-74). Home: 365 Kenilworth Pl Memphis TN 38112-5405

WALLIS, DIANA LYNN, artistic director; b. Windsor, Eng., Dec. 11, 1946; d. Dennis Blackwell and Joan Williamson (Gatcombe) W. Grad., Royal Ballet Sch., Eng., 1962-65. Dancer Royal Ballet Touring Co., London, 1965-68; ballet mistress Royal Ballet Sch., London, 1969-81, dep. ballet prin., 1981-84; artistic coord. Nat. Ballet of Can., Toronto, 1984-86, assoc. artistic dir., 1986-87, co-artistic dir., 1987-89; free-lance prod., tchr. London; dep. artistic dir. English Nat. Ballet, London, 1990-94; artistic dir. Royal Acad. Dance, 1994—. Fellow Imperial Soc. Tchrs. Dancing. Office Phone: 020 7326 8012. Business E-Mail: lwallis@rad.org.uk.

WALLIS, ERIC G., lawyer; b. Astoria, NY, Jan. 8, 1950; AB magna cum laude, U. Pacific, 1972; JD, U. Calif., Hasting Coll. of Law, 1975. Bar: Calif. 1975. Ptnr. Reed Smith LLP, Oakland, Calif., 1982—. Editl. assoc. Hastings Law Jour., 1974-75. Mem. ABA (sect. litigation), State Bar Calif., Alameda County Bar Assn. Office: Reed Smith LLP 1999 Harrison St Fl 26 Oakland CA 94612-3520 E-mail: ewallis@reedsmith.com.

WALLIS, M. CHAD, medical educator; b. Cin., Sept. 18, 1970; s. William Budge and Linda B. Wallis; m. Faith Stoddard; children: Michael, Henry, Ethan, Mason. MD, Ohio State U. Coll. Medicine, Columbus, 1999. Diplomate Am. Bd. Urology, 2008. Asst. prof. surgery U. Utah Sch. Medicine, Salt Lake City, 2006—. Office: Pediat Urology Assocs 100 Mario Capecchi Dr Salt Lake City UT 84113

WALLIS, MARY CAMILLA, civic leader; b. Albany, NY, Nov. 3, 1923; d. Huntington and Mary Camilla (McKim) Williams; m. Richard Fisher Wallis, Aug. 20, 1955; children: Maria Fisher, Sylvia Camilla. BA, Bryn Mawr Coll., 1946. Research asst. Cryogenic Lab Johns Hopkins U., Balt., 1946-52, research assoc. Applied Physics Lab. Silver Spring, Md., 1952-55; pres. Natural History Found. Orange County, Newport Beach, Calif., 1978. Docent Newport-Mesa Unified Sch. Dist., 1972-80, Smithsonian Inst., Washington, 1956-64. Contbr. articles profl. jours. Vol. curator Natural History Found. Orange County, 1980-91; bd. dirs. Orange County Natural History Mus., 1996—; pres. Carderock Springs (Md.) PTA, 1967; v.p. Newport Beach Parent Faculty Orgn., 1971; pres. U. Calif. Irvine Town and Gown, 1976-77. Mem. Geol. Soc. Am., Univ. Club (Irvine) Republican. Episcopalian. Avocations: fossil collecting, photography. Home: 2635 Alta Vista Dr Newport Beach CA 92660-4102

WALLIS, OLNEY GRAY, lawyer; b. Llano, Tex., July 27, 1940; s. Ben Alton and Jessie Ella (Longbotham) W.; m. Linda Lee Johnson, June 29, 1963; children: Anne, Brett. BA, U. Tex., 1962, JD, 1965. Bar: Tex. 1965, U.S. Dist. Ct. (so. dist.) Tex. 1966, U.S. Ct. Mil. Appeals 1968, U.S. Surpeme Ct. 1970, U.S. dist. Ct. (we. dist.) Tex. 1976, U.S. Ct. Appeals (5th cir.) 1977, U.S. Tax Ct. 1980, U.S. Ct. Appeals (10th cir.) 1981, U.S. Ct. Appeals (11th cir.) 1983, U.S. Dist. Ct. (no. dist.) Tex. 1985, U.S. Dist. Ct. (ea. and we. dists.) Ark. 1985, U.S. Ct. Appeals (8th cir.) 1985. Assoc. Brown & Cecil, Houston, 1965-66; asst. U.S. atty. Dept. Justice, Houston, 1971-74; mem. Jefferson, Wallis & Sherman, Houston, 1975-81, Wallis & Pruitt, Houston, 1981-87, Wallis and Short, Houston, 1987—. Instr. U. Md., Keflauik, Iceland, 1968-69; mem. faculty continuing legal edn. U. Houston, 1981-84. Capt. USAF, 1969-70. Decorated Air Force Commendation medal. Mem. Assn. Trial Lawyers Am., Am. Judicature Soc., Tex. Trial Lawyers Assn., Houston Bar Found., Phi Delta Phi, Phi Kappa Tau. Office: Wallis & Short 9535 S Hwy 16 Llano TX 78643 Office Phone: 325-248-0111. Personal E-mail: ogwlawyer@earthlink.net.

WALLMANN, JEFFREY MINER, author; b. Seattle, Dec. 5, 1941; s. George Rudolph and Elizabeth (Biggs) W. BS, Portland State U., 1962; MD, St. Johns U., 1977; PhD, U. Nev., 1998. Pvt. investigator Dale Sys., NYC, 1962-63; asst. buyer, mgr., pub. money bidder Dohrmann Co., San Francisco, 1966-69; dir. pub. rels. London Films, Cinelux-Universal, Trans-European Publs., 1970-75; editor-in-chief Riviera Life mag., 1975-77; instr. U. Nev., Reno, 1990—, Regis U., 2003—. Instr. U. Nev., Las Vegas, 1998—, chair gen. studies; instr. U. Phoenix, 2001—, Regis U., 2003—. Author: The Spiral Web, 1969, Judas Cross, 1974, Clean Sweep, 1976, Jamaica, 1977, Deathtrek, 1980, Blood and Passion, 1980, Brand of the Damned, 1981, The Manipulator, 1982, Return to Conta Lupe, 1983, The Celluloid Kid, 1984, Business Basic for Bunglers, 1984, Guide to Applications Basic, 1984, The Western: Parables of the American Dream, 1999, (under pseudonym Leon DaSilva) Green Hell, 1976, Breakout in Angola, 1977, (under pseudonym Nick Carger) Hour of the Wolf, 1973, Ice Trap Terror, 1974, (under pseudonym Margaret Maitland) The Trial, 1974, Come Slowly, Eden, 1974, How Deep My Cup, 1975, (under pseudonym Amanda Hart Douglass) First Rapture, 1972, Jamaica!, 1978, (under pseudonym Grant Roberts) The Reluctant Couple, 1969, Wayward Wives, 1970, (under pseudonym Gregory St. Germain) Resistance # 1: Night and Fog, 1982, Resistance #2: Magyar Massacre, 1983, (under pseudonym Wesley Ellis) Lonestar on the Treachery Trail, 1982, numerous others, (under pseudonym Tabor Evans) Longarm and the Lonestar Showdown, 1986, (under pseudonym Jon Sharpe) Trailsman 58: Slaughter Express, 1986, numerous others in Trailsman series, also others under pseudonyms; co-author: (under pseudonym William Jeffrey) Duel at Gold Buttes, 1980, Border Fever, 1982, Day of the Moon, 1983, The Western: Parables of the American Dream, 1999; contbr. articles and short stories to Argosy, Ellery Queen's Mystery Mag., Alfred Hitchcock's Mystery Mag., Zane Grey Western, Venture, Oui, TV Guide. Mem. Mystery Writers Am., Sci. Fiction Writers Am., We. Writers Am., Nat. Coun. Tchrs. English, Crime Writers Am., Nev. state Coun. Tchrs. English, Esperanto League N.Am., We. Lit. Assn., Internacia Soc. Amikeco Kaj Bonvolo, Sci. Fiction Rsch. Assn., Internat. Assn. Fantastic in the Arts, We. Lit. Assn. Office: care of Barry Malzberg PO Box 61 Teaneck NJ 07666-0061 Personal E-mail: msiinc@cox.net.

WALLOT, JEAN-PIERRE, archivist, historian; b. Valleyfield, Que., Can., May 22, 1935; s. Albert and Adrienne (Thibodeau) W.; m. Denyse Caron; children: Normand, Robert, Sylvie. BA, Coll. Valleyfield, 1954; lic. es lettres, U. Montreal, 1957, MA in History, 1957, PhD in History, 1965; D (hon.), U. Rennes, France, 1987, U. Ottawa, Can., 1996. Reporter Le Progres de Valleyfield, 1954—61; from lectr. to prof. dept. history U. Montreal, 1961—65, dept. chmn., 1973—75, vice-dean studies faculty arts and scis., 1975—78, vice-dean rsch. Faculty Arts and Scis., 1979—82, academic v.p., 1982—85. Nat. archivist, Can., 1985-97; historian Nat. Mus. Man, Ottawa, Ont., 1966-69; assoc. prof. U. Toronto, 1969-71; prof. Concordia U., Montreal, Que., 1971-73; vis. prof. U. Ottawa, 1997—, dir. Ctr. Rsch. en Civilisation Canadienne-Francaise, 2000-07; dir. Etude Assn. Ecole Pratique des Hautes Etudes en Scis. Sociales, Paris, 1975, 79, 81, 83, 85, 87, 89, 94. Author: French and American Intrigues in Canada, 1965; author: (with John Hare) Imprints in Lower Canada, 1967; author: Confrontations, 1971; author: (with G. Paquet) Patronage and Power in Lower Canada, 1973, A Quebec that Changed, 1973; co-author (with Gilles Paquat): Un Québec Moderne, 1760—1840, 2007; editor (with R. Girard): Memoires de J.E. McComber, bourgeois de Montréal, 1981; editor: (with J. Goy) Evolution and Ruptures in the Rural World, 1986; editor: Identity Constructs and Social Practices, 2002, The Non-Existent Debate: The Pepin-Robarts Commission, 2003, Linguistic Governance, 2005. Pres. internat. adv. com. on Memory of the World UNESCO, 1993—99. Decorated officer Order Arts et Lettres, France; recipient Marie Tremaine medal, 1973, Tyrrell medal, 1982, Royal Soc. Centenary medal, 1994, Jacques Ducharme prize, 1997, Queen's Jubilee medal, 2002; Faculty of Arts and Scis. U. de Montreal Merit medal, 2004. Fellow Royal Soc. Can. (sect. pres. 1985-87, pres. 1997-99); mem. Am. Antiquarian Soc., Acad. des Lettres du Quebec, Inst. d'Histoire l'Amerique Francaise (pres. 1973-77), Can. Hist. Assn. (pres. 1982), Assn. Can.-Francaise l'Avancement Scis. (pres. 1981-83, emeritus mem.), Assn. Archivists Que., Assn. Can. Archivists, Internat. Coun. on Archives (v.p. 1988-92, pres. 1992-96, pres. emeritus). Roman Catholic. E-mail: wallotcaron@rogers.com.

WALLS, MARTHA ANN WILLIAMS (MRS. B. CARMAGE WALLS), publishing executive; b. Gadsden, Ala., Apr. 21, 1927; d. Aubrey Joseph and Inez (Cooper) Williams; m. B. Carmage Walls, Jan. 2, 1954; children: Byrd Cooper, Lissa Walls Vahldiek. Student pub. schs., Gadsden. Pres., dir. Walls Newspapers, Inc., 1969-70; sec., treas., dir. Summer Camps, Inc., Guntersville, Ala., 1954-69; CEO, pres., dir. So. Newspapers, Inc., Houston, 1970—; pres., dir. So. Newspapers of Ala., Inc., Scottsboro. V.p., dir. Ft. Payne (Ala.) Newspapers, Inc., Galveston Newspapers, Inc.; dir. Monroe (Ga.) Newspapers, Inc.; bd. dirs. Jefferson Pilot Corp., Greensboro, N.C., 1990-98, Jefferson-Pilot Life Ins. Co., 1990-98, Jefferson Pilot Comm., 1990-98. Bd. dirs. Montgomery Acad., 1970-74. Mem.: Soc. Profl. Journalists. Episcopalian. Office: 5701 Woodway Ste 300 Houston TX 77057 Office Phone: 713-266-5481.

WALLS, WILLIAM WALTON, JR., management consultant; b. Phila., Oct. 3, 1932; s. William Walton and Mary Crown (Elliott) Walls; m. Nina Catherine deAngeli, July 1, 1961; 1 child, Deborah. BSME, Swarthmore Coll., 1959. With Boeing Helicopters, Phila., 1959-96, v.p. light helicopter joint venture, 1988-91, v.p. devel. programs, 1991-92, v.p. rsch. and engring., 1992-96; small high-tech. bus. cons. Ridley Park, Pa., 1996—. Cons. in field. Mem. NATO Indsl. Advisors Group, 1988—93; chmn. aerospace adv. coun. Pa. State Coll., 1974—79; mem. bd. advisors Rotocraft Ctr. Excellence Rensselaer Poly. Inst., 1982—84. Mem.: Am. Helicopter Soc. (pres. 1988—89, chmn. 1989—90). Republican. Avocations: travel, computers, classical music, exercise. Home: 502 Harrison St Ridley Park PA 19078-3208 Personal E-mail: wwwallsjr@comcast.net.

WALLS PERRY, J(OYCE) LORRAINE, elementary school educator; b. Washington, Pa., Aug. 23, 1948; d. William K. and Minnie (Crockett) W.; m: Robert L. Perry; 1 child, Lisa Michelle. BA, Point Park Coll., Pitts., 1971; MA in Teaching, U. Pitts., 1972, cert. in curriculum and supervision, 1995. Cert. elem. and early childhood tchr. Pa., elem. prin. Instructional teacher leader, elem tchr. Pitts. Bd. Edn., 1988-92, resource tchr. elem. and mid. sch. social studies, 1992—2000; v.p. Belmar Elem. Sch., Pitts., 2000—02; ednl. cons., 2002—; dir. edn. Greater Allen Christian Acad., Pitts., 2006—. Tchr.-in-Residence fellow U. Pitts., 1992-93. Holmes group scholar, 1992-93. Mem. TESA. Home: 3594 Harlow Pl Pittsburgh PA 15204-1143 Home Phone: 412-771-8737. Personal E-mail: raine823@msn.com.

WALL SPITZER, SILDA ALICE, hedge fund executive; b. Chapel Hill, NC, Dec. 10, 1957; m. Eliot Laurence Spitzer, Oct. 17, 1987; children: Elyssa, Sarabeth, Jenna. BA summa cum laude, Meredith Coll., 1980; JD, Harvard Law Sch., 1984. Atty., mergers, acquisitions, corp. fin. Skadden Arps Slate Meagher & Flom; atty., internat legal group Chase Manhattan Bank; mng. dir. Metropolitan Capital Advisors, Inc., NYC, 2008—. Founding chair Children for Children, 1996—; hon. chair Women's Leadership Forum NY, Eleanor Roosevelt Legacy Found.; founding co-chair Project Cicero; adv. bd. mem. NYCharities.org; mem. NY Blue Ribbon Commn. on Youth Leadership; bd. mem. Children's Museum Manhattan, 1995—99; trustee Horace Mann Sch.; chair NY State Commn. on Nat. & Cmt. Svc. Named one of The 50 Most Powerful Women in NYC, NY Post, 2007, 2008. Office: Metropolitan Capital Advisors Inc 660 Madison Ave 20th Fl New York NY 10021 also: Children for Children 6 E 43rd St 25th Fl New York NY 10017*

WALMER, EDWIN FITCH, retired lawyer; b. Chgo., Mar. 24, 1930; s. Hillard Wentz and Anna C. (Fitch) W.; m. Florence Poling, June 17, 1952; children: Linda Diane Walmer Dennis, Fred Fitch. BS with distinction, Ind. U., 1952, JD with high distinction, 1957. Bar: Wis. 1957, U.S. Dist. Ct. (ea. dist.) Wis. 1957. Assoc. Foley & Lardner, Milw., 1957-65, ptnr., 1965-90, ret., 1990. Served to 1st lt. U.S. Army, 1952-54. Recipient Cal. C. Chambers award Culver (Ind.) Mil. Acad., 1948. Fellow Am. Coll. Trust and Estate Counsel; mem. Order of Coif, Dairymen's Country Club (Boulder Junction, Wis.), Vineyards Country Club (Naples, Fla.), Phi Eta Sigma, Beta Gamma Sigma. Republican. Congregationalist. Avocations: golf, fishing.

WALMSLEY, JUDITH ABRAMS, chemistry professor; b. Oak Park, Ill., Feb. 6, 1936; d. Kenneth Frederick and Edna Martha (Grau) Abrams; m. Frank Walmsley, Aug. 29, 1959; children: Katherine Ellen, Susan Jennifer. BA in Chemistry, Fla. State U., 1958; PhD in Chemistry, U.N.C., 1962. Rsch. scientist Owens-Ill., Inc., Toledo, 1963-66; rsch. assoc., instr. Mich. State U., East Lansing, 1979-80; sr. rsch. assoc. U. Toledo, 1974-87; asst. prof. U. Tex., San Antonio, 1987-93, assoc. prof., 1993—2000, prof., 2000—, chair dept., 2001—05. Instr. U. Toledo, 1968-69, 75-77, 83-87. Patentee in field; author lab. manuals, 1985; contbr. over 40 articles to profl. jours. Recipient rsch. grants Rsch. Corp., U. Tex., 1988-90, NIH, 1990—2008, DeArce Biomed. Rsch., U. Toledo, 1984-87. Mem. Am. Chem. Soc., AAAS, Sigma Xi, Phi Beta Kappa, Phi Kappa Phi, Delta Gamma. Presbyterian. Avocations: reading, sewing, swimming. Office: Dept Chemistry U Tex San Antonio San Antonio TX 78249-0698 Business E-Mail: judith.walmsley@utsa.edu.

WALOCK, MICHAEL JAMES, research assistant; b. Dearborn, Mich., Oct. 13, 1977; s. Steven Carl Walock; m. Jennifer Ann Biladeau, Sept. 30, 2004. BS, Eastern Mich. U., Ypsilanti, 2001. SPC US Army, Mich., Ala., Afghanistan, 1995—2008; grad. rsch. asst. MINT Ctr., Tuscaloosa, Ala., 2004—. Decorated Joint Commendation medal Dept. Def. Mem.: Materials Rsch. Soc., U. Ala. Student Chpt. AVS (vice chair 2008—), Am. Phys. Soc., AVS. Roman Catholic. Achievements include research in surface and interfacial interactions of magnetic thin films and multilayers. Office: MINT Ctr PO Box 870209 Tuscaloosa AL 35487-0209 Office Fax: 205-348-2346. Business E-Mail: mwalock@mint.ua.edu.

WALRATH, PATRICIA A., state legislator; b. Brainerd, Minn., Aug. 11, 1941; d. Joseph James and Pansy Patricia (Drake) McCarvill; m. Robert Eugene Walrath, Sept. 1, 1961; children: Karen, Susan, David, Julie. BS, Bemidji State U., 1962; MS, SUNY, Oswego, 1975. Cert. secondary math. tchr., N.Y., Mass. Programmer analyst Control Data Corp., Mpls., 1962-65; crewleader dept. commerce U.S. Census, Middlesex County, Mass., 1979-80; selectman Town of Stow, Mass., 1980-85; tchr. math. Hale Jr. High Sch., Stow, 1981-82; instr. math. Johnson & Wale Coll. Hanscom AFB, Bedford, Mass., 1983-84, test examiner, 1983-84; state rep. 3d Middlesex dist. State of Mass., Boston, 1985—. Many coms. including most recently; chmn. com. long term debt and capital expenditures Mass. Ho. of Reps., 1997—2001, asst. whip, floor chair, 2001—04, chmn. healthcare financing com., 2005—. Chmn. Mass. Indoor Air Pollution Commn., Boston, 1987-88; mem. Stow Dem. Com., 1988—. Recipient Disting. Svc. award Auburn N.Y. Jaycees, 1976. Mem. LWV (pres. 1973-76, dir. fin. 1977-78), Mass. Legislators' Assn., Mass. Dem. Leadership Coun. (v.p. 1991-92, co-chmn. 1993-94, treas. 1995-99), Mass. Women's Legis. Caucus (chair 1986). Roman Catholic. Avocations: gardening, stamp collecting/philately, travel. Home: 20 Middlemost Way Stow MA 01775-1363 Office: State Capital RM 236 Boston MA 02133 Office Phone: 617-722-2430. Business E-Mail: Rep.PatriciaWalrath@hou.state.ma.us.

WALSDORF, MARISA, finance educator; d. Agustin and Juanita de los Santos; m. Louis Tom Waldsorf, Sept. 19, 1992; children: Christian Stuart Walsorf, Julia Maria. MBA, Dallas Bapt. U., 1998, degree in Bus Applied Bus. Admin - Mgmt., 1995. Team leader IBM, Dallas, 1984—99; instr. Brookhaven Coll., Farmers Br., Tex., 2000—. Leader Girl Scouts NE Tex., Dallas, 2005—09; youth religious edn. leader Mary Immaculate Ch., Farmers Branch, Tex., 2008—09, chair, parish festival, 2007—09. Mem.: Soc. Advancement Mgmt. - Brookhaven Coll. (sponsor, Campus Chpt. 2007—09). Office: Brookhaven Coll 3939 Valley View Ln Farmers Branch TX 75244-4997

WALSH, BRIDGET (MARY BRIDGET WALSH), legislative staff member; BA in govt. and internat. rels., U. Notre Dame; JD, Loyola U. Dep. legis. dir., counsel to Senator Bill Nelson US Senate, Washington, 2000—06, legis. dir., acting chief of staff to Senator Jon Tester, 2007—. Office: Office of Senator Jon Tester 204 Senate Russell Office Bldg Washington DC 20510-2604 Office Phone: 202-224-2644. E-mail: bridget_walsh@tester.senate.gov.*

WALSH, CARL E., economics professor; s. Eugene B. and Bessie E. Walsh; m. Judy Walsh, July 31, 1993; stepchildren: Deborah Newman, Michelle Newman. AB, Univ. Calif., Berkeley, 1971; PhD, Univ. Calif., 1976; degree, Lacturer Auckland U., NE, 1978. Asst. prof. Princeton U., NJ, 1979—85; sr. economist Fed. Res. Bank, San Francisco, 1985—87; vice provost Univ. Calif., Santa Cruz, Calif., 2005—07, prof., 1987—. Bd. editors Am. Econ. Rev., 1994—2000; assoc. editor Jour. Money, Credit, and banking, 2001—; co-editor Internat. Jour. Ctrl. Banking, 2008—. Author: (book) Monetary Theory and Policy; contbr. to profl. jours. Office: Dept Econ Univ Calif 1156 High St Santa Cruz CA 95064 Office Phone: 183-459-4082. Business E-Mail: walshe@ucsc.edu.

WALSH, CHARLES RICHARD, retired banker; b. Bklyn., Jan. 30, 1939; s. Charles John and Anna Ellen Walsh; m. Marie Anne Goulden, June 24, 1961; children: Kevin C., Brian R., Gregory M. BS, Fordham U., 1960; MBA, St. John's U., 1966, D of Comml. Scis. (hon.), 1985. V.p. Mfrs. Hanover Trust Co., Hicksville, NY, 1974-80, sr. v.p., 1980-86, exec. v.p., 1986-90, group exec., mem. mgmt. com., 1990-92; exec. v.p., group exec. Chem. Banking Corp., Hicksville, NY, 1992-95, The Chase Manhattan Corp., 1995-97; ret., 1997. Bd. dirs. Mastercard Internat.; bd. dirs., former chmn. Eastern States Monetary Svcs., Lake Success, NY, 1978-88; former pres., CEO, bd. dirs. The Bankcard Assn., Hicksville, 1988-91. Vice chmn. adv. bd. St. John's U., 1982—; sustaining mem. Rep. Nat. Com., 1978—. With USAR, 1960, 61-62. Mem. N.Y. State Bankers Assn. (former bd. dirs., mem. gov. coun., chmn. consumer banking divsn.), Am. Bankers Assn. (mem. govt. rels. coun., chmn. bank card divsn., mem. exec. com., former mem. comms. coun. and chmn. edn. com.), Am. Mgmt. Assn., N.Y. Credit and Fin. Mgmt. Assn., Soc. Cert. Consumer Credit Execs. (cert.), Beta Gamma Sigma, Omicron Delta Epsilon, North Hempstead Country Club, Gov.'s Club Kiawah Island (S.C.), Kiawah Island Club. Republican. Home: 31 Fieldstone Ln Oyster Bay NY 11771-3122 also: 107 Goldeneye Dr Kiawah Island SC 29455-5773

WALSH, DANIEL FRANCIS, bishop; b. San Francisco, Oct. 2, 1937; Grad., St. Joseph Sem., St. Patrick Sem., Catholic U. Am. Ordained priest Archdiocese of San Francisco, 1963, asst. chancellor, 1970—76, sec. to archbishop, 1976—78, chancellor, 1978—81, vicar gen., 1981—87; assoc. pastor St. Pius, Redwood City, 1963—64; tchr. Serra HS, San Mateo, Calif., 1966—70; ordained bishop, 1981; bishop Diocese of Reno, Nev., 1987—95, Diocese of Las Vegas, 1995—2000, Diocese of Santa Rosa, Calif., 2000—. Roman Catholic. Office: Diocese of Santa Rosa PO Box 1297 Santa Rosa CA 95402 Office Phone: 707-566-3325.

WALSH, DAVID JOSEPH, pediatric neurologist, educator; b. St. Louis, Oct. 5, 1946; s. Joseph Lloyd and Dorothy Ann Walsh. BS, Georgetown U., Washington, DC, 1968; MD, Med. U. SC, 1973. Diplomate Am. Bd. Psychiatry and Neurology, Am. Bd. Pediat. Asst. prof. neurology and pediat. Jacksonville Health Edn. Program, U. Fla., Jacksonville, 1981—82; asst. prof. pediat. and neurology U. Kans., Kansas City, 1982—88; pvt. practice Allegheny Neurol. Assoc., Pitts., 1988—90; asst. prof. neurology Med. Coll. Wis., Milw., 1990—2004; assoc. prof. neurology St. Louis U., St. Louis, 2004—. Program dir. pediat. residency U. Kans., Kansas City, 1982—87; program dir. pediat. neurology residency program Med. Coll. Wis., Milw., 2001—03; chief med. staff, divsn. neurology Children's Hosp. Wis., Milw., 2001—04; chief sect. child neurology St. Louis U., St. Louis, 2004—. Author: (short story) Upping the Ritalin. Chair profl. adv. bd. Epilepsy Found. S.E. Wis., Milw., 1992—2004, pres., 1994—2004; sec. profl. adv. bd. Epilepsy Found., 2006—; pres. profl. adv. bd. Epilepsy Found. Greater St. Louis area, 2008—. Lt. USNR, 1974—76. Fellow: Am. Acad. Neurology; mem.: Assn. U. Profs. Neurology, Harvard Med. Alumni Assn., Med. U. SC Alumni Assn., Child Neurology Soc. Independent. Roman Catholic. Avocations: Aikido, opera, travel. Office: Cardinal Glennon Children's Hosp 1465 S Grand Blvd Glennon Hall Rm 7514 Saint Louis MO 63104 Business E-Mail: walshdj@slu.edu.

WALSH, DAWNA HAMM, art educator; b. Tuscaloosa, Ala., Aug. 11, 1947; d. Jack Hamm and Dorisnel Alexander Hamm-Sims; m. John M. Walsh, III, Aug. 21, 1971; children: Grant, Whitney, Preston, Austin. BA, Dallas Bapt. U., 1971; MA, U. North Tex., 1977; PhD, Tex. Tech. U., 1993. Chair, prof. dept. art Dallas Bapt. U., 1978—. Juror art shows throughout Tex.; del. Washington Arts Task Force, Fulbright Orgn. Exhibitions include Hillcrest and Dallas Bapt. U. Gallery. Fellow, Fulbright Commn., 1970, 1975. Mem.: Leadership Tex., Delta Kappa Gamma. Avocations: art, museums. Home: 4015 University Blvd Dallas TX 75205 Office: Dallas Bapt U 3000 Mountain Creek Pkwy Dallas TX 75211

WALSH, DENNY JAY, reporter; b. Omaha, Nov. 23, 1935; s. Gerald Jerome and Muriel (Morton) W.; m. Peggy Marie Moore, Feb. 12, 1966; children from previous marriage: Catherine Camille, Colleen Cecile; 1 son, Sean Joseph. B.J., U. Mo., 1962. Staff writer St. Louis Globe-Democrat, 1961-68; asst. editor Life mag., NYC, 1968-70, assoc. editor, 1970-73; reporter N.Y. Times, 1973-74, Sacramento Bee, 1974—. Served with USMC, 1954-58. Recipient Con Lee Kelliher award St. Louis chpt. Sigma Delta Chi, 1962; award Am. Polit. Sci. Assn., 1963; award Sigma Delta Chi, 1968; Pulitzer prize spl. local reporting, 1969; 1st prize San Francisco Press Club, 1977; Beacon award for lifetime achievement, 1st Amendment Coalition, 2004. Office: Sacramento Bee 21st & Q Sts Sacramento CA 95816 Home Phone: 916-721-9624; Office Phone: 916-321-1189. Business E-Mail: dwalsh@sacbee.com.

WALSH, DIANA CHAPMAN, former academic administrator, sociologist, educator; b. Phila., July 30, 1944; d. Robert Francis and Gwen (Jenkins) Chapman; m. Christopher Thomas Walsh, June 18, 1966; 1 child, Allison Chapman. BA in English, Wellesley Coll., 1966; MS in Journalism, Boston U. Sch. of Pub. Comm., 1971; PhD in Health Policy, Boston U., 1983; LHD (hon.), Boston U, 1994, Amer. Coll. of Greece, Athens, 1995, U. Mass., Amherst, 1999; LHD, Northeastern U., 2003. Dir. info., edn. Planned Parenthood League, Newton, Mass., 1971—74; sr. program assoc. Dept Pub. Health, Boston, 1974—76; assoc. dir. Boston U. Health Policy Inst., 1985—90; prof. Sch. Pub. Health, Sch. Medicine, Boston U., 1987—90, adj. prof. pub. health, 1990—; Florence Sprague Norman and Laura Smart Norman prof., chair dept. health and social behavior Harvard Sch. Pub. Health, 1990—93, adj. prof., 1993—; pres. Wellesley Coll., 1993—2007. Trustee WGBH Edn. Found., Boston, 1993-2000, Amherst (Mass.) Coll., 1998—; dir. State St. Corp., Boston, 1997—; chair internat. commn. Am. Coun. on Edn., 1998; consortium on financing higher edn. Asian U. for Women. Author: Corporate Physicians, 1987; co-author: Payer, Provide, Consumer, 1977; editor: Women, Work and Health: Challenges to Corporate Policy, 1980; contbr. chpt. to book. Bd. dirs. Planned Parenthood League of Mass., 1974—79, 1981—85, bd. overseers, 1993—94; trustee Occupl. Physicians Scholarship Fund, 1987—94, WGBH Ednl. Found., 1993—2000. Recipient Book of the Yr. award Am. Jour. Nursing, 1980; Kellogg Nat. fellow, 1987-90. Mem. APHA, Am. Sociol. Assn., Soc. for the Study of Social Problems, Mass. Pub. Health Assn. Avocations: gender and health, social policy, writing, skiing. Office Phone: 781-283-2237.

WALSH, DOLORES ANN GONCZO (LORRY WALSH), special education educator; b. Detroit, Sept. 3, 1933; d. Joseph John and Dolores (Carey) Gonczo; m. Bernard Waldrup, Aug. 23, 1958 (div. 1980, dec. 2000); children: Elizabeth, Carey, Leslie, Bernard III; m. Deleon Walsh, Sept. 3, 1982 (dec. 1990). Student, Barat Coll., 1951-52; PhB, U. Detroit, 1955; MPS, Manhattanville Coll., 1978. Tchr. 2d grade East Detroit (Mich.) Pub. Schs., 1955-58; tchr. 4th grade Birmingham (Ala.) Schs., 1958-59, St. Franics Xavier Sch., Birmingham, 1959-62; homebound tchr. Greenburg Ctrl. 7, Hartsdale, NY, 1969-73, tchr. spl. edn., 1973-91; ret., 1991. Tchr. English, China, 1998; mem. Middle States Evaluating Team HS., 1982-90. Dist. leader Dem. Party Greenburgh, 1981-91; sec. Greenburgh Health Cen. Bd., Greenburgh, N.Y., 1986-91; leader Girl Scouts U.S., 1968-69; CCD tchr. Convent Sacred Heart (v.p. 2008-), Greenwich, Conn.; vol. West Valley Art Mus., 1992-2009, Cath. Ctr., 1998-; v.p. Ariz. Alumnae Sacred Heart, 2008-. Mem. NEA, NY State United Tchrs., Ariz. Alumnae of Sacred Heart (pres. 2001-03, 03-04), Delta Zeta Soc. E-mail: lorry2@azquick.com.

WALSH, DON, engineer, consultant; b. Berkeley, Calif., Nov. 2, 1931; s. J. Don and Marguerite Grace (Van Auker) W.; m. Joan A. Betzmer, Aug. 18, 1962; children: Kelly Drennan, Elizabeth McDonough BS, U.S. Naval Acad., 1954; MS, Tex. A&M U., 1967, PhD, 1968; MA, San Diego State U., 1968. Commd. ensign USN, 1954, advanced through grades to capt., 1974, officer-in-charge Bathyscaph Trieste Trieste, 1959-62, comdr. in USS Bashaw, 1968-69; dir. Inst. Marine and Coastal Studies, prof. ocean engring. U. So. Calif., LA, 1975-83; pres., CEO Internat. Maritime, Inc., 1976—; mng. dir. Deep Ocean Engring., Inc., 1990—2000, also bd. dirs. Dir. Ctr. for Marine Transp. Studies, U. So. Calif., 1980-83, Coastal Resources Ctr., 1990-94; trustee USN Mus. Found., 1989—; mem. Nat. Adv. Com. on Oceans and Atmosphere, 1979-85; bd. govs. Calif. Maritime Acad., 1985-95; pres. Parker Diving, 1989-94. Editor, contbr.: Law of the Sea: Issues in Ocean Resource Management, 1977, Energy and Resources Development of Continental Margins, 1980, Energy and Sea Power: Challenge for the Decade, 1981, Waste Disposal in the Oceans: Minimizing Impact, Maximizing Benefits, 1983; editor Jour. Marine Tech. Soc., 1975-80; mem. editorial bd. U.S. Naval Inst., 1974-75. Bd. dirs. Charles and Anne Lindbergh Found., 1996-2005. Decorated Legion of Merit (2); Woodrow Wilson Internat. Ctr. for Scholars fellow, 1973-74. Fellow Marine Tech. Soc., Acad. Underwater Arts and Scis., Explorers Club (hon. life, bd. dirs. 1994-2000, hon. pres. 2008-, Explorers Medal, 2001); mem. AAAS, Soc. Naval Archs. and Marine Engrs., Am. Soc. Naval Engrs., Navy Inst., Adventurers Club (hon. life), Am. Geog. Soc. (hon. life), Nat. Acad. Engring. Home and Office: Internat Maritime Inc 14758 Sitkum Ln Myrtle Point OR 97458-9726 Personal E-mail: imiwalsh@worldnet.att.net, imiwalsh@mac.com.

WALSH, DONNIE (JOSEPH DONALD WALSH JR.), professional sports team executive; b. NYC, Mar. 1, 1941; m. Judy McNamara; 5 children. B, law degree, U. NC. Bar: 1977. Draft pick Phila. Warriors; assoc. head coach U. NC Tar Heels; asst. coach U. SC Gamecocks, Denver Nuggets, head coach, 1979-81; asst. coach Ind. Pacers, 1984-86, gen. mgr., 1986-92; pres. Ind. Pacers Sports & Entertainment, 1988—2008, CEO, 1988—2008; pres. basketball ops. NY Knicks, 2008—. Office: NY Knicks Madison Sq Garden Two Pennsylvania Plz New York NY 10121-0091*

WALSH, EDWARD JOSEPH, food products and cosmetics executive; b. Mt. Vernon, NY, Mar. 18, 1932; s. Edward Aloysius and Charlotte Cecilia (Borup) W.; m. Patricia Ann Farrell, Sept. 16, 1961; children: Edward Joseph, Megan Simpson, John, Robert. BBA, Iona Coll., 1953; MBA, NYU, 1958. Sales rep. M & R Dietetic Labs., Columbus, Ohio, 1955-60; with Armour & Co., 1961-71, Greyhound Corp., 1971-87; v.p. toiletries div. Armour Dial Co., Phoenix, 1973-74, exec. v.p., 1975-77; pres., CEO Armour Internat. Co., Phoenix, 1978-84; pres. The Dial Corp. (formerly Armour-Dial Co.), Phoenix, 1984-87, chief exec. officer, 1984-87; pres., chief exec. officer Purex Corp., 1985; chmn., chief exec. officer The Sparta Group Ltd., Scottsdale, Ariz., 1988—2008. Bd. dirs. Nortrust Holding Corp., Phoenix, Matrixx Initiatives, Inc., Phoenix, 2000—07; mem. bd. advisors Brother to Brother Internat., 1988—2001, bd. dirs., 1988—2004; mem. bd. advisors Universal Tech. Inst., Phoenix, 1996—2004, No. Trust N.A., 2006—. Trustee Scottsdale Meml. Health Found., 1995-98; pres. Mt. Vernon Fire Dept. Mems. Assn., 1960-61. Served with U.S. Army, 1953-55, Germany. Recipient Loftus Lifetime Achievement award, Iona Coll., 2004. Mem. Am. Mgmt. Assn., Nat. Meat Canner Assn. (pres. 1971-72), Cosmetic, Toiletries and Fragrance Assn. (bd. dirs. 1985—87), Nat. Food Processors Assn. (bd. dirs.). Republican. Roman Catholic. Office: The Sparta Group Ltd 6623 N Scottsdale Rd Scottsdale AZ 85250-4421

WALSH, GEORGE WILLIAM, publishing company executive, editor, author; b. NYC, Jan. 16, 1931; s. William Francis and Madeline (Maass) W.; m. Joan Mary Dunn, May 20, 1961; children: Grail, Simon. BS, Fordham U., 1952; MS, Columbia U. Sch. Journalism, 1953. Copy editor, reporter Cape Cod Standard-Times, Hyannis, Mass., 1955; communications specialist IBM, NYC, 1955-58; editorial trainee Time, Inc., 1958-59; writer-reporter Sports Illus., NYC, 1959-62; book editor Cosmopolitan, NYC, 1962-65, mng. editor, 1965-74; editor-in-chief, v.p. Ballantine Books div. Random House, NYC, 1974-79, Macmillan Pub. Co., NYC, 1979-85; pub. cons., 1985—. Author: Gentleman Jimmy Walker, 1974, Public Enemies, 1980, Damage Them All You Can: Robert E. Lee's Army of Northern Virginia, 2002, Whip the Rebellion: Ulysses S. Grant's Rise to Command, 2004, Those Damn Horse Soldiers: True Tales of the Civil War Cavalry, 2006. Served with AUS, 1953-55. Mem. Assn. Am. Pubs. Clubs: Univ., NYC, Pamet Harbor Yacht and Tennis, Truro, Mass., Cosmos, Washington. Roman Catholic. Home and Office: 4000 Cathedral Ave NW Washington DC 20016 Office Phone: 202-944-3993. Personal E-mail: edchief@verizon.net.

WALSH, GERALD THOMAS, bishop; b. NYC, Apr. 25, 1942; s. Thomas and Anne Haggerty Walsh. MDiv, St. Joseph's Sem., NYC, 1967; MSW, Fordham U., NYC, 1983. Ordained priest Archdiocese of New York, NY, 1967; parochial vicar Holy Trinity Parish, NYC, 1967—80; dir. dept. family & children's svcs. Cath. Charities, NYC, 1980—89; named monsignor, 1990; pastor Incarnation Parish, NYC, 1989—96; priest sec. to John Cardinal O'Connor, 1996—98; pastor St. Elizabeth Parish, NYC, 1998—2007; vicar North Manhattan Vicariate, NYC, 1998—2007; vicar for devel. Archdiocese of New York, 2003—; ordained bishop, 2004; aux. bishop Archdiocese of New York, 2004—; rector, pres. St. Joseph's Sem., Yonkers, 2007—. Assoc. chaplain Knights of Columbus, NYC, 1980—. Roman Catholic. Office: Archdiocese of New York 1011 1st Ave New York NY 10022-4134 also: St Josephs Sem 201 Seminary Ave Yonkers NY 10704-1896 Office Phone: 914-968-6200.

WALSH, J. MICHAEL, wholesale distribution executive; BS in Indsl. Engring., Tex. Tech U., Lubbock; MBA, Tex. A&M U. Sr. v.p. ops. Core-Mark Holding Co., Inc., 1991—96, sr. v.p. US Distbn., 1996—99, exec. v.p. sales, 1999—2003, pres., CEO, 2003—, bd. dirs., 2004—. Office: Core-Mark Holding Co 395 Oyster Point Blvd Ste 415 South San Francisco CA 94080 Office Phone: 650-589-9445.

WALSH, JAMES THOMAS (JIM WALSH), lobbyist, former United States Representative from New York; b. Syracuse, NY, June 19, 1947; s. William F. Walsh; m. DeDe Ryan; 3 children. BA in Hist., St. Bonaventure U., NY, 1970. Agrl. ext. agt. Peace Corps, Nepal, 1970-72; mktg. exec. telecom. co., 1974-88; exec.-in-residence telecom. inst. SUNY Inst. Tech. Utica-Rome, 1986-87; mem. Common Coun., Syracuse, NY, 1977-85, pres., 1986-88; mem. US Congress from 25th NY dist., 1989—2009, dep. Republican whip, 1994—2006, chmn. Friends of Ireland, 1995—2009; mem. US House Agrl. Com., 1989—93, US House Appropriations Com., 1993—2009; ptnr. K&L Gates LLP, Washington, 2009—. Bd. mem. Erie Canal Mus., Vera Ho., Everson

Mus. Recipient Flax Trust award, 1997, Bobby Sands award, Ancient Order Hibernians, 1998, Disting. Svc. award, The Am. Ireland Fund, 2001, Capital award, Nat. Coun. of La Raza, 2001, Ellis Island Medal of Honor, Nat. Ethnic Coalition Organizations, 2002, Willis H. Carrier award, Ctr. Excellence in Environ. Systems, 2003, Exemplary Legislator award, Nat. Alliance on Mental Illness Veterans Coun., 2006, John Philip Sousa Disting. Svc. award, Assn. for the Preservation of Historic Congressional Cemetery, 2007; named Legislator of Yr., Congl. Fire Services Inst., 2003; named an Affordable Housing Champion, Nat. Coun. State Housing Agencies, 2000. Republican. Roman Catholic. Office: K&L Gates LLP 1601 K St NW Washington DC 20006 Office Phone: 202-778-9321. Office Fax: 202-778-9100. E-mail: jim.walsh@klgates.com.*

WALSH, JAN, library director; MLS, U. Pitts. With Wash. State Libr., Olympia, 1978—, acting state libr., 2002, state libr., 2002—. Mem.: Wash. Libr. Assn., Chief Officers of State Libr. Agys. (Continuing Edn. com., Stats. com.), Libr. Coun. Wash. Office: Wash State Libr Divsn Wash Sec State PO Box 42460 Olympia WA 98504-2460 Office Phone: 360-704-5253. Office Fax: 360-586-7575. E-mail: jwalsh@secstate.wa.gov.

WALSH, JENNIFER FITZGERALD, legislative staff member; b. Lancaster, Pa., Aug. 14, 1973; BA, U. Md., College Park, 1995. Dep. campaign mgr., field rep. for Rep. Vic Fazio, US House of Reps., 1995—98; chief of staff for Calif. State Assemblyman Thomas Calderon, 1999—2002; dep. chief of staff for Rep. Dennis Cardoza, US House of Reps., 2003—05, chief of staff, 2005—. Mem.: Omicron Delta Kappa, Alpha Omicron Pi. Office: Office of Congressman Dennis Cardoza 1224 Longworth Bldg Washington DC 20515 E-mail: jennifer.walsh@mail.house.gov.*

WALSH, JOANNE CLAIRE, school librarian, educator; b. Roslyn, NY, Sept. 1951; d. Gerard Paul and Constance Ann Walsh. BS, U. White Plains, NY, 1973; MLS, LI U., Brookville, NY, 1977. Lic. postgrad. profl. tchr. Va., 2000, initial tchr. NY, 2007, cert. Nat. Bd. Profl. Tchg. Standards, 2007. Ops. mgr. Brink's Inc, NYC, 1979—89; adminstrv. asst. Gulf Air Internat., NYC, 1989—90; ops. mgr. Fedex, Norfolk, Va., 1990—98, Via Mat Internat., NY, 1998—99, JFK Airport, Jamaica, 1998—99; tchr. Hampton City Schs., Va., 2000—, libr., 2000—. Grant adminstr. Bryan Elem. Sch., Hampton, Va., 2001—03, social studies instrnl. leader, 2003—06; media rep. Eaton Mid. Sch., Hampton, 2007—. Named Tchr. of Yr., Bryan Elem. Sch., 2004—05. Mem.: Va. State Reading Assn., Va. Ednl. Media Assn. Independent. Roman Catholic. Avocations: reading, travel, quilting. Home: 44 Cherry Ave Hampton VA 23661 Office: Hampton City Sch/Eaton Mid Sch 2108 Cunningham Dr Hampton VA 23666 Business E-Mail: jwalsh@sbo.hampton.k12.va.us.

WALSH, JOHN, television show host, missing children and victims' rights advocate; b. Auburn, NY, Dec. 26, 1945; m. Revé Drew Walsh, 1971; children: Adam(dec.), Megan, Callahan, Hayden. Co-founder Mus. of Crime & Punishment, Washington, 2008—. Author: Tears of Rage, 1997, No Mercy, 1998, Public Enemies: The Host of America's Most Wanted Targets the Nation's Most Notorious Criminals, 2001; host (TV series) America's Most Wanted, 1988—, The John Walsh Show, 2002—04, creator The New America's Most Wanted: America Fights Back, appeared in (TV) Springfield's Most Wanted, 1995, Safety Patrol, 1998, American Crime Fighter: E! True Hollywood Story, 2000, Inside TV Land: Cops on Camera, 2002, Laci Peterson: E! True Hollywood Story, 2004, co-host Hawaii's Missing Kids: Eyes of the Innocent, 2004, actor & exec. prodr. (TV films) Smart Kids, 1994, If Looks Could Kill: The John Hawkins Story, 1996; actor: (films) Jesuit Joe, 1991, Wrongfully Accused, 1998, Press Run, 1999, Grey Owl, 1999; narrator (films) The Safe Side, 2004. Founder Adam Walsh Child Resource Ctr., Straight Shooter; bd. dir. Nat. Ctr. for Missing and Exploited Children, chief exec. officers coun., nat. adv. bd., spokesperson. Recipient US Marshals Man of Yr. award, 1988, Spl. Recognition award, US Atty. Gen., honored in Rose Garden 4 times by 3 US Presidents, FBI Man of Yr. award, 2000; named one of 50 Most Beautiful People in World, People mag., 1996, 100 Americans Who Changed History, CBS Portraits. Achievements include being instrumental in the passage of the Missing Children Act of 1982, and the Missing Children's Assistance Act of 1984; testified over 55 times before Congress and state legislatures on crime, missing children and victims' issues. Office: Americas Most Wanted PO Box Crime TV Washington DC 20016-9126

WALSH, JOHN A., broadcast executive, editor; b. Scranton, Pa., Jan. 13, 1945; married; 2 children. BA in English, U. Scranton, 1966; M in Journalism, U. Mo., 1968. Sports editor Columbia Missourian, 1967—70; various editl. positions Newsday, 1970—73; mng. editor Rolling Stone, 1973—74, US News and World Report, 1985—86; editor, style sect. Wash. Post, 1977—78; founding editor Inside Sports Mag., 1979—82; cons. Esquire, 1982—83, Vanity Fair, 1983—84, CBS Sports' NFL Today, 1986—87, ESPN Inc., 1987—88, mgn. editor, 1988—90, sr. v.p., exec. editor, 1990—, ESPN Internet Group, 2000—. Recipient Frank J. O'Hara award, U. Scranton Nat. Alumni Assn., 1991; named one of The Most Influential People in the World of Sports, Bus. Week, 2007, 2008. Office: ESPN Internet Group ESPN Plz Bristol CT 06010

WALSH, JOHN ALFRED, retired social worker; b. NYC, June 4, 1927; s. Joseph Thomas and May Catherine (Moran) Walsh; m. Gwendolyn Ann Stockton, Apr. 13, 1952; children: Ralph, Carl, Nils. BA cum laude, St. Mary's U., Balt., 1949; M in Social Svc., Fordham U., 1954. Lic. clin. social worker, nursing home adminstr., marriage/family therapist. Social worker Cath. Charities, Bklyn., 1949—56; supr. after care clinics Ancora (N.J.) Psychiat. Hosp., 1956—57; dir. social svc. Trenton (N.J.) Psychiat. Hosp., 1958—68; asst. supt. Hunterdon Devel. Ctr., Clinton, NJ, 1968—91; ret. Author: (pamphlet) Fabulous Rosts, 1982. V.p. Warren County Hist. Soc., Belvidere, NJ, 1990—, Assn. Hunterdon Devel. Ctr., Clinton, 1991—; mem. bd. edn. Belvidere Sch. Dist., 1991—2001. Capt. US Army, 1953—66. Avocation: collecting stamps and post cards. Home: 703 Oxford St Belvidere NJ 07823 E-mail: jaw703@aol.com.

WALSH, JOHN BREFFNI, aerospace consultant; b. Bklyn., Aug. 20, 1927; s. George and Margaret Mary (Rigney) W.; m. Marie Louise Leclerc, June 18, 1955; children: George Breffni, John Leclerc, Darina Louise. BEE, Manhattan Coll., 1948; MS, Columbia U., 1950; postgrad., NYU, 1954-62. Asst., instr. Columbia U., NYC, 1948-51, asst. prof., asst. dir. Electronics Rsch. Labs., 1953-66; various positions through tech. dir. Intelligence and Reconnaissance Div., Rome Air Devel. Center, NY, 1951-53; dep. for rsch. to asst. sec. Air Force, 1966-71; sr. staff mem. Nat. Security Council, 1971-72, asst. to Pres.'s sci. advisor, 1971-72; dep. dir. Def. Research and Engring., 1972-77; asst. sec. gen. for def. support NATO, 1977-80; holder chair in systems acquisition mgmt., dean exec. inst. Def. Systems Mgmt. Coll., Ft. Belvoir, Va., 1981-82, prof. emeritus, 1982—; v.p., chief scientist Boeing Mil. Airplane Co., Wichita, Kans., 1982-89; v.p. rsch. and engring. programs Boeing Aerospace and Electronics div., Seattle, 1990-92; v.p. strategic analysis Boeing Defense and Space Group, Seattle, 1992-93; prin. John B. Walsh Assocs., 1993—. Mem. aeros. adv. com. NASA; mem. Congl. Adv. Com. on Aeros., 1984-85; assoc. Def. Sci. Bd.; mem. indsl. adv. bd. Wichita State U. Coll. Engring., adj. prof. elec. engring., 1989-90; chmn. tech. working group Def. Trade Adv. Group Dept. State, 1992-95; chmn. com. on adv. group on aeronautics R & D, NATO, 1981-82; cons. Def. Sci. Bd., 2003-. Author: Electromagnetic Theory and Engineering Applications, 1960; (with K.S. Miller): Introductory Electric Circuits, 1960, Elementary and Advanced Trigonometry, 1977; contbr. tech. papers to publs.; patentee in field. Mem. planning bd., Cresskill, N.J., 1964-66; commr. Kans. Advanced Tech. Commn., 1985-86; bd. dirs. Kans. Inc., 1986-90; mem. math. scis. edn. bd. NRC, 1989-92. Served with U.S. Army, 1946-47, USAR, 1947-52. Recipient Air Force Exceptional Civilian Service award, 1969; recipient Dept. Def. Meritorious Civilian Service award, 1971, Disting. Civilian Service award, 1977, Air Force Assn. citation of honor as outstanding Air Force civilian employee of year, 1971, Theodore von Karman award Air Force Assn., 1977. Fellow IEEE (life), AIAA (v.p. tech. 1987-89); mem. Internat. Inst. for Strategic Studies, N.Y. Acad. Scis., GPS Internat. Assn., Electromagnetics Acad., Sigma Xi, Eta Kappa Nu. Roman Catholic. Office: 8800 Prestwould Pl Mc Lean VA 22102-2231 Home Phone: 703-893-3610.

WALSH, JOHN CHARLES, investment company executive, director; b. Indpls., Sept. 8, 1924; s. John Charles; children: Michael S., Carolyn Ann, Anne D. BS, Notre Dame U., 1949. Auditor Herdrich Boggs & Co., Indpls., 1949—78; with P.R. Mallory & Co., Inc., 1978—; pres. Walgang Co. Inc., Indpls., 1970—. V.p., treas. P.R. Mallory & Co., 1971. With USMCR, 1943—45. Mem. Fin. Execs. Inst., Ind. Hist. Soc., Notre Dame Club. Home: 4974 Shadow Rock Cir Carmel IN 46033-9500 Office: 160 W Carmel Dr Ste 265 Carmel IN 46032

WALSH, JOHN E., JR., business educator, consultant; b. St. Louis, Apr. 28, 1927; s. John E. and Ann M. (Narkewicz) W. BS, U.S. Naval Acad., 1950; MBA, Washington U., St. Louis, 1957; DBA, Harvard U., 1960. Asst. prof. Washington U., St. Louis, 1959-60, assoc. prof., 1960-68, prof., 1968-2001, prof. emeritus, 2001—; vis. assoc. prof. Stanford U., 1964-65; vis. prof. INSEAD, Fontainebleau, France, 1970. Mem. exec. com. Econ. Strategy Inst. Author: Preparing Feasibility Studies in Asia, 1971, Guidelines for Management Consultants in Asia, 1973, Planning New Ventures in International Business, 1976, (with others) Strategies in Business, 1978, Management Tactics, 1980, International Business Case Studies: For the Multicultural Market Place, 1994, Joint Authoring: Managing Cultural Differences, 1994. Mem. State of Mo. leadership initiative to former Soviet Union, Poland, Hungary, 1990; mem. coun., chmn. bd. Kearny Alliance. 1st lt. USAF, 1950-54. Zurn Found. fellow, 1958; Presdl. fellow Am. Grad. Sch. Internat. Mgmt. Mem. Harvard Club N.Y.C. Personal E-mail: walshjejr@aol.com.

WALSH, JOHN EDWARD, political organization administrator, insurance company owner; b. Brockton, Mass., Apr. 14, 1958; s. John and Margaret Mary (Prendeville) Walsh; m. Donna Walsh; 1 child, Coleman. AB, Princeton U., NJ, 1980. Agt. John Hancock Ins. Co., Boston, 1980-81, pension mgr., 1981-82; owner, pres. Independence Ins. Agy., Abington, Mass., 1982—; campaign mgr. Deval Patrick's Gubernatorial Campaign, 2005—06; chmn. Mass. Dem. Party, 2007—. Democrat. Roman Catholic. Office: Mass Dem Party 56 Roaldn St Ste 203 Boston MA 02129 Office Phone: 617-776-2676. Office Fax: 617-776-2579. Business E-Mail: jwalsh@massdems.org.*

WALSH, JOHN L., energy executive; BA, MBA, Harvard Univ. Mgmt. positions through v.p. AmeriGas indsl. gas div. UGI Corp., 1981—86; v.p. spl. gases, pres. process gas solutions No. Am., pres. process Plants BOC Group PLC, 1986—2001, exec. dir., CEO indsl. & spl. products div., 2001—05; pres., COO UGI Corp., 2005—; pres., CEO UGI Utilities, 2009—. Bd. dir. UGI Utilities; vice chmn. Amerigas Propane. Office: UGI Corp 460 N Guelph Rd King Of Prussia PA 19406 Mailing: UGI Corp PO Box 858 Valley Forge PA 19482*

WALSH, JOSEPH BRENNAN, ophthalmologist; b. Troy, NY, Mar. 6, 1941; s. Joseph Edward and Edna Margaret (Molloy) W. BS in Biology, Georgetown U., 1962, MD, 1966. Diplomate Am. Bd. Ophthalmology. Intern SUNY Upstate Med. Ctr., Syracuse, 1966-67; resident in medicine Univ. Hosp., Boston, 1968—69; resident in ophthalmology The N.Y. Eye and Ear Infirmary, NYC, 1970-73; retina fellow Montefiore Hosp. and Med. Ctr./Albert Einstein Coll. Medicine, Bronx, 1973-74; from instr. to assoc. prof. dept. ophthalmology Montefiore Med. Ctr./Albert Einstein Coll. of Medicine, Bronx, N.Y., 1973-88; chmn., prof. dept. ophthalmology NY. Eye and Ear Infirmary, NY. Med. Coll., 1988—, pres., 2008—. Lectr. in field. Capt. M.C. USAF, 1968—70. Decorated Knight Hospitaller Am. Priory of the Most Venerable Order Hosp. St. John Jerusalem; recipient Chancellor award, 2002—05, Govs. award, 1993—2008. Fellow N.Y. Acad. Medicine (Charles H. May Meml. lectr. 1998—), N.Y. Acad. Scis., Royal Coll. Ophthalmologists, Am. Acad. Ophthalmology; mem. Assn. for Rsch. in Vision and Ophthalmology, Ophthalmic Laser Surg. Soc. (pres. 1992-94), Macula Soc., Retina Soc., N.Y. Soc. for Clin. Ophthalmology (pres. 1984-85, Schoenberg lectr. 1993—), N.Y. Ophthalmol. Soc. (sec. 2002, pres. 2008). Office: NY Eye and Ear Infirmary 310 E 14th St New York NY 10003-4201 Office Phone: 212-979-4447. Office Fax: 212-979-4268. Business E-Mail: jwalsh@mee.edu, jwalsh@nyee.com, jwalsh@nyee.edu. E-mail: rlewis212@aol.com.

WALSH, JOSEPH FIDLER (JOE WALSH), recording artist, record producer; b. Wichita, Kans., Nov. 20, 1947; s. George William and Helen Alice (Bowen) Walsh; m. Denise Driscoll; 3 children. Student, Kent State U., Ohio. Lead guitarist James Gang, 1968—71; with the Eagles, 1976—, Ringo Starr's All Star Band, 1990; disc jockey WXRK, NY, 1990. Musician (solo): (songs) Walk Away, Funk #49, In the City, Life's Been Good, (albums) Barnstorm, 1972, The Smoker You Drink, the Player You Get, 1973, So, What, 1975, But Seriously Folks, 1978, There Goes the Neighborhood, 1981, You Bought It: You Name It, 1983, The Confessor, 1985, Got Any Gum?, 1987, Ordinary Average Guy, 1991, Songs For A Dying Planet, 1992, Look What I Did, 1995, Little Did he Know..., 1997; musician: (with The James Gang) The James Gang, 1969, The James Gang Rides Again, 1970, (with The Eagles) Hotel California, 1976 (VH1's 100 Greatest Albums, 2001), The Long Run, 1979, Eagles Live, 1980, Hell Freezes Over, 1996 (Am. Music award, Favorite Rock Album, 1996), Long Road Out of Eden, 2007, (songs) Hotel California (Grammy award, Record of Yr., 1978), New Kid in Town (Grammy award, Best Arrangement for Voices, 1980), Heartache Tonight (Grammy award, Best Group Rock Vocal Performance, 1980), How Long (Grammy award, Best Group Rock Vocal Country Performance, 2008), I Dreamed There Was No War, 2007 (Grammy award for Best Pop Instrumental Performance, 2009); actor: (films) The Blues Brothers, 1980; (TV series) The Drew Carey Show, 1998—2001. Recipient Favorite Rock Group award, Am. Music Awards, 1981, 1996, Favorite Adult Contemporary Artist award, 1996, Favorite Rock Album award, 1996; named one of Greatest Artists of Rock & Roll, VH1, 1998, 100 Greatest Artists of All Time, Rolling Stone, 2004; named to Rock & Roll Hall of Fame, 1998. Mem.: Amateur Radio Relay League. Achievements include research in electronic music synthesizers.*

WALSH, JOSEPH HAYES, lawyer; b. Boston, Feb. 9, 1950; s. Joseph Henry and Eileen M. Walsh; m. Sandra A. Walsh; children: Catherine E., Christine A. AB cum laude, Boston Coll., 1972, JD cum laude, 1975. Bar: Mass. 1975, US Dist. Ct. Dist Mass. 1977, US Ct. Appeals (1st cir.), US Supreme Ct. Assoc. Crane, Inker & Oteri, Boston, 1975-80; ptnr. White, Inker & Aronson, Boston, 1984-92, Cuddy, Lynch & Bixby, Boston, 1992-94, Menard, Murphy & Walsh, Boston, 1994—. Named one of Top 100 Lawyers, Worth mag., 2005; named to New Eng. & Mass. Supper Lawyers. Office: Menard Murphy & Walsh 28 State St Boston MA 02109-1800

WALSH, JOSEPH MICHAEL, magazine distribution executive; b. NYC, Jan. 19, 1943; s. John Redmond and Bridget Judith (Donovan) W.; m. Theresa Rose Vericker, Oct. 3, 1964; children— Joseph, Matthew, Teresa Ann, John, James. BBA in Acctg., Iona Coll., 1964. With Peat, Marwick, Mitchell & Co., C.P.A.s, NYC, 1964-70, audit supr., until 1970; asst. to chmn. bd. and pres. Cadence Industries Corp., West Caldwell, NJ, 1970-71, v.p., 1971-74, exec. v.p., 1974-87; pres. subs. Curtis Circulation Co., 1972-74, chmn., chief exec. officer, 1982—; pres. Data Services for Health, 1976-77, U.S. Pencil and Stationery Co., 1977-79, Perfect Subscription Co. (parent Perfect Sch. Plans, Perfect Telephone Plan, Moore Cottrell and Keystone Readers Service), 1980-83. Mem. AICPA, N.Y. State Soc. CPAs, K.C. Office: Curtis Circulation Co 730 River Rd New Milford NJ 07646-3048 Home Phone: 561-694-1966; Office Phone: 201-634-7401. E-mail: jwalsh@curtiscirc.com.

WALSH, JOSEPH THOMAS, retired state supreme court justice; b. Wilmington, Del., May 18, 1930; s. Joseph Patrick and Mary Agnes (Bolton) W.; m. Madeline Maria Lamb, Oct. 6, 1955; children: Kevin, Lois, Patrick, Daniel, Thomas, Nancy. BA, LaSalle Coll., 1952; LLB, Georgetown U., 1955. Bar: D.C. 1955, Del. 1955. Atty. Ho. of Reps., Dover, Del., 1961-62; chief counsel Pub. Svc. Commn., Dover, 1964-72; judge Del. Superior Ct., Wilmington, 1972-84; vice chancellor Ct. of Chancery, Wilmington, 1984-85; justice Del. Supreme Ct., Wilmington, 1985—2003. Adjunct prof. Widener U. Sch. of Law, 2003—. Capt. U.S. Army, 1955-58. Democrat. Roman Catholic.

WALSH, JOY IRENE, literature and language educator; d. Lloyd Dice Tennies and Phyllis Cloe Wayland. AA in Elem. Edn., Butler County CC, Pa., 1987; BS in Elem. Edn., Houghton Coll., NY, 1989; MA in English, Slippery Rock U., Pa., 1992. Tutor Butler County CC, 1990—92, instr., 1993—; devel. specialist Lifesteps, Inc., Butler, 2000—02. Mem.: Nat. Coun. Tchrs. English. Office: Butler County CC College Dr Oak Hill Butler PA 16003

WALSH, KATE, actress; b. San Jose, Calif., Oct. 13, 1967; m. Alex Young, Sept. 1, 2007 (separated Nov. 22, 2008). Student, U. Ariz. Actor: (radio plays) Born Guilty; (plays) Moon Under Miami, Troilus and Cressida; (films) Normal Life, 1996, Peppermills, 1997, Night of the Lawyers, 1997, Three Below Zero, 1998, Heaven, 1998, Henry, Portrait of a Serial Killer II, 1998, The Family Man, 2000, Under the Tuscan Sun, 2003, After the Sunset, 2004, Kicking and Screaming, 2005, Inside Out, 2005, Bewitched, 2005, Veritas, Prince of Truth, 2006; (TV series) The Drew Carey Show, 1997—2002, The Mike O'Malley Show, 1999, Turks, 1999, The Norm Show, 2000—01, Mind of a Married Man, 2001, Joint Custody, 2004, Grey's Anatomy, 2005—07 (Outstanding Performance by an Ensemble in a Drama Series, SAG, 2007), Private Practice, 2007—; (TV films) Bobby Cannon, 2005. Mailing: Grey's Anatomy Los Feliz Tower 4th Fl 4151 Prospect Ave Los Angeles CA 90027*

WALSH, KATHERINE JEAN, physician; b. Deland, Fla., June 8, 1979; d. James Brian and Jennifer Walsh. BS with highest honors, U. Fla., Gainesville, 2001, MD, 2004. Diplomate Am. Bd. Internal Medicine, 2007. Tchg. asst. U. Fla., 2003, intern internal medicine, 2004—05, housestaff adv. coun. internal medicine residency program, 2004—, resident internal medicine, 2005—07, resident adv. bd. hosp. physician, 2006—, chief resident dept. medicine, 2007—, dept. medicine edn. com., 2007—08. Oncology fellow Duke U., Durham, NC, 2008—. Contact, mem. UF delegation healthcare lobbying ACP, Gainesville, Fla., 2005—07. Recipient Excellence in Ambulatory Care award, U. Fla., 2004, Tchg. Excellence award, U. Fla. Dept. of Medicine, 2007, Leighton Cluff award, U. Fla., 2007; named to Chapman Humanism Honor Soc., 2006; grantee, 1998-1999; scholar, Lockheed Martin, 1997; Anderson Scholar, U. Fla., 2000. Mem.: AMA (assoc.; mem. legislative action com. 2006—08), ACP (assoc. Chief Resident award 2007), Soc. Gen. Medicine, Fla. Med. Assn. (assoc.; del. ann. meeting 2005, pub. health com. 2006—07, sec. governing coun. 2006—08), Gold Humanism (Chapman chpt.), Alpha Omega Alpha, Golden Key Nat. Honor Soc. (hon.). Achievements include volunteer in neuroscience laboratory that led to a University of Florida scholarship and two publications; volunteer in aging and biochemistry laboratory that led to publication in Frontiers in Bioscience. Avocations: violin, ballroom dancing, tennis, football. Office: U Fla Dept Medicine PO Box 100277 1600 SW Archer Rd Gainesville FL 32608

WALSH, KERRI LEE, Olympic athlete; b. Santa Clara, Calif., Aug. 15, 1978; d. Tim and Margie; m. Casey Jennings, Feb. 4, 2005. BA in Am. studies, Stanford U., Calif., 1999. Player BVA Tour, 2001, FIVG Internat. Tour, 2001—, AVP Tour, 2003—; beach volleyball player, Team USA Sydney Olympic Games, 2000, Athens Olympic Games, 2004, Beijing Olympic Games, 2008. Recipient Gold medal, beach volleyball, Athens Olympic Games, 2004, Beijing Olympic Games, 2008; named First Team All-Am., NCAA, 1996—99, Pro Beach Volleyball Rookie of Yr., 2001, AVP Best Offensive Player, 2003, AVP Most Valuable Player, 2003—04, AVP Team of the Yr. (with Misty May), 2003—07, Sportswoman of Yr., FIVB, 2005—07, Best Offensive Player, 2007, Crocs Cup Champion (with Misty May), 2006—07. Achievements include winning FIVB World Championships (with partner Misty May-Treanor), 2003, 2005, 2007; becoming the first repeat gold medalist in Olympic women's beach volleyball history (with Misty May-Treanor), 2004, 2008. Office: c/o USOC One Olympic Plz Colorado Springs CO 80909

WALSH, KEVIN P., energy executive, financial services executive; BS cum laude in Fin., Bus. Mgmt., Fairfield Univ.; grad., GE Fin. Mgmt. Program. Region mgr., internat. credit, collections ops. GE, 1985—86; region mgr., customer fin. programs for comm. aircraft and indsl./power generation programs GE Aircraft Engines, 1986—88; program mgr., fin. mgmt. GE, 1988—90, asst. v.p., sales, 1990—92, v.p., project fin. sales Stamford, Conn., 1992—93, dir., structured fin. London, 1993—95, mng. dir., capital mkts, 1995—96, sales originator, structured fin., 1996—98, mng. dir., structured fin. printing, paper, forest products group, 1998—2000, mng. dir., structured fin. e-bus., 2000—04, mng. dir. of portfolio, comml. fin. energy fin. svcs. Stamford, Conn., 2004—. Past bd. dir. Southern Star Ctrl. Gas Pipeline, Inc., 2005. Named one of 50 Who Matter Now, Business 2.0, 2007. Office: GE Energy Fin Svcs 120 Long Ridge Rd Stamford CT 06927 Office Phone: 203-357-4880. Office Fax: 203-357-4942.

WALSH, LAURIE ANN, law educator; d. John Philip and Elsie Ann Ambrose; m. Robert Gerald Walsh, June 4, 1994; 1 child, Elise Meghan. BS Phys. Therapy, SUNY, Buffalo, 1982; JD, SUNY, Sch. Law, 1991. Bar: NY 1991. Phys. therapist BOCES, Lancaster, NY, 1985—91; atty. Damon & Morey, Buffalo, 1991—93; asst. prof. Daemen Coll., Amherst, NY, 1993—2000, assoc. prof., 2000—, chair, history & govt. dept., 2007—. Contbr. chapters to books. Recipient Merit award, NY Phys. Therapy Assn., 2006. Mem.: Am. Phys. Therapy Assn., NYS Bar Assn. Democrat. Roman Catholic. Office: Daemen Coll 4380 Main St Amherst NY 14226

WALSH, LAWRENCE EDWARD, lawyer; b. Port Maitland, NS, Can., Jan. 8, 1912; came to U.S., 1914, naturalized, 1922; s. Cornelius Edward and Lila May (Sanders) W.; m. Mary Alma Porter; children: Barbara Marie, Janet Maxine (Mrs. Alan Larson), Sara Porter, Dale Edward, Elizabeth Porter (Mrs. Peter LaColla). AB, Columbia U., 1932, LLB, 1935; LLD, Union U., 1959, St. John's U., 1975, Suffolk U., 1975, Waynesburg Coll., 1976, Vt. Law Sch., 1976. Bar: N.Y. 1936, D.C. 1981, Okla. 1981, U.S. Supreme Ct. 1951. Spl. asst. atty. gen. Drukman Investigation, 1936—38; dep. asst. dist. atty. N.Y. County, 1938—41; assoc. Davis Polk Wardwell Sunderland & Kiendl, 1941—43; asst. counsel to gov. State of NY, 1943—49, counsel to gov., 1950—51; counsel Pub. Svc. Commn., 1951—53; gen. counsel, exec. dir. Waterfront Commn. of N.Y. Harbor, 1953—54; judge US Dist. Ct. (so. dist.) NY, 1954—57; dep. atty. gen. US Dept. Justice, 1957—60; ptnr. Davis, Polk & Wardwell LLP, 1961—81; counsel Crowe & Dunlevy LLP, Oklahoma City, 1981—. Ind. counsel Iran/Contra investigation, 1986-93; chmn. N.Y. State Moreland Commn. Alcoholic Beverage Control Law, 1963-64; pres. Columbia Alumni Fedn., 1968-69; dep. head with rank of amb. U.S. del. meetings on Vietnam, Paris, 1969; counsel to N.Y. State Ct. on Judiciary, 1971-72; 2d cir. mem. U.S. Cir. Judge Nominating Commn., 1978-80. Author: (Book) Firewall The Iran-Contra Conspiracy and Cover-Up, 1997, The Gift of Insecurity, 2003. Trustee emeritus Columbia U., Mut. Life Ins. Co., N.Y. Recipient medal for excellence Columbia U., 1959, Law Sch., Columbia U., 1980, John Jay award Columbia Coll., 1989. Fellow Am. Bar Found., Am. Coll. Trial Lawyers; mem. Am. Law Inst., ABA (pres. 1975-76), N.Y. State Bar Assn. (pres. 1966-67), Oklahoma County Bar Assn., Okla. State Bar Assn., Internat. Bar Assn., Assn. of Bar of City of N.Y., N.Y. County Lawyers Assn., Fed. Bar Coun., Law Soc. Eng. and Wales (hon.), Can. Bar Assn. (hon.), Mex. Bar Assn. (hon.), Century Assn., Oklahoma City Golf and Country Club, Beta Theta Pi. Presbyterian. Home: 1902 Bedford Dr Oklahoma City OK 73116-5306 Office: 1800 Mid Am Towers Oklahoma City OK 73102 Office Phone: 405-235-7700. E-mail: legalew@sbcglobal.net.

WALSH, LOUISE JAQUELYN, literature and language professor; b. Wesson, Miss., July 13, 1954; d. Lewis Jackson and Hazel Juanita Weeks; m. Nicholas Joseph Walsh, Dec. 29, 1989. PhD, U. Miss., Oxford, 1988. Prof. English McNeese State U., Lake Charles, La., 1990—. Vol. coord. Banners Arts and Humanities Series, Lake Charles, 1998—2008, Bayou Blues and Zydeco Festival, Lake Charles, 1997—2001, Rouge et Blanc, Lake Charles, 2006—08. Fellowship, U. Miss., 1978—79. Mem.: Phi Kappa Phi. Democrat. Avocations: painting, swimming. Home: 1105 Oklahoma St Lake Charles LA 70607 Office: McNeese State Univ PO Box 92655 Lake Charles LA 70609

WALSH, M. EMMET, actor; b. Ogdensburg, NY, Mar. 22, 1935; BBA, Clarkson Coll., 1958; student, Am. Acad. Dramatic Arts, 1959-61. Appeared in films including Chasing 3000, The Man in the Chair, Raising Arizona, Ordinary People, The Milagro Beanfield War, Romeo and Juliet, Winterdance, My Best Friend's Wedding, Twilight, A Time To Kill, Albino Alligator, Free Willy II, Snow Dogs, Music of Chance, White Sands, Narrow Margin, The Mighty Quinn, Clean and Sober, Harry and The Hendersons, Fletch, Missing in Action, Back to School, Blood Simple, Blade Runner, Silkwood, Sundown, Brubaker, Raise the Titanic, Fast Walking, Reds, The Jerk, Straight Time, At Long Last Long, Serpico, What's Up Doc?, They Might Be Giants, Midnight Cowboy, End of the Road, Cannery Row, Slap Shot, Cold Turkey, The Traveling Executioner, Alice's Restaurant, Airport '77, Wild Wild West, Christmas in the Clouds, Poor White Trash, Random Hearts, Iron Giant, Skirty Winner, Queen of Hearts, Baggage, Me and Will, Erasable You, Carrot Top, A Time to Kill, Chairman of the Board, Retroactive, The Killing Jar, Portraits of Innocence, Criminal Hearts, Panther, Camp Nowhere, Dead Badge, Probable Cause, Glass Shield, Relative Fear, Cops and Robbersons, Bitter Harvest, Wilder Napalm, Equinox, Naked Truth, Killer Image, Red Scorpion, Chattahoochee, Thunderground, Catch Me If You Can, War Party, Sunset, No Man's Land, The Best of Times, Wildcats, Critters, The Pope of Greenwich Village, Grandview-USA, Raw Courage, Scandalous, Escape Artist, Back Roads, Bound for Glory, Nickelodeon, Mickey & Nicky, The Fish That Saved Pittsburgh, Kid Blue, Prisoner of 2nd Avenue, The Gambler, Get to Know Your Rabbit, Escape From the Planet of the Apes, Little Big Man, Loving, Stiletto, Christmas With The Kranks, Racing Stripes, Bitter Harvest, Greener Mountains, Inn Trouble, Man in the Chair, Big Stan, Your Name Here, Sherman's Way, Darkness Visible; (TV shows) include Frasier, Sandy Duncan Show, Bonanza, Mind of the Married Man, The Rockford Files, All in the Family, Bob Newhart Show, The Waltons, Little House on the Prairie, Early Edition, Tales from the Crypt, Home Improvement, The Outer Limits, X Files, The Abduction of Kari Swenson, Resting Place, The Woman Who Willed a Miracle, The Guardian, Tracy Ullman's Trailer Tales, Charlie Lawrence, Ed, Gideon's Crossing, Night Visions, Cover Me, NYPD Blue, Monster, Men in White, Nightmare in Big Sky Country, The Tracey Ullman Show, Dogs, The Lottery, The Mixed Up Files Of..., The Jackie Thomas Show, Wild Card, Four Eyes and Six Guns, Grey Fox, The Nerd, Love and Lies, Fourth Story, The Flash, Unsub, Brotherhood of the Rose II, Murder Ordained I & II, Amazing Stories, Broken Vows, Hero in the Family, The City, Deliberate Stranger, The Right of the People, Twighlight Zone, The Hitchhiker, You Are the Jury, Vanishing America, After Mash, Night Partners, High Noon Two, East of Eden I & II, Helinger's Law, French-Atlantic Affair, Countdown to Superdome, Dear Detective, Mrs. R's Daughter, James at Fifteen, Red Alert, A Question of Guilt, No Other Love, Panic On Page One, Skag, The Gift, Mississippi, Starsky and Hutch, Mary Hartman, Gibbsville, Tony Randall Show, Nancy Walker Show, Kate McShane, Joe & Sons, The Cop and the Kid, Brahmins, McMillan & Wife, N.Y.P.D., Baretta, Don Rickles Show, Nichols, Texas Wheeler, Crime Club, Prudential's "On Stage," The Doctors, Outlaws, Jimmy Stewart Show, Men at Law, Dr. Dan, Love of Life, Amy Prentiss, The Law, Arnie, Julia, Con Sawyer; HBO series includes The Mind of the Married Man; Broadway shows include That Championship Season, Does the Tiger Wear a Necktie?, Buried Child, Royal Nation Theatre, London, 2004; Off Broadway shows include Shepherds of the Shelf, Blackfriars Theatre, 1961, The Old Glory, The Outside Man, Am. Pl. Theatre, 1964, Death of the Well Loved Boy, St. Marks Playhouse, 1967, Three From Column "A", Theatre 73, 1968, Are You Now or Have You Ever Been, L.A. Ford's Theatre, D.C., 1975, Marathon '93, Ensemble Studio Theatre, 1993; Off-Off-Broadway shows at New Theatre Workshop, The Loft, Tamarack, Actors Studio, The Playbox,Ensemble Studio Theatre, The Pub. TheatreNYSF; regional theatre shows at Theatre of Living Arts, Phila., 1965, Studio Arena, Buffalo, 1966, Long Wharf Theatre, New Haven, 1967, Cin. Playhouse in Pk., 1995, La Jolla Playhouse, 1999, Arena Stage, D.C., 2000; summer stock shows at Coll. Theatre, Am. Acad. Dramatic Arts, 1954-61, Bucks County Playhouse, New Hope, Pa., 1962, Brattleboro Summer Theatre, Vt., 1963, Caravan Theatre, Dorset, Vt., 1964, U. Ky., 1966, Berkshire Theatre Festival, Stockbridge, Mass., 1967-70, Vt. Summer Theatre Festival, Johnson, 1974, U. Tulsa, 1983, Santa Barbara Theatre Festival, 1985, U. Vt., 1992; voices include The Civil War, Baseball, The Way West, The West, King of The Hill, Wild Thornberry, Muriel's Christmas Carol, Big Guy and Rusty, The Simpsons, The New Scooby Doo, BBC Radio Play, Squirrel Boy, the "X's", numerous others.

WALSH, MATTHEW M., construction executive; b. Chgo., Jan. 7, 1946; m. Joyce Walsh; children: Matt IV, Sean, Erin. BA in Bus., U. Notre Dame, Ind., 1968; JD, Loyola U., Chgo., 1972. CEO Walsh Group, Chgo. Bd. mem. Constrn. Industry Roundtable. Mem. bd. St. Ignatius Coll. Prep. Sch., Union League Club; mem. adv. coun. Sch. Architecture U. Notre Dame. Recipient Outstanding Achievement in Constrn. award, The Moles, 2005. Mem.: Union League Club. Office: Walsh Group 929 W Adams St Chicago IL 60607-3021 Office Phone: 312-563-5400. Office Fax: 312-563-5420.

WALSH, MICHAEL J., lawyer; b. Portland, Oreg., Sept. 4, 1932; s. Frank M.J. and Elisemary (Derbes) W.; m. June Griffin, Nov. 28, 1959; children: Molly, Erin, Kathryn (dec.), Anne. BA, U. Portland, 1954; JD, Georgetown U., 1959. Bar: D.C. 1959, Oreg. 1959, U.S. Ct. Appeals (fed. and 9th cirs.) 1959, U.S. Tax Ct. 1959, U.S. Supreme Ct. 1968. Law ck. to presiding justice Oreg. Supreme Ct., Salem, 1959-60; mng. ptnr. Rankin, Walsh, Ragen and Roberts, Portland, 1960-75; pvt. practice Portland, 1976—81; ptnr. Walsh and Connolly, Portland, 1982—83; of counsel McEwen, Hanna, Gisvold and Rankin, Portland, 1983-85, Bullivant, Houser, Bailey, Pendergrass, & Hoffman, Washington, 1985—. Chief Judge Employees Compensation Appeals Bd. US Dept. Labor, Washington, 1985—2003, sr. counsel Adminstrv. Appeals Bds., 2003—05; legal counsel Reagan-Bush '84, Nat. Hdqs., Washington, 1983—84; mem. US Congress, 1972. Chmn. legal dev. March of Dimes, 1967; chmn. admissions Georgetown U., Oreg., 1972-83; trustee Christie Sch., 1974-78; trustee Cath. Charities Oreg., 1966-72, pres. 1971; trustee Parry Ctr. for Children, 1967-73, v.p. 1970-71; trustee Portland Tennis Ctr. Assn., 1972-83, pres. 1976-82; bd. dirs. Portland Traffic Safety Commn., 1981-83. Served with JAGC, USAF, capt. res. Mem. Am. Judicature Soc., Am. Trial Lawyers Assn., Nat. Assn. Coll. and Uiv. Attys., Am. Arbitration Assn., D.C. Bar Assn., Oreg. Bar Assn. (mem. various coms.), Multnomah County Bar Assn., Portland C. of C. (bd. dirs. 1975-78, chmn. legis. coun. 1975), John Carroll Soc., Thomas More Soc. Clubs: Georgetown Univ. (Oreg.) (pres. 1966). Home: 3273 Sutton Pl NW # B Washington DC 20016-3537 Home Phone: 202-537-1789.

WALSH, MICHAEL P., mechanical engineer; b. Aug. 17, 1943; m. Evelyn Walsh; 3 children. BS, Manhattan Coll., 1966; postgrad., Princeton U., 1970. Dir. motor vehicle pollution control Dept. Air Resources, NYC, 1970—74; chief tech. support br., Office of Enforcement U.S. Environ. Protection Agy., 1974—77, spl. asst. to asst. adminstr. for Air, Noise and Radiation, 1977—78, dep. asst. adminstr., Mobile Source Air Pollution Control, 1978—81; independent technical cons., 1981—. Co-chair mobile source advisory subcom. EPA. Author: (bimonthly publ.) Car Lines. Recipient Thomas W. Zosel Outstanding Individual Achievement Award, U.S. Environ. Protection Agy., 2000, "Haagen Smit" award, Calif. Air Resources Bd., 2003; named MacArthur fellow, John D. and Catherine T. MacArthur Found., 2005. Mem.: Am. Assn. for the Advancement of Sci., Air and Waste Mgmt. Assn., Soc. Automotive Engineers (Lloyd L. Withrow Disting. Speaker Award 1999). E-mail: mpwalsh@igc.org.

WALSH, MICHAEL THOMAS, historian, musician; b. Balt., Dec. 1, 1978; s. John Michael and Annette Mary Walsh; m. Jennifer Trombetta, July 7, 2007. BA in History, magna cum laude, Loyola Coll., Balt., 2000; MA in Historical Studies, U. Md., Balt. County, 2002; PhD in Public Policy, U. Md., Balt., 2002—. Profl. musician self employed, Balt., 1998—; tchg. asst. history U. Md., 2002—03, tchg. asst. polit. sci., 2003—05, acadmic advisor, 2003—, tchg. asst. history, 2005—07; transfer student evaluator Towson U., 2007—. Contbr. ency. entries; musician: Whisky Train's Automatic Sin, 2004. Supporting mem. Colonial Williamsburg Found.; sustaining mem. Rep. Nat. Com., 2006; pres. Rep. Presdl. Task Force, 2006. Recipient Outstanding Achievement Jazz Performance, 1997—98. Mem.: Orgn. Am. hist., Am. Hist. Assn., Pi Sigma Alpha, Phi Alpha Theta. Republican. Roman Catholic. Avocations: music, reading, sports, swimming. Personal E-mail: mwalsh3@umbc.edu.

WALSH, NAN, artist, painter, sculptor, consultant; b. NYC, Nov. 4, 1932; d. Joseph Edward and Mary Ellen (White) Heinl; m. Albert Anthony Walsh, July 10, 1954 (dec. Oct. 9, 2002); children: Maryellen, Nanette, Mark, Gregg (dec.). BS in Elem. Edn., Fordham U., 1954; postgrad., Nat. Acad. Sch. Fine Arts, Art Life Studio Inc., White Plains and Portchester, NY, 1984-94, V.K. Jonynas, LI, NY, 1968-88, Art Ctr. No. N.J., 1996—2002. Fashion model Martha Clyde, NYC, 1951-54; tchr. Yonkers (N.Y.) Pub. Schs., 1953-55; gallery dir. Mamaroneck Artists Guild, Larchmont, NY, 1988-95; fine artist, art juror, cons., 1995—. Membership juror Mamaroneck Artists Guild, Larchmont, 1982-84, membership juror chair, 1996-98, mem. adv. bd., 1996-98; mem. Ctr. for Contemporary Printmaking, 1998—. One-woman shows and juried exhbns. Westchester and N.Y.C., 1976—; works represented in corp. and pvt. collecitons. Hostess chairperson Citizens for John Lindsay, Gracie Mansion, N.Y., 1970; mem. Studio Twelve, pres., show chair, 1972-80; mem. Katonah Mus. Art. Recipient numerous 1st place awards for art. Mem. Nat. League Am. Penwomen (corr. sec. and membership chair 1992-96), Nat. Mus. Women in the Arts, N.Y. Soc. Women Artists, Guild Creative Art, N.J. Artists Equity, Mamaroneck Artists Guild (v.p. 1982, 83, membership chair 1992-95 Fordham U. Art Club (show chair 1965-80). Avocations: gardening, bridge, tennis, swimming, travel.

WALSH, NICHOLAS C., insurance company executive; Joined Am. Internat. Underwriters (AIU), London, 1973, regional v.p. UK/Ireland divsn., 1989, 1996, pres., CEO; mng. dir. AIG Europe Am. Internat. Group, Inc. (AIG), London, 1989, 1996, regional pres. European gen. insurance ops. Paris, 1993, v.p. NYC, 1995, sr. v.p., 2002, exec. v.p. fgn. gen. insurance, 2005—. Spkr. in field. Office: Am Internat Group Inc (AIG) 70 Pine St New York NY 10270*

WALSH, NICOLAS EUGENE, rehabilitation services professional, educator; b. Mpls., July 1, 1947; s. Leonard Cyril and June Alice Walsh; m. Wendy Sarah Allnutt, June 1, 1973; children: Meghan, Rorey, Katlin, Alaine. BS, USAF Acad., 1969; MS, Marquette U., 1974; MD, U. Colo., 1979. Asst. prof. naval sci. Marquette U., Milw., 1972—74; from asst. prof. to assoc. prof. rehab. medicine U. Tex. Health Sci. Ctr., San Antonio, 1982—89, prof., chmn. rehab. medicine, 1989—, exec. assoc. dean Sch. Medicine, 1999—2000, disting. prof., 2001—. Dir. Am. Bd. Phys. Medicine and Rehab., Rochester, Minn., 1994—2006, sec., 1996—98, chmn., 1998—2005; pres., CEO Univ. Physician Group, 1998—2001. Author book chpts.; editor: Rehabilitation of Chronic Pain, 1991; editor-in-chief Archives of Phys. Medicine and Rehab., Chgo., 1994—2000; mng. editor: Rehabilitation Medicine: Principles and Practices, 2005. Recipient Excellence in Rsch. award, Am. Jour. Phys. Medicine and Rehab., 1991; named Health Care Profl. of Yr., Gov.'s Com. for Disabled Persons, 1989. Fellow: Am. Acad. Phys. Medicine and Rehab. (Richard and Hinda Rosenthal Found. award 1991, Zieter lectr. 2003), Am. Bd. Pain Medicine (v.p. 1993—94, sec. 1994—96); mem.: Phys. Medicine and Rehab. Edn. and Rsch. Found. (pres. 1993—2000, Excellence in Rsch. award 1991), Assn. Acad. Physiatrists (v.p. 1993—95, pres. 1996—98). Office: U Tex Health Sci Ctr Mail Code 7872 7703 Floyd Curl Dr San Antonio TX 78229-3900 Home Phone: 210-493-1174; Office Phone: 210-567-5350. Business E-Mail: walshn@uthscsa.edu.

WALSH, PATRICK CRAIG, urologist; b. Akron, Ohio, Feb. 13, 1938; s. Raymond Michael and Catherine N. (Rodden) W.; m. Margaret Campbell, May 23, 1964; children— Christopher, Jonathan, Alexander. AB, Case Western Res. U., 1960, MD, 1964. Intern in surgery Peter Bent Brigham Hosp., Boston, 1964-65, asst. resident in surgery, 1965-66; asst. resident in pediatric surgery Children's Hosp. Med. Center, Boston, 1966-67; resident in urology UCLA Med. Ctr., 1967-71; dir., chmn. James Buchanan Brady Urol. Inst., urologist-in-chief Johns Hopkins Hosp., Balt., 1974—2004; prof., dir. dept. urology Johns Hopkins U. Sch. Medicine, 1974—2004, prof. urology, 2004—. Contbr. articles to med. jours. Served to comdr. M.C. USN, 1971-73. Recipient Charles F. Kettering medal GM Cancer Rsch. Found., 1996, King Faisal Internat. prize, 2007. Mem. Am. Assn. Genitourinary Surgeons, Clin. Soc. Genitourinary Surgeons, Am. Urol. Assn., Am. Surg. Assn. Inst. Medicine of NAS, Alpha Omega Alpha. Roman Catholic. Office: Johns Hopkins Med Inst 600 N Wolfe St Baltimore MD 21287-0005 Office Phone: 410-955-6100.

WALSH, PATRICK M., career military officer; b. Va. Beach, Va., 1955; s. Jim and Betty Walsh; m. Andy Walsh; children: Jennifer, Matthew. BS, US Naval Acad., 1977; MA, Ph.D, Fletcher Sch. Law & Diplomacy, Tufts U. Advanced through ranks to admiral USN, 2007; with "Golden Dragons" Attack Squadron One Nine Two; comdr. Light Attack Wing Pacific; operational test dir. Air Test & Evaluation Squadron; ops. officer "Golden Warriors" Strike-Fighter Squadron Eight Seven; comdr. "Gunslingers" Strike Fighter Squadron One Zero Five, Carrier Air Wing One, Carrier Group Seven/USS John C. Stennis Strike Group; spl. asst. to dir. Office Mgmt. & Budget, Exec. Office of the Pres.; chair Dept. Leadership, Ethics, & Law US Naval Acad.; exec. asst. to Chief Naval Pers./Dep. Chief Naval Ops. for Manpower & Pers. USN; dep. dir. for strategy & policy (J-5) The Joint Staff, The Pentagon, 2001—05; dir. Navy Quadrennial Def. Review USN, 2005, dir. Navy Programming divsn., 2005; comdr. US 5th Fleet, Combined Maritime Forces, 2005—07, US Naval Forces, US Ctrl. Command (USNAVCENT), 2005—07; vice chief naval ops. USN, Washington, 2007—09. Decorated Def. Superior Svc. medal, Meritorious Svc medal, Air medal with Combat V, Strike/Flight medal (5), Navy Commendation medal (3) with Combat V, Navy Achievement medal, Presdl. Svc. badge; recipient Disting. Grad. award, Jesuit Coll. Preparatory, 1973, Disting. Alumnus award, 1995, Legion of Merit (4).

WALSH, PAUL HENRY, bishop; b. Bklyn., Aug. 17, 1937; Professed Order of Friars Preachers, 1963, ordained priest, 1966; head chaplain Providence Coll., RI, 1967—74; dir. formation Dominican House of Studies, Washington, 1974—78; pastor St. Vincent Ferrer Ch., NYC, 1978—83; assoc. pastor Our Lady Queen of Martyrs Ch., Centerport, NY, 1983—88; priest Diocese of Rockville Ctr., NY, 1984—2003, aux. bishop, 2003—; assoc. pastor St. Patrick's Ch., Smithtown, NY, 1988—90, pastor, 1990—2003; named monsignor, 1996; ordained bishop, 2003; pastor Queen of the Most Holy Rosary Ch., Roosevelt, NY, 2003—. Mem. admissions bd. Immaculate Conception Sem., Huntington, NY, 1997—2001; bd. dirs. Long Island Cath. newspaper, 1999—2001; chaplain Suffolk County Police Dept. Chaplain Suffolk County Police Dept., NY, 1995—. Roman Catholic. Office: Diocese of Rockville Ctr Western Vicariate PO Box 933 Roosevelt NY 11575-0933 Office Phone: 516-867-6340. E-mail: pualsh@drvc.org.

WALSH, PAUL S., beverage executive; b. Manchester, May 15, 1955; 1 child. Grad., Manchester Polytechnic. Fin. planning and acct. mgr. Grand Metropolitan, Watney, Mann and Truman Brewers, 1982—86; fin. dir. Grand Metropolitan (merged with Guinness UDV in 1997), Watney, Mann and Truman Brewers, 1986; CFO Inter-Continental Hotels, 1987—88, CFO, food divsn., 1989—92; chmn., pres., CEO Pillsbury Co., Mpls., 1992—2000; COO, CEO Guinness UDV Diageo plc, London, 2000—01, CEO, 2000—. Bd. dirs. Grand Metropolitan, 1995, Diageo, 1997—, Burger King Corp.; non-exec. dir. Centrica plc, 2003—, Fed. Express Corp., General Mills, Inc.; chair ct. of govs. Henley Mgmt. Coll.; non-exec. mem. bd. Unilever Plc; apptd. mem. Bus. Coun. Britain, 2008. Mem.: Prince of Wales Internat. Bus. Leaders Forum (bd. trustee mem.), Chartered Inst. Mgmt. Accountants, Scotch Whisky Assn. (chmn.). Office: Diageo plc 8 Henrietta Pl London W1G ONB England

WALSH, PETER JOSEPH, physics professor; b. NYC, Aug. 21, 1929; s. Peter and Mary Ellen (Kelly) W.; m. Rosemarie Imundo, May 13, 1952; children: Kathleen, Mary Ellen, Susan, Carole, Karen. BS, Fordham U., 1951; MS, N.Y.U., 1953, PhD, 1960. Research physicist Westinghouse Elec. Co., Bloomfield, NJ, 1951-60; supervisory physicist Am. Standard, Piscataway, NJ, 1960-62; prof. Fairleigh Dickinson U., 1962-93; prof. emeritus, 1993—. Vis. rsch. scientist MIT, 1977; vis. prof. electronics and elec. engring. U. Sheffield, 1978-79; NASA fellow U. Santa Clara, 1980; Am. Soc. Engring. Edn. Navy fellow Naval Rsch. Labs., 1981, 82, 86, NASA Langley, 1987, Air Force fellow Hanscom AFB, 1988, Kirtland AFB, 1990; vis. prof. U. Genoa, 1984; vis. scholar Stanford U., 1984-85, cons. physics to 20 labs., 1963—; chmn. bd. trustees EMS Ednl. Corp., 1982—. Author: Dark Side of Knowledge, articles in field; patentee in field. Mem. Am. Phys. Soc., AAAS, N.J. Acad. Sci., Sigma Xi (sec. 1969) Home: 40 Saint Josephs Dr Stirling NJ 07980-1224

WALSH, PHILIP CORNELIUS, retired mining executive; b. Harrison, NJ, May 23, 1921; s. Philip Cornelius and Frances (Prendergast) Walsh; m. Alexandra Somerville Tuck, May 19, 1945 (dec. Sept. 1993); children: Eugenie Philbin Flaherty, Philip C.C., Frances Cummings, Alexander Tuck, Nicholas Holladay, Elizabeth Lovering; m. Peggy Flanigan McDonnell, Oct. 13, 1996. BA, Yale U., 1943; member of the Class of 1944. With W.R. Grace & Co., Lima, Peru and NYC, 1946-71; v.p. parent co., chief operating officer Latin Am. group, 1961-71, group exec. corp. adminstrv. group, 1970-71; v.p. Cerro Corp., 1972-74, Newmont Mining Corp., 1974-80; chmn. bd. Foote Mineral Co., Exton, Pa., 1979-80; dir. Cyprus Minerals Co., 1980—85; vice chmn. St. Joe

Minerals Corp., 1980-85; chmn. bd. Chilean Lithium Co. Ltd., 1980-94; dir. T. Rowe Price Assocs., Inc., 1986—2000; ret., 2000. Past dir. Peabody Coal Co., Piedmont Mining Co.; bd. advisors Fond Elec.; mem. Nat. Strategic Minerals and Metals Program Adv. Commn. Mem. Harding Twp. Bd. Edn., NJ, 1960—66, Harding Twp. Com., 1966—72, police commr., 1966—72; trustee Morristown Meml. Hosp., 1969—79; vis. com. Colo. Sch. Mines, Global Sys. and Cultures. 1st lt. US Army. Decorated Silver Star, Purple Heart. Mem.: AIME (Saunders gold medal 1992, Disting. Mem. award 1993), Am. Soc. (hon. dir.), Pan Am. Soc. U.S. (past vice chmn.), Am. Assn. Order of Malta (past chancellor), Fed. Assn. Order of Malta, Edgartown Golf Club, Essex Hunt Club, Edgartown Yacht Club (commodore 1993—95), Racquet and Tennis Club, Somerset Hills Country Club, Sigma Xi, Phi Beta Kappa. Republican. Roman Catholic. Home: Pleasant Valley Peapack NJ 07977 Personal E-mail: knobbyiv@aol.com.

WALSH, R. MATTHEW, surgeon, gastroenterologist; Grad., Creighton U.; MD, Med. Coll. Wis. Intern & resident Loyola U. Med. Ctr. Foster G. McGaw Hosp.; fellow Mass. Gen. Hosp., Cleveland Clinic, hepato-pancreato-biliary & transplant surgeon. Office: Cleveland Clinic 9500 Euclid Ave MC-A80 Cleveland OH 44195 Office Phone: 216-445-7576.*

WALSH, ROBERT K., law educator, former dean; m. Kathie Walsh; 4 children. AB, Providence Coll., 1964; JD, Harvard U., 1967. Bar: Calif. 1967, Ark. 1979. Assoc. McCatchen, Black, Verleger & Shea, LA, 1967-70; asst. prof. Villanova U., Phila., 1970-71, assoc. prof., 1971-73, prof., 1973-76; dean U. Ark., Little Rock Sch. Law; ptnr. Friday, Eldredge & Clark, Little Rock, 1981-89; prof. law Wake Forest Sch. Law, Winston-Salem, NC, 1989—, dean, 1989—2007, dean emeritus. Bd. trustees Nat. Assn. Law Placement Found., Am. Inns of Ct. Found. Mem. ABA (chair Accreditation Com. 1984-86, chair Standards Rev. Com. Sect. Legal Edn. 1991—, Central European and Eurasian Law Initiative Adv. Coun.), N.C. Bar Assn. (chair bar bench and law schs. com. 1990-92, v.p., bd. govs. 1994-95). Office: Wake Forest Sch Law 1834 Wake Forest Rd Winston Salem NC 27109 Office Phone: 336-758-5770. Business E-Mail: walshrk@wfu.edu.*

WALSH, SHARI M., literature and language educator; b. Lawton, Okla., July 1, 1948; d. Porter Almus Hood and Mildred McCormack; m. Spencer Lee Walsh, Nov. 24, 1974 (dec.); children: Spencer Lee II, Cameron Grant. BA, U. Sci. and Arts of Okla., Chickasha, 1971; MA in Edn., Lesley U., Cambridge, Mass., 2004. Lic. tchr. Colo., cert. ESL 2006. Classroom tchr. English and French Davis Schs., Okla., 1974—76, Sterling HS/Mid. Sch., Colo., 1980—92; classroom tchr. English, and French Sterling HS, 1996—; classroom tchr. English Sterling Mid. Sch., 1992—96. Chaperone, sponsor Intercultural Student Experiences, 1996, 99, Sterling HS, 1993. Mem. curriculum com. Re-1 Valley Schs., Sterling, 1989—92; mem. bldg. accountability com. Sterling Mid. Sch., 1992—96, Sterling HS, 2003—06. Mem.: AAUW (co-pres.), Nat. Coun. Tchrs. English, Colo. Congress Fgn. Lang. Tchrs. Democrat. Methodist. Avocations: reading, sewing, cooking, gardening, writing. Office: Sterling HS 407 W Broadway Sterling CO 80751

WALSH, THOMAS CHARLES, lawyer; b. Mpls., July 6, 1940; s. William G. and Kathryne M. Walsh; m. Joyce Williams, Sept. 7, 1968; children: Brian Christopher, Timothy Daniel, Laura Elizabeth Smith. BS in Commerce magna cum laude, St. Louis U., 1962, LLB cum laude, 1964. Bar: Mo. 1964, U.S. Dist. Ct. (ea. dist.) Mo. 1964, U.S. Ct. Appeals (8th cir.) 1968, U.S. Supreme Ct. 1971, U.S. Ct. Appeals (6th cir.) 1972, U.S. Ct. Appeals (5th cir.) 1974, U.S. Ct. Appeals (D.C. cir.) 1980, U.S. Ct. Appeals (7th cir.) 1982, U.S. Ct. Appeals (9th cir.) 1987, U.S. Ct. Appeals (4th cir.) 1989, U.S. Ct. Appeals (11th and fed. cirs.) 1992, U.S. Ct. Appeals (2d and 10th cirs.) 1993. Jr. ptnr. Bryan, Cave, McPheeters & McRoberts, St. Louis, 1964-73; ptnr. Bryan Cave LLP, St. Louis, 1974—; mem. exec. com. Bryan Cave LLP, St. Louis, 1980-96. Mem. 8th Cir. Adv. Com., 1983-86. Bd. dirs. St. Louis Symphony Soc., 1983-95. With U.S. Army, 1965-66; lt. USNR, 1966-71. Fellow Am. Coll. Trial Lawyers, Am. Acad. Appellate Lawyers; mem. Mo. Bar Assn., St. Louis Bar Assn., Am. Law Inst., Mo. Athletic Club, Bellerive Country Club. Roman Catholic. Office: Bryan Cave LLP 1 Metropolitan Sq 211 N Broadway Saint Louis MO 63102-2750 Home Phone: 314-997-7871; Office Phone: 314-259-2284. Business E-Mail: tcwalsh@bryancave.com.

WALSH, THOMAS JOSEPH, ophthalmologist; b. NYC, Sept. 18, 1931; s. Thomas Joseph and Virginia (Hughes) W.; m. Sally Ann Maust, June 21, 1958; children: Thomas Raymond, Sara Ann, Mary Kelly, Kathleen Meghan. BA, Coll. Fordham, 1954; MD, Bowman Gray Med. Sch., 1958; degree in Mgmt., Yale U., 1998. Intern St. Vincent's Hosp., NYC, 1958-59; resident ophthalmology Bowman Gray Med. Sch., Winston-Salem, NC, 1961-64; fellow neuro-ophthalmology Bascom Palmer Eye Inst., Miami, Fla., 1964-65; practice medicine specializing in neuro-ophthalmology Stamford, Conn., 1965—; dir. neuro-ophthalmology service, asst. prof. ophthalmology and neurology Yale Sch. Medicine, New Haven, 1965-74, assoc. prof., 1974-79, prof., 1979—, also bd. permanent officers; dir. ophthalmology Stamford Hosp., 1978-83; mem. staff St. Joseph Hosp., Yale New Haven Hosp. Cons. to surgeon gen. army in neuro-ophthalmology Walter Reed Hosp., Washington, 1966—, VA Hosp., West Haven, 1965—, Silver Hill Found., New Canaan, Conn., 1974—; adj. prof. Dartmouth Med. Sch.; telemedicine bd. ORBIS Internat.; cons. mem. of bd. Orbis Internat.; lectr. in field. Contbr. articles to various publs. Adv. bd. Stamford Salvation Army, 1972-92; med. bd. Darien Nurses Assn., Conn., 1972—; surgeon Darien Fire Dept., 1969—. With AUS, 1959-61. Decorated Knight of Malta; Centennial fellow Johns Hopkins, 1976; named one of Top Opthalmologists, Best Doctors.com, 2004 Mem. AMA, Conn., Fairfield County med. socs., Acad. Ophthalmology, Oxford Ophthal. Congress, Acad. Neurology, Am. Assn. Neurol. Surgeons, Internat. Neuro-Ophthalmology Soc., Soc. Med. Cons. to Armed Forces, Cosmos Club (Washington), Darien County Club, Yale Club (N.Y.C.), Lions, Army-Navy Club, Orbis Internat. (cybermedicine bd. mem.). Office: Yale Dept Ophthalmology PO Box 208061 330 Cedar St Stamford CT 06520-8061 Home Phone: 203-866-0220; Office Phone: 203-785-6444. Personal E-mail: twalsh13@optonline.net. Business E-Mail: thomas.walsh@yale.edu.

WALSH, WILLIAM ALBERT, management consultant, retired military officer; b. Gilman, Ill., Aug. 15, 1933; s. Lawrence Eugene and Myrtle R. (Mulder) W.; m. Edith Leonora McGrath, Jan. 12, 2008, children: Kathryn, Michael, Julie. BS in Commerce, U. Notre Dame, 1955; MS in Mgmt. with distinction, U.S. Naval Postgrad. Sch., Monterey, Calif., 1962; MS in Internat. Affairs with honors, George Washington U., 1972. Commd. ensign U.S. Navy, 1955, advanced through grades to rear adm., 1981; exec. asst. to dep. chief naval ops. (Surface Warfare), Washington, 1974-76; comdg. officer USS Juneau, San Diego, 1976-78; comdr. Amphibious Squadron Three, San Diego, 1978-79; head plans and policy div., comdr. rapid deployment naval forces Comdr. in Chief U.S. Pacific Fleet, Honolulu, 1979-81; comdr. Amphibious Group Eastern Pacific, San Diego, 1981-82; dir. surface warfare div. Office Chief Naval Ops., Pentagon, Washington, 1983-85; ret., 1985; pres. Air/Space Am., San Diego, 1986-89, W.A. Walsh Enterprises, 1990—. Decorated Legion of Merit with 2 gold stars, Bronze Star, Navy Commendation medal U.S.; Disting. Service Order 2d Class Vietnam

WALSH, WILLIAM ARTHUR, JR., lawyer; b. Washington, Mar. 17, 1949; children: Jesse Creighton, Patrick McKay. BS in Econs. and Fin., U. Md., 1972; JD, U. Richmond, 1977. Bar: Va. Ptnr. Hunton & Williams LLP, Richmond, Va., 1977—. Adv. bd. for law rev. U. Richmond. Trustee, bd. dirs. Va. Commonwealth U. Real Estate Found.; mem. Va. Commonwealth U. Real Estate Circle of Excellence. Mem. Va. Bar Assn., Am. Coll. Real Estate Lawyers. Home: 4705 Leonard Pky Richmond VA 23226-1337 Office: Hunton & Williams LLP Riverfront Plz East Tower 951 E Byrd St Richmond VA 23219-4074 Home Phone: 804-359-2470; Office Phone: 804-788-8378. Business E-Mail: wwalsh@hunton.com.

WALSH, WILLIAM DESMOND, investor; b. NYC, Aug. 4, 1930; s. William J. and Catherine Grace (Desmond) W.; m. Mary Jane Gordon, Apr. 5, 1951 (dec. Jan. 18, 2008); children: Deborah, Caroline, Michael, Suzanne, Tara Jane, Peter. BA, Fordham U., 1951; JD, Harvard U., 1955. Bar: NY 1955. Asst. US atty. So. dist. NY, NYC, 1955-58; counsel NY Commn. Investigation, NYC, 1958-61; mgmt. cons. McKinsey & Co., NYC, 1961-67; sr. v.p. Arcata Corp., Menlo Park, Calif., 1967-82; chmn. Sequoia Assocs. LLC, 1982—; pres., CEO Atacra Liquidating Trust, 1982-88. Chmn. bd. dir. Neuroscis. Inst./Scripps, Ameriscape, Inc., Cornelius, Oreg., Creativity Inc., Van Nuys; bd. dir., lead dir. URS Corp., San Francisco; bd. dir. Am. Ireland Fund, Boston. Mem. bd. overseers, chmn. fin. com. Hoover Inst.; co-chmn. dean's adv. bd. Harvard Law Sch.; trustee emeritus Fordham U. Mem. NY State Bar Assn., Harvard Club (NYC and San Francisco), Fordham Club No. Calif., Knights of Malta. Office Phone: 650-321-4346. Office Fax: 650-321-4588.

WALSHE, AUBREY PETER, emeritus political science professor; b. Johannesburg, Jan. 12, 1934; s. Aubrey John and Joan Kathleen (Evans) W.; m. Catherine Ann Pettifer, Jan. 28, 1957; children: Sally, Jane, Dominic, Emma. BA, Wadham Coll., Oxford, Eng., 1956, MA, 1959; PhD, St. Antony's Coll., Oxford, 1968. Vis. asst. prof. U. Notre Dame, Ind., 1962-63, asst. prof. dept. govt. and internat. studies Ind., 1967-71, dir. African studies Ind., 1971-77, assoc. prof. Ind., 1971-77, prof. Ind., 1977—. Sr. assoc. fellow St. Antony's Coll., Oxford, 1972-73; dir. ann. Missionary Inst. on Sub-Saharan Africa, U.Notre Dame, 1969—; lectr. and cons. in field; found. mem. So. African Rsch. Archival Project;l mem. N.Am. Support Com., Ecumenical Dialogue of Third World Theologians. Contbr. articles to profl. jours.; author: The Rise of African Nationalism in South Africa, 1971, 2d edit. 1988, Black Nationalism in South Africa: A Short History, 1975, Church Versus State in South Africa, 1983, Prophetic Christianity and the Liberation Management in South Africa, 1997; contbr. revs. to numerous jours.; occasional reader: U. Calif. Press, U. Notre Dame Press, Rev. of Politics, Social Scis. and Humanities Rsch. Coun. of Can., Ottawa, Ind. U. African Studies Pubs. Com., Cath. Inst. for Internat. Rels., London, U. Queensland, Australia. Mem. edn. com. cath. Inst. for Internat. Rels., London; adv. bd. Storypoint Ctr., Presbyn. Ch. U.S.A., N.Y.C.; cons. Nat. Coun. of Chs. of Christ, Convocation of the Kairos Document: Challenge to the Ch. in South Africa. Walsh-Price fellow Ctr. for Mission Studies, Maryknoll, N.Y., 1980-81, Helen Kellogg Inst. for Internat. Studies fellow, 1983, Inst. for Internat. Peace Studies fellow, 1987; MacArthur Found. grantee, 1989-90; recipient Sheedy award for Excellence in Tchg, U. Notre Dame, 2004. Ecumenical Christian. Home: 1037 N Niles Ave South Bend IN 46617-1249 Office: Univ Notre Dame Dept Govt Notre Dame IN 46556

WALSH-HUNT, LINDA ANN, social worker, consultant, poet; b. Syracuse, May 24, 1952; d. Edmond Charles and Jane Kathleen (Hudson) Walsh; m. Francis Edward Hunt, Sr., June 11, 1976; children: Francis Hunt III, Patrick Hunt, Elizabeth Hunt, James Hunt. BS, MSW, Syracuse U. Patient svcs. dir. Am. Cancer Soc., Syracuse, NY, 1973—; therapist Dept. Mental Health, Syracuse, 1993—; social worker Syracuse City Sch. Dist., 1995—. Cons. in field. Author: numerous poems. Bd. dirs. Mental Health Assn., 1991—92. Mem.: NASW, Am. Group Psychotherapy Assn., Clin. Soc. Social Work. Democrat. Avocations: piano, poetry, writing. Home: 115 Ruskin Ave Syracuse NY 13207

WALSH-KELLY, CHRISTINE MARY, pediatrician, educator; d. Thomas Henry and Estelle Frances Walsh; m. Kevin Joseph Kelly, June 18, 1977; children: Brian Thomas Kelly, Christopher Vincent Kelly. MD, Loyola U., Stritch Sch. Medicine, Maywood, Ill., 1977. D Mo., 2005. Prof. pediat. & emergency medicine Med. Coll. Wis., Milw., 1980—2005; prof. pediat. Children's Mercy Hosp., Kans. City, Mo., 2005—. Fellow: Am. Acad. Pediat.; mem.: Alpha Omega Alpha Honor Soc. Office: Children's Mercy Hosp 2401 Gillham Rd Kansas City MO 64108 Business E-Mail: cwalshkelly@cmh.edu.

WALSH MITCHELL, DIANA, school psychologist, consultant; d. T. and D. Walsh. BA, Hofstra U., 1997; MA, Adelphi U., 1999; MS in Edn., Fordham U., 2002, Profl. Diploma in Sch. Psychology, 2002; D in Psychology, Fairleigh Dickinson U., 2005. Cert. sch. psychologist N.Y. State Edn. Dept., 2002. Sch. psychologist Pub. Sch., Hewlett, NY, 2002—03; psychometrician Schneider Children's Hosp., New Hyde Park, NY, 2002—04; cons. NY, 2004—; sch. psychologist NY, 2004—. Cons. Pvt. Sch., Kew Gardens, NY; presenter in field. Mem.: NASP, APA, N.Am. Assn. for the Study of Obesity, NY Assn. Sch. Psychologists.

WALSH-PIPER, KATHLEEN A., museum director; b. Chgo., Aug. 17, 1947; d. James Clement and Jane (Burnham) W.; m. Michael G. Rubin, May 17, 1969 (div. 1978); m. Rubin H. Piper, Dec. 19, 1987. BA, Washington U., St. Louis, 1969, MA in Art History, 1973; postgrad., St. Louis U. Cert. tchr., Mo. Tchr. St. Louis Archdiocesan Schs., 1970-73; asst. prof. Mo. Bapt. Coll., St. Louis, 1973; tchr. Hazelwood Jr. High Sch., St. Louis, 1974-77; mus. tchr. St. Louis Art. Mus., 1976, coord. rsch. ctr., 1977-80; asst. dir. mus. edn. Art. Inst. Chgo., 1980—85; dir. edn. Terra Mus. Am. Art, Chgo., 1985-88; head dept. tchr. and sch. programs Nat. Gallery Art, Washington, 1988—95; cultural specialist U.S. Info. Agency, 1995; dir. edn. and pub. progs. Dallas Mus. Art, Tex., 1995—2002; dir. U. Ky. Art Mus., Lexington, 2002—. Mus. guest scholar J. Paul Getty Mus., Malibu, Calif., 1997. Author: Image to Word: Art and Creative Writing, 2002; contbr. articles to profl. jours. Robert E. Smith fellow Nat. Gallery of Art, 1994. Mem. Nat. Art Edn. Assn. (regional mus. educator 1984, nat. mus. educator 1985, dir. mus. divsn. 1992—), Am. Assn. Mus. (chair midwest edn. ccom. 1983-84). Avocation: writing. Office: U Ky Art Mus 116 Singletary Ctr Rose St and Euclid Ave Lexington KY 40506-0241 Office Phone: 859-257-1152. Business E-Mail: kwpiper@email.uky.edu.

WALSTEDT, RUSSELL ERWIN, physicist; s. Erwin Leonard Walstedt and Maybelle Margaret MacGregor; m. Betty Jean Barcevac, Feb. 6, 1982 (div. Aug. 4, 2004); children: Eric, Kirsten Joyce, Alison Jean Guiseppe. PhD, U. Calif., Berkeley, 1961. Mem., tech. staff Bell Labs., Inc., Murray Hill, NJ, 1965—96; vis. scientist, physics dept. Rutgers U., Piscataway, 1996—2000, U. Mich., Ann Arbor, 2005—; group leader, uranium NMR group Advanced Sci. Rsch. Ctr., Japan Atomic Energy Agy., Tokai-Mura, Ibaraki, 2000—05. Contbr. scientific papers. Mem., bd. govs. Princeton Friends Sch., NJ, 1996—2000. Fellowship, Japan Soc. Promotion Sci., 2008, Am. Inst. Physics, 1974, NSF, 1961—62, Woodrow Wilson fellowship Found., 1958—59, Max Planck Inst., Dresden, Germany, 2006—07, 2009. Fellow: Am. Phys. Soc. Democrat. Avocations: skateboarding, golf.

WALSTON, RODERICK EUGENE, federal official; b. Gooding, Idaho, Dec. 15, 1935; s. Loren R. and Iva M. (Boyer) W.; m. Margaret D. Grandey; children: Gregory Scott W., Valerie Lynne W. AA, Boise Jr. Coll., 1956; BA cum laude, Columbia Coll., 1958; LL.B. scholar, Stanford U., 1961. Bar: Calif. 1961, U.S. Supreme Ct. 1973. Law clk to judge U.S. Ct. Appeals 9th Cir., 1961-62; dep. atty. gen State of Calif., San Francisco, 1963-91, head natural resources sect, 1969-91, chief asst. atty. gen. pub. rights div., 1991-99; spl. dep counsel Kings County, Calif., 1975-76; gen. counsel Metropolitan Water Dist. So. Calif., 2000—02; dep. solicitor U.S. Dept. Interior, 2002—; of counsel Best, Best and Krieger, LLP, Walnut Creek, Calif., 2005. Mem. environ. and natural resources adv. coun. Stanford (Calif.) Law Sch. Contbr. articles to profl. jours.; bd. editors: Stanford Law Rev., 1959-61, Western Natural Resources Litigation Digest, Calif. Water Law and Policy Reporter; spl. editor Jour. of the West. Co-chmn. Idaho campaign against Right-to-Work initiative, 1958; Calif. rep. Western States Water Coun., 1986—; environ. and natural resources adv. coun., Stanford Law Sch. Astor Found. scholar, 1956-58; Nat. Essay Contest winner Nat. Assn. Internat. Rels. Clubs, 1956, Stanford Law Rev. prize, 1961; recipient Best Brief award Nat. Assn. Attys. Gen., 1997, Burton award best article, 2007; named Pub. Lawyer of Yr., Calif. State Bar, 2004, Forensics Hall of Fame, Boise State U., 2009. Mem. ABA (chmn. water resources com. 1988-90, vice chmn. and conf. chmn. 1985-88, 90—, Best Lawyers of America, 2008), Contra Costa County Bar Assn., U.S. Supreme Ct., Hist. Soc., Federalist Soc., World Affairs Coun. No. Calif. Office: Best Best and Krieger LLP 2033 N Main St Walnut Creek CA 94596 Office Phone: 925-977-3304. Business E-Mail: roderick.walston@bbklaw.com.

WALT, MARTIN, physicist, educator; b. West Plains, Mo., June 1, 1926; s. Martin and Dorothy (Mantz) W.; m. Mary Estelle Thompson, Aug. 16, 1950; children: Susan Mary, Stephen Martin, Anne Elizabeth, Patricia Ruth. BS, Calif. Inst. Tech., 1950; MS, U. Wis., 1951, PhD, 1953. Staff mem. Los Alamos Sci. Lab., 1953-56; research scientist, mgr. physics Lockheed Missiles and Space Co., Palo Alto (Calif.) Rsch. Lab., 1956-71, dir. phys. scis., 1971-86, dir. research, 1986-93; cons. prof. Stanford U., 1986—. Mem. adv. com. NRC, NASA, Dept. Def., U. Calif. Lawrence Berkeley Lab. Author 2 books; contbr. articles to sci. jours. Served with USNR, 1944-46. Wis. Research Found. fellow, 1950-51; AEC fellow, 1951-53 Fellow Am. Geophys. Union, Am. Phys. Soc.; mem. Am. Inst. Physics (bd. govs.), Fremont Hills Country Club. Home: 12650 Viscaino Ct Los Altos Hills CA 94022-2517 Office: Stanford U Starlab Packard 352 Stanford CA 94305 Office Phone: 650-723-2690. Business E-Mail: walt@nova.stanford.edu.

WALT, STEVEN DAVID, law educator; b. Rochester, Minn., Mar. 10, 1954; s. Alexander Jeffrey and Irene (Lapping) W. BA cum laude, Kalamazoo Coll., 1976; MA in philosophy, U. Chgo., 1979, PhD in philosophy, 1984; JD, Yale U., 1988. Bar: NY 1988. Asst. prof. philosophy Calif. Inst. Tech., Pasadena, 1983-85; asst. prof. law Wharton Sch. Bus., U. Pa., Phila., 1988-90, U. San Diego, 1990-92, assoc. prof., 1992—93; prof. U. Va. Sch. Law, Charlottesville, 1992—. Vis. assoc. prof. U. Va. Sch. Law, 1992—93; mem. editl. bd. Legal Theory. Co-author (with R. Jordan and W. Warren): Commercial Law, 2000, Secured Transactions in Personal Property, 2000; co-author: (with C. Gillette) Sales Law: Domestic and International, 2002; co-editor (with J. Kraus): The Jurisprudential Foundations of Corporate and Commercial Law, 2000. Mem.: Am. Soc. Polit. & Legal Philosophy. Office: U Va Sch Law 580 Massie Rd Charlottesville VA 22903-1789 Office Phone: 434-924-7930. E-mail: sdw6a@virginia.edu.

WALTER, ARENSTEIN ALAN, environmental services administrator; s. Evelyn Langholz; m. Gina Facca, June 6, 1993. BS in Human Environment, Ramapo Coll. NY, Mahwah, NJ, 1976; MA in Environ. Sci., Edn., City U. NY, 1978. Qualified environ. profl. IPEP, 1995. Pres. Writrac Consulting, Pueblo, Colo., 1986—; air pollution control officer Placer County Air Pollution Control Dist., Auburn, 1992—94; instr. San Jose State U., Calif., 2004; staff specialist South Coast Air Quality Mgmt. Dist., Diamond Bar, Calif.; sr. environ. insp. City San Jose, 2007—08. Adv. bd. mem. Peublo Chem. Depot Adv. Bd., 2008. Mem.: Air & Waste Mgmt. Assn. (chair, nat. tech. com. 1996). Achievements include research in indirect source review. Home: PO Box 4202 Fairview Heights IL 62208 Personal E-mail: warenstein2@gmail.com.

WALTER, CARMEL MONICA, security consultant, writer; b. Dublin, July 24, 1943; arrived in U.S., 1961; d. Albert and Anastatia Woods; m. Michael William Walter, June 15, 1963; children: Coleen, Daniel, Eileen. BS magna cum laude, Madonna U., Livonia, Mich., 1987. Co-founder, co-owner Am. Security Alarm Co., Madison Heights, Mich., 1969—72, Alarm Supply Co., Inc., Livonia, Mich., 1969—89, founder, owner Milford, NJ, 2001—07. Intro.and product tng. for first wireless security sys. Resident Sentry, Madison Heights, 1967—72; co-owner CMD Co., Flemington, NJ, 1989—2002; established ongoing comprehensive tech. support sys. Alarm Supply Co., Milford, 2003—07. Co-author (with Michael Walter): (security products and application manual) The Security Store. Mem. cert. nat. emergency mgmt. teams emergency support function #13 public safety and security Am. Bd. Cert. in Homeland Security, Springfield, Mo., 2005—. Mem.: Am. Coll. Forensic Examiners Inst. (life; cert. homeland security-III), Kappa Gamma Pi. Roman Catholic. Avocations: travel, golf, theater, cooking, interior design. Personal E-mail: carmelwalter@aol.com.

WALTER, ELISSE BARBARA, commissioner; b. 1950; m. Ronald Alan Stern. BA in Math., cum laude, Yale U.; JD cum laude, Harvard Law Sch. Assoc. gen. coun. to dep. dir. divsn. corp. fin. SEC, 1977—94; sr. exec. v.p. policy and progs. Fin. Industry Regulatory Authority, 1994—2007; gen. coun. Commodity Futures Trading Commn.; commr. SEC, 2008—. Bd. trustees hist. soc. SEC. Bd. trustees Jewish Women Internat. Recipient Distinguished Presdl. Rank award, Chmns. award for excellence, SEC, Distinguished Svc. award. Mem.: ABA DirectWomen Inst. (inaugural class), Acad Women Achievers YWCA NYC. Office: SEC Hdqs 100 F St NE Washington DC 20549 Office Phone: 202-942-8088.*

WALTER, HUGO GÜNTHER, humanities educator, poet; b. Phila., Mar. 12, 1959; s. Elli R. Walter. BA, Princeton U., 1981; MA in Humanities, Old Dominion U., 1989; MA in Lit., Yale U., 1983, MPhil in Lit., 1984, PhD in Lit, 1985; PhD in Interdisciplinary Humanities, Drew U., 1996. Adj. instr. Yale U., New Haven, 1981-85, Old Dominion U., Norfolk, Va., 1988-89; asst. prof. Washington and Jefferson Coll., Washington, Pa., 1989-92, Fairleigh Dickinson U., Madison, NJ, 1992-

96, Kettering U., Flint, Mich., 1996-99; assoc. prof. Berkeley Coll., White Plains, 1999—. Vis. asst. prof. Rhodes Coll., Memphis, 1986-87, U. Mo., Columbia, 1987-88. Author: (poetry) The Fragile Edge, 1988, Velvet Rhythms, 1989, Amber Blossoms and Evening Shadows, 1990, Golden Thorns of Light and Sterling Silhouettes, 1991, Waiting for Babel Prophesies of Sunflower Dreams, 1992, Along the Maroon-Prismed Threshold of Bronze-Pealing Eternity, 1992, The Light of the Dance Is the Music of Eternity, 1993, Dusk-Gloaming Mirrors and Castle-Winding Dreams, 1994, Amaranth-Sage Epiphanies of Dusk-Weaving Paradise, 1995, 2d edit., 1996, A Purple-Golden Renascence of Eden-Exalting Rainbows, 2001, (monographs) The Apostrophic Moment in 19th and 20th Century Lyric Poetry, 1988, Space and Time on the Magic Mountain: Studies in the 19th and 20th Century European Literature, 1999. Recipient Faculty of Yr. award, Berkeley Coll., 2006. Mem. Acad. Am. Poets, Internat. Soc. Poets. Avocations: music, painting. Home: 157 Loomis CT Princeton NJ 08540-3438 Personal E-mail: hwalter2@optimum.net. Business E-Mail: hgw@berkeleycollege.edu.

WALTER, MICHAEL TODD, engineering educator; s. Michael Faiver and Dianne Lynn Walter; m. Christa Diane Salmon; children: Acadia Laurel, Juneau Rain. PhD, Wash. State U., Pullman, 1995. Instr. rsch. assoc. Cornell U., Ithaca, NY, 1995—99, sr. rsch. assoc., 2002—05, asst. prof., 2005—, Mont. State U. Northern, Havre, 1999—99, U. Alaska SE, Juneau, 2000—02. Recipient Outstanding Tchg. award, Cornell Coll. Engring., 2007. Mem.: ASCE, Am. Soc. Biol. and Environ. Engrs., Am. Soc. Engring. Educators, Soil and Water Conservation Soc., Am. Geophys. Union. Office: Cornell Univ Dept Biol and Environ Engring Ithaca NY 14853 Office Fax: 607-255-4080. Business E-Mail: mtw5@cornell.edu.

WALTER, PATRICIA L., psychotherapist, consultant; b. Logansport, Ind., Mar. 15, 1935; d. William Marion and Doris May (Duddleston) Sievers; m. Raymond C. Walter Jr., Mar. 28, 1968; m. Keith A. Erny (div.); children: Rodney Erny, Jeffrey Erny, Mark Erny, Troy Erny. BS in Edn., Ind. U., 1973, MS in Edn. & English, 1976, MS in Counseling, 1984. Cert. English tchr., lic. mental health counselor Ind., cert. nat. cert. addictions prevention specialist III, forensic counselors 1998, bd. profl. counselor Am. Psychtherapy Assn., 2007, grief recovery profl. 2007. Tchr. English Logansport Sch. Corp., Ind., 1973—97; psychotherapist Four County Counseling, Peru, 1993—2000; high sch. counselor Logansport Cmty. Schs., 1997—2003; mental health cons. Texas Migrant Headstart, Kokomo, 2004—; psychotherapist RAJ Clinic, Logansport, 2004—. Coord. Adminstrv. Counsel, Logansport, 2001—03; coach Acad. Competitions, 1987—98, Girls 6th Grade Basketball, 1975—78. Vol. First Call Home Health and Hospice, 2004. Mem.: APA, Cass County Carousel, Am. Mental Health Counselors Assn., Kiwanis (sec. 1997—98, pres. 2005—), Zeta Tau Chpt. Beta Sigma Phi. Republican. Avocations: golf, ballroom dancing, reading, exercise, gardening.

WALTER, PAUL HERMANN LAWRENCE, chemistry professor; b. Jersey City, Sept. 22, 1934; s. Helmuth Justus and Adelaide C. J. (Twardy) W.; m. Grace Louise Carpenter, Aug. 25, 1956; children: Katherine Elizabeth Walter Bousquet, Marjorie Allison Walter Moran. BS, MIT, 1956; PhD, U. Kans., 1960. Rsch. scientist DuPont Cen. Rsch. Dept., Wilmington, Del., 1960-67; prof. chemistry Skidmore Coll., Saratoga Springs, NY, 1967-96, chair chemistry and physics, 1975-85, prof. emeritus, 1996—. Translator: (book) Foundations of Crystal Chemistry, 1968; contbr. articles to profl. jours. Named Hall of Fame, Stamford, Conn. HS, 2009. Fellow Chem. Inst. Can.; mem. AAAS, AAUP (pres. 1984-86), Am. Chem. Soc. (bd. dirs. 1991-99, chmn. 1993-95, pres.-elect 1997, pres. 1998, Radding award 2002), Soc. Quimica de Mexico (hon.). Presbyterian. Achievements include patents in field. Home: 3 Benedictine Retreat Savannah GA 31411-1624 E-mail: phlw@alum.mit.edu.

WALTER, PETER, biochemist; b. Berlin; Diploma in Chemistry, Free U. Berlin, 1976; MSc in Organic Chemistry, Vanderbilt U., 1977; PhD in Cell Biology, Rockefeller U., 1981. Prof., chmn. dept. biochemistry & biophysics U. Calif., San Francisco; investigator Howard Hughes Medical Inst. Harvey lectr. Rockefeller U., 1996; Feodor-Lynen lectr. Mosbach Kolloquium, 1998. Co-author: Molecular Biology of the Cell, 2002, Essential Cell Biology, 2003. Recipient Searle Scholar award, 1983, Passano award, 1988, Eli Lilly award, 1988, Alfred P. Sloan award, 1989, Merit award, Nat. Insts. Health, 1990, Wiley Prize biomedical sciences, 2005, Gairdner Found. Internat. award, 2009. Fellow: Am. Acad. Microbiology, Am. Acad. Arts and Scis.; mem.: NAS, European Molecular Biology Orgn. (assoc.). Office: U Calif San Fransisco Dept Biochemistry & Biophysics Genentech Hall N312 600 16th St San Francisco CA 94143-2200 Office Phone: 415-476-5017. Office Fax: 415-476-5233. Business E-Mail: walter@cgl.ucsf.edu.*

WALTER, ROBERT D., health products executive; b. Columbus, Ohio, July 13, 1945; m. Peggy McGreevey, 1967; children: Matthew, Blane, Peter. BMechE, Ohio U., 1967; MBA, Harvard U., 1970; Ph.D (hon.), Ohio U., 1997. Engr. N. Am. Rockwell, 1968; founder Cardinal Foods Inc. (acquired by Roundy's Inc. 1988), Dublin, Ohio, 1971-88; founder, CEO Cardinal Distbn., Dublin, Ohio, 1979—94; CEO Cardinal Health, Inc. (formerly Cardinal Distbn.), Dublin, 1994—2006, chmn., 2006—07. Bd. dirs. Cardinal Health Inc., 1971—, Viacom Inc., 2000—06, American Express Co., 2002—, Yum! Brands, Inc., 2008—; bd. trustees Battelle Meml. Inst., Ohio U. Trustee Battelle Meml. Inst. Recipient Christopher Columbus award, Greater Columbus C of C, 2001. Avocations: golf, running, skiing. Office: Cardinal Health Inc 7000 Cardinal Pl Dublin OH 43017-1092*

WALTER, SHERYL LYNN, lawyer; b. Morris, Ill., July 18, 1956; d. C. Frank and Margaret (Juhl) W. BA in History cum laude, Grinnell Coll., Iowa, 1978; JD cum laude, U. Minn., 1984; MPA John F. Kennedy Sch. of Govt., Harvard U., 2003. Bar: Minn. 1984, U.S. Dist. Ct. Minn. 1987, U.S. Ct. Appeals (8th cir.) 1987, D.C. 1989, U.S. Dist. Ct. D.C. 1989, U.S. Ct. Appeals (D.C. cir.) 1989. Law clk. to presiding judge 3d Jud. Dist. of Minn., Rochester, 1984-85; law clk. to Chief Judge Donald P. Lay U.S. Ct. Appeals (8th cir.), St. Paul, 1985-87; assoc. Mayer, Brown & Platt, Washington, 1987-89; gen. counsel Nat. Security Archive, Washington, 1989-94, Assn. Records Review Bd., Washington, 1994-95, Commn. Protecting and Reducing Govt. Secrecy, Washington, 1995-97, dep. spl. counsel U.S. Senate Vets. Affairs com., 1997-98; minority staff dir., chief counsel U.S. Senate Jud. Com., Youth Violence Subcom., 1998-2000; with Office Legis. Affairs US Dept. Justice, Washington, 2000—03, acting asst. atty. gen., 2001, chief of staff Office Intelligence and Policy Rev., 2003—06, exec. officer Nat. Security Divsn., 2006—. Cons. Amnesty Internat., Washington, 1988-89. Sec., bd. dir Rosemont Ctr. Head Start Sch., 2004—, vice chair, 2005—07, chair, 2008—. Mem. ABA (vice chmn. adminstrv. law sect. govt. info. subcom. 1990-96), D.C. Bar Assn. (steering com., adminstrv. law sect. 1990-97), Am. Soc. Access Profls. (bd. dirs. 1990-98, pres. 1996-97), Brit.-Am. Security Info. Coun. (bd. dirs. 1994-2000), Lawyers Alliance for World Security (bd. dirs. 1994-2000). Office: US Dept Justice 9th and Pennsylvania Ave NW Washington DC 20530

WALTER, VIRGINIA LEE, psychologist, educator; b. Temple, Tex., Oct. 30, 1937; d. Luther Patterson and Virginia Lafayette (Wilkins) W.; m. Glen Ellis, 1958 (div.); children: Glen Edward, David Walter; m. Robert Reinehr, 1963 (div.); 1 son, Charles Allen; m. Robert Bruininks, 1975 (div.). BS, U. Tex., Austin, 1959, MEd, 1967; postgrad. internship program in spl. Edn. Adminstrn., 1970; EdD, U. Houston, 1973. Prof. ednl. psychology dept. ednl. psychology U. Minn., Mpls., 1973-85; pres. Sch. Resource Ctr., Austin, Tex., 1985-90; tchr. Llano Pub. Schs., 1988-97; dir. Walter Resources, 1998—. Chmn. State Adv. Coun. for Inservice Tng. Regular Classroom Tchrs., 1977-79; cons. spl. ednl. various sch. dists., state depts. and agys. Editl. cons.: Jour. Ednl. Psychology, 1979, Reading Rsch. Quar., 1982; assoc. editor: Exceptional Children, 1979-84; assoc. editor Teaching Exceptional Children, 1985-89; contbr. articles to profl. jours., papers to profl. confs. Named Minn. Spl. Educator of Yr., 1978; recipient Svc. award Internat. Coun. Exceptional Children, 1978; HEW Office of Human Devel. Svcs. grantee, 1976-80; Dept. Edn. contractee, 1980-83 Mem. Coun. for Exceptional Children, Nat. Assn. Children with Learning Disabilities (dir. Minn. chpt. 1978-80), Nat. Assn. Retarded Citizens, AAUP, Assn. Supervision and Curriculum Devel. Home and Office: 7108 Running Rope Austin TX 78731-2128

WALTER, W. EDWARD, hotel and corporate financial executive; Ptnr. Trammell Crow Residential Co.; pres. Bailey Capital Corp.; sr. v.p. acquisitions Host Hotels & Resorts Inc., Bethesda, Md., 1996—98, sr. v.p., treas., 1998—2000, exec. v.p., treas., 2000—01, exec. v.p., COO, 2001—03, exec. v.p., CFO, 2003—07, pres., CEO, 2007—. Treas. Friendship Pub. Charter Sch., Washington; bd. dir., past chmn. Nat. Capital Area Nat. Kidney Found. Office: Host Marriott Corp 6903 Rockledge Drive Ste 1500 Bethesda MD 20817

WALTER, WILLIAM G., consumer products company executive; V.p., gen. mgr., Specialty Chemicals Group FMC Corp., Phila., 1997—2000, exec. v.p., 2000—01, chmn., pres. CEO, 2001—. Dir. Internat. Paper Co., 2005—. Mem. The Business Roundtable; mem. exec. comm. The Philadelphia Chamber of Commerce. Office: c/o FMC 1735 Market St Philadelphia PA 19103

WALTERS, ARTHUR SCOTT, neurologist, educator, clinical research scientist; b. Balt., Feb. 20, 1943; s. Charles Henry and Jean Vivian (Scott) W.; m. Bokyun Kim, May 18, 1985 (div. Oct. 1992); m. Lesley J. Gill, Dec. 19, 1992. BA, Kalamazoo Coll., 1965; MS, Northwestern U., 1967; MD, Wayne State U., 1972. Diplomate Am. Bd. Psychiatry and Neurology; diplomate Am. Bd. Sleep Medicine. Intern Oakwood Hosp., Dearborn, Mich., 1972-73; resident in neurology SUNY Downstate Med. Ctr., Bklyn., 1976-79; movement disorder fellow Neurol. Inst., NYC, 1982-84; asst. prof. neurology Robert Wood Johnson Med. Sch., U. Medicine & Dentistry NJ, New Brunswick, 1984-91, assoc. prof. neurology, 1991-99, clin. prof. neurology, 1999—2008; asst. chief divsn. neurology Lyons VA Med. Ctr., NJ, 1985-89, neurology cons., 1984-99; prof. neurosci. Seton Hall U. Sch. Grad. Med. Edn., South Orange, NJ, 1999—2008, NJ Neurosci. Inst., Edison, 1999—2008; prof. neurology Vanderbilt U. Sch. Medicine, Nashville, 2008—. Nat. chmn. med. adv. bd. Restless Legs Syndrome Found., 1992-98; chair Internat. Restless Legs Study Group, 1992-2007; head Restless Legs Syndrome and Periodic Limb Movement Coun. for the Nat. Sleep Found., 1994-96; neurology cons. Coney Island Hosp., Bklyn., Bklyn. Jewish Hosp., 1980-81; presenter in field. Contbr. articles to profl. publs., chpts. to books; organizer symposia. Named Rschr. of Yr. in medicine Seton Hall U. Sch. Grad. Med. Edn., 2003-04, Michael S. Aldrich hon. lectr. in sleep medicine for outstanding contbns. to patient care, rsch. and edn. U. Mich., 2006, Best Vol. neurology faculty member UMDNJ-Robert Wood Johnson Med. Sch., 2007; recipient Disting. Svc, award Internat. Restless Legs Syndrome Study Group, 2007, Tchg. award, Sleep Fellows and Cmty. Sleep Physicians NJ Neurosci. Inst. JFK Med. Ctr., 2008; grantee UMDNJ, 1984-86, VA RAG, 1985-86, Sandoz Corp., 1985-88, VA Merit Rev., 1989-98, Clemente Found., 1994-95, Purdue Pharma, 2000—, NIH, 2002-07. Fellow Am. Acad. Neurology, Am. Acad. Sleep Medicine; editl. bd., (journal) Sleep, Sleep Medicine; mem. AAAS, Am. Neurol. Assn., Sleep Rsch. Soc., Movement Disorder Soc., NY Acad. Scis., NJ Sleep Soc. (sec. 1995-96, treas. 1996-97, v.p. 1998-99). Office: Dept Neurology Vanderbilt Univ Sch Medicine MCNA-0124 1161 21st Ave S Nashville TN 37232-2551 Office Phone: 615-322-0283. Personal E-mail: artumdnj@aol.com. Business E-Mail: arthur.walters@vanderbilt.edu.

WALTERS, BARBARA JILL, broadcast journalist; b. Boston, Sept. 25, 1931; d. Lou and Dena (Selett) Walters; m. Robert Katz, June 21, 1955 (div. 1958); m. Lee Gruber, 1963 (div. 1976); 1 adopted child, Jacqueline; m. Merv Adelson, 1986 (div. 1992). BA in English, Sarah Lawrence Coll., 1953, LHD (hon.), Ohio State U., Marymount Coll., 1975, Wheaton Coll., 1983, Temple U., Hofstra U., Ben-Gurion U. Former producer WNBC-TV; former writer CBS News; then with Stas. WPIX and CBS-TV; writer, reporter-at-large Today Show, 1961—63, regular panel mem., 1964—74, co-host, 1974—76; moderator syndicated program Not For Women Only, 1972—76; founder, pres. Barwall Productions, NYC, 1976—; newscaster ABC Evening News (now ABC World News Tonight), 1976—78; host The Barbara Walters Spls., 1976—; co-host ABC TV news show 20/20, 1984—99, anchor, 1999—2004; host The 10 Most Fascinating People, 1993—; co-exec. prodr., co-owner, co-host The View, ABC, NYC, 1997—; exec. prodr. The Iyanla Show, 2001. Contbr. NBC Radio Network. Author: (books) How to Talk With Practically Anybody About Practically Anything, 1970, Audition: A Memoir, 2008; contbr. ABC programs Issues and Answers, to Reader's Digest, Good Housekeeping, Family Weekly. Honorary chair Nat. Assn. Help for Mentally Retarded Children, 1970. Recipient Award Yr., Nat. Assn. TV Program Execs., 1975, Daytime Emmy award, Nat. Acad. TV Arts and Scis., 1975, Emmy award, 1980, 1982, 1983, Daytime Emmy award for outstanding talk show, 2003, Mass Media award, Am. Jewish Com. Inst. Human Relations, 1975, Barbara Walters' Coll. Scholarship in Broadcast Journalism established in her honor, Ill. Broadcasters Assn., 1975, Matrix award, N.Y. Women in Comm., 1977, Hubert H. Humphrey Freedom prize, Anti Defamation League B'nai B'rith, 1978, Pres.'s award, Overseas Press Club, 1988, inducted Hall of Fame, Acad. TV Arts and Scis., 1990, Lowell Thomas award, Marist Coll., 1990, Lifetime Achievement award, Internat. Women's Media Found., 1991, saluted, Am. Mus. Moving Image, 1992, Lifetime Achievement award, Women's Project and Prodn., 1993, honored for contbn. to broadcast journalism, Mus. TV and Radio, 1996, George Foster Peabody award for her interview with actor Christopher Reeve, 1996, Muse award, NY Women in Film and TV, 1997, Lifetime Achievement award, Daytime Emmy Awards, 2000, Nat. Acad. TV Arts and Scis., 2000, Silver Satellite award, Am. Women Radio and TV, Sherry Landing Leadership award, The Hollywood Reporter, 2005, Star on the Hollywood Walk of Fame, 2007, Media award, Gay and Lesbian Alliance Against Defamation, 2008; named Woman Yr. Comm., 1974, Broadcaster Yr., Internat. Radio and TV Soc., 1975, Woman Yr., Theta Sigma Phi; named an The 50 Most Powerful Women in NYC, NY Post, 2008; named one of Am.'s 75 Most Important Women, Ladies' Home Jour., 1970, 200 Leaders Future, Time Mag., 1974, 10 Women Decade, Ladies' Home Jour., 1979, Most Important Women, Roper Report, 1979, Women Most Admired Am. People, Gallup Poll, 1982, 1984, Am.'s 100 Most Important Women, Ladies' Home Jour., 1983, America's 100 Most Important Women of the Century, Good Housekeeping, 2000, Ladies' Home Journal, 2000, 100 Most Powerful Celebrities, Forbes.com, 2007, 100 Most Powerful Women, Forbes mag., 2008, The World's Most Influential People, TIME mag., 2009; named to 100 Women of Accomplishment, Harper's Bazaar, 1967, 1971, Museum of Television and Radio, Los Angeles, 2004. Achievements include first woman to co-anchor the Network News, 1976; interviewed every U.S. president and first lady since Nixon; conducted several historic interviews including the Nov. 1977 joint interview with Egyptian President Anwar Sadat and Israel's Prime Minister Menachem Begin; hour-long prime-time interview with Cuba's President Fidel Castro, June 9, 1977 and a second interview 25 years later in 2002; conducted the first interview with Monica Lewinsky, which became the highest-rated news program, 48.5 million viewers, ever broadcast by a single network, 1999. Office: The View 320 W 66th St New York NY 10023-6304*

WALTERS, BILL, retired state senator; b. Paris, Ark., Apr. 17, 1943; s. Peter Louis and Elizabeth Cecelia (Wilhelm) W.; m. Joyce Leslie Garrett Moore, Jan. 9, 1964 (div. 1970); children: Jamie, Sherry Ann; m. Shirley Ann Dixon, Aug. 20, 1971; 1 child, Sandra. BS, U. Ark., 1966, JD, 1971. Bar: Ark. 1971, U.S. Dist. Ct. Ark. 1971. Asst. prosecuting atty. 12th Jud. Dist. Ark., Ft. Smith, 1971-74; pvt. practice Greenwood, Ark., 1975—; mem. Ark. Senate, Little Rock, 1982-2000. Bd. dirs., sec.-treas. Mineral Owners Collective Assn. Inc., Greenwood; former v.p., bd. dirs. Sebastian County Abstract & Title Ins. Co., Greenwood and Ft. Smith, Ark.; mem. Ark. Real Estate Commn., Ark. Abstract and Title Commn. Committeeman Rep. Ctrl. Com. Ark., Ft. Smith, 1980; search pilot CAP, Ft. Smith. Decorated Silver Medal of Valor; recipient Cert. of Honor Justice for Crime's Victims, 1983. Mem. Ark. Bar Assn., South Sebastian County Bar Assn. (pres. 1991-94), Profl. Landmen's Assn. Roman Catholic. Home: PO Box 280 Greenwood AR 72936-0280 Office: 1405 W Center Greenwood AR 72936-3200 Home Phone: 479-996-4520; Office Phone: 479-996-2100. Business E-Mail: bwalters@waltlaw.net.

WALTERS, CLAYTON WILLIAM, health facility administrator, rehabilitation services professional, consultant; b. Jellico, Tenn., June 7, 1951; s. Phillip Gordon and Sarah Eileen Walters; m. Susan Louise Brandau; children: David Clayton, Christopher, Matthew, Cassandra. AA in Humanities, Dutchess C.C., Poughkeepsie, NY, 1979. Exec. dir. Baldwin Rsch. Inst., Amsterdam, NY, 2003—04, v.p. cons., 2004—06; v.p. ops. St. Jude Thaddeus Inc., Des Moines, 2006—08, St. Gregory Retreat Ctr., 2008—. Republican. Episcopalian. Avocations: reading, book collecting, sailing. Home: PO Box 310 Bayard IA 50029 Office: Saint Gregory Retreat Ctr 5875 Fleur Dr Des Moines IA 50321 Office Phone: 515-419-8788. Business E-Mail: clayton@stgregoryctr.com.

WALTERS, FARAH M., health services company administrator, former hospital administrator; b. Feb. 10, 1945; BS, Ohio State U., 1968; MS, Case Western Res. U., 1975, MBA, 1984. Sr. v.p., gen. mgr. Univs. Hosps., Cleve., 1987-89, exec. v.p., 1989-91, exec. dir., 1991-92, pres., CEO, 1992—2002, QualHealth LLC, 2005—. Mem. Ohio Commn. to Study the Ohio Econ. & Tax Structure; bd. dirs. PolyOne Corp., Celanese, 2007—. Recipient Ellis Medal of Honor; named to Bus. Hall of Fame, Bus. mag., 2000, Ohio Women's Hall of Fame, 2001.

WALTERS, GEORGE KAUFFMAN, retired business educator; b. Abilene, Kans., Oct. 10, 1929; s. Harry Elmer and Stella (Kauffman) W.; m. Martha Flo Kissell, June 27, 1954; 1 child, Jon K. BS, Ft. Hays State U., 1955; MA, U. No. Colo., 1958, EdD, 1968. Tchr. bus. Ashland (Kans.) High Sch., 1955-57, Norton (Kans.) High Sch., 1957-60; v.p. western div. Suttle Directory Co., Overland Park, Kans., 1960-62; asst. prof. No. State Coll., Aberdeen, S.D., 1962-64; prof. Emporia (Kans.) State U., 1964—94, assoc dean sch. bus., 1984-94, ret., 1994. Cons. editor Jour. Edn. for Bus., 1989—94; manuscript reviewer NABTE Rev. and Bulletin; honored by George K. Walters scholarship fund, 1994; contbr. articles to profl. jours. Usher coord. 1st United Meth. Ch.; docent William Allen White House Hist. Site; chair screening com. Nat. Tchrs. Hall of Fame. Recipient Leadership award, Boy Scouts Am., Empoira, 1974, Good Scout award, 2005; named Man of the Week, Emporia Gazette, 1994. Mem. Nat. Assn. Bus. Tchr. Edn. (pres. 1987-89), Nat. Bus. Edn. Assn., Kans. Bus. Edn. Assn., Mountain-Plains Bus. Edn. Assn., Am. Legion, VFW, Emporia Area Ret. Sch. Pers. (pres. 1997-98), Emporia Camera Club (pres. 1985-86), Outlook Study Club (pres. 1996-99, 2005-06), Lions Club (bd. dirs. 1986-89, newsletter editor, v.p. 1988, pres. 1989-90, Pres.'s award for Outstanding Leadership 1989-90), Pi Omega Pi (nat. pres. 1974-76), Delta Pi Epsilon, Phi Delta Kappa, Kappa Delta Pi. Avocations: travel, hiking, civic activity, photography, fishing. Home: 1029 West St Emporia KS 66801-2673

WALTERS, GLEN ROBERT, retired banker; b. Mpls., Sept. 11, 1943; s. Sterling Thomas and Mildred Eunice (Parkinson) W.; m. Gail Elvira Engelsen, June 11, 1966; children: Nicole Marie, Brent Aaron, Hillary Renee. BA, U. Minn., Mpls., 1965, postgrad., 1965-67; banking degree, Rutgers U., New Brunswick, NJ, 1982. Comml. banker 1st Nat. Bank, Mpls., 1967-83, sr. v.p. human resources, 1983-90; sr. v.p. Firstar Bank Minn., Mpls., 1990-2001, US Bank, Mpls., 2001—05. Served to sgt. USNG, 1967-73 Republican. Presbyterian.

WALTERS, JERRY B., retired art educator; b. Indpls., Jan. 25, 1942; s. Buford B. and Bitha Z. Walters; m. Linda B. Ball, Sept. 21, 1963; children: Andrew B., Rachel E. Walters-Ndiho. BS in Art Edn., Southern Ill. U., Carbondale, 1964; MS in Art Edn., U. Kans., Lawrence, 1969. Art instr. Jardine Jr. HS, Topeka, 1964—67, Lake Zurich HS, Ill., 1967; art grad. asst. U. Kans., Lawrence, 1967—69; prof. emeritus, fine arts dept. Mineral Area Coll., Pk. Hills, Mo., 1969—, head fine arts dept., instr., 1980—2001, dean evening divsn., 1985—2009. Brookhaven Coll. Art Workshop (Purchase award, 2001). Lectr. Mo. Coun. on Arts, Pk. Hills. Recipient Outstanding Faculty award, Mineral Area Coll., 1988, 2000, Mo. Gov.'s, 2000. Avocation: travel.

WALTERS, JOHN C., insurance company executive; BS in Bus. and Fin., U. NC, Chapel Hill; MBA, Duke U. Fuqua Sch. Bus., Durham. Assoc. Wheat First Butcher Singer, 1984—98; mgr. consulting services group First Union Securities, 1998—2000; various positions including v.p., exec. v.p., dir. investment products divsn. Hartford Fin. Services Group, Inc., 2000—06, pres. US wealth mgmt., 2006—07, co-COO life ops., 2007—08, pres., COO Hartford Life, Inc., 2008—. Mem., The Office of the Chmn. Hartford Fin. Services Group, Inc. Bd. governors Investment Co. Inst.; bd. trustees Wadsworth Atheneum Mus. Art, Hartford, Conn. Office: Hartford Fin Services Group Inc One Hartford Plz Hartford CT 06155 Office Phone: 860-547-5000. Office Fax: 860-547-2680.

WALTERS, JOHN P., think-tank executive, former federal official; b. Feb. 8, 1952; m. Mary Walters; children: Michaela, Rebecca. BA, Mich. State U.; MA, U. Toronto. Acting asst. dir., prog. officer divsn. edn. programs NEH, 1982—85; asst. to sec. US Dept. Edn., 1985—88; chief of staff Office Nat. Drug Control Policy (ONDCP), Washington, 1989—91, dep. dir. for supply reduction, 1991—93, dir., 2001—09; pres. Philanthropy Roundtable, Washington, 1996—2001; exec. v.p. The Hudson Inst., Washington, 2009—. Dir. Nat. Youth Anti-Drug Media Campaign; vis. fellow Hudson Inst., NY, 1993; instr. polit. sci. James Madison Coll. Mich. State U., Boston Coll.; sec.'s rep. Nat. Drug Policy Bd., Domestic Policy Coun.'s Health Policy Working Grp. Co-author (with William J. Bennett & John J. Di Iulio Jr.): Body Count: Moral Poverty and How to Win America's War Against Crime and Drugs, 1996. Pres. New Citizenship Prog. Republican. Achievements include releasing the National Drug Control Strategy which set aggressive goals of a ten percent reduction in teen and adult drug use in two years and a twenty five percent reduction in five years; Monitoring the Future Study showed a nineteen percent reduction in teen drug use over four years exceeding the President's goal and bringing drug use to its lowest levels since the early 1990s; lead a restructuring of the federal drug control budget so that it more accurately reflects the actual dollars spent on programs aimed at reducing drug use making it a more useful tool for policymaker; oversees the creation and implementation of the Access to Recovery treatment initiative announced by President Bush in his 2003 State of the Union Address; the Access to Recovery treatment initiative approach to drug treatment funding provides vouchers for hundreds of thousands of Americans struggling with addiction. Office: The Hudson Institute 1015 15th St NW 6th Fl Washington DC 20005 Office Phone: 202-974-2400. Office Fax: 202-974-2410.*

WALTERS, JOHNNIE MCKEIVER, lawyer; b. Hartsville, SC, Dec. 20, 1919; s. Tommie Ellis and Lizzie Lee (Grantham) W.; m. Donna Lucile Hall, Sept. 1, 1947; children: Donna Dianne Walters Gent, Lizbeth Kathern Walters Kukorowski, Hilton Horace, John Roy. AB, Furman U., 1942, LLD, 1973; LLB, U. Mich., 1948. Bar: Mich. 1948, N.Y. 1955, S.C. 1961, D.C. 1973. Atty. office chief counsel IRS, Washington, 1949-53; asst. mgr. tax div. law dept. Texaco, Inc., NYC, 1953-61; ptnr. firm Geer, Walters & Demo, Greenville, SC, 1961-69; asst. atty. gen. tax div. Dept. Justice, Washington, 1969-71; commr. IRS, 1971-73; ptnr. firm Hunton & Williams, Washington, 1973-79, Leatherwood Walker Todd & Mann, P.C., Greenville, 1979-95; exec. v.p., gen. counsel Colonial Trust Co., Greenville, 1996—2005; ret., 2006. Bd. dirs. Textile Hall Corp., Greenville, Colonial Trust Co. Mem. S.C. Coun. on Competitiveness, 1987—91, S.C. Ethics Commn., 2005—08. With USAF, 1942—45. Fellow Am. Coll. Tax Counsel (founding regent), Am. Coll. Trust and Estate Counsel, Am. Bar Found., S.C. Bar Found. (bd. dirs. 1988-92); mem. ABA (taxation sect.), S.C. Bar (chmn. taxation sect. 1983-84), Rotary (pres. local club 1968-69). Republican. Baptist. Home: 1438 Trailhead Ct Greenville SC 29617-6225 E-mail: jmac@wafres.org.

WALTERS, KAREN M., mathematics professor; married. BA, Dartmouth Coll., Hanover, NH, 1988; MS, U. Hartford, Conn., 1989; MEd, Harvard U., Cambridge, Mass., 1994; PhD, U. Ky., Lexington, 2003. Math prof. Northern Va. CC, Annandale, 2007—; math faculty Arapahoe CC. Office: Northern VA CC 8333 Little River Turnpike Annandale VA 22003

WALTERS, KENNETH, applied mathematics educator; b. Swansea, Wales, Sept. 14, 1934; s. Trevor Walters and Lilian (Price) Gullis; m. Mary Ross Eccles, July 27, 1963; children: Jeremy Ross, Jonathan Mark, Josephine Jane. BSc, Swansea Univ. Coll., Wales, 1956, MSc, 1957, PhD, 1959, DSc, 1984; doctorate (hon.), U. Joseph Fourier, Grenoble, France, 1998. Rsch. assoc. Brown U., Providence, 1959; asst. prof. San Diego State Coll., 1960; lectr. U. Coll. Wales, Aberystwyth, 1960-65, sr. lectr., 1965-70, reader, 1970-73, prof., 1973—2004, disting. rsch. prof., 2004—. Author: Rheometry, 1975, Rheometry: Industrial Applications, 1980; co-author: Numerical Simulation of Non-Newtonian Flow, 1984, An Introduction to Rheology, 1989, Rheological Phenomena in Focus, 1993, Rheology: An Historical Perspective, 1998, The Way It Was, 2003. Recipient Gold medal Brit. Soc. Rheology, 1984. Fellow Royal Soc.; mem. U.S. Nat. Acad. Engring. (fgn. assoc.), European Soc. Rheology (pres. 1996-2000, Weissenberg award 2002), Internat. Com. on Rheology (chmn. 2000-2004). Anglican. Home: 8 Pen y Graig Aberystwyth SY23 2JA Wales Office: Univ Aberystwyth Inst Math and Phys Penglais Aberystwyth SY23 3BZ Wales Home Phone: 44 1970 615276; Office Phone: 0197 062-2750. E-mail: kew@aber.ac.uk.

WALTERS, KIRK W., bank executive; b. 1955; Student, U. So. Calif., 1978. Audit supr. Coopers & Lybrand, LA, 1978-81; corp. fin. Atlantic Richfield Co., LA, 1981-84; sr. v.p., controller Calif. Fed. Savings & Loan Assn., 1984-89; pres., CEO, chmn. bd., CFO NE Fed. Corp., Hartford, Conn., 1990-96; exec. v.p., CFO & treas. Chittenden Corp., Burlington, Vt., 1997—2008; exec. v.p., CFO Sovereign Bancorp Inc., Boston, 2008—, acting pres., CEO, 2008—09, chief adminstrv. officer, 2009—. Office: Sovereign Bancorp Inc 75 State St Boston MA 02109 E-mail: kwalter1@sovereignbank.com.*

WALTERS, MARIAN R., research administrator; b. Washington, 1948; PhD, U. Houston, 1975. Prof. physiology Tulane U. Sch. Medicine, New Orleans, 1980—2004, dir. tuxcoe leadership core, 1999—2004, dir. of grad. studies in physiology, 1983—2004; assoc. dean rsch. and grad. studies Penn State U., Harrisburg, 2004—. Author: (book chapter) Encyclopedia of Hormones: Calcium Regulating Hormones. Mem.: Soc. Exptl. Biology and Medicine (coun. mem. 2001—08, treas. 2006—08). Office: Penn State Harrisburg 777 W Harrisburg Pike Middletown PA 17057

WALTERS, MARJORIE ANNE, interior designer, consultant; b. Flushing, NY, Dec. 5, 1925; d. Walter Bowne Williams, Florence Clara (Bach) Williams; m. Robert Leslie Walters, Sept. 17, 1949; children: Robert Bowne(dec.), Richard James. BS, Coll. William & Mary, 1947; AA, NY Sch. Interior Design, 1958. Owner, pres. M.W. Walters, Interiors, Hohokus, NJ, 1958—86; pres. NJ Ridgwood Art Inst., 1980—86; owner, pres. M.W. Walters, Interiors, Richfield Springs, NY, 1986—. Dir. Art & Program Commn., Richfield Springs, 1993—; chmn. Baker's Beach Art & Programs Commn., Richfield Springs; exec. dir. Cooperstown NY Art Assn., 1986—90. Smithy-Pioneer Gallery, Cooperstown, 2001—. Pres. Richfield Springs Hist. Assn., 1997—; v.p. Richfield Springs Libr. Bd., 1999—; sec. zoning bd. of appeals Town of Richfield Springs, 1999—; organizer of restoration and dedication of hist. town clock of 1918 Richfield Springs, NY, 2005. Recipient Cmty. Svc. award, Richfield C. of C., 1994, Good Citizenship award, DAR, 1994, Good Neighbor award, WBUG AM/FM, 1994, Ostego 2000 Historic Landmark award, Ostego County, 2006, Outstanding Achievement award, Richfield Springs Mayor and Bd. Trustees, 2006, Mayor's Spl. Commendation award for clock restoration, Richfield Springs, 2007. Mem.: Nat. Mus. Women in Arts (charter mem.), Internat. Visual Artists (Eng.), Lake and Valley Garden Club (pres. 1998—2000). Avocations: landscape painting, flower arranging, swimming. Home and Office: 217 Walters Way Richfield Springs NY 13439 Office Phone: 315-858-0027. Personal E-mail: mbwalt@aol.com.

WALTERS, MARTHA LEE, state supreme court justice; b. 1951; married; 2 children. JD, U. Oreg. Sch. Law, 1977. Pres. Walters, Chanti & Zennache, Eugene, Oreg.; assoc. justice Oreg. Supreme Ct., 2006—. Chmn. exec. com. Nat. Conf. Commrs. on Uniform State Laws, 1992—, pres., 2007—. Recipient Pub. Justice award, Oreg. Trial Lawyers Assn., 1998. Mem.: Am. Law Inst., Oreg. Law Commn. Office: Walters Chanti & Zennache 245 E 4th St Eugene OR 97401 Office Phone: 503-986-5668.*

WALTERS, MARY LYNN, nursing educator; m. Charles Walters. MS, Northern Ill. U., De Kalb. Assoc. prof. nursing Rock Valley Coll., Rockford, Ill., 2003—. Home: 323 E Royal Dekalb IL 60115 Office: Rock Valley Coll 3301 N Mulford Rd Rockford IL 61114 Business E-Mail: mwalters@ednet.rvc.cc.il.us.

WALTERS, MICHAEL W., social sciences educator; b. Darmstadt, Germany, Dec. 30, 1955; s. Blondina Hartenberger, adopted s. Marcus R. and Lillian V. Walters; m. Nancy B. Burney, Oct. 24, 1986; children: Courtney L. Eoff, Clinton Burney Skates. AA, U. Ctrl. Fla., Orlando, 1977; BS in Therapeutic Recreation, Fla. State U., Tallahassee, 1980; MA in Theol. Studies, Ref. Theol. Sem., Orlando, Fla., 2001. Ropes course coord. activity therapy dir. Lookout Mountain Cmty. Svcs., LaFayette, Ga., 1990—99; instr. & coord. coll. life Northwestern Tech. Coll., Rock Spring, Ga., 1999—. Asst. cons. Lookout Mountain Cmty. Svcs., LaFayette, 1993—99; counselor Stuart Heights Bibl. Counseling Ctr., Chattanooga, 1999—2008. Sch. instr. Stuart Heights Bapt. Ch., Chattanooga, 2000—. Recipient Outstanding Student award, Fla. State U., 1980, award, Nat. Honor Soc. Fla. State U., 1980, Outstanding Svc. award, State Ga., 2007. Conservative. Baptist. Avocations: hiking, running, gardening, reading. Home: 1211 Duane Rd Chattanooga TN 37405 Office: Northwestern Tech Coll 265 Bicentennial Trail Rock Spring GA 30739 Personal E-mail: mwalters@northwesterntech.edu.

WALTERS, MILTON JAMES, investment banker; b. Hornell, NY, May 21, 1942; s. James Henry and Frances Eleanor (Simmons) W.; m. Caroline Houck, May 24, 1963; children: Melissa Ann, Gregory Thomas, Timothy Allen. BA, Hamilton Coll., 1964. Trainee Mfrs. Hanover, 1964-65; with A.G. Becker Inc., NYC, 1965-84; mng. dir. Warburg Paribas Becker, NYC, 1978—84, Smith Barney, NYC, 1984—88, Prudential Securities, NYC, 1997-99; pres. Tri-River Capital, 1988—. Bd. dirs. Decision One, Frederick's of Hollywood, Sun Healthcare Group; former dir. Murray's Discount Auto, 2002—03. Former trustee Hamilton Coll., Clinton, NY, 1983-88, Friends Acad., Locust Valley, NY, 1981-91 Mem. Nat. Assn. Corp. Dirs., Nat. Assn. Cert. Valuation Analysis, Econ. Club NY. Republican. Presbyterian. Office: Tri-River Capital PO Box 128 New York NY 10150-0128 Office Phone: 212-581-5777. Business E-Mail: mjw@tririv.com.

WALTERS, RICHARD FRANCIS, computer science educator; b. Teleajen, Romania, Aug. 30, 1930; s. Ray Pearce and Gertrude (Gravett) W.; m. Shipley Newlin, Aug. 30, 1952; children: Leslie Walters Tuomi, David Todd. BA magna cum laude, Williams Coll., Williamstown, Mass., 1952; MA, U. Wyo., Laramie, 1953; Diplome superieur en scis. naturelles, U. Bordeaux, France, 1955; PhD, Stanford U., Calif., 1957. Geologist Humble Oil and Refining Co., Los Angeles, 1956-60, subsurface geologist Chico, Calif., 1960-63, sr. subsurface geologist New Orleans, 1963-66; sr. research geologist Esso Prodn. Research Co., Houston, 1966-67; lectr. computer sci. U. Calif., Davis, 1967-68, asst. prof. med. edn. and biomed. engring., 1968-73, assoc. prof. med. edn. and biomed. engring., 1973-78, assoc. prof. community health, 1978-79, prof. community health, 1979-83, prof. elec. and computer engring., 1980-83, prof. divsn. computer sci., 1983—, chair divsn. computer sci., 1983—89, prof. family practice, 1984-96, prof. med. informatics, 1996—; Edward A. Dickson prof. emeritus, 2006—07. Editorial cons. Soc. for Computer Simulations, 1970-76; editorial rev. bd. mem. Jour. of Computer Based Instrn., 1975-89, Med. Informatics, 1977—, MUMPS Users' Group Quarterly, 1981—, Computers in Biology and Medicine, 1982—, MD Computing, 1985-93; contbr. articles to profl. jours. Fellow Am. Geol. Soc., Am. Coll. Med. Informatics; mem. Am. Arbitration Assn. Computing Machinery (mem. spl. interest group on programming langs. 1980—, 1974—, mem. spl. interest group on mgmt. data base, 1981), MUMPS Users' Group (vice chmn. 1974-75, chmn. 1975-77, 81-83, devel. com. chmn. 1977-79, 80-82, hon. life mem. Europe and Japan), Am. Assn. Med. Systems and Informatics, IEEE (sr.), U. Calif. Davis Emeritus Assn. (pres. 2006-08). Democrat. Episcopalian. Avocation: music. Home: 647 Elmwood Dr Davis CA 95616-3514 Office: U Calif Dept Computer Sci One Shields Ave Davis CA 95616-8562 Office Phone: 530-752-3241. Business E-Mail: walters@cs.ucdavis.edu.

WALTERS, ROBERT ANCIL, physicist, mathematician; b. Russell Springs, Ky., Mar. 12, 1915; s. Robert Edmund Lee and Talitha Margaret (Wilson) W.; m. Etha Jane McKinley, Feb. 2, 1943; 1 child, Robert Ancil II; m. Sherry Walters, June 29, 1969; 1 child, Forrest Wayne. BS, Western Ky. U., 1941; postgrad., George Washington U., 1943-45, Agrl. Grad. Sch., 1947-48, Am. U., 1951-52. H.S. asst. prin. Russell County Bd. Edn., 1941-42; physicist, head exterior ballistics U.S. Naval Weapons Lab., Dahlgren, Va., 1942-59; pres. Walters Ins. and Investment Counselor, Dahlgren, 1948-80; engr., head systems planning U.S. Naval Space Surveillance, Dahlgren, Va., 1959-69; R&D specialist, physicist interdisplinary math. cons. U.S. Naval Warfare Lab., Dahlgren, 1969-75. Pres. Navel Weapons Lab. Fed. Credit Union, Dahlgren, 1968-74; bd. examiners Potomac River Naval Com., Washington, 1953-56; biology lab. instr. Western Ky. U., Bowling Green, 1935-36. Chmn. Old Dominion Eye Bank, Richmond, Va., 1975-76; co-chair Dem. Party, Ky., 1937-42; pres. Nat. Fedn. Fed. Employees, Washington, 1963-69. Recipient Nat. Quality award Nat. Assn. Life Underwriters, 1976; named Ky. Col., gov. of Ky., 1976, Outstanding Citizen of Yr., VFW, 1981, Guest of Honor King George County Fall Festival, 1994. Mem.: Lions Internat. (dep. dist. gov. 1976—77, Disting. Svc. award 1975, Melvin Jones fellow 2001, cert. for disting. leadership and svc. 2005). Baptist.

WALTERS, ROSS A., federal judge; BA in History, Pa. State U., 1971; JD with high distinction, U. Iowa, 1977. Law clk. to Judge William C. Hanson US Dist. Ct. (So. Dist. Iowa), 1977—79; assoc. Herrick and Langdon, Des Moines, 1979—82, ptnr., 1982—90; judge Iowa Dist. Ct. (Jud. Dist. 5-C), 1990—94; magistrate judge US Dist. Ct. (So. Dist.) Iowa, 1994—. Bd. editors, contemporary studies project leader Iowa Law Rev. Legal officer, adminstrv. div. officer US Navy Reserve, 1971—74, aboard USS Oklahoma City. Office: US Courthouse Rm 440 123 E Walnut St Des Moines IA 50309-2035

WALTERS, SUE FOX, broadcast executive, accountant; b. Louisville, June 9, 1941; d. Thomas Burke and Reva Crick Fox; m. Hugh Alexander Walters (dec. 2001); children: Thomas Wade Walters, Alexandra Walters Ebling. Student, N.C. State U., Ky. Wesleyan Coll. Acct., paralegal for fin. instns. and firms; ct. adminstr. 45th Jud. Cir. Ct., Ky.; v.p., treas. Alexander and Assocs., CATV cons. firm, Greenville, Ky.; corp. adminstr., pub. corp. Bellevue, Wash.; sr. acctg. specialist Japanese/Am. Automotive Mfg. Co., Bowling Green, Ky.; land developer. Pres., Jr. Woman's Club Greenville, 1964-65, Woman's Club of Greenville, 1976-78; vice gov. 2d dist. Ky. Fedn. Women's Clubs, 1980. Avocations: historical preservation, design, antiques, dogs, flying. Home: 151 N Main St Greenville KY 42345-1503 Home Phone: 270-338-4237.

WALTERS, SYLVIA SOLOCHEK, art educator; b. Milw., Aug. 24, 1938; d. Bernard and Becky (Perlstein) Solochek; m. James H. Walters, Aug. 26, 1963. BS, U. Wis., 1960, MS, 1961, MFA, 1962. Prof. painting Keuka (N.Y.) Coll., 1962-63; prof. printmaking Layton Sch. of Art, Milw., 1963-64; book designer U. Wis. Press, Madison, 1964-67; prof. art St. Louis U., 1968-69; prof. art, art dept. chair, gallery dir. U. Mo., St. Louis, 1969-84; prof., art dept. chair San Francisco State U., 1984—2004, acting dean creative arts, 1993-94, 1996—97; emerirus prof., 2009. Collections, St. Louis Mus., exhibitions include Chazen Mus. Art, Oakland Mus., San Francisco Fine Arts Mus., Achenbach Found. Graphic Arts, Judah Magnes Mus. Jewish Art. Bd. dirs. Art Coordinating Coun. for the Area, St. Louis, 1976-79, Bay Area Consortium for the Visual Arts, San Francisco, 1984-91, Calif. Printmakers Soc., no. Calif., 1985-86, 1989—, Kala Art Inst., 2006—; mem. nat. bd. Women's Caucus Art, 1978-80. Business E-Mail: swalters@sfsu.edu.

WALTERS, THOMAS R., gas and power company executive; b. Hammond, Ind. B in Mech. Engring., Vanderbilt U.; M in Ocean Engring., Tex. A&M U. Joined Exxon U.S.A., LA, 1978; v.p., Africa ExxonMobil Develop. Co., 1999, exec. v.p., 2007—09; v.p., US Exxon Prod. Co., 2002; pres. ExxonMobil Global Services Co., 2005; v.p. & pres. Exxon Gas & Power Mktg. Co., 2009—. Office: Exxon Mobil 5959 Las Colinas Blvd Irving TX 75039-2298*

WALTERS, WILLIAM BEN, chemistry professor; b. Highland, Kans., Apr. 26, 1938; s. Ben Guthrie and Dolly Varden (Shaw) W.; m. Barbara Lulu Sternaman, Aug. 5, 1962; children: Katharine, David. AS, Highland Coll., 1957; BS, Kans. State U., 1960; PhD, U. Ill., 1964. Asst. prof. MIT, Cambridge, 1965-70; assoc. prof. chemistry U. Md., College Park, 1970-77, prof., 1977—, assoc. chmn. dept., 1982-86, info. tech. coun., 2007—. Vis. prof. U. Louvain, Belgium, 1978; chair U. Senate, 1999-00; mem. physics adv. com. Grand Accelerateur Nat. d Ions Lourds, 2003-2006. Recipient Nuc. Chemistry award Am. Chemical Soc., 2001, Rsch. award U. Md., Sigma Xi, 1998; Guggenheim fellow Oxford U., 1986-87, Von Humboldt fellow Univ. Mainz, 2001-02, 06. Fellow U. Leuven, Belgium, 2008; mem. Am. Phys. Soc., European Phys. Soc., Am. Chem. Soc. (chmn. div. nuclear chemistry 1986), Rotary (bd. dirs. College Park 1990-91, 2000—). Office: U Md Dept Chemistry College Park MD 20742-0001 Office Phone: 301-405-1801. Business E-Mail: wwalters@umd.edu.

WALTHER, BARBARA ANN LANE, judge, former lawyer; b. San Angelo, Tex., Oct. 6, 1952; d. James Franklin and Dorothy Ann (Watson) Lane; m. Stevem Milton Walther, June 15, 1974; children: Katherine Ann, Stewart Lane. AA, Stephens Coll., 1972; BA, U. Tex., 1975; JD, Southern Meth. U., 1977. Bar: Tex. 1977, US Dist. Ct. (no. dist.) Tex. 1977. Law clk. Regional Atty. HEW, Dallas, 1976-77; pvt. law practice Dallas, 1977-83, San Angelo, Tex., 1985-87; assoc. Davis, Wardlas & Hay, San Angelo, 1983-85; family law master Tom Green County, San Angelo, 1987—92; dist. judge Tex. 51st Dist. Ct., 1992—. Mem. San Angelo Lake Bd., 1985-87; bd. dirs. San Angelo Nature Ctr., 1991—; v.p. El Camino Girl Scouts, San Angelo, 1988, Acad. Excellence Found., San Angelo, 1990. Mem. State Bar of Tex. (family law sect., litigation sect., Coll. of State Bar 1990), Carrolton Farmers Br. Lawyers Assn. (pres. 1982), Tom Green County Bar Assn. (sec.-treas. 1990), San Angelo Jr. League. Republican. Methodist. Avocation: scuba diving. Office: Tex 51st Dist Ct 112 W Beauregard San Angelo TX 76903-5850 Office Phone: 325-659-6571. Office Fax: 325-658-8046.

WALTHER, DANIEL JOSEPH, historian; b. Indpls., Nov. 4, 1965; s. Paul Philip Walther and Kathryn Anne (Spahr) Brocken. Student, U. Munich, 1986-87; BA in History, Northwestern U., 1988; postgrad., U. Bonn., Fed. Republic Germany, 1989-90; MA in History, Ind. U., 1990. Grad. asst. dept. history Ind. U., Bloomington, 1990, assoc. instr. German dept., 1991. Mem. People-to-People, Indpls., 1983-86. Max Kade fellow German dept. Ind. U., 1988-89, fellow German Fed. Parliament, 1990. Mem. German Studies Assn., Amnesty Internat., Delta Upsilon (scholar 1988). Avocations: swimming, biking. Home: 12711 S 84th Ave Palos Park IL 60464-2034

WALTHER, LARRY WOODROW, federal agency administrator; b. June 3, 1950; m. Janice Walther; children: Bill, Mandy. Grad., U. Ark., Monticello, 1970. Switching engr. Southwestern Bell, 1970, cost studies supr. St. Louis, 1975—78, dist. staff mgr. material mgmt., 1978, divsn. staff mgr. econ. analysis, 1979—83, divsn. mgr. rates and separations, divsn. staff mgr. regulatory affairs St. Louis, 1983, divsn. mgr. carrier mktg.; exec. dir. regulatory and industry rels. SBC Comm. (formerly Southwestern Bell), Ark., 1993—99, v.p. corp. svcs. San Antonio, 1999—2000; chmn. SBC Found., 1999—2000; appointed to US Dept. Treasury, 1989—90; pub. affairs cons. Pub. Strategies, Inc.; exec. dir. Ark. Dept. Econ. Devel., 2003—08; dir. US Trade & Devel. Agy., Arlington, Va., 2008—. Mem. bd. trustees Coll. Ozarks, Point Lookout, Mo., 1992—, bd. chmn., 2001—07; mem. bd. visitors U. Ark. Walton Sch. Bus.; mem. BioVentures adv. bd. U. Ark. Med. Sciences; mem. exec. bd. Ark. Policy Found., Southern Tech. Coun. Mem. Fellowship Bible Ch., Little Rock; mem. bd. dirs. Ark. Easter Seals; exec. bd. mem. Quapaw Area Boy Scouts, Downtown Little Rock Rotary. Mem.: Little Rock Sertoma Club (exec. bd. mem.). Republican. Office: US Trade and Devel Agy Ste 1600 1000 Wilson Blvd Arlington VA 22209-3901 Office Phone: 703-875-4357. Office Fax: 703-875-4009.*

WALTHER, PHILIP, physicist, researcher; b. Vienna, May 12, 1978; s. Gerd and Helga Walther. MS, Tech. U. Vienna, 2002; PhD, U. Vienna, 2005. Postdoctoral rschr. Harvard U., Cambridge, 2005—. Recipient Outstanding Acad. Performance award, Tech. U. Vienna, 2002, Loschmidt prize, Chem. Phys. Soc. Vienna, 2005, Outstanding Acad. Performance award, U. Vienna, 2006. Mem.: Young Acad. (Berlin-Brandenburg Acad. Scis.), German Acad. Natural Scientists. Achievements include research in quantum information processing using entangled photons. Office: Harvard Univ 17 Oxford St Cambridge MA 02138 Business E-Mail: pwalther@fas.harvard.edu.

WALTHER, STEVEN T., commissioner, lawyer; b. Reno, Nev., July 18, 1943; m. Diane Walther; children: Natalie, Mario, Wyatt. BA in Russian, U. Notre Dame, 1965; JD, U. Calif., Berkeley, 1968. Bar: Nev. 1968, US Dist. Ct. (Nev.) 1969, Calif. 1969, US Ct. Appeals (9th cir.) 1986, US Supreme Ct. 1991. Ptnr. Walther, Key, Maupin, Oats, Cox & LeGoy, Reno; commr. Fed. Election Commn., Washington, 2006—07, vice chmn., 2008—. Mem. US Commn. on Civil Rights, 1971—; chair Nev. Bd. CLE, 1982—90; panelist US Magistrate Judge Merit Selection Panel, 1990; pres. Western States Bar Conf., 1999—2000; mem. LexiNexis Martindale-Hubbell Legal Adv. Bd., 2001—; pres. Nat. Caucus State Bar Assn., 2002—03; guest lectr. Nat. Jud. Coll., Reno; mem. Nev. State Adv. Com.; chair internat. bus. task force Coll. Bus. Adminstrn., U. Nev., Reno; lectr., presenter on rule of law and human rights issues; mem. Am. Law Inst., mem. consultative group principles and rules of transnational civil procedures, mem. consultative group internat. jurisdiction and judgements. Author: The Globalization of the Rule of Law and Human Rights, 2000. Recipient Awards of Spl. Appreciation, 1991, 1999, Award of Spl. Appreciation, Am. Red Cross, Sierra, Nev. chpt., 1999, Pres. award, Scenic Nev., 2005. Fellow: World Acad. Art and Sci., Am. Bar Found. (chair 2003—04, del. leader, rule of law del. to Russia 2005); mem.: ABA (chair standing com.on world order under law 1993—95, bd. govs. 1995—97, fin. com. 1995—97, ho. del. 1995—97, chair spl. adv. com. on internat. activities 1997—98, mem. Cent. European and Eurasian Law Initiative 1997—98, mem. subcom. on internat. jud. relations 1997—98, rep. to UN 1998—2000, mem. UN and internat. instns. coord. com. 1998—, mem. internat. human rights com. 1999—, mem. Cent. European and Eurasian Law Initiative 2000—01, co-founder 2001, first chair 2001—03, exec. bd. mem. 2001—, coun. mem. 2002—, mem. sect. individual rights and responsibilities, mem. ctr. for human rights, mem. lit. sect., mem. exec. bd., mem. sect. on bus., mem. sect. internat. law), State Bar of Nev. (gov., bd. govs. 1978—91, pres. 1990—91), Human Rights First, Nat. Coun., State Bar of Calif., Washoe County Bar Assn., Am. Inns of Ct. (Bruce R. Thompson chpt.) (master emeritus), Am. Soc. Internat. Law, Nat. Conf. Bar Pres., Inc. (mem. sponsorship com. 1994—95), Nat. Conf. Bar Found. (trustee bd. trustees 2004—), Boalt Hall Alumni Assn., U. Calif. Law Sch. (pres. 2001—02). Democrat. Office: Fed Election Commn 999 E St NW Washington DC 20463*

WALTMAN, BOB RAY, coach, educator; s. Howard Lou and Cecilia Ann Waltman; children: Tricia Renee Brewster, Evan Rand Christensen, Kyle James Christensen, Vance Ryan Christensen. MS, Chadron State Coll., Nebr., 1997. Cert. tchr. Dept. Edn. Nebr., 1979. Tchr. Ctrl. City High Sch., Nebr., 1980—82, Hyannis High Sch., Nebr., 1983—98, coach, 1983—98, activities dir., 1983—98, counselor, 1983—98, Cross County Cmty. Sch., Stromsburg, Nebr., 1998—, tchr., 1998—, coach, 1998—. Mem.: Nat. Counselors Assn., Nebr. Counselors Assn., Nebr. Coaches Assn., NSEA. Office: Cross County Cmty Sch 1270 23rd Rd PO Box 525 Stromsburg NE 68666 E-mail: bwaltman@esu7.org.

WALTNER, BEVERLY RULAND, artist; b. Kansas City, Mo.; d. Harry George and Ruth Anna (Laitner) Waltner, Jr. Student Columbia U., 1950-51, Yale U., 1951-53; B.A., U. Miami, Fla., 1955; M.F.A., No. Ill. U., 1968; postgrad. Kent State U., summer 1968. Tchr. art pub. schs. N.Y., Fla., Mo., Ill., 1960-65; instr. art Barry Coll., Miami Shores, Fla., 1969-70; artist-designer, Coral Gables, Fla., 1972—; One-woman shows: Art Gallery, No. Ill. U., DeKalb, 1968, Lyons Meml. Library, Point Lookout, Mo., 1968, Jewish Community Ctr. Gallery, Kansas City, Mo., 1969; juried exhbns. include: New Horizons in Painting, North Shore Art League, 1966, 68, Chautauqua Exhbn. Am. Art, 1968-73, 78, 10th Midwestern Bienniel, Joslyn Mus., 1968, Mid-Am. I, Nelson Gallery and St. Louis Mus., 1968, Nat. Soc. Painters in Casein and Acrylic, 1969, 70, 72, 73, Ark. Nat., Ark. State U., 1970, 35th Ann. Mid-Yr. Show, Butler Inst. Am. Art, 1970, Ann. Exhbn. Am. Painting, Soc. Four Arts, 1971, 74, IV and V Ann. Pan. Am. Exhbns., 1972, 73; represented in permanent collections: No. Ill. U., Arlen Realty Mgmt., Inc., Alexander Muss and Sons, Equitable Life Assurance Soc. U.S., Gen. Devel. Corp., Zuckerman-Vernon Corp., also numerous pvt. collections. Recipient 1st place award Ann. Chautauqua Exhbn. of Am. Art, 1968, Louis E. Selden award, 1972; top award New Horizons in Painting Show, 1966, honorable mention, 1968. Mem. Artists Equity Assn., Cultural Execs. Council Profl. Artists Guild (treas. 1977-78, v.p. 1978-79, editorial staff newsletter 1977—79), Chautauqua Art Assn., Coral Gables C. of C. (cultural affairs com. 1979). E-mail: bob98@bellsouth.net.

WALTON, ALAN GEORGE, venture capitalist; b. Birmingham, Eng., Apr. 3, 1936; s. Thomas George and Hilda (Glover) W.; m. Jasmin Yvonne Christensen, Sept. 1, 1958 (dec. Nov. 1970); children: Kimm A., Keir D.A.; m. Elenor Jean McElliott, Aug. 6, 1977; children: Kristin M., Sherri L. PhD, U. Nottingham, Eng., 1960, DSc, 1973; LLD (hon.), U. Nottingham, Eng., 2005. Rsch. assoc. Ind. U., Bloomington, 1960-62; asst. prof. chemistry Case Western Res. U., Cleve., 1962-66, assoc. prof., 1966-69, assoc. prof. macromolecular sci., 1969-71, prof., 1971-81, dir. lab. for biol. macromolecules, 1972-81, disting. adj. univ. prof., 2007—; pres., CEO Univ. Genetics Co., 1981-86, chmn., 1986-87; sr. ptnr. Oxford Biosci Ptnrs., Westport, Conn., 1987—; chmn. Oxford Biosci. Corp., 1992—; pres. Com. Bus. Innovation, 2007—. Vis. lectr. biol. chemistry Harvard Med. Sch., 1971—72; mem. Pres. Carter's Task Force on Sci. and Tech.; U.S. project officer Rudjer Boskovic Inst., Zagreb, Yugoslavia, 1967—75; bd. dirs. Acadia Pharma, Alexandria R.E.I.T.; emeritus dir. Research!America; founder, past chmn. Gene Logic, Inc., Exelixis, Inc.; co-founder, past bd. mem. Human Genome Scis., Inc.; co-founder The Inst. for Genomic Rsch., 1994, Nat. Com. Bioscis. Innovation, 2008—, pres., 2008—; mem. and comm. adv. Pres. Obama's Policy Com. Sci. and Tech., 2008—09. Author: Formation and Properties of Precipitates, 1967, Biopolymers, 1973, Structure and Properties of Amorphous Polymers, 1980, Polypeptide and Protein Structure, 1981, Recombinant DNA, 1981, Yearbook of Genetic Engineering and Biotechnology, 1983, 85, 88, (biography) Beneath This Gruff Exterior There Beats a Heart of Plastic, 2000, How to Make Money Investing in Biotechnology, 2005. Bd. dirs. Friends of Nottingham U. Recipient Israel State medal, 1972, Case Inst. Centennial Scholar medal, 1981. Mem. Nat. Venture Capital Assn., Sigma Xi (Research award 1973), Pi Kappa Alpha. Home: 11 Beachside Common Westport CT 06880 Office: Oxford Biosci Corp 315 Post Rd W Westport CT 06880-4739 Business E-Mail: awalton@oxbio.com.

WALTON, ALICE LOUISE, bank executive; b. Newport, Ark., Oct. 7, 1949; d. Sam and Helen (Robson) Walton. BBA, Trinity U., 1971; D in Bus. Adminstrn. (hon.), S.W. Bapt. U., 1988. Investment analyst First Commerce Corp., New Orleans, 1972-75; dir., v.p. investments Walton Enterprises, Bentonville, Ark., 1975—; retail & investment broker E.F. Hutton Co., New Orleans, 1975-79; vice chair, investment dir. Walton Bank Group, Bentonville, Ark., 1982-88; founder, former pres., chair, CEO Llama Co./Llama Asset Mgmt. Co., Fayetteville, Ark. Mem. dean's adv. coun. U. Ark. Coll. Bus. Adminstrn., Fayetteville, 1989—90. Bd. trustees Amon Carter Mus., Ft. Worth. Named Arkansan of Yr., Ark. Easter Seals Soc., 1990; named a Disting. Bus. Lectr., Ctrl. State U., Edmond, Okla., 1989; named one of Top 100 Women in Ark., Ark. Bus., 1995, Top 200 Collectors, ARTnews mag., 2006—, Forbes 400, 1999—, World's Richest People, Forbes Mag., 2001—, Forbes Richest Americans, 2006—. Mem.: N.W. Ark. Coun. (first chairperson 1990). Avocation: horse racing.

WALTON, ANTHONY JOHN (TONY WALTON), set and costume designer, illustrator, writer; b. Walton on Thames, Eng., Oct. 24, 1934; s. Lancelot Henry Frederick and Hilda Betty (Drew) W.; m. Julie Andrews, May 10, 1959 (div. 1968); 1 child, Emma Kate; m. Genevieve LeRoy, Sept. 12, 1991; 1 stepchild, Bridget. Student, Oxford Sch. Tech. Art and Commerce, 1949-52, Slade Sch. Fine Art, London, 1954-55. Designer settings, costumes for theater prodns., London, off-Broadway, 1957-60, Broadway, 1961—; Broadway prodns. include Pippin, 1972 (Tony award 1972-73, Drama Desk award 1972-73), Shelter, 1973 (Drama Desk award 1972-73), Chicago, 1975, Sophisticated Ladies, 1981, The Real Thing, 1984, Hurlyburly, 1984, I'm Not Rappaport, 1985, House of Blue Leaves, 1986 (Tony award 1985-86), Drama Desk award 1985-86), Front Page, 1986, Social Security, 1986 (Drama Desk award 1985-86), Anything Goes, 1987, Grand Hotel, 1989, Six Degrees of Separation, 1990, The Will Rogers Follies, 1991, Death and the Maiden, 1992, Conversations with My Father, 1992, Four Baboons Adoring the Sun, 1992, Guys and Dolls, 1992 (Tony award 1991-92, Drama Desk award 1991-92), Tommy Tune Tonight, 1992, She Loves Me, 1993, A Grand Night for Singing, 1993, Laughter on the 23rd Floor, 1993, Picnic, 1994, A Christmas Carol, N.Y.C., 1994, Company, 1995, Moonlight, 1995, A Fair Country, 1996, A Funny Thing Happened on the Way to the Forum, 1996, The Shawl, 1996, Make Someone Happy, Bay St. Theater Festival, 1997, Not Waving, 1997, Steel Pier, 1997, King David, 1997, 1776, 1997; The Cripple of Inishmaan, 1998; Noel & Gertie, 1998; House, 1998; Ashes to Ashes, 1999; Annie Get Your Gun, 1999; On Raftery's Hill, 2000 (Dublin and London); If Love Were All, 1999; Taller Than a Dwarf, 2000, Uncle Vanya, 2000, The Man Who Came To Dinner, 2000, Our Town, 2002, Blithe Spirit, 2002, I'm Not Rappaport, 2002, Nobody don't Like Yogi, 2003, The Boy Friend, 2003, Princesses, 2004, Well, 2006, A Tale of Two Cities, 2008; dir., designer The Importance of Being Earnest, 1996, Major Barbara, 1997, Where's Charley?, 2004, After the Ball, 2004, The Devil's Disciple; dir. Noel Coward in Two Keys Bay St. Theatre Festival, 1996; dir. Missing Footage, 1999; dir., co-writer, costume designer Oops! The Big Apple Circus Stage Show, 1999; ballets, principally San Francisco Ballet Co., Am. Ballet Theatre, Peter and the Wolf, Sleeping Beauty, Dance Theatre of Harlem "St. Louis Woman", 2003, Lincoln Ctr., N.Y.C.; films include Mary Poppins, A Funny Thing Happened on the Way to the Forum, Murder on the Orient Express, The Wiz, All That Jazz (Acad. award with Philip Rosenberg 1980), Prince of the City, Star 80, The Glass Menagerie, 1987, Regarding Henry, 1991, Our Town, 2003; operas in London, 1963-68, Spoleto, Italy, 1965, Santa Fe, 1975, San Francisco, 1992, Chgo., 1993; author: Adelie Penguin in Wonders, 1981; illustrator (books) Wonders, 1981, The Importance of Being Earnest, 1973, Lady Windemere's Fan, 1973, Popcorn, 1972, God Is a Good friend, 1969, Witches Holiday, 1971, Dumpy the Dump Truck, 2000; (musical) The Great American, 2006, and 11 more books in the continuing series. Served with RAF, 1952-54. Recipient Emmy award Death of a Salesman, 1986; named to Theatre Hall of Fame, 1991; elected to Interior Design Hall of Fame, 1993. Mem.: Acad. Motion Picture Arts and Scis., Costume Designers Guild Calif., United Scenic Artists.

WALTON, CHARLES MICHAEL, civil engineering educator; b. Hickory, NC, July 28, 1941; s. Charles O. and Virginia Ruth (Hart) W.; m. Betty Grey Hughes; children: Susan, Camila, Michael, Gantt. BS, Va. Mil. Inst., 1963; MCE, N.C. State U., 1969, PhD, 1971. Research asst. N.C. State U., Raleigh, 1967-71; transp. planning engr. N.C. Hwy. Commn., Raleigh, 1970-71; asst. prof. civil engring. U. Tex., Austin, 1971-76, assoc. prof., 1976-83, prof., 1983—, Bess Harris Jones Centennial prof. natural resource policy studies, 1987-91, Paul D. and Betty Robertson Meek Centennial prof. engring., 1991-93, Ernest H. Cockrell Centennial chair engring., 1993—, chmn. dept. civil engring., 1988-96. Transp. cons., 1970—; assoc. dir. Ctr. for Transp. Rsch. U. Tex., 1980-88; chmn., exec. com. Transp. Rsch. Bd., NRC, 1991, Disting. Lectr., 1994. Contbr. articles to profl. jours. Past chmn. Urban Transp. Commn., Austin. Recipient Disting. Engring. award N.C. State U., 1995, Joe J. King Profl. Engring. Achievement award U. Tex. at Austin, 1995-96, W.N. Carey Jr. Disting. Svc. award Transp. Rsch. Bd., 1998, George S. Bartlett award AASHTO, Transp. Rsch. Bd., ARTBA, 2000, Disting. Contbns. to Univ. Transp. Edn. and Rsch. award Coun. Univ. Transp. Ctrs., 2005; named to Am.'s Top 100 Pvt. Sector Transp. Design and Constrn. Profls. of 20th Century, 2004, Am. Rd. and Transp. Builders Assn., 2005. Fellow ASCE (Harland Bartholomew urban planning award 1987, Frank M. Masters transp. engring. award 1987, James Laurie prize 1992, Francis C. Turner lectr. 1999, Outstanding Projects and Leaders award, 2005), Inst. Transp. Engrs.; mem. NSPE, NAE, Intelligent Transp. Soc. Am. (tech. coord. coun., past chair bd. dirs., past chair tech. coord. coun.), Am. Rd. and Transp. Assn. (western v.p., past pres. edn. divsn., 1st vice chair, named to Am.'s Top 100 Pvt. Sector Transp. Design and Constrn. Profls. of 20th Century), Am. Rd. and Transp. Builders Assn. (chmn.), Soc. Automotive Engrs., Urban Land Inst., Inst. for Ops. Rsch. and Mgmt. Scis., Soc. Am. Mil. Engrs., Internat. Rd. Fedn. (bd. dirs.), Internat. Rd. Ednl. Found. (bd. dirs.), Austin C. of C. (Leadership Austin program). Democrat. Methodist. Home: 3404 River Rd Austin TX 78703-1031 Office: U Tex Dept Civil Engring Dept Civil Engring ECJ Hall Ste 6 3 Austin TX 78712 Home Phone: 512-477-9258; Office Phone: 512-471-1414. Business E-Mail: cmwalton@mail.utexas.edu.

WALTON, CHRISTY R., philanthropist; b. Feb. 1949; m. John Thomas Walton (dec. June 27, 2005); 1 child, Lukas. Mem. bi-nat. adv. bd. San Diego Natural Hist. Mus.; former mem. bd. trustees San Diego Natural History Mus.; co-founder Harborside Sch., San Diego, 1996. Named one of Forbes Richest Americans (with family), 2005—, World's Richest People (with family), Forbes Mag., 2007, 2008.

WALTON, DAN GIBSON, lawyer; b. Houston, Mar. 26, 1950; s. Dan Edward and Lucy Frances (Gibson) W.; m. Martha Sandlin, June 24, 1972; children: Cole Gibson, Emily Wyatt. BA with honors, U. Va., 1972; JD with honors, U. Tex., 1975. Bar: Tex. 1975, U.S. Dist. Ct. (so. dist.) Tex. 1977, U.S. Ct. Appeals (D.C. cir.) 1975, U.S. Ct. Appeals (5th cir.) 1981, U.S. Supreme Ct. 2001; bd. cert. in civil trial law. Law clk. to hon. Malcolm R. Wilkey D.C. Ct. Appeals (D.C. cir.), 1975-76; assoc. Vinson & Elkins LLP, Houston, 1976-82, ptnr., 1982—. Bd. dirs., sec. The Meth. Hosp., Houston, 1993—2003; mem. admission commn. US Dist. Cts. (so. dist.) Tex., 2000—06; chair US Magistrate Judge Merit Selection Com. Bd. dirs. Tex. Equal Access to Justice Found., 2000-06, South Tex. Coll. Law, Houston, 1994—, Briarwood Sch./Brookwood Cmty., Houston, 1991—, Alley Theatre, 2003—; trustee St. John's Sch., Houston, 1997-2005, Good Samaritan Found., 1998—2006, Cullen Trust for Health Care, 2002—; chancellor Tex. Ann. Conf., United Meth. Ch., 1996—. Fellow Am. Bar Found., Tex. Bar Found.; mem. Houston Bar Found. (chair 1994), Houston Bar Assn. (pres. 1998-99), Am. Coll. Trial Lawyers, Garland Walker Am. Inn of Ct. (master), Am. Bd. Trial Advocates (assoc.), Internat. Soc. Barristers, Internat. Assn. Def. Counsel, Tex. Assn. Def. Counsel, State Bar Tex. (bd. dirs 1999-2002, pres. 2007—). Avocations: golf, skiing. Office: Vinson & Elkins LLP 2300 First City Tower 1001 Fannin St Ste 3201 Houston TX 77002-6706 Office Phone: 713-758-2026.

WALTON, GERALD WAYNE, retired university official, retired university official; b. Union, Miss., Sept. 11, 1934; s. Willie Jay and Ruby Elizabeth (Williamson) W.; m. Juliet Katherine Hart, Aug. 26, 1960; children: Katherine Hart, Dorothy Elizabeth, Margaret Stevens. AA, East Central Jr. Coll., 1954; BS, U. So. Miss., 1956; MA, U. Miss., 1959, PhD, 1967. Tchr. asst. U. Miss., 1956-59, instr. English, 1959-62, asst. prof., 1962-67, assoc. prof., 1967-70, prof., 1970-99, assoc. dean Coll. Liberal Arts, 1970-76, dean, 1976-82, assoc. vice chancellor for acad. affairs, 1982-94, interim vice chancellor for acad. affairs, 1994-96, provost, 1996-99. Contbr. articles to profl. jours. Vice-pres. Oxford Human Rels. Coun., 1968; mem. adminstrv. bd. Oxford U. Meth. Ch., chmn. bd. trustees, 1971-72, lay leader, 1999-2001; bd. dirs. Yoknapatawpha Arts Coun., 1980-81; sec.-treas. So. Lit. Festival, 1965; sec. U. Miss. Friends of Libr.; v.p. U. Miss. Friends Mus. bd. trustees Miss heritage Trust. Tri-Univ. fellow in linguistics U. Nebr., 1969-70. Mem. MLA, Am. Dialect Soc., Miss. Folklore Soc., Friends of Arts in Miss., Miss. Assn. English Tchrs. (sec. 1968), Miss. Inst. Arts and Letters (sec. 1979-80), Nat. Coun. Tchrs. English, William Faulkner Soc., Miss. Hist. Soc., Oxford-Lafayette County Heritage Soc., So. Studies Adv. Coun., Rotary (sec.), Golden Key, Phi Kappa Phi, Sigma Tau Delta, Omicron Delta Kappa. Home: 106 Ole Miss Dr Oxford MS 38655-2615 Office Phone: 662-915-1598. E-mail: gww@olemiss.edu.

WALTON, JAMES FARLEY, research and development company executive; b. 1950; MME, U. Fla., Gainesville, 1977. Capt., rsch. engr. rotordynamics USAF, Dayton, Ohio, 1977—81; program mgr. Mech. Tech. Inc., Latham, NY, 1981—95; v.p. program devel., dir., chmn. bd. Mohawk Innovative Tech., Inc., Albany, NY, 1995—. Dir. MiTiHeart Corp., Del., 2003—. Contbr. articles to tech. publs. (SAE Charles M. Manly Meml. medal, 1999). Elder Clifton Pk. Ch. Christ, NY, 2008. Fellow: ASME; mem.: AIAA, Profl. Ski Instrs. America. Achievements include patents for multi-plane balancing process and apparatus using powder metal for controlled material addition; hybrid foil magnetic bearing with improved load sharing; first to internal rotor friction instability in space shuttle main engine; design of small centrifugal blood pump with hybrid magnetic bearings; development of oil-free motorized turbocompressor for fuel cells. Office: Mohawk Innovative Tech Inc 1037 Watervliet-Shaker Rd Albany NY 12205

WALTON, JAMES MELLON, investment company executive; b. Pitts., Dec. 18, 1930; m. Ellen Carroll; 4 children. BA, Yale U.; MBA, Harvard U. With Gulf Oil Corp., Phila., Houston, Pitts., Tokyo, Rome, 1958-67; pres. Carnegie Inst., Pitts., 1968-84, Carnegie Mus. Natural History and Mus. of Art, Pitts., 1968-84, Carnegie Library, Pitts., 1968-84; life trustee, pres. emeritus Carnegie Inst. and Carnegie Library, Pitts. Bd. dirs. New Ireland Fund, Inc. Mem. sponsoring com. Penn's Southwest Assn.; trustee emeritus Carnegie-Mellon U.; treas. Carnegie Hero Fund Commn.; dir. World Affairs Coun. of Pitts., One Hundred Friends of Pitts. Art; trustee Sarah Scaife Found. Inc., Extra Mile Found.; chmn. Vira I. Heinz Endowment; mem. Cultural Dist. Devel. Com. Lt. U.S. Army, 1954-56. Office: 525 William Penn Way Ste 3902 Pittsburgh PA 15219-1710 E-mail: jmwa@earthlink.net.

WALTON, JIM, broadcast executive; BA in Radio, TV and Film, U. Md., College Park, 1981. Video journalist CNN, Atlanta, 1981-83; tape editor CNN Sports, Atlanta, 1983-85, exec. prodr., 1985—97; pres. CNN/Sports Illus., Atlanta, 1996—2000, CNN Networks/USA, Atlanta, 2000; pres., COO CNN News Group, Atlanta, chmn., CEO, 2003; pres., COO CNN Worldwide, pres. Olympic prodr. 1984 LA Games, remote prodr., sr. prodr. Office: CNN 1 CNN Ctr NW Atlanta GA 30303-2762*

WALTON, JIM CARR, bank executive; b. 1948; s. Sam Moore and Helen Walton; m. Lynne Walton; 4 children. Grad., U. Ark. Pres., chmn., CEO Arvest Bank, Bentonville, Ark. At-large exec. com. mem. Ark. Coun. Econ. Edn.; mem. dean's exec. adv. bd. Sam M. Walton Coll. Bus. Mem. nat. bd. advs. Children's Scholarship Fund. Named one of World's Richest People, Forbes Mag., 2001—, Forbes Richest Americans, 2006—. Office: 125 W Central Ste 218 Bentonville AR 72712

WALTON, JON DAVID, lawyer, metal products executive; b. Clairton, Pa., Sept. 18, 1942; s. Thomas Edward and Matilda Lucy (Sunday) W.; m. Carol Jeanne Rowland, Sept. 15, 1964; children: David Edward, Diane Elizabeth. BS, Purdue U., 1964; JD, Valparaiso U., 1969. Bar: Pa. 1969. Atty. U.S. Steel Corp. (now USX Corp.), Pitts., 1969-73; asst. gen. counsel Harbison-Walker Refractories, Pitts., 1973-75, gen. counsel, 1975-81, v.p., gen. counsel, 1981-83; regional gen. counsel Dresser Industries, Inc., Pitts., 1983-86; gen. counsel, sec. Allegheny Ludlum Corp., Pitts., 1986-90, v.p., gen. counsel, sec., 1990-96, Allegheny Techs. Inc., Pitts., sr. v.p., gen. counsel, sec., sr. v.p., chief legal and admin. officer, 2001—03, exec. v.p. human resources, chief legal and compliance officer, gen. counsel, corp. sec., 2003—. Trustee Westminster Coll., 1997—; pres., bd. dirs. Music for Mt. Lebanon, 1996-2002, Pitts. Youth Golf Found., 1991-2001, United Way of Allegheny County, 2002-, NAM, 2002-, Pitts. Symphony Orchestra, 2003-; clk. of session Southminster Presbyn. Ch., 1998-2001, 04-. Mem. ABA, Pa. Bar Assn., Allegheny County Bar Assn., Am. Soc. Corp. Secs. (former pres. regional group), Am. Corp. Counsel Assn., Am. Arbitration Assn. (panel arbitrators), Duquesne Club, Valley Brook Country Club, Rolling Rock Club. Home: 137 Hoodridge Dr Pittsburgh PA 15228-1803 Office: Allegheny Technologies Inc 1000 Six PPG Pl Pittsburgh PA 15222-5479 Office Phone: 412-394-2836. Business E-Mail: jwalton@alleghenytechnologies.com.

WALTON, MORGAN LAUCK, III, lawyer; b. Woodstock, Va., July 30, 1932; s. Morgan Lauck Jr. and Frances (Allen) W.; m. Jeannette Freeman Minor, Mar. 4, 1961; children: Morgan Lauck IV, Charles Lancelot Minor, Christopher Allen, Laura Cathlyn Hirschfeld. BA, Randolph-Macon Coll., 1953; LLB, U. Va., 1959. Bar: Va. 1959, N.Y. 1959, U.S. Ct. Appeals (2d cir.) 1959, U.S. Dist. Ct. (ea. and so. dists.) N.Y. 1960, U.S. Dist. Ct. (we. dist.) Va. 1988. Assoc. Donovan Leisure Newton & Irvine, NYC, 1959-68, ptnr., 1968-84; counsel FDIC, Washington, 1989-90, asst. gen. counsel, 1990-97; dir. Advice Co., Sausalito, Calif., 2005—; ret. Contbr. articles to profl. jours. Trustee Randolph-Macon Acad., Front Royal, Va., 1987-92, trustee emeritus, 2002—; trustee Unitarian Ch. Shenandoah Valley, Stephens City, Va., 1987-2007; mem. coun. Law Sch. U. Va., 1989-92; treas. Shenandoah Valley Music Festival, Woodstock, 1986-87; chmn. bd. All Souls Ch., NYC, 1974-76; active Shenandoah County Dem. Com., 1999—; assoc.dir. Lord Fairfax Soil and Water Dist., 2004-05, dir., 2005-06, 2008-. With US Army, 1953-56. Mem. Order of Coif, Phi Beta Kappa. Democrat. Home and Office: 908 Kern Springs Rd Woodstock VA 22664-3216 Personal E-mail: jwalton@shentel.net.

WALTON, REGGIE BARNETT, federal judge; b. North Charleroi, Pa., Feb. 8, 1949; m. Debra Walton; 1 child, Danon. BA, W.Va. State Coll., 1971; JD, Am. U., 1974. Staff atty. Defender Assn. Phila., 1974-76; asst. U.S. atty. US Dept. Justice, Washington, 1976-80, chief career criminal unit, 1979-80; assoc. judge Superior Ct. DC, 1981—89, 1991—2001, dep. presiding judge criminal divsn., 1986-89; exec. asst. US atty. US Dept. Justice, Washington, 1980-81; assoc. dir. Office Nat. Drug Control Policy, Exec. Office of Pres., Washington, 1989-91; sr. adv. for crime The White House, 1991; judge US Dist. Ct. (DC Cir.), Washington, 2001—, Fgn. Intelligence Surveillance Ct. (FISC), 2007—. Mem. US Dept. Justice and ABA Ctrl. and East European Law Initiative Reform Project, Irkutsk, Russia, 1996; instr. SEAK, Inc., 1993, 97, Criminal Practice Inst., Washington, 1996, 97, Ctrl. and East European Law Inst., ABA, 1996, Harvard U., 1994—; mem. faculty Nat. Jud. Coll., Reno, Nev., 1999—, George Washington U. Law Ctr., 1992—; instr. Nat. Inst. Trial Advocacy, Georgetown U. Law Sch., Washington, 1983—, US Dept. Justice, 1993, ABA Traffic Ct. Sem., Washington, 1984, 87; disting. guest lectr. Lincoln U., Jefferson City, Mo., 1991, Albany (Ga.) State Coll., 1991; lectr. US Atty.'s Office, Washington,

1979-81, DC Bar Assn., 1980, Graterford (Pa.) State Prison, 1974-76; mem. jud. coun. Cir. Ct. DC, 2004—; chmn. commn. Nat. Prison Rape Reduction, 2004— Contbr. article to profl. jours. Active Big Brothers; mem. task force on interscholastic programs DC Pub. Schs., 1987; hon. mem. Capital Ballet Guild, Inc., 1989; mem. DC Cares, Inc., 1990; mem. Nat. Ctr. for Missing and Exploited Children, bd dirs., 1990-91; bd. dirs. Robert A. Shuker Scholarship Fund., Inc., 1993—, Hillcrest Children's Ctr., 1994-96; co-chmn. pub. safety com. DC Agenda Project, Fed. City Coun., 1995—. Recipient Dean's award Washington Coll. Law, 1989, Disting. Svc. award Young Lawyers sect. Bar Assn. DC, 1989, H. Carl Moultrie award DC br. NAACP, 1989, Sec.'s award Dept. Vets. Affairs, 1990, James R. Waddy Meritorious Svc. award W.Va. State Coll. Nat. Alumni Assn., 1990, County Spotlight award Nat. Assn. Counties, 1990, William H. Hastie award Jud. coun. Nat. Bar Assn., 1993, Honorable Robert A. Shuker Meml. award Asst. US Attys. Assn., 1997, Friendship award Best Friends Found., 1998, Disting. Alumni award Am. U., 1999, Angel award Bridging the Gap Tri-County Inc., Mt. Sinai Bapt. Ch., 2000, North Star award Washington Coll. of Law, Am. U., 2000, among others. Mem. ABA (lawyer competency com. 1984-87, del. nat. conf. state trial judges 1986), DC Bar Assn. (criminal instrns. com. 1984-86), Washington Bar Assn., Nat. Inst. Trial Advocacy Advocates Assn., Am. Inns of Ct. Republican. Office: US Dist Ct E Barrett Prettman US Courthouse 333 Constitution Ave NW Washington DC 20001-2131 E-mail: waltonrb@dcsc.gov.*

WALTON, ROBERT LEE, plastic surgeon; b. Lawrence, Kans., May 30, 1946; s. Robert L. and Thelma B. (Morgan) W.; m. Elisabeth K. Beahm, Oct. 7, 2000; children: Marc, Morgan, Lindsey. BA, U. Kans., 1968; MD, U. Kans., Kansas City, 1972. Diplomate Am. Bd. Surgery, Am. Bd. Plastic Surgery. Resident in surgery Johns Hopkins Hosp., Balt., 1972-74, Yale-New Haven (Conn.) Hosp., 1974-78; chief of plastic surgery San Francisco Gen. Hosp., 1979-83; prof. and chmn. dept. plastic surgery U. Mass. Med. Ctr., Worcester, 1983-94; prof., chmn dept. plastic surgery U. Chgo., 1994—2004, prof. dept. plastic surgery, 2004—. Contbr. articles to profl. jours. Founder Projecto Mira Found. for Handicapped Children, Santurce, P.R., 1990. Mem. ACS, Am. Assn. Plastic Surgeons, Am. Soc. Plastic and Reconstructive Surgery, Am. Soc. Reconstructive Microsurgery, Alpha Omega Alpha. Office: Plastic Surgery Chgo 60 East Delaware Pl Ste 1430 Chicago IL 60611 Home Phone: 312-944-0972; Office Phone: 312-337-7795. Personal E-mail: notlaw72@sbcglobal.net. Business E-Mail: drrwalton@sbcglobal.net.

WALTON, (SAMUEL) ROB(SON), discount department store chain executive; b. Tulsa, 1944; s. Sam Moore and Helen Walton; m. Carolyn Walton (div.); 3 children. Student, Wooster Coll.; BA in Acctg., U. Ark., 1966; JD, Columbia U., 1969. Formerly with Conner, Winters, Ballaine, Barry & McGowen; with Wal-Mart Stores Inc., Bentonville, Ark., 1969, sr. v.p., 1978-82, bd. dirs., vice chmn. bd., 1982-92, chmn., 1992—. Trustee Wooster Coll. Named one of World's Richest People, Forbes Mag., 2005—, Forbes Richest Americans, 2006—. Avocations: bicycling, pheasant hunting. Office: Wal-Mart Stores Inc 702 SW 8th St Bentonville AR 72716-6299*

WALTON, RODNEY EARL, lawyer, historian; b. Corvallis, Oreg., Apr. 28, 1947; s. Ray Daniel Jr. and Carolyn Jane (Smith) W. BA, Coll. Wooster, Ohio, 1969; JD, Cornell U., Ithaca, NY, 1976; MA in History, Fla. Internat. U., Miami, 2001, attending in History, PhD in History, Fla. Internat. U., Miami, 2009. Bar: Fla. 1976, US Dist. Ct. (so. dist.) Fla. 1976, US Supreme Ct. 1980, US Ct. Appeals (11th cir.) 1981. Assoc. to jr. ptnr. Smathers & Thompson, Miami, Fla., 1976-87; ptnr. Kelley, Drye and Warren, Miami, 1987-93; atty. Heinrich Gordon Hargrove Weihe & James, P.A., Ft. Lauderdale, 1994-97. Adj. instr. US mil. history Fla. Internat. U., 2001, adj. instr. modern U.S. history, 2003—04, 2006, adj. instr. contemporary US history, 07, adj. instr. history of the US Supreme Ct., 07, adj. instr. World History and Origins of Modern Am., 08. Sec. bd. dirs. Kings Creek Condominium Assn., Miami, 1984-89, treas., 1984, pres., 1990-91. 1st lt. U.S. Army, 1969-73, Vietnam. Decorated Bronze Star. Mem. ABA, Fla. Bar Assn. Republican. Methodist. Avocations: travel, reading, tennis, history. Home: 7985 SW 86th St Apt 430 Miami FL 33143-7014 Personal E-mail: rodneyearlwalton@aol.com.

WALTON, SHIRLEY DAWN, retired medical technician; b. Jamestown, NY, Dec. 12, 1935; d. Kenneth Everett and Wilma Alene Lewis; m. Okley Homa Walton, May 3, 1963 (dec.); 1 child, William W. Cert. respiratory care practioner Fla., 1993. Trainee Women's Christian Hosp., Jamestown, 1956—61; nurse's aid St. Joseph's Hosp., Tampa, Fla., 1963—64, cardiology technician, 1964—74; cardiology tech. U. Hosp., Tampa, 1975—82, respiratory therapist, 1982—88; cardiology tech. East Pasco Med. Ctr., Zephyrhills, Fla., 1988—98; ret., 1998. Methodist. Home: 6801 Woodsman Dr Zephyrhills FL 33544 Home Phone: 813-929-3544.

WALTON, STANLEY ANTHONY, III, lawyer; b. Chgo., Dec. 10, 1939; s. Stanley Anthony and Emily Ann (Pouzar) W.; m. Karen Kayser, Aug. 10, 1963; children: Katherine, Anne, Alex. BA, Washington and Lee U., 1962, LLB, 1965. Bar: Ill. 1965, U.S. Dist. Ct. (no. dist.) Ill. 1966, U.S. Ct. Appeals (7th cir.) 1966. Ptnr. Winston & Strawn, Chgo., 1965-89, Sayfarth Shaw Fairweather, Chgo., 1989-96. Trustee Village of Hinsdale (Ill.), 1985-89; bd. dirs. Washington and Lee Law Sch., Lexington, Va., 1975-78, bd. dirs. univ. alumni, 1983-87, pres., 1986-87; bd. dirs. UNICEF, Chgo., 1983; pres. Hinsdale Hist. Soc., 1979-81, 2001—, St. Isaac Jogues PTA, 1980; sec. Hinsdale Cmty. Svc., 2000-07; bd. dirs. Hinsdale Ctrl. Found., 2000—. Mem. Ill. State Bar Assn., Phi Alpha Delta, Hinsdale Golf Club. Republican. Roman Catholic. Home and Office: 6679 Snug Harbor Dr Willowbrook IL 60527

WALTON, SURREY MAX, educator; b. Honolulu, Sept. 26, 1969; m. Lee Walton. PhD, U. Chgo., 1997. Asst. prof. UIC, Chgo., 1997—2004. Office: Univ Ill Chgo 833 South Wood St (M/C 871) Chicago IL 60612 Business E-Mail: walton@uic.edu.

WALTON, WILLIAM THEODORE, III, (BILL WALTON), sportscaster, former professional basketball player; b. San Diego, Calif., Nov. 5, 1952; s. Theodore and Gloria W.; m. Lori Walton; children: Adam, Nathan, Luke, Christopher. BA in History with honors, UCLA, 1974. Ctr. Portland Trail Blazers, 1974—79, San Diego Clippers, 1979—84, LA Clippers, 1985, Boston Celtics, 1985—88; broadcast analyst Prime Ticket Network, 1990, CBS Sports, 1990—92, NBC Sports, 1992—2002, ESPN, ABC Sports, 2002—. Actor: (films) Little Nicky, He's Got Game, Forget Paris, Celtic Pride, Ghostbusters, (reality show) Bill Walton's Long Strange Trip, 2003; author: Nothing But Net. Recipient James E. Sullivan Meml. award, 1974, James Naismith award, 1972, 73, 74, Adolph Rupp trophy, 1972, 73, 74, Emmy award, 1979, 2001, NBA Sixth Man award, 1986, Oscar Robertson Leadership award NBPA, 1991, Best TV Analyst/Commentator award Southern Calif. Sports Broadcasters Assn., 1992, 93, 95, 96, 98, 99, 2000, Silver Anniversary award NCAA 1999, Humanitarian award NBA Retired Player's Assn., 2002; named Most Valuable Player NBA, 1978; named to NBA All-Star Team, 1977, 78, Nat. Basketball Hall of Fame, 1993, Oreg. Sports Hall of Fame, 1993, Academic All-America Hall of Fame, 1994, Nat. HS Sports Hall of Fame, 1997, Grateful Dead Hall of Honor, 2001; named one of 50 Greatest Players in NBA History, 1996, Top 50 Sportscasters Am. Sportscasters Assn., 2009. Achievements include being a member of the NCAA Men's Basketball Championship winning UCLA Bruins, 1972, 1973; being the first overall pick in the NBA Draft by the Portland Trailblazers, 1974; member of the NBA Championship winning: Portland Trailblazers, 1977, Boston Celtics, 1986. Office: ESPN ESPN Plz Bristol CT 06010*

WALTON GRAY, ROCHELLE LAJOYCE, state legislator; b. St. Louis; d. Elbert A. and Juanita Head Walton (Stepmother); m. Alan Walton Gray; children: Alan II, Alana. B in Pub. Policy Adminstrn., U. Mo., St. Louis. Legal adminstr. for family owned law firm, 1984—; mem. Dist. 81 Mo. House of Reps., 2009—. Youth advisor Christ, Our Redeemer AME Ch., youth dir.; mem. and officer Hazelwood Sch. PTA. Recipient Annie Malone Child Advocate award. Mem.: Am. Legis. Exchange Coun. (ALEC), Mo. Legislative Black Caucus, Women's Democratic Caucus, Mo. Women's Coalition, Women Legislator's Mo., Nat. Black Caucus State Legislators (NBCSL), Nat. Conf. State Legislators (NCSL), NOBEL (Women), Unity PAC. Democrat. Office: House of Representatives 201 West Capitol Ave Rm 105H Jefferson City MO 65101 also: 2320 Chambers Rd Saint Louis MO 63136 Office Phone: 573-751-5538, 314-388-5849. Office Fax: 314-388-1325. E-mail: Rochelle.Gray@house.mo.gov.

WALTRIP, MICHAEL CURTIS, professional race car driver; b. Owensboro, Ky., Apr. 30, 1963; m. Elizabeth Buffy Waltrip; children: Caitlin Marie, Margaret Carol. Stock car racer, 1981—. Owner, pres. Michael Waltrip Racing, Inc. Appearances: (several televesion and radio commercials). Recipient Most Popular Driver awards, NASCAR Dash Series, 1983, 1984, Driver of the Race, Pocono 500, 2006. Achievements include Mini-Modified divsn. track championship Ky. Motor Speedway, 1981; NASCAR Touring Goody's Dash Series, 1982-84, including series title 1983; NASCAR Winston Cup Series, 1985—, including 2d-place in Rookie of Yr. race, 1986; 2d-place 1988 Miller 500 at Pocono; 1st place, Daytona 500, 2001, 2003, Pepsi 400, 2002; NASCAR Busch Series Grand Nat. divsn. career includes 11 victories. Avocations: golf, tennis.

WALTZ, JAMES RICHARD, physician; b. Massillon, Ohio, June 30, 1935; AB, Ohio U., 1957; MD, Ohio State U., 1962. Intern Milw. County Hosp., 1962-63; resident U. Ill. Rsch. Edn. Hosps., 1963-67; gen. surgeon Liberty Hosp. Mem. ACS. Office: 15724 Oakmont Dr Kearney MO 64060-9251 Office Phone: 816-628-6699.

WALTZ, JOSEPH MCKENDREE, neurosurgeon, educator; b. Detroit, July 23, 1931; s. Ralph McKinley and Bertha (Seelye) W.; m. Janet Maureen Journey, June 26, 1954; children: Jeffrey McKinley, Mary Elaine, David Seelye, Stephen McKendree; m. Marilyn Liska, June 5, 1967; 1 child, Tristana McKendree. Student, U. Mich., 1950; BS, U. Oreg., 1954, MD, 1956. Diplomate Am. Bd. Neurol. Surgery, Am. Bd. Forensic Medicine, Am. Bd. Forensic Examiners, lic. NY, 1963, Calif., 1960, NJ, 1969, Mich., 1958; cert. DABNS Bd. Surg. intern U. Mich. Hosp., 1956-57, gen. surg. resident, 1957-58, clin. instr. neurosurgery, 1960-63; neurosurg. assoc. St. Barnabas Hosp., NYC, 1963—; assoc. dir. Inst. Neurosci., 1974—, dir. dept. neurol. surgery, 1977—2002; attending Neurosci. Inst. Our Lady of Mercy, 1998—2009; with AANS CNS Joint Sections, 1993—, U. Mich. Med. Ctr., Ann Arbor, 2001—; attending neurosurgeon Neurosci. Inst., 1998—2008, St. Barnabas Hosp., dir., 1976—98, chief neurosurgery dept., 1998—2002, bd. trustees, 1976—2001, chmn. operating review bd., 1963—95, chmn. institutional review bd., 1975—90; asst. prof. NY Coll. Osteopathic Medicine, Old Westbury, NY, 1989—2002; bd. dirs. U. Mich. Med. ctr., Ann Arbor, 1995—2001, exec. bd., 1995—2001; bd. dir. alumni assn. U. Mich., 1996—99, presdl. club mem., 1977; clin. prof. dept. neurosurgery NYU Med. Ctr., 1974—79; student asst. dept. anatomy U. Oregon Dental Sch., Portland, Oreg., 1952—56; asst. resident dept. gen. surgery U. Mich. Med. Ctr., Ann Arbor, 1957—58, jr., sr. clin. instr., 1960—63. Assoc. cons. in neurosurgery Englewood (N.J.) Hosp., 1964—; assoc. prof. neurosurgery NYU Med. Str., 1974—; asst. prof. dept. surgery (neurosurgery) N.Y. Coll. Osteo. Medicine, 1989—; mem. alumni bd. U. Mich. Med. Ctr., 1995; dir. Med. Ct. Graphics; gen. surgery internship U. Mich. Med. Ctr., Ann Arbor, 1956—57. Author: (chpt.) Cryogenic Surgery, Neurology, 1982, Advances in Neurology, 1983, Textbook of Stereotactic and Functional Neurosurgery, 1997; contbr. 60 articles to profl. jours. Mem. sci. adv. bd. Dystonia Med. Research Found., 1980—2006; trustee St. Barnabas Hosp., 1980—. Served to capt. M.C. AUS, 1958-60. Capt. med. corps US Army, 1958—60, with US Army, 1960—62. Recipient Bronze award Am. Congress Rehab. Medicine, 1967, World Cmty. Svc. award Rotary, Disting. Trustee award United Hosp. Fund, 1995, Outstanding Contribution award, Neurostimulation Found., Appreciation NY State Supreme Ct., Med. Malpractice Mediation Panel, award, Electronics & Info. Scis., 1984, award, Inrternat. Biographical Ctr., Cambridge, fellow. Rsch. grant, Rockefeller Found., named, Yr. Book Sci. & Future, 1984, Notable Americans, Am. Biographical Inst., 1981, Best Doctors America, 1978, 2008, Top Doctors NY Metro Area, Americas Top Surgens, 2002-03. Mem. AMA, Am. Paralysis Assn., World Soc. Stereotactic and Functional Neurosurgery, Congress Neurol. Surgeons, Math. Assn. Am., Internat. Neural Network Soc., Soc. for Cryobiology, N.Y. State Med. Soc., Bronx County Med. Soc., N.Y. State Neurosurg Soc., Congress Neurological Surgeons, Joint Sect. Neurotrauma & Critical Care, Joint Sect. Stereotactic & Functional Neurosurgery, Joint Sect. Spine & Peripheral Nerves, Am. Acad. Pain Mgmt., Am. Acad. Spine Physicians, NY Med. Soc., Bronx County Med. Soc., Internat. Neural Network Soc., Math. Assn. America, NY Acad. Sci., Am. Assn. Advancement Sci., Nat. Ski Patrol, Phi Beta Pi. Achievements include spl. rsch. on neurophysiology and treatment of epilepsy, basal ganglia disorders, abnormal movement disorders, cerebral palsy, also neurosurg. application stereotactic thalamic surgery and spinal cord stimulation, patent for multi electrode catheter assembly for spinal cord stimulation. Office: 150 Purchase St Ste 7 Rye NY 10580 Office Phone: 914-967-6577. Personal E-mail: joemwaltz@aol.com.

WALTZ, KATHLEEN M., former publishing executive; b. Mar. 6, 1954; m. Bill Raffel, 1990; stepchildren: Jamie, Jenny. BA, DePaul U., 1985; postgrad., Northwestern U. Telemarketer Chgo. Tribune, 1973, mgr. recruitment advt., 1987, dir. customer satisfaction, 1989—90, dir. classified advt., 1990—95, v.p./dir. of developing bus., 1995—97; v.p., gen. mgr. Sun-Sentinel Co., Fla., 1997—98; CEO, pres., pub. Daily Press, Newport News, Va., 1998—2000; pub. Orlando Sentinel, 2000—08; pres. & CEO Orlando Sentinel Comm., 2000—08. Bd. dirs. United Way. of Va. Peninsula, Peninsula Allice for Econ. Devel. WHRO Found. and Greater Peninsula Now; bd. dirs., exec. com. Hampton Roads Partnership; ABC/NAA liaison com., sr. exec. resource corps. Coll. of William and Mary. Mem. So. Newspapers Pub. Assn. (diversity com.). Avocations: travel, golf, gardening.*

WALTZ, KENNETH NEAL, political science educator; b. Ann Arbor, Mich., June 8, 1924; s. Christian Benjamin and Luella (Braun) W.; m. Helen Elizabeth Lindsley, June 4, 1949; children: Kenneth L., Thomas E. (dec.), Daniel E. AB, Oberlin Coll., 1948, LLD (hon.), 2002; MA, Columbia U., 1950, PhD, 1954; D (hon.), Copenhagen U., 1995, Nankai U., 2003. Instr., then asst. prof. Columbia U., NYC, 1953-57, adj. prof., rsch. assoc. Inst. War and Peace Studies, 1997—; from assoc. prof. to prof. politics Swarthmore Coll., 1957-66; rsch. assoc. Harvard U. Ctr. Internat. Affairs, 1963-64, 68-69, 72; prof. politics Brandeis U., Waltham, Mass., 1966-71, Adlai E. Stevenson prof. internat. politics, 1967-71; Ford prof. polit. sci. U. Calif., Berkeley, 1971-94, Ford prof. emeritus, 1994—; vis. sr. rsch. assoc. King's Coll., U. London, 1986-87. Cons. govt. agys. Author: Man, The State and War, 1959, Foreign Policy and Democratic Politics, 1967, Theory of International Politics, 1979, The Spread of Nuclear Weapons, 1981; co-author: The Spread of Nuclear Weapons: A Debate, 1995, The Spread of Nuclear Weapons: A Debate Renewed, 2002; co-author, co-editor Conflict in World Politics, 1971, The Use of Force, 1971, 6th edit., 2003, mem. editl. bd. Jour. Strategic Studies, Jour. Chinese Polit. Sci. Served to 1st lt. AUS, 1944-46, 51-52. Recipient Heinz Eulau award for best article, Am. Polit. Sci. Rev., 1990, James Madison award disting. scholarly contbn. to polit. sci., 1999; grantee, NSF, 1968—71, Guggenheim, 1976—77, Woodrow Wilson Ctr., Internat. Ctr. Scholars, 1979—80; vis. scholar philosophy, London Sch. Econs., 1976—77, vis. scholar, Rsch. Sch. Pacific Studies, Australian Nat. U., 1978, U. Peking Dept. Internat. Politics, 1982, 1991, 1996, Fudan U., Shanghai, 1991, 2001, USAF Acad., 1991—92, U. Bologna, 2002. Fellow Am. Acad. Arts and Scis.; mem. Am. Polit. Sci. Assn. (sec. 1966-67, pres. 1987-88, James Madison award, 1999), Internat. Studies Assn. (pres. New Eng. sect. 1966-67), Coun. Fgn. Rels., Phi Beta Kappa. Office: Columbia Univ Inst War and Peace Studies 420 W 118th St 13th Fl Rm 1336 MC 3347 New York NY 10027*

WALTZ, SUSAN, political scientist, educator; Former chmn. Amnesty Internat., London, England, 1993-98; prof. internat. pub. policy Gerald Ford Sch. Pub. Policy U. Mich., Ann Arbor, 2001—. Bd. dirs. Am. Friends Svc. Com., 2000—08, Amnesty Internat.-USA, 2009—. Office: Ford Sch Public Policy Michigan Univ 3227 Weill Hall 735 S State St Ann Arbor MI 48109 Office Phone: 734-615-8683. Business E-Mail: swaltz@umich.edu.

WALZ, EDWARD GEORGE, protective services official; s. George Francis and Margaret Ellen Walz; m. Christine Ann Dallago, Apr. 23, 1992; life ptnr. Linda Periera; children: Kelly Ann, Edward George Jr., Christopher Joseph. Diploma, Big Bend CC, Washington, 1984. Police officer NYC Police Dept., 1988—2005, Dept Army Police, Fort Hamilton, NY, 2005—. Staff sgt. US Army, 1983—99. Decorated Army Achievment Medal US Army, SW Asian Svc. medal, Army Commedation Medal; recipient Cert. Achievment, Soc. Prevention Cruelty to Children, 2003, Nat. Law Enforcement Mus., 2006, Meritorious award, NYC Police Dept., 1986—2005, Excellant Police Duty award, 1988—2005, Silver Star For Bravery, Am. Fedn. Police, 1992, Cert. Achievment, Assn. US Army, 1986, Cert. Appreciation, Nat. World War II Mus., 2006, Cert. Commendation, Nat. Mus. US Army, 2007. Mem.: US Army Hist. Soc., NYC Patrolman Benevolent Assoc., Am. Legion, VFW (life; sr. vice comdr. 2005—06).

WALZ, JEFF (JEFFREY J. WALZ), women's college basketball coach; b. 1971; s. Roger and Janine Walz; m. Kim Kumfer, May 17, 2003; children: Kaeley Thöney, Jacob Joseph. BS in Secondary Edn. and Bus., No. Ky. U., 1995; MEd, Western Ky. U. Adminstrv. asst. Western Ky. U., asst. coach, 1995—97, U. Nebr., 1997—2001, U. Minn., 2001—02, U. Md., 2002—06, assoc. head coach, 2006—07; head coach U. Louisville, 2007—. Office: Univ Louisville Athletic Dept Womens Basketball 2100 S Floyd St Louisville KY 40292*

WALZ, TIM (TIMOTHY J. WALZ), United States Representative from Minnesota, former social science educator; b. West Point, Nebr., Apr. 6, 1964; m. Gwen Whipple, 1994; children: Hope, Gus. BS in Social Sci. Edn., Chadron State Coll., Nebr., 1989; MS in Edn. Leadership, St. Mary's U., Winona, Minn., 2001. High sch. tchr. People's Rep. China, 1989—90; tchr. Alliance Pub. Schools, 1991—96, Mankato West High Sch., Mankato, Minn., 1996—2006; mem. US Congress from 1st dist. Minn., 2007—, mem. agrl. com., vets affairs com., transp. & infrastructure com. Advanced to Sgt. Major US Army Nat. Guard, 1981—2005, served in Operation Enduring Freedom, 2005. Recipient Minn. Ethics in Edn. award, 2002; named Neb. Citizen Soldier of Yr., 1989, Outstanding Young Nebraskan, Nebr. Junior C. of C., 1993, Mankato Tchr. of Yr., 2003, Minn. Tchr. of Excellence, 2003. Dfl. Lutheran. Office: 1529 Longworth House Office Bldg Washington DC 20515 also: 1134 7th St NW Rochester MN 55901*

WALZER, NORMAN CHARLES, retired economics professor; b. Mendota, Ill., Mar. 17, 1943; s. Elmer J. and Anna L. Walzer; m. Dona Lee Maurer, Aug. 22, 1970; children: Steven, Mark. BS, Ill. State U., Normal, 1966; MA, U. Ill., 1969, PhD, 1970. Rsch. dir. Cities and Villages Mcpl. Problems Com., Springfield, Ill., 1974-84; vis. prof. U. Ill., Urbana, 1977-78; prof. econs. Western Ill. U., Macomb, 1978—2005, chmn. dept. econs., 1980-89, dir. Ill. Inst. Rural Affairs, 1988—2005, interim dean coll. bus. and tech., 1993-95; prof., dir. emeritus, 2005—. Author: Cities, Suburbs and Property Tax, 1981, Government Structure and Public Finance, 1984; editor: Financing State and Local Governments, 1981, Rural Community Economic Development, 1991; co-editor: Financing Local Infrastructure in Non Metro Areas, 1986, Financing Economic Development in The 1980s, 1986, Financing Rural Health Care, 1988, Rural Health Care, 1992, Rural Community Economic Development, 1992, Local Economic Development: International Trends and Issues, 1995, Community Visioning Programs: Practice and Principles, 1996, Public-Private Partnerships for Local Economic Development, 1998, Cooperative Approach to Community Economic Development, 2000, Local Government Innovations, 2000, American Midwest: Managing Change in Rural Transition, 2003, Cooperatives and Development: Applications for the 21st Century, 2003, Entrepreneurship and Local Development, 2007. Mem. Am. Econs. Assn., Ill. Cmty. Devel. Soc. (v.p. 2009-), Mid-Continent Regional Sci. Assn. (pres. 1985-86). Office: Northern Ill Univ Ctr Govtl Studies Dekalb IL 60115 Business E-Mail: nwalzer@niu.edu.

WAMBA, KOLO, physicist; b. Waltham, Mass., Apr. 30, 1974; s. Ernest Wamba-Dia-Wamba and Elaine Wamba; m. Alice Endamne, Feb. 29, 2000; children: Luezi Endamne-Wamba, Sana Endamne-Wamba. PhD, Stanford U., Calif., 2006. Sr. software engr. Sirf Tech., San Jose, Calif., 2006—07; sr. physicist Decision Scis. Corp., San Diego, 2007—. Office: Decision Scis Corp 3870 Murphy Canyon Rd San Diego CA 92123 Business E-Mail: kolo@dscresearch.com.

WAMBOLD, RICHARD LAWRENCE, manufacturing executive; b. Wilbraham, Mass., Jan. 19, 1952; s. Richard A. and Virginia M. (Reid) W.; m. Patricia Bentley, Aug. 24, 1974; children: Lauren, Carolyn, Robin. BA, U. Tex., 1974, MBA, 1977. From systems cons. to strategic planning mgr. Tenneco, Inc., Houston, 1977-81, asst. to chmn. and chief exec. officer, 1981-84, pres. Tenneco Ventures Inc., 1984-88, v.p. corp. planning and devel., 1988—; exec. v.p., gen. mgr. Internat. Bus. Group, J.I. Case Co., Racine, Wis., 1988—99; chmn. and CEO Pactiv Corp.,

1999—. Mem. Nat. Venture Capital Assn., Bus. Roundtable, Comml. Club Chgo. Avocation: sailing. Office: J I Case 700 State St Racine WI 53404-3392 also: Headquarters 1900 West Field Court Lake Forest IL 60045

WAMP, ZACHARY PAUL, United States Representative from Tennessee; b. Ft. Benning, Ga., Oct. 28, 1957; m. Kim Watts; 2 children. Student, U. NC, Chapel Hill, U. Tenn. Chmn. Hamilton County Rep. Party, 1987; regional dir. Tenn. Rep. Party, 1989; v.p. Charter Real Estate Corp., 1989-92; comml. and indsl. real estate broker Fletcher Bright Co., 1992-94; mem. US Congress from 3rd Tenn. dist., 1995—, mem. appropriations com., founder, co-chmn. Congl. Fitness Caucus. Bd. dirs. United Negro Coll. Fund, Am. Diabetes Assn., Boy Scouts Am., Chattanooga Urban League. Recipient Disting. Svc. award, Chattanooga C. of C., Brainerd-East Hamilton County Br., 1999, Energy Leadership award, US Energy Assn. and Johnson Controls, Inc., 2003; named Bus. Leader of Yr., Chattanooga Bus. Jour., 1993. Republican. Baptist. Office: US Ho Reps 1436 Longworth Ho Office Bldg Washington DC 20515 Office Phone: 202-225-3271.*

WAMUTOMBO, DIKEMBE MUTOMBO MPOLONDO MUKAMBA JEAN JACQUE See MUTOMBO, DIKEMBE

WAN, HUNG-DA, mechanical engineer, educator; b. Taiwan; married. PhD, Va. Poly. Inst. and State U., 2006. Postdoc. rschr. U. Tex., San Antonio, 2006—07, asst. prof., 2007—. Mem.: Soc. Mfg. Engring., Inst. Indsl. Engrs. Business E-Mail: hungda.wan@utsa.edu.

WAN, RONG-YU, metallurgist; b. China, Jan. 12, 1932; s. Zheng-Lin and Juan-Ying Yan Wan; m. KeZhong Wang, June 1, 1957; 1 child, Joseph J. BS in Chem. Engring., Chiao Tung U., Shanghai, China, 1952; PhD in Metallurgy and Metall. Engring., U. Utah, 1984. Metallurgy engr. engring. and design Inst. for Nonferrous Metall. Industries, Beijing, 1953-79; supervising chief Beijing Mining and Metall. Rsch. Inst., Beijing, 1958-79; rsch. assoc., asst. rsch. prof. U. Utah, 1980-87; sr. metallurgist Newmont Exploration Ltd., Metall. Svc., Salt Lake City, 1987-91, mgr. metall. rsch., 1992—. Adj. prof. metallurgy dept. U. Utah, 1987—. Contbr. articles to profl. jours. Recipient numerous awards from Chinese Govt., Ministry Metall. Industries, 1955-79. Mem. Minerals, Metals and Materials Soc. (vice chmn. aqueous processes com., vice chmn. precious metals com., honors and awards com., Extractive Metallurgy Tech. award 1989), Soc. for Mining, Metallurgy and Exploration, Mining Metall. Soc. Am. Achievements include 4 patents for new technologies of gold metallurgy, refractory gold ores treatment; research and development in innovative technologies and processes for gold recovery, gold recovery using noncyanide lixiviants, pressure oxidatioln of sulfide minerals fundamental and applications; technical contributions in the areas of nonferrouis extractive metallurgy and mineral processing.

WAN, SHUANGYI, research scientist; m. Ling Li. BS, Nanjing U., Jiangsu, China, 2000; MS, Nanjing U., 2003; PhD, U. Pitts., PA, 2008. Sr. rsch. scientist dept. medicinal chemistry Albany Molecular Rsch., Inc., NY, 2008—. Recipient Excellence Prize Chem. Experiments, Nanjing U., 2000. Mem.: Am. Chem. Soc., Sigma Xi. Achievements include research in developed a general and highly efficient approach to the synthesis of oxidized amides; Studied the structure/reactivity relationships between bicyclic epoxonium ions and tethered nucleophiles; completed the total synthesis of anti-tumor natural product (+)-dactylolide; synthesized the first 2D 4.8(2) threefold parallel interpenetrating metal-organic-framework from a flexible tripodal ligand; synthesized the first self-penetrated 3D metal-organic-framework from a flexible tripodal ligand with partial anion exchange property; observed for the first time the high catalytic activity of a series of zinc complexes with an S2N2 binding set toward the hydrolysis of 4-nitrophenyl acetate as carbonic anhydrase model complexes; synthesis of aldehydes and ketones from soluble polymeric supports; preparation of two honeycomb-like metal-organic-frameworks with different photoluminescent properties; synthesis of interpenetrating coordination polymers from benzenecarboxylate derivatives and rear earth metal salts. Office: Albany Molecular Rsch Inc 30 Corporate Cir Albany NY 12203 Personal E-mail: wan.shuangyi@gmail.com.

WAN, ZEHONG, research and development company executive; PhD, U. Pa., Phila., 2000. Prin. scientist investigator, medicinal chemistry Glaxo Smith Kline R & D, King of Prussia, Pa., 2000—08, mgr. Pudong, 2008—. Mem.: Am. Chem. Soc. Home and Office: GlaxoSmithKline R&D China 3F Bldg 3 898 Halei Rd Pudong Shanghai 201203 China Business E-Mail: zehong.2.wan@gsk.com.

WANCHOO, VISHAL K., electromedical equipment company executive; Undergraduate in Elec. Engring., Indian Inst. Tech.; MS in Computer Engring., U. So. Calif. V.p., gen.mgr., imaging & info. sys. orgn. GE Healthcare, 1997, v.p., gen. mgr., clin. info. tech., 2004, pres., CEO, integrated IT solutions; pres., CEO healthcare info. technologies GE Co., 2005—. Office: General Electric Co 3135 Easton Tpke Fairfield CT 06828 Office Phone: 203-373-2211. Office Fax: 203-373-3131.

WAND, KIMBERLY JOANNE, assistant principal; b. Colo. Springs, Calif., Feb. 21, 1957; d. William James and Joanne Alice Craig; m. Michael Floyd Wand, May 12, 1979; children: Emily, Steven, Maribeth. MusB, Delta State U., 1979, MusM, 1985; AA in Gifted Edn., 1993; EdS, Miss. State U., 2002. English Certification Hinds Cmty. Coll., 1999. Gen. music tchr. Ruleville Ctrl. Elem., Miss., 1979—81; kindergarten tchr. St. Luke Meth. Ch., Cleveland, Miss., 1981—83; gen. music tchr. grades 1-6 Parks Bell Elem., Cleveland, 1984—86; k-2d grade tchr. Ruleville Ctrl. Elem., 1988—94; music tchr. Brandon Mid. Sch., Miss., 1994—98; fine arts coord. Richland Mid. Sch., 1998—99; asst. fine arts coord. Brandon H.S., 1999—2001; reading specialist, gifted program coord., asst. fine arts coord. Rankin County Sch. Dist., Brandon, 2000—02; dir. of academics Miss. Sch. of the Arts, Brookhaven, 2002—04; asst. prin. grades 7-8 Brookhaven Sch. Dist., 2004—. Presenter in field. Recipient Karen Semple Tchr. of Yr., Brandon Mid. Sch., 1997, Leadership award, Miss. State U., 2002; named Star Tchr., Brandon H.S., 2002. Mem.: Miss. Sci. Tchrs. Assn., Miss. Coun. of Tchrs. of Math., Miss. Assn. for Children Under Six, Music Educators Nat. Conf., Miss. Music Tchrs. Assn., Nat. Coun. of Tchrs. of English, Miss. Coun. of Tchrs. of English, Nat. Assn. for Gifted Children, Miss. Assn. for Gifted Children, Miss. Alliance for Art Edn. (pres. elect 2005—), Mu Phi Epilson. Home: 135 Ken Dr Brandon MS 39042

WAND, MARTIN, ophthalmologist, educator; 3 children. BS, Yale U., New Haven, 1963, MD, 1968. Diplomate Am. Bd. of Ophthalmology, 1976, recertified 2003. Pres. New Eng. Ophthal. Soc., Boston, 1997—98; trustee McLean Health Ctr., Simsbury, Conn., 2000—05; councilor Am. Glaucoma Soc., San Francisco, 2000—05; clin. prof. ophthalmology U. Conn. Sch. Medicine, Farmington, Conn., 2000—; dir. and vice-chair Am. Bd. Ophthalmology, Phila., 2001—; trustee, vice chair coun. Am. Acad. Ophthalmology, San Francisco, 2006—. Contbr. over 130 articles to profl. jours., chapters to books. Lt. commdr. U. S. Pub. Health Svc., 1970—72, Ctr. for Disease Control. Fellow: Am. Acad. Ophthalmology (Honor award 1985, Sr. Honor award 1996, Secretariat award 2003); mem.: Chandler-Grant Soc., Am. Eye Study Club, Am. Glaucoma Soc., New Eng. Ophthal. Soc. Office: Cons Ophthalmologists 499 Farmington Ave Farmington CT 06032 Office Phone: 860-678-0202.

WANDEL, SHARON LEE, sculptor; b. Bemidji, Minn., Mar. 19, 1940; d. Roy J. and Bonnie (Englund) Opsahl; m. Thaddeus Ludwik Wandel, Oct. 17, 1970; children: Holly, Erika. BA, Gustavus Adolphus Coll., 1962; MSW, Columbia U., 1965; Cert. in Arts Mgmt., SUNY, Purchase, 1993. Caseworker Manhattan State Hosp., NYC, 1963-64; caseworker/rschr. Cmty. Svc. Soc., NYC, 1965-67; teaching asst. dept. medicine NYU Med. Ctr., NYC, 1967—71. Adv. bd. Lamia, Inc., NYC, 1999—2003. One-woman shows at Silvermine Guild of Artists, New Canaan, Conn., 1993, 97, 2000, Pen and Brush, NYC, 1994, Clark Whitney Gallery, Lenox, Mass., 1994, James Cox Gallery, Woodstock, NY, 1994, 96, Cortland Jessup Gallery, Provincetown, Mass., 1998, NYC, 2000, 02, Gallery Marya, Osaka, Japan, 1999, Laura Barton Gallery, Westport, Conn., 2000, Firehouse Gallery, Damaviscotta, Maine, 2000, Gallery Irohane, Osaka, Japan, 2001; exhibited in group shows at Nat. Acad. Design, NYC, 1988, 90, 92, 94-95, 97-2000, 08, 09, Cortland Jessup Gallery, Provincetown and NYC, 1998-2002, Canyon Ranch, Lenox, Mass. 1999-2003, Chesterwood, Lenox, Mass., 2000-01, Butler Inst. Am. Art., Youngstown, Ohio, 2000, Cavalier Gallery, Nantucket, Mass., 2001, Berkshires Bot. Garden, Mass., 2001, Paesaggio Gallery, West Hartford, Conn., 2001-04, Leighton Gallery, Blue Hill, Maine, 2001-09, Munson Gallery, Chatham, Mass., 2002-09, Sakai (Japan) City Mus., 2002, Craven Gallery, Martha's Vineyard, Mass., 2002-09, Berta Walker Gallery, Provincetown, Mass., 2002, Elan Fine Arts, Rockport, Maine, 2003-08, Clarke Galleries, Stowe, Vt., 2003-, Palm Beach, Fla., 2003-04, NYC, 2003-04, Westchester Arts Coun., White Plains, NY, 2004, Gallery Yellow, Cross River, N.Y., 2006-07, Flinn Gallery, Greenwich, Conn., 2006-07, Sculpture Baun, Fairfield, Ct., 2008-09, Wit Gallery, Lenox, Mass., 2008-09, Chace Randall Gallery, Andes, NY, 2008-09, ACA Galleries, NY, 2008-09. Permanent Collections at Art Students League, Westinghouse Corp. Collection, Pitts., Nat. Acad. Design, Housatonic Mus., CT, C. of C., Toyamura, Japan, Pfizer Corp. Collection, Armonk, NY; commns. include two 8' bronze figures for Ihilani Resort, Kapolei, Hawaii, 1993, 2 5" figures Silvermine Galleries, 1993, The Harrison Gallery Williamstown, Mass., 2009, The Handing Gallery, 2008-09, Ctr. Contemporary Printmaking, Norwach Ct., 2007,09. Mem. rsch. com. Arthritis Found., N.Y.C., 1968-69. Recipient N.Am. Sculpture Exhbn. 2d place, 1991, Three River Arts Festival (Carnegie Inst.) Purchase award, 1990, Hakone Open Air Mus. (Japan) 3d and 4th Rodin Grand Prize Exhbn. Excellent Maquettes, 1990, 92, Matrix Gallery 1st prize for sculpture, 1990, Ariel Gallery Internat. Competition Group Show award, 1989, Salmagundi Club McReynolds award, 1989, Barret Coleco award, 1988, 1st place nat. competition Sundance Gallery, Bridgehampton, N.Y., 1997; Vt. Studio Ctr. fellow, 2000; elected Nat. Academician Nat. Acad. Design, 1994, Elin T. Speyer prize, 2007. Mem. Silvermine Guild of Artists (Solo Show award 1992), N.Y. Soc. Woman Artists (past pres.), The Pen and Brush (Meisner award 1990, Solo Show award 1993), Nat. Acad. Design (elected nat. academician 1994, Cleo Hartwig award 1990), Nat. Sculpture Soc. (Meisner award 1994, Hexter award 1993, Spring award 1991, Meiselman award 1990), Audubon Artists (Chaim Gross Found. award 1993), Sculptors Guild (past bd. dirs.). Avocations: travel, cooking, reading. Studio: PO Box 314 Croton On Hudson NY 10520-0314 E-mail: wandel_s@hotmail.com.

WANDELL, KEITH E., motorcycle company executive; b. 1949; BBA, Ohio U., 1972; MBA, Dayton U., 1979. With Sheller Globe Corp., 1979—87, Farley Industries, 1987—88; mgmt. positions Johnson Controls, Inc., Milw., 1988—97, corp. v.p., 1997—2005, pres. battery group, 1997—2003, pres., automotive group, 2003—06, exec. v.p., 2005—06, pres., COO, 2006—09; pres., CEO Harley-Davidson, Inc., Milw., 2009—. Vice chmn. Mich. Minority Bus. Devel. Coun. Office: Harley-Davidson Inc PO Box 653 3700 W Juneau Ave Milwaukee WI 53201*

WANDELT, BENJAMIN DAN, physics and astronomy professor; b. Duesseldorf, Germany, Sept. 5, 1972; permanent resident, US, 2007; s. Hermann Sylvester Wilfried and Caroline Maria Franziska Wandelt; m. Sonja Julia Schoene, May 21, 2006. BSc in Physics, Imperial Coll., London, 1994, PhD in Astrophysics and Theoretical Physics, 1997, Diploma, 1997; associateship, Royal Coll. Sci., London, 1994. Postdoctoral rsch. fellow Theoretical Astrophysics Ctr., Copenhagen, 1997—99; rsch. assoc. Princeton U., NJ, 1999—2001; asst. prof. U. Ill., Urbana Champaign, 2001—06, assoc. prof., 2006—; vis. assoc. Caltech., 2009. Creator cosmology@home, (software) HEALPix. Recipient Sofja Kovalevskaja award, German Ministry Edn. and Rsch., 2006, Friedrich Wilhelm Bessel award, Alexander von Humboldt Found., 2007, Xerox award, 2009; grantee Bayesian Cosmostatistics, NSF, 2005—, Cosmic Beginning and Cosmic Fate, 2007—; Knowles Studentship, U. London, 1995—97, Beckman fellow, Ctr. for Advanced Studies, U. Ill., 2004, Faculty fellow, Nat. Ctr. for Supercomputing Applications, 2004, fellow, Marcel Grossman Conf., 2006. Mem.: Inst. Physics, Am. Astron. Soc., Am. Phys. Soc. Achievements include research in interpretation of cosmic microwave background data; theoretical Cosmology; invention of image reconstruction algorithm. Office: U Ill Urbana-Champaign 1110 W Green St Urbana IL 61801 Office Fax: 217-333-9819.

WANDER, HERBERT STANTON, lawyer; b. Cin., Mar. 17, 1935; s. Louis Marvin and Pauline (Schuster) W.; m. Karen Woloshin, Aug. 2004; children: Daniel Jerome, Susan Gail, Lois Marlene. AB, U. Mich., 1957; LLB, Yale U., 1960. Bar: Ill. 1960. Law clk. to judge US Dist. Ct. (no. dist.) Ill., 1960—61; ptnr. Pope Ballard Shepard & Fowle, Chgo., 1961—78, Katten Muchin Rosenman LLP, Chgo., 1978—. Chair Michael Reese Health Trust, 2006; bd. dirs. Tel. & Data Systems, Chgo.; mem. legal adv. com. to bd. govs. NY Stock Exch., 1989—92; mem. legal adv. bd. Nat. Assn. Securities Dealers, Inc., 1996—99; spkr. in field. Editor: (jour.) Bus. Law Today, 1992-93; editor-in-chief: (jour.) The Bus. Lawyer, 1993-94; contbr. numerous articles to profl. jour. Bd. dir. Jewish Fedn. Met. Chgo., 1972—, pres., 1981-83; bd. dir. Jewish United Fund, 1972—, pres., 1981-83, chmn. pub. affairs com., 1984-87, gen. campaign chmn., 1993 Mem.: ABA (sec. bus. law sect. 1992—93, vice-chair 1993—94, chair-elect 1994—95, chair 1995—96, apptd. to ABA commn. on multidisciplinary practice 1998, ABA task force on atty.-client privilege 2004, task force on fed. sentencing guidelines 2004, co-chair SEC adv. com. on smaller pub. cos. 2004), Chgo. Bar Assn., Ill. State Bar Assn., Yale Law Sch. Assn. (exec. com. 1982—86), Northmoor Country Club, Std. Club, Econ. Club, Phi Beta Kappa. Home: 70 Prospect Ave Highland Park IL 60035-3329 Office: Katten Muchin Rosenman LLP 525 W Monroe St Ste 1700 Chicago IL 60661-3693 Office Phone: 312-902-5267. Business E-Mail: hwander@kattenlaw.com.

WANDER, JOSEPH DAY, chemist; b. Columbus, Ohio, July 20, 1941; s. Clinton George Sr. and Joan Rosemary (Day) W.; m. Rosemary Casey, Sept. 2, 1967; children: Pandora Lucrezia, Ezekiel Robert, Jeremiah Day. BS, Case Inst. Tech., 1963; PhD, Ohio State U., 1970. Dir. CB Stout Neurosci. Lab., U. Tenn. Med. Units, Memphis, 1972-77; asst. prof. U. Ga., Athens, 1978-84, Columbus (Ga.) Coll., 1985-86; fuels chemist USAF Civil Engring. Support Ctr., Tyndall AFB, Fla., 1986-94, USAF Armstrong Lab., Tyndall AFB, 1994—. Mem. Am. Chem. Soc. (treas. divsn. carbohydrate chemistry 1982-85), Soc. Preservation Barbershop Singing in Am. (pres. Panama City Fla. chpt. 1990-91, cert. judge). Avocation: barbershop and string music.

WANDERS, HANS WALTER, banker; b. Aachen, Germany, Apr. 3, 1925; came to US, 1929, naturalized, 1943; s. Herbert and Anna Maria (Kusters) W.; m. Elizabeth Knox Kimball, Apr. 2, 1949; children: Crayton Kimball, David Gillette. BS, Yale U., 1947, Ga. Inst. Tech., 1945; postgrad., Rutgers U., 1961—64. With GE, 1947-48, Libbey-Owens-Ford Glass Co., 1948-53, Allied Chem. Co., 1953-55, McKinsey & Co., Inc., 1955-57; from asst. cashier to v.p. No. Trust Co., Chgo., 1957-65; v.p. Nat. Blvd. Bank, Chgo., 1965-66, pres., 1966-70; exec. v.p. Wachovia Bank & Trust Co., N.A., Winston-Salem, NC, 1970-74, chmn., 1977-85, vice chmn., 1985-88, also bd. dirs.; pres. Wachovia Corp., Winston-Salem, 1974-76, 85-87, chmn., 1977-85, vice chmn., 1987-88, also bd. dirs.; pres., chief exec. officer 1st Wachovia Corp. Services, Inc., Winston-Salem, 1986-88; dir. Exxon Supply Co., 1989-94, Goody's Mfg. Corp., 1989-94, Gulf Resources, Inc., 1989-92, Turnpike Properties, Inc., 2001—. Chmn. Winston-Salem Found. Com., 1981-82; bd. dirs. NC Textile Found., NC Engring. Found., Inc., 1971-88; trustee, mem. exec. com. Salem Coll. and Acad., 1986-91, Tax Found., 1982—, vice chmn., 1984-86, chmn., 1986-88, chmn. exec. com., 1989; mem. bd. visitors Fuqua Sch. Bus., Duke U., 1978-89, NC Japan Ctr., 1982—; mem. nat. corps. com. United Negro Coll. Fund; mem., chmn. NC Bd. Econ. Devel., 1989-93; corporator Belmont Hill Sch., 1996—. Lt. USNR, 1943-46, 51-53. Mem. Am. Bankers Assn. (chmn. mktg. divsn. 1979-80, dir. 1971-73), Assn. Res. City Bankers, Conf. Bd. (So. regional adv. coun.), Assn. Bank Holding Cos. (bd. dirs., exec. com. 1981-83), Chgo. Club, Commonwealth Club Chgo., Twin-City Club Winston Salem, Old Town Club Winston-Salem Home: 10 Graylyn Pl Winston Salem NC 27106 Office: Wachovia Corp 420 W 4th St Ste 202-A Winston Salem NC 27101-2837 Office Phone: 336-761-5016.

WANDS, BRUCE, academic administrator, musician, writer; s. Hoyland Archibald and Lillian Hannah Wands. BS, Lafayette Coll., Easton, Pa., 1971; MS, Syracuse U., NY, 1976. Artist, musician, writer Wands Studio, Verona, NJ, 1972—; chair, BFA computer art Sch. Visual Arts, NYC, 1994—98, chair, MFA computer art, 1998—. Author: (book) Art of the Digital Age, Digital Creativity. Mem. NYC Acm Siggraph, 1989—99. Grant, Rockefeller Found., 2003, Nat. Endowment Arts, 2003, NY State Coun. Arts, 2003—06. Mem.: Coll. Art Assn. Avocations: motorcycling, gardening. Office: MFA Computer Art Sch Visual Arts 209 E 23 St New York NY 10010 Office Fax: 212-592-2509. Personal E-mail: bruce@brucewands.com. Business E-Mail: bruce@mfaca.sva.edu.

WANDYCZ, PIOTR STEFAN, historian, educator; b. Krakow, Poland, Sept. 20, 1923; s. Damian Stanislaw and Stefania (Dunikowska) W.; m. Maria Teresa Chrzaszcz, Aug. 13, 1963; children: Anna, Joanna, Antoni. BA, Cambridge U., 1948, MA, 1952; PhD, London U., 1951; MA (hon.), Yale U., 1968; DHC, Wroclaw U., 1993, Sorbonne U., Paris, 1997, Jagiellonian U., 2000, Cath. U. Lublin, 2004. Instr. to assoc. prof. history Ind. U., 1954-66; fellow Harvard's Russian Rsch. Ctr., 1963-65; assoc. prof. history Yale U., 1966-68, prof., 1968-89, chmn. Russian and East European coun., 1974-76, 81-83, Bradford Durfee prof., 1989-97, prof. emeritus, 1997—. Vis. prof. history Columbia U., 1967, 69, 74 Author: Czechoslovak-Polish Confederation and Great Powers, 1956, France and Her Eastern Allies, 1962, Soviet-Polish Relations, 1969, The Lands of Partitioned Poland, 1974, United States and Poland, 1980, August Zaleski, 1980, Polska i Zagranica, 1986, The Twilight of French Eastern Alliances, 1988, Z Dziejow dyplomacji, 1988, Polish Diplomacy 1914-1945, 1988, The Price of Freedom, 1992, 2nd edit., 2001, Die Freiheit und ihr Preis, 1993, Pod zaborami, 1994, Cena wolnosci, 1995, 2d edit., 2003, Laisves Kaina, 1997, Stredni Evropa v Dejinach, 1998, Tsenata na svobodata, 1999, Z Pilsudskim i Sikorskim, 1999, Il prezzo della liberta, 2001, O Federalizmie i emigracji, 2003, Pax Europaea, 2003, O Czasach Dawniejszych i Blizszych, 2009; co-author: Historia Europy Srodkowo-Wschodniej, 2000, Histoire de l'Europe du Centre-Est 2004, Tsina Slobody, 2004, A Szabaeag Ara, 2004, Aleksander Skrzynski, 2006; co-editor: Wojna Polsko-Bolszewicka, 2003, Reflection on Polish Foreign Policy, 2007; contbr. articles to profl. jours.; mem. editl. bd. Slavic Rev., Internat. History Rev., Polish Rev., Polin., East European Politics and Society, Acta Poloniae Historica. Served as 2d lt. Polish Army, 1942-45. Decorated Comdr.'s Cross of Polonia Restituta; recipient Alfred Jurzykowski Found. award in history, 1977; fellow Guggenheim Found., Ford Found., Rockefeller Found., Am. Philos. Soc., Am. Coun. Learned Socs., Social Sci. Rsch. Coun., Internat. Rsch. and Exchs. Bd. Mem. AAAS (hon., Wayne Vucinich prize 1989), Am. Hist. Assn. (George Louis Beer prize 1962, 89), Polish Hist. Assn. (hon.), Polish Acad. Arts and Scis., Polish Acad. Scis., Polish Inst. Arts and Scis. (pres. 1999-2008), Polish Soc. Abroad (A. Lenkszewicz prize 1991, Oscar Halecki History award 1997), Czechoslovak Acad. of Scis. (Hlavka medal 1992, A. Gieysztor prize 2004, J. Nowak Jezioranski prize, 2006), Czechoslovak Soc. Arts and Scis. Home: 27 Spring Garden St Hamden CT 06517-1913 Office: Yale U Dept History New Haven CT 06520-8324 Office Phone: 203-432-1382. Business E-Mail: piotr.wandycz@yale.edu.

WANEBO, HAROLD J., surgeon, educator; b. Denver, Feb. 12, 1935; s. Clifford P. and JoAnn (Curtin) W.; m. Claire Anne Wanebo, Oct. 27, 1964; children: John Eric, Michael David, Jacqueline Elise. BS, Regis Coll., 1957; MD, U. Colo., 1961. Intern Cornell Med. divsn. Bellevue Hosp., N.Y., 1961-62, resident N.Y., 1962-63; surg. resident U. Calif. Med. Ctr., San Francisco, 1963-65, 67-69; fellow in tumor immunology Meml. Sloan-Kettering Cancer Ctr., N.Y., 1965-67, sr. surg. fellow N.Y., 1971-73, clin. asst. attending surgeon N.Y., 1973-74, assoc. N.Y., 1973-77, asst. attending surgeon N.Y., 1974-77, assoc. scientist N.Y., 1977-83, cons. clin. immunology svc. N.Y., 1977-90; instr. surgery Cornell U.-N.Y. Hosp. Med. Ctr., 1973-75, asst. prof. surgery, 1975-77; chief divsn. surg. oncology Med. Ctr., prof. surgery U. Va., Charlottesville, 1977-87; prof. surgery, dir. surg. oncology Brown U., Providence, R.I., 1987—; prof. surgery Boston U. Med. Sch., 2006—; editor (pelvic surgery) Clinics North Surgical, 2005. Editor: Hepatic and Biliary Cancer, 1987, Common Problems in Cancer Surgery, 1990, Colorectal Cancer, 1993, Surgery for Gastrointestinal Cancer, 1996, Surgical Clinic North America, Surgical Management Pelvic Malignancy, 2005, Surgical Clinic of North America Regional Therapy of Malignancy, 2008; numerous presentation papers to books and articles to profl. jours. Maj. U.S. Army, 1969-71, Vietnam. Decorated Bronze star; recipient Commendation medal with device. Mem. ACS, Am. Assn. Cancer Edn., Am. Assn. Cancer Rsch., Am. Assn. Immunologists, Am. Cancer Soc. (Jr. Faculty Clin. Fellowship award 1974-77), Am. Surg. Assn., Am. Soc. Clin. Oncology, Assn. Am. Vol. Physicians, Med. Soc. State of N.Y., Med. Soc. R.I., Med. Soc. Va., Nafzigger Surg. Soc., New Eng. Surg. Soc., N.Y. Acad. Scis., N.Y. Surg. Soc., Soc. Surgery of Alimentary Tract, Soc. Surg. Oncology, Soc. Univ. Surgeons, Southeastern Surg.

Congress, So. Surg. Assn., Soc. Head and Neck Surgery. Office: Landmark Med Ctr Divsn Surg Oncology 206 Cass Ave Woonsocket RI 02895 Office Phone: 401-767-1595. Business E-Mail: hwanebo@rwme.org.

WANER, MILTON, otolaryngologist, pediatric facial plastic surgeon; MD, U. Witwatersrand Med. Sch., Johannesburg, South Africa, 1977. Cert. Otolaryngology, South African Med. and Dental Coun., 1986. Resident, surgery U. Witwatersrand, Johannesburg, 1980, resident, otolaryngology, 1981—84; lectr. U. Sydney, Australia; resident, otolaryngology U. Ark. for Med. Sciences, Little Rock, 1984—85, prof. otolaryngology, 2001, dir., Laser Inst.; Benjamin and Milton Waner Endowed chair in pediat. facial plastic and reconstructive surgery Ark. Children's Hosp., Little Rock; dir. Vascular Anomalies Ctr., Ark. Children's Hosp.; fellow, otolaryngology and maxillofacial surgery U. Cin. Med. Ctr., Ohio, 1984—85; co-dir. Vascular Birthmarks Inst. NY, Beth Israel Med. Ctr. and St. Luke's-Roosevelt Hosp. Ctr. Author and co-author of several textbooks; contbr. chapters to books, med. papers. Recipient Power of One award, Vascular Birthmarks Found., Children's Miracle award, Children's Miracle Network, 2004; named one of Best Doctors, NY Mag., 2008, Top Doctors: New York Metro Area, Castle Connolly, 2008. Mem.: Am. Acad. Otolaryngology Head and Neck Surgery (award), Am. Acad. Facial Plastic and Reconstructive Surgery, Am. Soc. for Laser Medicine and Surgery (surgical rep. on bd. dirs.), British Acad. Aesthetic Plastic Surgeons (hon.). Achievements include being an internationally recognized authority on hemangiomas and vascular malformations; patents in field. Office: Vascular Birthmark Inst 126 W 60th St New York NY 10023 Office Phone: 212-636-3977. Office Fax: 212-636-3979. Business E-Mail: waner@NYHNI.org.*

WANG, ALBERT JAMES, violinist, educator; b. Ann Arbor, Mich., Nov. 19, 1958; s. James and Lydia (Ebenhoch) Wang; m. Bridget Renee Becker, June 30, 1987 (div. 2000); children: Ona Lenore, Kevin Lewis. MusB, Ind. U., 1979; MusM, U. Mich., 1981; DMA, Am. Conservatory, 1993. Prin. second violin Baton Rouge Symphony Orch., 1981-82; first violin Valcour String Quartet, Baton Rouge, 1981-82, Loyola String Quartet, 1982-83; mem. Lyric Opera Chgo. Orch., 1982—; mem. Orch. Ill., Chgo., 1982-88; prin. 2d violin Internat. Symphony Orch., Port Huron, Mich., 1984; 1st violin Internat. String Quartet, Port Huron, 1984; concertmaster, soloist Chgo. Chamber Orch., 1985-88, Chgo. Philharm., 1985—; mem. Grant Park Symphony Orch., Chgo., 1986-87; concertmaster, soloist Birch Creek Music Festival, Wis., Woodstock (Ill.) Mozart Festival Orch., 1988-90; concertmaster Rockford (Ill.) Symphony Orch., 1990-91, Northwestern Music Festival Orch., 1990—95; soloist, concertmaster Pro Musica Orch. of Mauritius, 1992-93; soloist, concertmaster China tour Classical Symphony Orch., 1994, 95; soloist, concertmaster Midwest Symphony Orch., 1995-96; music dir. Baroque Masterplayers, 1994—2007; soloist, concertmaster Met. Arts Orch., 1995-98. Artist-in-residence St. Clair Coll., Port Huron, 1984, Elgin C.C., 1994—97; lectr. Am. Conservatory Music, Chgo., 1989—92; Fulbright lectr. Francois Mitterand Conservatory of Music, Quatre Bornes, Mauritius, 1992—93; asst. prof. violin Roosevelt U., 1993—2002; adj. prof. violin Wheaton (Ill.) Coll., 1997—2000; adj. asst. prof. violin Moody Bible Inst., Chgo., 1997—2000; v.p. sales and mktg. Music Edn. Publs., Inc., Coral Springs, Fla., 1997—98. Numerous solo, recital and chamber music appearances and master classes throughout U.S., Can., France, Mauritius and China and Peru; recs. and broadcasts by Mauritian Nat. Radio and WFMT Chgo. Fine Arts Sta., PBS, Nat. Pub. Radio, and Chinese Nat. Radio and TV; numerous world premiers; recs. on New World Records and with Slavic Projection Ensemble; N.Y. recital debut at Carnegie Hall, 1998; adjudicator for state and nat. music competitions; contbr. articles and revs. to profl. jours. Vol. ARC, Literacy Vols. Am., Chgo. Pub. Librs., United Way; bd. advisors Prism Music Festival, 1984—, Am. Chamber Symphony, 1985, Symphony II, 1993-94. Fulbright grantee, 1992-93; recipient 1st prize Ann Arbor (Mich.) Symphony Competition, 1976, Soc. Am. Musicians Competition, Chgo., 1984, Internat. Concerts Atlantique Competition, N.Y.C., 1989, Chgo. Park Dist. Competition, 1991, 2nd prize Biennial Adult Artist Competition, 1992, Helmuth Fuchs Performance award 1998; selected to Arts Am. Touring Artist Roster, 1993; finalist Lilly Fellows Program in Humanities and the Arts, Valparaiso U., 1994, Harry and Sarah Zelzer Fellowship and prize; recipient Leo Sowerby medal, 1994; Christian Performing Artists' fellow. Mem. Am. Fedn. Musicians, Am. String Tchrs. Assn., Coll. Music Soc. Avocations: powerlifting, fishing, travel, woodworking. Home: 6110 N Glenwood Ave Chicago IL 60660-1804 Office: Lyric Opera Chgo 20 N Wacker Dr Chicago IL 60606-2806 Office Phone: 312-332-2244. Personal E-mail: aw_dma@hotmail.com.

WANG, ALEXANDER, apparel designer; b. San Francisco; Grad., Parsons Design Sch., NYC. Designer Alexander Wang collection, NYC, jewelry line, 2009—; launched Alexander Wang womens collection, 2007. Recipient Fashion Fund award, Coun. Fashion Designers of America, 2008, Emerging Talent award for Womenswear, 2009; nominee Swarovski Womens Wear Designer of Yr., 2008. Office: Alexander Wang Inc 386 Broadway 3rd Fl New York NY 10013 Office Phone: 212-532-3103. Office Fax: 212-532-3113.*

WANG, ANDREW HSING-JEN, marketing professional, information technology executive, journalist, librarian; b. Tainan, Taiwan, June 12, 1939; came to U.S., 1966. s. John Chin-Yuan and Ping Huang W. m. Miaw-Jen Lin Wang, Nov. 21, 1979; children: Sherry, Stanley, Jeffrey, Justina. BA in Journalism, Nat. Chengchi U., Taipei, Taiwan, 1962; MLS, Atlanta U., 1967; MBA, Ohio State U., 1984, News reporter and internat. news wire translator China Times, Taipei, Taiwan, 1964-66; head cataloging dept. St. Mary's (Md.) Coll., 1967-69; asst. univ. libr. Denison U., Granville, Ohio, 1969-76; exec. dir. Asia Pacific svcs. and new initiatives Online Computer Libr Ctr., Dublin, Ohio, 1976—2007; v.p. OCLC Asia Pacific, Dublin, 2007—. Advisor Nat. Ctrl. Libr., Taiwan, 1995-2000; master's degree examination com. mem. East China Normal U., Shanghai, 2000; cons., sr. tech. advisors recruitment UN Devel. Program Transfer of Knowledge Through Expatriate Nationals, 2002. Contbr. articles to profl. jours. Mem.: Beta Phi Mu. Office: OCLC Asia Pacific 6565 Kilgour Pl Dublin OH 43017-3395 Business E-Mail: wanga@oclc.org.

WANG, BAOLIANG (BOB WANG), applications scientist, researcher; b. Xinji, Hebei, China, Jan. 9, 1963; came to U.S., 1988; s. Yuzhuang and Shuyin (Yang) W.; m. Haiying Li, May 15, 1987; children: George, May. BS, Nankai U., 1982; PhD, U. Ill., Chgo., 1993. Lectr. Hebei Tchrs. U., 1985—88; postdoctoral rschr. U. Ill., Chgo., 1993—; sr. applications scientist, applications rsch. mgr. Hinds Instrument, Inc., Hillsboro, Oreg., 1995—. Recipient 2 R&D 100 awards. Achievements include research in polarization modulation instrumentation; investigation of vibrational Zeeman effect using magnetic vibrational circular dichroism; Fourier transform infrared-vibrational circular dichroism spectroscopy; invention of a highly sensitive birefringence measurement system known as EXICOR; measurement of optical rotation. Home: 16254 NW Joscelyn St Beaverton OR 97006-7258 Office Phone: 503-690-2000. E-mail: bwang@hindsintrument.com.

WANG, BIN, computer scientist, educator; PhD, Ohio State U., 2000. Asst. prof. Wright State U., Dayton, Ohio, 2000—05, assoc. prof., 2005—. Contbr. articles to profl. jours. Recipient Outstanding Faculty Mem., Coll. of Engring. and Computer Sci., 2004—05. Mem.: IEEE, Assn. Computing Machinery. Office: Department of Computer Science and Engr Wright State University 303 Russ Ctr Dayton OH 45435

WANG, BING, medical educator; b. Wuhan, China, Aug. 3, 1963; s. Shaoqun Wang and Yunxiu Ma; m. Ying Tang, Oct. 15, 1989; 1 child, Shiyu Sheri. MD, Tong Ji Med. U., Wuhan, 1986; PhD, Chinese Acad. Scis., Beijing, 1998. Physician in charge Tong Ji Med. U., Wuhan, China, 1991—94; assoc. prof. Inst. Virology, Chinese Acad. Scis., 1998—99; postdoc. fellow, dept. Biochemistry Hong Kong U. Sci. Tech., China, 1998—99; rsch. assoc., dept. MMG U. Pitts., 1999—2005, asst. prof., dept. orthop. surgery, 2006—; asst. prof., dept. neurology. Achievements include research in gene therapy for musculoskeletal diseases. Avocation: badminton. Office: Univ Pitts 200 Lothrop St E1642 BST Pittsburgh PA 15261 Office Fax: 412-648-8548. Business E-Mail: bingwang@pitt.edu.

WANG, BINGCHENG, oncologist, researcher; s. Xiongbin Wang and Yilan Zhang; m. Connie Wang; children: Albert Jening, Brandon. PhD, U. Wisconsin-Madison, 1991. Rsch. assoc. Burnham Inst., La Jolla, Calif., 1991—96; prof. Case Western Res. U., Cleve., 1997—, cancer rschr., 1997—. Contbr. articles to profl. jours. Grantee Heart Disease Rsch. Grant, Prostate Cancer Rsch. Found., Am. Heart Assn., 2001—04. Mem.: AACR. Achievements include patents for peptides & smalll molecules targeting eph kinases. Office: Case Western Res Univ 2500 MetroHealth Dr R421 Cleveland OH 44109

WANG, CAISHENG, engineering educator; m. Mingliu Zhang; 1 child, Harry. PhD, Mont. State U., Bozeman, 2006. Rsch. engr. Zhejiang Electric Power Test and Rsch. Inst., Hangzhou, Zhejiang, China, 1997—2001, vice dept. chair, 2001—02; asst. prof. Wayne State U., Detroit, 2002—. Contbr. articles to profl. jour. Mem.: IEEE (EDPG prize 2007). Independent. Achievements include research in fuel cell modeling. Office: Wayne State Univ 4855 4th St Detroit MI 48202 Office Fax: 313-577-1781. Business E-Mail: cwang@wayne.edu.

WANG, CECILIA CHIACHEH LOW, internist, educator; m. Michael Wang; 1 child, Maia. MD, U. Rochester, NY, 1996. Cert. Am. Bd. Internal Medicine, 2000, in endocrinology, metabolism and diabetes 2002. Staff physician Denver VA Med. Ctr., 2002—; instr. medicine, health scis. ctr. U. Colo., Denver, 2003—04, asst. prof. medicine Aurora, 2004—, assoc. dir., fellowship edn., Denver sch. medicine, 2007—. Mem., trainee devel. com. Endocrine Soc., Chevy Chase, Md., 2003—07, mem., sci. and ednl. programs core com., 2007. Recipient Assoc. Investigator award, Dept. Vets. Affairs Office R&D, 2002—04, Rsch. Career Devel. award, 2004—07, Career Devel. award, 2007—; Clin. Scholars fellowship, Diabetes Trust Found., 2004—05. Mem.: ACP, Am. Diabetes Assn., Endocrine Soc. (com. mem. 2003). Achievements include research in vascular cell biology. Office: Denver VA Med Ctr 1055 Clermont St 111H Denver CO 80220

WANG, CHARLES B., professional sports team executive, former computer company executive; b. Shanghai, Rep. China, Aug. 19, 1944; arrived in U.S., 1952; BS in Math., Queens Coll., 1967. Programming trainee Columbia U. Riverside Rsch. Inst., Islandia, NY; v.p. sales Std. Data Corp.; CEO Computer Assocs., Islandia, 1976—2000, chmn., 1980—2002, chmn. emeritus; owner, CEO NY Islanders, Uniondale, 1999—, Bridgeport Sound Tigers; co-owner NY Dragons (arena football). Author: Techno Vision, 1994, Techno Vision II: Every Executive's Guide to Understanding and Mastering Technology and the Internet, 1997. Founder The Smile Train; active Nat. Ctr. for Missing and Exploited Children, Make-A-Wish Found. Avocations: cooking, basketball. Office: NY Islanders Nassau Veterans Meml Coliseum 1255 Hempstead Turnpike Uniondale NY 11553

WANG, CHARLES PING, engineering executive; b. Shanghai, Apr. 25, 1937; came to U.S., 1962; s. Kuan-Ying and Ping-Lu (Ming) W.; m. Lily L. Lee, June 29, 1963. BS, Taiwan U., Republic of China, 1959; MS, Tsinghua U., Singchu, Republic of China, 1961; PhD, Calif. Inst. Tech., 1967. Mem. tech. staff Bellcomm, Washington, 1967-69; research engr. U. San Diego, 1969-74; sr. scientist Aerspace Corp., Los Angeles, 1976-86; pres. Optodyne, Inc., Compton, Calif., 1986—. Adj. prof. U. Calif., San Diego, 1979-90; pres. Chinese-Am. Engr. and Scientists Assn. So. Calif., LA, 1979-81; program chmn. Internation Conf. of Lasers, Shanghai, 1979-80; organizer and session chmn. Lasers Conf., LA, 1981-84, program chmn., Las Vegas, 1985. Editor in chief Series in Laser Tech., 1983-91; contbr. articles to profl. jours. Calif. Inst. Tech. scholar, 1965. Fellow Am. Optical Soc., AIAA (assoc., jour. editor 1981-83). Achievements include invention of discharge excimer laser and laser vector method for 3D volumetric positioning measurement. Office: Optodyne Inc 1180 W Mahalo Pl Compton CA 90220-5443 Office Phone: 310-635-7481. Personal E-mail: optodyne@aol.com.

WANG, CHEN CHI, electronics, real estate and diversified financial services company executive; b. Taipei, Taiwan, Aug. 10, 1932; came to U.S., 1959, naturalized, 1970; s. Chin-Ting and Chen-Kim Wang; m. Victoria Rebisoff, Mar. 5, 1965; children: Katherine Kim, Gregory Chen, John Christopher, Michael Edward. BA in Econs., Nat. Taiwan U., 1955; BSEE, San Jose State U., 1965; MBA, U. Calif., Berkeley, 1961. With IBM Corp., San Jose, Calif., 1965-72; founder, CEO Electronics Internat. Co., Santa Clara, Calif., 1968-72, owner, gen. mgr., 1972-81; reorganized as EIC Group, 1981-2000; chmn. bd., CEO EIC Investment Corp., 1982—2004; dir. Systek Electronics Corp., Santa Clara, 1970-73; founder, sr. ptnr. Wang Enterprises (name changed to Chen Kim Enterprises 1982), Santa Clara, 1974-75, Hanson & Wang Devel. Co., Woodside, Calif., 1977-85; chmn. bd. Golden Alpha Enterprises, San Mateo, Calif., 1979-99; mng. ptnr. Woodside Acres-Las Pulgas Estate, Woodside, 1980-85; founder, sr. ptnr. DeVine & Wang, Oakland, Calif., 1977-83, Van Heal & Wang, West Village, Calif., 1981-82; founder, chmn. bd. EIC Fin. Corp. (now EIC Investment Corp.), Redwood City, Calif., 1985-90; chmn. bd. Maritek Corp., Corpus Christi, Tex., 1988-89; chmn. EIC Internat. Trade Corp., Lancaster, Calif., 1989-90, EIC Capital Corp., Redwood City, 1990-91. Mng. mem. Sixtieth West, LLC, 1997—2004, Land Investment Co. Calif., LLC, 1998—, Aceh Capital, LLC, 1998—, Ameriland Capital, LLC, 2008—. Author: Monetary and Banking System of Taiwan, 1955, The Small Car Market in the U.S., 1961. Mem. nat. adv. coun. Brigham Young U. 2d lt. Nationalist Chinese Army, 1955—56. Mem. Internat. Platform Assn., Tau Beta Pi. Mem. Christian Ch. Home: 195 Brookwood Rd Woodside CA 94062-2302 Office: ACE Group Head Office Bldg 2055-2075 Woodside Rd Redwood City CA 94061-3355 Office Phone: 650-364-3330. Business E-Mail: cwang@ace4wealth.com.

WANG, CHEN-KU, retired library director; b. Peiping, China, July 18, 1924; s. Bing-fong Wang and Fong-gen Hsia; m. Shuo-fen Wang, Aug. 15, 1946; children: Pei-chi, Sheng-shiang, Sheng-Wen. MA, Peabody Coll. Tchrs., 1959; LLD (hon.), Ohio U., 1988. Prof. Nat. Taiwan Normal U., Taipei, 1960-94; dir. Nat. Ctrl. Libr. Republic of China, 1977-89, ret., 1994. Dir. Ctr. for Chinese Studies, 1977—89. Author: Selection and Acquisition of Library Materials, 1978; hon. editor Jour. Libr. and Info. Sci., 1975—. Decorated knight comdr. Silvestri, Vatican; recipient Disting. Svc. award Chinese-Am. Libr. Assn.and Libr. Assn. Republic of China, 1986, 87. Mem. Libr. Assn. Republic of China (pres. 1992-97, hon. pres. 2003-08).

WANG, CHIH, retired librarian, educator; s. Yung-Hsin and Ai-Chu Wang; m. Kwei-Yung Liu, Feb. 1, 1941; children: Marianne, Henry. PhD in Libr. Sci., U. Pitts., 1988. Asst. libr. to libr. Atlanta U. SLIS, 1972—87; pub. svc. libr. Asnuntuck CC, Enfield, Conn., 1987—89; dean and prof. Learning Resources U. Guam, Mangilao, 1989—99, east Asian libr./prof. Learning Resources, 1999—2006, prof. emeritus libr. sci. Officer Republic of China Army, Taiwan, 1950—70. Author: (monograph) Thirty-Years' Practice in Libraries, Micronesian Libraries, Patches of Light Clouds, Government of Guam: 1981-1996. Founding mem. Atlanta Chinese Christian Ch., 1972—2009, Guam Chinese Christian Ch., Mangilao, 1989—2005. Maj. ROC Army, 1950—70, Taiwan, China. Decorated Gold medal for Outstanding Svcs. Pres., Republic of China, Silver medal for Outstanding Svcs. Min., Nat. Def., Republic of China. Mem.: Chinese ALA. Achievements include installing and implementing library automation system at University of Guam in 1993, linking the University with the world; initiated and implemented Guam Governor's Conference on Library and Information Services. Office: U Guam Learning Resources Mangilao GU 96923 Office Fax: 671-734-6882. Business E-Mail: cwang@uguam.uog.edu.

WANG, DAVID, finance educator; BBA, Feng Chia U., Taiwan, 1994; MS in Bus. Adminstrn., San Francisco State U., 2000; D of Bus. Adminstrn., Golden Gate U., 2003. Adj. prof. of fin. Golden Gate U., San Francisco, Calif., 2002—04; asst. prof. of fin. Hsuan Chuang U., Hsinchu, Taiwan, 2004—, dir. of academic program devel., 2004—05. Internat. affairs com. mem. Decision Sciences Inst., 2005—; editl. adv. bd. mem. Internat. Rsch. Jour. of Fin. and Economics, 2005—, Internat. Bull. of Bus. Adminstrn., 2005—; cons. Info. Ctr. on Schools Abroad, Taipei Pub. Libr., Taiwan, 2005—. Author: (journal article) Journal of Academy of Business and Economics, Vol. 5, No. 2, pp. 53-61, Journal of American Academy of Business, Cambridge, Vol. 6, No. 1, pp. 272-277 (Best Author Award, 2005), Corporate Finance Review, Vol. 9, No. 3, pp. 33-38, Journal of Academy of Business and Economics, Vol. 3, No. 1, pp. 79-86, Journal of American Academy of Business, Cambridge, Vol. 5, No. 1&2, pp. 203-209. Recipient Rsch. Award, Hsuan Chuang U., Taiwan, 2005, Tutoring Award, 2005; grantee Rsch. Grant, 2004-2005, 2005-2006, Nat. Sci. Coun., Taiwan, 2004-2005. Mem.: Taiwan Fin. Assn., Fin. Engring. Assn. of Taiwan, Internat. Assn. of Fin. Engineers, Decision Sciences Inst., Global Assn. of Risk Professionals, Assn. for Fin. Professionals, Fin. Mgmt. Assn. Internat., Am. Fin. Assn. Achievements include research in Author of several journal articles in the field of financial engineering. Office: Hsuan Chuang University 48 Hsuan Chuang Road Hsinchu 300 Taiwan Office Fax: 886-3-5391235. E-mail: dwang@hcu.edu.tw.

WANG, DI, historian; married. PhD, Johns Hopkins U., Balt., 1998. Assoc. prof. Sichuan U., Chengdu, China, 1987—91; asst. prof. Tex. A&M U., Coll. Sta., 1998—2003, assoc. prof., 2004—08, prof., 2008—. Author: (book) Kuachu fengbi de shijie: Changjiang shangyu quyu she hui yanjiu, 1644-1911, 1993, Street Culture in Chengdu: Public Space, Urban Commoners, and Local Politics, 1870-1930, 2003 (Best Book award, Urban History Assn., 2006); editor: Shijian, Kongjian, Shuxie: Xin shehui shi, 2006; author: The Teahouse: Small Business, Everyday Culture, and Public Politics in Chengdu, 1900-1950, 2008. Fellow, Sun Yat-sen Culture and Edn. Found., Taiwan, 1998; Nat. Endowment Humanities grant, Am. Coun. Learned Soc., 2002, Bernadotte E. Schmitt grant, Am. Hist. Assn., 2004, grant, Japan Soc. Promotion Sci., 2004, NEH fellowship, Nat. Humanities Ctr., 2006. Fellow: Inst. Internat. Rsch., Hopkins-Nanjing Ctr.; mem.: Chinese Historians US (pres. 2003—05). Office: Tex A&M Univ Dept History College Station TX 77843-4236 Office Fax: 979-862-4314. Business E-Mail: di-wang@tamu.edu.

WANG, ER-JIA, drug safety researcher; m. Hong Song; children: Andrew R., Shirley. MD, BengBu Med. Coll., Anhui, China, 1982; postdoc. in Toxicology, Rutgers U., Piscataway, NJ. Med. cert. 1996. Resident, attending anesthesiologist Xiehe Hosp. Tongji Med. U., Wuhan, China, 1991; sr. scientist, dept. drug medicine Rhone-Poulenc, 1996—98; sr. scientist Schering-Plough Rsch. Inst., Summit, NJ, 2003—07, sr. drug safety rschr., 2008—. Contbr. articles to profl. jours. Achievements include research in mechanistic investigation of cellular or organ toxicology, drug metabolism and transporters, toxigenomics and biomarker evaluation; patents in field of pharmaceutical therapeutics. Office: Schering-Plough Research Inst 556 Morris Ave Summit NJ 07901 Business E-Mail: erjia.wang@spcorp.com.

WANG, FEI, pharmacist, educator; d. Ke-Chiang and Iok Meng Lee Wang; m. Cunegundo Manuel Vergara; children: Leander Vergara, Chiu Yen Vergara. BS in Pharmacy, St. John's U., Jamaica, NY, 1983, MS in Pharmacy, 1994, PharmD, 1996. Cert. pharmacotherapy specialist Am. Pharm. Assn., DC, 1998, smoking cessation specialist Nat. Smoking Cessation Program, U. Pitts., 1998. Cmty. pharmacist Genovese Drug Stores, Inc., Fort Lee, NJ, 1983—84, supervising pharmacist Astoria, NY, 1985—90; hosp. pharmacist Cornell Med. Ctr., NY Hosp., NYC, 1990—93, target drug clin. coord., 1993—95; specialty residency in adult internal medicine Med. U. SC, Charleston, 1996—97, clin. pharmacist in surgery & trauma, 1996—97; clin. specialist in ambulatory care Hartford Hosp., Conn., 1997—. Adj. preceptor St. John's U., NYH-CMC, 1993—94; adj. instr. Med. U. SC, 1996—97; clin. preceptor U. Conn., 1997—2005, asst. clin. prof. Sch. Pharmacy, 1997—, dir. ambulatory care residency and fellowship program, 2001—; presenter in field; lectr. in field. Contbr. articles to profl. jours. Grant, Hartford Hosp. & Boehringer Ingelheim, 2002—05. Mem.: Conn. Soc. Health Sys. Pharmacists, Am. Soc. Health Sys. Pharmacists, Am. Coll. Clin. Pharmacy. Office: U Conn Dept Pharmacy Practice 69 North Eagleville Rd Unit 3092 Storrs Mansfield CT 06269-3092 Business E-Mail: fwang@harthosp.org.

WANG, FEI, research scientist; s. Zudian Wang and Xiaoying Li; m. Lin Sun, Dec. 19, 2003. PhD, U. Fla., Gainesville, 2006. Rsch. staff mem. IBM Almaden Rsch. Ctr., San Jose, Calif., 2006—. Recipient Best Poster award, Computers Cardiology, Bologna, Italy., 2008, IBM Invention Achievement award, 2008. Mem.: IEEE (mem. 2002—), IEEE Computer Soc. (CVPR Travel grant 2006), Sigma Xi. Office: IBM Almaden Rsch Ctr 650 Harry Rd San Jose CA 95120

WANG, FREDERICK MARK, pediatrician, ophthalmologist, educator; b. NYC, Feb. 17, 1948; Student, Northwestern U., 1968; MD, Yeshiva U., 1972. Diplomate Am. Bd. Ophthalmology, Am. Bd. Pediats., Nat. Bd. Med. Examiners. Intern in pediats. H.C. Moffitt-U. Calif. San Francisco Hosps., 1972-73; resident in pediats. Bronx Mcpl. Hosp. Ctr.-Albert Einstein Coll. Medicine, 1973-74, resident in ophthalmology, 1976-79; Heed fellow in ophthalmology and strabismus Children's

Hosp. Nat. Med. Ctr., Washington, 1979-80; asst. prof. ophthalmology Albert Einstein Coll. Medicine, Bronx, 1980-82, asst. clin. prof., 1982-85, assoc. clin. prof., 1985-95, clin. prof., 1995—, asst. prof. pediats., 1980-82, asst. clin. prof. pediats., 1982-92; dir. pediat. ophthalmology and strabismus svc. Montefiore Med. Ctr., Bronx, 1980-90. Cons. ophthalmologist Children's Evaluation & Rehab. Ctr., Rose Kennedy Ctr. for Rsch. in Mental Retardation and Human Devel., Bronx, 1980—, Craniofacial Ctr., Montefiore Med. Ctr., Bronx, 1980—; attending physician in ophthalmology Bronx Mcpl. Hosp./Montefiore Med. Ctr., 1980—; asst. attending physician in ophthalmology North Ctrl. Bronx Hosp., 1980-98; attending physician Strabismus Svc., N.Y. Eye & Ear Infirmary, N.Y.C., 1982-99, attending surgeon, 1999—; mem. dept. ophthalmology Lenox Hill Hosp., N.Y.C., 1988—; sci. reviewer Jour. Am. Acad. Ophthalmology, 1980-86; mem. profl. adv. bd. Found. for Children with Learning Disabilities, N.Y.C., 1983-89; mem. sci. adv. bd. The Glaucoma Found., N.Y.C., 1986-92; mem. profl. adv. bd. Nat. Assn. for Visually Handicapped, N.Y.C., 1988—; coord. pediat. sect. Greater N.Y. Ophthalmology Clin. Lectr. Series, 1990-93; mem. Velo-Cardio-Facial Syndrome Ednl. Found., 1994—, nominating com., 1995—. Mem. editl. bd. Jour. Pediat. Ophthalmology and Strabismus, 1998—; contbr. articles to profl. jours., chpts. to books. Referee, U.S. Soccer Fedn. Maj. med. officer USAF, 1974-76. Mem. Am. Acad. Pediats., Am. Acad. Ophthalmology, Am. Assn. for Pediat. Ophthalmology and Strabismus, N.Y. Soc. for Pediat. Ophthalmology and Strabismus (program chmn. 1987-89, pres. 1990-92), N.Y. Soc. for Clin. Ophthalmology (corr. sec. 1988-90, membership chmn. 1990-91, program chmn. 1991-92, pres. 1992-93), N.Y. Acad. Medicine (sec. sect. on ophthalmology 1993-94, sect. chmn. 1995-96), Alpha Omega Alpha. Avocations: fishing, chess, swimming, soccer refereeing. Office: Pediat Ophthalmology NY 30 E 40th St New York NY 10016-1201 Home Phone: 914-723-7122; Office Phone: 212-684-3980.

WANG, GONGYAO, materials scientist; PhD, U. Tenn., Knoxville. Cert. MTS Co., Minn., 2004. Rsch. assoc. U. Tenn., 2007—; mgr. Shanghai Huazhong software devel. Co., Shanghai, 1996—2001. Author: (book) Bulk Metallic Glasses; contbr. articles to profl jours. Recipient Outstanding Grad. Rsch. asst., UTK Coll. Engring., 2004. Mem.: Minerals, Metals, & Materials Soc.

WANG, GUANGYA, ambassador; b. Jiangsu Province, China, Apr. 1950; married; 1 child. Studied, Student Ctr. of British Coun., Wales Atlantic Untied Coll. and London Sch. Econ. and Polit. Sci., United Kingdom of Great Britain and Northern Ireland, 1972—75, John Hopkins U., 1981—82. Sect. mem., dept. of translation and interpretation Ministry of Foreign Affairs, 1975—77, third sec. and then dep. divsn. chief, dept. internat. orgns. and conf., 1983—88, counselor and then dep. dir., dept. internat. orgns. and conf., 1992—93, dir., dept. of internat. orgns. and conf., 1993—98, asst. min. foreign affairs, 1998—99, vice min. foreign affairs, 1999—2003; staff mem. to attache Chinese Mission to UN, 1977—81, attache, 1982—83, counselor, 1988—92, amb. and perm. rep, 2003—08. Office: 350 East 35th St New York NY 10016 Office Phone: 212-655-6100, 212-655-6191. Office Fax: 212-634-7626, 212-481-2998.

WANG, GWO JAW, orthopedic surgery educator; Lillian T. Pratt prof. and chmn. orthopedic surgery U. Va. Sch. Medicine, Charlottesville, 1992—2000; pres. Kaohsiung Med. U., Taiwan, 2000—06; prof. emeritus Nat. Cheng-Kung U., 2008—, U. Va., 2009—. Vis. prof. orthop. surgery Kaohsiung Med. U., Taiwan, 2006—. Recipient U. Va. Pres.'s Report award, 1992, Otto Aufranc award, Hip Soc. and Am. Acad. Orthop. Surgeons, 1992, 1997, Stinchfield award, 1986, Nicholas Andry award, 1998, Va. career award, Va. Orthop. Soc., 2007. Office: Kaohsiung Med Univ 100 Shih Chuan 1st Rd Kaohsiung Taiwan Home Phone: 886-7-537-1179; Office Phone: 886-7-3121101 ext.5390. Business E-Mail: gwojaw@cc.kmu.edu.tw.

WANG, HAIBIN, systems administrator, consultant; b. Lianyungang, Jiangsu, China, Jan. 1, 1971; s. Jinhui and Yizhi Wang; m. Yihui Ji; children: Velda Shu, Sarah Yue. PhD, Ga. State U., Atlanta, 2005. Cert. in oracle 10g profl. 2007. Grad. tchg. asst. Ga. State U., Atlanta, 2000—05; database adminstr. Winship Cancer Inst., Atlanta, 2005—07, sr. database adminstr., 2007—. Database cons. Cedar Sinai, LA, 2009—. Contbr. articles to profl. jours.

WANG, HAIQIN, computer scientist; BS, U. Sci. & Tech. China, Hefei, Anhui, 1992; MS, Inst. Automation, Chinese Acad. Sci., Beijing, 1996; PhD, U. Pitts., 2004. Software engr. Inst. Automation, Chinese Acad. Sci., Beijing, 1992—94; advanced computing technologist Boeing Co., Seattle, 2001—. Mem.: IEEE, Inc., Assn. Computing Machinery, Assn. Advancement Artificial Intelligence.

WANG, HAOBIN, chemistry professor; b. Nanjing, Jiangsu, China, June 2, 1968; s. Jianmin Wang and Suzhen Hu; m. Qiao Fan; 1 child, Jerry Frank. BS, U. Sci. and Tech. China, Hefei, Anhui, 1991; PhD, Wayne State U., Detroit, 1996. Postdoc. assoc. U. Calif., Berkeley, 1996—2001; asst. prof. N.Mex State U., Las Cruces, 2001—06, assoc. prof., 2006—. Recipient Career award, NSF, 2004—. Mem.: Am. Chem. Soc. Home: 655 Stone Canyon Dr Las Cruces NM 88011 Office: N Mex State Univ Dept Chemistry and Biochemistry Las Cruces NM 88003 Office Fax: 575-646-2649. Business E-Mail: haobin@nmsu.edu.

WANG, HONGQING, ecologist, educator; married; children: Anna Q., Emma Y. PhD, SUNY Coll. Environ. Sci., Syracuse, 2001. Rsch. assoc. U. Md., Balt., 2001—04, Fla. A&M U., Tallahassee, 2004—07; asst. prof. rsch. U. La., Lafayette, 2007—. Fellowship, LTER-LUQ, NSF & USFS, 1997. Mem.: Sigma Xi, The Sci. Rsch. Soc., Internat. Assn. Landscape Ecology, ASPRS: The Imaging & Geospatial Info. Soc., Internat. Soc. Ecol. Modeling, Am. Geophys. Union, Ecol. Soc. Am. Achievements include research in climate, soil carbon & forest productivity in Luquillo Exsperimental Forest, Puerto Rico; long-term biogeochemical changes in China's anthropogenic landscapes; physical & ecological models for stress-response simulations of the apalachicola bay regional ecosystem; hydrodynamic & water quality modeling for the Loxahatchee refuge — everglades, Florida. Home: 249 Ivory St Lafayette LA 70506

WANG, HUAIHYU, philosopher, educator; PhD in Philosophy, Penn State U., Univ. Pk., 2006. Asst. prof. Ga. Coll. & State U., Milledgeville, 2008—. Contbr. articles to profl. jours. Office: Georgia Coll & State Univ Po Box 111 Milledgeville GA 31061 Business E-Mail: huaiyu.wang@gcsu.edu.

WANG, IGNATIUS CHUNG, bishop emeritus; b. Beijing, Feb. 27, 1934; arrived in US, 1974, naturalized; JCD, Urban U., Rome. Ordained priest, Hong Kong, 1959; parish priest, vicar general Diocese of St. George, Grenada, 1962—74; with Archdiocese of San Francisco, 1974—, coord. Chinese Apostolate, 1981; pastor St. Francis of Assisi, San Francisco, 1982—92; named monsignor, 1989; dir. Soc. for the Propagation of the Faith Archdiocese of San Francisco, 1994—2002, chancellor, 1998—2002; ordained bishop, 2003; aux. bishop Archdiocese of San Francisco, 2003—09, aux. bishop emeritus, 2009—. Roman Catholic. Achievements include first to becoming first US bishop of Asian ancestry. Office: Roman Cath Archdiocese of San Francisco 1 Peter Yorke Way San Francisco CA 94109 Office Phone: 415-614-5500. E-mail: wangi@sfarchdiocese.org.*

WANG, JAW-KAI, bioengineering educator; b. Nanjing, Jiangsu, China, Mar. 4, 1932; arrived in U.S., 1955; s. Shuling and Hsi-Ying (Lo) W.; m. Kwang Mei Chow, Sept. 7, 1957 (div. Oct. 1989); children: Angela C.C., Dora C.C., Lawrence C.Y.; m. Bichuan Li, Sept. 25, 1999. BS, Nat. Taiwan U., 1953; MS in Agrl. Engring., Mich. State U., 1956, PhD, 1958. Registered profl. engr., Hawaii. Faculty agrl. engring. dept. U. Hawaii, Honolulu, 1959-93, assoc. prof., chmn. dept. agrl. engring., 1964-68, prof., chmn. dept. agrl. engring., 1968-75, prof. biosys. engring., 1994—2000, prof. molecular bioscis. dept., 2000—02; prof. emeritus U. Hawaii-Manoa, Honolulu, 2004—, dir. Aquaculture Program, 1990-96; spl. asst., Internat. Rsch. Dept., Office of Internat. Cooperation and Devel. U.S. Dept. Agr., 1988; pres. Aquaculture Tech., Inc., 1990—; academic cons. Chinese Acad. Fishery Scis., 2004—, chief sci. advisor, fishery, machinery and instrument rsch. inst., 2004—, chief tech. expert, rsch. inst. fisheries machinery and instrument, 2005—, mem. nat. open lab. for control of aquaculture water quality, 2005—. Co-dir. internat. sci. and edn. coun. USDA; vis. assoc. dir. internat. programs and studies office Nat. Assn. State Univs. and Land-Grant Colls., 1979; vis. prof. Nat. Taiwan U., 1964-65, 2000-01, U. Calif., Davis, 1980; hon. prof. coll. pharmacology Tianjing U., China, 2003; cons. U.S. Army Civilian Adminstrn., Ryukus, Okinawa, 1965, Internat. Rice Rsch. Inst., Philippines, 1971, Pacific Concrete and Rock Co. Ltd., 1974, AID, 1974, Universe Tankships, Del., 1980-81, World Bank, 1981, 82, ABA Internat., 1981-85, Internat. Found. for Agrl. Devel./World Bank, 1981, Rockefeller Found., 1980, Orizaba, Inc., 1983, Agrisys./FAO, 1983, Info. Processing Assocs., 1984, County of Maui, 1984, 85, Dept. of State, 1985, Alexander and Baldwin, 1986; mem. expert panel on agrl. mechanization FAO/UN, 1984-90; sr. fellow East-West Ctr. Food Inst., 1973-74; dir. Info. Sys. and Svcs. Internat., Inc., 1986-90; mem. bd. on agr. and natural resources The Nat. Acads., 2004—; panel mem. Vietnam Edn. Found., 2004-06; acad. cons. Chinese Acad. Fishery Scis., 2004-06; mem. bd. agrl. and natural resources Nat. Acads., 2004-06. Author: Irrigated Rice Production Systems, 1980; editor: Taro-A Review of Colocasia Esculenta and its Potentials, 1983; mem. editl. bd. Aquacultural Engring., 1982—. Recipient Exemplary State Employee award State of Hawaii, 1986, State of Hawaii Disting. Svc. award Office of Gov., 1990. Fellow Am. Soc. Agrl. Engrs. (chmn. Hawaii sect. 1962-63, chmn. grad. instrn. com. 1971-73, various coms., Engr. of Yr. 1976, Tech. Paper award 1978, Kishida Internat. award 1991), Am. Inst. Med. and Biol. Engring.; mem. NAE, Aquaculture Engring. Soc. (pres. 1993-95), Sigma Xi, Gamma Sigma Delta (pres. Hawaii chpt. 1974-75), Pi Mu Epsilon. Office: U Hawaii MBBE Dept 1955 East West Rd Honolulu HI 96822 Home Phone: 808-377-5087; Office Phone: 808-956-8154. Personal E-mail: jawkai@gmail.com. Business E-Mail: jawkai@hawaii.edu. *To be allowed a continuing search for truth even when you are doubting its existence, is to be blessed.*

WANG, JEFFREY C., surgeon; b. Mitchell, SD, July 30, 1965; s. YuSan and Linda Wang; m. Christina Jennet Lee, June 28, 1992; children: Christopher Jeffrey, Benjamin Jeffrey. BS, Stanford U., Calif., 1987; MD, U. Pitts., 1991. Chief spine surgery UCLA Comprehensive Spine Ctr., 1997—. Office: UCLA Comprehensive Spine Center 1250 16th Street Suite 745 Santa Monica CA 90404 Office Phone: 310-319-3334. Office Fax: 310-319-5055.

WANG, JIAN, medical researcher, educator; arrived in US, 2001, permanent resident; s. Zhenshan Wang and Yafang Cui; m. Haiyang Jiang, Aug. 12, 1962; children: Elizabeth, Sabrina. MD, Inner Mongolia Med. Coll., China, 1985, MS in Urology and Physiology, 1994; PhD in Physiology, U. Western Ont., Can., 2002. Postdoc. fellow Med. Rsch. Coun. Can., 1999; rsch. assoc. Johns Hopkins U., Balt., 2002—04, instr. medicine, 2004—07, asst. prof., 2007—. Jour. peer reviewer: Circulation Rsch., 2003—; contbr. numerous sci. papers to profl. pubs. Recipient Best Paper award, Chinese Soc. Urology 1992, 1992, Excellent Scientist award, Directory Contemporary Chinese Scientists, 1993, Jr. Faculty award, Dept. Medicine Johns Hopkins U., 2003, Scientist Devel. award, 2007; grantee, NIH, 2006—, 2008, Am. Lung Assn., 2007—. Mem.: Am. Heart Assn., Am. Thoracic Soc., Am. Physiology Soc. (New Investigator award 2006). Achievements include patents for modified method of primary culture of human distal pulmonary arterial smooth muscle cells; modified method of primary culture of rat distal pulmonary endothelium cells. Avocations: football, tennis, running. Office: Johns Hopkins U Sch Medicine 5501 Hopkins Bayview Cir Rm 4B30 Baltimore MD 21224 Office Fax: 410-550-2612.

WANG, JIN, engineering educator; PhD, U. Tex., Austin, 2004. Registered profl. engr., Tex., 2005. Devel. engr. II Advanced Micro Devices, Inc., Austin, 2002—04, sr. devel. engr., 2004—06; asst. prof. Auburn U., Ala., 2006—. Contbr. articles to profl. jours. Recipient Ralph E. Powe Jr. Faculty Enhancement award, Oak Ridge Assoc. U., 2008. Achievements include 11 granted patents by USPTO.

WANG, JING, lawyer; BA in Economics, Shanghai Maritime Univ., 1982, Sun Yat-sen U., 1984, S. China Indsl. & Engring. U., 1985. Lic.: China 1987. With COSCO Guangzhou, 1982—90; pvt. practice atty., 1990—; founder, mng. ptnr. Wang Jing & Co, 1994—. Arbitrator China Maritime Arbitration Commn., 2002. Named AsiaLaw Leading Lawyer, 2004—07; named one of Hot 100 Lawyers in Asia, Asian Legal Bus. Mag., 2005. Mem.: All China Lawyer Assn. (exec. maritime com. 2006), Guangdong Lawyers Assn. (chmn. maritime com. 2003), China Maritime Law Assn. (dir. 1996). Avocation: languages. Office: Wang Jing & Co 14th Fl S Tower World Trade Ctr 371-375 Huanshi E Rd Guangzhou China Office Phone: (+86 20) 8760 0082. Business E-Mail: info@wjnco.com, wangjing@wjnco.com.

WANG, JINLIN, chemical engineer; b. Beijing, Apr. 12, 1957; s. Longji Wang and Enting Cai; m. Lifu Jiang, Mar. 15, 1986; children: Yuhong, John Yuming. BSE, Beijing Inst. Chem. Tech., 1982; PhD in Chem. Engring., Purdue U., 1995. Postdoctoral fellow Bisco Inc., Itasca, Ill., 1996—97; rsch. chemist Cargill Inc., Wayzata, Minn., 1997—98; sr. materials analyst Intel Corp., Chandler, Ariz., 1998—. Presenter in field. Contbr. articles to profl. jours. Mem.: The Soc. of Rheology. Achievements include research in packaging materials and processes developments for microelectronic packages, especially flip chip packaging technology; rheology and wettability of packaging materials; solder joint reliability; metrology developments; patents in field. Avocations: reading, table tennis. Office: Intel Corp CH5-232 5000 W Chandler Blvd Chandler AZ 85226 Business E-Mail: jinlin.wang@intel.com.

WANG, JOHN CHENG HWAI, communications engineer, researcher; b. Beijing, Feb. 12, 1934; s. Hwa Lung and Shu Shiang (Shia) W.; m. Rosa Jenny Chu, Sept. 9, 1967; children: Sophia, Maria, Nina, Amy. BS, U. Md., 1959; MS, U. Pitts., 1968. Engr. Chesapeake Instrument Corp., Shadyside, Md., 1959-64; rsch. scientist Rsch. Ctr. U.S. Steel Corp., Monroeville, Pa., 1964-67; asst. prof. Pa. State U., New Kensington, 1967-69; rsch. engr. FCC, Washington, 1969—. Cmn. working party ionospheric propogation, Internat. Telecom. Union (ITU), Geneva, 1983-. Contbr. articles to profl. jours. Fellow IEEE. Avocations: astronomy, bridge, Chinese history. Office: FCC 445 12 St SW Washington DC 20554-0001 Office Phone: 202-418-2435. Business E-Mail: john.wang@fcc.gov.

WANG, JOSEPHINE L. FEN, physician; b. Taiwan, China, Jan 2, 1948; came to U.S., 1974; d. Pao-San and Ann-Nam (Chen) Chao; m. Chang-Yang Wang, Dec. 20, 1973; children: Edward, Eileen. MD, Nat. Taiwan U., Taipei, 1974. Diplomate Am. Bd. Pediatrics, Am. Bd. Allergy and Immunology. Intern Nat. Taiwan U. Hosp., 1973-74; resident U. Ill. Hosp., Chgo., 1974-76; fellow Northwestern U. Med. Ctr., Chgo., 1976-78, instr. pediatrics, 1978—; cons. Holy Cross Hosp., Chgo., 1978—, Meth. Hosp. Ind., 1979—, St. Anthony Hosp., 1985—, Christ Hosp., 1995—. Fellow Am. Coll. Allergy; mem. AMA, Am. Acad. Allergy. Office: 9012 Connecticut Dr Merrillville IN 46410-7170 also: 4901 W 79th St Burbank IL 60459-1554 Office Phone: 708-425-1320, 219-769-6177.

WANG, JUE, veterinarian, educator; MS, SuZhou Med. Coll., China, 1990, MS, 1993. Diplomate Am. Bd. Internal Medicine, 2005, oncology 2007, lic. physician Nebr., 2007. Asst. prof. U. Nebr. Med. Ctr., Omaha, 2007—, attending physician, dept. vet. affairs, 2008—. Reviewer Jour. Infection, Kidlington, Conn., 2003—, Oxford, 2003—, Med. Prins. and Practice, Farmington, Conn., 2006—, Expert Rev. Respiratory Medicine, London, 2008—, Expert Rev. Anticancer Therapy, London, 2008—. Office: Univ Nebr Med Ctr 987680 Nebr Med Ctr Omaha NE 68198-7680 Office Fax: 402-559-6520. Business E-Mail: juewang@unmc.edu.

WANG, JULIAN XL, research scientist; s. Sugeng Wang and Yune Shen; m. Hualan Rui, Feb. 28, 1983; children: Jeffrey Y., Jennifer J. BS, Nanjing U. Info. Sci. & Tech., China, 1982; MS, U. Hawaii, Honolulu, 1986, PhD, 1988. Postdoc. rsch. scientist U. Md., Coll. Pk., Md., 1988—90; rsch. scientist NOAA Climate Prediction Ctr., Camp Spring, Md., 1990—98; sr. rsch. scientist NOAA Air Resources Lab., Silver Spring, 1998—. Office: NOAA Air Resources Lab 1315 East West Hwy Silver Spring MD 20910 Home Phone: 410-418-9584; Office Phone: 301-713-0295. Office Fax: 301-713-0119. E-mail: julian.wang@noaa.gov.

WANG, JUN, process engineer, materials scientist; s. Youfa Wang and Yulian Chen; m. Wenyun Yang, Dec. 23, 2002; 1 child, Barry K. BS, U. Sci. and Tech. China, Hefei, 1996; MS, Shanghai Inst. Ceramics, China, 1999; PhD, Pa. State U., University Park, 2004; MBA, U. Mass., Amherst, 2009. Adj. rsch. assoc. Pa. State U. Material Rsch. Inst., University Park, 2004—06; sr. rsch. engr. Saint-Gobain HPM Northboro R&D Ctr., Northboro, Mass., 2004—. Contbr. articles to profl. jours. Mem.: IEEE, Am. Chem. Soc., Materials Rsch. Soc., Am. Ceramic Soc. (program chair, sec. New England section 2005—). Achievements include patents pending for unagglomerated core-shell nanoparticles for functional applications; transition alumina nanoparticle abrasives for chemical mechanical planarization; improved stability of transition alumina slurry used for copper chemical mechanical planarization; methods and apparatus for minimizing the aging effect on alumina particles in slurry solutions; development of balidate HPLC as a powerful tool to separate and disperse nanoparticle for medical applications. A startup company called Keystone Nano was formed based on this core technology in 2005; developed and commercializing next generation of soft alumina abrasive for chemical mechanical planarization (CMP) application. Home: 47 Sheridan Dr #6 Shrewsbury MA 01545 Office: Saint-Gobain HPM Northboro R&D Ctr 9 Goddard Rd Northborough MA 01532 Office Fax: 508-351-7740. Business E-Mail: jun.wang@saint-gobain.com.

WANG, LAWRENCE K., engineering educator; m. Mu-Hao, 1968. BS, Nat. Cheng Kung U., Taiwan, 1962; M of Engring., U. Mo., 1965; MS, U. R.I., 1967; PhD, Rutgers U., 1972. Environ. engr. Veridan Engring., Buffalo, 1970-73; asst. prof. Rensselaer Poly. Inst., Troy, 1973—77; assoc. prof. Stevens Inst. Tech., Hoboken, NJ, 1977—80; dir. Lenox Inst. Water Tech., Lenox, Mass.; asst. pres. Krofta Engring. Corp., 1980—2002; v.p. Zerox Corp., Newtonville, NY, 1980—2002; sr. advisor UN, Vienna, 1995-96. Advisor EPA, Washington, 1977—, N.Y. State Dept. Environ. Conservation, 1973-78; adj. prof. Nat. Cheng Kung U., Taiwan, 1973-80; examiner Nat. Profl. Engrs., Bd., 1973-89; vis. prof. U. Ill., Urbana, 1993-95. Author 24 books; contbr. 700 articles to profl. jous.; inventor/patentee of 29 patents in field; chief editor Human Press, N.J. and CRC Press, Boca Raton, Fla., 2002—. Recipient Kenenth Rsch. award NY Water Environment Assn., NYC, 1978. Mem. AIChE, Am. Water Works Assn., Water Environ. Fedn., Assn. Environ. Engring. & Sci. Profs. Republican. Personal E-mail: lawrencekwang@gmail.com.

WANG, LEI, biochemist; b. China; BS in Organic Chemistry, Peking U., 1994, MS in Physical Chemistry, 1997; PhD in Bioorganic Chemistry, U. Calif., Berkeley, 2002. Postdoctoral rschr. biochemistry U. Calif., San Diego, 2002—. Contbr. articles to profl. jour. Recipient Grand prize, Collegiate Inventors Competition, Nat. Inventors Hall Fame, Young Scientist prize, Amersham Biosciences, 2003; named one of Top 100 Young Innovators, MIT Tech. Review, 2004; Merck fellow, Damon Runyon Cancer Rsch. Found., 2002. Office: The Salk Inst 10010 N Torrey Pines Rd La Jolla CA 92037 Business E-Mail: lewang@ucsd.edu.

WANG, LESLIE TSUN CHUNG, social sciences educator; b. Hong Kong, Nov. 20, 1962; m. Cristina Mary Golamb, Oct. 5, 2002. AB, Ulster County C.C., Stone Ridge, NY, 1983; B in History, SUNY, New Paltz, 1984, M in Sociology, 1987; PhD in Foundations of Edn., U. Toledo, 2005. Adminstrv. asst. in ESL program. SUNY, New Paltz, 1987—91; instr. social scis. U. Toledo C.C., 1991—99; instr. sociology U. Toledo, 1999—. Vol. spkr. diversity issues YWCA Rape Crisis Ctr., Toledo, 1995—. Mem.: N.Ctrl. Sociol. Assn. (tchg. com. chair 2001—04, coun. mem. 2002—). Office: Univ of Toledo Dept Sociology/Anthropology 2801 W Bancroft St Toledo OH 43606 Office Phone: 419-530-4076.

WANG, LI, business director; b. Shanghai, May 17, 1962; s. De-hua Wang and De-wei Zhang; m. Yu Shao, Mar. 15, 1988; 1 child, Anthony Ming. PhD, U. Minn., Mpls., 1992. Staff scientist Medtronic, Mpls., 1992—2000, project mgr., 1998—2000, sr. prin. scientist, 2000—02, sr. product planning mgr., 2003—06; mktg. dir. Medtronic CRDM Asia Pacific, Hong Kong, 2006—08, bus. dir. Shanghai, 2008—. Contbr. articles to profl. jours. Med. vol. Children's Heart Link, Mpls., 1999—2005. Recipient Star of Excellence awards, Medtronic Inc., 2003, 2007; Tech. fellowship, 2003. Mem.: Heart Rhythm Soc. Achievements include patents for implantable medical devices; first to use of impedance to measure and predict worsening heart failure in patients with implantable medical devices; development of multiple clinical relevant features in implantable medical devices. Office: Medtronic Inc S 8200 Coral Sea St Mounds View MN 55112 Office Phone: 862150800998-2278. Business E-Mail: li.wang@medtronic.com.

WANG, LICHANG, chemistry professor; b. Tianjin, China, Feb. 26, 1964; d. Changxiao Wang and Minghua Su; m. Qingfeng Ge; children: Shanshan Ge, Longmei Ge. BChE, Tianjin U., China, 1985, MChE, 1988; PhD, U. Copenhagen, 1993. Rsch. fellow U. Cambridge, England, 1994—98, U. Coll. London, 1996—97; postdoc. rschr. Ohio State U., Columbus, 1998—2001; prof. Southern Ill. U. Carbondale, 2001—. Mem.: AAAS, ACS. Achievements include research in theoretical and computational chemistry. Office: Southern Ill Univ Carbondale 1245 Lincon Dr Carbondale IL 62901 Business E-Mail: lwang@chem.siu.edu.

WANG, LINDSAY L., research and assessment director, principal; b. China, Nov. 24, 1962; d. Yifo Wang and Jiazen Ming; m. John Franklin Copper, Mar. 1, 1996; 1 child, Royce Wellington Copper. BA, Beijing Normal U., 1984; MA, Ark. Tech. U., 1992; EdD, U. Memphis, 1997. Adj. prof. U. Memphis, 1997—98; rschr. Ctr. Rsch. Ednl. Policy, Memphis, 1998—2002, sr. rschr., 2002—05; prin. Alamo Chinese Sch., San Antonio, 2004—; dir. Lady Lake U., San Antonio, 2005—. V.p. Heights Consulting, San Antonio, 2006—. Author: Dog's Daughter: My Life in Communist China and Liberal America, 2003; contbr. articles to profl. jours., chapters to books. Mem.: Instl. Rsch. Assn. Buddhist. Avocations: cooking, reading, writing. Office: Lady Lake Univ 411 SW 24th St San Antonio TX 78207 Office Phone: 210-434-6711. Office Fax: 210-431-3798. Business E-Mail: wangl@lake.ollusa.edu.

WANG, MARJORIE, medical educator; MD, Loyola Stritch Sch. Medicine, Maywood, Ill., 1996; MPH, U. Wash. Sch. Pub. Health, Seattle, 2005. Lic. Wis., 2005. Asst. prof. Med. Coll. Wis., Milw., 2006—. Office: Med Coll Wis 9200 W Wis Ave Milwaukee WI 53226 Office Fax: 414-955-0115.

WANG, MATTHEW NAI-HWEI, surgeon, educator; s. Shih-Ling Wang and Huan Wang-Lin; life ptnr. Sylvia Shun-Hui Kuo, Dec. 12, 1975; 1 child, Raymond Jen-Chih. MD, Kaohsiung Med. U., Taiwan, 1974. Diplomate Dept. of Health, Exec. Yuan, China, 1974. Chief divsn. pediat. orthop. Vet.'s Gen. Hosp., Taipei, Taiwan, 1985—96; supt. Tachia br. Kuang Tien Gen. Hosp., Taichung, 1996—. Prof. Hung Kuang U., Taichung, 2004—. Mem.: Taiwan Orthop. Assn. (com. mem. 1999—, editl. bd.), Pediat. Orthop. Soc. N.Am. (corr.). Avocation: golf. Office: Kuang Tien Gen Hosp 321 Chin-Kuo Rd Tachia Taichung 437 Taiwan Office Phone: 04-26888989. Business E-Mail: admin_tachia@ktgh.com.tw.

WANG, MIAN, education educator; s. Xiangyu He; m. Xiaohong Li, Oct. 6, 1988; 1 child, Yidi. PhD, U. Kans., Lawrence, 2004. Asst. prof. UC Santa Barbara, 2007—, Rowan U., Glassboro, NJ, 2004—07. Bd. mem. Divsn. Internat. Spl. Edn. & Svcs., Washington, 2008—. Recipient Early Career award, Am. Assn. Intellectual & Devel. Disabilities, 2009.

WANG, MICHAEL Y., neurosurgeon; s. Johnson and Lillian Wang; m. Amy Wang, Sept. 2, 1999; children: Patrick Taylor, Evan Nathaniel, Sarah Elizabeth. BS, Stanford U., Calif., 1991, MD, 1996. Asst. prof. U. Southern Calif., LA, 2003—07; assoc. prof. U. Miami, Fla., 2007—08. Mem. editl. rev. bd. Jour. Spinal Disorders, Madison, Wis., 2006—. Contbr. scientific papers (Mayfield Rsch. award, 2004, Sanford Larson Rsch. award, 2005). Mem.: Am. Assn. Neurosurgeons (mem. benefits com. 2006—08), Joint Spine Sect. (edn. chmn. 2005—08, publs. chmn. 2005—08), Congress Neurol. Surgeons (mem. edn. com. 2007—08). Achievements include patents for bone hemostasis materials & methods. Office: Univ Miami Sch Medicine 1095 NW 14th Ter D4-6 Miami FL 33136

WANG, MO, psychology professor; s. Dawu Wang and Honglin Li; m. Jing Zheng. PhD, Bowling Green State U., Ohio, 2005. Asst. prof. Portland State U., Oreg., 2005—08, U. Md., Coll Pk, 2009—. Contbr. articles to profl. jours. (Scholarly Achievement award, 2008). Personal E-mail: wangmo2008@gmail.com. Business E-Mail: mwang@psyc.umd.edu.

WANG, MORAN, physicist; s. Wei Wang and Mingyan Yang; m. Jingjing Li, Feb. 19, 2006. PhD, Tsinghua U., Beijing, 2004. Postdoc. fellow Johns Hopkins U., Balt., 2004—06; rsch. assoc. U. Calif., Davis, 2006—08; oppenheimer fellow Los Alamos Nat. Lab., N.Mex., 2008—. Contbr. articles to profl. jour. (NSK Sino-Japan Friendship Disting. Paper award, 2004). Mem.: ASME, Fiber Soc., APS. Office: Los Alamos Nat Lab MS T003 Los Alamos NM 87545

WANG, NANCY, pathologist, educator; b. An-Wei, China, Sept. 2, 1944; m. Tingchung Wang; children: Jessie, Melissa. BS, Nat. Taiwan U., 1966; MS, U. Minn., 1968, PhD, 1978. Diplomate Am. Bd. Med. Genetics. Instr. Dept. Pathology & Lab. Med. U. Minn., Mpls., 1978-79, asst. prof., 1980-82, Dept. Pathology, Tulane Med. Sch., 1982-83, assoc. prof., 1984-86, U. Rochester, NY, 1986-93, prof. NY, 1993—. Mem.: Am. Assn. Human Gennetics. Office Phone: 585-275-6597. Business E-Mail: nancy_wang@urmc.rochester.edu.

WANG, NING LIAN, geographer, educator; b. Xinping, Shanxi, China, Jan. 14, 1966; BS in Geography, NW U., Xianping, 1988; MS in Glaciology, Lanzhou Inst. Glaciology and Geocryology, Chinese Acad. Scis., 1991; PhD in Ice Core and Global Change, Cold and Arid Region Environment and Engring. Rsch. Inst., Chinese Acad. Scis., Lanzhou, Gansu, China, 2001. Prof., leader of divsn. of cryosphere and global change Cold and Arid Regions Environ. and Engring. Rsch. Inst., Lanzhou, Gansu, China, 2000—; postdoctoral rsch. fellow Byrd Polar Rsch. Ctr., Ohio State U., 2002—03. Recipient Nat. Sci. and Tech. award, Chinese Ministry Sci. and Tech., 2006, Honor of Nat. Experts award, State Coun. of People's Republic China, 2007. Mem.: Internat. Glaciological Soc. (coun. mem. 2007—), Coun. China Soc. Tibet Plateau (assoc.). Achievements include research in climatic and environmental records in ice cores. Office: Oklahoma State Univ 111 Ag Hall Stillwater OK 74078 Office Phone: 86-0931-4967353. Office Fax: 86-0931-8272814. Business E-Mail: nlwang@lzb.ac.cn.

WANG, PEI-LING, geochemist; b. Taipei, Taiwan, Apr. 30, 1971; d. Kai-Ying Wang and Lu-Mei Shao; m. Li-Hung Lin, May 7, 1971. PhD, Nat. Taiwan U., 1998. Postdoc. fellow Geophys. Lab., CIW, Washington, 2000—04; asst. prof. Inst. Oceanography, NTU, Taipei, 2004—. Office: Inst Oceanography NTU No 1 Sec 4 Roosevelt Rd Taipei 10617 Taiwan Business E-Mail: plwang@ntu.edu.tw.

WANG, PEIYUAN, scientist; b. Hangzhou, Zhejiang, China, Sept. 10, 1962; s. Jiong Wang and Shouying Tong; m. Huachun Chen, June 1987; 1 child, Yicheng. BS, Shanghai Med. U., 1984; MS in Medicinal Chemistry, Zhejiang U., China, 1990; PhD in Medicinal Chemistry, U. Ga., Athens, 1998. Asst. prof. Zhejiang U., 1985—90, lectr., 1990—92; postdoc. fellow Nat. Cancer Inst., NIH, Bethesda, Md., 1998—2000; sr. scientist Pharmasset, Inc., Tucker, Ga., 2000—07, group leader Princeton, NJ, 2007—. Contbr. articles to various sci. jours. including Jour. Med. Chemistry, Antiviral Rsch., Jour. Am. Chem. Soc., Jour. Organic Chemistry, Artimicrob Agents Chemother and others. Recipient Intramural Rsch. award, NIH, 1998—2000. Mem.: Am. Chem. Soc. Achievements include inventions, drug discoveries, publications and awards for the development of pharmaceuticals to treat diseases such as AIDS, hepatitis and cancer. Avocations: poetry, travel, reading. Office: Pharmasset Inc 303A College Rd East Princeton NJ 08540 Business E-Mail: pwang@pharmasset.com.

WANG, QIAN, physicist, educator; d. Yuqing Wang and Peirong Chen; m. Qiang Sun, July 4, 1987; 1 child, Tony Sun. PhD, Tohoku U., Sendai, Japan, 2001. Rsch. asst. prof. Va. Commonwealth U., Richmond, Va., 2003—04, rsch. assoc. prof., 2004—. Reviewer Funding Agys. US Dept. Energy, Washington DC, 2005—. Contbr. articles to peer review pubs. Recipient Rsch. award, Japan Inst. Metals., 2000. Mem.: Am. Phys. Soc. Home: 12433 Brightwater Ln Richmond VA 23233 Office: Va Commonwealth Univ 701 W Grace St Richmond VA 23284

WANG, RICHARD G., literature educator; b. Shanghai, Shanghai, China, Oct. 2, 1962; s. Muqun Wang and Chunling Shi; m. Xiaomei Zhao. PhD, U. Chgo., Chgo., 1999. Asst. rsch. fellow Inst. Lit. Shanghai Aca. Social Scis., Shanghai, 1987—90; asst. prof. Chinese U. Hong Kong, Shatin, New Territories, Hong Kong, 1999—. Grantee Competitive Earmarked Rsch. Grant, Hong Kong Rsch. Grants Coun., 2001-2003. Mem.: Am. Oriental Soc., Am. Acad. Religion, Assn. Asian Studies. Avocation: travel. Office Phone: (852)2609-6570. Office Fax: (852)2603-5280.

WANG, RUI, dean, educator; s. Jihong Wang and Qiwei Han; m. Ying Zhu; 1 child, Frances. BA, Xi'an Internat. Studies U., China, 1982; MA, Beijing U. Fgn. Studies, 1986; M in Libr. and Info. Sci., Northern Ill. U., DeKalb, 1992, EdD, 1993. Cert. in translation Gen. Secs., 1986. Dean, Humboldt Coll. Xi'an Internat. Studies U., Humboldt State U., Shaanxi, China, 2005—06; chair, info. svc. U. Libr., Humboldt State U., Arcata, Calif., 2004—05, dean, 2006—. Author: (novel) Homeland and Guest Country. Pres. Humbooldt Asian Soc., Arcata, 1998. Title VI grant, US Dept. Edn., 2004—06. Mem.: ALA. Office: Humboldt State Univ One Harpst St Arcata CA 95521 Office Phone: 707-826-3441. Business E-Mail: rw6@humboldt.edu.

WANG, SANGHAN, law educator; b. Seoul, Republic of Korea, July 25, 1963; s. Kyung-Ha Wang and Suk-Ki Ko; m. Woo-Young Byoun, June 7, 2002; children: Min, Yoo. JSD, Columbia U. Sch. Law, NY, 1996. Internat. assoc. Reid & Priest, NYC, 1993—95; summer assoc. Mayer, Browne & Platt, Washington, 1996; prof. internat. trade law Sogang U. Coll. Law, Seoul, 1996—; prof. Sogang U. Grad. Sch. Internat. Studies, Seoul, Republic of Korea, 1997—; working group mem. UN Commn. Internat. Trade Laws, NYC, 1997—; legal counsel Ministry Fgn. Affairs and Trade, Seoul, 1998—99, legal advisor, 2000—, Ministry Justice Internat. Trade Law Com., Kwacheon, Republic of Korea, 2002—; commr. Korean Internat. Trade Commn., Kwacheon, Republic of Korea, 2007—. Mem. APEC Electronic Commerce Steering Group, Bangkok, 1999—2002; vis. prof. George Wash. U. Sch. Law, 2003—04; Michaelle Wynne vis. prof. Loyola U. Sch. Law, New Orleans, 2008. Author: (book) Understand on Medical Conflicts, Principles of Medical Law, Principles of Electronic Contract, Critical Analysis of Concession by Korea to WTO, Technical Barrier to Trade at WTO, Principles of U.S. Trade Laws, Digital Broadcasting and Law, Electronic Commerce and International Law. Dir. Korea Internat. Trade Law Assn., Seoul, 2005—09, Korea Internat. Econ. Law Assn., Seoul, 2003—09, Korea Am. Studies Assn., Seoul, 1999—2009. Recipient award, Ministry Info. Tech., 2006; John M. Olin fellowship, Columbia U. Sch. of Law, 1995, Rsch. scholarship, Fulbright, 2003, Rsch. Grant, Korea Med. Assn., 2008. Mem.: NY Bar Assn. Home: 11-703 Shindongah Apt Yongsanku Sobinggo Seoul 140-752 Republic of Korea Office: Sogang Univ Coll Law 1 Mapoku Shinsudong Seoul 121-742 Republic of Korea Business E-Mail: shwang@sogang.ac.kr.

WANG, SEN, computer scientist, researcher; s. Congyao Wang and Zhijun Dong; m. Ying Qiao; 1 child, Alina Xinying. BE (hon.), Shandong U., Jinan, China, 2000; ME, Inst. Automation, Chinese Acad. Sci., Beijing, 2003; MS, Stony Brook U., NY, 2006, PhD, 2008. Rsch. asst. Stony Brook U., 2004—08; rsch. scientist Eastman Kodak Co., Rochester, NY, 2008—. Mem.: Assn. Computing Machinery, IEEE, Sigma Xi. Achievements include research in shape registration and analysis framework for computer vision and graphics; face reconstruction and recognition under varying pose and illumination condition; invention of fingerprint recognition. Avocations: travel, music, hiking. Office: Kodak Rsch Labs 1999 Lake Ave Rochester NY 14650

WANG, SHAOWEN, information scientist, geographer, educator; Sr. rsch. scientist Nat. Ctr. Supercomputing Applications, Urbana, Ill., 2007—; asst. prof. U. Ill., Urbana-Champaign, 2007—. Bd. dirs. U. Consortium Geog. Info. Sci., Washington, 2009—. Recipient Rsch. award, NSF, 2009. Achievements include research in cyber infrastructure & geographic information systems. Office: Univ Ill Urbana-Champai Rm 330 Davenport 607 S Mathews Ave Urbana IL 61801

WANG, SHENGQUAN, science educator; PhD, Tex. A&M U., Coll. Sta., 2006. Asst. prof. U. Mich. Dearborn, 2006—08. Recipient Career award, NSF, 2008—. Office: Univ Mich Dearborn 4901 Evergreen Rd Dearborn MI 48128 Office Fax: 313-593-4256. Business E-Mail: shqwang@umd.umich.edu.

WANG, SHIH-HO, electrical engineer, educator; b. Kiangsu, China, June 29, 1944; arrived in US, 1968; BEE, Nat. Taiwan U., Taipei, 1967; MEE, U. Calif., Berkeley, 1970, PhD in Elec. Engring., 1971. Asst. prof. elec. engring. U. Colo., Colo. Springs, 1973-76, Boulder, 1976-77; asst. prof. electrical engring. U. Md., College Park, 1977-78, assoc. prof., 1978-84; prof. U. Calif., Davis, 1984—. Cons. Lawrence Livermore (Calif.) Nat. Lab., 1986-88; scientific officer Office Naval Research, Arlington, Va., 1983-84. Assoc. editor Internat. Jour. Robotics and Automation, 1986—90. Served to 2d lt. China Air Force, Taiwan, 1967-68. Mem. IEEE (hon. mention award control systems soc. 1975). Office: Univ Calif Dept Elec Computer Engring Davis CA 95616 Business E-Mail: shwang@ucdavis.edu.

WANG, SHUANGQUAN, research scientist; s. Youmao Wang and Keqing Li; m. Hongyan Yang, Oct. 15, 2001; children: Andrea, Mandy. BS, Xi'an Inst. Posts and Telecom., Shaanxi, China, 1998; MS, Beijing U. Posts and Telecom., 2001; PhD, NJ Inst. Tech., Newark, 2006. Sys. engr. Siemens Ltd., Beijing, 2001—02; postdoc. scientist NEC Labs. America, Inc., Princeton, NJ, 2006—07; staff scientist Broadcom Corp., Matwan, NJ, 2007—. Contbr. articles to profl. jours. (EI Index prize, 2005, First pl., 2005). Recipient Hashimoto prize, NJ Inst. Tech., 2007, Grad. Student award, 2006; named to Hall of Fame, NJ Inventors. Mem.: IEEE. Achievements include patents for channel estimation in communication systems; multi-user detection method and apparatus for received-data-and-combined-CIR-based interference power estimation algorithm in TD-SCDMA; patents pending for two-stage low-complexity max-log bit-by-bit LLR calculator. Avocations: ping pong/table tennis, computers. Office: Broadcom Corp 14 Cliffwood Ave Metropark S II Ste 300 Matawan NJ 07747 Business E-Mail: shuangquan.wang@njit.edu.

WANG, SHUO, engineering researcher; arrived in USA, 2001; s. Congyi Wang and Yuefang Zeng; m. Xiang Gao, June 22, 2000; 1 child, William Henry. B in Elec. Engring., Southwest Jiaotong U., Chengdu, China, 1994; M in Elec. Engring., Zhejiang U., Hangzhou, China, 1997; PhD in Elec. Engring., Va. Tech., Blacksburg, 2005. Sr. engr. Zhongxing Telecom. Corp, Shenzhen, Guangdong, China, 1997—98; engr. UT Starcom. Telecomm. Corp., Hangzhou, Zhejiang, China, 1999—2000; rsch. asst. Ctr. Power Electronics Sys., Blacksburg, 2001—05, rsch. asst. prof., 2005—. Cons. LiteON Electronics Corp. Contbr. articles to profl. jours. Mem.: IEEE (sr.; jour. assoc editor, William Portnoy award 2004, Best Trans. Paper Award 2005). Achievements include patents for EMI filter self- and mutual-parastic cancellation, common mode EMI cancellaltion with balance, and common mode parasitic cancellation to reduce the common mode noise source; research in parasitic parameter's effects on EMI filter performance, establishing a novel parasitic model for EMI filters; the interaction of power interconnect and EMI filters to extract the parasitic parameters between components in filters; active EMI filters; hybrid EMI filters; development of separator to accurately separate common mode and differential mode noise; single-phase and three-phase circuits; ESL/EPC cancellation for capacitors/inductors; cancellation techniques for the coupling between inductor and capacitor, and capacitor and capicitor passive planer investigation, power conversions for renewable energy, high efficiency AC/DC & DC/DC; power electronics circuits; thermal analysis for HID ballast. Office: Ctr Power Electronics Sys 655 Whittemore Hall Blacksburg VA 24061 Personal E-mail: shuowang@ieee.org. Business E-Mail: shwang6@vt.edu.

WANG, SONA, venture capitalist; b. South Korea, 1958; naturalized, US; BS in Indsl. Engring., Stanford U., 1980; MBA magna cum laude, Northwestern U., 1986. Mgr., engr. Intel Corp., Calif.; investment mgr. Allstate Venture Capital; co-founder, gen. ptnr. Batterson, Johnson & Wang, Ill., 1988—2001, Inroads Capital Ptnrs., Evanston, Ill., 1995—; co-founder, mng. dir. Ceres Venture Fund, L.P., 2005—. Chmn. VIP-desk, Inc.; bd. dirs. IKOS Sys., Answer Systems (now subs. of Platinum Technologies), Sigmedics, Inc., Array Technologies, Success Lab., Inc., Ultimo Enterprises, Ltd., High Tower Software, Grand Eagle Cos., Wine.com, TrafficCast Internat., Inc., 2008—. Founding adv. coun. mem. Women's Bus. Devel. Ctr., Chgo.; mem. Coun. of 100, Northwestern U.; bd. trustees Northwestern U., Chgo. Symphony Orch.; bd. govs Met. Planning Coun.; mem. Chgo. Mayor's Coun. Tech. Adv.; bd. mem. Evanston Northwestern Healthcare & Blue Cross Blue Shield of Ill. Recipient Leadership award for Entrepreneurship, YWCA, 2001; named one of The 100 Most Influential Women in Chgo., Crain's Chgo. Bus., 2004. Office: Ceres Venture Fund LP 500 Davis St Ste 600 Evanston IL 60201 also: Inroads Capital Partners 500 Davis St Ste 600 Evanston IL 60201-4622 Office Phone: 847-864-2000. Office Fax: 847-864-9692.

WANG, TA-CHEN, economics professor; s. Cheng-Tung Wang and Chin-Er Ai. PhD, Stanford U., Calif., 2006. Asst. prof. Calif. State U., Sacramento, 2006—. Mem.: Cliometric Soc., Econ. History Assn., Am. Econ. Assn. Achievements include research in early American banking. Office: Calif State Univ 6000 J St Sacramento CA 95819-6082 Business E-Mail: tachen.wang@csus.edu.

WANG, TAYLOR GUNJIN, science administrator, educator, astronaut; b. Shanghai, June 16, 1940; came to U.S., 1963; m. Beverly Fung, 1966; children: Kenneth, Eric. BS, UCLA, 1967, MS, 1968, PhD, 1971. Mgr. microgravity sci. and applications program Jet Propulsion Lab., Pasadena, Calif., 1972-88, cons., 1987-89; Space Shuttle astronaut-scientist NASA, 1983-85; Centennial prof., dir. Ctr. for Microgravity Rsch. and Applications Vanderbilt U., Nashville, 1988—. Contbr. over 180 articles to profl. jours.; inventor living cellls encapsulation tech. as cure of hormone deficiency states in humans; over 20 patents in field. Bd. dirs. Com. of 100. Fellow Acoustical Soc. Am.; mem. AIAA, Am. Phys. Soc., Assn. Space Explorers-USA (pres. 1988), Sigma Xi. Office: Vanderbilt U Vanderbilt Pl Nashville TN 37235 Business E-Mail: taylor.g.wang@vanderbilt.edu.

WANG, TIAN, immunologist, educator; d. Hengqi Wang and Yanqiu Pan; m. Tong Han, 1995 (div. 1998); m. Thomas Welte, 2005. PhD, U. Tex., Galveston, 1995—2000. Postdoctoral fellow Yale U. Sch. Medicine, New Haven, 2000—04, assoc. rsch. scientist, 2004—05; asst. prof. Colo. State U., Ft. Collins, 2005—. Grantee Kempner Postdoctoral fellowship, U. Tex. Med. Br., 2001, 2003, Jr. Faculty award, Am. Fedn. Aging Rsch., 2005; Rsch. grant, NIH, 2006, Coll. Coun. grant, Colo. State U., 2006. Mem.: AAAS (corr.), Am. Assn. Virologist (assoc.), Am. Assn. Immunologist (life AAI Travel award 2005, 2006), Sigma Xi (assoc.). Achievements include patents for comprising West Nile Virus polypeptides. Office: Campus Delivery 1690 Colo State Univ Fort Collins CO 80523 Office Fax: 970-491-8707. Business E-Mail: tian.wang@colostate.edu.

WANG, TING, biomedical researcher; m. Wenli Ma, Dec. 18, 2001. PhD, U. SC, Columbia, 2005. Postdoc. scholar U. Chgo., 2005—. Contbr. articles to profl. jours. Recipient Grad. Tchg. Asst. award, U. SC, 2006; named Grad. of Yr., 2005; named to Best Translational Rsch. Abstract, U. Chgo. Dept. Medicine, 2008. Mem.: Am. Assn. Coll. Pharmacy, Am. Heart Assn., Sigma Xi Sci. Rsch. Soc. Achievements include patents for treatment of cardiovascular and respiratory disorders. Office: Univ Chgo 929 E 57th St Room W403R Chicago IL 60637 Office Fax: 773-834-2687. Business E-Mail: twang@medicine.bsd.uchicago.edu.

WANG, VERA, fashion designer; b. NYC, June 27, 1949; d. Cheng Ching Wang; m. Arthur Becker, June 22, 1989; children: Cecilia, Josephine. BA in Art History, Sarah Lawrence Coll., New York, 1978. Various positions including accessories editor, European editor, sr. fashion editor Vogue mag., NYC, 1969—85; design dir. Ralph Lauren Women's Wear, NYC, 1987-89; prin. Vera Wang Bridal House Ltd., NYC, 1990—; expanded to ready-to-wear, fragrance, eyewear, footwear, fine jewelry, and a home collection. Designer for Olympic figure skaters including Nancy Kerrigan's silver medal performance at the 1994 Olympics. Costume designer (films) The Parent Trap, 1998, First Daughter, 2004; author: Vera Wang on Weddings, 2001. Recipient Womenswear Designer of the Yr., Coun. Fashion Designers Am., 2005, André Leon Talley Lifetime Achievement award, Savannah Coll. Art and Design., 2006, Hall of Fame award, FiFi Awards, 2008. Achievements include first to successfully fuse high style and fashion with the tradition and symbolism of the bridal industry; designing wedding and red carpet gowns for Hollywood's elite. Office: Vera Wang Bridal House 225 W 39th St Fl 10 New York NY 10018-3103 Office Phone: 212-575-6400.

WANG, WANLIN, research scientist; b. July 12, 1976; PhD, Carnegie Mellon U., Pitts., 2007. Sr. rsch. scientist Reckitt Benckiser, Montvale, NJ, 2007—. Mem. ASM Internat., NACE Internat., TMS Internat.; reviewer Jour. Applied Electrochemistry, Colloids & Surfaces A, Physicochemical and Engring. Aspects, Chem. Engr. Comm.; organizer NACE Ann. Meeting, 2009. Contbr. scientific papers, articles to profl. jours. Recipient 1st prize, Baoshan Iron & Steel Co., Ltd., 1998, Champion award, TMS, 2006; grant, Reckitt Benckiser, 2008. Achievements include development of novel vapor phase corrosion estimation method to monitor and measure metal corrosion in the non-conductive vapor phase (hydrocarbon propellant) medium; design of develop and apply the advanced electrostatic spray technology to traditional aerosol spray system of Reckitt Benckiser product; develop the novel model to estimate the complex radiative heat transfer rate in the meniscus area; research; research in investigate the properties evolution of amorphous Lime-Silica-Alumina system with the addition of transient metal oxides. Office Phone: 201-573-6072. Personal E-mail: wanlin.wang@gmail.com. Business E-Mail: wanlin.wang@reckittbenckiser.com.

WANG, WILLIAM KAI-SHENG, law educator; b. NYC, Feb. 28, 1946; s. Yuan-Chao and Julia Ying-Ru (Li) W.; m. Kwan Kwan Tan, July 29, 1972; 1 child, Karen You-Chuan. BA, Amherst Coll., Mass., 1967; JD, Yale U., New Haven, Conn., 1971. Bar: Calif. 1972. Asst. to mng. partner Gruss & Co., NYC, 1971-72; asst. prof. law U. San Diego, 1972-74, asso. prof., 1974-77, prof., 1977-81, Hastings Coll. Law, U. Calif., San Francisco, 1981—. Vis. prof. law U. Calif., Davis, 1975—76, Hastings Coll. Law, U. Calif., 1980, UCLA, 1990, Villanova U., 1999, Bklyn. Law Sch., 2000, Leiden (Netherlands) U., 2004; cons. White Ho. Domestic Policy Staff, Washington, 1979; chair investment policy oversight group, bd. participant Law Sch. Admissions Coun.; nat. adjudicatory coun. FINRA, 2007—08, NASD, 2003—07; mem. then chair com. on audit and assn. investment policy Assn. Am. Law Schs., 1995—98. Co-author: Insider Trading, 2d edit., 2008; mem. editl. bd.: Internat. and Comparative Corp. Law Jour.; contbr. articles to newspapers, mags., profl. jours. Mem. State Bar Calif., Am. Law Inst. Home: 455 39th Ave San Francisco CA 94121-1507 Office: U Calif Hastings Coll Law 200 McAllister St San Francisco CA 94102-4978 Office Phone: 415-565-4666. Business E-Mail: wangw@uchastings.edu.

WANG, WILLIAM WEIQI, physician; b. Shanghai, June 3, 1962; arrived in U.S., 1989; s. Junmin Wang and Shanlai Gan; m. Lini Son-Will Wang. MD, Shanghai Med. U., 1985; PhD, U. Medicine and Dentistry N.J., Newark, 1995. Fellow NIMH, Bethesda, Md., 1995—96; rsch. assoc. Baylor Coll. Medicine, Houston, 1997—98; resident psychiatry Washington U., St. Louis, 1998—2002; attending psychiatrist SSM Healthcare, St. Louis, 2002—; clin. instr. St. Louis U. Med. Sch., 2003—. Dir. med. rsch. Advent Rsch. Inst., 2006—; bd. dir. Impact Group, LLC; med. dir. geriatric transitional program SSM St. Joseph Health Ctr., 2007—; dir. med. edn. Olivette Inst., 2008—. Author: Psychiatry Pearls of Wisdom, 1999, Psychiatry for the Boards, 2002, 2007, Comprehensive Psychiatry Review, 2009; contbr. articles to profl. jours. Recipient Clin. Rec. award, Shanghai Mpcl. Health Bur., 1988. Mem.: Am. Psychiat. Assn. Avocations: fine arts, history. Office: 255 Spencer Rd Saint Peters MO 63376 Office Phone: 636-939-2550. Personal E-mail: wwwang@rocketmail.com.

WANG, XIAO, language educator; arrived in US, 1990; d. ZhiYuan Wang and Yu Lang Huang. BA, NW Tchrs. U., China, 1979—83; MA, St. Cloud State U., Minn., 1990—92; PhD, Ball State U., Muncie, Ind., 1992—97. Cert. tchr. Xian Jiao Tong U., 1986. English instr. Ariz. State U., Tempe, 1997—98; prof. English Broward C, Ft. Lauderdale, Fla., 1998—. Program chair TYCA-SE Conf., Ft. Lauderdale, 2001—01. Author: (book) English Composition (Tchg. Excellence award, 2001). Donor Ball State U., Muncie, Ind., 2000—06. Mem.: NCTE. Achievements include research in interlanguage characteristcis in the texts by Chinese-American freshman composition students at UCLA. Home: 9230 Lagoon Pl #211 Davie FL 33324 Office: Broward CC 3501 SW Davie FL 33314 Home Phone: 754-422-9990; Office Phone: 954-201-6515. Office Fax: 954-202-6646. Business E-Mail: xwang@broward.edu.

WANG, XIN, engineering educator; b. Yangchun, Guangdong, China, June 22, 1974; s. Yangxi Wang and Zhengxiu Ouyang; m. Na Gao; children: Nancy S., Nathan S. PhD, Auburn U., Ala., 2004. Asst. prof. Fla. Atlantic U., Boca Raton, 2006—. Mem.: IEEE. Office: FL Atlantic Univ 777 Glades Rd Boca Raton FL 33431

WANG, XIN, geologist, researcher; s. B. Wang and F. Feng; m. H. Ma; 1 child, B. Y. PhD, U. Fla., Gainesville, 2004. Cert. rschr. Chinese Acad. Scis., 2007. Assoc. rsch. prof. Inst. Geology and Palaeontology, Nanjing, Jiangsu, China, 2007—. Contbr. scientific papers. Pres. Friendship Assn. Chinese Students Scholars, Gainesville, Fla., 1999—2000; senator Student Govt., 2000—01; mem. Internat. Student Consultative Bd., 2001—04. Recipient Excellent Grad., Peking U., 1990, Grad. Sch., CAS, 1991, Presdl., U. Fla., 2002. Mem.: Chinese Soc. Palaeontology, Sigma Xi Sci. Rsch. Soc., Bot. Soc. China, Bot. Soc. America (assoc.). Office: Nanjing Inst Geol Palaeontol 39 Beijing Dong Rd Jiangsu Nanjing 210008 China

WANG, XIN, computer engineer, researcher; PhD, U. Calif., Santa Cruz, 2009. Rschr. Computer Comm. Rsch. Group, U. Calif., Santa Cruz, 2005—. Contbr. articles to profl. jours. Chancellor Dissertation fellowship, U Calif. Santa Cruz, 2008. Mem.: ACM, IEEE. Office: Univ Calif Santa Cruz 1156 High St Santa Cruz CA 95064 Business E-Mail: wangxin@soe.ucsc.edu.

WANG, XINLEI, science educator; s. Linquan and Jinling Wang; m. Xiaohua Wang; children: Yiru Kathleen, Jonathan Yizhou, Kristine Yixin. PhD, U. Ill., Urbana, 2000. Asst. prof. Zhejiang U., Hangzhou, China, 1987—94; rsch. asst. U. Sask., Saskatoon, Canada, 1994—96, U. Ill., 1996—2000, postdoc. rsch. assoc., 2000, asst. prof., 2002—08, assoc. prof., 2008—; devel. engr. Internat. Truck and Engine Corp., Melrose Park, Ill., 2000—02. Assoc. editor Am. Soc. Agrl. and Biol. Engrs., St. Joseph, Mich., 2006—. Contbr. to numerous technical papers. Recipient J. Kent Mitchell Tchg. Excellence award, U. Ill., Dept. Agrl. and Biol. Engring., 2006, Ben and Georgeon Jones Excellence Tchg. awards, U. Ill. Dept. Agrl. and Biol. Engring., 2009; ACES Global Acad. fellow, U. Ill., 2006—08, Rsch. grant, US Dept. Agr., 2006—, US EPA, 2006—08. Mem.: ASHRAE (chair, tech. com. 2.2: environ. control for animal 2007—, Ann. Paper Award 2001), Am. Soc. for Engring. Edn., Internat. Soc. Automotive Engrs., Am. Soc. Agrl. and Biol. Engrs. (chair, se-302 environment animal structures com. 2007—08). Achievements include patents for control strategy for diesel particulate filter and de-sulfurization of a NOx adsorber catalyst in a diesel engine exhaust system; development of multi-point aerosol sampler using critical flow control devices. Office: Univ Illinois 1304 W Pennsylvania Ave Urbana IL 61801 Office Fax: 217-244-0323. Business E-Mail: xwang2@illinois.edu.

WANG, XINSHENG, lawyer; b. Da Tong, Shan Xi, China, May 20, 1975; arrived in US, 1997; d. Zhifang Wang and Fumei Zhang; m. Jiaher Tian, Jan. 9, 1999; 1 child, Caleb Y. Tian. BS, Peking U., Beijing, China, 1997; MS, U. Kans., Lawrence, 1999, JD, 2002. Rsch. asst. Higuchi Biosci. Ctr., Lawrence, 1997—99; patent atty. Lathrop & Gage, LC, Kansas City, Mo., 2002—05, NYC, 2005—. Corp. gen. counsel, dir. Christian Worldwide Worship Ministries, Omaha, 2002—05. Active Lawrence Chinese Evang. Ch., 2002—05. Mem.: ABA, US-China Lawyers Soc. (bd. dirs. 2005—06). Avocations: fishing, tai chi. Office: Ste 1847 230 Park Ave New York NY 10169 Office Phone: 212-650-6236. Personal E-mail: xinshengw@hotmail.com.

WANG, XIULING, engineering educator; d. Meiyin Wang and Yunying Li; m. Lijian Sun; 1 child, Emily Sun. PhD, U. Nev., Las Vegas, 2005. Lectr. Hebei U. Tech., Tianjin, China, 1998—2000; postdoc. fellow U. Nev., 2005—06, rsch. asst. prof., 2006—07; asst. prof. Purdue U. Calumet, Hammond, Ind., 2007—. Jour. reviewer, 2006—. Contbr. articles to profl. jours. Recipient Travel award, Ga. Tech U., 2004, Best Poster award, IHTC, 2006, award, Purdue U., 2007; Travel grant, NSF, 2007, grant, US BLM, 2008, Prudue Rsch. Found., 2008. Mem.: AIAA, ASME (k-20 numerical heat transfer com. mem., student advisor 2007—), ASEE, Sigma Xi. Achievements include development of hp-adaptive FEM algorithm. Office: Purdue Univ Calumet 2200 169th St Munster IN 46321

WANG, XUE MIN, biochemistry educator; b. Suzhou, Jiangsu, China, Oct. 30, 1945; s. Zhong Hua Wang and Zhi Fen Zhang; m. Xu Ling Tao, Oct. 1, 1972; 1 child, Qian. MD, 2nd Mil. Med. Coll. PLA, Shanghai, China, 1967. Physician 405 Mil. Hosp., Shandong, China, 1969-78; asst. 2nd Mil. Med. Coll., Shanghai, 1979-86, lectr., 1986-90, prof., 1990—. Vis. rschr. Heidelberg (Germany) U., 1988-90. Contbr. articles to profl. jours. Fellow WHO, Heidelberg, 1988; recipient Mil. Sci. and Tech. Programs prize Chinese Army, 1989, 97. Mem. Chinese Biochemistry and Molecular Biology Soc. (coun. mem. 1993—, standing coun. mem. 1997—). Avocation: collecting stamps. Office: Univ of Missouri Biology 1 University Blvd Saint Louis MO 63121

WANG, YANG, research scientist; b. Hefei, Anhui, China, Sept. 25, 1981; s. Bangjian and Ping Wang; m. Meiling Wang, May 28, 2004. BS, U. Sci. and Tech. China, Hefei, 2002; MS, Nat. U. Singapore, 2003; PHD, Lehigh U., Bethlehem, Pa., 2007. Rsch. assoc. Lehigh U., 2003—07; prin. investigator and scientist Opti Comp Corp., Zephyr Cove, Nev., 2007—. Contbr. articles to profl. jours. Recipient Newport Spectral-Physics Rsch. Excellence award, Internat. Soc. Optical Engring., 2006; SPIE scholarship, 2007. Mem.: IEEE, Phi Beta Delta Internat. Honor Soc., Sigma Xi Sci. Rsch. Soc. Office: OptiComp Corp 215 Elks Point Rd Carson City NV 89706

WANG, YE-YI, computer scientist; s. Wang and Shuqi; m. Xuebo Tang; 1 child, Susan. PhD, Carnegie Mellon U., Pitts., 1998. Rschr. Microsoft, Redmond, Wash., 1998—. Contbr. articles to profl. sci. jours., chapters to books. Mem.: IEEE, Assn. Computational Linguistics.

WANG, YING, chemist, researcher; m. Li Shen, Oct. 6, 2007. Postdoc. rschr. U. Calif., San Diego, 2007—08, U. Calif., LA, 2008—. Contbr. scientific papers.

WANG, YOURU, philosopher, educator; married. PhD, Temple U., Phila., 1998. Asst. prof. Chinese U. Hong Kong, 1997—2000; prof. Rowan U., Glassboro, NJ, 2000—. Author: Linguistic Strategies in Daoist Zhuangzi and Chan Buddhism; editor: (anthology) Deconstruction and the Ethical in Asian Thought.

WANG, YU, science educator; married. BEng, Tsinghua U., Beijing, 1998, MEng, 2000; PhD, Ill. Inst. Tech., Chgo., 2004. Asst. prof. U. NC, Charlotte, 2004—. Recipient Outstanding Faculty Rsch. award, Coll. Computing and Informatics, U. NC, 2008, Performance award, Mobile Ad-hoc Networking Interoperability and Coop., 2007, Ralph E. Powe Jr. Faculty Enhancement awards, Oak Ridge Assoc. Univs., 2006, Best Paper award, IEEE 35th Hawaii Internat. Conf. Sys. Scis., 2002. Mem.: IEEE, ACM. Business E-Mail: yu.wang@uncc.edu.

WANG, YUCONG, engineering executive; s. Hezhang and Lingmei Wang; m. Lin Cao, July 4, 1987; children: Linda J., Daniel J. BS, Shanghai Jiaotong U., 1982, MS, 1984; PhD, Mich. Tech., 1990; MBA, Ctrl. Mich. U., 2000. Faculty Shanghai Jiaotong U., 1984—87; sr. engr. advanced mfg. engring. GM Powertrain, Saginaw, Mich., 1990—96, staff engr. quality assurance, 1996—99; prin. engr., leader Surface Engring. and Tribology Ctr., GM, Pontiac, Mich., 1999—2006, program mgr. China tech. mgmt., 1999—2006; pres. Detroit Chinese Engrs. Assn., Detroit, 2005—06, GM CAG, Detroit, 2006—; dept. mgr. materials engring. GM Pontiac, 2006—. Adj. prof. engring. Oakland U., Mich.; guest prof. Shanghai Jiaotung U. Author over 60 articles to tech. publs. Vice chmn. Tri-City Am. Chinese Assn., Saginaw, Mich., 1992—93; pres. Detroit Chinese Engr. Assn., GM CAG. Recipient Appreciation award, U.S. Dept. of Energy, 2002, Herman H. Doehler award, N.Am. Diecasting Assn., 2005, Asian Am. Engr. of Yr. award, Chinese Inst. of Engrs., USA, 2006. Fellow: ASM Internat. (Saginaw Valley chpt. vice-chmn. 1998—99, chmn. 1999—2000, 5-Star chpt. award 2000); mem.: Soc. Automotive Engring., Am. Soc. Materials, Nat. Soc. of Collegiate Scholars (life), Beta Gamma Sigma (life). Achievements include invention of 35 Patents In Automotive Engineering, Materials Engineering, Surface Engineering And Tribology Areas. Office: Gen Motors Corp MC 483-730-312 823 Joslyn Ave Pontiac MI 48340 Business E-Mail: yucong.wang@gm.com.

WANG, YUEJIAN, research scientist; s. Gaoke Wang and Guimei Zhao; m. XinXin Liu; 1 child, Janice. MS, Stephen F. Austin State U., Nacogdoches, Tex., 2002; PhD, Tex. Christian U., Ft. Worth, 2006. Engr. 7th Rsch. and Design Inst., China Nat. Nuc. Corp., TaiYuan, 1996—2000; rsch./tchg. asst. Tex. Christian U., Los Alamos, 2002—06; rsch. assoc. Los Alamos Nat. Lab., N.Mex., 2006—07, postdoctoral rsch. assoc., 2007—. Presenter in field. Mem. editl. adv. bd.: Sci. Jours. Internat., 2007; contbr. articles to profl. jours. Nuc. Energy Qi-fei scholar, China Nat. Nuc. Corp., 1996. Mem.: Am. Phys. Soc. (assoc.). Home: Trinity Dr 3000 Apt 43 Los Alamos NM 87544 Office: Los Alamos National Laboratory Los Alamos NM 87545 Personal E-mail: wang_yuejian@hotmail.com.

WANG, YUFENG, science educator; d. Qiancai Wang and Jinzhu Chen; m. Hong Cai, Jan. 3, 2005. BS in Genetics, Fudan U., Shanghai, China, 1993; MS in Stats. and Genetics, Iowa State U., 1998, PhD in Bioinformatics and Computational Biology, 2001. Grad. asst. Iowa State U., Ames, 1995—2001; rsch. scientist Am. Type Culture Collection, Manassas, Va., 2001—03; asst. prof. U. of Tex., San Antonio, 2003—. Author to profl. jours. albums. Fellow James Cornette Rsch. fellowship, Iowa State U., 2001. Mem.: Am. Statis. Assn., Internat. Soc. Computational Biology, Genetics Soc. Am. Achievements include research in systems biology of infectious diseases functional divergence and age distribution of human gene families, computational approach in drug discovery, evolutionary and population genetics of infectious diseases. Office: University of Texas San Antonio Dept of Biology 6900 N Loop 1604 West San Antonio TX 78249 Business E-Mail: ywang@utsa.edu.

WANG, YUNG-HO OPHELIA, geographer, educator; b. Taipei, Taiwan, Jan. 1, 1978; PhD student, U. Tex., Austin, 2005—. Tchg. asst. U. Ill., Urbana, 2001—05; faculty project leader Internat. Student Vols., San Jose, Costa Rica, 2004; tchg. asst. U. Tex., 2005—, rsch. asst., 2006, academic mentor, 2009—. Dancer (tango) Cultural Festival Tango Performance. Robert E. Veselka Endowed fellowship, U. Tex., 2006, Grad. Dean's Prestigious fellowship, 2008, Dorothy and Jim Doyle fellowship, 2007. Mem.: Assn. Am. Geographers. E-mail: opheliawang@mail.utexas.edu.

WANG, ZHAOYANG, engineering educator; PhD, Tsinghua U., Beijing, 2000, U. Md., Coll. Pk., 2003. Prof. Cath. U. Am., Washington, 2004—. Office: Dept Mech Engring 620 Mich Ave NE Washington DC 20064

WANG, ZHENGANG, civil engineer, researcher; M, Tsinghua U., Beijing, China, 2000; PhD in Civil and Environ. Engring., Utah State U., Logan, 2005. Cert. prof. engr., Va., 2007, profl. civil engr., Calif., 2007, floodplain mgr., Assn. State Floodplain Mgrs., 2007. Resident civil engr. China Constrn. Corp., Tanggu, Tianjin, China, 1995—97; rsch. asst. Utah Water Rsch. Lab., Utah State U., 2000—05; hydrologist R. O. Anderson Engring., Inc., Minden, Nev., 2005—06; tech. specialist III Michael Baker Jr., Inc., Alexandria, Va., 2006—08, civil engr. I, 2008—. Contbr. articles to profl. jours. Mem.: ASCE (corr.), Assn. State Floodplain Mgrs. (corr.). Achievements include development of numerical, three-dimensional, non-cohesive earthen dam breach model; numerical method to predict the one-dimensional headcut migration of cohesive and zoned embankments. Home: 3045 Madden Ct Herndon VA 20171 Personal E-mail: zhengang_wang@hotmail.com, zwang@dambreach.com.

WANG, ZHI, biomedical researcher; b. Lanchou City, Ganshu, China, June 2, 1950; m. Xia Zhang, June 24, 1953; 1 child, Ruibing. MD, Xi'an Sch. Medicine, 1981. Action dir., asst. prof. Tufts U. Sch. Medicine, Boston, 1999—2000; dir., prof. Boston U. Sch. Medicine, 2001—. Recipient Assn. Rsch. award, Am. Laryngol. Assn., 1994; grantee, NIH, 2001. Fellow: Am. Acad. Otolaryngology Head and Neck Surgery. Achievements include research in less side-effects in cancer treatment/surgery. Office: Boston Univ Sch Medicine 88 E Newton St D616 Boston MA 02118 Home: 9 Hialeah Lane Framingham MA 01701-3585 Personal E-mail: zhiw@hotmail.com. Business E-Mail: zwang@bu.edu.

WANG, ZHI, environmental scientist, educator; s. T.D. Wang and Y.Y. Zhang; m. Chunfu Zhang; 1 child, Jinlin. PhD, U. Leuven, Belgium, 1997. Asst. prof. Calif. State U., Fresno, 2003—08, assoc. prof., 2008—. Postdoc. rschr. U. Calif., Riverside, 1998—2003. Contbr. articles to profl. jour. Pres. Chinese Student Assn. Leuven, 1995—96, Chinese Am. Faculty Assn., Fresno, 2005—06. Recipient award, Calif. Concerned Scientist Assn., 2006, Provost's Rsch. Activity award, Calif. State U., Fresno, 2008; named Outstanding Tchr., Northwestern Agrl. U., 1987—90. Mem.: AAAS, European Geophys. Soc., Soil Sci. Soc. America (grad. student award com. mem., sect. soil water conservation 2006), Am. Soc. Agronomy, Am. Geophys. Union. Achievements include research in unstable finger flow, watershed measurement and modeling. Office: Calif State Univ Fresno 2576 E San Ramon Ave St 24 Fresno CA 93740 Office Fax: 559-278-5980. Business E-Mail: zwang@csufresno.edu.

WANG, ZHI JIAN, aerospace engineer; b. Leiyang, Hunan, China, Oct. 3, 1964; came to U.S., 1991; s. Le Yao and Qiao Ying (Liu) W.; m. Xiao Jie Qu, Feb. 13, 1989; children: Diane Dian Li, Victor Wei. BSc, Changsha Inst. Tech., Hunan, 1985; PhD, U. Glasgow, Scotland, 1990. Rsch. fellow U. Glasgow, 1990-91; rsch. asst. Oxford (Eng.) U., 1991; rsch. engr., group leader CFD Rsch. Corp., Huntsville, Ala., 1991—. Contbr. articles to profl. publs. Mem. AIAA. Achievements include research on high-resolution schemes, conservative Chimera, adaptive Cartesian/Prism grid algorithims and parallel computing in computational fluid dynamics. Office: CFD Rsch Corp 215 Wynn Dr NW Huntsville AL 35805-1926

WANG, ZHIYONG, optical engineer, researcher; B of Engring., Beijing Inst. of Tech., China, 1995; MSEE, Va. Poly. Inst. and State U., 2000, PhD, 2005. Fiber optic engr. Bell Labs., Lucent Technologies, Murray Hill, NJ, 2000—01, OFS Labs. OFS Co., 2001—02; micro optical sys. devel. engr. GE Global Rsch., GE, Niskayuna, NY, 2006—. New Focus Student Travel grant, Optical Soc. of Am., 2005. Mem.: IEEE, Internat. Soc. for Optical Engring., Optical Soc. of Am. Achievements include patents pending for tunability of optical fiber long period grating by self-assembled layers and its use as a sensor or modulator; patents in field. Personal E-mail: zhwang@vt.edu.

WANGBERG, LARRY W., business consultant; b. 1944; married; 3 children. BS in Mech. Engring., U. Minn., MS in Indsl. Engring. Pres., COO, metro divsn Warner Amex Cable Comm., 1978—83; CEO, chmn. Times Mirror Cable TV, 1983—94; sr.v.p. Times Mirror Co., 1983—94; CEO, chmn. StarSight Telecast Inc., 1994—97, TechTV LLC (formerly ZDTV Inc.), 1997—2002; independent bus. cons., 2002—. Bd. dirs. USCS Internat. Inc., 1996—, StarSight Telecast, Inc., 1993—97, TechTV LLC, 1997—2004, Autodesk Inc., 2000—08, ADC Telecom. Inc., 2001—, Charter Comm. Inc., 2002—, Nat. Cable Satellite Corp., Zilog. Mem.: Nat. Cable TV Assn. (past chmn.), Nat. Acad. Cable Programming (past vice-chmn.). Office: ADC Telecommunications Inc 13625 Technology Drive Minneapolis MN 55440 Office Phone: 952-938-8080. Office Fax: 952-917-1717.*

WANGER, EUGENE GILKISON, retired lawyer; b. Chgo., May 16, 1933; s. Eugene Miles and Roka Gilkison Wanger; m. Marilyn Rose Morris, July 14, 1962. AB cum laude, Amherst Coll., Mass., 1955; JD, U. Mich., Ann Arbor, 1958. Bar: Mich. 1958, US Supreme Ct. 1968. Assoc. Fraser, Trebilcock, Davis & Foster, Lansing, Mich., 1958—61, Snyder Loomis & Ewert, Lansing, 1962—65; city atty. Lansing, 1965—67; prin. Wanger Law Offices, Lansing, 1968—95. Contbr. numerous articles and hist. bibliographies. Del. Mich Constl. Conv., 1961—62; nat. bd. dirs. Am. Truck Hist. Soc., 1987—2002; mem. Ingham County Bd. Commrs., Mich., 1965—73, chmn., 1972; co-chmn. Mich. Com. Against Capital Punishment, 1972—. Recipient Legacy of Life award, Ctrl. United Meth., Detroit, 2000, conf. rm. in state office bldg. named in his honor, 2001. Mem.: ABA (mem. death penalty com. sect. on individual rights and responsibilities), State Bar Mich. (past vice chmn. com. constl. law, Champion of Justice award 2005), Am. Judicature Soc., Hist. Soc. Mich. (life), Mich. Supreme Ct. Hist. Soc. (life), Mich. Bar Found. (life), Ingham County Hist. Commn. (pres. 1977—78). Republican. Congregational. Achievements include wrote Michigan's constitutional ban of death penalty. Avocation: history.

WANGIWANG, JULIUS BOLLA, mathematics professor; s. Raymundo Wangiwang and Rosita Bolla. BSCE, St. Louis U., Baguio City, 1989; MA, De La Salle U., Manila, 1994, EdD, 1998; diploma, Merit Tech. Inst. Sch. Allied Health, Harrison, NJ, 2006. Lic. practical nurse, NJ Bd. Nursing, 2006. Tchr. h.s. Letran Coll., Calamba, Laguna, Philippines, 1991—93, instr. Laguna, Calamba, 1993—96; assoc. prof. De La Salle U., Manila, 1998—2001; tchr. math. St. Dominic Acad., Jersey City, 2001—. Adj. instr. Bergen C.C., Paramus, NJ, 1994, CUNY, NYC, 2005. Mem. St. Aloysius Adult Choir, Jersey City, 2001—02. Mem.: Pi Gamma Mu. Office: Saint Dominic Academy 2572 Kennedy Blvd Jersey City NJ 07304 Home: 413-415 9th St Unit 301 Union City NJ 07087

WANGLER, WILLIAM CLARENCE, retired insurance company executive; b. Buffalo, Dec. 7, 1929; s. Emil A. and Viola M. (Roesser) W.; m. Carol B. Sullivan, Aug. 17, 1957; children: Jeffrey W., Eric J. BS, SUNY, Cortland, 1951. Claims adjuster Liberty Mut. Ins. Co., Buffalo, 1954-60, claims supr. Miami, Fla., 1960-65, home office examiner Boston, 1965-68, asst. claims mgr. Cleve., 1968-69, claims mgr. Cleve, 1969-73, div. claims service mgr. Pitts., 1973-79, div. claims mgr., 1979-86, v.p. asst. gen. claims mgr. adminstrn. Boston, 1986-94, ret., 1994. Pres. Claims Mgrs. Counsel, Cleve., 1970; chmn. Nationwide Intercompany Arbitration, Cleve., 1969-70. Loaned exec. Mass. Bay United Way, Boston, 1964; account exec. Pitts. United Way, 1985-86. Served to capt. USMC, 1951-54. Republican. Roman Catholic. Home: 64 Trout Farm Ln Duxbury MA 02332-4609 Home Phone: 781-585-3746. Personal E-mail: vcwangler@webtv.net.

WANGSNESS, GENNA STEAD, retired hotel executive, innkeeper; b. Detroit, Feb. 2, 1942; d. William Allen Stead and Genevieve Josephine Schreiber; m. Roger Carroll Wangsness, Dec. 1, 1967; children: Alison Lee Clement, Bijali Anne, Brian William. BA in Liberal Studies, Georgetown U., 1995. Vol. Peace Corps, Tehran, Iran, 1965—67; sec. Office of Pres. Georgetown U., Washington, 1984—86, coord. adminstrv. svcs. Office of Pres., 1986—89, adminstrv. officer dept. surgery, 1989—92, adminstrv. office Sch. Summer and Continuing Edn., 1992—95; exec. asst. to exec. v.p. Am. Soc. Clin. Oncology, Alexandria, Va., 1995—96; innkeeper The Inn at Folkston, Ga., 1997—2006; ret., 2006. Author: Folkston Then and Now 1881-2003, A Self-Guided Walking Tour of Historic Downtown, Folkston, Georgia, 2003. Mem.: Alpha Sigma Lambda. Achievements include establishment of womens studies section at Charlton Public Library.

WANI, MANSUKHLAL CHHAGANLAL, chemist; b. Nandurbar, Maharastra, India, Feb. 20, 1925; came to U.S., 1958, naturalized, 1977; s. Chhagnalal Kikabhai and Maniben Chhanganlal (Shah) W.; m. Ramila Mansukhlal Dalal, Dec. 4, 1954; 1 child, Bankim M. BS with honors, St. Xavier's Coll., Bombay U., 1947, MS, 1950; PhD, Ind. U., 1962. Lectr. chemistry Bhavan's Coll., Bombay, 1951-58; rsch. asst. Ind. U., Bloomington, 1958-61; rsch. assoc. U. Wis., Madison, 1961-62; prin. scientist Rsch. Triangle Inst., Rsch. Triangle Park, NC, 1962—. Inventor anticancer drugs. Recipient B.F. Cain Meml. award Am. Assn. Cancer Rsch., 1994, City of Medicine award Durham, N.C., 1994, Award of Recognition Nat. Cancer Inst., 1996, Charles E. Kettering prize GM Cancer Rsch. Found., 2000, Ranbaxy Rsch. award. Mem. AAAS, Am. Chem. Soc., Am. Soc. Pharmacognosy, N.Y. Acad. Scis., India Assn. (pres. 1970-72), Hindu Soc. (dir. 1976-81), Assn. Indians in Am., Indo-Am. Forum, Sigma Xi, Phi Lambda Upsilon. Democrat. Avocations: reading, travel, sports. Home: 2801 Legion Ave Durham NC 27707-1921 Office: Rsch Triangle Inst 3040 W Cornwallis Rd Research Triangle Park NC 27709-2194 Home Phone: 919-489-2573; Office Phone: 919-541-6685. Business E-Mail: mcw@rti.org.

WANK, GERALD SIDNEY, periodontist, educator; b. Bklyn., Jan. 20, 1925; s. Joseph and Sadie (Ikowitz) W.; m. Gloria Baum, June 4, 1949; children: David, Stephen, Daniel. BA, NYU, 1945, DDS, 1949; cert. in orthodontia, Columbia U., 1951, cert. in periodontia, 1956. Intern Bellevue Hosp., 1949-50; pvt. practice NYC, Great Neck, N.Y., 1949—; instr. dept. periodontia, oral medicine NYU Dental Sch., 1956-63, asst. clin. prof. dept. periodontia, 1963-67, asst. prof. periodontia, oral medicine, former postgrad. dir. periodontal-prosthesis dept. fixed partial prosthesis, 1970—, clin. assoc. prof. periodontia and oral medicine, 1970-77, clin. prof. dept. periodontia and implantology, 1977—, postgrad. dir. periodontia, 1968-71, Disting. prof. periodontics, 2002; lectr. periodontology Harvard U. Sch. Dental Medicine, 1971—74; vis. lectr. N.Y.C. C.C. Sch. Dental Hygiene, 1960-65, Albert Einstein Coll. Medicine, 1967-96; sr. asst. attending staff North Shore U. Hosp., 1974-77, sr. asst. attending divsn. surgery, 1977—. Cons. orthodontic panel N.Y. State, N.Y.C. depts. health, 1953-80; cons. periodontal prosthesis, Goldwater Meml. Hosp., N.Y.C.; former postgrad. instr. 1st Dist. Dental Soc. Postgrad. Sch., dist. claims com.; lectr. in field; mem. com. admissions N.Y. U. Coll. Dentistry, 1975-86, chmn. fund raising, 1976-77; cons. N.Y. VA Hosp., 1996—. Contbr. to: Practice of Periodontia, 1960, Dental Clinics of North America, 1972, 81, Manual of Clinical Periodontics, 1973; contbr. articles to profl. jours. Capt. USAF, 1953-55. Recipient Alumni Meritorious Service award NYU, 1981, Coll. Dentistry Alumni Achievement award NYU, 1983, Disting. Prof. Periodontics award NYU Coll. Dentistry, 2002, named to Leaders in Am. Sci., 1963-64. Fellow APHA, Am. Acad. Oral Medicine, Acad. Gen. Dentistry, N.Y. Acad. Dentistry (life), Internat. Coll. Dentists (life), Am. Coll. Dentistry (life), Am. Acad. Oral Medicine (pres. N.Y. sect. 1971-72); mem. N.Y. Coll. Dentists (dir.), ADA, Dental Soc. N.Y.C. (dir. 1st dist., chmn. ethics com. 1985-86, peer rev. com.), Fedn. Dentaire Internat., Am. Assn. Dental Schs., N.Y. State Pub. Health Assn., AAUP, Pan Am. Med. Assn. (life), AAAS, ADA, Am. Acad. Periodontology, Sci. Rsch. Soc. Am., Northeastern Soc. Periodontia (life), Am. Acad. Dental Medicine, Acad. Gen. Dentistry, Internat. Acad. Orthodontia, Am. Assn. Endodontists (life), Am. Acad. Periodontia (life), Am. Acad. Oral Medicine (life), NYU Coll. Dentistry Alumni Assn. (dir., sec. 1973-74, v.p. 1974-75, pres. 1976-77), Am. Assn. Endodontists, NYU Coll. Dentistry Dental Assocs. (charter), Acad. Oral Rehab. (hon.), First Dist. Dental Soc. (program chmn. 1984, chmn. continuing edn. 1983, sec., 1985, v.p. Eastern Dental Soc. br. 1986, pres.-elect 1987, pres. br. 1988, bd. dirs. 1989—, Meritorious Svc. award 1997), NY County Dental Soc. (peer rev. com.), Am. Acad. Osseointegration (life), NYU Gallatin Assocs., Alumni Fedn. NYU (dir. 1976-81), N.Y. County Dental Soc. (Dist. Claims Com.), Soc. of the Torch, Masons, Century Club, NYU Club, Fresh Meadow Country Club, Omicron Kappa Upsilon (life), Alpha Omega. Jewish. Home and Office: 40 Bayview Ave Great Neck NY 11021-2819 Office: 30 E 40th St New York NY 10016-1201 Office Phone: 516-487-7877. Personal E-mail: gwank@aol.com.

WANKAT, PHILLIP CHARLES, chemical engineering educator; b. Oak Park, Ill., July 11, 1944; s. Charles and Grace Wankat; m. Dorothy Nel Richardson, Dec. 13, 1980; children: Charles, Jennifer. BS in Chem. Engring., Purdue U., 1966, MS in Edn., 1982; PhD, Princeton U., 1970. From asst. prof. to C.L. Lovell disting. prof. chem. engring Purdue U., West Lafayette, Ind., 1970—, head freshman engring., 1987-95, interim dir. continuing engring. edn., 1996, head interdisciplinary engring., 2000—04. Cons. pharm. firm, 1985-94. Author: Large Scale Ads and Chromatog, 1986, Equil Staged Separations, 1988, Rate Controlled Separations, 1990, Teaching Engineering, 1993, The Effective, Efficient Professor, 2002, Separation Process Engineering, 2007. With AUS, 1962-64. Recipient award in Separations Sci. and Tech., Am. Chem. Soc., 1994. Mem. AIChE, Am. Soc. Engring. Edn. (Union Carbide Lectr. award 1997), Am. Chem. Soc. Achievements include patents in field. Avocations: fishing, canoeing, camping. Office: Purdue U Dept Chem Engring 480 Stadium Mall Dr West Lafayette IN 47907-2100

WANKEL, ROBERT EDMOND, performing arts organization administrator; b. Bklyn., Dec. 5, 1946; s. Ellery E. and Rose J. (Falco) W.; m. Helen Pfeiffer, Aug. 2, 1969; 1 child, Virginia. BBA, St. John's U., Jamaica, NY, 1968. CPA, NY. Acct. Laventhol & Horwath, NYC, 1968-75; contr., v.p. fin. The Shubert Orgn., Inc., NYC, 1975, exec. v.p., CFO, pres., co-CEO, 2008—, mem. bd. dirs., 2008—. Mem. exec. com. Broadway League, mem. bd. govs., Times Square Alliance, mem. exec. com.; chmn. emeritus, trustee Am. Acad. Dramatic Arts; officer, dir. Actors Studio. Office: The Shubert Orgn 234 W 44th St Fl 6 New York NY 10036-3979*

WANNER, ERIC, foundation executive; b. Wilmington, Del., Mar. 14, 1942; s. Edwin and Isabel Smith (Speakman) W.; m. Patricia Attix, June 13, 1964 (div. 1976); children: Noel Edwin, Erin Cole; m. Carla Francesca Seal, June 18, 1983; children: Lindzay Elizabeth. BA, Amherst Coll., 1963; PhD, Harvard U., 1969. Asst. to assoc. prof. Harvard U., Cambridge, Mass., 1968-76; behavioral sci. editor Harvard U. Press, Cambridge, Mass., 1976-82; program officer Alfred P. Sloan Found., NYC, 1982-84, v.p., 1984-86; pres. Russell Sage Found, NYC, 1986—. Trustee Ctr. for Advanced Study in Behavioral Scis., 1993-99; bd. dirs. Dogan Found., Paris, 2002-07, Am. Acad. Polit. Social Sci. 2003-09, Rockefeller Archive Ctr., 2009- Fulbright fellow Sussex U., Brighton, Eng., 1979, N.Y. Inst. for Humanities fellow, NYU, 1985-93, Am. Acad. Arts and Scis. fellow, 1994—. Mem.: Century Assn., Sigma Xi. Office: Russell Sage Found 112 E 64th St New York NY 10065-7383 Business E-Mail: ew@rsage.org.

WANNIER, MARIO MARC-ANTOINE, research scientist, multimedia specialist, director; b. Basle, Switzerland, Sept. 16, 1951; arrived in U.S., 2000; s. Willy Wannier and Aurelie Wannier-Bourquard; m. Clemencia Bello, Jan. 6, 1975; children: Catherine, Marianne. Vordiplomexamen, Basle U., Switzerland, 1973, Diplomexamen, 1975, PhD in Earth Scis., 1979. Asset mgr. Sarawak Shell Berhad, Miri, Malaysia, 1994—99; subsurface projects mgr. Shell Oil Co., Houston, 2000—07, head rsch. projects The Hague, Netherlands, 2007—. Author (dir.): Destination Miri: A Geological Tour, 1998 (Multimedia CD Title of Yr. award Pikom-Computimes IT, 1999), Northern Sarawak's National Parks and Giant Caves. Designer geol. exhbn. on the jura mountains Musee d'Histoire, Delemont, Switzerland, 1973—75. With Swiss AF, 1971—78. Personal E-mail: mwannier@yahoo.com.

WANNSTEDT, DAVID RAYMOND, college football coach, former professional football coach; b. Pitts., May 21, 1952; m. Jan Wannstedt; children: Keri, Jami. Grad., U. Pitts., 1974. Player Green Bay Packers, 1974; grad. asst. U. Pitts. Panthers, 1975—76, receivers & spl. teams coach, 1977—78; defensive line coach Okla. State U. Cowboys, 1979-82, U. So. Calif. Trojans, 1983-85; defensive. coord. U. Miami Hurricanes, 1986-89; def. coord. Dallas Cowboys, 1989-93; head coach Chgo. Bears, 1993-98; asst. head coach Miami Dolphins, 1999-2000, head coach, 2000—04, U. Pitts. Panthers, 2004—. Named to NCAA 2nd team All-East, NFL Coach of the Year UPI, Football News, 1994; inducted into Western Pa. Hall of Fame, 1990. Office: U Pitts Football Team PO Box 7436 Pittsburgh PA 15213 Office Phone: 412-648-8711.

WANSBROUGH, ANN, legal assistant; b. Ft. Worth, Mar. 1, 1952; d. Frank and Hazel S. Hilton; 1 child, Trenton Scott Smith; m. Aaron Gregory Wansbrough, July 7, 1995. BS in Edn., Baylor U., Waco, Tex., 1974. Merchandiser J C Penney Co., Dallas, 1974—76, sr. merchandiser, 1976—78, pers. mgr., 1978—81; nat. sales mgr. T. Cappelli Handbags, Dallas, 1986—97; sales rep. Ann Smith and Assocs., Dallas, 1986—2002; legal asst. Ferrer Poirot & Wansbrough, Dallas, 2002—. Office: 2603 Oak Lawn Ave Dallas TX 75219-4021

WANTA, WAYNE, communications educator; s. Edwin Lee and Alice May Wanta; m. Carol Ann Armbrust, Aug. 15, 1983; 1 child, Caitlin Anne. BA, U. Wis., Madison, 1980; MA, U. Tex., Austin, 1989; PhD, U. Tex., 1989. Sports writer Wis. State Jour., Madison, 1978—80; copy editor Post-Courier, Charleston, SC, 1980—81, Albuquerque Jour., 1981—82, Dallas Times Herald, 1982—83, Austin Am.-Statesman, 1983—86; asst. prof. So. Ill. U., Carbondale, 1989—92; assoc. prof. U. Oreg., Eugene, 1992—99, U. Fla., Gainesville, 1999—2001; prof. U. Mo., Columbia, 2001—. Author: (book) Public and the National Agenda: How People Learn about Important Issues; contbr. articles to profl. jours. Exec. dir. Ctr. Digital Globe, Columbia, Mo., 2004—08. Grantee Ford Found. grant, Ford Found., 1998, Internat. Travel grant, U. Mo., 2003, 2005, 2007, Spkr. and Specialists grant, US Dept. State, Office Internat. Programs, 2005. Mem.: World Assn. Pub. Opinion Rsch., Internat. Comm. Assn. (Top Faculty Paper award 1988—89), Assn. Edn. Journalism and Mass Comm. (pres. 2006—07, Top Faculty Paper award 1993, Krieghbaum Under-40 award 1998). Home: 2008 S Deerborn Cir Columbia MO 65203 Office: Univ Mo Sch Journalism Columbia MO 65211-1200 Business E-Mail: wantaw@missouri.edu.

WANTLAND, WILLIAM CHARLES, retired bishop, lawyer; b. Edmond, Okla., Apr. 14, 1934; s. William Lindsay and Edna Louise (Yost) W. BA, U. Hawaii, 1957; JD, Okla. City U., 1967; D in Religion, Geneva Theol. Coll., Knoxville, Tenn., 1976; DD (hon.), Nashotah House, Wis., 1983, Seabury-Western Sem., Evanston, Ill., 1983. With FBI, various locations, 1954-59, Ins. Co. of N.Am., Oklahoma City, 1960-62; law clk.-atty. Bishop & Wantland, Seminole, Okla., 1962-77; vicar St. Mark's Ch., Seminole, 1963-77, St. Paul's Ch., Holdenville, Okla., 1974-77; presiding judge Seminole Mcpl. Ct., 1970-77; atty. gen. Seminole Nation of Okla., 1969-72, 75-77; exec. dir. Okla. Indian Rights Assn., Norman, 1972-73; rector St. John's Ch., Oklahoma City, 1977-80; bishop Episcopal Diocese of Eau Claire, Wis., 1980-99; interim bishop of Navajoland, 1993-94; ret., 1999. Adj. prof. Law Sch. U. Okla., Norman, 1970-78; instr. canon law Nashotah House, 1983-97, 2004-09; nat. coun. Evang. and Cath. Mission, Chgo., 1977-90; mem. Episcopal Commn. on Racism, 1990-92, Episcopal Coun. Indian Ministries, 1990-95, Standing Commn. on Constn. and Canons, 1992-95; assisting bishop Diocese of Dallas, 2002—04, of Ft. Worth, 2000—. Author: Foundations of the Faith, 1982, Canon Law of the Episcopal Church, 1984, The Prayer Book and the Catholic Faith, 1994; The Catholic Faith, The Episcopal Church and the Ordination of Women, 1997; co-author: Oklahoma Probate Forms, 1971; contbr. articles to profl. jours. Pres. Okla. Conf. Mcpl. Judges, 1973; v.p. South African Ch. Union, 1985-95; trustee Nashotah House, Wis., 1981—, chmn., 1992-98; bd. dirs. SPEAK, Eureka Springs, Ark., 1983-89; Wis. adv. com. US Civil Rights Commn., 1990-91; support com. Native Am. Rights Fund, 1990—; coun. mem. City of Seminole, Okla., 2002—, vice mayor, 2003—; co-chmn. Luth.-Anglican-Roman Cath. Commn. of Wis., 1989-95; pres. Wis. Episc. Conf., 1995-97, Wis. Coun. Chs., 1985-86; active Living Ch. Found., 1981-02; bd. dirs. Seminole Nation Hist. Soc., 1999—, pres., 2006—; adv. bd. Seminole Hist. Soc., 2003—. Recipient Most Outstanding Contbn. to Law and Order award Okla. Supreme Ct., 1975, Outstanding Alumnus award Okla. City U., 1980, Wis. Equal Rights Coun. award, 1986, Manitou Ikwe award Indian Alcoholism Coun., 1988, Episcopal Synod Pres.'s award, 1995, 2004. Mem. Okla. Bar Assn., Okla. Indian Bar Assn., Oklahoma City Law Sch. Alumni Assn. (pres. 1968), Ct. Indian Offenses Seminole Nation Okla. (chief magistrate 2006—). Democrat. Episcopalian. Avocations: canoeing, skin-diving, cross country skiing. Personal E-mail: puca382@mbo.net. *If we truly believe that God reigns, we will so order our lives that such a belief is clearly reflected in all that we do and say; further, such a belief will shape our relations, not only with all other people, but all of God's created order.*

WAPIENNIK, CARL FRANCIS, manufacturing executive, planetarium and science institute administrator; b. Donora, Pa., Oct. 10, 1926; s. Karl and Rose (Kidzinski) W.; m. Elva Louise Bartron, Nov. 27, 1953; children: Carl Eric, Ellen Louise. BS, U. Pitts., 1953. Prodn. supr. RCA, Canonsburg, Pa., 1953—54; staff physicist Buhl Planetarium and Inst. Popular Sci., Pitts., 1954—64, exec. dir., 1964—82; owner, operator Work-O-Art Miniatures (small mfg. firm), 1983—2003. Patentee means for controlling liquid flow. Mem. Rostraver Twp. Planning Commn., 1965-67; mem. adv. bd. Allegheny C. of C. (formerly North Side Pitts. C. of C.), 1966-67, dir., 1968-73, pres., 1970; mem. adv. coun. Salvation Army, 1978-82; bd. dirs. Bapt. Homes, Pitts., 1982-94; chmn. Rostraver Twp. Mcpl. Water Authority, 1990-94. With USNR, 1945-46. Recipient Man of Yr. award in sci. Pitts. Jaycees, 1969. Mem. Pitts. Bapt. Assn. (bd. dirs. 1976-82), Phi Beta Kappa, Sigma Pi Sigma. Home: 602 Salem Church Rd Belle Vernon PA 15012-2906

WAPLES, JAN SUSAN (KLEIN WAPLES), priest; b. Seattle, Wash., Nov. 22, 1948; d. Jerry and Freda Klein; m. Douglas J. Waples, Dec. 29, 1971 (div. Feb. 9, 1998). MA in History, U. Nev., Las Vegas, 1972; BS in History, Calif. State U., Northridge, 1978; MDiv, Ripon Coll. Uddesdon, Univ Oxford, 2000, Ch. Div. Sch. Pacific, Grad. Theol. Union, Berkeley, Calif., 2001; degree in Clin. Residency, U. Iowa Hosps. & Clinics, 2003. Cert. ordained priest Episcopal Diocese Calif., 2001, in 5 precepts Kwan Um Sch. Zen, 2001. Priest-in-training St. Mary's Anglican Ch., Oxfordshire, England, 1999—2000; assoc. rector St. Francis Episcopal Ch., 2001—02; chaplain resident U. Iowa Hosps. & Clinics, 2002—03; bd. cert. chaplain St. Rose Dominican Hosps., Henderson, Nev., 2003—. Cons. Lee Pub. Rels., Redwood City, Calif.; faculty Oates Inst., Louisville, 2008—, columnist spirituality & fiction, 2008—. Contbr. chapters to books. Mem.: Assn. Profl. Chaplains, Iowa Rep. Party (co-chair 1991—93), Air Force Officers Wives Clubs (bd. govs. 1979—87). Non-Partisan. Episcopalian. Avocations: swimming, hiking, history, art, writing. Office: St Rose Dominican Hosps RDL Campus 102 E Lake Mead Pkwy Henderson NV 89015 Personal E-mail: janwaples@aol.com. Business E-Mail: jan.waples@chw.edu.

WAPNER, KEITH LESLIE, orthopedic surgeon, educator; b. Phila., Sept. 27, 1953; s. Paul Mordecai and Evelyn (Locke) W.; m. June Carosia, Jan. 16, 1982; children: Peter, Charles. BA, U. Pa., 1976; MD, Temple U., 1980. Diplomate Am. Bd. Orthopedic Surgery. Intern in surgery Hosp. of U. Pa., 1980-81, fellowship in orthop., 1981-82, resident in orthop. surgery, 1982-85, clin. prof. orthop. surgery, dir. orthop. foot and ankle surgery Phila., 2000—; asst. prof. Thomas Jefferson U., Phila., 1986-93, assoc. prof., 1993-95; prof. Allegheny U., Phila., 1996—2000. Adj. prof. orthop. Preyol Coll. Medicine, 2000-, clin. prof. U. Pa., 2000-. Mem. editl. bd. Seminars in Arthroplasty, 1990, Operative Techniques in Orthopaedics, 1990, Foot and Ankle, The Official Jour. of Am. Orthop. Foot and Ankle Soc., 1992, Clin. Orthops. and Related Rsch., 1993; reviewer Am. Jour. Sports Medicine, 1993; contbr. numerous articles to profl. jours. Bd. dirs. Ohev Shalom Hebrew Sch., Wallingford, Pa., 1995. Named one of Top Doctors, Phila. Mag., 2002, 2004-08. Fellow Am. Coll. Surgeons, Am. Acad. Orthop. Surgery, Am. Orthop. Foot and Ankle Soc.; mem. Am. Diabetes Soc., Pa. Med. Soc., Phila. Med. Soc., Phila. Orthop. Soc., Phila. Rheumatism Soc. Office: PennCare Farm Journal Bldg 5th Fl 230 W Washington Sq Philadelphia PA 19106

WARAB, KRISTI, librarian; b. Gary, Ind., Mar. 16, 1971; d. Jerry Dale White and Phyllis Esther Lindsay; m. Amirouche White, June 13, 1997; children: Amira Hanan, Johra Yasmin, Nadia Noor. MS in Bus. Mgmt., U. Mass., Boston, 1996; MLS, Simmons Coll., Boston, 2001. Serials & acquisitions asst. Mus. Fine Arts, Boston, 1999—2001; tech. svcs. libr. Wheelock Coll., Boston, 2001—. Independent. Muslim. Achievements include research in the Swiecikowski family of Chicago; descendants of Thomas Lindsey of Northern Ireland. Avocation: piano. Home: 36 Intrepid Cir Unit 106 Marblehead MA 01945 Office: Wheelock Coll 132 The Riverway Boston MA 02215 Business E-Mail: kwarab@wheelock.edu.

WARBERG, WILLETTA, concert pianist, music educator; b. Twin Falls, Idaho, June 2, 1932; d. George William Warberg and Ethel Margaret (Sargent) Warberg-Chandler; m. David Jacob Bar-Illan, Sept. 3, 1954 (div.); children: Daniela, Jeremy Oscar. Student, Colo. Women's Coll., 1950-51, Aspen Music Camp, 1951; studied with, Rudolph Firkusny, 1951-53; BS, Mannes Coll. New Sch. Music, NYC, 1954. Assoc. food editor Look mag., NYC, 1956-61; food editor Status mag., NYC, 1961-62, Ladie's Home Jour., NYC, 1964-66; photog. stylist Gourmet mag., NYC, 1961-64, freelance writer, photog. stylist, 1965-75; pres., owner Willetta Enterprises, advt. agy., Twin Falls, 1976-84; food columnist, music and arts critic Times News, 1978-87; duo-piano ptnr. with Robert Starer, NYC, Woodstock, 1991—2000; piano coach Saugerties, NY, 1991—. Made feasibility study of restaurant situation in Israel, U.S. Dept. State ICA Point 4 Program, Washington and Israel, 1960; artist-in-residence Holy Cross Concert Series, Kingston, N.Y., 1994—. Concert pianist, Idaho, Oreg., Utah, Wash., Colo., N.Y.C., N.Y. State, 1940—; author: Cooking from Scratch, 1976, Space Age Cookery, 1977; syndicated food columnist Willetta Says, 1978-87; contbr. food and sci. articles to Cosmopolitan, Modern Maturity, Esquire, Sun Valley, Sci. Digest, also other mags. Bd. dirs. N.W. Opera Assn., 1984-87; pres. bd. dirs. Woodstock Lyric Theatre, 1994-2000; v.p. bd. dirs. Woodstock Chamber Orch., 1993—; chmn. Friends of the Maverick Concerts Inc., Woodstock, N.Y., 1999—, bd. dirs., 2007-. Winner Rocky Mountain talent search contest Salt Lake Tribune and Salt Lake Telegram, 1949. Mem. Nat. Fedn. Music Clubs, Music Tchrs. Nat. Assn. (cert.), Kingston Music Soc. Avocations: designing and sewing clothes, painting still lifes, swimming, developing recipes, writing. Personal E-mail: wwarberg@hvc.rr.co.

WARBURTON, CHRISTOPHER EBUN, economics professor; s. Miriam Sarah Warburton; m. Nabia Andrea Taylor, July 3, 1993; children: Denise Samantha, Conrad Ebun. PhD in Economics, Fordham U., NY, 2003. Adj. prof. Monroe Coll., Bronx, NY, 2003—06, Bronx CC, 2003—06; non tchg. adj. prof. Lehman Coll., Bronx, 2004—06; upward bound instr. Fordham U., Bronx, 2004—06. Assoc. editor Common Ground, Altona, Australia, 2008—. Author: (book) The Evolution of Crises and Underdevelopment in Africa, Research and Profit Maximization in Finance and Economics; contbr. scientific papers to numerous profl. jours. Coord. UNESCO Club, Freetown, Sierra Leone, 1986—88. Grantee, CUNY, 2007—08. Mem.: Am. Soc. Internat. Law, Am. Soc. Internat. Law, Am. Econ. Soc., Omicron Delta Epsilon, Internat. Soc. Economics. Mem. Stroudsburg Wesleyan Ch. Avocations: soccer, travel. Office: John Jay Coll Criminal Justice 899 10th Ave New York NY 10019

WARBURTON, REED THOMAS, lawyer; b. Lexington, Va., Feb. 8, 1976; s. Roy David and Sally Ann Warburton; m. Sarah Oliver, Aug. 30, 2003; 1 child, Reed Thomas Jr. BA, Va. Mil. Inst., Lexington, 1998; JD, U. Va., Charlottesville, 2001. Bar: Fla. 2001, Ala. 2002, Ga. 2009, U.S. Dist. Ct. (no., so., mid. dists.) Ala. 2003, U.S. Ct. Appeals (11th and 5th cirs.) 2003, US Dist. Ct. (mid. dist.), Ga. 2009, US Dist. Ct. (no. dist.), Fla. 2009. Assoc. Bradley Arant Boult Cummings LLP, Birmingham, Ala., 2003—. Office: Bradley Arant Boult Cummings 1819 5th Ave N Birmingham AL 35203

WARCHOL, JUDITH MARIE, secretarial service company executive; b. Chgo., Apr. 20; d. Michael Henry and Rose Therese (Vito) Schmidt Fitpold; m. Daniel August Warchol, Aug. 17, 1963 (dec.); children— Kathleen Louise, Raymond Michael, Sherry Lynn. Exec. sec. N.W. Malt & Grain, Chgo., 1958-63; pres. Judy's Mailing & Secretarial Service, Northbrook, 1968—, Americano Motor Inn, Beaumont, Tex., 1976— mem. Northfield Twp. Human Svcs. Commn., 2002-, bd. dirs. Internat. Ctr. Def. & Arts, 2000-; owner Jovies Family Restaurant, Beaumont, 1977-78, Chances R, Beaumont, 1978-80; v.p. Golden Triangle Limo Service, Beaumont, 1982—; mng. ptnr. Warchol Investments, Beaumont, Tex., 1982—. V.p. Band Booster Club, Stanley Field Jr. High Sch., Northbrook, 1975-77; leader Blue Bird Group, Camp Fire Girls, Northbrook, 1971-76; bd. dirs. Stanley Field Jr. High Parent Tchr. Club, Northbrook, 1970-78; foster parent, Sierra Leone, 1978-85. Mem. Women in Mgmt., Nat. Assn. Secretarial Services, Mail Advertisers Assn., Northbrook C. of C. (bd. dirs. 1984-86), Northbrook Rotary Club(first Woman Pres. 1996-97). Republican. Roman Catholic. Avocations: fitness programs, self-improvement studies. Home: 3493 Techny Rd Northbrook IL 60062-5066 Office: Judy's Mailing & Secretarial Svc 3450 Commercial Ave Northbrook IL 60062-1833

WARCKEN, NANCY B., elementary school educator; d. Marvin and Geanice Bell; children: Mark, Lindsay, Jeff. BS in Elem. Edn., U. Tex.-Austin, 1973. Tchr. Old Town Elem., Round Rock, Tex., 1988—97; math. tchr. Cedar Valley Mid. Sch., Austin, Tex., 1998—; campus coord. Ptnrs. Edn. Cedar Valley Mid. Sch., 2000—07; chair, math dept. Cedar Valley Mid. Sch., 2007—. Recipient Tchr. of Yr., Cedar Valley Mid. Sch., 2002—03; named one of Outstanding Am. Tchrs., Nat. Honor Roll, 2007. Mem.: Austin Area Council Tchrs. Math., Tex. Council Tchrs. Math., Nat. Council Tchrs. Math. Avocations: hiking, travel, scrapbooks.

WARD, AARON, professional hockey player; b. Windsor, Ont., Can., Jan. 17, 1973; Attended, U. Mich. Defenseman Detroit Red Wings, 1993—2001, Carolina Hurricanes, 2001—06, 2009—, NY Rangers, 2006—07, Boston Bruins, 2007—09. Achievements include being a member of Stanley Cup Champion Detroit Red Wings, 1997, 1998, Carolina Hurricanes, 2006. Office: Carolina Hurricanes RBC Ctr 1400 Edwards Mill Rd Raleigh NC 27607*

WARD, ANNE STARR MINTON, musician, educator; d. James Royster and Bobbie Lee (Clegg) Minton; m. Benjamin Kirby Ward, June 19, 1966; children: David Alexander, Karen Virginia. MusB cum laude, U. N.C., Greensboro, 1965, M Music Edn., 1966. Tchr. orch. Dade County Schs., Miami, Fla., 1967—68, Jacksonville County Schs., Fla., 1968—69; pvt. violin tchr. Florence, SC, 1974—; mem. faculty N.C. Suzuki Inst., Greenville, 1986—2005. Violinist Florence Symphony Orch., 1974—2005, concert master, 2000—; violinist Piedmont Trio, SC, 1996—2000; co-chmn. Florence Ctr. Arts, Inc., 2000—05. Lay leader Ctrl. United Meth. Ch., Florence, 1996—2003; chmn. Evangelistic awards S.C. conf. United Meth. Ch., 1997—2003; mem. Florence Downtown Devel. Bd., 2002—05; bd. dirs. Florence 2010 Com., 2001—02. Mem.: Music Educators Nat. Conf., Florence-Darlington String Assn. (co-founder 1998, pres. 1998—2006), Suzuki Assn. Am., AMA Alliance. Avocation: travel.

WARD, ANTHONY, theatrical scenic and costume designer; Scenic & costume designer (Broadway plays) A Midsummer Night's Dream, 1996, Oklahoma!, 2002—03 (Olivier award & Outer Critics Circle award for Best Set Design), Gypsy, 2003—04, Chitty Chitty Bang Bang, 2005, production designer Macbeth, 2008, scenic & costume designer Mary Stuart, 2009 (Tony award for Best Costume Design of a Play, 2009), Uncle Vanya (Opie award for Best Set Design), (plays) Twelfth Night, (London West End plays) Oliver!, My Fair Lady, Royal Shakespeare Co., Nat. Theatre, Royal Ballet, Almeida Theatre, Donmar Warehouse, (Operas) The Makropoulos Case, Metropolitan Opera NYC, Peter Grimes, Opera North, (ballets) Nutcracker!, Matthew Bourne's New Adventures. Mailing: Broadhurst Theatre 235 W 44th St New York NY 10036*

WARD, CHESTER LAWRENCE, physician, consultant; b. Woodland, Calif., June 8, 1932; s. Benjamin Briggs and Nora Elizabeth Ward; m. Sally Diane Ward, Dec. 10, 1960; children: Katharine, Lynda. BA, U. Calif., Santa Barbara, 1955; MPH, U. Calif., Berkeley, 1966; MD, U. So. Calif., 1962; grad., Indsl. Coll. Armed Forces, 1978. Commd. 2d lt., inf. U.S. Army, 1954, advanced through grades to brig. gen., 1980; surgeon 5th Spl. Forces, Ft. Bragg, NC, Vietnam, 1963-64; chief aviation medicine, preventive medicine and aeromed. consultation service Ft. Rucker, Ala., 1967-68; surgeon Aviation Brigade and USA Vietnam Aviation Medicine Cons., 1968-69; flight surgeon Office of U.S. Army Surgeon Gen., 1970-71; physician The White House, Washington, 1971-75, 76; dir. environ. quality rsch. U.S. Army Med. Rsch. and Devel. Commd., 1975-76; comdr. Womack Cmty. Hosp., 1978—80; surgeon XVIII Airborne Corps, Ft. Bragg, 1978-80; comdr. William Beaumont Army Med. Ctr., El Paso, Tex., 1980-82; med. dir. Union Oil Co., Schaumburg, Ill., 1982-83, dir. domestic medicine LA, 1983-84; exec. dir. continuing med. edn. and clin. prof. emergency medicine U. So. Calif. Sch. Medicine, LA, 1984-85; dir., health officer Dept. Pub. Health, Butte County, Calif., 1985-95; cons., contractor, pvt. practice medicine, 1996—; med. dir. NorCal EMS, 2001—05. Trustee, pres. Oroville Union HS Dist., 1998—2002; chmn. Citizen's Bond Oversight Com., 2003—05; dir. The Estuary Owners' Assn., 2006—08, pres., 2007—08; mem. state bd. pilot commr. Pilot Fitness Cmty., 2009—; apptd. by Gov. Wilson Calif. Commn. Emergency Med. Svcs., past commr. Decorated DSM, Legion of Merit (2), Bronze Star, Air medal (5). Fellow: Aerospace Med. Assn., Am. Coll. Preventive Medicine (past regent); mem.: No. Calif. Emergency Med. Svcs. Inc. (governing bd. 1987—2006, dir.), Calif. Med. Assn. (past del.), Butte-Glenn County Med. Soc. (past pres.), Mil. Officers Assn. (past chpt. pres.). Personal E-mail: tvldoc@sbcglobal.net.

WARD, CHRISTOPHER, computer scientist, researcher; b. London, Eng., Aug. 17, 1959; s. Michael Ward and Jean Mary Potter; m. Kathleen M McWilliams, Sept. 1, 1990; children: Keegan D McWilliams-Ward, Eva J McWilliams-Ward, Christina C McWilliams-Ward. BSc in Computer Sci., U. Hertfordshire, Eng., 1983; MSc in Computer Sci., U. Fla., Gainesville, 1985, PhD in Computer Sci., 1987. Asst. prof. Auburn U., Ala., 1988—93; assoc. prof. Hunter Coll., CUNY, NYC, 1993—96; sr. mem., tech. staff and group head Sarnoff Corp., Princeton, NJ, 1996—2000; rsch. staff mem. and mgr. IBM T.J. Watson Rsch. Ctr., Hawthorne, NY, 2000—. Author: (textbook) Computer Organization and the MC 68000; contbr. articles to profl. jours. Mem. bd. edn. Glen Ridge Sch. Dist., NJ, 2001—07. Recipient Presdl. Recognition award, U. Fla., 1985, Authors award, Auburn U., 1993, Achievement award, Sarnoff Corp., 1998, Rsch. award, IBM Corp., 2005—08. Mem.: IEEE (sr.), Internat. Broadcasters Conv. (coun. mem. 1997—2000), Assn. Computing Machinery, Upsilon Pi Epsilon (chpt. pres. 1987—88). Achievements include papers and patents in field. Office: IBM TJ Watson Research 19 Skyline Drive 1S-D60 Hawthorne NY 10532 Personal E-mail: christopher_ward@ieee.org. Business E-Mail: cw1@us.ibm.com.

WARD, CHRISTOPHER O., transportation executive, director; BA, Macalester Coll., St. Paul; ThM, Harvard U. Divinity Sch., Cambridge, Mass. Sr. v.p. transp./commerce NYC Econ. Devel. Corp.; asst. commr. NYC Dept. Telecomm. and Energy; dir. rsch. NYC Dept. Consumer Affairs; chief planning/external affairs, dir. port redevel. Port Authority of NY/NJ, 1997—2002; commr. NYC Dept. Environ. Protection, 2002—05; CEO Am. Stevedoring, Inc., Bklyn., 2005—06; mng. dir. Gen. Contractors Assn. NY, Inc., 2006—08; exec. dir. Port Authority of NY/NJ, 2008—. Adj. prof. Columbia U. Sch. Internat. and Pub. Affairs; pres. Port Authority Trans-Hudson Corp., Newark Legal and Comm. Ctr. Urban Renewal Corp., NY/NJ Railroad Corp., 2008—. Office: Port Authority of NY & NJ Corp Hdqs 225 Park Ave S New York NY 10003 Office Phone: 212-435-7000.

WARD, DAVID, educational consultant, former educational association administrator, academic administrator; b. Manchester, Eng., July 8, 1938; arrived in US, 1960; s. Horace and Alice (Harwood) Ward; m. Judith B. Freifeld, June 11, 1964; children: Michael J.H., Peter F.B. BA, U. Leeds, Eng., 1959, MA, 1961; MS, U. Wis., 1961, PhD, 1963; LittD, U. Leeds, 1992. Lectr. Carleton U., Ottawa, Ont., 1963—64; asst. prof. U. Brit. Columbia, Vancouver, 1964—66, U. Wis., Madison, 1966—67, assoc. prof., 1967—70, prof., 1970—, chmn. geography dept., 1974—77, assoc. dean Grad. Sch., 1980—88, provost and vice chancellor acad. affairs, Andrew Clark prof. geography, 1989—94, chancellor, 1994—2000; pres. Am. Coun. Edn., Washington, 2000—08; cons., 2008—. Mem. exec. com. Argonne Nat. Lab., Ill., 1990—93; dir.-at-large Social Sci. Rsch. Coun., 1991—93; mem. Kellogg Commn. on Future of Land Grant Univs.; chair Internet 2, Consortium Advances Network Devel.; mem. coun. UN U., 2004—; mem. Sec. of Edn.'s Commn. on Future of Edn., 2005. Author: Cities and Immigrants, 1970, Geographic Perspectives on Americas Past, 1978, Poverty Ethnicity and the American City, 1989, Landscape of Modernity, 1992; contbr. articles to profl. jours. Fellow Guggenheim fellow, 1970, Einstein fellow, Hebrew U., 1980, Fulbright fellow, Australian Nat. U., 1979. Fellow: Am. Acad. Arts and Scis.; mem.: Assn. Am. Geographers (pres. 1989). Home: 1099 22nd St NW 410 Washington DC 20037

WARD, DAVID ALLEN, sociology educator; b. Dedham, Mass., June 21, 1933; s. Theodore Allen and Jessie Miller (Ketchum) W.; m. Carol Jane Barton, June 10, 1957 (div. 1964); children: Douglas Allen, Andrew Barton; m. Reneé Ellen Light, Mar. 10, 1967. BA, Colby Coll., 1955; PhD, U. Ill., 1960. Asst. prof. Wash. State U., Pullman, 1960-61; asst. research sociologist UCLA, 1961-64; assoc. prof. U. Minn., Mpls., 1965-68, prof., 1968—2002, chmn. dept. sociology, 1984-88, 92-95. Chmn. Salzburg (Austria) Seminar in Am. Studies, 1977; cons. jud. com. U.S. Ho. Reps., Washington, 1984. Co-author: Women's Prison, 1965, Prison Treatment, 1971; co-editor: Delinquency, Crime and Social Process, 1969, Confinement in Maximum Custody, 1981, Alcatraz: The Gangster Years, 2009. Mem. Mpls. Civilian Police Rev. Bd., 1991-94. Liberal Arts fellow Harvard U. Law Sch., 1968-69; Fulbright research fellow, 1971-72; research fellow Norwegian Fgn. Office, Oslo, 1976. Mem.: Am. Soc. Criminology, Am. Sociol. Assn. (chmn. sect. criminology 1976—77). Office: Univ of Minn Dept of Sociology 909 Social Sci Bldg Minneapolis MN 55455

WARD, DAVID CHRISTIAN, science association director; b. Sackville, NB, Canada, May 22, 1941; BS in Microbiology with honors, Meml. U. Newfoundland, Canada, 1961; MS in Biochemistry, U. BC Vancouver, 1963; PhD in Biochemistry, Rockefeller U., NY, 1969. Vis. worker Dept. Biochemistry, Standford U., Calif., 1966, Dept. Biophysics, Kings Coll., London, 1965—69; postdoc. fellow Imperial Cancer Rsch. Fund, London, 1969—71; asst. prof., dept. biophysics & biochemistry Yale U., Sch. Medicine, New Heaven, Conn., 1971—76, assoc. prof., dept. genetics, molecular biophysics & biochemistry, 1976—82, prof., dept. genetics, molecular biophysics & biochemistry, 1982—2004, acting chair, dept genetics, 1995—98; dep. dir. Navada Cancer Rsch. Inst., Las Vegas, 2004—; prof., personalized medicine & nutrition Utah State U., Logan, 2007—. Vis. worker dept. biochemistry Standford U., Calif., 1966, Kings Coll, London, 1969. Recipient Eastern Kodak prize, Am. Assn. Clin. Chemistry, 1989, Biochem. Analysis prize, 1992; fellow, Am. Assn. Advancement Sci., 1992, grant, NIH, 2003—08. Mem.: Histometrix Inc. (sci. adv. bd. mem. 2002—), Auren Biosci. Inc. (sci. adv. bd. mem. 2001—), Ikonysis Inc. (sci. adv. bd. mem. 1999—), Vion Pharm. (sci. adv. bd. mem. 1993—). Office: Navada Cancer Inst One Breakingthrough Way Las Vegas NV 89135 Office Phone: 702-822-5102. Office Fax: 702-944-2362.

WARD, DAVID SCHAD, scriptwriter, film director; b. Providence, Oct. 24, 1947; s. Robert McCollum and Miriam (Schad) W.; children: Joaquin Atwood, Sylvana Soto. BA, Pomona Coll., 1967; M.F.A., UCLA, 1970. Scriptwriter: films include Steelyard Blues, 1971, The Sting, 1973 (Acad. award best original screenplay 1973), The Milagro Beanfield War, 1988, (with Nora Ephron and Jeff Arch) Sleepless in Seattle, 1998 (Academy award nominee Best Original Screenplay 1998), (with John Eskow, Ted Elliott and Terry Rossio) The Mask of Zorro, 2006, (with Phil Sears and Blake T. Evans) Flyboys, 2006; writer, dir. films include Cannery Row, 1981, Major League, 1989, King Ralph, 1991, The Program, 1993, Major League II, 1995, Down Periscope, 1996. Mem.: Acad. Motion Picture Arts and Scis., Dirs. Guild Am. Office: Nate Ross 10250 Constellation Blvd Century City CA 90067

WARD, DOREE MAXINE, secondary school educator; b. Des Moines, Oct. 17, 1955; d. Jeane and Wesley Ward. BSE in Edn., Drake U., 1977, MSEd, 1997. Tchr. Thomas Jefferson HS, Council Bluffs, Iowa, 1978—82; tchr., coach Floyd Valley HS, Alton, Iowa, 1982—84, Newton HS, Iowa, 1987—. Del. Russia and Hungary People to People Internat., 1993. Mem.: APA, NEA, Iowa Assn. Safety Edn. (pres. 1994—2002), Iowa State Edn. Assn. Avocations: swimming, horseback riding, softball, basketball. Home: 515 E 10th St S Newton IA 50208 Office: Newton High School 800 E 4th St S Newton IA 50208 Business E-Mail: wardd@newton.k12.ia.us.

WARD, ELIZABETH, medical association administrator, director; PhD, Dana-Farber Cancer Inst., Boston. Rschr. cancer rsch. methods Nat. Inst. Occupational Safety and Health; rschr. Am. Cancer Soc., dir. surveillance rsch. Am. Cancer Soc. voting del. N.Am. Assn. Ctrl. Cancer Registries. Contbr. articles to prof. jours. Achievements include co-authoring a 2007 report with various government agencies concluding that cancer rates continue to drop among Americans. Office: Am Cancer Soc 1599 Clifton Rd Atlanta GA 30329 Office Phone: 404-327-6552. Office Fax: 404-327-6405. Business E-Mail: eward@cancer.org.

WARD, GEOFFREY CHAMPION, writer, editor; b. Newark, Ohio, Nov. 30, 1940; s. Frederick Champion and Rachel Duira (Baldinger) W.; m. Diane Raines; children: Nathan, Kelly; 1 stepchild, Garrett. BA, Oberlin Coll., 1962, DHL (hon.), 2004, Wilkes U., 1995. Sr. picture editor Ency. Britannica, Chgo., 1964-68; co-founder, editor Audience mag., Boston, 1969-73; mng. editor Am. Heritage Mag., NYC, 1976-78, editor, 1978-82. Author: Lincoln's Thought and the Present, 1978, Treasures of the Maharajas, 1983, Before the Trumpet: Young Franklin Roosevelt, 1882-1905, 1985, A First-Class Temperament: The Emergence of Franklin Roosevelt, 1989 (Nat. Book Critics Cir. award, Francis Parkman prize Soc. Am. Historians, L.A. Times biography prize, Ohioana award), The Civil War: An Illustrated History, 1990, American Originals: The Private Worlds of Some Singular Men and Women, 1991; (with Diane Raines Ward) Tiger Wallahs, Encounters with the Men Who Tried to Save the Greatest of the Great Cats, 1993, Baseball: An Illustrated History, 1994, Closest Companion: The Unknown Story of the Intimate Friendship between Franklin Roosevelt and Margaret Suckley, 1995, The West: An Illustrated History, 1996, (with Michael Nichols) The Year of the Tiger, 1998, Not for Ourselves Alone: Elizabeth Cady Stanton and Susan B. Anthony, 1999, Jazz: A History of America's Music, 2000, (with Dayton Duncan) Mark Twain, 2001, Unforgivable Blackness: The Rise and Fall of Jack Johnson, 2004 (Anisfield/Wolf Book award, 2005, William Hill Sports Book of Yr. 2006), The War: An Intimate History 1941-1945, 2007; editor: The Best American Essays of 1996; (TV documentaries) Huey Long, 1985, Thomas Hart Benton, 1989, Lindbergh, 1990, Nixon, 1990 (Writer's Guild Am. award), The Civil War, 1990 (Emmy award), Reminiscing in Tempo, 1991, Empire of the Air, 1992, The Kennedys, 1992 (Emmy award), George Marshall and the American Century, 1993, Baseball, 1994 (Emmy award), Daley: The Last Boss, 1995, The West, 1996, Theodore Roosevelt, 1996 (Emmy award), Thomas Jefferson, 1997, Frank Lloyd Wright, 1998, Not for Ourselves Alone, 1999, Jazz, 2000, (with Dayton Duncan) Mark Twain, 2001, Unforgivable Blackness: The Rise and Fall of Jack Johnson, 2005 (Emmy award, Writers Guild award), The War, 2007 (Emmy award); contbr. articles to mags., jours. Bd. dirs. Save the Tiger Fund. Recipient Christopher awards for The Statue of Liberty, Theodore Roosevelt, Not For Ourselves Alone, Mark Twain, The Civil War, The War, New Eng. Booksellers Assn. award, Am. Booksellers award, Lila Acheson Wallace Readers Digest writers award. Mem. Soc. Am. Historians, Orgn. Am. Historians (Friend of History award), Serengeti Club, Writers Guild Am., East Inc., Century Assn. Home: 17 C 290 W End Ave New York NY 10023-8106 Office: Brandt &Hochman care Carl Brandt 1501 Broadway Ste 2310 New York NY 10036-5689

WARD, GEORGE EDWARD, lawyer, law educator; b. Saginaw, Mich., Feb. 14, 1941; s. George E. and Mary Margaret (Hackett) W.; m. Margaret L. Barbour, June 13, 1968; children: Mary, William, Teresa, Anne, Thomas. AB, U. Detroit, 1963; JD, U. Mich., Ann Arbor, 1966. Bar: Mich. 1967. Rsch. atty. Mich. Supreme Ct., Lansing, 1966-67; assoc. Butzel, Long, Gust, Klein & VanZile, Detroit, 1967-71; exec. dir. Detroit Charter Commn., 1971-72; ptnr. Burgoyne, Kaufman, Roche & Ward, Detroit, 1972-82; pres. Wayne County Home Rule Charter Commn., 1981—82; of counsel Milmet, Vecchio, Ward & Carnago, Detroit, 1982-86; chief asst. pros. atty. Wayne County, 1986-2000; sole practice Detroit, 2000—. Adj. prof. U. Mich., MSU-DCL, WSU Law Sch., Dearborn, Mich. State U., Wayne State U. Law Sch.; cons. Pitts. Charter Commn., Pa., 1973, Pontiac Charter Commn., 1981; county pub. adminstr. State of Mich., Detroit, 1973—86; pres. Wayne Co. Charter Commn., 1981—82. Author: The Duties of Liberty, 1992, Cases and Materials on the Regulation of Business Franchises, 1997, Liberty and Law: Culture, Court, Consent of the Governed, 2001; contbr. articles to profl. jours. Mich. Law Revision Commn.; co-chmn. Gubernatorial Inaugural Com., 1983; bd. dirs. Wayne County Cath. Soc. Svcs., 1995—, Wayne County Neighborhood Legal Svcs., 1995—2002, Wayne Ctr., 1995—; chmn. bd. Wayne Ctr. for Developmentally Disabled, 2001; mem. pres.'s cabinet U. Detroit, 1980—. Mem.: State Bar Mich. (Rep. Assembly 1979—82, bd. commrs. 1990—96), Inc. Soc. Irish-Am. Lawyers (pres. 2000), Scribes Club, U. Mich. Pres. Club, Alpha Sigma Nu. Mailing: 13900 Sibley Rd Riverview MI 48193 Office Phone: 734-812-4173. Personal E-mail: geoward41@hotmail.com.

WARD, GEORGE FRANK, JR., international programs executive, ambassador; b. Jamaica, NY, Apr. 9, 1945; s. George Frank and Hildegard Louisa (Evans) W.; m. Peggy Elizabeth Coote, June 12, 1965; 1 child, Pamela Ward Priester. BA, U. Rochester, 1965; MPA, Harvard U., 1980. U.S. vice consul Am. Consulate, Hamburg, Germany, 1970-72; ops. officer Office Sec. State, Washington, 1972-74; U.S. consul Am. Consulate Gen., Genoa, Italy, 1974-76; polit. officer Am. Embassy, Rome, 1976-77, exec. asst., 1977-79, polit. officer Bonn, Germany, 1984—85, dep. chief mission, 1989—92; polit.-mil. officer US Dept. State, Washington, 1980-84, 1985—88, prin. dep. asst. sec. Bur. Internat. Orgn., 1992-96, US amb. to Namibia, 1996-99, US coord. for humanitarian assistance to Iraq, 2003; v.p., dir. profl. tng. program US Inst. Peace, Washington, 1999—2005; sr. v.p. internat. programs World Vision, 2005—. Capt. USMC, 1965—69, maj. USMCR, 1969—78. Decorated Vietnamese Cross Gallantry, Naval Commendation medal with combat V; recipient Presdl. Meritorious Svc. award, 1992, 1994, Disting. Honor award, U.S. State Dept., 1992. Fellow: Phi Beta Kappa; mem.: Am. Fgn. Svc. Assn., Washington Inst. Fgn. Affairs, Cosmos Club. Anglican. Home: 3404 Walnut Hill Ct Falls Church VA 22042-3546 Office Phone: 202-572-6318. Business E-Mail: gward@worldvision.org.

WARD, GEORGE TRUMAN, architect; b. Washington, July 24, 1927; s. Truman and Gladys Anna (Nutt) W.; m. Margaret Ann Hall, Sept. 10, 1949; children: Carol Ann Ward Dickson, Donna Lynne Ward Solomon, George Truman, Robert Stephen. BS, Va. Poly. Inst., 1951, MS, 1952; postgrad., George Washington U., 1966. Registered profl. arch., Va., Md., D.C., W.Va., N.C. Archtl. draftsman Charles A. Pearson, Radford, Va., 1950; head archtl. sect. Hayes, Seay, Mattern & Mattern, Radford and Roanoke, 1951-52; with Joseph Saunders & Assocs., Alexandria, Va., 1952-57, assoc. arch., 1955-57; ptnr. Vosbeck-Ward & Assocs., Alexandria, 1957-64, Ward/Hall Assocs., Fairfax, 1964—2008, emeritus, 2008. Dir. Crestar Bank/Greater Washington Region, 1967-99. Pres. PTA Burke (Va.) Sch., 1970-71; mem. bd. mgrs. Fairfax (Va.) County YMCA, 1964-76; chmn. adv. com. Coll. Arch., Va. Poly. Inst., 1984-90; bd. dirs., mem. investment com. Va. Tech. Found., Inc., 1986-91, 93-98; pres. Springfield Rotary Found,. 1978-79; chmn. county adv. bd. Salvation Army, 1978-79, 89-95, co-chmn. Fairfax County Salvation Army Capital Campaign, 1991-95; mem. Gen. Bd. Va. Bapts., deacon, moderator; mem. bd. vis. Va. Poly. Inst. & State U., 1984-87; trustee

Fairfax County Pub. Schs. Edn. Found., Inc. With AUS, 1946-47. Paul Harris fellow; recipient Disting. Svc. award Va. Tech. Alumni Assn., 1988; recipient William H. Ruffner medal Va. Tech., 1996, VSAIA William C. Noland award, 1998, Va. Tech. Coll. Arch. and Urban Studies Lifetime Contbn. award, 1998, 2007. Fellow Coll. AIA; mem. AIA (corp., charter Octagon Soc.), No. Va. Soc. AIA (chmn. polit. action com. 1991-93, Disting. Svc. award 1990, treas. Va. soc. 1994-98, Outstanding Achievement award 1996), Rowe Fellowship (charter mem. 1988), Alumni Assn. Va. Poly. Inst. & State U. (bd. dirs., v.p. 1992, pres. 1994), Interfaith Forum on Religion, Art and Arch., Va. Found. for Arch. (trustee), Va. Assn. Professions, Va. C. of C., No. Va. Angus Assn. (pres. 1987-88), Va. Tech. Alumni Assn. (hon., life, bd. dirs. Disting. Svc. award 1988), Masons, Shriners, KT, Rotary (charter mem., pres. Springfield 1973-74, Disting. Svc. award dist. 7610 1995), Tau Sigma Delta, Omicron Delta Kappa, Phi Kappa Phi, Pi Delta Epsilon, Ut Prosim. Baptist. Business E-Mail: gtward@wardhall.com.

WARD, HILEY HENRY, journalist, educator; b. Lafayette, Ind., July 30, 1929; s. Hiley Lemen and Agnes (Fuller) W.; m. Charlotte Burns, May 28, 1951 (div. 1971); children: Dianne, Carolee, Marceline, Laurel; m. Joan Bastel, Aug. 20, 1977. BA, William Jewell Coll., 1951; MA, Berkeley Bapt. Div. Sch., 1953; MDiv, McCormick Theol. Sem., Chgo., 1955; student, Northwestern U., 1948, 54, 56-57; PhD, U. Minn., 1977. News asst. Christian Advocate, 1953-55; editor jr. publs. David C. Cook Pub. Co., 1956-59; editor Record, Buchanan, Mich., 1960; religion editor Detroit Free Press, 1960-73; asst. prof. journalism Mankato (Minn.) State U., 1974-76; assoc. prof. journalism Wichita (Kans.) State U., 1976; prof. journalism Temple U., Phila., 1977-96, prof. emeritus, 1997—, dir. news-editorial sequence, journalism dept., 1977-80, chmn. dept., 1978-80. Instr. journalism Oakland U., Rochester, Mich., evenings 1963-66. Author: Creative Giving, 1958, Space-age Sunday, 1960, Documents of Dialogue, 1966, God and Marx Today, 1968, Ecumania, 1968, Rock 2000, 1969, Prophet of the Black Nation, 1969, The Far-out Saints of the Jesus Communes, 1972, Religion 2101 A.D., 1975, Feeling Good About Myself, 1983, Professional Newswriting, 1985, My Friend's Beliefs: A Young Reader's Guide to World Religions, 1988, Reporting in Depth, 1991, Magazine and Feature Writing, 1993, Mainstreams of American Media History, 1997; editor: Media History Digest, 1979-94; exec. editor: Kidbits, 1981-82; book editor: Editor and Publisher, 1989-98, Peters Rock, 2005-, Understanding Reality Religion, 2007-,; contbr. articles to profl. jours., feature articles to newspapers and mags.; also short stories and poems. Religious Pub. Rels. Coun. fellow, 1970; recipient citation Religious Heritage Am., 1962, Leidt award Epsic. Ch., 1969, citation U.S. Am. Revolution Bicentennial Adminstrn., 1976, Text and Acad. Authors citation, 1997. Mem. Religion Newswriters Assn. (pres. 1970-72), Am. Soc. Journalists and Authors, Am. Journalism Historians Assn. (bd. dirs. 1994-96, Kobre lifetime achievement award 1999), Overseas Press Club. Home: PO Box 399 1263 Folly Rd Warrington PA 18976-1422 E-mail: bastel@voicenet.com.

WARD, HINES, JR., professional football player; b. Seoul, Republic of Korea, Mar. 8, 1976; s. Hines Ward Sr. and Kim Young-hee; m. Simone Ward; 1 child, Jaden. BA in consumer economics, U. Ga., 1997. Wide receiver Pitts. Steelers, 1998—. Named Super Bowl XL MVP, 2006; named to NFL Pro-Bowl, 2001—04. Achievements include member of Super Bowl Championship winning Pittsburgh Steelers, 2006, 2009; being the first Korean-American Super Bowl MVP, 2006. Office: c/o Pittsburgh Steelers 3400 S Water St Pittsburgh PA 15203*

WARD, HORACE TALIAFERRO, federal judge; b. LaGrange, Ga., July 29, 1927; m. Ruth LeFlore (dec.); 1 son (dec.). AB, Morehouse Coll., 1949; MA, Atlanta U., 1950; JD, Northwestern U., 1959. Bar: Ga. 1960. Instr. polit. sci. Ark. A.M. and N. Coll., 1950-51, Ala. State Coll., 1951-53, 55-56; claims authorizer U.S. Social Security Adminstrn., 1959-60; assoc. firm Hollowell Ward Moore & Alexander (and successors), Atlanta, 1960-69; individual practice law Atlanta, 1971-74; judge Civil Ct. of Fulton County, 1974-77, Fulton Superior Ct., 1977-79; U.S. Dist. Ct. judge No. Dist. Ga., Atlanta, 1979-93; sr. judge U.S. Dist. Ct. No. Dist. Ga., Atlanta, 1993—. Lectr. bus. and sch. law Atlanta U., 1965-70; dep. city atty., Atlanta, 1969-70, asst. county atty., Fulton County, 1971-74 Former Trustee Friendship Baptist Ch., Atlanta; mem. Ga. adv. com. U.S. Civil Rights Commn., 1963-65; assisting lawyer NAACP Legal Def. and Edn. Fund, Inc., 1960-70; mem. Jud. Selection Commn., Atlanta, 1972-74, Charter Commn., 1971-72; mem. Ga. Senate, 1964-74, jud. com., rules com., county and urban affairs com.; mem. State Democratic Exec. com., 1966-74; former bd. dirs. Atlanta Legal Aid Soc.; bd. dirs. Atlanta Urban League, Fed. Defender Program, No. Dist. Ga.; trustee Met. Atlanta Commn. on Crime and Delinquency, Atlanta U., Fledgling Found. Mem. Am. Bar Assn., Nat. Bar Assn. (chmn. jud. council 1978-79), State Bar Ga., Atlanta Bar Assn., Gate City Bar Assn. (pres. 1972-74), Atlanta Lawyers Club, Phi Beta Kappa, Alpha Phi Alpha, Phi Alpha Delta, Sigma Pi Phi. Office: US Dist Court 1252 US Courthouse 75 Spring St SW Atlanta GA 30303-3309 Home Phone: 404-588-0641; Office Phone: 404-215-1330.

WARD, JACQUELINE ANN BEAS, nurse, healthcare administrator, legal nurse consultant; b. Somerset, Pa., Oct. 23, 1945; d. Donald C. and Thelma R. (Wable) Beas; divorced; children: Charles L. Jr., Shawn M. BSN, U. Pitts., 1966; MA in Counseling and Guidance, W.Va. Coll. Grad. Studies, 1976; MBA, Columbus Coll., 1983; AS in Health Svcs. Mgmt./Nursing Home Adminstrn., St. Petersburg Jr. Coll., 1997. Cert. advanced nursing adminstrn., legal nurse cons., 2007; adult living facility adminstr., nursing home adminstr. preceptor. Staff nurse W.Va. U. Hosp., Morgantown, 1966—67; staff nurse, head nurse Meml. Hosp, Charleston, W.Va., 1967—69; staff nurse Santa Rosa Hosp., San Antonio, 1969; staff nurse, supr. Bexar County Hosp., San Antonio, 1970; charge and staff nurse Rocky Mountain Osteo. Hosp., Denver, 1971; from staff nurse to asst. DON Charleston Area Med. Ctr., 1971—82; DON H.D. Cobb Meml. Hosp., Phenix City, Ala., 1982—84; v.p. nursing Venice Hosp., Fla., 1984—90, v.p. ops., 1990—94; exec. dir., v.p. Life Counseling Ctr., Osprey, Fla., 1994—95; dir. skilled unit and spl. projects Bon Secours/Venice Hosp., 1995—97; adj. clin. nursing faculty Manatee CC, Bradenton, 1998—99; interim adminstr. DON Contracting, Sarasota, 1999—2000; adminstr. Ctrs. for Long Term Care Venice Beach, 2000—01, Lake Towers-Sun Terrace Health Care Ctr., Sun City Center, Fla., 2002—05; exec. dir. Beneva Park Club, Sarasota, 2005, Tandem Health Care of Sarasota, 2005—07. Clin. instr. Chattahoochie Valley C.C., Phenix City, 1982—84; support svcs. cons. Bon Secours Healthcare, Venice, 1996—97, Long Term Care, 1997—98; legal nurse cons., 2007—. Office Phone: 941-377-7535.

WARD, JEANNETTE POOLE, retired psychologist, educator; b. Honolulu, June 19, 1932; d. Russell Masterton and Bessie Naomi (Hammett) Poole; children: John Russell Ward, Lisa Joy Ward. BA, Birmingham So. Coll., Ala., 1963; PhD in Psychology, Vanderbilt U., 1969. NSF summer rsch. asst. U. Iowa, Iowa City, 1962, Vanderbilt U., Nashville, 1963, NASA fellow, 1963-66, NIH postdoctoral fellow, 1966-67; spl. rsch. fellow Duke U., Durham, NC, 1970-71; asst. prof. psychology U. Memphis, 1967—72, assoc. prof., 1972—77, prof., 1977—2000; ret., 2001. Editor: Current Research in Primate Laterality, 1990, Primate Laterality, 1992; mem. editl. bd. Jour. Comparative Psychology, 1988-95, Internat. Jour. of Comparative Psychology, 1995—; contbr. chpts. to books and articles to profl. jours. Fellow APA; mem. Psychonomic Soc., Animal Behavior Soc., Am. Primatology Soc., Southeastern Psychol. Assn., Soc. for Neuroscis., Internat. Soc. for Comparative Psychology (treas. 1989-90, pres.-elect 1996-98, pres. 1998-2000), Sigma Xi (pres. Memphis State U. chpt. 1989-90, rsch. award 1985). Democrat. Avocations: reading, art, music.

WARD, JERI, automotive company executive, marketing professional; MS in Engring., Kettering U., Flint, Mich., 1995; MBA, Northwestern U. Kellogg Sch. Mgmt., Evanston, Ill., 2001; MS in Engring. Mgmt., Northwestern U. McCormick Sch. Engring., 2001. Various engring. positions, powertrain divsn. GM, 1990—99; various mktg. positions Ford Motor Co., 2001—05, mktg. mgr. Ford Edge, 2005—07; gen. mgr. mktg. & strategy Audi of America, LLC, 2007—. Named a Woman to Watch, Advt. Age, 2009. Office: Audi of America Inc 2200 Ferdinand Porsche Dr Herndon VA 20171*

WARD, JOE HENRY, JR., retired lawyer; b. Childress, Tex., Apr. 18, 1930; s. Joe Henry and Helen Ida (Chastain) W.; m. Carlotta Agnes Abreu, Feb. 7, 1959; children: James, Robert, William, John. BS in Acctg., Tex. Christian U., 1952; JD, So. Meth. U., 1964. Bar: Tex. 1964, Va. 1972, D.C. 1974; CPA, Tex. Mgr. Alexander Grant & Co. CPA's, Dallas, 1956-64; atty. U.S. Treasury, 1965-68; tax counsel U.S. Senate Fin. Com., 1968-72; pvt. practice Washington, 1972-83; asst. gen. counsel, tax mgr. Epic Holdings, Ltd. and Crysopt Corp., 1983-87; pvt. practice Washington and Va., 1987-95; ret., 1995. Lt. USNR, 1952-56. Mem.: AICPA, Univ. Club. Home: 2639 Mann Ct Falls Church VA 22046-2721

WARD, JOHN JAMES, bishop emeritus; b. LA, Sept. 28, 1920; Student, St. John's Sem., Camarillo, Calif., Catholic U. Am. Ordained priest Archdiocese of LA, 1946, aux. bishop, 1963—96; ordained bishop, 1963. Roman Catholic. Office: Archdiocese LA 3424 Wilshire Blvd Los Angeles CA 90010-2241

WARD, JOHN MILTON, music educator; b. Oakland, Calif., July 6, 1917; s. John Milton and Maud (Van Alstyne) W.; m. Ruth Marie Neils, Jan. 9, 1945. BA, San Francisco State Coll., 1941; MusM, U. Wash., Seattle, 1942; PhD, NYU, 1953; A.M. (hon.), Harvard U., Cambridge, Mass., 1955. Instr. lit. and fine arts Mich. State U., 1947-53; asst., later assoc. prof. music U. Ill., 1953-55; assoc. prof. music Harvard U., 1955-58, prof., 1958-61, chmn. dept., 1958-62, William Powell Mason prof., 1961-85, William Powell Mason prof. emeritus, 1985—. Author: The Dublin Virginal Manuscript, 1954, 3d edit., 1983, A Dowland Miscellany, 1977, Sprightly and Cheerful Musick, 1981, Music for Elizabethan Lutes, 1992, The Lute Music of John Johnson, 1994, (with Morris S. Levy) The King's Theatre Collection, 2003, Italian Ballet 1637-1977, 2003; contbr. articles to profl. jours. Hon. curator music and dance Harvard Theatre Collection. Mem. Am. Acad. Arts and Scis., Am. Musicol. Soc. (hon.), Internat. Musicological Soc., Royal Mus. Assn. (hon. fgn. mem.), Lute Soc. (hon.). Home: 20 Follen St Cambridge MA 02138-3503

WARD, JONATHAN P., investment banker; b. May 6, 1954; BSChemE, U. N.H., 1976; grad. advanced mgmt. program, Harvard Bus. Sch. With R.R. Donnelley, 1977—2001, pres. Merchandise Media and Fin. Svcs. bus. units, mgr. comml. printing operation, v.p., dir. Spartanburg, S.C., mfg. divsn., exec. v.p. Comml. Print Sector, 1995—97, pres., COO, 1997—2001; pres., CEO ServiceMaster, Downers Grove, Ill., 2001—02, chmn., CEO, 2002—06; mng. dir. investment banking, chmn. Chgo. office Lazard Ltd., Chgo., 2006—. Dir. Metromail Corp., Siegwerk Inc. USA, J. Jill Group Inc., First Horizon. Trustee Goodman Theatre, Chgo.; dir. Chgo. Youth Ctrs., Evanston Northwestern Hosp. Mem.: Nat. Assn. Mfr., Direct Mktg. Assn. Office: Lazard Freres 190 S La Salle St Fl 31 Chicago IL 60603-3498 Office Phone: 312-407-6600. Office Fax: 312-407-6620.

WARD, KEITH CHARLES, music educator; Instr. music Pa. State U., State Coll., 1981—86; asst., assoc. prof. music Denison U., Granville, Ohio, 1986—96, dir. academic support and freshman yr., 1992—95; chair, dept. of music Pitts. State U., Kans., 1996—98; dir., sch. music U. Puget Sound, Tacoma, 1998—. Office: Univ Puget Sound 1500 N Warner Tacoma WA 98416-1076 Business E-Mail: kward@ups.edu.

WARD, LLEWELLYN ORCUTT, III, oil industry executive; b. Oklahoma City, July 24, 1930; s. Llewellyn Orcutt II and Addie (Reisdorph) W.; m. Myra Beth Gungoll, Oct. 29, 1955; children: Casidy Ann, William Carlton. Student, Okla. Mil. Acad., 1948—50; BS, U. Okla., 1953; postgrad., Harvard U., 1986. Registered profl. engr., Okla. Dist. engr. Delhi-Taylor Oil Corp., Tulsa, 1955-56; ptnr. Ward-Gungoll Oil Investments, Enid, Okla., 1956—; owner L.O. Ward Oil Ops., Enid, 1963—; chmn., CEO Ward Petroleum Corp. Mem. Okla. Gov.'s Adv. Coun. on Energy; rep. to Interstate Oil Compact Commn.; dir. Hydril Corp; chmn., CEO Ward Petroleum Corp. Chmn. Indsl. Devel. Commn., Enid, 1968—; active YMCA; mem. bd. visitors Coll. Engring., U. Okla.; mem. adv. coun. Sch. Bus., trustee Phillips U., Enid, Univ. Bd., Pepperdine, Calif.; Okla. chmn. U.S. Olympic Com., 1986—; Rep. nat. committeeman from Okla., 1982-88; mem. Pres.'s adv. com. on arts Kennedy Ctr. Served with C.E., U.S. Army, 1953-55. Recipient Gov.'s. Arts award, 2006; named Chief Roughneck of Yr., Lone Star Steel, 1999, Disting. Alumnus, Okla. Mil. Acad., 1993; named to Hall of Fame, Enid Pub. Sch. Found., 2006. Mem. Ind. Petroleum Assn. Am. (chmn. 1996-98), Okla. Ind. Petroleum Assn. Am. (pres., bd. dirs.), Nat. Petroleum Coun., Enid C. of C. (Businessman of Yr. 1988, Citizen of Yr. 2006), U. Okla. Coll. Engring. Disting. Grads. Soc., Am. Bus. Club (pres. 1964), Masons, Shriners, Rotary (pres. Enid 1990-91), Alpha Tau Omega. Methodist. Home: 900 Brookside Dr Enid OK 73703-6941 Office: 502 S Fillmore St Enid OK 73703-5703 Home Phone: 580-234-8779; Office Phone: 580-234-3229.

WARD, LOUIS EMMERSON, retired physician; b. Mt. Vernon, Ill., Jan. 19, 1918; s. Henry Ben (Pope) and Aline (Emmerson) Ward; m. Nan Talbot, June 5, 1942; children: Nancy, Louis, Robert, Mark; m. Marian Mansfield, Jan. 27, 1979. AB, U. Ill., 1939; MD, Harvard, 1943; MS in Medicine, U. Minn., 1949. Intern Ill. Research and Ednl. Hosp., Chgo., 1943; fellow medicine Mayo Found., 1946—49; cons. medicine, rheumatology Mayo Clinic, 1950—83, chmn. bd. govs., 1964—75. Contbr. articles to profl. jours. Vice chmn. bd. trustees Mayo Found., 1964—76; past bd. dirs. Fund for Republic, Ctr. for Study Dem. Instns., Arthritis Found., Northwestern Bell Telephone Prin. Fin. Group; mem. Nat. Coun. Health Planning and Resource Devel., 1976—83. With M.C. US Army, 1944—46. Recipient Achievement award, U. Ill., 1968, Disting. Alumnus award, Mayo Found., 1983. Master: Am. Coll. Rheumatology; mem.: Inst. Medicine, So. Minn. Med. Assn., Zumbro Valley Med. Soc., Minn. Med. Soc., Ctrl. Soc. Clin. Rsch., Nat. Soc. Clin. Rheumatologists, AAAS, AMA, Phi Delta Theta, Alpha Omega Alpha, Sigma Xi, Phi Beta Kappa. Home: Apt 916 211 2nd St NW Rochester MN 55901-2820

WARD, MAL YVONNE, special education educator; d. John Alexander and Hattie Lee Miller; m. David Lee Ward, July 30, 2005; 1 child, Jocelyn Beth Harvey stepchildren: Darin, Pamela Trapp, Dennis, Dwayne. MA, Fayetteville State U., 1987; MEd, Harvard U., Cambridge, 1998. Handicap's tchr. Bd. Edn., Piscataway, NJ, 1972—2001, learning disabilities teacher-cons., 1992—2000, Newark, 2001—06, exceptional children's tchr. Fayetteville, NC, 1981—89; lectr. U. Fayetteville, 2006—. Early intervention specialist Mental Health, Fayetteville, 2006—08; cons., Fayetteville, 2006—. Contbr. scientific papers. Instr. Ch., Fayetteville, 2008; pres. Non-Profit, Fayetteville, 1998—2000. Mem.: Coun. Exceptional Children. Achievements include design of vocational, transitional program for disenfranchised youth; project renaissance, alternative educational placement for middle grades; technique resource manual for novice teachers. Avocations: travel, reading. Office Fax: 910-672-1941.

WARD, MEGAN MAE, yoga therapist; b. Hamilton, New Zealand, Jan. 19, 1962; d. John and Margaret Hayes; m. Rowan Trevor Ward, Oct. 5, 1985 (div. Sept. 21, 2008); children: Jessica Megan, Katharine Margaret, Jennifer Rowena, Brennan Rowan Trevor, Gareth Trevor. Degree in Sci., Auckland Tech. Coll., New Zealand, 1981; Degree in Naturopathy, Queensland Inst. Natural Therapies, Sunshine Coast, Australia, 1988; Degree in Advanced Yoga, Creative Health Inst., 1999. Cert. in feldenkrais Feldenkrais Assn., 1992, in dance Wu Tao Dance Acad., 2007. Yoga therapist Manasa Yoga, Brisbane, Queensland, 1998—, counsellor, 2000—, pub. spkr., 2006—; yoga tchr. tng. Sivannanda Yoga, 2009—. Yoga therapist Toowong Psychiat. Hosp., Brisbane, 1998—. Office: Manasa Yoga PO Box 2666 Queensland New Farm 4006 Australia Business E-Mail: contact@manasayoga.com.

WARD, MICHAEL J., rail transportation executive; b. Balt., Sept. 2, 1950; BS, U. Md., 1972; MBA, Harvard U., 1976. Rsch. analyst Chessie Sys., Balt., 1977—80, mgr., coord. analysis-fin., 1980—81, mgr. bus. rsch. Cleve., 1981—82, dir. nat. accts., 1982—84, asst. v.p. coal mktg., 1984—85, Balt., 1984—86; v.p. coal mktg. CSX Distbn. Svcs., Balt., 1986—88; v.p. coal CSX Transp., Jacksonville, 1988—94, gen. mgr. C&O Bus. Unit, v.p. coal Huntington, W.Va., 1994—95, sr. v.p. fin. Jacksonville, 1995—96, CFO, 1995—98, exec. v.p. fin., 1996—98, exec. v.p. coal and merger planning, 1998—99, exec. v.p. coal svc. group, 1999—2000, exec. v.p. ops., 2000, pres., 2000—03, CEO, 2002—03; pres. CSX Corp., Jacksonville, 2002—, chmn., pres., CEO, 2003—. Bd. dirs. Ky. Coal Coun., Ashland, Inc., CSX Corp. Bd. dirs. Ctr. Energy Econ. Devel., Take Stock in Children. Mem.: Fla. Coun. 100, Assn. Am. Railroads (bd. dirs.), Phi Kappa Phi, Beta Gamma Sigma. Office: CSX Corp 500 Water St C 900 Jacksonville FL 32202

WARD, MICHAEL T., classicist, educator; b. Ciudad de Panama, Panama, Mar. 30, 1955; s. Thurman L. and Sophia F. Ward; children: Alexander M., Nicholas R., Christopher S. PhD, U. Pa., Phila., 1986. Cert. oral proficiency examiner in Italian Am. Coun. Tchg. Fgn. Langs., 1985. Asst. prof. classics and Spanish Lawrence U., Appleton, Wis., 1984—87; asst. prof., assoc. prof. Italian and Spanish Trinity U., San Antonio, 1987—, chair linguistics program, 1997—2006. Advanced placement reader, table leader Spanish Coll. Bd., NYC, 1990—2000. Contbr. articles to profl. jour. on Italian renaissance and modern L.Am. linguistic historiography. Mem.: MLA, Am. Assn. Italian Studies, Am. Assn. Tchrs. Italian, Am. Italian Hist. Assn., Rocky Mountain Coun. L. Am. Studies, Southeastern Coun. L. Am. Studies, SW Coun. L. Am. Studies (pres. 1998—2003). Home: 4507 Green Acres Woods San Antonio TX 78249 Office: Trinity Univ One Stadium Dr San Antonio TX 78212 Office Fax: 210-999-8370. Business E-Mail: mward@trinity.edu.

WARD, NANCY L., federal agency administrator; Chief disaster assistance branch, dep. state coordinating officer Calif. Office Emergency Svcs.; various sr. mgmt. positions Fed. Emergency Mgmt. Agy. (FEMA), US Dept. Homeland Security, including adminstr. Response & Recovery Divsn., region IX, 2000—06, dep. dir. Recovery Directorate, 2004—05, regional adminstr., region IX, 2006—, acting adminstr., 2009. Recipient Sec.'s award for Excellence, US Dept. Homeland Security, 2007. Office: FEMA 500 C St SW Washington DC 20472 Office Phone: 202-646-2500.*

WARD, PATRICK J., manufacturing executive; HNC in acctg., Dundee Coll. Commerce, Scotland, 1981; MBA, Strathclyde Univ., Scotland, 1992. Acct. GRI Ltd., 1983—84, Babygro Ltd., 1984—85; mgmt. acct. British Rail Property, Scotland, 1985—87, Cummins Inc. (UK), 1987—88, plant acctg. mgr. Newage Internat., 1988—91, group acctg. mgr. Newage Internat., 1991—95; controller fuel systems bus. Cummins Inc., Columbus, Ind., 1995—96, dir. mgmt. info. & analysis, 1996—98, dir. fin. & info. tech., 1998—2000, exec. dir. Fleetguard bus. controller, 2000—03, exec. dir. power gen. bus. controller, 2003—05, exec. dir. engine bus. controller, 2005—06, v.p. engine bus. controller, 2006—08, v.p., CFO, 2008—. Mem.: Chartered Inst. Mgmt. Accountants (UK) (assoc.). Office: Cummins Inc 500 Jackson St Columbus IN 47202

WARD, R. LAWRENCE, lawyer; b. Kans. City, May 19, 1936; BBA, Univ. Mo., Kans. City, 1959, JD, 1961. Bar: Mo. 1961, US Dist. Ct. (Kans., we. Mo., ea. Mich. dist.), US Ct. Appeals (8th, 10th cir.), US Supreme Ct. Firm chmn. & chmn. bus. litigation group Shugart Thomson & Kilroy, Kans. City, Mo. Mem. Mo. 16th Cir. Judicial Commn., 1979—85, Mo. Appellate Judicial Commn., 1992—97. Trustee Donnelly Coll. Recipient Lon O. Hocker Mem. Trial Lawyer award, Mo. Bar Found., Purcell Professionalism award, 1997, Herbert Hartley award, Am. Judicial Soc., 2001; named one of Top Ten Trial Lawyers in Am., Nat. Law Jour., 1994, Top Ten Kans. City Legal Leaders, Daily Record, 2004. Fellow: Am. Bar Found., Am. Coll. Trial Lawyers; mem.: ABA (Mo. state del. to Ho. Del. 1992—98), Mo. Bar (mem. bd. gov. 1973—77), Kans. City Met. Bar Assn. (pres. 1983, Lifetime Achievement award 1997). Office: Shugart Thomson & Kilroy 12 Wyandotte Plz 120 W 12th St Kansas City MO 64105 Office Phone: 816-374-0571. Office Fax: 816-374-0509. Business E-Mail: lward@stklaw.com.

WARD, R. PARKER, cardiologist, educator; s. James and Mary Lee Ward; m. Sara K. Ward; children: Jack, Timothy, Sadie. BA, Middlebury Coll., Vt., 1989; MD, U. Pa., Phila., 1994. Cert. in cardiovasc. disease Am. Bd. Internal Medicine, 2001, physician Am. Soc. Echocardiography, 2001, Am. Soc. Nuc. Cardiology, 2002. Chief med. resident Hosp. U. Pa., 1997—98; cardiology fellow, med. ctr. U. Chgo., 1998—2001, asst. prof. Pritzker sch. medicine, 2001—07, dir., cardiology clinic med. ctr., 2002—06, assoc. prof. Pritzker sch. medicine, 2007—, dir., cardiovasc. fellowship program, 2007—. Editl. bd. mem Cardio Smart, 2008—. Recipient Tchg. sward, U. Chgo. Dept. Medicine, 2003—08, Postgrad. Tchg. award, 2008. Fellow: Am. Coll. Cardiology (Young Tchr. award 2005); mem.: Am. Soc. Nuc. Cardiology, Am. Soc. Echocardiography. Office: Univ Chgo Med Ctr 5841 S Maryland Ave MC 6080 Chicago IL 60305 Business E-Mail: pward@medicine.bsd.uchicago.edu.

WARD, RICHARD HURLEY, education educator, writer; b. NYC, Sept. 2, 1939; s. Hurley and Anna C. (Mittasch) W.; children from a previous marriage: Jeanne M., Jonathan B.; m. Michelle Pierczynski, June 15, 1987; 1 child: Michelle Sophia. BS, John Jay Coll., CUNY, 1968; M in Criminology, U. Calif., Berkeley, 1969, D in Criminology, 1971. Detective NYC Police Dept., 1962—70; coord. student activities John Jay Coll., NYC, 1970—71, dean students, 1971—75, v.p., 1975—77, vice chancellor, 1977—93; assoc. chancellor and prof. internat. criminology U. Ill., Chgo., 1993—98; exec. dir. Office Internat. Criminal Justice, 1985—99; exec. v.p. MBF Edn. Group, Malaysia, 1996—97; dean Coll. Criminal Justice, Sam Houston State U., Huntsville, Tex., 1999—2006, assoc. v.p. rsch. and spl. programs, 2006—08; dean Henry C. Lee Coll. Criminal Justice Forensic Scis., U. New Haven, Conn., 2008—. Vis. prof. Zagazig U., Egypt, Egyptian Police Acad., 1986, East China Inst. Politics and Law, Shanghai, 1990-91; lectr., various confs. in China, Egypt, Russia, Italy, Eng., Peru, Germany, Saudi Arabia, Finland, Taiwan, Vietnam, Turkey, Korea, United Arab Emirates and U.S., 1983—. Author: (with others) Police Robbery Control Manual, 1975; Introduction to Criminal Investigation, 1975, (with Robert McCormack) An Anti-Corruption Manual for Administrators in Law Enforcement; Quest for Quality, 1984; gen. editor Foundations of Criminal Justice, 46 vols., 1972-75; editor: (with Austin Fowler) Police and Law Enforcement, Vol. I, 1972; Police and Law Enforcement, Vol. II, 1975; (with Harold Smith) International Terrorism: The Domestic Response, 1982, International Terrorism: Operational Issues, 1988; co-author: (with James Osterburg) Criminal Investigation: A Method for Reconstructing the Past, 1992, 5th edit., 2007, (with K. Kiernan and D. Mabrey) Introduction to Homeland Security, 2006. Mem. Mayor of Chgo.'s Blue Ribbon Pannel on Police Promotion; varsity baseball coach U. Ill., Chgo., 1980-82, John Jay Coll. Criminal Justice, CUNY, 1971-72; chief investigator Mayor's Commn. Police Integrity, 1998; mem. Houston Crime Lab. Com., 2005. Cpl. USMC, 1957-61. Recipient Leonard Reisman award John Jay Coll. Criminal Justice, 1968, Alumni Achievement award, 1978, Richard McGee award U. Calif., Berkeley Sch. Criminology, 1971, Friendship medal Peoples Republic of China, 1994, Hans Mattick award Ill. Acad. Criminology, 1999; Justice Dept. fellow U. Calif., Berkeley, 1971. Mem. ASPA, Acad. Criminal Justice Scis. (pres. 1977-78, Founder's award 1985), Internat. Assn. Chiefs of Police (chmn. edn. and tng. sect. 1974-75), Sigma Delta Chi. Office: Sam Houston State U Coll Criminal Justice Huntsville TX 77341 Office Phone: 936-294-3621, 203-932-7260. Business E-Mail: ward@shsu.edu, rward@newhaven.edu.

WARD, RICHARD JOSEPH, university dean, educator, author; b. Beverly, Mass., Nov. 7, 1921; s. Ralph Woodbury and Margaret (Lyons) W.; m. Cecilia Butler, Sept. 1, 1951; children: Timothy, Mary, Richard, Christopher. BS, Harvard U., 1945; MA, U. Mich., 1948, PhD, 1958. Dir. planning AID Mission to Jordan, 1961-63; chmn. econ. dept. C.W. Post Coll., LI U., 1960-61, 63-65; chief planning Bur. for Near East and South Asia, AID, 1965-69; mgr. internat. cons. Peat, Marwick, Mitchell & Co., Washington, 1969-75; dean U. Mass. Coll. Bus., Dartmouth, 1975-87, assoc. dean, dir. rsch., prof., 1990—96, Chancellor prof. emeritus, 1996—; dir. US Internat. U. Sch. Bus., London, 1988-89; cons. in field. Author: Principles of Economics, 1967, Development Problems, 1973, The Palestine State French Translation, 1978, Development Horizon, 1980; editor: The Challenge of Development, 1967, Grampas Are For All Seasons, 2005, The Fragrance of Heliotrope the Presence of Cecilia, 2007, My Last Dungarees, 2009; contbr. articles to profl. jours. Bd. dirs. Indsl. Found., 1976-82; bd. dirs. pres. Jr. Achievement, 1977-99, exec. com. mem. World Congress on Violence and Human Co-existence. Lt. USNR, WWII. Recipient Disting. Svc. award AID, Jordan Mission, 1963, Univ. Svc. award U. Mass. Alumni Assn., 1983, Gov.'s Citation for Svc., 1987; Harvard fellow Ford Found., 1957. Mem. Assn. Social Econs. (pres. 1970-71), Ea. Am. Econ. Assn. (exec. com.), Harvard Club (pres. 1984-87, Harvard alumni assoc. regional bd. dirs. SE Mass. and RI 1989-92), Retirement Svc.(award 2009). Home: 20 Pleasant St South Dartmouth MA 02748-3813 Personal E-mail: wardjrichard@comcast.net.

WARD, RICHARD LEO, virologist; b. Bozeman, Mont., Nov. 16, 1942; s. Thomas S. and Loraine F. Ward; m. Shirley Ann Murphy, June 11, 1966; children: Christopher Corey, Stephanie Jill Deimling. PhD, U. Calif., Berkeley, 1969. Rsch. virologist UCLA, 1972—74; mem. tech. staff Sandia Nat. Labs., Albuquerque, 1974—80; divsn. leader US EPA, Cin., 1980—81; dir. clin. virology JN Gamble Inst. Med. Res., Cin., 1981—95; rsch. prof. Cin. Children's Hosp., 1995—. Achievements include invention of precursor to the rotavirus rotarix vaccine. Home: 2301 Estate Ridge Cincinnati OH 45244 Office: Cin Children's Hosp 3333 Burnet Ave Cincinnati OH 45229 Office Fax: 513-636-0950. Personal E-mail: rward_1796@fuse.net. Business E-Mail: dick.ward@cchmc.org.

WARD, ROBERT F., pediatric otolaryngologist; b. Bklyn., June 8, 1950; MD, Cornell Univ., 1981. Cert. Am. Bd. Otolaryngology, 1986. Intern NY Hosp., NYC, 1981—82, resident surgery, 1982—83, resident otolaryngology, 1983—86; fellow in pediatric otolaryngology Children's Hosp., Harvard Med. Coll., Boston, 1986; prof. otolaryngology Weill Med. Coll., Cornell Univ., NYC. Recipient Achievement award, Am. Acad. Otolaryngology-Head & Neck Surgery, 1996, Seymour Cohen award, Am. Bronchoesophagologic Assn., 1981; named one of Best Doctors, NY Mag., 2008—09. Office: Weill Cornell Med Coll 5th Fl 1305 York Ave New York NY 10021 Office Phone: 646-962-2224. Office Fax: 646-962-0100.

WARD, RODMAN, JR., lawyer, director; b. Wilmington, Del., Apr. 8, 1934; s. Rodman and Dorcas (Andrews) W.; m. Susan Speakman Hill, Oct. 10, 1959; children: Margery Ward Garnett, Emily Neilson, Levin, Rodman III, Jennifer Ward Oppenheimer. BA, Williams Coll., 1956; LLB, Harvard U., 1959. Bar: Del. 1959, D.C. 1959. Partner Prickett, Ward, Burt & Sanders, Wilmington, 1967-79, Skadden, Arps, Slate, Meagher & Flom, Wilmington, 1979—2002, of counsel, 2002—. Bd. dirs. WMB Holdings, Inc. Author: (with Folk and Welch) Folk on the Delaware General Corporation Law, 1987 Vice chmn. Winterthur Mus. Gardens and Libr.; exec. com., bd. dirs. The Garden Conservancy. Capt. USAF, 1960—63. Fellow: Am. Coll. Trial Lawyers; mem.: ABA, Am. Judicature Soc., Del. State Bar Assn. (pres. 1989—90), Am. Bar Found. (life), Am. Law Inst., Vicmead Hunt Club, Wilmington Country Club, Wilmington Club. Home: 52 Selborne Dr Wilmington DE 19807-1216 Office: PO Box 636 Wilmington DE 19899-0636 Office Phone: 302-651-3000. Business E-Mail: rod.ward@skadden.com.

WARD, RONALD R., lawyer; b. Sacramento, June 12, 1947; BA, Calif. State U., 1973; JD, U. Calif., 1976. Bar: Calif. 1977, Wash., U.S. Dist. Ct. Calif. (No. Dist.) 1979, U.S. Dist Ct. (We. Dist.) Wash., U.S. Ct. Appeals (9th cir.). Asst. atty. gen. State of Wash., 1979—82; atty., shareholder Levinson Friedman PS, Seattle, 1982—2005, Jones & Ward, PLLC, Seattle, 2005—. Vol. reading tutor, tchr. asst. Hawthorne Sch., Seattle, mem. parent bd., mem. annual giving steering com.; mem. long-range planning com. Holy Names Acad., Seattle; bd. trustees N.W. Chamber Orch. Recipient President's award, Washington State Trial Lawyers, 2006, Outstanding Plaintiff Trial Lawyer award, Washington Def. Trial Lawyers, 2006; named Super Lawyer, Washington Law & Politics Mag., 2003—; named one of Top 40 Who's Who in Washington Plaintiff's Personal Injury Law, 2006, Top 40 Lawyers, Seattle Mag., 2007. Mem.: ABA (mem. Ho. of Dels. 2004—, mem. commn. for renaissance of idealism in the profession, mem. standing com. on pro bono and pub. svc., Partnership award 2005), Am. Bd. Trial Advocates, Loren Miller Bar Assn., Nat. Bar Assn. (Disting Svc. award 1994), Assn. Trial Lawyers Am., Wash. State Trial Lawyers Assn. (mem. bd. govs. 1989—96, co-chmn. Seattle downtown roundtable 1993—96, v.p. west 1994—96, Spl. Pres. Recognition award 1995), State Bar Calif., Fed. Bar Assn., Wash. State Bar Assn. (mem. bd. govs. 2002—03, pres.-elect 2003—04, pres. 2004—05), King County Bar Assn. Office: Jones & Ward PLLC 1000 Second Ave Ste 4050 Seattle WA 98104-1023 Office Phone: 206-957-1272. Office Fax: 206-957-1275. Business E-Mail: rrw@joneswardlaw.com.

WARD, ROSCOE FREDRICK, engineering educator; b. Boise, Idaho, Dec. 5, 1930; s. Roscoe C. W. and Alice E. (Ward); m. Julia Duffy, June 8, 1963; children: Eric R., David C. Student, U. Oreg., 1949-50; BA, Coll. of Idaho, 1953; postgrad., U. Wash., 1955-57; BS, Oreg. State U., 1959; MS, Wash. State U., 1961; Sc.D., Washington U., St. Louis, 1964. Registered profl. engr., Ohio. Asst. prof. civil engring. U. Mo., Columbia, 1963-65, Robert Coll., Istanbul, Turkey, 1965-67; assoc. prof. civil engring. Asian Inst. Tech., Bangkok, 1967-68; assoc. prof. civil engring., assoc. dean Sch. Engring. U. Mass., Amherst, 1968-75; prof. Bogazici U., Istanbul, 1974-75; br. chief biomass energy Dept. Energy, Washington, 1975-79; interregional advisor UN/World Bank, NYC, 1979-83; dean Sch. Applied Scis. Miami U., Oxford, Ohio, 1983-88, prof. paper and chem. engring. Sch. Engring. and Applied Scis., 1983—2008, emeritus prof., 2008—. Vis. scientist Csir, Republic of South Africa, 1990-91. Contbr. chapters to books, articles to profl. jours. Fellow: ASCE. Home: 4818 Bonham Rd Oxford OH 45056-1423

WARD, SOLVEIG MARIA, marketing professional; b. Stockholm, Aug. 22, 1954; d. Ingvar Erik and Inga Kronman; m. Edward L. Ward, Jan. 20, 1997; children: Johan Fredrick Mahrs, Lars Richard Mahrs. MSEE, Royal Inst. of Tech., Stockholm, 1977. Sales engr. Asea Ab, Vasteras, Sweden, 1977—80; supr. dept. sales ASEA SA de CV, Mexico City, 1980—82; product mktg. mgr. Abb (Asea) Ab, Vasteras, 1982—92; mgr. consulting engring. ABB Inc., Coral Springs, Fla., 1992—99, product mgr. Allentown, Pa., 1999—2002; dir. product mktg. RFL Electronics Inc., Boonton Twp., NJ, 2002—. Mem.: IEEE. Achievements include patents for high speed single pole trip logic for use in protective relaying. Office: RFL Electronics Inc 353 Powerville Rd Boonton NJ 07005 Office Fax: 973-334-3863. Business E-Mail: solveig.ward@rflelect.com.

WARD, STEPHEN D., legislative staff member; b. Cleve., Aug. 12, 1950; m. Laura G. Hahn, 1987; 2 children. BA, Pa. State U., 1972, EdM, 1976. With Bill Wachob for Congress, 1983—86; polit. action com. dir. DC C. of C., 1986—89; v.p. Campaign Performance Group, 1989—91; dep. Washington dir. Nat. Com. for an Effective Congress, 1991—93; dir. govt. affairs EDS Corp., 1993—2003; chief of staff Senator Jeff Bingaman, 2003—. Congregationalist. Avocations: reading, politics, basketball, being a dad. Office: Office of Senator Jeff Bingaman 703 Senate Hart Office Bldg Washington DC 20510-3102 Office Phone: 202-224-5521. E-mail: stephen_ward@bingaman.senate.gov.*

WARD, STEPHEN M., JR., computer company executive; BSME, Calif. Polytech. State U., San Luis Obispo. Joined IBM Corp., Tucson, 1978; v.p. info. tech., gen. mgr. IBM ThinkPad; gen. mgr. IBM's Global Indsl. Sector; chief info. officer, v.p. bus. transformation IBM Corp., sr. v.p., gen. mgr. regional systems group Armonk, NY, 2003—04; sr. v.p., gen. mgr. personal sys. group IBM, Armonk, NY, 2004—05; CEO Lenovo Group Ltd., Purchase, NY, 2005, cons., 2005. Past bd. dir. e2open; bd. dir. Carpenter Technology Corp. Recipient NY Ten Award, Exec. Coun., 2005. Office: Lenovo 1009 Think Pl Morrisville NC 27560-9002

WARD, VERNON GRAVES, retired internist; b. Palisade, Nebr., Mar. 5, 1928; s. Charles Bennett and Mildred Belle (Graves) W.; m. Eleanore Mae Farstveet, Aug. 28, 1952; children: Margo, Alison, Barry. BA, Nebr. Wesleyan U., 1948; MD cum laude, U. Nebr., Omaha, 1954. Diplomate Am. Bd. Internal Medicine. Instr. in anatomy Columbia U., NYC, 1948—50; intern U. Wis., Madison, 1954—55, resident internal medicine, 1955—58, chief resident, physician, 1957—58; fellow in neurophysiology and psychosomatic medicine U. Okla., Oklahoma City, 1960—61; asst. clin. prof. medicine U. Wis., Madison, 1961—62; pvt. practice internal medicine Kearney, Nebr., 1962—67; asst. prof. U. Nebr. Coll. Medicine, Omaha, 1967—69; assoc. clin. prof. medicine U. Nebr., Omaha, 1969—; pvt. practice internal medicine Omaha, 1969—2005; ret. Chmn. dept. internal medicine Clarkson Hosp., Omaha, 1976-78, 96-98. Contbr. articles to profl. jours. including JAMA, Nebr. State Med. Jour., Wis. State Med. Jour., Am. Heart Jour., Postgrad. Medicine. Pres. Nebr. chpt. Arthritis Found., 1969-71. Lt. comdr. USNR, 1958-60. Recipient Cmty. Based Tchg. award ACP-ASIM, 2000; named Hutton Traveling Scholar Coll. of Physicians, 1965. Fellow ACP, Am. Coll. Rheumatology; mem. AMA, Nebr. State Med. Soc., Omaha Med. Soc., Am. Soc. Internal Medicine (Cmty.-Based Tchg. award 2000), Am. Psychosomatic Soc., Nebr. Soc. Internal Medicine (pres. 1980-82, Disting. Internist award 1990), Phi Kappa Phi, Alpha Omega Alpha (pres. Nebr. chpt. 1984-85), Phi Chi (grand sec.-treas. 1986—2006, co-chmn. nat. conv. Omaha 1953, emeritus trustee 2006—), Phi Kappa Tau. Republican. Lutheran. Home: 302 N 54th St Omaha NE 68132-2813 Home Phone: 402-558-7641.

WARD, WANDA LOUISE DOBBS, educational administrator; b. Hebron, Ill., Feb. 16, 1927; d. Willie S. and Ada S. (Burnett) Dobbs; m. William David Ward Sr., June 4, 1950; children— Susan Jean Ward Stare, William David Jr., Steven Carl. B.S., MacMurray Coll., 1969; M.S., SUNY-Geneseo, 1972; C.A.S., SUNY-Brockport, 1982. Tchr. grades 1 through 4, tchr. music 8 grades, two-room sch., Literberry, Ill., 1946-47; tchr. 1st and 3d grades, pub. schs., Creve Coeur, Ill., 1950-52; tchr. kindergarten classes, Barker Rd. Elem. Sch., Pittsford, N.Y., 1968-78; dir. Pittsford Tchr. Ctr., 1978-83, 84-90; supr. student tchrs. Nazareth Coll. of Rochester, 1990-92; dir. Pittsford Continuing Edn., 1981-90, liaison for overseas sch.-to-sch. programs in Belgrade and Zagreb, Yugoslavia, Pittsford schs., 1979-83; prin. Thornell Rd. Elem. Sch., 1983-84; regional cons. Instr. mag.; cons. mentor/intern program West Irondequoit Sch. Dist.; condr. local, state and nat. workshops on early childhood readiness, on starting tchr.-ctr. approach to staff devel.; cons. staff devel. programs State of N.Y.; dir., founder, pres. K Bd., Danville, Ill., 1965-66; coord., developer Greater Rochester Staff Devel. Coun., 1984-90; regional telecommunications trainer N.Y. State Tech. Com., 1985-90; mem. N.Y. State Higher Edn. Com., 1987—; co-chmn. State Tchr. Ctr. Conf.; chmn. N.Y. State Tchr. Ctr. Conf., 1989-91. Named Woman of Yr., Comml. News, 1965, Disting. Alumnae, MacMurray Coll., 1984; recipient Svc. award Phi Delta Kappa, 1988, N.Y. State Achievement award, 1990. Mem. Parent Tchr. Student Assn. (3 life membership awards 1963, 65, 69, Disting. Service award 1982), Pittsford Tchrs. Assn. (pres. 1976-77), N.Y. State Tchrs. Assn., Nat. Assn. Edn. Young Children, Assn. Supervision and Curriculum Devel. (pres. local exec. bd.), Delta Kappa Gamma Soc. Internat. (internat. communications com. 1988-90, internat. N.E. regional dir. 1990-92, pres. Alpha Xi chpt. 1980-82, pres. NY State 1987-89, internat. nominations com. 2004-, named Woman of Distinction 2007), Pittsford NY Women's Club (charter mem., pres. 2001-02, named State Women of Yr. 2000, recipient Wanda Ward Life Achievement award 2005). Republican. Methodist. Organizer, developer 10 kindergartens, Danville, Ill., 1965. Personal E-mail: wanward@rochester.rr.com.

WARD, WILLIAM E. (KIP WARD), career military officer; b. Balt., 1949; m. Joyce L. Ward; 2 children. BA in Polit. Sci., Morgan State U., 1971; student, US Army Infantry Sch., 1976; MA in Polit. Sci., Pa. State U., 1979; grad., US Army Command & Gen. Staff Coll., 1982—83, US Army War Coll., 1991—92. Commd. 2d lt. US Army, advanced through grades to gen., 2006; rifle platoon leader A Co., 3rd Bn. 325th Infantry 82nd Airborne Divsn., Ft. Bragg, NC, 1971—72, anti-tank platoon leader, 1972—74, liaison officer, 1974; rifle platoon leader B Co. 1st Bn., 17th Infantry, 2nd Infantry Divsn. Eighth Army, Republic of Korea, 1974—76; instr. then asst. prof. social scis. US Mil. Acad., West Point, NY, 1978—82; logistics staff officer 210th Field Arty. Group US Army Europe & 7th Army, Herzo Base, Germany, 1983-85, exec. officer US Army Community Activity Aschaffenburg, Germany, 1985—86, exec. officer 1st bn. (mechanized), 7th infantry, 3rd divsn., 1986—87; comdr. 5th bn. 9th Inf. Rgt. 6th Infantry Divsn., Ft. Wainwright, Alaska, 1988—91; comdr. 2d Commando Brigade 10th Mt. Divsn., Ft. Drum, 1992—94; exec. officer to vice chief of staff US Army, Washington, 1994—95; dep. dir. ops. Nat. Mil. Command Ctr., The Joint Staff (J-3), Washington, 1995-96; asst. divsn. comdr. for support 82d Airborne Divsn., Ft. Bragg, 1996-98; chief, Office Mil. Ops. Am. Embassy, Cairo, 1998—99; comdr. 25th Inf. Divsn. U.S. Army Hawaii, Ft. Shaffer, Hawaii, 1999—2000; vice dir. ops. The Joint Staff, Washington, 2000—02; comdr. Stabilisation Force, Operation Joint Force, Sarajevo, Bosnia-Herzegovina, 2002—03; dep. commdg. gen., chief of staff US Army Europe & 7th Army, 2003—05; spl. security coord. for Mid. East US Dept. State, 2005—06; dep. comdr. US European Command (USEUCOM), Stuttgart, Germany, 2006—07; comdr. US African Command (USAFRICOM), Stuttgart, Germany, 2007—. Decorated Def. Superior Svc. medal with oak leaf cluster,Def. Disting. Svc. medal, Disting. Svc. medal, Legion of Merit with 2 oak leaf clusters, Def. Meritorious Svc. medal, Meritorious Svc. medal with 6 oak leaf clusters, Joint Service Commendation medal, Army Commendation medal with three oak leaf clusters, Army Achievement medal with oak leaf cluster, Presdl. Order of Merit (Arab Rep. of Egypt). Achievements include participation in OPERATION RESTORE HOPE in Mogadishu, Somalia, 1992-93. Office: US African Command (USAFRICOM) Kelley Barracks 70567 Stuttgart Germany*

WARD, WILLIAM FRANCIS, JR., real estate investment broker; b. Everett, Mass., Aug. 23, 1928; s. William Francis and Helen (Schriber) W.; m. Elaine L. Wilson, June 11, 1950 (dec. Oct. 1993); children: Jeffrey W., Gary T., Michelle A., Gregory W., Suzanne M.; m. Marie-Louise Buchheit, Nov. 5, 1994. BS, US Mil. Acad., 1950; MBA, Harvard U., Cambridge, Mass., 1956; LLB, La Salle U., Chgo., 1966; LLD (hon.), So. Vt. U., Benington, 1996; HHD (hon.), NY Coll. Podiatric Medicine, 2003. Commd. 2d lt. US Army, 1950; resigned, 1956; econ. analyst E.I. duPont de Nemours & Co., Inc., Wilmington, Del., 1956-58; sec. N.Y. State Bridge Authority, Poughkeepsie, 1958-60; div. contr., dir. mktg. svcs. GAF Corp., NYC, 1960-63; asst. to pres. Grosset & Dunlap, Inc., 1963-65, v.p., 1965-67; contr. Dun & Bradstreet, 1967-71, v.p., 1968-71; chmn. bd., pres. Dun-Donnelley Pub. Corp., 1971-77; exec. v.p. Am. Cancer Soc.; from v.p., treas. to pres. Gestam, Inc., 1981-86; chief Army Res., 1986-91, comdr. US Army Res. Command, 1990—91; chmn., pres. Realicam, 1985—. Bd. dirs. Quotron Electronics, Inc., Empire Nat. Bank, Eastern Savs. Bank, Apple Bank for Savs., Corinthian Broadcasting, Greater NY Bank for Savs.; trustee All-City Funds; mem. adv. bd. Astoria Fin. Bank, Podia Ins. Co.; mem. faculty Dutchess C.C., 1958-60, NYU Sch. Commerce, 1960-64; trustee NYC Foot Clinics, 2004—; hon. col. 70th tank regiment US Army. Pres. Ramapo Central Sch. Dist., 1966-72, 1982-87; mem. facilities and planning bd. Good Samaritan Hosp., 1980-85; chmn. United Way, Rockland County, 1992-94; county chmn. Citizen for Kennedy and Johnson, 1960; Dem. candidate for Ho. of Reps., 1962; chmn. Young Citizens for Johnson and Humphrey, 55 counties NY, 1964; exec. v.p. Am. Cancer Soc., 1976-81; bd. dirs. NYC divsn. Aerospace Edn. Found., US Army War Coll. Found., West Point Fund, 1979, Franciscan Sisters of the Poor Found., 1980-92; trustee NY Mil. Acad., 1982-86, 91-96, trustee emeritus, 1996—; trustee Assn. Grads. US Mil. Acad., 1993-2003, trustee emeritus, 2003—, exec. com., 1996-2003, chmn. audit com., 1996-2004; trustee Hist. Soc. Rockland County, 1993-95, NY Coll. Podiatric Medicine, 2000, chmn. bd. trustees, 2004—. Capt. AUS, 1950-54; to maj. gen. 1978-91. Decorated D.S.M. with 1 oak leaf cluster, Legion of Merit, Meritorious Svc. medal with oak leaf cluster, Air medal with 3 oak leaf clusters, Army Commendation medal with oak leaf cluster, Purple Heart, Army Achievement medal. Mem. West Point Soc. (Washington chpt., Space Coast chpt., NY chpt., pres. 1974-76), Antrim Players, Soc. Harvard Engrs. and Scientists, Fin. Execs. Inst., Newcomen Soc., Res. Officers Assn., Am. Friends of Viet Nam (nat. chmn.), VFW, Am. Legion, Knight of Holy Sepluchre, Disabled Am. Vets., Pilgrim Soc., Army and Navy Club, Squadron "A" Club, Univ. Club (NY), Harvard Club (Washington), Nat. Press Club. Roman Catholic. Home: 1271 Continental Ave Melbourne FL 32940 also: 10 Debbie Ct Chester NY 10918 Personal E-mail: wward15@cfl.rr.com, wmfward@optonline.net.

WARD BLACK, JANET, lawyer; b. Kannapolis, NC; BA in Econs. cum laude, Davidson Coll., 1982; JD, Duke U., 1985. Asst. dist. atty. Cabarrus and Rowan Counties, 1985—88; atty. Wallace Whitley Pope & Black, Salisbury, NC, 1989—92, Donaldson & Black PA, Greensboro, NC, 1992—2006, Ward Black Law, Greensboro, NC, 2006—. Mem. Women's Profl. Forum, Greensboro; nat. adv. com. Win-Win Resolutions Inc., Greensboro; steering com. NC Inst. Govt. Judicial Edn. Fund; adv. panel mem. Legal Services NC, Greensboro, 2002—, co-chair Access to Justice, 2006. Bd. dirs. Women's Resource Ctr. Greensboro, Mercy Mission Teams, Greensboro; bd. trustees Hood Theological Seminary, Salisbury; vol. Appalachian Svc. Project, Save a Generation, Nicaragua, El Salvador, Habitat for Humanity, Honduras. Master: Joseph Branch Inn of Ct.; mem.: NC Assn. Women Attys., ABA, Acad. Catastrophic Injury Attys., NC Acad. Trial Lawyers (chair polit. action com. 2004—06), Assn. Trial Lawyers of Am. (bd. gov. 2005—), NC Bar Assn. (pres.-elect 2006—07). Office: Ward Black Law 208 W Wendover Ave Greensboro NC 27401 Office Phone: 800-531-9191. Office Fax: 336-379-9415. E-mail: jwblack@wardblacklaw.com.

WARDELL, DAVID A., lawyer, automotive executive; b. 1955; AB, Princeton U.; JD, Case Western Reserve U. Asst. dist. atty., NY; with legal dept. Bristol-Meyers Squibb Co.; assoc. counsel Clairol Inc.; various positions Abbott Labs., assoc. gen. counsel pharm. products group legal ops., 2005—07; sr. v.p., gen. counsel, corp. sec. Tenneco, Inc., Lake Forest, Ill., 2007—. Office: Tenneco Inc 500 North Field Dr Lake Forest IL 60045 Office Phone: 847-482-5000. Office Fax: 847-482-5940.*

WARDEN, JOHN LEHMAN, lawyer; b. Evansville, Ind., Sept. 22, 1941; s. Walter Wilson and Juanita (Veatch) W.; m. Phillis Ann Rodgers, Oct. 27, 1960; children: Anne W. Clark, John L., W. Carson. AB, Harvard U., 1962; LLB, U. Va., 1965. Bar: N.Y. 1966, U.S. Ct. Appeals (2d cir.) 1966, U.S. Dist. Ct. (so. and ea. dists.) N.Y. 1967, U.S. Ct. Appeals (10th cir.) 1971, U.S. Supreme Ct. 1972, U.S. Ct. Appeals (D.C. cir.) 1980. Assoc. Sullivan & Cromwell, NYC, 1965-73, ptnr., 1973—2008, of counsel, 2009—. Commr. US Antitrust Modernization Commn., 2004—07. Editor-in-chief: Va. Law Rev., 1964-65. Hon. trustee U. Va. Law Sch. Found., Am. Ballet Theatre. Fellow Am. Coll. Trial Lawyers; mem. ABA, Am. Law Inst., NY State Bar Assn., Assn. Bar City NY, NY County Lawyers Assn., Knickerbocker Club, Doubles Club, Bedford Golf and Tennis Club, Lyford Cay Club. Republican. Episcopalian. Office: Sullivan & Cromwell 125 Broad St Fl 28 New York NY 10004-2489 Office Phone: 212-558-3610. E-mail: wardenj@sullcrom.com.

WARDEN, RICHARD DANA, government labor union official; b. Great Falls, Mont., Dec. 10, 1931; s. Robert Dickinson and Helen (Leach) W.; m. Barbara Freeman; children from previous marriage: Denise, Michael, Joseph, Jerome. BA, U. Mont., 1957, MA, 1958. Reporter, then state editor Gt. Falls (Mont.) Tribune, 1959-61; legis. asst. to U.S. Senator Lee Metcalf of Mont., 1962-63; adminstrv. asst. to U.S. Congressman James G. O'Hara of Mich., 1963-67; dep. dir. Office Civil Rights, HEW, 1967-68; legis. rep. AFL-CIO, 1969-70; dir. Washington Research Project Action Council, 1970-72; asst. legis. dir. UAW, 1972—75, legis. dir., 1975-77, 79-91, ret., 1991. Asst. sec. legis. HEW, 1977-79 Served with USN, 1950-54. Congressional fellow, 1961-62; recipient Pub. Affairs Reporting award Am. Polit. Sci. Assn., 1960 Mem.: Am. Polit. Sci. Assn. Home: 211 Marina Dr Lewes DE 19958

WARDEN, WALDIA ANN, retired retreat center administrator, director; b. New Orleans, Jan. 15, 1933; d. Walter Emmer and Lydia Eugenie (LeBlanc) W BS, St. Mary's Dominican Coll., 1961; MS Dietetics, St. Louis U., 1964; JCL, Cath. U. Am., 1988. Joined Dominican Sisters, Congregation of St. Mary, Roman Cath. Ch., 1953, coun. mem., 1976-84, 96-2004. Tchr. elem. schs., 1954—62; instr. foods and nutrition Dominican Coll., New Orleans, 1964—66, chmn. dept. home econs., 1965—69, 1975—78, chmn. home econs. dept., 1966—69, asst. dean students, 1969—75, chmn. Coll. Planning Coun., 1972—76; dir. Rosaryville Ctr., Ponchatoula, La., 1979—81; pres. St. Mary's Dominican Coll., New Orleans, 1983—86; defender Bond for Tribunal Archdiocese of New Orleans, 1989—2005; dir. Rosaryville Spirit Life Ctr., Ponchatoula, 2005—08. Pres. St. Mary's Dominican H.S., 1990-94; coord. First Ct. Met. Tribunal, Archdiocese of New Orleans, 1994-2005 Trustee St. Mary's Dominican Coll., 1973-79, 83-86, 90-93; bd. regents Our Lady of Holy Cross Coll., New Orleans, 1992-98; bd. dirs. Henriette deLille Mid. Sch. for Girls, 2000-04, chair, 2004-05 Mem. La. Dietetic Assn. (editor jour. 1966-68), La. Leadership Conf. Women Religious, Am. Dietetic Assn., Am. Home Econs. Assn., Canon Law Soc. Am., Dominican Leadership; Dominican Cluster Union (cluster coord. com. 2002-06, chair reconfiguration subcom. 2002-06) Home: 2320 Airport Dr Columbus OH 43219-2098 Home Phone: 614-416-1093. Personal E-mail: dawaldia@aol.com.

WARDER, MICHAEL YOUNG, academic administrator; b. Buffalo, June 29, 1946; s. Thomas Grayston and Norma A. (Young) W.; m. Cheryl Lynn Gilkerson, Feb. 8, 1975; children: Maureen, Amy, Michael Jr. BA, Stanford U., 1968. Tchr. Drew Sch., San Francisco, 1968—69; pres. Internat. Re-edn. Found., San Francisco, 1970—73; sec.-gen. Internat. Conf. on Unity of Scis., NYC, 1974—79; pres., pub. Newsworld Comm., NYC, 1976—79; dir. adminstrn. Heritage Found., Washington, 1980—83; exec. v.p. Ethics and Pub. Policy Ctr., Washington, 1983—84, The Rockford Inst., Ill., 1985—95; v.p. devel. Claremont Inst., Calif., 1995—2001; exec. dir. So. Calif. Children's Scholarship Fund, 2001—05; vice chancellor Pepperdine U., Malibu, Calif., 2005—. Radio commentator (bi-weekly) Sta. WNIJ-FM NPR Affiliate, DeKalb, Ill., 1991—95; del. leader People to People, USSR, 1991, Rockford Inst., Lithuania, Latvia, Estonia, 1994; del. leader to London Claremont Inst., 1996, del. leader to Hong Kong, 97, del. leader to Israel, 98, del. leader to Rome, 2000, del. leader to China, 06; guest TV programs Politically Incorrect/ABC, Fox News Channel, MSNBC, others; spkr. in field; polit. analyst in field. Op-ed columnist The Wall Street Jour., USA Today, L.A. Times, The Chgo. Tribune, Chgo. Sun Times, San Francisco Chronicle, San Diego Union Tribune, St. Louis Post Dispatch, Indpls. Star, 1985—; host, prodr. (TV) Stateline Newsmakers, 1990-92; columnist (weekly) Rockford Register Star, 1991-92. Recipient Silver Dome award Ill. Broadcasters Assn., 1993, 95, 96; grantee Earhart Found., 1988. Mem.: Pacific Coun. Internat. Policy, L.A. World Affairs Coun., Phila. Soc., Coun. for Nat. Policy, Americanism Ednl. League (bd. dirs.). Republican. Avocations: travel, history, geography. Office: Pepperdine U 24255 Pacific Coast Hwy Malibu CA 90263 Office Phone: 310-506-4486. Business E-Mail: michael.warder@pepperdine.edu.

WARDER, RICHARD CURREY, JR., dean, mechanical aerospace engineering educator; b. Nitro, W.Va., Sept. 30, 1936; s. Richard Currey and Edith Irene (Moser) W.; m. Carolyn Strickler, Mar. 7, 1964 (div. Dec. 1978); children: Jennifer, Jeffrey W.; m. Marjorie Dianne Forney, Jan. 10, 1981. BS, S.D. Sch. Mines, 1958; MS, Northwestern U., 1959, PhD, 1963. Registered profl. engr., Mo., Tenn. Asst. prof. Northwestern U., Evanston, Ill., 1963-65; mgr. energy processes research Litton Industries, Beverly Hills, Calif., 1965-68; assoc. prof. mech. and aerospace engrng. U. Mo., Columbia, 1968-72, prof., 1972-94, James C. Dowell prof., 1989-94, chmn. mech. aerospace engrng., 1988-94; dean U. Memphis Herff Coll. Engrng., 1994—. Program mgr., head resources sect. NSF, Washington, 1974-76; mem. Engrng. Accreditation Commn., 2003-08; cons. to industry U.S. govt. Bd. dirs. Columbia Montessori Soc., 1971-73; bd. dirs. Columbia Soccer Club, 1976-80, pres., 1978-80; referee Maj. Indoor Soccer League, 1979-83. Fellow: AAAS, ASME, AIAA (assoc.); mem.: Am. Soc. Engrng. Edn., Am. Phys. Soc. Methodist. Office Phone: 901-678-4306.

WARDLAW, KIM A. MCLANE, federal judge; b. San Francisco, July 2, 1954; m. William M. Wardlaw Sr., Sept. 8, 1984. Student, Santa Clara U., 1972—73, Foothill C.C., Los Altos Hills, Calif., 1973—74; AB in Comm. summa cum laude, UCLA, 1976, JD with honors, 1979. Bar: Calif., US Dist. Ct. (ctrl. dist.) Calif. 1979, US Dist. Ct. (so. dist.) Calif. 1982, US Dist. Ct. Nev. 1985, US Dist. Ct. (no. dist.) Calif. 1992, US Dist. Ct. Mont. 1993, US Dist. Ct. Minn. 1994, US Dist. Ct. (no. dist.) Ala. 1994, US Dist. Ct. (so. dist.) Miss. 1995, US Supreme Ct. Law clk. US Dist. Ct. Ctrl. Dist. Calif., 1979—80; assoc. O'Melveny and Myers, 1980—87, ptnr., 1987—95; judge US Dist. Ct. Calif., LA, 1995—98, US Ct. Appeals (9th cir.), 1998—. Presdl. transition team Dept. Justice, Washington, 1993; mayoral transition team City of LA, 1995—; bd. govs. UCLA Ctr. for Comm. Policy, 1994—, vice-chair, 1994—; cons. in field. Co-author: The Encyclopedia of the American Constitution, 1986; contbr. articles to profl. jours. Pres. Women Lawyers Pub. Action Grant Found., 1986—87; founding mem. LA Chamber Orch., 1992—; active Legal Def. and Edn. Fund Calif. Leadership Coun., 1993—; active Blue Ribbon of LA Music Ctr., 1993—; del. Dem. Nat. Conv., 1992. Recipient Buddy award, NOW, 1995; named one of Most Prominent Bus. Attys. in LA County, LA Bus. Jour., 1995. Mem.: NOW, ABA, Orgn. Women Execs., Assn. Bus. Trial Lawyers (gov. 1988—), LA County Bar Assn. (trustee 1993—94), Women Lawyers Assn. LA, Calif. Women Lawyers, Mex.-Am. Bar Assn. LA County, Hollywood Womens Polit. Com., Downtown Women Ptnrs., City Club Bunker Hill, Breakfast Club, Chancery Club, Phi Beta Kappa. Office: US Ct Appeals 9th Cir 125 South Grand Ave Pasadena CA 91105*

WARDRIP, ELIZABETH JANE, retired librarian; b. Lawrenceburg, Ind., Dec. 12, 1925; d. Estal Joseph Ackerman and Dorothy Leona Unthank; m. Schuyler Clark Wardrip, Dec. 20, 1953 (div. Dec. 24, 1981); children: Gregory Clark, Elizabeth Jane, Margaret Louise, Laura Anne, Mary Ann. BS in Gen. Studies, Columbia U., 1951; MLS, U. Md., 1972. Cert. libr. Md., 1972. Libr. adult svcs. Prince George's County Meml. Libr. Sys., Hyattsville, Md., 1972—92, ret., 1992. Fellow, U. Rochester, 1951. Mem.: DAR (regent 1999—2001). Democrat. Roman Catholic. Avocations: reading, theater, travel, museums, art galleries. Home: 6103 Sutters Place Bowie MD 20720

WARDROPPER, IAN BRUCE, museum curator, educator; b. Balt., May 11, 1951; s. Bruce Wear and Joyce (Vaz) W.; stepmother: Nancy Hélène (Palmer) W.; m. Laurel Ellen Bradley, May 22, 1982 (div. 1996); 1 child, Chloe Bradley; m. Sarah Anne McNear, June 21, 1997. BA, Brown U., 1973; MA, NYU, 1976, PhD, 1985. Asst. curator European sculpture Art Inst. Chgo., 1982-85, assoc. curator European decorative arts and sculpture, 1985-89, Eloise W. Martin curator European decorative arts and sculpture, and classical art, 1989-2001; Iris and B. Gerald Cantor curator in charge dept. European sculpture and decorative arts Met. Mus. Art, NYC, 2001—05, chmn., 2005—. Adj. instr. Drew U., NJ, 1982; vis. asst. prof. Northwestern U., Evanston, Ill., 1986, Sch. of Art Inst. Chgo., 1988; guest scholar J. Paul Getty Mus., Malibu, Calif., 1995; Rhoades lectr. U. Chgo., 1997; exhbns. panelist NEA, 1993, creation and presentation panelist, 98, indemnity panelist, 1998—2001. Co-author: European Decorative Arts in the Art Institute of Chicago, 1991, Austrian Architecture and Design beyond Tradition in the 1990s, 1991, News from a Radiant Future: Soviet Porcelain from the Collection of Craig H. and Kay A. Tuber, 1992, Chiseled with a Brush: Italian Sculpture, 1860-1925, from The Gilgore Collections, 1994, From the Sculptor's Hand: Italian Baroque Terracottas from the State Hermitage Museum, 1998; contbr. articles to profl. jours. NEA fellow, 1976-77, Chester Dale fellow Met. Mus. Art, 1978-79; Kress Found. rsch. grantee, Paris, 1979-81, Am. Philos. Soc. grantee, 1991; named Chicagoan of the Yr. in Arts Chicago Tribune, 1994. Mem. Phi Beta Kappa. Office: Met Mus Art 1000 Fifth Ave New York NY 10028-0198 Office Phone: 212-879-5500 ext. 4980. Business E-Mail: Ian.wardropper@Metmuseum.org.

WARD-STEINMAN, DAVID, composer, music educator, pianist; b. Alexandria, La., Nov. 6, 1936; s. Irving Steinman and Daisy Leila (Ward) W.-S.; m. Susan Diana Lucas, Dec. 28, 1956 (div. 1993); children: Jenna, Matthew; m. Patrice Dawn Madura, May 28, 2001. MusB cum laude, Fla. State U., 1957; MusM, U. Ill., 1958, DMA, 1961; studies with Nadia Boulanger, Paris, 1958-59; postdoctoral vis. fellow, Princeton U., 1970. Grad. instr. U. Ill., 1957-58; mem. faculty San Diego State U., 1961—2003, prof. music, 1968—, disting. prof. music, emeritus prof., 2004, dir. comprehensive musicianship program, 1972—2003, composer in residence, 1961—, univ. rsch. lectr., 1986-87. Faculty Eastman Sch. Music Workshop, 1969, Coll. Music Soc. Nat. Inst. for Music in Gen. Studies, U. Colo., 1983-84, Calif. State Summer Sch. for the Arts, Loyola Marymount U., 1988; Ford Found. composer in residence Tampa Bay (Fla.) Area, 1970-72, Brevard Music Ctr., N.C., 1986; acad. cons. U. North Sumatra (Indonesia), 1982; concert and lecture tour U.S. Info. Agy., Indonesia, 1982; master tchr. in residence Atlantic Ctr. for the Arts, New Smyrna Beach, Fla., 1996; vis. artist in residence Victorian Ctr. for the Arts, Melbourne, Australia, 1997, faculty Coll. Mus. Soc. Nat. Insts., San Diego, 1999, 2001, 2003, Ind., 2003; adj. prof. music Ind. U., Bloomington, 2004—. Composer: Symphony, 1959, Prelude & Toccata for orch., 1962, Concerto No. 2 for chamber orch., 1962, ballet Western Orpheus, 1964, Cello Concerto, 1966, These Three ballet, 1966, The Tale of Issoumbochi chamber opera, 1968, Rituals for Dancers and Musicians, 1971, Antares, 1971, Arcturus, 1972, The Tracker, 1976, Brancusi's Brass Beds, 1977; oratorio Song of Moses, 1964; Jazz Tangents, 1967, Childs Play, 1968; 3-act opera Tamar, 1977; Golden Apples, 1981; choral suite Of Wind and Water, 1982; Christmas cantata And In These Times, 1982; Moiré for piano and chamber ensemble, 1983, And Waken Green, song cycle on poems by Douglas Worth, 1983, Olympics Overture for orchestra, 1984, Children's Corner Revisited, song cycle, 1984, Summer Suite for oboe and piano, 1984, Quintessence for double quintet and percussion, 1985, Chroma concerto for multiple keyboards, percussion and chamber orch., 1985, Winging It for chamber orchestra, 1986, Epilegy for Astronauts for orchestra, 1986, What's Left for piano, 1987, Gemini for 2 guitars, 1988, Intersections II: Borobudur, Under Capricorn, 1989, Voices from the Gallery, 1990, Cinnabar for viola and piano, 1991, Seasons Fantastic for chorus and harp, 1992, Cinnabar Concerto for Viola and Chamber Orchestra, 1993, Night Winds Quintet # 2 for woodwinds, 1993, Double Concerto for Two Violins and Orchestra, 1995, Prisms and Reflections (3rd Piano Sonata), 1996, Millennium Fanfare for symph. orch., 2000, Millennium Dances for symph. orch., 2001, FIESTA! for symphony orch., 2002, FLIGHT! for 2 Pianos, 2002, I Am the Wind for voice and chamber ensemble, 2002, Songs of the Seasons for voice and piano, 2006, Hildegrard's Apothecary for chorus and piano, 2007, Fantango No 2 for chorus and piano, 2007, incantation and dance Native Am. Flute and Prepared Piano, 2007, Taj Mahal Symphony Orch., 2008; recs. include Fragments from Sappho, 1969; Duo for cello and piano, 1974, Childs Play for bassoon and piano, 1974, The Tracker, 1989, Brancusi's Brass Beds, 1984, concert suite from Western Orpheus, 1987, Sonata for Piano Fortified, 1987, Moiré, 1987, 3 Songs for Clarinet and Piano, 1987, Concerto #2 for Chamber Orchestra, 1990, Prisms and Reflections, 1999, Cinnabar, 1999, Sonata for Piano Fortified, 1999, Night Winds, 1999, Borobudur, 1999, Cello Concerto, 2000, Cinnabar Concerto, 2000, Chroma Concerto, 2000, Skyline and Under Capricorn, 2005, Seasons Greetings for symphony orch, 2006; commd. by Chgo. Symphony, Joffrey Ballet, San Diego Ballet, San Diego Symphony, numerous others; author: (with Susan L. Ward-Steinman) Comparative Anthology of Musical Forms, 2 vols, 1976, Toward a Comparative Structural Theory of the Arts, 1989. Recipient Joseph H. Bearns prize in Music Columbia U., 1961, SAI Am. Music award, 1962, Dohnanyi award Fla. State U., 1965, ann. BMI awards, 1970—, Broadcast Music prize, 1954, 55, 60, 61; named Outstanding Prof., Calif. State Univs. and Colls., 1968, Outstanding Alumnus of Yr., Fla. State U., 1976; Fulbright sr. scholar La Trobe U. and Victorian Coll. Arts, Victorian Arts Ctr., Melbourne, Australia, 1989-90. Mem. Coll. Music Soc. (nat. bd. for composition 1991-93), Broadcast Music, Inc., Soc. of Composers, inc., Nat. Assn. of Composers U.S.A., Golden State Flying Club. Presbyterian. Home: 1159 E Winners Cir Bloomington IN 47401 Personal E-mail: dwardste@indiana.edu.

WARE, BILLY, musician; Mem. band BeauSoleil, 1976—. Albums include The Spirit of Cajun Music, 1976, Parlez Nous au Boire, 1984, Louisiana Cajun Music, 1984, Zydeco Gris Gris, 1985, Allons a Lafayette, 1986, Bayou Boogie, 1986, Bayou Cadillac, 1989, Live! From the Left Coast, 1989, Deja Vu, 1990, Cajun Conja, 1991, La Danse de la Vie, 1993, L'Echo, 1994, l'Amour ou la Folie, 1995 (Grammy award for Best Traditional Folk Album, 1997), Arc de Triomphe Two-Step, 1997, Looking Back Tomorrow, 2001, Gitane Cajun, 2004, Live at the 2008 New Orleans Jazz & Heritage Festival (Grammy award for Best Cajun Album, 2009), Live in Louisiana, 2006, Alligator Purse, 2009. Recipient Big Easy Entertainment award for Best Cajun Band, 2005. Office: care Rosebud Agy PO Box 170429 San Francisco CA 94117-0429*

WARE, D. CLIFTON, vocalist, educator; b. Newton, Miss., Mar. 15, 1937; s. Durward Clifton and Emma Edna (Blount) W.; m. Elizabeth Jean Oldham, June 20, 1958; children: Jon Clifton, David Michael, Stephen Alan. BA, Millsaps Coll., 1959; MusM, U. So. Miss., 1962; MusD, Northwestern U., 1970. Voice instr. U. So. Miss., Hattiesburg, 1964-69; prof. voice and pedagogy U. Minn., Mpls., 1970—2007, chmn. Roy A. Schuessler Vocal Arts Ctr., 1970—2007, prof. emeritus, 2007—. Clinician, cons., adjudicator. Author: (book, song collection and video) Voice Adventures, 1988, (text, song collection, audio cassette, CD) Adventures in Singing, 1995, 2d edit., 1998, 3rd edit., 2004, Basics of Vocal Pedagogy, 1998, The Singer's Life: Goals and Roles, 2005; made recs. St. Nicolas, 1977, Paul Bunyan, 1988, Vocal Explorations: The Bad, the Good, and the Other, 2003; tenor soloist opera, oratorio, recitals, The Aging Challange:Making the Most of Life After 50, 2009. Mem. Nat. Assn. Tchrs. Singing (pres. Minn. chpt. 1972-73, 81-82, found 1995-2006), Nat. Opera Assn. (pres. 1978-79), Pi Kappa Lambda, Phi Kappa Delta, Phi Mu Alpha Sinfonia, Pi Kappa Alpha. Avocations: travel, hiking, reading.

WARE, DEMARCUS, professional football player; b. Auburn, Ala., July 31, 1982; m. Taniqua Ware; 1 child, Marley. BS in Bus. Info. Systems, Troy U., Ala. Linebacker Dallas Cowboys, 2005—. Named 1st Team All-Pro, AP, 2007, 2008; named to Nat. Football Conf. Pro Bowl Team, NFL, 2006—08. Achievements include leading the NFL in: sacks (20), 2008. Office: Dallas Cowboys One Cowboys Pky Irving TX 75063*

WARE, GEORGE HENRY, botanist; b. Avery, Okla., Apr. 27, 1924; s. Charles and Mildred (Eshelman) W.; m. June Marie Gleason, Dec. 21, 1955; children: David, Daniel, Patrick, John. BS, U. Okla., 1945, MS, 1948; PhD, U. Wis., 1955. Asst. prof. Northwestern State U. of La., Natchitoches, 1948-56, assoc. prof., 1956-62, prof., 1962-67; dir. Conservation Sect., No. La. Supplementary Edn. Ctr., Natchitoches, 1967-68; dendrologist Morton Arboretum, Lisle, Ill., 1968-92; adminstr. Urban Vegetation Lab., 1986-92, rsch. fellow in dendrology, 1992-94, dendrologist emeritus, rsch. assoc., 1995—. Vis. prof. U. Okla., Norman, 1957, 61, 63-64; adj. prof. Western Ill. U., 1972-85; ext. faculty George Williams Coll., Downers Grove, Ill., 1969-76, Nat. Coll. Edn., Evanston, Ill., 1972-76, adj. prof. Aurora U., 2003—. Trustee nomination caucus Coll. of DuPage, Glen Ellyn, Ill., 1974-78; bd. dirs. Kane-DuPage Soil and Water Conservation Dist., 1969-81, DuPage Environ. Commn., 1992—, Openlands Project, 1996—; pres. La. Acad. Scis., 1966-67; dir. La. State Sci. Fair, 1966. With USN, 1942-46; hon. dir. Openlands, 2007-. Recipient Gold Seal award, Nat. Coun. State Garden Clubs, 1991, Am. Forests Urban Forestry Rsch. medal, 1994, Lifetime Svc. award, Nat. Urban and Cmty. Forestry Adv. Coun., 1995, Hutchinson medal, Chgo. Botanic Garden, 1997, Norman J. Colman award, Am. Nursery and Landscape Assn., 1998, award of merit, Am. Pub. Garden Assn., 2000, Liberty Hyde Bailey award, Am. Horticultural Soc., 2002, Conservation Leadership award, Openlands, 2005. Mem.: Am. Forests, Nature Conservancy, Ill. Arborist Assn. (pres. 1987—88), Am. Pub. Garden Assn., Internat. Soc. Arboriculture (Pres. Commendation award 2000, L.C. Chadwick Rsch. award 2008), Southwestern Assn. Naturalists (treas. 1963—69). Office: Morton Arboretum Lisle IL 60532-1293 Office Phone: 630-719-2413, 630-968-0074. Business E-Mail: gware@mortonarb.org.

WARE, GWENDOLYN C., retired counseling administrator; m. Roy Ware, Mar. 28; 1 child, Sonja. BA in English magna cum laude, U. Ark., Pine Buiff, 1970; MEd in Secondary Counseling with honors, U. Nev., Las Vegas, 1975. English instr. Clark County Sch. Dist., Las Vegas, 1971—77, guidance counselor, 1977—95, scholarship and coll. prep counselor, 1996—2003, ret., 2003. Fin. aid/scholarship workshop presenter Clark County Sch. Dist., Las Vegas, 1997—2003; coll. preparation workshop facilitator and presenter Kappa Alpha Psi Kappa League, Las Vegas, 2002—. Mem. Black Cmty. Orgn. Network, Las Vegas, 1988—. Mem.: AAUW, NAFE, Clark County Sch. Counselors' Assn., Western Assn. Coll. Admissions Counselors, Sickle Cell Anemia Found. (scholarship rev. and selection 1987—88), Phi Delta Kappa Internat., Phi Delta Kappa (2nd v.p. membership 1997—99, Mem. of Yr. 1997). Avocations: theater, literature, music, interior decorating.

WARE, MARILYN, former ambassador, former utilities company executive; b. Lancaster, Pa., Nov. 4, 1943; d. John III and Marian Ware; children: Mark Strode, Amy Strode, Scott Strode. D of Pub. Services, Thaddeus Stevens Coll. Tech., 1998; LittD (hon.), Franklin & Marshall Coll., 2003. Vice-chmn. Am. Water Works Co., Inc., Voorhees, NJ, 1984-88, chmn., 1988—2003, chmn. emeritus Vorhees, NJ, 2003; US amb. to Finland US Dept. State, Helsinki, 2005—08. CEO Ware Family Offices, Strasburg, Pa., 1991; dir. CIGNA Corp., Phila., 1993-2005, IKON Office Solutions, Malvern, Pa., 2000—2005, Am. Enterprise Inst., Washington, 1994, PENJERDEL Coun., Phila.; mem. Nat. Infrastructure Advisory Coun., 2002, Pew Oceans Commn., 2000-03 Editor: The Oxford Press, Lancaster, Pa., 1978-82. Trustee Nat. Osteoporosis Found., Washington, 1996-2000, U. Pa. Health Sys., Phila., 1991—, Gannon U., Erie, Pa., 1996-2000, Nat. Coun. of Conservation Fund, Washington, 1999—, Eisenhower Exch. Fellowships, Phila., 1995—, chmn. exec. com., 2000; founding mem., bd. dirs. Lancaster Farmland Trust, 1987—; founder, adv. bd. dirs. Janus Sch., Mt. Joy, Pa., 1991—; v.p., sec. Oxford Found., Strasburg, 1981—; chmn. Tom Ridge for Gov. Campaign, Harrisburg, Pa., 1993-94, Rep. Com. of Lancaster County, 1978-80, Woman for Bush, Pa., 1987-88; mem. Rep. State Com. of Pa., 1985-90. Recipient Samuel S. Baxter Meml. award Water Resources Assn., 2000, Paradigm award Greater Phila. C. of C., 1999, Dir.'s Choice award Nat. Women's Econ. Alliance Found., 1992; named Bus. Leader of Yr., Rep. Caucus, Pa. Ho. of Reps., 1993, Disting. Daus. of Pa., Gov. Tom Ridge, 2000.*

WARE, SUSAN W., historian; b. Washington, Aug. 22, 1950; d. Charles Kline and Charlotte McConnell Wolfe; m. Donald R. Ware, June 10, 1972. BA, Wellesley Coll., 1968—72; MA, Harvard U., 1973, PhD, 1978. Asst. to assoc. prof. NYU, 1986—95; hon. vis. scholar Radcliffe Coll., 1996—97; editor, Notable Am. Women Radcliffe Inst. for Advanced Study, Harvard U., 1997—2005; vis. lectr., history Harvard U., 2002—05. Adv. bd. Schlesinger Libr., Cambridge, Mass., 1988—97, Franklin and Eleanor Roosevelt Inst., Hyde Park, NY, 1986—; assoc. Clio, Inc., Charlotte, Vt., 1996—; exec. bd. Soc. of Am. Historians,

NYC, 1990—2002. Author: (books) Beyond Suffrage: Women in the New Deal, 1981, Letter to the World: Seven Women Who Shaped the Am. Century, 1998; editor: Forgotten Heroes: Inspiring Am. Portraits from our Leading Historians, 1998; author: Holding Their Own: Am. Women in the 1930s, 1982, Ptnr. and I: Molly Dewson, Feminism, and New Deal Politics, 1987, Still Missing: Amelia Earhart and the Search for Modern Feminism, 1993, It's One O'Clock and Here Is Mary Margaret McBride! A Radio Biography, 2005. Home: 16 Hilliard St Cambridge MA 02138 Home Phone: 617-492-5315. Personal E-mail: sdware@aol.com.

WARE, THADDEUS VAN, retired government official; b. High Point, NC, Mar. 31, 1935; s. Elsec and Irene (Myers) W.; m. Doretha Ardella Lee, June 18, 1960; children— Kimberly Melissa, Chrystal Lynn. BA cum laude, Va. Union U., 1957; JD, Howard U., 1960. Bar: Va. bar 1961, D.C. bar 1970, U.S. Supreme Ct. bar 1970. Gen. atty. Office of Solicitor, Dept. Labor, 1961—66; trial counsel Chief Counsel's Office, Fed. Hwy. Adminstrn., 1966—69; staff asst. to Pres. Richard M. Nixon, 1969—70; chief adminstrv. judge, chmn. Bd. Contract Appeals, Dept. Transp., 1987—2003; ret., 2003. Appt. bd. contract appeals Dept. Trans., 1970. Served with AUS, 1960-61. Mem. Va., D.C., U.S. Supreme Ct., Fed. Bar Assns., Urban League, NAACP, Bd. Contract Appeals Judges Assn. (pres. 1988-89), Alpha Phi Alpha, Sigma Delta Tau, Alpha Kappa Mu (Disting. Career Svc. award). Home: 2213 Parallel Ln Silver Spring MD 20904-5446 E-mail: tvanddlware@msn.com.

WAREHAM, ELLSWORTH EDWIN, cardiothoracic surgeon, educator; b. Avinger, Tex., Oct. 3, 1914; s. Dayton and Goldie Leah Wareham; m. Barbara Nell Nix, May 7, 1950; children: Martin, Robert, Julie, John, Scott. At, Can. Jr. Coll., Coll. Heights, Alta., 1931—33, at, 1935—36, Can. Union Coll., Lacombe, Alta., 1936; MD, Loma Linda U., Calif., 1942; LLD (hon.), Andrews U., Berrien Springs, Mich., 1971. Cert. Am. Bd. of Surgery, 1954, Am. Bd. of Thoracic Surgery, 1955. Intern Seattle Gen. Hosp., 1942; indsl. surgeon Good News Bay Mining Co., Platinum, Alaska, 1942—45; resident fellow in surgery Loma Linda U. Med. Ctr., Calif., 1947—50; resident surgery Bellevue Hosp. Columbia U., NYC, 1950—52; resident thoracic and cardiovasc. surgery Queens Med. Ctr., NYC, 1952—53; resident cardiovasc. surgery svcs. St. Francis Hosp. Cardiac Children, Roslyn, NY, 1954—55; prof. surgery Loma Linda U., 1964—2006, prof. emeritus surgery, 2006—; chief cardiothoracic surgery Loma Linda U. Med. Ctr., 1964—86; acting chmn. dept. of surgery Loma Linda U., 1973—75; staff Loma Linda U. Med. Ctr., 1964—86, Riverside Gen. Hosp., Calif., 1973—75; prof. cardiac surgery King Saud U., Riyadh, Saudi Arabia, 1986—88; admin. dir. Hong Kong Heart Ctr., 1988—. Surgeon and dir., Loma Linda U. mission to Pakistan, India, Thailand and Formosa U.S. Dept. of State, 1963; surgery team Govt. of Greece, Athens, 1967—73; organizer heart surgery affiliation Evangelismos Hosp. and Loma Linda U. Sch. Medicine, 1970—76; surgeon, heart team Loma Linda U., China, 1981. Performer: (films) Atrial Septal Defect, 1964 (Golden Eagle Cine award, Venice Film Festival, 1964); contbr. articles to profl. jours. Lt.(j.g.) USN, 1945—47, PTO. Recipient Outstanding Educator of Am., 1970, award for svc. to people of Pakistan, City of Karachi, 1963, Medallion award for svc. to Greek People, Evangelismos Hosp., Athens, 1967, Golden Medal of Health, Republic of Vietnam, 1974, Outstanding Alumnus, Loma Linda U. Sch. of Med., 1974, Outstanding Contbn. to Medicine, San Bernardino County Med. Soc., 1986, Outstanding Achievement award in medicine, Ministry of Def. and Aviation, Saudi Arabia, 1986, Pres. Commendation, US, 1984, Alumnus of the Yr., Loma Linda U., 1994, Outstanding Contbn., Pasadena divsn., Am. Heart Assn., 1999. Fellow: Am. Coll. of Cardiology, Am. Coll. Surgeons; mem.: AMA, Western Assn. of Thoracic Surgery, Pacific Coast Surg. Assn., Am. Assn. for Thoracic Surgery, San Bernardino County Med. Soc., Calif. Med. Assn., Soc. of Thoracic Surgeons, Alpha Omega Alpha. Republican. Adventist. Achievements include development of heart surgery programs in Greece, Saudi Arabia, Hong Kong, developing countries. Mailing: Box 1068 Loma Linda CA 92354

WAREHAM, L. MARIE, elementary school educator; BS, Mary Manse, Toledo, Ohio, 1966. Tchr. Gesu Sch., Toledo, 1964—66, Raymer Sch., Toledo, 1966—67, Dunham Sch., Maple Heights, Ohio, 1967, Solon Montessori Sch. Inc., Solon, Bainbridge, Ohio, 1971—84, St. Barnabas Sch., Northfield, Ohio, 1984—. Presenter in field. Eucharistic min. St. Barnabas Ch., mem. shepherd's svc. com. Named Outstanding Tchr. of Yr., Diocese Cleve., 1993. Mem.: Nat. Cath. Educators Assn., Walton Hills Women's Club. Home and Office: 18690 Dellwood Dr Walton Hills OH 44146 Office Phone: 440-467-7921. Personal E-mail: lwareham@earthlink.net.

WAREHAM, RAYMOND NOBLE, investment advisor; b. Rochester, NY, Nov. 20, 1948; s. Simon Harold and Barbara (Snell) W.; m. Cornelia Lee Clifford, June 28, 1975; children: Ellinor Park, Laura Stewart, Cornelia Ashley. BS in Indsl. Engring., Northwestern U., 1970; MBA, Harvard U., 1975. With J.P. Morgan & Co., NY, 1975-80, mgr. dir., head banking industry group NY, 1988-92, head-corp. fin. Tokyo, 1980-85; exec. dir. J.P. Morgan Securities Ltd., London, 1986-87; mng. dir. corp. fin. dept. J.P. Morgan Securities, NYC, 1992-98; sr. portfolio mgr. Sanford C. Bernstein Alliance Capital, NYC, 1999—, sr. mng. dir., 1999—. Trustee Am. Sch., Tokyo, 1982-85; bd. dir. Brick Ch. Day Sch., 1989-92, Juvenile Diabetes Found., 1997-98, Stanley Isaacs Neighborhood Ctr., 2006—; pres. bd. trustees Spence Sch., NYC, 1995-2003, life trustee, 2002—; dir. 1148 Corp., 2006—; elder Brick Presbyn. Ch., NYC, 1989-92. Lt. Supply Corps, USN, 1970-73. Mem. DERU (Northwestern hon.), Naval War Coll. Found., Union Club (NY), Duxbury (Mass.) Yacht Club, Century Club (Harvard Bus. hon.), Eagle Scout. Republican. Avocations: sports, antique furniture. Home: 1148 5th Ave New York NY 10128-0807 Office: Alliance Capital/Sanford C Bernstein 17th Fl 1345 Ave of Americas New York NY 10105-0096

WAREN, STANLEY ARNOLD, academic administrator, performing company executive; b. NYC, Mar. 22, 1919; s. Maurice and Minnie (Rosen) W.; m. Florence Rigal, Nov. 21, 1949; 1 child, Mark BSS., CCNY, 1938; MA, Columbia U., 1939, PhD, 1953. Exec. producer, dir. theatre, 1953-70; prof., chmn. dept. speech and theatre CCNY, 1967-72; prof., exec. officer Ph.D. program theatre CUNY, 1972-81, v.p., provost, dep. pres. Grad. Sch., 1981-84; dir. Ctr. for Advanced Study in Theatre Arts, NYC, 1979-82, 84-86. Reviewer NEH, 1978—91; advisor humanities com. Bklyn. Acad. Music, NYC, 1980—81; spl. edn. cons. Dougle Image Theatre, NYC, 1982—90; mem. adv. coun. Roundabout Theatre, NYC, 1985—93; Fulbright-Hayes vis. prof. Nat. Taiwan U., 1986—87; vis. prof. Shanghai Drama Inst., 1988; USIS grant, lectr., Hong Kong, 88, Ctr. for Living and Learning, Marymount Manhattan, 1998—2007, New Sch. U., 2000—03. Dir. musical The Chess King (Taiwan) 1987, Old B Hanging on the Wall (Shanghai), 1988, Judas, Mexico (NY), 1989, Seasoned Citizens Theatre Co., 2003-09. Bd. dirs. Women's Inter. Art Ctr., NYC, 1978-82; mem. grants panel NYC Dept. Cultural Affairs, 1979; bd. dirs. Frank Silvera Workshops for Writers, NYC, 1979-81. Served to capt. USAF, 1942-46 Grantee Herman Goldman Found., 1980-82, NEH, 1980-81, NY Coun. Humanities, USIA/Arts Am., Singapore, 1990. Mem. AAUP, Assn. Theatre in Higher Edn., Soc. Stage Dirs. and Choreographers, Actors Equity Assn., Profl. Staff Congress CUNY, The Drama League (mem. awards nominating com. 1997—). Clubs: The Century Assn. (resident 1984—, spkr. Humanities Coun. NY, 2009-). Democrat. Avocations: art, tennis, swimming. Home: 465 W End Ave #11D New York NY 10024-4926 Office: CUNY Theatre PhD Program Grad Sch 365 5th Ave New York NY 10016-4309

WARENSKJOLD, DOROTHY, singer, educator; d. William Earl and Mildred Lorrayne (Stombs) Warenskjold. BA, Mills Coll., 1943. Soprano San Francisco Opera Co., 1949—58, Columbia Artists Mgmt., NYC, 1950—72; adj. prof. UCLA, Westwood, 1984—97, 1999; master class instr. numerous orgns., 1999—. Master class instr. concert stage presentations. Singer numerous recs. Named Woman of Yr., Opera Guild, 1988. Mem.: Dorothy Warenskjold, UCLA Oval History, Nat. Assn. Tchrs. of Singing (adv. bd. 2004—). Achievements include 1st American singer asked to appear at the Rebild Festival in Denmark. Home: 7716 Oakview Ln Lenexa KS 66216 Personal E-mail: dwkc1@yahoo.com.

WAREY, ALOK, diesel engineer; BE in Mech. Engring., Nat. Inst. Tech., Trichy, Tiruchirappalli, India, 2000; MS in Mech. Engring., U. Tex., Austin, 2003, PhD in Mech. Engring., 2005. Sr. engr. emissions devel. Cummins, Inc., Columbus, Ind., 2005—06; project engr., diesel combustion FEV, Inc., Auburn Hills, Mich., 2006—. Mem.: Soc. Automotive Engr., Sigma Xi. Achievements include development of a new electronic sensor for on-board measurement of carbonaceous particulate matter emissions from diesel engines; research in cylinder wall wetting as a source of increased particulate matter emissions from direct-injection spark-ignition engines.

WARFEL, M(ARTHA) KAY, speech pathology/audiology services professional; b. Lancaster, Pa., Mar. 2, 1955; d. Orlene Dickenhart and Martha (Herr) W.; m. George Jay Malley, Jr., Sept. 21, 1978 (div. 1979); m. C. Robert Paul III, Aug. 15, 1987 (div. Mar. 2000); 1 child, Thomas Matthew Warfel Paul. BS in Speech Pathology/Audiology, Pa. State U., Univ. Pk., 1976; MEd in Speech Pathology, U. Oregon, Eugene, 1979; MBA in Mktg., Iona Coll., New Rochelle, NY, 1986; PhD in Health Adminstrn., Kennedy-Western U., Thousand Oaks, Calif., 2004. Cert. clinician. Speech lang. pathologist Lancaster-Lebanon #13, East Petersburg, Pa., 1970—78, Douglas ESD, Roseburg, Oreg., 1979—80, Bethel Sch. Dist. #52, Eugene, 1980—81, NY Bd. Edn., Bronx, 1981—93, Sch. Dist. Lancaster, Pa., 2003—04, Avon Grove Sch. Dist., West Grove, 2004—06; speech pathologist Hickory House Nursing Home, Honey Brook, Pa., 2006, Oxford Area Sch. Dist., Pa., 2006—. Speech pathologist Eugene Speech and Hearing Ctr., 1980; speech cons. Margaret Chapman Sch., Hawthorne, NY, 1988-89; instr. sensory impairments Manhattan Coll., Riverdale, NY, 1987-88; adj. instr. lang. disorders of children Coll. New Rochelle, NY, 1988-89; with press The Athletics Congress, Indpls., 1981-88; press officer 1988 USA Men's and Women's Olympic Track and Field Teams, 1988; bd. dirs. Pa. State U. Com. Scis. and Disorders, 2005—; liason to Pa. State. Am. Speech and Hearing Assn., 2006—. Contbr. dissertation. Vol. Rep. Nat. Com., Lancaster, 1972, Spl. Olympics, 1976-83, Lane County Prisons, Eugene, 1979; bd. dirs. Meml. Meth. Early Childhood Ctr., advt. chairperson, 1994—96. Mem. Am. Speech-Lang.-Hearing Assn., Am. Mktg. Assn., Coun. Exceptional Children, NY Speech-Lang.-Hearing Assn., Pa. Speech Hearing Assn. Republican. United Methodist. Avocations: gardening, jogging, reading, raising poultry, cross stitch. Personal E-mail: kaypsu76@kennett.net.

WARFEL, MICHAEL WILLIAM, bishop; b. Elkhart, Ind., Sept. 16, 1948; s. Robert and Josephine (Rumshas) Warfel. Attended, Ind. U.; BA in Philosophy, St. Gregory's Coll. Sem., Cin.; MDiv, Mount St. Mary's Sem. West, 1980; MA in Theology, St. Michael's Coll., Winnoski, Vt., 1990. Ordained priest Archdiocese of Anchorage, 1980; ordained bishop, 1996; bishop Diocese of Juneau, Alaska, 1996—2007; apostolic adminstr. Diocese of Fairbanks, Alaska, 2001—02; bishop Diocese of Great Falls-Billings, Mont., 2007—. With US Army, 1967—71. Mem.: US Conf. Cath. Bishops. Roman Catholic. Avocation: languages. Office: Diocese of Great Falls-Billings Chancery Office 121 23rd St S PO Box 1399 Great Falls MT 59403 Office Phone: 406-727-6683. Office Fax: 406-454-3480.

WARFIELD, GERALD ALEXANDER, composer, writer; b. Ft. Worth, Feb. 23, 1940; s. George Alexander and Geraldine (Spencer) Warfield. Student, Tex. Christian U., 1958-61; BA, N. Tex. State U., 1963, MMus, 1965; postgrad., Tanglewood, 1963—64; MFA, Princeton U., 1967. Instr. Princeton U., 1968-71; assoc. dir. Index New Mus. Notation, NYC, 1971-75. Lectr. contemporary music notation; mem. conf. com. Internat. Conf. New Mus. Notation, Belgium, 1974; chmn. program com. 2d Nat. Conf. Music Theory, 1977. Author: A Beginner's Manual of Music 4B, 1967, Layer Analysis: A Primer of Elementary Tonal Structures, 1976, Writings on Contemporary Music Notations, 1977, How to Write Music Manuscript, 1977, The Investor's Guide to Stock Quotations, 1982, How to Buy Foreign Stocks and Bonds, 1984, How to Read Financial News, 1986, No Nonsense Guides to the Stock Market, Mutual Funds, Tax-Free Bonds, 1999, Managing Your Stock Portfolio, Money Market Funds, 1993; co-author: Grove's Dictionary of Music and Musicians, 1976; author (with others): Layers Dictation, 1978, Export-Import Financing, 1986, Feng Shui Revealed, 1997; editor: Longman Music Series, 1976—85; contbr. articles to profl. jours.; composer: Variations and Metamorphoses, 1973 (1st prize Ariz. Cellos Soc.), Fantasy Quintet, 1978 (2d prize New Music Young Ensembles). Adv. bd. Boyce Ditto Pub. Libr., 2005—08, chmn. adv. bd., 2008—. Mem.: Mineral Wells Heritage Assn. (pres. 2009—), Broadcast Music Inc., Coll. Music Soc. (coun., conf. chmn. 1981), Am. Composers Alliance (treas. 1979—96), Soc. Composers, Inc. (chmn. exec. com. 1972—74, conf. chmn. 9th Ann. Conf. 1974, gen. mgr. 1977—2000, 2002—, founding editor Jour. Music Scores). Home: 410 SW 4th Ave # 4 Mineral Wells TX 76067-5840 Personal E-mail: geraldwarfield@suddenlink.net.

WARFORD, MARK KELLISON, language educator, consultant; s. Malcolm Lyle and Pamela Neal Warford; m. Cara Regan Regan, July 29, 2006. BA in English, Kenyon Coll., Gambier, OH, 1989; MA in Tchg., Brown U., Providence, 1990; PhD, U. Tenn., Knoxville, 2000. Cert. Spanish and English tchr. Ohio, 1991, RI, 1990. Primary sch. tchr. Colegio Intern. George Wash., Oviedo, Asturias, Spain, 1990—91; Spanish-lang. arts tchr. Mt. Vernon Mid. Sch., Ohio, 1991—92; upper sch. Spanish tchr. Webb Sch. Knoxville, 1992—95; adj. Spanish Pellissippi State Tech. CC, Knoxville, 1996—97; grad. tchg. asst. U. Tenn., 1997—2000; assoc. prof., for. lang. ed. & Spanish Buffalo State Coll.,SUNY. Speaker in fields Various sch. and cmty. organizations. Contbr. to numerous profl. jours.;, editor foreign language annals; dir.: (coordinating an irish music events). Co-director of the buffalo region NY State Assn. of Fgn. Lang. Teachers, NY. Recipient Anthony Papalia Professional Article award, NY State Assn. Language Tchrs., 2003; fellow Invited Facilitator,Honorarium, Nat. K-12 Fgn. Lang. Resource Ctr., 2003. Mem.: Am. Assn. Tchrs. Spanish and Portuguese, Am. Assn. Applied Linguistics, Phi Kappa Sigma (rush chair v.p. 1987—88). Independent. Office: Buffalo State Coll SUNY 1300 Elmwood Ave Webster NY 14580 Office Fax: 716-878-6730. Business E-Mail: warformk@buffalostate.edu.

WARFORD, PATRICIA, psychologist; d. Eldon J. Jameson and Rosa Kirschenman; m. Gary W. Warford, Sept. 5, 1955; children: Candice C. Zaniewski, Nathanael A. BS, S.D. State U., 1991; MS, George Fox Coll., 1993, D of Psychology, 1996. Lic. psychologist Oreg. Bd. Psychologist Examiners, 1998. Psychologist Western Psychol. & Counseling, Beaverton, Oreg., 1994—98, Yamhill County Adult Mental Health, McMinnville, 1998—2000, pvt. practice, Newberg, 2001—. Faculty State Victims Assistance Acad., Salem, Oreg., 2004—; presenter Boston Coll., Boston, 2002, George Fox U., Newberg, 2004, adj. faculty, 2006—. Co-author: (training manual chapter) Trauma Bonding. Oregon State Victims Assistance Academy Training Manual Number 2002-VF-GX-KO23 awarded by the Office for Victims of Crime, Office of Justice Programs, U.S. Department of Justic, 2004. Appointee Oreg. Gov.'s Coun. Domestic Violence, Salem, 2004. Mem.: APA, Tri-County Batterers Intervention Providers, Yamhill County Domestic Violence Task Force. Office: 901 Brutscher St Ste D Box 116 Newberg OR 97132 Office Fax: 877-892-6114.

WARGA, JACK, mathematician, educator; b. Warsaw, Dec. 5, 1922; came to U.S., 1943, naturalized, 1944; s. Herman and Czarna (Lichtenstein) W.; m. Faye Kleinman, Feb. 27, 1949; children: Charna Ruth Schakow, Arthur David. Student, Brussels U., 1939-40; BA, Carleton Coll., 1944; PhD, NYU, 1950. Assoc. mathematician Reeves Instrument Corp., NYC, 1951-52; Chief engring. computing sect. Republic Aviation Corp., Farmingdale, NY, 1952-53; head math dept. Burroughs Corp., Pasadena, Calif., 1954-56; mgr., math dept. Avco Research and Devel., Wilmington, Mass., 1957-66; prof. math. Northeastern U., Boston, 1966-93, prof. emeritus, 1993—. Author: Optimal Control of Differential and Functional Equations, 1972, expanded Russian transl., 1977; contbr. articles to profl. jours. Served with AUS, 1944-46. Weizmann Meml. fellow, 1956-57 Fellow AAAS; mem. Am. Math. Soc., Soc. Indsl. and Applied Math. (editor Jour. on Control and Optimization 1963-89). Home: 7356 Falls Rd W Boynton Beach FL 33437-6316 E-mail: warga@neu.edu.

WARIAN, CHRISTINE BARBARA, elementary school educator; b. Somerville, NJ, May 7, 1967; d. Terence and Loretta Warian. MusB in Music Edn. and Therapy, Immaculata Coll., 1989; MA in Reading Specialization, Kean U., 2003. Cert. reading specialist, elem. tchr. NJ. Tchr. Christ the King Sch., Manville, NJ, 1997—2000, Our Lady of Peace Sch., Fords, NJ, 2000—01; substitute tchr. Edison and Woodbridge Sch. Dists., 2001—04; reading specialist James Madison Intermediate Sch., Edison, 2004—05; tchr. Huntington Learning Ctr., Edison, NJ, 2005—06; substitute Woodbridge Sch. Dist., 2005—06; reading specialist Franklin Elem. Sch., South Plainfield, 2006—; adj. prof. Caldwell Coll., 2009. Mem.: NJ Reading Assoc., Kappa Delta Pi. Avocations: singing, exercise, reading. E-mail: readteacher228@optimum.net.

WARICHA, JOAN, publishing executive; BA, Boston U., 1967; MBA, Columbia U., 1980. V.p., editor-in-chief, assoc. pub. Scholastic, Inc., 1968-83; pres. Parachute Press, 1983-96; chmn., CEO Parachute Properties, 1996—; pres. Parachute Pub., 1996—, Parachute Entertainment, 1996—, Parachute Consumer Products, 1996—. Office: Parachute Properties 322 Eighth Ave Ste 500 New York NY 10001 Office Phone: 212-691-1421. Business E-Mail: jwaricha@parachuteproperties.com.

WARINER, JEREMY, Olympic track and field athlete; b. Irving, Tex., Jan. 31, 1984; Student, Baylor Univ. Mem. US Olympic Track & Field Team, Athens, Greece, 2004, Beijing, 2008; profl. runner, 2005—. Recipient Gold medal, 400m, 4x400m relay, Athens Olympic Games, 2004, Silver medal, 400m, Gold medal, 4x400m relay, Beijing Olympic Games, 2008, Gold medal, 400m, 4x400m relay, World Championships, 2005, 2007, ESPY award, Best Male Track Athlete, ESPN, 2007; named Mondo Outdoor Track Athlete of Yr., USA Track Coaches Assoc., 2004. Achievements include being NCAA Champion, Indoor 400m, 4x400m relay, Outdoor 400m, 4x400m relay, 2004. Office: c/o USOC 1 Olympic Plaza Colorado Springs CO 80909

WARING, GEORGE ORAL, III, ophthalmologist, surgeon; b. Buffalo, Feb. 21, 1941; s. George Oral Waring and Mary Jane Fitzpatrick-Waring; children from previous marriage: George Oral IV, John Timothy, Joy Waring-Harty, Matthew. BS cum laude, Wheaton Coll., Ill., 1963; MD, Baylor Med. Coll., Houston, 1967. Diplomate Am. Bd. Ophthalmology (assoc. examiner, 1980, 89). Rotating intern Ben Taub Gen. Hosp., Houston, 1967—68; resident Wills Eye Hosp. and Rsch. Inst., Phila., 1970—73, Heed fellow in corneal and external disease, 1973—74; staff physician Hosp. Ship Hope, Natal, Brazil, 1973; asst. prof. U. Calif., Davis, 1974—79, assoc. prof., 1979; surg. dir. Sacramento Valley Eye Bank, 1976—79; staff physician Emory Clinic, Inc., Atlanta, 1979—82, clinic ptnr., 1982—2002, with, 2002—04; mng. dir. Emory Vision Correction Ctr., 1994—2001; founding surgeon InView Vision (formerly Emory Vision), 2001—; pvt. practice Atlanta, 2004—. Affiliate scientist Yerkes Regional Primate Rsch. Ctr. Emory U. Sch. Medicine, Atlanta, 1982—92, assoc. prof., 1979—83, prof., dir. refractive surgery, 1983—2004, clin. prof., 2006—; rsch. assoc. French Ministry Rsch. & Tech., 1992; Fogarty sr. internat. fellow US NIH, 1992; vis. prof. Ain Shams U., Cairo, 1992—93; chmn. dept. ophthalmology, dir. rsch. dept. El-Magrabi Eye Hosp. and Med. Ctr., Jeddah, Saudi Arabia, 1992—95; cons. Summit Tech., 1990—95, Chiron Corp., 1993—2000, Nidek, Inc., 2001—, Bausch and Lomb, 2001—05, Advanced Med. Optics, 2005—, Schwind Corp., 2006—08; mem. sci. adv. bd. Calhoun Vision, 2002—; mem. sci. adv. bd., clin. investigator AcuFocus, 2005—; lectr. in field. Author 2 textbooks; mem. editl. bd.: Am. Jour. Ophthalmology, 1981—87, mem. consultative bd.:, 1987—97; mem. editl. bd. Jour. Refractive Surgery, 1985—87; assoc. editor: Jour. Refractive Surgery, 1987—88, editor-in-chief:, 1989—, mem. editl. bd.: numerous jours.; contbr. more than 50 chpts. to books, more than 500 articles to profl. jours. Lt. USPHS, 1968—70. Recipient Hon. medal, Ain Shams U., Ceiro, 1989, Barraquer prize, Internat. Soc. Refractive Keratoplasty, 1992, Gold medal, Pan Arab Coun. Ophthalmology, 1993, 1997, Gregg medal, Royal Assn. Coll. Ophthalmology, 1996, Buasch and Lomb Visionary award, 2004, Kritzinger medal, South Africa Cataract Refraction Surgery; co-recipient Emmy award, NATAS, 1977; grantee, NIH, 1978—81, 1980—, 1980—91, others, U. Calif., Davis, 1973—76, 1982—83, 1987—88, others, various industries; Pew Found. scholar, 1971—72, Training grantee, NIH, 1971. Fellow: ACS (mem. com. applicants 1991), Eye Bank Assn. Am. (mem. constitution and by-laws com. 1984—86, mem. program com. 1985, mem. adv. bd.), Royal Coll. Ophthalmologists, Am. Acad. Ophthalmology (mem. interprofessional edn. com. 1978—81, mem. instrn. adv. com. 1978—81, cons. 1983—, Honor, Sr. Honor and Life Achievement awards 2004), Explorer's Club; mem.: AMA (mem. ophthalmology program com. 1975—79, Physician's Recognition award 1989—95), Wills Eye Hosp. Ex-Resident's Soc., Soc. Heed Fellows (mem. Heed award nomination com. 1983—84, 2000—04, chmn. 2004, Outstanding Ophthalmologist

1978), Saudi Ophthal. Soc., Paton Corneal Transplant Soc., Internat. Soc. Refractive Surgery of Am. Acad. Ophthalmology (trustee 1981—89, editor Jour. Refractive Surgery 1989—, Lans award 1986, Berraguer award 1992, Lifetime Achievement award in Refractive Surgery 1997, Kvitzinger award 2003), Egyptian Soc. Ocular Implants and Refractive Surgery (hon.), Internat. Ophthalmic Microsurgery Study Group, Ga. Soc. Ophthalmology (mem. pub. edn. com. 1981—84, mem. govtl. com. 1988—89, mem. laser com. 1991—92), Dekalb Med. Soc., Coun. Refractive Surgery Quality Assurance, Castroviejo Cornea Soc. (mem. exec. com. 1981—85, program chmn. 1983—85, Castroviejo medal 2004), Assn. Rsch. Vision and Ophtalmology (mem. cornea sect. com. 1985—88, chmn. cornea sect. com. 1987—88, Weisenfeld award 2008), Am. Ophthal. Soc., Commd. Officers Assn. USPHS, Am. Eye Study Club (emeritus mem. 1988—). Avocations: art, kayaking, mountain climbing, scuba diving, sailing. Home: 36 Willow Glen Atlanta GA 30342 Office: INView 301 Perimeter Ctr N Ste 600 Atlanta GA 30346 Office Phone: 678-222-5102. Office Fax: 404-250-9006.

WARING, RICHARD HARVEY, retired research scientist; b. Chgo., May 17, 1935; s. Harvey Dwight and Mignon Hirsch Waring; m. Doris C. Carlson, June 16, 1957; children: Lance Eric, Lise Ellen. PhD, U. Calif., Berkeley, 1963. Prof. Oreg. State U., Corvallis, 1963—2000; guest prof. U. Innsbruck, Austria, 1969—70, U. Edinburgh, Scotland, 1976—77, Swedish U. Agr., Uppsala, 1982—83; vis. prof. Marine Biol. Lab., Woods Hole, Mass., 1986—87, U. Waikato, Hamilton, New Zealand, 1991—92; vis. sr. scientist NASA, Washington, 1992—93; vis. scientist CSIRO, Canberra, Australia, 1996—97, U. Western Australia, Perth, 2008—09. Office: Coll Forestry Oregon State Univ 30th & Jefferson Corvallis OR 97331

WARITZ, RICHARD STEFAN, toxicologist, researcher; b. Portland, Oreg., Apr. 1, 1929; s. Anton John and Theresa (Stegelmaier) W.; m. Ruth Evelyn White, June 7, 1950; children: Joyce E., Gary S., Sharon J., Carol L. BA, Reed Coll., 1951; PhD, Stanford U., 1957. Diplomate Am. Bd. Toxicology, Acad. Toxicological Scis. Sr. rsch. scientist E.I. DuPont de Nemours & Co., Wilmington, Del., 1957-64, mgr. inhalation toxicology, 1964-72, mgr. bio-scis., 1972-75; sr. toxicologist Hercules Inc., Wilmington, 1975-80, mgr. toxicology, 1980-92; pres. BioSante Internat., Inc., 1992—2005. Grad. toxicology edn. adv. bd. Rutgers U., Piscataway, N.J., 1980-2005, vis. prof. toxicology, 1993-2005; life scis. adv. bd. U.S. Army, Aberdeen, Md., 1982-92; toxicology peer rev. bd. U.S. Army Ctr. for Health Promotion and Preventive Medicine, 1992—2008. Contbr. articles to profl. jours. Mem.: Am. Chem. Soc., Am. Conf. Govtl. Indsl. Hygienists, Am. Indsl. Hygiene Assn., Internat. Union Toxicol. Socs. (councillor 1983—88), Soc. Toxicology (treas. 1981-85, pres. Mid-Atlantic chpt. 1989). Roman Catholic. Avocations: golf, fishing, bowling. Home: 2613 Turnstone Dr Wilmington DE 19808-1638 Personal E-mail: waritztox@verizon.net.

WARKENTIEN, MARK, professional sports team executive; m. Maureen Warkentien; children: Kreigh, Aubrie. Grad., Calif. State U., Fullerton, 1976. Coach Riverside City Coll., Saddleback Coll., U. Calif., Irvine, coach women's prog. Riverside; asst. coach Calif. State. U., Fullerton; asst. coach/recruiting coord., asst. athletic dir. UNLV, 1980—91; scout Seattle SuperSonics, 1991—94, Portland Trail Blazers, 1994—95, dir. scouting, 1995—98, asst. gen. mgr., 1998—2003, dir. player pers., 2003—04, Cleve. Cavaliers, 2004—05, interim gen. mgr., 2004—05; dir. player pers. Denver Nuggets, 2005—06, v.p. basketball ops., 2006—. Named NBA Exec. of Yr., 2009. Office: Denver Nuggets 1000 Chopper Cir Denver CO 80204*

WARMA, MAHAMADI JACOB, mathematics professor; s. Salam Warma and Limata Nonka; m. Koumba Maimouna Sankara, Jan. 10, 2008; 1 child, Sherry Rania. PhD, U. Ulm, Germany, 2003. Asst. prof. U. Eichstaett, Germany, 2003—05; vis. prof. U. Puerto Rico, San Juan, 2003, asst. & assoc. prof., 2005—. Fellow, DAAD, 1998.

WARMAN, GUY LEE, lawyer; b. Lambert, Pa., July 11, 1929; s. Guy B. and Ida Grace (Lee) W.; m. Katherine V. Baldridge, Nov. 6, 1954; children: Katherine L., Cynthia V. BA, Pa. State U., 1953; JD, U. Pitts., 1956. Bar: Pa. 1957, U.S. Dist. Ct. (we. dist.) Pa. 1957, U.S. Ct. Appeals (3d cir.) 1976, U.S. Supreme Ct. 1971. Assoc. Metz, Cook, Hanna & Kelly, Pitts., 1957-63, ptnr. 1963-78; mem. Guy L. Warman and Assocs., P.C., Pitts., 1978-82; ptnr. Warman, Crone and Studeny, Pitts., 1982-98; spl. counsel Reed Smith LLP, 1998—2006; pres. Guy L. Warman PC, 2006-. Republican county committeeman, 1970-80. Served with USAAF, 1946-49; 1st lt. USAFR 1953-56. Recipient Robert L. Vann award U. Pitts. Sch. Law, 1956. Mem. ABA, Pa. Bar Assn., Allegheny County Bar Assn. (chmn. membership com. 1968-69, chmn. ct. rules com. 1969-78, chmn. judiciary com. 1985). Republican. Presbyterian. Clubs: Longue Vue (Verona, Pa., pres. 1995-97), Duquesne Club (Pitts.), Masons, Shriners. Editor: The Allegheny County Common Pleas Court Manual, 1969-78. Contbr. articles to U. Pitts. Law Rev. Home and Office: 720 Shady Ave Pittsburgh PA 15232-2911 Office Phone: 412-956-0308. E-mail: gwarman@glwpc.com.

WARMAN, LINDA K., retired secondary school educator; b. Indiana, Pa., Mar. 25, 1942; d. James Edward and Elizabeth Josephine (Hawk) Warman. BA, Moravian Coll., Bethlehem, Pa., 1964. Tchr. Easton Area Sch. Dist., Pa., 1964—2001, chair dept. English, 1986—2001; ret., 2001. Contbr.: book Religious Literature of the West, 1970, mem.: Bach Choir of Bethlehem, 1963—78. Named Outstanding Instr. U. Honors Students, Pa. State U., 1985. Avocations: travel, reading, home decorating, gardening.

WARMAN, LYNNETTE R., lawyer; b. Willmar, Minn., Oct. 1, 1955; BA, U. Nebr., 1983; JD, Creighton U., 1986. Bar: Nebr. 1986, Tex. 1987, US Ct. Appeals 5th Cir., US Dist. Ct. No., Ea., We. & So. Districts Tex. Shareholder Jenkens & Gilchrist, P.C., Dallas, head bus. dept.; ptnr. Hunton & Williams LLP, 2007—. Mem.: ABA, Tex. Bar Assn., Dallas Bar Assn. (bankruptcy sect.), John C. Ford. Am. Inn of Ct., Am. Bankruptcy Inst. (bd. dirs.). Office: Hunton & Wiliams LLP Energy Plz 30th Fl 1601 Bryan St Dallas TX 75201-3402 Office Phone: 214-855-4792. Office Fax: 214-855-4300. Business E-Mail: lwarman@jenkens.com.

WARNASOORIYA, NILANTHI, research scientist; PhD, U. South Fla., Tampa. Lab. instr. U. Colombo, Sri Lanka, 2000—01; tchg. fellow Creighton U., Omaha, 2001—03; rsch. & tchg. asst. U. South Fla., 2003—08; postdoc. rschr. ESPCI, Paris, 2008—. Mem.: OSA Student Chpt., Optical Soc. America, Sigma Pi Sigma. Achievements include research in heterodyne holography applied to the photothermal detect quantitative phase imaging using three-wavelength optical phase unwrapping.

WARNATH, MAXINE AMMER, psychologist, arbitrator; b. NYC, Dec. 3, 1928; d. Philip and Jeanette Ammer; m. Charles Frederick Warnath, Aug. 20, 1952; children: Stephen Charles, Cindy Ruth. BA, Bklyn. Coll., 1949; MA, Columbia U., 1951, EdD, 1982. Lic. psychologist Oreg. Various profl. positions Hunter Coll., U. Minn., U. Nebr., U. Oreg., 1951-62; asst. prof. psychology Oreg. Coll. Edn., Monmouth, 1962-77; assoc. prof. psychology, chmn. dept. psychology & spl. edn. Western Oreg. U., Monmouth, 1978-83, prof., 1983—96, prof. emeritus, 1996—. Dir. organizational psychology program, 1983—96; pres. Profl. Perspective Internat., Salem, Oreg., 1987—; cons., dir. Orgn. R&D, Salem, Oreg., 1983—87; seminar leader Endeavors for Excellence program. Author: Power Dynamism, 1987. Mem.: APA (com. pre-coll. psychology 1970—74), Western Psychol. Assn., Oreg. Psychol. Assn. (pres. 1980—81, pres.-elect 1979—80, legis. liaison 1977—78), Oreg. Acad. Sci., N.Y. Acad. Scis., Am. Psychol. Soc. Home and Office: 658 Village Dr Pompano Beach FL 33060-7767 Office Phone: 954-786-3108, 954-707-0199. Business E-Mail: warnathm@wou.edu.

WARNE, ALAN M., continuing education educator, consultant; b. Pierre, SD, Aug. 24, 1945; s. Maynard L. and Ione P. Warne; m. Joan Caulfield, Sept. 7, 1996; children: Alan, Jr. M., Andrea W. White, Amy N. BA in Polit. Sci., Ariz. State U., 1963—67; MA in Ednl. Psychology, Ea. Ky. U., 1969—70; EdD in Continuing Edn., Temple U., 1972—78. Fgn. student advisor Ariz. State U., Tempe, 1966—68; dir. internat. student services U. of Ky., Lexington, 1968—71; dir. office internat. services Temple U., Phila., 1971—77; exec. dir. Phila. Coun. Internat. Visitors, 1977—81, Nat. Coun. Internat. Visitors, Washington, 1981—85; chief exec. officer/vice pres. for programs People to People Internat., Kans. City, Mo., 1986—99; pres. & ceo Entrepreneurial Edn. Found., Kans. City, 2000—01; sr. program mgr. Med. Ctr. U. Kans., Kans. City, 2002—07; v.p. ops. Silver Fox Assoc., Kans. City, 2007—. Mng. dir. The Brain Inc., Kans. City, Mo., 2000—; planning cons. Kauffman Ctr. for Entrepreneurial Leadership, Kans. City, Mo., 2000; academic program cons. Rockhurst U., Kans. City, Mo., 2000; mem. continuing med. edn. adv. com. U. Kans., 2002—, mem. continuing med. ctr. statewide adv. bd. and governing com., 2002—; peer grant reviewer U.S. Dept. Edn., 2005—. Contbr. curriculum guide Expo 92 (Kans. City-Seville), nat. profl. newsletter Mgmt./Program Planning Articles, admissions guide - internat. student A Model for the Edn. of Fgn. Students. Bd. mem./arts com. Mayor's UN Day Com., Kans. Citry, Mo., 1990—96; site planning com. Kans. City Sch. Dist., Kans. City, Mo., 1990—91; bd. mem./vice chair Nat. Coun. for Internat. Visitors, Washington, 1978—81; founding bd. mem. Consortium for Internat. Citizen Exch., Washington, 1981—85, Caruthers' Arts Alliance, Kans. City, Mo.; scholarship committees rep. U. of Mo., Kans. City, Mo., 1986—2005; pres./vice pres. Pk. U. Bd. of Visitors, Parkville, Mo., 1995—2001. Recipient Del. Leader - Baltic Nations, Ambassadors, Inc., 1999, Thematic Specialist -Citizen Initiatives (6-US Cities), Inst. of Internat. Edn., 1981; grantee Ednl. Travel Grant, Republic of China Ministry of Edn., 1975. Fellow: Rotary Club Internat. (ednl./scholarship/planning committees 1999—2006); mem.: Soc. Govt. Meeting Profls., Assn. of Internat. Educators (regional chair, coord. of nat. job registry, exec. com. 1967—2000), Kans. City Club (membership com. 1993—2006). Avocations: volunteerism, travel, cinema, theater, organizational development. Home: 431 West 70th St Kansas City MO 64113 Office: U Kans Med Ctr 3901 Rainbow Blvd Kansas City KS 66160-7108 Home Phone: 816-361-6192. Personal E-mail: kcawarne@aol.com.

WARNE, WILLIAM ROBERT, economist; b. Washington, Nov. 30, 1937; BA, Princeton U., N.J., 1960; MA, Johns Hopkins U., Balt., 1974. Provincial advisor U.S. Mission, Vinh Binh, Vinh Long, Vietnam, 1962-64; officer in charge trade, devel. and fin. policy U.S. Mission to European Communities, Brussels, 1974-77; dep. dir. E. Asian Econ. Policy, 1977-79; dir. Caribbean affairs U.S. Dept. State, Kingston, Jamaica, 1979-81, charge d'affaires, dep. chief mission, 1981-84, dir. Latin Am. Econ. Policy Washington, 1984-86; counselor for trade, energy, social affairs and agr. U.S. Delegation OECD, Paris, 1986-88; v.p. Midwest Ctr. Exec. Coun. Fgn. Diplomats, Indpls., 1988-89; pres. Korea Econ. Inst. Am., Washington, 1990-99; instr. Fgn. Svc. Inst., U.S. Dept. State, Washington, 2000—; prof. internat. studies Ewha Woman's U., Seoul, Republic of Korea, 2000—01; instr. Fgn. Svc. Inst. U.S. Dept. State, Washington, 2001—03. Prof. internat. studies Korea U., Seoul, Republic of Korea, 2003; instr. fgn. svc. Inst. U.S. Dept. State, Washington, 2004—. With US Army, 1960—62.

WARNECKE, HANS-JÜRGEN, retired engineering educator; b. Braunschweig, Germany, Apr. 2, 1934; s. Hans and Ella (Grobe) W. Diploma engring., Tech. U. Braunschweig, 1959, DEng, 1963; D (hon.), U. Ljubljana, Yugoslavia, 1989; DEng (hon.), Tech. U. Magdeburg, Germany, 1989; D (hon.), Tech. U. Timisoara, Romania, 1995, U. Žilina, Slovakia, 1998, U. Craiova, Romania, 2002. Rschr. Inst. Machine Tools, Braunschweig, 1959-65; dir. Rollei-Werke, Braunschweig, 1965-70; prof. U. Stuttgart, Germany, 1970-93; mng. dir. Fraunhofer Inst. IPA, Stuttgart, 1971-93; pres. Fraunhofer-Gesellschaft, Munich, 1993—2002, prof. emeritus, 2002—; hon. prof. Tongii U. Shanghai, 2001, Baotou U., 2002. KSB-Stiftung, Frankenthal, Anton-Klara Roser Stiftung, Stuttgart. Author: Der Produktionsbetrieb, Fertigunstechnik, 1985, The Fractal Co., 1993. Decorated officer's cross Order of Merit (Germany), Officer's Cross Order of Merit State Lower Saxony, and State Baden-Württenberg and State Bavaria Commdr.'s Cross of Merit (Germany); recipient Ring of Honor of Eduard-Rhein-Found Mem.: NAE, Assn. Dutch Engrs., Acad. Scis. Croatia, Internat. Assn. for Prodn. Rsch., Regional Soc. Engrs., Assn. German Engrs. (pres. 1995—97), Senate of Fraunhofer Assn. (hon.). Avocations: sailing, crafting. Office: Fraunhofer-Inst Manu & Automation Nobel St 12 D-70569 Stuttgart Germany Office Phone: +49-711-970-1201. Business E-Mail: warnecke@ipa.fraunhofer.de.

WARNEKE, JOEL, physics professor, mining engineer; s. Rick Warneke and Nancy Gaynor; m. Sarah Warneke, June 28, 2002. PhD in Mining Engring., U. Mo.-Rolla, 2004. Mining engr. Nat. Inst. Occupl. Safety & Health, Spokane, Wash., 2004—07; physics instr. Flathead Valley CC, Kalispell, Mont., 2007—. Owner GW & Assocs., Whitefish, Mont., 2007—. Fellow, NSF, 2002—04. Office: Flathead Valley CC 777 Grandview Dr Kalispell MT 59901

WARNER, BARRY GREGORY, ecologist, educator; b. Cambridge, Ont., July 20, 1955; s. Gregory O. and Alma (Jansen) W. B in Environ. Studies, U. Waterloo, 1978, MS, 1980; PhD, Simon Fraser U., Burnaby, Can., 1984. Rsch. asst. prof. U. Waterloo, Ont., 1985-89, rsch. assoc. prof., 1989-91, assoc. prof. geography, 1991-96, dir. Wetlands Rsch. Inst., 1991—2002, prof. biology and earth sci., 1996—, chair dept. earth and environ. scis., 2007—. Vis. prof. U. Neuchatel, 1993, U. Franche-Comte, Bescon, France, 2002; chair Can. Nat. Wetlands Working Group, 1993—; bd. dirs. Internat. Mire Conservation Group. Editor: Methods in Quaternary Ecology, 1990; co-editor: Wetlands: Envigradients, Boundaries and Buffers, 1996; contbr. articles to profl. jours. Postdoctoral fellow Natural Scis. and Engring. Rsch. Coun. of Can., 1984-85, rsch. fellow, 1985-90; fellow Suisse Nat. Res. Fond, 1993; Sr. Scientist Fellowship, Ministere de la Recherche, France. Fellow Geol. Assn. Can., Soc. Wetland Scientists (pres., v.p. 2000-2003). Office: Univ Waterloo Earth and Environ Scis Dept Waterloo ON Canada N2L 3G1 Home Phone: 519-884-9619. Business E-Mail: bwarner@uwaterloo.ca.

WARNER, CAROLYN G., musician, music educator; b. Winnipeg, Man., Can., Apr. 19, 1951; arrived in U.S., 1975; d. Alfred and Gertrude Gadiel; m. Stephen David Warner, June 1, 1980; 1 child, Ari M. BA, U. Toronto, Ont., Can., 1971, MA, 1972; postgrad., Paris Conservatory Music, 1975. Violinist, pianist Buffalo Philharm., 1975—79, Cleve. Orch., 1979—. Adj. prof. chamber music Cleve. Inst. Music, 1987—; artistic dir. Cleve. Duo and James Umble, 1994—, Agnon V young person's performing ensemble, Cleve., 1998—2003. Transcriber: classical music scores, musician: recordings Cappella, Dana and Klavier labels. Grantee, Ohio Arts Coun., 1984—, Arts Midwest, 1987—; Can. Coun. Career grantee, 1972—75. Mem.: Am. Fedn. Musicians, Coll. Music Soc., Chamber Music Am. Avocations: jogging, gardening, boating, organizing benefit concerts. Home: 17500 Shelburne Rd Cleveland Heights OH 44118 Office: Cleve Orch Severance Hall Euclid Ave Cleveland OH 44106

WARNER, CHARLES COLLINS, lawyer; b. Cambridge, Mass., June 19, 1942; s. Hoyt Landon and Charlotte (Collins) W.; m. Elizabeth Denny, Aug. 24, 1964; children: Peter, Andrew, Elizabeth. BA, Yale U., 1964; JD cum laude, Ohio State U., 1970. Bar: Ohio 1970. Assoc. Porter, Wright, Morris & Arthur and predecessor, Columbus, 1970-76, ptnr., 1976—, also mgr. labor and employment law dept., 1988-92. Pres. Peace Corps Svc. Coun., Columbus, 1974—76, Old Worthington (Ohio) Assn., 1976—78, Worthington Ednl. Found., 1994—96, Opera Columbus, 1999—2001, Alliance for Quality Edn., Worthington, 1987—89; chmn. lawyers sect. United Way, Columbus, 1983—84; mem. alumni adv. coun. Ohio State U., 1998—2004; pres. Chamber Music Columbus, 2007—. Recipient Disting. Svc. award, Ohio State U., 2003, Cmty. Svc. award, Columbus Bar Assn., 2003, Hon. Lifetime Fellowship award, Ohio State Bar Found., 2007. Fellow: Ohio State Bar Found., Coll. Labor and Employment Lawyers, Am. Bar Found., Columbus Bar Found. (trustee 1996—, pres. 2007—); mem.: Met. Club, Yale Club (pres. 1979—81), Lawyers Club, Capital Club, Nat. Coun. Ohio State U. Coll. Law (pres. 2002—04), Ohio State U. Law Alumni Assn. (pres. 1996—97, Disting. Svc. award 2003), FBA, Ohio Assn. Civil Trial Attys. (exec. bd. 1988—97, Frank Hurd Mem. of Yr. award 1998), Ohio Mgmt. Lawyers Assn. (chair 2004—06), Columbus Bar Assn. (bd. govs. 1982—93, pres. 1991—92, Cmty. Svc. award 2003), Ohio Met. Bar Assn. (pres. 1991—92), Ohio State Bar Assn. (chmn. fed. cts. com. 1992—94, coun. of dels. 1993—), ABA (exec. com. Met. Bar Caucus 1992—94, chmn. state and local bar ADR com. 1995—98, co-chair EEO com. 2000—02). Avocations: clarinet, singing, tennis. Home: 145 E South St Columbus OH 43085-4129 Office: Porter Wright Morris & Arthur 41 S High St Ste 2800 Columbus OH 43215-6194 Home Phone: 614-846-1160; Office Phone: 614-227-2013. E-mail: cwarner@porterwright.com.

WARNER, CHRISTOPHER HUGH, psychiatrist; b. Steubenville, Ohio, Apr. 2, 1974; s. William Norman and Diana Lynn Warner; m. Carolynn Marie Stocum, Mar. 3, 1997; children: Timothy Jordan children: Jacob Thomas, Aaron Christopher, Matthew Dylan. BS, U.S. Mil. Acad., West Point, NY., 1996; MD, Uniformed Svcs. U. of Health Sci., Bethesda, Md., 2000. Lic. physician Ind., 2000, diplomate Am. Bd. of Family Practice, 2005. Resident in family practice and psychiatry Walter Reed Army Hosp., Washington, 2000—05; chief resident NCC Family Practice-Psychiatry, Washington, 2003—05; divsn. psychiatry 3rd Inf. Divsn., Fort Stewart, Ga., 2005—. Maj. US Army, 1992—, Fort Stewart, GA. Decorated Bronze Star US Army; recipient Award for Outstanding Leadership in Psychiatry, Assn. of Acad. Psychiatry, 2004, George Ginsberg Award for Accomplishment in Edn. and Tng. in Psychiatry, Am. Assn. of Dirs. of Psychiat. Residency Tng., 2004, Gen. Graves B. Erskine Award for Most Outstanding Resident, Walter Reed Army Med. Ctr., 2005, Al Glass Award for Outstanding Leadership in Mil. Psychiatry, 2005, Physician Recognition award, US Army Surgeon Gen., 2006; named Martin Fenton Nat. Resident of the Yr., Assn. of Medicine and Psychiatry, 2005, Resident Tchr. of the Yr., Soc. of Tchrs. of Family Medicine, 2005. Mem.: Assn. for Acad. Psychiatry (assoc.), Am. Psychiat. Assn. (assoc.; regional chpt. jr. devel. officer 2005), Am. Acad. of Family Physicians (assoc.). Christian. Achievements include research in examining the ethics training of psychiatric residents; on eating disorders in military recruits; on depression in military recruits; on the characteristics and practices of FP/Psych trained individuals; on leadership development in medical residency training; psychological effects of combat exposure on soldiers. Home: 373 Steeple Chase Ln Richmond Hill GA 31324 Office: Division Mental Health Bldg 601E Fort Stewart GA 31314 Personal E-mail: christopher.h.warner@us.army.mil.

WARNER, DENNIS ALLAN, psychology professor; b. Idaho Falls, Idaho, Apr. 27, 1940; s. Perry and Marcia E. (Finlayson) W.; m. Charyl Ann DeHart, Dec. 12, 1962; children: Lisa Rae, Sara Michelle, David Perry, Matthew Arie. BS, Brigham Young U., 1964; MS with honors, U. Oreg., 1966, PhD, 1968. Asst. prof. edn. Wash. State U., Pullman, 1968-72, assoc. prof. edn., 1972-78, prof. edn., 1978-85, dir. tchr. edn., 1983-85, prof., chmn. ednl. counseling psychology, 1985-93, interim dir. Partnership Ctr., 1993—94, 2004—06, prof. edn. leadership and counseling psychology, 1994—, assoc. dean Coll. Edn., 1999—2005, exec. assoc. dean Coll. Edn., 2006—07, dir. H.S. equivalency program, 2004—. Vis. asst. prof. psychology U. Idaho, Moscow, 1971. Author: Interpreting and Improving Student Test Performance, 1982; contbr. articles to profl. jours. Postdoctoral research assoc. U. Kans., 1976-77. Fellow: APA. Mem. Lds Ch. Home: 645 SW Mies St Pullman WA 99163-2057 Office: Wash State Univ Coll Edn Cleveland Hl Rm 160B Pullman WA 99164-2114 Office Phone: 509-335-5652. Business E-Mail: dawarner@wsu.edu.

WARNER, DON LEE, dean emeritus; b. Norfolk, NB, Jan. 4, 1934; s. Donald A. and Cleo V. (Slagel) W.; m. Patricia Ann Walker, Feb. 24, 1957; children: Mark J., Scott Lee. BS in Geol. Engring., Colo. Sch. Mines, 1956, MSc in Geol. Engring., 1961; PhD in Engring. Sci., U. Calif., Berkeley, 1964. Registered profl. engr., Mo., geologist, Mo., Tex. Geol. engr. Gulf Oil Corp., Casper, Wyo., 1956, Calif. Exploration Co., Guatemala, 1957-58; civil engr. U.S. Forest Svc., Gunnison, Colo., 1958-59; teaching asst. Colo. Sch. Mines, Golden, 1959-61; rsch. asst. U. Calif., Berkeley, 1962-64; rsch. geologist and engr. U.S. Pub. Health Svc., Cin., 1964-67; chief, earth scis. Ohio Basin Region Fed. Water Pollution Control Adminstrn., 1967-69; prof. geol. engring. U. Mo., Rolla, 1969-92, prof. emeritus geol. engring., 1992—, dean emeritus Sch. Mines and Metallurgy, 1992—, chmn., geol. engring., 1980-81, dean Sch. Mines and Metallurgy, 1981-93. Bd. dirs. Underground Injection Practices Coun., 1985-89; mem. adv. com. to Sec. of Interior for Mineral Resources Rsch., 1985-92; vice chmn. Mo. Bd. Geologist Registration, 2006—. Author: Subsurface Wastewater Injection, 1977. Special award scholarship Colo. Sch. Mines, 1951-56, grad. fellowship Colo. Sch. Mines, 1959-51, rsch. fellowship U. Calif., 1962-64; recipient Best Paper award Am. Water Works Assn., 1971. Fellow Geol. Soc. Am.; mem. Am. Inst. Profl. Geologists (cert.), Am. Assn. Petroleum Geologists, Geol. Soc. Am., Nat. Ground Water Assn. (sci. award 1984, disting. lectr. 1986), Blue Key, Scabbard and Blade, Theta Tau, Tau Beta Pi. Avocations: fishing, boating, tennis, golf. Personal E-mail: dlw@fidmail.com.

WARNER, DOUGLAS ALEXANDER, III, (SANDY WARNER), retired diversified financial services company executive; b. Cin., June 9, 1946; s. Douglas Alexander Jr. and Eleanor (Wright) W.; m. Patricia G. Grant, May 13, 1977; children: Alexander, Katherine, Michael. BA, Yale U., 1968. Officer's asst. J.P. Morgan & Co. Inc., NYC, 1968-70; asst. treas. J.P. Morgan & Co., Inc., NYC, 1970-72, asst. v.p., 1972-75; v.p. Morgan Guaranty Trust Co., NYC, 1975-85, sr. v.p., 1983-87; exec. v.p. J.P. Morgan & Co., Inc. (formerly Morgan Guaranty Trust Co. N.Y.), NYC, 1987-89, mng. dir., 1989-90, pres., 1990-95, chmn., pres., CEO, 1995—2000; chmn. J.P. Morgan Chase & Co., NYC, 2000—01; financial adv. Pres. George H.W. Bush Transition Team, 2000. Bd. counselors Bechtel Group, Inc.; bd. dirs. J.P. Morgan & Co., Inc. 1990-2000, Gen. Electric Co., 1992-, Anheuser-Busch Companies, Inc., 1992-2008, J.P. Morgan Chase & Co., 2000-01, Motorola, Inc., 2002-; chmn. bd. of overseers and mgrs. Meml. Sloan-Kettering Cancer Ctr.; mem. The Bus. Coun. Trustee Yale U., 2008-; chmn. Yale Investment Com., 2008-. Mem. River Club, Meadowbrook Club (LI). Republican. Avocations: golf, skiing, shooting. Office Phone: 212-270-2323. Business E-Mail: warner_d_a@jpmorgan.com.

WARNER, H. TY, entrepreneur, manufacturing executive; b. Chgo., Sept. 3, 1944; s. Harold and Georgia Warner. Student, Kalamazoo Coll. Salesman Dakin Toys, Applause Inc., San Francisco; founder, owner, pres. Ty Inc., Westmont, Ill., 1985—; owner Four Seasons, NYC, 1999—, San Ysidro Ranch, 1999—, Four Seasons Biltmore, 2000—, Sandpiper Golf Course, 2003—. Founder Ty Warner Park, Ty Warner Sea Ctr. Named one of Forbes' Richest Americans, 1999—, World's Richest People, Forbes Mag., 2001—. Achievements include invention of Beanie Babies. Office: Ty Inc 280 Chestnut Ave Westmont IL 60559

WARNER, HAROLD CLAY, JR., banker, investment company executive; b. Knoxville, Tenn., Feb. 24, 1939; s. Harold Clay and Mary Frances (Waters) W.; m. Patricia Alice Rethorst, Sept. 1, 1961; children: Martha Lee, Carol Frances. BS in Econs, U. Tenn., 1961, PhD, 1965. Asst. to pres. First Fed. Savs., Savannah, Ga., 1965-67; v.p. and economist No. Trust Co., Chgo., 1967-73; sr. v.p. and chief economist Crocker Nat. Bank, San Francisco, 1974-79, sr. v.p. liability mgmt., 1979-82; exec. v.p., dir. fixed income mgmt. BA Investment Mgmt. Corp., 1982-84, dir., pres., COO, 1984-86; dir., pres. Montgomery St. Income Securities, Inc., 1984-86; sr. v.p. Bank of Am., San Francisco, 1982-86; chmn. BA Investment Mgmt. Internat., Ltd., 1985-86; pres. Arthur D. Gimbel, Inc., San Mateo, Calif., 1986-87; exec. v.p., chief investment officer Riggs Nat. Bank Washington, 1987-88; chmn. Riggs Investment Mgmt. Corp., 1988-89; sr. v.p., chief economist Bank of Calif., San Francisco, 1989-93; pres., chief investment officer MERUS Capital Mgmt., San Francisco, 1989-93; pres. Govett Asset Mgmt. Co., 1993-95, Govett Fin. Svcs. Ltd., 1993-95; pres., COO Fisher Investments, Inc., Woodside, Calif., 1996; pres. Warner Fiduciary Counsel, LLC, San Francisco, 1997; 1st v.p., sr. dir. portfolio mgmt. Mellon Pvt. Wealth Mgmt., San Francisco, 1998—2007; mng. dir. Mt. Eden Investment Advisors, San Francisco, 2007—. Lectr. dept. econs. U. Tenn., 1962-63, Grad. Sch. Bus., Loyola U., Chgo., 1969-73; lectr. Pacific Coast Banking Sch., U. Wash., 1978-79; bd. dirs. Children's Hosp. and Rsch. Ctr., 2007—. NDEA fellow, 1961-64 Mem. Burlingame Country Club, Pacific-Union Club, Phi Gamma Delta, Phi Eta Sigma, Beta Gamma Sigma, Omicron Delta Kappa, Phi Kappa Phi. Home: PO Box 2449 Yountville CA 94599-2449 Office: 343 Sansome St Ste 1600 San Francisco CA 94104 Home Phone: 650-347-7809; Office Phone: 415-288-3018. Business E-Mail: hcwarner@mtedeninvest.com.

WARNER, ISIAH MANUEL, chemistry professor; b. DeQuincy, La., July 20, 1946; s. Humphrey and Irma (St. Romain) W.; m. Della Blount, June 1, 1968; children: Isiah Jr., Chideha, Edward. BS chemistry, Southern U., 1968; PhD, U. Wash., 1977. Teaching asst. U. Wash., Seattle, 1973-75, rsch. asst., 1975-77; asst. prof. Tex. A&M U., College Station, Tex., 1977-82; assoc. prof. Emory U., Atlanta, 1982-86, prof., 1986, 1987-92; Philip W. West prof., analytical and environ. chem. La. State U., Baton Rouge, 1992—, chair, dept. chem., 1994—97, Boyd prof., chem., 2000—, vice chancellor, strategic initiatives, 2001—. Cons. Nat. Sci. Found., 1980—, Coca Cola, Atlanta, 1984-92, NIH, Bethesda, Md., 1979—, Eli Lilly & Co., Indpls., 1988, 89; rsch. prof., Howard Hughes Med. Inst., 2002-. Contbr. articles to profl. jours. Recipient Charles Holmes Herty award, 1992, Benedetti Pichler award, 1994, NY SAS Gold medal, 1991, Presdl. Young Investigator award, 1984, Outstanding Tchr. award, 1993, AAAS Lifetime Mentor award, Banneker Legacy award, 2006, AnaChem award, Assn. Analytical Chemists, 2007, Banneker Legacy award, 2006, Divsn. Aanalytical Chemistry award in Spectrochem. Analysis, Am. Chem. Soc., 2008; grantee, Howard Hughes Med. Inst., 2002; Fulbright fellow for rsch., tchg. in Kenya. Mem.: Internat. Chemometrics Soc. (N.Am. chpt.), Soc. Applied Spectroscopy, Nat. Orgn. Black Chemists and Chem. Engrs., Am. Chem. Soc. (So. Chemist award 2006, award for encouraging disadvantaged students into the scis. 2003), Sigma Xi. Avocations: racquetball, chess, cards. Office: La State Univ Dept Chemistry Baton Rouge LA 70803-0001 Office Phone: 225-578-2829. Office Fax: 225-578-3971. Business E-Mail: iwarner@lsu.edu.

WARNER, JOHN ARNAN, state supreme court justice; b. Great Falls, Mont., Jan. 22, 1943; s. James Arnan and Cleo (Schaedler) W.; m. Katherine Warner; children: Matthew, Marion, Ann, Jeffrey, Jonathan, Katherine. BA, U. Mont., 1965, LLB, 1967. Bar: Mont. 1967, U.S. Dist. Ct. Mont. 1967, U.S. Ct. Appeals (9th cir.) 1982. Law clk. Mont. Supreme Ct., Helena, Mont., 1967-68; ptnr. Bosch, Kuhr, et al, Havre, Mont., 1968-88; atty. City of Havre, 1984-88; dist. judge 12th Judicial Dist., Mont., 1988—2003; justice Mont. Supreme Ct., 2003—. Former chmn. Supreme Ct. Sentence Review Div.; former mem. Dist. Ct. Council; former chmn. Mont. Jud. Standards Commn.; mem. teaching staff Commn. on Cts. of Limited Jurisdiction; mem. Supreme Ct. Commn. to Review Canons of Jud. Ethics. Past pres. Mont. Swimming, Inc.; past chmn. Hill Top Recovery Bd.; past bd. dirs Mont. AAU; del. Mont. Officials Assn. Mem. ABA, Mont. Bar Assn. (trustee 1980-88, pres. 1987-88, mem. jud. relations com.), 12th Judicial Dist. Bar Assn. (past pres.), Def. Rsch. Inst., Lions (past pres. Havre chpt. swim team). Roman Catholic. Avocations: fishing, hunting, hiking. Office: Mont Supreme Ct Justice Bldg PO Box 203003 Helena MT 59620-3003 Office Phone: 406-444-5494. Business E-Mail: jwarner@mt.gov.*

WARNER, JOHN EDWARD, advertising executive; b. Troy, NY, Mar. 26, 1936; s. George Edward and Ann Frances (Teson) W.; m. Anne Elizabeth Hibbard, Sept. 19, 1959; children: Matthew J., Barbara A., Peter J., Christopher J. BS in Chemistry and Philosophy, Coll. Holy Cross, 1957. Promotion mgr. Union Carbide Corp., NYC, 1957-62; acct. exec. McCann-Erickson, Inc., NYC, 1962-64; pres. Warner, Bicking & Fenwick, Inc., NYC, 1964-84; chmn. Warner, Bicking, Morris & Ptnrs. Inc., 1984-97; pres. Transworld Advt. Agy. Network, 1987-97, Quatrefoil, Inc., 1998—. Bd. dirs. Thomas Pub. Co., N.Y.C. Author: (non-fiction) Decorating Time Savers by Jack Warner, 2001, (fiction) Tom Never's Ghost, 2006. Home: 706 Hillcrest Rd Ridgewood NJ 07450-1110 E-mail: jawarner@optonline.net.

WARNER, JOHN HILLIARD, JR., technical services company executive; b. Santa Monica, Calif., Mar. 2, 1941; s. John Hilliard and Irene Anne (Oliva) W.; m. Helga Magdalena Farrington, Sept. 4, 1961; children: Tania Renee, James Michael BS in Engring. with honors, UCLA, 1963, MS in Engring., 1965, PhD in Engring., 1967. Mem. staff Marquardt Corp., Van Nuys, Calif., 1963; mem. faculty West Coast U., LA, 1969-72; mem. staff TRW Sys. Group, Redondo Beach, Calif., 1967-70, sect. mgr., 1970-73; mem. staff Sci. Applications Internat. Corp., San Diego, 1973-75, asst. v.p., 1975-77, v.p., 1977-80, corp. v.p., 1980-81, sr. v.p., 1981-87, sector v.p., 1987-89, exec. v.p., 1989-96, bd. dirs., 1988—2006, corp. exec. v.p., 1996—2005, chief adminstrv. officer, 2003—06, exec. v.p., 2005—07. Cons. Rand Corp., Santa Monica, 1964—66; bd. dirs. AMSEC LLC, 1997—2007, Mimix Broadband, 2006—08, TREX Enterprises, ICW Group, Cubic Corp.; ptnr. Limestone Ventures. Contbr. articles to profl. jours. Trustee Scripps Health, 2001-06; bd. dirs. Corp. Dirs. Forum, 2001—. AEC fellow, 1963, 66, NSF fellow, 1964, 65. Mem. AIAA, NDIA, Nat. Assn. Corp. Dirs., Healthcare Info. and Mgmt. Sys. Soc., Assn. US Army, Air Force Assn., Armed Forces Comm. and Electronics Assn., Navy League US, La Jolla Chamber Music Soc. (bd. dirs. 1990-97, adv. bd. 1998-2001), San Diego C. of C. (bd. dirs. 2000-04, 07), Calif. C. of C. (bd. dirs. 2000—07), Calif. Bus. Roundtable, Sigma Nu, Tau Beta Pi. Methodist. Avocations: bicycling, golf, fishing, music, travel.

WARNER, JOHN WILLIAM, lawyer, former United States Senator from Virginia; b. Washington, Feb. 18, 1927; s. John William and Martha Stuart (Budd) W.; m. Catherine Conover Mellon, Aug. 7, 1957 (div. 1973) children: Mary Conover, Virginia Stuart, John William IV.; m. Elizabeth Taylor, Dec. 4, 1976 (div. Nov. 7, 1982); m. Jeanne Vander Myde, Dec. 15, 2003 BS in Engring., Washington and Lee U., 1949; LL.B., U. Va., 1953. Law clk. to Hon. E. Barrett Prettyman US Ct. Appeals (DC cir.), 1953-54; spl. asst. to US atty. US Dept. Justice, 1956-57, asst. US atty. (DC dist.), 1957-60; ptnr. Hogan & Hartson LLP, 1960-68; owner, operator Atoka Cattle Farm, 1961—94; under sec. Dept. Navy, US Dept. Def., Washington, 1969-72, sec., 1972-74; adminstr. Am. Revolution Bicentennial Adminstrn., 1974-76; US Senator from Va., 1979—2009; chmn. US Senate Rules & Adminstrn. Com., 1995—99, US Senate Armed Services Com., 1999—2001, 2001, 2003—07; ptnr. Hogan & Hartson LLP, 2009—. Rep. to sec. def., Law of the Sea Talks, 1969-73, prin. US negotiator & signatory, Incidents at Sea Exec. Agreement, 1970-72, exec. branch rep., Am. Revolution BiCentennial Adminstrn., 1974-76, US del. to 12th Spl. Session of UN Gen. Assembly, 1982, observer, Geneva Arms Control Talks, 1985 Served with USNR, 1944-46; USMC, 1951-52; USMCR, 1952-64. Recipient Edmund S. Muskie Disting. Pub. Svc. award, Ctr. for Nat. Policy, 1999, Harry S. Truman award, Nat. Guard Assn. of the US, 2000, James Forrestal Meml. award, Nat. Def. Industrial Assn., 2000, Wings of Liberty award, Aerospace Industries Assn., 2001, VFW Congl. award, VFW, 2001, Arthur T. Marix Congl. Leadership award, The Retired Officer Assn., 2001, Leadership award, Pvt. Sector Coun., 2003, Spirit of Hope award, United Svc. Organizations, 2003, Congl. Am. Spirit Medallion, Nat. D-Day Mus., 2004, Nat. Intelligence Disting. Pub. Svc. medal, 2008, Rule of Law award, Va. Holocaust Mus. & the Va. Law Found., 2009. Mem. DC Bar Assn., Am. Legion, Veterans Fgn. Wars (Va. chpt.) Republican. Episcopalian. Office: Hogan & Hartson LLP 555 Thirteenth St NW Washington DC 20004 Office Phone: 202-637-8875. Office Fax: 202-637-5910. E-mail: jwwarner@hhlaw.com.*

WARNER, KENNETH E(DGAR), dean, public health educator, consultant; b. Washington, Jan. 25, 1947; s. Edgar W. Jr. and Betty (Strasburger) W.; m. Patricia A. Hilty, Oct. 1, 1977; children— Peter, Andrew AB, Dartmouth Coll., 1968; MPhil, Yale U., 1970, PhD, 1974. Lectr. dept. health mgmt. and policy Sch. Pub. Health, U. Mich., Ann Arbor, Mich., 1972—74, asst. prof., 1974—77, assoc. prof., 1977—83, prof., 1983—, chmn., 1982—88, 1992—95, Richard D. Remington Collegiate prof. pub. health, 1995—2001, dir. Tobacco Rsch. Network, Avedis Donabedian Disting. Univ. prof. pub. health, 2001—, dean, 2005—. Cons., Washington, 1976—95, Office on Smoking and Health, USPHS, Rockville, Md., 1978—, Inst. Medicine, Nat. Acad. Scis., Washington, 1984—, numerous additional pub. and pvt. orgns.; mem. bd. sci. counselors divsn. cancer prevention and control Nat. Cancer Inst., Bethesda, Md., 1985—89. Author: (with Bryan Luce) Cost-Benefit & Cost Effectiveness Analysis in Health Care, 1982; contbr. articles to profl. jours. Trustee Am. Lung Assn., Mich., Lansing, 1982; mem. subcom. on smoking Am. Heart Assn., Dallas, 1983-87; mem. com. on tobacco and cancer Am. Cancer Soc., N.Y.C., 1984-92; bd. dirs. Am. Legacy Found., 1999-2003. Hon. Woodrow Wilson fellow, 1968; W.K. Kellog Found. fellow, 1980-83; vis. scholar Nat. Bur. Econ. Research, Stanford, Calif., 1975-76; recipient Surgeon Gen.'s medallion Dr. C. Everett Koop, 1989. Fellow Assn. Health Svcs. Rsch.; mem. APHA (leadership award 1990), Inst. Medicine, Phi Beta Kappa. Office: U Mich Dept Health Sch Pub Health 109 Observatory St Ann Arbor MI 48109-2029 Office Phone: 734-763-5454. Business E-Mail: kwarner@umich.edu.

WARNER, KENNETH WILSON, JR., editor, publishing executive; b. Chgo., Dec. 22, 1928; s. Kenneth Wilson and Ann S. (Knapp) W.; m. Deborah Ann Bollo, Dec. 28, 1982 (div. Apr. 1995); 1 child, Joseph; children by previous marriages: Sara, Seth, Katharin. BS Ed., No. Ill. State Teachers Coll., 1950. Staff editor Bldg. Supply News, Chgo., 1953-56; staff editor Elec. Merchandising, 1956-60; free-lance writer Sarasota, Fla., 1960-66; editor Gunsport Mag., Alexandria and Falls Church, Va., 1966-67, Gunfacts Mag., Arlington, Va., 1968-70, pub., 1968-70; exec. editor Am. Rifleman, Nat. Rifle Assn., Washington, 1971-78, asst. dir. publs. div., 1972-78; editor Am. Hunter, 1973-78, Am. Rifleman, 1976-78; dir. publs. NRA, Washington, 1977-78; editor in chief Gun Digest, Knives Annual-Krause Publs., Inc., Greenville, W.Va., 1979-99; editor, pub. Knives Digest Two Knife Guys Pub., Inc., Chattanooga, 2000—01; pres. Knifeware, Inc., Greenville, W.Va. Cons. firearms and cutlery cos.; co-founder Am. Knife and Tool Inst., 1997. Author: The Practical Book of Knives. 1976; The Practical Book of Guns, 1978. Editor: The Bolt Action, 1976. Contbr. articles to profl. jours. Cpl. U.S. Army. 1951-53. Recipient Cutlery Hall of Fame; inducted into Am. Bladesmith Soc. Hall of Fame, 1999. Mem.: NRA (life), Knifemaker's Guild Am. (assoc.). Office: Prin Office PO Box 52 Greenville WV 24945-0052 Office Phone: 304-832-6878. Personal E-mail: info@knifeware.com.

WARNER, KERSTIN JULIANNA, gifted and talented educator; d. Kerstin and John Warner; m. Louis Weinberg, June 23, 1995 (div. Apr. 11, 2008); 1 child, Sofia Weinberg. BS in Fine Art, Vassar Coll., Poughkeepsie, NY, 1986; MS in Spl. Edn., Bank St. Coll. Edn., 1994. Cert. tchr. K-8, spl. edn. 1-12, art 1-12 Conn., tchr. elem. K-6, art 1-12, spl. edn. 1 - 12 NY. Asst. tchr. St. Anne's Sch., Bklyn., 1987—90; tchr. spl. edn. preschool The League Sch., Bklyn., 1990—92; 2d grade tchr. Berkeley Carroll Sch., Bklyn., 1992—95; tchr. gifted St. Paul Pub. Schs., 1995—99, Bedford Mid. Sch., Westport, Conn., 1999—. Coach mock trial team Bedford Mid. Sch., Westport, 2002—06; book discussion trainer Westport Pub. Libr., 2001—; Conn. chair Nicholas Green award, 2005—. Pres. Vassar Club of Fairfield County, Westport, Conn., 2002—. Recipient Golden Apple Achiever award, Ashland, 1998, Honor Roll, Supporting Emotional Needs of the Gifted, 2007, Supporting Emotional Needs of Gifted Roll award, 2007; Inter-district Archaeology Program, Conn. Assn. for the Gifted, 2004—05. Mem.: ASCD, Westport Cmty. Emergency Response Team CC, Nat. Assn. for Gifted Children (Conn. chair Nicholas Green award selection 2006—), Conn. Assn. for the Gifted, Nat. Coun. Tchrs. Math., Vassar Club (pres. 2002—). Democrat. Avocations: creative writing, drawing, international travel. Office: Bedford Middle School 88 North Ave Westport CT 06880 Business E-Mail: kerstin_warner@westport.k12.ct.us.

WARNER, KURT (KURTIS EUGENE WARNER), professional football player; b. Burlington, Iowa, June 22, 1971; s. Gene and Sue Warner; m. Brenda Carney Meoni, Oct. 11, 1997; adopted children: Zachary, Jesse children: Elijah, Kade, Jadda, Sierra Rose, Sienna Rae. BA in Comm., No. Ill. U. Quarterback Green Bay Packers, 1994; quaterback Iowa Barnstormers (Arena Football League), 1995—97, Amsterdam Admirals (NFL Europe), 1998, St. Louis Rams, 1998—2004, NY Giants, 2004—05, Ariz. Cardinals, 2005—. Co-author (with Michael Silver): All Things Possible: My Story of Faith, Football and The Miracle Season, 2001. Co-founder First Things First Found., 2000—. Recipient Burt Bell award, Maxwell Football Club, 1999; named Gateway Conf. Offensive Player of Yr., NCAA, 1993, NFL MVP, AP, 1999, 2001, NFL All-Pro, 1999, 2001, Super Bowl XXXIV MVP, NFL, 2000; named to Nat. Football Conf. Pro Bowl Team, 1999—2001, 2008. Christian. Achievements include leading the NFL in: passing touchdowns, 1999, 2001, passer rating, 1999, 2001, passing yards per game, 2000, 2001, passing yards, 2001, pass completions, 2001, others; being a member of Super Bowl XXXIV winning St. Louis Rams, 2000; tying the NFL record with six consecutive 300-yard passing games, 2000; setting the Super Bowl record for passing yards and pass attempts without an interception, 2000. Office: 8701 S Hardy Dr Tempe AZ 85284*

WARNER, MALCOLM-JAMAL, actor, director, producer; b. Jersey City, Aug. 18, 1970; s. Robert and Pamela Warner; m. Karen Malina White. Grad. with honors, Profl. Children's Sch., NYC; grad., New York U. Founder record label The Wonder Factory, 1998. Actor TV series The Cosby Show, NBC, 1984-92, Here and Now, 1992, Malcolm & Eddie, 1996-2000, Jeremiah, 2002-, Listen Up, 2004-; co-starred numerous TV movies and series including NBC film The Father Clements Story, 1987, Tour of Duty, A Desperate Exit, 1986, Tyson, 1995, The Tuskegee Airmen, 1995; co-dir. episode The Cosby Show, 1989; dir. New Edition's hit music video N.E. Heartbreak; N.Y. stage debut in Off-Broadway prodn. Three Ways Home, 1988; author: (book) Theo and Me, 1988; host numerous instructional videos including Home Alone: A Kid's Guide to Playing Safe on Your Own, also a series on reading motivation; host TV shows: CBS Storybreak, 1993-95; voice in The Magic School Bus, 1994-98; feature films include Drop Zone, 1994, Restaurant, 1998, A Fare to Remember, 1998, Reflections: A Story of Redemption, 2004, The List, 2006, Contradictions of the Heart, 2006, Fool's Gold, 2008. Nat. chmn. Osmond Found.'s Miracle Network Telethon; hon. youth chairperson Nat. PTA; co-chair Black Family Reunion Celebration.

WARNER, MARK A., anesthesiologist; b. Greenville, Ohio, Oct. 7, 1953; s. Paul C. Jr. and Mildred G. Warner; m. Mary Ellen Bunch, Oct. 14, 1978; children: Paul, Mark, Matthew, Daniel. AB in Chemistry, Miami U., Oxford, Ohio, 1976; MD, Med. Coll. Ohio, 1979. Diplomate Am. Bd. Anesthesiology. Intern, resident Mayo Clinic, Rochester, 1979-82, prof. and chmn. dept. anes., 1999—2005, dir. hosp. ops., 1995-99, exec. bd., 2005—. Bd. dirs. Anesthesia Patient Safety Found., Boston, 1996—. Bd. dirs. Rochester Family YMCA, Rochester, 1998—, Rochester Airport Co., 1992—, Mayo Med. Transp. Sys., Rochester, 1995-2002, Gold Cross Ambulance, Rochester, 1995-2002. Mem. American Bd. Anesthesiology, Raleigh, N.C., (bd. dirs. 1999-, pres. 2009), American Soc. Anesthesiologists (bd. dirs. 1996-2008, 1st v.p., 2008-09). Office: Mayo Clinic 200 1st St SW Rochester MN 55905-0001 E-mail: warner.mark@mayo.edu.*

WARNER, MARK ROBERT, United States Senator from Virginia, former governor; b. Indpls., Ind., Dec. 15, 1954; s. Robert and Margaret Warner; m. Lisa Collis; children: Madison, Gillian, Eliza. BA, George Washington U., 1977; JD, Harvard U., 1980. Founding ptnr. Columbia Capital Corp., Alexandria, Va., 1989; gov. State of Va., Richmond, 2001—06; US Senator from Va., 2009—. Chmn. Va. State Dem. Party, 1993—95; mem. Dem. Nat. Com., 1993—95; chmn. Nat. Gov. Assn., 2004—05, Edn. Commn. of the States, Southern Tech. Coun. Founding chmn. Va. Health Care Found.; creator SeniorNavigator.com; founder TechRiders, Va. High-Tech Partnership; co-chmn. Va. Cmtys. in Schs. Found.; mem. Old Presbyn. Meeting House; past bd. dirs. Va. Union U., George Washington U., Appalachian Sch. Law, Va. Found. for Ind. Colls., Va. Math and Sci. Coalition. Mem.: Southern Govs. Assn. (1st vice chmn.), Dem. Govs. Assn. (recruitment chmn.). Democrat. Presbyn. Office: B40C Dirksen Senate Office Bldg Washington DC 20510 Office Phone: 202-224-2023.*

WARNER, MINER HILL, investment banker; b. NYC, Aug. 13, 1942; s. Bradford Arnold and Nancy (Hill) W.; m. Ellen C. Murphy, Mar. 18, 1972; children— Alix Mallet-Prevost, Lily Wolcott. AB, Harvard U., 1964; C.E.P., Institut d'Etudes Politiques, Paris, 1963; M.Sc. in Econs., London Sch. Econs., 1965; LL.B., U. Pa., 1968; postgrad., NYU. Grad. Sch. Bus. Adminstrn., 1971-73. Bar: N.Y. 1969. Assoc. Shearman & Sterling, NYC, 1968-71; assoc. Salomon Bros. Inc., NYC, 1971-73; v.p. Salomon Bros. Internat. Ltd., London, 1974-78; v.p., mgr. Salomon Bros. Inc., NYC, 1979-87; dir. Merrill Lynch & Co., NYC, 1988-92; pres. Pub. Resources Internat., NYC, 1992-95, chmn., 1996—. Adv. dir. Coun. of the Americas, 1991-93. Mem. Pres.'s Pvt. Sector Survey on Cost Control, Washington, 1982-83; mem. coun. Grad. Theol. Union, Berkeley, Calif., 1998-; vestryman St. John's Ch., Fishers Island, N.Y., 1980-99, sr. warden, 1994-99; trustee, mem. exec. com. Cathedral of St. John the Divine, N.Y., 1997—2008; English-Speaking Union U.S. bd. dirs., mem. exec. com., 2002-06, mem. task force Gen. Theol. Sem., N.Y., 2000-02; pres. Pilgrims of US; trustee N.Y. Hist. Soc., 1985-99, chmn. 1994-99, chmn. emeritus, 1999—; trustee Hispanic Soc. Am., 2005-. Decorated Order of St. John of Jerusalem. Mem. Pub. Securities Assn. (guaranteed loan com. 1980-86), Mayflower Soc. (former gov.), Brook Club (v.p.), River Club, Links Club, Met. Club (Washington), Fishers Island Club, Hay Harbor Club (Fishers Island) (former dir.). Republican. Episcopalian. Home: 148 E End Ave New York NY 10028-7503 Office: Pub Resources Internat 780 3d Ave Ste 2805 New York NY 10017-2024

WARNER, PAUL MICHAEL, federal judge, former prosecutor; b. 1952; BA, Brigham Young U., 1973, JD, 1976, MPA, 1984. Atty. judge advocate general's corps USN, 1976—82; asst. atty. gen. State of Utah, Salt Lake City, 1982—83; asst. US atty. Dist. Utah US Dept. Justice, Salt Lake City, 1983—96, US atty., 1996—2006; magistrate judge US Dist. Ct., Salt Lake City, 2006—. With USNR, 1976—82, advanced through ranks to col. Nat. Guard, 1983—, Utah. Office: US Dist Ct 350 S Main St Salt Lake City UT 84101

WARNER, ROBERTA ARLENE, retired accountant, financial services executive; b. Binghamton, NY, Dec. 31, 1938; d. Murrilan Earl and Ethel Margaret (Bell) W. BA, SUNY, Binghamton, 1960; MBA, Ind. U., 1962, MHA with highest distinction, 1973. CPA, N.Y.; lic. nursing home adminstr., N.Y. Sr. acct. Arthur Young & Co., CPA, Buffalo, 1962—66; acctg. supr. Children's Hosp., Buffalo, 1966—68; contr. King Manor Nursing Homes-Ave. Bldg. Corp., Buffalo, 1968—71; asst. dir. health fin. Hosp. Assn. N.Y. State, Albany, 1973—80, dir. health fin., 1980—93, Healthcare Assn. N.Y. State, Albany, 1994—97, dir. data analysis and stds., 1997—98; pres. Roberta A. Warner Co., 1999—2003, ret., 2003. Author articles in field. Trustee Ednl. Found. of Am. Women's Soc. CPA, Am. Soc. Women Accts., 1985-87; pres. hist. preservation com. Windsor Ctrl. Sch. Dist., 2006-. Fellow Healthcare Fin. Mgmt. Assn.; mem. AICPA, Am. Acctg. Assn., Am. Soc. Women Accts. (pres. Buffalo chpt. 1967-68), Am. Women's Soc. CPA, N.Y. State Soc. CPA, Ind. U. Alumni Assn. (life), SUNY Binghamton Alumni Assn. (life), Grange. Methodist. Home: 569 NY Rte 79 Windsor NY 13865-2714

WARNER, ROLLIN MILES, JR., economics educator, real estate broker; b. Evanston, Ill., Dec. 25, 1930; s. Rollin Miles Warner Sr. and Julia Herndon (Polk) Clarkson BA, Yale U., 1953; cert. in law, Harvard U., 1956; MBA, Stanford U., 1960; cert. in edn. adminstrn., U. San Francisco, 1974; cert., Coll. Fin. Planning, 1977. Lic. real estate broker Real Estate Cert. Inst., Calif. Asst. to v.p. fin. Stanford U., 1960—63; instr. history Town Sch., San Francisco, 1963—70, instr. econs. and history, dean, 1975—; prin. Mt. Tamalpais, Ross, Calif., 1972—74; dir. devel. Katharine Branson Sch., Ross, 1974—75. Author: America, 1986, Europe, 1986, Africa, Asia, Russia, 1986, Greece, Rome, 1981, Free Enterprise at Work, 1986 From scoutmaster to summer camp commr. Boy Scouts Am., San Francisco, 1956—2007. Served to lt. USNR, 1953—55, Korea, Pacific, Vietnam. Recipient Silver Beaver award Boy Scouts Am., 1986, medal Town Sch. for Boys Alumni Coun., 1995. Mem.: U.S. Naval Inst., Marines Meml. Assn., South End Rowing Club (San Francisco), San Francisco Yacht Club (Belvedere, Calif.), Grolier Club NY. Office: Town Sch 2750 Jackson St San Francisco CA 94115-1195 E-mail: warnerrollinm1960@alumni-gsb.stanford.edu.

WARNER, SCOTT DENNIS, investment banker; b. York, Pa., July 13, 1963; s. Earl Dennis and Sandra Glee (Barnhart) W. SB in Elec. Engring., MIT, 1986, SB in Computer Sci. and Engring., 1986, SM in Elec. Engring. and Computer Sci., 1986; MBA in Fin., U. Chgo., 1990. Intern IBM Corp., Yorktown Heights, NY, 1983-86; fin. analyst Merrill Lynch & Co., NYC, 1986-88, assoc., 1990-94, v.p., 1994-95; assoc. Goldman, Sachs & Co., NYC, 1989; v.p. Lipper & Co., L.P., NYC, 1995-98, Gerard Klauer Mattison & Co., Inc., NYC, 1998—2002; pres. Internat. Capital LLC, Luxembourg, 2003—05, Warner Capital, S.E.C.S., Luxembourg, 2003—05; sr. cons. avantage Capita Ltd., London, 2006—. Nat. Merit scholar, 1981, ROTC scholar, 1981, teaching asst. scholar MIT, 1985, 86; Leon C. Marshall scholar U. Chgo., 1988. Mem. Nat. Eagle Scout Assn., Delta Upsilon Frat. Republican. Presbyterian. Office: 17 Cranley Mews London SW7 3BX England Personal E-mail: scottdwarner@yahoo.com.

WARNER, SETH L., mathematician, educator; b. Muskegon, Mich., July 11, 1927; s. Seth LeMoyne and Agnes (Brustad) W.; m. Susan Emily Rose, June 16, 1962; children: Susan Emily, Sarah Southall, Seth Lawrence. BS, Yale U., 1950; MA, Harvard U., 1951, PhD, 1955. Rsch. instr. Duke U., 1955-57, asst. prof., 1957-61, asso. prof., 1961-65, prof. math., 1965-95, dir. grad. studies math., 1960-68; prof. emeritus math., 1995—; chmn. Duke U., 1968-70, 73-82; mem. Inst. Advanced Studies, 1959-60; vis. disting. prof. math. Reed Coll., 1970-71; visitor U. Paris, 1964-65, U. Oslo, 1982-83. Author: Modern Algebra, vols. I and II, 1965, re-issued, 1990, Classical Modern Algebra, 1971, Topological Fields, 1989, Topological Rings, 1993. Served with Med. Service Corps AUS, 1946-48. Mem. Phi Beta Kappa, Sigma Xi. Episcopalian. Office: Duke U Math Dept Box 90320 Durham NC 27708-0320 Home: 2708 Circle Dr Durham NC 27705-5727

WARNER, SUSAN, federal agency administrator; b. Rochester, NY, July 20, 1956; d. Harold J. and Jeannette (Nichols) Warner; divorced; children: Jennifer Lynn, Kathryn Alice. BA, Miami U., Oxford, Ohio, 1978; postgrad., Xavier U. Loan specialist HUD, Columbus, Ohio, 1978-79, Cin., 1979-83; fin. planner IDS Fin. Services, Inc., Cin., 1983-86, Manufacturer's Hanover Mortgage Corp., 1986, Shawmut Mortgage Corp., 1986-87, U.S. Dept. HUD, St. Louis, 1987—. Housing cons., Cin., 1985—. Author: Community Land Coop. Residents' Handbook, 1986. Adv. Cin. Tech. Coll., 1984—; mem. fin. com. Community Land Coop., Cin., 1985—; exhibits chair Conf. Cin. Women, 1985, corp. patrons chair, 1986, conf. coordinator, 1987; vol. Am. Cancer Soc., 1981-2008, March of Dimes, 1996-2008; leader Girl Scouts. Recipient Mercury awards IDS, Cin., 1984, award for superior performance U.S. Inspector Gen. HUD, 1990, Profl. Team 2003 Excellence in Govt. award The Greater St. Louis Fed. Exec. Bd., 2003. Republican. Roman Catholic. Avocations: reading, costume designing, making teddy bears, softball, theater.

WARNER, WILLIAM DEE, nursing consultant; b. El Reno, Okla., Jan. 13, 1942; s. Otto None and Cloney Lu Warner; m. Linda Gail Bolay, May 22, 1966; children: Michelle Diane Rohmfeld, Cynthia Ann, William Otto. BSN, West Tex. State U., Canyon, 1975. RN nurse, Tex., 1973. Instr. Howard Coll., Big Spring, Tex., 2001—. Nursing cons., examiner Tex. Nurses Assn., Austin, Tex., 1982—89. With Army N.G. US Army, 1980—81, Abilene, Tex. Home: 1902 Winston St Big Spring TX 79720 Office: Howard Coll 1001 Birdwell Ln Big Spring TX 79720 Office Fax: 432-263-0313; Home Fax: 432-263-0313. Personal E-mail: lndwarner@aol.com. Business E-Mail: bwarner@howardcollege.edu.

WARNER, WILLIAM HAMER, mathematician; b. Pitts., Oct. 6, 1929; s. John Christian and Louise (Hamer) W.; m. Janet Louise West, June 29, 1957; 1 dau., Katherine Patricia. Student, Haverford Coll., 1946-48; BS, Carnegie Inst. Tech., 1950, MS, 1951, PhD, 1953. Research asso. grad. div. applied math. Brown U., Providence, 1953-55; asst. prof. dept. aerospace engring. and mechanics U. Minn., Mpls., 1955-58, asso. prof., 1958-68, prof., 1968-95, prof. emeritus, 1995—. Author: (with L.E. Goodman) Statics, 1963, Dynamics, 1964; contbr. articles to profl. jours. Mem.: Soc. Natural Philosophy, Math. Assn. Am., Soc. Indsl. and Applied Math., Am. Math. Soc. E-mail: warner@aem.umn.edu.

WARNER, WILLIAM KENT, JR., religious organization administrator, consultant; b. Chgo., June 14, 1933; children: William Kent III, Robert David, Steven Bradley. BA in Biblical studies, Wheaton Coll., Ill., 1953; MA summa cum laude, Columbia Internat. U., SC, 1954; MS, U. Ill., Urbana, 1960; PhD, U. Iowa, Iowa City, 1972. Ordained Evang. Free Ch. Am., 1954. Missionary, tchr. and prin. Tchg. Tng. Inst., Zimbabwe, 1955—59; founder, dir. publ. house, 1961—67; founder, exec. dir. Christian Coll. So. Africa, Wheaton, Ill., 1969—. Prin. Tchg. Tng. Inst., Zimbabwe, 1959; founder, pub. Pub. House, Harare, 1961—67; founder, exec. dir. CCOSA, 1969—. Avocations: writing, speaking, table tennis. Office: CCOSA c/o M Mahoney CPA/MBA 416 E Roosevelt Rd Ste 110 Wheaton IL 60187 Business E-Mail: drwkwarner@hotmail.com.

WARNKE, GORDON E., lawyer; b. Wetaskiwin, Alta., Canada, Nov. 3, 1957; BS, U. Alta., 1978, LLB, 1981; SJD, Harvard Univ., 1984. Bar: NY 1984. Co-mng. ptnr., mem. exec. com., chmn. tax group Dewey LeBoevf LLP, NYC. Mem.: ABA (past chmn. com. on affiliated & related corp.), NY State Bar Assn. (mem. exec. com.), Assn. of the Bar of the City of NY. Office: Dewey LeBoevf LLP 1301 Ave of the Americas New York NY 10019-6092 Business E-Mail: gwarnke@dbllp.com.

WARNOCK, JOHN EDWARD, computer company executive; b. Salt Lake City, Oct. 6, 1940; BS in Math. and Philosophy, U. Utah, 1961, MS in Math., 1964, PhD in Elec. Engring. and Computer Sci., 1969; DSc (hon.), Univ. Utah. With Evans & Sutherland Computer Corp., Computer Scis. Corp., IBM; prin. scientist Xerox Palo Alto Rsch. Ctr., Calif., 1978-81; co-founder, chmn. Adobe Sys., Inc., San Jose, Calif., 1982—, CEO, 1982—2000. Bd. dir. Octavo Corp. Patentee in field; contbr. articles to profl. jours. and industry mags.; spkr. in field. Bd. mem., past chmn. Tech Mus. Innovation; mem. entrepreneurial bd. adv. com. Am. Film Inst. Recipient Computer Achievement award Assn. for Computing Machinery SIGGRAPH, 1989, Tech. Excellence award Nat. Graphics Assn., 1989, ACM Software Sys. award, 1989, Lifetime Achievement award for tech. excellence, PC Mag., 1989, J. Anderson Disting. Achievement award, 1991, Disting. Alumnus award U. Utah, 1995, Cary award Rochester Inst. Tech., 1995, Fellow award, Computer History Mus., 2002; named Entrepreneur of Yr. Ernst & Young, Merril Lynch, Inc., 1991; named to Computer Reseller News Hall of Fame, 1998. Fellow Assn. for Computing Machinery, Am. Acad. Arts & Scis.; mem. NAE, Utah Info. Tech. Assn. Office: Adobe Sys Inc 345 Park Ave San Jose CA 95110-2704

WARNSTADT, JACQUELINE RAE, elementary school educator; m. Steve Warnstadt. BA, Morningside Coll., 1972. Tchr., 1972—, Leeds Elem. Sch., Sioux City, Iowa. Named Iowa Tchr. of Yr., 2006. Mem.: Sioux City Mus. & Hist. Assn. Office: Leeds Elem Sch 3919 Jefferson St Sioux City IA 51108

WAROMG, RICHARD HARVEY, ecologist, educator; b. Chgo., May 17, 1935; m. Doris Jean Carlson, June 13, 1957; children: Lance Eric Waring, Lise Ellen Waring. PhD, U. Calif., Berkeley, 1963. Prof. emeritus Coll. Forestry, Corvallis, Oreg., 1963—. Acting program mgr., land atmosphere interactions NASA, Washington, 1992—93; disting. prof. Oreg. State U., 1995—2000. Achievements include research in process-based forest growth model. Office: Coll Forestry Jefferson & 30th St Corvallis OR 97331

WARPEHA, RAYMOND LEONARD, surgeon, educator; b. Mpls., Dec. 5, 1934; s. Frank Joseph and Sophie Helen (Fryzlewicz) Warpeha; m. Ivy Lee Kloth; children: Katherine, John, Joseph, Frank. BS, U. Minn., 1956, DDS, 1958; MD, Northwestern U., 1965, PhD in Anatomy, 1966. Cert. Am. Bd. Surgery, 1971, plastic surgery Am. Bd. Surgery, 1973. Instr. anatomy Northwestern U. Med. Sch., Chgo., 1963—65, instr. surgery, 1969—72; asst. prof. surgery and anatomy Loyola U. Stritch Sch. Medicine, Maywood, Fla., 1973—75, assoc. prof. surgery and anatomy, 1975—80, prof. surgery and anatomy, 1981—2000, prof. emeritus, 2000—. Cons. surgery Cook County Hosp., Chgo., 1970—72; founder, dir. Burn Ctr. Loyola U. Hosp., 1972—91; dir. surg. anatomy dept. surgery Loyola Med. Sch., 1972—2000. Author: 59 articles and 9 book chpts., Clinics of Plastic Surgery North America, 1981; mem. editl. bd.: Chgo. Medicine. Chmn. Ill. Burn Surgeons adv. group Ill. Dept. Med. Svcs., Springfield, 1973—80; chmn. burn surgeons adv. group Divsnl. Med. Svcs., Washington, 1975; mem. bd. trustees Ill. Trauma Soc.; trustee Am. Soc. Maxillofacial Surgery. Recipient award for Lifetime Med. Contbns. and Pub. Svc. to Burn and Fire Victims and Survivors, Knapp Burn Found., Chgo., 1999, Disting. Svcs. award, 2007, lectureship award, 2008; postdoctoral Am. Heart Assn. fellow, Northwestern Med. Sch., 1962—63. Fellow: Am. Coll. Surgeons (chmn. membership com. Dist. 3 1995—99); mem.: Am. Soc. Plastic and Reconstructive Surgeons, Soc. Head and Neck Surgeons, Am. Assn. Plastic Surgeons, Am. Soc. Maxillofacial Surgeons, Am. Burn Assn., Chgo. Soc. Plastic Surgery (pres. 1983—84, treas. 1981—82, v.p. 1982—83). Roman Catholic. Avocations: fishing, botany. Office: Loyola Med Ctr Dept Surgery 2160 S First Ave Maywood IL 60153

WARRASAK, SUKHUMA, ophthalmologist; d. Vudhi and Pramern Thamchaiprakarn. BSc, Mahidol U., 1972, MD, 1978, Grad. diploma in Clin. Sci., 1982. Intern Ramathibodi Hosp., 1979, resident dept. opthalmology Bangkok, asst. prof. dept. ophthalmology, 1989—95, assoc. prof. dept. ophthalmology, 1995—; asst. chief Pub. Health Ctr., Bangkok, 1979—81; attending staff Children Hosp., Ministry of Pub. Health, 1981; fellow retina-vitreous surgery U. Ottawa Sch. Medicine, Canada, 1987. Chief retina svc. dept. ophthalmology Ramathibodi Hosp., 2002—06; chmn. Thai Retina Soc., Royal Coll. Opthalmologists of Thailand, 2005—; adv. bd. Asia Pacific FFA Club, 2003—; program dir., chief retina unit Project React, 2005—06. Mem. editl. bd.: Ramathibodi Medicine Jour., 2002—04. Recipient Disting. Svc. award, Asia Pacific Acad. Ophthalmology, 2003. Mem.: Royal Coll. Ophthalmologists Thailand, Retina Soc., Am. Acad. Ophthalmology, Med. Coun. Thailand. Avocations: antiques, Western and Eastern civilization. Home: 180 Sukhumvit 49/6 Bangkok Thailand Office: Mahidol Univ Ramathibodi Hosp Dept Ophthalmology Bangkok 10400 Thailand Office Phone: 662-7125741. Office Fax: 662-7125743. E-mail: sukhuma@csloxinfo.com.

WARREN, ALICE LOUISE, artist; b. Springfield, Mass., May 7, 1927; d. Roland D. and Ella May (McGrath) Eaton Von Der Lancken; m. John Homer Warren, June 5, 1948 (dec. Jan. 1988); children: John David (dec.), Daniel Wayne. Student, N.Y. Sch. Writing, 1952-55, Mansion House Art Sch., 1969, 70, 71; grad., Nat. Landscape Inst., 1960, Famous Writers Sch., 1965; Cert., United UMA Sch., 1967. Home nursing cert.; cert. home health aide paramedical. Nurses aide ARC, Springfield, 1942-45; vol. nurses aid, 1943—44; hot-line councilor Check Line, West Springfield, Mass., 1945-46; freelance columnist New England Homestead, Springfield, 1960-63; freelance columnist, editor Garden Page Woman's Circle, Horticulture mags. Author, photographer: (booklet) Evergreen Shrubs, 1964. solo art exhbns. Mercy Hosp., Arts Unltd. Gallery, 1997, Bay State Med., Springfield, Mass., 1999; featured artist Barnes and Noble Bookstore, Oct. 1999, Westfield Antheneum, 2000; on-line exhbns. MindsIsland.com, 2002, ArtRepsart.com, 2002--, Art-Exchange.com, 2003--. Recipient Bill Curtin award for watercolor, 1983. Mem. Amherst Writers & Artists Inst., Springfield Art League, Scriptures Writers, Mass. Writers Guild (treas. 1963), Tobacco Valley Artists Assn. Avocations: painting, travel, photography, reading. E-mail: artislalw@comcast.net.

WARREN, ALVIN CLIFFORD, JR., law educator; b. Daytona Beach, Fla., May 14, 1944; s. Alvin Clifford and Barbara (Barnes) Warren; m. Judith Blatt, Aug. 20, 1966; children: Allison, Matthew. BA in English, Yale U., 1966; JD, U. Chgo., 1969. Bar: Conn. 1970, Pa. 1975. Asst. to assoc. prof. law U. Conn., West Hartford, 1969—73; assoc. prof. Duke U., Durham, NC, 1973—75; prof. U. Pa., Phila., 1975—80, Harvard Law Sch., Cambridge, Mass., 1980—98, Ropes & Gray prof., 1998—, dir. fund for tax and fiscal rsch. policy, 1985—. Vis. assoc. prof. U. Pa., 1974—75; vis. prof. law Harvard U., 1979—80. Author: Integration of Individual and Corporate Income Taxes, 1993; contbr. articles to law jours. Mem.: ABA (mem. tax. sect.). Office: Harvard Law Sch 1563 Massachusetts Ave Cambridge MA 02138 Office Phone: 617-495-3186. Office Fax: 617-496-4880. E-mail: warren@law.harvard.edu.

WARREN, ANDREW C., apparel executive; Joined GE Fin. Mgmt. Program; sr. v.p., CFO NBC Cable, 2002—04; exec. v.p., CFO NBC Universal TV Grp., 2004—06; sr. ops. leader Audit Staff Gen. Electric Co., 2006—07; CFO Liz Claiborne Inc., 2007—08, exec. v.p., CFO, 2008—. Office: Liz Claiborne Inc 1441 Broadway New York NY 10018 Office Phone: 212-354-4900. Office Fax: 212-626-1800.

WARREN, CHARLES DAVID, library consultant; b. Martin, Tenn., June 12, 1944; s. Charles Alton and Evelyn (Bell) W.; children: Aaron David, Meredith Hild, Julia Myers. BS, U. Tenn., 1967; MS, U. Ill., Urbana, 1969. cert. pub. library adminstr. Dir. Shiloh Regional Library, Jackson, Tenn., 1969-72, Cumberland County Pub. Library, Fayetteville, NC, 1973-79; exec. dir. Richland County Pub. Library, Columbia, SC, 1979—2009, exec. dir. emeritus, 2009—. Bd. dirs. Civic Music Assn., Fayetteville, N.C., 1973-79, Fayetteville Symphony, 1973-78, Fayetteville Arts Commn., 1975; v.p. Friends of Librs. U.S.A., 1994—2009; mem. Columbia Coord. Coun., 1987-88; chmn. Richland County History Commn., 1987-93; mem. John Cotton Dana Awards Commn., 1994-99. Recipient Lucy Hampton Bostick award, 1993, S.C. Pub. Adminstr. Yr. award, 1993; named Young Man of Yr., Fayetteville Jaycees, 1977, S.C. Libr. of Yr., 1991, Internat. Fedn. Librs., 1997-2001, Order of Silver Crescent, 1999. Mem. ALA (pres. Jr. Member Roundtable 1977, chmn. awards com. 1984), Southeastern Libr. Assn. (pres. pub. libr. sect. 1978), S.C. Libr. Assn. (bd. dirs. 1980), Friends Libraries USA (bd. dirs. 1992-), Southeastern Libr. Network (bd. dirs. 2002-), Rotary, Kiwanis, Beta Phi Mu. Democrat. Episcopalian. Office: Richland County Pub Libr 1431 Assembly St Columbia SC 29201-3101 Home: 7 West St C Charleston SC 29401 Business E-Mail: edwarrenlll@yahoo.com.

WARREN, DANIEL CHURCHMAN, health facility administrator; b. Washington, Sept. 23, 1939; s. Walter Thomas and Laura Katherine W.; m. C. Frederica Lescure, June 5, 1958(dec. Mar. 7, 2007), Elaina Gianatasio, Apr. 5, 2008; 1 child, Christopher C. BS, Roanoke Coll., 1960; MD, Med. Coll. Va., 1964; MPH, U. N.C., 1971; MMAS, U.S. Army Command & Gen. Coll., 1974. Diplomate Nat. Bd. Med. Examiners, Am. Bd. Preventive Medicine, lic. physician VA; ordained Anglican Cath. priest 2002. Intern Georgetown U. Hosp., 1964-65; resident in surgery Med. Coll. Va., 1967-68, William Beaumont Gen. Hosp., 1968-69; resident in preventive medicine Walter Reed Army Inst. Rsch., 1971-73; commd. 2d lt. U.S. Army, 1965, advanced through grades to col., 1986; asst. med. dir. HealthAm. Va., 1986; pvt. practice travel, 1987-89; dir. Peninsula Health Dist., Newport News, Va., 1990—2001; warden Holyrood Sem., 2001—03; rector St. Matthews Anglican Cath. Ch., 2002—09; priest-in-charge All Saints ACC, 2007—; warden Scott Sch. Theology, 2003—. Clin. asst. prof. family and cmty. medicine Ea. Va. Med. Sch., Norfolk; cons. Riverside Regional Med Ctr., Newport News. Active Gloucester County Rep. Com., 1987-96, chmn. 1992-95, Gloucester County Redistricting Adv. Com., 1991, 2001; hon. chmn. Combined Va. Campaign United Way the Va. Peninsula, 1992. Fellow: Am. Coll. Preventive Medicine; mem.: Knight of the Order St. Lazarus Jerusalem, Order Founders Patriots America, Jamestowne Soc., Med. Soc. Va. Republican. Anglican. Avocation: English and Virginia history. Business E-Mail: dwarrenmd@cox.net.

WARREN, DAVID HAROLD, religious studies educator; b. Detroit, Oct. 18, 1956; s. Harold Winford and Aimee Sue Warren; m. Bonnie Lynne Ramsey. AA, Freed-Hardeman Coll., Henderson, 1978; BA, Freed-Hardeman Coll., Henderson, Tennessee, 1975—78; ThM, Harding Grad. Sch. Religion, Memphis, 1983, Harvard U., Cambridge, 1993, ThD, 2001. Asst. prof. Bible Freed-Hardeman U., Tenn., 2001—02; prof. New Testament Heritage Christian U., Florence, Ala., 2002—. Editor: (book) Early Christian Voices; contbr. articles. Mem.: Evang. Theol. Soc., Am. Acad. Religion, Soc. Bibl. Lit., Alpha Chi. Office: Heritage Christian Univ 3625 Helton Dr (PO Box HCU) Florence AL 35630 Office Fax: 256-760-0981. Business E-Mail: dwarren@hcu.edu.

WARREN, DAVID LILES, educational association administrator; b. Goldsboro, NC, Sept. 15, 1943; s. James Hubert and Katherine (Liles) W.; m. Ellen Elizabeth LeGendre, Mar. 1, 1969; children— Jamison, Mackenzie, Katrin BA in English, Wash. State U., 1965; M in Urban Studies, Yale U., 1970, MDiv, 1970; PhD, U. Mich., 1976; LittD (hon.), Elmhurst Coll., 1994, Moravian Coll., 1994, Southwestern U., 2003, Middlebury Coll., 2001; LLD (hon.), Rider U., 1996, Mercer U., 1998, Franklin and Marshall Coll., 1999, Ky. Wesleyan Coll., 2000; LHD (hon.), Mt. Union Coll., 1997, Ctr. Coll., 1997, U. New Haven, 2001, Lyon Coll., 2008, St. Lawrence U., 2008; D in Pub. Svc. (hon.), Rocky Mountain Coll., 1999, Sage Colls., 2007; DCL, U. South, 2009. Gen. sec. Yale U. Dwight Hall, New Haven, 1969—76, bd. dirs., 1976; assoc. dir. cmty. rels. Yale U., New Haven, 1976—78; sr. v.p., provost Antioch U., NYC and Yellow Springs, Ohio, 1978—82; chief adminstrv. officer City of New Haven, 1982—84; pres. Ohio Wesleyan U., Delaware, 1984—93, Nat. Assn. Ind. Colls. and Univs., Washington, 1993—. Cons. to hosps., sch. systems, colls., univs.; bd. dirs. Delaware County Bank; chmn. NCAA Pres. Commn., Divsn. III, 1990-92. Contbr. chpts. to books, articles to Yale Alumni Mag. Mem. New Haven Bd. Alderman, 1973-75; vice chmn. New Haven Commn. Poverty, 1981-82; pres. North Coast Athletic Conf., 1988-90; justice of peace New Haven Dem. Party, 1974-76; state chmn. People to People, 1987; chmn. Gov.'s Task Force on Dep. Registrar, 1987; chmn. Ohio Five Coll. Commn., 1985-95, Campus Compact Nat. Exec. Com., 1987-88; bd. dirs. US Health Corp., Coun. Ethics and Econs.; exec. com. Great Lakes Colls. Assn., Ctrl. Ohio Symphony Orch.; chmn. Ohio Ethics commn. Fulbright scholar Wash. State U., 1965-66, disting. Centennial Alumnus; Rockefeller fellow Yale U., 1966. Mem. Am. Assn. Higher Edn., Assn. Ind. Colls. Univs. (sec. 1987-88), Univ. Club (Columbus, Ohio), Grad. Club (New Haven), Cosmos Club (Washington), Phi Beta Kappa. Democrat. Presbyterian. Avocations: running, writing, tennis. Office: Nat Assn Ind Colls & Univs 1025 Connecticut Ave NW Ste 700 Washington DC 20036-5409 Office Phone: 202-785-8866. Office Fax: 202-835-0003. E-mail: david@naicu.edu.

WARREN, DAVID P., stock exchange executive; b. 1954; BA, Wesleyan U.; MBA, Yale Sch. Mgmt., 1988. Investment banker CS First Boston, 1987—95; dep. treas. State of Conn., 1995—98; CFO Long Island Power Authority (LIPA), 1998—2000; chief adminstrv. officer

NASDAQ Stock Market, Inc., NYC, 2001, CFO, 2001—08; exec. v.p., CFO NASDAQ OMX Group, Inc., NYC, 2008—09. Office: NASDAQ OMX Group Inc 1 Liberty Plz New York NY 10006 Office Phone: 212-401-8912. Office Fax: 212-401-1014. Business E-Mail: david.warren@nasdaq.com.*

WARREN, DONALD WILLIAM, medical and dental educator; b. Bklyn., Mar. 22, 1935; s. Sol B. and Frances W.; m. Priscilla Girardi, June 10, 1956; children: Donald W. Jr., Michael C. BS, U. N.C., 1956, DDS, 1959; MS, U. Pa., 1961, PhD, 1963; D in Odontology (hon.), U. Kuopio, Finland, 1991. Asst. prof. dentistry U. N.C., Chapel Hill, 1963-65, dir. Craniofacial Ctr., 1963-2000, assoc. prof., 1965-69, prof., 1969-80, chmn. dept. dental ecology, 1970-85, Kenan prof., 1980—2004, Kenan prof. emeritus, 2004—, rsch. prof. otolaryngology, 1985—2004; ret. Cons. NIH, Bethesda, Md., 1967-2000, R. J. Reynolds-Nabisco, Winston-Salem, N.C., 1986-99. Contbr. articles to profl. jours. Recipient Honor award Am. Cleft Palate Assn./Craniofacial Assn., 1992, O. Max Garner award U. N.C. Bd. Govs., 1993, honors award Angle Orthodontic Soc., 1998. Fellow AAAS, Internat. Coll. Dentists, Am. Speech and Hearing Lang. Assn. (Editors award 1998, Honors award 2003), Internat. Assn. Dental Rsch., Acoustical Soc. Am., Am. Cleft Palate Assn. (pres. 1981-82, Disting. Svc. award 1984), Am. Cleft Palate Edn. Found. (pres. 1976-77), Am. Equest Trade Assn. (treas. 2008-, pres. 2009). Avocations: horse related activities, running, farming. Home: PO Box 1356 Southern Pines NC 28388-1356

WARREN, DWIGHT WILLIAM, III, physiology educator; b. LA, Dec. 21, 1942; s. Dwight William Jr. and Edna (Rainen) W.; m. Grace Anita Sturm, Nov. 24, 1965; 1 child, Jennifer Anne. AB, U. Calif., Berkeley, 1964; PhD, U. So. Calif., LA, 1972, MSEd, 2000. Asst. prof. U. So. Calif., LA, 1972-78, assoc. prof., 1978-88, prof. dept. physiology and biophysics, 1988—2006, prof. and acting chmn., dept. Pharmacology and Nutrition, 1992-94; prof. dept. cell and neurobiology Univ. So. Calif., LA, 1994—, prof. dept. ophthalmology, 1993—99, assoc. dean for curriculum, 1994—99; vice dean, chair dept. biomed. sci. Charles E. Schmitt Coll. Sci. Fla. Atlantic U., 1999—2006, emeritus prof. biomed. sci. Mem. editl. bd. Reproductive Scis., 1989-93, Biology of Reproduction, 1989-95; contbr. articles to profl. jours. Nat. rsch. svc. sr. fellow USPHS, 1980-81; Fulbright scholar USIA, Finland, 1990. Mem. AAAS, Endocrine Soc., Soc. Study Reproduction, Am. Soc. Andrology, N.Y. Acad. Scis., Assn. Rsch. in Vision and Ophthalmology. Business E-Mail: dwarren@usc.edu.

WARREN, ELIZABETH ANN, law educator; b. Okla., 1949; m. Bruce Mann; 1 child, Amelia Warren Tyagi. BS, U. Houston, 1970; JD, Rutgers U., 1976. Bar: NJ, Tex. Lectr. law Rutgers Sch. Law, Newark, 1977—78; asst. prof. law U. Houston Law Ctr., 1978—80, assoc. dean academic affairs, 1980—81, assoc. prof. law, 1981—83; rsch. assoc. Population Rsch. Ctr. U. Tex., Austin, 1983—87; prof. law U. Tex. Sch. Law, 1983—87, Conoco Faculty Fellow in Law, 1985—86, Jay H. Brown Centennial Fellow in Law, 1986—87; prof. law U. Pa. Law Sch., Phila., 1987—90, William A. Schnader Prof. Comml. Law, 1990—95; Leo Gottlieb prof. law Harvard Law Sch., Cambridge, Mass., 1995—; chair Congressional Oversight Panel overseeing Troubled Asset Relief Program (TARP), 2008—. Vis. assoc. prof. law U. Tex. Sch. Law, 1981—82; vis. prof. law U. Mich., 1985; Robert Braucher vis. prof. comml. law Harvard U., 1992—93; proposal reviewer NSF, 1985—; bd. editors Am. Bankruptcy Law Jour., 1989—92; editl. adv. bd. Little Brown & Co. Law Sch. Divsn. (now Aspen Press), 1990—; com. on jud. edn. Fed. Jud. Ctr., 1990—99; bd. trustees Am. Bankruptcy Bd. Certification, 1992—96; exec. com. Nat. Bankruptcy Conf., 1993—95, 2002—05; advisor German Govt. Task Force on Bankruptcy Reform, 1993; reporter, cons., sr. advisor Nat. Bankruptcy Rev. Commn., 1995—97; regular commentator All Things Considered program Nat. Pub. Radio. Co-author: As We Forgive Our Debtors: Consumer Credit and Bankruptcy in America, 1989 (Silver Gavel Award, ABA, 1990), The Law of Debtors and Creditors, 1991, Secured Transactions: A Systems Approach, 1995, Comml. Law: A Systems Approach, 1998, The Fragile Middle Class: Americans in Debt, 2000 (Scholarship Award, Am. Coll. Consumer Fin. Services Lawyers, 2000); co-author: (with Amelia Warren Tyagi) The Two-Income Trap: Why Middle-Class Mothers and Fathers Are Going Broke, 2003, All Your Worth: The Ultimate Lifetime Money Plan, 2005. Recipient Frankel Publ. Award for Outstanding Writing, 1982, Commedation for Svc., Am. Bankruptcy Bd. Certification, 1998, Brown Award for Jud. Scholarship and Edn., Fed. Jud. Ctr., 1998, Champion of Consumer Rights Award, Nat. Assn. Consumer Bankruptcy Attorneys, 2000, Excellence in Edn. Award, Nat. Conf. Bankruptcy Judges, 2001, Lawrence P. King Award, Comml. Law League Am., 2002, Outstanding Tchr. Award, U. Houston Law Ctr., 1981, L. Hart Wright Teaching Excellence Award, U. Mich. Sch. Law, 1986, Harvey Levin Award for Excellence in Tchg., U. Pa. Sch. Law, 1989, 1992, Lindback Award for Disting. Tch., U. Pa., 1994, Albert A. Sacks-Paul A. Freund Award for Tchg. Excellence, Harvard Law Sch., 1997; named one of The 50 Most Influential Women Lawyers in Am., Nat. Law Jour., 1998, 2007, The World's Most Influential People, TIME mag., 2009. Fellow: Am. Acad. Arts & Scis., Am. Coll. Bankruptcy (Commendation for Outstanding Pub. Svc. 1998); mem.: Assn. Am. Law Schools (chair comml. and related consumer law sect. 1983—84, chair comml. law workshop 1984, planning com. conf. on tchg. contract law 1989, profl. devel. com. 1988—91, chair debtor-creditor sect. 1989—90, chair legislation com. debtor-creditor sect. 1990—93), Am. Law Inst. (exec. com. coun. 1994—95, US Adviser, Transnat. Insolvency Project 1995—, mem. nominating com. 1995—, exec. com. coun. 1998—, 2nd v.p. coun. 2000—04). Office: Harvard Law School Hauser 310 Cambridge MA 02138 Office Phone: 617-495-3101. E-mail: ewarren@law.harvard.edu.*

WARREN, J. RICHARD, editor, retired humanities educator; b. Sanford, Apr. 27, 1925; s. Ralph Moore Warren and Demarius Kate Musson-Warren; m. Mabel Martin, Aug. 21, 1949; children: Barbara Anne Tucker, J. Richard Jr., Mary Jane Cowen. BA in French, Stetson U., Deland, Fla., 1949, MA in Secondary Sch. Guidance, 1951; PhD in Music Edn. Supervision and Adminstrn., Fla. State U., Tallahassee, 1961; at, Tex. A&M U., Bryan, U.Ill., Urbana, Ctrl. Signal Corps Sch., Camp Crowder, Mo., Marbach Tutoring Inst. Fgn. Langs., Frankfort, Germany, Biarritz Am. U., France, U. Fla., Gainesville, Fla. State u., Tallahassee, U. W. Fla., Pensacola. Cert. edn. adminstrn. and supervision Fla., 1951, music Fla., 1951, French Fla., 1951, coll. academic adminstrn. and supervision Fla., 1961. Tchr. music Washington County H.S., Chipley, Fla., 1950—53, Bay H.S., Panama City, 1952—59, Fla. State U., Tallahassee, 1959—61, Brevard C.C., Cocoa, 1961; cons. fine arts curriculum Fla. Dept. Edn. Instrnl. Svcs., Tallahassee, 1961—67; dean humanities Fla. Jr. Coll., Jacksonville, 1967—70; dir. continuing edn. Jacksonville U., 1970—72; dean humanities Piedmont C.C., Charlottesville, Va., 1972—73; dean humanities, divsn. dir. & chmn. fine & performing arts dept. Northwest Fla. State Coll. (former Okaloosa-Walton C.C.), Niceville, Fla., 1973—93; ret., 1993; exec. officer & editor Fla. League Arts Inc., 1993—. Min. music First Meth. Ch., New Smyrna Beach, Fla., 1950—51, First Baptist Ch., Chipley, 1951—53, First Meth. Ch., Panama City, 1953—59, First Baptist Ch., Merritt Island, 1961, Southside Baptist Ch., Jacksonville, 1970—72; tchr. summer sch. Fla. State U., Tallahassee, 1952—59; clinician music camp Bapt. Harmony Bay, 1952—59; cons. Duval Magnet Sch., Jacksonville, 1970—72, Mattie Kelly Arts Ctr., Destin, 1975—90; editor Arts & Humanities jour. of Fla. League Arts, Niceville, 1993—. Contbg. editor: Fla. Sch. Bull., 1961—68; contbr. articles to profl. jours. Deacon Southside Bapt. Ch., Jacksonville, Fla., First Bapt. Ch., Niceville, Fla.; ednl. and choir cons. Cath. Ch., Panama City, Fla., St. Augustine Diocese, Jacksonville, Fla. Sgt. Signal Corps US Army, 1943—47, ETO. Mem.: Fla. League Arts, Fla. Vocal Music Assn. (life; past pres.), Fla. Music Educators Assn. (life), Music Educators Nat. Conf. (life), Rotary (J.U. rep. 1970—72), Kiwanis (pres. Valparaiso chpt. 2005—, Cir. K advisor Okaloosa-Walton Coll. chpt., Legion of Honor), Lions, Lambda Chi Alpha (founder Stetson U. chpt.), Pi Kappa Lambda. Republican. Avocations: gardening, piano, writing. Home: 2408 Edgewater Dr Niceville FL 32578-2304

WARREN, JAMES RONALD, retired museum director, journalist; b. Goldendale, Wash., May 25, 1925; stepson H.S. W.; m. Gwen Davis, June 25, 1949; children: Gail, Jeffrey. BA, Wash. State U., 1949; MA, U. Wash., 1953, PhD, 1963. Adminstrv. v.p. Seattle Community Coll., 1965-69; pres. Edmonds Community Coll., Lynnwood, Wash., 1969-79; dir. Mus. of History and Industry, Seattle, 1979-89. Lectr. in field. Author history books; columnist Seattle Post Intelligencer, 1979-92, Seattle Times, 1992-96. Served with U.S. Army, 1943-45, ETO, prisoner-of-war, Germany. Mem. VFW, Am. Ex-POW Assn., 42d (Rainbow) Div. Vets., Rotary, also others. Home and Office: 3235 99th Ave NE Bellevue WA 98004-1803 Personal E-mail: jrgwarren@msn.com.

WARREN, JANE CAROL, psychologist; b. Dec. 25, 1938; d. George Stafford Harris and Helen Virginia (Swift) Swift-Harris; m. Philip Clinton Warren (div.); children: Charles, Susan Warren Sohn; m. Richard Karl Hertel, July 19, 2001. BA, U. Mich., Ann Arbor, 1961, MA, 1964, PhD, 1985. Lic. psychologist Mich. Tchg. asst. in botany U. Mich., Ann Arbor, 1960—61, asst. in counseling, 1967—68; sci. tchr. Belleville (Mich.) HS, 1961—63; clin. psychologist Huron Valley Cons. Ctr., Ann Arbor, 1980—85; pvt. practice Ann Arbor, 1985—. Past pres. Mich. Psychoanalytic Found., Farmington Hills; founding mem. Allen Creek Presch., Ann Arbor. Fellow, U. Mich., 1963—64. Mem.: APA, Mich. Psychol. Assn., Am. Psychoanalytic Assn. (assoc.; steering com. 2004—07, chair com. on psychotherapist assoc.). Office: 555 E William #16-I Ann Arbor MI 48104 Office Phone: 734-662-5110. Business E-Mail: jmail@umich.edu.

WARREN, JENNIFER ELIZABETH, family nurse practitioner; b. Clovis, N.Mex., Nov. 13, 1964; d. Ronald Dwayne and Lillian Ann (Reed) Carter; m. Johnny Lynn Warren Jr., May 18, 1991. BSN, West Tex. State U., 1988; MSN-FNP, West Tex. A&M U., 1998. RN, Tex.; cert. family nurse practitioner. Clin. asst. Northwest Tex. Hosp., Amarillo, 1987—88; neonatal ICU nurse Meth. Children's Hosp., Lubbock, Tex., 1988—98, Covenant Med. Ctr., Lubbock, 1999—2000; family nurse practitioner Covenant Family Health Care Ctr., 2000—03, Garza County Health Clinic, Post, Tex., 2003—05, Spur (Tex.) Clinic, 2005—. Family nurse practitioner Primestaff, 2004—, Physicians Network Svcs., 2001—05, Spur (Tex.) Clinic, 2005—. Mem. Am. Acad. Nurse Practitioners, Tex. Nursing Assn., Endometriosis Assn. (organizer/contact, Lubbock leader 1993—), South Plains Nurse Practitioners Assn. Democrat. Methodist. Avocations: gardening, cross stitch, latch hook, swimming. Office: Spur Clinic 907 E Hill Spur TX 79370 Home: 1425 W Harris St Spur TX 79370-2105 Office Phone: 806-271-3306. Office Fax: 806-271-4256. Personal E-mail: jewarren@caprock-spur.com.

WARREN, JOHN COOLIDGE, educational administrator; b. Boston, May 16, 1956; s. William Bradford and Mary-Elizabeth (Coolidge) W.; m. Laura Parker Appell, June 18, 1983; children: Ethan Reynolds Appell, Amanda Pfaltzgraff Appell. BA, Stanford U., 1978, MA, 1980; MEd, Harvard U., 1991, EdD, 1994. Tchr. history Robert Louis Stevenson Sch., Pebble Beach, Calif., 1979-81, Milton Acad., Mass., 1981, chmn. dept. history, 1992-95, acad. dean, 1995—2001, spl. asst. head sch., 2001—06; head sch. St. Mark's Sch., 2006—. Faculty cons. Ednl. Testing Svc., Princeton, 1990—, William Joiner Ctr., Boston, 1992—; editl. cons. Longman Inc., White Plains, NY, 1991—. Editor: America's Intervention in Vietnam, 1987. NEH fellow, 1985, advanced doctoral fellow, Harvard U., 1993. Mem. Am. Hist. Assn., Orgn. Am. Historians, Assn. Asian Studies, World History Assn., Boston Athaneum, Colonial Soc. Mass., Mass. Hist. Soc., Phi Beta Kappa. Avocations: canoeing, fishing. Home and Office: St Mark's Sch 25 Marlborough Rd Southborough MA 01772

WARREN, KAREN COHEN, librarian; b. Albuquerque, Mar. 19, 1944; d. Edward I. and Corinne Marie (Hall) C.; m. William Francis Warren, May 1, 1938; children: Lisa Marie, Leslie Gail. BA, U. N.Mex., 1966; MLS, U. Tex., 1972. Br. libr. Twin Oaks and Manchaca Rd. Br. Libraries, Austin, 1972-74; libr. assoc. Austin Travis County Collection, 1974-80; reader svcs. libr. Austin History Ctr., 1981—. Mem. Soc. of Southwest Archivists, Austin Heritage Alliance. Avocations: gardening, cooking. Office: Austin History Ctr PO Box 2287 Austin TX 78768-2287

WARREN, KELCY L., energy executive; b. Gladewater, Tex., Nov. 9, 1955; s. Hugh Brinson and Bertie (Robinson) W. BSCE, U. Tex., Arlington, 1978. Pipeline design engr. Lone Star Gas Co., Dallas, 1978-81; pres., chief oper. officer Cornerstone Natural Gas, Inc., Dallas, 1993—96; pres. Energy Transfer Partners, Energy Transfer Equity, Dallas, 1996—2004, co-chmn., co-CEO, 2004—07, chmn., CEO, 2007—. Mem. Natural Gas Transp. Assn., Natural Gas Soc. North Tex. (pres. 1981—), Energy Club Dallas (bd. dirs. 1985—). Office: Energy Transfer Company 3738 Oak Lawn Ave Dallas TX 75219-4333

WARREN, KENNETH R., federal agency administrator; Grad., City Coll. NY; D in Biochemistry, Mich. State U., 1970. Postdoc. fellow UCLA, U. Mich. Mental Health Rsch. Inst.; rschr. Walter Reed Army Inst. Rsch., Rockville, Md., 1974; staff mem. rsch. divsn. Nat. Inst. Alcohol Abuse & Alcoholism (NIAAA), NIH, Bethesda, Md., 1976, chief biomed. rsch. br., dep. dir. Divsn. Extramural Rsch., then dir. Office Sci. Affairs, 1984—2005, assoc. dir. Office Basic Rsch., 2002—07, acting dir. Office Sci. Policy & Comm., 2007—08, acting dir. NIAAA, 2008—. Contbr. articles to profl. jours. Recipient Superior Svc. award, USPHS, 1982, Seixas award, Rsch. Soc. Alcoholism, 1994, Henry Rosett award, 2002; named to Tom & Linda Daschle Hall of Fame, Nat. Orgn. Fetal Alcohol Syndrome, 2007. Achievements include research in the effects of alcohol use during pregnancy including fetal alcohol syndrome and fetal alcohol spectrum disorders. Office: NIAAA 5635 Fishers Ln MSC 9304 Bethesda MD 20892 Office Phone: 301-443-3885.

WARREN, LISA SOLOD, writer; b. Knoxville, Tenn., Jan. 3, 1956; d. Jay Lawrence and Fredlyn Kovitch Solod; m. Michael Warren, Feb. 14, 2007, John Addison Lambeth, June 23, 1985 (div.); children: Philip Stanhope Lambeth, Grace Amelia Lambeth. AB in Semiotics with honors, Brown U., 1978. Pub. info. officer Mus. Fine Arts, Boston, 1978-79; asst. editor Boston Mag., 1979-80; editor Moviegoer Mag. Whittle Comms., 1980-83; chief advt. copywriter Parsons, Friedman and Cen. Advt. Agy., Boston, 1984-85; pub. rels. dir. So. Va. Coll. for Women, Buena Vista, Va., 1985-86; pub. info. dir. The George C. Marshall Found., Lexington, Va., 1986-88. Instr. expository writing U. R.I., 1984; editl. cons. TeenAge Mag., Cambridge Free Press, The Illustrated, 1983-85; bd. dirs. Project Horizon, 1988-90. Editor: Desire: Women Write About Wanting, 2007. Bd. dirs. Montessori Ctr. for Children, Lexington, 1995-99, sec., 1996-98; bd. dirs. Lexington City Sch. Bd., 1997—2001, v.p., 1998—2001; sec. Valley region Va. Sch. Bd. Assn., 1997-98, v.p. Valley region, 1998-99, chmn. Valley region, 1999-2001, bd. dirs. Temple House of Israel, 2004-05, pres. 2006-08. Recipient 12 fellowships/residencies Va. Ctr. for Creative Arts, Mt. San Angelo, 1989-2004. Democrat. Jewish. Home: 101 Wetherwood St Staunton VA 24401 Personal E-mail: lisa.solod@gmail.com.

WARREN, MAREDIA DELOIS, music educator; d. Odis Franklin and Mary Velma Lewis; m. Charles Augustus Warren, July 9, 1966; children: John Charles, Maredia Dionne. B in Music Edn. magna cum laude, Howard U., 1965; MA, Columbia U., 1967, EdD, 1989. Tchr. elem. music Hartford Pub. Schs., 1965—66; adj. faculty Herbert H. Lehman Coll., CUNY, 1972—79, Fairleigh Dickinson U., 1975—79, Montclaire State U., 1984—93; tchr. music grades K-6 Teaneck Pub. Schs., NJ, 1979—87; dir. vocal music Teaneck H.S., 1987—99; asst. prof. music educator William Paterson U., Wayne, NJ, 1999—2000; assoc. prof., coord. music edn. N.J. City U., Jersey City, 2000—. Condr. N.J. All-State Chorus, N.J. State Music Tchrs. Assn., 1994, 2006, Mass. Am. Choral Dirs. Assn. Women's Honor Choir, Amherst, Mass., 2003, Cape Cod H.S. Festival, 2005; dir. music, organist Presbyn. Ch. Teaneck, 1995—; presenter Choral Music Workshop, Ghana, 1995; presenter in field. Bd. mem., cons. Bergen County Divsn. Hist. and Cultural Affairs, 2002—; People to People amb. to China, 1998. Recipient Trailblazer award in arts and culture, Nat. Coalition of 100 Black Women, 2005; named Disting. Secondary tchr., Princeton U., 1993. Mem.: NEA (life), Coll. Music Soc., N.J. Music Educators Assn., Am. Choral Dirs. Assn., Am. Orff Schulwerk Assn., Orgn. Am. Kodaly Educators, Music Educators Nat. Conf. (collegiate advisor 2003—), N.J. Am. Choral Dirs. Assn. (Repertoire and Standards chair multicultural 1999—2003, bd. mem.), N.J. Edn. Assn. (life), Alpha Kappa Alpha, Inc. (Women Who Make Difference Arts award 2007). Achievements include participating in Educational and Cultural exchange in Southern Africa. Office: NJ City Univ 2039 Kennedy Blvd Jersey City NJ 07305 Office Phone: 201-200-2158. E-mail: mdlwarren@aol.com.

WARREN, MARIE ANTOINETTE, elementary school educator; b. LA, July 21, 1965; d. Kazmer Anthony Wolkensperg and Janette Mary Hudgins; m. Brian Keith Warren, Sept. 26, 1983; children: Anthony Brian, Brianna Marie. AA, St. Clair County C.C.; BSc in Edn., Ctrl. Mich. U., 1990; MS in Child Devel., Mich. State U., 1995; degree in Ednl. Leadership, Oakland U.; EdS in Adminstrn., 2005. Cert. elem. tchr. Mich., 1990, in administrv. leadership in edn. Mich., 2005. Tchr. elem. sch. Port Huron (Mich.) Area Sch. Dist., 1991—. Mem. bd. edn. Trinity Luth. Sch., Port Huron. Mem.: Am. Youth Soccer Assn. (bd. dirs., child advocate).

WARREN, MICHELLE PALMIERI, internist, endocrinologist; b. NYC, 1939; MD, Cornell U. Med. Coll., 1965. Cert. Internal Medicine with subspecialty in endocrinology and reproductive endocrinology. Intern, medicine Bellevue Hosp. Ctr., NYC, 1965—66, resident, 1966—68; resident, endocrinology Meml. Hosp. Cancer, NYC, 1966—68; fellow Columbia U., Coll. Physicians & Surgeons, 1968—71, asst. prof., 1971—75, assoc. prof. clin. ob/gyn & clin. medicine, 1975—96, prof. ob/gyn & medicine, 1996—; attending St. Luke's Roosevelt Hosp., NYC, 1975; founder, med. dir., Ctr. for Menopause, Hormonal Disorders and Women's Health Columbia U. Med. Ctr., NYC, 1997—, prof. medicine and obstetrics and gynecology, Wyeth Ayerst prof. women. Cons. Wyeth Pharm.; lectr. in field. Contbr. articles to profl. jours., chapters to books; publ;ished a book on sports and hormones. Named Best Doctors in NYC, NY Mag.; named one of Best Doctors In America, 2004—05. Achievements include first to identify skeletal problems, including scoliosis and stress fractures that occur in young women because of menstrual irregularities. Address: Ctr for Menopause Hormonal Disorders and Women's Health Dept Ob/Gyn Columbia U Med Ctr 622 W 168th St PH 16 New York NY 10032 Office: 16 E 60th St Ste 490 New York NY 10022 Office Fax: 212-737-4664, 212-744-9353.

WARREN, NEIL CLARK, Internet company executive, psychologist; b. Iowa, Sept. 18, 1934; m. Marylyn Warren; 3 children. BS in Social Sci., Pepperdine U., 1956; MDiv, Princeton Theological Sem., 1959; PhD in Clin. Psych., U. Chgo., 1967. Asst. prof. Fuller Theological Sem. Grad. Sch. Psych., 1967, dean, 1975—82; pvt. practice Neil Clark Warren & Assocs., 1967—2000; co-founder, chmn. eHarmony, 2000—. Author: Finding the Love of Your Life, 1992, Finding Contentment, 1997, Make Anger Your Ally, 1998, Learning to Live with the Love of Your Life, 1998, The Triumphant Marriage, 1998, God Said It, Don't Sweat It, 1998, Catching the Rhythm of Love, 2000, Falling in Love for All the Right Reasons, 2005; co-author: Love the Life You Live, 2003. Office: eHarmony PO Box 60157 Pasadena CA 91116 Office Phone: 626-795-4814. E-mail: media@neilclarkwarren.com.

WARREN, PAMELA A., psychologist; d. James Herbert Trail, Jr. and Jacqueline Joann Trail; m. Bruce E. Warren, 1982; 1 child, Rachel M. B.A., MA, So. Ill. U., PhD, 1991. Lic. clin. psychologist Ill., 1993. Counselor So. Ill. U., Carbondale, 1986—89, instr., 1989—91; faculty U. Ill. Med. Sch., Dept. Psychiatry, 1994—; clin. supr. Resolutions Employee Assistance Program, Champaign, 1996—2001; faculty U. Ill., Psychology Dept., 2000—; head psychology dept. Carle Clinic Assn., Urbana, 2001—. Faculty SmithKline-Beecham Pharms., 1993—96; mem. work injury network steering com. Carle Clinic Assn., Urbana, 1999—; nat. psychol. cons. Work Injury Network, 1999—; cons. WebilityMD.com, Wayland, Md., 2001—04, Blue Cross Blue Shield Ins., Dallas, 2002—, CompPartners, Irvine, Calif., 2003—; psychol. cons. Ill. State Univs. Retirement Sys., Champaign, 2001—; mem. supported employment com. Disability Mgmt. Employer Coalitions, San Diego, 2002—; mem. complimentary and alternative medicine steering com. Carle Clinic Assn., Urbana, 2003—; adv. bd. Reed Group Med. Disability, Colo., 2004—; mem. adv. bd. Job Demands Project, Disability Rsch. Inst.; presenter in field. Author: The Management of Workplace Mental Health Issues and Appropriate Disability Prevention Strategies, 2005; contbr. articles to profl. jours. and newsletters. Hospice vol. Meml. Hospice, Carbondale, Ill., 1984—91; ticket to work adv. bd. Social Security Adminstrn., 2004—. Scholar, So. Ill. U., 1983—91. Mem.: APA, Disability Mgmt. Employee Coalition, Internat. Assn. Rehabilitation Profls. (bd. mem. Profl. Case Mgmt. sect.), Am. Coll. Occupational & Environ. Medicine (newsletter adv. bd., aadv. com.), Assn. Applied Psychophysiology and Biofeedback, Assn. Behavior Analysis, Prescribing Psychologists' Register (founding mem.), Psi Chi. Achievements include patents for state-of-the-art model to assess and manage psychological concerns in order to prevent psychological disability. Avocations: travel, art, reading, sports. Office: Carle Clinic Assn 602 W Univ E-6 Urbana IL 61801 E-mail: pawarren@mchsi.com.

WARREN, RICHARD, fashion photographer; b. Houston; married; 2 children. BA in Graphic Arts, We. Wash. Univ. Comml. fisherman; photo asst. to Bill King, Helmut Newton, Denis Piel, Robert Mapplethorpe, NYC; profl. photographer Milan, Paris, Sydney; opened photography studio NYC, 1990—. Photographer Italian Bazaar, Australian Vogue, Australian Harpers Bazaar, GQ, Allure, Marie Claire, US Cosmo, Style Monte Carlo, Muse mag., Victim (Italy), Lucire, Italian Cosmo, Greek Cosmo, Australian Cosmo, Nippon Vogue, Self, Mademoiselle, Glamour, French Glamour, Spanish AR, Ocean Drive, Vegas, 944, others. Office: Ste 802 336 W 37th St New York NY 10018 Office Phone: 917-623-5690. Business E-Mail: richard@richardwarrenphotos.com.

WARREN, RICHARD M., experimental psychologist, educator; b. NYC, Apr. 8, 1925; s. Morris and Rae (Greenberg) W.; m. Roslyn Pauker, Mar. 31, 1950. BS in Chemistry, CCNY, 1946; PhD in Organic Chemistry, NYU, 1951. Flavor chemist Gen. Foods Co., Hoboken, N.J., 1951-53; rsch. assoc. psychology Brown U., Providence, 1954-56; Carnegie sr. rsch. fellow NYU Coll. Medicine, 1956-57, Cambridge (Eng.) U., 1957-58, rsch. psychologist applied psychology rsch. unit, 1958-59; rsch. psychologist NIMH, Bethesda, Md., 1959-61; chmn. psychology Shimer Coll., Mt. Carroll, Ill., 1961-64; assoc. prof. psychology U. Wis., Milw., 1964-66, prof., 1966-73, rsch. prof., 1973-75, disting. prof., 1975-95, rsch. prof., disting. prof. emeritus, 1995—. Vis. scientist Inst. Exptl. Psychology, Oxford (Eng.) U., 1969-70, 77-78. Author: (with Roslyn Warren) Helmholtz on Perception: Its Physiology and Development, 1968, Auditory Perception: A New Analysis and Synthesis, 1999; contbr. articles to profl. jours. Fellow APA, Am. Psychol. Soc., Acoustical Soc. Am.; mem. AAAS, Am. Chem. Soc., Am. Speech and Hearing Assn., Sigma Xi. Office: Univ of Wisconsin-Milwaukee Dept Psychology PO Box 413 Milwaukee WI 53201 Office Phone: 414-229-5328. Business E-Mail: rmwarren@uwm.edu.

WARREN, RICHARD WAYNE, obstetrician, gynecologist; b. Puxico, Mo., Nov. 26, 1935; s. Martin R. and Sarah E. (Crump) W.; m. Rosalie J. Franzoia, Aug. 16, 1959; children: Lani Marie, Richard W., Paul D. BA, U. Calif., Berkeley, 1957; MD, Stanford U., Calif., 1961. Diplomate Am. Bd. Ob-Gyn. Intern Oakland Naval Hosp., Calif., 1961-62; resident on ob-gyn. Stanford Med. Ctr., 1964-67; pvt. practice specializing in ob-gyn. Mountain View, Calif., 1967—. Mem. staff Stanford Hosp., El Camino Hosp.; pres. Warren Medical Corp.; assoc. clin. prof. ob-gyn. Stanford Sch. Medicine. Contbr. articles to profl. jours. With USN, 1961-64. Fellow Am. Coll. Ob-Gyn.; mem. AMA, Am. Fertility Soc., Am. Assn. Gynecologic Laparoscopists, Calif. Med. Assn., San Francisco Gynecol. Soc., Peninsula Gynecol. Soc., Assn. Profs. Gynecology and Obstetrics, Royal Soc. Medicine, Shufelt Gynecol. Soc. Santa Clara Valley. Home: 102 Atherton Ave Menlo Park CA 94027-4021 Office: 2500 Hospital Dr Mountain View CA 94040-4106 Office Phone: 650-961-8111. Personal E-mail: warren423@sbcglobal.net.

WARREN, RICK (RICHARD DUANE WARREN), minister, writer; b. San Jose, Calif., Jan. 28, 1954; s. James Russell and Dorothy Nell (Armstrong) Warren; m. Elizabeth Kay Lewis, June 21, 1975; children: Amy Rebecca, Joshua James, Matthew David. BA, Calif. Bapt. Coll., 1977; MDiv, Southwestern Bapt. Theol. Sem., 1979; D in Ministry, Fuller Theol. Sem., 1989. Youth evangelist Calif. So. Bapt. Convention, Fresno, 1970-74; assoc. pastor First Bapt. Ch., Norwalk, Calif., 1974-76; asst. to pres. Internat. Evangelism Assn., Fort Worth, 1977-79; founding pastor Saddleback Valley Cmty. Ch., Mission Viejo, Calif., 1980—; founder Pastors Web site. Host Civil Forum on the Presidency, Lake Forest, Calif., 2008; keynote speaker Martin Luther King, Jr. Ann. Commemorative Svc., 2009. Author: The Purpose-Driven Church, 1995, Personal Bible Study Methods, 1997, The Power to Change Your Life, 1998, Answers to Life's Difficult Questions, 1999, Planned for God's Pleasure, 2002, The Purpose-Driven Life, 2002 (Gold Medallion award, ECPA Book of Yr., 2003), The Emerging Church, 2003, Daily Inspiration for the Purpose-Driven Life, 2004. Named an Outstanding Preacher, McGregor Found., 1977; named one of 15 World Leaders Who Mattered Most in 2004, TIME mag., The World's Most Influential People, 2005, 2008, America's Top 25 Leaders, US News & World Report, 2005, 15 People Who Make America Great, Newsweek, 2006. Baptist. Office: pastors.com 1 Saddleback Pky Lake Forest CA 92630-8700 also: Saddleback Valley Cmty Ch 24194 Alicia Pky Ste M San Juan Capistrano CA 92691-3927*

WARREN, ROBERT STEPHEN, lawyer; b. Pasadena, Calif., Dec. 9, 1931; s. Harry Ludwig and Maxine Winifred (Hopkins) W.; m. Betty Lou Soden, June 11, 1955 (dec. Sept. 1991); children: Kimberly Ann, Stephen Hopkins; m. Anna Marie Pretzel, Dec. 28, 1993. BA in Econs., U. Southern Calif., 1953, LLB, 1956. Bar: Calif. 1956, Del., U.S. Ct. Appeals (9th cir.), U.S. Dist. Ct. (ctrl. dist.) Calif., U.S. Ct. Mil. Appeals, U.S. Dist. Ct. (so. dist.) Calif., U.S. Dist. Ct. (ea. dist.) Calif., U.S. Dist. Ct. (no. dist.) Calif., U.S. Dist. Ct. Wyo., U.S. Dist. Ct. Colo., U.S. Dist. Ct. (ea. dist.) Wash., U.S. Supreme Ct. From assoc. to ptnr. Gibson, Dunn & Crutcher, LA, 1956, 59—. Contbr. articles to profl. jours.; assoc. editor Southern Calif. Law Rev.; speaker in field. Mem., former chair bd. councilors U. So. Calif. Law Ctr.; past pres., exec. com. mem. Western Justice Ctr. Found. 1st lt. US Army, 1957—59. Recipient Learned Hand award Am. Jewish Com., 1988, Shattuck-Price award Los Angeles County Bar Assn., 1989, Joseph A. Ball award Brennan Ctr. for Justice/NYU, 1997, Trial Lawyer Hall of Fame award Calif. State Bar Assn., 1998, Ninth Circuit John P Frank award, 2008. Mem. Am. Coll. Trial Lawyers, Assn. Bus. Trial Lawyers, Order of Coif, Phi Beta Kappa. Republican. Presbyterian. Avocations: hiking, reading, tennis. Office: Gibson Dunn & Crutcher 333 S Grand Ave Ste 4400 Los Angeles CA 90071-3197 Office Phone: 213-229-7326. Business E-Mail: rwarren@gibsondunn.com.

WARREN, RUSSELL FREDERICK, orthopedist; b. Burlington, Vt., June 18, 1939; MD, SUNY, Syracuse, 1966. Bd. cert. orthopedic surgery. Intern St. Lukes Hosp. Ctr., NYC, 1966—68; resident orthopedic surgery Hosp. for Spl. Surgery, NYC, 1970—73, surgeon in chief, 1993—2003, surgeon-in-chief emertius, 2003; fellow in shoulder surgery Columbia Presbyn. Med. Ctr., NYC, 1977; prof. surgery, chmn. divsn. orthopaedic surgery Weill Med. Coll., Cornell U.; physician New York Giants. Editor-in-chief Techniques in Shoulder and Elbow Surgery. Recipient Neer award for shoulder rsch., 1989, 1995, 2005, 2006, O'Donohue award for sports medicine rsch., 1982, 1991, 1994, Humana award for sports medicine, 1992, Mr. Sports Medicine award, Am. Orthopaedic Soc. Sports Medicine, 2003. Mem.: Am. Orthop. Soc. Sports Medicine (pres. 1994—95), Am. Shoulder and Elbow Soc. (pres. 1994—95). Achievements include research in shoulder and knee instability; ligament reconstruction and arthroscopy; joint replacement-knee and shoulder; rotator cuff disease and sports injuries. Mailing: Hosp for Spl Surgery 535 E 70th St New York NY 10021 Office: Belaire Bldg 1st Fl 525 E 71st St New York NY Office Phone: 212-606-1178. Business E-Mail: warrenr@hss.edu.

WARREN, RUSSELL GLEN, educational consultant; b. Balt., Apr. 29, 1942; s. Clarence N. and Kathryn (Butler) W. BBA, U. Richmond, 1964; PhD, Tulane U., 1968. Asst. prof. to assoc. prof. U. Richmond, Va., 1971—74, dean, 1974—76, asst. v.p. to asst. pres., 1976—78; v.p. acad. affairs U. Montevallo, Ala., 1978-84, James Madison U., Harrisonburg, Va., 1984-90, v.p. acad. affairs, acting pres., 1986—87; pres. N.E. Mo. State U., Kirksville, 1990—94; disting. prof. econs., mgmt. Hardin-Simmons U., Abilene, Tex., 1995-97, dir. Ctr. for Rsch. Tchg. and Learning, 1995-97; exec. v.p., provost Mercer U., Macon, Ga., 1997—2002; prof. econs. So. Wesleyan U., 2003—06; pvt. practice cons.; prodost Fla. Southern Coll., 2009—. Chmn. adv. bd. Coll. Humanities, Social Sci. Coll. Charleston, SC, 1999—2007. Author: Antitrust in Theory and Practice, 1976, Carpe Diem, 1995. Bd. dirs. Va. Rural Devel. Corp., Richmond, 1988-90, Am. Coll. Bldg. Arts, 2005—; v.p. Kiawah Island Cmty. Assn., 2006-07, chmn. bd., 2007-08. Capt. US Army, 1969—71. Named One of Outstanding Young Men of Va., Va. Jaycees, 1976. Mem.: Am. Coun. on Edn. (coun. of fellows), Am. Assn. Colls. and Univs. (bd. dirs. 1994—95). Methodist. Avocations: golf, collecting cars. Home and Office: 175 Marsh Island Dr Kiawah Island SC 29455 E-mail: rasswarr@bellsouth.net.

WARREN, STEPHEN MICHAEL, plastic surgeon; m. Constance Marian Chen. MD, UCLA, 1996. Cert. Am. Board Plastic Surgery, NY, 2008. Assoc. prof. plastic surgery NY U. Med. Ctr., 2006—. Office: Inst Reconstructive Plastic Surg 560 First Ave TH-169 New York NY 10016 Business E-Mail: stephen.warren.md@gmail.com.

WARREN, TODD, engineering educator, retired computer company executive; BA in Computer Sci. and Economics with honors, Northwestern U., Evanston, Ill. Product develop. positions through corp. v.p. Microsoft Corp., Redmond, Wash., 1987—2009, gen. mgr. embedded devices group, 2001, corp. v.p. devices, services & eXperiences group, 2004, corp. v.p. gen. embedded bus., corp. v.p. mobile comm. product group, 2007—09, ret., 2009; adj. prof. Northwestern U. McCormick Sch. Engring., 2009—. Office: Northwestern U McCormick Sch Engring 2145 Sheridan Rd Evanston IL 60208-4363

WARREN, WILLIAM BRADFORD, lawyer; b. Boston, July 25, 1934; s. Minton Machado and Sarah Ripley (Robbins) W.; children: John Coolidge, Sarah; m. Arete B. Swartz, Sept. 20, 1985. AB magna cum laude, Harvard U., 1956, LLB cum laude, 1959. Bar: N.Y. 1960. Assoc. Dewey Ballantine, NYC, 1959-68; ptnr. to of counsel Dewey Ballantine, LLP, 1968—. Lectr. Inst. Fed. Taxation, NYU, So. Fed. Tax Inst., Practicing Law Inst. Pres. Cintas Found., N.Y.C.; bd. dirs. St. John's Coll., Annapolis and Santa Fe; bd. dirs. John Carter Brown Libr., Providence; adv. bd. dirs. Met. Opera Assn., N.Y.C. Mem. Am. Law Inst., Am. Coll. Trust and Estate Counsel (former regent), Acad. Am. Poets (bd. dirs., vice chair), Internat. Acad. Estate and Trust Law (former exec. com.), N.Y. State Bar Assn. (chmn. com. taxation of trust and estates sect. 1980-83), Assn. Bar City N.Y., Soc. Mayflower Descs., Harvard Club, Knickerbocker Club, Century Club, Grolier Club (past pres.). Home: 520 E 86th St New York NY 10028-7534 Office: Dewey Ballantine LLP 1301 Avenue Of The Americas New York NY 10019-6022 Home Phone: 212-734-2779; Office Phone: 212-259-8700. Business E-Mail: wwarren@dbllp.com.

WARREN ELLISON, TASHEAYA L., lawyer, director; b. Portland, Oreg., Dec. 28, 1972; d. Johnnie R. and Ella F. Warren; m. Scott R. Ellison, June 21, 2002; 1 child, Thaddeus L. BA, U. of Oreg., 1994, JD, 1997; LLM in Taxation, Georgetown U., 1999. Bar: Calif. 2000, Oreg. 1997, D.C. 2000. Sr. assoc. PricewaterhouseCoopers LLP, Washington, 1999—2001; atty. advisor Assoc. Chief Counsel Internat. to the IRS, Washington, 2001—06; dir., corp. counsel Prudential Fin., Newark, 2006—08; tax attorney Internat. BP America Inc. Mem.: ABA (tax sect.), Nat. Bar Assn. (membership chair Greater Washington Area chpt. women lawyers divsn. 2002—04). Office: Prudential Fin Inc 213 Washington St 8th Fl Newark NJ 07102 Home: 5868 Westheimer Rd Houston TX 77057-5641 Office: Internat BP America Inc 501 Westlake Park Blvd Houston TX 77079

WARRICK, KIMBERLEY KAYE, language and social studies educator; b. Lake Wales, Fla., Apr. 13, 1963; d. Bonnie Dawn and Edward Milo Dunagin (Stepfather); m. Robert Kelly Warrick, Nov. 30, 1986 (div. Apr. 0, 1995); 1 child, Kalegh Rebekah. BA, Capital U., 1989; MA, Ohio State U., 1999. Sch. improvement specialist 1st Dist. RESA, Savannah, Ga., 2009; cert. elem. tchr. Mont., Ohio, learning disablities tchr. Mont., Ohio. Tchr. kindergarten/kindergarten afterschool program Columbus Torah Acad., Ohio, 1990—96, tchr. resource/ESL, 1990—96, tchr. 1st grade, 1990—96; tchr. 6th grade English/Social Studies Groveport Madison Local Schs., Ohio, 1996—2003; tchr. spl. edn. 8th grade Bozeman Pub. Schs., Mont., 2003—05, tchr. spl. edn. 9th grade, 2005—08, curriculum specialist, 2008—; mid. sch. and at-risk curriculum specialist Mont. Off. Pub. Instrn., 2008—. English curriculum com. Bozeman Pub. Schs., Mont., 2004—05; Ind. edn. lead tchr. Social Studies Curriculum Leadership Team, 2006. Facilitator Ctr. for Civic Edn., Bozeman, Mont., 2004—05; del. Mont. Rep. Party State Conv., Big Sky, 2004. Mem.: Phi Delta Kappa (pres. MSU chpt. 2006), Coun. Tchr. Cert. Profl. Develop. (state bd. pub. edn. 2005—), Nat. Coun. for History Edn., Bozeman Edn. Assn. (bldg. rep. 2004—08). Office: 1st Dist RESA 201 West Lee St Brooklet GA 30415 Office Phone: 406-444-0753, 912-842-5000. Office Fax: 406-444-1373. Business E-Mail: kwarrick@fdresa.org.

WARRICK, PAUL DAVID, otolaryngologist; b. May 15, 1972; MD, McMaster U., Hamilton, Ont., 1995—99. Diplomate Am. Bd. Otolaryngology, 2005. Intern dept. surgery U. Toronto, 1999—2000, resident dept. otolaryngology, 2000—04; otolaryngologist Affinity Med. Group, Appleton, Wis., 2004—08. Fellow: ACS, Royal Coll. Surgeons Can., Am. Acad. Otolaryngology-Head and Neck Surgery; mem.: Am. Acad. Otolaryngic Allergy. Achievements include research in vocal tremor. Avocations: golf, baseball, volleyball, stamp collecting/philately. Office: Piedmont Vista ENT Allergy & Sleep Assocs PLLC 1733 Connelly Spring Rd Lenoir NC 28645 Office Phone: 828-728-2188. Office Fax: 828-728-2215. Business E-Mail: pwarrick@piedmontvista.com.

WARRINER, KRISTIN PALMQUIST, retired public school educator; b. Seattle, July 2, 1938; d. Emil Eugene and Ingred Ostrom Palmquist; m. Philip Warriner, May 9, 1997; stepchildren: Elisabeth Warriner Waden, Craig, Matthew;children from previous marriage: Mark Foster Anton, Julie Anton Dunn, Elisabeth Anton McIntyre. BA in Am. Civilization, U. Calif., Berkeley, 1960, PhD in Edn., 1980; MA in Polit. Sci., San Francisco State U., 1974. Cert. secondary edn. tchr. Mills Coll., Calif., 1972. Rschr., adminstr. San Francisco State U., 1981—85; tchr. kindergarten US Navy Sta., Trinidad, West Indies, 1958; rschr., adminstr. Mills Coll. U., Berkeley, 1980—88; tchr. jr. high math. Oakland Pub. Schs., Calif., 1985—87; cons. Calif. Dept. Edn., Sacramento, 1989—2000. Contbr. articles to profl. pubs. Pres. Sac'to chpt. United Nations Assn., Sacramento, 2005—07; dir. vacation ch. sch. St. Paul Luth. Ch., Oakland, Calif., 1973—76; mem. profl. preparation commn. Luth. Ch. Am., Southwest Region, 1980—86. Mem.: Am. Ednl. Rsch. Assn., Am. Polit. Sci. Assn., Phi Beta Kappa. Democrat. Episcopalian. Avocations: politics, history, reading, travel, hiking. Home: 1132 Fremont Way Sacramento CA 95818 Home Phone: 916-443-1367. Personal E-mail: pwarriner@surewest.net.

WARRING, DOUGLAS FRANKLIN, education educator, psychologist; b. Braham, Minn., Aug. 16, 1949; s. Herbert Franklin and Maxine (Anderson) W.; children: Jana, Leah, Andrew. BA, Bethel Coll., St. Paul, 1971; MA in Tchg., Coll. St. Thomas, St. Paul, 1975; PhD, U. Minn., Mpls., 1983. Lic. social studies tchr., secondary sch. prin., Minn. Instr. bus. Inver Hills C.C., Inver Grove Heights, Minn., 1980-83; instr. psychology Concordia Coll., St. Paul, 1983; asst. prof. psychology U. Minn., 1982-84; asst. prof. edn. U. St. Thomas, St. Paul, 1984-90; dir. tchr. edn. Coll. St. Thomas, St. Paul, 1989-90, assoc. dean, 1990-95; prof. in edn. and psychology Univ. St. Thomas, 1996—, dir. continuing edn., 2005—, chair tchr. edn., 2006—. Mem. bd. examiners Nat. Coun. on Accreditation for Tchr. Edn., 1997—, Jour. Critical Issues in Curriculum & Instrn., 1999-2004, Jour. Action in Tchr. Edn., 2000—. Mem. editl. bd.: Internat. Jour. Critical Inquiry into Curriculum and Instrn., 2004—06. Mem. Curriculum Com., Bloomington, Minn., 1985-89; vice chair Planning, Evaluation and Reporting Com., Bloomington, 1985-87, chair, 1988-89. Master sgt. US Army, 1972—96, ret. Named one of Outstanding Young Men of Am., 1985. Mem. ASCD, Am. Assn. Tchr. Edn. (exec. bd., pres. Minn. chpt. 1985, nat. resolutions com. 1988, nat. rsch. com. 1997), Minn. Assn. Tchr. Edn. (exec. bd. 1984-93, pres. 1990-92), Minn. Human Rels. Assn., Internat. Coun. of Edn. for Teaching (life), Internat. Soc. for Tchr. Edn., Am. Legion, Met. Wrestling Ofcls. Assn. (v.p. 1982-86), Minn. Assn. Supervision and Curriculum Devel. (bd. dirs. 1994-2004), Soc. Psychol. Study of Social Issues, World Coun. Curriculum Instrn., Am. Edn. Rsch. Assn. Office: U St Thomas 1000 La Salle Ave Minneapolis MN 55403-2009 Business E-Mail: dfwarring@stthomas.edu.

WARRINGTON, WILLARD GLADE, retired university official; b. Macomb, Ill., Oct. 24, 1920; s. Henry K. and Farie V. (Prather) W.; m. A. Irene Windser, Aug. 9, 1945 (dec. 1969); m. Janette Moffatt Cooper, Apr. 26, 1972; children: David, Steven, Douglas, Jane Ann, Stephen Cooper. B.Ed., Western Ill. State Tchrs. Coll., 1941; MS, U. Ill., 1949, MS, 1950, Ed.D., 1952. Tchr. public high schs., Ill., 1941-42, 45-48; mem. faculty Mich. State U., 1952-58, dir. office evaluation services, 1958-74, asso. dean Univ. Coll., 1974-78, acting dean Univ. Coll., 1978-80, dir. undergrad. univ. div., 1980-85, dir., prof. emeritus, 1986—. Cons. edn.; Ford Found. cons. U. Philippines. Contbr. articles on ednl. measurement to profl. publs.; editorial bd.: Ednl. and Psychol. Measurement, 1968-85. Active Boy Scouts Am., 1957-68. Served to lt. col. USAAF, 1942-45. Mem. Nat. Council on Measurement in Edn. (pres. 1973-74), Am. Ednl. Research Assn., Assn. for Gen. and Liberal Studies (sec.-treas. 1973-79) Methodist. Home: 1312 Glenmeadow Lane East Lansing MI 48823

WARRIOR, DELLA C., academic administrator, art educator; BA in Sociology, Northeastern State U.; MA in Edn., Harvard U. Pres. Inst. Am. Indian Arts, Santa Fe, devel. dir. CEO Otoe-Missouria Tribe, 1989—92; exec. bd. mem. World Indigenous Nations Higher Edn. Consortium; mem. U.S. Pres. Bd. Adv. on Tribal Coll. & U., 2002—.

WARRIOR, PADMASREE Y., computer systems network executive; b. Oct. 22, 1960; m. Mohandas A. Warrior. BSChemE, Indian Inst. Tech., New Delhi, India; MSChemE, Cornell U. Joined Motorola, Inc., Schaumburg, Ill., 1984, v.p., gen. mgr., energy sys. grp., corp. v.p., chief tech. officer, semiconductor products sector, v.p., 1999, corp. officer, 2000, sr. v.p., 2003—05, chief tech. officer, 2003—07, exec. v.p., 2005—07; chief tech. officer Cisco Systems, Inc., San Jose, Calif., 2007—. Gen. mgr. Thoughtbeam, Inc. (subsidiary of Motorola); mem. coun. digital economy Tex. Gov.; mem. rev. panel Tex. Higher Edn. Bd.; dir. Ferro Corp.; mem. exec. bd. CTO Forum. Recipient Women Elevating Sci. and Tech. award, Working Woman Mag., 2001; named one of Top 25 Chief Tech. Officers, InfoWorld mag., 2007, Most Influential Women in Technology, Fast Company, 2009, 50 Women to Watch, The Wall St. Jour., 2008; named to The Women In Tech. Internat. Hall of Fame, 2007. Office: Cisco Systems Inc 170 W Tasman Dr San Jose CA 95134*

WARRO, EDWARD A., library director, dean; MLS, Simmons Coll., 1979. Libr. Simmons Coll., S.W. Tex. State U.; dean librs. Loyola U., Chgo.; dean univ. librs. Northeastern U., 2001—. Bd. mem. Boston Libr. Consortium Inc., New England Libr. Network (NELINET); dir. Ctrl. Libr., Qatar Found., Doha, 2007—. Office: Qatar Found PO Box 5825 Doha Qatar Office Fax: 974-454-0401. Business E-Mail: ewarro@qf.org.qa.

WARSAWER, HAROLD NEWTON, real estate appraiser, consultant; b. NYC; s. Sidney L. and Alice W.; m. Sally Kingsbury; children: Alice Cooper, Nancy Arkuss, Carole Warsawer-Greenblatt. BA, U. Mo.; MBA, Harvard. Property mgr. and real estate broker Sidney L. Warsawer & Son, NYC, 1950—; pres., dir. Consol. Capital, NYC, 1962-68; pres. Atlantic Appraisal Co., Inc., NYC, 1960—96; pres., dir. Contemporary Enterprises, NYC, 1974-76. Mem. editl. bd. The Appraisal Jour., 1970-85. Candidate Teaneck (N.J.) Sch. Bd., Town Coun.; chmn. bldg. com. Temple Emeth, Teaneck, 1954-64; bd. dirs. Friends Teaneck Libr. Capt. air corps. US Army, 1942—46. Mem. Appraisal Inst. (pres. N.Y. chpt. 1977, bd. dirs. 1970-80, 90-92, gov. counselor 1978), Nat. Assn. Rev. Appraisers, Real Estate Bd. N.Y. (chair com.), Nat. Realty Club (pres. 1992, bd. dirs.), Am. Arbitration Assn. Avocations: golf, clocks, library, coin collecting/numismatics. Home: 430 Rutland Ave Teaneck NJ 07666-2823

WARSH, KEVIN MAXWELL, federal official; b. Albany, Apr. 13, 1970; m. Jane Lauder. AB in Pub. Policy, with honors, Stanford U., Calif., 1992; JD cum laude, Harvard U., Cambridge, Mass., 1995. Exec. dir., v.p. mergers & acquisitions, investment banking divsn. Morgan Stanley & Co., Inc., NYC, 1996—2002; spl. asst. to Pres. for econ. policy, exec. sec. Nat. Econ. Coun., Washington, 2002—06; mem. bd. govs. Fed. Res. Sys., Washington, 2006—. Office: Federal Reserve System 20th St & Constitution Ave NW Rm 2010 Washington DC 20551 Home: 3259 N St NW Washington DC 20007-2845 Office Phone: 202-452-3200. Office Fax: 202-452-2271.*

WARSHAW, ALLEN CHARLES, lawyer; b. Harrisburg, Pa., Aug. 27, 1948; s. Julius and Miriam (Nepove) W.; m. Shirley Anne Nes, Aug. 23, 1970; children: Christopher James, Andrew Charles, William Robert. BA, U. Pa., 1970; JD, Villanova U., 1973. Bar: Pa. 1973, U.S. Dist. Ct. (ea. and mid. dists.) Pa. 1974, U.S. Ct. Appeals (3d cir.) 1975, U.S. Supreme Ct. 1977, Calif. 1978. Staff atty. Office Atty. Gen., State of Pa., Harrisburg, 1973-79, chief civil litig., 1979-85, dir. civil law, 1985-86; ptnr. Duane, Morris & Heckscher, Harrisburg, 1986—2002; shareholder Klett, Rooney, Lieber & Schorling, Harrisburg, 2002—06; chief counsel Dept. Pub. Welfare Commonwealth of Pa., 2006—. Past pres. Mechanicsburg Soccer Assn.; Dem. committeeperson Cumberland County; past bd. dirs. Mechanicsburg Area Sch. Dist. Fellow: Am. Bar Found.; mem.:

ABA, FBA, ABA Coun. Appellate Lawyers, Am. Bankruptcy Inst., Pa. Bar Assn., Dauphin County Bar Assn. Home: 1035 Mccormick Rd Mechanicsburg PA 17055-5970 Office: Dept Pub Welfare 7th and Foster Sts Harrisburg PA 17120 Office Phone: 717-783-2800. Business E-Mail: awarshaw@state.pa.us.

WARSHAW, STANLEY IRVING, federal official, consultant; b. Boston, Nov. 5, 1931; s. Alec and Sarah (Laserson) W.; m. Wanda Faye Capino, Feb., 12, 1992; 1 child from previous marriage, Karen Beth. BS in Ceramic Engring, Ga. Tech. Inst., 1957; Sc.D. in Ceramics, M.I.T., 1961; grad., Advanced Mgmt. Program, Harvard Bus. Sch., 1978. Sr. scientist research div. Raytheon Co., Waltham, Mass., 1961-64; with Am. Standard, Inc., New Brunswick, N.J., 1964-75, gen. mgr. engring. and devel., 1972-75; dir. Ctr. for Consumer Product Tech., Nat. Inst. Stds. and Tech. (formerly Nat. Bur. Stds.), Washington, 1975-80, dir. Office Product Standards Policy, 1981-86, assoc. dir., 1987-89, dir. Office Standards Svcs. Gaithersburg, Md., 1989-93; sr. policy advisor for stds. and tech. U.S. Dept. Commerce, Gaithersburg, 1994-99. Served to capt. U.S. Army, 1951-53. Fellow N.Y. Acad. Scis., Washington Acad. Scis. Home: 11783 Haddon Pkwy Boynton Beach FL 33437-1665 E-mail: swarshaw@comcast.net.

WARSHAWSKY, MARK JOEL, public finance and labor economist, former federal policy official; b. Chgo., Mar. 26, 1958; s. Arthur and Dorothy (Chislof) W.; m. Laura Beth Margolis, June 28, 1987; children: David, Hannah, Avi, Sarah. BA, Northwestern U., 1979; PhD, Harvard U., 1984. Actuary Combined Ins., Chgo., 1979-80; rsch. asst. Nat. Bur. Econ. Rsch., Cambridge, Mass., 1981—84; tutor Harvard U., Cambridge, 1983-84; economist Fed. Res. Bd., Washington, 1984-88, dir. Credit Union, 1988—89, sr. economist, 1989—92; sr. economist employee plans and exempt orgns. IRS, 1992—95; dir., strategic and pension rsch. Teachers Ins. & Annuity Assoc. Coll. Retirement Equity Fund, NYC, 1995—98; dir rsch. Teachers Ins. & Annuity Assoc. Coll. Retirement Equity Fund Inst., NYC, 1998—2001; dep. asst. sec. for econ. policy & microeconomic analysis US Dept. Treasury, Washington, 2002—04, asst. sec. for econ. policy, 2004—06; dir. retirement rsch. Watson Wyatt Worldwide, Inc., Arlington, Va., 2006—. Mem. Social Security Adv. Bd., 2006—. Contbr. dozens articles to profl. jours; author/editor several books. Trustee Actuarial Found., 2000—02. Sloan scholar Harvard U., 1983-84; recipient Brit. Inst. Actuaries prize, 2002. Mem. Am. Econ. Assn., Am. Risk and Ins. Assn., Nat. Assn. Bus. Economists. Republican. Jewish. Office: Watson Wyatt Worldwide Inc 901 N Glebe Rd Arlington VA 22203 Business E-Mail: mark.warshawsky@watsonwyatt.com.

WARTELL, SARAH ROSEN, think-tank executive; b. NYC, Dec. 22, 1961; d. Edward Arthur and Barbara Behrens Rosen. AB, Princeton U., 1983; JD, Yale U., 1988. Coord. analyst NY State Organized Crime Task Force, White Plains, 1983-85; assoc. Arnold & Porter, Washington, 1988-93; spl. asst. to FHA commr. US Dept. Housing & Urban Devel. Fed. Housing Adminstrn., Washington, 1993-96, deputy asst. sec. ops., 1996-97, assoc. gen. deputy asst. sec., 1997-98; sr. advisor Nat. Econ. Coun., White House, Washington, 1998-2000, spl. asst. to pres., 2000, dep. asst. to pres., 2000-01; gen. counsel Ctr. for Am. Progress, Washington, exec. v.p. Mgmt. of Am. Progress, acting CEO, 2008—. Adj. prof. law and tech. policy Georgetown U. Law Ctr. Avocation: tennis. Office: Ctr for Am Progress 1333 H St NW 10th Fl Washington DC 20005 Office Phone: 202-682-1611. E-mail: sarah_wartell@hotmail.com.*

WARTERS, T. ALISSA, political science professor, director; BA in Polit. Sci., Va. Tech, Blacksburg, 1996, MA in Polit. Sci., 1998; PhD in Polit. Sci., U. Tenn., Knoxville, 2004. Instr. polit. sci. High Point U., NC, 1999—2000; tchg. assoc. polit. sci. U. Tenn., Knoxville, 2000—04; asst. prof. polit. sci. Francis Marion U., Florence, SC, 2004—, dir. mcnair ctr. govt. and history, 2007—. Contbr. articles. Recipient Profl. Svc. Excellence award, Francis Marion U., 2008. Mem.: SC Polit. Sci. Assn., Midwest Polit. Sci. Assn., Am. Polit. Sci. Assn. Office: Francis Marion Univ 4822 Palmetto St Florence SC 29502

WARTH, JAMES ARTHUR, physician, researcher; b. NYC, Apr. 30, 1942; s. Peter and Anne Warth; m. Maria Archer Russell, May 3, 1969; children: David M., Andrew A. BS, Tufts U., 1963, MD, 1967. Diplomate Am. Bd. Internal Medicine, Am. Bd. Hematology, Am. Bd. Oncology. Hematologist Harvard Health Svc. Harvard U., Cambridge, Mass., 1976—77, officer, 1976—77; attending hematologist Harper Grace Hosp., Detroit, 1977—84; asst. prof. medicine Wayne State U., Detroit, 1977—84; rsch. scientist New Eng. Med. Ctr., Boston, 1984—86; attending hematologist, oncologist Faulkner Hosp., Boston, 1986—; asst. prof. medicine Tufts U. Sch. Medicine, Boston, 1986—, course dir. phys. diagnosis Faulkner Hosp., 1992—, assoc. course dir. phys. diagnosis, 1996; dir. dept. medicine, physician asst. program Faulkner Hosp., Boston, 1996—97, course dir., 2001—06; lectr. medicine Harvard Med. Sch., Boston, 2000—, patient Dr. II, 2001—06, sect. leader, tutor hematologic pathophysiology, 2004—. Guest appearance NBC affiliate NBC News, Detroit, 1980; cons. in hematology NIH, Bethesda, Md., 1980—83, 1987, rsch. lectr., NY, 86; invited lectr. Columbia U., 1982, Harvard U., 1984, SUNY, Syracuse, 1991, New Eng. Med. Ctr., Tufts Univ., 1992, Northwestern U., 2004, Brigham and Women's Hosp., 2004; vis. prof. Yale Univ., New Haven, 1986; faculty advisor Tufts U. Sch. Medicine, 1991—98; cons. in hematology Mass. Profl. Rev. Orgn., Waltham, 1991—93, Medfield State Hosp., Mass., 1993—99; Max Millman meml. lectr. in medicine Bay State Med. Ctr., Tufts U., Springfield, Mass., 2000; bd. dirs. Faulkner Physicians Assn., Inc., Boston, 1994—; mem. melanoma adv. bd. N.E. region Schering Plough Co., Kenilworth, NJ, 1995. Contbg. author: textbook Hematologic Disorders in Maternal-Fetal Medicine, 1990, reviewer: Am. Jour. Hematology, 1986, Jour. Andrology, 1990—92; contbr. articles to profl. jours. Preceptor Nat. Youth Forum, 1996—98. Maj. US Army, 1969—71. Recipient Mark Aisner M.D. Award for Excellence in Tchg. Physical Diagnosis, Tufts Univ. Sch. Medicine, 2001; named to Guide to America's Top Physicians, Consumer Rsch. Council of America, 2003, 2005; Spl. Fellow, NIH, 1974—76, rsch. grantee, 1980—83, 1983—86. Fellow: ACP; mem.: Bio-Membranes Sickle Cell Rsch. Group, Am. Fedn. Med. Rsch., Am. Soc. Hematology. Achievements include discovery of new human red blood cell, sequestrocyte accepted into Am. Soc. Hematology slide bank, 1995 and received in Textbooks of Hematology. Avocations: art, music, architecture, tennis. Office: Faulkner Hosp 1153 Centre St Rm 5950 Boston MA 02130-3446 Office Phone: 617-739-7776. Business E-Mail: james_warth@hms.harvard.edu.

WARTHEN, HARRY JUSTICE, III, lawyer; b. Richmond, Va., July 8, 1939; s. Harry Justice Jr. and Martha Winston (Alsop) W.; m. Sally Berkeley Trapnell, Sept. 7, 1968; children: Martha Alsop, William Trapnell. BA, U. Va., 1961, LLB, 1967. Bar: Va. 1967, U.S. Ct. Appeals (4th cir.) 1967, U.S. Dist. Ct. (ea. dist.) Va. 1969. Law clk. to judge US Ct. Appeals (4th cir.), Richmond, Va., 1967-68; assoc. Hunton & Williams, Richmond, 1968—2005, sr. counsel, 2005—. Lectr. in field U. Va. Law Sch., Charlottesville, 1975—77. Trustee exec. com. Hist. Richmond Found., 1986-95, 96—, pres., 2000-02; trustee Woodrow Wilson Presdl. Libr., 1997-2003, 05—; dir. exec. com. Preservation Alliance of Va. (now part of APVA Preservation Va.), 1991-97, pres., 1994-96; Va. rep. bd. advisors The Nat. Trust for Historic Preservation, 2003—; dir. The Corp. for Thomas Jefferson's Poplar Forest, 2005—; elder, trustee endowment fund Grace Covenant Presbyn. Ch.; moderator Hanover Presbytery, Presbyn. Ch. (USA), 1988. Lt. US Army, 1962—64. Fellow Am. Coll. Trust and Estate Counsel, Va. Law Found.; mem. Va. Bar Assn. (chmn. sect. on wills, trusts and estates 1981-89), Antiquarian Soc. Richmond (pres. 1977-78, 98-99), Country Club Va., Deep Run Hunt Club. Home: 1319 Shallow Well Rd Manakin Sabot VA 23103-2305 Office: Hunton & Williams Riverfront Plz E Tower 951 E Byrd St Richmond VA 23219 Home Phone: 804-784-5245; Office Phone: 804-788-8414. Business E-Mail: hwarthen@hunton.com.

WARTMAN, STEVEN A., medical association administrator; Grad., Cornell U., 1966; MD, Johns Hopkins U., 1970, PhD Sociology, 1979. Diplomate Am. Bd. Internal Medicine. Dir. med. svs., chmn. medicine Mount Sinai Med. Ctr., Miami Beach; prof. medicine U. Miami; sr. residency in internal medicine Baltimore City Hosp.; intern in internal medicine Stanford U. Med. Ctr.; resident in internal medicine Yale-New Haven Hosp.; prof. medicine Albert Einstein Coll. Medicine; physician-in-chief L.I. Jewish Med. Ctr.; with Edward Meilman Disting. Chair Medicine; dir. Ctr. Quality Rsch. North Shore-L.I. Jewish Health Sys.; dean U. Tex. Med. Sch. San Antonio, 2000—05; pres. Assn. Acad. Health Centers, Washington, 2005—. Contbr. more than 120 peer-reviewed jour. articles, abstracts, chapters to books. Recipient Leadership and Achievement award, Soc. Gen. Internal Medicine, 1997, Excellence award, U.S. Health Resources and Svcs. Adminstrn., 1999; fellow Internat. in Health Care, Yugoslavia, 1969, Primary Care Policy, USPHS, 1991; scholar Henry Luce, Indonesia, 1975—76, Robert Wood Johnson Clin., Johns Hopkins U., 1976—78. Fellow: ACP; mem.: Alpha Omega Alpha, Phi Beta Kappa. Office: Assn Academic Health Centers Ste 720 1400 Sixteenth St NW Washington DC 20036

WARTMANN, MICHAEL RUDI, chemical engineer, researcher; b. Nuertingen, Baden-Wuerttemberg, Germany, Jan. 2, 1980; s. Rudi and Monika Wartmann; m. Mangala Srinivas. Diploma in Engring., U. Stuttgart, 2005. Rschr. Carnegie Mellon U., Pitts., 2006—. Pres. Carnegie Mellon Tennis Club, Pitts., 2008—. Fellowship, Ernest Solvay Found., 2005. Mem.: Soc. Petroleum Engring., Am. Inst. Chem. Engring., Verein Deutscher Engr., Sigma Xi. Office: Carnegie Mellon Univ 5000 Forbes Ave Pittsburgh PA 15213 Business E-Mail: wartmann@cmu.edu.

WARWICK, MARGARET ANN, retired health science facility administrator, consultant; b. Camden, NJ, June 7, 1931; d. Ralph Arthur and Margaret Wilson (Dilworth) W. BS, Fairleigh Dickinson U., 1955. Staff mem., med. tech. Jefferson Med. Coll. Hosp., Phila., 1955—61; clin. chemist West Jersey Health System, Camden, NJ, 1961—68, lab. supr. Voorhees, 1968—80, mgr. clin. lab. services, 1980—85, quality assurance mgr. clin. lab svcs., 1985—96; founder, pres. Clin. Lab. Cons. Services, Inc., Cherry Hill, 1985—96; ret., 1996. Mem. faculty chemist dept. Harcum Jr. Coll., Bryn Mawr, Pa., 1958-64; ednl. coordinator West Jersey Hosp. Sch. of Med. Tech., Voorhees, 1963-81. Vice pres. Wilderness Acres Civic Assn., Cherry Hill, 1980-81; chmn. com. Respond Inc. at Asbury United Meth. Ch., Camden, 1985-94, trustee, 1984-93. Mem. Am. Assn. for Clin. Chemists (secret treas. 1966-70, chmn. elect 1971-72, chmn. 1972-73 Phila chpt.), Clin. Lab Mgmt. Assn., Am. Soc. of Clin. Pathologist, Am. Soc. for Med. Tech., N.J. Soc. for Med. Tech. (bd. dirs. 1978-79). Republican. Methodist. Avocations: golf, boating.

WARWICK, PAUL C., oil industry executive; b. Eng. MS, Cranfield Inst. Tech., Eng., 1978. Cert. chartered engr. 1981. Various large capital projects/ops. positions ConocoPhillips Co., Eng., Norway, 1981—97, mng. dir. Phoenix Park Gas Processors Ltd. Trinidad, West Indies, 1997—99, pres., CEO Gulfstream Resources Canada Ltd., 1999, pres., mng. dir. Conoco Energy Nigeria, 1999—2001, pres., CEO Gulf Indonesia Resources Ltd., 2001—02, pres. ConocoPhillips Indonesia, 2002—04, pres. Europe/West Africa upstream ops. Norway, 2004—. Past v.p. Am. C. of C. Trinidad & Tobago; past pres. Indonesian Petroleum Assn.; apptd. mem. World Bus. Coun. Sustainable Devel., 2007. Office: ConocoPhillips Norway PO Box 220 N 4098 Tananger Norway Office Phone: 47 52 02 0000.*

WARWICK, RANDALL JAMES, biology professor, writer; b. San Francisco, Calif., June 30, 1951; s. Franklin Waldo and Patricia Doyle Warwick; m. Alicia Barrera, Jan. 19, 1965; 1 child, Nigel Tristan. AS, San Francisco City Coll., CA, 1973; AB, U. Calif., Berkeley, 1975; MS, U. Calif., LA, 1981. Clk. Alexander and Alexander, Inc., San Francisco, 1967—69; anatomist Nat. Neurol. Rsch. Specimen Bank (West LA VA Brain Bank), 1975—98; quality control lab supr. Calif. Lab. Industries (Cal Labs), North Hollywood, Calif., 1982—83; quality assurance supr. Am. Hosp. Supply Corp, Am. Optics Divsn., Inglewood, Calif., 1983—84; quality engr. Pacific Optical Divsn. of Recon Optics, Torrance, Calif., 1984—89; quality assurance manger, dir. of quality Pearce Structures Inc., Chatsworth, Calif., 1989—91; adj. instr., anatomy Santa Monica Coll., Calif., 1984—92; prof. biology Coastline C.C., Fountain Valley, Calif., 1991—. Author textbook, co-author peer-reviewed neuroscience rsch. articles. Academic senator Coastline Coll. Academic Senate, Fountain Valley, Calif., 1992—2008. Recipient First prize, So. Cal Soc. Electron Microscopy, 1981, Outstanding Svc. award, West LA Veterans Adminstrn. Med. Ctr., 1985; scholar Cell Molecular Biology Tng. grant, NIH, 1977, 1978, 1979, 1980. Mem.: Am. Soc. Quality Control, Faculty Assn. Calif. Cmty. Coll. Avocations: architecture, gardening, music. Office: Coastline Community Coll 11460 Warner Ave Fountain Valley CA 92708 Business E-Mail: rwarwick@coastline.edu.

WARWICK, SHELLY, library director, researcher; b. Hartford, Conn., May 26, 1940; d. Nathan Hillman and Lillian Hillman nee Leibert. BFA, U. Conn., Storrs; PhD, Rutgers U., East Brunswick, NJ; MLS, Queens Coll., NY. Dir., Leon Ginzburg libr. Beth Israel Hosp., NYC, 1990—91; dir., Russell Hibbs meml. libr. Columbia Presbyn. Hosp., NYC, 1990—91; asst. prof., media libr. Baruch Coll., CUNY, NYC; asst. prof. GSLIS, Queens Coll., CUNY, NYC; dir. libr. svcs. Hastings Ctr., Garrison, NY; dir. libr. svcs., assoc. prof. Touro Coll. Osteo. Medicine, NYC. Dep. sig cabinet dir., bd. dirs. Am. Soc. Info. Sci. and Tech. Contbr. articles to profl. jours. Treas. NYC LWV, NYC, 2000—01; sec. BAMRA, NYC. Mem.: ALA (mem., intellectual property subcom. 1999—2003), ASIST (chair, metro NY chpt. 1993—94, chair, SIG TIS 2000—03, chair, SIG IFP 2006—08, dep. SIG cabinet dir. 2007—09). Avocations: travel, meditation, theater, yoga.

WARWICK, TANYA C., neurologist, educator, researcher; BS in Chemistry, W.Va. State U., Institute, 1996; MD, Marshall U. Sch. Medicine, Huntington, W.Va., 2000. Bd. cert. adult neurology Am. Bd. Psychiatry and Neurology, 2004, bd. cert. vascular neurology Am. Bd. Psychiatry and Neurology, 2004, cert. neurosonologist Am. Soc. Neuroimaging, 2005. Resident adult neurology Vanderbuilt U., Nashville, 2001—04; asst. prof. neurology W.Va. U., Charleston, 2004—06; asst. clin. prof. neurology U. Calif. San Francisco, Fresno, 2006—; med. dir. stroke svcs. Cmty. Regional Med. Ctr., 2006—. Bd. mem. Am. Heart Assn., Fresno, 2006—. Contbr. articles to profl. jours. Named one of Fresno's Best Drs., 2007. Mem.: AMA (assoc.), Am. Acad. Neurology (assoc.), Am. Stroke Assn. (assoc.). Office: 2828 Fresno St Fresno CA 93721

WAS, CHRISTOPHER A., psychology professor; s. Richard and Mary Was; m. Kyrstn Was. PhD, U. Utah, Salt Lake City. Asst. prof. ednl. psychology Kent State U., Ohio, 2005—. Office: Kent State Univ 405 White Hall Kent OH 44242

WASAN, DARSH TILAKCHAND, academic administrator, chemical engineer, educator; b. Sarai, Salah, West Pakistan, July 15, 1938; came to U.S., 1957, naturalized, 1974; s. Tilakchand Gokalchand and Ishari Devi (Obhan) W.; m. Usha Kapur, Aug. 21, 1966; children: Ajay, Kern. BSChemE, U. Ill., 1960; PhD, U. Calif., Berkeley, 1965. Asst. prof. chem. engring. Ill. Inst. Tech., Chgo., 1964-67, assoc. prof., 1967-70, prof., 1970—, chmn. dept., 1971-77, 78-87, acting dean, 1977-78, 87-88, v.p. rsch. and tech., 1988-91, provost, 1991—95, provost and sr. v.p., 1995-96, v.p., internat. and Motorola chair, 1996—. Cons. Inst. Gas Tech., 1965-70, Chgo. Bridge & Iron Co., 1967-71, Ill. EPA, 1971-72, NSF, 1971, 78-79, 87-89, Nelson Industries, 1976—, B.F. Goodrich Chem. Co., 1976-78, Exxon Rsch. & Engring. Co., 1977-89, Stauffer Chem. Co., 1980-88, ICI Ams., 1988-92, Westinghouse Savannah River Co., 1995-2004, Monsanto, 1999-2004, Dow Chem., 2006-07; Procter & Gamble lectr. U. Cin, lectr. U. Southern Calif., 2008 Editor-in-chief Jour. colloid and Interface sci.; mem. publs. bd. Chem. Engring. Edn. Jour.; mem. adv. bd. Jour. Separations Tech., Current Opinion in Colloid and Interface Sci., Jour. of Dispersion Sci. and Tech.; contbr. articles to profl. jours. Recipient ITT Excellence in Tchg. award, 1967, Donald Gage Stevens Disting. Lectureship award Syracuse U., 1991, Jakob J. Bikerman Lectureship award Case Western U., 1994, Robert Gilpin Lectr. award Clarkson U., 1995, MacMoran Disting. Lectureship award Tulane U., 1996, Sidney Ross lectr. award, 1996, Bonnet Dodge Disting. Lectureship award Yale U., 1998, Dinesh O. Shah Lectureship award U. Fla., 2004, Norman N. Li Disting. Lectureship award Wayne State U., 2005, Bird-Stewart-Lightfoot Lectureship award U. Wis., 2007, L. T. Fan Lecturship, Kansas State U., 2008; Spl. citation U.S. FDA, 2000, Lyman Handy Lectureship award, U. Southern Calif., 2008. Fellow AIChE (Ernest Thiele award 1989, Thomas Baron award in fluid-particle systems 2002, Alpha Chi Sigma award for chem. engring. rsch. 2005); mem. AAAS, NAE, Indian NAE, Am. Chem. Soc. (award in colloid chemistry 2000, Langmuir Lectureship award 2004), Am. Soc. Engring. Edn. (Western Electric award 1972, 3M Lectureship award chem. engring. divsn. 1991), Fine Particles Soc. (pres. 1976-77, Hausner award 1982). Home: 8705 Royal Swan Ln Darien IL 60561-8433 Office: Ill Inst Tech 3300 S Federal St Chicago IL 60616-3793 Office Phone: 630-985-8180. Business E-Mail: wasan@iit.edu.

WASDEN, LAWRENCE, state attorney general; m. Tracey Wasden; children: Sean, Ashley, Cassidy, Blake. BA, Brigham Young U., 1982; JD, U. Idaho, 1985. Bar: Idaho 1985. Dep. pros. atty. Canyon County, Idaho; dep. atty. gen. Idaho State Tax Commn.; dep. chief of staff State of Idaho, Boise, chief of staff to atty. gen., atty. gen., 2003—. Mem.: Idaho State Bar (founding mem., immediate past chmn. govt. and pub. lawyers sect.). Republican. Office: Office Atty Gen PO Box 83720 700 W Jefferson St Boise ID 83720 Office Phone: 208-334-2400.*

WASFI, SADIQ HASSAN, chemistry professor; b. Basrah, Iraq, July 1, 1936; established residency in the U.S., 1978; s. Hassan Mohammed and Seniye (Omar) W.; m. Ellen Olivia Schwarz, Nov. 15, 1968; children: Yasmine, Dahlia, Ammar. BS in Chemistry Edn., Baghdad U., Iraq, 1961; MS in Analytical Chemistry, Georgetown U., 1966, PhD in Inorganic Chemistry, 1971. Lectr. chemistry Basrah U., 1971-77; rsch. assoc. U. Hawaii, Honolulu, 1975-76, Georgetown U., Washington, 1977-78; assoc. prof. Montgomery Coll., Takoma Park, Md., 1978-79; prof. chemistry Del. State U., Dover, 1979—. Vis. assoc. prof. Georgetown U., 1980, 81; mng. editor Frontiers in Bio-Sci., 2003. Contbr. articles to profl. jours; patent in antimony oxometalate complexes having anti-viral activity, 1991. Mem. Am. Chem. Soc., Sigma Xi. Muslim. Home: 286 Pine Valley Rd Dover DE 19904-7111 Office: Del State Univ Dept Chemistry 1200 N Dupont Hwy Dover DE 19901-2202

WASHBURN, ANNE, playwright; Assoc. artist 13P, The Civilians, New Georges; mem. New Dramatists. Author: (plays) The Communist Dracula Pageant, 2000, Apparition, 2002, The Internationalist, 2003, The Ladies, 2003, Orestes, 2005, October/November, 2008. Fellow John Simon Guggenheim Meml. Found., 2009. Office: c/o Val Day William Morris Agy 1325 Ave of the Americas New York NY 10019 Office Phone: 212-903-1192. E-mail: vday@wma.com.*

WASHBURN, CAROLYN K., editor-in-chief; b. 1963; m. Perry Washburn; 3 children. Grad., Ind. U. Bus. reporter Lansing State Jour., Mich., 1984—87; bus. reporter, bus. editor, asst. mng. editor news, metro editor Rochester (NY) Democrat & Chronicle, 1987—93, mng. editor, 1995—99, Idaho Statesman, Boise, 1993—95, exec. editor, 1999—2005; v.p., editor Des Moines Register, 2005—. Recipient Pres.'s ring, Gannett Co., Inc., 2001. Mem.: Am. Soc. Newspaper Editors. Office: Des Moines Register PO Box 957 Des Moines IA 50306-0957 also: Des Moines Register 715 Locust St Des Moines IA 50309 Office Phone: 515-284-8502. E-mail: cwashburn@dmreg.com.

WASHBURN, DONALD ARTHUR, retired business executive, investor; b. Mankato, Minn., Sept. 24, 1944; s. Donald and Geraldine Helen (Pint) W.; m. Christine Carvell, Aug. 24, 1968; children: Timothy, Abigail. BBA cum laude, Loyola U., Chgo., 1971; MBA, Northwestern U., 1973, JD cum laude, 1978. Bar: Ill. 1978. With prodn. mgmt. dept. J.T. Ryerson/Inland Steel, Chgo., 1963-68; asst. to the pres. G.B. Frank, Inc., 1969-70; cons. Intec, Inc., 1970-72; mktg. mgmt., atty. Quaker Oats, Co., 1972-79; sr. cons. Booz, Allen & Hamilton, 1979-80; from corp. v.p. to exec. v.p. Marriott Corp., Washington, 1980-90; sr. v.p. N.W. Airlines, Mpls., 1990-94, exec. v.p., 1994-98; pres. chmn. N.W. Cargo, 1997—98; chmn. N.W. Aerospace Tng. Corp., 1996—98. Bd. dirs. LaSalle Hotel Properties, Greenbrier Cos., Inc., Key Tech., Inc., Amedisys, Inc., Draper & Kramer, Inc., LAI Co., Inc., Splty. Mfg., Inc.; law bd. Northwestern U., alumni adv. coun. Kellogg Grad. Sch.; adv. bd. Spell Capital Ptnrs. Fund II, LP. Contbr. articles to profl. jours. Mem. nat. bd. dirs. Friends of the Children; bd. dirs. Portland Citizens Crime Commn., Citizens Commn. on Homeless, Oreg. Bus. Assn.; dir. emeritus Childrens Cancer Rsch. Fund; chmn. nat. bd. Stand for Children. Mem.: ABA, Ill. Bar Assn., Alpha Sigma Nu, Beta Gamma Sigma. Unitarian Universalist.

WASHBURN, ERIC, lobbyist; m. Robin Washburn; 2 children. BS in Psychobiology, Bowdoin Coll.; MS in Forest Sci., Yale U. Cons. Natural Resources Defense Coun. (NRDC), Natural Resources Coun. of Maine (NRCM), Congl. Office of Tech. Assessment; legis. asst. energy and environ. issues to Senator Tom Daschle, sr. policy advisor, 2001—03; Dem. staff dir. Environ. and Pub. Works (EPW) Com., US Senate; sr. pub. policy advisor Baker, Donelson, Bearman, Caldwell, and Berkowitz; prin. BlueWater Strategies LLC, 2007—. Counsel Nat. Commn. on

Energy Policy, Bipartisan Policy Ctr., Am. Coalition for Ethanol. Office: BlueWater Strategies LLC 400 N Capitol St, NW Ste 475 Washington DC 20001 Office Phone: 202-589-0015. Office Fax: 202-589-1516.*

WASHBURN, GLADYS HAASE, retired church musician, educator, director; b. San Antonio, Feb. 19, 1919; d. Henry August and Rosa Sophie (Sundermeyer) Haase; m. Jost Brainard Washburn, Dec. 29, 1942 (dec.); children: Yvonne Rosalind, Henry Brainard, Diane Louise. Tchg. cert. in piano/organ, St. Louis Coll. Music, 1940. Cert. piano St. Louis Coll. Music, 1940. Ch. pianist Friedens Evang. Ch., 1932—38; organist, choir dir. St. Martin's Ch., High Ridge, Mo., 1939—40; choir dir. Bethany Evang. and Ref. Ch., San Antonio, 1940—42, organist, choir dir. New Orleans, 1952—55, St. Paul's Evang. and Ref. Ch., Corpus Christi, Tex., 1944—51, Bethlehem United Ch. of Christ, Buffalo, 1964—70, First Congl. United Ch. of Christ, Dwight, Ill., 1970—72, St. Michael's Episcopal Ch., Independence, Mo., 1985—92; dir. jr. choir Bethlehem Evang. and Ref. Ch., Buffalo, 1956—61; interim organist, choir dir. St. Paul's and St. Marks Ch., Buffalo, 1963, Village United Ch. of Christ, Blue Springs, Mo., 1992—93; interim organist chs. Greater Kansas City area, 1993—97; ret., 1997. Cons. chs. seeking organists, Buffalo, Blue Springs, Mo. Organ recitalist S.W. Conf. Nat. PTA Meeting, San Antonio, 1941, 1942; accompanist Harlandale Sch. Dist., San Antonio, 1941, 1942. Recipient Cert. in Ministry in Music, United Ch. Christ, 1992. Mem.: Am. Guild Organists. Republican. United Ch. Of Christ. Avocations: sewing, cooking, reading. Home: 300 SW 19th Terr Blue Springs MO 64015

WASHBURN, JARROD, professional baseball player; b. LaCrosse, Wis., Aug. 13, 1974; Attended, U. Wis., Oshkosh. Pitcher Anaheim Angels, Calif., 1998—2004, LA Angels of Anaheim, 2005, Seattle Mariners, 2006—09, Detroit Tigers, 2009—. Achievements include member of the World Series championship winning Anaheim Angels, 2002. Office: Detroit Tigers 2100 Woodward Ave Detroit MI 48201*

WASHBURN, JERRY MARTIN, accountant, corporate executive; b. Powell, Wyo., Dec. 31, 1943; s. Roland and Lavon (Martin) W.; divorced; children: Garth, Gavin, Kristina; m. Mary Scatterday. BS in Acctg., Brigham Young U., 1969. CPA, Wash., Idaho, Oreg. Staff acct. Arthur Andersen & Co., Seattle, 1969-70, from sr. auditor to audit mgr. Boise, Idaho, 1971—79; v.p. contr. Washburn Musicland, Inc., Phoenix, 1980-82; mgr., ptnr. Washburn Enterprises, Phoenix, 1977-90; pres. Total Info. Systems, Inc., Phoenix, 1984-90; v.p. KJ Mktg., Inc., Phoenix, 1990-91; dir. mktg. IPRO, Inc., Phoenix, 1991-94; assoc. Perfect Strategies, Inc., Phoenix, 1994—95; v.p., CFO Global Indsl. Products, Inc., Scottsdale, Ariz., 1995—96. Pres., CEO OneSource Techs., Inc., Scottsdale, 1996-2002, dir., chmn. 1999; ptnr. Tatum Ptnrs. LLP, 2002—; mng. mem. Ptnrs. Resource Mgmt., LLC, 2003-05; v.p., CFO Blue Sun Biodiesel, Inc., 2007; founding dir. Internat. and Commerce Bank, Phoenix, 1985-86; chmn. audit com. 1source Techs., 2000-03, AmeriFirst Found., 2004; bd. dirs. Emissions Tech. Inc., 2007-. Mem. AICPA, Inst. Internat. Auditors (pres. Boise chpt. 1974, bd. dirs. Boise and Portland chpts. 1975-77), Am. Mgmt. Soc., Wash. Soc. CPAs, Idaho Soc. CPAs. Independent. Office: Tatum Partners LLP PO Box 25881 4800 N Scottsdale Rd Scottsdale AZ 85255 Personal E-mail: washburn3@cox.net. Business E-Mail: jerry.washburn@tatumpartners.com.

WASHBURN, JOAN THOMAS, small business owner; b. NYC, Dec. 26, 1929; d. Frank B. and Josephine (Hartman) Thomas; m. Alan Lindsay Washburn, Sept. 26, 1953; children: Brian, Susan. BA, Middlebury Coll., Vt., 1951. Asst. Kraushaar Gallery, NYC, 1951—53; dir. pub. rels. Wadsworth Atheneum, Hartford, Conn., 1953—55; dir. contemporary art Graham Gallery, NYC, 1955—67; asst. Cordier-Ekstrom Gallery, NYC, 1967—69; dir. Am. painting dept. Sotheby Parke-Bernet, NYC, 1973—75; pres., dir. Washburn Gallery, NYC, 1971—. Mem. Art Dealers Assn. America Home: 20 W 57th St New York NY 10019-3917 Office Phone: 212-397-6780.

WASHBURN, JOHN ROSSER, entrepreneur; b. Hopewell, Va., July 24, 1943; s. Winthrop Doane and Mary Virginia (Overstreet) W.; m. Rebecca m. Wells, Sept. 1991; 1 child, Amanda Ashley Washburn; stepchildren: Eric Joseph Harrison, Leo M. Cicone, Suzann R. Weldon. Student, Louisburg Jr. Coll., 1963-64, U. Richmond Ext., 1967-69, Williams Coll., 1985, Stanford U., 1986-87. Asst. mgr. Liberty Loan Corp., Richmond, Va., 1965-67; loan interviewer Ctrl. Fidelity Bank, Richmond, Va., 1967-69; regional credit/sales supr. Moores Bldg Supplies, Inc., Roanoke, Va., 1969-74; corp. credit mgt. Owens & Minor, Inc., Richmond, 1974-88; fin., investment cons. JA-GO Enterprises, Richmond, 1982-98; prin. agt., owner Washburn Ins. and Fin. Svcs. Group, Richmond, 1996—2005. Instr., lectr. investment fin., credit mgmt. Washburn Enterprises, 1970—; sec.-treas. Multi-Enterprises, Inc., Richmond, 1988-98; ind. agt. N.Y. Life Ins. Co., Richmond, 1994-98; dir., v.p. Forbes Clin. Rsch. Group, Richmond, 1995-2005; exec. sr. v.p. E-Com Cons., Inc., Richmond, 1998—; charter mem., ptnr. Nations Bus. Cons. Group, Tysons Corner, Va., 1998-2003; pres., CEO Washburn & Assocs., 2003—; sr. v.p. Am. Wellness Alliance Immune Health Mgmt. Group LLC, 2005—; bd. mem. Greenwoods State Bank, Pharmacy Adv. Bd., 2007-, DaneVest Capital LLC, 2007-; vessel examiner officer Dept. Homeland Security US Coast Guard Aux., 2007—; flotilla comdr., 2009. Active YMCA, 1979—, Am. Mus. Nat. History, 1982—, Nat. Rep. Congl. Com., 1980—, U.S. Def. Com., 1981—; mem. Credit Rsch. Found. Mem. Internat. Platform Assn., Nat. Assn. Credit Mgmt. (Appreciation cert. for outstanding svc. 1980-81, pres. ctrl. Va. sect. 1979-80, chmn. legis. com. 1977-79, dir. 1983—), Am. Mgmt. Assn., Nat. Wildlife Fedn., Nat. Assn. Life underwriters (Nat. Quality award 1996, 97), Va. Assn. Life Underwriters, Am. Pharmacists Assn., Congressional Club, Hopewell Yacht Club, Mathews Yacht Club. Episcopalian. Office: Washburn Enterprises PO Box 477 Dutton VA 23050-0477 Home Phone: 804-725-1790; Office Phone: 804-725-2614. Business E-Mail: jack@washburnandassociates.com. E-mail: jrwashburn@wildblue.net.

WASHBURN, KEVIN, dean, law educator; BA, U. Okla., 1989; JD, Yale U., 1993. Bar: Minn., N.Mex. 1994. Law clk. for Judge William C. Canby Jr. US Ct. Appeals (9th Cir.); trial atty. US Dept. Justice, asst. US atty. Violent Crime Sect. N.Mex., 1997; gen. counsel Nat. Indian Gaming Commn., Washington; faculty mem. U. Minn. Law Sch., 2002—08; Rosenstiel disting. prof. law James E. Rogers Coll. Law, U. Ariz.; dean U. N.Mex. Sch. Law, Albuquerque, 2009—. Vis. Oneida Nation prof. Harvard Law Sch., 2007—08. Office: U NMex Sch Law 1117 Stanford NE / MSC11 6070 1 University of New Mexico Albuquerque NM 87131-0001 Office Phone: 505-277-4700. Office Fax: 505-277-1597. E-mail: washburn@law.unm.edu.*

WASHBURN, LAWRENCE ROBERT, manufacturing executive; b. Jackson, Mich., Aug. 5, 1941; s. Lawrence Merton and Elvina Marie W.; m. Kay Frances Wieczerzak, Nov. 21, 1970; children: Lawrence Robert II, Alexa Kay. BA in History, Govt., So. Calif. Coll., 1974. Supr., engr. Tool Rsch. & Engring., Inc., Santa Ana, Calif., 1968-77; ops. mgr. Knudsen Systems, Inc., Anaheim, Calif., 1977-86; plant mgr. Flourcarbon, Anaheim, Calif., 1986-88; dir. engring. Ricoh Electronics, Inc., Tustin, Calif., 1988-92; chmn., CEO TEQCOM Industries, Santa Ana, 1992—. Dist. commr. Boy Scouts Am., Orange County, Calif., 1982-90; exec. dir. Immanuel Luth. Ch. & Sch., 1987-92; bd. dirs. Luth. High Sch. Orange County, 1990-96. With USN, 1966-68. Decorated Navy Achievement medal; recipient Scouter medal Boy Scouts Am., 1986, Award of Merit, 1988. Mem. Soc. Mfg. Engrs., Balboa Bay Club, Ctr. Club, Club 33. Republican. Avocations: golf, body surfing, skiing. Office: TEQCOM Industries 1712 Newport Cir Ste O Santa Ana CA 92705-5118 Home Phone: 714-558-2826. Personal E-mail: teqcom@pacbell.net, lrwashbugn@att.net.

WASHIDA, HARUHIKO, botanist; married, 2007. PhD, Chiba U., Japan, 2000. Rsch. assoc. NIAS, Tsukuba, Ibaraki, Japan, 2000—02, Wash. State U., Pullman, 2002—. Achievements include research in plant biology. Office: Wash State Univ Inst Biol Chemistry Pullman WA 99164-6340 Business E-Mail: was@wsu.edu.

WASHINGTON, ALLYN JARVIS, writer; b. Manchester, Conn., July 15, 1930; s. Joseph Senior and Ruby Moore Washington; m. Mildred Irene Jones, June 7, 1958; 1 child, Joanne Washington Baron 1 stepchild, Margaret Ann Schroeder. BS, Trinity Coll., Hartford, Conn., 1953; ScM, Brown U., 1956. Instr. Trinity Coll., 1955—57, Boise Jr. Coll., Idaho, 1957—58; prof. Dutchess CC, Poughkeepsie, NY, 1958—79, acting exec. dean, 1974—75; textbook author Addison-Wesley pub., Boston, 1964—. Author: Basic Technical Mathematics with Calculus, 1964, 9th edit., 2009, Technical Calculus with Analytic Geometry, 1966, 4th edit., 2002, Introduction to Technical Mathematics, 1969, 5th edit., 2008. Sgt. US Army, 1950—51. Allyn J. Washington Ctr. Sci. and Art bldg. named in his honor, Dutchess C.C., 2000. Mem.: NY State Math. Assn. Two Yr. Colls. (pres. 1974—75, award for exemplary svc. 1978), Math. Assn. Am., Am. Math. Assn. Two Yr. Colls., Phi Beta Kappa. Avocations: bridge, travel, stamp collecting/philately. Home and Office: 160 Starling Cir Grass Valley CA 95945

WASHINGTON, DENNIS R., contracting company executive; b. Spokane, Wash., 1934; Equipment operator Guy F. Atkinson Co., Alaska; with King & McLaughlin Construction Co.; founder Washington Construction Co., Missoula, Mont., 1964; chmn., pres., CEO Morrison-Knudsen, 1999; chmn. Washington Group Internat., Inc. (formerly Morrison-Knudsen), Boise, Idaho. Founder Dennis & Phyllis Washington Found., 1998. Recipient Entrepreneurial award, Montana Ambassadors, Moles award outstanding achievement construction, Am. Soc. Civil Engineers, Lewis and Clark Pioneer award, Mont. Acad. Disting. Entrepreneurs, Golden Plate award, Acad. Achievement, Metal of Honor, Nat. Ethnic Coalition Organizations; named one of Forbes' RIchest Americans, 2006. Mem.: Horatio Alger Assn. (Norman Vincent Peale award), Am. Acad. Of Achievement. Office: Washington Group Internat Inc 720 Park Blvd Boise ID 83729 Mailing: The Dennis and Phyllis Washington Found PO Box 16630 Missoula MT 59808-6630 Office Phone: 208-386-5000. Office Fax: 208-386-7186.

WASHINGTON, DENZEL, actor; b. Mt. Vernon, NY, Dec. 28, 1954; s. Denzel and Lynn Washington; m. Pauletta Pearson, June 25, 1983; children: John David, Katia, Malcolm, Olivia. BA in Drama & Journalism, Fordham U., 1977; student, Am. Conservatory Theatre, San Francisco. With NY Shakespeare Festival, Manhattan Theatre Club, New Fed. Theatre. Stage appearances include Coriolanus, 1979, Spell No. 7, The Mighty Gents, Richard III, One Tiger to a Hill, Ceremonies in Old Dark Men, When the Chicken Comes Home to Roost (Audelco award), A Soldier's Play (Obie award 1981), Checkmates, 1988, Split Second, Julius Caesar, 2005; actor: (films) Carbon Copy, 1981, A Soldier's Story, 1981, Power, 1986, Cry Freedom (NAACP Image award, 1987), 1987, For Queen and Country, 1988, The Mighty Quinn, 1989, Glory, 1989 (Golden Globe award 1989, Acad. award for Best Supporting Actor, 1990, NAACP Image award, 1990), Heart Condition, 1990, Mo' Better Blues, 1990, Ricochet, 1991, Mississippi Masala, 1992, Malcolm X, 1992, Much Ado About Nothing, 1993, Philadelphia, 1993, The Pelican Brief, 1993, Crimson Tide, 1995, Virtuosity, 1995, Devil in a Blue Dress, 1995, Courage Under Fire, 1996 (NAACP Image award, 1997), The Preacher's Wife, 1996, Fallen, 1998, He Got Game, 1998, The Siege, 1998, The Bone Collector, 1999, The Hurricane, 2000 (nominee Best Actor Acad. award 2000, Golden Globe award for Best Performance by Actor in Motion Picture Drama 2000), Remember the Titans, 2000, Training Day, 2001 (Acad. award for Best Actor, 2002, nominee Golden Globe award for Best Performance by Actor in Motion Picture Drama 2002), John Q, 2002, Out Of Time, 2003, Man on Fire, 2004, The Manchurian Candidate, 2004, Inside Man, 2006, Déjà Vu, 2006, American Gangster, 2007, The Taking of Pelham 1 2 3, 2009; actor, dir., prodr. The Antwone Fisher Story, 2002; actor, dir. The Great Debaters, 2007 (Best Picture, African Am. Film Critics Assn., 2007, Outstanding Motion Picture, NAACP Image award, 2008, Outstanding Actor, 2008); actor (TV movies) Wilma, 1977, License to Kill, 1984, The George McKenna Story, 1986; (mini-series) Flesh and Blood, 1979; (TV series) St. Elsewhere, 1982-88; co-author (with Daniel Paisner) A Hand to Guide Me, 2006. Spokesperson Boys and Girls Clubs Am. Recipient Harvard Found. award, 1996, Whitmey M. Young award, L.A. Urban League, 1997, Herbert Hoover Humanitarian award, The Boys & Girls Clubs of America, 2004, Golden Plate award, Acad. Achievement, 2005, Stanley Kubrick Britannia award for Excellence in Film BAFTA/LA Cunard Britannia awards, 2007, Frederick D. Patterson award (with wife Pauletta), United Negro Coll. Fund, 2008; Am. Conservatory Theater scholar; named one of 50 Most Powerful People in Hollywood Premiere mag., 2002-06; named America's Favorite Movie Star, Harris Poll, 2007-08; named to Power 150 Ebony mag., 2008. Avocations: basketball, reading, cooking.*

WASHINGTON, DONALD W., prosecutor; b. 1955; m. Yvonna Malonson; children: Tiffany, Greg, Donny. BS in Mech. Engring., U.S. Mil. Acad., 1977; JD, S. Tex. Coll. Law, 1989. Assoc. Alexander & McEvily, Houston, 1990—91; gen. litig. counsel Conoco Inc., 1993—96, div. counsel, Gulf of Mex. divsn., 1993—96; ptnr. Jeansonne and Redmondet, Lafayette, La., 1996—2001; US atty. (we. dist.) La. US Dept. Justice, Shreveport, La., 2001—. With US Army, 1977—82, with USAR, 1983—87. Office: US Attys Office 300 Fannin St Ste 3201 Shreveport LA 71101-3068 Office Phone: 318-676-3600. Office Fax: 318-676-3641.

WASHINGTON, EDWARD T., literature and language professor; PhD, Boston U., Mass., 1990. Asst. prof. English Howard U., Washington, 1990—95; assoc. prof. English Mansfield U., Pa., 1995—. Mem. Folger Shakespeare Libr., Washington, 1990—95; chair African Am. Studies Minor, Mansfield U., 1997—. Mem.: MLA, Nat. Coun. Tchrs. English, Shakespeare Assn. Am., Coll. Lang. Assn. Achievements include research in fields of Shakespeare, African American Studies and Teaching. Office: English & Modern Languages Dept Mansfield Univ Mansfield PA 16933 Business E-Mail: ewashing@mansfield.edu.

WASHINGTON, ERIC T., judge; b. NJ, 1953; BA, Tufts U., 1976; JD, Columbia U. Sch. of Law, 1979. Assoc. Fulbright and Jaworski, Houston and Washington, 1979—82, 1985—87; legis. dir., counsel Rep. Michael Andrews, 1983—85; spl. corp. counsel Washington, 1987—88; prin. dep. corp. counsel, 1988—90; ptnr. Hogan & Hartson, Washington, 1990-95; judge Superior Ct., 1995—99, DC Ct. Appeals, 1999—2005, chief judge, 2005—. Former co-chair, strategic planning leadership council DC Courts; mem. Standing Com. on Fairness and Access to Courts, Access to Justice Commn. Mem.: DC Bar Assn. (mem. criminal justice act counsel for child abuse and neglect com., mem. standing com. on federal judiciary). Office: DC Ct Appeals 6th Fl 500 Indiana Ave NW Fl 6 Washington DC 20001-2138 Mailing: 3159 Tennyson St NW Washington DC 20015 E-mail: ewashington@dcca.state.da.us.*

WASHINGTON, GLORIA DUNN, secondary school educator; d. Percy and Eleanor McCoy Dunn; m. Leroy Roosevelt Washington; children: Cheryl Lynn Ford, Gloria Candacy, Daphne Dena Reddick. BA, Baber-Scotia Coll., 1966; MA, U. South Fla., 1978, Edn. Specialist, 1981. Tchr. Newfane Ctrl. Sch., NY, 1966—67, Auburndale H.S., Fla., 1976—97, North Ctrl. Adult Sch., Auburndale, 1980—88, Lakeland Sr. H.S., Fla., 1997—. Youth dir. St. Mark, Lakeland, Fla., 1985—; founder/sponsor Unified Culture Club, Lakeland, 1991—; co-chair English curriculum for English tchrs. Polk County, 1997; pres. Polk County Coun. Tchrs. English, 2002—04, Polk County Coun. Tchrs. English(parliamentarian), 2007. Editor: (poems) Polk County Poetry Contest Booklet; co-author: (curriculum) English Curriculum for North Central Adult School, 1984-1985. Chairperson adminstrv. coun. St. Mark United Meth. Ch., Lakeland, 1996—2004. Named English Tchr. Yr., Polk County Coun. Tchrs. English, 1995—96, 1999—2000, 2003—04, 2004—05, Tchr. of Excellence, Fla. Coun. Tchrs. English, 2005—06. Mem.: Delta Kappa Gamma (pres. 1998—2000, Plague-Outstanding Pres. 2000), Phi Delta Kappa (publicity 2003—, pres. 2008). St. Mark United Meth. Achievements include est. Peace and Unity Walk, 1999-. Avocations: reading, writing, playing the piano, collecting clocks. Office: Lakeland High School 726 Hollingsworth Rd Lakeland FL 33813 Office Fax: 863-499-2917. E-mail: gloria.washington@polk-fl.net.

WASHINGTON, KARA ELIZABETH, music educator; b. Jackson, Miss., Feb. 10, 1966; d. J. B. and Elizabeth Washington. MusB Edn. (hon.), Delta State U., Cleve., MS, 1988; MusM Edn., Jackson State U., 2004; PhD, U. So. Miss., Hattiesburg, 2007. Asst. band dir. Columbus Pub. Schs., Miss., 1988—90, Madison Pub. Schs., Miss., 1990—92; music tchr. Family Life Christian Schs., Brandon, Miss., 1990—99, Family Life Christian Acad., 1992—99; pvt. music tchr. Crossgates Sch. Fine Arts, 1999—2004; asst. prof. music edn., Ala. State U., Montgomery, Ala., 2007—. Mem.: Music Educators Nat. Conf. Office: Alabama State Univ 915 S Jackson St Montgomery AL 36101 Personal E-mail: karaew1@yahoo.com. Business E-Mail: kwashington@alasu.edu.

WASHINGTON, KERRY, actor; b. Bronx, NY, Jan. 31, 1977; BFA theatre, George Washington Univ., 1998. Actor: (TV films) Magical Make-Over, 1994; (films) Our Song, 2000, 3D, Save the Last Dance, 2001, Lift, 2001, Take the A Train, Bad Company, 2002, United States of Lelan, 2003, The Human Stain, 2003, Sin, 2003, Against the Ropes, 2004, Strip Search, 2004, She Hate Me, 2004, Ray, 2004, Sexual Life, 2005, Mr. & Mrs. Smith, 2005, Fantastic Four, 2005, Wait, 2005, Little Man, 2006, The Last King of Scotland, 2006, The Dead Girl, 2006, I Think I Love My Wife, 2007, Miracle at St. Anna, 2008, Lakeview Terrace, 2008. Nominee Best Female Actress, Ind. Spirit Awards, 2002. Office: c/o Washington Square Arts The Lot Writers Bldg 1041 North Formosa Ave West Hollywood CA 90046

WASHINGTON, LARISSA LENORE, educator; b. New Orleans, Tex., May 2, 1974; d. Oscar and Julia Irons Washington. BS, Grambling State U., LA, 1996, MA, 1997. Cert. in tchg. Md. State Dept. Edn. Instr. Paul Quinn Coll., Dallas, 1998—2002; prof. Eastfield Coll., Mesquite, Tex., 2004—. Organizer Pub. Sch. Sys., Dallas, 2005—09. Recipient Jean Sharon Griffith award, DCCCD Academic Advisement, 2004. Mem.: CCC, Tex. Folklore Soc., NCTE, Zeta Phi Beta Sorority (Tchr. of Yr. 2001), Alpha Kappa Alpha Sorority, Inc. Office: Eastfield Coll 3737 Motley Mesquite TX 75150 Office Fax: 972-860-7248. Business E-Mail: larissawashington@dcccd.edu.

WASHINGTON, LEON, professional football player; b. Jacksonville, Fla., Aug. 29, 1982; B in Social Scis., Fla. State U., Tallahassee, 2006. Running back, kick returner NY Jets, 2006—. Recipient Curtis Martin MVP award, NY Jets, 2007; named 1st Team All-Pro, AP, 2008; named to Am. Football Conf. Pro Bowl Team, NFL, 2008. Achievements include leading the National Football League in: all-purpose yards (2337), 2008. Office: NY Jets 1000 Fulton Ave Hempstead NY 11550*

WASHINGTON, LINDA JACOBS, federal agency administrator; b. Annapolis, Md., 1948; m. Mark Washington; 1 child, Lisa. BA, Morgan State U., 1970; MA, U. North Tex. Various sales mktg. positions Xerox Corp., 1982—94; chief of the photoduplication service Libr. of Congress, 1994—97, dir. of integrated support services (ISS), 1997—2003; dep. asst. sec. for adminstrn. US Dept. Transp., 2003—07, asst. sec. for adminstrn., 2007—. Apptd. Bd. Grad. Sch., US Dept. Agr., 2003—07; vice-chmn. Local Fed. Coord. Com. for the Combined Fed. Campagin's Nat. Capitol Region; rep. sec. of transp. Fed. Coun. on Arts and Humanities. Recipient Presdl. Rank award, 2007, Pres.'s Vol. Svc. award, 2008. Office: US Dept Transp 1200 New Jersey Ave SE Washington DC 20590 Office Phone: 202-366-4000.*

WASHINGTON, MARIO R., computer company executive; 2 children. AAS in Computer Engring., Queensboro Cmty. Coll., Bayside, NY, 1995. Cert. in Xsan adminstrn. NY, 2006. CEO Reboot Computer Svcs., Inc., Forest hills, NY, 1996—; owner Audion Reboot Techs., Mumbai, India, 2003—06. Dir. Sat- B Solution, Singapore, 2002—03. Achievements include development of multiple software applications for the medical industry; successful implementations of Xsan; succesful networking implementations. Office: Reboot Computer Svcs Inc 70-11 Austin St Ste 3L Flushing NY 11367 Personal E-mail: mariowashington@mac.com.

WASHINGTON, REGINALD LOUIS, pediatric cardiologist; b. Colorado Springs, Colo., Dec. 31, 1949; s. Lucius Louis and Brenette Y. (Wheeler) W.; m. Billye Faye Ned, Aug. 18, 1973; children: Danielle Larae, Reginald Quinn. BS in Zoology, Colo. State U., 1971; MD, U. Colo., 1975. Diplomate Nat. Bd. Med. Examiners, Am. Bd. Pediat., Pediatric Cardiology. Intern U. Colo. Med. Ctr., Denver, 1975—76, resident in pediat., 1976-78, chief resident, instr., 1978-79, fellow in pediatric cardiology, 1979-81, from asst. prof. pedit. to assoc. clin. prof. pediat., 1982—2005, clin. prof. pediat., 2005—; staff cardiologist Children's Hosp., Denver, 1981-90; v.p. We. Cardiology Assocs., Divsn. for Fetal, Pediatric and Adult Congential Heart Disease, Denver, 1990—2004; med. dir. Rocky Mountain Pediatrix Cardiology, Denver, 2004—08; chief med. officer Rocky Mountain Hosp. For Children, Denver, Colo., 2008—; chief of staff Presbyn./St. Lukes Med. Ctr., 1999-2001. Admissions com. U. Colo. Sch. Medicine, Denver, 1985-89; chmn., bd. dirs. Coop. Health Care Agreements, 1994-98; chmn. dept. pediatrics Presbyn./St. Lukes Med. Ctr, Denver, 1996-99, 2003-05, pres.-elect med. staff, 1997-99, chmn. ethics com., 2003-07; adv. coun.

Nat. Heart Lung Blood Inst., NIH, 1996-986 Cons. editor Your Patient and Fitness, 1989-92; mem. editl. bd. Jour. Pediats., 2004—, Congenital Heart Disease, 2006-. Chmn. Coop. Health Care Agreements Bd., State of Colo., 1994-98; adv. bd. dirs. Equitable Bank of Littleton, Colo., 1984-86; bd. dirs. Rocky Mountain Heart Fund for Children, 1984-89, Rainbo Ironkids, 1989-95, Ctrl. City Opera, 1989-95, Cleo Parker Robinson Dance Co., 1992-94, Nat. Coun. Patient Info. and Edn., 1992-98, Children's Heart Alliance, 1993-94, Colo. State U. Devel. Coun., 1994-2003, Caring for Colo. Found., 1999-2001; nat. bd. dirs. Am. Heart Assn., 1992-96; trustee Denver Ctr. Performing Arts, 1994—, Regis U., 1994-99; mem. Gov.'s Coun. Phys. Fitness, 1990-91; bd. govs. Colo. State U., 1996-2004, pres., 2001-03; trustee Colo. Trust, 2002-; trustee Helen Bonfils Found., 2003—, Temple Hoyne Buell Found., 2007-. Recipient William E. Morgan Alumnus Achievement award Colo. State U., 2004, Cardiologist of Yr., HCA, 2004; named Salute Vol. of Yr. Big Sisters of Colo., 1990; honoree NCCJ, 1994, Physician of Yr., Nat. Am. Heart Assn., 1995, Civis Princeps award Regis U., 2007, Gold heart award Nat. Am. Heart Assn., 2008. Fellow Am. Acad. Pediat. (cardiology subsect., chmn. sports medicine and fitness com. 2000-2004, chmn. task force on obesity 2003—08, Thomas Shaffer award 2007), Am. Coll. Cardiology, Am. Heart Assn. (coun. on cardiovasc. disease in the young, exec. com. 1988-91, nat. devel. program com. 1990-94, vol. of yr. 1989, pres. Colo. chpt. 1989-90, Torch of Hope 1987, Gold Heart award Colo. chpt. 1990, bd. dirs. Colo. chpt., exec. com. Colo. chpt. 1987-2000, grantee Colo. chpt. 1983-84, mem. editl. bd. Pediat. Exercise Scis. 1988-2002), Soc. Critical Care Medicine; mem. Am. Acad. Pediat. Perinatology, Am. Acad. Pediat./Pediat. Cardiology (exec. com. 1996-2004), N.Am. Soc. Pediat. Exercise Medicine (pres. 1986-87), Colo. Med. Soc. (chmn. sports medicine coun. 1993-94), Leadership Denver 1990, Glenmoor Golf Club. Democrat. Roman Catholic. Avocations: golf, fishing. Office: Rocky Mountain Hosp Children 1719 East 19th Ave Denver CO 80218 Office Phone: 303-839-6100. Business E-Mail: rlwash@aol.com.

WASHINGTON, ROBIN L., pharmaceutical executive; b. 1963; BA in Bus. Adminstrn., U. Mich.; MBA, Pepperdine U., Malibu, Calif. Sr. auditor Deloitte & Touche; acctg. analyst Fed. Res. Bank, Chgo.; fin. dir. Tandem Computers; with PeopleSoft, Inc., 1996, sr. v.p., corp. contr., 1999—2005; CFO Hyperion Solutions Corp., 2005—08; sr. v.p., CFO Gilead Sciences Inc., 2008—. Mailing: Gilead Sciences Inc Hdqs 333 Lakeside Dr San Mateo CA 94404 Office Phone: 650-574-3000. Office Fax: 650-578-9264.*

WASHINGTON, WARREN MORTON, meteorologist; b. Portland, Oreg., Aug. 28, 1936; s. Edwin and Dorothy Grace (Morton) W.; m. LaRae Herring, July 30, 1959 (div. Aug. 1975); children: Teri, Kim, Marc (dec.), Tracy; m. Jona Ann, July 3, 1978 (dec. Jan. 1987); m. Mary Elizabeth Washington, Apr., 1995. BS in Physics, Ore. State U., 1958, MS in Meteorology, 1960; PhD in Meteorology, Pa. State U., 1964; degree (hon.), Oreg. State U., 2006. Dir. of climate and global dynamics div. Nat. Center Atmospheric Research, Boulder, Colo., 1978-95; affiliate prof. meteorology oceanography U. Mich. at Ann Arbor, 1968-71; mem. Nat. Adv. Com. for Oceans and Atmospheres, 1978-84. Mem. sec. of energy adv. bd. U.S. Dept. Energy, 1990-93; mem. Nat. Sci. Bd., 1994-2006, chair, 2002-06. Contbr. articles to meteorol. jours. Mem. Boulder Human Rels. Commn., 1969-71; mem. Gov.'s Sci. Adv. Com., 1975-78. Recipient Disting. Alumni award Oreg. State U., 1991, E.B. Lemon Disting. Alumni award Pa. State U., 1991, Le Verrier medal Soc. Meteorol. France, 1995, Bonfils-Stanton Found. award, 2000, Vollum award Reed Coll., 2005; inductee NAS portrait collection African Am. in Sci., Engring., and Medicine, 1997; named Sigma Xi Disting. lectr., 1998-99. Fellow AAAS (bd. dirs.), Am. Meteorol. Soc. (pres. 1994, Anderson award 2000, Charles Brook award 2007); mem. NAE, Am. Philosophy Soc., Am. Geog. Union. Office: PO Box 3000 Boulder CO 80307-3000 Home: 8633 E Iliff Dr Denver CO 80231-3810

WASHKEWICZ, DONALD E., manufacturing executive; b. Cleve. m. Pam Washkewicz; children: Dawn, Tiffany, Bryan. BME, Cleve. State U., 1972; MBA, Case Western Res. U., Cleve., 1979. Lic. profl. engr., OH. With Parker Hannifin Corp., Cleve., 1972—, from engr. to gen. mgr. Parflex Divsn., 1972—82, v.p. ops. fluid connectors group, 1994-97, v.p., pres. hydraulics group, 1997-2000, COO, 2000—01, pres., 2000—04, 2007—, CEO, chmn., 2001—. Bd. Mfr. Alliance/MAPI. Bd. Greater Cleve. Growth Assn., Cleve. Tomorrow. Recipient George B. Davis Disting. Alumni award, Cleve. State U., 2002, Disting. Alumni award, Case Western Res. U., 2002, Ellis Island Medal of Honor, 2003. Mem.: Nat. Assn. Mfr., Nat. Soc. Profl. Engr. Office: Parker Hannifin Corp 6035 Parkland Blvd Cleveland OH 44124-4141

WASIELE, HARRY W., JR., diversified electrical manufacturing company executive; b. Chgo., June 29, 1926; s. Harry W. and Antoinette (Tuleja) W.; m. Loretta K. Anderson, Jan. 3, 1948; children: Kathleen Ann Wasiele Bach, Brian David, Larry Scott, Mark Thomas. Grad. high sch. Asst. sales mgr. Drake Mfg. Co., Chgo., 1950—55; sales engr. AMP, Inc., Chgo., 1955, Detroit, 1956—57, product mgr. Harrisburg, Pa., 1958—61, industry mgr., 1961—67, dir. marketing, 1967—68; gen. mgr. Brand-Rex divsn. Am. Enka Corp., Willimantic, Conn., 1968—70; pres. Brand-Rex Co., subs. Akzona Inc., 1967—83; ret., 1983. Chmn. Brand-Rex Ltd., Glenrothes, Scotland, 1974-83, Electronics SA, Iserables, Switzerland, Decollatage SA, Saint-Maurice, Switzerland, 1972-83, Pyle Nat. Ltd., Nottingham, Eng., 1974-83; v.p. sales and corp. devel. Cablec Corp., New City, N.Y., 1985—; bd. dirs. Berkel Inc.; chmn., pres. Tarpon Springs (Fla.) Internat. Tannery, Inc., 1990—. Bd. dirs. Ea. Conn. State Coll. Found., 1972-83; trustee Windham Cmty. Hosp., Willimantic, 1969-83, trustee emeritus, 1983—, pres. bd. trustees, 1981-83; trustee YMCA of Martin County Found. Served USN Air Corps., 1944-46. With air corps USN, 1944—46. Mem. Nat. Elec. Mfrs. Assn. (chmn. wire and cable div., bd. govs. 1982-84), Conn. Bus. and Industry Assn. (emeritus dir.), New Seabury Country Club, Mariner Sands Country Club. Republican. Roman Catholic. Home (Summer): PO Box 826 Mashpee MA 02649-0826 Home: Mariner Sands 6755 SE Barrington Dr Stuart FL 34997-8639 Personal E-mail: wasieles@aol.com.

WASIUDDIN, NAZIMUDDIN MOHAMMAD, engineering educator; b. Dhaka, Bangladesh, Dec. 10, 1975; s. Mohammad Nazim Uddin and Al-Marzia Begum; m. Mushfiqua Zaman, Oct. 10, 2002; 1 child, Anhaar Mohammad Wasi. PhD in Civil Engring., U. Okla., Norman, 2007; MS in Civil Engring., Dalhousie U., Halifax, Canada, 2002; BS in Civil Engring., Bangladesh U. Engring. and Tech., Dhaka, 2000. Rsch. and tchg. asst. Dalhousie U., Nova Scotia, 2001—02; rsch. asst. U. Okla., 2002—07; rsch. visitor Tech. U. Delft, Netherlands, 2006—06; asst. prof. La. Tech U., Ruston, 2007—. Standing com. mem. Transp. Rsch. Bd., DC, 2008—. Contbr. articles to numerous profl. jours. Recipient Nat. Dean's List, 2005—06. Mem.: ASCE (assoc.), Chi Epsilon. Home: 2501 Creekwood Dr Ruston LA 71270 Office: La Tech Univ 600 West Ariz Ave Ruston LA 71272 Office Fax: 318-257-2306. Personal E-mail: nmwasi@yahoo.com. Business E-Mail: wasi@latech.edu.

WASKIN, HETTY ANNE, epidemiologist, director; d. Richard Waskin and Lois Prance; children: Chunchun, Darah, Tessa, Andrew. MSPH, U. NC, Chapel Hill, 1973; BS, MD, U. Mich., Ann Arbor, 1978. Diplomate Am. Bd. Med. Examiners, 1978, Am. Bd. Internal Medicine, 1981, cert. in infectious diseases subspeciality Am. Bd. Internal Medicine, 1988. Worldwide med. dir. Liposome Co., Princeton, NJ, 1996—2002; sr. dir. clin. rsch. infectious diseases Schering Plough Rsch. Inst., Kenilworth, NJ, 2004—. Med. dir., cons., Princeton, 2002—04. Contbr. articles to profl. jours. Bd. mem. Montgomery Twp. Bd. Health, Belle Mead, NJ, 1998—2006. Epidemic intelligence svc. officer USPHS, 1985—87, Atlanta. Office: Schering Plough Rsch Inst 2015 Galloping Hill Rd Kenilworth NJ 07033 Business E-Mail: hetty.waskin@spcorp.com.

WASKO-FLOOD, SANDRA JEAN, artist, educator; b. NYC, Mar. 12, 1943; d. Peter Edmund and Margaret Dalores (Kubek) Wasko; m. Michael Timothy Flood, June 28, 1969. BA, UCLA, 1965, postgrad., 1968-69, Calif. State U., Northridge, summer 1968; student, Otis Art Inst., LA, 1969, Marie Kaufman, Rio de Janeiro, 1970-72, Museo de Arte Moderno, 1970-73, Foothill Coll., Los Altos, Calif., 1973-74, Claremont Coll., Calif., 1975, U. Wis., Janesville, 1977, Beloit Coll., Wis., 1977-78, U. Wis., 1977-78; grad. etching student, Warrington Colescott. Instr. printmaking Washington Women's Arts Ctr., 1983; artist-in-residence U. Md., College Park, 1985; instr. printmaking Arlington Arts Ctr., Va., 1984-85; prof. St. Mary's Coll., Md., 1985; instr. printmaking Arlington County Lee Arts Ctr., 1989-97; workshop coord. cultural affairs div. Arlington County Cultural Affairs, 1989-97; printmaking instr. Home Studio, Alexandria, Va., 1987—2005; founder, pres. Living Labyrinths Peace, Inc., 2005—. Condr. workshops Washington Performing Arts Soc., 2002—. One woman shows include Wisconsin Women in the Arts Gallery, Madison, 1977, Mbari Art, Washington, 1981, Miya Gallery, Washington, 1981, Slavin Gallery, Washington, 1982, Stuart Mott House, Washington, 1983, Washington Printmakers Gallery, 1986, 88, 91, St. Peter's Ch., NYC, 1989, Montana Gallery, Alexandria, Va., 1991, Montpelier Cultural Arts Ctr., Laurel, Md., 1992, Gallery 10, Washington, 1994, 96, Sch. 33, Balt., 1996, Sub-Basement Artist Studios, Balt., 2008-09; mus. and internat. shows include Boston Printmakers: The 39th North Am. Print Exhbn., Framingham, Mass., Jan.-Mar., 1986, Internat. Graphic Arts Found. and Silvermine Guild Arts Ctr., New Canaan, Conn., Feb., 1988, Prints: Washington, The Phillips Collection, Washington, Sept.-Oct., 1988, Contemporary Am. Graphics, Book Chamber Internat., Moscow, 1990, Gallery 10 Artists of Washington DC Vartai Gallery, Lithuania, 1994, Peninsula Fine Arts Ctr., Newport News, Va., 1995-96, Riva Sinistra Arte, Florence, Italy, 1997, Contemporary Art Ctr. Va., Virginia Beach, 2000, Charles Sumner Sch. Mus., Washington, DC, 2001, numerous others; numerous juried shows including most recently Cannon Rotunda, US House of Reps., Washington, 2000, Charles Sumner Sch. Mus., Washington, 2001, Washington Women Artists Marching into the Millennium, Women's Caucus for Art, 2001, Washington Women Artists, Women's Caucus for Art, 2001, Rockville Art Place, Md., 2002, Internat. Photography, 2003, Anne C. Fisher Gallery, Wash., 2005, Md. Printmakers Foundry Gallery, Washington, 2007; galleries: Slavin Gallery, Washington, D.C., 1981-83, Washington Printmakers Gallery, Washington, 1985-96, White Light Collaborative, Inc., NYC, 1988-89, Montana Gallery, Alexandria, Va., 1989-91, Gallery 10, Washington, 1992-97, Charleuoix Gallery, Albuquerque, NM, 1999, and numerous others; collections include Nat. Mus. of Women in the Arts, Washington, Corcoran Gallery of Art, Washington, Museo de Arte Moderno, Buenos Aires, Cultural Found., USSR, Coll. Notre Dame, Balt., Potomac Hosp., Woodbridge, Md.; dir. Labyrinths for Peace 2000, US Capitol, 2002; featured artist Kali Guide: A Directory of Resources for Women, 2d reprint, 2002. Pres. Washington Area Printmakers, Washington, D.C., 1985-86; pub. rels. dir. Washington Women's Arts Ctr., 1980; bd. dirs. Washington Women's Arts Ctr., 1981-82; program chair DC chpt. Women's Caucus for Art, 1998—; founding mem. the Labyrinth Soc., 1998-; spl. projects dir. Labryinth Soc., 2000; cons. Labyrinth Making and Products. Recipient Award of Honorable Mention Nat. Gallery of Art, 1989, Best of Show, Artists Equity Exhibit, Gallery 901, Washington, 1997; grantee Friends of the Torpedo Factory Art Ctr., Alexandria, Va., 1989, DC Commn. on Arts and Humanities Summer Edn. and Sports Program Artist in Schs., 2000, 01, 05, Wash. Performing Arts Soc., 2002-09; individual artists fellow Va. Commn. for Arts, 1994. Mem.: Md. Non-Profits, Theosophical Soc., Inst. Noetic Sci., Am. for the Arts Creative Alliance, Arts/Sci. Collaborative, Inc. (NYC), Artists Using Sci. and Tech. (San Francisco), YLEM, The Labyrinth Soc., Washington Sculpture Group, Am. Print Alliance, Md. Printmakers, Women's Caucus for Art, Pyramic Atlantic, Nat. Print Orgn., Corcoran Gallery/Washington Project for the Arts. Avocations: classical music, hiking, reading. Studio: Living Labyrinths Peace Ctr 57 N St NW Washington DC 20001-1254 Home: 2229 Lake Ave Baltimore MD 21213-1015 Home Phone: 410-243-1189; Office Phone: 703-217-6706. Personal E-mail: waskoart@comcast.net.

WASKOW, ARTHUR OCEAN, theologian, educator; b. Balt., Oct. 12, 1933; s. Henry B. and Hannah (Osnowitz) W.; m. Irene Elkin, 1956 (div. 1978); children: David, Shoshana; m. Phyllis Ocean Berman, 1986. BA, Johns Hopkins U., Balt., 1954; MA, U. Wis., 1956, PhD, 1963. Legis. asst. Ho. of Reps., Washington, 1959-61; sr. staff mem. Peace Rsch. Inst., Washington, 1961-63; fellow Inst. Policy Studies, Washington, 1963-77; colleague Pub. Resource Ctr., Washington, 1977-82; faculty Reconstructionist Rabbinical Coll., Phila., 1982-89; founder, dir. Shalom Ctr., 1983—. Fellow ALEPH Alliance for Jewish Renewal, 1990-93, pathfinder, 1993-2005; mem. adv. bd. Temple Understanding; vis. prof. religion Swarthmore Coll., 1982-83, Temple U., 1976-77, 87-88, Drew U., 1997-98, Vassar Coll., 1998, Hebrew Union Coll., 2008; sec.-treas. Conf. On Peace Rsch. in History, 1969-74. Author: The Limits of Defense, 1962, (with Stanley L. Newman) America in Hiding, 1962, Worried Man's Guide to World Peace, 1963, From Race Riot to Sit-In, 1966, The Freedom Seder, 1969, Running Riot, 1970, The Bush Is Burning, 1971, Godwrestling, 1978, Seasons of Our Joy, 1982, These Holy Sparks, 1983, (with David and Shoshana Waskow) Before There Was a Before, 1984, (with Howard Waskow) Becoming Brothers, 1993, Down-to-Earth Judaism: Food, Money, Sex, and the Rest of Life, 1995, Godwrestling—Round 2: Ancient Wisdom, Future Paths, 1996, (with Phyllis O. Berman) Tales of Tikkun: New Jewish Stories to Heal the Wounded World, 1996, (with Phyllis O. Berman) A Time for Every Purpose Under Heaven: The Jewish Life-Spiral as a Spiritual Path, 2002, (with Ari Elon and Naomi Mara Hyman) Trees, the Earth, and Torah: A To B'Shvat Anthology, 1999, Torah of the Earth: Exploring 4,000 Years of Ecology in Jewish Thought, 2000, (with Joan Chittister and Saadi Shakur Chisti) The Tent of Abraham: Stories of Hope and Peace for Jews, Christians and Muslims, 2006; editor: Debate Over Thermonuclear Strategy, 1965, Menorah Jour., 1979-2001; screenwriter: In Every Generation, 1988; editl. bd. Tikkun. Alt. del. Dem. Nat. Conv., 1968; fellow Chs. Ctr. for Theology and Pub. Policy, 1977-82; Gamaliel chair Luth. Student Ctr., Milw., 1996; wisdom-keeper UN Conf. on Habitat II, 1996; initiator A.J. Heschel 25th Yohrzeit Observance, 1998. Recipient Peace & Justice award Muslim Am. Soc., 2007, Rev. Richard Fernandez Religious Leadership award Neighborhood Interfaith Movement, 2007; Coolidge fellow Assn. Religion and Intellectual Life, 1983; named one of the Top 50 Rabbis in America, Newsweek Mag., 2007. Fellow Am. Acad. Arts and Scis. (colloquium on disarmament 1962); mem. Nat. Writers Union, Fabrangen, Nat. Havurah Com. (bd. dirs. 1979-80, 83-87), P'nai Or (bd. dirs. 1984-93, Aleph bd. dirs. 1993-95), Internat. Coord. Com. on Religion and Earth (steering com. 1990-93), Phi Beta Kappa. Address: 6711 Lincoln Dr Philadelphia PA 19119-3119 Office Phone: 215-844-8494. E-mail: awaskow@shalomctr.org. *For about 500 years the human race has made no "Sabbath" from ceaseless working, making, producing, doing and it therefore has raced to the brink of destroying itself and much of life on the planet. Just as individuals need rhythmic rest, so do societies—a spiritual truth that we should again learn from Torah. Time to be!.*

WASMER, DONALD J., finance educator, director; s. Donald H. Wasmer. MBA, Ind. State U., Terre Haute, 1982; DBA, Southern Ill. U., Carbondale, 1994. Chair dept. bus. and info. sys. St. Mary-of-the-Woods Coll., Ind., 1991—2006, dir., master leadership devel., 2006—. Pres. bd. dirs. Terre Haute Childrens Mus., Ind., 2001—05. Recipient Mary Joseph Pomeroy Faculty Excellence award, St. Mary-of-the-Woods Coll., 1994, 2003; Prochow fellowship, Grad. Sch. Banking, 1986, Lilly Distance Edn. fellow. Mem.: Am. Mktg. Assn. (pres. Wabash Valley chpt. 1994—95), Beta Gamma Sigma, Phi Kappa Phi. Office: St Mary-of-the-Woods Coll Saint Mary's Rd Saint Mary Of The Woods IN 47876 Business E-Mail: dwasmer@smwc.edu.

WASOW, OMAR, Internet company executive; b. 1971; BA in Race and Ethnic Rels., Stanford U., Calif., 1992. Coord. voter registration Freedom Summer '92, 1992; asst. dir. Strictly Bus., 1992—93; founder, owner New York Online, 1993—; internet analyst NewsChannel4, NYC, 1995—; co-founder, strategic advisor BlackPlanet.com at Cmty. Connect Inc., NYC, 1999—. Co-founder Brooklyn Excelsior Charter Sch., 2001. Co-chair Coalition for Ind. Pub. Charter Schs.; bd. mem. Black Alliance for Ednl. Options; bd, dirs. NY Software Industry Assn., WorldStudio, The Refugee Project. Named one of fifty most influential people to watch in cyberspace, Newsweek, 1995; fellow Next Generation Leadership program, Rockefeller Found. Office: NBC 30 Rockefeller Plz New York NY 10112 also: BlackPlanet Community Connect 205 Hudson St New York NY 10013

WASS, C(HARLES) THOMAS, anesthesiologist; b. Glendale, Calif., Apr. 11, 1961; s. Charles Wallace and Janice Lane (Buchanan) W.; m. Sharon Lorraine, Sep 1, 1966; children: Luke Thomas, Claire Elizabeth, Grant Taylor, Kate Lorraine, Scott Conner. BA in Chemistry, W.Va. U., 1984, MD, 1989. Diplomate Am. Bd. Anesthesiology. Intern W.Va. Univ. Hosp., Morgantown, 1989—90, resident, 1990—93; fellow in neurosurg. anesthesia Mayo Clinic, Rochester, Minn., 1993—95, sr. assoc. cons., 1995—97, instr. in anesthesiology, 1994—97, cons., asst. prof. anesthesiology, 1997—2002, assoc. prof. anesthesiology, 2002—. Mem. Mayo Rsch. and Human Studies Com., 1995—; mem. Mayo Exec. Edn. Com., Rochester, 1996—; mentor Mayo Neurosurg. Anesthesia Rsch., Rochester, 1996—; neuroanesthesia coord. Mayo Didactic Edn. Com., Rochester, 1996—. Co-author: Anesthesia Clinic North America, 1995; assoc. editor Anesthesiology Review, 1994, 2002, Mayo Clinic Proceedings, 2001, Epilepsia, 2001, Anesthesia and Analgesia, 2001, 2003, Anesthesiology, 2002-05, Transfusion, 2007; assoc. editor: Anesthesia: A Comprehensive Review, 1997, 2003, 2009; contbr. articles to profl. jours. Recipient Tchr. of Yr. award Mayo Found., 1995, 96, 97, 98, 99, Tchg. Recognition award Internat. Anesthesia Rsch. Soc., 2000; NIH rsch. tng. grantee, 1993-95; Am. Heart Assn. grantee, 1994-95. Mem. Am. Soc. of Anesthesiologists, Internat. Anesthesia Rsch. Soc. (Tchg. award 2000), Soc. of Neurol. Anesthesia and Critical Care, Minn. Soc. of Anesthesiologists, Soc. for Edn. in Anesthesia, Assn. U. Anesthesiologists. Achievements include patents for selective convective brain cooling apparatus and method invention. Avocations: bicycling, fishing, skiing, camping. Office: Mayo Clinic 200 1st St SW Rochester MN 55905-0002 Business E-Mail: wass.thomas@mayo.edu.

WASSENBERG, EVELYN M., retired medical/surgical nurse, educator; b. Oct. 8, 1933; d. Patrick A. and Mary A. (Kieffer) L'Ecuyer; m. Maurice P. Wassenberg, Oct. 29, 1955; children: Sherry Ann Gaines, Laura Marie O'Neil. Diploma in nursing, Marymount Sch. Nursing, Salina, Kans., 1955; BS in Nursing, Marymount Coll., Salina, 1982; MN, Wichita State U., Kans., 1987. Cert. nurse specialist. Dir. nursing svc. Community Meml. Hosp. Inc., Marysville, Kans., 1962-79; house supr. Luth. Hosp., Beatrice, Nebr., 1980-82; primary nurse Beatrice Cmty. Hosp., 1983; instr. Ft. Scott C.C., Kans., 1983-2001, 2001—06; nurse Girard Hosp., 2001; ICU nurse Nevada Regional Health Ctr., Mo., 2001—03, clin. instr., 2003—06, Ft. Scott CC Kans; ret., 2006. Mem. Mary Queen of Angels Cath. Ch. Named Nurse of Yr. Bourbon County Kans., 1992. Mem. Am. Nursing Assn., Kans. State Nursing Assn., Sigma Theta Tau. Address: 216 S Crawford St Fort Scott KS 66701-3231 Home Phone: 620-223-6994.

WASSENICH, LINDA PILCHER, retired health policy analyst, social worker; b. Washington, Aug. 27, 1943; d. Mason Johnson and Vera Bell (Stephenson) Pilcher; m. Mark Wassenich, May 14, 1965; children: Paul Mason, David Mark. BA magna cum laude with honors, Tex. Christian U., Fort Worth, 1965; MSW, U. N.C., Chapel Hill, 1970. Licensed advanced practitioner, cert. social worker, Tex. Counselor family ct. Dallas County Juvenile Dept., 1970-73, 75-76; dir. govt. rels. Vis. Nurse Assn., Dallas, 1980-84, exec. officer of hospice, 1984-85; exec. dir. Incest Recovery Assn., Dallas, 1985-86; assoc. exec. dir. Lone Star Coun. Camp Fire, Dallas, 1986-89; exec. v.p. Vis. Nurse Assn. Found., Dallas, 1989-91; dir. policy and resource devel. Vis. Nurse Assn. Tex., 1992-99; ret. Field instr. U. Tex. Arlington Sch. Social Work, 1993-99. Contbr. articles to profl. publs. Mem. Leadership Dallas, 1988—89; bd. dirs. Women's Coun. Dallas County, 1986—95, 1999—2001, pres., 1992—93; mem. adv. bd. Maternal Health and Family Planning Dallas, 1990—94; chmn. Dallas County Welfare Adv. Bd., 1991—95; bd. dirs. United Way of Met. Dallas, 1992—94, Youth Impact Ctrs., Dallas, 1993—94; trustee Simmons Family Found., Dallas, 2000—; mem. bd. dirs. Cmty. Coun. Greater Dallas, 2004—, sec., 2007, v.p., 2008; chair governance com. Human Rights Initiative of North Tex., Dallas, 2004—; chair adv. coun. Dallas Area Agy. on Aging, 2005—; bd. mem. Tex. Christianity U., Harris Coll. Nursing & Health Scis., 2008—. Recipient Heart award Lone Star Coun. Camp Fire USA, 1990, Laurel award AAUW, Dallas, 1995, Valuable Alumna award Tex. Christian U. Alumni Assn., 2003, Women of Spirit award Am. Jewish Congress, Dallas, 2005; named Field Inst. of Yr., U. Tex. Arlington Sch. Social Work, 1999, Golden Rule award finalist JC Penney, 2000. Mem.: LWV (bd. dirs. Dallas 1974—80, pres. 1995—99, bd. dirs. Tex. 1999—, Tex. v.p. pub. rels. 2001—, Myrtle Bales Bulkley award 2000, Pres. award 2005), NASW (co-chmn. Dallas unit 1981—82, chair Tex. nominating com. 1990—92, Tex. bd. dirs., Social Worker of Yr. award 1988, Lifetime Achievement in Social Work award 2002), Assn. Fundraising Profls. (bd. dirs. Dallas chpt. 1994—97, v.p. governance 1995—96, cert., Outstanding Fund Raising Exec. of Yr. 1999), Acad. Cert. Social Workers. Home: 5221 Pebblebrook Dallas TX 75229-5504

WASSENICH, RED, librarian; b. Austin, Tex., June 6, 1950; s. Paul Green and Ruth Seigfried Wassenich; m. Karen Pavelka, Nov. 5, 1988. BS, U. Tex., Austin, 1973, MLS, 1977. Libr. Am. Mus. Natural History, NYC, 1978—82; copy editor Putnam Pub., NYC, 1982—84; libr. Austin

CC, 1984—. Actor: (movie) The Hunger; author: (book) Keep Austin Weird: A Guide to the Odd Side of Town. Cmty. outreach mem. Met. Austin Interactive Network, Austin, 1992—2001. Mem.: Tex. CC Tchrs. Assn., Tex. Libr. Assn., Assn. Coll. & Rsch. Librs. Liberal. Avocations: travel, golf. Home: 1611 Waterston Austin TX 78703 Office: Austin CC 1212 Rio Grande Austin TX 78701

WASSER, DENNIS MATTHEW, lawyer; b. Bklyn., Aug. 27, 1942; BA with honors, U. Calif. LA, 1964; JD, U. So. Calif., 1967. Bar: Calif. 1968, cert.: State Bar Calif. Bd. Legal Specialization (specialist in family law). Ptnr. Wasser, Cooperman & Carter, LA. Lectr. in field; co-instr. advanced profl. program family law U. So. Calif., 1989; instr. U. Calif. LA. Contbr. articles to profl. jours. Mem.: ABA, Am. Acad. Matrimonial Lawyers, LA County Bar Assn. (chmn. 1984, mem. exec. com. family law sect. 1978—88), Beverly Hills Bar Assn. (chmn. family law sect. 1978—79). Office: Wasser Cooperman & Carter Ste 1200 One Century Plz 2029 Century Park E Los Angeles CA 90067 Office Phone: 310-277-7117. Office Fax: 310-553-1793.

WASSER, HENRY, retired American literature and sociology educator; b. Pitts., Apr. 13, 1919; s. Nathan and Mollie (Mendelson) W.; m. Solidelle Felicité Fortier, Aug. 20, 1942; children: Michael Frederick (dec.), Eric Anthony (dec.), Frederick Anthony, Felicity Louise. BA, MA, Ohio State U., 1940; PhD, Columbia U., 1951. Teaching fellow George Washington U., 1940-42; analyst USAAF intelligence, 1941-43; chemist Goodyear Synthetic Rubber Co., 1943-45; from tutor to assoc. prof. City Coll., CUNY, 1946-66; prof. English, dean faculties Richmond Coll., CUNY, 1966-73; v.p. for acad. affairs Calif. State U., Sacramento, 1973-74; prof. English Coll. S.I., CUNY, 1974-89; dir. Center for European Studies, Grad. Sch. CUNY, 1979-93, prof. emeritus of sociology and English, 1989—. Fulbright prof. U. Salonika, Greece, 1955-56; Higher Edn. Seminar assoc. Columbia U., 1961—, co-chair, 1982-87, chair, 1987-89; mem. Colloquium on Higher Edn., Yale U., 1974-75; Fulbright prof. Am. Lit. U. Oslo, 1962-64, dir., prof. Am. Inst., 1963-64; vis. prof. U. Warsaw, 1964, U. Sussex, Eng., 1972, U. Salonika, 1955-56; Fulbright prof. Am. Lit. and Civilization U. Bergen, Norway, 1989-90, U. Aveiro, Portugal, 1993; steering com. Internat. Conf. Higher Edn., 1989-; rsch. scholar comparative higher edn. CUNY, 1989—; lectr. in field. Author: The Scientific Thought of Henry Adams, 1956, (with others) Higher Education in Western Europe and North America: A Selected and Annotated Bibliography, 1979, American Literature and Language: A Selected and Annotated Bibliography, 1980; editor: (with Sigmund Skard) Americana Norvegica; Norwegian Contributions to American Studies, 1968, (with others) The Compleat University, 1983, Problems of the Urban University: A Comparative Perspective, 1984, Impact of Changing Labor Force on Higher Education, 1987, Higher Education Policy: Europe and USA, 2007; editor (with Ulrich Teichler) German and American Universities: Mutual Influences, 1992, Diversification in Higher Education: A Comparative View, 1999; mem. bd. editors History of European Ideas, 1986—, guest editor, summer, 1987; guest editor Higher Edn. Policy, spring, 1994, contbr. articles to newspapers and profl. jours. Faculty trustee CUNY, 1981-86, trustee emeritus, 1986—, chair senate; bd. dirs. Scandinavian Seminar, 1978-86, sec., 1980-83, vice chmn., 1983-86. Recipient Am. Scandinavian Found. award, 1969, 71, German Acad. Exch. Svc. award, 1973, 80, 2004, Swedish Info. Svc. award, 1979, Norwegian Ministry of Culture award, 1983, NEH award, 1984, Foscolo medal U. Pavia, Italy, 1986, German Marshall Fund award, 1985, 87, Atheneum medal U. Pavia, Italy, 1988, Disting. Senator award CUNY Faculty Senate, 1994. Mem. Am. Studies Assn. (pres. Met. N.Y. chpt. 1961-62, nat. exec. coun. 1968-74), Melville Soc. Am. (historian 1969-74), MLA, Am. Scandinavian Found. (fellow 1971), Internat. Assn. Univ. Profs. English, Assn. Upper Level Colls. and Univs. (2d v.p. 1971-72), Assn. for World Edn. (internat. coun.), Phi Beta Kappa (sec. City Coll. chpt. 1957-62, 1964-67, internat. advisory bd., U. Aegean, 1991-93, pres. CUNY Acad. for Humanities and Scis. 1991-2004, exec. dir. 2004-), Henry Adams Soc. (exec. coun. 1994—, pres. 1996-2003, dir. 2004-, exec. com. internat. conf. & higher edn. 2008-), Mass. Hist. Soc. (fellow 2001). Home: 333 E 34th St Apt 16C New York NY 10016-4950 also: 5517 Fieldston Rd Bronx NY 10471-2503 Office: CUNY Academy Grad Sch 365 Fifth Ave New York NY 10016-4309 Office Phone: 212-817-7944. Business E-Mail: hwasser@gccuny.edu.

WASSER, LAURA ALLISON, lawyer; b. LA, May 23, 1968; d. Dennis Wasser. BA, U. Calif. Berkeley, 1991; JD, Loyola Law Sch., 1994. Bar: Calif. 1994. Ptnr. Wasser, Cooperman & Carter, LA. V.p. fin. devel., bd. dirs. Harriet Buhai Ctr. Family Law. Mem.: Calif. State Bar Assn., LA County Bar Assn., Beverly Hills Bar Assn. Office: Wasser Cooperman & Carter Ste 1200 One Century Plz 2029 Century Park E Los Angeles CA 90067 Office Phone: 310-277-7117. Office Fax: 310-553-1793.

WASSER, MARILYN J., lawyer, real estate company executive; m. Eric Wasser; 3 children. AB in Govt., Smith Coll.; JD with honors, Case Western Reserve U. Atty. private practice; atty. AT&T Corp., 1983—91, chief atty., 1991—94, v.p. law, corp. sec., 1994—2002; exec. v.p., assoc. gen. counsel AT&T Wireless, 2002—05; exec. v.p., gen. counsel, corp. sec. Telcordia Technologies, 2005—07; exec. v.p., gen. counsel Realogy Corp., Parsippany, NJ, 2007—. Office: Realogy Corp 1 Campus Dr Parsippany NJ 07054

WASSERBURG, GERALD JOSEPH, geology and geophysics educator; b. New Brunswick, NJ, Mar. 25, 1927; s. Charles and Sarah (Levine) W.; m. Naomi Z. Orlick, Dec. 21, 1951; children: Charles David, Daniel Morris. Student, Rutgers U., 1946—48; BS in Physics, U. Chgo., 1951, MSc in Geology, 1952, PhD, 1954, DSc (hon.), 1992; D (hon.), Brussels U., 1985, U. Paris, 1986; DSc (hon.), Ariz. State U., 1987, U. Rennes, 1998, U. Turino, Italy, 2000. Rsch. assoc. Inst. Nuc. Studies U. Chgo., 1954-55; asst. prof. Calif. Inst. Tech., Pasadena, 1955-59, assoc. prof., 1959-62, prof. geology and geophysics, 1962-82, John D. MacArthur prof. geology and geophysics, 1982—2001, prof. emeritus, 2001—. Served on Juneau Ice Field Rsch. Project, 1950; cons. Argonne Nat. Lab., Lamont, Ill., 1952-55; former mem. U.S. Nat. Com. for Geochem., com. for Planetary Exploration Study, NRC, adv. coun. Petroleum Rsch. Fund, Am. Chem. Soc.; mem. lunar sample analysis planning team (LSAPT) manned Spacecraft Ctr., NASA, Houston, 1968-71, chmn., 1970; lunar sample rev. bd., 1970-72; mem. Facilities Working Group LSAPT, Johnson Space Ctr., 1972-82; mem. sci. working panel for Apollo missions, Johnson Space Ctr., 1971-73; advisor NASA, 1968-88, phys. scis. com., 1971-75, mem. lunar base steering com., 1984; chmn. com. for planetary and lunar exploration, mem. space sci. bd. NAS, 1975-78; chmn. divsn. Geol. and Planetary Scis., Calif. Inst. Tech., 1987-89; vis. prof. U. Kiel, Fed. Republic of Germany, 1960, Harvard U., 1962, U. Bern, Switzerland, 1966, Swiss Fed. Tech. Inst., 1967, Max Planck Inst., Mainz and Heidelberg, Fed. Republic of Germany, 1985, others; invited lectr., Vinton Hayes Sr. fellow Harvard U., 1980, Jaeger-Hales lectr. Australian Nat. U., 1980, Harold Jeffreys lectr. Royal Astron. Soc., 1981, Ernst Cloos lectr. Johns Hopkins U., 1984, H.L. Welsh Disting. lectr. U. Toronto, 1986, Danz lectr. U. Wash., 1989, Goldschmidt Centennial lectr. Norwegian Acad. Sci. and Letters, 1989, Lindsay lectr. Goddard Space Flight Ctr., 1996, other lectureshipss; plenary spkr. 125th Anniversary Geol. Soc. Sweden, 1996; 60th Anniversary Symposium spkr. Hebrew U., Jerusalem, 1985, 75th Anniversary Symposium spkr., 2000; Lezione Magistrale, Umbria Libri, Perugia, 2003. Rifleman U.S. Army, 1943-46. Decorated Combat Inf. badge, 2nd Divn.; recipient Group Achievement award NASA, 1969, Exceptional Sci. Achievement award NASA, 1970, Disting. Pub. Svc. medal NASA, 1973, J.F. Kemp medal Columbia U., 1973, Profl. Achievement award U. Chgo. Alumni Assn., 1978, Goldschmidt medal Geochem. Soc., 1978, Disting. Pub. Svc. medal with cluster NASA, 1978, Wollaston medal Geol. Soc. London, 1985, Sr. Scientist award Alexander von Humboldt-Stiftung, 1985, Crafoord prize Royal Swedish Acad. Scis., 1986, Holmes medal, 1987, European Union Geosar, Regents fellow Smithsonian Inst., Gold medal Royal Astron. Soc., 1991; named Hon. Fgn. fellow European Union Geoscis., 1983. Fellow Am. Acad. Arts and Scis., Geol. Soc. London (hon.), Geol. Soc. Am., Am. Geophys. Union (planetology sect., Harry H. Hess medal 1985, Bowie medal, 2008), Geol. Soc. Am. (life, Arthur L. Day medal 1970), Meteoritical Soc. (pres. 1987-88, Leonard medal 1975), Geochemical Society and the European Assn. for Geochemistry, 1996; mem. Nat. Acad. Scis. (Arthur L. Day prize and lectureship 1981, J. Lawrence Smith medal 1985), Norwegian Acad. Sci. and Letters, Am. Phil. Soc. Achievements include research in geochemistry and geophysics and the application of the methods of chemical physics to problems in the earth scis. Major researches have been the determination of the time scales of nucleosynthesis, connections between the interstellar medium and solar material, the time of the formation of the solar system, the chronology and evolution of the earth, moon and meteorites, the establishment of dating methods using long-lived natural radio-activities, the study of geologic and cosmic processes using nuclear and isotopic effects as a tracer in nature, the origin of natural gases, and the application of thermodynamic methods to geologic systems. Office: Calif Inst Tech Divsn Geol & Planetary Scis Pasadena CA 91125-2500 Home Phone: 541-997-9224. Business E-Mail: gjw@gps.caltech.edu.

WASSERHEIT, JUDITH N., social services administrator; b. NYC, 1954; m. Jeffrey Harris, 1981; one child. BA cum laude, Princeton U., 1974; MD, Harvard U., 1978; MPH, Johns Hopkins U., 1989. Co-dir., co-developer Harborview Med. Ctr., U. Wash., 1982-84; infectious disease physician Internat. Ctr. for Diarrheal Disease Rsch., 1984-86; asst. chief Sexually Transmitted Disease Clin. Svcs. Balt. City Health Dept., 1986-89; chief Sexually Transmitted Disease Br. Nat. Inst. Allergy and Infectious Diseases, NIH, 1989-92; dir. Sexually Transmitted Disease Prevention Disease Ctr. for Disease Control & Prevention, HHS, 1992—2001; dir. HIV Vaccine Trials Network, Seattle, 2001; prof. allergy and infectious disease U. Wash. Sch. Pub. Health, Seattle, vice chair, prof. global health. Affiliate investigator Fred Hutchinson Cancer Rsch. Ctr., Seattle; amb. Paul G. Rogers Soc. Global Health Rsch., 2007—. Editor: Reproductive Tract Infections: Global Impact and Priorities for Women's Health, 1992; contbr. articles to profl. jours. Recipient Spl. Recognition award Pub. Health Svc., 1990, 91, Young Profl. award Maternal-Child Health, APHA, 1991, Presdl. Meritorious Rank award, 1996; Pub. Health Leadership Inst. Scholar, 1993. Mem. Phi Beta Kappa, Sigma Xi. Office: U Washington Box 355065 1705 NE Pacific St Seattle WA 98195 also: Harborview Med Ctr 325 9th Ave Seattle WA 98109 Office Phone: 206-685-1894. Office Fax: 206-685-8519. E-mail: jwasserh@u.washington.edu.*

WASSERMAN, BARRY L(EE), architect; b. Cambridge, Mass., May 25, 1935; s. Theodore and Adelaide (Levin) Wasserman; m. Wilma Louise Greenfield, June 21, 1957 (div. 1971); children: Tim Andrew, Andrew Glenn; m. Judith Ella Michalowski, Apr. 22, 1979. BA, Harvard U., 1957, M. Arch., 1960. Registered arch., Calif. Assoc. John S. Bolles Assocs., San Francisco, 1960-69; prin. Wasserman-Herman Assocs., San Francisco, 1969-72; prin., dir. Office Lawrence Halprin U Assocs., San Francisco, 1972-76; dep. state architect State of Calif., Sacramento, 1976-78, state architect, 1978-83; prof. dept. architecture, dir. Inst. Environ. Design, Sch. Environ. Design Calif. State Poly. U., Pomona, 1983-87, chair dept. architecture, Coll. Environ. Design, 1988-96, prof. emeritus, 1997—. Program advisor Fla. A&M U., Tallahassee, 1981—83; adv. com. Interior Design Program Calif. State U., Sacramento, 2004—; bd. dirs. Environ. Coun. Sacramento; design rev. adminstr. Sacramento County, 2006—; cons. in field. Prin. works include Wasserman House, San Rafael, Calif., 1963 (AIA-Sunset Mag. award of Merit, 1965), Anna Waden Libr., San Francisco, 1969 (AIA award of Merit, 1970), Capitol Area Plan, Sacramento, 1977 (Ctrl. Valley chpt. AIA Honor award, 1979); co-author: Ethics and the Practice of Architecture, 2000. Mem. City of Sacramento Planning Commn., 2004—. Recipient awards citation, Prog. Architecture 26th Awards Program, 1979, Octavius Morgan award, Calif. Archs. Bd., 2000. Fellow: AIA (chmn. architecture govt. com. 1979, bd. dirs. environ. coun. Sacramento 2004—). Democrat. Jewish. Home: 6456 Fordham Way Sacramento CA 95831-2218 E-mail: blw2@mindspring.com.

WASSERMAN, DEBORAH L., medical researcher; b. Buffalo, Dec. 29, 1954; d. Bernard and Marcia Wasserman; 1 child, Luisa Max Canneto. PhD, Ohio State U., Columbus, 2002. Cert. women's health care specialist Calif., 1977. Clinician Planned Parenthood Assn. Utah, Salt Lake City, 1974—81; adminstrv. dir. Goldston Mime Found., Gambier, Ohio, 1981—85; dir. evaluation & assoc. dir. Cmty. Rsch. Partners, Columbus, 2002—05; postdoc. fellow Nationwide Children's Rsch. Inst., Columbus, 2005—06; evaluation & rsch. specialist Ohio State U. Ctr. Family Rsch., 2006—. Mem.: Am. Evaluation Assn. (program chair 1999—2006). Achievements include development of theory-based framework for creating evaluation logic models. Home: 1450 Roads End Pl Columbus OH 43209 Office: Ohio State Univ COSI 333 W Broad St Columbus OH 43215 Business E-Mail: wasserman.12@osu.edu.

WASSERMAN, RICHARD LEO, lawyer; b. Balt., Aug. 6, 1948; s. Jack B. and Claire (Gutman) W.; m. Manuele Delbourgo, May 13, 1973; children: Alexander E., Lauren E. AB, Princeton U., 1970; JD, Columbia U., 1973. Bar: N.Y. 1975, Md. 1978, U.S. Dist. Ct. (so. and ea. dists.) N.Y. 1975, U.S. Dist. Ct. Md. 1978, U.S. Ct. Appeals (2d cir.) 1975, U.S. Ct. Appeals (4th cir.) 1979, U.S. Supreme Ct. 1982. Law clk. to hon. Roszel C. Thomsen U.S. Dist. Ct. Md., Balt., 1973-74; assoc. Proskauer Rose Goetz & Mendelsohn, NYC, 1974-78, Venable LLP, Balt., 1978-81, ptnr., Bankruptcy & Creditors' Rights practice, 1982—. Bd. dirs. Legal Aid Bur., Inc., 2004—. Co-author, editor in chief: Bankruptcy Appeals Manual, 1998; editor: Bankruptcy Appeals Manual, 2d edit., 2005; contbr. chapters to books. Recipient Pro Bono Svc. award, US Dist. Ct. Md., 2005. Fellow Am. Coll. Bankruptcy, Md. Bar Found.; mem. ABA (bus. bankruptcy com.), Md. Bar Assn. (sec. coun. bus. law sect. 1989-92), Bar Assn. Balt. City (chmn. banking, bankruptcy and bus. law com. 1987-88), Bankruptcy Bar Assn. Dist. Md. (bd. dirs. 1988—, pres. 1990-91), Assn. Bar City N.Y., Am. Bankruptcy Inst., Princeton U. Alumni Assn. Md. (bd. dirs. 1980-98, pres. 1985-87), Suburban Club Baltimore County (bd. govs. 1982-89, 94-98, 2d v.p. 1986-87, sec. 1987-88, pres.-elect 1994-95, pres. 1995-97). Democrat. Jewish. Avocations: tennis, golf, bridge. Office: Venable LLP 750 East Pratt St Ste 900 Baltimore MD 21202 Office Phone: 410-244-7505. Office Fax: 410-244-7742. Business E-Mail: rlwasserman@venable.com.

WASSERMAN, ROBERT, Mayor, Fremont, California; b. Gary, Ind., Jan. 12, 1934; s. Morris K. and Alice Wasserman; m. Mary Linda Galantin, Sept. 13, 1958; children: Daniel Joseph, Jill Marie. BS Law Enforcement Adminstrn., Calif. State U., 1963; MPA, U. So. Calif., 1975. Chief of police City of San Carlos, Calif., 1969—72, City of Brea and Yorba Linda, Calif., 1972—76, City of Fremont, Calif., 1976—91; councilman Fremont City Council, 1992—2004; mayor Fremont, Calif., 1992—. Chmn. adv. com. Calif. Commn. on Peace Officer Stds. and Tng., 1979—83, mem., Pres.'s Adv. Com. Law Enforcement; cons. to police agys.; Contbr. articles to profl. jours. Bd. mgrs. Fremont-Newark YMCA, 1978—; mem. Internat. Assn. Chiefs of Police, Calif. Peace Officers Assn., 1980—. Served US Army, 1950—52, Korean War. Mem.: Rotary. Democrat. Avocations: sports, reading, travel. Office: City Hall 3300 Capitol Avenue PO Box 5006 Fremont CA 94537 Office Phone: 510-284-4011. Business E-Mail: bwasserman@ci.fremont.ca.us.*

WASSERMAN, ROBERT HAROLD, biology professor; b. Schenectady, Feb. 11, 1926; s. Joseph and Sylvia (Rosenberg) W.; m. Marilyn Mintz, June 11, 1950; children: Diane Jean, Arlene Lee, Judith Rose. BS, Cornell U., 1949, PhD, 1953; MS, Mich. State U., 1951. Research assoc. AEC project U. Tenn., Oak Ridge, 1953-55; sr. scientist med. div. Oak Ridge Inst. Nuclear Studies, 1955-57; assoc. prof. dept. phys. biology N.Y. State Vet. Coll., Cornell U., 1957-63, prof., 1963—, James Law prof. physiology, 1989-97, James Law prof. emeritus, 1998—, acting head phys. biology dept., 1963-64, 71, 75-76, chmn. dept. /sect. physiology, 1983-87, mem. exec. com. div. biol. sci., 1983-87. Vis. fellow Inst. Biol. Chemistry, Copenhagen, 1964-65; chmn. Conf. on Calcium Transport, 1962; co-chmn. Conf. on Cell Mechanisms for Calcium Transfer and Homeostasis, 1970; mem. adv. bd. Vitamin D Symposia, 1976—; adv. bd. Symposia Calcium-Binding Proteins, 1977-2001, chmn., 1977; food and nutrition bd. NRC; cons. NIH, Oak Ridge Inst. Nuclear Studies; pub. affairs com. Fedn. Am. Socs. Exptl. Biology, 1974-77; chmn. com. MPI, NRC; pre-doctoral fellowship panel Howard Hughes, 1999-2000, 03. Bd. editors: Calcified Tissue Research, 1977-80, Procs. Soc. Exptl. Biol. Medicine, 1970-76, Cornell Veterinarian, Jour. Nutrition; contbr.: articles to profl. jours. Served with U.S. Army, 1944-45. Recipient Mead Johnson award, 1969, Andre Lichtwitz prize INSERM, 1982, W.F. Neuman award Am. Soc. Bone and Mineral Rsch., 1990, Merit award NIH, 1993-96, Brown U. Rsch. award, 2004; Guggenheim fellow, 1964-65, 72, fellow NSF-OECD, 1964-65. Fellow Am. Inst. Nutrition, mem. Am. Physiol. Soc., Soc. Exptl. Biology and Medicine, AAAS, Nat. Acad. Scis., Sigma Xi, Phi Kappa Phi, Phi Zeta Home: 358 Savage Farm Dr Ithaca NY 14850-1758 Business E-Mail: rhw2@cornell.edu.

WASSERMAN, STEVE, literary agent; b. Vancouver, Wash., Aug. 3, 1952; s. Abraham and Ann (Dragoon) W.; m. Michelle Krisel, Mar. 7, 1982 (div. Dec. 2001); children: Claire, Paul, Isaac; m. Jodi Faith Cahn, Aug. 11, 2002; 1 child, Mira. AB in Criminology, U. Calif., Berkeley, 1974. Asst. editor City Mag. of San Francisco, 1975—76; dep. editor opinion sect. L.A. Times, 1977—83; editor-in-chief New Republic Books The New Republic, NYC, 1984—87; pub., editl. dir. Hill and Wang divsn. Farrar, Straus and Giroux Inc., NYC, 1987—90; pub. The Noonday Press divsn. Farrar, Straus and Giroux Inc., NYC, 1987—90; editl. dir. Times Books divsn. Random House, NYC, 1990—96; editor L.A. Times Book Rev., 1996—2005; mng. dir. Kneerim & Williams at Fish & Richardson, NYC, 2005—; lit. editor www.truthdig.com, 2007—. Cons. editor The Threepenny Rev., Berkeley, Calif., 1980—86, Tikkun, Oakland, Calif., 1986—90; founder, co-dir. L.A. Inst. for Humanities, U. So. Calif., 1998—2005; fellow NY Inst. for Humanities, NYU, 2006—; Donald and Doris Fischer lectr. Grad. Sch. of Journalism U. Calif. Berkeley, 1999; instr., master profl. writing program U. So. Calif., 2000—05; adj. prof. dept. journalism NYU, 2007—08; co-dir. L.A. Times Festival of Books, 1997—2005; chair Pulitzer Prize Nominating Jury for Gen. Nonfiction, 2001; mem. Pulitzer Prize Nominating Jury for Fiction, 2003; bd. dirs. Nat. Book Critics Cir., 1997—2005; mem. jury lit. prizes Commonwealth Club Calif., 2001—06. Contbr. articles and revs. to mags. and newspapers. Mem. PEN. Office: Kneerim & Williams at Fish & Richardson Citigroup Ctr 52nd Fl 601 Lexington Ave New York NY 10022-4611 Office Phone: 212-641-2267. Business E-Mail: wasserman@fr.com.

WASSERMANN, ERIC M., neurologist, department chairman; s. Felix E. and Hannah D. Wassermann; married. BA, Swarthmore Coll., PA, 1979; MA, U. Pa., Phila., 1981; MD, NY Med. Coll., Valhalla, 1985. Cert. neurology ABPN, 1992. Unit chief NIH/NINDS, Bethesda, Md., 1994—. Capt. USPHS. Avocation: sailing. Office: NIH/NINDS 10 Ctr Dr Msc 1440 Bethesda MD 20892-1440

WASSERMAN-SCHULTZ, DEBBIE, United States Representative from Florida; b. Forest Hills, NY, Sept. 27, 1966; BA in Polit. Sci., U. Fla., 1988, MA in Polit. Sci., 1990. Legis. aide office rep. Peter Deutsch State of Fla., 1989—92; mem. Fla. Ho. of Reps., 1992—2000, Dem. floor leader, 1998—99, Dem. leader pro tempore, 2000; mem. Fla. State Senate, 2001—04, US Congress from 20th Fla. dist., 2005—, sr. whip, 2005—06, chief dep. whip, 2008—; mem. US House Judiciary Com., US House Appropriations Com.; vice chair Dem. Nat. Com., 2009—; vice chair incumbent retention Democratic Congressional Campaign Com. (DCCC), 2009—. Mem. Classrooms First Task Force, 1993, Fla. Edn. Facilities Study Com., 1994, Gov.'s Commn. Edn., 1995—97, Fla. Supreme Ct. Gender Bias Study Implementation Commn., 1992—; second v.p. Gwen Cherry Women's Polit. Caucus, 1992—; mem. legis. adv. coun. So. Regional Edn. Bd., 1995—; chair South Fla. Dem. Caucus, 1998—. Sec. young leadership coun. Jewish Fedn. Greater Ft. Lauderdale, 1989—90; sec., v.p. Broward County Young Dems., 1990—92; bd. trustees Westside Regional Med. Ctr., Plantation, Fla., 1993—; bd. dirs. Fla. Distance Learning Network, 1995—97, South Fla. chpt. Nat. Safety Coun., Nat. Jewish Dem. Coun., S.E. Region Am. Jewish Congress. Recipient Giraffe award, Women's Advocacy Majority Minority (WAMM), 1993, Outstanding Family Advocacy award, Dade County Psychol. Assn., 1993, Rosemary Barkett award, Acad. Fla. Trial Lawyers, 1995; named Woman of Yr., AMIT, 1994, Outstanding Legislator of Yr., Fla. Fedn. Bus. & Profl. Women, 1994; named a Quality Floridian, Fla. League of Cities, 1994, Woman of Vision, Weizmann Inst. Sci.; named one of Six Most Unstoppable Women, South Fla. Mag., 1994. Mem.: NOW, Nat. Coun. Jewish Women, Hawkes Bluff Panel & Homeowner's Assn. (sec.), Weston C. of C., Pembroke Pines C. of C., Miramar C. of C., Omicron Delta Kappa. Democrat. Jewish. Avocations: bowling, golf, politics, old houses. Office: US Congress 118 Cannon House Office Bldg Washington DC 20515-0920 also: 10100 Pines Blvd Pembroke Pines FL 33026 Office Phone: 202-225-7931. Office Fax: 202-226-2052.*

WASSERSTEIN, BRUCE, investment banker; b. Bklyn., Dec. 25, 1947; s. Morris and Lola (Schleifer) Wasserstein; m. Laura Wasserstein (div. 1974); m. Christine Parrott (div. 1992); children: Ben, Pam; m. Claude Becker; children: Zack, Dash; 1 adopted child BA with honors, U. Mich., 1967; MBA with high distinction, Harvard U., 1971, JD cum laude, 1971; diploma in law, Cambridge U., 1972. Assoc. Cravath, Swaine & Moore, NYC, 1972-77; mng. dir. The First Boston Corp., NYC, 1977-88; pres. Wasserstein, Perella and Co., NYC, 1988—2000; exec. chmn. Dresdner Kleinwort Wasserstein, NYC, 2000—01; chmn., CEO Lazard Ltd., NYC, 2001—; chmn. Am. Lawyer Media, 1997—; owner The Daily Deal, 1999—, NY Mag., 2003—; chmn. Wasserstein & Co., 2001—. Author: Corporatwe Finance Law: A Guide for the Executive, 1978, Big Deal: Mergers and Acquisitions in the Digital Age, 1988 Mem. SEC Adv. Comm. Tender Offers; mem. vis. com. Harvard Law Sch., Harvard Bus. Sch., U. Mich., Columbia Journalism Sch., Cambridge U. Bus. Sch. Mem. Coun. on Fgn. Rels. Democrat. Office: Lazard Ltd 30 Rockefeller Plaza New York NY 10020*

WASSERSTEIN, RONALD L., statistics organization director; BA in Math., Washburn U., Topeka; MS in Stats., PhD in Stats., Kans. State U., Manhattan. Faculty mem. Washburn U., 1984—96, prof. stats., 1996—2007, v.p. acad. affairs, 2001—07; exec. dir. Am. Statis. Assn., Alexandria, Va., 2007—. Mem. Kans. Ratio Study Tech. Adv. Com., 1994. Fellow: Am. Statis. Assn. Office: Am Statis Assn 732 N Washington St Alexandria VA 22314-1943 Office Phone: 703-684-1221 ext. 1859. E-mail: ron@amstat.org.

WASSHAUSEN, DIETER CARL, botanist; b. Jena, Germany, Apr. 15, 1938; came to U.S., 1950, naturalized, 1957; s. Heinz P. and Elizabeth A. (Mueller) W.; m. Merrilee M. Locklin, Dec. 23, 1961; children— Lisa A., David B. BS, George Washington U., 1962, MS, 1965, PhD, 1972. Assoc. curator dept. botany Smithsonian Instn., Washington, 1969-76; chmn., curator dept. botany Nat. Mus. Natural History, Washington, 1976—2003, curator emeritus, 2003—, rsch. botanist, 2003—. Recipient Smithsonian Rsch. Found. award, 1974—75, Willdenow medal, 1979. Mem. Am. Soc. Plant Taxonomists, Internat. Assn. Plant Taxonomy, Neotropical Field Botanists Assn., Am. Inst. Biol. Scis., AAAS, Assn. Tropical Biology, Sigma Xi. Presbyterian. Achievements include research on systematics of neotropical Acanthaceae, floristic studies in Graminea of Brazil, floristic studies in Begoniaceae, revision of Nat. List Sci. Plant Names. Home: St James Plantation 2931 Legends Dr Southport NC 28461 Office: Nat Mus Natural History 10th St and Constitution Ave NW Washington DC 20560-0001 Office Phone: 202-633-0944. Personal E-mail: dmwasshausen@2khiway.net.

WASSMER, RUDOLF ANDREAS, entrepreneurial engineer; b. Berne, Switzerland, Nov. 27, 1941; s. Hans Erich and Margaretha Katharina (von Mandach) W.; m. Janine Antoinette Georgine Koch, Aug. 24, 1978; 1 child, Alexandra Janine. Diploma mech. engring., Fed. Inst. of Tech., 1967; diploma, European Inst. Bus. Adminstrn., 1971. Jr. project engr. internat. Polysius, Paris, 1968; del. project engr. SungShin Cement, Seoul, 1969-70; with Swiss Aluminium Ltd., Zuerich, 1971-72; cons. Portland Cement Werk, 1973; works engr. Würenlingen AG, 1973-74; tech. dir., rep., 1974-76; mem. staff Cementia Engring and Cons., Zurich, 1976-78, sr. engr. internat., 1981-87, 92; works dir., improvement plan Bamburi Portland Cement Co. Ltd., Kenya, 1978-81; enterpreneurial engr. Swiss secretariat Holdit, Leadership and Devel. Activities Internat., Zurich, 1987—. Capt. Swiss Army Res., 1964-91. Mem. INSEAD (alumnus), ETHZ, Swiss Engring. and Arch., Eur Ing Feani (cert.), Seoul Club, Mobasa Club. Avocation: sports. Office: Holdit & Studio P-C-W Hdqs 4th floor Asylstrasse 64 8032 Zurich Switzerland Office Fax: 41443830975.

WASSNER, STEVEN JOEL, pediatric nephrologist, educator; b. NYC, Dec. 16, 1946; s. Abraham and Clara (Weitzner) W.; m. Enid K. Kling, June 11, 1972; children: Adam Jacob, Nancy Shane. BS, CCNY, 1968; MD, NYU, 1972. Diplomate Am. Bd. Pediatrics, Am. Bd. Pediatrics Nephrology. Intern, resident Children's Hosp. L.A., 1972-74, fellow in pediatric nephrology, 1974-75; rsch. fellow in pediatric nephrology UCLA, 1975-77; asst. prof. pediat. Pa. State U. M.S. Hershey Med. Ctr., Hershey, 1978—83, chief divsn. pediat. nephrology and hypertension, 1978—, assoc. prof., 1983—91, dir. pediat. residency program, 1988—2006, dir. med./pediat residency program, 1989—94, vice chmn. dept., 1989—99, prof., 1991—, chief divsn. pediatric nephrology and diabetes, 1991—99, vice chmn. edn., 1999—, interim chief divsn. pediatric endocrinology, 2005—07, physician lead safety and quality, children hosp., 2006—. Vis. prof. human biochemistry Hebrew U., Hadassah Hosp., 1985-86; dir. Pediatric Diabetes Svc., 1998-99. Contbr. articles to med. jours. Mem. adv. bd. Kidney Found. South Ctrl. Pa., Harrisburg, 1980-90, sci. adv. coun. for pediatric nephrology/urology Nat. Kidney Found., 1986-92, Harrisburg com. for Hebrew U.; bd. dirs. Jewish Family Svc., Harrisburg, 1979-85, pres., 1983-85; bd. dirs. United Jewish Fedn., 1983-85, 94-97, Yeshiva Acad., 1987-90. Recipient Rsch. Career Devel. award NIH, 1983; Musclar Dystrophy Assn. grantee, 1979-81, Disting. Educator award, 2005; Sr. Internat. fellow Fogarty Internat. Ctr. NIH, 1985. Fellow Am. Acad. Pediatrics (exec. com. sect. on nephrology, chair program subcom. 1998-2002, chmn. exec. com. sect. on nephrology 2002-06); mem. Am. Bd. Pediatrics (fellow 1986-2003), Am. Pediatrics Soc., Am. Soc. Nephrology, Internat. Soc. Nephrology, Am. Soc. Pediatrics, Nephrology, Internat. Soc. Pediatric Nephrology, Internat. Pediatric Nephrology Assn. (counsellor 1989-95). Office: MS Hershey Med Ctr PO Box 850 Hershey PA 17033-0850 Office Phone: 717-531-5707. Business E-Mail: swassner@psu.edu.

WASSON, ELLIS ARCHER, history educator; b. Rye, NY, Dec. 31, 1947; s. Samuel Carson and Elizabeth (Ellis) W. BA, MA, Johns Hopkins U., 1972; PhD, Cambridge U., Eng., 1976. Dean of faculty The Rivers Sch., Weston, Mass., 1976-86; headmaster sr. sch. Shady Side Acad., Pitts., 1986-91; chmn. history dept. Tower Hill Sch., Wilmington, Del., 1991—. Test devel. com. Coll. Bd., N.Y.C., 1985-87, cons., 1981—; adj. prof. history U. Del., 2001—; vis. fellow Wolfson Coll., Cambridge (Eng.) U., 2004. Author: Whig Renaissance, 1987, AP European History, 1995, Born to Rule: British Political Elites, 2000, Aristocracy and the Modern World, 2006, Modern Britain: 1714 to the Present, 2009; contbr. articles to profl. jours., chpts. to books. Treas. New Eng. History Tchrs. Assn., Boston, 1978-79; chmn. history com. Ind. Sch. Assn. Mass., Boston, 1981-83, chmn. acad. deans, 1982-86; mem. alumni admissions com. Johns Hopkins U., Pitts. and Wilmington, 1987-2000; corporator The Rivers Sch., 1986-91; convenor Am. Friends of Cambridge U., Pitts., 1986-91. Gilman fellow Johns Hopkins U., 1972, NEH fellow, 1984, rsch. fellow English Speaking Union, 1994, 2000. Fellow Royal Hist. Soc., Royal Soc. Arts; mem. Inst. for Hist. Rsch. (U. London), Am. Hist. Assn. (Bernadotte Schmidt fellow 1993), Athenaeum of Phila., N. Am. Conf. on Brit. Studies. Avocation: travel. Office: Tower Hill Sch 2813 W 17th St Wilmington DE 19806-1198 Office Phone: 302-575-0550. Business E-Mail: ewasson@towerhill.org.

WASSON, GREGORY D., retail executive; b. 1958; BS in Pharmacy, Purdue U., 1981. Various positions Walgreen Co., Deerfield, Ill., 1980—86, dist. mgr., 1986—99, regional v.p. store ops., 1999—2001; exec. v.p. Walgreens Health Initiatives Inc. (WHI), 2001—02, pres., 2002; v.p. Walgreen Co., Deerfield, Ill., 2001—04, sr. v.p., 2004—05, exec. v.p., 2006—07, pres., COO, 2007—09, pres., CEO, 2009—. Bd. dirs. Walgreen Co., 2009—. Office: Walgreen Co 200 Wilmot Rd Deerfield IL 60015*

WASSON, JEFFREY, music educator; b. Evanston, Ill., Aug. 24, 1948; s. Newton Oliver and Hilda Crowell Wasson. MusB, Northwestern U., 1970, MusM, 1973, PhD, 1987. Instr. music Northwestern U., Evanston, Ill., 1980-85; asst. prof. music Barat Coll., Lake Forest, Ill., 1986-92; dir. music St. Mary of the Angels, Chgo., 1992-97, Barat Coll., Lake Forest, Ill., 1987—, assoc. prof. music, 1992-99, prof. music, 1999-2001, Barat Coll. DePaul U., 2001—02; prof. musicianship DePaul U., Chgo., 2002—. Vis. prof. music, Northwestern U., 1990, 93; bd. mem. New Music Chgo., 1987, 92-94, v.p., 1987-88, pres., 1988-92; bd. dirs. Mozart Sinfonia; bd. dirs. Ars Musica Chgo., 2000-05, v.p., 2003-04, pres., 2004—; NEH summer seminar participant Brandeis U., 1995, Boston U., 2000; lectr. Yale U., U. Leuven, Belgium, U. Mich., Ann Arbor, U. Minn., U. Pitts., Mich. State U., Loyola U. of Chgo., U. Nebr. Editor: A Compendium of American Musicology, 2000; contbr. articles to profl. jours., chpts. to books. Summer seminar grantee NEH, U. Rochester (declined). Mem. NARAS, Am. Musicol. Soc., Am. Guild Organists, Internat. Musicol. Soc., Coll. Music Soc., Organ Hist. Soc., Club Internationale, Phi Kappa Lambda. Episcopalian. Avocations: fine art collecting, Lionel trains. Office: DePaul U Sch Music 804 W Belden Ave Chicago IL 60614-3296 Office Phone: 773-325-4378. Business E-Mail: jwasson@depaul.edu.

WASTBERG, OLLE M., nation branding organization administrator; b. Stockholm, May 6, 1945; s. Erik and Greta (Hirsch) Wastberg; m. Inger Claesson, Feb. 21, 1968; children: David, Elias. BA, U. Stockholm, 1972. Tchr. polit. sci. U. Stockholm, 1967-68; journalist polit. dept. Expressen, 1968-71; editor-in-chief, 1994-95; rsch. fellow Bus. and Soc. Rsch. Ctr., 1971-76; pres. Aktieframjandet, 1976-82; mem. Parliament, 1976-82; pres. Swedish Newspaper Promotion Assn., 1983-91; undersec. of state for fin. affairs Ministry of Fin., Stockholm, 1991-93; pres. bd. Nordic Investment Bank, 1992-94, Swedish Broadcasting Corp., 1996-99; consul gen. for Sweden in NY, 1999—2004; dir. gen. Swedish Inst. Bd., 2005—. Bd. dirs. Swedish Inst., Alexandria, 2007, bd. govs. globalization coun., 09; group 10 deps. IMF, 1991—93; Swedish del. meeting mins. fin., 1992; mem. govt. com. South Africa consumer politis and stock market; pres. Bertil Ohlin Inst., 1996—2000. Author: books on African problems, immigration politics and econ. topics; contbr. articles to profl. jours. Bd. dirs. Friends Hebrew U. Jerusalem; polit. sec. Liberal Youth Sweden, 1966, v.p., 1969—71; bd. dirs. Liberal Party, 1972—93, 1997—2000, pres. exec. com., 1982—83. Recipient Gold medal, Swedish Mktg. Group, 1982; named Swedish Man of the Yr., NY, 2003. Mem.: Isaac Hirsch Found. (pres. 2008—). Home: Bellmansgatan 6 11820 Stockholm Sweden Office: Swedish Inst Skeppbron 2 16391 Stockholm Sweden Office Phone: 4684537810. Business E-Mail: olle@wastberg.se.

WASYNCZUK, OLEG, electrical engineer, educator; b. Chgo., June 26, 1954; s. Ludmila Wasynczuk; m. Anne Zinger, Aug. 12, 1978; children: Natalie, Kristina, Jacqueline. BSEE, Bradley U., Peoria, Ill., 1976; MSEE, Purdue U., West Lafayette, Ind., 1977, PhD, 1979. Vis. asst. prof. Purdue U., asst. prof., 1980—83, assoc. prof., 1983—89, prof. elec. communication engring., 1989—. Chief tech. officer PC Krause and Assocs., West Lafayette, 1985—. Recipient Manley Meml. medal, Soc. Automotive Engrs., 1995, Aerospace Power Sys. Conf. Best Paper award, 1998. Fellow: IEEE (chair, generator subcom. 2005—07). Home: 3242 Crawford St West Lafayette IN 47906 Office: Purdue Univ 465 Northwestern Ave West Lafayette IN 47907-2035 Business E-Mail: wasynczu@ecn.purdue.edu.

WATABE, NORIMITSU, marine biologist, educator; b. Kure, Hiroshima, Japan, Nov. 29, 1922; came to U.S., 1957; s. Isamu and Matsuko (Takamatsu) W.; m. Sakuko Kobayashi, Dec. 12, 1952; children: Shoichi, Sachiko. BS, 1st Nat. High Sch., Tokyo, 1945; MS, Tohoku U., Sendai, Japan, 1948, DSc, 1960. Rsch. investigator Fuji Pearl Co., Mie-ken, Japan, 1948-52; instr. Prefect U. Mie, Tsu, Mie-ken, 1952-55, asst. prof., 1955-59; rsch. assoc. Duke U., Durham, N.C., 1957-70; assoc. prof. U. S.C., Columbia, 1970-72, prof. biology and marine sci., 1972-93, disting. prof., 1993-94, disting. prof. emeritus, 1994—. Cons. Ford Found., 1968; vis. prof. U. Bonn, Germany, 1976-77; dir. Electron Microscipy Ctr., 19770-95; cons. in field. Author: Studies on Pearls, 1959; editor: Mechanisms of Mineralization, 1976, Mechanisms of Biomineralization, 1980, Hard Tissue Mineralization and Demineralization, 1991; assoc. editor, Jour. Morphology, 1999—; contbr. articles to profl. jours. Recipient Pearl Rsch. award Elmer W. Ellsworth, 1952, Alexander Von Humboldt award Govt. of Germany, Russel award U. SC, 1981; grantee NIH, 1971-76, NSF, 1973-95. Fellow AAAS; mem. Am. Micros. Soc. (life). Avocation: music.

WATANABE, AUGUST MASARU, physician, educator, retired pharmaceutical executive; b. Portland, Oreg., Aug. 17, 1941; s. Frank H. and Mary Y. W.; m. Margaret Whildin Reese, Mar. 14, 1964; children: Nan Reiko, Todd Franklin, Scott Masaru. BS, Wheaton Coll., Ill., 1963; MD, Ind. U., 1967. Diplomate Am. Bd. Internal Medicine. Intern Ind. U. Med. Center, Indpls., 1967-68, resident, 1968-69, 71-72, fellow in cardiology, 1972-74; clin. asso. NIH, 1969-71; clin. instr. medicine Georgetown U. Med. Sch., Washington, 1970-71; mem. faculty Ind. U. Sch. Medicine, Indpls., 1972—2003, prof. medicine and pharmacology, 1978—2003, chmn. dept. medicine, 1983-90; dir. Regenstrief Inst. for Health Care Ind. U. Sch. of Medicine, Indpls., 1984-90; from v.p. to group v.p. rsch. labs. Eli Lilly & Co., Indpls., 1990-94, v.p., pres. Lilly Res labs, 1994—2003; exec. v.p. sci. and tech. Eli Lilly and Co., Indpls., 1996—2003, mem. bd. dirs., 1996—2003; chmn. bd. BioCrossroads, 2003—. Mem. pharmacology study sect. NIH, 1979-81, chmn., 1981-83; cardiovasc.-renal adv. com. FDA, 1982-85; mem. com. A, Nat. Heart, Lung and Blood Inst., 1984-88, chmn., 1986-88; bd. dir. QuatRx, Endocyte, Kalypsys, Ambrx, Marcadia Biotech; cons. in field. Contbr. articles to profl. jours.; editorial bds. sci. jours. Bd. dir. Ind. U. Found., 1989—, Indpls. Symphony Orch., 1994—, Regenstrief Found., 1995—. NIH grantee, 1972-92. Fellow ACP, Am. Coll. Cardiology, Am. Heart Assn. (councils on clin. cardiology and circulation, research rev. com. Ind. affiliate 1978-82, research and adv. com. North Central region 1978-82, adv. com. cardiovascular drugs 1976-79, chmn. com. 1979-81, chmn. program com. council on basic sci. 1982-84, chmn. com. on sci. sessions programs 1985-88, bd. dirs. 1985-88), Am. Coll. Cardiology (govt. relations com. 1979-81, trustee 1982-87); mem. Am. Fedn. Clin. Research (councilor Midwest sect. 1976-77, chmn.-elect Midwest sect. 1977-78, chmn. sect. 1978-79, chmn. sect. nominating com. 1979-80), Am. Soc. Clin. Investigation, Am. Soc. Clin. Pharmacology and Therapeutics, Am. Soc. Pharmacology and Exptl. Therapeutics (exec. com. div. clin. pharmacology 1978-81), Cardiac Muscle Soc., Central Soc. Clin. Research (councillor 1983-86, pres.-elect 1989, pres. 1990), Internat. Soc. Heart Research, Assn. Am. Physicians, Assn. Profs. of Medicine, Sigma Xi. Office: BioCrossroads Baker and Daniels Bldg 300 N Meridian St Ste 950 Indianapolis IN 46204

WATANABE, KAZUHIDE, medical researcher; b. Yaita, Tochigi, Japan, July 2, 1973; MD, Tohoku U., PhD, 2005. Diplomate Japanese govt., 1998. Rschr. Nat. Cancer Inst., Bethesda, Md., 2005—. Office: Nat Cancer Inst 37 Convent Dr Rm1112 Bethesda MD 20892 Personal E-mail: kazuhidew@yahoo.com. Business E-Mail: watanabek@mail.nih.gov.

WATANABE, KYOICHI A(LOYSIUS), pharmacology educator, chemist; b. Amagasaki, Hyogo, Japan, Feb. 28, 1935; s. Yujiro and Yoshiko Francisca (Hashimoto) W.; m. Krystyna Lesiak; children: Kanna, Kay, Kenneth, Kim, Kelly, Katherine. BA, Hokkaido U., 1958, PhD, 1963. Lectr. Sophia U., Tokyo, 1963; rsch. assoc. Sloan-Kettering Inst., NYC, 1963—66, assoc., 1968—72, assoc. mem., 1972—81, mem., 1981—95; rsch. fellow U. Alta., Edmonton, Canada, 1966—68; assoc. prof. Cornell U. Med. Coll., NYC, 1972—81, prof. pharmacology, 1981—98; dir. organic chemistry Codon Pharm., Inc., Gaithersburg, Md., 1996—98; v.p. R&D Pharmasset Inc., Tucker, Ga., 1998—2003; vis. prof. U. Minn., 2003—. Study sect. NIH, Washington, 1981-84. Recipient Szalecki medal, Wojzkowa Akademia Medyczna, 1989, Marie Sklodowska Curie medal, Polish Chem. Soc., 1993, František Šorm Meml. award, Czech Acad. Scis., 2002. Mem. Polish Chem. Soc. (hon.), Russian Acad. Sci. (bd. sci. cons. Engelhardt Inst. Molecular Biology 1994-97). Achievements include rsch. in total synthesis of nucleoside antibiotics, novel heterocycle ring transformation, C-nucleoside chemistry, antiviral and anticancer nucleosides, intercalating agents, modified oligonucleotides, triplex DNA for gene repair.

WATANABE, MAKOTO, engineering educator; b. Fujioka, Gunma, Japan, Jan. 13, 1941; s. Satoshi and Fuji Watanabe; m. Kayoko Watanabe, May 3, 1969; 1 child, Chigusa. B in Engring., Nagoya Inst. Tech., Japan, 1965, M in Engring., 1967; D in Engring., Nagoya U., 1977. Rsch. assoc. Chubu Inst. Tech., Kasugai, Aichi, Japan, 1967—68, lectr., 1968—76, assoc. prof., 1976—84; prof. Chubu U., Kasugai, 1984—, dean of students, 1992—97, dean Coll. Engring., 1997—2002, adminstrv. asst. to pres., 2002—. Chair Chubu Com. Elec. Anticorr., Nagoya, 2006—. Fellow: Komaki Chamber of Commerce and Industry, Okazaki Chamber of Commerce and Industry, Kasugai Chamber of Commerce and Industry; mem.: Japanese Assn. Inorganic Phos. Chems. (pres. 2002—04, Sci. Hons. 1995), Soc. Inorganic Materials (dir. 1991—, Nagai Meml. prize 1984, Sci. Hons. 1994). Avocations: classical music, travel. Home: 30-10-1 Higashiyama-cho Kasugai 486-0811 Japan Office: Chubu U Coll Engring 1200 Matsumoto-cho Kasugai 487-8501 Japan Office Phone: 81/568 51 9646. Business E-Mail: watanabe@isc.chubu.ac.jp.

WATANABE, MARK DAVID, pharmacist, educator; b. Santa Monica, Calif., Dec. 7, 1955; s. Jack Shigeru and Rose Nobuko (Iida) W. BA in Chemistry, U. Calif., Irvine, 1977, BS in Biol. Sci., 1978; PharmD, U. Calif., San Francisco, 1982, PhD in Pharm. Chemistry, 1990. Lic. pharmacist Calif., Oreg., Ill., Mass. Pharmacy intern various locations, San Francisco, 1979-82; pharmacist Kaiser Permanente, San Francisco, 1981-87; clin. scis. rsch. fellow in psychiat. pharmacy U. Tex., Austin, 1987-89; clin. asst. prof. pharmacy practice U. Ill., Chgo., 1989-98. Rsch. asst. U. Calif., San Francisco, 1980-87; clin. pharmacy cons. Ill. Dept. Mental Health & Devel. Disabilities, 1994-98; med. sci. mgr. Bristol-Myers Squibb, 1998-99; clin. pharmacy specialist, Alameda Co., Calif., 1999-2003; asst. cli. prof. clin. pharmacy, U. Calif., San Francisco, 1999-2003; asst. clin. specialist Northeastern U., 2003-07, asst. clin. prof., 2007-08, clin pharm. cons. U. Mass. Med. Sch., 2008-. Regents scholar U. Calif., San Francisco, 1979-82; recipient Excellence in Teaching award Long Found., San Francisco, 1984. Mem.: Coll. Psychiatric Neurologic Pharmacists, Am. Pharm. Assn., Am. Soc. Health-Sys. Pharmacists, Am. Coll. Clin. Pharmacy, Mensa, Phi Lambda Sigma, Rho Chi. Unitarian Universalist. Avocations: individual and fitness sports, reading, travel, music. Office: Commonwealth Medicine Univ Mass Med Sch 333 South St Shrewsbury MA 01545 Office Phone: 508-856-4570. Business E-Mail: mark.watanabe@umassmed.edu.

WATANABE, SATOSHI PATTEN, economist, researcher; b. Koriyama, Fukushima, Japan, Oct. 19, 1966; s. Keiki Watanabe, Mieko Watanabe; m. Nicole Michelle Patten; children: Sean Lucas children: Daichi Joseph. BA, Weber State U., 1990, cert. in gerontology, 1990; MA in Econ., Columbia U., 1993, MEd, 1997, MA in Stats., 1999, MPhil, PhD, Columbia U., 2000. Lectr. Manhattan Coll., Riverdale, NY, 1998; stat. data analyst City of N.Y., 1998—99; rsch. assoc. Am. Inst. Rsch., Arlington, Va., 1999—2000, rsch. scientist, 2000—01, sr. rsch. scientist, 2001—02; asst. prof. Rsch. Ctr. for Univ. Studies, U. Tsukuba, Japan, 2002—04, assoc. prof. Rsch. Ctr. for Univ. Studies, 2004—. Bd. dirs. Policy Rsch. and Analysis Network for Japan, Washington, 1999—; cons. World Bank, Washington, 2000—01. Contbr. articles to profl. jours. Mem.: Soc. Labor Economists, Am. Econ. Assn., Phi Kappa Phi. Unitarian Universalist. Avocations: travel, guitar, marathons. Office: U Tsukuba 3-29-1 Otsuka Bankyo-ku Tokyo 112-0012 Japan Home Phone: 047-477-5525. Office Fax: 703-527-4661. E-mail: swatanabe@mbaib.gsbs.tsukuba.ac.jp.

WATANABE, SHIGERU, mathematician, researcher; s. Motosaburo Watanabe. BS in Math., Sophia U., Tokyo, 1986, MS in Math., 1988, DSc in Math., 1993. Asst. prof. U. Aizu, Aizu-Wakamatsu, Japan, 1994—. Reviewer Math. Reviews: pub. by Am. Math. Soc.; contbr. articles to profl. jours. Achievements include research in Watanabe unitary transform. Office: Univ Aizu Tsuruga Ikkimachi Fukushima Aizu-Wakamatsu 965-8580 Japan Business E-Mail: sigeru-w@u-aizu.ac.jp.

WATANABE, TAKAHIRO, medical educator; b. Kawaguchi-ko, Yamanashi, Japan, Mar. 24, 1967; s. Takao and Masuko Watanabe; m. Mariko Watanabe, May 11, 2003. MD, PhD, U. Tokyo, 1991. Lic. dermatologist Tokyo, 1996. Resident dept. dermotology Tokyo U., 1991—93, rsch. assoc. dept. dermatology, 1995—99, lectr. dept. dermatology, 2002—07; rsch. assoc. dept. dermatology Internat. Med. Ctr. Japan, 1993—95; rsch. fellow Nat. Cancer Inst., Bethesda, Md., 1999—2002. Office: Futaba Dermatology Clinic 3-7-2 Horikiri Katsushika Tokyo 124-0006 Japan

WATASHI, KOICHI, medical educator, researcher; b. Osaka, Japan, Oct. 13, 1975; s. Kenji and Midori Watashi; m. Ayako Watashi Fukutome, Apr. 2, 2006. PhD in Pharm. Scis., Kyoto U., Japan, 2003. Lic. pharmacist Ministry Health, Labor & Welfare, 1998. Rsch. fellow Japan Soc. Promotion Sci., Tokyo, 2002—03; instr. Inst. Virus Rsch., Kyoto U., 2003—04, asst. prof., 2004—. Vis. fellow NIH, Bethesda, Md., 2007—. Mem.: Molecular Biology Soc. Japan, Japanese Cancer Assn. (Incitement award 2007), Japanese Soc. Virology (Sugiura Meml. Incentive award 2007). Achievements include discovery of an immunosuppressant cyclosporin A (CsA) that suppresses hepatitis C virus (HCV) replication; the first report of non-immunosuppressive CsA analogs as potential anti-HCV agents. Avocation: driving. Office: NIH 9000 Rockville Pike Bldg 4 #304 Bethesda MD 20892 Business E-Mail: watashik@niaid.nih.gov.

WATERBURY, DEBORAH KAY, minister; b. Lakeland, Fla., Dec. 27, 1962; d. William Ray and Jacqueline Rosalie Willis; m. Jeffrey Paul Waterbury, Mar. 2, 1985; children: Jeffrey Spence, Gregory Miles. BS in English and History, Mid. Tenn. State U., Murfreesboro, 1984; MA in Tchg., Grand Canyon U., Tempe, Ariz., 2003. English and reading tchr. Lily Hill Mid. Sch., Philippines, 1986—89; reading tchr. NE Mid. Sch., Clarksville, Tenn., 1991—93; English tchr. Mt. Juliet HS, Mt. Juliet, Tenn., 1995—96; history tchr. Amphi Mid. Sch., Tucson, 1996—97, Catalina Foothills HS, Tucson, 1997—2006; dir. women's ministries Faith Com. Ch., 2006—. Dir. womens ministries Faith Cmty. Ch., Tucson, 2006—. Avocations: running, writing, singing. Office: Faith Com Church 2551 W Orange Grove Rd Tucson AZ 85741 Home: 6600 N Paseo De Gabriel Tucson AZ 85741-3049

WATERBURY, JOHN, political science professor, writer, former academic administrator; BA, Princeton U., 1961, LLD (hon.), 2008; PhD in Pub. Law and Govt., Columbia U., 1968. Asst. prof. polit. sci. U. Mich., 1968; mem. Am. Univs. Field Staff, Cairo, 1971—77; prof. politics and internat. affairs Woodrow Wilson Sch. Pub. and Internat. Affairs, Princeton U., NJ, dir. Ctr. Internat. Studies NJ; pres. Am. U. of Beirut, 1998—2008, disting. fellow Dept. Pub. Policy and Internat. Affairs, 2008—. Vis. prof. U. of Aix-Marseilles III, 1977—78; editor World Politics jour. Princeton U., 1992—98. Author: Commander of the Faithful: The Moroccan Political Elite-a Study in Segmented Politics, Vol. 2, 1970, North for the Trade: The Life and Times of a Berber Merchant, 1972, Egypt: Burdens of the past, Options for the Future, 1978, Hydropolitics of the Nile Valley, 1979, Egypt of Nasser and Sadat: The Political Economy of Two Regimes, 1983, Exposed to Innumerable Delusions: Public Enterprise and State Power in Egypt, India, Mexico, and Turkey, 1993, Nile Basin: National Determinants of Collective Action, 2002; co-editor: Patrons and Clients, 1977; co-author: Middle East in the Coming Decade: From Wellhead to Well-Being, 1978; co-editor: The Political Economy of Risk and Choice in Senegal, 1987; co-author: Political Economy of the Middle East: State, Class, and Economic Development, 1990; co-editor: Political Economy of Public Sector Reform and Privatization, 1990, Peasants and Politics in the Modern Middle East, 1991; co-author: Core and Periphery: A Comprehensive Approach to Middle Eastern Water, 1997; contbr. articles to profl. jours. Fellow: Am. Acad. Arts & Scis. Office: Am U of Beirut PO Box 11-0236 Riad El Solh Beirut 1107 2020 Lebanon also: 3 Dag Hammarskjold Plaza, 8th Fl New York NY 10017-2303 Office Phone: 961 1 350000. Office Fax: 961 1 744474. E-mail: waterbury@aub.edu.lb.

WATERHOUSE, KEITH, urologist, educator, retired surgeon; b. Derby, England, May 10, 1929; arrived in U.S., 1953, naturalized, 1964; s. Arthur Reginald and Marion (Tock) Waterhouse; m. Anne Therese Milotzky, Jan. 14, 1955; children: Katherine-Anne, Vincent, Maria-Ursula, Isabelle, Christopher. BA, Cambridge U., Eng., 1950; MD, Oxford U. Med. Sch., Eng., 1953; MA, Cambridge U., Eng., 1957. Cert. urology 1964. Intern Bklyn. Hosp., 1953—54; resident Kings County Hosp., Bklyn., 1957—59; instr. surgery SUNY, Bklyn., 1959—61, asst. prof. urology, 1961—62, assoc. prof. urology, 1962—65, prof. surgery, 1965—84, chmn. dept. urology, 1969—84, prof. emeritus, 1984—. Dir. urology Kings County Hosp., 1962—84; urologist-in-chief Downstate Med. Ctr., Bklyn., 1962—84; prof. Surg. Anatomy Ross U. Med. Sch., Domenica, 1984—85, Chancellor Inst. U. Health Sci., St. Kitts, 1985—88; chmn. Residency Rev. Com., 1975—76, Registry Genito Urinary Pathology, 1975—76. Contbr.: 86 articles to med. jours., mem. editl. bd.: 6 med. jours. including Jour. Urology, Urology, Nephrology, and Urologic Radiology. Capt. Royal Army Med. Corps, 1955—57, Berlin. Recipient Valentine medal, NY Acad. Medicine, 1992, William Burpeau award, NJ Acad. Medicine, 1973. Fellow: Royal Coll. Surgeons, Am. Coll. Pediatrics, Am. Coll. Surgeons; mem.: Clin. Soc. Genito Urinary Surgeons, Australian Urol. Soc. (hon.), Italian Urol. Soc. (hon.), Panamanian Urol. Soc. (hon.), Am. Soc. Genito Urinary Surgeons, Am. Urol. Soc., S.W. Fla. Archaeol. Soc. (pres. 1989—90, dir. 1987—93). Personal E-mail: rkwiuhs@aol.com.

WATERHOUSE, LYNETTE, mathematics educator; m. Robert Waterhouse; 1 child. BA in Sociology, Iona Coll., New Rochelle, NY, 1973; MS in Edn., Lehman Coll., Bronx, NY, 1987, Manhattan Coll., NY, 1991. Teacher NY State, 1984, Special Education Teacher NY State, 1991, Teacher 7-12 Social Studies NY State, 1995. Tchr. N.Y.C. Bd. Edn., 1984—93; math specialist Greenburgh Ctrl. Sch. Dist. 7, Hartsdale, NY, 1994—. Pres. Greenburgh Teachers Fedn., Hartsdale, NY, 2005—. Mem. Ethics Com., Yorktown, NY, 2005; pres., trustee John C. Hart Meml. Libr., Shrub Oak, NY, 2001—06; dir. NY State Theatre Inst., 2005—06. Scholarship, Manhattan Coll., 1989—91. Mem.: ASCD, Nat. Coun. for Social Studies, Nat. Coun. of Teachers of Math (assoc.), Kappa Delta Pi. Office: Greenburgh Ctrl Sch Dist#7 33 West HIllside Ave White Plains NY 10607 Business E-Mail: lwaterhouse@greenburgh7.com.

WATERMAN, CHRISTOPHER, dean; MusB in Composition and Electric Bass, Berklee Coll. Music; PhD in Anthropology, U. Ill. Assoc. prof. music U. Wash., head ethnomusicology program, chair African studies com.; prof. dept. world arts and cultures UCLA, 1996—, chair dept., 1997—2002, acting dean, 2002—03, dean Sch. Arts and Arch., 2003—. Author: Juju: A Social History and Ethnography of an African Popular Music, 1990; co-author: American Popular Music: From Minstrelsy to MP3, 2006. Recipient Ethel Curry Disting. Lectureship in Musicology, U. Mich. Achievements include cited by Rolling Stone magazine for his innovative course on world popular music, 1992. Office: UCLA Sch Arts and Arch Box 951427 Broad Art Ctr Los Angeles CA 90095-1427

WATERMAN, JASON, pediatrician; m. Diana Waterman. BS, U. Fla., Gainesville; DO, Western U. Health Sci., Pomona, Calif. Cert. Am. Bd. Osteo. Pediatricians, 2006. Pediat. resident Good Samaritan Hosp. Med. Ctr., West Islip, NY, 2002—06; attending pediatrician Friendly Med. Group, Stony Brook, NY, 2006—07, Mid-Suffolk Peds, Hauppauge, 2008, 54 Main St. Med., Hempstead, NY, 2008—. Contbr. articles to profl. jour. Office: 54 Main St Med Hempstead NY 11550

WATERMAN, MICHAEL SPENCER, mathematics and biology professor; b. Coquille, Oreg., 1942; s. Ray S. and Bessie E. Waterman; m. Vicki Lynn Buss, 1962 (div. 1977); 1 child, Tracey Lynn BS, Oreg. State U., 1964, MS, 1966; MA, Mich. State U., 1968, PhD, 1969. Assoc. prof. Idaho State U., Pocatello, 1969-75; mem. staff Los Alamos Nat. Lab., 1975-82, cons., 1982—; prof. math. and biology U. So. Calif., LA, 1982—, U. So. Calif. Assocs. Endowed Chair, 1991—. Vis. prof. math. U. Hawaii, Honolulu, 1979-80; vis. prof. structural biology U. Calif., San Francisco, 1982; vis. prof. Mt. Sinai Med. Sch., NYC, 1988; 150th anniversary vis. prof. Chalmers U., 2000; Aisenstadt chair U. Montreal, 2001 Author: Introduction to Computational Biology, 1995; editor: Mathematical Methods for DNA Sequences, Calculating the Secrets of Life, 1995, Genetic Mapping and DNA Sequencing, 1996, Mathematical Support for Molecular Biology, 1999; Annals of Combinatorics, Methodology and Computing in Applied Probability, Genomics, Computational Methods in Science and Technology, Acta Biochimica et Biophysica Sinca; editor-in-chief: Jour. Computational Biology; contbr. articles to profl. jours. Recipient Gardner Found. Internat. award, 2002; grantee, NSF, 1971, 1972, 1975, 1988—, Los Alamos Nat. Lab., 1976, 1981, Sys. Devel. Found., 1982—87, NIH, 1986—99, Sloan Found., 1990—91; fellow, Guggenheim Found., 1995. Fellow AAAS, Am. Acad. Arts and Scis., Inst. Math. Stats.; mem. NAS, French Acad. Sci., Am. Statis. Assn., Soc. Math. Biology, Soc. Indsl. and Applied Math. Office: U So Calif Dept Biol Sci Los Angeles CA 90089-1340

WATERMAN, ROBERT A., lawyer; b. LA, Jan. 4, 1954; m. Leslie Waterman; 2 children. BA summa cum laude, Calif. State U., Long Beach, 1976; JD, U. Calif., Berkeley, 1979. Bar: Calif. 1979. Mem. McCutchen, Doyle, Brown & Enersen, San Francisco; ptnr. Latham & Watkins, San Francisco, 1993—97; sr. v.p., gen. counsel HCA, Nashville, 1997—. Assoc. editor Calif. Law Rev., 1977-78, note and comment editor, 1978-79. Mem. State Bar Calif. Office: HCA Inc 1 Park Plaza Nashville TN 37203*

WATERS, ALICE L., executive chef, restaurant owner, writer; b. Chatham, NJ, Apr. 28, 1944; 1 child, Fanny. Grad. in French Cultural Studies, U. Calif., Berkeley, 1967; postgrad., Montessori Sch., London; degree (hon.), Mills Coll., Oakland, Calif., 1994. Exec. chef, owner Chez Panisse, Berkeley, Calif., 1971—, Chez Panisse Cafe, Berkeley, Calif., 1980—, Cafe Fanny, Berkeley, Calif., 1984—. Mem. adv. bd. U. Calif., Berkeley; founder, pres. bd. dirs. Martin Luther King Jr. Mid. Sch. Edible Schoolyard; active The Garden Project, San Francisco; spkr. in field of food safety and health; founder, dir. Chez Panisse Found.; internat. gov. Slow Food; vis. dean French Culinary Inst.; hon. trustee Am. Ctr. Food, Wine and the Arts, Napa; bd. mem. San Francisco Ferry Plz. Farmers Market, Land Inst., Nat. Com. for Mothers and Others for Pesticide Limits; advisor Pub. Voice on Food Safety and Health. Author: Chez Panisse Desserts, 1994, Chez Panisse Cooking, 1994, Chez Panisse Menu Cookbook, 1995, Chez Panisse Vegetables, 1996, Chez Panisse Pasta, Pizza, & Calzone, 1996, Fanny at Chez Panisse, 1997, Chez Panisse Café Cookbook, 1999, Chez Panisse Fruit, 2002, The Art of Simple Food, 2007. Recipient Spl. Achievement award, James Beard Found., 1985, Restaurant and Bus. Leadership award, Restaurants and Instns. Mag., 1987, Barbar Boxer Top Ten Women award, 1991, Le Tour du Monde en 80 Toques, Metziner & Varaut, 1991, Nat. Edn. Diplomate award, 1996, John Stanford Heroes award, US Sec. Edn., 1999, Lifetime Achievement award, Bon Appetit Mag., 2000; named Best Chef in America, James Beard Found., 1992, Best Restaurant in America, 1992, Humanitarian of Yr., 1997, Mother of Am. Cooking, NY Times, Best Restaurant in America, Gourmet Mag., 2001; named one of 10 Best Chefs in the World, Cuisine et Vins du France, 1986; named to Calif. Hall of Fame, 2008. Fellow: Am. Acad. Arts & Scis. Office: Chez Panisse 1517 Shattuck Ave Berkeley CA 94709-1598

WATERS, CHRIS HAROLD, literature and language professor, poet; b. Wilmington, NC, Nov. 8, 1926; s. Harold Carlton and Theodora Beatrice (Baring-Gould) Waters; m. Lenore Paley Waters (div.); children: Gwyneth, Jennifer; m. Dora Vera Mancinelli, Aug. 12, 1979; 1 child, Matthew. AB, Harvard Coll., Cambridge, Mass., 1949; MA, U. Wash., Seattle, 1954, PhD, 1956. Instr. Salisbury Sch., Conn., 1951—52; tchg. asst. U. Wash., Seattle, 1952—55; instr. to asst. prof. Coll. William and Mary, Williamsburg, Va., 1955—60; asst. prof. Carlton Coll., Northfield, Minn., 1960—62; prof. U. R.I., Kingston, 1962—91, prof. emeritus, 1991—. Co-founder, head South County French Speaking Union, RI, 1982—; co-founder Paul Claudel Soc. Author: Senegal, Poems on Africa, 1999, Hatteras Symphony, Poems, 2001, Outer Banks Sonata, Poems, 2005, Ghost Lighthouse Poems, 2009. Pfc. US Army, 1945—46. Mem.: R.I. Fgn. Lang. Assn., Am. Assn. Tchrs. French, African Lit. Assn. Avocations: tennis, bicycling, swimming. Home: PO Box 233 Saunderstown RI 02874

WATERS, DONALD JOSEPH, data processing executive; b. Balt., Sept. 16, 1952; s. Richard Hunter and Annette Catharine (Hannan) W.; m. Beverly Ann Brent, Apr. 5, 1974; children: Laura Elizabeth, Sarah Elizabeth. BA, U. Md., 1973; M Phil, Yale U., 1976, PhD, 1982. Resource specialist Yale Computer Ctr., New Haven, 1982-84; dir. computer services Yale Sch. Mgmt., New Haven, 1984-87; head, systems office Yale U. Library, New Haven, 1987-92, dir., libr. and adminstrv. systems, 1992-93, assoc. univ. librarian, 1993-97; dir. Digital Libr. Fedn., Coun. Libr. & Info. Resources, New Haven, 1997-99; program officer Andrew W. Mellon Found., N.Y., 1999—. Author: Strange Ways and Sweet Dreams: Afro-American Folklore From the Hampton Institute, 1983. Fellow AAAS; mem. Am. Soc. Info. Sci. Roman Catholic. Avocations: jazz, rowing, cabinet making. Home: 40 Overbrook Rd Madison CT 06443-1834 Office: 140 E 62nd St New York NY 10021-8124 Home Phone: 203-421-4320; Office Phone: 212-500-2470.

WATERS, FAITH H., retired education educator; b. Drexel Hill, Pa., Oct. 28, 1949; d. Ronald Mifflin and Anna Florence Hood; m. Edward Charles Kimes, Aug. 5, 1994; 1 child, Alexandra Kathryn Dickinson. BS, Bucknell U., Lewisburg, Pa., 1971; EdD, U. Pa., Phila., 1983; MEd, Trenton State Coll., 1974. Cert. adminstr. PDE, 1976, comm. supervsior PDE, 1977. Assoc. prof. Hatboro-Horsham HS, East Stroudsburg, Pa., 1989—94, prof., 1994—2008; disting. prof. profl. & secondary edn. East Stroudsburg U., Pa., 2008—09, prof. emeritus, 2008—; prin. Pocono Mountain HS, Swiftwater, Pa., 1983—89; dir. of secondary instrn. Ctrl. Bucks Sch. Dist., Doylestown, Pa., 1982—83, lang. arts supr., 1979—82; asst. prin. Springfield HS, Springfield, Pa., 1976—79; english tchr. Hatboro-Horsham H.S., Hatboro, Pa., 1971—76. Grant project dir. Ctr. Rsch. & Econ. Devel., East Stroudsburg, 2008—09. Contbr. articles to profl. jours. Bd. mem. Monroe County Children & Youth, Stroudsburg, Pa., 1986—89; cons. Ea. Pa. Conf. United Meth. Ch. Provisional Pastor Program, Vallley Forge, Pa., 2005—09; grants writer Family Promise, Stroudsburg, 2008—09; team mem. Hurricane Katrina Support Nat. Task Force, Arlington, Va., 2005—07; mentor Capers Found., Bethlehem, Pa., 2006—08; with KDP, 1991, 2005. Named one of Curriculum Developer of Yr., Nepa Ascd, 1999; grantee Statewide Study grant, Ctr. Rural Pa., 2004—06; Tchg. Excellence grant, PDE, 2006, Fed. grant, Virtual Edn. Acad., 2003—05. Mem.: ASCD, Phi Kappa Phi, Phi Delta Kappa. Liberal. Methodist. Achievements include co-development virtual education academy citizenship model for disaffected students. Avocations: reading, travel. Home: 10 Highland Rd East Stroudsburg PA 18301 Office: East Stroudsburg Univ 200 Prospect St East Stroudsburg PA 18301 Business E-Mail: fwaters@po-box.esu.edu.

WATERS, GUY PRENTISS, theology studies educator; b. Washington, Jan. 20, 1975; s. Elzberry and Karen Waters; m. Sarah Anne Vasaly, May 31, 1997; children: Phoebe Louise, Lydia Anne, Thomas Edward Elzberry. BA, U. Pa., Phila., 1995; MDiv, Westminster Theol. Sem., Phila., 1998; PhD, Duke U., Durham, NC, 2002. Cert. min. Presbyn. Ch. America, 2003. Asst. prof. bibl. studies Belhaven Coll., Jackson, Miss., 2002—07; assoc. prof. NT Ref. Theol. Sem., Jackson, 2007—. Author: (book) Justification and the New Perspectives on Paul (Finalist Christianity Today Book award, 2005), The Federal Vision and Covenant Theology: A Comparative Analysis, The End of Deuteronomy in the Epistles of Paul; co-editor: By Faith Alone: Answering Challenges To the Doctrine of Justification. Mem.: Inst. Bibl. Rsch., Soc. Bibl. Lit. Avocation: singing. Office: Reformed Theological Seminary 5422 Clinton Blvd Jackson MS 39209 Business E-Mail: gwaters@rts.edu.

WATERS, HARRY T., JR., theater educator, actor; b. Tulsa, Okla., Apr. 13, 1953; s. Harry T. and Betty Opal Waters; life ptnr. Thomas Carter Borrup; children: Jordon Theron Hatch, Tyler Matthew Hatch. MFA in Theater Directing, U. Wis., Madison, 2003. Asst. prof. Macalester Coll., St. Paul, 2003—. Dir. and cons., Mpls., 2003—08. Actor: (theater) Little Shop of Horrors. Dfl. Office: Macalester Coll 1600 Grand Ave Saint Paul MN 55105-1899 Office Fax: 651-696-6257. Business E-Mail: waters@macalester.edu.

WATERS, JENNIFER NASH, lawyer; b. Bridgeport, Conn., Dec. 21, 1951; d. Lewis William and Patricia (Cousins) W.; m. Todd David Peterson, Sept. 19, 1981; children: Elizabeth, Andrew. BA, Radcliffe, 1972; JD, Harvard, 1976. Bar: D.C. 1977, U.S. Supreme Ct. 1980. Clk. U.S. Ct. Appeals (D.C. cir.), Washington, 1976-77; assoc. Jones, Day, Reavis & Poque, Washington, 1977-79, Crowell & Moring, Washington, 1979-83, ptnr., 1983—. Mem. ABA (ho. of dels. 1997-99), Fed. Energy Bar Assn. (bd. dirs. 1988-99, v.p. 1994-95, pres. 1996-97). Office: Crowell & Moring LLP 1001 Pennsylvania Ave NW Fl 10 Washington DC 20004-2505

WATERS, JOHN B., lawyer; b. Sevierville, Tenn., July 15, 1929; s. J. B. and Myrtle (Paine) W.; m. Patsy Temple, Apr. 8, 1953; children: John B., Cynthia Beth BS, U. Tenn., 1952, JD, 1961; D in Environ. Sci. (hon.), Milligan Coll., 1993. Bar: Tenn. 1961, U.S. Dist. Ct. (ea. dist.) Tenn. 1961, U.S. Supreme Ct. 1969, U.S. Dist. Ct. D.C. 1970. Of counsel Long, Ragsdale & Waters, P.C., Knoxville, Tenn.; mng. ptnr. Waters and Co. Investment Mgmt., 1993—. Mem. hearing com. Bd. Profl. Responsibility Supreme Ct., 1974—80, 1995—2001, Fed. co-chmn. Appalachian Regional Commn., 1968—71; chmn. Sevier County Indsl. Bd., Sevierville Libr. Found.; mem. Gov.'s Com. Econ. Devel.; Tenn. rep. to So. Growth Policies Bd., 1970—74; appointed dir. by Pres. Reagan TVA, Knoxville, 1984, appointed chmn. bd. dirs. by Pres. Bush, 92; bd. dirs. Inst. Nuc. Power Ops., 1985—93; trustee East Tenn. Bapt. Hosp., Knoxville; mem. Tenn.-Tombigbee Waterway Authority, 1993—2000; bd. dirs. East Tenn. Found.; chmn. Leadership Sevier, 1996—2001. Author: Downbound, The Memoirs of John B. Waters, Jr., 2004. Dir. Friends of Great Smoky Mountain Nat. Pk., 1993—2006. Lt. USN, 1952—55. Fellow Am. Bar Found.; mem. Tenn. Bar Assn. (pres. 1983-84), Sevier County Bar Assn. (past pres.). Republican. Baptist. Home: Waters Edge 405 Burridge Dr Sevierville TN 37862-3202: 107 Joy St Sevierville TN 37862-3524 Home Phone: 865-453-3913; Office Phone: 865-453-1051. Business E-Mail: jbwaters@esper.com.

WATERS, JOHN CALDWELL, historic preservation professor; s. Caldwell Swain Waters and Belle Cochran Powell, William Griffith Powell (Stepfather); m. Charlotte Reasor Waters, Sept. 2, 1972. BLA, U. Ga., Athens, 1958, MLA, 1970. Environ. planning cons. Inst. Cmty. & Area Devel. UGA, Athens, 1966—82; prof. U. Ga., 1982—, dir., grad. studies hist. preservation, 1982—. Pres. and CEO Athens-Clarke Heritage Found., Ga., 1968—79; trustee & chair, hist. sites Ga. Conservancy Inc., 1969—71; mem., natural hist. resources adv. com. NE Ga. Regional Devel. Commn., Athens, 1972—90; bd. dirs. Preservation Action Inc., DC, 1978—79; trustee Ga. Trust Hist. Preservation, Atlanta, 1978—81, mem., scholarship com., 1984—90; chmn., edn. com. Nat. Alliance Preservation Commns., DC, 1983—85; mem., nat. register rev. bd. Ga. State Hist. Preservation Office, Atlanta, 1984—87; mem., hist. landscapes com. Internat. Fedn. Landscape Archs., Germany, 1984—88; with Nat. Coun. Preservation Edn. Task Force U. Ky., 1990; bd. mem. Shields-Ethridge Heritage Farm Inc., Ga., 1996—, Athens House Mus. Assn., 1999—, Henry Green Decorative Arts Com. Ga. Mus. Art, Athens, 2001—; hist. preservation degree cons. U. NC Greensboro, 1999. Contbr. chapters to books (Citation award, 1975), articles to profl. jours. Mem., vol. city commn. Athens Tree Commn., 1980—91; with Athens Tree Trust, 1992—2009. Recipient award, Nat. Coun. State Garden Clubs Sears, 1975, Disting. Faculty award, Environ. Design Alumni Assn., 1981, 2000, 2007, Mary Gregory Jewett award, Ga. Trust Hist. Preservation, 2003, Govs. award, Ga. Dept. Natural Resources, 2003, Ga. Humanities Coun., 2007, Citation award, Athens-Clarke Heritage Found., 2004, Phinizy Spalding award, 2007. Mem.: Nat. Trust Hist. Preservation. Episcopalian. Office: Univ Ga 609 Caldwell Hall Univ Ga Athens GA 30602

WATERS, MARY CATHERINE, sociology educator; b. Bronx, NY, Nov. 18, 1957; d. Michael Francis and Margaret Mary (O'Carroll) W.; m. Ric W. Bayly, Sept. 10, 1993. BA in Philosophy, Johns Hopkins U., 1978; MA in Sociology, U. Calif., Berkeley, 1981, MA in Demography, 1983, PhD in Sociology, 1986. Acting instr. dept. Sociol. U. Calif., Berkeley, 1983—85; asst. prof. dept. Sociol. Harvard U., Cambridge, Mass., 1986—90, John L. Loeb assoc. prof., 1991—93, prof., 1993—, chmn. dept. Sociol., 2001—05; prof. Harvard Coll., 1999—2004, M.E. Zukerman prof. sociology, 2006—. Mem. immigration com. Social Sci. Rsch. Coun., NYC, 1994; bd. dirs. Population Assn. Am., 2005—; cons. US Census Bur., Washington, 1993—95, adv. com. profl. associations, 1999—2005; cons. Bklyn. Children's Mus., 1994—98; cons. radio coverage of immigration WGBH Radio; cons. exhibits on African Am. history, immigration Strong Mus. of History, Rochester, NY, 1994; cons. project on social context of Puerto Rican child health and growth Wellesley Coll. Ctr. Rsch. on Women, 1995—97; internat. adv. bd. Ethnicities; consulting editor Am. Jour. Sociology, 1995—98; editl. bd. mem. Internat. Migration Rev. Author: (books) From Many Strands: Ethnic and Racial Groups in Contemporary America, 1990, Ethnic Options: Choosing Identities in America, 1990, Black Identities: West Indian Immigrant Dreams and American Realities, 1991 (Mira Komorovsky award Ea. Sociol. Soc., Otis Dudley Duncan award, Am. Sociol. Assn., Best Book in Ethnic Incorporation Am. Polit. Sci. Assn., Disting. Book award Cornell U. Ctr. Study Inequality, Thomas and Znaniecki award best book internat. migration Am. Sociol. Assn., 1999); co-editor (with Peggy Levitt): The Change Face of Home: The Transnational Lives of the Second Generation, 2002; co-editor: (with Joel Perlmann) The New Race Question: How the Census Counts Multiracial Individuals, 2002; co-editor: (with Fiona Devine) Social Inequalities in Comparative Perspective, 2003; co-editor: (with Philip Kasinitz and John H. Mollenkopf) Becoming New Yorkers: Ethnographies of the New Second Generation, 2004; contbr. articles to profl. jour., chapters to books. Bd. trustees Russell Sage Found., 2002—07; adv. bd. Ctr Rsch. on Immigration U. Houston; mem. Rsch. Network on Transition to Adulthood MacArthur Found., 2001—. Recipient Gertrude Jaeger prize, U. Calif. Berkeley, 1984, Hoopes award excellence in teaching, 1990, 1996, George R. Kharl award excellence in teaching, 1991, Shannon award, Nat. Inst. Child Health and Human Development, 1995—97; grantee Radcliffe Inst. Advanced Study, 2005—06; fellow Walter Channing Cabot Faculty, 2003—04; vis. scholar Russell Sage Found., 1991—92; Guggenheim fellow, 1993—94. Fellow: Am. Acad. Arts and Sciences; mem.: Regional Sci. Assn., Soc. for Study of Social Problems, Sociol. Rsch. Assn., Am. Philosophical Soc., Population Assn. Am., Ea. Sociol. Soc. (chair Candace Rogers award com. 1994, disting. contribution to scholarship com. 2002), Am. Sociol. Assn. (nom. com. mem. sect.

race and ethnic minorities 1992, coun. mem. sect. race and ethnic minorities 1994—96, nom. com. mem. sect. race and ethnic minorities 1995, coun. mem. sect. population 1995—97, nominations com. 1995—97, chair sect. internat. migration, Thomas and Znaniecky Book Award Com. 2000). Democrat. Office: Dept Sociology Harvard Univ 540 William James Hall Cambridge MA 02138-2044 Office Phone: 617-495-3947. Office Fax: 617-496-5794. E-mail: mcw@wjh.harvard.edu.

WATERS, MAXINE, United States Representative from California; b. St. Louis, Aug. 15, 1938; d. Remus and Velma (Moore) Carr; m. Sidney Williams, July 23, 1977; children: Edward, Karen. BA in Sociology, Calif. State U., LA; D (hon.), Spelman Coll., NC Agrl.& Tech. State U., Morgan State U. Vol. coord., tchr. Head Start prog.; mem. Calif. Assembly from dist. 48, 1976—91, US Congress from 35th Calif. dist., 1990—, chief dep. whip, 1990—, mem. house com. fin. svcs., chmn. subcom. housing and cmty. opportunity, mem. subcom. fin. instns. and consumer credit, mem. subcom. oversight and investigations, mem. subcom. domestic and internat. monetary policy, trade, tech., mem. com. on judiciary, subcoms. crime, terrorism, homeland security, immigration, border security and claims. Del. Minority AIDS Initiative, 1998; co-founder Black Women's Forum; mem. Congl. Children's Working Grp., Nat. Devel. & Voting Rights Inst., Progressive Caucus, Nat. Com. Econ. Conversion & Disarmament, Nat. Adv. Com. for Women, 1978—, Dem. Nat. Com., 1980—; chair Congl. Black Caucus, 1997—98; founding mem., chair Out of Iraq Congl. Caucus, 2005—. Founder Free South Africa Movement, Project Build; mem. Calif. Peer Counseling Assn., Nat. Com. Econ. Conversion and Disarmament; founder Maxine Waters Employment Preparation Ctr.; mem. bd. Ctr. Study Sport in Soc., LA Women's Found. Named one of 100 Most Influential Black Americans, Ebony mag., 2006; named to Power 150, 2008. Democrat. Office: US Ho Reps 2344 Rayburn Ho Office Bldg Washington DC 20515-0535 also: 10124 S Broadway Ste 1 Los Angeles CA 90003 Office Phone: 202-225-2201, 323-757-8900. Office Fax: 202-225-7854, 323-757-9506.*

WATERS, MICHAEL DEE, corporate scientific officer, consultant; s. Dee Howard and Mary Elizabeth Waters. PhD, U. NC Sch. Medicine, Chapel Hill, 1969. Dir., Genetic Toxicology Divsn. EPA, Health Effects Rsch. Lab., Research Triangle Park, NC, 1979—92, asst. nat. lab. dir., 1992—2002; asst. dir. NIEHS, Nat. Ctr. Toxicogenomics, 2002—07; chief sci. officer Integrated Lab. Systems, Inc., 2007—. Capt. USAR, 1969—71, Edgewood Arsenal. MD. Recipient Alexander Hollaender award sci. achievement, Environ. Mutagen Soc., 1996, Lifetime Achievement award, Genotoxicity and Environ. Mutagen Soc., 2000, Merit award, NIH, 2004, Bronze Commendable Svc. medal, EPA, 1980, 1987, 1997, 2001. Mem.: Rotary Club RTP (pres. 2008). Office: Integrated Lab Systems Inc PO Box 13501 Research Triangle Park NC 27709 Office Fax: 919-281-1118. E-mail: mwaters@ils-inc.com.

WATERS, RONALD W., theology studies educator, church administrator, pastor; b. Kokomo, Ind., July 23, 1951; s. Ronald Lee and Carolyn Elizabeth (Myers) W.; m. Norma Lee Grumbling Waters, June 16, 1973; 1 child, Melinda Ronee Layman. BA magna cum laude, Ashland U., Ohio, 1973; MA in Comms. with high honors, Wheaton Coll., Ill., 1975; MDiv with high honors, Ashland Theol. Sem., Ohio, 1985; postgrad., Asbury Theol. Seminary, 1993—2002. Ordained elder Brethren Ch., 1986; lic. minister, 1985-86. Asst. to dir. Bd. of Christian Edn. The Brethren Ch., Ashland, Ohio, 1971-74; mng. editor of publs. Brethren Pub. Co., Ashland, Ohio, 1975-78, asst. to dir. and gen. mgr., 1978-80, exec. dir., 1980-82; dir. of Denom. Bus. The Brethren Ch. Nat. Office, Ashland, Ohio, 1982-84; cons. in mgmt. and computer applications, 1984-85; pastor Mt. Olive Brethren Ch., McGaheysville, Va., 1985-89; dir. Brethren Ch. Ministries The Brethren Ch. Nat. Office, Ashland, Ohio, 1989-95; asst. prof. evangelism Ashland Theol. Sem., 1996-2001, interim dir. Dr. Ministries Program, 2008—09; cons. for evangelism and ch. growth The Brethren Ch. Nat. Office, Ashland, 1996—2001; pastor Hammond Ave. Brethren Ch., Waterloo, Iowa, 2002—08, 1st Brethren Ch., North Georgetown, Ohio, 2009—; mem. exec. bd. Brethren Ch., 2008—, mem. internat. ch., 2008—. Bd. dirs. corp. sec. Brethren Printing Co., Ashland, 1989-96; mem. mission bd. Brethren Ch. Southeastern Dist., 1987-89; mem., sec. exec. bd. Ctrl. Dist., The Brethren Ch., 2002—; mem. statement of faith task force Gen. Conf. Brethern Ch., 1981-84, polity com. 1986-91, 2004—; bd. ref. congl. adv. The Andrew Ctr., Elgin, Ill., 1994-97; founder, tchr. Young Adult Sunday Sch. class Park St Brethren Ch., Ashland, 1990-93; adv. com. Ashland Theol. Sem., 1990-95; mem. evangelism mgmt. team New Life Ministries, Mt. Joy, Pa., 1992-2001; adj. prof. Bethany Theological Seminary, 2002; spkr. in field. Author: Promise for the Future, 1993, Leader's Manual for Inviting and Welcoming New People, 1995; editor: The Brethren Evangelist mag., 1975-78, New Beginnings mag., 1995-97; contbg. editor LIFE process, 1998-99; contbr. numerous articles to religious jours.; webmaster, www.newlifeministries-nlm.org, 2000—. Mem. adv. coun. World Relief Corp., Wheaton, Ill., 1990-92; dir. vol. ministries Park St. Brethren Ch., 1998-99; sec.-treas. Ohio dist. Mission Bd., 1996-2001. Mem. Am. Soc. Ch. Growth, Nat. Assn. Brethern Ch. Elders, Black Hawk Assn. Evangelicals (pres. 2005-07). Mem. Brethren Ch. Office: Asland Theol Sem 910 Ctr St Ashland OH 44805

WATERS, ROSEMARY R., biology professor; d. Leon H. and Margaret M. Rockwell; m. Jerry Waters, July 3, 1964; children: Craig R., David W. BA in Zoology magna cum laude, Calif. State U., Fresno, 1966, MA in Microbiology with distinction, 1972. Cert. ALS instr. Am. Heart Assn., 1975; dental asst. ADAA, 1962, registered Calif., 1972, cert. CC instr. Calif., 1972. Asst. quality control dir. Burton Parsons Pharmaceuticals, Seat Pleasant, Md., 1966—69; HS biology tchr. Queen of the Valley Acad., Fresno, 1969—72; dental assisting coord. Reedley Coll., Calif., 1972—94; biology prof. Fresno City Coll., 1994—. Infection control cons., Fresno, 1989—94. Author: (manual) Microbiology-A Manual of Laboratory Experiments. Mem. Chancellors Cir. State Ctr. C.C. Dist., Fresno, 2003—06; marriage ministry facilitator St. Paul Parish Newman Ctr., Fresno, 1984—96. Mem.: Calif. State U. Fresno Alumni (life), Cath. Bus. and Profl. Breakfast Club, Kappa Alpha Theta (Gamma Chi facility corp. sec. 1998—2006), Phi Kappa Phi (life). Avocations: marriage ministry, travel. Home: 1754 West Dovewood Ln Fresno CA 93711 Office: Fresno City Coll 1101 East University Ave Fresno CA 93741 Personal E-mail: rwatersfcc@comcast.net. Business E-Mail: rosemary.waters@fresnocitycollege.edu.

WATERS, SYLVIA, performing company executive, dancer; b. NYC, Jan. 22, 1940; BS in Dance, Juilliard Sch.; studied with, Antony Tudor and Martha Graham; PhD (hon.), SUNY, Oswego, 1997. Prin. dancer Alvin Ailey Am. Dance Theater, NYC, 1968—74; artistic dir. Alvin Ailey Repertory Ensemble, NYC, 1974—. Panelist Nat. Endowment for the Arts, NY State Council on the Arts. Recipient NY Dance and Performance ("Bessie") award, Dance Theater Workshop, 2003, Legacy award, Internat. Assn. of Blacks in Dance, 2008, Women of Distinction award, Syracuse U., 2008, Dance Mag. award, 2008. Office: Ailey II Joan Weill Ctr for Dance 405 W 55th St New York NY 10019*

WATERS, WILLIAM CARTER, III, retired internist, educator; b. Atlanta, Dec. 12, 1929; s. William Carter and Nannie Ellen (Starr) W.; m. Sarah Ann Bankston; children: William Carter IV, Sarah Walker Waters McEntire. AB, Emory U., 1950, MD, 1958. Diplomate Am. Bd. Internal Medicine (internal medicine and nephrology). Resident in internal medicine Grady Meml. Hosp./Emory U., Atlanta, 1958-60, 61-62; fellow in nephrology New Eng. Med. Ctr., 1960-61; practice medicine specializing in internal medicine and nephrology, Atlanta, 1962—2002; from instr. to assoc. prof. Emory U. Sch. Medicine, 1962-70, clin. assoc. prof., 1970-85, clin. prof., 1985—. Chief staff internal medicine Piedmont Hosp., Atlanta, chmn. bd., 1991-94; 1st chmn. bd. Promina Health Sys., Atlanta, 1994-96; med. dir. internal. medicine divsn. Multiple Sclerosis Clinic, Atlanta, 2005—. Contbr. articles to med. jours.; author: three non fiction books, one novel. Chmn. Piedmont Hosp. Found., 2002—05, chmn. bd. visitors, 2004—. With USAF, 1951—52. Fellow ACP (master: gov. for Ga.); mem. AMA, Med. Assn. Ga., Med. Assn. Met. Atlanta, Am. Soc. Nephrology, S.E. Clin. Club, Atlanta, BCountry Club, Piedmont Driving Club. Methodist. Personal E-mail: drwaters@mindspring.com.

WATERS, ZENOBIA PETTUS, retired finance educator; b. Little Rock, Mar. 4, 1927; d. Henry Augustus and Lillie Liddell (Edwards) Pettus; m. Willie Waters, Jr., Jan. 29, 1949 (div. Feb. 1955); children: Pamela E. Reed, Zenobia W. Carter. BA cum laude, Philander Smith Coll., Little Rock, 1964; MEd, U. Wash., 1968. Cert. tchr. Ark., 1966. Office mgr. United Friends of Am., Little Rock, 1946—52; sec. State Dept. Edn., Little Rock, 1958—64; lectr. bus. Philander Smith Coll., Little Rock, 1965—67, asst. prof. bus., 1968—88, assoc. prof. bus. adminstrn., 1988—92, bd. dirs., faculty rep., 1976—80; asst. prof. bus. Ark. Bapt. Coll., Little Rock, 1970—84. Asst. bus. mgr. Philander Smith Coll., Little Rock, 1970—74, dir. summer sessions, 1970—81; spkr. in field. Mem. adv. bd.: Two Centuries of Methodism in Arkansas, 2000; contbr. articles to profl. jours. Dean West Gulf Regional Sch., 1975—77; founder Nat. Campaign Tolerance, Mont, Ala., 2005; vol. Dem. Party, Little Rock, 1986—92; contact person U.S. Presdl. Campaign, Little Rock, 1992; cert. lay spkr. United Meth. Ch., 1979—; pres. so. ctrl. juris United Meth. Women, 1984—88; bd. dirs. Gen. Bd. of Global Ministries, NYC, 1984—88, Aldersgate Camp, Little Rock, 1976—79, St. Paul Sch. Theology, Kansas City, Mo., 1984—88, Mount Sequoyah, Fayetteville, Ark., 1984—88. Recipient Svc. award, Gen. Bd. Global Ministries/Women's Divsn., 1988; named Legend, Union Am. Meth. Ch., 2005; grantee Ford Found. grantee, 1967; fellow, Nissan, 1989. Mem.: AAUW (Edn. Found. award 1983), Nat. Campaign for Tolerance (founding mem.), Nat. Trust for Historic Preservation, United Meth. Women (pres. recognition pins 1963—2004, recognition pins 1963—2005), Phi Delta Phi, Iota Phi Lambda. Methodist. Avocations: reading, walking, writing. Home: 1701 Westpark Dr Apt 219 Little Rock AR 72204

WATERSTON, ROBERT HUGH, medical educator, researcher, medical geneticist, department chairman; b. Detroit, Sept. 17, 1943; BSE, Princeton U., NJ, 1965; PhD, MD, U.Chgo., 1972. Postdoctoral fellow divsn. cell biology MRC Lab Molecular Biology, Cambridge, England, 1972—74; intern in pediatric medicine Children's Hosp. Med. Ctr., Boston, 1974—75; postdoctoral fellow divsn. cell biology MRC Lab Molecular Biology, Cambridge, England, 1975—76; asst. prof. dept. anatomy and neurobiology Washington U., St. Louis, 1976—89; asst. prof. genetics Washington U. Sch. Medicine, St. Louis, 1980—81, assoc. prof. genetics, 1981—87, prof. genetics, 1987—91, prof. and acting head dept. genetics, 1991—93, James S. McDonnell prof. and chmn. dept. genetics, 1993—2003, head, dept. genetics Seattle, dir., Genome Sequencing Ctr., chmn. dept. genome sci., 2002—, William B. Gates III endowed chair biomed. scis., 2003—. Founder Genome Sequencing Ctr., St. Louis; ad hoc mem. Molecular Cytology Study Sect., 1977, 83; regular mem. Molecular Cytology Study Sect., NIH, 1987—88, chmn., 1989—91; mem. NIH, 1985—86, mem. adv. coun., chmn. Molecular Cytology Study Sect., mem. nat. adv. coun. for human genome rsch., 1998—2002; mem. fellowship rev. subcom. Molecular Dystrophy Assn., 1982—87, mem task force on genetics, 1983; mem. organizing com. Fourth Internat. C. elegans Meeting, Cold Spring Habor, NY, 1985. Contbr. over 80 articles to profl. jours.; mem. editl. bd. Jour. Cell Biology, 1988—91. Recipient Beadle award, Gen. Soc. Am., Dan David Prize, Peter H. Raven Lifetime award, 2000, Gairdner Found. Internat. award, 2002, Alfred P. Sloan, Jr. prize, GM Cancer Rsch. Found., 2003, Genetics prize, Peter Gruber Found., 2005; named NIH predoctoral trainee, 1968—71, Am. Heart Assn. Established Investigator, 1980—85; grantee, NIH, 1997—99, 1998—2001, Merck & Co., 1994—99; fellow Am. Cancer Soc. (postdoctoral), 1972—74, Muscular Dystrophy Assn. (postdoctoral), 1975—76, John Simon Guggenheim, 1985—86. Fellow: Am. Acad. Arts & Sciences; mem.: NAS (coun. mem. Inst. Medicine 2006—), Am. Soc. Cell Biology: STS, Genetics Soc., Alpha Omega Alpha, Sigma Xi. Office: U Wash 1705 NE Pacific St HSB-K357 Seattle WA 98195-7730 Office Phone: 206-685-7347. Business E-Mail: waterston@gs.washington.edu.*

WATERSTON, SAM, actor; b. Cambridge, Mass., Nov. 15, 1940; s. George Chychele and Alice Tucker (Atkinson) W.; m. Lynn Louisa Woodruff, Jan. 26, 1976; children: Graham C., Elisabeth P., Katherine B.; child by previous marriage: James S. BA, Yale U., 1962; student, Sorbonne, Paris, 1960-61. Actor: (theatre) Indians, Oh Dad Poor Dad, Halfway Up the Tree, Lunch Hour, Hamlet, The Tempest, Measure for Measure, Much Ado About Nothing (Obie, Drama Desk awards), Benefactors, 1986, A Walk in the Woods, 1988, Abe Lincoln in Illinois, 1993-94 (Drama League award 1994), Shakespeare & Szekspir, 1994, Hamlet, 2008; (films) The Great Gatsby, 1975, Rancho Deluxe, 1976, Capricorn One, 1978, Interiors, 1978, Sweet William, 1978, Heaven's Gate, 1979, Eagle's Wing, 1983, The Killing Fields, 1984, Warning Sign, 1985, Savages, Hopscotch, 1980, Hannah and Her Sisters, 1986, Just Between Friends, 1986, The Devil's Paradise, September, 1987, Welcome Home, 1989, Crimes and Misdemeanors, 1990, Captive in the Land, 1990, Crimes and Misdemeanors, The Man in the Moon, 1991, Mindwalk, 1991, Serial Mom, 1994, Nixon, 1995, The Proprietor, 1996, Shadow Conspiracy, 1997, Le Divorce, 2003; (TV films) Much Ado About Nothing, 1974, The Glass Menagerie, 1975, Diabolique, 1975, Friendly Fire, 1978, Oppenheimer, 1982, Exiled, 1998, A House Divided, 2000, The Matthew Shepard Story, 2002; (TV series) Q.E.D., 1982, Terrorist on Trial: The United States vs. Salim Ajami; (TV miniseries) Oppenheimer, 1980, 82, Gore Vidal's Lincoln, 1988, Nightmare Years, 1989, Lost Civilizations, 1995 (Emmy award for best documentary 1996), Ken Burns' The Civil War, 1990, Thomas Jefferson, 1997; TV series Q.E.D., 1979, I'll Fly Away, 1991-93 (Emmy award nomination, Lead actor, Drama, 1993), I'll Fly Away: Then and Now, 1993 (Emmy nomination, Lead Actor - Special, 1994), Law and Order. 1994— (Screen Actors Guild award 1999), Miracle at Midnight, 1998. Law and Order: Special Victims Unit, 1999, (documentary) Unfinished Journey, 1999. Mem. Actors Equity Assn., Screen Actors Guild, AFTRA Address: care Addis/Wechsler & Assocs 955 Carrillo Dr Fl 3 Los Angeles CA 90048-5400

WATERWORTH, DAWN MARIE, research and development company executive, director; b. Belfast, Northern Ireland, Mar. 24, 1969; d. Norman and Isabel Waterworth; m. Parviz Gharagozloo; 1 child, Sienna Ariane Gharagozloo. BSc in Biology, U. Ulster, Coleraine, Northern Ireland, 1990; PhD, Imperial Coll., London, 1997. Post doc. fellow U. Coll. London, England, 1997—2000; asst. prof. Rutgers U., Piscataway, NJ, 2000—02; dir. genetics GlaxoSmithKline, King Prussia, Pa., 2002—. Contbr. to peer reviewed publication. Fellowship, Brit. Heart Found., 1997—2000, Rsch. Grant, 2000, Rsch. Autism, Mar. of Dimes, 2002—05, NJ. Governor's coun. autism, 2001—02. Mem.: Am. Soc. Human Genetics. Avocations: yoga, tennis, soccer, travel, reading. Office: GlaxoSmithKline 709 Swedeland Rd King Of Prussia PA 19406 Personal E-mail: dawn.waterworth@gmail.com.

WATFORD, DOLORES, elementary school educator; b. Feb. 26, 1951; BS in Edn., U. Hartford, 1973; MA in Psychol. Remedial Reading, Tchrs. Coll. Columbia U., 1974; MS in Spl. Edn., LI U., 1990, MS in Edn., 1993, profl. diploma in Sch. Adminstrn., 1997. Tchr. asst. Dalton Sch., Manhattan, NY, 1974—76; tchr. Pub. Sch., Conn., 1976—77; elem. tchr. Pub. Sch. 169, Bklyn., 1981—85; reading tchr. Pub. Sch. 167, Bklyn., 1981—85, Pub. Sch. 191, Bklyn., 1985—99, Pub. Sch. 255, Bklyn., 1999—. Sec. Sch. Leadership Team, Bklyn., 2004—05. Pres. Bklyn. Reading Council, 2002. Recipient Svc. award, Bklyn. Reading Coun., 2004. Mem.: Internat. Reading Assn., NY State Reading Assn. (v.p. 2005—, pres. 2007—). Avocations: singing, aerobics, volleyball, reading. Personal E-mail: doloresbrc2002@msn.com.

WATJEN, THOMAS ROS, insurance company executive; With investment and corp. fin. depts. Aetna Life and Casualty, 1981-84; ptnr. Conning and Co., ins. cons. firm, 1984-87; mng. dir. responsible for ins. practice group Morgan Stanley & Co., 1987-94; exec. v.p., CFO Provident Cos., Inc., Chattanooga, 1994—97, vice chmn., dir., 1997—99; exec. v.p., fin. UnumProvident Corp., Chattanooga, 1999—2002; vice chmn., COO UnumProvident Corp. (now Unum Group), Chattanooga, 2002—03; pres., CEO Unum Group, Chattanooga, 2003—. Office: Unum Group One Fountain Sq Chattanooga TN 37402 E-mail: twatjen@unumprovident.com.

WATKINS, ANN ESTHER, mathematics professor; b. LA, Jan. 10, 1949; d. Rex Devere and Burnice Gordine (Duckworth) Hamilton; m. William Earl Watkins, Oct. 5, 1973; children: Mary Ann, Barbara Lee. BA, Calif. State U., Northridge, 1970, MS, 1972; PhD, UCLA, 1977. Instr. math. Los Angeles Pierce Coll., Woodland Hills, Calif., 1975-90; prof. math. Calif. State U., Northridge, 1990—. Editor: (with Albers, Rodi) New Directions in Two Year College Mathematics, 1985; co-author: (with Landwehr) Exploring Data, 1986, 2d edit., 1994, (with Landwehr, Swift) Exploring Surveys, 1987, (with Albers, Loftsgaarden, Rung) Statistical Abstract of Undergraduate Programs in the Mathematical Sciences and Computer Science, 1992, (with Scheaffer, Gnanadesikan, Witmer) Activity-Based Statistics, 1996, 2d edit., 2004, (with Scheaffer, Cobb) Statistics in Action, 2d edit., 2007; assoc. editor: American Mathematical Monthly, 1996-00; editor Coll. Math. Jour., 1989-94; co-editor: (with Apostol, Mugler, Scott and Sterrett) A Century of Calculus, Part II, 1992; mem. editl. bd. Jour. Statis. Edn., 1992-95; mem. adv. bd. Math. Horizons mag., 1992-01. Grantee NSF, 1987-90, 92—. Fellow Am. Statis. Assn.; mem. Math. Assn. Am. (2d v.p. 1987-88, pres. 2001-03, chair So. Calif. sect. 1988-89, gov. So. Calif. sect. 1995-98), Nat. Coun. Tchrs. Math. Home Phone: 818-347-1509. Business E-Mail: ann.watkins@csun.edu.

WATKINS, BIRGE SWIFT, real estate investment executive; b. Grand Rapids, Mich., May 2, 1949; s. Robert Goodell and Betty Jane (Swift) W.; m. Elizabeth Beverly Price, Nov. 28, 1985; children: Elizabeth Porter, Benjamin Thorne Swift, Robert William MacIntosh. BA, Alma Coll., 1971; MBA, London Bus. Sch., 1981; MPA, Harvard U., 1989. Staff asst. to Pres. of U.S., Washington, 1974-77; congl. press sec. U.S. Ho. of Reps., Washington, 1977; v.p. Arbor Internat. Inc., McLean, Va., 1980-81; asst. office dir. AID, Washington, 1982-88; asst. dir. Pres.'s Task Force on Internal Pvt. Enterprise, Washington, 1983-85; dep. asst. sec. USDA, Washington, 1989-90; dir. investor outreach Resolution Trust Corp., Washington, 1991-94; ptnr. Benton Resources, Washington, 1994-95; mng. dir. Thornfalcon Internat., 1996-99; sr. v.p. Lifecare Mgmt. Ptnrs., 1999—2002, Friedman, Billings, Ramsey Group, Inc., 2002—03; v.p. Landmark Atlantic Holdings, LLC, 2003—07. Cons. Washington Campus Inc., 1977, Va. Med. Assocs. Inc., Springfield, 1988, U.S. C. of C. Mem. campaign staff Reagan-Bush campaign, Washington, 1980, Bush for President, 1988; mem. transition team office of Pres.-elect Bush, 1988; chmn. bd. trustees Partnership Warrenton Found.; bd. dirs., founder John Singleton Mosby Found. and Mus., Land Trust of Va.; coun. mem. Town of Warrenten, Va., 2002--. Avocations: skiing, running, contemporary art. Home: 832 Blackwell Rd Warrenton VA 20186-2216 Office: Arlington VA Office Phone: 703-998-5200.

WATKINS, CAROLE S., human resources specialist, medical products executive; b. 1960; BA in Bus., Franklin U., Columbus, Ohio. With O.M. Scott & Sons, Lazarus, Huntington Banks; mem. staff Ltd. Brands, Columbus, Ohio, 1989—96; v.p. human resources pharm. distbn. Cardinal Health, Inc., 1996—2000, sr. v.p. pharm. distbn. and provider svcs., 1999, exec. v.p. human resources, 2000, chief human resources officer, 2000—. Bd. pres. Action for Children, Ohio. Office: Cardinal Health 7000 Cardinal Pl Dublin OH 43017*

WATKINS, CHARLES REYNOLDS, medical equipment company executive; b. San Diego, Oct. 28, 1951; s. Charles R. and Edith A. (Muff) W.; children: Charles Devin, Gregory Michael, Joshua Tomas. BS, Lewis and Clark Coll., 1974; postgrad., U. Portland, 1976. Internat. salesman Hyster Co., Portland, Oreg., 1975-80, Hinds Internat. Corp., Portland, 1980-83; mgr. internat. sales Wade Mfg. Co., Tualatin, Oreg., 1983-84; regional sales mgr. U.S. Surg., Inc., Norwalk, Conn., 1984-86; nat. sales mgr. NeuroCom Internat., Inc., Clackamas, Oreg., 1986-87; pres. Wave Form Systems, Inc., Portland, 1987-98; pres., dir. Wave Form Mfg., Inc., Portland, 1998—; prin. Wave Form Lithotripsy LLC, Portland, 1998—; pres. Wave Form Mfg., Inc., 1998—. Bd. dirs. Portland World Affairs Coun., 1980. Mem. Am. Soc. Laser Medicine and Surgery, Am. Assn. Gynecol. Laparoscopists, Ind. Med. Distbrs. Assn., Portland City Club. Republican. Avocations: flying, photography, travel. Office: Wave Form Sys Inc PO Box 3195 Portland OR 97208-3195 Business E-Mail: chuckw@waveformsys.com.

WATKINS, CRAIG, prosecutor; b. Dallas, Nov. 16, 1967; m. Tanya Watkins; children: Taryn Michelle, Cale Marcus, Chad Marcus. BA, Prairie View A&M U., 1990; JD, Texas Wesleyan U., 1994. Dist. atty. intern. Tarrant County Dist. Atty., Tex.; prosecutor City Atty. Office, Dallas; atty. Dallas County Pub. Defender's Office; founder, prin. Craig Watkins Atty. at Law, Dallas, 1997—2007; dist. atty. Dallas, 2007—. Instr. El Centro Jr. Coll., Univ. Tex., Arlington. In numerous TV shows. Recipient Promenade Disting. award, 2009, Trumpet award, 2009; named Texan of Yr., Dallas Morning, 2008; named to Power 150, Ebony mag., 2008. Democrat. Office: Dallas Districy Atty Frank Crowley Courts Bldg LB19 133 N Industrial Blvd Dallas TX 75207-4399 Office Phone: 214-653-3600. Office Fax: 214-653-5774.

WATKINS, CURTIS WINTHROP, artist; b. Pontiac, Mich., Apr. 9, 1946; s. Robert James and Arvella Marquitta (Chenoweth) W.; m. Gayle Lynn Blom, Dec. 19, 1975; 1 dau., Darcy Ann. Student, Ann Arbor Art Ctr., 1964-66, Kendall Sch. Design, 1966-68, Kraus Hypnosis Ctr., 1966-70, Arons Ethical Hypnosis Tng. Ctr., 1977. Illustrator, instr. Ann Arbor Art Ctr., 1969-71; owner, dir. Hypno-Art Rsch. Ctr. and Studio, Howell, Mich., 1971—. Research on visualization process of subconscious by doing art work under hypnosis; lectr. hypnosis convs. and schs. One-man shows include LeVern's Gallery, 1969, Rackham Gallery, 1973, Hartland Gallery, 1974, Platt Gallery, 1975, Detroit Artists Guild Gallery, 1975, Golden Gallery, 1977, Cromaine Gallery, 1982, Driggett Gallery, 1982, Mill Gallery, 1983, Walnut Street Gallerya, 1983, Merrill Gallery, 1986, Corbino Gallery, 1986, VanAntwerp, 1991; group shows include Mich. All-State Show, 1980, Mich. State Fine Arts Exhibit, 1980, Washington Internat., 1981, Lansing (Mich.) Art Gallery, 1981, Capitol City Arts Show, 1981, Mich. Ann., 1981, Mich. Ann., 1982-83; illustrator: Handbook of Hypnotic Techniques, 1988. Bd. dirs. 9th Ann. Hartland Art Show, 1975, Livingston Arts and Crafts Assn., 1977-79, Hartland Art Coun., 1974-78. Recipient Dr. Garland H. Fross award, 1989, numerous awards of excellence in art. Mem. Internat. Soc. Artists, Assn. Advance Ethical Hypnosis, Am. Assn. Profl. Hypnologists, Internat. Soc. Profl. Hypnosis, Internat. Platform Assn. Presbyterian. Home: 1749 Pinckney Rd Howell MI 48843-7874 Office Phone: 517-546-6648.

WATKINS, DEAN ALLEN, electronics executive, educator; b. Omaha, Oct. 23, 1922; s. Ernest E. and Pauline (Simpson) W.; m. Bessie Ena Hansen, June 28, 1944; children— Clark Lynn, Alan Scott, Eric Ross. BS, Iowa State Coll., 1944; MS, Calif. Inst. Tech., 1947; PhD, Stanford, 1951. Engr. Collins Radio Co., 1947-48; mem. staff Los Alamos Lab., 1948-49; tech. staff Hughes Research Labs., 1951-53; asso. prof. elec. engring. Stanford, 1953-56; prof., dir. Electron Devices Lab., 1956-64, lectr. elec. engring., 1964-70; co-founder, pres., chief exec. officer, dir. Watkins Johnson Co., Palo Alto, Calif., 1957-67, chmn., chief exec. officer, dir., 1967-80, chmn., dir., 1980-2000. Cons. Dept. Def., 1956-66; mem. White House Sci. Coun., 1988-89. Patentee in field; contbr. articles to profl. jours. Legis. chmn., dir. San Meteo County Sch. Bds. Assn., 1959-69; gov. San Francisco Bay Area Coun., 1966-75; Rep. precinct capt. Portola Valley, 1964; vice chmn. San Mateo County Fin. Com., 1967-69; mem. Calif. Rep. Ctrl. Com., 1964-68; trustee Stanford, 1966-69; regent U. Calif., 1969-96, chmn., 1972-74; mem. governing bd. Sequoia Union H.S. Dist., 1964-68, chmn., 1967-68; mem. governing bd. Portola Valley Sch. Dist., 1958-66; mem. bd. overseers Hoover Instn. on War, Revolution and Peace, Stanford, 1969—, chmn., 1971-73, 85-86; adv. policy commn. Santa Clara County Jr. Achievement; trustee Nat. Security Indsl. Assn., 1965-78. Served from pvt. to 1st lt. C.E., O.R.C. AUS, 1943-46. Fellow IEEE (7th region Achievement award 1957, Frederik Philips award 1981), AAAS; mem. Am. Phys. Soc., Am. Mgmt. Assn., Western Electronic Mfrs. Assn. (chmn. San Francisco coun. 1967, v.p., dir.), Calif. C. of C. (dir. 1965-92, treas. 1978, pres. 1981), Nat. Acad. Engring., Mounted Patrol San Mateo County (spl. dep. sheriff 1960-70), San Mateo County Horseman's Assn., San Benito County Farm Bur., Calif. Cattlemen's Assn., Delta Upsilon. Clubs: Palo Alto (Palo Alto), University (Palo Alto); Shack Riders (San Mateo County); Commonwealth (San Francisco); Rancheros Visitadores.

WATKINS, DEBORAH KAREN, epidemiology investigator, educator; b. Mt. Pleasant, Pa., Sept. 10, 1950; d. Thomas Earl and Berniece Helen (Kapelewski) W. AB, George Washington U., 1972; MS, Georgetown U., 1990. Production editor Am. Pub. Health Assn., Washington, 1972-79; exec. dir. Soc. for Occupational and Evniron. Health, Washington, 1979-81; dir. legis. affairs Pa. Environ. Coun., Phila., 1982-83; rsch. asst. prof. dept. family medicine Georgetown U., Washington, 1983—2002, dep. dir. divsn. occupl. health studies, 1990—2002; mng. scientist Exponent, Inc., Washington, 2004—06; owner Watkins Consulting, Arlington, Va., 2007—. Adj. asst. prof. Georgetown U., Washington, 2002—. Mem. Soc. Occupl. and Eviron. Health (gov. coun. 1987-93), Soc. Epidemiologic Rsch., Soc. Profl. Journalists. Avocations: British history, needlepoint. Office: Watkins Consulting 4831 N 9th St Arlington VA 22203 Business E-Mail: dwatkins@ginevan.com.

WATKINS, EUGENE LEONARD, surgeon, educator; b. Worcester, Mass., Jan. 4, 1918; s. George Joseph and Marcella Katherine (Akels) W.; AB with honors in biology, Clark U., 1940; MD (Hood scholar), Harvard U., 1943; m. Victoria Peake, Sept. 23, 1944; children: Roswell Peake, Priscilla Welles. Intern, Roosevelt Hosp., NYC, 1944; resident in surgery, 1944-46, 49-50, asst. resident in surgery, 1948-49; fellow in surgery, clin. rsch. fellow Mass. Gen. Hosp., Boston, 1947-48; practice medicine specializing in surgery, NYC, 1950-56, Morristown, NJ, 1950-90, Denville, NJ, 1956-85, Boonton, NJ, 1961-85; mem. staff Morristown Meml. Hosp., 1950, vice chmn. dept. surgery, 1974-77, chmn., 1959-61, mem. corp.; cons. surgeon St. Clare's Hosp., Denville, NJ, Riverside Hosp., Boonton, NJ, Community Med. Ctr., Morristown; courtesy surg. staff St. Luke's-Roosevelt Hosp. Ctr., NYC; asst. clin. prof. surgery Rutgers U. Coll. Medicine and Dentistry, New Brunswick, NJ, 1972-85; asst. clin. prof. surgery Columbia U. Coll. Phys. and Surg., 1985-90; v.p. chmn. fin. com. Morristown Bd. Health, 1954-56. Served to 1st lt., AUS, 1946. Diplomate Am. Bd. Surgery. Fellow ACS (chmn. NJ Adv. Com. 1965-77, chmn. NJ State com. Trauma, 1960); mem. NJ, Morris County med. socs., AMA, Soc. Surgeons NJ (1st v.p. 1982, pres. 1983), Am. Thoracic Soc., AAAS, Harvard Med. Soc. NY (pres. 1960-61), West Side Med. Soc., Roosevelt Hosp. Alumni Assn. Republican. Presbyterian. Clubs: Harvard (NYC), Morristown, Morristown Field. Achievements include development of spring-loop surgical suture holder. Home: Unit 419 7501 E Thompson Peak Pkwy Scottsdale AZ 85255-4537

WATKINS, GEORGE DANIELS, physics professor; b. Evanston, Ill., Apr. 28, 1924; s. Paul F. and Lois V. (Daniels) W.; m. Carolyn Lenore Nevin, June 19, 1949; children: Lois Roberta, Paul Brent, Ann Romaine. BS, Randolph-Macon Coll., 1943; D.Sc. (hon.), 1976; MA, Harvard U., 1947, PhD, 1952. Research physicist Gen. Electric Research Lab., Schenectady, 1952-75; adj. prof. Rensselaer Poly. Inst., 1962-65, SUNY-Albany, 1969-72; Sherman Fairchild prof. physics Lehigh U., Bethlehem, Pa., 1975-95, prof. emeritus, 1995—; chmn. Gordon Research Conf. on Defects in Semiconductors, 1981; mem. solid state adv. com. Oak Ridge Nat. Lab., 1980-85. Mem. editl. bd. Phys. Rev. B, 1978-82; contbr. articles to profl. jours. Served to lt. (j.g.) USNR, 1943-46. NSF fellow, 1966-67; named Virginian of Yr. Va. Press Assn., 1980; recipient Alexander von Humboldt sr. U.S. Scientist award, 1983, 91. Fellow Am. Phys. Soc. (Oliver E. Buckley award 1978), AAAS, Nat. Acad. Scis. Democrat. Unitarian Universalist. Home Phone: 804-474-8654. Business E-Mail: gdw0@lehigh.edu.

WATKINS, HAROLD ROBERT, minister; b. Wauseon, Ohio, July 30, 1928; s. Orra Lynn and Florence Margaret (Bruner) W.; m. Evelyn Norma Earlywine, June 18, 1950; children: Mark Edwin, Nancy Jo Watkins. AB, Bethany Coll., 1950; MDiv, Lexington Theol. Sem., 1997; DD, Phillips U., 1985, Christian Theol. Sem., Indpls., 1995; BD, Coll. of Bible, 1953. Ordained minister Disciples of Christ, 1950. Min. Park Ave. Christian Ch., Tucson, 1953-56, First Christian Ch., Tuscaloosa, Ala., 1956-57; gen. ch. adminstr. Bd. Ch. Extension of Disciples of Christ, Indpls., 1958-95, pres., 1980-95, pres. emeritus, 2004—; mem. faculty Lexington Theol. Sem., 1996-97, 98-99, interim pres., 2001—02. Chmn. bd. dirs. Discipledata, Inc., Indpls., 1980—94; bd. dirs. United Church Ins. Co. Author: Continuity, Conservation and The Cutting Edge, 2005. Trustee Bethany (W.Va.) Coll., 1976—, Nat. City Christian Ch. Corp., Washington, 1981—; bd. dirs. Ecumenical Ch. Loan Fund, Geneva; pres. World Conv. Chs. of Christ, Nashville, 1988-92; bd. dirs. United Ch. of Christ Ins. Bd., 1997—. Recipient Outstanding Alumnus award Bethany Coll., 1975. Mem. Interfaith Forum on Religion, Art and Arch. (dir. officer 1979-95, pres. 1981-82, Elbert M. Conover award 1989). Home: 7601 Newport Bay Dr #118 Indianapolis IN 46240-3370 Office Phone: 317-251-2977. Personal E-mail: hwatkins28@aol.com.

WATKINS, HAYS THOMAS, retired railroad executive; b. Fern Creek, Ky., Jan. 26, 1926; s. Hays Thomas Sr. and Minnie Catherine (Whiteley) W.; m. Betty Jean Wright, Apr. 15, 1950; 1 son, Hays Thomas III. BS in Acctg., Western Ky. U., 1947; MBA, Northwestern U., 1948; LLD (hon.), Baldwin Wallace Coll., 1975, Alderson Broaddus Coll., 1980, Coll. of William and Mary, 1982, Va. Union U., 1987. CPA, Ill., Ohio. With C. & O. Ry. Cleve., 1949-80, v.p. fin., 1964-67, v.p. adminstrv. group, 1967-71, pres., CEO, 1971—73, chmn. bd., CEO, 1973—80; with B. & O. R.R., 1964-80, v.p. finance, 1964-71, pres., CEO, 1971—73, vice chmn. bd., CEO, 1973—80; chmn., CEO Chessie System, Inc., 1973—80; pres. and co-CEO CSX Corp. (merger of Chessie System, Inc. and Seaboard Coast Line Industries, Inc.), Richmond, Va., 1980—82, chmn. bd., CEO, 1982—89, chmn. bd., 1989-91; chmn. emeritus, 1991—. Vice-rector bd. visitors Coll. William & Mary, 1984-87, rector, 1987-93. With AUS, 1945-47. Named Man of Yr., Modern R.R. mag., 1984; recipient Excellence in Mgmt. award Industry Week mag., 1982. Mem. Nat. Assn. Accts., Am. Inst. C.P.A.'s. Clubs: Commonwealth (Richmond, Va.); Country of Va. (Richmond). Home: 22 Lower Tuckahoe Rd W Richmond VA 23238-6108 Office: CSX Corp 901 E Cary St Ste 1605 Richmond VA 23219 Office Phone: 804-782-1411.

WATKINS, JAMES DAVID, former United States Secretary of Energy, retired military officer; b. Alhambra, Calif., Mar. 7, 1927; s. Edward Francis and Louise Whipple (Ward) Watkins; m. Sheila Jo McKinney, Aug. 19, 1950 (dec. Sept. 1996); m. Janet L. McDonough, June 17, 2000; children: Katherine Marie, Laura Jo, Charles Lancaster, Susan Elizabeth, James David, Edward Francis stepchildren: John Christopher McDonough, Sean Charles McDonough, Robert Edward McDonough, Siobhan McDonough. BS, U.S. Naval Acad., 1949; MSME, Navy Postgrad. Sch., 1958; LHD (hon.), Marymount Coll., 1982, N.Y. Med. Coll., 1988; DSc (hon.), Dowling Coll., 1983, U. Ala., 1991; LLD (hon.), Cath. U. Am., 1985, Mt. Sinai Sch. Medicine, 1993, Calif. U. Pa., 1994; DS (hon.), Coll. William and Mary, 1999. Commd. ensign USN, 1949, advanced through grades to adm., 1979, comdg. officer U.S.S. Snook, 1964-66, exec. officer U.S.S. Long Beach, 1967-69; head submarine/nuclear power distbn. control br. Bur. Naval Pers., Dept. Navy, Washington, 1969-71, dir. enlisted pers. div., 1971-72, asst. chief naval pers. for enlisted pers. control, 1972-73; comdr. Cruiser-Destroyer Group 1 USN, 1973-75; dep. chief naval ops. manpower Dept. Navy, Washington, 1975-78, chief of naval pers., 1975-78, chief Bur. Naval Pers., 1975-78; comdr. U.S. Sixth Fleet USN, 1978-79; vice chief naval ops. Dept. Navy, Washington, 1979-81, comdr.-in-chief U.S. Pacific Fleet, 1981-82, chief naval ops., 1982-86; ret. USN, 1986; chmn. Presdl. Commn. Human Immunodeficiency Virus Epidemic, 1987-88; sec. US Dept. Energy, Washington, 1988—93; pres. Joint Oceanographic Instn., 1993-2000, Consortium Oceanographic Rsch. and Edn., 1993-2001. Chmn. Presidentially Apptd. Commn. Ocean Policy, 2001—04; co-chair Joint Ocean Commn., 2004—07. Decorated DSM with 1 gold star, Legion of Merit with 2 gold stars, Bronze Star medal with combat v; recipient Disting. Alumni award, Naval Postgrad. Sch., 1958, Chmn.'s award, Am. Assn. Engring. Socs., 1991, Disting. Grad. award, U.S. Naval Acad., 2001, Scientific Am. 50 award, 2004, Senator. John H. Chafee Coastal Stewardship award, 2005, Internat. Sea Keepers award, Lifetime Achievement award, Nat. Marine Sanctuary Found., 2006. Mem.: The Army Navy Country Club, The Alfalfa Club, Knights of Malta. Roman Catholic. Office Phone: 202-448-1249.

WATKINS, JEFFREY CLIFTON, neuroscientist; b. Perth, Australia, Dec. 20, 1929; s. Colin Hereward and Amelia Miriam (Smith) W.; m. Beatrice Joan Thacher, Apr. 5, 1973; children: Timothy Douglas, Katherine Helen. BS, U. Western Australia, Perth, 1949, BS with honors, 1950, MS, 1954; PhD, U. Cambridge, Eng., 1954. Rsch. fellow chemistry U. Cambridge, 1954-55, Yale U., New Haven, 1955-57; rsch. fellow in physiology Australian Nat. U., Canberra, 1958-61, fellow, 1961-65; vis. rsch. scientist Agrl. Rsch. Coun., Inst. Animal Physiology, Babraham, England, 1963—64, sci. officer, 1965-67; sci. staff mem. neuropsychiatry unit Med. Rsch. Coun., Carshalton, Surrey, England, 1968-73; sr. rsch. fellow in physiology/pharmacology U. Bristol, England, 1973-83, hon. sr. rsch. fellow in pharmacology, 1983-89, hon. prof. pharmacology, 1989-99, prof. emeritus, 1999—. Cons. Sandoz Pharma, Berne, Switzerland, 1983-94, Tocris Neuramin Ltd., Bristol, 1985-94, dir., 1992-94; cons. and dir. Tocris-Cookson Ltd., Bristol, 1994—2006. Co-editor: The NMDA Receptor, 1989, 2d edit. 1994; contbr. articles to profl. jours.; patentee in field. Recipient Wakeman Found. award, 1992, Charles A. Dana Found. award, 1994, Bristol-Myers Squibb award, 1995, Thudichum medal Brit. Biochem. Soc., 2000. Fellow Royal Soc. London, Inst. Biology London, Acad. Med. Sci. London, Brit. Pharm. Soc. (hon., Wellcome Gold medal 2001); mem. Brit. Physiol. Soc., Academia Europaea. Business E-Mail: jeffwatkins@onetel.com.

WATKINS, JOAN MARIE, retired osteopath, physician; b. Anderson, Ind., Mar. 9, 1943; d. Curtis David and Dorothy Ruth (Beckett) W.; m. Stanley G. Nodvik, Dec. 25, 1969 (div. Apr. 1974). BS, West Liberty State Coll., 1965; Cert. of Grad. Phys. Therapy, Ohio State U., 1966; DO, Phila. Coll. Osteo., 1972; M of Health Professions Edn., U. Ill., Chgo., 1986; MPH, U. Ill., 1989. Diplomate Osteo. Nat. Bds., Am. Bd. Preventive Medicine, Am. Bd. Occupl. and Environ. Medicine, Am. Bd. Emergency Medicine. Resident in phys. medicine and rehab. U. Pa., 1973—74; emergency osteo. physician Cooper Med. Ctr., Camden, 1974-79, Shore Meml. Hosp., Somers Point, NJ, 1979-81, St. Francis Hosp., Blue Island, Ill., 1981-82, Mercy Hosp. and Med. Ctr., Chgo., 1982-90, dir. emergency ctr., 1984-88; resident in occupl. and preventive medicine U. Ill., 1988-90; corp. med. dir. occupl. health svc. Univ. Cmty. Hosp., Tampa, 1992—2006; assoc. prof. environ. & occupl. health Coll. Pub. Health, USF; cons. in field, 2006—. Fellow Am. Coll. Occupl. and Environ. Medicine, Am. Soc. Preventive Medicine, Fla. Assn. Occupl. and Environ. Medicine (pres. 1999-2001). Avocations: sailing, needlecrafts, swimming. Home: 4306 Harbor House Dr Tampa FL 33615-5408 Office Phone: 813-390-6558. Business E-Mail: ywatkin9@tampabay.rr.com, jwatkins@health.usf.edu.

WATKINS, JOHN FRANCIS, management consultant; b. Alhambra, Calif., May 21, 1925; s. Edward F. and Louise (Ward) W.; divorced; children— Stephen, Katherine, John Francis, William. BSCE, U. Tex., Austin, 1947. With Earle M. Jorgensen Co., Lynwood, Calif., 1947-90, sr. v.p. adminstrn., 1978-90, ret.; owner John F. Watkins Assocs., Pasadena, Calif., 1990—. Pres. bd. Poly. Sch., Pasadena, 1978—80, Holy Family Sch., 1994—2002; adv. bd. mem. Serra H.S., Verbum Dei H.S., Dolores Mission Sch., 1996—; mem. Coll. Sci. and Engring. Coun. Loyola Marymount U., bd. visitors Sch. Edn.; adv. bd. Bishop Mora Salesian H.S., 1994—; mem. Cath. Edn. Found. Archdiocese L.A., 1995—; St. Gabriel pastoral region bd. dirs. Cath. Charities, 1994—; bd. dirs. Boys Republic, Chino Hills, Calif., 1970—, pres., 1977—80; bd. dirs. St. Luke Hosp., Pasadena, 1979—86, chmn. bd., 1982—86; bd. dirs. Econ. Literacy Coun. Calif., 1980—87, Pasadena Mus. of History, 1990—99. Mem. U.S. Navy League (nat. bd. dirs. 1989—, pres. Pasadena coun. 1992-93), Calif. Club, Annandale Golf Club, Serra Club (pres. 1995-97), Valley Club (San Marino, Calif.), Twilight Club (pres. 2002-03). Republican. Roman Catholic. Home and Office: 410 California Ter Pasadena CA 91105-2419 Home Phone: 626-432-4712; Office Phone: 626-432-4712. E-mail: jwatkins@pacificnet.net.

WATKINS, JOHN GOODRICH, psychologist, educator; b. Salmon, Idaho, Mar. 17, 1913; s. John Thomas and Ethel (Goodrich) W.; m. Evelyn Elizabeth Browne, Aug. 21, 1932; m. Doris Wade Tomlinson, June 8, 1946; m. Helen Verner Huth, Dec. 28, 1971; children: John Dean, Jonette Alison, Richard Douglas, Gregory Keith, Rodney Philip, Karen Stroobants, Marvin R. Huth; m. Paula Jean Etrick May 16, 2009. Student, Coll. Idaho, 1929-30, 31-32; BS, U. Idaho, 1933, MS, 1936; PhD, Columbia U., 1941. Instr. high sch., Idaho, 1933-39; faculty Ithaca Coll., 1940-41; prof. Auburn U., 1941-43; assoc. prof. Wash. State U., 1946-49; chief clin. psychologist U.S. Army Welch Hosp., 1945-46; clin. psychologist VA Hosp., American Lake, Wash., 1949-50; chief clin. psychologist VA Mental Hygiene Clinic, Chgo., 1950-53, VA Hosp., Portland, Oreg., 1953-64; prof. psychology U. Mont., Missoula, 1964-84, prof. emeritus, 1984—, dir. clin. tng., 1964-80. Lectr. numerous univs.; clin. asso. U. Oreg. Med. Sch., 1957; pres. Am. Bd. Examiners in Psychol. Hypnosis, 1960-62. Author: Objective Measurement of Instrumental Performance, 1942, Hypnotherapy of War Neuroses, 1949, General Psychotherapy, 1960, The Therapeutic Self, 1978, (with others) We, The Divided Self, 1982, Hypnotherapeutic Techniques, 1987, rev. edit., 2006, (with others) Hypnoanalytic Techniques, 1992, (with others) Ego States: Theory and Therapy, 1997, Adventures in Human Understanding, 2001, Emotional Resonance, 2005, (with others) Advanced Hypnotherapy: Hypnodynamic Techniques, Routledge, NY, 2007; contbr. articles to profl. jours. Recipient award, Am. Soc. Clin. Hypnosis, 2007. Mem. Internat. Soc. Clin. and Exptl. Hypnosis (co-founder, pres. 1965-67, awards 1960-65), Internat. Soc. Hypnosis (Benjamin Franklin Gold medal award), Soc. Clin. and Exptl. Hypnosis (pres. 1969-71, Morton Prince award), Am. Psychol. Assn. (pres. divsn. 30 1975-76, award 1993), Phi Delta Kappa. Home and Office: 8258 Greenwood Pl Longmont CO 80503 Home Phone: 303-652-6556. Office Fax: 303-652-6525. *For a complete life one needs a job, a home, a love, a friend, and an enemy. My "enemies" are injustice, war, poverty, illness, and suffering, not people. Make your existence as meaningful as possible. Enjoy life fully, and when it comes time to leave, have no fear or regrets. Seek to leave this world a little better off because you lived. These are my values. Would that I were mature enough always to live up to them.*

WATKINS, JULIA M., educational association administrator; b. Pocatello, Idaho, Sept. 24, 1941; d. Elaine (Steele) and Emory J. Herndon; m. Dennis A. Watkins, Sept. 20, 1963; children: Matthew T., Christopher J., Andrew J. BS, U. Utah, 1963, MSW, 1965, PhD, 1970; LHD (hon.), U. Maine, 2003. Social worker Children's Ctr, Salt Lake City, 1967—71; asst. prof. social welfare U. Maine, Orono, Maine, 1971—77, asst. prof. and coord. of social welfare program, 1977—84, prof. of social work, 1986—96, dean Coll. Social and Behavioral Scis. Orono, 1989-92, interim v.p. for acad. affairs, 1992—93; pres. Am. U. in Bulgaria, Blagoevgrad, 1993—2003; exec. dir. Coun. on Social Work Edn., Alexandria, Va., 2003—. Pres. Alliance of Univs. for Democracy (Internat.), Pecs, Hungary, 1999—2001, Assn. of Am. Internat. Coll. and Univs. (Internat.), Athens, Greece, 1998—2000; trustee Am. Univ. in Kyrgystan (now Am. Univ. of Central Asia), Bishkek, Kyrgyzstan, 1999—2003; mem., bd. gov. Les Roches Sch. of Hotel Mgmt., Bluche, Switzerland, 2005—. Author: (book) Social Policy and the Rural Setting, 1984, (reference handbook) Comprehensive Handbook of Social Work and Social Welfare/ Educating for Social Work, 2007, (ency.) The Encyclopedia of Social Work/Council on Social Work Education, 2008; contbr. articles to profl. jours. Mem. Rotary Club, Bangor Maine and Blagoevgrad, Bulgaria, 1990—2003; founding bd. mem. Am. C. of C., Sofia, Bulgaria, 1994—2000; bd. mem. Found. for Local Govt. Reform, Sofia, Bulgaria, 1995—2003; life hon. bd. mem. New Symphony Orchestra, Sofia, Bulgaria, 2001—03. Recipient Disting. Career Svc. award, Grad Sch. of Social work, U. Utah, 1992; grantee, HHS, Adminstrn. on Aging, Am. Assn. Ret. Person Andrus Found., USPHS, 1980—90. Mem.: NASW, Internat. Assn. of Schs. of Social Work (treas.), Phi Kappa Phi.

WATKINS, LESLIE M., academic administrator; d. Doug and Betty Jean Moseley; m. James Christopher Watkins, Dec. 16, 2000. BA, MA, Western Ky. U., Bowling Green. Sr. dir. devel. Western Ky. U., 1999—. Pres. Bowling Green Western Symphony Orch., 2008—. Mem.: Coun. Advancement and Support Edn., Bowling Green Jr. Woman's Club (pres. 1998—99, Woman of Yr. 1999). Office: Western Ky Univ 1906 College Heights Blvd Bowling Green KY 42101 Office Fax: 270-745-5300. Business E-Mail: leslie.watkins@wku.edu.

WATKINS, MARK CHARLES HENRY, finance educator; s. Ralph and Laura Watkins; m. Lesta Diane Swender; children: Christian, Blair. Cert. specialist Pittsburgh State U., Kans., 2004. Bus. instr. Neosho County CC, Chanute, 2005—. Office: Neosho County CC 800 West 14th St Chanute KS 66720

WATKINS, M(ARTHA) ANNE, family practice nurse practitioner; b. Vicksburg, Mich., Feb. 9, 1961; d. George H. and Coleene M. (Shearer) W. ADN, S.W. Mich. Coll., 1984; BSN, U. Mich., 1988, MSN, 2003. RN, Mich. Staff nurse Lee Meml. Hosp., Dowagiac, Mich.; clin. nurse II thoracic intensive care U. Mich. Hosps., Ann Arbor; emergency nurse Lee Meml. Hosp., Dowagiac, Mich.; critical care nurse Mercy Meml. Hosp., St. Joseph, Mich.; house supr. Lee Meml. Hosp., Dowagiac, Mich., dir. med. surg. pediat., 1995, v.p. patient care svcs., 1996—2001; family nurse practioner Planned Parenthood Mid Mich. Alliance, Benton Harbor, Mich., 2004—06, After Hours Clinic Watervliet Cmty. Hosp., Mich., 2006—. Mem. Phi Theta Kappa. Home: 303 Mcphil Dr Dowagiac MI 49047-1012 Office: After Hours Clinic Watervliet Cmty Hosp 420 Medical Park Dr Watervliet MI 49098 Office Phone: 269-463-3600. Business E-Mail: marthawatkins@borgess.com.

WATKINS, ROBERT G, surgeon; b. Memphis, Tenn., Feb. 5, 1964; MD, U. Tenn., Memphis, 1969. Orthop. spinesurgeon Watkins Spine, Marina del Rey, Calif., 2007—09. Office: Watkins Spine 3547 Ocean View Ave Marina Del Rey CA 90292 Business E-Mail: robertwatkinsmd@yahoo.com.

WATKINS, SHARON ELIZABETH, minister, religious organization administrator; b. 1954; m. Richard H. Lowery; children: Bethany, Christopher. BA in French & Economics, Butler U., Indpls., 1975;

MDiv, Yale Divinity Sch., New Haven, 1984; DMin, Phillips Theol. Seminary, Tulsa, Okla., DD (hon.), 2007. Ordained Hamden, Conn., 1984. Asst. min. Spring Glen Ch. (United Ch. of Christ), Hamden; pastor Boone Grove Christian Ch. (Disciples of Christ), Ind.; dir. student svcs. Phillips Theol. Seminary; assoc. v.p. Univ. rels. Phillips U., Enid, Okla.; sr. pastor, moderator Disciples Christian Ch., Bartlesville, Okla., 1997—2005; gen. min., pres. Christian Ch. (Disciples of Christ) US & Can., Indpls., 2005—. Mem. Gen. Bd. Task Force on Reconciliation Mission; mem. ctrl. com., permanent com. consensus and collaboration World Coun. of Churches, Geneva; rep. World Coun. Gen. Assembly, Porto Alegre, Brazil, 2006; mem. gov. bd. Nat. Coun. of Churches, NYC; bd. dirs. Sojourners/Call to Renewal, Washington; adj. prof. Phillips Theol. Seminary. Mem. Christian Ch. (Disciples Of Christ). Office: Gen Ministries Christian Ch US & Can PO Box 1986 Indianapolis IN 46206 Office Phone: 317-635-2410. Business E-Mail: swatkins@ogmp.disciples.org.*

WATKINS, STANLEY, legislative staff member; Grad., Monmouth Coll., Ill., 1978. Dist. dir., Rep. Bobby Rush US House of Reps., chief of staff to Rep. Bobby Rush Washington, 2007—. Office: 2416 Rayburn House Office Bldg Washington DC 20515 Office Phone: 202-225-4372. Office Fax: 202-225-0333.*

WATKINS, STEPHEN EDWARD, accountant, publishing executive; b. Oklahoma City, Sept. 1, 1922; s. Ralph Bushnell and Jane (Howell) W.; m. Suzanne Fowler, Aug. 16, 1976; children— Elizabeth Ann Watkins Racicot, Stephen Edward, Jr. BBA, U. N.Mex., 1944. C.P.A., N.Mex. With Peat, Marwick, Mitchell & Co., 1944-67; pres. The New Mexican daily newspaper, Santa Fe, 1967-78, 90—; pvt. practice pub. acctg. Santa Fe, 1978—. Vestryman Ch. of Holy Faith; trustee St. Vincent Hosp., 1979-85, Orchestra Santa Fe, 1976-82, Hist. Santa Fe Found. (pres. 1990). Mem. AICPA, Sons of Am. Revolution, Rotary. Home: 1325 Don Gaspar Ave Santa Fe NM 87505-4627 Office: 223 E Palace Ave Santa Fe NM 87501-1947

WATKINS, YELBERTON R. (YEBBIE WATKINS), legislative staff member; b. Columbia, SC; B, Duke U., Durham, NC; JD, Georgetown U., Washington. Staff mem., Senator Terry Sanford US Senate, Washington; legis. asst., Rep. James Clyburn US House of Reps., Washington, 1993—94, chief of staff to Rep. James Clyburn, 1994—, statutory, Dem. steering and policy com., 2003, receptionist, adminstrv. asst., Dem. employees, 2003—06, adminstrv. asst., Dem. Caucus, 2006—07, chief of staff, Office of the Majority Whip, 2007—. Named one of Fabulous 50, Roll Call. Democrat. Office: 2135 Rayburn House Office Bldg Washington DC 20515 Office Phone: 202-225-3315. Office Fax: 202-225-2313. Business E-Mail: yebbie.watkins@mail.house.gov.*

WATNE, DARLENE CLAIRE, county official; b. Minot, ND, Feb. 11, 1935; d. Charles A. and Anna Marie Widdel (Fjeld) W.; m. Clair A. Watne, Mar. 27, 1954; children: Carmen, Steven, Nancy, Matthew. Court reporting diploma, 1975; grad., Real Estate Inst., 1991. Cert. residential real estate specialist, N.D. Exec. sec. Grand Exalted Ruler Elks, Minot, ND, 1964-75; pres. Bus. Coll., Minot, 1974—76; ct. reporter NW Jud. Dist., Minot, 1976—90; real estate broker Watne Realtors Better Homes & Gardens, Minot, 1990—99; mem. ND Senate from 5th dist., Bismarck, 1994—2001; commr. Ward County, ND, 1994—. Active Joint Civil Svcs. to the Poor, 1995-2001. Commr. ND State Lottery, 2002—07; mem. Souris Basin Planning Coun., 2004—07, Ward County Libr. Bd., 2006—; dir. Minot Area Devel. Corp., 2006—; numerous state polit. interim senate coms.; bd. dirs. Salvation Army, Red Cross; bd. dir. ND Credit Union, 2007—. Named Minot Woman of Distinction in Bus. and Industry, 1993, Liberty award ND Bar Assn., 2000, named Citizen of Yr. ND Builders Assn., 2001. Republican. Avocations: reading, laking. Home: 520 28th Ave SW Minot ND 58701-7065

WATNE, DONALD ARTHUR, retired accountant, educator; b. Gt. Falls, Mont., Jan. 18, 1939; BA with high honors, U. Mont., 1960, MA, 1961; PhD, U. Calif., Berkeley, 1977. CPA, Oreg. Acct. Piquet & Minihan, Eugene, Oreg., 1961-65; mgr. capital investment analysis Weyerhaeuser Co., Tacoma, 1965-68; mktg. rep. IBM Corp., Portland, Oreg., 1968-70; dir. EDP Ctr. in Concejo Mcpl., Barquisimeto, Venezuela, 1971-72; prof. acctg. Portland State U., 1976-2001, prof. emeritus, 2001—. Vis. prof. Xiamen (Fujian, People's Rep. China), 1985-86, U. Otago, Dunedin, New Zealand, 1985-86, U. Newcastle, Australia, 1985-86; cons. in field; acctg. qualifications com. Oregon State Bd. Acctg., 1989-98, CPE com., 1998-2001 Author: (with Peter B.B. Turney) Auditing EDP Systems, 2d edit. 1990; contbr. chpts. to books, articles to profl. jours. Del. to Soviet Union citizen amb. program People to People Internat., 1990; active Tng. the Trainers Program, Vilnius, Lithuania, 1993; trustee, treas. First Unitarian Ch. of Portland, 2002-08; mem. bd. stewards First Unitarian Ch. of Portland Found., 2002-07, treas., 2004-07. Mem.: AICPA, Oreg. Soc. CPAs, Mensa, Mazamas Mountain Climbing Club. Home: 2826 NE 26th Ave Portland OR 97212-3503 E-mail: dawatne@msn.com.

WATROUS, ROBERT THOMAS, academic director; b. Cleveland, Apr. 20, 1952; s. Frank Thomas and Marie Anne (Kmeicik) W.; m. Robin Joyce (Braun), Mar. 14, 1981 (div. 1993); 1 child, Michael Francis; m. Susan J. (Rupp), Mar. 8, 2003. BS, U. Dayton, Ohio, 1974, MS, 1977. Dir. student ctr. for off campus cmty. rels. U. Dayton, Ohio, 1974—76, resident dir., 1976—78; dir. of housing St. Bonaventure U., Olean, NY, 1978—81; asst. dean of student life housing U. Pa., Kutztown, 1981—86, dir. commuter and jud. affairs, 1986—2004, dean, student svcs. & campus life, 2004—, assoc. v.p. student svcs. & campus life, 2007—. Faculty senate Kutztown U. Pa. 1986-89, 92-95; mem. Pa. Task Force on Intergroup Behavior in Higher Edn., 1991-94; trainer Pa. Interagy. Task Force on Civil Tension, Harrisburg, Pa., 1989-2001; exec. coun. Adult Learners Consortium, Bloomsburg, Pa., 1990-91; mem. Lehigh Valley Svc. Learning Consortium, 1994—. Bd. mgr. Tri Valley YMCA, Fleetwood, Pa., 1983-94; adv. bd. Crossroads, Kutztown, 1989-94; bd. dir. Jr. Achievement of Berks County, Reading, Pa., 1990, Reading, Pa., 1990, Reading and Berks Coun. YMCA, 1992-96; mem. Leadership Berks, Reading, 1990; bd. dir. Leadership Berks, 1995—, sec. 1998-99, pres., 2000-04; co-founder Leading Sch. Bd., 1994—; mem. Leadership Alliance Berks, 2004-, YMCA cultural diversity and internat. awareness com., 1994—; mem. Berks County Conflict Resolution Task Force, 1996-2004; v.p. Fleetwood Activities Booster Club, 1998-2002, pres., 1999-2001. Mem. Nat. Assn. Student Pers. Adminstr. (profl. affiliate), Hawk Mt. Coun. Boy Scouts Am. (sustaining mem.), Berks County C. of C. (sch. bd. governance com. 1993-2000), Fleetwood Youth Soccer Club (v.p., pres. 1999), Fleetwood Youth Basketball Assn. (coach 1995-96), Leadership Alliance of Berks, 2003-, Greater Reading Leadrership Alliance, 2004-. Avocations: golf, sports, gardening. Business E-Mail: watrous@kutztown.edu.

WATSON, ALLISON L., computer software company executive; d. Perry and Mona Lambird; 1 child. BA, Stanford U.; MBA, San Diego State U. With mid-Atlantic dist. & East region leadership teams Microsoft Corp., 1993—99, gen. mgr. mid-Atlantic dist., 1999—2001, chief of staff to sr. v.p. of Microsoft Americas, 2001—02, v.p. worldwide ptnr. group, 2002—06, corp. v.p. worldwide ptnr. group, 2006—. Named Channel Exec. of Yr., VARBus. Mag., 2004; named one of 10 Worldwide Agenda-Setters, 2006. Office: Microsoft Corp Worldwide Ptnr Group 1 Microsoft Way Redmond WA 98052-6399

WATSON, ANTHONY L., health facility executive; b. 1942; Supervising pub. health advisor dept.health edn. and welfare Ctr. for Disease Control, Pub. Health Svc., 1966-70; dep. dir. Comprehensive Health Planning Agy., NYC, 1970-76, Health Planning, NYC, 1976—85; exec. v.p., COO HIP Health Plan of NY, NYC, 1985—91, chmn., CEO, 1991—, Emblem Health, Inc., 2006—. Mem. Comty. Coun. Greater NY. Mem. Am. Health Planning Assn., Am. Hosp. Assn. Office: HIP Health Plan of NY 55 Water St New York NY 10041*

WATSON, ARTHUR DENNIS, federal official; b. Brownsville, Pa., May 11, 1950; s. Arthur Francis and Margaret Teresa (Mastile) Puglia, John Leslie Watson (Stepfather); m. Kathleen Frances Zaccardo, July 16, 1983; 1 child, Fiona Kathleen. BSBA, U. Richmond, 1972; MS in Bus.-Govt. Rels., Am. U., 1977, MA in Lit., 1979; PhD in English Lang. and Lit., Cath. U., 1987. Statis. asst. U.S. Postal Svc. Hdqrs., Washington, 1972—73, economist assoc., 1973—74, staff economist, 1974—77, mktg. analyst, 1977; rate analyst U.S. Postal Rate Commn., Washington, 1977—79, dir. pub. affairs, 1979—82; pub. affairs officer ICC, Washington, 1982—89, dep. dir. pub. affairs, 1989—93, assoc. dir. congl. and pub. affairs, 1993—95; dir. media affairs Dept. Transp., Washington, 1996—2008, dir. comm. surface transp., 2008—. Pres. Arthur D. Watson and Co., Clifton, Va., 1983—; Washington corr. Linn's Stamp News, Sidney, Ohio, 1983—84. Contbr. articles to profl. jours. With USCG, 1972—78. Recipient Meritorious Svc. medal, USCG Res., Pub. Svc. award, ICC, 1989, Spl. Achievement award, Surface Transp. Bd., 1999, Merger Response Team Performance award, 2000, Performance award for media and pub. affairs, 2000, Second Pl. award, Internat. Plastic Modelers Soc. (No. Va. divsn.), 2000, Merger Response Team Performance award, Surface Transp. Bd., 2001, Agy. Performance award Merger team, 2001, Performance award for website enhancements, 2002, Performance award for media and pub. affairs, 2002. Mem.: Assn. Transp. Law Profls., Nat. Assn. RR Passengers, E. Clairborne Robins Sch. Bus. Alumni Assn., Nat. Press Club. Avocations: classical music, reading, writing, model building, travel. Home: 6521 Rockland Dr Clifton VA 20124-2415 Office: Surface Transp Bd 395 E St SW Ste 1208 Washington DC 20423-0001 Office Phone: 202-245-0234.

WATSON, BRENDA BENNETT, insurance company executive; b. Decatur, Ga., Aug. 26, 1940; d. Robert Joseph and Clarissa Mae (Weekes) Bennett; m. James H. Pair Jr., Apr. 4, 1969 (div. Aug. 1993); children: Richard S. Pair, Randall J. Pair, Ronald G. Pair; m. James Leigh Watson, Sept. 9, 1995. Student, DeKalb Coll., 1971. Lic. property and casualty agt. Underwriter W. K. Stringer Co., Atlanta, 1961-65, Tharpe & Assocs., Atlanta, 1965-68; sr. v.p. Alexander - Howden, Atlanta, 1968-82; exec. v.p., ptnr. Pair Underwriting Mgrs. Inc., Atlanta, 1982-86; pres. Walkingstick-LaGere-Pair Underwriting Mgrs., Inc., Chandler, Okla., 1986-88; exec. v.p., dir. LaGere-Walkingstick Ins. Agy., Chandler, Okla., 1988—2002; exec. v.p., bd. dirs. Chandler Ins. Mgrs. Inc., 2003—06; pres., CEO, mng. ptnr. TIP Natl. Inc., 2007—. Exec. v.p. Nat. Am. Ins. Co., Chandler, Okla., 1987-2006, Austin, Tex., 1999-2003; exec. v.p., bd. dirs. Chandler Ins. Ltd., Cayman Islands, 1985-2004. Dir., past pres. Gateway to Prevention and Recovery, 1994-98. Mem. Nat. Assn. Ins. Women (pres. Atlanta chpt. 1978-79, Woman of Yr. 1979-80). Republican. Episcopalian. Office: 1900 NW Expressway Ste 860 Oklahoma City OK 73118 Home Phone: 405-340-1196; Office Phone: 405-848-8888. Business E-Mail: brenda.watson@tipnational.com.

WATSON, CAROL ELIZABETH, education educator; b. Sharon, Pa., Mar. 25, 1957; d. Dean Olin and Sylvia Leach Haney; m. Carl Ray Watson, Apr. 30, 1983; children: Nicholas, Alexander, Kyana. BA in Elem. Edn., Westminster Coll., New Wilmington, Pa., 1979; MA in Elem. Edn., W.Va. U., Morgantown, 1987; PhD in Curriculum and Instrn., Va. Tech., Blacksburg, 2005. Tchr. Tucker County Schs., Parsons, W.Va., 1979—84, Franklin Sch. Dist., NH, 1987—89, Shenandoah County Pub. Schs., Woodstock, Va., 1989—95, Alleghany County Pub. Schs., Covington, Va., 1995—2002; grad. asst. Va. Tech., 2002—04; asst. prof. W.Va. State U., Institute, 2004—05, Kutztown U., Pa., 2005—. Scholar, Fulbright-Hayes Found., Malawi, Africa, 2004. Mem.: Am. Assn. for Coll. Tchrs. Edn., Nat. Coun. for Social Studies, Nat. Reading Conf., Eastern Edn. Rsch. Assn., Nat. Assn. for Multicultural Edn. Avocations: singing, running, weightlifting, sewing. Office: Kutztown U 15200 Kutztown Rd Kutztown PA 19530

WATSON, CHARLES SCHOFF, psychology professor; b. Chgo., Aug. 16, 1932; s. Charles Burton Piatt and Anna Mary Schoff Frazer; m. Betty Unger Unger, May 5, 1970; children: Ann Bianco, Mary Stork, Katharine, Elizabeth. PhD, Ind. U., Bloomington, 1961. Prof. psychology Wash. U., St. Louis, 1965—77; prof. emeritus Ind. U., Bloomington, 1983—. Pres. Communication Disorders Tech., Inc., Bloomington, 1989—. Contbr. articles to profl. jours. Aviation electronics technician, 2nd class USN, 1951—55, USS Midway. Rsch. grant, NIH, ONR, AFOSR, NSF, 1965—2009. Fellow: APA, APS, Acoustical Soc. Am. (chmn. 1982—83); mem.: AAUP, ACLU. Achievements include research in perception of complex sounds, auditory learning, computer based perceptual training. Avocations: tennis, singing. Office: Communication Disorders Tech Inc 501 N Morton St Bloomington IN 47404

WATSON, CLAUDE ARMSTEAD, counselor; b. Marshall, Tex., Mar. 9, 1937; s. Andrew Polk and Lena Holloway Watson; m. Marie Ann Coleman, Jan. 21, 1994; children: Claudia Marie Coleman, Stephanie Colleen Swan, Andrea Maude Kelly, Mary Teresa Ricketts. BA, Wiley Coll., Marshall, Tex., 1955—61. Social ins. adminstr. Social Security Adminstrn., Dallas, 1964—87; exec. dir. Dallas County Cmty. Action Com., Inc., 1974—2006, 1989—90, Pvt. Industry Coun. Greater Dallas, Inc., 1990—91; spl. projects coord. Dallas Area Agy. Aging, 2003—. Bd. pres. Sickle Cell Anemia Found. Dallas, Inc., 1987—91; cons. to gen. supt. Wilmer-Hutchins Ind. Sch. Dist., Tex., 2002—03. Columnist (weekly newspaper) The Dallas Examiner, Perspectives. Founder, pres. Right Alternatives for People, Inc., Dallas, 1979—2001; mem. state bd. ACLU, Austin, 1994—96. Sp-4, e-4 US Army, 1958—61, Asian nations. Recipient Silver Beaver award, Boy Scouts Am., 1983, Whitney M. Young Svc. award, 1993, Regional Dirs. Quality award, US Bur. Census, 2000, For Polit. Commentary award, Nat. Newspaper Publishers Assn., 2005; finalist Quarter World Speech Competition, Toastmasters Internat., 1979. D-Liberal. Meth. Avocations: literature, bridge. Home: 1811 Dolores Way Dallas TX 75232-4102 Office Fax: 214-871-7442. Personal E-mail: kascole@sbcglobal.net. Business E-Mail: cwatson@ccgd.org.

WATSON, DAVID E., toxicologist, consultant; married. PhD, Duke U., Durham, NC, 1995. Post-doc. scientist NIEHS, Research Triangle Pk., NC, 1996—98; sr. toxicologist Eli Lilly & Co., Indpls., 1999—2002, prin. rsch. scientist, 2003—06, rsch. advisor, 2006—. Chief sci. officer Scienteur, Indpls., 2006—07. Mem.: Soc. Toxicology. Office: Eli Lilly & Co 355 E Merrill St DC0720 Indianapolis IN 46225 Business E-Mail: davewatson@lilly.com.

WATSON, DAVID H., physician; BS, Baylor U., Waco, Tex.; MD, Baylor Coll. Medicine, Houston, 1957. Rotating gen. internship Hermann Hosp., Houston; with Yoakum Med. Clinic, Tex., 1958—. Recipient Country Doctor of Yr., Staff Care, 2008. Avocations: crossword puzzles, reading, history. Office: Yoakum Medical Clinic 402 Hubbard St Yoakum TX 77995 Office Phone: 361-293-2371.*

WATSON, DAVID RIDDLE, literature and language professor; b. Chapel Hill, Nc., Jan. 10, 1981; s. William David and Gaye Dorothy Watson. BA in Philosophy and Religion, Appalachian State, Boone, NC, 2003, MA in English, 2005. English prof. Ctrl. Carolina CC, Sanford, 2005—. Ctrl. regional rep., English instructors NC Coll., 2007—. Contbr. articles to profl. jours. Music performer Animal Rescue and Shelter, Sanford, NC, 2009; musician Boys and Girls Club, Sanford, 2008. Home: 2627 Mallard Cove Sanford NC 27330 Office: Ctrl Carolina CC 1105 Kelly Dr Sanford NC 27330

WATSON, DENTON L., history professor; s. Audley Granville and Ivy Louise Watson; m. Rosa B Balfour, Sept. 1, 1962; children: Victor C, Dawn M Edwards. MSc, Columbia U. Grad. Sch. Journalism, NYC, 1965. Dir. pub. rels. NAACP, NYC, 1983—85; prof. SUNY Coll., Old Westbury, 1992—. Editl. writer Balt. Sun, 1979—81. Methodist. Avocation: photography. Home: 137 W Seaman Ave Freeport NY 11520 Office: SUNY Coll PO Box 210 Old Westbury NY 11568-0210 Personal E-mail: dennie.watson2@verizon.net. Business E-Mail: watsond@oldwestbury.edu.

WATSON, DIANE EDITH, United States Representative from California; b. LA, Nov. 12, 1933; d. William Allen Louis and Dorothy Elizabeth (O'Neal) Watson. Student, LA City Coll.; BA in Edn., UCLA, 1956; MA in Sch. Psychology, Calif. State U., LA, 1958; PhD in Edni. Adminstrn., Claremont Grad. Sch., 1987. Tchr., adminstr. LA Unified Sch. Dist., 1958—76, sch. psychologist LA, 1967—68; mem. Calif. Senate from dist. 26, 1979—98, mem. edn. com., budget & fiscal rev. com., criminal procedure com., housing & land use com., chairperson health & human svcs. com.; US amb. to Micronesia US Dept. of State, 1998—2001; mem. US Congress from 33d Calif. dist., 2001—, mem. oversight & govt. reform com., internat. rels. com., fgn. affairs com. Lectr. Calif. State U., LA, Long Beach; health occupations specialist Bur. Indsl. Edn. Calif. Dept. Edn., 1971—73; bd. mem. LA Unified Sch. Dist., 1975—78; mem. Calif. Commn. Status Women, Legis. Black Caucus, Dem. Nat. Com.; co-chair US-UK Caucus, Congl. Korea Caucus; chair Congl. Entertainment Industries Caucus; mem. exec. com. Nat. Conf. State Legislators; del. Dem. Nat. Conv., 1972—. Author: Health Occupations Instructional Units-Secondary Schools, 1975, Planning Guide for Health Occupations, 1975; co-author: Introduction to Health Care, 1976. Recipient Mary Church Terrell award, 1976, Brotherhood Crusade award, 1981; named Alumnus of Yr., UCLA, 1980, 1982; named to Power 150, Ebony mag., 2008. Mem.: NAACP (Black Woman of Achievement award 1988), Calif. Elected Women Edn. & Rsch., Nat. Orgn. Black Elected Legislators (pres.), United Tchrs. LA, Calif. Tchrs. Assn., LA Urban League, Calif. Assn. Sch. Psychologists, Alpha Kappa Alpha. Democrat. Roman Catholic. Office: US Ho Reps 125 Cannon HOB Washington DC 20515-0533 also: 4322 Wilshire Blvd Ste 302 Los Angeles CA 90010 Office Phone: 202-225-7084, 323-965-1422. Fax: 202-225-2422; Office Fax: 323-965-1113.*

WATSON, DOC (ARTHEL LANE WATSON), vocalist, guitarist, banjoist, recording artist; b. Deep Gap, NC, Mar. 2, 1923; s. General Dixon and Annie (Greer) Watson; m. Rosa Lee Carlton; children: Eddy Merle(dec.), Nancy Ellen. Ind. rec. artist, touring performer. First appearance Boone (N.C.) Fiddler's Conf., rec. artist Folkways in 1960's, signed with Vanguard Records, 1964, recorded for United Artists, Columbia, Poppy, Sugar Hill, Verve and Flying Fish labels; performer: Newport Folk Festival, 1963, Smithsonian Inst., White House, 1980, Carnegie Hall, 1985; toured in Africa for Dept. State, 1970, also Europe and Japan, albums (many with Merle Watson) Southbound, Red Rocking Chair, The Guitar Album, Riding the Midnight Train (Grammy award for Best Traditional Folk album, 1986), Portrait, Songs for Little Pickers, On Praying Ground, 1999 (Grammy award for Best Traditional Folk Album, 1990); performer (music): (films) Places in the Heart. Recipient Grammy award for Best Traditional Recording, 1973, 1974, 1986, 1990, Grammy award for Best Country Instrumental Performance, 1979, 2007, Grammy award for Best Traditional Folk Album, 2002, Grammy award for Lifetime Achievement, 2004, NC award, State of NC, 1985, Carolina prize NY Times Corp., 1985, Nat. Medal of Arts, Pres. of U.S. with NEA, 1997, Nat. Heritage award, NEH, 1988. Office: care Folklore Prodns 1671 Appian Way Santa Monica CA 90401-3258 Fax: 310-458-6005. E-mail: info@folkloreproductions.com.

WATSON, DONALD CHARLES, JR., cardiothoracic surgeon, educator; b. Fairfield, Ohio, Mar. 15, 1945; s. Donald Charles and Pricilla H. Watson; m. Susan Robertson Prince, June 23, 1973; children: Kea Huntington, Katherine Anne, Kirsten Prince. BA in Applied Sci., Lehigh U., 1968, BSME, 1969; MSME, Stanford U., 1969; MD, Duke U., 1972; MBA, Vanderbilt U., 1992. Diplomate Am. Bd. Thoracic Surgery, Am. Bd. Surgery. Intern Stanford U. Med. Ctr., Calif., 1972-73, resident in cardiovasc. surgery Calif., 1973-74, resident in surgery Calif., 1976-78, chief resident in heart transplant Calif., 1978-79, chief resident in cardiovasc. and gen. surgery Calif., 1978-80; clin. assoc. surgery br. Nat. Heart and Lung Inst., 1974-76, acting sr. surgeon, 1976; assoc. cardiovasc. surgeon dept. child health and devel. George Washington U., Washington, 1980-84, asst. prof. surgery, asst. prof. child health and devel., 1980-84, attending cardiovasc. surgeon dept. child health and devel., 1984-89, assoc. prof. surgery, 1984-89; assoc. prof. pediats. U. Tenn.-Memphis, 1984-90, prof. surgery, 1990—2006, prof. pediats., 1990—2006, chmn. cardiothoracic surgery, 1984-99, assoc. chief med. officer, 1999—2001. Mem. staff Le Bonheur Children's Med. Ctr., Memphis, 1984—2006, chmn. cardiothoracic surgery, 1984-99; cons. in field; instr. advanced trauma life support; profl. cons., program reviewer HHS. Contbr. chpts., numerous articles, revs. to profl. publs. Bd. dirs. Airlift Hope Am., Internat. Children's Heart Found., Child Health Alliance Mid-South. Served to lt. comdr. USPHS, 1974-76. Smith Kline & French fellow Lehigh U., 1967; NSF fellow Lehigh U., 1968; univ. interdepartmental scholar and univ. scholar Lehigh U., 1968. Fellow Am. Coll. Cardiology, ACS; mem. Am. Assn. Thoracic Surgery, Soc. Thoracic Surgeons, So. Thoracic Surg. Assn., Andrew G. Morrow Soc., Norman E. Shumway Soc. (multiple bd. dirs.), NIH Alumni Assn., Stanford U. Med. Alumni Assn., Stanford U. Alumni Assn., Lehigh U. Alumni Assn., Smithsonian Assocs., U. Tenn. Pres.'s Club, LeBonheur Pres's Club, Pilots Internat. Assn., Nat. Assn. Flight Instrs., Aircraft Owners and Pilots Assn., Biltmore Forest Country Club, Phi Beta Kappa, Tau Beta Pi, Pi Tau Sigma, Phi Gamma Delta. Republican. Presbyterian. Achievements include established a regional referral center for the treatment of congenital heart disease. Avocations: golf, sailing, mountain climbing, flying. Office Phone: 828-277-0677. Personal E-mail: dcwbusi@aol.com. Business E-Mail: dwutmem@aol.com.

WATSON, DONALD RALPH, architect, dean, writer, artist; b. Providence, Sept. 27, 1937; s. Ralph Giles W. and Ethel (Fletcher) Pastene; m. Marja Palmqvist, Sept. 8, 1966 (div. Jan. 1984); children: Petrik, Elise;

m. Judith Criste, Jan. 3, 1986 (dec. Oct. 8, 2000). AB, Yale U., 1959, BArch, 1962, MEd, 1969. Lic. architect Nat. Council Archtl. Registration Bds. Architect Peace Corps, Tunisia, 1962-64; archtl. cons. Govt. of Tunisia, 1964-65; pvt. practice, Trumbull, Conn., 1969—; cons. United Nations Devel. Program, 2009—; dean Sch. Architecture, Rensselaer Poly. Inst., Troy, NY, 1990-95, prof., 1990—2001. Frederick C. Baker vis. prof. U. Oreg., 1995; chmn. environ. design program, Yale U., 1979-90; vis. prof. Yale U., 1995-2000; cons. UN Devel. Program, 2009. Author: Designing and Building a Solar House, 1977, Energy Conservation Through Building Design, 1979, Climatic Design, 1983, Energy Design Handbook, 1993; editor-in-chief Time Saver Standards: Architectural Design Data, 1997, 2005, Time-Saver Standards: Urban Design, 2003. Bd. dirs. Save the Children Fedn., 1979-82. Recipient Honor Design award Conn. Soc. Architects, 1974, Honor Design award region AIA, 1978, 84, 1st award Owens Corning Energy Conservation Bldg. Design Program, 1983, Excellence in housing award Energy Efficient Bldg. Assn., 1988, Lifetime Achievement award Passive and Low Energy Architecture, 1990, Best in Show Watercolors, Soc. Creative Artists, 1999, Green Bldg. Design award NESEA, 2002, Disting. Prof. award ACSA, 2002, James Haecker Disting. Leadership award, Archtl. Rsch. Centers Consortium, 2004, US Green Bldg. Coun. Leadership award, 2008; Assn. of Collegiate Schs. of Archtecture/Am. Metals Climax rsch. fellow, 1967-69; rsch. fellow Rockefeller Found., 1978. Fellow: AIA. Home and Office: 54 Larkspur Dr Trumbull CT 06611-4652

WATSON, EMMA, actress; b. Oxford, England, Apr. 15, 1990; Actor: (films) Harry Potter and the Sorcerer's Stone, 2001, Harry Potter and the Chamber of Secrets, 2002, Harry Potter and the Prisoner of Azkaban, 2004, Harry Potter and the Goblet of Fire, 2005, Harry Potter and the Order of the Phoenix, 2007, Ballet Shoes, 2007, (voice) The Tale of Despereaux, 2008, Harry Potter and the Half-Blood Prince, 2009; appearances (TV) The Oprah Winfrey Show, 2002, The Tonight Show with Jay Leno, 2002. Office: c/o Leavesden Studios PO Box 3000 Leavesden WD2 7LT England*

WATSON, GEORGE HENRY, JR., broadcaster, journalist; b. Birmingham, Ala., July 27, 1936; s. George Henry and Grace Elizabeth (Carr) W.; m. Ellen Havican Bradley, July 13, 1979; children: George H., III, Ellen Havican (dec.). BA, Harvard U., 1959; MS, Columbia U., 1960. Reporter Washington Post, 1960-61; corr. ABC News, 1962-75, Moscow bur. chief, 1966-69, London bur. chief, 1969-75, v.p., Washington bur. chief, 1976-80; v.p., mng. editor Cable News Network, 1980; v.p. news ABC News, NYC, 1981-85, exec. in charge ABC News Viewpoint, 1981-85, v.p., Washington bur. chief, 1985-93, sr. contbg. editor, 1993-2001; freelance broadcast journalist. Served with U.S. Army, 1958. Recipient Peabody award, 1982, DuPont Columbia award, 1983, nat. news Emmy award, 1984. Mem. Radio Television News Dirs. Assn., Soc. Profl. Journalists, Nat. Press Club, Overseas Press Club (award for best television documentary 1971, citation for excellence 1974), Nat. Press Club, Com. to Protect Journalists, Fgn. Policy Assn., Cosmos Club. Personal E-mail: ghwjr727@hotmail.com.

WATSON, GEORGE WILLIAM, JR., science educator; b. Oxnard, Calif., Apr. 17, 1950; s. George Watson and Betty Jane Elizabeth Watson; m. Tracey Elisabeth Powers, Jan. 26, 2002; children: Jesse Presswood, Gabrielle Georgia, Matthew William. BA in Bus., U. Wash., Seattle, 1978; MBA, Calif. State Fullerton, 1980; MS, Naval Postgrad. Sch., Monterey, Calif., 1982; PhD, Va. Tech, Blacksburg, 1996. Capt. US MC, Quantico, Va., 1968—88; assoc. prof. Southern Ill. U., Edwardsville, 2003—. Bd. mem. Ctr. Against Spousal Abuse, St. Petersburg, Fla., 2000—02. Recipient Litschert Academic Achievement award, Va. Tech, 1996. Mem.: Acad. Mgmt. Achievements include research in organizational moral psychology. Home: 72 Annebriar Dr Maryville IL 62062 Office: Southern Ill Univ Edwardsville Sch Bus Edwardsville IL 62026

WATSON, GREGORY HARRISS, executive consultant, author; b. Englewood, N.J., July 16, 1948; s. Robert John and Anne Faye (Bellotte) Watson; m. Cynthia Sue Sandberg, June 6, 1971 (div. 1983); children: Andrew Daniel, Dina Belfer, Cristina Daniela Juola; m. Inessa Alexandra Belfer, June 14, 2003. BA cum laude, Taylor U., 1970; MS, U. So. Calif., LA, 1975, Okla. State U., Stillwater, 2003; MA, Antioch Sch. Law, Washington, 1985; Cert. six sigma black belt, reliability engr., Am. Soc. Quality, 2007, quality engr., 1991; project mgmt. profl., Project Mgmt. Inst., 2008; engring. mgr., Inst. Indsl. Engrs., 2008; registered engr., Tech. Acad. Finland, 2007; Lt. comdr. US Navy, Washington, 1971-83; mgr. quality leadership devel. Hewlett-Packard Co., Palo Alto, Calif., 1983-89; dir. rp. quality Compaq Computer Corp., Houston, 1989-91; v.p. Benchmarking, Am. Productivity & Quality Ctr., Houston, 1991-92; v.p. quality Xerox Corp., Rochester, NY, 1992-94; chmn. Bus. Excellence Solutions, Ltd., Espoo, Finland, 1994-. Adj. prof. indsl. engring. Okla. State U., Stillwater, 2003-. Author: (books) The Benchmarking Workbook, 1992, Strategic Benchmarking, 1993, Management Guide to Benchmarking, 1993, Business Systems Engineering, 1994, A World of Quality-The Timeless Passport, 1995, Six Sigma for Business Leaders, 2004, Design for Six Sigma, 2005, Strategic Benchmarking Reloaded with Six Sigma, 2007. Walter E. Masing medal Internat. Acad. Quality, 2007, Yoshio Kondo Academic Rsch. prize, 2009. Fellow Am. Soc. Quality, Australian Orgn. Quality, World Acad. Productivity Sci.; mem. IEEE (sr.), ASA (life), Internat. Statis. Inst., Mil. Ops. Research Soc., Ops. Research Soc. Am., Naval Inst., Asia Pacific Quality Orgn. (life), Am. Soc. Quality (E. Jack Lancaster medal 2001, Philip B. Crosby medal 2005), Profl. Assn. (Milw.) (bd. dirs. 1994-2002, v.p. 1996-99, pres. 2000-01, chmn. 2001-02), Internat. Acad. Quality, Profl. Assn. (pres. 2009-, v.p. 2006-08, sec.-treas. 2003-05), Inst. Indsl. Engrs. (sr; asst. sr. exec. v.p. Europe, Internat. Coun. 2008-, bd. dirs. 2008-), Russian Orgn. Quality (hon.), Am. Soc. Engring. Edn. (profl. mem.), Sigma Xi (hon.), Tau Beta Phi (hon.), Russian Benchmaking Club (hon.), Alpha Pi Mu (hon.)Phi Kappa Phi (hon.). Independent. Office: Bus Excellence Solutions Ltd Keilasatama 3 Ste 701 02150 Espoo Finland Home Phone: 358505779777. Personal E-mail: gregbss@aol.com. Business E-Mail: greg@excellence.fi.

WATSON, HARLAN L(EROY), federal agency administrator, physicist, economist; b. Macomb, Ill., Dec. 17, 1944; s. Joseph Carroll and Helen Louise (Sanders) Watson; m. Sharon Ann Rinkus Diguette, Apr. 22, 1977. BA in Physics, Western Ill. U., 1967; PhD in Physics, Iowa State U., 1973; MA in Econs., Georgetown U., 1981. Postdoctoral fellow Argonne (Ill.) Nat. Lab., 1973-75; project scientist, then sr. scientist B-K Dynamics, Inc., Rockville, Md., 1975-78; tech. staff TRW Energy Systems Planning Group, Mc Lean, Va., 1978-80; profl. staff mem. subcom. on energy nuclear proliferation and govt. processes Com. on Govtl. Affairs, U.S. Senate, Washington, 1980-81; tech. and sci. cons. Com. on Sci. and Tech., U.S. Ho. of Reps., 1981-86; rep. energy and environ., coord. Com. on Sci., Space and Tech., U.S. Ho. of Reps., 1986-89; sci. adviser to sec. Dept. Interior, Washington, 1989-93, dep. asst. sec. for sci.-water and sci., 1989-90, prin. dep. asst. to sec. for water and sci., 1990-93; rep. spl. asst. subcom. energy, com. sci., space, tech. U.S. Ho. of Reps., Washington, 1993-95, staff dir. subcom. energy and environment, com. sci., 1995—2001; sr climate negotiator, spec rep US Dept State, Washington, 2001—08; spl. envoy United Nation Framework Convention Climate Change US Dept. State, 2008—09; disting. profl. staff mem. Select Com. Energy Indepence & Global Warming, US House Reps., 2009—. Contbr. articles to profl jours. Home: 6719 Tomlinson Ter Cabin John MD 20818-1328 Office: 2201 C St NW Rm 2480 Washington DC 20520-0001 Office Phone: 202-647-3489, 202-225-3968. Business E-Mail: harlin.watson@mail.house.gov. E-mail: WatsonHL@state.gov.

WATSON, HARRY L., history professor, director; b. Greensboro, NC, July 10, 1949; s. John D. and Susannah T. Watson; m. Margot B. Stein, July 3, 1977; children: Adam S., Hannah S. AB, Brown U., Providence, 1971; PhD, Northwestern U., Evanston, Ill., 1976. Asst. prof. history U. NC, Chapel Hill, 1976—82, assoc. prof. history, 1982—90, prof. history, 1990—, dir., Ctr. Study Am. South, 1999—. Contbr. articles to numerous jours. Mem.: Hist. Soc. NC, Southern Intellectual History Assn., Soc. Historians Early Am. Republic, Southern Hist. Assn., Orgn. Am. Historians, Am. Hist. Assn. Democrat. Episcopalian. Avocations: running, swimming, hiking. Home: 107 Buck Taylor Trail Chapel Hill NC 27516 Office: Ctr Study Am South CB# 9127 410 E Franklin St Chapel Hill NC 27599 Office Fax: 919-962-4433. Business E-Mail: hwatson@email.unc.edu.

WATSON, JACK CROZIER, retired state supreme court justice; b. Jonesville, La., Sept. 17, 1928; s. Jesse Crozier and Gladys Lucille (Talbot) W.; m. Henrietta Sue Carter, Dec. 26, 1958; children: Carter Crozier (dec.), Wells Talbot. BA, U. Southwestern La., 1949; JD, La. State U., 1956; completed with honor, Appellate Judges Seminar, NYU, 1974, Sr. Appellate Judges Seminar, 1980. Bar: La. 1956. Atty. King, Anderson & Swift, Lake Charles, La., 1956—58; prosecutor City of Lake Charles, 1960; asst. dist. atty. Calcasieu Parish, La., 1961—64; ptnr. Watson & Watson, Lake Charles, 1961—64; judge 14th Jud. Dist., La., 1964—72; judge ad hoc Ct. Appeals, 1st Cir., Baton Rouge, 1972—73; judge Ct. Appeals, 3d Cir., Lake Charles, 1973—79; assoc. justice La. Supreme Ct., New Orleans, 1979—96, ret., 1996; of counsel Baggett, McCall, Burgess, Watson & Gaughan, Lake Charles, 2004—. Faculty advisor Nat. Coll. State Judiciary, Reno, 1970, 73; adj. prof. law summer sch. program in Greece, Tulane U., 1988-2000, 2005-09; adj. prof. law So. U., Baton Rouge, 1998-99; del. NEH Seminar, 1976; La. del to Internat. Conf. Appellate Magistrates, The Philippines, 1977; mem. La. Jud. Coun., 1986-92. 1st lt. USAF, 1950-54. Mem. ABA, La. Bar Assn., S.W. La. Bar Assn. (pres. 1963), Law Inst. State of La., La. Coun. Juvenile Ct. Judges (pres. 1969-70), Am. Judicature Soc., S.W. La. Camellia Soc. (pres. 1973-74), Am. Legion (post comdr. 1963), Lake Charles Yacht Club (commodore 1974), Blue Key, Sigma Alpha Epsilon, Phi Delta Phi, Pi Kappa Delta. Democrat. Baptist. Office Phone: 337-478-8888.

WATSON, JACK H., JR., lawyer, former White House chief of staff; b. El Paso, Tex., Oct. 24, 1938; children: Melissa Woodward, Lincoln Hearn. BA, Vanderbilt U., 1960; LLB, Harvard U., 1966. Bar: Ga. 1965, DC 1978. Assoc. King & Spalding, Atlanta, 1966-71, partner, 1972-77; asst. to Pres. for intergovernmental affairs and sec. to cabinet The White House, Washington, 1977-80, chief of staff to Pres., 1980-81; ptnr. Long, Aldridge & Norman, Atlanta, 1981-98; chief legal strategist global affairs Monsanto Co., Washington, 1998—2000. Mem. vis. com. Harvard Law Sch., 1987-93; chmn. Ga. Joint Commn. on Alt. Dispute Resolution, 1990-93, former chmn. Ga. Commn. on Dispute Resolution. Counsel Met. Atlanta Commn. Crime and Juvenile Delinquency, 1966-67; pres. Met. Atlanta Mental Health Assn., 1971-72; chmn. Gov.'s Study Commn. Alcohol, 1971-72, Ga. Alcoholism Adv. Council, 1972; chmn. bd. Ga. Dept. Human Resources, 1972-77; gubernatorial candidate Ga., 1982; mem. nat. adv. com. Ctr. Study the Presidency, 1983; bd. mem. Franklin D. Roosevelt Libr., Franklin & Eleanor Roosevelt Inst.; chmn. 20th Century Fund Task Force on the US Vice Presidency, 1987-88; bd. mem. Piedmont Environ. Council, 2001-04, Franklin & Eleanon Roosevelt Inst. Bd., 1985-2008, vice chair, 2000-2008, commr. Nat. Portrait Gallery Smithsonion Inst., 2002-. Capt. USMC. Recipient First Force Reconnaissance Co.Named One of Atlanta's Five Outstanding Young Men Jaycees, 1970 Mem. ABA (chmn. ABA task force on N.Am. Free Trade Agreement 1993), State Bar Ga., Atlanta Bar Assn., Atlanta Lawyers Club, Phi Beta Kappa, Phi Eta Sigma, Omicron Delta Kappa. Democrat.

WATSON, JAMES DEWEY, retired molecular biologist; b. Chgo., Apr. 6, 1928; s. James Dewey and Jean (Mitchell) W.; m. Elizabeth Lewis, 1968; children: Rufus Robert, Duncan James. BS, U. Chgo., 1947; PhD in Zoology, Ind. U., 1950; DSc (hon.), U. Chgo., 1961, Ind. U., 1963; LLD (hon.), U. Notre Dame, 1965; DSc (hon.), L.I. U., 1970, Adelphi U., 1972, Brandeis U., 1973, Albert Einstein Coll. Medicine, 1979, Hofstra U., 1976, Harvard U., 1978, Rockefeller U., 1980, Clarkson Coll., 1981, SUNY, 1983; MD (hon.), U. Buenos Aires, Argentina, 1986; DSc (hon.), Rutgers U., 1988, Bard Coll., 1991, U. Cambridge, 1993, Fairfield U., 1993, U. Stellenbosch, 1993, U. Oxford; MD, Charles Univ., Prague, 1998; DSc (hon.), Washington Coll., 1999, U. Judaism, 1999, U. Coll. London, 2000, Ill. Wesleyan U., 2000, Widener U., 2001, Dartmouth, 2001, Trinity Coll., Dublin, 2001. Rsch. fellow NRC, U. Copenhagen, 1950-51; Nat. Found. Infantile Paralysis fellow Cavendish Lab., Cambridge U., 1951-52, 55-56; sr. rsch. fellow biology Calif. Inst. Tech., 1953-55; asst. prof. biology Harvard U., 1955-58, assoc. prof., 1958-61, prof., 1961-76; dir. Cold Spring Harbor Lab., Watson Sch. Biol. Sci., NY, 1968—94, pres. NY, 1994—2004, chancellor NY, 2004—07; assoc. dir. Nat. Ctr. for Human Genome Rsch., NIH, 1988-89, dir. Nat. Ctr. for Human Genome Rsch., 1989-92. Newton-Abraham vis. prof. Oxford U., 1994; inst. advisor Allen Inst. for Brain Sci., Seattle, Washington. Author: Molecular Biology of the Gene, 1965, 4th edit., 1986, The Double Helix, 1968, (with John Tooze) The DNA Story, 1981, (with others) The Molecular Biology of the Cell, 1983, 2nd edit., 1989, 3rd edit. 1994, (with John Tooze and David Kurtz) Recombinant DNA, A Short Course, 1983, 2nd edit., 1992, A Passion for DNA, 2000, Genes, Girls and Gamow, 2001, DNA: The Secret of Life, 2003, Avoid Boring People: Lessons From a Life in Science, 2007 Named Hon. fellow Clare Coll., Cambridge U., hon. knight of Brit. Empire, 2002; recipient (with F.H.C. Crick) John Collins Warren prize Mass. Gen. Hosp., 1959, Eli Lilly award in biochemistry Am. Chem. Soc., 1959, Albert Lasker prize Am. Pub. Health Assn., 1960, (with F.H.C. Crick) Rsch. Corp. prize, 1962, (with F.H.C. Crick and M.H.F. Wilkins) Nobel prize in medicine, 1962, Presdl. Medal of Freedom, 1977, Kaul Found. award for excellence, 1993, Nat. Biotech. Venture award, 1993, Copley Medal, 1993, Charles A. Dana award, 1994, Lomonosov medal Russian Acad. Sci., 1995, Nat. medal of Sci., 1997, Liberty medal City of Phila., 2000, Benjamin Franklin medal for disting. achievement in scis. Am. Philos. Soc., 2001, Gairdner Found. award for merit, 2002, Lotos Club Medal of Merit, 2004. Mem. NAS (Carty medal 1971), Am. Philos. Soc., Am. Assn. Cancer Rsch., Am. Acad. Arts and Scis., Am. Soc. Biol. Chemistry, Royal Soc. (London), Acad. Scis. Russia, Danish Acad. Arts and Scis. Achievements include co-discovery of Double-Helix DNA; has become the first person to receive his own personal genome map in 2007.*

WATSON, JAMES RAYMOND, education educator; b. Blue Island, Ill., July 29, 1938; s. William James Henry Watson and Edna Mae Stucker; m. Suzette Marie Gehant, July 8, 1969. AB, Marquette Univ., Milw., 1966; MA, Univ. Wisc., Milw., 1969; PhD, So. Ill. Univ., Carbondale, Ill., 1973. Data analyst Clark Oil & Refining, Blue Island, Ill., 1958—59; photographic asst. Waltersheffer's Studio of Photography, Milw., 1960—61; photography instr. Layton Sch. of Art, Milw., 1960—61; asst. prof. Loyola Univ., New Orleans, 1973—77, assoc. prof., 1977—94, prof., 1994—2009, prof. emeritus, 2009—. Pres. SPSGH, 1996—; rsch. assoc. Pic. Univ. of Binghamton, NY, 2002—; assoc. editor Routledge Contintential Phila. Series, NY, 2001—; editor Rodopi Genocide & Holocaust Studies, 2009—. Author: Between Auschwitz and Tradition, 1994, Continental Philosophers in America, 1999, Contemporary Portrayals of Auschwitz, 2000. Exec. com. ACLU Miss., Jackson, 2002—06; bd. dirs. Picayune on Stage, Picayune, Miss., 2001—06. Pvt.1st. class US Army, 1961—63. Vis. scholar Max-Planck-Gesellschaft, Berlin, Germany, 1994. Mem.: Soc. Phenomenology and Existential Philosophy, Soc. for Philos. Study of Genocide and the Holocaust (pres.), Am. Philos. Assn. Avocations: photography, theater, painting. Office: Loyola U 6363 St Charles Ave New Orleans LA 70118 Home: 7 Pertusa Way Hot Springs Village AR 71909-8140 Office Phone: 504-865-3940. Personal E-mail: profjrwatson@me.com.

WATSON, JERRY CARROLL, advertising executive; b. Greenville, Ala., Aug. 22, 1943; s. William J. and Georgia Katherine (Mixon) W.; m. Judith Zeigler Brooks, Sept. 16, 1988; 2 child, Theodore William, Hunter Brooks. BS, U. Ala., Tuscaloosa, 1967; MS, U. Va., 1995. Staff writer Phillips, Eindhoven, The Netherlands, 1967-68; mgr. mktg. Fuller & Dees Mktg., Montgomery, Ala., 1968-70; v.p. Nat. Student Mktg., Washington, 1970-73; pres. Coll. & Univ. Press, Washington, 1973-80; ptnr. Direct Response Consulting Svcs., McLean, Va., 1981—2007. Bd. dirs. Foxhall Corp., Mustique Co. Founding mem. Am. Inst. Cancer Rsch. Mem. Direct Mktg. Assn., Non-Profit Mailer Fedn., Promotional Mktg. Assn., Nature Conservancy, Sierra Club, Falls Church (Va.) C. of C. (bd. dirs.). Avocations: forestry, gardening, astronomy, photography. Home: 850 Dolley Madison Blvd Mc Lean VA 22101-1821 Office: Direct Response Cons Svcs 6849 Old Dominion Dr Ste 300 Mc Lean VA 22101-3791 E-mail: watson@drcs.com, watson@mouselink.net.

WATSON, JESSICA LEWIS, writer; b. Urbana, Ill., June 16, 1964; d. Jane Eileen Lewis; m. Bruce S. Watson, Aug. 9, 1986 (div. Apr. 2003). BA in English, U. Ill., 1987; Diploma in Am. Lit., U. Liege, 1988; MA in English, Baylor U., 1994. Social worker Roundhouse, Champaign, Ill., 1988-89; cmty. liaison Krannert Ctr. for the Performing Arts, Urbana, Ill., 1989-90; freelance, writer and author Waco, also Champaign, Ill., 1990—; lectr. in English Baylor U., Waco, Tex., 1996-98; English instr. U. Ill., Urbana, 1988. Author: Illegitimacy Empowered, 1994, Bastardy as a Gifted Status in Chaucer and Malory, 1996; contbr. articles to profl. jours.; singer: Austin Civic Chorus, 1996—2000, Baroque Artists of Champaign-Urbana, 2007—08. Singer Austin Civic Chorus, Tex., 1996-2000. Recipient Literary Touring Program award Tex. Commn. on the Arts, Temple, Longview, Ft. Hood, 1994-97, Helen Chambers Poetry award Baylor U., Waco, 1994; grantee Aspen Writers Found., Colo., 1992. Avocations: modern dance, playing and singing classical music. Home: 1206 W Columbia Ave Champaign IL 61821 Personal E-mail: jessicabulty@yahoo.com.

WATSON, JOANN, Councilwoman; Degree in Journalism, U. Mich. Co-founder Coalition Health Care Equity; pub. policy liaison Congressman John Conyers; exec. dir. NAACP Detroit; vice chmn. Human Rights Commn.; councilwoman Detroit City Coun., pres. pro tempore. Mem. SE Mich. Coun. Govts. Talk show host: (TV miniseries, Wake Up Detroit). Chmn Women's Equality Day Celebrations; exec. YWCA; v.p. Detroit Wayne County Health Authority; mem. Every Ch. a Peace Ch.; bd. mem. NAACP, ACLU. Recipient Lifetime Achievement award, NAACP, YWCA, Detroit Human Rights Commn., Southern Christian Leadership Conf., Nat. award, Nat. Conf. Negro Women. Mailing: Detroit City Coun Coleman A Young Mcpl Bldg 2 Woodward Ave Ste 1340 Detroit MI 48226 Office Phone: 313-224-4535. Office Fax: 313-224-1524. Business E-Mail: watsonj@cnci.ci.detroit.mi.us.*

WATSON, JOANN FORD, theology studies educator; b. Ashland, Ohio, Apr. 11, 1956; d. Laurence Wesley and Edna Lucille (Garber) Ford; m. Duane Frederick Watson, June 2, 1984; 1 child, Christina Lucille. BA, DePauw U., 1978; MDiv, Princeton Theol. Sem., 1981; PhD, Northwestern U., 1984. Ordained to ministry Presbyn. Ch. Asst. prof. hist. theology Ashland (Ohio) Theol. Sem., 1984-86, assoc. prof. theology, 1989-95, chair dept. ch. history and theology, 1994—97, 2002—05, H.R. Gill prof. theology, 1996—; chaplain Grady Meml. Hosp., Atlanta, 1986-87; co-pastor Tri-Ch. Parish United Meth. Chs. Northwestern, NY, 1987-89; pastor Camroden Presbyn. Ch., Rome, NY, 1987-89; parish assoc. First Presbyn. Ch., 1985—86. Clergy commr. del. Gen. Assembly Presbyn. Ch., 1995; parish assoc. First Presbyn. Ch., Ashland, 2004—05. Author: Manna for Sisters in Christ, 1989, Mutuality in Christ, 1991, Meditations in Suffering, 1993, Study of Karl Barth's Doctrine of Man and Woman, 1995, Sister to Sister, 1998, Healed to Serve, 2001, Selected Spiritual Writings of Anne Dutton Vol. 1: Letters, 2003, Hymns, Poetry, Memoirs, Discourses, Vol. II, 2004, Vol. III, 2006, Vol. IV, 2007, V Correspondence, 2008. Mem. Hospice Ashland County chpt., 1989—93; assoc. mem. Women's Symphony League, Ashland Symphony Orch., 1989—94; missionary vol. Mother Teresa's Missionaries of Charity, Calcutta, 1988. Recipient Outstanding Faculty Mentor of Yr. award, Ashland Sem., 2003—04, Disting. Alumni Hall of Fame award, Ashland H.S., 2005;, Northwestern U. fellow, 1982—84. Mem.: Am. Acad. Religion, Soc. Bibl. Lit., Nat. Assn. Presbyn. Clergywomen, Presbyn. Women in Leadership, Internat. Assn. Women Mins. (mem. exec. bd., trustee 1990—95), Phi Beta Kappa (Outstanding Faculty Mentor award 2001, 2002, Women's Achievement award, Ashland County, Ohio 2003, Outstanding Faculty Mentor award 2004, 2005, 2007), Alpha Lambda Delta. Republican. Avocations: travel, music, water sports. Office: Ashland Theolog Sem 910 Center St Ashland OH 44805-4007 Office Phone: 419-289-5182. Business E-Mail: jwatson@ashland.edu.

WATSON, JOHN ALLAN, clergyman; b. Detroit, June 26, 1938; s. Roy Allan and Charlotte Luella (Piper) W.; m. Mary Louise Strawbridge, June 25, 1960; children: Paul Allan, Stephen John, Mark Andrew, Philip Scott. BA, Wheaton Coll., 1960; BD, Princeton Sem., 1964; MTh, U. Aberdeen, Scotland, 1971. Ordained minister Presbyn. Ch., 1964. Min. 1st Presbyn. Ch., Kentland, Ind., 1964—68, Bethel Presbyn. Ch., Columbus, Ohio, 1970—2003; pastor emeritus, 2004—. Dean Anselm Inst., Columbus, 1986—; moderator Presbytery of Scioto Valley, 2001-02; chmn. Ctr. Advanced Christian Edn., 2004-2008; theologian in residence Mandarin Presbyn. Ch., Jacksonville, Fla., 2005-08. Mem. Presbytery Scioto Valley (chmn. min. rels. 1982-85, jud. commn. 1987-96, chmn. Bills and Overtures, 1996-99, N.W. Presbyn. Urban Ministry, 1996-2003), Internat. Brotherhood Magicians. Independent. Home: 46 Winthrop Rd Columbus OH 43214 *One of the great mistakes of our time is living by a philosophy which has amended the great affirmation that "our chief end is to glorify God and enjoy Him forever" to "our chief end is to enjoy."*

WATSON, JOHN LAWRENCE, III, former trade association executive; b. Rome, Ga., Jan. 14, 1932; s. John Lawrence and Mary (Cowen) W.; m. Dorothy Palmer McLanahan, Aug. 9, 1958; children: Mary Palmer Watson Gard, Valerie Catherine Watson Bilbrough, John Lawrence IV. BS, Auburn U., 1954. Trader-over the counter J.C. Bradford & Co., Atlanta, 1957-58; with Robinson Humphrey & Co., Atlanta, 1958-64, dept. head-over the counter, 1964-74, dir. equity trading, 1974-83, dir. capital markets, 1983-85; pres. Security Traders Assn., NYC, 1985-96, ret., 1996. Past mem. bd. visitors Babcock Sch. Mgmt. Wake Forest U.; past chmn. Parent's Coun. Wofford Coll.; life trustee Pace Acad.; former trustee Securities Industry Found. for Econ. Edn.; pres. trustees The City Ch., N.Y., 2005-. Named Man of Yr., Equities mag. Mem. Nat. Assn. Securities Dealers (dist. chmn. 1982, bd. govs. 1983-85), Am. Mus. Fin. History (trustee), Capital City Club, Piedmont Driving Club (Atlanta), Ponte Vedra Club, Sawgrass Country Club (Ponte Vedra), Univ. Club (N.Y.C.). Home: 505 Ponte Vedra Blvd Ponte Vedra Beach FL 32082-2317

WATSON, JOHN S., oil industry executive; b. Calif., Oct. 1956; BA, U. Calif., Davis, 1978; MBA, U. Chgo., 1980. Fin. analyst to various fin. and analytical positions including supervisory positions in the comptroller's fin. and profit analysis groups Chevron Corp., 1980—90, mgr. investor rels., 1990—93; mgr. credit card enterprises Chevron USA Products Co., 1993—95, gen. mgr. strategic planning and quality, 1995—96; pres. Chevron Canada, Ltd., Vancouver, BC, Canada, 1996—98; v.p. strategic planning Chevron Corp., 1998—2001, v.p. fin., CFO, 2001—05, exec. v.p. strategy & devel., 2008—09, vice chmn., 2009—; pres. Chevron Internat. Exploration and Prodn., 2005—08. Merger integration exec. ChevronTexaco, 2001; bd. dirs. Chevron Corp., 2009—. Office: Chevron Corp 6001 Bollinger Canyon Rd San Ramon CA 94583-2324*

WATSON, KAROL ELIZABETH, internist, educator; b. Gary, Ind., Dec. 15, 1963; MD, Harvard Med. Sch., 1989. Cert. Am. Bd. Internal Medicine, 1993, Am. Bd. Internal Medicine, Cardiovascular Disease, 2004. Intern, internal medicine UCLA Sch. Medicine, 1990—91, resident, internal medicine, 1991—92, fellow, cardiology, 1992—97, assoc. prof. medicine; dir., Cholesterol and Lipid Mgmt. Ctr. UCLA CHAMP (Cholesterol, Hypertension, and Atherosclerosis Mgmt. Program); physician, medicine, endocrinology, diabetes and hypertension Gonda Diabetes Ctr. Office: UCLA Med-Cardio Mail Code 167917 Dept Code 1553 Box 951679 BH-307 CHS Los Angeles CA 90095-1679 Office Phone: 310-794-7121. Office Fax: 310-206-9133. Business E-Mail: kwatson@med.net.ucla.edu.*

WATSON, KENNETH MARSHALL, physics professor; b. Des Moines, Sept. 7, 1921; s. Louis Erwin and Irene Nellie (Marshall) W.; m. Elaine Carol Miller, Mar. 30, 1946; children: Ronald M., Mark Louis. BS, Iowa State U., Ames, 1943; PhD, U. Iowa, Iowa City, 1948; ScD (hon.), U. Ind., 1976. Rsch. engr. Naval Rsch. Lab., Washington, 1943-46; staff Inst. Advanced Study Princeton U., 1948-49; rsch. fellow Lawrence Berkeley Lab., Calif., 1949-52, staff Calif., 1957-81; asst. prof. physics U. Ind., Bloomington, 1952-54; assoc. prof. physics U. Wis., Madison, 1954-57; prof. physics U. Calif., Berkeley, 1957-81, prof. oceanography, dir. marine physics lab. San Diego, 1981-93. Cons. Sci. Application Corp., 1981-2004; mem. US Pres.'s Sci. Adv. Com. Panels, 1962-71; adviser Nat. Security Coun., 1972-75; mem. JASON Adv. Panel, 1959-2001; sci. adv. bd. George C. Marshall Inst., 1989—2005. Author: (with M.L. Goldberger) Collision Theory, 2004; (with J. Welch and J. Bond) Atomic Theory of Gas Dynamics, 1966; (with J. Nutall) Topics in Several Particle Dynamics, 1970; (with Flatté, Munk, Dashen) Sound Transmission Through a Fluctuating Ocean, 1979. Mem.: Nat. Acad. Scis. Home: Unit 2008 8515 Costa Verde Blvd San Diego CA 92122-1150 Office: Univ Calif San Diego 9500 Gilman Dr La Jolla CA 92093-0213 Office Phone: 858-634-6620. Business E-Mail: kmw@ucsd.edu.

WATSON, KIMBERLY, director, educator; b. Chattanooga, Jan. 22, 1969; d. John Arthur and Maureen Ellen McLean Watson. BA, NC State U., Raleigh, 1993; MA, East Carolina U., Greenville, NC, 1998; MS in Info. Tech., Am. InterContinental U., Plantation, FL, 1999; PhD, DePaul U., Chgo., 2004. MCSE 1999. Adj. faculty DePaul U., 2002—06; faculty Ctrl. Tex. Coll., Killeen, 2002—, U. Liverpool, England, 2002—. Cons., Raleigh, NC, 2000—. Contbr. articles to profl. jours. Mem.: Golden Key (life), Phi Kappa Phi (life), Alpha Phi Omega (life), Zeta Tau Alpha (life). Independent. Roman Catholic. Home: 2608 Van Dyke Ave Raleigh NC 27607 Personal E-mail: kimberlyswatson@nc.rr.com.

WATSON, MICHAEL S., medical geneticist, educator; BS, Am. U., Washington DC; MS in Med. Genetics, U. Ala., PhD in Physiology & Biophysics. Cert. Am. Bd. Med. Genetics. Exec. dir. Am. Coll. Med. Genetics; dir. clinical & molecular cytogenetics Wash. U., 1986—2000, adj. prof. pediatrics St. Louis. Office: 9650 Rockville Pike Bethesda MD 20814-3998 E-mail: mwatson@acmg.net.*

WATSON, NICHOLAS JAMES, literature and language professor; b. Bicester, Buckinghamshire, Eng., June 15, 1959; s. Angus James and Alison Watson; m. Amy Rose Appleford; children: Luke David Watson Savage, Connor Iain Watson Savage. MA, Cambridge U., Eng., 1980; MPhil, Oxford U., Eng., 1984; PhD, U. Toronto, Ont., Canada, 1987. Prof. english U. Western Ont., London, 1990—2000, Harvard U., Cambridge, Mass., 2001—. Author: (book) Richard Rolle and the Invention of Authority; translator: Anchoritic Spirituality: Ancrene Wisse and Associated Works; editor: The Idea of the Vernacular: An Anthology of Middle English Literary Theory, 1280-1520, The Vulgar Tongue: Medieval and Postmedieval Vernacularity, The Writings of Julian of Norwich. Recipient John Charles Polanyi prize, Govt. Ont., 1990; Postdoc. fellowship, Social Scis. & Humanities Rsch. Coun. Can., 1987—90, fellowship, Guggenheim Found., 2008—, Radcliffe Inst. Advanced Study, 2008—, Am. Coun. Learned Socs., 2008—. Mem.: New Chaucer Soc., Can. Soc. Medievalists, Early English Text Soc., Medieval Acad. Am. Office: Harvard Univ 12 Quincy St Cambridge MA 02138 Business E-Mail: nwatson@fas.harvard.edu.

WATSON, NOEL G., construction executive; b. Bison, SD, 1936; BSChemE, U. N.D., 1958; postgrad., Colo. Sch. Mines, 1958-60. With AMAX Inc., 1962-65, Jacobs Engring. Group, Pasadena, Calif., 1960-62, 1965—, pres., 1987—2002, CEO, 1992—2006, chmn., 2004—. Bd. dirs. Rotex Global LLC, GT Solar Internat., Inc., 2008—. Office: Jacobs Engineering Group PO Box 7084 1111 S Arroyo Pkwy Pasadena CA 91109 Office Phone: 626-578-3500. Office Fax: 626-568-7144.

WATSON, PATTY JO, anthropology educator; b. Superior, Nebr., Apr. 26, 1932; d. Ralph Clifton and Elaine Elizabeth (Lance) Andersen; m. Richard Allan Watson, July 30, 1955; 1 child, Anna Melissa MA, U. Chgo., 1956, PhD in Anthropology, 1959. Archaeologist-ethnographer Oriental Inst.-U. Chgo., 1959—60, rsch. assoc., archaeologist, 1964—70; instr. anthropology U. So. Calif., Los Angeles, 1961, UCLA, 1961, L.A. State U., 1961; asst. prof. anthropology Washington U., St. Louis, 1969—70, assoc. prof., 1970—73, prof., 1973—2004, Edward Mallinckrodt disting. univ. prof., 1993—2004, prof. emerita, 2004—; faculty affiliate anthropology U. Mont., 2003—. Mem. rev. panel NSF, Washington, 1974-76; fellow Ctr. Advanced Study in Behavioral Scis., Stanford, Calif., 1981-82, 91-92. Author: The Prehistory of Salts Cave, Kentucky, 1969, Archaeological Ethnography in Western Iran, 1979; author: (with others) Man and Nature, 1969, Explanation in Archeology, 1971, Archeological Explanation, 1984, Girikihaciyan, A Halafian Site in Southeastern Turkey; author: (editor) Archeology of the Mammoth Cave Area, 1974; co-editor: Prehistoric Archeology Along the Zagros Flanks, 1983, The Origins of Agriculture, 1992, Of Caves and Shell Mounds, 1996, Archaeology of the Middle Green River Region, Kentucky, 2005. Recipient Arthur Holly Compton Faculty Achievement award Washington U., St. Louis, 2000, Peter H. Raven award for lifetime achievement Acad. Sci. St. Louis, 2002; grantee NSF, 1959-60, 68, 70, 72-74, 78-79, NEH, 1977-78, Nat. Geog. Soc., 1969-75, Southeastern Arch. Conf. Lifetime Achievement award, 2004. Fellow Am. Anthropol. Assn. (editor archaeology 1973-77, Disting. Lectr. award 1994, Disting. Svc. award 1996), AAAS (chair sect. H 1991-92); mem. Cave Rsch. Found., Am. Acad. Arts and Scis., Am. Philos. Soc., Soc. Am. Archaeology (exec. com. 1974-76, 82-84, editor Am. Antiquity 1984-87, Fryxell medal 1990), Assn. Paleorient (sci. bd.), Nat. Speleological Soc. (hon. life, editorial bd. bull. 1979-2008, Sci. award), Archaeol. Inst. Am. (Gold medal Disting. Archaeol. Achievement 1999, Pomerance award 2007), Nat. Acad. Scis. Business E-Mail: pjwatson@artsci.wustl.edu.

WATSON, PAULA D., retired librarian; b. NYC, Mar. 6, 1945; d. Joseph Francis and Anna Julia (Miksza) De Simone; m. William Douglas Watson, Aug. 23, 1969; children— Lucia, Elizabeth AB, Barnard Coll., 1965; MA, Columbia U., 1966; MSLS, Syracuse U., 1972. Libr. reference U. Ill., Urbana, 1972—77, libr. city planning and landscape architecture, 1977—79, head documents libr., 1979—81; asst. dir. gen. svcs. U. Ill. Libr., Urbana, 1981—88, acting dir. gen. svcs., 1988—93, dir. ctrl. pub. svcs., 1989—93, asst. libr., 1993—95, dir. electronic info. svcs., 1995—2004, dir. scholarly comm., 2003—04; ret., 2004. Author: Electronic Journals: Acquisition and Management, 2003, E-Publishing Impact on Acquisition and Interlibrary Loan, 2004; contbr. articles to profl. jours. N.Y. State Regents fellow Columbia U., N.Y.C., 1965-66; Council on Library Resources profl. edn. and tng. for librarianship grantee, 1983 Mem. ALA (sec. univ. librs. sect. ALA-Assn. Coll. and Rsch. Librs. 1989-91, com. on instnl. coop., chair pub. svcs. dirs. group, 1997-99, mem. com. inst. coop./OCLC virtual electronic libr. steering com.), Ill. Library Assn. Avocation: gardening. Home: 715 W Delaware Ave Urbana IL 61801-4806

WATSON, RALPH EDWARD, internist, educator; b. Cin., Apr. 4, 1948; s. John Sherman and Evelyn (Moore) W.; m. Demetria Rencher, Sept. 9, 1972; children: Ralph Edward, Monifa. BS, Xavier U., 1970; MD, Mich. State U., East Lansing, 1976. Diplomate Am. Bd. Internal Medicine; cert. clin. hypertension specialist. Intern U. Cin. Med. Ctr., 1976-77, resident in internal medicine, 1977-79, asst. clin. prof. internal medicine, 1980-88; asst. prof. internal medicine Mich. State U., East Lansing, 1988-94, assoc. prof., 1994—. Attending physician in hypertension clinic Mich. State U., 1988-91, assoc. dir. hypertension clinic, 1991-94, dir. hypertension clinic, 1995—, program dir. transitional yr. residency, 1990-96, assoc. program dir. internal medicine residency, 1996-2003; mem. U.S. HHS Office Minority Health Resource Person Network. Fellow ACP, Internat. Soc. Hypertension in Blacks, Am Assn. Black Cardiologists; mem. Nat. Med. Assn., Am. Soc. Internal Medicine, Lansing Area Am. Heart Assn., Am. Black Cardiologists (chair rsch. com.), Am. Soc. Hypertension, Xavier U. Alumni Assn., Alpha Omega Alpha. Office: Mich State U 338B Clinical Ctr East Lansing MI 48824-1313 Office Phone: 517-353-4811.

WATSON, RICHARD THOMAS, lawyer; b. Lakewood, Ohio, Aug. 21, 1933; s. Thomas Earl Watson and Sara Lucille (Whapham) Hadfield; m. Judith C. Briggs, Aug. 6, 1960; children: David, Andrew, Susan (dec.). AB, Harvard U., 1954, JD, 1960. Bar: Ohio 1960. Assoc. Spieth, Bell, McCurdy & Newell, Cleve., 1960, ptnr., 1965, mng. ptnr., 1987—. Bd. dirs. numerous corps. Chancellor Episcopal Diocese of Ohio, Cleve., 1986—; mem. Harvard U. com. on univ. resources, 1992—; bd. trustees Cleve. Mus. Art, 1991—. Mem. Union Club Cleve. Office: Spieth Bell McCurdy & Newell 925 Euclid Ave Ste 2000 Cleveland OH 44115-1408 Office Phone: 216-696-4700. Personal E-mail: richardtwatson@att.net.

WATSON, ROBERT FRANCIS, lawyer; b. Houston, Jan. 9, 1936; s. Louis Leon and Lora Elizabeth (Hodges) W.; m. Marietta Kiser, Nov. 24, 1961; children: Julia, Melissa, Rebecca. BA, Vanderbilt U., 1957; JD, U. Denver, 1959. Bar: Colo. 1959, U.S. Dist. Ct. (no. dist.) Tex. 1967, U.S. Supreme Ct. 1968, Tex. 1973, U.S. Ct. Appeals (5th cir.) 1973, U.S. Dist. Ct. (so. dist.) Tex. 1980, U.S. Ct. Appeals (11th cir.) 1981. Law clk. U.S. Dist. Ct. Colo., 1960-61; trial atty. SEC, Denver, 1961-67, asst. regional adminstr. Ft. Worth, 1967-72, regional adminstr., 1972-75; ptnr. Law, Snakard & Gambill, P.C., Ft. Worth, 1975-98, of counsel, 1998—2005, shareholder, 2005—; exec. v.p., gen. counsel First Command Fin. Svcs., Inc., Ft. Worth, 1998—2005. Counsel City of Ft. Worth Police Investigation Commn., 1975; spl. counsel Office Atty. Gen. State Ariz., 1977-78. Contbr. articles to profl. jours. Mem. Ft. Worth Crime Commn., 1987-93. Honoree 27th Ann. Rocky Mountain State-Fed.-Provincial Securities Conf. Fellow: Coll. of State Bar Tex., U. Denver Law Sch. Alumni Coun., Colo. Bar Assn., Tex. Bar Found. (life), Tarrant County Bar Assn., Ft. Worth Club; mem.: ABA, Tarrant County Bar Found. (charter), Tex. Bus. Law Found. (bd.dirs. 1988—93), State Bar Tex., Fed. Bar Assn., Shady Oaks Country Club (Ft. Worth), Phi Delta Phi. Republican. Presbyterian. also: Law Snakard & Gambill PC 1600 W 7th St Ste 500 Fort Worth TX 76102-3819 Office Phone: 817-878-6374. Business E-Mail: bwatson@lawsnakard.com.

WATSON, ROBERT JOE, retired health facility administrator, retired career officer; b. Wellington, Kans., Nov. 12, 1934; s. Charles Bruce and Marguerite B. (Scholes) W.; m. Ursula Eschenroeder, Dec. 26, 1983; children: Stephanie Watson-Zollinger, Stacy Watson Bruce, Susannah Watson Gold; stepchildren: Jurgen Wanke, Claudia Beeck. MS in Edn., Kans. State Tchrs. Coll., 1963; MBA, U. Hawaii, 1969; MHA, George Washington U., 1973, EdD, 1976; student, Command-Gen. Staff Coll., 1973, U.S. Army War Coll., 1986. Commd. 2nd lt. U.S. Army, 1963, advanced through grades to col., 1989; stationed at Tripler Army Med. Ctr., Honolulu, 1967-69, USARV Surgeons Office, Long Binh, Vietnam, 1969-70, Surgeon Gen.'s Office, Washington, 1970-74, Walter Reed Med. Ctr., Washington, 1974-76, Acad. Health Svcs., Ft. Sam Houston, Tex., 1976—80, 68th Med. Group, Ziegenberg, Germany, 1980-82, U.S. Army Hosp., Ft. Riley, Kans., 1982-84, 34th Gen. Hosp., Augsburg, Germany, 1984-87; assoc. dean USA Med. Field Svc. Sch., Ft. Sam Houston, Tex., 1987—89; assoc. dir. Student Health Ctr. U. Fla., Gainesville, 1989—2005; ret., 2005. Fellow Am. Coll. Healthcare Execs. (adv., regent 1982-84). Episcopalian. Avocations: tennis, golf, gardening.

WATSON, ROBERT WINTHROP, poet; b. Passaic, NJ, Dec. 26, 1925; s. Winthrop and Laura Berdan (Trimble) W.; m. Elizabeth Ann Rean, Jan. 12, 1952; children: Winthrop, Caroline. BA, Williams Coll., 1946; postgrad., U. Zurich, 1947; MA, Johns Hopkins, 1950, PhD in English, 1955. Instr. English Williams Coll., 1946, 47-48, 52-53, Johns Hopkins, 1950-52; mem. faculty U. N.C., Greensboro, 1953—, prof. English, 1963-90. Vis. poet, prof. English Calif. State U., Northridge, 1968-69 Author: (poetry) A Paper Horse, 1962, Advantages of Dark, 1966 (Runner-up, Pulitzer prize), Christmas in Las Vegas, 1971, Selected Poems, 1974, Island of Bones, 1977, Night Blooming Cactus, 1980, The Pendulum: New and Selected Poems, 1995; (novels) Three Sides of the Mirror, 1966, Lily Lang, 1977, (art book) Betty Watson Paintings, 1999; co-founder The Greensboro Rev., 1966. Swiss-Am. exch. fellow, 1947; grantee Nat. Endowment for Arts, 1973; recipient Am. Scholar Poetry prize, 1959, Lit. award Am. Acad. Inst. Arts Letters, 1977. Home: 4321 Galax Trail Greensboro NC 27410

WATSON, ROBERTA CASPER, lawyer; b. Boise, Idaho, July 11, 1949; d. John Blaine and Joyce Lucile (Mercer) C.; m. Robert George Watson, July 22, 1972; 1 child, Rebecca Joyce. BA cum laude, U. Idaho, 1971; JD, Harvard U., 1974. Bar: Mass. 1974, U.S. Dist. Ct. Mass. 1975, U.S. Supreme Ct. 1979, U.S. Ct. Appeals (1st cir.) 1979, U.S. Tax Ct. 1979, Fla. 1985, U.S. Dist. Ct. (mid. dist.) Fla. 1985, U.S. Dist. Ct. (so. dist.) Fla. 1987. Assoc. Peabody & Brown, Boston, 1974-78, Mintz, Levin, Cohn, Ferris, Glovsky & Popeo, Boston, 1978-84; sr. dir. Wolper Ross & Co., Miami, 1983-85; assoc. Trenam, Kemker, Scharf, Barkin, Frye, O'Neill & Mullis, P.A., Tampa, Fla., 1985-87, ptnr., 1988—. Co-author: A Physician's Guide to Professional Corporations; co-editor-in-chief COBRA Adv. Newsletter, 1997-2000; contbr. articles to profl. jours. Pres. Performing Arts Ctr. Greater Framingham, Mass., 1983; bd. dirs., Northside Mental Health Ctr., 1987-2008, pres. 1999-2001; trustee Unitarian Universalist Found., Clearwater, Fla., 1986—; bd. dirs. Dist. 6 Cmty. Health Purchasing Alliance, pers. com. chair, 1998-2000. Named Bd. Mem. of Yr. Fla. Cmty. Mental Health, 1994; listed in Best Lawyers in Am., 1995-. Mem.: ABA (chair employee benefit com sect. taxation 1995—96, chair employee benefits interest group health law sect. 1998—2001, chair joint com. on employee benefits 2002—03), Fla. West Coast Employee Benefits Coun. (bd. dirs. 1996—2003, treas. 1997—98, v.p 1998—2001, pres. 2001—02), Am. Coll. Employee Benefits Counsel (charter mem.), Tampa Club (com. mem. 2006—08), Harvard Club (sec. 2007—, bd. dirs. West Coast Fla. chpt.), Order Ea. Star. Democrat. Avocations: music, metaphysics, Lincoln historian, genealogy. Home: 55 Martinique Ave Tampa FL 33606-4029 Office: Trenam Kemker Scharf Barkin Frye O'Neill & Mullis PA 2700 Bank of Am Plz 101 E Kennedy Blvd Tampa FL 33602 Office Phone: 813-227-7487. Business E-Mail: rcwatson@trenam.com.

WATSON, ROLLIN J., former academic administrator, educator, writer; m. Norma Osborne, May 20, 1967; children: David O., Juliana Watson-Dick, Jennifer Mary. PhD in Am. Studies, U. Md., College Park, 1975; DPA (hon.), Union Coll., Barbourville, Ky., 1992. V.p. to pres. Hiwassee Coll., Madisonville, Tenn., 1984—89; pres. Somerset CC, Ky., 1989—99, tenured assoc. prof., 1999—. Bd. mem. numerous agys. and assns. Author: (academic book) The School as a Safe Haven, (book) Spending a Lifetime: Careers of City Mangers. Cons. Safe Schs. America Inc., 1995—; libr. bd. U. Ky., Lexington, 1996—2007; mem. Somerset-Pulaski County Devel. Found., 1992—99. Recipient State Senate citation, Commonwealth of Ky., 1999, citation, U. Ky., 1999; fellow, U. Md., 1969, U. Ky., 1996. Mem.: hist. and Am. studies assns. Avocations: swimming, weightlifting, bicycling, reading. Office: Somerset CC 808 Monticello St Somerset KY 42501 Business E-Mail: rollin.watson@kctcs.edu.

WATSON, STANLEY ELLIS, clergyman, small business owner; b. New Orleans, July 25, 1957; s. Joseph and Dorothy (Jones) W. EdB, Jarvis Christian Coll., Hawkins, Tex., 1977; MRE, Tex. Christian U., Ft. Worth, 1979; spl. edn., So. U. A&M, Baton Rouge, 1986; grad., U.S. Acad. Pvt. Investigation, 1991; DD (hon.), Charter Ecumenical Ministries, 1994; student in Christian Counseling, Christian Bible Coll. and Sem., 2005—. Cert. tchr.; registered notary Mich.; lic. pvt. investigator, La. Asst. min. Jarvis Christian Coll., Hawkins, Tex., 1974-77; tchr. pub. sch., Daingerfield, Tex., 1977-78; sr. pastor Truevine Christian Ch., 1977—79; asst. min. Park Manor Christian Ch., Chgo., 1980-81; asst. mgr. K- Mart, Shreveport, La., 1981-82; min. United Christian Ch., Jackson, Miss., 1982-83; tchr. pub. sch., Napoleonville, La., 1986-87, Zachary, La., 1987-88; min. Vt. Christian Ch., Flint, Mich., 1988—92, sr. pastor, 1990; assoc. min. Buena Vista Bapt. Ch., St. James, La. Owner, mgr. Watson Diversified Fin. Co., 1989—, Watson Detective Agy., Donaldsonville, La., 1992—; v.p. DVY Sys., Inc., 1997—; CEO Watson and Julien Cmty. Mission, Inc., Donaldsonville, La.; clin. pastoral counseling, christian counseling, 2001.e Mem. NAACP, NEA. Recipient Presdl. citation Nat. Assn. for Equal Opportunity in Higher Edn.; Christian Women's fellow, 1975-77, St. Louis Bd. Edn. fellow, 1977-79, Tex. Christian U. Brite Div. Sch. scholar, 1977; Jarvis Christian Coll. cert. of Honor and Merit, 1974-77; named Rev. Stanley Watson Day City of Flint, Mich., 1989, Disting. Alumnus, Jarvis Christian Coll., 1995. Mem. Nat. Assn. Investigative Specialists, Am. Inst. Profl. Bookeepers, Am. Fin. Coord. Assn. (fin. coord.), Christian Counselors Assn., Nat. Assn Investigative Specialist, Nat. Assn. Federated Tax Preparers, Am. Soc. Notaries, Aircraft Owners and Pilots Assn. Coun. for Exceptional Children, Forgotten Man Ministries, Jarvis Christian Coll. Alumni Assn. (v.p.), NAACP, Urban League of Flint, Urban Coalition of Greater Flint, Flint C. of C., Internat. Reading Assn., NEA, Am. Sailing Assn., Phi Beta Sigma, Kappa Delta Pi. Mem. Tex. Christian U. Alumni Assn. Democrat. Avocations: beekeeping, collecting coins, stamps, sports cards, coffees. Home and Office: PO Box 668 Donaldsonville LA 70346-0668 Home Phone: 225-473-3364; Office Phone: 225-323-3025. Personal E-mail: jarvis19771@yahoo.com, jarvis19771@gmail.com.

WATSON, STEWART CHARLES, construction executive; b. Brock, Sask., Can., Sept. 17, 1922; s. Samuel Henry and Elva Jane (St. John) W.; m. Irene Lillian Ahrens, Aug. 4, 1943; children: Judith Gail (Mrs. David Stafford), Wendy Carolyn (Mrs. Rocco Amuso), Ronald James, Candyce Louise. Student, U. Buffalo. With Acme Steel & Malleable Iron Works, Buffalo, 1940—42, Acme Hwy. Products, Buffalo, 1946—55, internat. mktg. mgr., 1955—69; pres. Watson-Bowman Assocs. Inc., Buffalo, 1970—, Kinematics, 1984—. Chmn. bd. Air Stewart Inc.; Internat. lectr. on kinetics of civil engring. structures; mem. U.S. Transp. Rsch. Bd.; bd. dirs. Internat. Bridge of Peace for Bering Strait Crossing. With AUS, 1943-45, ETO. Fellow Am. concrete Inst. (dir. 1984—, Delmar Bloehm award 1984, Charles S. Whitney medal 1987, hon. mem.); mem. ASTM, NAS, Internat. Jts. and Bearings Rsch. Coun. (chmn. 1988—), Internat. Activities Commn., Masons (32 degree), Shriners. Home: 3 Chicory Ln East Amherst NY 14051

WATSON, TANYA PARTON, school system administrator, director; b. Rutherfordton, NC, Jan. 27, 1964; d. Reuben L. and Bonnie B. Parton; m. Jason M. Watson, Nov. 19, 1999. BA in Intermediate Edn., U. NC, Charlotte, 1985; MA in Sch. Adminstrn., Gardner-Webb U., Boiling Springs, NC, 1998, EdD in Ednl. Leadership, 2003. Cert. grant evaluator SC, tchr. Math and sci. tchr. East Rutherford HS, Forest City, NC, 1993—98; sci. tchr. Heritage Mid. Sch., Morganton, NC, 1998—99; asst. prin. Freedom HS, Morganton, 1998—99, Harris Elem. Sch., Forest

City, 2000—01; math tchr. R-S Ctrl. HS, Rutherfordton, NC, 2001—03; asst. prin. Chase Mid. Sch., Forest City, 2003—05; dir. fed. programs and profl. devel. Rutherford County Schs., Forest City, 2005—. Grant evaluator Rutherford Rsch. & Evaluation Svcs., Rutherfordton, 2006. Sec.-treas. Main St. Bapt. Ch., Spindale, NC, 2006. Mem.: ASCD (assoc.), Nat. Assn. Secondary Sch. Prins. (assoc.), Am. Ednl. Rsch. Assn. (assoc.), Am. Assn. Grant Profls. (assoc.), Am. Evaluation Assn. (assoc.). Office: Rutherford County Schs 382 W Main St Forest City NC 28043 Office Fax: 828-245-2990. Business E-Mail: twatson@rutherford.k12.nc.us.

WATSON, TERI L., insurance company executive; BS in bus. adminstrn.-acctg., Millersville U., Pa. Mgr. fin. reporting Skandia America; v.p. planning and budgeting GRE Ins. Group; asst. v.p. internat. rating divsn. A.M. Best Co.; asst. dir. rating agencies Am. Internat. Group, Inc. (AIG), 1999—2003, mng. dir. rating agencies, 2003—08, v.p. rating agy. rels., 2008—09, v.p. investor and rating agy. rels., 2009—. Office: Am Internat Group Inc 70 Pine St 27th Fl New York NY 10270 Office Phone: 212-770-7074. E-mail: teri.watson@aig.com.*

WATSON, WILLIE R., research scientist; s. Aaron L. Watson and Coletha Davis; m. Gretchen B. Beck; 1 child, Reginald C. PhD, George Wash. U., Washington, 1991. Aerospace technologist NASA Langley Rsch. Ctr., Hampton, Va., 1973—91, sr. rsch. scientist, 1991—. Contbr. scientific papers to profl. jours. V.p. Les Hommes Civic & Social Club, Hampton, 2008—. Fellow: AIAA (assoc.); mem.: Delta Beta Lambda Chpt. Alpha Phi Alpha Frat. (treas. 1998—2002). Achievements include research in impedance of sound absorbing structures. Office: NASA Langley Rsch Ctr Mail Stop 128 Hampton VA 23681 Office Fax: 757-864-8816. Business E-Mail: willie.r.watson@nasa.gov.

WATSON-BOONE, REBECCA A., dean, researcher, library and information scientist, educator; b. Springfield, Ohio, Mar. 7, 1946; d. Roger S. and Elizabeth Boone; m. Dennis David Ash, 1967 (div. 1975); m. Frederick Kellogg, 1979 (div. 1988); m. Peter G. Watson-Boone, May 26, 1989. Student, Earlham Coll., Richmond, Ind., 1964-67; BA, Case Western Res. U., Cleve., 1968; MLS, U. NC, Chapel Hill, 1971; PhD, U. Wis., Madison, 1995. Asst. reference libr. Princeton U., NJ, 1970-76; head cen. reference dept. U. Ariz., Tucson, 1976-83, assoc. dean Coll. Arts and Scis., 1984-89; co-dir. Placitas Cmty. Libr., N.Mex., 2007—. Loaned exec. Ariz. Bd. Regents, 1988-89; pres. Ctr. for Study of Info. Profls., 1995—2002. Author: Constancy and Change in the Worklife of Research University Librarians, 1998, A Good Match: Library Career Opportunities for Graduates of Liberal Arts Colleges, 2007; contbr. articles to profl. jours. Mem. ALA (div. pres. 1985-86, councilor 1988-92), Assn. Libr. and Info. Sci. Edn., N.Mex. Libr. Assn. Mem. Soc. Of Friends. Office: 30 Camino de la Vina Vieja Placitas NM 87043 Business E-Mail: rebeccawb@comcast.net.

WATT, (ARTHUR) DWIGHT, JR., computer programming and microcomputer specialist; b. Washington, Jan. 25, 1955; s. Arthur Dwight and Myrtle Lorraine (Putnam) W.; m. Shari Elizabeth Gambrell, July 30, 1988. BA, Winthrop U., Rock Hill, SC, 1977. MBA, 1979; EdD, U. Ga., Athens, 1989. Cert. computer and internet profl. Inst. Cert. Computer Profls., Microsoft; cert. home fire arms safety, NRA; cert. A+ personal computer technician, CompTIA; cert. sys. engr., sys. adminstr., office user specialist instr.; i-net plus cert. Comptia; Network + cert.; cert. network adminstr. and acad. instr., Cisco; Server + cert. CompTIA. Data processing instr. York Tech. Coll., Rock Hill, SC, 1977-78; computer ctr. asst. Winthrop U., Rock Hill, SC, 1976-79; data processing instr. Brunswick Coll., Ga., 1979-80; system operator, asst. programmer Sea Island Co., The Cloister, Ga., 1981; pvt. practice data processing cons. Swainsboro, Ga., 1981; computer programming/microcomputer specialist instr. Swainsboro Tech. Inst., 1981-96; sr. programmer/analyst Policy Mgmt. Sys. Corp., Columbia, SC, 1996-97; microcomputer specialist instr. Athens Tech. Coll.-Elbert County Campus, Elberton, Ga., 1997-2001; chmn. IT dept. Heart of Ga. Tech. Coll., Dublin, 2001—05; CIO Ga. Healthcare Sys., Atlanta, 2001; instr. Peirce Coll., Phila., 2005—07, So. Wesleyan U., Central, SC, 2005—06, Savannah River Coll., Augusta, Ga., 2006; dir./instr. database & networking program Northwestern Tech. Coll., Rock Spring, Ga., 2007—09, Ga. Northwestern Tech. Coll., Rock Spring, Ga., 2009—. Chmn. exec. bd. computer curriculum Ga. Dept. Tech. and Adult Edn., 1990-92, 2002-05, exec. bd. computer curriculum, 1994-96, 2002-05, 2007-, vice chair, 2000-02, CIS cons. for curriculum, 2006-07; chmn. East Ctrl. Ga. Consortium for Computer Occupations, 1990-96, networking curriculum, GDTAE, 2008-; co-facilitator CIS curriculum rev. and update Ga. Tech. Colls., 2001,2005; spkr. in field; cons. in field. Author: District Revenue Potential and Teachers Salaries in Georgia, 1989, Structured COBOL for Technical Students, 1998; co-author: District Property Wealth and Teachers Salaries in Georgia, 1990, Factors Influencing Teachers Salaries: An Examination of Alternative Models, 1991, Local Wealth and Teachers Salaries in Pennsylvania, 1992, School District Wealth and Teachers' Salaries in South Carolina, 1993, Test Yourself A+ Certification Practice Exams, 1998, GDTAE CIS Curriculum Standards and Guides Revision, 2001. Chmn. Emanuel County chpt. ARC, Swainsboro, 1989-90, 92-93, bd. dirs., 1989-96; pres. United Meth. Men. Swainsboro, 1984-86; trustee Greater Swainsboro Tech. Inst. Found., Inc., 1995-96; bd. dirs. Emanuel Arts Coun., 2004-07. Recipient Nat. Tech. Tchr. of Yr. finalist award Am. Tech. Edn. Assn., 1994; Olympic Cmty. Hero Torchbearer, 1996 Mem. Inst. Cert. Computing Profls., Ga. Bus. Edn. Assn. (dir. dist. 1 1986, 96, dist. sec.-treas. 1993-95, dist. 1 dir.-elect 1995-96, Dist. 1 Postsecondary Tchr. Yr. 1985, State Postsecondary Tchr. Yr. 1995), Profl. Assn. Ga. Educators, Swainsboro Jaycees (Outstanding Young Citizen 1985, treas. 1984-89, pres. 1987-88, pres. S.E. Ga. Jaycee Fair 1995, treas. S.E. Ga. Jaycee Fair 1993-94), Ga. Jaycees (v.p. area C 1988-89, chaplain 1989-90, dir. region 6 1990-91, chmn. state shooting edn. 1991-92, chair Internat. BB Gun Match Championship 1999, co-chair match 2000, treas. match 2002), US Jr. C. of C. (nat. rep. shooting edn. program 1992-95, Shooting Edn. State Program Mgr. Yr. 1992, webmaster Internat. BB Gun Championship match 1999—), Swainsboro-Emanuel County C. of C. (webmaster 2002-07), Ga. Kiwanis (tech. chair, webmaster 2002-), Emanuel Artist Guild (v.p. 2003—05), Swainsboro Kiwanis (bd. dirs., 2005—07, webmaster, 2003—), Kiwanis Club (Ft. Oglethorpe) (webmaster 2007-, v.p. 2009-), Walker County C. of C. (webmaster 2008-). Methodist. Home: PO Box 1637 206 Hereford Rd Swainsboro GA 30401 Office Phone: 706-764-3837. Personal E-mail: dwight-watt@att.net. E-mail: dwight@dwightwatt.com.

WATT, JAMES GAIUS, lawyer, former United States Secretary of the Interior; b. Lusk, Wyo., Jan. 31, 1938; s. William G. and Lois M. (Williams) W.; m. Leilani Bomgardner, Nov. 2, 1957; children: Erin Gaia, Eric Gaius. BS, U. Wyo., 1960, JD, 1962. Bar: Wyo. 1962, U.S. Supreme Ct. 1966. Legis. asst., counsel to Senator Simpson of Wyo., 1962-66; sec. to natural resources com. and environ. pollution adv. panel C. of C. of U.S., 1966-69; dep. asst. sec. water and power devel. US Dept. Interior, 1969-72; dir. Bur. Outdoor Recreation, Washington, 1972-75; mem., vice chmn. Fed. Power Commn., 1975-77; pres., chief legal officer Mountain States Legal Found., Denver, 1977-80; sec. US Dept. Interior, Washington, 1981-83; bus. cons. Washington, 1983-86, Jackson Hole, Wyo., 1986—; chmn. bd. Environ. Diagnostics, 1984-87, Disease Detection Internat., 1986-90. Instr. Coll. Commerce and Industry, U. Wyo. Author: (with Doug Wead) The Courage of a Conservative, 1985 Mem. Phi Kappa Phi, Delta Theta Phi.

WATT, JOSEPH MICHAEL, state supreme court justice; b. Austin, Tex., Mar. 8, 1947; m. Cathy Watt; children: Justin, Christopher, Jennifer, Michael. BA in Hist., Tex. Tech U., 1969; JD, U. Tex. Law Sch., 1972. Bar: Tex. 1972, Okla. 1974. Pvt. practice, Altus, Okla., 1972-85; judge Dist. Trial Ct., 1985-91; gen. counsel to gov. State of Okla., Oklahoma City, 1991-92; justice Okla. Supreme Ct., Okahoma City, 1992—, vice-chief justice, 2001—02, chief justice Okahoma City, 2003—04. Liaison to Okla. Bar Assn. Okla. Supreme Ct., 1997—98; mem. Appellate Divsn. Ct. on Judiciary, 1997—98, Truth in Sentencing Commn., Supreme Ct. Long Range Planning Commn.; chmn. Supreme Ct. Com. Time Standards. Mem.: Okla. Bar Assn. Office: Okla Supreme Ct State Capitol Rm 244 Oklahoma City OK 73105 Office Phone: 405-521-3848. Fax: 405-521-6982. E-mail: joseph.watt@oscn.net.*

WATT, MELVIN LUTHER, United States Representative from North Carolina, lawyer; b. Steele Creek, NC, Aug. 26, 1945; m. Eulada Paysour Watt; children: Brian, Jason. BS in Bus. Adminstrn., U. NC, Chapel Hill, 1967; JD, Yale U. Law Sch., 1970; degree (hon.), NC A&T State U., Johnson C. Smith U., Bennett Coll. Atty. Ferguson, Stein, Watt, Wallas, Adkins, & Gresham, 1971-92; mem. NC State Senate, 1985-86; co-owner East Towne Manor, 1989—; mem. US Congress from 12th NC dist., 1993—, mem. fin. svcs. com., 1993—, mem. judiciary com., 1993—, chmn. oversight and investigations subcommittee, chmn. Congl. Black Caucus, 2004—07, mem. joint econ. com. Pres. Mecklenburg County Bar. Active vol. Ctrl. Piedmont CC Found., Legal Aid So. Piedmont, NC Cmty. Devel. Corp., Auditorium-Coliseum-Civic Ctr. Authority, United Way, Mint Mus., Family Housing Svcs., Pub. Edn. Forum, Dilworth Cmty. Devel. Assn., Cities in Schs., Housing Authority Scholarship Bd., Morehead Scholarship Selection Com.; bd. dirs. Johnson C. Smith U. Named one of 100 Most Influential Black Americans, Ebony mag., 2006; named to Power 150, 2008. Mem.: NAACP (life), Inroads Inc., West Charlotte Bus. Incubator, Charlotte C. of C. (sports action coun.), NC Acad. Trial Lawyers, NC Assn. Black Lawyers, Phi Beta Kappa. Democrat. Presbyterian. Office: US House Reps 2236 Rayburn House Office Bldg Washington DC 20515-3312 Office Phone: 202-225-1510. Office Fax: 202-225-1512.*

WATT, RONALD G., archivist; b. Spring Canyon, Utah, Jan. 2, 1939; s. George L. and Norma L. Watt; m. Barbara Fluckiger, Jan. 1, 1940; children: Ronda Matthew, Andrew, Gardner, April, Kennan. BA, Utah State U., Logan, 1963; MA, Utah State U., 1967; PhD, U. Minn., Mpls., 1975. Cert. archivist 1989. Social studies tchr. Carbon HS, Price, Utah, 1964—65; history instr. So. Utah State Coll., Cedar City, 1966—68; archivist hist. dept. LDS Ch., Salt Lake City, 1972—2008. Author: (book) A History of Carbon County, 1997, City of Diversity, A History of Price, Utah, 2001. Mem.: Cert. Archivists (treas. 1991—93), Utah Manuscripts Assn. (Dr. Everett L. Cooley Distinguished Archival Career award 2005), Utah State Hist. Soc. (bd. editors 2000—, Nick Yengich Editors Choice award 2001), Soc. Am. Archivists (chmn. subcom. world mission records 1982—85, editl. com. religious archives newsletter 1983—87, program com. newsletter 1984—85), Conf. Intermountain Archivists (newsletter editor 1976—80, coun. mem. 1980—83, pres. 1983—84, chmn. nominating com. 1984—85, mem. nominating com. 1992—93). Democrat. Mem. Lds Ch. Avocations: photography, writing, travel. Home: 4493 Thayn Dr Salt Lake City UT 84120

WATT, STEPHANIE DENISE, musician, educator, department chairman; d. Edmund Hudson and Joan Elizabeth (Patterson) Watt. BFA in Music Performance, LI U., 1984, MA in Composition and Performance, 1988, MS in Computer Sci. and Engring., 1999. Adj. asst. prof. music LI U., C.W. Post Campus, Brookville, NY, 1988—97, assoc. prof. music, 1997—; adj. asst. prof. music Suffolk County CC, Ammerman Campus, Selden, NY, 1988—97; adj. asst. prof. music Dowling Coll., Oakdale, NY, 1989—91; guest lectr. in music history Alvin Ailey Am. Sch. Dance, NYC, 1996—98. Founder EastWest Sch. Performing Arts, NY, 1979—2006; coord. seminar divsn. LI U. Chamber Music Program, Brookville, 1994—97; dir. piano studies LI U., C.W. Post Campus, 1988—, co-dir. student concert series, 1990—96, dir. theory studies, 1999—; adjudicator LI Philharm. Young Artist Piano Competition, 1994—2004, Music Lovers Club Young Artist Competition, 1994—2006, 8th and 9th NY Young Artist Piano and Violin Competition, 2005, 06; piano master classes Művészeti Szakközepiskola és Gimnázium, Szombathely. Author: Information Theory Analyses of Bach Chorales and a Learning Classifier System, 1999; musician: (CD recording on Capstone Records) Duo for Cello and Piano by Allen Brings, 2006; dancer (dance exhbn.) Argentine Tango & Salsa Exhbn.; performer: Camerata Pro Musica, 2000, Carnegie Hall, 2005, The Hecksher Mus. Art, 2005, Park Ave. United Meth. Ch., 2005, Brick Gallery, 2005, LI U., C.W. Post Campus, 2005, 2006, Clarinet & Piano Concert, 2006, Concert Tour of Hungary, Communidad de Palermo Symphony Orch., 2006; guest artist, clinician LI Choral Festival and Inst., 2004, 2005, (DuoLeo performace) Weill Hall Carnegie Hall, NYC, 2005, Park Ave. United Meth. Ch., 2005, LI U., C.W. Post Campus, Brookville, 2005, 2006, (DuoLeo performace and solo performance) Brik Gallery, Catskills, NY, 2005, (Martino and Watt duo performace) Steinway Hall, NYC, 2006, Blueport Libr., 2006, LI Philharm. Choir, 2006, (DuoLeo performace one-woman shows) The Heckscher Mus. Art, Huntington, NY, 2005; dancer (dance exhbns.) Babylon Village Fair, NY, 2005, New Life Cmty. Ch., Sachem, NY, 2006, LI U., C.W. Post, 2006; featured Strings mag., 2002; contbr. articles to profl. confs. Recipient First Pl. award Foxtrot Exhbn., Kings Ball Dancesport Championships, SI, NY, 2001, First Pl. award Am. Tango Exhbn., 2001, First Pl. award Viennese Waltz Exhbn., Stardust Ball Competition, Melville, NY, 2002, First Pl. award Open Tango Exhbn., Stardust Ball, Melville, NY, 2002, Cert. of Recognition music performance, Mayor of Inc. Village of Hempstead, 1995, Second Pl. award slow waltz exhbn., NJ Open Championships, Rutherford, 2003, Third Pl. award Dance Team Exhbn., Northeastern Open Championships, Weston, Conn., 2003. Mem.: AAUW (assoc.), NY State Music Assn. (assoc.), Coll. Music Soc. (assoc.), Phi Eta Sigma. Achievements include research in the history of the tango and its political influence in Argentina. Office Fax: 516-299-2884. Personal E-mail: stefani1435@aol.com.

WATT, WILLIAM STEWART, retired physical chemist; b. Perth, Scotland, Feb. 25, 1937; BSc, U. St. Andrews, Scotland, 1959; PhD in Phys. Chemistry, U. Leeds, 1962. Fellow Cornell U., 1962-64; rsch. chemist Cornell Aeronautics Lab., Buffalo, 1964-71; head chem. laser sect. Naval Rsch. Lab., 1971-73, dep. head laser physics br., 1973-76, head laser physics br. optical sci. divsn., 1976-79; gen. mgr. wash ops. W. J. Schafer Assoc., Arlington, Va., 1979-80, v.p. program devel., 1980-90, sr. v.p., dir. programs, 1991-94; CEO Lawrence Assocs., Inc., Arlington, 1994-95; pres. WSW Consulting Inc., 1996—2002. Active U.S. Army Sci. Bd., 1992-98. Recipient J. B. Cohen Rsch. prize, 1962. Mem. IEEE (assoc. editor Jour. Quantum Electronics), Am. Phys. Soc., Combustion Inst., Sigma Xi. Achievements include research in laser physics and development, laser-induced chemistry, energy transfer and reaction rate measurements, optical diagnostics. E-mail: billswatt@bellsouth.net.

WATTA, DAVID ANTHONY, product manager; b. Detroit, Jan. 8, 1967; s. Watta D. Phillip and Elizabeth V. Watta. BA, We. Mich. U., Kalamazoo, 1993; MFA, Emerson Coll., Boston, 1996. Prodr. new media The Atlantic Monthly, Boston, 1993—97; mgr. internet program Banking website, North Palm Beach, Fla., 1997—99; exec. prodr. site Hard Rock Cafe Internat., Orlando, Fla., 1999—2000; sr. mgr. program Intel, Hillsboro, Oreg., 2000—06; dir. product mgmt. AARP, Washington, 2006—08; v.p. Sherman Travel Media, NYC, 2008—. Mem.: Mensa (life). Office Phone: 646-467-8112. Personal E-mail: davewatta@aol.com.

WATTERS, ANN OLIVA, psychologist, educator; d. George Verdelli II and Dorothy Austin Oliva; m. Thomas A. Watters, Aug. 30, 1975; children: Andrew George, Michael Thomas. BA in English, U. Calif., Berkeley, 1974; MA in English Lit., Washington U., St. Louis, 1976; MA in Health Psychology, Calif. Sch. Profl. Psychology, 1997, PhD in Psychology, 1999. Lectr. rhetoric and English Stanford U., Calif., 1987—; pvt. practice clin. psychology San Mateo, Calif., 1999—; asst. clin. prof. psychiatry U. Calif., San Francisco, 2005—. Author, editor: Global Exchange: Reading/Writing in a World Context, 2005; co-author: Creating America: Reading & Writing Arguments, 4th edit., 2005, Writing for Change: A Community Reader. Chair bd. dirs. San Mateo Med. Ctr. Found. Mem.: AAUP, APA, Calif. Psychol. Assn. Office Fax: 650-375-8398. Business E-Mail: watters@stanford.edu.

WATTERS, EDWARD MCLAIN, III, lawyer; b. 1943; s. Edward and Lucy F. (Disston) W.; m. Susan Secor, May 12, 1979; children: Jennifer Susan, Ann Elizabeth. BA cum laude, Yale U., 1965; JD cum laude, U. Pa., 1970. Bar: Pa. 1970. Ptnr. Pepper Hamilton LLP, Phila., 1977—. Lectr. programs on uniform trust act, estate planning and will drafting Pa. Bar Inst. Bd. dirs. Children's Cruise and Playground Soc. Pa., Sanitarium Playgrounds of NJ, others. Lt. USNR, 1965-75; chair Decedents Estate Adv. Com. to Pa. Legislature's Joint State Govt. Commn. Fellow Am. Coll. Trust and Estate Counsel; mem. ABA, Phila. Bar Assn., Pa. Bar Assn. (past chmn. legis. com. probate sect.), Phila. Estate Planning Coun. (past pres.), Yale Club of Phila., Penn Club, Merion Golf Club. Office: Pepper Hamilton LLP 400 Berwyn Park 899 Cassatt Rd Berwyn PA 19312-1183 Office Phone: 610-640-7809. Business E-Mail: watterse@pepperlaw.com.

WATTERS, KEVIN, bank executive; B, Lehigh U., Bethlehem, Pa.; MBA, U. Va. With Procter & Gamble, Pinnacle Brands, Vlasic Foods, WingspanBank.com; sr. v.p. corp. internet group Bank One (mearged with JP Morgan Chase & Co.), JP Morgan Chase & Co., CEO small bus. banking. Office: JP Morgan Chase & Co 270 Park Ave New York NY 10017*

WATTERS, LINDA A., former state banking agency administrator; m. Ronald E. Watters. BA in Bus. Adminstrn., Bowling Green State U.; MBA, U. Dayton. Analyst to positions in internat. mkt. and analysis group GM; various positions including loan analyst, corp. banking officer, asst. v.p. Comerica Bank, 1988—96, sr. loan analyst corp. banking, 1990, v.p. regional met. corp. banking, 1994—96; v.p., relationship mgr. comml. fin. svcs. Std. Fed. Bank, 1996—98; v.p., relationship mgr. Mich. Nat. Bank (now LaSalle Bank); pres., CEO Detroit Commerce Bank; commr. Mich. Office Fin. and Ins. Svcs., 2003—07. Bd. trustees Capital Region Cmty. Found., 2007—. Office Phone: 517-373-0220. Office Fax: 517-335-4978.

WATTLEWORTH, ROBERTA ANN, physician; b. Sioux City, Iowa, Dec. 26, 1955; d. Roland Joseph and Elizabeth Ann (Ahart) Eickholt; m. John Wade Wattleworth, Nov. 7, 1984; children: Adam, Ashley. BS, Morningside Coll., Sioux City, 1978; D of Osteopathy, Coll. Osteo. Medicine/Surgery, Des Moines, 1981; M.Healthcare Administrn., U. Osteo. Med. and Health Scis., Des Moines, 1999; MPH, Des Moines U., 2004. Intern Richmond Heights (Ohio) Gen. Hosp., 1981-82, resident in anesthesiology, 1982-84; anesthesiologist Doctor's Gen. Hosp., Plantation, Fla., 1984-85; resident in family practice J.F. Kennedy Hosp., Stratford, NJ, 1985-87; educator family practice U. Osteo. Medicine and Health Scis., Des Moines, 1987-89; family practitioner McFarland Clinic, P.C., Jewell, Iowa, 1989-94; lectr. family practice Osteopath. Med. Ctr., Des Moines U., 1999—, prof., chair dept. family medicine, 2003—. Med. dir. nursing home Bethany Manor, Story City, Iowa, 1990-99, Jewell Vol. Fire and Rescue Squad, 1990-99. Bd. dirs. Heartland Sr. Svcs., 1995—99, Iowa Rural Health Assn. Named Nat. Outstanding Osteo. Educator of Yr., Nat. Student Osteo. Med. Assn., 2001—02, Inaugural fellow, Nat. Acad. Osteopathic Med. Educators, 2009. Fellow Am. Coll. Osteo. Family Physicians; mem. Am. Osteo. Assn., Am. Med. Dirs. Assn. (sec.-treas. Iowa chpt. 1997-99), Am. Coll. Osteo. Family Physicians (pres. Iowa chpt. 1995-96), Iowa Osteo. Med. Assn. (trustee 1995-99, v.p. 1999—, pres.-elect 2000-01, pres. 2001-02, Physician of Yr. 2004-05), Soc. Tchrs. Family Medicine. Lutheran. Avocations: gardening, cooking, painting. Office: 3200 Grand Ave Des Moines IA 50312-4104 Office Phone: 515-271-7816. E-mail: Roberta.Wattleworth@dmu.edu.

WATTS, ANTHONY LEE, bank executive; b. Griffin, Ga., Jan. 24, 1947; s. Edgar Lee and Eula Mae (Benton) W.; m. Barbara Malinda Harp, Oct. 11, 1969; children: Natalie Paige, Barbara Leigh, Melanie Marie. AA, Gordon Mil. Coll., 1967; ABJ, U. Ga., Atlanta, 1969. Conventional loan rep. Fed. Nat. Mortgage Assn., Atlanta, from 1971, asst. regional appraiser, quality control and property mgr., to 1976; v.p., dir. ins. svcs. Ticor Mortgage Ins. Co., Atlanta, 1976-82; v.p., regional sales and exec. v.p. Ticor Indemnity Co., 1982-85; sr. v.p., regional mgr. Ticor Mortgage Ins. Co., Atlanta, 1984, sr. v.p., ea. divsn. mgr., 1984-85; pres. Mt. Vernon Fed. Savs. Bank, Dunwoody, Ga., 1985-95, Mt Vernon Fin. Corp., 1993-95; prin., dir. Banc Mortgage Fin. Corp., 1996-99, vice chmn., co-CEO, 1999—2002, co-pres., 2003—04; ret., 2004. Lectr. to trade assns. Founder, pres, co. registered Watts Family Enterprises, Inc., 1995; elder, bd. Peachtree Christian Ch.; bd. dirs. Ga. Spl. Olympics. With US Army, 1969—71. Recipient Bronze Star. Mem.: Phoenix Soc. (former bd. dirs.), Gridiron Club, Rotary Club (Paul Harris fellow 1987).

WATTS, CAROLYN SUE, nurse; b. Baxter, Tenn., Mar. 18, 1950; d. John D. and Bettye F. (Montgomery) McDaniel; m. Roy L. Watts, Oct. 27, 1973 (div. Sept. 1984); children: Eric, Allison. BS, Olivet Nazarene U., Kankakee, Ill., 1971; MS in Nursing, U. Tenn., 1978. RN, Tenn.; cert. wound/ostomy care nurse. Head nurse Martin Place Hosp., Madison Heights, Mich., 1971-75; nursing supr. Livingston Community Hosp., Tenn., 1975-78, dir. nursing, 1978-81; asst. dir. nursing DePaul Hosp., New Orleans, 1981-82; staff nurse Touro Infirmary Hosp., New Orleans, 1982-83; clin. nurse specialist, case mgr. Vanderbilt U. Med. Ctr., Nashville, 1983-2000; clin. edn. specialist Hollister, Inc., Libertyville, Ill., 2000—02; sr. assoc. surgery sch. medicine Vanderbilt U. Med. Ctr., Nashville, 2002—, instr. sch. Nursing, 2002—. Cons. dept.

nursing edn. Vanderbilt U. Sch. Nursing, 1983-2000, adj. faculty, 1984-2000, clin. instr., 2003—; assoc. in surgery Vanderbilt U. Sch. Medicine, 1986-2000; spkr. in field. Assoc. editor Jour. Urol. Nursing, 1985-91; contbr. articles to profl. jours. Mem. ANA, Tenn. Nurses Assn., Southeastern Surg. Nurses Assn. (counsellor 1983-91), AACN, Wound Ostomy Continence Nurses Soc., Assn. Advancement Wound Care, Mid. Tenn. Advanced Practice Nurse's Assn. (named Advanced Practice Nurse of Yr. 2006), Sigma Theta Tau. Avocations: reading, cooking. Home: 6236 Palomar Ct Nashville TN 37211-7482 Office: Vanderbilt Univ Med Ctr D-4316 MCN Nashville TN 37232-2730 Office Phone: 615-322-7836. Business E-Mail: carolyn.watts@vanderbilt.edu.

WATTS, CLAIRE A., retail executive; b. Feb. 26, 1960; BA in Mktg., U. Cin., 1982. With Limited Stores, Lands End, May Dept. Stores; divisional merchandising mgr. product devel. Wal-Mart Stores USA, Bentonville, Ark., 1997—2001, sr. v.p. product devel., 2001—03, exec. v.p., product devel., apparel, & home merchandising, 2003—07; pres. US Commerce QVC, Inc., West Chester, Pa., 2008—. Recipient Sam M. Walton Entrepreneur of Yr. award, 2003; named one of The 50 Most Powerful Women in Bus., Fortune mag., 2004—06. Office: QVC Inc 1200 Wilson Dr West Chester PA 19380

WATTS, COLIN F., retail executive; BA in History, Brown U., 1986; M in Internat. Rels., U. Pa., 1991, MBA, 1991. Pres., worldwide Johnson & Johnson (McNeil Nutritionals); pres., McNeil consumer healthcare worldwide Johnson & Johnson, 2005—07; v.p., gen. mgr. core US soup franchise Campbell Soup Co.; v.p., pres., Walgreens health & wellness disease mgmt. Walgreen Co., 2008—. Office: Walgreen Co 200 Wilmot Rd Deerfield IL 60015 Office Phone: 847-914-2500. Office Fax: 847-914-2804.

WATTS, D. WAYNE, telecommunications industry executive, lawyer; b. Abilene, Tex. BBA, U. Tex., Austin, 1976; JD, So. Meth. U., Dallas, 1980. Bar: US Dist. Ct. (no. dist. Tex.), US Dist. Ct. (ea. dist. Tex.), US Ct. Appeals (5th cir.), US Ct. Appeals (8th cir.). Atty. Southwestern Bell Telephone Co., Dallas, 1983—86, mergers and acquisitions staff, legal dept. St. Louis, 1988—89, v.p., asst. gen. counsel; gen. atty. Southwestern Bell Publs., St. Louis, 1986—88; v.p., gen. atty., sec. Southwestern Bell Mobile Systems, Dallas, 1989—95; gen. atty., asst. gen. counsel SBC Comm. Inc., counsel, mergers and acquisitions, wireless ops.; v.p., assoc. gen. counsel AT&T, Inc., sr. exec. v.p., gen. counsel, 2007—. Mem.: ABA, Mo. Bar Assn., State Bar Tex. Office: AT&T Inc 175 E Houston St San Antonio TX 78299 Office Phone: 210-821-4105.*

WATTS, EDWARD JAY, history professor; b. Princeton, NJ, Mar. 1, 1975; m. Manasi Watts, Aug. 11, 2001; children: Nathaniel, Zoe. PhD, Yale U., New Haven, 2002. Author: (book) City and School in Late Antique Athens and Alexandria (Outstanding Publ. award, 2007). Office: Ind Univ Ballantine Hall 742 1020 E Kirkwood Ave Bloomington IN 47403

WATTS, EMILY STIPES, retired English language educator; b. Urbana, Ill., Mar. 16, 1936; d. Royal Arthur and Virginia Louise (Schenck) Stipes; m. Robert Allan Watts, Aug. 30, 1958; children: Benjamin, Edward, Thomas. Student, Smith Coll., 1954-56; AB, U. Ill., 1958, MA (Woodrow Wilson Nat. fellow), 1959, PhD, 1963. Instr. English U. Ill., Urbana, 1963-67, asst. prof., 1967-73, assoc. prof., 1973-77, prof., dir. grad. studies dept. English, 1977—2005, prof. emerita, 2005—; bd. dirs. U. Ill. Athletic Assn., chmn., 1981-83; mem. faculty adv. com. Ill. Bd. Higher Edn., 1984—, vice chmn., 1986-87, chmn., 1987-88. Author: Ernest Hemingway and The Arts, 1971, The Poetry of American Women from 1632 to 1945, 1977, The Businessman in American Literature, 1982; contbg. editor: English Women Writers from the Middle Ages to the Present, 1990; contbr. articles on Jonathan Edwards, Anne Bradstreet to lit. jours. John Simon Guggenheim Meml. Found. fellow, 1973-74 Mem. Am. Inst. Archaeology, Assn. Lit. Scholars Critics, Authors Guild, Ill. Hist. Soc., The Phila. Soc., Phi Beta Kappa, Phi Kappa Phi. Presbyterian. Home: 937 Cheshire Dr Champaign IL 61821-3317

WATTS, EMMA, film company executive; Exec. v.p. prodn. 20th Century Fox, co-pres. prodn., 2007—. Named one of The 100 Most Powerful Women in Entertainment, Hollywood Reporter, 2007. Office: 20th Century Fox Film Corp 10201 W Pico Blvd Los Angeles CA 90064 Business E-Mail: emma.watts@fox.com.

WATTS, HAROLD WESLEY, economist, educator; b. Salem, Oreg., Sept. 30, 1932; s. Elton and Claire W.; m. Doris A. Roth, Sept. 28, 1951 (div. 1973); children— Michael Lee, Suzanne, Jane Marie, Kristin. BA, U. Oreg., 1954; MA, Yale U., 1956, PhD, 1957. From instr. to assoc. prof. Yale U., New Haven, 1957-63; from assoc. prof. to prof. econs. U. Wis., Madison, 1963-76, dir. Inst. Research on Poverty, 1966-71; prof. econs. and pub. policy Columbia U., NYC, 1976-98, prof. econs. and pub. policy emeritus, 1998—, dir. Pub. Policy Rsch. Ctr., 1988-93; sr. fellow Mathematica Policy Research Princeton, N.J., 1979-92; sr. rsch. assoc. Urban Inst., 1994-95. Recipient Paul Lazarsfeld award, 1980; Guggenheim fellow, 1975 Fellow Assn. Pub. Policy Analysis and Mgmt., Econometric Soc.; mem. Am. Econ. Assn., L.I. Wine Coun. (pres. 2000-02, sec. 2004-06). Democrat. Home: 144 Bay Ave Greenport NY 11944-1404 Office Phone: 516-384-7186. Personal E-mail: hwesleyw@aol.com.

WATTS, J. C. (JULIUS CAESAR WATTS JR.), lobbyist, former United States Representative from Oklahoma; b. Eufaula, Okla., Nov. 8, 1957; s. Julius Caesar and Helen Watts; m. Frankie Jones; children: LaKesha, Jerrell, Jennifer, Julia, J.C. BA in Journalism, U. Okla., 1981. Profl. football player Ottawa Roughriders, 1981—85, Toronto Argonauts, 1986; owner, pres. Watts Energy Corp., 1987—89; youth min. to assoc. pastor Sunnylane So. Bapt. Ch., Del City, 1987-94; mem. Okla. Corp. Commn., 1990—95, chmn., 1992—95; mem. US Congress from 4th Okla. Dist., 1995—2003, chmn. House Republican Conf., 1999—2003, mem. armed svcs. com., mem. spl. oversight panel on terrorism; chmn. GOPAC, 2003—07; founder, chmn. J.C. Watts Companies, Washington, 2003—; founder Black Television News Channel, 2009—. Mem. Nat. Drinking Water Adv. Coun.; mem. electricity com. Nat. Assn. Regulatory Utility Commrs; hon. co-chmn. Rep. Nat. Conv., 2000. Co-author (with Chriss Watson): What Color is a Conservative?: My Life and My Politics, 2002. Bd. of rep. Fellowship of Christian Athletes, Okla.; leader Orphan Found. of Am., Boy Scouts of Am.; guest preacher; co-chair Coalition for AIDS Relief in Africa. Recipient Black Achievement award, U. Okla., 1981; named Most Valuable Player (Orange Bowl), 1980, 1981; named one of The 50 Top Lobbyists, Washingtonian mag., 2007; named to Orange Bowl Hall of Fame, 1992. Republican. Baptist. Office: JC Watts Companies Ste 790 600 13th St NW Washington DC 20005 Office Phone: 202-207-2854. Office Fax: 202-207-2853.*

WATTS, JOHN RANSFORD, academic administrator; b. Boston, Feb. 9, 1930; s. Henry Fowler Ransford and Mary Marion (Macdonald) Watts; m. Joyce Lannom, Dec. 20, 1975; 1 child, David Allister. AB, Boston Coll., 1950, MEd, 1965; MFA, Yale U., 1953; PhD, Union Grad. Sch., 1978. Prof., ast. dean Boston U., 1958-74; prof., dean fine arts Calif. State U., Long Beach, 1974-79; dean and artistic dir. The Theatre Sch./Goodman Sch. Drama, DePaul U., Chgo., 1979-99, prof. and dean emeritus, 1999—. Mng. dir. DePaul U. Merle Reskin Theatre, 1988-99; gen. mgr. Boston Arts Festivals, 1955-64; adminstr. Arts Programs at Tanglewood, 1966-69; producing dir. Theatre Co. of Boston, 1973-75. Chmn. Mass. Coun. on Arts and Humanities, 1968-72; bd. dirs., v.p. Long Beach Pub. Cofp. for the Arts, 1975-79; mem. theatre panel Ill. Arts Coun., 1981-90. With U.S. Army, 1953-55. Recipient Lifetime Achievement award Joseph Jefferson Com., Chgo., 2000. Mem. Mass. Ednl. Comms. Commn., Am. Theatre Asasn., Nat. Coun. on Arts in Edn., Met. Cultural Alliance, U.S. Inst. Theatre Tech., League Chgo. Theatres, Chgo. Internat. Theatre Festival, St. Botolph Club (Boston), Univ. Club (Chgo.), Phi Beta Kappa, Phi Kappa Phi.

WATTS, JOHN S., JR., insurance company executive; BA in English, UCLA. Various mgmt. positions HealthNet, Northwestern Nat. Life Ins. Co.; regional dir. LA sales office Blue Cross of Calif., 1995—97, gen. mgr. large grp. svcs., 1997; acting sr. v.p. UNICARE comml. accounts large grp. divsn. ea., so. and ctrl. regions WellPoint Health Networks, Inc.; sr. v.p. large group divsn. Blue Cross and Blue Shield of Ga. (subs. WellPoint Health Networks, Inc.), 2001—03, pres., CEO, 2003—04; pres., CEO nat. accounts strategic bus. unit WellPoint, Inc, Indpls., 2004—06; pres., CEO comml. and consumer bus. strategic bus. unit WellPoint, Inc., Indpls., 2006—. Office: WellPoint Inc 120 Monument Cir Indianapolis IN 46204

WATTS, KISHA MANN, school system administrator, secondary school educator; b. Pensacola, Fla., June 3, 1980; d. Robert Darryl and Karen Theresa Watts. BA, Williams Coll., Williamstown, Mass., 2002. Membership intern Assn. Women in Sci., Washington, 2000; rsch. asst. Marine Biol. Lab., Woods Hole, Mass., 2001; sci. tchr., admissions coord., dir. diversity Thayer Acad., Braintree, Mass., 2002—09, dean girls, 2008—09. Del. for diversity Nat. Assn. Ind. Schs., India, China. Co-chair Nat. Assn. Ind. Schs. People Color Conf., 2007; chair Aisne HS Students Color Conf., 2009. Named to Wall of Tolerance, So. Poverty Law Ctr., 2003. Mem.: NAACP, Assn. Ind. Schs. in New Eng. (mem. diversity bd.), Tchg. Tolerance, Nat. Mus. Am. Indian Art, Nat. Scholars Honor Soc. Avocations: yoga, travel, reading, fitness. Office: Thayer Academy 745 Washington St Braintree MA 02184 Office Fax: 781-843-2916. Personal E-mail: kishamw2002@yahoo.com. Business E-Mail: kwatts@thayer.org.

WATTS, LINDA K., language educator; b. Columbus, Ohio, June 26, 1954; d. Admiral A. and Elizabeth A. Watts. BA in English, SUNY, Buffalo, 1976; MA in Linguistics, SUNY, Amherst, 1979; PhD in Anthropology, Ariz. State U., Tempe, 0192. Assoc. prof. U. Colo., Colo. Springs, 1993—. Author: The Social Semiotics of Relational Terminology at Zuni Pueblo. Clergy ECKANKAR, Chanhassen, Minn., 1990. Democrat. Avocations: writing, travel. Office: Univ Colo 1420 Austin Bluffs Pky Colorado Springs CO 80933-7150 Business E-Mail: lkwatts@uccs.edu.

WATTS, LINDA SUSAN, humanities educator; BA, U. Del., 1981, MA in History, 1983; MA in Am. Studies, Yale U., 1986, PhD in Am. Studies, 1989. Instr. history and Am. studies U. Del., Newark, 1981—83; instr. English and Am. studies Yale U., New Haven, 1984—86, coord. sr. essays and projects in Am. studies, 1987—89; vis. asst. prof. English, Am. studies, and Afro-Am. studies Wesleyan U., Middletown, Conn., 1989—90; asst. prof. Drake U., Des Moines, 1990—95, asst. prof., assoc. dir. women's studies program, 1992—93, assoc. prof. English, 1995—96, assoc. prof. English, assoc. dean Coll. of Arts and Scis., 1996—99; prof. Am. studies, dir. interdisciplinary arts and scis. program U. Wash., Bothell, 1999—2001, prof. Am. studies, interdisciplinary arts and scis. program, 2001—. Author: Rapture Untold: Gender, Mysticism, and 'The Moment of Recognition' in the Writings of Gertrude Stein, 1996, Gertrude Stein: A Study of the Short Fiction, 1999, Encyclopedia of American Folklore, 2006; contbg. author: The World Is Our Home: Society and Culture in Contemporary Southern Writing; co-author: Social History of the United States: The 1920's, 2008, Social History of the United States: The 1900's, 2008; contbr. articles to profl. jours. HIV/AIDS cmty. edn. instr. ARC, Des Moines, 1992—99, HIV/AIDS instr. trainer, 1996—99; vol. literacy tutor Adult Literacy Ctr., Des Moines, 1998—99; vol. mus. visitor svcs. Experience Music Project, Seattle, 2000—01; vol. AIDS Greater Des Moines, 1992—93, Selfhelp Crafts of the World, Des Moines, 1992—94; vol. curriculum cons., co-instr. Op. Peer Helper, ARC Youth Program, Des Moines, 1993—93; vol. edn. com. mem. AIDS Project of Greater Des Moines, 1993—95; chair HIV/AIDS edn. program com. ARC, Des Moines, 1994—95, vol. mem. HIV/AIDS edn. program com., 1995—99; vol. planning com. mem. World AIDS Day Observance, State of Iowa, Des Moines, 1997—98. Recipient Editor's Choice award for outstanding achievement in poetry, poetry.com, 2000, Open Poetry Competition award, King County Pub. Art Program, State of Wash., 2000, Internat. Poet of Merit award, Internat. Soc. Poets, 2002; named Semi-Finalist N.Am. Open Poetry Contest, Internat. Libr. of Poetry, 2000, Internat. Libr. Poetry, 2001; finalist Women's Studies grant, Woodrow Wilson Found., 1988, Manuscript award, Ill. Nat. Women's Studies Assn., 1990; nominee Poet of Yr., Internat. Soc. Poets, 2001. Mem.: Phi Beta Kappa, Phi Alpha Theta, Phi Kappa Phi. Office: Univ Wash Bothell Box 358511 11136 NE 180th St Bothell WA 98011-8246 Business E-Mail: lwatts@uwh.edu. E-mail: lswatts@u.washington.edu.

WATTS, MARY ANN, retired elementary school educator; b. Harrisburg, Pa., Sept. 13, 1927; d. Major Allan and Ellana Susan (Robinson) Brown; m. Spencer R. Watts, June 23, 1951; children: Shelley Lynn, Allison Dee, Howard Allan. BS, Cheyney U., 1949; postgrad., Temple U., 1965—67, Pa. State U., 1969—72, student, 2003—, BA in Profl. Writing, 2007. Tchr. Harrisburg Sch. Dist., 1949-51, 59-69, Balt. Sch. Dist., 1951-57, Reading (Pa.) Sch. Dist., 1969-89; keynote spkr. Martin Luther King Day East Stroudsburg U., 1998. Mem. sch. dist. dress and discipline code com., 1977-79. Corr. Hamburg Item. Bd. dirs. Pa. State Assn. Boroughs, mem. resolutions and policy com.; mem. Bernville Borough Coun., 1976-2003, v.p., 1988-93, 96-98; sec., treas. Berks County Borough Assn., 1977-2003; Reach to Recovery vol. Am. Cancer Soc., 1992-2007. Recipient Disting. Alumna award for achievement in govt. and politics Cheyney U., 1999, Achievement award Ctrl. Pa. African Am. Mus., 2009. Mem. NAACP, Pa. State Edn. Assn. (life), Pa. Assn. Sch. Retirees, Reading Assn. Sch. Retirees, Bernville Woman's Club (pres. 1978-80, 86-88, Woman of Yr. 1985, Grange Cmty. Svc. award 1988), Pa. State U. Alumni Assn., Cheyney Alumni Assn. Democrat.

WATTS, NAOMI, actress; b. Shoreham, Kent, Eng., Sept. 28, 1968; d. Peter and Myfanwy Watts; 2 children (with Liev Schreiber) Alexander Pete Schreiber, Samuel Kai Schreiber Spl. envoy on HIV/AIDS UN, 2006—. Spokesmodel Angel fragrance by Thierry Mugler, 2008. Actor: (films) For Love Alone, 1986, Flirting, 1991, Matinee, 1993, Wide Sargasso Sea, 1993, Gross Misconduct, 1993, The Custodian, 1993, Tank Girl, 1995, Children of the Corn IV: The Gathering, 1996, Persons Unknown, 1996, Under the Lighthouse Dreaming, 1997, Dangerous Beauty, 1998, A House Divided, 1998, Strange Planet, 2001, Ellie Parker, 2001, Down, 2001, Mulholland Drive, 2001, The Ring, 2002, Plots with a View, 2002, Rabbits, 2002, Ned Kelly, 2003, Le Divorce, 2003, 21 Grams, 2003 (Acad. Award nomination for best actress, 2004, Screen Actors Guild Award nomination for best actress, 2004), We Don't Live Here Anymore, 2004, The Assassination of Richard Nixon, 2004, I Heart Huckabees, 2004, Ellie Parker, 2005, The Ring Two, 2005, Stay, 2005, King Kong, 2005, The Painted Veil, 2006, (voice) Inland Empire, 2006, Eastern Promises, 2007, Funny Games, 2008, The International, 2009; (TV films) Bermuda Triangle, 1996, Timepiece, 1996, The Christmas Wish, 1998, The Hunt for the Unicorn Killer, 1999, The Wyvern Mystery, 2000, The Outsider, 2002; (TV miniseries) Brides of Christ, 1991; (TV series) Home and Away, 1991, Sleepwalkers, 1997. Office: c/o Untitled Entertainment 1801 Century Park E Los Angeles CA 90067

WATTS, OLIVER EDWARD, engineering company executive; b. Hayden, Colo., Sept. 22, 1939; s. Oliver Easton and Vera Irene (Hockett) W.; m. Charla Ann French, Aug. 12, 1962; children: Erik Sean, Oliver Eron, Sherilyn. BS, Colo. State U., 1962. Registered profl. engr., Colo., Calif.; profl. hand surveyor, Colo. Crew chief Colo. State U. Rsch. Found., Ft. Collins, 1962; with Calif. Dept. Water Resources, Gustine and Castaic, 1964-70; land and water engr. CF&I Steel Corp., Pueblo, Colo., 1970-71; engring. dir. United Western Engrs., Colorado Springs., Colo., 1971-76; ptnr. United Planning and Engring Co., Colorado Springs, 1976-79; owner Oliver E. Watts, Cons. Engr., Colorado Springs, 1979—. Dir. edn. local Ch. of Christ, 1969-71, deacon, 1977-87, elder, 1987-96. 1st lt. C.E., AUS, 1962-64. Recipient Individual Achievement award Colo. State U. Coll. Engring., 1981. Fellow ASCE (life; v.p. Colorado Springs br. 1975, pres. 1978); mem. NSPE (pres. Pike's Peak chpt. 1975, sec. Colo. sect. 1976, v.p. 1977, pres. 1978-79, Young Engr. award 1976, Pres.'s award 1979), Cons. Engrs. Coun. Colo. (bd. dirs. 1981-83), Am. Cons. Engrs. Coun., Profl. Land Surveyors Colo., Colo. Engrs. Coun. (del. 1980—), Colo. State U. Alumni Assn. (v.p., dir. Pike's Peak chpt. 1972-76), Lancers, Lambda Chi Alpha. Home: 7195 Dark Horse Pl Colorado Springs CO 80919-1442 Office: 614 Elkton Dr Colorado Springs CO 80907-3514

WATTS, ROBERT ALLAN, publisher, lawyer; b. July 4, 1936; s. Richard P. and Florence (Hooker) W.; m. Emily Stipes, Aug. 30, 1958; children: Benjamin H., Edward S., Thomas J. Student, DePauw U., 1954-55; BA, U. Ill., 1959, JD, 1961. Bar: (Ill.) 1961. Assoc. Stipes Pub. Co., Champaign, Ill., 1962-67, ptnr., editor, 1967—. Treas. Planned Parenthood, 1976—80; mem. Pres.'s Coun., U. Ill.; pres. Friends of Libr., U. Ill., 1980—82; treas. Campaign Rep. Party, 1976—80; bd. dirs. local United Way, 1972—81, City of Champaign Libr. Found., 1993—2007. Mem. Ill. Bar Assn., U. Ill. Found., Nat. Acad. Arts (bd. dirs. 1983-89), Champaign Country Club, Saugatuck Yacht Club (commodore), Lake Shore Bath & Tennis Club (pres. 1983-85). Home: 937 Cheshire Dr Champaign IL 61821-3317 Office: Stipes Publishing Co 204 W University Ave Champaign IL 61820-3912

WATTS, ROSS LESLIE, finance educator; b. Hamilton, Australia, Nov. 10, 1942; came to U.S., 1966; s. Leslie R. and Elsie B. (Horadam) W. m. Helen Clare Firkin, Jan. 15, 1966 (div. 2007); children: Andrew David, James Michael. B in Commerce with honors Commonwealth Govt. scholar 1960-65), U. Newcastle, Australia, 1966; MBA Ford Found. fellow 1967-68, U. Chgo., 1968, PhD, 1971. Audit clk. Forsythe & Co., Newcastle, Australia, 1960-64, acct., 1964-66; instr. Grad. Sch. Bus., U. Chgo., 1969-70; asst. prof. Simon Sch. Mgmt., U. Rochester, NY, 1971-78, assoc. prof. NY, 1978-84, prof. NY, 1984-86; endowed chair Rochester Telephone Corp., 1986-98; William H. Meckling prof. U. Rochester, NY, 1998—2005; prof. Sloan Sch. MIT, Cambridge, Mass., 2005—. Prof. commerce U. Newcastle, 1974-76; hon. prof. City U. Hong Kong, 1996-; disting. lectr. Hong Kong U. Sci. and Tech., 1994; vis. prof. MIT, 2002; cons. in field. Contbr. articles on acctg. rsch. to profl. jours.; assoc. editor Jour. Acctg. Rsch., 1972-78, Jour. Fin. Econs., 1974-89, Australian Jour. Mgmt., 1976-81; co-editor Jour. Acctg. and Econs., 1979—; editor Jour. Acctg. Abstracts, 1995-97; dir., editor Acctg. Rsch. Network, 1997—; mem. adv. bd. Midland Corp. Fin. Jour., 1983-88, Continental Bank Jour. of Applied Corp. Fin., 1988-94, Bank Am. Jour. Applied Corp. Fin., 1994—; mem. editorial bd. Contemporary Acctg. Rsch., 1983-85; cons. editor Asia Pacific Jour. Acctg. Econs., 1998-2005; cons. editor Jour. Contemporary Acctg. and Econs., 2005-. Recipient Notable Contbn. award AICPA, 1979, 80, award Alpha Kappa Psi Found., 1985. Mem. Am. Acctg. Assn. (Outstanding Educator award 2000, Seminal Rsch. award 2004), Am. Fin. Assn., Inst. Chartered Accts. in Australia. Home: 22 Park St Arlington MA 02474 Office: MIT Sloan Sch 50 Memorial Blvd Cambridge MA 02142-1347 Office Phone: 617-253-2668. Business E-Mail: rwatts@mit.edu.

WATTS, STEPHEN HURT, II, lawyer; b. Lynchburg, Va., Feb. 21, 1947; s. James Owen Jr. and Sarah Webb (Key) W.; m. Beverley Allan Brockenbrough, July 16, 1969 (div. 1986): children: Day Lowry, Stephen Hurt Jr.; m. Sally Yates Wood, May 24, 1986 (div. 1995); m. Mollie Crawford Talbott;, March 24, 1999. BA, Washington & Lee U., 1968; JD, U. Va., 1972. Bar: Va. 1972, W.Va. 1973. Law clk. Taylor, Michie & Callahan, Charlottesville, Va., 1970-72; assoc. Spilman, Thomas, Battle & Klostermeyer, Charleston, W.Va., 1972-75; ptnr. Watts & Watts, Lynchburg, Va., 1975-77; v.p., counsel Commonwealth Gas Pipeline Corp., Richmond, 1977-81; gen. counsel Commonwealth Natural Resources, Inc., Richmond, 1980-81; assoc. McGuire Woods LLP (formerly McGuire, Woods, Battle & Boothe, LLP), Richmond, 1981-83, ptnr., 1983—. Bd. dirs. Lower Fan Civic Assn., Richmond, 1987-91, TheatreVirginia, Richmond, 1992-93, Va. Oil and Gas Assn., 1993; pres., bd. dirs. Studio Theatre Richmond, 1991-93; chmn. outreach com. Grace and Holy Trinity Episcopal Ch., Richmond, 1993. Mem. ABA, Va. State Bar (dir. adminstrv. law sect., chmn. 1995-96), Fed. Energy Bar Assn. Office: McGuire Woods LLP One James Center 901 E Cary St Richmond VA 23219-4057 E-mail: swatts@mcguirewoods.com.

WATTS, SUSAN HELENE, theater educator; d. Howard Harold and Madelyn Rebecca (Moore) Watts. BA, Mich. State U., 1963; MS, U. Kans., 1984. Tchr. Douglas County Schs., Castle Rock, Colo., 1964—74; owner/mgr. Old Bank Cafe, Oskaloosa, Kans., 1976—80; tchr. Valley Falls H.S., 1984—86; instr. Highland C.C., 1986—89; tchr. Oskaloosa H.S., 1986—89; communication coord./actor Omaha Magic Theatre, 1989—90; instr./divsn. chair McCook C.C., 1990—. Charter mem. Leadership McCook, 1990—; bd. mem. S.W. Nebr. Cmty. Theater Assn., 1990—2001; del. Nebr. Transfer Initiative, 1995—; chair local integrity subcom. North Ctrl. Accreditation Com., 1998—2001; adv. bd. Bright Beginnings, 1997—2001; mem. Campus Pres.'s Adv. Coun., 1993—97. Actor: (plays) Marvin's Room, Pools Paradise, Morning's At Seven, (stand up comedy) An Evening with Cassandra; author: (humor column) Dear Cassandra; dir.: (over sixty plays and musicals) (Outstanding Kans. Theatre Tchr., 1983). Banquet com. writer/performer McCook C. of C., 1998—2002; mem. goal setting task force McCook City Coun., 1998—98; mem. McCook Humane Soc., McCook, 1995—2003; bd. dirs. SpringFest, 1998—2000. Named Outstanding Kans. Theatre Tchr., Assn. Kans. Theatre, 1983. Mem.: NEA, Soc. Stage Dir. Choregraphers,

Mid-Plains Edn. Assn., Nebr. State Edn. Assn., Kiwanis, Alpha Delta Kappa, Delta Kappa Gamma. Avocations: golf, gardening. Office: McCook Cmty Coll 1205 E Third Mc Cook NE 69001

WATTS, THOMAS PARRISH, history educator, consultant; m. Judy Marie Griffith, Nov. 24, 1968; 1 child, Shelly Dawn Watts-Dognazzi. BS, U. of So. Miss., Hattiesburg, 1971; MEd, U. of So. Calif., LA, 1978; M of Strategic Studies, Nat. Def. U., Washington, 1994. Nat. bd. cert. profl. tchr. Nat. Bd. for Profls. Tchg. Stds. Bn. comdr. 1313th Transp. Ocean Port Bn., Seattle, 1990—92; mil. adviser to sec. of def. Office of the Sec. of Def., Washington, 1992—93; mil. adviser to U.S. amb. U.S. Mission to NATO, Brussels, 1994—97; dir., instr. U.S. Army War Coll., Carlisle Barracks, Pa., 1997—99; dep. dir. Miss. Dept. of Human Svcs., Jackson, Miss., 1999—2000; tchr. Am. history Madison Mid. Sch., Miss., 2000—. Editor: (ednl. package) Tracing Our Trace (Nat. Geog. Soc. grant, 2002, Nissan Edn. grant, 2007). Col. US Army, 1971—99. Decorated Legion of Merit, Def. Meritorious Svc. Medal, Army Meritorious Medals (4), Joint Svc. Commendation Medal, Army Commendation Medal (4) US Def. Dept. and US Army; recipient John K. Bettersworth Hist. Tchr. Award, 2008; named Disting. Mem. of U.S. Army Transp. Corps' Rgt., 2006, 2002 - 2003 Tchr. of Yr., Madison County Sch. Dist., 2003, Gilda - Lehrman History Tchr. of Yr. for Miss., Gilda - Lehrman History Inst., 2005, Dar's Miss. History Tchr. of Yr., 2009. Mem.: VFW (life), Miss. Hist. Soc., Nat. Def. Transp. Assn., Am. Legion, Nat. Assn. of Social Studies Educators. Independent. Methodist. Avocations: history, travel. Office: Madison Midd Sch 1365 Mannsdale Rd Madison MS 39110 Office Fax: 601-853-2254; Home Fax: 601-853-2254. Personal E-mail: tomw1048@aol.com. Business E-Mail: twatts@madison-schools.com.

WATTS, VIRGINIA AGNES, retired special education educator; b. Hampstead, Md., Mar. 14, 1925; d. Thomas Leister and Anna (Freyer) Beam; m. Ervin Olman Watts., Sr., Feb. 9, 1946 (dec. 1972); 1 child, Ervin. RN, St. Agnes Hosp. Sch. Nursing, Balt., 1945; BS, U. Md., 1969, MS, 1974. Nurse St. Agnes Hosp., 1945-46; spl. edn. tchr. Anne Arundel Bd. Edn., Annapolis, Md., 1958-85; tchr. A. A. Co., 1998—99; pres. AARP Chpt., 1997—2006. Recipient Richard H. Carter award, Glen Burnie Improvement Assn., 2006. Mem. AARP (state housing coord. 1992-93, local health coord. 1993-96, bd. dirs. Capitol City task force 1997—, state legis. coun. 1997—, pres. Md. chpt. 2006), Anne Arundel County Retired Tchrs. Assn. (pres. elect 1997, pres. 1998), Md. Sr. Citizen Hall of Fame (bd. dirs. 1999-). Republican. Home: 714 Cotter Rd Glen Burnie MD 21060-7330

WATTS, WENDY HAZEL, wine consultant; b. York, Pa., Oct. 9, 1952; d. Alphonso Irving and Daphne Jean (Gainsford) Watts; m. Frederic Joseph Bonnie, (div. 1986); m. Kenneth Scott Herron, Feb. 14, 1987 (div. Jan. 1992). BS, U. Cin., 1975. Store mgr. The Grapevine, Inc., Birmingham, Ala., 1978-81; sales rep. Supreme Beverage Co., Birmingham, 1981-84, Internat. Wines Co., Birmingham, 1984-90; nat. sales exec. Kermit Lynch Wine Mcht., Berkeley, Calif., 1990-91; on-premise mgr., fine wine mgr. Premier Beverage Co., Birmingham, 1991-94; key accounts mgr. Ala. Crown Distbg. Co., Birmingham, 1994-95; dir. of wine Mountain Brook location Western Supermarkets, 1995—2001; dist. mgr. Winebow Italian Imports, 2001—05, state mgr., 2005—07; creative dir. Vintage Wine Shoppes, 2007—. Instr. ednl. wine tasting classes, 1996—; spkr., instr. various groups, Birmingham; co-chmn. Sonoma Wine Tour of Birmingham, 1987—88, chmn., 1989—90, Wine Tour of France, Birmingham, 1988—89; mem. exec. com. Taste of the Nation, 1992—98. Wine radio show host, 1992, Wine Edn. Videos, 2009—. Co-chmn. Multiple Sclerosis Wine Auction, 1992—93, mem. exec. com., 1997—; co-chair Share Our Strength Taste of the Nation, Birmingham, 1996-98; bd. dirs. Magic City Harvest, 1999—, vice chair, 2005—; mem. com. So. Environ. Ctr. Democrat. Avocations: wine and food tasting, designing, films, hiking, Italian language and culture. Home Phone: 205-467-7136; Office Phone: 205-980-9995. Personal E-mail: winewench@windstream.net.

WATTY URQUIDI, RICARDO, bishop; b. San Diego, Calif., July 16, 1938; Attended, Sem. of Missionaries of the Holy Spirit, Mexico City. Ordained priest Missionaries of the Holy Spirit, 1968; prof. Minor Seminary of Quetzaltenango, Mexico; vice superior, vicariate of Mexico Missionaries of the Holy Spirit; rector Seminary of the Missionaries of the Holy Spirit, Mexico City; ordained bishop, 1980; aux. bishop Archdiocese of Mexico, 1980—89; bishop Diocese of Nuevo Laredo, Tamaulipas, Mexico, 1989—2008, Diocese of Tepic, Nayarit, Mexico, 2008—. Roman Catholic. Office: Diocese of Tepic Apartado 15 Ave de las Flores 10 63137 Tepic Mexico

WAUD, ROGER NEIL, economist, educator; b. Detroit, Mar. 26, 1938; s. Othneil Stockwell and Mary Josephine (Gough) Waud; children: Heather, Neil. BA, Harvard U., 1960; MA, U. Calif., Berkeley, 1962; PhD (Ford Found. fellow), U. Calif., Berekley, 1965. Asst. prof. bus. econs. Grad. Sch. Bus. U. Chgo., 1964-69; assoc. prof. econs. U. N.C., Chapel Hill, 1969-72, prof., 1972-97, prof. emeritus, 1997—; sr. economist, bd. govs. Fed. Res. Sys., Washington, 1973-75; prof., dir. grad. econs. program Va. Tech., 1997—2002. Cons. Dept. Labor; mem. adv. bd. Taxpayers Ednl. Coalition, 1981; rsch. assoc. Nat. Bur. Econ. Rsch., 1982—92; vis. scholar Cambridge U., 1983; mem. N.C. Energy Policy Coun., 1986—92; vis. prof. Duke U., 1992—94. Author: Macroeconomics, 5th edit., 1992, Microeconomics, 5th edit., 1992; mem. editl. bd. So. Econ. Jour., 1970—73, Studies Econs. and Fin., 1995—97; contbr. articles to profl. jours. Mem.: So. Econ. Assn. (exec. com. 1977—79), Am. Econ. Assn.

WAUGH, JOHN STEWART, chemist, educator; b. Willimantic, Conn., Apr. 25, 1929; s. Albert E. and Edith (Stewart) W.; married 1983; children: Alice Collier, Frederick Pierce. AB, Dartmouth Coll., 1949; PhD, Calif. Inst. Tech., 1953; ScD (hon.), Dartmouth Coll., 1989. Rsch. fellow in physics Calif. Inst. Tech., 1952-53; mem. faculty MIT, Cambridge, 1953—, prof. chemistry, 1962—, Albert Amos Noyes prof. chemistry, 1973-88, inst. prof., 1989—, emeritus, 1996—. Vis. prof. U. Calif.-Berkeley, 1963-64, Max Planck Inst., Heidelberg, 1972; sr. fellow Alexander von Humboldt-Stiftung; vis. scientist Harvard U., 1976; mem. chemistry adv. panel NSF, 1966-69, vice chmn., 1968-69; mem. rev. com. Argonne Nat. Lab., 1970-74; mem. sci. and edn. adv. com. Lawrence Berkeley Lab., 1980-86; exchange visitor USSR Acad. Scis., 1962, 75; mem. vis. com. Tufts U., 1966-69, Princeton, 1973-78; mem. fellowship com. Alfred P. Sloan Found., 1977-82; Joliot-Curie prof. École Supérieure de Physique et Chemie, Paris, 1985, 96; lectr. in field. Author: New NMR Methods in Solid State Physics, 1978; editor: Advances in Magnetic Resonance, 1965-87; assoc. editor: Jour. Chem. Physics, 1965-67, Spectrochimica Acta, 1964-78; mem. editl. bd. Chem. Revs., 1978-82, Jour. Magnetic Resonance, 1989—, Applied Magnetic Resonance, 1989—. Recipient Irving Langmuir award, 1976, Gold Pick Axe award, 1976, Pitts. award Spectroscopic Soc. Pitts., 1979, Wolf prize in chemistry, Wolf Found., 1984, Pauling medal, 1985, Calif. Inst. Tech. disting. alumnus award, 1987, Killian award, 1988, ISMAR prize, 1989, Richards medal, 1992, Evans award, 1994, Ea. Analytical Symposium award 1996, Russell Varian prize, 2006; Sloan fellow, 1958-62, Guggenheim fellow, 1963-64, 72; Sherman Fairchild scholar Calif. Inst. Tech., 1989. Fellow: AAAS, Am. Phys. Soc. (chmn. divsn. chemistry and physics 1983—84), Sigma Xi; mem.: NAS, Slovenian Acad. Sci. and Arts (fgn. corr.), Nat. Magnetic Resonance Soc. India (hon.), Internat. Soc. Magnetic Resonance (coun. mem. 1989—95, exec. com. 1996—, v.p. 1997—, pres. 1999—2002), Phi Beta Kappa. Office: MIT 6-231 77 Massachusetts Ave Cambridge MA 02139-4307 Home Phone: 781-259-8030; Office Phone: 617-253-1901. Business E-Mail: jswaugh@mit.edu.

WAUGH, THEODORE ROGERS, orthopedic surgeon; b. Montreal, Sept. 21, 1926; s. Theodore Rogers and Anne Maude (Lawlor) W.; children: Susanne Rogers, Margaret Stewart, Theodore Rogers. BA, Yale U., 1949; MD, CM, McGill U., 1953; DMS, U. Goteborg, Sweden, 1968. Diplomate Am. Bd. Orthop. Surgery. Intern Royal Victoria Hosp., Montreal, 1953-54; asst. resident in pathology McGill U., 1954-55; asst. resident in surgery NYU Bellevue Med. Ctr., 1955-56; capt., M.C. USAF, 1956—58, lt. col., res., CMDR 695th MSCSU, 1959—66; asst. resident, resident, fellow N.Y. Orthop. Hosp., Columbia U., 1958-62, instr., clin. asst. prof. orthop. surgery, 1962-68; asst. attending Presbyn. Hosp., NYC, 1962-68; prof., chief divsn. orthop. surgery U. Calif., Irvine, 1966-78; prof., chmn. dept. orthop. surgery NYU Med. Ctr., 1978-96, emeritus prof., 1997—. Adj. prof. surgery Dartmouth U. Sch. Medicine, 1998-2003, adj. prof. orthopaedics, 2003—. Contbr. numerous articles to profl. jours. Fellow ACS, Royal Coll. Surgeons (Can.), Am. Acad. Orthop. Surgeons, Scoliosis Rsch. Soc., Assn. Bone and Joint Surgeons, Am. Orthop. Assn., Am. Orthop. Soc. Sports Medicine; mem. 20th Century Orthopedic Club, Alpha Omega Alpha. Presbyterian. Achievements include developing designer surgical devices used in orthopaedic surgery, in-vivo measurement of forces in correction of spinal deformity (scoliosis). E-mail: trwmd3@comcast.net.

WAUGH, WILLIAM HOWARD, physician, research scientist; b. NYC, May 13, 1925; s. Richey Laughlin and Lyda Pearl (Leamer) W.; m. Eileen Loretta Garrigan, Oct. 4, 1952; children: Mark Howard, Kathleen Cary, William Peter. Student, Boston U., 1943, W.Va. U., 1944; MD, Tufts U., 1948, postgrad., 1949—50. Cardiovascular rsch. trainee Med. Coll. Ga., Augusta, 1954-55, asst. rsch. prof. physiology, 1955-60, assoc. medicine, 1957-60; assoc. prof. medicine U. Ky., Lexington, 1960-69; Ky. Heart Assn. Chair in cardiovascular rsch. Ky. Heart Assn., Lexington, 1963-71; prof. medicine U. Ky., Lexington, 1969-71; prof. medicine and physiology East Carolina U., Greenville, 1971—2001, rsch. prof. physiology, 2001—04, prof. emeritus, 2001—. Head renal sect. U. Ky. Coll., Lexington, 1960-68; chmn. dept. clin. scis. East Carolina U., Greenville, 1971-75, chmn. policy and rev. com. on human rsch., 1972-90. Contbr. articles to profl. jours. With AUS, 1943-46; capt. USAF, 1952-54. Recipient NC Med. Soc. award, 1998. Fellow: ACP; mem.: AAAS, Microcirculatory Soc. (50-Yr. club), Am. Physiology Soc., NC Med. Soc. (life). Achievements include basic advances in excitation contraction coupling in vasc. smooth muscle; basic advances in autoregulation of renal blood flow and urine flow; adj. therapy in acute lung edema; noncovalent antisickling agents and amino acid nutrient in sickle cell hemoglobinopathy; oral citrulline as dietary supplement in man; daily intermittent peritoneal dialysis. Home: 119 Oxford Rd Greenville NC 27858-4954 Personal E-mail: ewwaugh@suddenlink.net.

WAUN, ROGER, small business owner, minister; b. Mount Clemens, Mich., Oct. 20, 1944; m. Vicki Waun; 5 children. BS, Eastern Mich. U., 1966, MA, 1968; attended, Pitts. Theol. Sem. Strategic intelligence officer US Army Reserves; co-owner regional wholesale distributorship bus.; pastor First Presbyn. Ch., Childress, Tex., Quanah. Democrat. Office: One Surrey Cir Wichita Falls TX 76309 Business E-Mail: roger@rogerwaun.com.*

WAUTISCHER, HELMUT, philosophy educator; s. Franz and Aloisia Wautischer. PhD, Karl Franzens U., Graz, Austria. Lectr. San Diego State U., 1988—91, Calif. State U., Long Beach, 1989—92; vis. asst. prof. Humboldt State U., Arcata, Calif., 1992—94; sr. lectr. Sonoma State U., Rohnert Park, Calif., 1995—. Editor: (book) Tribal Epistemologies, 1998, Ontology of Conciousness, 2008; contbr. articles to profl. jours. Mem.: Karl Jaspers Soc. North America (exec. bd. 2008—), Soc. for the Anthropology of Consciousness (exec. bd. 1991—99), Coun. of Philos. Socs. (exec. bd. 1997—). Office: Sonoma State U Dept Philosophy 1801 E Cotati Ave Rohnert Park CA 94928-3609 E-mail: wautisch@sonoma.edu.

WAVLE, JAMES EDWARD, JR., pharmaceutical company executive, lawyer; b. NYC, July 19, 1942; s. James Edward and Florence Marie (Kehoe) W.; children from previous marriage: James Edward, William Patrick, Robert Thomas, Stephanie Elizabeth; m. Elizabeth Edith Symons Tallett; 1 child, Christopher Andrew; stepchildren: James E. Tallett, Alexander M. Tallett. BA, Adelphi U., 1964; JD, Georgetown U., 1967; LLM, NYU, 1968. Bar: N.Y. bar 1967. With Warner-Lambert Co., Morris Plains, N.J., 1968-87, internat. counsel, 1971-74, assoc. gen. counsel, 1974-77, v.p., gen. counsel, 1977-80, sr. v.p., gen. counsel 1980-81; corp. sr. v.p. and pres. Parke-Davis Group, 1982-87; pres., CEO Centocor Inc., Malvern, Pa., 1987-92; chmn. Dioscor Inc., Stockton, N.J., 1993-97; chmn., pres., CEO Therics, Inc., Princeton, NJ, 1997—2003. Personal E-mail: jwavle@comcast.net.

WAWRYTKO, SANDRA ANN, humanities educator; b. Chgo., Oct. 18, 1951; d. Stanley Andrew Wawrytko and Alyce Valerie Cioch-Wawrytko; m. Charles Wei-hsun Fu, Sept. 29, 1994 (dec. Oct. 15, 1996). BA in Philosophy, Knox Coll., 1972; MA in Philosophy, Washington U., 1975, PhD in Philosophy, 1976. Instr. Washington U., St. Louis, 1973—77; prof. San Diego State U., 1980—. Vis. prof. Chinese Culture U., Yangmingshan, Taiwan, 1984, Fo Guang Buddhist Coll., Kaohsiung, Taiwan, 1990—2007; prin. investigator Lang. Acquisition Rsch. Ctr., San Diego State U., 1994—2003; vis. prof. U. San Diego, 1978—81; founder, exec. dir. Internat. Soc. for Philosophy and Psychotherapy. Author: The Undercurrent of Feminine Philosophy in Eastern and Western Thought, 1981, CRYSTAL: Spectrums of Chinese Culture Through Poetry, 1995; editor: North American Institute of Zen Buddhist Studies, Rethinking the Curriculum: Toward an Integrated Interdisciplinary Education, 1990, The Problem of Evil, 2000, (book series) Asian Thought and Culture, Philosophy and Psychotherapy; co-author: The Buddhist Religion, 1996; narrator: interactive CD-ROM Crystals of Chinese Culture, 2000, author, editor: Saving the Elephant: Asian Encounters with Imperialism, Orientalism, and Gloablization, 2004. Edn. rep. San Diego Sister City Program, Yantai, China, 1985; mem. editl. bd. Jour. Chinese Philosophy; mem. student Fulbright program nat. screening com.; bd. dirs. San Diego Chinese Hist. Soc. and Mus., 2002—; pres., founder Charles Wei-hsun Fu Found., San Diego, 1997—. Recipient Humanities Advancement Poetry Contest award, Humanities Advancement Com., 1983; fellow, Washington. U., 1974—75. Mem.: World Congress of Logotherapy (sec.-gen. 1982—85), Internat. Soc. for Chinese Philosophy (sec., exec. bd. mem. 1990—2003), Phi Beta Delta (governing bd. 2002—06), Phi Beta Kappa (Faculty Lectr. Nu chpt. 2002—03). Avocations: poetry, translating classical Chinese poetry, collecting Asian art and books, creating culinary adventures. Office: San Diego State U Dept Philosophy San Diego CA 92182-0303 E-mail: wawrytko@mail.sdsu.edu.

WAWRZASZEK, SUSAN V., university librarian; MSLS, SUNY Buffalo. With Brandeis U., Mass., 1995—, assoc. univ. libr. Mass., 2002—03, acting univ. libr. Mass., 2003—05, univ. libr. Mass., 2005—. Office: Brandeis U Mailstop 045 PO Box 549110 Waltham MA 02454-9110 Office Phone: 781-736-4700. Office Fax: 781-736-4719. E-mail: wawrzaszek@brandeis.edu.

WAX, ALAN S., language educator; s. Morton Leonard and Lois Mildred Wax. BA, No. Ill. U., Dekalb, 1971; Med, U. Ill., Champaign, 1979. French tchr. Sch. Dist. 123, Oak Lawn, Ill., 1972—2005; French instr. Moraine Valley CC, Palos Hills, Ill., 2002—, Sutherland Sch. Internat. Baccalaureate Sch., Chgo. Co-chair foreign lang. week com. State of Ill., Springfield, 1998—. Recipient Thanks to Tchrs. award, WBBM-TV, Chgo., 1994, Remarkable Promotion of French award, Montreal, 2005. Mem.: Am. Coun. Tchg. of Foreign Lang., Ill. Coun. Tchg. of Foreign Lang., Am. Assn. Tchrs. of French (Nat. Tchg. award 1995). Personal E-mail: awax@comcast.net.

WAX, MARTIN BRUCE, ophthalmologist; b. Bklyn., Aug. 17, 1951; s. Barbara and Harold Rothman (Stepfather); m. Lisa Gettinger, Aug. 11, 1973; 1 child, Sara. BA, U. Rochester, NY, 1973. Sr. dir. discovery rsch. Pfizer, Chesterfield, Mo., 2002—03; v.p. discovery rsch. & preclinical sciences Alcon Labs., Ft. Worth, 2003—08; prof., dept. ophthalmology U. Tex. Southwestern Med. Sch., Dallas; chief med. officer, exec v.p. R & D Pan Optica Inc. Mem. Glaucoma Rsch. Found., San Francisco, Ft. Worth Symphony Orch. Personal E-mail: mbw817@yahoo.com.

WAX, NADINE VIRGINIA, retired bank executive; b. Van Horne, Iowa, Dec. 7, 1927; d. Laurel Lloyd and Viola Henrietta (Schrader) Bobzien; divorced; 1 child, Sharlyn K. Wax Munns. Student, U. Iowa, 1970-71; grad. Nat. Sch. Real Estate and Fin., Ohio State U., 1980-81. Jr. acct. McGladrey, Hansen, Dunn (now McGladrey-Pullen Co., CPAs), Cedar Rapids, Iowa, 1944-47; office mgr. Iowa Securities Co. (now Wells Fargo Mortgage Co.), Cedar Rapids, 1954-55; asst. cashier Mchts. Nat. Bank (now U.S. Bancorp.), Cedar Rapids, 1956-75; asst. v.p. Mchts. Nat. Bank (now U.S. Bancorp), Cedar Rapids, 1976-78, v.p., 1979-90; ret., 1990. Vol. St. Luke's Hosp. Aux., Cedar Rapids, 1981—85, SCORE, 1999—2009; bd. dirs., v.p. Kirkwood C.C. Facilities Found., 1970—2009; bd. dirs., treas. Kirkwood C.C., 1984—91; trustee Indian Creek Nature Ctr., Cedar Rapids, 1974—2009, pres., 1980—81; mem. Linn County Regional Planning Commn., 1982—92, Cedar Rapids-Marion Fine Arts Coun., 1994—97; bd. suprs. Compensation Commn. for Condemnation, 1987—92; bd. dirs. Am. Heart Assn., Cedar Rapids, 1983—94; mem. Iowa Employment and Tng. Coun., Des Moines, 1982—83. Recipient Outstanding Woman award, Cedar Rapids Tribute to Women and Industry, 1984, Gold Mem. award, SCORE, 2009. Mem. Fin. Women Internat. (state edn. chmn. 1982-83), Am. Inst. Banking (bd. dirs. 1968-70), Soc. Real Estate Appraisers (treas. 1978-80), Linn County Bankers Assn. (pres. 1979-80), Cedar Rapids Bd. Realtors, Cedar Rapids C. of C. (bus.-edn. com. 1986-91), Cedar Rapids Country Club. Lutheran. Avocations: travel, reading, walking. Home: 147 Ashcombe SE Cedar Rapids IA 52403-1700

WAX, WILLIAM EDWARD, photojournalist; b. Miami, Fla., Dec. 7, 1956; s. Ira and Rita (Gunshor) W. AS, Berry Coll., Rome, Ga., 1976; BS in Engring., U. Fla., 1983. With Ind. Fla. Alligator, Gainesville, Fla., 1977-79; staff photographer Gainesville (Fla.) Sun, 1979-87; photo cons. N.Y. Times regional newspapers, 1984—; freelance photographer Miami, 1987—; pres. Wax & Co. Inc., Miami Beach, Fla., 1989—, Waxcom, Miami Beach, 1996—. Owner Studio SoBe, Miami Beach, 1992—; faculty So. Short Course in News Photography, 1985—; lectr. in field. Named Photographer of Yr., NPPA/U. Mo. and Nikon, 1980, So. Photographer of Yr., 1980, Regional Photographer of Yr., 1979, 82, 85; nominated Pulitzer prize, 1979, 89, STC Internat. Design, 1996-97; recipient Mark of Excellence, Sigma Delta Chi, 1978, Best of Show award Atlanta Seminar on Photojournalism, 1982, Best of Show and Silver medal Hearst awards, 1978, Design Gold award Fla. Tech. Writers Assn., 1992, Design award, Gold award, Excellence award Soc. Tech. Comm. Internat. Tech. Art Competition, 1993, 94, 97-03, Best of Show, 1994, 98, 01, Disting. Design award, 1993, 97, 99-03, Excellence Design award, 1993, 98, 99, Design Excellence awards and award of merit, 1995, 00, Best of Show award Ann. Report Fla. Pub. Rels., 1995, Gold, Silver and Bronze awards Fla. Mag. Assn., 1994, 96-04, Merit award STC, 1995, Apex Design awards 1996-06, Global award/Ann. Report, 1996, Maggie award Best Newsletter in the West, 2004, Healthcare Advt. award, 2002-06, Svc. Industry Advt. awards, 2004-06. Mem. Nat. Press Photographers Assn., Fla. Mag. Assn., Profl. Photographers Am., Nikon Profl. Svcs., Fla. Press Photographers Assn. Office: Wax & Co 350 Lincoln Rd Ste 516 Miami FL 33139-3148 Office Phone: 305-674-9542.

WAXENBERG, JAY DAVID, lawyer; b. NYC, Aug. 29, 1956; s. Milton J. and Edith (Balter) W.; m. Gayle D. Waxenberg, Mar. 3, 1985; children: Michael Ian, Alex Evan. BA, SUNY, Stony Brook, 1978; JD, Boston U., 1981; LLM in Taxation, NYU, 1987. Bar: NY 1982. Estate adminstr. US Trust Co., NY, 1981-84; assoc. personal planning dept. Proskauer Rose, LLP, NYC, 1984-90, partner, chmn. personal planning dept., 1991—, former exec. com. mem. Faculty mem. Fordham U. Sch. Law, continuing edn. prog. Estate Planning Beyond the Basics; faculty mem. Practising Law Inst. Intro. to the Adminstrn. of NY Estates; lectr. in will drafting. Contbr. articles to profl. jours. Mem. health sci. profl. advisor cir. Columbia U.; mem. Bankers and Lawyers adv. com. NY Philharmonic; mem. profl. adv. com. Mus. Arts and Design; mem. planning giving adv. com. Mus. Modern Art; mem. planning giving profl. adv. com. Blythedale Children's Hosp.; mem. planned giving adv. coun. NY-Presbyterian Hosp.; mem. planned giving adv. com. NY Pub. Libr.; mem. trust and estate adv. com. Meml. Sloan Kettering Cancer Ctr. Named Leader in Field, Chambers USA, NY Super Lawyer, Law and Politics, Best in Class Atty.; named one of Best Lawyers in Am., Top 100 Estate Planning Attys., Worth Mag., 2006. Fellow Am. Coll. of Trust & Estate Counsel; mem. Assn. Bar of City of NY, NY State Bar Assn. Office: Proskauer Rose LLP 1585 Broadway Fl 24 New York NY 10036-8299 Office Phone: 212-969-3606. Business E-Mail: jwaxenberg@proskauer.com.

WAXMAN, ALLEN PERRY, former pharmaceutical executive, lawyer; b. Mar. 7, 1962; m. Sharon L. Waxman. AB magna cum laude, Dartmouth Coll., 1984; JD magna cum laude, Harvard U., 1987. Law clk. for Hon. Thomas Penfield Jackson US Dist. Ct., Washington, 1987—88; assoc. Williams & Connolly, LLP, Washington, 1988—95, ptnr., 1995—2003; sr. asst. gen. counsel, chief litig. Pfizer, Inc., 2003—05, sr. v.p., assoc. gen. counsel, 2005—06, sr. v.p., gen. counsel, 2006—08. Chmn. bd. Thurgood Marshall Acad., Washington; adj. prof. law Georgetown U. Law Ctr., 1995—2003; mem. US policy governance com. Pfizer, Inc. Bd. dirs. Bus. Coun. NY State, NY Anti-Defamation

League. Recipient Champion of Children & Families Award, 2006, Corp. Leadership award, Legal Services NYC, 2007. Mem.: NY Legal Aid Soc. (bd. mem.), Equal Justice Works (vice chmn.).

WAXMAN, DOV, political science professor; b. London, June 6, 1974; s. Denis and Carole Waxman. BA, Oxford U., 1996; MA, Johns Hopkins U., Washington, 1998, PhD, 2002. Asst. prof. Bowdoin Coll., Brunswick, Maine, 2002—04, Baruch Coll. CUNY, NYC, 2004—. Author: (book) The Pursuit of Peace and the Crisis of Israeli Identity: Defending/Defining the Nation. Mem.: Am. Polit. Sci. Assn., Internat. Studies Assn., Israel Studies Assn. (mem. governing bd.). Office: Baruch Coll CUNY 1 Bernard Baruch Way New York NY 10010

WAXMAN, HENRY ARNOLD, United States Representative from California; b. L.A., Sept. 12, 1939; s. Louis and Esther (Silverman) Waxman; m. Janet Kessler, Oct. 17, 1971; children: Michael David, Shia. BA in Polit. Sci, UCLA, 1961, JD, 1964. Bar: Calif. 1965. Practicing atty., 1965—68; mem. Calif. State Assembly, 1969-74, US Congress from 24th Calif. Dist., 1975—93, US Congress from 29th Calif. Dist., 1993—2003, US Congress from 30th Calif. Dist., 2003—; chmn. US House Commerce subcommittee on Health & Environment, 1979-94; ranking minority mem. US House Oversight & Govt. Reform Com., 1997—2007, chmn., 2007—09, US House Energy & Commerce Com., 2009—. Mem. Congl. Children's Working Grp., H. Dem. Steering Com. Co-author (with Joshua Green): The Waxman Report: How Congress Really Works, 2009. Pres. Calif. Fedn. Young Dems., 1965—67. Recipient Excellence in Pub. Svc. award, Am. Acad. Pediat., 1983, Pub. Svc. award, Am. Assn. Pub. Health Dentistry, 1985, James Madison award, ALA, 1990, Leadership award, Nat. Gay & Lesbian Task Force, 1991, Leadership in Govt. award, Keystone Ctr., 2001, Health Leadership award, Nat. Orgn. Rare Disorders, 2002, Excellence in Immunization award, Nat. Partnership Immunization, 2002, Nat. Leadership award, Nat. Citizens' Coalition for Nursing Home Reform, 2002, Claude Pepper award, Nat. Inst. Cmty. Based Long-Term Care, 2004, Pub. Svc. award, Internat. Found. Employee Benefit Plans, 2004; named one of The 50 Most Powerful People in DC, GQ mag., 2007. Mem.: Am. Civil Liberties Union, Am. Jewish Congress, Guardians Jewish Home for Aged (Pub. Policy on Aging award 1992), Calif. Bar Assn., B'nai B'rith, Sierra Club, Phi Sigma Alpha. Democrat. Jewish. Office: US Congress 2204 Rayburn Ho Office Bldg Washington DC 20515-0530 also: 8436 W Third St Ste 600 Los Angeles CA 90048 Office Phone: 202-225-3976, 323-651-1040. Office Fax: 202-225-4099, 323-655-0502.*

WAXMAN, RONALD, computer engineer; b. Newark, Nov. 28, 1933; s. Benjamin and Rose (Lifson) Waxman; m. Pearl Latterman, June 19, 1955; children: David, Roberta, Benjamin. BSEE, NJ Inst. Tech., Newark, 1955; MEE, Syracuse U., NY, 1963. Engr. IBM, Poughkeepsie, NY, 1955-56, 58-64, East Fishkill, NY, 1964-70, Poughkeepsie and Kingston, NY, 1970-80, sr. engr. Manassas, Va., 1980-87; prin. scientist U. Va., Charlottesville, 1987-97; cons. pvt. practice, Reston, Va., 1997—. IEEE rep. and tech. advisor to Internat. Elec. Commn. US tech. activities group for internat. design automation stds., 1994—98; steering com. very high speed integrated circuits hardware description lang. VHDL Users Group, 1987—91; panel for assessment of Nat. Inst. Stds. and Tech. Measurement and Stds. Labs. NRC, 2002—; presenter in field. Contbr. articles to profl. jours. 1st lt. USAF, 1956-58. Fellow IEEE, IEEE Computer Soc. (bd. govs. 1989-94, 96-98, 2000-02, chmn. fellows evaluation com. 1995-96, chmn. audit com., 1997, founder, chmn. design automation stds. subcom. 1983-88, steering com. 1989-2003, chmn. design automation tech. com. 1988-90, steering com. 1991—, vice-chmn. tech. activities bd. 1991-92, 99, chmn. awards com. 1993, disting. visitor 1986-88, chmn. disting. visitor program 2004—, v.p. activities bd. 1994, v.p. tech. activities, 1998, Meritorious Svc. cert. 1988, Disting. Svc. cert. 1994, TAB Pioneer award 1989, 3d. Millennium medal 2000), Internat. Fedn. Info. Processing Orgns. (CS rep. 2000—, sec. tech. reps. com., 2000—; vice chmn. 2004—, Outstanding Svc. award 2005, tech. com. chmn. IFIP TC5, 2006—), Assn. for Computing Machinery (spl. interest group DA 1960-2007). Achievements include having Design Automation Standards Committee meritorious service award renamed the Ron Waxman meritorious service award; patents in field.

WAXMAN, SETH PAUL, lawyer; b. Hartford, Conn., Nov. 28, 1951; s. Felix H. and Frieda (Goodman) W.; m. Debra F. Goldberg, Mar. 20, 1977; children: Noah, Sarah, Ethan. AB summa cum laude, Harvard U., 1973; JD, Yale U., 1977. Bar: D.C. 1978, U.S. Dist. Ct. D.C. 1979, U.S. Ct. Appeals (D.C. cir.) 1979, U.S. Ct. Appeals (1st cir.) 2000, (2d cir.) 1998, (3d cir.) 1983, (4th cir.) 1982, (5th cir.) 1997, (6th cir.) 1998, (7th cir.) 1998, (8th cir.) 1998, (9th cir.) 1989, (10th cir.) 1998, (11th cir.) 1989, U.S. Ct. Appeals (fed. cir.) 1998, U.S. Supreme Ct. 1982. Law clk to Judge Gerhard A. Gesell US Dist. Ct. DC, Washington, 1977-78; ptnr. Miller Cassidy Larroca & Lewin, Washington, 1978-94; assoc. dep. atty. gen. US Dept. Justice, Washington, 1994-96, dep. solicitor gen., 1996-97, acting dep. atty. gen., 1997, solicitor gen., 1997-2001; ptnr. Wilmer, Cutler, Pickering, Hale and Dorr, LLP, 2001—. Disting. vis. from practice Georgetown U Law Ctr., 2001—; vis. prof. Georgetown U. Law Ctr., 2001; vis. fellow Harvard U. JFK Sch. Govt., 2001; dir. Supreme Ct. Inst., Georgetown U. Law Ctr.; chmn. Legal Affairs Mag., 2004—06. Editor Yale Law Jour., The Combatant Detention Trilogy Through the Lenses of History, 2005; contbr. articles to profl. jours. Trustee Supreme Ct. Hist. Soc.; overseer Harvard U. Recipient Pro Bono Publico award, ABA, 1988, Edmund J. Randolph award, U.S. Dept. Justic, 2001, Benjamin L. Cardozo Cert. of Merit, Anti-Defamation League, 1987, Thomas Jefferson Found. medal in law, U. Va., 2002, Pursuit of Justice award, Internat. Assn. Jewish Lawyers and Jurists, 2001, BYU Rex Lee Advocacy Award, 2002; named hon. spl. agt., FBI, 2001; named one of 75 Best Lawyers in Washington, Washingtonian mag., 2002, 100 Most Influential Lawyers, Nat. Law Jour., 2006; fellow Michael C. Rockefeller, Harvard U., 1973—74. Master: Edward Coke Appellate Inn Court; fellow: Am. Acad. Arts & Sciences, Am. Coll. Trial Lawyers, Am Acad. Appellate Attys., Am. Bar Found.; mem.: Am. Law Inst. Office: Wilmer Cutler Pickering Hale and Dorr LLP 1875 Pennsylvania Ave Washington DC 20006 Office Phone: 202-663-6000. Fax: 202-663-6000. E-mail: seth.waxman@wilmerhale.com.

WAXMAN, SHELDON ROBERT, lawyer; b. Chgo., Apr. 22, 1941; s. Henri and Ann (Sokolsky) W.; m. Katherine Slamski, Aug. 23, 1979; children: Josiah, Zoe. BA, U. Ill., 1963; JD, DePaul U., 1965. Bar: Ill. 1965, U.S. Supreme Ct. 1976, Mich. 1985. Staff atty. Argonne (Ill.) Nat. Lab., 1968-71; asst. U.S. Atty., Chgo., 1971-74; owner firm Waxman Tax & Legal Network, Chgo. and South Haven, Mich., 1976—. Owner Ind. Contractor Cons. Svcs. Artist: (screenplays) Black Messiah Murders, 2003, Chicago Piranhas, 2003; The Josephus Enigma, 2007; Author: In the Teeth of the Wind, 2002, All Anybody Needs to Know About Independent Contracting, 2003; co-author: Black Messiah Murders, A Sam Cohen Case Adventure, Number 1, 2003, Piranhas on the Loose, A Sam Cohen Case Adventure Number 2, 2003, The Josephus Enigma, A Sam Cohen Case Adventure, Number 3, 2007, The Case Adventures of Sam Cohen, J.D.; editor-in-chief New Z Letter; contbr. articles to profl. jours. Founder Freedom Lawyers of Am., People for Simplified Tax Law, Nukes to the Sun. Mem.: Mystery Writers Am. Office: PO Box 309 South Haven MI 49090-0309 Office Phone: 269-207-6219. Personal E-mail: sheldonw72@gmail.com.

WAXSE, DAVID JOHN, judge; b. Oswego, Kans., June 29, 1945; s. I. Joseph and Mary (Poole) W.; m. Linda Schilling (div.); children: Rachel, Ryan, Rebecca; m. Judy Pfannenstiel, May 29, 1982; 1 child, Elayna. BA, U. Kans., 1967; teaching cert., Columbia U., 1968, JD, 1971. Bar: Kans. 1971, U.S. Ct. Appeals (10th cir.) 1971, U.S. Supreme Ct. 1975, U.S. Ct. Appeals (8th Cir.) 1998. Dean of students Intermediate Sch. 88, NYC, 1968-70; spl. edn. tchr. Peter Cooper Sch., NYC, 1970-71; assoc. Payne & Jones, Olathe, Kans., 1971-74, ptnr., 1974-84; of counsel Shook, Hardy & Bacon, Overland Park, Kans., 1984-86, ptnr., 1986-95; shareholder Shook, Hardy & Bacon P.C., Overland Park, 1993-95; ptnr. Shook, Hardy & Bacon L.L.P., Overland Park, Kans., 1995-99; shareholder Shook, Hardy & Bacon P.C., Overland Park, 1993-95, v.p., asst. gen. counsel, 1995-99; U.S. magistrate judge Kansas City, 1999—. Mcpl. judge City of Shawnee, Kans., 1974-80; atty. City of DeSoto, Kans., 1972-79; adj. prof. U. Kans. Sch. Law, Lawrence, 1981-82; mem. juv. code adv. com. Kans. Jud. Coun., 1979-83, guardianship adv. com., 1982-83, atty. fees adv. com., 1986-87; mem. Civil Justice Reform Act Adv. Com., U.S. Dist. Ct. for Dist. Kans., 1991-95; mem. Kans. Commn. on Jud. Qualifications, 1992-99, vice-chmn. 1994-97, chair, 1997-99; v.p. Kans. Legal Svcs., Inc., 1980-82, pres., 1985-87; bd. advisors Kans. Coll. Advocacy, 1979-80; bd. trustees, Lawyer's Com. Civil Rights Under Law, 1997-99. Author: (with others) Kansas Employment Law, 1985, Litigating Employment Law Cases, 1987, Kansas Employment Law Handbook, 1991, supplements, 1992, 95, Kansas Annual Survey, 1990-2000; contbr. articles to profl. jours. Mem. Kan. Gov.'s Adv. Com. on Criminal Justice, 1974-77; mem. Kans. Justice Commn., 1997-99; gen. counsel Western Mo. Dist. ACLU, 1976-78, 86-97, v.p., 1983-86, nat. bd. dirs., 1979-86, 91-99, chmn. children's rights com., 1980-86; mem. AIDS Pol. Network, 1987-99, med. treatment issues com., 1991-96, constn. com., 1991-99; mem. med./tech. com. AIDS Coun. Greater Kans. City, 1986-98, ethics com. consortium Midwest Bioethics Ctr., 1990-2002; bd. dirs. Parents Anonymous Kans., 1978-83, pres., 1979; bd. dirs., mem. fin. com. Kans. Com. for Prevention Child Abuse, 1980-83. Fellow Am. Bar Found., Kans. Bar Found.; mem. ABA (chmn. children's rights com. and family law sects. 1985-86, mem. ho. of dels. 2000—, professionalism com. 2000-05, bd. of editors The Profl. Lawyer, 2000-05, mem. exec. com. nat. conf. fed. trial judges 2005—), Am. Judicature Soc. (bd. dirs. 1997-2003, adv. com. for ctr. for judicial conduct 1997—), Kans. Bar Assn. (chmn. legal aid com. 1978-83, bd. govs. 1988—, v.p. 1996-97, pres.-elect 1997-98, pres. 1998-99, mem. ABA ho. dels. 2000—, Pres.' Outstanding Svc. award 1982, 2006), Kans. City Met. Bar Assn., Johnson County Bar Assn. (chmn. legal aid com. 1975-82, 92-96), Earl E. O'Connor Am. Inn of Ct. (counselor, pres.-elect 2002, pres. 2003). Office: U S Courthouse 500 State Ave Rm 219 Kansas City KS 66101-2400 E-mail: judge_waxse@ksd.uscourts.gov.

WAY, BARBARA HAIGHT, retired dermatologist; b. Franklin, NJ, Dec. 27, 1941; d. Charles Padley and Alice Barbara (Haight) Shoemaker; m. Anthony Biden Way; children: Matthew Shoemaker Way, Sarah Shoemaker Way. AB in Music cum laude, Bryn Mawr Coll., 1962, postgrad., 1963-64; MD, U. Pa., 1968. Diplomate Am. Bd. Dermatology. Systems engr. IBM, Balt., 1962—63; mem. dean's staff Bryn Mawr (Pa.) Coll., 1963—64; med. intern U. Wis. Hosps., Madison, 1968—69, resident in dermatology, 1969—72; physician emergency rm. St. Francis Hosp., La Crosse, Wis., 1969—72, founder dept. dermatology, 1972; asst. prof. dept. dermatology Tex. Tech U. Sch. Medicine, Lubbock, 1972—73, from asst. clin. to assoc. clin. prof., 1973—74, asst. prof., assoc. chair, 1974—76, assoc. prof., chair, 1976—81, assoc. clin. prof., 1981—92; clin. prof. Tex. Tech. U. Health Scis. Ctr., Lubbock, 1995—2005, founder, dir. dermatology residency tng. program, 1978—81, pvt. practice, 1973—74, 1981—2006; acting dir. Lubbock City Health Dept., 1982—83; ret., 2006. Mem. credentials com. Covenant Hosp., Lubbock, 1990, 92, 94, 95, founding dir. phototherapy unit, 1990-91, 93, exec. com., 1991, 93, 98, chief dermatology sect., 1991, 93, 98, subsect. chief, 1992, 94. Alumna admissions rep. Bryn Mawr Coll., 1972-75, 87-96; mem. selection com. outstanding physician Lubbock chpt. Am. Cancer Soc., 1991-94, chmn., 1991; bd. dirs. Tex. Tech. U. Med. Found., 1987-89, Double T. Connection, 1988-90. Fellow Am. Acad. Dermatology (reviewer jour.); mem. Tex. Dermatol. Soc. (chmn. roster com. 1980), Tex. Med. Assn. (mem. sexually transmitted diseases com. 1986-90, mem. coun. pub. health 1990-92, vice councillor dist. III 1992-98, councillor dist III 1998-2000, chmn. reference com. fin. and orgnl. affairs ann. session 1992), Lubbock County-Garza County Med. Soc. (mem. various coms. 1980-2000, chmn. sch. and pub. health com. 1983, mem. bd. censors 1983-85, chair 1985, sec. 1986, v.p. 1987, liaison with Tex. Tech. U. Health Scis. Ctr. com. 1988-91, co-chmn. pub. rels. com. 1988-89, alt. Tex. Med. Assn. del. 1988-89, del. 1990-95, 98-2000, pres.-elect 1989, pres. 1990, chmn. ad hoc bylaws com. 1991-94, chmn. Hippocratic award 1991), Women's Dermatologic Soc. (founding sec.), Dallas County Medical Res. Corp. Personal E-mail: anthony.way@ttuhsc.edu.

WAY, E(DWARD) LEONG, pharmacologist, toxicologist, educator; b. Watsonville, Calif., July 10, 1916; s. Leong Man and Lai Har (Shew) Way; m. Madeline Li, Aug. 11, 1944; children: Eric, Linette. BS, U. Calif., Berkeley, 1938, MS, 1940; PhD, U. Calif., San Francisco, 1942. Pharm. chemist Merck & Co., Rahway, NJ, 1942; instr. pharmacology George Washington U., 1943-46, asst. prof., 1946-48; asst. prof. pharmacology U. Calif., San Francisco, 1949-52, assoc. prof., 1952-57, prof., 1957-87, prof. emeritus, 1987—, chmn. dept. pharmacology, 1973-78. USPHS spl. rsch. fellow U. Berne, Switzerland, 1955-56, China Med. Bd.; rsch. fellow, vis. prof. U. Hong Kong, 1962-63; Sterling Sullivan disting. vis. prof. Martin Luther King U., 1982; hon. prof. pharmacology and neurosci. Guangzhou Med. Coll., 1987; adv. com. Pharm. Rsch. Mfrs. Assn. Found., 1968-98; mem. coun. Am. Bur. for Med. Advancement in China, 1982; bd. dirs. Li Found., 1970—, pres., 1985-98, bd. dirs. Haight Ashbury Free Clinics, 1986-93; Tsumura prof. neuropsychopharmacology med. sch. Gunma U., Maebashi, Japan, 1989-90; sr. staff fellow Nat. Inst. on Drug Abuse, 1990-91; rschr. on drug metabolism, analgetics, devel. pharmacology, drug tolerance, drug dependence and Chinese materia medica; presenter in field. Editor: New Concepts in Pain, 1967, (with others) Fundamentals of Drug Metabolism and Drug Disposition, 1971, Endogenous and Exogenous Opiate Agonists and Antagonists, 1979; mem. editl. bd. Clin. Pharmacology, Therapeutics, 1975-87, Drug, Alcohol Dependence, 1976-87, Progress in Neuro-Psychopharmacology, 1977-91, Research Communications in Chem. Pathology and Pharmacology, 1978-91, Alcohol and Drug Dependence, 1986-91, Asian Pacific Jour. Pharm., 1985—, Jour. Chinese Medicine, 1993—; contbr. numerous articles and revs. to profl. publs. Recipient Faculty Rsch. Lectr. award, U. Calif., San Francisco, 1974, San Francisco Chinese Hosp. award, 1976, Cultural citation and Gold medal, Ministry of Edn., Republic of China, 1978, Nathan B. Eddy award, Coll. on Problems in Drug Dependence, 1979, Mentorship award, Coll. on Problems in Drug Dependence, San Juan, 2004, Chancellor's award, U. Calif., 1986, Disting. Alumnus award, U. Calif., San Francisco, 1990, Asian Pacific Am. Systemwide Alliance award, 1993, Lifetime Achievement award, Chinese Hist. Soc., 2001, Outstanding Overseas Chinese award, Chinese Cons. Benevolent Assn., Chinese Womens Assn., 2005, Cert. of Honor, Mayor Gavin Newsome, San Francisco, 2005. Fellow Am. Coll. Neuropsychopharmacology (life, emeritus), Am. Coll. Clin. Pharmacology (hon.), Coll. on Problems of Drug Dependence (exec. com. 1978-92, chmn. bd. dirs. 1978-82, Nathan B. Eddy award 1979, Mentorship award 2004); mem. AAAS, Am. Soc. Pharmacology, Exptl. Therapeutics (bd. editors 1957-65, pres. 1976-77, Torald Sollman award 1992), Fedn. Am. Socs. Exptl. Biology (exec. bd. 1975-79, pres. 1977-78), Am. Pharm. Assn. (life, Rsch. Achievement award 1962), AMA, Soc. Aid and Rehab. Drug Addicts (Hong Kong, life), Western Pharmacology Soc. (pres. 1963-64), Japanese Pharm. Soc. (hon.), Coun. Sci. Soc. Pres.' (exec. com. 1979-84, treas. 1980-84), Chinese Pharmacology Soc. (hon.), Academia Sinica (academician), Leong Man Way Found. (founder & pres. 1976-78). Office: Univ Calif Dept Cellular and Molecular Pharmacology U64 PBX 0622 San Francisco CA 94143-0001 Office Phone: 415-476-2722.

WAY, JACOB EDSON, III, museum director; b. Chgo., May 18, 1947; s. Jacob Edson Jr. and Amelia (Evans) W.; m. Jean Ellwood Chappell, Sept. 6, 1969; children: Sarah Chappell Quiroga, Rebecca Stoddard, Jacob Edson IV. BA, Beloit Coll., 1968; MA, U. Toronto, 1971, PhD, 1978; MDiv, Episcopal Theol. Sem. S.W., 2008. From instr. to assoc. prof. Beloit (Wis.) Coll., 1972—85; dir. Logan Mus. Anthropology, Beloit, 1980-85, Wheelwright Mus. Am. Indian, Santa Fe, 1985-89; interim dir. N.Mex. Mus. Natural History, Albuquerque, 1990-91; exec. dir. Space Ctr. Internat. Space Hall of Fame, Alamogorgo, N.Mex., 1991-94; dir. N.Mex. Farm and Ranch Heritage Mus., 1994-99; cultural affairs officer State of N.Mex., Santa Fe, 1997—2003; realtor Margo Cutler, Ltd., Santa Fe, 2003—05; rector St. Christopher Episcopal Ch., Lubbock, Tex., 2008—. Evaluator Nat. Park Service, Denver, 1986. Contbr. articles to profl. jours. Mem. Nuke Watch, Beloit, 1983-84; cultural affairs officer State of N.Mex., 1997-2003. Research grants Wis. Humanities Com., 1984, NSF, 1981; grantee Cullister Found., 1978-84; fellow U. Toronto, 1971. Mem. Am. Assn. Mus., Am. Assn. Phys. Anthropology, Can. Assn. for Phys. Anthropology, N.Mex. Assn. Mus. (pres. 1994-96), Soc. Am. Archaeology, Wis. Fedn. Mus. (adv. bd. 1982-85). Avocations: camping, skiing, fishing, reading, horseback riding. Office Phone: 806-799-8208. Personal E-mail: jeway@earthlink.net.

WAY, KRISTI, legislative staff member; Grad., Liberty U., 1999; MBA, Va. Commonwealth U., 2005. Legis. asst. Va. House of Del.; sr. adviser for Rep. Eric Cantor, US House of Reps., 2006—09, chief of staff, 2009—. Dep. campaign mgr. for Bill Bolling's Lt. Gov. Campaign, 2005. Office: Office of Congressman Eric Cantor 329 Cannon House Office Bldg Washington DC 20515*

WAYBOURN, KATHLEEN ANN, lawyer, consultant; BA magna cum laude, Queens Coll., Flushing, NY, 1978; JD, St. John's U. Law Sch., Jamaica, NY, 1984. Bar: N.Y. 1985, U.S. Supreme Ct. 2000, U.S. Dist. Ct. (so. dist.), NY 2002; cert. chemist Am. Chem. Soc., Ind. Ind. legal cons. Office of Corp. Counsel City N.Y., 1985—86; atty. Aaron J. Broder, PC, NYC, 1988—92; pvt. practice, 1991—; assoc. atty. Mangiatordi, Maher and Lemmo, LLC, 1998—99; contract atty. Steven R. Harris and Assocs., 2000—, Harris Law, 2000—, Fitzgerald & Fitzgerald, 2007—. Pres. Toxic Tort Cons., Inc., NYC, 2001—03. Author: St. John's Law Balance, 1984. Pro bono homeless shelter advocacy project NY County Lawyers Assn., 1991—92, sex discrimination clinic and no sweatshop coalition, 1994—98. Tchg. fellow scholarship, NYU Grad. Sch. Arts and Scis., 1978—79. Mem.: Am. Assn. for Justice, NY County Lawyers Assn. (recipient Appreciation certs.), Assn. Trial Lawyers Am., NY State Trial Lawyers' Assn., Beta Delta Chi. Avocations: photography, swimming, snorkeling. Office: 110 E 59th St Ste 3200 New York NY 10022

WAYDO, STEPHEN, aeronautical engineer, researcher; b. Berwick, Pa., Dec. 27, 1978; s. George and Mary Waydo; m. Jaime Dyk, July 15, 2005. BS in Aeronautics & Astronautics, U. Wash., Seattle, 2001; PhD in Control & Dynamical Sys., Calif. Inst. Tech., Pasadena, 2007. Staff engr. NASA Jet Propulsion Lab., Pasadena, 2000—08; mem. tech. staff C8 Medisensors, Los Gatos, Calif., 2008—. Grad. fellowship, Fannie & John Hertz Found., 2002—07. Mem.: IEEE, AIAA. Avocations: bicycling, running, skiing, travel. Office: C8 Medisensors Los Gatos CA 95030 Personal E-mail: swaydo@gmail.com.

WAYLAND-SMITH, ROBERT DEAN, retired banker; b. Oneida, NY, July 2, 1943; s. Robert and Prudence Cragin W.-S.; m. Kathleen Anne Schultz, Aug. 24, 1968 (dec. Oct. 1999), m. Linda M. Amendola, July 21, 2002; children: Kristin, Debra. BA in Econs., U. Rochester, 1965. Mgr. equipment svc. Strong Meml. Hosp., Rochester, NY, 1965-67; mgmt. trainee Chase Lincoln First Bank, N.A., Rochester, 1967-68, mgr. mcpl. securities, 1968-81, mgr. portfolio mgmt. depart., 1981-84, mgr. fin. and investment svc. dept., 1984-87, mgr. trust and fin. svc. dept., 1987-88; pres. and CEO Rochester region Chase Manhattan Bank, N.A., 1988-93, upstate trust and investment divsn. exec., 1993-98; ret., 1998. Mem. adv. bd. Roberts Wesleyan Coll., Rochester, 1989-99; mem. adv. coun. J.W. Jones Sch. Bus. SUNY, Geneseo, 1990-99. Trustee Ctr. for Govtl. Rsch., 1985-2009; dir. Greater Rochester Visitors Assn., 1990-93, Rochester Downtown Devel. Corp., 1991-93, United Neighborhood Ctrs., Greater Rochester Found., 1992-2002; mem. fin. execs. adv. bd. Coll. Bus. Rochester Inst. Tech., 1994-97; mem. United Way Greater Rochester Corp., 1998-2003; bd. dirs. Oneida Cmty. Mansion House, 1988—; bd. dir. Via Health, 1999-2001; bd. govs. The Genesee Hosp., 1992-2001; mem. bd. trustees Rochester Inst. Tech., 2003—; chair coll. coun. SUNY Coll. Geneseo, 1999—; bd. dirs. Greater Rochester Enterprise, 2004—. Fellow: Assn. for Investment Mgmt. and Rsch.; mem.: Greater Rochester Met. C. of C. (bd. dirs. 1992—95), Greater Rochester Ind. Practice Assn. (bd. dirs. 2000—), Rochester Soc. Security Analysts, Oak Hill Country Club, Genesee Valley Club (treas. 2002—05, pres. 2005—07). Avocations: golf, gardening, reading. Office: JP Morgan Chase One Chase Sq Rochester NY 14643 Home Phone: 585-381-1248; Office Phone: 585-797-1938. Business E-Mail: robert.d.wayland-smith@chase.com.

WAYMIRE, JACK CALVIN, medical educator; b. Dayton, Ohio, Jan. 10, 1941; s. Virgil Kniesley and Nellie Beatrice Waymire; 1 child, Kellie Suzan. BA, Earlham Coll., Richmond, Ind., 1963; PhD, Ohio State U., Columbus, 1969. Asst. prof. UC, Irvine, Calif., 1973—78; Levit family prof. UT-Health Sci. Ctr. Med. Sch., Houston, 1978—. Recipient Endowed Professorship award, UT Health Sci. Ctr., 2001—09; grant, US Pub. Health- NIH, 1973—2003, 1995—2004. Mem.: Am. Assn. Neurosci. Depts. & Programs (sec. 2002—03), Am. Soc. Neurosci. Democrat. Avocations: travel, painting, sculpting. Home: 2154 Southgate Houston TX 77030

WAYNE, EARL ANTHONY, ambassador; b. 1950; married; 2 children. BA in Polit. Sci., U. Calif., Berkeley, 1972; MA in Polit. Sci., Princeton U., 1975; MA, Stanford U., 1973; MPA, Harvard U., 1984. Joined Fgn. Svc., 1975, various positions; spl. asst. to sec. US Dept. State, 1981—83; first sec. US Embassy, Paris, 1984—87; nat. security corr. Christian Sci. Monitor, 1987—89; dir. regional affairs U.S. Amb. at Large for Counter-Terrorism, 1989—91; dir. Western European affairs Nat. Security Coun., 1991—93; dep. chief mission U.S. Mission to European Union, 1993—96; dept. asst. sec. for Europe and Can. US Dept. State, Washington, 1996—97, prin. dep. asst. sec. for European affairs, 1997—2000, asst. sec. for econ. & bus. affairs, 2000—06, interim under sec. for econ. bus. and agrl. affairs, 2005, US amb. to Argentina Buenos Aires, 2006—09, asst. amb. to Afghanistan, coordinating dir. for devel. & econ. affairs Kabul, 2009—. Recipient Presdl. Disting. Svc. award, 2001, Disting. Honor award, US Dept. State, 2005, Presdl. Meritorious Svc. award, Paul Wellstone Anti-Slavery Amb. of the Yr. award, 2008. Office: US Embassy 6180 Kabul Pl Dulles VA 20189 Office Phone: 57774533.*

WAYNE, JEFFREY D., surgeon; BA, Dartmouth Coll., Hanover, NH; MD, Boston U., Mass., 1992. Asst. prof. surgery Northwestrn U., Chgo., 2001—. Fellow: ACS. Office: Northwestern Univ 676 N St Clair St Ste 650 Chicago IL 60611 Office Fax: 312-695-1462.

WAYNE, JUNE CLAIRE, artist; b. Chgo., Mar. 7, 1918; d. Albert and Dorothy Alice (Kline) LaVine. DFA (hon.), Rutgers U., 2005. Indsl. designer, NYC, 1939-41; radio writer, mem. staff sta. WGN, Chgo., 1942-43; founder, 1959; since dir. Tamarind Lithography Workshop, Inc. (funded by Ford Found.), Los Angeles; Tamarind Inst., U. N.Mex., 1970—. Mem. vis. com. Sch. Visual and Environ. Studies, Harvard, 1972-74, chancellors adv. com., arts mgmt. program Grad. Sch. Adminstrn., U. Calif. at Los Angeles, 1969-80, Calif. Confederation of Arts adv. bd., 1988, Calif. State U. dept. of art adv. coun., Long Beach, 1988, Rutgers U. Mason Gross Sch. Arts prof. of rsch. printmaking and paper, New Brunswick, NJ, 2002-. Contbr. articles to profl. publs.; subject TV programs.; Numerous one-woman exhbns., 1935—, latest being, Art Mus., U. N.Mex., 1968, Cin. Art Mus., 1969, Iowa Art Mus., U. Iowa, 1970, Grunwald Graphics Arts Found., U. Calif. at Los Angeles, 1971, Municipal Art Gallery, Barnsdall Park, LA, 1973, Van Doren Gallery, San Francisco, 1974, La Demeure, Paris, 1974, Musée de Brest, France, 1976, Montgomery Gallery, Pomona Colls., Calif., 1978, Ariz. State U. Galleries, 1978, ICA travelling exhbn., Rennes, 1976, Nancy, 1977, Brussels, 1978, Reims, 1978, Lyons, 1979, Neuberger Mus., Purchase, NY, 1997, Skirball Mus., Cin., 1998, LA County Mus. Art, 1998, Palm Springs Desert Mus., Calif., 1999, A.R.T. Gallery, NY, 2003, Rutgers U., Newark, 2005, The Armory Ctr. for Arts, Pasadena, Calif., 2005, Stedman Gallery, Newark, 2005, Mason Gross Galleries, New Brunswick, NJ, 2006, Birmingham Mus. and Art Gallery, UK, 2006, Tama Art U. Mus., Tokyo, 2006; rep. permanent collections, Library of Congress, The British Mus., London, Mus. Modern Art, NYC, Art Inst. Chgo., Houghton Library at Harvard, Smithsonian Instn., Rosenwald Collection, The Victoria and Albert Mus., London, Nat. Gallery Art, NY Pub. Library, Cin. Art Mus., Pasadena (Calif.) Mus. Art, Phila. Mus. Art, Phila. Print Club, Birmingham Mus. and Art Gallery, Walker Art Center, Mpls., Zimmerli Art Mus., New Brunswick. Bd. dirs. Grunwald Center Graphic Arts, 1965-80. Recipient numerous prizes, 1950—, latest being Prix de la Biennal Internat. de L'Estampe d'Epinal, France, 1971; Purchase prize Biennal d'Epinal, 1973; Golden Eagle Cine award and Acad. award nomination for film Four Stones for Kanemitsu, 1974; Silver Life Achievement award YWCA, 1983; Communicator award Women in Media, 1983; Woman of the Year, Palm Springs Desert Mus., 1999; Zimmerli award Women in Arts Com., Coll. Arts Assn., 2003; Mason Gross Sch. Disting. Svc. Arts award, 2004; honoree, Nat. Women's History Project, Calif. Lawyers for Arts, 2008. Mem. Writers Guild Am., Women in Film, AFTRA, Women's Caucus for Art, Soc. Am. Graphic Artists, Soc. Washington Printmakers, LA Printmakers Soc., The Trusteeship, Internat. Women's Forum. Address: 1108 Tamarind Ave Los Angeles CA 90038-1906

WAYNE, KYRA PETROVSKAYA, writer; b. Crimea, USSR, Dec. 31, 1918; arrived in U.S., 1948, naturalized, 1951; d. Prince Vasily Sergeyevich and Baroness Zinaida Fedorovna (Fon-Haffenberg) Obbolensky; m. George J. Wayne, Apr. 21, 1961; 1 child, Ronald George. BA, Leningrad Inst. Theatre Arts, 1939, MA, 1940. Actress, concert singer, Russia, 1939-46; actress, 1948-59; enrichment lectr. Royal Viking Line cruises, Alaska-Can., Greek Islands-Black Sea, Russia/Europe, 1978-79, 81-82, 83-84, 86-8, 88. Author: Kyra, 1959, Kyra's Secrets of Russian Cooking, 1960, 1993, The Quest for the Golden Fleece, 1962, Shurik, 1971, 1992, 2007, The Awakening, 1972, The Witches of Barguzin, 1975, Max, The Dog that Refused to Die, 1979 (Best Fiction award Dog Writers Assn. Am., 1980), Rekindle the Dreams, 1979, Quest for Empire, 1986, Li'l Ol' Charlie, 1989, Quest for Bigfoot, 1996, Pepper's Ordeal, 2000, The Chaperone, 2006, Memoirs of a Piano, 2007. Founder, pres. Clean Air Program, Los Angeles County, 1971—72; mem. Seattle Art Mus.; mem. women's coun. Sta. KCET-Ednl. TV; mem. Monterey County Symphony Guild, 1989—91, Monterey Bay Aquarium, Monterey Peninsula Mus. Art, Friends of La Mirada, Fresno Art Mus., Fresno Met. Mus., Valley Children's Hosp. Served to lt. Russian Army, 1941—43. Decorated Red Star, numerous decorations USSR; recipient award, Crusade for Freedom, 1955—56, Los Angeles County, 1972, Merit award, Am. Lung Assn. Los Angeles County, 1988, award of Merit, Congress Russian Ams., 1999. Mem.: Seattle Art Mus., Idyllwild Sch. Music, Carmel Music Soc. (bd. dirs. 1992—94), Authors Guild, Soc. Children's Book Writers, PEN, Fresno Philharm., UCLA Affiliates (life), L.A. Lung Assn. (life; pres. and founder clean air program 1972—74), Art and Theatre Assn. (trustee 1987), Friends Lung Assn. (pres. 1988), UCLA Med. Faculty Wives (pres. 1970—71, dir. 1971—75), Club 25, Los Angelenos Club (life). *Personal philosophy: I believe in total loyalty. Loyalty to one's family and friends, to one's colleagues and to one's country. In my case - to my chosen country, the U.S.A.*

WAYNE, MICHAEL G., surgeon; s. Michael P. and Louise Wayne; m. Mylah DeLeon, June 13, 2003; 1 child, Michael A. DO, NY Coll. Osteo. Medicine, Old Westbury, 1994. Cert. Am. Bd. Surgery, 2004. Surgeon Biliary and Pancreatic Surgery, NYC, 2004—. Ssst. resident dir. St. Vincent Hosp., NYC, 2007—. Office: Biliary and Pancreatic Surgery NY 170 W12th St Cronin Bldg 454 New York NY 10011 Office Fax: 212-604-3383.

WAYNE, STEPHEN J., government educator, writer; b. NYC, Mar. 22, 1939; s. Arthur G. and Muriel Wayne; m. Cheryl Beil, May 22, 1982; children: Jared B., Jeremy B. BA with honors, U. Rochester, 1961; MA, Columbia U., 1963, PhD, 1968. Instr. polit. sci. U.S. Naval Postgrad. Sch., 1963-65; instr. politics and govt. Ohio Wesleyan U., 1966-68; asst. prof. to prof. polit. sci. and pub. affairs The George Washington U., 1968—88; prof. govt. Georgetown U., Washington, 1989—. Presenter and lectr. in field. Author: The Legislative Presidency, 1978, The Road to the White House, 1980, 8th edit., 2008, (with George C. Edwards) Presidential Leadership: Politics and Policy Making, 1985, 8th edit. 2009 (with Cal MacKenzie, David O'Brien and Richard L. Cole) The Politics of American Government, 1995, 3d edit., 1999; editor: Investigating the American Political System: Problems, Methods, and Projects, 1974, (with George C. Edwards) Studying the Presidency, 1983, (with Clyde Wilcox) The Quest for National Office, 1992, (with Wilcox) The Election of the Century and What It Tells Us About the Future of American Politics, 2002, Is This Any Way to Run a Democratic Government?, 2004, Is This Any Way To Run A Democratic Election?, 3rd. 2007, (with G. Cal Mackenzie) Conflict and Consensus in America, 2007; appeared on 3 one-hour programs on presidency Every Four Years, sta. WHYY-TV, PBS, 1980; election night analyst ARD-German TV, 1992, AP TV, 2008; contbr. numerous articles, chpts. and book revs. to books and profl. jours. Office: Georgetown U Dept Govt 37th And O NW Washington DC 20057-0001 Office Phone: 202-687-5908. Business E-Mail: waynes@georgetown.edu.

WAYTE, ALAN (PAUL), lawyer; b. Huntington Park, Calif., Dec. 30, 1936; s. Paul Henry and Helen Lucille (McCarthy) W.; m. Beverly A. Bruen, Feb. 19, 1959 (div. 1972); children: David Alan, Lawrence Andrew, Marcia Louise; m. Nancy Kelly Wayte, July 5, 1975. AB, Stanford U., 1958, JD, 1960. Bar: Calif. 1961, U.S. Dist. Ct. (so. dist.) Calif. 1961, U.S. Supreme Ct. 1984. Ptnr. Adams, Duque & Hazeltine, LA, 1966-85, Dewey Ballantine, LA, 1985—2004; of counsel DLA Piper LLP, LA, 2004—. Mem. L.A. County Bar Assn. (chmn. real property sect. 1981-82), Am. Coll. Real Estate Lawyers (bd. govs. 1989—, pres. 1994), Am. Coll. Mortgage Attys., Anglo-Am. Real Property Inst. (bd. govs. 1989-91), L.A. Philharm. Assn. (exec. com. bd. dirs. 1973—), Chancery Club, Calif. Club (L.A.), Valley Hunt Club (Pasadena). Office: DLA Piper LLP Suite 2300 550 S Hope St Los Angeles CA 90071 Home Phone: 626-792-8187; Office Phone: 213-330-7734. Office Fax: 213-330-7534. Business E-Mail: alan.wayte@dlapiper.com.

WBARCLAY, GERRY, biology professor; s. Berfield and Caroline Barclay; m. Julie; 1 child, Matthew Barclay. BS, CalPoly State U., San Luis Obispo, Calif., 1982; MS, Penn. State U., Univ Pk., 1984; PhD, Oreg. State U., Corvallis, ABD, 1990. Prof. dept. biology Highline CC, Des Moines, Wash., 1992—. Contbr. scientific papers to profl. jours. Mem.: Nat. Ctr. Sci. Edn., Skeptics Soc., Soc. Ethnobiology. Office: Highline CC 240th Des Moines WA 98198 Home Phone: 360-970-1870; Office Phone: 206-878-3710. Personal E-mail: ketchie1@gmail.com. E-mail: gbarclay@highline.edu.

WCELA, EMIL ALOYSIUS, bishop; b. Bay Shore, NY, May 1, 1931; MA, Cath. U. Am., Washington, 1963, Fordham U., NYC, 1963. Ordained priest Diocese of Bklyn., 1956; ordained bishop, 1988; aux. bishop Diocese of Rockville Ctr., NY, 1988—2007. Chmn. pastoral practices com. Nat. Conf. Catholic Bishops. Roman Catholic. Office: 50 N Park Ave Rockville Centre NY 11570-4184

WEABER, TERRY LEE, information scientist; b. Decatur, Ill., Feb. 9, 1961; s. Jerry Lee and Bonnie Lee Weaber; m. Genevieve Rose Lenertz, Sept. 26, 1987; children: Lauren Elizabeth, Elijah Lee. A in Avionics Tech., CC Air Force, Austin, Tex., 1984; BS in Info. Tech. with honors, U. Phoenix, 2003. Air res. technician Dept. Def., Austin, Tex., 1984—91; computer, electronics, info. tech. mgr. NOAA, Ft. Worth, 1991—. Leader Boy Scouts Am., Las Vegas, Nev., 2001—03; youth group leader Bapt. Ch., Las Vegas, 2001—03. Staff sgt. USAF, 1980—84. Mem.: Nat. Space Soc., Planetary Soc. Republican. Avocations: reading, art, computers, motorcycling. Office: Nat Weather Svc 819 Taylor St Rm 10A24 Fort Worth TX 76102

WEAKLAND, REMBERT GEORGE, archbishop emeritus; b. Patton, Pa., Apr. 2, 1927; s. Basil and Mary (Kane) Weakland. AB, St. Vincent Coll., Latrobe, Pa., 1948, DD (hon.), 1963, LHD (hon.), 1987; MS in Piano, Juilliard Sch. Music, 1954; postgrad., Columbia U., 1954—56, PhD in Musicology, 2000; LHD (hon.), Duquesne U., 1964, Belmont Coll., 1964, Cath. U. Am., 1975, Xavier U., Cin., 1988, DePaul U., 1989, Loyola U., New Orleans, 1991, Villanova U., 1992, Dayton U., 1993, Marian Coll., Fond du Lac, Wis., 1995, St. Anselm Coll., Manchester, NH, 1996, St. Norbert Coll., De Pere, Wis., 1996, U. San Francisco, 1997, Scholastica Coll., 1998; HHD (hon.), St. Ambrose U., Davenport, 1990, Aquinas Inst. Theology, St. Louis, 1991, St Mary's Coll., Notre Dame, Ind., 1994; LLD (hon.), Cardinal Stritch Coll., Milw., 1978, Marquette U., 1981, Loyola U., Chgo., 1986, U. Notre Dame, 1987, Mt. Mary Coll., Milw., 1989, John Carroll U., Cleve., 1992; LLD (hon.), Fairfield U., 1994; D of Sacred Music (hon.), St. Joseph's Coll., Rensselaer, Ind., 1979; DST of Sacred Music (hon.), Jesuit Sch. Theology, Berkeley, Calif., 1989; DST (hon.), St. John's U., Collegeville, Minn., 1991, Santa Clara U., 1991; DST (hon.), Yale U., 1993; DD (hon.), Lakeland Coll., Sheboygan, 1991, Ill. Benedictine Coll., Lisle, Ill., 1992, Regis Coll., Toronto, 1993, Trinity Coll., Hartford, 1996, Trinity Lutheran Sem., Columbus, Ohio, 1998; D of Ministry (hon.), Catholic Theol. Union, Chgo., 1999. Professed Order of St. Benedict, 1946, ordained priest, 1951; faculty music dept. St. Vincent Coll., 1957—63, chmn., 1961—63, chancellor chmn. of bd. of Coll., 1963—67; coadjutor archabbot St. Vincent Archabbey, 1963—67; abbot primate Benedictine Confederation, 1967—77; ordained bishop, 1977; archbishop Archdiocese of Milw., 1997—2002, archbishop emeritus, 2002—. Author: A Pilgrim in a Pilgrim Church: Memoirs of a Catholic Archbishop, 2009. Mem.: Ch. Music Assn. Am. (pres. 1964—66), Am. Guild Organists. Roman Catholic. Office: PO Box 070912 Milwaukee WI 53207-0912

WEAKLEY, CLARE GEORGE, JR., insurance company executive, theologian, entrepreneur; b. Dallas, Apr. 14, 1928; s. Clare George and Louise (Cunningham) Weakley; m. Jean C. Burrow, July 20, 1962; children from previous marriage: Clare George III, Carol J.(dec.), Charles E. BBA, So. Meth. U., 1948, ThM, 1967. Ordained to ministry Christian Cmty., 1977. With Employers Ins., Dallas, 1948-52; owner Weakley & Co., Dallas, 1952-2001. Founder, pres. Am. Svc. Found., Inc., 1967—, Cornerstone Ministries, 1982—, Small Bus. Assn., Inc., 1988—, Christian Cmty., 1977—, founder, leader; vis. prof. western bus. theory and Christian ethics St. Petersburg (Russia) Internat. Mgmt. Inst. (formerly Leningrad Internat. Mgmt. Inst.), 1990—. Author: In God We Trust, 1997, God 101, 1998; author, editor: The Wesley Library Series for Today's Reader, The Nature of the Kingdom, 1976, The Nature of Spiritual Growth, 1977, The Nature of Revival, 1987, The Nature of Salvation, 1988, The Nature Holiness, 1988. Republican. Home: 13731 Goldmark Dr Apt 1207 Dallas TX 75240-4220 Office: Christian Cmty 13731 Goldmark Dr #1207 Dallas TX 75240 E-mail: clare@christian-community.org, weakley_co@earthlink.net.

WEARLY, WILLIAM LEVI, retired manufacturing executive; b. Warren, Ind., Dec. 5, 1915; s. Purvis Gardner and Ethel Ada (Jones) W.; m. Mary Jane Riddle, Mar. 8, 1941, Margaret Wearly (Campbell), 1996; children: Patricia Ann, Susan, William Levi, Elizabeth. BS, Purdue U., 1937, Dr Engring. (hon.), 1959. Student career engr. C.A. Dunham Co., Michigan City, Ind., 1936; mem. elec. design staff Joy Mfg. Co., Franklin, Pa., 1937-39, v.p., gen. sales mgr., 1952-56, exec. v.p., 1956-57, pres., dir., 1957-62; v.p., dir. Ingersoll-Rand Co., 1964-66, exec. v.p., 1966-67, chmn., chief exec. officer, 1967-80, chmn. exec. com., 1981-85. Dir. ASA Ltd., Med. Care Am.; trustee LMI; speaker engring. groups. Author tech. publs. relating to mining; patentee in field. Bd. dirs. Boys Clubs Am. Mem. NAE, IEEE, AIME, Nat. Acad. of Engring., C. of C., Sky Club N.Y.C., Blind Brook Golf Club, Desert Forest Golf Club, Minikahda Golf Club, Ariz. Club, Masons, Shriners, Eta Kappa Nu, Tau Beta Pi, Beta Theta Pi. Republican. Methodist. Mailing: PO Box 1072 Carefree AZ 85377-1072 Home Phone: 480-488-9288. Personal E-mail: wwearly@peoplepc.com.

WEART, SPENCER RICHARD, historian; b. Detroit, Mar. 8, 1942; s. Spencer Augustus and Janet (Streng) W.; m. Carole Ege, June 30, 1971; children: Lara Kimi, Spencer Gen. BA, Cornell U., 1963; PhD, U. Colo., 1968. Postdoctoral fellow Calif. Inst. Tech., 1968-71, U. Calif., Berkeley, 1971-74; dir. Ctr. for History Physics, Am. Inst. Physics, College Park, Md., 1974—2009. Author: Scientists in Power, 1979, Nuclear Fear, 1988, Never at War, 1998, Discovery of Global Warming, 2003; contbr. articles to profl. jours. Recipient Andrew Gemant award Am. Inst. of Physics, 1994 Fellow AAAS. Home: 12 Buena Vista Dr Hastings On Hudson NY 10706-1104 Office: Am Inst Physics One Physics Ellipse College Park MD 20740-3843 Office Phone: 301-209-3174.

WEARY, PEYTON EDWIN, retired medical educator; b. Evanston, Ill., Jan. 10, 1930; s. Leslie Albert and Conway Christian (Fleming) W.; m. Janet Edsall Gregory, Aug. 23, 1952; children: Terry, Conway Christian, Carolyn Fielder. BA, Princeton U., 1970; MD, U. Va., 1955. Diplomate: Am. Bd. Dermatology (dir. 1978-88, pres. 1987-88). Intern, case Western Res. U. Hosps., Cleve., 1955-56; rotating intern Univ. Hosp. Cleve., 1955-56; asst. resident dermatology U. Va., Charlottesville, 1958-60, resident dermatology, 1960-61, instr. dept. dermatology, 1961-62, asst. prof., 1962-65, asso. prof., 1965-70, prof., chmn. dept. dermatology, 1970-93; mem. staff Univ. Hosp., mem. cancer com., 1979—98, ret., 2001, prof. emeritus, 2001—. Univ. Hosp. house staff, 1960-61, clin. staff, 1965-66, pres. clin. staff, 1966-67; co-chair Nat. Coun. on Skin Cancer Prevention, Fed. Coun. on Skin Cancer Prevention, 1997-2001, Ctr. for Disease Control, 1997-2000. Mem. editorial bd. Jour. Am. Acad. Dermatology, 1978-87; editorial adv. bd. Skin and Allergy News, 1978—; contbr. articles to profl. jours. Bd. dirs. Lupus Found. Am., 1980-84; trustee, mem. exec. com. Dermatology Found., 1975-79; pres. Albermarle County unit Am. Cancer Soc., 1967-69. Served from 1st lt. to capt., M.C. U.S. Army, 1956-58. Recipient Walter Reed Disting. Achievement award U. Va. Alumni Assn., 2001 Master: Am. Acad. Dermatology (hon. bd. dir. 1973—76, pres. 1993—95, elected master in dermatology 2000, Gold medal 1990); mem.: Coun. Med. Splty. Socs. (bd. dir. 1989—92, sec. 1992—95), Am. Bd. Med. Spltys. (v.p. 1988, pres.-elect 1989, pres. 1990—92, Disting. Svc. award 1999), Raven Soc., So. Med. Assn., Med. Soc. Va. (Cmty. Svc. award 2001), Albermarie County Med. Soc., Dermatology Found., Am. Dermatol. Assn. (bd. dir. 1987—93, pres. 1992—93), Assn. Profs. Dermatology (sec.-treas. 1976—79), Soc. Investigative Dermatology (bd. dir. 1976—81, v.p. 1985, hon. mem. 1996), Va. Dermatol. Soc. (sec.-treas. 1965—71), Nat. Assn. Physicians Environ. (pres. 1995—97), Alpha Omega Alpha, Sigma Xi. Presbyterian. Home: 500 Crestwood Dr Apt 1602 Charlottesville VA 22903-4861

WEATHERFORD, SHIRLEY DIANE, special education educator; b. Belton, Tex., June 26, 1951; d. John E. and Mary Lynn Wood; m. Rollie A. Weatherford, Jan. 8, 1972; children: Joy Michelle Howard, John Ray. BS, East Tex. State U., Commerce, 1972. Cert. in special edn. Tex., 1994. Consumer sci. tchr. Forney ISD, Tex., 1989—98; life skills, spl. edn. Mesquite ISD, Tex., 1999—2006. Mentor, life skills Mesquite, Poteet HS, 2004—05. Contbr. articles. Officer Forney Chamber Commerce, Tex., 1982—2009; sunday sch. tchr., meth. youth fellowship First Meth. Ch., Forney, 1978—90; sunday sch. tchr., spl. needs class Fellowship Forney, 2007—08. Mem.: Autism Advocacy. Achievements include research in improved quality of life for severe & profound students in life skills. Office: Forney Independent Sch Dist 600 Bois D Arc Forney TX 75126

WEATHERHEAD, ANDREW KINGSLEY, educator; b. Manchester, Eng., Oct. 8, 1923; came to U.S., 1951; s. Leslie Dixon and Evelyn (Triggs) W.; m. Ingrid Antonie Lien, Aug. 27, 1952; children: Lyn Kristin, Leslie Richard, Andrea Kathryn. BA, U. Cambridge, Eng., 1944, MA, 1947, U. Edinburgh, Scotland, 1950; PhD, U. Wash., Seattle, 1958. Assoc. prof. La. State U., New Orleans, 1958-60; with U. Oreg., Eugene, 1960—, assoc. prof., 1962-68, prof. 20th century lit., 1968-89, prof. emeritus, 1989—. Author: A Reading of Henry Green, 1961, The Edge of the Image, 1967, Stephen Spender and the Thirties, 1975, Leslie Weatherhead: A Personal Portrait, 1975, The British Dissonance, 1983, Upstairs, 2000; contbr. articles to profl. jours. Avocations: birdwatching, reading. Home: 2698 Fairmount Blvd Eugene OR 97403-1758 Home Phone: 541-344-1166. Business E-Mail: akw@uoregon.edu.

WEATHERLEY-WHITE, ROY CHRISTOPHER ANTHONY, surgeon, consultant; b. Peshawar, India, Dec. 1, 1931; S. Roy and Elfreda (Milward) Boehm, m. Dorian Jeanne Freeman Weatherley-White, Dec. 27, 1961; children: Carl Christopher, Matthew Richard, Larissa Chantal. MA, Cambridge U., 1953; MD, Harvard U., 1958. Surgeon Biomedical Cons., Denver, 1970—; pres. Plastic Surgery Group, Denver, 1992-97. Chmn. Plastic Surgery Rsch. Coun., 1975-76; pres. Rocky Mountain Assn. Plastic Surgeons, 1973-74; v.p. Am. Cleft Palate Assn. Author: Plastic Surgery of the Female Breast, 1982; contbr. over 45 articles to profl. jours. Cons. Colo. Biomedical Venture Ctr., Denver, 1993—; chmn. bd. trustees Colo. Venture Ctrs., 1999—; bd. chairperson Operation Smile, Colo., 2000—. Recipient Rsch. award Am. Soc. Plastic Surgery, 1962, 64. Mem. Harvard Club of N.Y., Oxford-Cambridge Club, Denver Country Club, Denver Athletic Club. Episcopalian. Avocations: flying, skiing, scuba diving, archaeology. Home: 2101 E Hawthorne Pl Denver CO 80206-4116 Office: 2101 E Hawthorne Pl Denver CO 80206-4116

WEATHERMAN, ELIZABETH H. (BESS WEATHERMAN), private equity firm executive; b. 1960; BA in English, summa cum laude, Mt. Holyoke Coll., South Hadley, Mass., 1982; MBA, Stanford U. Grad. Sch. Bus., Calif., 1988. Formerly with Donaldson, Lufkin & Jenrette Securities; mem. healthcare group to mng. dir. healthcare activities, mem. exec. mgmt. group Warburg Pincus LLC, NYC, 1988—. Bd. dirs. ev3 Inc., 2005—, Tornier, Inc., Keystone Dental, Adlens Beacon, Bausch & Lomb Inc., Bacchus Vascular, Inc.; past bd. dirs. Am. Med. Sys. Holdings Inc., Kyphon Inc., Micro Therapeutics Inc., SURx, Inc., SpineCore Inc., Velocimed Inc., Wright Med. Tech. Inc., EndiCOR Med., Inc., UroQuest Med. Corp. Named to Midas List of 100 most highly regarded dealmakers in venture capital industry, Forbes Mag., 2006, 2007. Mem.: Nat. Venture Capital Assn. (bd. dirs. 2001—). Office: Warburg Pincus LLC 466 Lexington Ave New York NY 10017 Office Phone: 212-878-0600. Office Fax: 212-878-9351.*

WEATHERMON, SIDNEY EARL, retired elementary school educator; b. Abilene, Tex., Jan. 20, 1937; s. Sidney Elliot Weathermon and Evelyn Marie (Landreth) Parker. BA, U. Colo., 1962, MA, 1968, EdD, 1976. Cert. K-12 reading tchr., elem. edn. tchr., K-12 reading specialist. Tchr. grades 4-6 Jefferson County Pub. Schs., Colo., 1963—66; tchr. grades 5-6 Boulder Valley Pub. Schs., Colo., 1962—63, tchr. reading, 1968—71, consortium dir. right-to-read project Louisville Mid. Sch., 1974—75, coord. comm. skills program Vocat.-Tech. H.S., 1976, K-12 dist. reading specialist, 1971—85, chpt. 1 tchr. grades 1-6, 1985—89, coord. chpt. 1 kindergarten project, 1985—89, tchr. grade 1, 1989—95;

ret., 1995. Instr. U. Colo., Boulder, 1971-72, U. No. Colo., Greeley, 1977; adj. faculty Regis U., Denver, 1972-95, dept. edn. instr., 1982. Contbr. articles to profl. jours. Recipient Celebrate Lit. award Boulder Coun. Internat. Reading Assn., 1986; named Tchr. of Yr., IBM Corp., 1989, Colo./Nat. Educator, Milkin Family Found., 1990; NDEA fellow, 1966-68. Mem. NEA, Internat. Reading Assn., Colo. Edn. Assn., Boulder Valley Edn. Assn. (chair tchr. adv coun., assoc. rep., tchrs. rights and activities commn., negotiations team, profl. leave com.), Phi Delta Kappa (certs. of recognition 1987, 90), Kappa Delta Pi. Democrat. Avocation: southwest Indian art. Home: 449 S Shore Dr Osprey FL 34229-9657 Office Phone: 941-966-7939. Personal E-mail: drsidw@comcast.net.

WEATHERS, DWIGHT RONALD, dental educator; b. Milledgeville, Ga., Aug. 14, 1938; s. Dwight Louis and Ruby Clyde (Watkins) W.; m. Patsy Ann Williams, Aug. 14, 1961 (div. 1974); children: Margo Elaine, Karen Ashley, Dwight Kendal; m. Betty Jean Adams, Apr. 29, 1975; 1 child, Jason Alan Martin. DDS, Emory U., 1962, MSD, 1966. Diplomate Am. Bd. Oral Pathology. Asst. prof. oral pathology Emory U. Sch. Dentistry, Atlanta, 1967-70, assoc. prof., 1970-79, prof., 1979—, chmn. dept. oral pathology, 1979—, dean, 1985—. Cons. VA Hosp., Atlanta, Grady Hosp. Atlanta, Emory Hosp., Atlanta. COntbr. over 40 articles to profl. jours. Served to capt. USAF, 1962-64. Recipient Oral Cancer Research grant Smokeless Tobacco Research Council, Inc., 1977-78. Fellow Am. Coll. Dentists, Ga. Dental Assn.; mem. Am. Bd. Oral Pathology (councillor 1986—, pres. 1987-88), ADA, Am. Bd. Oral Pathology (bd. dirs. 1981—), Ga. Assn. Pathologists. Baptist. Avocations: downhill skiing, hunting, fishing. Office: Emory U Sch of Dentistry 1462 Clifton Rd NE Atlanta GA 30322-1000

WEATHERS, MATTHEW, educator; b. Orange, Calif., Apr. 16, 1971; s. Mark and Esther Weathers. MS, U. Southern Calif., LA, 2005. Asst. prof. Biola U., La Mirada, Calif., 1999—. Conservative. Home: 14786 Fairvilla Dr La Mirada CA 90638 Office: Biola Univ 13800 Biola Ave La Mirada CA 90639

WEATHERSBY, GEORGE BYRON, management company executive; b. Albany, Calif., Dec. 9, 1944; s. Byron and Fannie A. Weathersby; m. Connie J. Titone, Mar. 31, 2007; children from previous marriage: Deborah Jane, Geoffrey Byron. BS, U. Calif., Berkeley, 1965, MS, 1966, MBA, 1967; MS, Harvard U., 1968, PhD, 1970; DHL (hon.), U. San Francisco, 1987; LLD (hon.), U. So. Ind., 1992. Mem. faculty, assoc. dir. analytical studies, dir. Ford Found. rsch. program U. Calif., Berkeley, 1969-72; spl. asst. to U.S. Sec. of State Washington, 1972-73; dir. rsch. Nat. Commn. on Financing Higher Edn., Washington, 1973-74; assoc. prof. mgmt. Harvard U., Cambridge, Mass., 1974-78; commr. higher edn. State of Ind., 1977-83; pres. Curtis Pub. Co., 1983-86, New UPI Inc., Washington, 1985-86; corp. v.p. fin. Ontario Corp., Muncie, Ind., 1986-88, pres., 1988-91, also bd. dirs.; ptnr. Founders Court Inc., Princeton, NJ, 1991-93; independant cons., 1975—; pres. Oxford Mgmt. Corp., 1993-98, Cambridge Parallel Processing, 1994-98, Electronic Retailing Syss. Internat., 1996-98; pres., CEO, bd. dirs. Am. Mgmt. Assn., NYC, 1998—2002; chmn., CEO Genesys Corp., LLC, 2002—. CEO, Quisic, Inc., 2001-02; chmn. bd. dirs. Otis Conner Cos., 1984-86, Curtis Media Corp., 1984-86, Curtis Internat. Ltd., 1985-86, Prince Gardner, Inc., 1991-93, Alma Industries, 1992-93, Hanes Holding Co., 1992-93; bd. dirs. Holcim (US), Inc., Farm Fans Inc., Delta Consol. Industries, Cambridge Parallel Processing, Advanced Retail Mktg., ERS, Inc., AOI Med., Inc., Bostwick Labs., Inc. Author: Financing Postsecondary Education in the U.S, 1974, Colleges and Money, 1976; contbr. numerous articles to profl. jours.; cons. editor: Jour. Higher Edn., 1974—; exec. editor: Change mag., 1980-84. Bd. dirs. Nat. Ctr. for Higher Edn Mgmt. Sys., 1980-83, U.S.A. Group, 1989—96; mem. steering com. Edn. Commn. of States, 1978-82; mem. Ind. Com. Humanities, 1981-87; trustee U. So. Ind., 1985-91, Park Tudor Sch. Indpls., 1986-91, Butler U., 1987-93; mem. adv. coun. Invest in New Zealand, 2001-, MicroNets, 2005-; mem. adv. coun. for leadership and mgmt. for U.S. Dept. State, 2004-06. Calif. Regents scholar, 1963-65; NSF fellow, 1966-67; AEC fellow, 1966-67; Kent fellow, 1967-70; White House fellow, 1972-73; named 1 of 100 Outstanding Young Leaders in Higher Edn. Change Mag., 1978, 1 of Top 100 CEOs, C10 Mag., 2000. Mem. Am. Mgmt. Assn., Am. Coun. Edn., Ops. Rsch. Soc. Am., Inst. Mgmt. Scis., Econometrica, Young Pres. Orgn. Republican. Office Phone: 908-400-2774. Business E-Mail: gweathersby@genesysllc.com.

WEATHERSBY, MICHAEL NELSON, lawyer; b. Columbus, Ga., Oct. 20, 1956; s. Nelson Jennings and Erma (Spann) W.; m. Phyllis Solomon, Nov. 30, 1973 (div. Dec. 1980); 1 child, James Michael; m. Risë Hegwood, Mar. 21, 1982; children, Alexander Hegwood, John Thomas. Lang. cert. Turkish, Presidio of Monterey (Calif.), 1976; BA summa cum laude, Ga. SW Coll., 1981; JD cum laude, U. Ga., 1984. Bar: Ga., D.C, Fla., Tex. Retail mgr. Benson Wholesale Co., Geneva, Ala., 1973-75; translater Ft. Meade, Md., 1976—79; sales mgr. Williams Office Equipment Co., Americus, Ga., 1980-81; law clk. Ga. Gov.'s Office, Atlanta, 1982; assoc. Neely & Player, Atlanta, 1984-87, Glass, McCullough, Sherrill & Harrold, Atlanta, 1987-89; ptnr. Evert Weathersby Houff, Atlanta, 1989—. Gen. counsel HDX-USA, Inc., Atlanta. Mem. and elder Intown Comty. Presbyterian Church. With USAF, 1975—79. Fellow Bryant T. Castellow Found., 1981-84. Mem. ABA, State Bar of Ga., D.C. Bar, Tex. Bar, Ga. Trial Lawyers Assn., Assn. Trial Lawyers Am., Druid Hills Golf Club, Sigma Tau Delta. Office: Evert Weathersby Houff Ste 200 3405 Piedmont Rd Atlanta GA 30305 Office Phone: 678-651-1222. Office Fax: 678-651-1201. Business E-Mail: mnweathersby@ewhlaw.com.

WEATHERUP, ROY GARFIELD, lawyer; b. Annapolis, Md., Apr. 20, 1947; s. Robert Alexander and Kathryn Crites (Hesser) W.; m. Wendy Gaines, Sept. 10, 1977; children: Jennifer, Christine. AB in Polit. Sci., Stanford U., 1968, JD, 1972. Bar: Calif. 1972, U.S. Dist. Ct. 1973, U.S. Ct. Appeals (9th cir.) 1975, U.S. Supreme Ct. 1980. Assoc. Haight, Brown & Bonesteel, LA, Santa Ana, 1972—78, ptnr., 1979—2003, Lewis Brisbois Bisgaard & Smith, LA, 2004—. Judge Moot Ct. UCLA, Loyola U., Pepperdine U.; arbitrator Am. Arbitration Assn.; mem. com. Book Approved Jury Instrns. LA Superior Ct. Mem. ABA, Calif. Acad. Appellate Lawyers, LA County Bar Assn., Town Hall Calif. Republican. Methodist. Home: 17260 Rayen St Northridge CA 91325-2919 Office: Lewis Brisbois Bisgaard & Smith 221 N Figueroa St Los Angeles CA 90012 Home Phone: 818-993-0542; Office Phone: 213-680-5130. E-mail: royweatherup@aol.com.

WEAVER, ANNE GENEVIEVE HERA, writer; d. George Edgar Zeigler and Ruth Roberts; m. Stephen Elliott Thompson, May 5, 1979; children: Jessica Weaver Thompson, James Scott Weaver Thompson. MS, PhD, U. N.Mex. Author: (non-fiction children's sci.) The Voyage of the Beetle (Zia award, 2008). Vol. Beetle NM State Library State Book, 2008; bd. officer Santa Fe Sci. Initiative, 2004—09. Mem.: Geol. Soc. Am., Paleoanthropological Soc., Brain Behavioral Sci.

WEAVER, CHARLES LYNDELL, JR., marketing executive, educational consultant; b. Canonsburg, Pa., July 5, 1945; s. Charles Lyndell and Georgia Lavelle (Gardner) W.; m. Ruth Marguerite Uxa, Feb. 27, 1982; children: Charles Lyndell III, John Francis. BArch, Pa. State U., 1969; cert. in assoc. studies, U. Florence, Italy, 1968. Registered architect, Pa., Mo., Va.; cert. Nat. Coun. Arch. Registration Bd.; cert. designee, Design Build Inst. Am., 2002. With Celento & Edson, Canonsburg, part-time 1966-71; project architect Meyers & D'Aleo, Balt., 1971-76, corp. dir., v.p., 1974-76; ptnr. Borrow Assocs.-Developers, Balt., 1976-79, Crowley/Weaver Constrn. Mgmt., Balt., 1976-79; pvt. practice arch. Balt., 1976-79; cons., project mgr. U. Md., College Park, 1979-80; corp. cons. architect Bank Bldg. & Equipment Corp., Am., St. Louis, 1980-83; dir. archtl. and engring. svcs. Ladue Bldg. and Engring. Inc., St. Louis, 1983-84; v.p., sec. Graphic Products Corp.; pres. CWCM Inc. Internat., 1987-2000. Dir. K-12 Edn. Market Ctr. and sr. program mgr. Sverdrup Corp., 1989-95; prin. Benham Internat. Eurasia, 1995, v.p., dir. mktg. and bus. devel. The Benham Group, St. Louis, 1995-96; v.p. Chiodini Assocs., 1997-98; asst. lectr. Washington U., 1997-2000, 01-; cons. Stifel Cap. Start Up Venture Capital Fund; ops. mgr., Stifel Capco Venture Capital, 1998, CERT Inst. Abu Dhabi, UAE, 2005; dir. mktg. sys. The Maiman Co., 1998-99; dir. edn. program mgmt. The Integral Group, Atlanta, 1999-2001; vis. Alpha Rho Chi lectr. Pa. State U., 1983; vis. lectr. Washington U. Lindenwood Coll., 1987, Wentworth Inst., Boston, Am. Assn. Cost Engrs., So. Fla., 1994, with U. Houston, 2002; mem. panel Assn. Univ. Architects Conv., 1983; v.p. program mgmt. and ednl. facilities Kennedy Assoc. Inc.; participant K-12 Nat. Summit, San Diego, 2002; URS Corp. dep. project mgmt. Phila. Sch. Improvement Team, 2003-04; demonstration ednl. facilities program svcs. coord.-design/build Joseph, Jingoli and Sons, 2004—, East Orange, Trenton & Vineland Abbott Demonstration Schs., 2004-09; spkr. and presenter in field. Contbr. Planning Guide for Maintaining Facilities, U.S. Dept. Edn.; author: (jour.) NY Construction Today, 2009 (BDYC Annual BLDG Team award), Learning By Design, 2009, Real Estate Construction And Review (Tri State Editionj)2009 (BDFC Spl. Recognition). Project bus. cons. Jr. Achievement, 1982-85, 2001-2003; mem. cluster com., advisor Explorer Program, 1982-85; mem. Design Build Inst. Am., 1998—, splty. contractor task force chmn., 2000-02. Recipient 5 brochure and graphic awards Nat. Assn. Indsl. Artists, 1973; 1st award Profl. Builder/Am. Plywood Assn., 1974; Honor award, 2 articles Balt. chpt. AIA, 1974; Better Homes and Gardens award Sensible Growth, Nat. Assn. Home Builders, 1975; winner Ridgely's Delight Competition, Balt., 1976. Mem. ASCD, AACE (conv. spkr. So. Fla. sect. 1994), Vitruvius Alumni Assn., Pa. State Alumni Assn., AIA, Constrn. Specifications Inst., Am. Assn. Sch. Adminstrs. (nat. coun., panel moderator 1994), Coun. Ednl. Facilities Planners, Assn. Sch. Bus. Ofcls., Alpha Rho Chi (nat. treas. 1980-82, dir. nat. found. treas. 1989-97), Optimists Internat. Office: 1 Lenox Dr Ste 100 Lawrenceville NJ 08648 Business E-Mail: cweaver@jingoli.com.

WEAVER, CLIFFORD LEE, retired lawyer, winery owner; b. Chgo., Mar. 11, 1945; s. Thomas E. and Thera A. (Ramey) Cash; m. Donna Rae Florence, Aug. 20, 1966; 1 child, Megan R. AB with honors, U. Chgo., 1966, JD with honors, 1969. Bar: Ill. 1969, U.S. Dist. Ct. (no. dist.) Ill. 1969, U.S. Ct. Appeals (7th cir.) 1969, U.S. Supreme Ct. 1975. Sr. clk. U.S. Ct. Appeals, Chgo., 1969-71; assoc. Ross & Hardies, Chgo., 1971-75, ptnr., 1976-83, Burke, Weaver & Prell, Chgo., 1983-99, mng. ptnr., 1990-99; owner, operator Azienda Agricola Le Miccine vineyard and winery, 1996—. Gen. counsel N.W. Water Commn., 1978—99, DuPage Water Commn., DuPage County, Ill., 1987—99, Lake County (Ill.) Forest Preserve, 1991—99; village atty. Village of Bannockburn, Ill., 1977—99, Village of Northbrook, 1977—99, Village of Glencoe, Ill., 1978—99, Village of Hinsdale, Ill., 1985—99, Village of Libertyville, Ill., 1990—99. Co-author: Special Districts in Illinois, 1977, City Zoning, 1979; contbr. numerous articles to profl. jours. Trustee Kenilworth (Ill.) Libr. Dist., 1987-89; mem. Kenilworth Zoning Bd., 1985-2006. Mem.: ABA, Order of Coif, Phi Beta Kappa. Republican. Home: 144 Woodstock Ave Kenilworth IL 60043-1262 Office Phone: 847-256-7258. E-mail: clw@lemiccine.com.

WEAVER, DAVE, Councilman; m. Linda Weaver; children: Noelani, Danny. BS in Civil Engring., USC, 1963. Cert. RCE. Councilman City of Glendale, Calif., 1997—, mayor, 2000—01, 2006—07. Vice chmn. Glendale Redevelopment Agy.; chmn. Glendale Housing Authority, 1997—98, former vice chmn.; chmn. Redevelopment Agy., 1999—2000, former vice chmn. Mem. Glendale C. of C.; bd. mem. Montrose C. of C.; former pres. LA Fed. Employees Credit Union League, Glendale Homeowners Coordinating Coun., chmn. Hillside Task Force. With Seabees USN, 1964—65, Construction Battalions Hdqs., ret. project mgr. CE US Army. Mem.: Filipino Bus. & Profl. Assn., Hispanic Bus. & Profl. Assn., Glenoaks Canyon Homeowners Assn. (former pres.), Rose Float Assn. (bd. mem., chmn. Dreaming of Roses Fundraiser), Bellarmine-Jefferson High Sch. Sports Booster Club (former pres.), USC Trojan Coaches Club (life), Glendale Cmty. Coll. Alumni Assn. Office: 613 E Broadway Rm 200 Glendale CA 91206 Office Phone: 818-548-4844. Fax: 818-547-6740. E-mail: dweaver@ci.glendale.ca.us.*

WEAVER, DENNIS RUSSELL, lawyer; b. Birmingham, Ala., Mar. 25, 1970; s. Dennis Michael and Pamela Wayland Weaver; m. Michelle Howell, Dec. 12, 1998; 1 child, Michael II. BS magna cum laude, U. Ala., Tuscaloosa, 1992, JD, 1995. Bar: Ala. 1995, US Dist. Ct. (no., mid. and so. dists.) Ala. 1995, US Ct. Appeals (11th cir.) 1995, US Dist. Ct. Wyo. 1998, Miss. 2000, US Dist. Ct. (no. and so. dists.) Miss. 2000, US Ct. Appeals (5th cir.) 2000, US Dist. Ct. (so. dist.) NY 2000, W.Va. 2003, US Dist. Ct. (so. dist.) W.Va. 2003. Assoc. Hollingsworth & Assocs., Birmingham, 1995—97; ptnr. Cory, Watson, Crowder & De Garis, Birmingham, 1997—2003; founding mem. Weaver Tidmore, LLC, Birmingham, 2003—. Legal advisor Ga. Mountain Vol. Fire Dept., Guntersville, Ala., 2005—. Coach Little League Soccer, Vestavia Hills, Ala., 2006—. Named Best of Bar, Birmingham Bus. Jour., 2005. Mem.: ATLA (advocate Nat. Coll. Advocacy 1996—), ABA, Miss. Trial Lawyers Assn., Ala. Trial Lawyers Assn. (com. chmn., bd. govs.), Nat. Crime Victim Bar Assn. (charter, Frank Carrington Champion of Civil Justice 2003), Nat. Transp. Safety Bd. Bar Assn., Birmingham Bar Assn., Farrah Law Soc., Million Dollar Advocates Forum. Baptist. Avocations: hunting, fishing, golf. Office: Weaver Tidmore LLC 200 Cahaba Park Cir Ste 214 Birmingham AL 35242

WEAVER, DIANNE JAY, lawyer; b. Kansas City, Mo., June 28, 1944; d. Thomas G. and Anna Jeanette Jay; m. Benjamin J. Weaver, Sept. 16, 1970; children: Jay, Jenny, Scott, Elizabeth. BS, U. Kans., 1965; JD, Ind. U., 1970. Bar: Ind., Fla., Colo.; bd. cert. trial lawyer. Ptnr. Weaver & Weaver, P.A., Ft. Lauderdale, Fla.; of counsel Krupnick Campbell Malone Roselli Buser Slama & Hancock P.A., Ft. Lauderdale; ptnr. Harrell & Narrel, P.A., Jacksonville, 2002—. Speaker in field. Contbr. articles to profl. jours. Trustee Civil Justice Found.; bd. dirs. Trial Lawyers for Pub. Justice; chmn. publicity com. Civil Justice Found. Fellow Roscoe Pound Found. (life); mem. ATLA (bd. govs., sec.), Acad. Fla. Trial Lawyers (bd. dirs.), So. Trial Lawyers Assn. (bd. govs.), Fla. Bar Assn. (chair trial advocacy com.),. Fed. Bar Assn., Broward County Women Lawyers Assn. (founding pres.). Office: Harrell & Harrell PA 4735 Sunbeam Rd Jacksonville FL 32257 Office Phone: 904-251-1111. Business E-Mail: dweaver@forjustice.com.

WEAVER, DONNA RAE, winery executive; b. Chgo., Oct. 15, 1945; d. Albert Louis and Gloria Elaine (Graffis) Florence; m. Clifford L. Weaver, Aug. 20, 1966; 1 child, Megan Rae. BS in Edn., No. Ill. U., 1966, EdD, 1977; MEd, De Paul U., 1974. Tchr. H.L. Richards High Sch., Oak Lawn, Ill., 1966-71, Sawyer Coll. Bus., Evanston, Ill., 1971-72; asst. prof. Oakton Community Coll., Morton Grove, Ill., 1972-75; vis. prof. U. Ill., Chgo., 1977-78; dir. devel. Mallinckrodt Coll., Wilmette, Ill., 1978-80, dean, 1980-83; campus dir. Nat.-Louis U., Chgo., 1983-90, dean div. applied behavioral scis., 1985-89; dean Coll. Mgmt. and Bus., 1989-90; pres. The Oliver Group, Inc., Kenilworth, Ill., 1993-97; mng. ptnr. Le Miccine, Gaiole-in-Chianti, Tuscany, Italy, 1996—. Cons. Nancy Lovely and Assocs., Wilmette, 1981-84, North Ctrl. Assn., Chgo., 1982-90. Contbr. articles to Am. Vocat. Jour., Ill. Bus. Edn. Assn. Monograph, Nat. Coll. Edn.'s ABS Rev., Nat. View. Mem. Ill. Quality of Work Life Coun., 1987-90, New Trier Twp. Health and Human Svcs. Adv. Bd., Winnetka, Ill., 1985-88; bd. dirs. Open Lands Project, 1985-87, Kenilworth (Ill.) Village House, 1986-87. Recipient Achievement award Women in Mgmt., 1981; Am. Bd. Master Educators charter disting. fellow, 1986. Mem. Nat. Bus. Edn. Assn., Delta Pi Epsilon (past pres.), Bears Care Gala Exec. Bd. Avocations: reading, travel, decorating. Home and Office: 144 Woodstock Ave Kenilworth IL 60043-1262 Address: Azienda Agricola Le Miccine S Traversa Chiantigiana 53013 Gaiole in Chianti Italy E-mail: drw@lemiccine.com.

WEAVER, ELIZABETH A., state supreme court justice; b. New Orleans; d. Louis and Mary Weaver. BA, Newcomb Coll.; JD, Tulane U. Elem. tchr. Glen Lake Cmty. Sch., Maple City, Mich.; French tchr. Leelanau Sch., Glen Arbor, Mich.; pvt. practice Glen Arbor, Mich.; law clk. Civil Dist. Ct., New Orleans; atty. Coleman, Dutrey & Thomson, New Orleans; atty., title specialist Chevron Oil Co., New Orleans; probate and juvenile judge Leelanau County, Mich., 1975—86; judge Mich. Ct. Appeals, 1987—94; justice Mich. Supreme Ct., Lansing, 1995—. Chief justice Mich. Supreme Ct., 1999—2000, re-elected, 2002—; chief justice Peter Rellected Superior Ct. Justice, 2002—; instr. edn. dept. Ctr. Mich. U.; mem. Mich. Com. on Juvenile Justice, Nat. Conv. State Adv. Groups on Juvenile Justice for U.S.; chair Gov.'s Task Force on Children's Justice, Trial Ct. Assessment Commn., Office Juvenile Justice and Delinquency Prevention; jud. adv. bd. mem. Law and Orgnl. Econs. Ctr. U. Kans.; treas. Children's Charter of Cts. of Mich. Chairperson Western Mich. U. CLE Adv. Bd.; mem. steering com. Grand Traverse/Leelanau Commn. on Youth; mem. Glen Arbor Twp. Zoning Bd.; mem. charter arts north Leelanau County; mem. citizen's adv. coun. Arnell Engstrom Children's Ctr.; mem. cmty. adv. com. Pathfinder Sch. Treaty Law Demonstration Project; active Grand Traverse/Leelanau Mental Health Found. Recipient Eastern award, Warren Easton Hall of Fame, Lifetime Dedication to Children award, Mich. Champions in Childhood Injury Prevention, 2000, Recognition award for outstanding svc. to Mich. children and families, Gov. Engler and Family Independence Agy., 2000, Profls. award, Mich. Assn. Drug Cts., 2002, Mary S. Coleman award, Ctr. for Civic Edn. Through Law, 2002; named Jurist of Yr., Police Officers Assn. of Mich.; named one of five Outstanding Young Women in Mich., Mich. Jaycees. Fellow: Mich. State Bar Found.; mem.: ABA, Antrim County Bar Assn., Leelanau County Bar Assn., Grand Traverse County Bar Assn., La. Bar Assn., Nat. Coun. Juvenile and Family Judges, Mich. Bar Assn. (chair CLE adv. bd., chair crime prevention ctr., chair juvenile law com.), Delta Kappa Gamma (hon.). Office: Mich Supreme Ct 10850 E Traverse Hwy Ste 4480 Traverse City MI 49684-1364*

WEAVER, ERIC JAMES, educational administrator; b. Purley, Surrey, Eng., May 14, 1938; came to U.S., 1947, naturalized, 1963; s. Edward Arthur and Amelia Cecily (Ealden) W.; m. Joyce Lynn McKean, Aug. 19, 1973; children: Stephanie Lynn, Heather Elizabeth, Jonathan Eric, Christopher James. AB, Princeton U., 1958; STB, Gen. Theol. Sem., 1961; MDiv, 1972; MS, CCNY, 1968; profl. diploma, Hofstra U., 1973; EdD, 1980. Rsch. assoc. Meadow Brook Nat. Bank, West Hempstead, N.Y., 1957-61; dir. Christian edn. and youth work Ch. Holy Cross, Bklyn., 1958-61; vicar Ch. Messiah, Ctrl. Islip, N.Y., 1961-63, St. Michael and All Angel's Ch., Gordon Heights, N.Y., 1961-63; tchr. spl. edn. Nassau County Vocat. Edn. and Extension Bd., N.Y., 1963-67; supr. ctrl. adminstrn. Nassau Bd. Coop. Ednl. Svcs., 1967-70; asst. prin. Rosemary Kennedy Sch. for Trainable Mentally Retarded, Wantagh, N.Y., 1970-73; dir. spl. edn. Middle County Schs., Suffolk County, N.Y., 1973-81, dir. spl. ednl. svcs., 1981—98. Vice chmn. Project EQUALS, 1983-86; ednl. cons., instr. Spl. Edn. Tng. Resource Ctr., 1986-98; impartial hearing officer State of N.Y., 1982-97; chmn. com. spl. edn. Middle County Schs., 1973-98, com. preschool spl. edn., 1990-98; mem. Spl. Edn. Adminstrv. Leadership Tng. Acad., 1989-98; adj. asst. prof. spl. edn. C.W. Post Coll., 1979-80; ednl. cons., 1998-2008. Author monographs: The Sources of the First Gospel, 1958, Rudolf Bultman and Entmythologisierung, 1961, Ocular, Manual and Podiatric Dominance in a Severely Retarded Older Adolescent Population, 1968, Efforts of Special Education Administrators to Meet the Needs of Special Education Teachers by Inservice Training, 1980. Capt. Aux Police, County of Suffolk, N.Y., 1962-69; bd. dirs. Traffic Safety Bd., County of Nassau, N.Y., 1969-71, RobinPark Civic Assn.,Huntington, N.Y., 1963-66; trustee Police Hall of Fame; hon. mem. steering com. ann. art auction Lake Grove (N.Y.) Sch., 1985-90; asst. to rector Grace Ch., Huntington Sta., N.Y., 1963-66, Trinity Episc. Ch., Northport, N.Y., 1966-99, rector 1999-2009, rector emeritus 2009-. Fellow Am. Assn. Mental Deficiency; mem. Interagy. Coun. on Recreation for Handicapped (dir. 1970-73), Coun. Exceptional Children (pres. 1973-74), Coun. Adminstrs. Spl. Edn. (treas. 1985-89), Internat. Assn. Sci. Study Mental Deficiency, Long Island Assn. Spl. Edn. Adminstrn. (sec. 1975-76, v.p. 1976-77, pres. 1977-78, exec. com. 1978-2008), Assn. to Help Retarded Children, Am. Ednl. Rsch. Assn., am. assn. sch. Adminstrs, Sch. Adminstrs. Assn. N.Y. State, Phi Delta Kappa. Republican. Episcopalian. Home: 8 Oceanside Ct Northport NY 11768-1301 E-mail: eweaver@optonline.net.

WEAVER, FRANKLIN THOMAS, retired newspaper executive; b. Johnstown, NY, Oct. 11, 1932; s. Edwin K. and Bertha J. (Wendt) W.; children: Thomas, James, Michael, David, Tammy, Kelly, Anna; m. Joyce W. Phelps, Oct. 23, 1991. BA with high honors in Journalism, Mich. State U., 1954. Advt. sales rep. Grand Rapids Press, Mich., 1955-64; controller Muskegon (Mich.) Chronicle, 1964-66; mgr. Bay City (Mich.) Times, 1966-73, Jackson (Mich.) Citizen Patriot, 1973-84, pub., 1984—99; ret. Mem.: Mich. Press Assn. (pres. 1991), Newspapers Assn. Am., Greater Jackson C. of C., Ella Sharp Mus. (pres. 1995—96), Jackson Country Club.

WEAVER, JACQUELYN KUNKEL IVEY, artist, educator; b. Richmond, Ky., Mar. 14, 1931; d. Marion David and Margaret Tabitha (Brandenburg) Kunkel; m. George Thomas Ivey Sr., 1951 (dec. 1989); children: George Thomas Ivey Jr., David Richard Ivey; m. Harrell Fuller Weaver, 1991. BFA, Wesleyan Coll., 1987. Owner J.K. Ivey Art, Macon, Ga., 1974-91, J.K. Ivey Bookkeeping and Tax Svc., Macon, Ga., 1976-84, J.K. Ivey-Weaver Art Studio, Macon, 1991—. Tchr. drawing, painting and sculpture, 1991—. Exhibitions include Mid. Ga. Art Assn. Gallery, Macon, 1980—2009, Stofko-Dixon Fine Arts, Bolingbroke, Ga., 1996—2001, Self Family Art Ctr., Hilton Head Island, SC, 2001, Mus. Arts and Scis., Macon, 2002, 2005, 2007, Brazier Art Gallery, Richmond, Va., 2002, Gallery 51, Forsyth, Ga., 2003—05, Roundtree Gallery, Seaside, Fla., 2003—04, Monroe County Arts Alliance, Forsyth, Ga., 2004—09, Richard Schmid Fine Art Auction, Bellvue, Colo., 2004, 2005, 2006, 2007, 2008—09, Macon Arts Alliance Gallery, Ga., 2005—09. Bd. dirs., treas. Mid. Ga. Art Assn., Macon, 1981-84, 92, publicity chmn., 1988-89, chmn. nominating com., 1997, mem. fin. com., 1998-99, audit com., 1998. Mem.: Monroe County Arts Alliance, Hilton Head Island Art League, Oil Painters of Am., Portrait Painters Am., Inc., Mid. Ga. Art Assn., Catherine Lorillard Wolf Art Club, Mus. Arts and Scis., Wesleyan Coll. Alumnae Assn., Nat. Mus. Women in Arts (charter). Presbyterian. Avocations: ballroom dancing, reading, walking, music. Office: JK Ivey-Weaver Art Studio 6183 Hwy 87 Macon GA 31210 Office Phone: 478-477-1385. Office Fax: 478-744-0983. Business E-Mail: jweav550@bellsouth.net.

WEAVER, JAMES HOWARD, former Congressman; b. Brookings, SD, Aug. 8, 1927; s. Leo C. and Alice (Flittie) W.; m. Katie Mason, 1998 BS in Polit. Sci, U. Oreg., 1952. Publisher's rep., 1954—58; builder & real estate developer Oreg.; staff dir. Oreg. Legis. Interim Com. on Agr., 1959—60; mem. US Congress from 4th Oreg. Dist., 1975—87. Del. to Dem. Nat. Convention, 1960—64. Author: Two Kinds: The Genetic Origin of Conservatives & Liberals. Served USN, 1945—46. Recipient numerous awards environ. orgns. and causes. Democrat.

WEAVER, JANET See COATS, JANET

WEAVER, JOHN, political strategist; Dep. campaign mgr., polit. dir. for Bill Clements Gubernatorial Campaign, Tex., 1986; exec. dir. Rep. Party of Tex., 1987—88; head Tex. campaign for V.p. George Bush, 1988; founder Campaign Svcs. Group (CSG), 1989; lead cons. Tex. campaign Pres. George Bush, 1992; chief polit. advisor to Senator John McCain, chief strategist to presdl. campaign, 2007; sr. ptnr. BreakPoint Pub. Affairs, LLC, Washington, 2007—, The Network, LLC, NYC, Washington. Head comm. NYC, 2001. Republican. Office: BreakPoint Public Affairs, LLC Ste 550 975 F St, NW Washington DC 20004 Office Phone: 202-552-5835. Office Fax: 202-552-5843.*

WEAVER, JOHN B., library director; b. Fayetteville, Ark., Apr. 16, 1973; m. Vivi Eugenia Washburn; children: Josephine Avril, Adela Breanne, Thessaly Laryn. PhD, Emory U., Atlanta, 2004. Reference libr. Pitts Theology Libr., Emory U., Atlanta, 2004—05, head pub. svcs., 2005—. Deacon Ch. Christ, Atlanta, 2006—08. Business E-Mail: jbweave@emory.edu.

WEAVER, JOHN BORLAND, musician, department chairman, composer; b. Palmerton, Pa., Apr. 27, 1937; s. David Williams and Bertha Brownlee (Borl) W.; m. Marianne Carol Gruhn, Apr. 30, 1942; children: Jonathan Kirk, Kirianne Elizabeth. Diploma, Curtis Inst. Music, Phila., 1959; M in Sacred Music, Union Theol. Sem., 1968; MusD (hon.), Westminster Coll., 1995, MusD (hon.), 1995, Curtis Inst. Music, 2003. Head organ dept. Curtis Inst. Music, 1972—2003; chmn. organ dept. Manhattan Sch. Music, 1983-84, Juilliard Sch. Music, NYC, 1986—2004. Mem. faculty Westminister Choir Coll., Princeton, N.J., 1970-72, Union Theol. Sem. Sch. Sacred Music, 1970-73 Organist, choirmaster, Holy Trinity Lutheran Ch., N.Y.C., 1959-70, Temple Beth-El, Manhattan Beach, N.Y., 1970-80; dir. music, Madison Ave. Presbyn. Ch., N.Y.C., 1970—2005; solo organ recitalist, U.S., Can., Western Europe, U.K., Brazil; composer: Psalm 100, 1958, Toccatafor Organ, 1959, Epiphany Alleluias, 1967, Rhapsody for Flute and Organ, 1968, Good Christian Men, Rejoice, 1978, Introit for Pentecost, Fantasia for Organ, Passacaglia on a Theme by Dunstable, all 1981, The Joyful Feast, 1988, Psalm 46, 1989, Dialogues for Flute and Organ, 1991, Prayer for Transfiguration Day, 1991, Prelude and Fugue in E Minor, 1994, Prayer From Psalm 139, 1995, Variations on Three Hymn Tunes, 1997, Restore Us, O Lord of Hosts, 1995; contbr. articles to jours. including Reformed Liturgy and Music. Served with AUS, 1961-63. Decorated Army Commendation medal; recipient Disting. Alumni award, Peabody Conservatory, 1989, Disting. Svc. in the Field of Music award, Peabody chpt. Johns Hopkins U., 1989, Disting. Alumni award, Union Theological Seminary, 2008; named the Performer of Yr., NYC Chpt. of Am. Guild, 2005, Hall of Fame, Balti. City Coll. Mem.: Presbyn. Assn. Musicians (pres. 1984—86), Am. Guild Organists, N.Am. Acad. Liturgy, St. Wilfrid Club (NYC). Home: 23 Rowell Rd West Glover VT 05875 Office Phone: 802-525-4491. Personal E-mail: marianneweaver@juno.com. *By hard work and good fortune I have been able to do that which I decided, at age ten, to do with my life.*

WEAVER, JOHN D. (BERT WEAVER), chemist, researcher; b. Louisville, Oct. 27, 1951; s. Gerald J. and Joyce M. Weaver; m. Sarah Springer, June 20, 1987. BA, Vanderbilt U., Nashville, 1973, PhD, 1977. Rsch. leader Dow Chem. Co., Freeport, Tex., 1978—. Mem.: Am. Chem. Soc. Achievements include patents and publications in field. Avocations: travel, baseball. Office: Dow Chem Co 2301 Brazosport Blvd B1603 Bldg Freeport TX 77541

WEAVER, KENNETH NEWCOMER, geologist, state agency administrator; b. Lancaster, Pa., Jan. 16, 1927; s. A. Ross and Cora (Newcomer) W.; m. Mary Elizabeth Hoover, Sept. 9, 1950; children: Wendy Elaine, Matthew Owen. BS, Franklin and Marshall Coll., 1950; MA, Johns Hopkins U., 1952, PhD, 1954. Instr. geology Johns Hopkins, 1953- 54; ops. analyst Ops. Rsch. Office, Washington, 1954-56; chief geologist, then mgr. geology and quarry dept. Medusa Portland Cement Co., Wampum, Pa., 1956-63; dir., state geologist Md. Geol. Survey, Balt., 1963-92; chmn. Md. Land Reclamation Com., 1978-92. Gov.'s rep. Interstate Oil Compact Commn., Interstate Mining Compact Commn.; mem. outer shelf adv. com. U.S. Dept. Interior; chmn. Md. Topographic Mapping Com.; mem. com. on surface mining and reclamation NAS, 1978, vice chmn. com. on disposal of excess spoil, 1980-81, mem. com. on geologic mapping, 1983, liaison mem. bd. earth scis., 1982-88, mem. com. on water resources rsch., 1989-92, chmn. com. on abandoned minelands rsch. priorities, 1987; mem. subcom. on mgmt. of maj. underground constrn. projects Nat. Acad. Engring.; mem. Md. Commn. on Artistic Property, 1988-92. With U.S. Maritime Svc., 1944—46, with AUS, 1954—56. Recipient John Wesley Powell award USGS, 1994; named hdqr. bldg. The Kenneth N. Weaver Bldg. Md. Geol. Survey, 1994. Fellow Geol. Soc. Am. (sec. N.E. sect. 1985-2001), AAAS (sr.); mem. Am. Assn. Petroleum Geologists (Ea. sect., George V. Cohee Pub. Svc. award 1991), Am. Inst. Mining Engrs., Am. Inst. Profl. Geologists (editor 1983-84, Martin Van Couvering Meml. award 1992), Am. Geol. Inst. (governing bd. 1973, exec. com. 1989-90, medal in memory of Ian Campbell 2001), Am. Water Rsch. Assn., Geol. Soc. Washington, Assn. Am. State Geologists (pres. 1973, hon. mem. 1992), Johns Hopkins Club (Balt.). Republican. Presbyterian (elder). Office: Md Geol Survey 2300 St Paul St Baltimore MD 21218-5210 Home: 2525 Pot Spring Rd Unit S322 Lutherville Timonium MD 21093-2862 Home Phone: 410-252-0181; Office Phone: 410-554-5532. Personal E-mail: kweaver418@aol.com.

WEAVER, LINDA MARIE, pharmacist, education educator; d. John William and Lorraine Marie Miller; m. Daniel Jacob Weaver. BA in Edn. and Spanish, Western Mich. U., 1974; BS in Pharmacy, Ferris State U., 1984; PharmD, Midwestern U., Chgo. Coll. of Pharmacy, 2000. Registered Pharmacist Mich., 1984. Ambulatory pharmacist Perry Drugs, Midland, Mich., 1984—87, Revco Drugs, Tucson, 1987—89, Walgreens Drug, Tucson, 1989—93; compliance officer Ariz. State Bd. of Pharmacy, Phoenix, 1993—99; clin. hosp. pharmacist John C. Lincoln Hosp., Phoenix, 1999—2001; med. sci. liaison Wyeth Pharmaceuticals, Scottsdale, 2001—03; med. liaison Abbott Labs., Scottsdale, 2003—04, clin. sci. mgr., 2004—07, sr. clin. sci. mgr., 2007—. Adj. faculty mem. Midwestern U. Coll. of Pharmacy, Glendale, Ariz.; instr. Rio Salado C.C., Phoenix, 1997—98, Ariz. Pharmacy Assn., 1987—; adv. bd. mem. SCP Comm., Inc., Phoenix, 2001—01. Vol. Am. Diabetes Assn., Scottsdale, 1994—2004, Am. Heart Assn., Scottsdale, 1994—2004, Am. Cancer Assn., Scottsdale, 1994—2004. Recipient Golden Key Nat. Honor Soc., Mich. State U., 1981, Rho Chi Honor Soc., Midwestern U., 2000. Mem.: Am. Soc. of Health Sys. Pharmacists (licentiate), Am. Colleges of Clin. Pharmacists (licentiate), Am. Pharmacists Assn. (licentiate; del. 2001—03), Ariz. Pharmacy Assn. (licentiate; co-chair profl. affairs com. 1999—2000, maricopa rep. 2001—02, 2nd v.p. 2002—03, cert. of appreciation for outstanding svc. to Ariz. pharmacy assn. 2000, exec. bd. mem. award 2003). Avocations: scuba diving, cooking, jazz, travel, wine tasting. Home: 6120 E Gold Dust Ave Scottsdale AZ 85253 Office: Abbott Laboratories 6120 E Gold Dust Ave Scottsdale AZ 85253 Personal E-mail: lwpharmd@juno.com.

WEAVER, LOIS JEAN, physician, educator; b. Wheeling, W.Va., May 23, 1944; d. Lewis Everett and Ann Weaver. BA, Oberlin Coll., 1966; MD, U. Chgo., 1970. Pulmonary fellow Northwestern U., Evanston, Ill., 1975-77; trauma fellow U. Wash. Harborview Hosp., Seattle, 1977-79, research assoc., instr. medicine, 1979-81, clin. asst. prof. medicine, 1983—; clin. research fellow Virginia Mason Med. Research Ctr., Seattle, 1981-82; mem. med. staff Swedish Hosp., Seattle, 1984-92. Pulmonary cons. Fred Hutchinson Cancer Research Inst., Seattle, 1984-86, regional med. advisor and med. cons., disability quality br. Social Security, Seattle, 1985—. Contbr. sci. articles to profl. jours. La Verne Noyes scholar U. Chgo., 1966; Parker B. Francis fellow Northwestern U., 1975. Mem. Sigma Xi. Avocations: gardening, music. Home: PO Box 2098 Kirkland WA 98083-2098 Office: 701 5th Ave Ste 2900 MIS 105 Seattle WA 98104-7075

WEAVER, LYNN EDWARD, academic administrator, consultant, editor; b. St. Louis, Jan. 12, 1930; s. Lienous E. and Estelle F. (Laspe) W.; m. JoAnn D., 1951 (div. 1981); children: Terry Sollenberger, Gwen, Bart, Stephen, Wes; m. Anita G. Gomez, Oct. 27, 1983. BSEE, U. Mo., 1951; MSEE, So. Meth. U., 1955; PhD, Purdue U., 1958. Devel. engr. McDonnell Aircraft, St. Louis, 1952-53; aerophysics engr. Convair Corp., Ft. Worth, 1953-55; instr. elec. engring. Purdue U., Lafayette, Ind., 1955-58; assoc. prof., then prof., dept. head U. Ariz., Tucson, 1959-69; assoc. dean coll. engring. U. Okla., Norman, 1969-70; exec. asst. to pres. Argonne Univs., Chgo., 1970-72; dir. sch. nuclear engring. and health physics Ga. Inst. Tech., 1972-82; dean engring., disting. prof. Auburn (Ala.) U., 1982-87; pres. Fla. Inst. Tech., Melbourne, 1987—2002, pres. emeritus, prof. elec. engring., 2002—. Cons. Ga. Power; bd. dirs. DBA Systems, Inc., Melbourne, Fla.; chmn. pub. affairs coun. Am. Assn. Engring. Soc., Washington, 1984-87; bd. adv. Ctr. for Sci., Tech. and Media, Washington; chmn. Ind. Colls. and Univs. Fla., 1999-2001. Author: (textbook) Reactor Dynamics & Control, State Space Techniques, 1968; exec. editor Annals of Nuclear Energy; contbr. numerous articles to tech. jours. U.S. rep. World Fedn., Engring. Orgn. Energy Com., 1981-86; bd. dirs. myregion.org, 2001-. Served to lt. USAF, 1951-53. Recipient U. Mo. Honors award for disting. svc. in engring., 1996. Fellow Am. Nuclear Soc.; mem. IEEE (sr.), Am. Soc. Engring. Edn., Sigma Xi, Eau Gallie Yacht Club. Republican. Roman Catholic. Avocations: tennis, jogging. Office: Fla Inst Tech 150 W University Blvd Melbourne FL 32901-6975 Office Phone: 321-674-8099. Business E-Mail: lweaver@fit.edu.

WEAVER, MAX ALLEN, chemist, consultant, inventor; b. Ashe County, NC, Mar. 26, 1936; s. Howard and Pearl Weaver; m. Helen Geraldine Moore, Dec. 21, 1957; children: Vickie Denise Weaver Barnes, Tod Allen. BA, King Coll., Bristol, Tenn., 1958, DSc, 1991; MA, East Tenn. State U., Johnson City, 1963. Chemist, rsch. chemist, sr. rsch. chemist, devel. and rsch. assoc. Eastman Kodak Co. Chem. Divsn., Kingsport, Tenn., 1958—87; cons. Eastern Kodak Co., Rochester, NY, 1987—2000; ret.; cons. Milliken Chem. Co., Spartanburg, SC, 1987—2008, Eastman Chem. Co., Kingsport, 1987—2008; asst. prof. chemistry King Coll., 1987—92. Contbr. articles to numerous sci. jours., chapters to books. Pastor Ch. Hill Ch. Nazarene, 1980—94, ordained as elder, 1991; pastor Kingsport Meth. Ch., 1994—2000; mem. Colour Index Editl. Com., 1979—2006. Recipient Patenting Distinction award, Eastman Chem. Co., 1994, Patenting Career Achievement award, 2007, Rsch. medal, Worshipful Co. Dyers, Soc. Dyers and Colorists, London, 2003. Mem.: Am. Assn. Textile Chemists and Colorists (Olney medal 2002, Henry E. Millson Invention award 2002), Am. Chem. Soc. (named Spkr. of Yr., NE Tenn. Sect. 1984—85). Avocations: gardening, music. Home: 125 Hill Rd Kingsport TN 37664

WEAVER, MICHAEL GLEN, pharmacist; b. Tuscola, Ill., Sept. 11, 1955; S. Glen and Margaret (Long) W.; m. Catherine (Paynic), 1978; children: Jennifer, Michelle, Gregory. BS in Pharmacy, St. Louis Coll. of Pharmacy, 1978; MBA, So. Ill. U., 1989. Registered pharmacist Ill. Clin. coordinator, staff pharmacist St. Elizabeth Med. Ctr., Granite City, Ill., 1975-87; dir. pharmacy Freeport Meml. Hosp. (now Freeport Health Network), Ill., 1987-92, dir. pharmacy and info. systems, 1992-97, dir. info. and telecom. svcs., 1997—2002; dir. pharmacy Freeport Health Network, 2002—. Dir. Ill. Bd. Pharmacy, 1995—99. Allocations com. United Way of NW Ill., 2000-, bd. dirs. 2006-; Girl Scouts, Green Hills, 2005-, bd. dirs., 2005-, exec. com., 2006- Mem.: Am. Coll. Healthcare Execs., Ill. Coun. Hosp. Pharmacists (dir. ednl. affairs 1991—94, dir. orgnl. affairs 2004—05, pres.-elect 2005—06, pres. 2006—07, treas. elect. 2008—), Am. Soc. Hosp. Pharmacists, Kiwanis (bd. dirs. Lincoln-Douglas chpt. 2002—, v.p. 2003—04, pres. elect 2004—05, pres. 2005—06), Delta Sigma Theta, Beta Gamma Sigma, Phi Kappa Phi. Republican. Avocations: computer, music. Home: 1346 Carriage Hill Ln Freeport IL 61032-6168 Office: Freeport Health Network 1045 W Stephenson St Freeport IL 61032-4899 Office Phone: 815-599-6113.

WEAVER, MICHAEL JAMES, lawyer; b. Bakersfield, Calif., Feb. 11, 1946; s. Kenneth James and Elsa Hope (Rogers) W.; m. Valerie Scott, Sept. 2, 1966; children: Christopher James, Brett Michael, Karen Ashley. AB, Calif. State U., Long Beach, 1968; JD magna cum laude, U. San Diego, 1973. Bar: Calif., 1973, U.S. Dist. Ct. (so. dist.) Calif. 1973, U.S. Ct. Appeals (9th cir.) 1975, U.S. Supreme Ct. 1977. Law clk. to chief judge U.S. Dist. Ct. (so. dist.) Calif., San Diego, 1973-75; with Latham & Watkins, San Diego. Judge pro tem San Diego Superior Ct.; master of the Bench of the Inn, Am. Inns of Ct., Louis M. Welch chpt.; lectr. Inn of Ct., San Diego, 1981—, Continuing Edn. of Bar, Calif., 1983—, Workshop for Judges U.S. Ct. Appeals (9th cir.), 1990; mem. task force on establishment of bus. cts. sys. Jud. Coun. Calif., 1996-97; adv. com. U.S. Ct. Appeals (9th cir.), 2006—. Editor-in-chief: San Diego Law Rev., 1973; contbr. articles to profl. jours. Bd. dirs., pres. San Diego Kidney Found., 1985-90; bd. dirs. San Diego Aerospace Mus., 1985-97; trustee La Jolla (Calif.) Playhouse, 1990-91. lt. USNR, 1968-74. Fellow Am. Coll. Trial Lawyers; mem. San Diego Assn. Bus. Trial Lawyers (founding mem., bd. govs.), San Diego Def. Lawyers Assn. (dir.), Am. Arbitration Assn., 9th Cir. Jud. Conf. (del. 1987-90, mem. adv. com. 2006—09), Calif. Supreme Ct. Hist. Assn. (bd. dirs. 1998—), Safari Club Internat. (San Diego chpt.), San Diego Sportsmen's Club, Coronado Yacht Club. Republican. Presbyterian. Avocations: reading, flying, skiing. Office: Latham & Watkins 600 West Broadway Ste 1800 San Diego CA 92101-8197 Office Phone: 619-238-3012. Business E-Mail: mike.weaver@lw.com.

WEAVER, MOLLIE LITTLE, lawyer; b. Alma, Ga., Mar. 11; d. Alfred Ross and Annis Mae (Bowles) Little; m. Jack Delano Nelson, Sept. 12, 1953 (div. May 1970); 1 dau., Cynthia Ann; m. 2d, Hobart Ayres Weaver, June 10, 1970; stepchildren: Hobart Jr., Mary Essa, Robert. BA in History, U. Richmond, 1978; JD, Wake Forest U., 1981. Bar; N.C. 1982, Fla. 1983; Cert. profl. sec.; cert. adminstrv. mgr. Supr., Western Electric Co., Richmond, Va., 1952-75; cons., owner Cert. Mgmt. Assocs., Richmond, 1975-76; sole practice, Ft. Lauderdale, Fla., 1982-86, Emerald Isle, N.C., 1986-89, Richmond, 1989—. Author: Secretary's Reference Manual, 1973. Mem. adv. coun. to Bus. and Office Edn., Greensboro, N.C., 1970-73, adv. com. to bus. edn. Va. Commonwealth U., Richmond, 1977. Recipient Key to City of Winston-Salem, N.C., 1963; Epps award for scholarship, 1978. Mem. ABA, N.C. Bar Assn., Fla. Bar Assn., Word Processing Assn. (v.p., founder Richmond 1973-75), Adminstrv. Mgmt. Soc. (com. chmn. Richmond, 1973-75), Phi Beta Kappa, Eta Sigma Phi, Phi Alpha Theta. Republican. Home: 12301 Renwick Pl Glen Allen VA 23059-6959 Home Phone: 804-360-2381. Personal E-mail: Legal311@aol.com.

WEAVER, PAMELA ANN, education educator; b. Little Falls, NY, July 7, 1947; d. Floyd Aron Weaver and Norma May (Putnam) Hoyer; m. Ken Ward McCleary, Mar. 2, 1947; children: Brian Wilson, Blake McCleary, Ryan McCleary. AA, Fulton Montgomery C.C., Amsterdam, NY, 1968; BA, SUNY, 1970; MA, U. South Fla., 1973; PhD, Mich. State U., East Lansing, 1978. Mem. math. dept. Riviera Jr. H.S., Miami, Fla., 1970-72; grad. asst. Office Med., Edn. R & D Mich. State U., East Lansing, 1973-74, grad. asst. dept. mktg., 1974-75, instr. mktg.; asst. prof. mktg., hospitality svcs. adminstrn. Ctrl. Mich. State U., Mt. Pleasant, 1978-79, 1982-86, chair acad. senate, 1985-86, prof. mktg., hospitality svcs. adminstrn., 1986-89; prof., undergrad. program coord. dept. hospitality and tourism mgmt. Va. Poly. Inst. and State U., Blacksburg, 1989—, undergrad. program coord., 2005—. Contbr. over 100 articles to profl. jours. Mem. Coun. on Hotel, Restaurant and Instl. Edn. (John Wiley & Sons, Inc. award for Litetime Achievement to Hospitality Industry 1994). Office: Va Poly Inst and State U Wallace Hall Blacksburg VA 24061-0429 Business E-Mail: weaver@vt.edu.

WEAVER, PEGGY (MARGUERITE MCKINNIE WEAVER), plantation owner; b. Jackson, Tenn., June 7, 1925; d. Franklin Allen and Mary Alice (Caradine) McKinnie; children: Elizabeth Lynn, Thomas Jackson III, Franklin A. McKinnie. Student, U. Colo., 1943-45, Am. Acad. Dramatic Arts, 1945-46, S. Meisner's Profl. Classes, 1949, Oxford U., 1990-91. Actress, 1946-52; mem. staff Mus. Modern Art, NYC, 1949-50; woman's editor radio sta. WTJS-AM-FM, Jackson, Tenn., 1952-55; editor, radio/TV Jackson Sun Newspaper, 1952-55; columnist Bolivar (Tenn.) Bulletin-Times, 1986—2000; chmn. Ho. of Reps. of Old Line Dist., Hardeman County, Tenn., 1986—91. Pres. Hardeman County chpt. Assn. Preservation of Tenn. Antiquities, 1991—95; charter mem. adv. bd. Tenn. Arts Commn., Nashville, 1967—74, Tenn. Performing Arts Ctr., Nashville, 1972—; chmn. trustees br. Tenn. Libr. Assn., Nashville, 1973—74; Henry County regional chmn. Opera Memphis, 1979—91; mem. nat. coun. Met. Opera, NYC, 1980—92, Tenn. Bicentennial Com., Hardeman County, 1993—96; bd. sec. Memphis Brooks Mus. League, 1997—98; docent Dixon Gallery and Gardens, Memphis; founder Paris-Henry County (Tenn.) Arts Coun., 1965. Mem. DAR, Nat. Soc. Colonial Dames Am. (chmn. Memphis Town com. 2002-04), Oxford Alumni Assn. NY, English Speaking Union (London chpt.), Jamestown Soc., Crescent Club, Dilettantes. Methodist. Avocations: horseback riding, travel, theater. Office: 402 Heritage Plantation Hickory Valley TN 38042 Business E-Mail: pweaver@heritagecompanies.net.

WEAVER, REG(INALD), educational association administrator; b. Danville, Ill. BS, Ill. State U.; MS, Roosevelt U., Chgo.; LHD (hon.), NC Shaw U.; D in Pub. Svc. (hon.), SC State U. Tchr. Danville HS, Ill.; local NEA pres. Harvey, Ill., 1967—71; pres. Ill Edn. Assn., 1981—87; mem. NEA exec. com., 1989—95; v.p. NEA, 1996—2002, pres., 2002—; v.p. Edn. Internat. Mem. exec. bd. Nat. Coun. for Accreditation of Tchr. Edn.; chair IEA Political Action Com. for Edn. (IPACE); appointed to Ill. Commn. for Improvement of Elementary and Secondary Edn., Ill. Project for Sch. Reform Adv. Coun., Ill. Literacy Coun., Task Force on At-Risk Youth; mem. Ill. State Bd. of Edn. Blue Ribbon Comm. on Improvement of Tchg. as a Profession; address conferences and forums sponsored by US Conf. Mayors, NAACP, Nat. Coun. LARaza, Rainbow Push Coalition, League United Latin Citizens, ASPIRA; advocate for public schs. Hon. mem. adv. bd. Dept. Edn. Leadership, Roosevelt U.; bd. govs. Joint Ctr. Polit. and Econ. Studies; bd. dirs. Nat. Bd. Profl. Tchg. Stds. Recipient Ebony Mag. Influential Black Educators award, Ill. Edn. Assn. Human Rels. award, People for Am. Way Spirit of Liberty award, 2005, Chmn. award for Ednl. Leadership, 100 Black Men in Am. Inc., 2006, Congl. Gt. Points of Light award, Congl. Black Caucus, 2006, George Meany Latino Leadership award, US Hispanic Leadership Inst., 2006, US Action Progressive Leadership award, Pres. award, Nat. Conf. Black Mayors, Excellence in Leadership award, MALDEF, 2007; named one of Outstanding Men of Am., Most Influential Black Ams., Ebony mag., 2006; named to Wall of Fame, Danville HS, Power 150, Ebony mag., 2007, 2008. Mem.: PTA (hon. life). Office: NEA 1201 16th St NW Washington DC 20036-3290 Office Phone: 202-802-7000. E-mail: rweaver@nea.org.

WEAVER, RICHARD J., state banking agency administrator; married; 1 child. B in Bus. Adminstrn. and Acctg., Lincoln U., Jefferson City, Mo.; grad., Grad. Sch. Banking, Boulder, Colo. With Mo. Divsn. Fin., Jefferson City, 1985—, dep. commr., 2004—09, commr., 2009. Office: Mo Divsn Fin 301 W Hight St PO Box 716 Jefferson City MO 65102 Office Phone: 573-751-3242. Office Fax: 573-751-9192. E-mail: rich.weaver@dof.mo.gov.

WEAVER, RICHARD L., II, writer, educator, lecturer; b. Hanover, NH, Dec. 5, 1941; s. Richard L. and Florence B. (Grow) W.; m. Andrea A. Willis; children: Richard Scott, Jacquelynn Michelle, Anthony Keith, Joanna Corinne. AB, U. Mich., 1964, MA, 1965; PhD, Ind. U., 1969. Asst. prof. U. Mass., 1968-74; assoc. prof. speech comm. Bowling Green State U., 1974-79, prof., 1979-96, dir., basic speech comm. course, 1974-96. Vis. prof. U. Hawaii-Manoa, 1981-82, Bond U., Queensland, Australia, 1990, St. Albans, Melbourne, Australia, 1990, Western Inst., Perth, Australia, 1990, pres. & CEO, And Then Some Publ. LLC. Author: (with Saundra Hybels) Speech/Communication,

1974, 2d edit., 1979, Speech/Communication: A Reader, 1975, 2d edit., 1979, Speech/Communication: A Student Manual, 1976, 2d edit., 1979, Understanding Interpersonal Communication, 1978, 7th edit., 1996, (with Raymond K. Tucker, Cynthia Berryman-Fink) Research in Speech Communication, 1981, Foundations of Speech Communication: Perspectives of a Discipline, 1982, Speech Communication Skills, 1982, Understanding Public Communication, 1983, Understanding Business Communication, 1985, Understanding Speech Communication Skills, 1985, Readings in Speech Communication, 1985, (with Saundra Hybels) Communicating Effectively, 1986, 89, 92, 95, 98, 2001, 04, 07, 09, Skills for Communicating Effectively, 1985, 4th edit., 1993, rev. edit., 1995, (with Howard W. Cotrell) Innovative Instructional Strategies, 1987, 6th edit., 1993, (with Curt Bechler) Listen to Win: A Guide to Effective Listening, 1994, Study Guide to Accompany Communicating Effectively, 1995, 2d edit., 1998, Essentials of Public Speaking, 1996, 2d edit., 2001, (with Edgar E. Willis) How to be Funny on Purpose: Creating and Consuming Humor, 2005, And Then Some: Essays to Entertain, Motivate & Inspire, book I, 2007, Public Speaking Rules: All You Need to Give a Great Speech, 2008, You Rules! All You Need for Self Improvement, 2008, SMOERs Self-Motivation, Optimism, Encouragement Rules: Daily reminders for Outstanding Living, 2009, Relationship Rules: For Long Term Happiness, Security, and Commitment, 2009. Mem. emeritus Nat. Comm. Assn., Ctrl. States Speech Assn., Ohio Speech Assn. Home and Office: 9583 Woodleigh Ct Perrysburg OH 43551-2669 Office Phone: 419-874-2124. Personal E-mail: rlweaverii@andthensomeworks.com. Business E-Mail: richard@weaverworks.net.

WEAVER, RICHARD LINDSAY NEWTON, financial services executive; b. Miami, Fla., Aug. 10, 1957; s. Robert Almon and Rita Margaret (Gaylord) W.; m. Christine Ann Curley, Sept. 28, 1991; children: Katherine Emory, Emily Price. BS in Econs., U. Pa., 1979; MBA, NYU, 1983. Internat. adminstr. Prudential-Bache, NYC, 1979—81, instnl. bond sales, 1981—82, assoc., internat. corp. fin. London, 1982—84; assoc. v.p., risk arbitrage Prudential Securities, Inc., NYC, 1984—87, v.p. managed futures, 1987—88, 1st v.p., pvt. client equity svcs., 1988—94, sr. v.p. exec. svcs., high net worth strategies/investments, 1994—2001, sr. v.p., dir., pvt. wealth mgmt., 2001—03; dir. wealth mgmt. group Bernstein Global Wealth Mgmt., NYC, 2004—. Mem. ctr. circle com. Lincoln Ctr., N.Y.C., 1993-96; mus. chmn., treas. Frances Tavern Mus., N.Y.C., 1994-96; trustee The Browning Sch., N.Y.C., 1995—, The Episc. Sch., N.Y.C., 2000—; jr. com. Sch. of Am. Ballet, N.Y.C., 1982-91. Mem. N.Y. Soc. Security Analysts, Assn. Investment Mgmt. Profls., Investment Assn. N.Y. Office: Bernstein Global Wealth Mgmt 1345 Ave of the Americas New York NY 10105 Business E-Mail: richard.weaver@bernstein.com.

WEAVER, SIGOURNEY (SUSAN ALEXANDRA WEAVER), actress; b. NYC, Oct. 8, 1949; d. Sylvester (Pat) Weaver and Elizabeth Inglis; m. Jim Simpson, Oct. 1, 1984; 1 child, Charlotte. BA in English, Stanford U., 1971; MA in Drama, Yale U., 1974. Actress: (theatre) including Watergate Classics, 1973, The Frogs, 1974 The Nature and Purpose of the Universe, 1974, Daryl and Carol and Kenny and Jenny, The Constant Wife, 1975, Titanic, 1976, Das Lusitania Songspiel (also co-writer), 1976, Marco Polo Sings a Song, 1977, A Flea in Her Ear, 1978, Conjuring an Event, 1978, Beyond Therapy, 1981, As You Like It, 1981, Hurlyburly, 1984-85, Sex and Longing, 1996, The Merchant of Venice, 1986, The Guys, 2002, The Mercy Seat, 2002, Mrs. Farnsworth, 2004, Crazy Mary, 2007; (films) Annie Hall, 1977, Madman, 1978, Alien, 1979, Eyewitness, 1981, The Year of Living Dangerously, 1982, Deal of the Century, 1983, Ghostbusters, 1984, Une femme ou deux, 1985, Aliens, 1986 (Acad. Award nomination for best actress, 1987), Half Moon Street, 1986, Gorillas in the Mist, 1988 (Acad. Award nomination for best actress, 1989, Golden Globe for best actress - drama, 1989), Working Girl, 1988 (Acad. Award nomination for best supporting actress, 1989, Golden Globe for best supporting actress in a motion picture, 1989), Ghostbusters II, 1989, 1492: Conquest of Paradise, 1992, Dave, 1993, Death and the Maiden, 1994, Jeffrey, 1995, Copycat, 1995, Snow White: A Tale of Terror, 1997, The Ice Storm, 1997 (BAFTA Film Award for best supporting actress, 1998), A Map of the World, 1999, Galaxy Quest, 1999, Airframe, 1999, Company Man, 2000, Speak Truth to Power, 2000, Heartbreakers, 2001, Big Bad Love (voice), 2001, Tadpole, 2002, The Guys, 2002, Holes, 2003, The Village, 2004, Imaginary Heroes, 2004, Snow Cake, 2006, The TV Set, 2006, Infamous, 2006, Happily N'Ever After (voice), 2007, Vantage Point, 2008, Baby Mama, 2008, WALL-E (voice), 2008, (TV series) Somerset, 1976, (TV miniseries) The Best of Families, 1977, (TV movies) 3 by Cheever: The Sorrows of Gin, 1979, 3 by Cheever: O Youth and Beauty!, 1979; co-prodr., actress: (films) Alien 3, 1992, Alien: Resurrection, 1997. Recipient Star on the Walk of Fame, 1999, Lifetime Achievement award, Chicago Internat. Film Festival, 2001, Women in Hollywood Tribute award, Elle Mag., 2008. Office: William Morris Agy One William Morris Pl Beverly Hills CA 90212

WEAVER, SUSAN JEANNE, sociology educator; b. Huntington, W.Va., Dec. 11, 1950; d. John Francis and Sherley Rae (Wells) Marnell; m. Douglas W. Weaver, Jan. 28, 1970; children: Sarah Marnell, Nathaniel Heath. BA in Sociology, Marshall U., 1975, MA in Sociology, 1980; EdD in Leadership Studies, W.Va. U., 2000. Instr. in sociology Marshall U., Huntington, 1984—99, Ashland (Ky.) C.C., 1985—99, Ky. Christian Coll., Grayson, 1988—89; asst. prof. sociology Miami U. Oxford, Ohio, 1999—2005; dir. tchg. and learning Univ. of the Cumberlands, Williamsburg, Ky., 2005—. Bd. dirs. Sojourner's Recovery Svcs. Inc. Vol. Contact of Huntington, 1992—99; leader Girl Scouts U.S., Proctorville, Ohio, 1985—92; cub scout den mother Boy Scouts Am., Proctorville, 1990—92; adv. bd. Whitley County Girls Ranch, 2006—. Mem. Am. Sociol. Assn., So. Sociol. Assn., Profl. Orgn. Devel. Network. Ky. Assn. Devel. Edn. Avocation: writing. Office: 6000 College Station Dr Williamsburg KY 40969

WEAVER, W(AYNE) DOUGLAS, cardiologist, researcher, medical educator; b. Ft. Fairfield, Maine, Mar. 14, 1945; 1 child, John. BA, U. Maine, 1967; MD, Tufts U., 1971. Diplomate Am. Bd. Internal Medicine, Am. Bd. Cardiovasc. Disease. Intern, then resident U. Wash., Seattle, 1971-74, fellow in cardiology, 1974-76, prof. medicine/cardiology, 1979-96; head divsn. cardiology, dir. Henry Ford Cardiovascular Inst. Henry Ford Health Sys., Detroit, 1996—, also Darin chair cardiology; prof. medicine Wayne State U. Contbr. over 350 articles to profl. jours. (articles), assoc. editor numerous jours. Named one of Am.'s Best Cardiologists; named to Top Doctors List, Hour Mag. Fellow: Am. Coll. Cardiology (pres. 2008—09, former v.p.), Am. Heart Assn. (bd. trustee-Metro Detroit). Avocations: skiing, boating, golf. Office: Henry Ford Hosp 2799 W Grand Blvd Detroit MI 48202-2689 Office Phone: 313-916-4420. Business E-Mail: wweaver1@hfhs.org.

WEAVER, WESLEY JAMES, III, literature and language professor; b. Schenectady, NY, Oct. 14, 1960; s. Wesley James Weaver Jr. and Joan Every Weaver; m. Maria de los Angeles Solana Lara, July 27, 1985; children: Wesley James IV, Maria Lara. BA summa cum laude, Hartwick Coll., Oneonta, NY, 1982; MA, U. Pa., Phila., 1985; PhD, U. Pa., 1989. Prof. spanish SUNY Coll. Cortland, NY. Author: (spanish criticism) Alvaro Pombo y la narrativa de la sustancia, Introduccion a la literatura de Jorge Marquez. Office: SUNY Coll Cortland ICC Dept Cortland NY 13045 Business E-Mail: wesley.weaver@cortland.edu.

WEAVER, WILLIAM CHARLES, manufacturing executive; b. Nov. 10, 1941; s. Curtis D. and Mary (Yahres) W.; m. Karla Lee Kottas, June 13, 1964; children: Michael, Kelli. BS in Bus. Edn., Indiana U. of Pa., 1963; postgrad. in acctg., Tex. Christian U., 1964-65. CPA, Pa. With Price Waterhouse & Co., Pitts., 1965-73, audit mgr., 1970-73; corp. contr. Kennametal Inc., Latrobe, Pa., 1973-78, v.p., contr., 1978-83, v.p., treas., 1983-86, v.p., CFO, 1987-89; sr. v.p., CFO Oak Industries, Inc., Waltham, Mass., 1990-95; ret., 1995. Bd. dirs. Gemini Precision Products, 1987—; chmn. bd. dirs. Weaver Enterprises, Inc., 1996—, Weaver Properties, LLC. Pres. Mountain View Parent Tchrs. Orgn., 1976—77; bd. dirs. East High Acres Civic Assn., 1976—77; treas. Greater Latrobe Hockey Club, 1982—87; chmn. bd. dirs., mem. adv. coun. Jr. Achievement, Latrobe, 1982—85; chmn. bd. trustees Latrobe United Way, 1988—89; trustee Hampton United Presbyn. Ch., 1972—73. 1st lt. US Army, 1963—65. Mem.: Fin. Execs. Inst., Palmetto Dunes Club Inc. (pres. 1998—2001). Home Phone: 843-785-2218. E-mail: kbweaver@hargray.com.

WEAVER, WILLIAM CLAIR, JR., (MIKE WEAVER), human resources development executive; b. Ind., Pa., Apr. 11, 1936; s. William Clair and Zaida (Bley) W.; m. Janet Marcelle Boyd, Sept. 18, 1963 (div. 1978); 1 child, William Michael; m. Donna June Hubbuch, Feb. 10, 1984. B Aero Engring., Rensselaer Poly. Inst., 1958; MBA, Washington U., St. Louis, 1971; postgrad., Rutgers U.; grad., Armed Forces Indsl. Coll. Registered profl. engr. Engr. aerodynamics N.Am. Aviation, LA, 1959-60; engr. flight test ops. Boeing/Vertol, Phila., 1963-66; engr. flight test project Lockheed Electronics, Plainfield, NJ, 1966—69; project engr. advanced systems, sr. staff engr. Emerson Electric Co., St. Louis, 1969—72; pres. Achievement Assocs., Inc., St. Louis, 1972—. Founder, charter mem. Catalyst, 1978—; faculty Leadership Mgmt., Inc.; spkr. in field. Author: Winning Selling, 1983; contbr. articles to profl. jours. Adv. com. Boy Scouts Am., Bridgeton, Mo., 1974. Capt. USAF, 1960-63, USAFR. Mem. AIAA, NSPE, Cato Inst., Am. Soc. Tng. and Devel., Am. Soc. Bus. and Mgmt. Cons., Am. Ordnance Soc., Assn. MBA Execs., Air Force Assn., Am. Helicopter Soc., Acacia Frat., St. Louis C. of C., Mensa, Mo. Athletic Club, Beta Gamma Sigma. Republican. Lutheran. Avocations: photography, music, sports. Home and Office: 1016 Evergreen Rd Yardley PA 19067-1018 Office Phone: 215-428-3400.

WEAVER, WILLIAM SCHILDECKER, retired electric power industry executive; b. Pitts., Jan. 15, 1944; s. Charles Henry and Louise (Schildecker) W.; m. Janet Kae Jones, Mar. 7, 1981. BA, Hamilton Coll., 1965; JD, U. Mich., 1968. Bar: Wash. 1968. Assoc. Perkins Coie, Seattle, 1968-74, ptnr., 1975-91; exec. v.p., CFO Puget Sound Power & Light Co., Bellevue, Wash., 1991-97; vice chmn., chmn. unregulated subs. Puget Sound Energy, 1997, pres., COO, 1997, pres., CEO, 1998—2002, chmn., 2001—02, ret. Bd. dirs. Wash. Rsch. Coun., Seattle, 1991-97, chmn., 1995-97; trustee Seattle Repertory Theatre, 1992-95, 99-00, chmn., 2000-02, Corp. Coun. Arts, 1995-02, Pacific Sci. Ctr., 1997-02; bd. dirs. Edison Electric Inst., 1998-02. Mem. ABA, Wash. State Bar Assn., Sovren, The Soc. of Vintage Racing Enthusiasts, Sports Car Club Am., Seattle Yacht Club, Flounder Bay Yacht Club.

WEAVER-STROH, JOANNE MATEER, education educator, consultant; b. May 21, 1930; d. Kenneth Hall and Jean (Weakley) Mateer; children: Karen, Mark, Laurie. BS in Edn., U. Pa., 1952, elem. and secondary prin. cert., 1979; MS in Psychology Reading, Temple U., 1968. Tchr. Paoli (Pa.) Sch., 1952-53, Somerville Sch., Ridgewood, NJ, 1953-55, Bryn Mawr (Pa.) Sch., 1955-57, Erdenheim Sch., Springfield, Pa., 1957-58; reading specialist Abington (Pa.) Sch. Dist., 1966-67, curriculum specialist, 1967-73, coord. human rels. programs, 1973-80; prin. Rydal Elem. Sch., Abington, 1980-88, Willow Hill Elem. Sch., 1988-96; ret., 1996. Cons., tchr. Marywood Coll., Scranton, Pa., 1972—; coord. drug and alcohol abuse program Abington Sch. Dist., 1989-96; cons. Conflict Resolution, 1996—. Chmn. Abington Human Rels. Adv. Coun., 1973-88; chmn. Cmty. Rels. Com. Abington Twp., 1978—; mem. Ea. Montgomery County Human Rels. Adv. Coun., 1981-83, 2006—; chmn. No Place for Hate project Abington Twp., 2003—; mediator Abington Twp.; leader Stephen Ministry program Abington Presbyn. Ch.; mem. ctr. internat. leadership and comm. bd. advisors Pa. State U., Abington, 2006—. Named Citizen of the Week Times Chronicle Newspaper, 1976; recipient award Four Chaplains Temple U., 1979, Disting. Citizens award Roslyn Jr. C. of C., 1981, Citizens for Progress Humanitarian award, 1982, Cmty. award Abington YMCA, 1987, Dr. Martin Luther King Jr. award Abington Twp., 1989, East Montgomery County/Pa. State Human Rels. Intergroup award, 2000, Citizens That Care award Abington Cmty. Taskforce, 2003, Disting. Cmty. Svc. award Intersvc. Clubs of Glenside, 2003, Cmty. Svc. award Willow Grove NAACP, 2008 Mem. ASCD, NASEP, Internat. Coop. Learning Assn., Pa. Assn. Elem. Prins., Phi Delta Kappa, Delta Kappa Gamma. Republican. Home: 35413 Anns Choice Way Warminster PA 18974 Business E-Mail: rwstroh@att.net.

WEBB, ADAM PAUL, librarian; BA in History, Coll. William & Mary, Williamsburg, VA, 2002; MSLS, UNC Chapel Hill, NC, 2005. Cert. Profl. Librarian Libr. Va., 2005. Reference libr. Tazewell County Pub. Libr., Va., 2005—07; regional libr. dir. Wythe Grayson Regional Libr., Independence, Va., 2007—. Mem.: ALA, Va. Libr. Assn. Office: Wythe-Grayson Regional Library 147 S Independence Ave Independence VA 24348 Office Phone: 276-773-3018. Business E-Mail: awebb@wythegrayson.lib.va.us.

WEBB, BRANDON (TYLER WEBB), professional baseball player; b. Ashland, Ky., May 9, 1979; s. Philip and Dreama Webb; m. Alicia Webb; 1 child, Reagan Lucille. Attended, U. Ky., Lexington. Pitcher Ariz. Diamondbacks, 2003—. Founder Brandon Webb K Found., 2005. Recipient Nat. League Cy Young award, 2006; named to Nat. League All-Star Team, MLB, 2006, 2007. Achievements include setting an Arizona Diamondbacks' franchise record with 42 1/3 scoreless innings; leading the National League in: starts, 2004, 2008; wins, 2006, 2008, shutouts, 2006, 2007; innings, 2007; complete games, 2007. Avocation: guitar. Mailing: c/o Arizona Diamondbacks Chase Field 401 E Jefferson St Phoenix AZ 85004

WEBB, CHARLES HAIZLIP, JR., retired dean; b. Dallas, Feb. 14, 1933; s. Charles Haizlip and Marion (Gilker) W.; m. Kenda McGibbon, June 21, 1958; children: Mark, Kent, Malcolm, Charles Haizlip III. AB, MMus, So. Meth. U., 1955; DMus, Ind. U., 1964; DMus (hon.), Anderson. U., Ind., 1978. Asst. to dean Sch. Music, So. Meth. U., 1957-58; mem. faculty Sch. Music, Ind. U., 1960-97, dean, 1973-97, Disting. prof., 1997—. Adv. bd. Classical Insites. Dir. Indpls. Symphony Choir, 1967-81; guest condr. chorus and orch. festivals throughout U.S.; duo-pianist with Wallace Hornibrook in U.S. and Australian tour, 1973; organist First Meth. Ch., Bloomington, 1961-, mem. hymnal revision com. Meth. Ch.; mem. jury Chopin competition; mem. jury internat. piano competitions in Munich, Budapest, South Africa, Paris, Chile, Warsaw, Bolzano, London, Cologne, Japan, Israel. Chmn. adv. bd. Internat. Music Festivals, Inc.; mem. Ind. Arts Commn., 1975-83, U.S.-USSR Commn. on Music Performance Edn., Am. Coun. Learned Socs./USSR Ministry of Culture; adv. panel Music Found.; recommendation bd. Avery Fisher Prize Program; bd. dirs. Busoni Found.; bd. adv. Van Cliburn Internat. Piano Competition; nat. adv. bd. Am. Guild Organists; trustee Indpls. Symphony Orch.; mem. Nat. Recording Preservation Found., 2002; adv. com. on cultural diplomacy U.S. Dept. State, 2004; active Nat. Rec. Preservation Found. With U.S. Army, 1955-57. Decorated D.S.M.; recipient Disting. Alumni award So. Meth. U., 1980, Sagamore of Wabash Gov. award, 1987, 89, 97, Thomas Hart Benton medal Ind. U., 1987, Disting. Alumni award Highland Park HS, Dallas, 1989, Disting Alumni award Ind. U., 2005, Ind. Gov. award for arts, 1989, Rocking Chair award, Ind. U., 1997, Sterling Patron award Mu Phi Epsilon Internat., 1989, Ind. Gen. Assembly House Resolution # 39 for meritorious svc., 1997, Pres.'s award Ind. U., 2000; subject of tribute in U.S. Congl. Record, 1997; Rockefeller scholar Bellagio Study Ctr., 1997; named Ind. Living Legend, 2004, named to Congl. Com. to Advise the Sec. of State on Cultural Diplomacy, 2004, Living Treasure Bloomington Area Arts Coun., 2007, Monroe County Arts Coun., 2007; Paul Harris fellow, Rotary Internat., 1997. Mem. Virtu Inc. (bd. dir. 2009), Ind. Acad., Century Assn. of N.Y., Pi Kappa Lambda, Phi Mu Alpha, Phi Delta Theta. Home: 648 S Woodcrest Dr Bloomington IN 47401-5417 Personal E-mail: webbc@indiana.edu.

WEBB, CHARLES RICHARD, retired university president; b. Berkeley, Calif., Oct. 4, 1919; s. Charles Richard and Adele (McDaniel) W.; m. Andrée Bonno; 1 child, Charles Richard III. AB, U. Calif., Berkeley, 1942, MA, 1944, Harvard U., 1947, PhD, 1949. Faculty San Diego State Coll., 1949-64, prof., 1958-64, chmn. dept. history, 1956-58; dean acad. affairs Stanislaus State Coll., Turlock, Calif., 1964-66; prof. history San Diego State Coll., 1966-70; pres. Eastern Conn. State U., Willimantic, 1970-88; ret., 1988; former assoc. dean acad. planning Calif. State Colls., 1966-69, former dep. state coll. dean acad. planning. Author: Workbook in Western Civilization, 2 vols, 1959, Western Civilization vol. 1 (with Schaefer), vol. 2 (with Palm), 1958, (with Crosby) The Past as Prologue, 2 vols, 1973; contbr. articles to profl. jours. Mem. pers. com. Santa Rosa Symphony Assn., New Eng. Program, Windham Meml. Cmty. Hosp.; mem. Commn. on Conn.'s Future. With USNR, 1941-45. Mem. AAUP, Am. Hist. Assn., Am. Fedn. Musicians, Nat. Pks. and Conservation, Sonoma Land Trust, Sierra Club, Nature Conservancy, New Eng. Hist. Assn., Assn. Calif. State Coll. Profs. (v.p. 1958-60), Save the Redwoods League, Conn. Employees Assn., Am. Assn. State Colls. and Univs., Phi Alpha Theta, Kappa Delta Pi, Omicron Delta Pi, Alpha Delta Phi. Clubs: University (San Diego), Commonwealth of Calif., Willimantic Country, Saddle Club, Santa Rosa, Montecito Heights Health & Racquet Club, Santa Rosa. Home: 6495 Timber Springs Dr Santa Rosa CA 95409-5900

WEBB, DAN K., lawyer; b. Bushnell, Ill., Sept. 5, 1945; s. Keith L. and Phyllis I. (Chow) Webb; m. Laura A. Buscemi, Mar. 15, 1973; children: Jeffrey, Maggie, Michael, Melanie, Megan. Attended, We. Ill. U., 1963—66; JD cum laude, Loyola U. Chgo. Sch. Law, 1970. Bar: Ill. 1970, lic.: US Dist. Ct. (no. dist.) Ill., US Ct. Appeals (6th Cir.), US Ct. Appeals (7th Cir.), US Ct. Appeals (8th Cir.), US Ct. Appeals (Fed. Cir.), US Supreme Ct. Chief spl. prosecutions divsn. US Attorney's Office US Dept. Justice, Chgo., 1970—76; ptnr. Cummins, Decker & Webb, Chgo., 1976—79; dir. Ill. Dept. Law Enforcement, Chgo., 1979—80; ptnr. Pierce, Webb, Lydon & Griffin, Chgo., 1980—81; US atty. (no. dist.) Ill. US Dept. Justice, Chgo., 1981—85; ptnr. Winston & Strawn LLP, Chgo., 1985—, chmn., 2006—. Instr. John Marshall Law Sch., 1975—, Loyola U. Sch. Law, 1980—; mem. Nat. Inst. Trial Advocacy, 1979—, Atty. General's Advisory Com., 1981—84; chmn. Governor's Chgo. Edn. Study Com., 1985—. Mem. Chgo. Metropolitan Fair & Exposition Authority, 1978—81; chmn. Ill. Hosp. Assn. Governing Bd. Council, 1983—. Recipient Spl. Commendation award, US Dept. Justice, 1975; named one of The 10 Outstanding Young Chicagoans, Chgo. Jaycees, 1979, The Nation's Top Litigators, The Nat. Law Jour., 1991, 2007, The 100 Most Influential Lawyers, 2006. Fellow: Internat. Acad. Trial Attorneys, Am. Coll. Trial Lawyers; mem.: ABA, Executives Club Chgo., Legal Club Chgo., Fed. Bar Assn., Ill. State Bar Assn., Chgo. Bar Assn. Republican. Office: Winston & Strawn LLP 35 W Wacker Dr Ste 4200 Chicago IL 60601-9703 Office Phone: 312-558-5856. Office Fax: 312-558-5700. E-mail: dwebb@winston.com.*

WEBB, DARRELL D., retail executive; MBA, Portland State U., 1980. Group v.p. procurement The Kroger Co.; pres. Quality Food Ctr., Inc., 1999—2002, Fred Meyer, Inc., 2002—06; chmn., pres., CEO Jo-Ann Stores, Inc., Hudson, Ohio, 2006—. Office: Jo-Ann Stores Inc 5555 Darrow Rd Hudson OH 44236-4011 Office Phone: 330-656-2600. Office Fax: 330-463-6675.

WEBB, DOYLE L., political organization administrator, former state legislator; b. Little Rock, Dec. 3, 1955; BA, JD, U. Ark. Atty., Benton, Ark.; mem. Dist. 14 Ark. State Senate, 1994—2002, mem. numerous coms. including hosp. and medicaid study; chief of staff to Lt. Gov. Win Rockefeller Office of the Lt. Gov., Ark., 2002—07; gen. counsel, exec. com. Republican Party of Ark., chmn., 2008—. Justice of peace 6th dist. Saline County Quorum Ct., 1986-92; bd. dirs. Discover Benton, Main St. Benton, Gann Mus. Mem. ABA, SAR, Ark. Bar Assn., Saline County Bar Assn., Benton-Bauxite Rotary Club, Benton Civitan Club (pres.), Gideon's Internat. (camp pres.), Benton Lodge, Benton C. of C. (bd. dirs.). Republican. Presbyterian. Office: Republican Party of Ark 1201 W 6th St Little Rock AR 72201 Office Phone: 501-372-7301. Office Fax: 501-372-1656.*

WEBB, EMILY, retired plant morphologist; b. Charleston, SC, Apr. 10, 1924; d. Malcolm Syfan and Emily Kirk (Moore) W.; m. John James Rosemond, Apr. 23, 1942 (div. 1953); 1 child, John Kirk; m. Julius Goldberg, Sept. 9, 1954; children: Michael, Judith. Student, Coll. Charleston, 1951—54; AB in Liberal Arts and Sci. with honors, U. Ill., Chgo., 1968, MS in Biol. Scis., 1972, PhD in Biol. Scis., 1985. Undergrad. fellow in bacteriology Med. Coll. S.C., Charleston, 1952-54; teaching asst. U. Ill., Chgo., 1969-72, 77-84, rsch. asst., 1977; teaching fellow W.Va. U., Morgantown, 1974, instr., 1975—76. Rsch. in N.Am. bot. needlework art, 1986—. Author: Studies in Several North American Species of Ophioglossum, 1986; translator Nat. Transl. Ctr., Chgo., 1976; contbr. articles to profl. jours. James scholar U. Ill., 1968-69. Mem. DAR, ACLU. Democrat. Episcopalian. Avocations: gardening, writing, money management. Home and Office: 1356 Mandel Ave Westchester IL 60154-3433

WEBB, EUGENE HENRY, real estate company executive; b. Red Level, Ala., Nov. 24, 1918; m. Danna Wood, 1999; 2 children. Attended, Columbia U., NYC, Pohs Inst., Miles Coll.; D (hon.), NY Podiatric Coll. of Medicine, Miles Coll. Co-founder, chmn. Webb & Brooker, Inc., 1968—. Bd. dirs. Greater Harlem Real Estate Bd. Former mem. bd. trustees Stillman Coll., Cambridge Coll.; chmn. exec. bd. Freedom Nat. Bank; bd. dirs. NYC C. of C. & Industry. With USN, WWII. Mem.: Nat. Assn. Real Estate Brokers, Bd. Associated Builders & Owners of Greater NY, Columbia Soc. Real Estate Appraisers, Real Estate Bd. NY

(Lifetime Real Estate Achievement award 2008). Office: Webb & Brooker Inc 2534 Adam Clayton Powell Blvd New York NY 10039 Office Phone: 212-926-7100. Office Fax: 212-862-0923.

WEBB, EVELYN DUNBAR, middle school educator; b. New Haven, Conn., Apr. 6, 1954; d. Marshall Nelson and Evelyn Louise (Clinton) Dunbar; m. John Henry Webb, Aug. 9, 1986; children: Jennifer Ann, Heather Merri. AAS, Ctrl. Va. C.C., Lynchburg, 2000; BA in English, Randolph-Macon Woman's Coll., Lynchburg, Va., 2002. Co-owner, v.p. Gremlin Systems, Ltd., Old Lyme, Conn., 1985—96; dir. of fiscal svcs. The Valley RR Co., Essex, Conn., 1993—96; client acctg. specialist First Step, Inc., New London, Conn., 1996—97; asst. office mgr. Old Va. Candle Co., Lynchburg, Va., 1997—99; tchr., tutor New Vistas Sch., Lynchburg, Va., 2002—03; writing workshop instr. Lynchburg Acad. Fine Arts Ctr., Va., 2003—04; tchr. James River Day Sch., Lynchburg, 2003—08; tchr. pregnant teens program Laurel Regional Sch. Alternate Edn., Lynchburg, 2008—. Pub. rels. dir. Triangle Prodns., Bridgeport, 1990; designer software Rental Realty Mgmt., Acctg. Systems Mgmt., 1986. Author: (short fiction) The Word Collector (Margaret I. Raynal Fiction Award, 2000), (poetry) Aunt Maude's Window (Margaret Walker Meml. Poetry Prize, 2002), (short fiction) The Gift (San Gabriel Writers' League Writing for Children Award, 2003), (poetry) The Gihon River Review Literary Journal, Cairn Literary Journal, (poetry, short fiction & plays) Hail, Muse! etc. Literary Journal, (essay) Alice Joins the Lobster Quadrille (Helen Calvert Award for Ekphrasis, 2001); contbr. articles to profl. jours. State of Conn. scholar, 1972; Conn. Coll. scholar, 1984, 86-87. Mem. NAFE, Conn. River Valley Women's Network (bd. dirs. 1989-90), Old Saybrook C. of C. Independent. Episcopalian. Avocations: yoga, reading, bicycling. Office: Regional Days Sch Alternate Edn 401 Monticello Ave Lynchburg VA 24501 Personal E-mail: aresti2007@gmail.com.

WEBB, GARFIELD, art educator; b. Wabash, Ind., Feb. 28, 1952; s. Garfield Webb and Mildred Rehm. HS, Plantation High, Fla., 1970. Tennis profl. USTA, NYC, 1976—90; respiratory therapist Hospitals, Fort Lauderdale, Fla., 1977—83; art tchr. Garfield Webb Art Gallery, Cocoa Beach, Fla., 1999—2008; tennis instr. Pvt. Lessons, Cocoa Beach. Surferamics art class Cocoa Beach Libr., 2001—01. Modern surreal absract cubistic dada, Garfield Webb Art Work. Recipient Tennis Champion, USTA, 1976—90. Mem.: Ea. Surfing Assn. Home: 102 N Brevard Ave Cocoa Beach FL 32931 Personal E-mail: gar_webb@yahoo.com.

WEBB, GARY DOUGLAS, cardiologist; s. John Douglas Webb and Jeannie Hardy Penman; m. Anne Michelle Phillips, Dec. 22, 1984; children: Laura Madeline, Natalie Anne. BS, McGill U., Montréal, 1965, MD, 1967. Chief cardiology Wellesley Hosp., Toronto, Ont, 1972—80; cardiologist Toronto Gen. Hosp., 1980—2004; dir., congenital cardiac ctr. adults U. Toronto, 1986—2004; dir., adult congenital heart ctr. U. Pa., Phila., 2004—. Chmn., med. adv. bd. Adult Congenital Heart Assn., Phila., 2007—; chair, adult congenital working group Am. Coll. Cardiology, Wash., 2005—; pres. Internat. Soc. Adult Congenital Cardiac Disease, Raleigh, NC, 1993—94, Can. Adult Congenital Heart Network, Toronto, 1992—2004; cochair, 32nd Bethesda conf. Am. Coll. Cardiology, Wash., 2000—01. Editor: (textbook) Diagnosis and Management of Adult Congenital Heart Disease, Cases in Adult Congenital Heart Disease. Recipient 700th Anniversary medal, Charles U., Prague, Czech Republic, 1998; named one of America's Top Doctors, Castle Connolly Med. Ltd., 2008; fellowship, RCPS, 1972, Am. Coll. Cardiology, 1976. Fellow: Am. Heart Assn. Office: Philadelphia Adult Congenital Heart Cntr 3400 Spruce St Philadelphia PA 19104-4283 Office Fax: 215-349-5927. Business E-Mail: gary.webb@uphs.upenn.edu.

WEBB, HELEN, literature and language professor; M in Labor and Indsl. Rels., Mich. State U., East Lansing, 1982; M in 2nd Lang. Acquisition and Hispanic Lit., U. Ark., Little Rock, 2000. Lectr. fgn. lang. U. Pa., Phila., 2003—. Pres. Ark. Fgn. Lang. Tchrs. Assn., 2000—01. Mem.: Am. Assn. Tchrs. Spanish and Portuguese, Phi Beta Kappa. Avocations: travel, writing, gardening, cooking, hiking. Office: Univ Penn 255 South 38th St Philadelphia PA 19104-6355 Business E-Mail: webbh@sas.upenn.edu.

WEBB, JACK D., Councilman; b. 1962; m. Elizabeth Webb; children: Michael, Eamon, Maura. BA in Hist., Iona Coll., 1984; MBA, U. Fla., 1987, JD, 1994. With Mahoney, Adams & Criser; dir. Labor & Employee Rels. CEVA Logistics, Inc.; councilman, Dist. 6 Jacksonville City Coun. Chmn. Dist. 6 Duval County Rep. Com.; mem. Land Use & Zoning Com.; chmn. Rules Com.; mem. Jacksonville Juvenile Justice Comprehensive Strategy Steering Com.; coun. liaison Jacksonville Transp. Authority; vice chmn. Jacksonville Waterways Commn.; mem. Personnel Com., Post-Employment Appeals Com. Bd. dirs. Divine Mercy House; vol. Jacksonville Basketball League; parish leader St. Joseph's Ch. Mem.: Mandarin Hist. Soc., St. Joseph's Men's Club (former pres.), Mandarin Cmty. Club. Republican. Office: 117 W Duval St Ste 425 Jacksonville FL 32202 Office Phone: 904-630-1386, 904-630-1388. Business E-Mail: webb@coj.net.*

WEBB, JACK M., lawyer; b. Monroe, La., Feb. 23, 1936; s. Sam L. and Lillian Etta (McCowen) W.; m. Diane Adele Waterman, Aug. 22, 1964; children: Julia Lillian Pogue, Kathryn Joy Shively, Samuel Logan. BS in Geology, Centenary Coll. La., 1957; JD, Tulane U., 1960; student, JFK Sch. Govt. Harvard U., 1999. Bar: La. 1960, Tex. 1962. Atty. Standard Oil Co. Tex., Houston, 1961-66; staff atty. Trunkline Gas. Co., Houston, 1966-71; sr. atty. M.W. Kellogg Co., Houston, 1971-73; sec., asst. gen. counsel Gulf Resources & Chem. Corp., Houston, 1973-78, v.p. govt. rels., adminstrv. asst. to chmn. bd., 1978-82; pres. Jack M. Webb & Assocs., 1983—; U.S. spl. amb. to Bolivia, 1985, to Finland, 1986, to Haiti, 1991, to Angola, 1992, to Ghana, 1993; hon. consul gen. Ghana, 1995—. Bd. dirs. Bradmark, Inc., Am. Meridian Ins. Co., Scotia Pacific Holding Co., Veri Med Rsch. Corp., Crystal Fuels, Inc., W.C.W. Internat. Bd. dirs. U.S. Peace Corps, 1985-86, Nat. Park Found., 1986-92, Boy Scouts Am., 1975—. Capt. U.S. Army, 1960-61. Mem. Tex. Bar Assn., La. Bar Assn. Methodist. Home: 3434 Locke Ln Houston TX 77027-4139 Office Phone: 281-586-7166. E-mail: jackw@jackwebb.com.

WEBB, JIM (JAMES HENRY WEBB JR.), United States Senator from Virginia; b. St. Joseph, Mo., Feb. 9, 1946; s. James Henry and Vera Lorraine (Hodges) Webb; m. Barbara Samorajczyk (div.); 1 child, Amy; m. Jo Ann Krukar (div.); children: Sarah C., James Robert, Julia A.; m. Hong Le Webb; 1 child, Georgia LeAnh 1 stepchild, Emily. Attended, U. Southern Calif., 1963—64; BA, US Naval Acad., 1968; JD, Georgetown U., 1972. Cons. to Gov. US Territory of Guam; asst. minority counsel House Com. on Veterans Affairs, Washington, 1977-78, chief minority counsel, 1979-81; asst. sec. for reserve affairs US Dept. Def., Washington, 1984-87, sec. Dept. Navy, 1987—88; US Senator from Va., 2007—; mem fgn. rels., armed services, & veterans affairs com. Instr. tactics and weapons Marine Corps Officer Candidates Sch.; vis. writer US Naval Acad. Journalist covering US Marines in Beirut, PBS, 1983 (Emmy award); author: Micronesia and US Pacific Strategy: A Blueprint for the 1980s, 1974, Fields of Fire, 1978, A Sense of Honor, 1981, A Country Such As This, 1983, Something To Die For, 1991, The Emperor's General, 1999, Lost Soldiers, 2001, Born Fighting: How the Scots-Irish Shaped America, 2004, A Time to Fight: Reclaiming a Fair and Just America, 2008; writer, exec. prodr. (films) Rules of Engagement, 2000. Served in USMC, 1968—72, 2nd lt., platoon comdr., Vietnam. Decorated Navy Cross, Silver Star, 2 Bronze Stars, 2 Purple Hearts, Mil. Order Iron Mike award US Marine Corp League; recipient Disting. Pub. Svc. award, US Dept. Def., Patriot award, Medal of Honor Soc., Nat. Commander's Pub. Svc. award, Am. Legion, Media Svc. award, VFW, John H. Russell Leader-ship award, Robert L. Denig Disting. Svc. award; fellow Harvard Inst. Politics, 1992. Democrat. Office: US Senate 144 Russell Senate Office Bldg Washington DC 20510 also: 507 E Franklin St Richmond VA 23219*

WEBB, JOHN GIBBON, III, lawyer; b. Flint, Mich., June 1, 1944; s. John Gibbon Jr. and Martha W.; m. Fain Murphey, July 6, 1968; children: Jennifer Horn, Philip, Andrew Aidan, John Matthew. AB, Davidson Coll., 1966; JD, Vanderbilt U., 1970. Bar: N.Y. 1971, N.J. 1981. Assoc. Curtis, Mallet-Prevost, Colt & Mosle, NYC, 1970—80; gen. counsel, v.p., sec. J.M. Huber Corp., Edison, NJ, 1980—95; pvt. bus. law practice Budd Lake, NJ, 1996—. Mem. exec. com. Sussex County CC Found., Episcopal Cmty. Devel. Inc. Mem.: ABA, Warren County C. of C., Mt. Olive C. of C., NJ State Bar Assn., NYC Bar Assn. Episcopalian. Office: Ste 125 500 International Dr N Budd Lake NJ 07828 Office Phone: 973-426-8435. Personal E-mail: webbgc@aol.com.

WEBB, JULIA JONES, elementary school educator, minister; b. Portsmouth, Va., Apr. 3, 1962; d. William Edward Jones Jr. and Fannie Ford Jones; m. Alexander Maurice Webb Sr., Nov. 17, 1990; children: Brittany Alexandria, Alexander Maurice II. BA in Early Childhood Edn., Norfolk State U., 1988; postgrad., Va. Union U., 2004—. Lic. early edn. Va. Educator Chesapeake (Va.) Pub. Schs., 1988—, chmn. grade level II Southwestern Elem., 2005—. Assoc. minister First Bapt. Ch. Gilmerton, Chesapeake, 1999—2002, New Hope Bapt. Ch., Chesapeake, 2002—05, Grove Bapt. Ch., Portsmouth, Va., 2005—. USAA All-Am. scholar, Norfolk State U., 1989. Mem.: Va. Edn. Assn. (del. 1990—91), Chesapeake Tchr. Forum. Democrat. Baptist. Avocations: coaching cheerleading, gardening, cooking, interior decorating, reading. Home: 2701 Dockside Ct Chesapeake VA 23323 Office: Southwestern Elem Sch 4410 Airline Blvd Chesapeake VA 23321 Office Phone: 757-465-6310.

WEBB, KARRIE, professional golfer; b. Ayr, Queensland, Australia, Dec. 21, 1974; Profl. golfer, 1994—; mem. LPGA Tour, 1996—; mem. Australian Team Women's World Cup of Golf, 2005. Recipient Vare Trophy, LPGA, 1997, 1999, 2000, Crowne Plaza Achievement award, 2000; named Rookie of Yr., Women Profl. Golfers' European Tour, 1995, Rolex Rookie of Yr., LPGA, 1996, Rolex Player of Yr., 1999, 2000, Outstanding Women's Golf Performer of Yr., ESPN Espy awards, 1997, 2001, Female Player of Yr., Golf Writers Assn. Am., 2000, Queesland Sportswomen of Yr., 2000—02, 2001, 2002. Achievements include winning LPGA Tour events including the Weetabix Women's Brit. Open, 1995, 97, 2002, Healthsouth Inaugural, 1996, Sprint Titleholders Championship, 1996, SAFECO Classic, 1996, 1997, ITT LPGA Tour Championship, 1996, Susan G. Koman Internat., 1997, Australian Ladies Masters, 1998, 99, 2000; winner, LPGA Tour events including the City of Hope Myrtle Beach Classic, 1998, Wegmans Rochester Internat., 1999, Mercury Titleholders Championship, 1999, Standard Register PING, 1999, The Office Depot, 1999, 2000; winner, LPGA Tour events including the du Maurier Classic, 1999, Nabisco Championship, 2000, Oldsmobile Classic, 2000, LPGA Takefuji Classic, 2000, AFLAC Champions presented by Southern Living, 2000, US Women's Open, 2000, 01; winner, LPGA Tour events including the McDonald's LPGA Championship presented by AIG, 2001, Tyco/ADT Championship, 2001, Wegmans Rochester LPGA, 2002, John Q. Hammons Hotel Classic, 2003, Kellogg-Keebler Classic, 2004, Kraft Nabisco Championship, 2006, Michelob Ultra Open, 2006, Evian Masters, 2006; winner, international events including the Women's Australian Open, 2000, 02, 07, ANZ Ladies Masters on the Robe di Kappa Ladies European Tour, 2005; inducted into World Golf Hall of Fame, 2005; first LPGA player to achieve the Super Career Grand Slam by winning all 5 majors available in her career, 2002. Avocations: reading, basketball, fishing. Office: c/o LPGA 100 Internat Golf Dr Daytona Beach FL 32124-1092*

WEBB, KATHARINE, counselor; b. Bklyn., Sept. 13, 1931; d. Joseph Norris and Thelma (Black) Norris Sharpton; m. John James Webb, May 25, 1956 (div. Aug. 1971); children: John, Tyra, Lori. BS in Home Econs., Hunter Coll., 1954, MS in Home Econs., 1957; MS in Guidance and Counseling, Western Mich. U., 1969; PhD in Guidance and Psychol. Svcs., Ind. State U., 1972. Tchr. home econs. N.Y.C. Bd. Edn., Bklyn., 1954-65, counselor, 1965-68, Ind. State U., Terre Haute, 1970-72; assoc. prof. counselor edn. SUNY-Brockport, 1972-79; commr. N.Y. State Commn. of Correction, Albany, 1979-85; dir. guidance and counseling N.Y. State Dept. Correctional Svcs., 1985-98. Mediator, arbitrator Cmty. Dispute Ctr., Rochester, N.Y., 1973-79; mediator, fact-finder N.Y. State Pub. Employees Rels. Bd., Albany, 1975-79; adj. prof. Maria Coll., Albany, N.Y., 1987-2004. Pres. bd. dirs. Brockport Childcare Ctr., N.Y., 1973-74, Nat. Migrant Found., Inc., Albany, 1983-84; bd. dirs. YWCA of Rochester, N.Y., 1975-77, YWCA of Albany, 1985-92, Albany Cath. Family and Cmty. Svcs., 1991-94, St. Casimir's Regional Sch., 1991-96; elected mem. Albany Sch. Bd., 1998, 2002; mem. N.Y.S. Regent's Adv. Coun. Inst. Accreditation, 2000—. Recipient cert. recognition YWCA of Rochester, 1975, cert. disting. svc. Urban League Rochester, 1976, award for disting. spl. programs SUNY Office Spl. Programs, Albany, 1978, award for support and contbns. Rochester Ednl. Opportunity Ctr., 1978, award for svc. Mental Health Assn. Rochester, 1979, Disting. Alumni award Ind. State U., 1986, Albany Humanitarian award, 1988. Mem. ACA, Am. Correctional Assn., N.Y. State Minorities in Criminal Justice, N.Y. State Pers. and Guidance Assn. (v.p. for profl. svcs. 1979-80), Pub. Offender Counselor Assn., Assn. for Non-White Concerns, Delta Kappa Gamma Soc. (past chpt. pres.), Delta Sigma Theta. Democrat. Roman Catholic.

WEBB, LISA MICHELLE, regulatory affairs manager; b. Ft. Irwin, Calif., Feb. 9, 1970; d. Albert Joseph Velasquez and Susan Jane Lindsey; m. Charles Haizlip Webb III, Sept. 18, 1993; children: Charles Haizlip IV children: Wesley Grant. BA in Human Biology, Stanford U., Palo Alto, Calf., 1993; MBA, Ind. Wesleyan U., Marion, 2000. Regulatory affairs cert., US Regulatory Affairs Profl. Soc., 1998, regulatory affairs cert., European Union Regulatory Affairs Profl. Soc., 2002, regulatory affairs cert., Can. Regulatory Affairs Profl. Soc., 2004, cert. regulatory affairs San Diego State U., 2004. Regulatory affairs specialist Cook Inc., 1997—2005, regulatory affairs mgr., 2005—. Presenter in field. Sunday sch. tchr. First United Meth. Ch., Bloomington, 2000—06. Mem.: Food and Drug Law Inst., Regulatory Affairs Profl. Soc., Sorosis Philanthropic Soc., Stanford U. Alumni Assn., Psi Iota Xi, Kappa Alpha Theta (mem. alumni assn.). Home: 1618 Greenfield Ct Bloomington IN 47401 Office: Cook Inc 750 Daniels Way Bloomington IN 47404 Business E-Mail: lisa.webb@cookmedical.com.

WEBB, MARTHA JEANNE, writer, educator, film producer; b. Grinnell, Iowa, Oct. 26, 1947; d. Frederick Winfield and Helen (Potter) W.; m. Bruce A. Clark; children: Marjorie, Paula, David. Student, St. Cloud State U., 1965-67, U. Minn., 1967-69, Coll. of St. Catherine, 1979-81. Personnel, pub. relations, drug abuse edn. NIH, 1967-77; account services Doremus & Co., Mpls., 1977-79; v.p. adminstrn. Webb Enterprises, Inc., Mpls., 1979-81; v.p. Russell-Manning Prodns., Mpls., 1981-86; pres. Clark Webb, Inc., Mpls., 1986-92. Pres. Minn. Film Bd., 1986-87, BCW Corp., 1988—. Author: Dress Your House for Success, 1997, Finding Home, 1998; co-prodr. Hubert H. Humphrey: A Passion for Justice, Whitney Mus., 1998. Recipient Summit awards, 1999, Distinction Communicator awards, 1998, Silver award Internat. Film and TV Festival of N.Y., 1983, 84, 85, 86, 87, Golden Eagle award CINE Festival, 1985, Gold award Telly Awards, 1987.

WEBB, MARTY FOX, principal; b. Des Moines, July 15, 1942; d. Joseph John and Jean (Way) Fox; m. Andrew H. Rudolph, Aug. 17, 1963 (div. Jan. 1988); children: Kristen Ann, Kevin Andrew; m. Eugene J. Webb, Nov. 23, 1991. BS, U. Mich., 1964; MEd, Houston Bapt. U., 1982; EdD, U. San Francisco, 1993. Cert. adminstr., Tex., elem. and spl. edn. educator, Mich., Tex. Tchr. spl. edn. Hawthorn Ctr., Northville, Mich., 1964-70; tchr. Bellaire (Tex.) Sch. for Children, 1977-80; prin. Corpus Christi Sch., Houston, 1980-97; founder, head of sch. The Monarch Sch., Houston, 1997—. Spkr. in field. Bd. dirs. DeBusk Found. Recipient Elem. Sch. Recognition award U.S. Dept. Edn., 1989-90, Blue Ribbon Sch. award, 1990, Outstanding Doctoral Student award, 1994. Mem. ASCD, U. Mich. Alumni Assn. Avocations: reading, fly fishing, camping, hiking, bodybuilding. Home: 3531 Sun Valley Dr Houston TX 77025-4148 Office: The Monarch Sch 1231 Wirt Rd Houston TX 77055-6852 Office Phone: 713-479-0800. Business E-Mail: mwebb@monarchschool.org.

WEBB, NATE, legislative staff member; Degree, U. Maine, Augusta; degree in Journalism, U. Ctrl. Okla. Mng. editor KTOK News Talk Sta., Okla.; comm. dir. Gubernatorial Campaign for Steve Largent; chief of staff for Lt. Gov. Mary Fallin State of Okla.; chief of staff for Rep. Mary Fallin US House of Reps., Washington, 2007—. With USN. Office: Office of Congresswoman Mary Fallin 1432 Longworth House Office Bldg Washington DC 20515*

WEBB, PAUL, physiologist, educator, researcher, consultant; b. Cleve., Dec. 2, 1923; s. Monte F. and Barbara (Webb) Bourjaily; m. Eileen Whalen, Mar. 13, 1948; children: Shaun P., Paula S. Womacks. BA, U. Va., 1943, MD, 1946; MS in Physiol., U. Wash., 1951. Asst. prof. physiology U. Okla. Sch. Medicine, Oklahoma City, 1952—54; chief environ. sect. Aeromed. Lab., Wright-Patterson AFB, Ohio, 1954-58; prin. assoc. Webb Assocs., Yellow Springs, Ohio, 1959-82; vis. scientist INSERM, Paris, 1983; vis. prof. U. Limburg, Maastricht, The Netherlands, 1986, U. Uppsala, Sweden, 1988-89; clin. prof. cmty. health Wright State U. Sch. Medicine, Dayton, Ohio, 1980—; rsch. prof. bioengring. Wright State U., Dayton, 2005—. Cons. aerospace and undersea medicine, energy balance and thermal physiology, Yellow Springs, 1980—. Author: Human Calorimeters, 1985; contbr. articles to profl. jours. Village councilman Village of Yellow Springs, Ohio, 1969-75; mem. Air Force Scientific Adv. Bd., Washington, 1984-88. Recipient Ely award Human Factors Soc., 1972. Fellow Aerospace Med. Assn. (Aerospace Indsl. Life Scis. Assn. award 1969), Am. Inst. Med. and Biol. Engring.; mem. Am. Physiol. Soc., Undersea & Hyperbaric Med. Soc. (oceaneering internat. award 1979, pres. 1980-81). Home and Office: 14 Cedar Ct Yellow Springs OH 45387-1958 Home Phone: 937-767-7843. Business E-Mail: paul.webb@wright.edu.

WEBB, RICHARD C., engineering company executive; b. Omaha, Sept. 2, 1915; m. Virginia; 1 son. BSE.E., U. Denver, 1937, DSc (hon.), 1996; MSE.E., Purdue U., 1944, PhD, 1951; DSc (hon.), U. Denver, 1996. Registered profl. engr., Colo. Traffic engr. Mountain States Telephone and Telegraph Co., Denver, 1937-39; research engr. RCA Labs. Div., Princeton, N.J., 1945-53; pres., founder, tech. dir. Colo. Research Corp. (subs. Carrier Corp.), Syracuse, N.Y., 1956-61; pres., founder. tech. dir. Colo. Instruments, Inc., Broomfield, Colo., 1961-71; pres., gen. mgr. Colo. Instruments div. Mohawk Data Scis. Corp., Utica, NYC, 1971-73; pres. Webb Engring. Co. (name changed to Data Ray Corp.), Boulder, Colo., 1973-85. Vis. lectr. U. Colo., 1962-82; prof. elec. engring. U. Denver, 1953-56, Iowa State Coll., 1950 Author: Tele-Visionaries: The People Behind the Invention of Television, 2005; contbr. articles pub. to profl. jours. Recipient Disting. Engring. Alumnus award Purdue U., 1970, Profl. Achievement award U. Denver Alumni Assn., 1983, Outstanding Elec. Engr. award Purdue U., 1992. Fellow IEEE; mem. Soc. Motion Picture and TV Engrs., Acoustical Soc. Am., Inst. Aerospace Scis., Am. Ordnance Assn., Western Electronics Mfrs. Assn. (past v.p., dir.), Sigma Xi, Tau Beta Pi, Eta Kappa Nu. Achievements include patents in field. Home: PO Box 3078 Estes Park CO 80517-3078

WEBB, ROBERT GRAVEM, retired biology professor; b. Long Beach, Calif., Feb. 18, 1927; s. Edward Walter and Eva Berg (Gravem) Webb; m. Patricia Ann Peden, May 25, 1985; 1 child, Christopher Michael. PhD, U. Kans., Lawrence, 1960. Prof. biol. scis. Dept Biol. Sci., U. Tex El Paso, 1966—91, emeritus prof. biol. sci., 1992—. Contbr. articles to profl. jours. (Faculty Rsch. award U. Tex El Paso, 1978). Seaman first class USN, 1945—46, Calif. Fellow: Soc. Study Amphibians & Reptiles. (pres. 1980—81). Home: 5701 Upper Valley Rd El Paso TX Office: Dept Biol Scis Univ Tex El Paso El Paso TX 79968-0519 Business E-Mail: rgwebb@utep.edu.

WEBB, TARA YVETTE, music educator; d. Harvey and Rachel Webb. BA in Music Edn., Baldwin Wallace Conservatory, Berea, Ohio, 1985. Cert. Orff Schulwerk level 1, 2, 3, Kodaly level 1. Music specialist Taft and Franklin Schs., Lakewood, Ohio, 1986—87; substitute tchr. Lakewood Pub. Schs., 1987—89; dir. children's choir and youth orch. Lakewood Presbyn. Ch., 1987—; music specialist K-8 Sts. Joseph and John Sch., Strongsville, Ohio, 1989—. Mem. guidance com. St. Joseph and John Sch., Strongsville, 2001—06. Singer, actress, orch. mem. Singing Angels, Cmty. Theater; goodwill amb. Ohio Light Opera, 1977—81; mem. West Surbon Philharm. Orch., Roots Rhythm World Percussion. Recipient Latin Am. Art and Music grant, Eva and Joseph M. Bruening Found., 1998, Native Am. Music grant, McGinty Found., 2001, 2006, 2008; grant, NAMN & House of Blue. Mem.: Smithsonian Nat. Mus. of the Am. Indian, Rock and Roll Hall of Fame and Mus., Am. Orff Schulwerk Assn., Orgn. Am. Kodaly Educators. Home: 1508 Bunts Rd Lakewood OH 44107 Office: Sts Joseph and John Sch 12580 Pearl Rd Strongsville OH 44136

WEBB, THOMAS IRWIN, JR., lawyer, director; b. Toledo, Sept. 16, 1948; s. Thomas Irwin and Marcia Davis (Winters) W.; m. Polly S. DeWitt, Oct. 11, 1986; 1 child, Elisabeth Hurst. BA, Williams Coll., 1970; postgrad., Boston U., 1970—71; JD, Case Western Res. U., 1973. Bar: Ohio, Mich. Assoc. Shumaker, Loop & Kendrick, Toledo, 1973—79, ptnr., 1979—, chmn. corp. law dept., 1992—94, 1994mgmt. com., 1994—99. Dir. Calphalon Corp., 1990-98, Yark Automotive Group, Inc. Coun. mem. Village of Ottawa Hills, Ohio, 1979-85, adviser

Ohio Divsn. Securities, 1979-85, Village of Ottawa Hills, 1999—; bd. dirs. Kiwanis Youth Found. Toledo, 1982-2002, Toledo Area Regional Transit Authority, 1989-91, Arts Commn. Greater Toledo, 1993-2003, exec. com., 1994-99, v.p., 1994-96, pres., 1996-97; bd. dirs. AAA Northwest Ohio Jr. Achievement of Northwestern Ohio, Inc., 1992-2005, Lourdes Coll. Found., 1995-2001, Toledo Orch. Assn., 1999—, Med. Coll. Ohio, 2001-05, Lourdes Coll., 2001-09, Maumee Valley Country Day Sch., 2005—. Mem. ABA, Ohio Bar Assn. (corp. law com. 1989—), Toledo Bar Assn., Benzie County Mich. Bar Assn., Northwestern Ohio Alumni Assn. of Williams Coll. (pres. 1974-83), Toledo-Rowing Found. (trustee 1985-2001), Toledo Area C. of C. (trustee 1991-98, exec. com. 1993-98, fin. com. 1993—), Order of Coif, Crystal Downs Country Club, Toledo Country Club, The Toledo Club (trustee 1984-90, pres. 1987-90), Williams Club NY, Crystal Lake Yacht Club. Republican. Episcopalian. Office: Shumaker Loop & Kendrick 1000 Jackson St Toledo OH 43604 Office Phone: 419-321-1237, 231-352-7542. Business E-Mail: twebb@slk-law.com.

WEBB, THOMAS J., utilities executive; b. Alexandria, Va., Oct. 3, 1952; m. Donna; 3 children. B in Fin. with honors, George Mason U.; MBA. Various fin. mgmt. positions Ford Motor Co. and subs.; controller Electronics divsn., Large Front-Wheel Drive Vehicle Ctr.; CFO Visteon Corp.; chief fin. info. officer Ford Motor Co.; exec. v.p., CFO Kellogg Co., Battle Creek, Mich., 2000—02, CMS Energy, Dearborn, Mich., 2002—. Bd. dirs. Conix, Can., Hall Climate Control, Korea, Halla Electronics, Korea, Samcor, South Africa, Yan Feng, China, Toledo (Ohio) Molding and Die, Climate Sys., India, others. Office: CMS Energy 1 Energy Plaza Dr Jackson MI 49201-2357

WEBB, TIMOTHY K., state official, school system administrator; AA, Columbia State CC; BA, Regent's Coll.; MA, Middle Tennessee State U.; PhD in Edn. Leadership, Nova Southeastern U. Math & social studies tchr. Lewis County Schs., Tenn., athletic dir. Tenn., asst. prin. Tenn., supt. Tenn., title II coord. Tenn.; dep. commr. Tenn. Dept. Edn., commr., 2008—. Mem. Nat. Assessment Governing Bd., Nat. Ctr. of Edn. Studies, Tenn. Info. Infrastructure (TNII) Steering Com. Office: Tenn Dept Edn Andrew Johnson Tower - 6th Fl 710 James Robertson Parkway Nashville TN 37243 Office Fax: 615-741-2731.*

WEBB, WATT WETMORE, physicist, researcher; b. Kansas City, Mo., Aug. 27, 1927; s. Watt Jr. and Anna (Wetmore) W.; m. Page Chapman, Nov., 1950; children: Watt III, Spahr C., Bucknell C. BS, MIT, 1947, ScD, 1955. Rsch. engr., asst. dir. rsch. Union Carbide Metals Co., Niagara Falls, N.Y., 1947-52, 55-61; prof. applied physics Cornell U., Ithaca, N.Y., 1961—, dir. Sch. Applied and Engring. Physics, 1983-88; dir. NIH-NSF Resource Biophysical Imaging and Opto-electronics, 1988—, dir. Biophysics Program, 1991-94; NIH scholar-in-residence Fogarty Internat. Ctr. for Advanced Study, 1988-92. Mem. adv. panels Materials Adv. Bd., 1958-59, 63-64, NSF, 1974—; co-chair NAS panel on sci. interfaces and tech. applications, Physics Through the 90s, 1983-86; bd. dirs., exec. com. Cornell Rsch. Found., 1983—. Mem. adv. com. Physics Today, 1991—; assoc. editor Phys. Rev. Letters, 1975-91; mem. editorial bd. Biophysics Jour., 1975-78, mem. publ. com., 1976-83; contbr. more than 250 articles to profl. jours. Recipient S.B. Eckert Prof. of Engring. award, Cornell U., 1998—, Michelson-Morley award, 1999, Ernst Abbe Lecture award 1997; Guggenheim fellow, 1974-75. Fellow AAAS, Am. Phys. Soc. (chmn. 1988-89, exec. com. divsn. biol. physics 1975-77, Biol. Physics prize 1991), Am. Inst. Med. and Biol. Engrs. (founding 1992); mem. Nat. Acad. Engring., Biophys. Soc. (mem. coun. 1972-75, 82-85), Nat. Acad. Scis., Am. Soc. Cell Biology, Am. Soc. Gen. Physiology, Optical Soc. Am., Ithaca Yacht Club, N.Y. Yacht Club. Achievements include patents in optical instruments, two photon laser microscopy, fluorescent probes, microcrystals, welding technology. Office: Cornell U 223 Clark Hall Ithaca NY 14853-2501

WEBB, WATTS RANKIN, surgeon; b. Columbia, Ky., Sept. 8, 1922; s. Frank Elbert and Susie Josephine (Rankin) W.; m. Frances Luella Cooke, Aug. 19, 1944; children: Michael Andrew, Paul Alan, Harvey Elbert, Gordon Lewis. BA, U. Miss., 1942; MD, Johns Hopkins U., 1945. Diplomate Am. Bd. Surgery, Am. Bd. Thoracic Surgery, Am. Bd. Surg. Critical Care. Intern Barnes Hosp., St. Louis, 1945-46; resident in surgery VA Hosp., Biloxi, Miss., 1946-48; resident in gen. and thoracic surgery Barnes Hosp., 1948-52; chief surgeon Miss. State Sanatorium, 1952-63; instr. surgery U. Miss., 1955-56, asst. prof. surgery, 1956-58, prof., 1958-63; prof., chmn. div. thoracic and cardiovascular surgery U. Tex. Southwestern Med. Sch., Dallas, 1964-70; prof., chmn. dept. surgery SUNY Upstate Med. Center, Syracuse, 1970-77; chmn. dept. Tulane U., New Orleans, 1977-89, prof. surgery, 1977-93, La. State U., New Orleans, 1993—, Huey P. Long Hosp., Alexandria, 2007. Author: Pulmonary Problems in Surgery, 1974, Surgery in Acute Coronary Problems, 1974, Aneurysms, 1983, Cardiovascular Emergencies, 1986, Atlas of Pulmonary Resections, 1988, (with others) Surgical Management for Chest Injuries, Vol. VII, 1990; mem. editl. bd.: Annals of Thoracic Surgery, 1968-79, Surg. Rounds, 1978-82, Surgery Clinics, 1980-82, Microcirculation, 1983-84, Brit. Jour. Surgery, 1981-89; contbr. articles to profl. jours. Recipient award Hadassah, 1965, Knockers Soc. Outstanding Tchr. award SUNY Upstate Med. Ctr., 1972, Owl Club Clin. Tchr. of Yr. award Tulane U. Med. Sch., 1978, 86, 88-93, Gloria P. Walsh award for best tchr. in Med. Sch., 1992, Aesculapian Tchr. of Yr. award La. State U., 1995, 96. Fellow ACS, Am. Coll. Chest Physicians; mem. AMA, Am. Assn. Thoracic Surgery, Am. Coll. Cardiology, Am. Fedn. Clin. Research, Am. Heart Assn. (Silver medal 1963), Am. Physiol. Soc., Am. Surg. Assn., Am. Thoracic Soc., Halsted Soc., La. Med. Soc., Orleans Parish Med. Soc., New Orleans Surg. Soc., Societe International de Chirurgie, Soc. Cryobiology, Soc. Thoracic Surgeons, Soc. Univ. Surgeons, Southeastern Surg. Congress, So. Med. Assn., So. Soc. Clin. Research, So. Surg. Assn. (Shipley medal 1961), So. Thoracic Soc., So. Thoracic Surg. Assn., Surg. Assn. La., Surg. Biology Club II, Internat. Soc. Heart Transplantation, Gulf Coast Vascular Soc., Sigma Xi, Alpha Omega Alpha, Pi Kappa Pi, Beta Beta Beta, Alpha Epsilon Delta. Methodist. Office: La State U Huey P Long Hosp PO Box 5352 Pineville LA 71361-5352 Office Phone: 318-542-1812. Personal E-mail: webbwatts@yahoo.com.

WEBB, WILLIAM YERICK, lawyer; b. Mont Estoril, Portugal, Apr. 13, 1935; came to U.S., 1939; s. Leslie A. and Laura E. (Detrich) W.; m. Jeannette L. Richardson, June 20, 1959; children: Elizabeth T., Douglas L., Philip N. AB, Dartmouth Coll., 1956; JD cum laude, U. Mich., 1961. Bar: Pa. 1961, U.S. Dist. Ct. (ea. dist.) Pa. 1961. Assoc. Ballard, Spahr, Andrews & Ingersoll, Phila., 1961-69, ptnr., 1969—2000; sr. v.p., gen. counsel Phila. Phillies, 2000—. Adj. prof. law Widener U. Law Sch., 1989; adj. prof. sports law Villanova Law Sch.; sec., dir. AMR Internat. Inc. and subs., 1971-81; gen. counsel Opera Co. Phila., 1975-81. Asst. editor U. Mich. Law Rev. Bd. dirs., sec., counsel Children's Country Week Assn., 1978-85; bd. dirs., chmn. Schuylkill Ctr. Environ. Edn, 1989-95; Natural Lands Trust(bd. trustee 2008-), pres., bd. dirs. Radnor A Better Chance, Inc., 1982-88; chmn., bd. dirs. History Ctr. in Phila., 1996. Lt. (j.g.) USNR, 1956-58. Mem. Sports Law Assn. (bd. dirs. 1984—, past pres.), Lake Paupac Club Greentown, Pa., (bd. dirs. 1990-2007, past pres.), Applebrook Golf Club. Episcopalian. Office: The Phillies One Citizens Bank Way Philadelphia PA 19148-5249

WEBB, YVONNE M., secondary school educator; b. Watertown, SD, May 27, 1954; d. Lloyd T. and Rose V. Hanks; m. Melvin R. Webb; children: Justin, Grant, Forrest, Grace. BSc, No. State U., 1974. Tchr. German S.D. Sch. Visually Handicapped, Aberdeen, SD, 1974—77; tchr. Roscoe (S.D.) H.S., 1977—79, Cheyenne Eagle Butte (S.D.) H.S., 1994—, chmn. Dept. English, 1994—. Adv. student coun. Cheyenne Eagle Butte (S.D.) H.S., 1990—92, adv. H.S. class, 1983—2006. Vol. YMCA, Eagle Butte, 1996—2004, All Saints Cath. Ch., Eagle Butte, 1996—2000. Named Tchr. of Yr., Indian Office Edn., 2000. Mem.: Eagle Butte (S.D.) Edn. Assn. (sec. 1995, treas. 1995). Democrat. Roman Cath. Avocations: reading, gardening. Home: Box 27 Eagle Butte SD 57625

WEBBER, ANDREA L., research scientist; d. Forrest C. and Sally A. Wealand; m. Nathan Webber, Dec. 28, 1991; children: Meredith L., Madison N., Macey E. BS, Bucknell U., Lewisburg, Pa., 1991; PhD, Princeton U., NJ, 1998. Postdoc. fellow U. Pa. Sch. Medicine, Phila., 1997—2002; sr. rsch. biologist Merck & Co. Inc., West Point, Pa., 2002—08, rsch. fellow, 2008—. Mem.: ARVO. Avocations: reading, walking. Office: Merck & Co Inc 770 Sumneytown Pike WP46-200 West Point PA 19486 Office Phone: 215-652-6295. Office Fax: 215-652-4692. Personal E-mail: andiwebber@comcast.net. Business E-Mail: andrea_webber@merck.com.

WEBBER, BONNY A., educational consultant; B, Cleary U., Ypsilanti, Mich., 1991; M, Jones U., Englewood, 2001. Real estate broker Shamrock Realty, Elk Rapids, 1973—80; mgr. procurement svcs. strategic contract mgmt. U. Mich., 1983—. Owner Webber Realty, Milan, 1981—83. Contbr. articles to profl. jours. Achievements include development of JIT desktop delivery tax free alcohol. Office: Univ Mich 3003 S State St Ann Arbor MI 48109-1282 Business E-Mail: bwebber@umich.edu.

WEBBER, CHRIS (MAYCE EDWARD CHRISTOPHER WEBBER III), sportscaster, retired professional basketball player; b. Detroit, Mar. 1, 1973; s. Mayce and Doris Webber. Student, U. Mich., 1991—93. Drafted Orlando Magic, Fla., 1993; forward Golden State Warriors, San Francisco, 1993—94, Washington Bullets, 1994—98, Sacramento Kings, 1998—2005, Phila. 76ers, 2005—07, Detroit Pistons, 2007, Golden State Warriors, Calif., 2008; ret., 2008; studio analyst NBA TV, 2008—. Rap album, 2 Much Drama, 1999. Founder Timeout Found. Named Nat. H.S. Player of Yr., 1990—91, Mr. Basketball, State of Mich., 1991, Coca-Cola Classic NBA Player of Yr., 1994, Brut Bullets Player of Yr., 1994—95; named to NBA All-Rookie 1st team, 1994, NBA All-Interview Team, 1999—2003, All-NBA First Team, 2001, All-NBA Second Team, 1999, 2002—03, All-NBA Third Team, 2000. Achievements include being drafted 1st round Orlando Magic, 1993; five-time NBA All-Star, 1997, 2000-03. Avocations: collecting signed historical documents of prominent African-Americans, water sports. Office: NBA TV c/o NBA Media Ventures LLC 450 Harmon Meadow Blvd Secaucus NJ 07094

WEBBER, DEREK, aerospace executive, space tourism entrepreneur; arrived in U.S., 1993, naturalized, 2000; s. George and Joan Webber; m. Freda Joyce Phillips (dec.); m. Sarah L. Fisher; 1 child, Grace Phillippa. BS with honors in Physics and Math., U. Newcastle upon Tyne, Eng., 1966; diploma in Space Sci., U. Coll. London, 1969; diploma in Mgmt. Studies, U. Westminster, London, 1973; Cdip in Acctg. and Fin., Assn. Cert. Accts., London, 1980. Satellite and launch vehicle design engr. EADS/Astrium, Stevenage, England, 1966—69; dir. satellite and launch vehicle procurement Internat. Mobile Satellite Orgn., London, 1982—93; pres., CEO, Intonations Cons., Inc., San Diego, 1993—2000; mng. dir. Tachyon Europe, Inc., Amsterdam, 2000—01; dir. Spaceport Assocs., Bethesda, Md., 2001—. Adj. prof. U.S. Internat. U., San Diego, 1996—97; vis. lectr. summer sch. Internat. Space U., 1989, 90, 1992—93, 2008; keynote spkr. Washington Space Bus. Roundtable, 2003; presenter TV series on satellite comm., England, 1988; lectr. in field. Contbr. articles to profl. jours.; co-author: Kids to Space, 2006, Beyond Earth, 2006, Space Enterprise, 2008. Mem. internat. trade coalition Greater San Diego C. of C., 1995—99. Recipient Formation of Space Tourism recognition, Orbit Awards, 2006. Fellow: Brit. Interplanetary Soc.; mem.: AIAA (sr.), United Socs. in Space (chair coun. of regents 1996), Space Tourism Soc. (life). Office: Spaceport Associates 5909 Rolston Rd Bethesda MD 20817 Office Phone: 301-493-2550. Personal E-mail: dwspace@aol.com.

WEBBER, JOHN BENTLEY, orthopedic surgeon; b. Morristown, NJ, Jan. 27, 1941; s. George Bentley and Gladys (Moody) W.; m. Mary Christina Thometz, Feb. 25, 1978; children: John Bentley, Edward Alan BA, Lehigh U., 1962; MD, Temple U., 1966. Intern Rochester Gen. Hosp., NY, 1966-67; resident Temple U. Med. Ctr., Phila., 1967-70; Stelrling Bunnell fellow in hand surgery Pacific Med. Ctr., San Francisco, 1971; assoc. prof. orthopedic surgery and rehab. Hahnemann Med. Coll. and Hosp., Phila., 1973—2001, chief sect. on hand surgery, 1973—2005; attending surgeon St. Christopher's Hosp. for Children, Phila., 1996—. Cons. in hand surgery Mcpl. Med. Svcs., Phila., 1973-87, USPHS, Phila., 1973-76, burn ctr. St. Agnes Med. Ctr., Phila., 1973—, Phila. unit Shriners' Hosp. for Crippled Children, 1979-95. Served to maj. USAF, 1971-73. Fellow ACS (Pa. com. on trauma), Am. Acad. Orthopedic Surgeons; mem. AMA, Am. Soc. for Surgery of Hand, Bunnell Hand Club (pres. 1978-80), Assn. for Acad. Surgery, Eastern Orthopedic Soc., Pa. Med. Soc., Phila. Orthopedic Soc., Phila. Hand Soc. (pres. 1987-89), Phila. County Med. Soc., Phila. Coll. Physicians, Meigs Med. Assn., Rotary, Union Leauge, Riverside Yacht Club (fleet surgeon), Phila. Country Club, Delaware Valley Ducks Unltd. (chmn. 1983-88), U.S. Coast Guard (cert. master). Republican. Congregationalist. Home: 138 Montrose Ave Town House 51 Bryn Mawr PA 19010 Personal E-mail: handweb@aol.com.

WEBBER, RICHARD JOHN, lawyer; b. Mpls., July 27, 1948; s. Richard John and Mary Lee (Moore) W.; m. Susan Barbara Listerman, Jan. 8, 1972; children: Hillary, Joanna. BA, Princeton U., 1970; JD, U. Mich., 1973. Bar: D.C. Ct. Appeals 1974, U.S. Ct. Appeals (9th and D.C. cirs.) 1980, U.S. Dist. Ct. D.C. 1980, U.S. Claims Ct. 1974, U.S. Supreme Ct. 1980. Law clk. U.S. Ct. Claims, Washington, 1973-75; trial atty. U.S. Dept. Justice, Washington, 1975-80; assoc. Arent, Fox et al, Washington, 1980-85, ptnr., 1985—. Mem. ABA (chmn. fed. contract claims and remedies com. sect. pub. contract law 1986-91), Fed. Bar Assn. (chmn. govt. contracts sect. 1992-94, 1994-96, chmn. ADR sect. 2002-03). Office: Arent Fox Washington Sq 1050 Connecticut Ave NW Ste 500 Washington DC 20036-5303 Office Phone: 202-857-6254. E-mail: webberr@arentfox.com.

WEBBER, ROBERT, medical researcher; s. I.R. and Fern Webber; m. Diane Faber, Aug. 24, 1968; 1 child, Douglas. BS, U. Calif., Berkeley, 1972; PhD, UCLA Sch. Medicine, 1978. Pres., CEO Rsch. & Diagnostic Antibodies, North Las Vegas, Nev., 1984—, DSX Therapeutics, North Las Vegas, 2005—. Mem.: AAAS, Internat. Order Moose, Protein Soc., Nitric Oxide Soc., Am. Peptide Soc. Avocations: swimming, hiking, travel, cooking. Office: Research & Diagnostic Antibodies 2645 W Cheyenne Ave North Las Vegas NV 89032

WEBBER, ROSS ARKELL, management educator; b. New Rochelle, NY, July 18, 1934; s. Richard and Muriel (Arkels) W.; m. Mary Louise Foradora, Sept. 29, 1956; children: Sarah Ruth, Judith Mary, Gregory Ross, Jennifer Louise, Stephen Andrew. BSE, Princeton U., 1956; PhD, Columbia U., 1966; MS (hon.), U. Pa., 1972. Indsl. engr. Eastman Kodak Co., Rochester, NY, 1959-61; instr. Columbia U., NYC, 1961-64; lectr. Wharton Sch. U. Pa., Phila., 1964-65, asst. prof., 1965-70, assoc. prof., 1970-76, prof., 1976-2000, chmn. dept. mgmt., 1992-95, prof. emeritus, 2000—; v.p. U. Pa., Phila., 1981-86. Dir. Wharton-Industry Exec. Program, U. Pa., 1966-68, chmn. Wharton Internat. Bus. com., 1968-69, coord. Orgn. Behavior and Mgmt. Group, 1968-75, asst. dept. chmn., PhD com., 1972-75, coord. Orgnl. and Mgmt. Component, Advanced Mgmt. Program in Health Care Adminstrn., 1973-74, mem. Univ. Coun., 1975-77, adv. com. Pub. Mgmt. Unit, The Wharton Sch., 1977-81, chmn. Grad. Admissions com.; mem. editl. bd. The Wharton Mag. Author: Organizational Behavior and the Practice of Management, 1968, 5th rev. edit., 1987; Spanish lang. edit., 1982, Culture and Management: Text and Reading in Comparative Management, 1969, Management: Basic Elements of Managing Organizations, 1979, 3rd rev. edit., 1984, Polish lang. edit., 1984, Management Pragmatics: Readings and Cases on Managing Organizations, 1979, Time is Money!: The Key to Managerial Success, 1980, Japanese lang. edit. 1983, Swedish edit. 1983, Spanish lang. edit., 1985, Portugese lang. edit., 1989, To Be a Manager, 1981, A Guide to Getting Things Done, 1984, Becoming a Courageous Manager: Overcoming Career Problems of New Managers, 1991, Breaking Your Time Barriers: Becoming a More Effective Strategic Time Manager, 1992, The Dog Ate My Budget: Tales About Teaching and Managing in the Ivy Tower, 2008; contbr. over 55 articles to profl. jours. Past mem. bd. dirs. United Way Southeastern Pa., Am. Water Sys., Arcadis, Netherlands; coach youth athletics, fund raiser for ch., religious educator. Lt. (j.g.) USN, 1956-59. Avocations: painting, tennis, skiing. Office: U Pa Wharton Sch 2000 Steinberg Hall Philadelphia PA 19104 Office Phone: 215-898-9368. Business E-Mail: webber@wharton.upenn.edu.

WEBB GIRARD, AMY, research scientist; b. Tifton, Ga., Jan. 18, 1975; d. Don Lee and Connie Webb; m. Daniel Benjamin Girard, May 19, 2007. BS, Mercer U., Macon, Ga., 1997; PhD, Emory U., Atlanta, 2006. HS biology tchr. Gatewood Schs., Eatonton, Ga., 1993—99, Westside HS, Macon, 1999—2000; postdoc. rsch. fellow Harvard Sch. Pub. Health, Boston, 2006—07; initiatives, global health, rsch. fellow U. Toronto, Canada, 2007—. Contbr. scientific papers to profl. jours. Recipient Rsch. award, Thrasher Rsch. Fund; Ruth L. Kirschstein Nat. Rsch. Svc. award, NIH, Rsch. fellowship, NSF. Mem.: Soc. Applied Anthropology. Avocations: international travel, running, cooking, organic gardening. Business E-Mail: aimee.webb@utoronto.ca.

WEBB JR., JAMES HENRY See **WEBB, JIM**

WEBEL, CHARLES PETER, human science and psychology educator; b. LA, Dec. 23, 1948; s. James Webel and Jeanne (Herbert). BA, U. Calif., Berkeley, 1969, PhD, 1976; postgrad. in pub. health/social medicine, Harvard U., 1989-91. Chair Ctr. Ednl. Change, Berkeley, 1968-70; filmmaker Nat. Ednl. TV, NYC, 1969-70; lectr. social scis. U. Calif., Berkeley, 1976-78; dir. grad. programs Western Inst. Social Rsch., Berkeley, 1977-78; asst. prof. sociology New Coll., Sarasota, Fla., 1978-79; exec. editor social scis. Columbia U. Press, NYC, 1980-83; asst. prof. philosophy Calif. State U., Chico, 1984-89; teaching fellow gen. edn. Harvard U., Cambridge, Mass., 1990-91; gen. editor scholarly book series Peter Lang Pub., NYC, 1990—. Rsch. assoc. dept. anthropology U. Calif., Berkeley, 1990—94, lectr. Sch. Social Welfare, 2000-01; prof. human sci. and psychology Saybrook Inst., San Francisco, 1990—2001; Fulbright prof. U. Heidelberg, Germany, 2002-031 dir. Ctr. for Peace Studies, prof. social scis. U. Tromso, Norway, 2004-05; UNESCO chair for the philosophy of people U. Castellon, Spain, 2005-06; Fulbright sr. specialist and prof. U. Rome; prof., dir., peace & conflict studies U. NY, Prague, Czech Republic. Author: Terror, Terrorism and the Human Condition, 2006-07; author, editor: Marcuse Critical Theory and The Promise of Utopia, 1988; co-author: Peace and Conflict Studies, 2008; co-editor: Handbook of Peace and Conflict Studies, 2007; filmmaker: Lifestyle, 1969. Organizer Congress Racial Equality, N.Y.C., 1965-66; West Coast sec. Internat. Philosophers for Prevention Nuclear Omnicide, 1985-89. Fulbright scholar Fulbright Commn., Germany, 1971-72; regents fellow U. Calif., Berkeley, 1972-73, dissertation fellow Social Sci. Rsch. Coun., N.Y.C., 1974-76, grad. fellow Harvard U., 1989-91, NEH summer fellow Harvard U., 1986, NEH fellow Cornell U., 1998. Mem. Am. Philos. Assn., Am. Sociol. Assn., Internat. Soc. Polit. Psychology, World Affairs Coun. Avocations: classical music, film, global travel, sports, humor. Personal E-mail: cwebel@aol.com.

WEBER, ALFONS, physicist; b. Dortmund, Germany, Oct. 8, 1927; PhD, Ill. Inst. Tech., 1956. Instr. physics Ill. Inst. Tech., Chgo., 1953-56; from asst. prof. physics to prof. Fordham U., Bronx, NY, 1957-81, prof. physics and chemistry, 1976-81, chmn. dept. physics, 1964-70; rsch. physicist Nat. Inst. Stds. and Tech., Gaithersburg, Md., 1977-98, acting chief molecular spectroscopy divsn., 1980-81, chief molecular physics divsn., 1982-95, sr. scientist physics lab., 1995-98, scientist emeritus, 1999—; program mgr. condensed matter physics divsn., materials rsch NSF, 1998—2001, program dir. exptl. phys. chemistry, chemistry divsn., 2001—04. With chem scis. divsn. U.S. Dept. Energy, 1991-92, chem. divsn. NSF, 1992-95. Editor: Raman Spectroscopy of Gases and Liquids, 1979; Structure and Dynamics of Weakly Bound Molecular Complexes, 1987, Spectroscopy of the Earth's Atmosphere and Interstellar Medium, 1992; former mem. editl. bd. Jour. of Raman Spectroscopy, Jour. Chem. and Phys. Reference Data. V.p. Union Free Dist. # 1 Sch. Bd., Eastchester, N.Y., 1970-73. Postdoctoral fellow NRC Can., U. Toronto, 1956-57. Fellow AAAS, Am. Phys. Soc. (councillor 1987-91); mem. Coblentz Soc., Soc. Applied Spectroscopy, Am. Chem. Soc. Office: Nat Inst Stds & Tech Gaithersburg MD 20899 Business E-Mail: aweber@nist.gov.

WEBER, ARNOLD I., lawyer; b. Little Cedar, Iowa, Oct. 4, 1926; divorced; children: Katherine Weber Hickle, Thomas, Margaret Weber Robertson. PhB magna cum laude, Marquette U., 1949; MA, Harvard U., 1950; JD, George Washington U., 1954, LLM, 1956. Bar: D.C. 1954, Md. 1961, Calif. 1962, U.S. Dist Ct. D.C. 1954, (no. dist.) Calif. 1962, (cen. dist.) Calif. 1992, U.S. Ct. Claims 1960, U.S. Tax Ct. 1965, U.S. Ct. Appeals (D.C. cir.) 1954, (9th cir.) 1962, (fed. cir.) 1991, U.S. Supreme Ct. 1959. Lawyer Housing and Home Fin., Washington, 1954; pvt. practice Washington, 1954-55; lawyer Tariff Commn., Washington, 1954-55, FCC, Washington, 1955-56, IRS, Washington, 1956-61; assoc. Brobeck, Phleger & Harrison, San Francisco, 1961-64; sr. gen. atty. So. Pacific Transp., San Francisco, 1964-84; western tax counsel Santa Fe Pacific Corp., San Francisco, 1985-88; pvt. practice San Francisco, 1988—. With USNR, 1944-54, PTO. Mem. ABA, Olympic Club, Bar Assn. San Francisco, State Bar of Calif. Office: 100 27th Ave San Francisco CA 94121-1034 Office Phone: 415-752-7465. Personal E-mail: aiweber@sbcglobal.net.

WEBER, ARNOLD ROBERT, academic administrator; b. NYC, Sept. 20, 1929; s. Jack and Lena (Smith) W.; m. Edna M. Files, Feb. 7, 1954; children: David, Paul, Robert. BA, U. Ill., 1951; MA, MIT, 1958, PhD in Econs., 1958; DHL (hon.), U. Notre Dame, 2005, U. Ill., 2005, Northwestern U., 2005, Loyola U., 2005, Ripon Coll., 2005, U. Colo., 2005. Instr., then asst. prof. econs. MIT, 1955-58; faculty U. Chgo. Grad. Sch. Bus., 1958-69, prof. indsl. relations, 1963-69; asst. sec. for manpower Dept. Labor, 1969-70; exec. dir. Cost of Living Council; also spl. asst. to Pres. Nixon, 1971; Gladys C. and Isidore Brown prof. urban and labor econs. U. Chgo., 1971-73; former provost Carnegie-Mellon U.; dean Carnegie-Mellon U. (Grad. Sch. Indsl. Adminstrn.), prof. labor econs. and pub. policy, 1973-80; pres. U. Colo., Boulder, 1980-85, Northwestern U., Evanston, Ill., 1985-95, chancellor, 1995-98, pres. emeritus, 1998—. Cons. union, mgmt. and govt. agys., 1960—; cons. Dept. Labor, 1965; mem. Pres.'s Adv. Com. Labor Mgmt. Policy, 1964, Orgn. Econ. Coop. and Devel., 1987; vice chmn. Sec. Labor Task Force Improving Employment Svcs., 1965; chmn. rsch. adv. com. US Employment Svc., 1966; assoc. dir. OMB Exec. Office of Pres., 1970—71, spl. asst. to pres., 1971; chmn. Presdl. R.R. Emergency Bd., 1982; trustee Com. for Econ. Devel., Nat. Multiple Sclerosis Soc.; bd. dirs. Diamond Cluster Inc.; asst. sec. manpower US Dept. Labor, 1969—70; bd. dirs. Burlington Northern Santa Fe, AON Corp. Contbr. articles to profl. jours. Lt. (j.g.) USCG, 1952—54. Laureate, Lincoln Acad. Ill.; Ford Found. Faculty Rsch. fellow, 1964-65. Mem. Am. Acad. Arts and Scis., Indsl. Rels. Rsch. Assn., Nat. Acad. Pub. Adminstrn., Comml. Club Chgo. (pres., civic com. 1995-2000), Econ. Club Chgo. (pres. 1995-97), Phi Beta Kappa. Jewish. Office: Northwestern U Office of Pres Emeritus 555 Clark St 209 Evanston IL 60208-0805 Business E-Mail: arnold-weber@northwestern.edu.

WEBER, BRUCE, photographer, filmmaker; b. Greensburg, Pa., Mar. 29, 1946; Studied, NYU, New School for Soc. Rsch., NYC, Princeton. Photographer Calvin Klein underware campaign, Ralph Lauren, Abercrombie & Fitch; owner Weberbilt clothing line. Prodr.: (films) Broken Noses, 1987 (recipient: Internat. Documentary Assn. award, 1988; nominee: Grand Jury prize, Sundance Film Festival, 1988), The Beauty Brothers, Parts I-IV, 1987, Beauty Brothers, 1987, Let's Get Lost, 1989 (recipient: Internat. Documentary Assn. award, 1989; nominee: Grand Jury prize, Sundance Film Festival, 1999, nominee: Acad. Award for Best Documentary, features, 1989), Backyard Movie, 1991, Gentle Giants, 1994, The Teddy Boys Of The Edwardian Draper Society, 1995, Chop Suey, 2001 (recipient: Teddy-Spl. Mention, Berlin Film Festival, 2001), A Letter to True, 2004; author: Bruce Weber, 1983, O Rio De Janeiro, 1986, The Andy Book, 1987, Let's Get Lost: A Film Journal, 1988, Bruce Weber, 1988, Sam, 1990, Bear Pond, 1991, Bruce Weber, 1991, Hotel Room with a View, 1992, No Valet Parking, 1994, Gentle Giants, 1994, A House is Not a Home, 1994, Branded Youth, 1997, The Chop Suey Club, 1999, Shufly, 2000, Mother's Days, 2002, Like a Moth to a Flame, 2003, Thank Your Lucky Stars, 2003, Heel to Heal, 2004, All American: Otherworldly, 2004, All American V: Is Love Enough, 2005, All American VI: Larger Than Life, 2006; dir.: (music videos) Chris Isaak, Pet Shop Boys; exhibitions include O Rio De Janeiro, Central Cultural Banco de Brasil, 2007. Recipient Eugenia Sheppard award for Excellence in Fashion Journalism, Coun. of Fashion Designers of Am., 2006. Achievements include being widely known for ad campaigns for Calvin Klein, Abercrombie & Fitch and Ralph Lauren. Mailing: c/o Arcana Books on the Arts 1229 Third St Promenade Santa Monica CA 90401 Business E-Mail: bwinfo@bruceweber.com.

WEBER, BRUCE, men's college basketball coach; b. Milw., Oct. 19, 1956; m. Megan Weber; children: Hannah, Christy, Emily. BS in Edn., U. Wis., Milw., 1978; MS in Edn. Adminstrn., Phys. Edn., Western Ky. U., Bowling Green, 1981. Vol. asst. coach Madison HS, Milw.; varsity asst. Marquette U. HS, Milw.; asst. coach Western Ky. U. Hilltoppers, 1979—80, Purdue U. Boilermakers, 1980—98; head coach Southern Ill. U. Salukis, 1998—2003, U. Ill. Fighting Illini, 2003—. Asst. coach, Team USA World Univ. Games, 1989; head ct. coach Pan Am. Team Trials, 1991. Active Coaches vs. Cancer. Recipient Naismith award, 2005, Henry Iba award, US Basketball Writers Assn., 2005, Adolph F. Rupp Cup, 2005, Coaches vs. Cancer Champion award, Coaches vs. Cancer Coun., 2007; named Coach of Yr., Mo. Valley Conf., 2003, Nat. Coach of Yr., NABC, AP, The Sporting News, Basketball Times, CBS/Chevrolet, Victor Awards, Nike Championship Basketball Clinic, 2005. Office: Univ Ill Divsn Intercollegiate Athletics Bielfeldt Athletic Adminstrn Bldg 1700 S Fourth St Champaign IL 61820*

WEBER, CRAIG P., meteorologist, newscaster; b. Buffalo, Oct. 3, 1948; m. Amanda Jane Weber; children: Pete, Michael, Jeremy, Samantha, Sophie. Attended, East Carolina U., Greenville, NC, 1972, Carteret CC, 1972—73; attended hurricanes and severe weather tng. program, USMC, 1978—82. Broadcaster Sta. WMBL Radio, Morehead City, NC, 1972—76; chief meteorologist Sta. WCTI TV 12, New Bern, NC, 1978—82; meteorologist The Weather Channel, 1982—83; chief meteorologist Sta. KHOU TV, Houston, 1983—87; news anchor Sta. KYW, CBS, Phila., 1992—96, 2000—02; chief meteorologist Sta. WOR Channel 9, NYC, 1996—97, Sta. WB 17, Phila., 1996—2000; news anchor Sta. CN-8, 2002—03. Active Heart Fund, March of Dimes; annual master of ceremonies Spl. Olympics. Served with USMC, 1967—71. Named Most Accurate Weatherman, Phila. Press Club. Mem.: NAACP, Nat. Weather Assn., Am. Fedn. TV and Radio Arts, Am. Meteorol. soc. Democrat. Mailing: 1413 Arendell St Morehead City NC 28557

WEBER, CURT MICHAEL, law educator; s. Curt Herbert and Lois Alice Weber. BA, Marquette U., Milw., 1978; JD, Duquesne U., Pitts., 1982. Instr. Milw. Area Tech. Coll., 1982—2002; adj. instr. Upper Iowa U., Fayette, 1994—, Concordia U. Wis., Mequon, 1996—; lectr. U. Wis., Whitewater, 2002—. Contbr. articles to profl. jour. Dir. Edn. Found. Wauwatosa, Wis., 2002—08; pres. Luth. A. Cappella Choir, Milw., 2003—. Recipient Hermsen Tchg. award, U. Wis.-Whitewater Coll. Bus. and Economics, 2004. Office: Univ Wis-Whitewater 800 W Main St Whitewater WI 53190-1790 Business E-Mail: weberc@uww.edu.

WEBER, DARRELL JACK, plant biochemistry educator; b. Thornton, Idaho, Nov. 16, 1933; s. John and Norma (Severson) W.; m. Carolyn Foremaster, Aug. 24, 1962; children:Becky, Brian, Todd, Kelly, Jason, Trent. BS, U. Idaho, 1958, MS, 1959; PhD, U. Calif., Davis, 1963. Postdoctoral fellow U. Wis., Madison, 1963-65; from assist. to assoc. prof. biology U. Houston, 1965-69; assoc. prof. botany Brigham Young U., Provo, Utah, 1969-74, prof. botany, 1976—; postdoctoral fellow Mich. State U., East Lansing, 1975-76. Author: (with others) Introductory Plant Biology Manual, 1973, Mechanisms of Pesticide Resistance in Non-Target Organisms, 1981; Principals and Application of Instrumentation in the Biological Sciences, 1976, Trees of Utah, 1993; contbr. numerous articles to profl. jours. Recipient Rsch. award Karl G. Maeser, 1974; Utah Acad. Sci. fellow, 1972; Fulbright grantee to U. Natal, South Africa, 1995. Mem. Am. Mycol. Soc. (editor), Sigma Xi (sec. Brigham Young U. chpt. 1982-85). Republican. Mem. Lds Ch. Avocations: skiing, growing fruit. Office: Brigham Young U 285 Widtsoe Provo UT 84602

WEBER, DARREN LEE, neuroscientist, researcher; arrived in US, 2003, permanent resident, 2005; s. Barry and Mary Weber; m. Elizabeth Bonner, Feb. 14, 2005; 1 child, Sophia. BS with honors in Psychology, Flinders U. South Australia, Adelaide, 1991, BA in Philosophy and English, 1998, PhD in Psychology, 2005. Assoc. mgr. cognitive neuroscience lab. Flinders U. South Australia, 1992—2003; postdoctoral scholar dept. radiology U. Calif., San Francisco, 2003—07. Mem.: Australasian Soc. Psychophysiology (student rep. 1996—2000, treas. 1996—2000), Soc. Neuroscience, Human Brain Mapping. Buddhist. Business E-Mail: darren.weber@radiology.ucsf.edu.

WEBER, DAVID J., history educator; b. Buffalo, Dec. 20, 1940; s. Theodore Carl and Frances (Maronska) W.; m. Carol Sue Bryant, June 16, 1962; children: Scott David, Amy Carol. BS in Social Sci., SUNY, Fredonia, 1962; MA in History, U. N.Mex., 1964, PhD in History, 1967. Asst. to full prof. history San Diego State U., 1967-76; prof. history So. Meth. U., Dallas, 1976-79, prof. history and dept. chmn., 1979-86, Robert and Nancy Dedman prof. history, 1986—; dir. Clements Ctr. SW Studies, 1995—. Fulbright-Hays lectr. Universidad de Costa Rica, 1970. Author: The Taos Trappers: The Fur Trade in the Far Southwest, 1540-1846, 1971, The Mexican Frontier, 1821-1846: The American Southwest Under Mexico, 1982 (Ray Billington award 1983), Richard H. Kern: Expeditionary Artist in the Far Southwest, 1848-1853, 1985 (Nat. Cowboy Hall of Fame 1985), The Spanish Frontier in North America, 1992, Barbaros: Spaniards and Their Savages in the Age of Enlightenment, 2005; contbr. articles to profl. jours. Recipient United Meth. U. Scholar/Tchr. of Yr. award, 1986, Spain and America prize Spanish Ministry of Culture, 1993, Real Orden de Isabel la Católica, King of Spain, Juan Carlos. 2003, Orden Mexicana del Aguila Azteca (the Order of the Aztec Eagle), Govt. Mexico, 2005; postdoctoral fellow Am. Philos. Soc., 1975, Huntington Libr., 1975, 2000-01, Am. Coun. Learned Socs., 1980, Ctr. for Adv. Study in Behavioral Scis., Stanford U., 1986-87, NEH, 1974-75, 90-91; Benicke sr. fellow, Yale, 2007-08. Fellow Soc. Am. Historians, Am. Acad. Arts & Scis.; mem. Academia Mexicana de la Historia, Tex. Inst. Letters, Tex. Hist. Assn. (lifetime fellow), Western History Assn. (pres. 1990-91), Mexico-U.S. Historians (pres. 1990), Am. Hist. Assn. (v.p. profl. divsn. 2008-), Orgn. Am. Historians (mem. exec. bd. 2006-09). Democrat. Avocations: running, bicycling, gardening, reading. Office: Dept History So Meth U Dallas TX 75275 Business E-Mail: dweber@mail.smu.edu.

WEBER, DEANNE, health science association administrator; b. NY; d. Donald and Donna Weber; married. BA, Bucknell U., Lewisburg, Pa., 1992; PhD, George Wash. U., 1999. Asst. dir., academic planning and assessment George Wash. U., 1997—2000; sr. v.p. Porter Novelli, Washington, 2000—. Contbr. numerous articles to profl. jours. Office: Porter Novelli 1900 K St NW Washington DC 20006 Business E-Mail: deanne.weber@porternovelli.com.

WEBER, DONALD B., advertising executive, marketing professional; s. John William and Rose Ann (Saroshi) Weber; m. Ann McDermaid, 1955 (div. 1975); children: Martha Elizabeth, Margaret Ann; m. Jean Host, 1980; children: Kimberly Elizabeth, Kristen Ann. BA, Rollins Coll., Winter Park, Fla.; MBA, Kellog/Northwestern U., Evanston, Ill. Account exec. Leo Burnett Co., Inc., Chgo., 1958-63; sr. v.p., mgmt. supr. Foote, Cone & Belding, Chgo., 1963-76; pres. Blau Bishop Assocs., 1976-79; v.p. Russell Reynolds Assocs., Chgo., 1979-82; sr. v.p., regional mgr. MSL Internat., Chgo., 1982-85; exec. v.p. Rumrill-Hoyt, Inc., Rochester, N.Y., 1985-88; sr. v.p. D'Arcy Masius Benton & Bowles, Chgo., 1988-95; sr. v.p., group mgmt. dir. Cramer-Krasselt, Chgo., 1996-99; pres. Intact, Inc., 1999—. Lectr. Northwestern U. Chmn. bd. Am. Cancer Soc., Chgo., 1996—99, pres., cons.; bd. dirs., chmn. comm. exec. com. Ill. divsn. Am. Cancer Soc., 1999—2001; bd. dirs. Am. Inst. Wine and Food, 1995—97; chmn. Chgo. coun. Boy Scouts Am., 1991—95. Lt. comdr. USNR, 1955—58. Mem.: Chgo. Advt. Fedn. (bd. dirs. 1988—93), Meadows Country Club. Republican. Episcopalian. Office Phone: 312-320-7400. Personal E-mail: intactdbw@aol.com.

WEBER, FREDRIC ALAN, lawyer; b. Paterson, NJ, July 31, 1948; s. Frederick Edward and Alida (Hessels) W.; m. Mary Elizabeth Cook, June 18, 1983. BA in History, Rice U., 1970; JD, Yale U., 1976. Bar: Tex. 1976, U.S. Dist. Ct. (so. dist.) Tex. Assoc. Fulbright & Jaworski LLP, Houston, 1976-80, participating assoc., 1980-83, ptnr., 1983—. Dir. Houston Symphony Soc., 1993—, v.p. devel., 2001-03, 2005-07. Mem. ABA, Am. Coll. Bond Counsel (treas. 2003-04, v.p. 2004-06, pres. 2006-08), Nat. Assn. Bond Lawyers (bd. dirs. 1988-89, treas. 1989-90, pres.-elect 1991, pres. 1991-92), Houston Bar Assn. Office: Fulbright & Jaworski LLP 1301 McKinney St Ste 5100 Houston TX 77010-3095 Office Phone: 713-651-5151. Office Fax: 713-651-5246. Business E-Mail: fweber@fulbright.com.

WEBER, GEORGE, oncology and pharmacology educator, researcher; b. Budapest, Hungary, Mar. 29; came to U.S., 1959; s. Salamon and Hajnalka (Arvai) W.; m. Catherine Elizabeth Forrest, June 30, 1958; children: Elizabeth Dolly Arvai, Julie Vibert Wallace, Jefferson James. BA, Queen's U., 1950, MD, 1952; MD (hon.), U. Chieti, Italy, 1979, Med. Faculty, Budapest, 1982, U. Leipzig, Fed. Republic of Germany, 1987, Tokushima U., Japan, 1988; degree, Kagawa U., Japan, 1992. Rsch. assoc. Montreal Cancer Inst., 1953-59; prof. pharmacology Ind. U. Sch. Medicine, Indpls., 1959—; dir. Lab for Exptl. Oncology Sch. Medicine, Ind. U., Indpls., 1974—; Milan Panič prof. oncology Ind. U., Indpls., 1994—, Wellcome prof., 1995—; prof. Lab. for Exptl. Oncology Sch. Medicine, Ind. U., Indpls., 1974-90, disting. prof. Lab. for Exptl. Oncology, 1990—. Chmn. study sect. USPHS, Washington, 1976-78; sci. adv. com. Am. Cancer Soc., N.Y.C., 1972-76, 94-98, Damon Runyon Fund, N.Y.C., 1971-76; mem. U.S. Nat. Com., Internat. Union Against Cancer, Washington, 1974-80, 90-94, NAS, Washington, 1974-80, 90-94, U.S. Army Med. Rsch. and Breast Cancer Rsch. Program, 1996-97; prof. Brit. cancer campaign U. Oxford, Oxford, Eng., 2001; vis. prof. U. Bologna, Italy, 2001—. Editor: Advances in Enzyme Regulation, Vols. 1-49, 1962—; assoc. editor Jour. Cancer Rsch., 1969—80, 1982—89. Recipient Alecce Prize for cancer rsch. Tiberine Acad., Rome, 1971, Best Prof. award Student AMA, Indpls., 1966, 68, G.F. Gallanti prize for enzymology Internat. Soc. Clin. Chemists, 1984, Outstanding Investigator award Nat. Cancer Inst., NIH, 1986-94, Semmelweis medal & diploma Budapest, Hungary, 2001, medal Gastroenterological Soc., Aliga, Hungary, 2001, Prestigious External Award Recognition Ind. U., Indpls., Ind., 2002. Mem. Am. Soc. for Pharmacology and Exptl. Therapeutics, Am. Assn. Cancer Rsch. (G.H.A. Clowes award 1982), Russian Acad. Sci. (hon.), Hungarian Cancer Soc. (hon.), Hungarian Acad. Scis. (hon.), Acad. Scis. Bologna (Italy) (hon.). Home: 7307 Lakeside Dr Indianapolis IN 46278-1618 Office: Ind U Sch Medicine Lab Exptl Oncology 699 West Dr Indianapolis IN 46202-5119 Office Phone: 317-274-7921.

WEBER, GEORGE RICHARD, financial and internet marketing executive, writer; b. The Dalles, Oreg., Feb. 7, 1929; s. Richard Merle and Maud (Winchell) W.; m. Nadine Hanson, Oct. 12, 1957; children: Elizabeth Ann Weber Katooli, Karen Louise Weber Zaro, Linda Marie. BS, Oreg. State U., 1950; MBA, U. Oreg., 1962. CPA, Oreg. Sr. trainee U.S. Nat. Bank of Portland (Oreg.), 1950-51; jr. acct. Ben Musa, CPA, The Dalles, Oreg., 1954; tax and audit asst. Price Waterhouse, Portland, 1955-59; sr. acct. Burton M. Smith, CPA, Portland, 1959-62; pvt. practice Portland, 1962-99; assoc. World Mktg. Alliance, 1996-99, Waterman and Assocs., 2000—01, Allstate Fin. Svcs., 2001—03, Legacy for Life, 2004—, Extras Casting, 2005—. Lectr. acctg. Portland State Coll.; expert witness fin. and tax matters. Author: Small Business Long-term Finance, 1962, A History of the Coroner and Medical Examiner Offices, 1963, CPA Litigation Service References, 1991, Letters to a Friend, 1995; contbr. to profl. publs. and poetry jours. Sec.-treas. Mt. Hood Kiwanis Camp, Inc., 1965; exec. counselor SBA; mem. fin. com., powerlifting team U.S. Powerlifting Fedn., 1984, amb. People to People, China, 1987. Arty. officer AUS, 1951-53. Decorated Bronze Star. Mem. AICPA, Internat. Platform Assn., Oreg. Hist. Soc., Oreg. City Traditional Jazz Soc., Order of the Holy Cross Jerusalem, Order St. Stephen the Martyr, Order St. Gregory the Illuminator, Knightly Assn. St. George the Martyr, World Literary Acad., Portland C.S. Lewis Soc., Beta Alpha Psi, Pi Kappa Alpha. Clubs: Kiwanis, Portland Track, City (Portland); Multnomah Athletic; Sunrise Toastmasters. Republican. Lutheran. Home and Office: 3715 NE Alberta Ct Portland OR 97211-8144 Home Phone: 503-288-3328; Office Phone: 503-288-3328. E-mail: grweber@earthlink.net. *My basic beliefs are in faith, family and freedom through limited government and personal responsibility, with personal responsibility including development and use of capabilities.*

WEBER, GLORIA RICHIE, retired minister, state legislator; married; 4 children. BA, Washington U., St. Louis; MA, MDiv, Eden Theol. Sem., Webster Groves, Mo. Ordained to ministry Evang. Luth. Ch. Am., 1974. Family life educator Luth. Family and Children's Svcs. Mo.; mem. Mo. Ho. of Reps., 1993-94. Mo. state organizer, dir. comm. Mainstream Voters C.A.R.E., 1995. Editor: Interfaith Voices for Peace and Justice, 1996—2000. Exec. dir. Older Women's League, 1990—95. Recipient Woman of Achievement award, St. Louis Globe-Dem., 1977, Unselfish Cmty. Svc. award, St. Louis Sentinel Newspaper, 1985, Faith in Action award, Luth. Svcs. St. Louis, 1994; named Woman of the Yr., Variety Club, 1978, Woman of Worth, Older Women's League, 1993. Mem.: Older Wiser Luths. in Svc. (devotion leader), Assn. Lutheran Older Adults (mem. nat. bd. 2004—09), N.Am. Interfaith Network (bd. dirs. 1993—2003), Phi Beta Kappa. Democrat. Personal E-mail: gloriaweber9@aol.com.

WEBER, HANNO, architect; b. Barranquilla, Colombia, Sept. 24, 1937; arrived in US, 1952; s. Hans and Ester (Oks) Weber. BA magna cum laude, Princeton U., 1959, MArch, 1961. Registered arch., Wis.; Ill., Fla., Mo., Pa., NJ, Va. Urban designer, rsch. assoc. Guayana project MIT and Harvard U., Caracas, Venezuela, 1961-63; project arch. Paul Schweikher Assocs., Pitts., 1963-67; asst. prof. architecture Princeton U., NJ, 1967-73; assoc. prof. Washington U., St. Louis, 1973-80; sr. design arch., studio head, assoc. Skidmore, Owings & Merrill, Chgo., 1980-83; prin. Hanno Weber & Assocs., Chgo., 1984—. Vis. lectr. Escuela Nacional de Arquitectura Universidad Nacional de Mex., 1975; rsch. assoc. Rsch. Ctr. Urban and Environ. Planning, Princeton; project dir. Cmty. Design Workshop Washington U. Sch. Architecture, St. Louis, 1973—78; prof. architecture U. Wis., Milw., 1983—. Contbr. articles to profl. jours. Mem. Pres.'s Commn. Edn. Women Princeton U., 1968—69. Recipient 1st prize winner, Flagler Dr. Waterfront Master Plan Design Competition, West Palm Beach, Fla., 1984, Mcpl. Ctr. Design Competition, Leesburg, Va., 1987, Chgo. AIA Disting. Bldg. award Citation of Merit, 1987, Urban Design award Mcpl. Govt. Ctr., Leesburg, AIA, 1992; finalist, Okla. City Meml. Internat. Design Competition, 1997, Green Homes for Chgo. Design Competition, 2000; fellow, NEH, 1970, Graham Found., 1973. Mem.: Nat. Coun. Arch. Registration Bds., Phi Beta Kappa. Office: Hanno Weber & Assocs 11 E Adams St # 702 Chicago IL 60603-6301 Home Phone: 312-664-7556; Office Phone: 312-922-5589. Business E-Mail: weber@hannoweber.com.

WEBER, HANS JÜRGEN, physics professor; b. Berlin, May 3, 1939; came to U.S., 1966; naturalized, 1993; s. Hans Gustav Wilhelm and Hedwig Bertha Elisabeth (Angermann) W.; m. Edith E. Enzian, Aug. 19, 1966; 1 child, Chris H. MS in Math., U. Frankfurt, Fed. Republic Germany, 1961, PhD in Physics, 1965. Postdoctoral rsch. assoc. U. Frankfurt, 1965-66, Duke U., Durham, NC, 1966-67, U. Va., Charlottesville, 1967, asst. prof. physics, 1968-71, assoc. prof., 1971-77, prof., 1977—2003. Vis. scientist U. Mainz, Fed. Republic Germany, 1972, 77, 91, U. Paris-Sud, Orsay, France, 1979; vis. prof. U. Lyon, France, 1978. Co-author: Mathematical Methods for Physicists, 1995, 2001, 2005, Essentials of Math Methods for Physicists, 2003; contbr. to Physics Reports, Springer Tracts, Phys. Letters, Phys. Rev. Rsch. grantee NSF, 1971-95. Mem. Am. Phys. Soc., Am. Assn. Physics Tchrs., Sigma Xi. Lutheran. Achievements include development of a nuclear force (NN interaction) from quark models and a possible connection between quantum chromodynamics and meson dynamics; rsch. on isobars in nuclei. Office: U Va Inst Nuclear and Particle Physics McCormick Rd Charlottesville VA 22904-0001 Business E-Mail: hw@virginia.edu.

WEBER, HERMAN JACOB, federal judge; b. Lima, Ohio, 1927; s. Herman Jacob and Ada Minola W.; m. Barbara L. Rice, 1948; children: Clayton, Deborah. BA, Otterbein Coll., 1949; JD summa cum laude, Ohio State U., 1951. Bar: Ohio 1952, U.S. Dist. Ct. (so. dist.) Ohio 1954. Ptnr. Weber & Hogue, Fairborn, Ohio, 1952-61; judge Fairborn Mayor's Ct., 1956-58; acting judge Fairborn Mcpl. Ct., 1958-60; judge Greene County Common Pleas Ct., Xenia, Ohio, 1961-82, Ohio Ct. Appeals (2d dist.), Dayton, 1982-85, U.S. Dist. Ct. (so. dist.) Ohio, Cin., 1985—2002, sr. judge, 2002—. Chmn. Sixth Cir. Dist. Judges Conf., 1988, Ohio Jud. Conf., Columbus, 1980-82; pres. Ohio Common Pleas Judges Assn., Columbus, 1975. Vice-mayor City of Fairborn, 1955-57, council mem., 1955-59. Served with USNR, 1945-46. Office: US Dist Ct 801 100 E 5th St Cincinnati OH 45202-3905

WEBER, HUGH, professional sports team executive; m. Julie Weber; children: Brenna, Zoë, Hugh III, Jackson. Grad., U. Puget Sound, Wash. Various positions in comml. products divsn. Proctor & Gamble; v.p. Ventura Foods; v.p. bus. ops. New Orleans Hornets (formerly Charlotte Hornets), COO, 2006—. Avocations: running, golf, reading. Office: New Orleans Hornets 1250 Poydras St # 19 New Orleans LA 70113-1804 Office Fax: 504-301-4000.*

WEBER, IDELLE, artist, educator; b. Chgo., Mar. 12, 1932; d. J. Earl and Min (Wallach) Feinberg; m. Julian L. Weber, Apr. 17, 1957; children: Jonathan Todd, Suzanne. BA, UCLA, 1954, MA, 1955. Adj. assoc. prof. art, grad. div. NYU, 1974-88; assoc. prof. Carpenter Ctr. Harvard U., 1988-91; prof. Nat. Acad., 2004-2006. Exhibited one-person shows: Bertha Schaefer Gallery, N.Y.C., 1963, 64, Hundred Acres Gallery, N.Y.C., 1973, 75, 77, Chatham Coll., Pitts., 1979, O.K. Harris Gallery, N.Y.C., 1979, 82, Ruth Siegel Gallery, N.Y.C., 1984, 85, 87, Anthony Ralph Gallery, NYC, 1989, Arts Club of Chgo., 1986, Homart, Houston, 1987, Barbara Fendrick Gallery, Washington, 1987, Jean Albano Gallery, Chgo., 1994, Victorian Coll. of Arts, Melbourne, U., Australia, 1995, Contemporary Arts Forum, Santa Barbara, 1995,

Nassau Mus. Art, 2004, Nevberger Mus. Art, 2004; group shows: Pa. Acad. Fine Arts, San Antonio Mus., Fort Collins U., Colo., Larry Aldrich Ctr. for Contemporary Arts, Ridgefield, Conn., 1981, Mus. Modern Art, N.Y.C., 1956, Guggeheim Mus., N.Y.C., 1964, Wadsworth Atheneum, Hartford, Conn., 1964, 66, Darnstadt (W.Ger.) Mus., Yale U. Mus., New Haven, 1975, Va. Mus., Richmond, Nat. Collection Fine Art, Washington, Butler Inst., Youngstown, Ohio, Fendrick Gallery, Washington, 1978, 85, Nat. Acad. 2002, 04, 05, 06, 07, 08, Danforth Mus., Framington, Mass, 1980, San Francisco Mus. Art, 1985-86, Contemporary Art Ctr., New Orleans, 1986, Indpls. Mus. Art, 1986, Graham Modern Mus., N.Y.C., 1986, Ft. Wayne Mus. Art, 1988, Carpenter Ctr. Harvard U., 1988, Met. Mus. Art, N.Y.C., 2001, U. Va. Art Mus., 2002, Gracie Mansion, Chelsea, N.Y.C., 2002, Nat. Acad. Design Mus., 2003, Neuberger Mus. Art, 2004, U. LA, Lafayette, 2005, Nelson-Atkins Mus. Art, 2006, Philoctetes Ctr., NYC, 2006, Gerald Peters Gallery, 2007, OK Harris, 2008, Katonah Mus. Art, 2008, Zipper, Sonoma, Calif., 2008, Scripps Coll., 2008, Boca Raton Mus. Art, 2008-09, Zimmerli Art Mus., Rutgers U., 2009; represented permanent collections: Nat. Collection Fine Art, Va. Mus., Sydney and Francis Lewis Found., Richmond, Yale U. Art Gallery, Albright Knox Gallery, Buffalo, Worcester (Mass.) Art Mus., Rochester (N.Y.) U. Mus., McNay Art Inst., N.Y. Pub. Library, Met. Mus. Art, N.Y.C., Pacific Bell, Calif., Bklyn Mus., Albright-Knox Gallery, Buffalo, Nelson -Atkins Mus. Art, Kansas City, Mo., Met. Mus. Art, Art Inst. Chgo., Krannert Art Mus., U. Ill., Urbana, Whitney Mus. Art, Nat. Acad. and Sch. Fine Arts, Archives Am. Art, Smithsoian Instn., Washington, Ark. Art Ctr., Little Rock, Boise Art Mus., Idaho, Del. Art Mus., Wilmington, Fogg Mus. Art, Harvard U., Melbourne U., Australia, Mus. Am. Fin. History, NYC, Nat Mus. Am. Art, NYC, Portland Art Mus., Oreg., San Francisco Mus. Art, Santa Barbara Mus. Art, Santa Fe Art Found., N.Mex. Tacoma Art Mus. UCLA Galleries. Recognized in various publs. including: Arts Mag., 1979, 82, 84, 86, Photo Realism (L. Meisel), 1980, San Antonio Mus. Catalogue (L. Nochlin), 1981, Art in Am. (E. Lubell), Am. Women Artists (C.S. Rubenstein), 1982, Wall St. Jour., 1985, Christian Sci. Monitor, 1985, 86, Art in America, 1986, Washington Post, 1986, Chgo. Tribune, 1986, Washington Post, 1986, 87, Art Examiner, 1986; subject of work: American Realist Painting, 1945-1980 (John L. Ward), 1989; Scholastic Arts mag. scholar, 1950. Mem. Coll. Art Assn., Women's Caucus for Art, Artists Equity, Nat. Acad. Business E-Mail: iweber@nyc.rr.com.

WEBER, JEAN MACPHAIL, retired museum director; b. Boston, Apr. 2, 1933; d. Harold Percy and Dorothy Norma (Mutch) Macphail; children: Julia Lee, Karin Macphail, Laurie Stewart. Student, Brown U. and R.I. Sch. Design, 1950-52, Edinburgh U., Scotland, 1952-53; BA magna cum laude, Brown U., 1954; postgrad. Danforth scholar, State U. Iowa, 1954-55. Mgr. Lane Bryant Splty. Shop, Denver, 1956-57; campus advisor Saratoga Springs Council Chs., Skidmore Coll., NY, 1960-64; art dir. Our Lady of Peace Hosp., Louisville, 1964-65; dir. Jr. Art Gallery, Louisville, 1965-69, Parrish Art Mus., Southampton, NY, 1969-79, Rochester Mus., NY, 1979-80, Rochester Mus. and Sci. Ctr., NY, 1979-80, Mus. N.Mex., Sante Fe, 1981-85; co-dir. Mus. Mgmt. Inst., U. Calif.-Berkeley, 1981; dir. hist. sites State Hist. Soc. Wis., 1985-90. Mem. mus. studies adv. com. Tufts U., Medford, Mass., 1993; dir. Maine Maritime Mus., 1990-94; interim dir. U. Maine Carnegie Mus. of Art, 1994; adv. bd. Maine Crafts Coun., 1995; exec. dir. Nantucket Hist. Assn., 1995-1999; mem. Maine State Archives Commn., Maine Arts Commn., 2000-04. Contbr. articles to profl. jours. Mem. cultural affairs adv. com. Suffolk County, NY, 1974; trustee Inter Pueblo Cultural Ctr., 1981-82, Brown U., 1983-88, trustee emeritus, 1989-; bd. dirs. Maine Community Cultural Alliance, 1991; bd. trustees ABBE Mus., 1999-2006, Hudson Mus., 1999-2003, Sir Andrew Macphail Found., 2000-. Met. Mus. grantee, 1971 Mem. Am. Assn. Mus. (accreditation commn. 1976-85, chmn. 1982-85, mem. coun. 1979-81, v.p. 1985, bd. dirs. 1993, named to Centennial Honor Roll, 2006), N.E. Mus. Conf. (v.p. 1978-79, pres. 1979-80), Internat. Coun. Mus., NY State Assn. Mus. (coun. 1977-80), Phi Beta Kappa. Home: R R 3 Eldon Belfast PE Canada COA-1AO Personal E-mail: ejmweber@gmail.com.

WEBER, JENNIFER LEE, historian, educator; b. Calif., Aug. 24, 1962; d. Emerson Allen and Henrietta E. Weber. PhD, Princeton U., NJ, 2003. Reporter Times-Adv., Escondido, Calif., 1988—92; legislative aide, chief cons. to women's caucus Assemblywoman Dede Alpert, Calif. State Legislaure, Secremento, 1993—95; press sec. State Senator Lucy Killea, San Diego, 1992—93; copy editor, celebrity gossip columnist Sacramento Bee, 1995—98; lectr. Princeton U., 2003—05; asst. prof. U. Kans., Lawrence, 2005—. Author: (book) Copperheads: The Rise and Fall of Lincoln's Opponents in the North. Recipient Hay-Nicolay prize, Abraham Lincoln Inst., 2005. Office: Univ Kans 3633 Wescoe 1445 Jayhawk Blvd Lawrence KS 66045 Business E-Mail: jlweber@ku.edu.

WEBER, JEROME CHARLES, human relations educator, retired academic administrator; b. Bklyn., Sept. 1, 1938; s. Meyer and Ethel (Shier) W.; m. Elizabeth Lynn Wiley, July 18, 1975; children: Amy Elizabeth, Jeffrey Glenn. BS, Bklyn. Coll., 1960; MA, Mich. State U., 1961, PhD, 1966. Mem. faculty U. Okla., Norman, 1964—, prof. edn., phys. edn., human rels. and social work, 1973—, Regents' prof. edn. and human rels., 1991—, asst. and acting dean, 1969-72, dean Univ. Coll., 1973-91, vice provost instructional svcs., 1979-91; chmn. ednl. leadership and policy studies, 1991-93. Author: (with D.R. Lamb) Statistics and Research in Physical Education, 1970, (with G. Henderson) College Survival for Student-Athletes, 1985, (with R. Cintron) Enduring Enigmas: Issues in Adult and Higher Education, 1997; contbr. chpts. to books; contbr. articles to profl. jours. Bd. dirs. Univ. div. United Way, 1970; pres. Norman Kindergarten Assn., 1968; commr. Norman Bd. Parks, 1971-79. Recipient Outstanding Faculty award, Okla. U., 2007; named to Higher Edn. Hall Fame, Okla., 2005. Fellow Am. Coun. Sports Medicine; mem. Am. Assn. Higher Edn., Coun. Sports Psychology, Am. Coun. on Edn. Democrat. Jewish. Home: 5 Pebble Creek Rd Norman OK 73072-2822 Office: 630 Parrington Oval Norman OK 73069-8813 Office Phone: 405-325-3629. E-mail: jcweber@ou.edu.

WEBER, JOHN BERTRAM, architect; b. Evanston, Ill., Oct. 15, 1930; s. Bertram Anton and Dorothea B. Weber; m. Sally Ann French; children: Suzanne French Roulston, Jane Marie McCarthy, Patricia Ann Blodgett, Nancy B. BArch, Princeton U., 1953; postgrad., Ill. Inst. Tech., 1959. Lic. arch.; registered energ profl. Chgo. Field engr. United Constrn. Co., Riverdale, ND, 1952; draftsman Bertram A. Weber Arch., Chgo., 1947, 53, arch., 1958-1973; field engr. Atkinson United Constrn. Co., Greenup and Ashland, Ky., 1956-58; ptnr., proprietor Weber & Weber Arch., Chgo., 1973—84; pvt. practice Northbrook, 1984—94, Winnetka, Northfield, 1994—. Mem. Ill. Architecture Act Revision Task Force, 1982—89; del. Ill. Arch.-Engr. Coun., 1976—87, chmn., 1981—82. Prin. works include Prestwick Country Club, 3175 Commercial Ave. Bldg., Northbrook, med. office bldg. and additions to Bi-County Hosp., Warren, Mich., additions and alterations to Detroit Osteopathic Hosp., addition to Duraclean Internat. Bldg., Deerfield, additions to The Admiral, Chgo., Villa Stresov, Borovets, Bulgaria, others. Active Winnetka Cmty. Caucus, 1965, 1974; mem. Mayor's Adv. Com. Bldg. Codes, Chgo., 1975—80; chmn. bldg. com. Winnetka Cmty. House, 1977—81; active Winnetka Zoning Bd. Appeals, 1983—88, chmn., 1987—88; active Winnetka Ad Hoc Zoning Com., 1995—96, Winnetka Design Rev. Bd., 2002—08, Winnetka Forestry Commn., 2003—08; deacon, elder Winnetka Presbyn. Ch. Officer USN, 1953—56. Fellow: Assn. Lic. Arch., Ill. Soc. Arch. (bd. dirs. 1969—84, pres. 1976—78, bd. dirs. 1991—99); mem.: VFW, AIA (health com. 1969—76), Constrn. Specifications Inst., Am. Legion, Dairymen's Country Club, Old Willow Club (pres. 1983), Builders Club Chgo. (bd. dirs. 1966—, pres. 1973—74), Architects Club Chgo. (bd. dirs. 1976—86, pres. 1981, bd. dirs. 1994). Office: John B Weber Architect 415 Berkeley Ave Winnetka IL 60093-2109 *Do what you should do, not what you have to do. In the end, it is only the things that we do that impact on other people's and other living being's lives that have real meaning.*

WEBER, JOHN WALTER, insurance company executive; b. Rochester, NY, Jan. 10, 1959; BS, U. Conn., 1984. Claims supr. Hartford Ins. Group, Southington, Conn., 1986-90; regional claims mgr. Housing Authority Risk Retention Group, Cheshire, Conn., 1990—2008, Chubb and Son, 2009—. Contbr. articles to tech. publs. Mem. U. Conn. Alumni Assn. Avocations: running, reading, softball, cooking. Office Phone: 860-408-2955.

WEBER, KATHLEEN M., sports medicine physician, orthopedist; BS in Nursing, Coll. Mt. Joseph, Cin., Oh.; MS in Exercise Physiology, George Williams Coll., Downers Grove, Ill.; Post-Baccalaureate in Health Sci., Loyola Univ., Chgo.; MD, Rush Med. Coll., Chgo., 1996. Cert. in sports medicine, in internal medicine, lic. Ill., Calif. Intern in health promotion Hinsdale Hosp. Cardiology Dept., Ill.; intern in corp. health promotion CF Industries, Inc., Long Grove, Ill., Amoco Corp. Hdqs., Chgo.; intern in cmty. health progrms Naperville YMCA, Naperville, Ill.; resident, internal medicine Rush Univ. Med. Ctr., Chgo., 1996—99, chief resident, internal medicine, 1999—2000; fellow in sports medicine U. Calif. San Diego Med. Ctr., 2000—01; health dir., cons. The LaSalle Club, Chgo.; cons., owner Leisure and Fitness Svcs., Evanston, Ill.; attending physician, dir. primary care/sports medicine and women's sports medicine Midwest Orthopaedics at Rush Univ. Med. Ctr. Team physician for various HS athletic departments; mem. med. staff for various sports competitions; team physician U. Calif. San Diego Athletic Dept., 2000—01, San Diego Spirits, 2001, Chgo. Blaze, WNBL, US Soccer, Chgo. White Sox, DePaul U. Athletic Dept. Contbr. articles to profl. jours., chapters to books. Recipient Outstanding Work as an Intern, Rush Univ. Med. Ctr. Dept. Medicine, 1997, Aesculapius award, Rush Med. Coll., 1998, Dept. Medicine award Resident Yr., Rush Univ. Med. Ctr., 1999, Dept. Medicine award Outstanding Tchr., 2000; named to Top Doctor's, Chgo. Mag., 2009. Mem.: Am. Soc. Internal Med., Am. Coll. Physicians, Am. Med. Soc. Sports Med., Am. Coll. Sports Med. Office: Midwest Orthopaedics at Rush Ste 1063 1725 W Harrison St Chicago IL 60612 Office Fax: 312-431-3400.*

WEBER, KATIE, retired special education educator; b. Delhi, La., Dec. 6, 1933; d. Sullivan and Teresa McClain Aytch; m. Hilliard Weber Jr., June 16, 1956; children: Barrett Renwick, Sandra Anita, Dawna Lynn, Thaddeus Marc. BA, So. U., 1957; MEd, Tex. So. U., 1982. Cert. elem. and spl. edn. tchr., La., Tex. Elem. tchr. Port Arthur Ind. Sch. Dist., Tex., 1957-73, elem. spl. edn. tchr. Tex., 1974-85, secondary spl. edn. tchr. Tex., 1985—93; ret., 1993. Part-time prin. Port Arthur Ind. Sch. Dist., 1976-83, interim prin., 1983-85; mem. Tex. assessment acad. skills test Tex. Edn. Agy., Austin, 1988-90, scorer master tchr. test, 1990; also curriculum writer; founder Weber Family Scholar Found., dir., 1990-2002; founder McClain Found. Incorporated, 2006. Candidate for city coun. City of Port Arthur, Tex., 1974; active Brentwood Bapt. Ch., Houston, Tex., 1998-, Bapt. Women Mission III, Sr. Adult Ministry, Class 10 Sunday Sch, Buchanan Cir., 1980—, Port Child Svc. League, Port Arthur, 1989—, Life PTA-Tex. PTA, 1985, Clean Cmty. Commn., Port Arthur, 1990—. Named One of Top 20 Tchrs. in Tex., Leadership Edn., 1984-85, Bus. Assoc. of Yr. plaque Energy City chpt. Am. Women Bus. Assn., 1984. Mem. Assn. Tex. Profl. Educators (Leadership cert. 1989), Zeta Phi Beta. Democrat. Avocations: walking, gardening, cooking, reading, classical music. Address: 1819 Thornbrook Dr Missouri City TX 77489-2207

WEBER, LARRY FRANCIS, retired electrical engineer; b. Anchorage, Alaska, July 9, 1947; s. Melvin Clemence and Bernice Leona Weber; m. Jane Ann Johnson, Aug. 22, 1970; children: Jason Frederick, Emily Kathleen. PhD in Elec. Engring., U. of Ill., Urbana-Champaign, Illinois, 1971—75, M. S. in Elec. Engring., 1969—71, B. S. in Elec. Engring., 1965—69. Prof. U. Ill., Urbana-Champaign, 1975—91; sr. v.p. and CTO Plasmaco Inc., Highland, NY, 1987—93, acting pres., 1993—96, pres. and CEO, Subs. Panasonic, 1996—2004; pres. Soc. Info. Display, San Jose, Calif., 2006—08. Contbr. chapters to books. Exec. com. Soc. Info. Display, 2004—. Recipient Spl. Recognition award, Soc. Info. Display, 1982, 1995, Karl Ferdinand Braun prize, 2000, award, Internat. Electrotechnical Commn., 2007, Daniel E. Noble award, Inst. Elec. and Electronic Engrs., 2009. Fellow: Soc. Info. Display (pres. 2006—08), Inst. Elec. and Electronic Engrs.; mem.: AAAS. Avocation: astronomy.

WEBER, LISA M., insurance company executive; b. 1963; BA in Psych., SUNY, Stony Brook. With Painewebber, 1988—98; exec. v.p. human resources MetLife, Inc., 1998—2001, sr. v.p., 1999, sr. exec. v.p., chief adminstrv. officer, 2001—04, pres. individual bus., 2004—. Bd. dirs. New Eng. Fin., Gt. Am. Fin., Reinsurance Grp. of Am.; bd. dirs. benefits com. MetLife, Inc.; dir. MetLife Found.; chair MetLife Bank, MetLife Auto and Home. Trustee Boys and Girls Clubs America NE Region. Named one of 50 Most Powerful Women in Bus., Fortune mag., 2006, 2007, 2008, Top 20 Nonbank Women in Fin., US Banker, 2007, 2008, The 100 Most Influential Women in NYC Bus., Crain's NY Bus., 2007, 100 Most Powerful Women, Forbes mag., 2008. Mem.: Phi Beta Kappa. Office: MetLife Inc 200 Park Ave New York NY 10166*

WEBER, MARGARET LAURA JANE, retired accountant; b. Fairview, Mo., Jan. 4, 1933; d. Mert James and Margaret Orr (Mortensen) Joel; m. James E. Jennings, Mar. 1953 (div.); children: James Edward Jennings, Janie Lea Franks, David Alan Jennings; m. Albert H. Weber, June 1956; children: Luhwanna Stonecipher, Margaret Anne Shadwick. AA, Crowder Coll., Mo., 1972; postgrad. Mo. So. Coll., 1988. Teller, First State Bank, Joplin, Mo., 1951-53; clk. Mo. Lic. Dept., Joplin, 1954-57, U. Mo. Ext. Dept., Neosho, 1967-68; cashier Crowder Coll., Neosho, Mo., 1968-83, acct., 1983-98m, ret., 1998. Mem., Newton County Welfare Com., 1984—. Mem. Am. Bus. Women's Assn. (Woman of Yr. 1982, Bus. Assoc. of Yr. 1987), Nat. Assn. Female Execs., Mo. Assn. Community Jr. Colls. (bd. dirs. 1978-82). Republican. Baptist. Home: 1205 Ozark Dr Neosho MO 64850-1363 Office: Crowder Coll 601 Laclede Ave Neosho MO 64850-9165 Office Phone: 417-451-2604.

WEBER, MARK, apparel executive; With Phillips-Van Heusen, NYC, 1972—2006, sr. v.p., gen. merchandise mgr., exec. v.p. merchandising, 1995—98, pres., COO, 1998—2005, CEO, 2005—06, LVMH Inc, NYC, 2006—; chmn., CEO Donna Karan Internat. Inc., NYC, 2006—. Office: LVMH Inc 19 E 57th St New York NY 10022

WEBER, MARK R., automotive executive; B in Indsl. Engring., Kettering U.; M in Mgmt. (Sloan fellow), MIT, 1983. Various pers. and labor rels. pos. GM Fisher Body, Elyria, Ohio, 1971—78, administr. pers. svcs. Columbus, Ohio, 1978—79, pers. dir. Syracuse, NY, 1979—82; adminstr. exec. compensation GM Pers. and Devel. Staff, Detroit, 1982—83, dir., classified employee compensation, 1983—85; dir. gen. offices pers. Chevrolet-Pontiac-GM of Can. Group, Warren, Mich., 1985—88, dir. human resources, salaried pers., 1985—88, dir. indsl. rels., 1988—91; gen. dir. pers. Inland Fisher Guide, Warren, Mich., 1991—93, gen. dir. pers. and pub. affairs, 1993—98; v.p. in charge human resources Delphi Corp., Troy, Mich., 1998—2000, exec. v.p., ops., human resource mgmt. and corp. affairs, 2000—06, exec. v.p. global bus. services, 2006—. Office: World Hdqrs Delphi Corp 5725 Delphi Dr Troy MI 48098-2815

WEBER, MARK W., library director, dean; BS, U. Wis., 1968, MLS, 1972; MA in Hist. and Edn., Colgate U., 1970. Dir. pub. svcs. Clifford Libr. and Learning Resources U. Evansville, 1975—79, tchr. reference and libr. mgmt., 1976—79; archives asst. Case Western Res. U., 1979—80; pub. svcs./outreach libr. Cuyahoga CC, 1981—85, tchr. labor hist. and collective bargaining, 1984—88, asst. pers. dir./EEOC officer, 1985—88; tchr. labor hist. Cleve. State U., 1983; asst. univ. libr. for pers. U. Cin., 1988—91; tchr. libr. mgmt. Ind. U., 1990; dir. staff svcs. Kent State U. Librs., 1991—2000, dean librs. and media svcs., 2001—. Contbr. articles to profl. jours. Founding bd. mem. Ethical Soc. of Cleve. Mem.: ALA, Assn. Jewish Librs., Greater Cleve. Labor Hist. Soc., Jewish Secular Cmty. Office: Kent State U Librs and Media Svcs PO Box 5190 Kent OH 44242-0001 Office Phone: 330-672-2962. E-mail: markw@lms.kent.edu.

WEBER, MATTHEW GEORGE, lawyer; s. Robert H. and Helena K. Weber; m. Ann Ralston Weber, Aug. 31, 1996; children: Caroline, Lindsey, Thomas. BA magna cum laude, Colo. Coll., Colorade Springs, 1985; JD, Northwestern U. Sch. Law, Evanston, Ill., 1988. Bar: US Dist. Ct., Dist. of Colo., DC Ct. Appeals 1988, US Dist. Ct., DC 1989, Colo. Supreme Ct. 1989, US Ct. Appeals, D.C. Circuit 1989, US Supreme Ct. 1992, US Ct. Appeals, 10th Circuit 1995. Assoc. atty. Dow, Lohnes & Albertson, Washington, 1988—90, Baker & Hostetler, Washington, 1991—94, Hoskin, Farina, Aldrich & Kampf, P.C., Grand Junction, Colo., 1994—99, shareholder, 1999—2003; atty. Holland & Hart, LLP, Denver, 2004—06, ptnr., 2007—. Chair of law day com. Mesa County Bar Assn., Grand Junction, 2002. Author: (68 den. u. l. rev. 57) Media Liability for the Publication of Advertising: When to Kill the Messenger; contbr. (ABA book) Managed Care Litigation. Bd. dirs. Mesa County Chpt. of ARC, Grand Junction, Colo., 1995—96; bd. trustees Mesa County Pub. Libr. Dist., Grand Junction, 1999—2003. Mem.: ABA, Am. Health Lawyers Assn., Denver Bar Assn. Office: Holland & Hart LLP 555 17th St Ste 3200 Denver CO 80202

WEBER, MICHAEL A., physician, researcher; m. Sandra Du Bro, Sept. 12, 1971; children: Mark S., David S. BS, Sydney U., Australia, 1967; MD, Sydney U. Sch. of Medicine, Australia, 1967. Cert. Medicine Royal Australasian Coll. of Physicians, 1977, ACP, 1977. Resident in medicine NYU Med. Ctr., 1968—71; rsch. fellow Sydney Hosp., U. Sydney, 1971—75; asst. prof. medicine Cardiovasc. Ctr., Cornell U. Med. Ctr., NYC, 1975—77; chief, sect. clin. pharmacology and hypertension, Irvine Coll. Medicine U. Calif., 1977—95, assoc. prof. medicine, 1977—82, prof. medicine, 1982—85; chmn., dept. medicine Brookdale U. Med. Ctr., Bklyn., 1995—2000; prof. medicine SUNY Downstate Coll. Medicine, Bklyn., 1995—, assoc. dean clin. rsch., 2000—04. Served on Cardiovascular and Renal Drugs Adv. Bd. FDA; cons. FDA; serves on steering committees of several nat. and internat. clin. outcomes trials; retained cons. and mem. speakers bur. Novartis, Merck, Boehringer Ingelheim, Bristol-Myers Squibb and Sanofi. Author: (jour. articles) Lancet; editor: (med. ref. book) Hypertension Medicine, Ambulatory Blood Pressure Monitorins; editor in chief (Jour. Clin. Hypertention); co-editor (mem. editl. bd.): Med Reviews; contbr. several articles to profl. jours. Pres. Am. Soc. of Hypertension, NYC, 1998—2000; chmn. ASH Specialists Program in Hypertension, NYC; cons., ctr. for drug evaluation and rsch. FDA, Washington, 1993—2009. Fellow: Am. Coll. Clin. Pharmacology, Am. Coll. Physicians, Am. Heart Assn. (fellow, coun. for high blood pressure rsch.), Am. Coll. of Cardiology; mem.: Am. Soc. Hypertension (founder, past pres., chair, hypertension specialists program). Office: SUNY Downstate Coll Medicine 450 Clarkson Ave Box 97 Brooklyn NY 11203 Office Fax: 212-584-9192. Personal E-mail: michaelwebermd@cs.com.

WEBER, MICHAEL F., physics professor; PhD, U. Mich., Ann Arbor, 1988. Physics prof. BYU, Laie, Hawaii, 1999—. Mem. Lds Ch. Office: BYU Hawaii 55-220 Kulanui St Laie HI 96762 Business E-Mail: weberm@byuh.edu.

WEBER, RANDAL SCOTT, head and neck surgeon, educator; b. Chattanooga, Feb. 14, 1952; s. Harry Nathan and Rosemary (Munsey) W.; m. Jane Covington Edmond, Sept. 1, 1984; children: Austin Edmond, Sophia Lyon. Student, U. Tenn., 1970-71; BA in Chemistry magna cum laude, U. Tenn., Chattanooga, 1975; MD, U. Tenn. Ctr. Health Scis., 1976. Diplomate Am. Bd. Otolaryngology; lic. physician, Tex., Tenn. Intern in surgery Nat. Naval Med. Ctr., Bethesda, Md., 1977-78; resident in surgery Baylor Coll. Medicine, Houston, 1981-82, resident in otolaryngology, 1982-85; fellow in head and neck surgery U. Tex. M. D. Anderson Cancer Ctr., Houston, 1985-86, faculty assoc., 1986, asst. prof. otolaryngology, 1987, assoc. prof. surgery, 1991—, vice chmn. dept. head and neck surgery, 1994. Adj. asst. prof. otolaryngology Baylor Coll. Medicine, Houston, 1990, adj. assoc. prof., 1992; mem. med. records com. U. Tex. M. D. Anderson Cancer Clinic, Houston, 1987-88, laser com., 1987—, surg. svcs. com., 1989-92, faculty senate, 1991-94, exec. com. faculty senate, 1993, dir. clin. rsch., 1993; mem. task force for new materials Am. Acad. Otolaryngology-Head and Neck Surgery/Am. Bd. Otolaryngology, 1992-96; guest examiner Ann. Oral Qualifying Exam., Am. Bd. Otolaryngology, 1992-93; dir., chmn., coord. numerous confs.; lectr. in field. Assoc. editor: Head and Neck, 1992-93, editor, 1994; assoc. editor: Cancer, 2000; mem. editl. bd. Cancer Bull., 1992-93; reviewer Archives of Otolaryngology-Head and Neck Surgery, 1992—; contbr. articles and abstracts to profl. publs., chpts. to books. Lt. comdr. USN, 1980-81. Recipient presdl. citation Am. Head and Neck Soc., 2000, Louis Durhing Outstanding Clin. Subspecialist award U. Pa. Health Sys., 2001. Health Professions scholar USN, 1973-76. Fellow ACS; mem. AMA, Am. Soc. Head and Neck Surgery (program chmn. 33d ann. meeting 1991), Soc. Head and Neck Surgeons, Am. Acad. Otolaryngology-Head and Neck Surgery (subcom. on endocrine surgery 1988-94), Soc. Univ. Otolaryngologists, Tex. Med. Assn., Houston Otolaryngologic Soc., Harris County Med. Soc., Alpha Omega Alpha.

WEBER, RICHARD MARTIN, theology studies educator; b. Columbus, Ohio, Feb. 28, 1970; s. Donald Eugene and Alma Louise Weber; m. Kathrin Suzanne Peterson, June 12, 1993; children: Charis Joy Peterson, Aren Edwards. MA, Trinity Internat. U., Deerfield, Ill., 1997; MDiv, Trinity Evang. Div. Sch., Deerfield, 1997; PhD, Marquette U., Milw., 2002. Lic. ministerial Meadowbrook Ch., Wis., 2003. Assoc. prof.

Moody Bible Inst., Chgo., 2002—. Contbr. chapters to books, articles to profl. jours. Mem.: Evang. Theol. Soc. Office: Moody Bible Inst 820 N LaSalle Blvd Chicago IL 60610 Business E-Mail: richard.weber@moody.edu.

WEBER, ROBERT CARL, lawyer; b. Chester, Pa., Dec. 18, 1950; s. Robert Francis and Lucille (Nobili) W.; m. Linda Brediger, June 30, 1972; children: Robert F., Mary Therese, David P., Joseph T. BA cum laude, Yale U., 1972; JD, Duke U., 1976. Bar: Ohio 1976, U.S. Dist. ct. (no. dist.) Ohio 1976, U.S. Ct. Claims 1980, U.S. Ct. Appeals (6th cir.) 1981, U.S. Ct. Appeals (5th cir.) 1995. Assoc. Jones, Day, Reavis & Pogue (now Jones Day), Cleve., 1976—83, ptnr., 1983—2006; sr. v.p. legal and regulatory affairs, gen. counsel IBM Corp., Armonk, NY, 2006—. Bd. dirs. United Way Svcs. of Cleve., 1992-2002. Named one of Top 10 Trial Lawyers in Am., Nat. Law Jour., 2000, 2004. Fellow Am. Coll. Trial Lawyers, Internat. Acad. Trial Lawyers; mem. Ohio Bar Assn., Am. Law Inst., Product Liability Adv. Coun., Cleve. Bar Assn. (chmn. jud. selection com. 1985-86, trustee 1990-93, pres.-elect 1994-95, pres. 1995-96), Jud. Conf. for 8th Jud. Dist. Ohio (life), Order of Coif. Roman Catholic. Office: IBM Corp 1 New Orchard Rd Armonk NY 10504-1722 Business E-Mail: rcweber@us.ibm.com.

WEBER, SHEA, professional hockey player; b. Sicamous, BC, Can., Aug. 14, 1985; s. James and Tracy Weber. Defenseman Nashville Predators, 2006—. Mem. Team Can., World Jr. Championships, Grand Forks, ND, 2005. Named to NHL YoungStars Game, 2007, NHL All-Star Game, 2009. Achievements include being a member of Gold Medal Team Canada, World Junior Championships, 2005. Avocations: baseball, golf, fishing, boating. Office: Nashville Predators Sommet Ctr 501 Broadway Nashville TN 37203*

WEBER, STEPHEN LEWIS, academic administrator; b. Boston, Mar. 17, 1942; s. Lewis F. and Catherine (Warns) W.; m. Susan M. Keim, June 27, 1965; children: Richard, Matthew. BA, Bowling Green State U., 1964; postgrad., U. Colo., 1964-66; PhD, U. Notre Dame, 1969; EdD (hon.), Capital Normal U., China, 1994. Asst. prof. philosophy U. Maine, Orono, 1969—74, assoc. prof., 1974—79, asst. to pres., 1976-79; dean arts and scis. Fairfield U., Conn., 1979-84; v.p. acad. affairs St. Cloud State U., Minn., 1984-88; pres. SUNY Oswego, 1988—96; interim provost SUNY Albany, 1995-96; pres. San Diego State U., 1996—. Contbr. numerous articles on philosophy and acad. adminstrn. to profl. jours. Mem. Commn. on Internat. Edn. and Commn. on Govtl. Rels.; bd. govs. The Peres Ctr. for Peace, San Diego Found.; bd. dirs. San Diego Regional Econ. Devel. Corp.; mem. internat. adv. bd. Found. for the Children of the Californias; bd. dirs. NCAA Divsn. 1 hon. mem. Asia Desk, San Diego Trade Ctr. Named Outstanding Humanities Tchr., U. Maine, 1975. Mem. Am. Philos. Assn., Am. Assn. Higher Edn. Democrat. Avocations: art, woodworking, swimming, boating. Office: San Diego State Univ Office Pres 5500 Campanile Dr San Diego CA 92182-8000 E-mail: presidents.office@sdsu.edu.

WEBER, SUSAN A., lawyer; b. 1958; BA, Drake U., 1984; JD, MBA, SUNY, Buffalo, 1989. Bar: Pa. 1990, D.C. 1992, Ill. 1993, U.S. Ct. Appeals (4th cir.) 1990, U.S. Ct. Appeals (3d cir.) 1991, U.S. Ct. Appeals (7th cir.) 1992. Clk. to Justice Byron White U.S. Supreme Ct.; clk. to Judge James Sprouse U.S. Ct. Appeals (4th cir.); with Sidley Austin Brown & Wood, Chgo., 1993—, ptnr., 1997—.

WEBER, THOMAS WILLIAM, chemical engineering professor; s. William A. and Dorothy (Negus) W.; m. Marianne S. Hartmann, June 4, 1966; children: Anne Louise, William Alois B.Chem. Engring., Cornell U., 1953, PhD, 1963; MS in Chem. Engring., Newark Coll. Engring., 1958. Chem. engr. econs. and planning Esso Research & Engring., Linden, NJ, 1955-58; instr. Cornell U., 1961-62; asst. prof. SUNY-Buffalo, 1963-66, assoc. prof. chem. engring., 1966-82, prof., 1982-2000, assoc. chmn. dept., 1980-82, chmn. dept., 1982-89, acting chmn., 1996-97, prof. emeritus, 2000—. Author: An Introduction to Process Dynamics and Control, 1973 Named Prof. of Yr., Tau Kappa Chi, 1965; recipient Chancellor's award for excellence in teaching, 1981, Tchr. of Yr. award Tau Beta Pi, 1982 Fellow AIChE (chmn. western N.Y. sect. 1969-70, Profl. Achievement award western N.Y. sect. 1978), Am. Soc. Engring. Edn. (chmn. instrumentation divsn. 1975-77, chmn. St. Lawrence sect. 1979-80, 92-94, chmn. divsn. experimentation and lab.-oriented studies 1985-86, chmn. Zone I 1999-2001, Outstanding Zone Campus Rep. award 1988, AT&T Found. award 1987-88); mem. Tech. Socs. Coun. Niagara Frontier (sec. 1973-75, pres. 1975-76, treas. 1978-2004), Swedish Club of Buffalo (pres. 1974-76), U.S. Masters Swimming Club, Sigma Xi, Phi Kappa Phi, Tau Beta Pi, Theta Xi. Presbyterian. Home: 617 Downing Ln Buffalo NY 14221-8058 Business E-Mail: twweber@buffalo.edu.

WEBER, VIN (JOHN VINCENT WEBER), lobbyist, former United States Representative from Minnesota; b. Slayton, Minn., July 24, 1952; m. Cheryl Weber; 2 children. Grad., U. Minn., Twin Cities, 1974. Former pres. Weber Publ. Co.; co-pub. Murray County Herald, 1976-78; press sec. to Congressman Tom Hagedorn, 1974-76; campaign mgr. for Rudy Boschwitz, 1978; sr. Minn. aide to Senator Rudy Boschwitz, 1979-80; mem. US Congress from 6th Minn. Dist., 1981—93; asst. minority whip; chaired election com., 1984; co-dir. Empower Am.; ptnr., CEO Clark & Weinstock, Washington, 1994—. Chmn. Nat. Endowment for Democracy; bd. mem. Coun. Fgn. Rels.; mem. US Sec. of Defense's Defense Policy Bd. Adv. Com.; sr. fellow, co-dir. policy forum Humphrey Inst., U. Minn.; Plains States regional chmn. Bush-Cheney '04; policy chmn. Romney for President, Inc., 2007—; bd. mem. ITT Ednl. Svcs., The Lenox Group, Aspen Inst. Named one of 50 Top Lobbyists, Washingtonian mag., 2007, 25 Most Influential Republicans, Newsmax mag., 2008. Republican. Office: Clark & Weinstock 601 13th St, NW, Ste 410 S Washington DC 20005 Office Phone: 202-621-4000.*

WEBER, YVONNE ROEBUCK, research administrator; educator; b. McKeesport, Pa., Oct. 22; d. Raymond Henry and Clara Maria (Roberts) Roebuck; B.A., U. Pitts., 1947, M.Litt., 1952, Ph.D., 1973; postgrad. Kent State U., 1950; Ecole Normale, Paris, 1953, Goethe Institut, 1960; m. William Frederick Weber, June 16, 1961; children: Laurel, Wendy. Tchr. French, German, English, history Carrollton (Ohio) HS, 1947-51, Canton, Ohio, 1951-52, Munhall (Pa.) HS, 1952-58, Wilkinsburg (Pa.) High Sch., 1958-61, Upper St. Clair (Pa.) HS, 1963-65; asst. prof. French and German, California (Pa.) State Coll., 1965-66, Point Park (Pa.) Coll., 1968-72; asst. prof., supr. edn. Washington and Jefferson Coll., 1976-79; scholar/discussion leader Pa. Humanities Coun., 1993. Recipient Good Citizenship award DAR, 1943, Doctoral Assn. Outstanding Svc. award U. Pitts., 1989; U. Pitts. scholar, 1943-47, Panhellenic Assn. scholar, 1946-47, disting. alumni award Sch. Edn., U. Pitts., 1985, Alumnae award, 1993; Fulbright grantee to Germany, 1960; program scholar Nat. Endowment for the Humanities, Am. Library Assn., 1986; named Disting. Alumna, U. Pitts., 1971-82; initial inductee hall of fame McKeesport High Sch., 1987. Mem. Modern Lang. Assn., Doctoral Assn. Educators, Pa. State Modern Lang. Assn., Pa. Assn. Tchr. Educators, U.Pitts. Alumni Council, Delta Kappa Gamma Soc. Internat. (Scholarship 1972-73, Eunah Temple Holden Golden Anniversary award 1979, head Delta Kappa Gamma internat. research project, 1979-82), Mensa Internat., Pi Lambda Theta, Phi Delta Gamma, Zeta Tau Alpha, Delta Kappa Gamma. Club: McKeesport Coll. Author: A Beacon to the Future: Charting a Course for Advancement; contbr. articles to profl. jours.

WEBER-LEVINE, PHYLLIS, secondary school educator; b. NYC, Dec. 27, 1952; d. William and Irene (Schafer) Weber; m. Edward Keleti Levine, Aug. 19, 1990. BA in Math. Edn., Bklyn. Coll., 1973, MS in Math. Edn., 1975; MA in Ednl. Adminstrn., Fordham U., NYC, 1978. Tchr. Bklyn. Tech. HS, 1973—75, Martin Luther King HS, NYC, 1975—79, HS of Performing Arts, NYC, 1979—2008, LaGuardia HS, NYC, 1985—2008, attendance coord., 1993; tchr. Bramson Tech. Coll., 1993—; asst. program chairperson Lehman Coll., NYC, asst. math. chairperson. Mem. 2d Conf. for State Edn. Dept. Curriculum and Assessment; attendee graphic calculating workshop; with Math. and Sci. Partnership Project, NYC. Contbr. articles to profl. jours., speaker at various orgns. Grantee Nat. Ctr. for Excellence in Edn., Calif., 1987, Woodrow Wilson Inst., 1988, 89. Mem. ASCD, United Fedn. Tchrs. (unity com. 1990—, exec. v.p. math. com. 1989—, math tchrs. com.), Nat. Coun. Tchrs. Math. (life), Assn. Tchrs. Math. NYC (1st v.p. 1988-90), Physics Club NYC (pres. 1977-78), Assn. Tchrs. Math. NY State, Alumni Assn. Bklyn. Coll. (exec. bd. mem., past corr. sec., life), Phi Delta Kappa, Kappa Delta Pi. Avocations: coin collecting/numismatics, swimming, biking, aerobics, tennis. Home: 67-76 Booth St Apt 6K Forest Hills NY 11375-3117

WEBRE, SEPTIME, performing company executive, choreographer; b. New Orleans, Dec. 7, 1961; s. Alfred L. and Juanita (Chisholm) Webre. BA, U. Tex., 1984. Dancer Merce Cunningham Dance Co., NYC, 1991, Am. Repertory Ballet/Princeton (N.J.) Ballet, 1987—99, choreographer, 1988—99, artistic dir., 1993-99, The Washington Ballet, 1999—. Freelance choreographer with Les Grands Ballets Canadienne, 1988—, Pacific N.W. Ballet, 1988—, Sacramento Ballet, 1988—, N.C. Dance Theatre, 1988—, Columbia City Ballet, 1988—, Ballet Austin, 1988—, Dayton Ballet, 1988—, Eglevsky Ballet, 1988—, The Aspen Ballet, the Carslile Project, 1988—, others, 1988—; guest master tchr. various ballet cos., 1990—. Former mem. exec. bd. Young Dems. Am., Austin. Choreographic fellow, N.J. Coun. on Arts, 1992. Roman Catholic. Office: The Washington Ballet 3515 Wisconsin Ave NW Washington DC 20016-3085

WEBSTER, CATHERINE T., telecommunications industry executive; B in Econs., NJ City U. CPA. Numerous fin. positions in internal auditing, security, fin. ops., corporate books and regulatory acctg. Bell Atlantic-NJ (formerly NJ Bell), 1978—93, dir. fin. planning & analysis for Telecom/Network, 1993—96, asst. v.p. fin. planning Corp. Fin. group, 1996; v.p. fin. network svcs./wholesale markets Verizon Comm. Inc., v.p. fin., then sr. v.p. investor rels., 2005, sr. v.p., treas., 2005—. Office: Verizon Comm 140 West St New York NY 10007 Office Phone: 212-395-1000. Business E-Mail: catherine.t.webster@verizon.com.*

WEBSTER, CHARLES M., political organization administrator; State Senator, minority leader Maine Senate, Augusta, 1991—94; gubernatorial candidate Maine, 1994; owner Webster Heating Co., Farmington, Maine; mem. Maine leadership team McCain 2008; chmn. Maine Republican Party, Augusta, 2009—. Republican. Office: Webster Heating Co 211 Perham St Farmington ME 04938 also: Maine Republican Party 9 Higgins St Augusta ME 04330 Office Phone: 207-778-9008, 207-622-6247. Office Fax: 207-623-5322. E-mail: websterheating@hotmail.com, webster@mainegop.com.*

WEBSTER, CHRISTOPHER WHITE, foreign service officer; b. Boston, Oct. 30, 1953; s. Henry deForest and Marion (Havas) W. BA cum laude, Amherst Coll., 1975; MA, Johns Hopkins U., 1977. Asst. comml. attache Am. Embassy, Buenos Aires, 1977-79; econ. comml. officer Georgetown, Guyana, 1979-81; desk officer for Jamaica and Guyana, 1982—84; econ. officer Office of Energy, Washington, 1984-86, fin. and devel. officer Lisbon, Portugal, 1986—89, econ. sect. chief Algiers, Algeria, 1989—92; dep. dir. Office of Pakistan, Afghanistan and Bangladesh Affairs, Washington, 1992—95; dep. chief of mission Khartoum, Sudan and Addis Ababa, Ethiopia, 1995-96; chief, developed Country Trade Divsn., Washington, 1996-98; dep. dir. Office of Ctrl. Am. and Panamanian Affairs, Washington, 1998-00, dep. chief of mission Dhaka, Bangladesh, 2000—03, Oslo, 2003—06; dir. Office of Devel. Fin., Washington, 2006—08, Ctrl. Am. and Panamanian Affairs, Washington, 2008—. Recipient Superior Honor award Dept. State, 1983, 91, 98-2000, Meritorious Honor award Dept. State, 2007. E-mail: webstercw@state.gov.

WEBSTER, DAVID MACPHERSON, lawyer; b. Chgo., June 22, 1950; s. Robert Fielden and Julia Orendorff (Macpherson) Webster; m. Lucia Maxwell Blair, Oct. 3, 1987; 1 child, Jessie Maxwell. BA in History magna cum laude with honors, Williams Coll., 1972; JD, U. Va., 1975; DD (hon.), Seabury-Western Theol. Sem., 2000. Bar: Ill. 1975. Assoc. Winston & Strawn, Chgo., 1975-81, ptnr., 1981-87; White House fellow Washington, 1987-88; spl. asst. to dir. FBI, Washington, 1988-89; asst. gen. counsel for multilateral negotiations U.S. Arms Control and Disarmament Agy., Washington, 1989—94; v.p., gen. counsel A.T. Kearney, Inc., Chgo., 1994—2002; of counsel Butler Rubin Saltarelli & Boyd, Chgo., 2002—03; sr. v.p., gen. counsel Hawaiian Airlines, Honolulu, 2003—05; v.p., gen. counsel, sec. DeVry Inc., Oakbrook Terrace, Ill., 2005—07; pvt. practice Webster Law Office, Winnetka, Ill., 2007—. Mem. adv. com. Ill. Bus. Corp. Ill. Sec. of State, Chgo., 1982—87. Bd. dirs. Ill. Soc. Prevention Blindness, Chgo., 1980—87, 1997—2004, pres., 1999—2001; trustee Village of Winnetka, Ill., 2003—05; bd. dirs. Better Govt. Assn., Chgo., 1997—99, Orchard Village, Skokie, Ill., 2009—; trustee Episc. Charities and Profl. Svcs., Chgo., 1980—87; bd. dirs. WBEZ Alliance, Inc., Chgo., 1996—2004; chair bd. trustees Seabury-Western Theol. Sem., Evanston, Ill., 1993—96, trustee, 1988—96, 2002—05. Mem.: Ill. State Hist. Soc. (life), White House Fellows Assn., Phi Beta Kappa (mem. exec. com. Chgo. chpt. 1996—98). Avocations: history, writing. Home: 596 Arbor Vitae Rd Winnetka IL 60093-2302 Office Phone: 847-826-6437. Personal E-mail: websterlawoffice@comcast.net. Business E-Mail: 50legal75@comcast.net.

WEBSTER, DOUGLAS WAYNE, federal agency administrator, management consultant; b. Huntington Park, Calif., Aug. 11, 1948; s. William Mac and Lorraine Marie (Browner) Webster; m. Concepcion Tumulak Bingco, Apr. 12, 1975; children: Kathy, Dawn. Grad., Air War Coll., Maxwell AFB, Ala., 1987; BS in Engring., UCLA, 1972; MS in Systems Mgmt., U. So. Calif., 1983; DBA, U.S. Internat. U., San Diego, 1991. Cert. credit union devel. educator; govt. fin. mgr., project mgmt. profl., Info. Tech. Infrastructure Libr. Commd. 2d lt. USAF, 1972, advanced through grades to lt. col., 1988, C-130 navigator Clark Air Base Philippines, 1973-77, C-130 instr. navigator McChord AFB Wash., 1977-79, chief ops. br. space divsn. LA, 1979-84, comdr. airlift control element 374th Tactical Airlift Wing Clark Air Base, 1984-87, dir. systems engring. space divsn. LA, 1987-90, ret., 1993; dep. concurrent engring. US Dept. Def., Washington, 1990-93; prin. Am. Mgmt. Systems, Fairfax, Va., 1992-97; dir. pub. sector cost mgmt. svcs. Price Waterhouse, Arlington, Va., 1997—2004; prin. fin. adv. Ministry Transp. Coalition Provisional Authority, Baghdad, Iraq, 2004; sr. mgr. Grant Thornton LLP, 2004—08; CFO US Dept. Labor, Washington, 2008—. Mgmt. cons. US Dept. Def., 1993—, NASA, 1994—. Author: Activity-Based Costing and Performance, 1994; co-author: Chasing Change: Building Organizational Capacity in a Turbulent Environment, 2008; mem. editl. adv. com. Concurrent Engring., 1992—, Quality Observer, 1992—. Decorated Defense Supr. Svc. medal, Meritorious Svc. medal (3), Air Force Commendation medal (3). Mem.: Am. Def. Preparedness Assn., Am. Soc. Quality Control (sr.). Avocations: genealogy, amateur radio, flying, teaching flying. Office: US Dept Labor Office of CFO 200 Constitution Ave NW Washington DC 20210*

WEBSTER, DUANE ERNES, retired librarian; b. Rochester, NY, Aug. 28, 1941; s. Laverne Judson and Evelyn (Bentley) Webster; m. Carol Elizabeth Webster, Oct. 15, 1964; 1 child, Christopher. BA, Heidelberg Coll., Tiffin, Ohio, 1963; MLS, U. Mich., 1964; student, U. Rochester. Libr. scholar U. Mich. Bus. Libr., Ann Arbor, 1963-64; sr. libr. Rochester Pub. Libr., 1965-67; tech. info. specialist Gen. Dynamics Elec. Div., Rochester, 1967-68; mgr. libr. sys. Svc. Tech. Corp., Cambridge, Mass., 1968-70; dir. office mgmt. svcs. Assn. Rsch. Librs., Washington, 1970-88, dep. exec. dir., 1984-88, exec. dir., 1988—2008, exec. dir. emeritus, 2008—. Bd. dirs. Nat. Humanities Alliance, Washington; cons. Australian Info. Mgmt. Assn. Author: Management Review and Analysis Program, 1973; contbr. articles to profl. jours. Recipient Disting. Alumni award, U. Mich. Libr. Sch., 1982, Disting. Svc. award, Assn. Rsch. Librs., 2008; named Rsch. Libr. of Yr., Chgo. Assn. Coll. & Rsch. Librs., 1987; named a Susan B. Anthony scholar, 1969. Mem.: ALA (Joseph W. Lippincott award 2008), Soc. Scholarly Publs. Avocations: tennis, sailing. Home: 8240 Windsor View Ter Potomac MD 20854-4028*

WEBSTER, ERNEST WESLEY, musician, educator; b. Mt. Vernon, Ill., Oct. 30, 1932; s. Melvin Harold and Nora Mae (Wimberley) Webster; m. Arlene Waite (div. 1972); children: Elizabeth Ann Webster Kennedy, Victoria Christina; m. Judith Ann Hichman (dec. 1995); m. Lindsey Carvalho Campos, Oct. 4, 2003. Diploma in ch./conducting, Moody Bible Inst., Chgo., 1953; student, Northwestern Schs., Mpls., 1953—54; diploma in music edn. and piano, U. Ariz., 1957. Owner Webster Sch. Music, Ft. Lauderdale, 1957—; concert pianist Ernest Wesley Website; chmn. Assn. Subjective Music Tchrs. Nat. Assn.; profl. accordionist mem. Am. Accordionist Assn. Instr. Barry U. Composer (music) piano, violin, viola and others. Mem.: Music Tchrs. Nat. Assn. (chmn., accordion subject area), Accordion Tchrs. Guild Internat. (v.p.), Fla. State Music Tchrs. Assn. (pres. dist. 6), Amer. Accordionist Assn. (prof. accordionist mem.). Office: Webster Sch Music 3058 N Federal Hwy Fort Lauderdale FL 33304 Home: 469 N Pine Island Rd Apt B203 Plantation FL 33324-1833

WEBSTER, HAROLD FRANK, physicist; b. Buffalo, June 25, 1919; s. Stephen and Florence Kathryn (Frank) W.; m. Helen Voorhis, Sept. 15, 1951; children: Sue Helen, Kenneth Harold, Jean Phyllis. BA magna cum laude, U. Buffalo, 1941, MA, 1944; PhD, Cornell U., 1953. Staff mem. Radiation Lab. MIT, Cambridge, 1943-45; rsch. assoc. Rsch. Lab. GE, Schenectady, N.Y., 1951-85, cons. R&D Ctr., 1985-90; ret. Contbg. author: Packaging of Power Semiconductor Devices, 1986, Advances in Electronics, Vol. 17, 1962; patentee in field. U.S. del. to XIII Gen. Assembly of Internat. Sci. Radio Union, London, 1960. Mem. IEEE (WRG Baker award 1958), Am. Phys. Soc., Phi Beta Kappa, Sigma Xi. Achievements include discovering vortex instability in electron sheet beams, deriving current/voltage characteristics of thermionic diodes from space charge distribution, measuring dependence of thermionic emission and wetting on crystal face of metal crystals in cesium vapor. Personal E-mail: websterh@gleneddy.com.

WEBSTER, HENRY DE FOREST, neuroscientist; b. NYC, Apr. 22, 1927; s. Leslie Tillotson and Emily (deForest) W.; m. Marion Havas, June 12, 1951; children: Christopher, Henry, Sally, David, Steven. AB cum laude, Amherst Coll., 1948; MD, Harvard U., 1952. Diplomate in Neurology Am. Bd. Psychiatry Neurology, 1959. Intern Boston City Hosp., 1952-53, resident, 1953-54; resident in neurology Mass. Gen. Hosp., 1954-56, rsch. fellow in neuropathology, 1956-59, prin. investigator NIH rsch. grants, electron micros. studies peripheral neuropathy, 1959-69, mem. staffs; instr. neurology Harvard Med. Sch., Boston, 1959-63, assoc. in neurology, 1963-66, asst. prof. neuropathology, 1966; assoc. prof. neurology U. Miami Sch. Medicine, Fla., 1966-69, prof., 1969; chief sect. cellular neuropathology Nat. Inst. Neurol. Diseases and Stroke, Bethesda, Md., 1969-97; chief Lab. Exptl. Neuropathology, 1984-97; scientist emeritus NIH, 1997—2009. Disting. scientist, lectr. dept. anatomy Tulane U. Sch. Medicine, 1973; Royal Coll. lectr. Can. Assn. Neuropathologists, 1982; Saul Korey lectr. Am. Assn. Neuropathologists, 1992; chmn. Winter Conf. on Brain Rsch., 1985-86; head neuropathology del. to visit China in 1990, Citizen Amb. Program, People to People Internat.; exec. com. rsch. group on neuromuscular disease World Fedn. Neurology, 1986-93. Author: (with A. Peters and S.L. Palay) The Fine Structure of the Nervous System, 1970, 3rd edit., 1991, Cellular Neuroscience: Projects and Images, 2006, (with K.E. Åström) Gliogenesis: Historical Perspectives, 1839-1985, 2009; contbr. sci. articles, revs. to profl. jours. and books. With USNR, 1945—46. Recipient Superior Svc. award USPHS, 1977, A. von Humboldt award Germany, 1985, Sci. award Peripheral Neuropathy Assn., 1994; named hon. prof. Norman Bethune U. of Med. Scis., Chanchun, China, 1991. Mem. Am. Assn. Neuropathologists (v.p. 1976-77, pres. 1978-79, Weil award 1960, Meritorious Contbns. to Neuropathology award 2001), Internat. Soc. Neuropathology (hon., councillor 1976-80, v.p. 1980-84, exec. com. 1980-84, 86-94, pres. 1986-90), Internat. Congress Neuropathology (sec. gen. VIII 1978), Peripheral Nerve Study Group (exec. com. 1975-93, chmn. 1977 meeting), Japanese Soc. Neuropathology (hon.), Am. Neurol. Assn., Am. Acad. Neurology, Royal Soc. Medicine, Am. Soc. Cell Biology, Soc. Neurosci., Rotary Internat., Ausable Club (exec. com.). E-mail: mhwebster@verizon.net.

WEBSTER, HUGH B., accountant, former state legislator; b. Caswell County, NC, Aug. 6, 1943; m. Patricia Webster; 2 children. BS, U. NC, 1968, postgrad., 1969, U. Ill., 1970. CPA NC. Farmer, NC, 1953-62; CPA, 1967—2003; constrn. project auditor; auditor, tax specialist Big Six Cert. Pub. Accountant Firms; auditor Dept. Def., Dept. Labor; mem., dist. 21 NC State Senate, Raleigh, 1995—2002, mem., dist. 24, 2003—06; accountant, 2003—. Mem. agr., environ. and natural resources com., fin. com., ins. com., ways and means com.; ranking minority mem. state and local govt. com. Former bd. mem. Caswell C. of C.; founding mem. Leasburg Vol. Fire Dept., former bd. pres. Mem.: Leasburg Ruritan Club. Republican. Methodist. Home: 700 Plum Tree Ln Yanceyville NC 27379-9272

WEBSTER, JAMES RANDOLPH, JR., physician; b. Chgo., Aug. 25, 1931; s. James Randolph and Ruth Marian (Burtis) W.; m. Joan Burchfield, Dec. 28, 1954; children: Susan, Donovan, John. BS, U. Chgo.-Northwestern U., 1953; MD, MS, Northwestern U., 1956. Diplomate: Am. Bd. Internal Medicine (sub bd. pulmonary disease and geriatrics). Intern Phila. Gen. Hosp., 1956-57; resident in medicine Northwestern U., 1957-60, NIH fellow in pulmonary disease, 1962-64;

chief medicine Northwestern Meml. Hosp., Chgo., 1976—88; prof. medicine Northwestern U. Med. Sch., 1977—, chief gen. med. sect. dept. medicine, 1987-88; chief exec. officer Northwestern Med. Group Practice, 1978-88; dir. Buehler Ctr. on Aging Northwestern U. Med. Ctr., 1988-2000. Chief staff Northwestern Meml. Hosp., 1988-90; pres. Chgo. Bd. Health, 2002—, Inst. Medicine, Chgo., Ill., 2002-04, exec. dir., 2004—; chair Ill. Ad Hoc Com. to Defend Health Care. Contbr. chpts. to books, articles to med. jours. Capt. U.S. Army, 1960-62. Recipient Outstanding Clin. tchr. award Northwestern U. Med. Sch., 1974, 77, 84, 86, Alumni Merit award Northwestern U., 1979, Henry P. Russe-Inst. of Medicine award for exemplary compassion in health care, 1997, Aeschulapian award as Physician of Yr., Anti Defamation League, 1998. Master: ACP (gov. for Ill. 1988—92, chair sub-com. on aging 1993, ClaypPole award 1994); mem.: Ill. Geriatrics Soc. (pres. 1992—94), Am. Geriatrics Soc., Alpha Omega Alpha. Office: Inst Medicine Chgo Ste 525 332 S Michigan Ave Chicago IL 60604 Home: PO Box 274 Lakeside MI 49116 Office Phone: 312-663-0040. Business E-Mail: j-webster@northwestern.edu. *Life should best be measured not by how long you live, but how well you function.*

WEBSTER, JEFFREY LEON, graphic designer; b. Idaho Falls, Idaho, Nov. 23, 1941; s. Leon A. and Marjory M. (McAllister) Webster; m. Judith Kess, Apr. 17, 1965; children: Eric J., Marjorie P. Student, Sch. Associated Arts, St. Paul, 1962. Sci. illustrator Mayo Clinic, Rochester, Minn., 1963—66; layout artist Brown & Bigelow, St. Paul, 1966; graphic designer U. Minn., Mpls., 1966—67, U. Calgary, Alta., Canada, 1967—68; sr. artist Control Data Corp., St. Paul, 1968—70; graphic designer Idaho State U., 1970—78; owner, operator studio, Harmony, Minn.; mktg. and advt. cons. to 45 regional and nat. firms, 1978—; dir. mktg., sr. driving program AAPP, Minn. Mem. Idaho State U. Meml. Lectureship Com.; artist pub. ednl. exhibits. Mem. Idaho Civic Symphony Bd.; chairperson pub. rels. Unitarian Ch. Rochester, 1991—; bd. dirs. Gift of Life Transplant Ho., Rochester, 1996, Rochester Orch. and Chorale, 1996, Rochester Music Guild, 2007. Recipient Profl. citation, Libr. Congress, 1976, 1st pl. best trucking ad, Overdrive Mag., 1990. Mem.: Sierra Club (nat. agrl. com. 2003—). Home and Office: 13020 241st Ave Harmony MN 55939 Home Phone: 507-937-3142. Personal E-mail: jlweb@mleaf.net.

WEBSTER, JOHN CROSBY BROWN, minister, educator; b. NYC, July 14, 1935; s. Leslie Tillotson and Emily Johnston (deForest) Webster; m. Ellen Low Purdy (div.); children: Elizabeth Low Webster Shillington, Marilyn White; m. Penelope Stearns, Jan. 3, 1988. BA, Amherst Coll., Mass., 1957; MDiv, Union Theol. Sem., NYC, 1960; MA, Lucknow U., India, 1962; PhD, U. Pa., Phila., 1971. Ordained minister Presbyn. Ch. Supply pastor La Bagh Meth. Ch., Lucknow, 1960—62; lectr. Baring Union Christian Coll., Batala, India, 1963—68, 1971—76; dir. Christian Inst. Sikh Studies, Batala, 1971—76; asst. prof., prof. United Theol. Coll., Bangalore, India, 1977—81; vis. prof. Pitts. Theol. Sem., 1981—83; pastor Crossroads Presbyn. Ch., Waterford, Conn., 1984—94; diaconal worker in India Presbyn. Ch. USA, Louisville, 1994—2001; ret., 2001. Lectr. in ecumenics Union Theol. Sem., 1985—; vice moderator Presbytery So. New England, Presbyn. Ch. (USA), 2003—04, moderator, 2004—05. Editor: The Study of History and College History Teaching, 1965, History for College Students, 1966, History and Contemporary India, 1971, Popular Religion in the Punjab Today, 1974; author: The Christian Community and Change in Nineteenth Century North India, 1976, An Introduction to History, 1977, 2d edit., 1981, The Nirankari Sikhs, 1979, The Dalit Christians: A History, 1992, 2d edit., 1994, Hindi edit., 2004, 3rd edit, 2009, The Pastor to Dalits, 1995, Studying History, 1997, Religion and Dalit Liberation: An Examination of Perspectives, 1999, 2d edit., 2002, A Social History of Christianity: Northwest India since 1800, 2007; co-author: From Role to Identity: Dalit Christian Women in Transition, 1997; co-editor: Local Dalit Christian History, 2002; editor: Bangalore Theol. Forum, 1977—81, Dalit Internat. Newsletter, 1996—2006. Bd. dirs. Drop-In Learning Ctr., New London, Conn., 1985—91, pres., 1990—91; bd. dirs. Habitat for Humanity Southeastern Conn., 1986—92, Union Theol. Sem., 1989—; mem. Waterford Housing Partnership, 1990—93; bd. dirs. Southeastern Conn. AIDS Project/Alliance for Living, New London, 1993—98, Opportunities Industrialization Ctr. New London County, 2004—; bd. mgrs. Am. Bapt. Hist. Soc., Valley Forge, Pa., 2005—. Recipient Human Rights award, Dalit Liberation Edn. Trust, Chennai, India, 1997; travel grantee, Am. Coun. Learned Socs., NEH, 1981. Mem.: Assn. Profs. Mission (v.p. 1991—92, pres. 1992—93), Assn. Presbyterians in Cross-Cultural Mission (pres. 1984—94). Democrat. Avocations: tennis, hiking.

WEBSTER, JOHN GOODWIN, biomedical engineering educator, researcher; b. Plainfield, NJ, May 27, 1932; s. Franklin Folger and Emily Sykes (Boody) W.; m. Nancy Egan, Dec. 27, 1954; children: Paul, Robin, Mark, Lark BEE, Cornell U., 1953; MSEE, U. Rochester, 1965, PhD, 1967. Engr. North American Aviation, Downey, Calif., 1954-55; engr. Boeing Airplane Co., Seattle, 1955-59, Radiation Inc., Melbourne, Fla., 1959-61; staff engr. Mitre Corp., Bedford, Mass., 1961-62, IBM Corp., Kingston, NY, 1962-63; asst. prof. elec. engring. U. Wis., Madison, 1967-70, assoc. prof. elec. engring., 1970-73, prof. elec. and computer engring., 1973-99, prof. biomed. engring., 1999—2001, prof. emeritus biomed. engring., 2001—. Author: (with others) Medicine and Clinical Engineering, 1977, Sensors and Signal Conditioning, 1991, 2d edit., 2001, Analog Signal Processing, 1999; editor: Medical Instrumentation: Application and Design, 4th edit., 2009, Clinical Engineering: Principles and Practices, 1979, Design of Microcomputer-Based Medical Instrumentation, 1981, Therapeutic Medical Devices: Application and Design, 1982; Electronic Devices for Rehabilitation, 1985; Interfacing Sensors to the IBM-PC, 1988, Encyclopedia of Medical Devices and Instrumentation, 2d edit., 2006, Tactile Sensors for Robotics and Medicine, 1988, Electrical Impedance Tomography, 1990, Teaching Design in Electrical Engineering, 1990, Prevention of Pressure Sores, 1991, Design of Cardiac Pacemakers, 1995, Design of Pulse Oximeters, 1997, The Measurement Instrumentation, and Sensors Handbook, 1999, Encyclopedia of Electrical and Electronics Engineering, 1999, Mechanical Variables Measurement, 2000, Minimally Invasive Medical Technology, 2001, Electrical Measurement, Signal Processing and Displays, 2004, Bioinstrumentation, 2004. Recipient Rsch. Career Devel. award NIH, 1971-76; NIH fellow, 1963-67; recipient Western Electric Fund award Am. Soc. Engring. Edn., 1978, Best Reference Work award, 1999, Theo C. Pilkington Outstanding Educator award, 1994. Fellow IEEE (3d Millennium medal 2000, IEEE-EMBS Career achievement award 2001), Am. Inst. Med. and Biol. Engring., Inst. Physics, Instrument Soc. Am. (Donald P. Eckman Edn. award 1974), Assn. for Advancement Med. Instrumentation (Found. Laufman-Greatbatch prize 1996). Democrat. Unitarian Universalist. Office: Univ Wis Dept Biomed Engring 1550 Engineering Dr Madison WI 53706-1609 Home Phone: 608-233-8410; Office Phone: 608-263-1574. Business E-Mail: webster@engr.wisc.edu.

WEBSTER, LESLIE TILLOTSON, JR., pharmacologist, educator; b. NYC, Mar. 31, 1926; s. Leslie Tillotson and Emily (de Forest) W.; m. Alice Katharine Holland, June 24, 1955; children: Katharine White, Susan Holland Webster Van Drie, Leslie Tillotson III, Romi Anne. BA, Amherst Coll., 1947, Sc.D. (hon.), 1982; student, Union Coll., 1944; MD, Harvard U., 1948. Diplomate: Am. Bd. Internal Medicine. Rotating intern Cleve. City Hosp., 1948-49, jr. asst. resident in medicine, 1949-50; asst. resident medicine Bellevue Hosp., NYC, 1952-53; research fellow medicine Harvard and Boston City Hosp. Thorndike Meml. Lab., 1953-55; from demonstrator to instr. medicine Sch. of Medicine Western Res. U., 1955-60; research assoc. to sr. instr. biochemistry Case Western Res. U. Sch. Medicine, 1957—60, asst. prof. medicine, 1960-70, asst. prof. biochemistry, 1960-65, asst. prof. pharmacology, 1965-67, assoc. prof., 1967—70, prof. pharmacology, 1976-92, chmn. pharmacology dept., 1976-91, prof. medicine, 1980-86, prof. emeritus pharmacology dept., 1992—2007, cons., pharmacology dept., 2007—; rsch. prof. pediat., divsn. pediat. pharmacology and critical care Rainbow Babies and Children's Hosp., Case Western Res. U. Sch. Medicine, 1992—2006, cons. dept. pharmacology, 2007—. Prof., chmn. pharmacology dept. Northwestern U. Med. and Dental Sch., 1970—76; dir. med. scientist tng. program Case Western Res. U. Sch. Medicine, 1979—92; mem. gastroenterology nutritional tng. grants com. NIAMD, NIH, 1965—69; mem. sci. working group on schistosomiasis WHO, 1977—83, chmn. subsect. on chemotherapy biochemistry, 1977—83; mem. exec. com. Gt. Neglected Diseases Network, Rockefeller Found., 1978—86; mem. cellular and molecular basis of disease rev. com. NIGMS, NIH, 1984—88; cons. World Bank, Laos, 2003. Contbr. articles to sci. jour. Served to lt. med. corps. USNR, 1950-52. Russell M. Wilder fellow Nat. Vitamin Found., 1956-59; Sr. USPHS Research fellow, 1959-61; USPHS Rsch. Career Devel. awardee, 1961-69; Macy faculty scholar, 1980-81. Mem. ACP (life), Central Soc. Clin. Rsch. Coalition (emeritus), Am. Soc. Clin. Investigation (emeritus), Am. Soc. Biochemistry and Molecular Biology (emeritus), Assn. Med. Sch. Pharmacology (emeritus), Am. Soc. Pharmacology and Exptl. Therapeutics (emeritus), Alpha Omega Alpha (hon.). Home: 12546 Cedar Rd No 4 Cleveland Heights OH 44106-3294 Office: Dept Pharmacology Case Western Res Univ 10900 Euclid Ave Cleveland OH 44106-4965 Office Phone: 216-368-0850. Business E-Mail: ltw2@case.edu.

WEBSTER, MURRAY ALEXANDER, JR., sociologist, educator; b. Manila, Philippines, Dec. 10, 1941; s. M.A. and Patricia (Morse) W. AB, Stanford U., 1963, MA, 1966, PhD, 1968. Asst. prof. social rels. Johns Hopkins U., Balt., 1968-74, assoc. prof., 1974-76; prof. sociology, adj. prof. psychology U. S.C., Columbia, 1976-86; vis. prof. sociology Stanford U., 1981-82, 85, 88-89; sr. lectr. San Jose State U., 1987-89; dir. sociology program NSF, 1989-91,99-2000; prof. sociology U. N.C., Charlotte, 1993—. Author (with Barbara Sobieszek): Soruces of Self-Evaluation, 1974; author: Actions and Actors, 1975; author: (with Martha Foschi) Status Generalization: New Theory and Research, 1988; author: (with Jane Sell) Laboratory Experiments in the Social Sciences, 2007. Recipient First Citizens Bank Scholars award, 2003; NIH fellow, 1966-68; grantee NSF, Nat. Inst. Edn. Mem.: Internat. Sociol. Assn., Sociol. Rsch. Assn., So. Sociol. Soc., Am. Sociol. Assn. Office: Univ NC Dept Sociology Charlotte NC 28223 Office Phone: 704-687-4079. Business E-Mail: mawebste@uncc.edu.

WEBSTER, NORMAN ERIC, journalist, foundation administrator; b. Summerside, PEI, Can., June 4, 1941; s. Eric and Elizabeth (Paterson) W.; m. Pat Roop, 1966; children: David, Andrew, Derek, Gillian, Hilary. BA, Bishop's U., Que., Can.; MA, St. John's Coll., Oxford, Eng. Corr. Globe and Mail, Que. and Ottawa, Ont., Canada; editor Globe Mag., Toronto, Ont.; corr. Globe and Mail, Peking, China, 1969-71, columnist Ont. affairs Toronto, European corr. London, editor-in-chief Toronto, 1983-89, Montreal (Que.) Gazette, 1989-93; pres. R. Howard Webster Found., Montreal, 1993—. Chancellor U. P.E.I., 1996-2005; chmn. North-South Inst., Ottawa, 1998-2000; bd. dirs. Internat. Press Inst., Vienna, Montreal Children's Hosp. Found., McGill U. Health Ctr. Found., Asia Pacific Found. Can., Commonwealth Journalists Assn., Can. Inst. for Advanced Rsch., Bishop's U., Michener Found. Recipient Nat. Newspaper award for Peking corr., 1971, for editl. writing, 1988; Can. Journalism Found. Lifetime Achievement award; Rhodes scholar; mem. Order of Can. Office: R Howard Webster Found Ste 2912 1155 Rene Levesque Blvd W Montreal PQ Canada H3B 2L5 Office Phone: 514-866-2424.

WEBSTER, OWEN WRIGHT, chemist; b. Devils Lake, ND, Mar. 25, 1929; s. Daniel Milton and Maude May (Wright) W.; m. Lillian Brostek; children: Ellen, Anne, John, James, Mary. BS in Chemistry, N.D. U., 1951, DSc (hon.), 1986; PhD in Chemistry, Pa. State U., 1955. Research chemist E.I. Du Pont de Nemours, Wilmington, Del., 1955-74, group leader, 1974-79, research supr., 1979-84, research leader, 1984-95, Du Pont fellow, 1986-95; ret., 1995. Adj. prof. dept. chemistry U. Ala., 2003. Patentee in field; contbr. articles to profl. jours. Recipient Chem. Pioneer award Am. Inst. Chemists, 1995. Fellow AAAS, Am. Chem. Soc. (chmn. Del. sect. 1975-76, Excellence in Resch. award 1987, Applied Polymer Sci. award 1993); mem. Sigma Xi. Republican. Roman Catholic. Avocations: chess, bridge, golf. Home Phone: 610-361-0933. Personal E-mail: owwebster@aol.com.

WEBSTER, PETER DAVID, judge; b. Framingham, Mass., Feb. 12, 1949; s. Waldo John and Helen Anne (Borovek) W.; m. Michele Page Hernandez, Jan. 13, 1989; 1 stepchild, Alana Perryman. BS, Georgetown U., 1971; JD, Duke U., 1974; LLM, U. Va., 1995. Bar: Fla. 1974, US Dist. Ct. (mid. dist.) Fla. 1975, US Ct. Appeals (5th cir.) 1975, US Dist. Ct. (so. dist.) Fla. 1977, US Dist. Ct. (no. dist.) Fla. 1978, US Supreme Ct. 1978, US Ct. Appeals (11th cir.) 1981. Law clk. U.S. Dist. Judge, Jacksonville, Fla., 1974-75; assoc. Bedell, Bedell, Dittmar, Smith & Zehmer, Jacksonville, 1975-78; ptnr. Bedell, Bedell, Dittmar & Zehmer, Jacksonville, 1978-85; cir. judge State Fla., Jacksonville, 1986-91; judge Dist. Ct. of Appeal, First Dist., State of Fla., Tallahassee, 1991—. Master of bench Chester Bedell Am. Inn Ct., 1988-91, Tallahassee Am. Inn Ct., 1992-2002, pres. 1999-2000; master of bench E. Robert Williams Am. Inn Ct., 2007, 1st Dist. Appellate Am. Inn. Ct., 2008-; adj. prof. Fla. Coastal Sch. Law, 1997-2006; Fla. Supreme Ct.: mem. com. standard jury instrns. civil cases, 1979-2001, chmn. 1999-2000; mem. com. trial ct. info. sys., 1986-91; mem. com. confidentiality records jud. br., 1993-95; mem. task force on complex litig., 2006-08, mem. Fla. Bd. of Bar Examiners Testing Comm., 2008-09; mem. jud. mgmt. coun. Fla., 2006-08; chmn. com. jud. evaluations, 2006-07. Contbg. author: Sanctions: Rule 11 and Other Powers, 1986, Florida Criminal Rules and Practice Manual, 1990. Bd. dirs. Jacksonville Area Legal Aid, Inc., 1978-82, River Region Human Svcs., Inc., Jacksonville, 1986-88; mem. adv. bd. P.A.C.E. Ctr. for Girls, Inc., Jacksonville, 1986-91; com. mem. Shawnee dist. North Fla. coun. Boy Scouts Am., 1974-78; mem. delinquency task force Mayor's Commn. on Children and Youth, City of Jacksonville, 1988-91; officer, mem. exec. bd. Suwanee River Area coun. Boy Scouts, 1991-96. Mem. Am. Judicature Soc. (bd. dirs. 2002—, sec. 2008-), Fla. Conf. Appellate Judges, Jacksonville Bar Assn., Tallahassee Bar Assn., Phi Beta Kappa, Phi Alpha Theta, Phi Eta Sigma, Am. Inns Ct. Found. (trustee 2009-). Office: 1st Dist Ct Appeal 301 Martin Luther King Blvd Tallahassee FL 32399-1850 Home Phone: 850-668-0079; Office Phone: 850-487-1000.

WEBSTER, ROBERT G., virologist, educator; b. Balclutha, New Zealand, July 5, 1932; BSc, Otago U., New Zealand, 1955, MSc, 1957; PhD, Australian Nat. U., Canberra, 1962. Virologist New Zealand Dept. Agr., 1958—59; postdoctoral fellow (Fulbright scholar) dept. epidemiology U. Mich. Sch. Pub. Health, Ann Arbor, Mich., 1962—63; rsch. fellow dept. microbiol. Australian Nat. U. John Curtain Med. Sch., Canberra, 1964—66, fellow dept. microbiol., 1966—67; assoc. prof. dept. microbiol. U. Tenn. Med. Units, Memphis, 1968—74; prof. dept. microbiol. U. Tenn. Ctr. Health Scis., Memphis, 1974—78, prof. depts. microbiol. and immunology, 1978—85; Rose Marie Thomas chair dept. virology and molecular biology St. Jude Children's Rsch. Hosp., Memphis, 1988—. Assoc. mem. lab. immunology St. Jude Children's Rsch. Hosp., Memphis, 1968—69, mem. labs. virology and immunology, 1969—75, mem. divsn. virology, 1975—78, mem. depts. virology and molecular biology, 1978—88; Fogarty internat. sr. fellow Nat. Inst. Med. Rsch., Med. Rsch. Coun., London, 1978—79; dir. WHO Collaborating Ctr. Studies on the Ecology of Influenza Viruses in Lower Animals and Birds. Contbr. articles to sci. jours. Recipient Bristol-Meyers Squibb award, 2002, Disting. Biotechnologist of Yr. award, New Zealand Biotechnology Assn., 2006; named a Rsch. Leader within Sci. Am. 50, 2005. Fellow: Royal Soc. Medicine, Royal Soc., London, Royal Soc., New Zealand (hon.); mem.: AAAS, Am. Soc. Virology, Am. Soc. Microbiol., NAS. Achievements include research in the emergence and control of influenza; viral immunology; discovery of link between human and avian influenza viruses. Office: St Jude Childrens Rsch Hosp 332 N Lauderdale St Memphis TN 38105-2794 Office Phone: 901-495-3400. E-mail: robert.webster@stjude.org.

WEBSTER, ROBERT KENLY, lawyer; b. NYC, May 16, 1933; s. Francis Kenly and Mary Louise (Rathbone) W.; m. Sally Irene Stratton, Apr. 16, 1960; children: Timothy Kenly, Kimberly Anne. AB, Princeton U., 1955; LLB, U. Va., 1960. Assoc. Cadwalader, Wickersham & Taft, NYC, 1960-65; asst. U.S. atty. Dept. of Justice, Washington, 1965-68; prin. dep. gen. counsel Dept. of Army, Washington, 1968-73; ptnr. Kennedy & Webster, Washington, 1973-81, Shaw, Pittman, Potts & Trowbridge, Washington, 1981-98; sole practice Washington, 1999—. Spl. investigator Iran FMS program Sec. of Def., Washington, 1977; advisor conflict of interest issues Watergate defendants Dept. Justice, Washington, 1977. Gen. counsel Princeton (N.J.) Project 55, Inc., 1989—. Lt. j.g. USN, 1955—57. Mem. ABA, ATLA, Fed. Bar Assn., Met. Club. Avocations: pottery, reading, travel, tennis.

WEBSTER, STEPHEN BURTIS, dermatologist, educator; b. Chgo., Dec. 3, 1935; s. James Randolph Webster and Ruth Marion (Burtis) Holmes; m. Katherine Griffith Webster, Apr. 4, 1959; children: David Randolph, Margaret Elizabeth, James Lucian. BS, Northwestern U., 1957, MD, 1960. Diplomate Am. Bd. Dermatology (bd. dirs. 1992—, v.p. 1997-98, pres.). Intern Colo. Gen. Hosp., Denver, 1960-61; resident Walter Reed Gen. Hosp., Washington, 1962-65; staff physician Henry Ford Hosp., Detroit, 1969-71, Gundersen Lutheran Med. Ctr., La Crosse, 1971—; assoc. clin. prof. U. Wis., Madison, 1976—; clin. prof. U. Minn., Mpls., 1978—. Lt. col. U.S. Army, 1962-69. Fellow Am. Acad. Dermatology (sec.-treas. 1985-88, pres. 1991); mem. AMA, Am. Dermatol. Assn. (pres. 1996-97), Am. Bd. Dermatology (v.p. 1997-98, pres. 1999-2000, assoc. exec. dir. 2001—08, asst. exec. dir., 2009-), Wis. Med. Soc., La Crosse County Med. Soc., Soc. Investigative Dermatology, Alpha Omega Alpha. Republican. Congregationalist. Avocations: bagpipes, model trains. Home: N2062 Wedgewood Dr E La Crosse WI 54601-7175 Office: Gundersen Clinic Ltd 1836 South Ave La Crosse WI 54601-5494 Business E-Mail: sbwebste@gundluth.org.

WEBSTER, TASHONNA, health services researcher; b. NYC, Dec. 9, 1976; d. Gregory and Lydia Webster; 1 child, Kai Hosein. BS, Rensselaer Poly. Inst., NY, 1998; MPH, SUNY, Albany, 2000; MS, Columbia U., NY, 2006. Health educator Settlement Health, NYC, 2000—01; rsch. assoc. Yale U., New Haven, 2001—07, 2009—, rsch. cons., 2007—. Recipient Norward C. Davis award, Rensselaer Poly. Inst., 1998, Academic Merit award, 1998; fellowship, LEND, 2009, Health Edn. fellowship, 2006. Office: Yale Univ 2 Church St S New Haven CT 06520 Office Fax: 203-764-9078. Business E-Mail: tashonna.webster@yale.edu.

WEBSTER, THOMAS JAY, engineering educator; b. Phila., Nov. 5, 1971; s. Thomas and Diane Webster; m. Karen Marie Haberstroh, July 28, 2001; children: Mia Rose, Zoe Lynne, Ava Belle. PhD, Rensselaer, Troy, NY, 2000. Eit, NY, 1997. Assoc. prof. Brown U., Providence, 2006—; founder Nanovis, Inc., West Lafayette, Ind., 2006—08, Nanorose, Inc., Providence, 2008. Author: (novels) Cancer Nanotechnology, Nanotechnology for the Regenerating Hard and Soft Tissues, Safety of Nanoparticles. Mem. Soc. Bio-Materials, 2005—08, Biomed. Engring. Soc., 2007—08. Recipient Career award, Coulter Found., Young Investigator award, Biomed. Engring. Soc., Purdue U. Fellow: Am. Acad. Nanomedicine. Achievements include patents for nanotechnology to regeneration tissue. Home: 7 Terrace Dr Barrington RI 02806 Office: Brown Univ 184 Hope St Providence RI 02912-9127 Office Fax: 401-863-9107. Business E-Mail: thomas_webster@brown.edu.

WEBSTER, WILLIAM G., JR., career military officer; b. Baton Rouge, July 3, 1951; BS, U.S. Mil. Acad., 1974. Commd. 2d lt. U.S. Army, 1974, advanced through grades to lt. gen., 2007, tank co. comdr. Fort Polk, La., 1974—78, ops. and plans officer Seventh Army Combined Arms Tng. Ctr., 1979—82, ops. officer 3-64 Armor, 3d Inf. Divsn. Germany, 1979—82, asst. G-3 and brigade ops. officer 24th Inf. Divsn. Ft. Stewart, Ga., 1984—87, joint staff War Plans Divsn. Washington, 1988—91, comdr. 3d bn., 77th armor in 4th inf. divsn., 1991-93; sr. armor observer contr. Cobra Team Nat. Tng. Ctr., Ft. Irwin, Calif., 1993-94; comdr. 1st brigade, 1st cavalry divsn. Ft. Hood, 1995-97; asst. divsn. comdr. 3d Inf. Divsn., Ft. Stewart, Ga., 1997-98; comdr. Ft. Irwin and Nat. Tng. Ctr., 1998—2000; deployed Ops. Desert Thunder U.S. Army, 1998, Army's dir. tng. Office Dep. Chief of Staff G-3, 2000—01, dep. J-3 U.S. Ctrl. Command Operation Enduring Freedom Afghanistan, 2001—02, dep. comdg. gen. for ops. Third U.S. Army, Combined Forces Land Component Command, Operation Iraqi Freedom Kuwait, 2002—03, Iraq, 2002—03, comdg. gen. 3d Inf. Divsn. Ft. Stewart and Hunter Army Airfield, 2003—06; comdr. Multi-Nat. Divsn. Baghdad, Task Force Baghdad, 2005—06; dir. ops. US No. Command, 2006—07, dep. comdr., 2007—; vice comdr. US Element Am. Aerospace Def. Command (NORAD), Peterson AFB, Colo., 2007—. Decorated Legion of Merit with 4 oak leaf clusters, Air Assault badge, Parachutist badge, Def. Superior Svc. medal, Armed Forces Expeditionary medal; recipient Bronze Star. Office: US No Command 250 Vandenburg Ste B016 Peterson AFB CO 80914

WEBSTER, WILLIAM HEDGCOCK, lawyer, federal agency administrator; b. St. Louis, Mar. 6, 1924; s. Thomas M. and Katherine (Hedgcock) W.; m. Drusilla Lane, May 5, 1950 (dec. 1984); children: Drusilla Lane Busch, William Hedgcock, Katherine Hagee Roessle; m. Lynda Clugston, Oct. 20, 1990. AB, Amherst Coll., 1947; JD, Washington U., 1949; LLD (hon.), Amherst Coll., 1975, Washington U., 1978, William Wood Coll., 1978, DePauw U., 1978, Drury Coll., Columbia Coll., U. Dayton, U. Notre Dame, Center Coll., Dickinson Coll., U. Miami, DePaul U., Am. U., John Jay Coll., Westminster Coll., Georgetown U., Rockhurst Coll., Pepperdine U. Bar: Mo. 1949, US Supreme Ct. 1960, DC 1981. With Armstrong, Teasdale, Kramer & Vaughan (and predecessors), St. Louis, 1949-50, 52-59, 61-70; US atty. (ea. dist.) Mo US Dept. Justice, 1960-61; judge US Dist. Ct. (ea. dist. Mo.), 1971-73, US Ct. Appeals (8th cir.), 1973-78; dir. FBI, 1978-87, CIA, 1987-91; sr. ptnr. Milbank, Tweed, Hadley & McCloy, LLP, Washington, 1991—2005, consulting ptnr., 2005—; chair Homeland Security Adv. Coun. US Dept. Homeland Security, 2006—. Mem. Mo. Bd. Law Examiners, 1964-69, mem. adv. com. on criminal rules, 1971-78, mem. ct. adminstrs. com., 1975-78; bd. dirs. Anheuser-Busch Cos., Maritz Inc., Pinkertons Inc., T.L.C. Beatrice Internat. Holdings Inc., Nextwave, Inc., Regulatory DataCorp Internat.; mem. adv. bd., Diligence LLC; chmn. Pub. Co. Acctg. Oversight Bd., 2002. Trustee Washington U., 1974; bd. dirs. Atlantic Coun., Nat. Legal Ctr. Pub. Interest, Nat. Symphony Assn., Coun. Fgn. Rels.; bd. dirs., chmn. Police Found.; hon. life pres. Big Bros. Orgn. St. Louis; bd. dirs. Big Bros. Am., 1966, hon. bd. dirs., 1978. Lt. USN, 1943—46, WWII, lt. USN, 1950—52, Korean War. Recipient Disting. Alumnus award Washington U., 1977, Stein award Fordham U., Law award U. Va., Theodore Roosevelt award for Excellence in Pub. Svc., Internat. Platform Assn., 1983, Jefferson award for the Greatest Pub. Svc. by an Elected or Apptd. Ofcl., 1984, Freedoms Found. Nat. Svc. medal, 1985, Disting. Intelligence medal, 1991, Presdl. Medal of Freedom, 1991, Nat. Security medal, 1991, Silver Buffalo award Boy Scouts Am., Disting. Svc. award, Am. Legion, Justice award, Am. Judicature Soc., 2001, Am. Bar Assn. medal, 2002; named Father of Yr., 1986, Man of Yr., St. Louis Globe Dem., 1980. Fellow Am. Bar Found., Am. Coll. Trial Lawyers (hon.); mem. ABA (chmn. sect. on corp. banking and bus. law 1977-78), FBA, Mo. Bar Assn., St. Louis Bar Assn., Am. Law Inst. (mem. coun. 1978), Wash. U. Alumni Fedn. (pres. 1956-57), Rotary, St. Louis Country Club, Nooday Club (St. Louis), Met. Club, Chevy Chase Club, Alfalfa Club, St. Alban's Tennis Club, Order of the Coif, Psi Upsilon, Delta Sigma Rho, Phi Delta Phi. Office: Milbank Tweed Hadley & McCloy LLP 1850 K St NW Ste 1100 Washington DC 20006-2213 also: US Dept Homeland Security 12th & C St SW Washington DC 20024 Office Phone: 202-835-7500. E-mail: wwebster@milbank.com.*

WEBSTER STRATTON, CAROLYN HINDE, psychology professor; b. Toronto, Ontario, Can., Oct. 7, 1947; d. Leonard and Mary Webster; m. John Russell Stratton, June 10, 1972; children: Seth Webster Stratton, Anna Allinson Webster-Stratton. PhD, U. Wash., Seattle, 1980. Cert. psychologist and nurse Wash., 1981. Lectr. Yale U., New Haven, 1972—73; prof. U. Wash., Seattle, 1976—, cons. spkr., 1990—2008. Cons. Incredible Years, Seattle, 1997—. Contbr. articles to profl. jours. (APA Rsch. Scientist award, 2001). Rsch. grants, NIH, 1984—2008. Achievements include research in inertventions for reducing childhood aggression and promoting social competence. Office: Univ Wash 1107 NE 45th Ste 304 Seattle WA 98195

WECHSLER, GIL, lighting designer; b. NYC, Feb. 5, 1942; s. Arnold J. and Miriam (Steinberg) W. Student, Rensselaer Poly. Inst., Troy, NY, 1958—61; BS, NYU, NYC, 1964; MFA, Yale U., New Haven, 1967. Lighting designer Harkness Ballet, NYC, 1967—69, Pa. Ballet, Phila., 1969—70, Stratford Shakespeare Festival, Ont., Canada, 1969—78, 1997—2006, Guthrie Theatre, Mpls., 1971, Lyric Opera, Chgo., 1972—76, Met. Opera, NYC, 1976—96, Equus, Stratford Shakespeare Festival, 1997, Macbeth, Stratford Festival, 2004, Coriolanus, Stratford Festival, 2006. Tchr. NYU, Rensselaer Poly. Inst., 1998; guest lectr. Teatro Colon, Buenos Aires, 1985, Yale U., 1980, Broadway Lighting Designers, 1994—98; guest lighting designer Am. Ballet Theatre, NYC, 1980, Paris Opera, 1983, Chatelet Theatre, Paris, 1991; dean's adv. coun. Rensselaer Poly. Inst. Cons. editor Opera Quar., 1983-90. Recipient Emmy award nominations, Illuminating Engring. Soc., United Scenic Artists. Avocations: collecting ocean liner memorabilia, gardening, kayaking. Home: PO Box 283 Upper Black Eddy PA 18972 E-mail: gillights@aol.com.

WECHSLER, MARY HEYRMAN, lawyer; b. Green Bay, Wis., Jan. 8, 1948; d. Donald Hubert and Helen (Polcyn) Heyrman; m. Roger Wechsler, Aug. 1971 (div. 1977); 1 child, Risa Heyrman; m. David Jay Sellinger, Aug. 15, 1981; 1 stepchild, Kirk Benjamin; 1 child, Michael Paul. Student, U. Chgo., 1966-67, 68-69; BA, U. Wash., Seattle, 1971; JD cum laude, U. Puget Sound, Tacoma, Wash., 1979. Bar: Wash. 1979. Assoc. Law Offices Ann Johnson, Seattle, 1979-81; ptnr. Johnson, Wechsler, Thompson, Seattle, 1981-83; pvt. practice Seattle, 1984-87; ptnr. Mussehl, Rosenberg et al, Seattle, 1987-88, Wechsler, Becker LLP, Seattle, 1988—. Mem. Bd. Ct. Edn., 1998—2007, sec., 2003—05, vice chair, 2006—07; bd. dirs. U. Wash. Law Sch. Child Advocacy Clinic, 1996—99; mem. Wash. State Commn. on Domestic Rels., 1996—97, 1999—2004; chair edn. com. Access to Justice Bd., 1996—99, mem. pub. trust and confidence com., 2000—05; chair Wash. State Coalition on Jud. Selection, 2005—07; mem. Jud. Coll. Bd. Trustees, 2005—; moderator Wash. State Summit on Jud. Independence and Jud. Selection, 2005; presenter in field. Author: Family Law in Washington, 1987, rev. edit., 1988, Marriage and Separation, Divorce and Your Rights, 1994; contbr. articles to legal publs. Mem. Wash. State Ethics Adv. Com., 1992-95; bd. dirs. Seattle LWV, 1991-92. Fellow Am. Acad. Matrimonial Lawyers (Wash. state chpt., sec.-treas. 1996, v.p. 1997-98, pres. 1999-2000, nat. arbitration com. 1999-2000, nat. interdisciplinary com. 1999-2000, nat. admissions procedure com. 2000-02, nat. long range planning com. 2003-05, chair 2003—05, nat. bylaws com. 2005, nat. budget com. 2004-09); mem. ABA (chmn. membership Wash. state 1987-88), Wash. State Bar Assn. (exec. com. family law sect. 1985-91, chair family law sect. 1988-89, Family Law Sect. Outstanding Atty. of Yr. 1988), profl. devel. com. 2002-03, media project com. 2001, ct. improvement com. 1998-2000, legs. com. 1991-96, disciplinary hearing officer 1998—), Wash. Women Lawyers, King County Bar Assn. (legis. com. 1985-2000, vice-chair 1990-91, chair family law sect. 1986-87, chair domestic violence com. 1986-87, trustee 1988-90, policy planning com. 1991-92, 2d v.p. 1992-93, 1st v.p. 1993-94, long-range planning com. 1998-99, awards com. 1997-99, nominations com. 2003, co-chair Bench-Bar Conf. 2003, pres. 1994-95, Outstanding Atty. award 1999), Nat. Conf. of Bar Pres., King County Bar Found. (trustee 1997-2000), Am. Judicature Soc. (v.p. Washington chpt. 2000-03, pres. 2003-05, 2008-09, nat. bd. dirs. 2006-09, membership com. 2007-09, fin. com. mem. 2007-09, gov. com. 2008-09), Seattle U. Law Sch. Alumni Bd. Office: Wechsler Becker LLP Ste 4550 701 5th Ave Seattle WA 98104-7097 Home Phone: 206-789-3657; Office Phone: 206-624-4900. Business E-Mail: mhwechsler@wechslerbecker.com.

WECHSLER, TONI, healthcare educator, writer; MPH, U. Calif., Los Angeles, 1985. Founder Fertility Awareness Counseling & Training Seminars (FACTS), 1986—. Author: Taking Charge of your Fertility, Cycle Savvy: The Smart Teen's Guide to the Mysteries of Her Body. Office: Ovusoft LLC 120 W Queens Way Ste 202 Hampton VA 23669 Office Phone: 757-722-0991, 757-722-7998. E-mail: info@ovusoft.com.*

WECHTER, CLARI ANN, manufacturing executive; b. Chgo., June 1, 1953; d. Norman Robert and Harriet Beverly (Golub) W.; m. Gordon Jay Siegel, Feb. 10, 1980; 1 child, Alix Jessica. BA, U. Ariz., 1975; BE, Loyola U., Chgo., 1977. Cert. tchr., Ill. Saleswoman, v.p. sales Federated Paint Mfg. Co., Chgo., 1979—. Republican. Jewish. Avocation: travel. Home: 25 E Cedar St Chicago IL 60611-1109 Office: Federated Paint and Pioneer Powder Mfg Co 1521 N 31st Ave Melrose Park IL 60160 Home Phone: 312-951-5991; Office Phone: 708-345-4848 x622.

WECHTLER, STEPHEN ROBERT, library director; b. East Orange, NJ, Nov. 13, 1946; s. Robert and Mary Wechtler; m. Nancy K. Kennedy, June 26, 1976; children: Eric S., Susan R. BA in History, Seton Hall U., South Orange, NJ, 1970; MLS, U. RI, Kingston, 1974. Jr. libr. Ft. Lee Pub. Libr., NJ, 1974—77, sr. libr., 1977—79, asst. libr. dir., 1979—82; libr. dir. Tenafly Pub. Libr., NJ, 1982—. Contbr. book. Sec. Tenafly Rotary Club, 2005—08, pres., 2001—02. Recipient Walter Head award, Rotary Club, 2002. Mem.: Centennial Book Com. (chmn.), NJ. Libr. Assn., ALA. Avocations: travel, skiing, hiking. Home: 103 Ralph Ave Hillsdale NJ 07642 Office: Tenafly Pub Libr 100 Riveredge Rd Tenafly NJ 07670 Personal E-mail: wechtlersr@yahoo.com. Business E-Mail: wechtler@bccls.org.

WECKLER, NORA, retired psychology educator, psychotherapist; b. Toronto, Ont., Can., Feb. 16, 1915; d. Bernard and Alice Emily (Heslewood) Weckler; m. Joseph E. Weckler, Oct. 25, 1941 (dec. 1963); children: Linda Ann, David Alan. BA, U. Toronto, 1937, MA, 1938, PhD, 1941. Lic. psychologist Calif. Instr. psychology U. Md., Coll. Pk., 1942—44; rsch. assoc. U. Chgo., 1944—45; lectr. U. Southern Calif., LA, 1951—55; prof. to assoc. prof. LA State Coll., 1955—58; prof. Calif. State U., Northridge, 1958—85; pvt. practice psychotherapy LA, 1968—2007; adj. prof. Pepperdine U., 1986—88. Mem.: Calif. State Psychol. Assn., Western Psychol. Assn., Am. Psychol. Assn.

WEDDING, CHARLES RANDOLPH, architect; b. St. Petersburg, Fla., Nov. 16, 1934; s. Charles Reid and L. Marion (Whitaker) W.; m. Audrey Whitsel, Aug. 18, 1956 (div. Apr. 1979); children: Daryl L., Douglas R., Dorian B.; m. Vonnie Sue Hayes, June 22, 1984 (div. Dec. 1991); stepchildren: Stephanie W., Brian E.; m. June A. Free, Mar. 31, 1993; stepchildren: Gregory, Kristine. BArch, U. Fla., 1957. Registered arch., Fla., Ga., N.C., S.C., Del., Va., Tex., Ill., Ind., Kans., La., Mo., Okla., Tenn. Arch. in tng. Harvard & Jolly AIA, St. Petersburg, 1957-60; arch., prin., pres. Wedding & Assocs., St. Petersburg, 1960—. Mayor City of St. Petersburg, 1973-75; past chmn. Pinellas County Com. of 100, Bldg. Dept. Survey Team, City of St. Petersburg; trustee All Children's Hosp., 1968-70; sect. leader St. Petersburg United Fund, 1965-70; mem. city coun. Action Team for Pier Redevel., 1967-68; mem. exec. com. Goals for City of St. Petersburg, 1970-72; den leader Webelos, Boy Scouts Am., 1971-72; chmn., trustee Canterbury Sch. YMCA, 1968-72; mem. adv. com. Tomlinson Vocat. Sch., 1969-79; past trustee Mus. Fine Arts; past bd. dirs. Neighborly Ctr., Jr. Achievement Pinellas County; chair Downtown Partnership, 2001—, Mcpl. Pier Task Force, City of Petersburg, 2009-; vice chair Pinelles County Local PLanning Agy., 2009-. Served to 1st lt. U.S. Army, 1958-60. Fellow AIA (5 Silver Spike awards, Merit of Honor, Medal of Honor); mem. Am. Soc. Landscape Archs., St. Petersburg Assn. Archs. (past pres.), Fla. Assn. Archs. (8 Merit Design awards), St. Petersburg Yacht Club, Suncoasters Club. Republican. Episcopalian. Avocations: sailing, hunting, golf, tennis. Home: 6900 10th Ave N Saint Petersburg FL 33710-6152 Office: Wedding & Stephenson Archs Inc 300 1st Ave S Saint Petersburg FL 33701-4209 Office Phone: 727-821-6610. Business E-Mail: randy@weddingarchitects.com.

WEDDINGTON, ELIZABETH GARDNER (LIZ GARDNER), actress; b. NYC, Oct. 13, 1932; d. A. Adolph and Anne Mary (Gardner) Blank; m. George Lee Weddington, Jr., Oct. 23, 1965; 1 child, Georgiana Marie. Student, Moravian Sem. for Girls. Freelance writer NYC Tribune, others. Columnist polit. commentary, 1984—; appeared in over 300 TV commls., also TV and radio voice-overs. Mem. County Com., Conservative Party, N.Y.C., 1988-90, 94-96, 17th Precinct Comty. Coun., N.Y.C., 1974-96; rep. Yorkville Area Cath. Coun., N.Y.C., 1986-93. Recipient Mayor's Vol. Action Ctr. award, N.Y.C., 1981-82, Cert. Recognition N.Y.C. Dept. Police Dep. Commr. Community Affairs, 1981. Mem.: Nat. League Am. Pen Women, Am. Fedn. Radio and TV Artists, Screen Actors Guild, Hereditary Order Descendants of Loyalists and Patriots Am. Revolution, Friends of Va. Archives, N.Y. State Soc. Children Am. Revolution (sr. historian 1988—90, sr. 2d v.p. 1990—92), Colonial Dames Am. (N.Y. claims com. 1993—96, chpt. XXIX N.C. 1999—, courtesy mem. parent chpt.), Daus. Colonial Wars, United Daus. of Confederacy (pres. N.Y. divsn. 1988—90, nat. chmn. revision of gen. bylaws com. 1989—91, McMath Scholar gen. com. 1991—92, nat. chmn. gen. bylaws com. 1992—96, gen. chmn. radio and TV com. 1998—2000, mem. Mrs. Simon Baruch Univ. award com. 2000—02, chmn. chpt. bylaws com. 2002—04, gen. bylaws com. 2004—09), N.Y. State Soc. Dames of Ct. of Honor (pres. 1984—88), N.Y. State Soc. Daus. 1812, Nat. Soc. U.S. Daus. of 1812 (organizing pres. Pres. James Madison chpt. 360 1988—98), Nat. Soc. Children of the Am. Revolution - Fraunces Tavern Soc. (sr. pres. 1985—89), Nat. Soc. DAR (assoc.; corr. sec. 1992—94, Washington colonial chpt. 1996—99, Mary Washington Colonial chpt. 1996—, mem. Warren chpt. 1996—, treas. 2001—09, chmn. nat. def. com. 2001—09, Warren chpt., chmn. com. Mary Washington Colonial chpt.). Republican. Roman Catholic. Avocations: genealogy, military, opera, antiques, porcelains, English, Am. constl. and religious hist. Home and Office: 316 N Main St Warrenton NC 27589-1826 Office Phone: 252-257-4663. Business E-Mail: betsy1013@vance.net.

WEDDINGTON, SARAH RAGLE, lawyer, educator; b. Abilene, Tex., Feb. 5, 1945; d. Herbert Doyle and Lena Catherine Ragle. BS magna cum laude, McMurry Coll., 1965, PhD (hon.), 1979; JD, U. Tex., 1967; PhD (hon.), Hamilton Coll., 1979, Southwestern U., 1989, Austin Coll., 1993, Nova Southeastern U., 1999; PhD in Human Letters (hon.), Fitchburg State Coll., 2004. Bar: Tex. 1967, D.C. 1979, U.S. Dist. Ct. (we., no. and ea. dists.) Tex., U.S. Ct. Appeals (5th cir.), U.S. Supreme Ct. Pvt. practice law, Austin, Tex., 1967-77, 1985—; gen. counsel USDA, Washington, 1977-78; spl. asst. to Pres. The White House, Washington, 1978—79, asst. to Pres., 1979—81; chmn. Interdepartmental Task Force on Women, 1978-81; mem. Pres.'s Commn. on Exec. Exchange, 1981; Carl Hatch prof. law and pub. adminstrn. U. N.Mex., Albuquerque, 1982-83; dir. Tex. Office State-Fed. Rels., Austin, Washington, 1983-85; founder The Weddington Ctr., Austin. Vis. prof. govt. Wheaton Coll., Norton, Mass., 1981-83; sr. lectr. Tex. Woman's U., Denton, 1981-90, 93, U. Tex., Austin, 1986-1989, adj. assoc. prof. 1989-2001, adj. prof., 2001-. Author: A Question of Choice, 1992; contbr. articles to various mags.; contbg. editor Glamour mag., 1981-83. Mem. Tex. Ho. of Reps., 1973-77; named hon. chair San Francisco Bar Assn. Breast Cancer Hotline/Network, 2001, named hon. chair ann. benefit for Breast Cancer Rsch. Ctr., Austin, 2002, named lecture showcase presenter Nat. Assn. Campus Activities, 2003. Recipient Woman of Yr. award, Tex. Women's Polit. Caucus, 1973, Outstanding Young Am. Leaders, Time Mag., 1979, Leadership award, Ladies Home Jour., 1980, Spl. Recognition award, Esquire mag., 1984, Elizabeth (Betty) Boyer award, Equity Action League, 1992, Woman Who Dares award, Nat. Coun. Jewish Women, 1993, Woman of Distinction award, Nat. Conf. for Coll. Women Student Leaders, 1993, Colby award for Pub. Svc., Sigma Kappa, 1996, Hummingbird award, Leadership Am., 1998, Tallest Texan award, Houston Chronicle, 2000, Speaking Out for Justice award, AAUW Legal Advocacy Fund, 2001, AAUW Ednl. Found., 2001, Ally award, Possible Woman Leadership Conf., 2001, Sarah Weddington Leadership Conf. named in her honor, Tex. Woman's U., 2001, Humanitarian of Yr. award, Planned Parenthood, Tex., 2003, Courage award, Women Lawyers LA, 2004, Reproductive Equity award, Lilith Orgn., 2005, Knowledge is Power award, Tex. Women Lawyers, 2007, Margaret Brent Women Lawyers of Achievement award, ABA, 2008; named Lectr. of Yr., Nat. Assn. Coll. Activities, 1990, Tex. Woman of Century, Tex. Women's C. of C., 1999, Face of Century, San Antonio Express News, 1999, 2000, Outstanding Alumnus, McMurry U., 2004, Nat. Pub. Health Hero, U. Calif., Berkeley, 2005, Keynote Spkr., China's Women Fedn., U.S. Conf. on Women in Leadership, Beijing, 2004; named one of Most Influential Lawyers of the 20th Century, Tex. Lawyer, 2000. Mem. Tex. Bar Assn. Office: The Weddington Ctr 709 W 14th St Austin TX 78701-1707 Business E-Mail: sw@weddingtoncenter.com.*

WEDDINGTON, STACEY LEE, not-for-profit developer; m. Jerry Leon Weddington; 1 child, Alexander. Dir. ann. giving Casady Sch., Okla. City, 2000—03; dir. devel. Okla. City Nat. Meml. & Mus., 2003—. Youth educator St. Elijah Orthodox Ch., Okla. City, 2002—07. Mem.: Okla. Mus. Assn., Assn. Fundraising Profls. (dir. 2006—), Jr. League Okla. City. Avocations: travel, reading. Office: Oklahoma City Nat Meml & Mus 620 North Harvey Ave Oklahoma City OK 73102

WEDEL, VOLEEN, police official; b. July 1956; d. Marissa and James Betesch; m. Mario Wedel; 1 adopted child, Barbara children: Robert, Allison, Rita. BA in Criminal Justice, N. Mex. State U., 1978, MA, 1980. Police officer Las Cruces Police Dept., N.Mex., 1983—87, police detective N.Mex., 1988—90, police lt. N.Mex., 1990—99, police capt. N.Mex., 2000—07; pvt. protection cons. Meriks Protection Firm, Las Cruces, N.Mex., 2007—. TA criminal justice dept. N. Mex. State U., 1977—80; intern Las Cruces police dept., 1981—82. Vol. educator D.A.R.E., 2000—; cheerleading coach Las Cruces High Sch., 2007—. Independent. Lutheran. Avocations: aquariums, yachting, keyboards. Office: Meriks Protection Firm 630 King James Ave Las Cruces NM 88007-5380

WEDEL-COWGILL, MILLIE REDMOND, secondary school, performing arts, communication and education educator; b. Harrisburg, Pa., Aug. 18, 1939; d. Clair L. and Florence (Heiges) Aungst; m. T.S. Redmond, 1956 (div. 1967); children: T.S. Redmond II; m. Frederick L. Wedel, Jr., 1974 (div. 1986); m. Paul R. Cowgill, May 19, 2001. BA, Alaska Meth. U., 1966; MEd, U. Alaska, Anchorage, 1972; postgrad. in comm., Stanford U., Calif., 1975-76. Lic. third class broadcasting, FCC. Profl. actress Charming Models & Models Guild of Phila., 1954-61; asst. dir. devel. in charge pub. rels. Alaska Meth. U., Anchorage, 1966, part-time lectr., 1966, 73; comm. tchr. Anchorage Sch. Dist., 1967-96; owner Wedel Prodns., Anchorage, 1976-86; cons. comms., media and edn., owner Cowgill Cons., 2003—. Pub. rels. staff Alaska Purchase Centennial Exhibit, U.S. Dept. Commerce, 1967; writer gubernatorial campaign, 1971; instr. Chapman Coll., 1990-93; adj. instr. U. Alaska, Anchorage, 1972, 77-79, 89-2001; cons. Cook Inlet Native Assn., 1978, No. Inst., 1979; judge Ark. Press Women's Writing Contest, 1990-91; sec. exec. bd. Alaska Dept. Edn. Profl. Tchg. Practices Commn., 1993-94. Bd. dirs. Sta. KAKM, Alaska Pub. TV, membership chmn., 1978-80, nat. lay rep. to Pub. Broadcasting Svc. and Nat. Assn. Pub. TV Stas., 1979; bd. dirs. Ednl. Telecom. Consortium for Alaska, 1979, Mid-Hillside Cmty. Coun., Municipality of Anchorage, 1979-80, 83-88, Hillside East Cmty. Coun., 1984-88, pres., 1984-85; rsch. writer, legal asst. Vinson & Elkins, Houston, 1981; v.p., bd. dirs. Inlet View ASD Cmty. Sch., 1994-95, pres., 1995-97; Valley Forge Freedoms Found., Murdoch Scholarships; bd. dirs. Rev. Richard Gay Trust, Alaska and Pa., 1992-2000. Recipient awards for newspapers, lit. mags.; award Nat. Scholastic Press Assn., 1981, 82, 83, 84; Alaska Coun. Econs., 1982, Merits award Alaska Dept. Edn., 1982-93, Legis. commendation State of Alaska, Nat. Blue Ribbon Outstanding Sch. award, 1993. Mem. NEA (AEA bldg. rep., state del. 70s, 80s, 94-95), Assn. Pub. Broadcasting (charter mem., nat. lay del. 1980), Indsl. TV Assn. (San Francisco and Houston 1975-81), Alaska Press Club (chmn. high sch. journalism workshops, 1968-69, 73, awards for sch. newspapers 1972, 74, 77), Alaska Fedn. Press Women (dir. 1978-86, 94-95, pres. 1995-96, h.s. journalism competition youth projects dir., award for brochures 1978, chair youth writing contest 1994-95), World Affairs Coun., Chugach Electric (chair 1990, nomination com. for bd. dirs. 1988-90), Hood Coll. Alaska Alumni Assn., Stanford U. Alumni Club (Alaska pres. 1982-84, 90-92, 99-2000, v.p. 1998-99), UAA Alumni & AMU, APU Alumni Anchorage, Rotary Club of Naples (photographer and asst. program chair 2003), Imperial Golf Course Country Club, Club at Pelican Bay, Naples (Fla.) Philharm. League (bd. dirs., 2006), Naples Fla. U. Pa. Club, English Speaking Union, Naples Press Club (Fla.). Presbyterian. Home: PO Box 111489 Anchorage AK 99511-1489 Office: Cowgill Cons PO Box 770662 Naples FL 34107-0662 Home Phone: 907-345-7793; Office Phone: 239-598-3770.

WEDEN, MARGARET, research and development company executive; m. Jan Kleissl. PhD, Johns Hopkins U., Balt., 2005. Robert Wood Johnson health & soc. scholar U. Wis.-Madison, 2004—06; assoc. social scientist RAND Corp., Santa Monica, Calif., 2007—. Office: RAND Corp 1776 Main St Santa Monica CA 90407

WEDEPOHL, LEONHARD MARTIN, electrical engineering educator; b. Pretoria, South Africa, Jan. 26, 1933; s. Martin Willie and Liselotte B.M. (Franz) W.; m. Sylvia A.L. St. Jean; children: Martin, Graham. BSc in Engring., Rand U., 1953; PhD, U. Manchester, Eng., 1957. Registered profl. engr., BC. Planning engr. Escom, Johannesburg, 1957-61; mgr. L.M. Erricson, Pretoria, South Africa, 1961-62; sect. leader Reyrolle, Newcastle, England, 1962-64; prof., head dept. Manchester U., 1964-74; dean engring. U. Man., Winnipeg, Canada, 1974-79; dean applied sci. U. BC, Vancouver, Canada, 1979-85, prof. elec. engring., 1985-97, prof. emeritus, 1998—, dean applied sci. emeritus, 1998—. Mem. Sci. Rsch. Coun., London, 1968-74; dir. Man. Hydro, Winnipeg, 1975-79, BC Hydro, Vancouver, 1980-84, BC Sci. Coun., 1982-84; cons. Horizon Robotics, Saskatoon, 1986; chmn. implementation team Sci. Place, Can., 1985; cons. CEPEL, Rio de Janeiro; adv. Man. High Voltage DC Rsch. Ctr.; tech. advisor RTDS Techs., Inc., Winnipeg, 1994—; head protection devel. Rolls Royce Indsl. Power Group, 1995-96; adj. prof. U. Man., 2002-; co-chair Knowledge Cluster, Okanagan Partnership, Kelowna, Can., 2004-08; bd. dirs. Okanagan Partnership; co-chair faculty engring. adv. com. UBC-O. Contbr. articles to sci. jours.; patentee in field. Named Hon. Citizen, City of Winnipeg, 1979. Fellow Instn. Elec. Engrs. (premium 1967), Engring. Inst. Can.; mem. Assn. Profl. Engrs. BC. Avocations: music, cross country skiing, hiking. Office: 1511 Chardonnay Pl West Kelowna BC Canada V4T 2P9 Business E-Mail: wedepohl@shaw.ca.

WEDGE, ERIC (MICHAEL WEDGE), professional baseball team manager; b. Ft. Wayne, Ind., Jan. 27, 1968; s. Tim and Nina Wedge; m. Kate Wedge; 1 child, Ava Catherine. Grad., Wichita St. U. Catcher Boston Red Sox, 1991—92, 1994, Colo. Rockies, 1993; mgr. Class A Columbus, 1998, A Kinston Indians, 1999, Akron Aeros, 2000, AAA

Buffalo Bison, 2001—02, Cleve. Indians, 2003—. Co-owner Strike One Sports Complex, Danvers, Mass. Vol. Ronald McDonald House, Multiple Myeloma Rsch. Found., Providence House, First Energy Grand Slam Summer Reading Literacy Program, Feed the Need, St. Augustines Ch., Cleve., YWCA, Cleve.; owner Motivated Sports. Named Triple A Mgr. of Yr., 2001, Minor League Mgr. of Yr., 2002, Am. League Mgr. of Yr., 2007; named to Ind. HS Baseball Coaches Assn. Hall of Fame, 2007. Office: Cleve Indians 2401 Ontario St Cleveland OH 44115-4003*

WEDGEWORTH, ANN, actress; b. Abilene, Tex., Jan. 21, 1935; m. Rip Torn, 1955 (div.); 1 child, Danae; m. Ernest Martin; 1 child, Dianna. Attended, U. Tex.; BA in Drama, So. Methodist U. Actor: (Broadway debut) Make A Million, 1958, (Broadway appearances) Chapter Two (Tony award), Thieves, Blues for Mr. Charlie, The Last Analysis, (off-Broadway appearances) Line, Chapparal, The Crucible, Days and Nights of Beebee Fenstermaker, Ludlow Fair, The Honest to God Shnozzola, A Lie of the Mind, Elba, The Aunts, The Debutante's Ball, (premiers) In the Moonlight Eddie at Pasadena Playhouse, Natural Affection in Pheonix, The Dream in Phila., (toured with nat. cos.) The Sign in Sidney Brustein's Window and Kennedy's Children, (appeared in TV series) Three's Company, The Edge of Night, Another World, Somerset, Filthy Rich, Evening Shade, (TV appearances) All That Glitters, The Equalizer, Roseanne, Bronk, Twilight Zone, Trapper John, M.D.; (TV films) The War Between the Tates, Right to Kill, Cooperstown, Fight for Justice: The Nancy Conn Story, Bogie, A Stranger Waits; (films) Handle With Care (Nat. Soc. Film Critics award), Thieves, Bang the Drum Slowly, Scarecrow, Catamount Killing, Law and Disorder, One Summer Love, Dragon-Fly, Birch Intervals, Soggy Bottom, USA, No Small Affair, Sweet Dreams, The Mens Club, A Tiger's Tale, Made in Heaven, Far North, Miss Firecracker, Green Card, Steel Magnolias, Love and a 45, The Whole Wide World, The Hunter's Moon, Hard Promises, Andy, My Science Project, The Hawk is Dying; (plays) Mother and Child, The Glass Menagerie, Period of Adjustment, Come Blow Your Horn, Goodbye Again, The Tender Trap; TV host Evening at the Improv, A&E.

WEDGWOOD, RUTH, law educator, international affairs expert; b. NYC; d. Morris P. and Anne (Williams) Glushien; m. Josiah Francis Wedgwood; May 29, 1982; 1 child, Josiah Ruskin Wedgwood. BA magna cum laude, Harvard U., 1972; fellow, London Sch. Econs., 1972—73; JD, Yale U., 1976. Bar: D.C., N.Y., U.S. Supreme Ct. Law clk. to judge Henry Friendly U.S. Ct. Appeals (2d cir.), NYC, 1976—77; law clk. to justice Harry Blackmun U.S. Supreme Ct., Washington, 1977—78; spl. asst. to asst. atty. gen. U.S. Dept. Justice, Washington, 1978—80; asst. U.S. atty. U.S. Dist. Ct. (so. dist.) N.Y., NYC, 1980—86; prof. law Yale U., New Haven, 1986—2002, fellow Inst. for Social and Policy Studies, 1989—2002; fellow Berkeley Coll., Yale U., 1989—. Mem. Sec. of State's Adv. Com. Internat. Law, 1993—; sr. fellow for internat orgns. and law Coun. Fgn. Rels., 1994—2004; Charles Stockton prof. internat. law U.S. Naval War Coll., Newport, RI, 1998—99; mem. Hart-Rudman Commn. on Nat. Security in the 21st Century, Nat. Sec. Study Group, Dept. Def. Adv. Comm., 1999—2001; mem. acad. adv. com. to spl. rep. UN Sec.-Gen. for Children and Armed Conflict, 1999—2002; dir. studies Am. Soc. Internat. Law, 2000—03; guest scholar U.S. Inst. Peace, 2001—02; dir. studies Hague Acad. Internat. Law, 2001—02; elected U.S. mem. UN Human Rights Com., Geneva, 2002—06, Geneva, 2006—; mem. Hist. Rev. Panel, adv. to dir. CIA, 2002—; mem. Def. Policy Bd., advisor to U.S. Sec. Def., 2002—; prof. du Droit Internat. U. Paris I (Sorbonne), 2004; Berlin Prize fellow Am. Acad., 2006. Exec. editor Yale Law Jour., 1975-76; author: The Revolutionary Martyrdom of Jonathan Robbins, 1990, The Use of Force in International Affairs, 1992, American National Interest and the United Nations, 1996, Toward an International Criminal Court?, 1999, After Dayton: Lessons of the Bosnian Peace Process, 1999; mem. bd. editors Yale Jour. Law and Humanities, 1988-98, Am. Jour. Internat. Law, 1998-, World Policy Jour. (New Sch. Social Rsch.), 2001—, Am. Interest, 2005—, The Nat. Interest, 2005—, adv. coun.; contbr. articles to profl jours. and popular publs. including N.Y. Times, Washington Post, Christian Sci. Monitor, Internat. Herald Tribune, Wall St. Jour., Washington Times, Fin. Times, L.A. Times, Die Zeit, Fgn. Affairs, Fgn. Policy, Nat. Interest, Time mag.; commentator for CNN, PBS, Fox, Nat. Pub. Radio, MSNBC, BBC, Lehrer News Hour, PBS. Prin. rapporteur U.S. Atty. Gen.'s Guidelines on FBI Undercover Ops., Informant Use and Racketeering and Gen. Crime Investigations, 1980; bd. dirs. Lawyers Com. for Human Rights, N.Y.C., 1988-94; mem. policy adv. com. UN Assn. U.S.A., 1998-2003; bd. dirs. Freedom House, 2003-, UN Watch, 2004—. Recipient Israel Peres prize, 1976, Disting. Contbn. to Internat. Law award N.Y. State Bar Assn., 2000; Ford Found. Rsch. grantee; Rockefeller Found. fellow; Am. Acad. Berlin prize fellow, 2006. Mem. ABA (standing com. on law and nat. security 2002—, coun. Internat. Law sect. 2003—), Am. Law Inst., Am. Soc. Internat. Law (exec. com. 1995-98, v.p. 2005—), Internat. Law Assn. (v.p. 1994—, program chmn. Am. br. 1992), Assn. Am. Law Sch. (chmn. sect. internat. law 1995-96), Assn. Bar City N.Y. (chmn. arms control and internat. security affairs com. 1989-92, chmn. internat. affairs coun. 1992-95, exec. com. 1995-99), Union Internationale des Avocats, U.S.A. (chpt. bd. govs. 1993-98), Women in Internat. Security (bd. dirs. 2006—), Ctr. for Global Prosperity (bd. dirs. 2006—), Coun. on Fgn. Rels., Internat. Inst. for Strategic Studies, Elizabethan Club, Mory's Assn., Yale Club (N.Y.C.). Office: Johns Hopkins Sch Advanced Internat Studies 1619 Massachusetts Ave NW Washington DC 20036 Office Phone: 202-663-5618. Business E-Mail: rwedgwood@jhu.edu. *Notable cases include: U.S. vs. Kostadinov, involving a Bulgarian spy traded for 25 East Bloc detainees; U.S. vs. Kampiles, involving government employee who gave satellite secrets to the Soviet Union; U.S. vs. Gold, Orosz, Egerhazi and Kompar, involving a million dollar racketeering/landlord arson ring in N.Y.C. that defrauded Lloyd's of London Sate Syndicate; U.S. vs. Kazemzadeh and DeVelasco, involving pub. corruption in N.Y.C. Health and Hospitals Corporation and the fed. WIC program.*

WEDIG, CHRISTOPHER P., environmental engineer; married. MS in Chem. Engring., MIT, Cambridge, Mass., 1972. Sr. tech. specialist, air quality control Shaw, Stoughton, Mass., 1973—. Contbr. scientific papers (Rsch. award, 2008). Achievements include design of fossil fired power plants. Office: Shaw 100 Tech Ctr Dr Stoughton MA 02072 Business E-Mail: christopher.wedig@shawgrp.com.

WEDNER, H. JAMES, physician, researcher; b. Pitts., May 12, 1941; s. Benjamin Mayer and Lucille Ruth (Jacobs) W.; m. Maureen Patricia Martin, June 18, 1978; children: Bryna Kimberly, Jason Oliver. BS, Cornell U., 1963; MD, Cornell Med. Coll., 1967. Intern Barnes Hosp., St. Louis, 1967—68; resident internal medicine Washington U. Med. Sch., St. Louis, 1970—71, fellow allergy and immunology, 1971—73; lt. comdr. USPHS, Govenor's Island, NY, 1968—70; prof. medicine Washington U. Med. Sch., St. Louis, 1990—, dir. tng. program allergy and immunology, 1986—95, 2001—, chief clin. allergy and immunology, 1988—, med. dir. The Asthma and Allergy Ctr., 2000—, acting chief Divsn. Allergy and Clin. Immunology, 2001—02, chief, 2002—. Vis. prof. Am. Coll. of Allergy and Immunology, Little Rock, 1991, U. Buffalo Med. Sch., 1999; William Pierson vis. prof. Ea. Va. Med. Sch., 2003; prin. investigator psychosocial aspects of asthma, St. Louis Asthma Study Unit; chmn. steering com. Nat. Coop. Inner City Asthma Study; prin. investigator Fungal Alleries Innercity Homes. Editor: Allergy: Theory and Practice, 1984, 2d rev. edit., 1991; mem. editl. bd. Jour. Immunology, 1980-82, Jour. Allergy and Clin. Immunology, 1991-96; assoc. editor Anaphylaxis and Drug Allergy Current Allergy Reports, 2000—; sect. editor Anaplylaxis and Drug Allergy, Current Allergy and Asthma Reports Fellow Am. Acad. Allergy Asthma Immunology; mem. Internat. Soc. Immunopharmacology, Am. Coll. Allergy Asthma Immunology, Am. Assn. Immunology, Clin. Immunology Soc., European Acad. Allergology and Clin. Immunology. Achievements include initial description of Parthenium hysterophruis allergy; research on asthma and the psychosocial aspects of asthma, molecular characterization of plant and fungal allergens and the role of fungi in asthma. Office: Washington U Med Sch Campus Box 8122 660 S Euclid Ave Saint Louis MO 63110-1010 Office Phone: 314-454-7937, 314-454-7376. Personal E-mail: wednerj@att.net. Business E-Mail: jwedner@im.wustl.edu, swedner@dom.wustl.edu.

WEED, DONALD T., otolaryngologist, educator; MD, Vanderbilt U. Sch. Medicine, Nashville, Tenn., 1989. Dir., head and neck site disease group, Sylvester Comprehensive Cancer Ctr. U. Miami Sch. Medicine, 2001—, dir., residency tng. program, dept. otolaryngology, 2004—, assoc. prof., dept. otolaryngology, 2005—, co-dir., head and neck divsn., dept. otolaryngology, 2006—. Recipient 1st Pl., Resident Rsch. Competition, Dept. Otolaryngology, Vanderbilt U. Med. Ctr., Faculty Tchg. award, U. Miami Sch. Medicine. Fellow: ACS, Am. Laryngol., Rhinol. and Otol. Soc. (hon.), Am. Acad. Otolaryngology- Head and Neck Surgery (hon.); mem.: Am. Acad. Facial Plastic and Reconstructive Surgery, Am. Assn. Cancer Rsch., Am. Head and Neck Soc. Office: Univ Miami Sylvester Comprehensive Cancer Ctr 1475 NW 12th Ave 4th Fl Rm 4027 Miami FL 33136 Office Fax: 305-243-1283.

WEED, ROGER OREN, rehabilitation services professional, educator; b. Bend, Oreg., Feb. 2, 1944; s. Chester Elbert and Ruth Marie (Urie) W.; m. Paula J. Keller BS in Sociology, U. Oreg., 1967, MS in Rehab. Counseling, 1969; PhD in Rehab. Counseling, U. Ga., 1986. Cert. rehab. counselor; cert. disability mgmt. specialist; lic. profl. counselor; cert. case mgr., cert. life care planner. Vocat. rehab. counselor State of Alaska, Anchorage, 1969-71; instr. U. Alaska, Anchorage, 1970-76; counselor Langdon Psychiat. Clinic, Anchorage, 1971-74; from asst. dir. to exec. dir. Hope Cottages, Anchorage, 1974-79; owner Profl. Resources Group, Anchorage, 1978-80; mng. ptnr. Collins, Weed & Assocs., 1980-84; assoc. dir. Ctr. for Rehab. Tech. Ga. Tech. U., Atlanta, 1986-87; catastrophic injury rehab. Weed & Assocs., Atlanta, 1984—; from asst. prof. to prof. Ga. State U., Atlanta, 1987—2002. Adj. faculty Ga. Inst. Tech.; courtesy faculty U. Fla., 1996-2004. Co-author: Vocational Expert Handbook, 1986, Transferable Work Skills, 1988, Life Care Planning: Spinal Cord Injured, 1989, 2d edit. 1994, Life Care Planning: Head Injured, 1994, Life Care Planning for the Amputee, 1992, Rehab Cons. Handbook, 1994, rev. edit., 2001; editor: Life Care Planning and Case Mgmt. Handbook, 1999 (rev., 2004), 3rd edit., 2009; assoc. editor Jour. Lifecare Planning, 2002—; mem. editl. bd. Jour. of Pvt. Sector Rehab., 1986—, Jour. Forensic Vocational Analysis; contbr. articles to profl. jour. Bd. dirs. Found. for Life Care Planning Rsch. Recipient Gov.'s award Gov.'s Com. on Employment, Alaska, 1982, Goldpan Svc. award Gov.'s Com. on Employment, Alaska, 1978, Profl. Svc. award Am. Rehab. Counselors Assn., 1993. Fellow Nat. Rehab. Assn. (chmn. legis. com., bd. dir. met. Atlanta chpt. 1987-89, pres. Pacific region 1983-85, Pres.'s award Pacific region 1986), Internat. Assn. Rehab. Profls. (chmn. resh. and tng. com. 1988-93, pres. 1994-95, named Educator of Yr. 1991, 97, Lifetime Achievement award 2004), Internat. Life Care Planning (Ann. Conf. Lifetime Achievement award 2005, Disting. Prof. award 2006), Pvt. Rehab. Suppliers Ga., Anchorage Amateur Radio Club, Ga. State U. Alumni Assn. (Disting. Prof. award, 2006). Republican. Methodist. Avocations: sailing, skiing, bicycling, flying, computers. Office: Ga State U Coll Edn Dept Counseling/Psychol Svc 9th Fl Atlanta GA 30302

WEEDIN, JAMES FRANK, biology professor, researcher; b. San Antonio, Tex., Dec. 17, 1949; m. Teresa Faye Johnson, Dec. 30, 1972. AS, San Antonio Coll., Tex., 1969; BA, U. Tex., Austin, 1975; MS, Sul Ross State U., Alpine, Tex., 1976. Prof. C.C. of Aurora, Colo., 1981—, sci. divsn. chair, 1985—93. Bot. cons. Tex. Natural Areas Survey, Austin, 1976—77; reviewer Sci. Jour., 2009. Sci. advisor: Chihuahuan Desert Trilogy Film Series, Nat. Edn. TV, 1980; author: (book) Cacti of the Trans-Pecos and Adjacent Areas, 2004 (SW Book award Border Regional Libr. Assn., 2005, Donovan S. Correll award Native Plant Soc. Tex., 2007), (profl. papers) American Jour. Botany, Southwestern Naturalist, Annals of the Mo. Botanical Gardens, (book) Cacti Of Texas - A Field Guide, 2008, Smithsonian Contribution to Botany. Mem. nursing adv. bd. Pickens Tech. Ctr., Aurora, 1982—2006. Recipient Excellence award, U. Tex. Nat. Inst. Staff and Orgnl. Devel., 1991, Master Tchr. award, U. Tex. Nat. Inst. Staff and Faculty Devel., 1991; named Faculty of Yr., C.C. of Aurora, 1990; grantee, U. Tex.-Austin, 1971, Chihuahuan Desert Rsch. Inst., 1975, Cmty. Colls. Colo., 1985. Mem.: Cactus and Succulent Soc. Am. (assoc.), Southwestern Assn. Naturalists (assoc.), Western Interior Paleontol. Soc. (assoc.), Colo. Cactus and Succulent Soc. (assoc.; v.p. 1988—89, grantee 1998, 2006). Avocations: hiking, camping, photography, travel. Home: 1189 Norfolk St Aurora CO 80011 Office: Cmty Coll of Aurora 16000 E CentreTech Pkwy Aurora CO 80011 Office Fax: 303-361-7374. Personal E-mail: weedin@comcast.net. Business E-Mail: jim.weedin@ccaurora.edu.

WEEDMAN, DANIEL WILSON, astronomy educator; b. Nashville, Oct. 19, 1942; BA, Vanderbilt U., 1964; PhD, U. Wis., 1967. Asst. prof. astronomy U. Tex., Austin, 1967-70; assoc. prof. physics and astronomy Vanderbilt U., Nashville, 1970-79, U. Minn., Mpls., 1974-75; prof. astronomy Pa. State U., University Park, 1979—. Councilor Am. Astron. Soc., 1978-81; vis. sr. scientist astrophysics NASA, Washington, 1990-92. Author: Quasar Astronomy, 1985; contbr. over 75 articles to profl. jours. Office: NASA Astrophysics Divsn Cod S # 2 Washington DC 20546-0001

WEEKES, KEVIN, professional hockey player; b. Toronto, Apr. 4, 1975; s. Carl and Vadney Weekes; m. Stephanie Weekes, Jan. 2008. Goaltender Fla. Panthers, 1997—98, Vancouver Canucks, 1999, NY Islanders, 1999—2000, Tampa Bay Lightning, 2000—02, Carolina Hurricanes, 2002—04, NY Rangers, 2005—07, NJ Devils, 2007—09. Guest appearance (TV series) Everybody Hates Chris, 2008.*

WEEKLEY, BOO (THOMAS BRENT WEEKLEY), professional golfer; b. Milton, Fla., July 23, 1973; m. Karyn Weekley; 1 child, Thomas Parker. Attended, Abraham Baldwin Agrl. Coll., Tilton, Ga., 1992—93. Laborer Monsanto chemical plant, Pensacola, Fla.; profl. golfer, 1997—; mem. Ryder Cup team, 2008. Achievements include winning Verizon Heritage, 2007, 2008, Ryder Cup, 2008. Avocations: hunting, fishing. Office: PGA Tour 100 PGA Tour Blvd Ponte Vedra FL 32082*

WEEKLEY, FREDERICK CLAY, JR., lawyer; b. San Antonio, Aug. 29, 1939; s. F. Clay and Topsy (Stevens) W.; m. Lynda Freeman; children: Amber Lee Carothers, Caroline Karazissis. BBA, Baylor U., 1962, JD, 1963; LLM, NYU, 1969. Bar: Tex. 1963. Ptnr. Bracewell & Patterson, Houston, 1974-90; atty. Bank One, Tex., N.A., 1990-98; ptnr./counsel Shannon, Gracey, Ratliff & Miller, LLP, Ft. Worth, 1999—. Mem. coun. real property, probate and trust law sect., State Bar of Tex., 1987-90; mem. adminstrv. coun. trust divsn. Tex. Bankers Assn., 1992-95, chmn. legis. com., 1992-95. Mem. Commn. Probate Law Examiners, Tex. Bd. Legal Specialization, 1978-82. Fellow Am. Coll. Trust and Estate Counsel. Home: 1821 Mossy Oak St Arlington TX 76012-5619 Office Phone: 817-882-7698. Business E-Mail: fweekley@shannongracey.com.

WEEKS, ALBERT LOREN, writer, educator, journalist; b. Highland Park, Mich., Mar. 28, 1923; s. Albert Loren and Vera Grace (Jarvis) W. Student, U. Mich., 1942-43; MA, U. Chgo., 1949; PhD, Columbia U., 1965; cert., Russian Inst., 1960. Reporter Chgo. City News Bur., 1946; polit. analyst U.S. Dept. State, 1950-53, Free Europe Com., Inc., 1953-56; editorial asst. Newsweek mag., 1957-58; Russian tech. glossary compiler McGraw-Hill Book Co., 1960-61; prof. continuing edn. NYU, 1959-89. Lectr. U.S. diplomatic history and soviet govt. Columbia U., 1951-52; mem. adv. coun. Nat. Strategy Info. Ctr., 1979-89; instr. Ringling Sch. Art and Design, 1991—; pub. spkr. S.W. Fla. Host: A Week's View of Red Press, Sta. WNBC, 1965-68; series Myths That Rule America, NBC-TV, 1979-82; author: Reading American History, 1963, The First Bolshevik: A Political Biography of Peter Tkachev, 1968, The Other Side of Coexistence: An Analysis of Russian Foreign Policy, 1970, Richard Hofstadter's The American Political Tradition and the Age of Reform, 1973, Andrei Sakharov and the Soviet Dissidents, 1975, The Troubled Detente, 1976, Solzhenitsyn's One Day in the Life of Ivan Denisovich, 1976, Myths That Rule America, 1980, War and Peace: Soviet Russia Speaks, 1983; editor/compiler Brassey's Soviet and Communist Quotations, 1987, The Soviet Nomenklatura, 1987-1991, Stalin's Other War: Soviet Grand Strategy 1939-1941, 2002, Russia's Life-Saver: Lend-Lease Aid to the USSR in World War II, The Choice of War, The Great Ruse: How Stalin Bluffed Hitler into Defeat, 2010; internat. affairs editor Def. Sci. mag., 1982-85; columnist Def. Report, 1982-90; contbr. articles to N.Y. Times, New Republic, New Leader, Annals, Russian, Slavic revs., Christian Sci. Monitor, Problems of Communism, Survey, Mil. Intelligence, Strategic Rev., World War II mag., Air Univ. Rev., L.A. Times, Washington Times, Orbis, Global Affairs, Panorama, Sarasota Herald-Tribune, Bradenton Herald, Defense and Diplomacy, Am. Intelligence Jour., USA Today, Rossiiskiye Vesti, Vechernii Vladimir, CityTempo mag., Modern Age mag. Home: 4884 Kestral Park Cir Sarasota FL 34231-3369 Personal E-mail: aweeks1@compuserve.com.

WEEKS, BRIGITTE, publishing executive; b. Whitchurch, Hants, Eng., Aug. 28, 1943; came to U.S., 1965; d. Jack and Margery May (Millett) W.; m. Edward A. Herscher, Sept. 6, 1969; children— Hilary, Charlotte, Daniel. Student, Univ. Coll. of North Wales, Bangor, 1962-65. Asst. editor Boston Mag., 1966-70; editor Kodansha Internat., Tokyo, 1969-72, Resources for the Future, 1973-74; asst. editor The Washington Post Book World, 1974-78, editor, 1978-88; sr. v.p., editor-in-chief Book-of-the-Month Club (now Bookspan), NYC, 1988-94; editor-in-chief Guideposts Books, NYC, 1994—2002, Crossings Book Club (divsn. of Bookspan), NYC, 2002—03, Bookspan, NYC, 2003—05, Crossings Book Club, 2007—. Pres. Nat. Book Critics Circle, 1990.

WEEKS, CLIFFORD MYERS, musician, academic administrator; b. NYC, Apr. 15, 1938; s. Vernal C. and Adeline (Campbell) W.; m. Ethel Lynn Fleming, Oct. 26, 1963 (dec. 1982); children: Clifford M. Jr., Michele Lynn. Diploma in Arranging and Composition, Berklee Coll. Music, 1962; MusB magna cum laude, Boston Conservatory Music, 1963, MusM, 1975; cert. in edn. adminstrn., Boston State Coll., 1977. Cert. secondary sch. adminstr. and tchr. music, Mass. Tchr. music Boston Pub. Schs., 1964-74, condr. All-City Stage Band, 1972-79, adminstrv. asst. to asst. supt., 1974-75, coordinator instrumental music, 1975-79, asst. prin., 1979, adminstrv. asst. to asst. supt., 1979-96, acting cmty. supt., 1983, cluster coord., 1996-2001, exec. asst. supt. office, 2001—03; fellow Boston U., 1989; ret., 2003. Arranger, composer, trombonist, 1963—; condr. Boston Coll. Jazz and Stage Band, Chestnut Hill, Mass., 1976-78; part-time city music faculty outreach coord., lead tchr. Berklee Coll. Music, 2006—. Composer Tryptych for tuba and piano, 1971, (oratorio) The King-Life and Teachings of Dr. Martin Luther King Jr., 1976; composer, arranger various jazz compositions, 1975. Mem. Medford (Mass.) Jaycees, 1975-76; adv. bd. Roxbury (Mass.) Boys and Girls Club, 1970—, Berklee Coll. Music, Boston, 1972. Recipient Mayor's Parkman Club award, 1999, Suskind Young at Art award, Wang Ctr. Boston Theatres, 2001; fellow, Boston U., 1989. Mem. Boston Assn. Sch. Adminstrs. and Suprs. (adminstrs. union 1997—), Boston Tchrs. Union, Black Educators Alliance Mass. (treas. 1972-76, award 1976), ASCAP, Adminstrv. Assts. Assn. (chmn. local chpt. 1982—), Assn. for Supervision and Curriculum Devel., Omega Psi Phi. Methodist.

WEEKS, GERALD, psychologist, educator; b. Morehead City, NC, Nov. 20, 1948; s. Marion G. and Ada (Willis) W. BA in Philosophy and Psychology, East Carolina U., 1971, MA in Gen. Psychology, 1973; PhD in Clin. Psychology, Ga. State U., 1977. Diplomate Am. Bd. Profl. Psychology (pres. 1987-88, bd. dirs. 1982-87), Am. Bd. Family Psychology, Am. Bd. Sexology; cert. marital and family therapist; lic. practicing psychologist, Nev., Pa.; bd. cert. sexologist. Intern in family therapy Harlem Valley Psychiat. Ctr., Wingdale, NY, 1978-79; assoc. prof. psychology U. N.C., Wilmington, 1979-85; dir. tng. Penn Coun. for Relationships, 1985—; clin. asst. prof. psychology Sch. Medicine U. Pa., Phila., 1985-87, clin. assoc. prof., 1988-98; chair, prof. dept. counseling U. Nev.-Las Vegas, 1999—. Pvt. practice Carolina Ob-gyn. Ctr., Wilmington, 1980-85. Author: Paradoxical Therapy, 1982, Treating Couples: The Intersystem Model of the Marriage Council of Philadelphia, 1989, Promoting Change through Paradoxical Therapy, 1991, Paradoxical Psychotherapy: Theory and Practice with Individuals, Couples, and Families, 1982; co-author: (with L. L'Abate) Family Therapy: Basic Concepts and Terms, 1985, (with L. L'Abate) Integrating Sex and Marital Therapy: A Clinicians Guide, 1987, Erectile Dysfunction, 2000, (with N. Gambescia) Couples in Treatment, 1992, rev. edit., 2001, Integrative Solutions: Treating Common Problems in Couple's Therapy, 1995, (with Hof and TREAT) Focused Genograms: Intergenerational Assessment of Individuals, Couples and Families, 1999, (with DeMaria & Hof) Hypoactive Sexual Desire, 2002, Treating Infidelity, (with Gambescia and Jenkins) Handbook of Family Therapy, 2003, (with Odell and Muthuen) If Only I Had Known: Common Mistakes in Couples Therapy, 2004, (with K. Hertlein & Mambescia) Muida to Systemic Sex Therapy, 2008, Systemic Sex Therapy, A Clinician's Guide to Systemic Sex Therapy; contbr. articles to profl. jours. Recipient Outstanding Family & Marriage Therapy award, AAMNFT, 2009. Fellow Am. Assn. Marital and Family Therapy (clin. mem., nat. adv. bd., approved supr.); mem. APA, Acad. Family Psychology, Interpersonal and Social Skills Assn. (founding mem.), Acad. Psychologists in Marital, Sex, and Family Therapy, Am. Assn. of Sex Educators (clin. mem.), Counselors of Therapists. Office: Dept Marriage and Family Therapy PO Box 453045 4505 S Maryland Pky Las Vegas NV 89154-3045 Office Phone: 702-895-1392. Business E-Mail: gerald.weeks@unlv.edu.

WEEKS, J. DAVID, state representative, lawyer; b. Sumter, SC, Sept. 24, 1953; s. Goliath Brunson Sr. and Eartha Lee Weeks Brunson; m. Cheryl Elaine Hannibal, July 31, 1985; children: Lynette, Davida. BA, Morris Coll., 1975, postgrad., 1996; JD, U. S.C., 1989; MEd, Howard U., 1996. Pvt. practice; mem. Dist. 51 S.C. House of Reps., 2001—. Bd. trustees Morris Coll., 2001—. Mcpl. ct. judge, Timmonsville, SC, 1996—2000; chmn. Sumter County Voter Registration Bd., 1994, Sumter City-County Planning Commn., 1998—2000; deacon Jehovah Missionary Bapt. Ch., ch. sch. tchr. Democrat. Office: State Capitol 328A Blatt Bldg Columbia SC 29211 Home: 2 Marlborough Ct Sumter SC 29154 E-mail: JDW@scstatehouse.net.*

WEEKS, JOHN ROBERT, geographer, social studies educator; b. Sacramento, June 1, 1944; s. Robert Louis and Thelma Hope (Evans) W.; m. Deanna Jean Hosea, May 16, 1965; children: John Robert, Gregory, Jennifer. AB, U. Calif., Berkeley, 1966, MA, 1969, PhD, 1972. Asst. prof. sociology Mich. State U., East Lansing, 1971-74, San Diego State U., 1974-78, assoc. prof., 1978-81, prof., 1981-92, prof. geography, 1992—, chmn. dept., 1978-85; adminstrv. dir. Internat. Population Ctr., 1985—; clin. prof. family & preventive medicine U. Calif. Sch. Medicine, San Diego, 1998—. Vis. rsch. demographer U. Calif., Berkeley, 1972; cons. Allied Home Health Assn., 1978-80, Area Agy. on Aging, San Diego, 1979-81, Los Angeles Regional Family Planning Coun., 1986—, East County Econ. Devel. Coun., 1986—, UN Food and Agrl. Orgn., 2002—. Author: Teenage Marriages, 1976, Population, 10th edit., 2008, Aging, 1984, Demography of Islamic Nations, 1988, High Fertility Among Indochinese Refuges, 1989, Demographic Dynamics of the U.S.-Mex. Border, 1992. Grantee USPHS, 1983-84, 87-88, 88-89, 90—, U.S. Administrn. on Aging, 1979-80, U.S. Bur. of Census, 1988-89, Andrew W. Mellon Found., 1998-2001, NSF, 2001-04, NICHD, 2004—; trainee USPHS, 1967-71. Mem. Population Assn. Am., Am. Sociol. Assn., Internat. Union for Sci. Study Population, Am. Assn. Geographers. Democrat. Office: San Diego State U Dept Geography San Diego CA 92182 Office Phone: 619-594-8040. E-mail: john.weeks@sdsu.edu.

WEEKS, LILLIAN DURRETT, law librarian; children: Katherine Durrett, Bradley Scott. BA in Polit. Sci., Miss. U. Women, Columbus, 1971; MLS, U. Ala., Tuscaloosa, 1973. Asst. law libr. U. Ala., 1973—95; asst. libr. dir. bounds law libr. U. Ala. Sch. Law, 1995—. Mem. Holy Spirit Sch. Bd., Tuscaloosa, 1993—96. Office: Univ Ala Sch Law 101 Paul Bryant Dr E Tuscaloosa AL 35487 Office Fax: 205-348-1112.

WEEKS, MARTA JOAN, retired priest; b. Buenos Aires, May 24, 1930; arrived in US, 1932; d. Frederick Albert and Anne (Newman) Sutton; m. Lewis Austin Weeks, Aug. 17, 1951 (dec. 2005); children: Kermit Austin, Leslie Anne; m. Karleton B. Wulf, Sept. 1, 2008. BA in Polit. Sci., Stanford U., 1951; MDiv, Episcopal Theol. Sem. S.W., 1991; LHD (hon.), U. Utah, 2005, Beloit Coll., 2009; DDiv (hon.), Episcop. Theol. Sem. of the S.W., 2006. Ordained priest Episcopal Ch., 1992. Legal libr., sec. Mene Grande Oil Co., Caracas, Venezuela, 1948; English tchr. Centro-Venezolano Americano, Caracas, 1948; sec. Household Fin. Corp., Salt Lake City, 1951; legal sec. McKelvey & McKelvey Attys., Durango, Colo., 1952; sec., dir. Weeks Air Mus., Miami, Fla., 1985—2001; chaplain Jackson Meml. Hosp., 1992-93; interim asst. St. James Episcopal Ch., Salt Lake City, 1994-95; assisting priest St. Andrew's Episcopal Ch., Miami, Fla., 1999—2002, 2007—; priest-at-large Episcopal Diocese of S.E. Fla., 2002—04. Honorary Canon in Episcopal Ch., 2008; trustee Beloit Coll., Wis., 1980—82, U. Miami, 1983—88, 1995—2007, bd. chmn., 2007—09; trustee Bishop Gray Inns, Lake Worth and Davenport, Fla., 1992—2002; advisor Ctr. for Sexuality and Religion, 1997—; nat. adv. coun. U. Utah, 1998—; trustee assoc. Am. Assn. Petroleum Geologists, 2005—; dir. S.E. Fla. Episcopal Found., 2002—05. Mem.: Am. Soc. Order St. John of Jerusalem. Address: 7350 SW 162nd St Palmetto Bay FL 33157-3820

WEEKS, PATSY ANN LANDRY, librarian, educator; b. Luling, Tex., Mar. 3, 1930; d. Lee and Mattie Wood (Callihan) Landry; m. Arnett S. Weeks, Dec. 2, 1950; children: Patsy Kate, Nancy Ann, Janie Marie. BS, Southwest Tex. State U., 1951; MLS, Tex. Woman's U., 1975. Tchr. art, reading, math. Grandview Ind. Sch. Dist., Tex., 1950—52; tchr. phys. edn. Beaumont Ind. Sch. Dist., Tex., 1953; tchr. art, coll. algebra Cisco Jr. Coll., Tex., 1957—58; tchr. remedial reading Taylor County Schs., Tuscola, Tex., 1965—66, Anson Ind. Sch. Dist., Tex., 1971—73; libr. Bangs Ind. Sch. Dist., Tex., 1973—79, learning resources coord., 1979—90; dir. Heart of Tex. Ctr. for the Rev. and Exam. of Children's and Young Adults' Lit., 1988—2001; cons. Heart of Tex. Lit. Ctr., 2001—03. Bd. dirs. Anson Pub. Libr., Tex., 1971—72, Brownwood Pub. Libr., 2003—; mem. adv. com. Edn. Svc. Ctr., 1978—83; coord. Reading is Fundamental Program, 1978—83; counsilor Children's Round Table, 1993—; cons. Heart of Tex. Lit. Ctr., 2000—03, dir. projects, 2003—. Exhibitions include oil paintings, pastels various Tex. Fairs (1st prize, 1952, 1960), Gary Air Force Base, San Marcos, 1952. Named Coming Home Queen, Howard Payne U., 2006. Mem.: ALA, Tex. Assn. Sch. Libr. Adminstrs., Teenage Libr. Assn. Tex. (chmn. audio-visual award com. 1984), Tex. Assn. Improvement Reading, Tex. Assn. Sch. Librs. (media prodns. award com. 1985—86), Tex. Libr. Assn. (mem. intellectual freedom and profl. responsibility com. 1979—81, mem. Tex. Bluebonnet award com. 1982—85, chair adv. com. 1987, chair children's round table 1987, sec. young adult round table 1991—92, publs. com. 1991—, round table coun. 1993—95), Intellectual Freedom Round Table, Am. Assn. Sch. Librs., Young Adult Libr. Svcs. Assn. (chair Baker and Taylor award jury com. 2006—, outstanding books for coll.bound-fine arts com., publ.'s liaison com.), Assn. Libr. Svc. to Children (Caldecott award com. 1986, Grosset and Dunlap Group award selection com. 1988, nominating com. 1989, chair 1989—91, Newbery award com. 1999, Disting. Svc. award com. 2002—, Disting. Svc. award com. chair 2003—, cons. priority gorup III profl. devel.), Tex. State Tchr. Assn. (life), Bangs Prog. Women's Club (treas. 1974—76), Delta Kappa Gamma, Beta Phi Mu, Alpha Chi, Kappa Pi, Phi Delta Kappa. Bapt. Office: Howard Payne Univ Sta Walker Memorial Library Heart of Tex Ctr Brownwood TX 76801 Home Phone: 325-752-7315; Office Phone: 325-649-8606. Business E-Mail: pweeks@hptux.edu.

WEEKS, ROBERT ANDREW, materials science researcher, educator; b. Birmingham, Ala., Aug. 23, 1924; s. William Andrew and Annie Bell (Hammond) W.; m. Jane Sutherland, Mar. 20, 1948; children: Kevin Dale, Robin Dee, Loren Hammond, Kerry Andrew. BS, Birmingham-So. Coll., 1947; MS, U. Tenn., 1951; PhD, Brown U., 1966. Sr. physicist Union Carbide Corp., Oak Ridge, Tenn., 1951-84; rsch. prof. material sci. Vanderbilt U., 1984-99, prof. emeritus, 1999—. Disting. vis. prof. Am. U, in Cairo, 1970-71; invited prof. Ecole Poly. Fed. de Lausanne, Switzerland, 1981; vis. prof. Cath. U., Leuven, Belgium, 1983; cons. numerous pvt. corps. and fed. agys.; prin. investigator lunar materials, 1966-74; co-prin. investigator expdn. Western desert of Egypt to desert glass site, 1981; CEO Oak Ridge Cons., 1993—. Co-editor: Effects of Modes of Formation on Structure of Glass, 1985, 88, Editing the Refereed Scientific Journal, 1994; assoc. editor Jour. Geophys. Rsch., 1968-74; editor Jour. Noncrystalline Solids, 1988-98; conf. editor Jour. Non-Crystalline Solids, 1998-2000; contbr. numerous articles to profl. jours. Served with U.S. Army, 1943-46. Union Carbide fellow, 1964; Fulbright lectr., 1980, Rsch. fellow Reading U., 1971, USIA Am. participant Egypt, India, Nepal and Sri Lanka, 1986; Sir Neville Mott award, Jour. Non-Crystalline Solids, 2006. Fellow Am. Ceramic Soc. (SiO_2, advanced diebeatrics and related devices conf. hon. chmn. 2004, 06, 08, R. A. Weeks Symposium named in his honor, Honolulu 1993, 2004, George W. Morey award 1998); mem. AAAS, Am. Phys. Soc., Sigma Xi. Avocation: photography. Home and Office: 509 Shannondale Way Maryville TN 37803 Personal E-mail: e1e2e4@bellsouth.net.

WEEKS, ROSS LEONARD, JR., museum executive; b. Jamestown, NY, Sept. 11, 1936; s. Ross Leonard and Cecile Forbes (Carrie) W.; m. Patricia Ann Earley, June 10, 1961 (div.); children: Susan Woodall, Ross Leonard III, William Andrew, David James; m. Ndeleshia C. Nanuwa, Oct. 15, 2007. AB, Colgate U., Hamilton, NY, 1958; MS, George Wash. U., Washington, DC, 1971; cert., Fed. Exec. Inst., 1988. Reporter Jamestown Post-Jour., Va., 1958-60, Richmond News Leader, 1960-65; dir. pub. info. Coll. William and Mary, Williamsburg, Va., 1965-71, asst. to exec. v.p., 1971-74, asst. to pres., dir. univ. comms., 1974-81; exec. dir. Jamestown-Yorktown Found., 1981-91, Hist. Crab Orchard Mus., Inc., Tazewell, Va., 1992—2002; ret., 2002; pres. Blue Ridge Concepts, Ltd., 1999—. Editor William and Mary Alumni Gazette, 1966-81; author: Virginia's Tazewell County: A Last Great Place, 2000; editor: 'Cause I'm Colored-The Black Heritage of Tazewell County, 2001; columnist: Clinch Valley News, 1998-2004. Chmn. Williamsburg-James City Bicentennial, 1975-77; treas. Coalfield Regional Tourism Devel. Authority S.W. Va., 1993-97; Va. S.W. Blue Ridge Highlands, Inc., 1993-97, v.p., 1996-97, pres., 1997-99; sec., treas. Frontier Culture Found., 1982-86; exec. dir. Va. Independence Bicentennial Commn., 1981-83; trustee coun. Thirteen Original States, 1982-87; chair Tazewell County Tourism Devel. Commn., 1993-97; mem. regional grant panel Va. Com. on the Arts, 1998—2002; mem. Gov.'s Va. History Initiative, 1995-2002; mem. parish coun., cluster adminstr. Tazewell-Buchanan Cath Ch., 2003-. Mem. Am. Assn. Mus., Am. Assn. State and Local History, Masons, Rotary (Paul Harris fellow 1987), Clan Ross Assn., SAR (pres. Clinch Mountain Militia chpt. 2001-03), Sigma Delta Chi, Kappa Delta Rho (Ordo Honora 1986). Roman Catholic. Avocations: travel, landscaping, antiques, history. Home: 205 View Hill Tazewell VA 24651 Personal E-mail: rossweeks@roadrunner.com.

WEEKS, SANDRA KENNEY, nursing administrator; b. Akron, Ohio; m. Theron Weeks, Jr.; children: Rebecca, Theron R. BSN, Stockton State Coll., 1990; MSN, The Coll. of N.J., 1996. RN, NJ, cert. rehab. registered nurse Assn. Rehab. Nurses, cert. in nursing adminstrn., advanced ANCC. Staff nurse Akron Childrens Hosp., Ohio, William Beaumont Hosp., Royal Oak, Mich.; elected pub. official Twp. of Cranford, NJ; rehab. nurse Kessler Inst. Rehab., West Orange, NJ; supr. HIP/HMO Ambulatory Care Ctr., Medford, NJ; rehab. nurse mgr. Lourdes Rehab. Ctr., Camden, NJ; assoc. dir. nursing Wake Forest U. Bapt. Med. Ctr., Winston-Salem, NC; dir. medicine and oncology nursing Pardee Hosp., Hendersonville, NC. Rschr. in nursing. Contbr. articles to profl. jours. Bd. dirs. United Way; trustee pub. libr.; mem. Twp. Com. Bd. Health. Recipient B'nai B'rith award Commn. Svc., 1980; named Citizen of Yr., Cranford C. of C., 1974; named one of The Great 100 Nurses N.C., 2000. Mem.: Oncology Nursing Soc., Assn. Rehab. Nurses, Sigma Theta Tau. Home: 2070 Golfside Ln Hendersonville NC 28739-8844 Office: Pardee Hosp Hendersonville NC 28791 Business E-Mail: sandy.weeks@pardeehospital.org.

WEEKS, STEVEN WILEY, lawyer; b. Topeka, Mar. 7, 1950; s. Glen Wiley and Grace Aileen (West) W.; m. Lee Nordgren, Aug. 1, 1974 (div. 1985); 1 child, Kirstin Nordgren. BS summa cum laude, Washburn U., 1972; JD cum laude, Harvard U., 1977. Bar: Ohio. Project leader Nat. Sanitation Found., Ann Arbor, Mich., 1972; engr. Kans. Dept. Health and Environ., Topeka, 1972-74; ptnr. Taft, Stettinius & Hollister, Cin., 1977—. Dir. The Myers Y. Cooper Co., Cin.; adj. faculty Chase Coll. Law, 1987-88. Mem. adv. com. prosecuting atty., Hamilton County, Cin., 1992; mem. Hamilton County Rep. Ctrl. Com., 1994—; bd. dirs. Chestnut Station II Condominium, 2007-. Mem. Ohio State Bar Assn., Cin. Bar Assn. Republican. Methodist. Avocations: computers, golf. Home: 3560 Traskwood Cir Cincinnati OH 45208

WEEKS, WILFORD FRANK, retired geophysics educator, glaciologist; b. Champaign, Ill., Jan. 8, 1929; married; 2 children. BS, U. Ill., 1951, MS, 1953; PhD in Geology, U. Chgo., 1956. Geologist mineral deposits br. U.S. Geol. Survey, 1952-55; glaciologist USAF Cambridge Research Ctr., 1955-57; asst. prof. Washington U., St. Louis, 1957-62; adj. prof. earth scis. Dartmouth Coll., Hanover, NH, 1962-85; glaciologist Cold Regions Rsch. and Engring. Lab., Hanover, 1962-89; chief scientist Alaska Synthetic Aperture Radar Facility, Fairbanks, 1986-93; prof. geophysics Geophys. Inst. U. Alaska, Fairbanks, 1986-96. Cons. in field, 1996—; vis. prof. Inst. Low Temperature Sci. Hokkaido U., Sapporo, Japan, 1973; chair Arctic marine sci. USN Postgrad. Sch., Monterey, Calif., 1978-79; mem. earth sys. sci. com. NASA, Washington, 1984-87; advisor U.S. Arctic Rsch. Commn., divsn. polar programs NSF, Washington, 1987-88; chmn. NAS Com. on Cooperation with Russia in Ice Mechanics, 1991-92; mem. environ. task force MEDEA Cons. Group, 1992-2002. Capt. USAF, 1955—57. Recipient Emil Usibelli Prize for Rsch., 1996, U. Ill. Dept. Geology Alumni Achievment award, 1999. Fellow Arctic Inst. N.Am., Am. Geophys. Union; mem. NAE, Internat. Glaciological Soc. (v.p. 1969-72, pres. 1973-75, Seligman Crystal award 1989), Am. Polar Soc. (hon.). Avocations: contrabassist, geophysics. Home and Office: 6533 SW 34th Ave Portland OR 97239-1077 Office Phone: 503-244-1695. E-mail: w-f-weeks@comcast.net.

WEEKS, WILLIAM RAWLE, JR., oil industry executive; b. Denver, Oct. 23, 1920; s. William Rawle Sr. and Besse Elizabeth (Griffith) W.; m. June Suzanne Stephens, Jan. 22, 1944 (div. 1980); children: Stephen R., Tacy A. Weeks Hahn. BA, Stanford U., 1943. With book prodn. divsn. Stanford U. Press, 1948-49; advt. exec. Palo Alto, Calif., 1949-50; with CIA, 1951—; gen. ptnr. Weeks, Brewer & Assocs., 1971; CEO Fort Collins Consol. Royalties, Inc., Cheyenne, Wyo., 1983—. Author: Knock and Wait Awhile, 1957 (Edgar Allan Poe award 1958, Commonwealth award 1958). Nat. press and media advance man Muskie Vice Presdl. Campaign, 1968. 2nd lt. U.S. Army, 1943-46. Mem. Nat. Press Club, Denver Petroleum Club. Avocations: flying, skiing, golf, hiking.

WEEMS, KERRY N., former federal agency administrator; b. Portales, N.Mex., 1956; BA in Philosophy, N.Mex. State U., 1978, BBA in Mgmt., 1978; MBA, U. N.Mex., 1981. Staff mem. Appropriations Com. US Senate, 1981—83; program & budget analyst US Dept. Health & Human Services, Washington, 1983—88, program analyst Office of Budget, 1988—91, chief budget planning br., 1991—96, dir. divsn. budget policy, execution & mgmt., 1996—2002, acting dep. asst. sec. budget, 2001—02, acting asst. sec. for budget, tech. & fin., 2003—05, dep. chief staff, 2005—07, adminstr. Centers for Medicare & Medicaid Services, 2007—09.*

WEENING, RICHARD WILLIAM, JR., venture capitalist, media communications executive, entrepreneur; b. San Bernardino, Calif., Dec. 24, 1945; s. Richard William and Alice Louise (Young) Weening; m. Elizabeth Louise Halmbacher, June, 1966 (div. Aug. 1971); children: Elicia Louise, Mia Lynn; M. Robin Lorraine Woodard, July, 1990 (div. 2008). BA in Classics and Polit. Sci., St. Johns U., 1965; student, U. Wis., 1966-68. Legis. asst. U.S. Congressman Henry S. Reuss, Washington, 1968-70; exec. sec., chief of staff Wis. Gov. Patrick J. Lucey, Madison, 1970-72; pres., pub., dir. Raintree Pubs., Inc., Milw., 1972-85; pres., chief exec. officer, dir. McDonald-Raintree, Inc., 1977-82, George Philip Raintree, Cartographers, Inc., 1978-82; chmn., dir. Raintree Pubs. Internat., Ltd., London, 1978-82, Raintree de Mexico Editores, SA, 1978-82; chief exec. officer AgriData Resources, Inc., 1981-87; pres., chief exec. officer RPI Holdings, Inc., 1985—; owner Northcote Vineyards, 1979—. Bd. dirs. CONNECT, Inc., Med. Electronic Records Exchange, Inc., Electronic Product Info. Corp., Dynatec Systems Corp. Bd. dirs. FFA Found., 19830-87; active Chenqua Police and Fire Commn. Mem. Info. Industry Assn., Young Pres.'s Orgn. Office: 1235 W Canal St Milwaukee WI 53233

WEER, CHRISTY HARRIS, finance educator; b. Dover, Del., Apr. 22, 1971; d. Joseph Richard and Phyllis Stubbs Harris; m. George Milton Weer, June 14, 1997; children: Loryn Ava, Landon Mitchel. BA, Wash. Coll., Chestertown, Md., 1993; MBA, Salisbury U., Md., 1996; PhD, Drexel U., Phila., 2006. Asst. prof. mgmt. Radford U., Va., 2006—08, Salisbury U., Md., 2009—. Mem.: Acad. Mgmt., Zeta Tau Alpha. Home: 3415 Redden Ferry Rd Eden MD 21822 Office: Salisbury Univ 1101 Camden Ave Salisbury MD 21801 Business E-Mail: chweer@salisbury.edu.

WEERACKODY, VIJITHA, electrical engineer, researcher; BSc in Engring. with 1st class honors, U. Moratuwa, Sri Lanka, 1983; PhD, U. Pa., Phila., 1984—89. Mem. tech. staff Bell Laboratories, Lucent Technologies, Murray Hill, NJ, 1990—2001; pres. PetaNetworks, NYC, 2002—05; sr. profl. staff Johns Hopkins U./APL, Laurel, Md., 2005—. Cons. TLVentures, Wayne, Pa., 2004—; adj. assoc. prof. U. Pa., Phila., 2004—. Achievements include patents for About 25 US Patents on Wireless/Communication Systems. Office: Johns Hopkins Univ/APL 11100 Johns Hopkins Rd Laurel MD 20723 Personal E-mail: vijitha@ieee.org. Business E-Mail: vijitha.weerackody@jhuapl.edu.

WEERASINGHE, KUMUDINI MANGALA (KELLY WEISE), science educator; arrived in U.S., 1984; d. Albert Arliss and Tilaka Sirimathi Weerasinghe. BSc in Biochemistry, U. London, 1979, PhD in Basic Med. Scis., 1983. Rsch. assoc. Temple U. Sch. Medicine, Phila., 1984—85; sr. lectr. North Colombo Med. Coll., 1986—88; rsch. assoc. N.C. State U., Raleigh, 1989—92, U. N.C., Chapel Hill, 1993—94; asst. rsch. prof. George Washington U. Med. Ctr., Washington, 1996; adj. faculty Marymount U., Arlington, Va., 1998; ind. piano tchr. Cool Enrichment, Montgomery County, Md., 1998—2003; hands-on-sci. tchr. Montgomery County Coun. PTA, 2000—03; ind. tchr. sci. and piano Cool Enrichment, Allentown, Pa., 2004—. Adj. faculty Northampton C.C., Bethlehem, Pa., 2004—, Lehigh Carbon C.C., Allentown, Pa., 2005, East Stroudsburg U., Pa.; adj. asst. prof. Temple U., Phila., 2006—07, adj. assoc. prof., 2008—; tchg. asst. U. Penn., Phila., 2007—; lectr. Pa. State. U., Abington, 2008—. Author (as Kelly Weise): (children's books) Granpa Knowall and his pupils, 2004, Count Yourself!, 2004, The Beginning of His Story, 2007, poetry; contbr. articles to sci. jours. Named Best Young Investigator, Brit. Soc. Thrombosis and Haemostasis, 1982; postgrad. scholar, King's Coll. Med. Sch., U. London, 1979—83. Mem.: AAAS (Sr. Scientists and Engrs. chpt. sci. fair judge 2001—), Music Tchrs. Assn., Music Tchrs. Nat. Assn. (assist with piano tests and recitals 2001—03, co-chair elem. recitals 2003). Achievements include development of method to purify human blood coagulation factor XII; research in ability of platelet factor-4 to inhibit the initial reactions of blood coagulation and inflammation; presence of glandular kallikrein in the placenta; development of a hands-on-science enrichment program for pre-K through grade 3. Avocations: cooking, arts and crafts, reading, sewing and hand embroidery, reviewing religions.

WEERS, VESTA L., secondary school educator, department chairman; m. Harlan T. Olson, June 8, 1968; children: Dianna W. Lambert, Brenda D. McKinney. BA, U. Minn., Morris, 1971; EdM, U. Southern Calif., LA, 1978; MSci in Supervion and Adminstrn., U. South Fla., Tampa, 1999. Cert. Nat. Bd. Cert. Tchr., 2002. Tchr., dept. chair Hillsborough County Pub. Schs., Tampa, 2002—.

WEERTMAN, JOHANNES, materials science educator; b. Fairfield, Ala., May 11, 1925; s. Roelof and Christina (van Vlaardingen) W.; m. Julia Ann Randall, Feb. 10, 1950; children: Julia Ann, Bruce Randall. Student, Pa. State Coll., 1943-44; BS, Carnegie Mellon U., 1948, DSc, 1951; postgrad., Ecole Normale Superieure, Paris, 1951-52. Solid State physicist U.S. Naval Rsch. Lab., Washington, 1952-58, cons., 1960-67; sci. liaison officer U.S. Office Naval Rsch., Am. Embassy, London, 1958-59; faculty Northwestern U., Evanston, Ill., 1959—, prof. materials sci. dept., 1961-68, chmn. dept., 1964-68, prof. geol. scis. dept., 1963—, Walter P. Murphy prof. materials sci. and engring. emeritus, 1999—. Vis. prof. geophysics Calif. Inst. Tech., 1964, Scott Polar Rsch. Inst., Cambridge (Eng.) U., 1970-71, Swiss Fed. Inst. Reactor Rsch., 1986; cons. Cold Regions Rsch. and Engring. Lab., U.S. Army, 1960-75, Oak Ridge (Tenn.) Nat. Lab., 1963-67, Los Alamos (N.Mex.) Sci. Lab., 1967—; co-editor materials sci. books MacMillan Co., 1962-76. Author: Dislocation Based Fracture Mechanics, 1996, (with Julia Weertman) Elementary Dislocation Theory, 1964, 2d edit., 1992; mem. editorial bd. Metal. Trans., 1967-75, Jour. Glaciology, 1972—; assoc. editor Jour. Geophys. Rsch., 1973-75, 2000-01; contbr. articles to profl. jours. With USMC, 1943-46. Honored with naming of Weertman Island in Antarctica.; Fulbright fellow, 1951-52; recipient Acta Metallurgica gold medal, 1980; Guggenheim fellow, 1970-71 Fellow Am. Acad. Arts and Scis., Am. Soc. Metals, Am. Phys. Soc., Geol. Soc. Am., Am. Geophys. Union (Horton award 1972, AIME Mathewson Gold medal 1977); mem. AAAS, NAE, Am. Inst. Physics, Internat. Glaciol. Soc. (Seligman Crystal award 1983), Arctic Inst., Am. Quaternary Assn., Explorers Club, Fulbright Assn., Sigma Xi, Tau Beta Pi, Phi Kappa Phi, Alpha Sigma Mu, Pi Mu Epsilon. Home: 834 Lincoln St Evanston IL 60201-2405 Office: Northwestern U Materials Sci Dept Evanston IL 60208-0001 Home Phone: 847-328-8718; Office Phone: 847-491-3197. Business E-Mail: j-weertman2@northwestern.edu.

WEERTMAN, JULIA RANDALL, materials engineering educator; b. Muskegon, Mich., Feb. 10, 1926; BS in Physics, Carnegie-Mellon U., 1946, MS in Physics, 1947, DSc in Physics, 1951. Physicist U.S. Naval Rsch. Lab., Washington, 1952-58; vis. asst. prof. dept. materials sci. and engring. Northwestern U., Evanston, Ill., 1972-73, asst. prof., 1973-78, from asst. prof. to assoc. prof., 1973-82, prof., 1982-99, Walter P. Murphy prof., 1989, chmn. dept., 1987-92, asst. to dean grad. studies and rsch. Tech. Inst., 1973-76, Walter P. Murphy prof. emeritus, 1999—. Mem. various NRC coms. and panels. Co-author: Elementary Dislocation Theory, 1964, 1992, also pub. in French, Japanese and Polish; contbr. numerous articles to profl. jours. Mem. Evanston Environ. Control Bd., 1972-79. Recipient Creativity award NSF, 1981, 86; Guggenheim Found. fellow, 1986-87. Fellow Am. Soc. Metals Internat. (Gold medal 2005), Minerals, Metals and Materials Soc. (leadership award 1997, Robert Mehl lectr. 2006); Neutron Scattering Soc. America, mem. NAE, Am. Acad. Arts and Scis., Am. Phys. Soc., Materials Rsch. Soc. (Von Hippel award 2003), Soc. Women Engrs. (Disting. Engring. Educator award 1989, Achievement award 1991). Home: 834 Lincoln St Evanston IL 60201-2405 Office: Northwestern U Dept Material Sci & Engring 2220 Campus Dr Evanston IL 60208-0876 Office Phone: 847-491-5353. Business E-Mail: jrweertman@northwestern.edu.

WEESE, JOHN AUGUSTUS, retired mechanical engineer; b. Topeka, July 24, 1933; s. Ray Augustus and Margaret Maureen (Richmond) Weese; m. Betty Kay Dietrich, June 5, 1955; children: Carol Ann, Katherine Lynn. BSME, Kans. State U., 1955; MS, Cornell U., 1958, PhD, 1959. Asst. prof. USAF Acad., Colo., 1960-62; assoc. prof. mech. engring. U. Denver, 1963-67, prof., 1967-74, chmn. mech. sci. and environ. engring., 1968-70, dean engring., 1970-74, Old Dominion U., Norfolk, Va., 1974-83; dir. mech. engring. and applied mechanics NSF, Washington, 1983-85, dir. mechanics structures and materials engring., 1985-86; prof. mech. engring. Tex. A&M U., College Station, 1986—2005, head dept. engring. tech., 1986-97, coord. accreditation, regents prof., 1997—2005, interim head mech. engring. dept., 2001—03, prof. emeritus, 2005—. Structural dynamics engr. Boeing Co., Wichita, Kans., 1959—60, rsch. specialist, 1962—63; rsch. engr. Martin-Marietta Corp., Denver, 1963. Co-author: (book) Mechanics of Materials, 4th edit., 1985; contbr. articles to profl. jours. Fellow: ASME (ad hoc visitor 1977—83, Ben C. Sparks medal 1994), Am. Soc. Engring. Edn. (projects bd. engring. rsch. coun. 1982—85, chmn. publs. com. 1983—86, exec. com. 1984—90, chmn. engring. rsch. coun. 1988—90, v.p. pub. affairs 1995—97, pres.-elect 1998—99, pres. 1999—2000, Outstanding Educator mechanics divsn. 1989, Frederick J. Berger award 1997, W. Leighton Collins award 2004, Presdl. Disting Svc. award 2005); mem.: Rotary Club Annapolis. Republican. Congregationalist. Avocations: fishing, photography. Home: 34 Harness Creek View Ct Annapolis MD 21403-1678

WEESE-MAYER, DEBRA ELLYN, pediatrician, educator; b. Chgo., Jan. 31, 1953; d. Dr. Carlisle and Florence Weese; m. Robert Nathan Mayer, June 17, 1976; children: Jennifer Mayer, Jaimie Mayer, Jonathan Mayer. MD, U. Chgo. Pritzker Sch. Medicine, Ill., 1978. Pediat. prof. Rush U., Chgo., 1995—2008, Northwestern U. Feinberg Sch. Medicine, Chgo., 2008—. Dir., pediatric respiratory medicine Rush U. Med. Ctr., Chgo., 1993—2008; dir. Ctr. Autonomic Medicine in Pediat. at Children's Meml. Hosp., Chgo., 2008—. Contbr. articles to profl. sci. jours. Trustee Nathan Cummings Found., NYC, 2001—08; trustee and treas. Am. Thoracic Soc. Found., NYC, 2006—08. Grant, NIH, ATS, Scottish Cot Death Trust, Rett Syndrome Rsch. Found., Dysautonomia Found. Inc, Mar. Dimes, CJ Found. SIDS. Mem.: Am. Acad. Pediat., Am. Autonomic Soc., Am. Thoracic Soc., Soc. Pediatric Rsch., Am. Physiol. Soc. Achievements include patents for PHOX2B screening test to diagnose congenital central hypoventilation syndrome. Office: Children's Meml Hosp 2300 Children's Plz Chicago IL 60614 Office Fax: 773-880-8100. Business E-Mail: dweese-mayer@childrensmemorial.org.

WEESNER, ANNA, composer, music educator; b. Iowa City, 1965; BA, Yale U.; MFA, Cornell U., DMA, 1995. Assoc. prof. music U. Pa. Dept. Music, Phila., dir. undergraduate study. Resident MacDowell Colony, 1994, 98, Found. Royaumont, France, 1996, Seal Bay Festival, Summit Inst., Park City, Utah, Blue Mt. Ctr.; vis. artist Am. Acad in Rome. Recipient Young Composers award, ASCAP, 1995, winner, Young American's Art Song Competition, 1995, Brian Israel prize, Soc. New Music, 1995, Excellence in the Arts award, Va. Ctr. Creative Arts, 2006, Acad. award, AAAL, 2008; fellow Bunting Found., 2002, Pew Found., 2003, Guggenheim Found., 2009; Lakond scholarship, AAAL, 1993. Office: U Penn Dept Music 201 34th St Philadelphia PA 19104-6313 Office Phone: 215-898-7544. E-mail: weesner@sas.upenn.edu.*

WEFALD, JON, former academic administrator; b. Nov. 24, 1937; s. Olav and Walma (Ovrum) W.; m. Ruth Ann; children— Skipp, Andy. BA, Pacific Lutheran U., Tacoma, 1959; MA, Wash. State U., Pullman, 1961; PhD, U. Mich., Ann Arbor, 1965. Teaching asst. Wash. State U., Pullman, 1959—61; teaching fellow U. Mich., Ann Arbor, 1961—64; assoc. prof. Gustavus Adolphus Coll., St. Peter, Minn., 1965—70; commnr. agr. State of Minn., St. Paul, 1971—77; pres. Southwest State U., Marshall, Minn., 1977—82; chancellor Minn. State Univ. System, St. Paul, 1982—86; pres. Kans. State U., Manhattan, 1986—2009. Author: A Voice of Protest: Norwegians in American Politics 1890-1917, 1971. Mem. Mid-Am. Internat. Agri-Trade Council (pres. 1974-75), Midwest Assn. State Depts. of Agr. (sec.treas. 1976-77), U.S. Dept. Agr. Joint Council on Food and Agrl. Scis.

WEG, JOHN GERARD, physician; b. NYC, Feb. 16, 1934; s. Leonard and Pauline M. (Kanzleiter) W.; m. Mary Loretta Flynn, June 2, 1956; children: Diane Marie, Kathryn Mary, Carol Ann, Loretta Louise, Veronica Susanne, Michelle Celeste. BA cum laude, Coll. Holy Cross, Worcester, Mass., 1955; MD, N.Y. Med. Coll., 1959. Diplomate: Am. Bd. Internal Medicine. Commd. 2nd lt. USAF, 1958, advanced through grades to capt., 1967; intern Walter Reed Gen. Hosp., Washington, 1959-60; resident, then chief resident in internal medicine Wilford Hall USAF Hosp., Lackland AFB, Tex., 1960-64, chief pulmonary sect., 1964-66, chief inhalation sect., 1964-66, chief pulmonary and infectious disease service, 1966-67; resigned, 1967; clin. dir. pulmonary disease div. Jefferson Davis Hosp., Houston, 1967-71; from asst. prof. to assoc. prof. medicine Baylor U. Coll. Medicine, Houston, 1967-71; assoc. prof. medicine U. Mich. Med. Sch. Univ. Hosp., Ann Arbor, 1971-74, prof., 1974—2001, prof. emeritus, 2001—. Physician-in-charge pulmonary divsn., 1971-81, physician-in-charge pulmonary and critical care med. divsn., 1981-85, co-chair instnl. review bd., 2004—; cons. Ann Arbor VA, 1971—, Wayne County Gen. Hosps., 1971-84; mem. adv. bd. Washtenaw County Health Dept., 1973—; mem. respiratory and nervous sys. panel, anesthesiology sect. Nat. Ctr. Devices and Radiol. Health, FDA, 1983—, chmn., 1985-88. Contbr. med. jours., reviewer, mem. editorial bds. Decorated Air Force Commendation medal; travelling fellow Nat. Tb and Respiratory Disease Assn., 1971; recipient Aesculpaius award Tex. Med. Assn., 1971 Master ACP (chmn. Mich. program com. 1974); fellow Am. Coll. Chest Physicians (chmn. bd. govs. 1976-79, gov. Mich. 1975-79, chmn. membership com. 1976-79, prof.-in-residence 1972—, chmn. critical care coun. 1982-85, chmn. ethics com. 1998, master fellow, 2002, master FCCP, 2002, master), Am. Coll. Chest Physicians and Internat. Acad. Chest Physicians (master, exec. council 1976-82, pres. 1980-81); mem. AAAS, Am. Fedn. Clin. Rsch., AMA, Am. Thoracic Soc. (sec.-treas. 1974-76), Am. Assn. Inhalation Therapy, Air Force Soc. Internists and Allied Specialists, Soc. Med. Consultants to Armed Forces, Internat. Union Against Tb, Mich. Thoracic Soc. (pres. 1976-78), Mich. Lung Assn. (dir., Bruce Douglas award 1981), Am. Lung Assn., Rsch. Club U. Mich., Assn. Advancement Med. Instrumentation, Central Soc. Clin. Rsch., Am. Bd. Internal Medicine (subsplty. com. on pulmonary disease 1980-86, critical care medicine test com. 1985-87, critical care medicine policy com. 1986-87), N.Y. Med. Coll. Alumni Assn. (medal of honor 1990), Alpha Omega Alpha. Home: 3060 Exmoor Rd Ann Arbor MI 48104-4132 Office: B I H 245 Box 0026 1500 E Medical Center Dr Ann Arbor MI 48109-0005 Home Phone: 734-971-6156; Office Phone: 734-763-2540. Business E-Mail: jweg@umich.edu.

WEGMAN, EDWARD JOSEPH, statistician, educator, researcher; b. Terre Haute, Ind., July 4, 1943; s. Andrew Joseph and Adelaide Mary Wegman; m. Patricia K. Joyce, Mar. 17, 1998; children: Lisa Anne, Katherine Dawn. BS St. Louis U., 1965; MS, U. Iowa, 1967, PhD, 1968. Prof. stats. U. N.C., Chapel Hill, 1968-78; vis. prof. math. Manchester (Eng.) U., 1976-77; head math. scis. div. Office Naval Rsch., Arlington, Va., 1978-86; dir. Ctr. Computational Data Scis., George Mason U., 1986—. NSF Sr. Faculty fellow, 1976; recipient Meritorious Civilian Service medal U.S. Navy, 1981. Fellow AAAS, Am. Statis. Assn., Royal Statis. Soc., Inst. Math. Stats., Washington Acad. Sci.; mem. IEEE (sr.), Math. Assn. Am., Internat. Statis. Inst., Soc. Indsl. and Applied Math. Author: (with dePriest) Statistical Design of Weather Modification Experiments, 1980, (with Smith) Statistical Signal Processing, 1984, (with De Priest) Statistical Image Processing and Graphics, 1986, (with Schwartz and Thomas) Topics in Nongaussina Signal Processing, 1988, (with Davis and Newburgh) Brain Structure, Learning and Memory, 1988. Office: Ctr Computational Data Scis George Mason U 368 Rsch 1 4400 University Dr Fairfax VA 22030-4422 Office Phone: 703-993-1691. Business E-Mail: ewegman@gmu.edu.

WEGNER, HAROLD CLAUS, lawyer, educator, consultant; b. Evanston, Ill., Aug. 9, 1943; s. Helmuth A. and Cordelia E. (Claussen) W.; m. Barbara A. Mock, Dec. 18, 1975; children: Kirsten Birgit, Peter Christopher. BA, Northwestern U., 1965; JD, Georgetown U., 1969. Bar: Va. 1969, D.C. 1971, U.S. Ct. Appeals (fed. cir.) 1982, U.S. Supreme Ct. 1980. Patent examiner Dept. Commerce, Washington, 1965-69; assoc. Stevens, Davis, Miller & Mosher, Washington, 1969-71; ptnr. Armstrong & Wegner, Washington, 1971-74; vis. scholar Max Planck Inst. for Fgn. and Internat. Patent, Copyright and Competition Law, Munich, W.Ger., 1974-76; Kenshuin law faculty Kyoto (Japan) U., 1977; ptnr. Stevens, Davis, Miller & Mosher, Washington, 1977-80; mem. Wegner & Bretschneider, Washington, 1980—; adj. prof. law Georgetown U., 1983—; cons. Japan tech. transfer. Max Planck Inst. Fgn. and Internat. Author: Japanese Patent Law, 1979; contbr. articles to various publs. Patent, Copyright and Competition Law fellow, 1974-76. Mem. ABA (chmn. sect. subcom. 1981-82, 86-87), Va. State Bar (chmn. sect. 1979-80), Am. Intellectual Property Law Assn. (chmn. internat. com. 1978-79, chmn. haas amicus com. 1978, chmn. chem. practice com. 1982-85, bd. dirs. 1985-88), Internat. Patent and Trademark Assn. (chmn. employed inventors law 1982-85, patent harmonization com. 1985—), Federation Internationale des Conseils en Propriété Industrielle, Intellectual Property Owners, Inc., Com. of Experts on Patent Harmonization, World Intellectual Property Orgn. Presbyterian.

WEGNER, JUDITH WELCH, lawyer, educator, dean; b. Hartford, Conn., Feb. 14, 1950; d. John Raymond and Ruth (Thulen) Welch; m. Warren W. Wegner, Oct. 13, 1972. BA with honors, U. Wis., 1972; JD, UCLA, 1976. Bar: Calif. 1976, D.C. 1977, N.C. 1988, U.S. Supreme Ct. 1980, U.S. Ct. Appeals. Law clk. to Judge Warren Ferguson, U.S. Dist. Ct. for So. Dist. Calif., LA, 1976-77; atty. Office Legal Counsel and Land & Natural Resources Divsn. U.S. Dept. Justice, Washington, 1977-79; spl. asst. to sec. U.S. Dept. Edn., Washington, 1979-80; vis. assoc. prof. U. Iowa Coll. Law, Iowa City, 1981; asst. prof. U. NC Sch. Law, Chapel Hill, 1981-84, assoc. prof., 1984-88, assoc. dean, 1986-88, prof., 1988—2007, dean, 1989-99, Burton Craige prof., 2007—; sr. scholar Carnegie Found. for Advancement of Tchg., 1999—2001; chmn. faculty U. NC, 2003—06. Spkr. in field. Chief comment editor UCLA Law Rev., 1975-76; co-author Educating Lawyers, 2007, State and Loval Government in a Federal System, 6th edit., 2007; contbr. articles to legal publs. Mem. Bd. Alderman, Carrboro, NC, 1984—89; mem. planning bd. Orange County, NC, 2006—. Recipient Ernest Bell award, NC Assn. Mcpl. Attys. Mem.: ABA, Assn. Am. Law Schs. (pres. 1995), Internat. Mcpl. Lawyers Assn., Women's Internat. Forum, NC Assn. Women Attys., NC State Bar Assn., Order of the Coif, Phi Beta Kappa. Democrat. Office: U NC Sch Law Van Hecke Wettach Hall Campus Box 3380 Chapel Hill NC 27599-3380 Home Phone: 919-929-5024; Office Phone: 919-962-4113. Business E-Mail: judith_wegner@unc.edu.

WEGNER, KARL HEINRICH, retired pathologist, educator, farmer; b. Pierre, SD, Jan. 5, 1930; s. Lester and Nell (Norbeck) W.; m. Mary Josephine Waddell, June 15, 1957 (dec. 2003); children: Madeleine Jean, Peter Norbeck, Mary Nell; m. Margaret Ann Cash, Apr. 28, 2004. BA, Yale U., 1952; MD, Harvard U., 1959. Intern, resident Mass. Gen. Hosp./Harvard U., 1959-62; pathologist Sioux Valley Hosp., Sioux Falls, S.D., 1962-90; pathologist, dir. Lab. Clin. Medicine, Sioux Falls, 1962-90; prof., chmn. dept. pathology U. SD, 1968-73, v.p. health affairs, founding dean Sch. Medicine, 1973-79, Regents Disting. prof. emeritus, 1992—2009; owner Meadowlark Farms, Montrose, S.D.; ret. Mem. Bd. of Regents for Higher Edn., State of S.D., pres. bd. regents, 1996-97. Bd. dirs. U. S.D. Found.; pres. bd. dirs. Sioux Valley Hosp. Found., Sioux Falls Area Cmty. Found. With USMC, 1952—54, capt. Reserves USMC, 1954—58. Karl H. Wegner Endowed Professorship, Bd. of Regents for Higher Edn., 1979; recipient Disting. Svc. award S.D. State Med. Assn., 1984, Community Svc. award, 1975, Philanthropist of Yr. award, S.D., 2002; inducted to S.D. Hall of Fame, 1987; Karl and Mary Jo Wegner Health Scis. Info. Ctr. named in their honor, 1998. Fellow Coll. Am. Pathologists, Internat. Acad. Pathologists, Am. Soc. Pathologists; mem. Am. Pathology Found. (pres. 1984-85, Am. Pathologist of Yr. award, 1989), Alpha Omega Alpha. Home: 5010 S Sunnymede Cir Sioux Falls SD 57108-2823

WEGNER, MARY, state librarian; Degree in Hist., Iowa State U., 1971; MLS, U. Iowa, 1973. Reference libr. Waterloo Pub. Libr.; caucus staffer Iowa Ho. of Reps.; dir. Iowa Meth. Libr., Iowa Luth. Libr., Blank Children's Hosp., Des Moines; asst. state libr. State Libr. Iowa, Des Moines, 2000, state libr., 2001—. Mem. bd. trustees Bibliog. Ctr. for Rsch., 2000—. Mem.: Chief Officers State Libraries Assn. (vice chair, legis. com.), Iowa Libr. Assn. (pres. 1999). Office: State Library of Iowa Ola Babcock Miller Bldg 1112 E Grand Ave Des Moines IA 50319-0233 Office Phone: 515-281-4105. Office Fax: 515-281-6191. Business E-Mail: mary.wegner@lib.state.ia.us.

WEGULO, STEPHEN NGAKHALA, plant pathologist, researcher; b. Kakamega, Kenya, Sept. 27, 1961; came to U.S., 1988; s. Gabriel and Florence Ngakhala; m. Consolatrix Akinyi, Aug. 4, 1989; children: Gibb, Maury, Marianne. BS, Davidson Coll., 1991; MS, Iowa State U., 1994, PhD, 1997. Tchr. Shikokho Secondary Sch., Kakakamega, 1985-88, dep. head master, 1985-86, headmaster, 1986-88; head math. dept. Vihiga (Kenya) H.S., 1991-92; rsch. asst. Iowa State U., Ames, 1992-97, rsch. assoc., 1997-99, asst. scientist, 1999—. Contbr. articles to profl. jours. Mem. AAAS, Am. Phytopathological Soc., Iowa Acad. Sci., Sigma Xi, Phi Kappa Phi, Gamma Sigma Delta. Avocations: classical music, soccer. Office: Iowa State U Dept Plant Pathology 351 Bessey Hl Ames IA 50011-0001

WEH, ALLEN EDWARD, aviation executive; b. Salem, Oreg., Nov. 17, 1942; s. Edward and Harriet Ann (Hicklin) W.; m. Rebecca Ann Roberton, July 5, 1968; children: Deborah Susan, Ashley Elizabeth, Brian Roberton. BS, U. N.Mex., 1966, MA, 1973. Asst. to chief adminstrv. officer Bank N.Mex., Albuquerque, 1973; pres. N.Mex. Airways, Inc., Albuquerque, 1974; dep. dir. N.Mex. Indochina Refugee Program, Santa Fe, 1975-76; dir. pub. affairs UNC Mining & Milling Co., Albuquerque, 1977-79; pres., CEO, CSI Aviation Svcs., Inc., Albuquerque, 1979—. Chmn. New Mex. State Republican Party, 2004—08. Bd. dir. N.Mex. Symphony Orch., Albuquerque Conv. and Visitors Bur., 1982; mem. Albuquerque Police Adv. Bd., 1977-78; mem. state fin. com. G.W. Bush for Pres.; co-chmn. N.Mex. Victory, 2000; mem. nat. adv. bd. U. N.Mex. Anderson Sch. Bus.; elected del. GOP Nat. Conv., 2000, 04, 08; chmn. def. bd. Employer Support of the Guard and Res., 2002-03. Capt. USMC, 1966-71, Vietnam; Col. USMCR, 1971-97, active duty, 1990-91, Persian Gulf, 1992-93, Somalia, 2003-04, Iraq. Decorated Silver Star, Legion of Merit, Bronze Star with V device, Purple Heart with two gold stars, Meritorious Svc. medal with gold star, five Air medals. Mem. Marine Corps Res. Assn. (life), Res. Officers Assn. U.S. (life), N.Mex. Retail Assn. (chmn. 1999-2000). Episcopalian. Office: CSI Aviation Svcs Inc 3700 Rio Grande Blvd NW Albuquerque NM 87107-2876 Office Phone: 505-761-9000.

WEHDE, ALBERT EDWARD, lawyer; b. Milw., Feb. 14, 1935; s. Albert Christian and Mary Hubbel (Dewey) W.; m. Joan M. Forney, Nov. 4, 1978; children: John C., Edward T., David Wilkins., Carol Michaels. BS, Marquette U., 1956, JD, 1960. Bar: Wis. 1960, Calif. 1968. Atty. AEC, Albuquerque, 1963-66; counsel Lockheed Aircraft Co., Sunnyvale and Redlands, Calif., 1966-73; assoc. Schultz & Manfield, Palo Alto, Calif., 1973-74; sr. counsel FMC Corp., Santa Clara, Calif., 1974-95; atty. AEW Internat. Cons., Sunnyvale, 1995—. Bd. dirs. Tech. Credit Union, San Jose, Calif., 1982—, chmn., 1994-96. Pres. Mountain View (Calif.) Babe Ruth League, 1976; trustee Mid-Peninsula Family Services Assn., Palo Alto, 1973-74. Served to capt. U.S. Army, 1960-63. Mem. ABA (chmn. region VII pub. contracts sect. 1977-81), Santa Clara County Bar Assn. (co-chmn. corp. counsel sect. 1983-84, mem. exec. com.), Am. Corp. Counsel Assn. (chpt. sec., pres. 1988, bd. dirs. 1983-93), Wis. Bar Assn. (bd. dirs. non resident lawyers divsn. 2002-, pres. 2004-05, bd. govs. 2003-06, 2008-). Democrat. Roman Catholic. Avocations: gourmet cooking, music, sports. Home: 1106 Lorne Way Sunnyvale CA 94087-5157 Personal E-mail: wehde@aol.com.

WEHN, KAREN SWANEY, education educator, consultant; b. Chillicotne, Ohio, Mar. 1, 1950; d. Glenn Warren and Joyce Wood Swaney; m. David Carl Wehn, Apr. 8, 1989; 1 child, Glenn Ian Taylor. BA, Ohio State Univ., Columbus, Ohio, 1980; MS, Kent State Univ., Kent, Ohio, 1986. Cert. Profl. Geologist 1996. Rsch. asst. Ohio State Univ., Columbus, Ohio, 1976—92; project geologist Conestaga Rover 3 Assoc., Niagara Falls, NY, 1992—97, Golder Assoc., Niagara Falls, NY, 1997—; lectr. Buffalo State Coll., Buffalo, 1997—; asst. prof. Erie CC, Buffalo, 2000—. Rschr., Antarctica, 1980—85; pres. Buffalo Assn. of profl. Geologists, Buffalo, 1997—98. Contbr. articles pub. to profl. jour. Lay leader Warrens Corners United Meth. Ch., 2004—05. Grantee travel to Australia, Nat. Sci. Found., 1982, travel and work in Nigeria, Earth Watch, 1990—91. Mem.: Air and Waste Mgmt. Assn. (bd. mem.). Meth. Business E-Mail: wehnks@bscmail.buffalostate.edu.

WEHNER, ANDRÉ, psychologist, educator; PhD, Utah State U., Logan, 2001. Asst. prof. Centre Coll., Danville, Ky., 2001—.

WEHNER, PETER HERMANN, political scientist, former federal official; b. 1961; m. Cindy Wehner; 3 children. BA in Polit. Sci., U. Wash., 1983. Speechwriter for sec. US Dept. Edn.; spl. asst. to dir. Office Nat. Drug Control Policy; exec. dir. policy Empower Am.; spl. asst. to pres., dep. dir. speechwriting The White House, Washington, 2001—02, dep. asst. to pres., dir. White House Office of Strategic Initiatives, 2002—07; sr. fellow Ethics & Pub. Policy Ctr., Washington, 2007—. Writer Nat. Review Online; commentator Fox News, CNN, MSNBC, C-SPAN. Contbr. Commentary, The Weekly Standard, Nat. Review, Washington Post, Fin. Times, Wall St. Jour. Office: Ethics and Pub Policy Ctr 1015 15th St NW, Ste 900 Washington DC 20005 Office Phone: 202-682-1200. Office Fax: 202-408-0632. E-mail: pwehner@eppc.org.*

WEHRING, BERNARD WILLIAM, nuclear engineering educator; b. Monroe, Mich, Aug. 3, 1937; s. Bernard Albert and Alma Christina (Graf) W.; m. Margaret Mary Robinson, Sept. 5, 1959; children: Mary Ann, James, Susan, Barbara. BSE. in Physics, U. Mich., 1959, BSE. in Math, 1959; MS in Physics, U. Ill., 1961, PhD in Nuclear Engring, 1966. Asst. prof. nuc. engring. U. Ill., Urbana, 1966-70, assoc. prof., 1970-77, prof., 1977-84, asst. dean engring., 1981-82; prof. nuc. engring. N.C. State U., Raleigh, 1984-89; dir. nuc. reactor program NC State U., Raleigh, 1984-89; prof. mech. engring. U. Tex., Austin, 1989-2000, dir. Nuc. Engring. Tchg. Lab., 1989-2000; adj. prof. nuc. engring. NC State U., Raleigh, 2000—. Cons. Argonne and Los Alamos nat. labs.; mem. crosssect. evaluation working group Brookhaven Nat. Lab. Contbr. sects. to books, articles to profl. publs. AEC fellow, 1963-65; NSF grantee, 1968— Fellow Am. Nuc. Soc.; mem. Am. Nuclear Soc. (standards com.), Am. Phys. Soc. Achievements include contributing in the generation of basic nuc. data and develop. of new instruments and exptl. techniques. Home: 516 Westbrook Dr Raleigh NC 27615-7321 Business E-Mail: bwwehrin@eos.ncsu.edu.

WEHRLE, LEROY SNYDER, economist, educator; b. St. Louis, Feb. 5, 1932; s. Fred Joseph and Eleanor (Snyder) W.; m. JoAnn Griffith, Aug. 29, 1959; children— Chandra Lee, Lon Joseph. BS, Washington U., St. Louis, 1953; MA in Econs, Yale, 1956, PhD with honors, 1959. Asst. instr. Yale, 1958-59; with econ. sect. AID mission to Laos, 1960-61; sr. staff economist President's Council Econ. Advisers, 1961-62; spl. econ. adviser to U.S. Ambassador Unger, Vientiane, 1962; dep. dir. AID mission to Laos, 1963-64; asst. dir. AID mission, also econ. counsellor to U.S. ambassador, Saigon, 1964-67; asso. dir. AID Mission, Saigon, 1964-67; dept. asst. adminstr. Vietnam, AID, Dept. State, 1967-68; univ. fellow Harvard, 1968-69; sr. fellow Brookings Instn., 1969-70; dir. Ill. Inst. for Social Policy, Springfield, 1970-72; aide to Lt. Gov. Paul Simon, 1972; prof. economics Sangamon State U., 1972-88; founding ptnr., chief exec. officer Health Econs. and Mkt. Analysis Inc., Springfield, 1987-94; pres. Healthcare Cost Analysis, Inc., 1994—. Chmn. bd. Tie Collar, Ltd. Mem. spl. study group Alliance Progress, 1962; mem. Rockefeller Latin Am. Mission, 1969; chmn. study team world food and nutrition study Nat. Acad. Sci., 1976-77. Served with AUS, 1953-55. Recipient William A. Jump meml. award, 1966 Home and Office: 2001 S Bates Ave Springfield IL 62704-3304 Home Phone: 217-546-0799; Office Phone: 217-206-7781. Personal E-mail: wehrle@5springnet7.com.

WEI, HENG, engineering educator; BS in Civil/Hwy. and Traffic Engring., Beijing U. Tech., 1985, ME in Civil/Hwy. and Traffic Engring., 1988; MS in Civil Engring., U. Kans., 1996, PhD, 1999. Cert. profl. engr., Mich. Lectr., scientist Beijing U. Tech., 1988—93; rsch. and tchg. asst. U. Kans., Lawrence, 1993—98; sr. its transp. sys. engr. Iteris, Inc.

and TranSmart Technologies, Inc., Anaheim, Calif., 1998—2004; lectr. Calif. State Poly. U. Pomona, 2003—04, U. So. Calif., LA, 2003—04; asst. prof. U. Cin., 2004—. Editor-in-chief U. Kans. Transp. Ctr., Lawrence, 1994—98; trb rep. U. Cin., Transp. Rsch. Bd., Washington, 2004—. Recipient Outstanding Undergrad. Student award, Beijing U. Tech., 1985; grantee, NSF, 2005, TEC Engring., Inc., 2005. Mem.: N.Am. China Overseas Transp. Assn., Internat. Chinese Transp. Profls. Assn., Engring. Soc. Detroit, Inst. Transp. Engrs. (corr.; advisor to UC student chpt.), Transp. Rsch. Bd. (corr.). Achievements include development of a new method using video-capture technique to extract vehicular trajectory and supportive software, Vehicle Video-Capture Data Collector (VEVID); strategies for large Urban Intermodal Hubs and Radiator Rodway Systems; research in methodology for prioritizing locations of Urban Transit Transfer Centers; planning on Beijing Urban Intermodal Transportational Systems; China Metropolitan Comprehensive Transportation System Planning Modes; Heuristic-Optimization Models for Service Request Vehicle/Crew Routing with Time Windows in a GIS Environment; Iteris Transportation Systems projects. Office: Dept of Civil & Environ Engring Univ of Cincinnati Cincinnati OH 45221 Office Fax: 513-556-2599. Business E-Mail: heng.wei@uc.edu.

WEI, JAMES, chemical engineering professor, academic dean; b. Macao, China, Aug. 14, 1930; came to U.S., 1949, naturalized, 1960; s. Hsiang-chen and Nuen (Kwok) W.; m. Virginia Hong, Nov. 4, 1956; children: Alexander, Christina, Natasha, Randolph (dec.). BS in Chem. Engring, Ga. Inst. Tech., 1952; MS, MIT, 1954, ScD, 1955; grad., Advanced Mgmt. Program Harvard, 1969. From rsch. engr. to rsch. assoc. Mobil Oil, Paulsboro, NJ, 1956-62, sr. scientist Princeton, NJ, 1963-68, mgr. corp. planning NYC, 1969-70; Allan P. Colburn prof. U. Del., Newark, 1971-77; Sherman Fairchild distinguished scholar Calif. Inst. Tech., 1977; Warren K. Lewis prof. MIT, Cambridge, 1977-91, head dept. chem. engring., 1977-88; Pomeroy and Betty Smith prof. chem. engring. Princeton (N.J.) U., 1991—, dean Sch. Engring. and Applied Sci., 1991—2002. Vis. prof. Princeton, 1962-63, Calif. Inst. Tech., 1965; cons. Mobil Oil Corp.; cons. com. on motor vehicle emissions Nat. Acad. Sci., 1972-74, 79-80; mem. sci. adv. bd. EPA, 1976-79; mem. Presdl. Pvt. Sector Survey Task Force on Dept. Energy, 1982-83. Bd. editors Chem. Tech, 1971-80, Chem. Engring. Communications, 1972—; cons. editor chem. engring. series, McGraw-Hill, 1964—; editor-in-chief: Advances in Chemical Engineering, 1980; Contbr. papers, monographs to profl. lit., The Structure of Chemical Processing Industries, 1979. Trustee Am. U. Beirut, 1998—, Smith Coll., 1999—. Recipient Am. Acad. Achievement Golden Plate award, 1966. Mem. AIChE (dir. 1970-72, Inst. lectr. 1968, Profl. Progress award 1970, Walker award 1980, Lewis award 1985, v.p. 1987, pres. 1988, Founders award 1990), Am. Chem. Soc. (award in petroleum chemistry 1966), Nat. Acad. Engring. (nominating com. 1981, 96, peer com. 1980-82, membership com. 1983-85, Draper award com. 1995-97, chair chem. engring. sect. 1998-99), AAAS, Am. Acad. Arts and Scis., Academica Sinica of Taiwan, Sigma Xi. Home: 571 Lake Dr Princeton NJ 08540 Office: Princeton U Engring Quadrangle Princeton NJ 08544-5263 E-mail: jameswei@princeton.edu.

WEI, JOHN THOMAS, urologist, educator; b. Hong Kong, Jan. 3, 1967; came to U.S., 1972; s. John K.C. and Lina Ko Wei; m. Mary Lee Wei, Sept. 25, 1993; children: Nicholas John, Katherine Britney. BS, Northwestern U., Chgo., 1989; MD, Northwestern U. Med. Sch., Chgo., 1991; MS, U. Mich. Sch. Pub. Health, 1999. Resident in surgery North Shore Univ. Hosp., Manhasset, NY, 1991-93; resident in urology Cornell-N.Y. Hosp., NYC, 1993-97; Robert Wood Johnson clin. scholar U. Mich., Ann Arbor, 1997-99, lectr. medicine and surgery, 1997-99, asst. prof. surgery, 1999—, assoc. prof., dept. urology, asst. prof. urology, dir., clin. rsch. and quality assurance, assoc. dir., Clin. Rsch. Tng. Program in Urology; staff urologist Ann Arbor VA Med. Ctr., 1997—. Voting mem. R&D com. Ann Arbor VA, 2000—. Chmn. prostate cancer com. Mich. Cancer Consortium, 1999. Am. Found. for Urologic Disease scholar, 1997. Mem. Am. Assn. Clin. Urologists, Am. Urol. Assn., Chinese Am. Med. Soc. Avocations: gardening, wood craft, aquariums. Office: Univ of Mich Taubman Ctr 3875 1500 E Medical Center Dr Ann Arbor MI 48109-0330 Mailing: Livonia Ctr for Specialty Care 19900 Haggerty Rd Fl 1 Ste 111 Livonia MI 48152-1052 Office Phone: 734-615-3040, 734-936-7030. E-mail: jtwei@umich.edu.*

WEI, LEI, telecommunications educator; b. NanJing, China, Feb. 5, 1964; s. Jia Kun and Yu Jie (Xie) W.; m. Honghui Qi, Oct., 1989; children: David M., Catherine Minming Wei. BE, NanJing Inst. of Posts, 1986; Me, U. NSW, 1993; PhD, U. South Australia, 1995. Rschr. NanJing Inst. of Post and Telecomms., China, 1985-90; rschr. fellow The ANU, Canberra, Australia, 1995-96; lectr. Australian Nat. U., Canberra, 1996-98, sr. lectr., 1998—. Cons. Coop. Rsch. Ctr. for Robust and Adaptive Control, Australia, 1995—. Patentee for a multiuser system for telecommunications, decoding method and apparatus. Commr. The Fedn. of Chinese Cmty. in Canberra, 1996. Grantee Australian Telecomm. Electronic Rsch. Bd., 1996, Australian Rsch. Coun., 1996. Mem. IEEE. Avocation: tai chi. Office: Univ of Central Florida 4000 Central Florida Blvd Orlando FL 32816

WEI, MARIA L., dermatologist, educator; Diplomate Am. Bd. Dermatology. Asst. prof. dermatology U. Calif., San Francisco, 2003—. Achievements include research in melanoma and melanocyte biology.

WEI, PAX S.P., research scientist; s. George C. and Alice B. G. Wei; m. Amy J. Wei; children: Pamela L., Oliver L., Regina L. BS, Nat. Taiwan U., Taipei, 1960; MS, U. Ill., Urbana, 1963; PhD, Calif. Inst. Tech., Pasadena, 1967. Tech. staff mem. Bell Telephone Lab., Murray Hill, NJ, 1967—69; rsch. scientist Boeing Co., Seattle, 1969—. Mem.: Antenna Measurement Technique Assn., Am. Chem. Soc., Am. Physical Soc. Office: Boeing Co PO Box 3707 M/S 4C-02 Seattle WA 98124

WEI, XIANGDONG, physicist, researcher; s. Bo and Jinzhi Wei. BS in Astrophysics, Peking U., Beijing, 1982; MS in Physics, Syracuse U., NY, 1992, PhD in Physics, 1994. From tchg. asst. to rsch. assoc. Syracuse U., 1988—98; asst. physicist Brookhaven Nat. Lab., Upton, NY, 1998—2000, assoc. physicist, 2000—03, physicist, 2003—. Presenter in field. Contbr. articles to profl. jours. Mem.: Am. Phys. Soc. Achievements include development of highly polarized frozen-sipn HD targets for both nuc. physics and inertial-confinement-fusion experiments; design of utilizing the polarized HD target sys. for nuc. physics measurements; research in spin-lattice relaxation time of HD-hydrogen deuteride. Office: Brookhaven Nat Lab 20 Pennsylvania Ave Upton NY 11973

WEI, XINZHOU, engineering educator; b. China; PhD, CUNY, NYC, 2002. Lectr. CUNY, Coll. Tech., Bklyn., 2002—03, asst. prof., 2003—. Program com. Internat. Symposium on Knowledge Comm. and Conf., Orlando, Fla., 2006—; session chair The 8th World Multi-Conf. on Systemics, Cybernetics and Informatics, Orlando, 2004; Asian Am. high edn. coun. Asian Rsch. Inst., NYC, 2004—; info. tech. com. CUNY Coll. Tech., Bklyn., 2003—; reviewer IEE Jour. of Info. Security, 2006—. Recipient Sue Rosenberg Zalk Student Rsch. and Travel award, CUNY, 2002, Best Paper award, 6th World Multi-Conf. Systemics, Cybernetics and Informatics, 2002, 8th World Multi-Conf. Systemics, Cybernetics and Informatics, 2004, 2d prize, Chinese Nat. Higher Edn. Com., 1991; grantee Perkins grantee, N.Y. State, 2006—, PSC-CUNY grantee, Rsch. Found. of the CUNY, 2006—, 2005—06, 2004—05. Mem.: Internat. Soc. of Systemics, Cybernetics and Informatics, Asian Rsch. Inst. (ny 2004—06), IEEE. Office: City University of New York / CityTech Dept of Electrical Eng 300 Jay Street Brooklyn NY 11201

WEI, YANZHANG, microbiologist, educator; s. Guoxun Wei and Shuyun Zhong; m. Jinhua Li, Apr. 21, 1966; children: Joshua Li, Catherine Li. PhD, Ohio U., 1996. Asst. dir. Greenville Hosp. Sys., SC; assoc. prof. Clemson U., SC, 2004—08. Mem.: AACR. Home: 209 S Ticonderoga Dr Greer SC 29650 Office: Clemson Univ 900 W Faris Rd Greenville SC 29605 Business E-Mail: ywei@clemson.edu.

WEICH, RONALD HARRIS, federal agency administrator; b. NYC, Nov. 19, 1959; Student, London Sch. Econs., 1979; BA, Columbia U., 1980; JD, Yale U., 1983. Bar: N.Y. 1984, U.S. Ct. Appeals (D.C. cir.) 1988. Asst. dist. atty. N.Y. Dist. Atty's Office, NYC, 1983-87; spl. counsel US Sentencing Commn., Washington, 1987-89; minority counsel US Senate Constitution Subcommittee, Washington, 1989; chief counsel drug policy US Senate Labor & Human Resources Com., Washington, 1990-95, gen. counsel, 1992-95; chief counsel to Senator Edward Kennedy US Senate Judiciary Com., Washington, 1995—97; ptnr. Zuckerman Spaeder LLP, 1997—2004; sr. counsel to Senator Harry Reid US Senate, Washington, 2005—07, chief counsel, 2007—09; asst. atty. gen. for legis. affairs US Dept. Justice, Washington, 2009—. Guest editor Federal Sentencing Reporter, 1991; contbr. articles to profl. jours. Named one of The 105 Most Influential Lawyers in the United States, The Nat. Law Jour., 1994. Office: US Dept Justice 950 Pennsylvania Ave NW Washington DC 20530 Office Phone: 202-514-2141. Business E-Mail: ron.weich@vgdo.gov.

WEICKER, MICHELINA EVA, biology professor, consultant; d. Paolo and Giovanna L'Episcopia Cardone; m. Ray F. Cardone, July 4, 1994; children: Raymond Paul, Stefan Robert. MD, La Sapienza U. Rome, 1988; MBA in Health Care, Alvernia U., Reading, Pa., 2004. Asst. prof. Alvernia U., 2001—, prof. biology, 2001—. Nutritional cons. Ctr. TMJ & Sleep Apnea, Reading, 2008—. Contbr. articles to profl. jours. Fellow Postdoc. rsch. pathology, NIH, 1990. Achievements include research in P53 & colon cancer. Office: Ctr TMJ & Sleep Apnea 2000 Morgantown Reading PA 19607 Business E-Mail: eva.weicker@alvernia.edu.

WEICKERT, WANDA OPAL, child welfare and attendance counselor, psychotherapist, educator; b. LaCygne, Kans., Apr. 10, 1941; d. Frank W and Opal M Weickert. BS in Phys. Edn., Kans. State Coll., 1959—63, MS in Phys. Edn., 1963—66; MA in Marriage and Family Therapy, Phillips Grad. Inst., 1983—85; Pupil Personnel Services Credential, Calif. Luth. Coll., 1987—89. Marriage Family Child Therapist Bd. of Behavioral Sciences-California, 1991; Teaching Credential Kans., 1963, Calif., 1969. Health phys. edn. tchr. Circle HS, Towanda, Kans., 1963—69; phys. edn. tchr. Nightingale Mid. Sch., LA, 1969—73; coach & phys. edn. tchr. Reseda Sr. HS, LA, 1973—81; career edn., coach, tchr. Kennedy Sr. HS, LA, 1981—89; child welfare & attendance counselor LA Unified Sch. Dist., 1989—; marriage family child therapist Self Employed, LA, 1991—; dist. counselor LA Unified Schs., 1994—2001. Coord. cheerleaders, kayettes and pep club Circle HS, Towanda, Kans., 1963—69; dir. camp waterfront Young Women's Christian Assn., Wichita, Kans.; counselor San Fernando Valley Mental Health Clinic, Van Nuys, Calif., 1985—88; drug prevention program dir. Kennedy HS, LA, 1987—89; counselor Valley Cmty. Clinic, North Hollywood, Calif., 1989—92; adv. bd. Sch. Attendance Rev. Bd. LAUSD, LA, 1991—2001; coach 1st pl. gymnast fl. exercise, city championships LA Unified Schs., 1976, coach 3d pl. volleyball team city championships, 79, coach 3d pl. gymnast all-around events, city championships, 80, crisis team leader, 1996—2001. Choreographer (drill team performance) LA Coliseum, 1977, Hollywood Christmas Parades, 1984—86, (1st pl. band and drill team championships) LA Unified Schs., 1978. Vol. Girl Scouts, LA, 1994—95; contbr. Civitan, Burbank, Calif.; presidents club contbr. Pitts. State U., Kans. Recipient Commendation for 32 years Pub. Sch. Svc., Mayor Jim Hahn, LA, 2001. Mem.: Calif. Assn. of Marriage and Family Therapists, Calif. Teachers Assn., Delta Psi Kappa (life), Alpha Sigma Alpha (life). Avocations: quilting, gardening, camping, swimming, walking. Personal E-mail: res1fosk@verizon.net.

WEIDEMANN, CELIA JEAN, social sciences educator, management consultant, financial consultant; b. Denver, Dec. 6, 1942; d. John Clement and Hazel (Van Tuyl) Kirlin; m. Wesley Clark Weidemann, July 1, 1972; 1 child, Stephanie Jean. BS, Iowa State U., 1964; MS, U. Wis., Madison, 1970, PhD, 1973; post grad., U. So. Calif., 1983. Advisor UN FAO, Ibadan, Nigeria, 1973—77; ind. rschr. Asia and Near East, 1977—78; program coord., asst. prof., rsch. assoc. U. Wis., Madison, Wis., 1979—81; chief inst. and human resources US AID, Washington, 1982—85; team leader, cons. Sumatra, Indonesia, 1984; dir. fed. econ. program Midwest Rsch. Inst., Washington, 1985—86; founder, pres. emeritus Weidemann Assoc., Arlington, Va., 1986—2000; pres. Weidemann Found., Arlington, Va., 2000—. Cons. U.S. Congress, Aspen Inst., Ford Found., World Bank, Egypt, Nigeria, Gambia, Pakistan, Indonesia, AID, Thailand, Jamaica, Panama, Philippines, Sierra Leone, Kenya, Jordon, Poland, India, Egypt, Russia, Finnish Internat. Devel. Agy., Namibia, pvt. client Estonia, Latvia, Russia, Japan, Internat. Ctr. Rsch. on Women, Zaire, UN FAO, Ghana, Internat. Statis. Inst., The Netherlands, Global Exch., 1986-87, Asian Devel. Bank, Mongolia, Nepal, Vietnam, Bangladesh, Indonesia, Philippines; peer reviewer NRC, NAS Author: (book) Planning Home Economics Curriculum for Social and Econ. Develop., Agrl. Ext. for Women Farmers in Africa, 1990, Fin. Services for Women, 1992, Egyptian Women and Micro.: The Invisible Entrepreneurs, 1992, Small Enterprise Development in Poland: Does Gender Matter?, 1994, Micro. and Gender in India, 1995, Supporting Women's Livelihoods: Micro Fin. That Works for the Majority, 2002; contbr. chapters to books and articles to profl. journals. Bd. visitors Sch. Human Ecology, U. Wis., 2002—; founding mem. Nat. Assn. Women Bus. Owners, Santa Barbara; bd. dirs. Women's Polit. Com., Santa Barbara, Calif., 2007—, Cmty. Counseling Ctr., Santa Barbara, 2004—, Women's Econ. Ventures, Santa Barbara, 2007—; mem Host Com. and Speaker, Women's Festival Calif. and Ariz., 2008. Am. Home Econ. Assn. Fellow, 1969-73; grantee Ford Found., 1987-89. Mem. Soc. Internat. Devel., Am. Sociol. Assn., Assn. for Women in Devel. (pres. 1989, founder, bd. dirs.), Women in Devel. (steering com.), Coalition for Women's Econ. Devel. and Global Equality, Internat. Devel. Conf. (bd. dirs., exec. com.), Internat. Platform Assn., Pi Lambda Theta, Omicron Nu. Avocations: mountain trekking, piano and pipe organ, canoeing, photography, poetry. Office: Weidemann Found 749 Westwood Drive Santa Barbara CA 93109 Home Phone: 805-637-7988; Office Phone: 805-965-2902. Personal E-mail: jweidemann@aol.com.

WEIDEMEYER, CARLETON LLOYD, lawyer; b. Hebbville, Md., June 12, 1933; BA in Polit. Sci., U. Md., 1958; JD, Stetson U., DeLand, Fla., 1961. Bar: Fla. 1961, DC 1971, US Dist. Ct. (mid. dist.) Fla. 1963, US Ct. Appeals (5th cir.) 1967, US Ct. Appeals (DC cir.) 1976, US Supreme Ct. 1966, US Ct. Appeals (11th cir.) 1982. Rsch. asst. Fla. 2d Dist. Ct. Appeals, 1961-65; ptnr. Kalle and Weidemeyer, St. Petersburg, Fla., 1965-68; asst. pub. defender 6th Jud. Cir., Fla., 1966-69, 81-83; ptnr. Wightman, Weidemeyer, Jones, Turnbull and Cobb, Clearwater, Fla., 1968-82; pres. Carleton L. Weidemeyer, P.A. Law Office, 1982—; pres. So. Mcpl. Corp., 1997—. Guest lectr. Stetson U., 1978—80; lectr. estate planning seminars. Author: (handbook) Arbitration of Entertainment Claims, Baltimore County's Second District, The Emerging Thirties, 1990, Area History, Baltimore County, 1990, History of Musicians' Association of Clearwater, Local 729, AFM, 1999; editor Ad Lib mag., 1978-81; pub. Weidemeyer World Quar., 2000—; contbr. articles to profl. jours.; performer This Is Your Navy Radio Show, Memphis, 1951-52; leader Polka Dots, The Jazz Notes, 1976—; mem. St. Paul Ch. Orch., Fla. Hist. Soc., 1973-1976, Md. Hist. Soc., 1990—, Pinellas County Estate Planning Assn., 1997-2005; performer Clearwater Jazz Holiday, 1980, 81. Bd. advisors Musician Ins. Trust; trustee Francis G. Prasse Meml. Scholarship Trust, 1984—, Jeanne Pisano Meml. Trust Young Musicians, 2008-; mem. planned giving com. Upper Pinellas Assn. Retarded Citizens, 1996-2001; trustee Tampa Bay Rsch. Inst., 2001—; adv. com. Fla. Sheriff Youth Ranches, 1997—2001; bd. dirs. Pinellas Ctr. for Visually Impaired, 1999-2000; bd. dirs. Watson Ctr. for the Blind, 2000-05; co-chmn. squadron VX-4, VW2 Navy Review Com., 1996-2009. Served with USN, 1951-54 Recipient Shriners Hosp. award, Upper Pinellas Assn. Retarded Citizens, 1992, Pres.'s award, 1998, Lighthouse for Blind, 2005, Patron of Jazz award, Suncoast Classic Jazz Soc., Inc., 2003, Sertoma Centurian award, Fla. Sheriff's Assn., 1991—95, Life Membership award, Loyal Order of Moose, 2005. Mem. Musicians Assn. Clearwater (pres. 1976-81, emeritus 1981), Fla.-Ga. Conf. Musicians (sec., treas. 1974-76), NRA, ABA (sr. bar sect.), Fed. Bar Assn., Fla. State Hist. Soc., Md. Hist. Soc., Greater St. Petersburg Musicians Assn., Clearwater Bar Assn. (probate divsn.), Am. Fedn. Musicians (internat. law com. pres. so. conf. musicians 1979-80), Nat. Geneal. Soc., Clearwater Genealogy Soc., Md. Geneal. Soc., Augustan Soc., Lancaster Geneal. Soc. (Pa.), Pinellas Geneal. Soc. (lectr. 1995—), Carroll County Geneal. Soc. (Md.), Balt. County Geneal. Soc. (Fla.), Lancaster Mennonite Hist. Soc., Navy Hurricane Hunters, Sons Am. Revolution, Sons Union Vets. Civil War, Md. Hist. Soc., Catonsville (Md.) Hist. Soc., Am. Legion, German Am. Geneal. Assn., DAV, Fleet Res., Masons, Scottish Rite (Tampa), Egypt Temple Shrine, Moose, Sertoma (bd. dirs. Clearwater chpt. 1984-2006, v.p. 1989-92), Phi Delta Phi, Sigma Pi, Kappa Kappa Psi Home: 2261 Belleair Rd Clearwater FL 33764-2761 Office: Legal Arts Bldg Ste 1 501 S Fort Harrison Ave Clearwater FL 33756-5317 Personal E-mail: clludee@aol.com.

WEIDENBAUM, MURRAY LEW, economist, educator; b. Bronx, NY, Feb. 10, 1927; s. David and Rose (Warshaw) Weidenbaum; m. Phyllis Green, June 13, 1954; children: Susan, James, Laurie. BBA, CCNY, 1948; MA, Columbia U., 1949; MPA, Princeton U., 1954, PhD, 1958; LLD, Baruch Coll., 1981, U. Evansville, 1983, McKendree Coll., 1993. Fiscal economist Bur. Budget, Washington, 1949—57; corp. economist Boeing Co., Seattle, 1958—62; sr. economist Stanford Rsch. Inst., Palo Alto, Calif., 1962—63; mem. faculty Washington U., St. Louis, 1964—, prof., chmn. dept. econs., 1966—69, Mallinckrodt prof., 1971—, dir. Ctr. for Study Am. Bus., 1974—81, Washingon U., St. Louis, 1982—95; chmn. Ctr. for Study Am. Bus. Washington U., St. Louis, 1995—2000; asst. sec. econ. policy US Dept. Treasury, Washington, 1969—71; chmn. Coun. of Econ. Advisors The White House, Washington, 1981—82; hon. chmn. Weidenbaum Ctr. on the Economy, Govt. and Pub. Policy, St. Louis, 2001—. Chmn. rsch. adv. com. St. Louis Regional Indsl. Devel. Corp., 1965—69; exec. sec. Pres.'s Com. on Econ. Impact of Def. and Disarmament, 1964; mem. U.S. Fin. Investment Adv. Panel, 1970—72; cons. various firms and instns.; chmn. U.S. Commn. to Rev. the Trade Deficit, 1999—2000. Author: Federal Budgeting, 1964, Modern Public Sector, 1969, Economics of Peacetime Defense, 1974, Economic Impact of the Vietnam War, 1967, Government-Mandated Price Increases, 1975, The Future of Business Regulation, 1980, Rendezvous With Reality: The American Economy After Reagan, 1988, Rendezvous With Reality: The American Economy After Reagan, paperback edit., 1990, Business, Government, and the Public, 1990, Small Wars, Big Defense, 1992, The Bamboo Network, 1996, Business and Government in the Global Marketplace, 2004, One-Armed Economist, 2004, Advising Reagan: Making Economic Policy, 1981-82, 2005, Competition of Ideas, 2008; mem. editl. bd.: Publius, 1971—2004, Jour. Econ. Issues, 1972—75, Challenge, 1974—81, 1983—, Business and the Contemporary World, 1997—2000. With US Army, 1945. Recipient Alexander Hamilton medal, U.S. Dept. Treasury, 1971, Disting. Writer award, Georgetown U., award for disting. tchg., Freedoms Found., 1980, award for best book in econs., Assn. Am. Pubs., 1993; named Banbury fellow, Princeton U., 1952—54; named to Free Market Hall of Fame, 1983. Fellow: Internat. Acad. Mgmt., Am. Acad. Arts & Scis., Assn. for Pvt. Enterprise Edn. (Adam Smith award 1986), City Coll. Alumni Assn. (Townsend Harris medal 1969), Soc. Tech. Comm., Nat. Assn. Bus. Economists, Cosmos. Office: Washington Univ Weidenbaum Ctr 1 Brookings Dr Saint Louis MO 63130-4899 Home Phone: 314-727-8950; Office Phone: 314-935-5662.

WEIDENBAUM, RHODA SUSSMAN, history educator, researcher; d. Carl and Celia Sussman; m. Sherman S. Weidenbaum, Oct. 30, 1948; children: Karen Tali Menkin, Mark, Abigail Eve Dishi. AB cum laude, Barnard Coll., NYC, 1951; MA in History of China, Columbia U., NYC, 1953; MA in US and European History, U. Conn., Storrs, 1974, PhD in Polit. Sci., 1981. Fellow Chinese history Yale U., New Haven, 1987—90; assoc. in rsch. Fairbank Ctr., Harvard U., Cambridge, Mass., 1990—2009; lect. US Coast Guard Acad., 1968—69. Rsch. scholar Beijng U., 1987—88, Qinghua U., Beijing, 1988; lectr. in field. Contbr. rsch. papers to profl. publs.; creator (TV series) China for Ednl. TV, 1960. Leader, synagogues svc. reader Torah scroll Beth El and Beth Jacob Synagogues, New London and Norwich, Conn. Recipient 1st prize ann. meeting, Psychohistory Assn., 1990; named most disting. fgn. scholar, Nankai U., Tianjin, China, 1998; Travel grantee, U. Alaska, Fairbanks, 1984. Mem.: Assn. Asian Studies (hon.; panel organizer, chmn. ann. meeting 1985). Jewish. Achievements include first woman to lecture at the US Coast Guard Academy. Avocations: vocal studies, musical composition for synagogue services, travel, cooking. Home: 17 Fifth Ave Waterford CT 06385 Home Phone: 860-442-2235. Personal E-mail: drrhoda81@sbcglobal.net.

WEIDENFELD, EDWARD LEE, lawyer; b. Akron, Ohio, July 15, 1943; s. Sam and Beatrice (Cooper) W.; m. Sheila Rabb, Aug. 11, 1968; children: Nicholas, Daniel. BS, U. Wis., 1965; JD, Columbia U., 1968. Bar: NY 1968, admitted to practice: US Supreme Ct. 1972, bar: DC 1973. Pvt. practice, NYC, 1969-71, 73-82, Washington, 1982—. Spl. cons. N.Y.C. Dept. Bldgs., 1967; counsel, dir. energy staff Com. on Interior and Insular Affairs, U.S. Ho. of Reps., 1971—73; mem. faculty Am. Law Inst.-ABA CLE Programs; mem. Internat. Del. to Observe Philippine Election, 1986, Internat. Del. to Observe Republic Korea Election, 1987, Pakistan Election, 1988, Chilean Election, 1989, Albanian Election, 1997; mem. D.C. Bar Task Force on the Omnibus Trusts and Estates Amendment Act of 2000, 1999—2001; lectr. to profl. groups. Editor in chief Atomic Energy Law Jour., 1975-76; contbg. author: Generations: Planning Your Legacy, 1999. Mem. Pres.'s Commn. on White House Fellowships, 1977; nat. chmn. Lawyers for Reagan/Bush, 1980; chief counsel Reagan/Bush Campaign, 1980; chmn. Reagan/Bush '84 Legal Adv. Bd., 1984; mem. D.C. Rep. Com., 1984-92, vice chmn., 1984-88; mem. Coun. Adminstrv. Conf. of U.S., 1981-92, sr. fellow, 1992-95; overseer dept. def. regional ctrs., sec. Salvation Army Adv. Bd.; trustee Danny Kaye and Sylvia Fine Kaye Found.; chmn. bd. visitors Nat. Def. U. Recipient medal of Peter the Great, Russian Fedn., 2000; named one of 75 Best Lawyers in Washington, Washingtonian mag., 2002. Mem. ABA, D.C. Bar Assn., Am. Law Inst. (life), Assn. Bar City N.Y., Met. Club (bd. govs., Washington). Office: 888 17th St NW Washington DC 20006 Office Phone: 202-785-2143. Business E-Mail: edward@weidenfeldlaw.com.

WEIDENFELD, SHEILA RABB, television producer, writer; b. Cambridge, Mass., Sept. 7, 1943; d. Maxwell M. and Ruth (Cryden) Rabb; m. Edward L. Weidenfeld, Aug. 11, 1968; children: Nicholas Rabb, Daniel Rabb. BA, Brandeis U., 1965. Assoc. prodr. Metromedia, Inc., Sta. WNEW-TV, NYC, 1965-68; talent coord. That Show with Joan Rivers, NBC, NYC, 1968-71; coord. NBC network game programs, NYC, 1968-71; prodr. Metromedia, Inc., Sta. WTTG-TV, Washington, 1971-73; creator/prodr. Take It From Here, NBC (WBC-TV), Washington, 1973-74; press sec. to first lady Betty Ford, spl. asst. to Pres. Gerald R. Ford, 1974-77; mem. Pres.'s Adv. Commn. on Hist. Preservation, 1977-81; TV prodr., moderator On the Record, NBC-TV, Sta. WRC-TV, Washington, 1978-79; pres. D.C. Prodns., Ltd., 1978; prodr., host Your Personal Decorator, 1987; mem. Sec. State's Adv. Commn. on Fgn. Svc. Inst., 1972-74; founding mem. Project Censured Panel of Judges, 1976—. Bd. dirs. First Star. Author: First Lady's Lady, 1979. Mem. US Holocaust Meml. Coun., 1987-97; corporator Dana Hall Sch., Wellesley, Mass.; bd. dirs. Wolf Trap Found., Women's Campaign Fund, 1978-79; bd. dirs. DC Contemporary Dance Theatre, 1986-88, DC Rep. Ctrl. Com., 1984—, DC Preservation League, 1987-90, Am. Univ. Rome, 1988—96, Friends of the Scuola San Rocco, 2002—, Ctr. for Sci. in the Pub. Interest, 2007—; chmn. C&O Canal Nat. Hist. Park Commn., 1988—. Recipient awards for outstanding achievement in the media AAUW, 1973, 74, Silver Screen award A Campaign to Remember for the U.S. Holocaust Meml. Coun., 1989, Bronze medal Internat. Film and Video Festival N.Y., 1990; named hon. consul gen. of Republic of San Marino to Washington; knighted by Order of St. Agatha, Republic of San Marino, 1986. Mem. NATAS (Emmy award 1972), Washington Press Club, Am. Newspaper Women's Club, Am. Women in Radio and TV, Cosmos Club, Consular Corps, Sigma Delta Chi. Home: 3059 Q St NW Washington DC 20007-3081 Personal E-mail: sheila.weidenfeld@gmail.com. E-mail: Sheila.Weidenfeld@verizon.net.

WEIDENKOPF, THOMAS W., human resources specialist; b. 1959; married; 2 children. BS, Cornell U. Various human resources positions Pepsi-Cola, Pizza Hut; mgr. orgn. and staffing GE, 1981—83; dir. global staffing and devel. Honeywell Internat., Inc., 1995—97; v.p. human resources Honeywell Aerospace, 1999—2002; sr. v.p. human resources and comm. Honeywell Internat., Inc., Morristown, NJ, 2002—. Office: Honeywell Internat 101 Columbia Rd Morristown NJ 07962

WEIDENTHAL, MAURICE DAVID (BUD WEIDENTHAL), academic administrator, journalist; b. Cleve., Nov. 26, 1925; s. William and Evelyn Kolinsky W.; m. Grace Schwartz, Apr. 14, 1957 (dec.); 1 child, Susan Elizabeth Weldenthal Saltzman. BA, U. Mich., 1950. Mem. staff Cleve. Press, 1950-81, editl. writer, 1950-51, asst. city editor, 1956-58, edn. editor, 1958-81; v.p. pub. affairs Cuyahoga C.C. Dist., Cleve., 1981-88; dir. Urban Colls. Project, Cleve., 1989—. Editor The Urban Report, Cleve., 1989-2005; writer, cons. Ranc Inc., Georgetown, Tex., 2007-. Pub. affairs com. Greater Cleve. Growth Assn., 1981-88; bd. advisors Coun. for Advancement and Support of Edn., 1981-88, Nat. Coun. Mktg. and Pub. Rels., 1981-2005; alt. bd. dirs. St. Vincent Quadrangle, 1983-88; trustee Hebrew Free Loan Assn., 1975-86. With AUS, 1944-45. Decorated Air medal. Mem. Edn. Writers Assn., Soc. Profl. Journalists, (bd. dirs. 1996-2003), Cleve. City Club (bd. dirs. 1969-76), Cleve. Press Club. Home: 25858 Fairmount Blvd Cleveland OH 44122-2214 Office: 4250 Richmond Rd Cleveland OH 44122-6104 Home Phone: 216-591-1911; Office Phone: 216-577-9743. Personal E-mail: u2w@roadrunner.com.

WEIDKNECHT, MARCIA E., chemistry professor; b. Pa. BSChemE, U. NH, Durham. Lectr. U. Akron, Ohio, 1978—89, instr., 1989—. Mem.: AAUP. Home: 921 Chaffin Rd Akron OH 44306 Office: Univ Akron Goodyear 213 Akron OH 44325 Business E-Mail: mweidknecht@uakron.edu.

WEIDMAN, DAVID N., chemicals executive; m. Rachel Weidman; 6 children. BSChE, Brigham Young Univ., 1978; MBA, Univ. Mich., 1980. Positions with Am. Cyanamid, 1980—87; mng. dir. Cyanamid Nordiska, Stockholm, 1987—89; v.p., gen. mgr. Cyanamid Canada, 1989—90; v.p., gen. mgr. fibers div. Am. Cyanamid, 1990—94; v.p., gen., mgr. performance additives Allied Signal, 1994—95, pres., gen. mgr. fluorine products, 1995—98, pres. performance polymers & mem. corp. exec. council, 1998—2000; CEO Celanese Chemicals, 2000—02; COO Celanese AG, 2002—04, vice-chmn. bd. mgmt., 2003—04; pres., CEO Celanese Corp., Dallas, 2004—07, chmn., CEO, 2007—. Bd. mem. Am. Chemistry Council. Mem. Nat. Adv. Council Marriott Sch. Mgmt. Mem.: Soc. Chem. Industry (hon. treas.). Office: Celanese Corp 1601 W LBJ Freeway Dallas TX 75234

WEIDMAN, JOHN CARL, II, education and sociology educator, consultant; b. Ephrata, Pa., Oct. 3, 1945; s. John Carl and Mary Elizabeth (Grube) W.; m. Carla Sue Fassnacht, Aug. 20, 1967; children: Jonathan Scott, Rebecca Mary. AB in Sociology cum laude, Princeton U., 1967; AM, U. Chgo., 1968, PhD, 1974. Acting asst. prof. edn. U. Minn., Mpls., 1970-74, asst. prof. edn., sociology and Am. studies, 1974-77; sr. rsch. assoc. Bur. Social Sci. Rsch., Inc., Washington, 1977-78; assoc. prof. edn. and sociology U. Pitts., 1979-86, prof. edn. and sociology, 1986—, chmn. dept. adminstrv. and policy studies, 1986-93, 2007—, dir. Inst. for Internat. Studies in Edn., 2004—07. Cons. Nat. Ctr. Adminstrv. Justice, Youthwork, Inc., Upper Midwest Tri-Racial Gen. Assistance Ctr., Acad. for Ednl. Devel., Egypt, Mongolia, Asian Devel. Bank, Indonesia, Laos, Kyrgyz Republic, Mongolia, German Acad. Exch. Svc., Mongolia, Sema-Belgium, Mongolia, Uzbekistan, CRA Internat., Saudi Arabia; UNESCO chair higher edn. rsch. Maseno U. Coll., Kenya; 1993, Guest Prof., Beijing Normal U., China, 2007-. Author: rsch. monographs; mem. editl. bd. Rev. of Higher Edn., 1984-88, Am. Ednl. Rsch. Jour., 1991-92, 96-98; co-author: Research on Higher Education in Developing Countries: Suggested Agendas and Research Strategies, 1991, Implementing a Faculty Assessment System: A Case Study of the University of Pittsburgh-USA, 1994, Higher Education Costs and Tuition, 1996, Higher Education in Korea: Tradition and Adaptation, 2000, Socialization of Graduate and Professional Students: A Perilous Passage?, 2001, Finance Higher Education, 2001; asst. editor Comparative Edn. Rev., 2003—; cons. editor Jour. Higher Edn., 1989—; contbr. chpts. to books, articles to profl. jours. Bd. dirs. Sch. Vol. Assn. Pitts., 1982-90, pres., 1984-87. Grantee U.S. Office Edn., 1971-73, Spencer Found., 1973-76, Nat. Inst. Edn., 1976-79, NEH, 1985-86, Asian Devel. Bank, Laos, 1995-96, Mongolia, 1997-2000, 2005, Indonesia, 2001, Krygyz Republic, 2003; Fulbright scholar U. Augsburg, Germany, 1986-87. Mem. Am. Ednl. Rsch. Assn. (sec. postsecondary divsn. 1987-89), Am. Sociol. Assn., Assn. Study of Higher Edn., Comparative and Internat. Edn. Soc., Sigma Psi, Phi Delta Kappa. Office: U Pitts 5910 Posvar Hall 230 S Bouquet St Pittsburgh PA 15260

WEIDNER, DONALD J., geophysicist educator; b. Dayton, Ohio, Apr. 26, 1945; s. Virgil Raymond and Aletha Winifred Weidner; m. Deborah Mary Ray, April 13, 1968; children: Raymond V., Jennifer L. AB in Physics cum laude, Harvard, 1967; PhD in Geophysics, Mass. Inst. Tech., 1972. Asst prof. SUNY, Stony Brook, N.Y., 1972-77, assoc. prof., 1977-82, prof. geophysics, 1982—, disting. prof., 1998—. Dir. Mineral Physics Inst., SUNY, 1988—, Ctr. for High Pressure Rsch, SUNY, 1991—. Am. Geophysical Union fellow, 1981; recipient James B. Macelwane award Am. Geophysical Union, 1981. Achievements include building (with others) the high pressure facility at Stony Brook SUNY; large volume high pressure studies with synchrotron radiation; determining the equation of state of earth materials; phase stability fields of minerals and has pioneered the use of this system to determine the yield strength of these materials; design team leader for the large volume experiments that the GeoCars program is preparing for the Advanced Photon Source. Office: Stony Brook University Dept of Geosciences Stony Brook NY 11794-2100

WEIDNER, DONALD J., dean, law educator; BS, Fordham U., 1966; JD, U. Tex., Austin, 1969. Bar: SC, U.S. Tax Ct., U.S. Dist. Cts. for No. Dist. Ohio and Dist. SC, Supreme Ct. U.S. Assoc. Willkie Farr & Gallagher, New York, NY, 1969—70; Bigelow Fellow U. Chgo. Law Sch., 1970—71; asst. prof. U. SC Sch. Law, 1971—74; assoc. prof. Cleveland State U., 1974—76, Fla. State U. Coll. Law, 1976—78, prof., 1978—, assoc. dean, 1984—85, dean, 1991—97, interim dean, 1998—2000; dean, 2000—. Vis. prof. U. Tex. Sch. Law, 1978, U. N.Mex, 1979, Stanford Law Sch., 1981, U. NC Sch. Law, 1991; prof in residence Ruden McClosky Smith Schuster & Russell, PA, 1997; reporter Uniform Partnership Act (1994) Nat. Conf. Commrs. on Uniform State Laws, 1987—94. Co-author: Real Estate: Taxation and Bankruptcy, 1979, General and Limited Liability Partnerships Under the Revised Uniform Partnership Act, 1996, The Revised Uniform Partnership Act, 1998—2009. Order of Coif. Mem.: Am. Law Inst., Assoc. Am. Law Schs. (mem. Membership Review (Accrediation) Com. 2001—03), Fla. Supreme Ct. Hist. Soc. (Bd. Trustees), Fla. Supreme Ct. Commn. on Professionalism. Avocations: boating, fishing, scuba diving, reading, exercise. Office: Coll Law Fla State U Rotunda Rm R201 Tallahassee FL 32306-1601 Office Phone: 850-644-3071. Office Fax: 850-644-5487. E-mail: dweidner@law.fsu.edu.*

WEIDNER, ROBERT WRIGHT, retired musician, musicologist, educator; b. Brookfield, Wis., Oct. 21, 1923; s. Oswald Frederick and Minnie Marie (Giencke) W.; m. Jean Dionne Rockwell; children: Robert Rockwell Weidner, Diane Jean Weidner. BS, Milw. State Tchrs. Coll., 1949; MA, Eastman Sch. of Music, 1951, PhD, 1960. Band dir., tchr. history North Divsn. H.S., Milw., 1949-50; music dir. Oostburg (Wis.) Pub. Schs., 1951—54; band dir., music prof. Ohio No. U., Ada, 1954—55; band dir., prof. music Tex. Luth. Coll., Seguin, 1955—57; dir. music Abbotsford Pub. Schs., Dorchester Pub. Schs., Wis., 1957—59; prof. music, dir. orchestra Nebr. Wesleyan U., Lincoln, 1959-62; prof. music, dept. head U. Dubuque (Iowa), 1962-65; coord. grad. studies in music Ea. Ill. U., Charleston, 1987-89, prof. music, 1965-93, retired, 1994. Composer: Tex. Luth. Coll. alma mater, 1956; editor: Christopher Tye: The Instrumental Music, 1965, Tye's Actes of the Apostles, 1970. Bd. mem. Charleston Civic Assn., Charleston, 1991-97. With U.S. Army, 1943-46, ETO. Mem. Am. Musicol. Soc. Mem. Dem. Socialists of Am. Avocation: reading. Home: 609 Ashby Dr Charleston IL 61920-3216 Personal E-mail: jweidnerc@aol.com.

WEIERSTALL, RICHARD PAUL, retired pharmaceutical chemist; b. Jersey City, Nov. 5, 1942; s. William August and Emily (Haughey) W.; m. Gail Janet Thomsen, Aug. 17, 1968; children: Eric, Kurt, Karen. BS, Rutgers U., 1966, MS, 1969; PhD, U. Calif., San Francisco, 1973. Unit head drug metabolism Sandoz Pharm., East Hanover, N.J., 1973-74; dir. tech. svc. Banner Gelatin Products, Chatsworth, Calif., 1974-76; v.p. tech. svc. Banner Gelatin Prod., Chatsworth, Calif., 1976-81; dir. pharm. sci. Ayerst Labs Inc., Rouses Point, N.Y., 1981-87; asst. v.p. Wyeth Ayerst Rsch., Rouses Point, 1987-95, asst. v.p. quality assurance, 1995-99; ret., 1999. Mem. Am. Assn. Pharm. Sci., Am. Pharm. Assn. Home: 7 Stewart St Rouses Point NY 12979-1511 E-mail: rweiers@northnet.org.

WEIGAND, ROBERT EUGENE, university educator; b. Terre Haute, Ind., Aug. 13, 1930; s. Arthur A. and Nora L. (Epler) W. Student, Eastern Ill. State Coll., 1948-50; BS in Commerce, U. Notre Dame, 1952; MS in Mktg., U. Ill., 1956, PhD in Bus., 1961. From instr. to assoc. prof. mktg. De Paul U., Chgo., 1959-67, chmn. dept., 1960-65, prof., 1967-69; head dept. mktg. U. Ill., Chgo., 1969-78, prof., 1969—98, prof. emeritus, 1998—. Vis. assoc. prof. bus. adminstrn. Grad. Sch. Bus., U. Ill., Urbana, 1967-68, lectr. mgmt. devel. program, 1970-75; com. mem. Am. Assembly Collegiate Schs. Bus. Adminstrn; external examiner, faculty Bus. Adminstrn. U. Lagos, Nigeria, 1976, 77, 78; internat. speaker, cons. in field; radio and TV guest. Co-author: Basic Retailing, 1976, rev. ed. 1982 with accompanying manual and workbook; editor Resource Book, 1974, Doing Business in Japan, 1963, Doing Business in France, 1964; mem. editl. bd. Jour. Mktg. Channels; cons. editor Review of Business and Economic Research, 1971—; contbr. book reviews, articles to profl. jours., chpts. to books. Served to cpl. U.S. Army, 1952-54, res. 1954-60. Am. Assn. Advt. Agys. fellow, 1964, Ford Found. fellow, 1965. Mem. AAUP, Am. Mktg. Assn. (internat. mktg. tchg. com. 1960-61, social concerns com. 1970-71, v.p. mktg. edn. Chgo. chpt. 1973-74), Acad. Internat. Bus., Assn. Japanese Bus. Studies. Roman Catholic. Home: 5455 N Sheridan Rd Chicago IL 60640-7440 Office: U Ill PO Box 802451 Chicago IL 60680-2451

WEIGAND, WILLIAM KENNETH, Bishop Emeritus; b. Bend, Calif., May 23, 1937; s. Harold and Alice Weigand. B in Philosophy, St. Edward's Sem., Kenmore, Wash., 1959; MDiv, St. Thomas Sem., Kenmore, 1963. Ordained priest Diocese of Boise City, Idaho, 1963, chancellor, 1964—68; missionary Cali, Colombia, 1968—78; pastor St. Hubert's Parish, Homedale, Idaho, 1978—80; ordained bishop Diocese of Salt Lake City, 1980, bishop, 1980—93, Diocese of Sacramento, 1993—2008, bishop emeritus Calif., 2008—. Roman Catholic. Office: Diocese Sacramento 2110 Broadway Sacramento CA 95818-2518 Office Phone: 916-733-0200. Office Fax: 916-733-0215.*

WEIGEL, GEORGE SHILLOW, JR., theologian; b. Balt. m. Joan Balcombe; children: Gwyneth, Monica, Stephen. BA, St. Mary's Seminary, Balt., 1973; MA, U. St. Michael's Coll., Toronto, Can., 1975. Asst. prof. theology, from asst. to dean of studies St. Thomas Sem. Sch. of Theology, Kenmore, 1975-77; scholar-in-residence World Without War Coun. Greater Seattle, 1977-84; founding pres. James Madison Found., 1986-89; pres. Ethics and Pub. Policy Ctr., Washington, 1989—96, disting. sr. fellow, 1996—. Author: Tranquillitas Ordinis: The Present Failure & Future Promise of American Catholic Thought on War & Peace, 1987, American Interests, American Purpose; Moral Reasoning & US Foreign Policy, 1989, Catholicism and the Renewal of American Democracy, 1989, Freedom and its Discontents, 1991, The Final Revolution: The Resistance Church and the Collapse of Communism, 1992, Idealism Without Illusions: US Foreign Policy in the Nineties, 1994, Soul of the World, 1996, Witness to Hope: The Biography of Pope John Paul II, 1999, The Truth of Catholicism, 2001, The Courage to Be Catholic, 2002, Letters to A Young Catholic, 2004, The Cube and the Cathedral, 2005, God's Choice: Pope Benedict XVI and the Future of the Catholic Church, 2005, Faith, Reason and the War Against Jihadism, 2007, Against the Corian: Christianity and Democracy, War and Peace, 2008; co-author (with James Turner Johnson): Just War and the Gulf War, 1991; co-editor (with Robert Royal): Building the Free Society, 1993; syndicated columnist, 1993—, mem. editl. bd. First Things. Recipient papal cross Pro Ecclesia et Pontifice, Gloria Artis Gold medal, Republic of Poland; fellow Woodrow Wilson Internat. Ctr. for Scholars, 1984—85. Achievements include eleven honorary doctorates. Office: Ethics and Pub Policy Ctr 1015 15th St NW Washington DC 20005-2605 Office Phone: 202-682-1200.

WEIGEL, KENNETH GEORGE, lawyer; b. Neptune, NJ, Aug. 28, 1954; s. Hugo Karl and Dolores May (Ambrose) W. BA, U. Mich., 1976; JD, George Washington U., 1979. Bar: DC 1979. Assoc. Barnes, Richardson & Colburn, Washington, 1979-83, Bayh, Tabbert & Capehart, Washington, 1983-85, Morgan, Lewis & Bockius, Washington, 1985-89; ptnr. Webster & Sheffield, Washington, 1989-1990, Baker & Hostetler, Washington, 1991—93, Kirkland & Ellis, 1993—2002; ptnr., co-chmn., internat. trade and regulatory group Alston & Bird LLP, Washington, 2002. Mem. ABA (chmn. customs law com., internat. law and practice sect. 1988-91). Office: Alston & Bird LLP 950 F St NW Washington DC 20004 Office Phone: 202-756-3431. Office Fax: 202-756-3333. Business E-Mail: ken.weigel@alston.com.

WEIGEL, OLLIE J, dentist, former mayor; b. Guthrie County, Iowa, Sept. 29, 1922; s. Verne Noble and Ethel Rebecca (Johnson) W.; m. Mary Kathryn Finnegan, June 3, 1944 (dec. Sept. 1999); children: John, Marilyn, Larry, Susan. DDS, U. Iowa, 1951. Practice dentistry, Ankeny, 1951-94; mayor City of Ankeny, 1974-93. Mem. Metro Planning Orgn., 1995-2000; bd. dirs. Neveln Resource Ctr., 1995-2000. Mem. Ankeny Bd. Adjustment, 1953-58, Ankeny Planning and Zoning Commn., 1953-65, Ankeny City Coun., 1966-73, Des Moines Area C.C. Found. Bd., 1993—, mem. emeritus; mem. Des Moines Area Metro Forum, 1985-93, found. bd. On With Life, 1994-2000; life mem. Ankeny Indsl. Devel. Corp.; mem. adv. bd. dirs. Brenton Bank of Ankeny, 1994-2000; mem. Polk County Aviation Authority, 2001-2003. 1st lt. USAAF, 1943-45, ETO. Recipient Person of Vision award, Ankeny Indsl. Devel. Corp. (1st recipient), 2001; named to Mayors Hall of Fame, 1993—96. Mem. ADA (life), Iowa Dental Assn. (life), Des Moines Dist. Dental Assn., Ankeny C. of C. (charter mem., life, pres. 1953, 70, Outstanding Citizen 1976, 93), Mid Iowa Assn. Local Govts. (chmn. 1983), League of Iowa Municipalities (pres. 1976-77), Ctrl. Iowa Regional Govts. (pres. 1978), Am. Legion (life), Ankeny Cmty. Dist. Sch. Found. (bd. dirs.)(named Hall of Fame 2007) Republican. Methodist. Avocation: fishing. Home and Office: 2506 NW 4th St Ankeny IA 50021-1002

WEIGEL, PAUL HENRY, biochemistry educator, researcher, consultant; b. NYC, Aug. 11, 1946; s. Helmut and Jeanne Weigel; m. Nancy Shulman, June 15, 1968 (div. Dec. 1987); 1 child, Dana J.; m. Janet Oka, May 17, 1992 BA in Chemistry, Cornell U., 1968; MS in Biochemistry, Johns Hopkins U., Balt., 1969, PhD in Biochemistry, 1975. NIH postdoctoral fellow Johns Hopkins U., Balt., 1975-78; asst. prof. U. Tex. Med. Br., Galveston, Tex., 1978-82, assoc. prof., 1982—87, prof. biochemistry and cell biology, 1987-94, vice chmn. dept. human biol. chemistry and genetics, 1990-93, acting chmn. dept. human biology, chemistry and genetics, 1992-93; prof., chmn. dept. biochemistry and molecular biology U. Okla. Health Scis. Ctr., Oklahoma City, 1994—, George Lynn Cross rsch. prof., 2004—, Ed Miller chair in molecular biology, 2006—; co-founder Hyalose LLC, 2000—. Mem. NIH Pathobiochemistry Study Sect., Washington, 1985-87; cons. Teltech, Mpls., 1985—, Hyalose LLC 2000—. Contbr. articles to profl. jours. Treas. Bayou Chateau Neighborhood Assn., Dickinson, Tex., 1981-83, v.p., 1983-84, pres., 1984-86. With U.S. Army, 1969-71. Grantee NIH, 1979—, Office Naval Rsch., 1983-87, Tex. Biotech., 1989-94, Okla. Ctr. Advancement Sci. and Tech., 2000-03; recipient Disting. Tchr. award U. Tex. Med. Br., 1989, Disting. Rsch. award, 1989. Mem.: Internat. Soc. for Hyaluronan Scis. (founding mem. 2004, sec. 2004—08, acting pres. 2007, treas. 2009—), Soc. for Glycobiology (mem. nominations com. 2004—08), Assn. Med. and Grad. Depts. Biochemistry (webmaster 2002—07, bd. dirs. 2002—, pres. 2007), Am. Soc. Biochemistry and Molecular Biology (mem. pub. affairs adv. com. 2000—03), Am. Soc. Cell Biology, Am. Chem. Soc. Democrat. Lutheran. Achievements include 26 US patents in field. Avocations: racquetball, basketball card collecting, poetry, camping. Home: 817 Hollowdale Edmond OK 73003-3022 Office: U Okla Health Scis Ctr Dept Biochem & Mol Biology Bmsb Rm 860 Oklahoma City OK 73190-0001 Office Phone: 405-271-2227. Business E-Mail: paul-weigel@ouhsc.edu.

WEIGELE, RICHARD SAYRE, police officer; b. Passaic, NJ, Oct. 5, 1949; s. Louis Charles and Marjorie (Sayre) W. BA, Hope Coll., Holland, Mich., 1972; MPA, Kean Coll. N.J., Union, 1989. Police officer Summit (N.J.) Police Dept., 1973-80; mobile intensive care paramedic Overlook Hosp., Summit, 1977—2006; first response tng. coord. Union County Police acad., Scotch Plains, NJ, 1980—2005; police sgt., 911 mcpl. coord. Mountainside Police Dept., NJ, 1980—2009, commdr. Emergency Svcs. Unit NJ, 1998—2003, lt. adminstrv. officer NJ, 2007—09. Paramedic preceptor Overlook Hosp., 1980-2003, pre-hosp. trauma life support instr., 1993-2001, pediatric prehosp. emergency care instr., 1995-2001; CPR instr. Am. Heart Assn., Summit, 1978; police instr. Union County Police Acad., 1980-2008; EMS text reviewer Brady Publishing, 1996. Officer Summit First Aid Squad, 1975-80; vol. Overlook Hosp., 1974-81; mem. Liberty Corner First Aid Squad, 1993-98; instr. ARC, Somerville, N.J., 1992-98. With N.J. Army NG, 1972-78, instr. Sommerset Hills YMCA, Basking Ridge, 2003-, govt. mktg. exec. Mack Camera & Video Svc. Springfield, NJ, 2009. Recipient Award of Merit N.J. State Police Benevolent Assn., 1974, Award of recognition, Union County Police Acad., 1990. Mem. Nat. Assn. EMT/Paramedics (charter), N.J. Police Honor Legion, Internat. Police Assn. (reception officer 1989-2006, Nat. Del. Conf. rep. 1990-, pres. 2002-), Mountainside Police Benevolent Assn. (Police Officer of the Yr. 1986), Pi Alpha Alpha. Ref. Ch. of Am. Avocations: skiing, biking, computers, community service. Home: 268 Crabtree Ct Basking Ridge NJ 07920-3154 Office: Mack Camera & Video Svc 200 Morris Ave Springfield NJ 07081 Office Phone: 973-467-2291 ext 107. Personal E-mail: rweigele@earthlink.net, richw@mackcam.com.

WEIGELT, JOHN AUGUST, surgeon; b. Chgo., July 4, 1947; s. John August and Brenda Doreen (Cornish) W.; m. Dorina Louise Dravis, Mar. 7, 1975; children: John Carey, Coby Elizabeth. DVM, Mich. State U., 1970; MD, Med. Coll. Wis., 1974; MA, U. Wis., 1994. From asst. prof. to prof. surgery U. Tex. Southwestern, Dallas, 1979-92; chmn. dept. surgery St. Paul-Ramsey Med. Ctr., 1992—. Author: Surgical Critical Care, 1996. Dir. surg. ICU U. Tex. Southwestern, Dallas, 1985-92, trauma dir., 1986-92; vice chair dept. surgery U. Minn., Mpls., 1992—, prof. surgery, 1992—, assoc. mem. grad. faculty, 1994—; chmn. U. Minn. surg. search com., Mpls. Bd. dirs. Life Link, St. Paul, Am. Trauma Soc., Minn. Safety Coun., St. Paul. Mem. Am. Coll. Surgeons, Am. Assn. Surgery of Trauma, Am. Surgical Assn., Ctrl. Surg. Assn., Western Surg. Assn. Avocations: pen collector, skiing, hiking. Office: St Paul-Ramsey Med Ctr 640 Jackson St Saint Paul MN 55101-2595

WEIGEND, GUIDO GUSTAV, geographer, educator; b. Zeltweg, Austria, Jan. 2, 1920; came to U.S., 1939, naturalized, 1943; s. Gustav F. and Paula (Sorgo) W.; m. Areta Kelble, June 26, 1947 (dec. 1993); children: Nina, Cynthia, Kenneth. BS, U. Chgo., 1942, MS, 1946, PhD, 1949. With OSS, 1943-45; with mil. intelligence U.S. War Dept., 1946; instr. geography U. Ill., Chgo., 1946-47; instr. then asst. prof. geography Beloit Coll., 1947-49; asst. prof. geography Rutgers U., 1949-51, assoc. prof., 1951-57, prof., 1957-76, acting dept. chmn., 1951-52, chmn. dept., 1953-67, assoc. dean, 1972-76; dean Coll. Liberal Arts, Prof. geography Ariz. State U., Tempe, 1976-84, prof. geography, 1976-89; ret., 1989. Fulbright lectr. U. Barcelona, 1960-61; vis. prof. geography Columbia U., 1963-67, NYU, 1967, U. Colo., summer 1968, U. Hawaii, summer 1969; liaison rep. Rutgers U. to UN, 1950-52; invited by Chinese Acad. Scis. to visit minority areas in Chinese Cent. Asia, 1988; mem. U.S. nat. com. Internat. Geog. Union, 1951-58, 61-65; chmn. Conf. on Polit. and Social Geography, 1968-69 Author articles, monographs, bulls. for profl. jours.; contbr.: (4th edit.) A Geography of Europe, 1977; geog. editor-in-chief: Odyssey World Atlas, 1966. Bd. adjustment Franklin Twp., N.J., 1959; mem. Highland Park (N.J.) Bd. Edn., 1973-75, v.p., 1975; mem. Ariz. Coun. on Humanities and Pub. Policy, 1976-80; vice chmn. Phoenix Com. on Fgn. Rels., 1976-79, chmn., 1979-81; mem. exec. com. Fedn. Pub. Programs in Humanities, 1977-82; bd. dirs. Coun. Colls. Arts and Scis., 1980-83; commr. N. Cen. Assn. Colls. and Schs., 1976-80, bd. dirs. commn. on instns. of higher edn., 1980-83. Research fellow Office Naval Research, 1952-55, Rutgers Research Council, 1970-71; grantee Social Sci. Research Council, 1956, Ford Found., 1966, Am. Philos. Soc., 1970-71, German Acad. Exchange Service, 1984; Fulbright travel grantee Netherlands, 1970-71. Mem. Assn. Am. Geographers (chmn. N.Y. Met. divsn. 1955-56, editl. bd. 1955-59, mem. coun. 1965-66, chmn. N.Y.-N.J. divsn. 1965-66), Am. Geog. Soc., Phoenix Chamber Mus. Soc. (bd. dirs. 1995-2003, pres. 2000-03), Sigma Xi (pres. Ariz. State U. chpt. 1989-91). Office: Ariz State U Dept Geography Tempe AZ 85287 Home: 7550 N 16th St Apt 3103 Phoenix AZ 85020-4618

WEIGER, ALAN W., theater director, educator; b. Chgo., Feb. 27, 1950; s. Walter John and Jeanne Dorothy Weiger; m. Natalie Horne, June 11, 1988; children: Alexander John, Erich Alan, Evan Eugene. MA, Northern Ill. U., DeKalb, 1977. Tchr. Lake Pk. HS, Roselle, Ill., 1973—75; prof. Elmhurst Coll., Ill., 1977—. Dir. Summer Pl., Naperville, Ill., 1987—2004; mem. Canterbury Carollers, Ill., 1988—. Com. mem. Boy Scouts Troop 82, Elmhurst. Mem.: Assn. Theatre Higher Edn. Office: Elmhurst Coll 190 Prospect Ave Elmhurst IL 60126 Office Fax: 630-617-6461. Business E-Mail: alanw@elmhurst.edu.

WEIGERT, ANDREW JOSEPH, sociology educator; b. NYC, Apr. 8, 1934; s. Andrew Joseph and Marie Teresa (Kollmer) W.; m. Kathleen Rose Maas, Aug. 31, 1967; children: Karen Rose, Sheila Marie. BA, St. Louis U., 1958, PhL, 1959, MA, 1960; BTh, Woodstock Coll, Md., 1964; PhD, U. Minn., 1968. NIMH trainee U. Minn., Mpls., 1965-67; asst. prof. sociology U. Notre Dame, Ind., 1968-72, assoc. prof. Ind., 1972-76, prof. Ind., 1976—, chmn. dept. Ind., 1980-84, 88-89. Vis. assoc. prof. Yale U., New Haven, 1973-74. Co-author: Family Socialization, 1974, Interpretive Sociology, 1978, Society and Identity, 1986; author: Everyday Life, 1981, Social Psychology, 1983, Life and Society, 1983, Mixed Emotions, 1991, Self, Interaction, and Natural Environment, 1997, Religious and Secular Views on Endtime, 2004; adv. editor various sociology jours.; contbr. articles to profl. jours., chpts. to books. Recipient tchg. awards, 1999, 2002, 05; NSF grantee, 1969. Avocation: woodlot and prairie management. Office: U Notre Dame Dept Sociology Notre Dame IN 46556 Office Phone: 574-631-7408. Business E-Mail: aweigert@nd.edu.

WEIGERT, LAURA, history professor; b. New Haven, Aug. 9, 1965; d. Martin and Shearer Weigert; m. Fabien Capeilleres, Sept. 5, 1996; children: Hector Weigert Capeilleres, Theo Weigert Capeilleres. BA, Swarthmore, 1987; Phd, Northwestern, Evanston, 1995. Assoc. prof. Reed Coll., Portland, Oreg., 2004—06, Rutgers U., New Brunswick, NJ, 2006—. V.p. TEAMS. Author: (book) Weaving Sacred Stories: The Performance of Clerical Identity in French Choir Tapestries, Judith et Holoferne. Fellowship, Fulbright, 1987, Sabbatical fellowship, Am. Philos. Soc., 2007. Office: Rutgers Univ 71 Hamilton St Princeton NJ 08540

WEIGHT, DOUG, professional hockey player; b. Warren, Mich., Jan. 21, 1971; Student, Lake Superior State Coll., Mich. Center NY Rangers, 1990-93, Edmonton Oilers, 1993—2001, St. Louis Blues, 2001—06, 2006—07, Carolina Hurricanes, 2006, Anaheim Ducks, 2007—08, NY Islanders, 2008—. Mem. U.S. Olympic Hockey Team, Nagano, Japan, 1998, Salt Lake City, 2002, Team U.S.A., World Cup of Hockey, 1996, 2004. Named to NHL All-Star Game, 1996, 1998, 2001, 2003. Achievements include being a member of World Cup Champion Team USA, 1996; being a member of silver medal winning USA Hockey Team, Salt Lake City Olympics, 2002; being a member of Stanley Cup Champion Carolina Hurricanes, 2006. Office: NY Islanders Nassau Veterans Meml Coliseum 1255 Hempstead Turnpike Uniondale NY 11553

WEIGNER, BRENT JAMES, secondary school educator; b. Pratt, Kans., Aug. 19, 1949; s. Doyle Dean and Elizabeth (Hanger) W.; m. Sue Ellen Weber Hume, Mar. 30, 1985; children: Russell John Hume, Scott William Hume. BA, U. No. Colo., 1972; MEd, U. Wyo., 1977, PhD, 1984. Cert. Nat. Bd. for Profl. Tchg. Stds. Counselor, coach Olympia Sport Village, Upson, Wis., 1968; dir. youth sports F.E. Warren AFB, Cheyenne, 1973—74; instr. geography Laramie County Comm. Coll., Cheyenne, 1974-75; tchr. social sci. McCormick Jr. HS, Cheyenne, 1975—, Laramie County Sch. Dist. 1, Cheyenne, 1975—; head social studies dept. McCormick Jr. HS, 1987-99, 2001—02; curriculum adv. coun. chmn. Laramie County Sch. Dist. No. 1, 1988-89. Lectr. ednl. methods U. Wyo., 1989, clin. faculty, 1992-94; nat. chmn. Jr. Olympic cross-country com. AAU, Indpls., 1980-81; pres. Wyo. Athletic Congress, 1981-87; tchr. cons. Nat. Geog. Soc. Geography Inst., 1991, North Pole Marathon cons. Global Expdns. 2002-03; South Pole marathon cons. and guide Adventure Network Internat., 2001-02; alt. cert. assessor Wyo. State Dept. Edn., 2001-02; cons. Adventure Network Internat., 1999-02; cons. North Pole marathon, Polar Running Adventures, 2003-04, Arctic Watch, 2004—, Antarctic Ice Marathon onsite race dir., 2007; presenter, cons. in field. Fgn. exch. student U. Munich, 1971-72; head coach Cheyenne Track Club, 1976—, pres., 1980; race dir. Wyo. Marathon, 1978—; deacon 1st Christian Ch., Cheyenne, 1987-90, elder, 1991-93; rep. candidate gen. election Wyo. Legis., 1991; bd. dirs. United Med. Ctr. of Wyo. Found., 1995—, Cheyenne Boys and Girls Club, 1999-2005; keynote spkr., Okla. Marathon, 2002. Named Wyoming State bd. edn. Disting. Educator, Wyo. U.S. West Outstanding Tchr., 1989, Wyo. Coun. for the Social Studies K-8 Tchr. of Yr., 1994-95, Jr. High Coach of Yr., Wyo. Coaches Assn., 1996, Vol. of Yr., office Youth Alternatives, 2000; fellow Taft Found., 1976, Earthwatch-Hearst fellow, Punta Allen, Mex., summer 1987, Christa McAuliffe fellow, 1991-92, Wyo. Christa Mcauliffe Fellowship Selection Com., 1994, 95, 01; Fulbright grantee, Israel, summer 1984; Fulbright scholar Ghana and Senegal, 1990; People-to-People Internat. Ambassador to Vietnam, 1993, Workshop grant, Korea Found., 2008; recipient Masons of Wyo. Disting. Tchr. award 1994. Mem. NEA, Nat. Network for Ednl. Renewal, Nat. Coun. Social Studies, Nat. Coun. Geog. Edn., Dominican Rep. Nat. Coun. for Geog. Edn. (Cram scholarship 1992), Wyo. Geog. Alliance (steering com., Amazon Workshop Fellowship 1998), Cheyenne Tchrs. Edn. Assn. (govtl. rels. com., instrn. and profl. devel. com.), U. No. Colo. Alumni Assn., Cheyenne C. of C., Wyo. Heritage Soc., Wyo. Edn. Assn. (World Book Ency. classroom rsch. project cons. 1976—, accountability task force 1989-90), Fulbright Alumni Assn. (life), U. Wyo. Alumni Assn. (life), Cheyenne Sunrise, Lions (bd. dirs. Cheyenne 1987, pres. 1995-96, 1st v.p. 1993-94, Melvin Jones Fellowship, 1995), Phi Delta Kappa (life, bd. dirs. Cheyenne 1989—, v.p., edn. award for rsch. 1990, pres. 1992-93, ednl. found. rep. 1993-94, area 4-D coord. 1994-95, Gerald Read Internat. Seminar scholar 1994; mem. outstanding doctoral dissertation com. 1994, 96), Phi Delta Kappa (Ed. award 2000). Achievements include first to run ultramarathon races on all seven continents, 1999; South Pole Ultramarathon champion, 2002; sr. men's nat. snowshoe champion, 2003, 05; North Pole Ultramarathon champion, 2003; only person in the world to run ultramarathons at both the North Pole, 2003, and the South Pole, 2002. Home: 402 W 31st St Cheyenne WY 82001-2527 Office: McCormick Jr HS 6000 Education Dr Cheyenne WY 82009-3991 Office Phone: 307-771-2650. Personal E-mail: runwyo@msn.com.

WEIHERER, PATRICIA DEE, retired librarian; b. West Reading, Pa., Sept. 17, 1933; d. Robert Peter and Marguerite (Sprout) Weiherer. BA, Albright Coll., Reading, Pa., 1955; MLS, Rutgers U., New Brunswick, NJ, 1961. English tchr. Manheim Ctrl., Pa., 1955—56; br. libr. Reading Pub. Libr., 1956—60, asst. ref. libr., 1961—95, ref. libr., 1995—. Democrat. United Ch. Of Crist. Avocations: piano, genealogy, needlepoint, reading. Home Phone: 610-376-7660.

WEIHRICH, HEINZ, management educator; b. Germany; came to US, 1959; s. Paul and Anna Weihrich; m. Ursula Weihrich, Aug. 3, 1963. BS, UCLA, 1966, MBA, 1967, PhD, 1973; Dr. (hon.), San Martin de Porres U., Peru, 2000. Assoc. Grad. Sch. Mgmt. UCLA, 1968-73; from asst. to assoc. prof. Ariz. State U., Tempe, 1973-80; prof. global mgmt. and behavioral sci. U. San Francisco, 1980—. Vis. prof. China Europe Internat. Bus. Sch., Shanghai, Grad. Sch. Bus. Adminstrsn., Switzerland, Peking U., Beijing; global mgmt. cons. in field; vis. prof. U. Applied Sci., Ludwigshafen, Germany. Author: Administración una perspectiva global, 1988 (best seller), Administracão Fundamentos da Teoriae da Cienca, Primeiro Volume, 1986, Administracão Organizacão Planejamento e Controle, Segundo Volume, 1987, Administracão Recursos Humanos: Desenvolvimento de Administradores, Terceiro Volume, 1; author: (with Harold Koontz and Cyril O'Donnell) Management, 1980, Japanese, Chinese and Indonesian edits., 1984, Singapore edit., 1985, Indonesian edit., 1986, Philippines edit., Bengali edit., 1989, Taiwan edit., 1985; author: (with Harold Koontz) 9th edit., 1988, Singapore edit., 1988, Chinese edit., 1989, Spanish edit., 1990 (best-seller Spanish speaking world), Korean edit., 1990, Pengurusan (Malaysian) edit., 1991, Czech edit., 1993, Hungarian edit., 1992; author: (with Harold Koontz and Cyril O'Donnell) Management: A Book of Readings, 1980, Essentials of Management, 1982, Taiwan, Philippines, Chinese and India edits., 1986, with Harold Koontz and Cyril O'Donnell: 6th edit., 2004, Chinese edit., Adminstracion Moderna, 1986; author: (with Harold Koontz) Management: A Global Perspective, 1993, Spanish edit., 1993 (best-seller Spanish speaking world), Singapore edit., 1993, Croatian edit., 1995, Chinese, 1998, Measuring Managers--A Double-Barreled Approach, 1981, Manajamen, Jilid 1, 1987, Manajamen, Jilid 2, 1986, Elementos de Administracion, 1983, with Harold Koontz: 6th edit., 2002, 7th edit., 2007, Management Excellence--Productivity through MBO, 1985, Japanese edit., 1990, Greek edit., Produttivita con L' Italian edit., 1987, Administracion, 1985, Management Basiswissen, 1986, Excelencia Administrativa (Mex.), 1987, Chinese edit., 1997, Management: A Global Perspective, internat. edit., 1993, 1993, Administración: Una Perspectiva Global, 1994, 12th edit., 2005 (best seller), Korean edit., 1996, 2006, Croatian edit., 1996, Czech edit., 1996, Elementos de Administracion - Enfoque Internacional, Exta Edicion, 2002; author: (with Harold Koontz & Mark Cannice) Administration - una Perspectiva Global Empresarial, 2008; author: (with George Odiorne and Jack Mendleson) Executive Skills: A Management by Objectives Approach, 1980, with George Odiorne and Jack Mendleson: 6th edit., 2002; author: (with Harold Koontz and A. Ramachandra Aryasri) Principles of Management, 2004; editor (with Jack Mendleson): Management: An MBO Approach, 1978; author (with Harold Koontz): Essentials of Management: Au International Perspective, 7th edit., 2007; contbr. articles to profl. jour. Grantee Am. Mgmt. Assn., 1970. Fellow Internat. Acad. Mgmt., mem. Acad. Mgmt., Assn. Mgmt. Excellence (trustee 1985-87), Assn. Bus. Simulation Exptl. Learning, Acad. Internat. Bus., Beta Gamma Sigma, Sigma Iota Epsilon. Roman Catholic. Office: U San Francisco 2130 Fulton St San Francisco CA 94117-1080

WEIKEL, MALCOLM KEITH, healthcare company executive; b. Shamokin, Pa., Mar. 9, 1938; s. Malcolm J. and Marian Eleanor (Faust) Weikel; m. Barbara Joan Davis, Dec. 17, 1960; children: Richard, Kristin. BSc, Phila. Coll. Pharmacy and Sci., 1960; MSc, U. Wis., 1962, PhD, 1966. Mgr. Roche Labs., 1966—70; commr. health svcs. HEW, Washington, 1970—77; v.p. Am. Med. Internat., 1978—82, pres., CEO, 1982—84; exec. v.p., COO, Manor Healthcare Corp., Silver Spring, Md., 1984—86; exec. v.p. Health Care & Retirement Corp., Toledo, 1986—88, sr. exec. v.p., COO, 1988—98, sr. exec. v.p., 1998—. Recipient Sec.'s Spl. citation, HEW, 1975, 1977. Mem.: Am. Health Care Assn. (v.p. 1990—, chmn. multifacility group 1990—93). Office: Health Care & Retirement Corp PO Box 10086 Toledo OH 43699-0086

WEIL, A. LORNE, computer company executive; B, U. Toronto, Ont., Can.; MS, London Sch. Econs.; MBA, Columbia U., NYC. Sr. profl. Boston Consulting Group; v.p. corp. devel. Gen. Instrument Corp.; chmn., CEO Autotote Corp., 1992—2000, Scientific Games Corp., NYC, 2000—. Office: Scientific Games Corp 750 Lexington Ave New York NY 10022 Office Phone: 212-754-2233. Office Fax: 212-754-2372.

WEIL, ANDREW THOMAS, physician, educator; b. Phila., June 8, 1942; s. Daniel Pythias and Jenny (Silverstein) Weil. BA, Harvard U., 1964, MD, 1968. Intern Mt. Zion Hosp. Med. Ctr., San Francisco, 1968-69; assoc. Harvard Bot. Mus., Cambridge, Mass., 1971-84; fellow Inst. Current World Affairs, NYC, 1971-75; lectr. U. Ariz., Tucson, 1983—96, clin. prof. medicine, founder and dir. program in integrative medicine, 1996—, Lovell-Jones endowed chair integrative rheumatology, 2005—; founder, chmn. Weil Found., Vail, Ariz., Weil Lifestyle, LLC, Phoenix. Dir. integrative health and healing Miraval Resort. Author: Natural Mind, 1972, Marriage of the Sun and Moon, 1980, From Chocolate to Morphine, 1983, Health and Healing, 1984, Natural Health, Natural Medicine, 1990, Spontaneous Healing, 1995, 8 Weeks to Optimum Health, 1997, Eating Well for Optimum Health, 2000, The Healthy Kitchen, 2002, Healthy Aging, 2005, (newsletter) Self-Healing, (website) drweil.com. Served to lt. USPHS, 1969-70. Recipient Inaugural award, Am. Acad. Osteopathy, 2001. Fellow Linnean Soc. London; mem. Am. Acad. Achievement, Sigma Xi. Democrat. Buddhist. Avocation: gardening. Home: 6700 S X9 Ranch Rd Vail AZ 85641-6202 Office: Ariz Health Scis Ctr PO Box 245153 Tucson AZ 85724-5153 also: Weil Found PO Box 922 Vail AZ 85641 Office Phone: 520-647-7865. Personal E-mail: nancy@x9ranch.com.*

WEIL, D(ONALD) WALLACE, business administration educator; b. Cleve., July 20, 1923; s. Laurence J. and Carol S. (Wallace) W.; m. Jane A. Bittel, Dec. 29, 1947; children— John Wallace, Charles Andrew, Margaret Jane, Carol Wyn. BA, Oberlin Coll., 1947; JD, Willamette U., 1950. Pres. James Foundry Corp., Fort Atkinson, Wis., 1960-70; faculty bus. adminstrn. U. Wis., Eau Claire, 1971-74, chmn. dept. bus. adminstrn., 1974-77, prof., 1985—2003, ret., prof. emeritis, 2003—; pres. Diversified Industries, Inc., St. Louis, 1977-81, UHI Corp., Los Angeles, 1981-85. Dir. U.H.I. Corp. Diversified Industries, Inc., St. Louis, Sales Investments, Mgmt. Inc., Elmwood, Wis., Jane B. Inc., Eau Claire Served with AUS, 1942-45. Mem. Nat. SAR (life), Wis. SAR, Am. Security Council, Nat. Council Small Bus. Mgmt. Devel., Phi Kappa Phi, Beta Gamma Sigma. Republican. Congregationalist. Office: U Wis-Eau Claire Dept Bus Adminstrn Eau Claire WI 54701 Home: 11201 Fairfield Rd Apt 300A Minnetonka MN 55305 Office Phone: 715-577-1704.

WEIL, EDWARD DAVID, chemist, researcher, consultant, inventor; b. Phila., June 13, 1928; s. Irving E. and Minna M. (Stainbrook) W.; m. Barbara Joy Hummel, Sept. 11, 1952; children: David L., Claudia E. BS in Chemistry, U. Pa., Phila., 1950; PhD in Organic Chemistry, U. Ill., 1953; MBA, Pace U., NYC, 1982. Chemist, supr. Hooker Chem. Co., Niagara Falls, NY, 1950-65; supr., sr. scientist Stauffer Chem. Co., Dobbs Ferry, NY, 1965-86; ind. cons., patent agt., propr. Intertech. Svcs., 1986—; dir. exploratory rsch. Adelphi Rsch. Ctr., Garden City, 1986-87; rsch. prof. Poly U., Bklyn., 1987—; IP fellow U. Akron Rsch. Found., 2006—; assoc. editor J. Fire Sci. Contbr. articles to Kirk-Othmer Ency., Ency. Polymer Sci., Rsch. Mgmt., others. Recipient IR-100 award Indsl. Rsch. Mag. Mem. Am. Chem. Soc. (chmn. profl. rels. com. NY sect. 1980-95), Assn. Cons. Chemists and Chem. Engrs., Sigma Xi. Achievements include more than 220 patents for commercial flame retardants, processes, agricultural chemicals, others. Home: 850 Sumner Pkwy Apt 301 Copley OH 44321 Office Phone: 330-664-1075. E-mail: eweil@poly.edu.

WEIL, FRANK A., investment banker, lawyer; b. Bedford, NY, Feb. 14, 1931; s. Sylvan and Ruth Alice (Norman) W.; m. Denie Sandison, Feb. 10, 1951; children: Deborah Weil Harrington, Amanda, Sandison, William. AB cum laude, Harvard U., 1953, LL.B., 1956. Bar: N.Y. 1956. Practiced in, NYC, 1957-60; gen. partner Loeb, Rhoades & Co., NYC, 1960-71; pres. Abacus Fund, Inc., 1968-72; chief fin. officer, dir. Paine, Webber, Jackson & Curtis, NYC, 1972-77; asst. sec. industry and trade Dept. Commerce, Washington, 1977-79; partner firm, bd. chmn., Ginsburg, Feldman, Weil & Bress, Washington, 1979-83, Wald, Harkrader & Ross, Washington, 1983-85; chmn., chief exec. officer, dir., Abacus and Assocs., Inc., 1985—; chmn. bd. SyVox Corp., Exxel/Atmos, Inc. Dir. Geico, Dorr-Oliver, Inc., Stamford, Conn., 1968-77, Hamburg Savs. Bank, N.Y.C., 1975-77, J.B. Lippincott Co., Phila., 1975-77, Govt. Research Corp., 1975-77, 79-85; dir., pres. Norman Found., 1953-77, 79, 92, chmn. bd. trustee, Ednl. Alliance. Trustee Tchrs. Coll., Columbia U., 1976-79, Montefiore Hosp., 1960-77; trustee, vice chmn. No. Westchester Hosp., 1971-77; past vice chmn. bd. govs. Atlantic Inst. Internat. Affairs; past pres. Ednl. Alliance, trustee, 1957-77; trustee, sec. Fedn. Jewish Philanthropies, N.Y.C., 1965-77; trustee, chmn. Harvey Sch., 1969-76; trustee Hurricane Island Outward Bound Sch., 1974—, Washington Opera, 1984-85, Asia Soc., 1993—; bd. dirs., pres., vice chmn., Hickrill Found., Inc., 1953-77, 79—; chmn. bd. dirs. Coun. Excellence in Govt., 1984—, chmn., 1988-93, Am. Assembly, 1992—, Smithsonian Inst., 1994—, chmn., 1997—; mem. vis. com. Kennedy Sch. Govt., Harvard U., chmn., 1998—; chmn. tax com., mem. N.Y. State Econ. Devel. Bd., 1975-77, mem. Appleseed Found. bd., 1995—; chmn., mem. N.Y. State Bd. Equalization and Assessment, 1976-77; adv. bd. Sch. Advanced Internat. Studies, Johns Hopkins U., 1979-88; mem. N.Y. State Council on Fiscal and Econ. Priorities, 1985-89, N.Y. Coun. Fgn. Rels.; mem. N.Y. State Adv. Commn. on Liability Ins., 1986. Mem. Century Assn., Harvard Club, Met. Club. Home: 1516 28th St NW Washington DC 20007-3058 Office: Abacus & Assocs Inc 147 E 48th St # 3fl New York NY 10017-1223 Home Phone: 202-338-6007; Office Phone: 212-230-9801. Business E-Mail: fweil2@abacusny.com.

WEIL, JEFFREY GEORGE, lawyer; b. Allentown, Pa., Apr. 28, 1951; s. Russel G.E. and Irene Marie (Kozlowski) W.; children: Michael, Stephen, Brooke, Lauren, Kristen. AB, Princeton U., 1973; JD, Harvard U., 1976. Bar: Pa. 1976, U.S. Dist. Ct. (ea. dist.) Pa. 1976, U.S. Ct. Appeals (3d cir.) 1976, U.S. Supreme Ct., 1988. Assoc. Dechert, Phila., 1976—84, ptnr., 1984—, chmn. firm hiring com., 1987—89, mem. firm exec. com., 1990—94. Chmn. com. United Way Southeastern Pa., Phila., 1982-85, trustee, 1983-89, funding policy com., 1987-90; participant Cmty. Leadership Seminar Program, Phila., 1986; bd. dirs. Hawk Mountain Sanctuary, 1993—, chmn. bd. dirs., 2000-05; bd. dirs. Pa. Wildlife Fedn., 1996-99. Mem. ABA (vice-chmn. adminstrn. law com. on pub. advs. and pub. representation 1985-88, antitrust sect. pvt. litig. subcom. 1991-2002), Pa. Bar Assn., Phila. Bar Assn. (fed. cts. com. 1985—), Princeton U. Alumni Schs. Com., Phila. Athenaeum, Princeton Club Phila. Avocations: fly fishing, reading. Home: 262 Pugh Rd Wayne PA 19087-5331 Office: Cira Snack Shop 646 Croft Dr Southampton PA 18966-4045 Home Phone: 610-935-0538; Office Phone: 215-994-2538. Business E-Mail: jeffrey.weil@dechert.com.

WEIL, JOHN WILLIAM, technology management consultant; b. NYC, Feb. 3, 1928; s. Frank Leopold and Henrietta Amelia Weil; m. Joan Leatrice Landis, June 15, 1950; children: Nancy Ellen, Linda Jill. BS, MIT, Cambridge, 1948; PhD, Cornell U., Ithaca, NY, 1953. Various positions in nuclear reactors and computers Gen. Electric Co. (various locations), 1953-70; v.p. advanced systems and tech. Honeywell Info. Systems, Inc., Waltham, Mass., 1970-74; v.p., chief tech. officer Bendix Corp., Southfield, Mich., 1974-77, sr. v.p., chief tech. officer, 1977-83; v.p. advanced tech. and engring. Allied Corp., Southfield, 1983; pres. Modular Bio Systems, Inc., 1983-85, Weil Assocs., Inc., Bloomfield Hills, Mich., 1985-97. Founder Met. Detroit Sci. and Engring. Coalition, 1977, sec., 1977-80, pres., 1980-82; chmn. Mich. Biotech. Inst., 1981-

85, trustee, 1985-92; mem. Army Sci. Bd., 1982-84. Contbr. articles to prof. jours. AEC fellow, 1950-51 Home and Office: 218 Guilford Rd Bloomfield Hills MI 48304-2737 Personal E-mail: johnww@weilhome.com.

WEIL, JOSEPH DAVID, editor, writer; b. Elizabeth, NJ, Mar. 24, 1958; s. Rocky John and Clare Irene Weil. BA, Empire State U., NY, 2008. Editor Black Swan Rev., Baron Art Ctr. Poetry Series, Woodbridge, NJ, 1988—2008, dir., 1988—2005; founder lit. mag. and dir. poetry series Black Swan Rev., Body Parts, Anti-Lawn, Cranford, NJ, 1988—2008. Poet sch. Geraldine R. Dodge Found., various cities, NJ, 1998—2008; editor NJ Poetry Resource Book, Paterson, 1999—2006; musician Mooks, Vestal, NY, 2006—08, composer, 2006—08. Author: (poetry book) Painting the Christmas trees. Home: 2221 Old Vestal Rd Vestal NY 13850 Business E-Mail: jweil@binghamton.edu.

WEIL, LAURA A., apparel executive; BA in Art History, Smith Coll., Northampton, Mass., 1979; MBA in Fin. and Mktg., Columbia U. V.p. restructuring and retailing industry groups Lehman Brothers, 1979—88; bus. mgr. L'Herbier de Provence, London, 1988—89; v.p. fin., CFO credit ops. R.H. Macy & Co., 1989—92; sr. v.p. investment banking CIBC Oppenheimer, 1992—95; exec. v.p., CFO American Eagle Outfitters, 1995—2005; exec. v.p., COO Ann Taylor Stores Corp., 2005—06; CEO Urban Brands, Inc., 2008—. Bd. dirs. Ultra Stores Corp., Aritizia, Carnival Corp., 2007—. Bd. mem. Girls Preparatory Sch. Office: Urban Brands Inc 100 Metro Way Secaucus NJ 07094*

WEIL, LYNNE AMY, communications executive, writer; b. Santa Monica, Calif., Apr. 29, 1963; d. Robert Harry and Miriam Ruth Weil; m. Nils Johan Axel Bruzelius, Aug. 10, 2002; 1 child, Emilie Anna Bruzelius. BA in Comm., U. Calif., LA, 1985; M in Pub. Policy, Princeton U., 2001. Freelance fgn. corr. Nat. Pub. Radio, Monitor Radio, Marketplace pub. radio, BBC, various others, Bonn, Germany, 1993—96; prodr., reporter Radio Deutsche Welle, Cologne, 1991—92; European corr. Cath. News Svc., Rome, 1996—99; reporter UPI, LA, 1986—88; prodr., reporter Calif. Pub. Radio Network, Long Beach, 1988—91; press sec. Senate Fgn. Rels. Com., Washington, 2001—03; comm. dir. Ho. Internat. Rels. Com. Dem. staff, 2003—. Cons. Woodrow Wilson Sch., Princeton U., NJ, 2003. Contbr. articles to profl. jours. Recipient Coll. journalism award with stipend, Pub. Interest Radio and TV Soc., 1985; scholar, Woodrow Wilson Sch., Princeton U., 2000—01; Congl. fellow, Am. Polit. Sci. Assn., 1999—2000. Mem.: Fgn. Corr. Assn. Germany (pres. 1995—96, v.p. 1994—95), Women in Internat. Security. Avocations: skiing, tennis, various musical instruments. Office Phone: 202-225-5021.

WEIL, PETER HENRY, retired lawyer; b. NYC, Nov. 20, 1933; s. Frank L. and Henrietta Amelia Weil; m. Helen Fay Kolodkin, Dec. 18, 1960; children: Karen L., Frank L. BA cum laude, Princeton U., 1954; LLB cum laude, Harvard U., 1957. Bar: N.Y. 1957, U.S. Dist. Ct. (so. and ea. dists.) N.Y. 1972. Assoc. Weil, Gotshal & Manges, NYC, 1958-62; from assoc. to ptnr. Kaye Scholer, NYC, 1962-95; ret., 1995. Lectr. SMU Inst. Comml. Financing, 1985—94, Banking Law Inst., 1987—89. Author: Asset Based Lending: An Introductory Guide to Secured Financing, P.L.I., 1989, 3d edit., 1996. Former chmn. N.Y. bd. overseers, former bd. govs. Hebrew Union Coll., Jewish Inst. Religion, Cin., NYC, LA, Jerusalem. With US Army, 1957—58. Recipient Gold medal, US Nat. Sr. Champions Ringwood Golden Master Volleyball Team, 1983. Mem.: ABA, Assn. Bar of City of N.Y. (mem. banking law com. 1975—78). Personal E-mail: phweil@aol.com.

WEIL, RANDOLPH ALLEN, executive; b. Champaign, Ill., Nov. 23, 1951; s. Nicholas Andrew and Audrey Florence W.; m. Susan Kay Rostad, Feb. 26, 1977; children: Alexandra, Aaron. BS in Econs., U. Ill., Chgo., 1973; MBA, U. Calif., Berkeley, 1974. Gen. sales mgr. Cummins Engine Co., Downers Grove, Ill., 1975—83; gen. mgr. ops. Sub of Cummins Engine. Co., Chgo., 1983-85; v.p., gen. mgr. Global Parts, Inc. (sub-co. of The Budd Co.), Dallas, 1985—87; dir. coastal ops. Allied Tube & Conduit, Harvey, Ill., 1987-88; dir. distbn. ops. Square D. Co., Florence, Ky., 1988-92; v.p. logistics AT&T Network Systems, Morristown, NJ, 1992-94; v.p. svc. logistics NCR Corp., Dayton, Ohio, 1994—2000; pres., COO IHS Engring., 2001—03; exec. v.p. IHS Group, 2003—04; pres., CEO Weil Operations West, LLC, 2004—; pres. Highlands Ranch Parks and Rec. Found., 2005—; dir. comm. St. Mary's Acad. Parents, 2005—; dir. Power Kure, Inc., 2005—. Dir. Jr. Achievement, Dayton, 1996—99, Boy Scouts Am., Columbus, 1978—80. Mem. Am. Prodn. & Inventory Control Soc., Coun. Logistics Mgrs. Avocations: bicycling, swimming, opera, remodelling, gardening.

WEIL, RICHARD, III, surgeon, medical educator; b. NYC, Feb. 22, 1936; s. Richard Jr. and Allene (Hall) W.; m. Polly Edgar, Aug. 22, 1959; children: Wendy, Richard. AB, Princeton U., 1957; MD, Columbia U. Coll. Physicians and Surgeons, 1961. Diplomate Am. Bd. Surgery, Nat. Bd. Med. Examiners. Intern in surgery Presbyn. Hosp., 1961-62, asst. resident in surgery, 1962-63, 65-67, chief resident in gen. surgery, 1968; chief resident in pediat. surgery Babies Hosp., 1969, chief resident in vasc. surgery, 1969, asst. attending surgeon, chmn. surg. house staff com., 1970-74, dir. kidney transplantation, 1973-74; asst. in surgery Columbia U. Coll. Physicians and Surgeons, 1967-68, instr. surgery, 1969, asst. prof. surgery, 1970-74; fellow in transplantation surgery U. Minn., 1970; assoc. prof. surgery U. Colo., 1974-79, prof. surgery, 1979-87, dir. transplantation, 1980-87; prof. surgery, dir. transplantation NYU, 1987-93; assoc. dean medicine, prof. surgery Brown U., Providence, 1993-98. Cons. surgeon Manhattan VA Hosp., 1989-92, Denver VA Hosp., 1980-87, Denver Gen. Hosp., 1980-87, St. Anthony-Ctrl. Hosp. Denver, 1980-87; attending surgeon Bellevue Hosp. Ctr., 1989-93 Contbr. more than 130 articles to profl. jours. including Surg. Forum, Am. Jour. Surgery, Transplantation, Surgery, Jour. Pediat. Surgery, Surgery, Gynecology & Obstets., among others. Capt. U.S. Army Med. Corps, 1963-65, Germany. Mem. Am. Assn. Tissue Banks, ACS, Am. Fedn. Clin. Rsch., Am. Soc. Transplant Surgeons, Am. Soc. for Artificial Internal Organs, Am. Surg. Assn., Assn. for Acad. Surgery, Allen O. Whipple Surg. Soc. (recorder 1976-78), Ctrl. Surg. Assn., Clin. Immunology Soc., Denver Acad. Surgery, Harvey Soc., Intermountain End-Stage Renal Disease Network (exec. com. 1975-79), Internat. Cardiovasc. Soc., N.Y. Ctr. for Liver Transplantation, N.Y. Clin. Soc., N.Y. Regional Transplant Program (pres. 1991-92), N.Y. Surg. Soc., Rocky Mountain Vasc. Surg. Soc., Soc. Internat. de Chirurgie, Soc. Vascular Surgery, Soc. U. Surgeons, Transplantation Soc., Western Assn. Transplant Surgeons, United Network for Organ Sharing (councilor for Colo., Wyo., Nebr., Kans., Iowa, Mo. 1986-87). Personal E-mail: rweiliii@msn.com.

WEIL, ROLF ALFRED, economist, retired university president; b. Pforzheim, Germany, Oct. 29, 1921; arrived in U.S., 1936, naturalized, 1944; s. Henry and Lina (Landauer) W.; m. Leni Metzger, Nov. 3, 1945; children: Susan Linda, Ronald Alan. BA, U. Chgo., 1942, PhD, 1950; D Hebrew Letters, Coll. Jewish Studies, 1967; DHL, Loyola U., 1970, Bowling Green State U., Ohio, 1986; LHD, Roosevelt U., 1988. Rsch. asst. Cowles Commn. for Rsch. in Econs., 1942-44; rsch. analyst Ill. Dept. Revenue, 1944-46; mem. faculty Roosevelt U., Chgo., 1946—, prof. fin. and econs., also chmn. dept. fin., 1954-65, dean Coll. Bus. Adminstrn., 1957-64, acting pres., 1965-66, pres., 1966-88, pres. emeritus, 1988—. Past pres. Selfhelp Home for the Aged, Chgo. Author: Through these Portals-from Immigrant to College President, 1991; contbr. articles on fin. to profl. jours. Bd. dirs. trustees Roosevelt U., Selfhelp of Chgo., Inc. Mem. Am. Econ. Assn., Cliff Dwellers Club. Office Phone: 312-341-4330. Personal E-mail: rolfleniweil@aol.com. Business E-Mail: rweil@roosevelt.edu.

WEIL, THOMAS ALEXANDER, retired electronics engineer; b. NYC, Jan. 22, 1930; s. Frank Leopold and Henrietta Amelia (Simons) W.; m. Dianne Isaacs; children: Deborah, Elizabeth, Alexander. BSEE, MIT, 1951. Engr. modulator sect. Raytheon Co., Watertown, Mass., 1951-55, sect. mgr. transmitters, 1955-69, dept. mgr. transmitters, 1969-77, staff scientist equipment devel. labs., 1972-95, lab. mgr. radar systems, 1977-79, lab. mgr. advanced devel., 1979-80, program mgr. oil shale program, 1980-84, sr. sci., 1985—95; ret., 1995. Cons. in field. Contbr. 3 chapters to books and 40 articles to profl. jours. Recipient Excellence in Tech. award Raytheon co., 1990; Raytheon Co. fellow, 1989. Fellow IEEE (tech. papers com. Modulator Symposia, Microwave Tube Symposia, Germeshausen award 1994). Unitarian. Achievements include 11 patents in field. Avocations: classical music, photography, mountain climbing, cosmology. Home: 14 Lanark Rd Wellesley MA 02481-3029 *Evolution and survival of the fittest have left mankind aggressive and prone to make war. Peace depends on finding how to overcome this heritage. Shouldn't we be working on how to resteer mankind's instincts?.*

WEIL, THOMAS P., retired health services consultant; b. Mount Vernon, NY, Oct. 2, 1932; s. H.M. and Alice (Franc) W.; m. Janet Whalen, Feb. 13, 1965. BA, Union Coll., 1954; MPH, Yale U., 1958; PhD, U. Mich., 1964. S.S. Goldwater fellow Mount Sinai Med. Ctr., NYC, 1957-58; assoc. cons. J.G. Steinle Assocs., Garden City, NY, 1958-61; asst. prof. UCLA, 1962-65; assoc. dir. Touro Infirmary, New Orleans, 1964-66; prof., dir. U. Mo., 1966—71; v.p. E.D. Rosenfeld Assocs., NYC, 1971-75; pres. Bedford Health Assocs. Inc., NY, NC, 1975-2000; ret. Chmn. Health Edn. & Applied Rsch. Found., Washington, 1981-83; bd. dirs. Albany Med. Ctr., Inc., NY, 1974-77; cons. to numerous hosps., med. schs., health related orgs., 1958-2000. Contbr. articles profl. jours. Named vis. prof. W.K. Kellogg Found., Sydney, Australia, 1969; recipient svc. award Am. Assn. Healthcare Cons., 1982; Weil Disting. Prof. in Health Svcs. Mgmt., U. Mo., 1991-2001. Fellow APHA (emeritus), Am. Assn. Healthcare Cons. (emeritus), Am. Coll. Healthcare Execs. (emeritus). Jewish. Avocations: Appaloosa and Quarter Horses, Pointers. Office Phone: 828-252-1616. Personal E-mail: tpweil@aol.com.

WEILAND, BARBARA J., neuroscientist; d. William Harold and Ruth Mary Yaeger; m. Jerauld P. Weilnad, Aug. 14, 1982; children: Maureen Romance, Eric Jerauld. BS in Chem. Engring., U. Mo., Rolla, 1983; PhD in Med. Physics, Oakland U., Rochester, Mich., 2006. Process engr. Gen. Motors Corp., Flint, Mich., 1983—89; regional mgr. LightSpeed Corp., Detroit, 2000—02; rsch. asst. Henry Ford Hosp., Detroit, 2002—06, postdoc. fellow, 2006—08, U. Mich., Ann Arbor, 2008—. Treas. Homeowners Assn., Davisburg, Mich., 2000—08. Mem.: Am. Assoc. Advancement Sci., Sigma Xi. Achievements include research in MEG measurement of sensory gating and tumor growth.

WEILAND, SCOTT RICHARD, singer; b. Santa Cruz, Calif., Oct. 28, 1967; m. Mary Forsberg, 2000 (div. 2003); children: Noah, Lucy Olivia. Founder, lead singer Mighty Joe Young, 1987—92; lead singer Stone Temple Pilots, 1992—, Velvet Revolver, 2003—08; founder Softdrive Records, 2003. Singer: (albums) (with Stone Temple Pilots) Core, 1992, Purple, 1994, Tiny Music...Songs From the Vatican Gift Shop, 1996, No. 4, 1999, Shangri-La Dee Da, 2001, Thank You, 2003, (solo) 12 Bar Blues, 1998, Happy in Galoshes, 2008, (with Velvet Revolver) Contraband, 2004, Libertad, 2007; co-prodr.: (albums) Break Your Silence, Cinder, 2003.

WEILER, JEFFRY LOUIS, lawyer; b. NYC, Dec. 31, 1942; s. Kurt and Elaine (Kabb) W.; m. Susan Karen Goodman, June 8, 1964; children: Philip K., June M. BS, Miami U., Oxford, Ohio, 1964; JD, Cleve. State U., 1970. Bar: Ohio 1970, Fla. 1981; CPA, Ohio 1968; bd. cert. specialist in estate planning trust and probate law, Ohio; bd. cert. tax specialist, Fla., 1983—. Acct. Meaden & Moore, CPAs, Cleve., 1964-65; IRS agt. U.S. Dept. Treasury, Cleve., 1965-70; assoc. Ulmer & Berne, Cleve., 1970-71; ptnr. Benesch, Friedlander, Coplan & Aronoff, LLP, Cleve., 1971—. Adj. assoc. prof. Cleve.-Marshall Coll. Law, Cleve. State U., 1980-87. Contbr. to profl. pubs. Named Disting. Estate Planner, Estate Planning Coun. Cleve., 2004; named one of Top 50 in Cleve., Ohio Super Lawyers, 2004—09, Top 100 in Ohio, 2004—08. Fellow Am. Coll. Trust and Estate Counsel; mem. ABA (sect. taxation), Ohio State Bar Assn. (coun. estate planning trust and probate law sect. 1999—), Cleve. Estate Planning Inst. (chmn. 1980), Cleve. Tax Inst. (chmn. 1983), Cleve. Bar Assn. (treas. 1993-96, trustee 1988-91), Tax Club of Cleve. (sec. 1996-97, v.p. 1997-99, pres. 1999-2000). Avocations: photography, sailing. Office: Benesch Friedlander Coplan & Aronoff LLP 200 Public Sq Str 2300 Cleveland OH 44114-2378 Home: 451 Muirfield Dr Highland Heights OH 44143 Home Phone: 440-446-8081; Office Phone: 216-363-4551. Business E-Mail: jweiler@beneschlaw.com.

WEILER, JOHN M., physician, educator, executive; b. Erie, Pa., Mar. 1945; s. Ad Richard and Ruth W.; m. Kay Lynn Boese, Dec. 23, 1971; children: Rebecca Lynn, James Michael. BS, U. Mich., Ann Arbor, 1967; MD, Temple U., Phila., 1971; MBA, U. Iowa, 2008. Research fellow Harvard U., Boston, 1975-77; instr. U. Iowa, Iowa City, 1977—78, asst. prof., 1978—83, assoc. prof., 1983-91, prof., 1991—2005, prof. emeritus, 2002—; pres. Comple Ware Corp. Visiting investigator Scripps Clinic and Research Found., La Jolla, Calif., 1986; program specialist immunology VA Cen. Office, Washington, 1985-88; mem. VA Merit Rev. Bd. for Immunology, 1989-91. Served as surgeon Pub. Health Service NIH, 1972-74. Recipient Research Career Devel. award Nat. Inst. Health, 1983, Clin. Investigator award VA, 1983-85, Research Assoc. award, 1980-83. Fellow ACP, Am. Coll. Rheumatology, Am. Acad. Allergy and Immunology (med. editor website 2001-08, chair ADT interest sect. 2009-); mem. Am. Assn. Immunologists, Am. Soc. Biochem. Molecular Biology, Am. Thoracic Soc., Ctrl. Soc. for Clin. Investigation, Drug Info. Assn. (clin. spl. interest area cmty. chair 2003-05, paitent reported outcomes & study endpoints SIACS 2007-). Avocations: amateur radio, computer software design.

WEILERT, MARY E., communications educator; b. Youngstown, Ohio, May 7, 1964; d. Chester E. Young and Sue E. Ayers; m. Tim D. Weilert, Nov. 17, 1984; children: Adam D., Amy M., Alex K. BA in Comm., Avila Coll., Kansas City, Mo., 1985; MA in English, Pitsburg State U., Kans., 1989. Tchr. Allen County CC, Iola, Kans., 1989—93; instr. Neosho County CC, Chantue, 1993—. Home: 802 S Highland Chanute KS 66720 Office: Neosho County CC 800 W 14 Chanute KS 66720

WEIL-GARRIS BRANDT, KATHLEEN (KATHLEEN BRANDT), art historian; b. Surrey, Eng. d. Kurt Hermann and Charlotte (Garris) Weil; m. Werner Brandt (dec. 1983). BA with honors, Vassar Coll., Poughkeepsie, NY, 1956; postgrad., U. Bonn, Germany, 1956-57; MA, Radcliffe U., 1958; PhD, Harvard, 1966; MA, Oxford U., 1998. Asst. prof. NYU, NYC, 1963-67, assoc. prof., 1967-72, prof., 1973—; asst. prof. NYU Inst. Fine Arts, NYC, 1966-67, assoc. prof., 1967-72, prof., 1973—; vis. prof. Harvard U., Cambridge, Mass., 1980; editor in chief The Art Bulletin, NYC, 1977-81; Slade prof. Oxford U., 1998. Cons. on Renaissance art Vatican Mus., 1987—; vis. fellow Bibliotheca Hertziana (Max-Planck Inst.) Rome; faculty fellow E. M. Remarque Inst., 2006. Author: Leonardo and Central Italian Art, 1974, Problems In Cinquecento Sculpture, 1977; author: (with J. d'Amico) The Renaissance Cardinal's Ideal Palace, 1981, (with C. d'Acidini, J. Draper, N. Penny) Giovinezza di Michelangelo, 1999-2000; editor: Michelangelo: la Cappella Sistina: documentazione e interpretazione, vol. III, 1996; contbr. articles to profl. jours. Mem. Am. com. Medici Archive Project, 1996—; bd. dirs. Raccolta Vinciana, 1997—. Decorated Officer, Order of Merit (Italy), 1993, Officer, Order of Arts and Letters, France, 2008; recipient Rsch. prize Humboldt Found., 1985, Disting. Tchg. award Lindback Found., 1967, Golden Dozen Tchr. award NYU, 1993, Alumni Great Tchr. award, 1996; Guggenheim fellow, 1976; grantee Henkel Found., 1987, Samuel H. Kress Found., 1999; Andrew W. Mellon fellowship Met. Mus., 2009, Fullbright scholarship. Mem. Coll. Art Assn. (bd. dirs. 1973-74, 77-81), Renaissance Soc. Am. (editl. bd. 1992—), Soc. Archtl. Historians, Friends of the Frances Lehman Loeb Art Ctr. (bd. mem. 2005-09); fellow NY Acad. Scis., Phi Beta Kappa (v.p. NYU chpt. 1979-81). Achievements include research in responses to art objects in relation to recent advances jn brain imaging. Avocations: art films, conservation, music, dance. Office: NYU Inst Fine Arts 1 E 78th St New York NY 10021-0119 Business E-Mail: kathleen.brandt@nyu.edu.

WEILL, HANS, medical educator; b. Berlin, Aug. 31, 1933; came to U.S., 1939; s. Kurt and Gerda (Philipp) W.; m. Kathleen Burton, Apr. 3, 1958; children: Judith, Leslie, David. BS, Tulane U., 1955, MD, 1958. Diplomate: Am. Bd. Internal Medicine. Intern Mt. Sinai Hosp., NYC, 1958-59; resident Tulane Med. Unit, Charity Hosp. La., New Orleans, 1959-60, chief resident, 1961-62, sr. vis. physician, 1972—; NIH research fellow dept. medicine and pulmonary lab. Sch. Medicine Tulane U., New Orleans, 1960-61, instr. medicine, 1962-64, asst. prof. medicine, 1964-67, assoc. prof., 1967-71, prof. medicine, 1971—, Schlieder Found. prof. pulmonary medicine, 1985-97; chief Environ. Medicine sect. Tulane Med. Center, 1980-96; dir. univ. Ctr. for Bioenviron. Rsch., 1989-93; dir. interdisciplinary research group in occupational lung diseases Nat. Heart, Lung and Blood Inst., 1972-92, mem. nat. adv. council, 1986-90, chmn. pulmonary disease adv. com., 1982-84; active staff Tulane Med. Center Hosp., 1976—; program dir. Nat. Inst. for Environ. Health Sci., 1992-96. Cons. pulmonary diseases Touro Infirmary, New Orleans, 1962—; cons. NIH, Nat. Inst. Occupational Safety and Health, Occupational Safety and Health Adminstrn., USN, NAS, EPA; lectr., participant workshops and confs. profl. groups in U.S., France, Can., U.K.; dir. Nat. Inst. Environ. Health Scis Superfund. Basic Rsch. Program, 1992-96. Mem. editorial bd. Am. Rev. of Respiratory Disease, 1980-85, CHEST, 1987-91; editor Respiratory Diseases Digest, 1981; guest editor Byssinosis conf. supplement, CHEST, 1981. Fellow Am. Acad. Allergy, Royal Soc. Medicine, ACP; mem. Am. Thoracic Soc. (pres. 1976), Am. Lung Assn. (bd. dirs. 1975-78), New Orleans Acad. Internal Medicine (sec., treas. 1973-75), Am. Coll. Chest Physicians (gov. for La. 1970-75), Am. Fedn. Clin. Research, So. Soc. Clin. Investigation, N.Y. Acad. Scis., Brit. Thoracic Assn., Internat. Epidemiol. Assn., Am. Heart Assn. (task force on environment and cardiovascular system 1978), Brit. Thoracic Soc., Phi Beta Kappa, Alpha Omega Alpha. Home and Office: 110 Bellshire Dr Flat Rock NC 28731 Personal E-mail: hweill@bellsouth.net.

WEILL, SANDY (SANFORD I. WEILL), retired diversified financial services company executive; b. Bklyn., Mar. 16, 1933; s. Max and Etta (Kalika) W.; m. Joan Mosher, June 20, 1955; children: Marc P., Jessica M. Bibliowicz. BA, Cornell U., 1955, student Grad. Sch. Bus. and Pub. Adminstrn., 1954-55. Chmn. bd., CEP Carter, Berlind & Weill (name changed to CBWL-Hayden, Stone, Inc. 1970, to Hayden Stone, Inc. 1972, to Shearson Hayden Stone 1974, to Shearson Loeb Rhoades), NYC, 1960-84, dir., chmn. exec. com., 1981-83, pres., 1983-85, Am. Express Co., 1983—85, chmn., CEO Fireman's Fund Ins. Co. subs., 1984-85; chmn., CEO Am. Express Ins. Services., Inc., 1984—85; chmn., pres., CEO Comml. Credit Co., Balt., 1986—88; chmn., CEO Primerica Corp., NYC, 1988—93, pres., 1988—92; chmn. Primerica Holdings Inc., NYC; chmn., CEO Travelers Group, NYC, 1986—98; CEO Citigroup, Inc., NYC, 1998—2003, chmn., 1998—2006, chmn. emeritus, 2006—. Bd. dirs. Citigroup, Inc., 1986-2006, AT&T Corp., 1998-2002, I. Du Pont Nemours & Co., 1998-2001, United Technologies Corp., 1999-2003, Fed. Res. Bank N.Y., 2001-06; vice chmn. adv. council The Johnson Grad. Sch. of Mgmt.; founder Acad. of Fin. Co-author (with Judah S. Kraushaar): The Real Deal: My Life in Business and Philanthropy, 2006. Mem. bd. overseers Joan and Sanford I. Weill Med. Coll. and Grad. Sch. Med. Scis. of Cornell U. (formerly Cornell Med. Coll.), 1982-, chmn., 1996-; chmn. bd. trustees Carnegie Hall, N.Y.C., 1991-; trustee N.Y. Presbyn. Hosp.; bd. overseers Meml. Sloan-Kettering Cancer Ctr.; bd. dirs. Balt. Symphony Orch.; bd. gov. NY Hosp.; mem. adv. coun. Cornell Univ. Johnson Grad. Sch. Mgmt.; mem. US Dept. Treasury Working Group on Child Care. Recipient NY State Gov.'s Art award, 1997; named one of the halls in honor of at Carnegie Hall, CEO of the Yr., Chief Exec. mag., 2002; named one of Top 25 Managers of Yr., BusinessWeek, 2001, 50 Most Generous Philanthropists, 2005, 400 Richest Americans, Forbes, 2006; named to Acad. of Achievement, Washington, D.C., 1997. Mem. N.Y. Soc. Security Analysts Clubs: Cornell (N.Y.C.), Century Country (Purchase, N.Y.), Harmonie (N.Y.C.); chmn. Nat. Acad. Found. Office: Citigroup Inc 399 Park Ave New York NY 10022-4614 also: Citigroup Inc 153 E 53rd St New York NY 10043-0001

WEIMER, JOHN L., state supreme court justice; b. Thibodaux, La., Oct. 2, 1954; m. Penny Hymel; 3 children. BS (with honors), Nicholls State U., 1976; JD, La. State U., 1980. Pvt. practice law, 1980—95; judge 17th Judicial Dist. Ct., 1995—98, 1st Cir. Ct. of Appeal, Dist. 1, Divsn. B, 1998—2001; assoc. justice La. Supreme Ct., 2001—. Adj. prof. law Nicholls State U., 1982—97; regional co-chmn. Citizens' Summit for Justice Reform, 1997. Mem. Thibodaux Vol. Fire Dept., Rotary Club, Nicholls State U. Alumni Bd., Thibodaux Chamber of Commerce, Houma-Terrebonne Chamber of Commerce, Assumption Chamber of Commerce; established Lafourche Parish Student Govt. Day Program. Recipient Crimefighter's Outstanding Jurist award, Outstanding Jud. award, Victims & Citizens Against Crime. Mem.: Lafourche Parish Bar Assn., La. State Bar Assn. (delegate). Achievements include development of Lafourche Parish Drug Treatment Court. Office: La Supreme Ct 400 Royal St New Orleans LA 70130*

WEIMER, ROBERT JAY, geology educator, energy consultant, civic leader; b. Glendo, Wyo., Sept. 4, 1926; s. John L. and Helen (Mowrey) Weimer; m. Ruth Carol Adams, Sept. 12, 1948; children: Robert Thomas, Loren Edward(dec.), Paul Christner, Carl Scott. BA, U. Wyo.,

Laramie, 1948, MA, 1949; PhD, Stanford U., Calif., 1953; DEng (hon.), CSM, 2008. Registered profl. engr., Colo. Geologist Union Oil Co. Calif., 1949-54; cons. geologist U.S. and fgn. petroleum exploration, 1954—; prof. geology Colo. Sch. Mines, 1957-83, prof. emeritus, 1983—, Getty prof. geology, 1978-83; vis. prof. U. Colo., 1961, U. Calgary, Can., 1970, Inst. Tech., Bandung, Indonesia, 1975; dir. dept. head Geol. Mus., 1965—70. Fulbright lectr. U. Adelaide, South Australia, 1967; disting. lectr. and continuing edn. lectr. Am. Assn. Petroleum Geologists, Soc. Expl. Geophysicists; ednl. cons. to petroleum cos., 1964—; mem. energy rsch. adv. bd. Dept. Energy, 1985-90, Bd. on Mineral and Energy Resources, Nat. Rsch. Coun., 1988. Editor: Guide to Geology of Colorado, 1960, Symposium on Cretaceous Rocks of Colorado and Adjacent Area, 1959, Denver Earthquakes, 1968, Fossil Fuel Exploration, 1974, Studies in Colorado Field Geology, 1976, Petroleum System, Denver Basin, 1996. Trustee Colo. Sch. Mines Research Found., 1967-70; pres. Rockland Found., 1982-83; bd. dirs. Foothills Art Ctr., 1997-2002. With USNR, 1944-46. Recipient Disting. Alumnus award U. Wyo., 1982, Mines medal Colo. Sch. Mines, 1984, Brown medal, 1990, Parker medal Am. Inst. Profl. Geologists, 1986, Exemplary Alumni award U. Wyo., 1994, ISEM Hedberg award, 2001, Carla Coleman Conservation award, 2005, Hall of Fame award IPAMS, 2006. Fellow Geol. Soc. Am. (chmn. Rocky Mountain sect. 1966-67, Sloss award 2003), AAAS; mem. Am. Assn. Petroleum Geologists (hon. pres. 1992, Sidney Powers medal 1983, Dist. Educator award 1996), Soc. for Sedimentary Geology (hon., sec.-treas. 1966-67, v.p. 1971, pres. 1972, Twenhofel medal 1995), Colo. Sci. Soc. (hon., pres. 1981), Rocky Mountain Assn. Geologists (hon., pres. 1969, found. bd. 1976-86, Scientist of Yr. 1982, Legend award 2003), Nigerian Mining and Geoscis. Soc. (hon.), Can. Soc. Petroleum Geologists (hon.), Wyo. Geol. Assn. (hon.), Colo. Sch. Mines Alumni Assn. (hon., Coolbaugh award 1996), Am. Geol. Inst. Found. (sec., treas. 1984-88, Legendary Geosci. award 2006-), Geol. Soc. Am. Found. (bd. dirs. 1999-04), Nat. Acad. Engring. (ch. sec. 11 1999), Northwoodside Inc. Land Conservancy Found. (v.p. 1995-96, pres. 1997—, Carla Coleman Conservation award 2005, Arthur Lakes Public Svc. award, 2008), Mt. Vernon Country Club (Golden, bd. dirs. 1956-59, 81-84, pres. 1983-84). Home: RR 3 25853 Mt Vernon Rd Golden CO 80401-9699 Office Phone: 303-526-0247. Business E-Mail: rweimer@mines.edu.

WEINBACH, ARTHUR FREDERIC, retired computer company executive; b. Waterbury, Conn., May 3, 1943; s. Max and Winifred (Eckstein) Weinbach; m. Joanne Kaplan, Nov. 22, 1970; children: Michael Scott, Jonathan David. BS in Econs., U. Pa., 1965, MS in Acctg., 1966. CPA. With Touche Ross & Co., NYC, 1966—75, ptnr. Stamford, Conn., 1976—79; from v.p. to pres. Automatic Data Processing, Inc., Roseland, 1980—98, CEO, 1996—2006, chmn., 1998—2007, Broadridge Fin. Solutions, Inc., 2007—. Bd. dirs. CA Inc., Schering-Plough Corp., Phoenix Companies, Inc., NJ Seeds; prior bd. dirs. 1st Data Health Plan Svcs., NJ Inst. Tech., Boys Hope, Overlook Hosp. Found., Metro NJ U. Pa. Club, United Way Tri-State. Jewish. Office: Broadridge Financial Solutions Inc 1981 Marcus Ave New Hyde Park NY 11042 Office Phone: 516-472-5400.*

WEINBACH, LAWRENCE ALLEN, computer services company executive, private equity managing director; b. NYC, Jan. 8, 1940; s. Max N. and Winifred E. Weinbach; m. Patricia Leiter, Dec. 1961; children: Wendy, Peter, Daniel. BS in Econs., Whrtin Sch. U. Pa., Phila., 1961. CPA. With Andersen Worldwide, NYC, 1961-97, mng. ptnr. Stamford, Conn., 1974-80, NYC, 1980-83, mng. ptnr. N.Y. Met. area, 1983-87, COO, 1987-89, mng. ptnr., CEO, 1989-97; pres. & CEO Unisys Corp., Blue Bell, Pa., 1997—2005, chmn., 2006—07; mng. dir. Yankee Hill Capital Mgmt. LLC, 2006—. Bd. dirs. Avon Products, Inc., Discover Fin. Svcs., Great Western Products LLC. Trustee Carnegie Hall; life trustee emeritus Northwestern U. Mem. Beta Gamma Sigma, Beta Alpha Psi. Business E-Mail: lawrence.weinbach@yankeehillcapital.com.

WEINBERG, ADAM D., museum director; b. NYC, Dec. 10, 1954; s. James Lionel and Edith (Zickerman) Weinberg; m. Lorraine Ferguson; children: Zoé, Kira. BA, Brandeis U., 1977; MFA, SUNY, Buffalo, 1981. Dir. edn., asst. curator Walker Art Ctr., Mpls., 1981-88; dir., equitable ctr. Whitney Mus. Am. Art, NYC, 1988-90, sr. curator, curator of permanent collection, 1993—99, mus. dir., 2003—; artistic and program dir. Am. Ctr., Paris, 1990—92; dir. Addison Gallery of American Art, Andover, Mass., 1999—2003. Author: (catalog) On the Line: The New Color Photojournalism, 1986, (book & catalog) Vanishing Presence, 1989, (exhbn. catalogs) Aldo Crommelynck: Master Prints with Am. Artists, 1989, Contingent Realms, 1990. Trustee Whitney Mus. Am. Art, Alice Pratt Brown Dir. Mem.: Coll. Art Assn., Am. Assn. Mus. Office: Whitney Mus Am Art 945 Madison Ave New York NY 10021 Business E-Mail: director@whitney.org.

WEINBERG, DAVID B., investor; b. Chgo., Feb. 19, 1952; s. Judd A. and Marjorie (Gottlieb) W.; m. Lynne Ellen Mesirow, July 6, 1980. AB cum laude, Harvard U., 1974; JD, Georgetown U., 1977. Bar: Ill. 1977, U.S. Dist. Ct. (no. dist.) Ill. 1977, U.S. Ct. Appeals (7th cir.) 1978. Law clerk to Hon. William G. Clark Supreme Ct. Ill., 1977-79; assoc. Lord, Bissell & Brook, Chgo., 1979-84, ptnr., 1985-89, Mayer, Brown & Platt, Chgo., 1989-96; chmn., CEO Judd Enterprises, Inc., Chgo., 1996—; pres. Digital BandWidth LLC, Chgo., 1996—. Ill. Supreme Ct. com. Profl. Responsibility, Chgo., 1984-94, chmn. subcom. lawyers certification. Chmn. bd. trustees Ravinia Festival Assn., Highland Park, Ill., 1998—2001; vice chmn. bd. trustees Northwestern U., 1999—. Mem. Chgo. Club, Econ. Club Chgo., Lake Shore Country Club, Arts Club Chgo. Office: Judd Enterprises Bank One Plz 21 S Clark St Ste 3140 Chicago IL 60603-2090

WEINBERG, DORON, lawyer; b. Israel, Sept. 13, 1944; JD, U. Chgo., 1968; AB, Cornell U., 1965. Bar: Calif. 1970, (US Court Appeals 9th cir.) 1973, cert.: (US Supreme Ct.) 1973. Articles editor U. Chgo. Law Review, 1967—68; instr. Stanford U. Law Sch., 1968—69; instr. criminal trial skills New Coll. Calif. Sch. Law, 1977—83; faculty Hastings Coll. Trial & Appellate Advocacy, 1977—78, Nat. Inst. Trial Advocacy, 1985—2000, Cardozo Advocacy Clinic, 1985—2000; ptnr. Weinberg & Wilder. Mem.: Nat. Assn. Criminal Defense Lawyers, Nat. Lawyers Guild (pres. 1974—76), Assn. Discipline Defense Counsel, Am. Arbitration Assn. (dispute resolution panel), Calif. Attys. for Criminal Justice (chmn. seminar com., bd. govs.), Am. Bar Assn. (white collar crime & criminal litigation subcom.), Bar Assn. San Francisco (chmn. criminal adv. com. 2006—08, bd. dirs. 2008—). Office: Weinberg & Wilder 523 Octavia St San Francisco CA 94102 Office Phone: 415-431-3472. Office Fax: 415-552-2703. E-mail: doronweinberg@aol.com.*

WEINBERG, EUGENE DAVID, microbiologist, educator; b. Chgo., Mar. 4, 1922; s. Philip and Lenore (Bergman) W.; m. Frances Murl Izen, Sept. 5, 1949; children— Barbara Ann, Marjorie Jean, Geoffrey Alan, Michael Benjamin. BS, U. Chgo., 1942, MA, 1948, PhD, 1950. Instr. dept. microbiology Ind. U., Bloomington, 1950-53, asst. prof., 1953-57, asso. prof., 1957-61, prof., 1961—, head microbiology sect., med. sci. program, 1978—92. Mem. sci. adv. bd., chair publs. Iron Disorders Inst., 1998—. Served with AUS, 1942-45. Mem.: Am. Soc. Microbiology. Office: Ind U Biology Dept Jordan Hall Bloomington IN 47405 Office Phone: 812-336-5556. Fax: 812-855-6705. Business E-Mail: eweinber@indiana.edu.

WEINBERG, FLORENCE MAY, retired modern language and literature educator; b. Alamogordo, N.Mex., Dec. 3, 1933; d. Steven Horace and Olive Gladys (Edgington) Byham; m. Kurt Weinberg, May 8, 1955 (dec. Feb. 1996). PhD, U. Rochester, 1968. Instr. modern langs. St. John Fisher Coll., Rochester, N.Y., 1967, asst. prof. modern langs., 1967-71, assoc. prof. modern langs., 1971-75, prof. modern langs., 1975-89, dept. chmn. modern langs., 1972-79, dir. internat. studies, 1983—86; prof. French and Spanish Trinity U., San Antonio, 1989—99, chair modern langs. and lits., 1989-95; ret., 1999; full-time writer, novels, 1999—. Resident Hambidge Ctr. for Writers, Artists, and Scientists, 1999—2001, 2003—07, 2009. Author: The Wine and the Will, 1972, Gargantua in a Convex Mirror, 1986, The Cave, 1986, Les Leçons du rire, 2000, Sonora Wind, Ill Wind, 2002, Longs désirs, 2002, I'll Come to Thee By Moonlight, 2002, The Storks of La Caridad, 2005, Apache Lance, Franciscan Cross, 2005, Seven Cities of Mud, 2008, Sonora Moonlight, 2008, Sonora Wind, 2009. Recipient Alumna of Yr. award Park U., 2008; finalist WILLA Literary award, Apache Lance Franciscan Cross, 2006, finalist N. Mex. Book award, Apache Lance Franciscan Cross, 2007, N.Mex. Book award, Seven Cities of Mud, 2008, finalist Eric Hoffer award 2009; grant-in-aid Am. Coun. Learned Socs., 1974-75, sr. fellowship NEH, 1979-80, grant NEH, 1983, Rsch. grant Ludwig Vogelstein Found., 1986. Mem. MLA, PEN, Renaissance Soc. Am., Women Writing the West. Democrat. Avocations: swimming, dressage horseback riding. Home: 331 Royal Oaks Dr San Antonio TX 78209-1623 Personal E-mail: florenceweinberg@juno.com.

WEINBERG, GERHARD LUDWIG, history professor, writer; b. Hannover, Germany, Jan. 1, 1928; arrived in UK, 1938, arrived in US, 1941, naturalized, 1949; s. Max Bendix and Kate Sarah (Gruenebaum) Weinberg; m. Janet Kabler White, Apr. 29, 1989. BA in Social Studies, SUNY, Albany, 1948, LHD (hon.), 1989; MA, U. Chgo., 1949, PhD in Hist., 1951; PhD (hon.), U. Hannover, 2001. Rsch. analyst, war documentation project Columbia U., NYC, 1951-54; vis. lectr. hist. U. Chgo., 1954-55, U. Ky., Lexington, 1955-56, asst. prof., 1957-59; faculty U. Mich., Ann Arbor, 1959—63, prof. hist., 1963-74, chmn. hist. dept., 1972-73; William Rand Kenan, Jr. prof. hist. U. NC, Chapel Hill, 1974-99, prof. emeritus, 1999—, acting chmn. hist. dept., 1989-90. Vis. U. Bonn, Germany, 1983, USAF Acad., 1990—91; Shapiro sr. scholar-in-residence US Holocaust Meml. Mus., Washington, 2001—02. Author: Guide to Captured German Documents, 1952, Germany and the Soviet Union, 1939-1941, 1954, The Foreign Policy of Hitler's Germany: Diplomatic Revolution in Europe, 1933-36, 1970, The Foreign Policy of Hitler's Germany: Starting World War II, 1937-1939, 1980, World in the Balance: Behind the Scenes of World War II, 1981, A World at Arms: A Global History of World War II, 1994, Germany, Hitler, and World War II: Essays in Modern German and World History, 1995, Visions of Victory: The Hopes of Eight World War II Leaders, 2005; editor, translator Hitler's Second Book: The Unpublished Sequel to Mein Kampf, 2003; contbr. numerous articles to various hist. jours., chapters to books; mem. bd. editors Jour. Modern Hist., 1970—72, Ctrl. European Hist., 1970—72, Internat. Hist. Rev., 1990—2000, Jour. Intelligence Hist., 2001. Chmn. Ann Arbor Dem. Com., 1961—63; mem. Mich. Dem. Ctrl. Com., 1963—67. Served with US Army, 1946—47. Recipient Pritzker Mil. Libr. Lit. award for lifetime achievement in mil. writing, Tawani Found., Chgo., 2009; fellow Am. Coun. Learned Societies, 1965—66, John Simon Guggenheim Meml. Found., 1971—72, NEH, 1978—79. Mem.: Am. Acad. Arts & Scis., WW II Studies Assn. (bd. dirs.), German Studies Assn. (exec. com. 1989—92, v.p. 1994—96, pres. 1996—98, Halverson prize 1981), So. Hist. Assn. (chmn. European sect. 1989), Am. Hist. Assn. (v.p. rsch. 1982—84, George Louis Beer prize 1971, 1995), Phi Beta Kappa. Jewish. E-mail: gweinber@email.unc.edu.*

WEINBERG, H. BARBARA, art historian, educator, curator; b. NYC, Jan. 23, 1942; d. Max and Evelyn Kallman; m. Michael B. Weinberg, Aug. 30, 1964. AB, Barnard Coll., 1962; MA, Columbia U., NYC, 1964, PhD, 1972. Prof. art history Queens Coll. Grad. Sch., CUNY, 1972—94; curator Am. paintings sculpture Met. Mus. Art., NYC, 1990—98; Alice Pratt Brown curator Am. paintings sculpture Met. Mus. Art, NYC, 1998—. Author: The Decorative Work of John La Farge, 1977, The American Pupils of Jean-Léon Gérome, 1984, The Lure of Paris: Nineteenth-Century American Painters and Their French Teachers, 1991, Thomas Eakins and the Metropolitan Museum of Art, 1994, co-author: American Impressionism and Realism: The Painting of Modern Life, 1885-1915, 1994, American Drawings and Watercolors in The Metropolitan Museum of Art: John Singer Sargent, 2000, John Singer Sargent in The Metropolitan Museum of Art, 2000, Childe Hassam, American Impressionist, 2004, Americans in Paris, 1860-1900, 2006, American Stories 1765-1915, 2009; mem. editl. bd. Am. Art Jour., 1984—. Mem.: Phi Beta Kappa. Office: Met Mus Art 1000 5th Ave New York NY 10028-0198 Office Phone: 212-879-5500 ext 8001.

WEINBERG, HELEN ARNSTEIN, retired literature and art educator; b. Orange, NJ, June 17, 1927; d. Morris Jerome and Jeannette (Tepperman) Arnstein; m. Kenneth Gene Weinberg, Sept. 11, 1949; children: Janet Sue Weinberg Strassner, Hugh Benjamin, John Arnstein. BA in English Lit., Wellesley Coll., Mass., 1949; MA in English Lit., Western Res. U., 1953, PhD in English Lit., 1966. Teaching fellow Ohio State U., Columbus, 1949-51, Western Res. U., Cleve., 1953-57; instr. to prof. Cleve. Inst. Art, 1958—2004; ret., 2004. Standing officer Coll. English Assn. Ohio, 1987-90; vis. tchr. NYU, 1985, Sch. Visual Art's, 1981; lecture tours Israel, 1968, 70, 71. Author: The New Novel in America: The Kafkan Mode in Contemporary Fiction, 1970. Recipient fellowship in art history NEH, Columbia U., N.Y.C., 1977-78; Recipient Am. Culture grantee NEH/Vassar Coll., 1993. Mem. AAUP, Modern Lang. Assn., Coll. Art Assn. Democrat. Jewish. Home: 3015 Huntington Rd Shaker Heights OH 44120-2407

WEINBERG, JEFFREY J., lawyer; b. NYC, Aug. 27, 1948; s. Arnold Mitchell and Lucile (Barton) W.; m. Bonnie J. Sandhaus, Aug. 23, 1970; children: Seth, Andrew. BA, SUNY, Stony Brook, 1969; JD, Georgetown U., 1973. Bar: N.Y., U.S. Dist. Ct. (so. and ea. dists.). Assoc. Weil, Gotshal & Manges, NYC, 1973-81, ptnr., 1981—. Acting judge Village of Roslyn Estates. Author: Sales of Troubled Business, 1991, 92, 93, 94. Former trustee Village of Roslyn Estate. Mem.: Friars Club. Avocation: sailing. Office: Weil Gotshal & Manges 767 5th Ave Fl Concl New York NY 10153-0119

WEINBERG, JERROLD G., lawyer; b. Norfolk, Va., Apr. 5, 1928; s. Charles Paul and Reba Gladstone Weinberg; m. Marcia Ellen Moress (dec.); children: Ellen Jane(dec.), Nancy Louise von Auersperg, Andrew Steven; m. Ruth A. Hofheimer, Feb. 6, 1999. BS in Comm., U. Va., Charlottesville, 1947, LLB, 1950. Bar: Va. 1949. Atty. pvt. practice, Norfolk, 1950—78; pres. Weinberg & Stein PC, Norfolk, 1978—. Lectr. law William & Mary Law Sch., Williamsburg, Va., 1980; mem. Jud. Conf. US Ct. Appeals (4th cir.). With US Army, 1951—53. Master: James Kent Am. Inn Ct. (pres. 1996—97); fellow: Va. Law Found., Am. Bar Found., Am. Coll. Trial Lawyers; mem.: ABA, Norfolk and Portsmouth Bar Assn. (pres. 1973—74), Va. Bar Assn., Norfolk Yacht and Country Club. Republican. Jewish. Home: 7310 Woodway Ln Norfolk VA 23505 Office: Weinberg Stein Pc 999 Waterside Dr Ste 1313 Norfolk VA 23510-3320

WEINBERG, JOHN LEE, federal judge; b. Chgo., Apr. 24, 1941; s. Louis Jr. and Jane Kitz (Goldstein) W.; m. Sarah Kibbee, July 6, 1963; children: Ruth, Leo. BA, Swarthmore Coll., 1962; JD, U. Chgo., 1965. Bar: Ill. 1966, Wash. 1967, U.S. Dist. Ct. (we. dist.) Wash. 1967, U.S. Ct. Appeals (9th cir.) 1967. Law clk. to Hon. Henry L. Burman Ill. Appellate Ct., Chgo., 1965-66; law clk. to Hon. Walter V. Schaefer Ill. Supreme Ct., Chgo., 1966; law clk. to Hon. William T. Beeks U.S. Dist. Ct. Wash., Seattle, 1967-68; atty. Perkins Coie Law Firm, Seattle, 1968-73; magistrate judge U.S. Dist. Ct.; U.S. Magistrate judge Seattle, 1973—2003; ret., 2003; recalled, 2003—. Author: Federal Bail and Detention Handbook, 1988. Mem. ABA, Am. Judicature Soc., Wash. State Bar Assn., Seattle-King County Bar Assn., Fed. Magistrate Judges Assn. (nat. pres. 1982-83). Avocations: sports and physical fitness activities, bridge, jazz piano. Office: US Magistrate Judge 12th Fl United States Courthouse 700 Stewart St Seattle WA 98101 Office Phone: 206-370-8910.

WEINBERG, JOHN SIDNEY, diversified financial services company executive; b. Feb. 18, 1957; m. Amy Marie Shepherd, Mar. 3, 1984. BA in History, Princeton U., 1979; MBA, Harvard U., 1983. Mgmt. trainee Knight-Ridder Newspapers, Miami; assoc. corp. fin. dept. Goldman, Sachs & Co., 1983, mng. dir., 1996, co-head of investment banking services NYC, 1997—2001; co-head of investment banking divsn. Americas Goldman Sachs & Co., NYC, 2002; mem. mgmt. com. The Goldman Sachs Group, Inc., NYC, 2002—, co-head global investment banking, 2002—, vice chmn., 2006—. Bd. dirs. Steppingstone Found.; trustee NY-Presbyterian Hosp., 2000—; mem. vis. com. Harvard Bus. Sch. Office: The Goldman Sachs Group Inc 85 Broad St New York NY 10004*

WEINBERG, LOUISE, law educator, writer; b. NYC; m. Steven Weinberg; 1 child, Elizabeth. AB summa cum laude, Cornell U.; JD, Harvard U., 1969, LLM, 1974. Bar: Mass. Sr. law clk. Hon. Chas. E. Wyzanski, Jr., Boston, 1971-72; assoc. in law Bingham, Dana & Gould, Boston, 1969-72; teaching fellow Harvard Law Sch., Boston, 1972-74; lectr. law Brandeis U., Waltham, Mass., 1974; assoc. prof. law Suffolk U., Boston, 1974-76, prof., 1977-80; vis. assoc. prof. law Stanford U., Palo Alto, Calif., 1976-77; vis. prof. law Sch. Law, U. Tex., Austin, 1979, prof. law, 1980-84, Thompson prof. law, 1984-90, Andrews and Kurth prof. law, 1990-92, Fulbright and Jaworski regents rsch. prof., 1991-92, Angus G. Wynne, Sr. prof., 1992-97, Fondren chair faculty excellence, 1995—, Eugene R. Smith Centennial rsch. prof. law, 1993-97, holder William B. Bates chair, 1997—. Vis. scholar Hebrew U., Jerusalem, 1989; Forum fellow World Econ. Forum, Davos, Switzerland, 1995—; cons. PBS; pub. spkr., lectr. in field. Author: Federal Courts: Judicial Federalism and Judicial Power, 1994; co-author: Conflict of Laws, 1990, 2d edit., 2002; contbr. chpts. to books and encyclopedias, articles to profl. jours. Bd. dirs. Ballet Austin, 1986-88, Austin Coun. on Fgn. Affairs, 1985—, Austin Civil War Round Table, 1998—. Recipient Disting. Educator award Tex. Exes Assn., 1996. Mem.: Supreme Ct. Hist. Soc., Am. Constn. Soc., Maritime Law Assn., Tex. Asian C. of C., Assn. Am. Law Schs. (chair sect. on conflict of laws 1991—93, chair sect. on fed. cts. 2003—05, chair sect. admiralty 2005—06), The Philos. Soc. Tex., Am. Law Inst. (life; consultative com. complex litigation 1989—93, consultative com. enterprise liability 1990—95, adv. group fed. judicial code revision project 1996—2001, mems.' consultative group, intellectual property 2004—, internat. jurisdiction and judgments 2004—, aggregate litigation 2006—), Phi Kappa Phi, Phi Beta Kappa. Office: U Tex Sch Law 727 Dean Keeton St Austin TX 78705-3224 Business E-Mail: lweinberg@law.utexas.edu. *Personal philosophy: The right thing is usually also the humane and liberal thing.*

WEINBERG, MORRIS (SANDY WEINBERG), lawyer; b. Chattanooga, Tenn., June 4, 1950; s. Morris Sr. and Jamie May (Stokely) W.; m. Rosemary Armstrong, Aug. 11, 1979; children: Stokely, Lilly, Antonio. BA, Princeton U., 1972; JD, Vanderbilt U., 1975. Assoc. Powell & Goldstein, Atlanta, 1975-79; asst. U.S. atty. US Dept. Justice, NYC, 1979-85; sr. ptnr. Carlton & Fields, Tampa, Fla., 1985-91; mng. ptnr. Zuckerman, Spaeder, Taylor & Evans, LLP, Tampa, Fla., 1991—. Mem. ABA (vice chmn. criminal justice section, white collar crime com., 2005-06), Ga. Bar Assn., D.C. Bar Assn., Fla. Bar Assn., Fla. Assn. Criminal Defense Lawyers, Nat. Assn. Criminal Defense Lawyers. Avocation: running. Office: Zuckerman Spaeder LLP 101 E Kennedy Blvd Ste 1200 Tampa FL 33602-5838

WEINBERG, RICHARD J., medical educator; b. Oak Ridge, Tenn., Apr. 16, 1947; s. Alvin M. and Margaret D. Weinberg; m. Clarice R. Weinberg, Nov. 19, 1980; 1 child, Anna M. PhD, U. Wash., Seattle. Prof. U. NC, Chapel Hill, 1999—. Office: Univ NC Taylor Bldg CB#7090 Chapel Hill NC 27599 Office Fax: 919-966-1856. Business E-Mail: rjw@med.unc.edu.

WEINBERG, RICHARD M., internist, pulmonary and critical care physician, consultant; b. NYC, July 13, 1946; s. Abraham and Grace F. Weinberg; m. Ellen L. Oberman, June 7, 1947; children: Joshua D., Aaron M., Jeremy O. BS, Rensselaer Poly. Inst., Troy, NY, 1966; MD, Albany Med. Coll., Union U., 1970. Diplomate Am. Bd. Internal Medicine, 1974, pulmonary disease Am. Bd. Internal Medicine, 1976, critical care medicine Am. Bd. Internal Medicine, 1987; cert. physician exec. Certifying Commn. in Med. Mgmt., 2003. Attending physician Overlook Hosp., Summit, NJ, 1975—2003, Morristown Meml. Hosp., NJ, 1975—2003, med. dir. dept. of respiratory therapy, 1978—95, sect. head, pulmonary and critical care medicine dept. medicine, 1978—95; med. dir. Morristown Meml. Physician-Hosp. Orgn., NJ, 1993—94, pres., CEO, 1995—97; sr. v.p. Morristown Meml. Hosp., NJ, 1995—97; v.p. physician network devel. Atlantic Health Sys., Florham Park, NJ, 1997—98; v.p. med. affairs Bayonne Hosp., NJ, 1999—2000; chief med. officer St. Francis Health Sys., Pitts., 2001—02; med. dir. quality improvement Univ. Hosp., Univ. Medicine and Dentistry of NJ, 2004—06; chief quality officer Stamford, Conn., 2006—. Mem. bd. Bayonne Behavioral Health Sys., NJ, 1999—2000; med. advisor N.J. Assn. for Respiratory Therapy; health care cons., Short Hills, NJ, 1999—2000, Short Hills, 2002—; mem. steering com. joint project in DVT prevention and treatment. Joint Commn. Accreditation Healthcare Orgns. and Nat. Quality Forum; mem. quality improvement adv. com. NJ Dept. Health and Sr. Svcs. Bd. mem. Congregation B'Nai Jeshurun, Short Hills, NJ, 1988—92. Fellow Pulmonary Medicine, Am. Lung Assn., 1974-1975. Mem.: Am. Coll. Physician Execs. Achievements include first to negotiate, secure and manage first two physician organization global risk managed care contracts in N.J; development and implementation of process to measure the cost-effectiveness of one of the most widely used new technology medications. Office Phone: 203-276-4156, 973-610-7814. E-mail: rmw@evisitmd.com.

WEINBERG, ROBERT ALLAN, biochemist, educator; b. Pitts., Nov. 11, 1942; s. Fritz E. and Lore (Reichhardt) Weinberg; m. Amy Schulman Weinberg, Nov. 19, 1976; children: Aron, Leah Rosa. BS, MIT, 1964, PhD, 1969; PhD (hon.), Northwestern U., Ill., 1984, Uppsala U., Sweden, 2007; DSc (hon.), Tufts U., 2009. Instr. Stillman Coll., Tuscaloosa, Ala., 1965—66; rsch. fellow Weizmann Inst., Rehovoth, Israel, 1969—70, Salk Inst., LaJolla, Calif., 1970—72; asst. prof. to assoc. prof. biology & ctr. cancer rsch. MIT, Cambridge, 1973—82, prof. biology, 1982—, Daniel K. Ludwig prof. cancer rsch., 1997—. Founding mem. Whitehead Inst., Cambridge, Mass., 1982—; rsch. prof. Am. Cancer Soc., 1985; mem. adv. bd. GM Cancer Rsch. Found. Author: (books) Racing to the Beginning of the Road: The Search for the Origin of Cancer, 1996, One Renegade Cell: How Cancer Begins, 1998, One Renegade Cell: The Quest for the Origin of Cancer, 1999, The Biology of Cancer, 2006; contbr. articles articles to profl. jours. Recipient Bristol Myers award, 1984, Brown-Hazen award, NY Dept. Health, 1984, Sloan prize, GM Cancer Rsch. Found., 1987, Rsch. Recognition award, Samuel Roberts Noble Found., 1990, Gairdner Found. Internat. award, 1992, Harvey Prize, Technion, 1994, G.H.A. Clowes Meml. award, 1996, Nat. Medal of Sci., 1997, Wolf Found. prize in medicine, 2004; named Scientist of Yr., Discover mag., 1982. Fellow: Am. Acad. Arts & Scis.; mem.: NAS, Inst. Medicine, Royal Swedish Acad. Scis. Avocations: genealogy, house building. Office: Whitehead Inst Biomed Rsch 9 Cambridge Ctr Cambridge MA 02142-1479 Office Phone: 617-258-5159. Fax: 617-258-5213. E-mail: weinberg@wi.mit.edu.*

WEINBERG, RUTHMARIE LOUISE, special education educator, researcher; b. Woodbury, NJ, Feb. 9, 1953; d. Louis Albert Schopfer, Sr. and Ruth Marie (Bilse) Schopfer; m. Robert Weinberg, June 26, 1982. AS Human Svcs., Camden County Coll., 1973; BA Tchr. of the Handicapped, Glassboro State Coll., 1975; MA Sch. Adminstrn., Rowan U., 1998. Cert. tchr. of the handicapped 1975, supr. 1998, prin./supr. 1998. Supr. of cottage life, tchr. and supr. of mentally retarded Am. Inst. Mental Studies, Vineland, NJ, 1975—79; spl. edn. tchr. Haddon Heights (N.J.) H.S., 1979—. Girl Scout leader for clients Am. Inst. Mental Studies, Vineland, NJ, 1975—79, supr. summer recreation program, 1975—79. Recipient Gov.'s award for excellence in tchg., Gov. Florio and Commr. John Ellis, N.J., 1991. Mem.: Haddon Heights Ednl. Assn., N.J. Ednl. Assn., Nat. Ednl. Assn. Avocations: music, dance, sports, nature walks, exploring new horizons. Home: 422 Austin Ave Barrington NJ 08007 Office: Haddon Heights Jr & Sr HS 301 2nd Ave Haddon Heights NJ 08035-1407

WEINBERG, STEVEN, physics professor; b. NYC, May 3, 1933; s. Fred and Eva (Israel) Weinberg; m. Louise Goldwasser, July 6, 1954; 1 child, Elizabeth. BA, Cornell U., 1954; postgrad., Copenhagen Inst. Theoretical Physics, 1954—55; PhD, Princeton U., 1957; AM (hon.), Harvard U., 1973; ScD (hon.), Knox Coll., 1978, U. Chgo., 1978, U. Rochester, 1979, Yale U., 1979, CUNY, 1980, Clark U., 1982, Dartmouth Coll., 1984, Columbia U., 1990, U. Salamanca, 1992, U. Padua, 1992, Bates Coll., 2002, McGill U., 2003, U. Waterloo, 2004; D (hon.), U. Barcelona, 1996; PhD (hon.), Weizmann Inst., 1985; DLitt (hon.), Washington Coll., 1985. Rsch. assoc., instr. Columbia U., 1957-59; rsch. physicist Lawrence Radiation Lab., Berkeley, Calif., 1959-60; mem. faculty U. Calif., Berkeley, 1960-69, prof. physics, 1964-69; vis. prof. MIT, 1967-69, prof. physics, 1969-73; Higgins prof. physics Harvard U., 1973-83; sr. scientist Smithsonian Astrophys. Lab., 1973-83; Josey prof. sci. U. Tex., Austin, 1982—; sr. cons. Smithsonian Astrophys. Obs., 1983—. Cons. Inst. Def. Analyses, Washington, 1960—73, ACDA, 1973; Sloan fellow, 1961—65; chair in physics Coll. France, 1971; mem. Pres.'s Com. Nat. Medal Sci., 1979—82, Coun. Scholars, Libr. of Congress, 1983—85; sr. adv. La Jolla Inst.; mem. Com. Internat. Security and Arms Control, NRC, 1981, Bd. Physics & Astronomy, 1989—90; adv. coun. Tex. Superconducting Supercollider High Energy Rsch. Facility, 1987; Loeb lectr. in physics Harvard U., 1966—67, Morris Loeb vis. prof. physics, 1983—; Richtmeyer lectr., 1974; Scott lectr. Cavendish Lab., 1975; Silliman lectr. Yale U., 1977; Lauritsen Meml. lectr. Calif. Inst. Tech., 1979; Bethe lectr. Cornell U., 1979; de Shalit lectr. Weizmann Inst., 1979; Cherwell-Simon lectr. Oxford U., 1983; Bampton lectr. Columbia U., 1983; Einstein lectr. Israel Acad. Arts and Sciences, 1984; Hilldale lectr. U. Wis., 1985; Clark lectr. U. Tex., Dallas, 1986; Dirac lectr. U. Cambridge, 1986; Klein lectr. U. Stockholm, 1989; Brittin lectr. U. Colo., 1994; Sackler lectr. U. Copenhagen, 1994; Gibbs lectr. Am. Math. Soc., 1996; Bochner lectr. Rice U., 1997; Sanchez lectr. Tex. A&M Internat. U., 1998; Witherspoon lectr. Washington U., 2001; messenger lectr. Cornell U., 2007, Phi Beta Kappa Oration, Harvard U., 2008; mem. Supercollider Sci. Policy Com., 1989—93; bd. dirs. Fedn. Am. Scientists. Author: Principles and Application of the General Theory of Relativity, 1972, The First Three Minutes: A Modern View of the Origin of the Universe, 1977, The Discovery of Subatomic Particles, 1982, Dreams of a Final Theory, 1992, The Quantum Theory of Fields - Vol. I: Foundations, 1995, Modern Applications, Vol. II, 1996, Supersymmetry, Vol. III, 2000, Facing Up: Science and Its Cultural Adversaries, 2001, revised edit., 2003, Glory and Terror: The Growing Nuclear Danger, 2004, Cosmology, 2008, Lake Views: This World and the Universe, 2009; co-author (with R. Feynman): Elementary Particles and the Laws of Physics; co-editor: monographs on math. physics Cambridge U. Press; rsch. and publs. on elementary particles, quantum field theory, cosmology, mem. adv. bd. Issues in Sci. and Tech., 1984—87, mem. sci. book bom. Sloan Found., 1985—91, editl. bd. Jour. Math. Physics, 1986—88, mem. bd. editors Daedalus, 1990—, Jour. Math. Physics, 1998—, mem. bd. assoc. editors Nuc. Physics B, —; cinematographer:. Bd. advisors Santa Barbara Inst. Theoretical Physics, 1983—86; bd. overseers SSC Accelerator, 1984—86; bd. dirs. Headliners Found., 1993—. Recipient J. Robert Oppenheimer Meml. prize, 1973, Dannie Heineman prize in math. physics, 1977, Am. Inst. Physics U.S. Steel Found. sci. writing award, 1977, Nobel prize Physics, 1979, Elliott Cresson medal, Franklin Inst., 1979, Madison medal, Princeton U., 1991, Nat. medal of Sci., NSF, 1991, Andrew Gemant prize, Am. Inst. Physics, 1997, Piazzi prize, Govts. Sicily and Palermo, 1998, Lewis Thomas prize, Rockefeller U., 1999, Trotter prize, Tex. A&M U., 2008, James Joyce award, Literacy & Hist. Soc. U. Coll., Dublin, 2009; named Hon. Citizen, Padua, Italy, 2007. Mem.: NAS, Royal Irish Acad. (Hamilton lectr. 2005), Tex. Inst. Letters, Philos. Soc. Tex., Royal Soc. London, Am. Philos. Soc. (Benjamin Franklin medal 2004), Coun. Fgn. Rels., Internat. Astron. Union, Am. Phys. Soc., Am. Acad. Arts and Sciences, Cambridge Sci. Soc., Headliners Club (Austin), Saturday Club (Boston), Tuesday Club (Austin), Phi Beta Kappa. Business E-Mail: weinberg@physics.utexas.edu.

WEINBERG, TERI ELLEN, former broadcast executive; b. June 29, 1960; TV talent agent Internat. Creative Mgmt., 1994—2002; exec. v.p. scripted programming Reveille Prodns., 2002—07; exec. v.p., head scripted programming NBC Entertainment, 2007—08. Prodr.: (TV series) Nashville Star, 2003, Coupling US, 2003; exec. prodr.: The Office, 2006—09, Ugly Betty, 2006—07; (TV miniseries) The Tudors, 2007. Named one of The 100 Most Powerful Women in Entertainment, The Hollywood Reporter, 2007, 2008.*

WEINBERG, THOMAS, legislative staff member; Sr. mgmt. positions Dept. Health & Rehabilitative Services, Fla.; dep. county adminstr. Orange County, Fla.; Fla. state dir., dep. chief of staff, Senator Mel Martinez US Senate, Washington, 2007—08, chief of staff to Senator Mel Martinez, 2008—. Republican. Office: 356 Russell Senate Office Bldg Washington DC 20510-0906 Office Phone: 202-224-3041. Business E-Mail: tom_weinberg@martinez.senate.gov.*

WEINBERG, THOMAS STEPHEN, social sciences educator; m. Bonnie Alane Beane, Apr. 30, 1988; 1 child, Eric Thomas. BA, Rutgers U., New Brunswick, NJ, 1965, MA, 1967; PhD, U. Conn., Storrs, 1977. Assoc. prof. sociology Buffalo State Coll., 1979—83, prof. sociology, 1983—. Assoc. editor Culture & Sexuality, Calif., 2007—. Author: (book) Gay Men, Gay Selves, S and M: Studies in Sadomasochism, Gay Men, Drinking and Alcoholism, S and M: Studies in Dominance and Submission. Bd. mem. Crime Resistance Exec. Bd., Town Tonawanda, NY, 1999—2009. Recipient Chancellor's award, SUNY, 1973. Office: Buffalo State Coll 1300 Elmwood Ave Buffalo NY 14222 Business E-Mail: weinbets@bscmail.buffalostate.edu.

WEINBERG, WALTER S., lawyer; b. Chgo., Sept. 12, 1956; BA in Econs., with hon., U. Chgo., 1978; JD cum laude, Northwestern U., 1981. Bar: Ill. 1981. Ptnr., Chmn. Corp. Group Katten Muchin Rosenman LLP, Chgo. Named one of Am. Leading Lawyers for Bus., Chambers USA, 2005—08, Ill. Super Lawyers, 2007. Mem.: ABA, Chgo. Bar Assn., Order of the Coif, Phi Beta Kappa. Office: Katten Muchin Rosenman LLP 525 W Monroe St Chicago IL 60661 Office Phone: 312-902-5405. Office Fax: 312-577-8771. Business E-Mail: walter.weinberg@kattenlaw.com.

WEINBERG, WILLIAM HENRY, chemical engineer, physicist, educator; b. Columbia, SC, Dec. 5, 1944; s. Ulrich Vivian and Ruth Ann (Duncan) W. BS, U. SC, 1966; PhD in Chem. Engring, U. Calif., Berkeley, 1970; NATO postdoctoral fellow in phys. chemistry, Cambridge U., Eng., 1971. Asst. prof. chem. engring. Calif. Inst. Tech., 1972-74, assoc. prof., 1974-77, prof. chem. engring. and chem. physics, 1977-89, Chevron disting. prof. chem. engring. and chem. physics, 1981-86; prof. chem. engring. and chemistry U. Calif., Santa Barbara, 1989—, assoc. dean Coll. Engring., 1992-96; chief sci. officer Symyx Techs., Santa Clara, Calif., 1996—. Vis. prof. chemistry Harvard U., 1980, U. Pitts., 1987-88, Oxford U., 1991; Alexander von Humboldt Found. fellow U. Munich, 1982; cons. E.I. DuPont Co. Author: (with Van Hove and Chan) Low-Energy Electron Diffraction, 1986; editor 4 books in field; mem. editl. bd. Jour. Applications Surface Sci., 1977-85, Handbook Surfaces and Interfaces, 1978-80, Surface Sci. Reports, 1980—, gen. editor, 1992—, Applied Surface Sci., 1985—, Langmuir, 1990-96, Surface Sci., 1992—, Jour. Combinatorial Chemistry, 1998—; contbr. articles to profl. jours., chpts. to books. Recipient Giuseppe Parravano award Mich. Catalysis Soc., 1989, Disting. Teaching award Coll. of Engring., U. Calif. Santa Barbara, 1995; fellow NSF, 1966-69, Alfred P. Sloan Found., 1976-78, Camille and Henry Dreyfus Found., 1976-81. Fellow AAAS, Am. Phys. Soc. (Nottingham prize 1972), Am. Vacuum Soc.; mem. AIChE (Colburn award 1981), Am. Chem. Soc. (LaMer award 1973, Kendall award 1991, Arthur W. Adamson award 1995), N.Am. Catalysis Soc., Nat. Acad. Engring., Phi Beta Kappa. Office: Symyx Technologies 415 Oakmead Pkwy Sunnyvale CA 94085 Office Phone: 408-764-2000. Business E-Mail: hweinberg@symyx.com.

WEINBERGER, ADRIENNE, artist, art appraiser; b. Washington, Apr. 28, 1948; d. Samuel Aaron and Marta (Barta) W.; m. Edward Herschel Egelman, Mar. 21, 1980; children: Serge Maurice, Liana Dora. BA, Goucher Coll., Balt., 1970; MEd, Johns Hopkins U., Balt., 1973; MA, Northwestern U., Evanston, Ill., 1974; postgrad., Sch. of Mus. of Fine Arts, Boston, 1979—82. Lectr. Art Inst. Chgo., 1973-75; lectr., docent trainer Mus. of Fine Arts, Boston, 1978-82; mus. educator Yale Ctr. Brit. Art, Yale Art Gallery, New Haven, 1984-86; instr., coord. alumni coll. Albertus Magnus Coll., New Haven, 1987-89; instr. Mpls. C.C., 1989-94; propr. Studio 95, Edina, Minn., 1995-99, Charlottesville, Va., 1999—. Panelist New England Regional Confs., Am. Assn. Muss., Mass., Conn., 1976-77; workshop leader New Haven Green Found., New Haven 350 Com., 1987-88; founder & pres. Cmty. Art Fund., 2000-07; bd. mem. Svc. Dogs Va., 2007-. Author, illustrator: New Haven Coloring Book, 1987, CulchaMan Visits New York City, 1988, CulchaMan Visits Washinton, D.C., 1988. Participant Edina Futures Forum, 1990; dir. Edina-Woodhill Assn., 1997—98; active State Affirmative Action Commn., 1996—98, VCom. Art Found., 2000—07; del. chair, mem. nominating com. Dem. State Conv., St. Paul, 1994, del., chair Rochester, 1996, St. Cloud, 1998, del. Norfolk, 2000, Roanoke, 2004; active Dem. State Exec. Com., 1997—99; sec. Dem.-Farmer Labor Party, Edina, Eden Prairie, 1990—94, chair, 1994—96, treas. 3d Congl. Dist., 1996—99; active Dem. State Cen. Com., 1994—99, Albemarle County Dem. Com., 2005; adv. bd. gifted edn. svcs. Edina Pub. Schs., 1993—96; bd. dirs. Consortium for Advancement of Arts, 2001—03, Leadership Charlottesville, 2002—, mem. leadership cir., 2002—; bd. dirs. Northwestern U. Alumni Club, 2003—, Northwestern U. Club Va., Svc. Dogs Va., 2007—09, leadership Charlottesville, 2006—08. Recipient Juror's award Berkshire Mus., Pittsfield, Mass., 1981, New Haven Brush & Palette Club, 1985, Edina Art Ctr., 1991. Mem. Am. Soc. Appraisers (accredited sr. appraiser; sec. Twin Cities chpt. 1997-99, pres. Richmond chpt. 2000-01, 3d v.p. Richmond chpt. 2001-03), Charlottesville C. of C. (Amb. Corps. 2000, legis. action com. 2000—2006, legal action com. 2000-2006), U. Va. Art Mus.(vol. bd. 2003-), Leadership Charlottesville Alumni Assn. (bd. dirs. 2006—08), Northwestern U. Alumni Club Va. (bd. dirs. 2003—, Vol. award 2007), Alumni Assn., Svc. Dogs Va. (bd. dirs., 2007-09). Avocations: travel, reading, politics. Office: Studio 95 3100 Waverly Dr Charlottesville VA 22901-9576 Office Phone: 434-297-0694. Business E-Mail: studio95@guanotronic.com.

WEINBERGER, ALAN DAVID, lawyer, business executive; b. Washington, July 31, 1945; s. Theodore George and Shirley Sunshine (Gross) W.; m. Lauren Myra Kaminski, Dec. 2, 1979; children: Mark Henry, Benjamin Charles. BA, NYU, 1967, JD, 1970; LLM, Harvard U., 1973. Bar: N.Y. 1971, D.C. 1978, U.S. Supreme Ct. 1980. Assoc. White & Case, NYC, 1970-72; founding law prof. Vt. Law Sch., South Royalton, 1973-75; atty. SEC and Fed. Home Loan Bank Bd., Washington, 1977-81; founder, chmn. bd. dirs., CEO The ASCII Group Inc., Washington, 1984—; founder, chmn. bd. dirs. Tech. Net, Inc., Bethesda, Md., 1995. Adv. bd. Ashton Tate Inc., Torrance, Calif., 1986—87; sponsor, agt. All Union Fgn. Trade Acad., Acad. Nat. Economy of USSR in USA, 1988—90; chmn. US adv. bd. Moscow State U. of Commerce, 1992—; chmn. govt. affairs com. Computer Tech. Industry Assn.; founder Internat. Tech. Channels Assn., Germany, 2007; cons. Hinduja Group, 2009. Author: White Paper to Reform Business Education in Russia, 1996; law rev. editor NYU Sch. Law, 1970. Named one of Top 25 Most Influential Execs. in Computer Industry, Computer Reseller News, 1988, Twelve Most Influential IT Execs., Ziff-Davis Enterprise, NYC, 2008; recipient CEO of Yr. award Cyber Chanels, 1999; named eInnovator of Yr. Cyber Channels Assn., 2000. Mem. Nat. Orgn. on Disability (CEO coun.), Internat. Tech. Channels Assn. (founder 2007), D.C. Bar Assn., Order of Coif, Kenwood Country Club. Avocation: tennis. Office: ASCII Group Inc 7101 Wisconsin Ave Bethesda MD 20814-4871

WEINBERGER, ARNOLD, retired electrical engineer; b. Bardejov, Czechoslovakia, Oct. 23, 1924; came to U.S., 1939; s. Henry C. and Bina (Shapira) W.; widowed; children: Paul I., Ronda B., Keith A. BSEE, CCNY, 1950. Engr. Nat. Bur. Standards, Washington, 1950-60; rsch. staff mem. IBM, Yorktown Heights, N.Y., 1960-66, engr., Poughkeepsie, N.Y., 1966-91, ret., 1991. Contbr. articles on computer arithmetic, logic, large-scale integration, system organization, memories, design automation. Patentee in field. With U.S. Army, 1944-46, ETO. Fellow IEEE (Outstanding sect. award 1981). Avocation: ping pong/table tennis. Home: 7113 E Mcdonald Dr Paradise Valley AZ 85253-5406

WEINBERGER, STEVEN, lawyer, educator; b. Bklyn., Apr. 13, 1953; s. Robert Ira and Elaine (Lichtenthal) W.; m. Maureen Susan Horan, Oct. 15, 1978 (div. 1998); children: John William, Matthew Lawrence; m. Maria DiBenedetto, Sept. 26, 1998. BA, SUNY, Binghamton, 1974; JD, U. Miami, 1977; MS, Hartford Grad. Ctr., 1989. Bar: N.Y. 1978, Conn. 1987, U.S. Dist. Ct. (no. dist.) N.Y. 1981, U.S. Dist. Ct. Conn. 1990. Legis. atty. N.Y. City Council, 1977-78; asst. atty. Westchester County, White Plains, N.Y., 1978-79; sr. asst. atty. Broome County, Binghamton, N.Y., 1979-81, dep. personnel officer, 1981-82; from labor rels. specialist to chief employee svcs. bur. State of Conn., Hartford, 1982-95, dir. retirement and benefit svcs. divsn., 1995—2004; exec. dir. United Faculty Fla., Tallahassee, 2004—06; asst. v.p., human resources U. Maine, Orono, 2006—. Adj. prof. Teikyo Post U., Waterbury, Conn., 1984-04, Albertus Magnus Coll., New Haven, 2000-04. Democrat. Jewish. Office Phone: 207-581-1581. Business E-Mail: steven.weinberger@maine.edu.

WEINBROT, HOWARD DAVID, language educator; b. Bklyn., May 14, 1936; s. William and Rose (Shapiro) W.; m. Dawn Simon. BA, Antioch Coll., Yellow Springs, Ohio, 1958; MA with honors (Woodrow Wilson fellow 1959, grad. fellow 1959-63), U. Chgo., 1959, PhD, 1963. Tchg. fellow U. Chgo., 1962-63; instr. English Yale U., 1963-66; asst. prof., then assoc. prof. U. Calif., Riverside, 1966-69; mem. faculty U. Wis., Madison, 1969—, prof. English, 1972-84, Ricardo Quintana prof., 1984-87, Vilas prof., 1987—. Andrew W. Mellon vis. prof. Inst. Advanced Study Princeton, 1993—94. Author: The Formal Strain, 1969, Augustus Caesar in Augustan England, 1978, Alexander Pope and the Traditions of Formal Verse Satire, 1982, Essays on 18th-Century Satire, 1988, paperback, 2007, Britannia's Issue, 1993, paperback, 2007, Aspects of Samuel Johnson, 2005, Menippean Satire Reconsidered, 2005, 07; also numerous articles, revs.; editor: New Aspects of Lexicography, 1972, Northrop Frye and 18th Century Studies; co-editor: The 18th Century: A Current Bibliography for 1973, 1975, Poetry in English, An Anthology, 1987, Eighteenth-Century Contexts, 2001. Named Clifford Lectr., ASECS, 2008; fellow, NEH, 1975—76; Guggenheim fellow, 1988—89, Andrew Mellon fellow, Huntington Libr., 2007, Mary and Donald Hyde Rsch. fellow, Houghton Libr., 2007—, Clark Libr. fellow, 2008, vis. mem., Inst. for Advanced Study, Princeton. Mem. Am. Soc. 18th Century Studies (mem. editl. bd. 1977-80, exec. com. 96-99), Internat. Soc. 18th Century Studies UCLA (planning com. 2003), Johnsonians, Johnson Soc. (sec.-treas. 1970-75, v.p. 2000-01, pres. 2002-03, 2009-), Midwest Am. Soc. Eighteenth Century Studies, Eighteenth Century Scottish Studies. Home: 1505 Wood Ln Madison WI 53705-1456 Office: U Wis English Dept 600 N Park St Madison WI 53706-1403 Office Phone: 608-263-3819. Business E-Mail: weinbrot@wisc.edu.

WEINE, SETH JOSEPH, architectural and graphic designer, writer; b. Bklyn., Mar. 21, 1956; s. Leo R. Weine and Rita A. Nadel. Student, Pratt Inst., 1973-76. Project mgr. Weisberg, Castro Assoc., Architects, NYC, 1976-83; art sales agt. Jack Gallery, NYC, 1981-83; mem. staff archtl. project Artec Cons., NYC, 1983-86; assoc. HRG+3 Assocs., NYC, 1986-87; designer Tom O'Toole, NYC, 1987-90; designer, project mgr. Harold Gross, Architect, NYC, 1990-94; archtl. and graphic designer Seth Joseph Weine Design Cons., NYC, 1987-95; mgr., designer, project mgr. Richard F. Sammons, Architect, NYC, 1995-98, Fairfax & Sammons, NYC, 1998—. Instr. H.S. arch. program Pratt Inst., N.Y.C., 1981-89. Designer various bldgs. including The Dairy, N.Y.C., Sutton Poolhouse, Braunstein Residence, N.Y.C., G.I.C. Corp. Showroom, N.Y.C., various residences and interiors; developer curriculum Introduction to Architecture, 1981, Introduction to Architectural Design, 1983; jewelry designer The Kestenbaum Collection, 1992; founding designer and art dir. The Classicist, 1994-97, art dir. emeritus, 1998—; photos published in jours., books and mags. Mem. Act Up Housing Com., N.Y., 1993-94; vol. G.& L. Switchboard, N.Y., 1977-86, N.Y.C. Aux. Police, 1992-96. Recipient Am. Graphic Design award, 1995, Soc. of Pub. Designers Merit award, 1995, Supon Design award, 1997. Fellow Inst. for Study of Classical Architecture (mem. comms. com.); mem. AIA (assoc.), OLGAD (co-founder, bd. dirs., chair outreach 1991—, newsletter editor 1995—, Golden Column award 1993), Soc. Archtl. Historians, Am. Printing History Assn., Classical America (bull. art dir.), The Folly Fellowship (U.K.), The Typophiles, U.S.S. Northstar (ship's counselor, sr. staff), APBA, ARICA, Am. Philos. Assn., Soc. for the Philosophy of Sex and Love, Type Dirs. Club. Democrat. Avocations: reading, design, correspondence, sketching, philosophy. Home: 224 Thompson St New York NY 10012-1363 E-mail: sethweine@aol.com.

WEINEL, PAMELA JEAN, nurse consultant; b. Olney, Md., Dec. 14, 1956; d. Clarence Dawson and Jean Elizabeth (Woodward) Weinel; m. Nathan Richards, May 6, 1995. AA in Edn., Montgomery Coll., Rockville, Md., 1976; BSN, U. Md., Balt., 1986, M in Sci. Adminstrn., 1998; MBA, U. Balt., 2001. Oncology staff nurse George Washington U. Med. Ctr., Washington, 1986—88, Bone Marrow Transplant coord., 1988—90; adminstrv. coord. Walter Reed Army Med Ctr., Washington, 1990—98; advice nurse Kaiser Permanente, Kensington, Md., 1991—98; rsch. program mgr. Clin. Rsch. and Protocol Mgmt. Office U. Md. Greenebaum Cancer Ctr., Balt., 1999—2002; IVF nurse Shady Grove Fertility Ctr., Rockville, Md., 2003—04; project mgr. Social and Sci. Sys., Inc. CODA Divsn. FDA MedSun Project, Silver Spring, Md., 2004—06; asst. dir., program ops. Crtr. Devices and Radiological Health, Food and Drug Adminstrn., Office Device Evaluation, Rockville, Divsn. Reproductive, Abdominal and Radiological Devices, 2006—; faculty assoc., grad. nursing prog. U. Md., Balt., 2006—. Cons., mem. People to People Internat., Russia, 1992, Vietnam, 93; roundtable facilitator Internat. BMT Symposium, Omaha, 1992; lectr. Contemporary Forums, San Francisco, 1994. Contbr., 1993—94. Sponsor for adults Resurrection Roman Cath. Ch., Burtonsville, Md., 1997—2000, CCD instr. 7th grade, 2001—02. Named an Outstanding Young Woman in Am., 1997. Mem.: Sigma Iota Epsilon, Phi Kappa Phi, Phi Theta Kappa, Sigma Theta Tau (scholar 1996). Avocations: travel, photography, writing, Tae Kwon Do. Office: FDA 10903 New Hampshire Ave Rm 2247 Silver Spring MD 20993-0002 Office Phone: 301-796-5074. Business E-Mail: pam.weinel@fda.hhs.gov.

WEINER, ANDREW JAY, lawyer; b. Hartford, Conn., Dec. 19, 1950; m. Debra Lewin, May 29, 1977; children: Joshua Isaac, Hannah Leah. BA, Yale Coll., 1972; JD, Harvard U., 1976. Bar: N.Y. 1977. Planner N.Y.C. Dept. City Planning, 1972-73; assoc. Shearman & Sterling, NYC, 1976-84; ptnr. Gordon Hurwitz Butowsky Weitzen Shalov & Wein, NYC, 1984-89, Morrison & Foerster LLP, NYC, 1990—. Office: Morrison & Foerster LLP 1290 Avenue Of The Americas Fl 40 New York NY 10104-0050 Office Phone: 212-468-8000. Office Fax: 212-468-7900. Business E-Mail: aweiner@mofo.com.

WEINER, ANTHONY DAVID, United States Representative from New York; b. Bklyn., Sept. 4, 1964; s. Morton and Francis Weiner. BA, SUNY, Plattsburgh, 1985. Budget dir., press-fgn. affairs asst., dist. office liaison to Rep. Charles E. Schumer US House Reps., 1985—91; city councilman Dist. 48 NYC, 1991-98; mem. US Congress from 9th NY dist., 1999—, US House Judiciary Com., US House Energy & Commerce Com. Bd. dirs. Bklyn. Bd. Boys Town Jerusalem, Shaare Zedek Hosp., Israel. Recipient Breaking the Silence award, Rachel's Children Reclamation Found., 2003, Friends of RESOLVE award, RESOLVE (Nat. Infertility Assn.), 2003; named Legislator of Yr., Jewish Cmty. Coun. Rockaway Peninsula, 2002, Friend of the Nat. Pks., Nat. Pks. Conservation Assn., 2003. Democrat. Jewish. Office: US House Reps 1122 Longworth House Office Bldg Washington DC 20515-3209 also: 80-02 Kew Gardens Rd Ste 5000 Kew Gardens NY 11415 Office Phone: 202-225-6616, 718-520-9001.*

WEINER, CARL DORIAN, retired historian; b. NYC, Mar. 26, 1934; s. Alexander and Ann (Goodson) Weiner; m. Ruth Ann Feinglass, Sept. 6, 1959; children: Nicholas, Kevin, Daniel. BA, Queens Coll., 1955; postgrad., U. Wis., 1958-61; MA, Columbia U., 1959. Instr. U. Pitts., 1961-62; mem. faculty Carleton Coll., Northfield, Minn., 1964—2004, chmn. dept. history, 1974-77, 95-98, prof., 1982—2002, William H. Laird prof. history and the liberal arts, 2002—04, prof. emeritus, 2004. With US Army, 1957. Recipient 2d Century award, Carleton Coll., 1968; Bush grantee, 1983—84. Jewish. Home: 403 Laurel Ave Saint Paul MN 55102-2015 Office Phone: 507-646-4209. Personal E-mail: cweiner@carleton.edu.

WEINER, CHARLES, historian, educator; b. Bklyn., Aug. 11, 1931; s. Louis and Minnie (Florman) W.; m. Shirley Marks (div. 1976); 1 child, Susan; m. JoAnn Hughes, 1993. BS, Case Inst. Tech., 1960, MA, 1963, PhD, 1965. Asst. editor Tooling and Production mag., Cleve., 1958-60, asso. editor, 1961; editor The Explorer, Cleve. Museum of Natural History, 1960-62; dir. Project on History of Recent Physics in the U.S., Am. Inst. Physics, NYC, 1964-65, Center for History of Physics, 1965-74; prof. history of sci. and tech. Mass. Inst. Tech., 1974—96, dir. oral history program, 1975—86, prof. emeritus, 1996—. Vis. prof. U. Calif., Berkeley, 2001, Regents lectr., 03; vis. prof. NYU, 2007—08. Co-editor: The Legacy of George Ellery Hale, 1972, Robert Oppenheimer: Letters and Recollections, 1980; editor: Exploring the History of Nuclear Physics, 1972, History of 20th Century Physics, 1977; mem. editorial council: Bull. of Atomic Scientists, 1979-84. Mem. com. social orgn. sci. Social Sci. Research Council, 1968-71; adv. com. to Library of Congress on Nat. Union Catalog of Manuscript Collections, 1965-71; mem. editorial adv. bd. Joseph Henry Papers, Smithsonian Instn., 1968-86; com. on history of recent biochemistry and molecular biology Am. Acad. Arts and Scis., 1968-80, project dir. com. history contemporary physics, 1966-74; mem. adv. bd. Center for the Study of Consumer Movement, Consumers Union; mem. humanities adv. bd. Sta. WGBH, Boston, 1978-79; mem. adv. bd. Sci. in Am. Life, Smithsonian Inst., 1990-94; cons. Pres. Adv. Com. Human Radiation Experiments, 1994-95; bd. dirs. Student Pugwash USA, 2008-. Served with U.S. Army, 1951-53. Recipient Disting. Service citation Am. Assn. Physics Tchrs., 1974; Case fellow, 1961-64; Guggenheim fellow, 1970-71; NSF grantee, 1965, 68, 70, 73, 75, 77, 81, 86; Nat. Endowment Humanities grantee, 1976, 77, 81, 86. Fellow AAAS (council 1969-75, com. on meetings 1969-72), History of Sci. Soc. (council 1968-70, chmn. Met. N.Y. Sect. 1969-70), Soc. for History of Tech. (adv. council 1977-79). Office: 56 Main St Yarmouth Port MA 02675

WEINER, CLAIRE ZUNDELL (CZ CAMERON), theatrical director; b. Worcester, Mass., June 19, 1933; d. Edward A. and Mary (Abramson) Shapiro; children: Aaryn Anne, Elliot Michael. Student, Clark U., SUNY, Miami-Dade Coll. Instr. fundamentals theatre Dade County Cmty. Sch. Sys., Fla., 1965—68; tchr. theatre arts Roberson Centre of Arts, Binghamton, NY, 1969—70; artist-in-theatre Colgate U., Hamilton, NY, 1968—70; freelance feature writer Norwich Evening Sun, NY, 1969—72; dir. Norwich Sr. High Theatre, 1968—72, Cultural Activities Youth Norwich Youth Commn., 1969—72; resident dir., actress Gold Crown Dinner Theatre & Touring Co., Downey, Calif., 1972—76; dir. Theatre for Youth City of Santa Clara, Calif., 1979—80; dir. Ctr. Players, Long Beach, Calif., 1977—78; resident dir./playwright Arrowhead Theatre, San Jose, Calif., 1990—, resident dir./actor, Reader's Theatre for Original Plays, 1992—94. Mem. Miami Actors Co., Fla., 1965-68, Gainesville (Fla.) Little Theatre, 1956-58, Jacksonville Little Theatre, 1958-62, Gallery Theatre, Coral Gables, Fla., 1961-62, Miami Beach Players, 1962-64, Arlington Players, Jacksonville, 1958-61; dir. Norwich Adult Weekly Summer Repertory Theatre, 1969-72, Norwich Weekly Children's Theatre in Mime, 1969-72; originator 1st area multi-sch. project Tino WorkShop Theatre, Fremont H.S. Dist., 1980—; guest dir. West Valley Civic Light Opera, 1982; advisor N.Y. State Coun. Arts, 1968-70; tchr. theatre arts Norwich Bd. Edn. 1970, Met. Edn. Dist., San Jose, 1998; spkr. in field Author: The Rabbi's Daughter, 1987, Between the Night Shadows, 1989, Thresholds, 1990, Billington's, Billington's Two, 1992, What Do I Wear Now? The Breast Cancer Legacy, 1995, Gettin On With It, 2001, The WaterStreet Diaries: a work in progress, 2001, Patterns of Life, 2003, New to America: A Family History, 2004; (novels) The Home, 2003, Redemption at Ringside, 2007 (Editor Choice award, Internat. Soc. Poets 2003-07); originator, leader, weekly memoir writers group, Santa Cruz, 2003—; playwright, dir.: Shadows on the Stair, 2004, Arrowhead Theatre, 2006; animation voice-overs E.J. Sound/Hosca Prodn., Inc., San Jose; featured poet Norwich Sun, N.Y., 2000— Youth leader B'nai B'rith; reader for the blind San Jose Pub. Libr Mem. AFTRA, Am. Ednl. Theatre Assn., Internat. Platform Assn Home: 1555 Merrill St #62 Santa Cruz CA 95062 Personal E-mail: seezie@yahoo.com.

WEINER, EARL DAVID, lawyer; b. Balt., Aug. 21, 1939; s. Jacob Joseph and Sophia Gertrude (Rachanow) W.; m. Gina Helen Priestley Ingoglia, Mar. 30, 1962; children: Melissa Danis Balmain, John Barlow. AB, Dickinson Coll., 1960; LL.B., Yale U., 1968. Bar: NY 1969. Assoc. Sullivan & Cromwell LLP, NYC, 1968—76, ptnr., 1976—2006, of counsel, 2007—; gen. coun. Mcpl. Art Soc. NY, NYC, 2007—, trustee, 2007—. Adj. prof. Rutgers U. Sch. Law, 1987—88; bd. dirs. Alliance-Bernstein Funds, 2007—, The Acting Co., vice chmn., 1992—2003, chmn., 2003—. Gov. Bklyn. Heights Assn., 1980—87, pres., 1985—87, adv. com., 1987—; gov. The Heights Casino, 1979—84, pres., 1981—84; trustee Green-Wood Cemetery, Bklyn., 1985—, vice chmn., 1991—96; trustee Bklyn. Hosp. Ctr., 1998—; bd. advisors Dickinson Coll., Carlisle, Pa., 1986—90, chmn., 1988—90, trustee, 1988—2002, vice chmn., 1998—2002; trustee Theatre Devel. Fund, 2005—, chmn., 2008—; mem. adv. com. East Rock Inst., 1988—; bd. visitors U. Md. Ctr. Environ. Sci., 2002—08. Lt. USN, 1961—65. Fellow Fgn. Policy Assn. (sr.); mem. ABA, N.Y. State Bar Assn., Assn. Bar City N.Y. Office: Sullivan & Cromwell 125 Broad St 3445 New York NY 10004-2498

WEINER, ELYSE, bank executive; married; 2 children. BA, MS, CUNY: Bklyn. Coll.; MBA, Adelphi U., Garden City, NY. Pub. sch. tchr., NYC; various positions Chase Manhattan Bank, 1984—97; dir. Bankers Trust, 1997—99, Deutsche Bank, 1999—2001; v.p. JP Morgan, 2001—04; mng. dir., global product head liquidity and investments Citigroup, Inc., 2004—. Active United Way. Named one of 25 Women to Watch, US Banker, 2008. Office: Citigroup Inc 388 Greenwich St New York NY 10013 Office Phone: 212-816-0470. Business E-Mail: elyse.weiner@citi.com.*

WEINER, FERNE, psychologist; b. NYC, June 14, 1928; d. Irving Kapp and Peggy (Finkelstein) Hessberg; m. Howard Weiner, July 20, 1948; children: Irving Kenneth, Laurie. BA, Skidmore Coll., 1965; MA, Sarah Lawrence Coll., 1971; PhD, U. Hawaii, 1975. Lic. psychologist, Calif., Hawaii. Asst. prof. West Oahu Coll. U. Hawaii, Honolulu, 1975—77; staff psychologist Cmty. Guidance Clinic, Manchester, Conn., 1978—83; chief cons. psychologist Consultation and Evaluation Ctr., Meriden, Conn., 1984—85; psychologist cons. Disability Determination Svcs., Hartford, Conn., 1986—87, Honolulu, 1988—; police psychologist Honolulu Police Dept., 1988. Pvt. practice, Greenwich, Conn., 1983-87, Honolulu, 1988—; cons. Adopt-A-Sch. Project, Honolulu, 1991-94; interviewer, therapist Sexual Abuse Treatment Team, Manchester, 1979-83; cons., trainer Conn. schs., day care, ch. groups, 1979-87. Contbr. articles to profl. jours. Active Disaster Assistance Mgmt. Team, Hawaii, 1994-95; v.p., sec. Queens Court at Kapiolani Bd., Honolulu, 1992-95; admissions rep. Hawaii Sarah Lawrence Coll., Honolulu, 1970-80; cons. to adoptees search Orphan Voyage, Conn., 1980-87; mentor Girl Scout Coun. Am., Oahu, 1993-94. Mem. Am. Psychol. Assn. (clin. psychotherapy and neuropsychology divsn.), Hawaii Psychol. Assn., Nat. Registry Health Svcs. Providers, Outrigger Canoe Club, Shiley Sports Club. Democrat. Jewish. Avocations: aerobics, interior design, property renovation, gourmet cooking, travel. Personal E-mail: wferne1@san.rr.com.

WEINER, GEORGE JAY, internist; b. Plainview, NY, Mar. 1, 1956; m. Teresa Emily Wilhelm, July 30, 1983; children: Aaron, Miriam, Nathan. BA, Johns Hopkins U., 1978; MD, Ohio State U., 1981. Cert. Am. Bd. Internal Medicine, 1985, in med. oncology Am. Bd. Internal Medicine, 1987, in hematology Am. Bd. Internal Medicine, 1988. Resident in internal medicine Med. Coll. Ohio, Toledo, 1981-85; hematology/oncology fellow U. Mich., Ann Arbor, 1985-89; asst. prof. medicine U. Iowa, Iowa City, 1989-94, assoc. prof., 1994-99, prof., 1999—, dir. Cancer Ctr., 1998—. Dir. Holden Comprehensive Cancer Ctr., U. Iowa. Contbr. articles to profl. jours. Chair subcom. A Nat. Cancer Inst., DC, 2007—; chair Iowa Consortium for Comprehensive Cancer Control, 2004—; dir. Iowa/Mayo Lymphoma Specialized Program of Rsch. Excellence. Achievements include devel. of new approaches to cancer immunotherapy. Office: Univ of Iowa 5970 JPP Iowa City IA 52242

WEINER, GERALD ARNE, stockbroker; b. Chgo., Dec. 20, 1941; s. Irwin S. and Lilyan (Stock) W.; m. Barbara I. Allen, June 18, 1967; children: Rachel Anne, Sara Naomi. BSS, Loyola U., Chgo., 1964; student, U. Vienna, 1962-63; MS, Georgetown U., 1966; postgrad., Ind. U., 1966-72, S.E. Asian Areas Cert., 1967. Pacification specialist AID, Laos, 1965; instr. polit. sci. Loyola U., Chgo., 1970-72; asst. v.p. A.G. Becker & Co., Chgo., 1973-78; sr. v.p. Oppenheimer & Co., Chgo., 1978-83, J. David Securities, Inc., Chgo., 1983-84, Morgan Stanley, Chgo., 1984—. Exec. edn. for securities industry Wharton Sch. Bus. U. Pa., 1988-90. Trustee Highland Park Police Pension Fund, 1991-2004. Mucia fellow, 1969. Mem. Midwest Bonsai Soc., Equinox Club. Republican. Jewish. Office: Morgan Stanley 70 W Madison St Ste 300 Chicago IL 60602-4278 Office Phone: 312-827-6634. Business E-Mail: gerald.weiner@morganstanley.com.

WEINER, HOWARD MARC, physician; b. Feb. 25, 1946; BSc, Marietta Coll., 1967; MD, U. Cin., 1971; MPH, Med. Coll. Wis., 1994. Diplomate Am.Bd. Allergy, Asthma and Immunology, Am. Bd. Preventive Medicine/Occupl. Medicine, Am. Bd. Ind. Med. Examiners. Intern medicine Temple U. Hosp., Phila., 1971—72, resident internal medicine, 1972—74; fellow allergy and clin. immunology Hosp. U. Pa., Phila., 1974—76; pres., physician Allergy & Asthma Assocs. West Boca, Boca Raton, Fla., 1988—; pres., med. dir. Med. Assessment Inst. Inc., Boca Raton, Fla., 1997—. Chmn. ethics com. Palm Beach County Med. Soc., West Palm Beach, Fla., 1994-97; bd. dirs. Primus Physicians Svcs., Inc., So. Fla. Mem. Omicron Delta Kappa Soc., Pi Kappa Epsilon. Office: Med Assessment Inst Inc 2385 NW Executive Ctr Dr Ste 100 Boca Raton FL 33431 Office Phone: 561-451-0200.

WEINER, IRVING BERNARD, psychologist; b. Grand Rapids, Mich., Aug. 16, 1933; s. Jacob H. and Mollie Jean (Laevin) W.; m. Frances Shair, June 9, 1963; children: Jeremy Harris, Seth Howard. BA, U. Mich., Ann Arbor, 1955, MA, 1957, PhD, 1959. Diplomate Am. Bd. Profl. Psychology. From instr. to prof. psychiatry and pediat. U. Rochester, NY, 1959-72; head divsn. psychology U. Rochester Med. Center, 1968-72; prof. psychology, chmn. dept. Case Western Res. U., 1972-77, dean grad. studies, 1976-79; vice chancellor for acad. affairs U. Denver, 1979-83, prof. psychology, 1979-85; v.p. for acad. affairs Fairleigh Dickinson U., Teaneck, NJ, 1985-89, prof. psychology, 1985-89; prof. psychiatry U. South Fla., Tampa, 1989—. Adv. editor John Wiley & Sons, 1967-93, 99—, Lawrence Erlbaum Assocs., 1993-99; psychology edn. rev. com. NIMH, 1977-81. Author: Psychodiagnosis in Schizophrenia, 1966, Psychological Disturbance in Adolescence, 1970, rev. edit., 1992, Rorschach Handbook, 1971, Child Development, 1972, Principles of Psychotherapy, 1975, rev. edit., 1998, 2009, Development of the Child, 1978, Child and Adolescent Psychopathology, 1982, Rorschach Assessment of Children and Adolescents, 1982, rev. edit., 1995, Adolescence, 1985, rev. edit., 1995, Handbook of Forensic Psychology, 1987, rev. edit., 1999, 2006, Principles of Rorschach Interpretation, 1998, rev. edit., 2003, Handbook of Psychology, 2003, Handbook of Personality Assessment, 2008; editor: Readings in Child Development, 1972, Clinical Methods in Psychology, 1976, 83, Adult Psychopathology Case Studies, 2004, Jour. Personality Assessment, 1985-93, Rorschachiana, 1989-96; mem. editl. bd. Profl. Psychology, 1971-76, Jour. Adolescent Health Care, 1979-87, Children and Youth Svcs. Rev., 1979-91, Jour. Pediat. Psychology, 1981-87, Devel. and Behavioral Pediat., 1985-96, Studi Rorschachiani, 1985-1996, European Jour. Psychol. Assessment, 1985—, Jour. Adolescent Rsch., 1986-91, Jour. Personality Disorders, 1986-92, Psychol. Assessment, 1994—2003, Jour. Personality Assessment, 2003—, Assessment, 2004—, Jour. Child Custody, 2005—. Recipient Disting. Profl. Achievement award Genesee Psychol. Assn., 1974 Fellow APA, Acad. Clin. Psychology, Acad. Forensic Psychology, Acad. of Assessment Psychology (Lifetime Achievement awrd 2001); mem. Assn. Advancement Psychology, Soc. Personality Assessment (pres. 1976-78, 2005-07, Disting. Contbn. award 1983), Assn. Internship Ctrs. (exec. com. 1971-76), Soc. Rsch. in Adolescence, Soc. for Rsch. in Child and Adolescent Psychopathology, Soc. for Exploration Psychotherapy Integration, Soc. Pediat. Psychology, Am. Psychol. Law Soc., Internat. Rorschach Soc. (pres. 1999-2005), Assn. Psychol. Sci., Soc. Clin. Psychology (pres. 2008), Phi Beta Kappa, Sigma Xi, Phi Kappa Phi. Home and Office: 13716 Halliford Dr Tampa FL 33624-6903 Office Phone: 813-961-8032. Business E-Mail: iweiner@health.usf.edu.

WEINER, JACK H., lawyer; b. Phila., Nov. 21, 1934; s. Samuel A. and Sophie S. (Snyderman) W.; m. Diana M. Wiess, June 12, 1960; children— Scott, Edward, Hope. A.B., U. Pa., 1956; LL.B., Yale U., 1959. Bar: D.C. 1959, Pa. 1960, N.Y. 1973. Trial atty. U.S. Dept. Labor, 1960-65, civil div., appellate sect. U.S. Dept. Justice, 1965-68, NLRB, 1970-72; v.p., counsel Bankers Trust Co., N.Y.C., 1973—99. Mem. ABA, N.Y. State Bar Assn., Assn. Bar City of N.Y. Republican. Club: Yale (N.Y.C.). Home: 1488 State Route 203 Chatham NY 12037-1706 Office Phone: 518-392-2426. E-mail: jackweiner@hotmail.com.

WEINER, JEFF, Internet company executive; BS in Econs., U. Pa., Phila. With Warner Bros., 1994—2000; head of corp. devel. Yahoo!, 2001—02, exec. v.p. network divsn.; exec. in residence Accel Ptnrs. and Greylock Ptnrs., 2008; interim pres. LinkedIn Corp., Mountain View, Calif., 2009, CEO, bd. dirs., 2009—. Bd. mem. DonorsChoose.org, Malaria No More. Office: LinkedIn Corp 2029 Stierlin Ct Mountain View CA 94043

WEINER, JENNIFER AGNES, writer; b. De Ridder, La., Mar. 28, 1970; m. Adam Bonin, Oct. 27, 2001; children: Lucy Jane, Phoebe. BA in English, summa cum laude, Princeton U., NJ, 1991. Intern Poynter Inst. Media Studies, St. Petersburg, Fla., 1991; reporter Centre Daily Times, State College, Pa., 1991—94; features writer Lexington Herald-Leader, Ky., 1994—95; gen. assignment, features reporter Phila. Inquirer, 1995—2001. Author: (novels) Good in Bed, 2001 (NY Times bestseller), In Her Shoes, 2002, Little Earthquakes, 2004 (Publishers Weekly bestseller), Goodnight Nobody, 2005 (Publishers Weekly bestseller), The Guy Not Taken, 2006—, Certain Girls, 2008—, Best Friends Forever, 2009 (#1 Publishers Weekly bestseller); contbg. editor Mademoiselle mag.; contbr. numerous short stories to mags. and anthologies. Mailing: c/o Atria Books divsn Simon & Schuster Inc 1230 Ave Americas 11th Fl New York NY 10020 Business E-Mail: jen@jenniferweiner.com.*

WEINER, JEROME HARRIS, mechanical engineering educator; b. NYC, Apr. 5, 1923; s. Barnet and Dora (Muchar) W.; m. Florence Mensch, June 24, 1950; children: Jonathan David, Eric Daniel. B. Mech. Engring., Cooper Union U., 1943; A.M., Columbia U., 1946, PhD, 1952. Mem. faculty Columbia U., NYC, 1952-68, prof. mech. engring., 1960-68, acting chmn. dept., 1961-62; L. Herbert Ballou Univ. prof. Brown U., Providence, 1968-93; L. Herbert Ballou Univ. prof. emeritus, 1993—. Author: (with B.A. Boley) Theory of Thermal Stresses, 1960, Statistical Mechanics of Elasticity, 1983. Fulbright research scholar Rome, Italy, 1958-59, Haifa, Israel, 1965- 66; Guggenheim fellow, 1965-66 Mem. Am. Phys. Soc., Am. Math. Soc., ASME Home: 24 Taber Ave Providence RI 02906-4113 Office: Brown U 79 Waterman St Providence RI 02912-9079 Business E-Mail: jerome_weiner@brown.edu.

WEINER, JONATHAN P., health policy and management educator; s. Myron E. and Ruth F. Weiner; m. Jennifer Churchill Beatty; children: Nathaniel B., Noah C. BA, U. Pa., Phila., 1975; MS, U. Mass., Amherst, 1977; PhD, Johns Hopkins U., 1981. From asst. to assoc. prof. Johns Hopkins U., Balt., 1982—94; faculty mem. dept. medicine Johns Hopkins Sch. Medicine, Balt., 1985—; prof. health policy & mgmt. Johns Hopkins Bloomberg Sch. Pub. Health, Balt., 1994—; faculty mem. Johns Hopkins Divsn. Health Informatics, Balt., 2005—. Sr. cons., advisor numerous pvt. & pub. health orgs., 1981—. Contbr. articles to profl. jours. Bd. dirs. Pk. Nicollet Inst., Mpls., 1995—2002; mem. Medicare Coverage Adv. Com., Balt., 2004—07. Atlantic fellow, UK, 1999—2000. Achievements include co-developer and team director of Johns Hopkins ACG case-mix software system used worldwide. Office: Johns Hopkins U 624 N Broadway - Rm 605 Baltimore MD 21205 Office Fax: 410-955-0470. Business E-Mail: jweiner@jhsph.edu.

WEINER, KAREN COLBY (KAREN LYNN COLBY), psychologist, lawyer; b. Oak Park, Ill., Oct. 28, 1943; d. Leonard L. and Mildred Irene (Berman) Colby; m. J. Laevin Weiner, July 26, 1964; children: Joel Laevin, Doren Robin, Anthony Justin. BA, Mich. State U., East Lansing, 1964; JD, U. Detroit, 1977, MA, 1986, PhD, 1988. Bar: Mich. 1977, D.C. 1978. Speech therapist Oak Park Sch. Dist., 1965-68; law clk. justice G. Mennen Williams Mich. Supreme Ct., Lansing, 1977-79; assoc. Dickinson, Wright, Moon, Van Dusen & Freeman, Detroit, 1979-83; intern in psychology Detroit Psychiat. Inst., 1986-88; psychologist Northland Clinic, Southfield, Mich., 1987-88; postdoctoral intern Wyandotte (Mich.) Hosp. and Health Ctr., 1988-90; psychologist Counseling Assocs., Southfield, 1988—2004, dir. psychol. svcs., quality assurance coord., 1991-99; bd. dirs. Mich. Psychoanalytic Inst. Found., 2004—. Hearing panelist Atty. Discipline Bd., Detroit, 1982-95; hearing referee Mich. Civil Rights Commn., Detroit, 1983-91; mem. Mich. Bd. Psychology, 1999—2007, vice chair, 2004-07; adj. prof. U. Detroit Mercy, 2001-03; Grad. Inst. Life Coach Tng. adj. prof. Inst. Life Coach Tng., 2008. Author: The Little Book of Ethics for Coaches, rev. edit., 2007; contbr. articles to profl. jours. Mem. adv. bd. Mich. chpt. Anti-Defamation League, 1981-90. Fellow Mich. Psychol. Assn. (mem. ethics com. 1992-2000, chmn. legis. com. 1993, chmn. ethics com. 1997-99, pres. 2008); mem. APA, Internat. Coach Fedn. (ethics and stds. com.), Mich. Soc. for Psychoanalytic Psychology (pres. 1995-97, sec. 1991-92, treas. 1992-94), Women Lawyers Assn. Mich. (pres. 1981-82, pres. Found. 1982-83), Mich. Bar Assn. Jewish. Home: 2501 Long Lake Rd West Bloomfield MI 48323 Office: 29260 Franklin Rd Ste 115 Southfield MI 48034-1144 Office Phone: 248-353-1020. Personal E-mail: drkcw@comcast.net.

WEINER, LAWRENCE, lawyer; b. Phila., Aug. 20, 1942; s. Robert A. and Goldie Weiner; m. Jane M. Coulthard, Feb. 28, 1976; 1 child, Kimberly. BS in Econs., U. Pa., 1964, JD, 1967. Bar: Pa. 1967, U.S. Dist. Ct. (ea. dist.) Pa. 1967, Fla. 1970, U.S. Dist. Ct. (so. dist.) Fla. 1976, U.S. Ct. Appeals (5th cir.) 1976, U.S. Tax Ct. 1984. Assoc., ptnr. Blank, Rome, Klaus & Comisky, Phila., 1967-71, 1975-77; ptnr. Weiner & Weisenfeld, P.A., Miami Beach, Fla., 1971-73, Pettigrew & Bailey, Miami, Fla., 1973-75; pres. Lawrence Weiner, P.A., Miami, 1977-83; ptnr. Spieler, Weiner & Spieler, P.A., Miami, 1983-89, Weiner & Cummings, P.A., Miami, 1989-94, Weiner, Cummings & Vittoria, Miami, 1994—. Lectr. Wharton Sch. U. Pa., Phila., 1968-70; instr. bus. law and acctg. Community Coll. Phila., 1967-70; lectr. estate planning various non-lawyer groups, Miami, 1972—. Mem. Fla. Bar (liaison non-lawyers groups 1980-87), Pa. Bar Assn., Phila. Bar Assn., Dade County Bar Assn. (chmn. ins. com. 1977-78, probate law com. 1992-2002). Democrat. Jewish. Office: Weiner Cummings & Vittoria 1428 Brickell Ave Ste 400 Miami FL 33131-3436 Office Phone: 305-371-7800. E-mail: lweiner@wcvlaw.com.

WEINER, LAWRENCE CHARLES, artist; b. Bronx, NY, Feb. 10, 1942; One-man shows include Hirshhorn Mus. and Sculpture Garden, Washington, 1990, San Francisco Mus. Modern Art, 1992, Walker Art Ctr., Mpls., 1994, Städtische Galerie Chemnitz, Germany, 1994, Phila. Mus. Art, 1994, Radio Düsseldorf, Germany, 1994, Leo Castelli Gallery, NY, 1994, NY Pub. libr., 1995, Mus. Ludwig Köln, 1995, Mus. Boijmans Van Beuningen, Rotterdam, 1996, The Lawrence Weiner Poster Archive, Kunsthalle Nüurnberg, 1998, Yvon Lambert Gallery, Paris, 2003, Galleri Susanne Ottesen, Copenhagen, 2003, The Wrong Gallery, 2004, Cristina Guerra Contemp. Art, 2004, Mus. Tamayo Arte Contemp., 2004, Davis Mus. Cult. Ctr., 2004, Mai 36 Gallery, 2004, Yvon Lambert Gallery, 2004, Gallery Rose Marie, 2004, Marian Goodman Gallery NYC, 2005, Regen Projects, LA, 2005, Lisson Gallery, London, 2005, Wolfsonian Mus., Miami, 2006, Nat. Maritime Mus., Greenwich, London, 2007, Parasite Art Space, Hong Kong, 2007, Whitney Mus. Am. Art, NY, 2007-08, CAC, Malaga, Spain, 2008, others; exhibited in group shows Mus. Modern Art, NY, 1970, 2009, Art Inst. Chgo., 1974, Tate Gallery, London, 1982, Mus. Contemporary Art, LA, 1983, Deutsche Guggenheim, Berlin, 2000, Kunstmuseum Rolfsburg, 2000, Reykjavik Arts Festival, 2005, Venice Biennale, 2007; represented in permanent collections Mus. Modern Art, NY, Guggenheim Mus., NY, Van Abbe Mus., Eindhoven, The Netherlands, Staatliches Mus. Mönchengladbach, Germany, Ctr. Georges Pompidou, Paris, Nat. Gallery Australia, Canberra, others. Recipient Arthur Köpcke prize, Copenhagen, 1991, Wolfgang Hahn prize, 1995, Skowhegan medal for painting, 1999; fellow Nat. Endowment Arts, 1976, 1983; John Simon Guggenheim fellow, 1994. Home: 297 W 4th St New York NY 10014-2207

WEINER, LOUIS MARC, oncologist; b. Phila., May 21, 1951; married. BA in Biology with honors, U. Pa., 1973; MD, Mt. Sinai Sch. Medicine, NYU, NYC, 1977. Diplomate Am. Bd. Internal Medicine, cert. Am. Bd. Internal Medicine, Med. Oncology. Intern U. Vt. Med. Ctr. Hosp., resident, chief resident; from assoc. mem. divsn. med. sci. to chmn. Fox Chase Cancer Ctr., Phila., 1985—94, chmn. med. oncology, 1994—, G. Morris Dorrance, Jr. endowed chair in med. sci., 2002—, v.p. translational rsch., 2002—; dir. Lombardi Comprehensive Med. Ctr. Georgetown U. Hosp., Washington, 2007—. Asst. prof. Temple U., Phila., 1987—95, prof., 1995—; sci. adv. bd. Merrimack Pharms., Cambridge, Mass., 2007—. Contbr. articles to profl. jours.; mem. editl. bd.: Cancer Rsch., Clin. Cancer Rsch. Steering com. translational rsch. working group Nat. Cancer Inst.; mem. cancer immunopathology and immunotherapy study sect. NIH. Recipient Clin. Investigtor award, Nat. Cancer Inst., 1986, Targeted Therapy award, Janssen Pharm. Found., 1998, Research award, American Cancer Soc.; grantee, NIH, 1986, 1989, 1990, 1993, 1996, 1999, 2000, Dept. of Defense, 1996, 1998—99, clin. and rsch. fellowships, Tufts U., Boston. Mem.: Am. Assn. Cancer Rsch. (chair immunology task force), Am. Soc. Clin. Oncology. Office Phone: 215-728-2480. Office Fax: 215-728-5338. Business E-Mail: louis.weiner@fccc.edu.

WEINER, LOUIS MAX, retired mathematics educator; b. Chgo., Nov. 11, 1926; s. Samuel and Lena (Adelman) W.; m. June Belmont, Aug. 18, 1957; children: Howard, Joel, Todd. BS, U. Chgo., 1947, MS, 1948, PhD, 1951. Examiner Civil Svc. Commn., Chgo., 1951-52; asst. prof. DePaul U., Chgo., 1952-58; rsch. engr. Gen. Am. Rsch. Divsn., Niles, Ill., 1958-64; prof. math. Northeastern Ill. U., Chgo., 1964-93, chmn. dept., 1968-74; ret., 1993. Instr. Oakton C.C., Des Plaines, Ill., 1974-92. Assoc. editor Math. mag., 1968-72; author: Introduction to Modern Algebra, 1970, Basic Mathematical Concepts, 1972. Mem. Am. Math. Soc., Math. Assn. Am., Sigma Xi, Phi Beta Kappa. Avocation: photography. Home: 13135 W Longleaf Dr New Berlin WI 53151-8344 Personal E-mail: lweiner1@comcast.net.

WEINER, MATTHEW, television producer, scriptwriter; b. LA; married; 4 children. Grad., Wesleyan U., Middletown, Conn., 1987; MFA, USC. Writer, dir. (films) What Do You Do All Day?, writer (TV series) Party Girl, The Naked Truth, 1995, prodr., writer Becker, 1999—2002, supervising prodr. Andy Richter Controls the Universe, 2002—03, writer, exec. prodr. The Sopranos, 2004—07 (Outstanding Drama Series Emmy award, 2004, 2007, TV Prodr. of Yr. award in Episodic Prodrs. Guild America, 2005, 2008, Best Dramatic Series Writers Guild America award, 2007), creator, exec. prodr. Mad Men, 2007— (Best New Series Writers Guild America award, 2008, Primetime Emmy for Outstanding Writing for a Drama Series, Acad. TV Arts and Scis., 2008, Primetime Emmy for Outstanding Drama Series, Acad. TV Arts and Scis., 2008, Best TV Series - Drama, Golden Globe award, Hollywood Fgn. Press Assn., 2009, Norman Felton Prodr. of Yr. award in TV - Drama, Prodrs. Guild America, 2009, Best Dramatic Series, Writers Guild America, 2009).

WEINER, MAX, psychology professor; b. Hartford, Conn., May 7, 1926; s. Harry Sam and Gertrude (Cohen) W.; m. Gloria Sall, Feb. 24, 1960; children: William Ronald, Jennifer Sharon. BA, U. Conn., 1950; MA, Trinity Coll., 1953; PhD, Yale U., 1957. Sci. tchr. Meriden (Conn.) Pub. Schs., 1952-55; guidance dir. White Plains (N.Y.) Pub. Schs., 1956-59; assoc. prof. Bklyn. Coll., CUNY, 1959-68; prof. Grad. Sch. CUNY, 1968-81, acting univ. dean, tchr. edn., 1973-74, exec. officer PhD program edn. psychology, 1970-76, dir. Ctr. for Advanced Study Edn., 1970-78, acting dean rsch. Grad. Sch., 1978-79; dean edn. Fordham U., NYC, 1981-93, prof. ednl. psychology, 1981-97, prof. and dean emeritus, 1997—. Cons. psychologist SUNY Health Sci. Ctr., Bklyn., 1967-89; mem. nat. commn. on excellence in edn. adminstrn. Univ. Coun. for Edn. Adminstrn., 1985-87; mem. nat. adv. commn. Coll. Bd. Equity 2000, 1993-2000. Contbr. articles to profl. jours. Treas. N.Y. Alliance for Pub. Schs., N.Y.C., 1987-93; mem. Mayor's Commn. on Spl. Edn., N.Y.C., 1984-85; bd. dirs. Arthritis Found., Atlanta, 1974-76; trustee Beth El Synagogue, New Rochelle, N.Y., 1985-2001, La Scuola, N.Y., 1986-2003; bd. visitors Scranton U. Sch. Edn., 1992-2002. Fellow, Japan Soc. Promotion Scis., 1978. Fellow APA, Am. Ednl. Rsch. Assn., Am. Psychol. Soc., N.Y. Acad. Scis.; mem. ACA (life), AAAS, Arthritis Health Professions Assn. (pres. 1974-75), Assn. Colls. and Schs. Edn. in State Univs. and Land Grant Colls. and Affiliated Pvt. Univs. (mem. exec. com. 1986-89, 92-93), Assn. for Measurement and Evaluation in Guidance (senator 1966-72, sec. 1973-75), Nat. Coun. Measurement in Edn., Westchester Assn. Hebrew Schs. (pres. 1982-84), Sigma Xi, Phi Delta Kappa, Kappa Delta Pi. Personal E-mail: maxglow22@aol.com.

WEINER, MICHAEL S., lawyer, labor union administrator; b. Paterson, NJ, 1961; s. Isaac Weiner; m. Diane Weiner; 3 children. B in Polit. Economy, Williams Coll., Williamstown, Mass., 1983; JD, Harvard U. Law Sch., Mass., 1986. Law clk., Judge H. Lee Sarokin US Dist Ct., Newark, 1986—88; union lawyer Maj. League Baseball Players Assn., 1988—, gen. counsel, 2004—. Counsel, salary arbitrations NHL Players Assn. Sunday sch. tchr. Jewish Ctr. Northwest Jersey. Office: Maj League Baseball Players Assn 12 E 49th St New York NY 10017*

WEINER, MICHAEL W., neuroscientist, researcher, educator; BA, Johns Hopkins U., Balt., 1961; MD, SUNY Upstate Med. Ctr., Syracuse, 1965. Diplomate in internal medicine and nephrology Am. Bd. Internal Medicine, 1972. Intern, asst. resident medicine Mt. Sinai Hosp., NYC, 1965—67; clin. fellow metabolism Yale-New Haven Med. Ctr., 1967—68; rsch. fellow Yale U. Sch. Medicine, 1968—70, U. Wis. Inst. Enzyme Rsch., Madison, 1970—72, joint appointment renal sect. dept. medicine, 1970—72, asst. prof., 1972—74; rsch. and edn. assoc. VA, 1971—74, clin. investigator, 1974—77; asst. prof. medicine U. Wis. Sch. Medicine, 1971—74, Stanford U. Sch. Medicine, 1974—80; asst. chief artificial kidney ctr. Palo Alto VA Hosp., Calif., 1974—80; chief metabolism svc. VA Hosp., Madison, 1973—74; assoc. prof. medicine in residence U. Calif., San Francisco, 1980—90, assoc. prof. radiology in residence, 1983—90, assoc. staff mem. Cardiovasc. Rsch. Inst., 1988—93, sr. staff mem. Cardiovasc. Rsch. Inst., 1994, prof. medicine, radiology and psychiatry, 1990—, mem. Alzheimer's Ctr. exec. com., 1994; chief hemodialysis unit San Francisco Vets. Affairs Med. Ctr., 1980—83, sci. dir. Magnetic Resonance Unit, 1985—, dir. Ctr. Imaging of Neurodegenerative Diseases, prin. investigator Neuroscience Ctr. Excellence. Mem. magnetic resonance com. Am. Coll. Radiology, 1989—; mem. sci. rev. bd. Alzheimer's Drug Discovery Found. (formerly Inst. for Study of Aging), 2000—; prin. investigator Alzheimer's Disease Neuroimaging Initiative. Contbr. articles to profl. publs., chapters to books; mem. editl. bd.: Nuc. Magnetic Resonance in Biomedicine, 1988—2003. Recipient Young Investigator award, Am. Coll. Cardiology, 1976, William S. Middleton award, Dept. Vets. Affairs, 2006. Fellow: Internat. Soc. Magnetic Resonance in Medicine (chair com. for affiliated sects. - SMRT 1997—98), Am. Coll. Physicians; mem.: AAAS, AAUP, Western Assn. Physicians, NY Acad. Scis., Radiol. Soc. N.Am. (Editor's Recognition award with Spl. Distinction 1993—95), Soc. Magnetic Resonance Imaging, Soc. Magnetic Resonance in Medicine, Internat. Soc. Magnetic Resonance, Internat. Soc. Artificial Organs, Western Soc. Clin. Investigation, Soc. Exptl. Biology and Medicine, Am. Soc. Pharmacology and Exptl. Therapeutics, Am. Soc. Biol. Chemists, Am. Physiol. Soc., Biophysical Soc., Am. Soc. Artificial Internal Organs, Am. Diabetes Assn., Am. Heart Assn. Coun. on Kidney in Cardiovasc. Disease, Internat. Soc. Nephrology, Am. Soc. Nephrology, Am. Fedn. Clin. Rsch., Bay Area Animal Resonance Club (founder), Mid-West Salt and Water Club, Sigma Xi. Achievements include patents in field. Office: VA Med Ctr MRS Unit 114M 4150 Clement St San Francisco CA 94121 Office Phone: 415-750-2146. Office Fax: 415-668-2864. E-mail: michael.weiner@ucsf.edu.

WEINER, MORTON DAVID, banker, insurance agent; b. Balt., Aug. 19, 1922; s. Max and Rose (Wolfe) W.; children: Bruce, Lori, Julie, Jeff. BS, Towson State Coll., 1942; grad. exec. program, UCLA, 1959. Pres., dir. AVNET, Inc., NYC, 1963-69; pres., owner Morton D. Weiner & Co., Inc., NYC, 1969-70; dir. USLIFE Corp., 1968-70; chmn. bd. Nat. Investors Life Ins. Cos., 1970-77; exec. v.p. Norris Grain Co., 1971-78; pres., chief exec. officer Norin Corp., 1971-78; chmn. bd. Maple Leaf Mills, Ltd., Toronto, Ont., Can., 1974-78; chmn., dir. South Atlantic Fin. Corp., 1978-80, Atico Fin. Corp., 1980-81; chmn. Morton D. Weiner & Co., 1981—. Bd. dirs. City Nat. Bank Fla. Served to capt. Signal Corps, U.S. Army, 1942-46, CBI. Office: 362 Minorca Ave Coral Gables FL 33134

WEINER, PERRIE M., lawyer; b. Beverly Hills, Calif., 1961; BA summa cum laude, UCLA, 1982; JD, Loyola Law Sch., 1985. Bar: Calif. 1988. Judicial extern Judge Ralph J. Geffen, US Dist. Ct. ctrl. dist. Calif., 1985; law clk. Judge John R. Kronenberg, US Dist. Ct. ctrl. dist. Calif., 1986—87; atty. Brobeck, Phleger & Harrison, 1988—2002; mng. ptnr., internat. co-chmn. securities litig. practice group DLA Piper LLP(US), LA, 2002—. Conf. spkr. in field. Contbr. articles to profl. jours. in field. Recipient Burton award, 2006; named a So. Calif. Super Lawyer, L.A. Mag., 2004—09; named one of Calif. Top Mega-Rainmakers, L.A. Daily Jour., 2004—07, Top 10 Securities Litigators in US, Securities Law 360, 2006, 500 Leading Lawyers in America, Law Dragon, 2007, 100 Lawyers, 2008. Mem.: LA County Bar Assn., Phi Beta Kappa. Office: DLA Piper LLP (US) 1999 Ave of the Stars 4th Fl Los Angeles CA 90067-6022 Office Phone: 310-595-3024. Office Fax: 310-595-3324. Business E-Mail: perrie.weiner@dlapiper.com.

WEINER, RICHARD, public relations executive; b. Bklyn., May 10, 1927; s. George M. and Sally (Kosover) W.; m. Florence Chaiken, Dec. 9, 1956; children: Jessica Weiner Lampert, Stephanie Weiner Iosbaker. BS, U. Wis., 1949, MS, 1950. Pres. Creative Radio Assocs., Madison, Wis., 1951-52, Weiner-Morton Assocs., Madison, 1952-53; sr. v.p. Ruder & Finn, Inc., NYC, 1953-68; pres. Richard Weiner, Inc., NYC, 1968-86; pres. N.Y. divsn. Porter/Novelli, NYC, 1987-88, sr. counselor, 1988—. Author: Professional's Guide to Public Relations Services, 1968, News Bureaus in the U.S., 1970, Syndicated Columnists, 1972, Professional's Guide to Publicity, 1979, Military Publications, 1979, College Alumni Publications, 1980, Investment Newsletters, 1981, Webster's New World Dictionary of Media and Communications, 1996, The Skinny About Best Boy: Dollies, Green Rooms, Leads and other Media Lingo, 2006. Bd. dirs. Shake-A-Leg Miami, Fla. Fellow Pub. Rels. Soc. Am. (accredited counselor, Silver Anvil award 1965, 84, 86, 87, John Hill award 1984, Gold Anvil award 1990). Jewish. Home Phone: 305-865-3262. Personal E-mail: rweiner522@aol.com. *The essence of life is growth, adaptation, change. I hope to continue to succeed in living vigorously.*

WEINER, ROBERT NEIL, lawyer; b. San Antonio, May 20, 1952; s. Arthur and Sheila (Freedman) W.; m. Cheryl Toubin, May 29, 1977; children: Courtney, Lindsay. AB summa cum laude, Princeton U., 1974; JD, Yale U., 1977. Bar: DC 1979, US Supreme Ct. 1983, NY 1993. Law clk. to Hon. Henry J. Friendly US Ct. Appeals (2nd Cir.), 1977—78; law clk. to Justice Thurgood Marshall US Supreme Ct., Washington, 1978—79; from assoc. to ptnr. Arnold & Porter LLP, Washington, 1979—97, ptnr., chair bus. litig. practice group, 1998—; sr. counsel to Pres. The White House, Washington, 1997—98. Adj. prof. Georgetown U. Law Ctr., Washington, 1984-86; lectr. U. Va. Law Sch., 1994; assoc. ind. counsel, 1987; chmn. hearing com. DC Bd. Profl. Responsibility. Recipient Servant of Justice award, Legal Aid Soc., William Reece Smith Jr. award, Nat. Assn. Pro Bono Profls. Mem. ABA (bd. govs. 2008-), DC Bar Assn. (co-chmn. ct., lawyers and adminstrn. of justice 1987-90, chmn. coun. on sects. 1989-90, bd. govs. 1990-92, gen. counsel 1992-94, pres 1995-96, bd. dir. product liability adv. coun., 2005), Am. Law Inst., Lawyers' Commn. on Civil Rights (bd. dir.), Am Bar Found., DC Bar Found. (pres.), Phi Beta Kappa. Home: 4248 50th St Washington DC 20016 Office: Arnold & Porter 555 12th St NW Washington DC 20004-1206 Office Phone: 202-942-5855. Office Fax: 202-942-5999. Business E-Mail: robert.weiner@aporter.com.

WEINER, ROBERT STEPHEN, federal agency administrator; b. Paterson, NJ, Apr. 3, 1947; s. Jess Joseph Weiner and Dorothea Violet (Slavin) Tabor. BA, Oberlin Coll., Ohio, 1969; MA, U. Mass., 1974. Student coord. Hampshire County, dir. telephone bank Kennedy for U.S. Senate, Amherst, Mass., 1970; dir. nat. voter registration Young Dems. Am., Washington, 1971-72; dir. voter registration, media dir. get out the vote Dem. Nat. Com., Washington, 1972; legis. asst. Congressman Edward Koch, Washington, 1974-75; staff dir. subcom. health and long-term care US Ho. of Reps., Washington, 1975-76, staff dir. com. aging, 1976-80; sr. assoc. Mgmt. Recruiters Internat., Springfield, Mass., 1981-83; dir. Robert Weiner Assocs., Amherst, 1983-86; media dir., press sec. com. narcotics US Ho. of Reps., Washington, 1987-90, press sec./comms. dir. com. on govt. ops., 1990-95; dir. comm. Ho. Judiciary com. Minority and Cong. John Conyers Jr., 1995; dir. pub. affairs White House Drug Policy Office, Washington, 1995—2002; pres. Robert Weiner Assocs., Pub. Affairs and Issues, 2002—. Dir. gen. press rm. Dem. Nat. Conv., Atlanta, 1988, NYC, 1992, Chgo., 1996, LA, 2000, Boston, 2004, Press Briefing Room, Denver, 2008; cons. Carter-Mondale Transition, Washington, 1976-77, Congressman Claude Pepper, Washington, 1975-89. Represented in permanent exhbns. Nat. Mus. Am. History, Smithsonian Instn., Washington; contbr. numerous articles to profl. jours. Dem. nominee for US Congress, Mass., 1986; chmn. Road Runners Am. Nat. 10 Mile Championship, Amherst, 1984; vice chmn. Dem. Town Com., Amherst, 1984-87; nat campaign aide Kennedy for Pres., Washington, 1980. Named Communicator of Yr., Washington Crime News Svcs., 1988, 89, 90; 2d place US Nat. Masters Track Championship, 1994, 97, 2003, 04, 06. Mem. Nat. Dem. Club (bd. govs. 2002—), Sugarloaf Mountain Athletic Club (pres. 1984-86), White House Athletic Ctr. (exec. bd. 1995-2001), Potomac Valley Track Club, Capitol Hill Runners (pres. 1991—), Nat. Press Club. Avocations: running, attending performing arts, hiking. Home: 1104 Sanford Ln Accokeek MD 20607-2324 Office: PO Box 28271 1750 Pennsylvania Ave NW Washington DC 20038-8271 Office Phone: 202-329-1700.

WEINER, RUTH FLEISCHMANN, science educator; d. Walter and Gertrude Fodor Fleischmann; m. Hubert Whitney Joy, Sept. 19, 1986; m. Eugene Robert Weiner, July 26, 1954 (div. July 31, 1974); children: Elisabeth, Ann Rebeccz, Sarah Susanne, Rachel. MS, U. Ill., Urbana, 1957; PhD, Johns Hopkins U., Balt., 1962. Postdoc. fellow U. Colo. Med. Sch., Denver, 1964—67; asst. prof. chemistry Colo. Women's Coll., 1967—71; assoc. prof. & chmn., dept. chemistry Fla. Internat. U., Miami, 1971—74; dean & prof. environ. studies Western Wash. U., Bellingham, 1974—93; prin. scientist Environ. Evaluation Group, Albuquerque, 1993—95; prin. mem. tech. staff Sandia Nat. Labs, 1995—. V.p. Oceanog. Inst., Olympia, Wash., 1978—82; adv. com. EPA, Washington, 1972—76; congl. sci. fellow AAAS, 1984; mem., adv. com. Nuc. Regulatory Commn., 2003—08; adj. prof. nuc. engring. U. Mich., Ann Arbor, 2003—. Chair, excom mem. Cascade Chpt. Sierra Club, Seattle, 1974—86; mem. Nat. Atomic Mus. Found., Albuquerque, 2001—07, Am. Lung Asssocication, 1975—92, Holocaust Mus., Washington, 2001—. Fellow: Am. Nuc. Soc. (profl. divsn. chair 1996—, Fellowship 2005); mem.: Health Physics Soc. Achievements include development of the risk analysis code RADTRAN to include a user friendly GUI, dynamic dispersion, economic model, and other refinements and downloadable code. Office Phone: 505-284-8406. Personal E-mail: ruthweiner@aol.com.

WEINER, SANDRA SAMUEL, critical care nurse, consultant; b. NYC, Jan. 12, 1947; d. Herbert A. and Ruth (Wallerstein) Samuel; m. Neil D. Weiner, June 15, 1969 (div. June 1980); 1 child, Jaime Michelle. BS in Nursing, SUNY, Buffalo, 1968; cert. in critical care, Golden West Coll., 1982; postgrad., UCLA, U. West L.A. Sch. Law, 1992—95. RN, Pa., Calif. Staff nurse N.Y. Hosp.-Cornell Med. Ctr., 1968-69; head nurse med.-surg. nursing Abington (Pa.) Hosp., 1969; assoc. prof. Sch. Nursing, U. Pa., Phila., 1970; instr. nursing Coll. Med. Assts., Long Beach, Calif., 1971-72; surg. staff nurse Med. Ctr. of Tarzana, Calif., 1978-79, Cedars-Sinai Med. Ctr., LA, 1979-81; supr. recovery rm. Beverly Hills Med. Ctr., LA, 1981-92; post anesthesia care unit nurse Westside Hosp., 1992-96, Midway Hosp., Beverly Hills, Calif., 1996-99, Encino (Calif.) - Tarzana Med. Ctr., 1996—, Four Seasons Surgery Ctr., 2001—. Med. cons. RJA & Assocs., Beverly Hills, Calif., 1984-92; instr. CPR, L.A., 1986-95. Mem. women's aux. Ctr. Theater Group Vols., L.A., 1986-94, Maple Ctr., Beverly HIlls, 1987-96. Mem. ANA, Am. Soc. Post-Anesthesia Nursing, Am. Assn. Critical Care Nurses, Heart and Lung Assn., Post Anesthesia Nurses Assn., U.S. Ski Assn. Democrat. Jewish. Avocations: skiing, aerobics, travel, theater, ballet. Home: 12633 Moorpark St Studio City CA 91604-4537 Office Phone: 818-793-2050.

WEINER, SANFORD ALAN, lawyer; b. Houston, Aug. 21, 1946; s. Abe I. and Zelda C. (Caplan) Weiner; m. Leslie Eve Grenadier, Aug. 16, 1970; children: Edward, David, Evan, Rebecca. BA, U. Tex., 1968; JD, Harvard U., 1971. Bar: Tex. 1971. Ptnr. Vinson & Elkins, Ltd. Liability Partnership, Houston, 1971—. Pres. Am. Coll. Real Estate Lawyers, 2003. Mem. Houston Bar Assn., Tex. Bar Assn. (Property, Probate and Trust Sect. Lifetime Achievement award, 2007), Houston Real Estate Lawyers Council, Anglo-Am. Real Property Inst. Jewish. Office: Vinson & Elkins LLP 1001 Fannin St Ste 2500 Houston TX 77002-6760 Office Phone: 713-758-2558. Business E-Mail: sweiner@velaw.com.

WEINER, STEPHEN ARTHUR, lawyer; b. Bklyn., Nov. 20, 1933; s. Joseph Lee W. and Ruth Lessall (Weiner); m. Mina Rieur, Sept. 1, 1958; children: Karen, James. BA summa cum laude, Harvard U., 1954; JD cum laude, Yale U., 1957. Bar: N.Y. 1958, U.S. Supreme Ct. 1963. Assoc. Winthrop, Stimson, Putnam & Roberts, NYC, 1958-65, ptnr., 1968—2000, vice chmn. mgmt. com., 1984-97; acting prof. law U. Calif., Berkeley, 1965-68; ptnr. Pillsbury Winthrop LLP, NYC, 2001, sr. counsel, 2002—04, Pillsbury Winthrop Shaw Pittman LLP, NYC, 2005—. Arbitrator FINRA, 2002—; mem. com. on character and fitness 1st dept. appellate divsn. N.Y. Supreme Ct., 1998—, spl. master, 1999—; mem. N.Y. State Jud. Inst. on Professionalism in the Law, 1999—; adj. prof. law Bklyn. Law Sch., 2003—, special prof. law Hofstra U., Sch. Law, 2008-. Contbr. articles to legal publs.; comment editor Yale Law Jour., 1956—57. Fellow Am. Coll. Trial Lawyers, Am. Bar Found., N.Y. Bar Found.; mem. Downstate Com. Assn. of Bar of City of N.Y. (chmn. recruitment of lawyers com., chmn. com. on Stimson medal), Fed. Bar Coun. (chmn. com. on 2d cir. cts., trustee), Order of Coif, Phi Beta Kappa. Home: 190 Harbor Rd Sands Point NY 11050-2636 Office: Pillsbury Winthrop Shaw Pittman LLP 1540 Broadway New York NY 10036 Office Phone: 212-858-1749. Business E-Mail: stephen.weiner@pillsburylaw.com.

WEINER, STEPHEN FRANCIS, academic administrator, communications educator; b. Bklyn., June 22, 1955; s. Martin Joseph and Phyllis (Barrett) W.; m. Mary Thelma Lanier, June 5, 1982; children: Sarah Jane, Abraham Joshua. BA, Gallandet U., 1978, MA, 1980; EdD, Am. U., 1992. Asst. to dean Gallandet U., Washington, 1982-84; coord. student life and tng. Tex. Sch. for the Deaf, Austin, 1984-87; dep. dir. NorCal Ctr. on Deafness, Sacramento, 1987-89; dir. The Career Ctr. Gallaudet U., Washington, 1990-93, exec. dir. student devel., 1993-94, dean Sch. Undergrad. Studies, 1995—2001, asst. prof., 1995—2001, assoc. prof. Dept. Comm. Studies, 2001—, provost, 2007—. Mem. Md. Assn. of the Deaf, Nat. Comm. Assn., Nat. Assn. of the Deaf. Avocations: radio controlled model airplane, boats and cars. Office: Gallaudet Univ 800 Florida Ave NE Washington DC 20002-3660 Office Phone: 202-651-5085. E-mail: Stephen.Weiner@gallaudet.edu.

WEINER, STEPHEN MARK, lawyer; b. Boston, Mar. 20, 1943; s. Meyer and Esther (Lowenstein) W.; m. Roslyn G. Weiner, Dec. 19, 1967 (div. 1992), Donald G. Cornuet, Mar 14, 2008; children: Jeremiah, Ben, Miriam, Isaac. AB magna cum laude, Harvard U., 1964; LLB, Yale U., 1968. Bar: Mass. 1968. Teaching fellow Boston Coll. Law Sch.,

Chestnut Hill, Mass., 1968-69; assoc. Goodwin, Proctor & Hoar, Boston, 1969-71; spl. asst. to Gov. Francis W. Sargent Commonwealth of Mass., Boston, 1971-74; chmn. Mass. Rate Setting Commn., Boston, 1972-78; assoc. prof. Boston U. Sch. Law, 1978-81, adj. prof. law, 1993—94, dir. Ctr. for Law and Health Scis., 1978; adj. prof. law Yale Law Sch., 1994—95, Suffolk U. Sch.Law, 1997—; mem. Goulston & Storrs, Boston, 1981-90, Mintz, Levin, Cohn, Ferris, Glovsky and Popeo, PC, Boston, 1990—, ptnr., chmn., health law practice. Mem. editl. bd. New Eng. Jour. Human Svcs., 1979-81; adv. bd. Hosp. Risk Mgmt., 1979-83; contbr. articles to profl. jours. Legal adv. com. AIDS Action Coun., Washington; dir., treas. AIDS Action Com., Mass., 1989—97; bd. dirs. GLAD, Inc., 1999—2000, Boston Film Video Found., 1986—2003; del. Mass. Easter Seal Soc.; trustee Beth Israel Hosp., Boston, 1979—95, Spaulding Rehab. Hosp., Boston, 1979—95, Corp. Ptnrs. Healthcare Sys., Inc., Boston, 1994—2001, Boston Ballet, dir., 2000—, treas., 2001—05; overseer Boston Lyric Opera, 2000—04; dir. New Eng. Conservatory Lab. Charter Sch. Found.; trustee Huntington Theater Co., Boston, 2004—05; pres. HealthWell Found., 2003—; trustee Opera Boston, 2006—; mem. govt. task force to evaluate Mass. Determination of Need Program, 1979—80; profl. adv. coun. Mass. Dept. Elder Affairs, 1979—81; Mass. atty. gen. Mass. Adv. Com. on Health Care and Tobacco Control. Mem.: Mass. Bar Assn., Nat. Health Lawyers Assn., ABA, Boston Bar Assn., Phi Beta Kappa. Office: Mintz Levin Cohn Ferris Glovsky and Popeo PC 1 Financial Ctr Boston MA 02111-2657 Home Phone: 508-660-7640; Office Phone: 617-348-1757. Office Fax: 617-542-2241. Business E-Mail: sweiner@mintz.com.

WEINER, TIMOTHY EMLYN, reporter, writer; b. June 20, 1956; s. Herbert and Dora B. Weiner. BA, Columbia U., 1978, MS in Journalism, 1979. Reporter, freelance writer, NYC, 1979-81; reporter Kansas City Times, Mo., 1981-82; investigative reporter Phila. Inquirer, 1982-93; reporter New York Times, NYC, 1993—, bur. reporter covering CIA Washington, 1993—99, nat.-security corr., fgn. corr. Mexico City. Author: Blank Check: The Pentagon's Black Budget, 1990, Legacy of Ashes: The History of the CIA, 2007 (Nat. Book Award for nonfiction, 2007); co-author: Betrayal: The Story of Aldrich Ames, an American Spy, 1995. Recipient Pulitzer Prize for national reporting, 1988. Office: New York Times 620 8th Ave New York NY 10018 Office Phone: 212-556-1234. Office Fax: 212-556-7614.

WEINER, TIMOTHY M., pediatric surgeon; b. Bethesda, Md., Jan. 9, 1961; BA in biology, Oberlin Coll., 1983; MD, Georgetown Univ., 1989. Cert. Am. Bd. Surgery, 1997, in Pediatric Surgery Am. Bd. Surgery, 2000. Intern in pediatric surgery Univ. NC Sch. Med., Chapel Hill, 1989—90, resident in pediatric surgery, 1990—93; rsch. fellow Lineberger Comprehensive Cancer Ctr., Univ NC, Chapel Hill, 1991—93; sr. resident pediatric surgery Univ. NC Sch. Med., Chapel Hill, 1993—95; fellow in pediatric surgery Children's Hosp. Pitts., Pa., 1995—97; asst. prof. pediatric surgery Univ. NC Sch. Med., Chapel Hill, 1997—2004, assoc. prof. pediatric surgery, 2004—. Contbr. articles to profl. jours. Recipient Nat. Rsch. Svc. award, 1992—93, James Ewing Travel award, Soc. Surgical Oncology, 1993. Office: UNC Sch Med Dept Surgery CB#7210 3010 Old Clinic Bldg Chapel Hill NC 27599-7210 Office Phone: 919-966-4220. Office Fax: 919-966-8806.

WEINFURTER, DANIEL JOSEPH, business services executive; b. Milw., Apr. 16, 1957; s. Joseph Thomas and Betty E. (Stanton) W.; m. Martha Marie Brennan, May 14, 1983; children: Amy Jordan, Andrea Taylor. BSBA, Marquette U., Milw., 1979, MBA, 1984; postgrad., George Wash. U., Washington, DC, 1984-85. Account rep. Gen. Electric Info. Svcs., Milw., 1979-81, sr. account rep., 1982-84, project mgr. Rockville, Md., 1984-86; acting regional sales mgr. Gen. Electric Corp., Morristown, N.J., 1986, dist. sales mgr. Bensonville, Ill., 1986-87; regional sales mgr. Intelogic Trace, Inc., Schaumburg, Ill., 1987-89, area sales mgr., 1989; dir. bus. devel. Alternative Resources Corp., Lincolnshire, Ill., 1989-90, v.p. ops., 1990-93; pres. Alternative Resources Corp. Ventures, Lincolnshire, Ill., 1993—; CEO and founder Parson Group, Chgo., 1995—2002; CEO Capital H Group, Chgo., 2003—. Ad-hoc com. Riverwoods (Ill.) Village Coun., 1990—; mem. YMCA. Named number 1 of INC 500, INC Mag., 2000. Democrat. Avocations: running, raquetball, bicycling, golf, reading. Office: Capital H Group 225 W Washington St Chicago IL 60606 Home: 123 W Delaware Pl Chicago IL 60610

WEINGAND, DARLENE ERNA, librarian, educator; b. Oak Park, Ill., Aug. 13, 1937; d. Edward Emil and Erna (Heidenway) W.,; m. Wayne Anthony Weston, Sept. 7, 1957 (div. June 1976); children: Kathleen Mary, Lynda Anne, Judith Diane, Barbara Jeanne; m. James Elberling, May 1977 (div. 1980); m. Roger Paul Couture, Apr. 7, 1984. BA in History and English, Elmhurst Coll., 1972; MALS, Rosary Coll., 1973; PhD in Adult Edn./Libr. Sci., U. Minn., 1980. Asst. prof. U. Wis., Madison, 1981-86, assoc. prof., 1986-92, prof., 1992-99, prof. emerita, 1999—, SLIS acting dir., 1991, summer 86, SLIS asst. dir., 1990-94, adminstr. SLIS Continuing Edn. Svcs., 1981-99; adj. prof. and mem. affiliate grad. faculty. U. Hawaii Manoa, Manoa, 1999—2006. Cons. in mktg., continuing edn., libr. futures, info. issues, and mgmt., 1980—; invited mentor Snowbird Leadership Inst., 1990, 92; vis. fellow Curtin U. Tech. Perth, Australia, 1990; Fulbright lectr. U. Iceland, 1988; lectr. 2d World Conf. on Continuing Edn. for Libr. and Info. Sci., Barcelona, 1993, Internat. Fedn. Libr. Assn. Author: Customer Svc. Excellence: A Concise Guide for Librarians, 1997, Future Driven Library Marketing, 1998, Marketing/Planning Library and Information Services, 1999, 4th edit., 2001, Administration of the Small Public Library, 4th edit., 2001, Budgeting and the political Process in Libraries, Simulation Games, 1992 (with others), Connections: Literacy and Cultural Heritage: Lessons from Iceland, 1992, Managing Today's Public Library: Blueprint for Change, 1994, author (with others) Continuing Professional Education and Internat. Fed. of Libr. Assoc.: Past, Present, and a Vision for the Future, 1992; contbr. articles to profl. jours. Recipient excellence award Nat. Univ. Continuing Edn. Assn., 1989, Econ. and Cmty. Devel. award, 1989, outanding achievement in audio applications award Internat. Teleconferencing Assn., 1991, LITA/Libr. Hi-Tech award, 1996, disting. alumna award Dominican U., 1998; Russia project fellow Assn. Libr. and Info. Sci., 1994. Mem. ALA, AAUW, Wis. Assn. for Adult and Continuing Edn. Personal E-mail: weingand@lava.net.

WEINGARTEN, JOSEPH LEONARD, aerospace engineer; b. NYC, June 5, 1944; s. Herman H. and Irene Jane (Binzer); m. Cindy L. Carter; 1 child, Toby stepchildren: Mark Carter, Jill Supancik. B Mech. Engring., NYU, 1966; postgrad., Air War Coll., 1976. Chief engr. Air Transportability Test Loading Agy. Wright-Patterson AFB, Wright-Patterson AFB, Ohio, 1972-74; project engr. dept. engring. USAF, Wright-Patterson AFB, 1966-72, sr. project engr. dept. engring., 1974-76, planning and project engr. dept. engring., 1976-81, chief mgmt. ops. dept. engring., 1981-83, sr. tech. planner dept. engring., 1983-92; tech. asst. DCS Engring. and Tech. Mgmt. Air Force Material Command, Wright-Patterson AFB, 1992-93; founder, CEO Huffman Wright Inst., 1993-98; cons. Main Net Inc., Urbana, Ohio, 1997—2002; exec. dir. MAC Reseller Assn., 2002—; pres. Weingarten & Winburn, LLC, Inc., 2005—. CEO Weingarten Gallery, Dayton, Ohio, 1967—; pres., v.p., sec., treas., bd. dirs. Ohio Designer Craftsmen, Columbus; sec. Ohio Designer Craftsmen Enterprise, Columbus, 1982-90; chmn. continuing edn. design dept. Affiliate Socs. Coun., Dayton, 1971-74, chmn. edn. coord. com. Kettering Inst., Wright State U., 1974-76, chmn. scientist and engr. awards panel, 1990-91, mem., 1992-94; cons. Gerson Lehrman Group, 2005-; scholar adv. Gerson Lehrman Group, 2006; bd. dirs. Geist United Opposition NW, 2006. Contbr. articles on systems engring. to Aeronautical Sys. divsn. Mech. Engring. Jour. (1st place award nat. contest 1970), Procs. 4th Intersoc. Conf. on Transp., Air Force Sys. Command, USAF Spl. Purpose Report, Gems and Minerals, Friends Jour. USAF Mus., Ceramics Monthly, The Crafts Report, Macintosh Software. Scoutmaster Troop 81, Boy Scouts Am., Kettering, Ohio, 1985—91, com. mem., 1991—93, dist. chmn. Wright Bros. Dist., 2000—04, dist. chmn. Sequoia Dist. Miami Valley Coun., 1991—93, asst. coun. commr., 1993—2000, exec. bd. Miami Valley Coun., 2004—; pres. Friends of Montessori Sch., South Dayton, Ohio, 1978—94; candidate Dem. party Ind. Ho. Reps., 2008. Capt. USAF, 1967—71. Recipient Disting. Eagle award Boy Scouts Am., 1992, Silver Beaver award Boy Scouts Am., 1995, Pinnacle award Eastern Region Microage, Inc., 1999; named as one of 5 bus. execs. of yr. Miami Valley Bus. Advisor/Cox Pub., 1998, Top 5% Cons., Gerson Lehrman Group; decorated with Meritous Civilian Svc. award, US Govt., 1973, Commendation Medal, USAF, 1971. Mem. AIAA (sr. mem., air transport systems tech. com. 1976-78, 80-82, Lawrence Sperry award 1977), ASME (sr. mem.), Am. Nat. Standards Inst. (materials handling 5 com. 1968-70), Soc. Automotive Engrs. (aircraft ground support equipment com. 1969-75). Achievements include 11 patents for expendable air cargo pallet, mail container, collapsible air cargo container, process for reinforcing extruded articles, process for large scale extrusions, air flotation cargo handling system, integral aircraft barrier net, load distributive cargo platform, laminated plastic packaging material, computer printer paper support, and investment casting mold base; development of 3g cargo restraint criteria used on aircraft/spacecraft/shuttles, rope extraction system for C-5A, system for large scale structural plastics extruxions, advanced planning documents for Air Force, report in new type of DOD procurement system; holds Department of Defense authorization for manufacture of military insignia. Personal E-mail: mrmac@aol.com.

WEINGARTEN, MARC, lawyer; b. Phila., Mar. 24, 1950; BS, U. Pa., 1971; JD, Georgetown U., 1974. Bar: NY 1975. Ptnr., corp. dept. Schultz Roth & Zabel LLP, NYC, mem. exec. com. Case & notes editor Georgetown Law Rev., 1973—74. Named a Dealmaker of Yr., Am. Lawyer mag., 2007. Mem.: Assn. of Bar of City of NY (corp. law com. 1984—87, 1989—92, spl. com. on mergers, acquisitions and corp. control contests 1995—2001), ABA (Bus Law Sect, com. on long range issues affecting bus. law practice 1991—95), NY State Bar Assn. Office: Schulte Roth & Zabel LLP 919 Third Ave New York NY 10022-3902 Office Phone: 212-756-2280. Office Fax: 212-593-5955. Business E-Mail: marc.weingarten@srz.com.

WEINGARTEN, MICHAEL S., surgeon, educator; m. Carol G. Toussie, June 2, 1974; 1 child, Robin. BS, SUNY, Binghamton, 1970; MD, Columia U., NYC, 1974; MBA, Villanova U., Penn., 1996. Diplomate in general surgery Am. Bd. Surgery, 1980, in vasc. surgery 1987. Prof. surgery Drexel U. Coll. Medicine, Phila., 2006—. Sculling Upper Merion Recreational Rowing Club, Bridgeport, Pa. Recipient Multiple Tchg. awards, Drexel U. Coll. Medicine, 2002—08. Achievements include research in near infra red imaging of diabetic wounds. Personal E-mail: michael.weingarten@drexelmed.edu.

WEINGARTEN, RANDI, labor union administrator, lawyer; b. NYC, Dec. 18, 1957; d. Gabriel and Edith (Appelbaum) Weingarten. BS in Labor Rels., Cornell U., NYC, 1980; JD cum laude, Benjamin N. Cardozo Sch. Law, Yeshiva U., NYC, 1983. Bar: NY 1984, US Dist. Ct. (so. and ea. dists.) NY 1984. Legis. asst. for labor com. NY State Senate, Albany, 1979-80; assoc. Stroock & Stroock & Lavan LLP, NYC, 1983-86; counsel to pres. United Fedn. Teachers, NYC, 1986—98, asst. sec., 1995—97, treas., 1997, pres., 1998—2009; v.p. Am. Fedn. Teachers, Washington, 1997—2008, pres., 2008—. Adj. instr. Benjamin N. Cardozo Sch. Law, 1986; tchr. Clara Barton HS, Crown Heights, NY, 1991—97; mem. State Commn. Edn. Reform, NY, 2003; bd. dirs. NY State United Tchrs., Justice Resource Ctr., Coun. for Unity, NY Com. Occupl. Safety & Health; mem. adv. bd. Operation Pub. Edn., U. Pa. Mediator Bklyn. Mediation Ctr. Victim Svcs. Agy., 1981—82; chair Health Insurance Plan (HIP) Greater NY; mem. Dem. Nat. Com.; bd. dirs. NYC Independent Budget Office; bd. dirs. United Way Greater NY, NY Region Anti-Defamation League, Justice Resource Ctr., Coun. for Unity, NY Com. Occupational Safety & Health. Recipient Cmty. Svc. award, Empire State Pride Agenda, 2007; named one of NY's Influentials, NY Mag., 2006, The 100 Most Influential Women in NYC Bus., Crain's NY Bus., 2007, The 50 Most Powerful Women in NYC, NY Post, 2007, 2008. Mem.: ABA, Women's Bar Assn., NYC Bar Assn., NY State Bar Assn., Am. Fedn. Labor & Congress of Indsl. Orgn. (v.p. NYC Ctrl. Labor Coun.), Cardozo Sch. Law Alumni Assn., NY Downtown Alliance. Democrat. Jewish. Avocations: gardening, running, music, theater. Office: Am Fedn Teachers 555 New Jersey Ave NW Washington DC 20001 Office Phone: 202-879-4400. Business E-Mail: rweingarten@aft.org.*

WEINGARTEN, REID H., lawyer; b. Newark, Mar. 9, 1950; divorced; 1 child, Ross. BS, Cornell U., 1971; cert., Hague Acad. Internat. Law, The Netherlands, 1974; JD, Dickinson Law Sch., 1975. Bar: Pa. 1975, DC 1981, US Ct. Appeals (4th, 5th, 11th, and DC cirs.) 1981. Dep. dist. atty. Dauphin County, Harrisburg, Pa., 1975-77; trial atty. Pub. Integrity Sect. US Dept. Justice, Washington, 1977-87; ptnr., head white collar def. group. Steptoe & Johnson LLP, Washington, 1987—. Instr. FBI, Washington, 1978; assoc. ind. counsel, Iran Contra Affair, 1988; spl. prosecutor, US Atty.'s Office (dist. Alaska), 1988; spl. counsel to the Senate fgn. rels. com. subcommittee on Near Eastern and South Asian Affairs, October Surprise Investigation, 1992; adj. prof. law, Georgetown U. Law Ctr.; spkr. in field. Contbr. articles to profl. jours. Co-founder, bd. dirs. See Forever Found., 1995—, chair, 1997—2003. Named one of 75 Best Lawyers in Washington, Washingtonian survey mag., 2002, 100 Most Influential Lawyers, Nat. Law Jour., 2006, The Nation's Top Litigators, The Nat. Law Jour., 2007, Best Lawyers in US, Chambers USA, 2009. Fellow Am. Coll. Trial Lawyers; mem. ABA (mem. coun. criminal justice sect. 1996-97, chair white collar crime com. 1992-94), Fed. Bar Assn. (Young Fed. Lawyer Award 1984), DC Bar Assn. Office: Steptoe & Johnson LLP 1330 Connecticut Ave NW Washington DC 20036 Office Phone: 202-429-6238. Office Fax: 202-429-3902. E-mail: rweingarten@steptoe.com.*

WEINGARTNER, H(ANS) MARTIN, finance educator; b. Heidelberg, Germany, Apr. 4, 1929; came to U.S., 1939, naturalized, 1944; s. Jacob and Grete Weingartner; m. Joyce Trellis, June 12, 1955; children— Steven M., Susan C. De La Paz, Eric H., Kenneth L. AB, SB, U. Chgo., 1950, AM, 1951; MS, Carnegie Mellon U., 1956, PhD, 1962. Economist Dept. Commerce, 1951—53; instr. Grad. Sch. Indsl. Adminstrn., Carnegie Mellon U., 1956—57; instr., then asst. prof. Grad. Sch. Bus., U. Chgo., 1957—63; assoc. prof. fin. Alfred P. Sloan Sch. Mgmt., Mass. Inst. Tech., 1963—66; prof. Grad. Sch. Mgmt., U. Rochester, NYC, 1966—77; Brownlee O. Currey prof. fin. Owen Grad. Sch. Mgmt., Vanderbilt U., Nashville, 1977—98, Brownlee O. Currey Prof. of Fin., emeritus, 1998—; dir. Computer Consoles, Inc., 1974—89. Cons. to industry. Author: Mathematical Programming and the Analysis of Capital Budgeting Problems, 3d edit, 1974, (with George Benston and Dan Horsky) An Empirical Study of Mortgage Redlining, 1978; also articles.; Deptl. editor: Mgmt. Sci, 1967-73. Served with AUS, 1953-54. With US Army, 1953—54. Mellon fellow, 1954-55; Ford Found. fellow, 1955-56, recipient first prize Dissertation Competition, 1963. Fellow: Inst. for Ops. Rsch. and the Mgmt. Scis.; mem.: Coun. Sci. Soc. Pres. (alumni mem.), Inst. Mgmt. Scis. (v.p. fn. 1978—84, pres. elect, pres., past pres. 1985—88), Harbor Island Yacht Club (bd. mem. 2005—08), Beta Gamma Sigma. Home: 1616 Ash Valley Dr Nashville TN 37215-4202 Office: Vanderbilt U Owen Grad Sch Mgmt 401 21st Ave S Nashville TN 37203

WEINGARTNER, RUDOLPH HERBERT, philosophy educator; b. Heidelberg, Germany, Feb. 12, 1927; came to U.S., 1939, naturalized, 1944; s. Jacob and Grete (Kahn) W.; m. Fannia Goldberg-Rudkowski, Dec. 28, 1952 (dec. Nov. 4, 1994); children: Mark H., Eleanor C.; m. Regitze E.G. Winkelhorn Hamburger, June 13, 1997. AB, Columbia U., 1950, MA, 1953, PhD, 1959. Fellow Inst. Philos. Rsch., San Francisco, 1953—55; instr. philosophy Columbia U., 1955—59; from asst. prof. to prof., chmn. dept. philosophy San Francisco State Coll., 1959—68; prof. philosophy Vassar Coll., Poughkeepsie, 1968—74, chmn. dept., 1969—74, Taylor prof. philosophy, 1973—74, dean Coll. Arts and Scis.; prof. philosophy Northwestern U., Evanston, Ill., 1974—87; provost U. Pitts., 1987—89, prof. philosophy, 1987—94, chmn. dept. philosophy, 1991—93. Author: Experience and Culture: The Philosophy of Georg Simmel, 1962, The Unity of the Platonic Dialogue: The Cratylus, The Protagoras, The Parmenides, 1973, Undergraduate Education: Goals and Means, 1992 (Frederick W. Ness book award 1993), Fitting Form to Function: A Primer on the Organization of Academic Institutions, 1996, The Moral Dimensions of Academic Administration, 1999, Mostly About Me: A Path Through Different Worlds, 2003, A Sixty-Year Ride through the World of Education, 2007; editor: (with Joseph Katz) Philosophy in the West, 1965; exhibited sculptures in Mendelson Gallery, 1992, 94, UP Gallery, 1992, Assoc. Artists Pitts. Gallery, 2000, Internat. Images Gallery, 2002-03; contbr. articles to profl. jours. Bd. dirs. Chamber Music Chgo., 1982—87, pres., 1986—87; mem. bd. advisors Pitts. Symphony, 1991—2000, bd. dirs., chmn. artistic com., mem. exec. com., 2000—05. Social Sci. Rsch. Coun. fellow, 1958—59, Guggenheim fellow, 1965—66, Am. Coun. Learned Socs. fellow, 1971—72, residency, Rockefeller Found. Study and Conf. Ctr. in Bellagio, 1994. Mem. Am. Philos. Assn., Assn. Am. Colls. (bd. dirs. 1985-89, task force on gen. edn. 1985-88, editl. bd. liberal edn. jours. 1986-94), Assoc. Artists Pitts. (artist, 1992-2009), Phi Beta Kappa. Home: 5448 Northumberland St Pittsburgh PA 15217-1129 E-mail: rudywein@comcast.net.

WEINGAST, MARVIN, laboratory executive; b. Bklyn., Jan. 1, 1943; s. Abe and Rose (Altein) W. BS, L.I. U., 1967, MS, 1971; postgrad., Poly. Inst., 1967-68. Analytic and pollution chemist Amerada Hess Corp., Pt. Reading, N.J., 1969-73; asst. lab. dir. Chem. Constrn., North Brunswick, N.J., 1973-74; dir. Indsl. Hygiene Lab. Nat. Starch and Chemical, Bridgewater, N.J., 1974—. Grant com. mem. Ctr. for Hazardous and Toxic Substance Mgmt., Newark, 1988—; mem. Sourland Regional Citizens Planning Coun., Neshanic, N.J., 1989—. Contbr. to book: Small Business Programs, 1980; contbr. articles to profl. jours. Recipient Chemistry Dept. award L.I. U., 1967, Teaching fellowship Poly. Inst., 1967, L.I. U., 1968. Mem. MENSA, Am. Chem. Soc., Am. Conf. Chem. Labeling, Soc. Toxicology. Achievements include development of improved system for identification of hazardous chemicals; organization of first global monitoring of indsl. workers to hazardous workplace chemicals. Office: Nat Starch & Chem Co 10 Finderne Ave Bridgewater NJ 08807-3355 Personal E-mail: weingast@weingast.com.

WEINGER, STEVEN MURRAY, lawyer; b. Chgo., Feb. 7, 1954; s. Paul and Joan (Taxay) W.; children: Blake, Paige, Haley. BA, Hampshire Coll., 1975; JD, U. Chgo., 1978. Bar: Fla. 1979, Ill. 1979, U.S. Dist. Ct. (so. dist.) Fla. 1979, U.S. Ct. Appeals (5th cir.) 1980, U.S. Ct. Appeals (11th cir.) 1981, U.S. Supreme Ct. 1982, U.S. Dist. Ct. (mid. dist.) Fla. 1989. Mem. faculty U. Miami Sch. Law, Coral Gables, Fla., 1978-79; ptnr. Kurzban, Kurzban & Weinger, P.A., Miami, Fla., 1979—. Bd. dirs. Sunrise Cmty. for Mentally Retarded, Miami, United Cerebral Palsy Tallahassee, Inc., Palmer-Trinity Sch., Miami, GobleStage, Inc., 1999—. Recipient Chmn.'s award Sunrise Cmty. for Mentally Retarded, 1987; honoree United Cerebral Palsy in South Fla., 1995, Fla. Assn. Rehab. Facilities, 1996, United Cerebral Palsy Assn., 1997. Mem. ABA, Assn. Trial Lawyers Am., Fla. Assn. Trial Lawyers. Office: Kurzban Kurzban & Weinger 2650 SW 27th Ave Fl 2D Miami FL 33133-3003 E-mail: swmiami@aol.com.

WEINGOLD, MARJORIE NASSAU, retired special education educator; b. Hartford, Conn., Oct. 27, 1929; d. Joseph Nassau and Ruth Klein; m. Allan Byrne Weingold, Dec. 21, 1952; children: Beth Plavner, Roberta Greenberg, Matthew, Daniel. BA, Oberlin Coll., 1951; MA, Columbia U., 1952; cert. diagnostic therapeutic reading disability, George Washington U., 1974. Elem. edn. tchr. Hartsdale (NY) Bd. Edn., 1952—55, USN Sch. Sys., San Juan, 1958—59; presch. tchr. White Plains (NY) Sch. Sys., 1959—60; diagnostician, remediator George Washington U. Reading Ctr., Washington, 1978—83. Pvt. tutor, Potomac, Md., 1981—90. Founder, chmn. Com. for George Washington Med. Ctr., Washington, 1992—2003; trustee George Washington U. Club, Washington, 1998—2003; chmn. host com. ACOG, Washington, 1984—88; mem. women's bd. George Washington Hosp., Washington, 1997—2006; trustee Contemporary Am. Theater, 1999—, Luther Brady Art Gallery, George Washington U., 2002—; bd. dirs. Literacy Vols. Am., Washington, 1988—97, Watergate East Inc., Washington, 1996—2001. Mem.: Heritage Soc. George Washington U. Avocations: reading, travel, tennis, swimming. Home: 2510 Virginia Ave NW Washington DC 20037-1904

WEINGROW, HOWARD LOUIS, finance company executive; b. NYC, Dec. 6, 1922; s. Nathan and Anna (Mintzes) W.; m. Muriel Corrine Franzblau, Nov. 24, 1946; children: Terry Vaccaro, Caron Abby Haim. DHL (hon.), Hofstra U., Hempstead, NY, 2004. Owner Legion Fluorescent Corp., NYC, 1946-56; ptnr. Hechler & Weingrow, Inc., NYC, 1956-58, Hechler, Lifton & Weingrow, Inc., NYC, 1958-78; exec. v.p. Tanscontinental Investing Corp., NYC, 1960-67, pres., 1967-70; prin. Lifton & Weingrow, NYC, 1958—; co-chmn. Marcade Group, Inc., NYC, 1986-91, bd. dirs., 1986-93; dep. chmn. Medis Techs., Ltd. (MDTL), 2002—07; pres. Wesak Internat., 1992-94, dep. chmn., 1992—94; chmn. Wesak Chrysler, 1992-94; pres. Medis Techs. Ltd., 1992—2006, 2007, dep. chmn., 2002—. Bd. dirs. Preferred Health Care, NYC, Four Winds Inc., NYC, Medis-El, Medis Techs. Ltd., Xilas Med., Inc.; founder Ctr. for Chilhood Asthma Schneider Children's Hosp., 2002, Weingrow Family Pediatric Urology Lab., LI Jewish Hosp., 1989, The Howard L. and Muriel Weingrow Collection of Avant-Garde Art and Lit., Hofstra U., 1972; chmn. Vision Telemedia, Inc., 1995-98; founder endowed scholarship program Hofstra U., 2005., Treas. Dem. Nat.

Com., Washington, 1970-72; bd. govs. Hofstra U. Law Sch., 1977-79; dep. fin. chmn. Pres. Carter, Washington, 1976, 80; trustee Hofstra U., 1973-76, James S. Brady Presdl. Found., 1982, Children's Med. Fund, L.I. Jewish Children's Hosp., Lake Success, NY, 1986—, Am. Jewish Congress, 1988-96; treas. Nassau County Mus. Fine Arts, 1988—, North Shore, LI Jewish Hosp. Sys., 1999—; advisor to Pres. Lyndon Johnson, OEO, Washington; fin. advisor Govt. of Grenada and Office of Prime Minister Gairy, 1977-79. Decorated DFC, Air medal, 2 bronze, 2 silver clusters; recipient Presdl. medal, Hofstra U., 1985. Office: Stanoff Corp 805 3rd Ave Fl 15 New York NY 10022-7513 Office Phone: 212-935-8484. Business E-Mail: hweingrow@stanoffcorp.com.

WEINGUST, DON, theater educator; PhD, U. Calif., Berkeley. Asst. prof. drama Tufts U., Medford, Mass., 2001—08; assoc. prof. Theatre Arts Ctr. Shakespeare Studies, Southern Oreg. U., Ashland, 2008—. Author: (book) Acting from Shakespeare's First Folio: Theory, Text and Performance; actor: (prof. stage). Mem.: Shakespeare Assn. America (seminar chair 2007), Am. Soc. Theatre Rsch. (founding chair, shakespearean performance rsch. group).

WEINHOLD, DAVID, library director; b. Sheboygan, Wis., July 21, 1949; s. Raymond D. and Cornelia J. Weinhold; m. Roseann Lebiedz, Sept. 10, 2005; children: Sarah M., Elizabeth C. R. BA, Valparaiso U., Ind., 1971; MLS, Southern Conn. State Coll., New Haven, 1977. Cert. libr. Dept. Pub. Instrn., Wis., 1977. Libr. dir. Sheboygan Falls Meml. Libr., Wis., 1977—80; libr. sys. coord. Eastern Shores Libr. Sys., Sheboygan, 1980—90, libr. sys. dir., 1990—. Pres. congregation St. Paul Luth. Ch., Sheboygan Falls, 1989—92. Mem.: ALA, Wis. Libr. Assn. (pres. 2006), Volkswagen Club Sheboygan, Inc. (pres. 2005), Volkswagen Club America, Vintage Volkswagen Club. Lutheran. Office: Eastern Shores Libr Sys 4632 S Taylor Dr Sheboygan WI 53081 Business E-Mail: weinhold@esls.lib.wi.us.

WEINHOLD, LINDA LILLIAN, psychologist, researcher; b. Reading, Pa., Nov. 9, 1948; d. Aaron Zerbe Weinhold and Nancy Louise (Spotts) Weikel; m. Jack Wayne Prisk, Jan. 21, 1967 (div. 1969). Lic. practical nurse, AVTS, 1970; BS, Penn State U., 1975; MS, C.W. Post Ctr., 1982; PhD, Fordham U., 1986. LPN; cert. profl. counselor. Instr., asst. prof. Gettysburg Coll., Pa., 1985-86; post doc. fellow John Hopkins U., Balt., 1986-88; staff fellow NIH NIDA Addiction Rsch. Ctr., Balt., 1988-93; cons. NIH NIDA Medications Devel., Rockville, Md., 1993-94; soc. sci. program coord. Med. Ctr. NIDA Rsch., Washington, 1994-95; cons. The Clin. Cons. Group Antech, Inc., Balt., 1995; substance abuse counselor Hope Village, Inc., Washington, 1996—. Various presentations. Mem. Am. Psychol. Assn., Am. Counseling Assn., Bah'a'i', Phi Kappa Phi, Sigma Xi. Avocations: singing, dance, painting, photography, reading. Home: 2611 Bowen Rd SE Apt 203 Washington DC 20020-6623 Office: Hope Village Inc 2840 Langston Pl SE Washington DC 20020-3241 Office Phone: 202-678-1077.

WEINHOLD, VIRGINIA BEAMER, interior designer; b. Elizabeth, N.J., June 21, 1932; d. Clayton Mitchell and Rosemary (Behrend) Beamer; divorced; children: Thomas Craig, Robert Scott, Amy Linette. BA, Cornell U., 1955; BFA summa cum laude, Ohio State U., 1969; MA in Design Mgmt., Ohio State U., 1982. Freelance interior designer, 1969-72; interior designer, dir. interior design Karlsberger and Assocs. Inc., Columbus, Ohio, 1972-82; assoc. prof. dept. design Ohio State U., 1982-2002, grad. studies chairperson, 1986-89, 1995-96; lectr. indsl. design Ohio State U., 1972, 79-80. Trustee Found. for Interior Design Edn. and Rsch., 1991-97. Mem. Inst. Bus. Designers (chpt. treas. 1977-79, nat. trustee 1979-81, nat. chmn. contract documents com. 1979-84, chpt. pres. 1981-83), Constrn. Specifications Inst., Interior Design Educator's Coun. (nat. treas. 1989-93), Interior Design Educator's Coun. Found. (nat. treas. 1992-94), Illuminating Engring. Soc. (chpt. v.p. 1997-98), AIA (assoc.), Internat. Interior Design Assn. (nat. dir. 1994-97). Prin. works include Grands Rapids (Mich.) Osteo. Hosp., Melrose (Mass.) Wakefield Hosp., Christopher Inn, Columbus, John W. Galbreath Hdqrs., Columbus, Guernsey Meml. Hosp., Cambridge, Ohio, Trinity Epis. Ch. and Parish House, Columbus, Hale Hosp., Haverhill, Mass., Ohio State U. Dept. Indsl. Design Lighting Lab., others. Author: IBD Forms and Documents Manual, Interior Finish Materials for Health Care Facilities, Subjective Impressions: Lighting Hotels and Resturants, 1989, Effects of Lighting on The Perception of Interior Spaces, 1993. Home: 112 Glen Dr Columbus OH 43085-4010 Office: Ohio State U Dept Design 128 N Oval Mall Columbus OH 43210-1318

WEININGER, MARKUS, radiologist; b. Wuerzburg, Germany; s. Erich and Gerlinde Weininger; m. Heidi Weininger. MD, U. Wuerzburg, Germany, 2000. Cons. KPMG Consulting, Frankfurt, Germany, 2001—02; mktg. mgr. Siemens Med. Solutions, Malvern, Pa., 2003—04, Erlangen, Germany, 2002—04; med. dir. Calyx Partners, LLC, Orlando, Fla., 2004; radiologist U. Hosp. Wuerzburg, 2004—. Home: 1650 William Hapton Way Mount Pleasant SC 29466 Personal E-mail: mweininger1@yahoo.com, markus@weiniger.us.

WEINKAUF, MARY LOUISE STANLEY, retired clergywoman, educator; b. Eau Claire, Wis., Sept. 22, 1938; d. Joseph Michael and Marie Barbara (Holzinger) Stanley; m. Alan D. Weinkauf, Oct. 12, 1962 (dec. Nov. 2000); children: Stephen, Xanti. BA, Wis. State U., 1961; MA, U. Tenn., 1962, PhD, 1966; MDiv, Luth. Sch. Theology, Chgo., 1993. Grad. asst., instr. U. Tenn., 1961-66; asst. prof. English Adrian Coll., 1966-69; prof., head dept. English Dakota Wesleyan U., Mitchell, SD, 1969-89; instr. Columbia Coll., 1989-91. Pastor Calvary Evang. Luth. Ch., Siloa Luth. Ch., Ontoragon Faith, White Pine, Mich., Gowrie, Iowa, dir. Lay Sch. for Mission, Sayner Campus, 2006—. Author: Hard-Boiled Heretic, 1994, Sermons in Science Fiction, 1994, Murder Most Poetic, 1996. Trustee Ednl. Found., 1986-90; bd. dirs. Ontonagon County Habitat for Humanity, 1995-97, Luth. Campus Ministry for Wis. and Upper Mich., 1996-2002, Lakeland Area Food Pantry, 2000—09, Fortune Lake Bible Camp, 2003-04, Pastime Club Adult Day Care Ctr., North Ctrl. Wis. Thrivent Fin. for Lutherans, 2006, pres., 2007-. Mem. AAUW (divsn. pres. 1978-80), Nat. Coun. Tchrs. English, S.D. Coun. Tchrs. English, Sci. Fiction Rsch. Assn., Popular Culture Assn., Milton Soc., S.D. Poetry Soc. (pres. 1982-83), Delta Kappa Gamma (pres. local chpt., mem. state bd. 1972-89, state v.p. 1979-83, state pres. 1983-85), Sigma Tau Delta, Pi Kappa Delta, Phi Kappa Phi, Alpha Eta (chpt. pres. 2008-). Personal E-mail: maryweinkauf@charter.net.

WEINMAN, HOWARD MARK, lawyer; b. NYC, May 6, 1947; s. Joseph and Kate (Dorn) Weinman; m. Pamela Eve Brodie, Jan. 6, 1980; children: David Lewis, Nathaniel Saul. BA magna cum laude, Columbia U., 1969; MPP, Harvard U., 1973, JD cum laude, 1973; LLM with highest hons. in Taxation, George Washington U., 1981. Bar: D.C. 1973. Assoc. Fried, Frank, Harris, Shriver & Kampelman, Washington and NYC, 1973—78; legis. atty. Joint Com. on Taxation U.S. Congress, Washington, 1978—80; assoc. Sachs, Greenebaum & Tayler, Washington, 1980—82, Crowell & Moring LLP, Washington, 1982—84, ptnr., 1984—. Adj. prof. internat. tax Georgetown U. Law Ctr., Washington, 1988—89. Contbr. articles to profl. jours. Mem.: ABA (taxation sect.), Phi Beta Kappa. Jewish. Home: 5404 Center St Chevy Chase MD 20815-7101 Office: Crowell & Moring LLP 1001 Pennsylvania Ave NW Fl 10 Washington DC 20004-2595

WEINMAN, STEVEN ALAN, emergency nurse practitioner, educator, writer, health facility administrator; b. St. Louis, July 17, 1962; s. Stanley I. Weinman and Diana Raye (Kessler) Schrader; m. Carol Angela Daiber, July 27, 1986; children: Erin Elizabeth, Sarah Katherine. Diploma in Nursing, Jewish Hosp. of St. Louis, 1986; BSN, Webster U., Kansas City, 1996. RN, Mo., NY, NJ; cert. emergency nurse. Emergency nurse Jewish Hosp. of St. Louis, 1986-87, Truman Med. Ctr.-West, Kansas City, Mo., 1987-93, clin. nurse mgr., 1987-93, clin. educator, 1993-95, St. Luke's Northland Hosp., Kans. City, Mo., 1996-97; prin. ptnr. Emergency Care Cons. Greater NY, Somerville, NJ, 1996—; instr. dept. emergency medicine NY Hosp.-Cornell Med. Ctr., NYC, 1997-2001; sr. dir. Med. Ed. and Custom Publ., Excepta Med. Elsevier, Hillsborough, NJ, 2001—02; dir. Office of Continuing Med. Edn. Elsevier Health Scis. Divsn., 2004; sr. dir. Ctr. for Accredited Healthcare Edn., Princeton, NJ, 2004—, Inst. Med. and Nursing Edn., Princeton, 2004—. Nurse rschr. Clin. Multiphase Rsch., 1991—2000; rsch. coord. dept. emergency medicine Truman Med. Ctr., Kansas City, 1991—96; mem. editl. adv. bd. Roadrunner Press/ENA, 1999—2001; per diem instr. in emergency and trauma care N.Y. Presbyn. Hosp.-Cornell Med. Ctr., NYC, 2001—; dept. health and human svcs. NNRT Region II, 2003—; deputy chief EMS & spl. operations Somerville Rescue Squad, NJ. Editor textbooks and monographs; mem. editl. bd. Clin. CORNERSTONE, 2001-03, Excerpta Medica, Inc.; contbg. author books and book chpt; contbr. articles to profl. jour. Adv. bd. Kansas City chpt. ARC, 1991-94; chief nurse EMS, Kansas City Spiritfest, 1989-95; emergency med. technician Somerville Rescue Squad, State of NJ, 2002, edn. and tng. officer, 2003—, crew chief, 2003—, EMS capt., 2006—, mem. exec. bd., 2004—. Recipient Spl. Recognition award Emergency Nursing Found., Spl. Recognition award Somerville Rescue Squad, Extrication Save award, 2004, Lifesaving awards, 2004-07, Rescue award, 2006-07. Mem.: Am. Orgn. Nurse Execs., NJ State Nurses Assn., Nat. Assn. EMS Educators, Global Alliance for Med. Edn., Alliance for Continuing Med. Edn., Soc. Trauma Nurses, Am. Trauma Soc., Emergency Nurses Assn. (treas. Greater Kansas City chpt. 1989—91, pres. 1994, state coun. exec. com. 1993—95, sec. 1991, state del. 1991—95, Recognition award 1991, 1993, Edn. award 1993, Recognition award 1994, Educator of Yr. 1994, 1996, Recognition award 2000—01, Disting. Svc. award 2000, 2003—04). Avocations: photography, writing, computers, travel. Home: 29 W Spring St Somerville NJ 08876-1627 Office: 201 Carnegie Ctr Ste 104 Princeton NJ 08540 Personal E-mail: rescsteve@aol.com.

WEINMANN, JOHN GIFFEN, lawyer, ambassador; b. New Orleans, Aug. 29, 1928; s. Rudolph John and Mary Victoria (Mills) W.; m. Virginia Lee Eason, June 11, 1955; children: Winston Eason, Robert St. George Tucker, John Giffen Jr., Mary Virginia Lewis, George Gustaf. BA, Tulane U., 1950, JD, 1952. Bar: La. 1952. Pvt. practice law Phelps Dunbar and predecessor firm, New Orleans, ptnr., 1955-80, of counsel, 1981-83, 85-89, 1993—; gen. counsel Times-Picayune Pub. Corp., Rathborne Land Co., 1968-80; pres., dir. Waverly Oil Corp., 1981-89; amb. to Finland Am. Embassy, Helsinki, 1989-91; amb., chief of protocol of White House Dept. of State, Washington, 1991-93. Lectr. bills and notes New Orleans chpt. Am. Inst. Banking, 1958-59; bd. dir. Eason Oil Co., 1961-81, chmn., 1977; bd. dir. 1st Nat. Bank of Oklahoma City, 1978-84, Am. Life Ins. Co. of N.Y., 1981-88, Allied Investment Corp., 1985-88; asst. sec. Am. Bar Endowment, 1971-74, bd. dirs., sec., 1975-80 Mem. adv. bd. Tulane Law Rev., 1965-92. Bd. govs. Tulane Med. Ctr., 1968-81; bd. adminstrs. Tulane Ednl. Fund, 1981-98, emeritus, 99—, chmn. devel. com., 1985-89, co-chmn. Tulane Parents Fund, 1980-81, bd. chmn., 1993-98; nat. chmn. ann. giving Campaign for Tulane, 1983-85; bd. dirs. Coun. for Better La., 1987-89, Tulane Children's Ctr., 1981-84, WYES Ednl. TV Sta., 1981-82; trustee S.W. Legal Found., 1978-80, Metairie Park Country Day Sch., vice chmn., 1976-77, chmn., 1978-80, U.S. commr. gen. for 1984 La. World Expn., 1983-85; U.S. del. Bur. Internat. Expositions, Paris, 1984-85, chmn. del., 1985; state fin. co-chmn. George Bush for Pres., and Victory La. '88, 1987-89. Named Outstanding Law Alumnus Tulane U., 1985, Outstanding Alumnus Class of 1950, Tulane Coll., 2000, Disting. Tulane U. Alumnus, 2002; selected Rex, King of Carnival, New Orleans, 1996. Mem. ABA (chmn. jr. bar conf. 1963-64, mem. ho. dels. 1964-66, 70, 72-76, sec. com. ethics evaluation 1965, rep. to conv. Union des Jeunes Avocats de France, 1964, chmn. sect. bar activities 1969-70), La. Bar Assn. (sec. treas. 1965-67, Outstanding Young Lawyer award), La. Soc. Colonial Wars (gov. 1976), Swiss-Am. Cultural Exch. Found. (hon. com. 1994—), Phi Beta Kappa, Order of Coif, Delta Kappa Epsilon, Omicron Delta Kappa. Episcopalian. Office: Waverly Enterprises 601 Poydras St Ste 2690 New Orleans LA 70130-6026 Home: 29 Nassau Dr Metairie LA 70005-4464 Office Phone: 504-566-1311. Office Fax: 504-568-9130.

WEINMANN, RONALD VINCENT, business educator; b. Harvey, N.D., Apr. 14, 1945; s. Vincent R. and Adeline C. (Muscha) W.; m. Loretta Jane Schmaltz, Dec. 28, 1973; children: Shannon, Shane, Shawn. AA, N.D. State Sch. Sci., 1971; BS, N.D. State U., 1974; MS in Adminstrn., Cen. Mich. U., Mt. Pleasant, 1989. Cert. nat. econ. devel. profl., 1994. Asst. mgr. Pierce Co., Fargo, N.D., 1974-76; spl. agt. Lincoln Nat. Life Ins. Co., Fargo, 1976-78; buyer Crane Johnson Co., West Fargo, N.D., 1978-79; small bus. mgmt. instr., coordinator small bus. mgmt. Lake Region Community Coll., Devil's Lake, N.D., 1979—; cons. SBA. Educator Lake Region State Coll., Devils Lake, ND, 1979-99, Embry Riddle U., Daytona Beech, FL, 1999-2005, Minot State U., ND, 2009-. Cons., tax prep pvt. practise, Devils Lake, 1975-. Contbr. articles to profl. jours. Pub. relations dir., past dist. commr. Boy Scouts Am., 1980—; commr. Devil's Lake Park Bd., 1986, Ramsey County Fair Bd., 1987; credit supervisory com. Citizens Cmty. Credit Union, Devils Lake, 1992-2000. With USAF, 1967-69. Decorated Air Force Commendation medal; recipient Dist. award of Merit, Boy Scouts Am., 1984. Mem. N.D. Assn. Small Bus. Mgmt. Instrs. (past pres.), Nat. Assn. Small Bus. Mgmt. Instrs. (past editor), Devil's Lake C. of C. (bd. dirs.), Jaycees (past state officer, mem. internat. senate), N.D. Assn. Acctg. Instrs., VFW, ND Soc. Pub. Accounts. Roman Catholic. Lodge: Eagles. Home: 1207 2nd Ave NW Devils Lake ND 58301 Office: Minot State Univ 500 W Ave Minot ND 58701 Office Phone: 701-858-3294. Business E-Mail: rweinmann@dvl.midco.net.

WEINREICH, GABRIEL, physicist, minister, educator; b. Vilnius, Lithuania, Feb. 12, 1928; came to U.S., 1941, naturalized, 1949; s. Max and Regina (Szabad) W.; m. Alisa Lourié, Apr. 19, 1951 (dec. 1970); m. Gerane Siemering Benamou, Oct. 23, 1971; children: Catherine, Marc, Daniel, Rebecca, Natalie. AB, Columbia U., 1948, MA, 1949, PhD, 1954. Ordained priest Episcopal Ch., 1986. Mem. staff Bell Telephone Labs., Murray Hill, NJ, 1953-60; mem. faculty U. Mich., Ann Arbor, 1960—, prof. physics, 1964-95; prof. emeritus, 1995—; Collegiate prof. U. Mich., 1974-76. Adj. min. St. Clare's Episcopal ch., Ann Arbor, 1985-90; rector St. Stephen's Episcopal Ch., Hamburg, Mich., 1993-96. Author: Solids: Elementary Theory for Advanced Students, 1965, Fundamental Thermodynamics, 1968, Notes for General Physics, 1972, Geometrical Vectors, 1998, Confessions of a Jewish Priest: From Secular Jewish War Refugee to Physicist and Episcopal Clergyman, 2005; editor: Mechanics of Musical Instruments, 1995. Recipient Disting. Teaching award U. Mich., 1968, Klopsteg award Am. Assn. Physics Tchrs., 1992, Internat. medal French Acoustical Soc., 1992, Hutchins Gold medal for lifetime achievement in mus. acoustics, 2002. Fellow Acoustical Soc. Am. (assoc. editor Jour. 1987-89, Silver medal, 2008). Home: 2116 Silver Maples Dr Chelsea MI 48118-1189 Home Phone: 734-433-1426. Business E-Mail: weinreic@umich.edu.

WEINRICH, BRIAN ERWIN, mathematician, computer scientist; b. Passaic, NJ, Jan. 8, 1952; s. Erwin H. and Ann E. (Gall) Weinrich. BS, Pa. State U., 1974, MA, 1978; MS, Shippensburg U., Pa., 1983; PhD, U. Fla., Gainesville, 2007. Mathematician US Dept. Agr., Agrl. Rsch. Svc., University Park, Pa., 1974-80; instr. math. and computer sci. Shippensburg U., 1980-84; assoc. prof. math. and computer sci. California U. of Pa., 1984-97, assoc. prof. emeritus math. and computer scis., 1997—. Cons. in field; mem. Wall St. Jour. Panel, 1990—; devel. articulation agreements in Malaysia California U. of Pa., 1992—2001; vis. sr. lectr. computer sci. Inti Coll., Subang Jaya, Malaysia, 1993—2001; cons. in math., sys. and database programming, 1981—2002; patent examiner US Patent and Trademark Office, Alexandria, Va., 2007—. Author (with A. S. Rogowski): (book) Water Movement and Quality on Strip-Mined Lands: A Compilation of Computer Programs, 1984; author: (with others) Surface Mining, 1990; contbr. articles to profl. jours. Mem. mission bd. Calvary Bapt. Ch., State College, Pa., 1975—80; visitation team Prince St. United Brethren Ch., Shippensburg, 1982—84; Bible study leader, asst. Sunday sch. tchr. Libr. Bapt. Ch., 1986—92; workshop leader, follow-up trainer Gator Christian Life, Cypress Ch., 2002—. Grantee, U.S. Dept. Age, 1982—89; fellow, U. Fla., 2002—. Mem.: Assn. Computing Machinery, Am. Biog. Inst. (bd. advisors 1989—), Computer Soc. of IEEE. Republican. Home: 9461 Russia Branch View Dr Apt 1311 Manassas Park VA 20111 Office: US Patent and Trademark Office Alexandria VA 22301 Office Phone: 571-270-3793. Personal E-mail: brianew@earthlink.net.

WEINSCHEL, ALAN JAY, lawyer; b. Bklyn., Feb. 9, 1946; m. Barbara Ellen Schure, Aug. 20, 1967; children: Lawrence, Adam, Naomi. BA, Bklyn. Coll., 1967; JD, NYU, 1969. Bar: N.Y. 1970, U.S. Dist. Ct. (so. and ea. dists.) N.Y. 1973, U.S. Ct. Appeals (2d cir.) 1979, U.S. Ct. Appeals (9th cir.) 1986, US Ct. Appeals (3d cir.) 1993, US Ct. Appeals (7th cir.) 1996, US Ct. Appeals (DC cir.) 2007. Assoc. Breed, Abbott & Morgan, NYC, 1969-74, Weil, Gotshal & Manges, NYC, 1974-78, ptnr., 1978—. Lectr. Practising Law Inst., Ohio Legal Ctr., Am. Mgmt. Assn., Law Jour. Seminars, Law and Bus. Seminars, Glasser Legalworks, Insight Seminars, Mfrs.' Alliance. Author: Antitrust Intellectual Property Handbook, 2000. Trustee N.Y. Inst. Tech., Old Westbury, N.Y., 1969-76, Temple Sinai, Roslyn, N.Y., 1981-87, 89-95. Capt. U.S. Army res., 1969-74. Mem. ABA (editl. bd. Antitrust Devels. 1981-87), NY State Bar Assn. (chmn. antitrust sect. 1993-95, Dting. Svc. award 2006), Assn. Bar of City of NY. Office: Weil Gotshal & Manges 767 5th Ave New York NY 10153-0119 Office Phone: 212-310-8550.

WEINSHENKER, NAOMI JOYCE, clinical psychiatrist, educator, researcher; b. Ridgewood, NJ, Mar. 28, 1961; d. Theodore and Anne Betty (Jaffe) W. BA summa cum laude, Yale U., 1983; MD, U. Pa., 1989. Diplomate Am. Bd. Psychiatry and Neurology. Rotating intern Overlook Hosp., Summit, NJ, 1989-90; resident in adult psychiatry Mass. Mental Health Ctr., Harvard U. Med. Sch., Boston, 1990-92, fellow in child and adolescent psychiatry, 1992-93, Boston Childrens Hosp., Harvard Med. Sch., 1993—94; staff psychiatrist Choate Health Systems, Woburn, Mass., 1994-96; asst. prof. clin. psychiatry U. Medicine and Dentistry of N.J., Newark, 1996-2000; asst. prof. clin. psychiatry Sch. Medicine NYU, 2000—; pvt. practice psychiatry, 2006—; freelance medical reporting News12, Norwalk, Conn., 2006—07; med. corr. Med. Missions Children, 2007—08. Staff psychiatrist Univ. Behavioral Health-Care, Newark, 1996—97; asst.dir. Univ.Hosp. Psychiat. Outpatient Ctr., 1998—2000; mem. faculty NYU Child Study Ctr., 2000—06; cons. child outpatient svcs. Tri-City Mental Health and Retardation Ctr., Inc., Medford, Mass., 1996; dir., young adult inpatient program Tisch Hosp., 2000—04. Contbr. articles to profl. jours.; editl. asst. Emergency Medicine mag., 1983-84. Vol. psychiatry unit, coord. psychiatry vols., Yale-New Haven Hosp., 1979-83; vol. recruitment coord. Phila. Adult Spl. Olympics, 1985. Mem. Am. Psychiat. Assn., Am. Acad. Child/Adolescent Psychiatry, NJ Psychiat. Assn. (Essex County rep. Tri-County chpt. 1997-98, treas. 1998-99, sec. 1999-00, v.p. 2000-2001, pres.-elect 2001-02), NJ Coun. Child/Adolescent Psychiatry, Phi Beta Kappa, Sigma Xi. Democrat. Jewish. Avocations: theater, nutrition, vegetarianism, weightlifting, aerobics. Office Phone: 973-471-4448. Personal E-mail: naomi_weinshenker@yahoo.com.

WEINSTEIN, ALAN EDWARD, lawyer; b. Bklyn., Apr. 20, 1945; s. John and Matilda W.; m. Patti Kantor, Dec. 18, 1965; children: Steven R., David A. AA, U. Fla., 1964; BBA, U. Miami, Fla., 1965, JD cum laude, 1968. Bar: Fla. 1968, U.S. Dist. Ct. (so. dist.) Fla. 1968, U.S. Ct. Appeals (5th cir.) 1969, U.S. Supreme Ct. 1973, U.S. Ct. Appeals (4th and 11th cirs,) 1981. Assoc. Cohen & Hogan, Miami Beach, Fla., 1968-71; pvt. practice Miami Beach, 1972-81; sr. ptnr. Weinstein & Preira, Miami Beach, 1981-92; prin. Law Offices of Alan E. Weinstein LLC, Miami, 1992—. Lectr. in field. Mem. ABA (criminal and family law sect. 1968—, white collar crime commn. 1986—), Nat. Assn. Criminal Def. Lawyers, 1st Family Law Am. Inn of Court, Fla. Bar Assn. (criminal and family law sect. 1968—, ethics com. 1987-88, bench/bar com. 1988-89, grievance com. 1999-2002, chmn. 2002, unlicensed practice of law com. 2002-05), Fla. Criminal Def. Attys. Assn. (pres. 1978-79), Fla. Assn. Criminal Def. Lawyers (treas. 1989-90), Miami Beach Bar Assn., Soc. Wig and Robe, Phi Kappa Phi. Avocations: marlin fishing, reading, travel. Office: 4500 Biscayne Blvd Ste 203 Miami FL 33137 Office Phone: 305-576-8666. Personal E-mail: defense1@bellsouth.net.

WEINSTEIN, ALLEN, archivist; b. NYC, Sept. 1, 1937; s. Samuel and Sarah (Popkoff) W.; m. Adrienne Dominguez, June 14, 1995; children: Andrew Samuel, David Meier. BA, CCNY; MA, Yale U., PhD, 1967. Prof. history Smith Coll., Northampton, Mass., 1966-81; editl. staff The Washington Post, 1981; exec. editor, The Washington Quarterly Georgetown Ctr. for Strategic and Internat. Studies, Washington, 1981—83; prof. Georgetown U., Washington, 1981—84; pres. Ctr. for the Study of Democratic Institutions, Santa Barbara, 1984; editor The Ctr. Magazine, 1984; prof. history Boston U., 1985-89; founder, pres. The Ctr. for Democracy, Washington, 1985—2003; sr. adv. for democratic institutions & dir. Internat. Found. for Elections Sys., Washington, 2003—; archivist of the US The Nat. Archives & Records Admin., Washington, 2005—. Author: Prelude to Populism:Origins of the Silver Issue, 1970, Freedom and Crisis: An American History, 1974, Perjury: The Hiss-Chambers Case, 1978 (NISC award 1978), new edit., 1998, Between the Wars: American Foreign Policy From Versailles to Pearl Harbor, 1978; co-author: The Haunted Wood: Soviet Espionage in America-The Stalin Era, 1999, The Story of America, 2002; editor: American Negro Slavery, 1968, 3d edit., 1981, Harry S Truman and the American Commitment to Israel, 1981. Exec. dir. The Democracy Program, Washington, 1982-83; acting pres. Nat. Endowment for Democracy, Washington, 1983-84;

chmn. edn. com. U.S. Inst. Peace, Washington, 1986-2001; mem. U.S. Observer del., Feb., 1986 Philippines election, co-author report; vice chmn. U.S. del. UNESCO World Conf. on Culture, 1982, UNESCO/IPDC meeting, 1983; chmn. Internat. IMPAC/Dublin Lit. award, 1996-2003. Recipient Meade prize in history CCNY, 1960, Egleston prize Yale U., 1967, Binkley-Stephenson prize Orgn. Am. Historians, 1968, UN Peace medal, 1986, Coun. of Europe Silver medal, 1990, 96; Fulbright lectr., Australia, 1968, 71; Commonwealth Fund lectr. U.S. History, U. London, 1981; Fourth of July Orator Fanueil Hall, Boston, 1987. Fellow Woodrow Wilson Ctr., NEH; mem. Soc. Am. Historians, Cosmos Club. Democrat. Jewish. From 1982-84 directed the rsch. study which led to the creation of the Nat. Endowment for Democracy (NED). Office: The Nat Archives & Records Adminstrn 8601 Adelphi Rd Rm 4200 College Park MD 20740*

WEINSTEIN, ANNA, music educator; arrived in US, 1993; d. Naum and Revekka Goykhman; m. David Weinstein, Dec. 30, 1972; children: Yana, Anthony. BS (hon.), Melitopol Pedagogical Inst., Melitopol, Ukraine, 1992. Lic. tchr. Ohio. Piano instr., pvt. piano tchr. Sch. Creative and Performing Arts, Cin., 1999—. Music dir. Russian Amateur Theatre Jewish Cmty. Ctr., Cin., 2004—06; judge World Piano Competition. Musician: (teaching piano) Regional Judge For World Piano Competition. Music dir. Jewish Cmty. Ctr., Cin., 2004—06. Recipient Talent award for tchg., World Piano Competition, 2000, Bronze medal, 2001. Mem.: Am. Music Scholarship Assn. Office: Sch Creative and Performing Arts 1310 Sycamore St Cincinnati OH 45202

WEINSTEIN, ARTHUR, rheumatologist, educator; b. Toronto, Ont., Can., Jan. 19, 1944; s. William and Ada (Bluestein) W. MD, U. Toronto, 1967. Diplomate Am. Bd. Rheumatology and Diagnostic Laboratory Immunology. Intern Toronto Gen. Hosp., 1967-68; resident, fellow Toronto Wellesley Hosp., Toronto Gen. Hosp., & Hammersmith Hosp. U. London, 1968-73; staff rheumatologist, asst. prof. medicine U. Toronto Med. Sch., 1974-76, U. Conn. Med. Sch., Farmington, 1976-80, assoc. prof. medicine, 1980-85; prof. medicine, chief div. rheumatic diseases, lab. dir. N.Y. Med. Coll., Valhalla, 1985—; chief rheumatology sect. Westchester Med. Ctr., Valhalla, 1985—. Chmn. med. adv. bd. Westchester chpt.Lupus Found. Am., 1988—; guest lectr. various orgns. U.S. and abroad; speaker in field. Contbr. chpts. to books, articles to profl. jours. Fellow ACP, Am. Coll. Rheumatology (editorial bd. for Jour. Rheumatology 1978—, program chmn. Northeastern regional meeting, Ottawa, Ont. 1988, edn. com. 1989—); mem. AAAS, N.Y. Rheumatism Assn. (exec. com. 1987—), Am. Assn. Pathology, Am. Assn. Immunologists, Am. Fedn. Clin. Rsch. Achievements include pioneering research and use of methotrexate for rheumatoid arthritis. Office: Div Rheumatic Diseases and Immunology NY Med Coll Valhalla NY 10595

WEINSTEIN, BARBARA, history professor; b. Bklyn., May 10, 1952; d. Lou and Esther Weinstein; m. Brian Erich Goode, Mar. 23, 1984; children: Sarah Rachel Goode, Lawrence Daniel Goode. PhD, Yale U., New Haven, 1979. Prof. history U. Md., Coll. Pk., 2000—06, Ny U., NYC, 2007—. Contbr. articles to numerous profl. jours. (LASA-Brazil prize, 2007). Fellowship, John Simon Guggenheim Meml. Found., 1998—99. Mem.: Am. Hist. Assn. (pres. 2007—08). Liberal. Avocations: travel, movies, walking. Office: NYU 53 Washington Sq S 7th Floor New York NY 10012-1098 Office Fax: 212-995-4017. Business E-Mail: bw52@nyu.edu.

WEINSTEIN, BOB (ROBERT WEINSTEIN), film company executive; b. Queens, NY, Oct. 18, 1954; s. Max and Miriam (Postel) Weinstein; m. Annie Clayton, Apr. 29, 2000. Student, SUNY, Fredonia, 1971—73. Co-founder, co-chmn. (with Harvey Weinstein) Miramax Films Corp., NYC, 1979—2005; co-founder (with Harvey Weinstein) The Weinstein Co., 2005—. Prodr. (films) Playing for Keeps (also dir.), 1986, Gandahar, 1988, Mimic, 1997, Reindeer Games, 2000; exec. prodr.: (films) Hardware, 1990, Strike It Rich, 1990, The Pope Must Die, 1991, Into the West, 1992, Benefit of the Doubt, 1993, Map of the Human Heart, 1993, The Night We Never Met, 1993, True Romance, 1993, Hour of the Pig, 1993, Mother's Boys, 1994, Road Killers, 1994, Prêt-à-Porter, 1994, The Englishman Who Went Up a Hill But Came Down a Mountain, 1995, Things to Do in Denver When You're Dead, 1995, Smoke, 1995, The Crossing Guard, 1995, A Month by the Lake, 1995, The Journey of August King, 1995, Blue in the Face, 1995, Beautiful Girls, 1996, Flirting with Disaster, 1996, The Pallbearer, 1996, Emma, 1996, I Love You, I Love You Not, 1996, The Crow: City of Angels, 1996, The English Patient, 1996, Scream, 1996, Sono pazzo di Iris Blond, 1996, Nightwatch, 1997, Addicted to Love, 1997, Robinson Crusoe, 1997, Mononoke-hime, 1997, Air Bud, 1997, Cop Land, 1997, Wings of the Dove, 1997, Good Will Hunting, 1997, Scream 2, 1997, Jackie Brown, 1997, Wishful Thinking, 1997, A Price Above Rubies, 1998, Phantoms, 1998, Senseless, 1998, Wide Awake, 1998, Ride, 1998, Velvet Goldmine, 1998, The Mighty, 1998, 54, 1998, Heaven, 1998, Rounders, 1998, Talk of Angels, 1998, The Faculty, 1998, Shakespeare in Love, 1998, Playing by Heart, 1998, She's All That, 1999, Guinevere, 1999, My Life So Far, 1999, Teaching Mrs. Tingle, 1999, Outside Providence, 1999, In Too Deep, 1999, Mansfield Park, 1999, Holy Smoke, 1999, Music of the Heart, 1999, Cider House Rules, 1999, Allied Forces, 1999, Down to You, 2000, Committed, 2000, The Crow: Salvation, 2000, Scream 3, 2000, Love's Labour's Lost, 2000, Takedown, 2000, The Yards, 2000, Boys and Girls, 2000, Scary Movie, 2000, Highlander: Endgame, 2000, Backstage, 2000, Malèna, 2000, Bounce, 2000, Chocolat, Dracula 2000, 2000, Spy Kids, 2001, Texas Rangers, 2001, Daddy and Them, 2001, Scary Movie 2, 2001, The Others, 2001, Shu shan zheng zhuan, 2001, Jay and Silent Bob Strike Back, 2001, Lord of the Rings: The Fellowship of the Ring, 2001, Shipping News, 2001, Kate & Leopold, 2001, Only the Strong Survive, 2002, Full Frontal, 2002, Spy Kids 2: Island of Lost Dreams, 2002, Below, 2002, Equilibrium, 2002, Waking Up in Reno, 2002, Lord of the Rings: The Two Towers, 2002, Gangs of New York, 2002, Chicago, 2002, Confessions of a Dangerous Mind, 2002, Spy Kids 3-D: Game Over, 2003, The Human Stain, 2003, Duplex, 2003, Kill Bill: Vol. 1, 2003, Scary Movie 3, 2003, Bad Santa, 2003, Lord of the Rings: The Return of the King, 2003, Cold Mountain, 2003, Ella Enchanted, 2004, Kill Bill: Vol. 2, 2004, Fahrenheit 9/11, 2004, Finding Neverland, 2004, Shall We Dance, 2004, The Aviator, 2004, Cursed, 2005, Sin City, 2005, The Adventures of Sharkboy and Lavagirl 3-D, 2005, The Great Raid, 2005, The Brothers Grimm, 2005, Proof, 2005, Derailed, 2005, Scary Movie 4, 2006, Pulse, 2006, Breaking and Entering, 2006, School for Scoundrels, 2006, Factory Girl, 2006, The Ex, 2007, Grindhouse, 2007, 1408, 2007, Who's Your Caddy?, 2007, The Nanny Diaries, 2007, Halloween, 2007, Rogue, 2007, The Mist, 2007, Awake, 2007, The Great Debaters, 2007, Hell Ride, 2007, Rambo, 2008, The Promorion, 2008, Superhero Movie, 2008, Fanboys, 2008, The Longshots, 2008, Zack and Miri Make a Porno, 2008, The Meerkats, 2008, Soul Men, 2008, Killshot, 2008, The Reader, 2008, Crossing Over, 2009; co-exec. prodr.: (films) Scandal, 1989, The Lemon Sisters, 1990, The Big Man, 1990, Dust Devil, 1992, Pulp Fiction, 1994, Victory, 1995, Jane Eyre, 1996, She's So Lovely, 1997, Halloween H20: 20 Years Later, 1998, B. Monkey, 1998, Halloween: Resurrection, 2002; prodr. (TV series) The Real Magees, 1973, Wasteland, 1999, Clerks, 2000, Project Greenlight, 2001, Glory Days, 2002, Tokyo Pig, 2002, Project Runway, 2004-; exec. prodr.: (TV movies) The No 1 Ladies' Detective Agency, 2008, Unstable Fables: 3 Pigs & a Baby, 2008 Named one of The 50 Most Powerful People in Hollywood, Premiere mag., 2004—06. Office: Weinstein Co 345 Hudson St 13th Fl New York NY 10014 Office Phone: 646-862-3400. Office Fax: 917-368-7000.

WEINSTEIN, CAROL, psychiatrist; b. NYC; BS, Cornell U., 1980; MD, SUNY, Buffalo, 1984. Cert. psychiatry. Psychiatrist, co-med. dir., med. dir. inpatients units Four Winds Hosp., Katonah, NY, 1988—92; asst. dir. psychiat. emergency svc. Montefiore Hosp. Ctr., Bronx, 1993—96, assoc. dir. psychiat. emergency svcs., 1996—97, assoc. dir. inpatient psychiatry, 1997—99; staff psychiatrist St. Vincents Westchester, Harrison, 1999—. Recipient Alumni award Contbn. Residency program, Cornell-N.Y. Hosp. Mem.: Am. Soc. Clin. Psychopharmacology, Am. Psychiat. Assn. Office: St Vincents Hosp 275 North St Harrison NY 10528

WEINSTEIN, EDWARD MICHAEL, architect, consultant; b. Bklyn., May 5, 1947; s. Hyman and Freda (Rochkes) W.; m. Melanie Jane Ross, June 22, 1969; children: Valerie, David. BS, CCNY, 1969. Registered architect; lic., NJ; NY. Jr. architect N.Y.C. Dept. Ports and Terminals, 1970-72, architect, 1972-75, sr. urban designer, 1975-80, dir. waterfront devel., 1980-84, asst. commr., 1984-87; pres. EMW Assocs., Hastings-On-Hudson, NY, 1984—; ptnr. The Hastings Design Group, Hastings-On-Hudson, 1987—2001; prin. Edward M. Weinstein, Planning and Architecture, 2001—02, Edward M. Weinstein, Architecture and Planning, P.C., 2002—. Adv. bd. Metro Marine Express Ltd., N.Y.C., 1989-91. Active Planning Bd., Hastings-on-Hudson, 1990-2000, Waterfront Ctr.; trustee Greenburgh Hebrew Ctr., Dobbs Ferry, N.Y., 1986-89, 92—; v.p. N.Y. Port Promotion Assn., N.Y.C., 1984-87; adv. com. on waterfront devel. N.Y. State Assembly; chair Village of Hastings-on-Hudson Waterfront Revitalization Com., 1999—. Recipient Gold Key award House Plan Assn., 1969. Mem. AIA, Am. Assn. Port Authority, N.Y. Soc. Architects, The Waterfront Ctr., CCNY Alumni Assn., Bklyn. Tech. H.S. Alumni Assn. (life), Am. Inst. of Cert. Planners, Mcpl. Art Soc. Democrat. Jewish. Avocations: tennis, art. Office: EMW Architecture and Planning PC 14 Spring St Hastings On Hudson NY 10706 Office Phone: 914-478-0800, 914-478-0800. Business E-Mail: edward@emweinsteinpc.com.

WEINSTEIN, HARRIS, lawyer; b. Providence, May 10, 1935; s. Joseph and Gertrude (Rusitzky) W.; m. Rosa Grunberg, June 3, 1956; children: Teme Ring, Joshua, Jacob. SB in Math., MIT, Cambridge, Mass., 1956, SM in Math., 1958; LLB, Columbia U., NYC, 1961. Bar: DC 1962. Law clk. to Judge William H. Hastie US Ct. Appeals (3d cir.), Phila., 1961-62; with Covington & Burling LLP, Washington, 1962-67, 69-90, 1993—; chief counsel Office of Thrift Supervision US Dept. Treasury, Washington, 1990-92; asst. to solicitor gen. US Dept. Justice, 1967-69. Pub. mem. Adminstrv. Conf. of US, 1982—90; lectr. U. Va. Law Sch., 1996; mgmt. com. Undiscovered Mgrs., LLC, 1998—2001; disting. lectr. Columbus Sch. Law, Cath. U. Am., 2007—. V.p. Jewish Social Svc. Agy., 1995—98; mem. MIT Corp., 1989—95; bd. dirs. Jewish Cmty. Rels. Coun. Greater Washington, 2004—08. Mem. Nat. Press Club. Home: 7717 Georgetown Pike Mc Lean VA 22102-1411 Office: Covington & Burling 1201 Pennsylvania Ave NW Washington DC 20004

WEINSTEIN, HARVEY, film company executive; b. Queens, NY, Mar. 19, 1952; s. Max and Miriam (Postel) Weinstein; m. Eva Chilton, 1987 (div. 2004); 3 children; m. Georgina Chapman, Dec. 15, 2007. Student, SUNY, Buffalo, 1969—73. With Harvey & Corkey Presents, Buffalo, 1973—79; co-founder, co-chmn. (with Bob Weinstein) Miramax Films Corp., NYC, 1979—2005; co-founder (with Bob Weinstein) The Weinstein Co., 2005—. Bd. dirs. Six Flags Inc., 2005—. Dir.: (films) Playing for Keeps, 1986, The Gnome's Great Adventure, 1987, Gandaharm, 1988; prodr.: (films) The Burning, 1981, Deep End, 1985, Playing for Keeps, 1986, Shakespeare in Love, 1998 (Acad. award for Best Picture, 1998, Golden Globe award best picture, 1998, Golden Satellite award Best Picture, 1998, BAFTA award best picture, 1999), Malena, 2000, Gangs of New York, 2002; exec. prodr.: (films) Hardware, 1990, Strike It Rich, 1990, The Pope Must Die, 1991, Benefit of the Doubt, 1993, Map of the Human Heart, 1993, The Night We Never Met, 1993, The Hour of the Pig, 1993, Mother's Boys, 1994, The Road Killers, 1994, Pret-a-Porter, 1994, The Englishman Who Went Up a Hill But Came Down a Mountain, 1995, Things to Do in Denver When You're Dead, 1995, Smoke, 1995, The Crossing Guard, 1995, A Month by the Lake, 1995, Blue in the Face, 1995, Beautiful Girls, 1996, Flirting With Disaster, 1996, The Pallbearer, 1996, Emma, 1996, I Love You, I Love You Not, 1996, The Crow: City of Angels, 1996, The English Patient, 1996, Nightwatch, 1997, Addicted to Love, 1997, Robinson Crusoe, 1997, Air Bud, 1997, Cop Land, 1997, The Wings of the Dove, 1997, Good Will Hunting, 1997, Scream 2, 1997, Jackie Brown, 1997, Wishful Thinking, 1997, The Prophecy II, 1998, A Price Above Rubies, 1998, Phantoms, 1998, Senseless, 1998, Wide Awake, 1998, Ride, 1998, Velvet Goldmine, 1998, The Mighty, 1998, 54, 1998, Heaven, 1998, Rounders, 1998, Talk of Angels, 1998, The Faculty, 1998, She's All That, 1999, Teaching Mrs. Tingle, 1999, Mansfield Park, 1999, Music of the Heart, 1999, The Cider House Rules, 1999, Down to You, 2000, The Crow: The Salvation, 2000, Scream 3, 2000, Love's Labour's Lost, 2000, Reindeer Games, 2000, Scary Movie, 2000, Highlander: Endgame, 2000, Bounce, 2000, Chocolat, 2000, Dracula, 2000, Spy Kids, 2001, Texas Rangers, 2001, Daddy and Them, 2001, Scary Movie 2, 2001, The Others, 2001, Jay and Silent Bob Strike Back, 2001, The Lord of the Rings: The Fellowship of the Ring, 2001, Iris, 2001, The Shipping News, 2001, Kate & Leopold, 2001, Spy Kids 2: Island of Lost Dreams, 2002, Waking Up in Reno, 2002, The Lord of the Rings: The Two Towers, 2002, Chicago, 2002, Confessions of a Dangerous Mind, 2002, Spy Kids 3-D: Game Over, 2003, The Human Stain, 2003, Duplex, 2003, Kill Bill: Vol. 1, 2003, Scary Movie 3, 2003, Bad Santa, 2003, The Lord of the Rings: The Return of the King, 2003, Cold Mountain, 2003, Ella Enchanted, 2004, The Aviator, 2004, Cursed, 2005, Sin City, 2005, The Adventures of Sharkboy and Lavagirl 3-D, 2005, The Great Raid, 2005, The Brothers Grimm, 2005, Proof, 2005, Derailed, 2005, Scary Movie 4, 2006, Pulse, 2006, Breaking and Entering, 2006, School for Scoundrels, 2006, Miss Potter, 2006, The Ex, 2007, Grindhouse, 2007, Sicko, 2007, 1408, 2007, Who's Your Caddy?, 2007, The Nanny Diaries, 2007, Halloween, 2007, Rogue, 2007, The Mist, 2007, Awake, 2007, The Great Debaters, 2007, Hell Ride, 2007, Rambo, 2008, The Promorion, 2008, Superhero Movie, 2008, Fanboys, 2008, The Longshots, 2008, Zack and Miri Make a Porno, 2008, The Meerkats, 2008, Soul Men, 2008, Killshot, 2008, The Reader, 2008, Crossing Over, 2009; co-exec. prodr.: (films) Scandal, 1989, The Lemon Sisters, 1990, Into the West, 1992, Pulp Fiction, 1994, Restoration, 1995, Jane Eyre, 1996, Scream, 1996, She's So Lovely, 1997, Mimic, 1997, Imposter, 2002; exec. prodr.: (TV movies) The No 1 Ladies' Detective Agency, 2008, Unstable Fables: 3 Pigs & a Baby, 2008; (TV series) Clerks, 2000, Project Greenlight, 2001, Glory Days, 2002, Tokyo Pig, 2002, Project Runway, 2004-; prodr.: (Broadway plays) The Real Thing, The Producers, 2001, Sweet Smell of Success, 2002, La Boheme, 2002, Gypsy, 2003, Wonderful Town, 2003, Never Gonna Dance, 2003, Dirty Rotten Scoundrels, 2005, All Shook Up, 2005, Chitty Chitty Bang Bang, 2005, Sweet Charity, 2005, The Color Purple, 2005. Recipient BAFTA Britannia award, 1996; named a Comdr. of the Order of the British Empire, Her Majesty Queen Elizabeth II, 2004; named one of The 50 Most Powerful People in Hollywood, Premiere mag., 2004—06. Democrat. Office: Weinstein Co 345 Hudson St 13 Fl New York NY 10014 Office Phone: 646-862-3400. Office Fax: 917-368-7000.*

WEINSTEIN, HERBERT, chemical engineer, educator; b. Bklyn., Mar. 10, 1933; s. Abraham and Pauline (Feldman) W.; m. Judith Cooper, Apr. 6, 1957; children: Michael Howard, Edward Marc, Ellen Rachel. B.Engring. in Chem. Engring, Coll. City N.Y., 1955; MS in Chem. Engring, Purdue U., 1957; PhD, Case Inst. Tech., 1963. Staff mem. Los Alamos Sci. Lab., 1956-58; research engr. NASA Lewis Research Center, Cleve., 1959-63; asst. prof. chem. engring. Ill. Inst. Tech., 1963-66, assoc. prof., 1966-72, prof., 1972-77; dir. Center for Biomed. Engring., 1973-77; prof. CUNY, 1977—2005, Herbert G. Kayser prof. of chem. engring., 1987—2003, dep. exec. officer PhD program, 2003—05, prof. emeritus, 2005—. Vis. rsch. assoc., mem. Med. Rsch. Inst. Michael Reese Hosp. and Med. Ctr., Chgo., 1965-77; vis. prof. mech. engring. Technion-Israel Inst. Tech., 1972-73; vis. prof. biomed. engring. Rush Med. Coll., Chgo., 1973-76; summer prof. Exxon Rsch. and Engring. Co., annually, 1981-92; Lady Davis vis. prof. Technion-Israel Inst. Tech., 1985; cons. to industry, rsch. labs. Mem.: Am. Inst. Chem. Engrs., Sigma Xi. Achievements include research publs. and patents on fluidization, chem. reactor engring., fluid mechanics, biomed. engring. Office: CUNY Dept Chem Engring New York NY 10031 Business E-Mail: hweinst@att.net, hweinst@ccny.cuny.edu.

WEINSTEIN, JACK BERTRAND, federal judge; b. Wichita, Kans., Aug. 10, 1921; s. Harry Louis and Bessie Helen (Brodach) W.; m. Evelyn Horowitz, Oct. 10, 1946; children: Seth George, Michael David, Howard Lewis. BA, Bklyn. Coll., 1943; LLB, Columbia U., 1948, LLD (hon.), 2004, Yeshiva U., Albany U., Hofstra U., L.I. U., Yale U., NYU, St. Francis Coll., 2007. Bar: N.Y. 1949. Assoc. Columbia Law Sch., 1948-49; law clk. N.Y. Ct. Appeals Judge Stanly H. Fuld, 1949-50; ptnr. William Rosenfeld, NYC, 1950-52; mem. faculty Columbia Law Sch., 1952-67, prof. law, 1956-67, adj. prof., 1967-97; U.S. judge (Eastern Dist. N.Y.), 1967-93, chief judge, 1980-88; sr. judge Ea. Dist. N.Y., 1993—. Vis. prof. U. Tex., 1957, U. Colo., 1961, Harvard U., 1982, Georgetown U., 1991, Bklyn. Law Sch., 1988-97, others; counsel N.Y. Joint Legis. Com. Motor Vehicle Problems, 1952-54, State Sen. Seymour Halpern, 1952-54; reporter adv. com. practice and procedure N.Y. State Temp. Commn. Cts., 1955-58; adv. com. practice N.Y. Judicial Conf., 1963-66; adv. com. rules of evidence U.S. Jud. Conf., 1965-75, mem. com. jurisdiction, 1969-75, mem., 1983-86; mem. 2d Cir. Jud. Coun., 1982-88, U.S. Jud. Conf., 1983-86, others in past. Author: (with Morgan and Maquire) Cases and Materials on Evidence, 4th edit, 1965, (with Maguire, Chadbourne and Mansfield, 5th edit.), 1971, 6th edit., 1975, (with Mansfield, Abrams and Berger), 9th edit., 1997, (with Rosenberg) Cases and Materials on Civil Procedure, 1961, rev. edit, (with Smit), 1971, (with Smit, Rosenberg and Korn), 1976, (with Korn and Miller) New York Civil Procedure, 9 vols., rev. edit, 1966, Manual of New York Civil Procedure, 1967, Basic Problems of State and Federal Evidence, 1976, (with Berger) Weinstein's Evidence, 7 vols., 1967, rev. edit., 1993, Revising Rule Making Procedures, 1977, A New York Constitution Meeting Today's Needs and Tomorrow's Challenges, 1967, Disaster, A Legal Allegory, 1988, (with Greenawalt) Readings for Seminar on Equality and Law, 1979, (with Murphy) Readings for Seminar in Individual Rights in a Mass Society, 1990-91, (with Berger) Readings for Seminar in Science and Law, (with Feinberg) Mass Torts, 1992, 94, Individual Justice in Mass Litigation, 1995. Chmn. N.Y. Dem. adv. com. on Constl. Conv., 1965; bd. dirs. N.Y. Civil Liberties Union, 1956-62, Cardozo Sch. Law, Conf. on Jewish Social Studies, 1980-88; nat. adv. bd. Am. Jewish Congress, 1960-67, CARE, 1985-90, Fedn. Jewish Philanthropies, 1985-94; chmn. lay bd. Riverside Hosp. Adolescent Drug Users, 1954-55. Lt. USNR, 1943-46. Mem. ABA, N.Y. State Bar Assn., Assn. of Bar of City of N.Y., Nassau County Bar Assn., Am. Law Inst., Soc. Pub. Tchrs. Law (Eng.), Am. Acad. Arts and Scis. Jewish. Office: US Dist Ct US Courthouse 225 Cadman Plz E Brooklyn NY 11201-1818 Office Phone: 718-613-2520.

WEINSTEIN, JAMES NEIL, orthopaedic surgeon; b. Chgo., June 7, 1950; s. Sheldon and Carolyn (Arkin) W.; m. Miriam Weinstein; 1 child, Brieanna. BS in Chemistry, Bradley U., 1972; postgrad., U. Ill. Med. Ctr., 1973; DO, Chgo. Coll. Osteopathic Medicine, 1977; postgrad., Rush-Presbyn. St. Luke's Med. Ctr., Chgo. Intern in orthopaedic surgery Rush-Presbyn. St. Luke's Med. Ctr., Chgo., 1978-79; resident in orthopaedic surgery St. Luke's Med. Ctr., Chgo., 1979-83, asst. instr. orthpaedic surgery, 1978-82, adj. attending orthopaedic surgeon, 1982-83; cons. VA Hosp., Iowa City, 1983—; asst. prof. orthopaedic surgery U. Iowa Hosps., Iowa City, 1983—. Instr., trainer CPR Am. Heart Assn., 1977-84; mem. med. sch. admissions com. Chgo. Coll. Osteopathic Medicine and Rush-Presbyn. St. Luke's Med. Ctr., 1977-82. Editorial advisor Iowa Orthopaedic Jour., 1984; contbr. numerous articles, abstracts and chpts. to books and profl. jours. Recipient Berkheiser award Inst. Medicine Chgo., 1980; Berg Sloat Traveling fellow, 1983-84; grantee Rehab. Engring. Ctr. U. Vt., 1984-85. Mem. N.Am. Spine Assn., Internat. Soc. Study Pain, N.Am. Research Inst., Sigma Sigma Phi. Home: PO Box 5249 Hanover NH 03755-5249

WEINSTEIN, JAY A., social sciences educator, researcher; b. Chgo., Feb. 23, 1942; s. Lawrence E. and Jacqueline L. (Caplan) W.; m. Diana S. Staffin, Sept. 16, 1961; m. Marilyn L. Schwartz, Nov. 25, 1972; children— Liza, Bennett. AB, U. Ill., 1963, PhD, 1973; MA, Washington U., St. Louis, 1965. Teaching fellow U. Ill., Urbana, 1963-64; teaching asst. McGill U., Montreal, Que., Canada, 1966-68; instr. Sir George Williams U., Montreal, Que., Canada, 1967-68; lectr. Simon Fraser U., Vancouver, B.C., Canada, 1968; asst. prof. North Central Coll., Naperville, Ill., 1970-71, U. Iowa, 1973-77; prof. social sci. Ga. Inst. Tech., Atlanta, 1977-86; head dept. sociology Eastern Mich. U., 1986-90, 2004—06, faculty rsch. fellow, 1990-91; grantee ednl. devel. project USIA-Soros Found., Albania, 1992—; dir. Applied Rsch. Unit, 1996—; vis. faculty, sociology U. North Fla., 2007—. Cons. World Bank Study Social and Econ. Vulnerability in Albania, 1997, World Bank Study on Closing the Vulnerability Gap, Albania, 1997—98; project dir. Ea. Mich.-U-Ypsilanti Cmty. Outreach Partnership Ctr.; cons. pvt. and pub. agencies; rschr. in field. Author: Madras: An Analysis of Urban Ecological Structure in India, 1974, Demographic Transition and Social Change, 1976, Sociology-Technology: Foundations of Postacademic Social Science, 1982, The Grammar of Social Relations: The Major Essays of Louis Schneider, 1984; editor: Paradox and Society, 1986; (with Vinod Tewari and V.L.S. Prakash Rao) Indian Cities: Ecological Perspectives, Social and Cultural Change: Social Science for a Dynamic World, 1997, 2005, The Holocaust: A Sociological Analysis, 1997, Demography: The Science of Population, 2000; Studies in Comparative International Development, 1978-88; mem. editorial bd. Social Development Issues, 1977-85; specialized contbr. Calcutta Mcpl. Gazette, 1979—; editor: Social and Cultural Change, 1974-75; editor Mich. Soc. Rev., 1997-2003, Jour. Applied Sociology, 2004—06; Applied Social Sci., 2006-, editl. reviewer Jour. Asian Studies, Social Devel. Issues, Tech. and Culture, Am. Sociologist, Technol. Forecasting and Social

Change; contbr. chpts. to book, articles to profl. jours. Recipient Charles Horton Cooley award for outstanding contbns. to sociology in Mich., 1998, Alex Boros award, 2005; Fulbright prof. Ahmedabad, India, 1975-76, Hyderabad, India, 1981-82; grantee Ga. Tech. Found., 1981-82, World Order Studies Course, 1994-97, State of Mich. Rsch. Excellence Fund; Steinberg fellow, 1967. Mem. Am. Sociol. Assn. (pres. 2002-03), Soc. for Applied Sociology (v.p. 1998-99, chair sociol. practice sect., 2004-05), mem. exec. bd. 2000, pres. 2002-03), Mich. Sociol. Assn. (pres. 1988-89, v.p. 1994-95), North Ctrl. Sociol. Assn. (pres. 2007-08, John F. Schnabel award for tchg. excellence), Sigma Xi, Phi Kappa Phi. Jewish. Office: Eastern Mich U Sociology Dept Ypsilanti MI 48197 Home Phone: 313-563-5292; Office Phone: 734-487-0012. E-mail: weinst@aol.com, jay.weinstein@emich.edu.

WEINSTEIN, JOYCE, artist; b. June 7, 1931; d. Sidney and Rose (Bier) W.; m. Stanley Boxer, Nov. 28, 1952. Student, CCNY, 1948-50, Art Students League, 1948-52. Exec. coord. Women in Arts Found., Inc., 1975-79, 81-82, coord. bd., 1983-87. One-person shows include Perdalma Gallery, NYC, 1953-56, L.I. U., Bklyn., 1969, U. Calif., Santa Cruz, 1969, T. Bortolazzo Gallery, Santa Barbara, Calif., 1972, Dorsky Gallery, NYC, 1972, 74, Galerie Ariadne, NYC, 1975, Gloria Cortella Gallery, NYC, 1976, Meredith Long Contemporary Gallery, NYC, 1978-79, 88-90, Martin Gerard Gallery, Edmonton, Alta., Can., 1981-82, 84, Galerie Wentzel, Cologne, Fed. Republic of Germany, 1982, 87, Haber Theodore Gallery, NYC, 1983, 95, Gallery One, Toronto, Ont., Can., 1983, 2002, Paul Kuhn Gallery, Calgary, 1985, Eva Cohn Gallery, Highland Park, Ill., 1985, Meredith Long & Co., Houston, 1988, 90, Alena Adlung Gallery, NYC, 1989, Flanders Contemporary Art, Mpls., 1999, 2005, Harmon-Meek Gallery, Naples, Fla., 2000, Gallery One, Toronto, 2002, Flanders Contemporary Art, Mpls., 2005, Ezair Gallery, NYC, 2007; exhibited in group shows at Marlborough Gallery, NYC, 1968, Bula Mus. Art, Calcutta, India, 1970, Phoenix Gallery, NYC, 1988, Provident Nat. Bank, 1988, Alena Adlung Gallery, 1989-90, Edmonton Art Mus., 1975, 77, 83, 85, 89, Rose Fried Gallery, NYC, 1970, Hudson River Mus., 1971, Dorsky Gallery, 1972, 94, Suffolk Mus., Stony Brook, NY, 1972, NY Cultural Ctr., 1973, Stamford (Conn.) Mus., 1973, Landmark Gallery, NYC, 1974, Women's Interart Ctr., NYC, 1974-75, 78, New Sch. Social Rsch., NYC, 1975, Bklyn. Mus., 1975, Galerie Ariadne, 1975, Mus. Modern Art, NYC, 1981, Queens Mus. NY, 1984, Centre de Creacio Contemporania, Barcelona, Spain, 1987, Fairleigh Dickinson U., Hackensack, NJ, 1976, Gloria Cortella, Inc., 1976, Northeastern U., Boston, 1977, Lehigh (Pa.) U., 1977, Meredith Long Contemporary Gallery, 1977, 78, 79, 80, Galerie Wentzel, 1981-85, Martin Gerard Gallery, 1981-84, Gallery One, 1983-84, Haber Theodore Gallery, 1982-85, Jerald Melberg Gallery, Charlotte, NC, 1984, Richard Green Gallery, NYC, 1986, Rosel Art Fair, Basel Switzerland, 1986, Meredith Long & Co., 1988-90, Broome St. Gallery, NYC, 1991, 97, Andre Zarre Gallery, NYC, 1990, Cork Gallery, NYC, 1990, Chgo. Internat. Art Exbn., 1990, Queens Coll., NYC, 1991, Miami Art Fair, 1993, Bklyn. Botanic Gardens, 1994, Dorothy Blau Gallery, Bay Harbor Islands, Fla., 1997-98, Harmon-Meek Gallery, Naples, Fla., 1998-99, Flanders Contemporary Art, Mpls., 1999, 2005, Hubert Gallery, NYC, 2003; represented in permanent collections: Pa. Acad. Fine Arts, NJ State Mus., Ciba-Geigy Corp., New Sch. Social Rsch., Bula Mus. Art, U. Calif., Mus. Modern Art, NYC, McMullen Gallery, Edmonton, Ga., De Spisset Mus., U. Santa Clara, Edmonton Art Gallery Mus., The Hines Collection, Boston, others; represented by Flanders Contemporary Art, Mpls., Gallery One, Toronto, Yellow Bird Gallery, Newburg, NY, Amy Simon Fine Art, Westport, Conn. Recipient Lambert Fund award Pa. Acad. Fine Arts, 1955, Susan B. Anthony award NOW, 1983. Home: 46 Fox Hill Rd Ancramdale NY 12503-5311 Office Phone: 518-329-0614. Personal E-mail: weinsteinjoyce@aol.com.

WEINSTEIN, KENNETH N., federal government administrator; b. NYC, Sept. 29, 1946; BS, Yale U., 1968, JD, 1974. Bar: Conn. 1974, DC 1980. Honors atty. Dept. Transp., Wash., DC, 1974—75; trial atty. (aeronautics) Fed. Aviation Adminstrn., 1975—78; trial atty. office of gen. counsel Dep. Transp., 1978—81; dep. asst. gen. counsel Dept. Transp., Wash., 1981—88, asst. chief, coun. for litig., 1988—97, assoc. adminstr. for enforcement, 1997—2005, NHTSA; counsel Mayer, Brown LLP, 2005—. Recipient SES Performance awards, 1990—2001, Presidential Rank award, 2002. Office: Mayer Brown LLP 1909 K Street NW Washington DC 20006-1101 Office Phone: 202-263-3259. Office Fax: 202-263-3300. Business E-Mail: kweinstein@mayerbrown.com.

WEINSTEIN, KENNETH R., think-tank executive; b. NYC, Nov. 4, 1961; s. Victor and Hannelore S. Weinstein; m. Amy B. Kauffman, Nov. 10, 1996; children: Raina, Harrison, Eden. BA, U. Chgo., 1984; DEA in Soviet Studies, Institut d'Etudes Politiques de Paris, 1987; PhD in Polit. Sci., Harvard U., 1992. Rsch. fellow Hudson Inst., Indpls., 1991—94; dir. rsch. The New Citizenship Project, Washington, 1994—96; dir. govt. reform project The Heritage Found., Washington, 1996—98; dir. Washington office Shalem Ctr., 1998—99; v.p. Hudson Inst., 1999—, CEO, 2003—. Adj. prof. govt. Georgetown U., Washington, 1999—2000. Fellow Carrere Travelling fellow, Harvard U., 1986, Chateaubriand Fellowship for Social Sci. Rsch., French Fgn. Ministry, 1989; scholar, Govt. France, 1986. Jewish. Home: 1426 35th St NW Washington DC 20007 Office: Hudson Inst 1015 15th St NW Ste 600 Washington DC 20005-2605 E-mail: ken@hudsondc.org.*

WEINSTEIN, LEE S., endocrinologist; BS, MIT, Cambridge, 1979; MD, Columbia U., NY, 1983. Lic. Md., diplomate in internal medicine Am. Bd. Internal Medicine, 1986, in endocrinology & metabolism 1989. Chief Signal Transduction Sect., NIDDK, NIH, Bethesda, Md., 2005—. Recipient Leo Davidoff award, Albert Einstein Coll. Medicine. Mem.: AAAS, Am. Soc. Clin. Investigation, Am. Soc. Bone & Mineral Rsch., Endocrine Soc., Am. Diabetes Assn., Alpha Omega Alpha, Phi Beta Kappa. Office: NIDDK Nat Inst Health Bldg 10 Rm 8C101 Bethesda MD 20892-1752 Office Fax: 301-402-0374. Business E-Mail: leew@mail.nih.gov.

WEINSTEIN, LEONARD HARLAN, institute program director, educator; b. Springfield, Mass., Apr. 11, 1926; s. Barney Willard Weinstein and Ida Pauline (Feinberg) Weinstein Clark; m. Sylvia Jane Sherman, Oct. 15, 1950; children: Beth Rachel, David Harold (dec.). BS, Pa. State U., 1949; MS, U. Mass., 1950; PhD, Rutgers U., 1953. Postdoctoral fellow Rutgers U., New Brunswick, N.J., 1953-55; plant physiologist Boyce Thompson Inst., Yonkers, N.Y., 1955-63, program dir. Ithaca, N.Y., 1963-91, bd. dirs., 1976-96; dir. ecosystem rsch. ctr. Cornell U., Ithaca, 1988-90, William Boyce Thompson scientist emeritus, 1993—, adj. prof. dept. natural resources, 1979—96. Mem. rsch. adv. com. Oak Ridge Nat. Lab, 1985-87. Author 2 books; contbr. over 175 articles to profl. jours., chpts. to books. Mem. sci. adv. bd. EPA, Washington, 1988-91; mem. com. natural resources NASULGC, 1986-89; cons. Problem Caused by Airbone Fluoride Plants, 1958-2008. Grantee NIH, NSF, HEW, Am. Cancer Soc., NASA, EPA, DOE, USDA. Mem. Am. Soc. Plant Physiologists, Sigma Xi, Pi Alpha Xi, Gamma Sigma Delta. Home: 608 Cayuga Heights Rd Ithaca NY 14850-1424 Office: Cornell U 125 Boyce Thompson Inst Tower Rd Ithaca NY 14853 Home Phone: 607-257-3389; Office Phone: 607-254-1229. Business E-Mail: lhw4@cornell.edu.

WEINSTEIN, MARK JAY, opera general director; b. NYC, Oct. 7, 1955; s. Lawrence and Rhoda Joy (Stucker) W.; m. Susanne Irene Marsee, May 15, 1987; 1 child, Zachary. BA, Carleton Coll.; MBA, Harvard U. Asst. product mgr. Gen. Mills, Inc., Mpls., 1979-81; assoc. Strategic Planning Assocs., Washington, 1981-83; pres. Pierre Deux, Pleasantville, N.Y., 1993; exec. dir. NYC Opera, 1983-96; v.p. ops. Nat. Artists Mgmt. Co., NYC, 1996-97; exec. dir. Pitts. Opera, 1997-99, gen. dir., v.p., 1999—2008; exec. dir. Washington Nat. Opera, Washington, 2008—. Co-chair Nat. Endowment Arts Challenge Grants Panel, Washington, 1994; chmn. AGMA Pension and Health Funds; on site evaluator Nat. Endowment Arts, Washington, 1995, 97, 99, 2001-02; chair Arts Leadership, 2000, 2001; bd. dirs. Greater Pitts. Arts Alliance; bd. dirs., treas. Opera Am., 1999--. Office: Washington Nat Opera Ste 301 2600 Virginia Ave Washington DC 20037 Office Phone: 202-295-2420. Office Fax: 202-295-2479.*

WEINSTEIN, MARTIN, aerospace transportation and manufacturing executive, materials scientist; b. Mar. 3, 1936; s. Benjamin and Dora (Lemo) Weinstein; m. Sandra Rebecca Yaffie, June 5, 1961; children: Hilary Ann, Sarah Elizabeth, Joshua Aaron. BS in Metals Engring., Rensselaer Poly. Inst., Troy, NY, 1957; MS, MIT, Cambridge, 1960, PhD, 1961. Mgr. materials sci. Tycolabs., Waltham, Mass., 1961-69; tech. dir. turbine support divsn. Chromalloy Am. Corp., San Antonio, 1968-71, v.p., asst. gen. mgr., 1971-74, pres., 1975-79, Chromalloy Compressor Techs., San Antonio, 1979-82; group pres. Chromalloy Gas Turbine, San Antonio, 1982-86, chmn., CEO NYC, 1986—; vice chmn., exec. officer SEQUA Corp., NYC, 2004—05, vice chmn., CEO, 2005—09. Supervisory mng. dir. Turbine Support Europe, Tilburg, Netherlands, 1975—2009; bd. dirs. Sequa Corp., NYC, 1999—2009, vice chmn., CEO, 2004; bd. dirs. Turbine Support Thailand, Bangkok, Chromalloy UK, Nottingham, England, Malichaud Orleans, France. Contbr. articles to profl. jours. Bd. dirs. Chamber Players San Antonio, 1979—83, NCCJ, 1982—85, Jewish Fedn., 1981—85; mem. vis. com. dept. metallurgy and materials sci. MIT, 1992—2001. Recipient Turner Meml. award, Electrochem. Soc., 1963, Achievement award, NASA, 1963, Fellows award, Rensselaer Alumni Assn., 2006; Am. Iron and Steel Inst. fellow, 1960. Mem.: NY Acad. Sci., Am. Inst. Metall. Engrs., Am. Soc. Metals, Sigma Xi. Achievements include patents for diffusion coating of jet engine materials. Home: 111 Sheffield San Antonio TX 78213-2626 Office: Chromalloy Gas Turbine Corp 4430 Director Dr San Antonio TX 78220 Home Phone: 210-344-0028; Office Phone: 210-359-5534. Personal E-mail: martin.weinsteintx@gmail.com.

WEINSTEIN, MELVIN PHILLIP, physician educator; b. Long Branch, NJ, Apr. 27, 1944; s. Joseph and Selma Joyce (Nathanson) W.; m. Dustra Lee Anderson, July 13, 1969; children: Joanna Lee, Michael Jacob. BA in Zoology with distinction, Rutgers U., 1966; MD, George Washington U., 1970. Diplomate Nat. Bd. Med. Examiners, Am. Bd. Internal Medicine, Am. Bd. Infectious Diseases, Am. Bd. Pathology (Med. Microbiology). Intern Hartford (Conn.) Hosp., 1970-71, resident, 1973-75; fellow in infectious diseases U. Colo. Health Sci. Ctr., Denver, 1975-77, fellow in clin. microbiology, 1983; asst. prof. medicine U. Medicine and Dentistry N.J., New Brunswick, 1977-83, assoc. prof. medicine and pathology, 1983-91, prof. medicine and pathology, 1991—; staff Robert Wood Johnson U. Hosp., New Brunswick, 1977—. Cons. staff St. Peter's U. Hosp., 1998-2005; cons. Roosevelt Hosp., Edison, N.J., 1986-89; vis. assoc. prof. Rutgers U., New Brunswick, 1986-98; vis. prof. Rutgers U. Coll. Pharmacy, 1998—; trustee Am. Bd. Med. Microbiology, Washington, 1991-97; mem. area com. on microbiology, 1997-2003, mem. subcom. antimicrobial susceptibility testing Clin. and Lab. Stds. Inst., Wayne, Pa., 1993—, vice chair area com. on microbiology, 1998-2002; dir. Microbiology Lab., Robert Wood Johnson U. Hosp., New Brunswick, 1983—, HIV-Antibody Counselling and Testing Svc., 1985-87, 91—; chief divsn. of allergy, immunology and infectious diseases Robert Wood Johnson Med. Sch., 2001—; lectr. in field. Mem. editl. bd. Jour. Clin. Microbiology, 1984-99, Am. Jour. Infection Control, 1987-2000, Diagnostic Microbiology and Infectious Disease, 1989—, Clin. Microbiol. Rev., 2002-; sect. editor Clin. Infectious Diseases, Manual Clin. Microbiology, 8th, 9th and 10th edit.; contbr. chpts. to books, articles to profl. jours. Comdr. USPHS, 1971-73. Henry Rutgers Rsch. fellow, 1965-66. Fellow ACP, Infectious Diseases Soc. Am., Am. Acad. Microbiology; mem. Am. Fedn. Clin. Rsch., Am. Soc. Microbiology (BD award for rsch. in Clin. Microbiology 2004), Soc. Hosp. Epidemiologists Am., N.J. Infectious Disease Soc. (founding mem.), Alpha Omega Alpha. Avocation: golf. Office: Robert Wood Johnson Med Sch 1 Robert Wood Johnson Pl New Brunswick NJ 08901-1928 Office Phone: 732-235-7713.

WEINSTEIN, MICHAEL ALAN, political science professor; b. Bklyn., Aug. 24, 1942; s. Aaron and Grace W.; m. Deena, May 31, 1964. BA summa cum laude, NYU, 1964; MA in Polit. Sci., Case Western Res. U., 1965, PhD, 1967. Asst. prof. polit. sci. Case Western Res. U., summer 1967, Va. Poly. Inst., 1967-68; asst. prof. Purdue U., 1968-70, assoc. prof., 1970-72, prof., 1972—; Milward Simpson disting. prof. polit. sci. U. Wyo., 1979; columnist Garoweonline.com, 2008—. Author: (with Deena Weinstein) Living Sociology, 1974, The Polarity of Mexican Thought, 1976, The Tragic Sense of Political Life, 1977, Meaning and Appreciation, 1978, The Structure of Human Life, 1979, The Wilderness and the City, 1982, Unity and Variety in the Philosophy of Samuel Alexander, 1984, Finite Perfection, 1985, Culture Critique: Fernand Dumont and New Quebec Sociology, 1985, (with Helmut Loiskandl and Deena Weinstein) Georg Simmel's Scopenhauer and Nietzsche, 1986; (with Deena Weinstein) Deconstruction as Cultural History/The Cultural History of Deconstruction, 1990, La Déconstruction un Jeu Symbolique, 1990, (with Deena Weinstein) Georg Simmel: Sociological Flâmeur/Bricoleur, 1991, Photographic Realism as a Moral Practice, 1992, (with Deena Weinstein) Postmodern(ized) Simmel, 1993, (with Arthur Kroker) Data Trash: The Theory of the Virtual Class, 1994, Culture/Flesh: Explorations of Postcivilized Modernity, 1995, Peter Viereck Reconciliation and Beyond, 1997, East/West: Globalizing Civilization, 2000, (with Deena Weinstein) Hail to the Shrub: Mediating the President, 2002, The Power of Silence and the Limits of Discourse at Oliver Wendell Holmes's Breakfast Table, 2005, The Imaginative Prose of Oliver Wendell Holmes, 2006; artist in residence Columbia Coll., 2002; mem. editl. bd. Humanitas, Social Philosophy Rsch. Book Series. Recipient Best Paper prize Midwest Polit. Sci. Assn., 1969; Guggenheim fellow, 1974-75; Rockefeller Found. humanities fellow, 1976; fellow Center Humanistic Studies, Purdue U., 1981, Lily Endowment Tchg. grant, 2001. Mem. Phi Beta Kappa. Home: 800 Princess Dr West Lafayette IN 47906-2038 Office: Dept Polit Sci Purdue U West Lafayette IN 47907 *And which is worse, to be arbitrary or to be contradictory? I have attempted to be the most consistent rationalist of all by refusing to harmonize what is irreconcilable in the name of reason.*

WEINSTEIN, MICHAEL P., marine scientist, administrator; s. Jack and Beatrice Weinstein; m. Yael Sisso, Dec. 22, 1991; children: Heather Ann Campbell, Lee Thomas. BA, Hofstra U., 1966; MS, Rutgers U., 1969; PhD, Fla. State U., 1975. Pres. TEVA Environ. Associates, Millburn, 1984—96; pres., CEO NJ. Marine Sciences Consortium, Fort Hancock, 1996—. Author: Concepts and Controversies in Tidal Marsh Ecology, 2000 (Gov.'s Tourism award, 2004, Coastal Am. Spirit award, 2006, Gov.'s Environ. Quality award, 2006); contbr. chapters to books, more than 150 articles to profl. jours. Mem. working group, bd. dirs. Nat. Transp. Rsch. Bd., Nat. Acads., Washington, 2003—04. Grantee, various fed. and state agys., 1970—.

WEINSTEIN, MILTON CHARLES, decision scientist, educator; b. Brookline, Mass., July 14, 1949; s. William and Ethel (Rosenbloom) W.; m. Rhonda Kruger, June 14, 1970; children: Jeffrey William, Daniel Jay. AB, AM, Harvard U., 1970, MPP, 1972, PhD, 1973. Asst. prof. John F. Kennedy Sch. Govt., Harvard U., Cambridge, Mass., 1973-76, assoc. prof., 1976-80; prof. policy and decision scis. Harvard Sch. Pub. Health, Boston, 1980-86, Henry J. Kaiser prof. health policy and mgmt., 1986—; prof. medicine Harvard Med. Sch., Boston, 1992—2005; v.p. Innovus Rsch. Inc., Medford, Mass., 1998—; prin. cons. i3 Innovus, Medford, 2005—. Adj. prof. cmty. and family medicine Dartmouth Med. Sch., Hanover, N.H., 1981-87; vis. lectr. Intermountain Health Care, Salt Lake City, 1997—; cons. U.S. Office Tech. Assessment, 1979-87, HHS, 1979—, VA, 1984-86, EPA, 1983—, New Eng. Med. Ctr., 1986-87, Intermountain Health Care, 1987—; mem. adult treatment panel Nat. Cholesterol Edn. Program, NIH; co-chair Panel on Cost-Effectiveness in Health and Medicine, USPHS, 1993-96. Author: Clinical Decision Analysis, 1980, Hypertension: A Policy Perspective, 1976, Cost-Effectiveness in Health and Medicine, 1996, Decision Making in Health and Medicine, 2001; mem. editl. bd. Med. Decision Making, 1981-94, Jour. Environ. Econs. and Mgmt., 1986-88, Jour. Clin. Oncology, 1996-99; assoc. editor Med. Decision Making, 1994-2001. NSF fellow, 1972. Mem. Inst. Medicine of NAS (com. on priorities new vaccine devel., com. to evaluate the NIH artificial heart program), Soc. Med. Decision Making (trustee 1980-82, pres. 1984-85), Internat. Health Econs. Assn., Internat. Soc. Pharmacoens. and Outcomes Rsch., Am. Med. Joggers Assn., US Speedskating (bd. dirs. 1996-00), Phi Beta Kappa.

WEINSTEIN, PHILIP, neurosurgeon, educator; b. Md. AB, Princeton U., NJ, 1961; MD, NYU Coll. Medicine, NYC, 1965. Diplomate Am. Bd. Neurol. Surgery, 1975. Chief, neurospinal disorders program U. Calif., chmn., resident edn. com., dept. neurosurgery, 1983—, prof. neurosurgery, 1984—, mem., Ad Hoc peer rev. com., 1988—, dir., neuro-spinal divsn., neurol. surgery, 2000—, mem., promotional and tenure com., 2003—. Staff surgeon USAF Regional Hosp., Mar. AFB, Calif., 1971—73; cons. neurosurgeon US Pub. Health Svc. Hosp., San Francisco, 1974—77; cons. neurosurgeon, Barrow Neurol. Inst. St. Joseph's Hosp., Phoenix, 1978—82, staff neurosurgeon, Tucson, 1980—82; staff, neurosurgeon Vets. Adminstrn. Hosp., San Francisco, 1982—, cons. neurosurgeon, Livermore, Fresno, Reno, 1982—, Children's Hosp. Med. Ctr., San Francisco, 1983—89; staff neurosurgeon Mt. Zion Hosp., San Francisco, 1990—. Contbr. articles to numerous med. jours. Grantee, VA Merit Rev. Program, San Francisco, 1983—98, U. Calif., Berkely, 1983—89, U. Calif. San Francisco, 1985—96, Neurogenesis After Focal Cerebral Ischemia, VA Merit Rev. Program, San Francisco, CA, 1999—2003; NINDBS grant, U. Ariz. Health Scis. Ctr., 1980—83, Extramural Faculty grant, NIH, U. Calif. San Francisco, 1996—2000, 1999—2004. Fellow: ACS; mem.: AMA, Am. Assn. Neurol. Surgeons, Internat. Soc. Study Pain, Congress Neurol. Surgeons, Calif. Assn. Neurol. Surgeons, Calif. Med. Soc., San Francisco Med. Soc., Internat. Soc. Cerebral Blood Flow and Metabolism, Internat. Soc. Neurovascular Surgery, Rsch. Soc. Neurol. Surgery, Soc. Neurosci., Am. Assn. Neurol. Surgeons and Joint Sect. Spinal Surgery, Am. Assn. Neurol. Surgeons Sect. Cerebrovascular Surgery, Soc. Neurol. Surgeons, Western Neurosurg. Soc., Rocky Mountain Neurol. Soc., Stroke Coun. Am. Heart Assn., San Francisco Neurol. Soc. Office: Univ Calif San Francisco 505 Parnassus Ave M780 San Francisco CA 94143 Office Fax: 415-353-3907.

WEINSTEIN, PHILIP MERRILL, lawyer; b. Providence, Nov. 12, 1942; s. Sidney and Isabelle W.; m. Nancy F. Freedman; children: Benjamin, Noah. BS, Boston U., 1965; JD, Howard U., 1968. Bar: Mass., R.I., U.S. Dist. Ct. Mass., U.S. Dist. Ct. R.I. Ptnr. Decof, Weinstein & Mandell, Providence, 1972-80; sole practice Providence, 1980-87; ptnr. Weinstein & Doren, Providence; pvt. practice. Mem. bd. trustees Gordon Sch., Providence, 1985—, Cmty. Prep Sch., Providence, 1999—; past pres. Temple Beth David. Fellow (life) RI Bar Found.; mem. ABA, Assn. Trial Lawyers Am., RI Trial Lawyers Assn, Mass. Bar Assn. (mem. exec. com., ho. of delegates, 1985-), RI Bar Assn. (mem. ho. of delegates, 1972-, mem. exec. com., v.p., pres.), Phi Sigma Delta. Avocations: sports, flute, cooking.

WEINSTEIN, ROBERT A., physician, medical educator, director, medical researcher; MD, Cornell U., 1972. COO CORE Ctr., Chgo., 1998—; interim chmn. dept. medicine Cook County Hosp., Chgo., 2008—; dir. infectious diseases Cook County Bur. Health Svcs., Chgo., 1996—; C. Anderson Hedberg prof. medicine Rush Med. Coll., Chgo., 2008—. Contbr. numerous articles to profl. jours., chpts. in books. Lt. cdr. Epidemic Intelligence Svc. Fellow: ACP, Infectious Disease Soc. of Am. Office: John Stroger Hosp Cook County 1900 Haurism St Rm 1509 Adminstrn Bldg Chicago IL 60612

WEINSTEIN, ROY, physics professor; b. NYC, Apr. 21, 1927; s. Harry and Lillian (Ehrenberg) W.; m. Janet E. Spiller, Mar. 26, 1954 (dec. 1995); children: Lee Davis, Sara Lynn; m. Gail A. Birdsell, July 26, 1996. BS, MIT, 1951, PhD, 1954; ScD (hon.), Lycoming Coll., 1981. Rsch. asst. Mass. Inst. Tech., 1951-54, asst. prof., 1956—59, Brandeis U., Waltham, Mass., 1954-56; assoc. prof. Northeastern U., Boston, 1960-63, prof. physics, 1963-82, exec. officer, chmn. grad. div. of physics dept., 1967-69, chmn. physics dept., 1974-81; spokesman MAC Detector Stanford U., 1981-82; dean Coll. Natural Scis. and Math. U. Houston, 1982-88; prof. physics, 1982—; dir. Inst. Beam Particle Dynamics U. Houston, 1985-95; assoc. dir., spokesman Tex. Ctr. for Superconductivity, 1987-89. Vis. scholar and physicist Stanford (Calif.) U., 1966-67, 81-82; bd. dirs. Perception Tech., Inc., Winchester, Mass., Omniwave Inc., Gloucester, Mass., Wincom Inc., Woburn, Mass.; cons. Visidyne Inc., Burlington, Mass., Houston Area Rsch. Ctr., Stanford U., Hodotector Inc., Houston, Park Square Engring., Marietta, Ga., Harvard U., Cambridge, Mass., Cambridge Electron Accelerator, mem. adv. com., 1967-69; adv. com. and portfolio evaluation com. Houston Venture Ptnrs., 1990-99; chmn. bd. dirs. Xytron Corp., 1986-91; dir., mem. exec. com. Houston Area Rsch. Ctr., 1984-87; chmn. organizing com. Internat. Conf. on Meson Spectroscopy, 1974, chmn. program com., 1977, mem. organizing com., 1980; chmn. mgmt. group Tex. Accelerator Ctr., Woodlands, 1985-90; chmn. Tex. High Energy Physicists, 1989-91; keynote spkr. MIT Alumni series, 1988; permanent mem. exec. com. Large Vol. Detector (Underground Neutrino Telescope, Italy), 1988—; organizer session High Temperature Superconducting Magnets 3d and 4th World Congress on Superconductivity, Munich, 1993, Orlando, 1994. Author: Atomic Physics, 1964, Nuclear Physics, 1964, Interactions of Radiation and Matter, 1964; editor: Nuclear Reactor Theory, 1964, Nuclear Materials, 1964; editor procs.: 5th Internat. Conf. on Mesons, 1977; contbr. over 200 articles to profl. jours. Mem. Lexington (Mass.) Town Meeting, 1973-84; vice chmn. Lexington Coun. on Aging, 1977-83. With USNR, 1945-46. Recipient Founders award World Congress Superconductivity, 1988, Materials/Devices award Internat. Superconductivity Technology Ctr., Japan, and Materials Rsch. Soc., 1995, High Current award, 1997, award Internat. Program Com. Processing and Applications of Large Superconducting Rare Earth Grains Worshop, 1999, NSF Rsch. awards, 1961-96, Tex. Rsch. award, 1986-87, 90—, US Dept. Energy award 1974, 77, 87-97, NASA award, 1990-98, 2004-2006, ARO award, 1994—, Elec. Power Rsch. Inst. award, 1990-95, Welch Found. award, 1997—, Nat. Cancer Inst. award, 2000-04; NSF fellow Bohr Inst., Copenhagen, 1959-60, Stanford U. 1969-70, Guggenheim fellow Harvard U., 1970-71. Fellow Am. Phys. Soc. (organizer session SSC and High Energy Physics 1984); mem. Am. Assn. Physics Tchrs., Masons, Sigma Xi, Phi Kappa Phi (chpt. pres. 1977-79, Nat. Triennial Disting. Scholar prize 1980-83), Pi Lambda Phi (pres. Theta chpt. 1949-50). Unitarian Universalist. Achievements include measurement of fine structure of positronium; first measurement of rho meson coupling to gamma rays, of phi meson decay to two muons; early observation of break down in SU3 symmetry; demonstration of electron-muon universality, discovery of non-applicability of Lorentz contraction to length measured by a single observer; disproof of splitting of A2 meson; independent discovery of upsilon meson (bottom quark); achievement of highest magnetic field for any permanent magnet, in YBa2Cu307, 10.1 Tesla; achievement of highest current density in textured superconductor, 0.8 megA/cm2 & encoated conductor 0.7 megA/cm2 at 1 Tesla; development of MILD pinning centers for high temperature superconductor. Home: 4368 Fiesta Ln Houston TX 77004-6603 Office: U Houston IBPD 632 SR1 Houston TX 77204-5005

WEINSTEIN, SAMUEL, thoracic surgeon, pediatrician, researcher; b. NYC, Oct. 9, 1962; children: Dalia Jordyn, Douglas Jacob. BA, U. Pa., Phila., 1984; MD, SUNY, 1989. Cardiothoracic surg. fellow Columbia Presbyn., NYC, 1996—97; congenital cardiothoracic surgery fellow Children's Hosp. Phila., 1998—99; attending physician Children's Hosp., Columbus, Ohio, 1999—. Bd. dirs. Heart Care Internat., Greenwhich, Conn. Mem.: Am. Bd. Surgery. Achievements include research in the effects of pulsatile perfusion on cardiac function; single ventricle revision with antiarrythmic surgery. Office: Childrens Hosp Columbus 700 Children's Dr Columbus OH 43205 Business E-Mail: weinstes@chi.osu.edu.

WEINSTEIN, SHARON SCHLEIN, corporate communications executive, educator; b. Newark, Apr. 15, 1942; d. Louis Charles and Ruth Margaret (Franzblau) Schlein; m. Elliott Henry Weinstein, May 7, 1978. BA, U. Pa., 1964; MA, New Sch. for Social Rsch., NYC, 1985. Sr. editor Merrill Lynch, NYC, 1972-74; pub. rels. officer Chase Manhattan Bank, NYC, 1974-79; mgr. corp. communication Sanford C. Berstein & Co., NYC, 1980-83; v.p. corp. affairs Nat. Westminster Bancorp, NYC, 1983-95; dir. corp. comms. Nat. Securities Cleaning Corp., NYC, 1995-98; asst. v.p. corp. comm. Guardian Life Ins. Co., NYC, 1998—2002; comms. mgr. Zurich N.Am., NYC, 2002—. Adj. asst. prof. NYU, 1988—. Home: 161 W 15th St New York NY 10011-6720

WEINSTEIN, STANLEY, Buddhist studies educator; b. Bklyn., Nov. 13, 1929; s. Louis Arthur and Ruth (Appleson) W.; m. Lucie Ruth Krebs, Sept. 23, 1951; 1 son, David Eli. BA, Komazawa U., Tokyo, 1954-58; MA, U. Tokyo, 1960; PhD, Harvard U., 1966; MAH (hon.), Yale U., 1974. Lectr. Sch. Oriental and African Studies, London, 1962-68; assoc. prof. Buddhist studies Yale U., New Haven, 1968-74, prof., 1974—2003, prof. emeritus, 2003—, chmn. coun. East Asian studies, 1982-85. Author: Buddhism under T'ang, 1987. Served with U.S. Army, 1952-54. Ford Found. fgn. area fellow, 1958-62; NEH sr. fellow, 1974-75 Mem. Am. Oriental Soc., Assn. Asian Studies Home: 270 Ridgewood Ave Hamden CT 06517-1426 Business E-Mail: stanley.weinstein@yale.edu.

WEINSTEIN-BLACKMAN, ELLEN DONNA, school psychologist; b. NYC, May 3, 1948; d. Bernard and Evelyn Estelle (Leifer) W. BA, Barnard Coll., 1969; MS in Psychology, Northeastern U., 1973; MS in Mgmt., Purdue U., 1980; EdS, Nat. Louis U., 1991. Instr. Hunter Coll. CUNY, 1973-75, Poly. Inst. N.Y., Bklyn., 1976-78; sr. cons. Bernard Kaufman Cons., Huntington Valley, Pa., 1978-82; mktg. rep. Radio Shack Computer Ctr., Aurora, Ill., 1981-82; contr. MEDX Incorp., Rolling Meadows, Ill., 1986-87; data processing mgr. IML MIL Imaging, Inc., Ill., 1983-88; instr. Nat. Louis U., 1993—99; sch. psychologist La Grange Dept. Special Edn., Ill., 1994—. Contbr. articles to profl. jours. Area rep. Barnard Coll. Mem. NASP, Columbia U. Club Chgo. (v.p. 1985-86), Ill. Sch. Psychologists Assn. (budget, fin. chair 1998-2009, treas. 2009-), Zonta Internat, Ill. Edn. Assn. (regional rep., 2007-). Avocations: tennis, travel, photography. Home: 400 Joseph Ct Oswego IL 60543-7315 Business E-Mail: ellenweinstein@ladse.org.

WEINSTOCK, LEONARD, lawyer; b. Bklyn., Aug. 18, 1935; s. Samuel Morris and Evelyn (Reiser) W.; m. Rita Lee Itkowitz, May 25, 1963; children: Gregg Douglas, Valerie Lisa, Tara Diane. BS, Bklyn. Coll., 1956; JD, St. John's U., Bklyn., 1959. Bar: N.Y. 1961, U.S. Supreme Ct. 1964, U.S. Ct. Appeals (2d cir.) 1963, U.S. Dist. Ct. (ea. and so. dists.) N.Y. 1963, U.S. Tax Ct. 1963. Assoc. Bernard Helfenstein law practice, Bklyn., 1962-63; supr. All State Ins. Co., Bklyn., 1963-64; atty. Hertz Corp., NYC, 1964-65; ptnr. Nicholas & Weinstock, Flushing, NY, 1965-68; v.p., ptnr. Garbarini & Scher, P.C., NYC, 1968—. Lectr. Practicing Law Inst., N.Y.C., 1975—; arbitrator Nassau County Dist. Ct., Mineola, N.Y., 1979—, U.S. Dist. Ct. (ea. dist.) N.Y. 1986—; mem. Med. Malpractice Mediation Panel, Mineola, 1978—. Legal counsel Massapequa Soccer Club, N.Y., 1981—; county committeeman Dem. Party, Massapequa Park, N.Y., 1979—. With U.S. Army, 1959-62. Mem. ABA, N.Y. State Bar Assn., Nassau County Bar Assn. (mem. med. jurisprudence ins. com. 1978), N.Y. Trial Lawyers Assn. Avocations: stamp collecting/philately, softball, racquetball. Office: Garbarini and Scher PC 432 Park Ave S New York NY 10016-8013 Home: 925 Roosevelt Way Westbury NY 11590 Office Phone: 212-689-1113.

WEINSTOCK, MARTIN ARTHUR, dermatologist, epidemiologist, educator; b. NYC, Oct. 31, 1956; s. Irvin and Mae Weinstock; m. Gail Gilkey, June, 1981; children: Hannah, Clara. BA in Math. summa cum laude, Williams Coll., 1977; MPhil in Epidemiology, Columbia U., 1981, PhD in Epidemiology, 1982, MD, 1983; MA (hon.), Brown U., 1995. Diplomate Am. Bd. Dermatology; lic. Mass., R.I. Resident in internal medicine U. Pitts. Hosps., 1983-84; resident in dermatology Harvard U. Hosps., Boston, 1984-87; Andrew W. Mellon Found. fellow in clin. epidemiology Harvard Med. Sch., Boston, 1987-88; chief of dermatology, staff physician Dept. Vets. Affairs Med. Ctr., Providence, 1988—; asst. prof. medicine (dermatology) Brown U., 1988—94, assoc. prof. medicine (dermatology), 1994—96, dir. rsch., divsn. dermatology, 1995—96, assoc. prof. dermatology, 1996—98, dir. rsch., dept. dermatology, 1996—, prof. dermatology, 1998—2003, prof. dermatology and cmty. health, 2003—. Staff physician Mass. Gen. Hosp. Chelsea Health Ctr., Boston, 1985-86, South Boston Community Health Ctr., 1986-88, Dept. Medicine Children's Hosp., Boston, 1987-88, Miriam Hosp., Providence, 1994-2002, RI Hosp., 1994-; dir. RI pigmented lesion unit, dir., photomedicine, Roger Williams Med. Ctr., Providence, 1988-97, 1997-, staff physician, 1988-98; vis. prof., Skin Diseases Rsch. Ctr., Case Western Reserve U., 2000; mem. med. faculty exec. com., Brown U., 2001-04, vice-chair, 2001-02, chair 2002-03, past chair, 2003-04; mem. exec. com., Brown U. 2002-03, and others. Mem. editl. bd. Jour. Am. Acad. Dermatology, 1993-98, asst. editor 1998-, Jour. Cutaneous Medicine and Surgery (also editor), 1995-97, Dermatology Lexicon Project, 2003-04, others; guest editl. bd. Health Edn. and Behavior, 1998; contbg. editor, Year Book of Dermatology, 1985-; assoc. editor Jour. Investigative Dermatology, 2002-, Jour. Am. Acad. Dermatology, 2004-; asst. sect. editor, Archives of Dermatology, 2004-; cons. editor, Sun and Skin News, 1991, 1994; contbr. articles to profl. jours.; reviewer for grants; reviewer for sci. jours. Grantee NIH, VA; recipient Benedict award-First prize in Math., 1974, Dept. Vet. Affairs Spl. Contbn. award, 1990, Diabled Am. Veterans Dept. RI Outstanding Physician award, 1993, Fed. Employee of Yr., Profl. Category (for RI), 1993. Mem. APHA, Am. Dermatological Assn., Assn. Professors of Dermatology, Am. DermatoEpidemiology Assn., Internat. DermatoEpidemiology Assn. (founder, pres. 2002-2003, bd. dirs. 2003-04, steering com., 2006-), Internat. Soc. Cutaneous Lymphomas, Med. Dermatology Soc.(bd. dirs. 2004-06, mentorship program com. 2004-05, pres.-elect, 2006-2008), Nat. Assn. VA Dermatologists (v.p. 1991-92, pres. 1992-93, nominating com. 1993-97, chair nominating com., 1996-97), Am. Acad. Dermatology(mem. epidemiology com., 1996-2000, environment coun., 1995-98, computer tech./computer and informatics com., 1996-2000, database develop. task force/task force on computers in edn. and rsch., 1996-2000), Soc. Epidemiologic Rsch., Soc. Investigative Dermatology (com. on sci. programs, abstract reviewer, 1993—), New Eng. Dermatol. Soc., Am. Cancer Soc. (Chair skin cancer adv. group, 1997-, bd. dirs. RI divsn. 1992-97, mem. exec. com. RI divsn. 1994-97), RI Dermatol. Soc., R.I. Med. Soc., Phi Beta Kappa, Sigma Xi. Office: VA Med Ctr 111D 830 Chalkstone Ave Providence RI 02908-4734 also: Warren Alpert Med Sc of Brown U Dept Dermatology Box G-A Providence RI 02912 Business E-Mail: MAW@brown.edu, Martin_Weinstock_MD@brown.edu.*

WEINSTOCK, WALTER WOLFE, systems engineer; b. Phila., Aug. 18, 1925; s. Abraham and Jeanne (Feldman) W.; m. Doris Alpert, Sept. 21, 1946; children— Steven Eric, Bruce Alan. BSE.E., U.Pa., 1946, MSE.E., 1954, PhD, 1964. Design engr. Philco, 1946-49; with RCA Corp., 1949-87; prin. scientist RCA Corp. (Missile and Surface Radar div.), Moorestown, N.J., 1979-87; cons., 1987—. Mem. planning and steering adv. group Surface Ship Security Panel, Dept. Navy, 1979-82 Contbg. author: Modern Radar, 1965, Practical Phased Array Antenna Systems, 1991; contbr. articles to profl. jours. Recipient David Sarnoff award for Outstanding Achievement in Enrging. RCA, 1972 Fellow IEEE (Pioneer Recognition award 2004); mem. Tau Beta Pi, Eta Kappa Nu, Sigma Tau, Pi Mu Epsilon. Achievements include patents in field. Home: 6 Beryl Rd Cheltenham PA 19012-1206 E-mail: walt1925@earthlink.net.

WEINSTOCK RAD, KATHERYN LOUISE, music educator; d. Henry Robert and Jeanallan Joyce Weinstock; m. Jalal Rad, Aug. 23, 1993; children: Jason Shyaan Rad, Sean Ryan Henry Rad. Aux. music study, U. Birmingham, England, 1983—84, U. Keele, Staffordshire/Newcastle, 1983—84; MusB, U. Tulsa, 1985, MusM, 1988. Cert. Okla. Tchr. Cert. State of Okla., 1988. Cellist Signature Symphony Okla. Sinfonia, Tulsa, 1982—2006, Tulsa (Okla.) Philharm., 1982—2002; adj. cello instr. Northeastern State U, Tahlequah, Okla., 1988—90; music tchr. Tulsa Pub. Schs., 1989—96, music curriculum coord., 1999—2002, fine arts adv. bd. mem., 2009—; dir. of strings, tchr. Broken Arrow (Okla.) Pub. Sch., 1996—99; music coord. Tulsa Cmty. Music Sch., 2003; adj. cello instr. Performing Arts Ctr. Edn. Tulsa C.C., 2000—; fine arts coord. Cent. High Sch. Acad. Arts, 2003—07; edn. cmty. engagement dir. Wisa Symphony Orchestra. Mem. bd. fine arts task force Tulsa Pub. Sch., 1996—2000; adv. Barthelmes Conservatory, 2000—02; bd. mem. Chamber Music Tulsa(Okla.), 2001—07; performer cellist Tulsa Philharmonic, Tulsa Signature Symphony, Tulsa Symphony Orch., Okla. City Philharmnic, Tulsa Opera, Tulsa Ballet; prin. cellist Light Opera Orchestra of Okla.; performer with many classical, pop/rock, jazz and blues artists, including a live performance on NPR.; edn. cmty. dir. Tulsa Symphony Orch., 2007—; assoc. prin. Cellist-Graz Internat. Orch.; with Melkus Chamber Ensemble Graz, Austria, Brady Orch. Grandstand, judge Vet. Day Parade, Tulsa, 1999—2002; mem. Tulsa Now Task Force - Mayor Bill Fortune, 2002—; fundraiser raised over one half million dollars music programs Tulsa Pub. Schs.; dir. Tulsa Honors Orch. Stardust Strolling String. Recipient Tchr. Touching Tomorrow Award, Tulsa Pub. Sch., 1996, Superior Civilian Svc. Award, Dept. of the U.S. Army, 1999—2000; grantee VH-1 save the Music Grant, VH-1, 2001, U.S. Dept. Edn., 2002, music study at Internat. Music Workshops in Graz, Austria, Found. for Tchrs., 2004. Mem.: Hyechka (civic com. mem.), Am. Federation of Musicians. Avocations: playing cello in variety of genres, cooking, exercise. Home: 630 Pioneer Rd Sapulpa OK 74066 Office: 111 E 1st St Tulsa OK 74103 Office Phone: 918-584-3461. Business E-Mail: kathy@tulsasymphony.org.

WEINTRAUB, ELLEN L., commissioner; b. NY, 1957; d. Edward Weintraub; m. William G. Dauster, May 10, 1986; children: Matthew, Natanya, Emma. BA cum laude, Yale Coll.; JD, Harvard U. Bar: NY, DC and Supreme Ct. Litigator Cahill Gordon & Reindel, NY, 1984—90; counsel Com. on Stds. of Ofcl. Conduct for US Ho. Reps., 1990—96; of counsel, mem. polit. law group Perkins Coie LLP, 1996—2002; commr. Fed. Election Commn., Washington, 2002—, chair, 2002—03. Office: Fed Election Commn 999 E St NW Washington DC 20463*

WEINTRAUB, RUSSELL JAY, lawyer, educator; b. NYC, Dec. 20, 1929; s. Harry and Alice (Lieberman) W.; m. Zelda Kresshover, Sept. 6, 1953; children: Sharon Hope, Harry David, Steven Ross. BA, NYU, 1950; JD, Harvard U., 1953. Bar: Tex. 1980. Tchg. fellow Harvard U. Law Sch., 1955-57; asst. prof. law U. Iowa, 1957-61, prof., 1961-65, U. Tex., 1965—, Marrs McLean prof. law, 1970-80, Bryant Smith chmn., 1980-82, John B. Connally chmn., 1982-98, Powell chmn., 1998—2003, emeritus, 2004—. Vis. prof. law U. Mich., 1965, UCLA, 1967, U. Calif., Berkeley, 1973-74, Bklyn. Law Sch., 1990, 95, Inst. Internat. Comparative Law, Paris, 1975, Florence, Italy, 1997, Barcelona, 1999, 2002, London, 2000, U. Houston, 1979-80, Inst. Internat. and Comparative Law, Oxford, Eng., 1982-83, 86-87, 92, 2003, Dublin, Ireland, 1989, La. State U., Aix-en-Provence, France, 1993, Tulane U., Spetses, Greece, 1998, Australian Nat. U., 2001; Ronald Graveson Meml. lectr. King's Coll., London, 2000; lectr. Hague Acad. Internat. Law, 1984; cons. U.S. Dept. State, 1995-2000, European Union Parliament, 2005; cons. in field. Author: International Litigation and Arbitration, 1994, 5th rev. edit., 2006, ann. supplement; (with Eugene Scoles) Cases and Materials on the Conflict of Laws, 1967, 2d rev. edit., 1972, supplement, 1978, Commentary on the Conflict of Laws, 1971, 5th rev. edit., 2006, ann. supplement; (with Hamilton and Rau) Cases and Materials on Contracts, 1984, 2d rev. edit., 1992; (with Hay and Borchers) Cases and Materials on the Conflict of Laws, 13th rev. edit., 2009, Comparative Conflict of Laws: Conventions, Regulations and Codes, 2009, annual supplement; contbr. articles to profl. jours. Trustee U. Iowa Sch. Religion, 1960-65. Ops. intelligence expert US Army, 1953—55. Recipient Disting. Prof. award U. Tex. Sch. Law, 1977, Teaching Excellence award, 1979, cert. of meritorious service Am. Bar Assn., 1977, cert. of meritorious service Tex. Bar Assn., 1978, Best Tchr. award U. Houston, 1980, Carl Fulda award scholarship in internat. law, 1993. Mem. Am. Law Inst. (life), Am. Bar Found. (life), Tex. Bar Found. (life), Scribes. Jewish. Office: U Tex Sch Law 727 E Dean Keeton Austin TX 78705-3224 Office Phone: 512-232-1370. E-mail: rweintraub@law.utexas.edu. *The only true happiness lies in useful work done to the best of your ability.*

WEINTRAUB, SAM, retired reading educator; b. St. Louis, Apr. 24, 1927; s. Julius and Jeannette (Schwartz) W.; 1 child, Robert. BA, Ohio State U., 1948, BS, 1950, MEd, 1954; EdD, U. Ill., 1960. Tchr. Wyandotte Pub. Schs., Mich., 1950-53, Campus Sch. Wis. STate Coll., La Crosse, 1953-54; asst. prof. Case Western Res. U., Cleve., 1960-61, U. Chgo., 1964-68; assoc. prof. Ind. U., Bloomington, 1968-74; prof. SUNY-Buffalo, Amherst, 1974-95, prof. emeritus, 1995—. Vis. prof. Tex. Woman's U., Denton, 1980-81; cons. in field. Author, editor: Ann. Summary of Investigations Relating to Reading, 1968-97; co-editor: Improving Reading Research, 1976; co-editor jour. Reading Rsch. Quar., 1969-79. Recipient Legacy Builder award Family and Children's Svc. of Niagara, Inc., 2003; named to Reading Hall of Fame. Fellow Nat. Conf. Rsch. in English (pres. 1978-79); mem. Internat. Reading Assn. (Spl. Svc. award 1987, Wm. S. Gray citation of merit 1997), Nat. Coun. Tchrs. English, Am. Ednl. Rsch. Assn., Niagara Frontier Reading Coun. (v.p. 1990-91, Spl. Svc. award 1990). Avocations: reading, travel.

WEINTRAUB, SIDNEY, economist, educator; b. NYC, May 18, 1922; s. Reuben and Anna Weintraub; m. Gladys Katz, Aug. 11, 1946; children: Jeffrey, Marcia Weintraub Plunkett, Deborah Weintraub Chilewich, M. Elizabeth Midgley, Dec. 29, 2005. BBA, CCNY, 1943; B, MA in Journalism, U. Mo., 1948; MA in Econs., Yale U., 1958; PhD in Econs., Am. U., 1966. Commd. fgn. svc. officer Dept. State, 1949, dep. asst. sec. of state for internat. fin. and devel. Washington, 1969-74; asst. adminstr. for interagy. devel. coordination AID, 1974-75, exec. dir. interagy. devel. coordination com., 1974-75; ret., 1975; sr. fellow Brookings Instn., Washington, 1978-79; Dean Rusk prof. Lyndon B. Johnson Sch. Pub. Affairs, U. Tex., Austin, 1976-96, prof. emeritus, 1996, also co-dir. Program for U.S.-Mex. Policy Studies; William E. Simon chair in polit. economy Ctr. Strategic and Internat. Studies, 1993—. Disting. vis. scholar Ctr. for Strategic and Internat. Studies, Washington, 1990. Author: Free Trade with Mexico, 1984, A Marriage of Convenience: Relations Between Mexico and The United States, 1990, NAFTA: What Comes Next, 1994, NAFTA at Three: A Progress Report, 1997, Financial Decision-Making in Mexico: To Bet a Nation, 2000, Commentaries on International Political Economy: Constructive Irreverence, 2004, NAFTA's Impact on North America: The First Decade, 2004, Energy Cooperation in the Western Hemisphere: Benefits and Impediments, 2007; contbr. articles to profl. jours. Served with U.S. Army, 1943-46. Recipient Disting. Career Svc. award AID, 1975, Aguila Azteca, Mex., 2006. Mem.: Am. Econ. Assn., Am. Fgn. Service Assn., Coun. on Fgn. Rels., Cosmos (Washington). Office: Ctr Strategic and Internat Studies 1800 K St NW Washington DC 20006-2202 Home: Apt 2E 3900B Watson Pl NW Washington DC 20016 Home Phone: 202-337-2715; Office Phone: 202-775-3292. Personal E-mail: sidney.weintraub@gmail.com. Business E-Mail: sweintraub@csis.org. *Once having been thrust into the Second World War, my main intellectual interest has been in foreign affairs. I had concluded, as President Kennedy did later, that domestic issues can hurt but misplaced foreign policy can kill. My drive has been to understand what motivates nations, what stimulates people within different nations, what is the U.S. national interest, and to become as expert as my talents would allow about such crucial issues as domestic security, international economic interaction, social mobility, and human development generally. This remains my ambition.*

WEINTRAUB, STANLEY, arts and humanities educator, writer; b. Phila., Apr. 17, 1929; s. Ben and Ray (Segal) W.; m. Rodelle Horwitz, June 6, 1954; children: Mark, David, Erica. BS, West Chester State Coll., Pa., 1949; MA, Temple U., 1951; PhD, Pa. State U., 1956. Instr. Pa. State U., University Park, 1953-59, asst. prof., 1959-62, asso. prof., 1962-65, prof. English, 1965-70, research prof., 1970-86, Evan Pugh prof. Arts and Humanities, 1986-99, Evan Pugh prof. Emeritus, 2000—; dir. Inst. for Arts and Humanistic Studies, 1970-90. Vis. prof. U. Calif. at Los Angeles, 1963, U. Hawaii, 1973, U. Malaya, 1977, Nat. U. Singapore, 1982 Author: Private Shaw and Public Shaw, 1963, The War in the Wards, 1964, Reggie, 1965, The Art of William Golding, 1965, Beardlsey, 1967, The Last Great Cause, The Intellectuals and the Spanish Civil War, 1968, Evolution of a Revolt: Early Postwar Writings of T.E. Lawrence, 1968, The Literary Criticism of Oscar Wilde, 1968, Journey to Heartbreak, 1971, Whistler: A Biography, 1974, Lawrence of Arabia: the Literary Impulse, 1975, Four Rossettis, A Victorian Biography, 1977, Aubrey Beardsley: Imp of the Perverse, 1976, The London Yankees: Portraits of American Writers and Artists in England, 1894-1914, 1979, The Unexpected Shaw. Biographical Approaches to G.B. Shaw and His Work, 1982, A Stillness Heard Round the World: The End of the Great War, 1985, Victoria. An Intimate Biography, 1987, Long Day's Journey into War: December 7, 1941, 1991, Bernard Shaw: A Guide to Research, 1992, Disraeli: A Biography, 1993, The Last Great Victory-The End of World War II, July/August 1945, 1995, Shaw's People. Victoria to Churchill, 1996, Uncrowned King: The Life of Prince Albert, 1997, MacArthur's War: Korea and the Undoing of an American Hero, 2000, The Importance of Being Edward. King in Waiting, 1841-1901, 2000, Silent Night. The Remarkable 1914 Christmas Truce, 2001, Charlotte and Lionel: A Rothschild Love Story, 2003, General Washington's Christmas Farewell: A Mount Vernon Homecoming, 1783, 2003, Iron Tears: America's Battle for Freedom, Britain's Quagmire: 1775-1783, 2005; editor: An Unfinished Novel by Bernard Shaw, 1958, C.P. Snow: A Spectrum, 1963, The Yellow Book: Quintessence of the Nineties, 1964, The Savoy: Nineties Experiment, 1966, The Court Theatre, 1966, Biography and Truth, 1967, Evolution of a Revolt: Early Postwar Writings of T.E. Lawrence, 1968, The Literary Criticism of Oscar Wilde, 1968, Shaw: An Autobiography 1856-1898, 1969, Shaw: An Autobiography, The Playwright Years, 1898-1950, 1970, Bernard Shaw's Nondramatic Literary Criticism, 1972, Directions in Literary Criticism, 1973, Saint Joan Fifty Years After: 1923/24-1973/74, 1973, The Portable Bernard Shaw, 1977, (with Anne Wright) Heartbreak House. A Facsimile of the Revised Typescript, 1979, (with Richard Aldington) The Portable Oscar Wilde, 1981, Modern British Dramatists, 1900-1945, 1982, The Playwright and the Pirate. Bernard Shaw and Frank Harris: A Correspondence, 1982, British Dramatists Since World War II, 1983, Bernard Shaw, the Diaries, 1885-1897, 1986, Bernard Shaw on the London Art Scene, 1885-1950, 1989, (with Rodelle Weintraub) Dear Young Friend. The Letters of American Presidents to Children, 2000, 11 Days in December. Christmas in the Bulge, 2006, 15 Stars. Eisenhower, MacArthur, Marshall: Three Generals Who Saved the American Century, 2007, General Sherman's Christmas Savannah, 1864: A Civil War Saga, 2009; also editor Comparative Literature Studies, 1987-92, Shaw, The Ann. of Bernard Shaw Studies, 1956-89. Pres. Jewish Community Council of Bellefonte (Pa.) State Coll., 1966-67. Served to 1st lt. AUS, 1951-53, Korea. Decorated Bronze Star medal.; Guggenheim fellow, 1968-69; recipient Disting. Humanist award Pa. Humanities Council, 1985 Mem. Internat. Shaw Soc. Home: 4 Winterfield Ct Newark DE 19711-2957 Office Phone: 302-235-2859.

Personal E-mail: sqw4@comcast.net. *I subscribe to Bernard Shaw's declaration in the Preface to Man and Superman that "This is the true joy in life, the being used for a purpose recognized by yourself as a mighty one; the being thoroughly worn out before you are thrown on the scrap heap; the being a force of Nature instead of a feverish selfish little clod of ailments and grievances complaining that the world will not devote itself to making you happy.".*

WEINTZ, JACOB FREDERICK, JR., retired investment banker; b. NYC, June 27, 1926; s. Jacob Frederick and Grace (Cortelyou) W.; m. Elisabeth Hamlin Brewer, Nov. 26, 1955; children: Elizabeth Weintz Cerf, Polly Weintz Sanna, Eric Cortelyou, Karl Frederick. Student, Norwich U., 1943—44, D (hon.) in Fin. Mgmt., 2001; BA, Stanford U., 1948; MBA, Harvard U., 1951. Salesman Vick Chem. Co., NYC, 1948-49; assoc. buying dept. Goldman, Sachs & Co., NYC, 1951-54, assoc. new bus. dept., 1954-65, ptnr., 1965-84; ltd. ptnr. Goldman, Sachs Group L.P., 1984—99; ret., 1999; with BCRS Assocs. LLC, NYC. Pres., chmn. bd. dirs. Stonebridge Condominium Assn., Snowmass Village, Colo., 1978-85; trustee Pace U., 1981-97, Norwich U., Stanford U., 1985-95, Sierra Club Found., 1984-90, 92—98; trustee Harbor Lights Found., N.Y.C., Nat. Lighthouse Mus., S.I.; leadership coun., Harvard Sch. Pub. Health, Pace U. Fin. and Audit and Investment com., 1997-, bd. vis., Stanford Inst. Internat. Studies; vice chmn. bd. dirs. Guiding Eyes for Blind, 1984-93; bd. dir. The Forum World Affairs, Stamford, Conn., 1988-94; pres. Harvard U. Bus. Sch. Alumni Assn., 1988-90; former del. Coun. Governing Bds., Albany, N.Y.; chmn. bd. dirs. N.Y. Young Rep. Club, 1957-58; mem. exec. com. Greenwich Rep. Town Com., Conn., 1962-69, The Task Force on Def. Spending, The Economy and the Nation's Security, BENS-ED Commn. on Fundamental Def. Mgmt. Issues, 1991-92; mem. Stanford in Washington Coun. With USAAF, 1944-45. Recipient La Medaille de la Ville de Paris, 1990, Stanford Gold Spike award, 1992. Mem. Ambs. Round Table (Stamford), Bond Club (N.Y.), Newcomen Soc. N.Am., Down Town Assn., Harvard Club (NYC), Riverside Yacht Club, Flying Scot Sailing Assn. (pres. 1968-69), Theta Chi. Republican. Episcopalian. Home: Harbor Lights 43 Jones Park Dr Riverside CT 06878-2205 Office: BCRS Assocs LLC 100 Wall St New York NY 10005 Home Phone: 203-637-3577; Office Phone: 212-440-0849. Business E-Mail: fweintz@mkllp.com, fweintz@bcrsllc.com.

WEIR, ALEXANDER, JR., chemical engineer, consultant; b. Crossett, Ark., Dec. 19, 1922; s. Alexander and Mary Eloise (Field) W.; m. Florence Forschner, Dec. 28, 1946; children: Alexander III, Carol Jean, Bruce Richard BSChemE, U. Ark., 1943; MChemE, Poly Inst. Bklyn., 1946; PhD, U. Mich., 1954; cert., U. So. Calif. Grad. Sch. Bus. Adminstrn., 1968. Chem. engr. Am. Cyanamid Co., Stamford Rsch. Labs., 1943-47; with U. Mich., 1948-58; rsch. assoc., project supr. Engring. Rsch. Inst., U. Mich., 1948-57; lectr. chem. and metall. engring. dept. U. Mich., 1954-56, asst. prof., 1956-58; cons. Ramo-Woolridge Corp., LA, 1956-57; mem. tech. staff, sect. head, asst. mgr. Ramo-Wooldridge Corp., LA, 1957-60, incharge Atlas Missile Captive test program, 1956-60; tech. adv. to pres. Northrop Corp., Beverly Hills, Calif., 1960-70; prin. scientist for air quality So. Calif. Edison Co., LA, 1970-76, mgr. chem. sys. R & D, 1976-86, chief rsch. scientist, 1986-88; utility cons. Playa Del Rey, Calif., 1988—. Rep. Am. Rocket Soc. to Detroit Nuc. Coun., 1954-57; chmn. session on chem. reactions Nuc. Sci. and Engring. Congress, Cleve., 1955; U.S. del. AGARD (NATO) Combustion Colloquium, Liege, Belgium, 1955; Western U.S. rep. task force on environ. R & D goals Electric Rsch. Coun., 1971; electric utility advisor Electric Power Rsch. Inst., 1974-78, 84-87; industry advisor dept. chemistry and biochemistry Calif. State U., L.A., 1981-88. Author: Two and Three Dimensional Flow of Air through Square-Edged Sonic Orifices, 1954; (with R.B. Morrison and T.C. Anderson) Notes on Combustion, 1955, also some 60 tech. papers; inventor acid rain prevention device used in 5 states. Sea scout leader, Greenwich, Conn., 1944-48, Marina del Rey, Calif., 1965-70; bd. govs., past pres. Civic Union Playa del Rey, chmn. sch., police and fire, nominating, civil def., army liaison coms.; mem. Senate, Westchester YMCA, chmn. Dads sponsoring com., active fundraising; chmn. nominating com. Paseo del Rey Sch. PTA, 1961; mem. LA Mayors Cmty. Adv. Com.; asst. chmn. advancement com., merit badge dean Cantinella dist. LA Area coun. Boy Scouts Am. Recipient Nat. Rsch. Coun. Flue Gas Desulfurization Industrials Scale Reliability award NAS, 1975, Power Environ. Achievement award EPA, 1980, Excellence in Sulfur Dioxide Control award EPA, 1985; named Arkansas Traveler by Gov. Bill Clinton, 1989; Cert. Appreciation, City of LA, 2008. Mem.: AIChE, St. Andrews Soc. LA, Clan Stewart Soc. America, Am. Geophys. Union, Navy League U.S. (v.p. Palos Verdes peninsula coun. 1961—62), NY Acad. Scis., Sci. Rsch. Soc. Am., Am. Chem. Soc., U.S. Power Squadron (navigator), Ark. Soc. Children of Am. Revolution (past pres.), Betty Washington Lewis Soc. Children of Am. Revolution (past pres.), Clan MacFarlane Soc., Clan Chattan of the US, Clan Farquharson Assn., Clan Buchanan Soc. Am., Clan Macnachtan Assn., St. Andrew Soc. So. Calif. (hon. capt. of fleet 1997, mem. bd. govs., chair scholarship com.), Santa Monica Yacht Club (lifetime hon. cannoneer, chief of protocol, vice chmn. marina mgmt. com.), Sigma Xi, Phi Kappa Phi, Phi Lambda Upsilon, Alpha Chi Sigma, Lambda Chi Alpha. Office: 8229 Billowvista Dr Playa Del Rey CA 90293-7807

WEIR, ANNE, writer; b. Boston, Feb. 9, 1942; d. John Weir and Martha (Kingman) Perry; children: Emily Weir, Sarah Noel, Katherine Joy. BA, Swarthmore Coll., Pa., 1964; MEd, U. Maine, Orono, 1984. Cert. elem. and secondary edn. tchr. Editor: Marlowe: Being In the Life of the Mind, 1996, A Book of Certainties, 1998, The Color Book, 1998, Marlowe, corrected and augmented, 1999, Christopher's Journey, Acts & Scenes, News, The Bird's Eye, 1996-2000, A Native Woman poems, 1999, American City, 2000, A Codebook for the Plays, 2000, Waking, An Academic Celebration, 2001, A Teacher's Holiday, "Streamlines" A Study in Bibliography, New Songs, 2001, The Reincarnation of Love, 2002, Literary Picture Notebooks, And in Aftertimes, 2003, Songs for the 20th Century, 2004, Summer Poems, Notes and Notice, 2005, Film, a study, 2006, Bulletins, A Preface, 2007, A Wordbook, 2008, The Portraits of Christ Marlone, 2009.

WEIR, BRYCE KEITH ALEXANDER, neurosurgeon, neurologist, educator; b. Edinburgh, Apr. 29, 1936; arrived in U.S., 1992, arrived in Can., 2002; s. Ernest John and Marion Weir; m. Mary Lou Lauber, Feb. 25, 1976; children: Leanora, Glyncora, Brocke. BSc, McGill U., Montreal, Que., Can., 1958, MD, CM, 1960, MSc, 1963. Diplomate Am. Bd. Neurol. Surgery, Nat. Bd. Med. Examiners. Intern Montreal Gen. Hosp., 1960-61; resident in neurosurgery Neurological Inst., Montreal, 1962-64, 65-66, NY Neurol. Inst., NYC, 1964—65; neurosurgeon U. Alta., Edmonton, Can., 1967-92, dir. div. neurosurgery, 1982-86, Walter Anderson prof., chmn. dept. surgery, 1986-92; surgeon-in-chief U. Alta. Hosps., 1986-92; Maurice Goldblatt prof. surgery and neurology U. Chgo., 1992—2002, dir. Brain Rsch. Inst., 1993—2001, interim dean biol. scis. divsn. and Pritzker Sch. Medicine, v.p. med. affairs, 2001—02. Past pres. V Internat. Symposium on Cerebral Vasospasm; mem. neurology A study sect. NIH, 1991—93; invited speaker at over 135 profl. meetings; vis. prof. over 68 univs., including Yale U., Cornell U., Columbia U., Duke U., U. Toronto, U. Calif., San Francisco; lectr. in field. Author: Aneurysms Affecting the Nervous System, 1987, Subarachnoid Hemorrhage-Causes and Cures, 1998, Cerebral Vasospasm, 2001; co-editor: Primer on Cerebrovascular Diseases, 1997, Stroke: Pathophysiology, Diagnosis and Management, 4th edit., 2004; mem. editl. bd. Jour. Neurosurgery, chmn. bd, 1993—94, mem. editl. bd. Neurosurgery Quar., Jour. Cerebrovascular Disease, Neurosurgery; contbr. over 275 articles to profl. jours. Named Officer of the Order of Can., 1995. Fellow: ACS, Royal Coll. Surgeons Can., Royal Coll. Surgeons Edinburgh (hon.); mem.: Can. Neurosurg. Soc. (Inaugural Lifetime Achievement award 2006), Interurban Neurosurg. Soc. (chmn.), Nat. Acad. Scis., Inst. Medicine, Japan Neurosurg. Soc. (hon.), Soc. Neurol. Surgeons (Grass gold medal 1992), Am. Acad. Neurol. Surgeons, James. IV Assn. Surgeons, Am. Surg. Assn. Achievements include rsch. in cerebral vasospasm and the surgical management of intracranial aneurysms. Home: 1262 Saturna Dr Parksville BC V9P 2X6 Canada

WEIR, EDWARD KENNETH, cardiologist, educator; b. Belfast, No. Ireland, Jan. 7, 1943; came to U.S. 1973; s. Thomas Kenneth and Violet Hilda (ffrench) W.; m. Elizabeth Vincent Pearman, May 29, 1971; children: Fergus G., Conor K. BA, U. Oxford, UK, 1964; MA, BM, BCh, U. Oxford, Eng., 1967, DM, 1976. Diplomate Am. Bd. Internal Medicine. Intern Churchill Hosp., Oxford, Eng., 1968, Radcliffe Infirmary, Oxford, 1968, resident, 1970-71, Hammersmith Hosp., London, 1969, Groot Schuur Hosp., Cape Town, South Africa, 1969-70, registrar in cardiology, 1971-73; postdoctoral rsch. fellow U. Colo., Denver, 1973-75; cons. pediatric cardiologist U. Cape Town Med. Sch., 1975-76; cons. cardiologist U. Natal Med. Sch., Durban, South Africa, 1976-77; assoc. prof. medicine U. Minn., Mpls., 1978-85, prof. medicine, 1985—, prof. physiology, 1999—. Staff physician VAMC, Mpls., 1978—, chief of cardiology, 2000—08; dir. Grover Confs. on Pulmonary Circulation, 1984—2000. Co-editor: Pulmonary Hypertension, 1984, The Pulmonary Circulation in Health and Disease, 1987, Pulmonary Vascular Physiology and Pathophysiology, 1989, The Diagnosis and Treatment of Pulmonary Hypertension, 1992, Ion Flux in Pulmonary Vascular Control, 1993, The Pulmonary Circulation and Gas Exchange, 1994, Nitric Oxide and Radicals in the Pulmonary Vasculature, 1996, Pulmonary Edema, 1998, Oxygen Regulation of Ion Channels and Gene Expression, 1998, The Fetal and Neonatal Pulmonary Circulations, 2000, Interactions of Blood and the Pulmonary Circulation, 2002. Fulbright scholar, 1973-75; Sr. Internat. Fogarty fellow, 1993, Disting. Scientist award Am. Heart Assn., 2008. Fellow Royal Coll. Physicians London, Am. Heart Assn. (Minn. affiliate bd. dirs. 1989-93, Nat. Cardiopulmonary Coun. (exec. com. 1992-2003), Pulmonary Circulation Found. (treas. 1985-2001). Office: VA Med Ctr 1 Veterans Dr # 111C Minneapolis MN 55417-2300 *What you "achieve" in life is much less important than what you do for those around you. One hundred years after their death, very few people are remembered for what they achieved.*

WEIR, DAME GILLIAN CONSTANCE, musician; b. Martinborough, New Zealand, Jan. 17, 1941; d. Cecil Alexander and Clarice M. Foy (Bignell) W. Grad., Royal Coll. Music, London, 1965; Mus D (hon.), U. Victoria of Wellington, New Zealand, 1983; DLitt (hon.), Huddersfield U., 1997; Mus D (hon.), Hull U., 1999, Exeter U., 2001; Doctorate (hon.), U. Ctrl. Eng., 2001; Mus D (hon.), Leicester Univ., 2003; MusD (hon.), U. Aberdeen, Scotland, 2004. Artist-in-residence numerous univs. including Yale U, Washington U., St. Louis, U. Western Australia, Johns Hopkins U., 2005, others; vis. lectr. Royal No. Coll. Music, Manchester, Eng., 1974-89; vis. prof. organ Royal Acad. Music, London, 1997-98; Prince Consort prof. Royal Coll. of Music, London, 1999—; spkr. BBC programs on music and performance; subject of Melvyn Bragg's TV documentary South Bank Show, 2000; apptd. Disting Artist-in-residence Peabody Inst., John Hopkins U., Balt., 2005; internat. chair in organ Royal No. Coll. Music, 2006-07. Concert appearances with leading Brit. Orchs. and Boston Orch., Seattle Orch., Australian ABC Orch., Wurttemberg Chamber and other fgn. orch.; appeared in major internat. festivals including Edinburgh, Flanders, Aldeburgh, Bath, Proms, Europalia; appeared at concert halls including Royal Festival Hall, Royal Albert Hall, Lincoln Ctr., NY, Sydney Opera House; numerous radio and TV appearances in Brit. and world-wide including Royal Festival Hall Jubilee; organ cons.; adjudicator internat. competitions; contbr. The Messiaen Companion, 1995; contbr. articles to profl. jour.; recs. include complete organ works of Olivier Messiaen, others; TV documentary film on career, 1982, BBC TV programs The King of Instruments, 1989. Decorated comdr., dame comdr. Order Brit. Empire; recipient Turnovsky award 1985, Evening Std. award for outstanding solo performance, 1998-99, Lifetime Achievement award The Link Found., London, 2005; winner 1st prize St. Albans Internat. Organ Competition, 1964. Fellow Royal Coll. Organists (hon., mem. coun. 1977—, mem. exec. 1981-85, pres. 1994-96, 1st Woman pres.), Royal Can. Coll. Organists (hon.), Royal Coll. Music (London); mem. Royal Acad. Music (hon.), Inc. Soc. Musicians (1st woman pres. 1992-93), Albert Schweitzer Assn. (Silver medal 1998). Office: Karen McFarlane Artists 33563 Seneca Dr Cleveland OH 44139-5578 Office Phone: 440-542-1882. Personal E-mail: gillianweir@gillianweir.com.

WEIR, JEFFREY MICHAEL, history professor, consultant; b. Corning, NY, Jan. 20, 1964; s. John Gruber Weir and Marcia Ann Sickel; life ptnr. Thomas Mark Siegrist. BS, Albright Coll., Reading, Pa., 1985; MA, George Mason U., Fairfax, Va., 2003, PhD, 2004. Sr. rsch. adminstr. George Wash. U., 2001—; asst. dir. Reading Pub. Mus., Pa., 1992—95; ops. dir. Winrock Internat., Arlington, Va., 1996—2001; adj. prof. history Northern VA CC, Alexandria, 2006—. Archival cons. Ind., Arlington, 2006—. Liberal. Achievements include design of home pages for history classes. Avocations: travel, reading. Personal E-mail: jweir@gmu.edu. Business E-Mail: jweir@biostat.bsc.gwu.edu.

WEIR, MARGARET, sociologist, political science professor; BA in Polit. Sci., Antioch Coll., 1975; MA, Brandeis Univ., 1978; PhD, Univ. Chgo., 1986. Asst. prof., govt. Harvard Univ., 1985—89, assoc. prof., 1989—90, John L. Loeb assoc. prof. social sci., 1990—92; sr. fellow, govtl. studies Brookings Inst., 1992—97, non-resident sr. fellow; and prof., dept. social, polit. sci. Univ. Calif., Berkeley, 1997—. Co-author (with Ira Katznelson): Schooling for All, 1985; author: Politics and Jobs, 1992. Fellow: Am. Acad. Arts & Scis. Office: Depts Sociology & Polit Sci 410 Barrows Hall #1980 Univ Calif Berkeley CA 94720 Office Phone: 510-643-1602. Business E-Mail: mweir@socrates.berkeley.edu, mweir@berkeley.edu.

WEIR, RITA MARY, retail executive; b. Ft. Dix, NJ, Aug. 28, 1955; d. Rynart Barnabas and Teruko (Yokota) Haling; m. Mark Adrian Weir, Oct. 25, 1986. AA, Austin C.C., 1988; BA summa cum laude, Granite State Coll., 1990; MBA cum laude, N.H. Coll., 1997. Store mgr. KFC, El Paso and Austin, Tex., 1973-86; asst. mgr. Stuart Shaines, Portsmouth, NH, 1989-90; mkt. human resources mgr. Wal-Mart, 1991—, human resource mgr. Bd. govs. Seacoast Learning Ctr., 2005—09. Mem. NAFE, Am. Bus. Women's Assn. (pres. 1992-93, bull. chair 1993-94, hospitality com. 1993-94, 94-95, membership com. 1993-94, 94-95, Woman of Yr. 1993, 95, v.p. 1994-95, chpt. del. 1994-95, program chair 1995), Top Ten 2000 (nominating chair 2006, 07), Phi Theta Kappa (leadership seacoast). Avocations: reading, walking, travel. Home: 44 Lamprey Ln Lee NH 03861-6552 Office: Wal-Mart 702 SW 8th St Bentonville AR 72716 Office Phone: 603-431-5313.

WEIR, SARA HART, science and health policy consultant; b. Omaha, Sept. 23, 1981; d. Scott James and Lucia Grace Weir; m. Thomas Bennett King, Oct. 11, 2008. Degree in Psychology, Westminster Coll., Fulton, MO, 2004; MS in Pub. Policy & Mgmt., Carnegie Mellon U., Pittsburgh, 2006. Sr. mgmt. analyst BearingPoint, Inc., Wash., 2006; asst. v.p. B&D Consulting, Wash., 2006—. Mem. Alumni Coun., Westminster Coll., 2008; sec. Carnegie Mellon U. DC Alumni Chpt.; pres. Westminster Coll. Alumni Chpt. Personal E-mail: sarahartweir@gmail.com.

WEIS, CHARLIE, college football coach; b. Trenton, NJ, Mar. 30, 1956; m. Maura Weis; 2 children. BA speech, drama, Notre Dame Univ, 1978; MA education, South Carolina Univ, 1989. Asst. coach Boonton High School, NJ, 1979, Morristown High School, NJ, 1980—84; grad. asst., defensive backs coach South Carolina U., 1985, 1986, defensive ends coach, 1987, asst. recruiting coord., 1988; head coach Franklin Township High School, 1989; def. asst., asst. special teams coach NY Giants, 1990, running backs coach, 1991—92; tight ends coach New England Patriots, 1993—94, running backs coach, 1995, wide receivers coach, 1996, NY Jets, 1997, offensive coord., wide receivers coach, 1998—99; offensive coord., running backs coach New England Patriots, 2000, offensive coord., quarterbacks coach, 2001—02, offensive coord., 2003—05; head football coach Notre Dame U., South Bend, Ind., 2005—. Co-author (with Vic Carucci): No Excuses: One Man's Incredible Rise Through the NFL to Head Coach of Notre Dame, 2006. Achievements include being a coach for Super Bowl Champion New York Giants, 1990, New England Patriots, 2000, 2003, 2004. Office: C112 Joyce Center Notre Dame IN 46556

WEIS, FREDERICK M., former academic administrator; m. Mary Fraser Weis; children: Matt, Marianna. Grad., Claremont McKenna Coll., 1965, MBA in Mgmt. and Fin., MA in Higher Edn. Dir. fin. and bus. affairs, treas. Scripps Coll., Claremont, Calif., 1980—82, interim pres., 2007—09, pres., 2009; v.p., treas. Claremont McKenna Coll., 1982—2002, exec. practitioner in residence, 2003—07. Bd. mem. EDFUND, Rancho Cordova, Calif. Contbr. articles to profl. jours.

WEIS, JODY P. (J.P. WEIS), police superintendent; b. 1957; BS in Chemistry, U. Tampa, 1979. With Houston divsn. Corpus Christi Resident Agy. FBI, investigator terrorism, narcotics and violent crimes Houston; bomb technician Houston SWAT team; with Bomb Data Ctr. FBI, 1992—94, with violent crimes/fugitive unit, 1994—96, mem. violent crimes squad Phoenix, 1996—2002, asst. spl. agent in charge Chgo. Field Office, 2002—03, dep. asst. dir. Office Profl. Responsibility, 2003—05, dep. asst. dir. for adminstrv. svcs. disvn. Office Profl. Responsibility, spl. agent in charge crime ops. LA Field Office, 2005—06, spl. agent in charge crime ops. Phila. Field Office, 2006—07; supt. Chgo. Police Dept., 2008—. 2d lt. explosive ordnance disposal US Army, ret. US Army, 1984. Office: Chgo Police Dept 3510 S Michigan Ave Chicago IL 60653 Office Phone: 312-746-6000. Business E-Mail: police@cityofchicago.com.

WEIS, JOSEPH FRANCIS, JR., federal judge; b. Pitts., Mar. 12, 1923; s. Joseph Francis and Mary (Flaherty) Weis; m. Margaret Horne Weis, Dec. 27, 1958; children: Maureen, Joseph Francis, Christine. BA, Duquesne U., 1947; JD, U. Pitts., 1950; LLD (hon.), Dickinson Coll., 1989. Bar: Pa. 1950. Pvt. practice, Pitts., 1950—68; judge Ct. Common Pleas, Allegheny County, Pa., 1968—70, US Dist. Ct. (we. dist.), Pa., 1970—73, US Ct. Appeals (3d cir.), Pitts., 1973—88, sr. judge, 1988—. Lectr. trial procedures, 1965—; adj. prof. law U. Pitts., 1986—; chmn. Fed. Cts. Study Com., Jud. Conf. Com. on Expt. to Videotape Trial Procs. within the 3rd Cir., Internat. Jud. Conf. the Joint Am.-Can. Appellate Judges Conf., Toronto, 1986, London, 85; futurist subcom. bicentennial com. Ct. Common Pleas, Allegheny County, Pa., 1988; participant programs legal medicine, Rome, London; mem. Am.-Can. Legal Exch., 1987; apptd. by Chief Justice Rehnquist US Jud. Conf., Com. on Internat. Jud. Rels., 1998—2004; com. on adminstrn. bankruptcy sys., subcom. on jud. improvements Jud. Conf. US, 1983—87, chmn. civil rules com., 1986—87, chmn. standing com. rules of practice and procedure, 1988. Contbr. articles to profl. jours. Active Mental Health and Mental Retardation Bd., Allegheny County, 1970—73, Leukemia Soc., 1970—73, Disabled Am. Vets., Cath. War Vets, Mil. Order of the World Wars; trustee Forbes Hosp. Sys., Pitts., 1969—74; bd. adminstrn. Cath. Diocese Pitts., 1971—83. Capt. US Army, 1943—48. Decorated Bronze Star, Purple Heart with oak leaf cluster, French War Cross with palm; recipient St. Thomas More award, 1971, Phillip Amram award, 1991, Edward J. Devitt Disting. Svc. to Justice award, 1993, History Makers award, 1997. Fellow: Am. Bar Found., Internat. Acad. Trial Lawyers (hon.); mem.: ABA (chmn. appellate judges' conf. 1981—83), Inst. Jud. Adminstrn., Am. Judicature Soc., Acad. Trial Lawyers Allegheny County (past pres., Disting. Svc. award 1997, Jud. Leadership and Excellence award 2004), Allegheny Bar Assn. (past v.p.), Pa. Bar Assn., French Legion of Honor (knight), 4th Armored Divsn. Assn., Am. Legion, Knights of Malta, KC. Office: US Ct Appeals 5200 US PO and Ct House 7th Ave & Grant St Pittsburgh PA 15219*

WEIS, MARGARET EDITH, writer, editor; b. Independence, Mo., Mar. 16, 1948; d. George Edward and Francis Irene (Reed) W.; m. Robert William Baldwin, Aug. 22, 1970 (div. 1981); children: David William (dec.), Elizabeth Lynn; m. Donald Bayne Stewart Perrin, 1996 (div. 2003). BA in Creative Writing, U. Mo., DC, 1966-70. Proofreader Herald Pub. House, Independence, Mo., 1970-73, advt. dir., 1973-82; dir. div. Independence Press, 1977-82; editor TSR Inc, Lake Geneva, Wis., 1982-86. Freelance writer; owner Sovereign Press, Williams Bay, Wis., margaretweis.com, Margaret Weis Prodns., Ltd. Author: (short story) The Test of the Twins, 1984, (books) The Endless Catacombs, 1984, Tower of Midnight Dreams, 1984, (with Tracy Hickman) The Dragonlance Chronicles, Vols. 1-3, 1984, 85, Dragonlance Legends, Vols. 1-3, 1985, 86, The Darksword Trilogy, Vols. 1-3, 1987, (with Roger Moore) Riddle of The Griffon, 1985, (under Margaret Baldwin) The Boys Who Saved The Children, 1982, Kisses of Death, 1983, (with Pat O'Brien) Wanted: Frank and Jesse James, The Real Story, 1981, (with Janet Pack) Children of The Holocaust, 1986, My First Thanksgiving, 1983, (with Gary Pack) Computer Graphics, 1984, Robots and Robotics, 1984, (short story) The Thirty Nine Buttons, 1987, (novella) (with Tracy Hickman) The Legacy, 1987, Wanna Bet?, 1987; editor: The Art of Dungeons and Dragons, 1985, Leaves of the Inn of the Last Home, 1987, The Art of Dragonlance, 1987, Dragonlance Tales, vol. 1, 2, 3, 1987, (with Tracy Hickman) The Rose of the Prophet, 1989, (with Tracy Hickman) Death's Gate, vol. 1, 1990, vols. 2, 3, 4, 5, 6, 7, Star of the Guardian, vol. 1, The Lost King, 1990, King's Test vol. 2, 1991, King's Sacrifice Vol. 3, 1991, Ghost Legion Vol. 4, 1991, Dragons of Summer Flame, 1996, (with Don Perrin), Doom Brigade, 1997, Mag Force 7 novels, 3 vols., The Soulforge, 1998, Brothers in Arms, 1999, (with Tracy Hickman) Starshield, Vols. 1-3, 1997, Legacy of the Darksword, 1997, War of Souls, 3 vols., 2000; editor: Kender, Gully Dwarves and Gnomes, 1989, Love and War, 1991, Reign of Istar, 1993,

Dragons of War, 1996, Dragons of Chaos, 1997, Relics and Omens, 1998, Sovereign Stone Role-Playing Games, 1999, Sovereign Stone novels, (with Tracy Hickman) vol. 1, Well of Darkness, 2000, vol. 2, Guardians of the Lost, 2001, Journey Into the Void, vol. 3, 2003, Mistress of Dragons, 2003, Draconian Measures, 2000, Dragon's Son, 2004, Ashes and Amber, 2004, Master of Dragons, 2005, Ashes and Iron, 2005, (with Tracy Hickman) The Lost Chronicles, vol. 1 Dragons of the Dwarven Depths, Lost Chronicles, Dragons of Highlord Skies, 2007, Dragonships, Bones of the Dragon, 2008, Dragons of the Hourglass Mage, 2009, (movie) Dragon of Autumn Twilight. Recipient Origins award, 2001; named to Writer's Hall of Fame, 2002, Adventure Gaming Hall of Fame, 2002. Avocations: flyball, agility.

WEIS, ROBERT FREEMAN, supermarket company executive; b. Sunbury, Pa. m. Patricia Ross; children: Jennifer, Colleen, Jonathan. Grad., Mercersburg Acad., 1937; BA, Yale U., 1941. With Weis Markets, Sunbury, Pa., 1946—, v.p., treas., bd. dirs., treas., 1995—, chmn. bd. dirs., 2002—. Chair steering com. capital campaign Susquehanna U., Selinsgrove, Pa., past vice chmn. bd. trustees; past pres. bd. trustees Sunbury Cmty. Hosp., trustee; bd. dirs. Lown Cardiovascular Rsch. Found., Brookline, Mass. Past pres. Sunbury C. of C.; past chmn. bd. dirs. First Nat. Trust Bank Sunbury, emeritus dir.; past dir. Susquehanna Bancshares; treas. Sunbury chpt. United Jewish Appeal. Office: Weis Markets Inc 1000 S 2d St PO Box 471 Sunbury PA 17801-0471

WEISBERG, BARBARA, writer, editor; b. Phila., Apr. 3, 1946; d. Samuel Weisberg and Miriam (Rosenbach) Weisberg-Kind; m. David Black, June 20, 1996; stepchildren: Susannah Black, Tobiah Black. BA, U. Pa., 1968; MPhil, Yale U., 1972; MFA, Bklyn. Coll., 1992. Prodr., writer Harcourt Brace Jovanovich, NYC, 1973-77; writer WNET/Thirteen, NYC, 1977-80; assoc. dir. TV devel. Scholastic, NYC, 1980-83; dir. TV devel. Consumer Reports, Mt. Vernon, N.Y., 1983-87; writer, prodr., editor NYC, 1987—. Poetry editor Bklyn. Review (lit. jour.), 1992. Co-creator (TV series) Charles in Charge, 1984; author: (children's books) Susan B. Anthony, 1989, Coronado's Golden Quest, 1993, Knights and Castles, 1994, (adult nonfiction) Talking to the Dead, Kate and Maggie Fox and the Rise of Spiritualism, 2004, paperback, 2005; editor: project McGraw-Hill Treasures, 2004-05, 2008-09. Mem. Hadassah, 1970—, NOW, 1970—, Planned Parenthood, 1985—. Recipient fellowship Yale U., 1971, MacArthur scholarship in poetry Bklyn. Coll., 1991, Wallace fellow for creative artists and writers Am. Antiquarian Soc., 1998, D. Scott Rogo award for Parapsychol. Lit., Parapsychology Found., 1998. Mem. Writers Guild of Am. East, Am. Antiquarian Soc., Authors Guild, Phi Beta Kappa, Am. Assoc. U. Women.

WEISBERG, HERBERT FRANK, political science professor; b. Mpls., Dec. 8, 1941; s. Nathan R. and Jean (Schlessinger) W.; m. Judith Ann Robinson, Dec. 16, 1979; 1 child, Bryan Bowen. BA, U. Minn., 1963; PhD, U. Mich., 1968. Asst. prof. polit. sci. U. Mich., Ann Arbor, 1967-73, assoc. prof. polit. sci., 1973-74, Ohio State U., Columbus, 1974-77, prof. polit. sci., 1977—, chmn. Dept. Polit. Sci., 2005—. Author: Central Tendency and Variation, 1992, The Total Survey Error Approach, 2005; co-author: Theory Building and Data Analysis, 1984, Controversies in Voting Behavior, 2001, Survey Research Polling and Data Analysis, 1996, Classics in Congressional Politics, 1999, The American Voter Revisited, 2008; editor: Political Science: Science of Politics, 1985, Democracy's Feast: Elections in America, 1995; co-editor Am. Jour. Polit. Sci., 1979-82, Great Theatre: The American Congress in the 1990's, 1998, Reelection 1996: How Americans Voted, 1999, Models of Voting in Presidential Elections, 2004. Mem.: Am. Polit. Sci. Assn. (program chmn. 1983), Midwest Polit. Sci. Assn. (pres. 2001—02), Phi Kappa Phi, Pi Sigma Alpha, Phi Beta Kappa. Home: 742 Gatehouse Ln Columbus OH 43235-1732 Office: Ohio State U Dept Polic Sci 2140 Derby Hall 154 N Oval Mall Columbus OH 43210-1330 Office Phone: 614-292-6572.

WEISBERG, JACOB, web magazine editor; b. Chgo., 1964; s. Bernard and Lois Weisberg. Attended, New Coll., Oxford; BA, Yale U., 1986. Contbg. editor Vanity Fair; reporter Newsweek, London, Washington D.C.; assoc., mng., dep., sr. editor New Republic, Washington D.C., 1989—94; contbg. writer NY Times Mag., 1994—96; editor Slate mag., 1996—. Freelance journalist; columnist Financial Times; commentator Nat. Pub. Radio. Co-editor: Bushisms, 1992; author: In Defense of Government, 1996, The Bush Tragedy, 2008; co-author (with Robert Rubin): In an Uncertain World: Tough Choices from Wall Street to Washington, 2003. Office: Slate Mag 251 W 57th St 19th Fl New York NY 10019 also: 1350 Conn Ave NW Ste 400 Washington DC 20036*

WEISBERG, JOSEPH SIMPSON, retired dean; b. Jersey City, June 7, 1937; s. Samuel and Augusta (Biel) W.; m. Gloria Helen Weisberg, June 21, 1964; children: Debra Susan, David Jeffrey. BA, Jersey City State Coll., 1960; MA, Montclair State Coll., 1964; EdD, Columbia U., NYC, 1969. Tchr. earth sci. Wayne (N.J.) Pub. Schs., 1960-64; prof. geosci. Jersey City State Coll., 1964—, chmn. geosci., 1973-83, dean arts and scis., 1983-93; prof. emeritus NJ City U. Cons. JSW Assocs., Parsippany, N.J., 1966—; cons. in field. Author: Oceanography, 1979, Meteorology, 1981; co-author: Science Investiguides, 1967, Earth Science, 1970; reviewer, author various encys., pubrs. Advisor environ. Mayor's Office, Jersey City, 1967—, Parsippany, 1975—; v.p. Bd. Edn., Parsippany, 1979-88; pres. Lake Hiawatha Jewish Ctr., 1981-83; trustee County Coll. Morris, 1983-88; mem. and pres. Town Coun., Parsippany, 1987-94, mayor, 1994; dir. Alliance for Creative Edn., 1994—; trustee County Coll. Morris, 1995—, Morris Tomorrow, 2009-. Jewish. Home: 4 Camelot Way Parsippany NJ 07054-1408 E-mail: jweisberg@aol.com.

WEISBERG, LEONARD R., retired engineering executive, researcher; b. NYC, Oct. 17, 1929; s. Emanuel E. and Esther (Raynes) W.; m. Frances Simon, Mar. 23, 1980; children: Glenna Weisberg Andersen, Orren Weisberg Falk, Frances Weisberg Brookner. BA magna cum laude, Clark U., 1950; MA, Columbia U., 1952. Rsch. asst. Watson Labs. IBM, NYC, 1953-55; with RCA Labs., Princeton, NJ, 1955-71, mem. tech. staff, 1955-66, head rsch. group, 1966-69, dir. semicondr. device rsch. lab., 1969-71; dir. materials rsch. lab. Itek Corp., Lexington, Mass., 1972-74, v.p., dir. ctrl. rsch. lab., 1974-75; dir. electronics tech U.S. Dept. Def., Washington, 1975-79; v.p. rsch. and engring. Honeywell Inc., Mpls., 1980-94, ret., 1994. Adv. group on electron devices US Dept. Def., 1981—99. Contbr. articles to profl. jours. Recipient award for initiating VHSIC program U.S. Dept. Def., 1979. Fellow IEEE; mem. Am. Phys. Soc., Sigma Xi. Home and Office: 1250 S Washington St # 202 Alexandria VA 22314-4441 Home Phone: 703-549-8151. Personal E-mail: LenW5678@aol.com.

WEISBERG, MORRIS L., retired lawyer; b. Phila., June 7, 1921; s. Alexander and Hilda (Lichtenstein) W.; m. Mildred Norma Lubich, July 7, 1948; children— Richard, James, John BA, U. Pa., 1943, LL.B., 1947; MA, Yale U., 1944. Bar: Pa. 1950, U.S. Dist. Ct. (ea. dist.) Pa. 1950, U.S. Supreme Ct. 1962. Bigelow teaching fellow U. Chgo. Law Sch., 1947-48, Raymond grad. fellow, 1948-49; Gowen fellow U. Pa. Law Sch., Phila., 1948-49; ptnr. Harry Norman Ball, Phila., 1950-56; assoc. Blank, Rome, Comisky & McCauley, and predecessor, Phila., 1956-60, ptnr., 1960-93. Permanent mem. Jud. Conf. 3d Cir. Fellow Am. Bar Found.; mem. Order of Coif, Phi Beta Kappa Assocs. Office: Blank Rome 1 Logan Sq Fl 3 Philadelphia PA 19103-6998

WEISBERG, ROBERT IRVING, former ambassador; b. Md., 1950; BA, Haverford Coll.; JD, U. NC Sch. Law; MA, Nat. War Coll. Bar: NY, NH. Devel. officer Dartmouth Coll., 1977—82; fgn. svc. officer US Consulate Gen., Bombay, 1982—84, US Embassy, Moscow, 1984—86, US Embassy various other cities including Milan, Geneva, Bishkek, Oslo, and Warsaw; counselor for adminstrv. affairs US Embassy, Jakarta, 2000—02, dep. chief mission Helsinki, Finland; US amb. to Republic of Congo US Dept. State, Brazzaville, 2006—08. Recipient Medal for Outstanding Y2K Svc., Pres.'s Coun. on Year 2000 Conversion, Ellis Island Medal of Honor, award, Estrella de Carabobo, Venezuela, Disting. Alumnus award, U. NC Law Sch., Presdl. award for Meritorious Svc.*

WEISBERGER, BARBARA, artistic director, advisor, educator; b. Bklyn., Feb. 28, 1926; d. Herman and Sally (Goldstein) Linshes; m. Sol Spiller, Sept. 3, 1945 (div. 1948); m. Ernest Weisberger, Nov. 15, 1949; children: Wendy, Steven. BS in Edn., Psychology, Pa. State U., 1945; L.H.D. (hon.), Swarthmore Coll., 1970; D.F.A. (hon.), Temple U., 1973, Kings Coll., 1978, Villanova U., 1978, U. New England, 1996. Founder, dir., tchr. Wilkes-Barre (Pa.) Ballet Theater, 1953-63; founder, dir. Pa. Ballet, Phila., 1962-82, Carlisle (Pa.) Project, 1984—96; artistic advisor Peabody Dance, Balt., 2001—. Vice chmn. dance panel Nat. Endowment for the Arts, Washington, 1975-79. Performed with Met. Opera Ballet, N.Y.C., 1937, 38, Mary Binney Montgomery Co., Phila., 1940-42, ballet mistress, choreographer, Ballet Co. of Phila. Lyric Opera, 1961-62; choreographic works include Italian Concerto, Bach, Symphonic Variations, Franck; also operas for, Phila. Lyric Opera Co. Named Disting. Dau. of Pa., 1972, Disting. Alumna, Pa. State U., 1972; recipient 46th ann. Gimbel Phila. award, 1978. Mem. Psi Chi. Home and Office: 571 Charles Ave Kingston PA 18704-4711 Home Phone: 570-287-8349; Office Phone: 570-287-8349.

WEISBERGER, JAMES DAVID, hematopathologist; b. Wilkes-Barre, Pa., Aug. 25, 1955; s. Seymour and Sally Weisberger; m. Linda Ellen Cohen, May 20, 1984; children: Nicholas, Laura. BS, Stanford U., 1977, MS, 1978; MD U. Pa., 1983. Intern, resident internal medicine Calif. Pacific Med. Ctr., San Francisco, 1983—86; internist Fairmount Med. Group, El Cerrito, Calif., 1986—89, Cmty. Health Care Plan, New Haven, 1988—89; resident pathology NY Med. Coll., Valhalla, NY, 1990—94; fellow hematopathology NY Hosp. Cornell Med. Ctr., NYC, 1994—95; asst. prof. pathology and medicine NY Med. Coll., Valhalla, 1995—99, clin. asst. prof. pathology, 1999—; dir. hematopathology IMPATH, Inc., NYC, 1999—2003; v.p. chief med. officer Bio-Reference Labs., Elmwood Park, NJ, 2003—. Contbr. articles various profl. jours. Office: Bio-Reference Labs 481 Edward Ross Dr Elmwood Park NJ 07407

WEISBERGER, JOSEPH ROBERT, retired state supreme court justice; b. Providence, Aug. 3, 1920; s. Samuel Joseph and Ann Elizabeth (Meighan) W.; m. Sylvia Blanche Pigeon, June 9, 1951; children: Joseph Robert, Paula Ann, Judith Marie. AB, Brown U., Providence, 1942, LLD (hon.), 1992; JD, Harvard U., Cambridge, Mass., 1949; LLD (hon.), RI Coll., Providence, Suffolk U., Boston, Mt. St. Joseph Coll.; DCL (hon.), Providence Coll.; DHL (hon.), Bryant Coll., Smithfield, RI; LLD (hon.), Roger Williams Coll., 1992, Constantine U., 1997; LLD, So. New England Sch. Law, 1998; DHL (hon.), Salve Regina U., Newport, RI, 2001. Bar: Mass. 1949, R.I. 1950. With Quinn & Quinn, Providence, 1951-56; solicitor Glocester, RI, 1953-56; judge Superior Ct. RI, Providence, 1956-72; presiding justice RI Superior Ct., Providence, 1972-78; justice RI Supreme Ct., Providence, 1978—, chief justice, 1993—2001; ret., 2001; vol. mediator, 2001—. Adj. prof. U. Nev., 1986—; mem. faculty Nat. Jud. Coll.; vis. lectr. Providence Coll., Suffolk Law Sch., Roger Williams Coll.; chmn. New Eng. Regional Conf. Trial Judges, 1962, 63, 65, New Eng. Regional Commn. Disordered Offender, 1968-71, RI Com. Adoption on Rules Criminal Procedure, 1968-72, RI Adv. Com. Corrections, 1973; bd. dirs. Nat. Ctr. for State Cts., 1975-81; chmn. bd. dirs., bd. overseers Roger Williams U.; chmn. bd. dirs. Roger Williams U. Sch. Law, Joseph R. Weisberger endowed faculty chair, 2007. Chmn. editl. bd. Judges Jour., 1973-75. Pres. RI Health Facilities Planning Coun., 1967-70; chmn. Gov. RI Coun. Mental Health, 1968-73; moderator Town of East Providence, 1954-56; mem. RI Senate, 1953-56, minority leader, 1955-56; vice chmn. bd. trustee RI Hosp., hon. trustee, 2006—, 1968-92, St. Joseph's Hosp., trustee, 1962—. Lt. comdr. USNR, 1941-46. Recipient Erwin Griswold award, Nat. Jud. Coll., 1989, Advancement Justice award, 2009; named to R.I. Hall of Fame; Paul Harris fellow, Rotary Internat. Fellow Am. Bar Found.; mem. ABA (ho. of dels., task force on criminal justice stds. 1977-79, exec. com. appellate judges' conf. 1979-95, nat. conf. state trial judges 1977-78, exec. com. appelate judges conf. 1979—, vice chmn., 1983-85, chmn., 1985-86), KC, RI Bar Assn. (Jud. Excellence award 2007), Am. Judges Assn. (gov.), Inst. Jud. Adminstrn., Am. Judicature Soc. (Herbert Harley award 1990), Am. Law Inst., Order of St. Gregory (knight comdr. with star 1989, Goodrich award for Svc. 1995), Phi Beta Kappa (past pres. Alpha chpt. Brown U.). Home: 60 Winthrop St Riverside RI 02915-2624 Home Phone: 401-433-0081; Office Phone: 401-222-7691. *My professional life for the last 53 years has been occupied with judicial duties. I have been blessed with the opportunity to meet ever changing challenges and to attempt to solve a myriad of problems. These opportunities have been rewarding and absorbing. I consider judicial work to be a great privilege.*

WEISBERG-SAMUELS, JANET S., psychologist; b. NYC, Mar. 21, 1940; d. Morris and Vivian (Wank) Weisberg; m. Richard Samuels, Jan. 16, 1983; children: Debra Samuels, David Samuels. BBA, CCNY, 1960; MS, CUNY, 1967; PhD, Yeshiva U., 1984. Lic. psychologist, cert. sch. psychologist N.Y. Psychologist, adminstr. Bklyn. Jewish Hosp., 1969—75, Beth Israel Hosp., NYC, 1975—87; dir. edn. Interfaith Med. Ctr., Bklyn., 1987—; pvt. practice psychology, NYC, 1985—. Program dir. Brotherhood Synagogue, NYC, 1968—75, dir. edn. and tng., 1987—, dept. psychiatry Interfaith Med. Ctr.; team leader N.Y. State Dept. Mental Hygiene, NYC, 1977; cons. N.Y.C. Bd. Edn., 1977, Parent-Child Consultation Ctr., 1980—, Westchester Jewish Comm. Svcs., 2000—06. Pres. singles divsn. Park Ave. Synagogue, NYC, 1980—83; bd. dirs. Couples Club, 1986—, pres., 1988—90. Mem.: APA, Manhattan Psychol. Assn. (exec. bd. 1993—, pres. 1997—98), Ea. Psychol. Assn., N.Y. State Psychol. Assn. (chair internship dirs. 2003—06). Avocations: opera, museums, ballet. Office: 160 E 89th St Apt 1B New York NY 10128-2306 Office Phone: 212-410-4391.

WEISBROD, BURTON ALLEN, economist, educator; b. Chgo., Feb. 13, 1931; s. Leon H. and Idelle C. (Chernoff) W.; m. Shirley Lindsay, Dec. 23, 1951; children: Glen, Linda. BS, U. Ill., 1951; MA in Econs, Northwestern U., 1952, PhD, 1958. Lectr. econs. Northwestern U., Evanston, Ill., 1954-55; instr. econs. Carleton Coll., Minn., 1955-57, Washington U., St. Louis, 1957-58, asst. prof. econs., 1958-62, assoc. prof. econs., 1962-64; vis. assoc. prof. Princeton (N.J.) U., 1962-63; sr. staff mem. Council of Econ. Advs., Pres. U.S., 1963-64; assoc. prof. dept. econs. U. Wis., Madison, 1964-66, prof., 1966-91, Evjue-Bascom prof. econs., 1985—91; dir. Ctr. for Urban Affairs and Policy Rsch. Northwestern U., Evanston, Ill., 1990-95, John Evans prof. econs., 1990—. Vis. prof. SUNY, Binghamton, 1972; sr. Fulbright lectr. U. Autonoma de Madrid, summer, 1970; vis. prof. Yale U., 1976-77; Ziskind vis. prof. Brandeis U., 1982-83; vis. scholar, Brotman fellow J.F. Kennedy Sch., Harvard U., 1982-83; tchg. fellow Australian Nat. U., 1986; mem. rsch. adv. com. Econ. Devel. Adminstrn., U.S. Dept. Commerce, 1967-69; mem. adv. com. Commn. on Pvt. Philanthropy and Pub. Needs, 1973-75; cons. various fed. and state govt. agys., 1964—; also IBM, Econ. Coun. Can., 1969, 71, 76, 78; mem. bd. econ. advs. Public Interest Econs. Ctr., 1973-86; mem. adv. com. med. care and med. econs. to 3d Nat. Cancer Survey, 1969-71; U.S. del. UN World Population Conf., Belgrade, Yugoslavia, 1965; bd. dirs. Nat. Bur. Econ. Rsch., Inc., 1979-90; vis. scholar Phi Beta Kappa Soc., 1998-99; mem. nat. rsch. resources coun. NIH, 1999-03; mem. panel on nonmarket activity NRC, 2002-04; chair com. on philanthropy and the nonprofit sector Social Sci. Rsch. Coun., 2002-04; mem. IRS stats income divsn. Users Adv. Group, 2004-. Author: Economics of Public Health, 1961, External Benefits of Public Education, 1964, (with W. Lee Hansen) Benefits, Costs, and Finance of Public Higher Education, 1969, (with Ralph L. Andreano) American Health Policy, 1974, The Voluntary Nonprofit Sector: An Economic Analysis, 1978, (with Joel F. Handler and Neil K. Komesar) Public Interest Law: An Economic and Institutional Analysis, 1978, (with Jeffrey Ballou and Evelyn Asch) Mission and Money: Understanding the University, 2008; contbg. author: (with others) Disease and Economic Development: The Case of Parasitic Diseases in St. Lucia, West Indies, 1974, Economics and Medical Research, 1983, The Nonprofit Economy, 1988; editor (with James Worthy) The Urban Crisis, 1997; author, editor: To Profit or Not to Profit, 1998; contbr. nearly 200 articles on econs. of edn., program evaluation, health care and econs. of pvt. non-profit sector to profl. jours.; mem. editl. bd.: Jour. Human Resources, 1966-86, Internat. Jour. Social Econs, 1972—, Jour. Public Econs, 1971-87, Pub. Fin. Rev., 1990—, Nonprofit and Voluntary Sector Quar., 1997—; assoc. editor: Public Fin. Quar, 1972-87. Guggenheim fellow, 1969-70; Ford Faculty fellow, 1971-72; Sr. research fellow Brookdale Inst., Jerusalem, 1978—; recipient Disting. Lifetime Rsch. award Assn. Rsch. Nonprofit Orgns. and Voluntary Assns., 1997; co-recipient Carl Taube award Disting. Rsch., APHA, 1992. Fellow AAAS; mem. Am. Econ. Assn. (exec. com. 1975-77, com. status of assn. jours. 1973-74, chmn. budget com. 1977), Midwest Econs. Assn. (pres. 1980-81), Nat. Acad. Scis. Inst. Medicine, Public Choice Soc., Internat. Inst. Public Finance, AAUP (exec. com. Washington U. chpt. 1961-62). Office: Northwestern U Econs Dept 2003 Sheridan Rd Evanston IL 60208-0826 Business E-Mail: b-weisbrod@northwestern.edu.

WEISBROD, CARL, lawyer, public official; b. NYC, Oct. 5, 1944; s. Walter and Hilda (Pelzer) W.; m. Jody Adams, Jan. 21, 1979; 1 child, William. BS, Cornell U., 1965; JD, NYU, 1968. Bar: N.Y., 1968; U.S. Dist. Ct. (so. dist.) N.Y., 1969. Asst. commr. N.Y.C. Housing Dept., 1970-72; counsel, chief exec. officer Wildcat Svc. Corp., NYC, 1972-77; gen. counsel Manpower Demonstration Rsch. Corp., NYC, 1977-78; dir. Mayor's Office of Midtown Enforcement, NYC, 1978-84; exec. dir. City Vol. Corps, NYC, 1984-86, N.Y.C. Planning Commn., 1986-87; pres. 42d St. Devel. Project, NYC, 1987-90; pres., chief exec. officer N.Y.C. Econ. Devel. Corp., 1990-94; pres. Alliance for Downtown N.Y., 1995—2005, Trinity Real Estate, NYC, 2005—. Chmn. N.Y.C. Loft Bd., 1982-84, Wildcat Svc. Corp., 2002-07, New York State Health Found., 2008 Contbr. articles to profl. jours. Trustee The Ford Found., 1996-2008, NYU Downtown Hosp., 1999-2005; Lower Manhattan Devel. Corp., Convention Ctr. Devel. Corp. Office: Trinity Real Estate 75 Varick St New York NY 10013 Office Phone: 212-602-0814. Business E-Mail: cweisbrod@trinitywallstreet.org.

WEISBROT, DEBORAH MARCIA, psychiatrist; BA (hons.), Cornell U. Coll. of Arts and Scis., 1975; MD, SUNY, 1979. Cert. diplomate adult, child and adolescent psychiatry 1991. Unit chief, long term treatment unit program Dept. Psychiatry Albert Einstein Coll. of Medicine, Bronx, 1986—91, assoc. dir. residency tng., 1988—91; child, adolescent and adult psychiatry pvt. practice, NYC and Long Island, 1986—98; dir. child and adolescent outpatient svcs. Univ. Hosp., 1998—. Dir. child and adolescent outpatient svcs. Univ. Hosp. Author multiple jour. articles on mood and anxiety disorders in chi. Mem.: Greater L.I. Psychiat. Soc. (bd. dirs.), Acad. Child and Adolescent Psychiatry, Am. Psychiatric. Office: Divsn Child and Adolescent Psychiatry Putnam Hall S Campus SUNY Stony Brook NY 11790-8794 Office Phone: 631-632-8840.

WEISBURGER, ELIZABETH KREISER, retired chemist; b. Greenlane, Pa., Apr. 9, 1924; d. Raymond Samuel and Amy Elizabeth (Snavely) Kreiser; m. John H. Weisburger, Apr. 7, 1947 (div. May 1974); children: William Raymond, Diane Susan, Andrew John. BS, Lebanon Valley Coll., 1944, DSc (hon.), 1989; PhD, U. Cin., 1947, DSc (hon.), 1981. Rsch. assoc. U. Cin., 1947-49; col. USPHS, 1951-89; postdoctoral fellow Nat. Cancer Inst., Bethesda, Md., 1949-51, chemist, 1951-73, chief carcinogen metabolism and toxicology br., 1972-75, chief Lab. Carcinogen Metabolism, 1975-81, asst. dir. chem. carcinogenesis, 1981-89, ret. Cons. in field; lectr. Found. for Advanced Edn. in Scis., Bethesda, 1980-95; adj. prof. Am. U., Washington, 1982-83. Asst. editor-in-chief Jour. Nat. Cancer Inst., 1971-87; mem. editl. adv. bd. Chem. Health and Safety, 1994-99, Jour. Applied Toxicology, 1996-2006; contbr. articles to profl. jours. Trustee Lebanon Valley Coll., 1970—, pres. bd. trustees, 1985—89. Recipient Meritorious Svc. medal USPHS, 1973, Disting. Svc. medal, 1985; Hillebrand prize Chem. Soc. Washington, 1981, Charles Gordon award, 1999, Cmty. Svc. award, 2008. Fellow AAAS (nominating com. 1978-81); mem. Am. Chem. Soc. (Garvan medal 1981, Tillmanns-Skolnick award divsn. chem. health and safety 2001), Am. Assn. Cancer Rsch., Soc. Toxicology, Am. Soc. Biochem. and Molecular Biology, Royal Soc. Chemistry, Am. Conf. Govtl. Indsl. Hygienists (Herbert Stokinger award 1996, William Wagner award 2003), Grad. Women in Sci. (hon.), Iota Sigma Pi. Lutheran. Office Phone: 301-309-0078.

WEISBURGER, JOHN HANS, retired medical researcher; b. Stuttgart, Germany, Sept. 15, 1921; came to U.S., 1943, naturalized, 1944; s. William and Selma (Barth) W.; children: William, Diane, Andrew. AB, U. Cin., 1947, MS, 1948, PhD, 1949; MD (hon.), U. Umeå, Sweden, 1980. Officer USPHS, 1950-72; mem. staff Nat. Cancer Inst., NIH, Bethesda, Md., 1950-61, head carcinogen screening sect., 1961-72; dir. bioassay segment, Carcinogenesis Programs Nat. Cancer Inst., Bethesda, Md., 1971-72; v.p. rsch. Am. Health Found., Valhalla, NY, 1972-87; dir. Naylor Dana Inst. for Disease Prevention, Valhalla, 1972—87; rsch. prof. pathology N.Y. Med. Coll., Valhalla, 1974—2008; pres. Weisburger Assocs., North White Plains, NY, 1987—2007. Mem. biochemistry and nutrition study sect. NIH, 1957—58; mem. interdepartmental panel on carcinogens FDA, USDA, USPHS, 1962—71; chmn. carcinogenesis subcom. Nat. Large Bowel Cancer Project, 1972—75; mem. expert panel on nitrites and nitrosamines USDA, 1973—77; mem. Nat. Cancer Inst. Clearinghouse on Environ. Carcinogens, 1976—78; co-chmn. organizing com. US-Japan Coop. Workshop on GI Tract Cancer, 1979; chmn. sci. rev. panel NJ State Commn. Cancer Rsch., 1988—90;

co-chmn. internat. symposium on health effects of tea, NY, 1991; chmn. nutrition and cancer sect. 3d Anticarcinogenesis & antimutagenesis conf., Italy, 1991; chmn. study sect. NIH-Nat. Cancer Inst., Bethesda, Md., 1991; rsch. fellow Japanese Found. for Promotion of Cancer Rsch. Nat. Cancer Ctr. Rsch. Inst., Tokyo, 1992; adv. com. rev. RDA Food & Nutrition Bd. NAS, 1993; lectr. numerous lectures in field; chmn. numerous confs. national & internat.; editl. bd. Internat. Jour. Tea Sci., 2006—. Assoc. editor Jour. Nat. Cancer Inst., 1960-62, Xenobiotica, 1971—2004, Archives of Toxicology, 1977-87, Internat. Jour. Toxicology, 1982-2002, Preventive Medicine, 1988-2004; mem. internat. editl. adv. bd. Food and Chem. Toxicology, 1967—2004; assoc. editor Cancer Rsch., 1969-80, mem. cover editl. bd., 1987-99; mem. editl. bd. Chemico-Biol. Interactions, 1969-88, Carcinogenesis, 1979-87, Inst. Sci. Info. Atlas of Sci., 1987-89, Cancer Epidemiology Biomarkers Prevention, 1991-98, Cancer Detection Prevention, 1994-2004; mem. guest editl. bd. Japanese Jour. Cancer Rsch., 1987—; hon. editor Protective Effects of Tea on Human Health, 2006; contbr. articles to profl. jours. With US Army, 1944—46, Italy, Austria, ret. col. USPHS. Decorated D.S.M.; recipient Meritorious Svc. medal USPHS HEW, 1970, Outstanding Service award Westchester div. Am. Cancer Soc., 1984, Meyer and Anna Prentis award Mich. Cancer Ctr., 1987; named one of 1000 most cited scientists, ISI List, 1981. Leadership plaque N.J. State Commn. Cancer Rsch., 1990. Fellow N.Y. Acad. Scis., Am. Coll. Nutrition; mem. Am. Assn. Cancer Rsch. (hon. mem., rep. to European Assn. Cancer Rsch. 1985-89), Am. Chem. Soc. (hon., com. environ. improvement 1992-94, chmn. lectr. chemistry and health 31st Middle Atlantic regional meeting 1997, chmn. symposium tea and health, N.Y., 2003), Am. Gastroent. Assn., Am. Soc. Biochem. Molecular Biologists, Am. Soc. Preventive Oncology (founding mem., bd. dirs. 1983-90, Disting. Svc. award 1990), Biochem. Soc. (London, emeritus), Environ. Mutagen Soc., European Assn. Cancer Rsch. (coun. 1985-90), Japan Cancer Assn. (hon. life), Soc. Exptl. Biol. Medicine, Soc. Toxicology (chmn. bd. publs. 1968-71, councilor 1972-74, amb. toxicology Mid-Atlantic divsn. 1990, hon. mem. 1995, Award of Merit 1981), Westchester Chem. Soc. (Disting. Scientist 1996), Sigma Xi, Alpha Chi Sigma (pres. Washington profl. chpt. 1967-68), Phi Lambda Upsilon. Achievements include rsch. in lifestyle and chronic disease prevention, relevant mechanisms, and medical care cost reduction. Home: 4 Whitewood Rd White Plains NY 10603-1137 Home Phone: 914-592-4037. Personal E-mail: johnweisburger@aol.com. *In my lifetime a revolutionary change occurred in our knowledge of the causes and the mechanisms involved in the major premature killing diseases—heart disease, hypertension, stroke, many forms of cancer. These key advances stemmed from the partnership between the federal government, public-supported societies and academic institutions that encourage health research. The impact of these diseases can be reduced in virtually all countries of the world provided their political bodies can agree that peaceful endeavors and cooperation in fostering better health for their people can be made a high priority goal. Medical science now can implement successful prevention efforts. I am glad I have lived through this period and have played a role in this development.*

WEISE, KELLY See WEERASINGHE, KUMUDINI

WEISEL, MICHAEL LLOYD, lawyer, educator; m. Deborah Lamm Weisel, June 6, 1987; children: Avery Christiana, Schuyler McFall. BS in Bus. Mgmt. and History, Guilford Coll., 1977; JD, Campbell U., 1980; postgrad., Duke U., 2002—; MA in History, N.C. State U., 2003. Bar: N.C. 1980; lic. securities arbitrator Fin. Industry Regulatory Authority. V.p. equity Wells Fargo Bank, NA, Washington, 1988—90; v.p., portfolio mgr. Kemper Fin. Svcs., Chgo., 1990—95; atty. Allen & Pinnix, Raleigh, 1996—2003, Taylor, Penry, Rash & Riemann PLLC, Raleigh, 2003—07; gen. counsel to spkr. pro tempore N.C. Ho. Reps., NC, 2006; atty. Bailey & Dixon LLP, Raleigh, 2007—. Bd. mem. NC State Banking Commn., Raleigh, 1993—97; trustee N.C. Tchrs. and State Employees' Retirement Systems, Raleigh, 1993—95, N.C. Local Govt. Employees' Retirement Sys., Raleigh, 1993—95; chair Fgn. Trade Zone #93, Raleigh, 1997—; sec. N.C. R.R. Co., 1999—2004, N.C. Devel. Fin. Corp., 2000—, bd. dirs. Local bd. dirs. US SSS, NC, 2003—; commn. mem. Legislative Sch. Capital Constrn. Study Commn., Raleigh, 1993—95; bd. dirs., vice chair fin. com. N.C. Bd. Cmty. Colls., Raleigh, 1997—2000; com. mem. NC Legislative Fin. Institutions Com., Raleigh, 1998—99; chair Wake County Smart Start, Inc., NC, 1997—2009; elected chair Wake County Dem. Party, NC, 1999—2003; mem. N.C. Dem. Party State Exec. Com., 1997—; candidate Office N.C. State Treas., 1995—96, NC, 2007—08. Named one of Outstanding Young Man of Am., Nat. Jaycees; fellow, Inst. Polit. Leadership; History Departmental fellow, Duke U., 2002—08, Mil. History fellow, West Point Mil. Acad., 2004. Mem.: Penn Club NY, Union League Club Chgo., Phi Alpha Theta. Office: Bailey & Dixon LLP PO Box 1351 Raleigh NC 27602

WEISENBERG, SHARI, broadcast executive, marketing professional; Grad., Boston U. Sales & mktg. positions DI Group/Editel Boston, 1990—93; dir. ops. & prodn. Telezign (TZ), NYC, 1993—99; sr. v.p. bus. devel. thoughtbubble Ltd., 1999—2001; mktg. dir. CNBC, NBC Universal, Inc., 2001—04, mktg. dir. Bravo, 2004—07, v.p. strategic mktg. Sci-Fi, 2007—. Vol. Morgan Stanley Children's Hosp., Good Dog Found. Named a Woman to Watch, Advt. Age, 2009. Mem.: Delta Gamma. Office: NBC Universal Inc Hdqs 30 Rockefeller Plaza New York NY 10112*

WEISENBERGER, ANDREW, lawyer; b. Cin., Sept. 12, 1977; BS, Miami U., Ohio, 1999; JD, Louis D. Brandeis Sch. Law, U. Louisville, 2002; LLM, Georgetown U., 2003. Bar: Ohio 2002, US Dist. Ct. Southern Dist. Ohio 2003, Ky. 2004. Assoc. Santen & Hughes, Cin. Named one of Ohio's Rising Stars, Super Lawyers, 2006. Office: Santen & Hughes STE 2700 600 Vine St Cincinnati OH 45202-2409 Office Phone: 513-721-4450. Office Fax: 513-721-0109.

WEISENBURGER, RANDALL J., advertising executive; b. 1958; With Coopers & Lybrand, 1980-85, First Boston Corp., 1987-88; mng. dir. to pres. & CEO Wasserstein Perella & Co., 1988-99; CEO Wickes Mfg. Co., Inc., Southfield, Mich., 1990-93; co-chmn. Collins & Aikman Corp., Charlotte, NC, 1993-99; exec. v.p. & CFO Omnicom Group, Inc., NYC, 1999—. Vice-chmn. Maybelline, Inc.; chmn. Yardley of London; bd. dirs. Alliance Entertainment Corp., CTS Corp. Office: Omnicom Group Inc 437 Madison Ave New York NY 10022 also: 701 Mccullough Dr Charlotte NC 28262-3318 Office Phone: 212-415-3600. Office Fax: 212-817-6551. E-mail: ir@omnicomgroup.com.

WEISENBURGER, THEODORE MAURICE, retired judge, poet, educator; b. Tuttle, ND, May 12, 1930; s. John and Emily (Rosenau) W.; children: Sam, Jennifer, Emily, Todd, Daniel, Dwight, Holly, Michael, Paul, Peter; m. Maylyne Chu, Sept. 19, 1985; 1 child, Irene. BA, U. N.D., 1952, LLB, 1956, JD, 1969; BFT, Am. Grad Sch. Internat. Mgmt., Phoenix, 1957. Bar: N.D. 1963, U.S. Dist. Ct. N.D. 1963. County judge, tchr. Bensen County, Minnewaukan, ND, 1968-75, Walsh County, Grafton, ND, 1975-87; trial judge Devils Lake Sioux, Ft. Totten, ND, 1968-84, Turtle Mountain Chippewa, Belcourt, ND, 1974-87; U.S. magistrate U.S. Dist. Ct., Minnewaukan, 1972-75; Justice of the Peace pro tem Maricopa County, Ariz., 1988-92; instr. Rio Salado C.C., 1992—. Tchr. in Ethiopia, 1958-59. Author: Poetry and Other Poems, 1991. 1st lt. U.S. Army, 1952-54. Recipient Humanitarian award U.S. Cath. Conf., 1978, 82, Right to Know award Sigma Delta Chi, 1980, Spirit of Am. award U.S. Conf. Bishops, 1982. Home: 4353 E Libby St Phoenix AZ 85032-1732 Office Phone: 602-992-0492. Personal E-mail: tweisenburger@cox.net.

WEISENFELD, CAROL ANN TRIMBLE, marketing executive, consultant; b. Port Arthur, Tex., Jan. 6, 1939; d. Vance Henry and Elzene Miller Trimble; m. Ronald John Nordheimer, Sept. 3, 1977; children: Diane Carol Nordheimer, David Douglas Nordheimer, Rex Robert Nordheimer. BA in Journalism, U. Pa., Phila., 1960; MA in Comm., Annenberg Sch. Comm. U. Pa., Phila., 1962. Cert. facilatator and bus. coach TAB, 2007. Wire editor Westchester County Pubs., Inc., Tarrytown, NY, 1960—61; interview asst. Samuel Lubell, NYC, 1961; editor U. City News Bartash Pubs., Phila., 1961—62; coord. cmty. rels. West Phila. Corp., 1962—71; comm. cons. Schnader Harrison Segal & Lewis, 1962—63; dir. comm. U. City Sci. Ctr., 1971—73; campaign cons. Heinz for U.S. Senate, 1976—77; dir. devel. Fox Chase Cancer Ctr., 1977—80; campaign cons. Holtzman for US Senate, NYC, 1980—81; asst. mng. dir. City of Phila., Philadelphia, Pa., 1981—83; dir. transition team Holtzman to N.Y.C. Comptr., NYC, 1990—91; chmn. and CEO Gauge Corp., Wilmington, Del., 1991—94; pres. and CEO Market Tech Assoc., Inc., 1994—. Adj. lectr. comm. Widener U. Brandywine Divsn., Wilmington, Del., 1988—89; mem. bd. dir. Forum Exec. Women, Phila., 1983—85, founder, pres., Wilmington, Del., 1993—94. Prodr.(host): (weekly radio program) Pathways to Service. Pres. Caesar Rodney Rotary Club, Wilmington, Del., 1996—97; gov. dist. 7630 Rotary Internat., 2001—02; regional vice chair Rotary Leadership Inst., 2004—08, faculty mem., 2004—; commr. Commn. Women, Del., 1994—; mem. Governor's Pub. Works and Procurement Coun., 2002—07; pres. Organized Classes of U. Pa., 1982—83; mem. bd. Pub. Allies (Del. chpt.), 1994—2004. Mem.: Del. Assn. Nonprofit Agencies (memb. bd. 2004—06), U. & Whist Club, Kappa Kappa Gamma. Office: Market Tech Assoc Inc 1304 Hilltop Ave Wilmington DE 19809-1628 Office Fax: 302-792-0111; Home Fax: 302-792-0111.

WEISER, RONALD, political organization administrator, former ambassador; b. South Bend, Ind., July 7, 1945; m. Eileen Weiser; 3 children. BBA, U. Mich., 1966, postgrad. Founder, chmn. bd. dirs., CEO McKinley Assocs., 1968—2001; US amb. to Slovak Republic US Dept. State, Bratislava, 2001—05; co-chmn. Mich. Republican Party, 2009—. Bd. dirs., former chmn. Quantumshift. Former mem., vice chmn. Mich. State Officer's Compensation Commn.; chmn. McKinley Found.; chmn. bd. trustees Mich. Theater; co-chmn. United Negro Coll. Fund of Washtenaw County, U. Mich. Ctr. for Cmty. Svc. and Learning; trustee, chmn. fin. com., treas. Henry Ford Mus. and Greenfield Village; bd. dirs. Purple Rose Theater; mem. Bus. Sch. nat. devel. Bd. U. Mich., mem. athletic dept. devel. and external rels. bd., former pres. adv. bd.; treas., chmn. Artrain USA. Republican. Office: Mich Republican Party Secchia-Weiser Mich Republican Ctr 520 Seymour St Lansing MI 48933 Office Phone: 517-487-5413. Office Fax: 517-487-0090.*

WEISFELD, SHELDON, lawyer; b. McAllen, Tex., Feb. 20, 1946; s. Morris and Pauline (Horwitz) W.; m. Eve F. Weisfeld, Jan. 23, 1994; 1 child, Raquel Paolina. BBA, U. Tex., 1967; postgrad., Nat. U. Mex., 1969; JD, U. Houston, 1970. Bar: Tex. 1971, U.S. Dist. Ct. (so. dist.) Tex. 1978, U.S. Dist. Ct. (we. dist.) Tex. 1995, U.S. Dist. Ct. (ea. dist.) Tex. 2001, U.S. Ct. Appeals (5th cir.) 1978, U.S. Ct. Appeals (11th cir.) 1981, U.S. Supreme Ct. 1982. Pvt. practice, Austin, Tex., 1973—77; pvt. practice law Brownsville, Tex., 1980—. Asst. fed. pub. defender U.S. Dist. Ct. (so. dist.) Tex., Brownsville, 1977-80. Fellow Tex. Bar Found. (life); mem. ABA, Nat. Assn. Criminal Def. Lawyers (life), Tex. Criminal Def. Lawyers (dir.), Fed. Bar Assn., State Bar Tex., Cameron County Bar Assn., Hidalgo County Bar Assn., B'nai B'rith. Democrat. Office: 855 E Harrison St Brownsville TX 78520-7173 Office Phone: 956-546-2727. Fax: 956-544-7446. E-mail: isweisfeld@aol.com.

WEISFELDT, MYRON LEE, cardiologist, educator; b. Milw., Apr. 25, 1940; s. Simon Charles and Sophia (Price) W.; m. Linda Nan Zaremski, Dec. 29, 1963; children— Ellyn Joy, Lisa Janel, Sara Michelle Student, Northwester U., 1958-60; BA, Johns Hopkins U., 1962, MD, 1965. Intern and resident Columbia-Presbyn. Med. Ctr., NYC, 1965-67; fellow in cardiology Mass. Gen. Hosp., Boston, 1970-72; asst. prof. medicine Johns Hopkins U., Balt., 1972-78, prof. medicine, 1978-91, Robert L. Levy prof. cardiology, 1979-91; Samuel Bard prof. medicine, chair dept. Columbia-Presbyn. Med. Ctr., NYC, 1991—2001; William Osler prof. medicine, dir. dept. medicine Johns Hopkins Med. Sch., 2001—; physician in chief Johns Hopkins Hosp., 2001. Dir. cardiology Johns Hopkins Med. Inst., Balt., 1975-91, Peter Belfer Lab. for Johns Hopkins, Ischemic Heart Disease Spl. Ctr. Rsch., 1977-91; nat. pres. Am. Heart Assn., 1989-90; cardiology adv. com. Nat. Heart, Lung and Blood Inst., 1986-90, chmn., 1988-90; mem. adv. coun. Nat. Inst. on Aging, 1999-2002; study chair resuscitation outcomes consortium Nat. Heart Lung and Blood Inst., 2004—. Editor: The Aging Heart, 1980; editorial bd. Jour. Clin. Investigation, 1984-88, Circulation, 1980-86, 88—2004, Jour. Am. Coll. Cardiology, 1987-93, Jour. Molecular and Cellular Cardiology, 1975-80, 86-89, Circulation Rsch., 1988-94. With USPHS, 1967—69. NIH grantee, 1977-91; recipient Golden Heart award Am. Heart Assn., 1998, Harrick award, 2004. Fellow AAAS, ACP (Phillips award in clin. medicine 2006), Am. Coll. Cardiology; mem. Assn. Univ. Cardiologists, Am. Soc. Clin. Investigation, Assn. Am. Physicians, Assn. Prof. Medicine (Diversity award, 2008), Inst. of Medicine, Phi Beta Kappa, Alpha Omega Alpha, Interurban Clin. Club. Jewish. Office: Johns Hopkins Medicine 1830 E Monument St Ste 9026 Baltimore MD 21287 Home Phone: 410-588-2481; Office Phone: 410-955-6642. Business E-Mail: mlw5@jhmi.edu.

WEISFUSE, ISAAC BRAM, city health department administrator; b. New Hyde Park, NY, Apr. 27, 1955; m. Evelyn Horn; children: Ari, Lois. MD, SUNY Downstate Med. Ctr., Bklyn., 1982; MPH in Health Policy and Mgmt., Columbia U., NYC, 1991. Diplomate Am. Bd. Internal Medicine. Intern/resident internal medicine LI Jewish Med. Ctr., 1982—85; fellow epidemiology & pub. health Epidemic Intelligence Svc., Ctr.'s for Disease Control & Prevention, 1985—87; with NYC Dept. Health & Mental Hygiene, 1987—, various positions including dir. Office AIDS Rsch., asst. commr. Bur. Sexually Transmitted Diseases, dir. emergency preparedness activities, 1999—, agy. incident comdr. for World Trade Ctr. disaster, dep. commr. disease control, 2002—. Assoc. prof. clin. pub. health of epidemiology Columbia U. Mailman Sch. Pub. Health; faculty Johns Hopkins Sch. Pub. Health, Balt. Contbr. articles to profl. jours. Office: NYC Dept Health & Mental Hygiene 125 Worth St Rm 326 CN#22 New York NY 10013 Business E-Mail: iweisfus@health.nyc.gov.*

WEISGALL, JONATHAN MICHAEL, lawyer; b. Balt., Mar. 17, 1949; s. Hugo David and Nathalie (Shulman) W.; m. Ruth Macdonald, June 3, 1979; children: Alison, Andrew, Benjamin. BA, Columbia Coll., 1970; JD, Stanford U., 1973. Bar: D.C. 1974, N.Y. 1974, U.S. Supreme Ct. 1982, Marshall Islands 1983. Law clk. to judge U.S. Ct. Appeals (9th cir.), San Francisco, 1973-74; assoc. Covington & Burling, Washington, 1974-79; from assoc. to ptnr. Ginsburg, Feldman, Weil & Bress, Washington, 1980-83; pvt. practice Washington, 1983-99; v.p. Legis. and Regulatory Affairs MidAmerican Energy Holdings Co., 1995—. Adj. prof. Georgetown U. Law Ctr. Author: Operation Crossroads: The Atomic Tests at Bikini Atoll, 1994; exec. prodr. documentary film Radio Bikini. Chmn. bd. dirs. Ctr. for Energy Efficiency and Renewable Techs.; trustee Arena Stage, Washington; bd. dirs. Meet the Composer, Geothermal Resources Coun. Mem. Geothermal Energy Assn. (past v.p., bd. dirs., pres.), Geothermal Resources Coun. (bd. dirs.), Phi Beta Kappa. Jewish. Home: 5309 Edgemoor Ln Bethesda MD 20814-1323 Office: Ste 330 N 1800 M St Washington DC 20036-5844 Office Phone: 202-828-1378. Personal E-mail: jmweisgall@midamerican.com.

WEISKOPF, WANDA, mezzo soprano, writer, poet; b. Jefferson City, Mo., Aug. 2, 1921; d. Elmer and Stella Jane (Buster) Connell; m. Herbert Weiskopf (dec.); children: Douglas McK., Marta Jane. Student, L.A. Conservatory, 1950—55. Pvt. practice, Portland, Oreg., 1970—80. Activities dir., editor Skylines Portland Ctr., 1970—85; adjudicator Met. Opera Auditions, Seattle, 1990. Singer: (Operas) Portland Cathedral and St. Michael's, 1970—85, appeared in maj. opera houses, leading roles in Mo., Calif., Oreg., Italy, San Remo; author: All Is Not Winter, 1976, On the Wings of Song: My Life with the Maestro, 1995, Listen To The River, 2001, My Song, 2009. Organizer meml. concert Am. Heart Assn., Portland, 1971; active Dem. Party, Burbank, Calif., 1990. With US Army, 1942. Mem.: Nat. Assn. Tchrs. Singing, Nat. Writers Assn. (sec. LA chpt. 1989—2005). Democrat. Avocation: walking. Home: 1207 N Cordova St #105 Burbank CA 91505-2218

WEISMAN, ERIC, music company executive; With Premier Artists Svcs., 1985, Bassin Distbr., 1985—90, Alliance Entertainment Corp., Minnetonka, Minn., 1990, pres., CEO, 1997—2003; CEO Musicland Holding Corp., 2003—05, advisor, 2005—. Office: Musicland STE 225 122 E 42nd St Rm 1014 New York NY 10168-1099

WEISMAN, GARY ANDREW, biochemist; b. Bklyn., June 18, 1951; s. Joseph Herman and Elaine (Melman) W.; m. Sandra Kay Hille, Aug. 4, 1979; children: Laura Joanne, Pamela Michelle, Veronica Evelyn. BS, Polytechnic U., 1972; postgrad., U. Bordeaux, France, 1972-74; PhD, U. Nebr., 1980. Postdoc. rsch. assoc. Cornell U., Ithaca, NY, 1980-85; asst. prof. U. Mo., Columbia, 1985-92, assoc. prof., 1992-98, prof., 1998—. Spl. reviewer NIH, mem. ODCS Study Section; reviewer NSF, Am. Jour. Physiology, Jour. Biol. Chemistry, Molec. Pharmacology, Euro. Jour. Pharmacol. GLIA; editl. bd. Purinergic Signalling. Contbr. articles to profl. jours. Grantee USDA, 1987—, NIH, 1988—, CF Found., 1994-2000, Am. Diabetes, 1995-2002, Am. Heart Assn. 1994-. Mem. AAAS, Am. Chem. Soc., Am. Soc. Biochem. and Molecular Biology, Am. Diabetes Assn., Am. Heart Assn., NY Acad. Scis., Soc. for Neurosci., Am. Soc. Nutr. Scis., Am. Soc. Pharmacol. and Exptl. Therapeut. Home: 1804 University Ave Columbia MO 65201-6004 Office: U Mo Dept Biochemistry 540E Life Scis Ctr Columbia MO 65211-7310 Business E-Mail: weismang@missouri.edu.

WEISMAN, JOEL, retired engineering educator; b. NYC, July 15, 1928; s. Abraham and Ethel (Marcus) W.; m. Bernice Newman, Feb. 6, 1955; 1 child, Jay (dec.) B.Ch.E., CCNY, 1948; MS, Columbia U., 1949; PhD, U. Pitts, 1968. Registered profl. engr., N.Y. Plant engr. Etched Products, NYC, 1950-51; from jr. engr. to assoc. engr. Brookhaven Nat. Lab., Upton, NY, 1951-54; from engr. to fellow engr. Westinghouse Nuclear Energy Systems, Pitts., 1954-59, from fellow engr. to mgr. thermal and hydraulic analysis, 1960-68; sr. engr. Nuclear Devel. Assocs., White Plains, NY, 1959-60; assoc. prof. nuclear engring. U. Cin., 1968—72, prof. nuclear engring., 1972-96, dir. nuclear engring. program, 1977-86, dir. lab. basic and applied nuclear research, 1984-94, prof. emeritus nuclear engring., 1996—. Co-author: Thermal Analysis of Pressurized Water Reactors, 1970, 2d edit., 1979, Chinese edit., 1981, 3rd edit., 1996, Introduction to Optimization Theory, 1973, Modern Power Plant Engineering, 1985; editor: Elements of Nuclear Reactor Design, 1977, Chinese edit., 1982, 2d edit., 1983; contbr. tech. articles to profl. jours.; patentee in field. Mem. Cin. Environ. Adv. Council, 1976-78; mem. Cin. Asian Art Soc., 1977—, v.p., 1980-82, pres., 1982-84; mem. exec. bd. Air Pollution League Greater Cin., 1980-90. Sr. NATO fellow, Winfrith Lab., U.K. Atomic Energy Authority, 1972; sr. fellow Argonne Nat. Lab., Ill., 1982; NSF research grantee, 1974-78, 82-85, 86-89; recipient Dean's award U. Cin. Coll. Engring., 1987. Fellow Am. Nuclear Soc. (v.p. Pitts. sect. 1957-58, mem. exec. com. thermal-hydraulics div. 1989-92); mem. Am. Inst. Chem. Engrs., Sigma Xi Democrat. Jewish. Avocation: Japanese art. Office: U Cin Dept Mech Ind & Nuclear Engr Cincinnati OH 45221-0001

WEISMAN, LEONARD E., medical educator; Prof. pediat. Baylor Coll. Medicine, Houston, 1994—.

WEISMAN, RICHARD SCOTT, lawyer; b. NYC, Nov. 3, 1956; s. Harold and Sarah (Delaney) Weisman. AB, Harvard Coll., 1978, JD, 1982. Bar: N.Y. 1983. Spl. asst. Senator Daniel Patrick Moynihan, Washington, 1978-79; assoc. Cahill Gordon & Reindel, NYC, 1982-84, Sidley & Austin, NYC, 1984-87, Winthrop Stimson Putnam & Roberts, NYC, 1987-90; atty. Richard S. Weisman, Esq., NYC and Westchester, N.Y., 1990-91, Beller & Keller, NYC, 1992-95; mng. ptnr. Weisman & Calderon LLP, Mt. Vernon, N.Y., 1996—. Mem.: Bronx County Bar Assn. (chmn., Surrogate's Ct. Com.), Westchester County Bar Assn., Nat. Guardianship Assn., Mt. Vernon Bar Assn., N.Y. State Trial Lawyers Assn., N.Y. State Bar Assn. Office: Weisman & Calderon LLP 6 Gramatan Ave Ste 206 Mount Vernon NY 10550-3209 Office Phone: 914-668-8900. E-mail: weismanr@erols.com.

WEISMAN, R(OBERT) BRUCE, physical chemist, educator, entrepreneur; b. Balt., Nov. 23, 1950; s. Samuel and Eva (Abramson) W.; m. Kathleen Mary Beckingham, July 25, 1986; 1 child, Caroline Mary. BA, Johns Hopkins U., 1971; PhD, U. Chgo., 1977. Postdoctoral fellow U. Pa., Phila., 1977-79; asst. prof. Rice U., Houston, 1979-84, assoc. prof., 1984-93, prof., 1993—. Founder, pres. Applied Nano Fluorescence, LLC. Mem. editl. bd. Rev. Sci. Instruments, 1991-93; co-editor Applied Physics A, 2004-; contbr. more than 120 articles to profl. and sci. jours. Grad. fellow Fannie and John Hertz Found., 1973-76, NSF, 1971-73; postdoctoral fellow NSF, 1977-78; rsch. fellow Alfred P. Sloan Found., 1985-89, fellow Am. Physical Soc., 2008. Mem. AAAS, Am. Chem. Soc., Am. Phys. Soc., Electrochem. Soc. (sec. Fullerenes Divsn. 2004-08, vice chair 2008—), Sigma Xi. Office: Rice U Dept Chemistry Houston TX 77005 Home Phone: 713-665-8845; Office Phone: 713-348-3709. Business E-Mail: weisman@rice.edu.

WEISMANTEL, GREGORY NELSON, management consultant, computer company executive; b. Houston, Sept. 8, 1940; s. Leo Joseph and Ellen Elizabeth (Zudis) W.; m. Marilyn Ann Fanger, June 18, 1966; children: Guy Gregory, Christopher Gregory, Andrea Rose. BA in English, U. Notre Dame, 1962; MBA in Internat. Bus., Loyola U., Chgo., 1979. With mgmt. staff Gen. Foods Corp., White Plains, NY, 1966-80; pres., chief exec. officer Manor House Foods, Inc., Addison,

Ill., 1980-82, Weismantel & Assocs., Downers Grove, Ill., 1982-84; v.p. perishable div. Profl. Marketers, Inc., Lombard, Ill., 1984-86, group v.p. sales and mktg. services, dir. corp. strategy, 1986-87; v.p. mng. prin. CPG Industry, Louis A. Allen Assoc. Inc., Palo Alto, Calif., 1987-88; pres., chief exec. officer The Vista Tech. Group, Ltd., St. Charles, Ill., 1989-2000, chmn. bd., 2001—02; pres. Epic Global Technol., 2002—. Bd. dirs. Epicurean Foods, Ltd., Chgo., 2004; pres. Aquitec, Inc., Chgo; pres., CEO Epic Group- Hawkeye Perfect Measure Sys., 2003-. Chmn. fin. St. Edward's High Sch. Jubilee, Elgin, Ill., 1982-85; bd. dirs. Dist. 301 Sch. Bd., Burlington, Ill., 1980-84, St. Edward's Found., Elgin, 1982—. Capt. U.S. Army, 1962-66. Recipient ICP/Chgo. Software Assoc. Re-Engring. award, 1994-96; State of Ill. grantee, 1989, Build Ill. Investment Fund, finalist KPMG Hi-tech. Entrepreneur award, Vista Technology, 2001. Mem. Grocery Mfg. Sales Execs., Chgo. Software Assn., Chg. C. of C. (small bus. com.). Clubs: Merchandising Execs., Food Products, Am. Mktg. (Chgo.), St. Charles Country Club (equity mem., fin. chmn.). Roman Catholic. *Success can only occur when a person realizes that life is not a rehearsal.*

WEISMILLER, ELEANOR KOVACS, library director; b. Perth Amboy, NJ, July 28, 1942; d. Louis T and Ethel D Kovacs; m. David L Weismiller (dec.); children: Chris, David. BA, Duquesne U., 1964; tchg. cert., Wash. Montessori Inst., 1967. Cert. Notary Public State of Calif. Tchr. Montessori Child Develop., West Covina, Calif., 1978—80; sch. libr. Rowland Unified Sch. Dist., Rowland Hts., Calif., 1981—87; libr. asst. County of Los Angeles Pub. Libr., 1987—96, cmty. libr. mgr. Whittier, Calif., 1996—. Founding mem. Friends of the Sorensen Libr., Whittier, Calif., 1989—. Mem. West Whittier Cmty. Coun., Population Stabilization, Washington. Avocation: art. Office: Sorensen Libr 11405 E Rose Hedge Dr Whittier CA 90606

WEISNER, TOM, Mayor, Aurora, Illinois; m. Marilyn Weisner. Mayor City of Aurora, Ill., 2005—. Vol. Peace Corps, Solomon Islands; mem. Afterschool Alliance. Democrat. Office: City Hall 44 E Downer Pl Aurora IL 60507 Office Phone: 630-264-4636. Business E-Mail: mayorsoffice@aurora-il.org.*

WEISS, ALLEN S., writer, educator, playwright; b. Bronx, NY, 1953; s. Lala and Leslie Weiss. BA, Queens Coll., CUNY, 1974; PhD, SUNY, Stony Brook, 1980; PhD in Cinema Studies, NYU, 1989. Prof. NYU, 1992—. Author: (books) Iconology and Perversion, 1988, The Aesthetics of Exces, 1989, Shattered Forms: Art Brut, Phantasms, Modernism, 1992, Perverse Desire and the Ambiguous Icon, 1994, Mirrors of Infinity: The French Formal Garden and 17th Century Metaphysics, 1995, Unnatural Horizons: Paradox and Contradiction in Landscape Architecture, 1998, Feast and Folly: Cuisine, Intoxication, and the Poetics of the Sublime, 2002, The Wind and the Source: In the Shadow of Mont Ventoux, 2005, Le Livre bouffon, 2009; editor (co-editor): Phantasm and Simulacra, 1985, Art Brut: Madness and Marginalia, 1988, New Paradigms in Film Theory, 1989, numerous books; playwright L'Indomptable, 1996, Danse Macabre I, 2004, Danse Macabre II, 2009; contbr. articles to profl. jours. Editl. and bd. mem. Adv. Com., IEHCA, France, 2008—09. Fulbright fellowship, Paris, 1978—79, Etants Donnes grant, 2001, 2004. Mem.: Phi Beta Kappa. Office: Performance Studies & Cinema Studies NYU 721 Broadway New York NY 10003 Office Phone: 212-998-1642.

WEISS, ALVIN HARVEY, chemical engineer, educator, research scientist, consultant; b. Phila., Apr. 28, 1928; s. Louis and Helen F. (Wilinsky) W.; m. Devorah Schwartz, June 10, 1979; child: Linda. BSChemE, U. Pa., 1949, PhD in Phys. Chemistry, 1965; MSChemE, Newark Coll. Engring., 1955. Registered profl. engr., Mass., Del. Chem. engr. Fiber Chem. Corp., Cliffwood, NJ, 1949-51, US Army Chem. Corps, Edgewood, Md., 1951—53, Colgate-Palmolive Co., Jersey City, 1953-55, Houdry Process and Chems. Co., Linwood, Pa., 1956-63; rsch. assoc., lectr. U. Pa., Phila., 1963-66; prof. chem. engring. Worcester (Mass.) Poly. Inst., 1966-94, prof. emeritus, 1994—. NASA-ASEE summer faculty fellow Stanford U. Ames Rsch. Ctr., 1967—68; affiliate scientist Worcester Found. Exptl. Biology, 1972—74; Fulbright-Hays sr. faculty fellow to dept. chem. engring. Ben-Gurion U. of Negev, Beersheva, Israel, 1973—74, vis. prof. chem. engring., 1974; U.S. coord. U.S.-USSR Coop. Sci. Program in Chem. Catalysis, Topic IV, 1973—76, prin. investigator (with M.M. Sakharov), 1976—78; prin. investigator (with K.I. Ione) U.S.-USSR Coop. Sci. Program in Chem. Catalysis, Topic III, 1978—80; Fulbright-Hays vis. lectr. dept. chem. engring. Mid. East Tech. U., Ankara, Turkey, 1974, vis. prof., 91; vis. rsch. scientist dept. organic chemistry Weizmann Inst., Rehovoth, Israel, 1974; vis. lectr. Inst. Isotopes and Ctrl. Inst. Chemistry, Hungarian Acad. Scis., Budapest, 1976; vis. prof. Inst. Cultural Rels. and Inst. Isotopes, Hungarian Acad. Scis., 1978—80; UNIDO chief tech. advisor to Petrochem Complex of Bahia Blanca, Argentina, 1980; sr. rsch. fellow chem. sys. lab. Army Chem. Ctr., Md., 1981; vis. prof. Inst. Organic Chemistry, Sofia, Bulgaria, 1982—89; UNIDO expert in chem. process devel. Rsch. Inst. for Chem. Industry, Beijing, 1982; UNIDO expert in catalysis to YARPET Petrochem. Complex, Yarimca, Turkey, 1986—87; bd. dirs. U.S. com. for sci. coop. with Vietnam; vis. lectr. Nat. Ctr. for Sci. Rsch., Hanoi Inst. of Indsl. Chemistry, Ho Chi Minh City, 1986; vis. prof., vis. scientist Ctr. for Advanced Microgravity Materials Processing, Northeastern U., Boston, 2000—02. Translator: (with M. Delleo, G. Dembinski and J. Happel) Catalysis by Non-Metals (O.V. Krylov), 1970; author (autobiography): Chemistry, Engineering and Other Stories, 2006; contbr. 125 articles to profl. jours.; patentee in field. With chem. corps US Army, 1951—53. Recipient Sci. Achievement award Worcester Engring. Soc., 1984, Founder's award, Catalysis Soc. New Eng., 1990, Outstanding Rschr. and Creative Scholar award, Worcester Poly. Inst., 1984; Rsch. grantee NSF, PRF, NASA, DOD, DOE, EPA. Fellow AIChE (rsch. com. 1968-80, symposia chmn. 1973-84); mem. AAUP, Catalysis Soc. (bd. dirs., sec. 1968-88), Catalysis Soc. New Eng. (founding pres. 1967-68, bd. dirs. 1968—), Am. Chem. Soc. (New Eng. petroleum divsn. rep. 1970-88, session chmn. 1973—), Deutsche Gesellschaft fur Chemische Apparatwesen Avocations: writing, photography. Personal E-mail: ahweiss@yahoo.com.

WEISS, ARMAND BERL, economist, association management executive; b. Richmond, Va., Apr. 2, 1931; s. Maurice Herbert and Henrietta (Shapiro) W.; m. Judith Bernstein, May 18, 1957; children: Jo Ann Michele, Rhett Louis. BS in Econs., Wharton Sch. Fin., U. Pa., 1953, MBA, 1954; DBA, George Washington U., 1971. Cert. assn. exec. Officer USN, 1954—65; spl. asst. to auditor gen. Dept. Navy, 1964—65; sr. economist Ctr. for Naval Analyses, Arlington, Va., 1965—68; project dir. Logistics Mgmt. Inst., Washington, 1966—74; dir. sys. integration Fed. Energy Adminstrn., Washington, 1974—76; sr. economist Nat. Commn. Supplies and Shortages, 1976—77; tech. asst. to v.p. Sys. Planning Corp., 1977—78; chmn. bd., pres., CEO Assns. Internat. Inc., 1978—; chmn. bd. dirs., CFO Rail Digital Corp., 1988—91; v.p., treas. Tech. Frontiers, Inc., 1978—80; sr. v.p. Weiss Pub. Co., Inc., Richmond, 1960—; co-founder US Strategic Petroleum Res.; adj. prof. Am. U., 1979—81, 1989—91. Treas. Nat. Jewish Youth Conf., 1948—52; del. White House Conservance on Children 2nd Youth, 1950; v.p. Condo News Internat., Inc., 1981; v.p., bd. dirs. Leaders Digest inc., 1987—88; sec., bd. dirs. Mgmt. Svcs. Internat. Inc., 1987—88, 1989—90; vis. lectr. George Washington U., 1971; assoc. prof. George Mason U., 1984; treas. Dranesville (Va.) Dist. Dem. Com., 1989—93, 2003—06, Fairfax County (Va.) Dist. Dem. Com., 1992—; assisted Pres. Clinton, v.p. Gore transition at White Ho., 1993; mem. Fairfax County(Va.) Budget Task Force, 2008—09; pres. Washington Mgmt. and Bus. Assn., 1993—; chmn. US del., session chmn. NATO Symposium on Cost-Benefit Analysis, The Hague, Netherlands, 1969, NATO Conf. on Operational Rsch. in Indsl. Sys., St. Louis, 1970, France, 70; pres. Nat. Coun. Assns. Policy Scis., 1971—77; chmn. adv. group Def. Econ. Adv. Coun. Dept. Def., 1970—74; resident assoc. Smithsonian Instn., 1973—; expert cons. Dept. State, GAO; undercover agt. FBI, 3 yrs.; del. conf. UN, 2004. Co-editor: Systems Analysis for Social Problems, 1970, The Relevance of Economic Analysis to Decision Making in the Department of Defense, 1972, Toward More Effective Public Programs: The Role of Analysis and Evaluation, 1975; editor: Cost-Effectiveness Newsletter, 1966-70, Operations Rsch./Systems Analysis Today, 1971-73, Operation Rsch./Mgmt. Sci. Today, 1974-87, Feedback, 1969-93, Condo World, 1981, The Democrat, 1997-2000; assoc. editor Ops. Rsch., 1971-75; pub. IEEE Scanner, 1983-89, Spl. and Individual Needs Tech. (SAINT) Newsletter, 1987-88, Jour. Parametrics, 1984-88. Del. Pres.'s Mid-Century White House Conf. on Children and Youth, 1950; scoutmaster Japan, U.S.; leader World Jamborees, France, Can., U.S., 1945-61; Eagle scout, 1947; U.S. del. Internat. Conf. on Ops. Rsch., Dublin, Ireland, 1972; organizing com. Internat. Cost-Effectiveness Symposium, Washington, 1970; spkr. Internat. Conf. Inst. Mgmt. Scis., Tel Aviv, 1973, del., Mexico City, 1967; mem. bus. com. Nat. Symphony Orch., 1968-70, Washington Performing Arts Soc., 1974-88; bus. mgr. Nat. Lyric Opera Co., 1983—, Internat. Assn. Med. Sci. Educators, 1997-98, Data Adminstrv. Mgmt. Assn. Nat. Capital, 1992-2001, Potomac Pedalers Touring Club, 1990-2001, Am. Friends of London Sch. Econs., 1988-97; mem. mktg. com. Fairfax Symphony Orch., 1984-91; bd. dirs. McLean (Va.) Orch., 1992-94; exec. com. Mid Atlantic coun. Union Am. Hebrew Congregations, 1970-79, treas., 1974-79, mem. nat. MUM com., 1974-79; mem. dist. com. Boy Scouts Am., 1972-75; bd. dirs. Nat. Coun. Career Women, 1975-79; pres. Temple Rodef Shalom, Falls Church, 1970-72; adminstr. Daniel Heumann Fund for Spinal Cord Rsch., 2000-07; treas. Quest for the Cure, 2000-07; mem. Coalition for Advancement of Med. Rsch., 2002-; del. UN Sci. Conf., 2004; mem. adv. bd. U. Pa. Mid. Atlantic Region, 2003-, U. Pa. Emeritus Soc., 2003-. Recipient Silver medal 50-yard free style and half mile swimming meet, No. Va. Sr. Olympics, 1990, Gold, 2 Silver, 3 Bronze medals, 2001; named Hero of Hope, Rutgers U. Rally for Cure, 2004. Fellow AAAS, Washington Acad. Scis. (gov. 1981-92, v.p. 1987-88, pres.-elect 1989-90, pres. 1990-91, past pres. 1991-92), Va. Acad. Scis., Nat. Assn. Acad. Sci. (del. 1991-93), Ops. Rsch. Soc. Am. (chmn. meetings com. 1969-71, chmn. cost-effectiveness sect. 1969-70), Washington Ops. Rsch./Mgmt. Sci. Coun. (editor newsletter 1969-93, sec. 1971-72, pres. 1973-74, trustee 1975-77, bus. mgr. 1976-93, Moving Spirit award 1994), Internat. Inst. Strategic Studies (London), Am. Soc. Assn. Execs. (membership com. 1981-82, assn. mgmt. co. sect. coun. 1995-98, cert.), Inst. Ops. Rsch. and Mgmt. Scis., Am. Econ. Assn., Wharton Grad. Sch. Alumni Assn. (exec. com. 1970-73), Nat. Eagle Scout Assn., VFW, Am. Legion, Navy League U.S., Greater Washington Soc. Assn. Execs. (new ventures com. 1995-97), Alumni Assn. George Washington U. (governing bd. 1974-82, chmn. univ. publs. com. 1976-78, Alumni Svc. award 1980), Alumni Assn. George Washington U. Sch. Govt. and Bus. Adminstrn. (exec. v.p. 1977-78, pres. 1978-79), George Washington U. Doctoral Assn. (sr. v.p. 1968-69), Wharton Sch. Washington (sec. 1967-69, pres. 1969-70, exec. dir. 1987-2001, Joseph Wharton award 1991, Lifetime Svc. award 2000, Founder's award, 2008). Home: 6516 Truman Ln Falls Church VA 22043-1821 Office Phone: 703-241-0333. Personal E-mail: aiboss@aol.com.

WEISS, AVERY H., ophthalmologist, educator; b. Gainesville, Fla., Dec. 23, 1948; s. Nathan Weiss and Elaine Slverman; children: Cameron, Colton. BS, U. Fla., Gainesville, 1970; MD, U. Miami, Fla., 1974. Diplomate Am. Bd. Ophthalmology, 1981. Inter and resident internal medicine and opthalmology Wash. U., St. Louis, 1974—80; prof. and divsn. chief pediat. ophthalmology Seattle Children's Hosp. and U. Wash., 1991—. Contbr. articles to profl. jours. Felowship, Children's Hosp. and Nat. Med. Ctr., Washington, 1980—81. Mem.: Am. Acad. Pediat., Am. Assn. Pediat. Ophthalmology and Strabismus, Am. Acad. Ophthalmoogy (hon.; editl. bd. mem. 2001—06). Achievements include development of cortical funcion in CNS malformations, eye movement disorders, ocular infections in childhood, ocular malformations, orbital disease in childhood, retinobla.

WEISS, BARRY, recording industry executive; b. 1958; Pres., CEO Jive Records, NYC, 1991—2008; pres., CEO Zomba Label Group Sony BMG Music Entertainment, 2004—08, chmn., CEO BMG Label Group, 2008—. Exec. prodr.: R. Kelly: The R. in R&B - The Video Collection, 2003, Trapped in the Closet: Chapters 1-12, 2005, Trapped in the Closet: Chapters 13-22, 2007. Office: Sony BMG Music 550 Madison Ave # 20 New York NY 10022

WEISS, CAROL JULIET, psychiatrist; b. NYC, Mar. 5, 1957; d. Eugene and Rose (Schwartz) Weiss. BA, Wesleyan U., 1977; MD, Johns Hopkins U., 1983. Diplomate Am. Bd. Psychiatry and Neurology. Intern N.Y. Hosp., NYC, 1983—84; resident Payne Whitney Clinic, N.Y. Hosp., NYC, 1984—87; asst. psychiatrist Payne Whitney Clinic - N.Y. Hosp., NYC, 1983—87; clin. fellow Cornell U., NYC, 1987—89, instr. and clin. affiliate in psychiatry and pub. health, 1989—, clin. asst. prof. in psychiatry and pub. health NYC, 1992—; pvt. practice NYC, 1987—. Cons. in field. Contbr. articles to profl. jours., chpts. to books. Mem. Am. Psychiat. Assn., Am. Soc. Addiction Medicine, Phi Beta Kappa. Office: 1044 Madison Ave New York NY 10075 Office Phone: 212-988-1209.

WEISS, CHARLES, JR., educator; b. San Francisco, Dec. 20, 1937; s. Charles and Dorothy (Wilkes) W.; m. Edith Gayle Brown, July 24, 1969; children: Jed Ariel, Tamara Ginger. BA summa cum laude, Harvard U., 1959, PhD, 1965. Post-doctoral fellow U. Calif., Berkeley, 1967-69; chemist Lawrence Berkeley Lab., U. Calif., Berkeley, 1969; staff scientist IBM Watson Lab., Columbia U., NYC, 1969-71; sci. and tech. advisor World Bank, Washington, 1971-86; prin. Internat. Tech. Mgmt. and Fin., 1987-91, Innovation Ptnrs., 1987-91; pres. Global Tech. Mgmt., 1991—. Lectr. U. Pa., Phila., 1986-90; vis. lectr. Woodrow Wilson Sch., Princeton U., 1989-94; professorial lectr. Sch. Advanced Internat. Studies, Johns Hopkins U., 1994-97; disting. prof. Sch. Fgn. Svc., Georgetown U., 1997—, chair sci., tech. and internat. affairs, 1997—2006, adj. prof. Georgetown U. Med. Ctr., 2006—; corp. bd. mem. Vols. in Tech. Assistance, Arlington, Va., 1974-85; mem. US Nat. Climate Adv. Com., Washington, 1978-81, Coun. of Fgn. Rels., 1985—; assoc. trustee Ctr. for Econ. Initatives, 2004-. Editor: (with Jairan Ramesh) Mobilizing Technology for World Development, 1979, Technology, Finance and Development, 1984, Choice and Management of Technology, 1987; Co-Author:(with William B. Bonvilliam) Structuring an Energy Technology Revolution, 2009; contbr. articles to profl. jours. Land use chmn. Bannockburn Cmty. Assn., 1990-94. Capt. U.S. Army, 1965-67. Fellow NSF, 1959-62, NIH, 1962-65, 67-69, Woodrow Wilson Found. (hon.); Internat. scholar Open Soc. Inst., U. Nat. and World Economy, Sofia, Bulgaria, 2005-06. Fellow AAAS; mem. Internat. Orgn. Chem. Scis. for Devel. (exec. officer biotic exploration fund 1995-06), Soc. Internat. Devel., Georgetown U. Faculty Senate, US State Dept. Adv. Com. on Internat. Comm. and Info. Policy, Phi Beta Kappa. Avocation: ethnographic art and music. Office: Sch Fgn Svc Georgetown Univ 37th & O Sts NW Washington DC 20057-0001 Office Phone: 202-687-9184. Business E-Mail: weissc@georgetown.edu.

WEISS, CHARLES ANDREW, lawyer; b. Perryville, Mo., Jan. 24, 1942; s. Wallace Francis and Iola Francis Weiss; m. Marie Suzanne Desloge, June 10, 1972; children: Christopher, Robert, Julie, Anne. BJ with highest honors, U. Mo., 1964, AB with hons. in History, 1965; JD cum laude, Notre Dame U., 1968. Bar: Mo. 1968, US Dist. Ct. (ea. dist.) Mo. 1968, US Ct. Appeals (8th cir.) 1968, U.S. Supreme Ct. 1972, US Ct. Appeals (9th cir.) 1974, U.S. Ct. Appeals (2d cir.) 1977, US Ct. Appeals (1st cir.) 1987, US Ct. Appeals (5th cir.) 1992, US Ct. Appeals (fed. cir.) 2003, US Ct. Appeals (7th cir.) 2003. Law clk. to chief judge U.S. Ct. Appeals (8th cir.), 1968; ptnr. Bryan Cave LLP, St. Louis, 1969—. Lectr. St. Louis U. Law Sch., 1970-73; chmn. Legal Aid Mo. Statewide, Inc., 2003—. Supr. Red Cross Water Safety Program, Perry County, Mo., 1962-64; dir. Neighborhood Youth Corps., Perry County, 1965-66; pres. Perry County Young Dems. Club, 1965-67; committeeman Boy Scouts Am., 1982-86; mem. St. Louis Met. Sewer Dist. Civil Svc. Commn., 1999—; bd. dirs. United Way of Greater St. Louis, 1988-90. Fellow Am. Coll. Trial Lawyers; mem. ABA (house dels. 1986-02, 04-, bd. govs. 2006-09), Met. Bar Assn. St. Louis (pres. 1984-85), Mo. Bar Assn. (bd. govs. 1985, v.p. 1994-95, pres.-elect 1995-96, pres. 1996-97), St. Louis Bar Found. (pres. 1983), Mo. Lawyers Trust Account Found. (pres. 1992), Mo. Athletic Club (St. Louis), The Riverlands Assn., Inc. (pres. 1991-93), Jefferson Nat. Parks Assn. (chmn. 1993-2000), Notre Dame Club St. Louis (dir.), Notre Dame Law Assn. (dir., pres. 1997—). Roman Catholic. Office: Bryan Cave 211 N Broadway, Ste 3600 Saint Louis MO 63102-2733 Home Phone: 314-991-2170; Office Phone: 314-259-2215. Business E-Mail: cweiss@bryancave.com.

WEISS, CHRISTOPHER JOHN, lawyer; b. Oswego, NY, Sept. 1, 1952; s. Robert Leo and Flora Elizabeth Weiss; children: Allison Ardis, Natalie Elizabeth, Christine Corinne, Kathryn Creigh. BS, Fla. State U., 1970, JD, 1977. Bar: Fla. 1977, U.S. Dist. Ct. (mid. and so. dists.) Fla. 1977, U.S. Supreme Ct. Ptnr. Holland and Knight (and predecessor firm), Orlando, Fla., 1977—. Lectr., author various constrn. litigation issues, 1977—. Mem. Orlando Rep. Com., 1975—. Mem. Fla. Bar, Orange County Bar Assn. (constrn. com. 1987—), Am. Arbitration Assn. (nat. panelist 1982—), Assoc. Gen. Contractors, Assoc. Builders and Contractors, Constrn. Fin. Mgrs. Assn. Avocations: reading, travel. Office: Holland & Knight PO Box 1526 Orlando FL 32802-1526 Office Phone: 407-244-1110. Business E-Mail: cweiss@hklaw.com.

WEISS, DANIEL, legislative staff member; b. NYC, 1962; married; 2 children. BA in Sociology, U. Calif, Santa Cruz, 1985. Reporter States News Svcs., press sec.; chief of staff for Rep. George Miller US House of Reps., 2009—; special asst. to chair US House Com. Edn. & Labor, 2009—. Jewish. Avocations: drums, music. Office: Office of Congressman George Miller 2313 Rayburn House Office Bldg Washington DC 20515*

WEISS, DANIEL H., academic administrator, former dean; m. Sandra Jarva; children: Teddy, Joel. BA, George Washington U., 1979; MA, Johns Hopkins U., 1982, PhD, 1992; MBA, Yale U., 1985. With Booz, Allen & Hamilton; chair Art Hist. Dept. Johns Hopkins U., Balt., 1998—2001, dean faculty, 2001—02, dean Zanvyl Krieger Sch. Arts and Scis., 2002—05; pres. Lafayette Coll., Easton, Pa., 2005—. Bd. mem. Walter Art Mus., John Hopkins, Shriver Hall Concert Series; trustee Park School, Baltimore. Office: Lafayette Coll 316 Markle Hall Easton PA 18042 Office Phone: 610-330-5200. E-mail: weiss@lafayette.edu.*

WEISS, DONALD S., real estate developer; b. St. Petersburg, Fla., Aug. 18, 1947; s. Jonas Weiss and Miriam Kahan; m. Anne M. Weiss, Feb. 1978 (div. Jan. 1991); children: Laurie Blumstein, Melissa, Jason. BSBA, U. Fla., 1969. Lic. real estate broker N.Y. Asst. portfolio mgr. Chase Manhattan Bank, NYC, 1969—70; office space leasing salesperson Williams & Co., NYC, 1971—74, Sylvan Lawrence & Co., NYC, 1974—78; pvt. real estate investor NYC, 1978—; developer, creator Sugar Hill Art Ctr., NYC, 2001—. Dir. Com. Living Ctrs. Orgn., Com. for Rational Housing Laws and Econ. Devel. NYC and NY State, various web sites. Exhibited in group shows. With US Army, 1969—73. Avocations: skiing, bridge, photography. Office: 555 W 151 St #26 New York NY 10031 Home: 8051 Mulholland Dr Los Angeles CA 90046 Home Phone: 917-923-2441; Office Phone: 212-283-1278. Personal E-mail: dweiss5348@aol.com.

WEISS, EARLE BURTON, physician; b. Waltham, Mass., Nov. 23, 1932; s. Murray E. and Ruth R. (Pill) W.; m. Ruth Lithwick, Dec. 1, 1963; children: Ilana, Joshua. BS with honors, Northeastern U., Boston, 1955; MS, MIT, Cambridge, 1957; MD, Albert Einstein Coll. Medicine, NYC, 1961. Intern King's County Hosp., Bklyn., 1961—62; resident Boston City Hosp., 1962—64, Nat. Heart Inst. fellow, 1964—66; sr. rsch. assoc. Tufts Lung Sta., 1964—71; founder/first dir. respiratory ICU, sr. attending physician pulmonary & med. svc. Boston City Hosp., 1964—71, dir. Pulmonary Physiology Lab., 1966—71; assoc. chief of medicine Tufts Med. Svc./Boston City Hosp., 1969—71; dir. divsn. respiratory diseases St. Vincent Hosp., Worcester, Mass., 1971—89, also acting med. dir., 1985—87; prof. medicine U. Mass. Med. Sch., 1977—; sr. pulmonary rsch. scientist, dept. anesthesia Rsch. Labs. Brigham and Womens Hosp., Boston, 1989—. Cons. medical devices adv. panel FDA, 1975-77; cons. in physiology Norfolk County Sanitorium, 1966-69; lectr. medicine Tufts Med. Sch., 1978-; assoc. prof. life scis. Worcester Poly. Inst., Mass., 1976—; vis. prof. Faculty of Medicine, dept. of anesthesia Harvard Med. Sch., 1990-2002, vis. prof. U. Guadalajara, Mexico, 1973, 77, prof. extraordinario faculty medicine, 1977, 82; med. dir. Found. Rsch. in Bronchial Asthma and Related Diseases, 1980—; Tb cons. Commonwealth of Mass., 1972-89; dir. regional inpatient Tb and outpatient Tb clinic, Worcester County, 1972-89 Author: Bronchial Asthma, 1976, 2d edit., 1985, 3d edit., 1993, Status Asthmaticus, 1978; contbr. (with artist Frank H. Netter) Ciba Collection: The Respiratory System Anatomy of Lung and Asthma Sections and Clinical Symposia Bronchial Asthma, Acute Respiratory Failure in COPD, 1969; contbr. over 90 articles to profl. jours., abstracts, audio tapes and book chpts. Capt. USAFR, 1965-70. Recipient 1st Dr. J. McKeever Meml. award for outstanding med. educator, 1970, The Acad. Honor Soc., Tchg. and Patient Care award, Boston City Hosp. (I-III), 1971; named one of Am.'s Top Physicians, 2003—. Fellow ACP, Am. Coll. Chest Physicians, Royal Coll. Physicians; mem. AAAS, AMA, Mass. Thoracic Soc. (pres. 1976-78, Chadwick medal for meritorious contbn. in Respiratory Diseases 1990), Am. Thoracic Soc. (co-founder clin. assembly, rep. councilor 1979-82, founder, chmn. med. devices com. 1972-79, rep. ANSI med. tech. adv. bd. 1973-75, med. edn. com. 1972-74), Am. Assn. Clin. Scientists, Am. Soc. Internal Medicine, Soc. Free Radical Rsch., NY Acad. Scis., Am. Acad. Med. Dirs., Interasthma, Astron. Soc. of the Pacific, Soc. for Astron. Scis., Royal Astron. Soc. Can., Planetary Soc., British Astron. Assn., Sigma Xi. Achievements include introduction and pioneering use of controlled mechanical ventilation in acute respiratory failure of chronic lung disease and asthma, arterial blood gas profiles in status asthma, "cross-over" point in status-severe asthma, recording of breath sounds, the theory of the role of calcium and oxygen toxic products in causing asthma and airways reactivity 1979, percutaneous lung biopsy for diagnosis of respiratory infections, effect thyroid hormones upon cerebral cortex maturation and first isolation of alpha-hydroxy acid oxidase; establishment student research fellowship at Albert Einstein College of Medicine. Home: 57 South St Natick MA 01760-5526 Office: Brigham and Womens Hosp Dept Anesthesia Rsch L Boston MA 02115 Personal E-mail: drwe@comcast.net. Business E-Mail: eweiss@bics.bwh.harvard.edu, eweiss@wellesley.edu.

WEISS, GEORGE HERBERT, senior scientist consultant; b. NYC, Feb. 19, 1930; s. Morris and Violet (Mayer) W.; m. Delia Esther Orgel, Dec. 20, 1961; children: Miriam Judith, Alan Keith, Daniel Jonathan. BA, Columbia U., 1951; MA, U. Md., 1953, PhD, 1958. Physicist USN White Oak, Md., 1951-61; asst. prof. U. Md., College Park, 1959-63; fellow Rockefeller U., NYC, 1963-64, Weizmann Inst., Rehovot, Israel, 1958-59; mathematician NIH, Bethesda, Md., 1964—. Cons. GM, IBM, GE. Author: Lattice Dynamics in the Harmonic Approximation, 1963, 2d edit., 1971, The Master Equation in Chemical Physics, 1977, Contemporary Problems in Statistical Physics, 1994, Aspects and Applications of the Random Walk, 1994, Introduction to Crystallographic Statistics, 1995. With U.S. Army, 1954-56. Recipient Disting. Svc. in Math. award Washington Acad. Sci., 1967, Disting. Svc. award NIH, 1970. Avocations: photography, music, chess, philately. Office: NIH Bethesda MD 20892 Business E-Mail: weissgh@mail.nih.gov.

WEISS, GERHARD HANS, German language educator; b. Berlin, Aug. 6, 1926; came to US, 1946; s. Curt Erich and Gertrud (Grothus) W.; m. Janet Marilyn Smith, Dec. 27, 1953; children: John Martin, Susan Elizabeth Weiss Spencer, James David. BA, Washington U., St. Louis, 1950, MA, 1952; PhD, U. Wis., 1956. Prof. German U. Minn., Mpls., 1956—98, assoc. dean, 1967—71, 1979, chmn. dept. German, 1987-95, prof. emeritus, 1998—, interim dir. Ctr. Austrian Studies, 1999-2001. Mem. German-Am. Textbook Commn., Braunschweig, Fed. Republic Germany, 1985-88. Author: Begegnung mit Deutschland, 1970; editor: Unterrichtspraxis, 1975-80, Minn. Monographs in the Humanities, 1964-75; contbr. articles to profl. jours. Served to lt. col. USAR, 1946-75. Recipient Cross Merit, Fed. Republic Germany, 1982, Austrian Cross of Honor 1st Class Sci. and Arts, Republic of Austria, 2004, Outstanding Achivement award, Soc. German-Am. Studies, 2008. Mem. MLA, Am. Assn. Tchrs. German (pres. 1982-83, cert. of merit 1981, Disting. German Educator award 1991, elected hon. mem. 1995), German Studies Assn. (v.p. 1997-98, pres. 1999-00), Am. Coun. Tchg. Fgn. Langs. (Nelson Brooks award 1987). Methodist. Home: 4101 Abbott Ave S Minneapolis MN 55410-1004

WEISS, GERSON, endocrinologist, educator; b. NYC, Aug. 1, 1939; s. Samuel and Lillian (Wolpe) Weiss; m. Linda Gordon, Dec. 24, 1959; children: Jonathan, David, Michele, Andrew. BA, NYU, 1960, MD, 1964. Diplomate Am. Bd. Ob-Gyn. Intern, fellow dept. medicine Johns Hopkins Sch. Medicine, 1964-65; resident ob-gyn NYU Med. Ctr., 1964-69; rsch. fellow physiology U. Pitts. Sch. Medicine, 1971-73; asst. prof. ob-gyn NYU Med. Ctr., 1971-76, assoc. prof., 1976-80, prof., 1980-85; dir. div. reproductive endocrinology NYU Med. Center, 1975-85; prof. ob-gyn U. Med. and Dentistry NJ-NJ Med. Sch., 1986—, chmn. dept., 1986—; dir. divsn. reproductive endocrinology Hackensack U. Med. Ctr., NJ, 1996—2002. Rep. Am. Bd. Med. Spltys., bd. dirs., 2004—. Mem. editl. bd.: Fertility and Sterility Jour., 1986—93, Gyn.-Ob. Investigation; contbr. scientific papers to profl. jours. Served to maj. MC US Army, 1969—71. Rsch. grantee, NIH, 1975—, United Cerebral Palsy Found., 1977—83, Mellon Found., 1982—85, Rsch. fellow, John Polachek Found. Mem.: ACOG, Liason Com. Ob-Gyn. (chair 2009—), Soc. Study Reprodn., NY Gynecol. Soc. (pres. 1989—90), NY Obstet. Soc. (pres. 1990—91), Soc. Gynecol. Investigation (pres. 2005—06), Endocrine Soc., Am. Bd. Ob-Gyn. (mem. divsn. reproductive endocrinology 1985—90, mem. ob-gyn. residency rev. com. 1995—2000, bd. dirs., treas. 1997—98, pres. 1998—2002, chmn. 2002—06), Am. Gyn.-Ob. Soc., Alpha Omega Alpha, Sigma Xi, Phi Beta Kappa. Home: 185 West End Ave Apt 7MN New York NY 10023 Office: UMDNJ NJ Med Sch Dept Ob-Gyn 185 S Orange Ave Newark NJ 07103-2757 Office Phone: 973-972-5266. Business E-Mail: weissge@umdnj.edu.

WEISS, GLENN P., television director; b. Long Island, NY, Sept. 6, 1961; s. Robert I. and Helen (Zuckerman) W. BA, U. Md., 1983. Dir. Am's. Most Wanted Fox Broadcasting Co. STF Prodns., Washington, 1988-90, Joan Rivers Show Tribune Broadcasting Co., NYC, 1989, This Evening Group W Productions, San Francisco, 1989, Attitudes-Lifetime TV, Astoria, N.Y., 1990-91, The Image Workshop-Lifetime TV, 1991, The Barbara DeAngelis Show-CBS, 1991, Totally Hidden Video-Fox Broadcasting Co., 1991. Director: (TV shows) CNN's July 4th from Nat. Mall, 1982-85, CNN State of the Union, 1983-85, dir. Crossfire CNN, 1983, Marine Corp Marathon Fox, 1987 (Emmy nominee 1987), American Interest PBS, 1988, White House Tennis Tournament, Tony Awards shows, 2001, 2002, 2005, 2006, 2007(Outstanding Directorial Achievement in Musical Variety for 2007, Directors Guild Am., 2008). Avocations: tennis, music.

WEISS, HOLLY ANNE, music educator, singer; b. Camden, NJ, Dec. 23, 1950; d. Nicholas John Weiss and Dorothy Lora Sloan; m. Ernest Libby Whitehouse, June 26, 1996. BS in Music Edn. summa cum laude, West Chester U., 1973; Master of Music, Northwestern U., 1974. Cert. tchr. music K-12 Pa., N.J. Instr. Northeastern Bible Coll., Essex Fells, NJ, 1974—79, choir dir. and tour dir., 1975—76; instr. Utica Coll., NY, 1999—2001; pvt. practice vocal studio NYC, 1974—96, NJ, 1974—96, New Hartford, NY, 1996—. Singer: (Operas) The Opening, 2003, A Game of Chance, 2005, Salvatore Rosa, Carmen, Don Giovanni, Il Trovatore, Madame Butterfly, La Boheme, (oratorio) Elijah, Festival Te Deum, Requiem, La Nativité, Requiem, Christmas Oratorio, La Fiesta de la Posada, Magnificat, (oratorio radio broadcast) Gloria, (oratorio) Magnificat, 1993, Messiah, 1995, 1996; singer: (appearances include) Everson Mus., 1999, Munson Williams Proctor Inst., 1999, 2003, Utica Symphony, 2001, numerous others; accompanist: for students in studio and performance, resident soloist: First Presbyn. and Trinity Ch., 1980—85, Temple Emanu-El, 1980—85; singer: (TV) State of the Arts, 1983. Active Post Polio Support Group; contbr. Compassion Internat., 1989—; chair Trinity Covenant Ch., Livingston, 1990—96; chair 2d svc. task force First United Meth. Ch., New Hartford, 1997—98. Mem.: Nat. Assn. Tchrs. of Singing, B-Sharp Musical Club, Phi Beta Kappa. Avocations: gardening, art, reading, cooking, lay speaking. Office: Holly Weiss Vocal Studio 43 South Hills Dr New Hartford NY 13413

WEISS, JACK MEYAR, academic administrator, law educator; b. New Orleans, Jan. 5, 1947; s. J.M. and Louise (Feitel) W.; m. Ann Robinson, June 21, 1969; children: David, Eli, Anne. AB cum laude, Yale Coll., 1968; JD magna cum laude, Harvard U., 1971. Bar: La. 1971, DC 1972, US Ct. Appeals (5th cir.) 1972, US Dist. Ct. (ea., mid. and we. dists.) La. 1975, US Supreme Ct. 1973. Law clk. to Hon. John M. Wisdom US Ct. Appeals, New Orleans, 1971-72; sr. law clk. chief justice Warren Burger US Supreme Ct., Washington, 1972-73; legis. asst. Office US Senator J.B. Johnston, Washington, 1973-75; assoc. Stone, Pigman, Walther, Wittmann & Hutchinson, New Orleans, 1975-77, ptnr., 1990—, Phelps Dunbar et al, New Orleans, 1977-90, Correro Fishman Haygood Phelps Weiss Walmsley & Casteix, L.L.P, New Orleans, Gibson, Dunn & Crutcher LLP, NYC, 1998—2007; chancellor, prof. law La. State U. Paul M. Herbert Law Ctr., Baton Rouge, 2007—. Adj. asst. prof. Law Sch. Tulane U., New Orleans, 1980-1988; adj. prof. La. State U., 1984-1998. Treas., mng. editor: Harvard Law Rev.; author: (ann. survey) La. Defamation and Privacy Law; co-author: (survey) La. Pub. Records and Open Meeting Law, 1988. Bd. governors Isidore Newman Sch., New Orleans, 1982-98; bd. trustees Children's Hosp., New Orleans, 1982-86. Named Am's. Leading Bus. Lawyers, by Chambers USA, 2006. Mem. ABA, DC, NYC, Am. Law Inst., NY State Bar Assn., La. State Bar Assn. (chmn. sect. corp., bus. law 1987-88), Phi Beta Kappa. Democrat. Jewish. Avocations: golf, photography. Office: Paul M Herbert Law Ctr La State Univ 1 E Campus Dr Baton Rouge LA 70803 Office Phone: 225-578-8491. Business E-Mail: jmweiss@law.lsu.edu.*

WEISS, JAMES LLOYD, cardiology educator; b. Chgo., Jan. 15, 1941; s. Edward Huhner and Ruth (Wingerhoff) W.; m. Susan Forscher Weiss. July 23, 1967; children: Ethan James, Lisa Fleur. BA, Harvard Coll., 1963; MD, Yale U., 1968. Intern, resident U. Mich. Hosp., Ann Arbor, 1968-70; staff fellow NIH, Bethesda, Md., 1970-72; resident medicine Johns Hopkins Hosp., Balt., 1972-73, fellow cardiology, 1973-75, dir. Heart Station, 1976—, asst. prof. Medicine, 1975-81, assoc. prof. Medicine, 1981-90, prof. Medicine, Cariology, 1990—, Michael J. Cudahy prof. of cardiology, 1992—, assoc. dean admissions and acad. affairs, 1999—, dir. cardiology fellowship and tng. program, 1999—. Mem. editl. bd.: Johns Hopkins Med. Letter, 1991—, Jour. Am. Coll. Cardiology, 1995—; contbr. 120 articles to profl. jours. Recipient Harvard Book prize, 1959. Fellow Am. Coll. Cardiology, AHA Coun. on Circulation; mem. Harvard Club N.Y.C., Ctr. Club. Office: Cardiology Divsn Johns Hopkins Hosp 600 N Wolfe St Baltimore MD 21287-0005 Home Phone: 410-321-1145; Office Phone: 410-955-6834. E-mail: jlweiss@jhmi.edu.

WEISS, JAMES MICHAEL, financial analyst, portfolio manager; b. Chgo., July 20, 1946; s. Harold Cornelius and Elizabeth Josephine (Jesse) W.; m. Kathleen Jane Postorino, July 18, 1970; children: Elizabeth, Ann, Jane, William. BA, Marquette U., 1968; MBA, U. Pa., Wharton Sch., 1972. CFA; chartered investment counselor. Credit analyst Provident Nat. Bank, Phila., 1972; ptnr., sr. portfolio mgr. Stein Roe & Farnham Investment Counsel, Chgo., 1972—87, 1st v.p., prin., sr. portfolio mgr., 1987—90, sr. v.p., prin., sr. portfolio mgr., 1991—92; exec. v.p., sr. portfolio mgr. IDS Adv. Group, Inc., Mpls., 1993—95; pres., chief investment officer IDS Equity Advisors, 1995; sr. v.p., dep. chief investment officer Equities, State St. Rsch. & Mgmt. Co., Boston, 1995—97, exec. v.p., mem. mgmt. com., dep. head of equities, 1998—99, exec. v.p. mem. mgmt. com., chief invest. officer, bd. dirs., 1999—2002; pres. Weiss Capital Mgmt., Inc., 2002—. Bd. dirs. Tropp & Co., Chgo.; v.p. Stein Roe Cash Reserves Fund, Chgo., 1982-87; mem. investment com. Pro Mutual Group, Boston, Mass., 2004—. Author: (with others) Handbook of Cash Flow and Treasury Management, 1987; contbr. articles to profl. jours. Commr. Glenview (Ill.) Zoning Bd., 1978-80; trustee Glenview Village Bd. Trustees, 1980-86; chmn. Marquette U. Exec. Senate, Chgo., 1984-87; active Glenview Bus. Area Redevel. Com., 1990-93; bus. adv. coun. Elmhurst (Ill.) Coll., 1986-93; founding bd. dirs. Glenview Edn. Found., 1990-93; bd. trustees Fenn Sch., Concord, Mass., 1996-2002, Fenn Sch. investment com., 1996-2007; co-chmn. Fenn Sch. Capital Campaign, 1997-2000; bd. dirs. Gaining Ground, Concord, 2003—, bd. mem. Wright Farm Condo Assn., 2007-, South Cove Assn., 2007-. With US Army, 1968—70. Recipient Cert. Merit Village of Glenview, 1987. Mem.: Investment Counsel Assn., CFA Inst., Boston Analysts Soc., Marquette U. Alumni Assn. (nat. bd. dirs. 1989—91, liberal arts bd. 2000—05, Nat. Svc. award 1995), Indian River Country Club (Vero Beach, Fla.), Boston Coll. Club, Wedgewood Pines Club (Stow, Mass.), North Shore Country Club (Glenview, Ill.). Avocations: golf, travel, writing. Office: Weiss Capital Mgmt PO Box 1128 Concord MA 01742-1128 Home: 13 Wright Farm Rd Concord MA 01742-1528 Home Phone: 978-369-9063; Office Phone: 978-505-5435. Business E-Mail: jweiss6@earthlink.net.

WEISS, JAY M(ICHAEL), psychologist, educator; b. Passaic, NJ, Mar. 20, 1941; s. Benjamin and Anne (Pearl) W.; m. Meryl Etta Levenson, June 9, 1963; children: Jennifer, Jason. BA, Lafayette Coll., 1962; PhD, Yale U., 1967. Asst. prof. Rockefeller U., NYC, 1969-73, assoc. prof., 1973-84; prof. dept. psychiatry Med. Ctr., Duke U., Durham, N.C., 1984-92; prof. dept psychiatry behavioral scis. Emory U. Sch. Medicine, Atlanta, Ga., 1992-95, Jenny Culbreth Adams prof. psychiatry and behavioral scis., 1995—. Adj. assoc. prof. NYU, 1973-84, CCNY, 1979-84. MacArthur Found. fellow, 1984-89. Fellow AAAS, Soc. for Behavioral Medicine, Am. Coll. Neuropsychopharmacology. Office: Emory West Campus Emory Univ 1256 Briarcliff Rd NE Atlanta GA 30306-2656

WEISS, JESSICA, history professor; d. Robert I. and Jean Weiss; m. Vladislav Luskin, 1992; 1 child, Sophie Luskin. PhD, U. Calif., Berkeley, 1994. Assoc. prof. CSU East Bay, Hayward, Calif., 1999—. Mem.: Western Assn. Women Historians. Office: Dept History CSU East Bay Hayward CA 94542 Business E-Mail: jessica.weiss@csueastbay.edu.

WEISS, JOAN OPPENHEIMER, social worker, educator; b. Balt., Apr. 10, 1930; d. Reuben and Selma (Levy) Oppenheimer; m. Milton Gottesman, Oct. 19, 1952 (div. 1958, dec.); m. Stanley Weiss, Nov. 6, 1960; children: Betsy, Michael, Jonathan (dec.). BA, Barnard Coll., 1952; MSW, Cath. U., Washington, 1956. Caseworker Jewish Social Svc. Agy., Washington, 1956-62, Family and Child Svcs., Washington, 1962-64; social worker divsn. med. genetics Johns Hopkins U., Balt., 1968-88; founding exec. dir. Alliance of Genetic Support Groups, Chevy Chase, Md., 1988-96; co-dir. Human Genome Edn. Model Project, 1993—2001; cons. in genetics support. Instr. Child Devel. Ctr., Georgetown U., Washington, 1981—95; cons. Genetics Ctr., Johns Hopkins U., 1988—90; chmn. GenEthics Consortium, 1997—98; chmn. genetic standards for clin. practice com. NASW. Co-author Starting and Sustaining Genetic Support Groups, 1996; co-editor: Genetic Disorders and Birth Defects in Families and Society, 1983, Genetic Support Groups: A Partnership of Volunteers and Professionals, 1986; contbr. articles to profl. jours. Mem. profl. adv. bds. several vol. genetic orgns., 1973—. Maternal and Child Health grantee, 1989-96, March of Dimes Birth Defects Found. grantee, 1991. Mem. NASW (vice-chmn.found. bd. dirs., pioneers steering com. mem.), Am. Soc. Human Genetics (social issues com.), Am. Coll. Med. Genetics, Nat. Soc. Human Genetics, Nat. Soc. Genetic Counselors, Genetic Alliance, Nat. Coalition Health Profl. Genetics in Edn. (bd. dirs.). Avocations: painting, travel, theater, reading, music.

WEISS, JOANNE MARION, writer; b. Wayne, NJ, Mar. 16, 1960; d. Henry Daniel and Florence Frances (Zaratkiewicz) W.; 1 child, David. BA, Bennington Coll., 1982; MA, U. Cambridge, Eng., 1988. Prodn. mgr. The Suburban News, N.J., 1982-83; gardener Artistic Landscaping, N.J., 1983; case mgr. Mid-Bergan Mental Health Ctr., N.J., 1985-86. Founder Isis Farm Writers, 1995—, Cambridge Actors, 1988—. Author, dir. play The Gift, 1987, 88; author: (plays) Catherine the Queen, 1997, Mother America, 1998; contbr.: (poetry) The Aurorean, 1998, Tears in the Fence, 2002, Decanto, 2008. Translator Solidarity, Poland, 1983; co-leader Vols. for Peace, 1986; mem., worker Pregnancy Adv. Svc., Cambridge, 1991-92. Recipient scholarship Inst. for Brit. and Irish Studies, Trinity Coll., Dublin, 1985, Chancellor's medal for poetry U. Cambridge, Eng., 1988, grants for Edinburgh, Sir John Gielgud, 1988, grant Judith Wilson Fund, U. Cambridge, Eng., 1988. Mem. Dramatists Guild, Jr. Whippet Rescue. Avocations: horse training, organic farming.

WEISS, JOHN ROBERT, lawyer; b. Chgo., May 7, 1961; s. Robert Gordon and Elizabeth Jean (Malecki) W.; m. Elizabeth Anne Zur, Dec. 5, 1987. BA, Northwestern U., 1982, JD, 1985. Bar: Ill. 1985, US Dist. Ct. (no. dist.) Ill. 1985, US Dist. Ct. (ctrl. dist.) Ill., 1997, US Ct. Appeals (7th cir.) 1987, US Ct. Appeals (8th cir.), 1999, US Supreme Ct. 1989. Assoc., ptnr. Chapman & Cutler, Chgo., 1985—96; ptnr. Katten Muchin Rosenman, Chgo., 1996—2006, Duane Morris LLP, Chgo., 2006—. Tchr. Chgo. Coalition for Law-Related Edn., 1985—; atty. Chgo. Vol. Legal Services, 1985—. Mem. ABA, 7th Cir. Bar Assn., Am. Judicature Soc., Ill. Bar Assn., Am. Bankruptcy Inst., Turnaround Mgmt. Assn. Roman Catholic. Avocations: golf, billiards, chess. Office: Duane Morris LLP 190 S LaSalle St Chicago IL 60603 Office Phone: 312-499-6700. Office Fax: 312-499-6701. Business E-Mail: jrweiss@duanemorris.com.

WEISS, JOSEPH JOEL, consulting company executive; b. Newark, July 27, 1931; s. Harry H. and Belle (Sass) W.; m. Leah Kneller, Apr. 10, 1954 (div. 1961); children: Sara, Daniel; m. Carol Lynn Seegott, Sept. 29, 1967; children: Laura, John. BSBA, Rutgers U., 1953, MBA, 1958. Dist. mgr. N.J. Bell Telephone Co., 1955-61; asst. comptroller ITT P.R. Telephone Co., San Juan, 1964-68; sr. cons. NYC, 1968-71; v.p. data services Rio De Janeiro, 1971-74; dir. ops. NYC, 1975-80; v.p. Control Data Corp., Rio De Janeiro, 1974-75; exec. v.p., chief adminstrv. officer Burger King Corp., Miami, 1980-89; chief oper. officer Goode, Olcott, Knight & Assocs., Coral Gables, Fla., 1989-90; pres. Contraband Detection Internat., Miami, Fla., 1990-92; sr. v.p. Seegott Inc., Streetsboro, Ohio, 1992—. Bd. dirs. Sta. WPB-TV. Author: How to Get from Cubicle to Corner Office, The Quotable Manager. Pres. Civic Betterment Assn., Franklin Twp., N.J., 1961; trustee U. Miami Citizens Bd., 1987—; bd. dirs. Boy Scouts Am., 1982—. Recipient Strategic Planning Achievement award Boy Scouts Am., 1985. Mem. Hist. Soc. Fla. (bd. dirs. 1986—). Clubs: Fisher Island. Republican. Presbyterian. Avocations: planning, tennis. Home: 6682 Brookside Woods Ct Se Ada MI 49301-8219

WEISS, KENNETH ANDREW, lawyer, educator; b. New Orleans, Jan. 16, 1951; s. Irving and Julia (Mayer) Weiss. BA, Tulane U., 1972, JD with honors, 1975; LLM in Taxation with highest honors, George Washington U., 1981. Bar: La. 1975, DC 1976. Editl. writer, Washington corr. The Times-Picayune, New Orleans and Washington, 1973-79; news editor Congl. Quarterly, Washington, 1979-81; mng. editor Reporters Com. for Freedom of the Press, Washington, 1981-82; assoc. McGlinchey Stafford, New Orleans, 1982-84, dir., 1984—. Prof. Tulane U. Law Sch., New Orleans, 1987—, La. State U. Law Sch., 2000—08; mem. trust code com. La. Law Inst., Baton Rouge, 1993—, mem. successions and donations com., 1996—; mem. planning com. Tulane Tax Inst., 1996—; chair Tulane U. Law Sch. Ann. Estate Planning Seminar, 1995—2001, Tulane U. Estate Planning Inst., 2002—; dean's adv. coun. Tulane Law Sch., 2003—. Co-author: Bankers' Guide to Establishing, Managing and Operating Common Trust Funds, 1986, Business Uses of Life Insurance, 1986, Executive Compensation, 1990; assoc. editor Tulane Law Rev., 1974-75, mem. bd. adv. editors, 1992—; contbr. articles to profl. jours. Bd. dirs. Longue Vue House and Gardens Adv. Corp., 1993-95, bd. dirs. Longue Vue Found., 1995—2003; trustee Greater New Orleans Ednl. TV Found., Sta. WYES-TV, 1994-98; bd. dirs. So. Repertory Theatre, 1996-2001, pres., 1998-99; bd. advisors Project Lazarus, 1996-2000, pres. 1997-99; mem. profl. adv. com., Jewish Endowment Found., 1982—; mem. planned gifts adv. com. Tulane U., 1989—; active Met. Area Com. Leadership Forum, New Orleans, 1983; fellow Inst. Politics Loyola U., New Orleans, 1989-90; mem. devel. com. Greater New Orleans Found., 1995—. bd. dirs., Innocence Project New Orleans, 2002-05, treas., 2002-04. Recipient Addy award for polit. advt., 1989, awards for investigative reporting; Phi Delta Phi scholar, 1972-73. Fellow Am. Coll. Trust and Estate Counsel; mem. La. State Bar Assn. (taxation sect., bd. cert. tax atty., bd. cert. estate planning and adminstrn. specialist), New Orleans Bar Assn. (chair taxation law com. 2003), Nat. Coun. Planned Giving (greater New Orleans chpt.), New Orleans Estate Planning Coun., Order of the Coif. Republican. Jewish. Office Phone: 504-596-2751.

WEISS, KENNETH R., newswriter; b. Calif. B in Folklore, U. Calif., Berkeley. Washington corr. NY Times Regional Newspapers; reporter States New Svc., Washington, LA Times, 1990—. Co-recipient John B. Oakes award for Outstanding Environmental Journalism, Columbia U. Grad. Sch. Journalism, 2006, George Polk award for Environmental Reporting, 2006, Walter Sullivan award for Excellence in Sci. Journalism, Am. Geophys. Union, 2007, Pub. Comm. award, Am. Soc. Microbiol., 2007, Print Media award, Am. Inst. Biol. Scis., 2007, Pulitzer Prize for Explanatory Reporting, 2007. Avocation: surfing. Office: LA Times 202 W 1st St Los Angeles CA 90012 E-mail: ken.weiss@latimes.com.

WEISS, KEVIN BARTON, epidemiologist, medical association administrator; b. Nov. 20, 1956; BA, Washington U., Mo., 1977; MS, MD, U. Chgo., 1981; MPH, Harvard U., 1985, MS, 1987. Bd. cert. internat medicine 1984. Intern internal medicine Cook County Hosp., Chgo., 1981—82, resident internal medicine, 1982—84, resident, 1984—85; tng. epidemiology US Nat. Inst. Allergy and Infectious Diseases, NIH, US Nat. Ctr. for Health Statistics, Ctrs. for Disease Control and Prevention; with Med. Ctr. George Washington U., DC, asst. prof. healthcare scis.; prof. divsn. gen. medicine, dir. Inst. for Healthcare Studies, co-dir. Inst. Health Svcs. & Policy Northwestern U.; dir. Medwest Ctr. for Health Svcs. and Policy Rsch. Hines VA Hosp. US Dept. Vets. Affairs, Ill., 2000—; pres., CEO Am. Bd. Med. Specialties, 2007—. Bd. regents ACP; initiator Nat. Cooperative Inner-City Asthma Study; prin. investigator Pediat. Asthma Care Patient Outcomes Rsch. Team Agy. for Healthcare Rsch. and Quality; prin. investigator Chgo. Initiative to Raise Asthma Health Equity Nat. Heart, Lung and Blood Inst.; mem. expert panel Asthmas Guidelines Nat. Heart, Lung and Blood Inst./Nat. Asthma Edn. and Prevention Program; chair Guideline Implementation panel Nat. Asthma Edn. and Prevention Program; chair asthma measure adv. panel NAt. Com. on Quality Assurance; chair various federally sponsored national asthma workshops. Contbr. articles to profl. pubs., chapters to books. Achievements include research in the epidemiology of asthma and asthma-related problems. Office: American Board Medical Specialties 1007 Church St Ste 404 Evanston IL 60201-5913 also: 675 N St Clair Ste 18-200 Chicago IL 60611 Office Phone: 847-491-9091. Office Fax: 847-328-3596. Business E-Mail: info@ambs.org. E-mail: k-weiss@northwestern.edu.*

WEISS, LAWRENCE N., lawyer; b. NYC, Aug. 9, 1942; s. Joseph and Martha (Guggenheimer) W. BA, CCNY, 1963; LLB summa cum laude, Columbia U., 1966. Bar: NY 1966, US Ct. Appeals (2d cir.) 1967, US Dist. Ct. (so. and ea. dists) NY 1968, US Supreme Ct. 1971, US Ct. Appeals (3d cir.) 1968, US Ct. Appeals (6th cir.) 1980, US Tax Ct. 1977. Assoc. Kaye, Scholer, Fierman, Hays & Handler, NYC, 1966-67, 67-73; law clk. to judge NY Ct. Appeals, Albany and NYC, 1967; assoc. Botein, Hays, Sklar & Herzberg, NYC, 1973-76, Weisman, Celler, Spett, Modlin & Wertheimer, NYC, 1976, ptnr., 1977-79, counsel, 1979-81; prin. Lawrence N. Weiss, P.C., NYC, 1981—, Pantaleoni & Weiss, NYC, 1993—2003. Arbitrator Civil Ct., NYC, 1985—; mediator US Dist. Ct. (ea. dist.) NY and NY Supreme Ct. Author: (newsletter) Review of the Shakespeare Wars, 2006. Mem. NY County Lawyers Assn. (arbitrator joint com. fee disputes), Assn. Bar of City of NY (com. on legal edn. and admission to bar, arbitrator joint com. fee disputes), NY State Bar Assn. (chair com. CLE, com. on fed. judiciary, spl. com. on copyright, vice chair com. on UN, subcom. internat. cts., litig. sect., judiciary com.), Shakespeare Assn. Am. Avocation: shakespearean studies. Home: 107 E 37th St New York NY 10016-3065 E-mail: larry@lweiss.net.

WEISS, LEONARD, mathematician, consultant, writer; b. NYC, Mar. 14, 1934; s. Max and Sadie (Albert) W.; m. Sandra Joyce Raynes, June 15, 1958; children: Madelyn, Eugene. B.E.E., CCNY, 1956; MS, Columbia U., 1959; PhD, Johns Hopkins U., 1962. Lectr. CCNY, 1956-59; staff scientist Research Inst. for Advanced Studies, Balt., 1962-64; asst. prof. Brown U., Providence, 1964-66, assoc. prof., 1966-68; prof. U. Md., College Park, 1968-78; legis. asst. to Senator John Glenn of Ohio, 1976-77; cons. Naval Research Lab., Washington, 1970-77; staff dir. Senate Subcom. on Energy, Nuclear Proliferation and Govt. Processes, 1977-86, Senate Com. Govtl. Affairs., 1987-99; sr. sci. fellow Ctr. Internat. Security and Cooperation, Stanford U., 2006—07; individual affiliate Ctr. Internat. Security Coop., Standford U., 2007—; bd. mem. Ctr. Nonproliferation and Arms Control, 2008. Cons. Lawrence Livermore Nat. Lab., 1999—. Editor: Ordinary Differential Equations, 1972; contbr. articles to profl. jours. and mags.; author legislation on nuclear proliferation, energy, health and safety, govt. orgn., and govt. mgmt. Alfred P. Sloan research fellow, 1966-68, IEEE Congl. fellow, 1976, Stennis Congl. fellow, 1997. Home: 101 Alma St Apt 507 Palo Alto CA 94301-1075 Office Phone: 650-324-7978.

WEISS, LYN DENISE, physician; b. Bethpage, NY, Apr. 13, 1959; d. Eugene and Lois Zanger; m. Jay M. Weiss, Apr. 7, 1984; children: Ari, Helene, Stefan, Richard. BA, U. Va., 1981; MD, SUNY, Bklyn., 1985. Diplomate Am. Bd. Electrodiagnostic Medicine, Nat. Bd. Med. Examiners, Am. Bd. Phys. Medicine and Rehab. Resident Dept. Phys. Medicine & Rehab. Nassau U. Med. Ctr., East Meadow, NY, 1985—89; attending physician Dept. Phys. Medicine & Rehab. Nassau U. Med. Ctr., 1989—94, dir. Electrodiagnostic Medicine Dept. Phys. Medicine Rehab., 1991—; dir. residency tng. Dept. Phys. Medicine & Rehab. Nassau U. Med. Ctr., 1993—; acting chmn. Dept. Phys. Medicine & Rehab. Nassau U. Med. Ctr., 1994—96; chmn. Dept. Phys. Medicine & Rehab. Nassau U. Med. Ctr., 1996—. Bd. dirs. Ctr. for Rehab. Rsch. Tech., Massapequa, N.Y., 1996— Author: Cumulative Trauma Disorders, 1997, Skin Care Triad, 2000, Easy EMG, 2004, Easy Injections, 2007, Oxford Handbook of PM&R, 2009.

WEISS, MARILYN ACKERMAN, artist; b. Bklyn., Sept. 4, 1932; d. Max and Anna (Haber) Ackerman; m. Howard Jerry Weiss, Nov. 24, 1972; children: Jodi Kim Magaliff Gittelman and Barry Todd Magaliff (twins). BS magna cum laude, NYU, 1953. One woman shows include Alper-Goldberg Gallery, Cedarhurst, NY, 1977, Fred Leighton Madison Ltd., 1975, Port Washington Libr., NY, 1974, Adelphi U., 1974, Hewlett Woodmere Libr., 1972, Bodley Gallery, NYC, 1983, Discovery Gallery, Glencove, NY, 1990, Z Gallery, NYC, 1995, Allen Sheppard Gallery, Piermont, NY, 1995, 97, Sundance Gallery, Bridgehampton, NY, 1998, Westhampton Libr., Westhampton Beach, NY, 1999, 2001, Shelter Rock Art Gallery, Manhasset, 2000, Omni Gallery, Uniondale, W.Va., 2003, Gayle Willson Gallery, Southampton, NY, 2003, Studio 389 A Ea., Quogue, NY, Harvest Gallery, East Dennis, Md., 2005, 06, Gayle Wilson Gallery, Southampton, NY 2004-06, Treasure Rm. Gallery, The Interchurch Ctr., NY, 2005, Madeline Hegeler Semerjian Gallery Rogers Nat. Libr., Southampton, NY, 2005, Graphic Eye Gallery, Port Washington, NY, 2009, others; exhibited in group shows at Firehouse Gallery Nassau CC, Garden City, 1971, Pallazzio Vechio, Florence, Italy, 1972, Palazzio Nat., Naples, Italy, 1972, Brockton (Mass.) Library, 1972, Roanoke (Va.) Fine Arts Ctr., 1972, Milliken U., 1972, U. Okla., 1973, Southeastern Ark. Art and Sci. Ctr., 1973, Tuskegee Inst., 1974, Albrecht Gallery, 1974, Bergen Community Mus., 1974, 84-85, Jesse Besser Mus., 1976, Cen. Wyo. Mus. Art, 1977, U. Wis., 1978, City Gallery, NYC, 1981, Community Mus., 1974, Equitable Gallery, NYC, 1979, Fed. Bldg., NYC, 1979, 81-92, U.S. Painting Exhbn., 1983-85, 85-88, 91-93, Traveling Painting Exhbn. U.S.A., 1972-74, 88-90, Traveling Watermedia Exhbn. U.S.A., 1976-78, Oil and Watermedia Exhbn., 1978-80, Cayuga Mus. History and Art, Auburn, ND, 1983, Stephanie Roper Gallery, 1985, Sarah Lawrence Coll., 1985-92, Lighthouse Gallery, Fla., 1986, McPherson Coll., 1986, Schenectady Mus., NY, 1987, Adelphi U., NY, 1987, Nabisco Art Gallery, NJ, 1987, Pace U. Art Gallery, NY, 1988, Maier Mus. Art, Va., 1988, Lever House, NYC, 1988, 91, Fine Arts Mus. Nassau County, 1988, Fine Arts Mus. L.I., 1988 (Bronze award 1988), Midge Karr Gallery L.I., 1989, Discovery Gallery, 1989-91, Cork Gallery, Lincoln Ctr., NYC, 1989, 91-92, 94, 98, Marbella Gallery, NYC, 1989, Firehouse Gallery, Garden City, 1990, Printmaking Exhbt. U.S.A., 1990-93, Adams State Coll. Co., 1991, Smithtown Twp. Arts Coun., NY, 1991, Jain Marunouchi Gallery, NYC, 1991-94, Broome St. Gallery, NYC, 1992-99, 2002-08, Richmond Art Mus., Ind., Concordia Gallery, NY, Thomas KJ Walsh Art Gallery, Conn., 1993, Mus. Southwest Tex., 1990, Cultural Ctr., Carmel, Calif., 1990, Lever House, NYC, Sarah Lawrence Coll., NY, 1992, Gallery 420 Broadway, NYC, 1995-96, Seagate, Princeton, NJ, 1995, Blue Hill Gallery, Hudson, NY 1995, Global Focus, Beijing, 1995, Millennium Gallery, East Hampton, NY, 1996, Morani Gallery, Phila., 1997, Shelter Rock (NY) Art Gallery, 1997, Gallery 54, NYC, 1997, Heckscher Mus. Art, Roslyn, NY, 1998, New World Art Ctr., NY, 1998, World Fine Art Ctr., NY, 1998-99, Salmagundi Club Gallery, NY, 1998, Sundance Gallery, Bridge Hampton, NY, 1998, New World Art Ctr., NYC, 1999, Cork Gallery, Lincoln Ctr., NYC, 1999, 2003, ISE Art Found., NYC, 2000, Sarah Lawrence Coll., Bronxville, NY, 2001, Gallery Fairlawn Libr., 2001, Elizabeth Found. for Arts, NYC, 2001, New Century Artists, NY, 2002, Freyberger Gallery, Pa. State U., Reading, 2002, Banana Factory, Bethlehem, Pa., 2002, Hiddenite (NC) Ctr., 2002, Paint Creek Ctr. Arts, Rochester, 2002, Long Beach Art Assn., 2002, BJ Spoke Gallery, Huntington Sta., NY, 2002, Gallery at 80 5th Ave, NYC, 2003, Art Trium, Melville NY, 2004, Goggle Works Ctr. Arts, Reading, Pa., 2006, Graphic Eye Gallery, Port Washington, NY, 2007-09, Guild Hall, East Hampton, NY, 2007, 08, 09, Blue Hill Cultural Ctr., Pearl River, NY, 2007-08, Noyes Mus. Art Ocean Ville, NJ, 2009, others; represented in permanent collections including Mus. Southwest, Midland, Tex., Nat. Mus. Women in Arts, Washington, Sarah Lawrence Coll., Bronxville, NY, Sloan Kettering Art Collection. Recipient maj. prize Suburban Art League Ann. Show, 1968, 71, Elizabeth Morse Genius Found. prize for water media, 1983, Cecil Shapiro Meml. award, 1988, Spl. award Innovation Drawing Show, 1989, Miriam E. Halpern Meml. award, 1991, Dr. Irving H. Silver award Nat. Assn. Women Artists, 2000, Donald Pierce Meml. award Am. Soc. Contemporary Artists, 2002, Excellence award Long Beach Art League, 2002-04, others. Mem. Contemporary Artists Guild, Nat. Assn. Women Artists (bd. dirs., Canady-Karasik Meml. award Work on Paper 1997, Cleo Hartwig award for sculpture 2004), Am. Soc. Contemporary Artists Guild (Harriet Febland Art Workshop award Work on Paper 1993, Bernard and Hortense Kassay Contemporary Art award 2006), Artists Equity. Home: 1100 Park Ave New York NY 10128-1202 Address: 35 Library Ave 7 I Westhampton Beach NY 11978 Personal E-mail: mawart1@yahoo.com.

WEISS, MARISA C., breast cancer oncologist, non-profit breast cancer organization executive; married; 3 children. Attended, U. Pa., MD, 1984. Intern radiological oncology Crozer-Chester Med. Ctr., Pa., 1984—85; resident radiological biology U. Pa. Hosp., 1985—88, fellow radiological oncology, 1988—90; practicing breast cancer oncologist Lankenau Hosp., part of Main Line Health Hospitals of the Thomas Jefferson U. Health System, 1992—; dir. breast radiation oncology, dir. breast health outreach Lankenau Hosp.; asst. prof. dept. radiation oncology U. Pa.; founder, past pres. Living Beyond Breast Cancer (LBBC), 1990—2007; pres., founder, spokesperson Breastcancer.org. Mem. director's consumer liaison group Nat. Cancer Inst., 2000—07; mem. profl. adv. bd. Mommy's Light Lives On, Phila. Wellness Cmty.; keynote spkr. on internat. women's health conference circuit, including Speaking of Women's Health, Europa Donna, Irish Cancer Soc., and John Hopkins; mem. Marine Biol. Lab., Woods Hole, Mass.; hosp. appointment Paoli Meml. Hosp., Pa., 1992—94, Chester Co. Hosp., Pa., 1992—94, Brandywine Hosp., Pa. Co-author (with mother Ellen Weiss): Living Beyond Breast Cancer, 1997, 1998; co-author: (with daughter Isabel Friedman) Taking Care of Your Girls: A Breast Health Guide for Girls, Teens and In-Betweens, 2008; author: 7 Minutes!: How to Get the Most from Your Doctor Visit, 2007; frequently consults by TV, print and radio media; performer: (ednl. video) Doctor, Doctor, Lend Me Your Ear: An Up-Close Look at Patient-Doctor Relationship; multiple guest appearances on Today Show, 1998—2007, Good Morning America and ABC News.com, 2007—08, guest appearances CNN House Call during Breast Cancer Awareness Month, 2003—06, (NPR) Fresh Air with Terry Gross, Radio Times with Mary Moss-Coane, CNN Radio, ABC Radio, CBS Radio, Washington Post Radio and the radio partner of Cosmopolitan Mag., med. editor (TV films) Why I Wore Lipstick to My Mastectomy, Lifetime TV, In Matters of Life and Dating, guest spkr. WebMD's spl. breast cancer feature, 2001—04, interviewed and regularly quoted in New York Times, USA Today, Wall Street Journal, Washington Post, Philadelphia Inquirer and articles for the AP newswire, People, Cosmopolitan, Ladies' Home Journal, Redbook, More, Shape, Self, Allure and O., serves on advisory bd. Women's Health mag. Recipient of several honors from Am. Cancer Soc., 2003 Professor of Survivorship award, Susan G. Komen Found. (now Susan G. Komen for the Cure); named Top Doc (cover story), Philadelphia Mag., 2005. Mem.: Am. Soc. Therapeutic Radiation Oncology, Am. Soc. Clin. Oncology. Office: Breastcancer.org 7 E Lancaster Ave 3rd Fl Ardmore PA 19003*

WEISS, MARK ANSCHEL, lawyer; b. NYC, June 20, 1937; s. George and Ida (Galin) W.; m. Joan Roth, June 8, 1958; children: Rebecca, Sarabeth, Jonathan, Deborah. AB, Columbia U., 1958; LLB magna cum laude, Harvard U., 1961. Bar: N.Y. 1961, D.C. 1962, U.S. Supreme Ct. 1965. Assoc. Covington & Burling, Washington, 1961-66, 69-70, ptnr., 1970—; spl. asst. to Under Sec. Treasury Dept. Washington, 1966-68; spl. asst. to sec., 1968-69. Mem. editl. adv. bd. Electronic Banking Law and Commerce Report. Mem. ABA, D.C. Bar, Fed. Bar Assn. (chmn. banking law com.). Office: Covington & Burling 1201 Pennsylvania Ave NW Washington DC 20004-2401 Home Phone: 301-657-4094; Office Phone: 202-662-5308. Business E-Mail: mweiss@cov.com.

WEISS, MARTIN HARVEY, neurosurgeon, educator; b. Newark, Feb. 2, 1939; s. Max and Rae W.; m. R. Debora Rosenthal, Aug. 20, 1961; children: Brad, Jessica, Elisabeth. AB magna cum laude, Dartmouth Coll., 1960, BMS, 1961; MD, Cornell U., 1963. Diplomate Am. Bd. Neurol. Surgery (bd. dirs. 1983-89, vice chmn. 1987-88, chmn. 1988-89). Intern Univ. Hosps., Cleve., 1963-64, resident in neurosurgery, 1966-70; sr. instr. to asst. prof. neurosurgery Case Western Res. U., 1970-73; asso. prof. neurosurgery U. So. Calif., 1973-76, prof., 1976-78, prof., chmn. dept., 1978—2004, Martin H. Weiss chair in neurol. surgery, 1997—. Chmn. neurology B study sect. NIH; mem. residency rev. com. for neurosurg. Accreditation Commn. for Grad. Med. Edn., 1989—, vice chmn., 1991—93, chmn., 1993—95, mem. appeals coun. in neurosurg., 1995—; vis. prof. U. Mich, 1987; vis. prof. Med. Sch. Harvard U., 1988; vis. prof. U. Wash., 1988, U. Calif., San Francisco, 1994, U. Oreg., 1995, Tufts U., 1996, U. Melbourne, 1996, U. Sydney, 1996, U. Erlangen/Nurnberg, 1999, U. Geneva, 1999, U. Tex., 2004, U. Oreg., 2004, Stanford U., 2005; vis. prof., Bronson Ray lectr. Cornell U., 2005—06; Afrox traveling prof. South African Congress Neurol. Surgeons, 1989; hon. guest Royal Coll. Physicians Endocrine Sect., London, 2001; lectr. in field. Author: Pituitary Diseases, 1980; assoc. editor Bull. L.A. Neurol. Socs., 1976-81, Jour. Clin. Neurosci., 1981—; mem. editl. bd. Neurosurgery, 1979-84, Neurol. Rsch., 1980—, Jour. Neurosurgery, 1987—, chmn., 1995—, assoc. editor, 1996—; editor-in-chief Clin. Neurosurgery, 1980-83, Neuro Sociological Focus, 1996-. Served to capt. USAR, 1964—66, assoc. in gen. surgery USAH, USMA, 1964—66, West Point, NY. Spl. fellow in neurosurgery NIH, 1969-70; recipient Jamieson medal Australasian Neurosurg. Soc., 1996, Pevehouse medal Calif. Assn. Neurol. Surgeons, 2008. Mem. ACS (adv. coun. neurosurgery 1985-88), Soc. Neurol. Surgeons (v.p. 1999, pres.-elect 2000—, pres. 2001-02), Neurosurg. Soc. Am., Am. Acad. Neurol. Surgery (exec. com. 1988-89, v.p. 1992-93, Cushing medal 2005), Rsch. Soc. Neurol. Surgeons, Am. Assn. Neurol. Surgeons (bd. dirs. 1988-91, sec. 1994-97, pres.-elect 1998-99, pres. 1999-00, past pres. 2000-01, Kurze Lectr. 2005, Cushing Medalist, 2005), Congress Neurol. Surgeons (v.p. 1982-83), Western Neurosurg. Soc. (Cloward medal 2006), Neurosurg. Forum, So. Calif. Neurosurg. Soc. (pres. 1983-84), Neurosurgeon Rsch. & Edn. Found. (chmn., exec. com. 2004-), Phi Beta Kappa, Alpha Omega Alpha. Home: 357 Georgian Rd La Canada Flintridge CA 91011-3520 Office: 1200 N State St Los Angeles CA 90033-1029 Home Phone: 818-790-7467; Office Phone: 323-226-7421. Business E-Mail: weiss@usc.edu.

WEISS, MITCHELL JOSEPH, librarian; b. Chgo., Nov. 12, 1942; s. Harry Edward and Gertrude Plotkin Weiss. ScB in Biology with high honors, Brown U., 1964; PhD in Zoology, U. Mich., 1970; MLS, Rutgers U., 1988. NIH postdoctoral rsch. fellow U. Wash., Seattle, 1970—73; postdoctoral instr. in zoology U. Iowa, Iowa City, 1973—74; asst. prof. biology Rutgers U., New Brunswick, NJ, 1974—81, vis. asst. prof., 1981—82, guest investigator, 1982—2000; sci. writer New Brunswick, 2001—02; reference libr., digital/global access libr. coord. Fairleigh Dickinson U., Teaneck, NJ, 2002—07, asst. univ. libr. online libr., 2007—. Cons. Oriel Corp., Stamford, Conn., 1983, Knoll Pharm. Co., Mt. Olive, NJ, 1999—2000. Contbr. articles to sci. jours. Grad. fellow, NSF, 1964—69, rsch. grantee, 1976—78. Mem.: Internat. Assn. Meiobenthologists, Am. Microscopical Soc. Achievements include research in structure and development of insect brain centers at microscopic and ultrastructural levels; biology of phylum Gastrotricha, with current emphasis on sexuality, life cycles and systematics of freshwater gastrotrichs. Avocations: classical music, swimming. Office: Fairleigh Dickinson U 1000 River Rd T-WL1-01 Teaneck NJ 07666 Office Phone: 201-692-2139. E-mail: mjweiss@fdu.edu.

WEISS, MORRY, greeting card company executive; b. Czechoslovakia, 1940; m. Judith Stone. Grad., Wayne State U. Salesman, field mgr. Am. Greetings Corp., Cleve., 1961-66, advt. mgr., 1966-68, v.p., 1969-73, group v.p. mktg. and sales, 1973-78, pres., 1978—2003, COO Cleve., 1978—87, bd. dir., chief exec. officer, 1987—2003, chmn., 1992—. Office: Am Greetings Corp 1 American Rd Cleveland OH 44144-2301

WEISS, MYRNA GRACE, management consultant; b. NYC, June 22, 1939; d. Herman and Blanche Ziegler; m. Arthur H. Weiss; children: Debra Anne Huddleston, Louise Esther Pennington. BA, Barnard Coll., 1958; MA, Hunter Coll., 1968; MPA, NYU, 1978; cert. in Mktg., U. Pa. Tchr., NYC and Vallejo, Calif., 1959-68; dir. admissions Columbia Prep. Sch., NYC, 1969-72; dir. PREP counselling NYU, NYC, 1973-74; dept. head Hewitt Sch., NYC, 1974-79; mgr. Met. Ins. Co., NYC, 1979-84; mktg. exec. Rothschild, Inc., NYC, 1984-85; pres. First Mktg. Capital Group Ltd., NYC, 1985—; mng. dir. Wrap Co. Internat. N.V., 1992-97; advisor Lared Group, NYC, 1987-97; CEO, pres., bd. dirs. Ibnet, 1998—2002; adj. prof. SUNY-FIT, 2004—. Adv. Gov.'s Hwy. Safety Com., NYC, 1985-88; pres. Fin. Women's Assn. NY, 1984-85; adj. prof. SUNY, Fashion Inst. Tech., 2005—. Bd. dirs. 92nd Y, NYC, 1972—90, ARC, NYC, 1989—2006, asst. treas., 1993—. Mem. Internat. Women's Forum (bd. dirs. 1990-92), Econ. Club N.Y., Women's Econ. Roundtable (bd. dirs. 1988-90). Office: 1st Mktg Capital Group Ltd 1056 5th Ave New York NY 10028-0112 Business E-Mail: myrna.weiss@fitnyc.edu. E-mail: mzweiss@nyc.rr.com.

WEISS, NANCY PASSMAN, artist; b. Chgo., June 12, 1938; d. Manny and Helen (Spero) Passman; m. Lenard Garsen Weiss, Aug. 30, 1958; children: Pamela Lee, Elizabeth Susan. Student, U. Colo., 1956-57, U. Calif., Berkeley, from 1958, CCAC, Oakland, Calif., 1980-81, San Francisco Art Inst., 1984-85. Artist, 1950—. Exhibited in shows at Jewett Gallery, San Francisco Main Libr., Bolinas Mus., Calif., 1992-2007, Galleria Le Logge, Assisi, Italy, 1997, 98, 99; contbr. to The Calif. Art Rev., 1990. Chair Berkeley Civic Arts Commn. City of Berkeley, 1980-85; mem. adv. bd. No. Calif. chpt. Nat. Mus. Women in the Arts; bd. dirs. Eureka Theatre Co., San Francisco, Mus. Performance & Design, 2005-. Democrat. Jewish. Avocations: walking, yoga, tennis. Office Phone: 415-834-5111. Personal E-mail: nancypassman@comcast.net.

WEISS, PAUL RICHARD, plastic surgeon; b. Bklyn., July 4, 1942; s. Murray and Belle (Edelman) W.; m. Linda Wayne, Aug. 23, 1964; children: Fredda Susan, Jonathan Michael. BS, Tufts U., Medford, Mass., 1964; MD, Tulane U., New Orleans, 1969. Diplomate Am. Bd. Plastic Surgery, 1977, Am. Bd. Surgery, 1975. Intern Bronx Muni Hosp Ctr., NY, 1969—70, resident surgery, 1970—72, Montefiore Hosp. Med. Ctr., NY, 1972—74, resident plastic surgery, 1974—76; attending plastic surgeon Montefiore Med. Ctr., NY, 1976—, Albert Einstein Coll. Med. Hosp., NY, 1976—, Beth Abraham Hosp., NY, 1976—, Jewish Home & Hosp., NY, 1976—, Beth Israel Med. Ctr., NY, 1986—2005; clin. prof. plastic surgery Albert Einstein Coll. Medicine, Bronx, NY, 1994—. Adv. bd. FOJP Medical Malpractice, N.Y.C., 1988—. Named one of Top Doctor, NY Mag. Fellow ACS (Bronx chpt., pres. 1995-96); Am. Soc. Plastic Surgeons, Am. Assn. Plastic Surgeons, Am. Soc. Aesthetic Plastic Surgery, NY Regional Soc. Plastic Surgeons (pres. 1992-93), Montefiore Med. Ctr. Staff Alumni Assn. (pres. 1994-97), Am. Assn. Hand Surgery, Northeastern Soc. Plastic Surgeons, World Profl. Assn. Transgender Health. Jewish. Avocations: landscape gardening, vintage automobiles, stamp collecting/philately, collecting and restoring antique furniture. Office: 1049 5th Ave Ste 2D New York NY 10028-0115 Office Phone: 212-861-8000. Office Fax: 212-861-8376. Personal E-mail: pweissmd@verizon.net.

WEISS, PENNY A., political science professor, director; b. Miami, Fla., Dec. 22, 1955; d. Leonard and Beatrice Brines Weiss; life ptnr. Robert Strikwerda; children: Linden Jesse Weiswerda, Brennin Emile Weiswerda, Avian Mason Weiswerda. BA, U. South Fla., Tampa, 1976; PhD, U. Notre Dame, Ind., 1987. Assoc. prof. polit. sci. Purdue U., West Lafayette, Ind., 1987—2008; dir. women's studies, prof. polit. sci. St. Louis U., 2008—. Editor: (anthology) Feminist Interpretations of Emma Goldman, Feminism and Community. Foster parent Divsn. Family Children, Lafayette, 2002—06; mentor Women in Transition, St. Louis, 2009—. Avocation: gardening. Office: St Louis Univ Women's Studies 3672 W Pine Mall Blvd Saint Louis MO 63108 Business E-Mail: pweiss1@slu.edu.

WEISS, RENEE E., accounting educator; d. Sam and Susan Weiss; m. Jeffrey N. Klein, Aug. 13, 1987; children: Sam A. Klein, Isabella J. Klein. PhD, Baruch Coll. CUNY, NY, 2005. V.P. Lane's Interiors Inc., NY, 1977; asst. prof. St. Thomas U., Mpls., 2007—. Trustee Temple Emanuel, NY, 2003—07. Com. mem. Am. Cancer Soc., NY, 1998—2004. Recipient Outstanding Achievement, NY State Soc. Cert. Pub. Accts., 1999. Mem.: Am. Acctg. Assn. Office: Univ St Thomas TMH343 1000 LaSalle Ave Minneapolis MN 55439 Office Phone: 651-962-4303. Office Fax: 651-962-4710. Business E-Mail: weis3696@stthomas.edu.

WEISS, RENÉE KAROL, editor, musician; b. Allentown, Pa., Sept. 11, 1923; d. Abraham S. and Elizabeth (Levitt) Karol; m. Theodore Weiss. BA, Bard Coll., 1951; student, Conn. Sch. Dance; studied violin with, Sascha Jacobinoff, Boris Koutzen, Emile Hauser, Ivan Galamian. Mem. Miami U. Symphony Orch., 1941, N.C. State Symphony, 1942-45, Oxford U. Symphony, Opera Orchs., Eng., 1953-54, Woodstock String Quartet, 1956-60, Bard Coll. Chamber Ensemble, 1950-66, Hudson Valley Philharmonic, 1960-66, Hudson Valley String Quartet, 1965, Princeton Orch., 1980—93; orchestral, chamber work, 1966—. Participant Theodore and Renée Weiss poetry writing workshops Princeton U., 1985, Hofstra Coll., 1985, modern poetry workshop Cooper Union, 1988, Princeton Adult Edn.; tchr. modern dance to children Bard Coll., Kindergarten Tivoli, NY Pub. Sch., 1955-58 Author: (children's books) To Win A Race, 1966, A Paper Zoo, 1968 (best books for children N.Y. Times, Book World 1968, N.J. Author's award 1968, 70, 88), The Bird From the Sea, 1970, Biography: David Schubert: Works and Days, 1984; co-editor, mgr. Quar. Rev. Lit., 1945-2005; co-author: (with Theodore Weiss) The Always Present Presents, 2005; opera from The Always Present, Present with music by Peter Westergaard, 2009. Mem.: PEN (Nora Magid Lifetime Achievement award with Theodore Weiss 1997). Office: Q R L Poetry Series Princeton U 185 Nassau St Princeton NJ 08544-4914 Business E-Mail: qrl@princeton.edu.

WEISS, RICHARD A., state official; b. Africa; m. Jan Weiss; 3 children. Grad. in liberal arts, Baylor U. Adminstr. Office of Budget, Dept. Fin. and Adminstrn., Little Rock, dep. dir., dir., 1994-97; CFO, State of Ark., Little Rock, 1994—; dir. Ark. Dept. Fin. and Adminstrn., Little Rock, 2001—. Office: Fin and Adminstrn Dept PO Box 3278 Little Rock AR 72203-3278 Office Phone: 501-682-2242. E-mail: richard.weiss@dfa.state.ar.us.

WEISS, RICK, reporter; married; 1 child. BS in Biology, Cornell U., 1974; M in Journalism, U. Calif. Berkeley, 1985. Lic. med. technologist various hosp. labs., 1974—84; biology and biomedicine writer Sci. News Mag., Wash.; staff writer Health Mag., San Francisco; sci. and med. reporter health sect. Wash. Post, 1993—96, sci. and med. reporter nat. news desk, 1996—. Contbg. writer: NY Times, L.A. Times, Science, Discover. Recipient Sci. Journalism award, AAAS, 2000, Sci. in Soc. Journalism award, Nat. Assn. Science Writers, Inc., 2002, Victor Cohn Prize for Excellence in Medical Science Reporting, 2005. Office: Wash Post 1150 15th St NW Washington DC 20071-0070 Office Phone: 202-334-5514. Business E-Mail: weissr@washpost.com.

WEISS, ROBERT FRANCIS, retired academic and religious organization administrator, consultant; b. St. Louis, Aug. 27, 1924; s. Frank L.G. and Helen M. (Beck) Weiss. BA, St. Louis U., 1951, Ph.L., MA, St. Louis U., 1953, S.T.L., 1961; PhD, U. Minn., 1964. Joined Soc. of Jesus, 1946; ordained priest Roman Cath. Ch., 1959; tchr. Rockhurst HS, Kansas City, Mo., 1953—56; adminstrv. asst. to pres. St. Louis U., 1961—62; asst. dean Rockhurst Coll., Kansas City, Mo., 1964—66, dean, v.p., asst. prof. edn., 1966—72, pres., 1977—88, St. Louis U. HS, 1973—77, interim pres., 1992; asst. higher edn. and continuing formation Mo. Province S.J., St. Louis, 1989—92, treas., 1992—2003, asst. higher edn. and continuing formation, 1997—2005, asst. to treas., 2003—05, del. higher edn., 2005—; assoc. dir. Advancement Office, 2007—. Mem. Commn. on Govtl. rels. Am. Coun. Edn., 1985—87; bd. dirs. Kansas City Regional Coun. for Higher Edn., 1987—88, Boys Hope Girls Hope, 1977—. Contbr. chapters to books, articles to profl. jours. Trustee St. Louis U., 1973—87, 1991—2003, Loyola U., New Orleans, 1973—82, 1985—88, United Student Aid Funds, Inc., 1977—94, U. San Francisco, 1987—99, Marymount Coll., Salina, Kans., 1986—88, St. Louis U. H.S., 1989—99, 2003—, Fontbonne Coll., St. Louis, 1973—77, Sacred Heart Program, Radio and TV Apostolate, St. Louis, 1990—96, pres., 1992—96, bd. mem., 2000—05; bd. dirs. Creighton U., Omaha, 1981—97, Our Little Haven, St. Louis, 1992—, St. Elizabeth Acad., St. Louis, 1997—2004, DeSmet Jesuit HS, 2003—09, Loyola Acad., St. Louis, 2003—, chmn. bd. mems., 2005—; bd. dirs. St. John's Coll., Belize City, Belize, 2003—; trustee St. Louis (Mo.) Archdiocesan Fund, 2006—; bd. regents Conception Sem. Coll., Mo., 2004—. 1st sgt. US Army, 1943—46. Decorated Bronze Star, Two Battle Stars, Combat Infantryman's Badge, Unit Presdl. Citation. Mem.: Am. Assn. for Higher Edn., Vets. Assn. Rainbow divsn. (nat. chaplain 1976—84, 1988—90, pres.-elect 1990—91, pres. 1991—92, assoc. nat. chaplain 1992—, found. pres. 2003—05), Alpha Phi Omega, Alpha Sigma Nu. Home: 3601 Lindell Blvd Saint Louis MO 63108-3393 Office: Mo Province SJ 4511 W Pine Blvd Saint Louis MO 63108-2109 Home Phone: 314-633-4425; Office Phone: 314-361-7765. Business E-Mail: rweiss@jesuits-mis.org. *The only way for me to look at life is in the light of faith, which I consider one of God's greatest gifts. Life for me is an opportunity to serve God and as many of my neighbors as I can. I am basically an optimist. There is so much beauty around us, so many good people, so many marvels to behold— that I thank the Lord for giving me the ability to know and experience this life and to look forward to eternal life with God, the Source of all life. Any success I have had I attribute to taking advantage of the opportunities that God has put in my path.*

WEISS, ROBERT M., urologist, educator; b. NYC, Jan. 13, 1936; s. David and Laura W.; m. Ilana Shemer, May 20, 1973; children: Erik Daniel, Dana Alexandra. BS magna cum laude, Franklin and Marshall Coll., Lancaster, Pa., 1957; MD, SUNY, Bklyn., 1960; MA (hon.), Yale U., New Haven, Conn., 1976. Diplomate: Am. Bd. Urology, Nat. Bd. Med. Examiners. Intern Cornell Med. Divsn., Bellevue Hosp., NYC, 1960-61; resident in gen. surgery Beth Israel Hosp., NYC, 1961-62; resident in urology Squier Urol. Clinic, Presbyn. Hosp., NYC, 1963-64, 65-67; vis. fellow Columbia U. Coll. Physicians and Surgeons, NYC, 1964-65, adj. assoc. prof. pharmacology, 1975-77, adj. prof. pharmacology, 1977—; mem. faculty Yale U. Med. Sch., New Haven, 1967—, prof. urology, 1976-88, prof., chief sect. of urology, 1988—, Donald Gutherie prof. surgery, 2001—, interim chmn. dept. surgery, 1999-2001; attending urology Yale-New Haven Hosp., New Haven, 1967-88, head sect. of urology, 1988—, interim chief dept. surgery, 1999—2001, pres. med. staff, 2004—06. Cons. West Haven VA Hosp. Contbr. articles to profl. jours. Trustee Am. Bd. Urology, 1998-2004. With USAR, 1962-63. Fellow ACS, Am. Acad. Pediat.; mem. AAAS, Am. Assn. Genito-Urinary Surgeons, Am. Surg. Assn., Am. Physiol. Soc., Soc. Gen. Physiologists, Assn. Univ. Urologists, Soc. Pediatric Urology, Am. Urol. Assn., Clin. Soc. Genito-Urinary Surgeons, New Eng. Surg. Soc., New Eng. Urol. Assn., Phi Beta Kappa, Sigma Xi. Office: Yale U Sch Medicine Dept Urology PO Box 208041 New Haven CT 06520-8041 Office Phone: 203-785-2815. Business E-Mail: robert.weiss@yale.edu.

WEISS, ROBERT ORR, speech educator; b. Kalamazoo, Apr. 8, 1926; s. Nicholas John and Ruth (Orr) W.; m. Ann Lenore Lawson, Sept. 16, 1951; children: Elizabeth Ann, John Lawson, James Robert, Virginia Lenore. BA, Albion Coll., 1948; MA, Northwestern U., 1949, PhD, 1954. Instr. speech Wayne State U., Detroit, 1949-51; instr. pub. speaking Northwestern U., Evanston, Ill., 1954-55; mem. faculty DePauw U., Greencastle, Ind., 1955—2002, H.B. Gough prof. speech, 1965-97, head comm. arts and scis., 1963-78, 85-86, 93. Author: Public Argument, 1995; editor: Speaker and Gavel, 1968-75, Speaking Across the Curriculum, 1990-2006; co-editor: Current Criticism, 1971; contbr. articles to profl. jours. Active A-Way Home Shelter Bd. Served in US Army, 1945—46. Recipient Fred C. Tucker Disting. Career award, 1995, Lifetime award, Nat. Ednl. Debate Assn., 1997, Presdl. citation Nat. Communication Assn., 1999. Mem. AAUP (pres. DePauw U. chpt. 1961-62), Nat. Comm. Assn. (legis. assembly 1966-68), Am. Forensic Assn. (sec.-treas. 1958-59), Ctrl. States Comm. Assn., Phi Beta Kappa, Delta Sigma Rho-Tau Kappa Alpha (nat. v.p. 1981-83, pres. 1983-85), Sigma Nu. Home: 210 W Poplar St Greencastle IN 46135-2638 Home Phone: 765-653-5487; Office Phone: 765-658-4490. Business E-Mail: robertweiss@depauw.edu.

WEISS, ROBERT STEPHEN, medical manufacturing company operating executive; b. Oct. 25, 1946; s. Stephen John and Anna Blanche (Lescinski) W.; m. Marilyn Annette Chesick, Oct. 29, 1970; children: Christopher Robert, Kim Marie, Douglas Paul. BS in Acctg. cum laude, U. Scranton, 1968. CPA, N.Y. Supr. KPMG (formerly Peat, Marwick, Mitchell & Co.), NYC, 1971-76; asst. corp. contr. Cooper Labs., Inc., Parsippany, N.J., 1977-78; group contr. Cooper Vision, Inc., 1980; v.p., corp. contr. Cooper Labs., Palo Alto, Calif., 1981-83, The Cooper Cos., Inc. (formerly CooperVision, Inc.), Palo Alto, Calif., 1984-89; v.p., treas., CFO The Cooper Cos., Inc., Pleasanton, Calif., 1989—2005, sr. v.p., 1992-95, exec. v.p. fin., 1995—2005, COO, 2005—07, CEO, 2007—, pres., 2007—. Bd. dirs. The Cooper Cos., Inc., Pleasanton, Calif, 1996-, Accuray Inc., Sunnyvale, Calif., 2007-. With U.S. Army, 1969-70. Decorated Bronze Star with oak leaf cluster, Army Commendation medal. Mem. AICPA, N.Y. State Soc. CPAs. Office: The Cooper Companies Inc Ste 590 6140 Stoneridge Mall Rd Pleasanton CA 94588

WEISS, RONALD DEAN, biology professor; b. Charter Oak, Iowa, June 14, 1936; s. Clarence Edward and Cleo Pauline Weiss; m. E. Verle Weiss, Dec. 27, 1957; children: Dana Rene Weiss-Petersen, Denton Dean, David Michael. BS, Iowa State U., Ames, 1958; MS, U. Nebr., Omaha, 1968. Cert. in profl. post secondary Iowa, 1968. Biology instr. Iowa Western CC, Sioux City, 1982—91, grant cons., 1989—91, asst. prof. biology Council Bluffs, 1991—2000, biology project and u. relationships rep., 1992—96, microbiologist, 1995, pres. coll. senate, 1996—98; asst. prof. biology Tidewater CC, Norfolk, Va., 2004—08, coop. biologist, open door project, asst. prof., 2004—. Mem. Nat. Biology Tchrs. Assn., 1992—2000; co-chair State Biology Tchrs. Conv., Council Bluffs, 1999—2000. 1st sgt. US Army, 1956—62, Iowa & Colo. Republican. Episcopalian. Avocations: reading, hunting, dance, sports, movies. Home: 201 North St Portsmouth VA 23704 Office Phone: 757-642-8095. Office Fax: 757-391-9290. Personal E-mail: weisspatriot@aol.com.

WEISS, RONALD PHILLIP, lawyer; b. Springfield, Mass., Apr. 28, 1947; s. Kermit Paul and Fay Roslyn (Robinovitz) W.; m. Janet Faye Landon, June 15, 1969; children: Emily, Katherine. BA, Dartmouth Coll., 1968; JD, U. Pa., 1972. Bar: Mass. 1972, U.S. Dist. Ct. Mass. 1975, U.S. Tax Ct. 1979, U.S. Ct. Appeals (1st cir.) 2000. Assoc. Bulkley, Richardson and Gelinas, Springfield, Mass., 1972-78; ptnr. Bulkley, Richardson and Gelinas, LLP, Springfield, 1978—. Pres. Estate Planning Coun. Hampden County, 1979-81; trustee Mass. Continuing Legal Edn. Inc., 1978-81. Author: (with others) Drafting Wills and Trusts in Massachusetts, 1990, 92, 94; editor: (with others) Massachusetts Corporate Tax Manual, 1986. Trustee Springfield Symphony Orch., 1986—, v.p., 1988—89, pres., 1989—91, chmn., 1991—94; mem. bd. advisors U. Mass. Family Bus. Ctr., 1992—; mem. adv. panel Hanson Initiative for Lang. and Literacy, MGH Inst. Health Professions, 2001—; counsel Cmty. Found. of Western Mass.; appropriations com. Town of Longmeadow, Mass., 1990—96, chmn., 1991—92, 1995—96; trustee Jewish Fedn. Greater Springfield, 1986—90. Mem. ABA, Mass. Bar Assn. (chmn. taxation sect. 1978-81, bd. dels. 1979-81), Mass. Bar Found., Hampden County Bar Assn., Rotary. Office: Bulkley Richardson and Gelinas LLP 1500 Main St Ste 2700 Springfield MA 01115-5507 Office Phone: 413-272-6259.

WEISS, SIMONA, retired paralegal; d. Leon and Rose Weiss; m. Morton B. Elliot, Apr. 14, 1951 (div. May 10, 1972); children: Russell Wayne Elliot, Linda Beth Elliot-Morris. Student, Columbia U., NYC, 1968—70; BA cum laude, Fairligh Dickinson U., Teaneck, NJ, 1974; postgrad., NYU, NYC, 1974—76, William Patterson U., Wayne, NJ, 2001—03. Cert. paralegal Upsala Coll. East Orange, NJ, 1980. Paralegal adminstr. Witco Chem. Corp., NYC, 1980—81; paralegal supr. Pitney, Hardin, Kipp & Szuch, Morristown, NJ, 1982—82; real estate paralegal Willkie Farr & Gallagher, NYC, 1983—84; real estate and corp. paralegal Robinson Silverman Pearce Aronsohn & Berman, NYC, 1984—90; real estate paralegal Freddie Mac, NYC, 1991—91; legal asst. Gen. Investment Sect. Legal Dept. The Prudential Ins. Co. of Am., Newark, 1992—94; comml. real estate paralegal Cleary, Gottlieb, Steen & Hamilton, NYC, 1994—96; real estate and corp. paralegal Hannoch Weisman, Roseland, NJ, 1996—98; comml. real estate paralegal Unilever Bestfoods, Englewood Cliffs, NJ, 1998—2002. Chmn. Haworth Parks & Playgrounds Com., NJ, 1972—78; county com. mcpl. chmn. Haworth Rep. Orgn., NJ, 1973—79; candidate Non-Partisan Bergen County NJ Charter Study Commn., 1973—74; primary candidate Bergen County Bd. of Chosen Freeholders, NJ, 1977—77; fin. and corr. sec. Temple Beth El, Closter, NJ, 1968—72; program and publicity chmn. 1st Bergen County Women's Ctr., Teaneck, NJ, 1972—74; v.p. fund raising Haworth Home and Sch. Assn., 1967—69. Recipient Mayor's Cert., Borough of Haworth, 1979; scholar, Fairleigh Dickinson U., 1971—74. Mem.: Nat. Coun. Jewish Women, Legal Asst. Mgmt. Assn., Nat. Paralegal Assn., Phi Omega Epsilon. Independent. Avocations: theater, movies, opera, ballet, reading. Home: 2000 Linwood Ave 19U Fort Lee NJ 07024 Personal E-mail: simona_wei@msn.com.

WEISS, STEPHEN J., lawyer; b. NYC, Sept. 12, 1938; s. Morris and Frances (Dinkin) Weiss; m. Madeline Adler, Aug. 12, 1962; children: Lowell Andrew, Valerie Elizabeth, Bradley Lawrence. BS, Queens Coll., 1959; LLB, Cornell U., 1962; LLM, Georgetown U., 1966. Bar: NY 1963, DC 1966, US Supreme Ct. 1975. Atty. SEC, Washington, 1962-65; assoc. firm Arent Fox Kintner Plotkin & Kahn, Washington, 1965-70, ptnr., 1971-94, Holland & Knight LLP, Washington, 1994—2009. Lectr. securities corp. law, dirs. and officers liability and ins. Am. Law Inst., ABA, Fed. Bar Assn., Practicing Law Inst., Bur. Nat. Affairs, Exec. Enterprises, Aspen Law & Bus. Orgn. Mgmt., Inc., Inst. Internat. Rsch., Profl. Liability Underwriting Soc.; mem. adv. bd. Securities Regulation and Law Report Bur. Nat. Affairs, 1980—95. Author: Regulation D-A Practical Guide, 1994, Navigating the D&O Maze: A Handbook for Purchasers of Employment Practices Liability Insurance, 1998; dirs. and officers liability ins. columnist: Dirs. & Bds. mag., 1998—2007; contbr. articles to profl. jours. Named to Best Lawyers in Am., 2003—. Mem.: ABA (fed. regulation securities com. 1970—, chmn. com. fgn. corrupt practices legislation 1976—77, chmn. Rule 10b-5 subcom. 1976—78, chmn. civil liabilities subcom. 1978—81, mem. devels. bus. financing com. 1982—, mem. Guiding Principles Task Force bus. ins. com. 1994—95), Fed. Bar Assn. (chmn. securities law comm. 1968—70, mem. coun. securities law com. 1971—, chmn. coun. financing and taxation 1971—72, chmn. publs. bd. 1977—78, mem. nat. coun. 1972—80, Leadership commendation 1973, Disting. Svc. award), Cornell Law Club Washington (pres. 1971—79). Business E-Mail: steve.weiss@hklaw.com.

WEISS, STEPHEN M., lawyer; b. Phila., Mar. 11, 1943; m. Sherry L. Weiss; children: Benjamin, Jessica. BA, U. Ariz., Tucson, 1965, JD, 1968. Bar: Ariz., US Ct. Appeals (9th cir.), US Supreme Ct. 1974. Ptnr. Karp & Weiss P.C., Tucson, 1995—2008, 2008—. Judge pro tempore Pima County Superior Ct., 1981—. Author: (chpt. to book) Domestic Torts, 1989. Mem. Pima County Commn. Trial Ct. Appts., 1985—89, Pima County Commn. Jud. Performance Rev., 1993—95, Supreme Ct. Com. Character and Fitness, 2000—06, co-chair, 2005—06. Named Trial Lawyer of Yr., Trial Lawyers for Pub. Justice, 1994. Mem.: ABA, Ariz. Attys. Criminal Justice, Pima County Bar Assn., State Bar Ariz., Am. Trial Lawyers Assn., Nat. Assn. Criminal Def. Lawyers, Nat. Conf. Bar Examiners (character and fitness com. 2006—07, state bar criminal law adv. com. 2007—), Fed. Bar Assn. (pres. Tucson chpt. 2001), Morris K. Udall Inn of Ct. (pres. 2002). Office: Karp Weiss PC 3060 N Swan Rd Tucson AZ 85712 Office Phone: 520-325-4200. Office Fax: 520-325-4224. Business E-Mail: sweiss@karpweiss.com.

WEISS, STEVEN ALLAN, lawyer; b. NYC; BA cum laude, Cornell U., 1977; JD cum laude, U. Mich., 1980. Bar: Ill. 1980, U.S. Dist. Ct. (N. Dist.) Ill. 1980, U.S. Ct. Appeals (7th Cir.) 1982. Assoc. Reuben & Proctor, Chgo., 1980-87; ptnr. Schopf & Weiss, Chgo., 1987—. Contbr. article to profl. publs. Mem. ABA. Office: Schopf & Weiss Ste 2800 One So Wacker Dr Chicago IL 60606

WEISS, SUSAN ELLEN, adult nurse practitioner, educator; b. Youngstown, Ohio, Oct. 25, 1951; d. Robert Cochran and Clara Olive (Cyphert) Stetson; m. Paul Wm. Weiss, Dec. 27, 1975; children: David, Rebecca, Noah, Simon, Solomon. AAS, Youngstown State U., 1971, BSN, 1975; cert. adult nurse practitioner, SUNY, 1981. Cert. adult nurse practitioner, legal nurse cons., 1998. Nurse practitioner St. Joseph Riverside Hosp., Warren, Ohio; emergency room nurse St. Elizabeth Hosp., Youngstown; ICU-CCU nurse Youngstown Osteo. Hosp.; dir. advanced nursing edn. NP Sch. Based Clinic, 1994. Pro-bono adult nurse practitioner Drs. James and Chris Ventresco, Family Practice, 2004—05. Mem.: AACN, Am. Acad. Nurse Practitioners, Cardiovascular Nursing Assn., Oncology Nursing Soc., Nat. League Nursing, Am. Coll. Cert. Legal Nurse Cons., Am. Coll. Nurse Practitioners. Home: 6131 Saint Andrews Dr Canfield OH 44406-9023 Personal E-mail: weissan@aol.com.

WEISS, WALTER STANLEY, lawyer; b. Newark, Mar. 12, 1929; s. Jack and Mollie (Orkin) W.; m. Misty M. Moore; children from previous marriage: Jack Stephen, Andrew Scott. AB, Rutgers U., 1949, JD, 1952. Bar: D.C. 1952, N.J. 1956, Calif. 1961. Trial atty. IRS, Phila., Los Angeles, 1957-62; asst. U.S. atty., chief tax div. Los Angeles, 1962-63; ptnr. firm Goodson & Hannam, Los Angeles, 1963-67; mng. ptnr. firm Long & Levit, Los Angeles, 1967-79; ptnr. firm Greenberg & Glusker, Los Angeles, 1979-81; ptnr. Rosenfeld, Meyer and Susman, Beverly Hills, Calif., 1981-93; prin. Law Office of Walter S. Weiss, LA, 1993—. Judge pro tem L.A. and Santa Monica (Calif.) Mcpl. Cts., 1994—. Contbr. articles to legal jours. Served to capt. JAGC USAF, 1953-56. Named Arbitrator Nat. Assn. Securities Dealers, 1974 Fellow Am. Coll. Trial Lawyers; mem. ABA, Los Angeles County Bar Assn., Beverly Hills Bar Assn. Home: 12349 Ridge Cir Los Angeles CA 90049-1183 Office: 1800 Century Pk E Ste 300 Los Angeles CA 90067 Home Phone: 310-471-4320. E-mail: waltersweiss@gmail.com.

WEISS, ZEV, corporate financial executive; s. Morry Weiss. BA, Yeshiva Univ.; MBA, Columbia Univ. With Am. Greetings Corp., Cleve., 1992—, exec. dir., Nat. Accounts, 1997—2000, v.p., Strategic Business Unit Division, 2000—01, sr. v.p. ventures, 2001, exec. v.p. ventures & enterprise mgmt., 2001—03, CEO, 2003—. Bd. mem. Yeshiva Univ. Office: American Greeting Corp 1 American Rd Cleveland OH 44144-2398

WEISSBACH, HERBERT, biochemist, researcher; b. NYC, Mar. 16, 1932; s. Louis and Vivian (Ruhalter) W.; m. Renee Kohl, Dec. 27, 1953; children— Lawrence, Nancy, Marjorie, Robert BS, CUNY, 1953; MS, George Washington U., 1955, PhD, 1957. Chemist Nat. Heart Inst., Bethesda, Md., 1953-68; acting chief NIH, Bethesda, 1968-69; assoc. dir. Roche Inst. Molecular Biology, Nutley, NJ, 1969-83, dir., 1983-96; v.p. Hoffmann-La Roche, Nutley, 1983-96; disting. rsch. prof., dir. ctr. for molecular biology and biotech. Fla. Atlantic U., Boca Raton, 1997—. Adj. prof. George Washington U., 1964-69, Columbia U., 1969-85, U. Medicine and Dentistry N.J., Newark, 1981-93, Princeton U., 1984-85. Editor: Molecular Mechanisms of Protein Biosynthesis, 1977, Archives of Biochemistry and Biophysics; contbr. articles to profl. jours. Recipient Superior Svc. award HEW, 1968, Enzyme award Am. Chem. Soc., 1970, Disting. Alumni award George Washington U., 1994. Mem. Am. Chem. Soc., Am. Soc. Biol. Chemists, Am. Soc. Pharmacology and Exptl. Therapeutics, Am. Soc. Microbiology, Nat. Acad. Scis., AAAS Home: 8008 Desmond Dr Boynton Beach FL 33437-5011 Office: Fla Atlantic U 777 Glades Rd Boca Raton FL 33431-6424 E-mail: herbweissbach@aol.com.

WEISSBLUTH, MARC, pediatrician, educator; b. 1943; MD, U. Wash., Seattle, 1970; grad., Stanford U. Cert. in pediat. Am. Bd. Med. Specialties, 1975. Intern St. Louis Children's Hosp., resident; prof. clinical pediat. Feinberg Sch. Medicine, Northwestern U.; pediatrician Children's Meml. Hosp., Chgo., Northwestern Children's Practice, Chgo. Author: Crybabies, Sweet Baby: How to Soothe Your Newborn, Your Fussy Baby, Healthy Sleep Habits, Happy Child. Mem.: Children's Cmty. Physicians Assn. Avocations: fishing, boating, golf, skiing, tennis. Office: Northwestern Childrens Practice 680 N Lake Shore Dr Ste 123 Chicago IL 60611 also: Childrens Meml Hosp Box 86 2300 Childrens Plz Chicago IL 60614 Office Phone: 312-642-5515, 773-880-4549. Office Fax: 312-642-0753.

WEISSENBERGER, GLEN, law educator, former dean; b. NYC, Jan. 19, 1946; s. Harold George and Helen Lillian (Hellmuth) W.; children: Kimberly, Geoffrey, Sarah. BA, U. Cin., 1969; JD, Harvard U., 1972. Bar: Ohio 1972, U.S. Dist. Ct. (so. dist.) Ohio 1972. Assoc. Taft, Stettinius & Hollister, Cin., 1972-75; of counsel Lloyd & Weissenberger, Cin., 1981—97; prof. law U. Cin. Law Sch., 1975—2002, DePaul U. Coll. Law, Chgo., 2002—, dean, 2002—09. Editl. cons. Anderson Pub. Co., Cin., 1980—; legal counsel Internat. Brotherhood of Magicians; chmn. editl. adv. bd. LexisNexis Legal Pub., 2005. Author: Weissenberger's Ohio Evidence, 1980, Weissenberger's Federal Evidence, 1987, Patients, Psychiatrists and Lawyers, 1989. Elder Presbyn. Ch., Cin., 1988—, trustee Glenn M. Weaver Found. and Glenn M. Weaver Inst. Law and Psychiatry, 1977. Recipient Jerome P. Goldman prize for Tchg. Excellence, 1977—80, U. Cin. Faculty Achievement award, 1995, Ohio State Bar Found. Outstanding Rsch. award, 2001. Mem. Cin. Bar Assn., U. Cin. Alumni Assn. (nat. v.p. 1975-83), Pi Kappa Alpha (nat. v.p., gen. counsel 1970-80), Phi Beta Kappa. Avocation: magic. Office: DePaul U Coll Law 25 E Jackson Blvd Chicago IL 60604 Office Phone: 312-362-8088. Office Fax: 312-362-5826. Business E-Mail: gweissen@depaul.edu.*

WEISSENBURGER, DAVID ALLEN, psychologist, educator, consultant; b. Anchorage, Sept. 7, 1953; s. Kenneth Albert and Dolores Jean Weissenburger; m. Barbara Jean Lyon, Nov. 28, 1998 (div. Apr. 2005); m. Jan Elizabeth Stone, Aug. 20, 1977 (div. Sept. 15, 1997); children: Jon Eric, Caryn Ann. AA, Sauk Valley Coll., 1973; BS, Western Ill. U., 1975; MA, Stephen F. Austin State U., 1979; PhD, Tex. Woman's U., 1994. Lic. psychol. assoc. Tex. State Bd. Examiners of Psychologists, 1980; cert. comprehensive diagnosis and evaluation - psychology Tex., 1980, qualified mental retardation profl. Tex., 1980. Unit dir., psychologist Tex. Dept. MHMR, Denton, 1976—87; dir. mental retardation svcs. Denton County MHMR Ctr., 1987—88; v.p. assessment and rsch. Behavioral Scis. Rsch. Press, Dallas, 1991—94; assoc. prof. U. Ctrl. Tex., Killeen, 1994—99, Tarleton State U., Killeen, 1999—2005, Stephenville, Tex., 2005—05, prof., 2005—, dept. head psychology and counseling, 2009—. Gen. ptnr. Weiss-Lyon Assocs., Copperas Cove, Tex., 1997—2004; faculty senate pres. Tarleton State U., Stephenville, Tex., 2002—03; v.p. West Tex. region Tex. Coun. Faculty Senates, Austin, 2002—04, pres.-elect, 2004—05, pres., 2005—; contract psychologist Pecan Valley MHMR, 2007—. Author: (psychological test)

Weiss-Lyon Scale. Mem. Ctrl. Tex. Coop. Workshop Coun., Killeen, 2001—02; asst. scoutmaster Boy Scouts, Roanoke, Tex., 1989—95; dir., past pres., v.p. Families in Crisis, Inc., Killeen, 1997—2005; mem. Texan Club - Tarleton State U., Stephenville, 2000—; pres. Student Govt. Assn. - Sauk Valley Coll., Dixon, Ill., 1972—73. Fellow Sr. fellow, Tex. Higher Edn. Coordinating Bd., 2002; scholar, State of Ill., 1971—75. Mem.: APA, Nat. Assn. Sch. Psychologists, Southwestern Psychol. Assn., Assn. Psychol. Sci., Optimist Club, Phi Theta Kappa, Psi Chi. Personal E-mail: dweissenburger@embarqmail.com.

WEISSINGER, THOMAS, librarian, educator; b. Silver Creek, NY, July 29, 1951; s. Tom and Hattie Weissinger; m. Maryann Hunter; children: Thomas Jr., Sandra Ellen. MA, U. Pitts., 1978, MLS, 1980. City hall libr. Newark Pub. Libr., 1980—82; reference libr. Rutgers U., NB, NJ, 1982—85. Head john henrik clarke africana libr. Cornell U., Ithaca, NY, 1985—2001; African Am. studies bibliographer U. Ill. Urbana Champaign, 2001—, assoc. prof. African Am. studies, 2003—. Contbr. articles to profl. jours. Adv. bd. mem. Champaign Pub. Libr., Ill., 2004—07. Recipient Mem., History Adv. Bd., Ebsco Pub., 2007. Mem.: ALA, Intellectual Freedom Round Table, Immroth award Com., African Am. Librs. Sect. (chair, conf. program planning com. 2004—06), Assn. Coll. Rsch. Librs. (assoc.; chair, african am. studies librarians sect. 2008—). Democrat. Office: Univ IL Urbana Champaign 1408 W Gregory Dr Urbana IL 61801 Office Fax: 217-333-0558. Business E-Mail: tweissin@illinois.edu.

WEISSMAN, ALLAN M., medical researcher; BS in biochemistry, SUNY, Stony Brook, 1977; MD, Albert Einstein Coll. Medicine, 1981. Resident in internal medicine Washington U.; postdoctoral fellow Cell Biology and Metabolism Br. Nat. Inst. Child Health & Human Devel., NIH, 1984; ind. investigator Nat. Cancer Inst., NIH, 1989, chief Regulation of Protein Functions Lab. Ctr. Cancer Rsch., 2001—03, acting chief Regulation of Cell Growth Lab., chief Lab. Protein Dynamics and Signaling, 2003—. Mem.: Assn. Am. Physicians, Am. Soc. Clin. Investigation, Alpha Omega Alpha. Office: Lab Protein Dynamics and Signaling Nat Cancer Inst Frederick 1050 Boyles St, Bldg 560, Rm 22-103 Frederick MD 21702-1201 Office Phone: 301-846-1222. Office Fax: 301-846-1666. E-mail: amw@nih.gov.*

WEISSMAN, JACK (GEORGE ANDERSON), retired editor; b. Chgo., June 6, 1921; s. Ben and Ida (Meyerson) W.; m. Bernice Platt, Nov. 13, 1949; children: Bruce, David, Ellen Weissman Montgomery. BA in Edn., Northwestern U., Evanston, Ill., 1943, MS in Journalism, 1944. Asst. editor Bankers Monthly, Chgo., 1944-45; mng. editor Practical Knowledge, Chgo., 1945-50; with pub. relations dept. Roosevelt U., Chgo., 1947-50; editor Opportunity Mag., Chgo., 1950-89, ret. Author: Make Money at Home, 1963, How to Make Correct Decisions, 1964, Money Making Businesses You Can Start for $500 Or Less, 1965, Making It Big in Selling, 1987. Served to cpl. USAAF, 1945-46 Mem. Sigma Delta Chi, Phi Delta Kappa. Jewish. Personal E-mail: j.b.weissman@att.net.

WEISSMAN, MICHAEL LEWIS, lawyer; b. Chgo., Sept. 11, 1934; s. Maurice and Sue (Goldberg) Weissman; m. Joanne Sherwin, Dec. 19, 1961; children: Mark Douglas, Greg Steven, Scott Adam, Brett Anthony. Student White scholar, U. Chgo., 1951-52; BS in Econs, Northwestern U., 1954; MBA in Acctg., U. Pa., 1956; JD, Harvard U., 1958; postgrad. Fulbright scholar, U. Sydney, Australia, 1958-59; postgrad., Hague Acad. Internat. Law, 1959. Bar: D.C. 1958, Ill. 1959. Asst. prof. bus. law Roosevelt U., Chgo., 1959-61; pvt. practice Chgo., 1959—; mem. firm Aaron, Aaron, Schimberg & Hess, 1969-78; sr. ptnr. Boorstein & Weissman, 1978-82, Weissman, Smolev & Solow, 1982-88, Foley & Lardner, 1988-92, McBride Baker & Coles, Chgo., 1992—2001; exec. v.p., gen. counsel Bridgeview Bank Group, Chgo., 2001—04; of counsel Holland & Knight LLP, 2001—, Levin Ginsburg, 2009—. Asst. prof. Roosevelt U., 1960—62; lectr. Lake Forest (Ill.) Coll., 1979—80; chmn. Banking Group, Union League Club Chgo.; panelist Risk Mgmt. Assn., Banking Law Inst., Midwest Fin. Conf., Greater O'Hare Assn., Miss. Law Inst., Bank Lending Inst., Chgo. Assn. Commerce and Industry, State of Art Seminars, Infocast Inc., SBA, Fed. Res. Bank Chgo., Lenders Ednl. Inst., Bank Adminstrn. Inst. Found., Lender's Forum, Clarion Legal; Fulbright sr. specialist Sch. Bus. Adminstrn., Turiba, Riga, Latvia, 2006, Nat. U. Laos, Vientiane, Laos, 2008; adj. prof. law John Marshall Law Sch., 2001—08; mem. Internat. Sr. Lawyers BLA Project, Capetown, 2009. Author: (book) Lender Liability, 1988, Commercial Loan Documentation and Secured Lending, 1990, How to Avoid Career-Ending Mistakes in Commercial Lending, 1996, The Lender's Edge, 1997; mem. editl. bd.: Commercial Damages, 1985—; contbr. articles to profl. jours. Mem. adv. bd. Affective Disorders Clinic, U. Ill. Med. Sch., 1979—81; instr. mentor program Risk Mgmt. Assn. White scholar, U. Chgo., 1951—52. Mem.: ABA, Comml. Fin. Assn. Ednl. Found. (adv. bd.), Turnaround Mgmt. Assn. (steering com. Chgo. chpt.), Harvard Law Soc. Ill., Assn. Comml. Fin. Attys. (bd. dirs.), Ill. Inst. CLE (bd. dirs. 1989—2001, chmn. 2001—02), Ill. Bankers Assn. (mem. com. bank counsel 1987—88, vice chmn. 1988—89), Chgo. Bar Assn., Ill. State Bar Assn., Beta Alpha Psi. Home: 2067 Old Briar Rd Highland Park IL 60035-4245 Office: Levin Ginsburg Ste 3200 180 N LaSalle St Chicago IL 60601-2800 Home Phone: 847-831-4331; Office Phone: 312-368-0100. Business E-Mail: mweissman@lgattorneys.com.

WEISSMAN, WILLIAM R., lawyer; b. NYC, Aug. 16, 1940; s. Emanuel and Gertrude (Halpern) Weissman; m. Barbra Phyllis Gershman; 1 child, Adam stepchildren: Eric, Jace, Julie Greenman. BA, Columbia U., 1962, JD cum laude, 1965. Bar: NY 1965, US Dist. Ct. (no. dist.) Tex. 1965, US Supreme Ct. 1968, DC 1969, US Ct. Appeals (DC cir.) 1969, US Ct. Appeals (9th cir.) 1973, US Ct. Appeals (2d and 3d cirs.) 1974, US Dist. Ct. (so. and ea. dists.) NY 1977, US Ct. Appeals (10th cir.) 1979, US Ct. Appeals (11th cir.) 1981. News dir., program dir. Sta. WKCR-FM, NYC, 1960-62; law clk. to US Dist. judge Dallas, 1965-66; trial atty. antitrust divsn. Dept. Justice, Washington, 1966-69; spl. asst. US atty. Washington, 1967; assoc. Wald, Harkrader & Ross, Washington, 1969-72, ptnr., 1973-85, Piper & Marbury LLP, Washington, 1986-99, Piper Rudnick LLP, Washington, 2000—04, DLA Piper US LLP, Washington, 2005—07, Venable LLP, Washington, 2007—. Instr. DC Bar continuing legal edn. program Georgetown U. Law Sch., Washington, 1980—89; instr. environ. regulation course Exec. Enterprises, Inc., 1985—95. Mem. editl. bd. Jour. Environ. Regulation, 1991—95, Environ. Regulation & Permitting, 1995—2000. Mem. Arlington County Tenant-Landlord Commn., Va., 1973—77, chmn., 1975—77; parliamentarian Arlington County Dem. Com., Va., 1971—75. Mem.: ASTM (E-50 com. environ. assessment 1996—, rec. sec. 1998—99, vice chmn. 2000—07, mem.-at-large 2008—), Columbia Law Sch. Alumni Assn. Washington (sec. 1982—84, pres. 1984—86, bd. dirs. 1984—88). Jewish. Home: 3802 Lakeview Ter Falls Church VA 22041-1313 Office: Venable LLP 575 7th St NW Washington DC 20004-1601 Office Phone: 202-344-4503. Business E-Mail: wweissman@venable.com.

WEISSMANN, ANDREW, lawyer, former prosecutor; b. NYC, Mar. 17, 1958; BA magna cum laude in Hist., Princeton U., 1980; JD, Columbia U. Law Sch., 1984. Bar: NY 1985, US Supreme Ct., US Ct. Appeals (2nd cir.), US Dist. Ct. (ea. dist.) NY, US Dist. Ct. (so. dist.) NY. Law clk. to Hon. Eugene Nickerson US Dist. Ct. (ea. dist.) NY, 1984—85; atty. Cleary, Gottlieb, Steen & Hamilton, LLP, NYC; asst. US atty. (ea. dist.) NY, chief criminal divsn. US Dept. Justice, Bklyn., 2000—03; ptnr., mem. white collar criminal defense and counseling practice Jenner & Block, LLP, NYC, 2006—. Dep. dir. Enron Task Force, US Dept. Justice, 2002—04, dir., 2004—05; spl. counsel to dir. FBI; bd. mem. Manhattan Legal Svcs., 2006—; spkr. in field. Recipient Spl. Achievement award, US Dept. Justice, 2003, 2004, Atty. General's award for Exceptional Svc., 2006, Dir. award for Superior Performance, 1994, 1996, 1999—2000; named one of The 100 Most Influential People in Bus. Ethics, Ethisphere mag., 2007; Harlan Fiske Stone Scholar. Mem.: Legal Services NY (mem. Bd. Mahattan Legal Services 2006—), Legal Aid Soc. (leader, Associate's Fund Raising Campaign 1988—90), Assn. of the Bar of the City of NY (sec., Com. on Legal Needs of the Poor 1989—90, mem., Com. on Criminal Advocacy 2006—). Office: Jenner & Block LLP 919 Third Ave, 37th Fl New York NY 10022-3908 Office Phone: 212-891-1650. Office Fax: 212-891-1699. E-mail: aweissmann@jenner.com.*

WEISSMANN, ARNIE, editor-in-chief, travel writer; married; 3 children. Creator Weissmann Travel Reports, group publisher, 1996; sr. advisor bus. devel. Cahners Travel Group, 1999; editor-in-chief Travel Weekly, 2001—. Mem. editl. com. Am. Bus. Media. Author: Weissmann Travel Planner for Western and Eastern Europe, 1994-1995, 1994, Travel around the World: A Complete Program for Learning about Geography, Destinations, and Selling Travel, 1996; editor: Travel Geography & Destinations, 1993, Ports of Call: The Caribbean and North America; contbr. articles to profl. jours. Office: Travel Weekly NORTHSTAR Travel Media, LLC 100 Lighting Way Secaucus NJ 07094-3626 Office Phone: 201-902-1954. E-mail: aweissmann@travelweekly.com.

WEISSMANN, CHARLES, molecular biologist, educator; b. 1931; MD, PhD, U. Zurich, Switzerland; D honoris causa, U. Verona, Italy, 1992, U. Ghent, Belgium, 1994, Swiss Fed. Inst. Tech., Zurich, 1998, U. Zurich, 2000, U. St. Andrews, 2000, Ecole Polytech. Fed. Lausanne, 2001. Prof., dir. Inst. Molecular Biology, U. Zurich, 1967-99; pres. Swiss Soc. for Cell and Molecular Biology; chmn. sci. bd. Biogen, 1984-86; pres. Ernst Hadorn-Stiftung, Zurich, 1986—; prof., chmn. dept. Scripps Rsch. Inst., Fla., 2004—. Bd. dirs. F. Hoffmann-LaRoche Ltd., Basel, 1988—2001; mem. sci. adv. bd. ZMB, Heidelberg, 1988—2001, Roche Inst. Molecular Biology, Nutley, NJ, 1993—95, Osaka Biosci. Inst., Japan, 1994—2000, Roche Molecular Sys., Alameda, Calif., 1994—98, Swiss Inst. for Cancer Rsch., Lausanne, 1994—98; mem. sci. coun. Swiss Nat. Fund, 1989—94, Internat. Human Frontiers Rsch. Program, 1994—98; mem. internat. sci. adv. bd. The Netherlands Cancer Inst., Amsterdam; bd. govs. Tel Aviv U., 1997—2004; chmn. European Com. Group on Bovine Spongiform Encephalopathy, 1996; Samuel Rudin disting. vis. prof. Columbia U., NYC, 1999; vis. prof. Imperial Coll., London, 2001—04. Assoc. editor Molecular Medicine, 1994-03; mem. editl. bd. Procs. Royal Soc. Decorated fgn. mem. Order for Merit for Sci. and Art (Germany); Hon. Sr. fellow Inst. Neurology, U. Coll., London; recipient Ruzicka prize in chemistry, 1996, Otto Warburg prize, 1980, H.P. Heineken prize, 1982, Sir. H. Krebs medal, 1974, Marcel Benoist prize, Bern, 1970, Scheele medal, Uppsala, 1982, Krebspreis Schweizerische Krebsliga, 1987, Jung prize for medicine, Hamburg, 1988, Gabor medal Royal Soc., London, 1993, Robert Koch medal, Bonn, 1995, Datta lectureship award FEBS, 1998, Charles Leopold Mayer prize French Acad. Sci., 1996, Royal Soc. Glaxo Wellcome prize, 1996, August Wilhelm von Hofmann Denkmünze, 1997, Klaus Joachim Zülch prize, 1997, Max Delbrück medal, Berlin, 1997, Wilhelm Exner medal, Vienna, 1997, Disting. Svc. award, Miami, 1998, Mendel medal Genetical Soc., London, 1998, Koetser prize, Zurich, 2001, Friedrich-Bauer prize for med. rsch., Munich, 2001, Warren Alpert Found. prize, Boston, 2004, Fifth Ann. Dart/NYU Biotech. award, NY, 2006. Fellow: Am. Acad. Microbiology; mem.: NAS (fgn. assoc.), Acad. Med. Scis. (London chpt.), Berlin-Brandenburgischen Acad. Sci. (extraordinary), Nordheim-Westfälischen Acad. Sci. (corr.), Human Genome Orgn., Academia Europaea, Weizmann Inst. Sci. (bd. govs. 1985—), Royal Soc. (fgn.), Deutsche Akademie Naturforscher Leopoldina, Swiss Acad. Med. Sci., Am. Acad. Arts and Scis., European Molecular Biology Orgn. Office: Scripps Fla 5353 Parkside Dr RF-2 Jupiter FL 33458 Office Phone: 561-799-8910, 561-799-8895. Office Fax: 561-799-8960. Business E-Mail: charlesw@scripps.edu.

WEISSTEIN, NAOMI, neuroscientist, psychology educator, writer; b. NYC, Oct. 16, 1939; d. Samuel and Mary (Menk) W.; m. Jesse Lemisch, June 14, 1965. BA with honors, Wellesley Coll., 1961; PhD with distinction, Harvard U., 1964; postgrad., U. Chgo., 1964-65. Rsch. assoc. Yale U., summer 1964; USPHS postdoctoral trainee in math. biology U. Chgo., fall 1964, lectr., rsch. assoc. dept. psychiatry, 1965-66; from asst. prof. to prof. psychology Loyola U., Chgo., 1966-73; tech. staff Bell Labs., Murray Hill, N.J., 1973; prof. psychology SUNY, Buffalo, 1973—2005, prof. emerita, 2005—. Founding mem. Chgo. Westside, Womens Liberation Group, 1967-71, Chgo. Women's Liberation Union, 1969-75, Women in Eye Rsch., 1979; organizer, layborist Chgo. Women's Liberation Rock Band, 1970-73; cons. Xerox Corp., Rochester, N.Y., 1973-74; vis. rsch. fellow dept. psychology Princeton U., 1979-80; mem. faculty exch. dept. psychology Moscow State U., 1978; presenter sci. meetings; spkr. Brown U., Stanford U., U. Pa., Princeton U., Rockefeller U., MIT, Moscow State U., others. Author: (with V. Blaisdell & J. Lemisch) The Godfathers: Freudians, Marxists, and the Scientific and Political Protection Societies, 1976, (biography in love, B.) Kinder, Kuche, Kirche as Scientific Law: Psychology Constructs the Female, 1969, Feminists who Changed America 1963-1975, 2006; cons. editor: Jour. Exptl. Psychology, 1973-75, Cognitive Psychology, Spatial Vision; mem. editl. bd.: Signs: A Jour. of Women in Culture and Soc.; contbr. articles to profl. jours. including Sci., Jour. Exptl. Psychology, Psychol. Rev., Vision Rsch., Perception & Psychophysics; rec. album: Mountain Moving Day, 1972, reissued as Papa don't lay that S--- on me, 2005; patentee in vision field. Recipient NIKE award for contbn. to women in soc., Europe, 1998, Vet. Feminists of Am. award for founders of women's liberation in U.S., 1997, Vet. Feminists of Am. award for Feminist Educators, 2001; Durant scholar; Hon. Woodrow Wilson fellow, 1961-64, NSF predoctoral fellow, 1961-64, NIMH postdoctoral fellow, 1979-80, Guggenheim fellow, 1980-81; Rsch. grantee NIH, NEI, NSF, others. Fellow AAAS (emerita), APA, NAS (nat. rsch. coun., com. on vision), Optical Soc. Am., Assn. for Rsch. in Vision and Ophthalmology (program com. 1977-80, program chair 1980), Am. Psychol. Soc., Ea. Psychol. Assn., Psychonomic Soc., Lake Ont. Visionary Establishment (program com. 1976-78, program chair 1978), Phi Beta Kappa, Sigma Xi, Women Psychonomic Soc. (founding mem. 1974). Home: 890 W End Ave Apt 8B New York NY 10025-3521 Office Phone: 212-222-6649. Personal E-mail: naomi.weisstein@verizon.com.

WEIST, WILLIAM BERNARD, lawyer; b. Lafayette, Ind., Dec. 23, 1938; s. Bernard Francis and Frances Loretta (Doyle) W.; m. Rosemary Elaine Anderson, Apr. 30, 1963; children: Sean M., Cynthia A. BBA, U. Notre Dame, 1961; JD, U. Louisville, 1970. Bar: Ky. 1971, Ind. 1971, U.S. Dist. Ct. (no. and so. dists.) Ind. 1971. Bank examiner Fed. Res. Bank, St. Louis, 1966-67; Trust officer Citizens Fidelity Bank, Louisville, 1967-71; pvt. practice Fowler, Ind., 1971—; sr. ptnr. Dumas, Weist and Mahnesmith. Bd. dirs. Benton Fin. Corp., Fowler, Fowler State Bank; pros. atty. 76th Jud. Cir., Benton County, Ind., 1975-98, 2006-. Capt. USAF, 1961-65. Fellow Ind. Bar Found. (charter mem.); mem. Ind. State Bar Assn., Ind. Pros. Attys. Assn. (pres. 1979), Ind. Pros. Attys. Coun. (chmn. 1989), Nat. Dist. Attys. Assn. (bd. dirs.), Columbia Club (Indpls.), Elks, KC. Avocations: golf, reading. Office: Weist Bldg Grant Ave Fowler IN 47944-0101 Home: 1302 E 12th St Fowler IN 47944-1707

WEISTROFFER, HEINZ ROLAND, information systems professional, educator; b. Herne, Germany, Jan. 24, 1950; came to the U.S., 1983; s. Rudolf Peter and Ursula (Krause) W.; m. Linda Massey Duke, June 8, 1974; children: George, Richard Peter, Charles. MA, Duke U., 1973; DSc, Free U. Berlin, 1976. Lectr., sr. lectr. Natal U., Durban, 1977-79; chief rsch. officer CSIR, Pretoria, South Africa, 1980-83; asst. prof. Va. Commonwealth U., Richmond, 1983-91, assoc. prof., 1991—. Mem. mgmt. info. systems commn. Cath. Diocese of Richmond, 1995—. Contbr. articles to profl. jours. Mem. Assn. Info. Tech. Profls. (v.p. membership com. 1997, v.p. publs. 1996—, v.p. meeting participation 1995, v.p. edn. 1994), INFORMS, Decision Scis. Inst., Internat. Soc. for Multiple Criteria Decision Making, others. Office: Va Commonwealth U Sch of Business Richmond VA 23284

WEISWASSER, STEPHEN, electronics executive; b. Detroit, Nov. 21, 1940; BA, Wayne State U.; postgrad., Johns Hopkins U.; JD magna cum laude, Harvard U. Ptnr. Wilmer, Cutler & Pickering; sr. v.p. Capital Cities/ABC, Inc.; pres., CEO Americast, 1995-98; ptnr. Covington & Burling, Washington, 1998-99; exec. v.p., gen. counsel Gemstar Internat. Group Ltd., Pasadena, Calif., 1999—, also bd. dirs. Woodrow Wilson Nat. fellow Johns Hopkins U. Office Fax: 626-792-0257.

WEISZ, DEBORAH, trombonist, music educator, composer; b. Chgo., June 20, 1962; d. Victor and Alice Weisz. AA in Music Performance, Mesa C.C., Ariz., 1982; BA in Music Performance, U. Nev., Las Vegas, 1984; MA in Music Composition, NY U., 2002. Trombonist, composer & band leader Deborah Weisz Small & Large Ensembles, New York, NY, 1986—; lead & sect. trombone Frank Sinatra Orch., Las Vegas, Nev., 1986—94; faculty - low brass instr., composition coach NY Pops Edn. Programs, New York, NY, 1994—; lead trombone Diva Jazz Orch., NYC, 1995—; adj. faculty - jazz arranging & composition, jazz trombone & jazz combo Rutgers U., New Brunswick, NJ, 2002—04; trombonist Roswell Rudd's Trombone Tribe Band, NYC, 2004—; trombone instr. & contbg music arranger Mid. Sch. Jazz Acad., Jazz at Lincoln Ctr., NYC, 2005—; adj. faculty - jazz trombone, jazz combo & music theory Western Conn. State U., Danbury, 2008—. Composer: (music composition) BAM! (finalist Charlie Parker award, 2002), Grace (Julius Hemphill Jazz Composition award, 2000), New Light (New Eng. Found. of the Arts Meet the Composer Grant, 2004). Vol. gardener Gen. Theol. Sem. - Landmark Bldg. & Garden, New York, NY, 1997—2003. Career Devel. grant, AAUW, 2001—02. Mem.: Internat. Trombone Assn., Musician's Union. Achievements include National Endowment of the Arts Grant 1989. Avocations: skiing, hiking, gardening, photography.

WEISZ, PAUL B(URG), physicist, researcher, chemical engineer; b. Pilsen, Czechoslovakia, July 2, 1919; naturalized, 1946; s. Alexander and Amalia (Sulc) Weisz; m. Rhoda A.M. Burg, Sept. 4, 1943; children: Ingrid B., P. Randall. Student, Tech. U. Berlin, 1937—39; BS, Auburn U., 1940; PhD, Swiss Fed. Inst. Tech., Zurich, 1966, ScD (hon.), 1980. Rsch. physicist Bartol Rsch. Found., Swarthmore, Pa., 1940—46; from rsch. assoc. to sr. scientist Mobil Oil Corp., 1946—61, mgr., corp. ctrl. rsch. lab. Princeton, NJ, 1969—84; disting. prof. chem. and bio-engring. sci. U. Pa., 1984—91, prof. emeritus, 1991—. Instr. elec. engring. Swarthmore Coll., 1942—43; with radiation lab. MIT, 1944—45; vis. prof. Princeton U., 1974—76, mem. adv. coun., dept. chem. engring., 1975—76, mem. adv. com., Sch. Engring., 1977—80, Pa. State U., 1996—99; chmn. ctr. policy bd. Ctr. for Catalytic Sci. and Tech., U. Del., 1977—81; cons. natural energy needs Pres. Coun. Sci. and Indsl. Rsch., South Africa, 1989; mem. energy rsch. adv. bd. U.S. Secretaries of Energy, 1985—90; cons. Ciba-Geigy Pharm. Ltd., Basel, Switzerland, 1990—92; adj. prof. Pa. State U., 1993—; mem. adv. com., future direction chem. related scis. Pres. Swiss Fed. Inst. Tech., 1992; cons. rsch. and tech. strategy. Editor: (ann. rev.) Advances in Catalysis, 1956—93; mem. editl. bd.:, 1985—, Jour. Catalysis, 1962—84; mem. editl. bd. Chem. Engring. Comms., 1972—78, Heterogeneous Chem. Revs., 1993—96; asst. editor: Semiconductor Surface Physics, 1957; editor: Kinetics and Catalysis, Chem. Engring. Progress Symposium Series, 1967, (book) Angiogenesis-Science, Technology, Medicine, 1992; author, column editor: Sci. of the Possible, Chemtech, 1980—81; contbr. (183 articles to sci. jours.). Recipient ann. award, Catalysis Club Phila., 1973, Lavoisier medal, Chem. Soc. France, 1983, Perkin medal, Internat. Soc. Chem. Industry, 1985, Nat. medal of Tech., Pres. U.S., 1992. Fellow: NAE (elected mem. 1977), AIChE (R.H. Wilhelm award 1978), Am. Inst. Chemistry (Chem. Pioneer award 1974), Am. Phys. Soc.; mem.: N.Y. Acad. Scis., Am. Chem. Soc. (sci. award South Jersey sect. 1963, E.V. Murphree award 1972, 1977, Chemistry of Contemporary Tech. Problems award 1986, Carothers award 1987), Nassau Club (Princeton). Mem. Soc. Of Friends. Achievements include 95 patents in field; research in radiation; electronics; solid state, energy, physics in all operating systems; angiogenesis; cell proliferation; R & D strategy, cross-disciplinary science, technology. Home Phone: 814-237-3160. Home Fax: 814-237-3202. Personal E-mail: pweisz@verizon.net. Business E-Mail: pbw5@psu.edu.

WEISZ, RACHEL, actress; b. London, Mar. 7, 1971; 1 child. BA, U. Cambridge, England. Motion picture and TV actress. Actor (films) Death Machine, 1995, Stealing Beauty, 1996, Chain Reaction, 1996, Going All the Way, 1997, Amy Foster, 1997, Land Girls, 1998, I Want You, 1998, Swept From the Sea, 1998, The Mummy, 1999, Sunshine, 1999, Beautiful Creatures, 2001, Enemy at the Gates, 2001, The Mummy Returns, 2001, About a Boy, 2002, The Shape of Things, 2003 (also prodr.), Confidence, 2003, Runaway Jury, 2003, She Died on Canvas, 2003, Envy, 2004, Constantine, 2005, The Constant Gardener, 2005 (Best Performance by an Actress in a Supporting Role in a Motion Picture, Hollywood Fgn. Press Assn., Golden Globe award, 2006, Outstanding Performance by a Female Actor in a Supporting Role, Screen Actors Guild award, 2006, Performance by an Actress in a Supporting Role, Acad. Motion Picture Arts & Sciences, 2006), The Fountain, 2006, Eragon, 2006, My Blueberry Nights, 2007, Fred Claus, 2007, Definitely, Maybe, 2008, The Brothers Bloom, 2009; (TV films) Scarlet and Black, 1993, My Summer with Des, 1998; (plays) Design For Living, 1994, Last Summer, 1999, The Shape of Things, 2001. Office: c/o Ind Talent Group Oxford House 76 Oxford St London W1D 1BS England*

WEISZ, VIRGINIA GRAVES, law educator; b. Charlottesville, Va., Nov. 1, 1945; d. Allen Willis and Helen Cannan Graves; m. John Richard Weisz, Sept. 3, 1967; children: Dawn Weisz Brown, Allison Weisz

Brettschneider, Daniel J., Tamara C. BA magna cum laude, Blue Mountain Coll., Miss., 1967; JD, Cornell U., Ithaca, 1978. Bar: N.C. 1979, Calif. 1992, U.S. Ct. Appeals (9th cir.) 1992, U.S. Dist. Ct. (ctrl. dist.) Calif. 1992, U.S. Dist. Ct. (ea. dist.) Calif. 1993, Mass. 2005. Pvt. practice, Chapel Hill, NC, 1979—83; state adminstr. Office of Guardian, Adminstrv. Office of Cts., Raleigh, NC, 1983—90; vis. prof. UCLA, 1990—92; directing atty. children's rights Pub. Counsel, LA, 1992—2004; exec. dir. Mass. Ct. Apptd. Spl. Adv., Newton, 2005—06; lectr. Tufts U., Medford, Mass., 2006—. Adj. prof. USC Sch. Law, LA, 1992—2004; mem. family adv. program Boston Med. Ctr., 2004—05; spkr. in field; cons. Co-author (with B. Kaban): Protecting Children & Adolescents in Need, 1995; editor: Legal Issues for Pregnant & Parenting Teens in California, 1998; author: Children and Adolescents in Need, 2008; contbr. articles to profl. jours. Vol. Peace Corps., Kenya, 1968—71; adv. com. Little Hoover Commn., Sacramento, 2001; tech. expert Nat. Abandoned Infants Resource, Berkeley, Calif., 2001—04; chair Kinship Care Coord. Coun., LA, 2002—03; cons. Jud. Coun. Calif., San Francisco, 1992—96, 2003—04. Recipient Child Adv. award, Am. Psychl. Assn., Hawaii, 2004; named Adv. of Yr., Calif. Mental Health Assn., 1996; grantee, Stuart Found., L.A., 1994—2004. Mem.: ABA, Nat. Assn. Counsel for Children, Nat. Children's Law Network. Baptist. Home: 96 Dexter Rd Newton MA 02460 Office Phone: 617-417-8183. Personal E-mail: jennyweisz@comcast.net.

WEITBERG, ALAN BARRY, physician, researcher, dean; b. Phila., Mar. 2, 1950; s. Sidney and Esther Weitberg; m. Katherine Raphaela Bick, Sept. 6, 1975 (div. Apr. 1993); children: Allison Ross, Seth Raphael. AB, Cornell U., Ithaca, NY, 1972; MD, Univ. Medicine and Dentistry NJ, Newark, 1976; MEd (hon.), Brown U., Providence, 1992. Lic. MD RI, 1978, Mass., 1982, cert. Nat. Bd. Med. Examiners, 1977, Internal Medicine, 1980, Med. Oncology, 1987, Hematology, 1988. Resident and chief resident in medicine Roger Williams Med. Ctr. and Brown Med. Sch., Providence, 1976—80; hematology fellow Mass. Gen. Hosp. and Harvard U., Boston, 1980—82; instr. med. sch. Harvard Med. Sch., Boston, 1982—85; chief divsn. hematology, oncology Brown Med. Sch. and Roger Williams Med. Ctr., Providence, 1985—91; prof. and chmn., dept. medicine Roger Williams Med. Ctr. and Boston U. Sch. Medicine, Providence, 1991—; asst. dean acad. affairs Boston U. Sch. Medicine, 2007—. Dir. divsn. med. oncology Brown U., 1988—; prof. medicine Boston U. Sch. Medicine, 1988—, asst. dean acad. affairs, 2007; bd. trustees Roger Williams Med. Ctr., 2002—04. Author: Cancer of the Lung, 2002; contbr. more than 75 sci. papers to profl. jours., chapters to books, articles to over 60 profl. jours. Critical care, med. appraisal, med. audit, med. rec. Roger Williams Hosp., 1979—80, infection control, nutritional support, patient care/greivence, 1979—80, intern selection, clin. competence com., 1985—, chmn. cancer com., 1986—99, chmn. credentials com., 1987—91, transfusion com., 1988—92, physician's adv. com., 1989—, exec. com., 1991—, strategic planning com., 1992—, joint conf. com., 1992—, quality improvement steering coun., 1992—, oncology task force, 1995—, pres., med. assoc., 1996—, bd. trustees, 2002—, Univ. Med. Group, 1999—, exec. com. bd., 2001—; chmn. admissions com. for an integrated med. residency program Brown U., 1990—; com. sectional chiefs Boston U., 1997—. Recipient Dean Charles L. Brown award, Univ. Medicine and Dentistry NJ, 1976, Tchr. of Yr. award, Brown U. Sch. Medicine, 1992, Eminent Scientist award, Internat. Rsch. Promotion Coun., Physician's Recognition award with commendation, AMA, 2005; named Top Dr. Am., 2009; named to Mu Eplison Delta Hon. Soc., Cornell U., 1971, Watts Scholarship Soc., Cornell Univ., 1971; nominee Ernesta Nuti Internat. prize for Cancer Rsch., Rome, 1992; Arts and Sci. Dean's scholar, Cornell U., 1969, over 30 rsch. grants from various colls. and univs. Fellow: ACP (exec. coun. RI chpt. 1992—); mem.: AMA (Physicians Recognition award 2005—), AAAS, Cancer Trials Support Unit, Assn. Acad. Med. Ctr., Clin. Oncology Group, Am. Soc. Hematology, Assn. Am. Med. Coll., Leukemia Soc. Am. (bd. dirs. 1989—), Am. Bd. Internal Medicine (recertification com. 1993—), Am. Soc. Cancer Rsch. (chmn. carcinogeneses sect. 1987—, state legis. com. 1992—), Am. Soc. Clin. Oncology (chmn. lung cancer sect. 1987—), Am. Cancer Soc. (chmn. nominating com. 1992, instl. rsch. grant rev. study sect. 1992—), Am. Fedn. for Clin. Rsch. (chmn. hematology sect. 1993—), Internat. Soc. Free Radical Rsch., Sigma Xi. Avocations: painting, opera, running, reading. Office: Roger Williams Med Ctr Dept Medicine 825 Chalkstone Ave Providence RI 02908 Office Phone: 401-456-2070, 401-456-2070. Business E-Mail: awietherg@rwmc.org.

WEITHORN, STANLEY STEPHEN, lawyer; b. NYC, Aug. 28, 1924; s. Louis W. and Florence O. (Mandel) W.; m. Corinne J. Breslow, Dec. 26, 1949 (dec. 1987); children: Lois Ann, Michael J.; m. Muriel Casper, Sept. 9, 1990; 1 stepchild, Corey Casper. BSBA, Hofstra U., 1947; JD, NYU Law Sch., 1954, LLM in Taxation, 1956. Bar: N.Y. 1955. Assoc. firm Olwine, Connelly, Chase O'Donnell & Weyher, NYC, 1956—61; ptnr. firm Lewis, McDonald & Varian, NYC, 1961—62; pvt. practice NYC, 1962—63, 1967—68; ptnr. firm Wormser, Koch, Keily & Alessandroni, NYC, 1963—66; sr. ptnr. firm Baer, Marks & Upham (successor to Upham, Meeker & Weithorn), NYC, 1968—88, Epstein, Becker & Green, NYC, 1988—89; sr. counsel Reid & Priest, NYC, 1989—94, Morrison & Foerster, Palo Alto, Calif., 1994—96, Fennemore Craig, Phoenix, 1996—2000, Roberts & Holland, NYC & Scottsdale, 1996—. Spl. prof. law Hofstra U., 1974-78; adj. prof. law U. Miami, Fla., 1975-79; mem. adv. com. U. Miami Law Ctr. Ann. Inst. Estate Planning, 1974-80; coordinator fed. budget and tax policy course nat. policy studies program New Sch. Social Rsch., N.Y.C., 1975; mem. fund raising mgmt. adv. com. Grad. Sch. Mgmt. and Urban professions, New Sch. for Social Rsch., N.Y.C., 1977-84; mem. adv. com. N.Y. U. Inst. on Fed. Taxation, 1980-90; program chmn. Practicing Law Inst. confs., N.Y.C., 1962-78, N.Y. Law Jour. confs., 1980, NYU Inst. on Fed. Taxation confs., 1955-88; tax cons. Pres's. Coun. on Environ. Quality, 1970; lectr. fed. taxation to univ. insts., non-profit org. confs., profl. bus. meetings. Author: Penalty Taxes on Accumulated Earnings and Personal Holding Companies, 1963, Tax Techniques for Foundations and Other Exempt Organizations, 7 vols, 1964, The Accumulated Earnings Tax, 1966; Contbg. editor, mem. adv. bd.: Tax Mgmt, 1959-68; feature columnist: Nat. Law Jour, 1978-79; Contbr. articles to profl. jours. Co-chmn. Port Washington-Manhasset (N.Y.) unit New Dem. Coalition, 1968-69; tax adviser nat. fin. com. McGovern for Pres., 1971-72, mem. N.Y. fin. com., 1971-72; bd. dirs., exec. com. Equal Employment Coun. Inc., N.Y.C., 1968-71; bd. dirs., sec. New Priorities Edn. Fund, 1969-70; bd. dirs., exec. com., sec., co-chmn., pres. Fund for New Priorities in Am., 1969-2004; bd. dirs., treas. Cow Bay Manpower Devel. Corp., Port Washington, 1969-71; bd. dirs., chmn. exec. com., pres. L.I. Pub. Affairs Coun., 1973-78; bd. dirs., pres. Mental Health Assn. Nassau County, N.Y., 1980-85, Herman and Amelia Ehrmann Found., 1977-95; pres. Weithorn and Ehrmann Families Found., 1995—, Am. Soc. Technion, 1992-2000, Social Venture Ptnrs. Ariz., 2003—; bd. dirs. Jewish Family and Children's Svcs., San Francisco; mem. legacy com. United Cerebral Palsy, N.Y.C., 1975-90; bd. dirs. Cmty. Action for Legal Svcs., 1976-78, Frederick and Amelia Schimper Found., 1977-94, Florence Weithorn Warner Found., N.Y.C., 1967-72, N.Y. Fedn. Reform Synagogues, 1973-78, Nat. Coalition for Children's Justice, 1980-90, Am. Inst. for Philanthropic Studies, L.A. and N.Y.C., 1981-92, Nat. Health Coun., 1984-92, Laurent and Alberta Gerschel Found., 1986-96, Interns for Peace, Am.-Israeli Civil Liberties Coalition, 1987-95, Inst. Am. Values, 1987-91, Fund for Human Dignity, 1989-90, Found. Fund, 1986-92, L.I. Cmty. Found., 1989-93, Cancer Prevention Rsch. Inst., 1989-96, Green Seal, 1989-92, New Israel Fund, 1996-2002, Albert L. Schultz Jewish Cmty. Ctr., 1996-2000, Nat. Ctr. Law & Social Justice, 1996-, Am. Jewish World Svc., 2001-, Internat. Edn. and Rsch. Network, 2002-, Heller Family Found., 1994-, Rouhana Family Found., 1990-, Scottsdale Cultural Coun., 2000-, Ariz. State U. Found., 1996-2004, Am. Com. for Weizmann Inst. Sci., 2000-, Piper Fund Proteus Found, 2000-; mem. Emergency Task Force on Juvenile Delinquency Prevention, 1976-79; mem. adv. panel N.Y. chpt. Am. Jewish Com., 1978-80; mem. com. on deferred giving Fedn. Jewish Philanthropies N.Y., 1978-86; mem. legal and tax panel United Jewish Appeal/Fedn. Jewish Philanthropies, N.Y., 1986-91; nat. chair Planned Giving Program, Am. Assocs. Ben-Gurion U. Negev, 1992-2000, mem. exec. com. N.W. region; mem. com. tax policy Nat. Assembly Vol. Health, Social Welfare Orgns. Inc., N.Y.C., 1961-73; mem. com. bequests and legacies Nat. Jewish Hosp., Denver, 1965-78; mem. estate planning com. ARC of Greater N.Y., 1970-98; mem. leadership coun. United Jewish Appeal, N.Y.C., 1966-70; mem. adv. com., project on ch., state and taxation NCCJ, 1980-85; mem. legacy adv. coun. Am. Jewish Congress, N.Y.C., 1968-72; mem. Internat. Coun. on Environ. Law, 1982-92; mem. Pres.'s adv. com. ACLU Found., 1983-2000; chmn. Uptown Tax Discussion Group, 1957-69, Exempt Orgns. Discussion Group, 1973-79, Fresh Meadows Civic Assn., 1961-63; mem. legal activities policy bd. Tax Analysts, 1974—. Served with AUS, 1943-46, ETO. Recipient Allard K. Lowenstein Meml. award Am. Jewish Congress, 1988; honoree Mental Health Assn. Nassau County, N.Y., 1991, Ariz. Citizen Action, 2000, Am. Com. for Weizmann Inst. Sci., 2002, Nat. Gay and Lesbian Task Force, 2003 Fellow Am. Coll. Tax Counsel, Am. Coll. Trust and Estate Counsel; mem. ABA (chmn. subcom. exempt orgns. 1965-69, subcom. charitable contbns. 1971-75), N.Y. State Bar Assn. (exec. com. 1967-69), Assn. of Bar of City of N.Y., Internat. Acad. Estate and Trust Law (exec. coun. 1974-78, 90-96), Univ. Club, Knickerbocker Yacht Club (bd. dirs. 1986-88). Jewish (trustee synagogue l970-74). Home (Winter): 10040 E Happy Valley Rd Lot 435 Scottsdale AZ 85255 Office: Roberts & Holland LLP 825 8th Ave 37th Fl New York NY 10019 also: 8655 E Via de Ventura G200 Scottsdale AZ 85258 Home: 10040 E Happy Valley Rd Unit 435 Scottsdale AZ 85255-2386 Office Phone: 212-903-8687. Personal E-mail: sweithorn@rhtax.com. *No one truly is an altruist. We all attempt to do what most fulfills us. For some this motivates apparently selfish behavior; for others it is quite the opposite. However, why we act as we do affects only the actor whereas what we do affects society. Look to the deed, not to the doer; good deeds make for a better world.*

WEITZ, HOWARD HY, cardiologist, educator; b. Phila., July 6, 1952; s. Thelma and Arnold Weitz; m. Barbara Malett, May 3, 1987; children: Aaron Richard, Benjamin Isaac, Hannah Sarah. BS, Muhlenberg Coll., Pa., 1974, DS (hon.), 2003; MD, Jefferson Med. Coll., Phila., 1978. Diplomate Am. Bd. Internal Medicine, 1981, cert. Cardiovascular Diseases Am. Bd. Internal Medicine, 1985. Dir. divsn. cardiology Jefferson Med. Coll., Phila., 1995—98, prof. medicine, 2005—, sr. vice-chmn., dept. of medicine, 2005—, dir. dept. cardiology, 2008; co-dir. Jefferson Heart Inst., Phila., 1998—, dir., 2008; commr. Fed. Medicaid Commn., Washington, 2005—06. Author: Medical Management of the Surgical Patient, 1992 (NBI Healthcare Found. Humanism in Medicine Faculty award, 1998), 2d edit., 1998, 3rd Edit., 2008, Peripheral Vascular Disorders, 2004. Fellow: Am. Coll. of Cardiology, ACP. Office: Jefferson Heart Inst 925 Chestnut St Philadelphia PA 19027 Business E-Mail: howard.weitz@jefferson.edu.

WEITZ, LESLEY ANNE, aerospace engineer, researcher; d. William Eugene and Debra Sue Weitz. BS in Mech. Engring., U. Buffalo, SUNY, 2002; MS in Aerospace Engring., Tex. A&M U., Coll. Sta., 2005. Product engr. Moog Inc., East Aurora, NY, 2002—03; grad. rsch. asst. Tex. A&M U., 2003—08, 2003—, grad. mentor robotics team, space engring. inst., 2006—08; vis. rschr. Nat. Inst. Aerospace, Hampton, Va., 2005. Mem. guidance, nav., and control tech. com. AIAA, Reston, Va., 2006—08. Contbr. articles to profl. jours. Recipient Guidance, Nav., and Control Grad. Student award, AIAA, 2007; fellow, NASA, 2007—08; Grad. Rsch. fellowship, NSF, 2004—07, Amelia Earhard fellowship, Zonta Internat., 2004—06, Lindbergh Found. grant, 2006—07. Avocations: running, bicycling, reading, travel, dance.

WEITZ, MELISSA, environmentalist; BS in Animal Sci., U. Del., Newark, MS in Environ. and Energy Policy. Environ. protection specialist US EPA, Washington, 2005—. Fellow, US EPA, 2004.

WEITZ, PERRY, lawyer; b. Bklyn., Aug. 5, 1959; BA, George Washington U., 1981; JD, Hofstra U., 1983. Bar: N.Y. 1985, U.S. Dist. Ct., Ea. and So. Dist. N.Y. 1986. Founding mem. Weitz & Luxenberg, New York, NY, 1986—. Faculty mem. Nat. Inst. for Trial Advocacy; liaison coun. N.Y. State Ct., Breast Implant Litig. Com., Ea. and So. Dist. Ct. on Asbestos Litig. Mem. bd. trustees North Shore U. Hosp.; mem. Dean's Counsel Hofstra U. Law Sch.; mem. exec. com. men's divsn. Children's Med. Fund, Schneider Children's Hosp. Named one of The 45 Under 45, The Am. Lawyer, 2003. Mem.: Jewish Lawyers Guild (bd. govs.), Trial Lawyers Pub. Justice, N.Y. State Trial Lawyers Assn., Assn. Trial Lawyers of Am., N.Y. County Lawyers Assn. (chairperson). Office: Weitz & Luxenberg 180 Maiden Lane New York NY 10038 Office Phone: 212-558-5500.

WEITZ, WILLIAM F. (BILL WEITZ), legislative staff member; Grad., SUNY, Albany, 1995. Chief dist. ops., Rep. Eliot Engel US House of Reps., NY, chief of staff to Rep. Eliot Engel NY, 2003—. Mem. Dem. State Com., NY. Democrat. Office: 2161 Rayburn House Office Bldg Washington DC 20515 Office Phone: 202-225-2464. Office Fax: 202-225-5513.*

WEITZEL, JOHN PATTERSON, lawyer; b. Pitts., Aug. 24, 1923; s. Albert Philip and Elizabeth (Patterson) W.; m. Elisabeth Swan, Mar. 20, 1965; children: Mary Middleton, Paul Patterson. AB, Yale U., 1946; LL.B., Harvard U., 1949. Bar: Mass. 1949, U.S. Supreme Ct. 1960. Asso. Herrick, Smith, Donald, Farley & Ketchum (now Herrick & Smith), Boston, 1949-53, ptnr., 1961-86, Palmer & Dodge, Boston, 1986-93, of counsel, 1993—2005; spl. asst. to asst. sec. treasury, 1953-55; asst. to under sec. treas, 1955-56; asst. gen. counsel Treasury Dept., 1956-59, dep. to sec. treasury, 1959-60, asst. sec. treasury, 1960-61; U.S. exec. dir. World Bank, 1960-61; of counsel Edwards, Angell, Palmer & Dodge, 2005—. Mem. planning bd. NSC, 1959-61; cons. to sec. def., 1973. Mem. Mass. Council Arts and Humanities, 1966-71; overseer, dir. sec. Boys and Girls Clubs, Boston; mem. corp. Mass. Gen. Hosp., Boston Mus. Sci.; trustee Roxbury Latin Sch. Served with USAAF, 1943-45. Mem. Am., Boston bar assns., Am. Law Inst. Clubs: Harvard (Boston), Union Boat (Boston). Home: 45 Devon Rd Chestnut Hill MA 02467-1851 Office: Edwards Angell Palmer & Dodge 111 Huntington Ave Boston MA 02199-7613

WEITZEL, JOHN QUINN, bishop; b. Chgo., May 10, 1928; s. Carl Joseph and Patricia (Quinn) Weitzel. BA, Maryknoll Sem., NY, 1951, M in Religious Edn., 1953; PMD, Harvard U. Ordained priest Cath. Fgn. Mission Soc. America, Maryknoll, NY, 1955, with ednl. devel., 1955—63, nat. dir. vocations for Maryknoll, dir. devel. dept. and info. services, 1963—72, mem. gen. coun., 1972—78; asst. parish priest Western Samoa, 1979—81; pastor, vicar gen., 1981—86; ordained bishop, 1986; bishop Diocese of Samoa-Pago Pago, 1986—. Roman Catholic. Office: Diocese Samoa-Pago Pago PO Box 596 Pago Pago AS 96799-3594 E-mail: QUINN@samoatelco.com.

WEITZEL, PAUL, finance educator; MBA, U. Wis., Madison, 1985. Asst. prof. U. Wis. Ctr., Janesville, 1993—97; assoc. prof. Ea. Shore CC, Melfa, Md., 1998—2008; vis. assoc. prof. U. Md., Princess Anne, Md., 2008—. Pres. Onley Recreation Assn., Va., 2004—06, bd. dirs., 2000—08; pres. Onancock Lions Club, Va., 2008—. Office: Eastern Shore CC 29300 Lankford Highway Melfa VA 23410

WEITZEL, WILLIAM CONRAD, JR., lawyer; b. Washington, Feb. 6, 1935; s. William Conrad and Pauline Lillian (Keeton) W.; m. Loretta LeVeck, Mar. 10, 1978; children: William Conrad III, Richard S., Sarah L., Andrew K. AB, Harvard U., 1956, LLB, 1959; postgrad., MIT, 1974. Bar: D.C. 1961. Law clk., chief judge U.S. Cts. Md., Balt., 1959-60; asst. U.S. atty., Washington, 1961-66; atty. Texaco, Inc., White Plains, N.Y., 1966-73, assoc. gen. counsel, 1973-76, gen. counsel, 1977-82, v.p., gen. counsel, 1982-84, sr. v.p., gen. counsel, 1984-90; pres. Texaco Philanthropic Found., Inc., 1980-90; ptnr. Cummings & Lockwood, Stamford, Conn., 1991—, chmn. bus. clients dept., 1991-94. Trustee Ctr. Am. Internat. Law Trustee Southwestern Legal Found., Forman Sch., 1998-2004. With USN, 1960-61. Mem. ABA, Am. Law Inst., Conn. Bar Assn., D.C. Bar Assn., Assn. Gen. Counsel (v.p., bd. dirs. 1988-90), Westchester-Fairfield Corp. Counsel Assn. (pres. 1981, chmn., chief legal officers com. 1982-90), Am. Petroleum Inst. (gen. com. on law, chmn. 1983-84), Harvard Club (dir. Harvard Alumni Assn. for Conn. 1990-93, pres. Fairfield County club 1987—2003). Republican. Episcopalian. Office: Cummings & Lockwood 6 Landmark Sq Stamford CT 06901

WEITZEN, JAY ALLEN, engineering educator; BSEE, U. Wis., Madison, 1977; MSEE, U. Wis., 1979, PhD, 1983. Prof. elec. engring. U. Mass. Lowell, 1986—. Contbr. to numerous scientific papers. Mem.: IEEE. Office: Univ of Mass Lowell 1 University Ave Lowell MA 01854 Business E-Mail: jay_weitzen@uml.edu.

WEITZMAN, ARTHUR JOSHUA, language educator; b. Newark, Sept. 13, 1933; s. Louis I. and Cecele W.; m. Catherine Ezell, Aug. 8, 1982; children: Peter A., Anne E. BA, U. Chgo., 1956, MA, 1957; PhD, NYU, 1964. Instr. English, Bklyn. Coll., 1960-63; asst. prof. Temple U., Phila., 1963-69; assoc. prof. Northeastern U., Boston, 1969-72, prof., 1972—2002, prof. emeritus, 2002—; mem. faculty Brookline Adult and Cmty. Edn., Mass., 2003—, Cambridge Ctr. Adult Edn., Mass., 2003—; lectr. Sarasota Inst. of Lifetime Learning, 2006—. Editor: Letters Writ by a Turkish Spy (G.P. Marana), 1970; founder, co-editor: The Scriblerian, 1968—2004; co-editor: Milton and the Romantics, 1980-81; contbr.: revs. and articles to profl. jours. and newspapers including Los Angeles Times, Boston Globe, Miami Herald NEH fellow, 1972-73, Mellon fellow, 1976; Rsch. grantee Temple U., Northeastern U. Mem.: MLA, Na. Assn. Scholars, Am. Soc. 18th Century Studies. Jewish. Home: 4 Bellis Ct Cambridge MA 02140-3240 Personal E-mail: ajwajwajw@hotmail.com.

WEITZMAN, HOWARD L., lawyer, former film company executive; b. LA, Sept. 21, 1939; BS, U. So. Calif., 1962, JD, 1965. Bar: Calif. 1966, U.S. Dist. Ct. (ctrl., ea. and so. dists.) Calif., U.S. Ct. Appeals (9th cir.), U.S. Supreme Ct. 1976, U.S. Ct. Appeals (6th cir.) 1983. Pvt. practice, 1965—86; mng. ptnr. Wyman Bautzer LLP, 1986—91; ptnr., chmn. exec. com. Katten Muchin Zavis & Weitzman, LA, 1991—2001; exec. v.p. corp. ops. Universal Studios (formerly MCA), 1995—98; ptnr. Proskauer Rose LLP, LA, 2001—04, Kinsella Weitzman Iser Kump & Aldisert LLP, Santa Monica, Calif., 2005—. Lectr. U. So. Calif., 1973-83. Recipient Jerry Gielser Memorial award, 1979, 1984; named Top 100 Outside Counsel, Hollywood Reporter, 2007, Power Lawyer, 2008; named one of Top 15 Lawyers in the country, Nat. Law Jour., So. Calif. Super Lawyers, 2009, So. Calif. Best Lawyers, LA Times, 2009. Mem. ABA, L.A. County Bar Assn., Beverly Hill Bar Assn., Foundres Cir. of the Fulfillment Fund Office: Kinsella Weitzman Iser Kump & Aldisert LLP 808 Wilshire Blvd 3rd Fl Santa Monica CA 90401 Office Fax: 310-566-9871. E-mail: hweitzman@kwikalaw.com.*

WEITZMAN, MARTIN L., economics educator; b. NYC, Apr. 1, 1942; s. Samuel and Fannie (Katzelnick) W.; m. Dorothy Earley, Dec. 27, 1964; 1 child, Rodica. BA, Swarthmore Coll., 1963; MS, Stanford U., 1964; PhD, MIT, 1967. Asst. prof. econs. Yale U., New Haven, 1967-70, assoc. prof., 1970-72, MIT, Cambridge, 1972-74, prof., 1974-89, Harvard U., Cambridge, 1989—. Cons. World Bank, others. Author: The Share Economy, 1984 (transl. to 7 langs.); editor, contbr. articles to profl. jours. NSF fellow, 1963-67, Guggenheim fellow, 1970-71. Fellow Am. Acad. Arts Scis., Econometric Soc.; mem. Am. Econ. Assn., Assn. for Comparative Econ. Systems (exec. bd.). Jewish. Avocations: gardening, outdoor sports. Office: Harvard U Dept Econs Cambridge MA 02138

WEITZMAN, RONALD ALFRED, psychology professor; b. Chgo., Apr. 29, 1930; s. Louis and Fanny Weitzman; m. Morley Brown, Aug. 8, 2008; children: Leora Sofia, Karen Maria; m. Brenda Barbara Aronowitz, Feb. 12, 1962 (div. Jan. 30, 1985). BA, 1952; MA, Stanford U., Palo Alto, Calif., 1954; PhD, Princeton U., NJ, 1959. Prof. U. South Calif., LA, 1969—71; tenured faculty mem. Naval Postgrad. Sch., Monterey, Calif., 1971—2009; asst. prof. CSU, Northridge, Calif., 1960—61, LA, 1962—64; sr. lectr. Bar Ilan U., Ramat Aviv, Israel, 1961—62; asst. prof. U. Minn., Mpls., 1964—68; assoc. prof. Am. U., Washington, 1968—69. Dir. test devel. Minn. Nat. Lab., Mlps., 1964—68; cons. CTB McGraw-Hill, Monterey, 1971—2008. Pres. of bd. Monterey Bay Symphony Assn., Carmel, Calif., 1986—2009; chmn. The Salvation Army, Monterey Peninsula Corps, Seaside, Calif., 1988—2009. Specialist 2 US Army, 1954—55, Tex. Fellowship, Stanford U., 1952—54, Princeton U., 1956—59, Postdoc. Fellowship, USPHS, 1959, Nat. Sci. Found., 1960. Mem.: Phi Beta Kappa. Achievements include patents pending for Bayesian estimation of population proportions; accounting for ttem discrimination in a single-parameter logistic model. Home: 23910 Fairfield Pl Carmel CA 93923

WEITZNER, STEVE, publishing executive; BA, York Coll., CUNY; MA, SUNY, Stony Brook. With Hearst Bus. Communications, CMP Tech. (formerly CMP Media, LLC), Manhasset, NY, 1984—, various positions, editor to pres., electronics group, exec. v.p., COO, 2002—05, pres., CEO, 2005—. Office: CMP Tech 600 Community Drive Manhasset NY 11030 Office Phone: 516-562-5000.

WEIXLMANN, JOSEPH NORMAN, JR., language educator, academic administrator; b. Buffalo, Dec. 16, 1946; s. Joseph Norman and Mary C. (Degenhart) W.; m. Sharron Pollack, Mar. 14, 1982; children: Seth Jacob, Adira Jenna, Benjamin Ari. AB, Canisius Coll., 1968; MA,

Kans. State U., 1970, PhD, 1973. Instr. U. Okla., Norman, 1973-74; asst. prof. Tex. Tech U., Lubbock, 1974-76; from asst. prof. to prof. Ind. State U., Terre Haute, 1976—2001, assoc. dean, 1987-92, acting dean, 1992-94, dean, 1994—2001; prof. St. Louis U., 2001—, dean, 2001—02, provost, 2002—. Author: John Barth, 1976, American Short-Fiction Criticism, 1982; co-editor: Black American Prose Theory, 1984, Belief vs. Theory in Black American Literary Criticism, 1986, Black Feminist Criticism, 1988, Studies in Black Am. Lit. Ann., 1984-88; editor African Am. Rev. jour., 1976-2004; contbg. editor High Plains Lit. Rev., 1987-2002; adv. editor Langston Hughes Rev., 1982—. Fellow NDEA, 1970-72, NEH, 1980; Nat. Endowment for Arts grantee, 1988-95; Disting. Editor award, Conf. Editors of Learned Jours., 2005, Disting. Alumni award Canisius Coll., 2008 Mem. Coll. Lang. Assn., Langston Hughes Soc., Zora Neale Hurston Soc. Office: Saint Louis U DuBourg Hall #444 Saint Louis MO 63103 Home: 6344 Wydown Blvd Saint Louis MO 63105-2213 Office Phone: 314-977-3718. Business E-Mail: weixlmj@slu.edu.

WEIZMANN, HOWARD CHARLES, consulting firm executive, former federal agency administrator; b. Akron, Ohio, June 12, 1948; s. Soloman and Ida Doris (Berkel) Bernson; m. Jane Kathleen Tice, Dec. 9, 1970; children: Brooke Suzanne, Haley Kathleen. AB Summa cum laude, Ohio U., 1970; MA, U. Mich., 1971, postgrad., 1973; JD, Georgetown Law Ctr., 1977. Bar: Pa. Assoc. atty Cohen, Shapiro et al., Phila., 1977-78, Dankner, Biddle & Reath LLP, Phila., 1978-81; sr. tax atty. Sun Co. Inc., Radnor, Pa., 1981-84, mgr., benefits planning & design, 1984-88; exec. dir. Assn. Pvt. Pension and Welfare Plans, Washington; v.p. pension & health benefits Aetna Life Insurance; mng. cons. Watson Wyatt Worldwide, Washington, 1994—2000; v.p. human resources Digex, Inc., 2000—01, sr. v.p. human resources, 2001—02, sr. v.p. human resources & comm., 2002—05; pres. Pvt. Sector Coun. (PSC), 2005—07; dep. dir. US Office Pers. Mgmt. (OPM), Washington, 2007—09; head Fed. Human Resources Practice EquaTerra, Inc., Houston, 2009—. Contbr. articles to profl. jours. Tchr. Temple Beth Shalom, Annapolis, Md., 1989-91. Columbia Downing Knight Found. scholar, 1967-70; Denforth Found. Grad. fellow, 1970-73. Mem. City Club Washington; co-author: Rewards and Business Strategy: People, Pay, and Performance Democrat. Jewish. Avocations: tennis, biking, reading.*

WEIZMANN, MARIA PIA, associate dean; b. Oslo, June 3, 1968; d. Liv Vigdis and Antonio Manchinu. AA, No. Va. C.C., 1992; BS in Criminal Justice, Fla. Met. U., 2000, MBA, 2002; BA in French, U. South Fla., 2002; postgrad., Capella U. Instr. ESL and coll. success courses Fla. Met. U., Tampa, 2000—06, program chmn., 2000—04, online learning coord., 2004—06, assoc. academic dean, 2006—. Author: The Grammar Reference: American English, 2002; editor: 101 Recipes: Escargots!, 2002. Vol., petitioner The Humane Soc., Washington, Tampa, 1996—2002; asst. to case mgrs. Hillsborough County Comprehensive Sanctions Ctr., Tampa, 2000—00; vol. academic tutor Northside Mental Health Ctr. (for female juveniles), Tampa, 1999—99. Mem.: Phi Sigma Iota. Avocations: writing, dance, swimming. Office: Everest Univ 3319 W Hillsborough Ave Tampa FL 33614 Office Phone: 813-879-6000.

WEK, ALEK, model; b. Wau, Sudan, 1977; Attended, London Coll. of Fashion. Model Models One agy., London, Ford Agy., Paris, 1996, D Mgmt. Grp., Milan, IMG Models, NYC. Panel mem. Internat. Black Caucus Fgn. Affairs; mem. adv. bd. US Com. for Refugees; designer Wek1933 handbags, 2001—. Actor: (films) Four Feathers, 2002; author: Alek: From Sudanese Refugee to International Supermodel, 2007. Involved with Bracelet of Life Campaign, Doctors Without Borders, NYC Spl. Olympics, UNICEF, London Refugee Week, Design Industries Found. Fighting AIDS; spokesperson World Vision; founder W.E.K. (Working to Educate Kids). Recipient Spirit of a Woman award, Am. Apparel and Footwear Assn., 2008; named Best New Model, Venus de la Mode Fashion awards, 1997 MTV model of yr., Model of Decade, i-D mag.; named one of 50 Most Beautiful People, People mag., 1999, 50 Most Influential Faces in Fashion, i-D mag. Office: IMG Models 304 Park Ave S 12th Fl New York NY 10010 Office Phone: 212-253-8884. Office Fax: 212-253-8883.

WELBORN, REICH LEE, lawyer; b. Winston-Salem, NC, Nov. 1, 1945; s. Bishop M. and Hazel (Weatherman) W.; m. Martha Huffstetler, Aug. 27, 1966; children: Judson Allen, Spencer Brooks. AB, U. NC, 1968, JD with honors, 1971. Bar: NC 1971. Assoc. Moore & Van Allen, PLLC and predecessor Powe Porter & Alphin, P.A., Durham, NC, 1971-76; ptnr. Moore & Van Allen and predecessor Powe Porter & Alphin, P.A., Durham, NC, 1976—. V.p. Family Counseling Svc., Durham, 1978-79; bd. trustees NC Sch. Sci. & Math., 2002—. Recipient Order of Long Leaf Pine award Gov. of NC, 1981, Spl. Citation, 1983. Mem. ABA, NC Bar Assn., Durham County Bar Assn. (pres. 1989-90), NC State Bar, Croasdaile Club (pres. 1989-90), Sertoma (pres. Durham chpt. 1987-88), NC Jaycees (pres. 1981-82), Durham C. of C. (bd. dirs. 1992-93). Home: 4422 Myers Park Dr Durham NC 27705 Office: Moore & Van Allen PLLC PO Box 13706 Research Triangle Park NC 27709-4658 Office Phone: 919-286-8000. Business E-Mail: welbornr@mvalaw.com.

WELBURN, EDWARD T., automotive executive; b. Phila., Dec. 14, 1950; BA, Howard U., 1972. Assoc. designer GM Advanced Design Studios, 1972, Buick Exterior Studio, 1973, Oldsmobile Exterior Studio, 1975—85, chief designer, 1989—98; with Saturn global design GM, Rüsselsheim, Germany, 1996—98, exec. dir. design body-on-frame architectures, 2002, v.p. design N. Am., 2003—05, v.p. global design, 2005—; dir. GM Corp. Brand Ctr., Warren, Mich., 1998—2001. Designer Indianapolis 500 Pace Car, 1985. Recipient The Best Concept Truck, North Am. Internat. Auto Show, 2003, Best Concept Car, Autoweek, 1995, Award of Design Excellence, Indsl. Designers Soc. America, 1988; named to Power 150, Ebony mag., 2008.*

WELCH, ALEX, Internet company executive, application developer; married. BS with emphasis in Computer Info. Sys., Colo. State U. Software engr. Level 3 Comm., Denver; co-founder, CEO Photobucket, Denver, 2003—. Spkr. in field. Finalist Ernst & Young Entrepreneur Of Yr. Award (Rocky Mountain Region), 2007. Office: Photobucket PO Box 13003 Denver CO 80201

WELCH, ASHLEY JAMES, engineering educator; b. Ft. Worth, May 3, 1933; married, 1952; 3 children. BS, Tex. Tech U., 1955; MS, So. Meth. U., 1959; PhD in Elec. Engring., Rice U., 1964. Cert. profl. engr., Tex. Aerophys. engr. Gen. Dynamics, Ft. Worth, 1957-60; instr. elec. engring. Rice U., 1960-64; asst. prof. elec. engr. U. Tex., Austin, 1964—70, dir. engring. computer facility, 1964—68, 1995—96, assoc. prof. elec. engr., 1970—75, prof. elec. engr. and biomedical engr., 1971—, Marion E. Forsman Centennial prof. engring., 1985—, faculty advisor undergraduate biomedical engring. students, 2002—03. Chmn. Gordon Conf. in Lasers in Medicine and Biology, Am. Soc. Lasers in Med. Surgery Annual Meeting; bd. dirs. Am. Soc. Lasers in Med. Surgery, 1989—92, 1999—2002. Editor, author Optical-Thermal Response of Laser-Irradiated Tissue; contbr. more than 500 articles to profl. jours. Lt. US Army, 1955—56. Recipient Best Dissertation award, Rice U., 1964, Hocott award, U. Tex., 2004, Human Effectiveness Directorate Ann. Excellence award, USAF, 2006, Rsch. Excellence award, 2006. Fellow: IEEE, Am. Inst. for Med. and Biol. Engring., Am. Soc. Lasers in Surgery and Medicine (W.B. Mark award 2002); mem.: Internat. Soc. Optical Engring. (chmn. sessions, Pioneers in Biomed. Optics award 2006, Biomed. Optics Lifetime Achievement award 2007). Achievements include research in laser-tissue interaction, application of lasers in medicine; patents in field; pioneer in optics. Office: U Tex at Austin Dept Biomedical Engring Austin TX 78712 Home: 108 Emeralds Dr Burnet TX 78611-2887 Office Phone: 512-471-1453. Business E-Mail: welch@mail.utexas.edu.

WELCH, AUDREY B., retired music educator; b. Johnson City, Tenn., Jan. 1, 1928; d. Houston and Ruth (Greene) Blevins; m. Thomas B. Welch, Aug. 22, 1953 (dec.); children: Thomas B. III, Rodney Patrick, Kevin Brooks. AA, Mars Hill Coll., NC, 1947; BS, East Tenn. State U., 1950; M.Mus. Edn., U. S.C., 1984; MA, Southwestern Sem., Ft. Worth, Tex., 1987. Choral dir. Cloudland H.S., Roan Mountain, Tenn., 1950—51, 1955—56, McLean Jr. H.S., Ft. Worth, 1953—55, Escambia County Schs., Pensacola, Fla., 1965—67, Bay County Schs., Panama City, Fla., 1968—73, Mullins H.S., SC, 1977—88; Spanish tchr. PeeDee Acad., Marion, SC, 1988—93; ret., 1988. Dir. music seminars Internat. Mission Bd., Richmond, Va., 1990—94, 1997; dir. and organist various chs.; dir. award-winning music groups Tex., SC; coord. God's Storehouse - A Food and Clothes Crisis Ministry, 2001—08. Co-author: Music Manual for Elementary Schools, 1969. Dir. Mullins Choral Soc., 1972—73. Recipient Recognition as Vol., Internat. Mission Bd., Richmond, 1990—94. Mem.: DAR, Music Educators Nat. Conf. Home: 129 Whitehurst Way Columbia SC 29229 Personal E-mail: adj1928@aol.com.

WELCH, BILLY E., retired government agency administrator, management consultant; b. West, Tex., Sept. 16, 1929; s. Perry S. and Elizabeth D. Welch; m. Dorothy J. Poling, Mar. 10, 1956; children: William, Rebecca Royse, Janet Dillard, Susan Glaeser. BS, Abilene Christian U., Tex., 1950; MS, Tex. A&M U., College Station, 1951, PhD, 1954. Sr. engr. Northrop Aircraft Corp., Hawthorne, Calif., 1957—59; dir. environ. scis. USAF Sch. Aerospace Medicine, San Antonio, 1959—72, dep. dir., 1977—81; spl. asst. for environ. quality Office of Sec. of Air Force, Washington, 1972—77; chief scientist Human Systems Ctr., San Antonio, 1981—89, program dir., 1989—90; dir. Armstrong Lab. Air Force Rsch. Lab., San Antonio, 1990—94; ret. Chair civilian exec. adv bd Air Force Material Command, Dayton, Ohio, 1988—94; Air Force sci. and engring. policy coun. Office of Sec. of Air Force, Washington, 1989—94; mem., vice-chair, chair adv. com. on rsch. Tex. Higher Edn. Coordinating Bd, Austin, 1994—2009; affiliate Los Alamos Nat. Lab., N.Mex., 1996—2004, Carlsbad Field Office US Dept. Energy, 2001—02. Various positions including mem., sec., v.p., pres. NE Ind. Sch. Dist., San Antonio, 1979—88; mem., pres. NE Ednl. Found., San Antonio, 1987—97; mem., chair Brooks Heritage Found., San Antonio, 1987—, Brooks Aerospace Found., San Antonio, 1997—; bd. mem. San Antonio New Schs. Found., 1991—95. Recipient Meritorious Exec. award, Pres. of US, 1988, Meritorious Civilian Svc. award, USAF, 1994. Fellow: Aerospace Med. Assn.; mem.: Internat. Acad. Astronautics, Am. Physiol. Soc., Sigma Xi. Avocations: golf, gardening, reading. Home: 122 Encino Blanco San Antonio TX 78232

WELCH, C. DAVID (CHARLES DAVID WELCH), former federal agency administrator; b. Munich, 1953; m. Gretchen Gerwe; children: Emma, Molly, Hannah. BA, Georgetown U., 1975; MA, Tufts U., 1977; student, London Sch. Econs., 1973—74. With Office of Under Sec. for Security Assistance, Sci. and Tech., 1977—79; polit. officer US Embassy, Islamabad, Pakistan, 1979—81, officer responsible for Syria Washington, 1981—82, officer responsible for Lebanon, 1982—83, chief polit. sect. Damascus, Syria, 1984—86, polit. officer Amman, Jordan, 1986—88; mem. staff NSC, Washington, 1989—91; exec. asst. to under sec. polit. affairs US Dept. State, Washington, 1991—92; charge d'affaires US Embassy, Riyadh, Saudi Arabia, 1992—94, dep. chief of mission, 1992—95; prin. dep. asst. sec. of state Bur. Near Ea. Affairs US Dept. State, Washington, 1996—97, asst. sec. for internat. orgn. affairs, 1998—2001, U.S. amb. to Egypt Cairo, 2001—05, asst. sec. Bur. Near Eastern Affairs Washington, 2005—08. Mem.: Am. Fgn. Svc. Assn., Coun. Fgn. Rels.*

WELCH, CHERIE LYNN, healthcare educator; b. Detroit, Feb. 5, 1966; d. Charles and Judith Welch. BS, Western Mich. U., 1990, MS, 1998. Secondary phys. edn. instr. Dept. Edn., Agana, Guam, 1992—93; secondary health, phys. edn. tchr. Hackett Cath. Ctrl. HS, Kalamazoo, 1994—96; secondary phys. edn. tchr. Our Lady of Mercy HS, Farmington Hills, Mich., 1996—97; phys. edn. instr. Western Mich. U., Kalamazoo, 1997—98; elem. and mid. sch. phys. edn. tchr. Grand Rapids Pub. Schs., Mich., 1998—2000; aquatic instr. Oakland CC, Farmington Hills, Mich., 2004—09; wellness instr. Rochester Cmty. Schs., Mich., 2000—09. 2nd elect pres. Mich. Assn. Health, Phys. Edu., Recreation and Dance, 2008—09. Home: 3721 Barberry Cir Wixom MI 48393 Office Phone: 248-726-4052. Business E-Mail: cwelch@rochester.k12.mi.us.

WELCH, DENNIS E., electric power industry executive; B in Environ., Health and Safety Mgmt., Ind. State U., Terre Haute; M in Bus. and Human Resource Mgmt., Rensselaer Poly. Inst., Troy, NY; grad. Environ. Leadership Program, Yale U. Sch. Forestry and Environ. Studies. Various positions Stone & Webster Engring.; positions including dir. environ. health and safety, mgr. occupational safety NE Utilities, v.p. environ., safety & ethics, pres., COO Yankee Energy Sys. subs., 2001; sr. v.p. environment, safety and health Am. Electric Power Svc. Corp., 2005—. Office: Am Electric Power Svc Corp 1 Riverside Plz Columbus OH 43215-2373 Office Phone: 614-716-1000.

WELCH, JAMES M., biology professor; BS, Coll. William and Mary, Williamsburg,Va., 1990; MS, U. Del., Lewes, 1994; PhD, Duke U., Durham, NC, 1998. Postdoc. fellow Harbor Br. Oceanog. Instn., Ft. Pierce, Fla., 1998—99; asst. prof. dept. biology Wittenberg U., Springfield, Ohio, 2000—, chair biology dept., 2008—. Contbr. articles to numerous profl. jours. Mem.: Sigma Xi. Avocations: hunting, golf. Office: Wittenberg Univ PO Box 720 Springfield OH 45501 Business E-Mail: jwelch@wittenberg.edu.

WELCH, JASPER ARTHUR, JR., security company executive, consultant; b. Baton Rouge, Jan. 5, 1931; s. Jasper Arthur and Oramay Ballinger (Young) W.; m. Frances Carroll Wright, Mar. 28, 1953 (div. Nov. 1984); children: Jasper Arthur III, Carroll Welch Pawlikowski, Brent Ballinger; m. Jane Ann Alford Tudor, Dec. 31, 1985. BS in Physics, La. State U., 1952; MA in Physics, U. Calif., Berkeley, 1954, PhD in Physics, 1958. Commd. officer 2d lt. USAF, 1952, advanced through grades to maj. gen., 1975; chief analyst Hdqs. USAF, Washington, 1969—71; chief strategic analysis Office Sec. Def., Washington, 1971—74; chief strategic concepts Hdqs. USAF, 1974—75, asst. chief staff for analysis, 1975—79; coord. def. policy NSC, 1979—81; asst. dept. chief staff Hdqs. USAF, 1981—83; ret., 1983. Tech. cons. Jasper Welch Assocs., Santa Fe, 1984—; mem. adv. coun. NASA, Washington, 1985-89; chmn. mil. adv. panel to dir. CIA, Washington, 1986-98; mem. nat. security panel U. Calif., 2000-07. Author: Atomic Theory of Gas Dynamics, 1965; contbr. articles to sci. jours., including Phys. Rev., Strategic Rev. Youth dir. St. Matthews Epis. Ch., Pacific Palisades, Calif., 1965-69, St. Andrews Epis. Ch., Arlington, 1969-74; mem. found. bd. Santa Fe Chamber Music Festival, 1998—2004. Decorated D.S.M. with oak leaf cluster, Legion of merit with two oak leaf clusters. Mem. NAE (found. bd. 1999—2005), Am. Geophys. Union, Am. Phys. Soc., Coun. on Fgn. Rels. Avocations: music, theater, gardening, hiking, racing sailboats. Office: 2129 Foothills Rd Santa Fe NM 87505

WELCH, JOHN, computer game company executive; BS in Math. and Computer Sci., MIT, Cambridge; MS, U. Mass. Sys. integration cons. Andersen Consulting; with Sega, 1998—99; v.p. games & product AtomShockwave Corp., 1999—2004; co-founder, pres., CEO PlayFirst Inc., San Francisco, 2004—. Chmn. online games steering com. Internat. Game Developers Assn., 2003—04. Office: 134 Ricardo Ave Piedmont CA 94611

WELCH, JOHN KIRTLAND, nuclear energy industry executive; b. Waltham, Mass., Mar. 8, 1950; s. Raymond Vincent and Justine Louise (Fairbank) W.; m. Michele Anne Mules, June 10, 1972; children: Nicole Kristen, Alison Corrinne. BA in Aero. Engring., U.S. Nav. Acad., 1972; MS in Aeronautics, Naval Postgrad. Sch., 1973; MBA in Fin., Loyola Coll., Balt., 1984. Registered profl. engr., Md. Commd. ens. USN, 1972, advanced through grades to lt., resigned, 1979; systems engr. Gen. Electric Co., Evendale, Ohio, 1979-80; div. dir. Gen. Physics Corp., Columbia, Md., 1980-84; ops. ctr. mgr. Advanced Tech., Inc., Reston, Va., 1984; various positions to exec. v.p. marine sys. group Gen. Dynamics Corp., 1989—2005; pres., CEO USEC Inc., 2005—. Lt. USNR, 1979—. Mem. ASME (chmn. plant engring. com. 1980—), Am. Soc. Naval Engrs. Avocations: swimming, photography, sailing. Office: USEC Inc 6903 Rockledge Dr Bethesda MD 20817

WELCH, LLOYD RICHARD, electrical and communications engineer, educator, consultant; b. Detroit, Sept. 28, 1927; s. Richard C. and Helen (Felt) W.; m. Irene Althea Main, Sept. 12, 1953; children: Pamela Irene Towery, Melinda Ann, Diana Lia Worthington. BS in Math., U. Ill., 1951; PhD in Math., Calif. Inst. Tech., 1958. Mathematician NASA-Jet Propulsion Lab., Pasadena, Calif., 1956-59; staff mathematician Inst. Def. Analyses, Princeton, NJ, 1959-65; prof. elec. engring. U. So. Calif., LA, 1965-99, prof. emeritus, 1999—. Cons. in field of elec. comms Contbr. articles to profl. jours. Served with USN, 1945-49, 51-52 Fellow IEEE (Shannon award Info. Theory Soc. of IEEE 2003); mem. Nat. Acad. Engring., Am. Math. Soc., Math. Assn. Am., Phi Beta Kappa, Sigma Xi, Phi Kappa Phi, Pi Mu Epsilon, Eta Kappa Nu Office: U So Calif Elec Engring Bldg 500A Los Angeles CA 90089-0001

WELCH, MARTHA LYNN, environmentalist, educator; d. Margaret Melvina Sandifer and Richard Charles O'Connell; m. John Tyler Welch II, Aug. 28, 1987. BA in Environ. Studies, U. N.C., Wilmington, NC, 1983; MS in Edn., Old Dominion U., 1996; EdD, Fla. Internat. U., 2004. Asst. edn., exhibits coord. N.C. Aquarium, Ft. Fisher, 1984—86; owner, operator Manatee Tours, Inc., Islamorada, Fla., 1990—93; marine edn. specialist Coll. William and Mary, Va. Inst. Marine Sci., Gloucester Point, 1996—97; field leader, instr. Audubon Fla., Miami, 1999—2003; dir. edn. Fla. Flora and Fauna, Inc., Hutchinson island, 1999—. Cons. Sch. Dist. Palm Beach County, Fla., 2002—; adj. prof. Palm Beach CC, 2008—. Author: Mandy the Manatee Saves the Day; contbr. articles to profl. jours. Mem.: ASCD, NSTA (assoc.), Fla. Assn. Sci. Tchrs., Nat. Marine Edn. Assn. (assoc.), Nat. Audubon Soc., Fla. Marine Sci. Edn. Assn., Phi Kappa Phi. Avocations: travel, snorkeling, boating. Home and Office: 137 Queens Rd Hutchinson Island FL 34949 Personal E-mail: jwelch261@sprintpcs.com. Business E-Mail: welchm@pbcc.edu.

WELCH, MARTIN E., III, investor, former rental company executive; b. Detroit, June 25, 1948; m. Anne Welch; children: Michele, James, Mary Beth, Brian. BS in Acctg., U. Detroit Mercy, 1970, MBA, 1973. Audit mgr. Arthur Young & Co., Detroit, 1970-77; dir. mktg. acctg. Fruehauf divsn. Fruehauf Corp., Detroit, 1977-82; mgr. corp. acctg. Chrysler Corp., Highland Park, Mich., 1982-83, asst. contr., 1983-86, gen. auditor, 1987-88, asst. treas., 1988-91; CFO Chrysler Can., Windsor, Ont., 1986-87; sr. v.p., CFO Federal-Mogul corp., Southfield, Mich., 1991-95; exec. v.p., CFO Kmart Corp, Troy, Mich., 1995—2001; bus. advisor, dir. York Mgmt. Svcs., Somerset, NJ, 2002—08; exec. v.p., CFO Oxford Automotive, Inc., Troy, Mich., 2003—04, United Rentals, Inc., Greenwich, Conn., 2005—08. Mem. nat. adv. bd. JP Morgan Bank, 1997—2000; bd. dirs. Delphi Corp., 2006—. Bd. dirs. U. Detroit-Mercy. Mem.: Fin. Execs. Internat. Personal E-mail: martywelch@yahoo.com.*

WELCH, MICHAEL R., sociologist, educator; b. Ogdensburg, NY, Feb. 8, 1947; s. Carlton Curtis Welch and Eleanor (Clary) Caruso; m. Helena Rose Kleist, Jan. 29, 1966; children: Kristen Reynolds, Michael Jr., Scott, Brian. BA, LeMoyne Coll., 1972; MA, U. N.C., 1975, PhD, 1980. Asst. prof. Fla. Atlantic U., Boca Raton, 1976—80, U. Cin., 1980—81; full prof. U. Notre Dame, 2006—. Contbr. articles to profl. jours. Mem.: Am. Soc. Criminology, Am. Sociol. Assn., Alpha Kappa Delta, Pi Gamma Mu. Roman Catholic. Office: Univ Notre Dame Sociology Dept 810 Flanner Hall Notre Dame IN 46556

WELCH, MILTON LAMONT, literature and language professor; b. Newport News, Va., July 6, 1977; s. Willie Mae and Milton Vann Welch. AB, Vassar Coll., Poughkeepsie, 1999; MA, St. John's Coll., Annapolis, 2001; D, U. Va., Charlottesville, 2006. Asst. prof. NC State U., Raleigh, 2006—. Office: Dept English NC State Tompkins Hall Box 8105 Raleigh NC 27695-8105 Business E-Mail: lamwelch@social.chass.ncsu.edu.

WELCH, MORGAN E., lawyer; b. Joplin, Mo., May 25, 1950; s. Morgan and Virginia Welch; m. Cheryl Welch, Oct. 23, 1982; children: Rick Martin, Ashley. BS, Westminster Coll., 1972; JD, U. Ark., 1975. Bar: Ark. 1975, U.S. Dist. Ct. (ea. dist. Ark.) 1975, U.S. Dist. Ct. (we. dist. Ark.) 1975, U.S. Ct. Appeals (8th cir.) 1984, U.S. Supreme Ct. 1990, U.S. Air Force Ct. Mil. Rev., U.S. Army Ct. Mil. Rev., Armed Forces Ct. Appeals. Jr. ptnr. Patterson and Welch, North Little Rock, Ark., 1976—80; owner Morgan Welch PA, North Little Rock, 1980—89; ptnr. Hurley Whitwell Shephard & Welch, North Little Rock, 1989—90, Welch & Adcock, Little Rock, 1990—95; owner Morgan Welch PA, Little Rock, 1995—2000; ptnr. Eubanks, Welch, Baker, Schulze, Little Rock, 2000—03; sr. ptnr. Welch and Kitchens LLC, Little Rock, 2003—. Counsel Ark. Legis., Little Rock, 1975—76. Pres. North Little Rock Jaycees, 1978—79; sec. North Pulaski County Bar Assn., North Little Rock, 1979—80; mem. 8th cir. Ark. Ho. Dels., 1994—96. Recipient Roxanne Wilson Trial Adv. award, 1997. Mem.: ATLA (bd. govs.), ABA, Am. Inns Ct. Found. (Master of Bench), Ark. Trial Lawyers Assn. (pres. 1991, Outstanding Trial Lawyer award 1990, President's award 2005). Democrat. Methodist. Office: One Riverfront Pl Ste 413 North Little Rock AR 72114 Office Phone: 501-978-3030.

WELCH, PETER F., United States Representative from Vermont, former state legislator; b. Springfield, Mass., May 2, 1947; s. Edward and Mart (Tracy) Welch; m. Joan Smith, Dec. 10, 1975 (dec. 2004); 5 children. AB, Holy Cross Coll., 1969; LLB, U. Calif., Berkeley, 1973. Bar: Vt. Pvt. practice law; mem. Vt. State Senate, 1981—89, 2002—07, minority leader, 1982—84, pres. pro tempre, 1985—89, 2003—07; mem.-at-large US Congress from Vt., 2007—, mem. oversight & govt. reform com., rules com., 2007—. Mem. Brain Injury Task Force, Congl. Arts Caucus, Congl. Prog. Caucus, Fire Svcs. Caucus, House Hunger Caucus, House Nursing Caucus, Nat. Guard and Res. Components Caucus, New England Congl. Caucus, Northeast Agr. Caucus, Northern Border Caucus, Rural Healthcare Coalition, Rural Working Group. Democrat. Roman Catholic. Office: 1404 Longworth House Office Bldg Washington DC 20515 also: 30 Main St Ste 350 Burlington VT 05401*

WELCH, RICHARD L., priest, lawyer; b. Naples, Italy, Dec. 22, 1953; s. Richard and Alice (Nevin) W. BA, St. Alphonsus Sem., Suffield, Conn., 1977; MRE, Mt. St. Alphonsus, Esopus, NY, 1979, MDiv, 1981; JCL, U. St. Thomas Aquinas, Rome, 1995, JCD, 1998. Parish priest, PR, 1981-87; rector Catholic cathedral Caguas, PR, 1987-93; rector Notre Dame Sch., 1987-93; pres. Human Life Internat., 1997—2000; judge, promoter of justice Archdiocese of NY, 2001—. Author: (books) Blood of the Martyrs, 1994, Culture of Death Vs. Culture of Life, 1995, The Manifestation of Conscience, 1998. Bd. dirs. For Human Life Internat, U.S., Can., Ireland, Australia, New Zealand, 1997, pres., 1997— Named Eagle Scout Boy Scouts of Am., 1968. Roman Catholic.

WELCH, ROBERT BOND, ophthalmologist, educator; b. Balt., May 24, 1927; s. Robert S.G. and Sally (Bond) W.; m. Elizabeth Truslow, May 30, 1953. AB, Princeton U., NJ, 1949; MD, Johns Hopkins U., Balt., 1953. Diplomate: Am. Bd. Ophthalmology. Intern in internal medicine Duke U. Hosp., 1953-54; resident in ophthalmology Wilmer Inst., Johns Hopkins U., 1954-57, chief resident in ophthalmology, 1959, co-dir. retina service, 1959-84, dir. retina service, 1984-85; retinal cons. in ophthalmology Walter Reed Army Hosp., 1961—2003, Bethesda Naval Hosp, 1976-99; assoc. prof. ophthalmology Johns Hopkins U.; chmn. dept. ophthalmology Greater Balt. Med. Ctr., 1985-91. Author: (with others) The Wilmer Institute 1925-1975, 1976; author: The Wilmer Opthalmological Institute 1925-2000, 2000; editor Transactions Am. Ophthal. Soc., 1984-91; mem. editorial staff Retina mag., 1980-86. Served with USNR, 1945-47. Recipient Disting. Alumnus award, Johns Hopkins U., 2001, Superior Civilian Svc. award, U.S. Army, 2004, Robert Bond Welch professorship in opthalmology, Johns Hopkins Medicine and Wilmer Eye Inst., 2006. Mem. Am. Ophthal. Soc. (v.p. 1992-93, pres. 1993-94, editor 1984-90), Retina Soc. (pres. 1981-83), Pan. Pacific Surg. Assn. (v.p. 1972-80), Md. Soc. Eye Physicians and Surgeons (pres. 1963-64), Md. Club., Elkridge Club, South River Club. Democrat. Episcopalian. Home: 4409 Atwick Rd Baltimore MD 21210-2811 Office: 86 State Cir Annapolis MD 21401-1906 Office Phone: 410-263-3492.

WELCH, STANTON, performing company executive; b. Melbourne, Australia, Oct. 15, 1969; s. Garth Welch and Marilyn Jones. Studied at, San Francisco Ballet Sch. Dancer to soloist Australian Ballet, 1989, resident choreographer, 1995—2003; artistic dir. Houston Ballet, 2003—. Artistic assoc. Ballet Met, Columbus, Ohio. Choreographer (ballets) Maninyas, San Francisco Ballet, 1996, Taiko, 1999, Tutu, 2003, Falling, 2005, Powder, Birmingham Royal Ballet, 1998, Ønsket, Royal Danish Ballet, 1998, Ander, 1999, Indigo, Houston Ballet, 1999, Bruiser, 2000, Tales of Texas, 2004, Blindness, 2004, Bolero, 2004, Nosotros, 2005, Brigade, 2006, Swan Lake, 2006, The Four Seasons, 2007, The Core, 2008, A Doll's House, 2008, Marie, 2009, Clear, Am. Ballet Theatre, 2001, Evolution, BalletMet, Don Quixote, A Dance in the Garden of Mirth, 2000, Green, Moscow Dance Theatre, 2000, OPUS X, 2001; created commissions for many of the world's best companies including American Ballet Theater, Houston Ballet, San Francisco Ballet, Royal Danish Ballet, Australian Ballet et al. Avocations: country music, country and western dancing. Office: Houston Ballet 1921 W Bell St Houston TX 77019*

WELCH, W(ALTER) SCOTT, III, lawyer; b. Jackson, Miss., Sept. 7, 1939; s. Walter Scott Jr. and Velma Lou (Hines) W.; m. Hermine McBee Copeland, Nov. 5, 1960 (div. Sept. 1981); children: Hermine, Walt; m. Mary Anne Kendrick, Dec. 6, 1981; children: Dennis, Kasi. BA cum laude, U. of South, 1961; LLB with distinction, U. Miss., 1964. Bar: Miss. 1964, U.S. Dist. Ct. (no. dist.) Miss. 1964, U.S. Dist. Ct. (so. dist.) Miss. 1967, U.S. Ct. Appeals 1968, U.S. Supreme Ct., 1970. Assoc. Welch, Gibbes & Graves, Attys., Laurel, Miss., 1964; chmn. litigation dept. Butler, Snow, O'Mara, Stevens & Cannada, Jackson, 2002—05, ptnr., 1967—2005; shareholder Baker, Donelson, Bearman, Caldwell & Berkowitz, PC, 2006—. Mem. Miss. Supreme Ct. Commn. on Impaired Lawyers, 2005—09; bd. dir. Harbor House Recovery Ctr., Jackson, Miss., 2004—. Capt. USAF, 1964—67. Fellow Am. Coll. Trial Lawyers, Am. Bar Found., Found. Am. Bd. Trial Advs. (trustee 1999-02, pres. 2001), Miss. Bar Found.; mem. ABA (house dels. 1994—, standing com. on public edn. 1998-00, 03-06, state del., nominating com. 2000-06, faculty tort and ins. practice sectin trial acad. 2003, bd. govs. 2006—09), Am. Bd. Trial Advs. (nat. dir. 1992—, local pres. 1987, v.p. 1999, pres.-elect 2000, nat. pres. 2001), Internat. Assn. Def. Counsel (faculty def. counsel trial acad. 1997), Trial Attys. Am., Trucking Industry Def. Assn., Miss. Def. Lawyers (past bd. dirs.), Miss. State Bar Assn. (commr. 1989-95, exec. com. 1991-92, pres.-elect 1993-94, pres. 1994-95, Disting. Svc. award 2004), Hinds County Bar Assn. (pres. 1979-80), Chambers Ptnrs. Am.'s Leading Attys., Best Lawyers America, Lawdragon 500. Republican. Episcopalian. Home: 6223 Waterford Dr Jackson MS 39211-2910 Office: PO Box 14167 Jackson MS 39236-4167 Home Phone: 601-957-1016; Office Phone: 601-351-2440. Business E-Mail: swelch@bakerdonelson.com.

WELCH, WAYNE WILLARD, educator; b. Clinton, Iowa, May 20, 1934; s. Willard Densmore and Evelyn Louise (Peterson) W.; m. Dorothy Geraldine Dunlap, Sept. 11, 1951; children: William Alan, Jean Carol, Mary Bethania. BS, U. Wis., 1956, PhD, 1966; MS, U. Pa., 1960, Purdue U., 1963. Rsch. assoc. Harvard U., 1965-69; prof. ednl. psychology U. Minn., 1969—98, prof. emeritus, 1998—, asst. dean, 1970-74. Vis. prof. U. Wash., 1976-77, Curtin U., Perth, Australia, 1984; head office studies and program assessment NSF, 1988-89; cons. in field. Mem. editl. adv. bd. Sci. Tchr, 1972-77, Jour. Rsch. in Sci. Tchg., 1969-76; contbr. numerous articles to profl. jours. Grantee NSF, 1971-78, 1980-84, 2008-; Fulbright-Hays lectr., Israel, 1979; Fulbright scholar, NZ, 1984-85. Fellow AAAS (councilman 1970-73); mem. Nat. Assn. Research in Sci. Teaching (pres. 1973-76, Disting. Rsch. award 1995). Home (Summer): 33837 Bonnie Point Rd Grand Rapids MN 55744

WELCH, WILLIAM JAMES, journalist, educator; b. Erie, Pa., Sept. 17, 1951; s. James C. and Margaret A. Welch; m. Patricia Marie Murray; children: Timothy M., Christopher W., Jennifer M. BA, Point Pk. U., Pitts., 1972; MA, Mercyhurst Coll., Erie, Pa., 2006—06. City editor Morning News, Erie, 1981—98, Erie Daily Times, 1998—2000; sports editor Erie Times-News, 2000—01, local news editor, 2001—01; instr. journalism, intelligence writing Mercyhurst Coll., 2002—, newspaper adviser, 2003—, dep. dir., ctr. intelligence rsch. & analysis tng., 2006—. Pres. Flagship Niagara League, Erie, 2006—08. Recipient Deadline News Writing award, Pa. AP Mng. Editors, 1979. Mem.: BPOE, Internat. Assn. Intelligence Edn. Office: Mercyhurst Coll 501 E 38th St Erie PA 16546-0001 Business E-Mail: wwelch@mercyhurst.edu.

WELD, JONATHAN MINOT, lawyer; b. Greenwich, Conn., Feb. 25, 1941; s. Alfred White and Sally Weld; m. Jane Paige, June 19, 1965; children: Elizabeth, Eric. AB in History cum laude, Harvard U., 1963; JD, Cornell U., 1967. Bar: NY 1967, U.S. Ct. Appeals (2d cir.) 1969, U.S. Dist. Ct. (ea. and so. dists.) NY 1970. Assoc. Shearman & Sterling, NYC, 1967-75, ptnr., 1976—2004, London, 1982-85, of counsel, 2005—. Bd. dirs. Bank of N.S. Internat.; chmn., bd. dirs. The Evergreens, Bklyn. Hosp. Bd. dirs. St. Ann's Sch., Bklyn. Bot. Garden, NY Presbyn. Healthcare Sys., Ctr. for Religious Inquiry; former bd. dirs. Bklyn. Home for Children, Harvard Coll. Fund, Winant and Clayton Vols. Mem.: ABA, NY State Bar Assn. Office: 599 Lexington Ave Fl C2 New York NY 10022-6030 Office Phone: 212-848-8075. Business E-Mail: jweld@shearman.com.

WELD, WILLIAM F., former governor; b. Smithtown, NY, July 31, 1945; s. David and Mary Blake (Nichols) W.; m. Susan Roosevelt (div. 2002), June 7, 1975; children: David Minot, Ethel Derby, Mary Blake, Quentin Roosevelt, Frances Wylie; m. Leslie Marshall, June 14, 2003. AB summa cum laude, Harvard U., 1966, JD cum laude, 1970; diploma with distinction, Oxford U., Eng., 1967. Bar: Mass. 1970. Law clk. to Hon. R.A. Cutter, Supreme Jud. Ct. Mass., 1970-71; ptnr. Hill & Barlow, Boston, 1971-81; assoc. minority counsel US Ho. of Reps. Judiciary Com. Impeachment Inquiry, Washington, 1973-74; US atty. (Dist. Mass.) US Dept. Justice, Boston, 1981-86, asst. atty. gen., criminal divsn. Washington, 1986-88; sr. ptnr. Hale & Dorr, Boston, Washington, 1988-90; gov. Commonwealth of Mass., Boston, 1991—97; ptnr. McDermott, Will & Emery LLP, NYC and Boston, 1997—; prin. Leeds Weld & Co., NYC, 2001—06. Author: Mackerel by Moonlight, 1998, Big Ugly, 1999, Stillwater, 2002; actor: (films) Traffic, 2000. Republican nominee for atty. gen., Mass., 1978, US Senate, Mass., 1996. Republican. Office: McDermott Will & Emery LLP 340 Madison Ave New York NY 10173 Business E-Mail: bweld@mwe.com.

WELDELE, EDDA HILDA TEMOCHE, language educator; Degree in Law, U. Nat. Federico Villarreal, Lima, Peru, 1975; MA in Hispanic Am. Lit., San Diego State U., 1981. Cert. child devel. tchr. Palomar Coll., 1978, Spanish tchr. CC, 1981, secondary tchr. San Diego State U., 1986. Tchr. Holy Trinity Sch., Lima, 1969—70, Whelan Elem. Sch., 1977, San Diego Statement U., 1979—86, Miramar Coll., 1982—83, San Diego Mesa CC, 1982—90, Clairemont HS, 1984, Intensive Lang. Study Program, 1988—95, Grossmont CC, 1988, 1989—92, 1989—. Lawyer Law Office Dr. Andres Echevarria Maurtua, Lima, 1972—76, Ministerio Economia & Fin., 1974—76, lawyer, nat. supervision bus., 1976; interpreter med. and law Betty Linguist Corp., 1981—87; interpreter comml. Spanish, legal and med. Congreso Internat. Sindicatos, 1982; mem. Coll. Recognition Com., 2001—; co-chair Coll. Wide Profl. Devel., 2004—; mem. Arabic Instr. Search Com., 2007; chair Profl. Devel. Com., 2005—06, co-chair, 2008; mem. Spanish Instr. Search Com., 2008. Contbr. to numerous profl. Recipient Tchg. Excellence award, 2003, Kudo's award, 2006, 2008; named one of Outstanding Interpreter, Ministry Edn., Caracas, Venezuela, 1982; Operacion Amigo fellowship, Palm Beach, Fla., 1963, grant, EDIC, 2001—02. Home: 5612 Delano Ave San Diego CA 92120

WELDON, CLODAGH, theology studies educator; d. Martin and Meg Brett; m. Timothy Weldon, Dec. 28, 2000; 1 child, Eamonn Martin. BA with honors, U. Oxford, 1994, MA, PhD, 1999. Assoc. prof. theology and chair theology and pastoral ministry Dominican U., River Forest, Ill., 2000—. Author: (book) Fr. Victor White O.P.: The Story of Jung's White Raven, 2007. Adv. coun. St Alexander Sch., Palos Heights, Ill., 2008—. Recipient Mother Evelyn Murphy Excellence Tchg. Award, Dominican U., 2005. Mem.: Am. Acad. Religion. Office: Dominican Univ 7900 W Division River Forest IL 60305

WELDON, DAVID JOSEPH, JR., former United States Representative from Florida; b. Amityville, NY, Aug. 31, 1953; s. David Joseph and Anna Weldon; m. Nancy Sourbeck, Aug. 18, 1979; children: Kathryn, David. BS, SUNY, Stony Brook, 1978; MD, SUNY, Buffalo, 1981. Intern Letterman Army Med. Ctr., 1981-82, resident in internal medicine, 1982-84; pvt. practice, Melbourne Internal Medical Assoc, 1987—94; mem. US Congress from 15th Fla. dist., Washington, 1995—2009; mem. appropriations com. Served in US Army, 1981—97 USAR, 1987—92. Fellow: ACP; mem.: AMA, Fla. Med. Assn. Republican. Protestant.*

WELDON, JEFFREY ALAN, lawyer; b. Billings, Mont., May 6, 1963; s. Richard Allen and Monica (Michaud) Weldon; m. Leslie Helen Boileau, July 7, 1990; 2 children. BA, U. Mont., 1986, MPA, 1994, JD, 1996. Assoc. atty. Moulton Bellingham, Longo & Mather, P.C., Billings, Mont., 1997-2000; chief legal counsel Office of Pub. Instrn., State of Mont., Helena, 2000—03; legal counsel, human resources dir. Billings Pub. Schs., 2003—04; share holder Felt, Martin, Frazier & Weldon PC, Billings, 2005—. State Senator, Mont., 1993—97. Office Phone: 406-248-7646. Business E-Mail: jweldon@feltmartinlaw.com.

WELDON, VIRGINIA V., retired food products executive, pediatrician; b. Toronto, Sept. 8, 1935; arrived in US, 1937; d. John Edward and Carolyn Edith (Swift) Vernal; children: Ann Weldon Doyle, Susan Weldon Erlinger. AB cum laude, Smith Coll., 1957; MD, SUNY-Buffalo, 1962; LHD (hon.), Rush U., 1985. Diplomate Am. Bd. Pediat., Am. Bd. Pediatric Endocrinology and Metabolism, Nat. Bd. Med. Examiners (bd. dirs. 1987-89). Intern Johns Hopkins Hosp., Balt., 1962-63, resident in pediat., 1963-64; fellow pediatric endocrinology Johns Hopkins U., Balt., 1964-67, instr. pediat., 1967-68; from instr. to assoc. prof. Wash. U., St. Louis, 1968—79, prof., 1979-89, v.p. Med. Ctr., 1980-89, dep. vice chancellor med. affairs, 1983-89, dir. Ctr. Study Am. Bus., 1998-99; v.p. sci. affairs Monsanto Co., St. Louis, 1989, v.p. pub. policy, 1989-93, sr. v.p. pub. policy, 1993-98. Mem. gen. clin. rsch. ctrs. adv. com. NIH, Bethesda, Md., 1976—80, mem. rsch. resources adv. coun., 1980—84; adv., dir. Monsanto Co., 1989—98. Contbr. articles to sci. jours. Mem. risk assessment mgmt. commn. EPA, 1992—97; commr. St. Louis Zool. Pk., 1983—92; mem. Pres.'s Com. Advs. Sci. and Tech., 1994—2000; trustee Calif. Inst. Tech., 1996—, Whitaker Found., 1997—99, St. Louis Sci. Ctr.; bd. dirs., vice chmn., chmn. St. Louis Symphony Orch., 1993—2005, hon. trustee, 2005—; bd. dirs. United Way Greater St. Louis, 1978—90, St. Louis Regional Health Care Corp., 1985—91; mem. adv. com. on agrl. biotech. USDA, 2000—01. Fellow: AAAS, Am. Acad. Pediat.; mem.: PT @ CC, St. Louis Med. Soc., Soc. Pediat. Rsch., Endocrine Soc., Am. Pediat. Soc., Assn. Am. Med. Colls. (disting. svc. mem., del., chmn. coun. acad. socs. 1984—85, chmn. assembly 1985—86), Nat. Acads. (nat. assoc.), Inst. Medicine, Alpha Omega Alpha, Sigma Xi. Roman Catholic. Home: 242 Carlyle Lake Dr Saint Louis MO 63141-7544

WELDON, WILLIAM CONRAD, pharmaceutical executive; b. Bklyn., Nov. 26, 1948; m. Barbara Weldon; 2 children. BS in Biology, Quinnipiac U., 1971. With sales and mktg. McNeil Pharm. Johnson & Johnson, 1971—82; mgr. ICOM Regional Develop. Ctr., 1982—84; v.p. mng. dir. Korea Mcneal Ltd., 1984—86; mng. dir. Orthro-Cilag Pharm., 1986—89; v.p. sales mktg. Janssen Pharm., 1989—92; pres. Ethicon Endo-Surgery, 1992, group chmn., 1995, chmn., pharm. group, 1998; vice-chmn., bd. dirs. Johnson & Johnson, New Brunswick, NJ, 2001—02, chmn., CEO, 2002—. Bd. dirs. J.P. Morgan Chase & Co., 2005—; chmn. Pharm. Rsch. & Manufacturers, 2005—. Serves Liberty Sci. Center Chmn.'s Adv. Coun.; mem. Sullivan Commn. on Diversity in the Healthcare Workforce; trustee Quinnipiac Univ. Avocation: basketball. Office: Johnson & Johnson 1 Johnson & Johnson Plaza New Brunswick NJ 08933*

WELGE, DONALD EDWARD, food manufacturing executive; b. St. Louis, July 11, 1935; s. William H. and Rudelle (Fritze) W.; m. Mary Alice Childers, Aug. 4, 1962; children: Robert, Tom. BS, La. State U., 1957. With Gilster-Mary Lee Corp., Chester, Ill., 1957—, pres., gen. mgr., 1965—. Dir. Buena Vista Bank of Chester; pres. Buena Vista Bankcorp. Former chmn. St. John's Luth. Bd. Edn. 1st lt. Transp. Corp, U.S. Army, 1958-63. Named So. Ill. Bus. Leader of Yr. So. Ill. U., 1988. Mem. Perryville C. of C. (pres. 1989), Chester, Ill. C. of C. (past pres.), Alpha Zeta, Phi Kappa Phi. Republican. Lutheran. Home: 5 Knollwood Dr Chester IL 62233-1416 Office: Gilster Mary Lee Co PO Box 227 Chester IL 62233-0227 Office Phone: 618-826-2361. Business E-Mail: dwelge@gilstermarylee.com.

WELGE, JACK HERMAN, JR., lawyer; b. Austin, Tex., Sept. 12, 1951; s. Jack Herman and Regina Victoria (Hunger) W.; m. Frances Ava Roddy Avent, Dec. 23, 1977; children: Kirsten Frances Page Welge, Kathleen Ava Regina Welge. BA, U. Tex., 1974; JD, St. Mary's U., 1977. Bar: Tex. 1977, U.S. Dist. Ct. (ea. dist.) Tex. 1979, U.S. Dist. Ct. (no. dist.) Tex. 1982, U.S. Ct. Appeals (5th cir.) 1983, U.S. Supreme Ct., 1984; cert. family law Tex. Bd. Legal Specialization 1984. Asst. dist. atty. Gregg County Criminal Dist. Atty., Longview, Tex., 1978-79; assoc. Law Office of G. Brockett Irwin, Longview, 1979-81; judge Mcpl. Ct. of Record, Longview, 1979-81; ptnr. Adams & Sheppard, Longview, 1981-83; pvt. practice, 1983—; mediation practice, 2005—. Of counsel East Tex. Assn. for Abused Families, Longview, 1985-90. Co-chair profl. divsn. Gregg County United Way, 1996—97; mem. bail bond bd. Gregg County, Tex., 2006—; mem. vestry Trinity Episcopal Ch., Longview, 1993—96, 2001—04, 2009—; bd. directors Longview Cmty. Theater, 1979—82, East Tex. Coun. on Alcoholism and Drug Abuse, Longview, 1981—83, East Tex. Assn. for Abused Families, Longview, 1983—85, Longview Mus. and Arts Ctr., 1991—94; bd. directors adv. com. Salvation Army, 1994—, chmn., 1997; mem. sch. bd. Trinity Sch. of Tex., 2001—04. Mem.: Gregg County Texas Exes (pres. 1993, 2008), Tex. Acad. Family Law Specialists, Gregg County Bar Assn. (pres. 1983), N.E. Tex. Bar Assn., State Bar of Tex. (pro bono coll., contested custody case panel, protective case panel, Gregg County lawyers pro bono project, Outstanding Contbn. award 1990, Disting. Svc. award 1993, Outstanding Pro Bono Atty. 1994, Disting. Svc. award 1995, Outstanding Pro Bono Atty. 1997), East Tex. Knife and Fork Club (pres. 1983—84), Rotary (pres. Longview Club 1987—88, Paul Harris fellow 1982, IFFR fellowship 2006—, 30 Yrs. Perfect Attendance 2008), Shriners, Scottish Rite (25 yr. pin), Mason, Delta Upsilon (Tex. chpt. found. bd. 1974—78), Delta Theta Phi (dean 1977, Bickett Senate). Office: 413-415 S Green St PO Box 3624 Longview TX 75606-3624 Office Phone: 903-753-5683. Personal E-mail: welgelaw@sbcglobal.net.

WELIKSON, JEFFREY ALAN, lawyer; b. Bklyn., Jan. 8, 1957; s. Bennet Joseph and Cynthia Ann Welikson; m. Laura Sanders, Aug. 19, 1979; children: Gregory Andrew, Joshua Stuart. BS, U. Pa., 1976, MBA, 1977; JD, Harvard U., 1980. Bar: N.Y. 1981; CPA, N.Y. Assoc. Shearman & Sterling, NYC, 1980-83; staff counsel Reliance Group Holdings Inc., NYC, 1983-84, dir. legal dept., 1984-85, asst. v.p., corp. counsel, 1985-88, v.p., asst. gen. counsel, asst. sec., 1988-94; exec. v.p., gen. counsel, sec. Reliance Nat. Ins. Co., NYC, 1994-2000; sr. v.p., corp. sec., head corp. law Lehman Bros., NYC, 2000—04, mng. dir., 2004—, corp. sec., 2004—, head corp. law, 2004—. Contbg. editor Harvard U. Internat. Law Jour., 1979-80. Mem.: Am. Soc. Corp. Secs. and Governance Profls., Am. Corp. Counsel Assn. Office: Lehman Brothers Holdings Inc 1301 Ave of the Americas New York NY 10019

WELK, THOMAS JOHN, lawyer; b. Hoven, SD, Aug. 12, 1950; s. Al John and Monica Rose (Coyle) W.; m. Genevieve T. Welk, 1975; children: Colleen, David, Kathleen. BS in Econs. with honors, U. S.D., 1972, MBA, JD, 1975. Bar: S.D. 1975, U.S. Dist. Ct. S.D. 1967, U.S. Ct. Appeals (8th cir.) 1977, U.S. Ct. Appeals (9th cir.) 1987, U.S. Tax Ct. 1981, U.S. Supreme Ct. 1981; bd. cert. civil advocacy Nat. Bd. Trial Advocacy 1995. Asst. atty. gen. State of S.D., Pierre, 1975-79, dep. atty. gen., 1979; ptnr. Boyce, Greenfield, Pashby & Welk, LLP (formerly Boyce, Murphy, McDowell & Greenfield), Sioux Falls, SD, 1979—. Mem. ABA (adminstrv. law, antitrust sect.), SD Bar Assn. (chmn., com. mem., pres. 2004-05), Am. Bd. Trial Advs., Internat. Assn. Def. Counsel, Fedn. Def. and Corp. Counsel, SD Def. Lawyers Assn. (past pres., leadership award Def. Rsch. Inst.), Westward House Country Club (pres.). Republican. Roman Catholic. Avocations: golf, hunting, travel. Office: Boyce, Greenfield, Pashby & Welk LLP 101 N Phillips Ave Ste 600 PO Box 5015 Sioux Falls SD 57117-5015 Office Phone: 605-336-2424. Office Fax: 605-334-0618. Business E-Mail: tjwelk@bgpw.com.

WELKER, JENNIFER CAROL MARIE, artist; b. Conroe, Tex., May 9, 1977; d. Pamela Diane and Ronald Vaughn Welker. AA in Fashion Design, Fashion Inst. Tech., NYC, 1999. Co-founder, designer IC3D, NYC, 1999—2002; mens designer Garren Inc., NYC, 2002; artist Briefly Stated Inc., NYC, 2003—. Co-founder D-Jeans, NYC, 2003—; founder War Angels, NYC, 2003—. Dir.: (documentary) Beyond The Ribbon. Mem. UNA-USA, NYC, 2005—06; rev. World Christianship Ministries, Fresno, Calif., 2006—06; sponsor, mentor Save the Children, NYC, 2005—06. Recipient Wall of Tolerance award, So. Poverty Law Ctr., 2005. Mem.: UN High Commn. for Refugees (life), Human Rights Watch (assoc.), Witness Orgn. (assoc.), Nat. Art Honor Soc. Achievements include design of digital custom clothing. Avocations: philanthropy, screen writing, human rights activist, sign language, actor. Home: 409 W 39th St Apt2A New York NY 10018 Personal E-mail: welker@beyondtheribbon.com.

WELKER, KRISTINA DIANE, psychotherapist; b. July 9, 1960; BA, U. Ctrl. Okla., Edmond, 1989; MA, Ottawa U., Phoenix, 2000; PsyD in Psychology, U. Southern Calif., 2006. Nat. cert. counselor 2003, lic. profl. counselor 2006. Pharm. sales rep. Mead Johnson Labs., Phoenix, 1992—94; profl. counselor, 2001—06; psychotherapist Well Within, LLC, 2006—. Contbr. articles to Ahwatukee foothills news. Mem.: Am. Assn. Christian Counselors, Nat. Bd. Cert. Counselors, Am. Counseling Assn., Am. Soc. Bariatric Physicians. Office: 12020 S Warner Elliot Loop Ste 104 Phoenix AZ 85044 Personal E-mail: drkristina@drkristinawelker.com.

WELKOWITZ, WALTER, biomedical engineer, educator; b. Bklyn., Aug. 3, 1926; s. Samuel and Shirley (Rosenblum) W.; m. Joan Horowitz, June 17, 1951; children: David, Lawrence, Julie. BS, The Cooper Union, NYC, 1948; MS, U. Ill., 1949, PhD, 1954. Profl. engr., N.J. Rsch. assoc. U. Ill., Urbana, 1948-54, Columbia U., NYC, 1954-55; asst. to pres., gen. mgr. Gulton Industries, Inc., Metuchen, NJ, 1955-64; prof., chmn. elec. engring. Rutgers U., Piscataway, NJ, 1964-86, prof. biomed. engring., 1986—, chmn. biomedical engring., 1986-90. Cons. Gulton Industries, Metuchen, N.J., 1964-74. Author: Engineering Hemodynamics: Application to Cardiac Assist Devices, 1977, 2d edit., 1987; co-author: Biomedical Instruments: Theory and Design, 1976, 2d edit., 1992; author numerous chpts. in books; contbr. more than 100 articles to profl. jours. With U.S. Navy, 1944-46. Rutgers U. Rsch. Coun. fellow, 1974-75; recipient Centennial medal IEEE, 1984, Excellence in Rsch. award Rutgers Bd. Trustees, 1985, IEEE Career Achievement award Soc. Engring. Med. Biology, 1991; Llewellyn Thomas vis. prof. U. Toronto, Can., 1989. Fellow IEEE (engring. in medicine and biol. soc. career achievement award 1991), N.Y. Acad. Medicine, Am. Inst. of Medicine and Biol. Engring. Achievements include 26 patents for Electron Tube, Ultrasonic Flowmeter, Ultrasonic Transducer, Piezoelectric Heart Assist Apparatus, Method and Apparatus for Non-Invasive Monitoring Dynamic Cardiac Performance, and others. Home: 37 Church St #4 Keene NH 03431 Home Phone: 603-903-0038; Office Phone: 813-626-8776. Personal E-mail: wwelkowitz@aol.com.

WELLBORN, W. CHRISTOPHER, construction executive; b. 1955; BA in Econ., Wake Forest U., 1977. CFO, sr. v.p. Lenox Inc., 1993—97; CFO, exec. v.p., asst. sec. Dal-Tile Inc., 1997—2002, pres., 2002—05; COO Mohawk Industries Inc., 2005—. Bd. dirs. Mohawk Industries Inc., 2002—, Palm Harbor Homes Inc., 2005—. Office: Palm Harbor Homes Inc Ste 800 15303 Dallas Pky Addison TX 75001 Office Phone: 972-991-2422. Office Fax: 972-991-5949.*

WELLEIN, MARSHA DIANE AKAU, military educator, director; d. George Herbert and Trude (Michelson) Akau; m. Daniel Navarro Atoigue; 1 child, Daniet Hokule'a; m. Lawrence Theodore Wellein (dec.); children: Geoffrey Michael, Nicholas Patrick. BA, U. Hawaii, 1966, tchg. cert., 1971; MEd, U. Guam, 1974; postgrad. in ednl. leadership, Argosy U., 2005. Instr. Hawaii Job Corps Ctr., 1969—71; tchr. spl. edn., reading, lang. arts, adults, pre-kindergarten to HS, U. Guam, 1972—80, Dept. Edn., Guam, 1972—80; reading specialist Waipahu Intermediate; instr. (full and part time) Leeward CC, U. Hawaii, 1981—85, instr. reading, 1983—85; full time guidance counselor US Army, Ft. Shafter Edn. Ctr., 1983—85, Larson Barracks, Germany, 1985—86; edn. svcs. officer, dir. Multinat. Force and Observers, North Camp, El Gorah, Sinai, Egypt, 1987—90; full time guidance counselor Dept. Army, Schofield Barracks, 1990; edn. svcs. officer Dept. Army, Soto Cano Air Base, Honduras, 1991—93, Ft. Kobbe, Panama, 1991—93; edn. svcs. specialist Dept. Army, Kuwait and Saudi Arabia (Desert Storm), 1993, Schofield Barracks Edn. Ctr. 25th Infantry, Hawaii, 1994—96, Camp Zama Edn. Ctr., Japan, 1996—98, 8th Army, Republic of Korea, 1998—99; dir. edn. and libr. svcs. US Army South, PR, 1999—2000; edn. svcs. specialist Dept. Army, Ft. Shafter, 2000—01; regional dir. Pacific and Asia USAR, Honolulu, 2001—. Author: (juvenile hardback novel) The Endless Summer, An Adventure Story of Guam, 1976; editor: Kalihi Kids Can Communicate, 1976. Bd. mem. Internat. Reading Assn., 1972—80, pres., 1980; mem. Oahu Com. Children and Youth, Honolulu, 1969. Recipient Multinat. Force and Observers medal, US State Dept, 1987—89, Achievement medal civilian svc., Kuwait, 1993, Japan, 1997, Comdr.'s award civilian svc., 1986, 1987, 1988, 1998, Sustained Superior Performance award, 1997—, Cold War cert., Dept. Def., 1998, Equal Opportunity award, Camp Zama, Japan, 1998, Unsung Heroes award, Dir. Army Edn., Hdqrs., Washington, 2005, Lamp Lighters award, USAR, 2005; named Outstanding Edn. Svcs. Officer, Dir. Edn., USAR, 2003. Mem.: Coun. Coll. and Mil. Educators, Am. Assn. Adult and Continuing Edn. Avocations: travel, reading, theater. Home: 95-086 Waihonu Pl Mililani HI 96789 Office: HQ G1 US Army Res 9RRC 1557 Pass St Honolulu HI 96819-2135 Office Fax: 808-438-1379. Personal E-mail: welleinmd@hotmail.com.

WELLEMS, THOMAS E., federal agency administrator; b. Anaconda, Mont., Aug. 2, 1951; PhD, U. Chgo., 1980; MD, U. Chgo. Pritzker Sch. Medicine, 1981. Cert. Internal Medicine. Intern, internal medicine Hosp. U. Pa., Phila., 1981—82, resident, tropical medicine, 1982—84; fellow NIH, Bethesda, Md., 1984—86; sr. staff fellow Nat. Inst. Allergy and Infectious Diseases/NIH, Bethesda, Md., 1987—91, head, GPS/LMR, 1991—95, chief, lab. malaria genetics sect. and vector rsch., 1995—. Frequent lectr., cons. and reviewer; serves on a number of adv. com. for founds. and pub.-private partnerships, including Medicines for Malaria Venture. Recipient sanofi-aventis US award, Am. Soc. Microbiology, 2007. Mem.: NAS. Address: NIAID Office of Communications and Pub Liaison 6610 Rockledge Dr MSC 6612 Bethesda MD 20892-6612 Office: NIAID Office Malaria and Vector Rsch Lab Twinbrook II 12441 Parklawn D 3E10A Bethesda MD 20892-0001 Office Phone: 301-496-2487. Business E-Mail: twellems@niais.nih.gov.

WELLEN, ROBERT HOWARD, lawyer; b. Jersey City, Aug. 19, 1946; s. Abraham Louis and Helen Rose (Krieger) W.; m. Anita Fass, June 16, 1968; children: Elizabeth, Judith Maria. BA, Yale Coll., 1968; JD, Yale U., 1971; LLM in Taxation, Georgetown U., 1975. Bar: Conn. 1971, D.C. 1972, Colo. 1982. Assoc. Fulbright & Jaworski, Washington, 1975-76, participating assoc., 1976-79, ptnr., 1979-93, Ivins, Phillips & Barker, Washington, 1993—. Adj. prof. law Georgetown U. Law Ctr., 1982-85. Contbr. articles to legal publs. Served to lt. JAGC, USNR, 1971-75. Mem. ABA (past asst. sec., past chmn. com. on corp. tax, sect. taxation, past supr. editor sect. taxation newsletter, vice chair law devel. com. on corp. tax), Fed. Bar Assn. (coun. taxation), Phi Beta Kappa. Jewish. Office: Ivins Phillips & Barker 1700 Pennsylvania Ave NW Ste 600 Washington DC 20006-4723 Office Phone: 202-662-3401. E-mail: rwellen@ipbtax.com.

WELLER, DAVID ALLEN, information technology executive, poet; b. Spartanburg, SC, May 2, 1962; s. LeGrand Joseph and Nancy Chapin (Gates) Weller. BBA, Tex. Christian U., Ft. Worth, 1984. Sec. officer Spartan Oil Corp., Abilene, Tex., 1985—92; v.p. Fine Books Co., Abilene, 1992—98; poet David Weller, Abilene, 1996—, info. profl., 2006—. Author: (poetry books) Sing Unto the Lord: Short Christian Lyrics, Classic and New, Bible Lights, (book) Reform Activist Hearts, Juxtapositions; prodr.: (internet radio sta.) Holy San Marco!, (website) Abilene Texas Local Daily Info; author: (website) BookUse, (weblog) All Things Reform. Nat. press sec. Reform Party, Hattiesburg, Miss., 2003—05, nat. campaign mgr., nominee Ted Weill for pres., 2004; county chmn. Reform Party Tex., Abilene, 1999—2005. Mem.: Friends of Libr. Methodist. Avocations: classical music, book collecting. Home: 982 Washington Blvd Abilene TX 79601-4643 Personal E-mail: cmptreas@yahoo.com.

WELLER, ELIZABETH BOGHOSSIAN, child and adolescent psychiatrist; b. Aug. 7, 1949; m. Ronald A. Weller, Feb. 18, 1978; children: Andrew, Christine. BS, Am. U., Beirut, Lebanon, 1971, MD, 1975. Lic. psychiatrist, Lebanon, Mo., Ohio, Pa. Intern Am. U. of Beirut, 1974-75; resident Renard Hosp./Washington U., St. Louis, 1975-78; fellow U. Kans. Med. Ctr., Kansas City, 1978-79; asst. prof. psychiatry U. Kans. Med. Sch., Kansas City, 1979-85; chief child/adolescent psychiatry Ohio State U., Columbus, 1985-94, assoc. chair dept. psychiatry, 1994-96; prof. psychiatry and pediat. U. Pa., 1996—, chmn. dept. psychiatry child and adolescent psychiatry, 1996-99, vice chmn. dept. psychiatry, prof. psychiatry/pediatrics, 1996—. Fred Allen chair dept. psychiatry Children's Hosp. of Phila., med. dir. Child Guidance Ctr., 1996-99; pres. Am. Bd. Psychiatry and Neurology, 2004. Co-author: Psychiatric Disorders in Child/Adolescent, 1990, Current Perspectives on Major Depressive Disorders in Children, 1984, Children's Interview for Psychiatric Syndromes, 1999. Fellow APA, Am. Acad. Child/Adolescent Psychiatry; mem. ACP, World Fedn. for Mental Health, Soc. Biol. Psychiatry, Am. Bd. Psychiatry and Neurology (pres. 2004). Office: 3440 Market St Philadelphia PA 19104-4399 Office Phone: 215-590-7573, 215-590-7574. Office Fax: 315-590-7537. Business E-Mail: weller@email.chop.edu.

WELLER, GERALD C. (JERRY WELLER), former United States Representative from Illinois; b. Streator, Ill., July 7, 1957; s. LaVern and Marilyn Weller; m. Zury Rios Sosa, Nov. 20, 2004; 1 child, Marizú Catherine. BS in Agrl., U. Ill., 1979. Aide to RepresentativeTom Corcoran US Congress, 1977-78; aide to sec USDA, 1981-85; active family farm, 1985-88; mem. Ill. House of Reps., 1987—93, US Congress from 11th Ill. dist., 1995—2009. Rep. Ho. Rep. steering com.; mem. Newt Gingrich's policy com., Ho. Rep. banking, vets. affairs, transp. and infrastructure coms. Mem. First Christian Ch., Morris, Ill. Mem.: Nat. Rep. Legis. Assn. Republican. Evangelical.*

WELLER, ROBERT STEPHEN, anesthesiologist; b. Syracuse, NY, Feb. 1, 1955; s. Elizabeth W Stein and Ralph N Weller; m. Elizabeth A McGowan, Nov. 30, 1991; children: Erin E Power, Jeffrey M McGowan, Kevin P McGowan. MD summa cum laude, Northwestern U., Chgo., 1979. Asst. prof. of anesthesiology U. of Conn. Sch. of Medicine, Farmington, Conn., 1984—91, assoc. prof. of anesthesiology, 1991—97, Wake Forest U. Sch. of Medicine, Winston-Salem, NC, 1997—2008, prof. anesthesiology, 2008—. Residency program dir. U. of Conn. Anesthesiology Dept., Farmington, Conn., 1986—96; cons. Am. Bd. Anesthesiology, 1984, 93, 2009. Recipient LB Arey award, Northwestern U. Sch. of Medicine, 1977, FK Rawson award, 1979, David Little award, Hartford Hosp. Anesthesiology Program, 1983; named Outstanding Tchr., Residents in Anesthesiology, 2001. Mem.: Internat. Anesthesia Rsch. Soc., Am. Soc. of Regional Anesthesia and Pain Medicine, Am. Soc. of Anesthesiologists. Office: Wake Forest University School of Med Medical Center Blvd Winston Salem NC 27157 Personal E-mail: rweller@triad.rr.com. E-mail: rweller@wfubmc.edu.

WELLES, FERNE BINGHAM MALCOLM, retired archivist; b. Fayetteville, Ark., June 2, 1921; d. William Thomas and Nellie E. (Coffey) Bingham; m. Eugene Glenn Malcolm, Sept. 5, 1940 (dec. 1975); children: Rebecca Malcolm Schubert, Rachel Malcolm-Woods, Eugene Glenn Malcolm Jr.; m. Edward Randolph Welles II, Nov. 2, 1984 (dec. 1991). AA, Penn Valley Coll., Kansas City, Mo., 1977; BA in Am. Culture, U. Mo., Kansas City, 1981, MA in History, 1986. Archival intern Regional Br. Nat. Archives, Kansas City, Mo., 1976; historian, archivist, hist. writer St. Luke's Hosp. Kansas City, 1975-85; archivist, historiographer, researcher Episc. Diocese West Mo., Kansas City, 1974-85; historian, archivist, writer Grace and Holy Trinity Cathedral, Kansas City, 1972-79, 86-87. Supr. grad students Emporia (Kans.) State U., 1983; presenter paper at history conf. Contbr. to numerous hist. publs. Pres. Kansas City Bus. and Profl. Women's Guild, 1982-83; mem. Women's C. of C., Kansas City, 1980-83; vestry mem. Grace and Holy Trinity Cathedral, 1982-84. Mem. AAUW (chmn. ednl. found. program 1989-92), Kansas City Area Archivists (edn. com.), Woman's City Club, Nat. Episc. Historians Assn., Phi Alpha Theta. Democrat. Episcopalian. Avocations: hiking, photography. Personal E-mail: fmwelles@aol.com.

WELLES, WANDA LIZAK, research scientist; b. Emsdetten, Germany, July 15, 1948; d. Michal and Helena Lizak; 1 child, Devon Michael. MS, Cornell U., Ithaca, NY, PhD, 1975. Project scientist Cleve. Clinic Found., Ohio, 1978—80; rsch. scientist NY State Dept. Health Ctr., Albany, 1980—2001; chief NY State Dept. Health, Troy, 2001—. Mem., vice chair Schenectady County Local Emergency Planning Com., NY, 1996—99; vol. Proctors, 1997—2008. Recipient Commrs. Recognition award, NY State Dept. Health, 2003. Achievements include development of NYSDOH chemical terrorism preparedness, response card and chemical terrorism wall chart. Avocations: gardening, reading, travel. Office: NY State Dept Health 547 River St Troy NY 12180-2216

WELLIN, KEITH SEARS, retired investment banker; b. Grand Rapids, Mich., Aug. 13, 1926; s. Elmer G. and Ruth (Chamberlin) W.; m. Carol D. Woodhouse, Sept. 5, 1951 (dec. 1970), m. Wendy C.H. Lane, Nov. 15, 2002; children: Cynthia Wellin Plum, Peter, Marjorie Wellin King. BA, Hamilton Coll., 1950; MBA, Harvard U., 1952. With E.F. Hutton & Co., Inc., Chgo., 1952-71, regional v.p., dir., 1962-66, pres. NYC, 1967-71; vice chmn., 1970-71; sr. v.p., treas., dir. Reynolds Securities Inc., 1971-74, pres., dir., 1974-78; exec. v.p., dir. Dean Witter Reynolds Orgn., 1978—2009; chmn. Dean Witter Reynolds Inter-Capital, 1978—2009; former vice chmn. Dean Witter Reynolds Inc. Chmn. bd. Moorco Internat., Houston; former gov., mem. exec. com. Assn. Stock Exchange Firms; mem. governing council Securities Industry Assn. Mem. investment com., trustee Hamilton Coll. Served to 2d lt., inf. AUS, 1945-47. Mem.: Knickerbocker (N.Y.C.); Clove Valley Rod and Gun (La Grangeville, N.Y.); Round Hill (Greenwich, Conn.); River Club. Home (Summer): Seaside Farm PO Box 335 Friendship ME 04547-0335 Office: c/o Dean Witter Reynolds 1345 Avenue Of The Americas New York NY 10105-0302 Home: John's Island 161 Coquille Way Vero Beach FL 32963

WELLINGHOFF, JON, commissioner; b. 1949; BS, U. Nev., 1971; MS, Howard U., 1972; JD, Antioch Coll., 1975. Dep. dist. atty. consumer fraud divisn., Washoe County, Nev., 1976—77; asst. majority staff counsel consumer com., commerce com. U.S. Senate, 1978; staff atty. energy and product info. divisn. FTC, 1978—79; adimstrv. asst. Pub. Utilities Commn., Nev., consumer advocate Nev., staff counsel Nev.; mng. prin. and regulatory atty. Efficiency Engergy Systems, Inc.; commr. Fed. Energy Regulatory Commn. (FERC), Washington, 2006—, acting chmn., 2009, chmn. Ptnr. Beckley Singleton. Office: Fed Energy Regulatory Commn 888 First St NE Washington DC 20426 Office Phone: 702-474-2629. Office Fax: 202-208-0064.*

WELLINGTON, HARRY HILLEL, lawyer, educator; b. New Haven, Aug. 13, 1926; s. Alex M. and Jean (Ripps) W.; m. Sheila Wacks, June 22, 1952; children: John, Thomas. AB, U. Pa., 1947; LLB, Harvard U., 1952; MA (hon.), Yale U., 1960; LLD, N.Y. Law Sch. Bar: D.C. 1952. Law clk. to U.S. Judge Magruder, 1953-54, Supreme Ct. Justice Frankfurter, 1955-56; asst. prof. law Stanford U., 1954-56; mem. faculty Yale U., 1956—, prof. law, 1960—, Edward J. Phelps prof. law, 1967-83, dean Law Sch., 1975-85, Sterling prof. law, 1983-92, Sterling prof. emeritus law, 1992—, Harry H. Wellington prof. lectr., 1995—; pres., dean, prof. law N.Y. Law Sch., NYC, 1992-2000, dean emeritus, prof., 2000—. Ford fellow London Sch. Econs., 1965; Guggenheim fellow; sr. fellow Brookings Instn., 1968-71; Rockefeller Found. fellow Bellagio Study and Conf. Ctr., 1984; faculty mem. Salzburg Seminar in Am. Studies, 1985; John M. Harlan disting. vis. prof. N.Y. Law Sch., 1985-86; review person ITT-SEC; moderator Asbestos-Wellington Group; cons. domestic and fgn. govtl. agys.; trustee N.Y. Law Sch.; bd. govs. Yale U. Press; mem. jud. panel, exec. com. Ctr. Public Resources Legal Program; Harry H. Wellington lectr., 1995—. Author: with Harold Shepherd) Contracts and Contract Remedies, 1957, Labor and the Legal Process, 1968, (with Clyde Summers) Labor Law, 1968, 2d edit., 1983, (with Ralph Winter) The Unions and the Cities, 1971, Interpreting the Constitution, 1990; contbr. articles to profl. jours. Mem. ABA, Bar Assn. Conn., Am. Law Inst., Am. Arbitration Assn., Am. Acad. Arts and Scis., Common Cause (nat governing bd.). Office: NY Law Sch 57 Worth St New York NY 10013-2959 also: Yale U Sch Law New Haven CT 06520

WELLINS, CORI, literary agent; m. Max Lagao, July 8, 2000. BA in History, UCLA, 1993. Head TV lit. FilmStew Inc.; asst. William Morris Agy., lit. agent, sr. v.p., head TV lit. devel. Actress (films) Arachnophobia, 1990. Named one of The 100 Most Powerful Women in Entertainment, Hollywood Reporter, 2006—07; named to Hollywood Reporters Next Generation List, 2004, Variety Womens Impact Report List, 2006, Broadcast & Cables Next Wave Women List, 2006. Office: WME Entertainment 9601 Wilshire Blvd 3rd Fl Beverly Hills CA 90210

WELLISZ, STANISLAW, economics professor; b. Warsaw, Mar. 28, 1925; came to U.S., 1941; s. Leopold and Jadwiga (Landau) W.; children: Tadeusz, Krzysztof. BA magna cum laude, Harvard Coll., 1946, MA, 1949; postgrad., U. Cambridge, England, 1949-52; PhD, Harvard U., 1953; D (hon.), Warsaw U., 1998. Asst. prof. U. Chgo., 1957-60, assoc. prof., 1960-63; prof. Columbia U., NYC, 1964-94, Kathryn and Shelby Cullom Davis prof. econs. and internat. affairs, 1994—2006, prof. emeritus, 2006—. Vis. prof. Warsaw U., 1989-97; adv. Polish Ministry Fin., 1989-91. Author: The Economics of the Soviet Bloc, 1964; co-author: The Political Economy of Growth, 1993; co-editor: Stabilization in Poland, 1993. NSF fellow, 1975, 82; named officer Polish Order Merit, Govt. Poland, 1997. Business E-Mail: sw11@columbia.edu.

WELLMAN, CARL PIERCE, philosophy educator; b. Lynn, Mass., Sept. 3, 1926; s. Frank and Carolyn (Heath) Wellman; m. Farnell Parsons, June 20, 1953; children: Timothy, Philip, Lesley, Christopher. BA, U. Ariz., 1949; MA, Harvard U., 1951, PhD, 1954; postgrad., U. Cambridge, Eng., 1951-52. Instr. Lawrence U., Appleton, Wis., 1953-57, asst. prof., 1957-62, assoc. prof., 1962-66, prof., chmn. dept. philosophy, 1966-68; prof. philosophy Washington U., St. Louis, 1968-88, Hortense and Tobias Lewin Disting. prof. humanities, 1988-99, Hortense and Tobias Lewin Disting. prof. emeritus, 1999—. Mem. rev. panel rsch. grants NEH, 1968—71. Author: The Language of Ethics, 1961, Challenge and Response: Justification in Ethics, 1971, Morals and Ethics, 1975, Welfare Rights, 1982, A Theory of Rights, 1985, Real Rights, 1995, An Approach to Rights, 1997, The Proliferation of Rights, 1999, Medical Law and Moral Rights, 2005. Recipient Uhrig Distinguished Teaching award Lawrence U., 1968; Am. Council Learned Socs. fellow, 1965-66; NEH sr. fellow, 1972-73; Nat. Humanities Center fellow, 1982-83 Mem.: Internat. Assn. for Philosophy Law and Social Philosophy (hon. pres.), Am. Philos. Assn. Home: 625 S Skinker Blvd # 902 Saint Louis MO 63105-2340 E-mail: cpwellma@artsci.wustl.edu.

WELLNER, JON AUGUST, statistician, educator; b. Portland, Oreg., Aug. 17, 1945; s. Charles August and Ethel Dorothy (Wolf) W.; m. Vera Dewey, Dec. 11, 1999. BS in Math., U. Idaho, 1968; PhD in Stats., U. Wash., 1975. Asst. prof. stats. U. Rochester, N.Y., 1975-78, assoc. prof. N.Y., 1978-83; prof. U. Wash., 1983—. Author: Empirical Processes with Applications to Statistics, 1986, Efficient and Adaptive Estimation for Semiparametric Models, 1993, Weak Convergence and Empirical Processes, 1996; contbr. articles to profl. jours. Served to lt. U.S. Army, 1969-71, Vietnam. Fellow John Simon Guggenheim Found., 1987-88. Fellow AAAS, Inst. Math. Stats. Am. Statis. Assn. (assoc. editor Annals of Stats. 1983-89, 92-94, editor 2001-03). Avocations: mountain climbing, skiing, photography. Home: 1947 14th Ave E Seattle WA 98112-2801 Office: U Wash Dept Stats Box 354322 Seattle WA 98195-4322 Office Phone: 206-543-6207. Business E-Mail: jaw@stat.washington.edu.

WELLNER, MARCEL NAHUM, research scientist, educator; b. Antwerp, Belgium, Feb. 8, 1930; came to U.S., 1949; s. Jules and Lucie (Rapoport) W.; m. Magdeleine Misselyn, Apr. 7, 1961; children: Pierre, Lucie. BS, MIT, 1952; PhD, Princeton U., 1958. Instr. Brandeis U., Waltham, Mass., 1957-59; mem. Inst. Advanced Study, Princeton, NJ, 1959-60; rsch. assoc. Ind. U., Bloomington, 1960-63; vis. scientist Atomic Energy Rsch. Establishment, Harwell, England, 1963-64; from asst. prof. to prof. Syracuse (N.Y.) U., 1964-95, prof. emeritus, 1995—; sr. rsch. scientist SUNY, Syracuse, 1995—. Author gen. physics textbook; contbr. numerous articles on quantum field theory, fractals and excitable media to profl. jours. Mem. Am. Phys. Soc. Office Phone: 315-464-8018. Business E-mail: wellnerm@upstate.edu.

WELLON, ROBERT G., lawyer; b. Port Jervis, NY, Apr. 18, 1948; s. Frank Lewis and Alice (Stevens) W.; m. Jan Montgomery, Aug. 12, 1972; children: Robert F., Alice Wynn. AB, Emory U., 1970; JD, Stetson Coll. Law, 1974. Assoc. Turner, Turner & Turner, Atlanta, 1974-78; ptnr. Ridley, Wellon, Schwieger & Brazier, Atlanta, 1978-86; of counsel Wilson, Strickland & Benson, Atlanta, 1987—2000; pvt. practice Atlanta, 2000—. Adj. prof. Atlanta Law Sch., 1981—94; adj. prof. law Emory U. Sch. of Law, 1995—. Gov.'s task force chmn. Atlanta 2000, 1978; exec. com., treas., 2nd v.p. Atlanta Easter Seals Soc., 1983-88; rep. Neighborhood Planning Unit, 1981-83; adminstrv. bd. Northside United Meth. Ch., 1996-99, Stephen min.; active Atlanta Sports Coun. With USAR, 1970-76. Named Super Lawyer, Atlanta Mag., 2004, 05, 06. Master: Charles Longstreet Weltner Family Law Inn of Ct. (founding pres. 1997—2000); fellow: Am. Bar Found.; mem.: Lawyers Found. of Ga., Atlanta Bar Found. (bd. dirs. 1996—), Am. Judicature Soc., Atlanta Bar Assn. (bd. dirs. 1978—88, pres. 1986—87, Atlanta continuing legal edn. bd. trustees 1994—97, del. to ho. of dels. 1999—2005, Charles E. Watkins Svc. award 1995, Disting. Svc. award 2005), State Bar. of Ga. (professionalism com. 1994—), Fla. Bar, Atlanta Found. for Psychoanalysis, Inc. (bd. dirs. 1994—, exec. com. 1997—), Old War Horse Lawyers Club, Lawyers Club Atlanta. Methodist. Office: Ste 1900 Promenade II 1230 Peachtree St NE Atlanta GA 30309 Home Phone: 404-355-4350; Office Phone: 404-942-3505. E-mail: rol@wellonfamilylaw.com.

WELLS, BARRY LEON, United States Ambassador to The Gambia; b. 1942; m. Winsome Wells; 2 children. BA in Psychology, MA in Social Work; attended, Fed. Exec. Inst.; attended exec. seminar, Aspen Inst. Country dir. US Peace Corps, Belize, Jamaica; joined Fgn. Svc. Inst., 1988—, assoc. dean, Sch. Profl. & Area Studies, assoc. dean Sr. Seminar & Leadership & Mgmt. Sch., dep. dir., 2001—05, acting dir., 2005—06; dir. Office Civil Rights US Dept. State, 2006—07, chief diversity officer, 2007, US amb. to The Gambia, 2008—. Assoc. prof., asst. dean Howard

U. Grad. Sch. Social Work, 1972—78; lectr. U. Pitts., Youngstown State U., U. West Indies; mem. Thursday Luncheon Group; bd. dirs. Nat. MultiCultural Inst. Recipient Superior Honor awards (3), US Dept. State, Meritorious Honor awards (2). Office: US Embassy 2070 Banjul Pl Washington DC 20521*

WELLS, BENJAMIN GLADNEY, lawyer; b. St. Louis, Nov. 13, 1943; s. Benjamin Harris and Katherine Emma (Gladney) W.; m. Nancy Kathryn Harpster, June 7, 1967; children: Barbara Gladney, Benjamin Harpster. BA magna cum laude, Amherst Coll., Mass., 1965; JD cum laude, Harvard U., 1968. Bar: Ill. 1968, Tex. 1973, U.S. Tax Ct. 1973, U.S. Ct. Claims 1975, U.S. Ct. Appeals (5th cir.) 1981, U.S. Dist. Ct. (so. dist.) Tex. 1985, U.S. Dist. Ct. (we. dist.) Tex. 1993. Assoc. Kirkland & Ellis, Chgo., 1968—69; assoc. to ptnr. Baker Botts, L.L.P., Houston, 1973—, chair, Firmwide Tax Dept., 2002—08. Contbr. articles to profl. jours. Mem. Harvard Legal Aid Bureau, 1966-68. Capt. US Army, JAGC, 1969-72. Fellow Am. Coll. Tax Counsel; mem. ABA (chair corp. tax com. sect. on taxation 2001-02), Houston Tax Roundtable (pres. 1994-95), The Forest Club, The Houston Club, Phi Beta Kappa. Presbyterian. Office: Baker Botts LLP One Shell Plaza 910 Louisiana St Ste 3330 Houston TX 77002-4995 Office Phone: 713-229-1210. Office Fax: 713-229-2810. Business E-Mail: benjamin.wells@bakerbotts.com.

WELLS, BUREN EARL, computer engineer, educator; b. Birmingham, Ala., Sept. 16, 1959; s. Buren Earl and Jane Wells; m. Jean Anne Haas, Dec. 30, 1983; children: Evelyn, Lillian, Buren Earl, Jane. BEE, U. Ala., Tuscaloosa, 1983, MEE, 1988, PhD, 1992. Grad. tchg. asst. U. Ala., 1983—84, grad. tchg., rsch. asst., 1988—92, asst. prof. Huntsville, 1992—98, assoc. prof., 1998—2005, prof., 2005—; engr. Harris Corp., Palm Bay, Fla., 1984—87. Prin. investigator NASA, Huntsville, 1999—2002, IPA constractor, 2003—04; prin. investigator Office Naval Rsch., Arlington, Va., 2003—06; cons. U. Space Rsch. Assn., Huntsville, 2005—06. Contbr. articles to sci. jours. Registered leader Boy Scouts America, Huntsville, 2007—08; sci. judge Weatherly Elem. Sch., Huntsville, 2007—08; deacon Southwood Presbyn. Ch., Huntsville, 2003—08. Named one of Best Paper awards, Internat. Symposium Performance Evaluation Computer and Telecom. Sys., 2005; Faculty fellowship, NASA, 1995—96, 2002. Mem.: IEEE, ACM. Avocations: tennis, hiking. Office: Univ Ala Huntsville 301 Sparkman Dr Huntsville AL 35899 Office Fax: 256-824-6803. Business E-Mail: wellsbe@uah.edu.

WELLS, CHARLES TALLEY, lawyer, retired state supreme court justice; b. Orlando, Fla., Mar. 4, 1939; BA, U. Fla., 1961, JD, 1964. Bar: Fla. 1965, US Dist. Ct. (mid. dist.) Fla., US Ct. Appeals (5th and 11th cirs.) 1966, US Supreme Ct. 1969, US Dist. Ct., US Dist. Ct. (so. dist.) Fla. 1976, US Ct. of Claims 1990. Trial atty. US dept justice, Washington, 1969; pvt. practice Maguire, Voohris and Wells, PA, Orlando, Fla., 1965—68, 1970—75, Wells, Gattis, Hollowes & Carpenter, PA, Orlando, Fla., 1976—94; justice Fla. Supreme Ct., Tallahassee, 1994—2009, chief justice, 2000—02; of counsel GrayRobinson PA, Orlando, Fla., 2009—. Active in Orange County Legal Aid Soc., 1968—94, mem. bd. trustees, 1988—89; bd. directors Conference of Chief Justices; mem. Federal Judicial Conference Standing Com. on Rules of Practice & Procedure. Former mem. bd. directors Orlando Area Chamber of Commerce, Orlando Jaycees, Orange County YMCA. Served in US Army. Fellow: Am. Bar Foundation; mem.: Tallahassee Bar Assn., ABA, Fla. Bar (bd. governors), Orange County Bar Assn. (pres. 1989—90). Methodist. Office: GrayRobinson PA Ste 1400 PO Box 3068 301 E Pine St Orlando FL 32802-3068 Office Phone: 407-843-8880. Office Fax: 407-244-5690.

WELLS, CHRISTINE LOUISE, physical education educator; b. Buffalo, Mar. 22, 1938; d. Harold Edward and Edythe Adelina (Burton) W. BS in Edn., U. Mich., 1959; MS, Smith Coll., 1964; PhD, Pa. State U., 1969. Phys. edn. tchr. Grosse Pointe (Mich.) Pub. Schs., 1959-62; instr. Smith Coll., Northampton, Mass., 1962-66; NDEA scholar Pa. State U., University Park, 1969-72; asst. prof. Dalhousie U., Halifax, N.S., Can., 1969-72; NIH postdoctoral fellow U. Calif., Santa Barbara, 1971-73; assoc. prof. Temple U., Phila., 1973-76, Ariz. State U., Tempe, 1976-80, prof., 1980—97. Lorraine C. Snell vis. prof. Northeastern U., Boston, 1984; mem. adv. bd. Rodale Press, Emmaus, Pa., The Women's Sports Found., Eisenhower Park, N.Y., 1992—98; presenter numerous papers in field, 1970—99; cons. U.S. Olympic Physiology Com., 1982-86, Granville Corp., 1982, Whittle Corp., 1986-91; mem. adv. bd. Internat. Dance-Exercise Assn., 1982-90, Melpomene Inst. Women's Health Rsch., 1983—97, Nat. Inst. Fitness and Sport, 1985-91. Author: Women, Sport and Performance: A Physiological Perspective, 1985, 2d edit., 1991, (with E.M. Haymes) Environment and Human Performance, 1986, (with others) Research and Practice in Physical Education, 1977, Female Endurance Athletes, 1986, Physical Activity and Human Well-Being, 1986, Future Directions in Exercise and Sport Science Research, 1989, Women in Sport, IOC Med. Com., Internat Fed. Sports Medicine, 2000, Healthy Hearts, Healthy Women, 2001; mem. editorial bd. Cycling Sci., 1990-94, Women in Sport and Phys. Activity Jour., 1990—96, biol. rev. editor; mem. adv. bd. Walking Mag., 1987—92, Time-Life Fitness Series, 1987, Moxie, 1989-90, Living Fit Mag., 1993-98, Fit Pregnancy Mag., 1993—96, Bicycling Mag., 1987—92, Runner's World, 1987-98; contbr. articles to profl. jours., chpts. to books; jour. reviewer in field. Alumni fellow Pa. State U., 1984; recipient Wonder Woman Found. award 1982, Women's Sport Found. Individual Contbn. to Women's Sports award 1983, Disting. Alumna award U. Mich., 1994. Fellow AAHPERD, Rsch. Consortium, (chmn. position statements 1976-77, pres. 1978-79, exec. v.p. search com. 1986, alliance scholar com. chair 1988-89), Am. Coll. Sports Medicine (trustee 1979-92, v.p. for edn. 1982-84, chmn. meetings evaluation 1976-77; pres. S.W. chpt. 1989-90, chmn. student breakfast 1984, position statements com. 1984, Citation award 1995, S.W. Chpt. Recognition award 1996); mem. Ariz. State Assn. of Health, Phys. Edn. and Recreation, Am. Acad. Kinesiology and Phys. Edn. (membership com. chairperson 1986-87, 93-94, program com. 1988-89), Mountaineers' Inc. (pres. 1995-98), Sigma Xi, Phi Lambda Theta, Phi Sigma. Avocations: bicycling, hiking, cross-country and downhill skiing, environmental activist. Personal E-mail: cwells@newmex.com.

WELLS, DAMON, investment company executive; b. Houston, May 20, 1937; s. Damon and Margaret Corinne W. BA magna cum laude, Yale U., 1958; BA, Oxford U., 1964, MA, 1968; PhD, Rice U., 1968. Owner, CEO Damon Wells Interests, Houston, 1958—; pres. Damon Wells Found., Houston, 1993—. Author: Stephen Douglas: The Last Years, 1857-61, 1971 (Tex. Writer's Roundup prize, 1971), paperback edit., 1990. Bd. dirs. Child Guidance Ctr. of Houston, 1970-73; trustee Christ Ch. Cathedral Endowment Fund, 1970-73, 84-88, chmn., 1987-88; trustee Kinkaid Sch., 1972-86, Camp Allen retreat of Episc. Diocese of Tex., 1976-78, Kinkaid Sch. Endowment Fund, 1981-86, Churchill Grave Trust, 2002—, Winston Churchill Found. U.S., 2003-; hon. friend of Somerville Coll., Oxford U., 1988—, mem. sr. common rm. Pembroke Coll., Oxford U., 1972-; founding bd. dirs. Brit. Inst. US, 1979-80; pres.'s coun. Tex. A&M U., 1983-89; hon. dir. Stephen A. Douglas Assn., 1975—; mem. Chancellors Ct. Benefactors, Oxford U., 2006—. Apptd. Hon. Comdr. Most Excellent Order of Brit. Empire by Her Majesty Queen Elizabeth II, 1991; named Outstanding Alumnus Yr. Kinkaid Sch., 1994; fellow Jonathan Edwards Coll. (assoc.), Yale U., 1982—, Sterling fellow Yale U., 2000—, hon. fellow Pembroke Coll., Oxford U., 1984—. Mem. English-Speaking Union (nat. dir. 1970-72, v.p. Houston br. 1966-73), Coun. Fgn. Rels., Houston Country Club, Houston Club, Yale Club (NYC), United Oxford and Cambridge U. Club (London), Cosmos Club (Washington), Buck's Club (London), Coronado Club (Houston), Little Ship Club (London). Phi Beta Kappa, Pi Sigma Alpha. Anglican. Home: 5555 Del Monte Dr Houston TX 77056-4100 Office: 2001 Kirby Dr Ste 806 Houston TX 77019-6088 Office Phone: 713-527-8966.

WELLS, DARREN R., manufacturing executive; b. Indpls., Dec. 25, 1965; 2 children. BA, DePauw U., Greencastle, Ind., 1987; MBA in Fin., Ind. U., Bloomington. Fin. analyst Ford Motor Credit Co., 1989—92, supr. fin. analysis, 1992—96, mgr. treasurer's office, 1996—97; contr. investment enterprises, fin. dir. Ford credit Ford Motor Co., Australia, 1998—2000; asst. treas. Visteon Corp., 2000—02; v.p., treas. Goodyear Tire & Rubber Co., 2002—05, sr. v.p. bus. devel., treas., 2005—07, sr. v.p. fin. and strategy, 2007—08, exec. v.p., CFO, 2008—. Office: Goodyear Tire & Rubber Co 1144 E Market St Akron OH 44316-0001 Office Phone: 330-796-2121. Office Fax: 330-796-2222.*

WELLS, DAVID LEE, sportscaster, retired professional baseball player; b. Torrance, Calif., May 20, 1963; Grad. high sch., San Diego. Pitcher Toronto Blue Jays, 1987—92, 1999—2001, Detroit Tigers, 1993-95, Cin. Reds, 1995, Balt. Orioles, 1996, NY Yankees, 1997-98, 2002—03, Chgo. White Sox, 2001, Boston Red Sox, 2005—06, San Diego Padres, 2004—05, 2006—07, LA Dodgers, 2007; Maj. League Baseball commentator, studio analyst TBS Sports, 2009—. Named to Am. League All-Star Team, 1995, 1998, 2000 Achievements include member of the World Series champion Toronto Blue Jays, 1992, NY Yankees, 1998; pitching a perfect game at Yankee Stadium against the Minnesota Twins, May 17, 1999. Office: c/o TBS Sports 10 Columbus Cir New York NY 10019*

WELLS, DENNIS J., dentist; Grad., Harvard U.; DDS, U. Tenn., 1983. Founder, dentist Nashville Ctr. for Aesthetic Dentistry. Dental cons. ABC's Extreme Makeover; clin. faculty PAC-Live, U. of the Pacific; lectr. in field. Mem.: Am. Acad. Cosmetic Dentistry (examiner in accreditation process, chpt. pres., President's Award 2001). Office: Nashville Ctr for Aesthetic Dentistry 105 Powell Ct Ste 101 Brentwood TN 37027 Office Phone: 614-371-8878. E-mail: info@drdenniswells.com.

WELLS, HUEY THOMAS, JR., lawyer; b. Gadsden, Ala., Mar. 22, 1950; s. Huey Thomas Sr. and Ruth (Allison) W.; m. Jan McKenzie, Dec. 29, 1972; children: Lynlee, Trey. BA with honors, U. Ala., Tuscaloosa, 1972, JD, 1975. Bar: Ala. 1975, US dist. Ct. (no. dist.) Ala. 1975, US Ct. Appeals (DC and 5th cirs.) 1977, US Supreme Ct. 1981, US Ct. Appeals (11th cir.) 1982, US Ct. Appeals Armed Forces, 2008; US Ct. Appeals (Fed. Ct.). Assoc. Cabaniss, Johnston, Gardner, Dumas & O'Neal, Birmingham, Ala., 1977-82, ptnr., 1983-84, Maynard, Cooper & Gale P.C., 1984—. Chmn. adv. com. on civil justice reform US Dist. (no. dist.) Ala., 1991-95. Legal co-chmn. championship Profl. Golf Assn., Birmingham, 1984, legal chmn., 1990; legal chmn. US Amateur Golf Championship, Birmingham, 1986. Served to capt. USAF, 1975-77. Mem. ABA (standing com. profl. disciple 1985-88, standing com. on environ. law 1988-94, chmn. environ. litig. com. of litig. sect. 1988-91, Ala. state del. 1992-2001, mem. coun. litig. sect. 1992-95, chair litig. sect. 1999-2000, chair house dels. 2002-04, pres. 2008-09, ex-officio mem. bd. govs. 2009-), Birmingham Bar Assn. (law day com., grievance com., divsn. dir. litig. sect. 1991-92), Ala. Bar Assn. (jud. liaison). Roman Catholic. Avocations: golf, softball, reading. Office: Maynard Cooper & Gale PC 2400 Regions Harbert Plz 1901 6th Ave N Ste 2400 Birmingham AL 35203-2618 Home Phone: 205-595-2095; Office Phone: 205-254-1062. Business E-Mail: twells@maynardcooper.com.

WELLS, JAMES M., III, bank executive; b. 1946; AB in English, U. NC, Chapel Hill, 1968; student, Rutgers U. Stonier Grad. Sch. Banking. Mgmt. trainee United Va. Bankshares, 1968-71, corp. adminstrv. officer, sec., 1971; br. officer, mgr. United Va. Bankshares/State-Planters, 1971-74; v.p., treas. United Va. Mortgage Corp., 1974-79; pres., CEO United Va. Leasing Corp., 1974-79; exec. v.p. United Va. Bank, Norfolk, Va., 1979-83, pres. Ea. region, 1983-85, exec. v.p. corp. banking, 1985-86, exec. v.p. banking group, 1986-88; pres. Crestar Fin. Corp, Richmond, Va., 1988—2000, CEO, 2000; vice chmn. SunTrust Banks Inc., Atlanta, 2000—04, pres., COO, 2004—06, pres., CEO, 2007—08, chmn., CEO, 2008—. Bd. dirs. Visa USA. Office: SunTrust Banks Inc PO Box 4418 Atlanta GA 30308-4418 Office Phone: 404-588-7711. Office Fax: 404-827-6173.*

WELLS, JAMES WAYNE, retired secondary school educator; b. Birmingham, Ala., Feb. 13, 1941; s. William Edward and Margaret Louise (Wainwright) W.; m. Jan. 30, 1965; children: Erin Elizabeth,Risa Kathryne. BS, U. Ala., 1963; postgrad., No. Ariz. U., 1975, U. Ala., 1987, Calif. State U., San Bernadino, 1994. Sci. tchr. Rockdale County HS, Conyers, Ga., 1964-67; Spanish tchr. Charlotte Country Day Sch., NC, 1967-69; tchr. math. Charles Hard Sch., Bessemer, Ala., 1970-72; sci. tchr. Hayes HS, Birmingham, Ala., 1973-74; biology tchr. Chinle HS, Ariz., 1974-87, Jess Lahier HS, Bessemer, 1987-88; dir. Scouting Report of Ariz., Phoenix, 1988-89; ESL tchr. Calif. Dept. Corrections, Blythe, Calif., 1990—2002; ret. Mem. Calif. Prof. Educator Assn., Scottsdale C. of C. (com. mem. pub. affairs 1988). Democrat. Lutheran. Avocations: basketball, golf, franklin mint collector. Home: 195 Eunice Cir Blythe CA 92225-1333 Office: Chuckawalla Valley State Prison PO Box 2289 Blythe CA 92226-2289 Office Phone: 602-692-9131. Personal E-mail: jwells9820@aol.com.

WELLS, JOHN TIMOTHY, pediatric neurologist; MD, Sch. Med. SUNY, Stony Brook, 1988. Cert. Am. Bd. Pediatrics, 1991, in Child Neurology Am. Bd. Pediatrics, 1996. Resident in pediatrics Long Island Jewish Med. Ctr., 1988—91; fellow in neurology NYU Med. Ctr., 1991—94; fellow in pediatric neurology Yale Univ., 1994—95; clinical assoc. prof., Dept. Neurology NYU Med. Ctr., NYC. Contbr. articles to profl. jours. Office: NYU Dept Neurology 109 E 67th St New York NY 10021 Office Phone: 212-772-6683. Office Fax: 212-452-3131.

WELLS, JULIA ELIZABETH See DAME ANDREWS, JULIE

WELLS, KAREN, food service company executive; Grad., Xavier U., Cin. Various positions including mktg. supr. Raleigh region to mktg mgr. McDonald's Corp. USA, 1992—2003, v.p. gen. mgr. Indpls. region, 2003—06, v.p. strategy/innovation, 2003—. Named a Woman to Watch, Fortune mag., 2008. Office: McDonald's Corp 2111 McDonald's Dr Oak Brook IL 60523*

WELLS, KELLY L., media specialist; b. Columbus, Ga., Feb. 16, 1974; d. James Thomas and Charlene Rose Lambert; m. Michael Keith Wells; children: Drew Keegan, Maddie Rose. MS, U. West Ga., Carrolton, 2007. Cert. tchr. Ga. Elem. sch. tchr. Brewer Elem., Columbu, 1997—2003, libr. media specialist, 2003—08, 2008—. Fund raiser Northern Little League, Columbus, 2008—. Home: 4135 Durwood Dr Columbus GA 31907 Office: Brewer Elem 2951 Martin Luther King Blvd Columbus GA 31906

WELLS, LESLEY, federal judge; b. Muskegon, Mich., Oct. 6, 1937; d. James Franklin and Inez Simpson Wells; m. Charles F. Clarke, Nov. 13, 1998; children: Lauren Elizabeth, Caryn Alison, Anne Kristin, Thomas Eliot. BA, Chatham Coll., 1959; JD cum laude, Cleve. State U., 1974. Bar: Ohio 1975, US Dist. Ct. (no. dist.) Ohio 1975, US Supreme Ct. 1989. Pvt. practice, Cleve., 1975; ptnr. Brooks & Moffet, Cleve., 1975—78; dir., atty. ABAR Litig. Ctr., Cleve., 1979—80; assoc. Schneider, Smeltz, Huston & Ranney, Cleve., 1980—83; judge Ct. Common Pleas, Cleve., 1983—94, US Dist. Ct. (no. dist.) Ohio, Cleve., 1994—2006, sr. judge, 2006—. Adj. prof. law and urban policy Cleve. State U., 1980-83, 90-93. Editor, author: Litigation Manual, 1980. Past pres. Cleve. Legal Aid Soc.; legal chmn. Nat. Women's Polit. Caucus, 1981-82; chmn. Gov.'s Task Force on Family Violence, Ohio, 1983-87; mem. biomed. ethics com. Case Western Res. U. Med. Sch., 1985-94; mem. NW Ordinance US Constn. Commn., Ohio, 1986-88; master William K. Thomas Inn of Ct., 1989—, counselor, 1993, pres., 1998-99; trustee Rosemary Ctr., 1986-92, Miami U., 1988-92, Urban League Cleve., 1989-90, Chatham Coll., 1989-94, mem. Cleve.-Marshall Coll. Law Nat. Av. Coun., 2003-, Aspen Inst. Justice and Soc. Program, 2006. Recipient Superior Jud. award Supreme Ct. Ohio, 1983, J. Irwin award Womenspace, Ohio, 1984, award Womens City Club, 1985, Disting. Alumna award Chatham Coll., 1988, Alumni Civic Achievement award Cleve. State U., 1992, Golden Gavel award Ohio Judges Assn., 1994, Outstanding Alumni award Cleve. Marshall Law Alumni Assn., 1994, Greater Cleve. Achievement award YWCA, 1995. Mem. ABA (coun. litigation sect. 1996-99), Am. Law Inst., Ohio Bar Assn., Ohio Womens Bar Assn., Cleve. Bar Assn. (Merit Svc. award 1983), Cuyahoga County Bar Assn., Nat. Assn. Women Judges, Philos. Club Cleve., Fed. Judges Assn. Office: 328 US Court House 201 Superior Ave Cleveland OH 44114-1234 Office Phone: 216-615-4480.

WELLS, LINDA ANN, editor-in-chief; b. NYC, Aug. 9, 1958; d. H. Wayne and Jean (Burchell) W.; m. Charles King Thompson, Nov., 1993. BA in English, Trinity Coll., 1980. Edit. asst. Vogue Mag., NYC, 1980-83, assoc. editor beauty, 1983-85; style reporter New York Times, NYC, 1985, beauty editor, food editor, 1985-90; founding editor, editor-in-chief Allure Mag., NYC, 1990—. Spkr. Am. Womens' Econ. Devel., NY, 1988-89, Brand Futures Group, NY, 1999. Contbr. numerous articles to NY Times Mag., Allure Mag., 1985—; appearances on Today Show, The View, Entertainment Tonight, E!, CNN. Chmn. NY Shakespeare Festival, 1993, 94; bd. fellows Trinity Coll., 1998—; bd. visitors Mary Inst. Country Day Sch., St. Louis. Recipient Fragrance Found. award 1991, 99, 2000, 2001, Nat. Mag. Design award, 1994, Legal Def. and Edn. Fund Equal Opportunity award NOW, 1994, Trinith Coll. Alumni Achievement award, 2000, Cosmetic Exec. Women Achiever award, 2001, Skin Sense Award, Skin Cancer Found., 2003; named one of Most Powerful Fashion Editors, Forbes, 2006. Mem. Am. Soc. Mag. Editors (bd. dirs. 1993-97). Office: Allure Mag Conde Nast Publs 4 Times Sq Fl 10 New York NY 10036-6522

WELLS, MARY ELIZABETH THOMPSON, deacon, chaplain, spiritual director, iconographer; b. Dallas, Oct. 9, 1936; d. Owen Perry and Ruth Marie Thompson; children: Tadd Whitney, Britony Ruth. BA in Sociology, Syracuse U., 1958; MA in Child Devel., Tufts U., 1964, MEd in Counseling Psychology, 1974; MA in Theology, St. Vincent de Paul Regional Sem., 2005. Ordained min. Diocese of Southeast Fla., 2002. Asst. dir. pub. rels. Inst. Crippled and Disabled, NYC, 1958-59; head tchr. Eliot-Pearson Children's Sch., Tufts U., Medford, Mass., 1964-66; psychotherapist Mental Health Ctr. Greater Cape Ann, Gloucester, Mass., 1974-89; deacon, chaplain, spiritual dir. St. Paul's Episcopal Ch., Delray Beach, Fla., 1999—2007, dir./dean Diocesan Sch. S.E. Fla., 2003—07; missioner ministry with aging Diocese Va., 2008—; Deacon Christ Episcopal Ch., Gordonsville, Va., 2009—. Mem.: APA, Spiritual Dirs. Internat., Assn. Profl. Chaplains, Assn. Clin. Pastoral Educators, Am. Orthopsychiatric Assn., Piedmont Sportsmen Club, Dolly Madison Garden Club. Home: 231 Spring Hill Dr Gordonsville VA 22942

WELLS, MARY JULIA, psychologist; b. Arlington, Va., Nov. 23, 1958; d. John Murrell and Rollene Sumner Wells. BS, Va. Commonwealth U., 1980; MPhil, George Wash. U., 1988, PhD, 1990. Lic. clin. psychologist Va., 1991. Psychology assoc. Wash. Pain and Rehab Ctr., Wash., DC, 1988—90; asst. prof. Med. Coll. Va., Richmond, Va., 1990—93; clin. psychologist Inst. Chronic Pain Mgmt., Richmond, 1993—96, pvt. practice, Richmond, 1996—2000, Sheltering Arm Hosp., Richmond, 2000—. Contbr. chapters to books. Pres. Richmond Acad. Clin. Psychologists, Richmond, Va., 1995—96, mem. chair, 2002—04, pres., 2005; anti racism trainer Unitarian, Universalist Assn., Richmond, Va., 1999. Mem.: Am. Psychological Assn., Va. Psychological Assn., Richmond Acad. Clin. Psychologists. Democrat. Unitarian. Avocations: music, dogs. Office: Sheltering Arms Physical Rehab Hosp 8254 Atlee Rd Mechanicsville VA 23116 Office Phone: 804-723-3275. Business E-Mail: mwells@shelteringarms.com.

WELLS, MELANIE KAY, marriage and family therapist, director; d. Charles Ronald and Dorothy Wells. BA in English, Southern Meth. U., Dallas, 1985; MS in Counseling Psychology, Our Lady Lake U., San Antonio, Tex., 1992; MA in Bibl. Studies, Dallas Theol. Sem., 1994. Lic. profl. counselor Tex. State Bd. Examiners, 1993, marriage & family therapist 1994. Pvt. practice therapist, Various, Tex., 1992—; founder & dir. LifeWorks Group, P.A., Dallas, 2000—. Supr. Tex. State Bd. Examiners Lic. Marriage & Family Therapist, Dallas, 1998—, Tex. State Bd. Examiners Lic. Profl. Counselor, Dallas, 1998—. Author: (novels) When the Day of Evil Comes, The Soul Hunter, My Soul to Keep. Bible study leader pvt., Dallas, Tex., 1986—2009. Mem.: Am. Assn. Marriage & Family Therapy (clin. mem. 1994—). Avocation: violin. Office: The LifeWorks Group PA 2515 Cedar Springs Rd Dallas TX 75201 Business E-Mail: writemelanie@earthlink.net.

WELLS, MELISSA FOELSCH, retired ambassador; b. Tallinn, Estonia, Nov. 18, 1932; emigrated to U.S., 1936, naturalized, 1941; d. Kuno Georg and Miliza (Korjus) Foelsch; m. Alfred Washburn Wells, 1960; children: Christopher, Gregory. BS in Fgn. Service, Georgetown U., 1956. Fgn. svc. officer Dept. State, Washington, 1958-61, consular officer Trinidad, 1961-64; econ. officer mission OECD, Paris, 1964-66; econ. officer London, 1966-71; internat. economist, 1971-73; dep. dir. maj. export projects Dept. Commerce, 1973-75; comml. counselor Brazil, 1975-76; amb. to Guinea-Bissau and Cape Verde Dept. of State, 1976-77; U.S. rep. ECOSOC, UN, NYC, 1977-79; resident rep. UNDP, Kampala, Uganda, 1979-81, dir. IMPACT program Geneva, 1982-86; amb. to Mozambique, 1987-90; amb. to Zaire, Kinshasa, 1991-93; under-sec. gen. for adminstrn. and mgmt. UN, NYC, 1993-94; consul gen. Sao Paulo, Brazil, 1995-97; amb. to Republic of Estonia, 1998—2001; ret., 2001. Bd. dirs. U.S.-Baltic Found. Mem. Am. Fgn. Service Assn., Am. Acad. Diplomacy. Office: Casa Wells Plz Leoncio Bento 7 38830 Agulo Gomera La Gomera Canary Islands Spain

WELLS, NINA MITCHELL, Secretary of State, New Jersey; b. 1950; m. Theodore V. Wells; 2 children. BA, Newton Coll. of Sacred Heart, 1973; JD, Suffolk U. Atty. Bell Comms. Rsch., 1985; dir. div. rate counsel NJ Pub. Advocate; dir. minority student program and fin. aid Rutgers U. Sch. Law, asst. dean, 1996—97; v.p. pub. affairs Schering-Plough Corp., Kenilworth, NJ, 1998—2004; sec. state State of NJ, Trenton, 2006—. Pres. Schering-Plough Found. Recipient Garden State Bar Assn. award, 2005. Democrat. Office: Office Sec of State PO Box 300 Trenton NJ 08625 Office Phone: 609-984-1900. Office Fax: 609-292-9897. E-mail: feedback@sos.state.nj.us.

WELLS, RAYMOND O'NEIL, JR., mathematics professor, researcher; b. Dallas, June 12, 1940; s. Raymond O. and Hazel (Rand) W.; m. Rena Schwarze, Aug. 1, 1963; children: Richard Andrew, René Michael. BA, Rice U., 1962; MS, NYU, 1964, PhD, 1965. Asst. prof. math. Rice U., Houston, 1965-69, assoc. prof., 1969-74, prof. math., 1974-2000, prof. edn., 1993-2000; chmn. dept. math., 1976-79; chmn. dept. edn. Rice U., Houston, 1994-98, dir. sch. math. project, 1987-2000, dir. computational math. lab., 1990-2000, prof. math emeritus, 2000—, asst. to pres., 2000-01; v.p. external affairs, prof. math. Internat. U., Bremen, 2001—05, disting. prof. math., 2005—06, Jacobs U., Bremen, 2007—. Vis. asst. prof. Brandeis U., Waltham, Mass., 1967-68; vis. prof. U. Göttingen, Germany, 1974-75, U. Colo., Boulder, 1983-84, U. Bremen, Germany, 1995-96, Internat. U. Bremen, 1998-2001; adj. prof. cmty. medicine Baylor Coll. Medicine, 1994-2000; active Inst. for Advanced Study, Princeton, N.J., 1970-71, 79-80; exch. visitor NAS, Sofia, Bulgaria, 1984; planning com. Internat. U., Bremen, 1997-99. Author: Differential Analysis on Complex Manifolds, 1973, Mathematics in Civilization, 1973, Twister Geometry and Field Theory, 1990, Wavelet Analysis: The Scaleable Structure of Information, 1998; editor: Mathematical Heritage of Herman Weyl, 1989, (book series) Expositions in Mathematics, 1988—2003, The Founding of International University Bremen: Perspectives for the Twenty First Century, 2003; contbr. numerous articles to sci. jours. Pres. Stages Repertory Theater, Houston, 1989-90; sec. bd. dirs. Jacobs U. Found. Am., Inc., 2004—, mem. bd. dirs., Jacobs U. Alumni & Friends Stiffing, GmbH, 2009-. Recipient Alexander von Humboldt Sr. U.S. Scientist award U. Göttingen, 1974-75; Fulbright fellow, 1968, Guggenheim fellow, 1974. Fellow AAAS (coun. 1989—); mem. Am. Math. Soc. (coun., editor 1978-88), Cosmos Club Washington, Carl Schurz Deutsch Am. Club (pres. 2002-). Home: Lüder-von-Bentheim Str 12 28209 Bremen Germany Office: Jacobs U Bremen PO Box 750561 28725 Bremen Germany Home Phone: 49 421 6520669; Office Phone: 49 421 200 4321. Business E-Mail: wells@jacobs-university.de.

WELLS, ROBERT HARTLEY, chemist, consultant; b. Springfield, Mass., Mar. 23, 1926; s. Cecil and Anna (Coates) W.; m. Mary G. Frinzi, May 30 1952 (wid. May 1969); children: Michael J., Brian H., Donald L.; m. Alice G. Asplund, June 20, 1970. BS in Chemistry, U. Maine, 1948, MS in Chemistry, 1950. Instr. in chemistry Lafayette Coll., Easton, Pa., 1950-51; rsch. chemist Celanese Corp., Summit, NJ, 1952-56, S.D. Warren, Westbrook, Maine, 1956-58; epoxy rsch. engr. CIBA Corp., Toms River, NJ, 1958-66; sect. head Foundry Products Borden Cem., Bainbridge, NY, 1966-70; sr. rsch. engr. Amoco Chem., Naperville, Ill., 1970-73; product mgr. epoxies Wilmington Chem., Del., 1973-76; product mgr. epoxy resins AZS Corp., Lakeland, Fla., 1976-83; cons. chemist Lakeland, 1983—. Contbr. articles to profl. jours.; photographer exhibits in field. Mem. Toms River Sch. Bd., 1962-66, Garden State Symphony, Toms River, 1963-66; pres. Toms River Jaycees, 1962; photographer SPCA, Lakeland, 1993-2001; vol. photographer Fla. Presbyn. Homes, 1997—; photographer Lakeland Vols. in Medicine, 2001—. Sgt. U.S. Army, 1944-46. Mem. AAAS, Am. Chem. Soc., Photog. Soc. (mem. chmn. 1993-95, Merit Svc. award 1994), Photog. Soc. Am., Am. Contract Bridge League, Polk County Camera Club (pres. 1988-91), Sigma Xi, Kappa Phi Kappa. Republican. Methodist. Achievements include patents in field. E-mail: aspwells@netzero.com.

WELLS, ROGER STANLEY, software engineer; b. Seattle, Apr. 13, 1949; s. Stanley A. and Margaret W. BA, Whitman Coll., 1971; postgrad., U. Tex., Austin, 1973—74; BS, Oreg. State U., 1977. Software evaluation engr. Tektronix, Beaverton, Oreg., 1979—83; computer engr. Aramco, Dhahran, Saudi Arabia, 1983—84; software engr. Conrac Corp., Clackamas, Oreg., 1984—85, Duarte, Calif., 1985; software analyst Lundy Fin. Systems, San Dimas, Calif., 1986—89; pvt. practice Seattle, 1989—92; sr. project engr. Illuminet, Olympia, Wash., 1993—2000; mgr. configuration New Edge Networks, Vancouver, Wash., 2000; sr. product engr. Wind River Systems, Beaverton, 2000—01; tech. advisor E-corps Wash. Svc. Corps, 2002—04; software builder Volt Tech. Resources, 2004—05; computer process specialist Boeing, 2005—. Adv. to chair Cascadia N.Am. Sci. Fiction Conf., 2003—05; mem. Exec. of Yr. com. Illuminet, Olympia, 1998—99. Bd. dirs. Lydia Whitney Found., Collinsville, Conn., Found. for Preservation Sci. Fiction and Fantasy Memorabilia, Salem, Oreg.; co-founder, bd. dirs., pres. Oreg. Sci. Fiction Conv., 1979-81; vol. Americorps, Yakima, Wash., 2002-03, Pasco, Wash., 2003-04, ARC, 2004-06; Boeing vol. disaster responder, 2006-. Recipient R. L. Fanthorpe grand prize, Write-Alike Contest, 2006. Mem. IEEE, Am. Philatelic Soc., Nat. Assn. Parliamentarians, Am. Inst. Parliamentarians (chpt. v.p. 1996-97, pres. 1997-98), Fantasy Amateur Press Assn., N.W. Sci. Fiction Soc., Mensa, Assn. Computing Machinery, L.A. Sci. Fantasy Soc., Melbourne (Australia) Sci. Fiction Club, Toastmasters Internat. (club pres. 1980, v.p. edn. 1994-95, area gov. 1994-95, dist. 32 parliamentarian 1996-99), Internat. Platform Assn. (2d place Monologue contest 1997, conv. com. 1998-99, bd. govs. 1999-2000, 2008-. Achievements include design of software program to transfer billing records for regional telephone companies. Avocations: travel, public speaking, science fiction, stamp collecting/philately. Home: PO Box 69254 Seatac WA 98168-9254 Office: PMB 178 15031 Military Rd S Ste B Seatac WA 98188 Personal E-mail: rswells@acm.org.

WELLS, ROGER W., lawyer; b. Sioux Falls, SD, May 7, 1957; BSBA summa cum laude, Creighton U., 1979, JD summa cum laude, 1981. Bar: Nebr. 1981, U.S. Dist. Ct. Nebr. 1981, U.S. Tax Ct. 1981. Gen. counsel ConAgra Foods Inc., Omaha, 2002; head, mergers and acquisitions McGrath, North, Mullin & Kratz, Omaha, 1981—. Mem. edtl. staff: Creighton U. Law Rev., 1980—81. Mem.: ABA (mem. corp., banking and bus. sect., mem. taxation sect., mem. internat. law sect.), Omaha Bar Assn., Nebr. Bar Assn., Beta Gamma Sigma. Office: McGrath North Mullin and Kratz PC Ste 3700 1st Nat Tower 1601 Dodge St Omaha NE 68102 Home Phone: 402-498-0941; Office Phone: 402-341-3070. Business E-Mail: rwells@mnmk.com.

WELLS, SAMUEL ALONZO, JR., surgeon, educator; b. Cuthbert, Ga., Mar. 16, 1936; s. Samuel Alonzo and Martha Steele W.; m. Barbara Anne Atwood, Feb. 13, 1964; children: Sarah, Susan. Student, Emory U., 1954—57, MD, 1961. Intern Johns Hopkins Hosp., Balt., 1961—62, resident in internal medicine, 1962—63; asst. resident in surgery Barnes Hosp., St. Louis, 1963—64; resident in surgery Duke U., Durham, NC, 1966—70; guest investigator dept. tumor biology Karolinska Inst., Stockholm, 1967—68; asst. prof. surgery Duke U., Durham, NC, 1970—72, assoc. prof., 1972—76, prof., 1976—81; clin. assoc. surgery br. Nat. Cancer Inst., NIH, Bethesda, Md., 1964—66, sr. investigator surgery br., 1970—72, cons. surgery br., 1975—; prof., chmn. dept. surgery Washington U., St. Louis, 1981—98; dir. ACS, Chgo., 1998—99, group chair, prin. investigator, oncology group, 1998—2005, exec. dir. internat. thyroid cancer study group, 2005—09; sr. clin. surgery br. Nat. Cancer Inst. Dir. Duke U. Clin. Rsch. Ctr., 1978—81; mem. Residency Rev. Com. Surgery, 1987—93, chmn., 1991—93; mem. bd. regents ACS, 1989—98, vice chmn. bd. regents, 1998—; prof. surgery Duke U. Sch. Medicine, 2001—07. Mem. editl. bd.: Annals of Surgery, 1975—93, Surgery, 1975—93, Jour. Surg. Rsch., 1981—93, editor in chief: World Jour. Surgery, 1983—92, Current Problems in Surgery, 1989—. Pres. GM Cancer Rsch. Found., 1996—2006. Lt. comdr. USPHS, 1964—66. Fellow: AAAS; mem.: ACS, Soc. Internationale de Chirurgie (pres. 2001), Soc. Surg. Oncology (pres. 1993—94), Halsted Soc. (pres. 1987), Nat. Cancer Adv. Bd., Inst. Medicine of NAS, Am. Soc. Clin. Investigation, Soc. Clin. Surgery (treas. 1980—86, v.p. 1986—88, pres. 1988—90), Soc. Univ. Surgeons (exec. coun. 1976—78), Am. Surg. Assn. (mem. coun. 1986—91, pres. 1995—96, recorder, Sci. Achievement medallion 2004), Am. Bd. Surgery (exec. com. 1986—89, vice chmn. 1987—88, chmn. 1988—89), Alpha Omega Alpha. Office: Nat Cancer Inst NIH Bldg 10 Room 3-2571 MSC 1206 9000 Rockville Pike Bethesda MD 20892 Office Phone: 301-435-7854. Business E-Mail: wellss@mail.nih.gov.

WELLS, STEPHEN MICHAEL, engineering educator; s. Wells; m. Sabrina Wells. MS, U. Tenn., Knoxville, 1980. Asst. prof. basic engring. Tenn. Tech U., Cookeville, 1980—. Engring. orientation fair coord. Coll. Engring., Cookeville, 1996—. Mem.: Am. Assn. Engring. Educators. Business E-Mail: mwells@tntech.edu.

WELLS, THEODORE V., JR., (TED WELLS), lawyer; b. Washington, Apr. 28, 1950; m. Nina Mitchell, 1972; 2 children. BA, Coll. Holy Cross, 1972; MBA, Harvard U., 1976; JD, Harvard Law Sch., 1976. Bar: NJ 1977, DC 2001, NY 2001, US Supreme Ct., US Ct. Appeals (3rd and 9th cirs.), DC Ct. Appeals, US Dist. Ct. (dist. NJ and so. dist. NY). Law clk. to Hon. John J. Gibbons US Ct. Appeals (3rd cir.), 1976-77; ptnr. Lowenstein, Sandler, Kohl, Fisher & Boylan, P.C., Roseland, NJ, 1977—2000; ptnr., co-chair litig. dept. Paul, Weiss, Rifkind, Wharton & Garrison, LLP, NYC, 2000—. Mem. adj. faculty trade regulation Sch. Law, Seton Hall U., 1980-81; mem. faculty trial advocacy Practicing Law Inst., 1982—; mem. lawyers adv. com. US Ct. Appeals (3rd cir.), 1982-85, 88—; former mem. bd. dirs. CIT Corp.; co-chair White Collar Criminal Sect. Nat. Assn. Criminal Def. Lawyers; gen. counsel NJ Dem. Party; tchg. team mem. Harvard Law Sch. Trial Advocacy Workshop; lectr. in field. Bd. trustees Coll. Holy Cross, 1977—, Newark Mus., 1979-82, NJ Performing Arts Ctr., NAACP Legal Def. Fund; bd. dirs. Essex County Urban League, 1979-88; NJ co-chairperson United Negro Coll. Fund; gen. counsel, NJ NAACP; fin. chmn. Bill Bradley's presdl. campaign, 2000. Named Lawyer of Yr., Nat. Law Jour., 2006; named one of 75 Best Lawyers in Washington, Washingtonian survey mag., 2002, America's Top Black Lawyers, Black Enterprise mag., 2003, 100 Most Influential Lawyers in America, Nat. Law Jour., 2006, 50 Most Influential Minority Lawyers in America, 2008; named to Power 150, Ebony mag., 2008. Fellow Am. Trial Lawyers Assn.; mem. ABA (antitrust law sect., state antitrust law subcommittee 1980—), Assn. Criminal Def. Lawyers (trustee 1984—), NJ State Bar Assn. (antitrust law com. 1980—) Office: Paul Weiss Rifkind Wharton & Garrison LLP 1285 Ave of the Americas New York NY 10019-6064 Office Phone: 212-373-3089. Office Fax: 212-373-2217. E-mail: twells@paulweiss.com.*

WELLS, THOMAS B., federal judge; b. Akron, Ohio, 1945; BS, Miami U., 1967; JD, Emory U., 1973; LLM, NYU, 1978. Atty. Graham & Wells, Vidalia, Ga., 1973—77; city atty. City of Vidalia, Ga., 1975—77; county atty. Toombs County, Ga., 1975—77; atty. Hurt, Richardson, Garner, Todd & Cadenhead, Atlanta, 1978—81, Shearer & Wells, Atlanta, 1981—86; judge US Tax Ct., Washington, 1986—, chief judge, 1997, 2000—04. With USNR, 1967—70. Recipient Disting. Alumnus award, Emory Law Alumni, 2001. Office: US Tax Ct 400 2nd St NW Washington DC 20217-0002 Office Phone: 202-521-0790.*

WELLS, W. DAVID, lawyer; b. Denver, Feb. 19, 1939; s. Warren C. and Ruth L. Wells; m. Rita Hirsch; children: Leslie, John, Peter. AB, Princeton U., NJ, 1961; JD, U. Nebr., Lincoln, 1964. Bar: Mo. 1965, Ill. 2000. Assoc. Thompson Mitchell, St. Louis, 1964—70; ptnr. Thompson Coburn, St. Louis, 1970—. Adj. prof. Washington U. Sch. Law, St. Louis. Trustee St. Louis Art Mus.; bd. dirs. Bi-state chpt. ARC, St. Louis. Fellow: Am. Coll. Trial Lawyers; mem.: Am. Bd. Trial Advocates, Best Lawyers in Am. Office: Thompson Coburn LLP 1 US Bank Plaza Saint Louis MO 63101

WELLS, WINSTON RAYMOND, political science professor; b. Radford, Va., Jan. 14, 1966; s. William Raymond and Margaret Santen Wells; m. Sara T. Meek, July 14, 2007; children: Matthew Flesher, Lynsey Flesher, Eric. BA, Northwestern U., Evanston, Ill., 1988; PhD in Polit. Sci., UCLA, 1997. Assoc. prof. Ill. Coll., Jacksonville, 1998—, coord. internat. studies program, 1998—. Mem. World Affairs Coun. West-Central Ill., Jacksonville, 2003—08. Recipient Harry Joy Dunbaugh Disting. Prof. award, Ill. coll., 2002, 2008; fellowship, 1993—94, Fullbright fellowship, 1993—94. Mem.: Ghana Studies Coun., African Studies Assn., Am. Polit. Sci. Assn., Pi Sigma Alpha. Office: Ill Coll 1101 W Coll Ave Jacksonville IL 62650 Business E-Mail: wwells@ic.edu.

WELLS-HENDERSON, RONALD JOHN, investment counselor; b. Jan. 28, 1934; s. William Noel and Sylvia Mary (Gowen) W.-H.; children: Anne, John; m. Maureen Davidson, Apr. 5, 2008. BA, U. Wash., 1955; MBA, Kellogg Sch. Mgmt., Northwestern U., 1957; grad., US Army Command & Gen. Staff Coll., 1969. CFA Chartered Fin. Analysts Inst., 1978. Security analyst Continental Bank, Chgo., 1957—59; fin. analyst Boeing Co., Seattle; trust investment mgr. Seattle Trust, 1970—80; prin. KAS Investment Cons., Seattle, 1980—. Contbr. articles to profl. jours. Mem. Seattle Art Mus., Bellevue Art Mus., 1957—; treas. Civil Affairs Assn., 1975—79; curator-treas. Seattle King County Mil. History Soc., 1978—80. Lt. col. USAR, 1955—83. Named Gazzam Found. scholar, 1952—55. Mem.: CFA Soc. Seattle, Washington Water Trails Assn., CFA Inst. (charter holder). Episcopalian. Home: 13005 SE 46th St Bellevue WA 98006-2042 Office: 13005 SE 46th St Bellevue WA 98006-2042 Office Phone: 425-641-7645. Personal E-mail: ronw-h@prodigy.net.

WELLS WULSIN, VICTORIA, epidemiologist; m. Lawson Wulsin; 4 children. BA, Harvard U., Cambridge, Mass., DPH in Epidemiology; MD, Case Western Res. U., Cleve. Lic. physician Ohio. Occupl. safety officer Internat. Chem. Workers, United Steel Workers; officer US Pub. Health Svc.; bd. mem. Health Resource Ctr., Over-the-Rhine, Ohio; city epidemiologist Cin. Health Dept.; founder Soteni Internat., Cin., 2003—. Mem. St. Andrew's Episc. Ch., Cin. Democrat. Office: Soteni Internat 2366 Kemper Ln Cincinnati OH 45206 Office Phone: 513-961-2100. Office Fax: 531-961-2101.

WELMAKER, GREGORY S., medical researcher; b. Greenville, Sc, June 9, 1967; s. Jerry G. and Susan Lovelace Welmaker; m. Elizabeth Dubil, May 28, 1994; children: Jason, Nathan. BS, Furman U., Greenville, 1988; PhD, U. SC., Columbia, 1992; Attending, Drexel U., Philadelphia, 2007—. Postdoc. fellow Am. Cancer Soc. U. Calif., Irvine, 1993—95; sr. rsch. scientist Ariad Pharmaceuticals, Cambridge, Mass., 1995—96; rsch. scientist III Wyeth Rsch., Princeton, NJ, 1996—98, sr. rsch. scientist i, 1999—2002, sr. rsch. scientist II Collegeville, Pa., 2002—03, prin. rsch. scientist, 2004—. Contbr. to numerous profl. jours. Serving elder First Presbyn. Ch., Phoenixville, Pa., 2005—07, United Presbyn. Ch. of Millstone, Perrineville, NJ, 2000—01. Recipient CSS Above and Beyond award, Wyeth Rsch., 2004, 2006; fellow Divsn. Organic Chemistry Grad. Fellowship, Am. Chem. Soc. Divsn. Organic Chemistry, 1991—92, Ethyl Corp. Fellowship, U. SC., 1988—89, Rsch. Corp. Summer Fellowship, Furman U., 1986, NSF Summer Fellowship, 1987; Fellowship, Am. Cancer Soc., 1993—94. Mem.: Am. Chem. Soc. Achievements include 21 patents; numerous patents pending. Personal E-mail: gwelmaker@gmail.com. Business E-Mail: welmakg@wyeth.com.

WELP, HERRAD SUSANNE, language educator; d. Egon Theodor and Edith Katharina Welp; m. Yamba-Yamba Mitanga, May 3, 1991; children: Myrtil Nioka Mitanga, Keanu Tambwe Mitanga. MA, U. Hamburg, Germany, 1995. Cert. methodology and didactics of German Goethe Inst. Internationes Paris, 2003, teaching Mandarin China Nat. Office Tchg. Chinese as a Fgn. Lang., 2005, Kodaly Level I Ga. State U. Sch. of Music, 2006. Tng. devel. cons. Hughes Raytheon, Ruesselsheim, Germany, 1995—98; tchr. Goethe Inst. Internat. Nat., Paris, 2002—03, Waldorf Sch., Atlanta, 2003—04, Atlanta Internat. Sch., 2004—. Office: Atlanta International School 2890 North Fulto Dr Atlanta GA 30305

WELSCH, ROY ELMER, statistician, educator; b. Kansas City, Mo., July 31, 1943; AB, Princeton U., 1965; MS, Stanford U., 1966, PhD in math., 1969. Asst. prof. ops. rsch. Sloan Sch. Mgmt. MIT, Cambridge, Mass., 1969-73, assoc. prof., 1973-79, prof. mgmt. sci. and stats. & engring. systems, 1979—, dir. statistics ctr., 1981—89. Sr. rsch. assoc. Nat. Bur. Econ. Rsch., 1973—79. Assoc. editor: Jour. Am. Statist. Assn. Fellow AAAS, Am. Statis. Assn., Inst. Math. Stats. Office: MIT Dept Mgmt & Stats Bldg E53-383 77 Massachusetts Ave Cambridge MA 02139-4307 Office Phone: 617-253-6601. Office Fax: 617-258-7579. E-mail: rwelsch@mit.edu.

WELSER-MÖST, FRANZ, conductor, music director; b. Linz, Austria, Aug. 16, 1960; LHD (hon.), Case Western Reserve U., 2003, Oberlin Coll., Cleve. Inst. Music. Chief condr. Sinfonieorkester Norrköping, Sweden, 1986-91, Stadtorchester Winterthur, Switzerland, 1987-90; prin. condr. London Philharm. Orch., 1990—96; music dir. Zurich Opera House, Switzerland, 1995—2000, prin. condr., 2002—05, gen. music dir., 2005—08; music dir. Cleve. Orch., 2002—. Guest condr. Berlin Philharm., Cleve. Youth Orch., Vienna Philharm., Bavarian Radio Symphony Orch., Gustav Mahler Youth Orch. Conducting debut Salzburg Festival, Austria, 1985; Am. debut St. Louis, 1989; appearances include Vienna biennial, Lucerne Festical, Carnegie Hall. Recipient Outstanding Achievement award, Western Law Ctr. Disability Rights, 1995, Silver medal, Region of Upper Austria, 2003; named Condr. of Yr., Musical America Internat. Directory Performing Arts, 2003; named an Academician, Yutse European Acad. Found., 2006. Mem.: Vienna Singverein (hon.). Office: Cleve Orch Severance Hall 11001 Euclid Ave Cleveland OH 44106*

WELSH, SIR ALFRED JOHN, lawyer, investment advisor; b. Louisville, May 10, 1947; s. Elvin Alfred and Carol (Kleymeyer) W.; m. Lee Mitchell, Aug. 1, 1970; children: Charles Kleymeyer, Kathryn Thomas. BA, Centre Coll., 1969; JD, U. Ky., 1972; LLM in Internat. Law cum laude, U. Brussels, 1973. Bar: Ky. 1972, U.S. Dist. Ct. (we. and ea. dists.) Ky. 1972, U.S. Ct. Appeals (6th cir.) 1972, U.S. Supreme Ct. Asst. atty. Ky. Atty. Gen. Office, Frankfort, 1973-74; legis. counsel to congressman Ho. of Reps., Washington, 1974-77; mng. ptnr. Adams, Hayward and Welsh, Louisville, 1977—, Boone Welsh and Hayward Internat. Law. Hon. counsel of Belgium, 1983—; econ. devel. advisor Kingdom of Belgium; mem. Ky. Econ. Adv. Coun., 1991-94; pres. Transcontinental Trading Cons., Ltd.; del. North African Mideast Econ. Summit Conf., Morocco, 1994; bd. dirs. Intervention Resources Ctr., Inc.; presenter in field. Bd. dirs. Greater Louisville Swim Found., 1983-94, exec. com., 1994—; bd. dirs. Melody Lake Ranch Inc.; bd. dirs. Louisville com. Coun. Fgn. Rels., 1981—, also pres.; chmn. Louisville Com. on Fgn. Rels.; bd. dirs. Am. Com. on Fgn. Rels.; bd. dirs. Jefferson County Alcohol and Drug Abuse Found., Louisville, 1986-98, Internat. Resolve, Louisville Internat. Cultural Ctr.; mem. econ. task force of Ky. Legis. Agts.; mem. Louisville Meml. Auditorium Commn.; bd. dirs. Am. Com. Fgn. Rels.; mem. Union Internat des Avocats. Decorated knight Order of the Crown (Belgium), Knight Order of Leopold. Mem. ABA (internat. law sect., commn. on impairment, com. on substance abuse), ATLA, Va. Bar Assn., Ky. Bar Assn. (bd. dirs. 1981-82, pres. young lawyers divsn. 1981-82), Ky. Acad. Trial Lawyers, Am. Judicature Soc., Louisville C. of C., Am. Ctr. Fgn. Rels. (chmn. Louisville com. on fgn. rels., treas., mem. exec. ct., bd. dirs.), Am. Com. on Fgn. Rels. (exec. com.). Democrat. Presbyterian. Avocations: swimming, water polo, soccer. Office: Barristers Hall 1009 S 4th St Louisville KY 40203-3207 Home Phone: 502-459-3648; Office Phone: 502-584-8583. Personal E-mail: bwbh@earthlink.net.

WELSH, CAROLINE MASTIN, museum director, curator, art historian; b. St. Louis, Nov. 30, 1948; d. Charles O'Fallon and Georgann Logsdon Mastin; m. Peter Corbett Welsh, Sept. 8, 1970; 1 child, James Munson Corbett. Degree cum laude, Kent Sch., 1966; AB in Art History, Wellesley Coll., Mass., 1970. Editl. asst. Smithsonian Jour. History, 1969; coord. exhibits Travelling Exbn. Svc. Smithsonian Instn., 1971—72; guest curator Albany Inst. History and Art, NY, 1975—76; dir. exhibits Marketechs Exhibit Design and Prodn., Inc., York, Pa., 1976—86; prin., owner Welsh Group, Camp Hill, Pa., 1984—88; from cons. curator to chief curator Adirondack Mus., Blue Mountain Lake, NY, 1986—92, chief curator, 1992—2007, dir. ops., 1994—2006, acting dir. pubs., 2002—07, dir., 2007—. Adv. bd. Adirondack Pk. Centennial Project WCFE Pub. TV, 1991—92; advisor film WMHT Ednl. Telecomms., 1993—95; mem. com. visual arts Hamilton Coll., 2002—; bd. dirs. Lake Placid Winter Olympic Mus., Lake Placid Ctr. Arts. Contbr. articles to profl. jours. Fellow, Smithsonian Instn., 1970—71; fellow, Getty Mus. Leadership Inst., 2007. Mem.: Am. Assn. Mus. (peer reviewer mus. assessment program 2002—), Soc. Preservation Am. Modernists (bd. dirs. 1994—), Century Assn. Home: 34 Second St Tupper Lake NY 12986 Office: Adirondack Mus PO Box 99 Blue Mountain Lake NY 12812 Office Phone: 518-352-7311. Office Fax: 518-352-7021. Business E-Mail: cwelsh@adkmuseum.org.

WELSH, CHRISTABEL JANE, neuroimmunologist; b. Dilston Hall, Northumberland, Eng., Nov. 3, 1954; d. Frank Reeson and Agnes Welsh; m. Colin Ruaraidh Young, Sept. 12, 1981; children: James MacFarlane Young, Robert Andrew Young. PhD, London U., 1979. Postdoc. rsch. fellow King's Coll. Hosp., London, 1979—81; postdoc. rsch. asst., dept. pathology Cambridge U., Cambridgeshire, 1981—89. Author: (book)

Neural and neuroendocrine mechanisms in host defense and autoimmunity. Grant, NIH, 1991—94, 2002—07, NSF, 1999—2001. Mem.: Internat. Soc. NeuroImmunoModulation (sec. treas. 2009—), Internat. Soc. Neuroimmunology, Brit. Soc. Immunology. Avocations: travel, photography.

WELSH, DONALD EMORY, publisher; b. Youngstown, Ohio, Oct. 6, 1943; s. Edward Francis and Clevelle Rose W.; m. Elizabeth Bourne Floyd, June 25, 1966; children: Leah Bourne, Emory Philip. AB, Columbia U., 1965; JD, Cleveland Marshall Sch. Law, 1969. Bar: Ohio 1969. Trust devel. officer Cleve. Trust Co., 1968-70; advt. sales rep. Fortune mag., Time, Inc., NYC, 1970-75; advt. dir. Rolling Stone mag., NYC, 1975-77, v.p., assoc. pub., 1977-78; pub. Muppet mag. and pres. Lorimar Pub. Group (formerly Telepictures Publs., Inc.), 1982-87; pres. Welsh Pub. Group, Inc., 1987-94; exec. v.p. Marvel Comics Group, NYC, 1994-96; chmn. Group XXVII Comms., NYC, 1997-2000; pres. pub. group Digital Convergence Inc., NYC, 2000-2001; chmn. Budget Living Commn., NYC, 2001—05; bus. chmn. DEW LLC, Millerson, NY. Global advisor Outward Bound, U.S.A.; bd. dirs. Cousteau Soc.; former bd. dirs. Big Apple Circus, B.P.A. Consumer Mags. Mem. ABA, Mag. Pubs. Assn. (past bd. dirs.), Century Assn., Sharon Country Club (Conn.), Ocean Reef Club (Fla.), Brook Club (N.Y.C.). Home: 415 Undermountain Rd Millerton NY 12546-5162 E-mail: DonaldEWelsh@aol.com.

WELSH, DOROTHY DELL, columnist, writer; d. Roland Fields and Martha Gladys (Sheppard) Butler; m. James Robert Welsh, June 26, 1965; children: Pamela Jeanne(dec.), James Michael, Julie Marie. BA, U. Okla., 1957, MA, 1964; postgrad., U. Tex., Austin, 1983-84, U. Tex., San Antonio, 1984. Newspaper reporter summer intern Pryor Jeffersonian, Okla., 1952—55; tchr. English and journalism Classen HS, Oklahoma City, 1957-61, Henderson Jr. HS, Nev., 1961-62, Desert HS, Edwards, Calif., 1965-66; dir. publs. Amarillo (Tex.) HS, 1962-64, coord. yearbook advt., 1962—64; tchr. English Palmdale HS, Calif., 1964-65; lectr. English San Antonio Coll., 1979-88; tchg. assoc. U. Tex., San Antonio, 1986-91; reporter Swimming World mag., Sedona, Ariz., 1980—2000; freelance writer, 1992—. Lectr. journalism John Brown U., 1992. Author: The Butlers of Oklahoma, 1957, A Good Man is Hard to Find, 1961, To Seattle for a Bone Marrow Transplant, 1982, Fact, Fiction and Poetic License, 1995, The Butlers: A Newspaper Family, 2003, Pre-Statehood Notes on the Coo-Wee-Scoo-Wee District Indian Territory and Mayes County, Oklahoma, 2007, Descendants of William Butler, Pendleton District, South Carolina with Allied Families, 2007; co-author: Pre-statehood Pioneers of Mayes County, Oklahoma, 2007; editor: Crescent News, 1974—80, 1983—86, The Swimmer's Ear, 1983—84, Off the Blocks, 1985—86; contbr. articles to profl. jours. Bd. dirs., publicity chmn. S. Tex. Swimming Assn., Austin, 1982—84; mem. info. com. Tex. Swimming Assn., Dallas, 1983—84; v.p. Mayes County Geneal. Soc., Okla., 2002; mem. Mayes County Hist. Soc., Okla., Rogers County Hist. Soc., Okla., Okla. Hist. Soc.; co-chair Mayes County Pre-Statehood Celebration, 2007; co-compiler Pre-Statehood Pioneers Mayes County 1850-1907, 2007. Recipient citation superior work journalism, U. Interscholastic League, Austin, 1964, Svc. award, San Antonio Aquatic Club, 1983, Outstanding Svc. award, U.S. Swimming/Phillips 66, 1989, Pres.'s award, Okla. Press Assn., 2003. Mem.: DAR, MLA, Cleve. Anthorp. Soc., Clan Grant Soc. U.S., Okla. Anthrop. Soc., Journalism Edn. Assn., Soc. Profl. Journalists, Okla. Hist. Soc., U. Okla. Assn., Tulsa Archeol. Soc., Indian Women's Pochohontas Club, Okla. Geneal. Soc., Elks, Pryor (Okla.) Red Hat Soc., First Families Okla., Gamma Phi Beta (internat. officer 1992—94, pres. San Antonio 1972—73, 1987—88, v.p. 1973—74, Svc. award 1977, Internat. Merit Roll 1986). Baptist. Office Phone: 405-872-7172.

WELSH, GEORGE FRANKLIN, plastic surgeon, educator; b. Charles City, Iowa, Oct. 13, 1940; s. George S. Welsh and Aldeen (Paris) Welsh Taylor; m. Rosemary Dahlen, June 23, 1973; children: Christopher Franklin, Penelope Cosette, Bradford Alexander. BA, Carleton Coll., 1962; BS, U. N.D., 1964; MD, Harvard U., 1966; M in Hosp. Adminstrn., Xavier U., 1994; cert. in Horticulture, U. Cin., 2002. Diplomate Am. Bd. Surgery, Am. Bd. Plastic Surgery; cert. physician exec; Health Care Garden Design, Chgo., 2004. Commd. officer USAF, 1966, advanced through grades to lt. col., 1974, intern Hosp. San Antonio, 1966—67, flight surgeon Takhli RTAFB Thailand, 1967—69, plastic surgeon Dayton, Ohio, 1975—78, flight surgeon, dir. base med. svcs. United Arab Emirates, 1991, Air War Coll., 1988; resident in surgery Mayo Clinic, Rochester, Minn., 1969—73; resident in plastic surgery U. Okla. Health Sci. Ctr., Oklahoma City, 1973—75; Maytag Fellow in plastic surgery U. Miami, Fla., 1976; ret. col. USAFR, 1996; pvt. practice Cin., 1978—. Cons. on healthcare adminstrn., Cin., 1994—; asst. clin. prof. surgery Wright State U. Sch. Medicine, Dayton, 1975-78; vol. asst. prof. surgery U. Cin. Sch. Medicine, 1978-. Contbr. chpt. to book; contbr. articles to profl. jours. including Surg. Clinics N.Am., Jour. Thoracic and Cardiovasc. Surgery, So. Med. Jour., Plastic and Reconstructive Surgery, Aesthetic Plastic Surgery, Brit. Jour. Plastic Surgery. Mem. Leadership Cin., 1981; citizen amb. People to People Internat., Albania, Russia, 1994, Cuba, 2000, Egypt, 2003, China, 2008. Fellow ACS, Am. Coll. Physician Execs.; mem. Am. Soc. Plastic Surgeons, Am. Soc. for Aesthetic Plastic Surgery, Millard Plastic Surg. Soc. (treas.), English Spkg. Union (past pres. Cin. br.), Gen. Soc. Colonial Wars (chmn. grants and contbns.) Ohio Soc., (sec.), Cin. Hort. Soc. (trustee), Harvard Alumni Assn. Avocations: medical missions, landscape design, fishing. Office: Aesthetic Plastic Surgery Ctr 6200 Pfeiffer Rd Ste 320 Cincinnati OH 45242-5861 Office Phone: 513-793-0302. Personal E-mail: aestheticps@aol.com.

WELSH, H. RONALD, lawyer; b. Orange, NJ, Jan. 9, 1950; s. Harry A. and Faye L. (Neal) W.; children: Austin, Ben. BS, Northwestern U., 1972; JD, U. Tex., 1975. Bar: Tex. 1975, U.S. Dist. Ct. (so. dist.) Tex. 1989, U.S. Ct. Appeals (5th and 11th cirs.) 1981; cert. in civil trial law and personal injury trial law Tex. Bd. Legal Specialization. Ptnr. Vinson & Elkins, Houston, 1982—2003, Cunningham, Welsh, Darlow, Zook & Chapoton, LLP, Houston, 2004—. Fellow Am. Coll. Trial Lawyers, Am. Bd. Trial Advs., Tex. Bar Found., Houston Bar Found. Office: Cunningham Welsh Darlow Zook & Chapoton LLP Ste 1700 600 Travis St Houston TX 77002 Home Phone: 713-850-1504; Office Phone: 713-255-5500. Business E-Mail: rwelsh@cdzc.com.

WELSH, JOHN BERESFORD, JR., retired lawyer; b. Seattle, Feb. 16, 1940; s. John B. and Rowena Morgan Welsh. Student, U. Hawaii, 1960, Georgetown U., Washington, DC, 1960; BA, U. Wash., Seattle, 1962; LLB, 1965. Bar: Wash. 1965. Staff counsel Joint Com. on Govtl. Cooperation, 1965-66; asst. atty gen. Dept. Labor and Industries, 1966-67; atty. Washington State Legis. Coun., 1967—73; acting as counsel Pub. Health Com., Labor Com., Pub. Employees Collective Bargaining Com., Com. on State Instns. and Youth Devel., State of Wash., 1967-73; sr. counsel Wash. Ho. of Reps., Ho. Com. on Social and Health Svcs., Olympia, WA, 1973-86; atty., parliamentarian, spkr. Ho. of Reps., 1973; counsel Ho. Com. Human Svcs., 1987-91, 93-95, Ho. Com. on Health Care, 1987—2003, ret., 2003. Counsel Ho. Com. Trade and Econ. Devel., 1995—98, Joint Select Com. Nurse Del., 1995—98, Joint Select Com. Oral Health, 1996; legal cons. Gov.'s Planning Commn. Vocat. Rehab., 1968, Gov.'s Commn. Youth Involvement, 1969; envoy from Gov. Wash. to investiture Prince of Wales, London, 69; fac. Nat. Conf. State Legislatures, Denver, 1977, New Orleans, 77, Coun. Licensure, Enforcement and Regulation, San Francisco, 1984, Orlando, Fla., 85, Denver, 86, Kansas City, Mo., 87, Washington, 88, Indpls., 89, Seattle, 90, Ft. Lauderdale, Fla., 91, Albuquerque, 92, Boston, 94, San Antonio, 95, Norfolk, 97; mem. suggested state legis. com. Coun. State Govts., 1988—95, mem. steering com., 1986—90, mem. legis. issues com., 1986—88. Vol. Hampton Rds. US Naval Mus., mem. gov.'s state medal merit com., 1986—2003. Recipient Gov.'s award for excellence in state health care policy, 2002, Spkr. of House award for dedicated pub. svc., 2002, Sec. of State award for pub. svc. to state legislature and people of state of Wash., 2003, Sec. of Health award for creating meaningful health policy change, 2003. Mem.: Wash. Bar Assn., Assn. Washington Gens. (lt. gen. bd.), Northwest Hist. Assn. (pres. 2003), Washington Nat. Rochambeau Hist. Revolutionary Rte. Assn. Bd., Friends Willie and Joe, Colonial Williamsburg Found., Napoleonic Hist. Soc. (exec. v.p. 2007, 2008—09), English Speaking Union, Soc. des Amis du Musee de l'Armee, Alliance Francaise, Soc. Napoleonienne (pres.), Custer Battlefield Hist. and Mus. Assn., Friends Old Ft. Stevens (bd. dirs.), Sons Union Vets. Civil War, Nat. Soc. SAR, French Soc. SAR. Personal E-mail: jbwelsh@comcast.net.

WELSH, KELLY RAYMOND, lawyer, investment company executive; b. Chgo., July 6, 1952; s. Raymond J. and Mary Jane (Kelly) W.; m. Ellen S. Alberding, June 28, 1985; children: Katherine A., Julia S. AB cum laude, Harvard U., 1974; MA, Sussex U., Eng., 1975; JD magna cum laude, Harvard U., 1978. Assoc. Mayer, Brown & Platt, Chgo., 1979-85, ptnr., 1985-89; corp. counsel City of Chgo., 1989-93; v.p., assoc. gen. counsel Ameritech Corp., Chgo., 1993-96, exec. v.p., gen. counsel, 1996—2001, Northern Trust Corp., Chgo., 2001—. Chmn. Met. Pier and Exposition Authority, Chgo., 1994—. Mem. ABA, Chgo. Bar Assn., Chgo. Coun. Lawyers, Chgo. Coun. Fgn. Rels. (mem. Chgo. com.), Legal Club Chgo. Office: Northern Trust Corp 50 S LaSalle Chicago IL 60675 Office Phone: 312-630-6000.

WELSH, PETER CORBETT, museum director, historian; b. Washington, Aug. 28, 1926; s. Arthur Brinkley and Susan Jane (Putney) W.; m. Catherine Beatrice Allen, Nov. 27, 1951 (div. 1969); children—Susan Jane, Peter Corbett; m. Caroline Levert Mastin, Sept. 8, 1970; 1 child, James Munson Corbett. BA, Mt. Union Coll., Alliance, Ohio, 1950; postgrad., U. Va., 1950-51; MA (Hagley fellow), U. Del., 1956. Research asst., fellowship coordinator Eleutherian Mills-Hagley Found., Wilmington, Del., 1956-59; assoc. curator dept. civil history Mus. History and Tech., Smithsonian Instn., 1959-61; curator Growth U.S., 1962-64, curator dept. civil history, 1964-69, asst. dir. gen. mus. of instn., 1969-70, dir. Office Mus. Programs, 1970-71; dir. N.Y. State Hist. Assn., Cooperstown, 1971-74; vis. prof. Cooperstown Grad. Program, N.Y. State Hist. Assn.; dir. Cooperstown Grad. Programs, 1971-74; dir. spl. projects N.Y. State Mus., Albany, 1975-76; dir. Bur. Mus., Pa. Hist. and Mus. Commn., 1976-84; pres. The Welsh Group, 1984-86; curator The Adirondack Mus., Blue Mountain Lake, N.Y., 1986-88, sr. historian, 1988-89; mus. cons., lectr., 1989—. Adj. prof. SUNY; cons. FDR Mus. and Little White House, Warm Springs, Ga., 1968-72; trustee Landon Sch., Bethesda, Md., 1964-70; bd. dirs., mem. exec. com. Ctr. for Conservation of Hist. Art and Artifacts, 1979-83; bd. dirs. Lake Placid Ctr. for the Arts, 1992-96; mem. publs. adv. com. The Adirondack Mus., 2002--. Author: Tanning in the United States: A Brief History, 1964, American Folk Art: The Art and Spirit of the People, 1967, Track and Road: The American Trotting Horse, 1820-1900, 1968, The Art of Enterprise: A Pennsylvania Tradition, 1983, Jacks, Jobbers and Kings: Logging the Adirondacks, 1850-1950, 1996; contbr. articles to profl. publs.; editor Smithsonian Jour. History, 1967-70. Served to 1st lt. AUS, 1951-54. Mem. Am. Hist. Assn., Am. Studies Assn., Am. Assn. Mus., N.Y. State Assn. Mus. (council 1971-75), Am. Assn. State and Local History (publ. com.), Soc. History of Tech., Sigma Nu. Clubs: Country of Harrisburg. Democrat. Roman Catholic. Office: 34 Second St Tupper Lake NY 12986-2011

WELSHIMER, MARK J., lawyer; b. Canton, Ohio, 1951; AB, Harvard U., 1973, JD, 1976. Bar: NY 1977. Assoc. Sullivan & Cromwell, NYC, ptnr., 1983—, and coord. asset-based fin. practice area. Named a Dealmakers of Yr., Am. Lawyer mag., 2008. Mem.: ABA. Office: Sullivan & Cromwell 125 Broad St Fl 28 New York NY 10004-2489 Office Phone: 212-558-4000. Office Fax: 212-558-3588. Business E-Mail: welshimerm@sullcrom.com.

WELSOME, EILEEN, journalist, writer; b. NYC, Mar. 12, 1951; d. Richard H. and Jane M. (Garity) Welsome; m. James R. Martin, Aug. 3, 1983. BJ with honors, U. Tex., 1980. Reporter Beaumont (Tex.) Enterprise, 1980—82, San Antonio Light, 1982—83, San Antonio Express-News, 1983—86, Albuquerque Tribune, 1987—94, Westword Newspaper, Denver, 2000—01; observer Tex., 2006—07. Author: The Plutonium Files, 1999 (PEN/Martha Albrand award for first nonfiction, 2000), The General and the Laguer, Little Brown, 2006. Recipient Clarion award, 1989, News Reporting award, Nat. Headliners, 1989, John Hancock award, 1991, Mng. Editors Pub. Svc. award, AP, 1991, 1994, Roy Howard award, 1994, James Aronson award, 1994, Gold Medal award, Investigative Reporters and Editors, 1994, Sigma Delta Chi award, 1994, Investigative Reporting award, Nat. Headliners, 1994, Selden Ring award, 1994, Heywood Broun award, 1994, George Polk award, 1994, Sidney Hillman Found. award, 1994, Pulitzer prize nat. reporting, 1994, PEN/West Lit. award rsch. nonfiction, PEN, 2000; John S. Knight fellow, Stanford U., 1991—92.

WELTER, WILLIAM MICHAEL, marketing and advertising executive; b. Evanston, Ill., Nov. 18, 1946; s. Roy Michael and Frances (DeShields) W.; m. Pamela Bassett, June 11, 1971; children: Barclay, Robert Michael. BS, Mo. Valley Coll., 1966. Account exec. Leo Burnett Co., Inc., Chgo., 1966-74; v.p., account supr. Needham Harper Worldwide, Chgo., 1974-80; v.p. mktg. Wendy's Internat., Inc., Dublin, Ohio, 1981, sr. v.p. mktg., 1981-84, exec. v.p., 1984-87; owner, chief exec. officer Haunty & Welter Advt. Agy., Worthington, Ohio, 1987-91; sr. exec. v.p. mktg. Rax Restaurants Inc., Dublin, 1992; exec. v.p. mktg. Metromedia Steakhouses, Inc., Dayton, 1992-93; sr. v.p. mktg. Metromedia Co., Dayton, 1993-95; exec. v.p., chief mktg. officer Heartland Foods Inc., Dublin, Ohio, 1995-96; exec. v.p. brand mgmt. Late Nite Magic, Inc., Las Vegas, Nev., 1996—99; pres., CEO W.M. Welter & Assocs., Las Vegas, 1996—; pres. Wings West LLC, Las Vegas, 1999—, Buffalo Wild Wings, Inc., Las Vegas, 2001—; cons. Natl. Restaurant, Sturgeon Bay, Wis., Wake Island, Las Vegas. Founder Santa's Silent Helpers, Columbus, Ohio, 1985 Mem. Advt. Fedn. Las Vegas.

WELTERS, ANTHONY, health services executive; BA in Econs., Manhattanville Coll.; JD, NYU. Atty. SEC; exec. asst. to Sen. Jacob Javits; sr.-level positions Amtrak and US Dept. Transp.; chmn. bd., pres., CEO Americhoice (subs. of UnitedHealth Grp.), 1989—; exec. v.p. UnitedHealth Group, Mpls., 2006—07, exec. v.p., pres. pub. & sr. markets group, 2007—. Bd. trustees Healthcare Leadership Coun.; vice chmn. bd. Morehouse Sch. Medicine; mem. bd. NYU Law Sch., Wolf Trap Found. Recipient Horatio Alger award, 1998. Mailing: UnitedHealth Group PO Box 1459 Minneapolis MN 55440-1459*

WELTMAN, EDWARD S., lawyer; AB cum laude, Brandeis U., 1972; JD, Washington U., 1975. Bar: NY 1976. Sr. ptnr. Schneck Weltman & Hashmall LLP, NYC; ptnr., litig. dept. Goodwin Procter LLP, NYC, chair, products liability group, mem., exec. com. Comment topics editor Wash. Univ. Law Quarterly. Mem.: Nat. Judicial Coll., Internat. Assn. Def. Counsel. Office: Goodwin Procter LLP 599 Lexington Ave New York NY 10022 Office Phone: 212-459-7420. Office Fax: 212-355-3333. Business E-Mail: eweltman@goodwinprocter.com.

WELTMAN, JOEL KENNETH, immunologist; b. NYC, May 22, 1933; s. Charles and Frances (Seasonwein) W.; m. K. Reulla Avatichi, June 28, 1956; children: Alica C., Orlee R. BA, NYU, 1954; MD, SUNY, Bklyn., 1958; PhD, U. Colo., 1963; MA, Brown U., Providence, 1972. Diplomate Am. Bd. Allergy and Immunology. Clin. emeritus prof. medicine Brown U., Providence, 2005—. Fellow Am. Soc. Biol. Chemists; mem. Am. Soc. Biol. Chemistry, Molecular Biology, New Eng. Soc. Allergy (treas. 1995—98, pres. 1999-2000). Achievements include patent for screening antibodies.

WELTON, SHARON MARIE, food service executive; b. Waterbury, Conn., Nov. 18, 1943; d. George Galvin Touponse and Catherine Marie Coon; m. Allen Richard Welton (div.); children: Catherine Welton-Pando, Douglas Allen Sr. AAS, Mattatuck Cmty. Coll., 1988; BS, U. Conn., 1996. Cert. dietary mgr. Nat. Dietary Managers Assn., 1992, instr. for Serv-Safe Course Nat. Restaurant Assn., 2002, food protection profl. 1996. Legal sec. Membrino/Fitzgerald, Waterbury, Conn., 1963—64; asst. mgr. Judy's Deli, Southbury, Conn., 1980—84; prin./mgr. Feasts by Sharon, Conn., 1981—2001; intern- affirmative action office Southbury Training Sch., Conn., 1995, supvr. food svc. Conn., 1984—. Cons./trainer State of Conn., 1990—, State of Conn. Nutritional Work Group, 1999—2003, Southbury Training Sch., 1992—. Polit. action com. mem. Dietary Managers Assn., 1993—95; mem./leader Girl Scouts, Watertown, Conn., 1951—61, 1977—81; com. mem. Christmas Town Festival, Bethlehem, 1999. Recipient State Achievement award, Dietary Managers Assn., 1994—95. Mem.: Dietary Managers Assn. (legis. coord. 1992—98, 2003—, pres. 1994—95). Independent. Avocations: clothing and jewlry design, sewing, wine tasting, water aerobics, book discussions. Home: 143 Pine Hill Rd 22B Thomaston CT 06787 Office: Southbury Training Sch Rte 172 Southbury CT 06488 Office Phone: 203-586-2193.

WELTS, RICK, professional sports team executive; Student, U. Wash. Dir. pub. rels. Seattle SuperSonics; v.p. Bob Walsh & Assocs., 1979; dir. nat. promotions NBA Properties NBA, NYC, 1982—83, v.p. mktg. NBA Properties, 1983—84, v.p. mktg. and comm. NYC, 1984—88, pres. NBA Properties, 1988—99, exec. v.p., chief mktg. officer, 1996—99; pres. Fox Sports Enterprises, 1999, First In Line; ptnr. ONSPORT, 2001; pres., COO Phoenix Suns, 2002—. Named Co-Marketer of Yr., Brandweek, 1998. Office: Phoenix Suns 201 E Jefferson St Phoenix AZ 85004*

WELTY, SARAH OSBORN, secondary school educator; d. James Leonard and Sharon Lea Osborn; m. William Howard Welty, Aug. 1997; children: Austin, Haley. BS in Edn., Va. Inst. Tech., Blacksburg, 1990; MS in Counseling, Western Md. Coll., Westminster, 1999. Cert. advanced profl. tchr., profl. horticulturalist. Agrl. educator Giles HS, Pearisburg, Va., 1991—92, North Carroll HS, Hampstead, Md., 1992—95, Walkersville HS, Md., 1995—. Mem. nat. bd. dirs., nat. bd. trustees Future Farmers Am. Recipient hon. degree, Future Farmers Am., 2001. Mem.: NEA, Nat. Coun. Agrl. Edn., Md. Agrl. Tchrs. Assn. (state pres. 1997—99, Leadership award 1999, Outstanding Tchr. award 2005), Nat. Assn. Agrl. Educators (life; regional v.p. 1999—2001, nat. pres. 2001—02). Office: Walkersville HS 81 Frederick St Walkersville MD 21793

WELTZ, MARTIN DAVID, hematologist; b. Phila., Jan. 18, 1948; children: Michael, Adam. BS in Biology, Bklyn. Coll., 1969; DO, Kans. City U. Medicine Biosci., 1973; MBA, Johns Hopkins U., 2002, MPH, 2003. Diplomate Nat. Bd. Med. Examiners for Osteo. Physicians and Surgeons, Am. Bd. Internal Medicine, (subspecialty of med. oncology, subspecialty of hematology, subspecialty hospice and palliative medicine). Commd. 2d lt. USMC, 1973, advanced through grades to lt. col., 1981; intern Walter Reed Army Med. Ctr., Washington, 1973-74, resident, 1974-76, fellow hematology and med. oncology sect., 1976-79, attending physician dept. internal medicine, 1979-81, staff hematologist, med. oncologist, dir. med. edn., 1979-80, chief divsn. head Clin. Cancer Chemo-Pharmacology Rsch. Lab., 1979-80, asst. chief, dir. clin. pharmacy hematology-med. oncology, 1980-81; resigned USMC, 1981; pvt. practice, sr. v.p., founder Hematology-Oncology Cons., Greenbelt, Md., 1983—, v.p., sec., 1986—; pres. med.-dental staff Laurel Regional Hosp., 1993-99; chmn. dept. internal medicine Washington Adventist Hosp., 1997-2001. V.p., sec., 1986—; attending med. staff AMI Drs. Hosp., Prince George's County, Lanham, Md., 1983, Washington Adventist Hosp., Takoma Park, Md., 1983—, sec.-treas. dept. internal medicine, 1991-94, asst. chmn., 1994-97; asst. chief hematology/med. oncology Prince Georges Hosp. Ctr., 1986—; staff Laurel Regional Hosp., 1983—, chmn. hematology-med. oncology, 1989-1998, med. dir. Hospice in Prince George's County, 1989—, chmn. dept. internal medicine, 1989-92, chmn. tumor bd., 1989—, chmn. employees ann. benefit med.-dental staff, 1990-2000, chmn. med. exec. com., 1993-2000, pres. med. and dental staff, 1993-99, trustee, 1993-99; bd. dirs. Dimensions Corp., Landover, Md., sec.-treas. bd. dirs., 1990-99; pres. Med. Dental Staff laurel Regional Hosp., 1993-99; vice chmn. Dept. Internal Medicine, Washington Adventist Hosp., 1994-96; chmn. Dimensions Health Care Network PHO, 1994-99; med. dir. Hospice in Prince Georges County, 1990-98, Hospice of the Chesapeake, 1999-; bd. dirs. Universal Health Care Network, Medi-Cen of Md.; bd. dirs., found. chmn. med. exec. com., pres. med.-dental staff Laurel Region Hosp., 1993—; bd. dirs. Dimensions Healthcare Network, Dimensions Health Care Corp. Medi-Cen of Md. and Universal Healthcare Corp., Cancer Care, Inc.; chmn., founder tumor bd. Laurel Regional Hosp. and Washington Adventist Hosp., 1988—; chmn. transfusion com. Washington Adventist Hosp., 1990—; sec. Laurel Hosp. Found., 2000-05. Contbr. articles to profl. jours. Bd. dirs. Am. Cancer Soc., Prince George's County, 1981—; med. advisor cansurmount program Am. Cancer Soc., Montgomery County, Md., 1982-90; ring dir. Ea. Regional Karate Tournament, Montgomery Coll., Rockville, Md., 1987—; mem. advisor Md. Blood Ctr., 1987-88; mem. med. adv. bd. Hospice Prince George's County, Largo, Md., 1991-99, active archtl. and design com., capital campaign com., bldg. com., 1992—; mem. com. Parent Fund and Centurion Campaign; bd. dirs. Found. Laurel Regional Hosp., 1993—, others. Fellow ACP, Acad. Medicine N.J.; mem. AMA, Am. Soc. Internal Medicine, Am. Soc. Clin. Oncology, Am. Soc. Hematology, Acad. Hospice and Palliative Medicine, Am. Coll. Clin. Pharmacology, Am. Coll. Osteo. Internists, Am. Soc. Clin. Oncologists, Am. Coll. Physician Execs., Am. Soc. Clin. Pharmacology and Therapeutics, Am. Soc. Contemporary Medicine and Surgery, Am. Fedn. for Clin. Rsch.,

Royal Soc. Medicine (London), Md. Osteo. Assn., Oncology Soc. N.J., N.J. Soc. Internal Medicine, N.Y. Acad. Scis., N.Y. Oncology Soc., Md. Soc. Clin. Oncology, George Washington U. Parent Assn., Luther Rice Soc., Johns Hopkins Alumni Assn. Office: Greenway Center Dr Greenbelt MD 20770 Personal E-mail: martinweitz@aol.com. Business E-Mail: martinweitz@jhsph.com.

WELU, JAMES A., museum director; b. Dubuque, Iowa, Dec. 15, 1943; s. Andrew L. and Anna E. (Riley) W. BA, Loras Coll., 1966; MA, U. Notre Dame, 1967, MFA, 1968; PhD, Boston U., 1977. Instr. St. Mary-of-the-Woods (Ind.) Coll., 1968-70; asst. curator Worcester Art Mus., Mass., 1974-76, assoc. curator Mass., 1976-80, instr. Mass., 1977-78, 80-81, chief curator Mass., 1980-86, dir. Mass., 1986—. Instr. Clark U., Worcester, 1980. Panelist Mass. Coun. on Arts and Humanities, Boston, 1981-82, 90, Utilization of Mus. Resources Nat. Endowment for the Arts, 1988; trustee Williamstown Regional Art Conservation Lab., Inc., Mass., 1981-86; mem. panel Utilization Mus. Resources, NEA, 1988. Boston U. grantee, 1973, NEA Mus.' Profl. grantee, 1976-81; Samuel H. Kress Found. fellow, 1973; recipient Netherland-Am. Found. award Netherland Found., 1973, Disting. Alumni award Boston U. Grad. Sch., 1986. Mem.: Historians Netherlandish Art, New Eng. Mus. Assn., Am. Assn. Mus. (accreditation commr. 2000—), Coll. Art Assn. Am., Am. Fedn. Arts, Assn. Art Mus. Dirs. (v.p. 1998—99, pres. 1999—2000, trustee 2000—01). Home: 10 Massachusetts Ave Worcester MA 01609-1649 Office: Worcester Art Mus 55 Salisbury St Worcester MA 01609-3196 Office Phone: 508-799-4406. E-mail: jimwelu@worcesterart.org.

WELZEL, TANIA M., physician; b. Stuttgart, Germany, Apr. 26, 1974; d. Edgar and Irene Welzel. MD, Heidelberg Sch. Medicine, Heib, 2000. Cert. master health scis. Duke U. Sch. Medicine, 2005. Resident LMU, Munich, 2001—03; physician dept. internal medicine, gastroenterology, hepatology, infectious diseases Katharinenhosp. Stuttgart, Stuttgart, 2007—; postdoc. fellow divsn. cancer epidemiology & genetics Nat. Cancer Inst., NIH, Bethesda, Md., 2003—06. Contbr. scientific papers to profl. jours. Fellowship, NIH, 2003—06, Nat. Cancer Inst., 2004. Personal E-mail: tmwelzel@web.de.

WEMPNER, GERALD ARTHUR, engineering professor; b. Waupun, Wis. s. Paul Christian and Thekla Nelda (Jung) W.; m. Lorraine Bischel, Sept. 6, 1952 (div. Apr. 1983); children: Susan K., Paul J. BS, U. Wis., 1952, MS, 1953; PhD, U. Ill., 1957. Instr. U. Ill., Urbana, 1953-57, asst. prof., 1957-59; assoc. prof. U. Ariz., Tucson, 1959-62; prof. U. Ala., Huntsville, 1964-73, Ga. Inst. Tech., Atlanta, 1973-91, prof. emeritus, 1991—. Vis. prof. U. Calif., Berkeley, 1962-63. Author: Mechanics of Solids, 1973; co-author: Mechanics of Deformable Bodies, 1961, Mechanics of Solids, 1995, Mechanics of Solids and Shells, 2003; contbr. articles to profl. jours. With US Army, 1946—48. NSF fellow, Stanford (Calif.) U., 1963-64, Sr. fellow Alexander von Humboldt Found., Germany, 1973, Killam fellow U. Calgary, Can., 1983. Fellow ASME (asssoc. editor 1976-83), Am. Acad. Mechanics. Avocations: art, sculpting, photography, woodwork. Home and Office: 3397 Hidden Acres Dr Doraville GA 30340-4445

WEN, CARSON, lawyer, legislator; b. Hong Kong, Apr. 16, 1953; s. Sir Yung and Tsi Fung Chu W.; m. Julia Yuet Shan Fung, Jan. 30, 1983; 1 child, Ho. BA, Columbia U., 1975, Oxford U., Eng., 1977, MA, 1980. Solicitor Supreme Ct. Hong Kong and Eng. and Wales; attesting officer, China. Assoc. D.W. Ling & Co., Hong Kong, 1977-81; fgn. law cons. Masuda & Ejiri, Tokyo, 1981; ptnr. Siao, Wen and Leung, 1982—2003; ptnr., chmn. China practice Heller Ehrman, 2003—06; ptnr. Jones Day, Hong Kong, 2006—07; chmn. Sancus Capital Ltd., 2007—08; of counsel Jones Day, Hong Kong, 2008—. Lectr. on Hong Kong law. Adviser on Hong Kong Affairs Govt. of China, 1993-97; vice chmn. Hong Kong Progressive Alliance, 1994-2004; mem. Selection Com. First Govt. of Hong Kong Spl. Adminstrv. Region, 1996; hon. pres. Hong Kong Indsl. Areas Industry and Trade Fedn., 1994-2005; dep. Nat. People's Congress, China, 1998—; vice chmn. Dem. Alliance Betterment and Progress Hong Kong, 2009-. Mem. Law Soc. Hong Kong, Law Soc. Eng., United Oxford and Cambridge Univs. Club (London). Avocation: reading. Office: 406 Fairmont House & Cotton Tree Dr Central Hong Kong Office Phone: 852-31028362. Business E-Mail: cwen@sancuscapital.com.

WEN, GEORGE WALTER SUN, publishing executive, editor; b. Seattle, Jan. 22, 1948; s. Herbert Jack Hsiu-jui and Rena Sun (Hsing-fang) Wen. BA magna cum laude, Dartmouth Coll., 1970; BA hon., Cambridge U., Eng., 1973; postgrad., Harvard U., 1970—71; MA, Cambridge U., Eng., 1976; Licence-ès-Lettres, Univ. Paris-VII, 1979; MS in Journalism, Columbia U., 1986. Sr. lectr. Inst. d'Etudes Politiques de Paris, Paris, 1982—85; sr. editor Attenzione Mag., NYC, 1986; editor N.Y. Mag., NYC, 1987; exec. mng. editor Macmillan Children's Pub. Group, NYC, 1990—. Trustee, bd. trustees Hemophilia Assn. of N.Y., 2002—. Yaddo residency, Saratoga Springs, NY, 2001, Reynolds scholar, 1972—73. Mem.: Phi Kappa Phi, Phi Beta Kappa. Office: Flatiron Bldg 175 Fifth Ave New York NY 10010

WEN, HONG, pharmaceutical executive; married. PhD, Purdue U., West Lafayette, 2002. Fellow Novartis Pharm. Corp., East Hanover, NJ, 2006—. Office: Novartis Pharm Corp One Health Plz East Hanover NJ 07936

WEN, SHIH-LIANG, mathematics professor; came to U.S., 1959; s. S.W. and C.F. (Hsiao) W.; m. Liang Tao; children: Dennis, Andy, Jue, Nannan. BS, Nat. Taiwan U., Taipei, 1956; MS, U. Utah, 1961; PhD, Purdue U., 1968. Assoc. research engr. The Boeing Co., Seattle, 1961-63; with dept. math. Ohio U., Athens, 1968—, successively asst. prof., assoc. prof. and prof., chmn. dept. math., 1985-93. Rsch. analyst Applied Math Rsch. Lab. USAF, Wright-Patterson AFB, Ohio, summer, 1972; vis. rsch. scientist Courant Inst. Math. Scis. NYU, 1978-79; hon. prof. Jiangxi U., People's Republic of China, 1985; disting. vis. prof. Lanzhou U., People's Republic of China, 1989. Mem. Am. Math. Soc., Soc. for Indsl. and Applied Math., Math. Assn. Am. Avocations: fishing, bridge, music. Office: Ohio Univ Dept Math Athens OH 45701

WEN, XIAN-HUAN, hydrogeologist; b. Yongdin, Fujian, China, Oct. 26, 1964; s. Biao-Lan Wen and Mei-Ying Shen; m. Xiaolin Xu, Nov. 22, 1995. B Engring., Hefei U. Technology, Anhui, China, 1984; M Engring., China U. Geoscis., Beijing, 1987; PhD, Royal Inst. Technology, Stockholm, 1995, Polytechnic U. Valencia, Spain, 1996. Rsch. assoc. Polytechnic U. Valencia, 1993-96; cons. prof. China U. of Geoscis., Beijing, 1995—; rsch. assoc. Stanford (Calif.) U., 1996—. Contbr. articles to profl. jours. Recipient Young Scientist Travel award European Geophys. Soc., Hamburg, 1995. Mem. Soc. Petroleum Engrs., Am. Geophys. Union, Internat. Assn. math. Geology. Avocation: sports. Office: Dept Petroleum Engring Stanford Univ Stanford CA 94305

WENDEBORN, RICHARD DONALD, retired manufacturing executive; b. Winnipeg, Man., Can. came to U.S., 1976; naturalized, 1988; s. Curtis and Rose (Lysecki) W.; m. Dorothy Ann Munn, Aug. 24, 1957; children: Margaret Gayle, Beverley Jane, Stephen Richard, Peter Donald, Ann Elizabeth. Diploma, Colo. Sch. Mines, 1952; grad. advanced mgmt. program, Harvard U., 1974. With Can. Ingersoll-Rand Co., Montreal, 1952—, gen. mgr., v.p., dir., 1968, pres., 1969-74, chmn. bd., 1976—; exec. v.p. Ingersoll-Rand Co., Woodcliff Lake, NJ, 1976-89; ret., 1989. Mem. Can Govt. Oil and Gas Tech. Exch. Program with former USSR, 1972—, Minerals and Metals Mission to China, 1972—. Mem. Resource Fund Colo. Sch. Mines; past pres., dir. Town and River Civic Assn; Stephen min. New Hope Presbyn. Ch., Ft. Myers, Fla., 2008. Recipient Disting. Achievement medal, Colo. Sch. Mines, 1973. Mem. Machinery and Equipment Mfrs. Assn. Can. (bd. dirs. 1974—, past chmn.), Royal Palm Yacht Club (commodore 1994), Internat. Order of Blue Gavel (past Commodore's Club, past pres. Royal Palm br. dist. 8), Tau Beta Pi. Home: 12998 Beacon Cove Ln Fort Myers FL 33919-8203 Personal E-mail: dickandda@aol.com.

WENDEL, CHARLES ALLEN, retired lawyer; b. Lockport, NY, Aug. 13, 1942; s. Harold Henry and Doris Lillian (Gardner) W.; m. Helen W. Roberts, June 23, 1973; children: William Charles, Jonathan David. BChem Engring., Rensselaer Poly Inst., 1964; JD, Am. U., 1968. Bar: N.Y. 1969, Va. 1971, D.C. 1980, U.S. Dist. Ct. Appeals (fed. and 4th cirs.), U.S. Dist. Ct. (ea. and we. dists.) Va., U.S. Supreme Ct. Patent examiner U.S. Patent and Trademark Office, Washington, 1964—66, assoc. solicitor, 1985—88; patent trainee Union Carbide Corp., Washington, 1966—68, patent atty. NYC, 1968—70; assoc., then ptnr. Stevens, Davis, Miller & Mosher, Arlington, Va., 1970—83; ptnr. firm Wegner & Bretschneider, Washington, 1983—85; assoc. Lyon & Lyon, Washington, 1988—90; founding ptnr. Parkhurst,& Wendel, Alexandria, Va., 1995—2005; of counsel Steptoe & Johnson, LLP, Washington, 2005—06; assoc. Oblon, Spivak, McClelland, Maier & Neustadt P.C., Alexandria, Va., 2006—07; of counsel Roberts Mardula Wertheim LLC, 2007—08. Contbr. articles to profl. jours. Mem. Va. State Bar (patent trademark copyright sect., chmn. 1977-78), Am. Intellectual Patent Law Assn., Patent Lawyers Club Washington (prs. 1982-83), Delta Theta Phi. Republican. Home Phone: 703-837-9047; Office Phone: 703-837-9047.

WENDEL, JOHN FREDRIC, lawyer, consultant; b. Newark, Nov. 8, 1936; s. John J. and Margaret D. (Mortimer) W.; m. Barbara Vaughn Smith, Dec. 17, 1960 (dec. July 1978); children: David I., Stephen F.; m. Carlene M. Arnoldini, 1 child, Carlene Margaret. BA, U. Fla., 1958; JD, Stetson U., 1963. Bar: Fla. 1963, U.S. Dist. Ct (so. and mid. dists.) 1964, U.S. Ct. Appeals (5th, 9th, and 11th cirs.) 1964, U.S. Supreme Ct. 1968. Chmn. Wendel & Chritton Chartered and predecessor firms, Lakeland, Fla., 1965—2007; of counsel sponsler Bennett Jacobs & Adams, Pa., 2007—. Town atty. Town of St. Leo, Fla., 1964-78, town judge, 1968; mcpl. judge Lakeland, Fla., 1966; county atty. Citrus County, Fla., 1976-81; of counsel, Whyte and Hirschboeck, Milw., 1989-90, gen. counsel and spl. counsel to various profl. baseball leagues, 1969-1998; vis. prof. law, dir. Nat. Sports Law Inst., Marquette U. Law Sch., Milw., 1989-90; adj. prof. law Marquette U. Law Sch., Milw., 1990-91, adj. prof. Stetson U. Coll. Law, 1992-93; adj. faculty mem. Fla. So. Coll., Lakeland, 1963-65; faculty mem. St. Leo Coll., 1963-73; del. 2d Internat. Conf. Ptnrs. for Alliance for Progress; mem. Fla. Columbia Alliance Coms. and Subco.; gen. counsel Sun 'n Fun Fly-In, Inc., 1998—. Mem. editorial bd. Sports Law and Fin., 1992-98. Assoc. mem. counsel Fla. Sports Adv. Coun. Served to 1st lt. USMC, 1957-59. Named one of Lakeland's Five Outstanding Young Men, Jaycees, 1967. Mem. Am. Arbitration Assn. (arbitrator alternative dispute resolution to settle sports disputes), Sports Lawyers Assn. (pres. 1986-93, sec., v.p., bd. dirs. 1974—, pres. and dir. emeritus, Award of Excellence 1993), The Fla. Bar (exec. coun. entertainment, arts and sports law sect.), Lakeland Bar Assn., Fla. Assn. County Attys. (pres. 1981), Nat. Assn. of Profl. Baseball Leagues, Inc. (gen. counsel 1971-82), KC. Republican. Roman Catholic. Office: Sponsler Bennett Jacobs & Addams Pa 336 W highland Dr Lakeland FL 33813 Office Phone: 863-603-7730. E-mail: jwendel@wendelchritton.com.

WENDEL, RICHARD FREDERICK, economist, educator, consultant; b. Chgo., Apr. 29, 1930; s. Elmer Carl and Victoria Matilda (Jeffrey) W.; m. Leslie Jane Travis, June 15, 1957; children: John Travis, Andrew Stewart. AB, Augustana Coll., 1951; MBA, U. Pa., 1957, PhD (fellow 1962-64), 1966. Asst. to pres. Flexonics Corp., Maywood, Ill., 1957-59; sales rep., product mgr. Kordite div. Nat. Distillers Corp., Macedon, N.Y., 1959-62; instr. Wharton Sch., U. Pa., 1964-65; asst. prof. mktg. Grad. Sch. Bus. Adminstrn., Washington U., St. Louis, 1965-69; assoc. prof. U. Conn., 1969-74, prof., 1974-90, prof. emeritus, 1990. Mem. U.S. Census Field Adv. Commn., 1967-69; mem. acad. adv. commn. Bur. Labor Stats., U.S. Bur. Census Survey of Consumer Expenditures, 1971-76; mem. Conn. Export Devel. Council, Dept. Commerce, 1972-76; dir. Neon Software Inc. Author: (with M.L. Bell) Economic Importance of Highway Advertising, 1966; (with W. Gorman) Selling: Preparation. Persuasion. Strategy., 1983, 88; editor: Readings in Marketing, 1973-74, 75-76, 77-78, 78-79, 79-80, 80-81, (with C.L. Lapp) Add to Your Selling Know-How, 1968; editorial staff: jour. Mktg., 1965-74. Bd. dirs. Roper Center. Served with USAF, 1951-55. Center for Real Estate and Urban Econs. grantee, 1969-70 Mem. Am. Mktg. Assn., N.Y. Acad. Scis. Democrat. Episcopalian. Home: 106 S Queen St Chestertown MD 21620-1522 Office Phone: 410-778-7185.

WENDELBURG, NORMA RUTH, composer, educator, pianist; b. Stafford, Kans. d. Henry and Anna Louise (Moeckel) W. MusB, Bethany Coll., 1943; MusM, U. Mich., 1947, Eastman Sch. Music, 1951, postgrad., 1964-65, 66-67, PhD in Composition, 1969; postgrd., Mozarteum, 1953-54, Vienna Acad. Music, 1955. Tchr. music edn., piano Wayne (Nebr.) State Coll., 1947-50; asst. prof. Bethany Coll., Lindsborg, Kans., 1952-53, U. Iowa, 1956-58; asst. prof. composition, theory, piano Hardin-Simmons U., Abilene, Tex., 1958-66, chmn. grad. com. Sch. Music, 1960-66, founder, chmn. ann. univ. festival contemporary music, 1959—; assoc. prof. music Dallas Bapt. Coll., 1973-75; rsch. asst. to dir. grad. studies Eastman Sch. Music, 1966-67; assoc. prof., chmn. dept. theory and composition S.W. Tex. State U., 1969-72; mem. faculty Friends Bible Coll., Haviland, Kans., 1977-83. Guest composer colls. including U. Ottawa, 1984; performed in Eng., Prague and Warsaw; performed Am. Conservatory Mus., Charles Ives Ctr. for Am. Music, 1990—; various solo recitals and festivals. Composer: Symphony, 1967, Suite for Violin and Piano, 1965, Song Cycle for Soprano, flutes, Piano, 1974, Music for Two Pianos, 1985, Affirmation, 1982, Interlacings (organ), 1983, (recorded) Suite No. 2 for Violin and Piano, 1989, Fantasy for Trumpet and Piano, 1990, Sonata for Clarinet and Piano, Sinfonietta, 1994, Concerto for Clarinet and Orch., (albums) Sinfonietta, 1997, Mosaic, 2001, Concerto for Clarinet and Oroh, 2002, (CD) Warsaw Rhapsody, Warsaw Nat. Philharm. Orch., 2006; performances Mosaic, 2001, Symphony Orch. of Prague, Smetana Hall, 1999, Symphony Hall, Boston, 1998, Concertino for Oboe and String Orch., Alice Tully Hall Lincoln Ctr., N.Y.C., 1999, Warsaw Rhapsody, Warsaw Philharm. Orch., Lutoslawski Hall, 1999, Warsaw Rhapsody, Warsaw, 1999, GALAXY, Bratislava, Slovakia, 2006; numerous recordings: of orchestral works on CD. Recipient Meet the Composer award N.Y. State Coun. Arts, 1979; named Kans. Composer of Yr., Kans. Fed. Music Clubs, 2000; Composition scholar Composers' Conf. Middlebury (Vt.), 1950, Berkshire Ctr., 1953; Fulbright awardee, 1953-55; Resident fellow Huntington Hartford Found., 1955-56, 58, 61; MacDowell Colony fellow, 1958, 60, 70; Nat. Festival Performing Arts fellow, 1989. Mem. ASCAP (Composition awards 1988-2009), Am. Soc. Univ. Composers, Minn. Composers Forum, Am. Women Composers, Music Club (Hutchinson), Sigma Alpha Iota. Republican. Avocations: travel, photography, gardening. Address: 2206 N Van Buren St Hutchinson KS 67502-3738

WENDER, PHYLLIS BELLOWS, literary agent; m. Ira Tensard Wender; children: Justin Bellows, Sarah Tensard. BA, Wells Coll. Publicity dir. Grove Press, NYC, Dell Pub. Co., NYC; theatrical agt. Artists Agy. Inc., NYC; prin. agt. Wender & Assocs., NYC; prin., agt., ptnr. Rosenstone/Wender, NYC; agent Gersh Agy., NYC, 2007—. Trustee Wells Coll., Aurora, N.Y., 1981-90. Mem. Women's Media Group (dir. 1988-90), Cosmopolitan Club. Office: The Gersh Agy 41 Madison Ave 33rd Fl New York NY 10010 Personal E-mail: pbwender@aol.com.

WENDLANDT, DOROTHEA SCHNEPF, artist, writer; b. Trenton, NJ, Aug. 17, 1927; d. Emil Ludwig Schnepf and Helen Dorothea Bruker, Cleveland A. Mulligan (Stepfather); m. Robert Jack Wendlandt, Aug. 14, 1974; children: Lynn Mioduszewski, Robert Jack Wendlandt, Jr., Leigh, Steven Daniel. Pictorial Illustration diploma, Newark Sch. of Fine and Indsl. Art, 1949. Artist Harold Pearson Advt., Edison, NJ, 1955—56; illustrator Joseph P. Schneider, NYC, 1957—58; asst. art dir. Batista Advt., NYC, 1959—60; ednl. exhibit designer/illustrator Binney and Smith, NYC, 1960—68; corp. dir. of advt. art Fedders Corp., Edison, NJ, 1968—74; artist, co-owner Bob's Art Ctr., Old Bridge, NJ/Sarasota, Fla., 1974—. Mem. NJ Art Dirs. Club, 1971—74; art tchr. Middlesex Jr. Coll., Edison, NJ, 1972—73; owner DS and W Creative Art Svc., Old Bridge, NJ, 1974—78. One-woman shows include Beaux Art Gallery, St. Petersburg, Fla., 1982, exhibitions include Phila. Mus. of Art Craft, 1966, Represented in permanent collections Fedders Exec. Offices, Edison, NJ, acrylic painting, Out of Gas (Meml. Award Nat. Soc. of Painters in Acrylics and Casein, 1983), Tools (Meml. Award Nat. Soc. of Painters in Acrylics and Casien, 1987), Birds in a Window (first prize Manatee Art League, 1983), acrylic and watercolor paintings, Four Artists, Bodies Of Work (Parade of Prize Winners, 1984), watercolor, Cactus Collection 1989 (Best of State Nat. League of Am. Penwomen State Show, 1989), Cactus Collection Two (Venice Art League Best of Show, 1990); author: An Artist's Life: A Tale of Love & Woe, 2006. Treas. Metuchen Arts Coun., NJ, 1970—74; pres. Art Uptown, Sarasota, Fla., 1982—83; bd. dirs. Sarasota Art Assn., Fla., 1981—88; dir. St. Boniface Conservatory of Visual Arts, Sarasota, Fla., 1984—86. Recipient Grumbacher award, Grumbacher Inc./ Sarasota Art Assn., 1983. Mem.: Nat. Soc. of Painters in Acrylics and Casein (life), Nat. League of Am. Penwomen (life; v.p. 1984—86). Democrat-Npl. Christian. Avocations: opera management, singing, writing, reading. Home: 5577 Burnt Branch Cir Sarasota FL 34232 Personal E-mail: lowerball243@aol.com.

WENDLANDT, GARY E., insurance company executive; married; 3 children. BS in applied math., computer sci., Wash. U., Mo. Various positions Mass. Mutual Life Ins. Co., 1972—92, exec. v.p., chief investment officer, 1992—99; exec. v.p., exec. mgmt. com. New York Life Ins. Co., NYC, 1999—2006, sr. exec. v.p., chief investment officer, 2006—07, vice-chmn., bd. dir., chief investment officer, 2007—. Fellow: Soc. of Actuaries; mem.: Am. Acad. of Actuaries. Office: NY Life Ins Co 51 Madison Ave New York NY 10010*

WENDLINGER, ROBERT MATTHEW, communications and memory consultant; b. NYC, 1922; s. Harry and Rose (Pollock) W.; m. Dalis Peralta, 1955 (div. 1973); children: David, Marcella, Marta; m. Joan Hays Cole, June 23, 1984. Student, U. Calif., Berkeley, 1942—43, Columbia U., 1947—52. Writer & critic review The Bandstand, Tempo, 1939—50; script editor Radio Free Europe, NYC, 1950—52; assoc. editor Ind. Film Jour., NYC, 1953—57; gen. mgr. Kermit Rolland and Assocs., Princeton, NJ, 1957—59; exec. asst. in charge editl. svcs. United Hosp. Fund of N.Y., NYC, 1959—60; editl. assoc. in pub. rels. N.Y. Life Ins. Co., NYC, 1960—65; mgr. info. sect. Com. for Air and Water Conservation Am. Petroleum Inst., NYC, 1965—66; with Bank of Am. NT & SA, San Francisco, 1966—78, adminstrv. officer, 1967—70, asst. v.p. comm., 1970—78; pres. Comm. Cons. and Svcs., Berkeley, Calif., 1978—82; pub. rels. Nestle Corp., White Plains, NY, 1983—84; pres. Proust Press, Oakland, Calif., 1994—. Mem. grad. faculty St. Mary's Coll., Moraga, Calif., 1975-78; mem. Astron Corp. Author: (with James M. Reid, Jr.) Effective Letters: A Program in Self-Instruction, 1964, 3d edit., 1978, Japanese edit., 1996, The Memory Triggering Book: Using Your Memories to Enhance Your Life and Your Relationships, 1995; contbr.: Everybody Wins: TA Applied to Organizations, 1973, Affirmative Action for Women, 1973, McGraw-Hill Ency. Professional Management, 1978. Fellow Am. Bus. Comm. Assn.; mem. Indsl. Comm. Coun. (past pres.). Office Phone: 510-845-5551.

WENDORF, RICHARD HAROLD, library director, scholar; b. Cedar Rapids, Iowa, Mar. 17, 1948; s. Harold Albert and Jeanne Ellen (Hamblin) Wendorf; m. Barbara Hilderman, 1970 (div. 1983); m. Diana Thanet French, 1984 (div. 1995); children: Reed Thanet Wendorf-French, Carolyn Thanet Wendorf-French; m. Elizabeth Morse, 1997. BA, Williams Coll., 1970; PhB, U. Oxford, Eng., 1972; MA, Princeton U., 1974, PhD, 1976. From asst. prof. English to assoc. prof. English Northwestern U., Evanston, Ill., 1976-86, assoc. dean, 1984-88, prof. English and art history, 1986-89; libr. dir. Houghton Libr., Harvard U., Cambridge, Mass., 1989-97; Stanford Calderwood dir. & libr. Boston Athenaeum, 1997—2009, dir. emeritus, 2009—. Sr. lectr. fine arts Harvard U., 1990—97, acting libr. Fine Arts Libr., 1991—92, dir. NEH summer seminars coll. tchrs., 1990, 92, 96; lectr. Phi Beta Kappa Assocs., 1992—96; dir. NEH summer seminars coll. tchrs. Northwestern U., 1987, Boston Anthenaeum, 2002, 04; Robert Sterling Clark vis. prof. art history Williams Coll., 1993; bd. mgrs. Lewis Walpole Libr., 2005—. Author: The Elements of Life: Biography and Portrait Painting in Stuart and Georgian England, 1990, William Collins and Eighteenth-Century English Poetry, 1981, papaerback edit., 1991, Sir Joshua Reynolds: The Painter in Society, 1996, The Scholar-Librarian, 2005, After Sir Joshua, 2005; editor: The Boston Athenaeum, 2009, Am. Membership Libraries, 2007, Articulate Images: The Sister Arts from Hogarth to Tennyson, 1983, Rare Book and Manuscript Libraries in the Twenty-First Century, 1993; editor: (with Charles Ryskamp) The Works of William Collins, 1979; contbr. essays in field; mem. editl. bd. Studies in 18th Century Culture, 1985—89, Word and Image, 1992—2000, Yale edit. Writings of Samuel Johnson, Old-Time New Eng., 1996—99. Trustee Mus. Fine Arts, Boston. Grantee, NEH, 1979; fellow, John Simon Guggenheim Meml. Found., 1989—90; Rsch. grantee, Folger Shakespeare Libr., Washington, 1976, Am. Philos. Soc., Phila., 1977, 1982, Henry E. Hungtinton Libr., 1979, 2003, Yale Ctr. Brit. Art, 1983, Brit. Acad., 2003, Jr. Rsch. fellow, Am. Coun. Learned Socs., 1978—79, Sr. Rsch. fellow, 1981—82, Rsch. fellow, NEH, 1988—89. Mem.: Soc. Antiquaries London, Mass. Hist. Soc, The Johnsonians (chmn. 1994—95, 1997—98, 2007—08), Nat. Com. Stds. Arts, Colonial Soc. Mass., Soc. Brit. Art Historians, Coll. Art Assn., Am. Soc. 18th Century Studies (pres. Midwest regional soc. 1986, Annibel Jenkins Biography prize 1998), Am. Antiquarian Soc., Keats-Shelley Assn. Am. (bd. dirs. 1993—98), Signet Soc. (assoc.), U. Club (NY), Union Club Boston,

Saturday Club, Cambridge Sci. Club, Grolier Club, Phi Beta Kappa (exec. bd. Chgo. 1984—87, nominating com. 1998—2002). Home: 24 Cedar St Cohasset MA 02025-1138

WENDT, CHARLES WILLIAM, soil scientist, educator; b. Plainview, Tex., July 12, 1931; s. Charles Gottlieb and Winnie Mae (Bean) W.; m. Clara Anne Diller, Oct. 15, 1955; children: Charles Diller, John William, Elaine Anne, Cynthia Lynne. BS in Agronomy, Tex. A&M U., 1951, PhD in Soil Physics, 1966; MS in Agronomy, Tex. Tech U., 1957. Research asst. Tex. Tech Coll., 1953-55, instr. agronomy, 1957-61, asst. prof., 1961-63; research asst. soil physics Tex. A&M U., 1963-65, research assoc., 1965-66; asst. prof. Tex. A&M U. (Agrl. Research and Extension Center), Lubbock, 1966-69, assoc. prof., 1969-74, prof., 1974-91, prof. emeritus, 1991—. Cons. cotton prodn. Ministry of Agr. Sudan, summer 1960; cons. Irrigation Assn., 1977-81, Office of Tech. and Assessment, 1982, S.E. Consortium for Internat. Devel., 1989, Rhone Poulenc Agrl. Co., 1992-93; prin. backstop scientist U.S. AID West African Rsch. Program on Soil-Plant0Water Mgmt., 1982-91; chmn. agrl. sect. Southwestern and Rocky Mountain divsn. AAAS, 1982-83. Contbr. articles to profl. jours., chpt. to book. Del. Lubbock County Rep. Conv., 1978; elder Westminster Presbyn. Ch.; Tex. rep. to Great Plains Coun. 1 com. on evapotranspiration; bd. dirs. Presbyn. Ctr., Inc., 1999—, The South Plains Food Bank, 1999—, bd. dirs. farm, orchard and garden divsn., 2002-. 1st lt. U.S. Army, 1951-53. Named Outstanding Researcher High Plains Research Found., 1982; recipient Superior Achievement award for rsch., soil and crop scis. dept. Tex. A&M Univ., 1987, Vice Chancellors award in excellence as mem. TROPSOILS Rsch. team Tex. A&M U., 1996; grantee industry and water dists. Dept. Interior, U.S. AID, EPA. Mem. Soil Sci. Soc. Am., Am. Soc. Agronomy, Optimist Club (1st v.p., bd. dirs. 2001-2004). Home: 4518 22nd St Lubbock TX 79407-2515 Office: Texas Agrl Expt Station RR 3 Lubbock TX 79403-9803 Business E-Mail: absendt@cox.net.

WENDT, E. ALLAN, international affairs consultant; b. Chgo., Nov. 8, 1935; s. John Arthur Frederic and Dorothy S. BA magna cum laude, Yale U., 1957; Cert. in Politics, Inst. d'Etudes Politques, 1958; MPA, Harvard U., 1967. Econ. comml. officer Am. Embassy, Saigon, Vietnam, 1967-71; fin. officer U.S. Mission to European Cmtys., Brussels, 1971-74; State Dept. fellow Coun. on Fgn. Rels., NYC, 1974-75; dir. Office Internat. Commodities Dept. State, Washington, 1975-79; counselor for econ. and comml. affairs Am. Embassy, Cairo, 1979-81; dep. asst. sec. of state for internat. energy and resources policy Dept. State, 1981-86, sr. rep. for strategic tech. policy, 1987-92, with rank of amb., 1988-92, U.S. amb. to Republic of Slovenia Ljubljana, 1993-95, spl. rep. Internat. Donor Activities in Kosovo, 1998-2000; internat. affairs cons., 2000—. Mem. Coun. Fgn. Rels. Washington Inst. Fgn. Affairs.; mem. adv. bd Nat Youth Leadership Forum; bd. dir Assn. Dip Tng. and Studies. Contbr. articles to profl. jours., radio stas. and newspapers. Recipient award for heroism Dept. State, 1968, Presdl. Meritorious Svc. award, 1986, Superior Honor award Dept. State, 1992. Episcopalian.

WENDT, OLIVER, special education educator; MA, U. Nebr. Lincoln, 1998; MS, U. Cologne, Germany, 2000; PhD, Purdue U., West Lafayette, Ind., 2006. Clin. instr. Purdue U., 2005—06, asst. prof. speech, lang., hearing scis. & spl. edn., 2006—. Recipient Editor award, Jour. Augmentative and Alternative Communication, 2005. Mem.: Campbell Collaboration, Edn. & Methods Groups, Assn. Behavior Analysis Internat., Am. Speech-Lang. Hearing Assn., Am. Assn. Intellectual & Devel. Disabilities, Sigma Xi, Sci. Rsch. Soc. Avocations: running, soccer, ping pong/table tennis. Office: Purdue Univ 100 N University St West Lafayette IN 47907-2098 Office Fax: 765-496-1228. Business E-Mail: olli@purdue.edu.

WENDT, RICHARD L., manufacturing executive; b. 1931; From mgr. frame factory to mgr. ops. Caradco; CEO Jeld-Wen Inc., Klamath Falls, Oreg., 1960—2003, chmn., 2003—. Address: Jeld Wen Inc PO Box 1329 Klamath Falls OR 97601-0268 Office: Jen Weld Inc 401 Harbor Isles Blvd Klamath Falls OR 97601

WENDT, THOMAS, finance company executive; CPA, Wis. Auditor Coopers & Lybrand, Milw., 1973-75; supr. Conley, McDonald, Sprague & Co., Milw., 1975-80; CFO E. Cen./Select Sires, Waupun, Wis., 1981—, also rec. sec., bd. dirs. Bd. dirs. Moravian Homes Inc., Mueller Apts., Inc., Marquardt Meml. Manor, Inc., Watertown, Wis., sec., treas. bd. dirs., 1986—; bd. dirs. Hus Apts., Inc., sec.-treas., 1993—. Mem. Marquardt Found., 1988—; bd. dirs. Zinsendorf Hall, 1989—, sec., treas., 1989—, forward campaign chmn., 1988; pres. bd. trustees Watertown Moravian Ch., 1981-84, bd. elders, 1990-93, ch. sec., 2000-03; adv. del. Western Dist. Synod, Wis., 1982, 86, 90, 96; bd. dirs. Moravian Homes of Sturgeon Bay, 1991—; bd. dirs. Hus Apts., Inc., 1993—, sec., treas., 1993—. Mem. AICPA, Wis. Inst. CPAs, Milw. Art Mus., Beaver Dam Lions Club (bd. dirs. 2005—, pres. 2009-). Office: E Central/Select Sires PO Box 191 Waupun WI 53963-0191

WENDT, VERNON EARL, internist, cardiologist; b. Cleve., Mar. 26, 1931; s. Raymond C. and Esther L. (Naujoks) Wendt; m. Hildegarde Caroline Moeller, Aug. 14, 1953; children: David, Frederick, Kathryn, Elizabeth, Doralyn, James, Vernon Earl Jr. BS in Zoology and Chemistry cum laude, Baldwin-Wallace Coll., 1952; MD, Columbia U., 1956. Diplomate Am. Bd. Internal Medicine. Intern Detroit Receiving Hosp., 1956—57, resident, 1959—62; USPHS postdoctoral fellow in cardiology Wayne State U. Sch. of Medicine, Detroit, 1962—65, from instr. to asst. prof. medicine, 1961—65; dir. rsch. Blodgett Meml. Med. Ctr., Grand Rapids, Mich., 1965—67; pvt. practice Grand Rapids, 1967—2000. Capt. M.C. USAF, 1957—59. Head Elder grant, Lauren Ch., Wyoming, Mich., 2008—. Fellow: ACP, Coun. Geriatric Cardiology, Am. Coll. Angiology, Am. Coll. Cardiology; mem.: AMA, Mich. State Med. Soc., Mich. Health Coun. (trustee 1998—), Am. Acad. Anti-Aging Medicine, Kent County Med. Soc., Mich. Soc. Internal Medicine (pres. 1991—92), Am. Lung Assn. Mich. (pres. 1978—80), Am. Heart Assn. Mich. (trustee 1973—93, pres. 1987—88). Lutheran. Avocations: golf, gardening, walking. Home and Office: 1620 Andover Rd SE Grand Rapids MI 49506 Office Phone: 616-949-6735. Personal E-mail: vhwendt@comcast.net.

WENER, BRIAN D., psychologist; s. Martin M. and Rachel Wener; 1 child, Sara. BA in Psychology with honors, Carleton U., 1971; MA in Psychology, SUNY, Plattsburgh, 1975; D of Psychology, Ctrl. Mich. U., 1982. Lic. psychologist NH, 1983, Mass., 1995, cert. sch. psychologist NH, 1981. Clin. psychologist Riverbend Counseling, Concord, NH, 1983—87; psychologist II Philbrook Ctr., 1975—78; clin. psychologist pvt. practice, Portsmouth, 1987—; sch. psychologist Hampton Schs., 2000—06. Cons., evaluator NH Medicaid Disability Unit, Concord, 1993—. Fellow: NH Psychol. Assn. (bd. dirs. 1992—94); mem.: APA, Nat. Assn. Sch. Psychologists. Avocations: photography, guitar. Office: 404 The Hill Portsmouth NH 03801-3736 Office Phone: 603-431-1294. Personal E-mail: shaman426@gmail.com.

WENG, DANIELLA, pharmacist, researcher; d. Kwok Soo and Zhao Quin Young. BS in Pharmacy, L.I. U., 1998, MS in Pharmaceutics, 2002. Intern in pharmacy N.Y. Hosp.-Cornell Med. Ctr., NYC, 1996—97; clin. pharmacy extern Meml. Sloan-Kettering Cancer Ctr., NYC, 1997; intern in pharmacy Vis. Nurse Svc. N.Y., NYC, 1998—99; rsch. project L.I. U., Bklyn., 1999—2002; pharmacist Kingsbrook Jewish Med. Ctr., Bklyn., 2001, Woodhull Med. Ctr., Bklyn., 2001—. Pharmacy Alumni scholar, Arnold & Marie Schwartz Coll. Of Pharmacy, 1993—98. Mem.: Am. Pharm. Assn., Am. Assn. Pharm. Scientists. Achievements include research in pharmacokinetics of acyclovir in rabbit estimated via microdialysis sampling after IV-bolus and iontophoretic administration. Avocations: hiking, ice skating, dance, reading, travel. Personal E-mail: daniella_weng@yahoo.com.

WENG, GEORGE JUENG-CIOUS, engineering educator; b. Oct. 8, 1944; s. Wan-Chung and Kuang-chieh (Hsieh) Weng; m. Jackie Li; children: Shawn, Cidney, Zoe;children from previous marriage: Bruce, Joyce. BS, Taiwan U., 1967; MPhil, Yale U., 1971, PhD, 1974. Rsch. fellow Delft U. Tech., Netherlands, 1973—74; postdoctoral fellow Yale U., UCLA, 1974—76; sr. rsch. engr. GM Rsch. Lab., Warren, Mich., 1976—77; asst. prof. mech. and aerospace engring. Rutgers U., New Brunswick, NJ, 1977—80, assoc. prof., 1980—84, prof., 1984—92, disting. prof., 1992—, grad. dir., 1995—98. Editor Acta Mechanica, 1985—, tech. editor Jour. Engring. Materials and Tech., trans. ASME, 1992—97, mem. editl. bd. Internat. Jour. Plasticity, 1985—, Acta Mechanica Solida Sinica, 1997—, JSME Internat. Jour., 1997—2002, Mechanics and Materials in Design, 2004—, Mechanics of Advanced Materials and Structures, 2004—, Mechanics of Materials, 2007—, Open Mech. Engring. Jour., 2007—, Open Mechanics Jour., 2007—; contbr. more than 160 articles to profl. jours. NSF grantee, 1978—. Fellow ASME, Am. Acad. Mechanics. Achievements include research in mechanics of materials, micromechanics of composite materials, shape-memory alloys, ferroelectric ceramics, nanocrystalline materials. Home: 65 Sycamore Way Warren NJ 07059 Office: Sch Engring Rutgers U New Brunswick NJ 08903 Home Phone: 908-822-8828; Office Phone: 732-445-2223. Business E-Mail: weng@jove.rutgers.edu.

WENGER, DIANE E., history professor; b. Lebanon, Pa., July 31, 1948; d. Doris M. West; m. Lynn R. Wenger, Apr. 27, 1967; children: Ethan Richard, Seth Jonathan, Laura Beth. PhD, U. Del., Newark, 2002. Author: (book) A Country Storekeeper in Pennsylvania. Chmn. Planning Commn., Heidelberg Twp., Pa., 2000—08. Mem.: Pa. German Soc. (bd. mem. 2008). Home: PO Box 148 Schaefferstown PA 17088 Office: Wilkes Univ 84 W South St Wilkes Barre PA 18766 Business E-Mail: dianewenger@verizon.net.

WENGER, JAMES L., education educator; b. Horton, Kans., Aug. 4, 1944; s. Donald and Edith Wenger; m. Phyllis C. Newton, June 2, 1973; children: Scott, Stacy. BSE, Emporia State U., Kans., 1967, MS, 1972. Cert. DP/CIS vocat. Kans. State Bd. Edn., 2008. Dir. data processing North Ctrl. Kans. Tech. Coll., Beloit, Kans., 1970—76; instr. Emporia State U., 1976—79, asst. prof., 1979—2004, assoc. prof., 2005—07, mem. emeritus faculty, 2007—. Contbr. articles pub. to profl. jour. Recipient Svc. award, Emporia State U., 1989, Pres. Equity award, 1997, 2003, Instrn. award, 2005, Disting. Rsch. award, Allied Academies, 2003; grantee Microsoft grant, Microsoft, 1997. Mem.: NEA, Kans. Nat. Edn. Assn., Assn. Info. Sys., Assn. Info. Tech. Profls., Mid Am. Assn. for Computers in Edn. (pres. 1982—83, bd. dirs. 1983—85, sec. 1985—2007), Beta Gamma Sigma. Lutheran. Avocations: golf, fishing.

WENGER, LARRY BRUCE, law librarian, educator; b. Everett, Wash., Dec. 21, 1941; s. Lester Edwin Wenger and Selma Marie (Norberg) W. Saterstrom; m. Marilyn Diane Watt, June 26, 1965; children: Bruce Daniel, Kathleen Marie. BA, U. Wash., 1964, JD, 1967; MLS, Simmons Coll., 1969. Reference libr. Sch. Law Harvard U., Cambridge, Mass., 1967-69; asst. law libr. SUNY, Buffalo, 1969-71, law libr., assoc. prof. law, 1971-76; law libr., prof. law U. Va., Charlottesville, 1976—. Cons. to law librs.; bd. dirs. Nat. Ctr. for Preservation Law. Editor: Marine Affairs Bibliography. Mem. Am. Assn. Law Librs., Internat. Assn. Law Librs. (pres. 1995-2001), Bibliog. Soc., Bibliog. Soc. Am. Home: 2630 Meriwether Dr Charlottesville VA 22901-9513 Office: U Va Law Libr 580 Massie Rd Charlottesville VA 22903-1739

WENGER, NANETTE KASS, cardiologist, medical researcher, educator; b. NYC, Sept. 3, 1930; d. Aaron Zelig and Edith (Malkin) Kass; m. Julius Wenger; children: Deborah, Judith, Beth. BA summa cum laude, Hunter Coll., 1951; MD, Harvard U., 1954. Intern Mt. Sinai Hosp., NYC, 1954—55, chief resident in cardiology, 1956—57; sr. resident in medicine Grady Meml. Hosp., Atlanta, 1958; fellow in cardiology Emory U. Sch. Medicine, Atlanta, 1958—59, instr. medicine, 1959—62, assoc. in medicine, 1962—64, asst. prof. cardiology, 1964—68, assoc. prof., 1968—71, prof. medicine Divsn. Cardiology, 1971—; cons. Emory Heart and Vascular Ctr., Atlanta; mem. med. staff Crawford W. Long Hosp., Atlanta, 1977—; chief cardiology Grady Meml. Hosp., Atlanta. Dir. cardiac clinics Grady Meml. Hosp., 1960—, chief cardiology, 1998—; cons. cardiology VA Med. Ctr., Atlanta, 1988—; participant numerous profl. symposiums and confs.; mem. cardiovas. and renal drugs adv. com. U.S. FDA, 1978-82; co-chair nat. plan for cardiac rehab. com. Div. Vocat. Rehab., Social and Rehab. Svcs., HEW, 1973-90; mem. Internat. Task Force for Prevention of Coronary Heart Disease, 1989—; founding fellow Soc. Geriatric Cardiology, 1986, bd. dirs., 1987—, pres., 1994-95; former chair, US Nat. Heart, Lung, and Blood Inst. Conf. on Cardiovascular Health and Disease in Women; cons. Emory Heart Ctr.; heads the Emory U. component of the Heart and Estrogen-Progestin Replacement Study (HERS). Mem. editl. bd. various profl. publs. including Cardiac Rehab. Quar., 1974-79, Primary Care, 1975-79, Internat. Jour. Sports Cardiology, 1983—, Med. Month, 1983-84, Jour. Cardiovasc. and Pulmonary Medicine, 1983—, Geriatric Cardiology, 1986—, Nutrition, Metabolism and Cardiovasc. Disease, 1989—; reviewer publs. including Am. Jour. Medicine, 1972—, Am. Jour. Cardiology, 1979—, Am. Heart Jour., 1975—, European Heart Jour., 1983—; editor Am. Jour. Geriatric Cardiology, editor-in-chief; assoc. editor The Heart; co-editor (with Peter Collins) Women and Heart Disease, 2005; contbr. articles to profl. jours.; contbr. book chpts. Chair Heart Sunday program, 1968-69, program chair Fulton County Heart Unit, 1969-71, bd. dirs., 1969-79, 80-82, pres., 1977-78; fellow coun. clin. cardiology, Am. Heart Assn., 1970, chair rehab. com., 1972-75, chair artherosclerosis task force, 1973-74, program v.p., 1975-76, pres., 1977-78, bd. dirs., 1975-79, mem./past mem. numerous other coms.; mem. med. adv. and cardiovasc. health coms. Butler St. YMCA, 1980-82; chair, WHO Expert Com. on Rehabilitation after Cardiovascular Disease; co-chair, Guideline Panel on Cardiac Rehabilitation, US Agy. for Healthcare Policy and Rsch. Recipient Myrtle Wreath award Atlanta Hadassah, 1967, award of Achievement, Nat. Ctr. for Vol. Action, 1978, Outstanding Profl. Achievement award, Hunter Coll., 1993, President's Women in Sci. award, Am. Med. Women's Assn., 1993, Citation, Am. Coll. Sports Medicine, 1994, Jan J. Kellermann Meml. award for Cardiovascular Prevention and Rehabilitation, Internat. Soc. Heart Failure, 1995, Juha P. Kokko award for Excellence in Cardiovascular Lecturing and Edu., Dept. Med. Housestaff, Emory Univ. Sch. Med., 1999-2000, Emory Williams Disting. Tchg. award, 2004, Evangeline Papageorge Alumni Tchg. award, 2004, Shining Star award Atlanta Women in Law and Medicine, 2000, Atlanta Bus. Chronicle Health-Care Heroes Lifetime Achievement award, 2005; Disting. Fellow Soc. Geriatric Cardiology, 2002; honoree Women of Yr. issue Time Mag., 1976; named Joseph B. Wolff Meml. Lectr., Am. Coll. Sports Medicine, 2001; named one of the 10 Most Important Women in Medicine, Ladies Home Jour., 1994; named to Best Doctors in Am.; recognized by McCall's Mag. for rsch. into causes and treatments for heart disease in women. Fellow Am. Heart Assn.(active Ga. affiliate 1960-, first woman president Ga. affiliate, fellow coun. clin. cardiology, 1970, chair rehab. com., 1972-75, chair artherosclerosis task force, 1973-74, program v.p., 1975-76, pres., 1977-78, bd. dirs., 1975-79, mem./past mem. numerous other coms., Bronze Disting. Svc. medallion Ga. affiliate Am. Heart Assn., 1970-71, Silver Disting. Svc. medallion, 1978, Gold Disting. Svc. medallion, 1979, named Physician of Yr., 1998, Disting. Achievement award, Sci. Coun., Women in Cardiol. Mentoring award, 1999, R. Bruce Logue award for Excellence in Medicine, 2001, Gold Heart award, 2004), Am. Coll. Cardiology (gov. for Ga. 1983-86, trustee 1987-89, various coms.), Am. Coll. Chest Physicians; master ACP (James D. Bruce Meml. award 2000); mem. AMA, WHO (expert adv. panel on cardiovasc. disease 1989—), Am. Assn. Cardiovasc. and Pulmonary Rehab. (trustee 1985-88, chairperson ethics com. 1985—, 2nd Ann. Lecture award 1987), Nat. Heart, Lung and Blood Inst., Internat. Soc. and Fedn. Cardiology (pres. sci. coun. on rehab. of cardiac patients 1984-88), Soc. Geriatric Cardiologists (officer, pres. 1994-95), Med. Assn. Ga., Med. Assn. Atlanta, Atlanta Clin. Soc.(emeritus), Soc. for Prevention of Heart Disease and Rehab. (hon.), Soc. Women's Health (bd. dirs. 2000—, vice chair 2002—), Philippine Heart Assn. (hon.), Philippine Coll. Cardiology (hon.), Omicron Delta Kappa. Office: Emory Univ Sch Medicine Grady Meml Hosp Glenn Bldg E278 49 Jesse Hill Jr Dr SE Atlanta GA 30303 Home Phone: 404-237-4802; Office Phone: 404-616-4420. Business E-Mail: nwenger@emory.edu.

WENGER, RONALD DAVID, surgeon; b. Phila., May 1, 1944; s. Christian Showalter and Helen Grace (Heisey) W.; m. Judith Kay Anderson, Jan. 24, 1970; children: Clayton, Lera. BA, Ohio Wesleyan U., 1966; MD, Case Western Res. U., 1970. Diplomate Am. Bd. Surgery. Intern U. Oreg. Med. Sch., Portland, 1970-71; fellow Mayo Clinic Surgery Dept., Rochester, Minn., 1973-77; clin. prof. surgery U. Wis. Med. Sch., Madison, 1977—; pvt. practice, Madison, 1977—; asst. chief surgery St. Mary's Hosp., Madison, 1980-00; chief surgery Dean Med. Ctr., Madison, 1988-93. Recipient Best Drs. in Dane County, Madison Mag., 2008; named one of, 2006. Mem. ACS (also Wis. chpt.), AMA, SAGES, Am. Assn. Endocrine Surgeons, Wis. State Med. Soc., Madison Surg. Soc., Wis. Surg. Soc. (pres. 2005—), Soc. for Surgery of Alimentary Tract. Avocations: skiing, bicycling, sailing, travel, reading. Home: 726 Farwell Dr Madison WI 53704-6032 Office: 1821 S Stoughton Rd Madison WI 53716-2257 Home Phone: 608-241-4216; Office Phone: 608-260-6853.

WENGER, SCOTT ANDREW, orthopedist, surgeon; b. Winter Park, Fla., Nov. 25, 1971; s. Thomas James and Katherine Wenger; m. Virginia Elliott, June 22, 1996; children: Luke Andrew, Adam Scott. BA in Bus. Adminstrn., So. Meth. U., 1994, BSc in Biology, 1994; MD, U. Tex. Southwestern Med. Sch., 1998. Lic. physician Tex. State Bd. of Med. Examiners, 2003, Med. Bd. Calif., 2003. Intern gen. surgery U. Tex. Southwestern Med. Ctr., Dallas, 1998—99, resident orthop. surgery, 1999—2003; sports medicine fellow Kerlan-Jobe Orthop. Clinic, LA, 2003—04; orthopaedic surgeon Coll. Sta. (Tex.) Orthopaedics, 2004—. Mem.: AMA, Tex. Orthop. Assn., Tex. Med. Assn., Brazos-Robertson County Med. Soc., Am. Orthop. Soc. Sports Medicine, Am. Acad. Orthop. Surgeons, Arthroscopy Assn. N.Am. (assoc.), Alpha Omega Alpha. Office: College Station Orthopaedics 1602 Rock Prairie Road STE #460 College Station TX 77845

WENGER, SHARON LOUISE, cytogeneticist, researcher, educator; b. Washington, Sept. 25, 1949; d. William Fred and Lois Helen (Compton) W.; m. George E. Fromlak Jr., Jan. 10, 1976; children: Nicholas Edward, Holly Louise, Andrea Lee. BA in Biology, Thiel Coll., 1971; MS in Human Genetics, U. Pitts., 1973, PhD in Human Genetics, 1976. Cert. in clin. cytogenetics Am. Bd. Med. Genetics. Asst. prof. U. Pitts. Sch. Med., 1980-89, assoc. prof., 1989—97; prof. pathology W. Va. U., 1997—. Contbr. articles to profl. jours. Mem. Am. Soc. Human Genetics, Am. Coll. Med. Genetics, Assn. Genetic Technologists, Assn. Molecular Pathology. Achievements include research of sister chromatid exchange and fragile sites, chromosome syndromes and mechanism of tissue limited mosaicism. Home: 50 Crescent Heights Morgantown WV 26505 Office: W Va U Dept Pathology PO Box 9203 Morgantown WV 26506-9203 Home Phone: 304-598-3872; Office Phone: 304-293-3212.

WENGLOWSKI, GARY MARTIN, economist; b. Rochester, NY, Sept. 2, 1942; s. Henry Bernard and Isabelle (Franc) W.; m. Joyce Richards, Oct. 3, 1964; children: Gary Martin, Catherine Jean. BS in Econs., U. Pa., 1964, MA, 1965, PhD in Econs., 1967. With Goldman Sachs & Co., NYC, 1967—, v.p., dir. econ. rsch., 1972-78, ptnr., 1978-86, ltd. ptnr., 1986-99; ret. ptnr., 1999—. Chmn. vis. com. econ. dept. U. Pa., 1985-98; adj. prof. Baruch Coll., 1998-02. Author: Industry Profit Forecasting, 1972, Industry Profit Forecasting— Progress Report, 1975. Trustee CARE Found., 1991—, Haystack Mountain Sch., 1993-2002. Named Best Economist on Wall St., Ann. Instnl. Investor Mag. Polls, 1976-86; NDEA fellow, 1965, 67. Fellow Nat. Assn. Bus. Economists; mem. Am. Econ. Assn., Deer Isle Yacht Club (vice commodore 1993-94, commodore 1994-2000). Home: 32 Partridge Ridge Rd Katonah NY 10536-3500

WENGLOWSKI, JOYCE, painter; b. Rochester, NY, Sept. 2, 1943; d. Harwin E. and Martha A. (Weit) Richards; m. Gary M. Wenglowski, Sept. 2, 1942; children: Gary M., Jr., Catherine J. Student, Rochester Inst. of Technology, 1961-63; BFA cum laude, Manhattanville Coll., 1980. Owner Joyce Wenglowski Gallery, Blue Hill, Maine, 1996-99; tchr. Artists Roster-Westchester Arts Coun., White Plains, 1995-2004; tchr., designer art program Waterview Hills Nursing Ctr., Purdy's, N.Y., 1989-99; tchr. painting, YMHA-YWHA, Pleasantville, N.Y., 1990-92; guest spkr. New Castle Pks. and Recreation, Chappaqua, N.Y.; tchr. artist-in.-residence New Rochelle Day Nursery, 2000-01, vis. artist, Empire State Partnership, Westchester Magnet Acad., 2005.; spkr. in field. One-woman shows include Studio Tour, Westchester County, NY, The Open Studio an Alternative Space for Contemporary Art, 2008, The Joyce Wenglowski Gallery, Blue Hill, Maine, 1996-99, Deer Isle (Maine) Artists Assn., Maine, 1993, 98, Landmark Gallery, Stamford, Conn., 1996, Island Fishermen's Wives Hardship Fund, Deer Isle, 1995, CARE, Pound Ridge, N.Y., 1993, The Annex., N.Y.C., 2002, Northern Westchester Hosp., 2000—, Katonah Mus. of Art, 2002, The Studio, Armonk, NY, 2007; exhibited in group shows at Westchester CC, Valhalla, NY, 2007, Newberger Mus. Art, Purchase, NY, 2008, Morgan Stanley Purchase NY, 2008, Northern Westchester Hosp. Cancer Care Ctr., 2006-, The Katonah Mus. of Art studio tour, 2002, Paramount Ctr. for the Arts, Peekskill, N.Y., 1999, Westchester Arts Coun., White Plains, N.Y., 1999, 2000, 03, 04, 05, Mus. Gallery, White Plains, 1999, The Gallery at Macy Pavilion, Valhalla, N.Y., 1998, The Walter Meade

Gallery, Roxbury, N.Y., 1997, Manhattanville Coll., Purchase, N.Y., 1997, Neiman Marcus, Westchester Art Coun., White Plains, N.Y., 1996, Silvermine Galleries, New Canaan, Conn., 1989, Mamaroneck Artists Guild, N.Y.C., 1994, Faber Birren Nat. Color Award Exhibit, Stamford, Conn., 1997, The Studio, Armonk, N.Y., 1999, 2000, 01, 02, 03, 05, 06, The Katonah Mus. Art, 2002, G. Watson Gallery, Stonington, Maine, 2001-08, The Hammond Mus. North Salem, N.Y., 2004, others; featured interview WFAS Radio, White Plains, 1999; represented in pvt. and corp. collectors, U.S. and Eng.; contbr. articles to profl. jours. Recipient Making a Difference award Westchester Arts Coun., 1993, Alumni Disting. in the Arts award Manhattanville Coll., 1991, Mixed Media award Stamford Conn., 1996, Katonah Mus. Artists' Assn., 2001; named NYNEX Patent Trader Vol. of Month, Westchester, 1992. Mem. Katonah Mus. Artsts Assn. (adv. bd. 1995—, pres. 2002-03, The Studio adv. bd., 2002—), Deer Isle Artists Assn. (adv. bd. 1993-97), Exhibiting Artists Ltd. (pres. 1982-83).

WENIG, CINDY L., lawyer; b. Queens, NY, Mar. 26, 1966; AB summa cum laude, Princeton U., 1988; JD, Columbia U., 1991. Bar: NY 1992. Ptnr., Real Estate Practice Group Chadbourne & Parke LLP, NYC, 1981—2007; gen. counsel Apollo Real Estate Advisors, 2007—. Adv. bd. Stewart Title Guaranty Co., Profl. Women's Alliance of NYC. Harlan Fiske Stone Scholar. Mem.: Real Estate Bd. NY, Women Exec. in Real Estate (WX) (sec.), Nat. Assn. Women Bus. Owners. Office: Apollo Real Estate Advisors 60 Columbus Cir 20th Fl New York NY 10023

WENK, EDWARD, JR., civil engineer, educator, writer, policy analyst; b. Balt., Jan. 24, 1920; s. Edward and Lillie (Heller) Wenk; m. Carolyn Frances Lyford, Dec. 27, 1941 (dec.); children: Lawrence Shelley, Robin Edward Alexander, Terry Allan(dec.). BE, Johns Hopkins U., 1940, DEng, 1950; MSc, Harvard U., 1947; DSc (hon.), U. R.I., 1968; LHD (hon.), Johns Hopkins U., 1989. Registered profl. engr. Head structures div. USN David Taylor Model Basin, Washington, 1942-56; chmn. dept. engring. mechanics S.W. Research Inst., San Antonio, 1956-59; sr. specialist sci. and tech. Legis. Reference Service, Library of Congress, Washington, 1959-61, chief sci. policy research div., 1964-66; tech. asst. to U.S. President's sci. adviser and exec. sec. Fed. Council for Sci. and Tech., White House, Washington, 1961-64; exec. sec. Nat. Council on Marine Resources and Engring. Devel., Exec. Office of Pres., Washington, 1966-70; prof. engring. and pub. affairs U. Wash., Seattle, 1970-83, prof. emeritus, 1983—, dir. program in social mgmt. tech., 1973-79; tech. advisor to gov. State of Wash., 1993-96; co-founder Blue Horizons Think Tank, Seattle, 2006. Nat. Adv. Com. on Oceans and Atmosphere, 1972-73; vice chmn. U.S. Congress Tech. Assessment Adv. Coun., 1973-79; adviser Congress, GAO, NSF, EPA, NOAA, White House, UN Secretariat, Wash. State, Alaska, U.K., Australia, Sweden, The Philippines, Alaska Oil Spill Commn., 1989, Wash. State Marine Oversight Bd., 1992, pub. interest groups, 1997, US Dept. Transportation; vis. scholar Woodrow Wilson Internat. Ctr. for Scholars, 1970-72, Harvard U., 1976, Woods Hole Oceanographic Instn., 1976, U. Sussex, 1977, Bellagio Ctr., Rockefeller Found., 1977, 90; lectr., cons. in field. Author: The Politics of the Oceans, 1972, Margins for Survival, 1979, Tradeoffs-Imperatives of Choice in a High-Tech World, 1986, Making Waves—Engineering, Politics and the Social Management of Technology, 1995, The Double Helix: Technology and Democracy in the American Future, 1999, How Safe is Safe? Coping with Mother Nature, Human Nature and Technology's Unintended Consequences, 2006; editor Exptl. Mechs. Jour., 1954-56, Engring. Mechs. Jour., 1958-60; mem. editl. bd. Tech. Forecasting, Tech. in Soc.; contbr. articles to profl. jours.; designer Aluminaut submarine. Bd. dir. Human Interaction Rsch. Inst., 1980-90, Smithsonian Sci. Info. Exch., 1977-82, URS Corp., 1973-88; mem. Interfaith Alliance. Ensign USNR, 1944-45. Recipient Navy Meritorious Civilian Svc. award, 1946, authors prize Gov. Wash., 1974, ann. prize Edn. Press Assn., 1997; named Disting. Alumnus Johns Hopkins U., 1979, Tchr. of Yr., Wash. State Engrs., 1980, Tchr. of Yr., Students in Pub. Adminstrn., 1986, Disting. Alumnus, Balt. Poly. Inst., 1991; Ford Found. grantee, 1970; Rockefeller Found. Bellagio fellow, 1976, 90; 1st Stuckenburg lectr. Wash. U., 1988; Regents lectr. U. Calif., Berkeley, 1989, Woodrow Wilson award Johns Hopkins U., 2004. Fellow ASME (exec., Ralph Coats Roe medal 1999), AAAS; mem. ASCE, NSPE, LWV, Soc. Exptl. Stress Analysis (past pres. and William M. Murray lectr.), Internat. Assn. Impact Assessment (pres. 1981-82), NAE (chmn. com. on pub. policy 1970-75), Nat. Acad. Pub. Adminstrn., Am. Soc. Pub. Adminstrn. (chmn. com. on sci. and tech. in govt. 1974-78), Assembly Engring. and Marine Bd. NRC, Nat. Oceanography Assn. (v.p. pub. affairs 1970-72), Cousteau Soc. (chmn. adv. bd. 1975-97), USA Club Rome (bd. dir. 1997-98), Explorers Club, Sigma Xi, Tau Beta Pi, Chi Epsilon. Home: 900 University St # 13G Seattle WA 98101 Business E-Mail: future@u.washington.edu. *Each of us has the opportunity, indeed responsibility, to contribute to the human experience and to enrich the lives of future generations. In a world of change, cultural diversity and uncertainty, we must be ourselves and not merely slaves of conventional thought. We must act on the basis of what we believe to be right rather than only from the desire to be loved.*

WENK, MICHAEL SCOTT, environmental services administrator; b. Livingston, NJ, Jan. 16, 1973; s. Robert Theodore and Georgia Irene Wenk; m. Cynde Lynn Hisel, Oct. 27, 1999; children: Andrew, Lauren. BS in Human Ecology, Rutgers U., New Brunswick, NJ, 1995; MS in Environ. Sci., NJ Inst. Tech., Newark, 2003; MBA, U. Md., College Park, 2006. Mgr. regulatory affairs Selig Industries, Atlanta, 1997—99, Eka Chems. Inc., Marietta, Ga., 1999—. Spkr. in field. The European Union's Eco-Management and Audit Scheme, 2005; contbr. articles to profl. jours. Mem.: Nat. Registry Environ. Profls. Office: Eka Chems Inc 1775 West Oak Commons Ct Marietta GA 30062

WENK, ROBERT E., pathologist; b. NYC, July 11, 1939; s. Sidney and Rita Wenk; m. Cheryl H. Parker; children: Harold M., Jonathan M. AB, NYU, NYC, 1959; MS in Human Genetics, U. Md., Balt.; MD cum laude, U. Louisville, 1967. Cert. Am. Bd. Pathology, 1968. Med. dir. BRT Labs., Balt., 1978—; clin. pathologist Hicken, Cranley, Taylor, P.A., Balt., 2002—. Prof. pathology Pa. State U., Hershey, 1980—2008. Contbr. scientific papers to profl. publs. Lt. comdr. USPHS, 1971—72, Boston. Named Best Tchr. Clin. Pathology Residents, Johns Hopkins U., Dept. Pathology, 1991; grantee, Weinberg Found. Mem.: Psi Chi, Beta Lambda Sigma.

WENNBERG, HANS-ERIK, communications educator; b. Mineola, NY, Feb. 13, 1946; s. Hans Jacob and Edith (Junker) W.; m. Linda Wright, Apr. 21, 1979; children: Steven Michael, Melissa Ann. BS in Edn., SUNY, Geneseo, 1969; MEd, Temple U., 1973; PhD, U. Conn., 1986. Cert. secondary math. tchr., N.Y. Jr. high sch. math. tchr. Rush Henrietta (N.Y.) Cen. Sch., 1969-72; asst. dir. audio-visual dept. R.I. Coll., Providence, 1973-84; dir. instnl. svcs. Elizabethtown (Pa.) Coll., 1984-90, asst. prof. communications, 1984-92, assoc. prof. communications, 1992—, chmn. dept., 1994-97. Presenter workshop in field. Producer multi-image presentation (Spectrum award, 1988-92, Capital awards, 1998-2008). Pres. Edn. Communications Found., Washington, 1992-2006. treas., 2007-08. Mem. Assn. Ednl. Communications and Tech., Assn. for Multi-Image Internat., Internat. Assn. Bus. Communicators (pres. Lancaster chpt. 1993-95, v.p. Harrisburg chpt., 1998-), Pa. Assn. Ednl. Communications and Tech. Am. Soc. Training and Devel., Nat. Assn. Photoshop Profls. Avocations: photography, woodworking, home improvements. Office: Elizabethtown Coll Comm Dept 1 Alpha Dr Elizabethtown PA 17022-2298 Business E-Mail: wennberg@etown.edu.

WENNER, CHARLES RODERICK, lawyer; b. New Haven, Jan. 10, 1947; s. Charles Bellew and Joan Rhoda (Morrison) Wenner; m. Jovita C. Vergara, June 11, 1999; children: Abigail Jessica, Charles Roderick Jr. BS, Coll. Charleston, 1969; JD, U. Conn., 1973. Bar: Conn. 1974, DC 1977. Law clk. Conn. Superior Ct., Hartford, 1973—74; staff atty. SEC, Washington, 1974—76, spl. counsel to chmn., 1976—77; assoc. Fulbright & Jaworski, 1977—81, ptnr., 1981—2005; of counsel Arnold & Porter LLP, 2005—. Lectr. law U. Conn. Sch. Law, 1973—74. Trustee United Meth. Ch., Arlington, Va., 1993—95, 1997—98; mentor Gospel Rescue Ministries Washington, 1991—. Recipient Am. Hist. award, DAR, 1969. Mem.: ABA, DC Bar Assn. Methodist. Avocation: running. Home: 1808 South Lynn St Arlington VA 22202 Office: Arnold & Porter LLP 555 Twelfth St Washington DC 20004 Home Phone: 703-979-1684; Office Phone: 202-942-6974. Office Fax: 202-942-5999. Business E-Mail: charles.wenner@aporter.com.

WENNER, GENE CHARLES, arts management executive; b. Catasauqua, Pa., Dec. 21, 1931; s. Clinton G. and Bertha (Taggert) W.; m. Carole Brunner, Aug. 15, 1953; children: Robert Larren, Laurel E. Wenner Carsell BS in Music, West Chester StateColl., Pa., 1953; M.Ed. in Music, Pa. State U., 1954. Tchr. music Phila. pub. schs., 1945-55, 56-60; assoc. prof. Kutztown (Pa.) State Coll., 1960-66, dir. coll. choir, 1960-66; fine arts adv. Pa. Dept. Edn., 1966-69, U.S. Office Edn., 1969-71; asst. dir. arts in edn. program John D. Rockefeller 3d Fund, 1971-78; arts edn. coordinator Office Commr., U.S. Office Edn., 1978-79; pres. Am. Music Conf., Wilmette, Ill., 1979-81; v.p. for programs Nat. Found. Advancement in Arts, Miami, Fla., 1983-87; pres. Arts and Edn. Cons., Inc., Reston, Va., 1987-91; sr. cons. Bus. & Industry for Arts Edn., 1990-91; exec. dir. Charlotte (N.C.) Community Sch. for the Arts, 1991-96; pres. Arts & Edn. Cons., Inc., Pittsfield, Mass., 1996—. Fund raising cons. Nat. Pub. Radio, Nat. Music Found., Mohawk Theater Capital Campaign, Goldman Meml. Band, Jacob's Pillow, Berkshire C.C. Non-Profit mgmt. Counsel, Mass. Coll. Liberal Arts; mus. dir. Allentown (Pa.) Mcpl. Oper, 1962-63, Allentown Civic Little Theatre, 1964, Little Theatre Alexandria, Va., 1971; dir. Hershey (Pa.) Little Theatre, 1967-68, Hershey Community Chorus, 1967-69 Composer: I'll Never Forget You, 1968, Chorale of Dedication, 1974, Great Things God Hath Done, 1986, In My Father's House, 1986; original music and script Adventures in the Arts, Hershey, 1968; also original TV music, I Am the Way, 1985, When You Remember, 1985; author papers, reports in field. Served with AUS, 1955-56. Named Best Mus. Dir. Little Theatre Alexandria Mem. Music Educators Nat. Conf., Network Performing and Visual Arts Schs. Clubs: Masons. Home and Office: 112 Doreen St Pittsfield MA 01201 Office Phone: 413-499-5311. Personal E-mail: gwenner@berkshire.rr.com.

WENNER, JANN SIMON, editor, publisher; b. NYC, Jan. 7, 1946; s. Edward and Ruth N. (Simmons) Wenner; m. Jane Ellen Schindelhiem, July 1, 1968 (separated 1995); children: Alexander Jann, Theodore Simon, Edward Augustus. Student, U. Calif., Berkeley. Editor, pub. Look mag., NYC, 1979, Record, NYC, 1981—86; editor in chief Outside Mag., San Francisco, 1977—79; pub. Family Life, 1993—95; co-founding editor, pub. Rolling Stone mag., NYC, 1967—; editor in chief US mag., NYC, 1985—, Men's Jour., 1992—, Wenner Media Inc., 1993—; founder Cease Fire Inc., 1995—. Vice chmn. Rock & Roll Hall of Fame. Author: Lennon Remembers, 1971, Garcia, 1972; actor: (films) Perfect, 1985, Jerry Maguire, 1996, Almost Famous, 2000, Breakfast with Hunter, 2003; co-author: (oral biography) Gonzo: The Life of Hunter S. Thompson, 2007. Bd. dirs. Robinhood Found. Recipient Disting. Achievement award, U. So. Calif. Sch. Journalism and Alumni Assn., 1976, Lifetime Achievement award, Rock and Roll Hall of Fame, 2004, Nat. Mag. award, 1970, 1977, 1986, 1987, 1988, 1989, 2007, Nat. Mag. award, 2009. Mem.: Am. Soc. Mag. Editors (Hall of Fame inductee 1997). Office: Rolling Stone 1290 Ave of Americas Fl 2 New York NY 10104-0295*

WENNERSTROM, ARTHUR JOHN, aeronautical engineer; b. NYC, Jan. 11, 1935; s. Albert Eugene and Adele (Trebus) W.; m. Bonita Gay Westenberg, Sept. 6, 1969 (div. Jan. 1989); children: Bjorn Erik, Erika Lindsay; m. Vicki Lynn Merrick, Feb. 17, 1990. BS in Mech. Engring., Duke U., 1956; MS in Aero. Engring., MIT, 1958; DSc of Tech., Swiss Fedn. Inst. Tech., Zurich, 1965. Sr. engr. Aircraft Armaments, Inc., Cockeysville, Md., 1958-59; rsch. engr. Sulzer Bros., Ltd., Winterthur, Switzerland, 1960-62; project engr. No. Rsch. and Engring. Corp., Cambridge, Mass., 1965-67; rsch. leader Air Force Aerospace Rsch. Lab., Dayton, Ohio, 1967-75, Air Force Aero Propulsion Lab., Dayton, 1975-91; dir. NATO Adv. Group for Aerospace R & D, Paris, 1991-94; engring. cons. Hillsborough, NC, 1994-95, Hot Springs Village, Ark., 1995—2003, Henderson, Nev., 2003—. Mem. tech. adv. com., von Karman Inst. for Fluid Dynamics, Rhode-St-Genese, Belgium, 1988-94, bd. dirs.; lectr. in field. Contbr. articles to profl. jours. 1st lt., USAF, 1962-65. Recipient Cliff Garrett Turbo Machinery award Soc. Automotive Engrs., 1986; named Fed. Profl. Employee of Yr. Dayton C. of C., 1975; fellow Air Force Wright Aeronautical Labs., 1987; named Hon. Prof., Inst. Engring. Thermophysics, Chinese Acad. Scis. and Beijing U. Aeronautics and Astronautics, 1994. Fellow AIAA (assoc. editor 1980-82, Air Breathing Propulsion award 1979), ASME (chmn. turbomachinery com. gas turbine divsn. 1973-75, mem. exec. com. 1977-82, chmn. 1980-81, program chmn. internat. gas turbine conf. 1976, Beijing internat. gas turbine symposium 1985, mem. nat. nominating com. 1985-87, mem. TOPC bd. on rsch. 1985-88, mem.-at-large energy conversion group 1986-88, mem. bd. comm. 1989-91, editor Jour. Engring. for Gas Turbines and Power 1983-88, chmn. bd. editors 1989-91, founder, editor Jour. Turbomachinery 1986-88, mem. internat. adv. com. 1995-96, R. Tom Sawyer award 1993). Achievements include introduction of wide-chord integrally-bladed fan, introduction of swept blading into mil. aircraft turbine engines; 5 patents in field. Home and Office: 363 Marlin Cove Rd Henderson NV 89012-4829 Home Phone: 702-837-1344; Office Phone: 702-837-1344. E-mail: wennco1@cox.net.

WENRICH, JOHN WILLIAM, college president; b. York, Pa., June 8, 1937; s. Ralph Chester and Helen Louise (McCollam) W.; m. Linda Larsen, June 23, 1961 (dec. Sept. 1966); 1 child, Thomas Allen; m. Martha Gail Lofberg, Sept. 1, 1967; 1 child, Margaret Ann AB, Princeton U., 1959; MA, U. Mich., 1961, PhD, 1968. Fgn. service officer Dept. State, Washington, 1962-65; rep. Internat. Devel. Found., NYC, 1965-66; project dir. U. Mich., Ann Arbor, 1966-69; asst. to pres. Coll. San Mateo, Calif., 1969-71; v.p. Ferris State U., Big Rapids, Mich., 1971-75, pres., 1984-88, Canada Coll., Redwood City, Calif., 1975-79, Santa Ana Coll., Calif., 1979-84; chancellor San Diego C.C. Dist., 1988-90, Dallas (Tex.) C.C., 1990—2003, chancellor emeritus, 2003—. Co-author: Leadership in Administration of Technical and Vocational Education, 1974, Administration of Vocational Education. Recipient Meritorious Service medal Dept. State, 1966; Hinsdale scholar Sch. Edn. U. Mich., 1968 Avocations: bridge, tennis, travel. Home: 3504 Springbrook St Dallas TX 75205-4337 Office: 4343 North Hwy 67 Mesquite TX 75150-2095 Home Phone: 214-521-9038; Office Phone: 972-860-7494. E-mail: bwenrich@dcccd.edu.

WENSINGER, ARTHUR STEVENS, literature and language professor, writer, translator; b. Grosse Pointe, Mich., Mar. 9, 1926; s. Carl Franklin and Suzanne (Stevens) W. Grad., Phillips Acad. Andover, 1944; BA, Dartmouth Coll., 1948; MA, U. Mich., 1951, PhD, 1958; postgrad., U. Munich, 1948, postgrad., 1950—51, U. Innsbruck, 1953—54. Instr., asst. prof., assoc. prof. Wesleyan U., Middletown, Conn., 1955-68, prof. German and humanities, 1968-93, Marcus Taft prof. German and humanities, 1977-93, prof. emeritus, 1994—, chmn. dept. German lang. and lit., 1971-93, also sr. tutor Coll. Letters; past pres. Friends of Davison Art Ctr.; co-editor Higganum Hill Books, 2003—. Mem. selection com. German Acad. Exch. Svc., 1980-92. Author: Hogarth on High Life, 1970, 2d edit., 2007, Plays by Arthur Schnitzler, 1982-1983, 1995; translator, editor (with W. Gropius): The Theater of the Bauhaus, 1961, rev. edit., 1996, translator, editor: The Letters and Journals of Paula Modersohn-Becker, 1983, 2d edit., 1990, Querelle: The Film Book, 1983, Franz Kafka: Pictures of a Life, 1984; translator: Marlene Dietrich: Portraits, 1984, Shabbat (Peter Stefan Jungk), 1985, Hanna Schygulla and R.W. Fassbinder, 1986, Kaethe Kollwitz: The Work in Color, 1988, Niklas Frank, In the Shadow of the Reich, 1991, (plays) Arthur Schnitzler; co-translator: Kafka: The Sons, 1989, Günter Grass, Two States-One Nation?, 1990; editor: Stone Island (Peter S. Boynton), 1973; co-editor: Hesse's Siddhartha, 1962; continuing co-editor: Correspondence of Norman Douglas, 1868-1952, 2008, continuing translator: plays of Schnitzler, contbr.: Columbia U. Database CD-ROM for quotations, aphorisms, 1995—, contbr. (DVD): Munich 1948/2005, 2007; performer: (presentation) Univ. of Munich, 2008; contbr. articles to profl. jours., exhbn. and symposium catalog articles; author: (exhbn. and symposium catalog articles) Norman Douglas, 2000, 2004, 2007, 2008, Douglas Forschungs Zentrum, W.H. Auden Newsletter. Wesleyan Ctr. for Humanities fellow, 1974, Reynolds fellow, 1950-51, Fulbright fellow, 1954-55, Danforth fellow, 1959, Ford Found. fellow, 1970-71; Inter Nations grantee, 1978, 82, NEH rsch. grantee, 1993. Mem. MLA, Am. Assn. Tchrs. German, Heinrich von Kleist Gesellschaft, Internat. Brecht Soc., Kafka Soc. Am., Auden Soc., Soc. Preservation New Eng. Antiquities, Conn. Acad. Arts and Scis., Yale Libr. Assocs., Haddam, Conn. Land Trust, Grosse Ile Nature and Land Conservancy, Phi Beta Kappa, Phi Kappa Phi(Mich), Delta Tau Delta, Candlewood Farm Arts Found. (founder trustee, 2009). Home: Candlewood Farm 95 Jacoby Rd Higganum CT 06441-4225 Office: Wesleyan U 406 Fisk Hall Middletown CT 06459-6082 Office Phone: 860-685-3357. Business E-Mail: awensinger@wesleyan.edu.

WENSKI, THOMAS GERARD, bishop; b. West Palm Beach, Fla., Oct. 18, 1950; s. Chester Stephen and Louise Mary (Zawacki) Wenski. AA, St. John Vianney Sem., Miami, Fla., 1970; BA, St. Vincent De Paul Sem., Boynton Beach, Fla., 1972, MDiv, 1975; MA, Fordham U. Ordained priest Archdiocese of Miami, Fla., 1976, aux. bishop Fla., 1997—2003; assoc. pastor Corpus Christi Ch., Miami, 1976-79; assoc. dir. Pierre Toussaint Haitian Cath. Ctr., Miami, 1979-84, dir., 1984-98; pastor Notre Dame d'Haiti, Miami, 1984-98; ordained bishop, 1997; coadjutor bishop Diocese of Orlando, Fla., 2003—04, bishop Fla., 2004—. Episcopal vicar to cultural groups, Miami, 1990-2003; dir. Cath. Charities Archdiocese Miami, 1996-2003; former chmn. migration com. US Conf. Cath. Bishops, chair Devel. and World Peace Internat. Policy Com., 2005; bd. dirs. Fla. Specialty Crop Found., 2007-. Roman Catholic. Office: Diocese of Orlando PO Box 1800 Orlando FL 32802 Office Phone: 407-246-4815.

WENTWORTH, BRENDA KATHRYN, theater educator; b. Ft. Worth, Jan. 25, 1950; d. Charles William Wentworth and Ellen Young Feagan. BA in Theater, Fredonia State U., NY, 1973; MA in Theater, U. SC., Columbia, 1978; PhD, U. Mo., Columbia, 1990. Prof. theatre St. Cloud State U., Minn., 1992—. Sec. bd. Theatre l'Homme Dieu, Alexandria, Minn., 2004—. Office: St Cloud State Univ 720 Fourth Ave S Saint Cloud MN 56301 Business E-Mail: bwentworth@stcloudstate.edu.

WENTWORTH, CHRISTOPHER DEAN, physics professor; b. Tallahassee, June 18, 1955; s. Aubrey Dean and Winifred Lane Wentworth; m. Sally Claire Fisher, Aug. 30, 1980; children: Brendan Kelly, Maira Brianna. BS in Physics, Duke U., Durham, NC, 1978; PhD in Physics, Fla. State U., Tallahassee, 1986. Rsch. assoc. Kamerling Onnes Lab., Leiden, Netherlands, 1987—88; postdoc. fellow Fla. State U., Tallahassee, 1988—89; asst. prof. physics Doane Coll., Crete, Nebr., 1989—95, assoc. prof. physics, 1995—2003, prof. physics, 2003—, chair, divsn. sci. & math., 2008—. Contbr. articles to profl. jours. Mem. exec. com. Nebr. Sect. Am. Assn. Physics Tchrs., 1997—2001; mem. parish coun. St. John Kronstandt Orthodox Ch., Lincoln, Nebr., 2002—08. Grantee, NASA Project NOVA, 1999—2000, NSF, 2001—04. Mem.: Am. Phys. Soc. Achievements include research in use of linked-cluster series expansion for quantum spin systems, magnetic properties of rare earth intermetallics. Office: Doane Coll 1014 Boswell Ave Crete NE 68333 Business E-Mail: chris.wentworth@doane.edu.

WENTWORTH, DIANA VON WELANETZ, author; b. LA, Mar. 4, 1941; d. Eugene and Marguerite (Rufi) Webb; m. Frederic Paul von Welanetz, Nov. 2, 1963 (dec. Mar. 19, 1989); 1 child, Lexi Welanetz Bursin; m. Theodore S. Wentworth, Dec. 9, 1989; stepchildren: Christina Wentworth Coyne, Kathryn Allison Wentworth Purdy. Student, UCLA, 1958-60. Ptnr. von Welanetz Cooking Workshop, LA, 1968-85; host TV series New Way Gourmet, 1983-86; founder Inside Edge Found. Edn., Calif., 1985-93. Spkr. in field. Author: The Pleasure of Your Company, 1976 (Cookbook of Yr.), With Love from Your Kitchen, 1976, The Art of Buffet Entertaining, 1978, The Von Welanetz Guide to Ethnic Ingredients, 1983, L.A. Cuisine, 1985, Celebrations, 1985, Chicken Soup for the Soul Cookbook, 1995, Send Me Someone, 2001, Chicken Soup to Inspire The Body and Soul, 2003. Mem. Les Dames D'Escoffier Internat, Internat. Food, Wine & Travel Writers Assn., Angels of Arts/Orange County Performing Arts Ctr., Ctr. Club, Confrérie de La Chaîne des Rôtisseurs. Avocations: painting, art, travel, design. Office: 4631 Teller Ave Ste 100 Newport Beach CA 92660-8105 E-mail: diana@dianawentworth.com.

WENTWORTH, EARL JEFFREY, state legislator, lawyer; b. San Antonio, Nov. 20, 1940; s. Earl and Margaret Wentworth; m. Karla Whitsitt; children: Jason, Matthew. BA, Tex. A&M U., 1962; JD, Tex. Tech. U., 1972. Bar: Tex. 1971, DC. 1972. Staff mem. U.S. Congressman Bob Price; pvt. practice law San Antonio; mem. Tex. Ho. of Reps., 1988-92, Tex. Senate, 1993—. County commr. Bexar County, 1977-82; bd. regents Tex. State U. Sys., 1987-88. Spl. agt. U.S. Army Counterintelligence Corps, 1962—65. Republican. Office: PO Box 12068 Austin TX 78711-2068 also: Ste 925 1250 NE Loop 410 San Antonio TX 78209-1500 Office Phone: 210-826-7800. Personal E-mail: ejeffrey@swbell.net. Business E-Mail: jeff.wentworth@senate.state.tx.us.

WENTWORTH, JACK ROBERTS, business educator, consultant; b. Elgin, Ill., June 11, 1928; s. William Franklin and Elizabeth (Roberts) W.; m. Rosemary Ann Pawlak, May 30, 1956 (dec. April 29, 2006); children: William, Barbara. Student, Carleton Coll., 1946-48; BS, Ind. U., 1950, MBA, 1954, DBA, 1959. Coord. displays Cadillac divsn., Gen. Motors Corp., Detroit, 1954-56; asst. prof. bus., assoc. dir. research Sch. of Bus. Ind. U., Bloomington, 1957-60, assoc. prof., dir. rsch., 1960-70, prof., 1970-93, chmn. MBA program, 1970-76, chmn. dept., faculty rep. NCAA, 1978-85, dean Sch. of Bus., 1984-93, Arthur M. Weimer prof., 1993-97, Arthur M. Weimer prof. emeritus, 1997—. Mktg. cons., Bloomington, 1960—; bd. dirs. Kimball Internat., Jasper, Ind. Editor: (monograph) Marketing Horizons, 1965; exec. editor Bus. Horizons, 1960-70 Served to 1st lt. USAF, 1950-53. Recipient Teaching award MBA Assn., 1973, 78, 81, 84, 85, Svc. award Assn. for Bus. and Econ. Rsch., 1983; Disting. Alumni Svc. award Ind. U., 1999. Mem. Am. Mktg. Assn. (v.p. 1971-73), Grad. Mgmt. Admissions Coun. (chmn. bd. trustees 1977-78), Univ. Club, Masons, Beta Gamma Sigma (pres. Alpha of Ind. chpt. 1971-72, bd. govs. 1986-98, nat. pres. 1994-96). Republican. Methodist. Avocations: travel, bicycling, magic, model railroading, sports. Office: Indiana Univ Kelley Sch Bus Bloomington IN 47405 Personal E-mail: lurojack@yahoo.com.

WENTWORTH, THEODORE SUMNER, lawyer; b. Bklyn., July 18, 1938; s. Theodore Sumner and Alice Ruth (Wortmann) W.; m. Sharon Linelle Arkush, 1965 (dec. 1987); children: Christina Linn, Kathryn Allison; m. Diana Webb von Welanetz, 1989; 1 stepchild, Lexi von Welanetz. AA, Am. River Coll., 1958; JD, U. Calif., Hastings, 1962. Bar: Calif. 1963, U.S. Dist. Ct. (no. and ctrl. dists.) Calif., U.S. Ct. Appeals (9th cir.), U.S. Supreme Ct.; diplomate Nat. Bd. Trial Advocacy; cert. trial lawyer Calif. State Bar. Assoc. Adams, Hunt & Martin, Santa Ana, Calif., 1963-66; ptnr. Hunt, Liljestrom & Wentworth, Santa Ana, 1967-77; pres. Solabs Corp.; chmn. bd., exec. v.p. Plant Warehouse, Inc., Hawaii, 1974-82; ptnr. Law Offices of Wentworth, Paoli & Purdy, Newport Beach & Temecula, Calif., 1979—; judge pro tem Superior Ct. Attys. Panel Harbor Mcpl. Ct.; owner, CEO Home Guardens, Inc., Murrietta, Calif., 2000—05. Owner Eagles Ridge Ranch, Temecula, 1977-2003. Author: Build a Better Spouse Trap, 2002. Pres., bd. dirs. Santa Ana-Tustin Cmty. Chest, 1972; v.p., trustee South Orange County United Way, 1973-75; pres. Orange County Fedn. Funds, 1972-73; bd. dirs. Orange County Mental Health Assn. Mem. ABA, Am. Bd. Trial Advs., State Bar Calif., Orange County Bar Assn. (dir. 1972-76), Calif. Trial Lawyers Assn. (bd. govs. 1968-70), Orange County Trial Lawyers Assn. (pres. 1967-68), Bahia Corinthian Yacht Club (founder). Achievements include research in vaidika principles, natural law, quantum physics and mechanics. Office: 4631 Teller Ave Ste 100 Newport Beach CA 92660-8105 also: 41530 Enterprise Cir S Temecula CA 92590-4816 Office Phone: 949-752-7711. Personal E-mail: tedruu@aol.com.

WENTWORTH, WILLIAM EDGAR, retired journalist; b. Newton, NH, Nov. 4, 1931; s. Charles Bertrand and Mildred Frances (Ingalls) Wentworth. BA in Journalism, U. Tenn., Knoxville, 1958. Reporter Rochester (N.H.) Courier, 1959; reporter, copy editor Foster's Daily Dem., Dover, NH, 1959-68; copy editor Fla. Today, Melbourne, Fla., 1968-93; ret., 1993. Author: (book) Vital Records, 1790-1829, 1995, Journals of Enoch Hayes Place, 1998, Historial Memoranda of Persons & Places in Old Dover, NH, vol. II, 2008; editor: (periodical) Genealogical Record, 1995—. Data entry-online Dover Pub. Libr., 1993—; libr. Woodman Inst. Mus., Dover. Sgt. USAF, 1950—54. Mem.: Strafford County Geneal. Soc., New Eng. Hist. Geneal. Soc., N.H. Soc. Genealogists, N.H. Hist. Soc. Republican. Baptist. Avocation: genealogy. Home: 1005 Cocheco Ct Dover NH 03820-4819 E-mail: edwent@comcast.net.

WENTZ, BLAKE E., engineering educator; b. Lincoln, Nebr., Oct. 19, 1976; s. Tim G. and Marsha A. Wentz. BS in Bus. Adminstrn., U. Nebr., Lincoln, 1999, MS in Engring., 2004. Cert. LEED profl. US Green Building Coun., 2006, contractor Am. Inst. Constructors, 2005. V.p. Wentz Plumbing and Heating, Lincoln, 1999—2004; asst. prof. Northern Ariz. U., Flagstaff, 2004—05, Milw. Sch. Engring., 2005—. Named Educator of Yr., Wis. Builder Mag., 2008; Excellence grant, Mech. Contractors Assn. America, 2005—08. Mem.: Am. Soc. Heating, Refrigerating and Air-Conditioning Engrs., Sigma Lambda Chi, Golden Key Soc., Phi Kappa Phi. Office: Milw Sch Engring 1025 N Broadway Milwaukee WI 53202 Office Fax: 414-277-7415. Business E-Mail: wentz@msoe.edu.

WENTZ, JEFFREY LEE, information systems executive; b. Philippi, W.Va., Nov. 29, 1956; s. William Henry and Edith Marie (McBee); m. Phuong Thi Thanh, Nov. 17, 2001; 1 child, Keith Thanh. AS in Data Processing, Fairmont State Coll., W.Va., 1978, BS in Acctg., 1978. Programmer/analyst U.S. Dept. Energy, Morgantown, W.Va., 1978-79; analyst Middle South Svcs., New Orleans, 1979-81; sr. analyst Bank of Am., San Francisco, 1981-83; pres., info. sys. cons. Wentz Cons. Inc., San Francisco, 1983-2000; dir. tech. solutions Charles Schwab & Co., San Francisco, 2000—. Personal E-mail: wentzcon@earthlink.net.

WENTZ, MARY H., gifted and talented educator; b. Troy, Ohio, Feb. 27, 1957; d. Victor C. and Wilma J. Drees; m. James R. Wentz, Sept. 13, 1978; 1 child, Alex J. BS, Wright State U., Dayton, Ohio, 1986; M, Ashland U., Ohio. Specialist in gifted intervention Logan Elm Local Schs., Circleville, Ohio, 1993—2002; gifted svcs. coord. Logan Elm, Westfall Schs., Circleville, 2002—. Recipient Presdl. award in Sci. Edn., State of Ohio, 1992. Mem.: Ohio Assn. for Gifted Children (assoc.). Office: Logan Elm Local Schs 9579 Tarlton Rd Circleville OH 43110 Business E-Mail: many.wente@logan-elk62.oh.us.

WENTZ, PETE (PETER LEWIS KINGSTON WENTZ III), musician; b. Wilmette, Ill., June 5, 1979; m. Ashlee Simpson, May 17, 2008; 1 child, Bronx Mowgli. Student, DePaul U. Bassist, vocalist & lyricist Fall Out Boy, 2001—; owner Clandestine Industries, Decaydence Records. Author: The Boy With the Thorn in His Side, 2005; musician: (albums) Fall Out Boy's Evening Out With Your Girl, 2002, Take This to Your Grave, 2003, From Under the Cork Tree, 2005, Infinity on High, 2007, Folie a Deux, 2008, (songs) Sugar, We're Going Down, 2003 (MTV2 award, MTV Video Music Awards, 2005), Dance, Dance, 2005 (Choice Music Single, Choice Rock Track, Teen Choice Awards, 2006, Viewer's Choice award, MTV Video Music Awards, 2006); actor: (films) Bedussey, 2005. Recipient Choice Music Rock Group award, Teen Choice Awards, 2006, Best Group award, MTV Video Music Awards, 2007. Office: Fall Out Boy Inc Box 219 1187 Wilmette Ave Wilmette IL 60091

WENTZ, WILLIAM HENRY, JR., aerospace engineer, educator; b. Wichita, Kans., Dec. 18, 1933; BS in Mech. Engring. cum laude, Wichita State U., 1955, MS in Aeronautical Engring., 1961; PhD in Engring. Mechanics, U. Kans., 1969. Lic. profl. engr., Kans. Liaison engr. Beech Aircraft, 1952-53; propulsion engr. Boeing Co., Wichita, Kans., 1955; instr. mech. engring. Wichita State U., 1957-58; aerodynamicist Boeing Co., Wichita, 1958-63; from asst. prof. to assoc. prof. aeronautical engring. Wichita State U., 1963-75, prof. aeronautical engring., 1975-83, Gates-Learjet prof. aeronautical engring., 1983-86, disting. prof. aerospace engring., 1986-98, dir. Ctr. Basic and Applied Rsch. Inst. Aviation Rsch., 1986-89, exec. dir. Nat. Inst. Aviation Rsch., 1988-97; sr. fellow Nat. Inst. Aviation Rsch., 1997-98; disting. prof. emeritus aerospace engring., exec. dir. emer. Nat. Inst. Aviation Rsch., 1999; ret. Dir. rsch. projects Boeing Co., 1960, 61, NASA, 1964-66, 66-68, 70-71, 71-83, 86-87, 86-88, 82-87, Dept. of Def., 1986-88, Kans. Tech. Enterprise Corp., 1988-96, FAA, 1986-96. Contbr. articles to profl. jours. With USAF, 1955-57. Recipient Disting. Engr. Svc. award Wichita State U., 1999, Kans. Aviation Honors award Gov. Bill Graves, 1999, Clean Air award City Wichita, 2009; Sci. Faculty fellow NSF, 1967-68. Fellow AIAA (assoc., past chmn. Wichita sect., Outstanding advisor student chpt. 1964, 65, 70, Gen. Aviation award 1981, Engr. of Yr. award Wichita sect. 1992, Engr. of Yr. award Region V 1991-92; mem. Soc. Automotive Engrs. (Ralph R. Teeter award 1973), Sigma Gamma Tau, Tau Beta Pi. Personal E-mail: william.wentz@cox.net.

WENZEL, JASON B., anthropologist, educator; b. Birmingham, Ala., Dec. 16, 1975; s. O. J. and Harlene Wehby. MA in Applied Sociology, U. Ctrl. Fla., Orlando, 2002. Adj. instr. Brevard CC, Cocoa, Fla., 2003—; anthropology prof. Valencia CC, Orlando, Fla., 2005—. Dir. Oakland Hist. Archeology Project, Fla., 2007—. Mem.: Am. Anthrop. Assn., Soc. Hist. Archeology, Fla. Anthrop. Soc. Office: Valencia CC 1800 S Kirkman Rd Orlando FL 32811 Business E-Mail: jwenzel@valenciacc.edu.

WENZEL, LARI BEA, psychologist; b. Milw., Dec. 3, 1955; d. Harry Bertran and Billie Diane (Schubert) W.; m. Timothy Lee Sams, Sept. 1, 1990; 1 child, Leah Rachelle Wenzel Sams. BA, U. Wis., 1978, MS, 1980; PhD, Ariz. State U., 1988. Lic. Psychologist. Psychology intern Boston VA Med. Ctr., 1987-88; psychologist Meml. Med. Ctr. Long Beach, 1988-92, Meml. Women's Specialty Group, Long Beach, Calif., 1992-93; prof. dept. medicine & program pub. health U. Calif., Irvine. Office: Ill Acad Ste 220 UC Irvine CA 92697 Office Phone: 949-824-3926. Business E-Mail: lwenzel@ual.edu.

WENZEL, LOREN ALVIN, accounting professor; b. Dec. 12, 1945; s. Alvin Karl Gustav and Lois LaVonne (Kuechenmeister) W.; children: Lisa Anne (Wenzel) Szumilas, Karl Louis, Sara Kirsten Wenzel; m. Nylah Onalee. DBA, U. Memphis, 1990. Asst. prof. acctg. Wichita State U., Kans., 1987-88; prof. acctg. Mankato State U., Minn., 1988-98, U. Md. European Divsn., Heidelberg, Germany, 1996-97, Buena Vista U., Storm Lake, Iowa, 1998-99, Austin Peay State U., Clarksville, Tenn., 1999-2000; prof. and head divsn. accountancy and legal environment Marshall U., 2000—09, Elizabeth McDowell Lewis endowed chair Lewis Coll. Bus., 2000—09, prof., 2005—09; prof. acctg., dean Coll. Bus. West Liberty U., 2009—; prof. Bharatiya Vidya Bhavan, Bangalore, India, 2005—. Founder, pres. W.Va. Acctg. Educators, 2003—05; dean Coll. Bus., West Liberty U., W.Va. Contbr. articles to profl. publs. Named W.Va. Outstanding Acctg. Educator of Yr., W.Va. Soc. CPAs, 2004. Office: Marshall U Lewis Coll Bus Div Acctancy/Legal Environ One John Marshall Dr Huntington WV 25545 Office Phone: 304-696-2660. Business E-Mail: wenzel@marshall.edu.

WEPRIN, DAVID I., city councilman, lawyer; b. Queens, NY, May 2, 1956; son of Saul Weprin; married to Ronni Weprin; children: five. BS cum laude, SUNY, Albany; JD, Hofstra Univ. Assoc. Julien, Schlesinger & Finz PC, 1980—83; sec. & dept. supt. banks NY State Banking Bd., 1983—87; mgmt. positions Donaldson Lufkin & Jenrette, Kidder Peabody, Paine Webber & Advest Inc., NYC, 1987—2002; ptnr. Sieratzki, Ceccarelli & Weprin, NYC, 2000—; city councilman Dist. 23 NY City Coun., 2002—. Chmn. Fin. com. NY City Coun. Bd. mem. Transitional Services for NY, Nat. Conf. Cmty. & Just., Respect for Law Alliance, Greater Jamaica Develop. Corp., Holliswood Civic. Assn., Brandeis Assn., Econ. Edn. Found., Securities Ind. Assn.; v.p. NE Queens Jewish Cmty. Coun.; bd. mem. Nat. Com. for Furtherance of Jewish Edn., Metro. Coun. on Jewish Poverty, Am. Jewish Congress. Recipient Mid-Queens Fresh Meadows Youth Alliance Cmty. Svc. award, Founders award, Metro. Coun. on Jewish Poverty. Democrat. Jewish. Mailing: Dist Off 205-07 Hillside Ave Ste 16 Queens NY 11423 Office Phone: 718-465-8202, 212-788-6984. Office Fax: 718-776-2302. Business E-Mail: weprin@council.nyc.ny.us.*

WERBA, GABRIEL, public relations consultant; b. Paris, Feb. 28, 1930; came to U.S., 1941; s. Aron and Dina (Lewin) W.; m. Barrie Celia Sakolsky, June 1, 1952; children: Dean Steffen, Annmarie Alexandra Bragdon. BA in Journalism, U. Tex., 1948; postgrad., NYU Grad. Sch. Bus., 1948-49, NYU Sch. Law, 1961-62. Account exec. Harold C. Meyers & Co., NYC, 1959-61; dir. pub. rels. and advt. Yardney Electric Corp., NYC, 1961-63, 57-59; sr. assoc. Shiefman & Assocs., Detroit, 1963-66; account exec. Merrill Lynch, Detroit, 1966-70; exec. v.p. Shiefman Werba & Assocs., Detroit, 1970-73; sr. v.p., exec. v.p., pres., chief oper. officer Anthony M. Franco, Inc., 1973-88; pres., chief exec. officer The Werba Group, Inc. and Gabriel Werba and Assocs., Inc., Detroit, 1988-94; prin. Durocher, Dixson, Werba, L.L.C., Detroit, 1994—2003; pres. Gabriel Werba & Assoc. LLC, Farmington Hills, Mich., 2004—05, Gabriel Werba & Assocs., Farmington Hills, 2005—. Contbr. articles to profl. jours. Bd. dirs. Oakland Citizens League, Detroit, 1970-93, Detroit Symphony Orch. Hall, Detroit Chamber Winds, 1985-91, The Common Ground Sanctuary, Mich., 1989-2007, vice chmn., Bloomfield Hills, 2000-06, adv. bd., 2007—; bd. dirs. The Attic Theatre, Detroit, 1989-93, The Children's Ctr., Detroit; mem. strategic planning oversight com., chair strategic planning com., chmn. comm. com., bd. dirs., 1989-95, 1996-2002, 03-05, adv. bd., 1995-96, 2002-03; bd. dirs. NATAS, Detroit, 1993-98, The Jewish Cmty. Coun. Met. Detroit, 1989-95, 2004-2007, co-chair commn. com., 2006-2007, Margaret W. Montgomery Hosp., 1993-95, adv. bd. 1988-93; bd. dirs. Lawrence P. Doss Found., 2002—, 1st vice-chmn., 2002—09; Detroit Inst. Arts Commn. Com., 1986-92, exhibits com., 1990-2001. Named to PRSA-Detroit Hall of Fame, 2001. Mem. Nat. Investor Rels. Inst. (founding pres. Mich. chpt., past dir., pres. Detroit chpt., spkr., panelist 1969-89), Pub. Rels. Soc. Am. (bd. dirs. Detroit chpt. 1988-94, pres. 1992-93, past treas. Detroit Counselors' sect., PRSA, past co-chair nat. sect. coun., past nat. chmn. fin. sect., mem. nat. bd. ethics and profl. stds. 2003-06, chair nat. audit com. 2005-07, spkr., panelist), Fin. Analysts Soc. Detroit (past chmn. pub. info. com.), Am. Mensa (bd. dirs. 1975-95, 2003-05, nat. chmn. 1979-83), Internat. Mensa (bd. dirs. 1975-83, 85-95). Avocations: art collecting, concerts, theater. Home: 21920 River Ridge Tr Farmington Hills MI 48335 Office: Gabriel Werba & Assoc 21920 River Ridge Tr Farmington MI 48335 Office Phone: 248-478-1281. Personal E-mail: gwerba@yahoo.com.

WERBELOW, LAWRENCE GLEN, chemistry educator, researcher; b. Ross, Calif., Dec. 19, 1948; s. Arnold Glen and Helen Corrine (Freeburg) W.; m. Catherine Elizabeth Fouques, Dec. 28, 1979; children: Prisca, Guilhem, Neil. B.Sc., Humboldt State U., 1970; Ph.D., U. B.C., 1974; D.Sc., U. Provence, Marseille, France, 1979. Rsch. assoc. U. Utah, Salt Lake City, 1974-78; vis. prof. U. Provence, Marseille, 1978-79, Mont. State U., Bozeman, 1979-80; prof. chemistry N.Mex. Inst. Mining and Tech., Socorro, 1980—, U. Provence Marseille, France, 1989-95; vis. scientist Los Alamos Nat. Lab., 1980-2000; vis. prof. U. Paris, 1987, Stockholms U., 1998, 2002. Contbr. chpts. to books, articles to profl. jours. Nat. Research Council Can. fellow, 1974; Am. Chem. Soc. grantee, 1980; NSF grantee, 1980; NATO grantee, 1982; Research Corp. grantee, 1983; Dept. Energy grantee, 1985, 89, CNRS grantee, 1980-87. Mem. Internat. Soc. Magnetic Resonance. Subspecialties: Nuclear magnetic resonance (chemistry); Nuclear magnetic resonance (biotechnology). Current work: Time-dependent aspects of nuclear paramagnetism; creation and dissipation of transient multipolar spin order; quantum theory angular momentum. Home: 907 Michigan Ave Socorro NM 87801-4021 Office: N Mex Inst Mining and Tech Dept Chemistry Socorro NM 87801 Business E-Mail: werbelow@nmt.edu.

WERBITT, WARREN, gastroenterologist, educator; b. Phila., Jan. 29, 1939; s. Saull Boris and Pearl (Weiner) W.; m. Drue Natalie Engman Werbitt, Aug. 30, 1964; children: Julie Michele, Jeffrey Brian. BS in Pharmacy, Temple U., 1960; D in Osteopathy, U. Osteo. Med. and Health Sci., Des Moines, 1966; MD, Drexel U. Coll. Med., 1973. Diplomate Am. Osteo. Bd. Internal Medicine, also sub-splty. bd. Gastroenterology; diplomate Am. Bd. Internal Medicine, also sub-splty. bd. Gastroenterology. Intern Doctor's Hosp., Columbus, Ohio, 1966-67, resident in internal medicine, 1967-68, Kennedy Meml. Hosps., Cherry Hill, NJ, 1968-69, Mercy Cath. Med. Ctr., Phila., 1969-70, Drexel U. Coll. Medicine, Phila., 1971—72, fellow in gastroenterology, 1970-71, 72-74, instr., 1973—, attending physician and cons. in gastroenterology, 1977-94; instr. Phila. Coll. Osteo. Medicine, Phila., 1973-75, chmn. divsn. gastroenterology, 1975-77; clin. assoc. prof. medicine U. Medicine and Dentistry, NJ, 1977—; attending physician and cons. in gastroenterology Vet. Adminstrn. Hosp., Phila., 1972-75; chmn. Div. Gastroenterology, Dept. Medicine Phila. Coll. Osteopathic Medicine, 1975-77; chmn. Dept. Medicine Kennedy Meml. Hosp. U. Med. Ctr., Cherry Hill, 1979-81, chmn. subsect. Gastroenterology, 1979-87; assoc. fellow AGAF Am. Gastroentology. Contbg. editor NJ Jour. for Osteo. Physicians and Surgeons, 1980—; mem. scientific adv. com. Phila. chpt. Nat. Found. Ileitis and Colitis, Inc., 1982—; contbr. articles to profl. jours. Recipient Profl. Svc. award Med. Soc. N.J., 1991., Named Top Dr. South Jersey Mag., 2007-08 Fellow Am. Coll. Physicians, Am. Coll. Gastroenterology, Am. Gastroenterol. Assn., Acad. Med. N.J.; mem. AMA, Am. Soc. Gastrointestinal Endoscopy, Am. Soc. Parenteral and Enteric Nutrition, Am. Inst. Ultrasound in Medicine, Am. Assn. Gynecologic Laparoscopists, Phila. Gastrointestinal Rsch. Forum, State Med. Soc. N.J., Camden County Med. Soc., N.J. Endoscopic Soc., Del. Valley Soc. for Gastrointestinal Endoscopy, South Jersey Gastroenterol. Soc., Am. Osteo. Assn., N.J. Soc. Osteo. Physicians and Surgeons, Am. Coll. Osteopathic Internists, Camden County Osteo. Assn., Am. Cancer Soc. (bd. dirs. N.J. chpt.), Crohn's and Colitis Found. Am. Inc. (Phila. and Del.), Pres.'s Circle Am. U., N.Y. Acad. Scis., John Sherman Myers Soc., Med. Club Phila., Lambda Omicron Gamma. Avocations: golf, running, music, reading, american history. Office: Profl Gastroenterology Assn 1939 Route 70 E Ste 250 Cherry Hill NJ 08003-4507 Office Phone: 856-429-4433. Business E-Mail: progastro@comcast.net.

WERCHNIAK, ANDREW EUGENE, dermatologist, educator; s. Wolodymyr and Anna Werchniak; m. Jeanine Courchesne Courchesne, Jan. 7, 1994; children: Andrew Morris, Anne, Alexander, Ethan, Elias, Kiernan. BS, U. Md., 1993; MD, U. Va., 2000. Diplomate Am. Acad. Dermatology, 2004. Internship internal medicine Dartmouth, Lebanon, NH, 2000—01, resident dermatology, 2001—04; instr. dermatology Harvard Med. Sch., Boston, 2004—. Clin. scholar, Brigham and Women's Hosp., 2004—. Fellow: Am. Acad. Dermatology; mem.: AMA. Office: Brigham Dermatology Associates 221 Longwood Ave Boston MA 02115

WERDEGAR, KATHRYN MICKLE, state supreme court justice; b. San Francisco; d. Benjamin Christie and Kathryn Marie (Clark) Mickle; m. David Werdegar; children: Maurice Clark, Matthew Mickle. Student, Wellesley Coll., 1954—55; AB with honors, U. Calif., Berkeley, 1957; JD with highest distinction, George Washington U., 1962; JD, U. Calif., Berkeley, 1990. Bar: Calif. 1964, U.S. Dist. Ct. (no. dist.) Calif. 1964, U.S. Ct. Appeals (9th cir.) 1964, Calif. Supreme Ct. 1964. Legal asst. civil rights divsn. U.S. Dept. Justice, Washington, 1962—63; rsch. atty., author Calif. State Study Commn. on Mental Retardation, 1963—64; assoc. U. Calif. Ctr. for Study of Law and Soc., Berkeley, 1965—67; spl. cons. State Dept. Mental Health, 1967—68; cons., author Calif. Coll. Trial Judges, 1968—71; dir. criminal law divsn. Calif. Continuing Edn. of Bar, 1971—78; assoc. dean acad. and student affairs, assoc. prof. Sch. Law, U. San Francisco, 1978—81; sr. staff atty. Calif. 1st Dist. Ct. Appeal, 1981—85, Calif. Supreme Ct., 1985—91; assoc. justice Calif. 1st Dist. Ct. Appeal, 1991—94, Calif. Supreme Ct., San Francisco, 1994—. Regents' lectr. U. Calif., Berkeley, 2000. Author: Benchbook: Misdemeanor Procedure, 1971, Misdemeanor Procedure Benchbook rev., 1975, Misdemeanor Procedure Benchbook, 1983; contbr. California Continuing Education of the Bar books; editor: California Criminal Law Practice series, Discovery, 1975, California Uninsured Motorist Practice, 1973, I California Civil Procedure Before Trial, 1977. Recipient 5 Am. Jurisprudence awards, 1960—62, Charles Glover award, George Washington U., 1962, J. William Fulbright award for disting. pub. svc., George Washington U. Law Sch. Alumni Assn., 1996, Excellence in Achievement award, Calif. Alumni Assn., 1996, Roger J. Traynor Appellate Justice of Yr. award, 1996, Justice of Yr. award, Consumer Attys. of Calif., 1998, Citation award, Boalt Hall Sch. Law U. Calif., Berkeley, 2002, Judge Learned Hand Human Rels. award, Am. Jewish Com., 2008. Mem.: Am. Law Inst., Nev./Calif. Women Judges Assn., Calif. Judges Assn., Nat. Assn. Women Judges, Calif. Supreme Ct. Hist. Soc. (bd. dir.), Order of the Coif. Office: Calif Supreme Court 350 McAllister St San Francisco CA 94102-4797 Office Phone: 415-865-7032.*

WERDENSCHLAG, LORI B., psychologist, educator; b. Livingston, NJ, Apr. 20, 1965; d. Stephen Robert and Sandra Joyce Werdenschlag; m. William Alden Barbour, Aug. 5, 2000; 1 child, Jordan Sara Barbour. BA in Psychology and Anthropology, Emory U., Atlanta, 1987; MS in Developmental Psychology, Tulane U., New Orleans, 1990; PhD in Developmental Psychology, Tulane U., 1992; postgrad., Lyndon State Coll. Prof. dept. psychology Lyndon State Coll., Lyndonville, Vt., 1992—; devel. home provider Washington County Mental Health, Vt., 1999—2006. Creator organizer Lyndon State Coll. Ann. Cultural Festival, 1996—; resource provider Coalition: Success by Six, Headstart, Vt. Dept. Health, 2003—, St. Johnsbury Daycare Provider Network, 2003—; condr. tng. workshops in field. Contbr. articles to profl. jours. Big sister Big Bro./Big Sisters, New Orleans, 1990—; sch. bd. mem. Barnet, Vt., 2008; exec. bd. dirs. AIDS Cmty. Awareness Project/Vt. Cares Orgn., 1996—2000. Fellow, PEW Found., 1991—92; Advanced Study grantee, Lyndon State Coll., 1995, 1999, 2000, 2007, Learning Cmtys. Fund grantee, Vt. State Colls., 1996—97, 2007—, Faculty fellow, 2002—04. Avocations: reading, travel, skiing. Office: Lyndon State Coll 1001 College Rd Lyndonville VT 05851 Office Phone: 802-626-6435. E-mail: lori.werdenschlag@lyndonstate.edu.

WERDER, OLAF H., communications educator, researcher; b. Dortmund, Northrhine-Westphalia, Germany, Apr. 24, 1967; s. Helmut O. and Erika M. Werder. Diploma in Bus., U. Dortmund, Germany, 1992; MS, U. Ill., Champaign, 1994; PhD, U. Fla., Gainesville, 2002. Media supr. The Hively Agy., Houston, 1994—96; media planner Fallon -McElligott Advt., Mpls., 1996—99; asst. instr. U. Fla., 1999—2002; asst. prof. U. N.Mex, Albuquerque, 2002—08, assoc. prof., 2008—, grant-funded health rsch., 2005—. Grant-funded health rsch. U. N.Mex, 2005—. Contbr. articles to profl. jour. Bd. mem. Luther Ho. Campus Ministry, Albuquerque, N.Mex., 2006—07. Cpl. Army German, 1986—87, Hannover. Recipient N.Mex Advt. President's award, N.Mex Advt. Fedn., 2006, Alec Courtalis award, U. Fla., 2001; grantee Disciplinary Large Grant Mechanism, Rsch. Allocation Com., U. N.Mex, 2008; Grinter Fellow, U. Fla., 2000, Bateman Fellow, Bateman Found., 2002. Mem.: U. Fla. Alumni Assn., U. Ill. Alumni Assn., European Advt. Acad., Assn. Edn. Journalism and Mass Comm. Lutheran. Achievements include research in NIH-funded project on obesity prevention. Avocations: skiing, travel, reading. Office: Univ NM MSC03 2240 1 Univ NM Albuquerque NM 87131 Office Fax: 505-277-4206. Business E-Mail: owerder@unm.edu.

WERDER, RICHARD I., JR., lawyer; b. White Plains, NY, 1957; BA magna cum laude, Canisius Coll., 1979; JD magna cum laude, U. Mich., 1982. Bar: Ohio 1984, NY 2003. Law clk. to Hon. Harry T. Edwards US Ct. Appeals (DC cir.), 1982; law clk. to Justice Byron White US Supreme Ct., 1983; assoc. Jones Day, NYC, 1984—89, ptnr., co-chmn. tech. issues practice; ptnr. Quinn, Emanuel, Urquhart, Oliver & Hedges, LLP, NYC, 2006—. Editor-in-chief Law Rev., 1982. Mem.: ABA, NY State Bar Assn., Cleve. Bar Assn., Ohio State Bar Assn., Prod. Liability Adv. Coun., Order of Coif. Office: Quinn Emanuel Urquhart Oliver & Hedges LLP 51 Madison Ave 22nd Fl New York NY 10010 Office Phone: 212-849-7231. E-mail: rickwerder@quinnemanuel.com.

WERFELMAN, WILLIAM HERMAN, JR., public relations executive; b. Bridgeport, Conn., July 11, 1953; s. William H. and Helen D. (Rainier) W.; m. Patricia Aileen Maytrott, Aug. 28, 1977; children: Lauren Aileen, Juliana Aileen. BA in English, St. Bonaventure U., 1975; postgrad., Georgetown U., 1975—76. Staff writer Post-Telegram newspapers, Bridgeport, 1976—79; product publicity specialist Dictaphone Corp., Rye, NY, 1979—81; supr. press rels. GE, Fairfield, Conn., 1981—84; mgr. corp. pub. rels. Olin Corp., Stamford, Conn., 1984—90, dir. pub. rels./comm., 1990—94; v.p. external comms. Home Ins. Co., NYC, 1994—95; v.p. media rels. N.Y. Life Ins. Co., NYC, 1995—2003; first v.p. N.Y Life Ins. Co., NYC, 2003—. Mem., chmn. Zoning Bd. Appeals, Redding, Conn., 1977-89, 92-99; party recruitment chmn. Rep. Town Com., Redding, 1976-90. Recipient Fin. World Bronze award for ann. report, 1992. Mem. Internat. Assn. Bus. Communicators (Best Pub. Rels. results 1982), Pub. Rels. Soc. Am., Nat. Assn. Investors (Best Ann Report 1988, 90). Republican. Roman Catholic. Avocations: writing, investments. Home: 195 Gallows Hill Rd Redding CT 06896-1423 Office: NY Life Ins Co Rm 516 51 Madison Ave New York NY 10010-1603

WERKMAN, ROSEMARIE ANNE, former public relations professional, volunteer; b. Washingtonville, NY, Apr. 21, 1926; d. Alexander and Michelina (Russo) Di Benedetto; m. Henry J. Werkman, June 29, 1947; children: Elizabeth, Kristine, Hendrik Student, U. Miami, Fla. Billing clk. Stern's Dept. Store, NYC, 1945; clk., typist Doubleday-Doran Book Pub., NYC, 1945—46; receptionist Moser & Cotins Advt. Agy., Utica, NY, 1947—48, Washingtonville Sch., NY, 1960—75. Instr. Personal Life History Class Orange County C.C. Author: (biography/autobiography) Love, War and Remembrance, 1992, Seminars: Personal Life History, Encore Program, OCCC, (poetry) P.S. I Love You; contbr. short stories, poetry to anthologies. Mem. Dem. Com., Blooming Grove; bd. dirs. Blooming Grove Hist. Assn.; mem. com. Update: Blooming Grove Master Plan; mem. Orange County Coun. Disabled; bd. dirs. Rehab. Support Svcs; charter mem. Orange County Citizens Found.; mem. steering com. Blooming Grove BiCentennial Celebration, 1999, 75th Anny's Wash. Sch.; participant restorations Habitat for Humanity, 2001—; mem. steering com. Hist. Brotherhood Winery, Inc., 2003— Named Poet of Merit, Am. Poetry Assn., 1989, Poet Laureate Orange County, NY, 2002; recipient Notable Civic Contbns. award Blooming Grove/Washingtonville C. of C., 1996, Rose award, 1996 Mem. Blooming Grove C. of C. (v.p.), Orange County Classic Choral Soc., Clearwater (Fla.) Chorus (personal life history class, 2008) Democrat. Roman Catholic. Avocations: reading, gardening, furniture refinishing, singing.

WERLEIN, EWING, JR., federal judge; b. Houston, Sept. 14, 1936; s. Ewing and Ruth (Storey) W.; m. Kay McGibbon Werlein, June 29, 1963; children: Ewing Kenneth, Emily Kay. BA, Southern Meth. U., 1958; LLB, U. Tex., 1961. Bar: Tex. 1961, US Dist. Ct. (so. dist.) Tex. 1965, US Dist. Ct. (ea. dist.) Tex. 1990, US Ct. Appeals (5th cir.) 1970, US Ct. Appeals (10th cir.) 1980, US Claims Ct. 1985, US Tax Ct. 1985, US Supreme Ct. 1983. Ptnr. Vinson & Elkins, Houston, 1964-92; dist. judge US Dist. Ct. (so. dist.) Tex., 1992—. Trustee So. Meth. U., Dallas, 1976-92, Asbury Theol. Sem., Wilmore, Ky., 1989—; mem. gen. bd. pub. United Meth. Ch., Nashville, 1974-84, chmn., 1980-84, chancellor Tex. ann. conf., 1977—; mem. exec. com. World Meth. Counh., 1981-96, treas, 1991-93. Capt. USAF, 1961-64. Fellow Am. Coll. Trial Lawyers, 1984, Internat. Soc. Barristers, 1987; recipient Disting. Alumni award SMU Alumni Assn., 1994. Fellow Am. Bar Found., Tex. Bar Found., Houston Bar Found.; mem. State Bar Tex. (dir. 1990-93), Nat. Conf. Bar Pres., Houston Bar Assn. (pres. 1988-89), Houston C. of C. (life), SAR, Order of Coif, Petroleum Club, Houston Club, Phi Beta Kappa. Office: US Dist Ct Tex US Courthouse 515 Rusk St Ste 9136 Houston TX 77002-2605

WERLIN, LAWRENCE B., obstetrician, gynecologist, reproductive endocrinologist; b. Albany, NY, 1948; s. Esther (Caplan) W.; m. Sally Rosso, Dec. 24, 1970; children: Rachel, Evan, Emma. BA, Boston U., 1970; MD, Mt. Sinai Sch. Medicine, NYC, 1976. Diplomate Am. Bd. Ob-Gyn. Intern Harbor Gen. Hosp., Torrance, Calif., 1976-77, resident in ob-gyn., 1977-80; fellow in reproductive endocrinology NIH, Bethesda, Md., 1980-82; mem. staff Hoag Meml. Hosp., Newport Beach, Calif. Nat. Reproductive Medicine fellow, 1980-82. Mem. AAAS, Am. Soc. Reproductive Medicine, Soc. for Assisted Reproductive Tech., Pacific Coast Fertility Soc. Office: Coastal Fertility Med Ctr 4900 Barranca Pky Ste 103 Irvine CA 92604-8603 E-mail: werlmd@coastalfertility.com.

WERLING, ROBERT LEWIS, law educator; b. Fort Wayne, Ind., Oct. 5, 1947; s. William Lewis and Betty Werling; m. Marsha Lynn Carnes, Dec. 8, 2004; children: David Michael, Daniel Robert. PhD in Criminal Justice, Sam Houston State U., Huntsville, Tex., 2006. Police officer Longview Police Dept., Longview, Tex., 1982—94; project coord. Sam Houston State U., Huntsville, 1997—2005; asst. prof. Calif. State U. Stanislaus, Turlock, Calif., 2005—. Contbr. articles to profl. publs. Advisor Neighborhood Watch Program, Waterford, Calif., 2006—09. Mem.: Alpha Chi Nat. Achievements include research in study police officers need for cognition as it relates to approval of community policing. Avocations: aerobics, travel. Office: California State Univ Stanislaus One University Cir Turlock CA 95382 Business E-Mail: rwerling@csustan.edu.

WERMAN, DAVID SANFORD, psychiatrist, psychoanalyst; b. NYC, Jan. 1, 1922; s. Morris and Blanche (Heftel) W.; m. Marjolijn R. de Jager, Oct. 25, 1958 (div. 1975); children: Marco W., Claudia J. BA, Queens Coll., 1942; postgrad., Columbia U., 1946-47; MD, Cert. d'Etudes Medicales, U. Lausanne, Switzerland, 1952. Diplomate Am. Bd. Obstetrics and Gynecology, Am. Bd. Psychiatry and Neurology. Intern Beth Israel Hosp., NYC, 1953-54, resident, 1954-57, Montefiore Hosp., Bronx, NY, 1964-67; pvt. practice specializing in ob-gyn. NYC, 1957-64; faculty acad. psychiatry U. NC, Chapel Hill, 1967-76, assoc. prof., instr. psychoanalytic tng. program, 1974—; prof. psychiatry Duke U. Med. Ctr., Durham, NC, 1976—, supervising and tng. analyst psychoanalytic tng. program, 1981-97, Honored prof. psychiatry, 1990—, prof. emeritus, 1992—, supervising and tng. analyst emeritus, 1997—. Cons. Durham VA Hosp. Author: The Practice of Supportive Psychotherapy, 1984. Contbr. chpts. to books, articles to profl. jours. With AUS, 1943-45 Named Outstanding Tchr. psychiatry U. N.C., 1975, honored tchr. psychiatry Duke U., 1978, hon. prof., 1990. Fellow ACS, Am. Psychiat. Assn., Am. Coll. Psychoanalysts, others Home and Office: 111 E 85th St 23G New York NY 10028 Office Phone: 212-722-0744. Home Fax: 212-722-0744. Personal E-mail: davidwerman@aol.com.

WERMAN, THOMAS EHRLICH, record producer; b. Newton, Mass., Mar. 2, 1945; s. Lester and Ruth (Ehrlich) W.; m. Susan Lynne Gould, Aug. 25, 1968; children: Julia Gould, Nina Eve, Daniel Lester. BA, Columbia U., 1967, MBA, 1969. Asst. account exec. Grey Advt., NYC, 1969-70; asst. to dir. Epic Records Artistes and Repertoire, 1970-73; dir. talent acquisition Epic Records, 1973-76, staff producer, 1976-80; v.p., exec. producer CBS Records, Inc., LA, 1980-81; sr. v.p. Elektra Records, 1981-82; pres. Julia's Music Inc., LA, 1981—; v.p. artists and repertoire EMI-Capitol Entertainment Properties, LA, 1997-98; owner, operator Stonover Farm Bed and Breakfast, Lenox, Mass., 2001—. Bd. trustees Berkshire Music Sch. Recipient N.Y.C. Civilian Commendation award for heroism, 1968, 14 platinum records awards Rec. Industry Assn. Am., 1977—, 10 Gold Record awards, 1977—. Mem.: Lenox C. of C. (bd. dirs. 2005), Country Club of Pittsfield. Democrat. Jewish. E-mail: werm1000@aol.com.

WERMUTH, PAUL CHARLES, retired language educator; b. Phila., Oct. 28, 1925; s. Paul C. and Susan (Manga) W.; m. Barbara Ethel Braun, Aug. 26, 1951; children— Geoffrey Paul, Paul Charles, Alan John, Stephen Mark. AB, MA, Boston U., 1951; PhD, Pa. State U., 1955. Instr. Clarkson Coll., Potsdam, N.Y., 1951-52; part-time instr., grad. asst. Pa. State U., 1952-55; asst. prof. Coll. William and Mary, 1955-57; mem. faculty Central Conn. State Coll., New Britain, 1957-68, asso. prof. English, 1966-68; prof. English Northeastern U., 1968-90, prof. emeritus, 1990—, chmn. dept., 1968-75. Vis. prof. Middlebury Coll., 1963-64 Author: Modern Essays on Writing and Style, 2d edit, 1969, Essays in English, 1967, Bayard Taylor, 1974, Selected Letters of Bayard Taylor, 1997, also articles. Served with USAAF, 1943-46. Danforth summer study grantee, 1961 Mem. Modern Lang. Assn., AAUP, Mensa. Home: 73 Mostyn St Swampscott MA 01907-1616 Office: English Dept Northeastern Univ Boston MA 02115 Personal E-mail: pwermuth@comcast.net.

WERNER, CLARENCE L., transportation executive; b. 1937; Asst. mgr. Larson Grain Co., Omaha, 1958-61; with Bus. Motor Express, Inc., Omaha, 1961-62; founder Werner Enterprises, Inc., Omaha, 1956-82, pres., 1982-84, chmn., CEO, 1984—2007, chmn., 2007—. Office: Werner Enterprises Inc 14507 Frontier Rd PO Box 45308 Omaha NE 68145-0308

WERNER, DAVID A., paper company executive; BS, MBA, U. So. Calif. CPA. With Peat, Marwick, Mitchell & Co., 1974-78; various mgmt. positions Lear Siegler's Telecomms. divsns./subsidiaries, Anaheim, Calif., 1978-86, v.p. fin. and adminstrn., 1986-90; v.p., CFO Microdot Components Group, 1990-94; exec. v.p., dir. Kaynar Technologies Inc. (formerly Microdot Components), Orange, Calif., 1994-99; exec. v.p., CFO Day Runner, Irvine, 1999—. Office: 101 Oneil Rd Sidney NY 13838-1055

WERNER, DAWN HETERICK, elementary school educator; b. Va. BA in Office Adminstrn., Va. Intermont Coll; MA in Edn., Eastern Tenn. State U., PhD in Edn., 2005. Worked in banking; Title I tchr., parent involvement coord., corrective reading dir. Fairmount Elem. Sch., Bristol, Tenn. Recipient E. Tenn. E. Grand Divsn. Tchr. of Yr., 2005; named Tenn. Tchr. of Yr., 2006. Office: Fairmount Elem Sch 500 Cypress St Bristol TN 37620 Business E-Mail: wernerd@btcs.org.

WERNER, ERIC JAMES, pediatrician, director; s. Howard M. and Marilyn G. Werner; m. Alice L. Laibstain, Aug. 20, 1977; children: Jacob S., Abby R., Andrew J. BS, Trinity Coll., Hartford, 1974; MD, Jefferson Med. Coll., Phila., PA, 1974—78. Diplomate pediatric hematology, oncology Am. Bd. Pediat., 1984, pediat. 1984. Prof. pediat. Eastern Va. Med. Sch., Norfolk, 1997—, pres., faculty senate, 2000—01, dir., pediatric hematology, oncology, 2003—; med. info. officer Children's Hosp. King's Daughters, Norfolk, 2006—, physician advisor informatics, 1998—2006. Sec. Hemophilia and Thrombosis Rsch. Soc., Milwaukee, 1996—2005; mem. Commonwealth Va. Hemophilia Adv. Bd., Richmond, 1988—2004. Editor: (book) Neonatal Hematology. Maj. USAF, 1983—87, Wright Patterson AFB. Decorated Commendation Medal USAF, Award Hampton Rds. Mag.; recipient Phi Beta Kappa, Trinity Coll., 1974, Tchr. of the Yr., Dept. Pediat., Wright State U. Sch. Medicine, 1987. Fellow: Am. Acad. Pediat.; mem.: Healthcare Info. and Mgmt. Sys. Soc., Am. Coll. Physician Execs., Am. Soc. Hematology, Am. Soc. Pediatric Hematology Oncology. Office: Children's Cancer and Blood Disorders Ce 601 Children's Ln Norfolk VA 23507

WERNER, GREGORY L., transportation executive; Treas. Werner Enterprises, Omaha, 1982—86, v.p., 1984—96, exec. v.p., 1996—97, pres., 1997—99, pres., COO, 1999—2007, pres., CEO, 2007—. Office: Werner Enterprises 14507 Frontier Rd PO Box 45308 Omaha NE 68145-0308

WERNER, JANE, museum administrator; m. Robert Rutkowski; 2 children. B. Synaesthetic Edn., Syracuse U. With Buhl Sci. Ctr., Franklin Inst. and Sci. Mus.; dep. dir. Pitts. Children's Mus., exec. dir. Carnegie-Mellon U./Studio for Creative Inquiry fellow. Office: Pittsburgh Childrens Mus Allegheny Sq North Side 10 Childrens Way Pittsburgh PA 15212

WERNER, LAURIE, science educator; BS in Physics, Le Moyne Coll., Syracuse, NY, 1971; MST in Biology, Binghamton U., NY, 1973; MS in Bioengring., Poly. Inst. NYU, Bklyn., 1978. Asst. prof. sys. analysis Miami U., Oxford, Ohio, 1979—86, assoc. prof. computer and info. tech., 1986—. Contbr. articles to profl. jour. on computer sci. Mem.: Consortium Computing Scis. Colls. (midwest regional membership chair 2002—). Office: Miami Univ 1601 University Blvd Hamilton OH 45011

WERNER, PATRICE (PATRICIA ANN WERNER), academic administrator; b. Jersey City, May 31, 1937; d. Louis and Ella Blanche (Smith) W. BA in French, Caldwell Coll., 1966; MA in French, McGill U., 1970; PhD in French, NYU, 1976; postgrad. Inst. Ednl. Mgmt., Harvard U., 1991. Joined Dominican Sisters of Caldwell, 1954. Sch. tchr. Archdiocesan Sch. Systems, N.J., Ala., 1954-62; tchr. French, Latin Jersey City, Caldwell, NJ, 1962-72; instr. French Caldwell (NJ) Coll., 1973-76, dir. continuing edn., 1976-79, chair dept. fgn. langs., assoc. prof. French, 1979-85, acad. dean, prof. French, 1985-94, pres., 1994—. Trustee Caldwell Coll.; mem. corp., trustee Providence Coll.; mem. Dominican Higher Edn. Coun.; mem. NJ Pres.' Coun. accountability com., liaison com. to NJ Higher Edn. Partnership for Sustainability. Recipient Woman of Achievement award, N. N.J. Coun. of Boy Scouts of Am., 1999, The Archbishop T.E. McCarrick award for Disting. Svc. to the Ch., 2000, Cmty. Woman of Achievement, West Caldwell Hist. Soc. and West Essex Women's Club, 2000, Caldwell Cup, Excellence in Edn. award, N. Essex C. of C. Found., 2003; named Salute to Policy Makers award, Exec. Women NJ, 2006, Outstanding Woman in Am. History, DAR Maj. Joseph Bloomfield Chpt.; scholar AATF Summer Grant. Mem.: Assn. Gov. Bds. of Univs. and Colls., N.J. C. of C., Assn. Cath. Colls. and Univs., Nat. Assn. Ind. Colls. and Univs. (bd. dirs., sec. bd. dirs., com. policy analysis and pub. rels.), Coun. Ind. Colls. (bd. dirs., pub. info. com.), Ind. Coll. Fund. N.J. (trustee, vice chmn. exec. com.), Assn. Ind. Colls. and Univs. in N.J. (chmn. bd. dirs.). Avocations: tennis, reading, avid sports fan, travel. Office: Caldwell Coll 120 Bloom Field Ave Caldwell NJ 07006-6195 Home Phone: 973-618-3283; Office Phone: 973-618-3217. Business E-Mail: spwerner@caldwell.edu.

WERNER, RAYMOND J., lawyer; b. Chgo., Aug. 25, 1944; s. Raymond and Marie (Vurpillat) W.; m. Lenore C. Werner, July 8, 1967; 1 child, Beth Anne. BS in Sci. and Commerce, DePaul U., 1967; JD, IIT Chgo. Kent Coll. Law, 1971. V.p., assoc. gen. counsel Chgo. Title Ins. Co., 1985; ptnr. Portes, Sharp, Herbst & Kravets Ltd., Chgo., 1985; now mng. ptnr. Arnstein & Lehr LLP, Chgo. Author: Modern Mortgage Law and Practice, 1981, Real Estate Law 10th Edition, 1992, Real Estate Closings, 1988. Mem. ABA (real property probate and trust law sect., bd. govs., 2006), Am. Coll. Real Estate Lawyers, Chgo. Bar Assn. (exec. council, real estate law com. 1985—) Anglo-Am. Real Property Inst.(chair, 2007), Clubs: Park Ridge (Ill.) Country Club Office: Arnstein & Lehr LLP Ste 1200 120 S Riverside Plz Chicago IL 60606-3910 Office Phone: 312-876-7152. Business E-Mail: rjwerner@arnstein.com.

WERNER, ROBERT JOSEPH, dean, music educator; b. Lackawanna, NY, Feb. 13, 1932; s. Edward Joseph and Marian L. (Geringer) W.; m. Sharon Lynne Mohrfeld, June 22, 1957; children: Mark J., Kurt M., Erik J. BME, Northwestern U., 1953, MusM, 1954, PhD, 1967. Dir. instrumental music Evanston (Ill.) Twp. H.S., 1956-66; assoc. prof. mus. Harpur Coll. SUNY, Binghamton, 1966-68, dir. Contemporary Music Project, 1968-73; dir. Sch. Mus. U. Ariz., Tucson, 1973-85, dean fine arts, 1981-82; dean Coll.-Conservatory of Music U. Cin., 1985-2000, dean emeritus, 2000—. Editor: Comprehensive Musicianship: An Anthology of Evolving Thought, 1971; author, editor: Musical Chairs: A Handbook for Music Executives in Higher Education, 2006; contbr. articles to profl. internat. and nat. jours. Mem. exec. bd. Tucson Symphony Orch., 1974-85; bd. dirs. Cultural Commn. Tucson, 1974-75, Cin. Symphony Orch., 1985-2000, Cin. Opera, 1985-2000, Cin. Ballet, 1985-2000; mem. artistic directorate Am. Classical Music Hall of Fame; pres. bd. dirs. The Coll. Music Soc. Fund, 2002-08. With U.S. Army, 1954-56. Mem. Nat. Assn. Schs. Music (pres. 1989-91), Coll. Music Soc. (pres. 1977-78), Internat. Soc. for Music Edn. (pres. 1984-86, treas. 1986-97), Music Educators Nat. Conf., McDowell Soc., Psi Upsilon, Phi Mu Alpha Sinfonia, Sigma Alpha Iota, Mu Phi Epsilon. E-mail: wernerrj@uc.edu.

WERNER, ROBERT L., lawyer, consultant; b. NYC, Feb. 28, 1913; s. Abraham L. and Elsa (Ludwig) W.; m. Raye Davies, Oct. 13, 1945; children: William, John. AB, Yale U., 1933; LLB, Harvard U., 1936. Bar: N.Y. 1936, U.S. Supreme Ct. 1936, also various fed. cts. and adminstrv. agys. 1936. Spl. asst. to U.S. atty. So. Dist. N.Y., 1936, asst. U.S. atty, 1937-40, confidential asst., 1940-42; dep. asst. atty. gen. U.S. Dept. Justice, Washington, 1946-47; spl. asst. to atty. gen. U.S., 1946-47; mem. law dept. RCA, NYC, 1947, v.p., gen. atty., 1951-62, exec. v.p., gen. atty., 1962-66, exec. v.p., gen. counsel, 1966-78, dir., 1963-79, cons., 1978-83. Mem. adv. bd. Internat. and Comparative Law Ctr. Southwestern Legal Found., Dallas, 1966—, treas., 1970-72, vice chmn., 1972-73, chmn. advisory bd., 1974-76, found. trustee 1976-88, hon. trustee 1988—; lectr. Conf. Bd., Practicing Law Inst., others; mem. nat. adv. council corp. law depts. Practising Law Inst., 1974-78; com. on restrictive bus. practices U.S. council Internat. C. of C., 1973-78; N.Y. Lawyers' Com. for Civil Rights under Law, 1972-78. Trustee Ithaca Coll., N.Y., 1968-88, hon. trustee, 1988—, chmn. bd., 1976-78; trustee Salisbury (Conn.) Sch., 1975-77, N.Y. Chiropractic Coll., 1986-89; bd. dirs. Midtown Arts Common at St. Peter's Ch., 1983-89. Capt. U.S. Army, 1942-44; to lt. col. USAAF, 1944-46, ETO. Recipient Disting. Service award Ithaca Coll., 1988. Fellow Am. Bar Found.; mem. Internat., Fed., Am., N.Y. State, City N.Y., FCC bar assns., IEEE (sr.), Am. Legion, Harvard Law Sch. Assn., Assn. Gen. Counsel (emeritus), U.S. Naval Inst., Internat. Law Assn. (Am. br.), Nat. Legal Aid and Defender Assn. (dir. 1974-79), Am. Judicature Soc., Newcomen Soc., N.Y. County Lawyers' Assn., Am. Soc. Internat. Law, Yale Club, Harvard Club N.Y., Army and Navy Club (Washington), Coral Beach Club (Bermuda). Home: 116 E 68th St New York NY 10021-5955

WERNER, SAMUEL ALFRED, physicist, educator; b. Elgin, Ill., Jan. 5, 1937; s. Charles August and Frances Agnes (Tasch) W.; m. Laura Louise Reed, Sept. 1, 1961; 1 dau., Catherine Louise. AB, Dartmouth Coll., 1959, MS, 1961; PhD, U. Mich., 1965. Staff scientist physics dept. Ford Motor Co., Dearborn, Mich., 1964-75; adj. prof. nuclear engring. U. Mich., Ann Arbor, 1968-75; prof. physics U. Mo., Columbia, 1975-2000, chmn. physics dept., 1981-83, Millsap Disting. prof., 1986—, Curator's prof., 1992—, prof. emeritus, 2000—; scientific cons.physics lab. Nat. Inst. Standards Tech., Gaithersburg, Md., 2000—. Vis. scientist A.B. Atomenergi, Studsvik, Sweden, 1970, Institut Laue-Langevin, Grenoble, France, 1977, Argonne Nat. Lab., Oak Ridge Nat. Lab., Brookhaven Nat. Lab.; cons. Argonne Nat. Lab., 1968—, mem. solid scis. div. rev. com., 1972-77, chmn. spl. com. Intense Pulsed Neutron Source, 1978-82; cons. Nat. Acad. Scis., 1977, 83; vis. scientist Nat. Bur. Stds, 1983-84; vis. scientist Nat. Inst. Stds. and Tech., 1996—, chmn. com. on assessment of physics lab., 1992-95. Contbr. numerous articles to profl. jours. Grantee NSF; fellow Swedish Rsch. Coun.; recipient outstanding alumni award U. Mich., 1980, Chancellor's award for Outstanding Rsch. U. Mo., 1980, Presdl. Rsch. award U. Mo., 1973. Fellow Am. Phys. Soc.,AAAS; mem. Sigma Xi Home: 7620 Augustine Way Gaithersburg MD 20879-4587 Office: Reactor Bldg 235 NIST Mail Stop 8461 Gaithersburg MD 20899 Personal E-mail: sam.werner@verizon.net.

WERNER, SHARON, legislative staff member, lawyer; Grad., Pa. State U.; JD, Stanford U. Law clk. to Hon. Barbara S. Jones US Dist. Ct. (so. dist.) NY; litig. assoc. Debevoise & Plimpton, LLP, NYC; fin. dir. for Jason Altmire's Congl. Campaign; chief of staff to Rep. Jason

Altmire US House of Reps. Fin. dir. Western Pa. Dem. Coordinated Campaign, 2004; worked at C-SPAN. Office: Office of Congressman Jason Altmire 332 Cannon House Office Bldg Washington DC 20515 Office Phone: 202-225-2565. Office Fax: 202-226-2274. E-mail: sharon.werner@mail.house.gov.*

WERNER, STUART LLOYD, computer services company executive; b. NYC, June 2, 1932; s. Leroy Louis and Frances Werner; m. Davideen Price, Jan. 6, 1990; children: Joan Leslie, Susan Lyn, Richard Wayne, Edgar Fredrick, Leslie Ann, Cassandre Lynn. BArch, Rensselaer Poly. Inst., 1954. Ptnr. in charge architecture Werner-Dyer & Assocs., Washington, 1959-68; v.p. Rentex Corp., Phila., 1968-70, ARA Svcs., Inc., 1981—83; pres. Werner & Assocs., Inc., Washington, 1970-81, Werner & Monk, Inc., 1983-90, STN, Inc., 1981-99, chmn. Falls Church, Va., 2000—04, chmn. emeritus, 2005—; pres. DRF, LLC, 2007—. Author: FilePro Developer's Reference, 4th edit., 2002; contbr. articles to tech. jours. Bd. dirs. Watergate South, 1984-90, Washington Opera Soc., Hampton West Condo, 2001—, Fla. Grand Opera Guild, Greater Miami Jewish Fedn., 2000-, exec. com. mem., 2005-; mem. Econ. Devel. Coun., City of Aventura, Fla., 2002. With AUS, 1955-57. Mem. AIA, Inst. Indsl. Engrs., Marinette Yacht Club, Masons, Scottish Rite, Tau Beta Pi. Democrat. Office Fax: 305-931-7028.

WERNER, VOLKER RALPH, physics professor; b. Cologne, NRW, Germany, Sept. 4, 1973; s. Peter and Waltraud Werner. Dr. rer. nat., U. Köln, Cologne, 2004. Postdoc U. Köln, 2004; postdoc. assoc. Yale U., New Haven, 2004—05, asst. prof. physics, 2005—. Fellow: Calhoun Coll. Yale; mem.: Am. Phys. Soc., Deutsche Physikalische Gesellschaft. Avocations: travel, piano, computers. Office: Yale Univ WNSL PO Box 208120 New Haven CT 06520-8120 Office Fax: 203-432-3522. Business E-Mail: volker.werner@yale.edu.

WERNER-JACOBSEN, EMMY ELISABETH, developmental psychologist; b. Eltville, Germany, May 26, 1929; came to U.S., 1952, naturalized, 1962; d. Peter Josef and Liesel (Kunz) W. BS, Johannes Gutenberg U., Germany, 1950; MA, U. Nebr., 1952, PhD, 1955; postgrad., U. Calif., Berkeley, 1953-54. Research asso. Inst. Child Welfare, U. Minn., 1956-59; vis. scientist NIH, 1959-62; asst. prof. to prof. human devel., rsch. child psychologist U. Calif., Davis, 1962-94, rsch. prof., 1995—. Sr. author: The Children of Kauai, 1971, Kauai's Children Come of Age, 1977; author: Cross-Cultural Child Development: A View from the Planet Earth, 1979, Vulnerable, but Invincible, 1982, 3d edit., 1998, Child Care: Kith, Kin and Hired Hands, 1984, Overcoming the Odds, 1992, Pioneer Children on the Journey West, 1995, Reluctant Witnesses: Children's Voices From the Civil War, 1998, Through the Eyes of Innocents: Children Witness World War II, 2000, Unschuldige Zeugen, 2001, Journeys From Childhood to Mid Life: Risk, Resilience and Recovery, 2001, A Conspiracy of Decency: The Rescue of the Danish Jews in World War II, 2002, In Pursuit of Liberty, 2006, Passages to America, 2009; contbr. articles to profl. jours. Recipient Disting. Sci. Contbn. to Child Devel. award, Soc. Rsch. Child Devel., 1999, Dolly Madison Presdl. award for outstanding lifelong contbns. to devel. and wellbeing of children and families, Zero to Three, 1999, Arnold Gesell award, German Soc. Pediat., 2001, award for disting. career contbns. to sci. study of lifespan devel., Soc. for Study of Human Devel., 2005. Fellow: Assn. Psychol. Scis., Soc. Rsch. Child Devel., German Acad. Social Pediats. (hon.). Business E-Mail: eewerner@ucdavis.edu.

WERNICK, RICHARD FRANK, composer, conductor, educator; b. Boston, Jan. 16, 1934; s. Louis and Irene (Prince) W.; m. Beatrice Messina, July 15, 1956; children: Lewis, Adam, Peter (dec.). BA, Brandeis U., 1955; MA, Mills Coll., 1957. Instr. music U. Buffalo, 1964-65; asst. prof. music, dir. univ. symphony U. Chgo., 1965-68; conductor Pa. Contemporary Players, 1968-93; prof. music U. Pa., 1968-96, prof. emeritus, 1996—. Co-founder Community Youth Orch. of Delaware County; cons. Contemporary Music, The Phil. Orch., 1983-89, spl. cons. to the music dir., 1989-93; bd. dirs. Theodore Presser Co. Music dir. Royal Winnipeg Ballet Can., 1957-58; composer: Haiku of Basho, 1967, A Prayer for Jerusalem, 1971 (Naumburg award 1975), Moonsongs from the Japanese, 1972, Kaddish Requiem, 1973, String Quartet 2, 1973, Songs of Remembrance, 1974, Visions of Terror and Wonder, 1976 (Pulitzer prize 1977), Contemplations of the Tenth Muse, Book I, 1976, Book II, 1978, Introits and Canons, 1977, A Poison Tree, 1979, Concerto for Cello and Ten Players, 1980, In Praise of Zephyrus, 1981, Piano Sonata: Reflections of a Dark Light, 1982, Sonata for cello and piano: Portraits of Antiquity, 1982, The Oracle of Shimon bar Yochai, 1983, Concerto for Violin and Orch., 1983-84 (Friedheim 1st prize 1986); Oracle II for soprano, oboe and piano, 1985, Concerto for Viola and Orch., 1985-86, Musica Ptolemeica brass quintet, 1987, Symphony #1, 1988, String Quartet #3, 1988, Concerto for Piano and Orch. (Friedheim award 1992), 1989-90, Fragments of Prophecy, 1990, String Quartet #4, 1991 (Friedheim 1st prize 1991), Concerto for Saxophone Quartet and Orch., 1991, Cello Concerto #2, 1992, Symphony #2, 1993, ...and a Time for Peace, 1994, String Quartet #5, 1995, Cassation-Music Tom Jefferson Knew, 1995, Trio for violin, cello, piano, 1996, Da'ase for solo guitar, 1996, Games of Menoretti for solo bassoon, 1997, Sonata for violin and piano, 1997, Duettino for violin and oboe, 1997, String Quartet 6, 1998, Musica da Camerata, 1999, Telino's Acrobats, (for solo bass clarinet), 1999, Piano Sonata # 2, 2000, The Name of the Game, 2000, Duo for cello and piano, 2001, Quintet for Horn & String Quartet, 2002, Suite #1 for Unaccompanied Cello, 2003, Sextet (for string quartet, double bass, piano), 2003, Double Duo for 2 pianos, 2 cellos, 2004, A Song for Phil, 2004, Woodwind Quintet, 2005, Tristam Redux for guitar and percussion, 2006, String Quartet #7, 2007, Suite #2 for Unaccompanied Cello, 2007, Songs of Joy and Blessing for Oboe, Guitar, Percussion and Piano, 2008. Recipient music award Nat. Inst. Arts and Letters, 1976, Nat. Endowment Arts grantee, 1975, 79, 82; Fellow Ford Found., 1962-64, Guggenheim Found., 1976. Mem. ASCAP. Home: 3300 Darby Rd C-901 Haverford PA 19041 Personal E-mail: rfwernick@aol.com.

WERNICK, SANDRA MARGOT, meeting event planner and public relations executive; b. Tampa, Fla., Sept. 13, 1944; d. Nathan and Sylvia (Bienstock) Rothstein. BA in English, U. Fla., 1966. Tchr. English Miami Beach Sr. HS, 1967; adminstrv. asst. pub. rels. Bozell & Jacobs, Inc., NYC, 1968-69; asst. to dir. pub. rels. Waldorf-Astoria, NYC, 1969-70; dir. advt. and pub. rels. Hyatt on Union Sq., San Francisco, 1974-82; pres. Wernick Mktg. Group, San Francisco, 1982—; exec. dir. Sales and Mktg. Execs. of the Bay Area, 1995-2000; mng. ptnr. The Stanford Group, 1998-99; pres. Auction Magic, San Francisco, 2003—. Bd. dirs. Nat. Kidney Assn., San Francisco, 1985-87; advisor Swords to Plowshares, San Francisco, 1988-89; mem. mktg. com. to bd. Boy Scouts of Greater East Bay, 1995-2000. Recipient Award of Merit, San Francisco Advt. and Cable Car Awards, 1979, Award of Excellence, San Francisco Art Dirs. 1978, Disting. Mktg. award Sales and Mktg. Internat., 1997, awards Am. Hotel and Motel Assn., 1981, 82. Mem. NAFE, Women in Comms. (bd. dirs. 1987-89), Am. Women in Radio and TV (bd. dirs. 1989-90), Pub. Rels. Soc. Am., San Francisco Publicity Club (pres. 1989, awards of excellence 1990, 94, 95-98), Variety Club, Profl. Bus. Women's Assn., Calif. Pacific Med. Ctr. (aux. 1988-95). Democrat. Jewish. Office: 1690 Broadway Ste 705 San Francisco CA 94109-2107 E-mail: sandie@wernickmarketinggroup.com.

WERREN, JOHN HAYNES, biology professor; b. Monroe, Wis., Dec. 11, 1952; PhD, U. Utah, Salt Lake City, 1980. Postdoc. rschr. U. Md., Coll. Pk., 1984—86; prof., biology U. Rochester, NY, 1986—. Capt. Med. Svc. Corps US Army, 1980—84, Landstuhl Germany & Washington, environ. sci. officer US Army, 1982—84, Washington. Recipient Humboldt prize, Germany Govt., 1995; Frontiers Integrative Biol. Rsch. grant, NSF, 2004—09, Indo-US Professorship fellow, Am. Soc. Microbiology, 2007, Vis. fellow, Japanese Soc. Promotion Sci., 2008, Inst. Advanced Study Ind. U., 2008. Fellow: AAAS; mem.: Phi Beta Kappa. Achievements include research in evolutionary genetics and genomics; nasonia genome sequencing project; discovery of gene transfers from bacteria to animals are common; research in insects alter sex of their offspring in adaptive manner. Office: Dept Biology Univ Rochester Rochester NY 14627 Business E-Mail: werr@mail.rochester.edu.

WERSHIL, BARRY KENT, pediatrician; s. Leo Wershil; m. Helen Beth Wanderstock, Oct. 14, 1996; 1 child, Sarah Jae ThuyHien. AB, Wash. U., St. Louis, 1975, MD, 1979. Instr. Harvard Med. Sch., Boston, 1986—91, asst. prof. pediat., 1991—98; prof. and vice chmn., dept. pediat. SUNY Downstate Med. Ctr., Bklyn., 1999—2003, chief, divsn. pediat. gastroenterology, 2001—03; prof. pediat. Albert Einstein Coll. Medicine, Bronx, NY, 2003—08, Feinberg Sch. Medicine at Northwestern, Chgo., 2008—. Chief, divsn. pediat. gastroenterology Children's Hosp. at Montefiore, Bronx, 2003—08, Children's Meml. Hosp., Chgo., 2008—. Ind. Investigator grant, NIH, 1995—2006. Mem.: Soc. Pediat. Rsch., Am. Gastroenterology Assn., Am. Assn. Immunologists, Children's Digestive Health and Nutrition Found., N. Am. Soc. Pediat. Gastroenterology, Hepatology, and Nutrition (mem. exec. coun. 1999—2002). Office: Children's Meml Hosp Box 65 2300 Children's Plz Chicago IL 60614

WERT, JONATHAN MAXWELL, II, management consultant; b. Port Royal, Pa., Nov. 8, 1939; s. Jonathan Maxwell and Helen Leona (Leonard) Wert; m. Wendy J. Mast; children: Jonathan Maxwell III, Kimberly Dee, Jon Adam, Justin Tyler, Amanda Elizabeth, Gabriel Chadwick, Emily Lauren. BS in Biology, Austin Peay State U., 1966, MS in Biology, 1968; PhD in Adminstrn., U. Ala., 1974. Park supt., chief interpretive services Bur. State Parks Pa. Dept. Environ. Resources, Harrisburg, 1968-69; chief naturalist Bays Mountain Park Environ. Edn. Ctr., Kingsport, Tenn., 1969-71; environ. and energy edn. specialist TVA, Knoxville, 1971-75; cons. energy, environment, conservation U. Tenn., Knoxville, 1975; sr. assoc.-energy Energy Extension Svc., Coop. Extension Svc., Pa. State U., 1977-80; pres. Energy-Environ. Consultants, Port Royal, Pa., 1981-85, Mgmt. Diagnostics, Inc., Port Royal, 1985—. Author: Writing Environmental Education Grant Proposals, 1974, Environmental Education Study Projects for High School Students, 1974, Environmental Education Study Projects for College Students, 1974, Developing Environmental Study Areas, 1974, Developing Environmental Education Curriculum Material, 1974, Finding Solutions to Environmental Problems... A Process Guide, 1975, Assessing an Issue in Relation to Environmental, Economic, and Social Impact... A Process Guide, 1976, Energy Conservation Measures for Mobile Home Dwellers, 1978, Selected Energy Conservation Options for the Home, 1978, Selected Energy Management Options for Small Business and Local Government, 1978, Life Lines: A Book of Poetry, Prose, and Axioms, 1983, Survivorship and Growth in Employment: A Question and Answer Guide, 1983; mem. adv. bd.: Environ. Edn. Report, 1974—; cons. editor: Jour. Environ. Edn, 1975; contbr. articles to profl. jours. Counselor Boy Scouts Am., 1975. Served with USMC, 1958-61. Recipient Conservation award Am. Motors Co., 1976 Mem. U.S. Energy Assn., Inst. Mgmt. Cons., Orgn. Devel. Inst., Inst. of Mgmt. Cons. (cert. mgmt. cons.), The Cons. Bur. (profl. mgmt. cons.). Lutheran. Office: Mgmt Diagnostics Inc PO Box 240 Port Royal PA 17082-0240 Home: 909 Main St Port Royal PA 17082-9528 Office Phone: 717-527-4399. Business E-Mail: jwert@mdi-wert.com.

WERTHAMER, NATHAN RICHARD, physicist; b. Milw., Feb. 9, 1935; BA, Harvard Coll., 1956; PhD in physics, U. Calif., 1961. Rsch. assoc. U. Calif., San Diego, 1961-62; mem. tech. staff Bell Labs, 1962-75; mem. corp. planning dept. AT&T, 1975-76; chmn. N.Y. State Energy Rsch. and Devel. Authority, 1976-78; sr. advisor sci. and tech. dept. Exxon Corp., 1978-83; exec. dir. Becton Dickinson Devel. Corp., 1983-89; exec. officer Am. Phys. Soc., 1990-93; mgmt. cons. Chelsea Technols, NYC, 1993—. Author: (book) Risk and Reward: The Science of Casino Blackjack, 2009 (Author of Yr.). Fellow AAAS, Am. Phys. Soc. Office: Chelsea Techs 43 W 16th St Apt 7D New York NY 10011-6321 Business E-Mail: chelseatechnologies@nyc.rr.com.

WERTHAN, JEFFREY MICHAEL, lawyer; b. NYC, Sept. 28, 1954; s. Fred and Evelyn (Rabinowitz) W.; m. Susan Elizabeth Miller, Aug. 27, 1978; children: David E., Benjamin J. Student, The Juilliard Sch., NYC, 1972-74; BA, Tufts U., 1976; JD, Boston U., 1979. Bar: D.C. 1979, N.Y. 1980, U.S. Ct. Appeals (1st, 6th and 9th cirs.). Staff atty. Fed. Home Loan Bank Bd./FSLIC, Washington, 1979—80, sr. asst. US atty., 1981, sr. atty., 1981-83; assoc. Silver, Freedman & Taff, L.L.P., Washington, 1983-85, ptnr., 1986—2001, Katten Muchin Rosenman LLP, Washington, 2001—. Mem. ABA (banking com. 1990—). Avocations: music, baseball, golf. Office Phone: 202-625-3500. Office Fax: 202-339-8281. Business E-Mail: jeff.werthan@kattenlaw.com.

WERTHEIM, JOHN V., lawyer, former political organization administrator; b. Santa Fe, Feb. 12, 1968; s. Jerry and Mary Carole Wertheim; m. Bianca Ortiz, Dec. 30, 1994. BA in History, Yale U., 1990; JD, U. N.Mex., 1995. Bar: New Mexico 1997. Fin. analyst, corp. fin. Alex. Brown & Sons, Inc., Balt., 1990-91; N.Mex. dir. Clinton for Pres., 1992; campaign mgr. Bruce King for Gov., Albuquerque, 1994; assoc. atty. The Jones Law Firm, Santa Fe, 1997—2003; mng. dir. Wertheim Doyle & Co., Albuquerque, 1998—2003; ptnr. Jones Snead Wertheim & Wentworth PA, Santa Fe, 2003—. NM Dir. Clinton for Pres. 1992, pres. Young Democrats of New Mexico 1994-96, guest political commentator KANW Public Radio for Ctrl. NM. Dem. Party nominee US Ho. of Reps. 1996, Dem. Candidate 2000 1st Congressional Dist. N.Mex.; former chmn. Dem. Party of N.Mex.; former mem. exec. com. Dem. nat. Com., 2005-07; pres., spkr. Yale Political Union Bd. Dirs., 2007-. 1st. American winner World Debating Championship U. Glasgow Scotland 1990, Pickens Prize for Outstanding Scholarship in African-American History, Yale U. Mem. AAJ, N.Mex. Bar Assn., N.Mex. Trial Lawyers Assn. (bd. dirs., 2007-). Jewish. Avocations: hiking, running, rafting, skiing. Office: Jones, Snead, Wertheim & Wentworth, PA 1800 Old Pecos Trail Santa Fe NM 87505 Office Phone: 505-982-0011. Business E-Mail: johnv@thejonesfirm.com.

WERTHEIM, MARY DANIELLE, educational coordinator; b. NYC; d. Daniel Leo and Helen Loretta (Sudimick) Conroy; m. Stanley Claude Wertheim, Mar. 9, 1963. BA in English with honors, CCNY, 1960, MA in Psychology, 1979. Coord. English and lang. arts Horace Mann Lower Sch., Riverdale, NY, 1969—. Pvt. investor Wertheim Trust, N.Y.C., 1985—; pres. winner's cir. Horace Mann Investment Club, Riverdale, 1989—. Founder, advisor Horace Mann Lower Sch. Cmty. Svc. Group, Riverdale, 1980—; active Rep. nat. Com., 1980—. Mem.: ASCD, Nat. Assn. Investors Corp., The Internat. Netsuke Soc. (sec. N.Y. chapter), Priory Scholars, Am. Firm, Mensa, The Grolier Club. Avocations: desk top publishing, manuscript collecting. Home: 180 Cabrini Blvd # 57 New York NY 10033-1138 Office: Horace Mann Lower Sch 4440 Tibbett Ave Bronx NY 10471-3416 Office Phone: 646-286-3592. Personal E-mail: herbieboo@aol.com.

WERTHEIM, MITZI MALLINA, information technology executive; b. NYC; d. Rudolf and Myrtle B. (McGraw) Mallina; m. Ronald P. Wertheim, Feb. 25, 1965 (div. July 1988); children: Carter, Tiana. BA, U. Mich., 1960. Asst. dir. div. research Peace Corps, Washington, 1961-66; sr. program officer Cafritz Found., Washington, 1970-76; dep. undersec. navy, 1977-81; with Fed. Sector Div. IBM, 1981-94; v.p. enterprise solutions SRA Corp., 1994-98, CNA Corp., 1998—2008; prof. sustainability & enterprises Cebrowski, Naval Postgrad. Sch., 2009—. Woodrow Wilson vis. fellow, 1979, 80. Founder, pres. The Energy Consensus, 2005—; founnder and dir., The Energy Conservation energyconservation.org, 2006—; bd. dirs. Nat. Coalition Sci. and Tech., 1983—86; mem. vis. com. MIT, 1983—89; bd. dirs. Youth Policy Inst., 1986—91, VITA, 1989—2001, Cebrowski Inst., 2001—, Naval Post Grad. Sch.; founder MIT Seminar XXI, 1985—. Recipient Federally Employed Women award Def. Dept., 1980; Disting. Pub. Svc. medal Navy Dept., 1981; fellow Maxwell Sch. Syracuse U., 1996-97. Mem.: Naval Studies Bd., Coun. on Fgn. Rels. Episcopalian. Home: 3113 38th St NW Washington DC 20016-3726 Business E-Mail: mitzi@ups.edu.

WERTHEIM, RAM D., lawyer; b. Tel Aviv, May 15, 1954; BA cum laude, City U., 1979; JD magna cum laude, Georgetown U., 1982. Bar: NY 1983. Atty. Simpson, Thacher & Bartlett, NYC; gen. counsel, chief adminstrn. officer CapMAC Holdings, Inc.; co-head structured fin. divsn. MBIA, Inc., Armonk, NY, 1998—2000, v.p., gen. counsel, sec., 2000—. Alt. mem. legal, regulatory, acctg., and tax. com. Am. Securitization Forum. Editor: Georgetown Law Jour., 1981—82. Office: MBIA Inc 113 King St Armonk NY 10504 Office Phone: 914-765-3945. Office Fax: 914-765-3163. E-mail: ram.wertheim@mbia.com.

WERTHEIM, ROBERT HALLEY, national security consultant; b. Carlsbad, N.Mex., Nov. 9, 1922; s. Joseph and Emma (Vorenberg) W.; m. Barbara Louise Selig, Dec. 26, 1946; children: Joseph Howard, David Andrew. Student, N.Mex. Mil. Inst., 1940-42; BS, U.S. Naval Acad., 1945; MS in Physics, M.I.T., 1954; postgrad., Harvard U., 1969. Commd. ensign U.S. Navy, 1945, advanced through grades to rear adm., 1972; assigned Spl. Projects Office, Washington, 1956-61, Naval Ordnance Test Sta., China Lake, 1961-62, Office Sec. Def., Washington, 1962-65; head Missile br. Strategic Systems Project Office, Washington, 1965-67, dep. tech. dir., 1967-68, tech. dir., 1968-77, dir., 1977-80; sr. v.p. Lockheed Corp., 1981-88; cons. nat. def., 1988—. Emeritus mem. Draper Lab., Inc.; sci. adv. group Dept. Def., Dept. Energy, U.S. Strategic Command; nat. security adv. Lawrence Livermore Nat. Lab. Decorated DSM with cluster, Legion of Merit, Navy Commendation medal, Joint Svc. Commendation medal; recipient Rear Adm. William S. Parsons award Navy League U.S., 1971, Chmn. Joint Chiefs of Staff Disting. Pub. Svc. award, 1996, Sec. of Def. medal, 1996, Disting. Grad. award U.S. Naval Acad., 2005; named Disting. Submariner, Naval Submarine League, 2006; named to Hall of Fame NMMI, 1987. Fellow AIAA, Calif. Coun. Sci. Tech.; mem. Am. Soc. Naval Engrs. (hon. mem., Gold medal 1972), Nat. Acad. Engring., U.S. Naval Inst., Bernardo Heights Country Club, Sigma Xi, Tau Beta Pi. Home: 17705 Devereux Rd San Diego CA 92128-2084 Office: Sci Applications Internat Corp 1074 Thornmint Rd San Diego CA 92127 E-mail: rhwertheim@aol.com.

WERTHEIM, SALLY HARRIS, director, academic administrator, dean, education educator, consultant; b. Cleve., Nov. 1, 1931; d. Arthur I. and Anne (Manheim) Harris; m. Stanley E. Wertheim, Aug. 6, 1950; children: Kathryn, Susan B., Carole J. BS, Flora Stone Mather Coll., 1953; MA, Case Western Res. U., 1967, PhD, 1970. Cert. elem. and secondary edn. tchr. Ohio. Social worker U. Hosps., Cleve., 1953-54; tchr. Fairmount Temple Religious Sch., Cleve., 1957-72; mem. faculty John Carroll U., Cleve., 1969—, chair dept. edn., 1969—86, dean Grad. Sch., 1986—99, dir. planning and assessment, 1999—2004, interim dean Coll. Arts and Scis., 2004—05, cons. Office of Acad. V.P., 2005—, interim dir. Career Ctr., 2005—06, interim dean Grad. Sch., 2007—08, emeritus dean and prof., 2008—. Cons. in field; cons. Jennings Found., Cleve.; chmn. sch. com. Cleve. Commn. on Higher Edn., 1987-99. Contbr. articles to profl. jours. Sec. Cuyahoga County Mental Health Bd., Cleve., 1978—82; pres. Montefiore Home, Cleve., 1987—90; bd. dir. Mt. Sinai Med. Ctr., Cleve., 1984—93; v.p. Mt. Sinai Health Care Found.; bd. dirs. Cleve. Edn. Fund, 1992—94, v.p., 2002—; chair edn. com. Cleve. Found. Commn. on Poverty, 1988—93, Cleve. Cmty. Bldg. Initiative, 1993—95, United Way Svcs., 1994—2001; trustee Gerson Found., 1998, Miller Found., 1998, Begun Found., 2001, Mandel Found., 2001; pres. Jewish Family Svc. Assn., Cleve., 1974—77; v.p. Jewish Cmty. Fedn., 1988—91, pres., 1994—97, life trustee, 1997—. Named One of 100 Most Influential Women, Cleve. mag., 1983, One of 29 Most Influential Women, Cleve. Mag., 1997; recipient award John Carroll U., Curtis Miles award for cmty. svc., 1997, Charles Eiseman award, 2008-09; grantee Jennings Found., 1984-87, Cleve. and Gund Found., 1987-90, Lilly Found., 1988; S.H. Wertheim scholarship and edn. excellence award established John Carroll U., 1997. Mem. Am. Assn. Colls. for Tchrs. Edn. (bd. dirs. 1982-85), Ohio Assn. Colls. for Tchrs. Edn. (pres. 1981-83), Coun. of Grad. Schs. Avocations: flower arranging, travel, antiques. Office: John Carroll Univ Cleveland OH 44118

WERTHEIMER, FREDRIC MICHAEL, public policy advocate; b. Bklyn., Jan. 9, 1939; s. Irving Wertheimer and Mildred (Klein) Van Brink; m. Linda Cozby, June 15, 1969. BA, U. Mich., 1959; LL.B., Harvard U., 1962. Bar: N.Y. bar 1963, D.C. bar 1971. Atty. SEC, 1963-66; legis. counsel Congressman Silvio Conte, 1967-68; counsel House Small Bus. Com., 1969-70; lobbyist, legis. dir., v.p. Common Cause, Washington, 1971-81, pres., 1981-95; news polit. analyst CBS News, Washington, 1996; pres. Democracy 21, 1997—. Fellow Press Politics and Policy Ctr. Harvard U., 1996; J. Skelly Wright fellow, vis. lectr. Yale Law Sch., 1997; polit. analyst ABC News, 1999-2000. Author: Common Cause Manual on Money and Politics. With U.S. Army, 1962-63. Fellow Inst. Politics Harvard U., 1972. Jewish. Home: 3502 Macomb St NW Washington DC 20016-3162

WERTHEIMER, MARILYN LOU, librarian, educator; b. Pueblo, Colo., Dec. 1, 1928; d. Louis Robert and Alice Erdine Schuman; m. Y. Ernest Satow, Jan. 4, 1953 (div. Oct. 1958); m. Michael M. Wertheimer, Sept. 12, 1970; stepchildren: Karen Anne, Mark David, John Benjamin. BA, Stanford U., Calif., 1950; MA and cert., Russian Inst. Columbia U., NYC, 1953; postgrad., U. Calif., Berkeley, 1961—62; MLS, U. Calif., LA, 1967. Sec., proofreader various publ. firms, NYC, 1953—56; sec. Rockefeller Bros. Fund, 1956—57; personal staff, sec. Nelson A. Rockefeller, 1957—58; sec. Gen. Dynamics Corp., San Diego,

1959—64; cataloguer U. Calif., 1965—68; reference libr. U. Colo., Boulder, 1968—93, prof. honors sem., 1972—91, prof. emeritus, 1993—. Mem. libr. del. U.S. Exch. China, 1985, U.S. Exch. U.S.S.R., 1988; cons. Archives of History Am. Psychology, Akron, Ohio, 1980. Co-author: Sources of Information in the Social Sciences, 1986; co-editor: History of Psychology: A Guide, 1979; photographer (one-woman shows) Boulder, Colo. Pub. Libr., 2004, Sun Microsystems, Broomfield, Colo., 2004, Norlin Libr. U. Colo., Boulder, 2005, Classical Acad., Colorado Springs, Colo., 2005. Mem. del. vis. Tibet, Boulder-Lhasa Sister Cities Program, 1988; vol. Christian Sci. Ch., 1986—; bd. dirs. U. Club, U. Colo., Boulder, 1976—79. Recipient 1st prize, Internat. Libr. Photography, Owings Mills, Md., 1999—2000. Mem.: ALA. Democrat. Home: 546 Geneva Ave Boulder CO 80302 Office: Norlin Libr U Colo Campus Box 184 Boulder CO 80309-0184 Business E-Mail: michael.wertheimer@colorado.edu.

WERTIME, TIMOTHY RAY, music educator; b. Chambersburg, Pa., Apr. 10, 1954; s. Rudolf Milton and Phyllis Jane Wertime. BA, Wittenberg U., 1976, M of Sacred Music, 1985. Cert. music/elem. tchr. Ohio Dept. Edn., water safety instr. Red Cross, 1990. Dir. youth choir Covenant Presbyn. Ch., 1975—76; substitute tchr. Springfield City Schs., Ohio, 1977—92, Clark County Schs., Springfield, 1977—92; organist Northminster Presbyn. Ch., Springfield, 1977—92; tchr. Wertime's Keyboard Studio, Greencastle, Pa., 1995—; organist/choirmaster St. John's Evang. Luth. Ch., Mercersburg, Pa., 1995—. Author: (rsch. project) English Liturgical Music of the Sixteenth Century, 1984; composer: (music anthem) Magnificat-Song of Mary, 1984. Singer Mercersburg Area Cmty. Chorus; deacon Northminster Presbyn. Ch., 1990. Fellowship of Christian Athletes, Wittenberg U., 1975—76. Mem.: Am. Guild Organists, Royal Sch. Ch. Music Eng., Music Educators Nat. Conf., Phi Delta Kappa. Republican. Presbyterian. Avocations: walking, hiking, music, camping, recitals. Home: 441 Leitersburg Rd Greencastle PA 17225 Studio: 207 Leitersburg St Greencastle PA 17225

WERTLIEB, DONALD LAWRENCE, psychologist, educator; b. Washington, Feb. 22, 1952; s. Norman N. and Helen (Rubin) W.; m. Lorre Beth Polinger, Aug. 12, 1973; children: Joshua Michael, Mollie Rebecca, Miriam Tamar. BS in Psychology summa cum laude, Tufts U., 1974, MA in Child Study, 1975; MA in Psychology, Boston U., PhD in Clin. and Cmty. Psychology, 1979. Instr. psychology Harvard U. Med. Sch., Boston, 1978-81; also staff psychologist Judge Baker Guidance Ctr., Boston, 1978-81; asst. prof. Eliot-Pearson dept. child study Tufts U., Medford, Mass., 1981-86, assoc. prof., 1986-89, chmn., 1989-96, prof., 1997—, chmn. dept. edn. interim, 1990-91, dir. Ctr. for Children, 1999—2002; vis. scholar Ctr. for Internat. Innovation, Leadership and Edn., Wheelock Coll., 2002—03. Sr. rsch. assoc. Harvard U. Community Health Plan, Boston, 1981-87; mem. faculty Inst. for Health Rsch., Harvard Sch. Pub. Health, 1983-87; lectr. dept. social medicine and health policy, Harvard Med. Sch., 1984-89; cons. mental health svcs. Mem. editl. bd. Profl. Psychology, 1981—, Jour. Clin. Child Psychology, 1981—2001; contbr. Carmichael prize scholar, 1973; NIMH tng. fellow, 1974-76; NIMH rsch. grantee, 1977-81, 83-86, Office Spl. Edn. tng. grantee, 1981-83, NIH Biomed. Rsch. grantee, 1982; W.T. Grant Found. grantee, 1982-86; lic. psychologist, Mass. Fellow Am. Orthopscyhiat. Assn., Am. Psychol. Soc. (charter); mem. APA, Assn. Advancement Psychology, New Eng. Psychol. Assn., Mass. Psychol. Assn., Boston Inst. Devel. Infants and Parents, Soc. Psychol. Study of Social Issues, Soc. Rsch. in Child Devel., Soc. Pediatric Psychology (pres. 1996-99), Phi Beta Kappa, Psi Chi.

WERTS, MERRILL HARMON, retired management consultant; b. Smith County, Kans., Nov. 17, 1922; s. Mack Allen and Ruth Martha (Badger) Werts; m. Dorothy Wilson, Mar. 22, 1946 (dec. Jan. 15, 2003); children: Stephen M., Riley J., Todd J., Kelly M. BS, Kans. State U., 1947; MS, Cornell U., 1948. Beef sales mgr. John Morrell & Co., Topeka, Memphis, 1948-53; dir. mktg. Kans. Dept. Agr., Topeka, 1953-55; sec.-treas. Falley's Markets, Inc., Topeka, 1955-58; v.p. S.W. State Bank, Topeka, 1958-65; pres. First Nat. Bank, Junction City, Kans., 1965-78; pvt. practice mgmt. cons. Junction City, 1978-98; ret., 1998. Pres. Junction City CC, 1975—76. Mem. adv. com. U.S. Comptroller Currency, 1971—72; mem. Topeka Bd. Edn., 1957—61, Kans. Bank Mgmt. Commn., 1967—71, Kans. Pub. Employees Rels. Bd., 1989—94, Kans. Commn. Future Health Care, 1991—94; trustee Kans. State U. Found., 1958—2001, Kans. Synod Presbyn. Westminster Found., 1965—72, Kans. Pub. Policy Inst., 1995—99; pres. Junction City Indsl. Devel., Inc., 1966—72, Junction City-Geary County United Fund, 1967—68; chmn. Kans. WWII Commemoration Com., 1995—96, Kans. Commn. Vets. Affairs, 1995—98, Geary County Pub. Bldg. Commn., 1996—99; civillian aide Sec. Army for Kans., 1991—95; pres., bd. govs. Ft. Riley Ctrl. Kansas chpt. AUSA, 1994—95; mem. Kans. Senate, 1978—88; bd. dirs. Kans. Hist. Soc., 1989—97. 1st lt. inf. US Army, 1943—46. Decorated Bronze Star, Purple Heart; named Outstanding State legis., Am. Legis. Exch. Coun., 1988; named to Inf. Officer Candidate Hall of Fame, 1981. Mem.: DAV, VFW, Kans. Livestock Assn., Kans. Farm Bur., Kans. Bankers Assn., Assn. U.S. Army (bd. govs., Gen. Creighton W. Abrams medal 1997), Kans. State U. Alumni Assn. (pres. 1957), Junction City Country Club (past pres.), Rotary (dist. gov. 1973—74), Am. Legion, Masons, Jesters, Shriners, Sigma Phi Epsilon. Republican. Presbyterian. Address: 1228 Miller Dr Junction City KS 66441-3312

WERTSMAN, VLADIMIR FILIP, librarian, writer, library and information scientist, translator; b. Secureni, Romania, Apr. 6, 1929; came to U.S., 1967; s. Filip and Anna Wertsman. LLM summa cum laude, U. A.I. Cuza, Romania, 1953; MLS, Columbia U., 1969. Judge lower and appellate cts., Romania, 1953-67; examiner stock certs. 1st Nat. City Bank, NYC, 1967-68; reference libr. sci. div. Bklyn. Pub. Libr., NYC, 1969-74, sr. libr. Canarsie br., 1974-77, sr. libr. Greenpoint br., 1977-80, sr. libr. Leonard br., 1980-82; sr. libr., Slavic and Romanian specialist Donnell Libr. Ctr. N.Y. Pub. Libr., 1982-86; sr. libr. Learner's Adv. and Job Info. Ctr., 1987-93. Author, editor: The Romanians in America, 1748-1974, 1974, The Ukrainians in America, 1608-1975, 1976, The Russians in America, 1727-1970, 1977, The Armenians in America, 1618-1976, 1978, The Romanians in America and Canada, 1980, Librarian's Companion: A Handbook of Thousands of Facts and Figures on Libraries/Librarians, 1987, 2d edit., 1996, Career Opportunities for Bilinguals and Multilinguals: A Directory of Resources in Education, Employment and Business, 1991, 2d eidt., 1994, What's Cooking in Multicultural America, 1996, New York: The City in Over 500 Memorable Quotations From American & Foreign Sources, 1996, paperback edit., 1999, Romanians in the United States and Canada: A Guide to Ancestry and Heritage Research, 2002, Directory of Ethnic and Multicultural Publishers, Distributors and Resource Organizations, 3d edit., 1995, 4th edit., 1999, 5th edit., 2003; co-author: Ukrainians in Canada and United States, 1981, Free Voices in Russian Literature, 1950s-1980s, 1986; editl. cons. Harvard Ency. Am. Ethnic Groups, 1980; contbr. Books, Libraries and Information in Slavic and East European Studies, 1986, Immigrant Labor Press in North America, 1840s-1970s, 1987, Through American Eyes, 1989, Ency. of N.Y.C., 1995; mem. adv. bd., contbr.: Gale Ency. Multicultural Am., 1995, 99; contbr. articles, book revs. to profl. jours. Recipient Disting. Lit. Achievement award Am. Soc. Writers, 1977, Cert. of Merit, Yeshiva U., 1981, Spl. Recognition award Pub. Libr. Assn. Am., 1990, Nominee Ellis Island Medal of Honor, 2009 Mem. ALA (chair multilingual libr. materials and svcs. com. 1976-88, chair pub. and multicultural material com. of Emie Round Table, Am. Libr. Assn. 1989—, ethnic and multicultural info. exchange roundtable, spl. merit award 1988, David Cohen Emiert Multicultural award 2003), Am. Assn. Advancement of Slavic Studies, Am. Romanian Acad. Arts and Scis., Delta Tau Kappa.(Outstanding Scholartic award), Am. Biographical Inst.(bd. advisors, 1998-2000) Avocations: chess playing, travel, stamp collecting/philately, dance, languages. Home Phone: 718-896-0212. Personal E-mail: vvladimirw@aol.com. *America is by its very nature of historical formation and development a multiethnic, multicultural and multilingual society. And if variety is the spice of life then American ethno-linguistic and cultural mosaique is the spice of our society. America's pluralism is also a microcosm of the entire world its citizens representing virtually all continents.*

WERTZ, CAROL R., education educator; d. Clarence R. and Janet L. Brunger; children: Lisa, Jim. BS in Edn., Ctrl. Mich. U., Mt. Pleasant, 1968; MA in Edn., Sonoma State U., Rohnert Park, Calif., 1985; EdD in Ednl. Leadership, U. So. Calif., LA, 2005. Multiple subject credential grades K-adult Calif. Tchr. Santa Rosa Christian Sch., Calif., 1980—89, Kumon Leysin Acad., Switzerland, 1990; ESL resource specialist Takanawa Gakuen, Tokyo, 1991—92; ESL instr. Shasta C.C., Redding, Calif., 1992—2001; tchr. Redding Christian Sch., 1993—97; instr. Nat. U., Redding, 1999—2001; adj. instr. Simpson U., Redding, 1999—2000, asst. prof., 2001—. Adult literacy coord., Shasta County, Calif., 1999—2000; v.p. Shasta Reading Coun., 2005—07; ednl. cons. Redding Christian Sch., 2006; presenter in field. Contbr. articles to profl. jours. Pianist, bd. mem., sec., youth leader Cornerstone Cmty. Ch., Redding. Office: Simpson Univ 2211 College View Dr Redding CA 96003 Home Phone: 530-221-7250; Office Phone: 530-226-4195.

WERTZ, GAIL WILLIAMS, microbiologist, educator; d. Henry Clay and Elsie Lunsford Williams; m. Laurence Andrew Ball, May 1987; children: Jennifer Ball Truitt, Katy Ball Lemuz. BS, Coll. William and Mary, Williamsburg, Va., 1966; PhD, U. Pitts., 1970. Prof. U. NC Sch. Medicine, Chapel Hill, 1973—87; prof., microbiology U. Ala. Birmingham Med. Sch., 1987—2005; prof., pathology and microbiology U. Va., Charlottesville, 2005—. Cons. WHO ARVD, Geneva, 1984—92; editl. bd. J. Virol Virus Rsch., 1984—2006; sci. adv. bd. Ctrs. Disease Control, Atlanta, 2003—06; adv. coun. NIAID NIH, Bethesda, Md., 2003—07. Contbr. numerous sci. papers and articles, chapters to books. Recipient NIH Merit award, 1986—2006, Infectious Disease Rsch. award, Bristol Myers Squibb, 1999—2004, Channock Lifetim award, Internat. RSV Colloquium, 2007. Fellow: Am. Acad. Microbiology; mem.: Soc. Gen. Microbiology, Am. Soc. Virology (pres. 1995—96), Am. Soc. Microbiology (divisional group rep. 1989—91, editl. bd., Jour. Virology 1986—2007). Achievements include patents for human respiratory syncytial virus vaccines; gene therapy vectors and vaccines; attenuation of negative stranded RNA viruses; manipulation of negative strand RNA viruses; recombinant respiratory syncytial viruses; nucleotide sequences encoding bovine respiratory syncytial virus immunogenic proteins; prevention and treatment of respiratory tract disease.

WERTZ, KENNETH DEAN, real estate company officer; b. Okla. City, July 14, 1946; s. Walter K. and Kathryn L. (Moore) W.; children: Adam Troy, Kirsten Paige. BS in Acctg., Okla. State U., 1968, MS in Acctg. and Econs., 1969; JD, U. San Francisco, 1978. CPA, Okla., Calif; lic. real estate broker, Okla. Sr. acct. Deloitte, Haskins & Sells, San Francisco, 1969-70, 71-75; v.p. acquisitions, mng. dir. Landsing Corp., Menlo Park, Calif., 1975-86; pres. Detrick Salsberry Mgmt. Inc., Tulsa, 1987-88; v.p. asset mgmt. Corporex Co., Cin., 1989-90; exec. v.p. real estate Brunner Cos., Dayton, Ohio, 1990-92; pres. Pillar Real Estate Advisors, Dayton, 1992—. Lt. col. Med. Svc. corps U.S. Army, 1968-98. Decorated Army Commendation medal with three oak leaf clusters, Meritorious Svc. medal. Mem. AICPA, Okla. Soc. CPAs, Calif. Soc. CPAs, Nat. Assn. Securities Dealers (fin. prin., registered sales rep.). Republican. Methodist. Avocations: bicycling, snow and water skiing, racquetball, camping, fishing. Home: 835 Huntersknoll Ln Cincinnati OH 45230-4343 Office: Pillar Real Estate Advisors 5335 Far Hills Ave Ste 318 Dayton OH 45429-2317 Home Phone: 513-232-1513; Office Phone: 937-434-4250. Personal E-mail: dw@okclighthouse.com.

WESBURY, STUART ARNOLD, JR., health science association administrator, educator; b. Phila., Dec. 13, 1933; s. Stuart Arnold and Jennie (Glazewska) W.; m. June Carol Davis, Feb. 23, 1957; children: Brian, Brent, Bruce, Bradford. BS, Temple U., 1955; MHA, U. Mich., 1960; PhD, U. Fla., 1972. Capt. USPHS, 1955, served as adminstrv. officer, hosp. and clinic pharmacist, resigned, 1958; adminstrv. asst. Del. Hosp., 1960-61; asst. adminstr. Bronson Meth. Hosp., 1961-66; assoc. dir., asst. prof. U. Fla. Tchg. Hosp., 1966-67, dir., assoc. prof., 1967-69; v.p. Computer Mgmt. Corp., Gainesville, Fla., 1969-72; dir., prof. grad. studies in health svcs. mgmt. U. Mo., Columbia, 1972-78; pres. Am. Coll. Healthcare Execs., Chgo., 1979-91; sr. v.p. TriBrook Group, Inc., Westmont, Ill., 1992-94; prof. Sch. of Health Adminstrn. and Policy Ariz. State U., Tempe, 1994-2000, dir., exec. edn. programs Coll. Bus., 1996-2000, prof. emeritus, 2000—. Chmn. bd. trustees, trustee emeritus Blood Sys., Inc., Scottsdale, Ariz. Co-author: Why We Spend Too Much on Health Care; contbr. articles to profl. jours. Bd. dirs. Health Task, Inc., Atlanta, Boys Clubs, Gainesville, Heartland Inst.; chmn. bd. dirs. Mid-Am. chpt. ARC, 1988-91, DuPage County Dist., 1984-87; active Boy Scouts Am.; chmn. adminstrv. bd. Meth. Ch.; trustee Nat. Blood Found.; Rep. Congl. candidate Dist. 13, Ill. Recipient Award of Honor, Temple U.; named to Health Care Hall of Fame, 2005, Gallery of Success, Temple U. Fellow Am. Coll. Health Care Adminstrs. (hon.), Am. Coll. Healthcare Execs. (Silver Medal award 1991); mem. APHA, Am. Hosp. Assn., Hosp. Mgmt. Sys. Soc., Assn. Univ. Programs in Health Adminstrn. (chmn. 1977-78), Am. Assn. Healthcare Cons. (hon.), Rotary (past pres.). Home and Office: 950 Willow Valley Lakes Dr H-312 Willow Street PA 17584 Home Phone: 717-464-4560. Business E-Mail: stu.wesbury@asu.edu.

WESCH, MICHAEL, anthropology educator, cultural anthropologist, media ecologist; b. June 22, 1975; BS in Anthropology summa cum laude, Kansas State U., 1997; PhD in Anthropology, U. Va., 2004. Rschr. social and cultural change Mountain Ok Region, Papua New Guinea, 1999—2003; asst. prof. cultural anthropology Kans. State U., 2004—. Responsible for launching Digital Ethnography Working Group Kansas State U., coord., Peer Review of Tchg. Project; working with Educause Ctr. for Applied Rsch. on "The Tower and the Cloud" project; spkr. in field. Creator (short video) Web 2.0...The Machine is Us/ing Us, released on YouTube, 2007 (most popular video in the blogosphere and has been viewed over 3 million times, Rave award-video, WIRED Mag., 2007, #1 featured YouTube video, 2007), (digital ethnography) Nekalimin.net, (on-line resource) Virtual Snow; contbr. articles to profl. publications; guest editor Spl. issue, Visual Anthropology Review, Beyond e-Text. Recipient US Professors of Yr. award for Doctoral and Rsch. Universities, Carnegie Found. for Advancement of Tchg. and Coun. for Advancement and Support of Edn., 2008; NSF Grad. Rsch. Fellowship, Jacob K. Javits Fellowship, Explorer's Club Grant, Fulbright-Hays Internat. Dissertation Rsch. Fellowship. Achievements include being active in the development of innovative teaching techniques, World Stimulation. Office: Kansas State U SASW 206 Waters Hall Manhattan KS 66506 Office Phone: 785-532-6866. Office Fax: 785-532-6978. Business E-Mail: mwesch@ksu.edu.*

WESCHLER, LAWRENCE MICHAEL, writer, journalist; b. Van Nuys, Calif., Feb. 13, 1952; s. Irving R. and Franzi (Toch) W.; m. Joanna S. Wegrzynowicz, Feb. 22, 1984; 1 child, Sara Alice. BA in Philosophy and Cultural History, U. Calif., Santa Cruz, 1974. Interviewer, editor Oral History Program UCLA, 1974-78; freelance writer LA, 1978-80; staff writer The New Yorker mag., NYC, 1981—. Author: Seeing is Forgetting the Name of the Thing One Sees: A Life of Contemporary Artist Robert Irwin, 1982, The Passion of Poland, 1984, David Hockney's Cameraworks, 1986 (Kodakpreis, 1986), Shapinsky's Karma, Boggs's Bills and Other True-Life Tales, 1988 (George Polk award, 1988), A Miracle, A Universe: Settling Accounts with Torturers, 1990, Mr. Wilson's Cabinet of Wonder, 1995, A Wanderer in the Perfect City: Selected Passion Pieces, 1998, Calamities of Exile: Three Nonfiction Novellas, 1998, Boggs: A Comedy of Values, 1999, Vermeer in Bosnia, 2004, Everything That Rises: A Book of Convergences, 2006 (Nat. Book Critics Circle award for Criticism, 2006); contbr. to Village Voice, L.A. Times, Internat. Herald Tribune, L.A. Weekly, Rolling Stone, N.Y. Times, Artforum, ArtNews, The Nation, others. Co-dir. Ernst Toch Archive & Soc., L.A., 1972—. Recipient Hemingway prize Overseas Press Club, 1982, Sidney Hillman award, 1989, George Polk award for best mag. reporting, 1992; Pointer fellow Yale U., 1982, Guggenheim fellow, 1986-87, N.Y. Inst. for Humanities fellow, 1991, Bard Ctr. fellow, 1992. Mem. PEN, Nat. Writers Union. Jewish. Office: The New Yorker 4 Times Sq New York NY 10036-6561

WESCOTT, HOWARD BLAKELY, retired humanities educator; b. Washington, June 18, 1940; s. James Blakely Wescott and Judith Leroy Steele; m. Julia Lupinacci Wescott, July 17, 1971. PhD, Brown U., Providence, 1972. Asst. prof. Smith Coll., Northampton, Mass., 1968—76; prof. emeritus SUNY, Fredonia, 1976—. Contbr. articles to profl. publs. Grantee, Brown U., 1979—80, SUNY, 1982, Spanish Ministry of Culture, 1985, Am. Coun. Learned Socs., 1990, Nat. Endowment Humanities, United U. Professions, 1990. Mem.: Modern Lang. Assn., Soc. Renaissance & Baroque Hispanic Poetry, Buffalo Yacht Club. Liberal. Avocations: sailing, reading. Home: 54 Ashland Ave Buffalo NY 14222 Office: SUNY Fredonia Central Ave Fredonia NY 14063 Business E-Mail: howard.wescott@fredonia.edu, wescott@fredonia.edu.

WESCOTT, JOSEPH WARREN, II, academic administrator, education educator; b. Wilmington, NC, July 19, 1959; s. James Warren and Delores (Pridgen) Wescott; m. Lisa Ann Blanton (div. Oct. 2002); children: Rachael, Joseph, Rose. BA, Wake Forest U., 1981, MA, 2000; MS, N.C. State U., 1998, EdD, 2005. Dir. alt. learning ctr. Beulaville Mid. Sch., NC, 1988; bus. mgr. Associated Ins. Agy., Wallace, NC, 1989—96; dir. grants and spl. projects Duplin County Hist. Assn., Rose Hill, NC, 1998—2000; coll. instr. James Sprunt C.C., Kenansville, NC, 1999—2001; fed. rels. analyst Duke U., Durham, NC, 2001—05; program specialist, grant approving agy., gen. admission U. NC, 2005—. Assoc. AAU Coun. on Fed. Rels., Washington, 2002—03; U. rep. The Sci. Coalition, Washington, 2001—03; com. mem. Edn. Adv. Com. and Ind. Agts., Raleigh, NC, 1998—2002. Editor: 1870 Fed. Census: The African Am. Population in Duplin County, 2000; author (contbr.): Ency. of N.C., 2005. Lay pastor Town Creek Christian Ch., Winabow, NC, 1990—; bd. dirs. Duplin County 250th Celebration, Kenansville, NC, 2000; bd. dirs., v.p. Duplin County Hist. Found., 2005—07. Capt. US Army, 1984—87. Rsch. grant, N.C. State U., 1998—2000, full fellowship, Wake Forest U., Winston-Salem, N.C., 1982—84. Mem.: Phi Alpha Theta, Phi Kappa Phi. Pentecostal. Avocations: reading, gardening, travel, public speaking. Home: 676 Wescott Rd SE Bolivia NC 28422-8562 Office: Dir Planning Policy & Edn Brunswick Cmty Coll PO Box 30 Supply NC 28462 Home Phone: 910-253-4257; Office Phone: 910-755-7486. Business E-Mail: westcottj@brunswickcc.edu. E-mail: history@post.com.

WESCOTT, WILLIAM BURNHAM, oral maxillofacial pathologist, educator; b. Pendleton, Oreg., Nov. 10, 1922; s. Merton Girard and Josephine (Creasey) W.; m. Barbara L., Dec. 31, 1944 (dec. June 12, 1969); children: William Douglas, Diane Elizabeth; m. Gloria Greer-Collins, Aug. 28, 1989. DMD, U. Oreg., Portland, 1951, MS, 1962. Asst. prof. to assoc. dean admin. U. Oreg. Dental Sch., Portland, 1953-72; co-dir. oral disease rsch. VA, Houston, 1972-75, dir. dental edn. ctr. LA, 1980-85; acting dir. Reg. Med. Edn. Ctr., Birmingham, Ala., 1978-80; chief dental svc. Dept. of Veteran's Affairs, San Francisco, 1985-94; clin. prof. U. Calif., San Francisco, 1994—2006; cons. Northern System of Clinics Dept. Vets. Affairs, 1994—. Dental surgeon, Oreg. Air N.G., Portland, 1954-68; cons. Madigan Army Med. Ctr., Ft. Lewis, W. Va., 1971-74, VA Med. Ctrs., No. Calif., 1985—, prof. pathology Duke U. Med. Sch., 1977-79; cons. U. Med. Ctr., Fresno, 1998—2006; mem. Enloe Hosp. Head and Neck Malignancy Tumor Bd. Contbr. 80 articles to profl. jours. and several chpts. to profl. books; 4 chtps. to books. Dist. chmn. Boys Scouts Am., Portland, 1965-67; bd. dirs. Am. Cancer Soc., Portland, 1964-67; comdr. Veterans Foreign Wars Post 5731, Gridley, Calif., 1994-95, comdr., 1996-98; chmn. Mil. Vets Ct. of Honor Meml., No. Calif., 1997—. With Oreg. N.G., 1938-40; with U.S. Army, 1940-42; lt. col. USAF, 1942-68. Decorated DFC with oak leaf cluster USAF, Oreg. N.G. Merit Svc. Medal, Portland, Fedn. des Anciens Combattants Français medal; named Man of Yr., Gridley C. of C., 2009. Fellow Am. Acad. Oral and Maxillofacial Pathology, Am. Coll. Dentists, Mil. Officers Assn. Am. (sec. 2000—05), Omicron Kappa Upsilon, Sigma Xi. Avocations: woodworking, fishing. Home: 437 Justeson Ave Gridley CA 95948-9434 Office: U Calif Sch Dentistry S 512 San Francisco 3rd & Parnassus San Francisco CA 94143-0424 Office Phone: 415-476-4866. Business E-Mail: wesco83@sbcglobal.net.

WESELY, EDWIN JOSEPH, lawyer; b. NYC, May 16, 1929; s. Joseph and Elizabeth (Bellas) W.; children: Marissa Celeste, Adrienne Lee; m. Marcy Brownson, Sept. 23, 1992. Ed., Deep Springs Coll., 1945-47; AB, Cornell U., 1949; JD, Columbia U., 1954. Bar: NY 1954, DC 1985, US Supreme Ct. 1960, others. Law clk. to judge US Dist. Ct. (so. dist.) NY, 1954-55; asst. US atty. So. Dist. NY, 1955-57; assoc. Winthrop, Stimson, Putnam & Roberts, NYC, 1957-63, ptnr., 1964-2000; sr. counsel Pillsbury Winthrop LLP, NYC, 2001—05, Pillsbury Winthrop Shaw Pittman LLP, NYC, 2005—. Spl. master numerous cases; chmn. spl. com. on effective discovery in civil cases US Dist. Ct. (ea. dist.) NY, 1982-84, com. on civil caseflow, 1985-88, com. on civil litigation, 1988-2002, chmn. emeritus, 2002—, civil justice reform adv. group, 1990-95; com. on pretrial phase civil cases Jud. Coun. 2d Cir., 1984-86, standing com. on improvement civil litigation, 1986-89; ex-officio Civil Justice Reform Act adv. group US Dist. Ct. (so. dist.) NY; pres. CARE, 1986-89, chmn., 1978-86, 89-90, internat. bd. dirs., 1981-90, pres., 1987-90; former bd. dirs. Internat. Rescue Com., bd. overseers, 2005—; bd. dirs., exec. com. Internat. Ctr. in NY, 1990—, chmn., 1998-2003, chmn. emeritus, 2003-. Trustee Deep Springs Coll.,

1991-2000; vice-chair, 1998-2000. Decorated Order of Civil Merit (Republic of Korea); recipient World Humanitarian award Fgn. Press Assn., 1988, Commendation Bd. Judges US Dist. Ct. (ea. dist.) NY, 1993, Deep Springs Medal, Deep Springs Coll., 2003. Fellow Am. Coll. Trial Lawyers; mem. ABA (spl. adv. com. on internat. activities 1990-93, litigation sect. chmn. com. on discovery 1977-78, spl. com. study discovery abuse 1977-82, chmn. task force on liaison with internat. profl. assns. on matters of mutual concern 1989-93, Civil Justice Reform Act task force 1991-93, task force on the state of the justice sys. 1993-95, fed. initiatives task force 1995-98, co-chmn. task force on fed. and local rules 1997-98), UN Assn. USA (bd. dirs. 1991-2004), Assn. of Bar of City of NY (com. chmn., organized demonstration observation panel), Coun. on Fgn. Rels. Office: Pillsbury Winthrop Shaw Pittman LLP 1540 Broadway New York NY 10036-4039 Office Phone: 212-858-1712. Business E-Mail: edwin.wesely@pillsburylaw.com.

WESELY, MARISSA CELESTE, lawyer; b. NYC, Apr. 25, 1955; d. Edwin Joseph and Yolanda Teresa (Pyles) W.; m. Frederick Hamerman; 1 child, Emma Elizabeth Wesely Allen. BA magna cum laude, Williams Coll., 1976; JD cum laude, Harvard U., 1980. Bar: N.Y. 1981. Assoc. Simpson Thacher & Bartlett, NYC, 1980-82, 84-88, London, 1982-84, ptnr., 1989—. Lectr., cons. Harvard Inst. Internat. Devel., Beijing, 1981, Jakarta, Indonesia, 1982; guest lectr. Yale Law Sch., New Haven, 1991; spkr. Am. Conf. Inst., Practicing Law Inst., Bankers Assn. for Fgn. Trade, N.Y. State Bar Assn. confs., 1993—, NY City Bar Assn., Harvard Law Sch. Bd. dirs. Legal Momentum. Mem.: ABA, Internat. Bar Assn., N.Y. State Bar Assn., N.Y.C. Bar Assn., Phi Beta Kappa. Office: Simpson Thacher & Bartlett LLP 425 Lexington Ave Fl 20 New York NY 10017-3954 Office Phone: 212-455-7173. Office Fax: 212-455-2502. Business E-Mail: mwesely@stblaw.com.

WESLER, OSCAR, retired mathematician, educator; b. Bklyn., July 12, 1921; s. Israel Edward and Sarah (Hartman) Wesler. BS, Coll. City N.Y., 1942; MS, N.Y. U., 1943; postgrad., Princeton U., 1943-46; PhD, Stanford U., 1955. Mem. faculty Stanford U., 1952-56, U. Mich., 1956-64; prof. stats. and math. N.C. State U., Raleigh, 1964—92, prof. emeritus, 1992—. Cons. Inst. Sci. and Tech., U. Mich., 1957—64, IBM, 1966; vis. prof. statis. Stanford U., 1962—63, 1973, 74, 78; vis. lectr. NSF, 1963—; vis. prof. statis. U. Calif., Berkeley, 1972—73. Author: Solutions to Problems in Theory of Games and Statistical Decisions, 1954; contbr. articles to profl. jours. Recipient Outstanding Tchr. award, N.C. State U., 1966. Mem.: Am. Math. Soc., Inst. Math. Stats., Sigma Xi, Phi Kappa Phi. Achievements include research in decision theory, probability, stochastic processes. Home: 1926 Smallwood Dr Raleigh NC 27605-1302

WESLEY, GLEN, retired professional hockey player; b. Red Deer, Alta., Can., Oct. 2, 1968; m. Barb Wesley; children: Amanda, Josh, Matthew. Defenseman Boston Bruins, 1987—94, Hartford Whalers, 1994—97, Carolina Hurricanes, 1997—2003, 2003—08, Toronto Maple Leafs, 2003; dir. defenseman devel. Carolina Hurricanes, 2008—. Player NHL All-Star Game, 1989. Achievements include being a member of Stanley Cup Champion Carolina Hurricanes, 2006. Office: Carolina Hurricanes RBC Ctr 1400 Edwards Mill Rd Raleigh NC 27607

WESLEY, JOHN E., photographer, educator; b. Seattle, Aug. 6, 1944; s. Jerome B. and Carol J. Ellingson; 1 child, Alisa N. BA, Minn. State U., 1967. Prof. photography, art Bellevue C.C., Wash., 1972—2004, prof. emeritus, 2005. Founding ptnr. Photoprintworks Gallery, Seattle, 1975—79. One-man shows include Libr. Gallery Bellevue (Wash.) C.C., 1983, Oreg. Gallery Mus. Art, U. Oreg., Eugene, Oreg., 1984, Seattle (Wash.) Art Mus., 1985, Edn. Access Channel 28, Bellevue, Wash., 1986, 1990, Arts and Humanities Divsn. Retreat, 1987, Cable Cmty. TV Channel 34, Eugene, Oreg., 1987, Libr. Gallery, Bellevue, Wash., 1990, Pacific Luth. U., Tacoma, Wash., 1994, exhibited in group shows at Libr. Gallery (Wash.) Bellevue C.C., 1990, 1991, Video 911 Gallery, Seattle, Wash., 1991, Green River C.C., Auburn, Wash., 1992, Bellevue (Wash.) C.C., 1994, many others, Represented in permanent collections Seattle Arts Commn., Wash. Arts Commn., Wash. State Arts Commn., photograph appeared in, B&W mag., Issue 56, 2008 (Merit award). Mem.: Kirkland Art Ctr., N.W. Soc. Photog. Edn. (treas. 1985—88). Avocations: music, jazz. Personal E-mail: johnwesleyphoto@mac.com. Business E-Mail: jwesley@bcc.ctc.edu.

WESLEY, NORMAN H., consumer products company executive; b. Dec. 11, 1949; m. Kim Wesley; 3 children. BA, U. Utah, 1972, MBA, 1973. With Crown Zellerbach Corp., San Francisco, 1973—83; v.p. corp. devel ACCO World Corp., Wheeling, Ill., 1983—87, COO, 1987—90, pres., 1987—97, CEO, 1990—97; chmn., CEO Fortune Brands Home & Office, Inc., 1997—99; pres., COO Fortune Brands, Inc., Lincolnshire, Ill., 1999, chmn, CEO, 1999—2007, chmn., 2008. Bd. dirs. Fortune Brands, Inc., 1999—, Pactiv Corp., 2001—, R.R. Donnelley & Sons, 2001—. Office: Fortune Brands Inc 520 Lake Cook Rd Ste 400 Deerfield IL 60015-5633

WESLEY, RICHARD C., federal judge; b. Canandaigua, NY, Aug. 1, 1949; s. Charles and Beatrice W.; m. Kathryn Rice; 2 children. BA summa cum laude, SUNY, Albany, 1971; JD, Cornell U., 1974. Bar: NY 1975. Assoc. Harris, Beach & Wilcox, 1974-76, Welch, Streb & Porter, 1976-77; ptnr. Streb, Porter, Meyer & Wesley, 1977—87; asst. counsel to minority NY State Assembly, 1979—82; justice Supreme Ct. 7th Jud. Dist., 1987—94; supervising judge Criminal Cts. 7th Jud. Dist., 1991; judge appellate div. Supreme Ct. 4th Dept., 1994—96; assoc. judge NY Ct. Appeals, Albany, 1997—2003; judge US Ct. Appeals (2nd cir.), NYC, 2003—. Creator Felony Screening Program, 1993; lectr. in field; bd. trustees Ctr. Dispute Resolution, Pre-Trial Svcs. Corp. Editor: Cornell Law Rev. Asst. counsel to Assembly Rep. leader James L. Emery, 1979-1982; assemblyman NY State 136th Assembly Dist., 1982-84, 84-86; chair Livingston County Alcohol and Drug Abuse Prevention Coun.; bd. trustees United Ch. Livonia, Chances and Changes, Charles Settlement House; bd. dirs. Myers' Found.; driver Livonia Vol. Ambulance. Named Legislator of Yr., Livingston-Wyoming Assn. Retarded Citizens, 1988; recipient Disting. SUNY Alumni award SUNY Alumni Assn., 1997. Fellow NY State Bar Found.; mem. Livingston County Bar Assn. (sec.), Supreme Ct. Justices Assn. (pres. 7th jud. dist.). Office: 1702 US Courthouse 40 Centre St New York NY 10007-1561*

WESLIN, ANNA THERESE, clinical nurse specialist, dance consultant; d. Norman Uno and Mary Lou Weslin. AA, El Paso CC, Colorado Springs, 1977; BA, Dance Minor, St. Mary's Coll., Kans., 1981; BS in Nursing, Beth-El Coll. of Nursing, Colorado Springs, 1995; MSN, U. Colo., Colorado Springs, 2004. RN Colo. State Bd. of Nursing, Colo., 1995, cert. Clinical Nurse Specialist, Colo. State Bd. of Nursing, Colo., 2006. Assoc. dir., sec. treas. Colo. Springs Ballet Acad., 1981—2005; RN, charge nurse Health South Rehab. Hosp., Colorado Springs, 1996—2000; pres., CEO, tchr. La Sante et la Danse, Inc., Colorado Springs, 2003—; RN Pikes Peak Hospice & Palliative Care, Colorado Springs, 2006—; rn cardiology staff nurse Parkview Episcopal Hosp., Pueblo, Colo.; R&D plant mgr. Brown Disc Mfg., Colorado Springs. Recipient Best of Springs award (Best Pl. for Dancer's with a Broken Pointe), Gazette Newspaper, 2005. Mem.: Colo. Springs BBB, Colo. Springs C. of C., Performing Arts Medicine Assn., Internat. Assn. Dance Medicine and Scis., Sigma Theta Tau Internat. Achievements include development of 1st nursing based dance medicine clinic in the State of Colo; research in common injuries of adolescent dance students. Office: La Sante et la Danse Inc 2935 N Prospect St Ste 200 Colorado Springs CO 80907 Business E-Mail: lasante@comcast.net.

WESSE, DAVID JOSEPH, higher education administrator, consultant; b. Chgo., May 5, 1951; s. Herman Theodore and Lorraine Joan (Holland) W.; m. Deborah Lynn Smith, Oct. 11, 1975; children: Jason David, Eric Joseph. AA, South Suburban Coll., 1971; student, Purdue U., 1971—72; BEd, Ill. State U., 1973; MS, Loyola U., Chgo., 1983. Cert. adminstrv. mgr. Adminstr. Reuben H. Donnelley Corp., Chgo., 1974-76; adminstrv. mgr. Loyola U., Maywood, 1976-79, Joint Commn. on Accreditation of Healthcare Orgns., Oakbrook Terrace, Ill., 1979-81; adminstrv. dir., asst. sec. Northwestern U., Evanston, Ill., 1981-97; higher edn. cons. KPMG Peat Marwick, LLP, Chgo., 1997—2000; exec. dir. U. Houston, 2000; prin. Joslyn Assocs., Alexandria, La., 2000—; asst. v.p. U. North Fla., Jacksonville, 2000—03; vice chancellor fin. and adminstrv. svcs. La. State U., Alexandria, 2003—. Seminar leader Nat. Assn. Coll. Aux. Svcs., 1998. Contbr. numerous articles to profl. publs. Pres., bd. dirs. Riverdale (Ill.) Libr. Dist., 1975, Riverdale Youth Commn., 1975; bd. dirs. Better Bus. Bur. Chgo. and No. Ill., 1991-97, Adminstrv. Mgmt. Soc. Found., 1998-07, Ctrl. La. Bus. Incubator, 2006-07; Alexandria Met. Found., 2008-; elder Redeemer Luth. Ch., 2006—. Recipient Svc. Recognition award Riverdale Libr. Dist., 1975, Excellence in Journalism award Nat. Assn. Coll. Aux. Svcs., 1989. Mem. Adminstrv. Mgmt. Soc. (bd. dirs. Chgo. chpt. 1983-88, pres. 1986-87, bd. regents 1986-88), Acad. Adminstrv. Mgmt. (bd. regents 1992-94), Profl. Office Mgmt. Assn. Chgo. (bd. dirs. 1992-93, sec. 1993-95, pres. 1995), Nat. Mgmt. Assn. (chpt. pres. 1995), Nat. Assn. Coll. and Univ. Bus. Officers (com. mem. 1986-87, 89-90, cost reduction awards 1986-88, 90, 92), Midwest Higher Edn. Commn. (com. mem. 1996-97), Assn. Coll. Adminstrn. Profls. (seminar leader 1995, 98, 99), Chgo. Area Bus. and Support Svc. Adminstrs. (founder 1988), Big Ten Bus. and Support Svc. Adminstrs. (founder 1992), Kiwanis Internat.(v.p. 2005-06, pres. 2006-07), Ctrl. La. C. of C., U. North Fla. Adminstrv. and Profl. Assn. (pres. 2002-03), Phi Theta Kappa, Lambda Epsilon. Lutheran. Avocations: reading, gardening, genealogy. Office: La State Univ 8100 Hwy 71 S Alexandria LA 71302-9121 Office Phone: 318-473-6409. Business E-Mail: dwesse@lsua.edu.

WESSEL, HENRY, photographer; b. Teaneck, NJ, July 28, 1942; s. Henry and Jennie (Cincotta) W.; children by previous marriage: Nicholas, Rider. BA, Pa. State U., 1966; M.F.A., SUNY, Buffalo, 1972. Propr., mgr. comml. photog. studio, State Coll., Pa., 1966-68; cinematographer for documentary film Dept. HEW, 1967; instr. dept. art Pa. State U., Phila., 1967-69; prof. dept. photography San Francisco Art Inst., 1973-98, chmn. grad. program photography, 1977-78, chmn. dept. photography, 1987-93; asst. prof. San Francisco State U., 1974-75; vis. lectr. photography various colls. and art schs., 1967-81; propr., dir. Photographic Resources, Point Richmond, Calif., 1977—. Vis. artist Mills Coll., 1987-88; resident faculty, San Francisco Art Inst. One-man show at Mus. Modern Art, NYC, 1973, Visual Studies Workshop, Rochester, NY, 1977, Fraenkel Gallery, San Francisco, 1981, 89, 92, Gallery Min, Tokyo, 1987, Gallery Ram, Santa Monica, Calif., 1996, Mus. Contemporary Art, LA, 1998, Rena Bransten Gallery, San Francisco, 2000, 02, Gallery Luisotti, Santa Monica, Calif., 2002, Palm Springs Art Mus., Calif., 2005, others; represented in permanent collections, Mus. Modern Art, NYC, Phila. Mus. Art, Boston Mus. Fine Arts, Library of Congress, Am. Arts Documentation Center, Exeter, Eng., Nat. Gallery of Can., Ottawa, Tokyo Met. Mus. Photography, Japan, Seattle Art Mus., Wash., Oakland Mus., Calif., Met. Mus. Art, NYC, Denver Art Mus., Colo., Australian Nat. Gallery, Canberra, Art Inst. Chgo., Ill., Charles Cowles Gallery, NYC, Robert Mann Gallery, NYC, others; retrospective exhbn: San Francisco Mus. Modern Art, 2007, Wolesburg Mus., Germany, 2009; author: Henry Wessel, 1987, House Pictures, 1992, Night Walk, 2000, Odd Photos, 2002, Five Books, 2006 Guggenheim fellow, 1971, 78; Nat. Endowment Arts fellow, 1975, 77, 78 Home: PO Box 70475 Richmond CA 94807-0475

WESSEL, MORRIS ARTHUR, retired pediatrician; b. Providence, Nov. 1, 1917; s. Morris Jacob and Bessie (Bloom) Wessel; m. Irmgard Rosenzweig, June 1, 1952; children: David, Bruce, Paul, Lois. BA, Johns Hopkins U., 1939; MD, Yale U., 1943. Diplomate Am. Bd. Pediat. Intern Babies Hosp., NYC, 1943-44; fellow in pediat. Mayo Found., Rochester, Minn., 1947-48; rooming-in fellow in pediat. Yale U. Sch. Medicine, 1948-51; asst. dir. pediatric outpatient clinic Yale-New Haven Hosp., 1951-52, dir. pediatric outpatient clinic, 1952-57; staff pediatrician, collaboration project Yale U. Sch. Medicine, 1957-62, instr. pediat., 1950-53, clin. asst. prof., 1963—71, clin. assoc. prof., 1961-75, clin. prof., 1975-97; ret., 2005. Bd. dirs. Clifford Beers Child Guidance Clinic, New Haven, 1950—55, cons. pediatrician, 1967—2005; bd. dirs. Women's Health Svc., New Haven, 1992—97, Child Welfare League, NYC, 1979—91. Author: Parents Book on Raising a Healthy Child, 1987. Maj. US Army, 1944—47, ETO. Mem.: New Haven County Med. Soc., Conn. Med. Soc., Soc. Adolescent Medicine, Am. Acad. Pediatrics (Practitioner Rsch. award 1994, C. Anderson Aldrich award 1997). Fax: 203-387-1927. E-mail: morriswessel@comcast.net.

WESSELINK, DAVID DUWAYNE, finance company executive; b. Webster City, Iowa, Sept. 5, 1942; s. William David and Lavina C. (Haahr) W.; m. Linda R. DeWitt, Dec. 27, 1971; children: Catherine, Bill. BA in Bus., Ctrl. Coll., 1964; MBA, Mich. State U., 1970. Tchr. Peace Corps, Turkey, 1964-66, Karabuk Koleji, Turkey, 1967-68, Robert Koleji, Turkey, 1969-70; rsch. analyst Household Fin. Corp., Chgo., 1971-73, asst. dir. rsch., 1973-77, asst. treas. Prospect Heights, Ill., 1977, v.p., dir. rsch., 1977-82, group v.p., CFO, 1982-86, sr. v.p., CFO, 1986—; v.p., treas. Household Internat., Prospect Heights, 1988-93; sr. v.p., CFO Advanta Corp., 1993-98; exec. v.p., CFO Metris Cos., Saint Louis Park, Minn., 1998-2000, vice chmn., 2000—02, chmn., CEO, 2002—05. Bd. dirs. Flex Fund Fin. Svcs., Irvine, Calif. Bd. dirs. Ctrl. Coll., Pella, Iowa, 1990—. Mem.: Fin. Execs. Inst., Econ. Club Chgo. E-mail: lrddw@juno.com.

WESSELLS, HUNTER, urologist, researcher; b. Bryn Mawr, Pa., May 24, 1963; s. Henry Walton Wessells III and Nancy Hunter Wessells; m. Bokgi Choi, Sept. 16, 1995; 1 child, Callista Lee. BS in Psychology, Georgetown U., 1984, MD, 1988. Diplomate Am. Bd. Urology, Nat. Bd. Med. Examiners. Surgical resident U. Pa., Phila., 1988—90, urology resident, 1990—94; fellow, reconstructive urology and trauma U. Calif., San Francisco, 1994—95; instr., dept. surgery U. Pa. Sch. Medicine, 1993—94; clin. instr. U. Calif., San Francisco, 1994—95; asst. prof., clin. surgery/urology U. Ariz. Coll. Medicine, Tucson, 1995—2000, assoc. prof., surgery, 2000—01; assoc. prof., urology U. Wash. Sch. Medicine, Seattle, 2001—03, prof., chair dept of urology, 2005—. Faculty mem. Biomedical Engring. Interdisciplinary Program Grad. Coll., U. Ariz., 1998—2001; com. mem. 1st and 2nd Internat. Consultation on Erectile and Sexual Dysfunction WHO, Paris, 1999, Paris, 2003; mem. panel NIH/Nat. Inst. Diabetes and Digestive and Kidney Diseases, Bethesda, Md., 2001—; affiliate Diabetes Endocrinology Rsch. Ctr., U. Wash. Sch. Medicine, Seattle, 2001—, Harborview Injury Prevention Rsch. Ctr., 2002—; hosp. appointments Harborview Med. Ctr., Seattle, 2001—, chief urology, 2002—, mem. med. exec. bd., 2002—, mem. trauma coun., 2002—, mem. ambulatory care adv. coun., 2002—, mem. surgical coun., 2004—; hosp. appointments U. Calif., San Francisco, 1994—95, San Francisco Gen. Hosp., 1994—95, U. Med. Ctr., Tucson, 1995—2000, So. Ariz. VA Health Care Sys., Tucson, 1995—2000, U. Wash. Med. Ctr., Seattle, 2001—, Puget Sound VA Health Care Sys., Seattle, 2001—; dir., urodynamics and sexual dysfunction unit U. Ariz. Health Sciences Ctr., 1996—99; several vis. professorships; invited lectr. in field. Contbr. chapters to books, articles to profl. jours.; Ad Hoc reviewer for several peer-related jours. Rsch. grantee, NIH/NIDDK, 2000, 2003. Fellow: ACS (mem. urology adv. com. 2002), Seattle Surgical Soc. (assoc.); mem.: Western Urologic Forum, Northwest Urol. Soc., Soc. Univ. Urologists, Sexual Medicine Soc. N. Am., Am. Assn. for the Surgery of Trauma, Am. Urol. Assn. (chair young urologists com. 2002), European Assn. Urology (assoc.), U. Barge Club (Founder's Cup 1991). Avocations: bicycling, swimming. Office: Harborview Med Ctr Dept Urology Box 359868 325 Ninth Ave Seattle WA 98104 Office Phone: 206-731-3205. Office Fax: 206-731-4709. E-mail: wessells@u.washington.edu.*

WESSELMANN, GLENN ALLEN, retired health facility administrator; b. Cleve., Mar. 21, 1932; s. Roy Arthur and Dorothy (Oakes) W.; m. Genevieve De Witt, Sept. 6, 1958; children: Debbie, Scott, Janet. AB, Dartmouth, 1954; MBA with distinction, Cornell U., 1959. Research aide Cornell U., Ithaca, NY, 1958-59; adminstrv. resident Meml. Hosp., NYC, 1957-58, adminstrv. asst., 1959-61, asst. adminstr., 1961-65, asst. v.p., 1965-68; v.p. for adminstrn. Meml. Hosp. for Cancer and Allied Diseases, NYC, 1968-79; exec. v.p., chief operating officer St. John Hosp., Detroit, 1979-84; pres., CEO St. John Health System, 1984-95, vice chmn., 1995-97; chmn., pres., CEO St. John Hosp. & Med. Ctr., 1984-94, ret., 1995. Mem. bus. adv. bd. City of Detroit, 1991-95, chmn., 1993-94; mem. exec. com. Greater Detroit Area Health Coun.; bd. dirs. Caymich Ins. Co. Ltd., Mich. Health Care Alliance, SelectCare, Detroit Econ. Growth Corp. Trustee Sisters of St. Joseph Health System 1981-94, Sisters of St. Joseph Health Svc., 1983-95, St. John Hosp. and Med. Ctr., 1979-95, St. John Health System, 1984-95, The Oxford Inst., 1984-95, Eastwood Clinics, 1992-95; pres. Providence Ch. Corp., Hilton Head Island, S.C., chmn. ch. fin. ocm., corp. pres. session; mem. bus. adv. bd.! City of Detroit, 1991-95, chmn. 1993-94. Served with MC AUS, 1955-57. Fellow ACHE; mem. Am. Hosp. Assn., Internat. Hosp. Fedn., Mich. Hosp. Assn. (trustee, chmn. 1994-95, mem. exec. com.), Assn. Am. Med. Colls. (Coth rep.), Am. Cancer Soc. (regional adv. bd. 1994-95), Med. Group Mgmt. Assn., Soc. Health Service Adminstrs., Sigma Phi Epsilon. Home: 63 Big Woods Dr Hilton Head Island SC 29926-2604 Personal E-mail: glengen@hargray.com.

WESSELS, BRUCE W., materials scientist, educator; b. NYC, Oct. 18, 1946; m. Beverly T. Wessels; children: David, Kirsten. BS in Metallurgy and Materials Sci., U. Pa., 1968; PhD in Materials Sci., MIT, 1973. Tech. staff GE R&D Ctr., 1972-77, acting br. mgr., 1976; from asst. prof. to assoc. prof. Northwestern U., Evanston, Ill., 1977-83, prof. materials sci. and engring., 1984—, prof. elec. and computer engring., 1987—, Walter P. Murphy prof., 1998—, dept. chair elec. engring. and computer sci., 2005—07. Vis. sci. Argonne Nat. Lab., 1978; mem. program com. Internat. Conf. Superlattices, Microdevices and Microstructures, 1987. Editor 5 books including (with G.Y. Chin) Advances in Electronic Materials, 1986; mem. editl. bd. Jour. Electronic Materials, 1982-88, 98—, Hour. Electroceramics, 2006—; contbr. articles to profl. jours.; patentee in field. Fellow ASM, Am. Phys. Soc., AIME (bd. trustees 1996-97); mem. TMS, The Minerals, Metals and Materials Soc. (chmn. electronic materials com. 1987-89, conf. program chmn. 1986-87, key reader Trans. of AIME 1985-92, bd. dirs. 1993-98, vice-chmn. exec. coun. electronic, magnetic and photonic materials divsn. 1991-92, chmn. 1993-95, v.p. 1995, pres. 1996), Electrochem. Soc. Materials Rsch. Soc. (symposium organizer 1993, 95), Optical Soc. Am., Electroceramics (internat. program com. 2000-09), Sigma Xi, Tau Beta Pi. Office: Materials Science-Engring Northwestern U 2220 Campus Dr Evanston IL 60208-3108 E-mail: b-wessels@northwestern.edu.

WESSELS, DANIEL L., lawyer; b. Sewickley, Pa., Feb. 21, 1953; BA summa cum laude, U. Pitts., 1976; JD, Harvard U., 1980. Bar: Pa. 1980. Assoc. Reed Smith Shaw & McClay; atty. Cohen & Grigsby, Pitts.; ptnr. Reed Smith LLP, Pitts., 2006—. Adj. prof. Duquesne U., John F. Donahue Grad. Sch. of Bus. Contbr. articles to profl. jours. Mem.: Phi Beta Kappa. Office: Reed Smith LLP 435 6th Ave Pittsburgh PA 15219 Office Phone: 412-288-5992. Office Fax: 412-288-3063. E-mail: dwessels@reedsmith.com.

WESSELS, IZAK FREDERICK, ophthalmologist; b. Johannesburg, Oct. 2, 1948; came to U.S., 1986; s. Hans Jacob and Anna Elizabeth (Van Heerden) W.; m. Elza Elaine Blake, Dec. 10, 1972; children: Gunter F., Delia A., Rhoda N. BSc, U. Witwaterstrand, Johannesburg, 1970, MD, 1973, M of Medicine Ophthalmology, 1985. Diplomate Am. Bd. Ophthalmology. Intern J.G. Strijdom Hosp., Johannesburg, 1974; resident in pathology U. Cape Town, 1975; resident in ob-gyn. U. Stellenbosch, 1976-77; supt. Maluti Adventist Hosp., Mapoteng, Lesotho, 1977-79; resident ophthalmology U. Witwaterstrand, 1979-83; pvt. practice Roodepoort, South Africa, 1983-86; asst. prof. Loma Linda (Calif.) U., 1989-91, fellow in cornea and ext. disease, 1986-88, assoc. prof., 1991—, U. Tenn., Chattanooga, 1995—. Adj. clin. faculty So. Coll. Optometry, Memphis, 1992—, Coll. Optometry Pacific U., 1995—; vis. prof. Kasturba Med. Coll., Manipal, India, 1990—. Contbr. articles to profl. jours. Bd. trustees Southern Adventist U. Fellow ACS, Royal Coll. Surgeons; mem. AMA, Royal Coll. Opthalmologists UC, Loma Linda U. Sch. Medicine Alumni Assn. Avocations: gardening, wind surfing, photography, classical music, astronomy. Home: 9616 Mountain Shadows Dr Chattanooga TN 37421-5353 Home Phone: 423-510-0330; Office Phone: 423-855-8522. Business E-Mail: izakfwessels@juno.com.

WESSLER, MELVIN DEAN, farmer, rancher; b. Dodge City, Kans., Feb. 11, 1932; s. Oscar Lewis and Clara (Reiss) W.; m. Laura Ethel Arbuthnot, Aug. 23, 1951; children: Monty Dean, Charla Cay, Virgil Lewis. Grad. high sch. Farmer, rancher, Springfield, Colo., 1950—. Dir., sec. bd. Springfield Co-op. Sales Co., 1964-80, pres. bd., 1980—; pres. Arkansas Valley Co-op Coun., SE Colo. Area, 1965-87, Colo. Co-op Coun., 1969-72, v.p. 1974, sec. 1980-86; cmty. com. chmn. Baca County, Agr. Stablzn. and Conservation Svc., Springfield, 1961-73, 79—, vice chmn. Baca County Com., 1980-90; mem. spl. com. on grain mktg. Far-Mar-Co; mem. com. for PROMARK, Hutchinson, Kans., 1978. Mem. adv. bd. Denver Bapt. Bible Coll., 1984-89; chmn. bd. dirs. Springfield Cemetery Bd., 1985—; apptd. spl. com. Farmland Industries spl. project Tomorrow, 1987—. Recipient The Colo. Cooperator award Colo. Coop. Coun., 1990. Mem. Colo. Cattlemen's Assn., Colo. Wheat Growers Assn., Southeast Farm Bus. Assn. (bd. dirs. 1991-95), Big Rock Grange (treas. 1964-76, master 1976-82), Southwest Kans. Farm Assn.

(dir. 1996—, pres. 1999-2001, v.p. 2007-), Southwest Kans. Farm Bus. Assn. (v.p. 2007-09), Big Rock Grange Master (2006-09). Address: 18363 County Road Pp Springfield CO 81073

WESSLER, SUSAN R., biologist, educator; b. NYC, 1953; BS in Biology, SUNY, Stony Brook, 1974; PhD, Cornell U., 1980. Postdoctoral fellow Am. Cancer Soc. Carnegie Inst. Dept. Embryology, Washington, 1980—82; asst. prof. botany U. Ga., Athens, 1983, Regents prof. botany and genetics, 1992—, disting. rsch. prof., 1994—. Editl. bd. Current Opinions in Plant Biology, Proceedings of NAS, assoc. editor Genetics; co-author (with M. Gerald Neuffer and Edward H. Coe): The Mutants of Maize. Fellow: Am. Acad. Arts & Scis.; mem.: NAS. Office: The Wessler Lab Univ Ga Dept Plant Biology 4505 Miller Plant Sciences Bldg Athens GA 30609 Office Phone: 706-542-1857. Office Fax: 706-542-1805. E-mail: sue@plantbio.uga.edu.

WESSLING, ROBERT BRUCE, retired lawyer; b. Chgo., Oct. 8, 1937; s. Robert Euans and Marguerite (Rickert) W.; m. Judith Ann Hanson, Aug. 26, 1961; children: Katherine, Jennifer, Carolyn. BA, DePauw U., 1959; JD, U. Mich., 1962. Bar: U.S. Ct. Appeals (9th cir.) 1965. Assoc. Latham & Watkins, LA, 1962-70, ptnr., 1970-94; ret., 1995. Bd. govs. Fin. Lawyers Conf., Los Angeles, 1974-2000. Mem. World Affairs Coun., L.A.; trustee DePauw U. Mem. Los Angeles Bar Assn., Phi Beta Kappa, Phi Delta Phi, Phi Eta Sigma, Order of Coif. Democrat. Methodist. Avocations: tennis, travel. Personal E-mail: bbwessling@aol.com.

WESSON, HERB J., councilman; b. Cleve. m. Fabian Wesson; children: Douglas, P.J., Herb III, Justin. BA in History, Lincoln U., Pa., 1999. Served as chief of staff LA County Supr. Yvonne Brathwaite Burke; served as chief dep. LA City Councilman Nate Holden; mem. Calif. State Assembly, 1998—2004, served on appropriations, health, utilities, and commerce com., served on bus. and professions com., chair govtl. orgn. com., speaker, 2002—04; councilman, Dist. 10 LA City Coun., 2005—. Mem. Exposition Metro Line Constrn. Authority. Mem. Mid-City C. of C., Culver City C. of C.; former mem. adv. bd. African Cmty. Resource Ctr.; bd. dirs. Martin Luther King, Jr. Gen. Hosp. Found., Second Dist. Edn. Found. Recipient Pub. Svc. award, Greater LA C. of C., Crusader State Leadership award, Calif. Alliance for Pride and Equality, Legis. of Yr. award, Youth Employment Sys., 1999—2000, Pub. Official award, Stonewall Dem. Club, 2000, Legis. of Yr. award, Planned Parenthood LA, 2001, Calif. Assessors' Assn., 2001. Democrat. Office: Dist Office 1819 S Western Ave Los Angeles CA 90006 also: City Hall 200 North Spring St Rm 430 Los Angeles CA 90012 Office Phone: 323-733-8233, 213-473-7010. Office Fax: 323-733-5833, 213-485-9829. Business E-Mail: councilmember.wesson@lacity.org.*

WEST, ALEXANDER BRIAN, pathologist; arrived in U.S., 1986; s. Timothy Roberts and Dorothy Trevor West; m. Lynda Tyrrell, June 25, 1970; children: Timothy Eoin, Stephanie Aoife. BA, U. Dublin, 1965, MB, BCh, BAO, 1979; MS, U. Calif., Davis, 1967. Cert. anatomic pathology Am. Bd. Pathology, 1989. Lectr. in zoology U. Dublin Trinity Coll., 1967—74, lectr. pathology, 1982—86; asst. prof. pathology Yale U., New Haven, 1988—91, assoc. prof. pathology, 1991—95, prof. pathology, 1995, U. Tex. Med. Br., Galveston, 1995—99, NYU, NYC, 1999—2005; dir. Ameripath N.Y. GI Diagnostics, NYC, 2005—. Adj. prof. pathology N.Y. U., NYC, 2005—. Fellow: Royal Coll. Pathologists, Royal Coll. Physicians Ireland; mem.: Binford-Dammin Soc. Infectious Disease Pathologists (pres. 2002—03), Gastrointestinal Pathology Soc. (pres. 1999—2000), US and Can. Acad. Pathology, Am. Assn. for the Study Liver Diseases, Am. Gastroent. Assn. Achievements include research in gastrointestinal, hepatic and pancreatic pathology; pathogenesis of infectious diseases. Avocation: fly fishing. Office: NYU Dept Pathology 560 First Ave (TH461) New York NY 10016 E-mail: bwest@ameripath.com.

WEST, ALISHA NICOLE, otolaryngologist, surgeon; b. San Francisco, Nov. 8, 1977; d. Robert Walker West Jr. and Pamela Leslie West. BS cum laude, U. Calif., San Diego, 1999, MS, 2001, MD, 2005. Dance instr. Calif. Acad. Performing Arts, Moraga, Calif., 1990—95; tchrs. asst. biology and chemistry U. Calif., San Diego, 1996—99, lab. technician, 1996—2001, rsch. scientist, neurosci., 1999—2001; gen. surgery intern U. NC, Chapel Hill, 2005—06, resident head and neck surgery, 2005—. Student coun. U. Calif., San Diego, 2001—02. Physician adv. Washington Advocacy Com., 2007; physician vol. Operation Smile, Mexico, 2000—05; vol. Habitat for Humanity, Mexico, 2001—05; med. student vol. Free Health Clinic, San Diego, 2004—05. Recipient Nat. Top Dancing Champion award, USA Dance, 1994, Selagi Rschr. Yr., U. Calif., LaJolla, 1999. Mem.: Am. Acad. Otolanyngic Allergy (scholar 2006—07), Am. acad. Otolaryngology Head and Neck Surgery, Am. Coll. Surgeons. Republican. Achievements include two-tim iron man finisher. Avocations: reading, skiing, surfing, flying, triathlon. Office: Univ NC 101 Manning Dr #7070 Chapel Hill NC 27515

WEST, ALLEN, retired military officer, civilian military employee; b. Atlanta, Feb. 7, 1961; m. Angela West; children: Aubrey, Austen. BS in Polit. Sci., U. Tenn., Knoxville, 1983; MS in Polit. Sci., Kansas State U., Manhattan, 1996; MS in Polit. Theory/ Mil. Hist. and Ops., US Command & Gen. Staff Officer Coll., Ft. Leavenworth, Kans., 1997. Served in US Army, 1982—2004, ret. as lt. col., 2004; tchr., track coach Deerfield Beach HS, Fla., 2004—05; sr. support adv. US Ctrl. Command, 2005—07; sr. analyst, chief ops. planner US Army Installation Mgmt. Command, 2007—. Decorated Bronze Star, 3 Meritorious Svc. medals, 3 Army Commendation medals, Valorous Unit award US Army; named Instr. of Yr., US Army ROTC, 1993. Republican. Mailing: 1641 Northwest 107 Ln Fort Lauderdale FL 33322

WEST, A(RNOLD) SUMNER, chemical engineer; b. Phila., Jan. 12, 1922; s. Arnold and Mary (Sumner) W.; m. Beverly Helen Lehman, Oct. 5, 1946; children: Barbara Ann, Richard Sumner. BSChemE, U. Pa., 1943; MS, Pa. State U., 1946. With Rohm and Haas Co., Phila., 1946—87, rsch. engr., 1946—62, rsch. supr., 1962—72, mgr. rsch. dept., 1972—77, sr. tech. specialist govt. and regulatory affairs, 1978—87; owner, prin. A.S. West Assocs., Huntingdon Valley, Pa., 1987—. Cons. dept. chem. engring. U. Pa., 1952-72; mem. indsl. and profl. adv. com. Coll. Engring., Pa. State U., 1978-84, chmn. chem. engring. divsn., 1980-81, chmn. com., 1982-83. Editor: AIChE Safety and Health News, 1996—. Mem. Lower Moreland Twp. (Montgomery County) Authority, 1970, sec., 1971—; vice-chmn. bd. dirs. Chemical Heritage Found., 1984-92; pres. United Engring. Trustees, 1986-87. Fellow Am. Inst. Chem. Engrs. (dir. 1964-66, treas. 1973-75, v.p. 1976, pres. 1977); mem. Engrs. Joint Council (dir. 1976-79), Am. Assn. Engring. Socs. (vice chmn. public affairs council 1981, chmn. council 1982-83), Am. Chem. Soc., Nat. Soc. Profl. Engrs., Soc. Automotive Engrs., Water Environ. Fedn. Clubs: The Valley (Huntingdon Valley). Home and Office: 3896 Sidney Rd Huntingdon Valley PA 19006-2347 Office Phone: 215-938-7181. Personal E-mail: aswest@worldnet.att.net.

WEST, BARRY J., telecommunications industry executive; With British Telecom, dir., value-added svcs.; dir., corp. mktg. Cellnet (subsidiary of British Telecom); exec. v.p. Nextel Comm., Inc., Reston, Va., 1996—2006, chief tech. officer, 2005—06; chief tech. officer, head Sprint Nextel, Reston, Va., 2006—. Office: Sprint Nextel 2001 Edmund Halley Dr Reston VA 20191 Office Phone: 703-433-4000.

WEST, BOB, pharmaceutical executive; b. Ellenville, NY, Mar. 7, 1931; s. Harry and Elsie May Wicentowsky; m. Betty Parker, May 9, 1957 (div.); children: Debra Ellen, Elizabeth Ann, Sharon Lynn; m. Jacqueline Cutler, Jan. 3, 1982. BS, Union U., 1952; MS, Purdue U., 1954, PhD, 1956; postgrad. mgmt. seminar, U. Chgo., 1972. Pres., dir. research Food, Drug, Chem. Svcs., Stamford, Conn., 1975—; pres., dir. research Bob West Assocs., Inc., Stamford, 1975—. Pres. Drug Info. Assn., Phila., 1974-75; sci. adv. bd. Fountain Pharms., Inc., Largo, Fla., 1993—, Dovetail Techs., Inc., College Park, Md., 1996—, Phytopede, Inc., Sarasota, Fla., 1999—. Mem. editl. bd. Drug Info. Assn. Jour., Phila., 1977-85; contbr. articles to profl. jours. Mem. ASPET, Soc. Toxicology, Acad. Pharm. Scis., Assn. Rsch. Dirs., Drug Info. Assn., Assn. Univ. Tech. Mgrs. Home and Office: Food Drug Chem Svcs 7925 Meadow Rush Loop Sarasota FL 34238-4319 Home Phone: 941-925-8325; Office Phone: 941-925-8958. Personal E-mail: bjwest22@verizon.net.

WEST, CAROLYN CHRISTENSEN, literature and language professor; b. Carlsbad, N.Mex., July 2, 1943; d. Christensen T. Ernst and Martha Eleanor Howard; m. Eric R. West, Jan. 10, 1981; 1 child, Randal Kristian. BA in English, Fla. State U., Tallahassee, 1965; MA in English, U. NC, Chapel Hill, 1970. Cert. ednl. specialist Harvard Grad. Sch. Edn., Cambridge, Mass., 1974. Learning lab. mgr. and English prof. Ctrl. Va. CC, Lynchburg, 1970—78; sr. prof. English Daytona State Coll., Fla., 1978—. Bd. mem. Sister Cities of Volusia County, Daytona Beach, 1998—2008; peace corps vol. US State Dept., San Jose, Philippines, 1965—68. Mem.: LWV, Volusia County. Democrat. Unitarian. Avocations: sailing, writing, photography. Office: Daytona State Coll 1200 Internat Speedway Blvd Daytona Beach FL 32120 Business E-Mail: westc@daytonastate.edu.

WEST, CATHERINE G., former retail executive; b. Sept. 6, 1959; BA, Lynchburg Coll., 1982. With People's Express Airline, 1981—85; v.p. credit card ops. Chevy Chase Bank FSB, 1985—91; sr. v.p. card mem. svcs. to exec. v.p. mktg. svcs. First USA Bank, 1991—2000; sr. v.p. U.S. consumer risk ops. Capital One, 2000—04, pres. U.S. card bus., 2004—06; exec. v.p., COO JC Penney Co., Inc., 2006. Named one of 50 Most Powerful Women in Business, Fortune mag., 2006.

WEST, CHARLES CONVERSE, retired theologian; b. Plainfield, NJ, Feb. 3, 1921; s. George Parsons and Florence (Farish) West; m. Ruth Floy Carson, Sept. 6, 1944; children: Russell Arthur, Walter Lawrence, Glenn Andrew. BA, Columbia U., 1942; B.D., Union Theol. Sem., NYC, 1945; PhD, Yale U., 1955. Ordained to ministry Presbyn. Ch. USA, 1946. Missionary, fraternal worker Bd. Fgn. Missions Presbyn. Ch. U.S.A., 1946-56; instr., chaplain Cheeloo U., Hangchow, China, 1948-49; instr. Nanking Theol. Sem., 1949-50; indsl. mission work Gossner Mission, Mainz-Kastel, Germany, 1950-51; lectr. Kirchliche Hochschule, Berlin, 1951-53; Lectr. Hartford Sem. Found., 1955-56; asso. dir. Ecumenical Inst., Bossey, Switzerland under World Council Chs., 1956-61; chargé de cours U. Geneva, 1956-61; instr. Peking Nat. U., 1948; assoc. prof. Christian ethics Princeton Theol. Sem., 1961-63, Stephen Colwell prof. Christian ethics, 1963-91, prof. emeritus, 1991—, acad. dean, 1979-84. Mem. commn. to form statement faith U. P. Ch. USA, 1961—67, chmn. internat. affairs adv. com., 1963—66; chmn. US Com. Christian Peace Conf., 1963—72; chmn. working com. dept. studies mission Evangelism World Coun. Chs., 1967—68; mem. commn. internat. affairs Nat. Coun. Chs., 1968—73. Author: Communism and the Theologians, 1958, Outside the Camp, 1959, Ethics, Violence and Revolution, 1969, The Power to be Human, 1971, Perspective on South Africa, 1985, Power, Truth and Community in Modern Culture, 1999, Storm Front, 2003; translator: J. Hamel - A Christian in East Germany, 1960; editor: The Sufficiency of God, Essays in Honor of Dr. W. A. Visser't Hooft, 1963; assoc. editor: Religion in Eastern Europe, 1985—2005. Mem.: Presbytery NYC, Am. Theol. Soc. (v.p. 1982—83, pres. 1983—84), Am. Soc. Christian Ethics (v.p. 1972—73, pres. 1973—74), Christian Associated Rels. with Eastern Europe (pres. 1988—92), Ams. Dem. Action. Presbyterian. Home: 9 Hedge Row Rd Princeton NJ 08540-5047 Office: Princeton Theological Seminary CN821 Princeton NJ 08542 Personal E-mail: randcwest@verizon.net.

WEST, CHARLES DAVID, chemistry professor; b. Riverside, Calif., July 25, 1937; s. Charle Cecil and Maurine (Kaylor) W.; m. Julia MacLaren, Dec. 20, 1964; children: Edward, Charles, Elizabeth. BA, Pomona U., 1959; PhD, MIT, 1965. Scientist Beckman Inst., Inc., Fullerton, Calif., 1964—67; prof. chemistry Occidental Coll., LA, 1967—2002, chair dept. chemistry, 1983—86, emeritus prof., 2002—. Sci. advisor U.S. FDA, 1995—2002. Author: Essentials of Quanititive Analysis, 1987; contbr. articles to profl. pubs. Mem. Am. Chem. Soc. (chair So. Calif. chpt. 1991-92), Soc. for Applied Spectroscopy (chair). Achievements include first to link photoelectric detection to a plasma, first in U.S. to use ultrasonic atomization for chemical analysis. Office: Occidental Coll 1600 Campus Rd Los Angeles CA 90041-3314

WEST, CLARK DARWIN, pediatric nephrologist, educator; b. Jamestown, NY, July 4, 1918; s. Clark Darwin and Frances Isabel (Blanchard) W.; m. Ruthann Asbury, Apr. 12, 1944 (div.); children: Charles Michael, John Clark, Lucy Frances; m. Dolores Lachenman, Mar. 1, 1986. AB, Coll. of Wooster, 1940; MD, U. Mich., 1943. Intern Univ. Hosp., Ann Arbor, Mich., 1943-44, resident in pediatrics, 1944-46; fellow in pediatrics Children's Hosp. Research Found., Cin., 1948-49, research asso., 1951-89, asso. dir., 1963-89, dir. div. immunology and nephrology, 1958-89; with cardiopulmonary lab. chest service Bellevue Hosp., NYC, 1949-51; attending pediatrician Children's Hosp., 1951-89; asst. prof. pediatrics U. Cin., 1951-55, asso. prof., 1955-62, prof., 1962-89. Mem. coms. NIH, 1965-69, 1972-73 Mem. editorial bd.: Jour. Pediatrics, 1960-79, Kidney Internat., 1977-89, Clin. Nephrology, 1989-96; contbr. articles to profl. jours. Served to capt. M.C., AUS, 1946-47. Decorated Army commendation medal; recipient recognition award Cin. Pediat. Soc., 1980, Mitchell Rubin award, 1986, Henry L. Barnett award, 1995, Daniel Drake medal, 1996, John P. Peters award, 1996; Founders award, 2008. Mem. Soc. Pediatric Research (sec.-treas. 1958-62, pres. 1963-64), Am. Pediatric Soc., Am. Soc. Pediatric Nephrologists (pres. 1973-74, Founders award 2008), Am. Physiol. Soc., Am. Assn. Immunologists, Am. Soc. Nephrology, Internat. Pediatric Nephrology Assn., Sigma Xi, Alpha Omega Alpha. Achievements include research on immunopathogenesis and treatment of glomerulonephritides and in the complement system. Home: 11688 Aristocrat Dr Harrison OH 45030-9753 Personal E-mail: CWest_2865@fuse.net.

WEST, CORNEL RONALD, humanities educator, writer; b. Tulsa, Okla., June 2, 1953; s. Clifton L. & Irene (Bias) W.; 1 child from previous marriage, Clifton; m. Elleni Gebre Amlak (separated) 1 child, Zeytun BA, Harvard U., 1973; PhD, Princeton U., 1977. Prof. religion Union Theol. Sem., NY, 1977-84, 87-88, Yale U. Divinity Sch., New Haven, 1984-87; prof. religion, dir. dept. Afro-Am. Studies Princeton U., 1988-94, Class of 1943 Univ. prof. religion, 2002—; prof. Afro-Am. studies, philosophy of religion Harvard U., Cambridge, Mass., 1994—99, Alphonse Fletcher jr. prof., 1999—2002. Am. corr. Le Monde Diplomatique; vis. prof. U. Paris; DuBois fellow Harvard U., 1994-99. Author: Black Theology and Marxist Thought, 1979, Prophesy Deliverance! An Afro-American Revolutionary Christianity, 1982, Prophetic Fragments, 1988, The American Evasion of Philosophy: A Genealogy of Pragmatism, 1989, Breaking Bread: Insurgent Black Intellectual Life, 1991, The Ethical Dimensions of Marxist Thought, 1991, Race Matters, 1993, Beyond Eurocentrism and Multiculturalism, Vol. I: Prophetic Thought in Postmodern Times. Vol. II: Prophetic Reflections: Notes on Race and Power in America, 1993, Keeping Faith: Philosophy and Race in America, 1994, (with Paula Giddings) Regarding Malcolm X, 1994, (with Michael Lerner) Jews and Blacks: Let the Healing Begin, 1995, (with Michael Lerner) Jews and Blacks: A Dialogue on Race, religion, and Culture in America, 1996, (with Henry Louis Gates Jr.) The Future of the Race, 1996, Restoring Hope: Conversations on the Future of Black America, 1998, (with Roberto Unger) The Future of American Progressivism, 1998, (with Sylvia Ann Hewlett) The War Against Parents, 1998, The Cornel West Reader, 1999, (with Henry Louis Gates Jr.) The African American Century: How Black Americans Have Shaped Our Century, 2000, Democracy Matters: Winning the Fight Against Imperialism, 2004, Hope on a Tightrope: Word and Wisdom by Cornel West, 2008; co-prodr. (with Derek "D.O.A." Allen, Clifton West & Mike Daily) album, Sketches of my Culture, 2001, (with Andre Benjamin, Jill Scott, Talib Kweli, et. al.) album, Never Forget: A Journey of Revelations, 2007. Recipient Literary Lion award, NY Pub. Libr., 1993; named one of 100 Most Influential Black Ams., Ebony mag., 2006; named to Power 150, 2007, 2008. Office: Princeton U Dept Religion Hall 208 Marx Hall Princeton NJ 08544-1066 Office Phone: 609-258-0021. E-mail: cwest@princeton.edu.*

WEST, DAVID J., food products executive; b. Mar. 26, 1963; married. BS in Bus. Adminstrn. cum laude, Bucknell U. V.p. corp. strategy and bus. planning Nabisco Biscuit Co., sr. v.p., CFO; sr. v.p. fin. Nabisco Biscuit, Confectionery and Snacks, Kraft Foods Inc.; v.p. bus. planning and devel. Hershey Foods Co., 2001—02, sr. v.p. bus. planning and devel., 2002, sr. v.p. sales, 2002—04, sr. v.p., chief customer officer, 2004; sr. v.p., CFO The Hershey Co., 2005—07, exec. v.p., COO, CFO, 2007, pres., CEO, 2007—. Bd. dirs. Hershey Foods Co., 2007—. Office: The Hershey Co 100 Crystal A Dr Hershey PA 17033

WEST, DAVID MOORER, professional basketball player; b. Teaneck, NJ, Aug. 29, 1980; s. Amos and Harriet West; m. Leslie West; 1 child, Dashia. BA in Comm., Xavier U., 2003. Power forward New Orleans Hornets, 2003—. Recipient Adolph Rupp Trophy, 2003, Oscar Robertson Trophy, 2003, Pete Newell Big Man award, 2003; named Atlantic 10 Player of Yr., 2001—03, 1st Team All-Am., AP, 2003, Nat. Player of Yr., US Basketball Writers Assn., 2003; named to Western Conf. All-Star Team, NBA, 2008, 2009. Avocation: tuba. Office: New Orleans Hornets 1250 Poydras St Fl 19 New Orleans LA 70113*

WEST, DOYLE THOMAS, retired music educator; b. Smithfield, Utah, May 10, 1932; s. Preston Dangerfield West and Eliza Genevieve Mecham; m. Ardyth Mae Hansen, July 13, 1962; children: MaryLynne Pope, Barbara Ann Livacich, David Hansen, Roger Hansen, Paul Hansen. BS, Utah State U., 1954. Cert. tchr. Utah, Calif. Jr. HS choral music tchr. Tooele Sch. Dist., Utah, 1954—58; asst. Brigham Young U., Provo, Utah, 1961—62; HS choral music tchr. San Lorenzo Unified Sch. Dist., Calif., 1962—92, dist. music chmn., supr.; ret., 1992. Pvt. voice tchr., 1958—2006. Prodr., music dir.: Temple Hill Pageant, 1964—2004, music dir.: annual Handel's Messiah, 1977—2006. Missionary to Cape Town, South Africa LDS Ch., 1958—60. Named Outstanding Tchr. of Yr., San Lorenzo H.S., 1963, Dist. Tchr. of Month, San Lorenzo Unified Sch. Dist., 1992. Mem.: NEA (life), Am. Choral Dirs. Assn. (life), Calif. Music Educator Assn. (life), Choral Music Nat. Assn. (life), Music Educators Nat. Conf. (life). Republican. Mem. Lds Ch. Home: 19535 Eagle St Castro Valley CA 94546

WEST, EILEEN C., general internal medicine physician, educator; b. Richmond, Va., Dec. 14, 1964; d. Peter and Mona West; m. S. Abbas Shobeiri, May 23, 1998; children: Sara Shadi Shobeiri, Sophie Rose Shobeiri, Susan Nava Shobeiri. BA, Yale U., New Haven, 1987; MD, U. Conn. Sch. Medicine, Farmington, 1998. Cert. Am. Bd. Internal Medicine, 2001, Internat. Soc. Clin. Densitometry, 2003, nat. practitioner North Am. Menopause Soc., 2006. Clin. assoc. prof., medicine, ob-gyn. U. Okla. Health Sci Ctr., Oklahoma City, 2002—, dir. internal medicine women's health. Singer various small ensemble. Mem. Civic Music Assn., Oklahoma City, 2004. Office: OU Health Scis Ctr 825 NE 10th St Oklahoma City OK 73104

WEST, GAIL BERRY, lawyer; b. Cin. d. Theodore Moody and Johnnie Mae (Newton) B.; m. Togo D. West, Jr., June 18, 1966; children: Tiffany Berry, Hilary Carter. BA magna cum laude, Fisk U., 1964; MA, U. Cin., 1965; JD, Howard U., 1968. Bar: D.C. 1969, U.S. Supreme Ct. 1978. Staff atty. IBM, 1969-76; spl. asst. to sec. HUD, 1977-78; staff asst. to spl. asst. to Pres., Washington, 1978-80; dep. asst. sec. for manpower res. affairs installations Dept. Air Force, 1980-81; atty. AT&T, Washington, 1983-84; exec. dir. govt. affairs Bell Comm. Rsch. Inc., Washington, 1984-95; dir. govt. rels. Armstrong World Industries, Inc., Washington, 1995—2003, cons., 2003—06. Mem. exec. com. ARC, Washington, 1974-85; bd. dirs. Family and Child Svcs., Washington, 1974-87; trustee Corcoran Gallery Art, 1983-00, Arena Stage, 1992-99, Decatur House, 1994-, WETA, 1995-01, Fisher House Found., Inc.; bd. dirs. Meridian House, 1994-00; mem. DC Commn. Fine Arts, 2003-; mem. cathedral chpt. Nat. Cathedral, 1997-06; bd. dirs. Nat. Mus. Am. History, Smithsonian, 2005-. Ford Found. fellow, 1965-68. Mem. ABA, D.C. Bar Assn., Unified Bar D.C. Democrat. Episcopalian. Home: 4934 Rockwood Pkwy NW Washington DC 20016-3211

WEST, GEOFFREY B., theoretical physicist, physics professor; b. England; BA in Physics, Cambridge U., 1961; PhD in Physics, Stanford U., 1966. Faculty Stanford U., 1970; high energy particle physics grp. leader Los Alamos Nat. Lab., N.Mex., 1974, high energy physicist, 1982—; prof. biology U. N.Mex, Albuquerque, 1999—; disting. prof. Santa Fe Inst., 2003—, pres., 2005—. Sr. lab. fellow Los Alamos Nat. Lab., 2003. Named one of 100 Most Influential People, Time Mag., 2006. Fellow: Am. Phys. Soc. Office: Santa Fe Inst 1399 Hyde Pk Rd Santa Fe NM 87501 Office Phone: 505-946-2701.

WEST, J. ROBINSON (ROBIN WEST), petroleum finance company executive, former government official; b. Bryn Mawr, Pa., Sept. 16, 1946; m. Eileen Shields, May 1992; children: Lily Eileen, Kate Cristy, Laura Shields, John Weyth. BA, U. NC, 1968; JD, Temple U., 1973. Bar: Pa. Staff mem. The White House, Washington, 1974-76; asst. to sec. US Dept. Def., Washington, 1976, dep. asst. sec. for internat. econ. affairs, 1976-77; v.p., 1st v.p. Blyth, Eastman, Dillon and Co., 1977-80; mem. Reagan Transition Team, 1980-81; asst. sec. US Dept. Interior, Washington, 1981-83, pvt. cons., 1983-84; pres., CEO, founder Petroleum Fin. Co. (now PFC Energy), Washington, 1984—. Mng. dir. Petroleum Intelligence Group, Ltd., 1988—; chmn. Generation Ventures Assocs., 1991—. Trustee German Marshall Fund of US, Nixon Ctr., Trans-Alaska Pipeline Liability Fund; mem. bd. advisors Nat. Interest Mag.; dir. Fr.-Am. Found.; pres. Weyth Endowment for Am. Art; chmn. bd. US Inst. for Peace, 2004-; mem. Nat. Adv. Com. on Oceans and Atmosphere, Chief of Naval Ops. Exec. Panel, Nat. Adv. Com. on Handicapped Children. Mem. Coun. Fgn. Rels., Internat. Inst. Strategic Studies. Office: PFC Energy 1300 Connecticut Ave NW Ste 800 Washington DC 20036-4011

WEST, JAMES HAROLD, finance company executive; b. San Diego, Oct. 11, 1926; s. Robert Reed and Clara Leona (Moses) W.; m. Norma Jean, 1953 (div.); 1 son, Timothy James; m. Jerel Lynn Smith, Nov. 16, 1976; 1 child, James Nelson. BS, U. So. Calif., 1949. CPA, Calif. Ptnr. McCracken & Co., San Diego, 1950-61; mgr. Ernst & Ernst, San Diego, 1961-64; ptnr. West Turnquist & Schmitt, San Diego, 1964—97, West, Rhode & Roberts, 1997—. Bd. govs. ARC, Washington, 1981-87; pres., bd. dirs. Combined Arts and Edn. Coun., San Diego, 1980-83; pres. Francis Parker Sch., 1988-90; bd. dirs. San Diego Hosp. Assn., 1981-95, 97-2007, San Diegans INc., 1989-92, Mus. Photographic Arts, 1990-92; trustee Calif. Western Sch. Law, 1985-2004; mem. bd. advisors U. So. Calif. Sch. Acctg., 1985-97; treas. San Diego Nat. Sports Tng. Found., 1988-92; mem. acctg. exec. bd. U. San Diego, 1992—. With AUS, 1945-46, PTO. Mem. AICPAs, Calif. Soc. CPAs (bd. dirs. 1963-64), Univ. Club (San Diego), Capital Hill Club (Washington), Masons. Republican. Home: 3311 Lucinda St San Diego CA 92106-2931 Home and Office: 3104 4th Ave San Diego CA 92103-5803 Business E-Mail: jhwest@wrr-cpa.com.

WEST, JAMES JOSEPH, lawyer; b. Tarentum, Pa., Nov. 26, 1945; s. Samuel Elwood and Rose (McIntyre) W.; m. Kathleen Geslak, Aug. 19, 1967; children: Joseph Allen, Yvonne Michelle, KaiLynn Ann. BS in Econs., St. Vincent Coll., 1967; JD, Duquesne U., 1970. Bar: Pa. 1971, U.S. Dist. Ct. (we. dist.) Pa. 1971, U.S. Ct. Appeals (3d cir.) 1971, U.S. Dist. Ct. (mid. dist.) Pa., 1980. Law clk. to presiding justice U.S. Dist. Ct., Pa., 1970-74; asst. U.S. atty. chief appellate sect. U.S. Atty.'s Office, Pitts., 1974-79; dep. dir. criminal law Pa. Atty. Gen.'s Office, Harrisburg, 1979-82; 1st asst. U.S. atty. U.S. Dist. Ct. (mid. dist.) Pa., Harrisburg, 1982-84, U.S. atty., 1984-93; assoc. Sprague & Sprague, Phila., 1993-95; pvt. practice Harrisburg, Pa., 1995—. Mem. Nat. Environ. Enforcement Coun. Recipient Outstanding Performance award U.S. Dept. Justice, 1974-78, Commendation Gov. of Pa., 1981. Mem. Pa. Bar Assn., Allegheny County Bar Assn., Dauphin County Bar Assn. Republican. Roman Catholic. Home: 1222 Cardinal Way Rd Hummelstown PA 17036-8548 Office: James West 105 N Front St Harrisburg PA 17101-1483 Office Phone: 717-233-5051. Personal E-mail: jwest@aol.com. Business E-Mail: jwest@jwestlaw.com.

WEST, JANET ELAINE OLSON, elementary school educator; d. Elmer Engebert and Mardell Avon Redfield Olson; m. Albert Newton West, Aug. 22, 1970; children: James Albert, Sarah Jo Faulkner. BEd, Ctrl. Mo. State U., Warrensburg, Miss., 1973. Elem. tchr. Lakeland R-3 Sch., Lowry City, Mo., 1974—77, Kingsville R-1 Sch., Mo., 1977—2005, elem. comm. arts tchr., 2005—. Edn. adv. com. mem. Powell Gardens, Kingsville, 2002—08. Recipient Above and Beyond award, Kingsville R-1 Schs., 2007. Mem.: Mo. Edn. Assn. (life; sec. west ctrl. unit coun. 2002—08), Delta Kappa Gamma (rsch. com. chair 2004—08, You Showed Us award 2007, Excellence in Edn. award 2007). Avocations: reading, cooking, quilting, camping.

WEST, JASON BROSSARD, education educator, consultant; b. Salt Lake City, Utah; PhD, U. Ga., 2002. Postdoctoral fellow U. Minn., St. Paul, 2002—04; rsch. assoc. U. Utah, 2004—05, rsch. asst. prof., 2006—. Sci. and tech. cons., Salt Lake City, 2005—. Postdoctoral fellowship, U. Minn., 2002—04, grant, NSF, 2000—02, Dissertation completion award, U. Ga., 2000—01. Mem.: AAAS, Ecol. Soc. of Am., Am. Geophys. Union. Office: Dept of Biology U of Utah 257 South 1400 East Salt Lake City UT 84112

WEST, JERRY ALAN, former professional sports team executive, retired professional basketball player; b. Chelyan, W.Va., May 28, 1938; s. Howard Stewart and Cecil Sue (Creasey) West; m. Martha Jane Kane, May 1960 (div. 1977); children: David, Michael, Mark; m. Karen Christine Bua, May 28, 1978; 1 child, Ryan. BS, W.Va. U., 1960; LHD (hon.), W.Va. Wesleyan Coll., W.Va. U., 2006. Player LA Lakers, 1960—74, head coach, 1976—79, spl. cons., 1979—82, gen. mgr., 1982—94, exec. v.p. basketball ops., 1994—2000; pres. basketball ops. Memphis Grizzlies, 2002—07. Author (with William Libby): Mr. Clutch: The Jerry West Story, 1969. Recipient Gold medal, Olympic Games, Rome, 1960; named NBA Finals MVP, 1969, NBA All-Star Game MVP, 1972, NBA Exec. of Yr., Sporting News, 1994—95, 1995, 2004; named to NBA All-Star Team, 1961—73, Naismith Meml. Basketball Hall of Fame, 1980, NBA 35th Anniversary All-Time Team, 1980. Achievements include being a member of the NBA Championship winning LA Lakers, 1972.

WEST, JOHN BURNARD, physiologist, educator; b. Adelaide, Australia, Dec. 27, 1928; came to U.S., 1969; s. Esmond Frank and Meta Pauline (Spehr) W.; m. Penelope Hall Banks, Oct. 28, 1967; children: Robert Burnard, Joanna Ruth. MB, BChir, Adelaide U., 1951, MD, 1958, DSc, 1980; PhD, London U., 1960; DSc (hon.), U. Barcelona, Spain, 1987, U. Ferrara, Italy, 2004, U. Athens, 2006. Resident Royal Adelaide Hosp., 1952, Hammersmith Hosp., London, 1953-55; physiologist Sir Edmund Hillary's Himalayan Expdn., 1960-61; dir. respiratory rsch. group Postgrad. Med. Sch., London, 1962-67, reader medicine, 1968; disting. prof. medicine and physiology U. Calif., San Diego, 1969—. Leader Am. Med. Rsch. Expdn. to Mt. Everest, 1981; U.S. organizer China-U.S. Conf. on respiratory failure, Nanjing, 1986; mem. life scis. adv. com. NASA, 1985-88, task force sci. uses of space sta., 1984-87, aerospace med. adv. com., 1988-89, chmn. sci. verification com. Spacelab SLS-1, 1983-92, commn. on respiratory physiol. Internat. Union Physiol. Scis., 1985—, commn. on clin. physiol., 1991—, commn. gravitation physiol., 1986—, study sect. NIH, chmn., 1973-75; prin. investigator Spacelabs SLS 1, 2, LMS, Neurolab, 1983—; co-investigator European Spacelabs, D2, Euromir, 1987—; external examiner Nat. U. Singpore, 1995; Wiltshire lectr., London, 1971, Schwidetzky lectr., 1975, Fleischner lectr., 1977, Robertson lectr. Adelaide U., 1978, I.J. Flance lectr. Washington U., 1978, W.A. Smith lectr. Med. Coll. SC, 1982, S. Kronheim lectr. Undersea Med. Soc., 1984, McClement lectr. NYU, 1996, Harry Fritts Jr. Lectr., Stony Brook U., 2007, Moran Campbell Lectr., Brit. Thoraic Soc., 2007. Author: Ventilation/Blood Flow and Gas Exchange, 1965, Respiratory Physiology-The Essentials, 1974, Translations in Respiratory Physiology, 1975, Pulmonary Pathophysiology-The Essentials, 1977, Translations in Respiratory Physiology, 1986—, Bioengineering Aspects of the Lung, 1977, Regional Differences in the Lung, 1977, Pulmonary Gas Exchange (2 vols.), 1980, High Altitude Physiology, 1981, High Altitude and Man, 1984, Everest-The Testing Place, 1985, Best and Taylor's Physiological Basis of Medical Practice, 1985, 91, Study Guide for Best and Taylor, 1985, High Altitude Medicine and Physiology, 1989, The Lung: Scientific Foundations, 1991, 2d edit., 1997, Lung Injury, 1992, Respiratory Physiology: People and Ideas, 1996, High Life: A History of High Altitude Physiology and Medicine, 1998; Pulmonary Physiology and Pathology: An Integrated, case-based approach, 2001, Gravity and the Lung, 2001; founder, editor-in-chief High Altitude Medicine and Biology, 2000-. Recipient Ernest Jung prize for medicine, Hamburg, 1977, Presdl. citation Am. Coll. Chest Physicians, 1977, Kaiser Tchg. award 1980; scholar Macy Found., 1974; Jeffries Med. Rsch. award AIAA, 1992. Fellow Royal Coll. Physicians (London), Royal Australasian Coll. Physicians, Royal Geog. Soc. (London), AAAS (med. sci. nominating com. 1987-93, coun. del. sect. med. scis.), Am. Inst. for Med. and Biol. Engring. (founding fellow 1992), Am. Heart Assn. (G.C. Griffith lectr. 1978, D.W. Richards lectr. 1980), Internat. Soc. for Mountain Medicine (pres. 1991-94), Am. Acad. Arts and Scis.; mem. NAS (com. space biology and medicine 1986-90, subcom. on space biology 1984-85, com. advanced space tech. 1992-94, panel on small spacecraft tech. 1994), Am. Assn. Thoracic Surgery (hon.), Nat. Bd. Med. Examiners (physiology test com. 1973-76), Am. Physiol. Soc. (pres. 1984-85, coun. 1981-86, chmn. sect. on history of physiology 1984-92, hist. pubs. adv. com., Reynolds prize for history 1987, Ray Daggs award 1998, Guyton Tchg. award 2002, Julius H. Comroe lectr. 2003), Inst. of Medicine of NAS, Am. Soc. Clin. Investigation, Physiol. Soc. Gt. Britain, Am. Thoracic Soc. (Edward Livingston Trudeau medal 2002), Royal Soc. of Medicine (Hickman medal, 2007), Assn. Am. Physicians, Western Assn. Physicians, Russian Acad. Sci. (elected fgn. mem.), Explorers Club, Fleischner Soc. (pres. 1985), Harveian Soc. (London), Royal Instn. Gt. Britain, Royal Soc. Medicine (London), Hurlingham Club (London), La Jolla Beach & Tennis Club. Home: 9626 Blackgold Rd La Jolla CA 92037-1110 Office: U Calif San Diego Sch Medicine 0623 Dept Medicine La Jolla CA 92093 Office Phone: 858-534-4192. Business E-Mail: jwest@ucsd.edu.

WEST, JOHN THOMAS, retired surgeon; b. Live Oak, Fla., June 23, 1924; s. James Whitaker and Lelah Eulalia (Moore) W.; m. Ruth Marita Blakely, June 18, 1948; children: Phyllis Ann, Rebecca Ruth, James Carl, Jeffrey Moore, Paul Blakely. BS, U. Mich., 1946; MD, Vanderbilt U., 1951. Diplomate Am. Bd. Surgery. Commd. officer USPHS, 1951, advanced through grades to capt., 1963; rotating intern USPHS Hosp., Seattle, 1951—52; chief surgery USPHS Alaska Native Hosp., Anchorage, 1957—60, resident gen. surgery, 1954—57; chief surgery USPHS Hosp., Seattle, 1963—69, USPHS Indian Hosp., Phoenix, 1969—71; sr. investigator surg. br. Nat. Cancer Inst. USPHS, Bethesda, Md., 1960—63, ret. Nat. Cancer Inst., 1971; clin. asst. prof. U. Wash., Seattle, 1964—68; clin. assoc. prof. Tex. Tech U., Lubbock, 1974—77; pvt. practice La Grange, Ga., 1971—74, 1977—94; ret., 1994. Mem. active staff West Ga. Med. Ctr., La Grange, 1971-74, 77-94. Bd. dirs. Ga. divsn. Am. Cancer Soc., 1972-77, 77-92. Recipient Meritorious Svc. medal USPHS, 1968. Fellow ACS, Soc. Surg. Oncology. Presbyterian. Achievements include report of facilitation of major hepatic resection by an innovation in the surgical exposure of the liver. Home: 134 Hickory Ln Lagrange GA 30240-8622 Home Phone: 706-884-1654. Personal E-mail: rutom@mindspring.com.

WEST, KANYE, rap artist; b. Atlanta, June 8, 1977; s. Ray and Donda West. Founder G.O.O.D. (Getting Out Our Dreams) Music, 2004—. Singer: (albums) The College Dropout, 2004 (Grammy award for Best Rap Album, 2005), Late Registration, 2005 (Grammy award for Best Rap Album, 2006), Graduation, 2007 (Grammy award for Best Rap Album, 2008, Favorite Rap/Hip-Hop Album award, Am. Music Awards, 2008), 808s & Heartbreak, 2008, (songs) Jesus Walks, 2004 (Best Male Video, MTV Video Music awards, 2005, Grammy award for Best Rap Song, 2005), Diamonds from Sierra Leone, 2005 (Grammy award for Best Rap Song, 2006), Gold Digger, 2005 (Grammy award for Best Rap Solo Performance, 2006, Soul Train Music award for Best Rap Video, 2006, 2 BET awards for Best Duet & Video of Yr., 2006), Stronger, 2007 (Grammy award for Best Rap Solo Peformance, 2008); singer: (with T-Pain) Good Life, 2007 (Grammy award for Best Rap Song, 2008, MTV Video Music award for Best Spl. Effects, 2008); singer: (with Common) Southside, 2007 (Grammy award for Best Duo Rap Performance, 2008); singer: (with Jay-Z and T.I.) Swagga Like Us, 2008 (Grammy award for Best Group Rap Performance, 2009); singer: (with Estelle) American Boy, 2008 (Grammy award for Best Rap/Sung Collaboration, 2009); composer (for Alicia Keys) You Don't Know My Name, 2003 (Grammy award for Best R&B Song, 2005); actor: (films) The Love Guru, 2008. Recipient Artist Achievement award, Billboard Music Awards, 2005, Vibe award, best rapper, 2005, 3 Grammy Awards, 2005, Image award for Outstanding New Artist, NAACP, 2005, 3 Grammy Awards, 2006, Best Hip Hop Entertainer, Internat. Reggae & World Music Awards, 2006, World's Best Rap/Hip Hop Artist, World Music Awards, 2007, Favorite Male Rap/Hip-Hop Artist award, Am. Music Awards, 2008, Internat. Male Solo Artist, BRIT Awards, 2009, Choice Music: Rap Artist, Teen Choice Awards, 2009; named Male New Artist of Yr., Billboard Music Awards, 2004, Best New R&B/Hip-Hop Artist of Yr., 2004, R&B/Hip-Hop Prodr. of Yr., 2004, Rap Artist of Yr., 2004; named one of Time Mag. 100 Most Influential People, 2005, The 10 Most Fascinating People of 2005, Barbara Walters Special, Top 25 Entertainers of Yr., Entertainment Weekly, 2007. Office: Roc A Fella Records 825 8th Ave 19th Floor New York NY 10019-7416 also: GOOD Records 2100 Colorado Ave Santa Monica CA 90404 also: c/o William Morris Agy 1 William Morris Pl Beverly Hills CA 90212*

WEST, KAZUKO ITO, mathematics educator, department chair; d. Hiroshi and Reiko Mori; m. Christopher Drane West, Sept. 5, 1998; 1 child, Shunsuke Ito. BS in Math., Waseda U., Tokyo, 1976, MS in Math., 1978; MEd, Harvard U., Cambridge, Mass., 1998; PhD in Math. Edn., Columbia U., NYC, 2005. Cert. tchr. math. high sch. Ministry of Edn., Japan, 1976. Math. tchr. Yokohama Tateno HS, Japan, 1978—81, Ikuta HS, Kawasaki, Japan, 1981—96; spl. edn. tchr. Takatsu HS, Kawasaki, 1996—97; math. tchr. Miss Hall's Sch., 1998—99, Keio Acad., Purchase, NY, 1999—, math. dept. chairperson, 2003—; math. edn. lectr. Manhattanville Coll., 2007—. Contbr. articles to profl. jours. Mem. Riverside Ch., NYC. Named Dewey Scholar, Columbia U. Tchrs. Coll. Mem.: Assn. Women in Math., Math. and Edn. Reform Forum, Internat. Cmty. Tchrs. Math. Modelling and Applications, Japan Soc. Math. Edn., Math. Assn. Am., Am. Math. Soc. Achievements include research in Japanese high school mathematics teacher competence. Home: 2900 Purchase St Purchase NY 10577 Office: Keio Academy of NY 3 College Rd Purchase NY 10577 E-mail: westc-k@post.harvard.edu.

WEST, LEE ROY, federal judge; b. Clayton, Okla., Nov. 26, 1929; s. Calvin and Nicie (Hill) W.; m. MaryAnn Ellis, Aug. 29, 1952; children: Kimberly Ellis, Jennifer Lee. BA, U. Okla., 1952, JD, 1956; LL.M. (Ford Found. fellow), Harvard U., 1963. Bar: Okla. 1956. Individual practice law, Ada, Okla., 1956-61, 63-65; faculty U. Okla. Coll. Law, 1961-62; Ford Found. fellow in law teaching Harvard U., Cambridge, Mass., 1962-63; judge 22d Jud. Dist. Okla., Ada, 1965-73; mem. CAB, Washington, 1973-78, acting chmn., 1977; practice law Tulsa, 1978-79; spl. justice Okla. Supreme Ct., 1965; judge U.S. Dist Ct. (we. dist.) Okla., 1979-94; sr. judge U.S. Dist. Ct. (we. dist.), Okla., 1994—. Editor: Okla. Law Rev. Served to capt. USMC, 1952-54. Named to Field Trial Hall of Fame, 2005; recipient Humanitarian award Nat. Conf. Cmty. and Justice, 2000, Jud. Excellence award Okla. Bar Assn., 2000, E.T. Dunlap medal and Lectureship award, 2006, Constn. Day award Rogers State U., 2006. Mem. U. Okla. Alumni Assn. (dir.), Phi Delta Phi (pres. 1956), Phi Eta Sigma, Order of Coif. Home: 6500 E Danforth Rd Edmond OK 73034-7601 Office: US Dist Ct 3001 US Courthouse 200 NW 4th St Oklahoma City OK 73102-3027 Home Phone: 405-348-0818; Office Phone: 405-609-5140.

WEST, MARC, information technology executive; B in Computer ci., U. Md.; M in Human Resource Mgmt., Golden State U., San Francisco. Various positions Quick & Reilly, Move.com, Oracle and Mobil Oil; sr. v.p. and global chief info. officer Electronic Arts, Redwood City, Calif., 2000—04; sr. v.p. & chief info. officer H&R Block, Kansas City, Mo., 2004—. Named one of Premier 100 IT Leaders, Computerworld, 2006. Office: SVP & CIO H&R Block Inc One H&R Block Way Kansas City MO 64105

WEST, MARK OTTO, psychology professor; b. Omaha, Jan. 16, 1948; s. Otto Cornelius and Cathryn Ann West; m. Carol Anne Christian, Aug. 12, 1984; children: Tivoli Anne, Heidi Cathryn, Whitney Caroline, Dane Mark, Skye Shannon, Dallas Kristin, Robert Edward. BS, U. of Calif., 1976; PhD, Wake Forest U., 1982. Postdoctoral rsch. assoc. U. of Tex. Southwestern Med. Sch., Dallas, 1982—86; prof. of psychology Rutgers U., New Brunswick, NJ, 1986—. Ad hoc reviewer NIH, Bethesda, Md., 1990—. Contbr. rsch. articles to sci. jours.; editl. reviewer: manuscripts for jours. With US Army, 1968—69, Vietnam. Grantee, NSF, 1987—90, Nat. Inst. on Drug Abuse, 1987—92, 1990—93, 1992—97, 1993—97, 1997—2001, 2001—05, 2006—. Mem.: Soc. for Neurosci. Achievements include discovery of functional reorganization of brain connections in basal ganglia in Parkinson's disease; First described somatotopic arrangement (functional organization) of the striatum in the basal ganglia of the rat brain; discovery of electrical activity in rat hippocampus correlated with updating (working) memory and activity in mesolimbic dopamine system correlated with relapse to cocaine abuse. Avocations: running, swimming, bicycling. Office: Rutgers U Busch Campus 152 Frelinghuysen Rd Piscataway NJ 08854 Business E-Mail: markwest@rci.rutgers.edu.

WEST, MARY BETH, food products executive; b. 1962; BS in Mgmt., Nazareth Coll., Rochester, NY, 1984; MBA, Columbia U., NYC, 1986. Various mgmt. positions Kraft Foods Inc., Northfield, Ill., 1986—98, v.p. bus. develop. N.Am., 1998—99, v.p. mktg., enhancers divsn., 1999—2001, sr. v.p., gen. mgr. meals divsn., 2001—04, group v.p., pres. US grocery sector, 2004—06, group v.p., pres. N.Am. beverages, 2006—07, exec. v.p., chief mktg. officer, 2007—. Bd. dirs. JC Penney Co., 2005—. Named a Woman to Watch, Advt. Age, 2008; named one of 40 Under 40, Chgo Bus. mag., 2001. Mem.: Exec. Leadership Council. Office: Kraft Foods Inc 3 Lakes Dr Northfield IL 60093*

WEST, MARY E., telecommunications industry executive; b. 1945; m. Gary L. West, 1968. Sec. Falstaff Brewing; founder Mardex, 1973; founder, v.p. of fin. WATS Mktg. of Am., 1978—86; co-founder, vice-chmn. West Corp., 1986—. Named one of 100 Most Powerful Women, Forbes mag., 2007. Avocation: Horse Racing. Office: West Corp Hdqs 11808 Miracle Hills Dr Omaha NE 68145 Office Phone: 800-232-0900.

WEST, MICHAEL ALAN, retired hospital administrator; b. Waseca, Minn., Aug. 4, 1938; s. Ralph Leland and Elizabeth Mary (Brann) W.; m. Mary Thissen, Jan. 21, 1961; children— Anne, Nancy, Douglas. BA, U. Minn., 1961, MHA, 1963. Sales corr. Physicians and Hosps. Supply Co., Mpls., 1959-60; adminstrv. resident R.I. Hosp., Providence, 1962-63, adminstrv. asst., 1963-65, asst. dir., 1965-68; exec. asst. dir. Med. Center U. Mo., Columbia, 1968-70, assoc. dir., 1970-74, asst. prof. community health and med. practice, 1968-74; v.p. for adminstrn. Luth. Gen. Hosp., Park Ridge, Ill., 1974-80, exec. v.p., 1980-84; pres., CEO Akron Gen. Med. Ctr., Ohio, 1984-97, Akron Gen. Health Sys., 1997—2002. Bd. dirs. Vol. Hosps. Am. Inc.; chair VHA-Ctrl., Inc. Bd. dirs. Great Trails Coun. Boy Scouts Am. Mem. Am. Coll. Healthcare Execs., Akron Regional Hosp. Assn. (chmn.), Portage Country Club, Akron City Club, Catawba Island Club, Noreaster Club. Home: 495 Woodbury Dr Akron OH 44333-2780

WEST, MICHAEL DAVIDSON, English educator; b. Morristown, NJ, Apr. 13, 1937; s. David Haller and Isabel Emily (Smith) W.; m. Deborah Hall Green, June 17, 1961; 1 child, Alexandra. AB, Harvard U., 1959, AM, 1961, PhD, 1965. Tchg. fellow Harvard U., Cambridge, Mass., 1961—64; instr. Wesleyan U., Middletown, Conn., 1964—65, asst. prof., 1965—72; instr. Middlesex C.C., Middletown, 1967—68; assoc. prof. English U. Pitts., 1972—76, prof. English, 1976—. Fulbright lectr. U. Copenhagen. Author: Transcendental Wordplay: America's Romantic Punsters and the Search for the Language of Nature, 2000; contbr. articles to profl. jours. Sr. fellow Wesleyan Ctr. for Humanities, Middletown, 1970, Am. Coun. Learned Socs. fellow, NY, 1978-79, Huntington-NEH fellow Huntington Libr., 1985-86, Newberry Libr. fellow, 1985-86, hon. fellow Inst. Advanced Studies in the Humanities, U. Edinburgh, Scotland, 1987; recipient DeGolyer prize SW Rev. So. Meth. U., 1987, 1st prize Frank O'Connor Essay Contest, 2002, 1st prize Anthony Trollope Essay Contest Harvard U., 2005. Mem. MLA (tchg. award 1972), N.E. MLA (Ohio U. Press Book award 1999, Thirtieth Anniversary award 2000), Renaissance Soc. Am., Am. Antiquarian Soc. (Peterson fellow 1985), Phi Beta Kappa (Christian Gauss award 2001). Home: 416 Morewood Ave Pittsburgh PA 15213-1814 Office: U Pitts English Dept CL 526 Pittsburgh PA 15260 Office Phone: 412-624-6543. Business E-Mail: mikewest@pitt.edu.

WEST, MICHAEL G., electric power industry executive; BS in Electronic Engring.; BS in Math., Oreg. State U.; MSEE, U. Ill. Integrated cir. designer Floating Point Sys., 1982—86; integrated cir. design engr. Bipolar Integrated Tech., 1986—87; chief scientist, sr. engr. In Focus Sys., 1988—96; co-founder, v.p. tech. Pixelworks, Inc., Tualatin, Oreg., 1997—, fellow, 2003—. Office: Pixelworks Inc Ste 300 8100 SW Nyberg Rd Tualatin OR 97062

WEST, MILDRED MARIE, art educator; b. Mill Creek, Okla., July 7, 1934; d. Minor Hubert and Audrey Eunice (Baker) Hughes; m. Joe Dean West, Dec. 18, 1954; children: Michael, Jared, Adam; stepchildren: Sue, Carla. BS Home Econs., East Ctrl. U., Ada, Okla., 1982. Cert. K-12 art edn., Okla., 6-12 home econs., Okla. Presenter in field of art edn. Columnist Ada Evening News, 1987-92; paintings exhibited Legis. Art Show, Oklahoma City, 1984-92. Chmn. Farm Bur. Womens Commn.; past pres. Ada Artists. Mem. AAUW (past pres.), Ada Artists Assn. (art show com.), Allied Arts Tanti Study Club (past pres.), Magic Brush Art Guild, Holdenville Soc. Painters and Sculptors, Beta Sigma Phi. Democrat. Member Church of Christ. Avocations: walking, aerobics, gourmet cooking, travel.

WEST, NORMAN ELLSWORTH, artist; b. Exeter, NH, May 16, 1952; s. Norman Ellsworth and Alice Marie West. BS, Plymouth State Coll., 1976; BFA, Maine Coll. of Art, 1980. Leader color workshops regional schs., York County, 1981—; artist in residence Holderness Acad., Plymouth, N.H., 1989-91; set designer Shenanigans Prodns., Portland, Boston, 1993-96; tchr. Heartwood Coll. of Art, Kennebunk, Maine, 1994—. Dir. Heartwood Coll. Art Gallery, 2002. One person shows include West Kuhn Gallery, Cape Neddick, Maine, 1988, Van Ward Gallery, Ogunquit, Maine, 1994, 98; group shows include Currier Gallery, Manchester, N.H., 1988, 89, Barn Gallery, Ogunquit, 1988, Mast Core Galleries, Kennebunkport, Maine, 1988, 89, Ogunquit Art Assn., 1988—, Maine Coast Artists, Rockport, Maine, 1989, 90. Bd. dirs. Shellfish Commn., Ogunquit, Maine, 1996—; clam warden Town of Ogunquit, 1997-99. Mem. Ogunquit Art Assn. (curator invited sculptor's exhibit 1996—), Ogunquit Arts Collaborative (v.p. 2000—), Ogunquit Rotary Club. Home: PO Box 1560 Ogunquit ME 03907

WEST, NORMAN R., history professor; b. Brooklyn, Jan. 1, 1932; BS, USCG Acad., New London, CT, 1955; MS, U. Stony Brook; MA in History, Boston U., 1963. Commd. officer USCG, Maine, 1955—65; prof. history Suffolk County CC, Selden, NY, 1965—. Democrat. Avocation: tennis. Office: Suffolk County CC College Rd Selden NY 11784 Business E-Mail: westn@sunysuffolk.edu.

WEST, PAUL NODEN, writer, playwright; b. Eckington, Derbyshire, Eng., Feb. 23, 1930; arrived in US, 1961, naturalized, 1971; s. Alfred Massick and Mildred (Noden) W. Student, Oxford U., 1950-53; MA, Columbia U., 1953. Asst. prof. English Meml. U. Nfld., Canada, 1957-58, assoc. prof., 1958-60; faculty Pa. State U., Pa., 1962-95, prof. English and comparative lit. Pa., 1968-95; prof. emeritus, 1995—. Crawshaw prof. Colgate U., 1972; Melvin Hill disting. vis. prof. Hobart and William Smith Coll., 1973; vis. English prof. Cornell U., 1986; disting. writer in residence Wichita State U., 1982; vis. prof. English Brown U., 1992; fiction judge Creative Artists Pub. Svc. Program, NYC, 1974, 81; writer-in-residence U. Ariz., 1984; judge Katherine Ann Porter Prize for Fiction, 1984, Artists Found. Author: Byron and the Spoiler's Art, 1960, rev. edit., 1990, I Said the Sparrow, 1963, The Snow Leopard, 1965, Tenement of Clay, 1965, The Wine of Absurdity, 1966, Alley Jaggers, 1967, libretta for opera, 1968, I'm Expecting to Live Quite Soon, 1970, Words for a Deaf Daughter, 1970, Caliban's Filibuster, 1972, Colonel Mint, 1973, Gala, 1976, The Very Rich Hours of Count von Stauffenberg, 1980, Out of My Depths: A Swimmer in the Universe, 1983, Rat Man of Paris, 1986, theatrical version, 1987, Sheer Fiction, 1987, The Universe and Other Fictions, 1988, The Place in Flowers Where Pollen Rests, 1988, Lord Byron's Doctor, 1989, Portable People, The Women of Whitechapel and Jack the Ripper, 1991, Sheer Fiction: II, 1991, James Ensor, 1991, Love's Mansion, 1992, Tenement of Clay, 2d edit., 1993, Sheer Fiction, III, 1994, A Stroke of Genius, 1995, The Tent of Orange Mist, 1995 (memoir) My Mother's Music, 1996, My Father's War, 2005; (novel) Sporting with Amaryllis, 1996, Terrestrials, 1997, Life With Swan, 1999, O.K.: The Corral, The Earps, and Doc Holliday, 2000, The Dry Danube: A Hitler Forgery, 2000, The Secret Lives of Words, 2000, A Fifth of November, 2001, Master Class, 2001, Oxford Days, 2002, Cheops: A Cupboard for the Sun, 2002, (play) Any Old How, 2002, (radio play) The Sacrifice, 1955, The Immensity of the Here and Now, 2003, Sheer Fiction IV, 2004, Samuel Beckett: Born Astride A Grave, 2004, My Father's War, 2005, Tea with Osiris, 2005, (TV) Sheer Fiction, IV, 2007, The Shadow factory, 2008; contbr. Washington Post and NY Times, 1962—, Harper's Mag., Paris Rev., Yale Rev., Parnassus, Agni, Conjunctions, War, Literature and the Arts, First Intensity, Tin Roof; translator Les Romanesques by Rostand, 1954 fiction judge NY Found. for the Arts, Nat. Book award, 1990. Served RAF, 1954—57. Decorated chevalier de l'Ordre des Arts et des Lettres (France); recipient Aga Khan Fiction prize, 1973, Hazlett Meml. award for Excellence in Arts (lit.), 1981, Lit. award Am. Acad. and Inst. Arts and Letters, 1985, Pushcart prize 1987, 91, 2003, The Best Am. Essays award, 1990, Outstanding Achievement medal Pa. State U., 1991, Grand Prix Halpérine Kaminsky award, 1992, Lannan Fiction award, 1993, Tchg. award Northeastern Assn. Grad. Sch., 1994, Art of Fact prize SUNY, 2000; named Lit. Lion NY Pub. Libr., 1987; Guggenheim fellow, 1963; NEA Creative Writing fellow, 1979, 84; nominated for Médicis, Femina and Meilleur Livre Étranger prizes, France, 1991, Lannan Lit. Videos 35, Nat. Book Critics award for fiction, 1996; named to Honor Roll The Yr. in Fiction, DLB Yearbook, 1996, Conf. on works of West, U. of Tours, France, 2003; manuscript collection at Pattee Libr., Pa. State U. Office: Elaine Markson Agy 44 Greenwich Ave Fl 3 New York NY 10011-8389 *The unexamined life may not be worth having, but the examined life is endurable only to an open mind, through which life holistically flows, keeping that mind as incomplete as our knowledge of the universe itself.*

WEST, REXFORD LEON, retired bank executive; b. Syracuse, NY, Feb. 18, 1938; s. Rexford A. and Nina (Crysler) W.; children: Lisa, Julie, Gregory, Kristen AAS, Auburn C.C., NYC, 1957; BS magna cum laude, Syracuse U., NYC, 1972; Advanced Mgmt. Program, Harvard Bus. Sch., Boston, 1984. Accountant Marine Midland Bank, Syracuse, NY, 1959-67, v.p., asst. treas., 1967-72; v.p., contr. Marine Midland Services Corp., Buffalo, 1972-76; v.p. ops. divsn. Marine Midland Bank, N.A., Buffalo, 1976-77, sr. v.p., sr. ops. officer, 1977-79, exec. v.p., sr. ops. officer, 1979-85, divsn. exec. ops., 1985-87, sector exec. ops. and fin. mgmt., 1987-90, sr. exec. v.p. corp. engring., 1990-92; exec. v.p. adminstrv. svc. Fleet Bank, Melville, NY, 1992-94; exec. v.p. loan servicing Fleet Mortgage Group, Columbia, SC, 1994-96; ret., 1996. Served with U.S. Army, 1957-61

WEST, ROBERT MACLELLAN, science educator, consultant; b. Appleton, Wis., Sept. 1, 1942; s. Clarence John and Elizabeth Ophelia (Moore) West; m. Jean Sydow, June 19, 1965; 1 child, Christopher. BA, Lawrence Coll., 1963; SM, U. Chgo., 1964, PhD, 1968. Rsch. assoc. Princeton (N.J.) U., 1968-69; asst. prof. Adelphi U., Garden City, NY, 1969-74; curator geology Milw. Pub. Mus., 1974-83; dir. Carnegie Mus. Natural History, Pitts., 1983-87, Cranbrook Inst. Sci., Bloomfield Hills, Mich., 1987-91; prin. RMW Sci. Action, Washington, 1992-95; pres. Informal Sci., Inc., Washington, 1993-98, Informal Learning Experiences, Inc., Washington, 1999—. Adj. prof. U. Wis., Milw., 1974—83. Contbr. articles to profl. jours. Bd. dirs. Friends New Zoo, Pitts., 1984—87; treas. E. Mich. Environ. Action Coun., Birmingham, 1987—92. Recipient Arnold Guyot prize, Nat. Geographic Soc., 1982; named Man of the Yr. in Sci., Vectors Pitts., 1988; NSF fellow, 1965—68, NSF Rsch. grantee, 1970—82, Nat. Geographic Soc. Rsch. grantee, 1973, 1976, 1977, 1979, 1980, 1982. Mem.: Visitor Study Assn. (bd. dirs. 2005—), Am. Assn. Mus., Mus. Group, Soc. Vertebrate Paleontology, Nat. Ctr. Sci. Edn. (bd. dirs. 1984—88, 1992—), Explorers Club, Rotary. Avocations: nature, history, sports. Office: Informal Learning Experiences Inc PO Box 42328 Washington DC 20015-0928 Home Phone: 202-686-1696; Office Phone: 202-362-5823. Business E-Mail: ile@informallearning.com.

WEST, STACY KATHLENA, athletic trainer; b. Flint, Mich., Sept. 22, 1979; d. Jay Robert and Sonia Kathleen Kelso; m. Aaron Michael West, May 3, 2003. BS, Cen. Mich. U., Mt. Pleasant, Mich., 2002. Cert. atletic trainer Nat. Athletic Trainers Assn. Cert. athletic trainer Mclaren Sports Medicine, Davison H.S., Mich., 2003—. Mem.: Nat. Athletic Trainers Assn. (assoc.). Home: 3106 Reid Rd Swartz Creek MI 48473 Office: Mclaren Sports Medicine 1240 Fairway Dr Davison MI 48423 Personal E-mail: kelso1sk@yahoo.com.

WEST, STEPHEN ALLAN, lawyer; b. Salt Lake City, Mar. 23, 1935; s. Allan Morrell and Ferne (Page) W.; m. Martha Sears, Mar. 21, 1960; children: Stephen Allan, Jr., Page, Adam. JD, U. Utah, Salt Lake City, 1961, BS in Philosophy, 1962. Law clk. to judge US Dist. Ct., Utah, 1961-62; assoc. Marr, Wilkins & Cannon, Salt Lake City, 1962-65, ptnr., 1965-67; atty. Jennings, Strouss, Salmon & Trask, Washington, 1967-68, Marriott Corp., Washington, 1968-71, asst. gen. counsel, 1971-74, v.p. and assoc. gen. counsel, 1974-87, v.p. and dep. gen. counsel, 1987-93; sr. v.p., gen. counsel Marriott Internat., Inc., Washington, 1993-94; pres. Tex. San Antonio Mission Ch. of Jesus Christ of Latter-day Saints, 1995-98, Gen. Authority, 1998—2004. Mem. exec. bd. Interfaith Conf. Met. Washington, 1989-93, vice chmn., 1992-93; mem. exec. bd. Christa McAuliffe Inst. Task Force of Nat. Found. for Improvement Edn.; mem. South Va. U. Nat. Adv. Coun., 2007-, Bringham Young U. Mus. Art Leadership Coun., 2007-, chmn., 2009-; trustee Utah State U. Found., 2007-. Mem. ABA (exec. coun. young lawyers sect. 1964-65), Utah Bar Assn. (exec. com. young lawyers sect. 1962-67), DC Bar Assn., Utah Profl. Rels. Com., U. Utah Alumni Assn. (Disting. Alumni award 1971), Skull and Bones, Owl and Key, Phi Delta Phi, Sigma Chi. Office: 1117 Fox Farm Rd Logan UT 84321 Office Phone: 435-753-4225.

WEST, STEPHEN KINGSBURY, lawyer, director; b. Pittsfield, Mass., Sept. 28, 1928; s. William Bradford and Ruth (Osteyee) W.; m. Ann Wick, Apr. 30, 1955; children: Timothy Wick, Lucy West Engebretson, Todd Kingsbury, Daniel Wick. BA, Yale U., 1950; LL.B., Harvard U., 1953. Assoc. Sullivan & Cromwell, NYC, 1957-64, ptnr., 1964-97, sr. counsel, 1997—. Bd. dirs. Pioneer Mut. Fund, Boston, Swiss Helvetina Fund, Inc. Trustee Morven Mus. and Garden, Princeton, NJ, Hancock (Mass.) Shaker Village; dir. Atlantic Salmon Fedn. Served to lst lt. inf. US Army, 1953—57. Mem.: N.Y. State Bar Assn., Assn. Bar City N.Y. Office: Sullivan & Cromwell 125 Broad St Fl 28 New York NY 10004-2489 Office Phone: 212-558-3522.

WEST, TERESA L. (TERRI WEST), electronics executive; BA in Journalism, U. North Tex., 1982. Student intern Tex. Instruments, Inc., 1978, mgr. media rels., v.p., mgr. strategic comm., sr. v.p. comm. and investor rels. Dallas. Dir. Dallas Pub. Broadcasting Sys. affiliate, KERA-TV; mem. Nat. Investor Rels. Inst. and Conf. Bd.; founding mem. Women of Tex. Instruments Fund; v.p. Tex. Instruments Found.; chair comm. com. (during renewal of US-Japan Semiconductor Trade Arrangement) Semiconductor Industry Assn., 1992, 96. Mem. chancellor's leadership coun. U. North Tex. Office: Tex Instruments Inc PO Box 660199 Dallas TX 75266-0199 Office Phone: 972-995-2011, 972-995-4360.

WEST, TOGO DENNIS, JR., lawyer, former United States Secretary of Veterans Affairs; b. Winston-Salem, NC, June 21, 1942; s. Togo Dennis and Evelyn (Carter) W.; m. Gail Estelle Berry, June 18, 1966; children: Tiffany Berry, Hilary Carter. BSEE, Howard U., 1965, JD cum laude, 1968; LLD (hon.), Winston-Salem U., 1996, Gannon U., 1998. Bar: D.C. 1968, N.Y. 1969, U.S. Ct. Mil. Appeals 1969, U.S. Supreme Ct. 1978, U.S. Ct. Claims 1981. Elec. engr. Duquesne Light and Power Co., 1965; patent researcher Sughrue, Rothwell, Mion, Zinn and McPeak, 1966-67; legal intern US EEOC, 1967; law clk. firm Covington & Burling LLP, Washington, 1967-68, summer assoc., 1968, assoc., 1973-75, 76-77, 2000—05; law clk. to Hon. Harold R. Tyler Jr. US Dist. Ct. (So. Dist.) NY, 1968-69; assoc. dep. atty. gen. US Dept. Justice, Washington, 1975-76; gen. counsel Dept. Navy, Washington, 1977-79; spl. asst. to sec. & dep. sec. US Dept. Def., Washington, 1979-80, gen. counsel, 1980-81; mng. ptnr. Patterson, Belknap, Webb & Tyler LLP, Washington, 1981-90; sr. v.p. govt. rels. Northrop Corp., Washington, 1990-93; sec. Dept. Army, Washington, 1993-98; chair Panama Canal Com., 1997; sec. US Dept. Veterans Affairs, Washington, 1998—2000; of counsel Covington & Burling LP, 2000—04; pres., CEO Joint Ctr. Polit. & Econ. Studies, 2004—06; chmn. TLI Leadership Group, Washington, 2006—. Adj. prof. Duke U. Sch. Law, 1980-81; bd. cons. Riggs Nat. Bank, Washington, 1990-93; bd. dirs. Krispy Kreme Doughnuts, Inc., Abitibi Bowater, Inc., Med Star Health; coun. trustees AUSA; chmn. bd. trustees Noblis, Inc., 2001—, Bristol-Myers Squibb, Fuel Cell Energy, Inc. Mng. editor: Howard Law Jour, 1968. Commr. D.C. Law Rev. Comm., 1982-89, chmn., 1985-89; treas., 1987-91; bd. govs. Antioch U. Sch. Law, 1983-87, vice chmn., 1986-87; bd. visitors Wake Forest U. Sch. Law, 1991-94; chmn. Greater Washington Bd. Trade, legis. bur., 1987-89, bd. dirs., 1987-93, mem. exec. com. 1987-92; mem. fed. legis. com., 1990-93; chmn. Kennedy Ctr. Community and Friends Bd., 1991-2001; mem. Washington Lawyers' Com. Civil Rights Under Law, 1987-93, D.C. Com. on Pub. Edn., 1988-93, chmn., 1990-91; trustee The Aerospace Corp., 1983-90, Ctr. for Strategic and Internat. Studies, 1987-90, Nat. Lawyers Com. for Civil Rights Under Law, 1987-93, Inst. for Def. Analyses, 1989-91, Protestant Episcopal Cathedral Found., 1989-95, Shakespeare Theatre at The Folger, 1990-93, N.C. Sch. Arts, 1990-2002, Aerospace Edn. Found. of Air Force Assn., 1991-93; bd. dirs. D.C. Law Students in Ct. Program, 1986-92, World Affairs Coun., 1991-93, 2000—, Atlantic Coun., 1991-93, 2000—; mem. fin. com. Episcopal Diocese of Washington, 1989—90, mem. standing com., 1990-92; sr. warden St. John's Ch., Lafayette Sq.; mem. Coun. Fgn. Rels., 1996—; chmn. trustee coun. YMCA Metro. Wash., 1990-92; mem. nat. adv. com. UN Assn. USA, 1991-93; D.C. Ct. Appeals Admissions Com., 1990-93; pres. Nat. Capital Area Coun. Boy Scouts Am.; chmn. Greater Washington Bd. of Trade; bd. trustees Assn. of U.S. Army, 2001—. Served to capt. Judge Adv. Gen. Corps U.S. Army, 1969-73. Decorated Legion of Merit, Meritorious Svc. medal; recipient Disting. Pub. Svc. medal Dept. Def., 1981, 88, Disting. Eagle Scout award Boy Scouts Am., 1995, Svc. to Howard U. award, 1965, Medal of Merit, Brazil, Disting. Civil Svc. medal, 1998, Dept. Vet. Affairs, 2000, Silver Buffalo award, 2000, Silver Beaver award, 2003; named one of Most Influential Black Americans, Ebony mag., 2006. Mem. ABA, Nat. Bar Assn., Washington Coun. Lawyers (dir. 1973-75), Sigma Pi Phi, Phi Alpha Delta, Omega Psi Psi, Alpha Phi Omega. Clubs: Metropolitan, University (Washington). Office: TLI Leadership Group 888 17th St NW Ste 302 Washington DC 20006 Business E-Mail: twest@tlileaders.com.

WEST, TONY (DEREK ANTHONY WEST), federal agency administrator, lawyer; b. 1965; AB, Harvard U., Cambridge, Mass., 1987; JD, Stanford U. Sch. Law, Calif., 1992. Bar: Calif. 1992. Asst. US atty. (no. dist.) Calif. US Dept. Justice, Washington, 1994—99; spl. asst. atty. gen. State of Calif., Sacramento, 1999—2001; ptnr. Morrison & Foerster LLP, San Francisco, 2001—09; asst. atty gen., civil divsn. US Dept. Justice, Washington, 2009—. Appearances as legal analyst include CNN-Headline News, ESPN, CBS-5, others. Bd. govs. No. Calif. Assn. Bus. Trial Lawyers. Recipient Exec. Office of US Attorneys Director's Award, US Dept. Justice, 1998, Bill Key Memorial Victim/Witness Assistance award, 1998, Centennial Leadership award, L.A. Consistory, 2008; named a New Star, Lawdragon Inc., 2006; named one of Calif.'s Top 20 Lawyers Under 40, Daily Jour., 2004, Northern Calif.'s Super Lawyers, 2006—08. Mem.: ABA, State Bar of Calif. Office: US Dept Justice 810 Seventh St NW Washington DC 20531*

WEST, W. RICHARD, JR., retired museum director; b. Okla., Jan. 6, 1943; s. W. Richard Sr. and Maribelle (McCrea) W.; m. Mary Beth Braden, June 29, 1968; children: Amy Elizabeth, Benjamin Braden. BA magna cum laude in Am. History, U. Redlands, 1965; AM in Am. History, Harvard U., 1968; JD, Stanford U., 1971; LHD (hon.), Bacone Coll., 1992, Ottawa U., 1994, U. Okla., 1995. Bar: Calif., DC, US Ct. Appeals (8th cir.), US Supreme Ct. Clk. to Hon. Benjamin C. Duniway U.S. Ct. Appeals (9th cir.), 1971-72; assoc. Fried, Frank, Harris, Shriver & Jacobson, Washington, 1973-79, ptnr., 1979-88; dir. direct support component Am. Indian Lawyer Tng. Program, Inc., 1976-77; ptnr. Gover, Stetson Williams & West P.C., Albuquerque, 1988-90; founding dir. Smithsonian Inst. Nat. Mus. Am. Indian, Washington, 1990—2007; ret., 2007. Treas. Am. Indian Lawyer Tng. Program, Inc., 1973—; adj. prof. Indian law Stanford U., 1977. Mem. edit. bd. Am. Indian Historian, 1969-71; note editor Stanford Law Review, 1970-71; contbr. articles to profl. jours. Coord., treas. Native Am. Coun. Regents Inst. Am. Indian Arts, 1975-80; bd. visitors Stanford Law Sch., 1978-81; trustee Phelps Stokes Fund, 1981-87, Bush Found., 1991—, Bacone Coll., 1986-89, chmn., 1988-89, Morning Star Found., 1987-93, U. Redlands, 1991—, alumni bd., 1987-89, Ednl. Found. Am., 1993-96; bd. dirs. Amerindian Circle, Inc., 1981-88, Nat. Indian Justice Ctr., 1982-89; cultural edn. com. Smithsonian Inst., 1987-90; nat. support com. Native Am. Rights Fund, 1990—; adv. com. Winslow Found., 1991—; hon. coun. Wings Am., 1993—; mem. Environ. Def. Fund, bd. trustees, 1986—. Recipient Career Achievement award U. Redlands, 1987, Disting. Svc. award, 1992, award Appreciation and Recognition, Cheyenne and Arapaho Tribes Okla., 1990, Spirit of the People award Okla. Inst. Indian Heritage, 1990; named (with another) Amb. of Yr. Red Earth Indian Ctr. Okla., 1993; named to Centennial Honor Roll, Am. Assn. Museums, 2006. Mem. Am. Indian Bar Assn. (charter pres. 1976-77). Mem. Cheyenne and Arapaho Tribes Okla.

WEST, III, WILLIAM CUSTIS, retired ancient language educator; b. Onancock, Va., Aug. 20, 1936; s. William Custis West, Jr and Hilda Thomas Belote; m. Jo Anne Garrett West, Aug. 22, 1964; children: Edward Garrett West, Amanda West Wallingford. PhD, U. NC, Chapel Hill, 1965. Instr. classics U. NC, 1966, prof. classics Chapel Hill, 1966—2003. Lt. USN, 1958—61, Little Creek, VA. Grant, Nat. Endowment Humanities, 1974—87. Home: 607 Yorktown Dr Chapel Hill NC 27516 Office: Univ of NC Chapel Hill NC 27599-3145 Business E-Mail: wwest@email.unc.edu.

WESTBERRY, ANITA PARRISH, education educator; b. Clewiston, Fla., Oct. 5, 1946; d. Virgil Ennis and Onetta Armour Parrish; m. Lawrence Ray Westberry, Sr., Nov. 5, 1966; children: Danita Westberry Thomas, Lawrence Ray Jr. AA, Edison Cmty., Fort Myers, Fla., 1978; BS, Nova S.E. U., Fort Lauderdale, Fla., 1988; MEd, Tenn. State U., Nashville, 1999. Elem. tchr. Glades County Schs., Moore Haven, Fla., 1988—89, Hendry County Schs., LaBelle, Fla., 1989—97; ESL tchr. Franklin County Schs., Winchester, Tenn., 1997—98, Rutherford County Schs., Murfreesboro, Tenn., 1998—2004; instr. U. Phoenix, Nashville, 2002—, online instr.; instr. Western Internat. U., Phoenix, 2004—, U. Phoenix, Nashville, Franklin, Chattanooga; online instr. Axia Coll., Western Internat. U. Rep. S.W. Fla. Tchr. Edn. Ctr., Fort Myers, 1995—97. Named Leader of Yr., 4-H, 1980. Church Of Christ. Avocations: reading, travel. Home: 256 White Oak Dr Manchester TN 37355 Office Phone: 931-570-5167. Personal E-mail: awestberry@charter.net. Business E-Mail: westberry03@email.phoenix.edu.

WESTBERRY, ROBERT KENT, lawyer; b. Marion, Ky., July 21, 1955; s. B.M. and Nancy Elizabeth (Kent) W.; m. Leslie Gail Fifield, Sept. 24, 1988. AB, Centre Coll., 1977; JD, Salmon P. Chase Coll., 1981. Bar: Ky. 1981, US Dist. Ct. (we. dist. Ky.) 1982, US Ct. Appeals (6th cir.) 1982, US Supreme Ct. Assoc. Westberry and Roberts, Marion, 1981; asst. US atty. US Dist. Ct. (we. dist. Ky.), Louisville, 1981-87; assoc. Greenebaum, Doll & McDonald, Louisville, 1987-89; spl. justice Ky. Supreme Ct., 1994; assoc. Landrum and Shouse, Louisville, 1989, ptnr. Moderator, lectr. Comprehensive Crime Criminal Act Seminar, 1985, Prosecution of Criminal RICO Action, 1986. Vice chmn. Jefferson County Rep. Party. Louisville, 1988; chmn. Civil Justice Reform Act Com., US Dist. Ct. (We. Dist. Ky.), 1991-95. Mem. Ky. Bar Assn. (chmn. younger lawyers sect., v.p. 2002-03, pres.-elect 2003-04, pres. 2004-05), ABA, Wong Sun Soc., Nat. Assn. Criminal Def. Atty. Episcopalian. Office: Landrum and Shouse Ste 1900 220 W Main St Louisville KY 40202 Office Phone: 502-589-7616. Office Fax: 502-589-2119. E-mail: kwestberry@landrumshouse.com.

WESTBIE, BARBARA JANE, retired graphics designer; b. Little Rock, Nov. 3, 1946; d. Freeman Bryant Davis and Virginia Lee Thompson; children: Suzanne Michelle, Derrek Christopher. Grad. in graphic design, U. Calif., Davis, 1992; student, Miramar Coll., San Diego, 1976, Chabot Coll., Hayward, Calif., 1974. Exec. dir. Ambiance, Danville, Calif., 1980—84; dir. Lake Gallery, Tahoe City, Calif., 1985—87; art cons. Reed Gallery, Tahoe City, 1988—90; ret., 1990. Art dir., creative cons. Associated Students Re-Entry Ctr. Chico State U., Calif., 2001—03. Inventor Fat Fuzzy/Iknonotrisc Family, 1981, artist (poster/logo) Project Mana Fundraising Event, 1988, (brochure/media kit) Chocolate Festival, 1989. Vol. crisis intervention counselor CIS/Tahoe Women's Svcs., Kings Beach, 1989—91; lead counselor Emotions Anonymous 12-Step Program, North Lake Tahoe Area, 1990—93; vol. pk. svc. Washoe Lake State Pk., Carson City, Nev., 1993—94; coord. new vols. ARC, Chico, 2000—01, vol. Butte County, 2000—, Emergency Animal Rescue Svcs., 2002—. Recipient Disting. Svc. award, CIS/Tahoe Women's Svcs., 1989—90; named Vol. of Yr., Tahoe Women's Svcs., 1989. Mem.: Smithsonian Instn. (assoc.). Protestant. Avocations: skiing, reading, gardening, writing, painting.

WESTBROCK, LEON E., energy and food products executive; B, St. Cloud State U., Minn. With Cenex, 1976, mgr. three local coops., with merchandising dept., mgr. lubricants dept., dir. retailing, v.p., exec. v.p. petroleum divsn., 1987; COO, exec. v.p. inputs CHS Inc. (merger of Cenex and Harvest States), Inver Grove Heights, Minn., 2000, exec. v.p., COO energy. Chmn. Nat. Coop. Refinery Assn. Vice chmn. Inver Grove Heights HS; mem. comml. devel. task force City of Inver Grove Heights. Served in US Army. Recipient Outstanding Alumni award, St. Cloud State U. Office: CHS Inc PO Box 64089 Saint Paul MN 55164-0089 Office Phone: 651-355-6000.*

WESTBROOK, BRIAN COLLINS, professional football player; b. Washington, DC, Sept. 2, 1979; s. Ronald and Zelda Westbrook. BS in Mgmt. Info Sys., Villanova U., Pa., 2001, grad. student, 2002. RB Phila. Eagles, 2002—. Organizer Variety Club, Phila.; host Police Athletic League Phila. Charity and Celebrity Weekend. Named First Team All-Pro, NFL, 2007; named to Nat. Football Conf. Pro Bowl Team,

2004, 2007. Achievements include leading the NFL in: punt return touchdowns, 2003, yards from scrimmage, 2007. Avocations: golf, pool. Office: CSMG Sports c/o Fletcher Smith 20 W Kinzie St Ste 1000 Chicago IL 60610*

WESTBROOK, CLINTON HOWARD, retired military petty officer, protective services official; b. Bklyn., Mar. 1, 1919; s. Alfred and Daisy (Gamble) Westbrook; m. Catherine Veronica Wetzel, Dec. 13, 1942 (dec. June 24, 2006); children: James Howard, Cathy Ann, John Alfred(dec.), Clinton Howard Jr., Robert Vincent(dec.). Enlisted USN, 1940, served on USS Maddox and USS Arizona, 1940—41, served on 23 campaigns in Atlantic and Pacific, 1941—45, served on USS Taylor, 1942—46, recalled to active duty, 1950—52, ret. chief petty officer, 1967; discharged to active reserve USNR, 1946; security patrol So. Pacific Railroad, San Francisco, 1946; with Parcel Post, NYC, 1947; X-ray svc. engr.; field engr., 1952—56; dir. emergency/civil def. County of Seminole, Fla., 1967—74; vet. svcs. officer Seminole County, 1967—84; ret., 1984. Hon. chmn. Golden Age Games, Sanford, 2003; vol. county resource lectr. Seminole County Schs., 1993—2007, Meml. Day Parade, Sanford, Fla., 2003—07, parade marshall, 2004, VIP guest, 2007. Recipient Order of the Eagle Feather plaque, numerous unit awards and citations, Presdl. Unit award; named State Vet. Svc. Officer of Yr. outstanding svc., Seminole County Commr., 1967—84, Purple Heart. Mem.: DAV (life), Pearl Harbor Survivors Assn. (life), Tin Can Sailor Assn. (life), USS Ariz. Reunion Assn. (life; bd. dirs. 1999—2002, v.p. 2003, 2005, 2006—07). Democrat. Roman Catholic. Achievements include being a survivor of the USS Arizona during the Pearl Harbor attack in 1941; led USS Missouri into Tokyo Bay for Japanese surrender while on board USS Taylor. Avocations: stamp collecting/philately, coin collecting/numismatics, photography, volunteering. Home: Lakeview Ter Blgd C Unit 2 PO Box 645 Windermere FL 34786-0645 Home Phone: 352-308-9485.

WESTBROOK, GARY L., neurologist; BA in Zoology, Miami U., Oxford, Ohio, 1970; MSE in Biomed. Engring., Case Western Res. U., Cleve., 1974, MD, 1976. Diplomate Am. Bd. Internal Medicine, 1979. Intern, resident in internal medicine Mt. Auburn Hosp., Harvard U., Cambridge, Mass., 1976—78; resident in neurology Barnes Hosp., Wash. U., St. Louis, 1978—81; PRAT fellow, pharmacology sci. program NIH Nat. Inst. Gen. Med. Sciences, Bethesda, Md., 1981—83; staff & sr. staff fellow, lab. devel. neurobiology NIH, Bethesda, 1983—87; asst. prof. neurology Oreg. Health Sci. U., Portland, 1987—88, assoc. prof. neurology, 1988—92, prof. neurology & physiology, pharmacology, 1992—; asst. scientist Vollum Inst., Portland, 1987—90, sr. scientist, 1990—, co-dir., 2005—; attending neurologist Univ. Hosp., Portland, 1988—, physician, epilepsy program, 1989—2003. Assoc. editor: Jour. Neurosci. Cellular Neurosci. Sect., 1988—93, editor:, 1995—97, sr. editor: Jour. Neurosci. Cellular and Molecular Neurosci., 1997—2002, editor-in-chief: Jour. Neurosci., 2003—07, mem. editl. bd.: Molecular Pharmacology, 1995—98; contbr. articles to profl. jours. Mem. Dana Alliance, 2005—; sci. adv. bd. Myelin Repair Found., 2004—, chmn., 2007—; chmn. ad hoc Max Planck Inst. Exptl. Medicine, 2006—; adv. coun. NINDS, NIH, 2006—. Recipient Devel. award, McKnight Endowment Fund Neurosci., 1988, Javits Neurosci. Investigator award, NINDS, NIH, 1993, MERIT award, 1997, Max Planck Rsch. award for internat. cooperation, 2003. Mem.: Inst. Medicine, Am. Acad. Arts & Sciences, Phi Beta Kappa, Omicron Delta Kappa. Office: Vollum Inst Oreg Health & Sci Univ 3181 SW Sam Jackson Park Rd Portland OR 97239-3098 Office Phone: 503-494-8311.*

WESTBROOK, JACK HALL, metallurgist, consultant; b. Troy, NY, Aug. 19, 1924; s. Russell Tippett and Grace Hall (Wager) W.; m. Elizabeth Kirkland, Sept. 20, 1947 (dec.); children: Nicholas, Kathryn, Melissa, Kirkland, Daniel; m. Jeanette (Sylvain) Hughson, July 26, 2003. B in Metall. Engring., Rensselaer Poly. Inst., 1944, M in Metall. Engring., 1947; ScD, MIT, 1949. Registered profl. engr., N.Y. Mem. staff Gen. Electric Corp., Schenectady, NY, 1949—85, mgr. materials info. svcs., 1971-82, cons. engring. and mfg., 1982-85; pres., prin., cons. Sci-Tech Knowledge Sys., Scotia, NY, 1985-91, Brookline Techs., Ballston Spa, NY, 1991—. Trustee Engring. Info. Inc., N.Y.C., 1977-80, chmn. indsl. data comm., mem. exec. com. Codata, 1988-94; cons. in field. Author: Material Memories of the Mohawk-Hudson Region, 2007; editor: Intermetallic Compounds, 1967, various other books; co-editor: Intermetallic Compounds: Principles and Practice, Vols. 1 and 2, 1994, Vol. 3, 2002; mem. editl. adv. bd. CRC Handbook of Chemistry and Physics, 1994-97; contbr. publs. and book reviews. Mem. zoning bd. Town of Ballston, N.Y., 1966-72; bd. edn. Ballston Spa Sch. Dist., 1970-76. With USN, 1944-46. Recipient Turner award Electrochem. Soc., 1957, Hofmann prize Lead Devel. Assn., 1971, Rensselaer Poly. Inst. Outstanding Career award, 1988; NAS traveling fellow to USSR, 1971. Fellow AAAS, Am. Ceramic Soc., Am. Soc. Metals (Campbell lectr. 1976, Jeffries lectr. 1979, Sauveur award 2001), Am. Inst. Chemists, Inst. Physics U.K.; mem. ASTM (Templin award 1959), AIME (New Eng. Regional Conf. award 1963), Inst. Materials (U.K.), Nat. Acad. Engring. Achievements include 6 patents in field. Avocations: old house restoration, history of science and technology. Home: 5 Brookline Rd Ballston Spa NY 12020 Office Phone: 518-309-3579. Personal E-mail: westbrookjh@earthlink.net.

WESTBROOK, JAMES EDWIN, law educator; b. Camden, Ark., Sept. 7, 1934; s. Loy Edwin and Helen Lucille (Bethea) W.; m. Elizabeth Kay Farris, Dec. 23, 1956; children: William Michael, Robert Bruce, Matthew David. BA with high honors, Hendrix Coll., 1956; JD with distinction, Duke U., 1959; LLM, Georgetown U., 1965. Bar: Ark. 1959, Okla. 1977, Mo. 1982. Assoc. Mehaffy, Smith & Williams, Little Rock, 1959-62; asst. counsel, subcom. of U.S. Senate Jud. Com., Washington, 1963; legis. asst. U.S. Senate, Washington, 1963-65; asst. prof. law U. Mo., Columbia, 1965-68, asst. dean, 1966-68, assoc. prof., 1968-70, prof., 1970-76, 80—, James S. Rollins prof. law, 1974-76, 80—, Earl F. Nelson prof. law, 1982-99, emeritus prof., 1999—, interim dean, 1981-82; dean U. Okla. Coll. Law, Norman, 1976-80. George Allen vis. prof. law, U. Richmond, 1987; vis. prof. law Duke U., 1988, Washington U., St. Louis, 1996, 2001; reporter Mid-Am. Assembly on Role of State in Urban Crisis, 1970; dir. Summer Internship Program in Local Govt., 1968; cons. various Mo. cities on drafting home-rule charters; mem. Gov.'s Adv. Coun. on Local Govt. Law, 1967-68, Fed. Practice Com. U.S. Dist. Ct. (we. dist.) Mo., 1986-90; chmn. Columbia Charter Revision Commn., 1973-74; mem. spl. com. labor relations Mo. Dept. Labor and Indsl. Rels., 1975; mem., chmn. subcom. on domestic violence Task Force on Gender and Justice, Mo. Jud. Conf., 1990-93; mem. com. to rev. govtl. structure of Boone County, Mo., 1991. Author: (with L. Riskin) Dispute Resolution and Lawyers, 1987, supplement, 1993, 3d edit., 2005, (with L. Riskin, C. Guthrie, T. Heintz, J. Robbennolt and R. Reuben); contbr. articles to profl. jours. Chair search com. for chancellor U. Mo., Columbia, 1992, chair search com. for provost, 1998; mem. fin. com. Roman Cath. Diocese of Jefferson City, 2003—. Mem. ABA, Nat. Acad. Arbitrators, Assn. Am. Law Schs. (chmn. local govt. law round table coun. 1972), Ctrl. States Law Sch. Assn. (pres. 1982-83), Mo. Bar Assn. (vice chmn. labor law com. 1986-87, chmn. 1987-88, Spurgeon Smithton award 1995), Order of Coif, Blue Key, Alpha Chi. Roman Catholic. Home: 3609 S Woods Edge Rd Columbia MO 65203-6606 Office: U Mo Sch Law Columbia MO 65211-0001 Home Phone: 573-446-0605. Personal E-mail: professorjwestbrook@gmail.com. Business E-Mail: westbrookje@missouri.edu.

WESTBROOK, JAY LAWRENCE, law educator; b. Morristown, NJ, Dec. 11, 1943; s. Joel W. and Elaine Frances (Summers) W.; m. Pauline June Travis, Feb. 15, 1969; 1 child, Joel Mastin. BA in Polit. Sci./Philosophy, U. Tex., 1965, JD, 1968. Bar: Tex. 1968, DC 1969, US Ct. Appeals (DC cir.) 1969, US Supreme Ct. 1976, US Ct. Appeals (4th cir.) 1978, US Ct. Appeals (2d cir.) 1979. Assoc. Surrey & Morse (now Jones, Day, Reavis & Pogue), Washington, 1969-74; ptnr. Surrey & Morse (now Jones, Day & Reavis), Washington, 1974-80; mem. law faculty U. Tex., Austin, 1980—, Benno C. Schmidt Chair Bus. Law, 1991—. Vis. prof. U. London, 1990, Harvard Law Sch., 1991-92; advisor Tex. Internat. Law Jour., 1985-91; reporter Am. Law Inst. Transnat. Insolvency Project, 1994-2000; co-leader US delegation to UN Commn. on Internat. Trade Law Working Group on Model Law Internat. Insolvency, 1995-97, 99; sr. advisor Nat. Bankruptcy Rev. Com., 1997; mem. State Dept. Adv. Com. on Pvt. Internat. Law, 1997-2000; vis. scholar Humboldt U., Berlin, 2002. Co-author: As We Forgive Our Debtors: Bankruptcy and Consumer Credit in America, 1989 (Silver Gavel award ABA 1989), The Law of Debtors and Creditors: Text, Cases and Problems, 5th edit., 2005, Teacher's Manual, The Law of Debtors and Creditors, 5th edit., 2005, The Fragile Middle Class: Americans in Debt(Ann. Writing award Am. Coll. Consumer Fin. Svcs. Lawyers), 2000; contbr. articles to profl. jours. Grantee U. Tex. Law Sch. Found., 1982, U. Rsch. Inst., 1982-83, NSF, 1983-86, Policy Rsch. Inst., Lyndon Johnson Sch. Pub. Affairs, 1984, Tex. Bar Found., 1985, Nat. Inst. Child Health and Human Devel., 1986, Nat. Conf. Bankruptcy Judges, 1991, 93, Am. Coll. Banker, 2004. Mem. ABA (bus. bankruptcy com., vice chair internat. bankruptcy subcom. 1999—, Meyer rsch. grant 1986), Am. Law Inst., Am. Coll. Bankruptcy, Nat. Bankruptcy Conf., State Bar Tex. (governing coun. internat. sect. 1987-89), Internat. Insolvency Inst. (bd. dirs. 2000—), Internat. Acad. Comml. and Consumer Law (pres. 2008—), Order of Coif. Office: U Tex Sch Law 727 E Dean Keeton St Austin TX 78705-3224

WESTBROOK, LYNDA A., bank executive; b. Jersey City, July 27, 1960; d. Nicholas and Mildred Lucarelli; m. Kevin J. Westbrook, Apr. 28, 2001; m. Erik Vikjaer, Apr. 7, 1984 (div. Mar. 30, 1991); children: Amanda Vikjaer, Andrew Vikjaer. Grad., Cliffside Park H.S., NJ, 1978. Asst. v.p. Fifth Third Bank, Cin., 2000—. Diversity bd. mem. Fifth Third Bank, Cin., 2006—. Office: Fifth Third Bank 38 Fountain Square Plz MD10907E Cincinnati OH 45263 E-mail: lynda.westbrook@53.com.

WESTBY, TIMOTHY SCOTT, lawyer, researcher; b. Fargo, ND, Apr. 16, 1957; s. Joseph Arlo and Dorothy Mae (Nye) W.; m. Ann Amoroso Westby, June 16, 2001. SBChemE, MIT, 1979; PhDChemE, U. Tex., 1984; JD, U. Houston, 1994. Bar: Tex., U.S. Dist. Ct. (so. dist.) Tex., eastern dist, U.S. Patent and Trademark Office, U.S. Ct. Appeals (fed. cir., 5th cir.). Researcher Energy Lab., MIT, Cambridge, 1976-79; rsch. asst. U. Tex., Austin, 1979-84, teaching asst., 1981-83; assoc. rsch. engr. Shell Devel. Co., Houston, 1984-87, rsch. engr., 1987-91, sr. rsch. engr., 1991-94; assoc. Conley, Rose & Tayon, P.C., Houston, 1994—2002; shareholder, dir. Conley Rose, PC, Houston, 2002—. Mem. adv. com. Ohio Combustion Rsch., Columbus, 1985-90, Pa. Coal Rsch. Coop., University Station, 1986-89; adj. prof. chemistry Rice U., 1998—; spl. asst. atty. gen. State of ND, 2005-09. Contbr. articles to profl. jours.; patentee method for in situ coal drilling, patentee coal blends having improved ash viscosity. Campaigner United Way, Houston, 1989-91. Scholar MIT, 1975-79; fellow U.S. dept. Energy, 1979-82, Getty Oil Co., 1983-84. Mem. ABA, AIChE, ASTM (com. D-5 1989-94), ASME (advisor rsch. com. on corrosion and deposits from flue gases 1988—), N.Am. Catalysis Soc., Southwestern Catalysis Soc., Am. Intellectual Property Law Assn., Fed. Cir. Bar Assn., Bar Assn. 5th Fed. Cir., State Bar of Tex., Houston Bar Assn., Houston Intellectual Property Law Assn., Coll. of State Bar of Tex., Porsche Club Am. (bd. dirs., treas. 2001—). Avocations: golf, sailing, skiing, auto racing. Office: Conley Rose 600 Travis Ste 7100 Houston TX 77002-2912 Office Phone: 713-238-8000. Business E-Mail: twestby@conleyrose.com.

WESTCOTT, BRIAN JOHN, manufacturing executive; b. Rexford, NY, June 19, 1957; s. John Campbell and Norma (Cornell) W.; children: Sarah Katharine, Paul Brian. BS, Lehigh U., 1979; MS, Stanford U., 1980, PhD, 1987. Engr. Combustion Engring., Windsor, Conn., 1980-81; rsch. engr. Gen. Electric Corp. Rsch., Niskayuna, NY, 1981-83; rsch. fellow Stanford (Calif.) Grad. Sch. Bus., 1987-88; mgr. Gen. Electric Corp. Mgmt., Bridgeport, Conn., 1988-89; prin. A.T. Kearney Tech. Inc., Redwood City, Calif., 1989—2005; CEO Westt, Inc., Menlo Park, Calif., 1990—2005, eInnovate, Menlo Park, Calif., 1999—2005, TTOC, Inc., 2005—. Author: (with others) Paradox and Transformation, 1988; contbr. articles to profl. jours.; inventor, patentee in field. Mem. Menlo Park Vitality Task Force, 1993-94; mem. Lehigh U. Leadership Coun., 2002—. Recipient Tech 500 award Westt, Inc., 1996, 97, 98, Inc. 500 award, 1997, Silicon Valley Tech fast 50 award, 1997, 98, San Francisco and San Jose award for top 100 fastest growing pvt. cos.; co. named among Top 50 Fastest Growing Pvt. Cos. in San Francisco and San Jose, 2001; postdoctoral rsch. fellow Stanford U. Grad. Sch. Bus., 1987, 88; rsch. fellow Electric Power Rsch., Stanford, 1983-87. Mem. ASME. Avocations: sports, politics. Office: eInnovate 325 Sharon Park Dr # 321 Menlo Park CA 94025 Personal E-mail: westcottbj@yahoo.com.

WESTER, J. MEREDITH, lawyer; b. Louisville, Ky., Nov. 26, 1953; d. Eugene and Emma Louise Meredith; m. James Clinton Wester, Jr., Sept. 28, 1974; children: James Clinton III, Bradley Eugene, Mitchell Lewis. Degree with honors in Bus. Adminstrn., U. South Fla., Tampa, 1988; JD, Stetson U., St. Petersburg, Fla., 1990. Bar: U.S. Ct. Appeals (11th cir.) Fla. 1991, U.S. Dist. Ct. (mid. dist.) Fla. 1991, U.S. Dist. Ct. (no. dist.) Fla. 1992, U.S. Dist. Ct. (so. dist.) Fla. 1992. Assoc. Ruden McCloskey Smith Schuster & Russell, Tampa, Fla., 1994—99; mng. ptnr. Litig. Mechanik Nuccio Hearne & Wester, P.A., Lutz, Fla., 2000—. Chmn. 13th jud. cir. grievance com. Fla. Bar, Tampa, 2003—06. Contbr. articles to profl. jours. Sec. FBI Nat. Citizens Acad., Washington, 2005—; dir. FBI Tampa Citizens Acad. Alumni, Tampa, 2003—; mem. water mgmt. basin bd. S.W. Fla. N.W. Hillsborough County, Tampa, 1995—99; pres. head start cmty. found. Hillsborough County, Tampa, 1997—2005, dir. PACE (Practical Academic and Cultural Edn.) for girls, 2001—06. Recipient Best Pub. Student Article award, Stetson Univ., 1990. Mem.: ATLA, ABA, Fla. Assn. Women Lawyers, Am. Inns Ct., Hillsborough Bar Assn. (dir. found. 1994—2004, dir. county chpt. 1998—2002). Office: Mechanik Nuccio Hearne & Wester PA 18560 N Dale Mabry Hwy Lutz FL 33548 Office Fax: 813-968-1502. Business E-Mail: jmw@mechaniknuccio.com.

WESTER, JOHN CHARLES, bishop; b. San Francisco, Nov. 5, 1950; B in Philosophy, St. Joseph's Coll., Mt. View, Calif.; M, St. Patrick's Coll.; M in Applied Spirituality, U. San Francisco; M in Pastoral Counseling, Holy Names Coll. Ordained priest Archdiocese of San Francisco, 1976, vicar for clergy, 1997-98, aux. bishop, 1998—2007; assoc. pastor St. Raphael Parish, San Rafael, Calif., 1976-79; tchr. Marin Cath. HS, 1979-82, asst. supt. schs., 1979, dir. campus ministry, 1982-84, pres., 1984-86; pastor St. Stephen Parish, San Francisco, 1993-97; ordained bishop, 1998; bishop Diocese of Salt Lake City, 2007—. Roman Catholic. Office: Diocese of Salt Lake City 27 C St Salt Lake City UT 84103 Office Phone: 801-328-8641. Office Fax: 801-328-9680.

WESTERBERG, GARY W., lawyer; b. Fergus Falls, Minn., Jan. 1, 1945; BA, Cornell U., 1968; JD, So. Meth. U., 1971. Bar: Ill. 1971, US Dist. Ct. (no. dist. Ill.) 1973, US Dist. Ct. (dist. Ariz.) 1997, US Ct. Appeals (3rd cir.) 1982, US Ct. Appeals (7th cir.) 1972, US Ct. Appeals (10th cir.) 1982, US Surpeme Ct. 2007. Ptnr. Lord, Bissell & Brook, Chgo. Editor: Jour. Air Law & Commerce, 1970—71. Mem.: NTSB Bar Assn., ABA, Lawyer-Pilots Bar Assn., Internat. Assn. Def. Counsel, Internat. Bar Assn., Order of the Coif. Office: Locke Lord Bissell & Liddell LLP 111 S Wacker Dr Chicago IL 60606 Office Phone: 312-443-0245. Office Fax: 312-896-6245. E-mail: gwesterberg@lockelord.com.

WESTERFIELD, PUTNEY, management consulting executive; b. New Haven, Feb. 9, 1930; s. Ray Bert and Mary Beatrice (Putney) W.; m. Anne Montgomery, Apr. 17, 1954; children: Bradford, Geoffrey, Clare. Grad., Choate Sch., 1942-47; BA, Yale, 1951. Co-founder, v.p. Careers, Inc., NYC, 1950-52; mgr. S.E. Asia Swen Publs., Inc., Manila, Philippines, 1952; mem. joint adv. commn. Korea, 1953-54; polit. officer Am. embassy, Saigon, Vietnam, 1955-57; asst. to pub. Time mag., NYC, 1957-59, asst. circulation dir., 1959-61, circulation dir., 1961-66, asst. pub., 1966-68, Life mag., NYC, 1968; pub. Fortune mag., NYC, 1969-73; pres. Chase World Info. Corp., NYC, 1973-75; v.p. Boyden Assocs. Internat., San Francisco, 1976-80, sr. v.p., western mgr., 1980-84, pres., chief exec. officer NYC, 1984-90, San Francisco, 1984—90, mng. dir. NYC, San Francisco, 1990—2005. Bd. dirs. Urban League, N.Y.C., 1969-71, Children's Village, 1968-71, Mediterranean Sch. Found., 1969-71, Nat. Boys Club, 1970-73, U.S. -S. Africa Leaders Exch. Program, 1971-03, Bus. Coun. Internat. Understanding, 1974-76, Yale-China Assn., 1975-78, East Meets West Found., 1991—2007; trustee Choate Sch., Wallingford, Conn., 1967-76, Westover Sch., Middlebury, Conn., 1975-79, Watch Hill Chapel Soc., 1963-77, Assn. Yale Alumni, 1972-75, 80-83. Mem. Burlingame Country Club, Pacific Union Club, Bohemian Club. Home and Office: 10 Greenview Ln Hillsborough CA 94010-6424 E-mail: putneyw@pacbell.net.

WESTERFIELD, RANDOLPH W., finance educator, former dean; BA in Econs., UCLA, 1963, MA in Econs., 1965, PhD in Fin., 1968. Asst. prof. fin. The Wharton Sch., U. Pa., Phila., 1968-73, assoc. prof. fin., 1973-81, sr. rsch. assoc., Rodney L. White Ctr. Fin. Rsch., 1977-88, prof. fin., 1981-88, chair fin. dept., 1986-88; Charles B. Thornton prof. fin., bus. econs. chair U. So. Calif. Sch. Bus. Adminstrn., LA, 1988-93; dean, Robert R. Dockson chair in bus. adminstrn. Marshall Sch. Bus., U. So. Calif., LA, 1993—2004. Bd. dirs. William Lyon Homes, 2000-, Health Mgmt. Assocs. Inc., 2000-, Nicholas Applegate Growth Equity Fund; vis. prof. fin. U. Nova de Lisbon, Portugal, 1981, Stanford U., Palo Alto, Calif., 1981-82, Claremont (Calif.) Grad. Sch., 1983; mem. trust com. Continental Bank, Phila., 1979-88; mem. pension rsch. coun., The Wharton Sch., 1979-88; mem. editl. adv. bd. John Wiley & Sons (Asia) Pte Ltd., 1996; mem. authors adv. coun., Times Mirror-Irwin Co., 1987-97; chmn. Consortium for Grad. Study in Mgmt., 1997; past cons. AT&T, Mobil Oil, UN, U.S. Depts. Labor and Justice. Co-author: (with Stephen A. Ross, Jeffrey Jaffe) Corporate Finance, 1988, 90, 93, 96 (including Can., Australian and internat. edits.), (with Stephen A. Ross, Bradford D. Jordan) Fundamentals of Corporate Finance, 1992, 93, 95, 97 (including South African, Can., Australian, Chinese, Dutch and Spanish edits.), (with Stephen A. Ross, Bradford D. Jordan) Essentials of Corporate Finance, 1996; author monographs; contbr. chpts. to books, numerous articles to profl. jours. and conf. procs.; assoc. editor Fin. Rev., 1985-92. Mem. Nat. Assn. Corp. Bds. (mem. bd. L.A. chpt. 1996). Office: Marshall Sch Bus Adminstrn U So Calif Hoffman Hall 800 701 Exposition Blvd Los Angeles CA 90089-0001

WESTERGAARD, GEORGE HENRY, secondary school educator; b. Sumas, Wash., Aug. 4, 1942; s. Henry C. and Mary T. Westergaard; m. Donna M. Westergaard, June 20, 1964; 1 child, Kristen. BA in Edn., Ctrl. Wash. State Coll., 1964; MS in Interdisciplinary Studies, U. Oreg., Eugene, 1969; DA in History, Carnegie Mellon U., Pitts., 1976. Cert. secondary edn. tchr., Wash. Tchr. social studies and English Woodrow Wilson Jr. H.S., Yakima, Wash., 1964-67, Cal Young Jr. H.S., Eugene, 1967-73; mem. staff, asst. rsch. historian Carnegie Mellon U., Pitts., 1971-73; tchr. social studies, counselor Thomas Jefferson Jr. H.S., Eugene, 1973-83; tchr. govt., econs., global studies, and psychology South Eugene H.S., 1983-88, tchr. social scis., chair social studies dept., 1988-94, tchr. advanced placement govt. and politics, 1994-99; tchr. advanced placement psychology, comp. govt., politics, US history Sammamish H.S., Bellevue, Wash., 1999—. Cons. AP Govt. and Politics workshops, 1990—; adj. prof. edn. U. Oreg., summer 1991; mem. social studies task force State of Oreg., 1997-99; nat. reader, question leader AP Gov. and Politics; adj. prof. Pacific Luth. U., 2001-05; editor, writer govt. and politics curricula and texts; chmn. program devel. Sammamish H.S., 2002-05 Mem. budget rev. com. Bellevue Sch. Dist. Fellow Ind. Study in the Humanities, 1986; Ednl. Cons. fellow. Avocations: photography, fishing, hiking, boating. Home: 6228 Sunlight Shores Ln Clinton WA 98236 Office Phone: 360-321-2609. Personal E-mail: westergg@comcast.net.

WESTERGARD, BILLIE, project engineer; b. Bingham City, Utah, Oct. 7, 1939; s. Orlee A. and Roma A. Westergaard; m. Sylvia Ann Devenney, July 25, 1942; children: Shelly Rene, Holly Lynn, William Lorin, Lara Lea. Design engr. DuPont Co., Wilmington, Del., 1962—80, project engr., 1980—93; cons. design engr. pvt. practice, 1994—2007, Bechtel Co., Richland, Wash., 2007—. Author: Hotson/Westergard Universe; contbr. scientific papers on particle spin and mass transfer. Trustee, sec. Mt. Cuba Astron. Obs., 1990—2007. Flight engr. USAF, 1960—80. Mem.: Del. Astron. Soc. (pres.), Nat. Philosophy Alliance. Avocations: astronomy, fishing, travel. Office: Bechtel Co 2435 Stevens Ctr Pl Richland WA 99354-1874 Home: 1499 Goddard Ave Seneca SC 29678-4673 Business E-Mail: westerb@udel.edu.

WESTERGREN, TIMOTHY BROOKS, music company executive; b. 1965; BA in Computer Acoustics & Recording Tech., Stanford U., 1988. CEO Nightfly Studios; co-founder Music Genome Project/Savage Beast Technologies, 2000—; founder, chief strategy officer Pandora, 2000—. Composer: (films) The Last Best Sunday, 1999, Now & Then: From Frosh to Seniors, 1999, (ballets) Defying Gravity, 1999. Named a Maverick, Details mag., 2007. Fellow: World Network Found. Office: Pandora 360 22nd St Ste 440 Oakland CA 94612 Office Phone: 510-451-4100. Office Fax: 510-451-4286.

WESTERHOFF, JOHN HENRY, III, priest, theologian, educator; b. Paterson, NJ, June 28, 1933; s. John Henry and Nona Celia (Walsh) W.; m. Alberta Louise Barnhart, Dec. 27, 1955 (div. 1991); childen: Jill Louise, John Jeffrey, Beth Anne; m. Caroline Askew Hughes, Oct. 27,

1991. BS, Ursinus Coll., 1955; STB, Harvard U., 1958; EdD, Columbia U., 1974; DD, Ursinus Coll., 1990. Ordained to ministry United Ch. of Christ, 1958. Episcopal Ch., 1978; pastor Congl. Ch., Presque Isle, Maine, 1958-60, assoc. pastor Needham, Mass., 1960-64; pastor 1st Congl. Ch., Williamstown, Mass., 1964-66; edn. sec., editor Colloquy (United Ch. Bd. for Homeland Ministries), NYC, 1966-73; Lentz lectr. Harvard U. Div. Sch., 1973-74; prof. Duke U. Div. Sch., Durham, NC, 1974-94; dir. Inst. Pastoral Studies, Atlanta, 1992—2003; interim rector St. Bartholomew Episcopal Ch., Atlanta, 1993-94; theologian in residence St. Lukes Episcopal Ch., Atlanta, 1994—2004; vis. prof. Gen. Theol. Sem., NYC, 2004—05; priest assoc., resident theologian St. Anne's Episc. Ch., Atlanta, 2005—. Author: Values for Tomorrows Children, 1970, A Colloquy on Christian Education, 1972, Generation to Generation, 1974, Tomorrow's Church, 1976, Will Our Children Have Faith?, 1976, McGuffey and His Readers, 1978, Who Are We?, 1978, Learning Through Liturgy, 1978, Inner Growth-Outer Change, 1979, The Church's Ministry in Higher Education, 1979, Liturgy and Learning Through the Life Cycle, 1980, Christian Believing, 1980, Bringing Up Children in The Christian Church, 1980, A Faithful Church, 1981, The Spiritual Life: Learning East and West, 1981, Building God's People, 1983, A Pilgrim People, 1984, Living the Faith Community, 1985, On the Threshold of God's Future, 1986, Living Into Our Baptism, 1990, Schooling Christians, 1992, The Spiritual Life: Foundation for Preaching and Teaching, 1994; A People Called Episcopalians, 1995, Holy Baptism: A Guide for Parents and Godparents, 1996, Grateful and Generous Hearts, 1997, To Love and to Cherich Till Death Do Us Part, 1998, Sensing Beauty, 1998, A Pilgrim People, 1999, Will Our Children Have Faith?, 2000, Living Faithfully as a Prayer Book People, 2005; editor: Religious Edn, 1979-89. Mem. Assn. Profs. and Researchers in Religious Edn., Religious Edn. Assn. Democrat. Episcopalian. Personal E-mail: johnwest33@bellsouth.net.

WESTERHOUT, GART, retired astronomer; b. The Hague, The Netherlands, June 15, 1927; arrived in U.S., 1962, naturalized, 1969; s. Gerrit and Magdalena (Foppe) W.; m. Judith Mary Monaghan, Nov. 14, 1956; children: Magda C., Gart T., Brigit M., Julian C. Drs., Leiden U., Netherlands, 1954, PhD, 1958. Asst. Leiden U. Observatory, 1952-56, sci. officer, 1956-59, chief sci. officer, 1959-62; prof., dir. astronomy U. Md., 1962-73, chmn. div. math. and phys. scis. and engring., 1972-73, prof. astronomy, 1973-77; sci. dir. U.S. Naval Observatory, Washington, 1977-93; vis. astronomer Max Planck Inst. Radio Astronomy, Bonn, Germany, 1973-74, mem. adv. bd., 1976-79. Mem. astronomy adv. bd. NSF, 1963-67; vice chmn. divsn. phys. sci. NRC, 1969-73; mem. com. on radio frequencies, 1971-92; trustee Assoc. Univs. Inc., 1971-74; mem. Inter Union Commn. on Allocation of Frequencies, 1974-82; mem. sci. coun. Stellar Data Ctr., Strasbourg, France, 1978-84, chmn., 1981; chmn. working group on astrometry, astronomy survey com. NAS, 1979-81; mem. adv. bd. Haystack-N.E. Radio Obs. Consortium, 1974-77; mem. Arecibo adv. bd. Nat. Astronomy and Ionosphere Ctr., 1977-80, chmn., 1979-80; mem. U.S. nat. com. CODATA, 1985-91. Contbr. on radio astronomy, spiral structure of our Galaxy and astrometry to profl. jours. Recipient citation for teaching excellence Washington Acad. Scis., 1972; U.S. Sr. Scientist award Alexander von Humboldt Stiftung, Ger., 1973; NATO fellow, 1959. Mem. Internat. Astron. Union (chmn. working group on astron. data 1985-91), Internat. Sci. Radio Union (pres. commn. on radio astronomy 1975-78), Am. Astron. Soc. (councillor 1975-78, v.p. 1985-87), Royal Astron. Soc. Roman Catholic.

WESTERLUND, LI, law educator; BSEE, Brännkyrka Upper Secondary Sch., Stockholm, 1986; JD, U. Uppsala, Sweden, 1993, LLM with Honors, 1993; LLD in Doctoral Biotech Patents, U. Stockholm, 2001. Bar: Calif. 2001, Uppsala U. (Jur Kand) 1993, Swedish Bar Assn. 2004, cert.: Adminstrv. Ct. Dist. Stockholm (jr. judge) 1996. Of counsel IMIR, Environ. Inst., Uppsala, 1992—94; law clk., jr. judge Adminstrv. Dist. Ct., Stockholm, 1994—96; legal rsch. asst. Stockholm U., 1997—2001; jud. intern Ct. Appeals Fed. Cir., Washington, 2000—01; European legal specialist McKenna Long and Aldridge, Washington, 2001—02; sr. assoc. RydinCarlsten, Stockholm, 2003—04; dir. intellectual property rights Bavarian Nordic A/S, Kvistgård, Denmark, 2004—07; v.p. global IP Bavarian Nordic Inc., Washington, 2007—. Lectr., examiner intellectual property law Stockholm U., 1997—2001, dir. master in law course, 2001; regular lectr. Karolinska Inst., Stockholm, 1999—2004; prof. intellectual property law Linköping U., Sweden, 2004—. Author: (books) Biotech Patents - Equivalency & Exclusions under European and U.S. Patent Law, 2001, Legal Reflections on Biological Material Stored in Bio Banks, 2001, Life Science Inventions - The Hurdles of Law, 2004; contbr. articles to profl. jours., chapters to books. Mem. supervisory bd. dirs. Zacco A/S, Hellerup, Denmark, 2005; mem. supervisory bd. dir. Nemoscience, Germany, 2005. Grantee, Bank Sweden Tercentenary Found., 1997—2001; fellow, RCAST Tokyo U.; vis. scholar, George Wash. U. Law Sch., 2000—01; Rsch. fellow, MaxPlanck Inst., Munich, 1999, Rsch. grant, STINT, 2000—01. Mem.: Swedish Intellectual Property Assn., Am. Intellectual Property Law Assn. (assoc.). Achievements include research in European and US patent laws: Biotech Inventions; bio-banks: interdisciplinary project; New Zealand study regarding sustainable development and the Rio-Convention; Malaysia study regarding EIA assessment. Avocations: scuba diving, writing. Office: Bavarian Nordic Inc 2900 K St NW S Bldg Ste 501 Washington DC 20007-5118 Office Fax: 202-536-1579. Business E-Mail: li.westerlund@bavarian-nordic.com.

WESTERMAN, DONNA DAY, artist; b. Detroit, June 22, 1940; d. James McAdam and Mary Elizabeth (McGibbon) Day; m. Jan Hendrik Westerman, Sept. 28, 1967 (div. May 2001); 1 child, Johanna Louise. Student, U. Mich., Ann Arbor, 1958—60, Boston Mus. Sch., 1962; BFA, MFA, Otis Art Inst., L.A., 1966. Tchr. art various mus. and schs., Mass. and Calif., 1960—76; emeritus prof. Orange Coast Coll., Costa Mesa, Calif., 1976—2007, founder, dir. computer graphics program, 1979—91, chmn. art dept., 1995—2005. Owner Saltlick Studios, Newport Beach, Calif., 1987—; curator confs. and symposiums; spkr. in field. Author: One-Of-A-Kind Artists Books; author, reviewer mag. Bookways, 1993; artist, creator cast glass, cast bronze and carved wood, archtl. commns.; exhibited in various shows nat. & internat., 1954-. Dir., vol. art program Santiago Sch., Santa Ana, 1976—78; mem. support group Big Bros./Big Sisters, Orange County, Calif., 1987—94; mem. edn. com. Bowers Mus., Santa Ana, 1975—80. Recipient Outstanding Calender Design award Printing Inst. Am., 1975; State of Calif. grantee, 1983-84. Mem.: Soc. Children's Book Writers and Illustrators, Guild Natural Sci. Illustrators, Wood Engravers' Network, Orange County Arts Alliance (officer, bd. dirs.), LA Women of Letters, LA Printmaking Soc. (bd. dirs., pres., chair 18th Nat. Printmaking Exhbn.). Avocations: photography, book binding, gardening, walking.

WESTERMANN, EDWARD BURTON, military officer, analyst, educator; b. Temple, Tex., Nov. 18, 1961; s. Francis X. and Suzann Westermann; m. Brigitte Angelika Engel, Dec. 16, 1991; children: Sarah E, Marie-Louise. BS, USAF Acad., 1984; MA in European History, Fla. State U., 1992; MA, Sch. Advanced Airpower Studies, Maxwell AFB, 1997; PhD in European History, U. N.C., 2000. Helicopter Pilot USAF, 1985. Commd. 2d lt. USAF, 1984, advanced through grades to col.; exch. instr. pilot with German air force Hubschraubertransportgeschwader 64, Ahlhorn, Germany, 1988—91; asst. prof. history U.S. Air Force Acad., Colorado Springs, 1992—95; strategy devel. officer Hdqs. European Command, Stuttgart, Germany, 2000—02; prof. comparative mil. theory Sch. Advance Air and Space Studies, Maxwell AFB, Ala., 2002—; sr. mil. prof. USAF Acad., 2006—08; comdr. USAF, Basic Mil. Training, 2008—. Selected mem. internat. adv. panel Royal Air force Ctr. for Air Power Studies, 2007. Author: (historical work) Hitler's Police Battalions: Enforcing Racial War in the East, Flak: German Anti-Aircraft Defenses, 1918-1945. Decorated Ehrenkreuz der Bundeswehr in Bronze Fed. Rep. Germany; recipient John L. Snell prize, 1998, League of WWI Aviation Historians Nat. award, 1999; fellow, German Academic Exch. Svc., U. Calif. Berkeley, 1993, Fulbright fellow, U.S. Govt., 1994—95, U.S. Holocaust Meml. Mus., 1999, German Academic Exch. Svc., 1999, 2003—04. Mem.: Soc. Mil. History (Mancado prize 2002), Am. Hist. Assn., German Studies Assn., Daedalians (life), Phi Alpha Theta. Independent. Roman Catholic. Home: 110 Yount Cir Lackland AFB TX 78236 Office: 737th Training Group Lackland AFB TX 78236 Office Phone: 210-671-4222. Personal E-mail: bawebw4@aol.com. Business E-Mail: edward.westermann@lackland.af.mil.

WESTERMEYER, JOSEPH JOHN, psychiatrist; b. Chgo., Apr. 8, 1937; m. Rachel Moga; children: Michelle, Joseph; 5 foster children. Student, U. Notre Dame and St. Thomas Coll., 1955-57; BS in Biology and Chemistry, U. Minn., 1959, MD, 1961, MA in Anthropology, 1969, MPH, PhD, 1970. Diplomate Am. Bd. Psychiatry and Neurology, Am. Bd. Family Practice. Rotating intern St. Paul-Ramsey Hosp., 1961-62; gen. practice medicine Payne Ave. Med. Clinic, St. Paul, 1962-65; dep. chief divsn. pub. health AID, Laos, 1965-67; resident in psychiatry U. Minn., Mpls., 1967-70, instr., 1970-71, asst. prof., 1971-74, assoc. prof., 1974-78, prof. psychiatry, 1978—, prof., chair, 1989, adj. prof. anthropology, 1979—89, 1993—, adj. prof. psychology, 1979—89, dir. med. student edn. dept. psychiatry, 1976-82; mem. psychiatry staff, outpatient psychiat. practice U. Minn. Hosps. and Clinics, Mpls., 1970-89; prof., chmn. dept. psychiatry and behavioral sci. Okla. U. Med. Ctr., Oklahoma City, 1989—92; founder, dir. acute in-patient service U. Minn. Hosps. and Clinics, Mpls., 1970-72, founder, dir. day hosp., 1971-73, cons. primary care clinic, 1970-83, founder, dir. outpatient clinic for refugees from S.E. Asia, 1977—89, founder, dir. program for alcohol and drug dependence, 1982—89, founder, dir. internat. clinic dept. psychiatry, 1984—89; chief psychiatry, dir. mental health Mpls. VA Med. Ctr., 1993—. Mem. ad hoc com. on Indochinese refugees Minn. Dept. Pub. Welfare, 1980-82; cons. methadone program Minn. VA Hosp., 1977-84, dept. psychiatry Mpls. VA Hosp., 1978-85; mem. case devel. com. for computer-based exam. Nat. Bd. Med. Examiners, 1983-88; mem. com. on mental and behavioral assessment and disorder in pilots FAA and AMA, 1984-85; chmn., co-editor devel. of a teaching manual on drug/alcohol dependence WHO, 1982-85, chmn., co-editor task force and report on methadone treatment in opiate dependence, 1982-85, research cons. internat. collaborative study of drug dependence intervention and treatment in primary health care, 1982-85; sec. Group for Advancement of psychiatry, 1999-2005, co-chair addiction psychiatry cert. Am. Bd. Psychiatry and Neurology, 2003-, Spl. Polulation Com. Health Svc Rsch VA, 2005-; cons. in field; vis. prof. various colls.; lectr. in field. Author: A Primer on Chemical Dependency: A Clinical Guide to Alcohol and Drug Problems, 1976, Poppies, Pipes and People: A Study of Opium and Its Use in Laos, 1983, (with C. Williams) Refugees Mental Health Issues in Resettlement Countries, 1986, A Clinical Guide to Drug and Alcohol Problems, 1986; (with A. Arif) A Manual for Substance Abuse Education, 1988, An Update on Methadone, 1988; The Psychiatric Care of Migrants, 1989; editor: Anthropology and Mental Health, 1976; co-editor: (with E. Foulks, R. Wintrob and A. Favazza) Transcultural Psychiatry, 1977, (with R. weiss and D. Ziedonis) Comorbid Affective Disorder and Substance Abuse, Johns Hopkins Press, 2003; contbr. revs. and articles to profl. jours., chpts. to books; mem. editorial bd. Am. Jour. Drug and Alcohol Abuse, 1973—, Jour. Operational Psychiatry, 1977-86, Am. Jour. Pub. Health, 1980-83, 83-87, Advances in Alcohol and Substance Abuse, 1980—, Alcoholism: Clin. and Exptl. Research, 1980-86, Alcohol and Research World, 1981—; social sci. editor Substance Abuse Newsletter, 1979-83; rev. reader Am. Jour. Psychiatry, 1978—, Transcultural Psychiat. Revs., 1980-84, Archives Gen. Psychiatry, 1981—, White Cloud Jour., 1981—, Jour. Nervous and Mental Disease, 1977—, Current Anthropology, 1979, 83, 85, Culture, Medicine and Psychiatry, 1979-80, various others. Recipient Meritorious Service award U.S. AID, 1967; Ginzburg fellow Group for Advancement of Psychiatry, 1969-70, NIH summer fellow Grad. Session in Epidemiology, U. Minn. Continuation Ctr., 1970, 72, 78; research grantee Office Internat. Programs, U. Minn., 1974-75, 78, 81, NIMH, 1973-74, 80-81, 82-84, Nat. Inst. Alcohol Abuse and Alcoholism, 1974-77, 78-79, Grad. Sch. U. Minn., 1977-78, Office Drug Abuse Prevention, U. Minn., 1977-78, Minn. Med. Found., 1974-75, 81, 82-83, Nat. Inst. Drug Abuse, 1977-78, 83-85, State Minn., 1979-80, Ctr. Urban and Regional Affairs, U. Minn., 1982-83, career tchr. grantee Alcohol, Drug Abuse and Mental Health Adminstrn., HEW, 1973-75, Biomed. research support grantee U. Minn. Med. Sch., 1977-78, Minn. Med. Found., 1977, tng. grantee Office Alcohol and Other Drug Abuse Programming, U. Minn., 1979-83, Indochinese Health Professionals, 1979-81, Archie; recipient neumerous other research grants. Fellow Am. Anthropol. Assn., Am. Assn. Family Practice, Am. Psychiat. Assn. (com. on drug abuse 1985—); mem. World Psychiat. Assn. (transcultural sect.), Am. Soc. Social Psychiatry, Soc. Med. Anthropology, Assn. Med. Educators and Researchers in Substance Abuse (award for disting. contributions to the field 1987), AAAS, Assn. Behavioral Sci. and Med. Edn., Assn. Acad. Psychiatrists, Am. Pub. Health Assn., Research Soc. on Alcoholism, World Psychiat. Assn. (sect. on transcultural psychiatry), Soc. for Study of Psychiatry and Culture (steering com. 1979—, secretariat 1984-85), Am. Med. Soc. on Alcoholism (state chmn. 1979—), Am. Acad. Psychiatrists in Alcoholism and Addictions, Soc. Traumatic Stress Studies, Minn. Psychiat. Assn. (mem. chem. dependency subcom. 1979—85, mem. Minn. mental health interdisciplinary interest group rep. 1980-85, pres. 1984-86), Minn. State Med. Assn. (resource group on alcoholism and other chem. dependencies 1976-81), Alpha Omega Alpha. Home: 1935 Summit Ave Saint Paul MN 55105-1430 Office Phone: 612-725-2037. Business E-Mail: joseph.westermeyer@med.va.gov, weste010@umn.edu.

WESTERN, BRUCE, sociologist, educator; BA with first class honors in Govt., Univ. Queensland, Australia, 1987; MA, UCLA, 1990, PhD, 1993. Asst. prof., sociology Princeton Univ., 1994—98, assoc. prof., 1998—2000, faculty assoc., Office Population Rsch., 1993—, prof., sociology, 2000—. Editl. bd. Political Analysis, 2001—, Sociological Methodology, 2001—, Socio-Economic Review, 2002—. Fellow: Am. Arts. & Scis.; mem.: Sociological Rsch. Assn., Soc. Advancement of Socio-Economics (exec. coun. 2002—05), Soc. Comparative Rsch. (exec. dir. 2002—05), Population Assn. Am., Australian Sociological Assn., Am. Statistical Assn., Am. Sociological Assn. Office: Dept Sociology Wallace Hall Princeton Univ Princeton NJ 08544 Office Phone: 609-258-2445. Office Fax: 609-258-2180. Business E-Mail: western@princeton.edu.

WESTERNOFF, TRENT H., surgeon; s. Philip H. and Dorothy A. Westernoff; m. Nazly Mehdizadeh, Aug. 29, 2003. BA with honors, U. Calif., Santa Barbara, 1994; MD, U. Calif., San Francisco, 2001; DMD cum laude, Harvard U., Boston, 1998. General Surgery Internship U. of Calif., 2002; Oral and Maxillofacial Surgery Univeristy of Calif., 2004. Oral and maxillofacial surgery resident U. Calif., San Francisco, 1998—2004, gen. surgery intern, 2001—02; commd. 2d lt. US Army, advanced through grades to maj., 2004, oral and maxillofacial surgeon El Paso, Tex., 2004—05, 2006—, combat maxillofacial surgeon Mosul, Iraq, 2005; credentialling com. mem., drug audit officer US Army Dentac, El Paso, 2006—. Mem. pharmacy and therapeutics com. William Beaumont Army Med. Ctr., El Paso, 2006—07. Steering com. mem. United Way Found., Santa Barbara, Calif., 1992—93; mem. big brother/big sister program Harvard Med./Dental Sch., Boston, 1994—97; participant Cambridge Children's Oral Health Program, Mass., 1997. Decorated Meritorious Svc. medal US Army, Order of the Combat Spur; recipient Student Scholarship award, Sigma Chi Found., 1993, Oral Biology award, Am. Assn. Oral Biologists, 1998; scholar, US Army, 1995—98. Fellow: Am. Dental Soc. Anesthesiology, Am. Assn. Oral and Maxillofacial Surgery, Nat. Dental Bd. Anesthesiology, Am. Bd. Oral and Maxillofacial Surgeons; mem.: Calif. Assn. Oral and Maxillofacial Surgeons (assoc.), Am. Coll. Oral and Maxillofacial Surgeons (assoc.), Am. Acad. Cosmetic Surgery (assoc.), Am. Legion, Thomas Barnes Hitchcock Soc., Golden Key Nat. Honor Soc. (life; sec. 1992—93), Sigma Chi Frat. (treas. 1992—93). Avocations: bicycling, running, skiing, travel.

WESTERVELT, GAYLE GAETANO, physical education educator; b. Utica, NY, Mar. 26, 1950; d. Felix Louis and Jeanne LaQuay Gaetano; m. Terry E. Westervelt, Aug. 3, 1975; 1 child, Marisa G. BS in Edn., SUNY, Cortland, 1973; postgrad., SUNY, Oneonta, 1976, St. Rose, Albany, NY, 1977—78. Cert. phys. edn. N.Y. Lifeguard and instr. swimming Town of Boonville, NY, 1967—73, Adirondack Ctrl. Sch., 1971—72; recreation instr. Cortland Dept. Pks. and Recreation, 1972—73; encore team facilitator Cobleskill-Richmondville Ctrl. Sch., Cobleskill, NY, 1993, phys. educator, 1973—, asst. athletic dir., 2001—, dist. health coord., 2004—. Chmn. health adv. com. Cobleskill-Richmondville Ctrl. Sch. Sch. and Cmty., Cobleskill, 2004—, coord. sch. health index, 2004—; mem. fit before 5 com. Bassett Hosp., Cobleskill, 2004—05; advisor Gymnastics Club, 1973—2002; coach girls basketball, girls tennis. Recipient N.Y. State Sportsmanship awards, 2002—05; Fitness grantee, BOCES, 1996, 1997, Health and Fitness grantee, BOCO and NYSPHERD, 2006. Mem.: Am. Assn. Health, Phys. Edn., Recreation and Dance, N.Y. Assn. Health, Phys. Edn., Recreation and Dance. Avocations: painting, swimming, gardening, interior decorating. Home: 244 Philip Schuyler Rd Cobleskill NY 12043 Office Phone: 518-234-8368 2030. Fax: 518-234-3950. E-mail: catboy@telenet.net.

WESTERVELT, ROBERT MOORE, physics educator; b. Phila., Oct. 9, 1949; s. Robert Moore and Marie Louise (Jefferson) W. BS in Physics with honors, Calif. Inst. Tech., 1971; PhD in Physics, U. Calif., Berkeley, 1977; AM (hon.), Harvard U., 1986. Prof. physics and applied physics Harvard U., Cambridge, Mass., 1979-84, assoc. prof. physics and applied physics, 1984-86, prof. physics, Gordon McKay prof. applied physics, 1986—. Co-chmn. Gordon Conf. on Condensed Matter Physics, 1988; bd. editors Physica D-Nonlinear Phenomena, 1986-90. Recipient Ross N. Tucker Meml. award Intel Corp., 1977; Chancellor's fellow U. Calif. Berkeley, 1971. Mem. Am. Phys. Soc. Office: SEAS Harvard U 29 Oxford St Cambridge MA 02138

WESTFALL, LYNN D., oil industry executive; B in Chem. Engring., U. Tex.; MBA, U. Houston. Process engr. Amoco Chems. Corp., 1975; v.p. strategy and strategic issues Ultramar Diamond Shamrock, San Antonio; v.p. devel. and bus. analysis Tesoro Corp., San Antonio, 2002—05, v.p., chief economist, 2005—06, sr. v.p. external affairs, chief economist, 2006—. Office: Tesoro Corp 300 Concord Plz San Antonio TX 78216-6999 Office Phone: 210-283-2000.

WESTFALL, SANDRA SOBIERAJ, journalist; d. John and Mary Lou Sobieraj; m. Franklin Edward Westfall Jr., Nov. 15, 2003. Grad., Princeton U.; M in Journalism, Stanford U. Assoc. press reporter Dole for Pres.; White House corr. Assoc. Press; Washington bur. chief People Mag. Recipient Merriman Smith award: Print Category, White House Correspondents Assn., 2001, 2009. Office: 1130 Connecticut Ave NW Ste 900 Washington DC 20036

WESTFIELD, FRED MEINHARD, economics professor; b. Essen, Germany, Nov. 7, 1926; came to U.S., 1940; s. Dietrich and Grete (Stern) W.; m. Joyce A. Horwitz Nochlin, Nov. 15, 1968; stepchildren: Steven Nochlin, Keith Nochlin. BA magna cum laude, Vanderbilt U., 1950; PhD in Indsl. Econs., MIT, 1957. Teaching asst., instr. MIT, Cambridge, 1952-53; lectr. Northwestern U., Evanston, Ill., 1953-57, asst. prof., 1957-60, assoc. prof., 1960-65; prof. econs. Vanderbilt U., Nashville, 1965-98, mem. faculty coun. Coll. Arts and Sci., 1974-76, mem. faculty senate, 1979-82, 94-95, dir. undergrad. studies dept. econs. and bus. adminstrn., 1984-87, mem. grad. faculty coun., 1991, prof. econs. emeritus, 1998—. Vis. prof. U. Colo., summers 1973-74; condr. seminars, lectr., participant univs. and rsch. orgns.; Fulbright sr. lectr. U. Nac. del Sur, Argentina, 1986; cons. Coun. Econ. Advisers, Exec. Office Pres., 1968, World Bank and Water and Power Devel. Authority, Pakistan, 1970-72, World Bank and East African Power and Light Co., Kenya, 1975, NSF, 1975, FTC, 1976-78, World Bank, UN Devel. Program and Econ. Planning Bd. South Korea, 1975-76; expert witness Tenn. Pub. Svc. Commn., 1980-89, Consumer Advocate Tenn. Atty. Gen., 1994; also others. Mem. editl. bd. Utilities Policy, 1990—2002, mem. bd. editors So. Econ. Jour., 1973—75, editl. referee Am. Econ. Rev., Jour. Polit. Economy, Econometrica, So. Econ. Jour., Econ. Inquiry; contbr. articles and book revs. to profl. jours. With US Army, 1945—46. Fellow Gen. Edn. Bd., MIT, Ford Found., 1958-59. Mem. Am. Econ. Assn., Econometric Soc. (program com. 1967, chmn. conf. sessions), So. Econ. Assn. (v.p. 1976-77, chmn. conf. sessions), Phi Beta Kappa. Home: 1097 Lynnwood Blvd Nashville TN 37215-4540

WESTHAUS, PAUL ANTHONY, retired physics professor; b. St. Louis, Dec. 10, 1938; s. Bernard Joseph and Florence Helen Westhaus; m. Wei Wang, July 5, 1995. BS, St. Louis U., 1961; PhD, Wash. U., St. Louis, 1966. Prof. physics Okla. State U., Stillwater, 1968—2008, emeritus prof. physics, 2008—. Contbr. articles to profl. jours. Treas. Birth Choice Stillwater, 1973—2008. Fellow, Woodrow Wilson Found., 1961—63, NASA, 1963—66. Roman Catholic. Avocations: travel, reading, music. Office: Dept Physics Okla State Univ Stillwater OK 74078 Office Fax: 405-744-6811. Business E-Mail: paul.westhaus@okstate.edu.

WESTHEAD, PAUL, former professional basketball coach; b. Phila., Feb. 21, 1939; m. Catherine Westhead; children: Monica, Patrice, Paul Jr., Julie. Grad., St. Joseph's Coll., Phila., 1961; MA, Villanova U. Head coach La Salle Coll., Phila., 1970-79; asst. coach LA Lakers, 1979, head coach, 1979—82, Chgo. Bulls, 1982-83, Loyola Marymount U., 1985-90, Denver Nuggets, 1990—92, George Mason U., 1993—97, Am.

Basketball Assn., 2000—01, Japanese Pro League, 2001—03; asst. coach Orlando Magic, 2003—05; head coach Phoenix Mercury, 2005—07; asst. coach Seattle Supersonics, 2007—08, Okla. City Thunder, 2008. Achievements include head coach of the NBA Championship winning Los Angeles Lakers, 1980; head coach of the WNBA Championship winning Phoenix Mercury, 2007.*

WESTHEIMER, GERALD, optometrist, educator; b. Berlin, May 13, 1924; naturalized, 1944, came to U.S., 1951; s. Isaak and Ilse (Cohn) W. Optometry diploma, Sydney Tech. Coll., Australia, 1943, fellowship diploma, 1950; BSc, U. Sydney, 1947; PhD, Ohio State U., 1953; DSc (hon.), U. NSW, Australia, 1988; ScD (hon.), SUNY, 1990; MD (hon.), U. Tubingen, 2005. Practice optometry, Sydney, 1945-51; research fellow Ohio State U., 1951-53; prof. physiol. optics U. Houston, 1953-54; asst. prof., then assoc. prof. physiol. optics Ohio State U., 1954-60; postdoctoral fellow neurophysiology Marine Biol. Lab., Woods Hole, Mass., 1957; vis. researcher Physiol. Lab., U. Cambridge, Eng., 1958-59; mem. faculty U. Calif. at Berkeley, 1960—, prof. physiol. optics, 1963-68, chmn. group physiol. optics, 1964-67, prof. physiology, 1968-89, prof. neurobiology, 1989—, head div. neurobiology, 1987-92; adj. prof. Rockefeller U., N.Y., 1992—. Sackler lectr. Tel Aviv U. Med. Sch., 1988, D.O. Hebb lectr. McGill U., 1991, Grass Found. lectr. U. Ill., 1991, Wertheimer lectr. U. Frankfort on the Main, 1998; mem. com. vision NRC, 1957-72; mem. visual scis. study sect. NIH, 1966-70, chmn. visual scis. B study sect., 1977-79; mem. vision, research and tng. com. Nat. Eye Inst., NIH, 1970-74, chmn. bd. sci. counselors, 1981-83; mem. exec. council com. vision NAS-NRC, 1969-72; mem. communicative scis. cluster Pres.'s Biomed. Rsch. Panel, 1975, Enuch Lectr., Wash. U. Med. Sch., 2009. Author rsch. papers; editor: Vision Rsch., 1972-79; editl. bd. Investigative Ophthalmology, 1973-77, Exptl. Brain Rsch., 1973-89, Optics Letters, 1977-78, Spatial Vision, 1985—, Ophthalmic and Physiological Optics, 1985—, Vision Rsch., 1985-92, Jour. of Physiology, 1987-94. Recipient Von Sallman prize Columbia U., 1986; Prentice medal Am. Acad. Optometry, 1986, Bicentennial medal Australian Optometric Assn., 1988, Named Order of Australia, 2009 Fellow AAAS, Royal Soc. London (Ferrier lectr. 1992, editl. bd. procs. 1990-96, 2000-06), Am. Acad. Arts and Scis., Optical Soc. Am. (Tillyer medal 1978, assoc. editor jour. 1980-83), Am. Acad. Optometry; mem. Royal Soc. New So. Wales, Soc. Neurosci., Assn. Rsch. in Vision and Ophthalmology (Proctor medal 1979), Internat. Brain Rsch. Orgn., Physiol. Soc. Gt. Britain, Sigma Xi, Gen. Divsn. AM (order of Australia 2009). Home: 582 Santa Barbara Rd Berkeley CA 94707-1746 Business E-Mail: gwestheimer@berkeley.edu.

WESTHOFF, CAROLYN LOUISE, obstetrician, gynecologist, epidemiologist, educator; b. Nov. 17, 1951; MD, U. Mich., 1977. Cert. Ob-Gyn., 1986. Intern in ob-gyn. Henry Ford Hosp., Detroit, 1977—78; resident in epidemiology SUNY Downstate, Bklyn., 1978—82; fellow London Sch. Hygiene and Tropical Medicine, 1982—83; prof. ob-gyn. Columbia U., NYC, prof. epidemiology and population and family, dir. family planning and preventive medicine. Mem.: Inst. Medicine. Office: Presbyn Hosp Rm 1669 630 W 168th St New York NY 10032 Office Phone: 212-305-9368. E-mail: clw3@columbia.edu.*

WESTIN, DAVID LAWRENCE, broadcast executive, lawyer; b. Flint, Mich., July 29, 1952; s. Lawrence Rae and Mary Louise (Holman) W.; m. Victoria Peters; children: Victoria, Elizabeth, Matthew. BA, U. Mich., 1974, JD, 1977. Bar: D.C. 1979. Law clk. U.S. Ct. Appeals (2d cir.), NYC, 1977-78, U.S. Supreme Ct., Washington, 1979; assoc. Wilmer, Cutler & Pickering, Washington, 1979-84, ptnr., 1985-91; sr. v.p., gen. counsel Capital Cities/ABC, Inc., NYC, 1991-93; pres. of prodn. ABC TV Network, NYC, 1993-94, pres., 1994-97, pres. of news, 1997—. Lectr. Harvard U. Law Sch., Cambridge, Mass., 1986; adj. prof. Georgetown U. Law Ctr., Washington, 1989-91. Bd. dirs. Lincoln Ctr. Film. Soc., 1994—, Am. Arbitration Assn., 1991—. Recipient duPont-Columbia U. award, 2009. Mem.: Chevy Chase (Md.). Democrat. Presbyterian. Office: ABC TV Network 47 W 66th St Fl 5 New York NY 10023-6201*

WESTLAKE, BLAIR, computer software company executive; JD, Whittier Law Sch., 1979. Bar: Calif. Atty. Great Western Fin. Corp., 1979—82, Universal Studios Inc., 1982—85, dir. bus. affairs studio ops., 1985—87, v.p. & sr. v.p. bus. & legal affairs home entertainment group, 1987—93, exec. v.p. home entertainment group, 1993—96, pres. worldwide pay TV, 1996—97, chmn. TV & Networks group, 1997—2001; corp. exec. v.p. Gemstar-TV Guide Internat., 2001; corp. v.p. media & entertainment group Microsoft Corp., Redmond, Wash., 2004—. Bd. dir. Digital Entertainment Group, ContentGuard Inc., Digital Coast Roundtable; media cons. Comcast Corp., NBC Universal. Recipient Alumni award for bus. excellence, Whittier Coll. Sch. Law, 2002, Spl. Founders award, Media & Entertainment Council, 2007. Mem.: Internat. Acad. Television Arts & Sciences (mem. exec. com.), Acad. of Television Arts & Sciences, Acad. of Motion Picture Arts & Sciences, Paley Ctr. for Media, Pacific Council on Internat. Policy. Office: Microsoft Corp 1 Microsoft Way Redmond WA 98052-6399

WESTLEY, JOHN RICHARD, economist; b. Fairmont, Minn., Feb. 25, 1939; s. Richard and Margaret (Kindschi) W.; m. Sidney Kathryn Bohanna, Mar. 26, 1966(div. Sept. 1977); children: Elizabeth Laura, Karen Margaret, Marian Bohanna; m. Joan Nancy Ehrlich, Apr. 12, 1980; 1 child, Katherine Matthea. BA in Philosophy, Yale U., 1961; MA in Econs., Columbia U., 1966; PhD in Econs., Am. Univ., 1983. Internat. economist U.S. Dept. Treasury, Washington, 1966-69; loan officer U.S. AID, Addis Ababa, Ethiopia, 1970-72, economist Nairobi, Kenya, 1973-75, Washington, 1976-78, program officer New Delhi, 1979-84, dir. mission to Bangladesh Dhaka, 1985-87, assoc. asst. adminstr. bur. Africa Washington, 1987-90, dir. mission to Kenya Nairobi, 1990-94; dir. Mission to Egypt US AID, Cairo, 1994-98; v.p. Internat. Fund Agrl. Devel., Rome, 1998—2002; adj. assoc. prof. econs. John Cabot U., Rome, 2002—. Author: Agriculture and Equitable Growth, 1986. With U.S. Army, 1961-64. Mem. Am. Econ. Assn., Phi Beta Kappa, Cosmos Club (Washington). Presbyterian. Office: John Cabot Univ Via Della Lungara 233 00165 Rome Italy Business E-Mail: jwestle@johncabot.edu.

WESTLING, JOHN T., retail executive; m. Donna Westling. With Nash Finch Co.; assoc. Wal-Mart Stores, Inc, 1988, dept. mgr., asst. mgr., asst. buyer, buyer, merchandise mgr., v.p. divisional merchandising mgr. household chemicals and papergoods, 1998—2001, sr. v.p. gen. merchandising mgr. consumables, 2001, sr. v.p. replenishment, pricing, & planning, now exec. v.p. replenishment, pricing, & planning. Bd. mem. Children's Miracle Network, Will Golf for Kids, 1st Tee, Global 20/20 program. Office: Wal-Mart Stores, Inc 702 SW 8th St Bentonville AR 72716-8611*

WESTLING, JON, university administrator; b. Yakima, Wash., June 7, 1942; s. Norman L. and Jean R. (Bergamini) W.; m. Elizabeth A. Wüthrich, Oct. 14, 1977; children: Emma E., Matthew R., Andrew N. BA, Reed Coll., 1964; postgrad., St. John's Coll. Oxford U., Eng., 1964-67, UCLA, 1971-74. Instr. history Centre Coll., Danville, Ky., 1967-68; asst. prof. history and humanities Reed Coll., Portland, Oreg., 1968-71; assoc. dir. Boston Univ. Prodns., 1974-76; asst. to pres. Boston U., 1976-79, assoc. provost, 1979-83, provost ad interim, 1983-84, provost, 1984-88, exec. v.p., 1988-90, interim pres., 1990, exec. v.p., provost, 1991-95, provost, pres.-elect, 1995-96, pres., 1996—2002, pres. emeritus, 2002—. Bd. dirs. Century Bank. Bd. dirs. Jobs for Mass., Inc., 1998—, Boston 2000, 1987—2000; trustee Boston Mus. Sci., 1990—; mem. corp. Nat. Braille Press, Inc., 1998—; trustee Am. Coll. Greece, 1998—; bd. dirs. Boston History Collaboration, 2000—, treas., 2001—. Gen. Motors Nat. scholar, 1960-64, Rhodes scholar, 1964-67. Office: Boston Univ Office Pres 147 Bay State Rd Boston MA 02215-1708 also: Boston Univ 121 Bay State Rd Boston MA 02215

WESTLUND, BEN (BERNARD JOHN WESTLUND II), state treasurer; b. Long Beach, Calif., Sept. 3, 1949; s. Bernard John and Dorothy W.; m. Libby Westlund; 2 children. BA in History, Whitman Coll., 1972; postgrad, U. Oreg., 1973. Corp. sec. Mgmt. Mktg. Assocs. Inc., 1973—77, Am. Fossil, 1977—78; pres. Westlund Wood, Republic, Wash., 1980; owner Juniper Butte Ranch, Mitchell, Oreg., 1980, High Country Herefords; ptnr. Westlund Investment Co., Lake Oswego, Oreg., 1980; mem. Dist. 53 Oreg. House of Reps., 1996—2004; mem. Dist. 27 Oreg. State Senate, 2003—08; treas. State of Oreg., 2009—. Mem.: Young Republicans, Multnomah Athletic, Sigma Chi. Club. Office: State Treasurer 350 Winter St NE Ste 100 Salem OR 97301-3896 Office Phone: 503-378-4329. Business E-Mail: Oregon.Treasurer@state.or.us.*

WESTMAN, CARL EDWARD, lawyer; b. Youngstown, Ohio, Dec. 12, 1943; s. Carl H. and Mary Lillis (Powell) W.; m. Carolyn J., July 17, 1965; children: C. Forrest, Stephanie A. BBA, Sam Houston State U., 1966; JD, U. Miami, 1969, LLM in Taxation, 1972. Bar: Fla. 1969. Ptnr. Frost & Jacobs, 1983-93, Roetzel & Andress, 1993-98; adminstrv. ptnr. Steel, Hector & Davis, Naples, Fla., 1999—2004, Cohen & Grigsby, 2004—08, Gary Robinson, 2009—. Trustee David Lawrence Found. for Mental Health, Inc., 1976-86, chmn., 1985-86; trustee Pikeville Coll., 1993-2005; trustee, 1991, chmn. NCH Healthcare Sys. Inc., 2005—, chmn. profl. capabilities com. physician credentialing, 1998—; trustee, chmn. Naples Cmty. Hosp., 2001; past pres. bd. trustees, elder Moorings Presbyn. Ch. Master lic. capt. USCG. Mem. Fla. Bar Assn., Collier County Bar Assn., Estate Planning Coun., Marco Island Marina Assn. (pres.). Home: 1952 Crayton Rd Naples FL 34102-5070 Office: Gray-robinson 5551 RidgeWood Dr Ste 101 Naples FL 34108 Office Phone: 239-430-1800. Business E-Mail: carl.westman@gray-robinson.com.

WESTMAN, CRAIG ELLERY, academic administrator; s. Franklin A. and Virginia Westman Vickers; m. Lee Ann Elliott Westman, Aug. 14, 1993; children: Madeleine Lee, Erica Grace, Jillian Grace, Paige Martha. BA, Fla. Atlantic U., 1988, MA, 1990; PhD, Fla. State U., 1997. Asst. registrar Fla. State U., Tallahassee, 1993—98; registrar Ferris State U., Big Rapids, Mich., 1998—2000, assoc. dean enrollment svcs., 2000—. Cons. enrollment mgmt. Ferris State U., Big Rapids, Mich., 2003—06. Author: AACRAO's Guide to Basic Enrollment Management, 2005, Gamers Go To College, 2006. V.p.bd. trustees Woodbridge Group, Big Rapids, Mich., 2000—06. Recipient Distinguished Staff award, Ferris State U., 2004. Office: Ferris State U 1201 South State St Ste 201 Big Rapids MI 49307 Business E-Mail: westmanc@ferris.edu.

WESTMAN, JACK CONRAD, child psychiatrist, educator; b. Cadillac, Mich., Oct. 28, 1927; s. Conrad A. and Alice (Pedersen) W.; m. Nancy K. Baehre, July 17, 1953; children— Daniel P., John C., Eric C. MD, U. Mich., 1952. Diplomate Am. Bd. Psychiatry and Neurology. Intern Duke Hosp., Durham, NC, 1952-53; resident U. Mich. Med. Ctr., 1955-59; dir. outpatient svcs. Children's Psychiat. Hosp., Ann Arbor, Mich., 1961-65; assoc. prof. U. Mich. Med. Sch., 1964-65; coord. diagnostic and treatment unit Waisman Ctr., U. Wis., Madison, 1966-74, prof. psychiatry, 1965-96, prof. emeritus, 1997—. Cons. Joint Commn. on Mental Health of Children, 1967-69, Madison Pub. Schs., 1965-74, Children's Treatment Ctr., Mendota Mental Health Inst., 1965-69 Author: Individual Differences in Children, 1973, Child Advocacy, 1979, Handbook of Learning Disabilities, 1990, Who Speaks for the Children?, 1991, Licensing Parents, 1994, Born to Belong, 1997, Parenthood in America, 2001; editor Child Psychiatry and Human Devel., 1984-99, Breaking the Adolescent Parent Cycle, 2009; contbr. articles to profl. jours. Vice-pres. Big Bros. of Dane County, 1970-73; v.p. Wis. Assn. Mental Health, 1968-72; co-chmn. Project Understanding, 1968-75; pres. Wis. Cares, 1998—. With USNR, 1953-55. Fellow Am. Psychiat. Assn., Am. Coll. Psychiatrists, Am. Acad. Child and Adolescent Psychiatry, Am. Orthopsychiat. Assn. (bd. dirs. 1973-76); mem. Am. Assn. Psychiat. Svcs. for Children (pres. 1978-80), Multidisciplinary Acad. Clin. Edn. (pres. 1992-98, Canyon scholars, trustee 2000-). Home: 1234 Dartmouth Rd Madison WI 53705-2214 E-mail: jwestman@wisc.edu.

WESTMORE, MICHAEL GEORGE, make-up artist, writer; b. Hollywood, Calif., Mar. 22, 1938; s. Montague George and Edith Adeline Westmore; m. Marion Christine Bergeson, Dec. 4, 1965; children: Michael George, Michele, McKenzie. BA, U. Calif., Santa Barbara, 1961. Apprentice make-up artist Universal City Studios, Universal City, Calif., 1961-63, staff make-up artist, 1964, asst. head dept. make-up lab., 1965-71; freelance make-up artist various studios, Hollywood, Calif., 1971-87; make-up supr. and designer Paramount Studios, Hollywood, 1987—2005. Instr. theatre arts dept. Los Angeles Valley Coll., 1966—71; pres. Cosmetic Control Ctrs., Inc., 1971—76, Hollywood Magic Cosmetics, 1985—87; rsch. cons., lectr. therapeutic cosmetics for med. assns. Author: The Art of Theatrical Make-Up for Stage and Screen, 1971; contbr. chapters to books; co-author: Star Trek Makeup FX Journal, Star Trek-Aliens & Artifacts; make-up artist TV spls. Eleanor and Franklin (Emmy award NATAS, 1976), Why Me? (Emmy award, 1984), Three Wishes of Billy Grier (Emmy award, 1985), Star Trek (Emmy award, 1988, 1992, 1993, 1995, 1996, Emmy nomination, 2005), Amazing Stories (Emmy award, 1987), make-up artist films 2010 (Acad. award nomination, 1985), Mask (Acad. award, 1986), Clan of the Cave Bear (Acad. award nomination, 1987), Star Trek First Contact (Acad. award nomination, 1996); contbr. articles to Make-Up Artists mag. Served with AUS, 1956. Recipient Best Spl. Effects Make-up on TV for Geppetto award, Hollywood Make-up Artists Guild, 2001, Emmy, 1977, 1985, 1987, 1990, 1992, 1993, 1995, 1996, 1997, 1998, 1999, 2001, 2002, 2003, 2004, 2005, Three Emmys, 1978, Two Emmys, 1986, 1988, 1989, 1991, 1994, 2000, Spl. Achievement award, Canadian Space Channel, 2007, Star on Hollywood Walk of Faure, 2008; nominee Emmy, 1973, 1976. Mem.: Archive of Am. TV, Internat. Alliance Theatrical Stage Employees, Knights of the Vine, Soc. Make-up Artists, Vikings of Scandia, Lambda Chi Alpha (life Order of Achievement award). Address: 4616 Balboa Blvd Encino CA 91316-4105

WESTMORELAND, ANDREW, academic administrator; m. Jeanna Westmoreland; 1 child, Riely. BA, Ouachita Baptist U., 1979; MA in Polit. Sci., U. Ark., Fayetteville; PhD in Higher Edn. Adminstrn., U. Ark., Little Rock. With Ouachita Baptist U., 1979—2006, prof. polit. sci. and edn., exec. v.p., v.p. devel., pres., 1998—2006, Samford U., Birmingham, Ala., 2006—. Cons., evaluator Higher Learning Commn. Author: Leading by Design, 2005. Office: Samford U 800 Lakeshore Dr Birmingham AL 35229 Office Phone: 205-726-2011.*

WESTMORELAND, LYNN A., United States Representative from Georgia; b. Atlanta, Apr. 2, 1950; m. Joan Eskew; children: Heather, Marcy, Trae. Attended, Ga. State U. Mem. Ga. Ho. Reps., Atlanta, 1992—2004, US Congress from 8th Ga. dist., 2005—07, mem. Govt. Reform com., Small Bus. com., transp. and Infrastructure com.; mem. US Congress from 3rd Ga. dist., 2007—. Mem. Fayette Bd. Realtors, Ga., Nat. Bd. Realtors. Mem.: Midwest Ga. Homebuilders Assn. Republican. Baptist. Office: US Ho Reps 1118 Longworth Ho Office Bldg Washington DC 20515-1008 also: 1601-B E Highway 34 Newnan GA 30265 Office Phone: 202-225-5901. Office Fax: 202-225-2515.*

WESTOFF, CHARLES FRANCIS, demographer, educator; b. NYC, July 23, 1927; s. Frank Barnett and Evelyn (Bales) Westoff; m. Joan P. Uszynski, Sept. 11, 1948 (div. Jan. 1969); children: David, Carol; m. Leslie Aldridge, Aug. 1969 (div. Feb. 1993); m. Jane DeLung, May 1997. AB, Syracuse U., NY, 1949, MA, 1950; PhD, U. Pa., Phila., 1953. Instr. sociology U. Pa., 1950—52; rsch. assoc. Milbank Meml. Fund, NYC, 1952—55; rsch. assoc. Office Population Rsch. Princeton U., NJ, 1955—62, Maurice P. During '22 prof. demographic studies and sociology, 1962—99, prof. emeritus, 1999—, sr. rsch. demographer, 1999—, chmn. dept. sociology, 1965—70, assoc. dir. Office Population Rsch., 1962—75, dir., 1975—92; assoc. prof. sociology NYU, also chmn. dept. sociology Washington Sq. Coll., 1959—62; vis. sr. fellow East-West Population Inst., Honolulu, 1979—81; Disting. vis. prof. Am. U., Cairo, 1979; mem. vis. com. Harvard-MIT Joint Ctr. for Urban Studies, 1980—83. Exec. dir. Commn. Population Growth and Am. Future, 1970—72; mem. adv. com. on population stats. US Bur. Census, 1973—79; chmn. Nat. Com. for Rsch. on 1980 Census, 1981—88; bd. dirs. Alan Guttmacher Inst., 1977—88, 1989—; sr. tech. advisor Demographic Health Surveys, 1984—; bd. dirs. Population Resource Ctr., 1985—, Population Ref. Bur., 1988—94, Population Commns. Internat., 1992—98; com. on population NAS, 1983—88. Co-author: Family Growth in Metropolitan America, 1961, The Third Child, 1963, College Women and Fertility Values, 1967, The Later Years of Childbearing, 1970, From Now to Zero, 1971, Reproduction in the United States, 1965, 1971, Toward the End of Growth: Population in America, 1973, The Contraceptive Revolution, 1976, Demographic Dynamics in America, 1977, Mass Media and Reproductive Behavior in Africa, 1997, New Estimate of Unmet Need and the Demand for Family Planning, 2006, Unmet Need at the End of the Century, 2002, Reproductive Preferences in Developing Countries at the Turn of the Century, 2002, Trends in Marriage and Early Childbearing in Developing Countries, 2006, Recent Trends in Contraception and Abortion in Twelve Countries, 2005, The Stall in the Fertility Transition in Kenya, 2006, Religion, Religiousness and Fertility in the US and in Europe, 2007, Religiousness and Fertility in the among European Muslims, 2007; contbr. articles on demography and sociology to profl. jours.; co-author: A New Approach to Estimating Abortion Rats, 2009. Recipient Irene Taueber award for Outstanding Rsch. Contbns., 1995. Fellow: Am. Acad. Arts and Scis.; mem.: Internat. Union Sci. Study Population (Laureate award 2007), Population Assn. Am. (bd. dirs. 1960—62, 1968—70, 1st v.p. 1972—73, pres. 1974—75), Planned Parenthood Fedn. Am. (dir. 1978—81), Inst. Medicine-NAS. Home: 1 Highland Rd Princeton NJ 08540 Office: Princeton U Wallace Hall Princeton NJ 08544 Business E-Mail: westoff@princeton.edu.

WEST-OLATUNJI, CIRECIE, science educator; b. Albany, NY; PhD, U. New Orleans, 1997. Asst. prof. Xavier U., New Orleans, 1998—2002, U. Fla., Gainesville, 2003—. Office: Univ Fla 1204 Norman Hall PO Box 117046 Gainesville FL 32611 Office Fax: 352-846-2697. Business E-Mail: cwestolatunji@coe.ufl.edu.

WESTON, ARTHUR WALTER, chemist, consultant, retired chemicals executive; b. Smith Falls, Ont., Can., Feb. 13, 1914; came to U.S., 1935, naturalized, 1952; s. Herbert W. and Alice M. (Houghton) W.; m. V. Dawn Thompson, Sept. 10, 1940; children: Roger L., Randall K., Cynthia B. BA, Queen's U., Kingston, Ont., 1934, MA, 1935; PhD, Northwestern U., 1938. Postdoctoral fellow Northwestern U., Evanston, Ill., 1938-40; with Abbott Labs., North Chgo., Ill., 1940-79, dir. rsch. and devel., 1959-61, v.p. rsch. and devel., 1961-68, dir. company, 1959-68, v.p. sci. affairs, 1968-77, v.p. corp. licensing, 1977-79; v.p., dir. San-Abbott, Japan, 1976-79; cons. Abbott Labs., North Chgo., Ill., 1979-85; pres. Arthur W. Weston & Assocs., Lake Forest, Ill., 1979—. Contbr. chapters to books, articles to profl. jours. Mem. Office Sci. Rsch. and Devel., War Manpower Commn., 1942-45; mem. exec. com. indsl. chemistry, div. chemistry and chem. tech. NRC, 1961-65; mem. indsl. panel on sci. and tech. NSF, 1974-80; mem. ad hoc com. chem. agts. Dept. Def., 1961-65. Mem. Rsch. Dirs. Assn. Chgo. (pres. 1965-66), Am. Chem. Soc. (trustee Chgo. 1965-2004, dir. Chgo. sect. 1952-59, nat. com. corp. assocs. 1967-72), Dirs. Indsl. Rsch., Indsl. Rsch. Inst. (bd. dirs. 1970-73), Phi Beta Kappa, Sigma Xi, Phi Lambda Upsilon. Achievements include patents in field. Home and Office: 349 Hilldale Pl Lake Forest IL 60045-3031 Personal E-mail: awweston@aol.com.

WESTON, FRANCINE EVANS, secondary school educator; b. Mt. Vernon, NY, Oct. 8, 1946; d. John Joseph and Frances (Fantino) Pisaniello. BA, Hunter Coll., NYC, 1968; MA, Lehman Coll., Bronx, NY, 1973; cert., Am. Acad. Dramatic Arts, NYC, 1976; PhD, NYU, 1991. Cert. elem., secondary tchr., NY; profl. devel. series completion cert. of achievement, Fed. Emergency Mgmt. Inst., US Dept. Homeland Security, 2006. Tchr. Yonkers Bd. Edn., NY, 1968—2007; aquatic dir. Woodlane Day Camp, Irvington-on-Hudson, NY, 1967—70, Yonkers Jewish Community Ctr., NY, 1971—75. Creative drama tchr. John Burroughs Jr. HS, Yonkers, 1971-77; stage lighting designer Iona Summer Theatre Festival, New Rochelle, NY, 1980-81, Yonkers Male Glee Club, 1981-89, Roosevelt HS, 1980-97; freelance, 1998—; rsch. specialist Scholarship Locating Svc., 1992-94, Yonkers Civil Def. Police Aux., 1994—; master electrician NYU Summer Mus. Theatre, 1979-80; appointed program developer for Cadet Acad. of Police & Fire Scis., Pub. Safety Magnet, Roosevelt HS, 2001-03, program dir., 2004-07. Actress in numerous comty. theater plays including A Touch of the Poet, 1979; dir. stage prodns. including I Remember Mama, 1973, The Man Who Came to Dinner, 1975; author: A Descriptive Comparison of Computerized Stage Lighting Memory Systems With Non-Computerized Systems, 1991, (short stories) A Hat for Louise, 1984, Old Memories: Beautiful and Otherwise, 1984; lit. editor: (story and poetry collection) Beautifully Old, 1984; editor: Command Post Dispatch quar., 1997—. Mem. Yonkers Civil Def. Police Aux., 1994—, adminstrv. asst. to comdg. officer, 1996—2004, capt. adminstrn., 2002—, capt., 2004—; steering com. chairperson Roosevelt H.S.-Middle States Assn. of Schs. and Colls. Self-Evaluation, 1985—88. Named Tchr. of Excellence, NY State English Coun., 1990, 95, 2000; recipient Monetary award for Tchg. Excellence, Carter-Wallace Products, 1992; President's Call to Svc. award, Lifetime award, USA Freedom Corps, 2005; named to Arrid Tchrs. Honor Roll, 1992. Republican. Roman Catholic. Avocations: swimming, theater.

WESTON, SIR JOHN (SIR PHILIP JOHN WESTON), retired diplomat; b. Apr. 13, 1938; s. Philip George and Edith Alice Bray (Ansell) W.; m. Margaret Sally Ehlers, 1967; 3 children. Grad. with 1st class honors, Worchester Coll., Eng.; student Chinese lang., Hong Kong, 1964-66, Peking, China, 1967-68. Joined diplomatic svc. Govt. of Gt. Britain, 1962, served Fgn. Office, 1962-63, 69-71, with Treasure Ctr. for Adminstrv. Studies, 1964, permanent rep. to EEC Brussels, 1972-74, asst. pvt. sec. to sec. state fgn. affairs and commonwealth affairs, 1974-76, counsellor, head EEC presidency secretariat Fgn. and Commonwealth Office, 1976-77, counsellor Brit. Embassy Washington, 1978-81, head def. dept. Fgn. and Commonwealth Office, 1981-84, asst. under-sec. state Fgn. and Commonwealth Office, 1984-85, min. Brit. Embassy Paris, 1985-88, dep. sec. to cabinet Cabinet Office, 1988-89, dep. under-sec. state def. Fgn. and Commonwealth Office, 1989-90, polit. dir. Fgn. and Commonwealth Office, 1990-92, amb., permanent rep. to NATO, also accredited to Western European Union Brussels, 1992-95; U.K. amb. to UN, U.K. permanent rep. UN Security Coun., NYC, 1995-98. Vis. fellow Old Souls Coll., Oxford (Eng.) U., 1977-78; hon. fellow Worcester Coll., Oxford, 2003. Chmn. governing body Sherborne Sch., 2001-07; trustee Nat. Portrait Gallery; Am. assoc. Royal Acad., 1999-2004; bd. govs. Ditchley Found., 2000-04; mem. coun. Internat. Inst. Strategic Studies, 2001-04; hon. pres. Cmty. Found. Network, 1999—. Served Royal Marines, 1956-58. Decorated knight comdr. St. Michael and St. George (Eng.); Order of Merit with star (Fed. Republic Germany). Address: 13 Denbigh Gardens Richmond Surrey TW10 6EN England

WESTON, JOHN FREDERICK, business educator, consultant; b. Ft. Wayne, Ind., Feb. 6, 1916; s. David Thomas and Bertha W.; children: Kenneth F., Byron L., Ellen J. BA, U. Chgo., 1937, MBA, 1943, PhD, 1948. Instr. U. Chgo. Sch. Bus., 1940-42, asst. prof., 1947-48; prof. The Anderson Sch. UCLA, 1949—, Cordner prof. The Anderson Sch., 1981-94, prof. emeritus recalled The Anderson Sch., 1986—, dir. rsch. program in competition and bus. policy, 1969—, dir. Ctr. for Managerial Econs. and Pub. Policy, 1983-86. Econ. cons. to pres. Am. Bankers Assn., 1945-46; disting. lecture series U. Okla., 1967, U. Utah, 1972, Miss. State U., 1972, Miami State U., 1975. Author: Scope and Methodology of Finance, 1966, International Managerial Finance, 1972, Impact of Large Firms on U.S. Economy, 1973, Financial Theory and Corporate Policy, 1979, 2d edit., 1983, 3d edit., 1988, Mergers, Restructuring and Corporate Control, 1990, Takeovers, Restructuring and Corporate Governance, 3d edit., 2000, Managerial Finance, 9th edit, 1992; assoc. editor: Jour. of Finance, 1948-55; mem. editorial bd., 1957-59; editorial bd. Bus. Econs., Jour. Fin. Rsch., Managerial and Decision Econs.; manuscript referee Am. Econ. Rev., Rev. of Econs. and Statistics, Engring. Economist, Bus. Econs., Fin. Mgmt. Bd. dirs. Bunker Hill Fund. Served with Ordnance Dept. AUS, 1943-45. Recipient Abramson Scroll award Bus. Econs., 1989-94; McKinsey Found. grantee, 1965-68; GE grantee, 1967; Ford Found. Faculty Rsch. fellow, 1961-62. Fellow Nat. Assn. Bus. Economists; mem. Am. Finance Assn. (pres. 1966, adv. bd. 1967-71), Am. Econ. Assn., Western Econ. Assn. (pres. 1962), Econometric Soc., Am. Statis. Assn., Royal Econ. Soc., Fin. Analysts Soc., Fin. Mgmt. Assn. (pres. 1979-80) Home and Office: UCLA 258 Tavistock Ave Los Angeles CA 90049-3229 Office Phone: 310-472-5110. Business E-Mail: jweston@anderson.ucla.edu.

WESTON, LOUANNE C., marriage and family therapist; Grad., Coll. William & Mary, Western Inst. for Social Rsch., Berkeley, Inst. Advanced Study Human Sexuality, San Francisco. Lic. Marriage & Family Therapist, diplomate Am. Coll. Sexologists, 1983, Am. Bd. Sexology, 1989. Marriage, family & child counselor pvt. practice. Fellow: Am. Acad. Clinical Sexologists; mem.: Am. Bd. Sexology (clinical supr.), Am. Assn. Marriage & Family Therapists, Calif. Assn. Marriage & Family Therapists, Soc. for the Scientific Study of Sexuality. Office: 5006 Sunrise Blvd Ste 106 Fair Oaks CA 95628 Office Phone: 916-961-2490. Office Fax: 916-965-1960. E-mail: louannecoleweston@sexmatters.com.*

WESTON, R. TIMOTHY, lawyer, government administrator; b. Los Angeles, Oct. 9, 1947; s. Robert Freidell and Thelma U. (Prince) W.; m. Mary T. Webber, May 3, 1986. BA cum laude in math., U. Calif., Santa Barbara, 1969; JD cum laude, Harvard U., 1972. Bar: Pa., US Dist. Ct. (ea. & mid. dist.) Pa., US Ct. Appeals (3rd & 4th cir.), US Supreme Ct. Asst. atty. gen. Pa. Dept. Environ. Resources, Harrisburg, 1972-79; assoc. dep. sec. Dept. Environ. Resources, 1979-87; ptnr. Kirkpatrick & Lockhart Preston Gates Ellis LLP. Bd. dirs. Interstate Conf. on Water Policy, Washington, chmn. 1984-85. Author: Public Rights in Pa. Waters, 1976, Ground Water Law in Pa., 1976; contbr. articles to profl. jours. Commr. Del. River Basin Commn., Trenton, NJ, 1979-87, Susquehanna River Basin Commn., Harrisburg, Pa., 1980-87, Ohio River Basin Commn., Lexington, Ky., 1979-87, Great Lakes Commn., Ann Arbor, Mich., 1987-88; mem. Am. Soc. Civil Engrs; bd. trustee Harrisburg U. Sci. & Tech., chair. Recipient Samuel Baxter Memorial award, by Water Resources Assn. of Delaware River Basin, 2001. Mem. ABA (sect. environ., energy & resources), ASCE, Phi Beta Kappa, Dauphin County Bar Assn., Pa. Bar Assn. Democrat. Editor-in-Chief, Harvard Civil Rights-Civil Liberties Law Review. Office: K&L Gates LLP 17 N 2nd St 18th Fl Harrisburg PA 17101-1507 Office Phone: 717-231-4504. Office Fax: 717-231-4501. Business E-Mail: tim.weston@klgates.com.

WESTON, RALPH EMERSON, JR., chemist; b. San Francisco, Nov. 9, 1923; s. Ralph E. and Ruth (Fields) W.; m. Virginia Louise Priest, May 26, 1951; children: Judith, Joan, Barbara. BS, U. Calif., Berkeley, 1946; PhD, Stanford U., 1950. Rsch. fellow Harvard U., Cambridge, Mass., 1949-51; from assoc. chemist to sr. chemist Brookhaven Nat. Lab., Upton, N.Y., 1951-94, guest scientist, 1994—. Vis. scientist Nuclear Rsch. Ctr., Saclay, France, 1960-61; vis. lectr. Columbia U., U. Calif. Co-author: Chemical Kinetics, 1972; contbr. numerous articles to profl. jours. 1st lt. USAF, 1943-46. Mem. Am. Chem. Soc., Sigma Xi, Phi Lambda Upsilon. Office: Brookhaven Nat Lab Chemistry Dept Upton NY 11973 Office Phone: 631-344-4373. Business E-Mail: weston@bnl.gov.

WESTON, ROGER LANCE, investment manager; b. Waukegan, Ill., Mar. 2, 1943; s. Arthur Walter and Vivian Dawn Weston; children: Cynthia Page, Kent Andrew, Arthur Eladio, Rebecca Dawn, Alice Sinclair, Elliot Churchill, Evan Walter, Spencer Lance. BS, MacMurray Coll., 1965; MBA, Washington U., St. Louis, 1967. Investment adviser Harris Trust & Savs. Bank, Chgo., 1967-69; sr. investment counselor Security Suprs., Chgo., 1969-70; gen. ptnr. Sierra Capital Group, Chgo., 1970-85; exec. v.p., treas., chief fin. officer Telemed Corp., Hoffman Estates, Ill., 1971-79; vice chmn. Bank Lincolnwood, Ill., 1979-85; pres., CEO, GSC Enterprises, Lincolnwood, 1979-85; chmn. bd. dirs., pres., CEO, GreatBanc, Inc., Chgo., 1986—. Mem. Barrington Hills (Ill.) Zoning Bd. Appeals, 1987-2003, com. Asian art, Antique Art Com., Art Inst. Chgo., 1987; mem. nat. coun. John M. Olin Sch. Bus., Washington U., bd. dirs. Art Inst. Chgo., 2009 Mem. Washington U. Eliot Soc. (Chgo. nat. com., chmn. membership com. 1996-92), Univ. Club. Republican. Presbyterian. Office: Great Banc Inc 1 N Wacker Dr Ste 4075 Chicago IL 60606

WESTPHAL, CAROL JEAN, media specialist; d. John Gerald and Florine Theresa Sapienza; m. Robert Michael Westphal, Aug. 11, 1979; 1 child, Christina Marie. BA in English, Iona Coll., 1976; MS in Spl. Edn., Coll. of New Rochelle, NY, 1979; MS in Libr. and Info. Sci., LI U., 2000. Montessori lic. St. Nicholas Tng. Ctr. Montessori tchr. New Rochelle Acad., 1976—87; 2d grade tchr. Christ the King, Yonkers, NY, 1987—88, computer tchr., 1988—96; libr. media specialist Ralph Waldo Emerson Mid. Sch., Yonkers, 1996—. Coun. mem. Yonkers Sch. Libr. Sys., 2003—. Grantee, Laura Bush Found., 2004. Mem.: ALA, Westchester Libr. Assn., Sch. Libr. Media Specialists of Southea. NY. Home: 2 E High St Valhalla NY 10595 Office: Ralph Waldo Emerson Mid Sch 160 Bolmer Ave Yonkers NY 10703 Office Phone: 914-376-8300 ext 254. Fax: 914-421-1825. E-mail: cwestphal@emerson.ypschools.org.

WESTPHAL, LYNN MARIE, obstetrician, gynecologist; b. Chgo., Apr. 26, 1961; MD, Stanford U., 1987. Diplomate Am. Bd. Ob-Gyn., Am. Bd. Reproductive Endocrinology and Infertility. Intern UCLA, 1987-88, resident, 1988-89, Stanford U., 1989-91, assoc. prof., 2005—; fellow in reproductive endrocrinology U. Calif., San Francisco, 1993-95. Dir. women's health Stanford U., 2005—. Mem. ACOG, Soc. Reproductive Medicine. Office: 300 Pasteur Dr Palo Alto CA 94305 Office Phone: 650-498-5478.

WESTPHAL, PAUL, professional basketball coach; b. Torrance, Calif., Nov. 30, 1950; m. Cindy Westphal; children: Victoria, Michael Paul. Degree in phys. edn., U. So. Calif., 1972. Guard Boston Celtics, 1972-75, Phoenix Suns, 1975-80, 83-84, asst. coach., 1988-92, head coach, 1992—95; guard Seattle Supersonics, 1980-81, head coach, 1998—2000; guard NY Knicks, 1981-83; coach Southwestern Coll. Eagles, Phoenix, 1985-86, Grand Canyon Coll. Antelopes, 1986-88; HS coach, 1995—98; head coach Pepperdine U. Waves, 2001—06; asst. coach Dallas Mavericks, 2007—08, exec. v.p. basketball ops., 2008—09; head coach Sacramento Kings, 2009—. Named First Team All-NBA, 1977, 1979, 1980, Comeback Player of Yr., NBA, 1983; named to Western Conf. All-Star Team, 1977—81. Achievements include being a member of the NBA Championship winning Boston Celtics, 1974. Office: Sacramento Kings Arco Arena One Sports Pky Sacramento CA 95834*

WESTRICH, GEOFFREY HOWARD, orthopaedic surgery; b. South Orange, NJ, May 26, 1964; BS in Engring. (with honors), Tufts U., 1986; MD, Tufts U. Sch. Medicine, 1990. Cert. Orthopaedic Surgery, NY. Intern, gen. surgery North Shore-Cornell U. Program, Manhasset, NY, 1990—91; resident, orthop. surgery Hosp. for Spl. Surgery-NY Hosp. Cornell Med. Ctr., NY, 1991—95; orthop. trauma fellowship AO fellowship Inselpital, Bern, Switzerland, 1995; hip/knee fellowship, adult reconstruction Hosp. Spl. Surgery, NY, asst. scientist NY, 1996—, asst. attending, orthop. surgery NY, 1996—2002, assoc. attending, orthop. suregery NY, 2002—; asst. attending, orthop. surgery NY Presbyterian Weill Cornell Med. Ctr., NY, 2001—02, assoc. attending, orthop. surgery NY, 2002—; asst. prof., orthop. surgery Weill Med. Coll. Cornell U., 1999, assoc. prof. clin. orthop. surgery. Mem. Orthop. Trauma Svc. Contbr. articles to profl. jours. Recipient Resident's award, NY Acad. Medicine, 1994, Resident award paper, Smith & Nephew Richards, Inc., 1995, Fellow award paper, Eastern Orthop. Assn., 1996, Hip Soc. Recipient, Orthop. Rsch. and Edn. Found., 1998; named one of Medical Marvels, New York Mag., 2006. Mem.: NY County Med. Soc., Am. Acad. Orthop. Surgeons, AMA, Alpha Omega Alpha. Avocations: boating, fishing, skiing, tennis, calligraphy. Office: Hosp for Spl Surgery 535 E 70th St New York NY 10021-4872 also: Affiliated Physician Offices 176-60 Union Turnpike Fresh Meadows NY 11366 Address: NY Presbyterian Weill Cornell Med Ctr 525 E 68th St Starr 2 New York NY 10021 Office Phone: 212-606-1510. Office Fax: 212-639-9266.

WESTRING, CHRISTIAN GUSTAV, geneticist, consultant; b. Copenhagen, Nov. 18, 1977; s. Peter Gustav and Jette Westring. PhD, U. Denver, Colo., 2008. Forensic geneticist, Inst. Forensic Genetics U. Denver, 2002—, Nat. Inst. Legal Medicine, Copenhagen, 2007—. Active mem., bd. dirs. Colo. Wildlife Fedn., Denver, 2005—08. Mem.: Internat. Soc. Forensic Genetics. Lutheran. Avocations: fly fishing, hunting, rugby, exercise, snowboarding. Personal E-mail: christian.westring@gmail.com.

WESTROPE, MARTHA RANDOLPH, psychologist, consultant; b. Gaffney, SC, May 19, 1922; d. Gordon Robert and Hannah (Brown) Westrope; 1 adopted child, Ashley Randolph. BS, Winthrop Coll., Rock Hill, SC, 1942; MA, U. NC, Chapel Hill, 1944; PhD, U. Iowa, Iowa City, 1952. Lic. psychologist SC. Pvt. practice, Greenville, S.C., 1960—; part-time pvt. practice, 1987-96; part-time staff mem. Spartanburg Mental Health Clinic, SC, 1971-73, Greenville Mental Health Ctr., 1974-85, Patrick B. Harris Psychiat. Hosp., Anderson, S.C., 1985-87; med. cons. SC Vocat. Rehab. Dept., Greenville, 1987-91, part-time med. cons., 1993-99. Cons. SC Parole Bd. Psychol. Evaluation SC Dept. Corrections, 1983—87. Mem.: Coun. Nat. Register Health Svc. Providers Psychology, Am. Group Psychotherapy Assn., Greenville County Mental Health Assn., Am. Assn. Advancement Psychology, SC Psychol. Assn., Southeastern Psychol. Assn., Am. Psychol. Assn. Democrat. Presbyterian. Avocations: wildlife preservation, fine arts. Home: 11 Darien Way Greenville SC 29615-3236

WESTWICK, ED, actor; b. Stevenage, Eng., June 27, 1987; Actor(guest appearances): (TV series) Doctors, 2006, Casualty, 2006, Afterlife, 2006,: (films) Children of Men, 2006, Breaking and Entering, 2006, Son of Rambow, 2007; (TV series) Gossip Girl, 2007— (Choice TV Villain, Teen Choice Awards, 2008, 2009). Office: c/o Silvercup Studios 42-22 22nd St Long Island City NY 11101 also: Emptage Hallett 14 Rathbone Place London W1T 1HT England*

WESTWICK, JOHN KEIRN, molecular cell biologist; b. Santa Barbara, Calif., July 24, 1963; s. Robert James and Dorothy (Keirn) W.; m. Dana Larios Baer, May 25, 1991; children: William Gray, Kurt Alexander. BA in Biology, U. Calif., San Diego, 1986, PhD in Molecular Pathology, 1994. Rsch. asst. VA Hosp., San Diego, 1986-88; postgrad. rschr. Sch. Medicine U. Calif., San Diego, 1988-92, U. N.C., Chapel Hill, 1993-94, rschr., lectr. dept. pharmacology and Lineberger Cancer Ctr., 1995—. Contbr. chpts. to books, articles to profl. jours. Vol. Crohns and Colitis Found. of Am., 1993-95. Grantee, fellow Ctr. for G.I. Biology and Disease, 1995, Lineberger Cancer Ctr., 1995, Am. Liver Found., 1995. Mem. AAAS. Achievements include description of crucial role for stress-activated protein kinases (SPKs) in liver injury and regeneration, and following cell stimulation by inflammatory cytokines and oncogenes; linked second messenger ceramide to activation of SAPKs. Office: Signal Pharm Inc 5555 Oberlin Dr San Diego CA 92121-3746

WESTWOOD, ALBERT RONALD CLIFTON, management consultant, researcher; b. Birmingham, Eng., June 9, 1932; came to US, 1958, naturalized, 1974; s. Albert Sydney and Ena Emily (Clifton) W.; m. Jean Mavis Bullock, 1956; children: Abigail, Andrea. BSc with honors, U. Birmingham, 1953, PhD in Phys. Metallurgy, 1956, DSc in Materials Sci., 1968. Chartered engr. and physicist, UK. Tech. officer research dept., metals div. Imperial Chem. Industries, Birmingham, 1956—58, successively scientist, sr. scientist, assoc. dir., head materials sci. dept., dep. dir., 1958—74; dir. Martin Marietta Labs., Balt., 1974—84, corp. dir. R & D, 1984—87; v.p. R & D Martin Marietta Corp., Bethesda, Md., 1987—90, v.p. sci., 1990, v.p. rsch. and tech., 1990—93; v.p. rsch. and exploratory tech. Sandia Nat. Labs. divsn. Lockheed Martin Corp., Albuquerque, 1993—96; v.p. emeritus Sandia Nat. Labs., 2002—; chmn., chief exec. Ctrl. Lab. of Rsch. Couns., England, 1998—2000; internat. cons. R. and D. Mgmt. Mem. numerous govt. and univ. adv. coms. including Office Sci. and Tech. Policy, NASA, NRC, NAS, NAE, NSF, Nat. Inst. Stds. and Tech., U. Md., U. Fla., MIT, Ga. Inst. Tech., Coun. on Competetiveness; bd. dir. Martin Marietta Energy Systems, Assn. Ind. Rsch. and Tech. Orgns. U.K., U.S. Civilian R&D Found.; mem. European rsch. coun. informatics and math. resources bd. Brit. Nat. Space Sci. Ctr.; mem. R&D coun. European Spallation Source; mem. coun. Found. Tech. Innovation and Soc. U.K.; lectr. in field. Contbr. over 120 articles to profl. jours. Chmn. Md. Humanities Coun., N.Mex. Humanities Coun., N.Mex. Symphony Orch.; bd. dirs. Santa Fe Opera; adv. com. Sci. and Tech. Corp., U. N.Mex., interim pres. Recipient Disting. Young Scientist award Md. Acad. Scis., 1966, Centennial award U. Md., 1994, Beilby gold medal Royal Inst. Chemistry, 1970, J. Herbert Holloman award Acta Metallurgica, 1996, Tewksbury lectr. U. Melbourne, 1974, Christie lectr., Johns Hopkins U., 1991, Wenk lectr. Johns Hopkins U., 1995, Herbert B. Chermside award, Soc. Rsch. Adminstrs. Internat., 2007. Fellow AAAS (chmn. indsl. sci. sect.), Am. Soc. Metals Internat. (Burgess lectr. 1984, Campbell meml. lectr. 1987, disting. lectr. materials and soc. 1995, medal for advancement rsch. 2006), Inst. of Physics, Inst. of Materials, The Minerals, Metals and Materials Soc. (dir., fin. officer, pres. 1990, Krumb lectr. 1988, leadership award 1992); mem. NRC (chmn. com. engring. and tech. sys. 1992-97), ASME (disting. lectr. 1989), NAE (elected), Acad. Engring. Ga. (elected), Royal Swedish Acad. Engring. Scis. (elected), Russian Acad. Engring. (elected), Royal Acad. Engring. (elected, UK), Md. Acad. Scis. (coun.), Md. Inst. Metals (pres.), Indsl. Rsch. Inst. (bd. dirs., pres. 1989-90). Avocations: theater, travel, accompanist and musical arranger for wife, singing, acting. Home: 13539 Canada Del Oso Pl NE Albuquerque NM 87111-8045 Personal E-mail: arwestwood@aol.com.

WESTWOOD, JAMES NICHOLSON, lawyer; b. Portland, Oreg., Dec. 3, 1944; s. Frederick Alton and Catherine (Nicholson) W.; m. Janet Sue Butler, Feb. 23, 1980; children: Laura, David. BA, Portland State U., 1967; JD, Columbia U., 1974. Bar: Oreg. 1974, U.S. Dist. Ct. Oreg. 1974, U.S. Ct. Appeals (9th cir.) 1978, U.S. Ct. Appeals (10th cir.), 2003, U.S. Ct. Appeals (fed. cir.) 1984, U.S. Ct. Appeals (D.C. cir.) 1997, U.S. Supreme Ct. 1981. Assoc. Miller, Anderson, Nash, Yerke & Wiener, Portland, 1974-76, 78-81; asst. to pres. Portland State U., 1976-78; ptnr. Miller, Nash, Wiener, Hager & Carlsen, Portland, 1981-99, Stoel Rives LLP, Portland, 1999—. Recipient Disting. Svc. award Portland State U. Found., 1984, Outstanding Alumni award Portland State U., 1992. Mem. ABA (chmn. forest resources com. 1987-89), Oreg. Bar Assn. (chmn. appellate practice sect. 1996-97, chmn. constnl. law sect. 2006), Am. Acad. Appellate Lawyers, Univ. Club (bd. govs. 1994), Park Blocks Found. (pres. 1999—), CASA for Children (bd. mem. 2006-), City Club (pres. 1991-92). Republican. Unitarian Universalist. Home: 3121 NE Thompson St Portland OR 97212-4908 Office: Stoel Rives LLP 900 SW 5th Ave Ste 2600 Portland OR 97204-1268 Office Phone: 503-294-9187. Business E-Mail: jnwestwood@stoel.com.

WESTWOOD, MELVIN NEIL, horticulturist, pomologist; b. Hiawatha, Utah, Mar. 25, 1923; s. Neil and Ida (Blake) Westwood; m. Wanda Mae Shields, Oct. 12, 1946; children: Rose Dawn, Nancy Gwen, Robert Melvin, Kathryn Mae. Student, U. Utah, 1948-50; BS in Pomology, Utah State U., 1952; PhD in Pomology, Wash. State U., 1956. Field botanist Utah State U., Logan, 1951-52, supt. Howell Field Sta., 1952-53; rsch. asst. State Coll. Wash., 1953-55; rsch. horticulturist Agrl. Rsch. Svc. USDA, Wenatchee, Wash., 1955-60; assoc. prof. Oreg. State U., Corvallis, 1960-67, prof., 1967-80, prof. emeritus, 1986—; rsch. dir. Nat. Clonal Germplasm Repository, Corvallis, 1980-83, nat. tech. advisor, 1984-86. Author: Deciduous Fruit and Nut Production, 1976, Temperate-Zone Pomology: Physiology and Culture, 1978, 3d edit., 1993, Contract Military Air Transport: From the Ground Up, 1995, Pear Varieties and Species, 1996, The Foods of Lewis and Clark, 2005; author: (with others) Cherry Nutrition, 1966, Pear Rootstocks, 1987, Management and Utilization of Plant Germplasm, 1988, Maintenance and Storage: Clonal Germplasm, 1989, Genetic Resources of Malus, 1991; contbr. articles to profl. jours. With US Air Transport Command, 1943—45, with USAAF, 1946—47. Recipient Hartman Cup award, Oreg. Hort. Soc., 1989, Earl Price Excellence in Rsch. award, Oreg. State U., 1989; grantee, NSF, 1966. Fellow: Am. Soc. Hort. Sci. (mem. pomology sect. 1967—74, chmn. com. environ. quality 1971, mem. publs. com. 1971—74, pres. Western region 1974, bd. dirs. 1974—75, adv. coun. 1974—79, Joseph Harvey Gourley award for Pomology 1958, Stark award for Pomology 1969, Joseph Harvey Gourley award for Pomology 1977, Stark award for Pomology 1977, Outstanding Rschr. award 1986); mem.: AAAS, Am. Pomological Soc. (mem. adbv. bd. 1970—75, mem. exec. bd. 1980—84, Paul Howe Shepard award 1968, 1982, Wilder medal 1980), Am. Soc. Plant Physiologists, Amnesty Internat., UN Assn. USA, Ams. United Separation of Ch. and State, Gamma Sigma Delta, Phi Kappa Phi. Baptist. Achievements include patents for Autumn Blaze ornamental pear; research in Pyrus (pear), Malus (apple) and Prunus (plum, cherry, peach); physiology of rootstock genera. Office: Oreg State U Dept Horticulture Corvallis OR 97331

WETCHER-HENDRICKS, DEBRA ELIZABETH, social sciences educator; b. Allentown, Pa., Oct. 19, 1970; d. Neil Steven and Judith Ann Wetcher; m. Glenn Thomas Hendricks, June 7, 1997; children: Mitchell Jack Hendricks, Joel Spencer Hendricks. BA, Glassboro State Coll., NJ, 1991; MA, PhD, Lehigh U., Bethlehem, Pa., 1998. Vis. prof. Northampton CC, Bethlehem, 1998—99, Moravian Coll., Bethlehem, 1999—2001, asst. prof., 2001—. Contbr. articles to profl. jours. Mem. adv. bd. Dept. of Children Youth and Families, Northampton County, Pa., 2005—. Mem.: Internat. Chinese Statis. Assn., Lehigh Valley Rsch. Consortium (mem. exec. bd.), Alpha Kappa Delta. Achievements include research in corrections for attenuation that do not assume independent error scores and applicable to partial and part correlation coefficients were derived; an error in Bohrnstedt's (1969) derivation of formulas to compute for partial and part coefficients implicitly corrected for attenuation was discovered and corrected; statistical analysis of behavior management variables imposed upon sports spectators. Office: Moravian College 1200 Main St Bethlehem PA 18018 Office Phone: 610-861-1415. Office Fax: 610-625-7811. Business E-Mail: medwh02@moravian.edu.

WETENHALL, JOHN, museum director; b. June 1, 1957; s. Jack Wetenhall and Jane (Rinaud) Keating; m. Tanya Williams, Aug. 28, 2004. AB cum laude, Dartmouth Coll., 1979; MA, Williams Coll., Williamstown, Mass., 1982, Stanford U., 1985, PhD, 1988; MBA, Vanderbilt U., 1999. Fellow Smithsonian Instn., Washington, 1986-87,

88-89; lectr. Santa Clara (Calif.) U., 1985, U. Minn., Mpls., 1988; curator painting and sculpture Birmingham (Ala.) Mus. Art, 1989-95; dir. Checkwood Mus. Art, Nashville, 1995-2001; exec. dir. John and Mable Ringling Mus. Art, Sarasota, Fla., 2001—. Founder Thomas Art Projects, Birmingham, 1992-95, Carell Woodland Sculpture Trail, Nashville, 1996-99; cons. Vietnam Women's Meml. Project, Washington, 1988-89, U. So. Calif. Pub. Art Program, 1991. Author: (with Karal Ann Marling) Iwo Jima: Monuments, Memories and the American Hero, 1991, (with David Cass) (catalogue) Italian Paintings, 1850-1910, 1982; editor: (catalogue) Splendors of the American West, 1990; contbr. articles to profl. jours.; appearance in Am. Masters: Alexander Calder, PBS, 1998. Chair Livelier City Ctr. com. Ops. New Birmingham, 1994—95, chair cultural dist. forum, 1992—94; nat. register peers, design excellence program Gen. Svcs. Adminstrn., 1998—; chair Nashville Rotary Adopt-A House Program; mem. Leadership Manatee, 2002, Leadership Fla., 2003; bd. Sarasota Conv. and Visitors Bur., 2006—. Recipient Award of Excellence Tenn. Assn. Mus., 1996, 2001, Gold and Silver medals for ednl. programming Southeastern Mus. Conf., 1999; B. Gerald Cantor fellow, 1986, Nat. Endowment for the Arts grantee, 1991, Lyndon Baines Johnson Found. Moody Travel grantee, 1986, John F. Kennedy Libr. Found. grantee, 1986, Inst. Mus. and Libr. Svcs. grantee. Mem. Am. Tchrs. Assn. of the Martial Arts (sensei), Rotary (Paul Harris fellow), Kiwanis, Sarasota C. of C. (bd. dirs. 2005—06), Beta Gamma Sigma, Assn. Art Mus. Dirs., Am. Assn. Mus. (bd. dirs. 2007-). Avocations: white water kayaking, flying, aiki ju jitsu (blackbelt). Office: Ringling Mus of Art 5401 Bay Shore Rd Sarasota FL 34243 Business E-Mail: john.wetenhall@ringling.org.

WETHERBE, HERBERT JOHN, pharmacist; b. Montague, Mass., Sept. 18, 1943; s. John Bond Wetherbe, Dorothy Mildred Wetherbe; m. Linda Ann Stines. MDiv, Trinity Evang. Div. Sch., 1979; PharmD, U. Ill., 1992. Registered pharmacist Ill., N.Y. Chemist Inmont Corp., Detroit, 1969—71; chief pharmacist Walgreens Drug Co., Deerfield, Ill., 1979—83; staff pharmacist VA Hosp., Danville, 1983—87, King Khaled Eye Specialist Hosp., Riyadh, Saudi Arabia, 1987—89; clin. pharmacist Northwestern Meml. Hosp., Chgo., 1992—93, Security Forces Hosp., Riyadh, 1993—96; pharmacist Kinney Drugs, Gouveneur, NY, 1996; clin. cons. hosp. info. sys. Nat. Consulting Bur. Huff Barrington Owens Alan Cooper, Inc., Safat, Kuwait, 1996—97, Integrated Solutions for Bus., Riyadh, 1998—2002, Nat. Consulting Bur. Huff Barrington Owens Alan Cooper, Inc., Safat, 2002—03, Kinney Drugs, Gouveneur, 2003—, supervising pharmacist, 2003—. Mem.: Northern NY Pharmacists Soc., Intravenous Nurses Soc., Pharmacists Soc. State N.Y., Am. Soc. Health Sys. Pharmacists, Am. Pharm. Assn., Am Inst. Chemists, Am. Chem. Soc., Gen. Soc. Mayflower Descs., N.Y. State Coun. Health Sys. Pharmacists. Republican. Avocation: travel. Personal E-mail: hjwetherbe@yahoo.com.

WETHERELL, ALBERT A., secondary school educator; b. Queens, NY; s. Albert M. and Hedwig D. Wetherell. BA, St. John's U., Queens, 1965, PhD, 1979; MA, Fordham U., 1967. Tchr. NYC Bd. Edn., 1967—2004. Recipient Bunzel award, United Fed. Tchrs., 1992, Achievement award, Am. Fedn. Tchrs., 2005. Mem.: Polish Inst. Arts and Sci., Am. Hist. Assn., Queens Hist. Soc., Equestrian Order of the Holy Sepulchre Jerusalem (eastern lieutenancy), Phi Alpha Theta, Phi Delta Kappa. Avocation: historical research.

WETHERELL, THOMAS KENT, academic administrator; b. Daytona Beach, Fla., Dec. 22, 1945; m. Virginia B. Wetherell; children: Kent, Blakely, Page. BS in Social Studies, Fla. State U., 1967, MS in Social Studies, 1968, PhD in Adminstrn., 1974. Pres. Wetherell Enterprises, Inc.; dir. housing and adminstrn., asst. v.p., asst. dean housing U. Ctrl. Fla.; assoc. prof. Bethune-Cookman Coll.; exec. asst. to pres. to dean of instrn. Daytona Beach CC, v.p., provost acad. and univ. transfer programs, dist. v.p., planning and devel.; pres. First Am. Mortgage and Investments, Inc., Tallahassee CC, 1975, Fla. State U., Tallahassee, 2003—. Mem. Fla. Ho. of Reps., 1980-92, spkr. 1990-92, chair appropriations com., 1989-90, chair appropriations edn. com., 1986-88, chair higher edn. com., 1984-86, majority fl. leader, 1982-84, chair Volusia county legis. delegation, 1981-83, 86-87. Bd. dirs. Econ. Devel. Coun., ARC, Canaveral Nat. Seashore Park, Southern Scholarship Found., United Way. Mem. Tallahassee C. of C. (bd. dirs.), Lions, Kiwanis, Blue Lodge, Shriners, Bahia Temple. Office: Office of Pres Fla State U 211 Westcott Bldg Tallahassee FL 32306-1470 Office Phone: 850-644-1085. E-mail: wetherell@mailer.fsu.edu.*

WETHERILL, EIKINS, lawyer, stock exchange executive; b. Phila., Oct. 3, 1919; s. A. Hecksher and Edwina (Brunner) W. LL.B., U. Pa., 1948. Practiced in, Phila., 1948-55, Norristown, 1955-98; assoc. firm Evans, Bayard & Frick, 1948-50; ptnr. Reilly, Hepburn, Earle & Wetherill, 1950-55; firm Henderson, Wetherill, O'Hey & Horsey, 1955-98; pres. Phila. Stock Exchange, Inc., 1965-81. Bd. dirs. Germantown Savs. Bank; fin. commentator CBS-TV News, 1966-68; chmn. bd. Sta. WHYY-TV, 1970-76, dir., 1976-90; dir. 1st Pa. Corp., 1st Pa. Bank, solicitor to lt. gov. Pa., 1951-55, asst. U.S. atty. gen., 1953-55, treas., Montgomery County, 1956-59; pres. Montgomery County Bd. Commrs., 1960-63; chmn. Pa. Securities Commn., 1963-65; commr. Delaware Valley Regional Planning Commn., 1965—, chmn., 1968-69, 70-71, 78-79. Former bd. dirs. Greater Phila. Partnership; chmn. Phila. Drama Guild, 1975-80, dir., 1980-87; trustee Davis and Elkins Coll., 1973-91, G.H. Montgomery County Open Space, 1994—. Served to capt., cav. Signal Corps, OSS, AUS, 1941-45. Mem. ABA, Phila. Bar Assn., Phila. Club, Racquet Club (Phila.), Sunnybrook Golf Club, Delta Psi. Episcopalian.

WETHERILL, LINDA MARIE, musician, educator, performing arts association administrator; b. Milw., Mar. 2, 1950; m. Joseph David Smith, July 7, 2000 (dec.). MusB, U. Rochester, 1972, performers cert., 1971; MusM, SUNY, Stony Brook, 1991. 1st flutist solo and ensemble Chamber Artists Garbarino of La Scala, Milan, 1973—76; solo and 1st flutist Frankfurt Radio Symphony Orch., 1975—76, IRCAM, Ensemble Intercontemporain, Paris, 1976—80; internat. soloist freelance, U.S.I.S. and McCann Artists, Ltd., London, 1973—; prof. music major Turkish univs., Istanbul, 1987—90; cultural amb. U.S. Info. Svc., Washington, 1985—; prof. music Adelphi U., Garden City, NY, 1994—; solo flutist Aspekte, 2006—, Salzburg Mozarteam, 2006—, Orch. of Our Time, NYC, 2006—, exec. dir., 2006—. Judge Internat. Competition, Salzburg, Austria, 2004—; solo performer, lectr. Internat. Soc. Cont. Music, Miami, 2004; performances and master classes in Argentina, Brazil, India, 2007—08; cons. various internat. programs, 1973—. Editor: LI Flute Notes, 1994—; editor, performer (solo CD) Sound and Repercussion, Far Amazon, 2000 (Amazon award, 2003), (book, CD) International Anthology of Solos for Alto and Bass Flutes, 2005, (concert, CD recording) George Rochterg Meml. Concert, 2006, editor, perfomer Indian Concerts/Master Classes, 2007—08, inaugarator Matrimandir Soul of World Peace Temple, Auroville, India; contbr. articles and interviews to profl. jours. Pres., founder Muzarte, Phila., NYC, 1980—. Grantee, NY State Coun. for the Arts, 1997—2005. Mem.: LI Flute Club (bd. dirs., adv. bd. 1994—2005), Sigma Alpha Iota. Achievements include first woman to perform publicly for mixed audiences in Saudi Arabia in 1986; first American flute soloist to perform and teach in Hunan province of China in 2002, to India, 2007-2008; solo inauguration of Matrimandir in Auroville, India, 2008. Avocations: travel, political diplomacy, world cultures. Home: 38 W 74th St Apt 3C New York NY 10023 Office: Adelphi U South Ave Garden City NY 11530 Address: 170 Via San Ginese di Compito Capannori 55012 Italy Office Phone: 917-861-4528. Personal E-mail: muzarte@msn.com. Business E-Mail: muzarte@lindawetherill.com.

WETHERINGTON, JIM, Mayor, Columbus, Georgia, former protective services official; m. Shirley Bell; 3 children. BS in Criminal Justice Adminstrn., Columbus State U.; MS in Edn., Ga. State U. Patrolman Columbus Police Dept., 1963, sgt. traffic div., lt. traffic div., dir. Alcohol Safety Action Project, comdr. patrol detective div., police chief, 1981—95; mem. State Bd. Pardons & Paroles, 1995—98; commr. Ga. Dept. Corrections, 1999—2003; headmaster Calvary Christian Sch., 2004—07; mayor City of Columbus, Ga., 2007—. Mil. police officer US Army, Walter Reed Army Hosp., Washington DC. Recipient Hispanic and Asian People of Columbus award, 1984, Am. Criminal Justice Assn. award, Lambda Alpha Epsilon Criminal Justice Frat., 1988, William Henry Shaw award for Svc. to Edn., Phi Delta Kappa Edn. Frat., 1992, Judge Aaron Cohn award, 1993, Liberty Bell award, Ga. Bar Assn., 1994; named Police Officer of Yr., Exchange Club of Columbus, 1967, Distinguished Alumni award, Columbus State U., 1984, Outstanding Man of Yr., Columbus Am. Legion, 1986, Police Chief of Yr., Ga. Police Chiefs Assn., 1994, Columbusite of Yr., Columbus and the Valley Mag., 1995, Boss of Yr., Sojourner Chpt. Am. Bus. Women's Assn., 1987. Baptist. Office: City Hall PO Box 1340 Columbus GA 31902-1340 Office Phone: 706-653-4712. Office Fax: 706-653-4970.*

WETHINGTON, AMY RENE, biology professor; b. Spartanburg, SC, Mar. 31, 1965; d. Charles Allen and Zelda Powell Wethington; m. James Martin Guthrie, June 5, 2008. BS, Clemson U., SC, 1987, Coll. Charleston, 1990, MS, 1992; MA, U. Ind., Bloomington, 1997; PhD, U. Ala., Tuscaloosa, 2004. Rsch. asst. Coll. Charleston, 1988, tchg. asst., 1991—92, U. Ala., 1999—2001, rsch. asst., 2002—03; assoc. instr. Ind. U., 1992—96; rsch. technician U. Ky., Lexington, 1997—98; postdoc. rsch. assoc. Purdue U., West Lafayette, Ind., 2004—05; asst. prof. Chowan U., Murfreesboro, NC, 2005—. With, snake river physa tech. team US Bur. Reclamation, Boise, Idaho, 2005—; rsch. assoc. Carnegie Mus. Natural History, Pitts., 2006—. Contbr. articles to profl. jours. Postdoc. Rsch. fellow, NIH, 2004—05. Mem.: Am. Malacological Soc. Office: Chowan Univ 1 Univ Pl Murfreesboro NC 27855 Office Fax: 252-398-1362. Business E-Mail: wethia@chowan.edu.

WETLE, TERRIE FOX, gerontologist, educator, dean; b. Bremerton, Wash., Nov. 7, 1946; d. Gerald Lee and Elinor Myrle (Martindale) Todd; m. Richard W. Besdine, July 2, 1981; children: Sarah, Molly. BS in Psychology, Portland State U., 1968, MS in Psychology, 1971, PhD of Urban Studies, 1976; doctorate (hon.), U. Geneva Sch. Medicine, 2005. Asst. prof. Portland (Oreg.) State U., 1976-78; social policy analyst Dept. Health, Edn. and Welfare, Washington, 1978-79; asst. prof. Yale U., New Haven, 1979-81, Harvard U., Boston, 1981-88; dir. Braceland Ctr., Hartford, Conn., 1988-95; assoc. prof. U. Conn. Health Ctr., Farmington, 1989—95; dep. dir. Nat. Inst. Aging, NIH, Bethesda, Md., 1995-2000; assoc. dean medicine, prof. cmty. health Brown U. Med. Sch., Providence, 2000—. Bd. dirs. Armed Forces Retirement Home, Washington. Editor: Handbook of Geriatric Care, 1982, Older Veterans, 1984, Medicare Coming of Age: A Proposal for Reform, 1986, The Patient Self Determination Act and Advance Directives: A Curriculum for Nursing Home Staff, 1995, Public and Private Responsibilities in Long-Term Care: Finding the Balance, 1998, End of Life In Nursing Homes: Experiences and Policy Recommendations, 2004, Improving Aging and Public Health Research: Qualitative and Mixed Methods, 2006; contbr. articles to profl. jours. Pres. Alzheimer's Assn. Greater Hartford, 1993-95; bd. trustees Perishable Theater, 2002-. Recipient Pres. award, Am. Coll. Health Care Adminstrs., DHHS Secs. Disting. Svc. award. Fellow: Gerontol. Soc. Am. (pres. 2003—04, chair com.); mem.: APHA (del., governing coun., Key award Outstanding Contbns. in Public Health and Aging), Am. Fedn. Aging Rsch. (pres. 2006—08), Am. Soc. Aging (Pres. award). Office: Brown Program in Public Health 121 S Main St G S121 Providence RI 02912

WETMORE, KEITH CHIDESTER, lawyer; b. Valparaiso, Ind., Oct. 17, 1956; s. Leonard Leander and Dorisann (Chidester) W. BA, Northwestern U., 1977; JD magna cum laude, U. Mich., 1980. Bar: Calif. 1981, U.S. Dist. Ct. (no. dist.) Calif. 1981. Law clk. to Hon. J. Edward Lumbard U.S. Ct. Appeals (2d cir.), 1980-81; assoc. Steinhart & Falconer, San Francisco, 1981-82, Morrison & Foerster LLP, San Francisco, 1982-86, ptnr., 1986—, chmn. NYC, 2000—. Articles editor U. Mich. Law Rev. 1980-81. Mem. ABA, Calif. Bar Assn., Bay Area Lawyers for Individual Freedom, San Francisco Bar Assn. Methodist. Office: Morrison & Foerster LLP 1290 Ave Americas New York NY 10104 Business E-Mail: kwetmore@mofo.com.

WETSCH, JOHN ROBERT, information scientist; b. Dickinson, ND, Aug. 27, 1959; s. Joseph John (dec.) and Florence Mae (Edwards) W.; m. Laura Jean Johnson, Aug. 29, 1981; children: Julie Elizabeth, Katherine Anne, John Michael, Joseph Harold. BS, Excelsior Coll., Albany, 1984; MA, Antioch U., 1989; PhD, Nova Southeastern U., 1994; BS, U. ND, 2001; M in Astronomy, U. Western Sydney, 2002; grad. in Theology, Australian Cath. U. Cert. project mgmt. profl. Project Mgmt. Inst. Radiation physics instr. Grand Forks Clinic, ND, 1983-85; sr. programmer PRC, Inc., Cavalier Air Force Sta., ND, 1987-91, PARCS project-SAFEGUARD sys.; pres. Dakota Sci. Inc., Langdon, ND, 1988-95; instr. U. N.D.-Lake Region, Devils Lake, 1988-91; systems adminstr. U.S. Courts Nat. Fine Ctr., Raleigh, NC, 1991-94; project leader U.S. Postal Svc., Raleigh Integrated Bus. Sys. Solution Ctr., 1994—2001, program mgmt. info. tech. enabling portfolio, 2001—03; sr. tech. fellow Litton/PRC, 1997—2002; tech. fellow Northrop Grumman Info. Tech., 2002—06, sys. engr., 2004—06; program dir. NC Window of Info. on Student Edn. NC Dept. Pub. Instrn., 2006—08, IT dir. acad. svcs., 2009—. Cons. on Wave Obs./ND Proposal, Gov.'s Office, Bismarck, 1991; founder, developer Dakota Sci., Inc., Langdon, 1988-95; instr. divsn. continuing edn. Wake Tech. CC, 1993-99; adj. faculty computer info. systems NC Wesleyan Coll., 1997—; adj. faculty NC State U., 1999-2000, Capella U., Mpls., 2000-02, U. Phoenix, 1998-2001. Author: Distributed UNIX System Administration, 1998; (with others) COMPUTE!'s 2nd Book of Amiga, 1988; contbr. articles to COMPUTE! Jour. of Progressive Computing, 1987, other profl. jours. Program coord. Lake Region Outreach, U. ND, Cavalier Air Force Sta., 1988—91; mem. bd. alumni trustees USNY-Regents Coll., Albany, 1995—2000, v.p., 1996—97, pres., 1997—2000, ex-officio mem. bd. overseers, 1997; pres. Zeta Rho chpt. Pi Kappa Alpha, Grand Forks, 1981; pres. Alumni Assn. Excelsior Coll., 1999—2001; ex-officio voting Excelsior Coll. Bd. Trustees, 1999—2001, bd. trustees, 2001—, elected vice chair, 2008—. Decorated knight comdr. Order of St. Gregory the Great (Vatican); recipient Westinghouse Sci. Talent Search award, 1978, Nova Southeastern U. Leadership award, Internat. Alumni Assn., 1998, Excelsior Coll. Founder's award, 2001; named Larimore-Mathews scholar, U. ND, Grand Forks, 1978, ND Acad. Sci. scholar, 1978, SMITS scholar, ND Acad. Sci., 1990; named one of Premiere 100 IT Leaders, Computer World Mag., 2009; named to Hon. Order of Ky. Cols., 2007. Mem.: Project Mgmt. Inst., Dakota Astron. Soc. (pres. 1987—91, co-founder). Roman Catholic. Achievements include research in missile simulation; microcomputer short range weather forecasting algorithm, study in astronomy and culture, astronomy information systems, large scale system integration to government information systems. Office: 301 N Wilmington St Raleigh NC 27601 Personal E-mail: drwetsch@msn.com.

WETTELAND, JOHN KARL, professional baseball coach, retired professional baseball player; b. San Mateo, Calif., Aug. 21, 1966; m. Michele Wetteland; 4 children. Student, Coll. San Mateo. Pitcher LA Dodgers, 1989-91, Montreal Expos, 1992-94, NY Yankees, 1995-96, Tex. Rangers, 1996—2000; bullpen coach Washington Nationals, 2006; asst. baseball coach Liberty Christian Sch., Argyle, Tex., 2007; bullpen coach Seattle Mariners, 2008—. Recipient Rolaids Relief award, 1996; named Am. League Fireman of Yr., The Sporting News, 1996, World Series MVP, 1996; named to Am. League All-star Team, 1996, 98, 99, Tex. Rangers Hall of Fame, 2005. Achievements include leading the American League in saves (43), 1996; member of the World Series Championship winning New York Yankees, 1996. Office: Seattle Mariners Safeco Field PO Box 4100 Seattle WA 98104*

WETTELS, NICHOLAS BENJAMIN, biomedical engineer; b. Fairfield, Calif., Nov. 29, 1977; s. Nancy Jo and Ron Dean Wettels. BS in Physics, Tulane U., New Orleans, LA, 2000; MS in Engring. Mgmt., Old Dominion U., Norfolk, Va., 2005; MS in Biomedical Engring., U. Southern Calif., LA, 2008, attending in Biomedical Engring., 2006—. Scientist, CFO Syntouch LLC, South Pasadena, Calif., 2008—. Disaster relief vol. ARC, LA, 2007—08. Lt. USN, 2000—06, San Diego. Decorated Navy Achievement medal USN, Navy Commendation medal; NROTC scholarship, 1997. Buddhist. Achievements include patents for biomimetic tactile sensor. Personal E-mail: nick.wettels@gmail.com. Business E-Mail: wettels@usc.edu.

WETTER, VIRGINIA FORWOOD PATE, broadcast executive; b. Havre De Grace, Md., Aug. 10, 1919; BA, Coll. William and Mary, 1940, PhD (hon.) in Pub. Svc., 2006. Pub. rels. Std. Oil Co. of Pa., 1940, Irwin and Leighton Contractor, 1941; pres., gen. mgr. WASA and WHDG radio Havre de Grace, MD, 1960—85; pres. Multiview Cable Co. (later Comcast), 1966—82; chmn. bd. Chesapeake Broadcasting Corp., 1985—. Trustee Harford CC Bd. of Trustees, 1959—69, chmn., 1966—69; pres. Md. Assn. Bds. of Edn., 1963—64, Md. Dist. of Columbia Del. Broadcaster's Assn., 1965—66; mem. Harford County Bd. Edn., 1959—69, pres., 1966—69; mem. radio code bd. Nat. Assn. of Broadcasters, 1966—71; libr. bd. Broadcast Pioneers, 1980—2004. Dir. Harford County Heart Assn. and Cancer Soc., Susquehanna Coun. of Girl Scouts; county chmn. Pres.'s Com. to Promote Employment of Physically Handicapped; plans bd. United Way; dir. Blood Bank of Md.; vol. Harford Meml. Hosp. Aux.; chmn. ann. fund drive Coll. William and Mary, 1985, endowment assn. trustee, pres.'s coun.; vestry St. John's Episcopal Ch., chair 150th anniversary celebration, co-chair bldg. com. Recipient Alumni Medallion award, Coll. William and Mary, 1969, Am. Broadcast Pioneer award, Broadcasters' Found., 2001, Disting. Svc. to Broadcasting award, Broadcast Pioneers of Washington Area, 2001. Mem.: Am. Women in Radio and Television (life; nat. pres. 1970—71, Bd. Dirs. award 1991, Radio Leadership award 2000), Md. Congress of Parents and Tchrs. (life), Delta Kappa Gamma (hon.). Home: 1000 Chesapeake Dr Havre De Grace MD 21078 Personal E-mail: vwetter@aol.com.

WETZEL, BETTY PREAT, writer; b. Roundup, Mont., Nov. 7, 1915; d. Alfred William and Rachel Preat (Johnston) Eiselein; m. Winston Warren Wetzel, June 5, 1940; children: Susan Hinman, Kurt, Gretchen Grafin von Rittberg, Rebecca. BA in Journalism, U. Mont., 1937. Columnist, reporter Roundup (Mont.) Rec.-Tribume, 1938-46; sec. SEATO Cholera Rsch. Lab. and Hosp., Dacca, Bangladesh, 1965-67; adminstrv. asst. to v.p. Wellesley (Mass.) U., 1969-73; dir. pub. rels. Oxfam-Am., Boston, 1973-77; book rev. editor Mont. Mag., Helena, 1989-91. Author: The Making of a Montanan, 1986, Missoula, The Town and The People, 1988, After You, Mark Twain, 1990; co-author: Older Women in the Outdoors, 1996. Bd. dirs. Flathead Lake Biol. Sta., Bigfork, Mont., 1980-86. Democrat. Avocations: mountain hiking, tennis, reading, politics. Home: 189 Pierce Ln PO Box 693 Bigfork MT 59911-0693 Personal E-mail: bwetzel@digisys.net.

WEXELBAUM, MICHAEL, lawyer; b. Bklyn., Aug. 12, 1946; s. Joseph and Beatrice (Skurnick) W.; m. Cynthia Debra Schorr, Apr. 15, 1973 (dec. 1984); children: Joshua David, Stephanie Faye; m. Joan Brenda Math, Aug. 21, 1994; stepchildren: Jonathan David Kaye, Matthew Lawrence Kaye, Julie Dana Kaye. BA in Econs., Bucknell U., 1968; JD, NYU, 1971. Bar: N.Y. 1972, U.S. Dist. Ct. (so. and ea. dists.) N.Y. 1973, U.S. Dist. Ct. (ea. dist.) Wis. 1998. Assoc. Sherman, Citron & Karasik, P.C., NYC, 1972-80, ptnr., head litigation dept., 1980-2001; ptnr. litigation dept. Snow Becker Krauss P.C., NYC, 2001—, co-chair litigation dept., 2003—. Arbitrator Nat. Arbitration Forum, 1999—. Arbitrator Am. Arbitration Assn. and Gen. Arbitration Coun. of Textile and Apparel Industries, N.Y.C., 1982—. Named a N.Y. Super Lawyer, 2006, 2007, 2008. Mem. Bankruptcy Lawyers Bar Assn., Lawyers Assn. Textile and Apparel Industries (bd. govs.), Am. Arbitration Assn. (arbitrator), Nat. Arbitration Forum (arbitrator), Assn. Comml. Fin. Attys. Democratic. Jewish. Avocations: tennis, skiing, biking, theater. Home: 85 Norrans Ridge Dr Ridgefield CT 06877-4237 Office: Snow Becker Krauss PC 605 Third Ave New York NY 10158-0125 Office Phone: 212-455-0486. Office Fax: 212-455-0455. Personal E-mail: jmwex@hotmail.com. Business E-Mail: mwexelbaum@sbklaw.com.

WEXLER, DAVID B., law educator; b. NYC, Apr. 4, 1941; s. Irving Wexler and Lillian Heiden; m. Ghislaine Laraque, Nov. 13, 2004; children: Nancy, Douglas. BA, Binghamton U., NY, 1961; JD, NYU, NY, 1964. Atty., criminal divsn. US Dept. Justice, Washington, 1965—67; Lyons prof. law and psychology U. Ariz., Tucson, 1967—. Dir. Internat. Network Therapeutic Jurisprudence, San Juan, 1997—; prof. law U. PR, San Juan, 1997—; cons. in field. Author: Mental Health Law: Major Issues, 1981, Essays in Therapeutic Jurisprudence, 1991; author: (editor) Therapeutic Jurisprudence: The Law as a Therapeutic Agent, 1990, Law in a Therapeutic Key, 1996, Practicing Therapeutic Jurisprudence: Law as a Helping Profession, 2000, Judging in a Therapeutic Key: Therapeutic Jurisprudence and the Courts, 2003, Rehabilitating Lawyers: Principles of Therapeutic Jurisprudence for Criminal Law Practice, 2008. Mem. legal task panel Pres.'s Commn. Mental Health, Washington, 1977—88; mem. rsch. network mental health and law MacArthur Found., Chco., 1987—97. Recipient Guttmacher Forensic Psychiatry award, Am. Psychiat. Assn., 1972, Outstanding Svc. award, Nat. Assn. for Mental Health, 1974, Creative Tchg. award, U. Ariz. Pres.'s Club, 1975, Disting. Tchg. Scholarship award, NYU Sch. Law, 1989, Disting. Svc. award, Nat. Ctr. State Cts., 2000; fellow, Fulbright Found., Australia, 2002. Mem.: Am. Psychology-Law Soc. (disting.). Achievements include development of the field of therapeutic jurisprudence. Office: PO Box 23349 San Juan PR 00931-3349 Personal E-mail: davidbwexler@yahoo.com.

WEXLER, DEBORAH LEE, physician; b. Minn., Mar. 16, 1950; MD, U. Minn., 1982. Exec. dir. & founder Immunization Action Coalition. Editor Needle Tips, Vaccinate Adults, Vaccinate Women, IAC Express, Hep Express. Office: Immunization Action Coalition 1573 Selby Ave Ste 234 Saint Paul MN 55104 Office Phone: 651-647-9009. Office Fax: 651-647-9131. E-mail: admin@immunize.org.*

WEXLER, HASKELL, film producer; b. Chgo., 1922; s. Simon Wexler; m. Nancy Ashenhurst (div.); two children; m. Marian Witt (div.); 1 son, Mark; m. Rita Taggart. Ednl. documentaries, Chgo., for eleven years; cinematographer films: The Hoodlum Priest, The Best Man, America America, The Loved One, In the Heat of the Night, Who's Afraid of Virginia Woolf? (Acad. award), The Thomas Crown Affair, American Graffiti, One Flew Over the Cuckoo's Nest, Introduction to the Enemy, Bound for Glory (Acad. award), Coming Home, Colors, Three Fugitives, 1988, Blaze, 1989, Lookin' to Get Out, Matewan, Other People's Money, The Babe, Mulholland Falls, 1995, Rich Man's Wife, 1995, (with others) Days of Heaven, (with others) Rolling Stones-IMAX, The Secret of Roan Inish, Canadian Bacon, Limbo, 1999, HBO 61—, 2001, Silver City, 2004; writer, dir., photographer: Medium Cool, 1969; wrote and directed Latino, 1985; feature documentary Bus Riders Union, Five Days in March, From Wharf Rats to Lords of the Docks, Who Needs Sleep?. Received star on Hollywood's Walk of Fame, 1996. Mem. Acad. Motion Picture Arts and Scis. (bd. govs. cinematographers br.). Address: 201 Ocean Ave # 904B Santa Monica CA 90402

WEXLER, JOAN G., dean, law educator; b. NYC, Nov. 25, 1946; m. Leonard Orland, Aug. 20, 2005; children: Matthew Eric, Laura Page. BS (hons. and distinction), Cornell U., 1968; MAT in tchg., Harvard U., 1970; JD, Yale, 1974. Bar: N.Y. 1976. Jud. law clk. for Judge Jack B. Weinstein US Dist. Ct. (ea. dist.), NY, 1974-75; assoc. Debevoise & Plimpton, NYC, 1975-77; asst. prof. law NYU Sch. Law, 1978-81, assoc. prof. law, 1981-85; prof. law Bklyn. Law Sch., 1985—87, assoc. dean acad. affairs, prof. law, 1987—93, acting dean, 1994, Joseph Crea dean, prof. law, pres., 1994—. Spkr. in field; evaluator trust adminstrn. and estate adminstrn. atty. mem. Jud. Conf. of State of NY. 2000-02; with Bklyn. Legal Svcs. Corp. (mem. adv. com. 1994-). Contbr. articles to profl. jours. Bd. dirs. Assn. Bar City of NY Fund, 1994-96, Fund Modern Cts., 1994-2007, Task Force Ct. Facilities, 2001, Children's Law Ctr., 2004-07, Am. Law Dean's Assn., 2007-; bd. trustees Practising Law Inst., 1998-, exec. com. mem., 2003-, Progs & Pub. Com., 1998-. Fellow Am. Bar Found., NY Bar Found.; mem. ABA (mem. Ind. Law Schs. Forum Com., 1996-97, 2000-, mem. continuing legal edn. com. 1997-98, 99-2001, new deans sem ping com. legal edn. & admissions to bar sect., 2001-04), Am. Law Inst., Fed. Bar Coun. (exec. com. mem. 2002-, pres. 2004-06, v.p. 2001-2002, chair Winter Bench and Bar Conf. 2001-2002), Fed. Bar Found. (bd. mem. 1993-98, pres. 1998-99), NY State Bar Assn. (mem. com. on children and law 1993-97, com. legal edn. and admission to bar 1994—), N.Y. Women's Bar Assn. (v.p. 1987-88, 92-93, bd. dirs. 1998-91, Pres.'s Spl. award 2002, Spl. Recognition award 1996), Greater Boy Scouts Coun. NY, Greater Boy Scouts Coun. NY (Good Scout award 1999), Soc. Adolescent Psychiatry (William Schoenfeld award 1999), NYS Ct. Officers Assn. (Pres.'s award 2009), NY County Lawyers' Assn. (honoree, named Outstanding Women of Bar 2004), Jud. Conf. State N.Y. (atty. mem. 2000-2002), Downtown Bklyn. Coun. (mem. exec. com. 2000-06, exec. com. mem. Downtown Bklyn. Partnership 2006-), State N.Y. Office of Ct. Adminstrn. (commn. on alcohol and substance abuse in profession 1999-), NYS Office Ct. Adminstrn. (mem. Com. Alcohol and Substance Abuse Prosessions 1999-2002), Assn. Bar City NY (com. matrimonial law 1985-89, 92-95, long range planning com. 1992-95, com. on family ct. and family law, 1989-92, ad hoc com. on AIDS 1987-88, ad hoc com. surrogate parenting 1986-88), Pres. Coun. Cornell Women (PCCW com. on univ. rels. 1995-2006, PCCW Affinito-Stewart Grants Program com. 2007-), KKG Cornell Edn. Found. (bd. mem. 2004-), Com. to Restore Thurgood Marshall Landmark Courthouse, Cornell U. (mem. Cornell Coun. 2002-06, 08-, admissions and Fini aid 2003-), Second Cir. Task Force on Gender, Racial and Ethnic Fairness in Cts., N.Y. State Supreme Ct.(adv. com. 18-B family ct. panel 1987-92, appellate divsn. first dept.), Jud. Conf. 2nd Cir. (planning and programming com. 1992-2000, 04-06). Home: 1045 Nine Acres Ln Mamaroneck NY 10543-4706 Office: Bklyn Law Sch 250 Joralemon St Brooklyn NY 11201-3700 Business E-Mail: joan.wexler@brooklaw.edu.*

WEXLER, LAURA F., cardiologist, academic administrator; b. Washington, Jan. 26, 1947; d. Michael and Helen (Fooner) Wexler; m. David N. Glass, Nov. 9, 1980; children: Stephanie, Eleanor, Benjamin. BA, Barnard Coll., NYC, 1967; MD, Washington U. Sch. Medicine, St. Louis, 1971. Diplomate Am. Bd. Internal Medicine, cert. in Cardiology. Intern, resident Boston City Hosp./Harvard Med. Sch.; fellow internal medicine/cardiology Mass. Gen. Hosp., Boston; asst. prof. medicine Boston U. Sch. Medicine, 1976-87; assoc. prof. medicine U. Cin. Coll. Medicine, 1987—91, prof. medicine, 1991—99, interim dir. divsn. cardiology, 1999—2001, assoc. dean student affairs/admissions, 2001—. Chief cardiology Cin. Vets. Affairs Med. Ctr., 1987—98; chair clin. biennium curriculum com., reappointment, promotions and tenure com. U. Cin. Coll. Medicine. Editor: Cardiology Alert, 1978—87; contbr. articles to profl. jours. Fellow: Am. Heart Assn., Coun. Clin. Cardiology, Am. Coll. Cardiology. Achievements include research in heart disease in women; sleep apnea in patients with heart failure. Office: U Cin Coll Medicine Divsn Cardiovasc Diseases 231 Albert Sabin Way Cincinnati OH 45267-0001 Office Phone: 513-558-4721. Office Fax: 513-558-3116. Business E-Mail: wexlerl@ucmail.uc.edu.*

WEXLER, LEONARD HOWARD, pediatric oncologist; b. Bklyn., Nov. 21, 1961; s. Theodore and Florence Wexler; m. Beth Sue Brown, Sept. 1999. BA, Boston U.; MD, Boston U. Sch. Medicine, 1985. Cert. Pediatrics, Pediatric Hematology-Oncology. Intern, pediatrics Albert Einstein/Montefiore, Bronx, NY, 1985—88, resident, pediatrics, 1985—88; fellow, pediatric hematology and oncology NIH-Nat. Cancer Inst., Bethesda, Md., 1988—92, sr. clin. investigator, pediatric branch, 1992—96; dir. clin. services Babies & Children's Hosp., NYC, 1996—99; assoc. mem. dept. pediatrics Meml. Sloan-Kettering Cancer Ctr., NY, 1999—; asst. prof. pediatrics Uniformed Services Univ. of the Health Sciences; assoc. prof. pediatrics, divsn. pediatric oncology Columbia U., NY, 1996—99; assoc. prof. pediatrics Weill Med. Coll.-Cornell U., NY, 1999. Co-chair of internat. study to evaluate the effectiveness of chemotherapy for the treatment of children with osteosarcoma; co-investigator clin. trial that evaluates a novel combination of chemotherapy agents & radiotherapy techniques for the treatment of children with rhabdomyosarcoma, Meml. Sloan-Kettering. Med. editl. adv. bd. Libby Shriver Sarcoma Initiative. Named one of Medical Marvels, New York Mag., 2006. Office: Dept Pediatrics #210 Meml Sloan Kettering Cancer Ctr 1275 York Ave New York NY 10021 Office Phone: 212-639-7990. Business E-Mail: wexlerl@mskcc.org.

WEXLER, PATRICIA SUSAN, dermatologist, surgeon; b. 1951; MD, U. Libre de Bruxelles, Belgium, 1979. Diplomate Am. Bd. Internal Medicine 1983, Am. Bd. Dermatology 1986. Intern Beth Israel Med. Ctr., N.Y.C., 1979—80, resident in internal medicine, 1980—82, fellow in infectious disease, 1982—83, attending physician, Mt. Sinai Hosp., N.Y.C.; private practice Wexler Dermatology, N.Y.C. Assoc. clin. prof. dept. dermatology Mt. Sinai Med. Ctr., N.Y.C.; cons. in devel. of several skin care and make-up lines. Author medical rsch. publs. Recipient Am. Acad. Cosmetic Surgery award for Excellence in Cosmetic Surgery. Fellow: Am. Soc. Dermatologic Surgery. Office: 145 E 32nd St 7th Fl New York NY 10016-6055 Office Phone: 212-684-2626. E-mail: crespi666@aol.com.

WEXLER, PETER JOHN, artist, sculptor, photographer, theatre designer, producer, director; b. NYC, 1936; s. S. David and Berda (Sarnoff) W.; m. Constance Ann Ross, Nov. 30, 1962. BS in Design, U. Mich., 1958; student, Yale Sch. Drama, 1958. Designs include White House stage, 1961, War and Peace, 1964, The White Devil, 1965, A Joyful Noise, 1966, The Happy Time, 1967, In the Matter of J. Robert Oppenheimer, 1968, Merv Griffin TV show, 1965, Terra Nova, 1979 (L.A. Dramalogue Critics award); prin. designer, Mark Taper Forum, Ctr. Theatre Group, L.A., 1967-70, designer, N.Y. Philharm. Promenades, 1965-78; play and film The Trial of the Catonsville 9, 1971-72; Leonard Bernstein's Mass, L.A., 1973, N.Y. Philharm. Rug Concerts, 1973-77, Les Troyens, Met. Opera Co., 1973, Le Prophète, Met. Opera Co., 1977, Un Ballo in Maschera, Met. Opera Co., 1980, Theatre Space, Prodns., Pitts. Pub. Theatre, 1975-81; mem. design team for Frank O. Gehry & Assocs., redesign Hollywood Bowl; designer: Albert Herring, Savonlinna Opera Festival, Finland, 1981; centennial prodn. Les Troyens, Met. Opera, 1983; directed: Cold Storage, Ariz. Theatre Co., 1978, Terra Nova, Pitts. Public Theatre, 1981; producer, Dallas Symphony Orch.'s Star Fest 80; producer Rocky Mountain Music Festival, Denver Symphony Orch., 1983-84, Star Spangled Banner, Permanent Exhbn. U.S. Nat. Emblem, Smithsonian Instn., Washington, 1982; prodr., design exhbn. Am. Anthem, LTV Ctr., Dallas/Smithsonian Instn., 1985; designer, broker exhbn. Liberties with Liberty, Trammell Crow Co./Mus. Am. Folk Art, 1985; designer Horizons '86, N.Y. Philharm., 1986; co-prodr., designer video, exhbn. and space Albany Urban Cultural Park, Albany, N.Y., 1986; prodr., dir. Pletka, multimedia theatre piece for orch., Dallas Symphony Orch., 1987; programmer, interior designer Trans-Hudson Ferry for the Port Authority of N.Y. and N.J., 1987-88; prodr. The Search for Life, Smithsonian Inst., 1987; prodr. Mstislav Rostropovich 60th Anniv. Gala Concert, Nat. Symphony Orch., Kennedy Ctr., Washington, 1987, Navy 87, Navy 89, USN multi-media orchestral prodn., Washington, 1987; founder, prodr., artistic dir. Spring Creek Music Festival, Garland, Tex. Dallas Ft. Worth Metroplex, 1992-94; dir. Lost in the Stars, A.C.O., Carnegie Hall, 1989; visual cons. Lifetime Med. (cable TV), 1989-90; design cons. Reebok River Stage - Radio City Music Hall Prodns, 1989; program designer Mega-Mall, Oxford Devel. Co., Pitts., 1990; designer Unfinished Stories, 1994; prodr. A Salute to Slava, Kennedy Ctr., Washington, 1994; cons. (TV project) Music in America Nat. Symphony Orch., Kennedy Ctr., Washington, 1997; creator Boston Pops Environment, 1995-97; cons. Boston Symphony Hall Sys. Update Plan, 1995-98; design cons. ABC News-Good Morning Am., 20/20, World News Tonight, 1997-98; cons., devel. new material Nextstage Entertainment Corp., 1999-2000; cons. concert environment, hall update and lighting, Midland Ctr. Arts, 2001-02, Concert Shell and Lighting, Orch. Hall, Detroit, 2002, Performance and Event Planning, Campus Martius Pk., Detroit, 2004; author, designer, photographer "The Remarkable Adventures of Texas and Bubba in Venice", 2003; designer scenery and projections The Talking Cure, Mark Taper Forum, 2004; con. design tent graphics, Big Apple Circus, 2005; one-man exhbn. Chgo. Cultural Ctr., US Equities, Wentz Arts Ctr., Naperville, Ill., Reflections, 2009; author, photographer (book) Reflections-Riflessioni, 2007, Reflections Wentz Arts Ctr. Naperville, Ill., 2009; featured artist Lincoln Ctr. 50th Anniversary Exhbn., NY, 2009-. Project leader, design, planning, Outdoor Performance Facility, Met. Opera Co., N.Y. Philharm. Orch., Dept. Cultural Affairs City of N.Y., 1980-2004; cons. Temp. Quarters Project San Francisco Ballet, 1994. Recipient Internat. Theatre Inst. competition award ANTA, 1965, most imaginative use of scene design award Saturday Rev., 1965, Drama Desk-Joseph Maharam award for The Happy Time as best designer of mus., 1968, L.A. Drama Critics Circle award, 1971, Bard award for Excellence in Architecture & Urban Design, 1996. Address: 277 W End Ave New York NY 10023-2604 Office Phone: 212-877-9494. Business E-Mail: peterwexler@mindspring.com.

WEXLER, RAYMOND P., lawyer, automotive executive; b. St. Louis, May 17, 1942; s. Morris J. and Augusta W.; m. Mary Anne Lacks, Mar. 5, 1967; Children: Jennifer, Randy, Colin. BA, Washington U., St. Louis, 1964, JD, 1967; LLM, N.Y.U., 1972. Bar: Mo. 1967, Ill. 1972. Ptnr. Kirkland & Ellis, Chgo., 1972—2006; chief tax officer General Motors Corp., 2006—. Dir. Internat. Tax Forum, Chgo., 1989—. Lt. USN, 1967-71. Mem.: ABA. Mailing: General Motors Corp PO Box 300 Detroit MI 48265-3000 Office: General Motors Corp 300 Renaissance Ctr Detroit MI 48243*

WEXLER, ROBERT, academic administrator; m. Hannah Wexler. BA summa cum laude, UCLA, MA, PhD, UCLA; MBA, Baruch Coll. Ordained rabbi Jewish Theol. Seminary. Lectr. Near Eastern Studies Princeton U.; prof. Am. Jewish U., LA, 1978—, Colen Disting. Lectr. in Bible, pres., 1992—. Named one of The Top 50 Rabbis in America, Newsweek Mag., 2007, 2008, 2009. Mem.: Israel Democracy Inst., World Coun.of Synagogues, Am. Jewish Com. Office: American Jewish Univ 15600 Mulholland Dr Los Angeles CA 90077-1599 Office Phone: 310-476-9777. Business E-Mail: rwexler@ajula.edu.

WEXLER, ROBERT, United States Representative from Florida; b. NYC, Jan. 2, 1961; m. Laurie Cohen; children: Rachel, Zachary, Hannah. Student, Emory U., Atlanta; BA in Polit. Sci., U. Fla., 1982; JD, George Washington U. Law Sch., 1985. Mem. Fla. State Senate, 1991—96, US Congress from 19th Fla. dist., 1997—, mem. internat. rels. com., judiciary com., fgn. affairs com. (chmn. Europe subcom.). Mem. New Dem. Coalition, India Caucus, Congl. Friends of Animals, Serbia Caucus, Silk Road Caucus; co-founder US-Turkish Rels. Caucus, Taiwan Caucus, Indonesia Caucus; co-founder, co-chair Intellectual Property Promotion & Piracy Prevention Caucus; Am. rep. NATO Parliamentary Assembly. Co-author (with David Fisher): Fire-Breathing Liberal: How I Learned to Survive (and Thrive) in the Contact Sport of Congress, 2008. Mem. Calusa Elem. Sch. PTA, Miami; bd. dirs. Caldwell Theater Co., Boca Raton, Boca Raton Mus. Art. Recipient Senatorial Leadership award, Fla. Prosecutor's Assn.; named Top Environ. Senator, Fla. League Conservation Voters, 1996, Legislator of Yr., Palm Beach Police Benevolent Assn. Mem.: Fla. Bar Assn. Democrat. Jewish. Office: Ho Rep 213 Cannon Ho Office Bldg Washington DC 20515-0919 Office Phone: 202-225-3001.*

WEXLER, SANDRA M., artist, medical illustrator; b. NYC, Dec. 17, 1945; d. Irving and Sophie Engel; children: Jason, David. AA, Fashion Inst. Tech., 1965. Cert. medical asst. Balt., 1996. CMA Johns Hopkins Hosp., Lutherville, Md., 1996—97; CMA, clin. coord. Drs. Stanley Klatsky & Adam Basner, Balt., 1997—2000; CMA Dr. Eve Bruce, Lutherville, 2001—03, Dr. Seth Goldberg, Rockville, Md., 2004—06, Dr. Maria Lundquist, Rockville, 2006—. Exhibitions include Am. Inst. Architects Gallery, Sch. 33, Katzenstein Gallery, Slayton House Gallery, Women's Resource Ctr, Greater Balt. Med. Ctr., Gormley Gallery, Coll. Notre Dame, one-woman shows include Shainberg Gallery, Gallerie Elan, 2005, Represented in permanent collections The Art Resource, Balt., limited edit. greeting cards, Balt. Mus. Art Shop, corporate collections, Bloomingdales, NYC, Hyatt Regency, Balt., The Hammers Co., Greenbelt, Md., Wharton, Levin, Ehrmantraut, Klein & Nash, Bethesda, Md., Edward Friedman, CPA, Balt., Signature Mgmt., Balt., Levindale Hebrew Geriatric Ctr. & Hosp., Balt., Ampersand Inc., Reiserstown, Md., Penan & Scott, P.A., Rockville, Md., Martin, Junghans, Snyder & Bernstein, Balt., TCAG, Rockville, Potts & Potts, P.A., Balt., Royal Ins. Co., Balt., Cooper Wingard, Balt., Wiley, Rein & Fielding LLC, DC, Art Forms Gallery, Red Bank, NJ, A. Lee Dellon, MD, Balt., Arles Mgmt., Inc., NY, Gallerie Elan, Bethesda, Ellicott City, Md., Maslow Media Group, Inc. Vol. surg. holding area Sinai Hosp., Balt., 1993—2000. Fellow, Vt. Studio Colony, 1990. Jewish. Avocations: art, reading, travel, cooking, photography.

WEXNER, ABIGAIL, apparel executive; m. Leslie H. Wexner. Dir. Ltd. Brands, Inc., Columbus, Ohio, 1997—. Past chair governing com. Columbus Found.; chair Ctr. for Child and Family Advocacy; mem. bd. trustees Children's Hosp., Inc, The Columbus Acad., The Wexner Ctr. Found.; founder, chair Columbus Coalition Against Family Violence. Named one of Top 200 Collectors, ARTnews Mag., 2004—08. Avocation: Collector of Modern and Contemporary Art; British Sporting Pictures. Office: Ltd Brands Inc Three Limited Pky PO Box 16000 Columbus OH 43216

WEXNER, LESLIE HERBERT, retail executive; b. Dayton, Ohio, 1937; m. Abigail Wexner; 4 children. BSBA, Ohio State U., 1959, HHD (hon.), 1986; LLD (hon.), Hofstra U., 1987; LHD (hon.), Brandeis U., 1990; PhD (hon.), Jewish Theol. Sem. Founder, pres., chmn. bd. The Limited, Inc., fashion chain, Columbus, 1963—. Dir., mem. exec. com. Banc One Corp., Sotheby's Holdings Inc., vis. com. Grad. Sch. Design Harvard U.; mem. bus. adminstrn. adv. coun. Ohio State U.; chmn. Retail Industry Trade Action Coalition. Bd. dirs. Columbus Urban League, 1982-84, Hebrew Immigrant Aid Soc., NYC, 1982—; co-chmn. Internat. United Jewish Appeal Com.; nat. vice chmn., treas. United Jewish Appeal; bd. dirs., mem. exec. com. Am. Jewish Joint Distbn. Com., Inc.; trustee Columbus Jewish Fedn., 1972, Columbus Jewish Found., Aspen Inst., Ohio State U., Columbus Capital Corp. for Civic Improvement; former trustee Columbus Mus. Art, Columbus Symphony Orch., Whitney Mus. Am. Art, Capitol South Community Urban Redevel. Corp.; former mem. Governing Com. Columbus Found.; founding mem., first chair The Ohio State U. Found; exec. com. Am. Israel Pub. Affairs Com. Decorated cavaliere Republic of Italy; named Man of Yr., Am. Mktg. Assn., 1974; named one of Top 200 Collectors, ARTnews Mag., 2004—08, Forbes' Richest Americans, 1999—, Forbes' Exec. Pay, 1999—, World's Richest People, Forbes mag., 2001—. Mem. Young Presidents Orgn., Sigma Alpha Mu. Clubs: B'nai B'rith; fellow Am. Acad. Arts & Sciences Jewish. Avocation: Collector of Modern and Contemporary Art; British Sporting Pictures. Office: Limited Inc PO Box 16000 3 Limited Pkwy Columbus OH 43230-1450

WEYAND, CORNELIA MARITTA, medical educator; Prof., medicine and immunology Mayo Med. and Grad. Sch., Rochester, Minn., 1990—2003; prof., medicine Emory U., Atlanta, 2004—. Office: Emory Univ 101 Woodruff Cir #1003 Atlanta GA 30322

WEYDT, ERIC CHARLES, private school educator; b. Sheboygan, Wis., Mar. 3, 1963; s. Charles Harry Weydt and Elenore Marie Prokash; m. Bonita Beth LeLou, June 30, 1990; children: Robert, Samantha, Claire. AA, U. Wis., Marinette, 1984; BS, U. Wis., Stevens Point, 1986; postgrad., St. John's U., NYC, 2005—. Cert. tchr. Mich. Tchr., adminstr. Menomenie Cath. Ctr. Sch., Mich., 1986—2004; adminstr. Holy Name Cath. Sch., Escanaba, Mich., 2004—. Regional rep. Mich. Assn. Non-Pub. Schs., Lansing, 1997—98, cons.; mem. Escanaba Cath. Bd. Edn., 2004—; tchr. leader Delta/Schoolcraft Intermediate Sch. Dist. Mem.: Escanaba C. of C., KC, Elks. Roman Catholic. Avocations: music, films, reading, outdoor activities. Office: Holy Name Ctrl Grade Sch 409 S 27th St Escanaba MI 49829

WEYER, DIANNE SUE, health facility administrator; b. Anchorage, Aug. 15, 1954; d. Vernon H. and Myrtle M. Larson; m. Merlin D. Weyer; 1 child, Alison. BSW magna cum laude, Augustana Coll., Sioux Falls, SD, 1976; MPA, U. S.D., Vermillion, 1989. LCSW 1996. Program dir. Threshold, Sioux Falls, SD, 1976—78; policy analyst S.D. Divsn. Law Enforcement Assistance, Pierre, SD; coord. youth projects Mountain Plains Youth Svcs. Coalition, Pierre, 1980—82; social worker S.D. Dept. Social Svcs., Pierre, 1983—85; child and adolescent program specialist S.D. Divsn. Mental Health, Pierre, 1985—96; mgr. Social Svcs. St. Mary's Healthcare Ctr., Pierre, 1996—2000, dir. outreach, 2002—. Social work adv. bd., adj. faculty Augustana Coll., Sioux Falls, 1977—79; interagy. coord. coun., state bd. mem. S.D. Dept. Edn., Pierre, 1989—96; state rep. for children and youth Nat. Assn. State Mental Health Program Dirs., Washington, 1985—96; chair S.D. Interagy. Coordination Network Coun., Pierre, 1991—96; social work adv. bd. Presentation Coll., Aberdeen, SD; adj. faculty Capital U., Pierre, 2000—09; exec. bd., past pres. S.D. Social Work Leaders in Health Care, Sioux Falls, 1999—2001. Healthcare com. Pierre C. of C., 1999—2003; tchr., confirmation guide Luth. Meml. Ch., Pierre, 1985—2001; bd. dirs. Missouri Shores Resource Ctr., Pierre, 1980—82; exec. bd. Healthy Cmtys./Healthy Youth, Pierre, 1999—. Recipient Spl. Recognition award, Capitol Area Counseling Svc., 2001, S.D. Family-Based Svcs. Assn., 1994, Outstanding Svc. award, S.D. Corrections Assn., 1990; grantee S.D. CASSP-Local Infrastructure Demonstration, Ctr. Mental Health Svcs., 1993—96, Rural Mental Health Demonstration, NIH, 1987—89, HHS Adminstrn., Children, Youth and Family Svcs., 1987—90. Mem.: NASW, S.D. Alliance for the Mentally Ill, S.D. Social Work Leadership in Healthcare (sec., v.p., pres. 1998—2001, Spl. Recognition award 1996), Nat. Social Work Leadership in Healthcare, Optimist Club (sec. bd. dirs. 2006). Home: 1217 Hilgers Dr Pierre SD 57501 Office: St Mary's Healthcare Ctr 801 E Sioux Pierre SD 57501 Personal E-mail: mdweyer@pic.midco.net. Business E-Mail: dianneweyer@catholichealth.net.

WEYERS, LARRY LEE, energy executive; b. Nebr. BA, Doane Coll., 1967; MS, Columbia U., 1971; MBA, Harvard U., 1975. Registered profl. engr. With Babcock & Wilcox, 1971—73, Commonwealth Edison, 1975—84; mgmt. cons. Towers Perrin, 1984—85; dir. fuel svc. WPS Resources Corp., Green Bay, 1985—89, asst. v.p. energy supply, 1989—92, v.p. energy supply, 1992—94, v.p. power supply & engring., 1994—95, sr. v.p. power supply & engring., 1995, pres., COO, 1995—97, bd. dir., 1996—, pres., CEO, 1997, chmn., pres., CEO, 1998—2007; pres., CEO Integrys Energy Group (merger of WPS Resources & Peoples Energy), 2007—08; exec. chmn. Integrys Energy Group, 2009—. Bd. dir. WS Packaging Corp., Wis. Pub. Svc. Corp., 1996—; bd. mem. Edison Elec. Inst., Am. Gas Assn., 2004, Assn. Edison Illuminating Cos., 2003. Bd. mem. Bellin Health, Green Bay Packers, Wis. Manufacturers & Comm., Competitive Wis., UTECH Ventures, Utility Bus. Edn. Coalition. Office: Integrys Energy Group PO Box 19001 Green Bay WI 54307-9001*

WEYLAND, JACK ARNOLD, physics educator, writer; b. Butte, Mont., June 12, 1940; s. Arnold Clive and Lolita Teckla Weyland; m. Sheryl Raner, Aug. 21, 1965; children: Barbara Dawn Yanish, Dan Auty, Bradley Jack, Jed Raner, Josie Marie. BS, Mont. State U., Bozeman, 1962; PhD, Brigham Young U., Provo, Utah, 1969. Physics prof. SD Sch. Mines and Tech., Rapid City, 1968—93, Brigham Young U. Idaho, Rexburg, 1993—2005. Author: (novels) Charly. Home: 369 Yale Rexburg ID 83440 Business E-Mail: weylandj@byui.edu.

WEYMAN, STEVEN ALOYSIUS, retired military officer; b. Fort Thomas, Ky., May 31, 1957; s. Edward Joseph Weyman and Carol Jean (Steffen) Jackson; m. Kathleen Anne Bradford, June 2, 1990; 1 child, Jennifer Elizabeth. BS in Math., No. Ky. U., 1978; MS in Comm. Sys. Tech., Naval Postgrad. Sch., 1988. Commd. 2d lt. U.S. Army, 1978, advanced through grades to lt. col., 1995; bn. signal officer 8th Engr. Bn., 1st Cav. Divsn., Ft. Hood, Tex., 1979-81, 2nd M.I. Bn., Pirmasens, Germany, 1982-85; co. comdr. B Co., 307th M.I. Bn., Ludwigsburg, Germany, 1985-86; signal combat devel. project officer Combined Arms Command, Ft. Leavenworth, Kans., 1988-91; student U.S. Army Command Gen. Staff Coll., Ft. Leavenworth, 1991-92; bn. exec. officer 123rd Signal Bn., 3rd Inf. Divsn., Kitzingen, Germany, 1992-94; asst. divsn. signal officer 3rd Inf. Divsn., Wuerzburg, Germany, 1994-95; operational readiness evaluation team chief 5th U.S. Army (West), Ft. Lewis, Wash., 1995-97; def. info. sys. network deployed program mgmt. chief Def. Info. Sys. Agy., Arlington, Va., 1997-2000, ret., 2000; student Armed Forces Staff Coll., Norfolk, Va., 1998; tech. acct. mgr. Intel Online Svcs., 2000—01; teleport installation program mgr., prin. engr. Arrowhead Global Solutions Inc., 2001—03; project leader, network sys. lead engr. Mitre Corp., 2003—. Decorated Legion of Merit. Mem. U.S. Signal Corps Assn. (Bronze Order of Mercury 1995), Armed Forces Comm. Electronics Assn. Avocations: computers, travel, reading, sports. E-mail: steve@weyman.net, sweyman@mitre.org.

WEYMOUTH, KATHARINE BOUCHAGE, publishing executive; b. 1966; d. Elizabeth Morris (Graham) Weymouth and Yann R. Weymoth; children: Madeleine, Beckett, Bridget. BA magna cum laude, Harvard Coll., 1988; JD, Stanford Law Sch., 1992. Clk. US Ct. Appeals (9th Cir.), 1992—93; assoc. Williams & Connolly LLP, Washington, 1993—96; asst. counsel The Washington Post, 1996—98, advt. liaison, 2000—02, dir. advt. jobs unit, 2002—04, dir. advt. sales, 2004—05, v.p. advt., 2005—08, pub., 2008—; assoc. counsel Washingtonpost.Newsweek Interactive Co., LLC, 1998—2000; CEO Washington Post Media, 2008—. Bd. dirs. Online Publishers Assn. Office: The Washington Post 1150 15 St NW Washington DC 20071 Office Phone: 202-334-6000. E-mail: weymouth@washpost.com.*

WEYMULLER, BRUNO, oil and gas industry executive; Formerly chief fin. officer Elf Aquitaine, Courbevoie, France; now exec. v.p. Total S.A. (formerly TotalFinaElf S.A.), Courbevoie; also pres. strategy and risk assessment. Office: Total SA 2 Pl de la Coupole-La Défense 6 Paris 92078 France Business E-Mail: bruno.weymuller@total.com.

WHALE, ARTHUR RICHARD, retired lawyer; b. Detroit, Oct. 28, 1923; s. Arthur B. and Orpha Louella (Doak) W.; m. Roberta Lou Donaldson, Oct. 29, 1949; children: Richard Donaldson, Linda Jean. BSChemE, Northwestern U., 1945; JD, George Washington U., 1956. Bar: D.C. 1957, Mich. 1957, Ind. 1977, U.S. Patent and Trademark Office 1957. Chem. engr. Ansul Chem. Co., Marinette, Wis., 1946-47, Parke, Davis & Co., Detroit, 1947-50, writer med. lit., 1950-52; chem. engr. Bur. Ships, U.S. Dept. Navy, Washington, 1952-55, dep. sect. head, indsl. gas sect., 1954-55; patent engr. Swift & Co., Washington, 1955-56; patent atty. Upjohn Co., Kalamazoo, 1956-65; asst. mgr. organic chems. sect. patent dept. Dow Chem. Co., Midland, Mich., 1965-66, mgr., 1967-73, mng. counsel, 1973-75; asst. sec., gen. patent counsel Eli Lilly & Co., Indpls., 1975-86; of counsel Miller, Morriss, & Pappas, Lansing, Mich., 1986-89, Baker & Daniels, Indpls., 1987—2003; ret., 2003. Bd. dirs. Wyckoff Chem. Co., South Haven, Mich., 1985-99; lectr. Practicing Law Inst., John Marshall Law Sch. Contbr. articles to profl. jours. Pres. Nat. Inventors Hall of Fame Found., 1978-79; bd. dirs. Holcomb Rsch. Inst., Indpls., 1982-86. Served to lt. (j.g.) USNR, 1943-46. Mem. State Bar Mich. (chmn. patent trademark copyright sect. 1967-69), D.C. Bar Assn., Midland County Bar Assn. (pres. 1974-75), Am. Bar Assn. (mem. patent trademark copyright sect.), Assn. Corp. Patent Counsel, Nat. Coun. Patent Law Assns. (chmn. 1979-80), Am. Intellectual Property Law Assn. (pres. 1974-75), Ashlar Lodge, Masons, Shriners. Republican. Presbyterian. Avocation: golf. Office Phone: 239-262-8561. Business E-Mail: arwhale@bakerd.com.

WHALEN, CHARLES WILLIAM, JR., writer, retail executive, Former United States Representative, Ohio; b. Dayton, Ohio, July 31, 1920; s. Charles William and Colette (Kelleher) W.; m. Mary Barbara Gleason, Dec. 27, 1958; children— Charles E., Daniel D., Edward J., Joseph M., Anne E., Mary B. BS, U. Dayton, 1942, HHD (hon.), 1980; MBA, Harvard U., 1946; postgrad., Ohio State U., 1959-60; LLD, Central State U., Ohio, 1966. Vice pres. Dayton Dress Co., 1946-52; faculty U. Dayton, 1952-66; mem. 90th-95th Congresses 3d Dist. Ohio; pres. New Directions, Washington, 1978-79; fellow Woodrow Wilson Internat. Center for Scholars, 1980; adj. prof. Sch. Internat. Service, Am. U., 1981. Mem. Ohio Ho. of Reps., 1954-60, Ohio Senate, 1960-66; mem. Internat. Vol. Svcs., Inc., 1985-95; v.p. Washington Inst. Fgn. Affairs, 1982-98; mem. U. Dayton adv. bd. Ctr. for Internat. Studies, 1990-96; bd. dirs. Harvard Bus. Sch., Washington, 1982-84, 91-94. 1st lt. AUS, 1943-46. Recipient Disting. Alumnus award U. Dayton Alumni Assn., 1975, Alumni Lifetime Achievement award U. Dayton Sch. Bus. Adminstrn., 2001. Mem.: Dayton Bicycle Club, Kenwood Country Club, Capitol Hill Club. Roman Catholic.

WHALEN, DANIEL JAMES, astrophysicist; s. Robert Paul and Carol Ann Whalen. BS, Brigham Young U., Provo, Utah, 1989; PhD, U. Ill. Urbana-Champaign, 2000. Course prof. physics dept. U. Calif. San Diego, La Jolla, 2001—04; postdoc. rsch. assoc. Los Alamos Nat. Lab., N.Mex., 2006—. Leader Ch. Jesus Christ LDS, Champaign, Ill., 1994—2000. Named Outstanding Tchr. of Freshmen, Tau Beta Pi, 1997. Mem.: Am. Astron. Soc. Office: Los Alamos Nat Lab T-2 MS B227 Los Alamos NM 87545 Office Fax: 505-667-1931. Business E-Mail: dwhalen@lanl.gov.

WHALEN, JOHN SYDNEY, management consultant; b. Moncton, NB, Can., Sept. 26, 1934; s. Harry Edward and Sarah Maude (Bourgeois) W.; m. Margaret Joan Carruthers, May 3, 1958; children: Bradley Graham, Elizabeth Ann. Grad., Can. Inst. Chartered Accts., 1959. Chartered acct. Coopers & Lybrand (formerly McDonald, Currie & Co.), St. John, N.B., 1954-63; with Kaiser Services, Oakland, Calif., 1963-75, telecommunications mgr., 1966-69, asst. controller, 1969-70, controller, 1970-74; mgr. corp. acctg. Kaiser Industries Corp., Oakland, 1975; controller Kaiser Engrs., Inc., Oakland, 1975-76, v.p. fin. and adminstrn., 1976-82; mgmt. cons., owner Whalen & Assocs., Inc., Alamo, Calif., 1983—. Pres. Round Hill Holdings, Inc., 1993-99. Mem. Rancho Cañada Golf Club. Home: PO Box 709 Alamo CA 94507-0709 Office Phone: 925-820-3506. Personal E-mail: sydwhalen@aol.com.

WHALEN, LAURENCE J., federal judge; b. Pa., 1944; BA, Georgetown Coll., 1967; JD, Georgetown U., 1970, LLM in Taxation, 1971. Spl. asst. to asst. atty. gen. tax divsn. US Dept. Justice, Washington, 1971—72, trial atty tax divsn., 1971—75; atty. Hopkins, Sutter, Hamel and Park (formerly Hamel & Park), Washington, 1977—84, Crowe & Dunlevy, Oklahoma City, 1984—87; judge US Tax Ct., Washington, 1987—2002, sr. judge, 2002—. With USAR, 1971. Mem. ABA (taxation, litig. and bus. law sects.), Fed. Bar Assn. Office: US Tax Ct 400 2nd St NW Washington DC 20217-0002*

WHALEN, LUCILLE, retired academic administrator; b. LA, July 26, 1925; d. Edward Cleveland and Mary Lucille (Perrault) W. BA in English, Immaculate Heart Coll., LA, 1949; MSLS, Catholic U. Am., 1955; DLS, Columbia U., 1965. Tchr. elem. and secondary parochial schs., LA, 1945—52; tchr., libr. Conaty Meml. HS, LA, 1950—52; reference/serials libr., instr. in libr. sci. Immaculate Heart Coll., 1955—58; dean Immaculate Heart Coll. (Sch. Libr. Sci.), 1958-60, 65-70; assoc. dean, prof. SUNY, Albany, 1971-78, 84-87, prof. Sch. Info. Sci. and Policy, 1979—84; dean grad. programs, libr. Immaculate Heart Coll. Ctr., LA, 1987—90; ref. libr. (part-time) Glendale CC, 1990—2008. Dir. US Office Edn. Instn. Author, editor (with others): Reference Services in Archives, 1986; author: Human Rights: A Reference Handbook, 1989; author: (with Nina Redman) Human Rights: A Reference Handbook, 2d edit., 1998. Mem. ACLU, Common Cause, Amnesty Internat. Democrat. Roman Catholic. Home: 320 S Gramercy Pl Apt 101 Los Angeles CA 90020-4542 Home Phone: 213-383-4046. Personal E-mail: lucillew213@sbcglobal.net.

WHALEN, NORMA JEAN, retired special education educator; b. Albuquerque, N. Mex., Nov. 26, 1936; d. Ervin O'dell and Louise (Harcrow) Betts; m. Thomas Leo Whalen; children: Timothy, Patrick, Anna, Emily Wells, Kevin. BEd, Carson-Newman Coll., Jefferson City, Tenn., 1959. Cert. Tchr Secondary Edn. Fla., 1959, Tchr. - History Fla., 1959. Sec. sch. tchr. La Puente Jr. HS, La Puente, Calif., 1959—62; tchr. Umatilla Elem. Sch., Fla., 1969—70; substitute tchr. Lake County Schs., Leesburg, 1969—70, 1975—79; tchr., evening class Lee Adult H.S., Leesburg, Fla., 1979—80; elem. sch. tchr. St. Paul's Cath. Ch., Leesburg, Fla., 1980—81; spl. edn. tchr. Lee Opportunity Ctr. Lifestream Behavioral Ctr., Leeburg, Fla., 1990—2003; ret. Cons. curriculum devel. St. Paul's Cath. Ch., Leesburg, 1986—89, tchr. 1st communion and confession classes, 1986—2006. Dir. learning resource ctr. St. Paul Cath. Ch., Leesbug, 1986—89, sunshine lady; Bd. dirs. Melon Patch Theater, Leesburg, Fla., 1976—81. Recipient Best Supporting actress award, Melon Patch Theater, 1979, Disting. Svc. award, 1980, Svc. award, Lake County Bd. Edn., 1999, Nat. Assn. Mentally Ill Parents Org., 2000. Mem.: NEA, Leesburg Edn. Assn. Roman Catholic. Avocations: crocheting, reading, swimming, cooking, travel.

WHALEY, BETH DOWLING, retired elementary school educator; b. Providence, Apr. 24, 1926; d. Henry Joseph and Agnes Josephine Dowling; m. Richard Charles Whaley, Apr. 28, 1951; children: Mark Michael, Richard Sean, Brian Timothy, Karen Marie. BEd, RI Coll., Providence, 1948; M in Adminstrn. and Reading, Loyola Coll., Balt., 1967. Tchr. Anne Arundel County Pub. Schs., Annapolis, Md., reading resource tchr., vice prin.; cons. Anne Arundel County Bd. Edn., 1987—88; ret., 1988. Founder Annapolis Fine Arts Festival, 1963, Md. Hall Story Theatre, 1981; founding bd. mem. Annapolis Arts Alliance, 2003; co-founder Md. Hall Creative Arts, 1979, Remember Inc., 1990. Author: (book) The Best I Can Be, 1988; editor-in-chief: book Annapolis Faces, 1965, For the Love of It, 1999. Vol. book recorder, narrator Md. Libr. Blind Handicapped; vol. St. Vincent dePaul Soc., St. Mary's Ch., Annapolis. Recipient, County Exec. Citation, Carolyn Brady award, 1980, Arts Achievement award, Anne Arundel County Comm. Culture Arts, 1990, D.A.R. Cmty. Svc. award, 1994, Lifetime Achievement in Arts award, Arts Coun. Anne Arundel County, 2004; named to Md. Hall Fame, 1985. Mem.: Friends Arts, Annapolis Arts Alliance, Colonial Players (pres. 1962—64, 1991—92). Roman Catholic. Avocations: theater, reading, travel, walking, painting. Home: 31 Wilelinor Dr Edgewater MD 21037 Personal E-mail: bduhale@verizon.net.

WHALEY, FRANK, actor; b. Syracuse, NY, July 20, 1963; m. Heather Bucha; children: Buster, Tallulah. Grad., State U. NY. Film appearances include: Ironweed, 1987, Field of Dreams, 1989, Little Monsters, 1989, Born on the Fourth of July, 1989, The Freshman, 1990, JFK, 1991, The Doors, 1991, Career Opportunities, 1991, Back in the U.S.S.R., 1992, A Midnight Clear, 1992, Hoffa, 1992, Swing Kids, 1993, Pulp Fiction, 1994, Swimming With Sharks, 1995, Homage, 1995, Cafe Society, 1995, The Winner, 1996, Broken Arrow, 1996, Retroactive, 1997, Went to Coney Island on a Mission from God: Be Back by Five, 1998, Curtain Call, 1999, Glam, 2001, Pursuit of Happiness, 2001, Chelsea Walls, 2001, A Good Night to Die, 2003, World Trade Center, 2006, The System Within, 2006, The Hottest State, 2006, Crazy Eights, 2006, Vacancy, 2007, Drillbit Taylor, 2008, The Cell 2, 2009; TV films include: Unconquered, 1989, Flying Blind, 1990, To Dance with the White Dog, 1993, Fatal Deception: Mrs. Lee Harvey Oswald, 1993, Dead Man's Gun, 1997, The Wall, 1998, When Trumpets Fade, 1998, Shake, Rattle and Roll: An American Love Story, 1999, Bad News Mr. Swanson, 2001, Sun Gods, 2002, Detective, 2005, Mrs. Harris, 2005, Where There's a Will, 2006, Ruffian, 2007; writer, dir. Joe the King, 1999, The Jimmy Show, 2001, New York City Serenade, 2007; stage appearances include: Tigers Wild, 1986, The Years, 1993; guest appearances include Spenser: For Hire, 1987, Law & Order, 2002, Navy NCIS, 2004, Law & Order: Criminal Intent, 2004, Curb Your Enthusiasm, 2005, Psych, 2006, Boston Legal, 2007, House MD, 2007, Law & Order: Special Victims Unit, 2008, CSI, 2009. Office: Agency for the Performing Arts 405 S Beverly Dr Beverly Hills CA 90212*

WHALEY, KATHARINE BIRGITTA, chemistry professor; b. Barnehurst, Kent, Eng., Mar. 20, 1956; d. John Whaley and ElseLore Anna Maria Johanna Whaley nee Runge; m. Marcin Michal Majda, Mar. 20, 1987; children: Eva Apollonia Whaley-Mayda, Lukas Vincenty Whaley-Mayda. BA, Oxford U., Eng., 1978; PhD, U. Chgo., 1984. Postdoc. fellow Hebrew U. Jerusalem, 1984—86, Tel Aviv U., 1984—86; prof. U. Calif., Berkeley, 1986—; sr. scientist Alexander Von Humboldt Found., Bonn, Germany, 1996—97. Editl. bd. Chem. Physics, Burlington, Mass., 1996—, Jour. Phys. Chemistry, Washington, 1998—2003, Quantum Info. Processing, NYC, 2002—; internat. adv. bd. Australian Rsch. Coun., Sydney, 2001—; com., atomic, molecular and optical sci. NRC, Washington, 2004—06, NAS, Washington, 2005—06; physics divsn. rev. com. Los Alamos Nat. Lab., N.Mex., 2002—06; dir. Berkeley Quantum Info. and Computation Ctr., 2004—; external adv. bd., inst. quantum info. sci. U. Calgary, Alta., Canada, 2007—; functional mgmt. rev. com. Lawrence Livermore Nat. Lab., Livermore, Calif., 2008—. Contbr. more than 160 articles to jours. Recipient Bergmann Meml. Rsch. award, Tel Aviv & Hebrew U., Israel, 1986, award, Alfred P. Sloan Found., 1991—93, Sr. Scientist Rsch. award, Alexander Von Humboldt Found., 1996—97, Continuation award, 2004; Rsch. fellowship, J. F. Kennedy Found. and Harvard U., 1978—79, Golda Meir Rsch. fellow, Hebrew U. Jerusalem, 1984—85. Fellow: Am. Phys. Soc.; mem.: SW Quantum Info. Sci. and Tech. Network, Am. Chem. Soc. Achievements include patents for quantum computation; discovery of molecule induced non-superfluidity in helium, de coherence free and universal spaces; incoherently generated quantum coherences. Avocations: music, hiking, swimming, travel. Office: Dept Chemistry Univ Calif Berkeley CA 94720-1460 Office Fax: 510-643-0003. Business E-Mail: whaley@berkeley.edu.

WHALEY, MICHAEL JOSEPH, history professor; s. Joseph and Evelyn Whaley; m. Cricket Ferguson, June 17, 1983. PhD, Southern Ill. U., Carbondale, 2008. History prof. Lindenwood U., St. Charles, Mo., 2002—, dir, honors coll., 2005—. Mem.: Phi Alpha Theta (faculty advisor 2008—). Office: Lindenwood Univ 209 S Kingshighway Saint Charles MO 63301 Business E-Mail: mwhaley@lindenwood.edu.

WHALEY, ROSS SAMUEL, environmentalist, educator; b. Detroit, Nov. 7, 1937; s. Lyle John and Margaret Nielson (Semple) W.; m. Beverly Mae Heemstra, June 14, 1958; children: Heather Jean, Susan Lesli, Lindsay John. BS, U. Mich., 1959, PhD, 1969; MS, Colo. State U., 1961. Asst. prof., assoc. prof., prof. Utah State U., Logan, 1965—70, dept. head, 1967—70; assoc. dean Colo. State U., Ft. Collins, 1970—73; dept. head U. Mass., Amherst, 1973—76, dean, 1976—78; dir. econ. research USDA Forest Service, Washington, 1978—84; pres. SUNY Coll. Environ. Sci. and Forestry, Syracuse, 1984—2000; prof. SUNY Coll. Environ. Scis. and Forestry, 2000—03; chair Adirondack Park Agy., 2003—07; sr. advisor Adirondack Landowners. Cons. UN FAO, Rome, 1983-84, UN, Budapest, Hungary, 1974, U.S. Peace Corps., South Am., 1972, Geddes, Brecher, Qualls & Cunningham, Denver, 1971-72. Contbr. articles to profl. jours. Bd. dirs. Audubon NY, Adirondack North Country Assn., Single Shanty Preserve & Rsch. Sta. Fellow Soc. Am. Foresters (pres. 1991). Mem. Christian Ref. Ch. Avocations: reading, swimming, hiking, fly fishing, cross country skiing.

WHALEY, STEVEN P., retail executive; BBA, U. Okla., Norman, 1981. CPA 1985. Assoc. KPMG; v.p., controller Southwest Airlines Co., 2001—05; v.p., asst. controller Wal-Mart Stores, Inc., Bentonville, Ark., 2005—06, v.p., controller, 2006—07, sr. v.p., controller, prin. acctg. officer, 2007—. Mem.: Fin. Execs. Internat., Am. Inst. Cert. Pub. Accts. Office: Wal-Mart Stores Inc 702 SW 8th St Bentonville AR 72716-8611*

WHALEY, STORM HAMMOND, retired federal agency administrator; b. Sulphur Springs, Ark., Mar. 15, 1916; s. Storm Onus and Mabel Etta (Prater) W.; m. Jane Florence Bucy, Oct. 6, 1935; children: Carroll Jean Whaley Anderson, Ann Marie Whaley Adams, Rebecca Glenn Whaley. BA, John Brown U., 1935; LL.D. (hon.), 1959; postgrad., Am. U. Law Sch., 1954; D.Sc. hon., U. Ark. for Med. Scis., 1983. Mgr. Sta. KUOA, Siloam Springs, Ark., 1935-53, Sta. KGER, Long Beach, 1948-53, KOME, Tulsa, 1951-53; asst. to Congressman J.W. Trimble, 1953-54; asst. to pres. U. Ark., 1954-59, acting pres., 1959-60, v.p. health scis., 1960-70; assoc. dir. communications NIH, Bethesda, Md., 1970-92; ret., 1992. Mem. U.S. del. World Health Assembly, 1962-64; nat. adv. health coun. USPHS, 1963-66; chmn. ad hoc com. Report to Pres. and Congress Regional Med. Programs, 1967; mem. U.S. Sr. Exec. Service, 1979 Author: They Call It, 1951. Del. Democratic Nat. Conv., 1940, 44, 48, 52. Recipient Superior Service award HEW, 1974, SES Performance award, 1982, Superior Service award USPHS, 1987; named Outstanding Alumnus, John Brown U., 2001. Fellow AAAS; mem. Broadcast Pioneers, Ark. Broadcasters Assn. (life), Masons (33d deg.), Omicron Delta Kappa, Lambda Chi Alpha. Home and Office: 849 Coast Blvd CN105 La Jolla CA 92037 Personal E-mail: stormwhaley@yahoo.com.

WHAM, DAVID BUFFINGTON, secondary school educator; b. Evanston, Ill., May 25, 1937; s. Benjamin and Virginia (Buffington) W.; m. Joan Field Wilber, Mar. 9, 1968 (div. May, 1972); children: Benjamin, Rachel. AB cum laude, Harvard U., 1959; MA, So. Ill. U., Carbondale, 1967. Instr. U. Wyo., Powell, 1963-65, So. Ill. U., Carbondale, 1965-67; legis. asst. U.S. Congress, Washington, 1969-78; freelance writer Chgo., 1980-89; tchr. Chgo. Pub. Schs., 1994—. Speechwriter Adlai Stevenson for Gov. campaign, 1986, Dawn Netsch for Gov. campaign, 1994. Author: My Farewell to Bohemia, 1968, The Comic Genuflection, 1984, A Wave of Bright Boys, 1994. With US Army, 1959-62. Recipient fiction award Columbia Pacific U., 1994. Mem. Harvard Club Chgo. (interviewer 1984—), Spee Club Harvard, Hasty Pudding Club Harvard. Democrat. Episcopalian. Office: 125 S Clark St Chicago IL 60603-5200 Home: 625 E Fourth St Centralia IL 62801

WHANG, MATTHEW IHN SEONG, urologist; b. Seoul, Republic of Korea, June 28, 1960; s. Mike Dae Yun and Ok Joo Whang; m. Margaret K. Nam, June 18, 1988; children: Dana Youngha, Nicole Yoonha, Michael Joonha. BA in Biochemistry, Duke U., 1983; MD, Columbia U., NYC, 1987. Diplomate Am. Bd. Urology, 1995. Surgery resident Columbia Presbyn. Med. Ctr., 1987—89, urology resident, 1989—93; physician Physicians in Urology, Livingston, NJ, 1993—99; pres. Modern Urology, West Orange, NJ, 2000—. Dir. transplant urology St. Barnabas Med. Ctr., Livingston, NJ, 1999—. Contbr. articles to profl. jours., chapters to books. Fellow: ACS; mem.: Assn. Korean Am. Med. Graduates (v.p. 1997—99, pres. 1999—2001), Korean AMA (chmn. membership com. 1998—99, chmn. sci. and edn. com. 1999—2000, sec. gen. 2000—02, exec. v.p. 2002—04). Roman Catholic. Avocation: golf. Office: Modern Urology 1001 Pleasant Valley Way West Orange NJ 07052 Personal E-mail: matthewmd@msn.com.

WHANG, WILLIAM, cardiologist; MD, Columbia U. Coll. Physicians & Surgeons. Cert. cardiovascular disease, clinical cardiac electrophysiology. Intern & resident Columbia U. Med. Ctr.; fellow Mass. Gen. Hosp.; cardiologist NY-Presbyterian Hosp. Office: 622 W 168th St New York NY 10032 Office Phone: 212-305-8559. Office Fax: 212-305-3137.*

WHARTON, ARTHUR EMRIE, pharmacist, director; b. Bethune, SC, July 2, 1934; s. Arthur Emrie Wharton and Janie Artemus Gilmer; m. Jan Kathleen Hankins, Apr. 28, 1984; children: Lesley Ladonis, Arthur Emrie III, Robert Arthur; m. Helen Ludie Summerour, July 23, 1955 (div. Aug. 1983); 1 child, Helen Elaine. BS in Pharmacy, Mercer U. Southern Sch. Pharmacy, Atlanta, 1956, PharmM in Adminstrn., 1990. Lic. practice pharmacy Ga., 1956, Fla., 1973. Pharmacy scis. liaison Upjohn Co., Kalamazoo, 1962—94; dir. continuing edn. U. Fla. Coll. Pharmacy, Gainesville, 1998—. Oil painting. Chmn. Alunmi Assn., Mercer U., Macon, Ga., 1986—88. Lt. comdr. USN, 1956—60. Mem.: APhA, ASHP. Home: 6357 SW 88th Ter Gainesville FL 32608 Office: Univ Fla Coll Pharmacy PO Box 113195 Gainesville FL 32608

WHARTON, KRISTI ANNA, biology professor; b. Walnut Creek, Calif., Feb. 19, 1957; d. Charles Benjamin and Gloria Jean Dorris Wharton; m. David McNear Rand, Aug. 23, 1986; children: Katherine McClain Rand, Laura McNear Rand. PhD, Yale U., New Haven, 1986. Postdoc. fellow IMBB, U. Crete, Heraklion, Crete, Greece, 1987—87, Harvard U., Cambridge, Mass., 1988—91; assoc. prof. Brown U., Providence, 2001—; vis. prof. Biozentrum, Basel, Switzerland, 2003.

Investigator Am. Heart Assn., 1994—99. Recipient Elizabeth Leduc award, 2005. Office: Brown Univ 185 Meeting St Providence RI 02912 Office Fax: 401-863-1348. Business E-Mail: kristi_wharton@brown.edu.

WHARTON, LENNARD, engineering company executive; b. Boston, Dec. 10, 1933; s. Nathaniel Philip and Deeda (Levine) W.; m. Judith R. Gordon, Dec. 26, 1957; children: Ruth, Rebecca, Nathaniel. BS in Chem. Engring, MIT, 1955; BA, MA, Cambridge U., 1957; A.M., Harvard U.; A.M. (NSF fellow 1957-60), 1960, PhD (Jr. fellow Soc. of Fellows 1960-63), 1963. Registered profl. engr., N.J., Ill. Prof. dept. chemistry U. Chgo., 1963-80; v.p. engring. ITE Imperial Corp., 1972-73; v.p. tech. Studebaker-Worthington, Barrington, Ill., 1978-79, McGraw Edison Co., Rolling Meadows, Ill., 1979-80, v.p. engring. and tech. Worthington group Mountainside, NJ, 1980-85; corp. v.p. tech. Material Research Corp., Pearl River, NY, 1985-87; v.p. Packer Engring. Inc., Naperville, Ill., 1987-95, chmn. bd., 1994-95; pres. Evidentia Engring. Inc., Short Hills, NJ, 1995—. Sloan fellow, 1964-66; named Outstanding Young Man of Chgo. Chgo. Jr. Assn. Commerce and Industry, 1968 Mem. IEEE (sr.), Nat. Fire Protection Assn., Am. Inst. Chem. Engrs. Office: 10 Park Pl Short Hills NJ 07078-2826

WHARTON, MARGARET MARY, nun, educator; b. San Diego, Sept. 2, 1948; d. John Philip Wharton and Mary Elizabeth Roundtree. BA in Math., Salve Regina Univ., Newport, RI, 1976; MA in Math., Appalachian Univ., 1997. Cert. tchg. math/secondary N.C, 1994, R.I., 1982. Tchr. St. Anthony Sch., Guam, 1969—72, Cathedral Grade Sch., Guam, 1972—74, 1978—82, vice prin., 1973—74, Santa Barbara Sch., Guam, 1983—84, tchr., 1982—85; sub. tchr. Gaston/Charlotte-Mecklenburg Sch., 1990; tchr. St. Michael's Sch., Gastonia, NC, 1990—94, Acad. of Our Lady, Guam, 1976—78, 1985—88; tchg. asst. Appalachian State Univ., 1996; prof. Southern W.Va. Cmty. & Tech. Coll., 1998—2000, Marshall Univ., 2000—01, Shenandoah Univ., 2001—. Author: Tutor-Training Manual for Shenandoah University, 2003, Learning Styles, 2003, Study Skills, 2003, Math Anxiety, 2003; contbr. scientific papers; co-author: Collabrorative Learning Activties Manual, 2006, Introductory and Intermediate Algebra, 2006, Beginning Algebra with Critical Thinking, 2008. Mem.: Kellogg Inst. Developmental Educators, Coll. Reading & Learning Assn., N.C. Coun. of Tchrs. of Math., Math. Assn. of Am., Nat. Assn. of Devel. Educators, Va. Assn. of Devel. Educators, Nat. Coun. of Tchrs. of Math. Democrat. Roman Cath. Avocations: astronomy, research, medicine. Home Phone: 540-465-9368. Business E-Mail: mwharton@su.edu.

WHARTON, RALPH NATHANIEL, psychiatrist, educator; b. Boston, June 15, 1932; s. Nathaniel Philip and Deeda (Levine) W.; children: Naida, Philip, Laura. AB cum laude, Harvard U., 1953; MD, Columbia U., 1957, degree in psychoanalysis, 1970. Cert. Neurology and Psychiatry 1969. Intern Cornell divsn. Bellevue Hosp., NYC, 1957—58; resident Columbia-Presbyn. Med. Ctr., 1961—64; pvt. practice psychiatry/pharm., 1964—; assoc. psychiatry Coll. Physicians and Surgeons, 1964—69, asst. prof. clin. psychiatry, 1969—72, assoc. prof., 1972—83, prof., 1984—; sr. rsch. psychiatrist NY State Psychiat. Inst., 1964—70; assoc. attending psychiatry Columbia-Presbyn. Hosp., 1970—80, attending psychiatrist, 1980—; sr. cons. supr. psychiatric svc. NY Presbyteriuan Hosp. Ex-officio mem. bd. trustees Columbia-Presbyn. Med. Ctr., pres. soc. practitioners, 1980—82, attending, 1984—; exec. dir. Wharton Fund for Brain Rsch.; med. dir. Black Sea project Macalester Coll., 1994—98; co-dir. Reiner for Behaviour and Psychosomatic Rsch. and Tchg. Columbia U. Med. Ctr., 2004—; exec. dir. Wharton Fund Brain Rsch., 1993—; assoc. dir. Reiner Ctr. Psychosomatic Medicine, Columbia Med. Ctr. Author: Landmark Papers, Lithium Carbonate for Affective Disorders, 1966; contbr. Mood and Anxiety chapters, Merritt's Textbook of Neurology, 2005, 08, AARP chapter, Art of Aging, 2006, numerous papers, publs. in profl. jours. and chpts. to books. Mem. alumni campaign com. Coll. Physicians and Surgeons, Columbia U., 2001—. Served to Capt. M.C., US Army, 1958-60, US Army Hosp. Orleans, France, 1960-61 Capt. med. corp US Army, 1958—60. Named one of Best Drs., NY Mag. Fellow: Am. Coll. Psychoanalysts (pres. 1996, bd. dirs. 1996—), NY Acad. Medicine, Am. Psychiat. Assn. (life Hon. Life fellow 2002); mem.: AMA, Group for Advancement Psychiatry, Internat. Assn. Study of Pain (founding mem.), Royal Soc. Medicine, Soc. Practitioners (exec. com. 1990—), Harmonie Club, Harvard Club (class agent 1953—), Salon de Virtuosi (founding bd. mem. 1991—, treas. 1991—), Lotos Club. Achievements include sponsor of Wharton Professorship in Psychiatry at Columbia U. Health Ctr., 2008. Avocations: skiing, sailing, literature. Office: Columbia-Presbyn Med Ctr Atchley Pavilion Ste 209 161 Ft Washington Ave New York NY 10032-3713 Office Phone: 212-860-2666.

WHATLEY, JACQUELINE BELTRAM, lawyer; b. West Orange, NJ, Sept. 26, 1944; d. Quirino and Eliane (Gruet) Beltram; m. John W. Whatley, June 25, 1966 (dec. July 1998). BA, U. Tampa, 1966; JD, Stetson U., 1969. Bar: Fla. 1969, Alaska 1971; cert.: (real estate law specialist). Assoc. Tucker, McEwen, Smith & Cofer, Tampa, Fla., 1969-71; pvt. practice Anchorage, Alaska, 1971-73; ptnr. Gibbons, Tucker, Miller, Whatley & Stein, P.A., Tampa, 1973—; pres., 1981—. Bd. dirs. Travelers Aid Soc., 1982-94; trustee Humana Women's Hosp., Tampa, 1987-93, Keystone United Meth. Ch., 1986-89, 99—. Mem. ABA, Fla. Bar Assn. (real estate cert. com. 1993-95), Alaska Bar Assn., Tenn. Walking Horse Breeders and Exhibitors Assn. (v.p. 1984-87, dir. Fla. 1981-87, 90-93, 97-99, adv. com. Tenn. Walking Horse Celebrateion 1994-97), Fla. Walking and Racking Horse Assn. (bd. dirs. 1988-89, pres. 1980-82), Athena Soc. Republican. Methodist. Home: PO Box 17595 Tampa FL 33682-7595 Office: 101 E Kennedy Blvd Ste 2190 Tampa FL 33602-5146 Office Phone: 813-228-7841. Business E-Mail: whatley@gte.net.

WHATLEY, JILLIAN KATRI, physiologist, educator; b. Birmingham, Ala., June 29, 1977; d. Charles Alan and Ruby Smith Whatley. M.S., U. Tenn., Knoxville, 2001; MA, Gallaudet U., Washington, 2005, EdS, 2007. Cert. Nat. Assn. Sch. Psychologist, 2007. Case mgr. Founds. First Home Care, Washington, 2004—06; adj. prof. Prince George's C.C., Upper Marlboro, Md., 2005—08, Ga. Perimeter Coll., Dunwoody, 2008—; recruiter, trainer foster families Nat. Ctr. Children & Families, Washington, 2006—07; sch. psychologist Prince George's County Pub. Schs., Upper Marlboro, 2006—08, Gwinnett County Pub. Schs., Suwanee, Ga., 2008—. Mem. Md. Sch. Psychologist Assn., 2006—08. Recipient Elizabeth Peete award, Gallaudet U., 2007; named one of Most Outstanding Tchr., Marietta City Schools, 2003; fellowship, AEL, 2004. Fellow: Alpha Kappa Alpha; mem.: Nat. Assn. Sch. Psychologist (student mem. to bd. 2006—07), Ga. Assn. Sch. Psychologist. Personal E-mail: jillian.whatley@gmail.com.

WHATMORE, GEORGE BERNARD, research scientist, writer, internist, neurophysiologist; b. Seattle, Aug. 31, 1917; s. Harry Joseph and Delia (Frolich) Whatmore; m. Frances Maxwell Beatty, May 28, 1942; children: Pamela Frances, David Blake, Nancy Janice. BS, U. Wash., 1940, MS, 1941; PhD, U. Chgo., 1946, MD, 1948. Intern King County Hosp., Seattle, 1948—49, resident, 1949—50, Lab. Clin. Physiology, Chgo., 1950—51; pvt. practice and rsch. in internal medicine, clin. neurophysiology, functional disorders Seattle, 1951—. Mem. staff Virginia Mason Hosp., Seattle, 1951—, Swedish Hosp., Seattle, 1951—, Med.-Dental Bldg. Hosp., Seattle, 1951—, Eastern State Hosp., Medical Lake, Wash., 1955—58; prin. investigator Pacific N.W. Rsch. Found. and Inst., Seattle, 1966—. Author (with Daniel R. Kohli): Dysponesis: A Neurophysiologic Factor in Functional Disorders, 1968, The Physiopathology and Treatment of Functional Disorders, 1974; author: A Scientist Looks at Christianity, A Probability Analysis, 1993, 2d edit., 1995, A Scientist Looks at Religion, Based on Evidence Plus Logic, 3d edit., 2003, De-contaminating The New Testament, Based on Lessons Learned from The Galileo Scandal, 2004; contbr. articles to profl. jours.; author (with Patricia A. Huggins): High Probability Christianity The Most Probable Teachings of jesus Christ Based on Existance Plus Logic, 2009. Recipient Ginsburg award, U. Chgo., 1946; Univ. fellow, 1941—45, Rawson fellow, 1945—46, Sheldon fellow, 1945—46. Mem.: AMA, AAAS (life), Western Acad. Beaux Arts, King County Med. Soc., Wash. State Med. Assn., Assn. for Applied Psychophysiology and Biofeedback, Acad. Psychosomatic Medicine, Behavior Therapy and Rsch. Soc., Biofeedback Rsch. Soc., Internat. Stress and Tension Control Assn., Am. Physicians Soc. for Physiologic Tension Control, N.Y. Acad. Sci., Sigma Xi. Home and Office: 10524 SE 27th St Bellevue WA 98004-7231 Office Phone: 425-454-7273.

WHEALEY, LOIS DEIMEL, humanities scholar; b. NYC, June 20, 1932; d. Edgar Bertram Deimel and Lois Elizabeth (Hatch) Washburn; m. Robert Howard Whealey, July 2, 1954; children: Richard William, David John, Alice Ann. BA in History, Stanford U., 1951; MA in Edn., U. Mich., 1955; MA in Polit. Sci., Ohio U., 1975, M in Social Sci., 2007. Tchr. 5th grade Swayne Sch., Owyhee, Nev., 1952-53; tchr. 7th grade Ft. Knox (Ky.) Dependent's Sch., 1955-56; tchr. adult basic edn. USAF, Oxford, 1956-57; tchr. 6th grade Amerman Sch., Northville, Mich., 1957-58; tchr. 8th grade English, social studies Slauson Jr. High Sch., Ann Arbor, Mich., 1958-59; adminstrv. asst. humanities conf. Ohio U., Athens, 1974-76, 83. Part-time instr. Ohio U., Athens, 1966—68, 1975, VISTA with Rural Action, 1996—98. Contbr. articles to profl. jours. Mem. Athens County Regional Planning Commn., 1974—78, treas., 1976—78; mem. Ohio coord. com. Internat. Women's Yr., 1977; v.p. Black Diamond Girl Scout Coun., 1980—86; chair New Day for Equal Rights Amendment, Athens, 1982; mem. Athens City Bd. Edn., 1984—90, v.p., 1984, pres., 1985; mem. Tri-County Vocat. Sch. Bd., Nelsonville, Ohio, 1984—90, v.p., 1988—89; mem. adv. com. Ohio River Valley Water Sanitation Commn., 1986—95; Ohio outreach liaison Nat. Town Meeting for Sustainable Am., 1999; bd. dirs. Ohio Environ. Coun., 1984—90, sec., 1986—90; bd. dirs. Ohio Alliance for Environ., 1994—98, v.p., 1998; bd. dirs. Organize Ohio, 1999—2007, bd. pres., 2001—07; bd. dirs. Ohio Women, Inc., 1995—, sec., 1997—; bd. dirs. Unitarian Universalist Svc. Com., 2001—03, Ohio Meadville Dist. Unitarian-Universalist Assn., 1975—81; co-chair nat. vol. network Unitarian Universalist Svc. Com., 2003—05. Recipient Unsung Unitarian Universalist award, Ohio-Meadville Dist. Unitarian Universalist Assn., 1984, How-to award, Ednl. Press Assn. Am., 1990, Donna Chen Women's Equity award, Ohio U., 1994, Cmty. Svc. award, Athens County Cmty. Svcs. Coun., 1998, award for individual contbn. over a lifetime, Ohio Alliance Environment, 2002, Thanks badge, Black Diamond Girl Scout Coun., 1986, Social Justice award, UCM, Ohio U., 2007; named Woman of Achievement, Black Diamond Girl Scout Coun., 1987, Peacemaker, Appalachian Peace and Justice Network, 1998, Outstanding Feminist, Athens Herstory Celebration, 2002. Mem.: LWV (pres. Athens 1975—77), AAUW (pres.Athens br. 1969—70, 1989—90, 1993—2001, AAUW/Ohio bd. 1995—2004), Phi Kappa Phi, Pi Lambda Theta. Democrat. Avocation: genealogy. Home: 14 Oak St Athens OH 45701-2605

WHEAT, ALAN DUPREE, former Congressman, political consultant; b. San Antonio, Tex., Oct. 16, 1951; s. James and Emogene Wheat; children: Alynda, Christopher, Nicholas. BA, Grinnell Coll., 1972. Economist HUD, Kansas City, Mo., 1972-73, Mid.-Am. Regional Council, Kansas City, 1973-75; aide County Exec.'s Office, Kansas City, 1975-76; mem. Mo. Ho. of Reps., Jefferson City, 1977-82, US Congress from 5th Dist. Mo., Washington, 1983—95; v.p. Fed. Rels. SmithKline Beecham; ptnr. Winburn, Jenkins & Wheat; v.p. public policy & govt. rels. CARE, 1994—98; founder, pres. Wheat Govt. Relations, Arlington, Va., 1998—. Bd. dir. CARE; Dem. candidate for US Senate from Mo., 1994; dep. campaign mgr., dir. public liason Clinton-Gore 1996. Named Best Freshman Legislator St. Louisan Mag., 1977-78; 1 of 10 Best Legislators Jefferson City News Tribune, 1979-80; 1 of 10 Best Legislators Mo. Times Newspaper, 1979-80 Democrat. Office: Wheat Govt Relations Inc Ste 2 1201 S Eads St Arlington VA 22202 Office Phone: 703-271-8770. Office Fax: 703-271-9594. Business E-Mail: awheat@wheatgr.com.

WHEAT, BILL W., construction executive; BBA in Acctg. and Fin., Baylor U., Waco, Tex. CPA. Auditor Price Waterhouse LLP (now PricewaterhouseCoopers LLP); various positions including fin. planning mgr. and asst. contr. The Bombay Co., 1991—98; acctg. mgr. D.R. Horton, Inc., Fort Worth, 1998—2000, sr. v.p., contr., 2000—03, exec. v.p., CFO, bd. dirs., 2003—. Office: DR Horton Inc DR Horton Tower 301 Commerce St Ste 500 Fort Worth TX 76102

WHEAT, MYRON WILLIAM, JR., cardiothoracic surgeon; b. Sapulpa, Okla., Mar. 24, 1924; s. Myron William and Mary Lee (Hudiburg) W.; m. Erlene Adele Plank, June 12, 1949 (div. June 1970); children: Penelope Louise, Myron William III, Pamela Lynn, Douglas Plank; m. Carol Ann Karmgard, June 18, 1970 (div. Apr. 1996); 1 child, Christopher West. AB, Washington U., St. Louis, 1949; MD cum laude, Washington U., 1951. Diplomate Am. Bd. Surgery, Am. Bd. Thoracic Surgery. Instr., clin. fellow Washington U., St. Louis, 1956—58; asst. prof. surgery U. Fla., Gainesville, 1958—65, prof. surgery, 1965—72; dir. profl. svcs., chief clin. physician U. Fla. Shands Tchg. Hosp., Gainesville, 1968—72; prof. surgery, dir. thoracic and cardiothoracic surgery U. Louisville Sch. Medicine, 1972—75, clin. prof. surgery, 1975—; cardiothoracic surgeon Cardiac Surg. Assocs., P.A., St. Petersburg, Fla., 1975—91; cons., thoracic surgery Bay Pine VA Hosp., St. Petersburg, 1994—; clin. prof. surgery U. So. Fla. Sch. Medicine, Tampa, 1995—; cardiothoracic surgeon Cardiac Surg. Assocs., P.A., Clearwater, Fla., 1991—. Clin. prof. surgery U. South Fla., 1995—; cons. Bay Pines VA Hosp., St. Petersburg, 1991—; mem. Am. Bd. Thoracic Surgery, 1969-75 Author (with others) 18 books; mem. editl. bd. Am. Heart Jour., 1971; contbr. over 100 articles to profl. jours.; developed drug therapy for acute dissecting aneurysms of the aorta 1st lt. USAF, 1943-46, ETO Decorated DFC Air medal (4), Presdl. Citation; named First Howard W. Lillenthal Meml. lectr. Mt. Sinai Hosp., 1963. Fellow ACS (gov.), Am. Coll. Cardiology (chmn. bd. govs. 1968-69); mem. Am. Surg. Assn., Am. Assn. Thoracic Surgery (sec. 1972-78), So. Surg. Assn., So. Thoracic Surg. Assn., Soc. Thoracic Surgeons, Soc. Thoracic Surgeons Gr. Britain and Ireland, Alpha Omega Alpha Republican. Home and Office: 8413 SW 55th Pk Gainesville FL 32608 Personal E-mail: myronwheat@msn.com.

WHEATER, ASHLEY C., former dancer, performing company executive; b. Cutler, Scotland; Student, Royal Ballet Sch. Mem. Royal Ballet, prin. dancer; mem. London Festival Ballet, Australian Ballet, 1982, Joffrey Ballet, 1985—89; soloist San Francisco Ballet, 1989-90, prin. dancer, 1990—96, ballet master, 1996, asst. to artistic dir., 2002—07; artistic dir. Joffrey Ballet, Chgo., 2007—. Performances with the San Francisco Ballet include The Sleeping Beauty, Swan Lake, Romeo and Juliet, Menuetto, Valses Poeticos (Love Letters), Handel-a Celebration, Forevermore, Bugaku, Who Cares?, The Four Temperaments, Duo Concertant, Symphony in C, Company B, In G Major, In the Night, In the middle, somewhat elevated, New Sleep, Maelstrom, Tagore, The End, La Fille mal gardée, La Sylphide, Nutcracker, Forgotten Land, Pulcinella, Connotations, Job, The Son of Horus, The Wanderer Fantasy; with other cos. include La Fille mal gardée, Monotones II, The Dream, Wedding Bouquet, Romeo and Juliet, La Sylphide, Love Songs, Remembrances, Return to the Strange Land, Etudes, Echoing of Trumpets, Sphinx, Greening; performed at Reykjavik Arts Festivals, Iceland, 1990, Jacob's Pillow, 1990. Office: Joffrey Ballet 10 East Randolph St Chicago IL 60601*

WHEATLAND, RICHARD, II, fiduciary services executive, museum executive; b. Boston, Nov. 25, 1923; s. Stephen and Dorothy (Parker) W.; m. Cynthia McAdoo, Feb. 13, 1954; 1 child, Sarah Wheatland Fisher. AB, Harvard U., 1944, postgrad., 1946-47; JD, Columbia U., 1949. Various positions with Marshall Plan adminstrn. Office Spl. Rep. in Europe, Dept. State, Paris, 1950-53; v.p. N.Y. Airways, NYC, 1953-68; pres. Acadia Mgmt. Co., Inc., Boston, 1968-93, chmn., 1993—. Bd. dirs., v.p. Pingree Assocs., Bangor, Maine. Mem. Mayor's Com. Insl. Leaders for Youth, N.Y.C., 1963-66; mem. corp. New Eng. Forestry Found.; mem., former chmn. Fund for Preservation of Wild Life and Natural Areas, Boston, 1980-92, bd. dirs. 1980-91; trustee Penobscot Marine Mus., Searsport, Maine, 1968-90, hon. trustee, 1990—,; bd. dirs. Friends of Pub. Garden, Boston, 1972-89, 90-96, 97—, Beacon Hill Civic Assn., Boston, 1985-89, Boston Natural Areas Fund, 1987—, asst. treas., 1993-94, treas. 1994-96, bd. dirs. 1997, acting chair, 1997—; treas. Frank Hatch for Gov. com., Boston, 1977-78; chmn., bd. trustees & overseers Peabody Essex Mus. (formerly Peabody Mus. of Salem), Salem, Mass., 1992—, trustee, 1972-92, pres., 1983-92. Lt. (j.g.) USN, 1943-46, PTO. Mem. Am. Assn. Mus. (bd. dirs. trustee com. 1976-86, govt. affairs com. 1985-89), Mus. Trustee Assn. (founder, bd. dirs. 1986—, sec. 1986-92), City Club Corp. (former bd. mgrs., former treas.). Avocations: jogging, sailing, travel.

WHEATLEY, DEBORAH A., music educator; b. Mt. Clemens, Mich., Oct. 28, 1954; d. Ernest William Wheatley and Joanne Smith. AA with honors, Miami-Dade CC, 1975; BA magna cum laude, U. Ctrl. Fla., 1978; grad., US Army Element Sch. Music, 1984. Music tchr. Lecanto Primary, Fla., 1978—81; band dir. Lecanto Mid. Sch., 1981—83, fine arts tchr., 1986—96, band dir., 1996—; with signal corps band U.S. Army Elem. Sch. Music, Ft. Gordon, Ga., 1984; summer duty U.S. Army, 1986—92. With Signal Corps Band US Army, 1984—86. Recipient U.S. Army Commendation medal, 1986. Republican. Avocations: running, promoting healthy lifestyle to middle school students. Home: 1801 Silverwood St Inverness FL 34453 Office: Lecanto Mid Sch 3800 W Educational Path Lecanto FL 34461 Office Phone: 352-746-2050. Personal E-mail: debwheat@mailstation.com.

WHEATLEY, SEAGAL V., lawyer, legal association administrator; b. Houston, May 24, 1935; s. Seagal V.and Hilda (Guess) W.; m. Wanda Jean Wheatley, Dec. 15, 1978; children: Jill Wilder, Julie. BA in Govt., North Tex. U., 1957; JD, U. Tex., 1960. Bar: Tex. 1960. Ptnr. Beckman, Standard, Wood & Vance, San Antonio, 1960-69; atty. U.S. Dept. of Justice, Tex., 1969-71; pres. Oppenheimer, Rosenberg, Kelleher & Wheatley Inc., San Antonio, 1971—97; ptnr., litig. practice Jenkens & Gilchrist, San Antonio, 1997—. Adj. prof. U. Tex. Sch. of Law, Austin, 1985, 86, 89. Contbr. articles to profl. jours. Del. Rep. Nat. Conv., Miami, Fla., 1968; chmn. Bexar City Reps., San Antonio, 1968. Fellow Tex. Bar Found.; mem. ABA, Assn. Trial Lawyers Am., Tex. Bar Assn., San Antonio Bar Assn., Fed. Bar Assn., 5th Cir. Bar Assn. (past pres.), Internat. Soc. of Barristers. Avocations: golf, tennis. Office: Jenkens & Gilchrist Ste 900 Weston Ctr 1445 Ross Ave Ste 3700 Dallas TX 75202-2755 Office Phone: 210-246-5635. Office Fax: 210-246-5999. Business E-Mail: swheatley@jenkens.com.

WHEATON, DOUGLAS B., city manager, lawyer; b. Milw., July 21, 1972; s. Frank and Doreen Wheaton. BS in criminal justice, Carroll Coll., 1994; JD, Marquette U. Law Sch., 1998; MA in polit. sci., Marquette U. Grad. Sch., 1999; attended program of inst. for law, Harvard Law Sch., 2000. Bar: Wis. 1998, US Ct. of Appeals, 7th Circuit, US Dist. Ct., Ea. Dist. Wis., US Dist. Ct., Western Dist. Wis. Legis. asst. Wis. State Legis., Madison, 1999—2002; govt. affairs dir. Wis. Realtors Assn., Madison, 2002—05; dir. city devel. City of Franklin, Wis., 2005—08. Recipient CALI Excellence for the Future award, Ctr. for Computer Assisted Legal Instr., 1997. Mem.: Internat. Econ. Devel. Coun., Am. Polit. Sci. Assn. Avocations: travel, reading.

WHEATON, MARILYN, musician; b. Warren, Ohio, Feb. 1, 1933; d. Russell and Donabelle Irene Donehue; m. Warren Randall Wheaton, June 20, 1953; 1 child, Janean Renee Vaupel-Wilson. BS in Music Edn. cum laude, Kent State U., 1955. Cert. Yamaha music instr. Pvt. piano and organ tchr., Ohio and Ariz., 1950—; profl. pianist, organist, accompanist, 1946—; elem. music supr. Austintown Pub. Schs., Youngstown, Ohio, 1955-61. Founder, dir. Potter's Clay Christian singing group, Phoenix, 1981-85; choir dir., organist, pianist at various chs., Ohio and Ariz., 1942—; rep. for elem. music texts and programs Mahoning County Schs., Youngstown, 1959-60; tchr., organizer student trips to numerous concerts; tchr., dir. choirs and soloists for dist. and state competitions, 1955—. Composer (poems to music) Seven Last Words of Christ, also anthems, introits, reponses; arranges music for beginning and handicapped students. Dir., accompanist Terry's Variety Show, Austintown, 1951, Potter's Clay, 1980-85; pianist at various sr. citizens' groups Kent State U. and Youngstown U. scholar, 1951-55. Mem. Music Tchrs. Nat. Assn., Delta Omicron (life, charter mem., pres. Delta Upsilon chpt.). Avocations: travel, camping, reading, walking, piano recitals. Home and Office: 3245 W Yucca St Phoenix AZ 85029-4133

WHEELAN, BELLE S., educational association administrator; 1 child, Reginald. BA in Psychology and Sociology, Trinity U., San Antonio, 1972; MA in Devel./Ednl. Psychology, La. State U., Baton Rouge, 1974; D in Ednl. Adminstrn., U. Tex., Austin, 1984. Asst. prof. psychology, dir. devel. edn., dir. acad. support svcs. San Antonio Coll., 1974—87; dean student svcs. Thomas Nelson C.C., Hampton, Va., 1987—89; provost Tidewater C.C., Portsmouth, Va., 1989—92; pres. Ctrl. Va. C.C., 1992—97, No. Va. C.C., 1998—2001; sec. of edn. Commonwealth of Va., Richmond, 2002—05; pres. Commn. on Colls. So. Assn. for Colls. and Schs., Decatur, Ga., 2005—. Mem. Am. Coll. Testing Bd., Nat. Commn. on NAEP 12th Grade Assessment and Reporting, 2003—. Recipient Disting. Grad. award, U. Tex., 1992, Outstanding Alumnus award, Trinity U., 2002, Strong Men and Women award, 2003. Mem.:

Nat. Coun. on Black Am. Affairs (pres. roundtable). Roman Catholic. Office: Commn on Colls So Assn Colls and Schs 1866 Southern Lane Decatur GA 30033 Office Phone: 404-679-4512. Business E-Mail: belle.wheelan@sacscoc.org.

WHEELDON, CHRISTOPHER, performing company executive, choreographer; b. Yeovil, Somerset, England, 1973; s. Peter and Judy Wheeldon. Student, West Coker Ballet Sch., Somerset, Royal Ballet Sch., London, 1981-89, student higher sch., 1989-91. Dancer Royal Ballet, 1991-93; dancer-corps de ballet NYC Ballet, 1993—98, soloist, 1998—2001; resident choreographer, 2001—08; founder Morphoses the Wheeldon Co., 2007—. Early roles include Fritz in The Nutcracker, Royal Ballet, Covent Garden, 1984; choreographer The Syncopated Clock, Royal Ballet Sch., 1984, more recently Le Voyage, Royal Ballet, 1995, Danses Bohémiennes, NYC Ballet, 1995 (Mae L. Wien award for Young Choregrapher 1995), Souvenir, Royal Ballet, 1996, A Midsummer Night's Dream, Colo. Ballet, 1996, Diversions, Royal Ballet Sch., 1996; choreographer Ctr. Stage (film), 2000, Variations Serieuses, 2001, Polyphonia, 2001 (Nat. Dance award for Best Classical Choreography, London Critics' Cir., 2004, Dance Mag. award for Best New Ballet, 2005), Sweet Smell of Success, 2002, Tryst, 2002, Continuum, 2002, Tryst, 2002, Morphoses, 2002, Carousel, 2002, Sweet Smell of Success (Broadway play), 2002, Carnival of the Animals, 2003, Swan Lake, 2004, Liturgy, 2003, After the Rain, 2005, An American in Paris, 2005, Klavier, 2006, DGV, 2006, Dance of the Hours, 2006, The Nightingale and the Rose, 2007, Misericors, 2007 Electric Counterpoint, 2008 (Critics' Cir. Nat. Dance award for Best Classical Choreography, 2008). Recipient Gold Medal for dance (original choreography), Prix de Lausanne, 1991, Martin E. Segal award, Lincoln Ctr., Am. Choreography award, Olivier award; named one of 40 Under 40, Crain's NY Bus., 2006. Office: Morphoses 800 5th Ave Ste 18F New York NY 10065 Office Phone: 212-588-9001. Office Fax: 888-391-1110. E-mail: info@morphoses.org.*

WHEELER, ALBIN GRAY, retired military officer, educator; b. Huntington, W.Va., Mar. 16, 1935; s. Harvey Gray and Hattie Benson (Weddle) W.; m. Beatrice Thomas, May 17, 1958; children: Dianne, Michelle, Patrice. BA, Marshall U., 1958; MBA, Pepperdine U., 1975; student, Army War Coll., 1976, Harvard U., 1990; DHL (hon.), Marshall U., 2004. Enlisted U.S. Army, 1952, commd. 2d lt., 1959, advanced through grades to maj. gen., 1982; comdr. divsn. spt. command, chief of staff 1st Inf. Divsn., Ft. Riley, Kans., 1978-80; CEO Army AF Exch. Svc.-Europe/Middle East, Munich, 1981-83; comdr. 2d Spt. Command, VII U.S. Corps, Germany, 1983-85; pres. Indsl. Coll. Armed Forces, Washington, 1985-89; CEO Army and Air Force Exch. Svc., Dallas, 1991-93; ret. U.S. Army, 1993; exec. dir. Arent Fox, Washington, 1993-96. Exec. com. Soc. Yeager Scholars, Marshall U. Decorated Def. and Army D.S.M., Bronze Star with two oak leaf clusters, Legion of Merit with two oak leaf clusters; inducted into Army Quartermaster Hall of Fame, 1999. Mem. Marshall U. Alumni Assn. (disting. alumnus 1983).

WHEELER, ALFRED GEORGE, JR., retired entomologist, biology professor, researcher; s. Alfred George and Frances (Rudisill) W. BA, Grinnell Coll., Iowa, 1966; PhD, Cornell U., Ithaca, NY, 1971. Instr. Cornell U., 1971; entomologist Pa. Dept. Agr., Harrisburg, 1971—96; adj. prof. Clemson U., 1995—. Adj. asst. prof. Pa. State U., University Park, 1973-81, adj. assoc. prof., 1981-88, adj. prof., 1988—; cons. Dames & Moore, Cranford, N.J., 1974, U.S. Congress, Office of Tech. Assessment, Washington, 1991. Sr. author: A Synthesis of the Holarctic Miridae (Heteroptera): Distribution, Biology, and Origin, with Emphasis on North America, 1992; editor: Regulatory Horticulture, 1975-96, Melsheimer Entomological Series, 1978-82, Biota of South Caroling, 2000-; assoc. editor Fla. Entomologist, 1997-99; contbr. more than 200 articles to profl. jours., chpts. to books. V.p. Hershey Jaycees, Pa., 1977. NSF Undergrad. Rsch. participant, 1964. Mem. Entomol. Soc. Am. (Disting. Achievement award in regulatory entomology 1986, Ea. Br. L.O. Howard Disting. Achievement award in entomology 1996, Ea. Br. Meritorious Svc. award 1993), Entomol. Soc. Wash., Entomol. Soc. Pa. (pres. 1977). Office: Clemson Univ Divsn Entomology 114 Long Hall Clemson SC 29634-0315 Office Phone: 864-656-5061. Business E-Mail: awhlr@clemson.edu.

WHEELER, BARBARA J., management consultant; b. Coral Gables, Fla., June 1, 1960; d. Robert Henry and Mary Jean (Seiler) W. BA, Miami U., 1982. Commd. 2nd lt. USAF, 1984, advanced through grades to capt., 1988, chief command control comm., def. sect., XIDB project mgr., intelligence agency; resigned, 1992; prin. cons. Litton-PRC, McLean, Va., 1994-97; dir. TRW Mgmt. Cons., Reston, Va., 1998-2000; strategic and program mgmt. cons., writer Md., 2000—. Mem. Project Mgmt. Inst. (cert.). Avocations: reading, lecturing, travel, ice skating.

WHEELER, BRUCE C., engineering educator; BS, MIT, Cambridge, 1971; MS, Cornell U., Ithaca, NY, 1977, PhD, 1981. Prof. elect. and computer engring. U. Ill., Urbana, 1980—2008, prof. bioengring.; prof. biomed. engring. U. Fla., 2008—. Fellow, IEEE, 2008. Achievements include research in technology for neuroscience and engineering. Office: Univ Fla Pruitt Biomed Engring Dept 130 BME Bldg Gainesville FL 32611 Office Phone: 352-846-2950. Office Fax: 352-392-9791. Business E-Mail: bwheeler@uiuc.edu, bwheeler@ufl.edu.

WHEELER, BURTON M., language educator, dean; b. Mullins, SC, Mar. 12, 1927; s. Paul and Elizabeth (Cleveland) W.; m. Jacquelyn Mulkey, Aug. 20, 1950; children— Paul, Geoffrey, Kristin AB, U. S.C., 1948, MA, 1951; PhD, Harvard U., 1961. Teaching fellow Harvard U., Cambridge, Mass., 1953-56; mem. faculty Washington U., St. Louis, 1956-96, prof., 1974-96; prof. emeritus, 1996—; dean Coll. Arts and Scis. Washington U., St. Louis, 1966-78, interim dean univ. librs., 1988-89. Cons., panelist Danforth Found., St. Louis, 1958-82; mem. GPEP panel Assn. Am. Med. Colls., Washington, 1981-84; cons.-evaluator North Cen. Assn., Chgo. Author: Close to Me, But Far Away, 2001; contbr. articles to profl. jours. Mem. spkrs. bur. Alzheimers Assn. Eli Lilly Found. fellow, 1965-66 Mem. Alzheimer's Assn., Phi Beta Kappa (senator 1992-2004, chmn. qualifications com., chmn. com. on chpts.). Business E-Mail: bwheeler@artsci.wustl.edu.

WHEELER, CASS (M. CASS. WHEELER), healthcare consultant, former health science association administrator; b. Tex. BA in Bus., U. Texas, Austin, 1963. Stockbroker NY Stock Exch. firm, Dallas, 1969—73; with Am. Heart Assn., Austin, Tex., 1973—82, COO Dallas, 1982—96, sr. v.p., field ops., 1996—97, CEO, 1997—2008, ret., 2008. Guest lectr. Harvard U. Sch. Bus. & Pub. Health, U. Texas Sch. Mgmt., Dallas, U. Texas Lyndon B. Johnson Sch. Pub. Affairs, Austin; former bd. chmn. Nat. Health Coun.; bd. mem. Partnership for Prevention, Research! America, Nat. Ctr. Tobacco-Free Kids, Nat. Assembly Health & Human Svc. Organizations; advisory bd. mem. Discovery Health Media, Inc.; former mem. President's Commn. Improving Econ. Opportunity in Communities Dependent on Tobacco Production While Protecting Pub. Health; bd. dirs. Am. Legacy Found. Avocations: running, skiing, bicycling.*

WHEELER, DARREN THOMAS, pathologist; s. Pearl Wheeler. MD, U. Wash. Sch. Medicine, Seattle, 1995. Diplomate anatomic pathology Am. Bd. Pathology, 1998, cert. gynecologic pathology Johns Hopkins U., 1999. Cons. pathologist Armed Forces Inst. Pathology, Divsn. Gynecologic and Breast Pathology, Washington, 2002—04, Quest Diagnostics Inc., Las Vegas, Nev., 2004—, med. dir. anatomic pathology, 2004—. Contbr. scientific papers to profl. jours. (Young Investigator award, 2006). Lt. col. US Army, 1999—2004, Wash. and DC. Decorated DSM US Army; named one of Top Dr., Nev. Woman's Mag., 2008. Fellow: Coll. Am. Pathologists; mem.: Internat. Soc. Breast Pathology, Internat. Soc. Gynecologic Pathologists (webmaster 2000—09). Achievements include research in gynecologic and breast cancer. Office: Quest Diagnostics Inc 4230 Burnham Ave Las Vegas NV 89119

WHEELER, DAVID LAURIE, university dean; b. Saginaw, Mich., July 30, 1934; s. Clayton Final and Blanche Beatrice (Hunt) W.; m. Jane Louise Manchester, Sept. 6, 1958; children: Elizabeth, Anne. AB, U. Mich., 1956, AM, 1958, PhD, 1962. Asst. dean student service Ill. State U., Normal, 1967-68, assoc. dean, 1968-69, assoc. dean grad. sch., 1969-72; dean grad. sch. West Tex. State U., Canyon, 1972-79, Ball State U., Muncie, Ind., 1979-96, dean emeritus, 1996—. Cons. McGraw-Hill Pub. Co., N.Y.C., Van Nostrand Reinhold Pub. Co., N.Y.C. Editor: The Human Habitat: Contemporary Readings, 1971. Woodrow Wilson fellow, 1961; recipient Commdrs. Pub. Svc. award Dept. of Army, 1996. Mem. Assn. Am. Geographers, Nat. Coun. Univ. Rsch. Adminstrs., Western History Assn., Tex. State Hist. Assn., U.S. Army War Coll. Found., Rotary (Paul Harris fellow), Sigma Xi, Phi Kappa Phi, Kappa Sigma. Republican. Presbyterian. Personal E-mail: wheeler2@bresnan.net.

WHEELER, DENNIS EARL, mining company executive, lawyer; b. Wallace, Idaho, Dec. 17, 1942; s. Earl L. and Virginia (Rice) W.; m. Jacquline Rae, May 16, 1971; children: Michelle, Maura, Wendy, Brad. BS in Bus., U. Idaho, 1965, JD, 1967. Bar: Idaho 1967. Ptnr. Hull, Hull & Wheeler, Wallace, 1967-78; sr. v.p., gen. counsel Coeur d'Alene (Idaho) Mines Corp., 1978-80, pres., 1980-86, CEO, 1986—, chmn., 1992—. Bd. dirs. Sierra Pacific Resources; vice chmn., dir. Ctr. for Democracy; dir. World Gold Coun., Geneva, 1994—. Pres. Idaho Bd. Edn., 1984-87; founder Jobs Plus, Coeur d'Alene, 1987—; bd. dirs. Ctr. for Democracy, Washington, 1992—, Children's Village, Coeur d'Alene, 1994—, Wildlife Habitat Enhancement Coun., Silver Spring, Md., 1992—, Idaho chpt. Nature Conservancy, Sun Valley, Idaho, 1992—; mem. exec. bd. Boy Scouts Am., Coeur d'Alene, 1994—.=. Recipient Environ. Conservation Disting. Svc. award Soc. for Mining, Metallurgy and Exploration, 1993. Mem. ABA, Idaho Bar Assn., Silver Inst. (pres. 1992-94), Am. Mining Congress (chmn. western bd. govs. 1993—), Elks, Sigma Chi (Significant Sig award 1992). Avocations: fishing, skiing, boating. Office: Coeur D'Alene Mines Corp PO Box 1 Coeur D' Alene ID 83816-0316

WHEELER, DOUGLAS PAUL, conservationist, state agency administrator, lawyer; b. Bklyn., Jan. 10, 1942; s. Robert S. and Lottie (Neubauer) W.; m. Heather A. Campbell, Aug. 28, 1965; children: Clay Campbell, Christopher Campbell. AB in Govt. with honors, Hamilton Coll., Clinton, NY, 1963; LLB, Duke U., 1966. Bar: NC 1966, DC 1999. Assoc. Levine, Goodman & Murchison, Charlotte, NC, 1966-69; legis. atty. to asst. legis. counsel US Dept. Interior, Washington, 1969-72, dep. asst. sec. Fish and Wildlife and Pks., 1972-77; exec. v.p. Nat. Trust for Hist. Preservation, Washington, 1977-80; pres. Am. Farmland Trust, Washington, 1980-85; now life mem.; exec. dir. Sierra Club, San Francisco, 1985-86; v.p. Conservation Found., Washington, 1986-88, exec. v.p., 1989-91; sec. resources State of Calif., Sacramento, 1991—99; ptnr. Hogan & Hartson LLP, Washington, 1999—. Bd. mem. Lincoln Inst. Land Use Policy, Am. Farmland Trust, Nat. Conservation Sys. Found. Contbr. chapters to books. Hon. life mem. bd. visitors Duke U. Sch. Law; mem. adv. coun. The Conservation Fund; mem. biodiversity conservation working group N.Am. Commn. Environ. Cooperation; trustee Colo. Conservation Trust; mem. coun. Yosemite Fund; candidate NC House of Reps., 1968; mem. DC Rep. Ctrl. Com., 1984-85; chmn. adv. bd. Nat. Park Sys. Lt. JAGC, USNR, 1969-75. Recipient commendation US Dept. Interior, 1976, Achievement award, 1980, Conservation award Gulf Oil Corp., 1985, Charles S. Murphy award for pub. svc, 1995, Presdl. award for sustainable devel., 1996, Nat. Conservation Leadership award The Conservation Fund, 1997. Mem. ABA, DC Bar Assn., NC Bar Assn., Sierra Club (life), Am. Farmland Trust (life). Episcopalian. Home: 4541 45th St NW Washington DC 20016-4473 Business E-Mail: dpwheeler@hhlaw.com.

WHEELER, ELTON SAMUEL, financial executive; b. Salinas, Calif., Oct. 25, 1943; s. Luther Elton and Naomi E. (Beatty) W.; m. Moretha Jean Miller, June 17, 1995; children: Pamela Kathleen, Leslie Elizabeth-Anne, Deborah Suzanne, Jonathan Samuel. BS, Calif. State U., 1966. CPA, Calif. Acct. Pricewaterhouse Coopers, Oakland, Calif., 1967-70, Adams Properties, Inc., San Francisco, 1970-71, treas., 1972-75, v.p., CFO, 1976-77, Adams Capital Mgmt. Co., San Francisco, 1977-79, pres., CEO, 1979-87; pres., CEO, bd. dirs. Calif. Real Estate Investment Trust, 1980-88, Franklin Select Real Estate Income Trust, 1989-2000, Franklin Advantage Real Estate Income Trust, 1990-96; owner E. Samuel Wheeler, CPA, 1992—. Chair audit com. Mother Lode Bank, Sonora, Calif., 2004—, bd. dirs. Bd. trustees Sierra Repertory Theatre, 2006—. With USMCR, 1966-72. Mem. Nat. Assn. Real Estate Investment Trusts, Inc. (sec., treas., bd. govs. 1984-89), Am. Inst. CPAs, Calif. Soc. CPAs, United Way of Tuolumne-Calaveras Counties (pres., dir., treas. 1989-98), Rotary (Sonora, Calif., pres. 1994-95), Rotary Internat. (dist. 5220 dir. 1998-99, asst. gov. 2000-2001, dist. conf. chair 2001-2002, youth exch. officer 2005—). Home: 16399 Crestridge Ave Sonora CA 95370-8752 Office: PO Box 3718 Sonora CA 95370-3718 Business E-Mail: swheeler@samwheelercpa.com.

WHEELER, FLOYD LARRY, education educator; b. Reagan County, Tex., Aug. 25, 1947; s. Floyd L and Rita Marie Wheeler; m. Pamela Sue Wilkerson, Aug. 2, 1969; children: Melissa Dawn, Andrew Lawrence. BA, Austin Coll., 1969; MABS, Dallas Theol. Sem., 1983. Commn. tech. USN, 1970—74; assoc. pastor Marsh Lane Bapt. Ch., Dallas, 1975—81; carpenter Calvin Justice Corp., Lewisville, Tex., 1981—84; instr. Wayland Bapt. U., Plainview, Tex., 1984—88; asst. prof. Hardin Simmons U., 1988—, chmn. Dept. Theatre, 2004, assoc. prof. theatre, 2006—. Lighting/set design cons. First Bapt. Ch., Plainview, Tex., 1984—88, Elmcrest Bapt. Ch., Abilene, Tex., 1988—95, Pioneer Dr. Bapt. Ch., Abilene, 1995—, Abilene Opera Assn., Abilene, 1988—93. Rosa Parks exhibit contbr. Nat. Ctr. for Children's Illustrated Lit., 2006. E-5 USN, 1970—74, Iceland, Spain. Recipient Cullen Tchg. award, Hardin Simmons U., 1995; named Faculty Mem. of Yr., Hardin-Simmons U., 2000. Mem.: Am. Univ. Prof. Assn. Republican. Bapt. Office: Hardin Simmons U Box 14864 Abilene TX 79698 Office Phone: 325-670-1511.

WHEELER, GEORGE CHARLES, JR., materials and process engineer; b. Balt., Oct. 9, 1923; s. George Charles and Julia Elizabeth (Watrous) Wheeler; m. Dorothy W. Whittemore, Sept. 13, 1947; children: Scott, Craig, Mark, Matthew, Tracy, Bruce; m. Clare Frances Weiner, Jan. 21, 1978. BS in Metall. Engring., Lehigh U., 1944. Various engring. and supervisory positions GE, Mass. and N.Y., 1944-62; mgr. materials, welding and nondestructive test engring. Knolls Atomic Power Lab., G.E., Schenectady, NY, 1962-68; mgr. nondestructive testing G.E. Power Sys., Schenectady, NY, 1968-85; pres., CEO Wheeler Nondestructive Testing, Inc., Schenectady, 1985-95, Materials and Processes Cons., Schenectady, 1995—; mgr. tech. svcs. Am. Soc. for Nondestructive Testing, Columbus, Ohio, 1993-94. Cons. UN, NYC, 1985—98, IAEA, Vienna, 1985—98, ASNT, 1997—, others; guest lectr. Rennsselaer Poly. Inst., Troy, NY, Union Coll., Schenectady, 1978—87; mem. math. sci. and tech. com. Schenectady County CC, 1978—85, adj. prof., 1987—97; US del. Internat. Stds. Orgn., mem. com. TC 135/SC7 NDT Pers. Qualification, 1987—97, convenor working group #2 ISO-9712; mem. ASNT Cert. Mgmt. Bd., 1994—98, chmn., 1976—80, 1986—89; founding chmn. SNT-TC-IA Interpretation Com., 1975—76. Author: Guide to Personnel Certification, 1990, rev. edit., 2003, Guide to Developing Certification Exams, 1992; co-author: rev. edit., 2005, Level II Study Guide: Radiographic Testing, 1998, Level II Study Guide: Ultrasonic Testing, 1999; contbg. editor: Materials Evaluation Jour. ASNT, tech. editor: Nondestructive Testing Handbook, 3d edit., vol. 3. Fellow: Am. Soc. Nondestructive Tsting (hon.; bd. dirs. 1976—85, pres. 1983—84, chmn. 1984—85, chmn. cert. com. 1976—80, 1986—89, Gold medal); mem.: ASTM (mem. com. internat. stds., mem. com. nondestructive testing), NRA (life), Nature Conservancy (life), Am. Soc. Metals (life), Trout Unlimited (life), Adirondack Mountain Club, Adirondack Forty-Sixers. Achievements include pioneering personnel certifications for nondestructive testing work worldwide for ASTM, ISO and ASNT. Avocations: mountain climbing, flying, firearms, photography, cross country skiing, golf, fishing.

WHEELER, GERALDINE HARTSHORN, historian, writer; b. Pomona, Calif., Feb. 5, 1919; d. Albion True and Beatrice Osa (Barnes) Hartshorn; m. Lloyd Franklyn Wheeler, Dec. 2, 1938 (dec. Mar. 1996); children: Russell Lloyd, Robert Gerald. AA, Santa Barbara City Coll., Calif., 1950s. Co-owner Atheling's, Santa Barbara, Calif., 1971-76, Pomona, 1976-90; chmn. bd. trustees Atheling Heritage Trust, Claremont, Calif., 1994—. Pub., editor: mag. Atheling's, 1974—75, newsletter Grand Priory of America Order of St. Lazarus, 1974—86; editor: St. Margaret's Jour., 1975—; author: (essays) A World Full in 1891, 1975—, President John Adams-A Profile, 1975—, Ralph Waldo Emerson-A Profile, 1975, The Many Masks of Communism, 1975, A Tale of St. Nicholas, 1995, Post Cards and Postal Cards, 1996, Pocahontas Kinships, 1996. Vol. PTA, Fontana and Santa Barbara, 1945-60; mem. various coms. and choir First Congl. Ch., Santa Barbara, 1952-72; leader Cub Scouts Am., Santa Barbara, 1953-56; grey lady unit chmn. Santa Barbara chpt.-ARC, 1958-62; women's project bd. v.p., activities chmn., active various coms. Santa Barbara Hist. Soc., 1960-74; exec. sec. 1960 Nixon for Pres. Campaign, Santa Barbara, 1960; mem. spkrs. bur. Nixon for Gov. Campaign, Santa Barbara, 1962; mem. Rep. state ctrl. com. State of Calif., 1962-64; blitz chmn. Rockefeller for Pres. Campaign, Santa Barbara, 1964; coord. vol. svcs. Office of Civil Def., City of Santa Barbara, 1965-76; coord. tv series on earthquakes Sta. KEYT, Office of Civil Def., Santa Barbara, 1968; bd. dirs. Calif. Ctrl. Coast Area, U.S.O., 1968-76, treas. bd., 1970-76; supporter Vis. Nurses and Hospice Assn., 1994—; others. Decorated Dame of Grace, Mil. and Hospitaller Order of St. Lazarus of Jerusalem, Cert. of Merit, 1973, The Alan Weaver Hazelton award; recipient Cert. of Merit, Santa Barbara Jr. Coll., 1954-55, Medal of Appreciation SAR, 1972, Cert. of Award Nat. Soc. Daus. of Founders and Patriots of Am., 1977. Mem. Acad. Polit. Sci., Calif. Hist. Soc., New Eng. Hist. and Geneal. Soc., The Pomona Ebell (pres. 1998-2000), Wilson Ctr. Assocs., Smithsonian Assocs., Nat. Trust for Hist. Preservation, Am. Farmland Trust, Nat. Woman's History Mus., Nat. Arbor Day Found., Pomona Valley Hist. Soc., La Verne Hist. Soc., La Salle County Hist. Soc., Nat. Wildlife Fedn., Colonial Williamsburg Found., The Postcard Soc. (founder), Musicians Club Pomona Valley, Shakespeare Club Pomona Valley, Nat. Soc. DAR (past regent chpts.), Calif. Huguenot Soc., Nat. Soc. Daus. Founders and Patriots (past nat. officer, orgn. pres. So. Calif. chpt.), Colonial Dames Am. (orgn. pres. chpt. XX), Nat. Soc. Daus. Colonial Wars (state officer), Nat. Soc. Women Desc. Ancient and Honorable Artillery Co. (past nat. chaplain and state officer), Soc. Mayflower Desc. (past colony gov.), Nat. Soc. Dames of the Ct. of Honor, Nat. Soc. New Eng. Women, Hereditary Order Desc. Colonial Govs. (past nat. officer), Soc. Desc. Most Noble Order of the Garter, Ams. Armorial Ancestry, Ams. Royal Descent, Colonial Order of the Crown, The Plantagenet Soc., Nat. Soc. Magna Charta Dames, Order of the Crown of Charlemagne in USA, Nat. Soc. Ams. Royal Descent, Nat. Soc. Desc. Early Quakers (founding nat. clk.), Nat. Guild St. Margaret of Scotland (founder), Nat. Gavel Club, Mt. Vernon Ladies' Assn., Order of the Merovingian Dynasty. Republican. Avocations: book collecting, reading, genealogy, classical music, needlecrafts. Home: 1047 E Baseline Rd Claremont CA 91711-1577

WHEELER, HEWITT BROWNELL, surgeon, educator; b. Louisville, July 21, 1929; s. Arville and Lois (Vance) W.; m. Elizabeth Jane Maxwell, July 21, 1956; children: Stephen, Elizabeth, Jane, Mary. Student, Vanderbilt U., 1945-48; MD, Harvard U., 1952. Diplomate Am. Bd. Surgery (bd. dirs. 1984-90). Cushing fellow Harvard Med. Sch., Boston, 1953, Peters fellow, 1956, research fellow, 1959-60, instr. surgery, 1961-64, clin. assoc. surgery, 1964-67, asst. clin. prof. surgery, 1967-70, assoc. prof. surgery, 1970-71; asst. in surgery Peter Bent Brigham Hosp., Boston, 1959-60, jr. assoc. surgery, 1961-64, assoc. surgery, 1964-69, sr. assoc. surgery, 1969-71; asst. chief surgery Roxbury VA Hosp., Boston, 1961-62, chief surgery, 1962-71, chief of staff, 1968-71; cons. surgery U. Mass. Med. Sch., Worcester, 1966-71; prof., chmn. dept. surgery U. Mass. Med. Sch. at Worcester, 1971-96, Harry M. Haidak disting. prof. surgery, 1985-98, prof. emeritus, 1998—; chief staff U. Mass. Hosp., 1974-76, surgeon-in-chief, 1976-96; exec. dir. Ctr. for Advanced Clin. Tech., 1995—; affiliate prof. biomed. engring. Worcester Poly. Inst., 1974—; lectr. surgery Harvard Med. Sch., 1974-96; chief surgery St. Vincent Hosp., Worcester, 1971-75. Cons. Meml. Hosp., Worcester City Hosp., 1970-96, Worcester Hahnemann Hosp., 1974-94, Peter Bent Brigham Hosp., 1973-96; chmn. surg. research program com. VA, Washington, 1965-67, nat. participant surg. cons., 1965-69, chmn. ad hoc adv. com. surgery, 1969-71. Pres. Mass. Compassionate Care Coalition, 2000—04; trustee Ctrl. Mass. Health Care Found., 1975—77, Worcester Found. for Biomed. Rsch., 1996—2004, Hospice Ctrl. Mass. Inc., 1997—2000, U. Mass. Meml. Found., 1998—2005, Boston Med. Libr., 1996—2002. 1st lt. M.C. AUS, 1953—55. Mem. ACS (bd. govs. 1984-90, coun. Mass. chpt. 1973-76, pres. 1980), AAAS, AMA, Am. Surg. Assn., Soc. Univ. Surgeons, Internat. Cardiovascular Soc., New Eng. Surg. Soc. (treas. 1977-84, v.p. 1986-87, pres. 1989-91), Boston Surg. Soc. (pres. 1995-96), Worcester Surg. Soc. (pres. 1973-75), Transplantation Soc., Mass. Med. Soc. (100th Shattuck lectr. 1990; lifetime achievement award 2005), Worcester Dist. Med. Soc. (sec. 1996-99, v.p. 1999-00, pres. 2000-01), New Eng. Vascular Soc. (v.p. 1985-86, pres. 1988-89). Achievements include rsch. in exptl. transplantation, blood vessel surgery, method to detect blood clots, improving end-of-life care. Home: 52 Stockton Rd South Portland ME 04106-5110 E-mail: bwheele1@maine.rr.com.

WHEELER, HOYT NOLAND, management educator, arbitrator; b. Ravenswood, W.Va., Jan. 21, 1937; s. Harold Lee and Virginia Laura Wheeler; m. Elizabeth Dawson Scrivener, May 30, 1996; children: Jeffrey Smith, Jonathan Philip. BA cum laude, Marshall U., Huntington, W.Va., 1958; JD, U. Va., Charlottesville, 1961; PhD, U. Wis., 1974. Bar: W.Va. 1961. Assoc. Kay, Casto & Chaney, Charleston, W.Va., 1961—65, ptnr., 1966—70; instr. in bus. adminstrn. U. Wyo., Laramie, 1973—74, asst. prof. of bus. adminstrn., 1974—76; assoc. prof. of indsl. rels. U. Minn., Mpls., 1976—81; prof. of mgmt. U. SC, Columbia, 1981—2009, dist. prof. emeritus, 2009—. Labor arbitrator, Columbia, SC, 1974—. Author: (scholarly book) Workplace Justice Without Unions, (scholarly/trade book) The Future of the American Labor Movement, (scholarly book) Workplace Justice: Employment Obligations in International Perspective, Industrial Conflict: An Integrative Theory. Mem.: Internat. Indsl. Rels. Assn. (exec. bd. 2006—), Internat. Soc. for Labor Law and Social Security (exec. bd. 2003—04), Nat. Acad. of Arbitrators (chair, rsch. com. 2003—04), Indsl. Rels. Rsch. Assn. (pres. 1996—97). Episcopalian. Avocations: tennis, reading, swimming. Home: 109 Saluda View Ct West Columbia SC 29169 Office: 109 Saluda View Ct West Columbia SC 29169 Business E-Mail: hwheeler@sc.rr.com.

WHEELER, JANE, investment banker; Grad., U. Va. Various positions to mng. dir. Morgan Stanley, NYC, 1993—2005; sr. mng. dir. Evercore Ptnrs. Inc., NYC, 2005—. Bd. trustees Brearley Sch. Named one of The Top 50 Rainmakers, Dealmaker mag., 2006—07; named to Online Fin. 40, Instl. Investor, 2005, 2006. Mem.: Phi Beta Kappa. Office: Evercore Ptnrs 43rd Fl 55 East 52nd St New York NY 10055 Office Phone: 212-857-3100. Office Fax: 212-857-3101.

WHEELER, JOHN OLIVER, retired geologist; b. Mussoorie, India, Dec. 19, 1924; s. Edward Oliver and Dorothea Sophie (Danielsen) W.; m. Nora Jean Hughes, May 17, 1952; children: Kathleen Anna Wheeler Hunter, Jennifer Margaret Wheeler Crompton. BASc in Geol. Engring., U. BC, 1947, DSc (hon.), 2000; PhD in Geology, Columbia U., NYC, 1956. Geologist Geol. Survey Can., Ottawa, Ont., 1951-61, Vancouver, BC, 1961-65, rsch. scientist, 1965-70, rsch. mgr. Ottawa, 1970—, chief regional and econ. geology divsn., 1970-73, dep. dir. gen., 1973-79; rsch. scientist Geol. Survey Can. (Cordilleran divsn.), 1979-90, rsch. scientist emeritus, 1990—2006; ret., 2006. Gen. editor: Geology of Canada, 8 vols., 1989-2006; compiler of regional geol. maps of we. Can., Can. and no. N.Am. and Greenland; contbr. articles to profl. jours.; chpts. to books. Recipient Queen's Silver Jubilee medal, 1977, Can. 125 medal, 1994, Earth Sci. Sector and Dept. awards Nat. Resources Can., 1996, Spl. award of BC-Yukon Chamber of Mines for outstanding contbn. to Can. Cordilleran geology, 2000, Massey medal Royal Can. Geog. Soc., 2002, hon. fellow 2003. Fellow Royal Soc. Can., Geol. Assn. Can. (pres. 1970-71, Logan medal 1983, Disting. fellow 1996), Geol. Soc. Am. (councillor 1971-74), Can. Geosci. Coun. (pres. 1981); mem. Can. Inst. Mining and Metallurgy, Can. Geol. Found. (pres. 1974-79), Can. Alpine Club (hon.), Am. Alpine Club. Anglican.

WHEELER, JOHN S., JR., urologist; s. John S. Wheeler Sr. and Virginia S. Wheeler; m. Michele A. Marganski, June 4, 1977; children: Nicholas, Anne. BA, Dartmouth Coll., 1972; MD, Georgetown U., 1977. Lic. physician Ill., cert. Mass. Resident gen. surgery Boston Med. Ctr., 1977—79, resident urology, 1979—82, urodynamics fellowship, 1983; faculty Loyola U. Med. Ctr., Maywood, Ill., 1983—; staff urologist Hines VA Hosp., 1983—, RML Hosp., Hinsdale, 2003—. Cons. in field. Contbr. articles to profl. jours., chapters to books. Fellow, Boston U. Med. Ctr., 1982—83. Mem.: Am. Paraplegia Soc. (rsch. com. 1984—), Am. Coll. Surgeons, Am. Urological Assn., Alpha Omega Alpha. Roman Catholic. Avocations: golf, skiing. Office: Loyola U Med Ctr Dept Urology 2160 S First Ave Maywood IL 60153 Office Phone: 708-216-4076. Business E-Mail: jwheeler@lumc.edu.

WHEELER, JOHN WATSON, lawyer; b. Murfreesboro, Tenn., Sept. 11, 1938; s. James William and Grace (Fann) W.; m. Dorothy Anita Pressgrove, Aug. 5, 1959; children: Jeffrey William, John Harold. BS in Journalism, U. Tenn., 1960, JD, 1968. Bar: Tenn. 1968, U.S. Dist. Ct. (ea. dist.) Tenn. 1968, U.S. Dist. Ct. (mid. dist.) Tenn., U.S. Dist. Ct. (we. dist.) Tenn., U.S. Supreme Ct. 1974, U.S. Ct. Appeals (6th cir.) 1975. Editor The Covington (Tenn.) Leader, 1963-65; adminstrv. asst. to lab. dir. UT-AEC Rsch. Lab., Oak Ridge, Tenn., 1965-68; assoc. Hodges, Doughty & Carson, Knoxville, Tenn., 1968-72, ptnr., 1972—2005, of counsel, 2005—. Mem. commn. to study Applellate Cts. in Tenn.; chair U.S. magistrate merit selection panel, U.S. Dist. Ct. (ea. dist.) Tenn., 1991, 2002, 03, mem. bankruptcy judge merit selection panel, 1992-94; chmn. hist. soc., U.S. Dist. Ct. (ea. dist.) Tenn., 1993-2004. Mem. organizing com. Tenn. Supreme Ct. Hist. Soc. Lt. U.S. Army, 1961-63, capt. Res. Fellow Am. Bar Found. (life, Tenn. chair 1999-2008), Tenn. Bar Found. (life); mem. ABA (ho. of dels. 1986-2000), Tenn. Bar Assn. (pres. 1989-90, bd. govs. 1981-91), Nat. Conf. Bar Pres., Am. Inns. of Ct. (master of bench, emeritus), Internat. Assn. Def. Counsel, So. Conf. Bar Pres., 6th Cir. Jud. Conf. (life), Fox Den Country Club (bd. dirs. 2001-04). Republican. Lutheran. Avocations: golf, travel. Home: 12009 N Fox Den Dr Knoxville TN 37934 Office: Hodges Doughty & Carson PO Box 869 Knoxville TN 37901-0869 Home Phone: 865-966-5323; Office Phone: 865-546-9611. Business E-Mail: jwheeler@hdclaw.com.

WHEELER, LAWRENCE JEFFERSON, museum director; BA in History and French cum laude, Pfeiffer Coll., 1965; MA in European History, U. Ga., 1969, PhD in European History, 1972; cert., Fed. Execs. Inst., Charlottesville, Va., 1977, U. N.C., 1982. Asst. prof. European history Pfeiffer Coll., Misenheimer, N.C., 1970-74; dep. sec. NC Dept. Cultural Resources, Raleigh, 1977-85; asst. dir. mus. and dir. devel. Cleve. Mus. Art, 1985-94; staff liaison for bldg. and staffing NC Mus. Art, Raleigh, 1977-83, dir., 1994—. Cons. on fundraising and pub. rels. N.C. Mus. History, Raleigh; coord. 400th anniversary celebration Sir Walter Raleigh's voyages festival, 1984. Bd. dirs. Am. Arts Alliance, 1991-92. Named N.C. Man of Yr., News and Observer newspaper, Raleigh, N.C. Mem. Am. Assn. Mus. (chmn. dvel. and membership profl. com. 1990-92, sr. reviewer mus. assessment program 1992—), Inst. Mus. Svcs. (reviewer 1988—), Art Mus. Devel. Assn. (pres. 1987-88). Home: 44 Cedar St Chapel Hill NC 27514-2712 Office: NC Mus Art 4630 Mail Service Ctr Raleigh NC 27699-4630 Fax: 919-733-8034.

WHEELER, LORNA RAVEN, literature and language educator; d. Charles Wheeler and Doris Joanne Perry; life ptnr. Lara Raven Lara Bishop; children: Elena Ruth Raven, Tobin Daniel Raven. PhD, U. Colo., Boulder, 2006. Asst. prof. dept. English Pa. State U., Hazleton, 2006—07; asst. prof. Met. State Coll. Denver, 2007—; instr. Kaplan U., Boca Raton, Fla., 2007—, South U. Online, Savannah, Ga., 2008—. Chef & owner Basil's Cafe, Denver, 1989—93. Home: 4290 Hill St Port Townsend WA 98368

WHEELER, MALCOLM EDWARD, lawyer, educator; b. Berkeley, Calif., Nov. 29, 1944; s. Malcolm Ross and Frances Dolores (Kane) W.; m. Donna Marie Stambaugh, July 25, 1981; children: Jessica Ross, M. Connor. SB, MIT, 1966; JD, Stanford U., 1969. Bar: Calif. 1970, Colo. 1992, U.S. Dist. Ct (cen. dist.) Calif. 1970, U.S. Ct. Appeals (9th cir.) 1970, U.S. Ct. Appeals (10th cir.) 1973, U.S. Dist. Ct. (no., so., ea. and cen. dists.) Calif. 1975, U.S. Ct. Appeals (11th cir.) 1987, U.S. Ct. Appeals (D.C. cir.) 1987, U.S. Supreme Ct. 1976, U.S. Ct. Appeals (3d cir.) 1989, (4th cir.) 1992, (8th cir.) 1993, (5th cir.) 1995, (Fed. cir.) 1998. Assoc. Howard, Prim, Smith, Rice & Downs, San Francisco, 1969-71; assoc. prof. law U. Kans., Lawrence, 1971-74; assoc. Hughes Hubbard & Reed, Los Angeles, 1974-77, ptnr., 1977-81, 83-85, cons., 1981-83; ptnr. Skadden, Arps, Slate, Meagher & Flom, Los Angeles, 1985-91; dir. Parcel, Mauro, Hultin & Spaanstra P.C., Denver, 1991-98, Wheeler Trigg & Kennedy, P.C., Denver, 1998—. Vis. prof. U. Iowa, 1978, prof., 1979; prof. U. Kans., Lawrence, 1981-83; chief counsel U.S. Senate Select Com. to Study Law Enforcement Undercover Activities, Washington, 1982-83. Mem. editl. bd. Jour. Products Liability, 1984-90, Fed. Litigation Guide Reporter, 1986-90; contbr. articles to profl. jours. Fellow Am. Coll. Trial Lawyers; mem. ABA, Calif. Bar Assn., Colo. Bar Assn., Am. Law Inst. Home: 100 Humboldt St Denver CO 80218-3932 Office Phone: 303-292-2525. Business E-Mail: wheeler@wtklaw.com.

WHEELER, MARGARET JANE, actress, soprano, voice educator; b. Apr. 16, 1925; d. William Henry and Ruth Bond Wheeler. BA in Voice, George Peabody Coll. (now Vanderbilt U.), Nashville, 1947; grad. study in voice and opera with L. Vaida, St. Louis Inst. Music, 1950; grad. study with Oren Brown, 1976—77; studied voice, Franco Iglesias, Aida Favia Artsay, Thomas Houser, Thomas Cultice, Willard Young, Julia Drobner, Anthony Frisell, 1960—90; acting study, Stella Adler Studio, 1964—65, David LeGrant Sudio, 1965—69; MA in Voice Performance, Hunter Coll., NYC, 1976. Louis Nicholas voice tchr. Peabody Coll., 1943—47; tchr. Army Dependents Sch., La Rochelle, France, 1955—56; tchr. music Rockland County Pub. Schs., NY, Westchester County Pub. Schs.; tchr.music L.I. Pub. Schs., St. Louis Pub. Schs.; asst. prof. music dept. Millersville State Coll., Pa. Dir. adult choir Asbury Meth. Ch., Croton-on-Hudson, NY; dir. Cmty. Chorus, Croton-on-Hudson, NY; dir. choirs Evang. Ch., Overland, Mo.; voice tchr. Bronx Conservatory of Music, NY, 1990—; tchr. sr. citizen singing classes Co-op City, 2001—04; voice tchr. Bronx Music Ho., Bennett Conservatory of Music, Croton-on-Hudson; tchr. continuing edn. opera appreciation Briarcliff Manor, NYC, White Plains. Performer: (classical and light opera) Brunswick Summer Playhouse, 1961, Lake George Opera Co., 1965, Pitts. Civic Light Opera Co., 1967, Phila. Grand Opera Co., 1971, Assoc. Concert Artists, 1972, 1973, Sycamore Performing Arts Festival, 1973, (classical and light opera conducted by Thomas Cultice) The Medium, 1975, (classical and light opera) Staten Island Opera Co., 1976, (sacred music) Peabody Coll., 1947, Park Ave. Meth. Ch., 1960, St. Matthew's Luth. Ch., 1980, North Yonkers Cmty. Ch., 1985—94; soloist: sacred music Park Ave. Meth. Ch., 1961—67, Christian Sci. Ch., 1968—72, 1974—75, Cmty. Synagogue, 1968—72, soloist: First Westminster Presbyn. Ch., 1976, St. Paul's Episcopal Ch., 1976—77; performer: (showcases) Gunda Morden, 1960, Opera Club of Am., 1960, Messina Opera Co., 1960, Gim Game, 2009; soloist and recitalist: Bronx Conservatory of Music, 1970—90, Grad. Recital Hunter Coll. Playhouse, 1976, Westchester Conservatory Music, 1977, Faculty Recitals Millersville (Pa.) Coll., 1977—78, Stewart Smith Singers Concert, 1985, North Yonkers Cmty. Ch., 1985—94, Warner Libr., 1986, Bennett Conservatory, 1986, Westchester CC, 1991; soloist and recitalist Westchester CC, 1994; soloist and recitalist: Sigma Alpha Iota Am. Musicales, 1999—2002; performer: Met. Opera Extra Chorus, 1962, Schola Cantorum NY, 1962—70, Camerata Singers, 1970; dir.: Children's Wing Croton Shakespeare Festival; performer: (musical theater) The Sound of Music, 1971, (multimedia) A Weapon Most Unusual!, 2005, (caberet show) Entertainment Express, 2006, (sang 4 concerts) Westchester Concert Singers, 2006—08, The Part of Fonsia Dorsey in a Scene from the Gin Game for the Forthill Players Showcase, 2009. Mem. delegation music tchrs. People to People, China, 1988, Hong Kong, 1988. Mem.: Nat. Assn. Tchrs Singing, Am. Guild Musical Artists, Actor's Equity, Sigma Alpha Iota. Home: 786 Sleepy Hollow Rd Briarcliff Manor NY 10510-2525

WHEELER, MICHAEL JOSEPH, protective services official, educator; b. Evergreen Pk., Ill., June 9, 1948; s. John Patrick Wheeler and Mary (Dalton) Dolores; m. Mary Anne Letkey, May 22, 1973; children: Christopher Michael, Erin Michelle Hisel, Jennifer Lynn Nimmons; 1 child, Michael Sean. AAS, Prairie State Coll., Chgo. Heights, Ill., 2005. Cert. engring. technician, ICET, 1974; advanced emergency med. technician Ill. Dept. Pub. Health, 1975; catechist Archdiocese of Chgo., 1996; advanced cert. fire fighter III Office of Ill. State Fire Marshal, 1982, cert. hazardous materials first responder 1992, fire officer II 1995, rescue specialist 2002, fire apparatus engr. 2004, in vehicle machinery ops. 2005, fire investigator 2006, fire prevention insp. II Nat. Bd. Fire Svc. Profl. Qualifications, 1998. Capt. Pk. Forest Fire Dept., Ill., 1973—; fire prevention bur. coord. Village Pk. Forest Fire Dept., 1982—; prof. Prairie State Coll., Chgo. Heights, 1998—. Fire and police commr. Village Richton Pk., Richton Pk., Ill., 1994—2004. Catechist St. Lawrence O'Toole, Matteson, Ill., 1985—2004. Recipient Disting. Svc. award, Pk. Forest Jaycees, 1989, 1998, Meritorious Unit Commendation award, Village Pk. Forest Fire Dept., 2007, Award of Merit, 2008, Cmty. Svc. award, Nina Coun., 2008, Fire Achievement award, Ill. Fire Insps., 1999, Catechetical Ministries Recognition award, Archdiocese Chgo., 2003, Fire Achievement award, Ill. Fire Insps., 2008; named Firefighter of Yr., Nat. Assn. Profl. Ins. Adjusters, 1987. Mem.: Internat. Assn. Fire Fighters, Ill. Fire Insps. Assn., Nat. Fire Protection Assn., Internat. Code Coun. Roman Catholic. Office: Pk Forest Fire Dept 156 Indianwood Blvd Park Forest IL 60466 Personal E-mail: wheeler_m@att.net. Business E-Mail: mwheeler@vopf.com.

WHEELER, R(ICHARD) KENNETH, lawyer, educator; b. Washington, July 25, 1934; s. Nathaniel Dudley and Ruth Lee (Matthews) W.; m. Christine Kandris, Jan. 11, 1990; children by previous marriage: Jennifer L., Ruth E. BA, Emory and Henry Coll., U. Richmond, 1957; LLB, U. Richmond, 1964. Bar: Va. 1963, D.C. 1977, U.S. Tax Ct. 1978. Assoc., then ptnr. Hunton, Williams, Gay, Powell & Gibson and successor firms, Richmond, 1963-88; sr. ptnr. Kane, Wheeler, Fenderson & Jeffries, Richmond, 1988-90; counsel Durrette, Irvin, Lemons & Fenderson, P.C., Richmond, 1990-94; sr. ptnr. Wallace, Harris & Wheeler, Richmond, 1994-95. Adj. prof. law T.C. Williams Sch. Law, U. Richmond, 1966, 83, bd. dirs., 1977-79; adj. prof. law Va. Commonwealth U., 1970; lectr. trial practice U. Va., 1981-82, 85, 87; arbitrator Am. Arbitration Assn. Served to capt. USMCR, 1957-61. Williams scholar U. Richmond, 1961-63. Mem. Am. Law Inst., Va. State Bar (chmn. com. liaison with law schs. 1977-78, chmn. com. legal edn. and admission to bar 1978-80, spcl. com. on professionalism 1987-88), Web Soc., McNeill Law Soc., Marine Corps League (life), Rector's Club (U. Richmond, life), Pi Sigma Alpha, Phi Delta Phi, Omicron Delta Kappa (hon.).

WHEELER, RURIC E., mathematics professor; b. Clarkson, Ky., Nov. 30, 1923; s. Mark H. and Mary (Sullivan) Wheeler; m. Joyce Ray, May 31, 1946; children: Eddy Ray, Paul Warren. AB, We. Ky. U., 1947; MS, U. Ky., 1948, PhD, 1952. Instr. math. U. Ky., Lexington, 1948—52; asst. prof. stats. Fla. State U., 1952—53; assoc. prof. math. Samford U., 1953—55, prof., head math. dept., 1955—65, chmn. natural scis. divsn., 1965—67, asst. to dean, 1967—68; dean Howard Coll. Arts and Scis., 1968—70, v.p. acad. affairs, 1970—87, univ. prof., 1987—94, rsch. prof., 1994—. Cons. in field; dir. NSF Inst., 1961, Ala. Vis. Scientist Program, 1962—67. Author: Modern Math., 1966, 12th edit., 2005, Fundamental Concepts of Math, 1968, 2d edit., 1976, Modern Math for Business, 1969, 4th edit., 1986, A Programmed Study of Number Systems, 1972, Finite Mathematics, 1974, 3d edit., 1985, Intuitive Geometry, 1975, Introduccion a los Conjuntos Numericos, 1976, Mathematics, an Everyday Language, 1979, Student Activities Manual, Elementary Mathematics, 1984, Mathematicas un Lenguaje Cotidiano, 1982, Activities Manual for Elementary School Teachers, 1988, Modern Mathematics for Elementary School Teachers, 1994, Finite Mathematics (A Problem Solving Approach), 1991, College Mathematics (a Graphing Calculator Approach), 1996, Brief Calculus (a Graphing Calculator Approach), 1996, Chinese Translation of Brief Calculus, 1997, (novels) All Because of Polly, 2002, Modern Mathematics: Fundamentals and Concepts, 2005, Modern Mathematics for Elementary Educators, 2005. Mem. Birmingham Manpower Area Planning Coun., 1972—75; trustee Gorgas Found., 1968—94, chmn., 1988—92; mem. Jefferson County Ednl. Consortium, 1981—93, pres., 1986—90; mem. Com. to Upgrade Jefferson County Schs., 1982—86; deacon Bapt. Ch. Lt. USAAF, 1943—46. Mem.: Conf. Acad. Deans So. States (pres. 1985—86), So. Conf. Deans Faculties and Acad. V.P. (pres. 1982), Am. Conf. Acad. Deans, Am. Assn. Univ. Adminstrs. (exec. com. Ala. sect. 1972—74, v.p. 1974—76, pres. 1976—77), Assn. Ala. Coll. Adminstrs. (exec. com. 1976—80, pres. 1978—79), Am. Assn. Higher Edn., Ala. Acad. Sci. (pres. 1967—69), Assn. So. Bapt. Colls. and Schs. (sec. 1973, v.p. 1974, pres. 1975, deans sect.), Assn. Math. Tchrs. Ala. (pres. 1963), Nat. Coun. Tchrs. Math., Am. Math. Assn. (chmn. SE sect. 1966—67, vis. lecture program 1989—93), Am. Math. Soc., Am. Edn. Assn., Rotary (pres. of Vestavia rotary club 1983—84). Home: 173 University Park Dr Birmingham AL 35209-6770 Office Phone: 205-726-2389. Business E-Mail: rewheele@samford.edu.

WHEELER, SHARON, legislative staff member; d. Kirk and Carolyn Wheeler. Degree in journalism, U. Ala., degree in law. Law clk., Justice Sonny Hornsby Ala. Supreme Ct., 1988—89; with Ala. Power Co.; intern, Senator James Sasser US Senate; chief of staff to Senator Lowell Barron Ala. State Senate, legis. dir., Dem. Caucus; chief of staff to Rep. Parker Griffith US House of Reps., Washington, 2008—. Democrat. Office: 417 Cannon House Office Bldg Washington DC 20515 Office Phone: 202-225-4801. Office Fax: 202-225-4392.*

WHEELER, STEPHEN FREDERICK, legal administrator; BA in Polit. Sci., Mt. Union Coll., Alliance, Ohio, 1968; MS in Adminstrn. of Justice, Am. U., 1974. Probation officer 19th Dist. Juvenile and Domestic Rels. Ct. Prince William County, Manassas, Va., 1972-75; ct. systems planner Office of Jud. Planning Ky. Jud. Coun., Frankfort, 1975-76; co-dir. Ky. pretrial svcs. Adminstrv. Office of Cts. Ky. Ct. of Justice, Frankfort, 1976-81; ct. adminstr. Jud. Dist. 27A, Gastonia, N.C., 1982-87, Colorado Springs (Colo.) Mcpl. Ct., 1987—2005; ret. Ct. systems cons. Nat. Criminal Justice Collaborative, Sea Island, Ga., 1981-85. E-mail: stvwhlr@cs.com.

WHEELER, STEVE DEREAL, neurologist; b. Chgo., Sept. 15, 1951; s. Clarence and Tommie L. (Andrews) W.; m. Debra B. Buckingham; children: Winter N., Ryan S., Gabrielle S. Student, Mich. State U., 1970-73; MD, Dartmouth Coll., 1976. Diplomate Am. Bd. Psychiatry and Neurology, Nat. Bd. Med. Examiners; lic. Mich., Ohio, Fla. Intern Thomas Jefferson U., Phila., 1976-77; emergency physician River Dist. Hosp. Emergency Cons., Inc., St. Clair, Mich., 1977-78; fellow Dartmouth Med. Sch., 1978; resident U. Miami, Fla., 1978-81; fellow Washington U., St. Louis, 1981-82; instr. in neurology Med. Coll. Pa., Phila., 1982-83; electroencephalograph reader, attending neurologist VA Med. Ctr., Phila., 1982-83; asst. neurologist, attending neurologist Muscle Clinic U. Hosps. Cleve., 1983-86; electromyographer Rainbow Babies and Children's Hosp., U. Hosps. Cleve., 1983-86; chief neuromuscular diseases divsn., asst. prof. neurology Case Western Res. U., Cleve., 1983-86, co-dir. muscle disease ctr. and lab., 1985-86; clin. assoc. prof. of neurology U. Miami, 1987-89; pvt. practice Miami, 1987—; dir., co-founder Ryan Wheeler Headache Treatment Ctr., Miami, 2001—. Lectr. Myasthenia Gravis Found., Vermillion, Ohio, 1984, Cleve., 1983—86; vol. assoc. prof. U. Miami Sch., 1992—97, 2004—, vis. lectr., 1993—2001; chief headache divsn. Neurologic Ctr. for South Fla.; neurology cons. Low Back Pain Team U. Hosps. Cleve., 1984—86; mem. quality assurance com. Coral Reef Hosp., Miami, 1987—88; cons. dir. planning Bapt. Headache Clinic Bapt. Hosp., Miami, 1993—95; mem. adminstrv. com. Deering Hosp. Pain Mgmt. Ctr., Miami, 1993—94; mem. sleep diagnostic ctr. com. Bapt. Hosp., 1990—92, 1994—98, advisor to headache support group, 1995—; lectr. in field; co-founder, dir. Ryan Wheeler Headache Treatment Ctr. Author: (chpt.) Intensive Care For Neurological Trauma and Disease, 1982, (chpt.) Migraine and the Primary Headaches, 2002; mem. editl. bd.: Headache, 2001—02, ad hoc reviewer:, 2000—, Cephalalgia, 1999—, Jour. Nat. Med. Assn., 2001—, contbr. chpt.: Miscellaneous Primary Headache, 2004. Named Internat. Man Yr., 1991-92; recipient Celebration Excellence Black Achiever award Family Christian Assn. Am., 1992. Fellow Royal Soc. Medicine, Am. Acad. Neurology; mem. ACP, Am. Headache Soc., So. Med. Assn. (chmn. psychiatry and neurology sect. 2000-02), Nat. Headache Found., Internat. Headache Soc., Fla. Soc. Neurology, Muscular Disease Soc. Northeastern Ohio (trustee 1984-86), Dade County Med. Assn., So. Pain Soc., Dartmouth Club Greater Miami, Am. Coun. for Headache Edn. Achievements include research in plasmaphereses in treatment of acute Guillain-Barre Syndrome; repeat neuroimaging in headache when first study normal, migraine with cluster features, hemicrania continua, migraine-associated gluten sensitivity, secondary headaches, novel phenotype-driven strategies for headache and migraine prevention. Office: Ryan Wheeler Headache Treatment Ctr 5975 Sunset Drive Ste 501 Miami FL 33143 Office Phone: 305-661-2022. Office Fax: 305-661-2133.

WHEELER, THOMAS CRAIG, federal judge; b. Chgo., Mar. 18, 1948; married; 2 children. BA, Gettysburg Coll., 1970; JD, Georgetown U., 1973. Bar: DC, US Dist. Ct. DC, US Ct. Appeals 4th, 10th, DC, and Fed. Circuits, US Ct. Fed. Claims, US Supreme Ct. Ptnr. DLA Piper Rudnick Gray Cary (formerly Piper & Marbury), Washington, 1995—2005; judge US Ct. Fed. Claims, Washington, 2005—. Mem.: DC Bar Assn., Nat. Def. Indsl. Assn., Boards of Contract Appeals Bar Assn., ABA (public contract law sect., litig. sect.). Avocations: skiing, photography, writing, softball, hiking. Office: US Ct Fed Claims 717 Madison Pl NW Washington DC 20005*

WHEELER, THOMAS EDGAR, private equity executive; b. Redlands, Calif., Apr. 5, 1946; s. Charles Taylor and Martha (Edgar) W.; married; children: Nicole Fraser, Maxwell. BS, Ohio State U., 1968. Asst. dir. Ohio State U. Alumni Assn., Columbus, 1968-69; v.p. Grocery Mfrs. Am., Inc., Washington, 1969-76; exec. v.p. Nat. Cable TV Assn., Washington, 1976-79, pres., CEO, 1979-85, NABU: The Home Computer Network, 1985-86; chmn., CEO, NuCable Resources Corp., Washington, 1986-94; pres., CEO, Cellular Telecom. Industry Assn., Washington, 1992—2003; pres. Shiloh Group, LLC, 2003—; ptnr. Core

Capital Ptnrs., 2004—. Author: Leadership Lessons from the Civil War, 1999, Mr. Lincoln's T-Mails, 2006. Bd. dirs. Earthlink; pres. Found. for Nat. Archives. Democrat. Office: Core Capital 1401 I St NW Ste 1000 Washington DC 20005

WHEELER, TONY (ANTHONY IAN WHEELER), travel publishing executive; b. Dec. 20, 1946; s. Ian James and Hilary Audrey Wheeler; m. Maureen Dixon, 1971; 2 children. BS in Engring., Warwick Univ., 1969; MBA, London Bus. Sch., 1972. Engr. Rootes Cars, 1969—70; co-founder, joint dir. Lonely Planet Publications, 1973—. Co-author: Across Asia on the Cheap, 1972, South East Asia on a Shoestring, 1975, Nepal and Trekking in the Himalayas, 1976, Australia, 1977, New Zealand, 1977, Africa, 1977, Europe, 1977, India, 1981; publishes over 600 titles including specialist activity guides, shoestring guides, world food guides and phrasebooks. Office: Lonely Planet Publications 90 Maribyrnong St Footscray Victoria 3011 Australia also: 150 Linden St Oakland CA 94607 Office Phone: 510-893-8555. Office Fax: 510-893-8572.

WHEELER, WILLIAM J., insurance company executive; AB, Wabash Coll., 1983; MBA, Harvard Univ. Sr. v.p. Donaldson Lufkin Jenrette, MetLife, Inc., NYC, 1997—2003, exec. v.p., CFO, 2003—. Bd. dir. LIMRA. Trustee Wabash Coll. Mem.: Phi Beta Kappa. Office: MetLife Inc 200 Park Ave New York NY 10166*

WHEELER, WILLIAM JOE, retired research scientist; s. Joe G. and Lois M. Wheeler; m. Arlene Moss; children: Sherri L. Hendrich, Derek S. BS, Purdue U., West Lafayette, Ind., 1962; MS, Butler U., Indpls., 1967; PhD, Purdue U., Indpls., 1970. Rsch. fellow Eli Lilly & Co., Indpls., 1967—2007; N.Am. editor J. Labelled Cmpds. Radiopharm, 2006—; adj. prof. Ivy Tech. CC, 2008—. Contbr. scientific papers to profl. publs. Mem.: Internat. Soc. Heterocyclic Chemists, Am. Chem. Soc., Internat. Isotope Soc. (pres., bd. of trustees 2007—09).

WHEELER, W(ILLIAM) SCOTT, composer, conductor, music educator; b. Washington, Feb. 24, 1952; s. Malcolm Frederick and Aurora Dorothy (Anas) W.; m. Christen Struthers Frothingham, Jan. 5, 1985; children: Margaret Lee, Catherine Elizabeth. BA, Amherst Coll., 1973; MFA, Brandeis U., 1978, PhD, 1984. Artistic dir. Dinosaur Annex Music Ensemble, Boston, 1975—; dir. Cambridge (Mass.) Chorale, 1976-78; tchr. music, condr. Emerson Coll., Boston, 1978—. Composer (choral) A Babe is Born, 1979, (chamber) Winter Hills, 1987 (Somerville Arts Coun. Commn.), (symphony) Northern Lights, 1987 (Koussevitzky commn.), (operas) The Construction of Boston (libretto by Kenneth Koch), 1989, Democracy, 2004, (choral) The Angle of the Sun, 1994 (Nat. Endowment for the Arts). Guggenheim fellow, 1988-89. Mem. Am. Music Ctr., ASCAP. Episcopalian. Home: 6 Sunset Ave North Reading MA 01864-1427 Office: Emerson Coll Div Performing Arts 120 Boylston St Boston MA 02116-4624 Office Phone: 617-824-8385. Business E-Mail: scott_wheeler@emerson.edu.

WHEELESS, CHARLOTTE ANN, science educator; m. Gene Wheeless, May 12, 1990; children: Patrick, Nicholas, Jessica. BS in Edn. summa cum laude, Williams Bapt. Coll., Walnut Ridge, Ark., 1994; MEd, Grand Canyon U., Phoenix, 2006. Cert. nat. bd. tchr E.A. Sci., 2007. Sci. tchr. Walnut Ridge Mid. Sch., Ark., 1996—. Tchr. tng. workshop facilitator Interactive Tng. Media, Orlando, Fla., 2003—05; tchr. adv. bd. mem. Williams Bapt. Coll., Walnut Ridge, 2000—01. Adult leader 4-H Western Wranglers Horse & Pony Club, Black Rock, Ark., 2001—09, Ark. 4-H State Tech. Team, Little Rock, 2005—09; bd. mem. Lawrence County Hist. Soc., Powhatan, 2000—07. Recipient Tchr. Yr., Walnut Ridge Pub. Sch., 1999, Wal-Mart Tchr. Yr., Wal-Mart Corp., 1999, Young Achievement award, Williams Bapt. Coll., 1999—2000; grantee, Ark. Sci. and Tech. Authority, 2002—09; scholar, Walnut Ridge Bus. & Profl. Women Assn., 2005; Japan Fulbright tchr. participant, 2006. Mem.: Ark. Sci. Tchrs. Assn., Nat. Sci. Tchrs. Assn., Bus. & Profl. Women Assn. Avocations: travel, reading. Office: Walnut Ridge Public School 508 East Free Street Walnut Ridge AR 72476

WHEELOCK, BRYAN KING, lawyer, educator; b. NYC, Sept. 1, 1958; m. Victoria Ann Vonder Haar; children: Brigham King, Kathryn Patricia. JD, Wash. U., St. Louis, MO, 1982. Bar: 1982, lic.: U.S. Patent Trademark Office 1984. Adj. prof. Wash. U., 1998—; ptnr. Harness, Dickey & Pierce PLC, St, Louis, 2000—. Mem.: Bar Assn. of Met. St. Louis (chair, patent sect.). Home: 7727 Davis Dr Saint Louis MO 63105 Office: Patent Atty 7700 Bonhomme Ste 400 Saint Louis MO 63105 Office Fax: 314-726-7501. E-mail: bwheelock@hdp.com.

WHEELOCK, DOUGLAS H., astronaut, military officer; b. Binghamton, NY, May 5, 1960; s. Olin and Margaret Wheelock; m. Cathleen Hollen; 1 child. BS in Applied Sciences and Engring., U.S. Mil. Acad., West Point, NY, 1983; MS in Aerospace Engring, Ga. Inst. Tech., 1992. Commd 2d lt. U.S. Army, West Point, NY, 1983; student Army Aviation Sch., Ft. Rucker, Ala., 1983—84; from combat sect. leader, platoon leader, co. exec. officer, battalion ops. officer and comdr. officer Pacific Theater, Air Cavalry Troop. 9th U.S. Cavalry; advanced weapons rsch. and devel. engr. Aviation Directorate of Combat Developments, Fort Rucker, Ala.; mem. class 104 U.S. Naval Test Pilot Sch.; from exptl. test pilot to divsn. chief for fixed wing testing of airborne signal and imagery intelligence systems. U.S. Army Aviation Tech. Test Ctr., 1997—98; astronaut NASA Johnson Space Ctr., Houston, 1998—. Crew support astronaut Internat. Space Station Expedition 2, 2001, Internat. Space Station Expedition 4, 2001—02; spacecraft communicator (CAPCOM) Mission Control Ctr., Houston, 2002; lead CAPCOM Internat. Space Station Expedition 8; NASA's dir. ops. Gagarin Cosmonaut Tng. Ctr., Star City, Russia, 2005; mission specialist conducting both EVA and robotics ops. during the 3 spacewalks STS-120 Discovery Mission to Internat. Space Station, 2007. Decorated Meritorious Svc. medal (1st Oak Leaf Cluster), Army Commendation medal, Army Achievement medal (2nd Oak Leaf Cluster), Nat. Def. Svc. medal, Global War on Terrorism Svc. medal, Korea Def. Svc. medal, Army Good Conduct medal, Overseas Svc. Ribbon, Army Svc. Ribbon, Airborne Wings, Air Assault Wings, Master Aviator Wings, Air Force Space and Missle Badge; recipient Gamble award, U.S. Naval Test Pilot Sch., 1995, Group Acheivement award, NASA, 1997, NASA Group Achievement awards: Global Positioning System, 1997, Russian Liaison Support Team, 2001, NASA Superior Accomplishment award, 2002, 2004, 2005, Air Force Master Space Badge; named Outstanding Spokesman for Freedom, VFW, 1990, Disting. Grad., U.S. Army Initial Entry Flight Tng. Course, 1984. Mem.: Army Aviation Assn. Am., Assn. U.S. Army, Soc. Am. Military Engineers, Soc. Exptl. Test Pilots, West Point Assn. Graduates. Avocations: baseball, flying, coaching youth sports, hiking, sports. Office: Astronaut Office/CB Johnson Space Ctr Houston TX 77058

WHEELON, ALBERT DEWELL, physicist; b. Moline, Ill., Jan. 18, 1929; s. Orville Albert and Alice Geltz (Dewell) W.; m. Nancy Helen Hermanson, Feb. 28, 1953 (dec. May 1980); children: Elizabeth Anne (dec. Mar. 2006), Cynthia Helen; m. Cicely J. Evans, Feb. 4, 1984. BSc, Stanford U., 1949; PhD, MIT, 1952. Tchg. fellow, then rsch. assoc. physics MIT, Boston, 1949-52; with Douglas Aircraft Co., 1952-53, Ramo-Wooldridge Corp., 1953-62; dep. dir. sci. and tech. CIA, Washington, 1962-66; with Hughes Aircraft Co., LA, 1966-88, chmn., CEO, 1987-88. Vis. prof. MIT, 1989; mem. Def. Sci. Bd., 1968-76; mem. Pres.'s Fgn. Intelligence, 1983-88; mem. Presdl. Commn. on Space Shuttle Challenger Accident, 1986; trustee Aerospace Corp., 1990-93, Calif. Inst. Tech., 1985-, Rand Corp., 1993-2001. Author Electromagnetic Scintillation: Vol. 1 and 2, 2001, 03; contbr. 36 papers on radiowave propagation and guidance systems. Recipient R.V. Jones Intelligence award, 1994. Fellow IEEE, AIAA (Von Karman medal 1986, Goddard Astronautics award 1997), Am. Phys. Soc.; mem. NAE, Sigma Chi. Episcopalian. Independent. Address: 181 Sheffield Dr Montecito CA 93108-2242

WHELAN, ANDREW T., legislative staff member; Staff asst., resources com. US House of Reps., Washington, 2005—06, press sec., Rep. Greg Walden, 2006—. Republican. Office: 2352 Rayburn House Office Bldg Washington DC 20515 Office Phone: 202-225-6730. Office Fax: 202-225-5774.*

WHELAN, HARRY T., neurologist, educator; b. Milw., Nov. 3, 1953; s. Patrick E. and Marion P. Whelan; m. Melissa Whelan; children: Noel, Perry. BA cum laude, U. Wis., Madison, 1975, MD, 1979. Diplomate in neurology and spl. child neurology Am. Bd. Psychiatry and Neurology, 1986. Prof. neurology Med. Coll. Wis., Milw., 1988—, dir. hyperbaric medicine, 1998—, prin. investigator, Def. Advanced Rsch. Projects Agy., 2002; commdg. officer, PRIMUS Unit, Gt. Lakes Naval Hosp. USN, Ill., 1998—2000, capt. Milw., 2002—, diving med. officer, Deep Submergence Unit San Diego, 2006—. Chief neurology Children's Hosp. Wis., Milw., 1992—97; Bleser Endowed Prof. Bleser Found., 2001—; hon. prof. U. Wis., 2004—, U. Ill., Chgo., 2004—; disting. rsch. prof. Ctr. Tech. and Nat. Security Policy Nat. Def. U., Washington, 2004—06. Author: (textbook) Hyperbaric Medicine Practice, 2nd edit., 3rd edit.; contbr. articles to numerous neurol. jours. Recipient Clin. Oncology Career Devel. award, Am. Cancer Soc., 1987—90, 1st in Class award, USN-Officer Tng. Sch., 1994, 1st Class award, USN-Diving Casualties Sch., 1995, Achievement Rsch. medal, USN, 1995, Commendation medal, Navy & Marine Corps., 1997, Technol. Innovation award, Discover Mag., 2001; grantee, NASA, Quantum Devices, 2001—05, NASA, 2005—09, NIH, 2006—09, Hyperbaric Oxygen Therapy Stroke, Clin. and Transl. Sci. Inst., 2007—, USN Exptl. Diving Unit, 2007; Rsch. Found. grant, Chad Bauman Fund, 2000—, Rsch. grant, Def. Advanced Rsch. Projects Agy., 2001—06. Mem.: UDT-SEAL Assn., Assn. M.C. Officers Navy (founding mem.), US Naval Inst., Undersea & Hyperbaric Med. Soc., Pediat. Oncology Group Neurosci. Com., Soc. Neurosci., Am. Acad. Neurology, Child Neurology Soc., Naval Submarine League (life). Achievements include patents for red to near-infrared photobiomodulation treatment of the visual system in visual system disease or injury; system and method for convergent light therapy having controllable dosimetry; method and apparatus for treating neurological disorders by light stimulation; research in photodynamic therapy for brain tumors; amelioration of oral mucositis pain by NASA near infra red LED's in bone marrow transplant patients; near-infrared light (NIR) therapy for diabetic macular edema. Avocations: sailing, scuba diving, skiing. Office: Med Coll Wis 8701 W Watertown Plank Rd Milwaukee WI 53226

WHELAN, JAMES ROBERT, investor, mining company executive; b. Buffalo, July 27, 1933; s. Robert and Margaret (Southard) Whelan; children from previous marriage: Robert J., Heather Elizabeth. Student, U. Buffalo, 1951-53, U. RI, 1955-57; BA, Fla. Internat. U., 1974. Staff corr. UPI, Buffalo, 1952—53, bur. mgr. Providence, 1955—57, divsn. news editor Boston, 1957—58, fgn. corr. Buenos Aires, 1958—61, country mgr. Caracas, Venezuela, 1961—66, divsn. mgr San Juan, 1966, divsn. mgr., 1968; regional dir. corp. rels., then v.p. ops. ITT World Directories, San Juan, 1968—70; Latin Am. corr. Scripps-Howard Newspaper Alliance, Washington, 1970-71; mng. editor Miami News, Fla., 1971-73; free-lance writer, 1973-74; pres., editor, pub. Hialeah Pub. Co., Fla., 1975-77; v.p., editl. dir. Panax Corp., Washington, 1977-80; v.p., editor Sacramento Union, 1980-82; editor, pub. Washington Times, 1982-84; mng. dir. CBN News, 1985-86; pres. Capital Comm. Internat., 1986—; editor-in-chief Conservative Digest, 1988-89; vice chmn. Inter-Am. Found., Arlington, Va., 1991-94; external affairs advisor Inter-Am. Investment Corp., 1992-93; dir. strategic planning Cocetel Holding, Santiago, Chile, 1993-94; pres. Minera Silver Standard S.A., 1994—, Silver Std. Resources, Mexico, 1995—2000, advisor to bd., 2001—04, advisor to pres., 2004—. Freelance writer; guest lectr. Boston U., U. Miami, Ctrl. U., Venezuela, Cath. U., Washington, Andrès Bello U., Chile, U. Chile, U. Tex., Austin, U. Concepcion, Chile, U. Santiago; guest prof. U. Fla., 1973; adj. prof. U. Md., 1992—93; vis. prof. Polit. Sci. Inst. U. Chile, 1993—95; assoc. prof. Finis Terrae U., 1993—; scholar World Assn. Internat. Studies Stanford U., 1999—; adj. scholar Inst. World Politics, Washington, 2003—. Author: Through the American Looking Glass; Central America's Crisis, 1980, Allende: Death of a Marxist Dream, 1981, Catastrophe in the Caribbean: The Failure of America's Human Rights Policy in Central America, 1984, The Soviet Assault on America's Southern Flank, 1988, Out of the Ashes: Life, Death and Transfiguration of Democracy in Chile, 1833-1988, 1989, Hunters in the Sky, 1991, Desde las Cenizas: Vida, Muerte y Transfiguracion de la Democracia en Chile, 1833-1988, 1993, 2nd edit., 1995. Bd. dir. Christian Cmty. Svc. Agy., Miami, 1973, Hialeah-Miami Springs C. of C., 1976-77, Wolf Trap Found., 1984-87; bd. dirs. Nat. Coun. for Better Edn.; chmn. print media div. United Way campaign, Sacramento, 1981; bd. govs. Council on Nat. Policy, Washington, 1981-87; del. Commn. of Californias, 1981; chmn. Coun. for Inter-Am. Security Ednl. Inst., 1986-90; mem. spl. task force on pub. safety Greater Washington Bd. Trade; mem. Nat. Commn. on Free and Responsible Media, 1983-84; bd. dir. Nat. Bus. Consortium for Gifted and Talented Children, 1985-87; bd. govs. Internat. Policy Forum, 1985—; mem. Presdl. Bd. Fgn. Scholarships (Fulbright Commn.), 1986-92, exec. planning com., 1987-92. With Signal Corps U.S. Army, 1953-55. Nieman fellow Harvard U., 1966-67; recipient citation of excellence Overseas Press Club, 1971, Unity award Lincoln U., 1976, Golden Press award Am. Legion Aux., 1977, Freedom award Valley Forge Found., 1981, Bernardo O'Higgins award Chilean Govt., 1990, presented at Chilean Embassy by Amb. Octavio Errazuriz. Mem.: Instituto O'Higginiano de Chile, Harvard Club (NYC), Cosmos Club, Georgetown Club. Personal E-mail: jamesrwhelan@hotmail.com.

WHELAN, ROGER MICHAEL, lawyer, educator; b. Montclair, NJ, Nov. 12, 1936; s. John Leslie and Helen Louise (Callahan) W.; m. Rosemary Bogdan, Aug. 26, 1961; children: Helen, Theresa, John, James, Kathleen (dec.), Julie, Jennifer. AB cum laude, Georgetown U., Washington, DC, 1959, JD, 1962. Bar: DC 1962, US Dist. Ct. DC 1962, US Ct. Appeals (DC cir.) 1962, US Supreme Ct. 1968. Assoc. Fried, Rogers & Ritz, Washington, 1961—66; ptnr. Doctor & Whelan, Washington, 1967—72; judge US Bankruptcy Ct., Washington, 1972—83; sr. mem. Verner, Liipfert, Bernhard, McPherson & Hand, Chartered, Washington, 1984—89; ptnr., sr. counsel Shaw, Pittman, Potts & Trowbridge, Washington, 1989—2000; outside counsel to several Washington & Md. law firms, 2000—09; resident scholar Am. Bankruptcy Inst., 2004; sr. counsel Cooter, Mangold, Tompert & Karas LLP. Dir. Lincoln Ctr. for Legal Studies, Arlington, Va., 1974-84; disting. lectr. Columbus Sch. Law, Cath. U. Am., Washington, 1975—; bd. govs. Conf. on Consumer Fin. Law, 1995-2005; resident scholar Am. Bankruptcy Inst., 2004. Sec. local campaign com., Alexandria, Va., 1964; trustee YMCAA, Silver Spring, Md., 1972-74. Recipient award DC Cir. Jud. Conf., 1984. Fellow: Am. Coll. Bankruptcy (bd. regents 1989—95, bd. dirs. 1995—2002); mem.: FBA (chmn. bankruptcy subcom. 1988, exec. com. 1993—96, pres. 1999—2000), Assn. Former Bankruptcy Judges (sec.-treas. 1996—), Am. Bankruptcy Inst. (bd. dirs. 1991—97, chmn. legis. com. 1991—99, exec. com. 1993—95, apptd. resident scholar 2004), Walter Chandler Inn of Ct. (master emeritus 1990—). Republican. Roman Catholic. Avocations: fishing, hunting, boating. Office: Cooter Mangold Tompert & Karas LLP 5301 Wisconsin Ave NW Washington DC 20015 Office Phone: 301-260-7707, 202-537-0700. Personal E-mail: rmwhelan@verizon.net.

WHELAN, STEPHEN THOMAS, JR., lawyer; b. Phila., July 28, 1947; s. Stephen Thomas and Virginia King (Ball) W.; m. Elizabeth Ann Murphy, Apr. 3, 1971; children: Christine B. Whelan. BA magna cum laude, Princeton U., 1968; JD, Harvard U., 1971. Bar: N.Y. 1972, U.S. Dist. Ct. (so. dist.) N.Y. 1975. Assoc. Mudge Rose Guthrie & Alexander, NYC, 1971-75, Thacher Proffitt & Wood, NYC, 1975-77; ptnr. Thacher Proffitt & Wood LLP, NYC, 1978—2008, Sonnenschein Nath & Rosenthal LLP, 2009—; exec. com. Thacher Proffitt & Wood LLP, 1982—88, 2003—05, chmn. corp. dept., 1992-97; lectr. politics dept. Princeton U., 1999—. Chmn. Witherspoon Inst., Princeton, NJ, 2006—. Author: New York's Uniform Commercial Code Article 2A, 1994, The ABCs of the UCC: Article 2A (Leases), 1997, The ABCs of the UCC: Amended Article 2A, 2005; contbr. articles to profl. jours. Bd. dir. Atlantic Legal Found., 1997—; active N.Y. County Rep. Com., 1985—; active Princeton U. Alumni Coun., 1993—; trustee The Cloister Inn of Princeton U., 1996—, mem. adv. coun. James Madison program, 2000-. Fellow Am. Coll. Investment Counsel; mem. ABA (chmn. subcom. on leasing 1994-04), Am. Law Inst., NY State Bar Assn., Equipment Leasing and Fin. Assn. (fed. govt. rels. com. 1992-97, legal com. 1995-97, Excellence in Leasing award 2006), S.R. (bd. dirs. NY 1979—). Roman Catholic. Avocations: road racing, golf. Office Phone: 212-768-5333. Business E-Mail: swhelan@sonnenschein.com.

WHELCHEL, SANDRA JANE, writer; b. Denver, May 31, 1944; d. Ralph Earl and Janette Isabelle (March) Everitt; m. Andrew Jackson Whelchel, June 27, 1965; children: Andrew Jackson, Anita Earlyn. BA in Elem. Edn., U. No. Colo., 1966; postgrad., Pepperdine Coll., 1971, UCLA, 1971. Elem. tchr. Douglas County Schs., Castle Rock, Colo., 1966-68, El Monte (Calif.) schs., 1968-72; br. libr. Douglas County Librs., Parker, Colo., 1973-78; zone writer Denver Post, 1979-81; reporter The Express newspapers, Castle Rock, 1979-81; history columnist Parker Trail newspapers, 1985-93; columnist Authorship Mag., 1991—, Gothic Jour., 1994; writing tchr. Aurora Parks and Recreation, 1985-91; writing instr. Arapahoe C.C., 1991-2000; exec. dir. Nat. Writers Assn., 1991—. Lectr. writing and history Durango Writer's Workshop, 1996-97, Estes Park Writer's Retreat, 1996-97, Pikes Peak Writer's Workshop, 1997, Sinipee Writer's Workshop, 1998, Oasis for Seniors, 2000, Denver Women's Press Club, 1999, Rocky Mountain Gold Conf., 1999, Colo. Writers Fellowship, 2000, Colo. Ind. Publishers, 2000; spkr. in field. Editor Authorship mag., 1992-98; lit. agent NWLA, 1996-99; contbr. short stories and articles to various publs. including: The Writer, Writer's Open Forum, Writer's Jour., Reunions, Fresno Bee, Ancestry Newsletter, Calif. Horse Rev., Jack and Jill, Child Life, Children's Digest, Peak to Peak mag.; author: (non-fiction) Your Air Force Academy, 1982, A Guide to the U.S. Air Force Acad., 1990, Parker, Colorado: A Folk History, 1990, The Beginning Writer's Writing Book, 1996, Guide for Begining Writers, Nat. Writers Assn., 2008, A Folk History of Parker and Hilltop, 1996; co-author: The Writer's Office, 1998, Writing for Beginners, Nat. Writers Assn., 2006, 08, What's In a Name? Parker's Past Today, 2009, The Register, 1989, (coloring books) A Day at the Cave, 1985, A Day in Blue, 1984, Pro Rodeo Hall of Champions and Museum of the American Cowboy, 1985, Pikes Peak Country, 1986, Mile High Denver, 1987, (novel) Hide & Seek, 2006, Check & Mate, 2007; contbr. chpts. to books. Mem.: Nat. Writers Assn. (pres. 1990, 1991, 2003—04), Colo. Author's League (awards com. 1999—2000, who's who com. 2001), Parker Landmark Commn., Parker Area Hist. Soc. (pres. 1987—89), Nat. Writer's Club (treas. Denver Metro chpt. 1985—86, v.p. membership 1987, sec, 1990, bd. dirs., pres. 1990—91, v.p. programs 1992, v.p. membership 2002, bd. dirs., pres. 2003). Office Phone: 303-841-0246. *Personal philosophy: Tenacity and perseverance are keys to success. Optimism and self-belief open the door. The goals achieved through these elements are the most thrilling and savory.*

WHELDON, DAN (DANIEL CLIVE WHELDON), race car driver; b. Emberton, Eng., June 22, 1978; s. Clive and Sue Wheldon. Race car driver IndyCar Series Andretti Green, 2003—05, Ganassi, 2006—. 1st pl. Indy Japan 300 Twin Ring Motegi, 2004, 05, 2nd pl. Indy Japan 300, 06, 07; 1st pl. SunTrust Indy Challenge Richmond Internat. Raceway, 2004; 1st pl. Firestone Indy 225 Nazareth Speedway, 2004; 1st pl. Toyota Indy 300 Homestead-Miami Speedway, 2005, 06, 1st pl. XM Satellite Radio Indy 300, 07; 1st pl. Honda Grand Prix St. Petersburg, 2005; 1st pl. Indy 500 Indpls. Motor Speedway, 2005; 2nd pl. Argent Mortgage Indy 300 Kans. Speedway, 2005, 2nd pl. Kans. Lottery Indy 300, 06, 1st pl. Kans. Lottery Indy 300, 07, 1st pl. Kans. 300, 08; 2nd pl. Firestone Indy 400 Mich. Internat. Speedway, 2005; 1st pl. Honda Indy 225 Pikes Peak Internat. Raceway, 2005; 1st pl. Peak Antifreeze Indy 300 Chicagoland Speedway, 2005, 06; 2nd pl. Firestone Indy 200 Nashville Super Speedway, 2006; 1st pl. Iowa Corn Indy 250 Iowa Speedway, 2008. Named Rookie of Yr., Indy Racing League, 2004, IndyCar Series Champion, 2005. Achievements include becoming the first two-time IndyCar winner at Kansas Speedway, 2008. Avocations: travel, music. Mailing: Ganassi Racing 7777 Woodland Dr Indianapolis IN 46278

WHELIHAN, ALAN STUART, real estate developer, automotive executive; b. Phila., Sept. 17, 1932; s. John Franklin and Dorothy Dodge W.; m. Joan Murrell, June 20, 1959; children: Pamela, Deborah, Linda, Jacqueline. BS in Engring., Princeton U., 1954; MBA, U. Pa., 1960. Elect. engr. Philco Corp., Phila., 1954-55; product line mgr. govt. and indsl. divsn. RCA, Camden, NJ, 1959-65; gen. mgr. Chem. Micromilling Co., Pensauken, NJ, 1965-66; mgmt. cons. Peat Marwick Mitchell & Co., Washington, NJ, 1966-72; asst. commr. Fed. Supply Svc., Arlington, Va., 1973-79; dir. planning and coordination U.S. Metric Bd., Arlington, Va., 1979-82; dir. metric program U.S. Dept. Commerce, Washington, 1983-94; pres. VAW, LLC, Frederick, Md., 1994—, W Properties, L.L.C., Frederick, 1994. Dir. Am. Nat. Stds. Inst., 1973-75, Am. Nat. Metric Coun., Washington, 1990-92; consumer adv. coun. Underwriters Labs., 1973-2008. Lt. Comdr. USNR, 1955-57. Mem. IEEE (life), Congl. Country Club. Republican. Avocation: collecting antique automobiles. Office: W Properties LLC Stanford Indsl Park 4975 Winchester Blvd Frederick MD 21703-7400 Home: PO Box 221 Adamstown MD 21710-0221

WHELLEY, PATRICK LIAM, geologist; b. Ohio, 1981; married. BS, Ariz. State U., Tempe, 2005, MS, 2007; student, U. Buffalo, 2007—. Grad. rsch. fellow NASA GSFC GSRP, Greenbelt, Md., 2008—. MER sci. team mem. Athena Sci. Team, Pasadena, Calif., 2003—07. Achievements include research in global distribution of dust devil activity on mars. Avocations: music, soccer, hiking, travel. Office: Univ Buffalo SUNY Dept Geology Buffalo NY 14260 Business E-Mail: pwhelley@buffalo.edu.

WHELPLEY, DENNIS PORTER, lawyer; b. Mpls., Feb. 16, 1951; s. John Olsen and Harriet Marie (Porter) W.; m. Patricia Jan Adamy, Nov. 27, 1976; children: Heather Nicolle, Christopher Eric. BA, U. Minn., 1973, JD magna cum laude, 1976. Bar: Minn. 1976. Assoc. Oppenheimer Wolff & Donnelly, St. Paul, 1976-83, ptnr., 1983—. Mem. Order of Coif (Minn. chpt.), Phi Beta Kappa (Alpha of Minn. chpt.), Psi Upsilon (Mu chpt.), Dellwood Hills Golf & Country Club. Avocations: golf, tennis, squash, bridge. Home: 49 Locust St Mahtomedi MN 55115-1542 Office: Oppenheimer Wolff & Donnelly 45 S 7th St Ste 3300 Minneapolis MN 55402-1614 Home Phone: 651-426-0949; Office Phone: 612-607-7397. Business E-Mail: dwhelpley@oppenheimer.com.

WHELTON, BEVERLY JEAN, philosopher, educator; BA in Biology, Northeastern U., Boston, 1972; MS in Nursing, Cath. U. Am., Washington, DC, 1978, PhD in Philosophy, 1996. Assoc. prof. philosophy Wheeling SJ U., W.Va., 2001—. Book rev. editor Nursing Philosophy, Internat. Jour. Wiley Blackwell, 2004—; v.p. Internat. Philosophy Nursing Soc., Internat. Based UK, 2005—. Office: Wheeling Jesuit Univ 316 Washington Ave Wheeling WV 26003 Office Fax: 304-243-4441. Personal E-mail: bevwhelton@sbcglobal.net. Business E-Mail: bwhelton@wju.edu.

WHERRY, ROBERT ALLEN, JR., federal judge, lawyer; b. Langley Field, Va., Apr. 7, 1944; s. Robert Allen and Lorene Fletcher (Ivy) W.; m. Leslie Anne Ross, June 23, 1943; children: Richard Washburn, Marsha Ivy. Student, Ohio State U., 1962-63; BS, U. Colo., 1966, JD, 1969; LLM in Taxation, NYU, 1972. Bar: Colo. 1969, US Dist. ct. (fed. dist.) 1969, US Tax Ct. 1973, US Ct. Appeals (10th circuit) 1976, US Ct. Claims, 1978, US Ct. Appeals (fed. circuit) 1991, US Supreme Ct. 1992. Constrn. laborer EBY Constrn. Co., Denver, 1965; acct. CF&I Steele, Pueblo, Colo., 1966; jr. acct. Ernst & Ernst, Denver, 1967-69; tax analyst Colo. Atty. Gen. Office (Inheritance Tax Divsn.), Denver, 1972; atty. Lentz, Evans & King P.C., Denver, 1973—; judge US Tax Ct., Washington, 2003—. Spkr. continuing edn. U. Denver, Tulane U. Tax Inst., Colo. Soc. CPA's, Englewood, 1984—; correspondant State Tax Notes, Tax Analysts, Arlington, Va., 1991—. Tax coun. Colo. Assn. Commerce & Industry, 1978—; mem. Colo. Dept. Revenue Advisory Com., 1989-82, 89-90, Denver Mayor's Tax Com., Denver, 1992-93. Served in US Army, 1970—71. Fellow American Coll. Tax Counsel (regent); mem. ABA (former chmn. adminstrv. practice com. tax sect.), Colo. Bar Assn. (tax sect., chmn. 1981-82), Greater Denver Tax Counsel (chmn. 1986). Republican. Methodist. Avocations: bridge, chess. Office: US Tax Ct 400 2nd St NW Washington DC 20217*

WHETSTONE, JONI LEE, music educator; b. Cumberland, Md., July 25, 1955; d. John Moyer and Eleanor Mae Shambach; 1 child, Leanna Lynn. MusB in Edn., Lee U., 1977; MusM, Ind. U. Pa., 1982. Instr. vocal music Everett Area Middle/Sr. HS, 1983—. Lectr. music Pa. State U., Altoona, Pa., 1986—; instr. vocal music Everett (Pa.) Christian Academy, 1977—78, 1980—83; dir. music First Evang. Luth. Ch., Altoona, 1987—89. Named Claes Nobel Educator Distinction, Nat. Soc. H.S. Scholars, 2004; named one of Outstanding Am. Tchrs., Nat. Honor Roll, 2006, 2007. Mem.: NEA, Pa. State Educators Assn., Am. Choral Dirs. Assn., Pa. Music Educators Assn., Music Educators Nat. Conf. Republican. Home: PO Box 1495 Altoona PA 16603 Office: Everett Area Middle/Sr HS 1 Renaissance Cir Everett PA 15537-1406 Office Phone: 814-652-9114 1302. Business E-Mail: jwhetstone@everett.k12.pa.us.

WHICHARD, WILLIS PADGETT, lawyer, retired educator, judge; b. Durham, NC, May 24, 1940; s. Willis Guilford and Beulah (Padgett) W.; m. Leona Irene Paschal, June 4, 1961; children: Jennifer Diane, Ida Gilbert. AB, U. N.C., 1962, JD, 1965; LLM, U. Va., 1984, SJD, 1994. Bar: N.C. 1965. Law clk. NC Supreme Ct., Raleigh, 1965-66, assoc. justice, 1986-98; assoc. judge NC Ct. Appeals, Raleigh, 1980-86; ptnr. Powe, Porter, Alphin & Whichard, Durham, 1966-80; dean, prof. law Campbell U., 1999—2006, Moore and Van Allen Law Firm, 2006—. Instr. grad. sch. bus. adminstrn. Duke U., 1978; vis. lectr. U. N.C. Sch. Law, 1986-98. Contbr. articles to profl. jours. Rep. N.C. Ho. of Reps., Raleigh, 1970-74; senator N.C. Senate, 1974-80, chair numerous coms. and commns.; N.C. legis. rsch. commn., 1971-73, 75-77, land policy coun., 1975-79; bd. dirs. Sr. Citizens Coordinating Coun., 1972-74; chair local crusade Am. Cancer Soc., 1977, state crusade chair, 1980, chair pub. issues com., 1980-84; pres., bd. chmn. Downtown Durham Devel. Corp., 1980-84; bd. dirs. Durham County chpt. ARC, 1971-79; Durham county campaign dir. March of Dimes, 1968, 69, chmn., 1969-74, bd. dirs. Triangle chpt., 1974-79; bd. advisors Duke Hosp., 1982-85, U. N.C. Sch. Pub. Health, 1985-96, U. N.C. Sch. Social Work, 1989—; bd. visitors N.C. Ctrl. U. Sch. Law, 1987—; mem. law sch. dean search com. U. N.C., 1978-79, 88-89, self-study com., 1985-86; pres. N.C. Inst. Justice, 1984-94; bd. dirs. N.C. Ctr. Crime and Punishment, 1984-94. Staff sgt. N.C. Army NG, 1966-72. Recipient Disting. Service award Durham Jaycees, 1971, Outstanding Legis. award N.C. Acad. Trial Lawyers, 1975, Outstanding Youth Svc. award N.C. Juvenile Correctional Assn., 1975, named Citizen of Yr. Eno Valley Civitan Club, Durham, 1982, Faith Active in Pub. Life award N.C. Coun. of Churches, 1983, Outstanding Appellate Judge award N.C. Acad. Trial Lawyers, 1983; named to Durham H.S. Hall of Fame, 1987. Mem. ABA, N.C. Bar Assn. (v.p. 1983-84, 2001-02), Durham County Bar Assn., U. N.C. Law Alumni Assn. (pres. 1978-79, bd. dirs. 1979-82), Nat. Guard Assn. (judge adv. 1972-73, legis. com. 1974-76), Order of Golden Fleece, Order of Grail, Order of Old Well, Amphoterothen Soc., Order of Coif, Phi Alpha Theta, Phi Kappa Alpha, Durham-Chapel Hill Torch Club (pres. 1984-85), Watauga Club (Raleigh, pres. 1994-95). Democrat. Baptist. Home: 84402 Winslow Chapel Hill NC 27517 Office: Moore and Van Allen Attys PO Box 13076 Research Triangle Park NC 27709 Office Phone: 919-286-8054. Business E-Mail: williswhichard@mvalaw.com.

WHIFFEN, JAMES DOUGLASS, surgeon, educator; b. NYC, Jan. 16, 1931; s. John Phillips and Lorna Elizabeth (Douglass) W.; child from a previous marriage, Gregory James; m. Sally Vilas Runge, Aug. 21, 1993. BS, U. Wis., 1952, MD, 1955. Diplomate: Am. Bd. Surgery. Intern Ohio State U. Hosp., 1955-56; resident U. Wis. Hosp., 1956-57, 59-61; instr. dept. surgery U. Wis. Med. Sch., 1962-64, asst. prof., 1964-67, asso. prof., 1967-71, prof., 1971-96, vice chmn. dept., 1970-72, acting chmn., 1972-74; asst. dean Med. Sch., 1975-96; prof. emeritus U. Wis. Med. Sch., 1996—; mem. exam. council State of Wis. Emergency Med. Services, 1974-77. Bd. dirs. Wis. Heart Assn. Served to lt. comdr. USNR, 1957-59. John and Mary R. Markle scholar in acad. medicine, also; Research Career Devel. award NIH, 1965-75 Fellow A.C.S., Am. Soc. Artificial Internal Organs. Clubs: Maple Bluff Country. Achievements include research publs. on biomaterials, thrombo-resistant surfaces and the physiology of heart-lung bypass procedures. Home: 17 Cambridge Ct Madison WI 53704-5906 Office: 600 Highland Ave Madison WI 53792-0001 E-mail: jwhiffen@wisc.edu.

WHIGHAM, MARK ANTHONY, computer scientist; b. Mobile, Ala., Jan. 14, 1959; s. Tommie Lee Sr. and Callie Mae (Molette) W. BS in Computer Sci., Ala. A&M U., 1983, MS in Computer Sci., 1990; postgrad., Ala. A&M Univ., 1995; student in Religious Edn., Andersonville Theological Sem., Camilla, GA, 2003—; cert., Am. C.C. Leadership Acad., U. Ala., 2005. Cert. Microsoft cert. profl., A+ cert CompTIA, i-Net+ cert. profl. CompTIA, network + cert. profl. CompTIA, Microsoft Office specialist cert. 2003, others. Computer programmer U.S. Army Corps of Engrs., Huntsville, Ala., 1985-88; programmer analyst, coord. acad. computing Ala. A&M U., Normal, Ala., 1988-89, programmer analyst II, DEC systems coord., instr. part-time computer sci. dept., 1989-91; systems engr. Advanced Bus. Cons. Inc.-La. div. Dow Chem. Co., 1991-93; owner Whigham's Computer Cons., 1990—; sys. engr. DOW Chem. Co.-USA La. Divsn., Plaquemine, La., 1991-93; instr. computer info. system Calhoun C.C., Decatur, Ala., 1993-97; network specialist/cons. Ala. A&M U., Normal, 1994—; computer info. sys. instr. Calhoun C.C., Decatur, Ala., 1994—; mgmt. info. sys. dir., CIO J.F. Drake Tech. Coll., Huntsville, Ala., 1997-98; software engr. Colsa Corp., Huntsville, Ala., 1998—99; dir. info. tech. Lane Coll., 1999—2000; instr. computer sci. Lawson State CC, 2000—. Instr. computer sci. dept. Ala. A&M U., 1989-91; network specialist, cons. Ala. A&M U., Normal, 1994—. Active Huntsville Interdenominational Ministerial Fellowship, Huntsville, 1984. Mem. Nat. Assn. Sys. Programmers, Computer Sci. Tchrs. Assn., Ala. Info. Tech. Assn. (adv-.com.), Ala. Coun. for Computer Edn., Assn. for Computing Machinery, Huntsville Jaycees, Nat. Soc. Black Engrs., Assn. Info. Tech. Profls., So. Poetry Assn., Nat. Arts Soc., Internat. Black Writers and Artists Assn., Optimists, U.S. Chess Fedn. (cert. chess coach), Future Bus. Leaders of Am.-Phi Beta Lambda, Sigma Tau Epsilon, Alpha Phi Omega. Democrat. Baptist. Avocations: chess, skating, reading, playing piano. Office: Lawson State CC 3060 Wilson Rd ACATT Ste 250 Birmingham AL 35209-1542 Home: 827 Tyler CT APT E Birmingham AL 35226-1352 Office Phone: 205-929-2023. Business E-Mail: mark_whigham@msn.com, mwhigham@lawsonstate.edu.

WHILDIN, LEONORA PORRECA, retired nursing educator; b. Boston, Mass., Dec. 7, 1926; d. John and Anna (Annunziata) Porreca; m. William Miller Whildin; children: Susan Lee, Robert Miller, Walter Thomas. BS, Boston U., 1954; MS, Columbia U., 1971. RN, Mass., N.Y., N.J.; cert. nurse midwife, N.Y. Cadet nurse corps. Boston City Hosp., 1943-46, staff, asst. head nurse neurology, neurosurgery, 1946-48, scrub nurse neurosurgery, 1948-50; civilian nurse Dept. of Army, Bremerhaven, Germany, 1948; pub. health nurse Bklyn. Vis. Nurse Assn., 1954-56; instr. Helene Fulde Sch. of Practical Nursing, NYC, 1956-57; pub. health nurse V.N.A. Morris Co., Morristown, NJ, 1967; instr. All Souls Hosp. Sch. of Nursing, Morristown, NJ, 1968-69; guest lectr. Seton Hall U., South Orange, NJ, 1978. Del. Am. Nurses Assn, Mass., 1954; By-Laws Com. Am. Coll. Nurse Midwives, N.Y., 1972, By-Laws Com. Am. Coll. Nurse Midwives (N.J. chpt.), 1980; bd. mem. V.N.A. Morris Co., Morristown, N.J., 1977-78; v.p. bd. health, Randolph Twp., Randolph, N.J., 1972-74. Coun. woman Randolph Twp., 1972-78; mayor (1st woman mayor) Randolph Twp., 1977; Dem. party county com., Morris Co., Morristown, N.J., 1972-96; Dem. party state com., N.J., 1992-98; vol. United Way of Morris County. Mem. APHA, ANA, LWV, Mass., N.Y., N.J. (bd. mem. 1964-66), Sigma Theta Tau. Democrat. Avocations: ice skating, knitting, crafts, baking. Home: 82 Radtke Rd Randolph NJ 07869-3815

WHINNERY, PETER B., design educator; married. BA in Math., Albion Coll., Mich., 1979; MA in Theater, U. Mich., Ann Arbor, 1982. Tech. advisor U. Pa., Phila., 1982—, faculty, 1986—. Resident designer InterAct Theatre Co., Phila., 1989—. Office: Univ Pa 4100 Walnut St Philadelphia PA 19104

WHINSTON, MICHAEL D., economics professor; b. NYC, Feb. 3, 1959; BS in Economics, Wharton Sch., U. Pa., 1980, MBA in Fin., 1984; PhD in Economics, MIT, 1984. Asst. prof. economics Harvard U., 1984—88, Frederick S. Danziger assoc. prof. economics, 1988—91, prof. economics, 1991—98; Robert E. and Emily H. King prof. bus. institutions, dept. economics Northwestern U., 1998—, by courtesy, Sch. Law, 1998—, by courtesy, Kellogg Grad. Sch. Mgmt., Dept. Mgmt. and Strategy, 2003—. Vis. position, dept. economics Northwestern U., 1997—98; vis. position, Antitrust Divsn. US Dept. Justice, 1988; vis. position, dept. economics Yale U., 1989; Olin vis. prof. and fellow at the Ctr. for the Study of the Economy and the State, Grad. Sch. Bus. U. Chgo., 1999—2000, vis. adj. prof., grad. sch. bus., 2002; mem. program com. Utah Bus. Economics Conf., 2007—; rsch. assoc. Nat. Bur. Econ. Rsch.; co-organizer Duke/Northwestern/Tex/ IO Theory Conf.; co-dir., Ctr. for the Study Indsl. Orgn. Northwestern U.; invited lectr. in field. Contbr. articles to profl. jours.; co-editor: RAND Journal Economics, 1991—97, Microeconomic Theory, 1995; bd. editors mem. American Economic Journals: Microeconomics, 2007—; author: Lectures on Antitrust Economics, 2006; co-author (with B.D. Bernheim): Microeconomics, 2007. Alfred P. Sloan Rsch. Fellow, 1990—92, Ctr. for Advanced Studies in the Behavioral Scis. Fellow, 1993—94, NSF Rsch. Grants, 1986—88, 1990—94, 2000—03, 2003—06. Fellow: Econometric Soc. (mem. program com. for Winter meetings 1989, mem. program com. for Summer World Congress 2000), Am. Acad. Arts & Scis.; mem.: Am. Econ. Assn. (mem. program com. for ann. meetings 2001). Office: Dept Economics Northwestern U Rm 3230 Arthur Anderson Hall 2001 Sheridan Rd Evanston IL 60208 Office Phone: 847-491-8260. Office Fax: 847-491-7001. Business E-Mail: mwhinston@northwestern.edu.

WHIPPLE, DEAN, federal judge; b. 1938; BS, Drury Coll., 1961; postgrad., U. Tulsa, 1961-62; JD, postgrad., U. Mo., Kansas City, 1965. Pvt. practice, Lebanon, Mo., 1965-75; cir. judge div. II 26th Jud. Cir. Mo., 1975-87; judge US Dist. Ct. (we. dist.) Mo., Kansas City, 1987—2007, chief judge, 2000—07, sr. judge, 2007—. Prosecuting atty. Laclede County, Mo., 1967-71. With Mo. N.G., 1956-61; USAR, 1961-66. Mem. Mo. Bar Assn. (mem. bd. govs. 1975-87, mem. exec. com. 1983-84, 86-87), Mo. Trial Judges Assn., 26th Jud. Bar Assn., Laclede County Bar Assn. (pres. 1968-69, 72-73), Kansas City Met. Bar Assn., Kansas City Inn of Ct. (instr. 1988-93), Mo. Hist. Soc., Phi Delta Phi. Office: US Courthouse 400 E 9th St Kansas City MO 64106-2607

WHIPPLE, JACQUELINE CONANT, writer, media specialist; b. Columbus, Ohio, Mar. 31, 1921; d. William Horace and Gertrude Virginia (Bryant) Conant; AB magna cum laude, Mt. Holyoke Coll., 1943; postgrad. Art. Inst. Boston, 1974-79; MA Lesley Coll., 1991; m. David Collins Whipple, Sept. 6, 1944; children: Nancy, Roger, Leah, Benjamin. Reporter, Scarsdale Inquirer, NY, 1939-43; scriptwriter radio dept. J. Walter Thompson Co., NY, 1943-45; reporter Washington Daily News, 1945-47; broadcast journalist, chief editorial writer Sta. WCRB-AM-FM, Waltham, Mass. and Boston, 1960-67; with sch. divsn. Houghton Mifflin Co., Boston, 1967-86; freelance all media; jury chmn. excellence in pub. writing/support of edn. Council for Advancement and Support of Edn., Washington, 1981. Chmn. Know Your Town-Waltham LWV, 1951, v.p., 1953; pres. Cohasset (Mass.) PTA, 1963. Recipient Tom Phillips award, UPI Broadcasters of Mass., 1963; cert. of merit Art Inst. Boston, 1976, Cohasset Yacht Club. Democrat. Unitarian. Contbr. articles to popular mags. Home and Office: 119 N Main St Cohasset MA 02025-1317

WHIPPLE, JUDITH ROY, retired editor; b. NYC, May 14, 1935; d. Edwin Paul and Elizabeth (Levis) Roy; m. William Whipple, Oct. 26, 1963. AB, Mount Holyoke Coll., 1957. Head libr. Am. Sch. Lima (Peru), S.A., 1957-59; asst. editor children's books G.P. Putnam's Sons, NYC, 1959-62; assoc. editor W.W. Norton & Co., Inc., NYC, 1962-68; editor Four Winds Press, 1968-75; editor-in-chief Scholastic Gen. Book Divsn., 1975-77; pub. Four Winds Press subs. Scholastic Inc., NYC, 1977-82; pub., v.p. Macmillan Pub. Co., NYC, 1982-89, exec. editor, 1989-94; editl. dir. Cavendish Children's Books, Tarrytown, NY, 1994—2002, ret., 2002. Mem.: PEN, Children's Book Coun. (pres. 1977, bd. dirs. 1970—79), Women's Nat. Book Assn., Soc. Children's Book Writers and Illustrators. Avocations: gardening, swimming, piano, travel. Personal E-mail: jrwhipple@stny.rr.com.

WHIPPLE, KENNETH, utilities executive; b. 1934; BS, MIT, 1958. With Ford Motor Co., Dearborn, Mich., 1958—, systems mgr. Ford Credit, 1966-69, mgr. mgmt. svcs. dept. fin. staff, 1969-71, systems analysis mgr. fin. staff, 1971-74, asst. contr. internat. fin. staff, 1974-75, v.p. fin. Ford Credit, 1975-77, exec. v.p. Ford Credit, 1977-80, pres. Ford Credit, 1980-84, v.p. corp. strategy, 1984-86; v.p. chmn. Ford of Europe, 1986-88; exec. v.p., pres. Ford Fin. Svcs. Group, Dearborn, 1988—99; chmn., CEO CMS Energy, Dearborn, Mich., 2002—04, chmn., 2004—. Office: CMS Energy 1 Energy Plaza Drive Jackson MI 49201

WHIPPS, EDWARD FRANKLIN, lawyer; b. Columbus, Ohio, Dec. 17, 1936; s. Rusk Henry and Agnes Lucille (Green) W.; children: Edward Scott, Rusk Huot, Sylvia Louise, Rudyard Christian. BA, Ohio Wesleyan U., 1958; JD, Ohio State U., 1961. Bar: Ohio 1961, U.S. Dist. Ct. (so. dist.) Ohio 1962, U.S. Dist. Ct. (no. dist.) Ohio 1964, U.S. Ct. Claims 1963, U.S. Supreme Ct. 1963, Miss. 1965, U.S. Ct. Appeals (6th cir.) 1980. Assoc. George, Greek, King & McMahon, Columbus, 1961-66; ptnr. George, Greek, King, McMahon & McConnaughey, Columbus, 1966-79, McConnaughey, Stradley, Mone & Moul, Columbus, 1979-81, Thompson, Hine & Flory, Columbus, 1981-93; prin. Edward F. Whipps & Assocs., Columbus, 1993-94, 2000—; ptnr. Whipps & Wistner, Columbus, 1995-99. Founder, trustee Creative Living, Inc., 1969—; trustee, v.p. Unverferth House, Inc., 1989; trustee Eagle Scholarship Trust. Host: (TV) Upper Arlington Plain Talk, 1979-82, Bridging Disability, 1981-82, Lawyers on Call, 1982—, U.A. Today, 1982-86, The Ohio Wesleyan Experience, 1984—. Mem. Ohio Bd. Psychology, 1992-02, pres. 2001-02; active Upper Arlington (Ohio) Bd. Edn., 1971-80, pres., 1978-79; bd. alumni dirs. Ohio Wesleyan U., 1975-79; trustee Walden Ravines Assn., 1992-96, pres. 1993-96. Mem. ABA, Columbus Bar Assn., Ohio State Bar Assn., Assn. Trial Lawyers Am., Ohio Acad. Trial Lawyers, Franklin County Trial Lawyers Assn., Columbus Bar Found., Columbus C. of C., Upper Arlington Area C. of C. (trustee 1978-80), Lawyers Club, Barrister Club, Columbus Athletic Club, Nat. Football Found. & Hall of Fame, Columbus Touchdown Club, Downtown Quarterback Club, Ohio State U. Faculty (Columbus) Club, Ohio State U. Golf Club, Highlands Golf Club (dir. 2001—, v.p. 2005—), Delta Tau Delta (nat. v.p. 1976-78). Republican. Home: 51 Highland Ct Pataskala OH 43062-8910 Office: Edward F Whipps & Assocs 500 S Front St Columbus OH 43215-7619 Office Phone: 614-461-6006. Personal E-mail: efwhipp@aol.com. *Personal philosophy: Commitment to personal growth, the development of interpersonal relationships, the rule of law and a firm belief in the unique value of every individual in a holographic universe are the primary factors seen in my approach to life.*

WHISENANT, JOHN, professional basketball coach; b. Gore, Okla. m. Joyce Mowery; children: Stan, Daniel, Johnette, Justin, Jordyn. Attended, Connors State Coll., Warner, Okla.; BS in Phys. Edn., N.Mex. State U.; MA in History, Pittsburg State U., Kans. Asst. coach Coffeyville Cmty. Jr. Coll. Red Ravens, Kans., 1967—69; head basketball coach Ariz. Western Jr. Coll. Matadors, 1969—72; head asst. coach U. N.Mex. Lobos, 1972—79; businessman in comml. real estate, home constrn. and horse racing; head coach AAU, Albuquerque, IBL/CBA; v.p. basketball N.Mex. Slam, AAA Pro League, 1999—2000; asst. gen. mgr. Sacramento Monarchs, 2003, head coach, 2003—06, 2009—, gen. mgr., 2004—. Cons. to the Maloof family, Sacramento. Named Coach of Yr., WNBA, 2005. Achievements include head coach of the WNBA Finals championship winning Sacramento Monarchs, 2005. Office: Sacramento Monarchs 1 Sports Pky Sacramento CA 95834*

WHISENHUNT, DONALD WAYNE, retired historian, dean, educator; b. Meadow, Tex., May 16, 1938; s. William Alexander Whisenhunt and Beulah (Johnson) King; m. Betsy Ann Baker, Aug. 27, 1960; children: Donald Wayne Jr., William Benton. BA, McMurry Coll., 1960; MA, Tex. Tech U., 1962, PhD, 1966. Tchr. Elida (N.Mex.) High Sch., 1961-63; from asst. to assoc. prof. history Murray (Ky.) State U., 1966-69; assoc. prof., chmn. dept. Thiel Coll., Greenville, Pa., 1969-73; Dean Sch. Liberal Arts and Scis., Ea. N.Mex. U., Portales, 1973-77; v.p. acad. affairs U. Tex., Tyler, 1977-83; v.p., provost Wayne (Nebr.) State Coll., 1983-91, interim pres., 1985; prof. history, chmn. dept. Western Wash. U., Bellingham, 1991—2003. Fulbright lectr. Peoples Republic of China, 1995, Republic of Korea, 1994, Belarus, 2004. Author: Environment and American Experience, 1974, Depression in the Southwest, 1979, Chronological History of Texas, Vol. 1, 1982, Vol.2, 1987, Texas: Sesquicentennial Celebration, 1984; editor: Encyclopedia USA, 1988—, Poetry of the People: Poems to the President, 1929-1945, 1996, Tent Show: Arthur Names and His Famous Players, 2000, It Seems to Me: Selected Letters of Eleanor Roosevelt, 2001. Democrat. Methodist. Home: 1139 Martin St Sycamore IL 60178

WHISENHUNT, KEN, professional football coach; b. Atlanta, Feb. 28, 1962; m. Alice Whisenhunt; children: Kenneth Jr., Mary Ashley. BS in Civil Engring., Ga. Tech. U., 1990. Tight end Atlanta Falcons, 1985—88, Washington Redskins, 1990, NY Jets, 1991—92; spl. teams, half backs, & tight ends coach Vanderbilt U., 1995—96; tight ends coach Balt. Ravens, 1997—98; spl. teams coach Cleve. Browns, 1999; tight ends coach NY Jets, 2000, Pitts. Steelers, 2001—03, offensive coord., 2004—06; head coach Ariz. Cardinals, 2007—. Achievements include being a member of Super Bowl XL winning Pittsburgh Steelers, 2006. Office: Ariz Cardinals 8701 S Hardy Dr Tempe AZ 85284*

WHISLER, JAMES STEVEN, retired mining executive, lawyer, rancher; b. Centerville, Iowa, Nov. 23, 1954; s. James Thomas and Betty Lou (Clark) W.; m. Ardyce Dawn Christensen, Jan. 20, 1979; children: James Kyle, Kristen Elyse. BS, U. Colo., Boulder, 1975; JD, U. Denver, 1978; MS, Colo. Sch. Mines, 1984, DSc (hon.), 2001; AMP, Harvard Bus. Sch., 1998. Bar: Colo. 1978; CPA, Ariz. Assoc. gen. counsel, sec. We. Nuc., Inc., Denver, 1979—81; exploration counsel Phelps Dodge Corp., NYC, 1981—85, legal and adminstrv. mgr. Phoenix, 1985—87, v.p., gen. counsel, 1987—88, sr. v.p., gen. counsel, 1988—91; pres. Phelps Dodge Mining Co., 1991—98; pres., COO Phelps Dodge Corp.,

Phoenix, 1997—99, chmn., pres., CEO, 2000—03, chmn., CEO, 2003—07. Bd. dir. Am. West Holdings Corp., 2001—05, Phelps Dodge Corp., 1995—2007, Burlington No. Santa Fe Corp., U.S. Airways Group, Inc., Brunswick Corp., Internat. Paper Corp., 2007—. Mem.: AIME, AICPA, Nat. Cowboy and Western Heritage Mus., Mining and Metall. Soc. Am., Colo. Bar Assn., Soc. Mining Engrs., Mont. Stock Growers' Assn. E-mail: jswhisler@gmail.com.

WHISLER, JOE B., lawyer; b. Nevada, Mo., May 31, 1947; BA, Ctrl. Meth. Coll., 1969; JD, So. Meth. Univ., Dallas, 1972. Bar: Mo. 1972, US Ct. Appeals (8th Cir.) 1980, US Ct. Appeals (10th Cir.). Mem., atty. Cooling & Herbers PC, Kans. City, Mo. Bd. of editors: Jour. of Air Law and Commerce, 1971—72. Mem.: ABA, Lawyers Assn. of Kans. City (pres., jr. sect. 1977—78), Kans. City Met. Bar Assn., Bar Assn. of Met. St. Louis (chmn. aviatin law com. 1998, mem. planning commn. City Westwood, Kans. 1998), Barristers, Mo. Bar (bd. gov. 1979—83, 1996—, pres.-elect 2003, pres. 2004), Phi Alpha Delta. Office: Cooling & Herbers PC 2400 City Center Sq 1100 Main St Kansas City MO 64105

WHISNANT, JACK PAGE, neurologist; b. Little Rock, Oct. 26, 1924; s. John Clifton and Zula I. (Page) W.; m. Patricia Anne Rimmey, May 12, 1944; children: Elizabeth Anne, John David, James Michael. BS, U. Ark., 1948, MD, 1951; MS, U. Minn., 1955; MD (hon.), U. Edinburgh, Scotland, 1996. Intern Balt. City Hosp., 1951-52; resident in medicine and neurology Mayo Grad. Sch. Medicine, Rochester, Minn., 1952-55, instr. neurology, 1956-60, asst. prof., 1960-64, asso. prof., 1964-69, prof., 1969—; Meyer prof. neurosci. Mayo Med. Sch.; chmn. dept. neurology Mayo Clinic, Mayo Med. Sch., Mayo Grad. Sch. Medicine, 1971-81; chmn. dept. health scis. research Mayo Clinic and Mayo Med. Sch., 1987-93. Cons. neurology Mayo Clinic, 1955-96, head sect. neurology, 1963-71; dir. Mayo Cerebrovascular Clin. Rsch. Ctr., 1975-96. Contbr. articles on neurology and cerebrovascular disease to med. jours. Trustee YMCA, Rochester, pres., 1977. With USAAF, 1942-45. Decorated Air medal. NIH grantee, 1959-96. Fellow Am. Heart Assn., Am. Acad. Neurology (pres. 1993-95); mem. AMA, Am. Neurol. Assn. (pres. 1981-82), Am. Bd. Psychiatry and Neurology (bd. dirs. 1983-90, pres. 1989), Zumbro Valley Med. Soc., Minn. Med. Assn., Minn. Soc. Neurol. Scis., Ctrl. Soc. Neurol. Rsch. (pres. 1964), Alumni Assn. Mayo Found. (Disting. Alumnus award 2003). Presbyterian. Office: Mayo Clinic Dept Health Scis Rsch 200 1st St SW Rochester MN 55905-0001 Home: 211 2nd St NW Apt 716 Rochester MN 55901-2813 Personal E-mail: whisnant24@charter.net. Business E-Mail: whisnant@mayo.edu.

WHISNER, MARY, librarian; d. Jack E. and Ethel C. Whisner; life ptnr. Mary A. Hotchkiss. BA, U. Wash., Seattle, 1977; JD, Harvard Law Sch., Cambridge, Mass., 1982; MLIS, La. State U., Baton Rouge, 1987. Law clk. Hon. Stephanie K. Seymour, 10th Cir., Tulsa, Okla., 1982—83; atty. Nat. Labor Rels. Bd. Appellate Ct. Br., Washington, 1983—84; fellow, women's law & pub. policy fellowship program Lawyers' Comm. Civil Rights Under Law, Washington, 1984—85; lib. asst. Loyola U. Sch. Law Libr., New Orleans, 1985—86; grad. asst. Law Libr., Paul M. Hebert Law Ctr., La. State U., 1986—87; reference libr. Gallagher Law Lib., U. Wash. Sch. Law, 1988—. Author: (book) Practicing Reference: Thoughts for Librarians and Legal Researchers. Tutor Youth Tutoring Program, Seattle, 2004—. Mem.: Wash. State Bar Assn., Am. Assn. Law Librs., Ballard Sedentary Sousa Band, Phi Beta Kappa. Office: Univ Wash Sch Law Box 353025 Seattle WA 98195-3025 Business E-Mail: whisner@u.washington.edu.

WHITACRE, EDWARD E., JR., automotive executive, retired telecommunications industry executive; b. Ennis, Tex., Nov. 4, 1941; m. Linda Whitacre; 2 children. BS in Indsl. Engring., Tex. Tech U., 1964. Various positions ops. dept. Southwestern Bell Tel. Co., 1963-85, pres. Kans. divsn. Topeka, 1982-85; group pres. Southwestern Bell Corp., 1985-86, v.p. revenues/pub. affairs, vice-chmn., CFO St. Louis, 1986-88, pres., COO, 1988-89; chmn., CEO SBC Comm. (now AT&T, Inc.), San Antonio, 1990—2007; chmn. Gen. Motors Corp., Detroit, 2009—. Bd. dirs. Anheuser Busch, Inc., 1988—2008, May Dept. Stores, 1989—2004, Emerson Electric Co., 1990—2004, Burlington No. Santa Fe, Inc., 1993—, ExxonMobil Corp., 2008—, Gen. Motors Corp., 2009—. Pres. Boy Scouts of America, 1999—2000; campaign chmn. United Way, San Antonio, 1998; mem. gov. bus. coun. State of Tex.; chmn. bd. regents Tex. Tech U. Health Sci. Ctr., Lubbock, Tex., 1992—98; bd. govs. S.W. Found. Bio Med. Rsch. Recipient Internat. Citizen of Yr. award, World Affairs Coun., San Antonio, 1997, Freeman award, San Antonio C. of C., 1997, Spirit of Achievement award, Nat. Jewish Med. & Rsch. Ctr., 1998; named one of 50 Who Matter Now, CNNMoney.com Bus. 2.0, 2006; named to Tex. Bus. Hall of Fame, 1997. Presbyterian. Avocations: golf, hunting, cooking, reading. Office: General Motors Corp 300 Renaissance Ctr Detroit MI 48265*

WHITAKER, DARLA, electronics executive; BSEE, So. Meth. U., 1989; MBA, U. Dallas, 1997. With Tex. Instruments, Inc., 1984—, compensation mgr. Asia region Taipei and Singapore, human resources mgr. ASIC orgn., dir. human resources for application specific products bus. unit, v.p., mgr. compensation and human resource systems and svcs., sr. v.p., dir. worldwide human resources, mem. strategy leadership team. Office: Tex Instruments Inc PO Box 660199 Dallas TX 75266-0199 Office Phone: 972-995-2011. Office Fax: 972-995-4360.

WHITAKER, ELAINE EMANUEL, humanities educator; b. Oklahoma City, Nov. 23, 1942; d. Alfred Thorn and Cora Emma (Cocke) Emanuel; m. John Nicholas Whitaker, June 14, 1964; children: John Jeffrey, Amy Clare, Stacey Nicole. BA, Hendrix Coll., Conway, Ark., 1964; MA, PhD, NYU, 1971. Tchr. Memphis City Schs., 1964-67, Rhodes Coll., Memphis, 1978-85, U. Ala., Birmingham, 1985—. Lectr. Ala. Shakespeare Festival, Montgomery, 1990—. Contbr. articles and revs. to profl. jours. Mem. U. Ala. Birmingham Faculty Women's Club (pres. 1988-89), Alpha Psi Omega. Episcopalian. Home: 4312 Glenwood Ave Birmingham AL 35222-4303 Office: U Ala Birmingham Dept English University Sta Birmingham AL 35294-0001

WHITAKER, ERIC E., academic administrator, former state agency administrator; b. Chgo. m. Cheryl Whitaker; children: Caleb, Caitlin. BS, Grinnell Coll., 1987; MPH, Harvard Univ., 1991; MD, Univ. Chgo., 1993. Attending physician internal med. John H. Stroger Jr. Hosp. (Cook County Hosp.), Chgo.; asst. prof. Rush Med. Coll., Chgo.; dir. Ill. Dept. Public Health, Springfield, 2003—07; exec. v.p. strategic affiliations U. Chgo. Med. Ctr., 2007—, assoc. dean cmty. based rsch., 2007—. Co-founder Project Brotherhood Black Men's Clinic, Chgo., 1998; past pres. Am. Med. Student Assn. Office: Univ Chgo Med Ctr 5841 S Maryland Ave Chicago IL 60637*

WHITAKER, EWEN ADAIR, retired astronomer; b. London, Eng., June 22, 1922; arrived in US, 1958; s. George Frederick and Gladys Emily (Johnstone) Whitaker; m. Beryl Joyce Horswell, June 22, 1946; children: Malcolm John, Graham David, Fiona Carolyn. Higher Nat. Cert. in Mech. Engring., Woolwich Polytechnic, Eng., 1944. Spectrographer Siemens Bros. & Co. Ltd., London, 1940—49; asst. exptl. officer Royal Greenwich Obs., London, 1949—58; rsch. assoc. U. Chicago, Yerkes Obs., Williams Bay, Wis., 1958—60; assoc. rsch scientist U. Arizona, Lunar & Planetary Lab., Tucson, 1960—87; retired, 1987. Cons. Air Force Chart & Info. Ctr., St. Louis, 1958—72; co-investigator NASA Ranger Lunar Missions, 1963—66; team mem. NASA Lunar Surveyor TV, 1965—68, NASA Apollo Orbital Sci. Photog. Team, 1970—73. Author: Mapping & Naming the Moon, 1999, The University of Arizona's Lunar & Planetary Laboratory - Its Founding & Early Years, 1985; co-author: Orthographic Atlas of the Moon, 1960—61, Photographic Lunar Atlas, 1960, Rectified Lunar Atlas, 1963, Consolidated Lunar Atlas, 1967. Recipient Goodacre Gold Medal & Gift, British Astron. Assoc., 1982. Fellow: Royal Astron. Soc.; mem.: Internat. Astron. Union, Natl. Assoc. of Watch & Clock Collectors. Achievements include first to be able to produce differential bi-spectral imagery of moon; use of coronagraphic techniques to stars; discovery of orbital inclination and eccentricity of Uranus' satellite Miranda; chose impact location for Ranger 7, NASA's first successful moonshot; discovery of landing location of Surveyor 3 on the moon to which Apollo 12 was later targeted; received international approval for choosing two separate groups of 7 craters in the lunar farside Apollo basin to receive the names of the deceased Challenger and Columbia Space Shuttle astronauts; asteroid 7948 named Whitaker for contributions to NASA lunar programs and lunar science, Internat. Astron. Union; scheme for lettering lunar farside craters adopted internationally. Avocation: clock repair and restoration. Home: 4332 E 6th St Tucson AZ 85711

WHITAKER, FOREST, actor; b. Longview, Tex., July 15, 1961; m. Keisha Nash, May 4, 1996; children: Sonnet, True Isabella 1 stepchild, Autumn; 1 child, Ocean Alexander. Attended, U. So. Calif. Pres. Spirit Dance Entertainment; exec. dir. Nodance Film Festival, 2003—. Stage appearances (London) Swan, Romeo and Juliet, Hamlet, Ring Around the Moon, Craig's Wife, Whose Life Is It Anyway?, The Greeks, Patchwork Shakespeare, Beggar's Opera, Jesus Christ Superstar; actor: (films) TAG: The Assassination Game, 1982, Fast Times at Ridgemont High, 1982, Vision Quest, 1985, The Color of Money, 1986, Platoon, 1986, Stakeout, 1987, Good Morning, Vietnam, 1987, Bloodsport, 1988, Bird, 1988 (Best Actor Cannes Film Festival 1988), Johnny Handsome, 1989, Downtown, 1990, Rage in Harlem, 1991, Article 99, 1992, Diary of a Hit Man, 1992, Consenting Adults, 1992, Body Snatchers, 1993, The Crying Game, 1993, Bank Robber, 1993, Blown Away, 1994, Jason's Lyric, 1994, Prêt-à-Porter, 1994, Species, 1995, Smoke, 1995, Phenomenon, 1996, Body Count, 1998, Ghost Dog: The Way of the Samuai, 1999, Light It Up, 1999, Battlefield Earth, 2000, Four Dogs Playing Poker, 2000, Green Dragon, 2001, The Follow, 2001, The Fourth Angel, 2001, Panic Room, 2002, Phone Booth, 2002, Jiminy Glick in La La Wood, 2004, Mary, 2005, A Little Trip to Heaven, 2005, Even Money, 2006, The Marsh, 2006, The Last King of Scotland (Hollywood Actor of the Yr. award, Hollywood Awards, 2006, Best Actor award, LA Film Critics Assn. (Tie) & NY Film Critics Circle awards, 2006, Best Actor, Nat. Bd. Review, 2006, African-American Film Critics Assn., 2006, Nat. Soc. Film Critics, 2007, 2006 Critics Choice award, Broadcast Film Critics Assn., 2007, Best Performance by an Actor in a Motion Picture-Drama, Golden Globe award, Hollywood Fgn. Press Assn., 2007, Outstanding Performance by a Male Actor in a Leading Role, SAG, 2007, Actor in a Leading Role, British Acad. Film and TV Arts, 2007, Acad. award best actor in a leading role, 2007, Actor in a Motion Picture, NAACP Image Awards, 2007), 2006, (voice only) Everyone's Hero, 2006, Vantage Point, 2008, Street Kings, 2008; (TV movies) Grand Baby, 1985, Hands of a Stranger, 1987, Criminal Justice, 1990, Last Light, 1993, Lush Life, 1993, The Enemy Within, 1994, Rebound: The Legend of Earl "The Great" Manigault, 1996, The Split, 1998, Witness Protection, 1999, Deacons for Defense, 2003; (TV mini-series) North & South, 1985, North and South Book II, 1986; (TV series) The Shield, 2006-2007; (TV appearances) Making the Grade, 1982, Cagney & Lacey, 1983, Trapper John, M.D., 1984, Hill Street Blues, 1984, The Fall Guy, 1985, Diff'rent Strokes, 1985, Amazing Stories, 1986, Feast of All Saints, 2001, The Twilight Zone, 2003, ER, 2006; actor, dir., exec. prodr.: (films) First Daughter, 2004; actor, exec. prodr.: (films) Green Dragon, 2001, American Gun, 2005; (TV movies) Feast of All Saints, 2001; dir.: (films) Waiting to Exhale, 1995, Hope Floats, 1998; (TV films) Strapped (Toronto Film Festival award for best new dir.), 1993, Black Jaq, 1998; prodr. (films) Chasing Papi, 2003; co-exec. prodr. (TV films) Door to Door, 2002 Recipient of a star on the Hollywood Walk of Fame, 2007; named Best Actor, Black Entertainment TV (BET) Awards, 2007. Office: care DGA 7920 W Sunset Blvd Los Angeles CA 90046-3300*

WHITAKER, G(EORGE) WARREN, lawyer; b. NYC, Oct. 13, 1950; s. George Warren Jr. and Stella S. (Stann) W.; m. Marian Kramer, Sept. 15, 1982; children: Alexander Stuart, Emily Kate. BA, Rutgers U., 1972; JD, Columbia U., 1976. Bar: NJ 1976, NY 1977, US Tax Ct. 1991. Assoc. Davidson, Dawson, NYC, 1977-80, Curtis, Mallet, NYC, 1980-83; sr. atty. Breed, Abbott, NYC, 1983-91; assoc. Chadbourne & Parke, NYC, 1991-94; sr. atty. Jones, Day, Reavis & Pogue, NYC, 1994-96; ptnr. Law Offices James E. Hughes Jr., NYC, 1996-98, Hughes and Whitaker, NYC, 1998—2001, Day, Berry & Howard, LLP, NYC, 2002—06, Day Pitney LLP, NYC, 2007—. Counsel Pelham Art Ctr., NY, 1995-2001; bd. dirs. Shakespeare's Globe, USA; mem. banker lawyer adv. com. NY Philharmonic, 2003-; counsel, bd. dirs. Picture Ho. Regional Theater, 2005—. Named one of Top 100 Attys., Worth mag., 2005—06. Fellow NY Bar Found.; mem. ABA (vice chair internat. estate planning com. 1996—), Soc. Trust and Estate Practioners (chmn. NY chpt. 1998-06, US chmn. 2005-), NY State Bar Assn. (chair internat. estate planning com. 1996-98, 1st dist. rep. 1999-01, treas. 2001-02, sec. 2002-03, chair-elect 2003—04, chair 2004-05), NYC Bar Assn. (estate tax com. 1996—). Republican. Avocations: bicycling, book collecting. Home: 514 Esplanade Pelham NY 10803-2400 Office: Day Pitney LLP 7 Times Sq Fl 20 New York NY 10036 Office Phone: 212-297-2468. Business E-Mail: gwwhitaker@daypitney.com.

WHITAKER, JOEL, publishing executive, public official; b. Indpls., May 27, 1942; s. Quincy Myers and Sigur Elizabeth (Moore) W.; m. Donna Kay, Apr. 27, 1986. BS in Bus. Journalism, Ind. U., 1964, MA in Journalism, 1971; JD, Temple U., 1979. Reporter St. Petersburg (Fla.) Times, 1964, copy editor, 1966-68, Wall St. Journal, NYC, 1968-73; bus. news editor Phila. Evening and Sunday Bull., 1973-78; law clk. Fellheimer, Krakower & Eiclen, Phila., 1978—79; mng. editor Bank Letter, NYC, 1979-80; editor, pres. Whitaker Newsletters Inc., Silver Spring, Md., 1980—. Chmn. Fanwood Planning Bd., 1981-85; trustee Fanwood cmty. Found. 1998-2004; mem. Downtown Redevel. Commn., Fanwood, 1983-85; mem. Union County (N.J.) local adv. commn. on alcoholism and drug abuse, 1993-97, chmn., 1994-95, vice chmn. 1997; councilman Borough of Fanwood, 1998-2003, coun. pres., 2000-03. Mem. Newsletter Publishers Assn. (bd. dirs. 1983-92, found. trustee 1986—2006, treas. 1989-93, found. treas. 2005-06), Soc. Profl. Journalists (treas. N.J. profl. chpt. 1997-2005), Nat. Press Club (Washington), Rotary (bd. dirs. Fanwood-Scotch Plains club 1996-98), Army and Navy Club (Washington). Republican. Roman Catholic. Office: Whitaker Newsletters Inc PO Box 224 Spencerville MD 20868-0224 Home Phone: 301-879-8802; Office Phone: 301-384-1573. Personal E-mail: joelwhitaker1@verizon.net.

WHITAKER, JOHN KING, retired economics professor; b. Burnley, Lancashire, Eng., Jan. 30, 1933; arrived in US, 1967; s. Ben and Mary Whitaker; m. Sally Bell Cross, Aug. 24, 1957; children: Ann Elizabeth, Jane Claire, David John. BA in Econs., U. Manchester, 1956; AM, Johns Hopkins U., 1957; PhD, Cambridge U., 1962. Lectr. U. Bristol, England, 1960-66, prof., 1966-69; vis. prof. U. Va., Charlottesville, 1967-68, prof. econs., 1969-86, chmn. dept. econs., 1979-82, Paul Goodloe McIntire prof. econs., 1986-92, Georgia Bankard prof. econs., 1992—2003, Georgia Bankard prof. econs. emeritus, 2003—. Author: The Early Economic Writings of Alfred Marshall, 1867-1890, 2 vols., 1975, The Correspondence of Alfred Marshall, Economist, 3 vols., 1996. Fellow: History Econs. Soc. (disting.). Home: 1615 Yorktown Dr Charlottesville VA 22901-3046 Business E-Mail: jw9s@virginia.edu.

WHITAKER, LINTON ANDIN, plastic surgeon; b. Navasota, Tex., Nov. 16, 1936; s. Ira Andin and Lena Rivers (Stedman) W.; m. Renata Grasmanis, Dec. 20, 1963; children: Derek Andin (dec.), Ingrid Marlena, Brandon Andrew. BA, U. Tex., 1958; MD, Tulane U., 1962. Diplomate Am. Bd. Surgery, Am. Bd. Plastic Surgery. Founder, dir. ctr. human appearance U. Pa. Med. Ctr., Phila., 1988—; resident in gen. surgery Dartmouth Affiliated Hosps., Hanover, NH, 1965-69; resident in plastic surgery U. Pa. Hosp., Phila., 1969-71; chief plastic surgery Grad. Hosp., 1971-77, U. Pa. Hosp., Phila., 1987—2005, attending surgeon, 1971—; chief plastic surgery Children's Hosp. Phila., 1981—2001, attending surgeon, 1971—; v.p. med. staff Children's Hosp., Phila., 1992-94, pres. med. staff, 1994-96; attending physician VA Hosp., 1971—, Phila. Gen. Hosp., 1971-77; assoc. in plastic surgery Sch. Medicine, U. Pa., Phila., 1971-73, asst. prof. in plastic surgery, 1973-76, assoc. prof., 1976-81, prof., 1981—; founder, dir. ctr. human appearance U. Pa. Med. Ctr., Phila., 1988—. Vis. prof. South Australia Craniofacial Unit, Adelaide, Australia and New Zealand, 1981, U. Hawaii, 1983, Brown U., Providence, 1983, Mass. Gen. Hosp., Boston, 1984, U. Utah, Salt Lake City, 1984, U. B.C., Vancouver, 1986, U. Pitts., 1988, U. Calif., San Diego, 1992, Ohio Valley Soc. for Plastic and Reconstructive Surgery, 1992, N.Y. U., 1994; Curts vis. prof. Dartmouth U. Med. Ctr., Hanover, N.H., 1990, Kazanjian vis. prof. Mass. Gen. Hosp., Boston, 1990; First Seiichi Ohmori Meml. lectr. All Asiatic Congress on Aesthetic Surgery, Tokyo, 1988; vis. speaker Inst. Cosmotology and Inst. Stomatology, Moskow, Russia, 1985, vis. prof. Seoul Nat. U. and vis. speaker Korean Soc. for Plastic Surgeons, 1994; hon. vis. spkr. Chinese Plastic Surgery Soc., Beijing, 1996; lectr., speaker at univs., assns. in field. Co-author: Atlas of Cranio-maxillofacial Surgery, 1982, Aesthetic Surgery of the Facial Skelton, 1992; editor (with P. Randall): Symposium on the Reconstruction of Jaw Deformity, Clinics in Plastic Surgery, 1987, 1991; co-editor: Yearbook of Plastic and Reconstructive Surgery, 1980—97; assoc. editor: Seminars in Complementary Medicine, 2001—, mem. editl. bd.: Jour. Cutaneous Aging and Cosmetic Dermatology, 1988—; contbr. articles to profl. jours. Capt. M.C., U.S. Army, 1963-65. Foederer fellow Foederer Fund for Excellence, 1985-88; NIH grantee, 1976-79, 81-87, 82-85, 89, Plastic Surgery Edn. Found. Rsch. grantee, 1980-82; recipient James IV Surg. Traveller award, 1979. Fellow ACS, Am. Soc. Ophthalmic Plastic and Reconstructive Surgery (hon.); mem. AMA, Am. Assn. Plastic Surgeons (mem. program com. 1988, chmn. 1989, Rsch. grantee 1984-85), Am. Surg. Assn., Am. Alpine Workshop in Plastic Surgery (founding mem.), Am. Cleft Palate Assn. (chmn. com. classification craniofacial anomalies 1976-80, mem. program com. for 1978 mtg. 1977, mem. long-range planning com. 1980, mem. coun. 1981-84, chmn. internat. rels. com. 1981-83), Am. Cleft Palate Ednl. Found. (bd. dirs. 1975-84, chmn. rsch. com. 1975-78, chmn. instrl. courses 1980-81), Am. Soc. Aesthetic Plastic Surgery, Am. Soc. Craniofacial Surgery (mem. coun. 1992—), Am. Soc. Maxillofacial Surgeons (Spl. Honors 2003, bd. dirs. 2003—), Am. Soc. Plastic and Reconstructive Surgeons, mem. plastic surgery speakers bur. 1977—), Am. Soc. Plastic and Reconstructive Surgeons Ednl. Found. (chmn. ednl. assessment com., maxillofacial truama and craniofacial anomalies 1975-78, mem. clin. symposia com. 1978-82, chmn. clin. symposia com. 1981-82), Internat. Cleft Palate and Related Craniofacial Anomalies Soc., Internat. Soc. Aesthetic Surgery, Internat. Soc. Craniofacial Surgeons (founding mem., organizer, mem. exec. com. 1987—, sec and treas. 1993-95, pres. 1995-97), Phila. Med. Soc., Phila. Acad. Surgery, Coll. Physicians Phila., Assn. Acad. Surgery, Northeastern Soc. Plastic Surgeons N.Y. (chmn. program com. 1987, mem. programcom. 1988), Plastic Surgery Rsch. Coun., John Morgan Soc., Robert H. Ivy Soc., The Columbian Soc. Plastic, Maxillofacial and Hand Surgery (hon.), Academia Medica Lombarda (Italy, hon.), Sociedad Jamie Planas de Cirugia Plastica (Spain, hon.), Mt. Kenya Safari Club (hon.), Japan Soc. Craniomaxillofacial Surgeons (hon.), Asian Pacific Cranofacial Assn., Japan Soc. Plastic and Reconstructive Surgery (hon.), Phila. Club, Merion Cricket Club, Confrerie des chevaliers du Tastevin, Grand Senechat. Avocations: mountain climbing, skiing, wines. Office: U Pa Med Ctr 10 Penn Tower 3400 Spruce St Philadelphia PA 19104-4206 Office Phone: 215-662-2048. Business E-Mail: linton.whitaker@uphs.upenn.edu.

WHITAKER, MARK THEIS, broadcast executive, editor; b. Lower Merion, Pa., Sept. 7, 1957; s. Cleophus Sylvester and Jeanne (Theis) W.; m. Alexis Lynn Gelber, May 5, 1985; children: Rachel Eva, Matthew Edward. BA summa cum laude, Harvard U., 1979; postgrad., Oxford U., Eng., 1979-81; LLD (hon.), Wheaton Coll. Assoc. editor Newsweek mag., NYC, 1981-83, gen. editor, 1983, sr. writer, 1984-86, sr. editor, bus. editor, 1987-91, asst. mng. editor, 1991-95, mng. editor, 1996-98, corp. editor, editor NYC, 1998—2006; v.p., editor in chief new ventures Washingtonpost Newsweek Interactive Co., LLC Washington Post Co., 2006—07; sr. v.p. news NBC News, 2007—, Washington bur. chief, 2008—. Featured in Ebony mag., 2007. Bd. dir. Literacy Partners, NYC. Marshall scholar Brit. Marshall Fund, Oxford U., 1979-81. Mem. Nat. Assn. Black Journalists, Am. Soc. Mag. Editors (bd. dirs., 1999-, pres., 2004-2006), Coun. on Fgn. Rels., Century Assn., Phi Beta Kappa. Achievements include first African-American editor of a newsweekly; Newsweek won two National Magazine Awards for General Excellence during his tenure as editor. Office: NBC News 4001 Nebraska Ave NW Washington DC 20016 also: 30 Rockefeller Plz New York NY 10112

WHITAKER, MATTHEW GEORGE, prosecutor; Grad., U. Iowa, 1991, JD, MBA, 1995. Corp. counsel SUPERVALU; atty. Briggs & Morgan, Finley Alt Smith, Des Moines; US atty. (so. dist.) Iowa US Dept. Justice, Des Moines, 2004—. Office: US Courthouse Annex Ste 286 110 E Court Ave Des Moines IA 50309 Office Phone: 515-474-9300. Office Fax: 515-284-6288.*

WHITAKER, RUTH REED, state legislator, retired publishing executive; b. Blytheville, Ark., Dec. 13, 1936; d. Lawrence Neill and Ruth Shipton (Weidemeyer) Reed; m. Thomas Jefferson Whitaker, dec. 29, 1961; children: Steven Bryan, Alicia Morrow. BA, Hendrix Coll., 1958. Copywriter, weather person KTVE TV, El Dorado, Ark., 1958-59; nat. bridal cons. Treasure House, El Dorado, 1959; bridal cons. Pfeifers of Ark., Little Rock, 1959-60; dir. of continuity S. M. Brooks Advt. Agy.,

Little Rock, 1960-61; layout artist C. V. Mosby Co., St. Louis, 1961-62; editor, owner Razorback Am. Newspaper, Ft. Smith, Ark., 1979-81; ret., 1981; mem. Dist. 3 Ark. State Senate, 2001—. Host Crawford Conversations TV show; contbr. author indsl. catalog, 1979 (Addy award). State sec. Rep. Party of Ark., 1992-94, mem. Ark. Electoral Coll., 1996, del. Rep. Nat. Conv., 1996; mem. Ben Geren Regional Park Commn., Sebastian County, Ark., 1984-89, pres., 1990; past pres. Jr. Civic League; mem. Ft. Smith Orchid Com.; mem. com. of 21 United Way; publicity chmn. Sebastian County Rep. Com., 1983-84; state press officer Reagan-Bush Campaign, 1984; exec. dir. Ark. Dole for Pres., 1995-96; pres. Women's Aux. Sebastian County Med. Soc., 1974; mem. Razorback Scholarship Fund; class agt. alumni fund Hendrix Coll., 1990, 91, 92; mem. Sparks Woman's Bd.; 1st vice chmn. 3d Dist. Rep. Party; state committeewoman Rep. Party Ark.; chmn. Crawford County Rep. Com.; apptd. by Gov. of Ark. to Commr. Ark. Ednl. TV Network Commn., sec. 1998-99; mem. city coun. City of Cedarville, Ark., 1998; dist. panelist NOW in Bux., 2003. Recipient Disting. Vol. Leadership award Nat. Found. March of Dimes, 1973, Appreciation award Ft. Smith Advt. Fedn., 1977, 78, Recognition award United Cerebral Palsy, 1980, Hon. Parents of Yr. award U. Ark., 1984, Firekeeper award Sparks Hosp. Women's Ctr., 2003. Mem. AAUW, Alden Soc. Am. (life), Ft. Smith C. of C., Ark. Nature Conservancy, Am. Legion Aux., Frontier Rschrs. Soc. (pres. 1995-96), Daus. Union Vets. Presbyterian. Avocations: philanthropy, genealogy, writing, photography, ornithology. Mailing: PO Box 349 Cedarville AR 72932-0349 Office Phone: 479-474-0911. Business E-Mail: whitakerr@arkleg.state.ar.us.*

WHITAKER, STEPHEN TAYLOR, geologist, oil exploration consultant; b. Cleve., Dec. 12, 1953; s. Clay Westerfield and Karen Lee (Taylor) W.; m. Teri Teruko Nakazawa, Dec. 30, 1976; children: Laura, Daniel, Christopher. BS in Geology, U. So. Calif., 1976; MS in Geology, U. Colo., 1978. Geol. asst. U.S. Geol. Survey, Denver, 1976-78; staff geologist Texaco, Denver, 1978-80, Ill. State Geol. Survey, Champaign, 1986-92; exploration geologist Apache Corp., Denver, 1980-82; sr. exploration geologist K&E Petroleum, Denver, 1982-85; pres. IBEX Geol. Cons., Inc., Champaign, 1992—; geology mgr. Rex Energy Corp., 2008—. Bd. dirs. Ill. Petroleum Resources, Ill. Oil & Gas Assn. Author: Silurian Pinnacle Reef Distribution in Illinois: Model for Hydrocarbon Exploration, 1988; Fluvial-Estuarine Valley Fills at the Mississippian-Pennsylvanian Unconformity in Sandstone Petroleum Reservoirs, 1990; contbr. articles to profl. jours. Mem. Am. Assn. Petroleum Geologists (cert., del. 1986-90, Outstanding Poster Presentation 1988, Cert. of Merit 1993), Ill. Geol. Soc. Achievements include encouraging oil exploration in Illinois through lectures, publications, and the development of exploration programs, i.e. potential for additional oil-bearing Silurian reefs; importance of paleovalley system at base of Pa. System as hydrocarbon traps; shallow Silurian reservoirs in western Illinois; application of microgravity data for Silurian reef exploration; application of sequence stratigraphy; potential of Waulsortian mounds in Illinois; additional reserves through use of improved oil recovery techniques, ASP flooding. Office Phone: 618-943-8700. Personal E-mail: stevewhitaker@earthlink.net.

WHITAKER, SUSANNE KANIS, veterinary medical librarian; b. Clinton, Mass., Sept. 10, 1947; AB in Biology, Clark U., 1969; MS in Library Sci., Case Western Res. U., 1970. Regional reference libr. Yale Med. Libr., New Haven, 1970-72; med. libr. Hartford Hosp., Conn., 1972-77; asst. libr. Cornell U., Ithaca, NY, 1977-78; vet. med. libr. Coll. Vet. Medicine, Cornell U., 1978-98, vet. pub. svcs. libr., 1998—. Mem. Med. Libr. Assn. (vet. med. librs. sect. 1983-84, chmn. 1984-85, chmn. pub. rels. com. 2000—), Med. Libr. Assn. (Upstate NY and Ont. chpt.), Acad. Health Info. Profls. (disting. mem.), Am. Vet. Med. History Soc. (sec.-treas. 2004—). Home: 23 Wedgewood Dr Ithaca NY 14850-1064 Office: Cornell U Coll Vet Medicine Flower-Sprecher Libr Ithaca NY 14853-6401 Home Phone: 607-257-9248; Office Phone: 607-253-3499. Business E-Mail: skw2@cornell.edu.

WHITAKER, THOMAS KENNETH, former university chancellor; b. Rostrevor, Ireland, Dec. 8, 1916; s. Edward and Jane (O'Connor) W.; m. Nora Fogarty (dec.); children: Kenneth, Gerald (dec.), Raymond, David, Catherine (dec.), Brian; m. Mary Moore (dec.). MS in Econs., U. London, 1953; DEconSc, Nat. U. Ireland, Dublin, 1962; LLD (hon.), U. Dublin, 1976, Queen's U., Belfast, 1981; DSc (hon.), U. Ulster, 1983. Sec. Irish Dept. Fin., 1956—69; gov. Ctrl. Bank Ireland, 1969—76; mem. Senate of Republic of Ireland, 1977—82, Coun. of State, 1991—98; dir. A. Guinness & Sons, 1976—84, Bank of Ireland, 1976—86; chancellor Nat. U. Ireland, Dublin, 1976—96. Pres.Constitution Review Group, 1995-96. Author: Financing by Credit Creation, 1947, Interests, 1983, Protection or Free Trade--The Final Battle, 2006, Retrospect, 2006-1916, 2006; editor, contbg. author: Economic Development, 1958. Decorated Freeman of Drogheda (Ireland); comdr. Legion of Honor (France). Mem. Royal Irish Acad. (pres. 1985-87), Econ. and Social Rsch. Inst. (pres. 1970-87), Dublin Inst. Advanced Studies (chmn. coun. 1980-95). Roman Catholic. Avocation: fishing. Home Phone: 01-2693474. Personal E-mail: kandmwhitaker@eircom.net.

WHITAKER, THOMAS O'HARA, theater educator, director; s. Thomas Russell and Dorothy Whitaker. BA, Oberlin Coll., Ohio, 1975; MFA, Carnegie-Mellon U., Pitts., 1983. Instr. acting Carnegie-Mellon U., Coll. Fine Arts, 1982—83; instr. SW Mo. State U., Springfield, 1983—84; asst. prof. Ind. State U., Terre Haute, 1984—87, U. Tex., Austin, 1987—92, U. Calif., Santa Barbara, 1992—96, assoc. prof., 1996—. Cons. dir., tchr. Conn. Humanities Coun., Hartford, 1980—81; cons. Ctr. Theatre Techniques Edn., Stratford, 1980—81, Comprehensive Arts Program, New Haven, 1980—81; guest artist Oberlin Theater Inst., 1987; tenured dir. Tex. Shakespeare Festival, Kilgore, 1989—; cons. Beijing Inst. World Theater and Film, 2005—; guest prof. Nanjing U., China, 2006—. Musician: (puppet theater) Young Woman's Sorrow, Man is Man, Loot, The Misanthrope, Advice to the Players, Love's Labor's Lost; actor: King Lear; dir.: Tartuffe, Taming of the Shrew; actor: Heartbreak House, (puppet theater) Grey Lady Cantata; dir.: (theater) The Bourgeois Gentleman, Two Gentlement of Verona; dir., dir.: As You Like It; actor: Henry IV, part 1; dir.: Big Love, Arms and the Man, The Merchant of Venice, Life's a Dream, Cyrano de Bergerac, bobrauschenbergamerica Woyzeck Reckless; actor: (film) The Meadow's Green; dir.: (theater) Revel's World of Shakespeare; actor: The Marilyn Project, The Forced Marriage; dir.: Time Play, Misalliance, Fool for Love, Buried Child, Man of La Mancha, 2007, Loves Labor's Lost, 2009. Recipient Boettcher award Directing, Carnegie-Mellon U., 1983; grantee, Conn. Humanities Coun., 1980; scholar, Carnegie-Mellon U., 1982—83. Mem.: Phi Beta Kappa.

WHITAKER, THOMAS PATRICK, lawyer; b. Washington, Sept. 22, 1944; s. Thomas J. and Mary K. (Finn) W.; m. Donna Mae Brenish, Feb. 16, 1974; children: Laura, Kevin. BA, George Washington U., 1966, MPA, 1973, JD, 1979; postgrad., Naval War Coll., 1984, Nat. Def. U., 2005. Bar: Va. 1979. Staff asst. Adminstrn. Office of U.S. Cts., Washington, 1972-73, analyst, 1975-77; cons. Planning Research Corp., McLean, Va., 1973-75; program analyst Social Security Adminstrn., Falls Church, Va., 1982—; congrl. aide Rep. Abercrombie, 2005. Served to lt. (j.g.) USNR, 1966-71, Vietnam, capt. with Res. 1983-97. Asst. U.S. Naval Attache, Egypt, 1988, Malaysia, 1992. Home: 9817 Days Farm Dr Vienna VA 22182-7306 Office Phone: 703-605-8292. Personal E-mail: twhitake@hotmail.com.

WHITAKER, THOMAS RUSSELL, English literature educator; b. Marquette, Mich., Aug. 7, 1925; s. Joe Russell and Sarah Genevieve (Houk) W.; m. Dorothy Vera Barnes, June 17, 1950 (dec. Dec. 1995); children: Thomas O'Hara, Sarah Mae, Mary Beth, Gwendolyn Anne; m. Joan Bower Horwitt, Oct. 4, 1997 (div. Sept. 2002); m. Lillian Ann Traub, Jul. 26, 2003. BA summa cum laude, Oberlin Coll., 1949; MA, Yale U., 1950, PhD, 1953. Instr. English Oberlin (Ohio) Coll., 1952-55, asst. prof., 1955-59, assoc. prof., 1959-63, prof., 1963-64; tchr. lit. Goddard Coll., Plainfield, Vt., 1964-66; prof. English U. Iowa, Iowa City, 1966-75, Yale U., New Haven, Conn., 1975-95, prof. theater studies, 1986-95, chmn. dept. English, 1979-85, Frederick W. Hilles prof. English, 1989-95; Frederick W. Hilles prof. emeritus English, 1995—. Author: Swan and Shadow: Yeats's Dialogue with History, 1964, 2d edit. with new preface, 1989, William Carlos Williams, 1968, rev. edit., 1989, Fields of Play in Modern Drama, 1977, Tom Stoppard, 1983, augmented edit., 1984, Mirrors of Our Playing: Paradigms and Presences in Modern Drama, 1999; editor: Twentieth Century Interpretations of the Playboy of the Western World, 1969, Teaching in New Haven: The Common Challenge, 1991; editor Iowa Rev., 1974-77; chmn. editorial bd. On Common Ground, 1993-2009; author, narrator video script: Excellence in Teaching: Agenda for Partnership, 1997; writer, advisor Yale-New Haven Tchrs. Inst. Nat. Demonstration Project, 1998-02, Yale Nat. Initiative, 2002—. Served with C.E. U.S. Army, 1944-46. Recipient Harbison award for gifted teaching Danforth Found., 1972, Seton Elm and Ivy award, City of New Haven and Yale U., 2005; fellow, Am. Council Learned Socs., 1969—70, NEH-Huntington, 1981. Mem. MLA. Home: 38 Wilford Rd Branford CT 06405-5321

WHITAKER, URBAN GEORGE, JR., educational consultant, former dean; b. Colony, Kans., May 19, 1924; s. Urban George and Flora Gladys (Fackler) W.; m. Rebekah Jean Knox, Mar. 18, 1950; children: Susan Whitaker Wittwer, Bruce, Keith. AB, Occidental Coll., 1946; PhD, U. Wash., 1954. Mem. faculty San Francisco State U., 1954-79, prof. internat. relations, dean undergrad. studies, 1969-79, dir. all-univ. programs, 1976-78, assoc. dean grad. div., 1978-79; Far West regional mgr. Council for Advancement of Experiential Learning, 1981-86, regional exec. officer, 1986—. Vis. research asso. Columbia U., 1960-61; vis. prof. U. SC, 1965-66; radio commentator UN corr., Pacifica Network, Berkeley, Calif., 1958-65; mem. exec. com. Commn. to Study Orgn. of Peace, 1963—; nat. bd. dirs. Nat. Soc. for Internships and Experiential Edn. Author: Propaganda and International Relations, 1960, (with Paul Breen and Thomas Donlon) Teaching and Assessing Interpersonal Competence, 1976, Democracies and International Relations, 1960, Politics and Power: A Text in International Law, 1964, (with Bruce Davis) The World and Ridgeway, South Carolina, 1968, (with Paul Breen) Bridging the Gap: A Learner's Guide to Transferable Skills, 1983, Assessing Learning: Standards, Principles and Procedures, 1989. Pres. Peninsula Democratic Forum, San Mateo County, 1967-68, 70-72; Dem. candidate U.S. Ho. Reps., 1968; Trustee San Bruno (Calif.) Elementary Schs., 1958-60, New Coll. Calif., San Francisco, 1971-76, 79-84; nat. bd. dirs. UN Assn. U.S., 1962-70. Served with USNR, 1943-46, 50-52. Ford Found. fellow summer 1955; Rockefeller fellow Columbia U. and UN, 1960-61 Mem. Internat. Studies Assn. (pres. 1966-67). Unitarian Universalist. Home: 656 Lytton Ave Apt C336 Palo Alto CA 94301-1379 Home Phone: 650-566-8914. Personal E-mail: jeanurban@gmail.com. *Law and Order without Justice is tyranny. But Justice without Law and Order is impossible. I try to work for the ideals of world Law and Order, with Justice, by planning all of my projects in three stages: first, taking the time to dream about what is desirable; second, making an estimate of what seems possible; and then setting my course some place in between.*

WHITAKER, WILLIAM L., physiologist, educator; s. Derwood L. Whitaker; m. Tina M. Shannon, Apr. 14, 1962; 1 child, Susan Y. Johnson. MDiv., Trinity Evang. Div. Sch., Deerfield, IL, 1977. Physiology instr. Western Nebr. CC, Scottsbluff, 2006—. Office: Western Nebr CC 1601 E 27th St Scottsbluff NE 69361

WHITBREAD, THOMAS BACON, language educator, writer; b. Bronxville, NY, Aug. 22, 1931; s. Thomas Francis and Caroline Nancy (Bacon) W. BA, Amherst Coll., 1952; A.M., Harvard U., 1953, PhD, 1959. Instr. English, U. Tex. at Austin, 1959-62, asst. prof., 1962-65, asso. prof., 1965-71, prof., 1971—. Vis. asso. prof. Rice U., 1969-70; mem. lit. adv. panel Tex. Commn. on Arts and Humanities, 1972-76 Author (poetry): Four Infinitives, 1964, Whomp and Moonshiver, 1982, The Structures Minds Erect, 2007; co-author: Prize Stories, 1962, The O. Henry Awards, 1962; editor: Seven Contemporary Authors, 1966. Recipient third Aga Khan prize for fiction Paris Rev., 1960, Lit. Anthology Program award Nat. Endowment for Arts, 1968, Outstanding Freshman Tchr. award Phi Eta Sigma, 1972-73 Mem. AAUP, Tex. Inst. Letters (Poetry award 1965, 83), Nat., Am. amateur press assns., Phi Beta Kappa. Democrat. Home: 1014 E 38th St Austin TX 78705-1835 Office: U Tex Dept English 1 Univ Station B5000 Austin TX 78712 Business E-Mail: whitbread@mail.utexas.edu.

WHITBURN, MERRILL DUANE, English literature educator; b. Mpls., Apr. 29, 1938; s. George and Marie Ellen (Carlstedt) W.; m. Diane Robertson, June 15, 1960; children: Stephen, Mark, Elizabeth. AB, U. Mich., 1960, AM, 1968; PhD, U. Iowa, 1973. With Western Electric Co., NYC and Indpls., 1965-67; asst. prof. Tex. A&M U., College Station, 1973-77, assoc. prof., 1977-79; assoc. prof. English Rensselaer Poly. Inst., Troy, NY, 1979-83, prof., 1983-89, Louis Ellsworth Laflin prof., 1989—, chmn. dept., 1979-85, 88-95; rsch. fellow Yale U. Divinity Sch., New Haven, 2003; Rensselaer Poly. Inst. Exch. prof. humanities and social sci. SUNY-Albany U., 2005. Co-owner Pride and Prejudice Books, Ballston Lake, N.Y., 1985—. Author: Rhetorical Scope and Performance: The Example of Technical Communication, 2000; co-author: (booklet) Guide for Departments of English, 1985; contbr. articles to profl. publs. Recipient Disting. Svc. award Tex. A&M U., 1976, Disting. Teaching award, 1979, Jay R. Gould award for excellence in tchg. tech. comm. Soc. Tech. Comm., 1995, Trustee's Outstanding Tchr. award Rensselaer Poly. Inst., 2002; grantee Fund for the Improvement of Postsecondary Edn., 1983. Mem. Nat. Coun. Tchrs. English (best article in tech. writing award 1981), Coun. for Programs in Tech. and Sci. Communication.

WHITCOMB, JAMES HALL, geophysicist, foundation administrator; b. Sterling, Colo., Dec. 10, 1940; s. Clay Thane and Julia Melvina Whitcomb; m. Sandra Lynn McMurdo, July 13, 1965 (div. 1978); m. Teresa R. Idoni, Feb. 3, 1989; children: Lisa Michelle, Marisa Giulia, Sabina Maria. Geophysics engring. degree, Colo. Sch. of Mines, 1962; MS in Oceanography, Geophysics, Oreg. State U., 1964; PhD in Geophysics, Calif. Inst. Tech., 1973. Grad. rsch. asst. dept. oceanography Oreg. State U., Corvallis, 1962-64; geophysicist Ctr. Astrogeology U.S. Geol. Survey, Flagstaff, Ariz., 1964-66; Fulbright-Hayes program rsch. fellow Seismol. Inst. U. Uppsala, Sweden, 1966-67; grad. rsch. asst. seismol. lab. Calif. Inst. Tech., Pasadena, 1967-73, sr. rsch. fellow seismol. lab., 1973-79; assoc. prof. attendant rank dept. geol. scis. U. Colo., Boulder, 1979-82, fellow Coop. Inst. Rsch. in Environ. Scis., 1979-84; v.p. technical applications and mktg. ISTAC, Inc., Pasadena, 1984-88; program dir. seismology NSF, Washington, 1989-99, acting dep. divsn. dir., 1999—2002, sect. head, 2002—07, acting divsn. dir., 2008—. Expert witness U.S. Ho. Reps. Com. on Sci. and Tech., 1977; mem. geodynamics rev. bd. Jet Propulsion Lab., 1980-82, com. on geodesy Nat. Acad. Scis., 1982-85; pres. Boulder Systems, Inc., Pasadena, 1987-88. Recipient Outstanding Achievement award U.S. Geol. Survey, 1964, Dir.'s award for mgmt. excellence NSF, 1995, 2003; scholar State of Colo., 1958-62, Mobil Oil Co., 1960; fellow Sweden-Am. Found., 1966. Mem. AAAS, Am. Geophysical Union, Seismol. Soc. Am., Soc. Exploration Geophysicists (scholar 1963), Tau Beta Pi, Phi Kappa Phi, Sigma Xi. Office: Nat Sci Found Geosciences 4201 Wilson Blvd Arlington VA 22230-0002

WHITE, ALAN FREDERICK, academic administrator; b. Evansville, Ind., Dec. 17, 1937; s. Hubert Ruben and Nota Lizzee (Culver) W.; m. Patricia Lynn Townsend, Nov. 7, 1959; children: Gregory Townsend, Samuel Townsend. AB, Miami U., Oxford, Ohio, 1963; MS, MIT, 1971. Dir. U. Hawaii Ctr. Crosscultural Tng. and Rsch., Hilo, 1967-70, exec. asst. to pres. Honolulu, 1971-73; Alfred P. Sloan fellow MIT, Cambridge, 1970-71, assoc. dir. exec. edn., 1973-78, dir. exec. edn., 1978-85, assoc. dean for exec. edn., 1985-95, sr. assoc. dean, COO, sr. lectr., 1991; vis. prof. Hong Kong U.; hon. prof. Fudan U., China, 2009. Cons. AT&T, Brit. Petroleum, Alcoa Young Pres. Orgn.; bd. dirs. Internat. Consortium for Exec. Edn. Rsch.; bd. advisors Toffler Assoc., Lingnan U., China; mem. Internat. Mgmt. Devel., 1985—; vis. prof. Hong Kong U., 2006. Contbr. articles to profl. jours. Recipient Gordon Y. Billard award for Disting. Svc. to MIT, 2005. Mem. Consortium of Univ. Dirs. of Exec. Edn. Avocations: painting, tennis, swimming, golf, gardening. Home: 13 Pickman Dr Bedford MA 01730-1009 Office Phone: 617-253-7189.

WHITE, ALICE VIRGINIA, academic administrator; b. Wichita, Kans., June 30, 1946; d. Harry Houston White and Margaret V. Milligan. BA in Spanish with distinction and with honors in Russian, U. Kans., 1967; MS in Counseling, Ft. Hays State U., 1973; PhD in Journalism, U. Tex., 1991. Tchr. Russian and Spanish Ingalls Sch. Dist., Kansas City, Mo., 1967-72; instr. Dodge City (Kans.) C.C., 1972-73, 84; tchr. Arrowhead West, Inc., 1984-85; asst. dir. Ctr. for Bus. & Industry Dodge City C.C., Kans., 1984-85, dir. community rels. and resource devel., 1985-87; co-founder, treas. Breitenbach Farms, Inc., Dodge City, Kans., 1970-79, pres., 1979-85; asst. to dean for devel. Coll. Comm., U. Tex., Austin, 1990-93, asst. instr. journalism, 1988-90, lectr. pub. rels., 1992; asst. coord. Shots Across Tex. coord. Tex. Dept. Health, Austin, 1993-95, coord. spl. health initiatives, 1995-96; mgr. Tex. Vol. Health Corps, 1996—2002; liaison Tex. Alliance for Healthy Communities, 1999—2002; program dir., Tex. higher edn. coordinating bd., interim campaign dir. Coll. for Texans Campaign, 2002—04; dir. pub. rels. Tex. Tech U. System, 2005—06; transfer coord. GO Ctrs. Liaison, Tex. Tech. U., 2006—07, relationship creator, 2007—08, Go Ctrs. Liasons, 2008—. Media judge Headliners Found., Austin, 1989, Tex. Hosp. Assn., 1990, 91; dir. job placement Kans. Elks Tng. Ctr. for Handicapped, 1984-85; mgr., chairside asst. dental office, 1973-83; bd. dirs. Dispute Resolution Ctr., 1992-93; adv. bd. N.E. Caregivers of Austin, 2002-04; mem. chancellor's coun. Tex. Tech. U. Sys., 2005—; founder Endowed Scholarships Tex. Tech. U. Chancellor's Coun., 2005, 06; founding sec. Breedlove Foods Inc., 2008-09. Treas. Ford County Hist. Soc., 1972—77, Ofcl. Bicentennial Com. Ford County, 1975—77; active Leadership Austin, 1990—91, Leadership Tex., 1999; co-founder Leadership Dodge, 1987, Tex. Leadership Inst. Lower Colo. River Authority, 1999—2004; active Leadership Lubbock, 2006—07, Leadership Lubbock Alumni, 2007—; founder Walk-a-Dog project Williamson County SPCA, Austin State Sch., 1991—92; media judge Tex. PTA, 1992, Tex. Med. Assn., 1993; life mem. chancellors coun. U. Tex. Sys., 1990—; mem. endowment com. United Way Capital Area, 1994; mem. Ready Teddy, the Emergency Med. Svcs. Bear-A-Medic Mascot, 1994—2001, Wiley the Crab mascot Coll. for Texans Campaign, 2005—08, Gov.'s Blue Ribbon Selection Com. for Tex. Vol. awards, 1998, 1999; mem. Vols. of Yr. selection com. Tex. Commn. on Volunteerism and Cmty. Svcs., 2000—03; mem. Gov.'s Unified State Planning/Cmty. Svc. Com., 1997, 1998; 2d v.p. Pub. Health Mus. of Tex., 1999—2002, bd. dirs., 2003—04; treas. Pet Helpers, Inc., 2000—04; mem. Animal Trustees of Austin's Vol. Spotlight, 2000; mem. selection com. for Tex. vol. awards Tex. Dept. Human Svcs., 2001; hon. life. laboratorian Tex. Dept. Health, 2000—; 5th grade mentor Gullett Elem. Sch., 2001—03; mem. founding adv. bd. Women's Giving Network, 2003—04; Goodwill Amb. to Turkey, Interfaith Dialog, 2006; mem. adv. coun. South Plains Tech. Prep., 2006—, founder endowment, 2006, endowment, 2008; mem. dean's adv. coun. Tex. Tech. U. Coll. Edn., 2006—, founder endowment, 2007; founder Lubbock Animal Svcs. endowment Lubbock Area Found., 2007; founder Dog & Cat Welfare endowment Wichita Cmty. Found., 2007; vol. Feeder Io TTU Feral cat Sta., 2007—; CEO Comm. Liaison Roundable, 2008—. Recipient Most Creative Vol. Project award Tex. Mental Health and Mental Retardation, 1992, Athena winner Women's C. of C., 1987, Kans. PRIDE honoree, 1988; U. Tex. fellowship, 1987-89; named of one of 100 Best-Managed Farms in U.S., Farm Futures Mag., 1983; named endowments at Austin Cmty. Found., Arthur E. and Cornelia Scroggins Found., Dodge City. Fellow: Tex. Pub. Health Assn.; mem.: AAUW (treas. 1977—78, pres. Kans. 1979—81, gift honoree 1973, 1981, 1991), Understand Our World (adv. bd. 2009), African-Am. Hispanic Internat., TTU Sys. Chancellor's Enrollment Taskforces, African Am., TTU, Pres.'s Diversity Coun., Lambda Tex. Phi Beta Kappa (founding mem. 2007, historian 2009—), South Plains P-20 Edn. Inst. (bd. mem. & sec. closing gap coun. 2008—), Tex. Tech. Alumni Assn. (founder, two EASI endowments 2009), South Plains Coll. Found. Board, Cmty. Partnership Com. Wheatley Elementary Sch. (Raiders Rojos Nat. Alumuni 2007, hon. Charter mem.), Humane Soc. West Tex. Tech. U. (mem. ferat cat program 2007—08), Wayland Bapt. U. (devel. planning com. mem. 2008), Rotary (Paul Harris fellow 2008—), Lubbock Lions Club, Austin C. of C., Women in Comm. (liaison to student chpt. 1989—91), Tex. Pub. Rels. Soc. (bd. dirs. 1993), Pub. Rels. Soc. Am. (mentor, profl. advisor U. Tex. 1987—93), Tex. Health Found. (life), Better Investing (life), Tex. Tech. Alumni Assn., Lone Star Cir. (State Employee Charitable Campaign 2001—02, 2004—05, 2005—06, 2006—07, 2007—08), KLRU Pub. TV Prodrs. Cir., Leave a Legacy Tex. Style, U. Tex. Littlefield Soc., U. Kans. Alumni Assn. (nat. bd. dirs. 1977—82), Tex. Exes Alumni Assn. (life), Austin-Travis County Humane Soc. (life), Leadership Kans. Alumni (life), U. Tex. Pres.'s Assocs., Waterloo Benevolent Soc. of United Way Capital Area, Lubbock Rotary Club (newsletter editor 2007—, bd. mem. 2008—), U. Kans. Chancellor's Club (founding mem. 1980), Phi Kappa Phi, Phi Beta Kappa (treas. 2000—01, Austin Alumni Assoc., pres. 2008—09, founder endowments, WTX&E NM Assoc.), Chi Omega Alumnae Austin (life). Home: 403 Topeka Lubbock TX 79416-4906 Office: Tex Tech U Box 45005 Lubbock TX 79409 Office Phone: 806-742-1480 Ext. 258. Business E-Mail: alice.white@ttu.edu.

WHITE, ALLEN BRADLEY, meteorologist; s. Donald D. and Sharon L. White; m. Pamela B. Brown, Oct. 3, 1992; children: Jeffrey A. Barnes, Laura E. Barnes, Kaitlin E. BS in Mech. Engring., Brown U., Providence, 1984; MS in Meteorology, PhD in Meteorology, Pa. State U., U. Pk., 1989. Power plant peformance engr. Knolls Atomic Power Lab., Niskayuna, NY, 1984—86; rsch. scientist CIRES, U. Colo., Boulder, 1889—2007; meteorologist NOAA Earth Sys. Rsch. Lab., Boulder, 2007—. Contbr. articles to profl. jours. (NOAA Outstanding Paper award, 2004). Treas. Episcoal Ch. Ressurrection, Broomfield, Colo., 2006—. Avocations: squash, swimming, golf, running, bridge.

WHITE, ANN MARIE, medical educator; d. Domenick and Beatrice H. White; m. David Robert Mowry; 2 children. BS with honors, Cornell U., 1992; MA, Columbia U. Tchrs. Coll., 1993; EdD, Harvard U., 2002. Rsch. asst. Cornell U., Ithaca, NY, 1991—92, Tchrs. Coll., Columbia U., NYC, 1992—93, Harvard U., Cambridge, Mass., 1993—95; data analyst Wellesley Coll., 1993—99; rsch. assoc. Harvard Grad. Sch. Edn., 1998—2001; sr. instr., dir. dept. psychiatry U. Rochester Med. Ctr., NY, 2004—. Rsch. cons. in field. Fellow, U.S. Senate, Washington, 2002—03, NIH. Bethesda, Md., 2003—04. Mem.: Soc. Rsch. Child Devel. (student rep. to policy com. 1997—99). Roman Catholic. Office: U Rochester Med Ctr 300 Crittenden Blvd Rochester NY

WHITE, AUGUSTUS AARON, III, orthopaedic surgeon; b. Memphis, June 4, 1936; s. Augustus Aaron and Vivian (Dandridge) White; m. Anita Ottemo; children: Alissa Alexandra, Atina Andrea, Annica Akila. BA cum laude in Psychology, Brown U., Providence, 1957, DMS (hon.), 1997; MD, Stanford U., Calif., 1961; PhD, Karolinska Inst., Sweden, 1969; degree in Mgmt., Harvard U., Cambridge, Mass., 1984; DHL (hon.), U. New Haven, Conn., 1987; DS (hon.), So. Conn. State U., New Haven, 2000. Diplomate Nat. Bd. Examiners, Am. Bd. Orthopaedic Surgery. Intern U. Mich. Hosp., Ann Arbor, 1961-62; asst. resident in gen. surgery Presbyn. Med. Center, San Francisco, 1962-63; asst. resident in orthopaedic surgery Yale Med. Center, New Haven, 1963-65, sr. instr., resident orthopaedic surgery, 1965-66; asst. prof. orthopaedic surgery Yale Med. Sch., 1969-72, assoc. prof., 1972-76, prof., 1977-78, dir. biomech. rsch. dept. orthopaedics, 1970-78; prof. orthopaedic surgery Harvard Med. Sch., 1978—; orthopaedic surgeon-in-chief Beth Israel Deaconess Med. Ctr., Boston, 1978-92, orthopaedic surgeon-in-chief emeritus, 1996—; sr. assoc. orthopaedic surgery Children's Hosp. Med. Ctr., Boston, 1979-89; assoc. in orthopaedic surgery Brigham & Women's Hosp., Boston, 1980-89; cons. div. surgery Sidney Farber Cancer Inst., Boston, 1980—; Ellen and Melvin Gordon disting. prof. med. edn., prof. orthopaedic surgery Harvard Med. Sch., 2002—. Rschr. biomechanics lab. Beth Israel Deaconess Med. Ctr.; chair sci. adv. bd., dir. OrthoLogic, Inc., Phoenix; sci. adv. bd. Am. Shared Hosp. Svcs., San Francisco; chair sci. adv. bd., bd. dirs. Zimmer Holding, Inc.; cons. orthop. surgery West Haven VA Hosp., Conn., 1970—78, Hill Health Ctr., New Haven, 1970—78; chief orthop. surgery Conn. Health Care Plan, 1976—78; adv. coun. Nat. Inst. Arthritis, Metabolism and Digestive Disease, NIH, 1979—82; mem. admissions com. Yale Med. Sch., 1970—72; presenter, moderator Symposium on Cervical Myelopathy, San Francisco, 1987; chmn. grant rev. com. NIH, 1985; founding mem., bd. overseers Brown U. Sch. Medicine, 1996—99; bd. overseers WGBH Radio/TV, Boston, 1996—98, trustee, 1998—2007, mem. adv. bd., bd. overseers, 2007—; Alfred R. Shands Jr. lectr. Am. Orthop. Assn., 2001; W. Montague Cobb lectr. W. Montague Cobb/ Nat. Med. Assn. Health Inst., 2008; pres. guest lectr. Scoliosis Rsch. Soc., 2001; chair com. culturally competence care Harvard Med. Sch., 2002—06; hon. staff orthopaedics Beth Israel Deaconess Med. Ctr., 2005—09; mem. adv. coun. biology and medicine Brown U., 2005; mem. adv. coun. Nat. Ctr. for Minority Health and Health Disparities, NIH, 2001—06. Author: Clinical Biomechanics of the Spine, 1978, 2d edit., 1990, (with M. Panjabi) Biomechanics in the Musculoskeletal System, 2001, Symposium on Idiopathic Low Back Pain, 1982, Your Aching Back-A Doctor's Guide to Relief, 1983, rev. edit., 1990, translated in German, 1992; guest editor Clin. Orthop. and Related Rsch., 1999; contbr. articles to profl. jours., chpts. to books. Trustee Brown U., Providence, 1971-76, bd. fellows, 1981-92, fellow emeritus, 1992—, chmn. corp. com. on minority affairs, 1981-86, chmn. corp. com. on med. edn., 1989-96, chmn. vis. com. on diversity; trustee Northfield Mt. Hermon Sch., Northfield, Mass., 1976-81; bd. dirs. The Partnership, Boston, 1984—. Capt. AUS, 1966-68. Decorated Bronze Star medal; named one of 10 Outstanding Young Men US Jr. C. of C., 1969, Selected for Exceptional Black Scientist poster series CIBA-GEIGY Corp., 1982; recipient Martin Luther King, Jr. Med. Achievement award, 1972, Kappa Delta award, nat. prize for outstanding rsch. in orthopaedics field, 1975; nat. award for spinal rsch. Eastern Orthopaedic Assn., 1980, Disting. Svc. award Northfield Mt. Hermon Sch. Alumni Assn., 1983; William Rogers award Associated Alumni Brown U., 1984, Outstanding Achievement award Delta Upsilon, 1986, Brown Bear award Brown Alumni Assn., Lifetime Achievement award Beth Israel Deaconess Med. Ctr., 2005, Candle in the Dark in Medicine award Morehouse Coll., 2006, J.E. Wallace Sterling Lifetime Achievement award Stanford Med. Sch., 2006, Smith and Nephew Disting. Clin. Educator award Am. Orthop. Assn., 2006; Am.-Brit.-Canadian Travelling fellow Am. Orthopedic Assn., 1975, Disting. Clin. Educator award, 2006; Ann. Spine Symposium named in his honor Beth Israel Deaconess Med. Ctr., 2004. Fellow Am. Acad. Orthopaedic Surgeons (chmn. diversity com. 1997-2001, Diversity award 2006), Scoliosis Rsch. Soc.; mem. The Acad. Harvard Med. Sch., Orthopaedic Rsch. Soc., Cervical Spine Rsch. Soc., Internat. Soc. for Study Lumbar Spine, Internat. Soc. Orthopaedic Surgery and Traumatology, Nat. Med. Assn. (Orthopaedic Scholar award 1994), Cervical Spine Rsch. Soc. (pres. 1988), N.Am. Spine Soc., Acad. Orthopaedic Soc. (co-chmn. com. on diversity), Clin. Orthopedic Soc. (Nix Ethics award 2002), J. Robert Gladden Orthopaedic Soc. (founding pres. 2000-03), Fedn. of Spine Assns. (pres. 1998), Sigma Xi, Sigma Pi Phi, Delta Upsilon (pres. Brown U. chpt. 1956, Charles Evan Hughes award for advancement of justice 2006, Augustus White III award for excellence in medicine established 2006, 09). Office: HMS Landmark East 401 Park Dr Boston MA 02215 Office Phone: 617-998-8802. Business E-Mail: augustus_white@hms.harvard.edu.

WHITE, BARBARA ANN, composer; b. Boston; AB, Harvard/Radcliffe Colleges, 1987; MA, U. Pitts., 1994, PhD., 1997. Co-founder Momentum Interdisciplinary Arts, 1996; lectr. Pa. State U., Erie, 1997—98; asst. prof. music Princeton U., 1998—2004, Harold Willis Dodds Univ. preceptor, 2001—04, assoc. prof. music, 2004—. Composer, musician: albums When the Smoke Clears, Apocryphal Stories. Recipient Acad. award in Music, AAAL, 2009; fellow NJ State Coun. Arts, 2000, John S. Guggenheim Meml. Found., 2003; Charles Ives scholar, AAAL, 1997, Charles Ives fellow, 2003, Bunting fellow, Radcliffe Inst. Advanced Study, 2000—01. Office: 220 Woolworth Music Ctr Princeton U Dept Music Princeton NJ 08544-1007 Office Phone: 609-258-1443. Office Fax: 609-258-6793. E-mail: bwhite@princeton.edu.*

WHITE, BARRY BENNETT, lawyer; b. Boston, Feb. 13, 1943; s. Harold and Rosalyn (Schneider) W.; m. Eleanor Greenberg; children: Joshua S., Adam J., Benjamin D. AB magna cum laude, Harvard U., 1964, JD magna cum laude, 1967. Bar: Mass. 1967, U.S. Dist. Ct. Mass. 1967, U.S. Ct. Appeals (1st cir.) 1967. Assoc. Foley Hoag & Eliot, Boston, 1969—74, chmn. exec. com., 1987—91, mng. ptnr., 1991—92, 1993—2001, ptnr., 1975—. Chmn. Lex Mundi, 1994; bd. dirs. Edgewater Tech., Inc., 2005—. Editor Harvard Law Rev., 1965-67. Sec., gen. counsel, exec. com. Greater Boston C. of C., 1998—, Initiative for Competitive Inner City, 1995—; bd. dirs., exec. com. Mass. Assn. Mental Health, 1985—, pres., 1993-95; bd. dirs., exec. com. Boston Mcpl. Rsch. Bur., 2003—, Vol. Lawyers Project, 1987-93, Support Ctr. of Mass., 1988-95; active Jewish Family and Children's Svcs., Boston, 1979-87; bd. visitors Boston U. Grad. Sch. Dentistry, 1981—; bd. trustees Jewish Cmty. Rels. Coun., 1988-92; chmn. com. for Clinton/Gore New Eng. Lawyers, 1992-96; chmn. Tsongas for Pres. Com., 1991-98; co-chair Mass. Lawyers for Kerry for Pres., 2004. With USPHS, 1967-69. Mem. ABA, Mass. Bar Assn., Boston Bar Assn., Internat. Bar Assn., Am. Acad. Hosp. Attys., Am. Hosp. Assn. (adj. task force on health planning 1982-84, contbg. editor hosp. law manual 1981-84), Harvard Club Boston, Badminton and Tennis Club. Democrat. Office: Foley Hoag LLP 155 Seaport Blvd Boston MA 02210 Office Phone: 617-832-1254. Business E-Mail: bbwhite@foleyhoag.com.

WHITE, BETTY, actress, comedienne; b. Oak Park, Ill., Jan. 17, 1922; m. Dick Barker 1945 (div. 1945), m. Lane Allen 1947 (div. 1949), m. Allen Ludden, 1963 (dec. 1981). Student pub. schs., Beverly Hills, Calif. Appearances on radio shows This Is Your FBI, Blondie, The Great Gildersleeve; actress: (TV series) including Hollywood on Television, The Betty White Show, 1954-58, Life With Elizabeth, 1953-55, A Date With The Angels, 1957-58, The Pet Set, 1971, Mary Tyler Moore Show, 1974-77, The Betty White Show, 1977, Mama's Family, 1983-86, The Golden Girls, 1985-92 (Emmy award for best actress 1986), Another World, 1988, The Golden Palace, 1992-93, Maybe This Time, 1995, (TV films) With This Ring, 1978, The Best Place to Be, 1979, Before and After, 1979, Eunice, 1982, Chance of a Lifetime, 1991, The Story of Santa Claus, 1996, A Weekend in the Country, 1996, The Retrievers, 2001, Annie's Point, 2005, (films) Advise and Consent, 1962, Dennis the Menace 2, 1998, Hard Rain, 1998, The Story of Us, 1999, Bringing Down the House, 2003, The Third Wish, 2004, The Proposal, 2009; guest appearances include Petticoat Junction, 1969, The Odd Couple, 1972, Fame, 1983, St. Elsewhere, 1985, Who's the Boss, 1985, Matlock, 1987, Empty Nest, 1989, 92, Carol & Company, 1990, Nurses, 1991, Diagnosis Murder, 1994, The Naked Truth, 1995, Suddenly Susan, 1996, (voice) King of the Hill, 1999, 2002, Ally McBeal, 1999, (voice) The Simpsons, 2000, Yes, Dear, 2002, Providence, 2002, That 70s Show, 2002, 03, Everwood, 2003, 04, The Practice, 2004, My Wife and Kids, 2004, Malcolm in the Middle, 2004, (voice) Father of the Pride, 2004, Boston Legal, 2005; frequent celebrity guest on numerous game shows including Hollywood Squares, Match Game; summer stock appearances Guys and Dolls, Take Me Along, The King and I, Who Was That Lady?, Critic's Choice, Bells are Ringing; author (book) Betty White's Pet-Lovers: How Pets Take Care of Us, 1987, Here We Go Again: My Life in Television, 1995; contbr. to forward(book) The Irrepressible Toy Dog, Dr. Fisher's Life on the Ark: Green Alligators, Bushman and Other "Hare Raising" Tales from America's Most Popular Zoo and Around the World, 2004, (preface) The Pets are Wonderful Family Album. Mem. Morris Animal Found., 1976—; zoo commr. Greater LA Zoo, 1998—. Recipient Emmy award NATAS, 1975, 76, 86; LA Area Emmy award, 1952, Living Legacy award, Women's Internat. Ctr., 1988, star on the Hollywood Walk of Fame; inducted into TV Hall of Fame, 1995; named Amb. to the Animals, Greater LA Zoo, 2006. Mem. AFTRA, Am. Humane Assn., Greater LA Zoo Assn. (dir.). Office: c/o William Morris Agy Betty Fanning 151 S El Camino Dr Beverly Hills CA 90212-2704*

WHITE, BEVERLY JANE, retired cytogeneticist; b. Seattle, Oct. 9, 1938; Grad., U. Wash., 1959, MD, 1963. Diplomate Nat. Bd. Med. Examiners, Am. Bd. Pediatrics, Am. Bd. Med. Genetics; lic physician and surgeon, Wash., Calif. Rsch. trainee dept. anatomy Sch. Medicine U. Wash., Seattle, 1960-62, pediatric resident dept. pediatrics, 1967-69; rotating intern Phila. Gen. Hosp., 1963-64; rsch. fellow med. ob-gyn. unit Cardiovascular Rsch. Inst. U. Calif. Med. Ctr., San Francisco, 1964-65; staff fellow lab. biomed. scis. Nat. Inst. Child Health and Human Devel. NIH, Bethesda, Md., 1965-67, sr. staff fellow, attending physician lab. exptl. pathology Nat. Inst. Arthritis, Metabolism and Digestive Diseases, 1969-74, acting chief sect. cytogenetics, 1975-76, rsch. med. officer, attending physician sect. cytogenetics lab. cellular biology and genetics, 1974-86, dir. cytogenetics unit, interinstitute med. genetics program clin. ctr., 1987-95; dir. cytogenetics Corning Clin. Labs., Teterboro, NJ, 1995-96; assoc. med. dir. cytogenetics Nichols Inst.-Quest Diagnostics, San Juan Capistrano, Calif., 1996-97, med. dir. cytogenetics, 1998—2008, med. dir. genetics divsn., 2000—02. Vis. scientist dept. pediat. divsn. genetics U. Wash. Sch. Medicine, 1983-84; intramural cons. NIH, 1975-95; cons. to assoc. editor Jour. Nat. Cancer Inst., 1976; cons. dept. ob-gyn. Naval Hosp., Bethesda, 1988-89; lectr., presenter in field. Recipient Mosby Book award, 1963, Women of Excellence award U. Wash. and Seattle Profl. chpt. Women in Comm., 1959, Reuben award Am. Soc. for Study Sterility, 1963. Fellow Am. Coll. Med. Genetics (founding), Am. Acad. Pediatrics; mem. AMA. Am. Soc. Human Genetics, Assn. Genetic Technologists (program com. 1989). Personal E-mail: bjwsur@comcast.net.

WHITE, BILL (WILLIAM HOWARD WHITE), Mayor, Houston; b. San Antonio, June 16, 1954; m. Andrea White; 3 children. BS in Econs. magna cum laude, Harvard U., 1976; JD, U. Tex., 1979. Atty. Susaman Godfrey LLP, Houston, 1979—93; instr. antitrust law and voting rights U. Tex., Austin; dep. sec., COO US Dept. Energy, Washington, 1993—95; chmn. Howe-Baker Internat., Tyler, Tex., 1997—2000; pres., CEO The Wedge Group, Houston, 1997—2003; mayor City of Houston, 2004—. Recipient Profile in Courage award, John F. Kennedy Libr. Found., 2007. Office: City Hall 901 Bagby St 3rd Fl Houston TX 77002 also: PO Box 1562 Houston TX 77251 Office Phone: 713-247-2200. E-mail: mayor@cityofhouston.net.

WHITE, BRAD, political organization administrator; Chmn. Simpson County Rep. Party, 1996; chmn. candidate recruitment, get-out-the-vote dir. Miss. Rep. Party, 2007, chmn., 2008—. Former pres. Mendenhall Area C. of C., Simpson County Devel. Found.; founder, charter pres. Co-Lin College Rep.; deacon Jupiter Bapt. Ch. Republican. Office: Miss Rep Party 415 Yazoo St Jackson MS 39201 Office Phone: 601-948-5191, 601-354-0972.*

WHITE, BRETT, real estate company executive; BA, U. Calif., Santa Barbara. Sales trainee, indsl. salesperson CB Richard Ellis, LA, 1984—91, sales mgr. San Diego, 1991—2001, mng. dir. Newport Beach LA, 1991—2001, regional mgr. L.A., 1991—2001, pres. brokerage, 1991—2001, chmn. The Ams., 1991—2001, pres., 2001—05, pres., CEO, 2005—, bd. dirs., 1998—, mem. exec. com., 1999—. Bd. dirs. Edison Internat., Southern Calif. Edison. Mem. LA Mus. Contemporary Art, Jr. Achievement. Named Brokerage Exec. of Yr., 2005, Real Estate Industry Exec. of Yr., 2006, Brokerage Exec. of Yr., Comml. Property News, 2006. Office: CB Richard Ellis 11150 Santa Monica Blvd Los Angeles CA 90025 Office Phone: 310-405-8919. Office Fax: 310-405-8950. Business E-Mail: brett.white@cbre.com.*

WHITE, BURTON LEONARD, retired educational psychologist, writer, consultant; b. Boston, June 27, 1929; s. Jack J. and Evelyn S. W.; m. Janet Hodgson-White; children— Laura, Emily, David, Daniel. BSM.E., Tufts Coll., 1949; BA, Boston U., 1956, MA, 1957; PhD, Brandeis U., 1960. Research assoc. Brandeis U., 1960-62, M.I.T., 1962-65; sr. research assoc. Harvard Grad. Sch. Edn., 1965-78; head Center Parent Edn., Newton, Mass., 1978-99, ret., 1999. Author: books including Human Infants, 1971, Experience and Environment, Vol. I, 1973, Vol. II, 1978, The First Three Years of Life, 1975, latest edit. 1995, The Origins of Competence, 1979, Educating the Infant and Toddler, 1988, Raising A Happy, Unspoiled Child, 1994, The New First Three Years of Life, 1995; contbr. articles to profl. jours. Served with AUS, 1951-53. Home: 115 Pine Ridge Rd Newton MA 02468-1616 Personal E-mail: todours1@aol.com.

WHITE, C. VANESSA, director; d. Robert Lee White and Doris Jean Redd White Foster, Herbert Randolph Foster (Stepfather). BS, No. Ill. U., DeKalb, 1978; M in Theol. Studies, Cath. Theol. Union, Chgo., 1990, D in Ministry, 2005. Cert. master catechist Xavier U. La., 1991. Child life specialist Michael Reese Hosp., Chgo., 1979—85; dir. Claretian vols. and lay missionaries Claretian Missionaries, Chgo., 1986—94; dir. retreat program and staff Christian Brother's LaSalle Manor Retreat Ctr., Plano, Ill., 1994—97; dir. Augustus Tolton scholar's program Cath. Theol. Union, Chgo., 1998—. Faculty Inst. for Black Cath. Studies Xavier U., New Orleans; bd. dirs. US Conf. Cath. Bishops Commn. on Certification and Accreditation, Washington; adv. bd. Fullerton Cenacle Retreat Ctr., Chgo. Editor: Songs of Our Hearts and Meditations of Our Souls; contbr. documentary film, articles to profl. jours. Active Secular Franciscan Order, Chgo., 1985—2006. Recipient Fr. Augustus Tolton Archdiocesan award, Archdiocese of Chgo., 1998. Mem.: Cath. Theol. Union Alumni Assn., Nat. Assn. for Lay Ministry, Knights of Peter Claver - Ladies Aux. (Sr. Thea Bowman award 1992, Adele Stadeker Svc. award 2003). Independent. Roman Catholic. Office: Catholic Theological Union 5401 S Cornell Chicago IL 60615 Business E-Mail: tolton@ctu.edu.

WHITE, CALVIN JOHN, zoo executive, zoological association executive, financial manager; b. Twillingate, Nfld., Can., Feb. 28, 1948; s. Harold and Meta Blanche (Abbott) W.; m. Lorna Joan Maclachlan; children: Chelsea Elizabeth, Evan Alexander. B in Commerce, U. Toronto, Ont., Can., 1971. Fin. analyst Can. GE Co. Ltd., Toronto, 1971-72, Ford Motor Co. Can., Oakville, Ont., 1972-74; sr. fin. analyst Municipality of Met. Toronto, 1974-77, asst. dir. budget and ops. analysis, 1977-81, dir. budget analysis and internal control, 1981-86; CEO Toronto Zoo, 1986—. Bd. dirs. Borealis Hydro Elec. Holdings Inc., Can. Assn. Zoos and Aquariums, Ctr. for Endangered Reptilia, 1989-91, Rouge Pk. Alliance, Toronto Chongqing Assn., Textile Mus. Can., Tourism Toronto; pres. Greenposer Can. Fellow Am. Zoo and Aquarium Assn.; mem. Am. Assn. Zoo Keepers, Inst. Pub. Adminstrn. Can. (bd. dirs. 1989-91), Toronto Zoo Found., World Conservation Union, World Zoo Orgn., Toronto Sportmen's Assn., Mensa. Office: Toronto Zoo 361A Old Finch Ave Scarborough ON Canada M1B 5K7 Office Phone: 416-392-5909. Business E-Mail: cwhite@torontozoo.ca.

WHITE, CECIL RAY, librarian, consultant; b. Hammond, Ind., Oct. 15, 1937; s. Cecil Valentine and Vesta Ivern (Bradley) W.; m. Frances Ann Gee, Dec. 23, 1960 (div. 1987); children: Timothy Wayne, Stephen Patrick. BS in Edn., So. Ill. U., 1959; postgrad., Syracuse U., 1961; MDiv, Southwestern Bapt. Sem., 1969; MLS, No. Tex. State U., 1970, PhD, 1984. Libr. Herrin (Ill.) H.S., 1964-66; acting reference libr. Southwestern Sem., Ft. Worth, 1968-70, asst. libr., 1970-80; head libr. Golden Gate Bapt. Sem., Mill Valley, Calif., 1980-88, West Oahu Coll., Pearl City, Hawaii, 1988-89; dir. spl. projects North State Coop. Libr. System, Yreka, Calif., 1989-90; dir. libr. St. Patrick's Sem., Menlo Park, Calif., 1990—. Libr. cons. Hist. Commn., So. Bapt. Conv., Nashville, 1983-84, Internat. Bapt. Sem., Prague, Czech Republic, 1996; mem. Thesaurus Com., 1974-84; adv. bd. Cath. Periodical and Lit. Index, 1995—, chair, 1999-2008. Bd. dirs. Hope and Help Ctr., 1986-88, vice chmn., 1987-88. With USAF, 1960—64. Lilly Found. grantee Am. theol. Assn., 1969, Mary A. grant, recipient Vol. Svc. award, Cath. Lib. Assn., 2009. Mem. ALA, Am. Theol. Libr. Assn. (coord. cons. svc. 1973-78, program planning com. 1985-88, chmn. 1986-88), Nat. Assn. Profs. Hebrew (archivist 1985—), Assn. Coll. and Rsch. Librs., Cath. Libr. Assn. (mem. exec. bd. 1999-2005, Mary A. Grant Svc. award, 2009), Phi Kappa Phi, Beta Phi Mu. Democrat. Baptist. Home: 229 Rome Place Hayward CA 94544 Office: St Patricks Sem 320 Middlefield Rd Menlo Park CA 94025-3563 Home Phone: 510-429-1955; Office Phone: 650-321-5655. E-mail: cecilrwhite@hotmail.com, stpats@ix.netcom.com. *Personal philosophy: Except for the gift of life and faith, the best gift that has been given to me, and which I can give, is the unique gift of oneself in friendship. No one else can give it, and it cannot be bought at any price.*

WHITE, CHARLES SIDNEY JOHN, retired humanities educator; b. New Richmond, Wis., Sept. 25, 1929; s. Ferne Rosemary Holt. BA in English with honors, U. Wis., Madison, 1951; MA magna cum laude, U. de las Am. Mexico City Coll., Mexico City, 1957; MA, U. Chgo., 1962, PhD with distinction, 1964. Staff pub. rels. and advt. Wallace Supplies Mfg. Co., Chgo., 1957—61; asst. prof. Indian studies U. Wis., Madison, 1965—66; asst. prof. religious thought U. Pa., 1966—71; assoc. prof. philosophy and religion Am. U., Washington, 1971—78, prof. philosophy and religion, 1978—94, prof. emeritus philosophy and religion, 1995—; dir. Asia Ctr. Sch. Internat. Svc., 1976—78, chmn. dept. philosophy and religion, 1984—87, 1988—94. Vis. lectr. history of religions Princeton (N.J.) U., 1968; vis. prof. world religions Lakehead U., Thunder Bay, Ont., Canada, 1974—88; vis. prof. Wesley Seminary, 1985, 86; lectr. in field; vis. prof. Hindu studies faculty theology Oxford U., England, 2002; mem. program adv. com. diploma in Buddhist studies U. Hyderabad, 2006. Author: The Caurāsī Pad of Śrī Hit Harivaṁś, 1977, Ramakrishna's Americans, 1979, The Adyar Library, The Institute for Vaisnava Studies and The American University Microfilm Collection of Vaisnava Literature, 2001, Teaching Saranagati: A Dialogue with HH Sri Sathguru Swami Gnanananda Sarasvathi, 2002, Catalogue of Vaisnava Literature, 2004, The Garden of Loneliness, Jay Shankar Prasad's Tears, 2006, Roses from the Desert of my Heart, A Book of Poetry, 2007; co-author: The Religious Quest, 1983, 2d edit., 1985, Joseph Campbell: Transformations of Myth Through Time, 1990; contbr. chapters to books, articles to profl. jours. and encyclopedias, numerous book reviews. With USN, 1951—55. Grantee, Smithsonian Instn., India, 1982—83; fellow, Hindi-Urdu U., Chgo., 1961—64, Am. Inst. Indian Studies, India, 1964, 1968, 1974, 1978, 1995. Mem.: Am. Inst. Indian Studies (exec. com. 1988—90). Office Phone: 202-885-2925. Business E-Mail: philrel@american.edu.

WHITE, CHRISTOPHER, engineering educator; s. Edward and Denise White; m. Rowena White; children: Kyle, Isabel, Maia. BME in Mech. Engring., Stony Brook U., NYC, 1994; PhD in Mech. Engring., Yale U., Conn., 2001—01. Postdoc. fellow Stanford U., Calif., 2001—03; sr. mem. tech. staff Sandia Nat. Labs., Calif., 2003—06, faculty, 2007—; asst. prof. mech. engring. U. NH. Contbr. scientific papers. Endowed fellowship, Yale U., 1997, Northrop Grumman fellow, 1999—2001. Mem.: Am. Phys. Soc. Office: Univ NH S254 Kingsbury Hall 33 Academic Way Durham NH 03824

WHITE, CHRISTOPHER TODD, language educator, anthropologist; b. Columbia, Mo., Dec. 7, 1965; s. Eric B. and Barbara K. White; life ptnr. Ryan C. Reiss. BA, U. Nebr., Lincoln, 1990; MA, U. Mo., Kansas City, 1994, U. Nev., Las Vegas, 1998; PhD, U. So. Calif., LA, 2005. Adj. lectr. Rockhurst Coll., Kansas City, Mo., 1994—95; editl. asst. BkMk Press, Kansas City, 1993—95; adj. lectr. English U. Mo., Kansas City, 1993—95; acad. advisor Ednl. Talent Search, Las Vegas, Nev., 1995—96; asst. prof./lectr. U. Nev., Las Vegas, 1996—98; instr. Glendale C.C., Calif., 1998—2003; tchr., rsch. asst. dept. anthropology U. So. Calif., LA, 1998—2005; asst. prof. anthropology SUNY, Brockport, NY, 2005—06; staff anthropologist, Digital Initiatives Unit, U. Rochester, 2007—08; lead ethnographer Colo. State U. Librs., 2007, Rutgers U. Librs., 2009—; vis. asst. prof.,dept sociology & anthropology James Madison U., 2008—09. Dir. Homosexual Info. Ctr., LA, 2001—, ONE Inst. and Archives, LA, 2001—02; mem. adv. bd. GLBTQ history website project CUNY, Ctr. Lesbian and Gay Studies, 2008—. Editor: U. Nev.-Las Vegas Jour. Anthropology, 1995—2005, San Dieguito and La Jolla: The Collected Works of Claude N. Warren on the Archaeology af Southern California, 2006; asst. editor Before Stonewell: Activists for Gay and Lesbian Rights in Historical Context, 2002, mem. editl. bd. Collegiate Press, 2002, referee Popular Culture Rev.; columnist: Orange County/Long Beach Blade Mag., 2006—07; author: Pre Gay L.A.: A Social History of the Movement for Homosexual Rights, 2009; contbr. articles to profl. jours. Recipient Patricia Roccio Award in Anthropology, U. Nev.-Las Vegas, 1997, Dissertation Fellowship award, U. So. Calif., 2005; scholar Hal Call Mattachine scholar, Inst. for Study of Human Resources, 2000—01. Mem.: Assn. for Psychol. Anthropology, Homosexual Info. Ctr. (sec.-treas. 2001—), Southwestern Anthropol. Assn., Soc. of Lesbian and Gay Anthropologists (sec.-treas. 1998—2005), Soc. of Linguistic Anthropology, Am. Anthropol. Assn. Democrat. Avocations: camping, book collecting, piano, running, bicycling. Office: James Madison Univ Dept Anthropology Harrisonburg VA 22807 Personal E-mail: ctgrant@mac.com.

WHITE, CLARA JO, small business owner, consultant; b. County Cherokee, Tex., June 26; children: Anita, Jackie, Mona Lisa, Jeris, Gina. Diploma, Ft. Worth Bus. Coll., Tex., 1947; AA in Social Sci., Riverside City Coll., 1986; degree magma cum laude, Am. Biog. Inst. Cert. graphoanalyst 1977, master graphoanalyst Internat. Graphanalysis Soc., Inc., 1979, mus. docent 1977, diploma IGAS Congress Inst. Training, 1979, cert. mgmt. supr. devel. U. Calif., Riverside, 1986, counseling skills U. Riverside, 1990. Owner, pres. White Handwriting Analysis Svc., Riverside, Calif., 1982—. Instr. Internat. Congress and Resident Inst., Internat. Graphoanalysis Soc., 1989, discussion group leader, 88; analyzed handwriting Lady Margaret Beaufort, 1992, Mary Queen of Scots, 1994, Hillary Rodham Clinton, 1994, Pres. Bill Clinton, 1997, Georgia O'Keeffe, 1999, presidents George Washington, Abraham Lincoln, John F. Kennedy, 2000; presenter, cons., spkr. in field. Editor (asst. editor): Reflections, 1986; author: numerous poems. Mem. children's conf. planning com. Riverside Mental Health Assn., 1981—; v.p. Heritage Ho. Mus., Riverside, Calif., 1981—, co-pres., 1985—86, pres; historian Riverside Juvenile Hall Aux., 1984—, pres., 1987—; mem. U.S. Olympic Com., 1984; bd. dir. Riverside Mus. Assoc., 1985—87, vol., 1985—88, aux. historian, 1984—, pres., 1987—88; bd. mem. KCET TV PBS, LA, 2005—. Recipient cert. of Appreciation, Riverside County Probation Dept., 1986, County Riverside Suprs., 1988, Riverside Mental Health, 1990, Nat. Law enforcement Officers Meml. Fund, 1998, award, F. H. Butterfield Sch., 1980, Golden Post award, Homer Honor Soc., 1987, 1990, cert., Libr. of Congress, 1998, cmty. svc. cert., Riverside City Coll., 1982, 1st pl. writing-poetry, Am. Biog. Rsch. Assn., 1991, trophy Outstanding Svc. to Cmty., Sta. KQLH-FM, trophy, Vol. Ctr. Riverside, 1991, trophy and Individual Svc. award, Riverside County Juvenile Hall of Fame, 1990—91, cert. of Recognition, Riverside County Probation Dept., 1991, Calif. Legis.-State Assembly, 1991, So. Calif. chpt. IGAS, 1990—91, Riverside County Bd. Suprs. and Riverside County Probation Dept., 1993, 26th Children's Conf. Com., 1999, Internat. Gold medal of Honor for Disting. Participation, ABI/IBC 26th Congress Arts and Comm., 1999, Graphoanalysts of the Yr. award, So. Calif. chpt. Graphoanalysts, 2000, Disting. Svc. award, City of Riverside, 2004, Order of Ambs. Sovereign award, ABI/IBC Inaugural World Forum, 2006; named Vol. of the Yr., Genius Laureate, ABI Inst., 2009; named to Hall of Fame, Riverside Juvenile Hall Aux., 1984. Master: Internat. Graphoanalysis Soc. (life; 2d then 1st v.p. so. Calif. chpt. 1984, Merit cert. 1981, Pres. Excellence award 1982, 1983, 1984, Pres. Merit citation 1988, Achievement cert. 1995); mem.: NAFE, AAUW, DAV Aux. (life), YWCA, US Olympic USA Sixth Ring, US Olympic Com. Sixth Ring (vol. CANDA 2009), Nat. Mus. Women in Arts, KCET TV PBS, Nat. Geographic Soc., Met. Mus. Assocs., World War II Meml. Soc. (charter mem.), Top Cops Nat. Assn. Police Orgns., Rsch. Coun. of Scripps Clinic and Rsch. Found., Smithsonian Assocs., Calif. Probation, Parole, and Corrections Assn. (cert. of tng. 1995), US Olympic Soc. (U.S. Olympic Team, U.S.A Olympic Com. Sixth Ring 2004, Replica Bronze medal 2004, Vancouner award 2009), Women's Networking Club (Riverside chpt.), Confederation of Chivalry (life; grand coun., dame officer). Avocations: sewing, music, collecting antiques, dance, exercise. Home and Office: 7965 Helena Ave Riverside CA 92504-3513

WHITE, DALE ANDREW, journalist; b. Jacksonville, Fla., Feb. 17, 1958; s. John Andrew and Jeannelle Corinne White. B in Journalism, U. Fla., 1983. Reporter UPI, Miami, Fla., 1980, Orlando (Fla.) Sentinel Star, 1981; corr. Fla. Times-Union, Gainesville, 1982; reporter, columnist, editl. writer, editor Sarasota Herald-Tribune, Fla., 1983—. Contbr. short stories to profl. publs. Recipient Chmn.'s award N.Y. Times, 1987, 2004, 3d place Editorial Writing award Fla. Soc. Newspaper Editors, 1993, 1st place Ind. Reporter Media award Fla. Sch. Bds. Assn., 1996. Office: PO Box 1695 Bradenton FL 34206-1695

WHITE, DALE TIMOTHY (TIM WHITE), television journalist, producer; b. Mt. Pleasant, Mich., May 12, 1949; s. Dale Glenn and Norma Jean (Lessender) W.; m. Basha Banczyk, Sept. 12, 1991 (div. Sept. 17, 1993); 1 child, Elizabeth Natalia. BA in Film and TV, Mich. State U., 1971; MA in Polit. Sci., U. So. Calif., 1975; PhD in Comm., U. Md., 1994. Exec. prodr. film and TV svc. U.S. State Dept./U.S. Info. Agy., Worldwide, 1975-80; pres. T White Comms., Arlington, Va., 1985—. Chmn. Lives and Legacies Films, McLean, Va., 1994—; pres. First Person Films Inc., McLean, 1994—. Moderator PBS-TV Techno-Politics, 1991-95; host Fox Morning News, 1990-92, FOX-TV Sightings, 1991-95, Network Cable, 1996—; Gannett/ NBC, 1999-2008; host for CBS News, Turner Broadcasting, WorldNet, CNN, Knowledge TV. Bd. dirs. WAVE Inc., 1990—, Coun. on Internat. Non-Theatrical Events, 1995—. With USAF, 1971-75; col. USAFR, 1976-2006; brig gen. (ret). Recipient CINE Golden Eagle awards, 1976-80, Emmy awards, 1991, 92; Television and Radio Broadcasting Hall of Fame, inducted 2005 Mem. NATAS, AFTRA, VFW, Screen Actors Guild, Army Navy Country Club, Air Force Assn., Am. Legion, Reserve Officers Assn., Potomac Club, Cosmos Club, Nat. Press. Club, Wash. Literary Soc. Union Club, The Country Club (pepper Pike, Ohio) Congregationalist. Avocations: golf, tennis, theater, wilderness, hiking. Home: 1200 N Nash St Arlington VA 22209-3616 Business E-Mail: twhitecom@aol.com.

WHITE, DANIEL BOWMAN, lawyer; b. Charlotte, NC, Apr. 12, 1948; s. William Garner and Elizabeth (Bowman) W.; m. Sarah de Saussure Peterson, May 29, 1976; children: Bentley Parker, Sarah de Saussure. AB, Davidson Coll., 1970; JD, U. S.C., 1976. Bar: S.C. 1976, U.S. Dist. Ct. S.C. 1976, U.S. Ct. Appeals (4th cir.) 1978, U.S. Ct. Appeals (fed. cir.) 1990. Ptnr. Gallivan, White & Boyd P.A., Greenville, SC, 1976—. Mem. Fed. Cir. Jud. Conf. Comments editor U. S.C. Law Rev., 1975-76. Commr. Greenville Zoning Commn., 1980-85; mem. Supreme Ct. Bd. Commrs. on Grievances and Discipline, 1988-91. 1st lt. U.S. Army, 1971-73. Decorated Bronze Star; Dana scholar Davidson Coll., N.C., 1966-70, Named one of Best Lawyers in Am., SC Super Lawyers; State Co-chair & Charter fellow Litig. Counsel Am., named Leading Lawyers Chambers USA. Mem.: Assn. Def. Trial Attys., Internat. Assn. Def. Counsel, Nat. Assn. R.R. Trial Counsel, S.C. Bar (ho. dels. 1986—, chmn. ho. dels. 2000—02, bd. govs. 1992—95, 2000—, sec. 2002—03, treas. 2003—04, pres.-elect 2004—05, pres. 2005—06), Def. Rsch. Inst., Greenville Young Lawyers Club (pres. 1981). Episcopalian. Office: Gallivan White & Boyd PO Box 10589 Greenville SC 29603-2804 Office Phone: 864-271-5342. Business E-Mail: dwhite@gwblawfirm.com.

WHITE, DANIEL EUGENE, lawyer; b. Cheyenne, Wyo., Sept. 6, 1950; s. Philip and Rita Ann (Moran) W.; m. Diane Dreher McInerney, Oct. 4, 1986; children: Caroline M., Stephanie M. BA in Polit. Sci., U. Wyo., 1972, JD, 1976. Bar: Wyo. 1976. Asst. atty. gen. State of Wyo., Cheyenne, 1976-79; dep. county atty. Converse County, Wyo., 1979-80; exec. dir. Wyo. State Bar, Cheyenne, 1980-83; ptnr. Gusea, Pattno & White, P.C., Cheyenne, 1983—2000, Woodard & White, P.C., Cheyenne, 2001—. Co-founder, organizer Wyo. High Sch. Mock Trial Tournament, 1985-95. Mem. ABA, Wyo. Bar Assn. Democrat. Roman Catholic. Avocations: swimming, gardening, biking, camping. Home: 304 Carriage Dr Cheyenne WY 82009-2008 Office Phone: 307-634-2731. Personal E-mail: bwomail@qwest.net.

WHITE, DANNY LEVIUS, counselor, consultant, educator; b. Temple, Tex., Oct. 9, 1956; s. Chester Allen and Elizabeth (Jimmerson) W.; m. Phemonia Lyvette Miller, July 23, 1988; children: Amadi, Sakilae. AA, Mesa CC, Ariz., 1976; BA, Ottawa U., Kans., 1982; postgrad., Chapman Coll., 1989-90; MEd magna cum laude, No. Ariz. U., 1993. Clinician V Phoenix South Mental Health, 1982-85; therapist I Ariz. Dept. of Correction, Tucson, 1985-87; cons. Tucson Urban League, 1987-88; counselor, assessment specialist Pima County Atty.'s Office, Tucson, 1988-96; pres., CEO Family Matters Counseling and Cons. Svcs., Tucson, 1996—2001; counselor, spl. group coord. Jewish Family and Children's Svcs., 2001—02; adj. prof. dept. counseling, social and cultural devel. Mesa C.C., 2002—. Adj. faculty Pima C.C., 1993-95; mem. com. So. Ariz. Task Force Against Domestic Violence, Tucson, 1989—, outreach coord., Day of Unity chair, 1993, 94, 95; chair MCC Day of Unity and Week Without Violence, 2003—; psychology assoc. II minor's unit Ariz. Dept Corrections, 1996. Dem. precinct committeeman, Tucson, 1988-92; del. 1988 Nat. Dem. Conv.; dep. registrar Pima & Maricopa County Recorders Office, Phoenix and Tucson, 1983-90; mem. citizens adv. coun. Phoenix Elem. Sch. Dist. 1, 1983-85; chair radiothon membership drive com. Tucson chpt. NAACP, 1990-93, chair health fair drive, 1992-93; pres. bd. dirs. P.A.S.A.R., Tucson, 1989-91; booster Spl. Olympics, 1980-90; spl. friend Ariz. Children's Home Foster Care, 1990; implemented Will to Win and Stay In Sch. drive programs, 1987-91; vol., blood drive coord. United Blood Svcs., Phoenix, 1983-87; pres. bd. dirs. United Parent and Youth League, Inc., 2004—. Named Outstanding West Campus Adj. Faculty Mem., Pima C.C., 1994-95; recipient Robert L. Horn Outstanding Cmty. Svc. award NAACP, 1996, Tucson NAACP Presidents award, 1998, Mesa C.C. Alumni Achievement award, 2004; named No. Ariz. U. Alumni Citizen of Yr., 1998. Mem. United Parent and Youth League Inc. (pres. bd. dirs. 1984-85), Gov.'s Alliance Against Drugs (bd. dirs. 1989-91), Omega Psi Phi (named Man of Yr. Ariz. chpts. 1983, 85, 92, pres. Tucson grad. chpt. 1991-95), Delta Alpha Alpha. Avocations: photography, music, plants, people. Home: PO Box 8627 Phoenix AZ 85066-8627 Office Phone: 480-461-7588. E-mail: dwhite@mcmail.maricopa.edu.

WHITE, DARREN P., protective services official; b. Suffern, NY, 1963; married; 1 child. BA in Mgmt., U. Phoenix. Police officer City of Houston, City of Albuquerque; cabinet sect. N.Mex. Dept. of Pub. Safety, Sante Fe; sherriff Bernalillo County, N.Mex., 2002—. Sr. mgmt. team S.W. Border States Project; joint command group Operation Alliance; bd. dirs. Rocky Mountain Info. Network; chmn. N.Mex. High Intensity Drug Trafficking Area exec. com. Served with 82nd Airborne Divsn. US Army. Recipient Jefferson award Am. Inst. for Pub. Svc. Republican. Office: Bernalillo County Sherriff's Dept 400 Roma NW Albuquerque NM 87102

WHITE, DAVID CALVIN, electrical engineer, educator, energy executive, consultant; b. Sunnyside, Wash., Feb. 18, 1922; s. David Calvin Sr. and Leafie Eloise (Scott) W.; m. Glorianna Guilii, July 30, 1949 (dec. Dec. 1965); 1 child, Julie Anne White Coman (dec.); m. Margot Ann Fuller, June 4, 1966; 1 child, Constance Anne. BS, Stanford U., 1946, MS, 1947, PhD, 1949. Registered profl. engr. Elec. engr. Kaiser Industries, Vancouver, Wash., 1941-42, 43-45; assoc. prof. elec. engring. U. Fla., Gainesville, 1949-52; asst. prof. elec. engring. MIT, Cambridge, 1952-54, assoc. prof., 1954-58, prof., 1958-62, Ford prof. engring., 1962-92, dir. energy lab., 1972-89, Ford prof. engring. emeritus, 1992—. Pres., dir. Energy Conversion, Inc., 1961-64; cons. Gulf Oil, 1976-84, Johnson Controls, 1980-98; sr. advisor and vis. prof. Birla Inst., India, 1968-70; mem. council U. Benin, Nigeria, 1972; trustee Lowell Tech. Inst., Mass., 1972-74; mem. corp. Woods Hole Oceanographic Inst., Mass., 1977-84; mem. research coordinating panel Gas Research Inst., Chgo., 1977-85; chmn. adv. council Electric Power Research Inst., Palo Alto, Calif., 1984-86, mem., 1980-87. Author: (with others) Electromechanical Energy Conversion, 1959 Commr. Electric Light Plant, Concord, Mass., 1959-64, Kalmia Woods Water Dist., Concord, 1960-63 Named hon. prof. Instituto Politecnico Nacional, Mex., 1961 Fellow IEEE; mem. Nat. Acad. Engring., Am. Acad. Arts and Scis., Am. Soc. Engring. Edn. (George Westinghouse award 1961), Country Club Boca Raton, Phi Beta Kappa, Sigma Xi, Tau Beta Pi, Eta Kappa Nu. Republican. Avocations: golf, boating. Office: MIT 77 Massachusetts Ave Rm E40-473 Cambridge MA 02139-4307 Home: 15961 N 111 Way Scottsdale AZ 85255 Personal E-mail: dcmfwhite@aol.com.

WHITE, DAVID HYWEL, physics professor, researcher; b. Cardiff, Wales, June 4, 1931; arrived in US, 1959, naturalized, 1966; s. William Richard and Bessie (Morgan) W.; m. Frances Mary Shearman, July 23, 1954; children: Richard Gerwyn, Christopher David. BS, U. Wales, 1953; PhD, Birmingham U., 1956. Asst. lectr. Birmingham U., 1958—59; asst. prof. U. Pa., 1961—64; asso. prof. Cornell U., Ithaca, NY, 1964—69, prof., 1969—78; sr. physicist, head exptl. facilities div. Isabelle Project, Brookhaven Nat. Lab., Upton, L.I., NY, 1978—86; group leader nuclear and particle physics rsch. P divsn. Los Alamos Nat. Lab., N.Mex., 1986—98, lab. fellow N.Mex., 1996—. Cons., 1967-69, 76-78, 99—. Author: Elementary Electronics, 1967; Editor: Scintillation Counters, 1966. NSF sr. postdoctoral fellow, 1970; JSPS fellow, 1981 Fellow Am. Phys. Soc. Home: 913 Calle Vistoso Santa Fe NM 87501-1031 Personal E-mail: hywelwhite@comcast.net.

WHITE, DAVID LAWRENCE, mechanical engineer, marketing professional; b. Cheverly, Md., June 16, 1965; s. Kenneth William and Betty Mary (Brunacci) White; m. Reena Shah-White, May 21, 1994; children: Savanah, Brianna. BS in mech. engring., Va. Polythech. Inst., 1987; MBA, Case Western Reserve U., 1993. Cert. EIT, 1987. Dist. sales engr. Torrington Ingersoll-Rand, Cleveland, 1987-92; free market devel. advisor USAID, Washington, 1992-93; internat. bus. devel. RELTEC Corp., Cleveland, 1993—95, internat. sales Delhi and Chennai, India, 1995—97; area mgr. Torrington Ingersoll-Rand, Mumbai, India, 1997—2001; mktg. mgr. Ingersoll-Rand, Shippensburg, Pa., 2002—04, mgr. global product mktg., 2004—05; dir. sales and mktg. Timken, Bangalore, India, 2005—07; gen. mgr. Timken Indsl. Services, 2008—. Roman Catholic. Office: 267 Brentwood Dr Hudson OH 44236 Office Phone: 330-471-6051. Personal E-mail: pinhead_dave@hotmail.com.

WHITE, DAVID R., healthcare company executive; Grad., Univ. Tenn.; M healthcare adminstrn., Trinity Univ., San Antonio. Regional v.p. Republic Health Corp.; exec. v.p., COO Cmty. Health Systems Inc.; pres. Atlantic group HCA/Columbia, 1994—98; pres., CEO LifeTrust, 1998—2000; non-exec. chmn. IASIS Healthcare, Franklin, Tenn., 1999—2000, CEO, 2000—04, pres., 2001—04, chmn., CEO, 2004—. Bd. dir. Am. Fedn. Hospitals. Office: IASIS Healthcare Corp Bldg E 117 Seaboard Ln Franklin TN 37067

WHITE, DAWN ROBERTA, energy executive; b. Urbana, Ill., May 29, 1958; d. Robert Allan and Wilma Ethel White; m. James Walter Fash, Oct. 30, 1999; 1 child, Annika Fash-White. BS in Metall. Engring., U. Ill., Urbana-Champaign, 1979, MS in Metall. Engring., 1981, PhD in Mech. Engring., 1986. Dir., program devel. MTS Sys., Eden Prairie, Minn., 1986—92; staff tech. specialist Ford Motor Co., Dearborn, Mich., 1993—99; founder Solidica Inc., Ann Arbor, Mich., 1999—2007; pres. Accio Energy Inc., Ann Arbor, 2007—. Achievements include patents for improving uniformity in additive manufacturing processes; electrical resistance based object consolidation, fabricating low distortion lap weld construction; self-aligining end effector for friction soldering metals to glass plate; producing a mandrel for use in hot isostatic pressed powder metallurgy rapid tool making; friction welding non-metallics to metallics, making spray formed rapid tools; ultrasonic object consolidation system and method. Office: Accio Energy 3600 Green Ct Ste 300 Ann Arbor MI 48105

WHITE, DENISE, multimedia company executive; b. 1954; Human resources leader Pan Am. World Airways; joined Microsoft Corp., Redmond, Wash., 1990, sr. human resources mgr., gen. mgr. Entertainment & Devices Divsn.; exec. v.p. human resources & adminstrn. Viacom Inc., NYC, 2007—. Achievements include establishing and managing two non-profit foundations directed at supporting at-risk youth and animal welfare. Office: Viacom Inc 1515 Broadway New York NY 10036

WHITE, DENNIS J., lawyer; b. Waterbury, Conn., Apr. 10, 1947; s. Alfred and Emily W.; m. Judith A. Biondi, June 30, 1973; children: Lindsey, Christopher. BA summa cum laude, Coll. of the Holy Cross, 1969; JD cum laude, Harvard U., 1975. Bar: Mass. 1975. Ptnr. Herrick & Smith, Boston, 1983-86, Sullivan & Worcester, Boston, 1986—2003, McDermott Will & Emery. Woodrow Wilson Found. fellow 1969, leading lawyer by Chambers USA 2008. Mem. Boston Bar Assn. (chmn., global bd. dir.), Assn. Corporate Growth (MSA com. mem.), ABA. Avocations: golf, reading. Office: McDermott Will & Emery 28 State St Boston MA 02109-1775 Office Phone: 617-535-4011. Office Fax: 617-535-3800. Business E-Mail: dwhite@mwe.com.

WHITE, DORINDA, legislative staff member; CEO Rindi Media Internat. Inc.; pres. Women in Film and Video, Washington; comm. dir. to Rep. Diane Watson US House of Reps., Washington, 2007—. Assoc. editor: Africa Comm. Mag.; prodr., host (radio program) Women in the Media. Named Next Generation Leader Honoree, Congl Black Caucus Annual Legis. Conf., 2006. Mem.: Nat. Assn. Multi-Ethnicity in Comm. (pres., Mid-Atlantic chpt. 2005, 2006), Nat. Assn. Black Female Execs. in Music and Entertainment, Women in Cable and Telecomm., Nat. Ass. Black Journalists. Democrat. Office: 2430 Rayburn House Office Bldg Washington DC 20515 Office Phone: 202-225-7084. Office Fax: 202-225-2422.*

WHITE, DOUGLAS JAMES, JR., lawyer; b. NYC, Mar. 20, 1934; s. Douglas James and Margaret (Stillman) W.; m. Denise Beale, May 28, 1960; children: Brian Douglas, James Roderick. BA, U. Oreg., 1955; LLB, Willamette U., 1958. Bar: Oreg. 1958. Law clk. to assoc. justice Oreg. Supreme Ct., Salem, 1958-59; assoc. Schwabe, Williamson & Wyatt (formerly known as Mautz, Souther, Spaulding, Kinsey & Williamson), Portland, Oreg., 1959-69; shareholder, gen. ptnr. Schwabe, Williamson & Wyatt, P.C. (formerly known as Schwabe, Williamson, Wyatt, Moore & Roberts), Portland, Oreg., 1969-79, sr. ptnr., 1979-93; shareholder, 1994—98; ret., 1998; of counsel, 1999—2008. Trustee Jesuit H.S., Beaverton, 1991-94; bd. dirs. St. Vincent de Paul Child Devel. Ctr., Portland, 1979-90, Portland Coun., Soc. St. Vincent de Paul, 1989-92, Portland House of Umoja, 1995—, Friends Sat. Acad., 2006—; bd. dirs., officer Maryville Nursing Home, Beaverton, 1993-99, St. Vincent de Paul Conf. of St. Thomas More, Portland, 1966—; adv. bd. Saturday Acad., Portland, 1982-2005. Mem.: Oreg. State Bar Assn. (real estate and land use sect. exec. com. 1984—85), Flyfisher Club Oreg., Multnomah Athletic Club. Republican. Roman Catholic. Avocations: fly fishing, bridge, walking, hiking, travel. Home: 6725 SW Preslynn Dr Portland OR 97225-2668 Office: Schwabe Williamson & Wyatt 1211 SW 5th Ave Ste 1800 Portland OR 97204-3713 Office Phone: 503-222-9981.

WHITE, EDWARD ALFRED, lawyer; b. Elizabeth, NJ, Nov. 23, 1934; BS in Indsl. Engring., U. Mich., 1957, JD, 1963. Bar: Fla. 1963, US Ct. Appeals (5th cir.) 1971, US Ct. Appeals (11th cir.) 1981, US Supreme Ct. 1976. Assoc. Jennings, Watts, Clarke & Hamilton, Jacksonville, Fla., 1963-66, ptnr., 1966-69, Wayman & White, Jacksonville, Fla., 1969-72; pvt. practice Jacksonville, Fla., 1972—. Mem. aviation law com. Fla. Bar, 1972-94, chmn., 1979-81, bd. govs., 1984-88, admiralty com., 1984—, chmn., 1990-91, chmn. pub. relations com., 1986-88, exec. coun. trial lawyers sect., 1986-91, chmn. admiralty cert. com., 1995-97. Fellow Am. Bar Found.; mem. ABA (vice chmn. admiralty law com. 1995—), Fla. Bar Assn. (bd. cert. civil trial lawyer, bd. cert. admiralty lawyer), Jacksonville Bar Assn. (chmn. legal ethics com. 1975-76, bd. govs. 1976-78, pres. 1979-80), Assn. Trial Lawyers Am. (sustaining mem. 1984—), Acad. Fla. Trial Lawyers (diplomate), Fla. Coun. Bar Assn. Pres.'s, Lawyer-Pilots Bar Assn., Am. Judicature

Soc., Maritime Law Assn. (proctor in admiralty), Southeastern Admiralty Law Inst. (bd. dirs. 1982-84, chmn., pres. 1994), Am. Bd. Trial Advocates (city of Jacksonville Mpl. code enforcement bd., 2006—). Home: 1959 Largo Rd Jacksonville FL 32207-3926 Office: 901 Blackstone Bldg 233 E Bay St Jacksonville FL 32202-3452 Office Phone: 904-356-6500. Office Fax: 904-356-6508.

WHITE, EDWARD ALLEN, electronics executive; b. Jan. 1, 1928; s. Joseph and Bessie (Allen) W.; m. Joan Dixon, Dec. 22, 1949 (div. Aug. 1978); children: Leslie Ann Lollar; m. Nancy Rhoads, Oct. 6, 1979. BS, Tufts U., 1947. Chmn. bd. White Electronic Designs Corp., Phoenix, 1951—. Pres. Ariz. Digital Corp., Phoenix, 1975—91, Interactive Digital Corp., Phoenix, 1992—. Patentee in field. Bd. dirs. Gov.'s Coun. Children, Youth and Families, Phoenix, 1982-84, Planned Parenthood Fedn. Am., 1984-88; pres., bd. dirs. Planned Parenthood. Sanfrancisco, Calif.; trustee Internat. House, N.Y.C., 1973-75, Tufts U., 1973-83. Recipient Horatio Alger award, 1962. Mem.: World Pres.'s Orgn., Bohemian Club, Paradise Valley Country Club, Tau Beta Pi. Home: 5786 N Echo Canyon Cir Phoenix AZ 85018-1242 Office: White Electronic Designs Corp 3601 E University Dr Phoenix AZ 85034-7254 Home Phone: 602-840-0704; Office Phone: 602-437-1520 x111. Business E-Mail: ewhite@whiteedc.com.

WHITE, EDWARD C., chemicals executive; Fin. dir. affiliates in Finland and Poland Owens-Ill. Inc., 1996—97, v.p., dir. fin., planning, and adminstrn. Internat. Ops. Perrysburg, Ohio, 1997—99, contr., 1999—2004, v.p., 2002—03, sr. v.p., 2003—, sr. v.p. fin. and adminstrn., 2003—04, sr. v.p., dir. sales and mktg. O-I Europe, 2004—05, CFO, 2005—; contr. Owens Ill. Group Inc., pres., CFO, prin. acctg. officer. Office: Owen Ill Inc One Michael Owens Way Perrysburg OH 43551-2999 Office Phone: 567-336-5000. Fax: 419-247-1132.

WHITE, ELIZABETH NICHOLE, lab administrator, educator; b. May 5, 1964; m. Laura Jean Bell, Apr. 19, 1995. Cert. in ordination ministry Coun. Ind. Churches, 2000. Worship min. Lavender Rd. MCC, Santa Cruz, Calif., 1992—2000; lab. instrnl. asst. Cabrillo Coll., Aptos, Calif., 1995—; assoc. pastor Celebration of Faith, San Jose, Calif., 2002—04, Grace Inclusive Ch., Santa Cruz. Lectr., sex work UCSC, Santa Cruz, 1990—97. Office: Cabrillo Coll 6500 Soquel Dr Aptos CA 95003

WHITE, EMMET, JR., retirement community administrator; b. Newark, Oct. 18, 1946; s. Emmet, Sr. and June (Howlett) White; m. Betty Orr, June 7, 1970; children: Benjamin, Suzanne, George. BA, Lafayette Coll., 1968; JD, Coll. William and Mary, 1971. Bar: Hawaii 1972; nursing home adminstr., Hawaii. Law ptnr. Mau and White, AAL, Honolulu, 1975-83, White and Tom, AAL, Honolulu, 1983-95; pres., CEO Arcadia Retirement Residence, Honolulu, 1996—. Trustee Ctrl. Union Ch., Honolulu, 1980-84, chmn. 1983-84, moderator, 1987, also deacon; mem. Health Planning Coun. Honolulu, Am. Oahu Workforce Investment Bd. Col. USAR, 1968-94. Mem.: Nat. Com. Employer Support of Guard and Res. (ombudsman), Hawaii Long Term Care Assn. (chmn. 2001—03, 2007—), Hawaii Bar Assn. Avocation: physical activities. Office: Arcadia Retirement Residence 1434 Punahou St Honolulu HI 96822-4754 Office Phone: 808-983-1823. E-mail: ewhite@arcadia-hi.org.

WHITE, EUGENE G., school system administrator; b. Phenix City, Ala., Dec. 1947; m. Jetties White; children: Reginald E., Kimberly R. BS with honors in Social Studies, Health and Phys. Edn., Ala. A&M U., Normal, 1970; MS in Sch. Health, U. Tenn., Knoxville, 1971; EdS in Superintendency, Ball State U., Muncie, Ind., 1977, EdD in Edn. Adminstrn. and Supervision, 1982. Tchr., coach, sch. adminstr. Ft. Wayne Cmty. Schs.; prin. Wayne HS, 1985—90, North Ctrl. HS, Indpls., 1990—92; dep. supt. Indpls. Pub. Schs., 1992—94, supt., 2005—, Met. Sch. Dist. Washington Twp., 1992—2003. Author: Leadership Beyond Excuses: The Courage to Hold the Rope. Recipient Ctr. for Leadership Devel. Edn. Award, 1995, Modern Red Schoolhouse Disting. Svc. Award, 2006; named Outstanding Supt. of Yr., Ind. Music Educators Assn., 1997, Ind. Supt. of Yr., 2002, 2008, Supt. of Yr., Nat. Assn. Black Sch. Educators, 2007; named a Visonary Leader, Redbook mag., 1992; named to Ala. A&M U. Athletic Hall of Fame, 2001. Mem.: Am. Assn. Sch. Adminstrs. (pres. 2006—07), Ind. Assn. Pub. Sch. Supts. (past pres.), North Ctrl. Assn. (pres. commn. accreditation and sch. improvement). Office: Indianapolis Public Schools Office of the Superintendent 120 E Walnut St Indianapolis IN 46204 Office Phone: 317-226-4000.*

WHITE, FLORENCE MAY, retired special education educator; b. Ottawa, Kans., Sept. 1, 1936; d. O.C. Robert and Effie Lynne (Walker) Arnold; m. Donald L. White, June 1, 1958 (dec. Jan. 1996); children: Tab Vincent, Jacque Sue, Michelle May. BA, Ottawa U., 1958; MS, Kans. U., 1974; postgrad., Kans. U. Med. Ctr., 1975—76. Cert. reading specialist, learning disabilities specialist; cert. elem. and mid. sch. edn.: lang. arts, social studies, elem. curriculum. Classroom tchr. 2d grade Wellsville Elem., Kans., 1958-59; learning disabilities tchr. Olatha Spl. Edn. Coop., Kans., 1971-74; learning disabilities specialist, tchr. 7-9 Ottawa Mid. Sch., 1974-77; learning disabilities specialist, tchr. Paola Spl. Edn. Coop., Richmond, Kans., 1980-95; tchr. learning disabilities classes elem. level Ctrl. Heights Elem. Sch., Richmond, Kans., 2001—02. Pub. rep., speaker on learning disabilities to civic groups and local orgns., 1972-75. Den mother Boy Scouts Am. and Brownies, Ottawa, 1968-70; chair state GOP women's polit. activities Rep. State Party, Topeka, 1964-67; chair scholarship contest DAR, Ottawa dist., 1984-96; Sunday sch. tchr. Meth. Ch., Ottawa; crafts tchr. local 4-H, Ottawa; mem. Central Heights PTA (projects com. 1980-95); mem. Ottawa Arts Coun. State of Kans. scholar State Spl. Edn. Dept., 1976. Mem.: PEO, Kans. Assn. Ret. Sch. Employees, Franklin County Reading Coun. (pres.-elect 1989—91, pres. 1991—92, v.p.), Kans. Reading Assn., Internat. Reading Assn., Garden Club, Soroptimist, Ottawa Area C. of C., Alpha Delta Kappa. Roman Catholic. Avocations: oil painting, reading, travel, music, volunteer work.

WHITE, FREDERICK, literature and language professor, researcher; b. Prince Rupert, BC, Can., Mar. 21, 1960; s. Edmund Franz and Margaret Cherie Bernhard; m. Teresa White, Nov. 27, 1986; children: Elias Reyns, Hasia Nicole, Aleksander Jeremy, Adriela Isannah. PhD, U. Calif., LA, 2001. Cert. in tchg. ESL Azusa Pacific U., Calif., 1992. Asst. prof. English Azusa Pacific U., 2000—01; assoc. prof. English Slippery Rock U., Pa., 2002—. Author: (novels) Welcome to the City of Rainbows (Native Writers' Cir. Americas 1st Book award, 2006), (book) Ancestral Language Acquisition Among Native Americans: A study of a Haida Language Class. Recipient Rev. Dr. Martin Luther King Civil Leadership award, Slippery Rock U., 2006; Faculty Profl. Devel. grant, Pa. State Sys. Higher Edn., 2008—. Mem.: MLA (del. assembly 2005—07), Soc. Study Indigenous Langs. Americas. Office: Slippery Rock Univ 312 H Spotts 1 Morrow Way Slippery Rock PA 16057 Office Fax: 724-738-4839. Business E-Mail: frederick.white@sru.edu.

WHITE, GARY A., automotive executive; b. Akron, Ohio, Nov. 29, 1950; BS in Mech. Engring., Kettering U. (formerly GM Inst.), 1973; MS in Mgmt., Stanford U., 1991. Joined Fisher Body Divsn. GM Corp., Lordstown, Ohio, with Buick Motor Divsn., 1969—82; mgr. program mgmt. Flint Automotive Divsn. Buick-Oldsmobile-Cadillac Group, 1985—87, mgr. chassis/HVAC sys., 1987—91, planning dir., 1991; program dir. large luxury cars Cadillac Luxury Divsn. GM Corp., 1993—94, gen. engring. and planning mgr. Oldsmobile Divsn., 1994, vehicle line exec. high-midsize cars, 1995—99, vehicle line exec. full size trucks, 1999—, v.p. GM N.Am., 2002—. Office: GM Corp PO Box 33170 Detroit MI 48232-5170*

WHITE, GARY RICHARD, electrical engineer; b. Detroit, Nov. 15, 1962; s. Thomas Richard and Davene (Reynolds) White. BSEE, Wayne State U., 1986; MBA, MS in Info. Systems, Hawaii Pacific U., 2006. Electronics engr. U.S. Army Info. Sys. Engring. Command, Ft. Belvoir, Va., 1987-88, Ft. Shafter, Hawaii, 1988-92; elec. worker U.S. Navy Pub. Works Ctr., Pearl Harbor, Hawaii, 1992-96, plant operator, 1996—. Mem. IEEE, Air Force Assn., NSPE, Assn. Computing Machinery, US Naval Inst., Am. Mgmt. Assn. Avocations: weightlifting, bicycling, computers, music, movies. Office: PO Box 19055 Honolulu HI 96817-8055 Home Phone: 808-847-7416; Office Phone: 808-474-2202. Personal E-mail: garywhite4me@yahoo.com.

WHITE, GEORGE COOKE, theater director, foundation administrator; b. New London, Conn., Aug. 16, 1935; s. Nelson Cooke and Aida (Rovetti) W.; m. Elizabeth Conant Darling, July 5, 1958; children: George Conant, Caleb Ensign, Juliette Darling. Student, U. Paris, 1956; BA, Yale U., 1957, MFA, 1961; student, Shakespeare Inst., 1959; ArtsD (hon.), Conn. Coll., 1994. Stage mgr. Imperial Japanese Azumakabuki Co., 1955; asst. mgr. Internat. Ballet Festival, Nervi, Italy, 1955; prodn. coordinator Talent Assos., 1961-63; adminstrv. v.p. score prodns. Paramount Pictures, 1963-65; founder, pres. Eugene O'Neill Meml. Theatre Found., 1965—2000; adviser, dir. Theatre One, Conn. Coll. Women, 1967-70; exec. dir. The Johnny Mercer Found., 1999; regional theater cons. Nat. Ednl. TV Network; guest lectr. Wagner Coll., 1970; acting dir. Hunter Coll. Hunter Arts, 1972-73; chmn. Florence Acad. Art, 2004—. Adj. prof. U. NC; prof. theater adminstrn. program Yale U., 1978-91; co-chmn. Yale Drama Sch.; mem. exec. com. Theatre Libr. Assn., 1967; bd. govs. Am. Playwrights Theatre; mem. bd. ANTA, 1967-68; mem. Mayor NYC's. Theatre Adv. Com.; advisory bd. Internat. Theatre Inst.; panel mem. Exptl. Theatre; US State Dept. cultural exchange grantee to Australia; guest adminstr. Australian Nat. Playwrights Conf., 1973; US del. Internat. Theatre Inst. Congress, Moscow, 1973; mem. Conn. Commn. on Arts, 1978-93, mem. exec. com., 1979-83, vice chair, 1992-93; co-founder Caribbean-US Theatre Exchange; dir. Actors Theatre St. Paul, 1979, 80, 82, 83, 86, Hartman Repertory Theatre, 1980; guest dir. Chinese Theater Assn., Beijing, 1984, 87, Hedgerow Theatre, 1986; mem. nominating com. Antoinette Perry Awards, 1984-86, 88, 94-96, 98-2002, adminstrv. com. Am. Theater Wing, 1997; dir. Anna Christie Beijing Cen. Dramatic Theater, 1984, 87; bd. dirs. New London Day. Appeared in TV series Citizen Soldier, 1959-61; appeared in off-Broadway prodn. John Brown's Body. Trustee Goodspeed Opera House, 1966-68, Nat. Theatre Conf., 1973—, Eastern Conn. Symphony, Dance Arts Coun., Conn. Opera Assn., Conn. Pub. TV, 1973-83, Mitchell Coll., 1994—, Arts & Bus. Coun., 1994—, Arts Internat., 2001, 02, Boston Conservatory, 2000-; trustee Conn. Edn. Telecommunications Corp., 1973-83, chmn., 1982; mem. planning bd. Op. Rescue; bd. dirs. Rehearsal Club, Centre for Inter-Am. Rels., Theater of Latin Am., Manhattan Theatre Club, 1970-80, Met. Opera Guild; Performance mag.; exec. com. Yale Drama Alumni, 1963-73; mem. Yale Alumni Bd.; bd. overseers drama dept. Brandeis U.; adv. bd. Am. Musical Theatre Program, Hartford Conservatory, Bd. Arts & Bus. Coun., Brandeis Creative Arts Award Jury, Theater and New Music Theatre Works Panel, NEA; mem. Waterford (Conn.) Rep. Town Meeting, 1975-77, 2001—; presdl. appointment to Nat. Coun. NEA, 1992; mem. Nat. Coun. Arts, 1992-97; trustee Arts Internat.; bd. dirs. Day Pub. Co., RKO Pictures, American Acad. Dramatic Arts; bd. mem. Boston Conservatory; mem. Coast Guard Auxillary, watch q.m. US Coast Guard Barque Eagle. Served with AUS, 1957-59; Flotilla Cmdr., US Coast Auxillary, 1998-99, divsn. comdr., 2008-. Recipient spl. citation, New England Theatre Conf., 1968, 1998, Margo Jones award, 1968, Pub. Svc. award, New London County Bar Assn., 1975, Disting. Citizen's award, Town of Waterford, 1976, Distin. Svc. award, Conn. mag., 1981, Contbns. to State award, 1981, Lifetime Contbn. to Theatre award, Am. Theater Assn., 1989, Contbn. to Conn. Arts award, Quinnipiac Coll., 1989, Medal of Arts, Russian Federation, Chevalier des artes et des lettres (France), 1983, gold medal, Cairo Internat. Experimental Theater Festival, Cavalieri, Order of St. Maurice and Lazarus; named Officer first class, Royal Swedish Order of Polar Star; grantee Internat. Communications Agy. cultural exch. grantee to People's Republic of China, 1980. Fellow Royal Soc. Arts, Coll. of Am. Theatre; mem. Chinese Theatre Assn. (hon.). Clubs: Century; Cosmos (Washington); Thames (New London); White's Point Yacht. Office: 234 W 44th St New York NY 10036 Office Phone: 212-382-2790, 860-439-0667. Personal E-mail: whitebg@att.net.

WHITE, GEORGE EDWARD, lawyer, educator; b. Northampton, Mass., Mar. 19, 1941; s. George LeRoy and Frances Dorothy (McCafferty) W.; m. Susan Valre Davis, Dec. 31, 1966; children: Alexandra V., Elisabeth McC. BA, Amherst Coll., Mass., 1963; MA, Yale U., New Haven, Conn., 1964, PhD, 1967; JD, Harvard U., Cambridge, Mass., 1970. Bar: DC 1970, Va. 1975, US Supreme Ct. 1973. Vis. scholar Am. Bar Found., 1970—71; law clk. to Chief Justice Warren US Supreme Ct., 1971—72; asst. prof. law U. Va., 1972—74, assoc. prof., 1974—77, prof., 1977—86, John B. Minor prof. law and history, 1987—2003, disting. univ. prof., John B. Minor prof. law and history, 1992—2003, David and Mary Harrison disting. prof. law, 2003—. Vis. prof. Marshall-Wythe Law Sch. spring 1988, NY Law Sch., fall 1988; acad. visitor London Sch. Econs. and Polit. Sci., 2005. Author: The American Judicial Tradition, 1976, 3d edit., 2007, Tort Law in America: An Intellectual History, 1980 (Gavel award ABA, 1981), 2nd edit., 2003, Earl Warren: A Public Life, 1982 (Gavel award ABA, 1983), The Marshall Court and Cultural Change, 1988, 2nd edit., 1991 (James Willard Hurst prize, 1990), Justice Oliver Wendell Holmes: Law and the Inner Self, 1993 (Gavel award ABA, 1994, Scribes award, 1994, Littleton-Griswold prize, 1994, Triennial Order of the Coif award, 1996), Intervention and Detachment: Essays in Legal History and Jurisprudence, 1994, Creating the National Pastime: Baseball Transforms Itself, 1903-1953, 1996, The Constitution and the New Deal, 2000, Alger Hiss's Looking-Glass Wars, 2004, Oliver Wendell Holmes, 2006 (Green Bag award, 2008), History and the Constitution, 2007, others; editor: Oxford University Board of Syndics, The Common Law, John Harvard Libraiyed, 2009, Studies in Legal History, 1980—86, Delegate in Law, 1986—97, The Common Law, 2009. Mem. AAAS, Am. Law Inst., Am. Soc. Legal History (bd. dirs. 1978-81), Soc. Am. Historians. Office: Law Sch U Va 580 Massie Rd Charlottesville VA 22903-1789 Office Phone: 434-924-3455. Business E-Mail: gew@virginia.edu.

WHITE, GEORGE WILLIAM, theater educator; b. Dayton, Ohio, July 1, 1947; s. Raleigh Arch and Fannie Irene White; m. Joy Johnson, Mar. 18, 1972; children: Raleigh Dale, Adam Patrick. MA, Bowling Green State U., Ohio, 1989. Prof. theatre arts and chair theatre Hastings Coll., Nebr., 1976—. Past potentate Tehama Shriners, Hastings, 2006. Office: Hastings Coll 710 Turner Hastings NE 68901 Business E-Mail: gwhite@hastings.edu.

WHITE, GERALD ANDREW, retired chemical company executive; b. L.I., NY, Aug. 2, 1934; s. Charles Eugene and Grace Mary (Trojan) W.; m. Mary Alice Turvey, June 8, 1957; children— Kevin, Patricia, Timothy, Megan B in Chem. Engring., Villanova U., 1957; cert. advanced mgmt. program, Harvard Bus. Sch., 1975. Staff engr. Air Products and Chems., Inc., Allentown, Pa., 1962-65, mgr. systems devel., 1965-66, group controller, 1969-72, corp. controller, 1974-76, v.p. planning, 1977-82, v.p. fin., chief fin. officer, 1982-92, sr. v.p. fin., chief fin. officer, 1992-95. Pres. United Way in Lehigh County, 1981; bd. dirs. Pa. Coun. on Econ. Edn., 1981-95; trustee, treas. Allentown Art Mus., 1984; trustee, chmn. bd. trustees De Sales U, Center Valley, 1983. Lt. USN, 1957-62. Recipient J. Stanley Morehouse Meml. award Villanova U. Coll. Engring., 1983 Mem. AIChE, Fin. Execs. Inst. (pres. northeastern Pa. chpt. 1974-75), Fin. Execs. Rsch. Found. (trustee 1992-96), Tau Beta Pi. Avocation: squash.

WHITE, GORDON ELIOT, historian, writer; b. Glen Ridge, NJ, Oct. 25, 1933; s. Maurice Brewster and Sarah Fullilove (Gordon) W.; m. Nancy Johnson, 1955 (div. 1957); m. Mary Joan Briggs, Aug. 6, 1960 (dec. Nov. 1987); children: Sarah Elizabeth and Gordon O'Neal Brewster (twins), David McIntyre; m. Francis C. Barrineau, 1989 (div. 1996); m. Angela Tyler, Mar. 27, 1999 (dec. Mar., 2009). BA, Cornell U., 1955; MS in Journalism, Columbia U., 1957. Lic. master mariner USCG; lic. pilot FAA. Stringer Nassau Daily Rev.-Star, Rockville Centre, L.I., NY, 1948-50, Freeport (N.Y.) Leader, 1949-50; sports writer Morris County (N.J.) Citizen, 1950-51; stringer Ithaca (N.Y.) Evening News, 1951-55; photo editor, editl. writer Cornell Daily Sun, 1951-55; copy editor Am. Banker, NYC, 1958; Washington corr. Chgo. Am., 1958-61; chief Washington bur. Deseret News, Salt Lake City, 1961-88. Also corr. in Europe, U.S. and Antarctic for WJR, Detroit; KSL-KSL-TV, Salt Lake City, also KGMB, Honolulu; free lance writer with U.S. Navy, Army and Air Force, 1959; cons. Nat. Air and Space Mus.; auto racing, mil. aviation electronics historian. Author: Offenhauser, the Legendary American Racing Engine and the Men Who Built It, 1996, The Indianapolis Racing Cars of Frank Kurtis, 1940-1963, 2000, Kurtis-Kraft: Masterworks of Speed & Style, 2001, Lost Race Tracks, 2003, The Marvelous Mechanical Designs of Harry A. Miller, 2004, Ab and Marvin Jenkins and the Mormon Meteors, 2006, Leader Card Racers, Three Times Winners at Indianapolis, A History of Moore's Creek Middlesex Country, 1608—2008. Advisor auto racing Nat. Mus. Am. History, Smithsonian Instn., 1989—; curator Miller-Offenhauser Archive of historic race engine blueprints. Recipient Raymond Clapper Meml. award White House Corrs. Assn., 1978; award for excellence in reporting Exec. Dept. and White House; Roy W. Howard award for outstanding pub. svc. by a newspaper corr., 1979; award for disting. investigative reporting Investigative Reporters and Editors, 1980, Reser-Tuthill award for writing on history of automobile racing, Indpls., 1985. Mem. Nat. Press Club (Washington, Excellence in Reporting award 1979), Sigma Delta Chi (1st prize for newsphoto, 1954, Nat. award 1979), Pi Kappa Phi, Pi Delta Epsilon Episcopalian. Home and Office: PO Box 129 Hardyville VA 23070 Office Phone: 804-776-7947. Personal E-mail: gewhite@crosslink.net.

WHITE, GREGORY A., federal judge, former prosecutor; b. Nov. 1949; BA in Criminal Justice and Police Adminstrn., Kent State U., 1973; JD magna cum laude, Cleveland Marshall Coll., 1976. Atty. Wilcox and White Law Firm, 1977—84; law dir. City of Elyria, 1979; prosecutor Lorain County, Ohio, 1981—2002; US atty. US Dept. Justice, Ohio, ND, 2003—08; magistrate judge US Dist. Ct. Ohio, ND, 2008—. With USMC, Vietnam. Office: Carl B Stokes US Ct House 801 W Superior Ave Cleveland OH 44113-1845 Office Phone: 216-357-7135.

WHITE, H. KATHERINE, lawyer; b. Salina, Kans., May 21, 1945; BS, MIT, 1967; JD, Rutgers U., 1975. Bar: Calif. 1975, NJ 1982. Joined Sealed Air Corp., Elmwood Park, NJ, 1982, v.p., gen. counsel, sec., 1998—. Mem.: ABA, Soc. Corp. Secretaries and Governance Profls., NJ Corp. Counsel Assn. (dir. 1994—96), Assn. Corp. Counsel, State Bar Calif., NJ State Bar Assn. Office: Sealed Air Corp 200 Riverfront Blvd Elmwood Park NJ 07407

WHITE, HAROLD JACK, pathologist; b. Bklyn., Jan. 4, 1920; s. Abraham and Jennie (Warshawsky) W.; m. Lucette Darby, July 19, 1962; children: Elizabeth, Darby, Matthew, Esther. BS, Harvard U., 1941; MD, U. Geneva, 1952. Diplomate Am. Bd. Pathology. Intern, resident in pathology Yale U. Sch. Medicine, New Haven, 1953-58, fellow, 1957-58; assoc. pathologist Brigham and Women's Hosp., Boston, 1962-66; chief lab. svc. VA Hosp., West Roxbury, Mass., 1962-66, Little Rock, 1966-80; sr. scientist, acting head biomed. sci. dept. GM Rsch. Labs., Warren, Mich., 1980-85, cons., 1985—. Prof. pathology, microbiology U. Ark. Med. Sch., Little Rock, 1966—; vis. scientist dept. comparative medicine, MIT, Cambridge, 1988—. Contbr. over 100 articles, abstracts in pathology, microbiology, immunology, toxicology, biomedicine to profl. jours. 1st lt. USAAF, 1942-46. Fellow Coll. Am. Pathologists, Internat. Coll. Pathology. Home: 24 Bass Rocks Rd Gloucester MA 01930-3276 Office: 35 Main St Gloucester MA 01930-5730 Office Phone: 978-281-3531. Personal E-mail: hjwriverrun@aol.com.

WHITE, HELENE NITA, federal judge; b. Jackson Heights, NY, Dec. 2, 1954; d. Frank William and Ruth (Gruber) White. AB, Columbia U., 1978; JD, U. Pa., 1978. Bar: Pa. 1979, Mich. 1979. Law clk. to Justice Charles L. Levin Mich. Supreme Ct., Southfield, 1978—80; judge Common Pleas Ct., Detroit, 1981, 36th Dist Ct., Detroit, 1981—83, Wayne Cir. Ct., Detroit, 1983—93, Mich. Ct. Appeals, Detroit, 1993—2008, US Ct. Appeals (6th Cir.), 2008—. Bd. dirs., chmn. bylaws com. Met. Detroit YWCA, 1986—87, Coalition Temporary Shelter, 1986—, chmn. nominating com., 1988—; program com. bus. and profl. divsn. Jewish Welfare Fedn., 1987—; bd. advisors Sojourner Found., 1988, Detroit Women's Forum, 1988—. Mem.: ABA, Women Lawyers Assn. Mich., Nat. Assn. Women Judges (chmn. publicity 1984, membership com. 1985—), Detroit Bar Assn., Pa. Bar Assn. Jewish. Office: US Ct Appeals Theodore Levin Courthouse 231 W Lafayette Blvd Detroit MI 48226*

WHITE, HENRY F., JR., legal association administrator, retired military officer; b. NYC; BS, US Naval Acad., Annapolis, Md.; JD, Fordham U., NYC, 1976. Mem. adv. com. on comml. ops. customs and border protection US Dept. Homeland Security; mem. Hill, Betts & Nash, LLP, NYC; dep. commr. transp. City of NY, counsel to Mayor; mng. mem. Barger & Wolen LLP, NYC, 1992; pres. Inst. Internat. Container Lessors, 1999; exec. dir., COO ABA, Chgo., 2006—. Rear admiral, vice comdr., US Fleet Forces Command USNR. Office: ABA 321 N Clark St Chicago IL 60610-7598 Office Phone: 312-988-5000. Office Fax: 312-988-6281.*

WHITE, HENRY J., engineering educator, consultant; b. NYC, Nov. 20, 1965; s. Henry and Dolores White; m. Yuxie P. White, Dec. 26, 1998; children: Hillary X., Francis H. BS, Poly. U., Bklyn., 1987; MS, U. Tenn., 1992; PhD, Stony Brook U., 1999. Registered profl. engr., NY. Metall. technician Lucius Pitkin Inc., NYC, 1985—87, LI Testing Lab., North Babylon, NY, 1986—87; metallurgist ABB Lummus Global, Bloomfield, NJ, 1987—90; materials engr. Misonix Inc., Farmingdale, NY, 1993—94; mgr. heat treating ops. Skyo Industries Inc., Deer Park, NY, 1994—2000; prof. Stony Brook (NY) U., 2000—. Cons. NSF, Arlington, Va., 2000—, Air Force Office Sci. Rsch., Arlington, 2005—; ABET program evaluator Metall. Soc., Warrendale, Pa., 2002—, profl. registration com., 2003—, faculty fellow. Grantee, NSF, 2004; fellow, Am. Soc. for Engring. Edn./ NASA, 2001. Mem.: Assn. Iron and Steel Tech., Metall. Soc., Materials Rsch. Soc., Am. Soc. Engring. Edn., Am. Soc. Materials Internat. (chmn. LI chpt. 2002—03, bd. dirs. metro NY/NJ chpt. 2003—, vice chmn. metro NY/NJ chpt. 2006—. Quality Performance Program award 2002, 2003), Soc. Mfg. Engrs. Achievements include patents for densification of thermal spray coatings. Office: Stony Brook Univ Dept Materials Sci Stony Brook NY 11794-2275 Home: 12487 Windbush Way Carmel IN 46033-9174 Personal E-mail: hwhite@notes.cc.sunysb.edu.

WHITE, HERBERT SPENCER, library and information scientist, educator, dean; b. Vienna, Sept. 5, 1927; came to U.S., 1938, naturalized, 1944; s. Leon and Ernestine (Lichteneger) Hochweis; m. Mary Virginia Dyer, Feb. 19, 1953 (dec.); 1 son, Jerome; m. Nancy J. Cornell, May 1, 2002. BS in Chemistry, CCNY, 1949; MSLS, Syracuse U., 1950; PhD in Humane Letters (hon.), Ind. U., 2003. Intern Libr. of Congress, Washington, 1950, mem. tech. info. divsn., 1950-53; tech. libr. AEC, Oak Ridge, Tenn., 1953-54; organizer, mgr. corp. libr. Chance Vought Aircraft, Dallas, 1954-59; mgr. engring. libr. IBM Corp., Kingston, N.Y., 1959-62, mgr. tech. info. ctr. Poughkeepsie, N.Y., 1962-64; exec. dir. NASA Sci. and Tech. Info. Facility, College Park, Md., 1964-68; v.p. info. mgmt. Leasco Systems & Rsch. Corp., Bethesda, Md., 1968-70; sr. v.p. Inst. Sci. Info., Phila., 1970-74, corp. dir., 1971-74; pres. Stechert-Macmillan, Inc., Pennsaucken, N.J., 1974-75; prof., dir. Rsch. Ctr. Grad. Libr. Sch. Ind. U., Bloomington, 1975-80, dean Sch. Libr. and Info. Scis., 1980-90, disting. prof., 1991-95; prof. emeritus, 1995—. Adj. prof. U. Ariz. Sch. Libr. Scis., 1995—; vis. prof. Alberta, San Jose State, Hawaii; cons., lectr. Author: Librarianship Quo Vadis?, 2000, others; contbr. articles to profl. publs.; columnist Libr. Jour. Mem. Pres.'s Adv. Com. for Adminstrn. Title II-B Higher Edn. Act, 1965-68, Libr. Rsch. Planning Com. for 1980s, U.S. Dept. Edn., v.p. Green Valley Cmty. Coordinating Coun., 1997—; grant reviewer Inst. Mus. and Librs., 1998—. Spl. honoree, U. of Essen (Germany) Conf., 1992. Fellow Spl. Libraries Assn. (pres. 1969-70, J.C. Dana award 1985, Hall of Fame 1994); mem. ALA (councillor 1988-92, planning com. 1989-91, Dewey medal 1987), Am. Soc. Info. Sci. (pres. 1973-74, W. Davis award 1977, award of merit 1981, named Pioneer, 1987), Assn. Libr. and Info. Sci. Edn. (chmn. govtl. rels. com. 1980-88), Am. Fedn. Info. Processing Socs. (dir. 1972-78), Federation Internationale de Documentation (Netherlands, bd. dir. 1976-78, treas. 1978-82), Soc. for Scholarly Pub. (bd. dirs. 1981-82), Assn. Rsch. Libraries (com. on libr. edn, 1983-85), Coun. Libr. Resources (rsch. priorities task force 1984-88, Ind. Libr. Lifetime Achievement award 1990), Beta Phi Mu (Svc. award 1995). Address: 13500 N Rancho Vistoso Blvd # 523 Tucson AZ 85755-5951

WHITE, HOWARD D., information science educator; b. 1936; PhD in Librarianship, U. Calif., Berkeley, 1974. With Coll. Info. Sci. and Tech. Drexel U., Phila., 1974—, prof. libr. sci., disting. prof., 1998—2002, prof. emeritus, 2002—. Contbr. articles to profl. publs.; co-author (with Marcia Bates and Patrick Wilson): For Information Specialists: Interpretations of Reference and Bibliographic Work, 1992; author: Brief Tests of Collection Strength, 1995. Recipient Rsch. award, Am. Soc. Info. Sci. and Tech., 1993, Award of Merit, 2004, Derek John de Solla Price Meml. medal, Internat. Soc. Scientometrics and Informetrics, 2005. Office: Drexel U Coll Info Sci & Tech Rush Bldg 421 33rd and Market St Philadelphia PA 19104 Office Phone: 215-895-2484. Office Fax: 215-895-2494. E-mail: whitehd@drexel.edu.

WHITE, IAN, information technology executive; m. Ellen White; 3 children. Grad. in Elec. Engring., U. Nottingham, Eng.; grad. in Electronic Engring., Derby Tech. Coll., Eng. With Rolls Royce; rsch. & devel. engr. telecom. co.; with Computervision, Sun Microsystems, Inc., 1989—, dir. UK customer svc. ops. & customer edn., dir. UK Installed Base Sales & Sales Support, v.p. Europe, Mid. East and Africa, v.p. Internat. Ams., v.p. Sun Svcs. Ams., sr. v.p. global customer svcs. Office: Sun Microsystems Inc 4150 Network Cir Santa Clara CA 95054 Office Phone: 650-960-1300.

WHITE, JACK (JOHN ANTHONY GILLIS), musician; b. Detroit, July 9, 1975; m. Meg White, Sept. 21, 1996 (div. Mar. 24, 2000); m. Karen Elson, June 1, 2005; children: Scarlett Teresa, Henry Lee. Former drummer Goober and the Peas, The Go, The Upholsterers, Jack White and The Bricks; singer, guitarist The White Stripes, 1997—, The Raconteurs, 2005—, The Dead Weather, 2009—; founder Third Man Records, Nashville, 2009—. Singer: (albums with The White Stripes) The White Stripes, 1999, De Stijl, 2000, White Blood Cells, 2001, Elephant, 2003 (Grammy award for best alternative music album, 2003, Grammy award for best rock song, 2003), Get Behind Me Satan, 2005, Icky Thump, 2007 (Grammy award for best alternative music album, 2008, Grammy award for best duo rock performance with vocals, 2008), (songs with The Whites Stripes) Conquest, 2007 (Best Cinematography, MTV Video Music Awards, 2008), (albums with The Raconteurs) Broken Boy Soldiers, 2006, Consolers of the Lonely, 2008 (Grammy award for best engineered non-classical album, 2009), (albums with The Dead Weather) Horehound, 2009; prodr.: (albums) Lack of Communication, 2001, Do Rabbits Wonder?, 2003; prodr., contbr. (Loretta Lynne albums) Van Lear Rose, 2004 (Grammy award for best country album, 2004), actor, composer (films) Cold Mountain, 2003; actor: (films) Coffee and Cigarettes, 2003, Walk Hard: The Dewey Cox Story, 2007; (documentaries) Shine a Light, 2008. Office: Press Here Publicity 138 W 25th St New York NY 10001*

WHITE, JAMES BOYD, law educator; b. Boston, July 28, 1938; s. Benjamin Vroom and Charlotte Green (Conover) W.; m. Mary Louise Fitch, Jan. 1, 1978; children: Emma Lillian, Henry Alfred; children by previous marriage: Catherine Conover, John Southworth. AB, Amherst Coll., 1960; AM, Harvard U., 1961, LLB, 1964. Assoc. Foley, Hoag & Eliot, Boston, 1964-67; asst. prof. law U. Colo., 1967-69, assoc. prof., 1969-73, prof., 1973-75; prof. law U. Chgo., 1975-83; Hart Wright prof. law and English U. Mich., Ann Arbor, 1984—. Vis. assoc. prof. Stanford U., 1972 Author: The Legal Imagination, 1973, (with Scarboro) Constitutional Criminal Procedure, 1976, When Words Lose Their Meaning, 1981, Heracles' Bow, 1985, Justice as Translation, 1990, "This Book of Starres", 1994, Acts of Hope, 1994, From Expectation to Experience, 1999, How Should We Talk About Religion?, 2006, The Edge of Meaning, 2001, Living Speech, 2006, Law and Democracy in the Empire of Force, 2009. Sinclair Kennedy Traveling fellow, 1964-65; Nat. Endowment for Humanities fellow, 1979-80, 92; Guggenheim fellow, 1993; vis. scholar Phi Beta Kappa, 1997-98. Mem. AAAS, Am. Law Inst. Office: U Mich Law Sch 1035 Legal Research 625 S State St Ann Arbor MI 48109-1215 Office Phone: 743-936-2989. Business E-Mail: jbwhite@umich.edu.

WHITE, JAMES EDMUND, architect, educator; b. Anson, Tex., Feb. 21, 1933; s. Victor Philemon and Lucy Alice (Baker) W.; m. Wanda Sue Sandlin, Aug. 6, 1970. B.Arch., U. Tex., 1957; M.S., Tex. Tech U., 1973. Registered architect, Tex. Draftsman, F.C. Olds., Abilene, Tex., 1957; draftsman, ptnr. Peters and Fields, Odessa, Tex., 1962-71; mem. faculty Tex. Tech U., Lubbock, 1971—; pres. White Assocs., Lubbock, 1971—; dean Coll. Architecture Tex. Tech. U. 1997-2002; mem. intern devel. com. Nat. Council Archtl. Registrations Bd., Washington, 1984-86, regional dir. Intern Devel. Program; Served with USAF, 1957-61. Mem. AIA (sec. Lubbock chpt. 1974, 1977, treas. chpt. 1979), Tex. Soc. Architects (state coordinator intern devel. 1982-84, bd. dirs. 1986-87), Tau Kappa Epsilon (chpt. advisor 1981—2003). Democrat. Methodist. Avocations: painting; golf.

WHITE, JAMES PATRICK, law educator; b. Iowa City, Sept. 29, 1931; s. Raymond Patrick and Besse (Kanak) W.; m. Anna R. Seim, July 2, 1964. BA, U. Iowa, 1953, JD, 1956; LLM, George Washington U., 1959; LLD (hon.), U. Pacific, 1984, John Marshall Law Sch., 1989, Weidner U., 1989, Campbell U., 1993; Jur D (hon.), Whittier Coll., 1992; LLD (hon.), Campbell U., 1993, Southwestern U., 1995, Quinnipiac U., 1995, Calif. Western Law Sch., 1997; LLD, Roger Williams U., 1999, New England Sch. of Law, 2001, Seattle U., 2001, We. New Eng. Coll., 2002; LHD (hon.), Barry U., 2005. Bar: Iowa 1956, D.C. 1959, U.S. Supreme Ct. 1959. Teaching fellow George Washington U. Law Sch., 1958-59; asst. prof. U. N.D. Law Sch., Grand Forks, 1959-62, asso. prof., acting dean, 1962-63, prof., asst. dean, 1963-67; dir. agrl. law rsch. program, prof. law Ind. U. Law Sch., Indpls., 1967—2002, also dir. urban legal studies program, 1971-74, prof. emeritus, 2002—; dean acad. devel. and planning, spl. asst. to chancellor Ind. U., Indpls., 1974-83. Mem. for N.D., Commn. on Uniform State Laws, 1961-66; cons. legal edn. ABA, 1974-2001, cons. emeritus, 2001—. Contbr. papers to tech. lit. Trustee Butler U., John Marshall Law Sch., Atlanta, Indpls. Mus. Art. Capt. JAGC, 1st lt. USAF, 1956—58. Recipient Thomas More award, St. Mary's U., 1965, Sagamore of the Wabash award, State of Ind.; Carnegie postdoctoral fellow, U. Mich. Ctr. for Study Higher Edn., 1964—65. Fellow: China-US Commn. Legal Edn. (commr.), Soc. for Advanced Legal Studies (Eng.) (chair Fulbright com. awards in law 1989—92), Am. Bar Found. (life), Indpls. Bar Found. (disting. fellow); mem.: ABA (Kutak award medal 2001), Indpls. Bar Assn., Am. Law Inst. (life), Iowa Bar Assn., Ind. Bar Assn., Woodstock Club (Indpls.), Order of Coif. Roman Catholic. Home: 7707 N Meridian St Indianapolis IN 46260-3651 Office: Ind U 530 W New York St Indianapolis IN 46202-3225 Home Phone: 317-253-4066; Office Phone: 317-278-9690. Business E-Mail: jwhite@iupui.edu.

WHITE, JAMES RICHARD, lawyer; b. McKinney, Tex., Jan. 22, 1948; s. James Ray and Maxine (Brown) White; children: Nicole Olivia, Mandi Leigh, James Derek. BBA, So. Meth. U., 1969, MBA, 1970, JD, 1973, LLM, 1977. Bar: Tex. 1973, US Tax Ct. 1975, US Supreme Ct. 1989, US Ct. Appeals (5th cir.) 1989); cert. Comml. Real Estate Law Tex. Bd. Legal Specialization. Assoc. Elliot, Meer, Vetter, Denton & Bates, Dallas, 1973-74, Atwell, Cain & Davenport, Dallas, 1974-75; atty. Sabine Corp., Dallas, 1975-77; assoc. Brice & Barron, Dallas, 1977-79; ptnr. Millard & Olson, Dallas, 1979-82, Johnson & Swanson, Dallas, 1982-83, Winstead, Sechrest & Minick P.C., Dallas, 1983—, hiring ptnr., 1987-2001, exec. com., 2000-01. Mem. staff Southwestern Law Jour., Dallas, 1971-73; mem. So. Meth. U. Moot Ct. Bd., Order Barristers, Dallas, 1972-73; prof. North Lake Coll., Dallas, 1985; bd. dirs. Tex. Assn. Young Lawyers, Austin, 1980-82; sec. bd. dirs. Dallas Assn. Young Lawyers, 1976-80; adv. bd. Sports Source Inc., 2007-. Contbr. articles to profl. jours. Chmn. bd. dir. Tex. Lawyers Credit Union, Austin, 1980-82; pres. North Tex. Premier Soccer Assn., Dallas, 1979-81; v.p. Lake Highlands Soccer Assn., 1995-96, pres., 1996—; North Tex. State Soccer Assn., Volunteer of the Year, 2003; mem. regional mobility task force Real Estate Coun., City of Dallas, 1991-92, mem. downtown revitalization com., 1995-97; mem. Dallas Indsl. Devel. Bd., 1992-93, Dallas Higher Edn. Authority Bd., 1994-96; spkr.'s bur. and accreditation divsn. World Cup USA '94; mem. exec. coun. Recreational Interleague Assn. Dallas, 2002—; pres. Storm Soccer Club, 2003-05; founding mem. Premiere Acad. League, 2004—; mem. outstanding sr. man selection com. dad's club So. Meth. U., 2007, bd. mem., 2007-, pres. 2009-. Staff sgt. 49th Armored Divsn. Tex. Nat. Guard, 1969—75. Named Vol. of the Yr., North Tex. State Soccer Assn., 2003; named a Texas Super Lawyer, 2003—; named to Best Lawyers in Am., 2003—. Mem. ABA (mem. title ins. and survey, mortgage loan origination and structure com., mortgage financing and opinion, non-traditional comml. real estate fin. coms.), Tex. Bar Assn. (cert. 1973, mem. mortgage loan opinion com.), Tex. Coll. Real Estate Attys., Coll. State Bar Tex., Storm Soccer Club (pres. 2003-05). Methodist. Avocations: soccer, golf, skiing, racquetball. Home: 8003 Hundley Ct Dallas TX 75231-4728 Office Phone: 214-745-5126. Business E-Mail: jrwhite@winstead.com.

WHITE, JEFFERY LANE, chemistry professor, researcher; b. Houston; s. Wesley Buren and Shelia Ann (Cortines) White; m. Stacie Suzanne Bratz, Aug. 23, 1986; children: Lane, Hannah, Elissa. BSc, Stephen F. Austin U., 1987; PhD, Tex. A&M U., 1992. Postdoctoral fellow AT&T Bell Labs., Murray Hill, NJ, 1992—93; rsch. chemist Exxon Chem., Houston, 1993—98; group leader ExxonMobil Rsch., Houston, 1998—2000; asst. prof. N.C. State U., Raleigh, 2000—04, assoc. prof., 2004—. Contbr. articles to profl. jours.; patentee in field. Deacon Kingwood (Tex.) 1st Bapt. Ch., 1996—2000; Royal Amb. leader Forest Hills Bapt. Ch., Raleigh, 2003—05; mem. Bible Study Fellowship Internat., Apex, NC, 2003—05. Divsn. materials rsch. grantee, NSF, 2002—. Mem.: Am. Phys. Soc., Am. Chem. Soc. (PRF Type G grantee 2002—04), Sigma Xi. Office: Oklahoma St Univ Phys Sci I Stillwater OK 74078

WHITE, JEFFREY MUNROE, lawyer; b. Lewiston, Maine, Jan. 16, 1948; BS in Applied Physics magna cum laude, Tufts U., Medford, Mass., 1970; JD, Boston Coll., 1975. Bar: Maine 1975, US Ct. Appeals (1st cir.) 1979. Semiconductor engr. Fairchild Semiconductor, 1970—72; ptnr., head litig. group and antitrust and trade regulation group Pierce Atwood, Portland, Maine, 1975—. Lectr., contbr. to profl. publs. on antitrust, litig., and intellectual property topics. Chmn. Cape Elizabeth Sch. Study Com., 1990-91, Corporator Hospice of So. Maine, 2004-; mem. IS Eng. adv. coun. U. Maine, 2006-. Mem. ABA (antitrust, intellectual property and litig. sects.), N.E. Bar Assn. (dir. 1982-85), Maine Bar Found., Maine State Bar Assn. (co-chmn. com. CLE 1981-83), Maine Trial Lawyers Assn., Cumberland County Bar Assn. Office: Pierce Atwood Monument Sq Portland ME 04101 Office Phone: 207-791-1100. Business E-Mail: jwhite@pierceatwood.com.

WHITE, JENNIFER ELIZABETH BELK, corporate training specialist; b. Houston, July 29, 1967; d. Joe Harvey and Joan Pardue Belk; m. Thomas Roger White, Apr. 28, 2007. BA, U. Tex., Austin, 1988; postgrad., U. Houston, Clear Lake, 1990—91, U. So. Calif., LA, 2007. Admissions counselor U. Tex., Austin, 1988—90; coll. field rep. Prentice Hall, Houston, 1990—92; trainer Kaplan Test Prep and Admissions, NYC, 1993—97, master tchr. LA, 1997—2001, dir. of tng., 2001—04; mgr. internal communication and instrnl. design Pub. Storage, Glendale, Calif., 2004—07, corp. tng. mgr., 2007—08; sr. mgr. tng. and devel. Internat. Coffee & Tea LLC, 2007—08, dir. tng. & devel., 2008—. Vol. L.A. Chamber Orch., 2004—; mem. Angel City Chorale, LA, 2004—, mng. dir., 2005—08; deacon St. Philip Presbyn. Ch., Houston, 1991—93. Recipient People's Choice award, Pub. Storage, 2005, 2006; named Tchr. of Yr., Kaplan Test Prep and Admissions, 1994. Mem.: ASTD, Coun. Hotel and Restaurant Trainers, Internat. Soc. Performance Improvement, Mensa, Golden Key, Alpha Lambda Delta, Phi Eta Sigma. Office: Coffee Bean and Tea Leaf 1945 S La Cienega Blvd Los Angeles CA 90034 Personal E-mail: jenbelkwhite@gmail.com.

WHITE, JESSE, Secretary of State, Ill; b. Alton, Ill., June 23, 1934; BS, Ala. State Coll., 1957. Profl. baseball player Chgo. Cubs; tchr., adminstr. Chgo. Pub. Sch. Sys.; mem. Ill. Gen. Assembly, Springfield, 1972—74, 1976—92, chmn. com. human svcs., mem. edn. com., mem. select com. children and aging; recorder of deeds Cook County, Chgo., 1992—98; sec. state State of Ill., Springfield, 1999—. Founder Jesse White Tumbling Team, 1959; Dem. committeeman 27th Ward, Chgo., 1996—; libr. State of Ill. State Libr.; archivist State of Ill. Served in Ill. Nat. Guard, paratrooper 101st Airborne Divsn. US Army. Recipient Archbishop Richard Chenevix Trench award, 1999; Inductee Southwestern Athletic Conf. Hall of Fame, 1995, Chgo. Pub. League Basketball Coaches Assn. Hall of Fame, 1995, Ala. State U. Sports Hall of Fame, 1999; named one of 100 Most Influential Black Americans, Ebony mag., 2006. Democrat. Office: Sec of State 213 State Capitol Springfield IL 62706 Office Phone: 217-782-2201. Office Fax: 217-785-0358. E-mail: jessewhite@ilsos.net.

WHITE, JILL CAROLYN, lawyer; b. Santa Barbara, Calif., Mar. 20, 1934; d. Douglas Cameron and Gladys Louise (Ashley) W.; m. Walter Otto Weyrauch, Mar. 17, 1973. BA, Occidental Coll., LA, 1955; JD, U. Calif., Berkeley, 1972. Bar: Fla. 1974, Calif. 1975, U.S. Supreme Ct. Staff mem. U.S. Dept. State, Am. Embassy, Rio de Janeiro, 1956-58; with psychol. rsch. units Inst. Human Devel., Inst. Personality Assessment and Rsch., U. Calif., Berkeley, 1961-68; adj. prof. criminal justice program U. Fla., Gainesville, Fla., 1976-78; pvt. practice immigration and nationality law, Gainesville, 1976—2002. Contbr. articles to profl. jours. Mem.: Fla. Bar (immigration and nationality law cert. com. 1994—99, chmn. cert. com. 1997—98, cert. in immigration and nationality law 1995—), Bar Assn. 8th Jud. Cir. Fla., Am. Immigration Lawyers Assn. (bd. dirs. Ctrl. Fla. chpt. 1985—94, 1995—96, 1997—2000, chmn. Ctrl. Fla. chpt. 1988—89, co-chmn. so. regional liaison com. 1990—92, nat. bd. dirs. 1988—89), Altrusa. Democrat. Home Phone: 352-375-6205; Office Phone: 352-380-9122. Personal E-mail: jwhite49@earthlink.net.

WHITE, JOHN, JR., lawyer; b. St. Louis, Oct. 20, 1943; s. John Aaron and Helen Inez (Stewart) White; children: Dorian, Cameron, Lauren, John Aaron III. BA, U. Nev., 1965; JD, George Washington U., 1968. Bar: DC 1969, Nev. 1969, US Dist. Ct. (DC cir.) 1969, US Supreme Ct. 1979. Atty. City Atty.'s Office, Reno, 1969—74; sole practice Reno, 1974—78; ptnr. White Law Chartered, Reno, 1978—. Adj. prof. in bankruptcy Old Coll. Nev. Sch. Law, 1986—87; lectr. computers and law Nev. State Bar Conv., 1986. Co-author: Nevada Civil Practice Manual, 1986—88. Mem. Gov.'s Commn. on Status People, 1975—78; founder Family Ch. Jesus. With USMC, 1961—68. Mem.: ABA, Washoe County Bar Assn., Am. Bankruptcy Inst., DC Bar Assn., Nev. State Bar Assn., Reno Host Lions (past pres.). Republican. Achievements include pioneer in litigating early cases against Dow Corning and Dow Chemical involving silicone breast implants. Office: White Law Chartered 335 W 1st St Reno NV 89503-5344 Office Fax: 775-322-1228. E-mail: john@whitelawchartered.com.

WHITE, JOHN ARNOLD, physics professor, research scientist; b. Chgo., Jan. 30, 1933; s. Maxwell Richard and Dorothy Edith (Arnold) W.; m. Rebecca Anne Cotten, June 20, 1964; children: Lauren, Thomas, Julia. BA, Oberlin Coll., 1954; MS, Yale U., 1955, PhD, 1959. Instr. physics Yale U., 1958-59, Harvard U., 1959-62; research assoc. Yale U., 1962-63; research physicist Nat. Bur. Standards, Washington, 1963-64; research assoc. U. Md., College Park, 1965-66; assoc. prof. Am. U., Washington, 1966-68, prof., 1968-97, prof. emeritus, 1997—. Cons. Nat. Bur. Standards, 1965-72; mem. tech. staff Bell Telephone Labs., summers 1954, 60-62; vis. scientist MIT, fall 1972, Nat. Bur. Standards, Washington, summer 1981; vis. prof. Inst. for Phys. Sci. and Tech., U. Md., College Park, fall 1993. Author sci. papers on atomic structure and fluorescence, magnetism, lasers, speed of light, thermodynamic fluctuations, critical point phenomena, extended renormalization group theory of fluids. Recipient (with Zoltan Bay) Boyden Premium Franklin Inst., Phila., 1980; honor scholar, 1950-54; Noyes Clark fellow, 1954-57; NSF fellow, 1957-58; grantee NSF, 1966, 67, 69, 71; grantee Office Naval Research, 1973, 74; Am. Soc. Engring. Edn. faculty fellow Naval Research Lab., Washington, summer 1985; Dept. Energy Office Basic Energy Scis. grantee, 1986, 88, 90. Fellow Am. Phys. Soc.; mem. AAUP, Washington Philos. Soc., Phi Beta Kappa, Sigma Xi. Home: 7107 Fairfax Rd Bethesda MD 20814-1234 Office: Am U Dept Physics Washington DC 20016-8058 E-mail: jwhite@american.edu.

WHITE, JOHN AUSTIN, JR., engineering educator, retired academic administrator; b. Portland, Ark., Dec. 5, 1939; s. John Austin and Ella Mae (McDermott) W.; m. Mary Elizabeth Quarles, Apr. 13, 1963; children: Kimberly Elizabeth White Brakmann, John Austin III. BS in Indsl. Engring., U. Ark., 1962; MS in Indsl. Engring., Va. Poly. Inst., 1966; PhD, Ohio State U., 1970; PhD (hon.), Cath. U. of Leuven, Belgium, 1985, George Washington U., 1991. Registered profl. engr., Va. Indsl. engr. Tenn. Eastman Co., Kingsport, 1961-63, Ethyl Corp., Baton Rouge, 1965; tchg. assoc. Ohio State U., Columbus, 1966-70; instr. Va. Poly. Inst. and State U., Blacksburg, 1963-66, asst. prof., 1970-72, assoc. prof., 1972-75, Ga. Inst. Tech., Atlanta, 1975-77, prof., 1977-84, Regents' prof., 1984-97, Gwaltney prof., 1988-97, dean engring., 1991-97; disting. prof. indsl. engring. U. Ark., Fayetteville, 1997—, chancellor, 1997—2008. Asst. dir. engring. NSF, 1988-90, acting dep. dir., 1990-91; founder, chmn. SysteCon Inc., Duluth, Ga., 1977-84; exec. cons. Coopers & Lybrand, N.Y.C., 1984-93; mem. mfg. studies bd. NRC, Washington, 1986-88; bd. dirs. Russell Corp., 1992-2006, Eastman Chem. Co., 1994-2004, Motorola Corp., 1995-, Logility Inc., 1997-2009, J.B. Hunt Transport Svcs., Inc., 1998-, Nat. Sci. Bd., 1995-2006, Malcolm Baldrige Nat Quality Award Found., 1999-2008; pres. Southeastern U. Rsch. Assn., 2003-04, chair coun. presidents 2004; pres. Nat. Consortium for Grad. Degrees for Minorities in Engring. and Sci., Inc., 1993-95; bd. dirs. Nat. Collegiate Athletic Assn.; mem. exec. com. NCAA, 2002—05; apptd. U.S. del. to the Internat. Steering Com. of the Intelligent Mfg. System, 1995-97; dir. Ark. Sci. and Tech. Authority, 2002-08, chair, 2004-05; dir. Ark. Biosciences Inst. 2002-; pres. S.E. Conf., 2002—04, pres. NW Ark. Regional Airport Authority, 2005-08; co-chair NW Ark. Coun., 2005-08. Co-author: Facility Layout and Location: An Analytical Approach, 1974 (Book of Yr. award Inst. Indsl. Engrs. 1974), 2d edit., 1991, Analysis of Queueing Systems, 1975, Principles of Engineering Economic Analysis, 4th edit., 1998, Capital Investment Decision Analysis for Management and Engineering, 1980, 3d edit., 2005, Facilities Planning, 1984 (Book of Yr. award Inst. Indsl. Engrs. 1984), 3rd edit., 2003; editor: Production Handbook, 1987; co-editor: Progress in Materials Handling and Logistics, Vol. 1, 1989; also numerous articles to profl. jours., chpts. to books and handbooks in field, conf. procs. Recipient Outstanding Tchr. award Ga. Inst. Tech., 1982, Disting. Alumnus award Ohio State U. Coll. Engring., 1984, Disting. Indsl. Engring. alumnus award Va. Polytech. Inst. and State U., 1993, Reed-Apple award Material Handling Edn. Found., 1985, Disting. Svc. award NSF, 1991, Rodney D. Chipp Meml. award Soc. Women Engrs., 1994, Disting. Alumnus award U. Ark. Alumni Assn., 2005, Humanitarian of Yr. award NW Ark. chpt. Nat. Coalition for Cmty. and Justice, 2005. Fellow Am. Inst. Indsl. Engrs. (pres. 1983-84, facilities planning and design award 1980, outstanding indsl. engr. award region III 1974, region IV 1984, Albert G. Holzman disting. educator award 1988, outstanding pub. award 1988, David F. Baker disting. rsch. award 1990, Frank and Lillian Gilbreth award 1994), Am. Soc. Engring. Edn. (Donald E. Marlowe award 1994), Inst. Ops. Rsch. & Mgmt. Scis., 2002, Nat. Soc. Profl. Engrs. Inst. for Ops. Rsch. and the Mgmt. Scis. (hon.), Am. Assn. Engring. Socs. (bd. govs., chmn. 1986, Kenneth Andrew Roe award 1989); mem. Nat. Acad. Engring., Ark. Acad. Indsl. Engring. (John L. Imhoff Global Excellence award 2006), Internat. Material Mgmt. Soc. (material mgr. of yr. 1989), Soc. Mfg. Engrs. (mfg. educator award 1990), Golden Key, Sigma Nu (Regent's medallion of Merit 2005), Alpha Pi Mu, Omicron Delta Kappa, Phi Kappa Phi, Tau Beta Pi, Omega Rho. Baptist. Avocations: reading, golf, writing. Office: U Ark Engr 308 Fayetteville AR 72701 Office Phone: 479-575-2773. E-mail: jawhite@uark.edu.

WHITE, JOHN D., legislative staff member; Legis. dir. to congressman Mazie Hirono US House of Reps., Washington, 2007, chief of staff, 2008—. Democrat. Mailing: US House Reps 1524 Longworth HOB Washington DC 20515 Office Phone: 202-225-4906. Office Fax: 202-225-4987. Business E-Mail: john.white@mail.house.gov.*

WHITE, JOHN DAVID, composer, author; b. Rochester, Minn., Nov. 28, 1931; s. Leslie David and Millie (Solum) W.; m. Marjorie Manuel, Dec. 27, 1952; children: Jeffrey Alan, Michele Kay, David Eliot. BA magna cum laude, U. Minn., 1953; MA, U. Rochester, 1954, PhD, 1960, performance cert., 1960. Mem. faculty Kent (Ohio) State U., 1956-58, 60-63, 65-73, prof. music, assoc. dean Grad. Sch., 1967-73; asst. prof. U. Mich., 1963-65; dean Sch. Music, Ithaca (N.Y.) Coll., 1973-74; vis. prof. U. Wis., 1975-78; chmn. music dept. Whitman Coll., 1978-80; prof. U. Fla., 1980-97, prof. emeritus, 1997—; prof. U. Innsbruck, 1994; dist. chair U. Vienna, 2003—04. Prin. cellist Eastman Philharmonia, 1959, Akron Symphony Orch., 1969-73; cellist Fla. Baroque Ensemble, 1980-97, Fla. Arts Trio, 1986-93; dir. Fla. Musica Nova, 1991-97; author: (with A. Cohen) Anthology of Music for Analysis, 1965, Understanding and Enjoying Music, 1968 (pub. in Japanese 1978), Music in Western Culture, 1972, The Analysis of Music, 1976, 2d edit., 1984, Guidelines for College Teaching of Music Theory, 1981, 2d edit., 2002, Comprehensive Musical Analysis, 1994, Theories of Musical Texture in Western History, 1995, New Music of the Nordic Countries, 2002; editor: Music and Man; editl. bd. Jour. for Musicological Research, Jour. Music Theory Pedagogy; contbr. articles to profl. jours.; Composer: Symphony No. 2, 1960, Blake Songs, 1961; Divertimento for Flute, Violin and Viola, 1961; opera The Legend of Sleepy Hollow, 1962; Three Choruses From Goethe's Faust, 1965, Three Joyce Songs, 1966, Ode to Darkness, 1967, Cantos of the Year, 1969; (for clarinet and piano) Variations, 1971, Whitman Music, 1970, Three Madrigals, 1971, Russian Songs for Voices and Winds, 1972, Prayer (Solzhenytsin), 1973, String Quartet 1, 1975, Variations, 1976, Suite, 2001; Ode on the Morning of Christ's Nativity (Donne), 1977, Music for Oriana, 1978, Pied Beauty, 1980; (for cello and piano) Sonata, 1981, Zodiac, 1981, Music for violin and piano, 1982, The Soft Voice, 1983, Concerto for Flute and Wind Ensemble, 1983, Dialogues, 1984, Sonata for Piano, 2001, Symphony for Wind Band (3rd Symphony), 1985, Concerto da Camera, 1985, Symphony for a Saint (4th Symphony), 1986, Music for Cello and Percussion, 1988, Songs of the Shulamite, 1989, Mirrors, 1990, But God's Own Descent (5th Symphony), 1991, Music of the Open Road, 1993, Daylight and Moonlight, 1993, O Sing to the Lord a New Song, 1993, Illusions for Three, 1994, Tryptich, 1994, Ars Poetica, 1995, Colors of Earth and Sky (6th Symphony), 1995, Summer Storm Madrigals, 1996, Time and the Water, 1996, O Sing to the Lord a New Song, 1997, Maria Laudata, 1998, God's Own Descent, 1998, The Song of Ruth, 1999, Symbolic Interaction for Orchestra, 1999; Suite for for Harpsichord, 1999, The Heavens are Telling, 1999, Flower Songs, 2000, Concerto, 2000 for Piano and Winds, Sonata da Camera for Piano, 2001, Music for 2 Cellos, 2002, Pindar Hymns for Choir and Orch., 2003, Abraham Lincoln walks at Midnight 2003, Olympiad for Chorus, Brass, Percussion and Piano, 2004, The Canonical Hours for Chorus, 2005, Music for Victims of our Earth, 2005, Echoes and Airs for Soprano, Viola and Piano, Mass for Chorus, 2006, Alone and not Alone, 2006, The Divine Image, 2007, Daystar(Lincoln), 2008, O Captain, My Captain, Credo Trifarium, 2008; recs. on Advent, Mark, Capstone, Cygnus and Opus One Labels. With AUS, 1954-56. Recipient Benjamin award, 1960, award Nat. Fedn. Music Clubs, 1962, internat. composition award U. Wis.-Oriana Trio, 1979, composition award Am. Choral Dirs. Assn., 1984; grantee NEA; Fulbright rsch. fellow, 1995-96; Fulbright Disting. Lectr., 2003-04. Fellow Am. Scandinavian Found., 1997; mem. ASCAP (awards 1965—), Soc. Composers, Inc. (nat. coun. 1987-89, 93-96), Coll. Music Soc. (Seqorbe Choral Festival 1st prize, 2008), Soc. Music Theory, Pi Kappa Lambda, Delta Omicron (nat. patron), Phi Mu Alpha, Phi Beta Delta. Home: 10599 N Osceola Dr Westminster CO 80031 Personal E-mail: jwhite48@earthlink.net.

WHITE, JOHN DAVID, social sciences educator; s. Clarence Everet and Elwanda June White. BS, Ea. Ill. U., Charleston, 1978; MDiv, United Theol. Sem., Dayton, 1982; MA in History, Western Ill. U., Macomb, 2008. Assoc. pastor First United Meth. Ch., East Peoria, Ill., 1982—86; pastor Oquawka United Meth. Ch., Ill., 1986—88; dist. exec. Southeast Iowa Coun. Boy Scouts Am., Burlington, 1989—93; sr. dist. exec. Miss. Valley Coun. Boy Scouts Am., Quincy, Ill., 1993—95; custodian Trinity United Meth. Ch., Keokuk, Iowa, 1996—2002; social sci. instr. Southeastern CC, Keokuk, 2002—. River valley dist. tng. chair., commr Miss. Valley Coun. Boy Scouts Am., Keokuk, 1996—2008; com. chair Venture Crew 43, Keokuk, 2007—08; foster care rev. bd. chair South Lee County, Iowa Citizens Vol. Foster Care Rev. Bd., Keokuk, 1995—2002; mem., Foster Care Rev. Bd. South Lee County, Iowa Citizens, 2002—08; ct. apptd. spl. adv. Iowa Child Advocacy Bd., Keokuk, 2005—08; com. chair Boy Scout Troop 43, Keokuk, 2005—08, Cub Scout Pack 43, Keokuk, 2005—08; lead tchr. Learning Life Group 143, Keokuk, 2005—08; sunday sch. tchr. Trinity United Meth. Ch., Keokuk, 2000—08, scouting coord. Mem.: Golden Key Internat. Avocations: travel, reading. Home: 3 South Oak Ct Keokuk IA 52632

WHITE, JOHN P., consulting firm executive, public policy educator; b. Syracuse, NY, Feb. 27, 1937; BS in Indsl. & Labor Rels., Cornell U., 1954; MA in Economics, Syracuse U., 1964, PhD in Economics, 1969. Dir. manpower, pers., & training rsch. The RAND Corp., 1969—71, v.p. rsch., 1971—75, sr. v.p. nat. security rsch. programs, 1975—77; asst. sec. for manpower, reserve affairs & logistics US Dept. Def., 1977-78; dep. dir. Office Mgmt. & Budget, Exec. Office of the Pres., 1978-81; CEO, chmn. Interactive Sys. Corp., 1981-88; gen. mgr. integration and sys. products divsn., v.p. Eastman Kodak Co., 1988-92; faculty dir. Ctr. for Bus. and Govt. John F. Kennedy Sch. Govt., Harvard U., 1992-95, Robert & Renee Belfer lectr., 1998—; dep. sec. US Dept. Def., Washington, 1995-97; mng. ptnr. Global Tech. Partners LLC, Washington, 1998—. Bd. dirs. L-3 Communications Corp., 2004—, IRG Internat. Inc., Inst. Def. Analyses, The Concord Coalition; mem. policy & global affairs oversight com. Nat. Rsch. Coun. Bd. trustees The RAND Corp., 1973—. Served in USMC, 1959—61. Recipient Medal for Disting Pub. Svc. (2), US Dept. Def. Mem.: Coun. Fgn. Rels. Office: Global Technology Partners LLC PO Box 290825 Charlestown MA 02129 also: John F Kennedy Sch Govt Harvard U Mailbox 58 79 JFK St Cambridge MA 02138 E-mail: John_White@ksg.harvard.edu.*

WHITE, JOHN PATRICK, lawyer; b. Boston, Oct. 14, 1946; s. John Marion and Margaret Patricia (Gannon) W.; m. Gemma Mary Flattly, Feb. 9, 1980; 1 son, John Myles. BS in Chem. Engring., Columbia U., 1968, MA in Biochemistry, 1971, MPh in Molecular Biology, 1975; JD, Fordham U., 1977. Bar: NY 1978, US dist. ct. (ea. and so. dists.) NY 1978, US Ct. Customs and Patent Appeals 1979, US Ct. Appeals (Fed. cir.) 1982, US Supreme Ct. 2006. Legis. dir. Cmty. Coun. Greater N.Y., 1971-77; assoc. Cooper, Dunham, Clark, Griffin & Moran, NYC, 1977-81, ptnr., 1981-88, Cooper & Dunham, LLP, NYC, 1988—. Owner Shallow Brook Farm, Stillwater, N.J.; breeder Reg Angus Cattle, Ringneck Pheasants and Carriage Horses; dir. OSI Pharm., Inc., Bio-Tech. Gen. Corp., Thioltech, Inc.; instr. Practicing Law Inst., Fordham Law Sch. Internat. IP Conf. Contbr. articles to sci. and legal jours. Democratic dist. leader, 1975-81; vice chmn. Dem. Com. N.Y. County, 1977-81; jud. del. 1st jud. dept., 1975, 76, 77, 79; adminstr. screening panel 2d Mcpl. Ct. Dist.; pub. mem. Columbia U. Recombinant DNA Biosafety Com. Columbia U. faculty fellow, 1969-71; NIH grantee, 1969-71. Mem. ABA, Am. Chem. Soc., Am. Intellectual Property Law Assn. (com. patents), NY Intellectual Property Law Assn., Assn. Bar City NY(com. patents), Fed. Bar Coun. (conver Inn Coust), Fedn. Cir. Bar Assn., Lic. Exec. Soc., Rockefeller U. Coun, Columbia U. Sci. Rsch. Adv. Com., Club: Columbia of NYC, Four In Hand Club (exec. com. mem.), Newton (NJ) Country Club, NY Coaching Club. Office: Cooper & Dunham LLP 20th Fl 30 Rocksfeller Plz New York NY 10112-2202 Office Phone: 212-278-0421. Business E-Mail: jwhite@cooperdunham.com.

WHITE, JOHN VALERY, dean; BA, Southern U.; JD, Yale U., 1991. Orville Schell fellow Human Rights Watch, NYC; J. Dawson Gasquet Meml. prof. law La. State U.; disting. vis. prof. U. Insubria, Como, Italy; dean, prof. law U. Nev. Las Vegas Boyd Sch. Law. Dir. summer prog. La. State U., Lyon, France. Office: U Nev Las Vegas 4505 S Maryland Pkwy Box 451003 Las Vegas NV 89154 Office Phone: 702-895-1876. Business E-Mail: john.white@unlv.edu.*

WHITE, JOHN VINCENT, surgeon, consultant; b. Chgo., May 7, 1952; s. Ralph and Angela White. BS, Northwestern U., 1974; MD, Columbia U., 1978. Diplomate Am. Bd. Surgery. Instr. surgery Columbia U., NYC, 1982-83; asst. prof. surgery Temple U., Phila., 1984-88, assoc. prof. surgery, 1988-94, prof. surgery, 1994-99; clin. prof. surgery U. Ill. Sch. Medicine; chmn. dept. surgery Luth. Gen. Hosp., Park Ridge, Ill., 1999—. Adj. sr. fellow Sch. Health Econs. U. Pa., Phila., 1994—; tech. cons. Boston Scientific Corp., Natick, Mass., 1995—; surg. cons. Dept. of Health N.Y. State, 1993; surg. tech. cons. Congl. Office of Tech. Assessment, Washington, 1995; laser tech. cons. Office of Naval Rsch., Washington, 1993-97, cons. NSF Biomed. Engring. Program, 2007-09. Editor: Hemodilution in Patient Care, 1989, Alternatives to Open Vascular Surgery, 1995, Surgical Clinics of North America, 1998; founding editor: Jour. Laparoendoscopic Surgery, 1990. Recipient Samuel D. Gross award Phila. Acad. Surgery, 1992. Mem. Am. Soc. Laser Medicine and Surgery, Soc. Univ. Surgeons (mem. found. bd. dirs. 1994-98), Del. Valley Vascular Soc. (pres. 1995—), Soc. Vascular Surgery (mem. com. outcomes analysis 1994—), Midwestern Vascular Soc., Alpha Omega Alpha. Office: Lutheran Gen Hosp 1775 Dempster St Park Ridge IL 60068-1173 Office Phone: 847-723-7200. Office Fax: 847-696-3394. Business E-Mail: john.white-md@advocatehealth.com.

WHITE, JOHN WESLEY, JR., retired academic administrator; b. Nashville, Oct. 20, 1933; s. John W. and Ernestine (Engle) W.; m. Martha Ellen Bragg, June 24, 1956; children: Marcus Wesley, Michelle Suzanne. Student, Martin Jr. Coll., 1952-54; BA, Vanderbilt U., 1956, BD, 1959; MA, George Peabody Coll., 1966, PhD, 1968; LHD, U. Nebr., 1983; LLD, Kwansai Gakuin U., Japan, 1991. Dean admissions, dir. student affairs Martin Coll., 1960-65; asst. to acad. v.p. George Peabody Coll., 1965-67; assoc. dean for humanities Oklahoma City U., 1968-70, dean Coll. Arts and Scis., 1970-77, assoc. prof. English, 1968-73, prof., 1973-77; pres. Nebr. Wesleyan U., 1977-97, chancellor, 1997-98, pres. emeritus, 1998—. Cons., spkr. in field; chmn. Nebr. Ednl. Temecom. Commn., 1996-97. Past pres. U. Senate, United Meth. Ch.; bd. dirs. Cooper Found. Eli Lilly Sr. scholar Vanderbilt U., 1959. Mem. Nat. Assn. Ind. Colls. and Univs. (bd. dirs. 1989-93, 95-97), Lincoln C. of C. (bd. dirs. 1990-93), Rotary (pres. West Oklahoma City 1976), Kappa Delta Pi, Phi Kappa Phi, Alpha Mu Gamma, Blue Key. *Two principles have been paramount in my life: One, related to the attitude toward myself, is that we can help to shape life, not simply endure it. We are "creative" creatures, not just "surviving" creatures. The second principle, related to the attitude toward others, is that communication is essential to coexistence; and only as we make a real effort to hear what is meant, rather than simply what is said or written, are we able to communicate effectively.*

WHITE, JOSEPH CHARLES, manufacturing and retailing company executive; b. Toronto, Aug. 14, 1922; s. Joseph Cleveland and Edith Parker (Johnson) W.; m. G. Evelyn Vipond, July 15, 1944; children—Ronald, Richard, JoAnne. Chartered acct., Queens U., Kingston, Ont.; B.Commerce, U. Toronto. Vice-pres., dir. Agnew-Surpass, Inc., Brantford, Ont., Can., 1964-78; v.p., dir. Genesco Can., Inc., Cambridge, Ont., Can., 1978-82, exec. v.p., dir., 1982-87, pres., gen. mgr. retail op., 1986-87. Dir., v.p. Genesco Group Inc.; dir. Genesco Fin. Ltd.; pres. Brantford Art Gallery, 1994-95, Brantford Probus Club, 1995-96. Chmn. Ross MacDonald Found., Brantford, Ont., 1983-86; pres. YMCA, Brantford, 1968-69; chmn. Brant County Post-Secondary Edn. Corp., Brantford, 1973-76. Served with Royal Can. Air Force, 1943-45 Mem. Ont. Inst. Chartered Accts., Can. Council Distbn. (pres. 1972-73), Brant County C. of C. (treas. 1966-68) Mem. United Ch. of Can. Avocations: skiing, tennis. Office: Genesco Can Inc 401 Fountain St Cambridge ON Canada N3H 4V5

WHITE, JOY MIEKO, retired communications executive; b. Yokohama, Japan, May 1, 1951; (parents Am. citizens); d. Frank Deforest and Wanda Mieko Mellen; m. George William White, June 5, 1948; 1 child, Karen. BA in Comm., Calif. State U., Fullerton, 1974, student Secondary Teaching Credential in Journalism/English, 1977; student, Orange Coast CC, Costa Mesa, Calif., 1981, Golden West CC, Westminster, Calif., 1990. Cert. secondary tchr., Calif.; cert. tchr. higher edn. Coast CC Dist. Secondary tchr. Anaheim Union H.S. Dist., Calif., 1977—80; tech. writer Pertec Computer Corp., Irvine, Calif., 1980—81; supr. large sys. disvn. Burroughs, Mission Viejo, Calif., 1981—83; mgr. Lockheed divsn. CalComp, Anaheim, 1983—86; owner, pres. Communicator's Connection, Irvine, 1986—90; pres. Info Team, Inc., 1989—2004; ret., 2004. Adj. faculty, coord. tech. comm. program Golden West Coll., Westminster, Calif., 1987-90; instr. U. Calif., Irvine, 1987-89, Calif. State U., Fullerton, 1988-91; sec. Santa Ana Dist. chpt. US SBA Assn. for Minority-Owned Bus., 1991-96; presenter in field, 1981—. Active Performing Arts, Costa Mesa, 1986— Recipient Achievement Pin, Girl Scouts San Gorgonio Coun., 2002, Silver award, Points Light Found., Vol. Ctr. Nat. Network. Fellow Soc. Tech. Comm. (assoc., internat. assoc., sr., Orange County chpt. 1987, Mem. of Yr.); mem. NAFE, Soc. Profl. Journalists, Women in Comm. (pres. Orange County Profl. chpt. 1989-90), Nat. Assn. Women Bus. Owners, Rembrandts Wine Club (Yorba Linda), Girl Scouts USA (life, active 1958—, troop leader 1995-2003, vol. 1994—). Republican. Avocations: writing short stories, travel, needlecrafts. Home: 3531 Brentridge Dr Corona CA 92881-8445 Office Phone: 951-818-3891. Personal E-mail: joywhitemk@ca.rr.com. Business E-Mail: infoteam@ca.rr.com.

WHITE, JOYCE LOUISE, librarian; b. Phila., June 7, 1927; d. George William and Louisa (Adams) W. BA, U. Pa., 1949; MLS, Drexel U., 1963; MA in Religion, Episc. Sem. S.W., 1978. Head libr. Penniman Libr. Edn. U. Pa., Phila., 1960-76; archivist St. Francis Boys' Home, Salina, Kans., 1982-84; libr. Brown Mackie Coll., Salina, 1983-86; libr., dir. St. Thomas Theol. Sem., Denver, 1986-95; libr., dir. Archbishop Vehr Theol. Libr. Archdiocese of Denver, 1995-96. Author: Biographical and Historial Yarnall Library, 1979, Colorado Episcopal Clergy in the 19th Century: A Biographical Register, 2003; asst. editor: Women Religious History Sources, 1983; contbr. articles to profl. jours. and chpts. to books. Vol. libr. St. John's Cath., Denver, 1993—. Mem. Ch. and Synagogue Libr. Assn. (life, founding, pres. 1969-70, exec. sec. 1970-72, exec. bd. 1967-76, ann. conf. chair 1996). Avocations: gardening, cats, church libraries. Office: 1350 Washington St Denver CO 80203-2008

WHITE, JUDITH MIRIAM, biology professor; PhD, Harvard U., Cambridge, MA, 1979. Asst. prof. U. Calif., San Francisco, 1985—91, assoc. prof., 1991—93; prof. U. Va., Charlottesville, 1994—. Sci. adv. bd. Trimeris, Durham, NC, 1996—2003. Contbr. articles to sci. jours. Grant, NIH, 1985—. Fellow: Am. Assn. Advancement Sci. Achievements include research in biomedical sciences.

WHITE, JULIE M., bank executive; BA in English and Polit. Sci., Bethel U.; attended U. Minn. Training mgr. CENEX; joined Wells Fargo & Co., 1987, sr. v.p. human resources Norwest Svcs., Inc., 1994, human resources Norwest Ops. and Norwest Tech. Svcs., exec. v.p. human resources and comm. Home and Consumer Fin., 1998—2007, exec. v.p., dir. human resources, 2007—. Mem. Wells Fargo Housing Found. Bd. mem. Best Buddies Ctrl. Iowa. Office: Wells Fargo & Co 420 Montgomery St San Francisco CA 94163*

WHITE, KATE, editor-in-chief; m. Brad Holbrooke; 2 children. BA, Union Coll. Editl. asst. to feature writer Glamour mag.; editor Child mag., 1988—89; editor-in-chief Working Woman mag., NYC, 1989—91, McCall's mag., NYC, 1991—94, Redbook, NYC, 1994—98, Cosmopolitan mag., NYC, 1998—. Author: Why Good Girls Don't Get Ahead and Gutsy Girls Do, 1995, (novels) If Looks Could Kill, 2002, A Body to Die For, 2003, 'Til Death Do Us Part, 2004, Over Her Dead Body, 2005, Lethally Blonde, 2009. Recipient Matrix award, Women in Comm., 2003. Office: Cosmopolitan Hearst Corp 300 W 57th St New York NY 10019-3299 also: Sandra Dijkstra Lit Agy 1237 Camino Del Mar Del Mar CA 92014 Office Phone: 212-649-3561. Office Fax: 212-397-7581.*

WHITE, KATHERINE RUSSELL, lawyer; b. Washington, 1949; m. Thomas W. Urquhart. BA, Goucher Coll., 1971; JD, U. Md., 1976. Bar: Md. 1976, N.C. 1986. Clk. Hon. Marshall Levin, Balt., 1974-76, Hon. Richard A. Gilbert, Annapolis, Md., 1976-77; reporter The Sun, Balt., 1977-80, The Charlotte (N.C.) Observer, 1981-86; asst. atty. gen. Dept. Justice, Raleigh, N.C., 1986-89; atty. pvt. practice, Raleigh, NC, 1989—98; vis. lectr., comms. law N.C. State U., 1992—98, N.C. office of Info. Tech. Svcs., 1999—2009; gen. counsel NC Dept. Transp., 2009—. Contbg. author: North Carolina Focus, 1989, 96, State Government, 1996, N.C. Insight, 2005. Mem. Nat. Freedom of Info. Coalition, Dallas, 1990— (Achievement award 1995).

WHITE, KENDRED ALAN, lawyer; b. Madisonville, Tenn., Oct. 2, 1938; s. Leonard A. and Nora (Clyde) W.; m. Peggy Ann Cowling, Aug. 24, 1963; children: Jonathan C., Erik K., Lauren A. BS, U. Tenn., 1961, JD, 1964. Bar: Tenn. 1964, U.S. Dist. Ct. (ea. dist.) Tenn. 1966, U.S. Supreme Ct. 1971. Pvt. practice law, Madisonville, 1964—. Hearing com. Bd. of Profl. Responsibility, Tenn. Supreme Ct., 1982-85; bd. dirs. Vol. Fed. S&L, Madisonville. With USAF, 1958-64. Fellow Tenn. Bar Found.; mem. ABA, Tenn. Bar Assn., Phi Delta Phi (province pres. 1996-2004). Republican. Baptist. Avocation: travel.

WHITE, KENNETH SPENCER, SR., lawyer; b. Lynchburg, Va., Oct. 31, 1939; s. Kenneth L. and Bertha (Spencer) W.; m. Jane Stafford Baber, June 23, 1962; children: Virginia White O'Keefe, Kenneth Spencer Jr., Charles B. BS, U. Va., 1962, JD, 1965. Bar: Va. 1965. Ptnr. Edmunds & Williams, P.C., Lynchburg, 1966—2000, of counsel, 2000—08. Chmn. bd. dirs. Bank of James Fin. Group, Inc., 2000—, Centra Health, Inc., 2009—. Pres. Va. Bd. of Edn., 1983-86; chmn. Va. Pub. Sch. Authority, 1990-94; mem. Commonwealth Transp. Bd., 2002—. Fellow Am. Bar Found., Va. Law Found. (trustee 1981-86); mem. ABA (chmn. standing com. on profl. utilization and career devel. 1978-80), Va. Bar Assn. (exec. com. 1977-80), Lynchburg Bar Assn. (pres. 1977). Episcopalian. Home: 1616 Langhorne Rd Lynchburg VA 24503-3118

WHITE, KERR LACHLAN, retired physician, foundation administrator; b. Winnipeg, Man., Can., Jan. 23, 1917; s. John Alexander and Ruth Cecelia (Preston) Stevenson; m. Isabel Anne Pennefather, Nov. 26, 1943; children: Susan Isabel, Margot Edith. BA with honors (Oliver Gold medal), McGill U., 1940, MD, CM, 1949; DM (hon.), U. Leuven, 1978; postgrad., London Sch. Hygiene and Tropical Medicine, 1960; DSc (hon.), McMaster U., 1983. Intern, resident in medicine Mary Hitchcock Meml. Hosp., Hanover, NH, 1949—52; Hosmer fellow McGill U. and Royal Victoria Hosp., Montreal, Que., Canada, 1952—53; asst. prof. medicine U. N.C. Sch. Medicine, Chapel Hill, 1953—57, assoc. prof. medicine and preventive medicine, 1957—62;

Commonwealth advanced fellow Med. Rsch. Coun., Social Medicine Rsch. unit London Hosp., 1959—60; chmn., prof. epidemiology and community medicine U. Vt., Burlington, 1962—64; prof. Sch. Hygiene and Pub. Health Johns Hopkins U., Balt., 1965—76, chmn. dept. health care orgn., 1965—72; dir. Inst. Health Care Studies United Hosp. Fund N.Y., 1977—78; dep. dir. health scis. Rockefeller Found., NYC, 1978—97, ret., 1997. Chmn. U.S. Nat. Com. Vital and Health Stats., 1975—79; mem. health adv. panel Office of Tech. Assessment, U.S. Congress, 1975—82; cons. Nat. Ctr. Health Stats., 1967—83, WHO, 1967—. Editor: Manual for Examination of Patients, 1960, Medical Care Research, 1965, Health Care: An International Study, 1976, Epidemiology as a Fundamental Science, 1976, Task of Medicine, 1988, Healing the Schism, 1991; mem. editl. bd.: Med. Care, 1962—73, Inquiry, 1967—79, Internat. Jour. Epidemiology, 1971—81, Internat. Jour. Health Svcs., 1971—; contbr. chapters to books, articles to profl. jours. Trustee Case-Western Res. U., 1974—79; bd. dirs. Found. for Child Devel., 1969—80. With Can. Army, 1942—45. Recipient Pew Primary Care Achievement award, 1995, Baxter Found. award, 1996, Wood award for lifetime contbns. to primary care rsch., 1999. Fellow: APHA (gov. coun. 1964—68, 1971—73, coun. med. care sect. 1962—65), NAS (Inst. Medicine coun. 1974—76, chmn. membership com. 1975—77), ACP, AAAS, Am. Heart Assn., Am. Acad. Preventive Medicine, Royal Soc. Medicine (hon.); mem.: AMA, Kerr L. White Inst. Health Svcs. Rsch. (hon. dir. 1995—), Internat. Epidemiol. Assn. (hon.; life, pres. 1974—77, treas., exec. com. 1964—71, 1974—77, coun. 1971—81), Am. Hosp. Assn. (adv. coun. ednl. and rsch. trust 1965—68), Assn. Tchrs. Preventive Medicine (coun. 1963—68), Century Club (N.Y.C.), Cosmos Club (Washington), Alpha Omega Alpha, Sigma Xi. Office Phone: 434-972-2499. Business E-Mail: klw2j@virginia.edu.

WHITE, KEVIN M., athletic director; b. Amityville, NY, Sept. 25, 1950; m. Jane Gartland; children: Maureen, Michael, Daniel, Brian, Mariah. BBA, St. Joseph's Coll., 1972; B in Bus. Athletic Adminstrn., Ctrl. Mich. U.; PhD, So. Ill. U.; postdoctoral, Harvard U., 1985. Coach Gulf HS, New Port Richey, Fla., Southeast Mo. State U., Ctrl. Mich. U.; athletic dir., v.p. devel. Loras Coll., Dubuque, Iowa, 1982-87; athletic dir. U. Maine, Orono, 1987-91, Tulane U., New Orleans, 1991-96, Ariz. State U., Tempe, 1996-2000, Notre Dame U., Ind., 2000—08, Duke U., Durham, NC, 2008—. Office: Duke Univ Athletic Dept Box 90555 Durham NC 27708

WHITE, LAWRENCE J., economics professor; b. NYC, June 1, 1943; s. Martin H. and Florence M. (Meiman) W. AB, Harvard U., 1964, PhD, 1969; MS in Econs., London Sch. Econs., 1965. Econ. adviser Harvard Devel. Adv. Svc., Pakistan and Indonesia, 1969-70; asst. prof. econs. Princeton U., NJ, 1970-76; mem. faculty Stern Sch. Bus., NYU, 1976—, prof. econs., 1979—, chmn. dept., 1990-95, dep. chmn. dept., 2005—; sr. staff economist U.S. Coun. Econ. Advisers, 1978-79; dir. econ. policy office, antitrust div. Dept. Justice, Washington, 1982-83. Mem. Fed. Home Loan Bank Bd., 1986-89; cons. in field. Author: The Automobile Industry Since 1945, 1971, Industrial Concentration and Economic Power in Pakistan, 1974, Reforming Regulation: Processes and Problems, 1981, The Regulation: Processes and Problems, 1981, The Regulation of Air Pollutant Emissions from Motor Vehicles, 1982, The Public Library in the 1980s: The Problems of Choice, 1983, International Trade in Ocean Shipping Services: The U.S. and the World, 1988, The S&L Debacle: Public Policy Lessons for Bank and Thrift Regulation, 1991; editor or co-editor: The Deregulation of the Banking and Securities Industries, 1979, Mergers and Acquisitions: Current Problems in Perspective, 1982, Technology and the Regulation of Financial Markets: Securities, Futures and Banking, 1986, Private Antitrust Litigation: New Evidence, New Learning, 1988, The Antitrust Revolution, 1989, Bank Management and Regulation, 1992, Structural Change in Banking, 1993, The Antitrust Revolution: The Role of Economics, 2d edit., 1994, The Antitrust Revolution: Economics, Competition, and Policy, 3d edit., 1999, 4th edit., 2004; 5th edit., 2009; N.Am. editor Jour. Indsl. Econs., 1984-87, 90-95; co-editor Rev. of Indsl. Orgn., 2003-04, gen. editor, 2004-. NSF fellow, 1965—69. Mem. Am. Econ. Assn., Western Econ. Assn. Internat. (bd. mem., treas. 2006—), Phi Beta Kappa. Office: NYU Stern Sch Bus 44 W 4th St New York NY 10012-1126 Office Phone: 212-998-0880. Business E-Mail: lwhite@stern.nyu.edu.

WHITE, LINDA DIANE, lawyer; b. NYC, Apr. 1, 1952; d. Bernard and Elaine (Simons) Schwartz; m. Thomas M. White, Aug. 16, 1975; 1 child, Alexandra Nicole. AB, U. Pa., Phila., 1973; JD, Northwestern U., Chgo., 1976. Bar: Ill. 1976. Assoc. Walsh, Case, Coale & Brown, Chgo., 1976-77, Greenberger & Kaufmann (merged into Katten, Muchin), Chgo., 1977-82, ptnr., 1982—85, Sonnenschein Nath & Rosenthal LLP, 1985—, chair fin. com., 2007—. Mem. law bd. Northwestern U. Sch. Law; mem. trustees coun. Penn Women. Fellow: Am. Bar. Found.; mem.: ABA (mem. real property, probate and trust law sect. 1987—, mem. real property fin. com., mem. comml. leasing com.), Practical Real Estate Lawyer (editl. bd.), Practicing Law Inst. (chmn. program negotiating comml. leases 1995—99, mem. real estate law adv. com.), Chgo. Bar Assn., Ill. Bar Assn. Office: Sonnenschein Nath & Rosenthal LLP 7800 Sears Tower 233 S Wacker Dr Ste 7800 Chicago IL 60606-6491 Home Phone: 312-943-5108; Office Phone: 312-876-8950. Business E-Mail: lwhite@sonnenschein.com.

WHITE, LISA L., diversified financial services company executive; 2 children. BA in Journalism, U. Ga., Athens, 1983. Mgmt. assoc. Columbus Bank and Trust, Ga.; sr. v.p. direct customer solutions, Synovus Technologies Synovus Fin. Corp., Columbus, Ga., pres., CEO synovusbank.com, sr. v.p., sr. dir. Innovative Solutions divsn. Active United Way. Named one of 25 Women to Watch, US Banker, 2008. Office: Synovus PO Box 120 Columbus GA 31902*

WHITE, LONNIE JOE, retired history educator; b. Knox City, Tex., Feb. 12, 1931; s. John Alexander and Fannie Coates White; m. Nancy Louella Evans, June 23, 1951; children: John Evans, Brenda Jo White Holman. BA in History, W. Tex. State Coll., 1950; MA in History, Tex. Tech. Coll., 1955; PhD in History, U. Tex., Austin, 1961. Tchg. asst. history U. Tex., Austin, 1957—61; prof. history Memphis State Univ. (now U. Memphis), 1961—89; prof. emeritus U. Memphis, 1989—. Editl. adv. bd. Jour. of the West, Manhattan, Kans., 1963—88; assoc. edit. Military History of Texas and the Southwest, Austin, Tex., 1977—88. Author: Politics on the Southwestern Frontier: Arkansas Territory, 1819-1836, 1964, Panthers to Arrowheads: The 36th (Texas-Oklahoma) Division in World War I, 1984, The 90th Division in World War I: The Texas-Oklahoma Draft Division in the Great War, 1996; co-author: Hostiles and Horse Soldiers: Indian Battles and Campaigns In the West, 1972; co-editor: By Sea to San Francisco, 1849-50: The Journal of Dr. James Morison, 1977, 2nd edit., 2000; editor: Old Mobeetie, 1877-1885: Texas Panhandle News Items from the Dodge City Times, 1967, The Miles Expedition of 1874-1875: An Eyewitness Account of the Red River War, 1971, Chronicle of a Congressional Journey: The Doolittle Committee in the Southwest, 1865, 1975; contbr. more than 45 articles to profl. jour., book reviews over 97 pub. to prof. jour. Sgt. US Army, 1951—53. Grantee Rsch. Grant, Am. Philos. Soc., 1963. Mem.: So. Hist. Assn., Am. Hist. Assn. Republican. Baptist. Avocations: history, writing, travel, flying, genealogy.

WHITE, LOWELL ELMOND, JR., retired medical educator; b. Tacoma, Wash., Jan. 16, 1928; s. Lowell E. and Hazel (Conley) W.; m. Margie Mae Lamb, June 21, 1947; children: Henry, Leanna White Maynes, Inger-Britt White Peterson. BS in Pharm., U. Wash., 1951, MD, 1953. Diplomate Am. Bd. Neurol. Surgery. Intern N.C. Meml. Hosp., Chapel Hill, 1953-54; resident neurosurgery, asst. to instr. U. Wash., 1954-60, asst. prof., 1960-64, assoc. prof., 1964—68; asso. dean U. Wash. Sch. Medicine, 1965-68; prof. surgery & neurosic., chief divsn. neurol. surgery U. Fla., 1968—72; prof. neurosci. U. South Ala., 1972—94, chmn. divsn. neurosci., 1972-77, ret., 1994. Adj. prof. speech pathology audiology Ala. Sch. Math. and Sci., 1993-94; chmn. nat. adv. com. Animal Resources NIH, 1966-70; cons. rsch. facilities and resources NIH; cons. divsn. hosp. and med. facilities USPHS; cons. grants adminstrn. policy U.S. Dept. HEW. Contbr. articles profl. jours. Bd. dirs. Mobile County Emergency Med. Svcs. Com., 1973-82, Epilepsy chpt. Mobile, 1973-89, Mobile cpt. Myasthenia Gravis Found. Am., 1974-90, Mobile, Ala. Mental Health Assn., 1979-89, Spl. Edn. Action Com., 1985-97, pres. 1996; vol. Homeland Security Med. Res. Corps and ARC, 2005-. With USN, 1946—47, with USNR, 1948—66. Guggenheim fellow, 1958-59 Mem. AMA, Am. Assn. Neurol. Surgeons, Am. Assn. Neuropathologists, Am. Acad. Neurol. Surgeons, Soc. for Neurosci., Assn. Am. Med. Colls., Am. Assn. Anatomists, Rsch. Soc. Neurol. Surgeons, Neurosurg. Soc. Ala. (pres. 1975), Am. Physicians Poetry Assn., Odyssey U. South Ala., Soc. for Arts in Healthcare, Snohomish County Med. Soc., Sigma Xi. Home: 11009 E Villa Monte Dr Mukilteo WA 98275-4881

WHITE, LUTHER G., finance educator; b. Sanford, NC, June 14, 1945; s. Robert Glenn and Elsie Riddle White; m. Carlene Meacham, June 8, 1969; 1 child, Kristin White del Rosso. BS in Bus. Adminstrn., U. NC, Chapel Hill, 1967; MBA, East Carolina U., Greenville, North Carolina, 1969; PhD, U. SC., Columbia, 1972. Lectr. East Carolina U., Greenville, NC, 1969; rsch. fellow U. SC., Columbia, 1971—72, asst. prof., 1976—77, Marshall U., Huntington, W.Va., 1972—76, 1979—86, Clemson U., SC, 1977—79, cons., 1978—79; evening dir. Beaufort CC, Washington, NC, 1986—87; bus. dept. chmn. Ctrl. Carolina Cmty., Sanford, NC, 1987—2003; instr. Ctrl. Carolina CC, Sanford, 2003—. Cons. Greenville Chamber of Commerce, Greenville, SC, 1978—79. Contbr. articles to rsch. jours. V.p. Optimists, Huntington, W.Va., 1972—83. Named Coll. Advisor of Yr., U. SC., Columbia, 1970—71, Prof. of Yr., Marshall U., 1981—82, Coll. Employee of Yr., Ctrl. Carolina CC, Sanford, 1988; Faculty Rsch. grants, Marshall U., 1975—76. Avocations: gardening, sports. Business E-Mail: lwhite@cccc.edu.

WHITE, LYNN H., psychology professor, researcher; d. Robert D. and Shirley White; m. Andrew R. Milner, May 11, 1996; children: Burgess A Milner, Troilus R. BA in Applied Psychology, Bishop's U., Lennoxville, Que., Can., 1990; MA in Physiol. Psychology, McGill U., Montreal, Que., Can., 1993, PhD in Physiol. Psychology, 1997. Asst. prof. psychology Southern Utah U., Cedar City, 1997—2003, assoc. prof. psychology, 2003—09, prof. psychology, 2009—. Dir. behavioral neuroscience lab Southern Utah U., 1998—, dir. psychology undergraduate rsch. lab, 1999—, instl. rev. bd. dir., 2000—06, dir. undergraduate rsch., 2006—; liaison officer Coun. on Undergraduate Rsch., Washington, 2002—03. Mem. Human Rights Com. Danville Svcs., Cedar City, 1999—; vice chair Iron Parke Corp., Cedar City, Utah, 1997—2002. Mem.: Rocky Mountain Psychol. Assn. (assoc.), Alpha Chi (hon.; Utah beta faculty sponsor 1998—, region vii v.p. 2002—04, region vii pres. 2004—06). Avocations: fossil collecting, camping, hiking, Karate. Office: Southern Utah Univ 351 West University Blvd Cedar City UT 84720 Office Fax: 435-865-8289. Business E-Mail: white_l@suu.edu.

WHITE, MARTHA VETTER, allergist, immunologist; b. Richmond, Va., Oct. 23, 1951; d. Robert Joseph and Miriam Ernestine (Thomas) Vetter; m. Frederick Joseph Kozub, Oct. 11, 1975 (div. June 1982); m. John Irving White, Feb. 18, 1984; children: Josh, Christie. Student, Vanderbilt U., Nashville, 1969-71; BA, U. Richmond, 1973; MD, Va. Commonwealth U., Richmond, 1978. Cert. m. Bd. Pediatrics, Am. Bd. Allergy and Immunology. Pediatric intern and resident Va. Commonwealth U., Richmond, 1978-81; locum tenans Pub. Health, Richmond, Va., 1981-82; fellow Allergy and Immunology U. Southern Calif., LA, 1983-84, Georgetown U., 1983-84; sr. staff fellow Food and Drug Adminstrn., Bethesda, Md., 1984-85; NSRA fellow Nat. Inst. Allergy and Infectious Diseases, Bethesda, Md., 1985-88; sr. staff fellow, 1988-93; rsch. dir. Inst. for Asthma and Allergy, Wheaton, Md., 1993—. Cons. Sandoz Pharms., Marion Merrell Dow, Glaxo, Boehringer Ingleheim, Ciba-Geigy, Miles Genentech; rschr. Glaxo, Abbott, Pfizer, Marion Merrell Dow, Miles, Rhône Poulenc Rhoen, Sanofi, Adams, Astra, Merck, Neurbiol. Techs., 3M, Zeneca, Wyeth, Smith-Kline Beecham; bd. dirs. Allery & Asthma Network/Mothers of Asthmatics, 1987—; med. editor MA Report, 1986—; assoc. editor Allergy, Asthma and Immunology Guide, 1989-90. Contbr. numerous scientific papers, abstracts, chpts. and reviews in field. Recipient Norwich Eaton Rsch. award, 1987; Merrell Dow scholar in allergy, 1989; Geigy fellow, 1984. Mem.: Soc. Prin. Investigators (pres. 2002—03), Am. Thoracic Soc., Am. Coll. Allergy and Immunology, Adm. Acad. Allergy and Immunology, Am. Acad. Pediat., Am. Assn. Immunologists, Gamma Sigma Epsilon, Psi Chi, Beta Beta Beta. Office: Inst Asthma and Allergy 11002 Veirs Mill Rd # 414 Wheaton MD 20902 Home Phone: 301-962-1600; Office Phone: 301-962-5800.

WHITE, MARTIN CHRISTOPHER, academic administrator; b. Anderson, SC, Oct. 16, 1943; s. Jesse Martin and Christine Freida (Powell) W.; m. Linda Ann Fleming, July 31, 1965; children: Martin Lynn, Andrew Christopher. AB, Mercer U., 1965; MDiv, So. Bapt. Theol. Sem., 1968; PhD, Emory U., 1972. Prof. Elon Coll. (N.C.), 1972-76, dean acad. affairs, 1976-82, v.p. for acad. and student affairs, 1982-86; pres. Gardner-Webb U., Boiling Springs, NC, 1986—2002, Chowan U., Murfreesboro, NC, 2002—. Cons. So. Assn. Colls. and Schs., Atlanta, 1982—. Contbr. articles in field. Bd. dirs. United Way, Shelby, N.C., 1987. Woodrow Wilson fellow, 1971. Mem. Soc. Bibl. Lit., Nat. Assn. Bapt. Profs. of Religion, N.C. Ind. Coll. Assn., Alpha Chi, Omicron Delta Kappa. Lodges: Rotary (bd. dirs. Burlington, N.C. chpt. 1986). Democrat. Baptist. Avocations: golf, tennis, music, travel. Home: 100 Jones Dr Murfreesboro NC 27855-1800 Office: One University Dr Murfreesboro NC 27855 Home Phone: 252-398-5266; Office Phone: 252-398-6221. E-mail: whitec@chowan.edu.

WHITE, MARY JO, lawyer, former prosecutor; b. Kansas City, Mo., Dec. 27, 1947; d. Carl and Ruth King Monk; m. John W. White, Jan. 24, 1970. BA, Coll. William and Mary, 1970; MA in Psychology, New Sch. for Social Rsch., 1971; JD, Columbia U., 1974. Bar: NY 1975. Law clk. to Hon. Marvin E. Frankel US Dist. Ct. (So. dist.) NY, 1975—76; assoc. Debevoise & Plimpton LLP, 1976—78, litig. ptnr., 1983—90, ptnr., chair litig. dept., 2002—; asst. U.S. atty., chief appellate atty. criminal divsn. (So. dist.) NY US Dept. Justice, 1978—81; instr. in profl. responsibility and ethics Columbia Law Sch., 1981—; chief asst., acting U.S. Atty. (ea. dist.) NY US Dept. Justice, Bklyn., 1990—93, US atty. (so. dist.) NY Manhattan, 1993—2002. Chair Atty. Gen. Janet Reno's Adv. Com. of U.S. Attys., 1993—94; dir. mem. Exec., Audit, and Policy Committees Nasdaq Stock Exchange, 2002—06. Recipient Magnificent 7 award, Bus. & Profl. Women USA, Law Enforcement Person of Yr. award, Soc. Profl. Investigators, Human Relations award, Anti-Defamation League Lawyer's Divsn., 1996, Edward Weinfeld award, NY County Lawyers' Assn., 1998, John P. O'Neill Pillar of Justice award, Respect for Law Alliance, 2002, Sandra Day O'Connor award for distinction in pub. svc., 2002, Jefferson Cup award, FBI, 2002, George H. W. Bush award, CIA, 2002, Agency Seal Medallion, 2002, Women of Power and Influence award, NOW; named one of Top Women Litigators, Nat. Law Jour., 2002, 100 Most Influential Lawyers in America, 2006, 50 Most Influential Women Lawyers in America, 2007. Fellow: Am. Coll. Trial Lawyers; mem.: ABA (Vice-Chair Comm. on Discretionary Justice, Adminstrv. Law Sect. 1980—81), N.Y. State Bar Assn., Assn. Bar City of N.Y., Phi Beta Kappa. Achievements include being first women to serve as US Attorney for Southern District of NY. Office: Debevoise & Plimpton LLP 919 Third Ave 46t Fl New York NY 10022 Office Phone: 212-909-6260. Office Fax: 212-909-6836. Business E-Mail: mjwhite@debevoise.com.*

WHITE, MEG(AN) (MARTHA), musician, vocalist; b. Grosse Pointe, Mich., Dec. 10, 1974; m. John Gillis, 1996 (div. 2000). Drummer, vocalist The White Stripes, 1997—; toured with Pavement and Sleater-Kinney, 1999, 2000. Performer: (albums) The White Stripes, 1999, De Stijl, 2000, White Blood Cells, 2001, Maximum, 2002, Elephant, 2003, Get Behind Me Satan, 2005, Icky Thump, 2007 (Grammy award for Best Alternative Music Album, 2008, Grammy award for Best Duo Rock Performance with Vocals, 2008), (songs) Conquest, 2008 (Best Cinematography, MTV Video Music Awards, 2008); actor: (films) Coffee and Cigarettes, 2003, Cold Mountain, 2003. Office: Monotone Inc 150 S Rodeo Dr # 200 Beverly Hills CA 90212-2408

WHITE, MICHAEL DENNIS, food products executive; b. Norwood, Mass., Jan. 11, 1952; s. Thomas Michael and Sally (Davenport) W.; m. Susan Lee Burns, June 30, 1972; children: Larissa, Paul, Jennifer. BA, Boston Coll., Newton, Mass., 1974; cert. of proficiency, Leningrad U., Russia, 1974; MA in Internat. Rels., Johns Hopkins U., 1976. CPA, Mass. Cons. Arthur Andersen & Co., Mgmt. Info. Cons. Div., Washington, Boston, 1976-80, mgr., 1980-81; cons. Bain & Co., Boston, 1981-84, mgr., 1984-86; v.p. planning, devel. Avon Products, NYC, 1986-87, v.p. retail devel., 1987-88; sr. v.p., gen. mgr. internat. Parfums Stern Inc. (subs. Avon Products), NYC, 1988-90; v.p. planning Frito-Lay Inc., Plano, Tex., 1990—91, sr. v.p. fin., CFO; exec. v.p., CFO PepsiCo, Intern. Snack div.; sr. v.p., CFO Pepsi-Cola Co., 1996—98, PepsiCo, Inc., 1998—2000; pres., CEO Frito-Lay, Europe/Africa/Middle East division, 2000—03; chmn., CEO PepsiCo Internat., 2003—; vice chmn. PepsiCo, Inc., 2006—. Active Tri-State United Way, N.Y.C.; v.p. Westport (Conn.)-Weston United Way, 1988-90. Office: PepsiCo Inc 700 Anderson Hill Rd Purchase NY 10577*

WHITE, MICHAEL LEE, executive producer, writer; b. Rochester, Minn., Aug. 2, 1967; s. Floyd Leroy and Yvonne Cecile (Jarrett) W.; m. Tatyana Nayda, Sept. 17, 1996. Student, U. Ariz., 1984-85; BS, U. Berkley, 1997, MBA, 1999. Glazier Sunset Glass & Mirror, Tucson, 1980-84; assoc. astronomer Flandrau Planetarium, Tucson, 1984-85; owner W.A.V. Enterprises, Hemet, Calif., 1985-88; programming cons. TMJ Stations, Temecula, Calif., 1988-91; exec.producer, writer Nine Star-Domestic, Hemet, 1989-95; news/program dir. Buffalo Comms., San Jacinto, Calif., 1992, gen. mgr., 1993; co-owner Mail Depot, Hemet, 1994-97; owner Aeropig Systems, Downey, Calif., 1995—; co-owner, producer, writer Misha Prodns., Downey, 1995—. Editor Hemet Valley Bull. Bd. List, 1990-96, Tucson Bull. Bd. List, 1987-96; contbr., author: Computer Phone Book, 1986; author screenplay Summer Breeze, 1996, Summer Breeze: The Series, 1997; exec. prodr. Computer Doctor, 1992-94, Spirit of Television, 1992-93; exec. prodr., writer Computer Doctor, Russian ed., 1996-99. Founder, spokesperson Pro-Am. Found., Tucson, 1985—, internat. pres., 1986-88, 92, 95-97; pres. Tucson Jr. Civitan, 1982-83. Republican. Lutheran. Avocations: basketball, football, hockey, sailing, astronomy.

WHITE, MILDRED VIRGINIA, secondary school educator, retired counseling administrator; d. Stanis Augustus and Elsie Emma Watkins; m. Richard Clarence White, Jan. 1, 1949; children: Michael Kenneth, Valerie Clarissa. BSc, Tuskegee Inst., 1948; MA, Atlanta U., 1965. Cert. counseling Ala., 1965. H.S. health and phys. edn. tchr. Macon County Tng. Sch./Macon County Bd. Edn., Tuskegee, Ala., 1950—65; career counselor for adult students Manpower Tng. Act/Labor Dept. Fed. Govt., Tuskegee, Ala., 1965—66; guidance dir. /job developer H.S. equivalency program OEO, Tuskegee, 1966—67, 1968—69; program dir. for rsch. and demonstrational program Adult Edn. Rsch. Program HEW, Tuskegee, 1967—68; career devel. specialist for head start teachers Head Start Supplementary Program for Tchrs., Tuskegee, 1970—71; world history instr. for headstart tchrs. Tuskegee Inst. Fed. Govt., 1971—72; h.s. guidance counselor Deborah Cannon Wolfe H.S./Macon County Bd. Edn., Shorter, Ala., 1972—81; coord. health program Tuskagee Inst. Health, Edn. and Welfare, 1984; career coord. Explorer Pk., Tuskagee, 1994—95. Cons. Adult Edn. State Workshop for Tchrs., Tuskegee, 1970—70; coun. mem. for tng. program Tng. and Preparation for Employment, Montgomery, Ala., 1970—72; dir. Consortium Minorities in Engring., 1984—86; mem. state retirement com. representing Macon County State Retirement and Membership Com./Ala. Tchrs. Assn., Tuskegee, 1995—97. Co-author: Handbook for Counselors for Disadvantaged Adults, 1956. Den mother Macon County Cub Scout Pack, Tuskegee Inst., 1962—64; rsch. coord. Tuskegee Inst./HEW, 1974; explorer career coord. Explorer Post of Tuskegee, 1995—95; neighborhood chmn. United Way, Tuskegee, 1998—2003. Fellow, Tuskegee Inst., 1944, Kellogg Found./Tuskegee Inst. Resource Devel. Ctr., Ohio State U., Columbus, 1969. Mem.: NEA, Ret. Tchrs. Assn., Ala. Ednl. Assn., Macon County Ret. Tchrs. Assn. (v.p. 1992—94, pres. 1994—96), Tuskegee Optimist Mrs. Club (pres. 1997—98), Delta Sigma Theta (life; founder, dir. Delteen youth club 1984—91, pres. 1990—91). Home: 903 N Marable Dr Tuskegee AL 36083 Personal E-mail: mildredgreta@aol.com.

WHITE, MILES D., pharmaceutical executive; b. Mpls., Mar. 10, 1955; m. Kim White. BS in Mech. Engring., Stanford U., 1978, MBA, 1980. Mgmt. cons. McKinsey & Co.; with Abbott Labs., 1984—, v.p. diagnostic sys. and ops., 1993-94, sr. v.p. diagnostic ops., 1994-98, exec. v.p., 1998-99, chmn., CEO, 1999—. Bd. dirs. Abbott Labs., 1998—, Motorola Inc., 2005—, The Tribune Co., 2005—06, Fed. Res. Bank, Chgo., 2002—, chmn., 2002—04, 2005—07. Bd. trustee Field Mus., Chicago, Northwestern U., Joffrey Ballet, Chicago, Culver Ednl. Found.; mem. Stanford Grad. Sch. of Bus. Adv. Coun., Stanford Adv. Coun. on Interdisciplinary Biosciences. Mem.: Econ. Club of Chgo., Executives' Club of Chgo. (chmn.). Office: Abbott Labs 100 Abbott Park Rd Abbott Park IL 60064-6400*

WHITE, MORTON GABRIEL, philosopher, writer, historian, retired educator; b. NYC, Apr. 29, 1917; s. Robert and Esther (Levine) Weisberger; m. Lucia Perry, Aug. 29, 1940 (dec.); children: Nicholas Perry, Stephen Daniel; m. Helen Starobin, June 30, 1997. BS, CCNY, 1936; L.H.D., CUNY, 1975; A.M., Columbia U., 1938, PhD, 1942. Instr. philosophy Columbia U., 1942—46; instr. physics CCNY, 1942—43; asst. prof. philosophy U. Pa., 1946—48, Harvard U., 1948—50, assoc. prof., 1950—53, prof., 1953—70, chmn. dept., 1954—57, acting chmn. dept., 1967—69; prof. Inst. Advanced Study, 1970—87; prof. emeritus, 1987—; ret., 1987. Guggenheim research fellow, 1950-51; vis. prof. Tokyo U., 1952, 60, 66, U. Oslo, 1977-78; Neesima lectr. Doshisha U., Kyoto, 1985, CUNY, 1968-69, Rutgers U., 1987-88, 88-89 Keio U., Tokyo, 2002-03; mem. Inst. Advanced Study, 1953-54, 62-63, 67-68, 68-69. Author: The Origin of Dewey's Instrumentalism, 1943, Social Thought in America, 1949, The Age of Analysis, 1955, Toward Reunion in Philosophy, 1956, Religion, Politics, and the Higher Learning, 1959; (with Lucia White) The Intellectual Versus the City, 1962; Editor: (with Arthur M. Schlesinger, Jr.) Paths of American Thought, 1963, Foundations of Historical Knowledge, 1965, Science and Sentiment in America, 1972, Documents in the History of American Philosophy, 1972, Pragmatism and the American Mind, 1973, The Philosophy of the American Revolution, 1978, What Is and What Ought to Be Done, 1981; (with Lucia White) Journeys to the Japanese, 1952-79, 1986, Philosophy, The Federalist and the Constitution, 1987, The Question of Free Will, 1993, A Philosopher's Story, 1999, A Philosophy of Culture, 2002, From a Philosophical Point of View, 2005. Fellow Center Advanced Study Behavioral Scis., 1959-60; fellow Am. Council Learned Socs., 1962-63 Mem. Am. Acad. Arts and Scis., Am. Antiquarian Soc., Am. Philos. Soc. Office: Inst for Advanced Study Princeton NJ 08540

WHITE, NICHOLAS JOHN, musician, director, composer; b. London, Aug. 9, 1967; arrived in USA, 1990, permanent resident, 1991; s. Ronald John and Andre Bernice White; 1 child, Samuel Dempsey. MA, Cambridge U., 1986—89. Organ scholar Clare Coll., Cambridge, England, 1986—89; dir. of choral music McMurry U., Abilene, Tex., 1992—94; asst. organist and choirmaster Wash. Nat. Cathedral, Washington, 1994—98; music dir. Woodley Ensemble, Washington, 1997—2000; dir. of music St. Michael's Ch., NYC, 1998—2005; music dir. Tiffany Consort, NYC, 2003. Composer: (choral work) Magnificat, 1997, Full Freedom, 2002, Alleluia! Puer Natus Est Nobis, 2003, In Sure and Certain Hope, 2007; musician: (cd recording) The Amsterdam Bach, 1999, O Magnum Mysterium, 2004 (Grammy nominee, 2006). Bd. mem. St. Wilfrid's Club, NYC, 2001—04. Mem.: Am. Guild of Organists (advtg. dir. 1998—2005, exec. bd. mem. 1998—2003), Assn. of Anglican Musicians, Royal Coll. of Organists (assoc.), St. Wilfrid's Club. Anglican. Avocations: theater, travel, cooking. Home: 100 W 87TH ST Apt 1A New York NY 10024-2954 Personal E-mail: nicholaswhite@earthlink.net.

WHITE, NORVAL CRAWFORD, architect; b. NYC, June 12, 1926; s. William Crawford and Caroline Ruth (Taylor) W.; m. Joyce Leslie Lee, May 24, 1958 (div.); children: William Crawford, Thomas Taylor, Gordon Crawford, Alistair David; m. Camilla Cecilia Crowe, June 7, 1992. BS, Mass. Inst. Tech., 1949; student, Sch. Fine Arts, Fontainbleau, 1954; M.F.A., Princeton, 1955. Designer, assoc. Lathrop Douglass (Architect), 1955-59; prin. Norval C. White (Architect), NYC, 1959-62, 66-67; partner Rowan & White (Architects), NYC, 1962-66, Gruzen & Partners, NYC, 1967-70; prin. Norval C. White & Assos., NYC, 1970-74; ptnr. Levien, Deliso & White, 1974-80, Levien Deliso White Songer, 1980-86. Asst. prof. architecture Cooper Union, 1961-67; prof. architecture City Coll., CUNY, 1970-95, prof. emeritus, 1995—, chmn. dept. 1970-77. Author (with E. Willensky): AIA Guide to New York City, 1968, AIA Guide to New York City, 4th edit., 2000; author: The Architecture Book, 1976, New York: A Physical HIstory, 1987, The Guide to the Architecture of Paris, 1991; prin. works include Seiden House, Tenafly, N.J., 1960, Essex Terrace (housing), Bklyn., 1970, N.Y.C. Police Hdqrs., 1973, Brookhaven Parks (L.I.) Sanitary Landfill, 1971, Forsgate Indsl. Park, South Brunswick, N.J., 1978—86, Del Vista Condominiums, Miami, 1981, 61 Christopher Street, Greenwich Village, 1987, White House, Salisbury, Conn., 1998, Goodman House, Oyster Bay Cove, NY, 2003, White House, Mouchan, France, 2004. Trustee Bklyn. Inst. Arts and Scis., 1973-82, Bklyn. Pub. Libr., 1993-96; gov. Bklyn. Mus., 1973-82, adv. com., 1982-2006; mem. NYC Art Commn., 1975-86, sec., 1975-77, v.p., 1978-80. With USNR, 1944—46. Fellow AIA; mem. Soc. Archtl. Historians, N.Y. State Assn. Architects. Clubs: Century Assn. (N.Y.C.). Democrat. Home and Office: Village 32310 Roques France E-mail: norvalwhite@mac.com.

WHITE, ORA DADE, educational consultant, writer, activist, counselor, community volunteer; b. Algoma, W.Va., Apr. 1945; d. Alexander and Ora Dee Dade; m. Huey White, 1972; children: Candace, Tarik. BS in Speech and English, Ohio State U., 1970, MA in Guidance and Counseling, 1975; PhD in Edn. Adminstrn., Belford U., 2007. Cert. tchr., counselor, prin., supr., vocal counselor. Pres., CEO Old Ade Enterprises, LLC; spkr., panelist, tchr., advisor, Former Tea counselor, Prin., Pres. Franklin County Alliance Black Sch. Educators. Author: (book) Think on Those Things That are Good, 1998; commentator (commentator) Educational Issues, Community needs Concernsin Cols. Dispatch, Call & Post, Newspaper. Del. Dem. Nat. Convention, 2000. Mem. Alpha Kappa Alpha (co founder), Alpha Sigma Omega Edn. Found. (exec. dir, chmn.), OSU, Otterbein, Ohio Wesleyan, Ohio Bd. Regents, Nat. Alliance Black Sch. Educators, Phi Delta Kappa, Top Lady of Distinction, Phi Kappa Phi, Ray Miller, Mayor Tom Moody, Cols. City Schs. & First Ch. of God (commendations). Democrat. Avocations: dance, singing, reading. Home: 6320 Peach Tree Rd Columbus OH 43213-3420 Office: 1005 Mr Vernon Ave Columbus OH 42203 Office Phone: 614-863-1901.

WHITE, PAMELA JANICE, lawyer; b. Elizabeth, NJ, July 13, 1952; d. Emmet Talmadge and June (Howlett) W. BA, Mary Wash. Coll., 1974; JD, Wash. and Lee U., 1977. Bar: Md. 1977, US Supreme Ct. 1981. Assoc. Ober, Grimes & Shriver, Balt., 1977-84; prin. Ober, Kaler, Grimes & Shriver PC, Balt., 1985—2007, Band Visitors, U. Mary, Washington, 2009—; assoc. judge Cir. Ct. Balt. City, 2007—; eight circuit ADR supervisory judge Pro Bosio Com. Liason. Chair Employment Grp., 1994—2007; mem. bd. law examiners, 1986-94, select com. on Gender Equality, 1989-2000, chair, 1997-99, judiciary pub. trust and confidence com., 2001-05, spl. com. on ethics 2002-04, jud. campaign conduct com., 2005—07; mem. fed. dist. ct. adv. grp. Civil Justice Reform Act, 1990; exec. com. Md. Inst. Continuing Profl. Edn. Lawyers, 2000-02, vol. faculty; adv. bd. Md. Mediation and Conflict Resolution Ctr., 2001-02; equal justice coun. Legal Aid Bur., 2000-06; mem. Md. Conf. Cir. Judges, cicuit judge, ADR Com., 2009-. Note and comment editor Wash. and Lee Law Rev. 1976-77, Wash. and Lee Law Council 1983-87, pres. 1991-92. Mem. Fed. Ct. Bicentennial Com., 1988-90; vol. Profl. Gov.'s Drug-Free Workplace Initiative, 1990-93; trustee Wash. and Lee U., 1995-2004, Balt. Hist. Soc., 2002—07. Recipient Leadership in Law award Md. Daily Record, 2001, Exemplary Svc. award Legal Aid Bur. 2002, Outstanding Pro Bono Cert., 2004; named Disting. Alumna, Wash. and Lee U., 1994, Mary Wash. Coll., 2001, Mayland Top 100 Woman, Cir. Excellence, 2007. Fellow Am. Bar Found., Md. Bar Found. (award for excellence 1996, bd. dirs. 2000-07); mem. ABA (chair tort and ins. practice employer/employee rels. com. 1999-2000, del. 2000-02), Am. Arbitration Assn. (arbitrator, mediator employment and comml., large complex case panels), Nat. Assn. Women Judges, Balt. Bar Found. (bd. dirs. 2003—), Fed. Bar Assn., Md. State Bar Assn. (coun. legal edn. sect. 1987-96, chmn. 1992-93, labor sect. coun. 1992-96, professionalism com. 1991—, chmn. 1994-97, bd. govs. 1993-95, 1998-2003, exec. com. 1994-95, 99-01, pres. 2001-02, immediate past pres. 2002-03, task force on professionalism chair 1996-97), D.C. Bar Assn., Balt. City Bar Assn. (exec. coun. 1995-96, 1997-98), Md. Legal Svcs. Corp. (bd. mem. 2006-), U. Mary Wash. Alumni Assn. (bd. dirs. 2006—), Women's Bar Assn. Md. (treas. 1986-87, v.p. 1987-88, pres.-elect 1988-89, pres. 1989-90, bd. dirs. 1984-86, Rita C. Davidson award 2000), Judicial Selection WOA Task Force on Discrimination, Pro Bono Resource Ctr. (exec. com. 2000-02, trustee 2002-03, Leaders of Equal Justice award 2002), Order of Coif, Phi Beta Kappa (hon. alumni), Omicron Delta Kappa (hon. alumni). Presbyterian. Avocation: baseball. Office: Circuit Ct Balt City 111 N Calvert St Baltimore MD 21202

WHITE, PAMELA JO, elementary school educator; b. Lynchburg, Va., June 20, 1943; d. Robert E. and Josephine T. (Patterson) W. BA in Art and Elem. Edn., Lynchburg Coll., 1968, MA in Teaching, 1969; postgrad., U. Va., Kent State U. Elem. tchr. Baltimore County Pub. Schs., Towson, Md., Bedford County Pub. Schs., Bedford, Va., Appomattox County Pub. Schs., Appomattox, Va.; ret., 1990. Recipient Outstanding Vol. award 4-H Club, Cystic Fibrosis Found. Mem. Am. Fedn. Tchrs., Nat. Trust for Hist. Preservation, Smithsonian Assocs., Kappa Delta Pi, Delta Kappa Gamma, Beta Sigma Phi.

WHITE, PATRICIA DENISE, dean, law educator; b. Syracuse, NY, July 8, 1949; d. Theodore C. and Kathleen (Cowles) Denise; m. Nicholas P. White, Feb. 20, 1971 (div. 1997); children: Olivia Lawrence, Alexander Cowles; m. James W. Nickel, Sept. 15, 2005. BA, U. Mich., 1971, MA, 1974, JD cum laude, 1974. Bar: D.C. 1975, Mich. 1988, Utah 1995. Assoc. Steptoe & Johnson LLP, Washington, 1975-76; vis. asst. prof. Coll. of Law U. Toledo, 1976-77; assoc. Caplin & Drysdale, Washington, 1977-79; vis. assoc. prof. Law Ctr. Georgetown U., 1979—80, asst. prof., 1980—84, assoc. prof. Law Ctr., 1985-88; vis. prof. Law Sch. U. Mich., Ann Arbor, 1988-94; counsel Bodman, Longley and Dahling, Detroit, Ann Arbor, 1990—95; prof. U. Utah, Salt Lake City, 1994-98; counsel Parsons, Behle and Latimer, Salt Lake City, 1995—98; dean, prof. Sandra Day O'Connor Coll. Law, Ariz. State U., 1999—2008, Jack Brown prof., 2008—09, dean emeritus, 2008—; spl. counsel Steptoe & Johnson LLP, Wash., 2008—09; vis. prof. Georgetown U. Law Ctr., 2008—09; dean, prof. U. Miami Sch. Law, 2009—. Affiliated prof, Dept. Philosophy Ariz. State U., faculty fellow, Ctr. Study of Law, Sci., & Tech. Contbr. articles to profl. jours. Recipient Judge Learned Hand award for Disting. Pub. Svc., Am. Jewish Com., 2009. Fellow: Am. Coll. Tax Coun.; mem.: Mich. Bar Assn., Utah Bar Assn., Law Sch. Admission Coun. (bd. dirs. 2003—07, chair audit com. 2003—04, chair test devel. and rsch. com. 2005—07), Am. Law Deans Assn. (bd. dirs. 2001—08). Office: U Miami Sch Law 1311 Miller Dr Coral Gables FL 33146 Home Phone: 480-838-6550; Office Phone: 305-284-2394. Office Fax: 305-284-3210. Business E-Mail: pwhite@law.miami.edu.*

WHITE, PATRICIA MARIE, psychology professor, researcher; d. Robert Amos and Margaret Agnes White; m. William Tate Troyer, Aug. 17, 1997; 1 child, Dylan Jon Troyer. BA, Stanford U., 1981, BS, 1986; PhD, UCLA, 2001. Asst. prof. U. Oreg., Eugene, 2001—. Recipient Michael Goldstein Disting. Dissertation award, UCLA, 2001. Mem.: APA, Assn. Behavioral and Cognitive Therapies, Soc. Psychophysiological Rsch. Achievements include research in ERP, P50 suppression. Office: U Oregon 1227 University of Oregon Eugene OR 97403-1227 Office Fax: 541-346-4911; Home Fax: 541-346-4911. Personal E-mail: troyer@uoregon.edu. Business E-Mail: pmwhite@uoregon.edu.

WHITE, PATRICK E., academic administrator; m. Chris White; children: Katie, Molly, Paddy. Grad. with honors, U. Chgo., 1971; MA in English and Am. Lit., PhD in English and Am. Lit., U. Iowa. Tchr. Westmar Coll., 1976—85; chair Dept. Language and Lit. Pfieffer U., 1985—88; assoc. dean faculty St. Mary's Coll., Notre Dame, Ind., 1988—2002, v.p., dean faculty, 2002—06, co-founder Ctr. for Academic Innovation; pres. Wabash Coll., Crawfordsville, Ind., 2006—. Office: Wabash Coll Office of Pres PO Box 352 Crawfordsville IN 47933 Office Phone: 765-361-6221. Office Fax: 765-361-6461. E-mail: president@wabash.edu.*

WHITE, PERRY MERRILL, JR., orthopedic surgeon; b. Texarkana, Ark., Oct. 11, 1925; s. Perry Merrill and Mary Gladys (Shelton) W.; m. Lucy Katherine Freeman, Dec. 23, 1947; children: Perry Merrill III, MD., Georgia Lynette, Katherine Landis White Long, John David. BS, Baylor U., 1948, MD, 1953; postgrad., Vanderbilt U., 1948-49. Diplomate Am. Bd. Orthopedic Surgery. Intern VA Hosp., Houston, 1953-54; gen. practice medicine Spearman, Tex., 1955-57; resident orthopedic surgery Eugene Talmadge Meml. Hosp., Augusta, Ga., 1957-61; pvt. practice orthopedic surgery Atlanta, 1961-83; chief Ga. Adult Amputee Clinic, 1965-79; active staff Scottish Rite Hosp. for Crippled Children, Decatur, Ga., 1965-73; instr. orthopedic surgery residency program Ga. Bapt. Hosp., 1965-83; orthopedic panelist Ga. Dept. Vocat. Rehab. Cons. Ga. Crippled Children's Service, 1965-76 Former mem. bd. dirs. Haggai Inst., Atlanta, London, Singapore. Served with USNR, 1944-46. Fellow ACS, Am. Acad. Orthopedic Surgeons; mem. So., Ga., Atlanta med. assns., Eastern Orthopedic Assn., Ga., Atlanta orthopedic socs., Alpha Kappa Kappa. Republican. Baptist (deacon). Home: 1547 Cave Rd NW Atlanta GA 30327-3119 E-mail: kaper1947@bellsouth.net.

WHITE, RALPH PAUL, automotive executive, consultant; b. Watertown, Mass., Aug. 1, 1926; s. Irving William and Margaret Sarah (McGowan) W.; m. Shirley Irene Christie, Nov. 22, 1947; children: Karin Ann, Eric John. BS in Indsl. Engring., Columbia U., 1951; postgrad., Yale U., 1958-59. Instr. engring. mechanics U. Conn., Torrington, 1956-57; mgr. data processing. B.F. Goodrich Co., Shelton, Conn., 1956—61; ptnr., mgmt. cons. Bavier, Bulger & Goodyear, New Haven, 1961-66; v.p. Davidson Rubber Co., Dover, NH, 1966-69, pres., 1969-80; group v.p. parent co. Ex-Cell-O, Troy, Mich., 1980-83; pres. Troy (N.H.) Mills Inc., 1983-86, chief exec. officer, 1983-89, chmn., 1987-89. Bd. dirs. J.A. Wright Co., Keene, NH, J.D. Cahill Co., Hampton, NH, Exeter Trust Co., D.G. O'Brien Co., Seabrook, NH. Mem. N.H. Indsl. Devel. Authority, 1972-80, 85-88, Pease Devel. Authority, State of N.H., 1990-93, N.H. Bus. Fin. Authority, 1992-2004; exec. bd. Whittemore Sch. Bus., U. N.H., Durham, 1984-2002. Mem. Am. Inst. Indsl. Engrs., Soc. Automotive Engrs., N.H. Bus. and Industry Assn. (bd. dirs. 1970-80, pres. 1972-73, vice chmn. 1984-86), Abenaqui Country Club, Rye Beach Club. Republican. Roman Catholic. Avocations: skiing, golf. Home Phone: 603-964-5271. Personal E-mail: rpw99@aol.com.

WHITE, RAYMOND LESLIE, geneticist; b. Orlando, Fla., Oct. 23, 1943; s. Lawrence and Marjorie White; m. Joan Palmer Distin, June 1, 1968; children: Juliette, Jeremy. BS in Microbiology, U. Oreg., 1965; PhD in Microbiology, MIT, 1971; postdoctoral studies, Stanford. Rsch. assoc., instr. MIT, Cambridge, 1971-72; postdoctoral fellow Sch. Medicine Stanford U., Calif., 1972-75; asst. prof. Dept. Microbiology U. Mass. Sch. Medicine, Worcester, 1975-78, assoc. prof. Dept. Microbiology, 1978-80; investigator Howard Hughes Med. Inst. U. Utah Med. Ctr., 1980-94; assoc. prof. Dept. Cellular, Viral and Molecular Biology U. Utah Sch. Medicine, 1980-84, co-chmn. Dept. Human Genetics, 1984-94, prof. Dept. Oncological Scis., 1985—; prof. Dept. of Human Genetics U. Utah Sch. of Medicine, 1985—; chmn. Dept. Oncological Scis. U. Utah Sch. Medicine, 1994—, dir. Huntsman Cancer Inst., 1994—2000; chief sci. officer DNA Scis., Inc., Fremont, Calif., 2000—02; dir. Ernest Gallo Clinic & Rsch. Ctr. U. Calif. San Francisco, Emeryville, Calif., 2002—, vice chair, prof. neurology, 2002—. Ad hoc mem. NIH Gen. Med. Sci. Inst. Coun., 1984, mem. NIH study sect., 1979-83. Consulting editor Jour. Clin. Investigation; subject area editor Genomics, 1987-90; contbr. articles to profl. jours. Woodrow Wilson fellow, 1965-66, NIH grad. fellow, 1966-71, Jane Coffins Childs Found. fellow, 1971-75; Nat. Cancer Inst. Cancer Ctr. Support grantee, 1995—; recipient Sword Hope award Am. Cancer Soc., 1995, Lewis S. Rosenstiel award Disting. Work Basic Med. Scis., Brandeis U., 1992, Rosenblatt award for excellence, 1993, Nat. Med. Rsch. award Nat. Health Coun., 1991, Friedrich von Recklinghausen award Nat. Neurofibromatosis Found., 1990, Charles S. Mott prize Gen. Motors Cancer Rsch. Found., 1990, Raymond Bourfine award, Paris, 2002. Mem. NAS, Am. Soc. Human Genetics (Allen Cancer Rsch. award 1989, assoc. editor Cancer Rsch.), Utah Acad. Scis., Inst. Medicine. Achievements include the development of a new technology for mapping and ultimately identifying human genes causing disease and the discovery of fundamental genes and genetic mechanisms important in the inherited and cellular pathways to cancer. Office: Ernest Gallo Clinic & Rsch Ctr Ste 200 5858 Horton St Emeryville CA 94608 Office Phone: 510-985-3102. Office Fax: 510-985-3101. E-mail: rayw@egcrc.net.

WHITE, RAYMOND PETRIE, JR., dentist, educator, dean; b. NYC, Feb. 13, 1937; s. Raymond Petrie and Mabel Sarah (Shutze) White; m. Betty Pritchett, Dec. 27, 1961; children: Karen Elizabeth, Michael Wood. Student, Washington and Lee U., 1955—58; DDS, Med. Coll. Va., 1962, PhD, 1967. Diplomate Am. Bd. Oral and Maxillofacial Surgery. Postdoctoral fellow anatomy Med. Coll. Va., Richmond, 1962—67, resident in oral surgery, 1964—67; asst. prof. U. Ky., Lexington, 1967—70, assoc. prof., 1970—71, chmn. dept. oral surgery, 1969—71; prof., asst. dean adminstrn. Va. Commonwealth U., Richmond, 1971—74; prof. Sch. Dentistry U. N.C., Chapel Hill, 1974—, Dalton L. McMichael disting. prof., 1993—, dean Sch. Dentistry, 1974—81, assoc. dean Sch. Medicine, Sch. Dentistry, 1981—92. Mem. staff U. N.C. Hosps., mem. exec. com., 1974—98, sec., 1977—78, assoc. chief staff, 1981—92; mem. adv. panel on dentistry U.S. Pharmacopial Conv., 1985—; sr. program cons. The Robert Wood Johnson Found., 1982—90. Author (with E.R. Costich): Fundamentals of Oral Surgery, 1971; author: (with Bell and Proffit) Surgical Correction of Dentofacial Deformities, 1980; author: (with W.R. Proffit) Surgical Orthodontic Treatment, 1990; author: (with M.R. Tucker, B.C. Terry, J.E. Van Sickels) Rigid Fixations for Maxillofacial Surgery, 1991; co-editor: Internat. Jour. Adult Orthodontics and Orthodontic Surgery, 1985—2002; asst. editor: Jour. Oral and Maxillofacial Surgery, 1993—; author (with W.R. Profit, R.P. Jr., and D. Sarver): Contemporary Treatment of Dentofacial Deformity, 2002; contbr. sci. articles to profl. jours. Bd. dirs. Am. Fund for Dental Health, 1978—86, v.p., 1982—85. Recipient Disting. Svc. award, Am. Fund Dental Health, 1987, Dental Found. N.C., 1981, John C. Brauer award for acad. distinction, U. N.C. Alumni Assn., 2000, Daniel M. Laskin award, 2002, Rsch. Excellence award, Oral and Maxillofacial Surgery Found., 2003. Mem.: AAAS, ADA, N.C. Assn. Oral and Maxillofacial Surgeons, Am. Assn. Oral and Maxillofacial Surgeons (gen. chmn. sci. sessions com. 1974—76, chmn. strategic planning com. 1990—96, Outstanding Svc. award as committeeman 1976, William Gies award 2000, Disting. Svc. award 2003), Chalmers J. Lyons Acad. Oral Surgery, Inst. Medicine of NAS, Internat. Assn. Dental Rsch. (pres. Ky. sect. 1970), N.C. Dental Soc., Sigma Xi, Omicron Kappa Upsilon, Sigma Zeta, Alpha Sigma Chi, Delta Tau Delta, Psi Omega. Roman Catholic. Home: 1506 Velma Rd Chapel Hill NC 27514-7601 Office: U NC Sch Dentistry Dept Oral/Maxillofacial Surgery Chapel Hill NC 27599-7450 Office Phone: 919-966-1126. Business E-Mail: ray_white@dentistry.unc.edu.

WHITE, REBECCA E., advocate; b. Washington, Nov. 17, 1945; d. Edward and Anna Pendleton White. BS, D.C. Tchrs. Coll., 1971; postgrad., Pepperdine U., Malibu, Calif., 1993, Calif. State U., LA, 2003—04. Cert. tchr., D.C., Calif. Tchr. English D.C. Pub. Schs., Washington, 1971-73; paralegal specialist U.S. Dept. Justice, Washington, 1973-81; adminstr. U.S. Dept. Vet. Affairs VA Med. Ctr., LA, 1982-89, 94-96, Sepulveda, Calif., 1992-94; patient/employee advocate U.S. Dept. Vet. Affairs, LA, 1982-89, 92-96; tchr. English L.A. Unified Sch. Dist., 1989-91, children's advocate, 1989—2005; tchr. English Inglewood (Calif.) Unified Sch. Dist., 1996-97, children's advocate, 1996—98; tchr. spl. edn. East San Gabriel Valley Sch., Calif., 2002—03, Gladstone St. Elem. Sch., Azusa, Calif., 2003—04; freelance writer, 2005—; tchr. English Mpls. Pub. Schs., 2005—08. Cmty. advocate Baldwin Hills Cmty., L.A., 1983—2004; children's advocate L.A. County Schs., 1999-2004; Children's adv. Mpls. Schs., 2006-08, Children's Adv. DC Pub. Schs., 2009-; mem. L.A. World Affairs Coun., 1999-2004; mem. Nat. Campaign For Tolerance, 2006-. Mem. NEA, Calif. Tchrs. Assn. Avocations: writing, hiking, entertaining, reading.

WHITE, REBECCA HANNER, dean, law educator; BA, Ea. Ky. U.; JD, U. Ky. Jud. law clerk to Chief Judge George C. Edwards US Ct. Appeals (6th cir.); atty. Dinsmore & Shohl, Cincinnati; prof. U. Ga. Sch. Law, 1989—, assoc. provost and assoc. v.p. academic affairs, interim dean, 2003—04, dean, 2004—, J. Alton Hosch prof. law. Co-author: Employment Discrimination, 2002, Cases and Materials on Employment Discrimination, 2003; editl. bd. The Labor Law Jour. Recipient Josiah Meigs Award, 2000, John C. O'Byrne Award, Woman of Distinction award, State Bar Ga. Younger Lawyers Div., 2004, Faculty Book Award for Excellence in Teaching. Fellow: Foundation Fellows, U. Ga. (sr.); mem.: Teaching Acad., U. Ga. Office: University of Georgia Law School Office of the Dean Athens GA 30602 Office Phone: 706-542-7140. Office Fax: 706-542-5556. E-mail: rhwhite@uga.edu.*

WHITE, RICHARD BOOTH, management consultant; b. NYC, Aug. 26, 1930; s. Frank K. and Doris (Booth) W.; m. Mary Kane Russell, Dec. 9, 1961; children: Katherine Learned, Richard Booth (dec.), Anne Tristram, Leslie Russell. BA, Yale U., 1952. Asst. account exec. Batten, Barton, Durstine & Osborn, NYC, 1955, account exec., 1956—58, account supr., 1958—63, v.p., 1959—70, mgmt. supr., 1963—76, sr. v.p., 1970—76, exec. v.p., 1976—83, also dir., chmn. exec. com.; dir. BBDO Worldwide Inc.; sr. dir., ptnr. Spencer Stuart & Assocs., NYC, 1984—98; ind. cons., 1998—. Mem. New Canaan (Conn.) Town Coun.;

bd. dirs. Waveny Care Network, New Canaan. 1st lt. USMCR, 1952-55. Mem. Yale Club N.Y.C., Country Club of New Canaan, Sankaty Golf and Beach Club (Nantucket, Mass.). Presbyterian. Home: 27 Bank St New Canaan CT 06840-6202

WHITE, RICHARD EDMUND, human resources specialist; b. Reading, Pa., June 8, 1944; s. Carl Marshall and Miriam Elizabeth (Curry) W.; m. Kristen Margaret Lloyd, June 17, 1967; children: Ross, Peter, Andrew. BS in Econs., U. Pa., 1967; MBA with distinction, U. Mich., 1968. Gen. mgr. mktg. H. J. Heinz Co., Pitts., 1970-81; dir. mktg. Seven Up Co., St. Louis, 1981-83; v.p. mktg. & sales Herr Foods, Inc., Nottingham, Pa., 1984—2006, sr. v.p. human resources, 2006—. Bd. dirs. Conard-Pyle Co. Chmn. fin. com. Sewickley Borough Coun., Pa., 1977—81; pres. So. Chester County Devel. Found., Jennersville, Pa., 1988—94, So. Chester County YMCA, West Grove, Pa., 1988—93, bd. mgrs., 1988—93, Avon Grove United Way, 1988—93, pres., 1988—93; chmn. Health and Welfare Found. So. Chester County, 2001—, So. Chester County Med. Ctr., 1988—2001, bd. dirs., 1988—2001, Brandywine YMCA Assn.; chmn. bd. dirs. Jenners Pond, 2001—03. Mem. Am. Mgmt. Assn. (mktg. coun.), Soc. Human Resource Mgrs. Republican. Avocations: physical fitness, reading. Home: 7 Sullivan Chase Dr Avondale PA 19311-9347 Office: Herr Foods Inc PO Box 300 Nottingham PA 19362-0300 Business E-Mail: richard.white@herrs.com.

WHITE, RICHARD LEE, astronomer; b. Maryville, Tenn., 1953; s. Elmer and Oneda White; m. Barbara Jean Engelke, 1985; children: Travis, Mia. BS in Engring. Physics, U. Tenn., Knoxville, 1974; PhD in Astrophysics, U. Wis., Madison, 1978. Postdoc. rsch. assoc. Columbia U., NYC, 1978—81, Lawrence Livermore Nat. Lab., Calif., 1981—82; adj. asst. prof. UCLA, 1981—82; astronomer Space Telescope Sci. Inst., Baltimore, 1982—. Contbr. scientific papers to profl. jours. Mem.: Internat. Astron. Union. Achievements include patents in field. Office: Space Telescope Sci Inst 3700 San Martin Dr Baltimore MD 21218

WHITE, RICHARD MANNING, electrical engineering educator; b. Denver, Apr. 25, 1930; s. Rolland Manning and Freeda Blanche (Behny) W.; m. Chissie Lee Chamberlain, Feb. 1, 1964 (div. 1975); children: Rolland Kenneth, William Brendan. AB, Harvard U., 1951, AM, 1952, PhD in Applied Physics, 1956. Rsch. assoc. Harvard U., Cambridge, Mass., 1956; mem. tech. staff GE Microwave Lab., Palo Alto, Calif., 1956-63; prof. elec. engring. U. Calif., Berkeley, 1963—2003, Chancellor's prof., 1996-99, prof., graduate sch., 2006—. Chmn. Grad. Group on Sci. and Math. Edn., U. Calif. at Berkeley, 1981-85; co-dir. Berkeley Sensor and Actuator Ctr., 1986—, Co-author: Solar Cells: From Basics to Advanced Systems, Microsensors, 1991, Electrical Engineering Uncovered, 1997, Acoustic Wave Sensors, 1997; editor ElectroTechnology Rev.; patentee in field. Guggenheim fellow, 1968. Fellow AAAS, IEEE (Cledo Brunetto award 1986, Achievement award 1988, Disting. lectr. 1989, Cady award 2000, Rayleigh award 2003); mem. Nat. Acad. Engring., Acoustical Soc. Am., Am. Phys. Soc., Phi Beta Kappa, Sigma Xi. Avocations: photography, hiking, skiing, running, music. Office: U Calif Sensor & Actuator Ctr EECS Dept Ctr Berkeley CA 94720-1774

WHITE, RICHARD THOMAS, radiologist; b. Binghamton, NY, May 10, 1941; s. William Joseph and Winifred (Murphy) W.; 1 child by previous marriage, Kevin Michael; m. Rory Lynn Leyman. BS, SUNY, Binghamton, 1967; DO, Chgo. Coll. Osteo. Medicine, 1972. Intern Bi County Hosp., Warren, Mich.; staff radiologist Bi-County Hosp., 1977-79; resident Detroit Hosp., Children's Hosp., Detroit, 1973-76; fellow Johns Hopkins Hosp., Balt., 1976; asst. prof. radiology Mich. State U., East Lansing, 1980-84, cons. ultra-sound rsch., 1980-83, cons. nuclear magnetic rsch., 1982-83; asst. prof. radiology U. Tex., Houston, 1984-85, U. Ill., Chgo., 1985-88; chief radiology VA Med. Ctr., Bath, NY, 1988—2009; clin. prof. radiology U. Rochester, Sch. Medicine and Dentistry, NY, 1989—2009, prof. imaging scis., 2009—. Cons. varsity sports, 1980-84, handicapped athletes Spl. Olympics, Washington, 1978-84, Detroit Red Wings hockey team, 1977-84; cons. in radiology St. James Hosp., Hornell, N.Y., 1989-2009. Med. dir. Mich. Spl. Olympics Ctrl. Mich. U., Mt. Pleasant, 1977-84; bd. dirs. Spl. Olympics, Mich., 1980-84, N.Y. Spl. Olympics, 1996-2000; med. advisor Amateur Hockey Assn. USA, Colorado Springs, Colo., 1980-84. With U.S. Army, 1960-66; lt. col. USAR, 1990-96, ret. Recipient Outstanding Contbn. award Spl. Olympics, 1980; named Team Physician U.S. Nat. Hockey Team, Mich. Amateur Hockey Assn., 1979, 81, 83. Mem. AMA, Am. Osteo. Assn., Am. Osteo. Coll. Radiology, Assn. Mil. Physicians and Surgeons, Am. Osteopath Assn., Radiol. Soc. N.Am., Am. Coll. Radiology, Am. Inst. Ultrasound in Medicine, Am. Acad. Sci., Soc. Med. Cons. to U.S. Armed Forces, Kiwanis, Am. Legion. Office: PO Box 750 Bath NY 14810-0750 Office Phone: 607-664-4408.

WHITE, ROBERT EDWARD, think-tank executive; b. Melrose, Mass., Sept. 21, 1926; s. Edward V. and Emily G. (McGuire) W.; m. MaryAnne Cahill, June 4, 1955; children: Christopher, Kevin, Claire, MaryLouise, Laura. BA, St. Michael's Coll., Winooski, Vt., 1952, DHL (hon.), 1978; MA, Tufts U., 1954; DHL (hon.), Simmons Coll., 1985. Joined Fgn. Svc., Dept. State; dir. Latin Am. Peace Corps, Washington, 1968-70; dep. chief mission Am. Embassy, Managua, Nicaragua, 1970-72, Bogota, Colombia, 1972-75; dep. rep. Orgn. Am. States, Washington, 1975-77; US amb. to Paraguay US Dept. State, Asuncion, 1977-79, US amb. to El Salvador San Salvador, 1979-81; sr. assoc. Carnegie Endowment for Internat. Peace, Washington, 1981-83; prof. internat. rels. Simmons Coll., Boston, 1983-85; pres. Ctr. for Internat. Policy, Washington, 1985—. Pres.'s spl. rep. Inter-Am. Conf. on Edn., Sci. and Culture, 1977-79. Contbr. numerous articles to Commonweal, Atlantic, N.Y. Times. With USN, 1944-46; PTO. Fulbright scholar U. Bristol, Eng., 1953. Mem. Fgn. Svc. Assn., Fund for Constl. Govt. (bd. dirs.), Cosmos Club. Office: Ctr for Internat Policy 1717 Massachusetts Ave NW Washington DC 20036-2102 Office Phone: 202-232-3317.

WHITE, ROBERT JAMES, retired columnist; b. Mpls., Nov. 6, 1927; s. Robert Howard and Claire Lillian (Horner) W.; m. Adrienne Hoffman, Sept. 24, 1955; children: Claire, Pamela, Sarah. BS, U.S. Naval Acad., 1950. V.p. White Investment Co., Mpls., 1957-67; editl. writer Mpls. Tribune, 1967-73, assoc. editor, 1973-82; editor editl. pages Mpls. Star Tribune, 1982-93, columnist, 1993-95, contbg. columnist, 1996—2006. Trustee Refugee Policy Group, Washington, 1985—95. Destroyer officer, fighter pilot, flight instr., aide and flag lt. to cmdr. Fleet Air Jacksonville USN, 1950—58. Recipient cert. of excellence Overseas Press Club, 1981. Mem. Coun. Fgn. Rels., Mpls. Club. Congregationalist. Home: Summit House 400 Groveland Ave #2212 Minneapolis MN 55403 Personal E-mail: rjw823@aol.com.

WHITE, ROBERT JOEL, lawyer; b. Chgo., Nov. 1, 1946; s. Melvin and Margaret (Hoffman) W.; m. Gail Janet Edenson, June 29, 1969 (div. Dec. 1982); m. Penelope K. Bloch, Dec. 22, 1985. BS in Accountancy, U. Ill., 1968; JD, U. Mich., 1972. Bar: Calif. 1972, N.Y. 1985, U.S. Dist. Ct. (ctrl., ea., so. dists.) Calif. 1972, U.S. Ct. Appeals (9th cir.) 1978, U.S. Ct. Appeals (5th cir.) 1983, U.S. Ct. Appeals (6th cir.) 1984, U.S. Supreme Ct. 1977. Staff auditor Haskin & Sells, Chgo., 1968-69; assoc. O'Melveny & Myers, LA, 1972-79, ptnr., 1980—2007, chair reorgn. and restructuring dept., 1986—2001; CEO O'Melvey Cons. LLC, 2001—03; bd. dirs. Image Doc, 2007—, Syncora Holdings Ltd., 2008—, FPC PropCo, LLC, 2009—. Vis. lectr. U. Mich. Law Sch., Ann Arbor, 1986; lectr. Profl. Edn. Sys., Inc., Dallas, 1987, L.A., 1987, 89, Phoenix, 1990, Practicing Law Inst., San Francisco and N.Y.C., 1989-93, 2001-, Southwestern Legal Found., Dallas, 1991, UCLA Bankruptcy Inst., 1993, UCLA, 1993; mem. L.A. Productivity Commn., 1993-96. Contbr. articles to profl. jours. Active Constl. Rights Found., 1980—; active Am. Cancer Soc., 1989—, mem. L.A. bd. dirs., 1995—, vice chair, partnership com., 2003-; chair chpt. 11 com. Nat. Bankruptcy Conf., 2004-. Fellow Am. Coll. Brankruptcy; mem. ABA (litig. sect., mem. comml. law and bankruptcy com. 1972—), L.A. County Bar Assn. (comml. law and bankruptcy sect., chmn. fed. cts. com. 1981-82, exec. com. 1982—), Assn. Bus. Trial Lawyers (bd. govs. 1983-85), Fin. Lawyers Conf. (bd. govs. 1986—, pres. 1990-91), Am. Bankruptcy Inst. Avocations: skiing, running, history. Office: O'Melveny & Myers 1999 Ave of Stars Los Angeles CA 90067-6035 Office Phone: 310-246-8485. Business E-Mail: rwhite@omm.com.

WHITE, ROBERT LEE, electrical engineer, educator; b. Plainfield, NJ, Feb. 14, 1927; s. Claude and Ruby Hemsworth Emerson (Levick) W.; m. Phyllis Lillian Arlt, June 14, 1952; children: Lauren A., Kimberly A., Christopher L., Matthew P. BA in Physics, Columbia U., 1949, MA, 1951, PhD, 1954. Assoc. head atomic physics dept. Hughes Rsch. Labs., Malibu, Calif., 1954-61; head magnetics dept. Gen. Tel. and Electronics Rsch. Lab., Palo Alto, Calif., 1961-63; prof. elec. engring., materials sci. and engring. Stanford U., Palo Alto, 1963, chmn. elec. engring. dept., 1981-86, William E. Ayer prof. elec. engring., 1985-88, prof. emeritus, 1988—; exec. dir. The Exploratorium, San Francisco, 1987-89; dir. Inst. Electronics in Medicine, San Francisco, 1973—87, Stanford Ctr. Rsch. on Info. Storage Materials, 1991—2003; initial ltd. ptnr. Mayfield Fund, Mayfield II and Alpha II Fund, Rainbow Co-Investment Ptnrs., Halo Ptnrs.; pres. MacArray, Inc., 2005—. Vis. prof. Tokyo U., 1975, Nat. U. Singapore, 2002; Sony sabbatical chair, 1994; cons. in field. Author: (with K.A. Wickersheim) Magnetism and Magnetic Materials, 1965, Basic Quantum Mechanics, 1967; contbr. numerous articles to profl. jours. With USN, 1945-46. Fellow Guggenheim Oxford U., 1969-70, Canton Hosp., Swiss Fed. Inst. Tech., Zurich, 1977-78, Christensen fellow Oxford U., 1986, IEEE Magnetics Soc. Disting. lectr., 1998. Fellow IEEE, Am. Phys. Soc.; mem. Sigma Xi, Phi Beta Kappa. Home: 450 El Escarpado Stanford CA 94305-8431 Office: Stanford U Dept Material Sci Engr Stanford CA 94305 Office Phone: 650-799-4650. Personal E-mail: rlwhite450@sbcglobal.net.

WHITE, ROBERT LESLIE GORDON, JR., aerospace transportation executive; b. Orange, NJ, Dec. 20, 1941; s. Robert L.G. and Gertrude Marie (Wilson) W.; m. Joan Adam, May 9, 1970; children: Robert L.G. III, Sonya Lynn. BS in Metallurgical Engring., Lafayette Coll., 1964. Sr. engr. Crucible Steel Co., 1964-68; various positions Curtiss-Wright Corp., Woodridge, NJ, 1968-76, plant mgr. nuclear facility, 1976-80, dir. gas turbine overhaul, 1980-83; v.p., gen. mgr. Curtiss-Wright/Marquette, Inc., Fountain Inn, SC, 1983-87; pres. GEC-Marconi Aerospace Inc., Whippany, NJ, 1987-94, Breeze-Eastern, Union, NJ, 1994—98; pres., Breeze-Eastern divsn. Breeze-Eastern Corp., 1994; pres. aerospace products group Transtechnology Corp., Union, NJ, 1998—2003, pres., CEO, 2003, Breeze-Eastern Corp., 2003—. Bd. dirs. Breeze-Eastern Corp., 2003—. Office: Breeze-Eastern Corp 700 Liberty Ave Union NJ 07083-4115 Office Phone: 908-686-4000. Office Fax: 908-686-9292.

WHITE, ROBERT MARSHALL, retired physicist, educator, government official, consultant; b. Reading, Pa., Oct. 2, 1938; s. Carl M. and Miriam E. White; m. Sara Tolles; children: Victoria, Jonathan. BS in Physics, MIT, 1960; PhD, Stanford U., 1964. Vis. scientist Osaka (Japan) U., 1963; NSF postdoctoral fellow U. Calif., Berkeley, 1965-66; asst. prof. physics Stanford U., Palo Alto, Calif., 1966-70; NSF sr. postdoctoral fellow Cambridge U., England, 1970-71; mgr. solid state rsch. area XEROX PARC, 1971-78, mgr. storage tech., 1978-83, prin. scientist, 1983-84; v.p. rsch. and tech. Control Data Corp. Data Storage Products Group, Mpls., 1984-86; chief tech. officer, v.p. rsch. and engring. Control Data Corp., Mpls., 1986-89; v.p., dir. advanced computer techs. Microelectronics & Computer Tech. Corp., Austin, Tex., 1989-90; undersec. of commerce for tech. Dept. Commerce, Washington, 1990-93; prof., head dept. elec.l and computer engring. Carnegie Mellon U., Pitts., 1993-99, prof., dir. Data Storage Sys. Ctr., 1999—2004, prof. emeritus, 2004—; cons. prof. materials sci. & engring. Stanford U., 2004—. Vis. scientist Ecole Polytechnique, Paris, 1976-78, U. Pernambuco, Brazil, 1978, Max Planck Inst., Stuttgart, 1981; cons. prof. applied physics Stanford U., 1982-93; adj. prof. dept. physics U. Minn., 1987-89; bd. dirs. Found. Nat. Medals Sci. and Tech., Scientists and Engrs. America, Silicon Graphics, STMicroelectronics, ENSCO; sci. adv. bd. Data Storage Inst., Singapore, 2002-06; adv. bd. Pacific Enterprise Capital, LLC; mem. Nat. Adv. Com. on Semicondrs., 1990-92, Mfg. Forum, 1991, Nat. Critical Techs. Panel, 1990-91. Author: Quantum Theory of Magnetism, 1970 (Russian transl., 1972, Polish transl., 1979); Long Range Order in Solids, 1979 (Russian transl., 1982); Quantum Theory of Magnetism, 1983, 3d edit., 2007; Introduction to Magnetic Recording, 1985; contbr. articles to profl. jours. Recipient Alexander von Humboldt prize, Fed. Republic of Germany, 1981. Fellow AAAS, IEEE (disting. lectr. Magnetics Soc., mem. editl. bd. SPECTRUM, IEEE Disting. Pub. Svc. award 1993), Am. Phys. Soc. (George E. Pake prize 2004); mem. NAE, NRC (mem. nat. materials adv. bd., chmn. com. magnetic materials 1984, material sci. and engring., vice chmn. IUPAP commn. on magnetism), Conf. Magnetism and Magnetic Materials (adv. com. 1976-78, 80-95, program com. 1973-75, chmn. 1981, chmn. Intermag. Conf. 1991), Internat. Conf. Magnetism (program chmn. 1985). Office: Carnegie Mellon U Elec & Computer Engring Dep Pittsburgh PA 15213-3890 Business E-Mail: white@ece.cmu.edu.

WHITE, ROBERT MAYER, meteorologist; b. Boston, Feb. 13, 1923; s. David and Mary (Winkeller) W.; m. Mavis Seagle, Apr. 18, 1948; children: Richard Harry, Edwina Janet. BA, Harvard, 1944; MS, Mass. Inst. Tech., 1949, Sc.D., 1950; D.Sc., L.I. U., 1976; D.Sc. (hon.), Rensselaer Poly. Inst., 1977, U. Wis., Milw., 1978; ScD (hon.), U. Bridgeport, 1984, U. R.I., 1986, Clarkson U.; PhD (hon.), Johns Hopkins U., 1982, Drexel U., 1985, Ill. Inst. Tech., 1994. Project scientist Air Force Cambridge Rsch. Ctr., 1950-58, chief meteorol. devel. lab., 1958-59; asso. dir. research dept. Travelers Ins. Co., 1959-60; pres. Travelers Rsch. Ctr., Inc., 1960-63; chief US Weather Bur., 1963-65; adminstr. Environ. Sci. Svcs. Adminstrn., 1965-70, NOAA, 1970-77; pres. Joint Oceanographic Inst., Inc., 1977-79; chmn. Climate Research Bd., exec. officer Nat. Acad. Scis., 1977-79; Washington; adminstr. NRC, 1979-80; pres. Univ. Corp. Atmospheric Rsch., 1980-83, Nat. Acad. Eng., 1983-95; Karl T. Compton lectr. MIT, Cambridge, 1995-96; sr. fellow U. Corp. Atmospheric Rsch., 1995—. Sr. fellow H. John Heinz III Ctr. for Sci., Econs. and Environment, 1996—2000; pres. Wash. Adv. Group, 1996—. Author: articles in field; mem. editl. bd.: Am. Soc. Engring. Edn. Jour. Bd. overseers Harvard U., 1977—79; mem. vis. com. Kennedy Sch. Govt., Harvard U.; bd. dirs. Resources for the Future, 1980—. Capt. USAF, World War II. Decorated Legion of Honor France; recipient Godfrey L. Cabot award, Aero Club Boston, 1966, Cleveland Abbe award, Am. Meteorol. Soc., 1969, Jesse L. Rosenberger medal, U. Chgo., 1971, Rockefeller Pub. Svc. award, 1974, David B. Stone award, New Eng. Aquarium, 1975, Neptune award, Am. Oceanic Orgn., 1977, Matthew Fontaine Maury award, Smithsonian Instn., 1976, Internat. Conservation award, Nat. Wildlife Fedn., 1976, Internat. Meteorol. Orgn. prize, 1980, Tyler prize for Environ. Achievement, U. Calif., 1992, Vannevar Bush award, Nat. Sci. Bd., 1998, Centenary medal, Australia, 2003, Milennium award, Australian Acad. Engring., 2003. Fellow: Am. Acad. Arts and Scis., Australian Acad. Tech. Scis. and Engring., Am. Geophys. Union, World Acad. Art and Scis., AAAS, UCAR (sr.), Am. Meteorol. Soc. (coun. 1965—67, 1977—, pres. 1980, Charles Franklin Brooks award1978); mem.: Royal Acad. Engring. (U.K.), Russian Acad. Engring., Royal Acad. Engring. (hon.), Engring. Acad. Japan (fgn. assoc.), Am. Philos. Soc., Finnish Acad. Tech. (fgn.), Nat. Action Coun. Minorities in Engring. Inc., Coun. Fgn. Rels., Marine Tech. Soc., NAE (coun. 1977, pres. 1983—95), Cosmos Club (Washington). Home: Somerset House II 5610 Wisconsin Ave Apt 1506 Bethesda MD 20815-4439 Office: 888 16th St NW Washington DC 20005 Office Phone: 202-682-0164. Business E-Mail: rmw@theadvisorygroup.com.

WHITE, ROBERT STEPHEN, retired physics professor; b. Ellsworth, Kans., Dec. 28, 1920; s. Byron F. and Sebina (Leighty) White; m. Freda Marie Bridgewater, Aug. 30, 1942; children: Nancy Lynn, Margaret Diane, John Stephen, David Bruce. AB, Southwestern Coll., 1942, DSc (hon.), 1971; MS, U. Ill., 1943; PhD, U. Calif., Berkeley, 1951. Physicist Lawrence Radiation Lab., Berkeley, Livermore, Calif., 1948-61; head dept. particles and fields Space Physics Lab. Aerospace Corp., El Segundo, Calif., 1962-67; physics prof. U. Calif., Riverside, 1967-92, prof. emeritus physics dept., rsch. physicist, 1992—, dir. Inst. Geophysics and Planetary Physics, 1967-92, chmn. dept. physics, 1970-73. Lectr. U. Calif., Berkeley, 1953—54, Berkeley, 1957—59. Author: Space Physics, 1970, Why Science?, 1998, Energy for the Public: The Case for Increased Nuclear Fission Energy, 2006; contbr. articles to profl. jours. Officer USNR, 1944—46. Grantee, NASA, NSF, USAF, numerous others; Sr. Postdoctoral fellow, NSF, 1961—62. Fellow: AAAS, Am. Phys. Soc. (mem. exec. com. 1972—74); mem.: Am. Astron. Soc., Am. Geophys. Union. Home: 5225 Austin Rd Santa Barbara CA 93111-2905 Personal E-mail: stevewhite2@cox.net.

WHITE, RODNEY, general and vascular surgeon; b. Punxsutawney, Pa., Mar. 22, 1949; s. Forrest Dale and Bernice (Gaston) W.; m. Deanna White; children: Brittlyn Lee, Ryan Alan, Carissa Michelle, Cameron Allen. B.S., Syracuse U., 1970; M.D., Upstate Med. Ctr. NYU, 1970-74. Diplomate Am. Bd. Surgery. Intern, Harbor/UCLA Med. Ctr., Torrance, 1974-75, resident in surgery, 1975-79, vascular fellow, 1979-80, instr. surgery, 1979-80, chief vascular surgery, 1980—; cons., dir. Interpore Internat., Irvine, Calif., 1976-84. Contbr. articles to profl. jours., chpts. to books. Patentee in field. Mem. Council for Ethical Animal Research, Los Angeles, 1980—. Fellow Am. Coll. Surgeons; mem. Am. Heart Assn., Assn. Acad. Surgeons, Internat. Soc. Cardiovascular Surgery, Soc. Vascular Surgery, Soc. Biomaterials, Am. Assn. Med. Instrumentation (vascular graft standards com. N.J. 1980—), Med. Research Assn. Calif. (bd. dirs. 1980—), Phi Beta Kappa, Alpha Omega Alpha. Office: Harbor/UCLA Med Ctr Box 11 1000 W Carson St Torrance CA 90502-2004

WHITE, RONALD JOSEPH, biomedical researcher, physiologist, educator; b. Opelousas, La., Dec. 4, 1940; s. John Wesley and Alma Louise (LaSalle) White; m. Margaret Helen Launey, June 8, 1963; children: Joseph LaSalle, Angela Alma, Margaret Leslie. BS in Chemistry, U. S.W. La., 1963; PhD in Phys. Chemistry, U. Wis., 1968. NSF postdoctoral fellow in theoretical chemistry U. Oxford, England, 1967-68; rsch. assoc. Bell Tel. Labs., Murray Hill, NJ, 1968-70; from asst. prof. to assoc. prof. math. U. S.W. La., Lafayette, 1970—76, prof. math., dir. Univ. Honors Program, 1976—80; rsch. assoc. dept. physiology and biophysics U. Miss. Med. Ctr., Jackson, 1973-75; sr. scientist GE Co./Mgmt. and Tech. Svcs. Co., Washington and Houston, 1980-85; chief scientist Life/Biomed. Scis. and Applications Divsn. NASA, Washington, 1985—96; rsch. prof. physiology Uniformed Svcs. U. Health Scis., Bethesda, Md., 1985—96; prof. dept. otorhinolaryngology Baylor Coll. Medicine, Houston, 1996—2003; assoc. dir. Nat. Space Biomed. Rsch. Inst., 1997—2003; sr. fellow Univs. Space Rsch. Assn., Houston, 2003—09; v.p. rsch. SD Sch. Mines & Tech., Rapid City, 2009—. V.p. Assn. Gifted and Talented Students, La., 1977—80; pres. La. Collegiate Honors Coun., 1978—79. Editor (assoc. life scis.): Simulation, 1974—75; editor: (spl.) Medicine and Sci. in Sports and Exercise, 1996; contbr. numerous chpts. to books, papers to profl. jours. Recipient NASA traineeship, 1963—66, Am. Inst. Chemists award, 1963, Disting. Prof. award, 1978, Med. Info. Processing Best Paper award, 15th ann. Hawaii Internat. Conf. on Systems Sci., 1982, Hon. Mem. award, Soc. NASA Flight Surgeons, 1992, Exceptional Achievement medal, NASA, 1992; fellow, Woodrow Wilson Found., 1963. Mem.: Internat. Soc. Computational Biology, Internat. Acad. Astronautics (bd. trustees 1997—2009, commr. space life scis. 2001—03, chair life scis. 2001—09, Luigi Napolitano Lit. award 1996), Am. Soc. Gravitational and Space Biology (charter mem.), Am. Phys. Soc., Aerospace Med. Assn., Sigma Xi (rsch. award 1976), Phi Kappa Phi. Office: SD Sch Mines & Tech 501 E Saint Joseph St Rapid City SD 57701 Home: 764 Fox Run Dr Rapid City SD 57701 Office Phone: 605-394-2493. Personal E-mail: ronwhite@earthlink.net. Business E-Mail: ronald.white@sdsmt.edu.

WHITE, RONALD LEON, retired business executive; b. West York, Pa., July 14, 1930; s. Clarence William and Grace Elizabeth (Gingerich) W.; m. Estheranne Wieder, June 16, 1951; children: Bradford William, Clifford Allen, Erick David. BS in Econs, U. Pa., 1952, MBA, 1957. Cost analysis supr. Air Products & Chem. Corp., Allentown, Pa., 1957-60; cost control mgr. Mack Trucks, Inc., Allentown, 1960-64; mgmt. cons. Peat, Marwick, Mitchell & Co., Phila., 1964-66; mgr. profit planning Monroe, The Calculator Co. (divsn. Litton Industries), Orange, NJ, 1966-67, contr., 1967-68; v.p. fin. Bus. Sys. Group of Litton Industries, Beverly Hills, Calif., 1968-70; pres. Royal Typewriter Co. (divsn. Litton Industries), Hartford, Conn., 1970-73; exec. v.p., COO, treas., dir. Tenna Corp., Cleve., 1973-75, pres.,COO dir., 1975-77; v.p. fin. Arby's, Inc., Youngstown, Ohio, 1978-79; exec. v.p., dir. Roxbury Am., Inc., Beverly Hill, Calif., 1979—81; v.p. fin., treas. Royal Crown Cos., Inc., Atlanta and Miami Beach, Fla., 1981-86; v.p. fin. TDS Healthcare Sys. Corp., Atlanta, 1987-88; v.p. Corp. Fin. Assocs., Atlanta, 1988-90; prin. The Janelle Co., Atlanta, 1991—2006; ret., 2006. Vice chmn. Ga. Mental Health, Mental Retardation, Substance Abuse Regional Bd. #6, 1994-2002, chmn., Ga. State Regional Bds. Leadership Coun., 1999-2000; v.p. and dir. Ga. Alliance for Mentally Ill, 1997-2003; instr. acctg. Wharton Sch. U. Pa., 1952-53, instr. industry, 1953-54. Deacon United Ch. of Christ. Lt. USNR, 1954-57. Mem. Am. Mgmt. Assn., Inst. Mgmt. Accts., Nat. Assn. Corp. Dirs., Fin. Execs. Internat., Acacia, Masons, Rotary. Personal E-mail: rlwea@comcast.net.

WHITE, ROSCOE BERYL, research physicist, educator; b. Freeport, Ill., Dec. 20, 1937; s. Beryl Roscoe and Merlyn (Worth) W.; m. Laura Sanguinet, July 11, 1966; 1 child, Veronica Maria. BS, U. Minn., 1959; PhD, Princeton U., 1963. Rsch. asst. Princeton (N.J.) U., 1962, instr.,

1962-63, full prof., 1984—; rsch. assoc. U. Minn., 1963; exch. scientist U.S. Acad. Scis., Lebedev Inst., Moscow, 1963-64; vis. scientist Internat. Ctr. Theoretical Physics, Trieste, Italy, 1964-66; asst. prof. UCLA, 1966-72; mem. Inst. Advanced Study, Princeton, 1972-74; physicist Princeton Plasma Physics Lab., 1974—, prin. rsch. physicist, 1980—, head theory divsn., 1986-93. Vis. lectr. New Delhi U., Udaipur, 1966; vis. scientist U. Chile, Santiago, 1969; cons. Trecani Encyclopedia, Italy, 1992-93. Author: Theory of Tokamak Plasmas North Holland, 1989, 2d edit., 2002. Avocations: windsurfing, Karate, music, chess. Office: Princeton Plasma Physic Lab Princeton Univ Princeton NJ 08543

WHITE, ROY BERNARD, performing arts association administrator; b. Cin. s. Maurice and Anna (Rudin) W.; m. Sally White, June 17, 1951; children: Maurice, Barbara Dee, Daniel Robert. BA, U. Cin., 1949. Sales staff Twentieth Century Fox Films, Cin.; pres. Mid-States Theatres; dir. Nat. Assn. Theatre Owners, nat. pres., exec. com., chmn. bd. Mem. film adv. panel Ohio Arts Coun.; bd. dirs. Will Rogers Meml. Fund, Found. Motion Picture Pioneers, Inc.; mem. media arts panel Nat. Endowment for Arts. Served with USAAF, 1944-45. Named Exhibitor of Year Internat. Film Importers and Distbrs. Am. Mem. Nat. Assn. Theater Owners (pres.), Am. Film Inst. (trustee 1972-75, exec. com. 1972-75, trustee emeritus), Fedn. Motion Picture Pioneers (v.p.), Masons, Queen City Racquet, Amberley Village (Ohio) Tennis Club (pres. 1972-73), Bankers Club, Quail Creek Country Club, Bay Colony Country Club, Bay Colony Golf Club, Morrings Country Club, Forum Club(Naples-)(dir.) Home: 1274 Waggle Way Naples FL 34108-1994 Personal E-mail: royb3140@aol.com.

WHITE, SARA KATHRYN, literature and language professor; b. Scranton, Pa., Apr. 29, 1972; BA in English, Marywood U., Scranton, 1994; MA in English, U. Scranton, Pa., 1998. Cert. in secondary English Pa., 1998. Newspaper reporter Susquehanna County Ind., Montrose, Pa., 1990—99; English instr. Keystone Coll., La Plume, Pa., 1999—. Office: Keystone Coll One College Green La Plume PA 18440 Business E-Mail: sara.white@keystone.edu.

WHITE, SCOTT, federal agency administrator; Leadership and staff positions Directorate of Intelligence, Washington, Office Congl. Affairs, Washington, Nat. Intelligence Coun., Washington, assoc. dep. dir. intelligence, 2002—04; sr. posts including dir. source ops. & mgmt. Nat. Geospatial-Intelligence Agency, Washington; dir. of support CIA, Washington, assoc. dep. dir., 2008—. Office: Ctrl Intelligence Agency Office of Assoc Dep Dir c/o Office Pub Affairs Washington DC 20505*

WHITE, SHARMAN LYNELL, lawyer; b. Albany, Ga., Aug. 19, 1968; d. Frank Irvin and Annette Jones White; 1 child, Andrew Franklin White Cleary. BA in Govt. cum laude, Harvard Coll., Cambridge, Mass., 1990; JD, U. Tex., Austin, 1995. Bar: NY 1996. Assoc. Beveridge & Diamond, PC, Washington, 1995—97; atty., adviser U.S. Dept. Agr., 1997—. Mem. unexploded ordnance panel US Dept. Interior, Conf. Environment, Albuquerque, 2001; spkr. pub. lands and natural resources seminar US Dept. Justice, Nat. Advocacy Ctr., Columbia, SC, 2000; appointee Fed. Natural Resource Damage Assessment and Restoration Adv. Com.; mem. legal rsch. bd. U. Tex. Law Sch. Lead articles editor: Tex. Environ. Law Jour., 1994—95. Sponsor Christian Children's Fund. Recipient Performance awards, USDA Office Gen. Counsel, 1998—2004, On the Spot award, 1999, Extra Effort award, 2000, Departmental awards, USDA Hazardous Materials Mgmt. Group, 2001, 2005. Mem.: ACLU, Harvard Crimson, Harvard Club Washington, Potomac Pedalers Touring Club, MENSA. Avocations: travel, writing, bicycling, movies, boating. Office: US Department of Agriculture 1400 Independence Ave SW Washington DC 20250 Personal E-mail: sharmian.white@post.harvard.edu. E-mail: sharmian.white@usda.gov.

WHITE, SHAUN ROGER, Olympic athlete, professional snowboarder, professional skateboarder; b. San Diego, Sept. 3, 1986; s. Kathy and Roger White. Profl. snowboarder Burton Snowboarding team, 1999—; skateboarder Tony Hawk Gigantic Skatepark Tour, 2002; profl. Skateboarder, 2003—; designer The White Collection. Snowboarder US Olympic Team, Torino, Italy, 2006. Actor: (films) The White Album, 2004. Recipient ESPY award, Best Male Action Sports Athlete, ESPN, 2003, 2006, 2008, ESPY award, Best US Olympian, 2006; named Sports-Choice Action Sports, Teen Choice Awards, 2006. Achievements include being the youngest snowboarder to win the US Open Slopestyle Championship, 2004; being the first athlete to compete in both Winter and Summer X Games, 2003; winning the gold medal at Winter X Games, Slopestyle, 2003-2006, Halfpipe, 2003, 2006; winning the gold metal at Summer X Games, Vert, 2005; winning all 5 Grand Prix Superpipes, 2005-2006; winning a gold metal at Torino Olympic Games, Men's Halfpipe, 2006. Office: c/o USSA Box 100 1500 Kearns Blvd Park City UT 84060

WHITE, SHELBY, art association administrator; m. Leon Levy (dec. 2003). BA, Mount Holyoke Coll; MA, Columbia U. Chmn. Shelby White-Leon Levy Prog. for Archaeol. Publs., 1997—. Mem. Cultural Property Adv. Com., 2000; bd. dirs. Alliance Capital Money Market Funds. Bd. dirs. Met. Mus. Art, NYC; cofounder New Initiative Program Inst. Advanced Studies, Princeton, NJ; cofounder Leon Levy Biogenetics Ctr. Rockefeller U.; chair White-Levy Program for Archaeological Publications. Named one of Top 200 Collectors, ARTnews Mag., 2004, 2006, 2007. Avocation: Collector of Antiquities. Office: Semitic Mus Harvard U 6 Divinity Ave Cambridge MA 02138 Office Phone: 617-495-9317. E-mail: info@whitelevy.org.

WHITE, STANLEY ARCHIBALD, electrical engineer, researcher; b. Providence, Sept. 25, 1931; s. Clarence Archibald White and Lou Ella (Givens) Arford; m. Edda María Castaño-Benítez, June 6, 1956; children: Dianne, Stanley Jr., Paul, John. BSEE, Purdue U., 1957, MSEE, 1959, PhD in Elec. Engring. and Aero. and Engring. Scis., 1965. Registered profl. engr., Ind., Calif. Engr. Rockwell Internat., Anaheim, Calif., 1959-68, mgr., 1968-84, sr. scientist, 1984-90; pres. Signal Processing and Controls Engring. Space Corp., 1990—2003; pvt. practice San Clemente, Calif., 2000—03. Lectr. in elec. engring. U. Calif., 1959-84, adj. prof., 1984-97; cons. and lectr. in field; bd. dirs. Asilomar Signals, Systems and Computers Conf. Corp., 1988-02. Contbr. chpts. to books; contbr. articles to encys. and profl. jours. With USAF, 1951-55. N.Am. Aviation Sci. Engring. fellow, 1963-65; recipient Disting. Lectr. award Nat. Electronics Conf., Chgo., 1973, Engr. of Yr. award Orange County (Calif.) Engring. Coun., 1984, Engr. of Yr. award Rockwell Internat., 1985, Leonardo da Vinci Medallion, 1986, Sci. Achievement award, 1987, Disting. Engring. Alumnus award Purdue U., 1988, Meritorious Inventor's award Rockwell Internat. Corp., 1989, Outstanding Elec. Engr. award Purdue U., 1992, Boeing N.Am. Aviation Top Inventor award, 1998. Fellow AAAS (life), AIAA, IEEE (life; Centennial medal, Millenium medal, chair of ICASSP and ISCAS, Signal Processing Soc. disting. lect. and founding chmn. L.A. coun. chpt., Circuits and Sys. Soc. Tech. Achievement award 1996, Golden Jubilee medal 1999), Inst. for Advancement Engring., N.Y. Acad. Scis. (life); mem. VFW (life), Air Force Assn. (life), Am. Legion (life), Sigma Xi (life; founding pres. Orange County chpt., pres. 1988-00, 05—), Eta Kappa Nu (Paul K. Hudson disting. fellow, internat. dir. emeritus, Vladimir Karapetoff award 2005), Tau Beta Pi. Achievements include 82 US and over 20 foreign patents in field. Avocation: choral music. Office Phone: 949-498-5519. Business E-Mail: stan.white@ieee.org.

WHITE, STANLEY V., legislative staff member; b. Ft. Bragg, NC, Sept. 10, 1956; Exec. dir. for Rep. Thomas Foglietta, US House of Reps., Washington, 1992—96, sr. legis. asst., 1996—97; adminstr. Office of First Congl. Dist. of Pa., 1997—98; chief of staff Rep. Robert Brady, US House of Reps., 1998—. Avocations: skiing, reading. Office: Office of Congressman Robert Brady 206 Cannon House Office Bldg Washington DC 20515-0001 also: 1907-09 S Broad St Philadelphia PA 19148 Office Phone: 202-225-4731. E-mail: stan.white@mail.house.gov.*

WHITE, STEPHANIE, computer science educator; life ptnr. William White; 1 child, Michele. MS, PhD, Poly. U., Bklyn., 1987. Prin. engr. Grumman Corp., Bethpage, NY, 1979—95, Northrop Grumman, Bethpage, 1995—99; prof. LI U., Brookville, NY, 1999—. Contbr. scientific papers. Mem. IEEE Computer Soc., 2006—08, v.p., tech. activities, 2005—07; chair Audit Com., Washington, 2008. Fellowship, Woodrow Wilson Found., 1958—60. Mem.: IEEE Computer Soc. (sr.; bd. govs. 2006—08, Golden Core 2006), Phi Beta Kappa, Pi Mu Epsilon, Sigma Xi. Achievements include advances in requirements definition modeling and verification; development of process centered environment for complex systems. Office: Long Island Univ CW Post Campus 720 Northern Blvd Brookville NY 11548

WHITE, STEPHEN HALLEY, biophysicist, educator; b. Wewoka, Okla., May 14, 1940; s. James Halley and Gertrude June (Wyatt) W.; m. Buff Ertl, Aug. 20, 1961 (div. 1982); children: Saill, Shell, Storn, Sharr, Skye, Sunde; m. Jackie Marie Dooley, Apr. 14, 1984. BS in Physics, U. Colo., 1963; MS in Physics, U. Wash., 1965, PhD in Physiology and Biophysics, 1969; PhD (hon.), Stockholm U., 2008. USPHS postdoctoral fellow biochemistry U. Va., Charlottesville, 1971-72; asst. prof. physiology and biophysics U. Calif., Irvine, 1972-75, assoc. prof. physiology and biophysics, 1975-78, prof. physiology and biophysics, 1978—, vice chmn. physiology and biophysics, 1974-75, chmn. physiology and biophysics, 1977-89. Guest biophysicist Brookhaven Nat. Lab., Upton, L.I., N.Y., 1977-99; mem. NIH BBM study sect., 2005—. Contbr. numerous articles to profl. jours. Served to capt. USAR, 1969-71. Recipient Research Career Devel. award USPHS, 1975-80, Kaiser-Permanente Tchg. award, 1975, 92; fellow Biophysical Soc., 2002; grantee NIH, 1971—, NSF, 1971—. Mem. NSF (adv. panel for molecular biology 1982-85, mem. nat. steering com. advanced neutron source 1992-95), Internat. Union Pure and Applied Biophysics (U.S. nat. com. 1997—2004, chmn. 2000-04), Fedn. Am. Soc. for Exptl. Biology (bd. dirs. 1998-2002), Biophys. Soc. (chmn. membrane biophysics subgroup 1977-78, acting sec., treas. 1979-80, coun. 1981-84, exec. bd. 1981-83, program chmn. 1985, ann. meeting, sec. 1987-95, pres. 1996-97, Disting. Svc. award 1999, Avanti award 2009), Am. Physiol. Soc. (editl. bd. 1981-93, membership com. 1985-86, publ. com. 1987-91), Assn. Chmn. Depts. Physiology (rep. to coun. acad. socs. 1981-82, councilor 1982-83, pres. 1986-87), Soc. Gen. Physiologists (treas. 1985-88), The Protein Soc. (electronic pub. coord. 1993-2007, NIH BBM study section 2005—). Avocations: skiing, cooking, travel. Office: U Calif Dept Physiology & Biophysics Med Sci I-D346 Irvine CA 92697-4560

WHITE, SUZANNE MARIE, medical educator; d. J. W. and Grace Jean Baptiste White. M, NY U., 1991. Cert. occupl. therapist NBCOT, 1975. Clin. asst. prof. SUNY Downstate Med. Ctr., Bklyn., 2000—. Contbr. scientific papers. Recipient DR. Donald Scherl Faculty Excellence award, SUNY Downstate Med. Ctr., 2008, Janet Bair Writer's award, Am. Occupl. Therapy Assn., 2008. Mem.: NY State Occupl. Therapy Assn. (mental health SIS chair 2007—, Merit Practice award 2007). Achievements include research in mental health advocacy OT and lets get organized time management(cognitive adaptation for persons with mental illness and or substance use disorders co-occurring conditions). Avocations: gardening, travel, cooking. Office: SUNY Downstate Med Ctr 450 Clarkson Ave Box 81 Brooklyn NY 11203 Office Fax: 718-270-7464. Business E-Mail: suzanne.white@downstate.edu.

WHITE, TAYLOE MCDONALD, artist; d. Frank Bartow and Margaret Forkin McDonald; m. Jonathan Michael White, Dec. 20, 1997; 1 child, William Sheldon. BS in Psychology with high honors, U. Fla., Gainesville, 1997. Dir. training and develop. Kesler Mentoring Connection, 1999—2002; owner Tayloe White Portaiture and Fine Art, 2004—; Artist R. Roberts Gallery, Jacksonville, Fla., 2009. Pres. Shift*Eight, 2008—. Exhibitions include, Jacksonville Mus. Contemporary Art, one-woman shows include, R. Roberts Gallery, Rohm Gallery, New Orleans, La. Mentor Take Stock in Children, Jacksonville, 1998—2007. Recipient Mentor of Yr. award, Delores Barr Weaver Found., 2001. Mem.: NAACP (assoc.), Zonta Internat., Thalias Writer's Salon (life), Golden Key Honory Soc. (life). Democrat-Npl. Avocations: art, travel, literature, music, writing. Personal E-mail: tayloewhite@mac.com.

WHITE, TERESA LYNNE, insurance company executive; married; 2 children. BBA, U. Tex., Arlington; M in Mgmt., Troy U., Ala. Second v.p. policy/payroll account svcs. AFLAC Inc., Columbus, Ga., 1998—2000, v.p. client svcs., 2000—04, sr. v.p. sales support and adminstrn., 2004—07, sr. v.p., dep. chief adminstrv. officer, 2007—08, exec. v.p., chief adminstrv. officer, 2008—. Bd. dirs. Communicorp, Columbus. Bd. mem. Columbus Housing Initiative; mem. bd. pensions South Ga. Conf. of United Meth. Ch. Named one of Top 77 Women in Exec. Leadership Worth Watching in 2006, Profiles in Diversity Jour.; named to 2006 Divas List, Bus.-to-Bus. mag. Fellow: Life Mgmt. Inst. Office: AFLAC Inc 1932 Wynnton Rd Columbus GA 31999 Office Phone: 706-323-3431.

WHITE, THOMAS, JR., city councilman; b. South Jamaica, NY; City councilman Dist. 28 NY City Coun., 1992—2001, 2006—. Chmn. Econ. Develop. com. NY City Coun. Co-founder, exec. dir. J-CAP. Recipient Outstanding Contbn. citation, Gov. Hugh Carey, Disting. Svc. award NY State Black and Puerto Rican Legis. Caucus. Democrat. Office: 145-40 Rockaway Blvd South Ozone Park NY 11436 Office Phone: 718-843-0792, 212-788-6850. Office Fax: 718-845-0817. Business E-Mail: twhite@council.nyc.gov.*

WHITE, THOMAS EDWARD, lawyer; b. NYC, July 11, 1933; s. Thomas Aubrey and Gladys Mary (Piper) W.; m. Joan Carolyn Olsen, Dec. 2, 1967 (dec.); children: Charles Garret, Nancy Carolyn, Linda Marie, Penelope Lindsay, Elizabeth Ann. AB, Princeton U., 1955; LLB, Columbia U., 1960; BA summa cum laude, SUNY-Purchase Coll., 2002; student in Fine Arts, NYU, 2002—04. Bar: NY 1961. Atty. Seward & Kissel, NYC, 1960-69; gen. counsel Howmet Corp., NYC, 1969-70; v.p., gen. counsel, sec. Howmedica, Inc., NYC, 1970-74, sr. v.p., dir., 1974-83; pvt. practice NYC, 1983-97. Ptnr. Westmed Venture Ptnrs. (formerly Integrated Med. Venture Ptnrs.), NYC, 1987-99; chmn. Shoreside Cons. Ltd., Miami, Fla., 1987-98. Mem. Mamaroneck Town Coun., 1971-75; mem. vestry Episcopalian Ch., 1987-90; mem. diocesan coun. Episcopal Ch. NY, 2001-07; bd. trustees, SUNY Purchase Coll. Found., 2008-. Served to 1st lt. US Army, 1955-57. Mem.: Larchmont (NY) Yacht; Princeton (NYC). Republican. Home: 260 Barnard Rd Larchmont NY 10538-1941

WHITE, TIMOTHY PAUL, brokerage house executive; b. Ft. Sill, Okla., Jan. 9, 1963; s. Paul R. and Lucille (Mattison) White; m. Susan Gertrude Foreman, Dec. 29, 1984; children: Jessica Lynn, Rebecca Anne, Kathleen Marie. BS in Fin., Pa. State U., 1985; MS, Coll. Fin. Planning, 2009. Cert. fin. planner Colo. Assoc. planner, agt. Pa. Fin. Group, Harrisburg, Pa., 1988-92; mgr. mktg. and sales Meridian Securities, Inc., Reading, Pa., 1992-96; v.p. products and sales mgr. Core States Securities Corp., Reading, 1996-98; regional sales mgr. First Union Brokerage Svcs. Inc., 1998-2001; fin. advisor, v.p. First Union Securities Inc., 2001—02; pres. Investors Ctrl. Comm. Inc.; mng. dir., co-founder, owner Guidon, LLC, 2001—; fin. advisor Wachovia Securities LLC, 2002—, sr. v.p., 2002—. Spkr. Nat. Mut. Fund Conf., 1995, Cmty. Bank Investment Program Symposium, 1996, Nat. Investment Products Conf., 1996. Author: Money Smart Records, 2002; contbg. editor: Bank Securities Jour.; contbr. articles to profl. jours. Program cons. Jr. Achievement, Lancaster, Pa., 1990—91; pres. Adamstown Recreation Bd., 1996; bd. dirs. Dollars for Scholars, Lancaster, Pa., 2006—08. 1st lt. US Army, 1985—88, capt. USAR, 1989—92. Decorated Commendation medal, Achievement medal; recipient George C. Marshal award, U.S. Army, 1985; scholar ROTC, 1981—85. Mem.: Fin. Planning Assn., Ctrl. Pa. Soc. Inst. CFP (bd. dirs. 1996—, pres.-elect 1998, pres. 1999), U.S. Cav. Assn. (fundraising com. 1994—96), Inst. CFP. Republican. Lutheran. Avocations: military and political history, reading, gardening, woodworking. Office: Wachovia Securities LLC 3411 Concard Rd York PA 17402 Home Phone: 717-336-5663; Office Phone: 717-751-1280. Business E-Mail: tim.white@wachovia.com.

WHITE, TIMOTHY PETER, academic administrator; b. Buenos Aires, July 9, 1949; came to US, 1957; s. Anthony Robert and Mary (Weston) White; m. Karen N. White; children: Randall Patrick, Timothy Anthony, Alexander John, Logan. Student, Diablo Valley Community Coll., 1966-67; BA magna cum laude, Fresno State U., 1970; MS, Calif. State U., Hayward, 1972; PhD, U. Calif., Berkeley, 1977. Asst. prof. phys. edn. U. Mich., Ann Arbor, 1978-82, assoc. prof., 1982-84, assoc. prof., chmn. dept. kinesiology, 1985-89; rsch. scientist Inst. Gerontology, 1986-91; prof., chmn. U. Mich., Ann Arbor, 1989-91; dept. chmn., prof. dept. human dynamics U. Calif., Berkeley, 1991—2000; provost, exec. v.p. Oreg. State U., 2000—04, interim pres., 2002—03; pres. U. Idaho, 2004—08; chancellor U. Calif., Riverside, 2008—. Editor: (with others) Frontiers of Exercise Biology, 1983; contbr. articles to profl. jours. and chpts. to books on exercise and muscle. Fellow Am. Coll. Sports Medicine (trustee, v.p. 1991—, New Investigator award 1981), Am. Acad. Phys. Edn.; mem. AAAS, AAHPERD, Gerontol. Soc. Am., Am. Physiol. Soc., Sigma Xi, Phi Kappa Phi. Avocations: woodworking, nordic skiing, sailing, swimming, running. Office: U Calif Riverside 4108 Hinderaker Hall 900 University Ave Riverside CA 92521 Office Phone: 951-827-5201. Office Fax: 951-827-3866. E-mail: chancellor@ucr.edu.*

WHITE, TONY L., former health and medical products executive; BA, We. Carolina U., 1969. Sales rep. Baxter Internat. Inc., 1970-74, dist. mgr., 1974-76, export mgr. Latin Am., 1976-82, v.p. AMPAC, pres. Travenol-Can., 1982-85, pres. Fenwal divsn., 1985-86, pres. scientific products, biomedical divsn., 1986, v.p. diagnostics, 1986-92, exec. vp, 1992-95; chmn., pres., CEO Applied Biosystems Inc. (formerly Applera Corp.), Foster City, Calif., 1995—2008. With USAR, 1968-74.*

WHITE, W. CHRISTOPHER, lawyer; b. Boston, Dec. 30, 1951; s. William George and Patricia Elizabeth (Brophy) W.; m. Anne Marie Cosgriff, Aug. 19, 1972; children: Jennifer, Andrew, Meghan. BA, U. Notre Dame, 1973; postgrad., London Sch. Econs., 1974; JD, U. Mich., 1977. Bar: N.Y. 1981, Mass 1978. Atty. Ryan & White, Springfield, Mass., 1977—78, Fred F. French Co., NYC, 1978—80, Breed Abbot & Morgan, NYC, 1980—87; ptnr. Breed, Abbott & Morgan, NYC, 1984-87; ptnr., chmn. global fin. dept. Cadwalader Wickersham & Taft LLP, NYC, 1987—, chmn., 2008—. Mem. Univ. Club. Office: Cadwalader Wickersham & Taft LLP 1 World Fin Ctr New York NY 10281 Office Phone: 212-504-6633. Office Fax: 212-504-6666. Business E-Mail: christopher.white@cwt.com.

WHITE, WALTER HIAWATHA, JR., lawyer; b. Milw., Aug. 21, 1954; s. Walter H. and Winifred (Parker) W.; m. Sonja Athene Rein, Dec. 30, 1977. Student, Leningrad Pedagogical Inst., USSR, 1976; BA, Amherst Coll., 1977; JD, U. Calif., Berkeley, 1980. Bar: Wis. 1980, U.S. Dist. Ct. (ea. dist.) Wis. 1980, U.S. Ct. Appeals (7th cir.) 1980, U.S. Supreme Ct. 1983. Assoc. Michael, Best & Friedrich, Milw., 1980-88; commr. securities State of Wis., 1988-91; ptnr. Quarles & Brady, Milw., 1991-94; mng. dir. Steptoe & Johnson Internat., Moscow, 1994-99; ptnr. Bryan Cave, London, 1999—2001, White & Jones LLP (merged with Grundberg Mocatta Rakison LLP), London, 2001—06, Grundberg Mocatta Rakison LLP, London, 2006—. Trustee Milw. Found., 1992-94; vice chmn. dist. com. Bd. Attys. Profl. Responsibility, Milw., 1984-87; bd. dirs. Wis. Trust Found., Madison, Church Mut. Ins. Co., Merrill, Wis., Ctrl. Asian Am. Enterprise Fund; bd. adv. Law & Policy Group Inc. Editor Black Law Jour., 1978-80; mem. editorial bd. Barrister Mag.; contbr. articles to profl. jours. Mem. Cardinal Stritch Coll. Bus. Adv. Bd., Milw., 1982-85, health law com. Wis. Civil Liberties Union, Milw., 1985-88, Gov.'s Adv. Bd. to Legal Services Corp., Madison, 1982-87; sec. Milw. Forum Inc., 1982-88; pres. Milw. Urban League, 1985; bd. dirs. WUWM Pub. Radio Sta., Milw., 1983-86, Family Service Milw., Inc., 1987-89, Neighborhood House of Milw., Inc., 1987-94. John Woodruff Simpson fellow, 1977; Named one of the 86 most interesting people in Milw., Milw. Mag., 1986. Mem. ABA (chair young lawyers div. 1989-90, commn. on opportunities for minorities in the profession, del. assn. Soviet lawyers, co-chair commonwealth of ind. states law com. of internat. law and practice sect. 1990-91, bd. govs. 2002—2005), Nat. Bar Assn., Assn. Internat. des Jeunes Avocats, Milw. Bar Assn., Wis. Black Lawyers Assn. (bd. dirs. 1982-83), Milw. Young Lawyers Assn. (pres. 1984-85, pres.'s award 1985), Bd. Bar Examiners, Milw. Found. Avocations: Russian lit., rowing, squash. Office: Grundberg Mocatta Rakison LLP 13 Loraine Road London N7 6EZ England Business E-Mail: whw@whiteandjones.com.

WHITE, WESLEY MATTHEW, urologist; BA, U. Tenn., Knoxville, 1999; MD, U. Tenn., Memphis, 2003. Resident, divsn. urologic surgery U. of Tenn., Med. Ctr. Knoxville, 2003—08; fellow laparoscopic and robotic urologic surgery Cleve. Clinic Found., 2008—. Office: Univ Tenn Med Ctr 1924 Alcoa Hwy Knoxville TN 37920

WHITE, WILL WALTER, III, public relations consultant, writer; b. Glen Ridge, NJ, July 3, 1930; s. Will Walter and Miriam Chandler (Milburn) W.; m. Phyllis Marcia DuFlocq, Dec. 28, 1951 (div. 1971); children: Will Walter IV, Scott, Alan; m. Anne Elizabeth Levenson, Nov. 21, 1971 (div. 1992); children: Duncan, Christopher; stepchildren: Michael, Susan; m. Catherine Laur, Aug. 26, 1992. BA, Cornell U.,

1952. Supr. Union Carbide Corp., NYC, 1954-59; account exec. Ketchum, MacLeod & Grove, NYC, 1959-62; sr. v.p. Wilson, Haight & Welch, Hartford, Conn., 1962-72; chmn., chief exec. officer Lowengard & Brotherhood, Hartford, 1972-83; pres., chief exec. officer Harland & Tine & White, Hartford, 1983-87; chmn. Donahue Inc., Hartford, 1987-89; ptnr. Laur White & White, Heathsville, Va., 1992—2000; owner Omega Cubed Press, 1996—. Exec. com. Conn. Dist. Export Council, 1979-88. Author: The Sunfish Book, 1983, 96; contbg. editor Mid-Gulf Sailing mag., 1994-95; sailing columnist, Waterline Mag., 2007-. Mem. exec. com. Hartford Stage Co., 1982-86; pres. Vis. Nurse Assn., Hartford, 1979; fin. chmn. Vis. Nurse and Home Care, Inc., Hartford and Waterbury, 1982-91; mem. pub. rels. com. Fairfield County Rep. Com., 1961; chmn. S.W. Fla. Regional Harbor Bd., 1995-2000. 1st lt. U.S. Army, 1952-54. Nat. champion Sunfish Racing Class, 1966, 68 Mem. Pub. Rels. Soc. Am. (accredited, chmn. investor rels. sect. 1983, charter mem. Hall of Fame 1990), Bus. Profl. Advt. Assn. (cert. bus. communicator), Nat. Investor Rels. Inst., U.S. Sunfish Class Assn. (pres. 1985-88, charter mem. Hall of Fame 1991), Boaters Action and Info. League (exec. v.p. 1992-2000), Hist. Soc. Sarasota County (bd. dirs. 1995-2000). Address: 3220 S E Hansel Ave Arcadia FL 34266-3143 Personal E-mail: omegacubed@embarqmail.com.

WHITE, WILLIAM B., medical educator, researcher; b. Oceanside, NY, Aug. 28, 1953; s. Eli D. and Irene (Silberman) W.; m. Kari Ostvik, Oct. 1, 1978; children: Bjornulf Ostvik-White, Marte Ostvik-White, Elin Ostvik-White. BS, Emory Coll., 1974; MD, Med. Coll. Ga., 1978. Asst. prof. U. Conn. Sch. Medicine, Farmington, 1981-86, assoc. prof., 1986-91, prof., 1991—, chief divsn. internal medicine, 1992—. Author: Physician's Guide to Hypertension, 1990; contbr. 138 articles to profl. jours.; mem. editl. bd. Jour. Hypertension, 1991-94, Am. Jour. Cardiology, 1992—, Clin. Pharmacology Therapeutics, 1987—, Jour. Human Hypertension, 1993—. Chmn. health site task force, Am. Heart Assn., Conn., 1986-88. Prin. investigator State of Conn., 1993—. Fellow ACP, High Blood Pressure Coun., Soc. Vascular Medicine; mem. Am. Soc. Clin. Pharmacology (chair hypertension sect. 1990—), Internat. Soc. Hypertension. Office: Univ Conn Health Ctr 263 Farmington Ave Farmington CT 06030-0001

WHITE, WILLIAM BLAINE, geochemist, researcher; b. Huntingdon, Pa., Jan. 5, 1934; s. William Bruce and Eleanor Mae (Barr) W.; m. Elizabeth Loczi, Mar. 27, 1959; children: Nikki Elizabeth White Vezendi, William Brion (dec.). BS, Juniata Coll., 1954; PhD, Pa. State U., 1962. Rsch. assoc. Mellon Inst., Pitts., 1954-58; asst. prof. Pa. State U., University Park, 1963-67, assoc. prof., 1967-72, prof. geochemistry, 1972—2002, emeritus prof., 2002—, chmn. grad. program in materials, 1990-93. Assoc. editor Am. Mineralogist, 1972-75, Materials Rsch. Bull., 1979-93, Jour. Am. Ceramic Soc., 1985-93, Water Resources Bull., 1992-93; editor earth scis. Nat. Speleological Soc. Bull., 1964-94; author: Geomorphology and Hydrology of Karst Terrains, 1988; (with Elizabeth L. White) Karst Hydrology: Concepts from the Mammoth Cave Area, 1989; (with Susan Barger) Daguerreotype: Nineteenth-Century Technology and Modern Science, 1991; (with David C. Culver) Encyclopedia of Caves, 2004, Benchmark Papers in Karst Science, 2007; contbr. articles to profl. jours. Home: 4538 Miller Rd Petersburg PA 16669-2711 Office: Pa State U Materials Rsch Lab University Park PA 16802 Home Phone: 814-667-2709; Office Phone: 814-865-1152. Business E-Mail: wbw2@psu.edu.

WHITE, WILLIAM NORTH, retired chemistry professor; b. Walton, NY, Sept. 16, 1925; s. George Fitch and Frances (Peck) W.; m. Hilda R. Sauter, Sept. 8, 1951; children: Carla Ann, Eric Jeffrey. AB, Cornell U., 1950; MA, Harvard U., 1951, PhD, 1953. NRC postdoctoral fellow Calif. Inst. Tech., Pasadena, 1953-54; asst. prof. Ohio State U., Columbus, 1954-59, asso. prof., 1959-63; prof. chemistry U. Vt., Burlington, 1963-76, 77-95, prof. emeritus, 1995—, chmn. dept., 1963-70, acting chmn. dept., 1975-76; prof. chemistry U. Tex. at Arlington, 1976-77, chmn. dept., 1976-77; ret., 1995. NSF sr. postdoctoral fellow Brookhaven Nat. Lab., Upton, N.Y., 1963-64, Harvard U., 1965; vis. scholar Brandeis U., 1974-75; chmn. arrangements com. Nat. Organic Chemistry Symposium, 1965-67 Contbr. articles on organic chemistry profl. jours. Selectman Town of Shelburne, Vt., 1968-74, water commr., 1973-74, justice of the peace, 1981-2009, sewer commr., 1991-93, Natural Resources and Conservation com., 1970-74, 2004-; mem. Chittenden County Regional Planning Commn., 1983-91; mem. bd. suprs. Winooski (Vt.) Natural Resources Conservation Dist., 1999-2004. With AUS, 1943-46. Recipient Outstanding Forest Stewardship award Winooski Conservation Dist., 1997. Mem. Am. Chem. Soc. (chmn. Western Vt. sect. 1966-67), Royal Soc. Chemistry, New Eng. Assn. Chemistry Tchrs., AAAS, N.Y. Acad. Scis., Phi Beta Kappa, Sigma Xi, Phi Kappa Phi, Phi Lambda Upsilon. Home: 226 Pierson Dr Shelburne VT 05482 Business E-Mail: wnwhite@uvm.edu.

WHITE, WILLIAM SAMUEL, foundation executive; b. Cin., May 8, 1937; s. Nathaniel Ridgway and Mary White; m. Claire Mott, July 1, 1961; children: Tiffany, Ridgway Harding. BA, Dartmouth Coll., 1959, MBA, 1960; degree (hon.), GMI Engrng. and Mgmt. Inst., 1996; LLD (hon.), Eastern Mich. U., 1975, U. Mich., 2006. With Barrett & Williams, NYC, 1961-62; sr. assoc. Bruce Payne & Assos., NYC, 1962-71; v.p. C. S. Mott Found., Flint, Mich., 1971-75, pres., 1976—, trustee, 1971—, also chmn. bd. dirs. Chmn. bd. dirs. U.S. Sugar Corp.; bd. dirs. Am. Water Works, 1999—2003. Mem. exec. com. Daycroft Sch., Greenwich, Conn., 1966-70; bd. dirs. Flint Area Conf., 1971-84, Coun. on Founds., 1985-90, Independent Sector, 1994-99, 2004—, Am. Friends Czech Republic, 1999-2004, European Found. Centre, 1994—, Civicus, 1995-2001; citizens adv. task force U. Mich., Flint, 1974-79; chmn. Coun. of Mich. Founds., 1979-81, Flint Area Focus Coun., 1988—98, Afterschool Allstars, 2004-; mem. Pres.'s Task Force on Pvt. Sector Initiatives, 1982; trustee GMI Engring. and Mgmt. Inst., 1982-86, Network European Founds., 2000—, Madriaga Found., 2004—. With U.S. Army, 1960-62. Office: C S Mott Foundation 1200 Mott Foundation Bldg Flint MI 48502-1807

WHITE, YONSENIA S., artist, educator; BA, Va. Tech, Blacksburg, 1996, BFA, 1997; MFA, Rutgers U., New Brunswick, NJ, 1999. Instr. dept. art and art history Va. Tech., Blacksburg, 1999—2000, asst. prof. dept. art and art history, 2000—06, assoc. prof., 2006—. Manna from the Marquis: Spiritual Guidance from the Side of the Road, visual art exhibitions, Stereotypes & Catharsis, Hard to Ingest, Race (Enter Personal Politics), As I Am, 3rd Annual Women's Art Show. Prayer team leader St. Paul AME Ch., Blacksburg, Va., 2003—05. Recipient Minority Blueprint award, Rutgers U., Dept. Art, Mason Gross Sch. Arts, 1999; grantee, Peninsula Fine Arts Ctr., 1999, Va. Tech., U. Writing Program, 2003. Mem.: Women's Caucus Art, Nat. Mus.Women Arts, Southeastern Coll. Art Conf., Founds. Art Theory and Edn., Coll. Art Assn. Liberal. Avocations: fine and performing arts, poetry, sports, travel, jazz. Personal E-mail: yonsenia@yahoo.com.

WHITEHEAD, DAVID BARRY, lawyer; b. San Francisco, Oct. 14, 1946; s. Barry and Fritzi-Beth (Bowman) W.; m. René Dayan, May 26, 1990. AB in History, Stanford U., 1968, JD, 1971. Bar: Calif. 1972, U.S. Dist. Ct. (no. dist.) Calif. 1972, U.S. Ct. Appeals (9th cir.) 1972, U.S. Dist. Ct. (cen. dist.) Calif. 1974. Assoc. Cullinan Hancock Rothert & Burns, San Francisco, 1972-74, Cullinan Burns & Helmer, San Francisco, 1975-77, ptnr., 1977-78, Burns & Whitehead, San Francisco, 1979-85, Whitehead & Porter, San Francisco, 1986—. Bd. dirs. Rainbow Music, Inc., San Francisco, ITP, Inc., Sunnyvale, Calif.; founding dir. A. Lincoln High Sch. San Francisco, 1989—. Mem. San Francisco Rep. Steering Com., 1984—89; bd. dirs. Enterprise for High Sch. Students, San Francisco, 1982—86; bd. dirs. San Francisco chpt. Easter Seal Soc., 1986—90; bd. dirs. Opera West Found., San Francisco, 1986—2006, Traveler's Aid Soc., San Francisco, 1989—90, Hosp. de la Familia, 1995—2000, Gold Rush Trail Found., 1998, Calif. Hist. Soc. Found., 1998. Mem. ABA, Calif. Bar Assn., San Francisco Bar Assn., Calif. Scholarship Fedn. (life) Family Club San Francisco (bd. dirs. 1986-89, 93-95), World Trade Club, Abraham Lincoln High Sch. San Francisco Alumni Assn. (founding dir.). Roman Catholic. Avocations: writing, art, directing, singing. Office: Whitehead Porter LLP 220 Montgomery St Fl 18 San Francisco CA 94104-3402 Office Phone: 415-781-6070. Business E-Mail: dbw@wpglaw.com.

WHITEHEAD, ELIZABETH PHILLIPS, lawyer; b. Mobile, Ala., Apr. 20, 1976; d. James L. Philips and Frances R. Phillips; m. Jeff Whitehead; 1 child, Porter. BA, Troy State U., Ala., 1997; JD, Loyola U., New Orleans, 2001. Bar: La. 2001, Fla. 2002, US Dist. Ct. (no. dist.) Fla. 2005. Atty. Pub. Def. Office 6th Jud. Cir., New Port Richey, Fla., 2002, Pub. Def. Office 19th Jud. Cir., Fort Pierce, Fla., 2002—03, Pub. Def. Office 14th Jud. Cir., Panama City, Fla., 2003—04, Hoot Crawford, P.A., Panama City, 2004—05, Elizabeth P. Whitehead, P.A., Panama City, 2005—. Fellow: Am. Bar Found.; mem.: ABA, Nat. Coll. DUI Def., Fla. Assn. Criminal Def. Lawyers, Am. Immigration Lawyers Assn., Bay County Bar Assn. (sec. 2004—06, pres. 2006—, treas. 2004—06), Bay County C. of C., St. Andrews Bay Inn Ct. (assoc.). Home: Elizabeth P Whitehead Pa 1244 Mountain Air Trl Fort Worth TX 76131-5445 Office Fax: 850-215-6238; Home Fax: 850-215-6238. Business E-Mail: attorney@elizabethpwhitehead.com.

WHITEHEAD, J. RENNIE, science administrator, consultant; s. William and Beatrice Cora (Fenning) W.; m. Nesta Doone James, Nov. 1, 1944; children— Valerie Lesley (dec.), Michael James Rennie. B.Sc. in Physics, Manchester U., Lancashire, Eng., 1939; PhD in Phys. Chemistry, Cambridge U., Eng., 1949. Cert. profl. engr., Ont.; chartered engr., U.K. Sci. officer TRE (UK Radar), England, 1939-51; assoc. prof. McGill U., Montreal, P.Q., Canada, 1951-55; dir. research RCA Victor Co Ltd., Montreal, 1955-65; prin. sci. adviser Govt. of Can., Ottawa, Ont., 1965-75; sr. v.p. Philip A. Lapp Ltd., Ottawa, 1975-82; pvt. practice sci. cons. Ottawa, 1982-86. Author: Superregenerative Receivers, 1949. Bd. dirs. Found. for Internat. Tng., Toronto, 1976—86. Fellow Royal Soc. Can., Inst. Physics, Instn. Elec. Engrs., Can. Aeronautics and Space Inst., Can. Assn. for Club of Rome (chmn. 1976-81, editor and pub. newsletter and procs. 1987-99). Anglican. Avocations: automobiles, stamp collecting/philately, carpentry, computers. Home and Office: 1368 Chattaway Ave Ottawa ON Canada K1H 7S3 E-mail: drrennie@sympatico.ca.

WHITEHEAD, JANE KATHARINE, archaeologist, educator; b. New Haven, Dec. 15, 1944; d. George Goethals Whitehead and Norma Noreen Wiersig. BA, Wellesley Coll., Mass., 1966; MA, Trinity Coll., Hartford, Cin., 1970; PhD, Yale, New Haven, 1984. Cert. in tchg. K-12 State Conn., 1969. Dir. Archaeological Excavation Etruscan Settlement, La Piana, Italy, 1982—2002; founding editor Etruscan Studies, 1994—2000, Etruscan News, NYC, 2002—; assoc. prof. Valdosta State U., Ga., 2001—; dir. Archaeological Excavation Roman Baths, Carsulae, Italy, 2004—. Recipient Merrill Presdl. Scholar Tchg. award, Cornell U., 1994, Faculty Excellence award Profl. Devel., Valdosta State U., 2008; grant, Italy Fulbright, 1979—80. Fellow: Explorers Club (fellow, nat. 1994); mem.: US Sect. Istituto di Studi Etruschi ed Italici (founding editor of newsletter 2002), Phi Kappa Phi Honor Soc. Avocations: singing, travel. Home: 200 East Cranford Ave Valdosta GA 31602 Office: Valdosta State Univ Modern and Classical Lang Dept Valdosta GA 31698 Business E-Mail: jwhitehe@valdosta.edu.

WHITEHEAD, JOHN CUNNINGHAM, former bank executive; b. Evanston, Ill., Apr. 2, 1922; s. Eugene C. and Winifred W.; m. Helene E. Shannon, Sept. 28, 1946 (div. Dec. 1971); children: Anne Elizabeth, John Gregory; m. Jaan W. Chartener, Oct. 22, 1972 (div. 1986); 1 child, Sarah; m. Nancy Dickerson, 1989 (dec. 1997); m. Cynthia Matthews, Feb. 7, 2007. BA, Haverford Coll., 1943; MBA, Harvard U., 1947; LLD (hon.), Pace. U., Rutgers U., Haverford Coll., Harvard U., Amherst Coll., Seton Hall U.; LLD, Bates Coll., 2004; Gen. Theological Seminary, Berea Coll. With Goldman, Sachs & Co., NYC, 1947-84, ptnr., 1956-76, sr. ptnr., co-chmn., 1976-84; dep. sec. US Dept. State, Washington, 1985-89; chmn. Fed. Res. Bank NY, NYC, 1996—2000, Lower Manhattan Devel. Corp., NYC, 2001—06. Trustee Haverford Coll.; past pres. bd. overseers Harvard U.; co-chmn. greater N.Y. coun. Boy Scouts Am.; past chmn. Internat. Rescue Com., UN Assn. U.S.A.; Andrew Mellon Found; founding chmn. World Trade Ctr. Meml. Found., 2005-, former chmn. Brookings Instn., Internat. House, Nat. Gallery of Art; dir. Nature Conservancy, East West Inst., Eisenhower Exch. Fellowship. With USNR, 1943—46. Mem. Coun. on Fgn. Rels., Links Club, Univ. Club, Knicks Broken Club.

WHITEHEAD, JOHN WAYNE, lawyer, educator, writer; b. Pulaski, Tenn., July 14, 1946; s. John M. and Alatha (Wiser) W.; m. Virginia Carolyn Nichols, Aug. 26, 1967; children: Jayson Reau, Jonathan Mathew, Elisabeth Anne, Joel Christofer, Joshua Benjamen. BA, U. Ark., 1969, JD, 1974. Bar: Ark. 1974, U.S. Dist. Ct. (ea. and we. dists.) Ark. 1974, U.S. Supreme Ct. 1977, U.S. Ct. Appeals (9th cir.) 1980, Va. 1981, U.S. Ct. Appeals (7th cir.) 1981, U.S. Ct Appeals (4th and 5th cirs.). Spl. counsel Christian Legal Soc., Oak Park, Ill., 1977-78; assoc. Gibbs & Craze, Cleve., 1978-79; sole practice law Manassas, Va., 1979-82; pres. The Rutherford Inst., Charlottesville, Va., 1982—, also bd. dirs. Frequent lectr. colls., law schs.; past adj. prof. O.W. Coburn Sch. Law. Author: Schools on Fire, 1980, The New Tyranny, 1982, The Second American Revolution, 1982, The Stealing of America, 1983, The Freedom of Religious Expression in Public High Schools, 1983, The End of Man, 1986, An American Dream, 1987, The Rights of Religious Persons in Public Education, 1991, Home Education: Rights and Reasons, 1993, Religious Apartheid, 1994, Slaying Dragons, 1999, Grasping For the Wind, 2001, others; writer, dir.: (video series) Grasping for the Wind (Silver World medal N.Y. Film Festival), 1998-99; contbr. articles to profl. jours., chpts. to books. 1st lt. U.S. Army, 1969-71. Named Christian Leader of Yr. Christian World Affairs Conf., Washington, 1986; recipient Bus. and Profl. award Religious Heritage Am., 1990, Hungarian Freedom medal, Budapest, 1991. Mem. ABA, Ark. Bar Assn., Va. Bar Assn. Office: The Rutherford Inst PO Box 7482 Charlottesville VA 22906-7482 Office Phone: 434-978-3888. Business E-Mail: johnw@rutherford.org.

WHITEHEAD, KENNETH DEAN, writer, translator, retired federal agency administrator, editor; b. Rupert, Idaho, Dec. 14, 1930; s. Clarence Christian and May Bell (Allen) W.; m. Margaret Mary O'Donohue, Aug. 2, 1958; children: Paul Daniel, Steven Francis, Matthew Patrick, David Joseph. BA in French, U. Utah, 1955; postgrad., U. Paris, 1956-57; cert. in Arabic and Middle East studies, Fgn. Service Inst., Beirut, 1962; LittD (hon.), Franciscan U., Steubenville, Oho, 2003. Instr. English U. Utah, Salt Lake City, 1955-56; fgn. service officer Dept. State, Rome, Beirut and Tripoli, Libya, 1957-65; chief Arabic service Voice of Am., Washington, 1965-67; dep. dir. fgn. currency program Smithsonian Instn., Washington, 1967-72; exec. v.p. Caths. United for Faith Inc., New Rochelle, NY, 1972-81; dir. Ctr. for Internat. Edn. U.S. Dept. Edn., Washington, 1982-86, dep. asst. sec. for higher edn. programs, 1986-88, asst. sec. for postsecondary edn., 1988-89. Author: Respectable Killing: The New Abortion Imperative, 1972, Agenda for the Sexual Revolution, 1981, Catholic Colleges and Federal Funding, 1988, DOA: The Ambush of the Universal Catechism, 1993, Political Orphan? The Prolife Cause after 25 Years of Roe v. Wade, 1998, One, Holy, Catholic, and Apostolic: The Early Church Was the Catholic Church, 2000, The New Ecumenism, 2009, Mass Misunderstandings: The Mixed Legacy of the Vatican II Liturgical Reforms, 2009; co-author: The Pope, The Council and the Mass, 1981, rev. edit., 2006, Flawed Expectations: The Reception of the Catechism of the Catholic Church, 1996; sr. editor: World Almanac Book of Dates, 1982, Macmillan Concise Dictionary of World History, 1983; editor: Marriage and the Common Good, 2001, Pope John Paul II--Witness to Truth, 2001, The Catholic Imagination, 2003, Voices of the New Springtime, 2004, The Catholic Citizen: Debating the Issues of Justice, 2004, The Church, Marriage, and the Family, 2007, Vatican Council II's Diverse Legacy, 2007, Sacro Sanctumn Concilium & the Reform of the Liturgy, 2009; co-editor: The Battle for the Catholic Mind, 2001; translator 20 books from French, German, Italian, 1980—. Bd. dir. Notre Dame Inst. for Advanced Study, Arlington, Va., 1986-95, Philosophy Edn. Soc., 1995—, Christas Magister Found., 1997-2001. Fulbright scholar U.S. Dept. State, 1956-57. Mem. Fellowship Cath. Scholars (bd. dir. 1990-2000, 04—), Brent Soc. Cath. Profls. (bd. dir. 1992-98), Cath. League for Religious and Civil Rights (bd. dir. 1992—), KC. Republican. Home: 809 Ridge Pl Falls Church VA 22046-3631 Office Phone: 703-538-5085. Fax: (703) 534-3015. E-mail: whiteheadz@msn.com.

WHITEHEAD, KIMBERLY B., lawyer; Grad., George Mason U. Sch. Law; BS in Biomed. Engrng., U. Pa., Phila., 2000; JD, Georgetown U., Washington, 2003. Bar: Va. 2003, DC 2005, US Ct. Appeals (4th cir.) 2004, registered: US Patent and Trademark Office (patent atty.) 2004. Assoc. Law Office of Eric M. May, PC, Washington, 2003—04; intellectual property assoc. Burns & Levinson LLP, Washington, 2004—07; with Baker & Hostetler LLP, 2007—; atty., intellectual property group Dickstein Shapiro LLP, Wash., DC; sr. counsel PCT Law Group, 2009—, atty., 2009—. Vol. Habitat for Humanity, Fairfax, Va., 2003—05. Recipient Sr. award, Nat. Soc. Black Engrs., 2000, W.E.B. DuBois Legacy award for commitment and svc., U. Pa., 2000. Mem.: ABA (judge DC regional for nat. law sch. appellate advocacy competition 2004), Inspiration Alumni Found. (founder, chair 2007—), Am. Intellectual Property Assn. (brief grader appellate advocacy competition 2004—05), Nat. Bar Assn. Women Lawyers Divsn., Bar Assn. DC, Biomed. Engrng. Soc. (assoc.), Toastmasters Internat., Giles S. Rich Inn of Ct. Office: PCT Law Group 818 Connecticut Ave NW Washington DC 20006 Office Phone: 202-683-8929. Office Fax: 202-280-1393. Business E-Mail: kwhitehead@bakerlaw.com.

WHITEHEAD, MICHAEL ANTHONY, chemistry professor; b. London, June 30, 1935; arrived in Can., 1962, naturalized, 2003; s. Francis Henry and Edith Downes (Rotherham) W.; 1 son, Christopher Mark. B.Sc. in Chemistry with honors, Queen Mary Coll., U. London, 1956, PhD, 1960, D.Sc., 1974. Asst. lectr. Queen Mary Coll., U. London, 1958-60; postdoctoral fellow U. Cin., 1960, asst. prof., 1961; asst. prof. theoretical chemistry McGill U., Montreal, Que., Canada, 1962-66, asso. prof., 1966-74, prof., 1974-99, prof. emeritus, 1999—. Vis. prof. U. Cambridge, Eng., 1971-72, U. Oxford, Eng., 1972-74; vis. professorial fellow Univ. Coll. Wales, Aberystwyth, 1980, U. Oxford, 1990-91; invited prof. U. Geneva, 1983-84; life guest prof. Nat. U. Def. Tech., Changsha, People's Republic of China; vis. Erskine fellow chemistry dept. U. Canterbury, Christchurch, N.Z., 2000, co-chair history and advanced in quantum chemistry 84th conf., Montreal, 2001; mem. Internat. Com. on Nuclear Quadrupole Resonance.; co-chmn. 7th Internat. Symposium on Nuclear Quadrapole Resonance, Kingston, Ont., Can., 1983; convenor Can. and Internat. N.E. Symposium of Montreal, 2004; mem. Ctr. for Molecular Modelling, Concordia U., Montreal, 2005—; joint chmn. 1st Applied Pulp and Paper Molecular Modelling Symposium, 2005; honorary chair, Fundamental Applied Pulp and Paper Modelling Symposium, 2008. Contbr. articles to profl. jours. Mem. parish coun. St. John the Evangelist; exec. coun. Can. Sci. and Christian Affiliation; chmn. Montreal Sch. Theology; mem. Planned Giving Com. Montreal Anglican Diocese; mem. Stewardship Environ. Com. Fellow Royal Chem. Soc., Chem. Inst. Can., Royal Soc. Arts; mem. Am. Chem. Soc., Am. Phys. Soc., James McGill Soc. (pres. 1993-95), Sigma Xi (pres. McGill chpt. 1971-72, 81-82, 92-95, 97-99, dir. Can. and internat. constituency group 2000—06, pres. 2007-, chair awards com. 2001—06, ad hoc mem. internat. com. 2001-05, Nominations Comm. Mem.), McGill Savoy Soc. (founder, life), Phi Lambda Upsilon. Anglican. Office: McGill U Dept Chemistry 801 Sherbrooke St W Montreal PQ Canada H3A 2K6 Office Phone: 514-398-6239. Business E-Mail: tony.whitehead@mcgill.ca. *My faith in God and belief in Christ.*

WHITEHEAD, PAUL, law educator, former labor union administrator; b. 1951; BA, U. Wis., 1973, MA in Industrial Rels., 1975; JD, Harvard U., 1978. Bar: Pa. 1980. Asst. gen. counsel United Steelworkers America, Pitts., 1980—2000, assoc. gen. counsel, 2000—01, gen. counsel, 2001—08; prof. practice in labor studies, employment rels. & law Pa. State U., University Park, Pa., 2009—. Adj. prof. Carnegie Mellon U.; chmn. bd. CC Allegheny County, 1994—. Office: Pa State U Dept Labor Studies & Employment Rels 133 Willard Bldg University Park PA 16802 Office Phone: 412-562-2400. Office Fax: 412-562-2484. E-mail: pvw11@psu.edu.*

WHITEHEAD, TANYA DIANNE GRUBBS, psychologist, educator, researcher; b. Scottsbuff, Nebr., June 23, 1953; d. William Elliott Grubbs and Esther Mary Cooper Grubbs; m. William Downing Whitehead, Aug. 12, 1971; children: Shana Alexandra, Thomas William, Bethany Rose. B in Psychology summa cum laude, Ottawa U., 1990; M in Clin. Psychology, Avila U., 1992; D in Psychology, U. Mo., 2001. Cert. specialist, developmental and handicapping conditions U. Kans. Sch. Medicine, 1993. Clin. instr. U. Kans. Sch. Medicine, Kansas City, 1987—96; rsch. prof. U. Mo., Kansas City, 1996—. Psychol. consulting burn unit, craniofacial team, spina bifida clinic, pediatric gastroenterology Sch. Medicine, U. Kans., Kansas City, 1987—96; state, regional and nat. advisor People First Self Advocacy Tng. Adults With Devel. Disabilities, 1997—2001; peer grant rev. facilitator and chair US Depts Health and Human Svcs., Corp. for Nat. Svc., Washington, 1999—; program evaluator, impact of asset bldg. on youth from disadvantaged circumstances Office of Cmty. Svc., US Dept. Health and Human Svs.; program evaluation: promoting higher edn. partnerships for global devel. US AID, Assn. Liaison Office for U. Cooperation in Devel., Cape Town, South Africa; dir. AmeriCorps VISTA Project in Self Advocacy,

Statewide, Mo., 1998—2000; cons.: cmty. movement for urban progress cmty. devel. corp. Urban Core Cmty. Devel. Project, Kansas City, 2002—04; sr. program evaluator; assets for independence demonstration project, us hhs, office cmty. svcs. PeopleWorks, Inc., Washington, 2000—01. Author: (Self Determination Workshops) New Media Workshops for Adults with DD, (book) Exploring Self Advocacy from a Social Power Perspective, Disability Accommodations from a Person Centered Perspective, (film) Enslaved Minds: Final Barrier to Freedom and Justice; contbr. new media toolkit (Crystal Communicator Award, 2001); author: (disability accommodation guide) Exchange City Accommodation Guide. Recipient Sr. Specialist Fulbright, Sr. Devel. Specialist, USAID; fellow Ctr. for the City, U. Mo., 2004-2005; fellow, Studies in Cmty. Change, 2000. Mem.: ANA (mem. commn. accreditation 2006—08), AAUP, AAUW, APA, LWV, Am. Nurses Credentialing Ctr. (bd. Commn. on Accreditation). Business E-Mail: whiteheadt@umkc.edu.

WHITEHILL, ANGELA ELIZABETH, artistic director; b. Leeds, Yorkshire, Eng., Oct. 21, 1938; arrived in US, 1963, naturalized, 1995; d. Donald Paul and Audrey May (Clayforth) Warner; m. Norman James Whitehill, Jr., Dec. 23, 1959; children: Norman James III, Pamela Elizabeth; m. William Parker Noble, Dec. 27, 1998. Student, Arts Ednl. Sch., London, 1955-59. With corps de ballet Ballet Paris, 1958-59; dir. London Sch. Ballet, St. Thomas, V.I., 1960-63; asst. dir. Ocean County Ballet Co., Toms River, NJ, 1965-68; founder, dir. Shore Ballet Sch., Toms River, 1968-76; artistic dir. Shore Ballet Co., Toms River, 1971-76; artist in residence Castleton State Coll., Rutland, Vt., 1977-79; founder, artistic dir. Burklyn Ballet Theatre, Johnson, Vt., 1977—2003; coord., tchr. Burlington Vocational Tchg. Performing Arts, 1988—92; founding artistic dir. Burklyn Ballet Theatre, 2003—; dir. Ballet Umbrella, Dance Coun., Burklyn Designs, 2003—; artistic dir. Paradise Ballet Theatre, Key West, Fla., 2005—07. Vis. prof. Colby Sawyer Coll., New London, N.H., 1978-80; resident designer Atlanta Ballet Co., 1981-83; designer, pub. relations N.J. Ballet Co., 1983-85; artistic dir. Vt. Ballet Theatre, Burlington, 1985-94; master tchr. 1st Congress Internat. de Ballet Classico Contemporaneo, Mex., 2000, Ft. Wayne Ballet, 2005, Regional Dance Am. SW Festival, 2006; interim artistic dir. Huntington Ballet Theatre, 2006, artistic dir., 2006-07, 2009-. Choreographer Arensky Dances, 1983, A Deux, 1984, 4 Plus 2, 1986, Twins From A Time Gone By, 1987, Heart of the Island, 2002; co-author: Parent's Book of Ballet, 1988, 2d edit., 2003, The Young Professional's Book of Ballet, 1990, The Dancer's Book of Ballet, 2000, Ballet Magic, The Burklyn Story, 2001, Nutcracker Backstage, 2004; dir. artistic advisor Paradise Ballet Theatre, Nutcracker Key West, 2005-07; costumer designer Grand Rapids Ballet Swan Lake Act III, 1984, Scottish Am. Ballet, La Sylphide, 1984, Legend of Ench. Bird, 1994, Burklyn Youth Ballet, 1999-07, Hansel & Gretel, Alice in Wonderland, Cinderella & The Flower Fairies, Little Mermaid, Beauty and the Beast, Aladdin, Huntington Ballet Theatre, Cinderella, 2005, Nutcracker Key West ACT II, 2005, Sleeping Beauty, 2007, Designs Classical Acad. Ballet, 2008; adjudicator, SW Regional Dance Am. Festival, 2008. Dir. Vt. Ballet Theatre Found., Calledonia County, 1986-96. Recipient Francis Hopkins award Ocean County, N.J., 1976, Woman of Achievement award Vt. Woman, 1989, Author's award N.J. Inst. Tech., 1989. Mem. Vt. Council on the Arts, Regional Dance Am. Mem. Soc. Of Friends. Home: 218 Ocean Ave Island Heights NJ 08732 Home (Winter): PO Box 907 Island Heights NJ 08732-0907 Office: Dance Counsel PO Box 493 Johnson VT 05656-0493 Home Phone: 723-288-2660; Office Phone: 732-288-2660. Personal E-mail: awhitehill@aol.com.

WHITEHOUSE, DAVID BRYN, museum director; b. Worksop, Nottinghamshire, Eng., Oct. 15, 1941; came to U.S., 1984; s. Brindley Charles and Alice Margaret (Dobson) W.; m. Ruth Delamain Ainger, 1963; children: Sarah, Susan, Peter; m. Elizabeth-Anne Ollemans, 1975; children: Julia, Simon, Nicola. BA, Cambridge U., 1963, MA, 1965, PhD in Archaeology, 1967. Dir. Brit. Inst. Afghan Studies, Kabul, Afghanistan, 1973-74, Brit. Sch., Rome, 1974-84; chief curator Corning Mus. Glass, NY, 1984-87, dep. dir., 1988-92, dir., 1992-99, exec. dir., 1999—. Dir. Siraf expdn. Brit. Inst. Persian Studies, Tehran, Iran, 1966-73. Author: (with Ruth Whitehouse) Archaeological Atlas of the World, 1975, (with David Andrews and John Osborne) Aspects of Medieval Lazio, 1982, (with Donald B. Harden and others) Glass of the Caesars, 1987, Glass of the Roman Empire, 1988, (with Richard Hodges) Mohammed, Charlemagne and the Origins of Europe, 1983, Glass: A Pocket Dictionary, 1993, English Cameo Glass, 1994, Roman Glass in The Corning Museum of Glass, Vol. 1, 1997, Vol. 2, 2001, Vol. 3, 2003, Excavations at ed-Dur (Umm al-Qaiwan, UAE), Vol. 1, The Glass Vessels, 1998, The Corning Museum of Glass, A Decade of Glass Collecting, 1990-1999, 2000, (with Stefano Carboni) Glass of the Sultans, 2001, Sasanian and Post-Sasanian Glass in the Corning Museum of Glass, 2005 (with Susan Rossi-Wilcox) Drawing upon Nature: Studies for the Blaschkas' Glass Models, 2007, Reflecting Antiquity, 2007; editor: Jour. Glass Studies, 1988-; contbr. numerous articles and revs. to profl. jours. Trustee Corning Mus. Glass, Rockwell Mus. Western Art. Wainwright fellow, Oxford U., 1966—73. Fellow Soc. Antiquaries (London), Royal Geog. Soc., Pontificia Accademia Romana di Archeologia; mem. Accademia Fiorentina delle Arti del Disegno, Accademia di Archeologia, Lettere e Belle Arti di Napoli, Deutsches Archaologisches Inst., Am. Assn. Mus. (mem. accreditation visiting com. 1998-), Internat. Assn. for the History of Glass (pres. 1991-95, bd. dirs.), Athenaeum Club (London). Office: Corning Mus Glass One Museum Way Corning NY 14830-2253 Office Phone: 607-974-8424. Business E-Mail: whitehoudb@cmog.org.

WHITEHOUSE, FRED WAITE, endocrinologist, researcher; b. Chgo., May 6, 1926; s. Fred Trafton Waite and Grace Caroline (Peters) W.; m. Iris Jean Dawson, June 6, 1953; children: Martha, Amy, Sarah. Student, Northwestern U., 1943-45; BS, U. Ill., Chgo., 1947, MD, 1949. Diplomate Am. Bd. Internal Medicine; cert. endocrinology and metabolism. Intern, then resident Henry Ford Hosp., Detroit, 1949-53, staff physician, 1955—, chief divsn. metabolism, 1962-88, chief divsn. endocrinology and metabolism, 1988-95; divsn. head emeritus, 1995—; fellow Joslin Clinic, Boston, 1954-55. Cons. FDA, Washington, 1980—; mem. Coalition on Diabetes Edn. and Minority Health, 1989-91. Contbr. articles to profl. jours. Bd. dirs. Wheat Ridge Found., 1984-93. Lt. USNR, 1951-53. Master ACP; mem. NIH (nat. diabetes adv. bd. 1984-88), Am. Diabetes Assn. (pres. 1978-79, Banting medal 1979, Outstanding Clinician award 1989, Outstanding Physician Educators award 1994, Best award 1994), Detroit Med. Club (pres. 1976), Detroit Acad. Medicine (pres. 1991-92). Lutheran. Avocations: bicycling, gardening. Home: 1265 Blairmoor Ct Grosse Pointe Woods MI 48236-1230 Office: Henry Ford Med Group 3031 W Grand Blvd Ste 800 Detroit MI 48202 Home Phone: 313-884-1324; Office Phone: 313-916-2131. Office Fax: 313-916-8343. Business E-Mail: fwhiteh1@hfhs.org.

WHITEHOUSE, JOHN HARLAN, JR., systems software consultant, diagnostician; b. Lakewood, Ohio, Sept. 12, 1951; s. John Harlan and Frances Elizabeth (Nation) W.; divorced; 1 child, John Harlan III. BA magma cum laude, Ohio Wesleyan U., 1973; postgrad., U. Chgo., 1974; MBA, Cleve. State U., 1976; PhD, Columbia Pacific U., San Rafael, Calif., 1988; postgrad., Vedic U. of Am., 1996—. Cert. computing profl.; cert. info. sys. auditor; cert. in Visual Basic. Programmer San Antonio Express-News, 1977; programming mgr. S.W. Info. Mgmt. Sys., San Antonio, 1977, Utility Data Corp., Houston, 1978; sr. data sys. auditor Nat. City Corp., Cleve., 1978-81; sys. programmer Std. Oil Co., Cleve., 1981-84; adv. sys. engr. IBM, Cleve., 1984-92; pres. Semiotica Corp., 1992—. Mem. exams. editl. coun. Inst. for Cert. Computer Profls., Des Plaines, 1990—, test deployment mgr., 1996-2001, dir. certification, 1999—. Author: CICS Problem Determination Workshop, 1990; co-author: ICCP Guidelines for Recertification, 1990, ICCP Official Study Guide, 1991-95; editor Clifton-Gaston Allen Light, 1994-2004; also numerous articles, columnist. Mem. Assn. for Computing Machinery (sr; chmn. Greater Cleve. chpt. 1982-83, Svc. Recognition award 1984), Assn. of Inst. for Cert. Computer Profls. (regional dir. 1989-93, nominating com. 1991), Masons (dist. edn. officer 2001-02, dist. dep. Grand Master 2002-05), Philalethes Soc. (pres. Western Res. chpt. 2005-06), Phi Beta Kappa. Unitarian Universalist. Home: 22291 Berry Dr Rocky River OH 44116-2013 Office: Semiotica Corp Software Ohio PMB 241 25935 Detroit Rd Westlake OH 44145-2449 Office Phone: 440-356-8738. Business E-Mail: sales@softwareohio.com.

WHITEHOUSE, SHELDON, United States Senator from Rhode Island, former state attorney general; b. NYC, Oct. 20, 1955; s. Charles Sheldon and Mary (Rand) Whitehouse; m. Sandra Christine Thornton, Sept. 20, 1986; 2 children. BA, Yale U., 1978; JD, U. Va., 1982. Bar: W.Va. 1982, RI 1983, US Dist. Ct. RI 1984, US Supreme Ct. 1986, US Ct. Appeals (1st cir.) 1984. Atty. State of RI, Providence, 1983—84, spl. asst. atty. gen., 1985—90, chief regulatory unit, 1988—90, asst. atty. gen., 1989—90, exec. counsel to Gov., 1991, dir. gov. policy office, 1991—92, dir., Dept. Bus. Regulation, 1992—94; US atty. Dist. RI US Dept. Justice, Providence, 1994—98; atty. gen. State of RI, Providence, 1999—2003; US Senator-elect from RI, 2007—. Recipient Robert M. Goodrich award for Outstanding Pub. Employee, RI Pub. Expenditure Coun., 1993, Secret Svc. Honor award, US Dept. Treasury, 1998, Pub. Achievement award, Common Cause, 1999. Democrat. Office: US Senate B-40D Dirksen Senate Office Bldg Washington DC 20510*

WHITEHURST, BROOKS MORRIS, chemical engineer; b. Apr. 9, 1930; s. David Brooks and Bessie Ann (Lowry) W.; m. Carolyn Sue Boyer, July 4, 1951; children: Garnett, Anita, Robert. BS, Va. Poly. Inst. and State U., 1951. Registered profl. engr., NC. Sr. process asst. Am. Enka Corp., Lowland, Tenn., 1951-56; sr. process devel. engr. Va.-Carolina Chem. Corp., Richmond, Va., 1956-63; project engr. Texaco Inc., Richmond, 1963-66; mgr. engring. svcs. Texasgulf, Inc., Aurora, NC, 1967-80, mgr. spl. projects, long range planning, 1980-81; pres. Whitehurst Assocs., Inc., New Bern, NC, 1981—. Instr., lectr., cons. alt. sources of energy comty. colls. and univs.; presenter paper Solar World Forum, Brighton, Eng., 1981. Co-chmn. NC state supt. task force on secondary edn., 1974—; mem. NC state adv. com. on trade and indsl. edn, 1971-77; chmn. Gov.'s Task Force Vols. in Workplace, 1981; chmn. State Adv. Coun. Career Edn., 1977—; gov.'s liaison for edn. and bus., 1978-79. Recipient commendation Pres. US, 1981 Mem. AIChE, Am. Inst. Chemists (cert., bd. dirs. 1980-84), NC Inst. Chemists (pres. 1975-77), Nat. Soc. Profl. Engrs., NC Soc. Profl. Engrs., Royal Soc. Chemistry. Achievements include patents and current work on biodegradable chelate systems, municipal yard waste disposal, micronutrients for agriculture, waste rubber recycling, conversion of industrial by-products containing manganese and phosphorous to useful non-toxic materials for use in agriculture for environmental clean-up; development of environmentally friendly products for forest fertilization and chelates for organic agriculture, and a process for purification of impure phosphoric acid, patent for the development of products and processes to minimize ammonia volatilization from urea. Home: 1983 Hoods Creek Rd New Bern NC 28562-9103 Office: PO Box 3335 New Bern NC 28564-3335

WHITEHURST, GROVER JAY (RUSS WHITEHURST), psychologist, former federal agency administrator; b. Washington, NC, Sept. 28, 1944; s. Grover J. and Dixie (Daniel) W.; m. Janet E. Fischel, June 7, 1981; children: Owen E., Adam E. BA in Psychology, East Carolina U., Greenville, 1966; MA in Clinical Psychology, U. Ill., 1968, PhD in Child Psychology, 1970. Lic. psychologist, N.Y. Asst. prof. SUNY, Stony Brook, 1970—74, assoc. prof., 1975—79, prof. psychology, 1981—2002, chair dept. psychology, 1998—2002; sr. lectr. U. N.S.W., Sydney, 1974—75; acad. v.p. Merrill-Palmer Inst., Detroit, 1979—81; asst. sec. for ednl. rsch. & improvement US Dept. Edn., Washington, 2001—02, acting commr. edn. statistics, 2006, dir. Inst. Edn. Sciences (IES), 2002—08; sr. fellow governance studies, dir. Brown Ctr. on Edn. Policy The Brookings Instn., Washington, 2009—. Author: Child Behavior, 1977; editor Developmental Rev., 1981-2000; contbr. over 100 articles to profl. jours. Grantee NIH, 1985, Smith Richardson Found., 1990, Pew Charitable Trusts, 1992, US Adminstrn. Children & Families, 1996, 2000; recipient Microsoft Innovators in Higher Edn. award, 1996, SUNY Great Web Page award Edn;. Tech. Category, 1996, Outstanding Alumni award, East Carolina U., 1999, Comeback Alumni award, U. Ill Urbana Champaign, 2004, Northwestern U. Inst. for Policy Rsch.award, 2004, Edward L. Meyen Disting Lecture award, U. Kans. 2007, Peter H. Rosso award, Assn. Pub. Policy Analysis & Mgmt., 2008 Fellow APA, Am. Assn. Profl. and Applied Psychology; Nat. Rsch. Coun. (commn. early childhood); Head Start, Nat. Adv. Bd. on Rsch. Avocation: sailing. Office: The Brookings Instn 1775 Massachusetts Ave Washington DC 20036 Office Phone: 202-797-6090. E-mail: gwhitehurst@brookings.edu.*

WHITEHURST, JIM (JAMES M. WHITEHURST), former air transportation executive; b. Columbus, Ga., 1967; m. Lauren N.; 2 children. BS in Computer Sci. and Econs., Rice U., Houston, 1989; student, Friedrich-Alexander U., Erlangen, Germany, London Sch. Econs.; MBA, Harvard Bus. Sch. V.p., dir. Boston Consulting Group, 2001; sr. v.p. fin., treasury & bus. devel. Delta Air Lines, Inc., Atlanta, 2002—04, sr. v.p., chief network and planning officer, 2004—05, COO, 2005—07; pres., CEO Red Hat, Inc., 2008—. Bd. dirs. Red Hat, Inc., 2008—. Office: Red Hat Inc 1801 Varsity Dr Raleigh NC 27606-2072 Office Phone: 919-754-3700. Office Fax: 919-547-0024.*

WHITEHURST, WILLIAM WILFRED, JR., management consultant; b. Balt., Mar. 4, 1937; s. William Wilfred and Elizabeth (Hogg) Whitehurst; m. Linda Joan Potter, July 1, 1961; children: Catherine Elizabeth, William Wilfred III. BA, Princeton U., 1958; MS with distinction, Carnegie Inst. Tech., 1963. Mathematician Nat. Security Agy., Fort George G. Meade, Md., 1961—63; mgmt. cons. McKinsey & Co., Inc., Washington, 1963—66; ptnr. L.E. Peabody & Assocs., Washington, 1966—69, exec. v.p., dir. Lanham, Md., 1969—82, pres., dir., 1983—86; pres. W.W. Whitehurst & Assoc., Inc., Cockeysville, Md., 1986—. Contbr. Code of Fed. Regulations 49 C.F.R. Sect. 1157. Comdr. USNR, 1958—65. Recipient Diploma De Honor 14th Pan Am. Rwy. Congress. Mem.: CFA Inst., Washington Soc. Investment Analysts, Am. Rwy. Engring. Assn. Home and Office: 12421 Happy Hollow Rd Cockeysville Hunt Valley MD 21030-1711

WHITEKER, ROY ARCHIE, retired chemistry professor; b. Long Beach, Calif., Aug. 22, 1927; s. Ewing Harris and Mabel Mary (Williams) W.; m. Jean Fiske MacLean, June 3, 1960; 1 son, Scott MacLean. BS, UCLA, 1950, MS, 1952; PhD, Calif. Inst. Tech., 1956. Instr. chemistry M.I.T., 1955-57; asst. prof. Harvey Mudd Coll., Claremont, Calif., 1957-61, assoc. prof., 1961-67, prof. chemistry, 1967-73; assoc. dir. fellowships Nat. Acad. Scis., Washington, 1967-68; dep. exec. sec. Com. on Internat. Exch. of Persons, Washington, 1971—72, exec. sec., 1972—75; dir. Coun. Internat. Exchange Scholar, 1975-76; prof. chemistry U. Pacific, Stockton, Calif., 1976-92, dean Coll. Pacific, 1976-89; ret., 1992. Bd. dirs. Stockton Symphony Assn., 1978-80; dir. cmty. adv. bd. Sta. KUOP, 1981-89; bd. dirs. Stockton Chorale, 1989-97; pres. U. of the Pacific Emeriti Soc., 1992-94, 2000-02. With USNR, 1945-46. Dow Chem. Co. fellow, 1953-54, DuPont Tchg. fellow, 1954-55, NSF Sci. Faculty fellow Royal Inst. Tech., Stockholm, Sweden, 1963-64 Mem. Am. Chem. Soc., Alpha Chi Sigma, Phi Beta Kappa, Phi Kappa Phi, Sigma Xi. Home: 3400 Wagner Hts Rd # 30 Stockton CA 95209 Office Phone: 209-946-2606. Business E-Mail: rwhiteker@pacific.edu.

WHITELEY, BENJAMIN ROBERT, retired insurance company executive; b. Des Moines, July 13, 1929; s. Hiram Everett and Martha Jane (Walker) W.; m. Elaine Marie Yunker, June 14, 1953; children—Stephen Robert, Benjamin Walker BS, Oreg. State U., 1951; MS, U. Mich., 1952; postgrad. advanced mgmt. program, Harvard U.; DHL (hon.), Pacific U., 2001. Clk. group dept. Standard Ins. Co., Portland, Oreg., 1956-59, asst. actuary group dept. then asst. actuary actuarial dept., 1959-63, asst. v.p., asst. actuary, 1963-64, asst. v.p., assoc. actuary, 1964-70, v.p. group ins. adminstrn., 1970-72, v.p. group ins. div., 1972-80, exec. v.p. group ins., 1980-81, exec. v.p., 1981-83, pres., CEO, 1983-92, chmn. bd. dirs., CEO, 1993-94, chmn. bd. dirs., 1994—98; ret., 2000. Bd. dir. The Greenbriar Cos., chmn. bd., 2004—. Past pres. Columbia Pacific coun. Boy Scouts Am.; past chmn. bd., trustee Pacific U., Forest Grove, Oreg.; past chmn. Oreg. Health Scis. Found., Oreg. Trail Coordinating Coun., Portland Opera Assn.; trustee Oreg. Cmty. Found., 1998—2006, chmn., 2004-06; campaign chair, bd. dir. United Way Portland, 1994. 1st. lt. USAF, 1952—55. Recipient Silver Beaver award Cascade Pacific coun. Boy Scouts Am., 1993, Harvey and Emiline Clark medal Pacific U., 1991, Alumni fellow award Oreg. State U., 1991, Aubrey R. Watzek award Lewis and Clark Coll., 1994, Lifetime Achievement award Bus. Youth Exch., Portland, Oreg., 1995. Fellow Soc. Actuaries; mem. Arlington Club (pres. 1991), Waverley Country Club, Multnomah Athletic Club. Republican. Methodist.

WHITELEY, EMILY C., biology professor; b. Charlevoix, Mich., Oct. 10, 1962; d. Daniel G. and Ruth O. Axt; m. Stephen J. Whiteley, May 25, 1986. AS, Western Piedmont C.C., Morganton, NC, 1995; BA in Biology, U. NC, Asheville, NC, 1997; MS, Western Carolina U., Cullowhee, NC, 2000. Biology instr. Catawba Valley C.C., Hickory, NC, 2001—. Mem.: Nat. Assn. of Biology Teachers (assoc.). Achievements include discovery of a new spider species in 1999, Spider was named Anthrobia whiteleyae in 2005. Avocations: hiking, horse rescue. Office: Catawba Valley Cmty Coll 2550 Hwy 70 SE Hickory NC 28602 Personal E-mail: dunhorse2003@yahoo.com. E-mail: ewhitele@cvcc.edu.

WHITEMAN, DOUGLAS E., publishing executive; b. Emporia, Kans., Mar. 4, 1961; s. Floyd E. and Phyllis E. (Troyer) Whiteman; m. Susan R. Anderson, Sept. 14, 1985; 1 child, Aaron Anderson Douglas. BSBA, U. Kans., 1983. With Putnam Pub. Group, Denver and NYC, 1983—, dir. trade sales and mktg., internat. sales mgr. NYC, 1987—89, v.p. sales and mktg., 1989—94; sr. v.p., pub. Putnam and Grosset Book Group, NYC, 1994—95, pres., pub., 1995—97; pres. Young Readers Grp. Penguin Group USA, NYC, 1997—2008, exec. v.p. bus. ops., 2008—. Vice chmn., bd. dirs. Eric Carle Mus. of Picture Book Art, 2001—07, 2009—; bd. dirs. Children's Book Coun., 2004—08; bd. chair Acelero Learning, Monmouth County, NJ, 2007—. Mem.: Pub.'s Lunch Club NYC (pres. 2004—05). Methodist. Avocations: literature, tennis, fantasy baseball. Office: Penguin Group USA 375 Hudson St Fl 5 New York NY 10014-4592 Office Phone: 212-366-2500. Business E-Mail: doug.whiteman@us.penguingroup.com.

WHITEMAN, JOSEPH DAVID, retired lawyer, manufacturing company executive; b. Sioux Falls, SD, Sept. 12, 1933; s. Samuel D. and Margaret (Wallace) W.; m. Mary Kelly, Dec. 29, 1962; children: Anne Margaret, Mary Ellen, Joseph David, Sarah Kelly, Jane. BA, U. Mich., 1955, JD, 1960. Bar: D.C. 1960, Ohio 1976. Assoc. Cox, Langford, Stoddard & Cutler, Washington, 1959-64; sec., gen. counsel Studebaker group Studebaker Worthington, Inc., NYC, 1964-71; asst. gen. counsel. United Telecommunications, Inc., Kansas City, Mo., 1971-74; v.p., gen. counsel, sec. Weatherhead Co., Cleve., 1974-77, Parker Hannifin Corp., Cleve., 1977-98; ret., 1998. Immediate past chmn. bd. dirs. St. Lukes Med. Ctr. Served as lt. USNR, 1955-57. Mem. ABA, Beta Theta Pi, Phi Delta Phi. Republican. Roman Catholic. Home and Office: 2508 Robinson Springs Rd Stowe VT 05672

WHITEMAN, RICHARD FRANK, architect; b. Mankato, Minn., Mar. 24, 1925; s. Lester Raymond and Mary Grace (Dawald) W.; m. Jean Frances Waite, June 20, 1948 (dec. May 1980); children: David, Sarah, Lynn, Ann, Carol, Frank, Marie, Steven; m. Mavis Patricia Knutsen, May 30, 1982. BArch, U. Minn., 1945; MArch, Harvard U., 1948. Registered architect, Minn. Designer Ellerbe Co., St. Paul, Minn., 1946; architect Thorshov and Cerny, Mpls., 1948-53; ptnr. Jyring and Whiteman, Hibbing, Minn., 1953-62; pres. AJWM Inc., Hibbing and Duluth, Minn., 1963-72, Architects Four, Duluth, 1972-83; owner Richard Whiteman, Duluth, 1983-95; sr. architect U. Minn., Duluth. Chmn. Architect Sect. Registration Bd., Minn., 1972-80. Prin. works include Washington Sch., Hibbing, 1957 (Minn. Soc. Architects Design award 1957), Whiteman Summer Home, Pengilly, Minn. (Minn. Soc. Architects Design award 1959), Bemidji State Coll. Phys. Edn. Bldg. (Minn. Soc. Architects Design award 1960), Whiteman Residence, Griggs Hall UMD, 1990. Pres. U. for Srs., 1993-94, 2000-01; chair Duluth Housing Authority, 2001-06, vice chair, 2006—07. With USNR, 1943—45. Mem. Minn. Soc. Architects (pres. 1972), Northeast Minn. Architects (pres. 1962), Minn. Designer Selection Bd. (chmn. 1990). Clubs: Kitchi Gammi (Duluth). Lodges: Kiwanis. Democrat. Roman Catholic. Avocations: photography, fishing, cross country skiing, travel. Home: 3500 E 3rd St Duluth MN 55804-1812 Personal E-mail: arch032425@aol.com.

WHITE-MEANS, SHELLEY, healthcare educator; PhD, Northwestern U., Evanston, Ill., 1983. Asst. prof. Cornell U., Ithaca, NY, 1981—88; prof. U. Memphis, 1988—2004, U. Tenn. Health Sci. Ctr., Memphis, 2004—. Mem. of class Leadership Memphis, 1997—98; mem. Mustard Seed Inc., Memphis, 2004—09; bd. dir. & exec. com. Memphis Health Ctr., 1994—2003; bd. chair Bluff City Christian Coll., Memphis, 2002—05. Named Convocation Spkr., Spelman Coll., 2000; Health & Econ. Productivity grant, Milbank Found., 1988—89, Cost Caregiving grant, Retirement Rsch. Found., 1996, Grant, Dept Health & Cmty. Svcs., State Tenn., 2004—05, Nat. Acad. Social Ins. & Rockefeller Found., 2008—09. Mem.: Internat. Soc. Pharmacoeconomics &

Outcomes Rsch., Gerontol. Soc. America, Am. Econ. Assn., Nat. Acad. Social Ins., Nat. Econ. Assn. (pres. 1996—96). Home Fax: 901-448-1640. Business E-Mail: swhiteme@utmem.edu.

WHITENECK, GALE, medical researcher; b. Kans., Dec. 4, 1948; s. Wray and Irene Whiteneck; m. Ann Vivian Kraetzer, Jan. 6, 1979; children: Colin Kraetzer, Ryan Kraetzer. PhD, U. Denver, 1981. Rsch. asst., dept. instns. tng. ctr. State Colo., Denver, 1972—73; grad. tchg. asst., dept. speech communication U. Denver, 1973—74, rsch. analyst ctr. social R & D, 1973—74, rsch. social scientist, ctr. social R & D, 1974—77, adj. prof. dept. speech communication, 1975—79; rsch. cons. Denver, 1977—86; asst. clin. prof. dept. preventive medicine & biometrics U. Colo., Health Sci. Ctr., Denver, 1984—, asst. clin. prof. dept. rehab. medicine, 1997—; dir. rsch. dept. Craig Hosp., Englewood, Colo., 1986—. Contbr. scientific papers to numerous profl. jours. Recipient Disability Achievement award, APHA, 2004; fellowship, Congress Rehab. Medicine, 2002. Mem.: ICIDH Revision Team, Med. Outcomes Trust, Am. Disability & Wellness Assn., APHA, Am. Assn. Health & Disability, Am. Paraplegia Soc., Am. Congress Rehab. Medicine (Disting. Mem. award 2005), Am. Spinal Injury Assn. (Excellence award 1986). Office: Craig Hosp 3425 S Clarkson St Englewood CO 80113 Office Phone: 303-789-8204. Office Fax: 303-789-8441. Business E-Mail: gale@craighospital.org.

WHITENER, JEANETTE (JEANETTE PENNY FORCASH WHITENER), legislative staff member; Grad., De Paul U., Chgo., 1994; M in Pub. Policy, Georgetown U., Washington. Legis. asst., policy advisor US House of Reps., legis dir., Rep. Jerry Weller, chief of staff to Rep. Jerry Weller, 2001—07, chief of staff to Rep. Randy Neugebauer, 2007—. Republican. Office: 1424 Longworth House Office Bldg Washington DC 20515 Office Phone: 202-225-4005. Office Fax: 202-225-9615.*

WHITENER, RONNIE DALE, physics professor; s. Jessie Ray and Betty Jean Whitener; m. Sue B. Stewart, Nov. 24, 1979; 1 child, Tiffany Charise Goebel. MS, Western Carolina U., Cullowhee, NC, 2003. Chem. mgr. Nalco Chem. Co., Naperville, Ill., 1998—2000; astronomy educator and lectr. Tri-County CC, Murphy, tchr., 2000—. Hazardous waste mgmt. Clifton Precision, Murphy, 1974—94. Contbr. scientific papers. Recipient Excellence Tchg. award, Tri-County CC, 2006. Master: Nat. Tech. Honor Soc. (head 2000—08).

WHITENER, SCOTT, music educator, researcher; b. Wash., DC, July 17, 1940; m. Cathryn L. Hetman, Oct. 18, 1980; children: Richard DeWitt, Alexandra, Diana Maye. Diploma in Performance, Juilliard Sch., NYC, 1962; MusM, U. Mich., Ann Arbor, 1966; EdD, Rutgers U., New Brunswick, NJ, 1974. Prof. music Mason Gross Sch. Arts Rutgers U., New Brunswick, NJ, 1966—. Author: A Complete Guide to Brass: Instruments and Technique, 3rd edit., 2007. Mem.: Brit. Horn Soc. Anglican. Avocation: bicycling. Home: 21 Buffa Dr Somerset NJ 08873 Office: Rutgers Univ Marryott Music Bldg 81 George St New Brunswick NJ 08901-1411 Business E-Mail: swhiten@rci.rutgers.edu.

WHITENER, WILLIAM GARNETT, dancer, choreographer; b. Seattle, Aug. 17, 1951; s. Warren G. and Virginia Louise (Garnett) Whitener. Student, Cornish Sch. Allied Arts, Seattle, 1958-69. Dancer NYC Opera, 1969, Joffrey Ballet, NYC, 1969-77, Twyla Tharp Dance, NYC, 1978-87; asst. to choreographer Jerome Robbins for Robbins' Broadway, NYC, 1988; artistic dir. Les Ballets Jazz de Montréal, 1991-93, Royal Winnipeg Ballet, 1993-95, Kansas City Ballet, 1996—. Coord. dance dept. Concord Acad., Mass., 1988; vis. artist U. Wash., 1989—91; dance faculty mem. Harvard U. Summer Dance, 1989—90, NYU, 1985; mem. jury panel Internat. Ballet Prize Benois de la Danse, Moscow, 2008. Dancer (Broadway plays) Dancin', 1978, choreographer Princeton Ballet, Joffrey II, John Curry Ice Theatre, Ballet Hispanico of NY, Boston Ballet Internat. Choreography Competition, Tommy Tune, Martine van Hamel/Kevin McKenzie, Ann Reinking, Seattle Repertory Theatre, Am. Ballroom Theatre, NYC, Hartford Ballet, Conn., On the Boards with Bill Irwin, PBS-TV Alive From Off Center, (Operas) A Little Night Music, Pacific Northwest Ballet, Rusalka, Seattle Opera, (Operas) Aida, Kansas City Repartory Theatre, The Pearlfishers Eugene Oreg., Lyric Opera Kans. City, dancer (films) Amadeus, Zelig, (TV films) The Catherine Wheel, Dance in America; performer: Garden of Earthly Delights, 1988. Bd. trustees DanceUSA, 2000—. Ford Found. scholar, 1963—64. Mem.: Am. Guild Musical Artists, Actor's Equity. Office: Kansas City Ballet 1616 Broadway Kansas City MO 64108-1207

WHITENER, WILLIAM JACKSON, retired military officer, dean; b. Mount Holly, NC, Apr. 21, 1922; s. David Henry and Elizabeth Jane (Barrett) Whitener; m. Martha Pacolette Sarratt, June 28, 1952; 1 child, Martha Sarratt Whitener Walker. BSc, US Mil. Acad., West Point, NY, 1946; MA, Columbia U., NYC, 1966; MSc, George Washington U., DC, 1967; HHD (hon.), Lander U., Greenwood, SC, 1992. Col. US Army, USA, Germany, Korea, Vietnam, 1946—75, brigade comdr. Aschaffenburg, Germany, 1969—70, G-3, ctrl. army group Mannhein, Germany, 1970—72, army advisor, Air U. Maxwell AFB, Ala., 1972—75; dean U. SC, Union, SC, 1977—84, interim chancellor Spartanburg, 1993—94; chief of staff US Mil. Acad., West Point, 1967—69; ret., 1975. Chmn. SC Commn. Higher Edn., Columbia, SC, 1989—93. Editor: Some Reminiscences For My Nieces and Nephews, 2005. Pres. Union County Hist. Soc., 2003—06; chmn. Union Cmty. Found., 2006. Republican. Methodist. Avocation: historic preservation. Home: 203 Thomson Blvd Union SC 29379

WHITESCARVER, JACK EDWARD, federal agency administrator; b. Palestine, Tex., May 16, 1937; s. A.B. and Elizabeth Lorraine (Kimball) Whitescarver. BS, Sam Houston State U., Huntsville, Tex., 1959, MS, 1965; PhD, U. Medicine Dentistry NJ, 1974. Rsch. assoc. Harvard U. Sch. Pub. Health, Boston, 1976-77; grants assoc. NIH, Bethesda, Md., 1977, spl. asst. to dir., Nat. Inst. Allergy & Infectious Diseases (NIAID), 1978-84, dep. dir., Office AIDS Rsch. (OAR), 1988—2000, acting dir. OAR, 2000—02, dir. OAR, assoc. dir. AIDS rsch., 2002—; asst. dean rsch. & devel. Emory U. Sch. Medicine, Atlanta, 1984-86, assoc. dean, 1986-88, asst. prof. pathology, 1985-88. Contbr. numerous articles to profl. jours., chapters to books. Recipient Disting. Svc. award, HHS; named Alumnus of Yr., UMDNJ Grad. Sch. Biomed. Scis., 1991; fellow Albert Soiland Cancer Found., 1967—70. Mem.: Internat. AIDS Soc., Infectious Diseases Soc. America, Am. Acad. Allergy & Immunology. Office: OAR NIH 5635 Fishers Ln MSC 9310 Rockville MD 20892 Office Phone: 301-496-0357. Office Fax: 301-496-2119. Business E-Mail: jack.whitescarver@nih.hhs.gov.*

WHITESELL, ANN THERESE, elementary school educator; b. Ipswich, Mass., Oct. 3, 1967; d. William Howard and Adelaide Ann (Auckley) Lindquist; m. Anthony David Whitesell, May 20, 2006. BS in Early Childhood Edn., Salem State Coll., Mass., 1985—90. Cert. early childhood edn. tchr. Mass., 1990, NH, 2006. K-1 tchr. St. Mary's Sch., Boston, 1990—92; preschool tchr. Stoneybrook Children's Ctr., Georgetown, Mass., 1999—2006; spl. edn. asst. N. Londonderry Elem. Sch., NH, 2006—. Mem.: Nat. Assn. Edn. Young Children, Assn. Childhood Edn. Internat. Independent. Cath. Home: 85 Cote Dr Epping NH 03042 Personal E-mail: anntlind1003@aol.com.

WHITESELL, JOHN EDWIN, retired motion picture company executive; b. DuBois, Pa., Feb. 23, 1938; s. Guy Roosevelt and Grace Ethlyn (Brisbin) W.; m. Amy H. Jacobs, June 12, 1960; 1 child, Scott Howard; m. Martha Kathlyn Hall, Sept. 3, 1975; m. Phyllis Doyle, May 8, 1993. BA, Pa. State U., 1962. Asst. mgr. non-theatrical div. Columbia Pictures Corp., NYC, 1963-66; with Warner Bros., Inc., 1966—2003, nat. sales mgr. non-theatrical div. Burbank, Calif., 1968-75, v.p., 1975-76; v.p. internat. sales adminstrn. Warner Bros. Internat. TV Distbn., 1976-2001, cons., 2001—03, ret., 2003. Bd. dirs. Mastermedia Internat. Inc.; past bd. dirs. Found. for Entertainment Programming in Higher Edn.; mem. self-study com. Nat. Entertainment Conf., 1974-75. Served with USNR, 1956-58. Recipient Alumni Fellow award Pa. State U., 2001, Outstanding Alumnus award Pa. State U. DuBois Campus, 1995, Founders award Nat. Entertainment Conf., 1975. Mem. Nat. Audio-Visual Assn. (motion picture coun. 1973-76, exec. com. film coun. 1969-76, ednl. materials producers coun. 1970-76), Acad. TV Arts and Scis. 1976-80, Nat. Assn. Media Educators (adv. com. 1973-76)

WHITESELL, PATRICK, talent agency executive; b. 1965; m. Lauren Sanchez, Aug. 20, 2005; children: Schuyler, Nikko, Evan, Ella. Previously with Intertalent; agent United Talent Agy. (UTA); with Creative Artists Agy. (CAA), 1995—2000, co-head motion picture talent dept., 2000—01; ptnr. Endeavor Agy., Beverly Hills, Calif., 2001—09; co-CEO William Morris Endeavor Entertainment (WME), Beverly Hills, Calif., 2009—. Mem. Calif. Film Commn., 2006—. Named one of The 50 Most Powerful People in Hollywood, Premiere mag., 2004—06.*

WHITESIDE, CAROL GORDON, foundation executive; b. Chgo., Dec. 15, 1942; d. Paul George and Helen Louise G.; m. John Gregory Whiteside, Aug. 15, 1964; children: Brian Paul, Derek James. BA, U. Calif., Davis, 1964. Pers. mgr. Emporium Capwell Co., Santa Rosa, 1964-67; pers. asst. Levi Strauss & Co., San Francisco, 1967-69; project leader Interdatum, San Francisco, 1983-88; with City Coun. Modesto, 1983-87; mayor City of Modesto, 1987-91; asst. sec. for intergovtl. rels. The Resources Agy., State of Calif., Sacramento, 1991-93; dir. intergovtl. affairs Gov.'s Office, Sacramento, 1993-97; pres. Great Valley Ctr., Modesto, Calif., 1997—. Bd. dirs. Lincoln Inst. Land Policy. Trustee Modesto City Schs., 1979-83; nat. pres. Rep. Mayors and Local Ofcls., 1990; mem. Sierra Nev. Conservancy Bd., 2005—; chmn. bd. Sierra Health Found. Recipient Lifetime Achievement award League of Calif. Cities, 2002, Excellence in Pub. Svc. award, Fresno Bus. Coun., 2004, Olmstead medal Am. Soc. Landscape Archs., 2007; named Outstanding Woman of Yr. Women's Commn., Stanislaus County, Calif., 1988, Woman of Yr., 27th Assembly Dist., 1991; Toll fellow Coun. of State Govts., 1996, Champion of Am. Dream, Calif. State U., Stanislaus, 2002. Republican. Lutheran. Office: Great Valley Ctr 201 Needham St Modesto CA 95354-0903 Home Phone: 209-521-0485. E-mail: carol@greatvalley.org.

WHITESIDE, CHARLES B., III, investment company executive; b. Ft. Smith, Ark., Mar. 17, 1941; s. Charles B. Jr. and R. Evelyn cindy Whiteside; m. Catherine Ware, Jan. 29, 1966; children: Carrie H., Charles B. IV. BSBA, U. Ark., Fayetteville, 1963. 1st v.p. Merrill Lynch & Co., Little Rock, 1965—. Trustee Ark. Children's Hosp., 1974—, chmn., treas., 1983—88; vice chmn. bd. dirs. Ark. Children's Hosp. Found., 1983—; trustee Ark. Children's Rsch. Inst., 1989—2000, chmn., 1990—; trustee, treas. Lyon Coll., Batesville, Ark., 1992—; bd. advisors U. Ark., Fayetteville, 2006. 1st lt. US Army, 1963—65. Recipient Outstanding Vol. Fundraising award for State of Ark., Nat. Soc. Fund Raising Execs., 2000; Sr. Paul Harris fellow, Rotary. Mem.: Kappa Sigma Alumni Assn. (pres. bd. dirs. 1974—). Episcopalian. Avocations: hunting, fishing. Office: Merrill Lynch 2200 Rodney Parham Ste 300 Little Rock AR 72212 Office Phone: 501-312-7285.

WHITESIDE, JOAN ROBINSON, administrative assistant, music educator; b. Dayton, Tenn., Jan. 9, 1954; d. William Eugene and Elsie Beene Robinson; m. Harry Woodrow Whiteside, Nov. 23, 1978; children: Emily Whiteside McCoy, Katherine Grace, Benjamin Burch. MusM, U. Tenn., Knoxville, 1978. Flute instr. Maryville Coll., Tenn., 1995—98, Pellissippi State, Knoxville, Tenn., 2007—. Music theory & appreciation instr. Thursday Connection Homeschool Classes, Knoxville, 2004—09. Home: 3705 Dyestone Gap Rd Knoxville TN 37931

WHITESIDE, RUTH A., federal agency administrator; m. James Shelhamer; 1 child. BA, Austin Coll.; MA, Univ. Tex.; PhD, Rice Univ. Asst. dir. SW Ctr. for Urban Rsch. & Inst. for Urban Studies Univ. Houston; various Fgn.Svc. positions US State Dept., 1978—84, mem. policy planning staff, bureau European Affairs, & bureau of Diplomatic Security, exec. asst. to undersecretary for mgmt., dep. dir. Fgn. Svc. Inst. Washington, 1997—2001, prin. dep. asst. sec. Bureau of Human Resources, 2001—06, dir. Fgn. Svc. Inst., 2006—. Recipient Disting. Presdl. Rank award, 2 Meritorious Presdl. Rank awards. Office: US State Dept 2201 C St NW Washington DC 20520*

WHITESIDE, WILLIAM ANTHONY, JR., retired lawyer; b. Phila., Feb. 23, 1929; s. William Anthony and Ellen T. (Hensler) Whiteside; m. Eileen Ann Ferrick, Feb. 27, 1954 (dec. July 24, 2008); children: William Anthony III, Michael P., Eileen A., Richard F.(dec.), Christopher J., Mary P. BS, Notre Dame U., 1951; LLB, U. Pa., 1954. Bar: Pa. 1955. Assoc. Speiser, Satinsky, Gilliland & Packel, Phila., 1956—58, ptnr., 1958—61, Fox, Rothschild, O'Brien & Frankel, Phila., 1961—2001; ret., 2001. Past chmn. Police Athletic League, Phila.; trustee LaSalle Coll. HS, Phila., Am. Coll. Mgmt. and Tech., Dubrovnik, Croatia, emeritus trustee; chmn. emeritus bd. trustees, emeritus trustee Rochester Inst. Tech.; emeritus trustee CC Phila. Found.; pres. adv. coun. U. Notre Dame; emeritus trustee Germantown Acad., past pres. 1st lt. USAF, 1954—56. Recipient Hall of Fame, LaSalle Coll. HS, 2008; named Man of Yr., Notre Dame Club Phila., 1967. Mem.: ABA, Pa. Soc., Phila. Bar Assn., Pa. Bar Assn., Wissahickon Skating Club, Union League Club Phila. Republican. Roman Catholic. Office: Fox Rothschild LLP 2000 Market St Ste 10 Philadelphia PA 19103-3231 Home: 7808 Cobden Rd Glenside PA 19038-7256 Office Phone: 215-299-2032.

WHITESIDES, GEORGE MCCLELLAND, chemistry professor; b. Louisville, Aug. 3, 1939; m. Barbara Breasted; children: George Thomas, Benjamin Haile. AB, Harvard U., 1960; PhD, Calif. Inst. Tech., 1964; D Honoris Causa (hon.), U. Twente, The Netherlands, 2001. Asst. prof. dept. chemistry MIT, Cambridge, 1963—69, assoc. prof., 1969—71, prof., 1971—75, Arthur C. Cope prof., 1975—80, Haslam and Dewey prof., 1980—82; prof. dept. chemistry Harvard U., Cambridge, 1982—86, Mallinckrodt prof., 1986—2004, Woodford L. and Ann A. Flowers U. prof., 2004—. Adv. position NRC, NSF, Dept. Def. Advanced Rsch. Projects Agy. Recipient Pure Chemistry award, Am. Chem. Soc., 1975, Harrison Howe award, Rochester sect., 1979, Disting. Alumni award, Calif. Inst. Tech., 1980, Remsen award, 1983, Arthur C. Cope Scholar award, 1989, James Flack Norris award, 1994, Arthur C. Cope award, 1995, Def. Advanced Rsch. Projects Agy. award for Significant Technical Achievement, 1996, Madison Marshall award, Am. Chem. Soc., 1996, Nat. Medal of Sci., 1998, Disting. Chemist award, Sierra Nev. sect. Am. Chem. Soc., 1999, Wallac Oy Innovation award, Soc. Biomolecular Screening, 1999, Excellence award in Surface Sci., Surfaces Biomaterials Found., 1999, Von Hippel award, Material Rsch. Soc., 2000, World Tech. award for materials, World Tech. Network, 2001, Rschr. of Yr. award, Small Times Mag., 2002, Pitts. Analytical Chemistry award, Soc. Analytical Chemists of Pitts., 2003, Kyoto prize for advanced tech., Inamori Found., 2003, Paracelsus prize, Swiss Chem. Soc., 2004, Ralph and Helen Oesper award, Cin. sect. Am. Chem. Soc., 2004, Jacob Heskel Gabbay award in biotech. and medicine, 2004, Dickson Prize in Sci., 2005, Dan David Found. prize, 2005, Emanuel Merk Lect. prize, 2005, Linus Pauling medal, 2005, Welch award in Chemistry, 2005, Emanuel Merck Lecture prize, 2005, Linus Pauling Medal award, 2005, Welch award, 2005; Alfred P. Sloan fellow, 1968. Fellow: AAAS, Indian Nat. Sci. Acad., World Tech. Network, Chem. Rsch. Soc. India (hon.); mem.: NAE, NAS, Academia Sinica (chmn. internat. sci. adv. bd. Genomics Rsch. Ctr. 2006—), Royal Netherlands Acad. Arts and Scis., Materials Rsch. Soc. India (hon.), Am. Philos. Soc., Am. Acad. Arts and Scis. Office: Harvard U Dept of Chemistry 12 Oxford St Cambridge MA 02138-2902 Business E-Mail: gwhites.des@gmwgroup.harvard.edu.

WHITESIDES, JOHN LINDSEY, JR., aerospace engineering educator, researcher; b. San Antonio, Feb. 27, 1943; s. John Lindsey and Florene Lyndelle (Wheelis) W.; m. Sheila LaVerne Beadle, May 30, 1964 (div. 1975); children: Lisa Diane, John Gregory; m. Andrea Martina Chavez Lewis, Mar. 26, 1994. BS in Aerospace Engring., U. Tex., 1965, PhD, 1968. Asst. prof. George Washington U., Hampton, Va., 1968-74, assoc. prof., 1974-80, prof., 1980—2005, prof. emeritus, 2006—; assoc. dir. Joint Inst. for Advancement of Flight Scis., Hampton, 1986—2005. Contbr. articles to profl. jours. Mem. Sigma Series Lectures, Hampton, 1990-2000. Recipient disting. pub. svc. medal NASA, 1993, Malina medal Internat. Astronautical Fedn., 1995. Fellow AIAA (dir. 1987-93, nat. faculty advisor 1989, v.p. mem. svcs. 1999-2002, v.p. publs. 2006—09); mem. Am. Soc. Engring. Edn., Soc. Engring. Sci. (organizing com. 1975, 76, 77), Tau Beta Pi, Phi Eta Sigma, Sigma Gamma Tau. Avocations: sports, art. Home: 670 Anns Way Blanco TX 78606 Office: George Washington U MAE Dept Washington DC 20052 Home Phone: 830-833-0516. Business E-Mail: jlw@gwu.edu.

WHITE-THOMSON, IAN LEONARD, retired mining executive; b. Halstead, Eng., May 3, 1936; came to U.S., 1969; s. Walter Norman and Leonore (Turney) W-T.; m. Barbara Montgomery, Nov. 24, 1971. BA with 1st class honors, New Coll., Oxford U., 1960, MA, 1969. Mgmt. trainee Borax Consol. Ltd., London, 1960-61, asst. to sales mgr., 1961-64, asst. to sales dir., 1964; comml. dir. Hardman & Holden Ltd., Manchester, Eng., 1965-67, joint mng. dir., 1967-69; v.p. mktg. dept. U.S. Borax Inc., Los Angeles, 1969-73, exec. v.p. mktg., 1973-88, pres., 1988-98, also dir., chmn., 1996-99; group exec. Pa. Glass Sand Corp., Ottawa Silica Co., U.S. Silica Co., 1985-87; exec. dir. L.A. Opera, 2000—01. Bd. dirs. Canpotex Ltd., chmn. bd., 1974-76. Bd. dirs. Colburn Sch.; bd. dirs. Thornton Sch. U. So. Calif. With Brit. Army, 1954—56. Named Mfr. of Yr., Calif. Mfrs. Assn., 1997. Mem. Can. Potash Prodrs. Assn. (v.p. 1976-77, dir. 1972-77), Chem. Industry Coun. of Calif. (bd. dirs. 1982-85, chmn. 1984), Am. Mining Congress (bd. dirs. 1989), RTZ Borax and Minerals (bd. dirs. 1992, chief exec. 1995-99), Kerr-McGee Corp. (bd. dirs. 1999-2006), Calif. Club (bd. dirs. 2007), Valley Hunt Club. Home: 1897 Braemar Rd Pasadena CA 91103-3712 Personal E-mail: iwhitethom@aol.com.

WHITFIELD, EDWARD (WAYNE), United States Representative from Kentucky; b. Hopkinsville, Ky., May 25, 1943; m. Constance Harriman; 1 child, Kate. BS in Bus., U. Ky., 1965; JD, U. Ky. Coll. of Law, 1969. Mem. Ky. Ho. of Reps., 1974-75; pvt. practice law, 1970-79; govt. affairs counsel Seaboard Sys. R.R. subs. CSX Corp., 1979-83, counsel to pres., 1983-85; v.p. state rels. CSX Corp., 1986-88, v.p. fed. r.r. affairs, 1988-91; legal counsel to chmn. Interstate Commerce Commn., 1991-93; mem. US Congress from 1st Ky. dist., 1995—; mem. energy and commerce com. 1st lt. USAR. Republican. Office: US Ho Reps 2411 Rayburn House Office Bldg Washington DC 20515 also: 1403 S Main St Hopkinsville KY 42240 Office Phone: 202-225-3115.*

WHITFIELD, ERICA SHARON, director, career planning administrator; b. Roanoke, Va., July 5, 1980; d. Edith Cookie (Peirce) and David James Whitfield. BS with honors, Lynchburg Coll., Va., 2001, MEd, 2004. Hall dir., grad. asst. residence life Lynchburg Coll., 2002—04, career counseling intern, 2003; counselor intern New Land Jobs, Lynchburg, 2003, Ctrl. Va. CC, Lynchburg, 2003—04; counselor Region 2000 Workforce Ctr., Lynchburg, 2003—04; dir. career devel. svcs. Mary Baldwin Coll., Staunton, Va., 2004—06; event planner, edn. coord. Alpha Sigma Alpha Sorority, Indpls., 2006—. Conf. chair Consortium of Va. Women's Coll. and Univ., Staunton, Va., 2005. Scholar, Mary Baldwin Coll., 2006. Mem.: ACA, Va. Found. for Ind. Coll., Va. Assn. Colleges and Employers, Nat. Assn. Colleges and Employers, Am. Coll. and Pers. Assn., Nat. Career Devel. Assn. (field editor for career convergence 2005—06), Alpha Psi Omega, Psi Chi, Kappa Delta Pi, Omicron Delta Kappa, Alpha Sigma Alpha (chpt. advisor 2004—06). Home: 502 PINE SONG LN APT 101 Virginia Beach VA 23451-5342 Personal E-mail: eryielle@yahoo.com. Business E-Mail: ewhitfield@alphasigmaalpha.org.

WHITFIELD, FRED, JR., professional sports team executive; s. Fred Whitfield; m. Mary Whitfield. BBA in Econs., Campbell U., Buies Creek, NC, 1980, MBA in Mktg.; JD, NC Ctrl. U., Durham. Pvt. practice lawyer, Greensboro, NC; dir. Carolinas region Falk Assocs. Mgmt. Enterprises; dir. player devel. basketball divsn. Nike, dir. bus. and legal affairs Brand Jordan divsn., 2003—06; dir. player pers., asst. legal counsel Washington Wizards, 2000—03; pres., COO Bobcats Sports & Entertainment, Charlotte, NC, 2006—. Founder, dir. Achievements Unlimited Basketball Sch., Greensboro, NC, 1985—. Named to Campbell U. Sports Hall of Fame, 1995. Office: Charlotte Bobcats 333 E Trade St Charlotte NC 28202*

WHITFIELD, GRAHAM FRANK, orthopedic surgeon; b. Eng., 1942; arrived in U.S., 1969, naturalized, 1975; BSc, King's Coll., U. London, 1963; PhD, Queen Mary Coll., U. London, 1969; MD, NY Med. Coll., 1976. Rsch. scientist Unilever Rsch. Lab., England, 1963-66; postdoctoral fellow dept. chemistry Temple U., 1969-71, instr., 1971-72, asst. prof., 1972-73; resident in surgery NY Med. Coll. Affiliated Hosps., NYC, 1976-78, resident in orthopedics, 1978-79, sr. resident in orthop. surgery, 1979-80, chief resident, 1980-81; attending orthop. surgeon Good Samaritan Hosp., West Palm Beach, Fla., 1981-87, St. Mary's Hosp., West Palm Beach, 1981—82, JFK Med. Ctr., Lake Worth, Fla., 1981—, Palms Wellington Surg. Ctr., West Palm Beach, 1994-96, Wellington Regional Med. Ctr., West Palm Beach, 1996—, Bethesda Health City, Boynton Beach, Fla., 1996—2009, Palms West Hosp., Loxahatchee, Fla., 1997—2004, Columbia Hosp., West Palm Beach, 1997—2002. Instr. health professions divsn. Nova Southeastern U., North Miami, Fla., 1994-95, clin. asst. prof. dept. surgery, Coll.

Osteo. Medicine, Nova Southeastern U., Ft. Lauderdale, Fla., 1995—. Author: (with Joseph Cohn and Louis Del Guercio) Critical Care Readings, 1981; editl. bd., contbg. editor Hosp. Physician, 1978-82; cons. editor Physician Asst. and Health Practitioner, 1979-82; orthop. cons. Conv. Reporter, 1980-82; assoc. editor-in-chief Critical Care Monitor, 1980-82; editl. bd. Complications in Orthopedics, 1986-96; practice panel cons. in orthop. surgery Complications in Surgery, 1982-96. Recipient N.Y. Med. Coll. Surg. Soc. award, 1976. Fellow: Internat. Coll. Surgeons; mem.: AMA, Fla. Orthop. Soc., So. Orthop. Assn., Royal Inst. Chemistry (Eng.), Palm Beach County Med. Soc., Fla. Med. Assn., Soc. the Four Arts, Rotary, Explorer's Club (N.Y.C.), Brit. Schs. and Univs. Club, Soc. Sons of St. George (N.Y.C.), Sigma Xi. Office: 2150 S Congress Ave West Palm Beach FL 33406-7604 Office Phone: 561-965-5200. Business E-Mail: doctorwhitfield@aol.com.

WHITFIELD, STEPHEN JACK, history educator; b. Houston, Dec. 3, 1942; s. Bert and Joan (Schwarz) W.; m. Donna Elaine Arzt, Aug. 21, 1977 (div. 1983); m. Lee Cone, Dec. 15, 1984; children: Kimberly, Andrea. BA, Tulane U., 1964; MA, Yale U., 1966; PhD, Brandeis U., 1972. Instr. So. U., New Orleans, 1966-68; from asst. prof. to assoc. prof. Brandeis U., Waltham, Mass., 72-85, prof., 1985—. Vis. prof. Hebrew U., Jerusalem, Israel, 1983-84, Cath. U. Leuven & Louvainla, Neuve Fall, 1993, Sarbonne, Paris Spring, 1994, Spring, 1998, U. Munich, 2004. Author: Scott Nearing: Apostle of American Radicalism, 1974, Into the Dark: Hannah Arendt and Totalitarianism, 1980, Voices of Jacob, Hands of Esau, 1984, A Critical American: The Politics of Dwight Macdonald, 1984, A Death in the Delta: The Story of Emmett Till, 1988, American Space, Jewish Time, 1988, The Culture of the Cold War, 1991, In Search of American Jewish Culture, 1999. Recipient Kayden prize U. Colo., Boulder, 1981, Fulbright Found. professorship, 1983-84, 93. Mem. Am. Jewish Hist. Soc. (mem. academic coun.). Home: 3 Ewell Ave Lexington MA 02421-7507 Office: Brandeis U 415 South St Waltham MA 02454-9110 Office Phone: 781-736-3035. Business E-Mail: swhitfie@brandeis.edu.

WHITFORD, BRADLEY, actor; b. Madison, Wis., Oct. 10, 1959; m. Jane Kaczmarek, Aug. 15, 1992; children: Frances, George, Mary. BA, Wesleyan U., 1981. Actor: (plays) Curse of the Starving Class, Three Days of Rain, Measure for Measure, Corionlanus; (Broadway plays) A Few Good Men, 1990—91, Boeing-Boeing, 2008 (Drama Desk award for Outstanding Revival of a Play, 2008); (films) Dead as a Doorman, 1986, Adventures in Babysitting, 1987, Revenge of the Nerds II, 1987, Vital Signs, 1990, Presumed Innocent, 1990, Young Guns II, 1990, Awakenings, 1990, Scent of a Woman, 1992, The Silent Alarm, 1993, RoboCop 3, 1993, My Life, 1993, A Perfect World, 1993, Philadelphia, 1993, The Client, 1994, Cobb, 1994, Billy Madison, 1995, My Fellow Americans, 1996, The Spittin' Image, 1997, The People, 1997, Masterminds, 1997, Red Corner, 1997, Wildly Available, 1999, The Muse, 1999, Bicentennial Man, 1999, Kate & Leopold, 2001, The Sisterhood of the Traveling Pants, 2005, Little Manhattan, 2005; (TV films) C.A.T. Squad, 1986, The Betty Ford Story, 1987, Web of Deception, 1994, Nothing But the Truth, 1995, The Desperate Trail, 1995, In the Line of Duty: Blaze of Glory, 1997, Cloned, 1997, The Sky's on Fire, 1998, Behind the Mask, 1999, Fathers & Sons, 2005; (TV series) NYPD Blue, 1994, The West Wing, 1999—2006, Studio 60 on the Sunset Strip, 2006—07. Co-founder Clothes Off Our Back Found. Office: Endeavor Agy 10th Fl 9601 Wilshire Blvd Beverly Hills CA 90212

WHITFORD, WALTER GEORGE, retired biology professor; b. Providence, June 12, 1936; s. Walter Albert and Helen Whitford; m. Linda Claire Grist, June 16, 1969; children: William Brett, Eric Ian. PhD, U. RI, Kingston, 1964. Prof. biology N. Mex State U., Las Cruces, 1964—93; sr. rsch. ecologist US EPA, Las Vegas, Nev. Cons. Whitford Consultants, Las Cruces, 1971—2008. Contbr. article to numerous jours. Rep. Zoning Code Bd., Las Cruces, 1972—77. With US Army, 1954—57, Great Britain. Rsch. grant, NSF, 1970—92, Internat. Arid Lands Consortium, 2001—. Avocations: swimming, golf, birdwatching. Home: 4210 Tesota Rd Las Cruces NM 88011 Personal E-mail: wlawhit@zianet.com.

WHITING, ALBERT NATHANIEL, former university chancellor; b. Jersey City, July 3, 1917; s. Hezekiah Oliver and Hildegarde Freida (Lyons) W.; m. Charlotte Luck, June 10, 1950; 1 dau., Brooke Elizabeth. AB, Amherst Coll., 1938; student, Columbia, summer 1938, U. Pitts., 1938-39; MA in Sociology, Fisk U., 1941, L.H.D. (hon.), 1980; PhD in Sociology, Am. U., 1952; LL.D., Amherst Coll., 1968, Western Mich. U., 1974, Duke, 1974, Kyung Hee U., Seoul, Korea, 1981; L.H.D. (hon.), N.C. Central U., 1983. Research and teaching asst. Fisk U., 1939-41; instr. sociology, dir. rural community study Bennett Coll., Greensboro, NC, 1941-43, 46-47; asst. prof. sociology Atlanta U., 1948-53; dean coll., prof. sociology Morris Brown Coll., Atlanta, 1953-57; asst. dean coll. Morgan State Coll., Balt., 1957-59, dean of college, 1960-67; pres. N.C. Central U., Durham, 1967-72, chancellor, 1972-83. Mem. bd. regents U. Md. Sys., 1988-95. Contbr. articles profl. jours. Bd. dirs. Am. Coun. Edn., Ednl. Testing Svc.; bd. dirs., past pres. Assn. State Colls. and Univs.; v.p. Internat. Assn. Univ. Pres.; bd. dirs. Research Triangle (N.C.) Inst.; mem. Md. Higher Edn. Commn., 1995-98. 1st lt. AUS, 1943-46. Episcopalian. Home: 11253B Slalom Ln Columbia MD 21044-2810

WHITING, ANTHONY, executive search consultant; b. Saigon, Indochina, Nov. 6, 1951; s. Dinty Warmington and Lorraine (Yarborough) W. BA summa cum laude, Tulane U., 1973; MA with honors, Columbia U., 1974, MPhil, 1977, PhD, 1984. V.p. Columbia Consulting Group, NYC, 1987-92; partner Johnson, Smith, and Knisely, NYC, 1993-99; mng. dir. Illsley Bourbonnais, NYC, 1999-2000; mng. ptnr. The Waterman Group, NYC, 2000—. Vis. scholar Columbia U., 2001—03; apptd. vis. scholar Union Theol. Sem., 2006—. Author: The Never Resting Mind: Wallace Stevens' Romantic Irony, 1996, Edward Thomas, 1996; contbg. author: Wallace Stevens: Comprehensive Research and Study Guide, 2003. Mem. SAR, Soc. of Mayflower Descendants, Order of Crown of Charlemagne, Baronial Order of Magna Carta, Soc. of the Cinn., Hereditary Order of Descendants of Colonial Govs., Soc. of Order of Founders and Patriots of Am., Soc. of Descendants of Colonial Clergy, Phi Beta Kappa. Office: 267 Fifth Ave New York NY 10016

WHITING, GARY BRIAN, design educator; b. Fontana, Calif., Aug. 19, 1957; s. Fred Leon Whiting and Gladys Annetta Green; m. Debra Eve Greenwood. AS, Victor Valley Coll., Victorville, Calif., AA, 2001. Owner Whiting Enterprises, Victorville, 1998—2006; prof. Victor Valley Coll., 2005—. Youth, Calif., 1998—2008; scout., 1998—2008. With USN, 1976—87. Decorated Many Letters Commendation USN. Mem.: AFT. Home: 7416 Oak Hill Rd Oak Hills CA 92345 Personal E-mail: whiting2@verizon.net.

WHITING, GORDON JAMES, investment banker; b. Bronxville, NY, Nov. 17, 1965; s. William Gordon Whiting and Doris (Chubb) Whiting Simmons; m. Cornelia Conway Cabot, Aug. 30, 2003. BS, Cornell U., 1988; MBA, Columbia U., 1994. Sales and mktg. mgr. Epcot Ltd., Tsim Sha Tsui, Kowloon, Hong Kong, 1989-90; mng. dir. Stapenhurst Ltd., Victoria, Hong Kong, 1990-92; acquisitions assoc. W. P. Carey & Co. LLC, NYC, 1993-94, 2d v.p., 1994-95, v.p., 1995-97, 1st v.p., 1997-98, sr. v.p., 1998-2000, dep. dir. of acquistions, 1999—2003, exec. dir., 2000—; exec. v.p. and portfolio mgr. Corp. Property Assocs.: 14 Inc., NYC, 1998-2000, pres. and portfolio mgr., 2000—. Bd. dir. Fed. Ret. Thrift Investment Bd.; mem. coun. Cornell U., 2002—. Local bd. mem. Selective Svc. Sys., Eagle Scout. Mem. Profl. Assn. Diving Instrs., Bronxville Field Club, Constant Spring Golf Club (Jamaica), Holland Lodge No. 8 F&AM, Leander Club (U.K.), The Camp Fire Club Am., Mashomack Preserve Club (Pine Plains, N.Y.), The Order of St. John, The Pilgrims, Hon. Order Ky. Cols., Racquet and Tennis Club, Royal Hong Kong Yacht Club, Sigma Chi. Republican. Episcopalian. Avocations: fly fishing, golf, scuba diving, skiing, squash. Home: 70 E 96th St Apt 11b New York NY 10128-0752 E-mail: gwhiting@angelogordon.com.

WHITING, HUGH RICHARD, lawyer; b. East Chgo., Ind., Dec. 8, 1945; s. Harold C. and Nina (Hofstetter) W.; m. Sherry Ballast, July 2, 1965; 1 child, Kristin Anne. BA, U. Mich., 1967; JD, Ohio State U., 1974. Bar: Ohio 1974, Tex. 1981. Salesman, adminstr. Procter & Gamble, Cin., 1967-71; law clk. to Judge George Edwards U.S. Ct. Appeals (6th cir.) Ohio, Cin., 1974-75; assoc. Jones, Day, Reavis & Pogue, Cleve., 1975-81, ptnr., 1982—; mng. ptnr. Houston office Jones Day. Chmn. Firmwide Profl. Svcs. Com.; mem. civil justice reform act adv. com. No. Dist. Ohio Adv. Com., Cleve., 1990—; mem. Ohio State U. Coll. Law Nat. Coun., Columbus, 1984—; speaker, presenter on legal practice and practice mgmt. various confs. and seminars. Co-chmn. Gen. Bus. Campaign Cleve. Orch., 1992. Mem. ABA (litigation sect., sect. bus. law), Tex. Bar Assn., Cleve. Bar Assn., Mayfield Country Club, Order of Coif. Avocations: golf, travel, reading. Office: Jones Day Ste 3300 717 Texas Houston TX 77002-2712 Office Fax: 832-239-3600. Business E-Mail: hrwhiting@jonesday.com.

WHITING, RICHARD ALBERT, lawyer; b. Cambridge, Mass., Dec. 2, 1922; s. Albert S. and Jessie (Coleman) W.; m. Marvelene Nash, Feb. 22, 1948 (div. 1984); children— Richard A. Jr., Stephen C., Jeffrey D., Gary S., Kimberly G.; m. Joanne Sherry, Oct. 14, 1984 (div., 2007). AB, Dartmouth Coll., 1944; JD, Yale U., 1949. Bar: D.C. 1949. Assoc. Steptoe & Johnson, Washington, 1949-55, ptnr., 1956-86, of counsel, 1987—. Adj. prof. Vt. Law Sch., South Royalton, 1985-90; mem. exec. com. Yale Law Sch. Assn., New Haven, 1985-88; mem. adv. bd. The Antitrust Bull., N.Y.C., 1975-99. Contbr. articles to profl. jours. Trustee Colby-Sawyer Coll., 1987-97. 1st lt. U.S. Army, 1945-46. Mem. ABA (council mem. Antitrust Law sect. 1977-85, del. to Ho. Dels. 1982-83, chmn. 1984-85) Presbyterian. Office: 1330 Connecticut Ave NW Washington DC 20036-1704 Office Phone: 202-429-8080.

WHITING, S. CAROL, music educator; b. Bryan, Tex., Sept. 1, 1948; d. Robert Louis and Helen Sharon Whiting. MusB, U. Tex., Austin, 1970. Strings instr. Houston Ind. Sch. Dist., 1976—85, Spring Branch Ind. Sch. Dist., Houston, 1985—93, 2006—07, Arlington Ind. Sch. Dist., Tex., 1993—95; orch. instr. Bryan Ind. Sch. Dist., 1995—99, Richardson Ind. Sch. Dist., Tex., 1999—2000, Garland Ind. Sch. Dist., Tex., 2000—01. Mem.: Suzuki Assn. Ams., Am. String Tchr. Assn., Tex. Music Educator Assn. Avocations: crafts, gardening. Home: 207 Fireside College Station TX 77840 Office: 625 Brittmore Houston TX 77079

WHITING, SUSAN DICKINSON, media research company executive; b. Chgo., Aug. 1, 1956; d. Lawrence H. Whiting Jr.; BA in Econs. cum laude, Denison U., 1978. Mgmt. devel. program Nielsen Media Rsch., Dunedin, Fla., 1979-86, v.p. Nielsen Homevideo Index, 1986-87, mktg. mgr., 1987-93, sr. v.p., dir. mktg., 1993-97, gen. mgr. nat. svcs. & emerging markets, 1997—2001, pres., COO NYC, 2001—02, pres., CEO, 2002—; exec. v.p., Media Measurement & Info. Group VNU Bus. Media, 2005—. Named an Outstanding Female Role Model, NBA Wives Awards Luncheon, 2005; named one of 50 Women to Watch, Wall St. Jour., 2006, The 100 Most Influential Women in NYC Bus., Crain's NY Bus., 2007. Mem.: NY Radio and TV Rsch. Coun. (past pres.), Conn. Women's Forum (pres.), Women in Cable & Telecomm., Cable TV Adminstrv. and Mktg. Assn. Office: Nielsen Media Rsch Inc 770 Broadway New York NY 10003

WHITING-SORRELL, ANNA, state agency administrator; b. Hot Springs, Mont., July 1, 1957; m. Gene Whiting-Sorrell; 1 child, Katy. BA in Polit. Sci. with honors, U. Mont., Missoula, 1980, MPA, 1993. Instr. Two Eagle River Sch., Mont., 1980—82, academic supr., curriculum devel. specialist, 1982—83; adminstr., Alcohol and Substance Abuse Program Confederated Salish and Kootenai Tribes Tribal Adminstrn., 1984—92, social services adminstr., Alcohol and Substance Abuse Program, 1991—93, health systems planner, 1993—94, program analyst, 1994—2002, dir. office support services, 2002—05; dir. Native Am. Outreach Senator John Kerry's Presdl. Campaign, 2004; dep. policy dir. Gov. Elect. Schweitzer and Lt. Gov. Elect Bohlinger Transition Team, 2004; policy advisor on families to Gov. Brian Schweitzer Office of the Gov., Mont., 2005—08; dir. Mont. Dept. Pub. Health and Human Services, Helena, 2008—. Mem. Ronan Sch. Dist. Indian Parent Com., chairwoman, 1995—97; co-chair, cmty. partnership com. Ronan Sch. Office civil Rights, 2003; mem. Kellogg Leadership Cmty. Change Program, 2004; enrolled mem. Confederated Salish and Kootenai Tribes; mem. Salish Kootenai Devel. Bd. Dirs. Recipient Cert. Disting. Svc., Tribal Coun., Confederated Salish and Kootenai Tribes, 1987, Outstanding Performance award, 1992, 1998, Group Citation award, US Dept. Health and Human Services Indian Health Service, 1988, Outstanding Svc. award, Ctr. Substance Abuse Prevention, 1997, 25 Yrs. Honoring 25 Individuals award, Nat. Assn. Children of Alcoholics, 2008. Democrat. Office: Mont Dept Pub Health and Human Services 111 N Sanders Rm 301 Helena MT 59620 Office Phone: 406-444-5622. Office Fax: 406-444-1970.*

WHITINGTON, PETER FRANK, pediatric hepatologist, educator; b. Memphis, May 8, 1947; s. Frank Everett and Mary Lena (Hollingsworth) Whitington; m. Susan Maurine Hoagland, June 6, 1967; children: Helen Frances Josephic, Mary Louise, Katherine Daphne, Patrick M. BA in Econs., Tulane U., 1968; MD, U. Tenn., Memphis, 1971. Diplomate Am. Bd. Pediat., Am. Bd. Pediatric Gastroenterology. Resident in pediat., then chief resident U. Tenn. Ctr. for Health Scis., 1972—74, instr., 1975, asst. prof., 1978—81, assoc. prof., 1981—84, chief divsn. pediatric gastroenterology, 1978—84; rsch. fellow in gastroenterology Johns Hopkins Hosp., Balt., 1975—77; rsch. fellow in gastroenterology dept. pediatrics U. Wis., Madison, 1977—78; assoc. prof. dept. pediat. U. Chgo. Pritzker Sch. Medicine, 1984—87, assoc. prof. depts. pediat. and medicine, 1987—92, prof., 1992—97; prof. pediat. Northwestern U. Med. Sch., 1997—, Sally Burnett Searle prof. pediat. and transplantation; dir. divsn. gastroenterology, hepatology & nutrition Children's Meml. Hosp., Chgo., 1997—, dir. organ transplantation, Siragusa Transplantation Ctr., 1997—; co-dir. Northwestern U. Affiliated Transplant Ctrs., 1997—. Chief gastroenterology LeBonheur Children's Med. Ctr., Memphis, 1978—84; numerous invited lectures and guest spkr. at profl. meetings, workshops, symposia, hosps., confs.; mem. pediatric transplantation com. United Network for Organ Sharing, Nat. Organ Procurement and Transplantation Network, 1992—94; reviewer numerous med. jours. including New Eng. Jour. Medicine, Gastroenterology, Hepatology, Jour. Pediat., Digestive Diseases and Scis., Pediat., Transplant. Editl. bd. Jour. Pediatric Gastroenterology and Nutrition, 1991—96, Liver Transplantation, 1994—. Pediatric Transplantation, 1997—, sect. editor Birth Defects Compendium, 1987—90, contbr. numerous articles and abstracts to med. jours. Mem. sci. adv. bd. Mid-South chpt. Nat. Found. for Ileitis and Colitis, Memphis, 1983—84; chmn. med. adv. com. Ill. chpt. Am. Liver Found., 1996—, mem., med. adv. on bd. dirs., 1993—; med. dir. The Johnny Genna Found., Chgo., 1987—; bd. dirs. Parents for Ctrl. H.S., Memphis, 1983—84, Liver/Organ Transplant Fund, Memphis, 1983—84. Recipient Cmty. Svc. award, NCCJ, Memphis, 1983; fellow postdoctoral rsch. NIH, 1977. Mem.: Am. Assn. Transplantation, N.A.m Soc. for Pediatric Gastroenterology and Nutrition, Soc. for Pediatric Rsch., Am. Gastroenterol. Assn., Gastroenterology Rsch. Group, Am. Assn. for Study of Liver Diseases. Avocations: making furniture, fly fishing. Home: 5490 S South Shore Dr Apt 8 Chicago IL 60615-5984 Office: Childrens Meml Hosp Box 57 2300 Childrens Plaza Chicago IL 60614-3394 Business E-Mail: p-whitington@northwestern.edu.

WHITLEY, JOE DALLY (JOE DALLY WHITLEY), lawyer; s. Thomas Youngie and Mary Jo (Dally) W.; m. Kathleen Pinion, Sept. 27, 1975; children: Lauren Jacqueline, Thomas McMillan. BA, U. Ga., 1972, JD, 1975. Bar: Ga. 1975, DC, 1990, US Supreme Ct. 1989. Assoc. Kelly, Denney, Pease & Allison, Columbus, Ga., 1975-78; asst. dist. atty. Chattahoochee Jud. Cir., Columbus, 1978-79; assoc. Hirsch, Beil & Partin, P.C., Columbus, 1979-81; US atty. (mid. dist.) GA US Dept. Justice, Macon, 1981-87, dep. asst. atty. gen., criminal divsn. Washington, 1987-88, dep. assoc. atty. gen., 1988-89, acting assoc. atty. gen., 1989; ptnr. Smith, Gambrell & Russell, Atlanta, 1989-90; US atty. (no. dist.) GA US Dept. Justice, Atlanta, 1990-93; ptnr. Kilpatrick Stockton, Atlanta, 1993-97, Alston & Bird, Atlanta, 1997—2003, 2005—08; gen. counsel US Dept. Homeland Security, Washington, 2003—05; shareholder Greenberg Traurig LLP, Atlanta, 2008. Mem. Atty. Gen.'s adv. com. dept. justice, Washington, 1982-85; chmn. organized crime and violent crime subcom. Atty. Gen.'s adv. com., 1990-93; mem. investigative subcom.; chmn. white collar crime subcom., 1993-99; program chmn. Ga. Inst. of Continuing Legal Edn. Programs; lectr. in field. Contbr. articles to profl. jours. Treas. Muscogee County Young Reps., Columbus, 1979-80. Mem. ABA (mem. criminal justice dect. voun., vice-chmn. govt. affairs 2002-03), Ga. Bar Assn., Macon Bar Assn., Young Lawyers Club (pres. Columbus chpt. 1980-81), Lawyers Club of Atlanta. Republican. Presbyterian. Office: Greenberg Traurig LLP 3290 Northside Pky Ste 400 Atlanta GA 30327 also: Greenberg Traurig LLP 2101 L St NW Ste 1000 Washington DC 20037 Office Phone: 678-553-7339, 202-331-3131. Business E-Mail: whitleyj@gtlaw.com.

WHITLEY, RICHARD, state agency administrator; BA, Willamette U., Oreg.; MS in Counseling Psychology, Oreg. State U., Corvallis. Sr. psychologist Nev. Women's Correctional Facility; chief, bur. cmty. health Nev. Dept. Health and Human Services, Carson City, dep. adminstr., health divsn., 2004—08, adminstr., health divsn., 2008—. Office: Nev Dept Health and Human Services Health Divsn 4150 Technology Way Ste 300 Carson City NV 89706 Office Phone: 775-684-4200. Office Fax: 775-684-4211.*

WHITLOCK, CHARLES PRESTON, former university dean; b. Highland Park, NJ, June 19, 1919; s. Frank Boudinot and Rosena Craig (Foster) W.; m. Patricia Hamilton Hoey, Mar. 10, 1960; children: Carol Foster, Adam Hoey, Susan Boudinot, Matthew Fitzsimmons, Beth Brewer. BA, Rutgers U., 1941; MA, Harvard U., 1947. Assoc. dir. Bur. Study Counsel Harvard U., 1948-52, Allston Burr sr. tutor, 1952-58, lectr. social psychology, 1955-72, asst. to pres., 1958-70, assoc. dean of coll., 1970-72, dean of coll., 1972-76, assoc. dean faculty, 1976-82, master Dudley House, 1976-82. Dir. Cambridgeport Savs. Bank.; Mem. Mass. Higher Edn. Facilities Commn. Co-author: Harvard University Reading Films. Trustee Charity of Edward Hopkins, Lesley Coll.; bd. corporators New Eng. Deaconess Hosp.; treas. Annisquam Village Ch. Col. USAF. Decorated Silver Star, D.F.C., Air medal. Mem. Phi Beta Kappa. Home: 9 Barberry Heights Rd Gloucester MA 01930-1201 Office: Harvard U Cambridge MA 02138

WHITLOCK, GARY L., energy executive; b. Houston, 1950; B in Bus. Adminstrn. Acctg., Sam Houston State U., 1972. CPA. Joined Dow Chem. Co., 1972, responsible for worldwide fin. consolidation and mgmt. reporting, 1981, fin. dir. UK and Ireland, 1984; v.p. fin., CFO Dow AgroScis. subs. Dow Chem. Co., 1998—2001; exec. v.p., CFO delivery group Reliant Energy, 2001—02; exec. v.p., CFO CenterPoint Energy, Houston, 2002—. Mem.: AICPA, Tex. Soc. CPAs, Inst. Mgmt. Accts. Office: CenterPoint Energy PO Box 1700 Houston TX 77251-1700

WHITLOCK, JAMES ALAN, pediatrics educator; b. Kingsport, Tenn., July 19, 1958; s. James M. and Ethel E. (Hawk) Wh.; m. Deborah A. Wrenn, Apr. 26, 1986; 1 child, Christopher. BS, Southwestern U., Memphis, 1980; MD, Vanderbilt U., 1984. Diplomate Am. Bd. Pediatrics, Nat. Bd. Med. Examiners. Intern Vanderbilt U. Med. Ctr., Nashville, 1984-85, resident, 1985-87, fellow, 1987-90, asst. prof., 1990-97, assoc. prof., 1997—, dir. pediat. hematology and oncology, 1997—. Mem. AMA, Am. Assn. for Cancer Rsch., Am. Soc. Hematology, Am. Soc. Pediatric Hematology-Oncology, Phi Beta Kappa. Office: Vanderbilt U Med Ctr 525 MRB II 220 Pierce Ave Nashville TN 37232-0001

WHITLON, DONNA SUE, neuroscientist, researcher; b. Flushing, NY, Oct. 24, 1952; d. Leonard E. and Eileen S. W.; m. Jack M. Rozental, Jan. 6, 1980; two children. BS, Mich. State U., 1974; PhD, U. Wis., 1979. Rsch. asst., NIH predoctoral trainee U. Wis. Dept. Biochemistry, Madison, 1974-79; biol. lab. scientist Manufactaras Arriol, Santo Domingo, Dominican Republic, 1980; high sch. sci. tchr. Carol Morgan Sch., Santo Domingo, Dominican Republic, 1981; postdoctoral fellow McArdle Lab. for Cancer Rsch. U. Wis., Madison, 1981-84, asst. scientist, 1985-91, assoc. scientist Waisman Cntr., 1991—. Contbr. articles to profl. jours. Mem. Assn. for Rsch. in Otolaryngology, Soc. for Neuroscience. Office: U Wis Rm 636 Waisman Ctr 1500 Highland Ave Madison WI 53705-2274

WHITMAN, BRIAN E., engineering educator; Degree in Environ. Engrng., Mich. Technol. U., Houghton, 1998. Assoc. prof. Wilkes U., Wilkes-Barre, Pa., 1997—2008. Author: (book) Wastewater Collection System Modeling and Design, Computer Applications in Hydraulic Engineering, Introduction to Environmental Engineering, Security and Emergency Management for Water Systems. Recipient Outstanding Faculty award, Wilkes U., 2002, 2005, Outstanding Alumnus award, Adrian Schs Ednl. Found., 2008; named to Outstanding Grad. Student of the Yr., Grad. Student Govt., Mich. Technol. U., 1997. Mem.: Internat. Water Assn., Assn. Environ. Engrng. and Sci. Profs., Am. Soc. Engrng. Edn., ASCE, Am. Soc. for Microbiology, Am. Chem. Soc. Achievements include research in bioremediation technologies, water distribution systems, wastewater collection systems, wastewater treatment technologies. Office: Wilkes Univ 150 S River St Wilkes Barre PA 18766 Business E-Mail: brian.whitman@wilkes.edu.

WHITMAN, CHRISTINE TODD (CHRISTIE WHITMAN), consulting firm executive, former federal agency administrator, former governor; b. NYC, Sept. 26, 1946; d. Webster Bray and Eleanor Prentice Schley Todd; m. John Russell Whitman, Apr. 21, 1974; children: Kate, Taylor. BA in Govt., Wheaton Coll., 1968. Staff mem. US Office of Economic Opportunity; freeholder Somerset County, 1982—87; pres. NJ State Bd. Pub. Utilities, 1988—90; host radio talk show Sta. WKXW, Trenton, NJ; gov. State of NJ, Trenton, 1994-2001; adminstr. EPA, Washington, 2001—03; founder, pres. Whitman Strategy Group, Princeton, NJ, 2004—; co-chair CASEnergy Coalition, 2006—. Bd. dirs. Texas Instruments Inc., 2003-, S.C. Johnson and Son, Inc., 2003-, United Tech. Corp., 2003-; mem. steering com. Cancer Inst. NJ Leadership Coun.; chmn. Com. for an Affordable N.J.; co-chair Nat. Smart Growth Coun., Smart Growth Am.; mem. leadership coun. Rep. Pro-Choice Coalition, gov.'s bd. Oquirrh Inst., S&T presdl. and fed. adv. com. Appointments of Nat. Acads. Author: It's My Party Too: The Battle for the Heart of the GOP and the Future of America, 2005. Columnist newspapers. Rep. candidate for senator State of NJ, 1990.; mem. Ctr. Civic Engagement and Volunteerism adv. bd. Raritan Cmty. Coll., UN sec-gen. adv. bd. Water and Sanitation. Republican. Achievements include first female governor in N.J.; delivered Republican response to President Clinton's 1995 State of the Union address. Office: Whitman Strategy Group 116 Village Blvd Ste 200 Princeton NJ 08540 E-mail: christie.whitman@whitmanstrategygroup.com.

WHITMAN, GREGORY THEODORE, neurologist; b. Lansdale, Pa., Oct. 16, 1966; s. Steven and Sheila Whitman. BA, Cornell Univ., Ithaca, NY, 1985—89; MD, Univ. of Conn., Farmington, 1990—94. Cert. in Neurology Am. Bd. of Psychiatry and Neurology, 2000. Intern medicine Boston City Hosp., Boston U., 1994—95, resident neurology, 1995—97, Tufts U., Boston, 1997—98; clin. instr. neurology U. Calif., LA, 1998—2000, asst. prof. neurology Irvine, 2000—. Dir. neurology residency program U. Calif., Irvine, 2002—05; asst. clin. prof. neurology UCLA, 2006—. Co-author: (journal articles) Neurology, Archives of Neurology, Jour. of Neuroimaging, Stroke, Neurobiology of Aging. Mem.: Am. Acad. of Neurology.

WHITMAN, MARINA VON NEUMANN, economist, educator; b. NYC, Mar. 6, 1935; d. John and Mariette (Kovesi) von Neumann; m. Robert Freeman Whitman, June 23, 1956; children: Malcolm Russell, Laura Mariette. BA summa cum laude, Harvard U., 1956; MA, Columbia U., 1959, PhD, 1962; DHL (hon.), U. Mass., 1975; LittD (hon.), Williams Coll., 1980; LLD (hon.), Mount Holyoke Coll., 1980, Lehigh U., 1981; LHD (hon.), Clemson U., 1984; LLD (hon.), U. Notre Dame, 1984, Ea. Mich. U., 1992. Mem. faculty U. Pitts., 1962-79, prof. econs., 1971-73, disting. pub. svc. prof. econs., 1973-79; v.p., chief economist Gen. Motors Corp., NYC, 1979-85, group v.p. pub. affairs, 1985-92; disting. vis. prof. bus. adminstrn., pub. policy U. Mich., Ann Arbor, 1992-94, prof. bus. adminstrn., pub. policy, 1994—. Mem. Trilateral Commn., 1973-84, 88-95; mem. Pres. Adv. Com. on Trade Policy and Negotiations, 1987-93; mem. tech. assessment adv. coun. U.S. Congress Office of Tech. Assessment, 1990-95; mem. Consultative Group on Internat. Econs. and Monetary Affairs, 1979—; mem. U.S. Price Commn., 1971-72, Coun. Econ. Advisers, Exec. Office of Pres., 1972-73. Author: Government Risk-Sharing in Foreign Investment, 1965, International and Interregional Payments Adjustment, 1967, Economic Goals and Policy Instruments, 1970, Reflections of Interdependence: Issues for Economic Theory and U.S. Policy, 1979, New World, New Rules: The Changing Role of the American Corporation, 1999, American Capitalism and Global Convergence, 2003; bd. editors: Am. Econ. Rev., 1974-77; mem. editl. bd. Fgn. Policy; contbr. articles to profl. jours. Trustee Nat. Bur. Econ. Rsch., 1993—, Princeton U., 1980-90, Inst. Advanced Study, 1999—; bd. dirs. Peterson Inst. for Internat. Econs., 1986—, Salzburg Seminar, 1994—, Eurasia Found., 1992-95; bd. overseers Harvard U., 1972-78, mem. vis. com. Kennedy Sch., 1992-98. Fellow Earhart Found., 1959-60, AAUW, 1960-61, NSF, 1968-70, Social Security Rsch. Coun.; recipient Columbia medal for excellence, 1973, George Washington award Am. Hungarian Found., 1975. Mem. Am. Econ. Assn. (exec. com. 1977-80), Am. Acad. Arts and Scis., Coun. Fgn. Rels. (dir. 1977-87), Phi Beta Kappa. Office: U Mich Gerald Ford Sch Pub Policy Joan and Sanford Weill Hall Rm 3228 Ann Arbor MI 48109-3091 Office Phone: 734-763-4173. Business E-Mail: marinaw@umich.edu.

WHITMAN, MARTIN J., portfolio manager; b. NYC, Sept. 30, 1924; s. Irving and Dora (Cukier) W.; m. Lois M. Quick, Mar. 10, 1956; children: James Q., Barbara E., Thomas I. Chartered fin. analyst. Rsch. analyst, buyer Shearson Hammill & Co., NYC, 1950—56; analyst William Rosenwald Co., NYC, 1956—58; head rsch. Ladenburg, Thalmann & Co., NYC, 1958—60; gen. ptnr. Gerstley Sunstein & Co., Phila., 1960—67; v.p., dir. Blair & Co., Inc., NYC, 1967—68; pres., founder M.J. Whitman & Co. (now Inc.), NYC, 1969—84; pres., CEO Equity Strategies Fund, Inc., NYC, 1984—90; founder, chmn. Third Ave. Value Fund, Inc. (now Third Ave. Mgmt. LLC), NYC, 1990—. CEO, Third Ave. Mgmt. LLC, 1990—95; dir. Nabors Industries, Inc.; past chmn. bd. Danielson Holding Corp.; Disting. Mgmt. Fellow in Fin. Yale U., New Haven, 1972—; mem. adv. bd. Yale Sch. Mgmt., New Haven, 1994—95; cons. disclosure study SEC, 1968; cons. Pres.'s Commn. on Accident at Three Mile Island, 1979; adj. prof. Sch. Bus. Columbia U., NYC, 2001—; adj. prof. Whitman Sch., Syracuse U. Author: Value Investing: A Balanced Approach, 1999; co-author: The Agressive Conservative Investor, 1979, new edit., 2005, Distress Investing: Principles and Techniques, 2009; contbr. articles to profl. publs. Chmn. 3d Ave. Fund, 1991. Served with USNR, 1942-46. Named in his hon. Martin J. Whitman Sch. of Mgmt., Syracuse Univ. named its bus. sch., 2003. Mem. N.Y. Soc. Security Analysts, Phila. Econ. Soc. Jewish.

WHITMAN, MEG (MARGARET CUSHING WHITMAN), former Internet company executive; b. LI, NY, Aug. 4, 1956; m. Griffith Rutherford Harsh IV; children: Griff, Will. BA in Economics, Princeton U., 1977; MBA, Harvard U., 1979. Brand asst. Procter & Gamble, 1979—81; v.p. Bain & Co., 1982—89; sr. v.p. mktg. & consumer products divsn. Walt Disney Co, Burbank, Calif., 1989—92; corp. v.p. strategic planning Stride Rite Corp., 1992—93, exec. v.p. Keds divsn., 1993—94, pres. Stride Rite Divsn., 1994—95; pres., CEO Florists' Transworld Delivery (FTD), 1995—97; gen. mgr. preschool divsn. Hasbro Inc., 1997—98; pres., CEO eBay, Inc., San Jose, Calif., 1998—2008; co-chair Republican Victory '08, 2008—; running for the 2010 Rep. nomination for Calif. gov., 2009—. Bd. dirs. eBay, Inc., 1998—2009, Staples Inc., 1999—2008, The Goldman Sachs Group Inc., 2001—02, Procter & Gamble Co., 2003—08, The Gap Inc., 2003—06, DreamWorks Animation SKG, Inc., 2005—08. Bd. trustees Princeton U. Recipient Webby Lifetime Achievement award (eBay), 2007; named Number One on List of Best CEO's, Worth, 2002; named one of 25 Most Powerful Bus. Mgrs., Bus. Week, 2000—, Most Powerful Women in Am. Bus., Fortune mag., 25 Most Powerful People in Bus., 2004, 50 Most Powerful Women in Bus., 2006, 2007, World's 100 Most Influential People, Time Mag., 2004, 2005, 100 Most Powerful Women, Forbes mag., 2005—07, 50 Women to Watch, Wall St. Jour., 2005, 2006, 50 Most Important People on the Web, PC World, 2007. Fellow: Am. Acad. Arts & Scis. Republican. Avocation: fly fishing.*

WHITMAN, ROBERT VAN DUYNE, civil engineer, educator; b. Pitts., Feb. 2, 1928; s. Edwin A. and Elsie (Van Duyne) W.; m. Elizabeth Cushman, June 19, 1954; children: Jill Martyne Whitman Marsee, Martha Allerton (dec.), Gweneth Giles Whitman Kaebnick. BS, Swarthmore Coll., 1948, DSc (hon.), 1990; SM, MIT, 1949, ScD, 1951. Faculty MIT, 1953—, prof. civil engring., 1963-93, head structural engring., 1970-74, head soil mechanics divsn., 1970-72; prof. emeritus, 1993—. Vis. scholar U. Cambridge, Eng., 1976-77; cons. to govt. and industry, 1953—; mem. adv. com. for nat. earthquake hazard reduction program Fed. Emergency Mgmt. Agy., 1991-94, mem. commn. engring. and tech. systems NRC, 1992-97. Author: (with T. W. Lambe) Soil Mechanics. Mem. Town Meeting Lexington, Mass., 1962-76, 85—, mem. permanent bldg. com., 1968-75, mem. bd. appeals, 1979-81, 84-2000. Lt. (j.g.) USNR, 1954-56. Recipient U.S. Scientist award Humboldt Found., 1984-90; Norwegian Geotech. Inst. Rsch. fellow, 1984. Mem. NAE, ASCE (Rsch. award 1962, Terzaghi Lecture 1981, Terzaghi award 1987, C. Martin Duke Lifeline Earthquake Engring. award 1992, James Croes medal 1994, H. Bolton Seed medal, 2006), Boston Soc. Civil Engrs. (Structural Sect. prize 1963, Desmond Fitzgerald medal 1973, Ralph W. Horne Fund award 1977), Internat. Soc. Soil Mechanics and Found. Engrs., Mex. Soc. Soil Mechanics (hon., Nabor Carrillo lectr. 2000), Earthquake Engring. Rsch. Inst. (dir. 1978-81, 84-88, v.p. 1979-81, pres. 1985-87, Disting. lectr. 1994, hon. 1997—). Achievements include research in soil mechanics, soil dynamics, earthquake engineering and earthquake loss estimation. Home: 1010 Waltham St 346 Lexington MA 02421 Office: MIT Dept Civil and Environ Engring Cambridge MA 02139

WHITMAN, SHAWN R., legislative staff member; m. Kristin Phillips. BS in Agrl. Bus., U. Wyo., Laramie, 1994. Staff asst., Senator Alan Simpson US Senate, Washington, 1994, press asst., Senator Craig Thomas, 1995—2004, chief of staff to Senator Craig Thomas, 2004—07, chief of staff to Senator John Barrasso, 2007—. Mem. Wyo. State Soc., 1994—2004; bd. mem. Hope Rising, Fairlington Green, U. Wyo. Nat. Ambs. Sr. Stennis Congl. fellow. Mem.: Alpha Tau Omega. Republican. Baptist. Avocations: hunting, golf. Office: 307 Dirksen Senate Office Bldg Washington DC 20510 Office Phone: 202-224-6441. Business E-Mail: shawn_whitman@barrasso.senate.gov.*

WHITMER, FREDERICK LEE, lawyer; b. Terre Haute, Ind., Nov. 5, 1947; s. Lee Arthur and Ella (Diekhoff) W.; m. Valeri Cade; children: Caitlin Margaret, Meghan Connors, Christian Frederick. BA, Wabash Coll., 1969; JD, Columbia U., 1973. Bar: N.Y. 1975, U.S. Dist. Ct. (so. dist.) N.Y. 1975, N.J. 1976, U.S. Dist. Ct. N.J. 1976, U.S. Ct. Appeals (3d cir.) 1977, U.S. Ct. Appeals (fed. cir.) 1983, U.S. Ct. Appeals (2d cir.) 1987, U.S. Supreme Ct. 1988, U.S. Ct. Appeals (7th cir.) 1994. Assoc. Kaye, Scholer, Fierman, Hays & Handler, NYC, 1973-76, Pitney Hardin and Kipp, Morristown, NJ, 1976—78; ptnr. Pitney Hardin LLP, Morristown, 1979—2004, Brown, Raysman, Millstein, Felder & Steiner, NYC, 2004—06, Thelen Reid Brown Raysman & Steiner, LLP, NYC, 2006—. Mem. ABA, N.J. Bar Assn., Phi Beta Kappa. Republican. Episcopalian. Home: 190 Hurlbutt St Wilton CT 06897-2706 Office: Thelen Reid Brown Raysman & Steiner LLP 875 3d Ave New York NY 10022 Office Phone: 212-603-2074. Business E-Mail: fwhitmer@thelen.com.

WHITMEYER, STEVEN J., geologist, educator; b. Akron, Ohio, Jan. 28, 1966; s. Eugene j. and Rebecca K. Whitmeyer; m. Shelley J. Johnston, Jan. 7, 2006; 1 child, Catherine E. PhD in Earth Sci., Boston U., MA, 2004. Vis. prof. U. Tenn., Knoxville, 2004—05; asst. prof. James Madison U., Harrisonburg, Va., 2005—. Contbr. articles to profl. jours. Rsch. grant, US Geol. Survey, 2007—, NSF, 2008—. Mem.: Nat. Assn. Geo Sci. Tchr., Am. Geophys. Union, Geol. Soc. Am., Sigma Xi, Phi Beta Kappa. Avocations: travel, music, mountain climbing. Office: James Madison Univ MSC 6903 Harrisonburg VA 22807 Office Fax: 540-568-8058. Business E-Mail: whitmesj@jmu.edu.

WHITMORE, DOUGLAS MICHAEL, physician; b. Cambridge, Mass., Oct. 30, 1947; s. Donald Herbert and Marcela (Klein) W.; m. Ana Maria Lopez. BS, MS in Physics, U. Ill., Champaign-Urbana, 1969; MS in Physics, Stanford U., 1970, PhD in Physics, 1975; MD, U. Miami, 1978. Diplomate Am. Bd. Internal Medicine, Am. Bd. Pulmonary Disease, Am. Bd. Critical Care Medicine, Am. Bd. Geriatric Medicine. Physician Holy Cross Hosp., Ft. Lauderdale, Fla., 1983—. Pres. med. staff Holy Cross Hosp., 1996-97, chief of medicine, 1995-98. Trustee Holy Cross Hosp., 1995-98. Fellow ACP, Am. Coll. Chest Physicians; mem. Caducean Med. Soc. (pres. 1996-97), Am. Thoracic Soc., Royal Soc. Medicine. Office: Med Complex West 1930 NE 47th St Ste 205 Fort Lauderdale FL 33308-7728

WHITMORE, FRANK CLIFFORD, JR., retired geologist; b. Cambridge, Mass., Nov. 17, 1915; s. Frank Clifford and Marion Gertrude (Mason) W.; m. Martha Burling Kremers, June 24, 1939; children: Geoffrey, John, Katherine, Susan. BA, Amherst Coll., 1938; MS, Pa. State U., 1939; MA, Harvard U., 1941, PhD, 1942. Instr. geology R.I. State Coll., Kingston, 1942-44; geologist U.S. Geol. Survey, Washington, 1944-84, chief mil. geology br., 1946—59, rsch. paleontologist, 1959—84, scientist emeritus, 1984—; mem. com. rsch. and exploration Nat. Geog. Soc., 1970-96, vice chmn., 1990-96, emeritus, 1997—; rsch. assoc. dept. paleobiology Smithsonian Instn., Washington, 1967—97; ret., 1997. Sci. cons. U.S. Army, Philippines, Japan, Korea, 1945-46; mem. adv. bd. Ctr. for Study of Early Man, U. Maine, Orono, 1985-90. Editor: Resources for 21st Century, 1982; contbr. articles to profl. jours. Bd. dirs. Prince Georges County Boys Clubs, Md., 1954-56; mem. program com. Nat. Capital coun. Girl Scouts U.S.A., Washington, 1967-69; pres. Thornton Soc., Washington, 1977-84. Recipient medal of Freedom U.S. Army, 1946, spl. achievement award U.S. Geol. Survey, 1980, Meritorious Svc. award U.S. Dept. Interior, 1981, Arnold Guyot Meml. award Nat. Geog. Soc., 1993, Thomas Jefferson medal Va. Mus. Natural History, 2002; Tchg. fellow Harvard U., Cambridge, 1940-42. Fellow AAAS, Geol. Soc. Am.; mem. Soc. Vertebrate Paleontology (hon. life, exec. com. 1960-62), Midriver Club, Harvard Club. Democrat. Avocation: architectural history. Home: 20 Woodmoor Dr Silver Spring MD 20901-2447

WHITMORE, JON SCOTT, academic administrator, play director; b. Seattle, Mar. 22, 1945; s. Walter James and Eurma (Thody) W.; m. Jennifer Gean Gross, Aug. 17, 1985; children: Ian Scott, Amy Lee. BA in Speech and Theatre, Wash. State U., 1967, MA in Speech and Theatre, 1968; PhD in Dramatic Arts, U. Calif., Santa Barbara, 1974. Instr. theatre Highline Coll., Seattle, 1968-71; grad. asst. U. Calif., Santa Barbara, 1971-74; asst. prof. theatre W.Va. U., Morgantown, 1974-78, assoc. prof., 1978-82, prof., 1979-85, chmn. dept., 1979-84, interim dean, 1984-85; prof., dean faculty arts and letters SUNY, Buffalo, 1985-90; dean Coll. Fine Arts, U. Tex., Austin, 1990-96; provost, prof. theater arts U. Iowa, Iowa City, 1996—2003; pres. Tex. Tech U., Lubbock, 2003—08, San José State U., 2008—. Mem. exec. com. Big XII Athletic Conf., 2006—07. Dir. plays including Suddenly Last Summer, The Miracle Worker, Equus, Romeo and Juliet, Long Days Journey Into Night, The Sea Gull, The Comedy of Errors, The Glass Menagerie, Blithe Spirit, The Tavern, Black Comedy, You're a Good Man Charlie Brown, Vanities, The Effect of Gamma Rays on Man-In-The-Moon Marigolds, Epiphany, Endgame, The Miser, J.B., The Mousetrap, Knapp's Last Tape, Miss Julie, Servant of Two Masters, Before We Were; actor various classical, modern and contemporary plays, and performance pieces; author: Directing Postmodern Theater, 1994, William Saroyan, 1994. Mem. Erie County (N.Y.) Cultural Resources Adv. Bd., 1986-89, long range planning com. Studio Arena Theatre, Buffalo, 1986-90, trustee, 1987-90; mem. coun. fellows Am. Coun. Edn., 1984—; pres. W.Va. Theater Conf., 1978-80, pres.-elect, 1977-78, founding mem., bd. dirs., 1975-81. Recipient ACE Fellow award Am. Council Edn., 1983-84; fellow U. Calif., Santa Barbara, 1973-74, Lilly Found., 1976-77; Maynard Lee Daggy scholar Wash. State U., 1967. Mem. Internat. Coun. Fine Arts Deans, Am. Coun. Arts, Assn. Theatre in Higher Edn. (v.p. adminstrn. 1991—, chmn. nat. conf. planning com. chief adminstrs. program, 1987), Assn. Comm. Adminstrn. (elected to exec. com. 1982-85, chmn. task force theatre adminstrn., 1982-84), Speech Comm. Assn., Coun. Colls. Arts and Scis., Assn. Coll., Univ. and Cmty. Arts Adminstrs., Nat. Assn. State Univs. and Land-Grant Colls. (chair elect commn. arts, 1990-92, chair 1992-93, chair coun. on acad. affairs 2001—). Office: San Jose State U Office of Pres / Tower Hall 207 One Washington Sq San Jose CA 95192-0002 Office Phone: 408-924-1177. E-mail: Jon.Whitmore@sjsu.edu.

WHITMORE, MICHAEL RAYMOND, science educator; b. Prince George, Va., Oct. 16, 1953; s. Francis and Kahryn Whitmore. D in Chiropractic, Life U., Marietta, Ga., 2000. Prof. C. Tech. Coll., Marietta, 2004—08. Recipient Tchr. of yr., Career Inst., 2003—04. Home: 209 Bennett Farms Trail Acworth GA 30102 Personal E-mail: michael.whitmore1@gmail.com.

WHITNEY, BENSON K., United States Ambassador to Norway; m. Mary Whitney; 4 children. BA magna cum laude, Vassar Coll.; JD, U. Minn. Atty. Popham, Halk, Schnobrich, Kaufman and Doty. Ltd.; mng. gen. ptnr. Gideon Hixon Fund; pres. Minn. Venture Capital Assn.; CEO Whitney Mgmt. Co.; U.S. amb. to Norway US Dept. State, Oslo, 2005—. Exec. dir., fin. chair Bush-Cheney '04 Rep. Nat. Com., Minn. Former trustee, dir., chmn., advisor numerous nonprofit orgns. including Guthrie Theater, Wilderness Inquiry, Minnesotans for Term Limits, Mpls. Acad., Persephone Fund, Headwaters Fund. Office: Am Embassy 5460 Oslo Pl Washington DC 20521*

WHITNEY, BRET MEYERS, travel company executive; s. Charles H. and Jeanne Meyers Whitney. BA, Earlham Coll., Richmond, IN, 1978. Birding tour guide Victor Emanuel Nature Tours, Austin, Tex., 1979—85; co founder, tour guide Field Guides Inc., Austin, Tex., 1985—. Ornithol. field coord. Nature Conservancy & SOS Amazônia, Brasília, DF, & Rio Branco, Acre, Brasil, 1996—97. Contbr. articles to profl. jours. Recipient Elective Mem. award, Am. Ornithologists' Union, 2003—, Hon. Rsch. Assoc. award, Mus. Natural Sci., La. State U., 1995—. Mem.: Cooper Ornithol. Soc., Comitê Brasileiro de Registros Ornitológicos (consulting mem.), South Am. Checklist Com. Am. Ornithologists' Union (consulting mem.), Sociedade Brasileira de Ornitologia, Wilson Ornithol. Soc. (Ernest G. Edwards award 1994), Am. Birding Assn. Avocations: bicycling, photography. Home: 2202 Euclid Ave Austin TX 78704-5126 Office: Field Guides Inc 9433 Bee Cave Rd Bldg 1 Ste 150 Austin TX 78733 Business E-Mail: fieldguides@fieldguides.com.

WHITNEY, CRAIG RICHARD, journalist; b. Milford, Mass., Oct. 12, 1943; s. A. Gordon and Carol Alma (Kennison) W.; m. Heidi Witt, May 11, 1974; children: Alexandra Kennison, Stefan Robert. AB, Harvard, 1965. Reporter New York Times, Washington, 1965-66, NYC, 1969-70, Saigon, Vietnam, 1971-72, Bonn, West Germany, 1973-77, Moscow, USSR, 1977-80, dep. fgn. editor, 1980-82, fgn. editor, 1982-83, asst. mng. editor, 1983-86, Washington Bur. chief, 1986-88, London bur. chief, 1988-92, European diplomatic corr., 1992-2000, asst. mng. editor, 2000—. Author: Spy Trader, 1993, All the Stops, 2003, The WMD Mirage, 2005. Served with USNR, 1966-69. Mem. Coun. Fgn. Rels., Harvard Club (N.Y.C.). Home: 1 Pierrepont St Brooklyn NY 11201-3302 Office: NY Times 620 Eight Ave New York NY 10018 Office Phone: 212-556-3909. Personal E-mail: crwhitney65@gmail.com. Business E-Mail: whitney@nytimes.com.

WHITNEY, DANIEL LAWRENCE See LARRY THE CABLE GUY

WHITNEY, DAVID See MALICK, TERRENCE

WHITNEY, EDWARD BONNER, retired investment banker; b. Glen Cove, NY, June 6, 1945; s. Edward Farley and Millicent Bonner (Bowring) W.; m. Martha Congleton Howell, Aug. 17, 1974; children: William Howell, John Howell. BA, Harvard U., 1966, MBA, 1969. Systems engr. IBM, Cambridge, Mass., 1966-67; assoc. Dillon, Read & Co. Inc., NYC, 1969-74, v.p., 1975-79, sr. v.p., 1980-83, mng. dir., 1984-97, also bd. dirs.; mng. dir. UBS Warburg, London, 1997—2002. Bd. dirs., IRRC Inst.; bd. dirs., chmn. Am. Rivers. Trustee Butler Fund for the Environment; pres. coun. Wilderness Soc. Mem. Harvard Club NYC E-mail: Nedwhitney@aol.com.

WHITNEY, FRANK DEARMON, federal judge, former prosecutor; b. Charlotte, NC, Nov. 22, 1959; s. A. Grant and Lillian (DeArmon) Whitney; m. Catherine Whitney; children: Anne Stone, Frances Hunter. BA, Wake Forest U., 1982; MBA, JD, U. NC, 1987. Bar: NC 1987, DC 1988. Assoc. McKenna Conner Cuneo, Washington, 1987—90; law clk. to Hon. David B. Sentelle US Ct. Appeals (DC Cir.), 1988—89; asst. US atty. (we. dist.) NC US Dept. Justice, Charlotte, 1990—2001, US atty. (ea. dist.) NC Raleigh, 2002—06; counsel Kilpatrick Stockton LLP, Charlotte, 2001—02; judge US Dist. Ct. (we. dist.) NC, 2006—. Col., military judge Judge Advocate Corps. Serves in USAR, 1982—, paratrooper USAR, military intelligence officer USAR. Presbyterian. Office: US Dist Ct Charles R Jonas Bldg 401 W Trade St Charlotte NC 28202 Office Phone: 704-350-7480.

WHITNEY, JANE, foreign service officer; b. July 15, 1941; d. Robert F. and Mussette (Cary) W. BA, Beloit Coll., 1963; CD, U. Aix, Marseille, France, 1962. Joined Fgn. Svc., U.S. Dept. State, 1965; vice consul Saigon, Vietnam, 1966—68; career counselor, 1968—70; spl. asst. Office of Dir. Gen., 1970—72; consul Stuttgart, Germany, 1972—74, Ankara, Turkey, 1974—76; spl. asst. Office of Asst. Sec. for Consular Affairs, 1976—77; mem. Bd. Examiners Fgn. Svc., 1977—78, 1979—81; consul Munich, 1978—79, Buenos Aires, 1981—82; ethics officer Office of Legal Adviser, 1982—85; advisor Office of Asst. Sec. for Diplomatic Security, 1985—86; dep. prin. officer, consul Stuttgart, 1986—90; prin. officer, consul gen. Perth, Australia, 1990—91. Presbyterian. Recipient awards U.S. Dept. State, 1968, 70, 81, 85, 87, 90.

WHITNEY, KENT R.E., securities trader; b. Chgo., Feb. 7, 1979; s. Kent R.N. and Arlene M. Whitney; m. Kiva R. Cosson, Mar. 21, 2004 (div. Apr. 18, 2006); 1 child, Kent E.E. Options market maker Chgo. Bd. Options Exchage, 1997—2000, COMEX, NYC, 1999—2000; mem.

Chgo. Bd. Trade, 2000—. Named Entrepreneur of Yr., Ernst & Young, 1997. Mem.: Plz. Club (life). Office: 141W Jackson Blvd Chicago IL Home: 400 E Randolph St Apt 3429 Chicago IL 60601-5062 Personal E-mail: krwoptions@yahoo.com.

WHITNEY, LORI ANN, legislative staff member; b. Rhinelander, Wis, Feb. 20, 1968; d. Larry R. and Mary E. (Gaffney) Whitney. BA in Spanish/Polit. Sci. cum laude, U. Wis., Eau Claire, 1990. Messenger Wis. State Assembly, Madison, 1991—95, postal clk., 1995—2003, postmistress, 2003—. Fundraiser State Employees Combined Campaign, Madison, 1992—, mem. state coordinating com., 1996—; fundraiser Multiple Sclerosis Soc., 1993—2005; mem. Amnesty Internat., 1991—2005; monthly donor Planned Parenthood Nat. Leadership Coun.; fundraiser, vol. Am. Diabetes Assn., 1993—2004; vol., donor Planned Parenthood Advocates of Wis.; mem., donor YWCA; blood donor ARC; vol. Prevent Child Abuse Wis., 1994—; mem., donor So. Poverty Law Ctr., 1994—, People for the Am. Way, 1996—, Wis. Coalition Against the Death Penalty, 1993—; mem. Hoop Troop Booster Club U. Wis. Madison Women's Basketball, 1993—2005; campaign vol. David Clarenbach and Tammy Baldwin, Madison, 1992, State Rep. Tammy Baldwin, 1994, 1996, 1998, Fred Risser, 1996, 2000, 2004, Russ Feingold, 1998, 2004, Tammy Baldwin and Al Gore, 2000, Tammy Baldwin, Jim Doyle, Kathleen Falk, Barbara Lawton, 2002, 2004, Tammy Baldwin, John Kerry, Kathleen Falk, 2006, Change Barack Obama, 2008. Recipient Hopebuilder Habitat for Humanity award, 1995, 10 SECC Fundraising awards, Cmty. Vol. award, United Way, 2002, Hannah Needham Rogers award, Planned Parenthood Advocates of Wis., 2002, Backyard Hero award, Prevent Child Abuse Wis., 2004, Know Your Wis. State Jour. award, 2004, Top Fundraiser award, Madison Walk for Diabetes, 2004, Bob Alesch award, (Ptnrs. in Giving) State Employees Combined Campaign, 2005. Mem.: NOW and Emily's List. Democrat. Avocations: reading, sports, rock music, movies (comedy), travel. Home: 4322 Melody Ln # 211 Madison WI 53704

WHITNEY, MEREDITH ANN, financial analyst; b. Md., Nov. 20, 1969; d. Richard P. Whitney and Barbara Gentry; m. John Charles Layfield, Feb. 12, 2005. BA in History, Brown U., 1992. Jr. analyst Oppenheimer & Co. Inc., NYC, 1993—98; head fin. institutions rsch. Wachovia Securities (formerly First Union), 1998—2001; analyst Front-Point Partners, 2001—04; sr. fin. instns. analyst CIBC World Markets (formerly Oppenheimer & Co. Inc.), 2004—07, mng. dir., sr. fin. instns. analyst, 2008—09; founder Meredith Whitney Advisory Group, LLC, 2009—. Bus. contbr. Fox News, 2003. Named Power Player of the Yr., CNBC, 2008; named one of The 50 Most Powerful Women in NYC, NY Post, 2008, The 50 Most Powerful Women in Bus., Fortune mag., 2008, The Top 25 Market Movers, US News & World Report, 2009, The 50 Women to Watch, The Wall St. Jour., 2008, The 40 Under 40, Crain's NY Bus., 2009, The World's Most Influential People, TIME mag., 2009; named to The Power 30, Smart Money, 2008. Office: Meredith Whitney Adv Group LLC 50 W 57th St 2d Fl New York NY 10019 Office Phone: 212-542-4320. E-mail: info@meredithwhitneyllc.com.*

WHITNEY, PATRICK FOSTER, design educator; b. Edmonton, Alta., Can., Sept. 5, 1951; came to US, 1974; s. Gordon and Geraldine (Walker) W.; m. Cheryl Kent. BFA in Design with distinction, U. Alta., 1974; MFA in Design, Cranbrook Acad. Art, Bloomfield Hills, Mich., 1976. Designer RVI Corp., Chgo., 1976-79; chmn. Div. of Design Mpls. Coll. Art and Design, 1979-83; chmn. Inst. of Design, Ill. Inst. Tech., Chgo., 1983-87, dir., 1987—, Steelcase/Robert C. Pew Prof. Design. Lectr. in the field; mem., disting. advisor bd. Assn. Computing Machinery's Special Interest Group in Computer Human Interaction; chmn. US Conf. of Internat. Coun. on Graphic Design Assns., 1978; juror Presdl. Design Awards, 1995; mem. White House Council on Design; pres. Am. Ctr. for Design (ACD); principal investigator for a rsch. project called Global Companies in Local Markets. Editor Design in the Information Environment, 1984, Design Journal; author numerous published articles on design and communications. Mem. Am. Ctr. for Design (bd. dirs. 1984-86, v.p. 1986-90, pres. 1992-94), Arts Club. Office: Ill Inst Tech Inst Design 350 N LaSalle St Chicago IL 60610 Office Phone: 312-595-4900. Business E-Mail: whitney@id.iit.edu.

WHITNEY, RICHARD BUCKNER, lawyer; b. Corpus Christi, Tex., Mar. 1, 1948; s. Franklyn Loren and Betty Wolcott (Fish) Whitney; m. Chantal Marie Gindt, Aug. 18, 1972; children: Jennifer L, James R, Katherine E. BA in Polit. Sci., Union Coll., 1970; JD, Case Western Res. U., 1973. Bar: Ohio 1973, N.Y. 1998, US Ct Appeals (6th cir) 1974, US Ct Appeals (3d cir) 1987, US Dist Ct (so dist) NY 2000, U.S. Dist. Ct. (no. dist.) Ohio 1974, US Supreme Ct. 2006. From assoc. to ptnr. Jones Day, Cleve., 1973—. Dir., bd. chmn. Hospice of the We. Res. Mem.: Fed. Bar Assn., Am Inns of Ct., Cleve. Bar Assn., Order of Coif. Home: 2750 Southington Rd Shaker Heights OH 44120-1603 Office: Jones Day 901 Lakeside Ave Cleveland OH 44114-1190 Business E-Mail: rbwhitney@jonesday.com.

WHITNEY, RICHARD K., health products executive; CFO Specialty Laboratories, Inc., 2000—04, bd. dirs., 2004—06, chmn. bd., 2005—06; founder, mng. mem. Whitney Capital, LLC, 2005—; venture ptnr. New Enterprise Assocs., 2006—; CFO DaVita Inc., El Segundo, Calif., 2008—. Office: DaVita Inc 601 Hawaii St El Segundo CA 90245 Office Phone: 310-536-2400. Office Fax: 310-792-8928.

WHITNEY, RODGER FRANKLIN, academic administrator; b. Dallas, Feb. 2, 1948; s. Roger Albert and Genevieve Mae (Mohr) W. Cert. higher studies, U. Lausanne, Switzerland, 1970; BA, So. Meth. U., 1971, M Liberal Arts, 1973; EdD, Harvard U., 1978. Dir. upperclass residences So. Meth. U., Dallas, 1971-73, mem. faculty, 1973-75; dir. Mohr Edn. Found., Dallas, 1975-77; dir. North Park East, Raymond D. Nasher Co., Dallas, 1977-79; dir. Stanford Housing Ctr., asst. dean student affairs Stanford (Calif.) U., 1979-91, sr. exec. dir. student housing, chief housing officer, 1991—. Dir. Camp Grady Spruce, YMCA, Dallas, 1971-76, bd. dirs., 1976-80. Bd. dirs. Kentfield Commons, Redwood City, Calif., 1989-91. Mem. Assn. Coll. and Univ. Housing Officers, Harvard Club San Francisco, Phi Beta Kappa. Avocations: swimming, travel, history, reading, music. Home: 861 Whitehall Ln Redwood City CA 94061-3685 Office: Stanford U Housing 565 Cowell Ln Stanford CA 94305-8512 Business E-Mail: rwhitney@stanford.edu.

WHITNEY, SHARRY JAN, science educator; b. Houston, Tex., Aug. 6, 1960; d. Lonie Gene and Elizabeth Janet Cook; m. Michael William Whitney, Nov. 15, 1997; children: Jennifer, Stephanie, Richard, David, Allie, Carson. BS, Baylor U., Waco, Tex., 1982. Cert. Tchr. grades 1-8 (sci. emphasis) Tex. Dept. Edn. 2d grade tchr. Hurst-Euless-Bedford Ind. Sch. Dist., Hurst, Tex., 1982—83, Gravette Pub. Schs., Ark., 1984—86; 5th grade tchr. Nashville Pub. Schs., Tenn., 1990—99; 7th grade sci. tchr. Lewisville Ind. Sch. Dist., Tex., 1999—2006, AIS instrnl. specialist, 2006—. Recipient Tchr. of Yr., Rosepark Mid. Sch., Nashville, 1998, Tchr. Who Makes a Difference award, Griffin Mid. Sch., The Colony, Tex., 2004, 2005. Mem.: NSTA, ASCD. Avocations: mountain biking, reading, skiing, hiking. Office: Delay Middle Sch Lewisville TX 75057

WHITNEY, WILLIAM ELLIOT, JR., advertising agency executive; b. Albany, NY, Feb. 22, 1933; s. William Elliot and Louise E. (Goldsmith) W.; m. Nancy B. Bivings, Mar. 1, 1958; children— Susan, James, Douglas. BA cum laude, Amherst Coll., 1954; MBA, Harvard U., 1956. Account exec. McCann-Erickson, NYC, 1956-58, Marschalk Co., NYC, 1958-60; v.p., then sr. v.p. Ogilvy & Mather, NYC, 1960-80, sr. v.p., mng. dir. Chgo., 1980-85, exec. v.p., 1985-87, pres., 1987-89, chmn., 1990-91; cons. ptnr. Redirections, Inc., 1991-98. Lectr. U. Chgo. Grad. Sch. Bus., 1991-98. Bd. dirs., v.p. Chgo. Coun. Boy Scouts Am., 1978-81, 88—, Off-the-St. Club, Chgo., 1979—, pres., 1988-89; bd. dirs. Hinsdale (Ill.) Cmty. House, 1981, King-Bruwaert House, 1988-2004; v.p. civic adv. bd. Hinsdale Hosp., 1989-93; bd. dirs. Exec. Svc. Corps of Chgo., 1996-2004, life dir., 2005-; trustee Village of Hinsdale, 1993-97, pres., 1997-2001; bd. dirs. Hinsdale Area United Way, 2001-04; life dir.2006-. Mem. Econs. Club, Hinsdale Golf Club. Home: 736 S Park Ave Hinsdale IL 60521-4646

WHITSEL, RICHARD HARRY, retired biologist, entomologist; b. Denver, Feb. 23, 1931; s. Richard Elstun and Edith Muriel (Harry) W.; m. Laurie Pearson, May 25, 1997; children by previous marriages: Russell David, Robert Alan, Michael Dale, Steven Deane. BA, U. Calif., Berkeley, 1954; MA, San Jose State Coll., 1962. Sr. rsch. biologist San Mateo County Mosquito Abatement Dist., Burlingame, Calif., 1959—72; mgr. environ. program, chief watershed mgmt., chief planning, chief wetlands planning office Calif. Regional Water Quality Control Bd., Oakland, 1972—2000; ret., 2000. Trustee Alameda County Mosquito Abatement Dist., 1999-2001; mem. grad. faculty water resource mgmt. U. San Francisco, 1987-89. Served with Med. Svc. Corps, U.S. Army, 1954-56. Mem. Soc. Wetland Scientists, Entomol. Soc. Am., Calif. Alumni Assn., The Benjamin Ide Wheeler Soc., Nat. Parks and Conservation Assn. (life), Sierra Club. Democrat. Episcopalian. Home: 17901 Minnow Way Penn Valley CA 95946 Personal E-mail: lauriewhitsel@comcast.net.

WHITSELL, JOHN CRAWFORD, II, general surgeon; b. St. Joseph, Mo., Dec. 21, 1929; s. Ora Earl and Lorena (Spratt) W. AB, Grinnell Coll., Iowa, 1950; MD, Washington U., St. Louis, 1954. Diplomate Am. Bd. Surgery, Am. Bd. Thoracic Surgery. From instr. to clin. prof. surgery Cornell U. Med. Ctr., NYC, 1963—70; from asst. attending to attending in surgery NY Hosp., 1964—70; surg. dir. Rogosin Kidney Ctr. NY Hosp.-Cornell Med. Ctr., NYC, 1973—75; attending in surgery NY Hosp., 1970—98, hon. attending surgeon, 2001—; clin. prof. surgery Cornell Med. Coll., 1970—98, clin. prof. surgery emeritus, 1998—. Surg. cons. Rogosin Kidney Ctr., 1975—, Sharon Hosp., Conn., 1976-2001. Contbr. articles to profl. jours. Capt. USAF, 1961-63, Eng. Fellow ACS; mem. Transplantation Soc., NY Surg. Soc., Am. Soc. Transplant Surgeons, NY Soc. for Thoracic Surgery, Soc. Thoracic Surgeons, NY Acad. Medicine, Union Club of NY, Phi Beta Kappa. Avocations: golf, fishing, auto racing, antique cars. Personal E-mail: rmwhitsell@aol.com.

WHITT, GREGORY SIDNEY, evolution educator; b. Detroit, June 13, 1938; s. Sidney Abram and Millicent (Ward) W.; m. Dixie Lee Dailey, Aug. 25, 1963. BS, Colo. State U., 1962, MS, 1965; PhD, Yale U., 1970. Asst. prof. zoology U. Ill., Urbana, 1969-72, asso. prof. genetics and devel., 1972-77, prof., 1977-87, prof. ecology, ethology and evolution, 1987-2000, prof. animal biology, 2000—. Affiliate Ill. Natural History Survey, 1981—; mem. NIH study sect., 1975-76 Co-editor: Isozymes: Current Topics in Biological and Medical Research, 1977-87; editor: Isozyme Bull., 1978-81; mem. editl. bd. Biochem. Genetics, 1975—, Devel. Genetics, 1978-83, Jour. Molecular Evolution, 1979-2000, Molecular Biology and Evolution, 1983-93, Molecular Phylogenetics and Evolution, 1992-2000; contbr. articles to profl. jours. Fellow AAAS; mem. Am. Soc. Microbiology, Soc. Protection Old Fishes, Archaeol. Inst. Am. Office: U Ill Dept Animal Biology 515 Morrill Hall 505 S Goodwin Ave Urbana IL 61801-3707 Home: 3108 Earle Ct Urbana IL 61802-7091

WHITT, JOHN J., legislative staff member; Legis. dir., chief of staff for Rep. Madeleine Bordallo, US House of Reps., Washington, 2003—05, chief of staff, 2005—. Office: Office of Congresswoman Madeleine Bordallo 427 Cannon House Office Bldg Washington DC 20515-5301 Office Phone: 202-225-1188. Office Fax: 202-226-0341. E-mail: john.whitt@mail.house.gov.*

WHITT, MARCUS CALVIN, marketing executive, public relations executive; b. Paintsville, Ky., Feb. 5, 1960; s. Calvin Leo and Dora Sue (Spears) W.; m. Jennifer Marie McGuire, Jan. 4, 1986; children: Emily Marie, Elizabeth Anne, Jacob Robert. BA in Speech Communication & Human Rels., Eastern Ky. U., 1982, MA in Sociology, 1985. Intern, dir. student rels. dept. music Eastern Ky. U., Richmond, 1982-85; assoc. for ch. rels. Cumberland Coll., Williamsburg, Ky., 1985-87; dir. communications Conv. & Visitors Bur., Louisville, 1987; staff corr. The Western Recorder, Louisville, 1987—90; dir. pub. rels. Georgetown (Ky.) Coll., 1988-92; dir. pub. rels. and mktg. Campbellsville (Ky.) U., 1992-95, asst. to pres., 1995-97, v.p. advancement, 1997-2001, v.p. comms. and mktg., 2001—03, acting dir. Am. Civil War Inst., 2000—03; assoc. v.p. for pub. rels. and mktg. Eastern Ky. U., Richmond, 2003—; vice chair Am. Assn. State Coll., 2009—. Bd. dirs. Coun. Advancement and Support of Edn., Ky., 1990-96, pres.-elect, 1992, pres., 1993, 94, program co-chair, 1989-91, chair III pub. and promotion, 1994, mem. program com., 1997-98, co-chair sr. profl. track, 2003; mem. program com. Bapt. Pub. Rels. Assn., Louisville, 1987; program com. co-chair CASE III Conf., 1998, 05, bd. dirs., 1999-01, 07-; lectr. higher edn. instrl. advancement. Contbr. articles to profl. jours. Co-founder Assn. Communicators in Bapt. Edn., pres., 2002—03; chair Ky. Heartland Civil War Trls. Commn., 1997—2003; bd. dirs. Taylor County Tourism Commn., 1995—97, Campbellsville/Taylor County Adult Edn.Commn., 2001—03, Taylor County Mid. Sch. Site Base Decision Making Coun., 2002—03; comm. chair Taylor County United; mem. tourism and econ. devel. adv. coun. U.S. 2d Congl. Dist. Ky., 2003—; pres. Madison Ctrl. H.S. Band Parents Assn., 2005—; mem. stewardship com. First Bapt. Ch., Richmond, 2003—04, chmn. pub. rels. com., 2004—06. Recipient Gold award for Instnl. Rels., Mktg. Higher Edn., 1991, Silver medal Coun. for Advancement and Support of Edn., 1991, award of excellence, 1992, 94, 95, 2000-03, 05, Spl. Merit award, 1991, 94, 95, 2001, 05, Grand award, 1991, 94, 2000, 02, 03, Silver medal, 1991, 92, 2000-02, 05, Gold medal Image Improvement Mktg. Higher Edn., 1991, Gold award Outdoor Transit Billboard, Admissions Advt. awards, 1990, 91, Merit award in TV advt., hon. alumnus award Campbellsville U., 2003, Beth K. Fields Lifetime Achieve. award CASE Ky., 2005, Mem. Campbellsville/Taylor County C. of C. (bd. dirs. 1995-99, pres.-elect 1996-97, pres. 1997-98, program chair 1997-01), Leadership Scott County (publicity 1990-92), Scott County Adult Lit., Scott County Cmty. Showcase (publicity chair 1989-92), Ky. Bapt. Communicators Forum (co-founder 1991), Richmond C. of C. (bd. dirs. 2007-), Madison Ctrl. HS Band Parents Assn. Republican. Baptist. Avocations: music, southern and Kentucky history, baseball, public speaking. Home: 601 Augusta Dr Richmond KY 40475 Office: Eastern Ky U Div PR and Mktg Coates Adminstrn Bldg CPO 7A 521 Lancaster Ave Richmond KY 40475 Office Phone: 859-622-2301. Business E-Mail: marc.whitt@eku.edu.

WHITT, MARGARET EARLEY, retired literature and language professor; b. Jacksonville, Fla., Aug. 16, 1946; d. Vuron Thomas and Ruth Meriwether Earley; children: Charles, Wintry Whitt Smith. PhD, U. Denver, 1986. Dir. 1st yr. English U. Denver, 1987—2004, prof. emeritus, 2008—. Editor short stories to anthology. Sunday sch. tchr., chair, ch. coms. St Andrew United Meth. Ch., Littleton, Colo., 1977—2008. Recipient Driscoll Master Tchr. award, U. Denver, 1990, Disting. Tchg. award, 1993, Pioneer award, 2007; named Faculty Advisor of Yr., 2008. Democrat. United Methodist. Home: PO Box 123 Gerton NC 28735 E-mail: mwhitt@du.edu.

WHITTAKER, BILL DOUGLAS, minister; b. Bowling Green, Ky., June 14, 1943; s. Ewing A. and Lois (Jenkins) W.; m. Rebecca Kaye Howard, June 18, 1966; children: John, Karen, Mary. BA, Western Ky. U., 1965; MDiv, So. Bapt. Theol. Sem., Louisville, 1969, D of Ministry, 1974; MA, Union Coll., 2004. Ordained to ministry So. Bapt. Conv., 1964. Pastor 1st Bapt. Ch., Sturgis, Ky., 1969-76, Murray, Ky., 1976-82; missionary Internat. Mission Bd., So. Bapt. Conv., The Philippines, 1983-86; pastor Downtown Bapt. Ch., Orlando, Fla., 1986-88; pres. Clear Creek Bapt. Bible Coll., Pineville, Ky., 1988—2007; pastor Glasgow Bapt. Ch., Ky., 2007—. Author: Preparing to Preach, 1999, Korean edit. 2002; columnist Western Recorder newspaper, 1988—07; editor: Ky. Bapt. Heritage, 2001—. Bd. dirs. Coalition for the Homeless, Cen. Fla. YMCA, Orlando, 1986-88; mem. Ky. Bapt. Archives Adv. Bd. Mem. Assn. Bible Colls. (accredited, del. 1988—07), Assn. So. Bapt. Colls. and Schs. (del. 1988—07), So. Assn. Coll. and Schs. (del. 1999-06), Kiwanis (pres. Pineville chpt. 1994-95, dist. 6 lt. gov. 1997-98), Ky. Bapt. Conv. (pres. 1980). Baptist. Home: 105 Terrace Manor Glasgow KY 42141 Office Phone: 270-651-2186. Business E-Mail: bill@glasgowbaptist.org.

WHITTELL, POLLY (MARY K.), editor, journalist; b. Washington, Oct. 20; d. Alfred Whittell Jr. and Mary Halsey (Patchin) Hopper. BA in English, U. Calif., Berkeley; postgrad., Radcliffe Coll.; postgrad. in journalism, Columbia U. Rschr. Nat. Rev. Mag., NYC, 1970-71; asst. to presdl. speech writer The White House, Washington, 1971-72; asst. editor TravelAge East Mag., Dun & Bradstreet Publs., NYC, 1973-75; copy editor Ski Mag. Skier's Guides, Times Mirror Mags. and Am. Express, NYC, 1975-76; asst. editor to sr. editor Hearst Mags., Motor Boating & Sailing Mag., NYC, 1977-2000; contbg. editor Powerboat Mag., 2000—01, Hearst Mags., 2002—04. Contbg. author: (anthology) Against the Sea, 1998, 2001; contbr. articles to other nat. and internat. consumer mags. Mem. charity benefit com. Youth Counseling League, N.Y.C., 1975-85, Am. Cancer Soc., 1998-99, and others; v.p. Knickerbocker Rep. Club, N.Y.C., 1979-80; elected mem. N.Y. Rep. County Com., N.Y.C., 1980-84; v.p. membership SandBar Beach Club, 1980-82. Mem. Boating Writers Internat. (award for environ. article 1995), Soc. Profl. Journalists (NYC chpt. exec. coun. co-chair 2009), Princeton Club (NY). Episcopalian. Avocations: photography, travel, boating, skiing. Personal E-mail: pollywhittell@aol.com.

WHITTEMORE, ANNE MARIE, lawyer; b. Southampton, Eng., Mar. 19, 1946; (parents Am. citizens); d. Robert R. and Vera (McMullen) Grimes; m. F. Case Whittemore, June 22, 1968; 1 child, Robert Pendleton. AB, Vassar Coll., 1967; LLB, Yale U., 1970. Bar: Va. 1970. Law clk. to presiding judge U.S. Ct. Appeals (4th cir.), Alexandria, Va., 1970-71; assoc. McGuireWoods LLP (formerly McGuire, Woods, Battle & Boothe), Richmond, Va., 1971-77, ptnr., 1977—. Bd. dirs. Fed. Res. Bank of Richmond. Bd. of govs. Greater Richmond Community Found., 1978—; bd. advisors Va. Commonwealth U., Richmond, 1981—; trustee Confederate Meml. Library Soc., Richmond, 1988—. Named one of Best Lawyers in Am., Woodward/White, Inc., The 50 Most Influential Women Lawyers in Am., Nat. Law Jour., 2007; named to Leading Lawyers in Am. list, Lawdragon 3000, 2006. Mem. Richmond Bar Assn. (exec. com. 1986—), Va. Law Found. (bd. of govs. 1986—), Downtown Club (bd. dirs.). Republican. Roman Catholic. Office: McGuireWoods LLP 1 James Ctr 6th Fl 901 E Cary St Richmond VA 23219 Home: 403 Moodys Run Williamsburg VA 23185-6563 Office Phone: 804-775-4359. Office Fax: 804-698-2206. Business E-Mail: awhittemore@mcguirewoods.com.*

WHITTEMORE, ANTHONY DUNSTER, vascular surgeon, chief medical officer; b. Boston, Nov. 5, 1944; s. Anthony Rogers Whittemore and Kathrine Gansevoort Binnian Howe; m. Rhoda Belknap Stetson, June 18, 1966; children: Anthony Rogers, Joshua Stetson, Sarah Belknap. BS, Trinity Coll., 1966; MD, Columbia U., 1970. Resident surgery Columbia Presbyn. Med. Ctr., 1970—76; rsch. assoc. Columbia U., NYC, 1972—73; trainee NIH, 1975—76; vascular fellow Peter Bent Brigham Hosp., Boston, 1976—77; chief vascular surgery Naval Regional Med. Ctr., Portsmouth, Va., 1977—79; instr. surgery Harvard Med. Sch./Peter Bent Brigham Hosp., Boston, 1979—80; asst. prof. surgery Harvard U., 1981—87, assoc. prof. surgery, 1987—93, prof. surgery Med. Sch., 1993—. Dir. surg. tng. program Harvard Med. Sch./Brigham and Women's Hosp., 1979; mem. med. staff. Brigham and Women's Hosp., 1979—, chief divsn. vascular surgery, 1990—99, apptd. dir. Vascular Ctr., 1991, chief med. officer, 1999—; grant investigator NIH, 1979, 83; cons. Bard CardioSurgery, Billerica, Mass., 1982—, Meadox Meds., Oakland, NJ, 1983—, Instrumentation Labs., North Andover, Mass., 1980—. Contbr. articles to profl. pubs. Served to lt. comdr. USN, 1977—79. Decorated Commendation award USN. Fellow: ACS; mem.: Soc. Internat. de Chirurgie, New Eng. Soc. Vascular Surgery, New Eng. Surg. Soc., Soc. Vascular Surgey, Internat. Cardiovascular Soc., Boston Surg. Soc., Soc. U. Surgeons, Am. Surg. Soc., Am. Soc. for Artificial Internal Organs (program com. 1982—), Am. Surg. Assn., Assn. Acad. Surgery, Country Club. Achievements include patents in field. Home: 148 Farm Rd Sherborn MA 01770-1622 Office: Brigham & Women's Hosp 75 Francis St Boston MA 02115-6106 Office Phone: 617-732-8515.

WHITTEMORE, EDWARD REED, II, poet, retired educator; b. New Haven, Sept. 11, 1919; s. Edward Reed and Margaret Eleanor (Carr) W.; m. Helen Lundeen, Oct. 3, 1952; children: Catherine Carr, Edward Reed III, John Lundeen (dec.), Margaret Goodhue. AB, Yale U., New Haven, Conn., 1941; postgrad., Princeton U., NJ, 1945-46; LittD., Carleton Coll., Northfield, Minn., 1971. Mem. faculty Carleton Coll., 1947-67, prof. English, 1962-67, chmn. dept., 1962-64; program assoc. Nat. Inst. Pub. Affairs, 1966-68; cons. in poetry Libr. of Congress, 1964-65, 84-85; Bain-Swiggett lectr. Princeton, 1967; prof. U. Md., 1968-84, prof. emeritus, 1984—; poet laureate State of Md., 1985-88. Lit. editor New Republic, 1969-74. Author: Heroes and Heroines, 1947, An American Takes a Walk, 1956, The Self-Made Man, 1959, The Boy From Iowa, 1962, The Fascination of the Abomination, 1963, Poems, New and Selected, 1967, From Zero to the Absolute, 1967, 50 Poems 50, 1970, The Mother's Breast and the Father's House, 1974, William Carlos Williams: Poet from Jersey, 1975, The Poet as Journalist, 1976, The Feel of Rock, 1982, Pure Lives, 1988, Whole Lives, 1989, The Past, the Future, the Present, 1990, Six Literary Lives, 1993, A Literary Life of a Poet, Against the Grain, 2007; editor: Furioso, 1939-53, Browning, 1960, Carleton Miscellany, 1960-64, Delos mag., 1988-91. Capt. USAAF, 1941-45. Decorated Bronze star, 1945. Home: Chevy Chase House 5420 Connecticut Ave NW # 304 Washington DC 20015-2832

WHITTEMORE, GAIL FARNSWORTH, law librarian; b. Washington, Mar. 12, 1951; d. Carl Davis and Margaret Smith Farnsworth; children: Diana Margaret, Laura Ann. MusB, U. Conn., Storrs, 1973; JD cum laude, NY Law Sch., 1982; MLIS magna cum laude, LI U., Purchase, NY, 2003. Bar admission: NY 1983, NJ 1983. Assoc. Mudge Rose Guthrie Alexander & Ferdon, NYC, 1982—84; litig. atty. NY Tel. Co., NYC, 1984—86; assoc. Brandeis, Bernstein, Pollack & Greene, NYC, 1989—93. Mem. AALL, Govt. Docs. SIS, NYC, 2003—. Mem.: Am. Assn. Law Librs. Avocation: music. Office: Pace Univ Sch Law 78 N Broadway White Plains NY 10603 Office Fax: 914-422-4412. Business E-Mail: gwhittemore@law.pace.edu.

WHITTEMORE, PAUL BAXTER, psychologist; s. Harry Ballou and Margaret B. Whittemore; m. Jane Moore, Apr. 22, 1995. BA in Religion, Ea. Nazarene Coll., 1970; MDiv., Nazarene Theol. Sem., 1973; MA in Theology, Vanderbilt U., 1975, PhD in Theology, 1978; PhD in Clin. Psychology, U. Tenn., 1987. Cert. in clin. psychology Am. Bd. Profl. Psychology, lic. psychologist Calif. Asst. prof. philosophy Trevecca Nazarene Coll., Nashville, 1973—76; asst. prof. philosophy and religion Point Loma Coll., San Diego, 1976—80; asst. prof. philosophy Mid. Tenn. State U., Murfreesboro, 1980—83; clin. psychology intern LA County/U. So. Calif. Med. Ctr., LA, 1986—87; coord. behavior health ctr. Calif. Med. Ctr., LA, 1987—88; clin. asst. prof. family medicine U. So. Calif. Sch. Medicine, LA, 1988—; pvt. practice Newport Beach, Calif., 1991—. Mem. behavioral sci. faculty Glendale Adventist Family Practice Residency Program, Glendale, Calif., 1989—90; inpatient group therapist Ingleside Hosp., Rosemead, Calif., 1990—92; founder, pres. Date Coach, 1992—2000. Contbr. articles to profl. jours. Recipient Andrew W. Mellon Postdoctoral Faculty Devel. award, Vanderbilt U., 1981. Mem.: AAUP (chpt. v.p. 1982—83), APA, Orange County Psychol. Assn. (bd. dirs. 1996—2001), Calif. Psychol. Assn. (media divsn. sec.-treas. 1997—98), Am. Philos. Assn., Am. Acad. Religion. Achievements include discovery of link between phenylthiocarbamide tasting and depression. Office: 1001 Dove St Ste 145 Newport Beach CA 92660-2123

WHITTEMORE, RONALD PAUL, hospital administrator, retired army officer, nursing educator; b. Saco, Maine, Aug. 10, 1946; s. Ronald B. and Pauline L. (Larson) W.; m. Judy D. McDonald, Feb. 17, 1967; 1 child, Leicia Michelle. BGS, U. S.C., 1974, MEd, 1977; BSN, Med. Coll. Ga., 1975. Enlisted U.S. Army, 1968, advanced through ranks to maj., 1985, ret., 1991; adult/oncology nurse practitioner Martin Army Cmty. Hosp.; asst. head nurse SICU, infection control practitioner Moncrief Army Cmty. Hosp.; infection control practitioner U.S. Army Hosp., Seoul, Republic of Korea; chief nurse 2nd Combat Support Hosp., Ft. Benning, Ga.; cmty. health nurse Brooke Army Med. Ctr., Ft. Sam Houston, Tex.; comty. health nurse Giessen (Germany) Mil. Cmty.; clin. instr. Eisenhower Army Med. Ctr., Ft. Gordon, Ga.; chief nursing adminstrn. E/N Frankfurt (Germany) Army Med. Ctr.; adminstr., dir. quality improvement Gracewood (Ga.) State Sch. and Hosp., 1995-97; clin. nurse analyst Southeastern Regional Med. Commd., Ft. Gordon, Ga., 2005—; head nurse pulmonary medicine Eisenhower Army Med. Ctr., Ft. Gordon, Ga., 2006—. Instr. Augusta (Ga.) Tech. Inst., 1991-95; nurse epidemiologist Med. Coll. Ga., Augusta. Mem. ANA, Ga. ANA (3rd Dist. honoree, pres. 1983-85), Assn. Practitioners in Infection Control, Am. Holistic Nurses Assn., Nat. Assn. Health Care Quality Profls., Assn. for Profls. in Infection Control and Epidemiology, Sigma Theta Tau. Office: Eisenhower Army Med Ctr Fort Gordon GA 30905 Office Phone: 706-787-8410. E-mail: ron.whittemore@us.army.mil.

WHITTEN, CHARLES ALEXANDER, JR., physics professor; b. Harrisburg, Pa., Jan. 20, 1940; s. Charles Alexander and Helen (Shoop) W.; m. Joan Emann, Nov. 20, 1965; 1 son, Charles Alexander III. BS summa cum laude, Yale U., 1961; PhD in Physics, Princeton U., 1966. Rsch. assoc. A.W. Wright Nuclear Structure Lab., Yale U., 1966-68; asst. prof. physics UCLA, 1968-74, assoc. prof., 1974-80, prof., 1980—, vice chmn. physics dept., 1982-86. Vis. scientist Centre d'Etudes Nucléaires de Saclay-Moyenne Energie, France, 1980—81, 1986—87; Vis. prof. U. Sci. and Tech., Hefei, China, 2007, Tsinghua U., Beijing, 2008. Contbr. articles to profl. jours. Mem. Am. Phys. Soc., Sigma Pi Sigma, Phi Beta Kappa. Home: 9844 Vicar St Los Angeles CA 90034-2719 Office: U Calif Dept Physics Los Angeles CA 90024 Office Phone: 310-825-1691. Business E-Mail: whitten@physics.ucla.edu.

WHITTEN, JERRY LYNN, chemistry professor; b. Bartow, Fla., Aug. 13, 1937; s. John Graves and Dorothy Iola (Jordan) W.; m. Mary Hill (div. Sept. 1977); 1 child, Jerrard John; m. Adela Chrzeszczyk, June 21, 1980; 1 child, Christina. BS in Chemistry, Ga. Inst. Tech., 1960, PhD, 1964. Cert. chemist. Rsch. assoc. to instr. Princeton (N.J.) U., 1963-65; asst. prof. chemistry Mich. State U., East Lansing, 1965-67, SUNY, Stony Brook, 1967-68, assoc. prof., 1968-73, prof., 1973-89, chmn. chemistry dept., 1985-89; prof. chemistry, dean Coll. Phys. and Math. Scis. N.C. State U., Raleigh, 1989-99. Vis. prof. Centre Europèen de Calcul Atomique et Molèculaire, Orsay, France, 1974-75, Univ. Bonn and Wuppertal, Fed. Republic Germany, 1979-80, Eidgenossische Technische Hochschule, Zurich, Switzerland, 1984, U. Wuppertel, 2005 Contbr. more than 190 articles to profl. jours. Bd. dirs. N.C. Sch. Sci. and Math Found., chair; bd. dirs. Burroughs Wellcome Fund. Recipient Alexander von Humboldt U.S. Sr. Scientist award, 1979; grantee Petroleum Rsch. Fund, 1966-67, 74-76, 77-81, NSF, 1967-72, U.S. Dept. Energy, 1977—; SDIO/ONR grantee, 1991-92; Alfred P. Sloan fellow, 1969-71. Mem. AAAS, Am. Phys. Soc., Am. Chem. Soc., N.Y. Acad. Scis., Sigma Xi (pres. N.C. chpt.), Phi Beta Kappa, Phi Kappa Phi. Episcopalian. Avocations: boating, tennis, skiing. Office: NC State U Coll Dept Chemistry PO Box 8204 Raleigh NC 27695-0001 Office Phone: 919-515-7960. E-mail: j_whitten@ncsu.edu.

WHITTEN, LESLIE HUNTER, JR., writer, poet, reporter; b. Jacksonville, Fla., Feb. 21, 1928; s. Leslie Hunter and Linnora (Harvey) W.; m. Phyllis Webber, Nov. 11, 1951; children: Leslie Hunter III, Andrew, Daniel, Deborah Wilson Engle. BA in Journalism/English magna cum laude, Lehigh U., 1950, LHD, 1989. Journalist Radio Free Europe, 1952-57, I.N.S., 1957-58, U.P.I., 1958, Washington Post, 1958-63; with Hearst Newspapers, 1963-66, asst. bur. chief Washington, 1966-69; sr. investigator Jack Anderson's Washington Merry-Go-Round, 1969-92; pres. Athanor Inc., 1977-93. Vis. assoc. prof. Lehigh U., 1967-69; adj. prof. So. Ill. U., 1984. Author: Progeny of the Adder, 1965, Moon of the Wolf, 1967, Pinion the Golden Eagle, 1968, The Abyss, 1970, F. Lee Bailey, 1971, The Alchemist, 1973, Conflict of Interest, 1976, Washington Cycle, 1979, Sometimes a Hero, 1979, A Killing Pace, 1983, A Day Without Sunshine, 1985, The Lost Disciple, 1989, The Fangs of Morning, 1994, Sad Madrigals, 1997, Moses, the Lost Book of the Bible, 1999, The Rebel, 2005; contbr. numerous poems to anthologies and other publs. Vol. Hospice, 1987-2003. Served with AUS, 1946-48. Recipient hon. mention pub. service Washington Newspaper Guild, 1963, Edgerton award ACLU, 1974 Home: 3142 Gracefield Rd Apt 303 Silver Spring MD 20904-5856 Home Phone: 301-593-5943. Personal E-mail: lhwhitjr@aol.com.

WHITTEN, MAURICE MASON, chemistry professor; b. Providence, Oct. 1, 1923; s. Albert Ernest and Caroline A. (Steere) W.; m. Doris Ruth Meserve, May 21, 1983; 7 stepchildren. AB, Colby Coll., 1945; MA, Columbia Tchrs. Coll., 1949; PhD, Ohio State U., 1971. Sci. tchr., Wilton, Maine, 1945-48; chemistry and physics tchr. Lewiston (Maine) H.S., 1948-55; instr., then asst. prof. phys. sci. Gorham (Maine) State Coll., 1955-70; assoc. prof., then prof. chemistry U. So. Maine, Gorham, 1970-83, prof. emeritus chemistry, 1983—. TV master sci. tchr. Maine State Dept. Edn., Augusta and Portland, 1959-60. Author: The Gunpowder Mills of Maine, 1990. Pres. Gorham Hist. Soc., 1985-87; bd. dirs. Gorham Land Trust, 1989-92. Recipient E. Thompson Outstanding Sci. Tchg. award Am. Acad. Arts and Scis., 1954. Mem. AAAS, Am. Chem. Soc., New Eng. Assn. Chemistry Tchrs. (hon., chair no. sect. 1958-60), Maine Hist. Soc. Democrat. Methodist. Avocations: hymn histories, travel, collecting coins, stamps, rocks and minerals. Home: 11 Lincoln St Gorham ME 04038-1703 Personal E-mail: dwhitten13@maine.rr.com.

WHITTENBURG, JUSTIN M., lawyer; b. Amarillo, Tex., Nov. 8, 1974; s. Mack Whittenburg and Catherine Leftwich Reavis; m. Blythe Dayne Martindale, Feb. 27, 1999; children: Mack, David Earl, Dane. BA in Econs., U. Tex., Austin, 1998; JD, U. Houston, 2004. Project mgr. Zachry Constrn. Corp., San Antonio, 1998—2001, ABB Lummus Global, Houston, 2001—02; atty. Baker & McKenzie LLP, 2004—. Office: Baker & McKenzie LLP 711 Louisiana St Ste 3400 Houston TX 77002 Business E-Mail: justin.m.whittenburg@bakernet.com.

WHITTERS, JAMES PAYTON, III, lawyer, educator; b. Boston, Oct. 23, 1939; s. James P. Jr. and Norene (Jones) W.; m. Elizabeth Robertson, July 19, 1969; children: James P. IV, Catharine A. BA in History, Trinity Coll., Hartford, Conn., 1962; JD, Boston Coll., 1969; MA in Am. studies, U. Mass., Boston, 2002. Bar: Mass. 1969, US Dist. Ct. Mass. 1970, US Ct. Appeals (1st cir.) 1972. Assoc. Ely, Bartlett, Brown & Proctor, Boston, 1969-74, Gaston Snow & Ely Bartlett, Boston, 1974-79, ptnr., 1979-88, Gaston & Snow, Boston, 1988-91; of counsel Peabody & Brown, Boston, 1991-95; dir. Office Career Devel., Suffolk U. Law Sch., Boston, 1995—2004, adj. prof. Am. legal history, 1997—. Bd. dirs., sec. Robertson Factories, Inc., Taunton, Mass., 1979-04; v.p. The Alkalol Co., Boston, 1976-97, sr. v.p., 1997-05, pres., treas., gen. counsel, dir., 2005—; vis. tchr. Groton Sch., Mass., 1993-94; mem. Mass. Conflict Intervention Mediation Team, 1995—. Bd. dirs. New Eng. com. NAACP Legal Def. Fund, 1982-2006, Beacon Hill Nursery Sch., 1976-78, Mass. Appleseed Ctr. Law and Justice, 1997—, The Esplanade Assn., 2005-, New Workplace Inst., 2006-; chmn. Mass. Outdoor Advt. Bd., Boston, 1975-81; vice chmn. Mass. Jud. Nominating Coun., Boston, 1983-87; trustee Trinity Coll., 1984-95; trustee, sec. Hurricane Island Outward Bound Sch., 1977-87; bd. dirs. Mass. affiliate Am. Heart Assn., 1979-98, chmn., 1989-91; bd. dirs. Greater Boston Legal Svcs., 1982-84, 93-99, Mass. Assn. Mediation Programs and Practitioners, 1993-98; founder Beacon Hill Seminars, 2000-2001, bd. dirs., 2001-02; facilitator Boston City Wide Dialogues on Racial and Ethnic Diversity, 2003-08. Lt. (j.g.) USN, 1962-65. Recipient Alumni Excellence award Trinity Coll., 1987, Touchdown Club award Trinity Coll., 2006. Mem.: ABA, Boston Bar Assn. (standing com. on work-life balance, children's outreach task force, pub. svc. and criminal justice task force, Pres.'s award 2007), The Country Club (Brookline, Mass.). Democrat. Unitarian Universalist. Avocations: mountain climbing, jogging, yoga, reading. Home: 44 Mount Vernon St Boston MA 02108-1302 Home Phone: 617-742-9467; Office Phone: 617-248-8822. Business E-Mail: jpwhit3@comcast.net.

WHITTIER, BARBARA J (BOBBIE), retired biology and chemistry educator; b. New Rochelle, NY, July 13, 1943; d. Gordon F. and Elinor E. Whittier. BS, Cornell U., Ithaca, NY, 1965; MAT, Harvard U., Cambridge, Mass., 1966. Postgraduate Professional License Va. State Bd. of Edn., 1968, Collegiate Professional Va. State Bd. of Edn., 1966. Sci. educator Wakefield HS, Arlington, Va., 1966—98, sci. dept. chair, 1990—95; ret., 1998. Softball coach Wakefield HS, 1983—90; cons. Arlington Pub. Schools, 1998—2003; project asst. Biotechnology Inst., Arlington, 2003—. Mem., elder, clk. of session, meals on wheels Arlington Presbyn. Ch., 1980—2006; pnc liaison and mem., com. on ministry Nat. Capital Presbytery, Washington, 2000—08; com. mem. Va. Jr. Acad. Sci., Richmond, 1982—2008, sponsor, 1982—2006; mem. Wakefield Alumni Assn., Arlington, 2003—08. Recipient Outstanding Educator award, Joint Bd. Sci. and Engring. Edn. and Wash. Acad. Sci., 1984, Presdl. award for excellence in sci. and math. tchg., NSF, 1986, Disting. Svc. award, Va. Jr. Acad. Sci., 2006; named to Wakefield HS Hall of Fame, 2005. Mem.: Va. Assn. Sci. Tchrs. (Va. Jr. Acad. Sci. rep. 2005—08), Nat. Assn. Biology Tchrs. (life), Delta Delta Delta. Presbyn. Avocation: sports. Home: 2424B S Walter Reed Dr Arlington VA 22206-4086 Personal E-mail: bwhittier@aol.com.

WHITTINGHAM, CHARLES ARTHUR, library director, publishing executive; b. Chgo., Feb. 11, 1930; s. Charles Arthur and Virginia (Hartke) W.; m. Jean Bragger Whittingham, June 4, 1955; children: Mary Elizabeth, Charles Arthur III, Philip Alexander, Leigh Ann. BS in English Lit. cum laude, Loyola U., Chgo., 1951. With McCall Corp., Chgo., 1956-59, Time, Inc., Chgo., 1959-62; pub.'s rep. Fortune mag., Time, Inc., NYC, 1962-65, mgr. San Francisco, 1965-69; asst. to pub. Fortune, NYC, 1969-70, asst. pub., 1970-78; pub. Life mag., NYC, 1978-88; sr. v.p. N.Y. Pub. Libr., 1989-92; exec. prodr. Kunhardt Prodns., Inc., 1995—. Lt. j.g. USNR, 1951—55. Named to Athletic Hall of Fame Loyola U., Loyola Acad. Mem.: Century Assn., The Pilgrims, Grolier Club, Brook Club. Home and Office: 800 Fifth Ave 8C New York NY 10021

WHITTINGHAM, KENNETH, television director; Dir.: (TV series) The Amanda Show, 2000—01, Girlfriends, 2001—03, Mano a Mano, 2005, The Bernie Mac Show, 2002—06, The King of Queens, 2003—06, One on One, 2001—06, Everybody Hates Chris, 2005—07, My Name is Earl, 2006—07, The Office, 2005—07 (Outstanding Directing in a Comedy Series, NAACP Image award, 2007, 2008), Scrubs, 2002—07. Office: c/o NBC Network 30 Rockefeller Plz New York NY 10112

WHITTINGHAM, KYLE, college football coach; b. Provo, Utah, Nov. 21, 1959; m. Jamie Daniels; children: Tyler, Melissa, Alex, Kylie. B in Ednl. Psychology, Brigham Young U., Provo, Utah, 1984, M in Athletic Adminstrn., 1987. Linebacker, tng. camp. Denver Broncos, 1982; linebacker Denver Gold, New Orleans Breakers, US Football League, 1983—85; replacement squad LA Rams, 1987; grad. asst. Brigham Young U. Cougars, 1985—86; defensive coord. Coll. Ea. Utah Eagles, 1987; asst. coach Idaho State U. Bengals, 1988—91, defensive coord., 1991—93; defensive line coach U. Utah Utes, 1994, defensive coord., 1995—2004, head football coach, 2004—. Recipient Paul "Bear" Bryant award, Nat. Sportscasters & Sportswriters Assn., 2008; named Mountain West Conf. Co-Defensive Coord. of Yr., Las Vegas Rev. Jour., 2002, Mountain West Coach of Yr., Sporting News, 2008. Office: Univ Utah Athletics Dept 1825 E South Campus Dr Salt Lake City UT 84112-0900*

WHITTINGHAM, M(ICHAEL) STANLEY, chemist; b. Nottingham, Eng., Dec. 22, 1941; came to U.S., 1968, naturalized, 1980; s. William Stanley and Dorothy Mary (Findlay) W.; m. Georgina Judith Andai, Mar. 23, 1969; children: Jenniffer Judith, Michael Stanley. BA in Chemistry, Oxford U., 1964, MA, DPhil, 1968. Rsch. assoc., head solid state electrochemistry group Materials Ctr., Stanford U., 1968-72; mem. staff Exxon Rsch. Co., Linden, N.J., 1972—; group head solid state chem. physics, 1975-78; dir. solid state scis., 1978-80; mgr. chem. engring. tech., 1980-84; dir. phys. scis. Schlumberger Co., Ridgefield, Conn., 1984-88; prof. chemistry and materials sci. and engring., dir. The Inst. for Materials Rsch., SUNY, 1988—; vice provost for rsch. SUNY, 1994-2000; vice-chair bd. dirs. Rsch. Found., 1995-2001. Cons., lectr. in field; JSPS fellow U. Tokyo. Author, editor papers in field; author 5 books. Recipient Gas Coun. scholarship, Oxford U., 1964-67. Mem. Electrochem. Soc. (Young Author award 1971, N.Y. chmn. 1980-81, Battery Rsch. award 2002, fellow 2004), Am. Chem. Soc. (chmn. solid state sect. 1987, chmn. Binghamton sect. 1991), Am. Phys. Soc., Materials Rsch. Soc. Achievements include patents in field; reversible (rechargeable) lithium batteries and methods for making intercalation batteries; method for making TiS_2 mixed material cathodes, high briteness luminescent displays. Home: 396 Meeker Rd Vestal NY 13850-3230 Office: SUNY Dept Chemistry Binghamton NY 13902 Office Phone: 607-777-4623. E-mail: stanwhit@binghamton.edu.

WHITTINGTON, CHRISTOPHER L., lawyer, political organization administrator; children: Lauren, Lucy. BS in Fin., La. Tech. U., 1987; JD, So. U. Law Ctr., 1992. Ptnr. Whittington & Reynolds, Baton Rouge, The Whittington Law Firm. Legal counsel La. Dem. Party, chmn., 2006—. Mem.: ABA, Am. Assn. Justice, La. Assn. Justice (bd. govs.), Baton Rouge Bar Assn., La. Bar Assn., Am. Assn. Trial Lawyers, La. Assn. Trials Lawyers. Democrat. Avocations: reading, golf, trivia, hunting. Office: PO Box 3035 Baton Rouge LA 70821 also: La Dem Party 701 Government St Baton Rouge LA 70802 Office Phone: 225-346-8777, 225-336-4155. Office Fax: 225-346-0009. Business E-Mail: cwhittington@lademo.org. E-mail: chris@whittingtonlawfirm.com.*

WHITTINGTON, E. MICHAEL, museum director; Cur. Pre-Columbian and African Art Mint Mus. Art, Charlotte, NC; exec. dir. Monterey Mus. Art, Calif., 2005—. Author: Sport of Life and Death: The MesoAmerican Ballgame, 2001. Office: Menterey Mus Art 559 Pacific St Monterey CA 93940 Office Phone: 831-372-5477. Business E-Mail: emwhittington@montereyart.org.

WHITTINGTON, LORIN DALE, retired music educator; b. Balt., Nov. 1, 1951; s. Cicero Edward Whittington and Dorothy Virginia Peters. MusB, Appalachian State U., 1979. Cert. tchr. music k-12 N.C. Tchr. Hall Fletcher Mid. Sch., Asheville, NC, 1979—81, Hill St. Mid. Sch., Asheville, 1979—81, Owen H.S., Swannanoa, NC, 1981—97, Owen Mid. Sch., Swannanoa, 1997—2006. Chorus master Mid-Atlantic Opera Co., Asheville, 1985—86. Composer: (sound recording) Rochelle, 1972. Mem.: Music Educators Nat. Conf. Achievements include performance by Owen Middle School Chorus at Carnegie Hall, 2005. Avocations: genealogy, art, computer graphics, guitar, travel. Office: Owen Mid Schl 730 Old US 70 Swannanoa NC 28778 Home: 3964 Mountain View Cir Lenoir NC 28645-8713 Personal E-mail: vytiense@att.net.

WHITTINGTON, RALPH EDWARD, retired curator, librarian; b. Washington, Jan. 13, 1945; s. Ralph John and Mildred May Whittington; m. Jennifer Kay Rutland, June 7, 1969 (div.); 1 child, Amanda Anne. Grad., Surrattsville HS, Clinton, Md., 1963. Deck attendant Libr. of Congress, Washington, 1963—76, searcher libr. materials locator, 1976—85, curator main reading rm., 1985—2000; cons. Mus. Sex, NYC, 2001—; ret. Author: Dictionary of International Biography, 2008—09. Avocation: vinyl record collector. Home: 9204 Greenfield Ln Clinton MD 20735 Home Phone: 301-868-3974.

WHITTINGTON, ROBERT BRUCE, retired publishing company executive; b. Oakland, Calif., Mar. 5, 1927; s. Edward and Loretta (Edalgo) W.; m. Marie D. Sanguinetti, June 18, 1950; children: Mark, Lynn. Student, Stockton Jr. Coll., 1946-48; BA in Journalism and Polit. Sci. (Friend W. Richardson fellow), U. Calif., Berkeley, 1950. Reporter Stockton (Calif.) Record, 1950-60, exec. news editor, 1965-68, asso. pub., 1968-69, pub., 1969-72; v.p., dir. Speidel Newspapers, Reno, 1972-77; regional pres., dir. Gannett Co., Inc., 1977-82; publ. Reno (Nev.) newspapers, 1980-82; v.p., trustee Gannett Found., 1982-85. Dir. Sierra Pacific Resources, 1985-99; pres. Speidel Newspapers Charitable Found. With PTO USNR, 1944—46. Roman Catholic. Home: 8721 Bainbridge Pl Stockton CA 95209

WHITTINGTON, STEPHEN LUNN, museum director; b. Washington, Jan. 31, 1956; s. Charles Lunn and Alice Marie (Doyle) W.; m. Christine Ann Carlson, Aug. 18, 1979; children: Daniel, Joseph. AB in Anthropology, U. Chgo., 1977; MA, Pa. State U., 1981, PhD, 1989. Dir. Proyecto Arqueologico Ostuman, Copan, Honduras, 1989, U. Maine Hudson Mus., 1991—2002, Teozacoalco Archaeol. Project, 2002, Iximche Osteological Project, 1992—95; asst. curator collections Wyo. Hist. and Geol. Soc., Wilkes-Barre, Pa., 1989-90; cooperating assoc. prof. dept. anthropology, dir. Hudson Mus., U. Maine, 1991—2002. Adj. assoc. prof. dept. anthropology Wake Forest U., dir. Mus. Anthropology, 2002—. Author: Archaeology and Ethnohistory of Iximche, 2003; editor: Bones of the Maya, 1997; contbr. articles to profl. jours. Active Maine State Mus. Commn., 1998—2002; treas. Southeastern Mus. Conf., 2006—08; chair Hispanic Arts Initiative Steering Com., 2005; bd. dirs. Assn. Coll. & U. Mus. & Galleries, 2009—. Grantee Wenner-Gren Found. for Anthrop. Rsch., 1992-93, NSF, 1989, Inst. Internat. Edn., 1988, Found. for the Advancement of Mesoamerican Studies, 1995, 99, 2002, NEH, 1997, 2005, Inst. Mus. and Lib. Svcs., 1991, 94, 96-98, 2001, 04, 06, 08, 09, Dumbarton Oaks, 2009. Mem. Am. Assn. Mus., N.C. Mus. Coun., Soc. for Am. Archaeology, Southeastern Mus. Conf. Avocations: jogging, fencing, bicycling. Home: 1307 Brookwood Dr Winston Salem NC 27106 Office: Wake Forest Univ Mus Anthropology PO Box 7267 Winston Salem NC 27109 Office Phone: 336-758-5827. E-mail: whittisl@wfu.edu.

WHITTINGTON, THOMAS LEE, lawyer; b. Waukesha, Wis., July 14, 1943; s. Floyd Leon and Winifred Carol (McDonald) W.; m. Ashley J. Whittington; children: Erin, Hilary, Eric Cartner, Ryan Cartner, Kyle Sanders. BA, Coll. of Wooster, 1965; JD, U. Mich., 1967. Bar: Trust Terr. of Pacific Islands 1967, Mich. 1969, Wash. 1974, U.S. Dist. Ct. (wc. dist.) Wash. 1974. Vol. Peace Corps, Micronesia, 1967-69; staff asst. legis. office Dept. Interior, Washington, 1969-74; ptnr. Thomas, Whittington, Anderson, Bergan & Studebaker, Issaquah, Wash., 1974—2000, Scottsdale, Ariz., 2000—05, Carefree, Ariz., 2005—. Mailing: PO Box 5827 Carefree AZ 85377

WHITWORTH, HALL BAKER, forest products company executive; b. St. Paul, NC, Feb. 15, 1919; s. A. Frederick and Maude Ethel (Baker) W.; m. Mary Margaret Mease, May 18, 1946; children: Hall Baker,

Laura Ellen, David Allen. Student, Miss. So. Coll., 1942, U. N.C., 1957. With Champion Internat., Canton, NC, 1936-62, mgr. materials, 1956-62, dir. materials packages div. Chgo., 1962-65, dir. purchase U.S. Plywood-Champion Papers, Inc. (now champion Internat. Corp.) Hamilton, Ohio, 1965-68, dep. dir. corporate materials services, 1966, v.p., dir. purchase, 1968-75, v.p. materials Stamford, Conn., 1975—, dir., 1975—, now ret.; v.p., dir. So. Agrl. Co., 1985—; pres., dir. H. Whitworth Enterprises, Cin., 1985—. Bd. dirs. Pathfork-Harlan Coal Co., Elmac Corp. Served with U.S. Army, 1942-46. Recipient Thomas award Carolina-Va. Purchasing Agts. Assn., 1963 Mem. Am. Paper Inst. (chmn. energy subcom.), Am. Mgmt. Assn. (v.p. purchasing, transp. and phys. distbn. div. council) Clubs: Canton Toastmakers (founder, 1st pres.). Lodges: Elks. Methodist. Home and Office: 1111 S Lakemont Ave Ste 102 Winter Park FL 32792-5469 Personal E-mail: hall_whitworth@msn.com.

WHITWORTH, HORACE ALGERNON, mechanical engineer; b. Kingston, Jamaica, W.I., Mar. 24, 1953; came to U.S., 1967; s. Egbert Leopold and Violet Cecilia (Trouth) W. BSME, U. Mass., 1975; MS, George Washington U., 1977, DSc, 1983. Asst. prof. Howard U., Washington, 1983-89, dir. grad. studies dept. mech. engring., 1988-96, assoc. prof. mech. engring., 1989-99, prof. mech. engring., 1999—, chmn. dept. mech. engring., 2004—. Contbr. articles to profl. jours. Bd. dirs. Jamaica Support Found., Washington, 1991-95. Recipient Sr. Fellows Found. award Pacific Telesis Found., 1988, Prof. Acad. award Honeywell Corp., 1992; rsch. grantee in field. Mem. ASME (bd. dirs. Washington chpt. 1994—, Instr. of Yr. student chpt. 1985-86, 87-89), Am. Soc. Metals, Soc. for Exptl. Mechanics. Democrat. Methodist. Achievements include development of mathematical models to evaluate fatigue damage development in fibrous composite materials. Office: Howard U 2300 6th St NW Washington DC 20059-2323 Home Phone: 301-871-2711; Office Phone: 202-806-6600. Business E-Mail: hwhitworth@howard.edu.

WHITWORTH, KATHRYNNE ANN, professional golfer; b. Monahans, Tex., Sept. 27, 1939; d. Morris Clark and Dama Ann (Robinson) W. Student, Odessa Jr. Coll., tex., 1958. Joined tour Ladies Profl. Golf Assn., 1959—. Named to Hall of Fame Ladies Profl. Golf Assn., Tex. Sports Hall of Fame, Tex. Golf Hall of Fame, World Golf Hall of Fame; Capt. of Solhiem Cup, 1990-92. Mem. Ladies Profl. Golf Assn. (sec. 1962-63, v.p. 1965, 73, 88, pres. 1967, 68, 71, 89, 1st mem. to win over $1,000,000). Office: care Ladies Profl Golf Assn 2570 Volusia Ave Daytona Beach FL 32114-8144

WHITWORTH, WILLIAM A., magazine editor; b. Hot Springs, Ark., Feb. 13, 1937; s. William C. and Lois Virginia (McNabb) W.; m. Carolyn Hubbard, Dec. 27, 1969; children— Matthew, Katherine. BA, U. Okla., 1960. Reporter Ark. Gazette, Little Rock, 1960—63; reporter N.Y. Herald Tribune, 1963—65; staff writer The New Yorker, 1966—72, assoc. editor, 1973—80; editor-in-chief The Atlantic Monthly, Boston, 1981—99, editor emeritus, 1999—; editor-at-large The American Scholar, Washington, 2002—04. Office: 600 New Hampshire Ave NW Washington DC 20037 Personal E-mail: ww131@comcast.net.

WHOLEY, MARK H., radiologist, director; m. Roseanne Wholey. MD, U. Pitts. Dir., interventional radiology U. Pierre et Marie Curie Shadyside, Pitts., 1969—. Office: Univ Pierre et Marie Curie Shadyside 5230 Ctr Ave Ste EG-01 Pittsburgh PA 15232 Office Fax: 412-623-0011.

WHORTON, M. DONALD, physician, epidemiologist; b. Las Vegas, N.Mex., Jan. 25, 1943; s. R. H. and Rachel (Siegal) Whorton; m. Diana L. Obrinsky, Apr. 9, 1972; children: Matthew Richard, Laura Elizabeth, Julie Hannah. Student, U.S. Naval Acad., 1961—62; B of Biology, N.Mex. Highlands U., 1964; MD, U. N.Mex., 1968; MPH, Johns Hopkins U., 1973. Intern Boston City Hosp., 1968—69; resident in pathology U. N.Mex., Albuquerque, 1969—71; instr., resident in medicine Balt. City Hosp., 1972—74; instr. Johns Hopkins U., Balt.; assoc. dir. divsn. emergency medicine Balt. City Hosps., 1974—75; clin. asst. prof. divsn. ambulatory and cmty. medicine U. Calif. Sch. Medicine, San Francisco, 1975—77; lectr. U. Calif. Sch. Pub. Health, San Francisco, 1975—79; med. dir. labor occup. health program Inst. Indsl. Rels., Ctr. for Labor Rsch. and Edn., 1975—79, assoc. clin. prof. occup. medicine, 1979—87; prin. Environ. Health Assocs., Inc., Oakland, 1978—88; v.p. ENSR Health Scis., 1988—94; pvt. practice Alameda, Calif., 1994—2001; with WorkCare, 2001—. Chmn. adv. com. for hazard evaluation svc. and info. system Indsl. Relations Dept., State of Calif., 1979—84; cons. in field; chmn. statewide adv. com. on occupl. and environ. health U. Calif. Ctrs., 1996—. Contbr. articles to profl. jours. Recipient Upjohn Achievement award, 1968; scholar, Robert Wood Johnson Found., 1972—74. Fellow: Am. Coll. Occupl. and Environ. Medicine, Am. Coll. Epidemiology; mem.: APHA, Inst. Medicine NAS, Calif. Med. Assn. (adv. panel on occupl. and environ. medicine), Soc. for Occupl. and Environ. Health, Alpha Omega Alpha. Office: WorkCare 1320 Harbor Bay Pkwy # 115 Alameda CA 94502-6556 Office Phone: 510-748-6900 ext. 201. Personal E-mail: whobrin@lmi.net. Business E-Mail: dwhorton@workcare.com.

WHOULEY, MICHAEL J., communications specialist, political strategist; b. Mass., 1959; m. Sally Kerans. BA, Boston Coll., 1981. Founder, polit. strategist Whouley & Associates; dir., office priority placement The White House; founder, polit. strategist Dewey Square Group (DSG), Boston, 1993—. Nat. field dir. Clinton/Gore Presdl. Campaign, 1992; nat. campaign mgr., Vice Pres. Al Gore Clinton/Gore Re-election Campaign, 1996; advisor Vice Pres. Al Gore's Presdl. Campaign, 2000; chief polit. strategist Dem. Nat. Com., 2000, gen. election dir., 04; sr. advisor Senator John Kerry's Presdl. Campaign, 2004; head, nat. GOTV activities Dem. Congl. Campaign Com., 2006. Democrat. Office: Dewey Square Group 100 Cambridge St Ste 1301 Boston MA 02114 Office Phone: 617-367-9929. Office Fax: 617-742-6880.*

WHYBARK, DAVID CLAY, business educator, researcher; b. Tacoma, Sept. 18, 1935; s. Clay Alfred and Irene (Stanton) W.; m. Neva Jo Richardson, July 6, 1957; children: Michael David, Suzanne Marie (dec.). BS, U. Wash., 1957; MBA, Cornell U., 1960; PhD, Stanford U., 1967. Rsch. assoc. Stanford (Calif.) U., 1962-67; asst. prof. Ariz. State U., Tempe, 1965-66; assoc. prof. Purdue U., West Lafayette, Ind., 1967-76; prof. Ind. U., Bloomington, 1976—90; Macon G. Patton disting. prof. U. NC, Chapel Hill, 1990—2008, emeritus prof., 2008—; academic advisor Inst. Defense & Bus., 2005—. Vis. prof. Shanghai Inst. Mech. Engring., 1986-87, Chinese U. of Hong Kong, 1996, Victoria U., New Zealand, 1996, Canterbury U., New Zealand, 1996; adj. prof. Inst. for Mgmt. Devel., Lausanne, Switzerland, 1981-82, 85-90; dir., founder Global Mfg. Rsch. Group, 1990—; cons. in field. Author: Master Production Scheduling: Theory and Practice, 1979, Manufacturing Planning Control Systems, 1984, International Operations Management, 1989, Integrated Production and Inventory Management, 1993, Why ERP?, 2000, Manufacturing Planning and Control Systems for Supply Chain Management, 2004; editor: Internat. Jour. Prodn. Econs., 1991-95, Global Manufacturing Practices, 1993. Recipient Lilly Alumni MBA Tchg. Excellence award, 1990, Disting. Rsch. award, Kenan-Flagler Sch., 1998. Fellow: Pan Pacific Bus. Assn. (mem. coun., Disting. Global Leadership award 2007), Ops. Mgmt. Assn. (pres. 1992—93), Internat. Soc. Inventory Rsch. (mem. coun., pres. 2000—02), Decision Scis. Inst. (past pres., Disting. Svc. award 1984). Avocations: travel, winemaking. Office: U NC Kenan-Flagler Sch Chapel Hill NC 27599-3490 Office Phone: 919-962-3206. Business E-Mail: clay_whybark@unc.edu.

WHYBROW, PETER CHARLES, psychiatrist, educator, director, author; b. Hertfordshire, Eng., June 13, 1939; U.S. citizenship, 1975; s. Charles Ernest and Doris Beatrice (Abbott) W.; children: Katherine, Helen Student, U. Coll., London, 1956—59; MB BS, U. Coll., 1962; diploma psychol. medicine, Conjoint Bd., London, 1968; MA (hon.), Dartmouth Coll., 1974, U. Pa., 1994. House officer endocrinology U. Coll. Hosp., 1962, sr. house physician psychiatry, 1963—64; house surgeon St. Helier Hosp., Surrey, England, 1963; house officer pediat. Prince of Wales Hosp., London, 1964; resident psychiatry U. N.C. Hosp., 1965—67, instr., rsch. fellow, 1967—68; mem. sci. staff neuropsychiat. rsch. unit Charshalton, Surrey, 1968—69; dir. residency tng. psychiatry Dartmouth Med. Sch., Hanover, NH, 1969—71, prof. psychiatry, 1970—84, chmn. dept., 1970—78, exec. dean, 1980—83; prof., chmn. dept. psychiatry U. Pa., Phila., 1984—96, Ruth Meltzer prof. psychiatry, 1992; chief psychiatrist Hosp. U. Pa., 1984—96; prof. psychiatry and biobehavioral scis., chmn. dept. psychiatry Sch. Medicine UCLA, 1996—, dir. Semel Inst. for Neurosci. and Human Behavior, 1996—, physician-in-chief Neuropsychiat. Hosp., 1996—, Judson Braun disting. prof. psychiatry, 1999—. Dir. psychiatry Dartmouth Hitchock Affiliated Hosp., 1970-78; vis. scientist NIMH, 1978-79; cons. VA, 1970—, NIMH, 1972—; chmn. test com. Nat. Bd. Med. Examiners, 1977-84; rschr. psychoendrocrinology Author: Mood Disorders: Toward a New Psychobiology, 1984, The Hibernation Response, 1988, A Mood Apart, 1997, American Mania: When More Is Not Enough, 2005 (Gradiva Book award, Nat. Assn. Advancement Psychoanalysis, 2006); editor: Psychosomatic Medicine, 1977 (Ann. Book award NAMI 2005); mem. editl. bd. Cmty. Psychiatry, Psychiat. Times, Directions in Psychiatry, Neuropsychopharmacology, Depression; contbr. articles to profl. jours Recipient Anclote Manor award psychiat. rsch. U. N.C., 1967, Sr. Investigator award Nat. Alliance for Rsch. into Schizophrenia and Depression, 1989; scholar Josiah Macy Jr. Found., 1978-79, vis. scholar Oxford U., 2009-; fellow Ctr. Advanced Studies in Behavioral Sci., Stanford, 1993-94; recipient Lifetime Investigator award NDMDA, 1996; decorated Knight of Merit, Sovereign Order of St. John of Jerusalem, 1993; Disting. Prof. U. Calif., 2004, Silver Ribbon award Pw Sci. Leadership NARSAD, 2008. Fellow AAAS, Am. Psychiat. Assn., Royal Coll. Psychiatrists (founder), Am. Coll. Psychiatrists, Ctr. Advanced Study of Behavioral Scis. (hon.), Soc. Psychosomatic Rsch. London (hon.); mem. Am. Assn. Chmn. Depts. Psychiatry (pres. 1977-78), Royal Soc. Medicine, Am. Psychopath Assn., Am. Coll. Neuropsychopharmacology, Soc. Biol. Psychiatry, N.Y. Acad. Scis., Soc. Neurosci., Sigma Xi, Alpha Omega Alpha Office: UCLA Semel Inst Neuroscience & Human Behavior 760 Westwood Plz Los Angeles CA 90095-8353 Office Phone: 310-206-1233. Fax: 310-825-3942. Business E-Mail: pwhybrow@mednet.ucla.edu.

WHYTE, BRUCE LINCOLN, management executive, Marketing Consultant; b. NYC, Mar. 13, 1941; s. Lincoln Dodge and Louise (Connor) W. BS, Fordham U., NY, 1962; MS, NYU, 1963; PhD in Bus. Adminstrn., San Francisco Internat. U., 2005. Editor corp. planning Am. Airlines, NYC, 1963—65; sr. mktg. analyst Ea. Airlines, NYC, 1965—67; ptnr. Internat. Devel. Corp., NYC, 1966—69; chmn. Crossley-Whyte Aircraft, London, 1967—70; v.p. Deckcraft Corp., NYC, 1967—69; pres. Hunter-Whyte Prodns., NYC, 1969—72; founder, pres. Original Print Collectors Group, NYC, 1972; chmn. bd. OPCG (Subs. Reader's Digest), NYC, 1980—84; pres. Bruce Whyte Enterprises, internat. fine arts bus., NYC, 1984—92, Bruce Whyte Bus. Devel. Co., 1998—, Bruce Whyte Cons., 1998—. Cons. mktg. The Prudential Co., N.Y.C., 1986, Am. Express, 1987; sr. mktg. cons. A.R.T. Corp., 1988; bus. cons. Mystic Seaport Mus., Mass., 1990-; Am. Art liaison Dr. of the World, Paris, 1992; chmn. Bus. Incubator Group Corp. Kingston, N.Y., 1993-; gen. mgr. Sherpa's Pet Trading Co., N.Y.C., 1996; exec. v.p. Sanctuary, Inc., 1996-99, chmn. nat. bd. advisors, 2000-, v.p. bd. dir., 2004-; cons. N.Y. State coun. on the Arts, 1996-97; registered expert witness Dept. Treasury, 1983-; mng. dir. Venture Capital Forum, 1995-96; tech. assistance program cons. N.Y. State Govt., 1996-; trustee Integrity Global Asset Mgmt., 1999-2001; gen. devel. dir. First Alert, Rockville Centre, N.Y., 1998-2002; pres. disaster recovery plans and response devel. Disaster Recovery Experts, Inc., Rockville Centre, 1999-2002; trustee Dow Jones Internet Index Fund/Dow Jones, Global Biotech. Index Fund, Dow Jones Global Wireless Commn. Fund Index, Wakefield, RI, 1999-2001; hon. chmn. Congl. Bus. Adv. Coun., 2002, spkr. Congress, 2003—; dep. dir. gen. Am.'s Internat. Biog. Ctr., 2000—. Editor: Art Newsletter OPCG Newsletter, 1972-84 (Best award in U.S.A. 1983-84). Sr. advisor U.S. Congl. Adv. Bd., Washington, 1981-83; chmn. Com. U.S. Senatorial Bus. Adv. Bd., Washington, 1981-83, 2002—; advisor NY Dept. State, 1993; trustee, v.p. Hist. Preservation Soc., NYC 1986-92, U.S. art liaison Found. Mitterand (The Universal Declaration of Human Rights) on behalf of Amnesty Internat., UN, UNESCO, High Commn. on Refugees, Nat. Mus., Heads of State, Paris, NYC, 1989; consumer art protection legis. advisor, atty. gen. NY State Senate and Assembly, 1981; pres. Ulster Arts Alliance, 1993-96; chmn. Kingston Carnegie Libr./Pub. Mus., 1993, Mus. Arts and Tech. Old City Hall, 1994-95; trustee Entrepreneurial Catalyst Forum, 1994-96; advisor Congl. Bus. Commn., 2002—, sustaining hon. chmn., 2003—; Conn. Congl. Com. voting del. to U.S. Congress, The White House and IRS, 2002—; Silver Anniversary mem. Rep. Presdl. Task Force, 1981-2008; mem. nat. adv. bd. Am. Security Coun., 1981-2005; dep. dir. gen. Ams. Internat. Biog. Ctr., 2002—, presenter of NYC homeland security awards to former NYC police commr. Bernard Kerrick on behalf of Sept. 11 disaster recovery efforts, 2002, and police commr. Raymond Kelly, 2003; dep. dir. gen. for Americas of the Internat. Biog. Ctr., Eng., 2002-; hon. co-chmn. Ann. Formal Pres.'s Dinner, 2003, Ann. Bus. Adv. Coun. Bd. Meeting honoring Pres. George W. Bush, 2003. Recipient Best of Art Catalogues award, Sroge Colorado Springs, 1983, Gold medal Congress Majority Whip Tom DeLay, 2002-03, Internat. Order of Merit, 2003, U.S. Senate Medal of Freedom, Century Proclamation and Gold medal Internat. Biog. Ctr., Cambridge, Eng., 2003; named to U.S. Congl. Bus. Honor Roll, 2002, Nat. Rep. Exec. Com. Congl. Spkrs. Cir., 2002; Artist fellow, 1988—; named U.S. Businessman of Yr. Congl. Bus. Adv. Coun., 2003, 2004. Mem. Fine Arts Publ. Assn. (bd. dirs. 1984—), Nat. Arts Club (gov., treas. 1972-74, 86—), U.S. C. of C. Home and Office: 109 Grace St Fairfield CT 06825 Personal E-mail: bruce.whyte@snet.net.

WHYTE, MARY CHRISTINA, pediatrician; b. Waterford, Ireland, Apr. 2, 1962; d. Jack and Catherine Claire Merry; m. Joseph M. Whyte, Aug. 14, 1997; children: Campbell Claire, Killian Gerard. MB, BAO, U. Coll. Dublin, BCh, 1985, MD, 2000. Specialist physician European Union, 1999. Rsch. fellow, Children's Rsch. Ctr. Our Lady's Children's Hosp., Dublin, 1994—95, sr. registrar pediat. surgery, 1996—99; fellow pediat. laparoscopy U. Tenn., Memphis, 1997; attending pediat. surgeon Meml. Hosp., Colo. Springs, 2000—01, Children's Hosp. Montefiore, Albert Einstein Coll. Medicine, Bronx, NY, 2001—. Contbr. articles to profl. jours. Fellow: RCS (Ireland) (gen. surgery resident 1985—93, Accreditation in Pediat. Surgery 1998), ACS; mem.: NY Pediat. Soc., Internat. Pediatric Endosurg. Group, Am. Pediat. Surg. Assn. Office: Children's Hosp Montefiore 111 E 210 St Bronx NY 10467

WHYTE, MICHAEL P., genetics educator, researcher, director; b. NYC, Dec. 19, 1946; s. Michael Paul and Sophie (Dziuk) W.; m. Gloria Frances Golenda, Oct. 26, 1974; 1 child, Catherine Alexandra. BA in Chemistry, NYU, 1968; MD, SUNY, Bklyn., 1972. Diplomate Am. Bd. Internal Medicine, Nat. Bd. Med. Examiners. Intern, 1st yr. resident dept. medicine NYU Sch. Medicine Bellevue Hosp., NYC, 1972-74; clin. assoc. devel. and metabolic neurology br. Nat. Inst. Neurol. and Communicative Disorders and Stroke NIH, Bethesda, Md., 1974-76; fellow divsn. bone and mineral metabolism dept. medicine Washington U. Sch. Medicine, 1976-79, instr. dept. medicine, 1979-80, asst. sci. dir. Clin. Rsch. Ctr., 1979—; asst. physician Barnes Hosp., 1979—; staff physician St. Louis Children's Hosp., 1979—; NIH clin. assoc. physician Clin. Rsch. Ctr. Washington U. Sch. Medicine, 1980-82, asst. prof. medicine dept. medicine, 1980-86, assoc. prof. medicine dept. medicine, 1986-91, asst. prof. pediat. Edward Mallinckrodt dept. pediat., 1982-89, assoc. prof. pediat. Edward Mallinckrodt dept. pediat., 1989-92, prof. medicine dept. medicine, 1991—, prof. pediat. Edward Mallinckrodt dept. pediat., 1992—, prof. genetics James S. McDonell dept. genetics, 1997—; med. dir. Metabolic Rsch. Unit Shriners Hosp. for Children, St. Louis, 1982-2000, mem. staff, 1983—; assoc. attending physician Jewish Hosp., 1983—. Mem. editl. bd. Calcified Tissue Internat., 1995-2000, Jour. Bone and Mineral Rsch., 1994—; med. adv. bd. Osteogenesis Imperfecta Found., 1986—, med. adv. panel Paget's Disease Found., 1986—; chmn. med. adv. com., bd. dirs. Osteogenesis Found., 1995—; med.-sci. dir. Ctr. for Metabolic Bone Disease and Molecular Rsch. Shriners Hosp. for Children, St. Louis, 2000—. Assoc. editor: Primer on Metabolic Bone Diseases and Disorders of Mineral Metabolism, 1990, 93, 96, 99, 2003, 06; assoc. editor Calcified Tissue Internat., 1989-2000; contbr. chpts. to books, articles to profl. jours. Lt. comdr. USPHS, 1974-76. Fellow Am. Coll. Endocrinology; mem. ACP (assoc.), Assn. Am. Physicians, Am. Soc. Cell Biology, Am. Soc. Clin. Investigation, Am. Fedn. Clin. Rsch., Am. Soc. Advancement Sci., Am. Soc. Bone and Mineral Rsch. (ednl. com. 1987—, Fuller Albright award 1987, Young Investigator award 1983, Dr. Boy Frame award 1997, Frederic C. Bartter award, 2007), Am. Soc. Human Genetics, Endocrine Soc., Soc. Exptl. Biology and Medicine, Japanese Soc. Inherited Metabolic Disease (hon.), NY Acad. Scis. Office: Shrinens Hosp Children 2001 S Lindbergh Blvd Saint Louis MO 63131 Office Phone: 314-872-8305. Business E-Mail: mwhyte@shrinenet.org.

WHYTE, NANCY MARIE, performing arts educator; b. Myrtlepoint, Oreg., Mar. 12, 1948; d. Lawrence Edward and Carol Elizabeth (Johnson) Guderian; m. Anthony John Whyte, Aug. 7, 1967 (div. Sept. 1968); 1 child, Charles Lawrence; m. Douglas Brian Graff, June 27, 1971 (div. Oct. 1974); m. Lawrence Hanson, Mar. 12, 1976 (div. Aug. 1984); m. Joseph Paul Deacon, Aug. 10, 1985; 1 child, Nina Alexandra. Student, U. Wash., 1969-72, Am. Sch. Dance, 1972; BA, Evergreen State Coll., 1987. Owner, dir. Nancy Whyte Sch. Ballet, Bellingham, Wash., 1969—; artistic dir. Garden Street Dance Players, Bellingham, 1969-72, MT Baker Ballet, Bellingham, 1975—, Alpha and Omega Worship Dancers, 2003—07; co-dir. Exptl. Performance Workshop, Bellingham, 1975-77; instr. creative dance St. Paul's Primary Sch., Bellingham, 1993-97; facilitator dance workshop Allied Arts/Whatcom Co., Bellingham, 1995—. Guest lectr. Western Wash. U., Bellingham, 1976—83, 1996—2003; guest faculty Dance Theatre N.W., Tacoma, 1995—2001; liturgical dance cons. Assumption Cath. Sch., 2001—05; artistic dir. Alpha and Omega Worship Dancers, 2003—07. Author: Memoirs of a Child of Theatre Street, 1993; soloist Raduga Folk Ballet/N.Y. Character Ballet, N.Y.C., 1978-79; choreographer numerous ballets, 1972—. Mem. Nat. Dance Assn., Dancers Over 40, Sacred Dance Guild, Vancouver Ballet Soc. Democrat. Avocations: voice, writing. Office: MT Baker Ballet 1412 Cornwall Ave PO Box 2393 Bellingham WA 98227-2393 Office Phone: 360-734-9141. Personal E-mail: isadorables@msn.com.

WHYTE, RICHARD IAN, surgeon; b. Brighton, England, July 4, 1958; MD, U. Of Pitts., 1979—83; MBA, Wharton Sch. U. Pa., 2006. Head divsn. thoracic surgery Stanford U. Med. Ctr., Calif., 1997—2008, prof. cardiothoracic surgery, 2008—. Med. dir. operating rooms Stanford U. Med. Ctr., 2001—06, dir. med. informatics, 2006—08. Office: Cvrb 205 300 Pasteur Dr Stanford CA 94305 E-mail: riwhyte@stanford.edu.

WIANT, SARAH KIRSTEN, law librarian, educator, director; b. Waverly, Iowa, Nov. 20, 1946; d. James Allen and Eva (Jorgensen) Wiant; m. Robert E. Akins (dec.). BA, Western State Coll., 1968; MLS, U. North Tex., 1970; JD, Washington & Lee U., 1978. Asst. law libr. Tex. Tech. U., 1970—72, Washington & Lee U., Lexington, Va., 1972—78, dir. Law Libr., 1978—, asst. prof. law, 1978-83, assoc. prof. law, 1984-92, prof. law, 1993—. Participant Conf. on Fair Use, NII, 1995—98; visitor U. Melbourne, Monash U., 2001. Co-author: Copyright Handbook, 1984, Libraries and Copyright: A Guide to Copyright Law in the 1990s, 1994, UCITA Encyclopedia of Lib. and Information Science, 2009; co-author: (Va. sect.) Legal Research in the District of Columbia, Maryland and Virginia, 2005; co-author: (admiralty chpt.) Specialized Legal Research, 2009; co-author: Developments on Copyright Law, Bowker Annual, 2009; mem. adv. bd. Westlaw, 1988—93, 2003—; contbr. chapters to books. Mem.: ABA (com. on librs. 1987—93), U.S. Trademark Assn., Maritime Law Assn., Spl. Librs. Assn. (chair copyright com. 1990—96, John Cotton Dana award 1997), Am. Assn. Law Schs. (chmn. sec. on librs. 1990—92, accreditation com. 1991—94), Am. Assn. Law Librs. (mem. exec. bd. 1981—84, mem. copyright com. 1990—94, chmn. 2003—04, copyright office rep., Pres.' award 2001, Spl. Dist. Svc. award Southeastern chpt. 1997). Office: Washington & Lee U Law Libr Lewis Hall Lexington VA 24450 Office Phone: 540-458-8543. Business E-Mail: wiants@wlu.edu.

WIARDA, IÊDA SIQUEIRA, political scientist, educator; b. Belo Horizonte, Brazil, Nov. 3, 1939; came to U.S., 1957, naturalized, 1968; d. Elvindo Dutra and Maria (Barros) S.; B.A., Nebr. Wesleyan U., 1960; M.A., U. Fla., 1962, Ph.D., 1968; m. Howard J. Wiarda, Feb. 4, 1964; children: Kristy Lynn, Howard Elvindo, Jonathan Siqueira. Research assoc. U. Mass., Amherst, 1972; faculty assoc. Smith Coll., 1978; now professorial lectr., course chmn. U. Mass., 1968-69, Fgn. Service Inst./Dept. State, 1983-84, George Washington U., 1986-87, Libr. Congress, Washington, 1990—; lectr. Bus. Council for Internat. Understanding, Am. U.; guest lectr. Nebr. Wesleyan U., U. Fla., New Coll., Fla., Mt. Holyoke Coll., Smith Coll.; cons. population policies. Grantee Ford Found., Rockefeller Found., NIH. Mem. Am. Polit. Sci. Assn., Latin Am. Studies Assn., Population Assn. Am., Am. Public Health Assn., New Eng. Council Latin Am. Studies, World Population Soc., World Future Soc., Conselho Nacional de Mulheres, Nat. Council Hispanic Women, Assn. for Women in Devel., Internat. Women's Health Coalition (dir.), Amherst Growth Com., Kestrel Fund, AAUW (v.p. Conn. Valley br.). Republican. Contbr. articles, chpts. to profl. publs. Office: Libr Congress Hispanic Dv Washington DC 20540-0001

WIATT, JIM (JAMES ANTHONY WIATT), talent agency executive; b. L.A., Oct. 18, 1946; s. Norman and Catherine (Sonners) W.; m. Elizabeth Wiatt; children: Isabel, Caroline BA in History & Philosophy, U. So. Calif., 1969. Campaign coord. Tunney for Senate, LA, 1969-71; adminstrv. asst. to Senator John V. Tunney US Senate, LA, 1972-75; agt. FCA, LA, 1976-78; lit. agt. Internat. Creative Mgmt. Inc., LA, 1978-81, motion picture agt., 1981-83, head, motion picture dept., 1983-85, pres., co-CEO, 1985—98; pres., CEO William Morris Agy., Beverly Hills, Calif., 1999—2009; chmn. William Morris Endeavor Entertainment (WME), Beverly Hills, Calif., 2009. Mem. bd. councilors USC Sch. Cinema-TV; mem. bd. govs. Music Ctr. L.A., Am. Film Inst.; mem. exec. bd. med. scis. UCLA; exec. coun. The Quills; bd. dirs. William Morris Agy. Inc., 2004—. Named one of The 50 Most Powerful People in Hollywood, Premiere mag., 2004—06.*

WIBERG, DONALD MARTIN, electrical engineering educator, consultant; b. Battle Creek, Mich., Sept. 20, 1936; s. Martin and Lina (Havstein) W.; children: Erik M., Kristin A., Kenneth C. BS, Calif. Inst. Tech., 1959, MS, 1960, PhD, 1965. Registered profl. engr., Calif. Sr. design engr. Convair, San Diego, 1964-65; asst. prof. elec. engring. UCLA, 1965-71, assoc. prof., 1971-77, prof., 1977-94, prof. anesthesiology, 1979-94, vice chmn. dept. elec. engring., 1985-86, prof. emeritus, 1994-2001; prof. emeritus dept. elec. engring. U. Calif., Santa Cruz, 2001—, rsch. prof. Ctr. for Adaptive Optics, 2002—, prof. emeritus dept. computer engring., 2009—. Cons. in field; vis. prof. German Rsch. Orgn. for Air and Space Flight, Munich, 1969-70, dept. elec. engring. and computer sci. U. Newcastle, Australia, 1989-90, Inst. Sys. Rsch., U. Md., College Park, 1994, Ajou U., Suwon, Korea, 2006. Author: State Space and Linear Systems, 1971; co-editor: Regulation of Breathing, 1983. Mem. adv. bd. Parthenia Sch., Los Angeles, 1971-74. Sr. NATO research fellow KFZ Karlsruhe, W.Ger., 1973; sr. Fulbright fellow, Copenhagen, 1976-77, Trondheim, Norway, 1983-84 Fellow IEEE (applications assoc. editor Trans. on Automatic Control 1983, assoc. editor-at-large 1987-89, 92-94, named Congl. fellow legis. asst. office Senator Tom Harkin, D-IA 1995), Am. Physiol. Soc. (assoc. editor Modelling Methodology Forum 1980-91), Sigma Xi. Home: 2395 Delaware Ave #153 Santa Cruz CA 95060-5716

WIBERG, LARS-ERIK, occupational compatibility consultant; b. Wakefield, Mass., June 1, 1928; s. Sverker Claesson and Ingrid (Heurlin) W.; m. Elizabeth Margaret (Allenbrook), Oct. 18, 1957; children: Kirsten, Margaret, Brenda. BS in Geology, MIT, 1950; MAT, Harvard U., 1952. From engr. to dir. corp. comm. EG and G Inc., Boston and Bedford, Mass., 1956—69; from asst. v.p. to v.p. compensation, orgnl. planning and ombudsman for officers First Nat. Bank of Boston, 1969—81; cons. Rockport, Mass., 1981—. Lectr. human resources mgmt. Boston U., 1988—92; lectr. job search and career planning U. Karlstad, Sweden, 1992; corporator Granite Savs. Bank, Rockport, Mass., 1981—. Author: It's Your Move, 1991; inventor in the field of Occupl. Compatibility; interviewed in Rockport Recollected. Mem. Gov. John A. Volpe's Mgmt. Engring. Task Force, 1965; mem. planning bd., Rockport, 1965-72, chmn., 1969-72; pres. ch. coun. Swedenborg Chapel, Cambridge, Mass., 1984-2004; dir. Mass. New Ch. Union, 1990-2004; mem. zoning bd. appeals, Rockport, 1986-, chmn., 2006-07, chmn. Rockport site rev. com., 1999-2001; v.p., founder The Uses Trust, Ltd., 2005—09, pres. 2009-. 1st lt. USAF, 1953—55. Mem. Affiliated New Eng. Cons. (founding mem. Lexington, Mass. 1985), Life Ext. Found., Heritage Found., Swedenborg Sci. Assn. Avocations: church work, home repair, music, cooking, reading. Home and Office: 90 South St Rockport MA 01966-1916 Business E-Mail: bjara@gis.net.

WIBLE, ANDY, philosopher, educator; b. North Manchester, Ind., Feb. 25, 1970; s. Dan and Nancy Wible; life ptnr. Oliver Songlinco. PhD, Wayne State U., Detroit, 2000. Instr. philosophy Muskegon CC, Mich., 2000—, dir. Ethics Inst., 2006—. Bd. mem. ACLU, Grand Rapids, Mich., 2005—08. GPA Fulbright grant, US Govt., 2003. Mem.: Soc. Lesbian and Gay Philosophy (co-chair 2004—08). Home: 1977 Addison St Muskegon MI 49441 Office: Muskegon CC 221 S Quarterline Dr Muskegon MI 49441 Business E-Mail: andy.wible@muskegoncc.edu.

WICHA, MAX S., oncologist, educator; b. NYC, Mar. 24, 1949; m. Sheila Crowley; children: Jason, Allyson. BS in Biology summa cum laude with honors, SUNY, Stony Brook, 1970; MD, Stanford U., 1974. Diplomate Am. Bd. Internal Medicine; lic. physician, Mich., Ill. Intern in internal medicine U. Chgo. Hosps. and Clinics, 1974-75, jr., sr. resident in internal medicine, 1975-77; rsch. assoc. lab. pathophysiology Nat. Cancer Inst./NIH, Bethesda, Md., 1977-79, fellow in clin. oncology, 1978-80, investigator lab. pathophysiology, 1979-80; asst. prof. internal medicine divsn. hematology and oncology U. Mich., Ann Arbor, 1980-83, assoc. prof., 1983-88, prof. internal medicine, disting. prof. oncology, 1988—, mem. tumor metastasis, extracellular matrix, reproductive endocrinology programs, 1982—, chief, divsn. hematology and oncology, dept. internal medcine, dir. Simpson Meml. Rsch. Inst., 1984-93, mem. program in cellular and molecular biology, 1984—, founding dir. Comprehensive Cancer Ctr., 1987—. Mem. cancer rsch. com. U. Mich., 1981—, sci. adv. bd. dental rsch. inst., 1983—, dean's adv., 1988—, reproductive endocrinology selection com., breast care ctr. exec. com., 1988—, exec. dir.'s adv. coun., 1992—, chair instl. rev. com. gene therapy program project., 1992—, dean's adv. com. Howard Hughes Med. Inst., 1992—, strategic planning policy and organizational com. health scis. info. tech. and networking, 1992—; vis. prof. Mich. State U., 1985, Harvard U., Boston, 1986, Wash. State U., 1986, Boston U., 1986, Wayne State U./Harper Grace Hosps., 1987, U. Ill., 1987, Med. Coll. Wis., 1987., U. Chgo., 1987, Eppley Inst. for Rsch. in Cancer and Allied Diseases, Omaha, 1988, U. Nebr., Omaha, 1988, U. Minn./Minn. VA Hosp., 1988, MD Anderson Cancer Ctr., Houston., Mt. Sinai Med. Ctr., N.Y.C., Am. Cancer Soc., Kalamazoo, 1989, Gainesville, Fla., 1990, Orlando, Fla., 1990, Pezcoller Symposium, Rovereto, Italy, 1990, Prince Henry's Hosp., Melbourne, Australia, 1990, Northwestern U. Med. Ctr., Chgo., 1990, Meml. Sloan-Kettering Cancer Ctr., N.Y.C., 1990, Tex. S.W. U., Dallas, 1990, Mich. State U., 1991; lectr. U. Mich., 1990; mem. NIH Site Visit team U. Calif. Cancer Rsch. Lab., Berkeley, 1985; ad hoc mem. cell biology and physiology study sect. NIH, 1985, 86, study sect., Bethesda, 1991; mem. NCI Site Visit team Norris Cotton Dartmouth Cancer Ctr, 1989, Howard U., Wash., 1989, Howard U. Parent Com., 1989, MD Anderson Cancer Ctr., Houston, 1992; sci. advisor U. Colo. Cancer Ctr., Denver, 1990, Samuel Waxman Cancer Rsch. Found., Mt. Sinai Med. Ctr., N.Y.C., 1988-93; mem. NCI Adv. Panel, Bethesda, 1991; mem. sci. adv. com. U. Tex. San Antonio Cancer Ctr., U. Miami Sylvester Cancer Ctr., Mich. State U., East Lansing, Norris-Cotton Cancer Ctr., Dartmouth-Hitchcock Med. Ctr., Hanover, N.H., Mich. Cancer Found., Detroit, V. T. Lombardi Cancer Rsch. Ctr., Georgetown U., Washington, 1992—, MD Anderson Cancer Ctr., Houston, 1992—; mem. extramural sci. adv. bd. UCI Clin. Cancer Ctr., U. Calif. Irvine, Orange, 1992—; mem. NCI SPORE in Prostate Cancer Study Sect., 1992; chair NCI Cancer Ctr. Support Rev. Com., 1993; NCI Site Visit chair Jefferson Cancer Ctr., Phila., 1992, Worcester (Mass.) Cancer Found., 1993, Duke U. Cancer Ctr., Durham, N.C., 1993, Lineberger Comprehensive Ctr., Chapel Hill, N.C., 1993; mem. NCI Comprehensive Cancer Ctrs. Review, 1993, chmn. parent com. Cancer Ctr. Support Rev. Com., 1992—; cons. Warner Lambert Co., 1980—. Assoc. editor: Molecular and Cellular Differentiation, 1993; co-editor: The Hematopoietic Microenvironment, 1993; mem. editorial bd. Blood, Molecular and Cellular Differentiation, Jour. Lab. and Clin. Medicine, Cancer Rsch., 1993—, Oncology, Cancer Prevention Internat.; reviewer Nature, Science, Proceedings of NAS, Jour. Clin. Investigation, Jour. Cell Biology, Exptl. Cell Rsch., Exptl. Hematology, Cancer., Clin. and Exptl. Metastasis, Jour. Nat. Cancer Inst., Tissue & Cell, Am. Inst. Biol. Scis., Am. Jour. Pathology, Jour Immunology, Jour. Med. Scis., NSF, Oncology Rsch., Lab. Investigation, Breast Cancer Rsch. and Treatment; contbr. over 110 articles and to profl. jours., chpts. to books.; invited lectr. in field. With USPHS, 1977-80. Recipient NSF RSch. award SUNY, 1969, Eli Luke and David Jacob Rsch. award Stanford U. Sch. Medicine, 1974, Upjohn Achievement Excellence in Medicine award, Outstanding Med. Resident award U. Chgo. Hosps., 1977, Jerome Conn Excellence in Rsch. award, 1983; grantee NIH, 1991—, 93—, Am. Cancer Soc., 1992—, Suntory Rsch. Inst., 1992-93. Mem. AAASN, Am. Assn. for Cancer Rsch. (state legis. com. 1992—, finance com. 1992—), Am. Fedn. for Clin. Rsch. (selections com. midwest sect. 1986—, comm. com., 1986—, awards com., 1986—), Am. Soc. for Cell Biology, Am. Soc. Hematology (com. on publs. 1991-93), Assn. Am. Cancer Insts. (bd. dirs. 1993—), Am. Soc. for Clin. Investigation, Am. Soc. Clin. Oncology (award selection com. 1992—), Ctrl. Soc. for Clin. Rsch., Mich. Soc. Hematology and Oncology, Southwest Oncology Group, Assn. Community Cancer Ctrs. Achievements include patents for antibodies to human mammary cell growth inhibitor and methods of production and use, human mammary cell growth inhibitor and methods of production and use; research in regulation of cell growth and differentiation, molecular mechanisms of tumor metastasis. Mailing: U Mich Cancer Ctr Rm 6302 1500 E Medical Ctr Dr Ann Arbor MI 48109-0942 Office Phone: 734-936-1831. Office Fax: 734-615-3947. Business E-Mail: mwicha@umich.edu.

WICHER, CAMILLE PHYLLIS, nursing administrator; b. Buffalo, Dec. 11, 1955; m. Donald J. Wicher; 1 child, Christopher James. M.S. in Nursing, SUNY-Buffalo, 1983; postgrad. Sch. of Law, 1985-88. Registered nurse, N.Y. Charge nurse intensive care unit Roswell Park Meml. Inst., Buffalo, 1977-79; dir. inservice edn. Buffalo Columbus Hosp., 1979-82, dir. nursing, 1982-85; clin. instr. SUNY-Buffalo, 1981-82; law clk., 1985-88; Mem. Soc. Nursing Service Adminstrs. Democrat. Roman Catholic. Office: Offerman Cassano Pigott & Greco 1776 Statler Towers Buffalo NY 14202-7502

WICHERN, DEAN WILLIAM, business educator; b. Medford, Wis., Apr. 29, 1942; s. Arthur William and Rebecca Ann (Ambler) W.; m. Dorothy Jean Rutkowski, Dec. 7, 1968; children: Michael, Andrew. BS in Math., U. Wis., 1964, MS in Stats., 1965, PhD in Stats., 1969. Instr. Sch. Bus. U. Wis., Madison, 1967-69, asst. prof., 1969-72, assoc. prof., 1972-76, prof., 1976-84, chmn. quantitative analysis dept., 1975-78; prof. Mays Bus. Sch. Tex. A&M U., 1984—2006, head info. and ops. mgmt. dept., 1984—88, 1997—98, 2004—06, assoc. dean, 1988-95, John E. Pearson prof. bus. adminstrn., 1985—2006, prof. emeritus, 2006—. Vis. prof. Math. Rsch. Ctr., 1978-79. Co-author: Intermediate Business Statistics, 1977, Applied Multivariate Statistical Analysis, 6th edit., 2007, Business Statistics: Decision Making With Data, 1997, Business Forecasting, 9th edit., 2008; mem. editl. bd. Jour. Bus. and Econ. Stats., 1983—91. Mem. Beta Gamma Sigma, Phi Kappa Phi. Office: Tex A&M U Mays Bus Sch 4217 TAMU College Station TX 77843-4217 Home: 4782 Stonebriar Cir College Station TX 77845-8987 Business E-Mail: d-wichern@tamu.edu.

WICHMANN, DAVID S., health care services executive; Ptnr. Arthur Andersen; sr. v.p. corp. develop. UnitedHealth Group, Minnetonka, Minn., 1998—2004, pres., COO specialized care services, 2001—03, CEO specialized care services, 2003—04, pres., COO UnitedHealthcare, 2004—06, exec. v.p., pres. comml. group, 2006—08, exec. v.p., pres. group ops., 2008—. Office: UnitedHealth Group PO Box 1459 Minneapolis MN 55440-1459*

WICK, DOUGLAS, producer; m. Lucy Fisher; 3 children. Grad. cum laude, Yale U. Owner Red Wagon Prodns., Culver City, Calif. Assoc. prodr. Starting Over 1979; prodr. Wolf, 1994, The Craft, 1996, Hush, 1998, Working Girl (six Acad. Award Nomiations, five Golden Globes including Best Picture), 1988, Stuart Little, 1999, Girl, Interrupted, 1999, Gladiator, 2000, The Hollow Man, 2000, Stuart Little 2, 2002, Peter Pan, 2003, Win A Date With Tad Hamilton, 2004, Bewitched, 2005, Memoirs Of A Geisha, 2005, Jarhead, 2005. Recipient David O. Selznick Achievement award in Theatrical Motion Pictures, Producers Guild Am., 2007. Office: Red Wagon Prodns Hepburn West Bldg 10202 W Washington Blvd Culver City CA 90232 Fax: 310-244-1480.

WICK, MITCHELL A., physician; b. NYC, July 15, 1954; s. Edwin and Doris Wick. BA in Chemistry, U. South Fla., 1976; postgrad., U. Miami, Coral Gables, Fla., 1972—73; D.O., Kirksville Coll. Osteo. Medicine, Mo., 1980. Diplomate Am. Osteo. Bd. Family Physicians, Am. Acad. Pain Mgmt., Am. Assn. Integrative Medicine. Intern Southeastern Med. Ctr., N. Miami, Fla., 1980—81; resident Parkview Hosp., Toledo, 1981—83; staff physician Walk-in Family Medicine Ctr., Boynton Beach, Fla., 1983—86; physician Davie-Dania Med. Ctr., Fla., 1986—96; staff physician Meml. Pembroke Hosp., Pembroke Pines, Fla., 1991—. Author: Megaphysics, A New Look at the Universe, 2003. Mem.: Fla. Osteo. Med. Assn., Am. Osteo. Assn. Achievements include research and copywrite on physics theory regarding the fractal nature of spacetime manifolds and how matter and energy interact with thereof utilizing string theory. Avocations: physics, tensor calculus. Home: 25399 The Old Rd Unit 13110 Stevenson Ranch CA 91381-1627 Personal E-mail: mitchell598@comcast.net, wickmitchell@gmail.com.

WICK, ROBERT THOMAS, retired supermarket executive; b. St. Louis, Nov. 26, 1927; s. Robert Berninger and Katherine (Burke) W.; m. Virginia Rose Allen, Sept. 6, 1952; children: Susan, Patrick, Nancy, Robert J. BS, St. Louis U., 1955; cert. in food distbn., Mich. State U., 1956. Sales mgr. Nat. Tea Co., St. Louis, 1966-68, asst. div. mgr., 1968-69, div. mgr. Sioux City, Iowa, 1969-71, Milw., 1971-73, Chgo., 1973-74; v.p., gen. mgr. A&P Food Stores, Indpls., 1975-77; div. v.p. Colonial Food Stores- Grand Union, Norfolk, Va., 1977-79; pres., chief exec. officer Bonnie Be-Lo Markets, Inc., Norfolk, 1979-90, ret., 1990. Bd. dirs. Virginia Beach (Va.) Community Svcs. Bd., 1985-89; mem. adv. bd. Straight, Inc., Chesapeake, Va., 1987-91; dir. Community Alternatives, Inc., Virginia Beach, 1991-92. Tech. cpl. U.S. Army, 1946-48. Recipient Citizen of Yr. award St. Louis Argus Newspaper, 1968. Mem. Food Mktg. Inst. (bd. dirs. 1982-89), Va. Food Dealers Assn. (bd. dirs. 1981-87), Tidewater Retail Mchts. Assn. (pres., bd. dirs. 1981-91). Conservative. Roman Catholic. Avocations: travel, golf. Home: 801 Winthrope Dr Virginia Beach VA 23452-3940

WICK, WILLIAM SHINN, clergyman, chaplain, pastor; b. West Chester, Pa. s. William R. and Barbara (Shinn) W.; m. Debra R. Smith, Apr. 1, 1989; 1 child, Christopher R. BA, Trinity Internat. U., Deerfield, Ill., 1975; MDiv, Trinity Evang. Div. Sch., Deerfield, 1978. Ordained to ministry Evang. Free Ch. Am., 1978. Pastor Bradford (Vt.) Evang. Free Ch., 1978-85, Cornerstone Evangelical Fee Ch., Vt., 1985-89, Grace Evang. Free Ch., Northfield, Vt., 1989-96; chaplain Norwich U., Northfield, 1989—; interim pastor First Bapt. Ch., Barre, Vt., 2001—03, Resurrection Bapt. Ch., Montpelier, Vt., 2003—04, Orange Christian and Missionary Alliance Ch., 2004—05, Websterville Baptist Ch., 2006. Mem. bd. govs. Trinity Western U., Langley, B.C., Can., 1999-2008; mem. Evangelical Free Ch. Am. Chaplain's Commn., 2006—. Capt. CAP, 2005—. Mem.: Profl. Ski Instrs. Am. Avocations: alpine skiing, racquetball, tennis, scuba diving, sailing, astronomy. Home: 763 S Main St Northfield VT 05663-5718 Office: White Chapel Norwich U 158 Harmon Dr Northfield VT 05663-1035 Office Phone: 802-485-2128. Personal E-mail: theskiingrev@hotmail.com. Business E-Mail: chaplain@norwich.edu, wwick@norwich.edu.

WICKE, JASON, biochemist, educator; b. Kathmandu, Nepal, Nov. 11, 1972; m. Jo-Elle Wicke. PhD, Queen's U., Kingston, Ontario, Canada, 2006. Asst. prof. Tex. A&M-Commerce, Tex., 2006—. Office: Texas A&M Univ - Commerce 2600 South Neal St Commerce TX 75428 Office Fax: 903-886-5365. Business E-Mail: jason_wicke@tamu-commerce.edu.

WICKER, DOROTHY BALDWIN, physicist; b. Buffalo, Jan. 27, 1943; d. August A. and Dorothy (Smith) Cenkner; m. Frank J. Baldwin, Feb. 10, 1973 (dec. 1994); m. James E. Wicker, Aug. 9, 1996. BA in Physics (magna cum laude), Hartwick Coll., 1965; MA in Physics, Kent State U., 1968; PhD in Applied Mgmt. Decision Scis., Walden U., 1999. Cert. physics educator, N.J., Fla; cert. modeling and simulation profl. Nat. Tng. Sys. Assn./Nat. Def. Indsl. Assn., 2003. Physics instr. Kent (Ohio) State U., 1968-70; physics tchr. Watchung Hills (N.J.) High Sch., 1970-73, Edgewater High Sch., Orlando, Fla., 1973-77; adj. physics instr. Valencia Community Coll., Orlando, 1977, Fla. Tech. U., Orlando, 1975, 73; physicist Naval Tng. Equipment Ctr., Orlando, 1977-84; sr. engring. specialist Gen. Dynamics Corp. (now Lockheed Martin), Fort Worth, 1984-90; engring. project mgr. Gen. Dynamics Corp., Fort Worth, 1990-96, staff specialist, mgr., 1997—2001, prin. sys. engr., 2001—. Tech. program com. Inter Svc. Industry Tng. System Conf., 1987, 91, 92, 93. Contbr. articles to profl. jours. Co-founder Friendship Force Ft. Worth Metroplex, 1985, pres., 1990-93. Recipient Cost Savs. award Gen. Dynamics, 1986. Mem. NAFE, Nat. Def. Indsl. Assn. (life mem.), Nat. Mgmt. Assn., Women in Defense, Mensa, Friendship Force Internat., Sigma Xi. Achievements include patents in field. Home: 3436 Clayton Rd E Fort Worth TX 76116-7342 Office: Lockheed Martin Tactical Aircraft Sys MZ 8848 PO Box 748 Fort Worth TX 76101-0748 Office Phone: 817-935-4543. Business E-Mail: dorothy.b.wicker@lmco.com.

WICKER, JAMES EUGENE, retired psychologist; b. Whittenburg, Tex., Jan. 26, 1935; s. ELbert Shelton and Mrytle Blanche (Brown) W.; children: Tamra Michelle, David Andrew; m. Dorothy Baldwin, Aug. 9, 1996. AA, Del Mar Coll., 1955; BA in Psychology, U. Tex., 1960, MA, 1962; PhD in Clin. Psychology, Clayton U., 1989. Electronics technician various cos., Austin, Tex., 1953—57; tech. staff asst. II, rsch. scientist asst. Radiobiol. Lab. U. Tex. and USAF, 1957—64; cons. psychologist Austin and Ft. Worth, 1962—70; pvt. practice psychology Ft. Worth, 1970—2005; ret., 2005. Spl. instr. psychology U. Tex., 1964; human factors engr. Gen. Dynamics, Ft. Worth, 1964-65, sr. human factors psychologist, 1966-67; dir. Human Factors Lab., 1967-86; psychologist III Counseling Ctr. Tex. Christian U., Ft. Worth, 1987-89; clin. dir. Cherry Ln. Hosp., 1990-91; condr. seminars, lectr., cons. in field. Contbr. articles to profl. jours. Mem. APA (life), Tex. Psychol. Assn., Tarrant County Psychol. Assn. (pres. 1990-91), Mensa. Republican. Episcopalian. Avocations: hiking, camping, tennis, chess. Address: 3436 Clayton Rd E Fort Worth TX 76116-7342 Office Phone: 817-738-2339.

WICKER, ROGER FREDERICK, United States Senator from Mississippi; b. Pontotoc, Miss., July 5, 1951; s. Fred and Wordna Wicker; m. Gayle Long; children: Margaret, Caroline, McDaniel. BA in Polit. Sci. & Journalism, U. Miss., 1973; JD, Ole Miss Law Sch., 1975. Judge adv. USAF, 1976—80; mem. staff rules com. Staff of US Rep. Trent Lott, 1980-82; ptnr. Sparks, Wicker, and Colburn, 1982—94; pub. defender Lee County, Miss., 1984—87; judge pro tem Mcpl. Ct. City of Tupelo, 1986—87; mem. Miss. State Senate, 1987—94, US Congress from 1st Miss. dist., 1995—2007, dep. majority whip; mem. appropriations com., 1995—2007, budget com., 2003—07, Rep. Policy Com., 2001—07, House Task Force for a Drug Free America; US Senator from Miss., 2007—. Mem. Cmty. Devel. Found., Lions Club, Tupelo First Baptist Church, Miss. With USAF, 1976—80, positions up to lt. col. USAFR, 1980—2004. Recipient Nat. Pub. Svc. award, Am. Heart Assn., 1998, Capitol Dome award, Am. Cancer Soc., 2003, Award, Mfg. Excellence, NAM, 2003. Republican. Baptist. Office: US Senate 487 Russell Senate Office Bldg Washington DC 20510*

WICKERT, JONATHAN ADAM, engineering educator; b. El Paso, Tex. BS, U. Calif.-Berkeley, 1985, MS, 1987, PhD, 1989. Rsch. fellow U. Cambridge, England, 1989—90; prof. mech. engring. Carnegie Mellon U., Pitts., 1990—2007; prof. Iowa State U., Ames, 2007—, mech. engring. dept. chair, 2007—09, chair, coll. engr., 2009—. Mem. Wickert Consulting Svcs. LLC, Allison Park, Pa., 2003—. Author: (textbook) An Introduction to Mechanical Engineering, (articles) Applied Mechanics Revs., Internat. Jour. Nonlinear Mechanics, Jour. Acoustical Soc. Am., Shock and Vibration Digest, Jour. Vibration and Acoustics, Jour. Manufacturing Sci. and Engring., Jour. Tribology, Jour. Micromechanics and Microengring.; associate editor Jour. Info. Storage Systems. Recipient George Tallman Ladd Rsch. award, Carnegie Mellon U., 1993, Ralph Teetor Ednl. award, Soc. Automotive Engrs., 1996, Marsha and Philip Dowd Faculty Fellowship, Carnegie Mellon U., 1998, Benjamin Teare Ednl. award, 2000, Curtis McGraw Rsch. award, Am. Soc. for Engring. Edn., 2002, Tech. Achievement award, Info. Storage Industry Consortium, 2003, Curriculum Innovation award, ASME, 2005; grantee rsch. in dynamics, applied mechanics, and vibration, NSF, 1991—2006; fellow, NSF/NATO, 1989—90. Fellow: ASME; mem.: AAUP, Soc. Automotive Engrs., Am. Soc. Engring. Edn. Achievements include patents for damper for brake noise reduction; research in high-density computer data storage; machine dynamics; manufacture of sheet metal, fiberglass, polymer materials; design of automotive disk brakes. Avocations: long distance running, woodworking. Office: Iowa State Univ Coll Engring 104 Marston Ames IA 50011 Business E-Mail: wickert@iastate.edu.

WICKESBERG, ALBERT KLUMB, retired management consultant; b. Neenah, Wis., Apr. 2, 1921; s. Albert Henry and Lydia (Klumb) W.; m. Dorothy Louise Ahrensfeld, Oct. 28, 1944; children— Robert, William, James. BA, Lawrence Coll., 1943; MBA, Stanford U., 1948; PhD, Ohio State U., 1955. Staff accountant S.C. Johnson & Son, Inc., Racine, Wis., 1948-50; asst. prof. Sacramento State Coll., 1950-51; prof. U. Minn., Mpls., 1953-86, prof. emeritus, 1987—, chmn. dept. bus. adminstrn., 1959-62, dir. grad. studies, 1963-66, chmn. dept. mgmt. and transp., 1971-77. Author: Management Organization, 1966. Served with AUS, 1943-46, 51-52. Soc. Advancement Mgmt. fellow, 1972 Mem. Acad. Mgmt., Soc. Advancement Mgmt. (pres. Twin Cities chpt. 1961-62). Congregationalist. Home: 3663 Park Ctr Blvd #413 St Louis Pk Minneapolis MN 55416-2585

WICKESSER, THOMAS A., finance company executive; s. Robert and Eleanor A. Wickesser; 1 child, Thomas A. AS in Electronics, Merced Coll., Calif.; BA in Mgmt., NW Christian U., Eugene, Oreg., 2003, MBA, 2005. Cert. biomed. equipment technician AAMI, 1989. Asst. front line mgr. Legacy Health Sys., Portland, Oreg., 2005—06; dir., biomed. engring. Med1Online, Golden, Colo., 2006—07; fin. mgr. Exempla St. Joseph Hosp., Denver, 2007—. Sergant USMC, 1974—76, Camp Lejeune. Fellow: Am. Soc. Healthcare Engrs. Home: 15916 W 60th Cir Golden CO 80403 Personal E-mail: twickesser@hotmail.com.

WICKHAM, JOHN ADAMS, JR., retired army officer; b. Dobbs Ferry, NY, June 25, 1928; s. John Adams and Jean Gordon (Koch) W.; m. Ann Lindsley Prior, June 18, 1955; children: Lindsley, John Adams, Matthew. BS, U.S. Mil. Acad., 1950; MA, Harvard U., 1955, MPA, 1956; grad., Nat. War Coll., 1967. Commd. 2d lt. U.S. Army, 1950, advanced through grades to gen., 1979; asst. prof. social scis. U.S. Mil. Acad., 1956-60; bn. comdr. 1st Cavalry Div., Republic of Vietnam, 1967; brigade comdr., chief of staff 3d Inf. Div., Fed. Republic of Germany, 1969-70; army mem. chmn.'s staff group Office of Chmn. Joint Chiefs of Staff, Washington, 1970-71; dep. chief of staff for econ. affairs Mil. Assistance Command, Republic of Vietnam, 1971-73; dep. chief, negotiator U.S. del. Four Party Joint Mil. Commn., Republic of Vietnam, 1973; sr. mil. asst. to Sec. Def. Washington, 1973-76; comdr. 101st Airborne Div. (Air Assault), Ft. Campbell, Ky., 1976-78; dir. Joint Staff Orgn. Washington, 1978-79; comdr. in chief UN Command, Republic of Korea-U.S. Combined Forces Command, Korea, 1979-82; vice chief of staff U.S. Army, Washington, 1982-83, chief of staff, 1983-87, ret., 1987; pres., chief exec. officer Armed Forces Communications and Electronics Assn., Fairfax, Va., 1987-92. Bd. dirs. Cooper Inst. for Aerobic Rsch., Xsirius, Inc., Honeywell Fed. Sys., Advanced Photonics, Nortel Inc. Author: Korea on the Brink, 2000. Pres. Sun City Town Coun., 1996—99, Sun City Found., 2001—03; elder St. Andrews Presbyn. Ch., 2001—. Decorated D.S.M. (8), Silver Star (2), Legion of Merit (4), Bronze Star with V device, Air medal (11), Purple Heart, Legion of Honor (France), Order of Mil. Merit (Rep. of Korea), Royal Order of Polar Star (Sweden); recipient Disting. Grad. award West Point, 2005, Infanry Doughboy award, 2006. Mem. Assn. U.S. Army, 101st Airborne Assn., Retired Officers Assn. Home: 13500 N Rancho Vistoso Blvd No 519 Tucson AZ 85755-5801 Personal E-mail: j55wick@comcast.net.

WICKHAM, MADELEINE SOPHIE See KINSELLA, SOPHIE

WICKLEIN, JOHN FREDERICK, journalist, educator; b. Reading, Pa., July 20, 1924; s. Raymond Roland and Parmilla Catherine (Miller) W.; m. Myra Jane Winchester, July 31, 1948 (dec. 2002); children: Elizabeth, Peter, Joanna. LittB, Rutgers U., 1947; MS in Journalism, Columbia, 1948. Reporter Newark (N.J.) Evening News, 1947-51; news mng. editor Elec. World (McGraw-Hill weekly), NYC, 1951-54; reporter, editor N.Y. Times, 1954-62; news dir. Sta. WNET-TV, NYC, 1962-64; exec. producer news Sta. WABC-TV, NYC, 1964-67; exec. producer Washington Bur. chief Pub. Broadcast Lab. (Nat. Ednl. TV), 1967-70; mng. news and pub. affairs broadcasts Sta. WCBS-TV, NYC, 1970-71; gen. mgr. Sta. WRVR, NYC, 1971-74; prof. journalism and broadcasting Boston U., 1974-80; dean Sch. Public Communication Boston U., 1974-78; vis. prof. communication Meth. U., São Paulo, Brazil, 1979; program officer for news and pub. affairs programs Corp. for Pub. Broadcasting, 1980-84; Willard M. Kiplinger chair in pub. affairs reporting, dir. Kiplinger mid-career program for journalists Ohio State U., 1984-89, mem. adv. bd. Kiplinger program, 2004—; Fulbright rsch. scholar Charles Sturt Univ., Bathurst, NSW, Australia, 1990. Lectr., cons. Rutgers U. Media Resources Ctr., Cracow, Poland, 1992, 94; Ayers vis. prof. journalism Jacksonville (Ala.) State U., 1992-93; prodr. news documentaries for pub. and comml. TV; ind. writing, reporting and editing coach for newspapers including Washington Post, Buffalo News, Memphis Comml. Appeal, 1994—; coord. Working Group for Pub. Broadcasting, 1987-89; spl. com. on regulation of media ACLU, 1988-92; adj. faculty Poynter Inst. for Media Studies, 1988; adj. prof. journalism for rsch. Ohio State U., 1991-93; media ethics com. Nat. Coun. Chs., 1975-92; fellow Inst. Dem. Comm. Boston U., 1975-78; newsroom trainers group Poynter Inst., 1995—; lectr., cons. in field. Author: (with Monroe Price) Cable Television: A Guide for Citizen Action, 1972, Electronic Nightmare: The New Communications and Freedom, 1981; editor: Investigative Reporting: The Lessons of Watergate, 1975; contgb. editor The Washington Monthly, 1969-72; contbr. to Am. Journalism Review, The Progressive, TV Quar., Atlantic Monthly, Columbia Journalism Rev., Archeology, Quill, Australian Journalism Rev., others. Recipient George Polk award, 1963, documentary award, Venice Film Festival, 1968, DuPont award, 1973, Brechner Freedom Info. prize, 1987. Mem.: ACLU, Soc. Profl. Journalists, Amnesty Internat. USA, Phi Beta Kappa. Democrat. Home and Office: 7 Riverwoods Dr C116 Exeter NH 03833 Office Phone: 603-772-4032. Personal E-mail: jfwicklein@comcast.net.

WICKLIFFE, CHARLES WALTON, cardiologist; b. Gaffney, SC, Mar. 17, 1943; s. Charles Walton and Maude W. Badgett; m. Melody Anne Craig, Mar. 25, 1965; children: Charles, Andrew. MD cum laude, Emory U., 1967. Cert. Am. Bd. Internal Med., 1973, Am. Bd. Cardiovascular Diseases, 1975. Fellow cardiology Emory U. Sch. of Medicine, Atlanta, 1973-75, asst. prof. medicine, cardiology faculty, 1975-76; co-dir. cardiac cath lab. Grady Meml., Atlanta, 1975—76; clin. asst. prof. of medicine, cardiology Emory U. Sch. of Medicine, Atlanta, 1976-87, clin. assoc. prof., 1987—; pvt. practice internal med., cardiovascular diseases Cardiology of Ga., P.C., Atlanta, 1976—. Chmn., bd. trustees West Paces Ferry Hosp., Atlanta, 1984, bd. trustees, 1981—84; chmn. credentials Piedmont Hosp., Atlanta, 1995, pres. elect-med. staff, 1996—97, pres. med. staff, 1998—2000, trustee, bd. dirs., 1996—; chmn. Specialty Physician Orgn. Piedmont Clin.; chmn. bd. dirs. Piedmont Healthcare, 2002—. Editor: (of profl. jours.) Med. Assn., 1985—89. Venue med. officer ACOG; com. Olympic games, 1995—96. Flight surgeon USN, 1969, lt. comdr., flight surgeon USN, 1969—72. Fellow: Am. Coll. Clinical Cardiology, Am. Heart Assn., Atlanta Diabetes Assn., Am. Coll. Cardiology; mem.: Med. Assn. Atlanta, Med. Assn. Ga., Am. Med. Assn., Atlanta Clinical Soc., Atlanta Cardiology Forum. Democrat. Methodist. Avocations: reading, horseback riding, golf, fishing. Office: 275 Collier Rd NW Ste 500 Atlanta GA 30309-1749 Personal E-mail: docwickliffe@aol.com.

WICKLUND, DAVID WAYNE, lawyer; b. St. Paul, Aug. 7, 1949; s. Wayne Glenwood and Elna Katherine (Buresh) W.; m. Susan Marie Bubenko, Nov. 17, 1973; children: David Jr., Kurt, Edward. BA cum laude, Williams Coll., 1971; JD cum laude, U. Toledo, 1974. Bar: Ohio 1974. Assoc. Shumaker, Loop & Kendrick, Toledo, 1974-80, ptnr., 1981—. Adj. instr. law, U. Toledo, 1988. Editor-in-chief U. Toledo Law Rev. 1973-74. Mem.: ABA, Toledo Bar Assn., Ohio State Bar Assn. (bd. govs. antitrust sect. 1994—2001), U. Toledo Coll. Law Alumni Assn. (pres. 1999—2000), Inverness Club. Office: Shumaker Loop & Kendrick N Courthouse Sq 1000 Jackson St Toledo OH 43604-5573 Office Phone: 419-321-1213. Business E-Mail: dwicklund@slk-law.com.

WICKLUND, LEE ARTHUR, retired school system administrator; b. Fort Atkinson, Wis., Aug. 10, 1938; s. Verner F. and Ellen V. (Anderson) W.; m. Georganne Emilie Trumbull, June 27, 1964; children: Eric Trumbull, Lance Frederick. BEd, Chgo. Teachers Coll., 1961; MEd, Loyola U., Chgo., 1964; DEd, U. Oreg., Eugene, 1969. Cert. std. adminstr., supt., prin., Oreg. Elem., secondary tchr., asst. prin. Chgo. Bd. Edn., 1961—67; rsch. asst. Bur. Ednl. Rsch. and Svc., U. Oreg. Coll. Edn., 1967—69; dir. lab. sch., asst. prof. edn. Idaho State U. Grad. Faculty, Pocatello, 1969—71; R&D specialist NW Regional Edn. Lab., Portland, Oreg., 1971—72, supt. in residence, 1994—95; assoc. prof. ednl. adminstrn. U. Wis. Grad. Faculty, Superior, 1972—75; dir. curriculum and instrnl. svcs. North Bend Sch. Dist., Oreg., 1975—89; assoc. supt., instrnl. & pers. svcs. Mercer Island Sch. Dist., Wash., 1989—92; supt., prin. Riverdale Sch. Dist., Portland, 1992—94; asst. supt. instrn. Racine Unified Sch. Dist., Wis., 1995—2003. Pres. elect Idaho ASCD, 1971; sr. fellow Inst. for Devel. of Edn. Activities, Kettering, Ohio, 1977-2000; chmn. Oreg. State Textbook Commn., Salem, 1980-87; mem. instrnl tech. edn. com. Am. Assn. Sch. Adminstrs., 1985-88, chmn. internat. edn. com., 1990-93; rep. alumni bd. Alumni Soc. Coll. Edn. U. Oreg., 1987-88, 1994-95; past chair Inter-Luth. Commn. for Continuing Edn., Tacoma, 1982-89; adj. prof. U. Oreg. Coll. Edn., 1984-88; alumni pres. coll. edn., U. Oreg., 1986-87, 1993-94; adj. instr. U. Wash. Coll. Edn., 1991. Chmn. budget com. North Bay Rural Fire Dist., North Bend, 1984-89; mem. adv. com. South Slough Natural Estuarine Res., Coos Bay, Oreg., 1984-89; sec. exec. com. United Way of S.W. Oreg., Coos Bay, 1978-83; mem. exec. com. Music Enrichment Assn., Coos Bay, 1977-81; trustee Lake Oswego (Oreg.) Libr. Bd., 1993-95; bd. dirs. Slingerland Inst., vice chmn., Bellevue, Washington, 1989-94; bd. dirs., U.S. dir.-at-large alumni bd. U. Oreg., 1998-2004; exec. com., area dir., planning com. mem. Palisades Neighborhood Assn., Lake Oswego, Oreg., 2004-07; v.p., treas. Greentree Swimming Pool Assn., Lake Oswego, 2004-07; mem. budget com. Lake Oswego Sch. Dist., 2004-09, mem. reconfiguration com., 2006-, respectful culture com., 2005-2008. Staff sgt. Hdqs. Ill. Air NG, 1956—65. Recipient Honor Recognition Svc. award, Oreg. State Bd. Edn., 1988, Svc. award, Oreg. Supt. Pub. Instrn., 1988, Presdl. citation, Nat. Assn. Equal Opportunity in Higher Edn., 1998; rsch. asst., U. Oreg., 1967—69. Fellow, Paul Harris, Rotary Internat.; mem. ASCD, Am. Ednl. Rsch. Assn., Am. Assn. Sch. Adminstrs., U. Oreg. Alumni Assn. (charter, life), Arnold Bennett Hall Soc., Pres. Assn., Oreg. Club Portland, Lake Oswego Rotary, Phil Delta Kappa. Lutheran. Achievements include co-author of over $3 million of funded proposals. Avocations: travel, boating, reading. Home: 16860 Lakeridge Dr Lake Oswego OR 97034-6819 Home Phone: 503-636-1985. Personal E-mail: lgwicklund@comcast.net.

WICKRAMASINGHE, HEMANTHA KUMAR, electrical engineer, physicist; b. Colombo, Sri Lanka, May 31, 1949; naturalized U.S. citizen, 1996; s. Percival Herbert and Therese Elizabeth (Soysa) W.; m. Sophie Marie de La Porte, Nov. 17, 1973; children: Lucille Samantha, Anita Elizabeth. BSc in Electronic Engring., U. London, 1970, PhD in Electronic and Elec. Engring., 1974. Assoc. rsch. asst. dept. electronic and elec. engring. U. Coll. London, 1974-75, lectr. dept. electronic and elec. engring., 1978-83; rsch. assoc. E.L. Ginzton Lab. Stanford (Calif.) U., 1975-78; from mgr. phys. measurements T.J. Watson Rsch. Ctr. to fellow IBM, Yorktown Heights, NY, 1984—2000, fellow T.J. Watson Rsch. Ctr., 2000—, sr. mgr. nanoscale and quantum studies Almaden Rsch. Ctr. San Jose, Calif., 2002—03, sr. mgr. nanoscale sci. and tech., 2003—05, chief tech. officer sci. and tech., 2005—07; Henry Samueli endowed chair, dept. elec. engring. & comuter sci. & dept. biomed. engring. U. Calif., Irvine, 2007—. Cons. Hirst Rsch. Ctr. GE Co., London, 1980-83, U.K. Atomic Energy Authority, Harwell, Eng., 1980-82; adj. prof. Poly. Inst. N.Y., Bklyn., 1985-87; mem. editl. bds. Nanotech., 1991-96, Advances in Nanoscale Physics, electonics and Engring., 1991—, Rev. of Sci. Instruments, 1996—; prof. Editor: Scanned Probe Microscopy, 1992; co-editor: Determining Nanoscale Properties of Materials by Microscopy and Spectroscopy, 1994; contbr. over 150 articles to profl. jours.; holder numerous patents in field. Recipient V.K. Zworykin premium, Inst. Elec. Engrs., 1983, Disting. Corp. Inventor award, Nat. Inventors Hall of Fame, 1998, Morris E. Leeds award, IEEE, 1992, Joseph F. Keithley award, Am. Phys. Soc., 2000; Emeritus fellow, IBM, 2007—. Fellow: IBM, Royal Microscopical Soc., Inst. of Physics, IEEE, Am. Phys. Soc. (centennial spkr. 1999); mem.: Nat. Acad. Engring. Achievements include first introduction of vibrating mode atomic force microscopes, atomic force microscopes into manufacturing lines, first deployment of a magnetic force microscope capable of imaging nanometer scale magnetic properties, work in areas of optics, acoustics, photoacoustics, metrology and scanning probe microscopy. Office: Univ Calif Henry Samueli Sch Engring Dept Elec Engring and Computer Sci 616F Engring Tower Irvine CA 92697 Home Phone: 949-823-9276; Office Phone: 949-824-0378. Personal E-mail: wickla@sbcglobal.net. Business E-Mail: hkwick@uci.edu.

WICKS, DAVID O., JR., communications executive; b. Boston, May 17, 1941; s. David O. and Elizabeth L. Wicks; m. Joan Gagnebin, Sept. 7, 1963; children: Perrin, Sara. BA, Trinity Coll., Hartford, Conn., 1963; MBA, U. Va., 1968. With nat. divsn. Chem. Bank, 1963—66; specialist in venture capital and cable TV Warburg Paribas Becker, NYC, 1968—83, mng. dir., 1979—83; gen. ptnr. Becker Venture Assoc., Becker Comms. Assoc. II; sr. ptnr. Criterion Venture Ptnr., Houston, 1983—88. Mng. dir. Criterion Investments, Inc., 1983-88; pres. Criterion Investments, Inc., 1985-88; v.p. Cablevision Sys. Corp., Bethpage, NY, 1996-2002; pres. Devonshire Comms. Assocs., cons., 2002-; ptnr. The Alwyn Group, LLC, 2002—; exec. NASA Mid Continent Tech. Transfer Ctr., 1992-95; adj. prof. Columbia U., N.Y.C., 2004-08; mem. NY Mayor's Broadband Com., 2007—; expert witness on cable TV, US Congress and state regulatory bodies. Contbr. articles to profl. jour. Chmn. Cable Positive, Inc., 2003—05; elected pioneer CATV, 2000, Omicron Delta Kappa, 1968; bd. dirs. Vis. Nurse Assn. NY, Union Chapel Shelter Island, Friends of Cath. Univ. in Chile. Recipient Vanguard award Nat. Cable TV Assn., 1978. Mem.: Shelter Island Yacht Club, Univ. Club. Office Phone: 516-695-2951. Personal E-mail: dwicksjr@aol.com.

WICKS, JUDY, restaurant manager; Owner, founder White Dog Cafe, Phila.; pres. White Dog Cmty. Enterprises, Phila.; co-founder Free People's Store (now Urban Outfitters), 1970; gen. mgr., co-proprietor Restaurant La Terrasse, 1974—84; co-founder, pres. Synapse, Inc. Founder White Dog mentoring program, 1992—; co-founder, bd. dirs. Bus. Alliance for Local Living Economics; founder, mem. emeritus bd. dirs. Sustainable Bus. Network of Greater Phila.; vice chair, emeritus adv. bd. mem. Social Venture Network. Editor, art dir. Whole City Catalog, 1972, 1974, Philadelphia Resource Guide, 1982; co-author: White Dog Cafe Cookbook: Multicultural Recipes and Tales of Adventure from Philadelphia's Revolutionary Restaurant, 1998; contbg. author Girls Like Us, 1999, Families of Women, 1999, Focus on Leadership: Servant-Leadership for the 21st Century, 2001. Recipient Human Rights award, Phila. Commn. on Human Rels., 1991, Shining Example award, PhilaPride. Inc., 1992, Mother-Friendly Bus. award, UNICEF, 1993, Women in Leadership award, Women's Way, 1993, Disting. Alumni award, Lake Erie Coll., 1994, Mellon Bank Good Neighbor award, 1994, Human Soc. award for Humane & Sustainable Food Choices, 1994, Paradigm award, Greater Phila. C. of C., 1994, Am. Jewish Congress award, 1995, Bus. Enterprise Trust award, 1995, Humanitarian award, Prisoners' Family Welfare Assn., 1996, award for Philanthropy, Bread & Roses Cmty. Fund, 1996, Brotherhood/Sisterhood award, Greater Phila. Region Nat. Conf., 1998, Domestic Partnership award, US Agy. Internat. Devel., 1998, Making a Difference for Women award, Soroptimist Internat. Phila., 1999, Peace Maker award, Women's Internat. League for Peace and Freedom, 1999, Lifetime Achievement award, Girl Scouts Am., 1999, Civic Leadership award, League Women Voters, 1999, Green Power award for Commitment to Sustainable Energy, 2000, Clean Water Fund award for Outstanding Environ. Activism, 2000, Wind Powering America award, US Dept. Energy, 2002, Champion for Justice award, Citizens for Consumer Justice, 2002, Caring Bus. award, Bus. Leaders for Sensible Priorities, 2002, Environ. Edn. Corp. Sponsor award, Pa. Alliance Environ. Edn., 2002, Living Economy award, Bus. Ethics mag., 2002, Partnership for the Del. Estuary Visionary award, 2003, Investing for the Common Good award, Phila. Area Coalition for Responsible Investment, 2003, Arts & Cmty. award, InterAct Theatre Co., 2004, Bus. Leadership award, Pa. Assn. Sustainable Agr., 2004, First Ann. Interdependence award, Democracy Collaborative, 2004, Breastfeeding-Friendly Bus. award, Maternity Care Coalition, 2004, Althea Gibson Cmty. award, 2005, Spirit of Phila. award, Phila. Cares, 2005, Humanitarian of Yr. award, James Beard Found., 2005, Bus. award, Pa. Resources Coun., 2005, Living the Chance We Wish to See award, Phila. Student Union, 2005, New Prophetic Voice award, Shalom Ctr., 2006, Lifetime Achievement award, Phila. Sustainability Awards, 2007, George Bailey award, Reinvestment Fund, 2007, Humanitarian award, Internat. Assn. Culinary Professionals, 2008; named a Bus. Adv. for the Arts, Great Phila. C. of C., 1993; named to Philly Hall of Fame, Phila. Mag., 1993. Office: White Dog Cafe 3420 Sansom St Philadelphia PA 19104 Office Phone: 215-386-9224 ext. 101. Business E-Mail: judy@whitedog.com.

WICKS, ROBERT S., museum director, educator; B in the History of Art, U. Wash., Seattle, 1975; PhD, Cornell U., 1983. Various positions through affiliate prof., art history Miami U., Oxford, Ohio, 1983—, dir. Art Mus. Fulbright lectr. Silpakorn U., Bangkok, 1987; vis. prof. Asian studies Kansai Gaidai U., Osaka, Japan, 1992. Author: (books) Money, Markets, and Trade in Early Southeast Asia, 1992, rev. edit., 1996; co-author: Buried Cities, Forgotten Gods, 1999. Office: Miami University Art Mus 801 S Patterson Ave Oxford OH 45056 Office Phone: 513-529-2238. Business E-Mail: wicksrs@muohio.edu.

WICKS, SHEILA M., hospital administrator, research scientist, educator; b. Chgo., Mar. 9, 1965; BS, U. Ill., Chgo., 1989; MS, Chgo. State U., 1992; MS in Acupuncture, Midwest Coll. Oriental Medicine, Wis., 1993; MD, Guangzhou Med. U., China, 1996; MBA in Health Svcs., Keller Grad. Sch. Mgmt., Ill., 2003; PhD in Pain Mgmt. and Nutrition, Walden U., Md., 2007. Cert. med. rev. officer Am. Soc. Addiction Medicine, 2006, in profl. clin. rsch. Nat. Inst. Health, 2006, in acupuncture Ill., Md. Vol. attending, faculty, anesthesiology, pain mgmt. John Stroger Hosp. Cook County, Chgo., 2000—; nutritional cons. MERZ Apothecary, Chgo., 2004; rsch. assoc., anesthesia, critical care, pharmacology, herbal medicine U. Chgo., 2005—; CEO, pres. Dr. Sheila's Oriental Hosp. & Nutrition Svcs. Ltd., Chgo., 2006—; rsch. cons., collaborator, pain studies Rehab. Inst. Chgo., 2006—; adj. faculty prof., health. scis. Malcom X City Wide Coll. Chgo., 2006—. Co-author: (book) Textbook of Complementary and Alternative Medicine, 2006; contbr. articles to med. jours. Mem. Trinity United Ch. Christ, 1983—. Recipient Collaboration and Transl. award, China, 1994. Fellow: Am. Acad. Pain Mgmt., Med. Acupuncture Soc.; mem.: Royal Coll. Physicians and Surgeons Can., Am. Pain Soc., Am. Soc. Addiction Medicine, Internat. Assn. Pain Mgmt., Chgo. Neurol. Soc., Nat. Assn. Black Journalists. Avocations: aerobics, cooking, dance, golf, travel. Home: 4800 S Chicago Beach Dr Unit 311 Chicago IL 60615 also: 9734 S Greenwood Ave Chicago IL 60628 Home Phone: 773-624-8461, 773-768-3509. Personal E-mail: docshe95@hotmail.com.

WICKS, WILLIAM WITHINGTON, retired public relations executive; b. Chgo., Dec. 20, 1923; s. William and Alice (Withington) W.; m. Frances M. Horner, Nov. 29, 1947; children: Barbara Anne, Christine Frances. BNS, U. Notre Dame, Ind., 1944, AB in Journalism magna cum laude, 1947. Staff corr. United Press Assn., Milw., 1947; pub. rels. mgr. Internat. Harvester Co., Louisville, 1948-58; mgr. field svcs. pub. rels. Std. Oil Co. (Ind.), Chgo., 1959—60; v.p. pub. rels. Griswold-Eshleman Co., Chgo., 1961-68; dir. pub. rels. G. D. Searle & Co., Chgo., 1968-74; from dir. pub. rels./investor rels. to v.p. Kimberly-Clark Corp., Neenah, Wis., 1974—89, v.p. Dallas, 1989-92, asst. to CEO, 1989—92, ret., 1992. Chmn. pub. relations sect. Pharm. Mfrs. Assn., Washington, 1974. Pres. Jr. Achievement Neenah-Menasha, 1978-81; bd. mem. Friends of the Irving Pub. Libr., 1997-99. Served to lt. (j.g.) USNR, 1942-46, PTO. Recipient Silver Anvil award Pub. Rels. Soc. Am., 1963, 79, J. Sinnott Meyers Burse for Journalism award, U. Notre Dame, 1946-47. Mem. PRSA (founder, pres. Bluegrass chpt. 1957-58), Optimist (pres. South End Club in Louisville 1957), Publicity Club of Chgo. (pres. 1967-68), Las Colinas Sports Club (Irving), USN Meml. Found. (plank owner), Navy League U.S., Patrol Craft Sailors Assn, Notre Dame Club Dallas. Republican. Roman Catholic. Home: 1312 Travis Cir S Irving TX 75038-6243

WICKWIRE, PATRICIA JOANNE NELLOR, psychologist, educator; d. William McKinley and Clara Rose (Pautsch) Nellor; m. Robert James Wickwire, Sept. 7, 1957; 1 child, William James. BA cum laude, U. No. Iowa, Cedar Falls, 1951; MA, U. Iowa, Iowa City, 1959; PhD, U. Tex., Austin, 1971; postgrad., U. So. Calif., LA, UCLA, Calif. State U., Long Beach. Lic. ednl. psychologist, marriage and family therapist, Calif.; nat. cert. counselor. Tchr. Ricketts Ind. Schs., Iowa, 1946-48; tchr., counselor Waverly-Shell Rock Ind. Schs., Iowa, 1951-55; reading cons., head dormitory counselor U. Iowa, Iowa City, 1955-57; tchr., sch. psychologist, adminstr. S. Bay Union H.S. Dist., Redondo Beach, Calif., 1962-82, dir. student svcs. and spl. edn. Cons. mgmt. and edn.; pres. Nellor Wickwire Group, 1981—; mem. exec. bd. Calif. Interagy. Mental Health Coun., 1968-72, Beach Cities Symphony Assn., 1970-82; chmn. Friends of Dominguez Hills, Calif., 1981-85. Contbr. articles in field to profl. jours. Pres. Calif. Women's Caucus, 1993-95, 2003-06. Mem. APA, AAUW (exec. bd., chpt. pres. 1962-72), Nat. Career Devel. Assn. (media chair 1992-98), Am. Assn. Career Edn. (pres. 1991—), LA County Dirs. Pupil Svcs. (chmn. 1974-79), LA County Pers. and Guidance Assn. (pres. 1977-78), Assn. Calif. Sch. Adminstrs. (dir. 1977-81), LA County SW Bd. Dist. Adminstrs. for Spl. Edn. (chmn. 1976-81), Calif. Assn. Sch. Psychologists (bd. dirs. 1981-83), Am. Assn. Sch. Adminstrs., Calif. Assn. for Measurement and Evaluation in Guidance (dir. 1981, pres. 1984-85, 98-2000, 04-05), ACA (chmn. Coun. Newsletter Editors 1989-91, mem. com. on women 1989-92, mem. com. on rsch. and knowledge 1994-97, chmn. 1995-97, mem. and chmn. bylaws com. 1998-2001, rep. to joint com. on testing practices 2001-07), Assn. Measurement and Eval. in Guidance (Western regional editor 1985-87, conv. chair 1986, editor 1987-90, exec. bd. dirs. 1987-91, chair position statements and standards 2001—), Calif. Assn. Counseling and Devel. (exec. bd. 1984—, pres. 1988-89, jour. editor 1990-2002), Nat.

Assn. for Ind.-Edn. Coop. (bd. dirs. 2002-05), Internat. Career Assn. Network (chair 1985—), Internat. Women's Rev. Bd. (Women's Inner Cir. of Achievement 2008-), Calif. Edn. Found. (bd. dirs. 1987—), World Future Soc., Pi Lambda Theta, Alpha Phi Gamma, Psi Chi, Kappa Delta Pi, Sigma Alpha Iota, Phi Delta Kappa. Office: The Nellor Wickwire Group 2900 Amby Pl Hermosa Beach CA 90254-2216 Office Phone: 310-376-7378.

WICZYK, MODI, media company executive; Degree, Harvard Coll., 1993; grad., Harvard Bus. Sch., 1999. Head prodn. Summit Films, 2000—02; ptnr. Endeavor Agy.; co-founder, co-CEO Media Rights Capital, LA, 2003—. Named one of 50 Smartest People in Hollywood, Entertainment Weekly, 2007. Home: 2037 Desford Dr Beverly Hills CA 90210

WIDBIN, ROBERT BRYAN, theology studies educator; b. St. Louis, Sept. 8, 1948; s. John Robert and Lois Evelyn Widbin; m. Karen Dianne Hanson; children: Lydia Hanson, Zachary Hanson. PhD, Brandeis U., Waltham, Mass., 1985. Cert. ordination Christian and Missionary Alliance, 1994, guide credentials Notre Dame Ctr., Jerusalem, 1988. Prof. Nyack Coll., NY, 1985—; dean Alliance Theol. Sem., Nyack, 1995—2003. Office: Alliance Theol Sem 350 N Highland Ave Nyack NY 10960 Business E-Mail: bryan.widbin@nyack.edub.

WIDDEL, JOHN EARL, JR., lawyer; b. Minot, ND, Nov. 17, 1936; s. John Earl Sr. and Angela Victoria W.; m. Yvonne J. Haugen, Dec. 21, 1973; children: John P., James M., Suianne N., Andrea K. PhB, U. ND, 1966, BSBA, 1966, JD, 1971. Bar: ND 1971, US Dist. Ct. ND, 1971, US Ct. Appeals (8th cir.) 1989, Minn. 2004. Ptnr. Thorsen & Widdel, Grand Forks, ND, 1971-97; shareholder Law Offices ND, PC. Mcpl. judge City of Grand Forks, 1972—; ct. magistrate Grand Forks County, 1975. Mem. N.D. Foster Parent Program, 1974-87, Nat. Conf. of Bar Pres., 1986-87; mem. bd. dirs. YMCA, Grand Forks, 1982; dist. chmn. Boy Scouts Am., 1987-88; corp. mem. ALTRU Hosp. With U.S. Army, 1960-62. Mem.: Greater Grand Forks Sr. Citizens Ctr. (v.p. 2009), ND Mcpl. Judges Assn. (dir. 1993—), Nat. Assn. Estate Planning Coun. (accredited estate planner 1994—), Grand Forks Jaycees, Grand Forks Hist. Soc. (pres. 1983), Grand Forks Cemetery Assn. (bd. dirs. 1984—96, pres. 1989—94), NE Ctrl. Jud. Dist. (pres. 1983), Greater Grand Forks County Bar Assn. (pres. 1982), State Bar Assn. ND (bd. govs. 1983—88, pres. 1986—87), Minn. State Bar Assn., Antique Automobile Club Am. (pres. ND region 1977—78, 1983—84, nat. bd. dirs. 1984—2000, v.p. 1985—89, sec.-treas. 1989), Sertoma Grand Forks (bd. dirs. 1994—99, pres. 1997—98, ND dist. gov. 2001—05, Sertoma Internat. 2001—05), Am. Legion (comdr. ND Post 201 2006—09), Masons (Kem Temple Potentate 1995), Elks (exalted ruler 1985—86). Office: Law Offices North Dakota PC PO Box 5624 Grand Forks ND 58206-5624 Home: 215A S 4th St Grand Forks ND 58201 Office Phone: 701-746-7485. Business E-Mail: ndljw@msn.com.

WIDDER, EDITH ANNE, biologist; b. Boston, June 11, 1951; d. David Vernon and Vera Adela (Ames) Widder; m. David Charles Smith, Feb. 9, 1972. BS magna cum laude in Biology, Tufts U., Medford, Mass., 1973; MS in Biochemistry, U. Calif., Santa Barbara, 1977, PhD in Neurobiology, 1982. Cert. sci. rsch. pilot for atmospheric diving sys. submersibles 1984. Lab. asst. phycology U. Mass. Field Sta. Environ. Scis., 1968—69; rsch. assoc. NIH Resource Lab. Electron Probe Microanalysis Harvard U. Med. Sch., Boston, 1973-75; assoc. rschr. ONR bioluminescence prog. U. Calif., Santa Barbara, 1977-83, post-doctoral rsch. biologist, 1983-85, asst. rsch. biologist, co-prin. investigator Marine Sci. Inst. and Neuroscience Rsch. Inst., 1985-89; asst. scientist, prin. investigator Harbor Br. Oceanog. Instn., Ft. Pierce, Fla., 1989-91, assoc. scientist, prin. investigator, 1991—93, acting divsn. dir., 1993—94, sr. scientist, prin. investigator, 1993—2005; prof. biol. scis. Fla. Inst. Tech., 1991—; pres., sr. scientist Ocean Rsch. & Conservation Assn., 2005—. Sci. cons. Dynamics Tech., Inc., LA, 1987—89; disting. scientist adj. Monterey Bay Aquarium Rsch. Inst., 1998—; adj. rsch. prof. earth and planetary scis. dept. Johns Hopkins U., 2000—; affiliate prof. dept. biol. sci. Fla. Atlantic U., 2000—; adj. sr. rsch. scientist Bigelow Lab. Ocean Scis., 2005—. Contbr. articles to profl. jours.; mem. editl. bd.: Marine Tech. Soc. Recipient Women of Discovery award, Sea, Wings WorldQuest, 2006; named Earle C. Anthony fellow, 1978; grantee, NSF, 1986—88, 1990—91, 1991—; MacArthur Fellow, John D. and Catherine T. MacArthur Found., 2006. Mem. AAAS, Am. Soc. Limnology and Oceanography, Am. Soc. Zoologists, Soc. Neuroscience, Soc. Photo-Optical and Instrumentation Engrs., Internat. Soc. Bioluminescence and Chemiluminescence (councilor), Am. Acad. Underwater Scis., Explorers Club. Achievements include patents in field; first to make video recordings of bioluminescence in the ocean, 1985. Office: Ocean Rsch & Conservation Assn 1420 Seaway Dr Fort Pierce FL 34949 Office Phone: 772-467-1600. Business E-Mail: ewidder@oceanrecon.org.

WIDDICOMBE, RICHARD PALMER, librarian; b. Paterson, NJ, Apr. 12, 1941; s. Robert Lord and Elvira Barbara (Guttilla) W.; m. Martha Elizabeth Bruyn, Feb. 26, 1972 BA, Alfred U., 1963; MS L.S., Syracuse U., 1964. Asst. librarian Yonkers Pub. Library, NY, 1964-65; asst. librarian Cooper Union, NYC, 1965-66, Stevens Inst., Hoboken, NJ, 1966-72, dir. library, 1973—2006; curator Frederick Winslow Taylor Collection, 2007—. Trustee Alfred U., NY, The Sagamore Inst., 2006—; trustee, chmn. bd. Hoboken Hist. Mus., 2002—04; bd. dirs. Sculpture Space, Utica, NY, 2009—. Episcopalian. Office: SC Williams Libr Stevens Inst Hoboken NJ 07030 Home: 1711 Sherman Dr Utica NY 13501-5839 Home Phone: 315-749-8528; Office Phone: 201-216-5421. Business E-Mail: richard.widdicombe@gmail.com.

WIDDOWS, MARIANNE SHUTA, orchestra director; b. Wilkes-Barre, Pa., June 18, 1960; d. Joseph and Matilda Marie Shuta; m. Donald Richard Widdows. B of Music Edn., Coll. Misericordia, Dallas, Pa., 1982; M of Music Edn. in String Pedagogy, U. NC, Greensboro, 1990. Orch. dir. Southview Jr. H.S., Fayetteville, NC, 1984—86, Terry Sanford H.S., Fayetteville, 1989—97, Ashley Elem., Fayetteville, 1985—, Van Story Elem., Fayetteville, 1986—, Max Abbott Mid. Sch., Fayetteville, 1986—. Violin coach Cumberland County Youth Orch., Fayetteville, 1984—; assoc. dir. Snyder Bapt. Ch. Youth Orch., Fayetteville, 2004—; violinist Cumberland Quartet, Fayetteville, 1984—. Mem.: Am. Fedn. Musicians, Am. String Tchrs. Assn., Nat. Sch. Orch. Assn., Music Educators Nat. Conf. Avocations: collecting nesting dolls, reading, animals. Office: Max Abbott Mid Sch 590 Winding Creek Rd Fayetteville NC 28305 E-mail: dwiddows@aol.com.

WIDEMAN, IDA DEVLIN, science educator; d. John Cole and Lillie Alma Devlin; m. Leroy Wideman, May 12, 1945; children: Michael Andre, Leroy Maurice. BS, SC State U., 1964—68; MAT, U. of SC, 1976—77. Sci. tchr. West Side H.S., Newark, 1971—73, Hopkins Jr. H.S., Hopkins, SC, 1976—83, St. Andrews Mid. Sch., Columbia, SC, 1983—. Co-dir. NSF grant Ctr. for Sci. Edn., U. S.C.; master tchr. sci. U. S.C., Columbia, Aiken; presenter in field. Mem. Nat. Assn. of U. Women, Columbia, SC, 1990. Named Tchr. of Yr., St. Andrews Middle Sch., state winner, Presdl. Awards for Excellence in Math. and Sci. Tchg. Mem.: Richland County Edn. Assn., SC Edn. Assn., NEA, SC Earth Sci. Teachers Assn. (past pres., v.p. 1988—90), SC Sci. Coun., NSTA, Delta Sigma Theta Sorority (life). United Methodist. Avocations: walking, reading. Home: 446 Koon Store Rd Columbia SC 29203 Office: St Andrews Middle Sch 1231 Bluefield Rd Columbia SC 29210 Office Fax: 803-731-8913; Home Fax: 803-333-0542. Personal E-mail: lwideman@sc.rr.com. E-mail: iwideman@richlandone.org.

WIDEMAN, JOHN EDGAR, English literature educator, novelist; b. Washington, June 14, 1941; m. Judith Ann Goldman, 1965 (div. 2000); children: Daniel, Jacob, Jamila; m. Catherine Nedonchelle, 2004; 1 stepchild, Romeo Alexander. BA, U. Pa., 1963; BPhil, Oxford U., Eng., 1966; grad., U. Iowa Writers Workshop, 1967; DLitt (hon.), U. Pa., 1985, Rutgers U., NJ. Mem. faculty U. Wyo., Laramie, prof. English, 1974—85, U. Mass., Amherst, 1986—2001, disting. prof. English, 2001—; prof. dept. African studies Brown U, Providence. USIS lectr. in Ea. Europe. Author: A Glance Away, 1967, Hurry Home, 1969, The Lynchers, 1973, Hiding Place, 1981, Damballah, 1981, Sent for You Yesterday, 1983 (PEN Faulkner award for fiction, 1984), Brothers and Keepers, 1984, The Homewood Trilogy, 1985, Reuben, 1987, Fever, 1989, Philadelphia Fire, 1990 (PEN Faulkner award for fiction, 1991), All Stories Are True, 1993, Fatheralong: A Meditation on Fathers and Sons, Race and Society, 1994, The Cattle Killing, 1996, Two Cities, 1998, Hoop Roots: Basketball, Race, and Love, 2001, God's Gym, 2005, Fanon, 2008; co-author (with Mumia Abu-Jamal): Live from Death Row, 1995; co-author: (with Bonnie TuSmith) Conversations with John Edgar Wideman, 1998; author: (short stories) Weight, 2000 (O. Henry award, 2000); contbr. articles and revs. to profl. jours., mags. Recipient Nat. Endowment for Humanities grant, Lannan Lit. award, 1991, MacArthur genius grant, 1993, Rea Award for the short story, 1998, Katherine Anne Porter award for lit., AAAL, 2008; named a Kent fellow, Ben Franklin scholar, Rhodes scholar. Mem.: MLA, Am. Acad. Arts Scis., Am. Studies Assn. (mem. coun. 1980—81), Am. Assn. Rhodes Scholars (dir.). Office: Brown U Dept African Studies Providence RI 02912

WIDENER, MARY LEE, non-profit financial executive; b. Schaal, Ark., July 6, 1938; d. Mert and Johnnie (Newton) Thomas; children: Warren Jr., Michael, Stephen. Diploma, Heald Bus. Coll., 1956; Pub. Adminstrn. Program, U. San Francisco Sch. Profl. Studies, 1978; LLD (hon.), John F. Kennedy U., 1979. Adminstrv. asst. to exec. v.p. U. Calif., Berkeley, 1959-69, office mgr. gifts and endowments, 1959-69; urban program coord. Fed. Home Loan Bank Bd., Washington, 1972-73; housing cons. Ford Found., NYC, 1973-74; exec. dir. Oakland Neighborhood Housing Svcs., Oakland, 1973-76; program cons. Urban Reinvestment Task Force, Washington, 1974-76; pres., CEO Neighborhood Housing Svcs. of Am., Inc., Oakland, 1974—. Chmn., Fed. Home Loan Bank, San Francisco, 1994-2003, Social Compact, 2004-; bd. dirs. The PMI Group, S.H. Cowell Found., The First Am. Corp.; bd. trustees Nat. Housing Conf., 2000—. Author: (with others) Housing America, 1993. Trustee, San Francisco Found., 1988-98, chair, 1996-98; trustee Ptnrs. for Livable Cmtys.; adv. bd. PEW Charitable Trusts Partnership for Civic Change, Phila.; former dir. KQED, San Francisco, United Way Bay Area, Univ. YWCA, BRIDGE Housing Corp., John F. Kennedy U., program adv. coun. Inst. Nonprofit Orgn. Mgmt., U. San Francisco; former state chair Calif. Dem. Ctrl. Com., former mem. at large, Democratic Nat. Com., San Francisco; former mem. U.S. Senate Housing Task Force, Washington, Commn. on Homelessness, Oakland; former chair affordable housing adv. coun. Fed. Home Loan Bank, San Francisco; mem. Fannie Mae's Adv. Coun.; former participant Internat. Exch. Housing Profls. Recipient award Nat. Coalition of 100 Black Women, N.Y., 1989, San Francisco LWV Women who could be Pres. award, 1996; named Housing Person of Yr., Nat. Housing Conf., Washington, 2000. Democratic. Methodist. Avocations: tennis, travel, golf. Office: Neighborhood Housing Svc Am 1970 Broadway Fl 4 Oakland CA 94612-2212 Office Phone: 510-287-4201.

WIDERA, GEORG ERNST OTTO, mechanical engineering educator, consultant; b. Dortmund, Germany, Feb. 16, 1938; arrived in U.S., 1950; s. Otto and Gertrude (Yzermann) Widera; m. Kristel Kornas, June 21, 1974; children: Erika, Nicholas. BS, U. Wis., 1960, MS, 1962, PhD, 1965. Asst. prof. then prof. dept. materials engring. U. Ill., Chgo., 1965-82, prof. mech. engring., 1982-91, head dept., 1983-91, acting head indsl. sys. engring. dept., 1985-86, dir off-campus engring. programs, 1987-88; prof., chmn. mech. and indsl. engring. dept. Marquette U., Milw., 1991—2002, co-dir. Ctr. Joining and Mfg. Assembly, 2002—, dir. Discovery Learning Ctr., 2000—07, sr. assoc. dean Coll. Engring., 1999—2007, interim dean Coll. Engring., 1998—99, 2003, prof., sr. scholar, 2007—. Gastdozent U. Stuttgart, Germany, 1968; vis. prof. U. Wis.-Milw., 1973—74, Marquette U., Milw., 1979—80; cons. Ladish Co., Cudahy, Wis., 1967—76, Howmedica, Inc., Chgo., 1972—75, Sargent & Lundy, 1970—88, Nat. Bur. Stds., 1980; bd. dirs. Engrs. and Scientists Milw., 1996—98; vis. scientist Argonne Nat. Lab., Ill., 1968. Editor: Procs. Innovations in Structural Engring., 1974, Pressure Vessel Design, 1982, Jour. Pressure Vessel Tech., 1982—93, 2005—; co-editor: SME Handbook of Metalforming, 1985, 1994, Design and Analysis of Plates and Shells, 1986; assoc. editor: Pressure Vessel Tech., 1977—81, 2003—05, Applied Mechanics Revs., 1987—94, Mfg. Rev., 1991—95, mem. editl. adv. bd.: Acta Mechanica Sinica, 1990—98, mem. editl. bd.: Pressure Vessels and Piping Design Technology, 1982. Fellow Std. Oil Co. Calif., 1961—63, NASA, 1966, von Humboldt, Fed. Republic Germany, 1968—69. Fellow: WRC (chmn. subcom. design procedures for shell intersections 1983—87, chmn. com. reinforced openings and external loads 1987—91, vice chmn. com. polymer pressure components 1991—99, chmn. com. shells and ligaments 1994—97, pressure vessel rsch. coun.), ASCE (sec.-treas. structural divsn. Ill. sect. 1972—73, chmn. divsn. 1976—77, chmn. peer rev. com., tech. coun. rsch. 1984, coun. structural plastics), ASME (chmn. machine design div. Chgo. sect. 1967—68, exec. com. Chgo. sect. 1970—73, editor newsletter Chgo. sect. 1971—73, chmn. jr. awards com. applied mechanics divsn. 1973—76, chmn. design and analysis com. pressure vessel and piping divsn. 1980—83, chmn. pressure vessel rsch. com. 1982—87, bd. editors 1983—93, mem. exec. com. and program chmn. pressure vessel and piping divsn. 1985—89, vice-chmn., sec. pressure vessel and piping divsn. 1989—90, mem. bd. pressure tech. codes and stds. 1989—94, mem. materials and structures group 1990—91, historian, senate pressure vessel and piping divsn. 1992—93, honors and awards chmn. Milw. sect. 1992—95, mem. coun. engring. 1992—96, v.p., chair materials and structures group 1993—96, mem. tech. execs. com. 1993—96, bd. editors 2005—, mem. bd. pressure tech. codes and stds. 2009—, Pressure Vessel and Piping medalist 1995), 2d China Nat. Stds. Com. Pressure Vessels (hon. cons. 1989—94), Internat. Coun. Pressure Vessel Tech. (chmn. Am. regional com. 1988—, internat. chmn. 1992—96, 2003—06), French Pressure Vessel Assn., Wis. Mfg. Curriculum Com. (life; vice-chmn. exec. com. 1998—2002), Soc. Mfg. Engrs. (sr.; life mem., co-chair NAMRC 34), Am. Soc. Engring. Edn.; mem.: Wis. Assn. Rsch. Mgmt. (v.p. 2003—04, pres. 2004—05), Tau Beta Pi. Achievements include research in mechanics of composite materials, plate and shell structures, stress analysis, pressure vessels, mechanics of deformation processing. Office: Marquette U Coll Engring PO Box 1881 Milwaukee WI 53201-1881 Office Phone: 414-288-3543. Business E-Mail: jpvt@marquette.edu.

WIDHELM, JENNIFER COCHRAN, theater educator; b. Cin., Jan. 6, 1958; d. George Robert and Jane Louise Kramer; m. William John Widhelm, Mar. 11, 2000; m. Randall George Cochran, June 16, 1986 (div. July 10, 1994); children: Hannah Lee Cochran, Hayley Jane Cochran. BFA in Theatre summa cum laude, San Marcos, Tex. Cert. tchr. Tex., 2000. Music tchr. Sunshine Cottage Sch. Deaf, San Antonio, Tex., 2001—05; theatre arts tchr. Kazen Mid. Sch., San Antonio, 2005—07. Actress Equity Assn., 1980—86. Actor: (musical theatre) College Competition (Coll. Performing Arts Kennedy Ctr., 1979). Liberal. Lutheran. Avocations: singing, travel. Office: Cole Middle Sch Fort Sam Houston ISD 1902 Wianas Rd San Antonio TX 78234 Personal E-mail: jenniferwidhelm@aol.com.

WIDING, ERIC P., auction specialist; BA in Art History, Williams Coll. Head, american paintings dept. Christie's, NYC, sr. v.p. Contbr. articles to art jours. Mem.: Phi Beta Kappa. Office: Christie's NY 20 Rockefeller Plz New York NY 10020 Office Phone: 212-636-2140. Office Fax: 212-636-4924. Business E-Mail: ewiding@christies.com.

WIDLUND, OLOF BERTIL, computer science educator, mathematician; b. Stockholm, Feb. 11, 1938; s. Sten O. and Dagmar W.; m. Nadine H. Taub, June 13, 1972. MS in Engring., Royal Inst. Tech., Stockholm, 1960, PhD, 1964; habilitation, Uppsala U., Sweden, 1966. Asst. prof. NYU, NYC, 1968-72, assoc. prof., 1972-75, prof. computer sci., 1975—, chmn. dept. computer sci., 1980-86. Contbr. articles to profl. jours. and a rsch. monograph. Achievements include research in numerical solutions of partial differential equations. Office: NYU Courant Inst 251 Mercer St New York NY 10012-1110 Business E-Mail: widlund@cims.nyu.edu.

WIDMAN, GARY LEE, lawyer; b. Fremont, Nebr., June 1, 1936; s. Benjamin H. and Alice C. (Negley) W.; m. Mary Margaret Donnelly, Mar. 5, 1972(div. 1988); children: Andrew Scott, Natalie Claire. BS, U. Nebr., 1957; JD, Hastings Coll. Law U. Calif., 1962; LLM, U. Mich., 1966. Bar: Calif. 1962, D.C. 1982. Assoc. Thelen, Marrin, Johnson & Bridges, San Francisco, 1962-65; assoc. prof. law U. Denver, 1966-69; prof., dir. resource and environ. law program Hastings Coll. Law, U. Calif., San Francisco, 1969-80; gen. counsel Coun. Environ. Quality, Exec. Office Pres., Washington, 1974-76; lectr. U. Calif. at Davis, 1978, Boalt Hall, 1977-79; assoc. solicitor Dept. Interior, Washington, 1980-81; of counsel Fulbright & Jaworski, 1981-85; dir. staff attys. U.S. Ct. of Appeals (9th cir.), San Francisco, 1985-87; atty. Bronson, Bronson & McKinnon, San Francisco, 1988-95; chief counsel State Dept. Parks and Recreation, Sacramento, 1995-96; prof. law Santa Clara (Calif.) U. Law Sch., 1998-99; sr. mediator Concur Inc., Berkeley, Calif., 2001—04. Trustee Rocky Mountain Mineral Law Found., 1969-74, 77-80; apptd. by gov. P. Wilson to Bay-Delta Oversight Coun., 1993-95. Author and project dir.: Legal Study of Oil Shale on Public Lands, 1969-07. Bd. dir. Sustainable Bus. Inst., 2004-08, Achenbach Graphic Arts Coun.,mem. Fine Arts Mus. San Francisco, 2004—, vice chair, 2008. Served with U.S. Army, 1957-59. Mem. ABA (coun. sect. natural resources 1975-77, spl. com. energy law 1977-82, coun. lawyers and scientists 1984-90), Fed. Bar Assn. (chmn. com. natural resources 1977), Calif. Bar Assn., Trout Unltd. Calif. (pres. 1986-90), Calif. Heritage Coun. (pres. 2004-06, bd. chair 2006-08), Presidio Hist. Assn (v.p 2004-06, pres. 2006—). Home: 28 Marinero Cir Apt 31 Tiburon CA 94920-1644 Personal E-mail: gwidman@mindspring.com.

WIDMAN, PHILLIP C., machinery manufacturing executive; Fin. and opers. positions Asea Brown Boveri Ltd., 1987—98; v.p., CFO, supply mgmt., 1997—98; exec. v.p., CFO Philip Svcs. Corp., 1998—2001, ind. cons., 2001—02; sr. v.p., CFO Terex Corp., Westport, Conn., 2002—. Office: Terex Corporation 200 Nyala Farms Rd Westport CT 06880-6261

WIDMAN, RUDOLPH PAUL, college administrator; b. Abington, Pa., Sept. 19, 1940; s. Rudolph Paul and Sara (Brinker) W.; m. Alberta Elanora Sabino, May 20, 1963; children— Rudi Paul, Karl Albert. A.B., Eastern Nazarene Coll., Wollaston, Mass., 1963; M.S., Northeastern U., 1965, Ph.D., 1971; M.B.A., Fla. Inst. Tech., Jensen Beach, 1982. Tchr., Plymouth-Carver High Sch. (Mass.), 1964-66; prof. chemistry Curry Coll., Milton, Mass., 1966-68; research fellow U. Va., Charlottesville, 1971-73; adminstrv. asst. Piedmont Va. Community Coll., Charlottesville, 1974-2003; dean of librs. Indian River Community Coll., Ft. Pierce, Fla., 1974—2003. Pres. bd. dirs. Sun Grove Montessori Sch., Ft. Pierce, 1975—; bd. dirs. St. Michael's Sch., Stuart, Fla., 1977—, Fla. Found. Future Scientists, Gainesville, 1977—, Community Action Orgn., Ft. Pierce, 1975-78. Recipient 4th Annual award Soc. Applied Spectroscopy, 1970. Mem. Fla. Atlantic U. (mem. lib. adv. com. 2006-), St. Lucie County Lib. (mem. adv. bd. 1996-), Fla. Assn. Community Colls., Sigma Xi, Phi Kappa Phi, Phi Delta Kappa. Contbr. articles to profl. publs.

WIDMANN, R L., literature and language professor; b. Watertown, Wis., Nov. 16, 1941; d. William Edward and Evelyn Bernice Zastrow Widmann. BA, U. Wis., Madison, 1963; AM, U. Ill., Champaign Urbana, 1964, PhD, 1967. English prof. U. Pa., Phila., 1974, U. Colo., Boulder, 1975—, chair cu faculty coun. Denver, 2006—08, past chair cu faculty coun., 2008—. Advisor SEED Found., Washington, 2000—. Mem. bd. Consenting Adults, Washington, 1980—86. Recipient Numerous Tchg. awards, U. Colo. Boulder, 1976, Svc. award, U.Colo. Pres. Office, 1987, U. Colo. Boulder, 1988, U. Colo. Faculty Coun., 2003, award, U. Colo., 1978, 1986, 1993, 2000; fellowships, Folger Shakespeare Libr., 1969, 1972, 1974—75. Mem.: MLA, U. Ill. Alumni Assn., U. Wis. Alumni Assn., Renaissance English Text Soc. Liberal. Achievements include development of creation of numerous courses for English dept at UCB. Avocations: reading, travel. Home: 109 7th St SE Washington DC 20003 Office: U Colorado Boulder English Dept 226 UCB-101 Hellems Boulder CO 80309-0226 Office Fax: 303-492-8904; Home Fax: 202-675-0313. Personal E-mail: rlw109@gmail.com. Business E-Mail: r.widmann@colorado.edu.

WIDMANN, ROGER FRANKLIN, Pediatric Orthopaedic Surgeon; m. Miriam A. Leventhal, Mar. 1988. B summa cum laude, Yale Univ., 1985, MD, 1989. Cert. Am. Bd. Orthopaedic Surgery, 1997. Resident in pediatric orthopaedic surgery Mass. Gen. Hosp., Harvard Univ., 1989—94; fellowship in pediatric orthopaedic surgery Children's Hosp., Boston, 1994—95; assoc. attending orthopaedic surgeon, Pediatric Orthopaedic Surgery Svc. Hosp. for Spl. Surgery, NYC, 1995—, chief, Pediatric Orthopaedic Surgery Svc., 2004—, co-chief, Limb-Lengthening Svc. & mem. Scoliosis Svc.; dir. pediatric orthopaedic trauma NY Hosp.; assoc. prof., clinical orthopaedic surgery Weill Cornell Med. Coll., NYC. Contbr. articles to profl. jours. Recipient Doniger Prize for MD Thesis, Yale Sch. Med., 1989. Mem.: AMA, Am. Bd. Orthopaedic Surgery, Am. Acad. Pediatrics, Am. Acad. Orthopaedic Surgeons, Am. Acad. Cerebral Palsy & Develop. Med., Phi Beta Kappa, Sigma Xi. Office: Hosp for Spl Surgery 535 E 70th St New York NY 10021 also: Burke Rehabilitation Office 785 Mamaroneck Ave White Plains NY 10605 Office Phone: 212-606-1325. Office Fax: 212-717-0673.

WIDNALL, SHEILA EVANS, aeronautical educator, former secretary of air force, university official; b. Tacoma, July 13, 1938; d. Rolland John and Genievieve Alice (Krause) Evans; m. William Soule Widnall, June 11, 1960; children: William, Ann. BS in Aero. and Astronautics, MIT, 1960, MS in Aero. and Astronautics, 1961, DSc, 1964; PhD (hon.), New Eng. Coll., 1975, Lawrence U., 1987, Cedar Crest Coll., 1988, Smith Coll., 1990, Mt. Holyoke Coll., 1991, Ill. Inst. Tech., 1991, Columbia U., 1994, Simmons Coll., 1994, Suffolk U., 1994, Princeton U., 1994. Asst. prof. aeros. and astronautics MIT, Cambridge, 1964-70, assoc. prof., 1970-74, prof., 1974-93, head divsn. fluid mechanics, 1975-79; dir. Fluid Dynamics Rsch. Lab., MIT, Cambridge, 1979-90; chmn. faculty MIT, Cambridge, 1979-80, chair com. on acad. responsibility, 1991-92, assoc. provost, 1992-93; sec. USAF, 1993-97; Inst. prof. MIT, Cambridge, 1997—. Bd. dirs. Gen. Corp., Chemfab Inc., Bennington, Vt., Aerospace Corp., L.A., Draper Labs., Cambridge, Gencorp; past trustee Carnegie Corp., 1984-92, Charles Stark Draper Lab. Inc.; mem. Carnegie Commn. Sci., Tech. and Govt, mem. Columbia Accident Investigation Bd, 2003-. Co-author: Lean Enterprise Value: Insights from MIT's Lean Aerospace Initiative, 2002 (Engring. Sci. Book award Internat. Acad. Astronautics 2003); contbr. articles to profl. jours.; patentee in field; assoc. editor AIAA Jour. Aircraft, 1972-75, Physics of Fluids, 1981-88, Jour. Applied Mechanics, 1983-87; mem. editorial bd. Sci., 1984-86. Bd. visitors USAF Acad., Colorado Springs, Colo., 1978-84, bd. chair, 1980-82; trustee Boston Mus. Sci., 1989-93, Sloan Found., 1998-. Recipient Washburn award, Boston Mus. Sci., 1987; named to Nat. Women's Hall of Fame, 2003. Fellow AAAS (bd. dirs. 1982-89, pres. 1987-88, chmn. 1988-89), AIAA (bd. dirs. 1975-77, Lawrence Sperry award 1972, Durand Lectureship for Pub. Svc. award 1996, pres. 2000-01), Am. Phys. Soc. (exec. com. 1979-82); mem. ASME (Applied Mechs. award 1995, Pres. award 1999), NAE (coun. 1992-93, v.p. 1998—), NAS (panel on sci. responsibility), Am. Acad. Arts and Scis., Soc. Women Engrs. (Outstanding Achievement award 1975), Internat. Acad. Astronautics, Seattle Mountaineers. Office: MIT Bldg 33-411 77 Massachussetts Ave Cambridge MA 02139 Office Phone: 617-253-3595. E-mail: sheila@mit.edu.

WIDNER, RALPH RANDOLPH, retired public administrator; b. Phila., Oct. 21, 1930; s. Ralph Litteer and Viola (Cunningham) W.; m. Joan Sundelius Ziegler, July 9, 1955; children: Jennifer Anne, Wendy Widner Ducharme. BA, Duke U., 1952; postgrad., NYU, 1957, Georgetown U., 1958; DHL (hon.), Union Coll., Ky., 1970, Capital U., Columbus, Ohio, 1971. Journalist Paterson (N.J.) Evening News, 1955-56, N.Y. Times, 1956-58; Congressional fellow Am. Polit. Sci. Assn., 1958; dir. pub. affairs Pa. Dept. Forests and Waters, 1959-60; asst. dir. Pa. Planning Bd., 1960-62; legis. asst. to U.S. Senator Clark, 1962-65; exec. dir. Appalachian Regional Commn., 1965-71; pres. Acad. for contemporary problems, 1971-82; adj. prof. pub. adminstrn. and city planning Ohio State U., 1971-82; pres. Nat. Tng. and Devel. Service for State and Local Govt., 1979-81; staff v.p. Urban Land Inst., 1982-83; exec. dir. Greater Phila. First Corp., 1983-88; chmn. emeritus Fairfax House Internat. Author: Forests and Forestry in the American States, Regional Development in the United States; co-author: Revitalizing the Industrial City. Bd. dir. Am. Forestry Assn., Landscape Architecture Found., Am. Soc. Public Adminstrn., Nature Conservancy, Va., Northeast-Midwest Inst. Lt. jr. grade USN, 1952—55. Rsch. fellow, Urban Land Inst., 1975. Fellow Nat. Acad. Pub. Adminstrn. (sr.). Democrat. Personal E-mail: ralph.widner@comcast.net.

WIDNER, ROBERTA ANN, accountant, artist; b. El Paso, Tex., Sept. 27, 1940; d. Wilburn Alton and Frances (Martin) Leavelle; m. Jerry Wesley Widner, Jan. 21, 1959; children: Kim, Mark. Attended, Fechin Inst., 1986. Civil svc. Fed. Govt., 1958, cert. state merit system State of N.Mex, 1958. Stenographer Employment Security Commn. Legal Dept., Albuquerque, 1958, Cannon AFB Comdr.'s Office, Clovis, 1958; sec. to pres. Walker Wholesale Hardware, Jacksonville, 1959; stenographer Household Fin. Corp., San Diego, 1960—61; temp. clk. U.S. Post Office, Clovis, 1974; sec./acctg. Coop. Ext. Svc./Dir. - 4-H - NMSU Rodeo Dept., Las Cruces, 1977—. Sec. N.Mex Employment Security Commn., Albuquerque, 1958; state triticale sec. N.Mex Triticale Assn., Clovis; profl. improvement com. Coop. Ext. Svc., Las Cruces, 1983—84. Oils, pastels, watercolors. Planning com. fashion fund raisers Am. Cancer Soc., Las Cruces, 1991—92; planning com. ann. renaissance fair Dona Ana Arts Coun., Las Cruces, 1985—85; planning com. nat. maid of cotton fashion show Cotton Inc., Las Cruces. Recipient Pres.'s Star Performer award, NMSU, 2002. Mem.: Border Book Festival, Dona Arts Coun., Mesilla Valley Arts Guild (treas. 1985). Achievements include juried Exhibit - El Paso Museum of Art, 1987; juried - Internat. Penwomens' Mex./U.S. Exhibit; juried Art - Cinco Pintores - Linda Lundeen Gallery/Las Cruces; juried - Southern New Mexico Arts Profls., 1999; juried - Rio Grande Arts Invitational, 1998. Avocations: painting, Mexican/European travel, ballooning, sewing, water-skiing. Business E-Mail: rwidner@nmsu.edu.

WIDOM, BENJAMIN, chemistry professor; b. Newark, Oct. 13, 1927; s. Morris and Rebecca (Hertz) W.; m. Joanne McCurdy, Dec. 21, 1953; children: Jonathan, Michael, Elisabeth. AB, Columbia U., NYC, 1949; PhD, Cornell U., Ithaca, NY, 1953; DSc (hon.), U. Chgo., 1991; Dr. honoris causa, U. Utrecht, 1999. Rsch. assoc. U. N.C., Chapel Hill, 1952-54; instr. chemistry Cornell U., Ithaca, NY, 1954-55, asst. prof., 1955-59, assoc. prof., 1959-63, prof., 1963-83, Goldwin Smith prof., 1983—2007, prof. emeritus, 2007—; van der Waals prof. U. Amsterdam, Netherlands, 1972; vis. prof. Harvard U., Cambridge, Mass., 1975; IBM vis. prof. Oxford U., England, 1978. Lorentz prof. U. Leiden, The Netherlands, 1985; vis. prof. Kath. U. Leuven, Belgium, 1988, U. Aix Marseille, France, 1995; Kramers/Debye prof. U. Utrecht, 1999. Co-author: (with J.S. Rowlinson) Molecular Theory of Capillarity, 1982; author: Statistical Mechanics, 2002. With US Army, 1946-47. Recipient Clark disting. tchg. award Cornell U., 1973, Dickson prize for sci. Carnegie-Mellon U., 1986, Hirschfelder Prize in Theoretical Chemistry U. Wis., 1991, Bakhuis Roozeboom medal Royal Netherlands Acad. Arts & Scis., 1994, Onsager medal U. Trondheim, Norway, 1994, Boltzmann medal Internat. Union of Pure and Applied Physics, Commn. on Statis. Physics, 1998. Fellow Am. Phys. Soc., Am. Acad. Arts and Scis., NY Acad. Scis. (Boris Pregel award for chem. physics rsch. 1976); mem. NAS, Am. Philos. Soc., Am. Chem. Soc. (Langmuir award in chem. physics 1982, Hildebrand award in theoretical and exptl. chemistry of liquids 1992, Theoretical Chemistry award 1999). Home: 204 The Parkway Ithaca NY 14850-2247 Office: Cornell U Chemistry Dept Ithaca NY 14853 Office Phone: 607-255-3363. Business E-Mail: bw24@cornell.edu.

WIDOM, HAROLD, mathematician, educator; b. Newark, Sept. 23, 1932; s. Morris and Rebecca (Hertz) W.; m. Lois Sanow, Mar. 20, 1955 (div. Sept. 1976); children: Barbara, Jennifer, Steven; m. Linda Novick, May 26, 1985. Attended, CUNY, 1951; MS, U. Chgo., 1952, PhD, 1955. From instr. to prof. Cornell U., Ithaca, NY, 1955-68; with U. Calif., Santa Cruz, 1968—, prof. emeritus. Author: (book) Lectures on Measure and Integration, 1969, Lectures on Integral Equations, 1969; assoc. editor Jour. Integral Equations Operator Theory, Asymptotic Analysis, Mathematical Physics, Analysis and Geometry; hon. editor Integral Equations and Operator Theory; contbr. over 130 articles to profl. jours. NSF postdoctoral fellow, 1959-60, Alfred P. Sloan Found. fellow, 1964-65, J.S. Guggenheim Found. fellow, 1967-68, 72-73; NSF grantee, 1970—; co-recipient with Craig Tracy, George Polya prize, Soc. Indsl. and Applied Math., 2002 Fellow: Am. Acad. Arts and Sciences; mem.: Am. Math. Soc. (and the Soc. for Indsl. and Applied Math., Norbert Wiener prize in Applied Math. with Craig Tracy 2007). Office: Professor Emeritus Math Dept 133B Kerr Hall 353B Baskin Engineering Santa Cruz CA 95064 Office Phone: 831-459-2652. Office Fax: 831-459-3260. E-mail: widom@math.ucsc.edu.

WIDOM, MICHAEL, physicist, researcher; b. Ithaca, NY, Oct. 29, 1958; s. Benjamin and Joanne Widom; m. Mary Reed, Feb. 4, 1984; children: Julia, Theodore, Anne. BA, Cornell U., 1980; PhD, U. Chgo., 1983. Postdoctoral assoc. Harvard U., Cambridge, Mass., 1983-85; asst. prof., assoc. prof. Carnegie Mellon U., Pitts., 1985-94, prof., 1994—. Vis. assoc. prof. Cornell U., Ithaca, 1991-92; vis. prof. U. Paris-Sud, Orsay, 1993, U. Paris VII, 1996. Contbr. articles to profl. jours. Fellow A.P. Sloan Found., 1991; grantee NSF, 1987—, Petroleum Rsch. Fund, 1988. Fellow Am. Phys. Soc. Achievements include research of thermodynamics and structure of quasicrystals, phase transitions in ferrofluids. Home: 5549 Darlington Rd Pittsburgh PA 15217-1507 Office: Dept Physics Carnegie Mellon Univ Pittsburgh PA 15213

WIE, MICHELLE SUNG, professional golfer; b. Honolulu, Oct. 11, 1989; d. Byung-Wook and Hyun-Kyong Sung Wie. Attended, Stanford U., 2007—08. Profl. golfer, 2005—, LPGA Tour, 2009—. Mem. US nat. team Solheim Cup, 2009. Named one of The 100 Most Influential People in the World, TIME mag., 2006. Mem.: Hawaii State Jr. Golf Assn. Achievements include winner amatuer tournaments: Hawaii State Women's Stroke Play Championship, 2001, USGA Women's Amateur Pub. Links Championship, 2003, Jennie K. Wilson Invitational 2004; youngest player to make a LPGA major cut (13 years old), playing in the Kraft Nabisco Championship, 2003; member of Solheim Cup winning US national team, 2009. Avocations: reading, drawing, computers. Office: c/o LPGA 100 Internat Golf Dr Daytona Beach FL 32124-1092*

WIEAND, LOU ANN, psychology educator, psychotherapist; b. South Bend, Ind. d. Cassel B. and Martha Grace (Kurtz) W.; children: Joel Brent, Brian Randal, Darin Michael. BA, Manchester Coll., Ind., 1963; MA, Ball State U., Ind., 1977; PhD, U. Calif.-Riverside, 1983. Asst. prof. U. Redland, Calif., 1979-80; research assoc. Loma Linda VA Hosp., Calif., 1980-82; prof. Humboldt State U., Arcata, Calif., 1982—. Cons. mental health agys.; pvt. practice psychotherapy, 1980—. Contbr. chpt. to book. Mem. APA, Soc. Psychol. Study Social Issues, APS, SSSS. Office Phone: 707-826-5263. Business E-Mail: law3@humboldt.edu.

WIEBENSON, DORA LOUISE, architectural historian, editor, writer; b. Cleve., July 29, 1926; d. Edward Ralph and Jeannette (Rodier) W. BA, Vassar Coll., 1946; MArch, Harvard U., 1951; MA, NYU, 1958, PhD, 1964. Architect, N.Y., 1951-66; lectr. Columbia U., 1966-68; assoc. prof. U. Md., 1968-72, prof., 1972-77; vis. prof. Cornell U., 1974; prof. U. Va., Charlottesville, 1977-92, prof. emeritus, 1992—, chmn. div. archtl. history, 1977-79, assoc. fellow U. Va. Ctr. Advanced Studies, 1982-83; pres. Archtl. Publs., NYC, 1982—; editor-in-chief Centropa, 2000—. Editor: Marsyas XI: 1962-64, 1965, Essays in Honor of Walter Friedlaender, 1965; Architectural Theory and Practice from Alberti to Ledoux, 1982, rev., 1983, Spanish transl., 1988; Guide to Graduate Degree Programs in Architectural History, 1982, rev., 1984, 86, 88, 90; co-editor: The Architecture of Historic Hungary, 1998, Hungarian transl., 1998; author: Sources of Greek Revival Architecture, 1969, Tony Garnier: The Cité Industrielle, 1969, Japanese transl., 1983, The Picturesque Garden in France, 1978, Mark J. Millard Architectural Collection, Vol. I: French Books: Sixteenth through Nineteenth Centuries, 1993; contbr. articles to profl. jours. Student fellow Inst. Fine Arts, 1961-62, 62-63; grantee Am. Philos. Soc., 1964-65, 70, Samuel H. Kress Found., 1966, 72-73, 98, Gen. Rsch. Fund, U. Md., 1969, 74, 76, NEH, 1972-73, Am. Coun. Learned Socs., 1976, 81, 85, Ctr. Advanced Studies, U. Va., 1980, 81, 97, Graham Found. Advanced Studies Fine Arts, 1982, 93, Archtl. History Found., 1996; fellow Yale Ctr. Brit. Art, 1983; sr. rsch. fellow NEH, 1986-87. Mem. Soc. Archtl. Historians (bd. dirs. 1974-77, 80-83, chair edn. com. 1976-90), Coll. Art Assn., Am. Assn. Advancement Slavic Studies, Am. Soc. Eighteenth Century (mem. exec. bd. 1991-94). Business E-Mail: centropa@rcn.com.

WIEBERS, TODD, psychology professor; BA, Ohio State U., Columbus, 1984, MA, 1988, PhD, 1992. Cert. Bailey & Bailey Workshop, Animal Behavior Enterprises, 2002. Dir. undergrad. rsch. Henderson State U., Arkadelphia, 1994—99, chair & prof. psychology, 1992—. Grant, Ark. Dept. Higher Edn., 1993—95. Mem.: Southwestern Psychol. Assn., Psi Chi Nat. Honor Soc. (advisor 1992—). Achievements include research in animal behavior. Office: Henderson State Univ 1100 Henderson St Arkadelphia AR 71999 Business E-Mail: wiebert@hsu.edu.

WIECHA, JOSEPH AUGUSTINE, language educator; b. Chorzów II, Poland, Sept. 20, 1926; came to U.S., 1955, naturalized, 1958; s. Karol and Gertruda (Rudzki) W.; m. Mary Ruth Moore, 1953; children: Joseph Damian, Charles Francis, John Moore. BA with first class honors, Nat. U. Ireland, 1950; PhD with distinction, NYU, 1963. Instr. fgn. langs. U.S. Third Air Force, London, 1951-55; instr. German and Spanish U. Md., London, 1951-55; tchr. Spanish and math. Bklyn. Friends Sch., 1955-56; instr. German NYU, NYC, summer, 1958; lectr. German and humanities Harvard U., Boston, 1959-63; lectr. German lit. Colby Coll., summer 1963; prof. German SUNY, Oswego, 1963-69, chmn. dept. fgn. langs. and lit., 1963-69, chmn. dept. Germanic and Slavic langs. and lit., 1969-72, disting. teaching prof., 1973-92, disting. tchg. prof. emeritus, 1992—; chmn. SUNY Fgn. Studies Ctr., 1972-73. Lectr. and cons. methodology of tchg. fgn. langs., 1959—; condr. seminars tchg. methodology fgn. langs. Nat. U. Pedro Enriquez Ureña, Santo Domingo, 1973, U. Pisa, Italy, 1974, Moscow State Pedagogical Inst.; Fgn. Langs., USSR, 1976; vis. prof. U. Wroctaw, Poland, 1977. Served as officer 2d Polish Corps Brit. VIII Army, 1944-47. Decorated Bronze medal Polish Army, Brit. Def. medal; French Star; Star of Italy; recipient diploma of spl. recognition U. Nat. Pedro Enriquez Ureña, 1973; Galileo medal U. Pisa, 1974; Ogden Butler fellow, 1958-59, Fels fellow, 1956-59, Kosciuszko Found. fellow, 1959. Mem. MLA, N.Y. State Assn. Fgn. Lang. Tchrs. (dir. 1975-78, Disting. Tchr. award 1975, Disting. Bd. Dirs. award 1978, Spl. Contbn. to Teaching Fgn. Langs. award 1979), Am. Assn. Tchrs. of German, Polish Inst. Arts and Scis. in Am., Nat. Spanish Honors Soc. (hon.), Am. Coun. on Edn. (nat. honor roll), Delta Phi Alpha (hon.), Dobro Slovo (hon.) Achievements include development of Wiecha Progressive-Reflex method of teaching fgn. langs. Home: 710 Copa De Oro Marathon FL 33050-5406 also: 45 Tall Oaks Dr Northport ME 04849-4435 Personal E-mail: joemarywiecha@att.net.

WIECHMANN, ERIC WATT, lawyer; b. Schenectady, NY, June 12, 1948; s. Richard Jerdone and Ann (Watt) W.; m. Merrill Metzger, May 22, 1971. BA, Hamilton Coll., Clinton, NY, 1970; JD, Cornell U., Ithaca, NY, 1974. Bar: Conn. 1974, US Dist. Ct. (so. and ea. dists.) NY 1975, US Dist. Ct. Conn. 1975, US Dist. Ct. D.C. 1981, US Ct. Appeals (2nd cir.) 1975, US Ct. Appeals (9th cir.) 1980, US Ct. Appeals DC 1982, US Ct. Appeals (5th cir.) 1986, US Ct. Appeals (10th cir.) 1989, US Supreme Ct. 1978. Assoc. Cummings & Lockwood LLC, Stamford, Conn., 1974—82, ptnr., 1982—2003, mng. ptnr. Hartford office, bd. dirs., 1996—2003, bus. clients exec. com., 2003; ptnr. McCarter & English LLP, Hartford, Conn., 2003—, mng. ptnr., Hartford office, 2003—04, mem. exec. com., 2003—, mem. compensation com., 2004—, firm mng. ptnr., 2007—. Spl. pretrial master US Dist. Ct. Conn., 1984—; state atty. trial referee, 1986—, mem. evidence code oversight com., 2002—; civil task force, 1995—, civil jury instrn. com. Conn. Superior Ct., 1996-2000, docket control com., 2001—; comml. arbitrator Am. Arbitration Assn. Contbr. articles to profl. jours. Mem. Zoning Bd. Appeals, New Canaan, Conn., 1984-85; bd. dirs. Conn. Rivers coun. Boy Scouts Am., trustee; bd. dirs. Internat. Assn. Def. Counsel Found., pres., 2005—09. Mem. ABA (vice-chmn. toxics and hazardous law com. TIPS sect.), Def. Rsch. Inst., Internat. Assn. Def. Counsel (faculty Def. Trial Acad. 1996, chmn. toxic and hazardous substance com. 1998-99, chmn. CLE bd. 2000-02, bd. dirs. 2006-), Internat. Soc. Barristers, Conn. Bar Assn. (life fellow; exec. com. antitrust sect. 1982—, ct. rules adv. com, chmn. 1991-93), Conn. Bar Found. (life fellow) Home: 705 Weed St Apt A New Canaan CT 06840-4000 Office Phone: 860-275-6731. Personal E-mail: ewiech@yahoo.com. Business E-Mail: ewiechmann@mccarter.com.

WIECKERT, STEVEN KELLY, real estate developer, former state legislator; b. Appleton, Wis., Oct. 26, 1954; s. Carlton Albert and Betty Jane (Marx) Wieckert. BS in Polit. Sci., Am. U., Washington, 1978, MPA, 1981. Congrl. aide to representative Thomas Petri, Washington, 1979-83; realtor, broker Madison, Wis., 1990—; CEO Wieckert Real Estate, Appleton, 1983—; mem. from Dist. 57 Wis. House of Reps., Madison, 1997—2008. Named Legislator of Yr., Wis. Ind. Bus. Assn., 1999. Mem.: Wis. Soc. Ornithology, Am. Soc. Pub. Adminstrn., Fox Cities C. of C., Valley Home Builders Assn., Wis. Realtors Assn., Ducks Unltd., Madison Athletic Club, Phi Alpha Alpha. Avocations: birkebeiner ski race, ornithology. Office: Wieckert Real Estate 3033 W Spencer St Appleton WI 54914 E-mail: swieckert@aol.com.*

WIECZOREK, JOHN RICHARD, application developer, systems analyst; b. River Falls, Wis., Mar. 8, 1963; s. John Richard Vichorek and Sara Ellen Wieczorek; life ptnr. Eileen Anne Lacey. AB in Physics, Cornell U., 1984. Programmer, analyst Mus. of Vertebrate Zoology, U. Calif., Berkeley, 1997—. Mem. sci. subcom. data access and database interoperability Global Biodiversity Info. Facility, Copenhagen, 2004—; co-convenor of geospatial interest group Taxonomic Databases Working Group, 2004—. Co-developer (distributed database protocol) Distributed Generic Information Retrieval. Recipient Ebbe Nielsen prize, Global Biodiversity Info. Facility, 2006. Avocations: volleyball, travel. Office: U Calif Mus Vertebrate Zoology 3101 VLSB Berkeley CA 94720 Office Fax: 510-643-8238. Business E-Mail: tuco@berkeley.edu.

WIED, GEORGE LUDWIG, physician; b. Carlsbad, Czechoslovakia, Feb. 7, 1921; came to U.S., 1953, naturalized, 1960; s. Ernst George and Anna (Travnicek) W.; m. Kayoko Y. Yamauchi, 1980; 1 child, George. MD, Charles U., Prague, 1945, Hon. Med. Degree, 1995. Intern County Hosp., Carlsbad, Czechoslovakia, 1945; intern U. Chgo. Hosps., 1955; resident in ob-gyn U. Munich, Fed. Republic Germany, 1946-48; practice medicine specializing in ob-gyn West Berlin, 1948-53; asst. ob-gyn Free U., West Berlin, 1948-52; assoc. chmn. dept. ob-gyn Moabit Hosp., Free U., West Berlin, 1953; asst. prof., dir. cytology U. Chgo., 1954-59, assoc. prof., 1959-65, prof., 1965-91, mem. bd. adult edn., 1964-68, prof. pathology, 1967-91, Blum-Riese prof. ob-gyn, 1968-91, acting chmn. dept. ob-gyn, 1974-75. Editor-in-chief Jour. Reproductive Medicine, Acta Cytologica, Analytical and Quantitative Cytology, Clinical Cytology; editor: Introduction to Quantitative Cytochemistry, Automated Cell Identification and Cell Sorting, Compendium on Clinical Cytology, Compendium on the Computerized Cytology and Histology Laboratory, Compendium on Quality Assurance in Clinical Cytology; sr. editor Gen. and Diagnostic Pathology. Hon. dir. Chgo. Cancer Prevention Ctr., 1959-83; chmn. jury Maurice Goldblatt Cytology award, 1963-92. Recipient Cert. of Merit, U.S. Surgeon Gen., 1952, Maurice Goldblatt Cytology award, 1961, George N. Papanicolaou Cytology award, 1970, Masubuchi Gold Medal award 13th Internat. Cytology Congress, 1998, Kazumsa Masubuchi Lifetime Achievement award, 1998. Mem. Am. Soc. Cytology (pres. 1965-66), Mex. Soc. Cytology (hon.), Spanish Soc. Cytology (hon.), Brazilian Soc. Cytology (fgn. corr.), Indian Acad. Cytology (hon., Lifetime Achievement award 1998), Latin-Am. Soc. Cytology (hon.), Japanese Soc. Cytology (hon.), Internat. Acad. Cytology (pres. 1977-80), German Soc. Cytology (hon.), Ctrl. Soc. Clin. Rsch., Chgo. Path. Soc., Chgo. Gynecol. Soc. (hon.), Am. Soc. Cell Biology, German Soc. Ob-Gyn, Bavarian Soc. Ob-Gyn, German Soc. Endocrinology, Russian Assn. Cytologists (hon.), Swedish Soc. Medicine (hon.), Austrian Soc. Clin. Cytology (hon.), Sigma Xi. Home and Office: 1640 E 50th St Chicago IL 60615-3161 E-mail: wied@cytology.

WIEDEBUSCH, MARY KATHRYNE, dance educator; b. Clarksburg, W.Va. d. Danton Leon and Mary Margaret (Dixon) Caussin; m. Charles Edward Wiedebusch, July 12, 1952 (dec.); children: Carole Jean, Charles Edward II. BS, W.Va. U., 1951, MA, 1974; postgrad., Radford Coll., 1975, Am. U., 1979, Duke U., 1980. Tchr., choreographer Morgantown (W.Va.) H.S., 1951; asst. prof., choreographer Orchesis Modern Dance Ensemble W.Va. U., Morgantown, 1955-90, assoc. prof., dir., choreographer, 1990-93, prof. dance, coord. dance program, 1993—, dir. Orchesis Dance Ensemble, 1993—. Mem. faculty fine arts music camp W.Va. U., 1976, dir. fund raiser project/residency program, 1978—, founder, dir. dance artist-in-residence program, 1978—; mem. faculty Governors Honor Acad., Morgantown, 1997; bd. dir. Metro. Theatre Found., mem. commn. bd., 2003, Metro Theatre Commn., WVU Honor Dance Gala, 2005, Honor P.E. Gala, 2006 (WVU Paul Martin Alumni Svc. award, 2006), WVU the order of Vandalia. Choreographer gala performances W.Va. State Dance Festivals, 1975-95; choreographer, dir. theatrical dance prodns. W.Va. U. Creative ARts Ctr., 1976—. Chair Golf Classic, 1993-95. Named to Hall of Fame, Sch. of Phys. Edn., W.Va. U., 1994. Mem. Am. Coll. Dance Festival Assn. (founding bd. dirs. 1973-87, nat. awards 1990-91). Avocations: golf, boating. Office: WVA U Coll Creative Arts PO Box 6111 Morgantown WV 26506-6111 Office Phone: 304-293-8623. Personal E-mail: cgwiede@aol.com.

WIEDEGREEN, ERIC ALBERT, interior designer, educator; b. Newark, Jan. 27, 1947; s. Albert Henry and Lucille Elsa Wiedegreen; m. Sanda Jane Reiser, Aug. 9, 1969; children: Kristiaan Erik, Karl Walter. BA, Stetson U., DeLand, Fla., 1969; B in Design, U. Fla., Gainesville, 1973, MArch, 1975. Asst. prof. U. Fla., Gainesville, 1975—80; v.p. Edward Snowden d'Avi Archs., Ocala, Fla., 1980—89; assoc. prof. interior design Va. Tech, Blacksburg, 1989—2000; program dir. Internat. Acad. Design & Tech., Chgo., 2000—04; prof. & chair, interior design Fla. State U., Tallahassee, 2004—. Elder Presbyn. Ch. Fellow: Interior Design Educators Coun. (pres. 2006—07). Presbyterian. Home: 630 E 6th Ave Tallahassee FL 32303 Office: Floirda State Univ 302 Eppes Hall Tallahassee FL 32306-1231 Office Fax: 850-644-3112. Business E-Mail: ewiedegr@fsu.edu.

WIEDEMANN, CHARLES LOUIS, dentist; b. Belvidere, NJ, May 6, 1936; s. Charles and Clothilde Paulina (Fischer) W.; m. Jacqueline Burdzy, June 11, 1960; children: Lorraine Carol, Julie Patricia. BA in Biol. Sci., Rutgers U., 1957; DDS with honors, Fairleigh Dickinson U., 1962; grad., U.S. Army Med. Field Svc. Sch., 1962; postgrad. student, Inst. for Grad. Dentists, 1968-69, St. Clare's Hosp. Continuing Edn., NJ, 1972—, U. Pa., 1974-75, Boston U. Sch. Grad. Dentistry, 1991. Pvt. practice dentistry, Hackettstown, N.J., 1966—. Founder dental sect. staff dept. surgery Hackettstown Regional Med. Ctr., chief dentistry, 1973-75, 77-78, chief of staff dental sect. dept. surgery, 1974, 80, 85; dental health dir. Clarence W. Sickles Med. Ctr., Hackettstown, 1970-90; co-dir. Stargazer, Bd. of Ed, Online Mag. telecomm. sys., 1985-86; pres. Rexxcom Sys. Electronic Pub. and Computer Software, Co., 1990—; lectr. in field. Author: The Now Philosophy for Dentistry, 1972, Fantastic Facts About Dental Health, 1975, (computer software) The Format Machine, 1987, Autofont, 1990, The Magic Font Machine (Magifont, Magivue, Magishow), 1990, News 1, 1991, Digipad, 1993, The Autofont Titler, 1994; co-author: Autodoc, 1990, rev. edit., 1993, Font Mania, 1991;: rev. edit., 1996, XL1000, 1993, XL2000, 1993, XL2001, 1994, rev. edit., 1995, E-Z Book, 1995, Autofont Titler, 1995; editl. adv. panel: Dental Econs. Jour., 1979—80; editor: DPA News, 1993—95; contbr. articles to profl. jours. and mags.; columnist: Hackettstown Gazette, 1983—85. Chmn. Bd. of Health, Washington Twp., Morris County, N.J., 1975-78; co-dir. telecomm. sys. Hunterdon Ctrl. Regional H.S., 1989-98; presentations to Morris, Warren, and Sussex Counties, N.J. elem. schs. ann., 1966-93. Capt. Dental Corps., U.S. Army, 1962-65. Recipient cert. Stuart L. Isler Found. for Preventive Dentistry, 1986. Fellow Acad. Gen. Dentistry, Am. Endodontic Soc. (Harold Katz Meml. award 1983); mem. ADA (panel on quar. survey of pvt. practitioners 1990-93), Digital Pub. Assn. (founder, bd. dirs.), Am. Analgesia Soc., Internat. Analgesia Soc., N.J. Dental Assn., Warren-Sussex Dental Soc., Tri-County Dental Soc. (tchr. dental practice adminstrn. 1970-71), Hackettstown Dental Study Group (co-founder 1974-2006), Found. for Motivation in Dentistry (founder, chmn., bd. dirs.), Hosp. Assn. Neighborhood Dentists. Republican. Achievements include design of computer fonts, modules, graphics simulations; giant talking toothbrush, talking molar; development of painless dental injections; improved nerve-block anesthesia technique; first to develop electronic publishing software; invention of Rexxcom character set; Gentle Numb an injection syringe for dental anesthesia. Office: 110 Mill St Hackettstown NJ 07840-2343 Office Phone: 908-852-0880.

WIEDERSCHAIN, DMITRI, research scientist; b. Moscow, May 10, 1970; s. Gherman and Mila Wiederschain. ALB, Harvard U., Cambridge, Mass., 1998, PhD, 2003. Presdl. fellow Novartis, Cambridge, 2004—07, rschr., 2007—, lab. head, 2007—. Recipient Ruth L. Kirschstein Nat. Rsch. Svc. award, NIH, 2003—04, award, Am. Assn. Cancer Rsch., 2003; fellowship, Harvard U., 2002—03. Office: Novartis 250 Mass Ave Cambridge MA 02139 Personal E-mail: dwiederschain@yahoo.com.

WIEGAND, ELIZABETH GRIEGER, musician, educator; b. Michigan City, Ind., Sept. 25, 1931; d. Leo Theodore and Ella Martha Grieger; m. Lee Paul Wiegand, June 17, 1950; children: David Lee, Elaine Martha Johnson, Susan Elizabeth, Christine Mary. Cert. music tchr., Valparaiso U. Cert. Nat. Cert. Music Tchrs., permanent cert. Music Tchrs. Nat. Assn. Organist Queen All Sts. Ch., Michigan City, 1954—92; spl. Eucharistic min. St. Stanislaus Kostka, Michigan City, 1998—; chapel organist St. Anthony Meml. Hosp., Michigan City, 1998—2009. Competition judge Nat. Tchrs. Music Conf., Nat. Assn. Organ Tchrs. Musician: Tex. Women's U. Repository, 1999, Cath. of Antwerp, 1998, St. Williams Ch. Music dir., organist St. Peter's Ch., LaPorte, Ind.; pictorial profile on self Blagg Huey Libr. Recipient Elizabeth Grieger Wieg Sached Music Faiths Scholarship, Nat. Federation Music Clues, 1984; named Music Educator of the Yr., Am. Music Conf., 1995—2005. Fellow: Nat. Fedn. Music Clubs; mem.: ASCAP (Popularity award 1980—2009), Am. Guild Organists Nat. (Fla. chpt.), Am. Coll. Musicians (faculty mem., 1st Pl. gold medal Internat. Rec. Competition), Sigma Alpha Iota. Roman Catholic. Avocations: embroidery, art, photography. Home: 7421 W Johnson Rd Michigan City IN 46360

WIEGEL, ROBERT LOUIS, consulting engineering executive; b. San Francisco, Oct. 17, 1922; s. Louis Henry and Antionette L. (Decker) W.; m. Anne Pearce, Dec. 10, 1948; children: John M., Carol E., Diana L. BS, U. Calif., Berkeley, 1943, MS, 1949. Mem. faculty U. Calif. at Berkeley, 1946—, prof. civil engring., 1963-87, prof. emeritus, 1987—, asst. dean Coll. Engring., 1963-72, acting dean, 1972-73; dir. state tech. svcs. program for Calif. U. Calif., 1965-68, sec. acad. senate, 1988-89; vis. prof. Nat. U. Mex., summer 1965, Polish Acad. Sci., 1976, 88, U. Cairo, 1978; sr. Queen's fellow in marine sci. Australia, 1977; cons. to govt. and industry, 1946—. Chmn. U.S. com. for internat. com. oceanic resources, mem. marine bd. Nat. Acad. Engring., 1975-81; pres. Internat. Engring. Com. on Oceanic Resources, 1972-75, hon. mem., 1988; mem. coastal engring. research bd. Dept. Army, 1974-85; mem. IDOE adv. panel NSF, 1974-77, Gov. Calif. Adv. Commn. Ocean Resources, 1967, Calif. Adv. Commn. on Marine and Coastal Resources, 1967-73, Tsunami Tech. Adv. Council, Hawaii, 1964-66; U.S. del. U.S.-Japan coop. sci. programs, 1964, 65 Author publs. in field; editor Shore and Beach jour., 1988-96; patentee in field. V.p., bd. dirs. Am. Shore and Beach Preservation Assn., 1988-95, dir. emeritus, 1995—; mem. Nat. Rsch. Coun. com. on Beach Nourishment and Protection, 1992-95. 1st lt. U.S. Army, 1942-46. Recipient Outstanding Civilian Svc. medal Dept. Army, 1985, Berkeley citation U. Calif., 1987, Joe W. Johnson Outstanding Beach Preservation award Calif. Shore and Beach Preservation Assn., 1993, Coastal Zone Found. award, 1993, Morrough P. O'Brien award Am. Shore and Beach Preservation Assn., 1995, Oral History award Bancroft Libr., U. Calif., 1997; Robert L. Wiegel scholar, 2001—. Fellow AAAS; mem. NAE, ASCE (hon., disting. mems. 2008, chmn. exec. com. waterways, harbors, coastal engring. div. 1974-75, vice chmn. coastal engring. rsch. coun. 1964-78, chmn. 1978-92, chmn. task com. wave forces on structures 1960-67, chmn. com. on coastal engring. 1970-71, Rsch. prize 1962, Moffatt-Nichol Coastal Engring. award 1978, Internat. Coastal Engring. award 1985), Japan Soc. Civil Engrs. (hon.), Sigma Xi. Home: 1030 Keeler Ave Berkeley CA 94708-1404 Office Phone: 510-642-7340.

WIEGERINK, ROBIN L., medical association administrator; CAE. Exec. dir, CEO Am. Soc. Echocardiography, 2001—. Office: Am Soc Echocardiogrphy 2100 Gateway Centre Blvd Ste 310 Morrisville NC 27560 Office Phone: 919-297-7164. Office Fax: 919-882-9900. Business E-Mail: rwiegerink@asecho.org.*

WIEGLEY, ROGER DOUGLAS, lawyer; b. Buffalo, Dec. 8, 1948; s. Richard John and Georgianna (Eggleston) W. BA, SUNY, Buffalo, 1970; JD magna cum laude, U. Wis., 1977. Bar: Wis. 1977, Hawaii 1978, N.Y. 1982, D.C. 1982, Calif. 1986. Spl. asst. U.S. atty. U.S. Justice Dept., Honolulu, 1978-81; spl. asst. to gen. counsel Dept. of the Navy, Washington, 1981-82; assoc. Sullivan & Cromwell, Washington, 1982-88; ptnr. Sidley & Austin, Washington, 1988-94, Winthrop, Stimson, Putnam & Roberts, Washington, 1994-98; dir. Credit Suisse First Boston, NYC, 1999—2001, Winterthur Ins. Group, NYC, 2001—. Arbitrator nat. panel Am. Arbitration Assn., 1988—98. Co-author: Trade and Export Finance, 2d edit., 2000; contbr. numerous articles to profl. jours. Served with USN, 1973-82. Mem. Assn. of Bar City of N.Y. (chmn. banking law com. 2000-03). Address: Harrington Intl Ins Ltd 8 Par la Ville Rd Hamilton Bermuda Office Phone: 441-296-0757.

WIEGMAN, EUGENE WILLIAM, minister, academic administrator; b. Fort Wayne, Ind., Oct. 27, 1929; s. A. Henry and E. Catherine (McDonald) W.; m. Kathleen Wyatt, Apr. 26, 1952; children: Kathryn, Rose Marie, Mark, Jeanine, Gretchen, Matthew. BS, Concordia Coll., 1953; MS, U. Kans., Lawrence, 1956, EdD, 1962; grad., Pacific Luth. Theol. Sem., 1985. Tchr., coach Trinity Luth. Sch., Atchison, Kans., 1954-58; prin. tchr. St. John's Coll., Winfield, Kans., 1958-61; prof. Concordia Coll., Seward, Nebr., 1961-65; adminstrv. asst. to Rep. Clair Callan, Lincoln, Nebr., 1965-66; asst. to adminstr. fed. extension service Dept. Agr., Washington, 1966-67; dean community edn. Fed. City Coll., Washington, 1967-69; pres. Pacific Luth. U., Tacoma, 1969-75, Independent Colls. Wash., 1975-76; dir. Wash. Office Community Devel., 1977-78; commr. Dept. of Employment Security, 1978-81; exec. dir., pres., CEO emeritus Family Counseling Service of Tacoma and Pierce County, Wash., 1987-97; assoc. pastor Luther Meml. Ch., Tacoma, 1987-90; pastor Gethsemane Luth. Ch., Tacoma, 1990-98, Luther Meml. Ch., Tacoma, 1998—2002; dean clin. pastoral edn. Grad. Sch. of Korea, 1992—. Mem. Wash. State Employment and Tng. Council; mem. cabinet Gov. of Wash., 1977-81. Candidate for U.S. Congress from 6th dist. Wash., 1976; mem. Council on Washington's Future; exec. bd. dirs. Pacific Harbors Coun. Boy Scouts Am.; bd. dirs. Tacoma Area Urban Coalition; past chmn. Wash. Friends Higher Edn.; bd. dirs. Tacoma Urban League, Bellarmine Prep. Sch., Tacoma, Camp Brotherhood, Nativity House; trustee Tacoma Gen. Hosp., Pacific Sci. Center; mem. Commn. on Children, Youth and Families for Tacoma and Pierce County; mem. com. Faith Homes for Young Women; pres. Second City chamber of Tacoma. Recipient Disting. Teaching award City Winfield, Kans., 1960, Freedom Found. Teaching award, 1961, Disting. Eagle Scout award, 1982, Pres. award St. Martins Coll., 1980. Mem. Kiwanis, Phi Delta Kappa. Home: 405 N Stadium Way Tacoma WA 98403-3228 Personal E-mail: eugenewiegman@msn.com.

WIEGNER, EDWARD ALEX, financial and energy executive; b. Waukesha, Wis., Dec. 13, 1939; s. Roy Edward and Margaret (Kuehnlein) Wiegner; m. Cathryn J. Mullens, Oct. 16, 1970; children: Carlin, Ryan; 1 child from previous marriage, Christine. BBA, U. Wis., Madison, 1961, MS in Econs., 1965, PhD in Econs., 1969. Asst. prof. bus. adminstrn. Marquette U., Milw., 1965-71; assoc. prof U. Wis., Madison, 1972-73; sec. Wis. Dept. Revenue, Madison, 1971-74; sr. v.p. fin., bd. dirs. Wis. Power and Light Co., Madison, 1974-76, sr. v.p. consumer, pub. and fin. affairs, dir., 1976-80, exec. v.p., bd. dirs., 1980-82; sr. v.p., CFO, bd. dirs. Am. Natural Resources Co., 1982-85, exec. v.p., chief adminstrv. officer, bd. dirs., 1985-86; sr. v.p. Coastal Corp., 1985-86; sr. v.p., chief fin. officer Household Internat., Inc., 1986-88; exec. v.p., CFO Progressive Corp., Mayfield Heights, Ohio, 1988-91, pres. fin. svcs. div., 1989-93; gen. ptnr. Aurora Ptnrs., 1994-96; vice chmn. 1st Am. Ins. Co., Kansas City, Mo., 1994-97; chmn., CEO First Am. Fin. Corp., 1997-98; chmn. Geologix, Inc., Placerville, Calif., 1998—, Ins. Distbn. Solutions, LLC, Jacksonville, Fla., 1999—. Contbr. articles to profl. jours. Mem.: Grand Harbor Country Club. Home and Office: 151 Shores Dr Indian River Shores FL 32963 Personal E-mail: edward@wiegner.com.

WIEHL, LIS W., legal analyst, educator; b. Seattle, Aug. 9, 1961; d. Richard Lloyd and Inga (Wolfsberg); 2 children. BA, U. Helsinki, Finland, 1979, Columbia U, 1983; MA, U. Queensland, Brisbane, Australia, 1985; JD, Harvard U., 1987. Bar: Wash., (US Dist. Ct.), (US Ct. Appeals (9th cir.)). Assoc. Perkins Coie Law Firm, Seattle, 1987-90; fed. prosecutor U.S. Attys. Office, Seattle, 1990-95; assoc. prof. Law Sch., dir. of trial advocacy program U. Washington, Seattle, 1995. Prin. dep. chief investigative counsel US House of Reps. Com. on Judiciary, 1998—99; legal commentator Nat. Pub. Radio NBC News, 2000—01, Sta. KIRO (CBS) News, 2001—02; legal analyst Fox-TV News Channel, 2001—; vis. prof., law and journalism dir. NY Law Sch. Contbr. articles New York Times, ABA Jour., Jour. Trial Advocacy, Harvard Blackletter Law Jour., U. Mich Law Rev. U. Wash. Law Rev. Treas. Lawyers Students Engaged in Resolution, Seattle, 1995—99. Recipient Distinction in Teaching award, Harvard U., 1987, Emil Gumpert award, Am. Coll. Trial Lawyers, Richardson S. Jacobson award for Excellence in Tchg., Trial Advocacy Roscoe Pound Inst., 2001. Mem.: Fed. Bar Assn., Order of the Coif, Phi Beta Kappa. Business E-Mail: lis.wiehl@foxnews.com.*

WIEHOFF, JOHN P., trucking executive; With Arthur Anderson, 1984—92; contr., treas. C.H. Robinson Worldwide, 1992—98, sr. v.p., CFO, 1998—99, pres., 1999—2006, CEO, 2002—06, chmn., CEO, 2006—. Office: 8100 Mitchell Rd Eden Prairie MN 55344

WIELAND, GILBERT DARRYL, medical researcher, anthropologist, gerontologist; b. Hagerstown, Md., Oct. 31, 1951; s. Gilbert Hugh and Joan Kanaga Wieland; m. Manhal A. Wieland, Apr. 26, 1980; 1 child, Christopher. BA cum laude in Anthropology, Am. U., Washington, DC, 1972; PhD in Anthropology, U. Rochester, NY, 1982; MPH in Health Svcs., UCLA, 1983. Sr. rsch. scientist VA Geriatric Rsch., Edn. and Clin. Ctr., Sepulveda, Calif., 1982—96; rsch. dir. Beverly Found., Pasadena, Calif., 1987—90; assoc. rsch. prof. divsn. geriat. UCLA, 1991—96; prof. USC Sch. Medicine, Columbia, 1996—; rsch. dir. geriat. Palmetto Health Richland, Columbia, 1998—. Dep. editor Journal of Gerontology: Medical Sciences, 2005—, assoc. editor Aging: Clinical and Experimental Research, 2005—, mem. editl. bd., reviewer 30 med. and sci. jours., —. Fellow: Soc. Applied Anthropology, Gerontol. Soc. Am. (chair pub. policy com. 2000—02, chair rsch. task force), Am. Geriatrics Soc. (mem. rsch. com. 2000—05, mem. publ. ed. com. 2008—). Office Fax: 803-434-4331. Business E-Mail: darryl.wieland@palmettohealth.org.

WIELAND, PAUL OTTO, environmental control systems engineer; b. Louisville, Apr. 9, 1954; s. Otto George and Flora Carolyn (Wolf) W. BS in Botany, U. Louisville, 1982, BS in Applied Sci., 1985, M. in Engring., 1987. Lic. profl. engr., Ala., Va.; cert. indoor air quality profl. Assn. of Energy Engrs. Leed AP. Paper carrier Courier-Jour., Louisville, 1976-77; youth program dir. UNICORN, Louisville, 1978; recreation worker Met. Parks Dept., Louisville, 1978-80; retail sales clk. Lose Bros. Lawn and Garden, Louisville, 1980-82; trainee engr. Sealand Svc., Inc., Elizabeth, NJ, 1982; engr. NASA Marshall Space Flight Ctr., Huntsville, Ala., 1983—2005; pres. Wiseland Svcs., Huntsville, 1996—. Author: Designing for Human Presence in Space: An Introduction to Environmental Control and Life Support Systems, 1994, Living Together in Space: The Design and Operation of the Life Support Systems on the International Space Station, 1996, rev. edit., 1998, A Guidebook to a Healthier House, 1999, Living Together in Space: The International Space Station Internal Active Thermal Control System Issues and Solutions - Sustaining Engineering Activities at the Marshall Space Flight Center from 1998 to 2005, 2007; contbg. author: Space Launch and Transportation Systems, 2005; contbr. articles to profl. jours. Vol. advocate R.A.P.E. Relief Ctr., Louisville, 1977-80; vol. tutor Adult Basic Edn. Program, Huntsville, 1988-89; vol. projectionist Film Co-op., Huntsville, 1990-91; vol. tech. advisor Am. Lung Assn. Health House '96, Huntsville. Mem. ASME, ASHRAE, AIAA (chmn. student chpt. 1984-85), NSPE (mathcounts vol. 1990-91), Inst. for Advanced Studies in Life Support (treas. 1990-92), USGBC Avocations: nature, art, dance. Home and Office: 4212 9th Ave SW Huntsville AL 35805-3408 Office Phone: 256-426-4325.

WIELUNSKI, LESZEK STANISLAW, materials scientist; b. Lublin, Poland, July 28, 1943; arrived in Australia, 1986; s. Stefan and Alicia Sabina (Gosiewska) W.; m. Aleksandra Anna Gorgon, Feb. 7, 1967; children: Andrzei, Alicia. MS in Physics, Moscow U., 1968; PhD of Physics, Inst. Nuclear Rsch., Warsaw, Poland, 1972. Rsch. scientist Inst. Nuclear Rsch., Warsaw, 1973-80; rsch. assoc. Calif. Inst. Tech., Pasadena, 1980-82, SUNY, Albany, 1982-84, asst. prof. Plattsburgh, 1984-85; scientist instrumentation Electro-Scan Corp., Boston, 1985-86; rsch. scientist CSIRO, Sydney, Australia, 1986—. Author: Ion Beams for Materials Analysis, 1986; contbr. articles to profl. jours. Fellow Australian Inst. Physics. Office: Rutgers Univ 136 Frelinghusen Rd Piscataway NJ 08854 Home: 52 Davidson Rd Apt A Piscataway NJ 08854

WIEMAN, CARL E., physics professor; b. Corvallis, Oreg., Mar. 26, 1951; s. N. Orr and Alison W.; m. Sarah Gilbert. BS, MIT, 1973; PhD, Stanford U., 1977; DS (hon.), U. Chgo., 1997. Asst. rsch. physicist dept. physics U. Mich., Ann Arbor, 1977—79, asst. prof. physics, 1979—84; assoc. prof. physics U. Colo., Boulder, 1984—87, prof., 1987—97, disting. rsch. prof., 1997—; fellow Joint Inst. for Lab. Astrophysics, Boulder, 1985—; prof. Physics and Astronomy Dept. U. BC, Vancouver, 2007—, dir. Carl Wieman Sci. Edn. Initiative (CWSEI), 2007—. Loeb lectr. Harvard U., 1990—91; Rosenthal Meml. lectr. Yale U., 1988, Columbia U., 1988; Cherwell-Simon Meml. lectr. Oxford U., 1999; vis. scholar Phi Beta Kappa, 1999—2000. Recipient Ernest Orlando Lawrence Meml. award, U.S. Dept. Energy, 1993, Einstein medal for laser sci., Soc. Optical and Quantum Electronics, 1995, Fritz London prize for low temperature physics, 1996, Newcomb Cleveland prize, AAAS, 1996, King Faisal Internat. prize for Sci., 1997, Sci. award, Bonfils Stanton Found., 1998, Lorentz medal, Netherlands Royal Acad. Sci., 1998, Benjamin Franklin Medal in Physics, 2000, The Nobel Prize in Physics, 2001, Nat. Sci. Found. Dir. Award for Dist. Teaching Scholars, 2001, U.S. Outstanding Doctoral and Rsch. Univ. Prof., Coun. for Advancement and Support of Edn. & Carnegie Found. for Advancement of Tchg., 2004, U.S. Prof. of Yr., Carnegie Found. for the Advancement of Teaching & the Coun. for Advancement & Support of Edn., 2004, Vollum Award, Reed Coll., 2009. Fellow: Guggenheim, 1990-1991, Hertz Found., 1973-1977, Am. Phys. Soc. (Davisson-Germer prize 1994, Schawlow prize in laser sci. 1998); mem.: NAS, 1995, Am. Physical Soc. (fellow, 1990), Am. Acad. Arts and Sci., 1998, Am. Assn. Physics Tchrs. (Richtmyer lectr. award 1996), Optical Soc. Am. (R.W. Wood prize 1999). Achievements include first to achieve Bose-Einstein condensation, 1995. Office: U BC 2146 Health Sciences Mall Vancouver BC Canada V6T 1Z3 Office Phone: 604-822-1732. E-mail: carl.wieman@phas.ubc.ca.*

WIEMANN, MARION RUSSELL, JR., (BARON OF CAMSTER), biologist, ambassador general; b. Sept. 7, 1929; s. Marion Russell and Verda (Peek) W.; 1 child from previous marriage, Tamara Lee (Mrs. Donald D. Kelley). BS, Ind. U., 1959; PhD (hon.), World U. Roundtable, 1991; ScD (hon.), The London Inst. Applied Rsch., 1994, ScD (hon.), 1995, World Acad., Germany, 1995. Histo-rsch. technician U. Chgo., 1959, rsch. asst., 1959-62, rsch. technician, 1962-64; tchr. sci. Westchester Twp. Sch., Chesterton, Ind., 1964-66; with U. Chgo., 1965-79, sr. rsch. technician, 1967-70, rsch. technologist, 1970-79; prin. Marion Wiemann & Assocs., cons. R&D, Chesterton, Ind., 1979-89. Advisor Porter County Health Bd., 1989-91; mem. consultive faculty World U., 1991-99, SkyWarn, Nat. Weather Svc., 1993—. Author: Tooth Decay, Its Cause and Prevention Through Controlled Soil Composition and Soil pH, 1985; contbr. articles to profl. jours. and newspapers. Vice-chmn. The Duneland 4th of July Com., 1987-91; v.p. State Microscopical Soc. Ill., 1969-70, pres., 1970-71. With USN, 1951-53. Recipient Disting. Tech. Communicator award Soc. for Tech. Communication, 1974, Internat. Order Merit (Eng.), 1991; ennobled Royal Coll. Heraldry, Australia, 1991, Highland Laird, Scotland, 1995; named Sagamore of the Wabash Gov. Ind., 1985; McCrone Rsch. Inst. scholar, 1968; named Prof. of Sci. Australian Inst. for Co-Ordinated Rsch., Australia, 1995; recipient Scouters Key award Boy Scouts Am., 1968, Arrowhead honor, 1968, Albert Einstein Silver medal, Huguenin, Le Locke, Switzerland, Henri Dunant Silver medal with silver bars, 1995, Henri Dunant Silver medal, 1995, medal of honor, England, 1996. Fellow: Australian Inst. Co-Ordinated Rsch., World Lit. Acad.; mem.: World Explorers Club, Order Internat. Fellowship, World Acad., Assn. Masters Universe, Govs. Club, Order Am. Ambassadors (sovereign ambassador 2006), VFW (post judge adv. 1986—99, apptd. post adj. 1986—99, charter mem., bd. dirs., Cross of Malta 1986). Achievements include demonstration that radiation does not produce dental caries; proved that soil calcium, magnesium, potassium and phosphorous, with soil PH, controls population size and longevity of earthworms and humans and the incidence of dental caries; demonstrated that fluoride neither reduces or prevents dental caries. Address: PO Box 1016 Chesterton IN 46304-0016 Office: Am Embassy 418 S Ninth St Chesterton IN 46304 Office Phone: 219-926-1295. *Personal philosphy: Leadership founded upon trust, perpetuated by participation, example and instruction, dedicated to wise use, protection or improvement of health and environment. If you put in an hour of real work you get an hour of results. There is no other way to do it.*

WIENER, HESH (HAROLD FREDERIC WIENER), publishing executive, consultant; b. Bklyn., July 20, 1946; s. Jesse Leonard and Regina (Rappaport) W. BS in Polit. Sci., MIT, 1969; LLB with honors, Open U., London, 2002. Mem. staff systems devel. Data Gen. Corp., Southboro, Mass., 1969-70; dir. computer edn. project U. Calif., Berkeley, 1970-72; editor Computer Decisions Mag., Rochelle Park, NJ, 1973-78; editor, pub. Tech. News Am., NYC, 1976-88; pres. Tech. News of Am. Co., Inc., NYC, 1982—; mng. dir. Tech. News Ltd., London, 1992—. Pub. Computer and Comms. Buyer Newsletter, 1979-95, Mainstream Newsletter, 1980-82, Infoperspectives Newsletter, 1982—, Storage Tech. Monitor, 1984-87, Infoperspectives Internat., UK, 1989—, Mid. East, 1991—, The Four Hundred Newsletter, UK, 1990-97, The Four Hundred Newsletter, US, 1990-97; editor Infoperspectives Internat., Italy, 1991-98, The Four Hundred Newsletter, Italy, 1995—; pub. US edit. Computergram Internat. Newsletter, 1985-90; corr. Processeurs mag., 1989-99; cons. Hewlett-Packard Co., Paris, 1971-72, Xerox Corp., 1972-73; advisor NSF, 1975; columnist 451.com, 2000—06. Author: Big Blue and You, The IBM Atlas, The Mainframe; corr. Computer Weekly, UK, 1975-81, Computable, Amsterdam, 1976-87, Computing Can., 1977-78, Ordinateurs, Paris, 1977-89, Data News, Brussels, 1979-86, Informatics, UK, 1981-85, Datanytt, Copenhagen, 1982-89, Mgmt. Tech. mag., 1983-85; editor BusinessWeek Newsletter for Info. Execs., 1987-90, Datamation Mag., 1983-90, Infoperspectives Internat., Milan, 1991—; contbg. editor Bus. and Soc. Rev., 1978-85; contbr. NY Times Syndicate, Los Angeles Times Syndicate, N.Am. Newspaper Alliance Wireservice, Newsday, Manhattan, Inc., Rom Mag.,

Informatique, Paris, The Economist, London, Dun's Bus. Month, Software News, Intermedia, Digital News, Data Communications, Bus. Week Newsletter for Info. Execs., Bus. Strategy Internat., Nikkei Watcher on IBM, Tokyo, 1989-96; contbg. editor Midrange Svc. Pubs., 2002-05, IT Jungle Publs., 2003—; contbg. editor Big Iron News, 2005—; webmaster tech-news.com, 1995—, PrimroseHill.com, 1997—, luminum.com, 1999—, SongLakeBooks.com, 2000-, The Guild Cos., 2005-, Spuyten Duyvil Preschool, 2005-, Thinks Rsch., 2007-, Schlamstone.com, 2007-, Primrose Hill Books, 2007-, Maatbarlow.com, 2008-, rpsupport.com, 2008-, rpresellers.com, 2009-. Mem.: Overseas Press. Office: Tech News Am 123 7th Ave #171 Brooklyn NY 11215-1383

WIENER, JACQUES LOEB, JR., federal judge; b. Shreveport, La., Oct. 2, 1934; s. Jacques L. and Betty (Eichenbaum) Wiener; m. Sandra Mills Feingerts; children: Patricia Wiener Shifke, Jacques L. III, Betty Ellen Wiener Spomer, Donald B. BA, Tulane U., 1956, JD, 1961. Bar: La. 1961, US Dist. Ct. (we. dist.) La. 1961. Ptnr. Wiener, Weiss & Madison, Shreveport, 1961—90; judge US Ct. Appeals (5th cir.), New Orleans, 1990—. Mem. coun. La. State Law Inst., 1963—; master of the bench Am. Inn of Ct., 1990—98. Pres. United Way N.W. La., 1975, Shreveport Jewish Fedn., 1969—70. Fellow: La. Bar Found., Am. Bar Found., Am. Coll. Trust and Estates Counsel; mem.: ABA, Am. Law Inst., Shreveport Bar Assn. (pres. 1982), La. Bar Assn., Internat. Acad. Estate and Trust Law (academician). Avocations: fly fishing, upland game bird hunting, photography, travel. Office: Court of Appeals Building 600 Camp St Rm 244 New Orleans LA 70130-3425*

WIENER, JOEL HOWARD, historian, educator; b. NYC, Aug. 23, 1937; s. Philip Wiener and Elizabeth Weissman; m. Suzanne Wolff Wiener, Sept. 4, 1961; children: Paul, Deborah, Jane. BA, NYU, 1959; postgrad., U. Glasgow, Scotland, 1961—63; PhD, Cornell U., Ithaca, NY, 1965. Asst. prof. history Skidmore Coll., Saratoga Springs, NY, 1964—67, CUNY, 1967—71, assoc. prof. history, 1972—78, prof. history, 1978—2000, emeritus prof. history, 2000—. Dir. study abroad program in Eng. CUNY, 1971—73, prof. history doctoral program, 1980—2000, chmn. dept. history, 1981—85; cons., advisor Cornell U. Press, U. NC Press, Victorian Studies, NEH, English Lit. in Transition, 1880-1920, Princeton U. Press, Greenwood Press, UK Social Sci. Rsch. Coun., Ill. U. Press, Victorian Periodicals Rev., Am. Journalism, Albion, Jour. Brit. Studies, Rutgers U. Press, PSC-CUNY, Dictionary Labour Biography, Harvester Press, Broadview Press, Jour. Interdisciplinary History; mem. editl. bd. Media History, Jour. Victorian Culture. Author: The War of the Unstamped, 1969, A Descriptive Finding List of Unstamped British Periodicals, 1830-1836, 1970, William Lovett, 1989, Radicalism and Freethought in Nineteenth-Century Britain, 1983; editor: Great Britain: Foreign Policy and the Span of Empire, 4 vols., 1972, Great Britain: The Lion at Home, 4 vols., 1974, Innovators and Preachers, 1985, Papers for the Millions, 1988; co-editor (with Mark Hampton): Anglo-American Media Interactions, 1850-2000, 2007; assoc. editor Dictionary of National Biography, 1999—2004; mem. adv. bd.: Dictionary of Nineteenth-Century Journalism; contbr. articles to profl. jours. Grantee, Oxford Bibliog. Soc., 1971—72, Am. Philos. Soc., 1971—72. Fellow: Royal Hist. Soc.; mem.: Am. Journalism Historians Assn. (rsch. com. 1998—), Rsch. Soc. for Victorian Periodicals (v.p., pres. 1981—85). Avocations: travel, theater, cinema. Home: 267 Glen Ct Teaneck NJ 07666 Office Phone: 201-837-5452. Home Fax: 201-837-8658. Personal E-mail: jwiener267@aol.com.

WIENER, JOSEPH, pathologist, educator; b. Toronto, Can., Sept. 21, 1927; arrived in U.S., 1949, naturalized, 1960; s. Louis and Minnie (Salem) W.; m. Judith Hesta Ross, June 20, 1954; children: Carolyn L., Adam L. MD, U. Toronto, 1953. Intern Detroit Receiving Hosp., 1953-54; resident to chief resident pathology Mallory Inst. Pathology, 1954-55, 57-60; from asst. to assoc. prof. pathology Columbia U., NYC, 1960-68; prof. pathology N.Y. Med. Coll., NYC, 1968-78, Wayne State U., Detroit, 1978—, chmn. dept., 1978-90. Cons. NIH, 1970— Served to capt. M.C. U.S. Army, 1955-57. Grantee Heart, Lung and Blood Inst., 1971-93; fellow Coun. for High Blood Pressure Rsch., 1982. Fellow Am. Heart Assn., Am. Stroke Assn., Coll. Am. Pathologists; mem. AAAS, Am. Soc. Investigative Pathology, Am. Soc. Cell Biology, Mich. Path. Soc., Internat. Acad. Pathology, Am. Heart Assn., U.S./Can. Acad. Pathology, Mich. Heart Assn. (dir.), Internat. Soc. Hypertension. Achievements include rsch. on cellular/molecular biology of experimental hypertension. Office: 540 E Canfield St Detroit MI 48201-1928 Home Phone: 248-626-2421; Office Phone: 313-577-1157. Business E-Mail: j.wiener@wayne.med.edu.

WIENER, MARVIN S., rabbi, editor, executive; b. NYC, Mar. 16, 1925; s. Max and Rebecca (Dodell) W.; m. Sylvia Bodek, Mar. 2, 1952; children: David Hillel, Judith Rachel. BS, CCNY, 1944, MS, 1945; BHL, Jewish Theol. Sem. Am., 1947, MHL, Rabbi, 1951, DD (hon.), 1977. Registrar, sec. faculty Rabbinical Sch., Jewish Theol. Sem. Am., 1951-57; cons. Frontiers of Faith TV Series, NBC, 1951-57; dir., instr. liturgy Cantors Inst.-Sem. Coll. Jewish Music, Jewish Theol. Sem. Am., 1954-58; faculty coord. Sem. Sch. and Women's Inst., 1958-64; dir. Nat. Acad. for Adult Jewish Studies, United Synagogue Am., NYC, 1958-78; editor Burning Bush Press, 1958-78, United Synagogue Rev., 1978-86; dir. com. congrl. stds. United Synagogue Am., 1976-86, cons. cmty. rels. and social action, 1981-82, editor, exec. joint retirement bd., 1986—. Mem. Joint Commn. on Rabbinic Placement, 1951-57, Joint Prayer Book Commn., 1957-62; mem. exec. coun. Rabbinical Assembly, 1958-86, summer Rabbi, Forest Hills Jewish Ctr., 1961-64; editl. cons. N.Y. Bd. Rabbi, 1987-89; trustee joint retirement bd. Jewish Theol. Sem. Am. Rabbinical Assembly and United Synagogue Am., 1959-86, sec. 1968-76, 84-85, vice chmn., 1976-82, 85-86, chmn. 1982, treas., 1983-84; co-chmn. Jewish Bible Assn., 1960-64; chmn. bd. rev. Nat. Coun. Jewish Audio-Visual Materials, 1968-69; mem. exec. com. Nat. Coun. Adult Jewish Edn., 1966—; mem. exec. bd., editl. adv. bd., v.p. Jewish Book Couns., 1976-96; chmn. Internat. Conf. Adult Jewish Edn., Jerusalem, 1972. Editor: Nat. Acad. Adult Jewish Studies Bull., 1958-78, The High Holy Days, Book I (Herman Kieval), 1959, The Jewish Dietary Laws (Samuel H. Dresner and Seymour Siegel), 1959, Past and Present: Selected Essays (Israel Friedlaender), 1961, Heart of Wisdom, Book I (Bernard S. Raskas), 1962, Book II, 1979, Judaism: Profile of a Faith (Ben Zion Bokser), 1963, The Wisdom of Solomon Schechter (Bernard Mandelbaum), 1963, Jewish Tract Series, 1964-78 (15 titles), Foundations of A Faith (Simon Greenberg), 1967, Judaism and the Christian Predicament (Ben Zion Bokser), 1967, The Maturing of the Conservative Movement (Bernard Mandelbaum), 1968, The Sabbath (Samuel L. Dresner), 1970, Adult Jewish Edn., 1958-78, Talmudic Law and the Modern State (Moshe Silberg), 1973, Self-Incrimination in Jewish Law (Aaron Kirschenbaum), 1970, Sex and the Family in the Jewish Tradition (Robert Gordis), 1970; contbr. articles to numerous periodicals. Mem. Am. Acad. Jewish Rsch., Assn. Jewish Studies, N.Y. Bd. Rabbis, Rabbinical Assembly. Home: 67-66 108th St Apt D-46 Forest Hills NY 11375-2974 Office: Joint Retirement Bd Ste 1515 One Penn Plaza New York NY 10119 Office Phone: 212-947-2400.

WIENER, THOMAS ELI, lawyer; b. Dallas, Nov. 29, 1940; s. Samson and Fan (Gardner) W.; m. Felice Gloria Goodwin, Jan. 24, 1970; children: Gary Allen, Debra Roslyn, Allison Beth, Todd David. BA, U. Tex., 1962, JD with honors, 1968. Bar: Tex. 1968, D.C. 1969, Pa. 1972, U.S. Supreme Ct. 1972. Atty.-advisor office chief counsel IRS, Washington, 1968-72; assoc. Pepper Hamilton & Scheetz, Phila., 1972-74, Abrahams & Loewenstein, Phila., 1974-76, Goodis, Greenfield, Henry & Edelstein, Phila., 1976-77, Mesirov, Gelman, Jaffe, Cramer & Jamieson, Phila., 1977-78; prin. Franklin, Margulies & Huntington, 1978-91, Riley & DeFalice, P.C., Phila., 1991-92, Wiener & Caplan, P.C., Phila., 1992-95; pvt. practice Bala Cynwyd, Pa., 1995—. Bd. dirs. Lufkin (Tex.) Industries, Inc. Author: (with others) Tax Problems of Fiduciaries, 1977. Trustee Golden Slipper Club; pres. Main Line Reform Temple, 1992-94, pres. brotherhood 1981-83; pres. Rotary Gundaker Found., 1986-87; 1st v.p. N. Am. Fedn. Temple Brotherhoods, 1999-01; v.p. Phila. Fedn. Reform Synagogues, 1993-98; chmn. Synagogue Fedn. Coun. of Phila., 1994-97; trustee Union Reform Judaism, 1995—, exec. com., 2001-05, ARZA/World Union N.Am. Mem. Pa. Bar Assn., Tex. Bar Assn., Phila. Bar Assn., Am. Law Inst. (life), Order of Coif, Masons (32 degree K.C.C.H., past master), Rotary (pres. chpt. 1985-86). Home: 1233 Remington Rd Wynnewood PA 19096-2329 Office: One Belmont Ave Ste 605 Bala Cynwyd PA 19004-1609 Office Phone: 610-667-8999. Personal E-mail: twiener@aol.com.

WIENER, VALERIE, state senator, communications executive, writer; BJ, U. Mo., 1971, MA, 1972, U. Ill., Springfield, 1974; postgrad., McGeorge Sch. Law, 1976—79. Prodr. Checkpoint Sta. KOMU-TV, Columbia, Mo., 1972-73; v.p., owner Broadcast Assocs., Inc., Las Vegas, 1972-86; pub. affairs dir. First Ill. Cable TV, Springfield, 1973-74; editor Ill. State Register, Springfield, 1973-74; prodr. and talent Nev. Realities Sta. KLVX-TV, Las Vegas, 1974-75; account exec. Sta. KBMI (now KFMS), Las Vegas, 1975-79; nat. traffic dir. six radio stas., Las Vegas, Albuquerque and El Paso, Tex., 1979-80; exec. v.p., gen. mgr. Stas. KXKS and KKJY, Albuquerque, 1980-81; exec. adminstr. Stas. KSET AM/FM, KVEG, KFMS and KKJY, 1981—86; press sec., Rep. Harry Reid US House of Reps., Washington; adminstrv. asst. Friends for Harry Reid, Nev., 1986; press sec., Senator Harry Reid US Senate, Washington, 1987-88; owner Wiener Comm. Group, Las Vegas, 1988—; mem., Clark County No. 3 Nev. State Senate, Carson City, 1996—; owner PowerMark Pub., Las Vegas, 1998—. Mem. Nev. Drug Commn., 1997—2000, Nev. Commn. on Aging, 1997—; chair Commn. on Sch. Safety and Jevenile Violence, 1999—2000; mem. Nev. Technol. Crimes Task Force, 2001—03, Nev. Anti-Bullying Task Force, 2001—03, Gov.'s Task Force on Corrections, 2002; chair legis. com. on obesity Nev. State Senate, 2003—04, minority whip, 2001—08, majority whip, 2008—. Author: Power Communications: Positioning Yourself for High Visibility (Fortune Book Club main selection 1994, Money Book Club selection 1995, Communicator award of distinction 2000), Gang Free: Friendship Choices for Today's Youth, 1995, 2d edit., 1996, The Nesting Syndrome: Grown Children Living at Home, 1997, Winning the War Against Youth Gangs, 1999, Power Positioning: Advancing Yourself as The Expert, 2000 (Nat. awards), PowerMaster HandBook Series, 2000— (11 nat. awards); contbg. writer The Pacesetter, ASAE's Comm. News. Sponsor Futures for Children, Las Vegas, Albuquerque, El Paso, 1979—83; mem. El Paso Exec. Women's Coun., 1981—83, Clark Coun. Sch. Dist. and Bus. Cmty. PAYBAC Spkrs. and Partnership Programs, 1989—, chair legis. com. on juvenile justice, 1999—2000; steering com. Youth Recovery Network, 2001—02; founding mem. Nev. team Action Healthy Kids; media chmn. Gov.'s Coun. Small Bus., 1989—93; vice chmn. Congl. Awards Coun., 1989—93; med. dir. Gov.'s Conf. on Women, 1990; vice chmn. Gov.'s Commn. on Postsecondary Edn., 1992—96; mem. VIP bd. Easter Seals, El Paso, 1982; bd. dirs. BBB So. Nev., 1994—, Pub. Edn. Found., 1997—. Recipient 208 Comm. awards, 1989—, Outstanding Achievement award, Nat. Fedn. Press Women, 1991, Disting. Leader award, Nat. Assn. Cmty. Leadership, 1993, Gold medals in swimming, Nev. Sr. Olympics, 2002—03, 2005—07, Gold medals in fitness and weightlifting, 1998—2003, 2005—07, Walking Silver medal, 2005, Outstanding Women Adv. for Edn. award, Va. Commonwealth U., 2000, Internat. Cmty. Svc. award, Internat. New Thought Alliance, 2001, Winner Nev. 100 Fitness Challenge, Nev. State Legis. Session, 2005, Special Svc. award, Nev. Athletic Trainers Assn., 2007, NV Sec. of State's Participatory Democracy award, 2009; named Outstanding Vol., United Way, El Paso, 1983, SBA Nev. Small Bus. Media Adv. of Yr., 1992, Nev.'s Disting. Sr. Athlete, 2000, So. Nev. Health Care Policy Hero, 2003, Nev. Legislator of Yr., Soc. Pub. Health Educators, 2004; named one of 27 Healthy Sch. Heroes in U.S., 2002; named to Hall Fame, Leadership Las Vegas, 2006. Mem. Nat. Assn. Women Bus. Owners (media chmn., nat. rep. So. Nev. 1990-91, Nev. Adv. of Yr. award 1992), Nev. Press Women, Nat. Spkrs. Assn., Small Pubs. Assn. N.Am., Dem. Press Secs. Assn., El Paso Assn. Radio Stas., U.S. Senate Staff Club, Las Vegas C. of C. (Circle of Excellence award 1993), Soc. Profl. Journalists. Democrat. Avocations: reading, writing, fitness and weighlifting training and competition, public speaking, community involvement. Office: Nev Senate 401 S Carson St Rm 2132 Carson City NV 89701 Office Phone: 775-684-1422. Business E-Mail: vwiener@sen.state.nv.us.

WIENS, ARTHUR NICHOLAI, psychology professor; b. McPherson, Kans., Sept. 7, 1926; s. Jacob T. and Helen E. (Kroeker) W.; m. Ruth Helen Avery, June 11, 1949; children: Barbara, Bradley, Donald. BA, U. Kans., 1948, MA, 1952; PhD, U. Portland, 1956. Diplomate: Am. Bd. Examiners Profl. Psychology. Clin. psychologist Topeka State Hosp., 1949-53; sr. psychologist outpatient dept. Oreg. State Hosp., Salem, 1954-58, chief psychologist, 1958-61, dir. clin. psychology internship program, 1958-61; clin. instr. U. Oreg. Med. Sch., Portland, 1958-61, asst. prof., 1961-65, assoc. prof., 1965-66; prof. med. psychology, 1966—96; prof. emeritus med. psychology, 1997—. Field assessment officer Peace Corps, 1965; cons. psychologist Portland Ctr. for Hearing and Speech, 1964—67, Dammasch State Hosp., 1967—69, Raleigh Hills Hosp., 1968—84, Oreg. Vocat. Rehab. Divsn., 1973—2001, mem. state adv. com., 1976—93; cons. William Temple Rehab. House, Episcopal Laymen's Mission Soc., 1968—88; chmn. State Oreg. Bd. Social Protection, 1971—84, State of Oreg. Bd. Psychologist Examiners, 1963—66, 1974—77; v.p. bd. dirs. Raleigh Hills Rsch. Found., 1974—80. Contbr. articles to profl. jour. Fellow AAAS, APA (chmn. com. on vis. psychologist program 1972-76, chmn. accreditation com. 1978, mem. task force edn. and credentialing 1979-84); mem. Am. Assn. State Psychology Bd. (pres. 1978-79), Nat. Register Health Svc. Providers in Psychology (bd. dirs. 1985-92, chmn. 1989-92), Profl. Exam. Svc. (bd. dirs. 1982-88, 90-96, chmn. 1986-88), Sigma Xi. Home: 74 Condolea Way Lake Oswego OR 97035-1010 Office: Oreg Health Scis U Portland OR 97201

WIER, LEANNE MAY, life sciences educator; b. San Antonio, Aug. 29, 1977; adopted d. Glen W. and Shirley Diane Latimer Wier. BS in Agrl. Devel., Tex. A&M U., College Station, 2000; MS Animal Sci., Okla. State U., Stillwater, 2004. Lab. technician Okla. State U., Stillwater, 2001—05; lab. tech. Ultimate Genetics, Franklin, Tex., 2000—01; prof. Rose State Coll., Midwest City, Okla., 2005—. Lab. tech. OvaGenix, Bryan, Tex., 2001—05. With U. Ctrl. Okla. Educators Leadership Acad. Class, 2008—. Tchg. in Cmty. grantee, Rose State Coll., 2006. Mem.: Am. Physiol. Soc., Human Anatomy and Physiology Soc., Okla. Microscopy Soc., Nat. Sci. Tchrs. Assn., Classic Motorcycle and Scooter Riders Okla., Phi Kappa Phi. Achievements include research in evaluation of gene expression during development of the neonatal porcine uterus using suppression subtractive hybridization. Office: Rose State College 6420 SE 15th Street Midwest City OK 73110 Home: 1212 N Country Club Rd Stillwater OK 74075-9574

WIER, PATRICIA ANN, publishing executive, consultant; b. Coal Hill, Ark., Nov. 10, 1937; d. Horace L. and Bridget B. (McMahon) Norton; m. Richard A. Wier, Feb. 24, 1962; 1 child, Rebecca Ann. BA, U. Mo., Kansas City, 1964; MBA, U. Chgo., 1978. Computer programmer AT&T, 1960-62; lead programmer City of Kansas City, Mo., 1963-65; with Playboy Enterprises, Chgo., 1965-71, mgr. systems and programming, 1971; with Ency. Britannica, Inc., Chgo., 1971—; v.p. mgmt. svcs. Ency. Britannica USA, 1975-83, exec. v.p. adminstrn., 1983-84; v.p. planning and devel. Ency. Britannica, Inc., 1985, pres. Compton's Learning Co. divsn., 1985; pres. Ency. Britannica (USA), 1986-91, Ency. Britannica N.A., 1986—94; exec. v.p. Ency. Britannica, Inc., 1986-94; pres. Ency. Britannica N.Am., 1986—94. Cons. pvt. practice, Chgo., 1994—; bd. dirs. Alcas Corp., Mannatech Inc. Life mem. coun. Grad. Sch. Bus., U. Chgo. Mem. Direct Selling Assn. (bd. dirs. 1984-93, chmn. 1987-88, named to Hall of Fame 1991), Women's Coun. U. Mo. Kansas City (hon. life), Com. 200, The Chgo. Network. Roman Catholic. Office: Patricia A Wier Inc 175 E Delaware Pl Ste 8305 Chicago IL 60611-7748 Personal E-mail: wier@prodigy.net.

WIERINGA, JEFFREY A., federal agency administrator, military officer; BS, Univ. Kans., 1975. Commissioned as ensign US Navy, 1976, naval aviator with over 4000 flight hours & 534 carrier landings, 1977—; A-6 Intruder pilot USS Ranger (CV 61), USS Kitty Hawk (CV 63); operational test pilot, engring. test pilot US Navy, aeronautical engring. duty officer A-12 prog., avionics systems project officer & asst. prog. mgr. AX prog., comdr. F/A-18 prog., exec. dir. ops. rsch. & engring. group, RAdm., comdr. Naval Air Warfare Ctr. Aircraft Div., asst. comdr. rsch. & engring. Naval Air Systems Command, chief test pilot & chief engr. Naval Aviation, aerospace engring. duty officer, dep. asst. sec. for internat. programs; VAdm, dir. Def. Security Cooperation Agy., US Dept. Def., Washington, 2007—. Decorated Legion of Merit (3), Meritorious Svc. medal (4), Navy & Marine Commendation medal (2), Navy & Marine Corps Achievement medal, Lean Six Sigma Green Belt. Office: Def Security Cooperation Agy 2800 Defense Pentagon Washington DC 20301-2800*

WIERMAN, JOHN CHARLES, mathematician, educator; b. Prosser, Wash., June 30, 1949; s. John Nathaniel and Edith Elizabeth (Ashley) W.; m. Susan Shelley Graupmann, Aug. 13, 1971; 1 child, Adam Christopher. BS in Math., U. Wash., 1971, PhD in Math., 1976. Asst. prof. math. U. Minn., Mpls., 1976-81; asst. prof. Johns Hopkins U., Balt., 1981-82, assoc. prof., 1982-87, prof., 1987—, chmn. math. scis. dept., 1988-2000, dir. entrepreneurship and mgmt. program, 1996—2009, dir. Ctr. for Leadership Edn., 2004—09. Sr. rsch. fellow Inst. Math. and Its Applications, Mpls., 1987—88; rsch. fellow Mittag-Leffler Inst., Sweden, 2009; Navy ASEE fellow Naval Surface Warfare Ctr., 2001—02. Co-author: First-Passage Percolation on the Square Lattice, 1978; contbr. articles to profl. jours. Grad. fellow, NSF, 1971—74, NSF rsch. grantee, 1976—93, sabbatical fellow, Navy-ASEE, 2001—02. Fellow Inst. Math. Stats. (organizer spl. session on percolation theory 1982, organizer spl. session on probability and math. stats. 1986), Inst. of Combinatorics and its Applications; mem. Southern Regional Coun. Statistics (pres. elect 2003-05, pres. 2005-07, treas. 2007-), Am. Soc. Quality, Inst. Math. Stats., Am. Math. Soc., Am. Statis. Assn., Math. Assn. Am., Sigma Xi, Phi Beta Kappa. Office: Johns Hopkins U Dept Applied Math and Stats 34th & Charles Sts Baltimore MD 21218 Office Phone: 410-516-7211. Business E-Mail: wierman@jhu.edu.

WIERNIK, PETER HARRIS, oncologist, educator; b. Crocket, Tex., June 16, 1939; s. Harris and Molly (Emmerman) W.; m. Roberta Joan Fuller, Sept. 6, 1961; children: Julie Anne, Lisa Britt, Peter Harrison. BA with distinction, U. Va., 1961, MD, 1965; Dr. honoris causa, U. Republic, Montevideo, Uruguay, 1982. Diplomate Am. Bd. Internal Medicine, Am. Bd. Med. Oncology (mem. writing com. 1981-87). Intern Cleve. Met. Gen. Hosp., 1965—66, resident, 1969—70; resident Osler Svc. Johns Hopkins Hosp., Balt., 1970—71; sr. asst. surgeon USPHS, 1966, advanced through grades to med. dir., 1976; sr. staff assoc. Balt. Cancer Rsch. Ctr., 1966—71, chief med. oncology sect., 1971—76, chief clin. oncology br., 1976—82, dir., 1976—82; assoc. dir. cancer treatment divsn. Nat. Cancer Inst., 1976—82; assoc. dir. Albert Einstein Cancer Ctr., Bronx, 1982—98, prof. medicine, 1983—98, prof. radiation oncology, 1996—98, head med. oncology divsn. Asst. prof. medicine U. Md. Sch. Medicine, Balt., 1971-74, assoc. prof., 1974-76, prof., 1976-82; prof. medicine and radiation oncology NY Med. Coll., 1998—; cons. hematology med. oncology Union Meml. Hosp., Greater Balt. Med. Ctr., Franklin Sq. Hosp.; bd. dirs. Balt. City unit Am. Cancer Soc., 1971-78; chmn. patient care com., 1972-75, profl. edn. grants com., NYC divsn., 1983-90, nat. clin. fellowship com., 1984-96; med. adv. com. Nat. Leukemia Assn., 1976-88, chmn. med. adv. com., 1989—; chmn. adult leukemia com. Cancer Leukemia Group B, 1976-83; prin. investigator Ea. Coop. Oncology Group, 1982-94, 96—; chmn. gynecol. oncology com., 1986-88, chmn. leukemia com., 1988-94; sci. cons. Vt. Regional Cancer Ctr., 1987—; dir. OLM Comprehensive Cancer Ctr., NY Med. Coll., 1998—2008, dir. Cancer Ctr. Montefine Med. Ctr., North Divsn., 2008-, editor-in-chief Jour. Clin. Medicine Oncology, 2007-. Editor: Controversies in Oncology, 1982, Supportive Care of the Cancer Patient, 1983, Neoplastic Diseases of the Blood, 1985, 4th edit., 2003, Adult Leukemias, 2001; editor: (assoc.) Medical Oncology and Tumor Pharmacotherapy, 1987—91; editor: (sr.), 1991—; editor: (assoc.) Am. Jour. Therapeutics, 1994—; co-editor: Year Book of Hematology, 1986—98, Handbook of Hematologic and Oncologic Emergencies, 1988—98, Bone Marrow Transplantation (textbook), 1995, Am. Jour. Medical Scis., 1976—81; editor: Jour. of Cancer Rsch. and Clin/ Oncology, 1986—89, Jour. Clin. Pharmacology, 1985—; mem. editl. bd. Cancer Treatment Reports, 1972—76, Leukemia Rsch., 1977—86, 1991—2005, Leukemia, 1986—2003, Cancer Clin. Trials, 1977—, Jour. of Therapeutic Rsch., 1994—, Hospital Practice, 1979—, Jour. of Clin. Oncology, 1989—91, Leukemia and Lymphoma, 1989—, PDQ National Cancer Inst., 1987—94, Cancer Investigation, 1998—2007, Serbian Archives Medicine, 2005—; contbr. articles to profl. jours., chapters to books. Recipient Z Soc. award U. Va., 1961, Byrd S. Leavell Hematology award U. Va. Sch. Medicine, 1965, Gold medal 1st Polish Congress Oncology, 2002, Statesman award Am. Soc. Clin. Oncology, 2008. Fellow AAAS, ACP, Am. Coll. Clin. Pharmacology (awards com. 1999—), Internat. Soc. Hematology, Royal Soc. Medicine (London), NY Acad. Medicine; mem. Am. Soc. Clin. Investigation (instl. rep. 1997—), Am. Soc. Clin. Oncology (chmn. edn. tng. com. 1976-79, 84, subcom. clin. investigation 1980-82, program com. 1990, pub. issues com., 1990-95, com. rsch. awards 1996-2000, com. health svcs. rsch. 2000-2003), Am. Assn. Cancer Rsch. (clin. cancer rsch. com. 2002—), Am. Soc. Hematology, Am. Fedn. Clin. Rsch., Am. Acad. Clin. Toxicology, Internat. Soc. Exptl. Hematology, NY Acad. Sci., Am. Soc. Hosp. Pharmacy, Am. Soc. Clin. Pharmacology Therapeutics, Am. Radium Soc. (program com. 1987-93, exec. com. 1988-95, publ. com. 1988-92, sec. 1990-91, pres.-elect, 1992-93; pres. 1993-94, Janeway medalist,

1996), Polish Oncology Soc. (hon., finalist Gold medal), Harvey Soc., Uruguayan Hematology Soc. (hon.), Acad. Medicine Uruguay (corr.), European Assn. Cancer Rsch., European Soc. Hematology, Phi Beta Kappa (assoc.), Sigma Xi, Alpha Omega Alpha, Phi Sigma (award 1961), FDA Grand Application Review Panel, Faculty 1000 Biology (faculty mem. 2007-). Office Phone: 718-304-7220. Personal E-mail: pwiernik@aol.com. Business E-Mail: wiernik@jimmy.harvard.edu, pwiernik@montefiore.org. *Always remember why you entered a profession in the first place. Leave the politics to those who have forgotten.*

WIERSBE, WARREN WENDELL, clergyman, writer, lecturer; b. East Chgo., May 16, 1929; s. Fred and Gladys Anna (Forsberg) W.; m. Betty Lorraine Warren, June 20, 1953; children: David, Carolyn, Robert, Judy. B.Th., No. Baptist Sem., 1953; D.D. (hon.), Temple Sem., Chattanooga, 1965, Trinity Ev-Div. Sch., 1986; LittD (hon.), Cedarville U., 1987. Ordained to ministry, Bapt. Ch., 1951. Pastor Central Bapt. Ch., East Chicago, 1951-57; editl. dir. Youth for Christ Internat., Wheaton, Ill., 1957-61; pastor Calvary Bapt. Ch., Covington, Ky., 1961-71; sr. min. Moody Ch., Chgo., 1971-78; bd. dirs. Slavic Gospel Assn., Wheaton, 1973-87; columnist Moody Monthly, Chgo., 1971-77; author, conf. minister, 1978-80; pres. ScripTex, Inc., Lincoln, Nebr., 1982—. Vis. instr. pastoral theology Trinity Div. Sch., Deerfield, Ill.; gen. dir. Back to the Bible Radio Ministries, Lincoln, Nebr., 1984-89; writer-in-residence Cornerstone Coll., Grand Rapids, Mich.; disting. prof. preaching Grand Rapids Bapt. Sem. Author: over 150 books including William Culbertson, A Man of God, 1974, Live Like a King, 1976, Walking with the Giants, 1976, Be Right, 1977, (with David Wiersbe) Making Sense of the Ministry, 1983, Why Us? Why Bad Things Happen to God's People, 1984, Real Worship: It Can Transform Your Life, 1986, The Integrity Crisis, 1988, Be What You Are, 1988, The New Pilgrim's Progress, 1989, Living With the Giants, 1993, Preaching and Teaching with Imagination, 1994, Be Myself, 1994, The Bible Exposition Commentary, 6 vols., 2004. Home and Office: 441 Lakewood Dr Lincoln NE 68510-2419

WIERSMA, G. BRUCE, dean, forester, educator; b. Paterson, NJ, Oct. 26, 1942; s. George and Marjorie (Zeedyk) W.; m. Ann Becker, Aug. 15, 1964; children: Heather, Robin, Jennifer, Joshua. BS, U. Maine, 1964; MF in Forestry, Yale U., 1965; PhD Coll. Environ. Sci. & Forestry, SUNY, 1968. Cert. flight instr., lic. comml. pilot. Teaching asst., 1965-66; rsch. biologist Coll. Environ. Sci. and Forestry SUNY, 1968; combat devels. staff officer U.S. Army Inst. Land Combat, Alexandria, Va., 1968-70; head monitoring sect. EPA, Washington, 1970-72, chief ecol. monitoring branch, 1972-74, chief pollutant pathways br. Las Vegas, Nev., 1974-79, sr. ecologist, 1979-80; mgr. environ. earth scis. group, Idaho Nat. Engring. Lab. EG&G Idaho, Inc., 1980-87; instr. Idaho Falls Campus of Higher Edn. U. Idaho, 1981-90, affiliate grad. faculty Coll. Forestry Wildlife and Range Scis., 1988-90; mgr., dir. Ctr. Environ. Monitoring and Assesment Environ. Sci. and Tech. Group, 1989-90; dir. Ctr. Environ. Monitoring and Assesment Idaho Nat. Engring. Lab., EG&G Idaho, Inc., Idaho Falls, 1988-90; dean Coll. Forest Resources, assoc. dir. Maine Agrl. Experiment Sta., prof. Forest Resources U. Maine, Orono, 1991-93, dean Coll. Natural Scis., Forestry and Agr., dir. Maine Agrl. and Forest Exptl. Sta., 1993—2006, dir. Ctr. for Rsch. on Sustainable Forests, 2006—. Dir. Ctr. Environ. Monitoring and Assessment, Idaho Falls, Idaho, 1980-90; ad-hoc task force to plan global environ. monitoring sys., 1993-95; trustee Nature Conservancy, 1993-95; UN ad hoc task force to plan global terrestrial observing sys., 1993-95; bd. dirs. Maine Forest Products Coun., 1993—; U.S. Nat. Com. on Data for Sci. and Tech., 1990-92; chmn. com. on databased NRC, 1990-94, com. on marine monitoring, 1986-90; forest resources adv. com. U.S. Sec. Agr., 1998-2005; mem. Gov. Maine's Com. on Sawmill Biomass Conversion, 1999. Contbr. chpts. to books, articles to profl. jours; editor, founder Jour. Environ. Monitoring and Assesment. Pilot, Maine wing CAP. Capt. U.S. Army, 1968-70. Recipient numerous rsch. grants from various orgns. Mem. NRC (chair com. on databases, 1990-94, com. on marine monitoring, 1986-90, Nat. Assn. Profl. Forestry Schs. (exec. com. 1993-98), Assn. Expt. Sta. Dirs. (exec. com. N.E. region 1996-2000, chmn. 1998-99, com. on policy 1997-2000). Avocations: jogging, swimming, cross country skiing, backpacking. Home: 103 Wildwood Estates Dr Holden ME 04429-7344 Office: U Maine Ctr Rsch on Sustainable Forests 5755 Nutting Hall Orono ME 04473 Home Phone: 207-843-5885; Office Phone: 207-581-3794. Business E-Mail: bruce_wiersma@umenfa.edu.

WIERSMA, SUSAN RENEE, pediatrician; b. Milw., Wis., May 5, 1958; MD, Case Western Reserve Univ., 1984. Cert. Am. Bd. Pediatrics, 1989, in Pediatric Hematology-Oncology Am. Bd. Pediatrics, 1992. Intern in pediatrics Univ. Minn., Mpls., 1985, resident in pediatrics, 1986—87; fellowship in pediatric hematology-oncology Children's Hosp., LA, 1987—90; assoc. prof. Case Western Reserve Univ., Cleve.; dir., pediatric stem cell transplant program Univ. Hospitals, Cleve. Contbr. articles to profl. jours. Office: UH Rainbow Babies & Children's Hosp RBC 6054 11100 Euclid Ave Cleveland OH 44106 Office Phone: 216-844-3345. Office Fax: 216-844-5431.

WIERZCHOLSKI, WUNSCHIK CHRISTOPH, mechanical engineer, mathematician, information scientist; b. Znin, Poland, Mar. 18, 1939; s. Henryk and Kanarkowska Maria Wunschik; m. Anna Poznanska, Apr. 27, 1974; 1 child, Michalina. M of Engring., Tech. U., Poznań, Poland, 1961; MSc in Math., U. Poznań, 1967; ScD, Tech. U., Poznań, Poland, 1970, PhD. Asst. prof. Tech. U., Lublin, Poland, 1983-85, Szczecin, Poland, 1985-90, prof., 1990—, Maritime U. Gdynia, 2000, Gdansk U. Tech., 2003—. Head dept. applied math. U. Szczecin, 1986-88; head dept. tech. mechanics Agrl. Acad. Szczecin, 1990-94; lectr., Tech. U. Hannover, Germany, 1992, guest prof. mech. engr., Tech. U. Essen, Germany DFG, German Rsch. Found., 1997; coord. European Union Grantee Transfer of Knowledge, MTKD-CT-2004-517226, 2005-08. Contbr. over 400 articles to profl. sci. jours. in field of tech. mechanics tribology. Polish grant, 1990, 94, 97, 99, 2001, 2003, German grantee DLR-Berlin-POL, 1980-96; recipient Sci. State award in topic hydrodynamic lubrication, 1981. Mem. Polish Math. Soc., Polish Acad. Scis. (sect. of biomechanics 1999—), Polish Tribological Soc. (mem. mgmt. 1997—), Am. Bibliographic Inst., Scientific Soc. of Szczecin, N.Y. Acad. Roman Catholic. Avocations: numerical and analytical applications in biomechanics, micro and nano biotribiology. Office: Seledynowa St 9/7 PL70-781 Szczecin Poland Address: Seledynowastr 9/7 PL70781 Szczecin Poland

WIESCHAUS, ERIC F., molecular biologist, educator; b. South Bend, Ind., June 8, 1947; m. Gertrud Schüpbach; 3 children. BS, U. Notre Dame, 1969; PhD in Biology, Yale U., 1974. Rsch. fellow Zool. Inst., U. Zurich, Switzerland, 1975-78; group leader European Molecular Biol. Lab., Germany, 1978-81; from asst. prof. to assoc. prof. Princeton U., 1981-87; Squibb prof. molecular biology Princeton U., 1987—; and adj. prof. biochemistry Univ. Medicine & Dentistry of NJ-Robert Wood Johnson Med. Sch. Fellow Lab. de Genetique Moleculaire, France, 1976; vis. rschr. Ctr. Pathobiology, U. Calif., Irvine, 1977; mem. sci. adv. coun. Damon Runyon-Walter Winchell Cancer Fund, 1987-92. Contbr. articles to numerous profl. jours. Recipient Nobel prize in physiology or medicine, 1995. Fellow Am. Acad. Arts and Scis.; mem. NAS. Office: Princeton U MOF 435 Dept Molecular Biology Washington Rd Princeton NJ 08544-0001*

WIESE, JOHN PAUL, federal judge; b. Bklyn., Apr. 19, 1934; s. Gustav and Margaret W.; m. Alice Mary Donoghue, June 1961; 1 child, John Patrick. BA cum laude, Hobart College, Geneva, NY, 1962; LLB, U. Va., Charlottesville, 1965. With Cox, Langford & Brown, Washington, 1967-1969, Hudson & Creyke, 1969-74; trial commr. US Claims Ct., Washington, 1974-1986; judge US Ct. Fed. Claims, Washington, 1986—2001, sr. judge, 2001—. Mem. Phi Beta Kappa, Bar Assn. DC. Office: US Ct of Federal Claims 717 Madison Pl NW Washington DC 20439-0002*

WIESE, RICHARD, explorer, field scientist, journalist; BSc in Geology and Biology, Brown U., 1982; studied applied physiology, Columbia U., 1988. Anchor, reporter Network of the World, 2000—01; reporter, prodr., weather anchor WWOR-TV, NJ; explorer in residence Am. Mus. Natural History Expeditions; host Exploration with Richard Wiese, 2005—. US rep. to the Moussem de Tan Tan, Morocco, 2004; organizer, founder Central Park Bio Blitz, 2003; spkr. in field. Featured in several publications including People, Travel and Leisure, New York Sun, Esquire, New York Times, Business Week, USA Today, Wine Spectator, Life, Sports Illustrated, New Yorker, Star-Ledger, Newsday, Star-Telegram.com, Fox News, The Magazine Antiques, Men's Journal, Daily News, Dan's Papers, Science, National Geographic, LA Times, Forbes and Beretta, host Earth and Science, columnist UK column covering earth events and environ. issues, 2000—01, columnist (monthly adventure travel advice) Men's Journal, Ask the Explorer, 2004, guest appearances include Late Night with Craig Ferguson, CNN, Dateline, FOX News, BBC, MSNBC, ABC News, CBS Morning Show, Good Morning America, WB11, Morning Show and others; actor: Club Paradise, 1986; corr. Beyond Tomorrow, 1988, narrator (TV films) The Waterkeepers, 2000. Recipient Nat. Genesis award for excellence in wildlife advocacy, 1992, Associated Press Folio award, Golden Halo Advertising award for best environ./wildlife campaign, 2004, Sci. Mus. LI Sci. Achievement award, 2006; named one of Hottest Bachelors Alive, People Mag., 2003. Fellow: Royal Geographical Soc.-London, Explorer's Club (pres. (youngest to serve) 2002, founder of film festival 2003); mem.: Am. Alpine Club, Am. Meteorological Soc. Achievements include travelled to all seven continents; tagged jaguars in the Yucatan Jungle; being a expedition leader to the Northern Territory of Australia to look for basis of the Aboriginal myth of the Rainbow Serpent; being a team member of the largest medical expedition ever conducted on Mt. Everest; achieved the first ascent of an unclimbed peak in the Wrangell Mountains of Alaska in 2005; discovered 29 new life forms on Mt. Kilimanjaro in Africa; Cross country skiing to the North Pole in 2006; travelled to the hottest place on earth in Ethiopia to attempt to extract DNA fragments from molten lava to look for evidence of microbial life in conditions never thought to be able to support life; honored at the 2005 Boy Scout National Jamboree, addressed 90,000 people and had camp named in honor. E-mail: Explorer@NewsWeather.com.*

WIESE, WILLIAM D., lawyer; s. Ray and Beverly Wiese; children: Jackson, Carter. BSChemE, U.Iowa, Iowa City, 1981; MBA, St. Thomas U., St. Paul, 1987; JD, U. Tex., Austin, 1999. Bar: US Patent Office 1999, US Dist. Ct (no., we., ea., so. dists.) Tex. 2006. Atty. Jenkens & Gilchrist, Austin, Tex., 1999—2005; ptnr. DuBois, Bryant, Campbell & Schwartz, LLP, Austin, Tex., 2005—. Office: DuBois Bryant Campbell & Schwartz LLP 700 Lavaca St Ste 1300 Austin TX 78701 Business E-Mail: bwiese@dbcslaw.com.

WIESE, WOLFGANG LOTHAR, physicist, researcher; b. Tilsit, Germany, Apr. 21, 1931; came to U.S., 1957; naturalized, 1965; s. Werner Max and Charlotte (Donath) W.; m. Gesa Ladehoff, Oct. 12, 1957; children: Margrit, Cosima. BS, U. Kiel, Fed. Republic Germany, 1954, PhD, 1957, PhD (hon.), 1993. Rsch. assoc. U. Md., College Park, 1958-59; rsch. physicist Nat. Bur. Standards, Gaithersburg, Md., 1960-62, chief plasma spectrosc. sect., 1962-77, chief atomic and plasma radiation div., 1978-91, chief atomic physics div., 1991—2004; ret., 2004; NIST rsch. assoc., 2005—. Lectr. U. Calif., 1963, 64. Author: Atomic Transition Probabilities, Vol. I., 1966, Vol. II, 1969, Vol. III, 1988, Vol. IV, 1988, Atomic Transition Probabilities for C, N, and O, 1996, Spectral Data for Highly Ionized Atoms, 2000. Recipient Silver Medal award Dept. Commerce, 1962, Gold Medal award, 1971, Humboldt award, 1986, A.S. Fleming award U.S. C. of C., 1971, Disting. Career in Sci. award Wash. Acad. Sci., 1992, Disting. Postdoctoral award U. Md., 2003; Guggenheim fellow, 1966. Fellow Am. Phys. Soc., Optical Soc. Am., Wash. Acad. Sci.; mem. Internat. Astron. Union. Lutheran. Home: 8229 Stone Trail Dr Bethesda MD 20817-4555 Home Phone: 301-365-2863; Office Phone: 301-975-3201. Business E-Mail: wiese@nist.gov.

WIESEL, ELIE, writer, educator; b. Sighet, Romania, Sept. 30, 1928; arrived in Paris, 1945; came to US, 1956, naturalized, 1963; s. Shlomo and Sarah (Feig) W.; m. Marion Erster, 1969; 1 son, Shlomo Elisha; 1 stepchild, Jennifer. Student, The Sorbonne, Paris, 1948-51; LittD (hon.), Jewish Theol. Sem., NYC, 1967; LHD (hon.), Hebrew Union Coll., 1968, Manhattanville Coll., Purchase, NY, 1972, Yeshiva U., NYC, 1973; D of Hebrew Letters (hon.), Spertus Coll. Judaica, 1973; PhD (hon.), Bar-Ilan U., 1973; LHD (hon.), Boston U., 1974; LLD (hon.), Hofstra U., Hempstead, NY, 1975; LittD (hon.), Marquette U., Wis., 1975, Simmons Coll., Boston, 1976; LHD (hon.), Coll. St. Scholastica, 1978; LLD (hon.), Talmudic U. Fla., 1979; LHD (hon.), Wesleyan U., 1979; LLD (hon.), U. Notre Dame, Ind., 1980; LHD (hon.), Brandeis U., Waltham, Mass., 1980; LittD (hon.), Anna Maria Coll., 1980, Yale U., New Haven, Conn., 1981; LHD (hon.), Kenyon Coll., 1982, Hobart/William Smith Coll., 1982, Emory U., Atlanta, 1983, Siena Heights Coll., 1983, Fla. Internat. U., Miami, 1983, Fairfield U., Conn., 1983, Dropsie Coll., 1983, Moravian Coll., Bethlehem, Pa., 1983, Colgate U., Hamilton, NY, 1984; LittD (hon.), Wake Forest U., Chgo., 1985; LHD (hon.), SUNY, Binghamton, 1985, Lehigh U., Pa., 1985; LittD (hon.), Haverford Coll., Pa., 1985; HHD (hon.), U. Hartford, 1985; LHD (hon.), Coll. New Rochelle, 1986, Tufts U., Medford, Mass., 1986, Georgetown U., Washington, DC, 1986; LittD (hon.), Capital U., 1986; LHD (hon.), Hamilton Coll., 1986, Rockford Coll., 1986; PhD (hon.), U. Haifa, 1986; LittD (hon.), LI U., 1986; LHD (hon.), Villanova U., Pa., 1987, Coll. St. Thomas, 1987, U. Denver, 1987, Walsh Coll., Troy, Mich., 1987, Loyola Coll., Balt., 1987; LittD (hon.), U. Paris, Sorbonne, 1987; HHD (hon.), Lycoming Coll., Williamsport, Pa., 1987; LittD (hon.), U. Conn., Storrs, 1988; PhD (hon.), Ben Gurion U., 1988; LittD (hon.), U. Ctrl. Fla., Orlando, 1988; LLD (hon.), La Salle U., 1988; LHD (hon.), Ohio U., 1988; HHD (hon.), U. Miami, 1988; LittD (hon.), Wheeling Jesuit Coll., 1989, Wittenberg U., Springfield, Ohio, 1989; HHD (hon.), Brigham Young U., Provo, Utah, 1989; DSc (hon.), U. Health Scis./Chgo. Med. Sch., 1989; LHD (hon.), Concordia Coll., 1990, NYU, 1990, Fordham U., Bronx, NY, 1990, Conn. Coll., New London, 1990; ThD (hon.), U. Åbo Akadem, 1990; LHD (hon.), Upsala Coll., 1991, Duquesne U., Pitts., 1991, Roosevelt U., 1991, Hunter Coll., NYC, 1992, Susquehanna U., Selinsgrove, Pa., 1992, Am. U., 1992; LittD (hon.), Fairleigh Dickinson U., Teaneck, NJ, 1993; LHD (hon.), Millersville U., Pa., 1993; degree (hon.), U. Dayton, 1993, U. Mich., 1993, U. Bordeaux, 1993; LHD (hon.), Gustavus Adolphus Coll., 1994, McGill U., Montreal, 1994, Mt. Sinai Med. Sch., 1994, Spelman Coll., Atlanta, 1995; Doctorat (hon.), U. Catholique de Louvain, 1995; LLD (hon.), Bates Coll., Lewiston, Maine, 1995; LHD (hon.), Sacred Heart U., Fairfield, Conn., 1995; D (hon.), U. Buenos Aires, 1995; Docteur (hon.), U. de Picardie Jules Verne, Amiens, France, 1996; LHD (hon.), Briar Cliff Coll., Sioux City, Iowa, 1996, Clark U., Worcester, Mass., 1996, Phila. Coll. Textiles, 1996, U. Mass., Dartmouth, 1997, U. South Fla., Tampa, 1997, Fla. Atlantic U., Boca Raton, 1997, U. RI, Kingston, 1997, U. Mass., Lowell, 1997; LLD (hon.), U. Guelph, 1997; LHD (hon.), De Paul U., Chgo., 1997, Seton Hall U., South Orange, NJ, 1998; LittD (hon.), St. John's U., 1998; LHD (hon.), Eckerd Coll., St. Petersburg, Fla., 1998, Appalachian State U., Boone, NC, 1998, Merrimack U., 1998; D. (hon.), Cedar Crest Coll., Allentown, Pa., 1998; LHD (hon.), Gettysburg Coll., Pa., 1998, Loyola U., Chgo., 1999; HHD (hon.), Mich. State U., East Lansing, 1999; Doutor (hon.), U. do Estado do Rio de Janeiro, 1999; Docteur (hon.), U. Montreal, 1999; LHD (hon.), St. Norbert Coll., De Pere, Wis., 1999, St. Joseph's U., 2000, U. Fla., Gainesville, 2000; PhD (hon.), Hebrew U., Israel, 2000, U. Bologna, 2000; EdD (hon.), Regis U., 2001; Docteur (hon.), U. Paris, Sorbonne, 2001; LHD (hon.), Hebrew Coll., 2001; EdD (hon.), Stockton Coll., 2003, Meredith Coll., Raleigh, NC, 2003, Old Dominion U., Norfolk, Va., 2003, Elon U., 2004, Case Western Reserve U., Cleve., 2004; LHD (hon.), Chapman U., Orange, Calif., 2005, Israel Inst. Tech., 2005, Snow Coll., Ephraim, Utah, 2006, Dartmouth Coll., Hanover, NH, 2006; HHD (hon.), McDaniel Coll., 2005; DHL (hon.), Cabrini Coll., Radnor, Pa., 2006, U. Vt., 2007. Disting. prof. Judaic studies CCNY, 1972-76; Andrew W. Mellon prof. in the humanities Boston U., 1976—, prof. religious studies and univ. prof., 1976—, prof. philosophy, 1988—. Disting. vis. prof. Henry Luce, 1982-83, Yale U.; lectr. Andrew W. Mellon Ann. Lecture Series Boston U., 92d St. YMHA, YWHA Ann. Lectr. Series, ann. radio broadcast series, 1966-86, advisory bd. Rena Costa Ctr. for Yiddish Studies at Bar-Ilan U., 1994, advisory coun. Carnegie Commn. on Preventing Deadly Conflict, 1994; chmn. US Pres.'s Commn. on the Holocaust, 1979-80, US Holocaust Meml. Coun., 1980-86; hon. chmn. Holocaust Studies Ctr. of Bronx HS Sci., Nat. Jewish Resource Ctr., NYC; hon. coun. Vancouver Holocaust Ctr. Soc., 1992—, Ctr. Christian-Jewish Understanding, Sacred Heart U., Am. Friends of Ghetto Fighter's House; co-chmn. Children of Chernobyl/Children at Heart, 1995—; steering com. The Balkan Inst., 1996—; mem. Nat. hon. com. Darius Milhaud Soc.; mem. coun. Ethic Accord Project on Ethic Rels., (hon.) Am. Friends of Neve Shalom/Wahat al-Salam, 1996—; leadership coun. Tanenbsum Ctr. Interreligious Understanding, 1997—; founder Elie Wiesel Found. for Humanity, 1987; founding pres. Paris-based Universal Acad. Cultures, 1993; pres. Comité Français Pour "Yad Vashem," Am. Gathering of Jewish Holocaust Survivors, 1985, Am. Kurdish Info. Network, 1997, adv. bd., 1997; v.p. Internat. Rescue Com., 1985—; adv. bd. The Raoul Wallenberg Commn. of US, 1981—, Friends of LeChambon, 1982, Boston U. Inst. for Philosophy & Religion, 1986, Boston U. Students for a Free Tibet, Nat. Inst. Against Prejudice & Violence, Internat. Ctr. in NY, 1986—, Friends of Akim USA, 1991, Sholom Aleichem Meml. Found., Nat. Jewish Law Students Assn., 1995—, AmeriCares, 1995, React Take Action Awards, 1996—, No Greater Love, 1996—, Inst. Study of Violence, 1996—, Global Lawyers and Physicians: Working Together for Human Rights, 1997; internat. adv. bd. Elmhurst Coll. Holocaust Edn. Project, 1996—; Am. bd. adv. The Moscow Ctr.; adv. coun. US Com. Refugees, 1996—, Nat. Endowmet for Democracy, 1996—; Helsinki adv. com. Human Rights Watch; bd. govs. Haifa U., (mem. emeritus) Tel Aviv U. 1976—, Massuah - Inst. Study of Holocaust, Israel; bd. dirs. Nat. Com. on Am. Fgn. Policy, Elaine Kaufman Cultural Ctr., Humanitas, Am. Assocs. Ben-Gurion U. of the Negev, Mut. of Am., France Libertés; hon. dir. HIAS; bd. trustees Annenberg Rsch. Inst., 1983-89, Am. Jour. World Svc., 1985—, Haifa U., Tel-Aviv U., Yeshiva U., 1977—, Am. Jewish Heritage Ctr., Mus. Jewish Heritage, NY; patron Internat. Peace U., Berlin, 1995—; colleague Cathedral St. John the Divine, 1975—; mem. jury Neustadt Internat. Prize Lit., 1984; mem. Task Force Apprehending Indicted War Criminals, 1998—. Author: Night (Oprah's Book Club 2006), 1960, Dawn, 1961, The Accident, 1962, The Town Beyond the Wall, 1964, The Gates of the Forest, 1966, The Jews of Silence, 1966, Legends of Our Time, 1968, A Beggar in Jerusalem, 1970, One Generation After, 1970, Souls on Fire, 1972, The Oath, 1973, Ani Maamin, 1973, Zalmen, or the Madness of God, 1974, Messengers of God, 1976, A Jew Today, 1978, Four Hasidic Masters, 1978, The Trial of God, 1979, The Testament, 1980, Le Testament D'Un Poète Juif Assassiné (France's Prix Livre-Inter 1980, Bourse Goncourt, 1980, Prix des Bibliothécaires, 1981), 1985, Images from the Bible, 1980, Five Biblical Portraits, 1981, Somewhere A Master, 1982, Paroles d'Étranger, 1982, The Golem, 1983, The Fifth Son (Grand Prix de la Littérature, City of Paris), 1985, Signes d'Exode, 1985, Against Silence (3 vols., ed. Irving Abrahamson), 1985, Job ou Dieu dans la Tempête, 1986, A Song for Hope, 1987, The Nobel Address, 1987, Twilight, 1988, Un desir fou de danser, 2006; (essays) Silences et Mémoire d'hommes, 1989, L'Oublié, 1989, From the Kingdom of Memory, 1990, Célébration Talmudique, 1991, Sages and Dreamers, 1991, The Forgotten, 1992, (with John Cardinal O'Connor) A Journey of Faith, 1990, (with Albert Friedlander) The Six Days of Destruction, 1988, (with Kofi A. Annan) Confronting Anti-Semitism, 2006; (novels) Un désir fou de danser, 2006, (dialogues with Philippe-Michaël Saint-Cheron) Evil and Exile, 1990, commentaries to A Passover Haggadah, 1993, All Rivers Run To The Sea (a memoir), 1995, (with Jorge Semprun) Se taire est impossible, 1995, (with François Mitterand) Memoir in Two Voices, 1996, Et la Mer N'est Pas Remplie, Memoirs II, 1996, Célébration Prophétique, Portraits et Légendes, 1998, Les juges, 1999, King Solomon and His Magic Ring, 1999, And the Sea is Never Full (English transl. of Et la mer n'est pas remplie, Memoirs II 1999), The Judges, 2002, (dialogues with Michael de Saint Cheron) Le Mal et L'Exil/Dix ans après, 1999, (essays) D'où viens-tu? (pub. by Le Seuil), 2001, After the Darkness, 2002, Wise Men and Their Tales, 2003, The Time of the Uprooted, 2005, A Mad Desire to Dance, 2009; (essays) Et où vas-tu?, 2004, Confronting Anti-Semitism, 2006; mem. editl. and adv. bds. Midstream, Religion and Lit. (U. Notre Dame), Sh'ma: Jour. of Responsibility, Hadassah Mag., Acad. of the Air for Jewish Studies, Holocaust and Genocide Studies: An Internat. Jour., Passages, Religion and the Arts; subject of more than 55 books; journalist Israeli, French and Am. newspapers. Chmn. adv. bd. World Union Jewish Students, 1985—; comité d'Honneur Ligue International Contre le Racisme et l'Antisemitisme, 1985—; founder Nat. Jewish Ctr. Learning and Leadership, 1974; mem. soc. fellows Ctr. Judaic Studies, U. Denver, 1980, bd. overseer Bar-Ilan U., 1970—. Recipient Prix Rivarol, 1963, Prix de l'Universite de la langue Francaise, 1963, Ingram Merrill award, 1964, Jewish Heritage award, Haifa U., 1975, Remembrance award, 1965, Prix du Souvenir, 1965, Nat. Jewish Book Council award, 1965, 1973, Prix Médicis, 1968, Prix Bordin, French Acad., 1972, Eleanor Roosevelt Meml. award, NY United Jewish Appeal, 1972, Am. Liberties medallion, Am. Jewish Com., 1972, Martin Luther King Jr. medallion, CCNY, 1973, Ann. award for Disting. Service to Am. Jewry, Nat. Fedn. of Jewish Men's Clubs, 1973, Faculty Disting. Scholar award, Hofstra U., 1974, Rambam award, Am. Mizrachi Women, 1974, Meml. award, NY Soc. Clin. Psychologists, 1975, First Spertus Internat. award, 1976,

Myrtle Wreath award, Hadassah, 1977, King Solomon award, 1977, Liberty award, HIAS, 1977, Jewish Heritage award, B'nai B'rith, 1966, Avodah award, Jewish Tchrs. Assn., Jewish Tchrs. Assn., 1972, Humanitarian award, B'rith Sholom, 1978, Joseph Prize for Human Rights, Anti-Defamation League, 1978, Zalman Shazar award, State of Israel, 1979, Presdl. Citation, NYU, 1979, Inaugural award for Lit., Israel Bonds Prime Minister's Com., 1979, Jabotinsky medal, S.Y. Agnon medal, State of Israel, 1980, Rabbanit Sarah Herzog award, Emunah Women of Am., 1981, Le Grand Prix Littéraire du Festival Internat. Deauville, 1983, Internat. Lit. prize for Peace, Royal Acad. Belgium, 1983, Lit. Lions award, NY Pub. Libr., 1983, Jordan Davidson Humanitarian award, Fla. Internat. U., 1983, Anatoly Scharansky Humanitarian award, 1983, Grand Officer, Legion of Honor, France, Congl. gold medal, 1985, Voice of Conscience award, Am. Jewish Congress, 1985, Remembrance award, Israel Bonds, 1985, Anne Frank award, 1985, 4 Freedoms award, FDR 4 Freedoms Found., 1985, Medal of Liberty award, Statue of Liberty Presentation, 1986, Nobel Peace Prize, 1986, First Herzl Lit. award, First David Ben-Gurion award, Nat. UJA, Gov.'s award, Shaarei Tzedek, Internat. Kaplun Found. award, Hebrew U. Jerusalem, Scopus award, 1974, Am.-Israeli Friendship award, Disting. Writers award, Lincolnwood Library, 1984, First Chancellor Joseph H. Lookstein award, Bar-Ilan U., 1984, Sam Levenson Meml. award, Jewish Cmty. Rels. Coun., 1984, Comenius award, Moravian Coll., 1985, Henrietta Szold award, Hadassah, 1985, Disting. Cmty. Svc. award, Mut. Am., 1985, Covenant Peace award, Synagogue Coun. Am., 1985, Jacob Pat award, World Congress Jewish Culture, 1985, Humanitarian award, Internat. League Human Rights, 1985, Disting. Fgn.-Born Am. award, Internat. Ctr. NY, Inc., 1986, Freedom Cup award, Women's League Israel, 1986, First Jacob Javits Humanitarian award, UJA Young Leadership, 1986, Boston City Coun. Commendation, 1986, medal of Jerusalem, 1986, Freedom award, Internat. Rescue Com., 1987, Achievement award, Artist and Writers for Peace in the Mid. East, 1987, La Grande Médaille de Vermeil de la Ville de Paris, 1987, La Médaille de la Chancellerie de l'Université de Paris, 1987, La Médaille de l'Université de Paris, 1987, First Eitinger prize, U. Oslo, 1987, Lifetime Achievment award, Present Tense mag., 1987, Spl. Christopher award, The Christophers, 1987, Achievement award, State Israel, 1987, Sem. medal, Jewish Theol. Sem. Am., 1987, Metcalf Cup and Prize for Excellence in Teaching, Boston U., 1987, Spl. award, Nat. Com. on Am. Fgn. Policy, 1987, Grã-Cruz da Ordem Nacional do Cruzeiro do Sul, Brazil's highest distinction, 1987, Profiles in Courage award, B'nai B'rith, 1987, Centennial medal, U. Scranton, 1987, Citation from Religious Edn. Assn., 1987, Golda Meir Sr. Humanitarian award, 1987, Presdl. medal, Hofstra U., 1988, Bicentennial medal, Georgetown U., 1988, Human Rights Law award, Internat. Human Rights Law Group, 1988, Janus Korczak Humanitarian award, INTERPHIL, 1989, Count Sforza award in Philanthropy, Am. Hungarian Found., 1989, Lily Edelman award for Excellence in Continuing Jewish Edn., B'nai B'rith Internat., 1989, George Washington award, NAHE, Kent State U., 1989, Bicentennial medal, NYU, 1989, Humanitarian award, Human Rights Campaign Fund, 1989, Internat. Brotherhood award, C.O.R.E., 1990, Frank Weil award for Disting. Contbn. to Adv. of N.Am., Jewish Culture Jewish Cmty. Ctrs. Assn. N.Am., 1990—, 1st Raoul Wallenberg medal, U. Mich., 1990, Award of Highest Honor, Soka U., 1991, Facing History and Ourselves Humanity award, 1991, La Medaille de la Ville de Toulouse, 1991, 1st Internat. Primo Levi award, 1992, Lit. Arts award, Nat. Found. for Jewish Culture, 1992, Ellis Island Medal of Honor, 1992, Guardian of the Children award, AKIM USA, 1992, Bishop Francis J. Mugavero award for religious and racial harmony Cath. Newman Ctr. Queens Coll., 1994, Golden Slipper Humanitarian award, 1994, Interfaith Coun. on the Holocaust Humanitarian award, 1994, Crystal award Davos World Economic Forum, 1995, First Niebuhr award, Elmhurst Coll., 1995, Mathilde Schecter award Women's League Conservative Judaism, 2000, Manhattan award Nat. Arts Club, 2000, Benediction medal The Delbarton Sch., 2001, Humanitarian award Israel Cancer Rsch. Fund, 2004, Inaugural award Louise T. Blouin Found., 2005, Grifo d'Oro award Mayor of Genoa, Italy, 2005, Light of Truth award Internat. Campaign Tibet, 2005; named Humanitarian of the Century Coun. Jewish Orgns., Presdl. medal Freedom, 1992; Beth Hatefutsoth hon. fellow, 1988; honors established in his name: Elie Wiesel award for Holocaust Rsch., U. Haifa, Elie Wiesel Chair in Holocaust Studies, Bar-Ilan U., Elie Wiesel Endowment Fund for Jewish Culture, U. Denver, 1987, Elie Wiesel Disting. Svc. award, U. Fla., 1988, Elie Wiesel awards for Jewish Arts and Culture B'nai B'rith Hillel Founds., 1988, Elie Wiesel Chair in Judaic Studies Conn. Coll., 1990, Disting. Libery award NYC Refugee Employment Project, 1995, Freedom award Nat. Civil Rights Mus., 1995, Humanitarian award Queensborough Comty. Coll./Holocaust Resource Ctr. Archives, 1995, Socio Honorario de la Sociedad Hebrai ca Argentina, 1995, Pres. award Quinnipac Coll., 1996, Golden Plate award Am. Acad. Achievement, 1996, Lotos medal of Merit, The Lotos Club, 1996, Guardian of Zion award Ingeborg Rennert Ctr. Jerusalem Studies, Bar-Ilan U., 1997, Eisenhower Leadership prize Eisenhower World Affairs Inst. Gettysburg Coll., 1997, Canterbury medalist Becket Fund for Religious Liberty, 1998, ABA ann. award, 1998, Rabbi Marc H. Tanenbaum award for Advancement Interreligious Understanding, 1998, Yitzhak Rabin Peacemaker award Merrimack Coll., 1998, Aesop prize Children's Am. Folklore Soc. for King Solomon and His Magic Ring (Children's Folklore sect. 1999), Raoul Wallenberg Internat. Humanitarian award The Am. Jewish Joint Distbn. Com., 1999, Comdr.'s Cross, Order of Merit, Republic of Hungary, 2004, King Hussein award, Hashemite Kingdom of Jordan, 2005, Hon. Citizen City of Santa Margherita, Italy, 2005, Cosmos Club award, 2006, Literary Lions award NY Pub. Libr., 2006, Chubb Fellowship award Timothy Dwight Ho., Yale U., 2006, La Grande Médaille de la Ville de Paris, 2006; named Man of Year Tel Aviv Mus. Art, 2005, Hon. Citizen, City of Aix-en-Provence, France, 2006; named one of 100 Most Influential People, Time Mag., 2006; named Honorary Knight in the Most Excellent Order of the Brit. Empire, 2006. Fellow Jewish Acad. Arts and Scis., Am. Acad. Arts and Letters (dept. lit.), Am. Acad. Arts and Scis., Modern Lang. Assn. Am. (hon.), Timothy Dwight Coll., Yale U.; mem. Fgn. Press Assn. (hon. life), Amnesty Internat., PEN (New England coun. 1993—), Writers and Artists for Peace in Middle East, Writers Guild of Am. East, The Author's Guild, Royal Norwegian Soc. Scis. and Letters, Soc. des auteurs Paris, European Acad. of Arts, Sci. and Humanities, Albert Einstein Soc. (hon., Phila.), Phi Beta Kappa (Assocs. award 1994). Office: Boston U 147 Bay State Rd Boston MA 02215 Office Phone: 617-353-4561.*

WIESEL, TORSTEN NILS, neurobiologist, educator; b. Upsala, Sweden, June 3, 1924; arrived in U.S., 1955; s. Fritz Samuel and Anna-Lisa Elisabet (Bentzer) Wiesel; 1 child, Sara Elisabet. MD, Karolinska Inst., Stockholm, 1954; D Medicine (hon.), Karolinska Inst, Stockholm, 1989; AM (hon.), Harvard U., 1967; D Medicine (hon.), Linköping U., 1982; ScD (hon.), NYU, 1987, U. Bergen, 1987. Instr. physiology Karolinska Inst., 1954—55; asst. dept. child psychiatry Karolinska Hosp., 1954—55; fellow in ophthalmology Johns Hopkins U., 1955—58, asst. prof. ophthalmic physiology, 1958—59; assoc. in neurophysiology and neuropharmacology Harvard U. Med. Sch., Boston, 1959—60, asst. prof. neurophysiology and neuropharmacology, 1960—64, asst. prof. neurophysiology, dept. psychiatry, 1964—67, prof. physiology, 1967—68, prof. neurobiology, 1968—74, Robert Winthrop prof. neurobiology, 1974—83, chmn. dept. neurobiology, 1973—82; Vincent and Brooke Astor prof. neurobiology, head lab. Rockefeller U., NYC, 1982—98, pres., 1991—98, pres. emeritus, 1998—, dir. Shelby White and Leon Levy Ctr. for Mind, Brain & Behavior, 1998—; sec. gen. Human Frontier Sci. Program, 2000. Ferrier lectr. Royal Soc. London, 1972, NIH lectr., 75; Grass lectr. Soc. Neurosci., 1976; lectr. Coll. de France, 1977; Hitchcock prof. U. Calif.-Berkeley, 1980; Sharpey-Schafer lectr. Phys. Soc. London; George Cotzias lectr. Am. Acad. Neurology, 1983; chmn. bd. govs. NY Acad Scis., 2001—. Contbr. numerous articles to profl. jours. Recipient Jules Stein award, Trustees for Prevention of Blindness, 1971, Lewis S. Rosenstiel prize, Brandeis U., 1972, Friedenwald award, Assn. Rsch. in Vision and Ophthalmology, 1975, Karl Spencer Lashley prize, Am. Philos. Soc., 1977, Louisa Gross Horwitz prize, Columbia U., 1978, Dickson prize, U. Pitts., 1979, Nobel prize in physiology or medicine, 1981, W.H. Helmerich III award, 1989, 2005 Nat. Medal Sci., NSF, 2007. Mem.: AAAS, Inst. Medicine (chmn. com. on human rights 1994—2004, David Rall medal 2005), Royal Swedish Acad. Scis. (fgn.), Royal Soc. (fgn.), Soc. Neurosci. (pres. 1978—79), Swedish Physiol. Soc., Nat. Acad. Arts and Scis., Am. Acad. Arts and Scis., Am. Philos. Soc., Am. Physiol. Soc., Physiol. Soc. (Eng.) (hon.). Office: Rockefeller U 1230 York Ave New York NY 10021-6399 E-mail: wiesel@mail.rockefeller.edu.*

WIESELTHIER, JEFFREY E., electronics engineer, researcher; SB, MIT, Cambridge, Mass., 1969; MS, Johns Hopkins U., Balt., 1971; PhD, U. Md., Coll. Pk., 1979. Electronics engr. Naval Surface Warfare Ctr., Silver Spring, Md., 1969—79; rsch. engr. Naval Rsch. Lab., Washington, 1979—2007; pres. Wieselthier Rsch., Silver Spring, 2007—. Contbr. articles to engring. jours., scientific papers to numerous confs. Fellow: IEEE. Achievements include patents for group-division multiple access concept. Personal E-mail: wieselthier@verizon.net. Business E-Mail: jeff@wieselthier.com.

WIESEN, DONALD GUY, retired diversified manufacturing company executive; b. NYC, July 4, 1928; s. Benjamin and Grace (Heath) W.; m. Patricia Ann Elfers, Apr. 29, 1950; children: Mara, Caitlin, Elizabeth, Anne, Megan. BS, Columbia U., 1948, MS, 1954. C.P.A., N.Y. Sr. tax specialist Price Waterhouse & Co., NYC, 1950-58; with Chesebrough-Pond's Inc., Greenwich, Conn., 1958-87, gen. mgr. ops. Europe, 1965-70, treas., 1970-72, group v.p., chief fin. officer, 1972-77, group v.p., internat., 1977-82, sr. group v.p., 1982-84, vice chmn., chief fin. officer, 1984-87, also dir., ret., 1987. Bd. dirs. Skandia Am. Corp., 1985-91. Trustee Greenwich Libr., 1974-80; bd. govs. St. Bernard Coll., Cullman, Ala., 1973-75; rep. Columbia U. Alumni, Geneva, 1968; bd. dirs. Inner-City Found. for Charity and Edn., Bridgeport, Conn., 1992-93. Capt. USMC, 1951-54. Mem. AICPA, Indian Harbor Yacht Club, Univ. Club (N.Y.). Roman Catholic.

WIESENBERG, RUSSEL JOHN, statistician; b. Kaukauna, Wis., Apr. 9, 1924; s. Emil Martin and Josephine (Appelbaker) W.; m. Jacqueline Leonardi, Nov. 23; children: James Wynne, Deborann Donna. BS, U. Wis., 1951; postgrad. Cornell U., 1960-61, U. Mich., 1969, George Washington U., 1976. Analyst, GE, West Lynn, Mass., 1951-56; specialist Internat. GE, Rio de Janeiro, 1956-59; statistician Gen. Motors Corp., Lockport, NY, 1959-65, sr. statistician, Harrison Radiator divsn., 1965-78, sr. reliability engr., 1978-82, sr. reliability statistician, 1982-87. Auditor Cmty. Chest Fund, 1952-55; umpire Little League Baseball, 1962-65; committeeman Buffalo Area coun. Boy Scouts Am., 1962—, Cub Scout committeeman, 1962-64, Webelos cubmaster, 1963-64; mem. Nat. Congress Parents and Tchrs., 1963—; heart fund Vol. Heart Assn., 1968; tournament dir. Am. Legion Baseball, 1975; vol. United Way campaign, 1983, nat. telethon March of Dimes, 1983-84. Served with AUS, 1943-46. Decorated Bronze Star. Mem. AAAS, Am. Statis. Assn., Nat. Register Sci. and Tech. Pers., U. Wis. Alumni Assn., Artus, Internat. Platform Assn., Phi Kappa Phi. Lutheran. com.). Contbr. articles to profl. jours. Home: 14 Norman Pl Buffalo NY 14226-4233

WIESENFARTH, JOSEPH JOHN, retired literature educator; b. Bklyn., Aug. 20, 1933; s. Charles Adam and Elizabeth Wiesenfarth; m. Louise Halpin, 1971; 1 child, Adam Joseph Halpin. BA, Cath. U. Am., 1956, PhD, 1962; MA, U. Detroit, 1959. Asst. prof. English LaSalle U., Phila., 1962—64, Manhattan Coll., Bronx, NY, 1964—67, assoc. prof. English, 1967—70, U. Wis., Madison, 1970—76, prof. English, 1976—2000, prof. emeritus, 2000—08. Author: Henry James and the Dramatic Analogy, 1963, Errand of Form: Jane Austen's Art, 1967, George Eliot's Mythmaking, 1977, George Eliot: A Writer's Notebook, 1981, Gothic Manners and the Classic English Novel, 1988, Ford Madox Ford and the Arts, 1989, Jane Austen's Jack & Alice, 2001, History and Representation in Ford Madox Wrintings, 2004, Jane Austen's The Three Sisters, 2004, Ford Madox Ford and the Regiment of Women, 2005. Grantee, Am. Philos. Soc., 1976; fellow, NEH, 1967—68, Fulbright Found., 1981—82. Mem.: Istituto di Studi Avanzati Bologna. Home: 5401 Greening Ln Madison WI 53705

WIESENTHAL, ROBERT S., Entertainment Company Executive; BA in Polit. Sci., U. of Rochester, 1987. Mem., mergers & acquisitions group First Boston, 1986—93, mem., media group, 1993—99; mng. dir. to mng. dir. of credit Credit Suisse First Boston, 1999—2000; exec. v.p. & CFO Sony Corp. of America, 2000—; exec. v.p. & chief strategy officer Sony Broadband Entertainment, 2000—; group exec. Sony Corp. Bd. mem. Panavision, Inc., Entercom Comm. Corp. Bd. mem. Hamptons Internat. Film Festival. Office: Sony Corp of America 550 Madison Ave New York NY 10022*

WIESER, HELMUT, metal products executive; b. Steyr, Austra, Oct. 11, 1953; M in Mech. Engring. and Econs., U. Graz, Austria, 1981. Various sr. mgmt. positions including pres. Voest Alpine Venezuela Voest Alpine; various mgmt. positions in rolled products unit up to mem. exec. bd., COO Austria Metal Group; v.p. ops. Flat-rolled products group Alcoa, Inc., Geneva, 2000—01, pres. Flat-rolled products group, 2001—04, pres. North Am. and European Mill Products, v.p., 2004—05, group pres. global mill products, rigid packaging and hard alloy extrusion businesses, exec. v.p. NYC, 2005—. Bd. govs. Internat. Grad. U., Washington. Achievements include representing Austria in the Modern Pentathlon event at the 1980 Summer Olympics in Moscow. Office: Alcoa Inc 390 Park Ave New York NY 10022 Office Phone: 212-836-2600.

WIESLER, JAMES BALLARD, retired banker; b. San Diego, July 25, 1927; s. Harry J. and Della B. (Ballard) W.; m. Mary Jane Hall, Oct. 3, 1953; children: Tom, Ann, Larry. BS, U. Colo., 1949; postgrad., Rutgers U., 1962, Advanced Mgmt. Program, Harvard U., 1973. With Bank of Am., NT & SA, 1949-87; v.p., mgr. main office San Jose, Calif., 1964-69; regional v.p. Cen. Coast adminstrn., 1969-74; sr. v.p., head No. European Area office Frankfurt, Fed. Republic of Germany, 1974-78; exec. v.p., head Asia div. Tokyo, 1978-81; exec. v.p., head N.Am. div. Los Angeles, 1981-82; vice chmn., head retail banking San Francisco, 1982-87; ret., 1987. Bd. dirs. Visa USA, Visa Internat., Sci. Applications Internat. Corp.; bd. dirs., chmn. Bank Adminstrn. Inst., 1986-87. Pres. Santa Clara County United Fund, 1969, 70, San Jose C. of C., 1968; fin. chmn. Santa Clara County Reps., 1967-74; bd. dirs. San Diego Armed Svcs., YMCA, Sidney Kimmell Cancer Ctr.; trustee Borrego Cmty. Health Found., 2002-06; trustee, chmn. bd. dirs. Sharp Meml. Hosp.; hon. consul-gen. for Japan, 1990-95. With USN, 1945-46. Mem. San Diego Hosp. Assn. (bd. dirs., treas.), San Diego Zool. Soc., Greater San Diego C. of C. (pres., CEO 1998-99), Bohemian Club, San Diego Yacht Club. Presbyterian. Home: 605 San Fernando St San Diego CA 92106-3312 Office: Bank Am Nat Trust & Savs 450 B St San Diego CA 92101-8001

WIESNER, DAVID, illustrator, children's writer; b. Bridgewater, NJ; m. Kim Khang; 2 children. BFA in Illustration, R.I. Sch. Design. Illustrator Houghton Mifflin, NYC. Author (illustrator): (books) Free Fall, 1988 (Caldecott Honor book), Hurricane, 1990, Tuesday, 1991 (Caldecott medal, 1992), June 29, 1999, 1991 (Reading Rainbow book), Sector 7, 1999, Three Pigs, 2001 (Caldecott medal, 2002, Prix Sorcières); illustrator (books) Kite Flier, 1986, The Sorcerer's Apprentice, 1989, The Rainbow People, 1989, Tongues of Jade, 1991, Man From the Sky, 1992, Night of the Gargoyles, 1994, Flotsam, 2006 (Caldecott medal, 2007), creator (CD-ROM) The Day the World Broke; one-man shows include Nat. Ctr. for Children's Illustrated Lit., Abilene, Tex., 1999. Office: Houghton Mifflin 222 Berkeley St Boston MA 02116

WIESSLER, DAVID ALBERT, news correspondent; b. Cambridge, Mass., July 20, 1942; s. Albert Francis and Vivian Mary Wiessler; m. Mary Judith Burton, Dec. 28, 1968. AB, Princeton U., 1964; MA, U. Tex., 1968. Editor UPI, Dallas, NYC, Washington, 1966-82; assoc. editor U.S. News & World Report, Washington, 1982-84; Washington Bur. chief UPI, Washington, 1984-90, sr. polit. editor, 1990-93; news editor Bloomberg News Svc., 1994-95; editor nat. news Reuters, Washington, 1995-98, sr. Wash. corr., 1998—2009. Recipient Best Feature Writer award, Dallas Press Club, 1970. Mem.: Washington Gridiron Club. Avocations: reading, travel, cooking.

WIEST, DIANNE, actress; b. Kansas City, Mo., Mar. 28, 1948; Student, U. Md. Appearances in Broadway and off-Broadway plays including Ashes, 1976, Leave It to Beaver is Dead, The Art of Dining (Obie award, 1979, Theatre World award, 1983), Bonjour La Bonjour, Three Sisters, Serenading Louie (Obie award, 1983), After the Fall, Heartbreak House, Our Town, Hunting Cockroaches, 1987, Blue Light, 1994, Memory House, 2005, Third, 2005, The Seagull, 2008, (Broadway plays) Othello, 1982, In the Summer House, 1993, Salome, 2003, All My Sons, 2008, actress (films) It's My Turn, 1980, I'm Dancing as Fast as I Can, 1982, Independence Day, 1982, Footloose, 1984, Falling in Love, 1984, The Purple Rose of Cairo, 1985, Hannah and Her Sisters, 1986 (Acad. award for Best Supporting Actress, 1987), Radio Days, 1987, Lost Boys, 1987, September, 1987, Bright Lights, Big City, 1988, Parenthood, 1989 (Acad. award nominee), Cookie, 1989, Edward Scissorhands, 1990, Little Man Tate, 1991, Cops and Robbersons, 1994, The Scout, 1994, Bullets Over Broadway, 1994 (Golden Globe award Best Supporting Actress-Drama, 1995, Acad. award for Best Supporting Actress, 1995), Drunks, 1995, The Birdcage, 1996, The Associate, 1996, Practical Magic, 1998, The Horse Whisperer, 1998, Portofino, 1999, I Am Sam, 2001, Dr. Rey!, 2002, Robots (voice only), 2005, A Guide to Recognizing Your Saints, 2006, Dedication, 2007, Dan in Real Life, 2007, Synechdoche, New York, 2008, Passengers, 2008, (TV films) The Wall, 1982, The Face of Rage, 1983, Simple Life of Noah Dearborn, 1999, (TV miniseries) The 10th Kingdom, 2000, (TV series) Law & Order, 2000—02, In Treatment, 2008 (Primetime Emmy for Outstanding Supporting Actress in a Drama Series, Acad. TV Arts and Scis., 2008).*

WIET, RICHARD JAMES, otolargynologist; b. Chgo., Oct. 6, 1945; s. John Florian and Othelia Catherine Wiet; m. Jamee Denise, Sept. 11, 1970; children: Elizabeth, Mark, Marie. MD, Loyola U., Chgo., 1971. Prof., chief otolaryngology Evanston Northwestern Healthcare, Evanston, Ill., 1997-2002. Surg. instrument designer; author books on surgery of the ear. Mem. ACS (gov.), Am. Otological Soc., Triological Soc., Am. Neurotology Soc. (past pres.). Office: Ear Inst of Chicago LLC 11 Salt Creek Hinsdale IL 60521

WIETHOLTER, JON PATRICK, pharmacist, educator; b. Findlay, Ohio, Oct. 8, 1982; s. Bradley Dean and RoseMary Wietholter; m. Carrie Anne Kindred, July 23, 2005; 1 child, Caleb James. PharmD, U. Pitts., Pa., 2007. Registered pharmacist W.Va., 2008. Pharmacy practice resident Pitt County Meml. Hosp., Greenville, NC, 2007—08; clin. asst. prof. W.Va. U., Morgantown, 2008—; internal medicine clin. pharmacist Cabell Huntington Hosp., Huntington, W.Va., 2008—. Contbr. articles to profl. jours. Mem.: Am. Assn. Coll. Pharmacy, Am. Soc. Health-Sys. Pharmacists. Conservative. Roman Catholic. Avocations: sports, travel. Office: Cabell Huntington Hosp 1340 Hal Greer Blvd Huntington WV 25701 Office Fax: 304-526-2101. Business E-Mail: jwietholter@hsc.wvu.edu.

WIEU, ANDREW W. RIANG, government agency administrator; b. Malakal, Sudan, Jan. 1, 1928; arrived in US, 1976; s. Riak Wieu Riak and Abok Jok Radol; m. Teresa Nyagi Kuok (dec.); children: Helena, Bol, Abei; m. Nyanbeny Akom Deng (dec.); children: Ding, Anying; m. Mary Nyandeng Obuti; children: Jiel, Riak. Diploma, Khartoum U., Sudan, 1954; LLD, Wheaton Coll., Ill., 1977; MA in Polit. Sci., Am. U., Washington, 1978, postgrad., 1978. Mem. treasury staff Province Adminstrn., Malakal, 1951; police profl., adminstr. Province Police, Malakal, 1951; field adminstr. Western Nuer Dist., Bentiu, Sudan, 1952—53; adminstr. sch. law Khartoum U. Coll., 1954; adminstr. officer Bor Dist. Adminstrn., Sudan, 1954—55, Western Darfur Dist., Zelinge, Sudan, 1956; asst. dist. commr. Lakes Dist., Kumbek, Sudan, 1957—58, Dar Hamar Dist., Nahud, Sudan, 1959—61; asst. local govt. Kasala Province, Sudan, 1962; inspector local govt. No. Region Adminstrn., Marowe, Sudan, 1962; ret. Dep. spkr. Nat. Assembly, Khartoum, 1972—74, leader ho., 1994; min. state Rep. Palace, Khartoum, 1974—76; min. agrl. Sudan Govt., Khartoum, 1955; founder, pres. Devel. Ext. Consultancy Svcs. Internat. Co. Ltf., Trinity Ch. Sudan; Social Care and Humanitarian Agy. Mem.: Concerned Scientists, Americans for the Arts, Sierra Club, Oxford Investment Club (premier mem.). Democrat. Avocations: reading, history, politics, anthropology. Office: Trinity United Ch Sudan Thora Jalaba Malakal Sudan Office Phone: 315 876 9074.

WIGAND, ROBERT CHARLES, JR., retired civil engineer, retired aerospace engineer; b. SI, NY, June 17, 1924; s. Robert Charles Wigand Sr. and Marion Carolyn (Waner) Wigand; m. Wanda Constance Beelick, Mar. 10, 1952 (dec. 2008); children: Gwendolyn Mary Bolling, James Robert, John Theodore. BS in Civil Engring., U. Colo., Boulder, 1944. Lic. profl. engr. and land surveyor. Messenger Sullivan and Cromwell Law Firm, 1941; miner Climax Molybdenum Co., Colo., 1943; supt. trainee Callan Builders Inc., Manhasset, NY, 1946; constrn. supt. Johns-Manville Corp., NY, 1947—50; real estate supr. N.E. region Household Fin. Corp., NYC, 1953—55; engr. Franki Found. Co., NYC, 1955, Worcester, Mass., 1956; engr., field supr. power plant constrn. Burns and Roe Inc., NYC, 1957—58, siting engr. project Mercury tracking stas., 1959—60, Indonesia, 1961, Europe, 1962; project mgr., engr. Alaska tracking sta. NASA Goddard Space Flight Ctr., Fairbanks, Alaska, 1963—64, project mgr. Apollo tracking antennas worldwide network, 1965—70, supr. tracking network facilities Greenbelt,

1971—95. Contbr. articles to profl. jours. Pvt. to lt. col. USMCR, 1942—77. Recipient Project Team awards, NASA, 1967—95. Fellow: ASCE, Am. Congress Suveying and Mapping; mem.: NSPE, Res. Officers Assn., Am. Soc. Mil. Engrs., Goddard Retirees and Alumni Assn. (bd. dirs.), Am. Geophys. Union. Home: 4210 Sellman Rd Beltsville MD 20705 Office Phone: 301-937-1178.

WIGDOR, HARVEY ALAN, dentist, educator; b. Chgo., Nov. 9, 1949; s. Ben and Charlotte Wigdor; m. Pamela Waltz, May 3, 1998; children: Jennifer Hale, Charla Ruth, Benjamin Eisenberg. BS, Northern Ill. U., Dekalb, 1971; DDS, U. Ill., Chgo., 1976, MS, 1984. Dentistry Ill., 1976. Adj. assoc. prof. Dept Biomedical Engring., Northwestern U., Evanston, Ill., 2000—; chair, dir. dental residency program, dept. dentistry Adv. Ill. Masonic Med. Ctr., Chgo., 2001—; clincal prof., dept. oral medicine and diagnostic sci. U. Ill. Coll. Dentistry, Chgo., 2001—. Musician: (north shore chamber orchestra) Double Bassist. Chair Masonic Rels. Com., Chgo., 2003—09; mem. Ill. Masonic Charitable Found., Chgo., 2006—09. Sp4th class Ill. N.G., 1969—73, Chgo. Fellow: Acad. Osseointegration, Am. Soc. Lasers Medicine and Surgery. Home: 2639 W Morse Ave Chicago IL 60645 Office: Adv Illinois Masonic Med Ctr Dept Dentistry 811 W Wellington Chicago IL 60657 Office Fax: 773-871-6353. Personal E-mail: grizzlyb@aol.com.

WIGGINS, BARBARA SUE, pharmacist, educator; b. St. Louis, Va., Mar. 5, 1969; d. Earl Leonard and Carrie Sue Pigg; m. John Wesley Wiggins, Nov. 4, 1962; children: Luke James, Lauren Grace. BS in Pharmacy, St. Louis Coll. Pharmacy, 1992; PharmD, Va. Commonwealth U./Med. Coll. Va., 1998. Bd. cert. pharmacotherapy specialist with added qualifications in cardiology. Clin. specialist - cardiology U. Wash. Med. Ctr., Seattle, 1999—2002; clin. instr. U. Wash. Sch. Pharmacy, Seattle, 1999—2002; ACLS instr. Am. Heart Assn., Seattle, 1999—2002; pharmacy clin. specialist- cardiology U. Va. Health Sys., Charlottesville, 2002—; clin. instr. Sch. Nursing U. Va., Charlottesville, 2002—; ACLS instr. Am. Heart Assn., Richmond, Va., 2002—; clin. instr. Sch. Medicine U. Va., 2003. Contbg. editor and reviewer Springhouse (Pa.) Pub., 1998. Contbr. chapters to books, articles to profl. jours. Chair profl. affairs Wash. Soc. Health Sys. Pharmacists, Seattle, 2002—02. Lt. USN, 1993—99. Recipient Merck Award for Clin. Rsch., 1998. Mem.: Am. Soc. Health Sys. Pharmacists, Va. Soc. Health Sys. Pharmacists (assoc.), Am. Heart Assn. (assoc.), Rho Chi. Achievements include 1996 United States Olympic Marathon Trials Qualifier. Avocations: running, tennis, bicycling, hiking. Office: Univ Va PO Box 800674 Charlottesville VA 22908-0674 E-mail: bsw4v@virginia.edu.

WIGGINS, CANDICE DANA, professional basketball player; b. Balt., Feb. 14, 1987; d. Alan and Angela Wiggins. Grad. in Comm., Stanford U., Calif., 2008. Guard Stanford U. Cardinal, 2004—08, Minn. Lynx, 2008—. Injury replacement US Sr. Nat. Team. Recipient Wade Trophy award, 2008; named Player of Yr., PAC-10 Conf., 2005, 2006, 2008, US Basketball Female Athlete of Yr., 2007; named a Kodak/WBCA All-Am., 2004—08, First Team All-Am., AP, Sports Illustrated, ESPN.com, and CBSSportsline.com, 2008; named to John R. Wooden Award All-America Team, 2008; finalist John R. Wooden award, 2007, 2008, Wade Trophy award, 2007, Naismith Trophy, 2008. Mem.: Delta Sigma Theta. Achievements include being the third overall pick in the WNBA draft, 2008. Office: Minn Lynx 600 First Ave N Minneapolis MN 55403 Office Phone: 612-673-1600.

WIGGINS, CHARLES HENRY, JR., lawyer; b. Balt., July 15, 1939; s. Charles Henry and Kathryn Wilson (Walker) W.; m. Wendy Jane Horn, June 20, 1964 (div. 1996); children: Charles Hunter, Rebecca Rae, Melinda Marie; m. Karen Ann Kowal, Apr. 26, 1997 (div. 2002). BSEE, U. Ill., Urbana, 1962; JD with honors, U. Ill., 1965. Bar: Ill. 1965, U.S. Dist. (no. dist.) Ill. 1970, U.S. Tax Ct. 1974, U.S. Ct. Appeals (7th cir.) 1983. Assoc. Vedder, Price, Kaufman & Kammholz, Chgo., 1969-73, ptnr., 1974—. Mem. zoning bd. appeals Village of Indian Head Pk., Ill., 1984-91. Capt. U.S. Army, 1965-68. Mem. Chgo. Bar Assn., University Club (Chgo.), Edgewood Valley Country Club (LaGrange, Ill., bd. dirs. 1991-98), SAR. Avocations: golf, tennis, bridge. Office Phone: 312-609-7525. Business E-Mail: cwiggins@vedderprice.com.

WIGGINS, DAVID STEWART, state supreme court justice; b. Chgo., Oct. 19, 1951; s. Kalman G. and Joan (Feldman) W.; m. Marsha Wiggins, Dec. 23, 1973; children: Samantha, Sydney, Taylor. BA in Philosophy, U. Ill., Chgo., 1973; JD, Drake U., 1976. Bar: Iowa 1976, U.S. Dist. Ct. (no. and so. dists.) Iowa 1976, U.S. Ct. Appeals (8th cir.) 1976, U.S. Ct. Claims, 1979, D.C. Ct. Appeals, 1979, U.S. Supreme Ct. 1979. Assoc. to ptnr. Williams, Hart, Lavorato & Kirtley, 1976—79; ptnr. Wiggins & Anderson P.C. (now Anderson & Tully), West Des Moines, 1979—2003; justice Iowa Supreme Ct., 2003—. Mem. Iowa Jud. Com. Cost of Litig., 1988, Iowa Jud. Adv. Com. Rules of Civil Procedure, 1991—97; chair Iowa Jud. Qualifications Commn., 2000—03; mem. Iowa Jud. Redistricting Commn., 2002. Fellow C. Edwin Moore Am. Inn of Ct. (master emeritus). Office: Jud Br Bldg 1111 East Ct Ave Des Moines IA 50319 Office Phone: 515-281-5175. Business E-Mail: david.wiggins@iowacourts.gov.*

WIGGINS, DEWAYNE LEE, financial executive; b. Stillwater, Okla., Jan. 6, 1949; s. Lloyd Lee Wiggins and Joyce Yvonne Blair; m. Susan Sochinski, Sept. 9, 1978. BS in Acctg., Okla. State U., 1972; MBA, Ind. U., 1984. Pilot Braniff Internat., Dallas, 1977-82; investment analyst Duff & Phelps, Inc., Chgo., 1984-86; portfolio mgr. Centerre Trust Co., St. Louis, 1986-88; pres. Lindbergh Capital Mgmt., Inc., St. Louis, 1988—; founder, pres. Lindbergh Signature Fund, St. Louis, 1999—2005. Capt. USAF, 1972-76. Mem. Ind. U. Alumni Assn., Beta Gamma Sigma. Roman Catholic. Avocations: reading, tennis, gardening. Office: Lindbergh Capital Mgmt Inc 5520 Telegraph Rd Ste 204 Saint Louis MO 63129-3570

WIGGINS, JAMES BRYAN, religion educator; b. Mexia, Tex., Aug. 24, 1935; m. Elizabeth R. Wiggins, May 27, 1995; children: Bryan, Karis. BA, Tex. Wesleyan U., 1957; BD, So. Meth. U., 1959; PhD, Drew U., 1963; postgrad., Tübingen U., Fed. Republic Germany, 1968-69. Ordained to ministry Meth. Ch., 1959. Instr. humanities Union Jr. Coll., Cranford, NJ, 1960-63; asst. prof. religion Syracuse U., NY, 1963-69, assoc. prof., 1969-75, prof., 1975, dir. grad. studies, 1975-80, chair dept., 1980—2000, Eliphalet Remington prof. religion, 1999—2001, Eliphalet Remington prof. religion emeritus, 2001—; exec. dir. Am. Acad. Religion, 1983—92, dir., 1973-75, 83-91; exec. dir. Interreligious Coun. of Ctrl. NY, Syracuse, 2002—. Cons. in field; People to People del. leader to former Soviet Union, 1992. Author: The Embattled Saint, 1966, Foundations of Christianity, 1970; editor: Religion as Story, 1975, Christianity: A Cultural Perspective, 1987, In Praise of Religious Diversity, 1996; contbr. articles to profl. jours. Trustee Scholars Press, Atlanta, 1983-91, chmn., 1986-91; chair, bd. dirs. Onondaga Pastoral Counseling Ctr., 1997-99; bd. dirs. Inter-religious Coun. Ctrl. N.Y., 1997-2001. Rockefeller Found. fellow, 1962-63; Lilly Endowment rsch. grantee, 1992-93. Fellow Soc. for Arts (bd. dirs. 1976—), Religion and Culture; mem. AAUP, Am. Acad. Religion. Democrat. Methodist. Avocations: golf, tennis, music, reading, travel. Office: 3049 E Genesee St Syracuse NY 13244-0001 also: 700 University Ave Syracuse NY 13244 Office Phone: 315-449-3552, 315-443-2241. Business E-Mail: jbwiggin@syr.edu. E-mail: jwiggins@twcny.rr.com.

WIGGINS, MARY ANN WISE, small business owner, educator; b. Coushatta, La., Dec. 25, 1940; d. George Wilkinson and Maitland (Allums) Wise; m. Gerald D. Paul (div. Nov. 1977); children: John Barron, James Gordon, Brenda Michelle; m. Billy J. Wiggins, Oct. 3, 1981; children: Marshall Wade, Brian Alan Paul, William Joshua, George Justin; stepchildren: Joseph James, Winona Gail. BA, Northwestern State U., Natchitoches, La., 1964, postgrad., 1994, Weatherford Coll., 1967, North Tex. State U., 1968; MA in Principalship and Supervision, La. Tech. U., Ruston, 2005. Lic. ins. agt., real estate agt., La., pvt. pilot. Tchr. US Army Schs., Nuremberg, Germany, 1964—66, Mineral Wells Ind. Sch. Dist., 1967—70; bookkeeper Wise Dept. Store, Coushatta, La., 1966—67; amb. of good will Vietnam, 1971; owner, mgr. Mary Ann's Furniture & Hardware, Coushatta, 1977—97; tchr. Springville Mid. Sch., 1994—96, Red River Parish Alternative Sch., 1996—98, tchr. Ware Youth Ctr., 1998—. Com. mem. Instrn. and Profl. Devel. Com. La. Assn. Educators, 1998-2000, vice chmn. 1999-2002; v.p. La. Juvenile Detention Tchrs. Assn., 1999—; tchr. leader La. Tech., 2002-03. Columnist: Wise Old Owl Coushatta Citizen, 2004—. Chmn. Am. Cancer Soc., Conway, Ark., 1972, Red River Parish United Way, Coushatta, 1987-88; treas., bd. dirs. Hall Summit United Meth. Ch.; pres. Red River Parish Assn. Educators Polit. Action Com; candidate La. House of Reps., Dist. 24. Recipient German-Am. hospitality award Orgn. German-Am. Women, Nuremberg, 1965. Mem. NEA, La. Assn. Educators (chmn. legis. com. 2000-04), Red River Assn. Educators (v.p. 1994, pres. 1998-2001), U.S. C. of C., Coushatta-Red River C. of C. (charter, bd. dirs. 2007), Pi Kappa Sigma, Sigma Kappa. Democrat. Methodist. Avocations: gardening, swimming, horseback riding, computers, week-enders with family, landscaping. Home: 2217 E Carrol St Coushatta LA 71019-8567

WIGGINS, STEPHEN EDWARD, physician; b. Phila., May 7, 1951; s. Ralph Cannon and Bernice J. (Maslovitz) W.; m. Rebecca del Carmen, Oct. 3, 1992; children: Daniel Stephen, Elizabeth Rebekah. BA, Rutgers U., 1973; MD, Med. Coll. Va., 1977. Diplomate Am. Bd. Family Practice. Resident in family practice Riverside Hosp., Newport News, Va., 1977-80; staff emergency physician North Arundal Hosp., Glen Burnie, Md., 1980-81, So. Md. Hosp. Ctr., Clinton, 1982-84; med. dir. Convenient Health Care, Waldorf, Md., 1984—. Ptnr. Old Line Med. Partnership, Waldorf, 1990-97, Convenient Health Care Mgmt., Waldorf, 1989-97; instr. family practice Georgetown U. Sch. Medicine, Washington, 1995—2005; pres. 640 Old Line Ctr. L.P., 1997—; pres. Old Line Med. Svcs. P.C., 1997—. Vol. physician and citizen diplomat Gesundheit Inst., Russia, 1991; citizen diplomat U.S.-China Peoples Friendship Assn., China, 1988; vol. physician March of Dimes Walk-a-thon, Md., 1985-86. William Demarest scholar, Rutgers U., New Brunswick, N.J., 1969-73. Fellow Am. Acad. Family Physicians; mem. Med. and Chirurg. Faculty of the State of Md., Md. Acad. Family Physicians, Charles County Med. Soc. Avocation: scuba diving. Office: Convenient Health Care 12090 Old Line Ctr Waldorf MD 20602-2556

WIGGLESWORTH, MARGARET, real estate company executive; b. Potomac, Md. BA, U. Md. Staff for Senator Charles McC. Mathias Jr. US Senate, Washington; asst. dir. nat. affairs Nat. Pub. Radio; exec. dir. US Coalition of Svc. Industries, Inc., Washington; pres. Colliers Internat. USA, Boston, 1998—, CEO. Office: Colliers International USA 50 Milk St 20th Floor Boston MA 02109 Office Phone: 617-722-0221. Office Fax: 617-722-0224. E-mail: margaret@colliers.com, mwigglesworth@colliers.com.

WIGHTMAN, ALEC, lawyer; b. Cleve., Jan. 23, 1951; s. John and Betty Jane (Follis) W.; m. Kathleen A. Little, June 19, 1976; children: Nora, Emily. BA, Duke U., 1972; JD, Ohio State U., 1975. Bar: Ohio 1975, U.S. Tax Ct. 1982, U.S. Ct. Appeals (6th cir.) 1983. Assoc. Krupman, Fromson & Henson, Columbus, Ohio, 1975-77; ptnr. Krupman, Fromson, Bownas & Wightman, Columbus, 1978-82; assoc. Baker & Hostetler, Columbus, 1982-83, ptnr., 1984—, exec. ptnr., 2004—08. Bd. trustees The Arthur G. James Cancer Hosp., Richard J. Solove Rsch. Inst.; bd. dirs. Cleve. Rock & Roll., Inc. Mem. ABA, Ohio Bar Assn., Columbus Bar Assn., Ohio Oil and Gas Assn. Avocation: tennis. Office: Baker & Hostetler 65 E State St Ste 2100 Columbus OH 43215-4260 Home Phone: 614-222-0999; Office Phone: 614-462-2636. Business E-Mail: awightman@bakerlaw.com.

WIGHTMAN, SHARON LEILANI, retired librarian; d. Frank Bacon and Hazel Elizabeth Drake; m. James Ernest Wightman, Oct. 9, 1965; children: Wendy Joy, Kim Diane, Dawn Lyn, Robin Gail. BS in Liberal Arts, Cazenovia Coll., 1995; MLS, Syracuse U., 1996. Cert. pub. libr. N.Y. State. Tailor, owner Wightman Tailoring, Cazenovia, NY, 1982—88; admissions rep. Cazenovia Coll., 1988—95; sales lead coord. Inchcape Testing, Cortland, NY, 1995—97; children's libr. Fayetteville Free Libr., NY, 1996—; libr. ITT Tech. Inst., Liverpool, 2001—08. Bd. trustees Ctrl. NY Libr. Resources Coun., 2006—, sec. bd. trustees, 2007—. Bd. dirs. 4-H Found., Madison County, 2001—04. Recipient Achievement in Profl. Devel., Reference Adult Svc. Sect., N.Y. Libr. Assn., 2004; named Employee of the Quar., ITT Tech. Inst., 2002, Employee of the Yr., 2002, Women Pioneers, New Woodstock Hist. Soc. Cmty. Mem.: ALA, NY Libr. Assn. Republican. Avocations: travel, reading, gardening, surf fishing. Personal E-mail: swightma@hotmail.com.

WIGINGTON, RONALD LEE, retired chemical information services executive; b. Topeka, May 11, 1932; s. Oscar and Virginia C. (Ritchie) W.; m. Margaret E. Willey, Aug. 17, 1951; children: Linda (dec.), Carol, David, Brian. BS in Engring. Physics, U. Kans., 1953; MEE, U. Md., 1959; PhD in Elec. Engring., U. Kans., 1964; postgrad. in Advanced Mgmt., Harvard Bus. Sch., 1976-77. Tech. staff Bell Telephone Labs., Murray Hill, NJ, 1953-54; divsn. chief Dept. Def., Washington, 1956-68, cons., 1968—86, Battelle Meml. Inst., Columbus, Ohio, 1968—75; dir. R & D Chem. Abstracts Svc., Am. Chem. Soc., Columbus, Ohio, 1968-84; dir. Washington ops. Am. Chem. Soc., 1984-86; CEO, dir. Chem. Abstracts Svc., Am. Chem. Soc., Columbus, 1986-91; dir. info. tech. Am. Chem. Soc., Columbus, 1991-94. Chmn. bd. Online Computer Libr. Ctr., Dublin, Ohio, 1985-87, trustee, 1978-92; lectr. Am. U., Washington, 1967-68; adj. assoc. prof. Ohio State U., 1969-78, mem. computer sci. & engring. bd. Nat. Acad. Sci., 1969-72 Contbr. chpts. to books; contbr. articles to profl. jours. Pres., various positions PTA Prince George's County, Md., 1966-68; moderator, treas. Cmty. Assn. Upper Arlington (Ohio) Schs., 1970-74; mem. Upper Arlington Civic Orch., 1970-84, pres., 1973-76, Nat. Libr. Medicine Long Range Planning Panel, 1985-86; bd. dirs. Material Property Data Network, 1987-94, Ohio Ctr. of Sci. and Industry, 1988-93; trustee Health Coalition of Ctrl. Ohio, Columbus, 1991-99, treas., 1994-99, vice-chmn., 1996-99. With US Army, 1954—56. Recipient Nat. Capital award, D.C. Coun. Engring. and Archtl. Socs., 1967, Meritorious Civilian Svc. award, Dept. Def., 1967; named Honor Man of U. Kans, 1953; named to, Topeka H.S. Hall of Fame, 2001; Summerfield scholar, U. Kans., 1949—53. Fellow: Internat. Coun. Sci. and Tech. Info. (exec. bd. and treas. 1992—94, fellow 1995—), Nat. Fedn. Abstracting and Info. Svcs. (bd. dirs. 1979—84, pres. 1982—83, hon. fellow 1995—); mem.: IEEE (sr.), Am. Chem. Soc., Sigma Xi. Avocations: gardening, music, genealogy. Home: 2470 Wimbledon Rd Columbus OH 43220-4212 Personal E-mail: rwigingt@columbus.rr.com.

WIGINTON, LARRY MICHEAL, chemistry professor; b. Memphis, Tex., Sept. 26, 1954; s. L.M. and Floye Wiginton; m. Dianna Mae Cantrell, May 18, 1976; children: Deborah Diane McAnear, Lee Michael. BS, West Tex. State U., Canyon, 1978; MS, Tex. Tech. U., Lubbock, 1980. HS sci. tchr. Memphis ISD, Tex., 1985—95; prof. chemistry Clarendon Coll., Tex., 1995—. Mem.: ACS. Conservative. Baptist. Office: Clarendon Coll PO Box 968 Clarendon TX 79226 Office Fax: 806-874-5080.

WIGLER, ANDREW JEFFREY, lawyer; b. Bklyn., Aug. 11, 1965; s. Jerome L. and Florence (Hoffstein) W.; m. Nancy D. Wigler, Feb. 22, 1992. BA, Albany State U., 1987; JD, Yeshiva U., NYC, 1990. Bar: NJ 1990, US Dist. Ct. NJ 1990, NY 1991, US Dist. Ct. (so. and ea. dists.) NY 1991, US Ct. Appeals (2nd cir.) 1991, DC 1993. Legis. intern Hon. Thomas J. Bartosiewicz, Albany, NY, 1986; legis. aide Hon. Anthony J. Genovesi, Albany, 1987; assoc. Reisman, Peirez, Reisman & Calica, Garden City, NY, 1993-94, Berger & Ackman, P.C., NYC, 1990-93, ptnr., 1994-95, Law Offices of Andrew J. Wigler, Esq., Great Neck, NY, 1995—; atty. in pvt. practice Advanced Mortgage Sys., L.L.C., Great Neck, NY, 1995—2005. Bd. dirs. Advanced Mortgage Sys., LLC, NYC, Advanced Informatics, Inc., CancerMD.com, Inc. Mem. bd. zoning appeals Village of Great Neck Estates, 2001-05; bd. dirs. Westhampton Bath and Tennis Club, 2005—; committeeman Queens County Dem. Com., 1993, Kings County Dem. Com., 1999, Nassau County Dem. Com., 2000—. Recipient First Place Brief award Phillip C. Jessup Moot Ct. Competition, NY, 1989, Best Brief award Cardozo Advocacy Competition, NYC, 1988. Mem. ABA, NY State Women's Bar Assn., Nassau County Bar Assn., NY State Bar Assn., NY County Lawyers Assn., Washington Bar Assn. Democrat. Office Phone: 516-466-4767. Personal E-mail: andrew516@aol.com. Business E-Mail: greatnecklaw@aol.com.

WIGLESWORTH, MICHAEL BLAND, advertising executive; b. Balt., Apr. 13, 1949; s. Reginal A. and Janice (Peppler) W.; m. Barbara Atkinson, Aug. 5, 1972 (div. Apr. 1980); m. Shari Kulik, Dec. 7, 1997. BS, Va. Commonwealth U., 1975. Account exec. Richmond Newspapers, Va., 1973—75; v.p. mktg. Bunch & Laughon Advt., Richmond, 1975—76; pres. Collier & Wiglesworth, Inc., Richmond, 1976—80; v.p. account svcs. Brand Edmonds Bolio, Richmond, 1980—82; v.p. sales promotion Eisner & Assocs., Balt., 1983—85; dir. promotion J. Walter Thompson, LA, 1985—87; mgmt. supr. Einson Freeman, Paramus, NJ, 1987—89; sr. v.p., mgmt. supr. SAI/Earle Palmer Brown Promotions, Phila., 1989—94; sr. v.p. acct. svc. Hadley, NYC, 1994—96; ptnr. Allegis Mktg., 1996—2000; sr. v.p. acct. svcs. SAI Mktg., 1996—2000; v.p. promotional mktg. Marketsource, Cranbury, NJ, 2000—01; group dir., relationship mktg. Carlson Mktg. Group, Phila., 2001—03; sr. v.p. Mastermind Mktg., Phila., 2003—06; ptnr. Dreamscapes Builders, LP, Houston, 2004—, Galveston Bay Redevel. Authority; pres. Dreamscape Ventures LLC, 2009—. Pres. M & W Ventures, Richmond, 1977-83; ptnr. Recreation Unltd., Inc., Richmond, 1979-80. Recipient best in Show award Am. Newspaper Assn., N.Y.C., 1979, Maxi award Direct Mail Assn., 1992, Reggie award Promotional Marketers Assn. Am., 1993, Pro award Coun. of Sales Promotion Agencies, 1994. Mem. Am. Advt. Fedn. (Retail Advt. award 1979), Am. Mktg. Assn. (Effie award 1980, Spire award 1992, GHBA Prism award, Best Website Builder, 2008), Phi Kappa Sigma. Democrat. Avocations: jogging, skiing, scuba diving, travel, music. Home and Office: 1814 B Binz St Houston TX 77004 Office Phone: 713-529-2335. Personal E-mail: mwiglesworth@comcast.net.

WIGLEY, DIANA GAIL, respiratory therapist; d. Roland Eugene and Jewel Maxine Box; children: Trent Matthew, Kyle Brandon. Diploma, Ind. Voc. Tech Sch., 1984. Registered respiratory therapist Ind., 1997, EEG Tech & Evoked Potenial Tech Ind., 2003. Staff therapist Bedford Med. Ctr., Ind., 1980—90; staff therapist, lead therapist James W. Riley Children's Hosp., Indpls., 1990—92; area supr. Golden Care, 1993—96; staff therapist, EEG tech Wash. County Hosp., Washington, 1996—97; registered respiratory therapist Bloomington Hosp., 1997—, registered EEG tech, IOM tech, 2000—. Office: Bloomington Hosp 402 West 2nd St Bloomington IN 47402 Office Fax: 812-353-5220. Personal E-mail: blmgtneeg@verizon.net.

WIGSMOEN, SUSAN CATANIA, elementary school educator; b. Chgo., Sept. 13, 1964; d. Anthony Edward and Susan Catherine (Kmetty) Catania; m. David Andrew Wigsmoen, July 10, 1993. BA, St. Xavier Coll., 1986; MA, St. Xavier U., 1995. Tchr. kindergarten Bridgeport Cath. Acad., Chgo., 1986—99; tchr. Luther Burbank Elem. Dist. 111, Ill., 2004—, reading specialist dist. III, 1999—2004. Mem. pub. rels. com. Epilepsy Found. of Greater Chgo. 1994. Mem. Ill. Assn. for Supervision and Curriculum Devel. Republican. Roman Catholic. Avocation: piano. Home: 8745 S Utica Ave Evergreen Park IL 60805-1034 Home Phone: 708-499-2320; Office Phone: 312-376-6223, 708-499-0838. Personal E-mail: schwigs@msn.com.

WIGTON, ROBERT SWIFT, medical educator; b. Phila., Jan. 22, 1942; s. Robert Spencer and Marcia Catherine (Swift) W.; m. Deborah Ann Adkins, Jan. 9, 1976. BA, Harvard Coll., 1965; BS, U. Nebr., 1967, MD, 1969, MS, 1973. Diplomate Am. Bd. Internal Medicine. Cert. Nebr. State Bd. Med. Examiners, 1969. Instr. Dept. Physiology U. Nebr. Coll. Medicine, Omaha, 1969-71, residency med., 1971—74, asst. prof. Dept. Internal Medicine, 1974-81, dir. House Officer Program, 1976-79, asst. dean for grad. med. edn., 1976-87, assoc. prof. Dept. Internal Medicine, 1981-89, assoc. dean for acad. affairs and grad. med. edn., 1986-93, prof. Dept. Internal Medicine, 1989—, chief Sect. Gen. Internal Medicine, 1993—2002, assoc. dean for grad. med. edn., 1993—. Vis. scholar Dept. Medicine U. Pa. Sch. Medicine, Phila., 1982-83; editl. bds. Med. Decision Making, MD Computing, Jour. Gen. Internal Medicine. Editor: (CD-ROM multimedia text) Procedures in Internal Medicine, 1996; contbr. articles to profl. jours. Fellow ACP (Tchg. and Rsch. scholar 1973-76, Nebr. Laureate award 2006), Am. Coll. Med. Informatics; mem. Soc. for Med. Decision Making (v.p. 1988-89, trustee 1985-88, Eugene Saenger award 1996), Soc. Gen. Internal Medicine (coun. 1985-88, Elnora Rhodes award, 2005), Assn. Am. Med. Colls. (regional chair group on ednl. affairs 1994-95), Alpha Omega Alpha (pres. Alpha chpt. 1996-97, counselor 1997—), Phi Rho Sigma (Irving Cutter medal, 2007). Avocations: music, drawing, computers, photography, hiking. Office: U Nebr Med Ctr 984285 Nebraska Med Ctr Omaha NE 68198-5524 E-mail: wigton@unmc.edu.

WIJNBERG, SANDRA S., investment company executive; b. Aug. 1, 1956; BA English, UCLA; MBA, U. So. Calif., LA. With Morgan Stanley & Co. Inc.; joined PepsiCo as v.p., treas., 1994; sr. v.p., CFO KFC Corp. Divsn.; sr. v.p., treas. Tricon Global Restaurants Inc, 1997—2000; sr. v.p., CFO Marsh & McLennan Cos., NYC, 2000—06;

chief adminstrv. officer Aquiline Holdings LLC, 2007—. Bd. dirs. Pvt. Sector Coun., 2001—, Tyco Internat. Ltd., 2003—. Corp. adv. bd. N.Y.C. Ballet. Office: Aquiline Holdings LLC 535 Madison Ave 27th Fl New York NY 10022

WIKE, D. ELAINE, small business owner; b. Ridgecrest, Calif., Sept. 26, 1954; d. Robert G. and Jimmie Mae (Sallee) Field; m. Mike Wike, Oct. 14, 1978; children: Mike II, Angelina Elaine, William Willy V., Danielle Elizabeth, Edward Lawrence, Windy Gale. Student, U. Houston, 1975—77. Legal sec. Morgan, Lewis & Bockius, Washington, 1977—78; legal asst. Alfred C. Schlosser & Co., Houston, 1972—77, 1978—81, Jerry Sadler, atty., Houston, 1982—83; founder, owner DEW Profl. & Bus. Svcs., Houston, 1979—; office mgr. Law Offices Mike Wike, Houston, 1983—. Contbr. poetry to publs. including Internat. Libr. of Poetry, 2001. Treas. Wilhelm Schole Parents Orgn, 1981—82; mem. Free, Inc.; vol. campaign worker Ron Paul for Congress and Reagan for Pres., 1975, 1976. Recipient 3d place, Nassau Bay Tex. Christmas Boat Lane Parade First Ann. Photography Contest, 1990. Mem.: Nat. Paralegal Assn., Am. Soc. Notaries, Nat. Assn. Female Execs., Nat. Notary Assn., Young Ams. for Freedom. Republican. Libertarian. Mem. Christian Ch. Office: 2421 S Wayside Dr Houston TX 77023-5318

WIKINA, SUANU BLISS, human resources specialist; BS in Biochemistry, U. Port Harcourt, Nigeria; grad. in Sys. Analysis, U. Md., Adelphi, 2002, MS in MIS, 2002, MBA, 2006; PhD in Tech. Mgmt., Ind. State U., Terre Haute, 2007—. Profl. in human resources HR Certification Inst. Soc. Human Resource Mgmt., 2000. Counselor Embassy Nigeria, Tokyo, 1993—98; chief fgn. affairs officer Ministry Fgn. Affairs, Abuja, Nigeria; human resources US Postal Svc., Greensboro, NC, 2004—. Contbr. articles to profl. jours. Mem.: ASTD (assoc.), Golden Key Internat. (mem.). Business E-Mail: swikina@mymail.indstate.edu, swikina@indstate.edu.

WIKLIND, TOMMY GERT, astrophysicist; b. Gothenburg, Sweden, Oct. 2, 1957; s. Gert Roland and Inger Jane Wiklind; m. Duilia Fernandes de Mello, July 10, 1997. PhD, Chalmers U. Tech., Gothenburg, Sweden, 1990. Assoc. prof. Chalmers U. Tech., Gothenburg, Sweden, 1997—2002; esa astronomer European Space Agy., Balt., 2002—. Recipient Stromer-Fernerska prize, Swedish Royal Acad. Sci., 1995. Mem.: Internat. Astron. Union, Am. Astron. Soc., Airplane Owners and Pilots Assn. Achievements include research in molecular gas content of external galaxies.

WIKOFF, KARIN, school librarian; b. Detroit, Sept. 24, 1964; d. Judy Ann and Birt Kirby Hurlbert; life ptnr. Sean Lacey; m. Jack Wikoff, Sept. 28, 1985 (div. Jan. 6, 2000); children: Michael Dietrich, Garret Duncan. BA in German, Wells Coll., Aurora, NY, 1986. Cert. sec. tchr. NY State Bd. Edn., 1986, Zertifikat Deutsch Goethe Inst., 1986, technician NY State Preservation Conservation Program and Cornell U., 1997, Toastmasters Internat., 2006. Libr. asst. cataloging Wells Coll., Aurora, 1986—2003; wide receiver, cornerback Syracuse Sting Women's Profl. Football Team, 2003; electronic resources libr. Ithaca Coll., NY, 2004—06, electronic svcs. libr., 2006—, tech. svcs. libr., 2006—. Sec. Genoa Comprehensive Planning Group, NY, 2008. Recipient H. T. Lowe-Porter Transl. prize, Wells Coll., 1985—86. Mem.: Ithaca Coll. Toastmasters (v.p. edn. 2005—08, Competent Toastmaster 2006), Phi Beta Kappa. Office: Ithaca Coll Libr 953 Danby Rd Ithaca NY 14850 Business E-Mail: kwikoff@ithaca.edu.

WIKSTROM, LORETTA WERMERSKIRCHEN, artist; b. Willow River, Minn., Mar. 2, 1938; d. Jacob Joseph and Anna Bertha (Doege) Wermerskirchen; m. Donovan Carl Wikstrom, Aug. 16, 1958; children: Bradley Donovan, Kendra Kay, Brock Karl. Student, St. Paul Sch. of Art, 1956-57, U. Minn., 1957-58, Honolulu Acad. of Art, 1963-66, Dayton Art Inst., 1985-87. Exhibited in group shows at Sinclair Coll., 1985, Arts Venture, 1985, one-woman shows include Bevercreek Libr., 1986, City of Englewood, 1986. Vol. artist Boy Scouts Am., Charleston, SC, Minn., 1967—74; vol. artist, tchr. Girl Scouts U.S., O'Fallon, Ill., 1975—76; vol. art judge pub. elem., jr. and sr. HS, Charleston, Mascoutah, Ill., 1969—78, Ill. State Hist. Libr., Belleville, 1979, Belbrook (Ohio) HS, 1988, 1989. Recipient 2d pl., hon. mention, Nat. Nature and Wildfowl Show, 1987, hon. mention, Wyoming (Ohio) Pub. Arts Comm. show, 1987, 1st Pl. award, West End Art Fair, Toledo, Ohio, 2007. Mem.: Dayton Soc. Painters and Sculptors, Beavercreek Creative Artists Assn. (sec. 1987—, v.p. 1988—90), St. Louis Artists Guild, Gateway East Artists Guild, Minn. Artists Assn., Charleston Artists Guild, Guild S.C. Artists. Home: 395 12 Oaks Trl Dayton OH 45434-5873 Personal E-mail: lwikstrom@aol.com.

WILBANKS, DONNIE JO, healthcare educator; b. Oklahoma City, Okla., Feb. 21, 1950; s. James Henry and Laura Aneice (Henderson) Wilbanks; m. Sandra Kay Smith, Aug. 6, 1977; children: Kimberly Lynn, Eric Leslie. BA, Mo. Bapt. Coll., St. Louis, 1976; MA in Tchg., Webster U., St. Louis, 1991. Vocat. instr. State of Mo. and State of Ill. Assoc. pastor Fourth Bapt. Ch., St. Louis, 1972—76; alcoholism counselor Project Promised Land, St. Louis, 1972—75; bus. agt. Svc. Employees Internat. Union, St. Louis, 1985—86; children's svc. worker Mo. Family Svcs., 1986—93; in-home family therapist Mo., 1993—98; instr. psychology, anatomy, physiology St. Louis Coll. Health Careers, 1998—. Author: (textbook) Applied Psychology in Health Care, 2008. Vol. fund raising ARC, St. Louis, 2006. Cpl. USMC, 1968—71. Recipient Outstanding Svc. award, St. Louis Coll. of Health Careers, 2004; named Instr. of the Quarter, 2004, Instr. of the Yr., 2005. Mem.: MENSA, Am. Assn. of Profl. Hypnotherapists. Office: St Louis Coll of Health Careers 909 S Taylor Saint Louis MO 63110 Personal E-mail: donnie.wilbanks@yahoo.com.

WILBANKS, JAN JOSEPH, retired philosopher; b. Lynchburg, Ohio, Dec. 17, 1928; s. James Odell and Bernice Elizabeth (Daugherty) W.; m. Alice Ramona Pacheco, Nov. 14, 1953; children— Elise, Anita, Jennifer. BS, Cin. Coll. Pharmacy, 1951; PhD in Philosophy, Ohio State U., 1964. Instr. philosophy Purdue U., 1961-64; mem. faculty Marietta (Ohio) Coll., 1964-89, prof. philosophy, 1973-89. Author: Hume's Theory of Imagination, 1968, also articles. With AUS, 1951-53. Home: 122 High St Marietta OH 45750-2636

WILBUR, E. PACKER, investment company executive; b. Bridgeport, Conn., Sept. 9, 1936; s. E. Packer and Elizabeth (Wells) Wilbur; m. Laura Mary Ferrier, Sept. 17, 1965; children: Alison Mary Thompson, Andrew Packer, Gillian Elizabeth Stratmann. BA, Yale U., New Haven, Conn., 1959; MBA, Harvard U., Cambridge, Mass., 1965. Cons. McKinsey & Co. Inc., NYC, 1964-67; dir. corp. planning Am. Express Co., NYC, 1967-69; v.p. Van Alstyne Noel & Co., NYC, 1969-70; exec. v.p., dir., mem. exec. com. Newburger Loeb & Co. Inc., NYC, 1970-73; pres. E. P. Wilbur & Co., Inc., Southport, Conn., 1973—, Southport Properties Corp., 1986—. Chmn. bd. dirs. Criterion Mgmt., Inc., Trend Mgmt., Inc., Fairfield Advisors, Inc., EPW Securities, Inc.; gen. ptnr. Embankment Properties Ltd., London, others; former allied mem. N.Y. Stock Exch., NYC. Contbr. articles to fin. jours. Bd. dirs. Winthrop Corp., Discovery Mus., Bridgeport, Wakeman Meml. Boys/Girls Club, Southport, Greater Bridgeport Jr. Hockey League, Pequot Libr., Southport, Northfield-Mt. Hermon Sch., Mass., Charter Revision Commn., Harbor Mgmt. Commn., Fairfield, Conn.; mem. dean's coun. John F. Kennedy Sch. Govt Harvard U., mem. bd. Inst. Social and Econ. Policy in Mid. East; mem. dean's internat. coun. Harris Sch. Pub. Policy Studies U. Chgo. With US Army, 1959—60. Mem.: Royal Victorian Aero. Club, Royal No. Yacht Club (Scotland), Yale Club (NYC), Country Club Fairfield, Pequot Running Club (Southport, founder), Pequot Yacht Club (Southport). Office: 2507 Post Rd Southport CT 06890-1259 Home: PO Box 669 227 Main St Southport CT 06890

WILBUR, LESLIE CLIFFORD, mechanical engineering educator; b. Johnston, RI, May 12, 1924; s. Clifford Elwood and Isabel (Winsor) W.; m. Gertrude Monica Widmer, Sept. 9, 1950; children— Clifford Leslie, Kenneth Charles, Ted Winsor, Christopher Francis. BS in Mech. Engring, U. RI, Kingston, 1948; MS, Stevens Inst. Tech., Hoboken, NJ, 1949. Registered profl. engr., Mass. Instr., then asst. prof. Duke, 1949-57; mem. faculty Worcester Poly. Inst., 1957—, prof. mech. engring., 1961—, dir. nuclear reactor facility, 1959-86, prof. and chmn. nuc. reactor facility emeritus, 1987—. Mem. N.E. adv. council Atomic Indsl. Forum, 1972— Editor-in-chief: Handbook of Energy Systems. Served with AUS, 1943-46, ETO. Fellow ASME (vice chmn. Eastern NC sect. 1956-57); mem. Am. Nuc. Soc. (mem. at large exec. com. Northeastern sect. 1961-62, 66-67, chmn. Northeastern sect. 1968-69), Am. Soc. Engring. Edn., AAAS, Sigma Xi, Tau Beta Pi, Phi Kappa Phi, Pi Tau Sigma. Baptist (deacon 1962-65). Home: 94 Parkway N Brewer ME 04412-1235 Office: Worcester Poly Inst Dept Mech Engring Ed Worcester MA 01609 Personal E-mail: yazcat@aol.com.

WILBUR, RICHARD PURDY, writer, educator; b. NYC, Mar. 1, 1921; s. Lawrence L. and Helen (Purdy) W.; m. Mary Charlotte Hayes Ward, June 20, 1942; children: Ellen Dickinson, Christopher Hayes, Nathan Lord, Aaron Hammond. AB, Amherst Coll., 1942, AM, 1952, DLitt (hon.), 1967; AM, Harvard U., 1947; LHD (hon.), Lawrence Coll., Washington U., Williams Coll., U. Rochester, SUNY, Potsdam, 1986, Skidmore Coll., 1987, U. Lowell, 1990; LHD (hon.), Mass. Coll. Liberal Arts, 2002; DLitt (hon.), Clark U., Am. Internat. Coll., Marquette U., Wesleyan U., Carnegie-Mellon U.; DLitt. (hon.), Lake Forest Coll., 1982, Smith Coll., 1996, Sewanee U., 1996; DD (hon.), St. Mary's Sem. and U., 2001. Jr. fellow Harvard U., Cambridge, Mass., 1947-50, Asst. prof. English, 1950-54; assoc. prof. Wellesley Coll., 1955-57; prof. Wesleyan U., 1957-77; writer in residence Smith Coll., 1977-86; Simpson lectr. Amherst Coll., 2008—. Author: The Beautiful Changes, 1947, Ceremony, 1950, A Bestiary, 1955, 2d edit., 1993, Things of This World, 1956, Poems 1943-56, 1957, Advice to a Prophet, 1961, Poems of Richard Wilbur, 1963, Walking to Sleep, 1969, The Mind-Reader, 1976, Seven Poems, 1981, The Whale, 1982, New and Collected Poems, 1988 (Pulitzer prize for poetry, 1989), Bone Key and Other Poems, 1998, Mayflies: New Poems and Translations, 2000, Collected Poems 1943-2004, 2004, (children's books) Loudmouse, 1963, Opposites, 1973, More Opposites, 1991, A Game of Catch, 1994, Runaway Opposites, 1995, The Disappearing Alphabet, 1998, Opposites, More Opposites and Some Differences, 2000, The Pig in the Spigot, 2000, (criticism) Responses, 1976, expanded edit., 2000, (prose pieces) The Catbird's Song, 1997; co-author (with Lillian Hellman): (comic opera) Candide, 1957; co-author: (with William Schuman) (cantata) On Freedom's Ground, 1986; translator (Moliere): The Misanthrope, 1955, Tartuffe, 1963 (co-recipient Bollingen Translation prize, 1963), The School for Wives, 1971, The Learned Ladies, 1978, Four Comedies, 1982, Lovers' Quarrels, 2006; translator: (Racine) Andromache, 1982, Phaedra, 1986, The Suitors, 2001; translator: Moliere's The School for Husbands, 1992, Imaginary Cuckold, 1993, Molière's Amphitryon, 1995, Don Juan, 1998, Molière's The Bungler, 2000, Pierre Corneille's Theatre of Illusion, 2007; editor: Complete Poems of Poe, 1959, Poems of Shakespeare, 1966, Selected Poems of Witter Bynner, 1978, Edgar Allan Poe: Poems and Poetics, 2003; author: Corneille's Le Lid and the Liar, 2009. Decorated chevalier Ordre des Palmes Academiques; recipient Harriet Monroe prize Poetry mag., 1948, Oscar Blumenthal prize, 1950, Prix de Rome, Am. Acad. Arts and Letters, 1954, Edna St. Vincent Millay Meml. award, 1957, Nat. Book award, 1957, Pulitzer prize, 1957, Sarah Josepha Hale award, 1968, Bollingen prize, 1971, Brandeis U. Creative Arts award, 1971, Prix Henri Desfeuilles, 1971, Shelley Meml. award, 1973, Harriet Monroe Poetry award, 1978, St. Botolph's Club Found. award, 1983, Drama Desk award, 1983, Aiken-Taylor award, 1988, Bunn award, 1988, Washington Coll. Lit. award, 1988, St. Louis Lit. award, 1989, Grand Master award Birmingham-So. Coll., 1989, Gold Medal for Poetry, Am. Acad. Inst. Arts and Letters, 1991, Edward MacDowell medal, 1992, Nat. Arts Club Medal of Honor for Lit., 1994, PEN/Manheim Medal for Translation, 1994, Milton Ctr. prize, 1995, Acad. Am. Achievement award, 1995, Robert Frost medal Poetry Soc. Am., 1996, T.S. Eliot award, 1996, Wallace Stevens award, 2003, Ruth Lilly prize, 2006; Guggenheim fellow, 1952-53, 63, Ford fellow, 1960-61, Camargo Found. fellow, 1985; named U.S. Poet Laureate, Libr. Congress, 1987, Nat. Medal of the Arts, 1994; named to Theater Hall of Fame, 2003. Fellow: MLA (hon.); mem.: PEN (Transl. award 1983), ASCAP, AAAL (pres. 1974—76, chancellor 1976—78, 1980—81), Dramatists Guild, Acad. Am. Poets (chancellor emeritus), Am. Acad. Arts and Scis. Home: 87 Dodwells Rd Cummington MA 01026-9705

WILBUR, RICHARD SLOAN, medical association administrator, physician; s. Blake Colburn and Mary Caldwell (Sloan) Wilbur; m. Betty Lou Fannin, Jan. 20, 1951; children: Andrew, Peter, Thomas. BA, Stanford U., 1943, MD, 1946; JD, John Marshall, 1990. Cert. ABIM (Gastroenterology Am. Bd. Internal Medicine, 1954. Intern San Francisco County Hosp., 1946—47; resident Stanford Hosp., 1949—51, U. Pa. Hosp., 1951—52; postgrad. tng. U. Mich. Hosp., 1957, Karolinska Sjukhuset, Stockholm, 1960; staff Palo Alto (Calif.) Med. Clinic, 1952—69; dep. exec. v.p. AMA, Chgo., 1969—71, 1973—74; asst. sec. for health and environment dept. def., 1971—73; sr. v.p. Baxter Labs., Inc., Deerfield, Ill., 1974—76; exec. v.p. Council Med. Splty. Socs., 1976—91, sec. accreditation coun. for continuing med. edn., 1979—91; assoc. prof. medicine Georgetown U. Med. Sch., 1971—77, Stanford Med. Sch., 1952—69; pres. Nat. Resident Matching Plan, 1991—92. Chmn. bd., CEO Inst. Clin. Info., 1994—99; sr. v.p. healthcare Buckeye Corp. Pte, Ltd., Singapore, 1997—2000; CEO Medic Alert, 1992—94; pres. Am. Bd. Med. Mgmt., 1992; mem. Am. Bd. Electrodiagnostic Medicine, 1993—98; chmn. med. adv. bd. Med. City, Bangalore, India, 1997—2000; bd. visitors Drew U. Postgrad. Med. Sch. Contbr. articles to profl. jours. Bd. govs. ARC; chmn. Mid-Am. Blood Svcs. Bd., Lifesource Blood Bank, 1996—98; vice-chmn. Rep. Cen. Com. Santa Clara County, Calif., 1966—89; bd. dir. Nat. Adv. Cancer Coun., Nat. Health Coun., 1993—95; chmn. bd. dir. Medic Alert Found.; chmn. bd. Calif. Med. Assn., 1968—69, Calif. Blue Shield, 1966—68, Am. Med. Found., 1987—; pres. Royal Soc. Medicine Found., 1998—2004. With USNR, 1942—58. Recipient Disting. Svc. medal, Dept. Def., 1973, Scroll of merit, Nat. Med. Assn., 1971. Fellow: ACP, Am. Coll. Physician Execs. (bd. regents 1985—89, pres. 1988—89), Am. Coll. Legal Medicine (pres. 2006—07), Internat. Coll. Dentistry (hon.); mem.: Am. Soc. Internal Medicine, Am. Gastroent. Assn., Santa Clara County Med. Soc. (hon.), Lake County Med. Soc., Ill. Med. Assn., Inst. Medicine, Union League Phila., Cedars Club, Pacific Interurban Clin. Club, Alpha Omega Alpha, Phi Beta Kappa. Home: 985 Hawthorne Pl Lake Forest IL 60045-2217 Office: APT Management Inc 736 N Western Ave #222 Lake Forest IL 60045 E-mail: aptmgmnt@aol.com.

WILBURN, NANCY, accounting educator; m. Bob Kilpatrick, 1984; children: Tiffany Kilpatrick, Kayla Kilpatrick. BS in Acctg. summa cum laude, Ctrl. State U., Edmond, Okla., 1980; MS in Acctg., Okla. State U., Stillwater, 1983; PhD in Acctg., Tex. A&M U., Coll. Sta., 1987. CPA Okla., 1981. Staff acct. Deloitte, Haskins & Sells, Okla. City, Okla., 1980—81; grad. instr. Okla. State U., Stillwater, 1982—83; lectr. Tex. A&M U., Coll. Sta., 1983—86, asst. prof., 1987, Northern Ariz. U., Flagstaff, 1988—93, assoc. prof., 1993—99, prof. acctg., 1999—, acctg. area coord., 2002—05. Bd. trustees Ariz. Soc. CPAs Found. Edn. & Innovation, 2007—. Contbr. articles to profl. jours. on acctg. Vol. Flagstaff Alpine Ski Team, 1996—2008; parent vol. Knoles Elem. Sch., Flagstaff, 1998—2002; asst. coach Flagstaff Girls' Softball League, 1999—2007; asst. coach, HS girls' fastpitch softball team Northland Prep. Acad., Flagstaff, 2006—. Recipient Excellence in Tchg. award, AZ CPA Found. Edn. & Innovation, 1994, Edn. Innovation award, 2001—02, Best Prof., NAU Delta Sigma Pi Profl. Bus. Frat., 1997, Outstanding Tchg. award, NAU Acctg. Adv. Coun., 1998, 2006—07, Outstanding Tchr. award, NAU Coll. Bus. Adminstrn., 2004, Faculty Advisor award, Northern Ariz. U., 2005, Lifetime Achievement award, Flagstaff Alpine Ski & Snowboard Team, 2008, Tchg. Scholar award, NAU, 1997, Parent of Yr. award, Northland Prep. Acad., 2009. Mem.: Am. Acctg. Assn. Avocations: softball, skiing, travel, scuba diving. Office: Northern Ariz Univ W A Franke Coll Bus Flagstaff AZ 86011-5066 Business E-Mail: nancy.wilburn@nau.edu.

WILCHEK, MEIR, biochemist, educator; b. Warsaw, Oct. 17, 1935; arrived in Israel, 1949; s. Eliezer Nechemia and Rachel (Zaidenberg) Wilchek; m. Esther Edlis, Mar. 14, 1960; children: Eliezer Yizhak, Yael Zvia, Hagit Zipora. BS, Bar-Ilan U., Ramat Gan, Israel, 1960, PhD (hon.), 1995; PhD in Biochemistry, Weizmann Inst. Sci., Rehovot, Israel, 1965; DSc (hon.), U. Waterloo, Can., 1989; PhD (hon.), U. Jyvaskyla, Finland, 2000, Ben-Gurion U., Beer-Sheva, Israel, 2000. Chief chemist Yeda Co., Rehovot, 1960-62; rsch. assoc. dept. biophysics Weizmann Inst. Sci., 1965-66, sr. scientist, 1968-71, assoc. prof., 1971-74, prof., 1974—, head dept. biophysics, 1977-78, 83-87; vis. fellow NIH, Bethesda, Md., 1966-67, rsch. assoc., 1967-68. Vis. scientist NIH, 1972, 1974—75. Contbr. articles to profl. jours., chapters to books;, editor various med. texts. Recipient Rothschild prize in chemistry, Israel, 1984, Pierce prize for biorecognition tech., Ill., 1987, Israel prize in life scis., 1990, Sarstedt prize, Germany, 1990, Disting. Clin. Chemist award, Internat. Fedn. Clin. Chemistry, 1996, Christian B. Anfinsen award, Protein Soc., 2004, Wilhelm-Exner medal, Austria, 2004, Emet prize, Israel, 2005; co-recipient Wolf Found. prize in medicine, 1987; named an Hon. Citizen, City of Rehovot, 2004; Fogarty Internat. Scholar, 1981—82. Mem.: Israeli Acad. Scis. & Humanities, Israel Immunological Soc., Israel Chem. Soc., Israel Biochem. Soc., European Acad. Sci. & Art, European Molecular Biology Orgn., Inst. Medicine, Am. Chem. Soc., Am. Soc. Biol. Chemistry (hon.). Office Phone: 893 438 08. E-mail: meir.wilchek@weizmann.ac.il.

WILCHINS, HOWARD MARTIN, lawyer; b. Paterson, NJ, Mar. 6, 1945; s. Philip Aaron and Esther (Blake) Wilchins; m. Margaret Mandon, Sept. 6, 1970 (dec. July 2001); children: Julie, Daniel; m. Sue Renay Rubinstein, Mar. 21, 2004. AB, Mich. State U., 1966; JD, U. Chgo., 1969. BAR: DC 1969, US Supreme Ct. 1975. Trial atty. FPC, Washington, 1969-70; spl. asst. to N.Y. Public Service Commn., Albany, 1970-72; dep. sect. chief AEC, Washington, 1972-75; dep. gen. counsel-litigation U.S. Ry. Assn., Washington, 1975-81, gen. counsel, 1981-84; dep. chief enforcement div. FCC Common Carrier Bur., Washington, 1984-90; v.p. Arnold S. Tesh Advisors, Washington, 1990-92; sr. litigation atty. Office Nuclear Safety Enforcement, U.S. Dept. Energy, Washington, 1992—2007; exec. cons. Epsilon Sys. Solutions Inc., 2007—. Mem. faculty Trial Practice Inst., US CSC, 1977-79 Bd. dirs. United Jewish Appeal Greater Washington, 1984-90, 92-96; bd. dirs. Charles E. Smith Jewish Day Sch., 1983—, v.p., 1986-88, pres., 1988-90; mem. Hillel of Greater Washington, 1990-2006, v.p., 1992-94, pres., 1994-96; bd. dirs., mem. Capital Camps, 1990-96; bd. dir. Jewish Edn. Svc. N.Am., 1996—, asst. treas., 2000-02, treas., 2003-05, v.p., 2005—; bd. dirs. Tikvat Israel Congregation, Rockville, Md., 2000-04, Gesher Jewish Day Sch., 2005-. Mem. ABA, DC Bar Assn., Fed. Comm. Bar Assn. (co-chmn. com. on arbitration and mediation 1991-94). Home: 10308 Snowpine Way Potomac MD 20854-3940 Office: Epsilon Sys Solutions Inc 1660 Internat Dr Ste 400 Mc Lean VA 22102 Business E-Mail: hwilchins@wilchins.com.

WILCKE, SAM LEWIS, financial analyst, consultant; b. Escondido, Calif., Aug. 8, 1975; s. Brent Edward and Loree Nancy Wilcke. BA, Reed Coll., Portland, OR, 1995; BS, Calif. Inst. Tech., Pasadena, CA, 2000; PhD, U. Calif., Berkeley, 2006. Lead bus. analyst DemandTec, San Carlos, Calif., 2006—07; decision engr.-analytical cons. Rapt-Microsoft, San Francisco, 2007—08. Luce Fellowship, Henry Luce Found., 2000—01, Nat. Sci. Fellowship, NSF, 2002—05. Mem.: Phi Beta Kappa. Home: 1113 Keppler Ct Unit E San Francisco CA 94130 Personal E-mail: swilcke@gmail.com.

WILCOX, C. JAYNE, chemistry professor; PhD, U. Pa., Phila., 1971. Prof. chemistry Harper Coll., Palatine, Ill., 1991—2008. Prin. donor Otter Chemistry Endowment, Harper Coll., 1993—2008. Lt. USN, 1972—76, Bethesda, Md. Office: Harper Coll 1200 W Algonquin Rd Palatine IL 60062

WILCOX, DAVID ERIC, electrical engineering, educator, consultant, business owner; b. Cortland, NY, Sept. 4, 1939; s. James A. and Lucille (Fiske) C.; m. Phillipa Ann Wilcox, Jan. 23, 1977; children: Terri L., Cindy A., Jana L. 0postgrad., Syracuse U., 1965; BSEE, U. Buffalo, 1961; 0postgrad., Marist Coll., Rutgers U.; MS, U. Bridgeport, 1977. Registered profl. engr., N.Y. Rsch. engring. mgr. input/output devices Rome (NY) Air Devel. Ctr., 1966—70; dir. sales Mercom Inc., Winsooki, Vt., 1970-73; pres. Wilcox Tng. Sys., Newburgh, NY, 1973—98; pres., CEO Global Skills Exch., Alexandria, Va., 2003—. Exec. dep. dir., Nat. Skill Stds. Bd., 1998-2003, bd. dirs.; prin. Exec. Effectiveness, Inc., NYC; instr. Dale Carnegie courses. Author: Information System Sciences, 1965; contbr. articles to profl. jours.; patentee in field. Pres. N.Y. State Jaycees, 1972-73, chmn., 1973-74; dir. U.S. Jaycees, 1970-71; bd. dirs., v.p. N.Y. State Spl. Olympics, 1972-73; bd. dirs., treas. Family Counseling Svc., Inc.; mem. Orange County Pvt. Industry Coun., N.Y. State Excelsior Examiner, 1995. Lt. USAF, 1961-65. Mem. IEEE, Soc. Info. Display, N.Y. State Soc. Profl. Engrs., Internat. Transactional Analysis Assn., Internat. Platform Assn., Am. Soc. Quality Control. Methodist. also: 30 W 60th St New York NY 10023-7902 Office: Global Skills Exch 1410 King St Alexandria VA 22314 Home: 413 N Fairfax St Alexandria VA 22314-2321 Home Phone: 703-836-1189; Office Phone: 703-684-5067. Business E-Mail: dwilcox@gskillsxchange.com.

WILCOX, HARRY HAMMOND, retired anatomist; b. Canton, Ohio, May 31, 1918; s. Harry Hammond and Hattie Estelle (Richner) W.; m. D. June Freed., June 21, 1941; children: Joyce L. Wilcox Graff, Margaret J. (Mrs. Grayson S. Smith), James Hammond. BS, U. Mich., 1939, MS, 1940, PhD, 1948. Asso. prof. biology Morningside Coll., Sioux City, Iowa, 1947-48; asso. in anatomy U. Pa., 1948-52; mem. faculty U. Tenn. Center for Health Scis., 1952-83, Goodman prof. anatomy, 1966-83, emeritus prof. anatomy, 1983—. Assoc. editor: Anat. Record, 1968-83. Docent Memphis Zoo, 1983—, emeritus, 2005. With US Army, 1945—46. Mem.: AAAS, Soc. for Integrative and Comparative Biology, Am.Assn. Anatomists, Sigma Xi. Home: 1031 Marcia Rd Memphis TN 38117-5513

WILCOX, HARRY WILBUR, JR., retired manufacturing executive; b. Phila., Feb. 13, 1925; s. Harry Wilbur and Justine Elizabeth (Doolittle) Wilcox; m. Colleen Ann Cerra, Apr. 6, 1946 (dec. 2004); children: Justine, Harry Wilbur III; m. Elizabeth W. Crowther, 2006. BS, Yale U., New Haven, Conn., 1949. With GE Co., NY, 1949-50; mfg. supt. Sylvania Electric Products, 1951-67; v.p., gen. mgr. Granger Assocs., Palo Alto, Calif., 1967-70; gen. mgr. ITT-Cannon Electric Co., Phoenix, 1970-72; pres. Hills McCanna Co., Carpentersville, Ill., 1972-75, VSI, and group v.p. IU Internat. Corp., 1975-78; exec. v.p. ITT-Grinnell, 1978-85; pres. ITT Indsl. and Constrn. Divsn., Lancaster, Pa., 1985-88; ret., 1988. Bd. dirs. Meyer Industries, Nat. Temperature Control Ctrs., Paul N. Howard Co.; former chmn. VSI, VSI-UK. Mem. adv. com. Town of Sherborn, Mass. With US Army, 1943—46. Decorated Bronze Star. Mem.: Madison Beach Club (Conn.), Grand Harbor Golf and Beach Club (Vero Beach), Yale Club of Treasure Coast. Achievements include patents in field of electroluminescence. Home: 1135 Harbor Links Cir Vero Beach FL 32967 Personal E-mail: harcon13@comcast.net.

WILCOX, HARVEY JOHN, lawyer; b. Elyria, Ohio, Nov. 1, 1937; s. Hubbard Clyde and Sylvia (Wahter) W.; m. Leslie Louise Coleman, Apr. 11, 1970. BA cum laude, Amherst Coll., 1959; LLB, Yale U., 1962. Bar: Ohio 1962, Va. 1994. Mem. firm Wilcox & Wilcox, 1962-78; with office gen. counsel Dept. Navy, Washington, 1966-94, asst. to gen. counsel, 1969-72, counsel Naval Air Systems Command, 1972-76, Navy dep. gen. counsel, 1976-94, cons. atty., arbitrator, 1994—. Guest lectr. US Army Logistics Mgmt. Ctr.; mem. Navy Contract Adjustment Bd., 1968-72 Designed Arlington County (Va.) flag, 1983. Bd. dirs. Navy Fed. Credit Union, 1974-77, sec.-treas., 1974-75, 2d v.p., 1975-77; mem. Def. Adv. Panel on Streamlining Acquisition Laws, 1991-92. Lt. USNR, 1963-66. Recipient Meritorious Exec. rank 1980, Disting Exec. rank, 1981, 89, Navy Disting. Civilian Svc. award, 1989, Defense Disting. Civilian Svc. award, 1994. Mem. Ohio Bar Assn., Va. State Bar, Charlottesville-Albemarle Bar Assn., Nat. Trust Hist. Preservation, Nature Conservancy, Piedmont Environ. Coun., Waynesboro Symphony Orch. Home: PO Box 338 Turner Mountain Rd Ivy VA 22945-0338 Personal E-mail: wilcoxivy@earthlink.net.

WILCOX, HELENA MARGUERITA (HELENA RITA WILCOX), music educator; b. Manhattan, Kans., Feb. 16, 1930; d. Virgil Otis Jones and Helena Mary Viers-Jones; children: Charles E., Marguerita E., Patricia A. MusB, State U. Iowa, 1952, MA, 1959. Cert. music tchr. Ariz., 1959, Calif., 1967, Jr. Coll. Calif., 1972. Pvt. kindergarten, Springerville, Ariz., 1959—60; art supr. Yuma (Ariz.) Elem. Sch. Dist., 1960—67; violin tchr. Ariz. Western Cmty. Coll., Yuma, 1965—67; string instrument tchr. Stockton (Calif.) Unified Sch. Dist., 1967—2002; Suzuki violin tchr. San Joaquin Delta Coll., Stockton, 1972—; musician Stockton (Calif.) Symphony, 1967—; tchr. summer arts Stockton (Calif.) Arts Commn.; organ. Symphony Orch., Yuma, 1962—67. Recipient Music Edn. award, Stockton Arts Commn., 2007; Production grant, Stockton Unified Sch. Dist., 1980. Mem.: Nat. Music Educators, Calif. Tchrs. Assn., Suzuki Assn. of the Am., Music Tchrs. Assn. of Calif., Stockton Br. (pres. 2003—), Am. String Tchrs. Assn. (pres. 1975). Democrat. Unitarian. Home: 2348 W Alpine Ave Stockton CA 95204 Home Phone: 209-464-2456. Personal E-mail: ritaviola@sbcglobal.net.

WILCOX, JOHN CAVEN, lawyer, financial executive; b. NYC, Nov. 12, 1942; s. Daniel A. and Jessie Alexandra (Caven) W.; m. Vanessa Guerrini-Maraldi, Sept. 30, 1983; children Daniel D.G., William G.M., Julia G.M. BA magna cum laude, Harvard U., 1964; MA, U. Calif., Berkeley, 1965; JD, Harvard U., 1968; LLM, NYU, 1981. Bar: N.Y. 1973. Account exec. Georgeson & Co. Inc., NYC, 1973-79, mng. dir., 1979-90, chmn., 1990—2005; sr. v.p. head corp. governance TIAA-CREF, 2005—08, sr. cons., 2008—09; chmn. Sodali Ltd., 2006—. Dir. GSC Proxitalia, 1999-05; bd. govs. Internat. Corp. Governance Network, 2002- 05; chair ICGN com. on cross-border voting practices; dir. Shareowners Edn. Network, 2008-. Trustee Woodrow Wilson Nat. Fellowship Found., 1996, vice chmn., 2002-08; trustee Family Dynamics, Inc., NYC, 1979-96, Bennington Coll., 1998—. With US Army, 1968-70, Vietnam. Woodrow Wilson fellow. Mem. ABA (com. corp. laws), NYSE (shareholders comm. com. 1989-95), Am. Soc. Corp. Secs., Nat. Assn. Security Dealers (issuer affairs com 1990-05), Nat. Assn. Corp. Dirs. (adv. bd. NY chpt.), Nat. Investor rels. Inst., Com. Econ. Devel. (subcom. on corporate govs.), The Brook, Harvard Club (NYC), Phi Beta Kappa. Democrat. Home: 580 West End Ave New York NY 10024-1723 Office: Sodali 9 West 57th St 26th Fl New York NY 10019 Home Phone: 212-877-3413; Office Phone: 212-825-1600. Business E-Mail: j.wilcox@sodali.com.

WILCOX, MARK DEAN, lawyer; b. May 25, 1952; s. Fabian Joseph and Zeryle Lucille (Tase) W.; m. Catherine J. Wertjes, Mar. 12, 1983; children: Glenna Lynn, Joanna Tessie, Andrew Fabian Joseph. BBA, U. Notre Dame, 1973; JD, Northwestern U., 1976; CLU, Am. Coll., 1979, ChFC, 1992. Bar: Ill. 1976, Tex. 2009, U.S. Dist. Ct. (no. dist.) Ill. 1976, Trial Bar 1982, U.S. Ct. Appeals (7th cir.) 1987, U.S. Supreme Ct. 1989, Tex., 2008. Staff asst. Nat. Dist. Attys. Assn., Chgo., 1974-75; trial asst. Cook County States Atty., Chgo., 1975; intern U.S. Atty. No. Dist. Ill., Chgo., 1975-76; assoc. Lord, Bissell & Brook, LLP, Chgo., 1976-85, ptnr., 1986—2005; founding ptnr. Walker Wilcox Matousek, LLP, Chgo., 2005—. Venue ofcl. Internat. Spl. Olympics; bd. mgrs. YMCA Met. Chgo., exec. com.; active No Bats Baseball Club, Hall of Fame; bd. trustees YMCA, Chgo.; past trustee Trinity United Meth. Ch.; v.p., bd. trustees YMCA Chgo.; bd. dirs., past chair Irving Park YMCA. Fellow Am. Bar Found.; mem. ABA (tort and ins. practice sect.), Am. Soc. CLU and ChFC, Chgo. Bar Assn. (ins. law com.), State Bar Tex. (sect. ins. com. mem.), Am. Health Lawyers Assn., Nat. Assn. Ins. and Fin. Advisors, Def. Rsch. Inst., Soc. Fin. Svc. Profls., Trial Lawyers Club Chgo., Notre Dame Nat. Monogram Club, Union League Club, Chgo. Lions Rugby Football Club, Beta Gamma Sigma. Office Phone: 312-244-6722.

WILCOX, MARY MARKS, retired Christian education consultant, educator; b. Madison, Wis., Apr. 23, 1921; d. Roy and Mary Celia (Leary) Marks; m. Ray Everett Wilcox, Nov. 28, 1942; children: Peter, Anne, Susan, Steven. BA, U. Wis., 1942; MRE, Iliff Sch. Theology, Denver, 1968. Cert. Christian educator. Cons. local chs., Lakewood, Littleton, Wheat Ridge, Colo., 1963-74; instr., leader numerous seminars throughout U.S. and Can., 1963—; interim parish cons. 1st Presbyn. Ch., Lakewood, 1988-90, profl. assoc. for faith devel., 1993-97; adj. prof. Iliff Sch. Theology, 1970—; ret., 2002. Author: Developmental Journey, 1979; co-author: Viewpoints, 1998; contbr. articles to various publs., chpts. to books. Trustee, mem. exec. bd. Nat. Ghost Ranch Found., Abiquiu, N. Mex., 1983-93. Recipient award Iliff Alumni Assn., 1989. Mem.: Assn. Presbyn. Christian Educators (past mem. exec. bd.). Democrat. Presbyterian. Home: 2119 Wadsworth Blvd 1 Lakewood CO 80214-5706

WILCOX, MAUD, editor; b. NYC, Feb. 14, 1923; d. Thor Fredrik and Gerda (Ysberg) Eckert; m. Edward T. Wilcox, Feb. 9, 1944 (dec. 1998); children: Thor(dec.), Bruce, Eric, Karen. AB summa cum laude, Smith Coll., 1944; A.M., Harvard U., 1945. Teaching fellow Harvard U., 1945-46, 48-51; instr. English Smith Coll., Northampton, Mass., 1947-48, Wellesley Coll., Mass., 1951-52; exec. editor Harvard U. Press, 1958-66, humanities editor, 1966-73, editor-in-chief, 1973—89; freelance editorial cons. Cambridge, 1989—; ret. Cons., panelist NEH, Washington, 1974-76, 82-84; cons. Radcliffe Pub. Course, 1991. Mem. MLA (com. scholarly edits. 1982-86), Assn. Am. Univ. Presses (chair com. admissions and standards 1976-77, v.p. 1978-79, chair program com. 1981-82), Phi Beta Kappa. Democrat. Episcopalian. Home and Office: 63 Francis Ave Cambridge MA 02138-1911 Home Phone: 617-864-3625; Office Phone: 617-864-3625. Personal E-mail: maudwilcox@post.harvard.edu.

WILCOX, RAND ROGER, psychology professor; b. Niagara Falls, NY, July 6, 1946; s. Howard Clinton and Phyllis Hope (Stevens) W.; m. Karen Lesley Thompson, Apr. 25, 1986; children: Quinn Alexander, Bryce Colin. BA, U. Calif., Santa Barbara, 1968, MA in Math., 1976, PhD in Ednl. Psychology, 1976. Sr. rsch. assoc. UCLA, 1976-81; prof. psychology U. So. Calif., LA, 1981—. Author: New Statistical Procedures for Social Sciences, 1987, Statistics for Social Sciences, 1996, Robust Estimation and Hypothesis Testing, 1997, 2d edit., 2005, Fundamentals of Modern Statistical Methods, 2001, Applying Contemporary Statistical Techniques, 2003, Basic Statistics Understanding Conventional Methods and Modern Insights, 2009; assoc. editor Psychometrika, Computational Stats. and Data Analysis, Comms. in Stats.; mem. editl. bd. Brit. Jour. Math. and Statis. Psychology, Jour. Math. and Mgmt. Sci., Jour. Edn. in Psychol. Methods; contbr. articles to profl. jours. Recipient T.L. Saaty award Am. Jour. Math. & Mgmt. Scis., 1984. Fellow: Ctr. Excellence Rsch., Royal Statis. Soc., Am. Psychol. Soc.; mem.: Internat. Assn. Statis. Computing, Am. Ednl. Rsch. Assn., Inst. Math. Stats., Am. Statis. Assn., Psychometric Soc. Achievements include research on improved methods for comparing groups and measuring achievement; resistant measures of correlation and regression; substantial gains in power when testing hypotheses. Office: U So Calif Dept Psychology Los Angeles CA 90089-0001 Office Phone: 213-740-2258. Business E-Mail: rwilcox@usc.edu.

WILCOX, RAYMOND I., oil industry executive; b. Mar. 19; BSME cum laude, U. Mich., 1968; postgrad., London Bus. Sch., 1994. Design and constrn. engr. Chevron, 1968—81, mem. fgn. ops. staff, 1981—86, ops. supt. Lafayette, La., 1986—90; mng. dir. Chevron Asiatic, Melbourne, Australia, 1990—96; v.p., gen. mgr. marine transp. Chevron Shipping Co., San Ramon, Calif., 1996—99; gen. mgr. asset mgmt. Chevron Nigeria Ltd., 1999—2000, chmn., mng. dir., 2000—01; mng. dir. Nigeria/Mid-Africa strategic bus. unit ChevronTexaco Corp., 2001—02; pres. ChevronTexaco Exploration and Prodn. Co., 2002—06; v.p. ChevronTexaco Corp., Houston; pres., CEO Chevron Phillips Chem. Co. LLC, 2006—. Bd. dirs. Dynergy Inc., 2003—. Bd. dirs. Spindletop Charities, Greater Houston Partnership; chmn. Century divsn. United Way of Tex. Gulf Coast, 2003. Mem.: Am. Petroleum Inst. (mem. upstream com.). Office: Chevron Phillips Chem Co 10001 Six Pines Dr The Woodlands TX 77380

WILCOX, SHIRLEY JEAN LANGDON, genealogist; b. Arcata, Calif., Dec. 10, 1942; d. Elmore Harold and Alberta May (Starkey) Langdon; m. Wayne Kent Wilcox, June 22, 1963; 1 child, Harold Bonner. BS, U. Md., 1964. Cert. Bd. for Certification of Genealogists. Tchr. Prince George's County (Md.) Sch. System, 1964-67, substitute tchr., 1968-73; profl. genealogist Lanham, Md., Arlington, Va., 1973—; genealogy tchr. Fairfax County Pub. Schs., 1995-99. Level II coord. Mid-Atlantic Genealogy and History Inst., George Mason U., Fairfax, Va., 1986; trustee Bd. for Certification of Genealogists, 2000—09. Editor: A Bibliography of Published Genealogical Source Records, Prince George's County, Maryland, 1975, Prince George's County Land Records, Vol. A, 1696-1702, 1976, 1850 Census Prince George's County, Maryland, 1978, 1828 Tax List Prince George's County, Maryland, 1985; author: The National Genealogical Society: A Look at Its First One Hundred Years, 2003. Elder Presbyn. Ch., 1970-73, 95-98. Fellow: Nat. Geneal. Soc. (chmn. conf. program subcom. 1990, 2d v.p. 1990—94, councilor 1994—96, pres. 1996—2000); mem.: DAR (libr. Gov. Robert Bowie chpt. 1985—, Outstanding Jr. Mem. award 1979), Fairfax Geneal. Soc. (pres. 1986—89), Prince George's County Geneal. Soc. (pres. 1973, 1975—76, book rev. editor 1976—96, Jane Roush McCafferty award of excellence 1985), Va. Geneal. Soc. (gov. 2001—07, pres. 2007—), Assn. Profl. Genealogists (pres. 1991—93, pres. Nat. Capital area chpt. 1994—96, dir. region 3 2004—06, Grahame Thomas Smallwood Jr. award of merit 1995), Clay Family Soc. (dir. 2002—06), Soc. Mayflower Descs. in DC (bd. assts. 2007—), Paperweight Collectors Assn. (pres. Md.-DC-Va. chpt. 1988—90), numerous others. Avocation: collecting paperweights. Home: 1500 23rd St S Arlington VA 22202-1523

WILCOX, STEVEN ALAN, lawyer; b. RI, 1955; s. Donald and Edna Wilcox; m. Nancy Wilcox, 1980. BA summa cum laude, Boston Coll., 1977, JD cum laude, 1980. Bar: Mass. 1980. Assoc. Ropes & Gray, Boston, 1980-89, ptnr. corp. dept., 1989—, head life sci. practice grp. Mem. ABA, Mass. Bar Assn., Boston Bar Assn. Office: Ropes & Gray 1 International Pl Boston MA 02110-2624 Office Phone: 617-951-7319. Office Fax: 617-951-7050. Business E-Mail: swilcox@ropesgray.com.

WILCOXSON-UECKERT, CATHERINE ANN, science educator, consultant; b. Lemmon, SD, Nov. 13, 1948; d. Alvin Herman and Myra V. (Eggers) Thies; m. Dale Arthur Wilcoxson, Dec. 13, 1969 (div.); children: Blaine, Erik; m. Warren Ueckert, May 19, 2001 BS, Midland Luth. Coll., 1971; Masters, U. Nebr., Omaha, 1989; PhD, U. Nebr., 1994; D (hon.), Midland Coll., 2003. Tchr. North Bend (Nebr.) Ctrl. Sch., 1971-78, Fremont (Nebr.) H.S., 1978-81, 84-92; project coord. N.E. Dept. Edn., Lincoln, 1993-95; assoc. prof. No. Ariz. U., Flagstaff, 1995—. Cons. La. Dept. Edn., 1994, 95, Coun. Chief State Sch. Officers, Washington, 1994, 96, Ark. Dept. of Edn., 1996. Editor: N.E. Math/Science Frameworks, 1994, Guidelines for Teacher Preparation: Mathematics and Science, 1995, Middle School Idea Book, 1996. Recipient Master Tchr. award Midland Luth. Coll., 1993. Mem. Nat. Sci. Tchrs. (manuscript reveiw com. Jour. Coll. Sci. Tchrs. 1995-98), Am. Ednl. Rsch. Assn., Nat. Assn. Biology Tchrs. (sec./treas. 1996-2000, pres. 2003 Outstanding Biology Tchr. 1991, Excellence in Encouraging Equity award 1994), Nat. Assn. for Rsch. in Sci. Tchg., Ariz. Sci. Tchrs. Assn., Phi Delta Kappa Office: No Ariz Univ PO Box 5640 Flagstaff AZ 86011-0001 Office Phone: 928-523-7026. Business E-Mail: catherine.ueckert@nau.edu.

WILCZEK, FRANK ANTHONY, physics professor; b. Mineola, NY, May 15, 1951; s. Frank John and Mary Rose (Cona) W.; m. Elizabeth Jordan Devine, July 3, 1973; children: Amity, Mira. BS in Math., U. Chgo., 1970; MA in Math., Princeton U., 1972, PhD in Physics, 1974; Doctorate degree (hon.), Universitè de Montrèal, 2001; Doctorate degree, Clark U., 2007, Ohio State U., 2007. Instr. Princeton U., NJ, 1974, asst. prof. NJ, 1974-76, Princeton, NJ, 1977—78, assoc. prof., 1978—80, prof., 1980-81; prof., Sch. of Natural Scis. Inst. for Advanced Study, Princeton, NJ, 1989—2000; prof. U. Calif., Santa Barbara, Calif., 1980—88, Inst. for Theoretical Physics, Santa Barbara, Calif., 1981-88; Herman Feshbach Prof. Physics MIT, Cambridge, Mass., 2000—. Vis. fellow Inst. Advanced Study, Princeton, 1976-77; Chancellor Robert Huttenback prof. of physics U. Calif., Santa Barbara, 1984-90; vis. prof. Harvard U., 1987-88; J. Robert Oppenheimer prof. Inst. for Advanced Study, 1997-2000; adj. prof. Centros Estudios Cientificos, 2002-; vis. Schrodinger-prof. City of Vienna, Austria, 2002; Leland J. Haworth Disting. Scientist, Brookhaven Nat. Lab., 1994-97; lectr. several univs. and socs.; serves several adv. bds. Author: Longing for the Harmonies, 1988, Geometric Phases in Physics, 1989, Fractional Statistics and Anyon Superconductivity, 1990, Fantastic Realities, 2006; editor-in-chief Annals of Physics, 2001-; editl. advisor, Daedalus, 2002-; contbr. articles to profl. jours. Trustee U. Chgo., 1998—2004. Recipient J.J. Sakurai prize Am. Phys. Soc., 1986, Dirac medal UNESCO, 1994, Michelson-Morley prize Case Western Res. U., 2002, Lorentz medal, 2002, Lilienfield prize Am. Physics Soc., 2003, Europhysics prize, 2003; named A.P. Sloan fellow, 1975-77, MacArthur fellow, 1982-87, Regent's Fellow, Smithsonian Astrophysical Observatory, 1986-88; co-recipient High Energy and Particle Physics prize, European Physical Soc., 2003, Nobel Prize in Physics, 2004, King Faisal prize (Sci.), King Faisal Found., 2005. Fellow: AAAS, Am. Philos. Soc., Am. Philos. Soc.; fgn. mem. Royal Netherlands Acad. Arts and Sci.; mem. NAS, Am. Acad. Arts and Scis. Achievements include discovery of asymptotic freedom in the theory of the strong interaction. Avocations: chess, music, logic puzzles. Office: MIT-NE25-4010 Ctr for Theoretical Physics 6-301 5 Cambridge Center Cambridge MA 02142 Business E-Mail: wilczek@mit.edu.*

WILCZYNSKI, JANUSZ S., manufacturing executive, retired physicist; b. Warsaw, May 12, 1929; came to US, 1962; m. Brahna Lauger. Diploma in Indsl. Mechanics, Mining Acad., Cracow, Poland, 1954; MSc in Physics, Jagellonian U., Cracow, Poland, 1957; PhD in Physics and Optics, Imperial Coll. U. London, 1961. Physicist Watson, Ltd., London, 1961-62; rsch. staff mem. T.J. Watson Rsch. Ctr., IBM, Yorktown Heights, NY, 1962-63, mgr. tech. optics, 1963-83, 2d level mgr., 1983-84, sr. mgr., 1984-86, dir., 1986-93; gen. ptnr. Wilc Instruments LLP, 1995. Contbr. over 60 articles to profl. jours. Recipient 13 Invention awards, 1966-98, 7 Outstanding Innovation awards IBM, 1968-91; IBM fellow, 1981. Fellow Optical Soc. Am. (Richardson medal 1988); mem. NAE. Avocation: astronomical optics. Home: PO Box 790 Sandia Park NM 87047-0790 Office Phone: 505-286-8285. Office Fax: 505-286-8272. Personal E-mail: wilczyn@swcp.com.

WILD, JAMES ROBERT, biochemistry and genetics professor; b. Sedalia, Mo., Nov. 24, 1945; s. Robert Lee and Frances Elleta (Wheeler) W.; m. Ann Lynn Brenner, Aug. 1, 1973; 1 child, Kalli Ann. BA in Zoology, U. Calif., Davis, 1967; PhD in Cell Biology, U. Calif., Riverside, 1971, post doctoral fellow, 1972. From asst. to assoc. prof. genetics and biochemistry Tex. A&M U., Coll. Sta., Tex., 1975-84, prof., chair genetics faculty, 1984—, prof. biochemistry & genetics, 1984—2000, head biochemistry and biophysics dept., 1986-90, exec. assoc. dean Coll. Agr. and Life Scis., 1987—92, prof., head dept. biochemistry and biophysics Coll. Agr. and Life Scis., 1994—2000, chmn. faculty genetics. Fellow faculty Tex. Agrl. Experiment Sta., 1999. With USN, 1972-75. Recipient So. Regional award for excellence in coll. anduniv. tchg. in food and agrl. scis., Higher Edn. program USDA, 1992. Fellow AAAS. Methodist. Office: Tex A&M U 2128 Biochemistry Bldg Rm 332 College Station TX 77843-2128 Office Phone: 979-845-6539. Business E-Mail: j-wild@tamu.edu.

WILD, JOHN JULIAN, surgeon, researcher, medical educator; b. Sydenham, Kent, Eng., Aug. 11, 1914; came to U.S., 1946; s. Ovid Frederick and Ellen Louise (Cuttance) W.; m. Nancy Wallace, Nov. 14, 1949 (div. 1966); children: John O., Douglas J.; m. Valerie Claudia Grosenick, Aug. 9, 1968; 1 child, Ellen Louise. BA, U. Cambridge, Eng., 1936, MA, 1940, MD, 1942, PhD, 1971. Intern, resident U. Coll. Hosp., London, 1938-42; intern U. College Hosp., London, 1938-42; staff surgeon Miller Gen., St. Charles and North Middlesex Hosps., London, 1942-44; venereologist Royal Army Med. Corps, 1944-45; rsch. fellow, instr. depts. surgery and elec. engring., prin. investigator U. Minn., Mpls., 1946-51; dir. rsch. Medico.-Technol. Rsch. Dept. St. Barnabas Hosp., Mpls., 1953-60; dir. Medico-Technol. Rsch. Unit Minn. Found., St. Paul, 1960-63; pvt. practice Mpls., 1966—90; dir. Medico-Technol. Rsch. Inst. Mpls., St. Louis Park, Minn., 1965—2006. Lectr. in field of medical instruments, ultrasound. Contbr. articles to profl. jours. Recipient Japan prize in Medical Imaging, Sci. and Tech. Found. Japan, 1991, 1st Frank Annunzio award Christopher Columbus Fellowship Found., 1998, lifetime achievement award U. Minn. Med. Sch., 2000, Ian Donald Tech. Achievement aard ISUOG, 2000. Fellow Am. Inst. Ultrasound in Medicine (Pioneer award 1978); mem. AMA, World Fedn. Ultrasound in Medicine and Biology, Minn. State Med. Assn., Hennepin County Med. Soc., N.Am. Alvis Owners Club; hon. mem. Brit. Inst. Radiology, Japan Soc. of Ultrasound in Medicine. Achievements include patents in field; origination of ultrasonic medical imaging instruments and diagnostic techniques; origination of the field of pulse-echo ultrasonic diagnostic medicine. Home and Office: Medico-Technol Rsch Inst 4262 Alabama Ave S Minneapolis MN 55416-3105

WILD, NELSON HOPKINS, lawyer; b. Milw., July 16, 1933; s. Henry Goetseels and Virginia Douglas (Weller) W.; m. Joan Ruth Miles, Apr. 12, 1969; children: Mark, Eric; m. Diana Morris, Sept. 7, 2002. AB, Princeton U., 1955; LL.B., U. Wis., 1961. Bar: Wis. 1962, Calif. 1967; cert. specialist in probate, estate planning and trust law State Bar of Calif. Research assoc. Wis. Legis. Council, Madison, 1955-56; assoc. Whyte, Hirschboeck, Minahan, Harding & Harland, Milw., 1961-67, Thelen, Marin, Johnson & Bridges, San Francisco, 1967-70; sole practice law San Francisco, 1970—. Mem. State Bar Calif. Client Trust Fund Commn., 1983, mem. exec. com. conf. dels., 1985-88. Contbr. articles to legal jours. Bd. dirs. Neighborhood Legal Assistance Found., San Francisco, 1974-85, chmn. bd., 1978-81. Served with USAF, 1956-58. Mem. ABA, Calif. Bar Assn., San Francisco Bar Assn., Am. Bar Found., Lawyers of San Francisco Club (gov. 1975, treas. 1981, v.p. 1982, pres.-elect 1983, pres. 1984), Calif. Tennis Club (bd. dirs. 1995-97, pres. 1997). Office: 332 Pine St Ste 710 San Francisco CA 94104-3230 Personal E-mail: nwildlaw@aol.com.

WILD, RICHARD, music educator, musician; b. Santa Monica, Calif., Dec. 15, 1954; s. Caryll Harris and Marguerite Grunseth Wild; m. Julie Marie Ahern, Sept. 19, 1981; children: Eve Noel, Benjamin Caryll. BA in Music, UCLA, 1976; BA in Elem. Edn., Coll. Santa Fe, 1995. Nat. bd. cert. tchr. 2005. Gen. organ builder Abbott and Sieker Organ Builders, LA, 1977—79; proprietor Rick Wild Organbuilder, Albuquerque,

1984—; organist 1st Prebyn. Ch., Albuquerque, 1988—2001; tchr. Sandia Prep. Sch., Albuquerque, 1988—89, Manzano Boys Sch., Albuquerque, 1988—94; music specialist Albuquerque Pub. Schs., 1998—; organist Ctrl. United Meth. Ch., Albuquerque, 2001—. Composer: How Can I Deny God's Grace, 2003. Mem. fine arts adv. bd. Albuquerque Arts Alliance, 2004—07; bd. dirs. University Heights Assn., Albuquerque, 1992—93. Mem.: Am. Orff-Schulwerk Assn., N.Mex. Music Educators Assn. (John Batchellor award for excellence in tchg. elem. music 2005), Am. Guild Organists (N.Mex. dist. convenor 2001—07, past dean 2003—04), PI Lambda Theta. Methodist. Avocations: amateur radio, sailing, bicycling. Home: 205 Cornell SE Albuquerque NM 87106 E-mail: wild@aps.edu.

WILD, ROBERT ANTHONY, academic administrator; b. Chgo., Mar. 30, 1940; s. John Hopkins and Mary Dorothy (Colnon) Wild. BA in Latin, Loyola U., Chgo., 1962, MA in Classical Lang., 1967; STL, Jesuit Sch. Theology, Chgo., 1970; PhD in Study of Religion, Harvard U., 1977. Ordained priest 1970. From asst. to assoc. prof. Marquette U., Milw., 1975—83; vis. prof. Pont. Istituto Biblico, Rome, 1983—84; dir. Jesuit philosophate program Loyola U., Chgo., 1984—85, assoc. prof. theology, 1985—92; provincial superior Chgo. Province S.J., 1985—91; pres. Weston Jesuit Sch. Theology, Cambridge, Mass., 1992—96, Marquette U., Milw., 1996—. Trustee Jesuit Sch. Theology, Berkeley, 1985—90, Weston Sch. Theology, Cambridge, Mass., 1985—96, Marquette U., 1990—, St. Louis U., 1994—2002, Milw. Rsch. Park, 2002—05, Greater Milw. Commn., 2002—, Wis. Assn. Ind. Colls. and Univs., 1996—, chmn., 2001—07, St. Joseph's U., Pa., 2004—, U. Detroit Mercy, 2008—. Author: Water in the Cultic Worship of Isis and Sarapis, 1981; co-editor: Sentences of Sextus, 1981; contbr. articles to profl. jours. Mem.: Cath. Bibl. Soc., Soc. Bibl. Lit. Office: Marquette Univ O'Hara Hall PO Box 1881 Milwaukee WI 53201-1881 Home Phone: 414-288-5000; Office Phone: 414-288-7223. Business E-Mail: robert.wild@marquette.edu.

WILDASIN, DAVID E(ARL), economics professor; m. Kathleen Ann Preslin, 1973. BA in Econs., U. Va., Charlottesville, 1972; PhD in Econs., U. Iowa, Iowa City, 1976. Asst. prof. U. Ill., Chgo., 1976—79, Ind. U., Bloomington, 1979—82, assoc. prof., 1982—86, prof. econs., 1986—93, prof. West European studies, 1993; prof. econs. Vanderbilt U., Nashville, 1993—2000; endowed prof. pub. fin. Martin Sch. Pub. Policy and Adminstrn., prof. econs. U. Ky., Lexington, 2000—, dir. Inst. Federalism and Intergovtl. Rels., 2005—. Cons. World Bank, 1992—2002, long-term cons. policy rsch. dept. pub. econs. divsn., 1995—96; vis. assoc. prof. Queen's U., Kingston, Ont., Canada, 1982—83; vis. prof. U. Cath. Louvain, Louvain-la-Neuve, Belgium, 1986—87, Sch. of Higher Studies in Social Scis., Marseille, France, 1995; summer fellow U. Bonn, Germany, 1990; vis. scholar Interuniv. Ctr. for Econ. Studies, Gadjah Mada U., Indonesia, 1990, Ctr. for Econ. Studies U. Munich, 1991, U. B.C., Canada, 1992; econ. policy rsch. unit Copenhagen Bus. Inst., 1996; cons. Ky. C. of C., 2002—03; internat. rsch. fellow Oxford U. Ctr. for Bus. Taxation, 2007—; lectr. in field; cons. in field; keynote spkr. several confs. Author: Urban Public Finance, 1986; co-author: Public Sector Economics, 1984; editor: Fiscal Aspects of Evolving Federations, 1997; assoc. editor: Regional Sci. and Urban Econs., 1987—2004, Jour. Regional Sci., 1989—, Jour. Urban Econs., 1991—, Internat. Tax and Pub. Fin., 1993—, Rev. Internat. Econs., 1994—, Nat. Tax Jour., 1998—, Jour. Pub. Econ. Theory, 1999—, Jour. Pub. Econs., 1999—2003, Papers in Regional Sci., 1999—2001, German Econ. Rev., 2000—, Finanzarchiv, 2000—, CESifo Econ. Studies, 2003—, Contbns. to Econ. Analysis, 2004—, Founds. and Trends in Microecons., 2005—06, referee: profl. jours.; contbr. over 100 articles to Am. Econ. Rev., Econ. Jour., others. Mem Consensus Forecasting Group Commonwealth of Ky., 2007—. Grantee, NSF, 1978—81; fellow, Ctr. Ops. Rsch. and Econometrics, U. Cath. de Louvain, Belgium, 1986—87, Inst. Study of Labor, U. Bonn, Germany, 2000—; Ameritech fellow, Ind. U., 1988—89, U. Bonn, Germany, 1990. Mem. Am. Econ. Assn., Econometric Soc, Nat. Tax Assn., Tax Inst. Am. Office: U Ky Martin Sch Pub Policy Lexington KY 40506-0027 Office Phone: 859-257-2456. Business E-Mail: dew@davidwildasin.us.

WILDE, DANIEL UNDERWOOD, computer engineering educator; b. Wilmington, Ohio, Dec. 27, 1937; s. Arthur John and Ruby Dale (Underwood) Wilde. BSEE, U. Ill., 1960; MS, M.I.T., 1962, PhD, 1966. Rsch. instr. medicine Boston U. Med. Sch., 1964-66; asst. prof. info. adminstrn. U. Conn., 1966-69, assoc. prof., 1970-75, prof., 1976-85; assoc. dir. New Eng. Rsch. Application Ctr., Storrs, Conn., 1966-72, dir., 1973-85, NASA Indsl. Application Ctr., 1972-91; pres. NERAC, Inc., Tolland, Conn., 1985-99. Cons. NERAC Inc., 1999-2004; trustee Engring. Index, Inc.; cons. Am. Soc. Metals, 1973-76; bd. dirs. Internat. Coun. Sci. Info. Author: Author: Introduction to Computing: Problem Solving, Algorithms and Data Structures, 1973; contbr. articles to profl. jours. With USAF. Recipient NASA Public Service award, 1975 Fellow Nat. Fedn. Abstracting and Indexing Svcs. (hon.), Internat. Coun. Sci. Info. (hon.); mem. IEEE, Am. Soc. Info. Sci., Assn. Computing Machinery, Assn. Info. and Dissemination Centers (sec.-treas. 1976-79, pres. 1979-81).

WILDE, EDWIN FREDERICK, retired mathematics professor; b. Lombard, Ill., Jan. 14, 1931; s. Edwin Frederick and Carrie Belle (Hammond) W.; m. Connie Mae Rawlings, Aug. 23, 1952 (dec. July 2002); children— Brad Alan, Bruce Ramon, Elizabeth Lynn; m. Kathleen Wright, Sept. 25, 2004. BS, Ill. State U., Normal, 1952, MS, 1953; MA, U. Ill., Champaign-Urbana, 1955, PhD, 1959; postgrad., U. Wis., Madison, part time, 1955-58, Stanford U., Calif., 1964-65; PhD in Edn. (hon.), Roger Williams Coll., 1980. With Beloit Coll., Wis., 1955-76, prof. math., dean faculty Wis., 1969-71, v.p. for planning Wis., 1971-75; dean Roger Williams Coll., Bristol, RI, 1976-80; provost, dean of faculty U. Tampa, Fla., 1980-86; vice chancellor U. S.C., Spartanburg, 1986-91, prof. math., 1991-99; ret., 1999. Cons. AID insts., India, 1964, Insts. Internat. Edn., East Pakistan, 1969 NSF Sr. Sci. Faculty fellow, 1964—65, Endowed Professorship in his honor, Beloit Coll., 2008. Mem. Math. Assn. Am. (bd. govs. 1968-69, 72-75). Home: 409 Summit Lake Ct Spartanburg SC 29307 Personal E-mail: efw1931@yahoo.com.

WILDE, HAROLD RICHARD, college president; b. Wauwatosa, Wis., May 14, 1945; s. Harold Richard and Winifred (Wiley) W.; m. Benna Brecher, Feb. 4, 1970; children: Anna, Henry, Elizabeth Ty. BA, Amherst Coll., 1967; MA, PhD, Harvard U., Cambridge, Mass., 1973. Spl. asst. to gov. Office of Gov., State of Wis., Madison, 1972-75; ins. commr. Office of Commr. of Ins., State of Wis., Madison, 1975-79; spl. asst. to pres. U. Wis. System, Madison, 1979-81; v.p. for external affairs Beloit (Wis.) Coll., 1981-91; pres. North Ctrl. Coll., Naperville, Ill., 1991—. Bd. dirs. Ctr. for Pub. Representation, Inc., Madison, 1981-87, Beloit Community Found., 1988-91, Budget Funding Corp., 1993-99, Naperville Devel. Partnership, 1996—. Mem.: Phi Beta Kappa. Home: 329 S Brainard St Naperville IL 60540-5401 Office: North Ctrl Coll 30 N Brainard St Naperville IL 60540-4607 Office Phone: 630-637-5454. Business E-Mail: hrwilde@noctrl.edu.

WILDE, WILLIAM KEY, lawyer; b. Houston, May 3, 1933; s. Henry Dayton and Louise (Key) W.; m. Ann Jeannine Austin, Aug. 3, 1957; children— William Key, Austin, Adrienne, Michael Degree, Coll. William and Mary, Williamsburg, Va., 1955; JD, U. Tex., Austin, 1958. Bar: Tex. 1958. Assoc. Bracewell & Patterson, Houston, 1958-61, ptnr., 1961—. Bd. trustees Montreat Coll. Bd. dirs. Goodwill Industries Houston, 1972—; elder 1st Presbyn. Ch.; trustee Presbyn. Found. U.S.A., Ky., 1983-91; chmn. bd. trustees Schriener Coll., 1991-2000. Fellow ABA, Am. Bar Found., Am. Coll. Trial Lawyers; mem. Tex. Bar Assn. (bd. dirs. 1984-87), Houston Bar Assn. (pres. 1982-83), Houston Club (pres. 1981-82), Houston Country Club (bd. dirs., pres. 1989-90). Republican. Avocations: golf, skiing, scuba diving. Home: 6206 Woods Bridge Way Houston TX 77007-7041 Office: Bracewell & Giuliani 2900 S Tower Pennzoil Pl Houston TX 77002 Home Phone: 713-862-1077; Office Phone: 713-221-1128. Business E-Mail: william.wilde@bgllp.com.

WILDENTHAL, C(LAUD) KERN, physician, educator; b. San Marcos, Tex., July 1, 1941; s. Bryan and Doris (Kellam) W.; m. Margaret Dehlinger, Oct. 15, 1964; children: Pamela, Catharine. BA, Sul Ross Coll., 1960; MD, U. Tex. Southwestern Med. Ctr., Dallas, 1964; PhD, U. Cambridge, Eng., 1970. Intern Bellevue Hosp., NYC, 1964-65; resident in medicine, fellow cardiology Parkland Hosp., Dallas, 1965-67; rsch. fellow Nat. Heart Inst., Bethesda, Md., 1967-68; vis. rsch. fellow Strangeways Rsch. Lab., Cambridge, 1968-70; asst. prof. to prof. internal medicine and physiology U. Tex. Southwestern Med. Ctr., Dallas, 1970-76, prof., dean grad. sch., 1976-80, prof., dean Southwestern Med. Sch., 1980-86, prof., pres., 1986—2008, prof., 2008—; pres. Southwestern Med. Found., 2008—. Hon. fellow Hughes Hall, U. Cambridge, 1994—. Author: Regulation of Cardiac Metabolism, 1976, Degradative Processes in Heart and Skeletal Muscle, 1980; contbr. articles to profl. jours. Bd. dirs. Lasker Found., Dallas Ctr. Performing Arts, Dallas Symphony, Dallas Opera, Dallas Mus. Art, Dallas Citizen's Coun., Dallas Regional C. of C., Cambridge in Am., Hoblitzelle Found., Reves Found. Recipient rsch. career devel. award NIH, 1972; spl. rsch. fellow USPHS, 1968-70; Guggenheim fellow, 1975-76. Mem. AMA, Inst. Medicine/NAS, Am. Soc. Clin. Investigation, Royal Soc. Medicine Gt. Britain, Am. Physiol. Soc., Internat. Soc. Heart Rsch. (past pres. Am. sect.), Am. Fedn. Clin. Rsch., Assn. Am. Physicians, Am. Heart Assn. (past chmn. sci. policy com.), Assn. Acad. Health Ctrs. (past chmn. sci. policy com.), Brit. N.Am. Com. Home: 4001 Hanover Ave Dallas TX 75225-7010 Office: Southwestern Med Found 2305 Cedar Springs Rd Dallas TX 75201-7805 Office Phone: 214-351-6143.

WILDER, BRENDA, music specialist; b. Macon, Miss., Oct. 4, 1951; d. Roy Thomas and Martha Loraine Box; m. Donald Krecker Wilder, Jan. 29, 1983; children: Susannah, Joey. BA in music edn., Miss. State Univ., Starkville, MS, 1973; MA in music edn., Miss. Univ. for Women, Columbus, MS, 1977; PhD in Edn. Admin., Univ. Miss., Oxford, MS, 1991. Staff musician Mt. Sales Presbyterian Ch., Clinton, 1995-99, music cons., 1955-99; piano instr. pvt., Clinton, MS, 1984-99; adj. music instr. Belhaven Coll., Jackson, MS, 1997-99, Hinds Com. Coll., Pearl, MS, 1997-99. Adjudicator, Nat. Piano Guild, Austin, TX, 1995-99, fac. mem. So. Bapt. Convention, Glorieta, New Mexico, 1995, 98, Ridgecrest, NC, 1996, Hinds Piano Camp, Raymond, Miss., 1996. Freelance author; contbr. articles to profl. jours. Commnr. Clinton Baseball Assn., Clinton, MS, 1990, chmn. MMTA Festival, Raymond, MS, 1994, 96, Nat. Fedn. of Music Clubs, Clinton, MS, 1985, 86. Mem. Nat. Guild of Piano Tchrs. (adjudicator), 1994-99, Music Forum of Jackson (bd. mem.), 1991-99, Nat. Music Tchrs. Assn., 1991-99, Metro Piano Tchrs. League, 1995-99, Miss. Music Tchrs. Assn., 1991-99, Phi Kappa Phi, 1991-99. Republican. Baptist. Avocations: playing piano, singing, computer, family. Home: 1735 Clinton Raymond Rd Clinton MS 39056-9622 E-mail: dbwilder@worldnet.att.net.

WILDER, CHARLES DAVID, lawyer; b. Orlando, Fla., Aug. 6, 1948; s. Thomas Vaughn and Virginia (McKinney) W. BA, U. South Fla., 1970; JD cum laude, Nova Southeastern U. Ctr. for Study of Law, 1980; LLM in Taxation, U. Fla., 1981. Bar: Fla. 1980, US Dist. Ct. (mid. dist. Fla.) 1980, US Supreme Ct., 2007; cert. Fla. Bar (wills, trusts and estates). Mgr. So. Bell Tel. Co., Miami, Fla., 1970-77; assoc. Broad & Cassel, Orlando, Fla., 1981-84; pvt. practice Orlando, 1984-85; ptnr. Johnson & Wilder, Orlando, 1985-88, Dittmer & Wilder, Maitland, Fla., 1988-92, Wilder & Culton, Maitland, Fla., 1992-94, Wilder & Assocs., Winter Park, Fla., 1994-95, Wilder & Berkson, Winter Park, Fla., 1995; founder, sr. atty. Estate Planning & Legacy Law Ctr., Maitland, Fla. Named one of Top 100 Attys., Worth mag., 2005. Mem. Fla. Bar Assn. (exec. coun. real property probate & trust law sect. 1994), Orange County Bar Assn. (estate planning com. 1984), Estate Planning Discussion Grp. (chmn. 1985). Republican. Avocations: water sports, photography, dance. Office: Estate Planning and Legacy Law Ctr PLC 159 Lookout Pl Ste 101 Maitland FL 32751 Office Phone: 407-647-7526. Office Fax: 407-644-2194. Business E-Mail: cwilder@epllc-plc.com.

WILDER, DAVID RANDOLPH, retired materials engineer; b. Lorimor, Iowa, June 11, 1929; s. Rex Marshall and Ethel Marie (Busch) W.; m. Donna Jean Moore, June 17, 1951; children: Susan, Michael, Margaret, Bruce. BS, Iowa State U., 1951, MS, 1952, PhD, 1958. Registered profl. engr., Iowa (inactive). Engr. Ames Lab., 1951-81; faculty mem. dept. materials sci. and engring. Iowa State U., Ames, 1955—, prof. engring., chmn. dept., 1961-89, prof. engring., 1989-91, prof. emeritus, 1991—; cons. to various industries, fed. agys, 1955—. Contbr. numerous tech. paper to profl. lit.; patentee in field. Fellow Am. Ceramic Soc., Accreditation Bd. for Engring. and Tech.; mem. Nat. Inst. Ceramic Engrs., Am. Soc. for Engring. Edn., Keramos. Home: 1214 Ridgewood Ave Ames IA 50010-5208

WILDER, DOUG (LAWRENCE DOUGLAS WILDER), Mayor, Richmond, Virginia, former governor; b. Richmond, Va., Jan. 17, 1931; children: Lynn, Larry, Loren. BS, Va. Union U., 1951; JD, Howard U., 1959; Ph.D (hon.), Ariz. State U., 2004. Bar: Va. Mem. Va. State Senate, 1969-85; lt. gov. State of Va., 1986-89, gov., 1989-93; Al Douglas Wilder Disting. prof. Va. Commonwealth U., 1988—; mayor City of Richmond, 2005—. Del. Democratic Nat. Conv., 1980; agt. NAACP Legal Def. Fund. Bd. dirs. United Givers Fund; chmn. bd. Red Shield Boys' Club. Served with U.S. Army, 1952-53 Decorated Bronze Star; recipient Spingarn Medal, NAACP, 1990, Anna Eleanor Roosevelt Medallion of Honor, Thurgood Marshall Award of Excellence; named one of 100 Most Influential Black Americans, Ebony mag., 2006; named to Power 150, 2008. Mem. ABA, Va. Bar Assn., Nat. Bar Assn., Am. Judicature Soc., C. of C., Urban League (bd. dirs. Richmond), Omega Psi Phi. Clubs: Masons; Shriners. Democrat. Baptist. Achievements include becoming the first African-American to be elected governor in the U.S., 1989. Office: Virginia Commonwealth Univ 919 W Franklin St PO Box 842028 Richmond VA 23284-2028 also: Mayor's Office Rm 201 900 E Broad St Richmond VA 23219 Office Phone: 804-828-4971, 804-646-7970. Office Fax: 804-646-7987.

WILDER, DWIGHT SAFFORD, academic administrator; b. Plainfield, NJ, Dec. 24, 1946; s. Glenn Safford and Marion Seaver (Fiske) W.; children: Thomas, Douglas; m. Margaret Ruth Holland, Sept. 9, 1995. BA, Johns Hopkins U., 1969; postgrad., Harvard U., 1969-70; MBA, So. N.H. U., 1981; postgrad., Rivier Coll., 2002—03. Mem. faculty Hebron (Maine) Acad., 1969-70; assoc. dir. continuing edn. N.H. Coll., Manchester, 1975-78, seminar adminstr., 1978-80, asst. to dean, 1980-84; program design specialist N.H. Job Tng. Council, Concord, 1984-89; apprentice program mgr. Portsmouth Naval Shipyard, 1989-92; coord. Seacoast Tech. Prep. Consortium, 1992-96; sch.-to-career coord. Timberlane Sch. Dist., Plaistow, NH, 1996—2004, asst. prin., 2004—. Mng. editor Jour. Ednl. Computing Research, 1983-84. Mem. Cold River Camp Com., 1999— Mem. Appalachian Mountain Club (vol. educator and cons., 1975—, sec. North Country bd. 1980-87), N.H. Sch. Prins. Assn., Chatham Trails Assn. (pres. 2002-05), Old Johannian Assn. (U.S. rep. 2001—), Toastmasters (pres. Navy Brunswick chpt. 1973-74, pres. Manchester chpt. 1982-83), Nat. Assn. Sec. Sch. Prins. Avocations: hiking, painting. Home: 15 Pinecrest Dr Somersworth NH 03878 Office: Timberlane Sch Dist 36 Greenough Rd Plaistow NH 03865 Home Phone: 603-692-6898; Office Phone: 603-382-6541. Personal E-mail: dwilder@timberlanehs.com.

WILDER, ELMON, retired university administrator; b. Macon, Ga., July 23, 1937; s. Elmer and Ethel M. (Harris) W. BA, U. Buffalo, 1970, MBA, JD, 1975. Fiscal and budget analyst pub. services and careers Model Cities Program, Buffalo, 1972-73; legal asst. Stevens & Berger, Buffalo, 1974-75; spl. asst. to pres. N.Y. State Civil Service Commn., Albany, NY, 1975-76; paralegal, fin. and mgmt. analyst Harambee House, Washington, 1978; fiscal and bus. mgr. phys. facility mgmt. Howard U., Washington, 1978—2004, dir. program control adminstrn., 1994—99, program mgr., 1998—2004. Mem. Shiloh Bapt. Ch. Mem. NB/MBA Assn., Piano Technicians Guild, NAACP, Phi Alpha Delta, Alpha Phi Alpha, Fin. and Tax Analysts. Home: 6305 Juanita Ct Suitland MD 20746-3769 Personal E-mail: emon6305@aol.com.

WILDER, GENE (JERRY SILBERMAN), actor, film director, writer; b. Milw., June 11, 1935; s. William J. and Jeanne (Baer) Silberman; m. Mary Joan Schutz, Oct. 27, 1967 (div. 1974); 1 child, Katharine Anastasia; m. Gilda Radner, 1984 (dec.); m. Karen Boyer, Sept. 8, 1991. BA, U. Iowa, 1955; postgrad., Bristol Old Vic Theatre Sch., 1955-56. Appeared in Broadway play: The Complaisant Lover, 1962 (Clarence Derwent award); appeared in London production of Laughter on the 23rd Floor, 1996; actor: (films) Bonnie and Clyde, 1967, The Producers, 1967 (Acad. award nom. best supporting actor), Start the Revolution Without Me, 1968, Quackser Fortune Has a Cousin in the Bronx, 1969, Willy Wonka and the Chocolate Factory, 1970, Everything You Always Wanted to Know About Sex But Were Afraid to Ask, 1972, Rhinoceros, 1972, Blazing Saddles, 1973, The Little Prince, 1974, Silver Streak, 1976, The Frisco Kid, 1979, Stir Crazy, 1980, Hanky Panky, 1982, See No Evil, Hear No Evil, 1989, Funny About Love, 1990, Another You, 1991; (TV films) Murder in a Small Town, 1999, Alice in Wonderland, 1999, The Lady in Question, 1999; dir., writer, actor: (films) The Adventures of Sherlock Holmes' Smarter Brother, 1975, The World's Greatest Lover, 1977, Sunday Lovers, 1980, The Woman in Red, 1984, Haunted Honeymoon, 1986; actor, co-writer: (films): Young Frankenstein, 1974; actor: (TV appearances) The Defenders, 1962, The DuPont Show of the Week, 1962-63, The Scarecrow, 1972, The Trouble With People, 1973, Marlo Thomas Spl., 1973, Thursday's Games, 1973,The Frank Skinner Show, 1997, Will & Grace, 2002-03 (Emmy award best guest actor 2003); (TV series) Something Wilder, 1994-95; author: Kiss Me Like a Stranger: My Search for Love and Art, 2005, My French Whore, 2006, The Woman Who Wouldn't, 2008 Campaigned with Elaine May and Rene Taylor for Eugene McCarthy, Allard Lowenstein and Paul O'Dwyer, 1968. Served with U.S. Army, 1956-58. Actors Equity Assn., Am. Federation of Television & Radio Artists, DGA, WGA.

WILDER, JANET MARY, performing company executive; d. Robert and Jean; m. Ward Wilder; children: Suzanne, Robert. BS, U. Colo., 1966. Cecchetti tchr. cert. Cecchetti Coun. Am., tchr. cert. Chgo. Nat. Dance Masters Assn., tchg. cert. Calif. Tchr. Santa Venetia Mid. Sch., San Rafael, Calif., 1967—68; fitness/dance instr. Am. Wives' Club, Ghedi, Brescia, Italy, 1969—71; instr. Julie Ward Sch. Dance, Rapid City, SD, 1972—77, Spokane Ballet, Wash., 1981—83, Capitol City Ballet, Sacramento, 1985—87, Marguerite Phares Sch. Dance, Sacramento, 1985—87; artistic dir. Dakota Repertory Dance Co., Rapid City, 1975—77, San Antonio Dance Theatre, 1983—85, Dance Theatre NW, Spokane, 1994—2004, Ballet Spokane, 2003—; instr., co-dir. Entenman Sch. Dance, Bellvue, Nebr., 1978—81; dancer Omaha Ballet, 1979—81; dir. Ballet Arts, San Antonio, 1983—85; co-dir. Ballet Arts Acad., Spokane, 1987—94; co-founder, dir. Theatre Ballet Spokane, 1987—94; choreographer/prodr./dir. Coeur d'Alene (Idaho) Summer Theatre, 1991—96; resident choreographer Spokane/Coeur d'Alene Opera, 1987—; owner, dir. Acad. Dance, Spokane Valley, Wash., 1994—. Founder/mem. Inland NW Dance Assn., Spokane, 1989—; ballet adv. bd. mem. Greater Spokane Music & Allied Arts Festival, 1988—2000, MusicFest NW, Spokane, 2000—; dance edn. del. to China People to People, Bejing, 1996. Author: (book) Terms Every Dancer Should Know; writer, prodr., dir.: (ballets) The Toy Shelf; choreographer (over 150 ballets, operas & musicals). Mem. Rapid City Svc. League, 1975—77; mem./officer PTA, Rapid City, 1975—77; com. mem. First Night Spokane, 2003; mem. entertainment com. Diamonds & Divas, Spokane, 2000—05. Recipient Outstanding Mem., Ghedi Air Force Wives' Club, 1971, Ellsworth Officer's Wives' Club, 1977, Outstanding Young Women of Am., Outstanding Young Women of Am. program, 1973, Wash. State Dance Sch. Dir., Dance Excellence Internat. Festival for Young Dancers, 1992—95, Bowl Games of Am./CocaCola Olympic City, 1996, Jim Chase Asset builder, Chase Youth Commn., 1997, Dir. in charge - Teen Group Creativity Award, 2000, Dir. in charge - Teen Group Cmty. Svc. Hon. Mention, 2001. Mem.: Nat. Dance Edn. Orgn., Nat. Dance Assn., MusicFest NW, Inland NW Dance Assn. (v.p. 2002—04). Avocations: writing, scuba diving, skiing, boating. Personal E-mail: janetwilder123@aol.com.

WILDER, JOHN SHELTON, state legislator, former lieutenant governor; b. Fayette City, Tenn., June 3, 1921; s. John Chamblee and Martha (Shelton) W.; m. Marcelle Morton, Dec. 31, 1941; children: John Shelton Wilder, II, David Morton. Student, U. Tenn.; LLB, U. Memphis, 1957. Bar: Tenn. 1957. Engaged in farming, Longtown, Tenn., 1943—; supr. mgmt. Longtown Supply Co.; judge Fayette County Ct.; mem. Tenn. Senate, 1959—60, 1966—; lt. gov., spkr. senate State of Tenn., 1971—2006. Past pres. Nat. Assn. Soil Conservation Dists., Tenn. Soil Conservation Assn., Tenn. Agrl. Council; exec. com. So. Legis. Conf., Conf. Lt. Govs.; dir. Bank Tenn., Cumberland Bank; chmn. Cumberland BanCorp, Inc. Served with U.S. Army, 1942-43. Mem. Tenn. Cotton Ginners Assn. (past pres.), Shriner, Scottish Rite, Mason, Delta Theta Phi. Clubs: Shriners. Democrat. Methodist. Office: Tenn State Senate 4020 Highway 59 Mason TN 38049

WILDER, LYNN K., education educator; d. E. W. Wieting and Elizabeth L. (Bets) Schneider; m. Michael D. Wilder, Dec. 28, 1974; children: Joshua, Matthias, Micah; 1 child, Katie Warren. PhD in Edn., Ball State U., Muncie, Ind., 1999. Lic. tchr. Ind., 1975. Assoc. prof. spl. edn. Brigham Young U., Provo, Utah, 1999—2007, dir. culturally responsive spl. edn. English as 2nd lang. program, 2004—07; program leader, spl. edn. and early childhood edn. Fla. Gulf Coast U., Fort Myers, 2007—. Contbr. articles to profl. jours. Named Excelencia in Edn., ESL Program, 2007; grantee, Office Spl. Edn. Programs, 2004—08. Mem.: Nat. Assn. Multicultural Edn., Coun. Exceptional Children. Achievements include research in Numerous publications. Office: Fla Gulf Coast Univ 10501 FGCU Blvd S Fort Myers FL 33965 Office Fax: 239-590-7801. Business E-Mail: lwilder@fgcu.edu.

WILDER, RONALD PARKER, economics professor; b. Freeport, Tex., Jan. 15, 1941; s. J. Barton and Lois (Parker) W.; m. Charlotte D. Pearson, Sept. 4, 1965; children: Erika, Rachel, David. BA, Rice U., 1963, MA, 1964; PhD, Vanderbilt U., 1969. Asst. prof. econs. U. S.C., Columbia, 1970-75, assoc. prof., 1975-80, prof., 1980—2006, prof. emeritus, 2006—, chmn. dept. econs., 1987—2002. Co-author: Stock Life Insurance Profitability, 1986; mem. editorial bd. So. Econ. J., 1978-80; contbr. articles to profl. jours. Capt. U.S. Army, 1968-70. Fellow Ford Found., Vanderbilt U., 1964-65. Mem. Am. Econ. Assn., So. Econ. Assn., Omicron Delta Epsilon. United Methodist. Avocations: hiking, canoeing. Office: U of SC Dept Of Econs Columbia SC 29208-0001

WILDEROTTER, JAMES ARTHUR, lawyer; b. Newark, July 25, 1944; s. Arthur Walter and Dorothy Theresa (King) W.; children: James, Kristin, Kathryn. BA, Georgetown U., 1966; JD, U. Ill., 1969. Bar: D.C. 1969, U.S. Supreme Ct. 1974. Assoc. Covington & Burling, Washington, 1969-71; spl. asst. to Under Sec. Commerce, Washington, 1971-73; exec. asst. to Sec. HUD, Washington, 1973-74; assoc. dept. atty. gen. U.S. Washington, 1974-75; assoc. counsel to Pres. U.S., 1975-76; gen. counsel U.S. Energy Research and Devel. Adminstrn., Washington, 1976-77; of counsel Morgan, Lewis & Bockius, Washington, 1977-78; ptnr. Jones, Day, Reavis & Pogue, Washington, 1978—91, 1995—2006; v.p., gen. counsel Internat. Paper Co., Purchase, NY, 1991-94; gen. counsel U. S. Trade and Devel. Agy., Washington, 2006—. Editor in chief: U. Ill. Law Rev., 1968-69. Gen. counsel rules com. Rep. Nat. Conv., 1980; sec. James S. Brady Presdl. Found., 1982-88; gen. counsel Nat. Sudden Infant Death Syndrome Found., 1986-90, sec. Sudden Infant Death Syndrome Alliance, 1990-93. With USN, 1962-68. Mem. ABA Republican. Roman Catholic. Home: 5903 Mount Eagle Dr Alexandria VA 22303 Office: US Trade and Devel Agy 1000 Wilson Blvd Ste 1600 Arlington VA 22209 Office Phone: 202-879-3832. Personal E-mail: jawilder@yahoo.com. Business E-Mail: jwilderotter@ustda.gov.

WILDEROTTER, MAGGIE (MARY AGNES WILDEROTTER), software company executive, former cable television executive; b. Neptune, NJ, Feb. 9, 1955; d. Denis James and Constance Rosemary (Shields) Sullivan; m. Philip Jay Wilderotter; children: Christopher, Daniel. BA in Economics and Bus. Adminstrn., Holy Cross Coll., 1977. Accts. receivable supr. CableData, Sacramento, 1979-80, mgr. acctg. svcs., 1980-82, mgr. reg. support, 1982, mktg. mgr., 1982-83, dir. mktg., 1983, dir. nat. accts., 1983-85, v.p., 1985—87, sr. v.p., sales & mktg., 1987—91; sr. v.p. McCaw Cellular Communications, 1991—95; exec. v.p., nat. ops. & CEO, Aviation Communications div. AT&T Wireless Svcs., Inc., 1995—97; pres., CEO Wink Communications, 1997—2002; sr. v.p., worldwide pub. sector Microsoft Corp., 2002—04; pres., CEO Frontier Communications Co., 2004—06, chmn., CEO, 2006—. Bd. dirs. McClatchy Co., Phoenix Cable Ptnrs., San Rafael, Calif., 1988-, Satellite Video Ctr., Rancho Cordova, Calif., 1988-, CableData Europe Ltd., Leeds, Eng., 1989-, Tribune Co., Catalyst Inc., Frontier Communications Co., 2004-, Xerox Corp., 2006-, Yahoo! Inc., 2007-, bd. dirs. Procter & Gamble Co., 2009- Trustee Coll. of the Holy Cross. Recipient Top 10 Women in Cable & Telecommunications award, Women in Cable and Telecommunications Found., 1989, Outstanding Mentor award, 1999, Vanguard award for Disting. Leadership, Nat. Cable TV Assn., 1989, 2000 (one of only 20 individuals to have received two of these awards since its inception). Mem. Nat. Cable TV Assn. (bd. dirs. 1987-), Women in Cable (exec. mem.), Cable TV Adminstrn. & Mktg. Soc., Calif. Cable TV Assn., Nat. Acad. Cable Programming. Republican. Roman Catholic. Office: Frontier Communications 3 High Ridge Park Stamford CT 06905-1390 Office Phone: 203-614-5600. Office Fax: 203-614-4602. Business E-Mail: mwilderotter@czn.com.*

WILDERSON, FRANK B., III, performing arts educator, writer; b. New Orleans, Apr. 11, 1956; s. Frank B. and Ida-Lorraine Wilderson; life ptnr. Anita Delores Wilkins; m. Kamogelo Lekubu, July 7, 1990 (div. Dec. 2, 2000); 1 child, Rebaabetswe Khanya. AB, Dartmouth Coll., Hanover, NH, 1980; MFA in Fiction Writing, Columbia U., NYC, 1991; PhD in Rhetoric, Film Studies, U. Calif., Berkeley, 2004. Elected ofcl., cadre African Nat. Congress, Johannesburg, 1991—96; cmty. organizer, trainer Khanya Coll., Soweto, Johannesburg, 1992—93; lectr. U. Witwatersrand, Johannesburg, 1992, Vista U., Soweto, Transvaal, South Africa, 1993—95; writer Berkeley, 1997—2005; asst. prof. U. Calif., Irvine, 2005—09, assoc. prof., 2009—. Author: (book) Incognegro: a Memoir of Exile and Apartheid (Am. Book award, Before Columbus Found., 2008), Red, White & Black: Cinema and the Structure of US Antagonisms, 2010. Mem.: Cinema Studies Assn., Am. Studies Assn. Office: Univ Calif Irvine 3226 Humanities Gateway Irvine CA 92697-6850 Office Fax: 949-824-7006. Business E-Mail: fwilders@uci.edu.

WILDHACK, WILLIAM AUGUST, JR., lawyer; b. Takoma Park, Md., Nov. 28, 1935; s. William August and Martha Elizabeth (Parks) W.; m. Martha Moore Allston, Aug. 1, 1959; children: William A. III, Elizabeth L. BS, Miami U., Oxford, Ohio, 1957; JD, George Washington U., 1963. Bar: Va. 1963, D.C. 1965, Md. 1983, U.S. Supreme Ct. 1967. Agt. IRS, Va., 1957-65; pvt. prac. Washington, 1965—69; v.p., corp. counsel B.F. Saul Co. and affiliates, Chevy Chase, Md., 1969-87, Chevy Chase Bank, F.S.B. and affiliates, 1987-90; atty. pvt. practice, Arlington, Va., 1990—. Sec. B.F. Saul Real Estate Investment Trust, Chevy Chase, 1972-87. Mem. ABA, Md. Bar Assn., D.C. Bar, Va. Bar, Arlington County Bar Assn. (chmn. trusts and estates sect. 2002—), Nat. Acad. Elder Law Attys., Soc. Corp. Secretaries and Governance Profls. Business E-Mail: waw@wildhacklaw.com.

WILDIN, ROBERT, medical geneticist; BS, MIT, Cambridge, 1981; MD, U. Calif San Francisco, 1985. Diplomate Am. Bd. Pediat., 1989, Am. Bd. Med. Genetics, 1993. Owner Epintell LLC, Portland, Oreg., 2006—; clin. geneticist Idaho Dept. Health & Welfare, Boise, 2004—. Office: Robert Wildin MD Epintell LLC 6140 SW 41st Ave Portland OR 97221 Business E-Mail: bob@epintell.com.

WILDING, DIANE, computer scientist, consultant; b. Chgo. Heights, Nov. 7, 1942; d. Michael Edward and Katherine Surian; m. Manfred Georg Wilding, May 7, 1975 (div. 1980). BSBA in Acctg. magna cum laude, No. Ill. U., DeKalb, 1963; postgrad., U. Chgo., 1972—74; cert. in German lang., Goethe Inst., Rothenburg, Germany, 1984; cert. in internat. bus. German, Goethe Inst., Atlanta, 1994; cert. in Web page design, Kennesaw State U., Ga., 2000. Lic. cosmetologist. Sys. engr. IBM, Chgo., 1963-68, SAP cons. Atlanta, 1993—; data processing mgr. Am. Res. Corp., Chgo., 1969-72; system R & D project mgr. Continental Bank, Chgo., 1972-75; fin. industry mktg. rep. IBM Can., Ltd., Toronto, Ont., 1976-79; regional telecom. mktg. exec. Control Data Corp., Atlanta, 1980-84; gen. mgr. The Plant Plant, Atlanta, 1985-92. Pioneer installer on-line automatic teller machines Pos Equipment. Author: The Canadian Payment System: An International Perspective, 1977. Mem. Chgo. Coun. Fgn. Rels.; bd. dirs. Easter House Adoption Agy., Chgo., 1974—76. Mem.: Internat. Brass Soc., Mensa, Goethe Inst., Libertyville Racquet Club, Royal Ont. Yacht Club, Ponte Verde Club (Fla.). Avocations: travel, gourmet cooking, languages, antiques. Office Phone: 770-850-9161. Personal E-mail: diane.wilding@gmail.com.

WILDING, GREGORY EDWARD, statistician, educator; b. Batavia, NY, May 12, 1974; PhD in Stats., U. Rochester, NY, 2002. Asst. prof. SUNY, Buffalo, 2003—; asst. chair Roswell Pk. Cancer Inst., Buffalo, 2005—. Office: State Univ NY Buffalo 3435 Main St Buffalo NY 14214-3000

WILDMAN, IRIS J., retired law librarian; b. Chgo., May 10, 1930; d. Isadore and Stella (Stark) W. BS, Northwestern U., Evanston, Ill., 1952; MLS, Case Western Res. U., 1954; JD, Santa Clara U., 1978. Asst. cataloger U. Chgo. Law Libr., 1952-53; cataloger Copyright Office/Libr. of Congress, 1954; law cataloger U.S. Army Libr./Pentagon, 1954-56; cataloger U.S. Dept. of Justice Libr., Washington, 1956-57; head tech. svcs. Ohio State U. Law Libr., Columbus, 1957-59, Skokie (Ill.) Pub. Libr., 1959-60; head cataloging and classification Northwestern U. Law Libr., Chgo., 1961-64; chief acquisitions and binding Yale Law Libr., New Haven, 1965-74; pub. svcs. libr. Stanford U. Law Libr., 1976-85; sr. reference and spl. projects libr. Robert Crown Law Libr. Stanford (Calif.) U., 1985-95; ret. Cons. Corp. Counsel, Govt., Washington D.C. Libr., 1957, U. P.R. Law Libr., 1968; faculty/dir. AALL Institutes on Cataloging, Classification and Acquisitions, 1966, 70, 73; libr./lectr. Stanford Law Sch., 1978-82, 85-93. Compiler: Federal Judges and Justices, 1987-2001; editor: Law Libraries in the U.S. and Can., 1958, Directory of Law Librs., 1964, 66; indexer: Index to Foreign Legal Periodicals, 1983-2000; contbr. articles to profl. jours. Mem. No. Calif. Assn. Law Librs. (v.p., pres. elect 1980-82, Profl. Achievement award, 1999), Am. Assn. Law Librs. Avocations: writing, reading, photography, gardening. Home: 22399 Cupertino Rd #11 Cupertino CA 95014 Business E-Mail: iwildman@stanford.edu.

WILDMAN, KENNETH N., professor emeritus of psychology; b. NYC, 1942; s. P. and S. Wildman; married; children: Kevin, Jason. PhD, Fla. State U., Tallahassee, 1969. Asst. prof. psychology Fla. A & M U., Tallahassee, 1967—71; assoc. prof. psychology Nathaniel Hawthorne Coll., Antrim, NH, 1971—74; prof., chair emeritus psychology Ohio Northern U., Ada, Ohio, 1974—2001. Cons. Monadnock Workshop, Peterborough, NH, 1972—74, Crotched Mountain Rehab. Ctr., Peterborough, 1972—74, State Dept. Edn., Concord, NH, 1973—74, NH. State Hosp., Concord; v.p. Personal HealthCare Sys., Inc., Lima, Ohio, 1978—81; ednl. cons. Timex Computer Corp., 1981—82; mem. Steering Com., Nat. Coun. Undergrad. Psychology Programs, 1988—90; mediator, arbitrator, prin. Positive Negotiations, Ada, 1997—. Contbr. scientific papers. Mem. Drug Abuse Prevention Adv. Coun., Corcord, 1974—74; cons. Area Agy. Aging, Lima, 1976—77; bd. dirs. Tri-Star Cmty. Mental Health Ctr., Lima, 1982—2002; commr. Village Planning Commn., Ada, 2007—09; mem. Ceara Brazil Prtnrs. Americas, Concord, NH, 1973—74, Family Resource Ctr. Mental Health Ctr., Lima, 2000—04; reviewer- drug abuse mental health standards Joint Commn. Accreditation Hosps., 1975—75; mem. arbitration com. Nfld. Club Am., 2008—09. Recipient Commendation award, Gov. NH., 1973. Mem.: Ohio Mediation Assn. Office: Positive Negotiations 419 N Johnson St Ada OH 45810

WILDMAN, PETER ROBERTS, mathematics professor; b. Glendale, Calif., Aug. 18, 1959; s. Neol Roberts and Maria Anna Wildman; m. Karen Louise Muehl, June 15, 1985; children: Daniel, Andrew, Matthew. BA, Occidental Coll., 1981; MS, N.Mex. State U., 1992. Instr. Murlborough Sch., LA, 1982—90; asst. N.Mex. State U., Las Cruces, N.Mex., 1990—92; instr. math. Casper (Wyo.) Coll., 1992—. Co-dir. Wyo. Math and Sci. Coalition, Casper, 1995—2003. Bd. dirs., fundraiser Sci. Zone Mus., Casper, 2004—; cubmaster, den leader Boy Scouts Am., Casper, 1997—. Mem.: Nat. Coun. Tchrs. Math., Math. Asn. Am., Wyo. Math. Assn. Two Yr. Colls. (pres. 2000—02), Am. Math. Tchrs. Two Yr. Coll. (v.p. ctrl. region 2004—, Tchr. Excellence award 2001), Phi Theta Kappa (Tchg. award 2004). Democrat. Baptist. Office: Casper Coll 125 College Dr Casper WY 82601 Home: 37 E 26th Ave Spokane WA 99203-2421 Office Phone: 307-268-2506.

WILDNAUER, RICHARD HARRY, pharmaceutical executive; b. New Kensington, Pa., Feb. 14, 1940; s. Richard Michael and Rosemary Elizabeth (Moore) Wildnauer; m. Sharon Ann Novick, Jan. 22, 1966; 1 child, Tara Lynne. BS in Chemistry, St. Vincent Coll., 1962; PhD in BioChemistry, W.Va. U., 1966; MBA in Mgmt., Rider U., 1974. NIH trainee W.Va. U., 1963—66; sr. rsch. assoc. in skin biology, exploratory rsch. divsn. Johnson & Johnson Domestic Operating Co., New Brunswick, NJ, 1967—75, assoc. mgr. tech. planning, exploratory rsch. divsn., 1975—77; sr. project coord. new products, pharm. divsn. McNeil Labs., Ft. Washington, Pa., 1977—79; dir. new product devel. Janssen Pharmaceutica Inc., New Brunswick, 1979—82, v.p. R&D, 1982—88; v.p. tech. and bus. devel. Johnson & Johnson Corp., New Brunswick, 1988—92; pres. Baker Cummins Dermatologicals, Inc., Lakewood, NJ, 1992—95; pres., CEO NeoStrata Co., Inc., Princeton, NJ, 1995—2007; founder RHW Assoc. LLC, East Brunswick, NJ, 2007—. Contbr. articles to profl. jours. Trustee, bd. dirs. United Way Ctrl. N.J., 1988—95, pres., 1991—93. Mem.: Nat. Assn. Corp. Dirs., Soc. Co. Chemists, NY Acad. Scis., Soc. Investigative Dermatology, Am. Acad. Dermatology (life), Sigma Xi. Roman Catholic. Office: RHW Assoc LLC 6 Pilgrim Run East Brunswick NJ 08816 Business E-Mail: rhwildnauer@aol.com.

WILDONER, NANCY SCHAMU, music educator, fine arts department chairman; b. Syracuse, NY, June 8, 1957; d. Frederick William and Marlyn Meyer Schamu; m. Robert Sterling Wildoner, Aug. 15, 1987; children: Melody June, Robert Sterling III. BA in Music Edn., Fredonia State U., 1979; MusM, Binghamton U., 1983; studied organ with M. Searle Wright and Paul Jordan. Tchng. Cert. NY. Music tchr. Norwich Sch. Dist., NY, 1979—81; grad. asst. Binghamton U., NY, 1981—83; substitute tchr. Broome County, Binghamton, NY, 1983—85; K-12 music tchr., chair fine arts dept. Chenango Forks Sch., Binghamton, NY, 1984—; choir dir., organist First Congregational Ch., Binghamton, NY, 2002—. Church organist various chs., 1977—2005; pvt. piano and organ tchr., Binghamton, NY, 2001—. Womens aux. mem. Sanitaria Springs Fire Dept., NY, 1989—2005. Mem.: Broome County Music Educators Assn. (mem. exec. coun. 2000—), NY Sch. Music Assn., Music Educators Nat. Conf., Am. Guild of Organists. Protestant. Avocations: theater, travel. Home: 778 Brotzman Rd Binghamton NY 13901 Office: Chenango Forks HS 1 Gordon Dr Binghamton NY 13901 Business E-Mail: wildonern@cforks.org.

WILDS, DANIEL O., health products executive; BA, Calif. State U., LA; MBA, Northwestern U., Evanston, Ill. With Baxter Internat., 1968—92, pres. chemotherapy svc. divsn., pres., COO diagnostic joint venture with Genentech, gen. mgr. Mexico City ops., gen. mgr. Container Devel. Bus. Ctr., dir. strategy devel., v.p. corp. alliances; pres., CEO Medisense, Inc., Adeza Biomed. Corp., 1992—96, Shiloov Biotechnologies (USA) Inc., 1997—98; pres., CEO, dir. Northwest Biotherapeutics, Inc., Boethell, Wash., 1998—.

WILE, JOAN, composer, lyricist, singer, author; b. Rochester, NY, July 17, 1931; d. Louis and Janet Louise (Wile) Meltzer; children: Ron Wasserman, Diana Wasserman McCloskey. BA, U. Chgo., 1952. Freelance composer, lyricist, singer, mus. book writer. Author: Grandmothers Against the War: Getting Off Our Fannies and Standing Up for Peace, 2008; rec. artist Vanguard Records, 1954; singer Storyville, 1954, The Crystal Palace, 1957; mem. vocal-revue act The Neighbors performances include The Village Vanguard, Le Ruban Bleu, The Bon Soir and The Living Room; singer, lyricist feature film The Happy Hooker, 1974; singer radio and TV jingles, movie sound tracks, supper clubs, hotels, TV music spls. and variety shows; lyricist, composer mus. Tobacco Road, 1974, Seven Ages of Woman, 1987 (named most promising new musical); writer, producer When They Turned on the Tap at the Watergate, The Truth Come Pourin' Out; lyricist songs for Romper Room, 1983; lyricist, composer, writer People is People, 1983; lyricist, composer script for children's albums for Golden and Peter Pan Records, others; lyricist, composer material in Julius Monk's Upstairs at the Downstairs, 1958; lyricist, composer, performer Nancy's Economic Plan, 1980; lyricist, composer Mothers and Daughters, 1984; lyricist, composer; librettist The Symposium, 1987; lyricist, composer From There to Here, 1987; writer Rhyme, Women and Song; lyricist, librettist, composer Museum of Natural Sex History, 1992; composer Women Walking, 1997, composer-lyricist What A Woman (Homage to Peggy Lee), 2003; founder, singer The NY Granny Chicks, 2005. Organizer Women in Def. Eleanor Roosevelt, NYC, 1989—; founder, dir. Grandmothers Against the War, 2003; founder, organizer Revolt Against the Tax Refund, 2001; founder Granny Peace Brigade, 2005. Runner-up Am. Song Festival, 1976 Mem.: ASCAP (Popular award 1970—2008), AFTRA, SAG, Theatre Artists Workshop, Dramatists Guild, Soc. of Singers (bd. dirs.). Avocations: politics, singing, writing. Home and Office: 263 West End Ave Apt 4B New York NY 10023-2613 E-mail: joanwile@grandmothersagainstthewar.org.

WILENCHIK, DENNIS I., lawyer; b. NYC, Sept. 27, 1952; s. Eugene and Shirley (Lassoff) W.; m. Becky Ann Bartness, Aug. 30, 1978; children: John Douglas, Caitlin Bartness. BA magna cum laude, CUNY, 1974; JD, S. Tex. Coll. of Law, 1977. Bar: Ariz. 1978, US Dist. Ct. Ariz. 1978, US Ct. Appeals (9th cir.) 1978, US Supreme Ct. 1988, US Dist. Ct. (no. dist.) Tex. 1990, cert. Civil Trial adv., Nat. bd. Trial Advocacy. Bailiff to presiding criminal judge Ariz. Superior Ct., Phoenix, 1977; clk. intern, under Chief Staff atty. Ariz. Supreme Ct., Phoenix, 1977; ptnr. Squire Sanders & Dempsey, Phoenix, 1979—81; dep. atty. Maricopa County (Trial Bureau and assigned to Spl. Ops.), 1978—80; editor treatises Evidence in Ariz., Michie Co., 1989, Toxic Mold Litig., Michie Co., 1989, Lawyers and Judges' Pub., Michie Co., 1989; instr. MCBA/NITA faculty, 1987; mem. The Wilenchik & Bartness PC, Phoenix. Judge pro tem Maricopa County Superior Ct. 1986-1990., Phoenix, 1989—; mem. civil study com. Ariz. Superior Ct., 1983-87. State committeeman Ariz. Dem. Party, Phoenix, 1984; bd. dirs. Phoenix Little Theatre, 1984, St. Bd. Phys. Therapist Examiners, Phoenix, 1985-90, Mem. Ari. Bar Journal Editorial bd., 1984-1987., Naturopathic bd. Medical Examiners, 1992-1994., Ariz. bd. Physical Therapist Examiners, 1986-1990; Treasurer, 1990. Recipient: E.E. Townes award, C.R. Stanton Moot Ct award; named one of the Top Bus. Litigators, Superlawyers, 2007, Preeminent Lawyers, Martindale Hubbell, AV rated. Mem. Fellow Ariz. Bar Found.; mem. State Bar Ariz. (sec. civil rules com. 1987-88, chmn. trial practice sect 1988., Town of Cave Creek Planning & Zoning commn. practice manual com.), Maricopa County Bar Assn. (chmn. jud. evaluation poll com. 1985-90, pres. young lawyers sect. 1981-92, CLE com. 1989, sr. editor), Nat. Bd. Trial Advocacy (cert. civil trial specialist), Am. Bar Assn. (Mem., Trial Evidence Com., Sec. on Litigation), Phoenix Country Club, Mission Bay Yacht Club, La Jolla Tennis Club. Republican. Avocations: tennis, golf, horseback riding, boating. Office: Wilenchik & Bartness PC The Wilenchik & Bartness bldg 2810 N 3rd St Phoenix AZ 85004 Office Phone: 602-606-2810. Office Fax: 602-606-2811. Business E-Mail: diw@wb-law.com.

WILENSKY, GAIL ROGGIN, economist, researcher; b. Detroit, June 14, 1943; d. Albert Alan and Sophia (Blitz) Roggin; m. Robert Joel Wilensky, Aug. 4, 1963; children: Peter Benjamin, Sara Elizabeth. AB (hon.), U. Mich., 1964, MA in Econs., 1965, PhD in Econs., 1968; degree (hon.), Hahnemann U., 1993, Rush U., 1997, U. Scis., Phila., 2002. Economist President's Commn. on Income Maintenance Programs; exec. dir. Md. Coun. of Econ. Advs., 1969-71; sr. rschr. Urban Inst., Washington, 1971-73; assoc. rsch. scientist, pub. policy and pub. health U. Mich., Ann Arbor, 1973-75, vis. asst. prof. econs., 1973-75; sr. rsch. mgr. Nat Ctr. for Health Svcs. Rsch., Hyattsville, Md., 1975-83; assoc. profl. lectr. George Washington U., 1976-78; v.p. div. health affairs Project HOPE, Millwood, Va., 1983-90; adminstr. Health Care Fin. Adminstrn., Washington, 1990-92; dep. asst. to the pres. for policy devel. White House, 1992-93; sr. fellow Project HOPE, Bethesda, Md., 1993—, chair phys. payment rev. com., 1995-97; chmn. Medicare Payment Adv. Commn., 1997—2001; co-chair Pres.'s Task Force to Improve Healthcare Delivery for Vets., 2001—03, Dept. Def. Task Force on Future of Mil. Health Care, 2006—. Contbr. 25 articles in field to profl. jours. Dir. Am. Heart Assn., 1980-85, bd. dirs., 2002—; mem. health adv. com. Compt. Gen. U.S., 1987-90; bd. dirs. United Healthcare Corp., Cephalon, Gentiva Health Svcs., Inc., Quest Diagnostics; mem. vis. com. med. sch. U. Mich., 1993-97; trustee United Mine Workers Am. Retirement Fund, 1993—; commr. WHO Commn. on the Social Determinants of Health, 2005-. Flinn Found. disting. scholar, 1985; recipient Dean Conley award Am. Coll. Healthcare Execs., 1989. Mem. NAS Inst. Medicine (coun. mem. 2006-), Am. Econ. Assn. (women's com. 1982-84), Fedn. Orgn. of Profl. Women (chmn. econ. task force 1981-83), Am. Statis. Assn., Nat. Tax Assn., Washington Women Economists, Assn. Health Svc. Rsch. (dir. 1984-87), Found. Health Svc. Rsch. (bd. dir. 1987-90), Acad. Health (chair bd. dir. 2000—, Cosmos Club (Washington). Home: 2807 Battery Pl NW Washington DC 20016-3439 Office Phone: 301-656-7401. Business E-Mail: gwilensky@projecthope.org.

WILENSKY, HAROLD L., political science professor, sociologist, researcher; b. New Rochelle, NY, Mar. 3, 1923; s. Joseph and Mary Jane (Wainsten) W.; children: Stephen David, Michael Alan, Daniel Lewis. Student, Goddard Coll., 1940-42; AB, Antioch Coll., 1947; MA, U. Chgo., 1949, PhD, 1955. Asst. prof. sociology U. Chgo., 1951-53, asst. prof. indsl. relations, 1953-54; asst. prof. sociology U. Mich., Ann Arbor, 1954-57, assoc. prof., 1957-61, prof., 1961-62, U. Calif., Berkeley, 1963-82, prof. polit. sci., 1982—, research sociologist Inst. Indsl. Relations, 1963—, project dir. Inst. Internat. Studies, 1970-90; project dir. Ctr. for German and European Studies, Berkeley, 1994-96, Inst. Govtl. Studies, 1996—. Mem. rsch. career awards com. Nat. Inst. Mental Health, 1964—67; cons. in field. Author: Industrial Relations: A Guide to Reading and Research, 1954, Intellectuals in Labor Unions: Organizational Pressures on Professional Roles, 1956, Organizational Intelligence: Knowledge and Policy in Government and Industry, 1967, The Welfare State and Equality: Structural and Ideological Roots of Public Expenditures, 1975, The New Corporatism, Centralization, and the Welfare State, 1976, Rich Democracies: Political Economy, Public Policy, and Performance, 2002, (with C.N. Lebeaux) Industrial Society and Social Welfare, 1965, (with others) Comparative Social Policy, 1985, (with L. Turner) Democratic Corporatism and Policy Linkages, 1987; editor: (with C. Arensberg and others) Research in Industrial Human Relations, 1957, (with P.F. Lazarsfeld and W. H. Sewell) The Uses of Sociology, 1967; contbr. articles to profl. jours. Pilot USAAF, 1943—45. Recipient aux. award Social Sci. Rsch. Coun., 1962, Book award McKinsey Found., 1967; fellow Ctr. for Advanced Study in Behavioral Scis., 1956-57, 62-63, German Marshall Fund, 1978-79; Harry A. Millis rsch. awardee U. Chgo., 1950-51. Fellow AAAS; mem. AAUP, Internat. Sociol. Assn., Internat. Polit. Sci. Assn., Indsl. Relations Research Assn. (exec. com. 1965-68), Soc. for Study Social Problems (chmn. editorial com.), Am. Polit. Sci. Assn., Am. Sociol. Assn. (exec. council 1969-72, chmn. com. on info. tech. and privacy 1970-72), Council European Studies (steering com. 1980-83). Democrat. Jewish. Avocations: music, trumpet, skiing. Office: U Calif Dept Polit Sci 1950-210 Barrows Hall Berkeley CA 94720-1902 E-mail: hwilensk@socrates.berkeley.edu.

WILENTZ, AMY, literature educator; b. NYC; d. Robert Nathan Wilentz and Jacqueline Malino; m. Nicholas J. Goldberg; children: Raphael J. Goldberg, Gabriel T. Goldberg, Noah Malino Goldberg. BA, Harvard, Cambridge, Mass., 1976. Contbg. editor Nation Mag., NYC, 1989—; prof. lit. journalism U. Calif., Irvine, 2006—. Author: (non-fiction book) The Rainy Season: Haiti Since Duvalier (Whiting Writers award, 1990), I Feel Earthquakes More Often Than They Happen: Coming to California in the Age of Schwarzenegger, (novel) Martyrs' Crossing (Rosenthal award, 2001); translator: (non-fiction book) In the Parish of the Poor. Office: Univ Calif 410 HIB Irvine CA 92697 Personal E-mail: amywilentz@mac.com. Business E-Mail: awilentz@uci.edu.

WILENTZ, SEAN, historian, educator, writer; b. NYC, Feb. 20, 1951; s. Elias and Jeanne Marie (Campbell) W.; m. Christine Stansell, Jan. 30, 1980; children: James Thomas Farrell, Hannah Cady Rose. BA, Columbia Coll., 1972, U. Oxford, Eng., 1974; MA, Yale U., New Haven, Conn., 1975, MPhil, 1976, PhD, 1980. Asst. prof. Princeton U., NJ, 1979-85, assoc. prof., 1985-87, Dayton-Stockon prof., history, 1987—2004, dir. program in Am. studies, 1995—2006, George Henry Davis 1886 prof. Am. history, 2004—07, Sidney and Ruth Lapidus prof. Am. revolutionary era, 2007—. Author: Chants Democratic, 1984, anniversary edition, 2004, The Rise of American Democracy, 2005 (Bancroft prize for history, Columbia Univ., 2006), Andrew Jackson: The Seventh President, 1829-1837, 2005, The Age of Reagan, 2008; editor: Rites of Power: Symbolism, Ritual and Politics Since the Middle Ages, 1985; co-author: The Kingdom of Matthias, 1994; co-editor: The Key of Liberty, 1993, The Rose & the Briar: Death, Love and Liberty in the American Ballad, 2004; editl. bd. Dissent, NYC, 1992—; contbg. editor The New Republic, Washington, 1995—. Recipient Alfred Beveridge award Am. History Assn., 1984, Frederick Jackson Turner award Orgn. Am. Historians, 1985; nominee Grammy award, 2004; finalist Pulitzer Prize, 2006; Guggenheim fellow John Simon Guggenheim Meml. Found., 1990-91; fellow Dorothy and Lewis Cullman Ctr. for Scholars and Writers, NY Pub. Libr., 2006-07.George Henry Davis 188 Fellow Soc. Am. Historians (exec. bd. 1986-96). Democrat. Avocations: baseball, American music. Office: Dept History Princeton U Princeton NJ 08544-0001

WILES, ANDREW J., mathematician, educator; b. England, Apr. 11, 1953; s. M. F. Wiles; married; 2 children. BS in Math., Oxford U., England, 1974; PhD in Math., Cambridge U., England, 1980; DSc (hon.), Yale Univ., 2005. Asst. prof. math. Harvard U., Cambridge, Mass., 1977—80; lectr. Inst. Advanced Studies Princeton U., Princeton, NJ, 1981, prof. math., 1982—88, 1990—. Chair dept. math Princeton U. Recipient Wolf prize in math., Wolf Found., Israel, 1995, NAS award in Math., 1996, Royal medal, Royal Soc., 1996, Frank Nelson Cole prize in algebra, Am. Math. Soc., 1996, Frank Nelson Cole prize in number theory, 1997; fellow John D. and Catherine T. MacArthur Found. fellow, 1997. Achievements include solving (with Richard Taylor) Pierre de Fermat's last theory of 1637. Office: Princeton U Dept Math Fine Hall Washington Rd Princeton NJ 08544-0001

WILES, CHARLES PRESTON, minister; b. Frederick, Md., Aug. 5, 1918; s. Charles Wesley and Nellie (Burgess) W.; m. Mary McCallum; children: Mary Margaret, Charles Preston, Wade Burgess. AB, Washington Coll., Chestertown, Md., 1939; postgrad., U. Va., Charlottesville, 1940; MA, Duke U., Durham, NC, 1945, PhD (Univ. fellow 1947-51, Kearns Honor fellow 1949-50), 1951; B.D., Va. Theol. Sem., Alexandria, 1947. Ordained to ministry Episc. Ch., 1947. Priest-in-charge St. Joseph's Ch., Durham, NC, 1947-51; rector St. Mary's Episcopal Ch., Burlington, NJ, 1951-64; pres., trustee Burlington Coll., 1951-64, faculty cons., 1956-64; mem. faculty Phila. Div. Sch., 1959-62, lectr. ch. history, 1960-62; dean St. Matthew's Episcopal Cathedral, Dallas, 1964-87, dean emeritus, 1989; assoc. priest St. Luke's, Dallas, 1987—. Faculty US Army War Coll., Carlisle, Pa., 1964; dep. gen. Conv. from Diocese Dallas, 1967, 69, 70, 73, 76, 79; del. Provincial Synod from Diocese Dallas, 1966, 69, 72, 75, 78; mem. exec. coun. Diocese Dallas, 1967—77, 1984—86, pres. mem. standing com., 1970—73, pres., 1971—73, bd. missions, 1967—69, chmn. dept. coll. work, 1965—71, bd. examining chaplains, 1965—71, mem. standing liturgical commn.; dean, warden Cathedral Ctr. for Continuing Edn. and Pastoral Concern, 1971—87, Commn. Ministry, 1971—76; dean Dallas Deanery, 1965—69, 1984—86, Bicentennial preacher, 1975; pres. convocation and clericus Diocese of NJ, 1961—64, examining chaplain, bd. missions,bd. Christian edn., dean Burlington-Trenton convocation; instr., dean Drew Conf. for Adults in NJ, 1952—56; retreat condr. St. Martin's Ho., Bernardsville, NJ, St. John Bapt. Convent, Mendham, NJ; dean Diocesan Sch. Religion, NJ, 1962—63; founding dean Anglican Sch. Theology, 1971—75; parish life lab. and weekend condr. Nat. Dept. Christian Edn., 1962; co-founder, dean Princeton Conf., NJ, 1956—64; mem. Goals for Dallas Com.; co-chmn. N.Am. Cathedral Deans' Conf., 1980—81. Author: Sacrament and Sacrifice, 2d edit., 1973, Lancelot Andrews, Caroline Divine, 1951, Lift Up Your Hearts, 1956, A Manual of Prayers, 1975, The Holy Eucharist: Word and Sacrament, 1993, The Gate of Heaven, 1993, A Centennial Narrative History of the Episcopal Diocese of Dallas, 1995, Troubadours of God, 1998, Windows for Faith, 2000. Trustee Gen. Theol. Sem., 1968-80; bd. dirs. Evergreen Home for Aging, St. Philip's Community Center, Overseas Mission Soc. Named Priest of Yr., 1969. Mem.: Ch. Hist. Soc. (dir. 1960—68), Navy League, Burlington Country Club, Vesper Club (Phila.), Dallas Athletic Club, Kiwanian Club (Disting. Svc. award 1951, Disting. Citizen award Brunswick, Md. 1986). Home: 7023 Northwood Rd Dallas TX 75225-2439 Home Phone: 214-691-5915. Personal E-mail: dr.cpwiles@dallastexas.com.

WILES, DAVID MCKEEN, chemist; b. Springhill, NS, Can., Dec. 28, 1932; s. Roy McKeen and Olwen Gertrude (Jones) W.; m. Valerie Joan Rowlands, June 8, 1957; children: Gordon Stuart, Sandra Lorraine. BSc with honors, McMaster U., 1954, MSc, 1955; PhD in Chemistry, McGill U., 1957. Rsch. officer chemistry divsn. NRC Can., Ottawa, 1959-66, head textile chemistry sect. chemistry divsn., 1966-75, dir. chemistry divsn., 1975-90; pres. Plastichem Cons., Victoria, B.C., Canada, 1990—. Chmn. Can. High Polymer Forum, 1967—69; v.p. N.Am. Chem. Congress, Mexico City, 1975. Contbr. articles to profl. jours.; mem. editl. adv. bd. numerous profl. jours.; patentee in field. Can. Ramsay Meml. fellow, 1957-59. Fellow Chem. Inst. Can. (chmn. bd. dirs. 1972-74, pres. 1975-76, Dunlop Lectr. award 1981), Royal Soc. Chem. London, Royal Soc. Can.; mem. Am. Chem. Soc. (Polymer Chem. divsn.). Home and Office: 3965 Juan Fuca Terr Victoria BC Canada V8N 5W9 Home Phone: 250-731-0732; Office Phone: 250-721-0732. Personal E-mail: dmwiles@telus.net.

WILES, EDWIN MCKINLEY, education educator, librarian; b. Ponca City, Okla., Sept. 14, 1948; s. William McKinley and Lova Mildred (Rau) Wiles. BA, Ctrl. State U., Edmond, Okla., 1970; MA, Ctrl. State U., 1973; MS, U. Ill., Urbana, 1971. Asst. cataloger, instr. U. Ill., Chgo., 1971—72; catalog libr. Okla. Dept. Libr., Okla. City, 1974—75; lectr. libr. sci. Ctrl. State U., Edmond, 1975—76; libr. Southwestern Libr. Assn., Dallas; dir. Edmond Libr., Edmond, 1977—84; info. svcs. coord. Dulaney-Browne Libr. Okla. City U., 1986—. Cons. Maua Meth. Hosp., Maua, Meru, Kenya, 1998, Electric Generating Authority of Thailand, Bangkok, 1999. Recipient Appreciation Cert., Internat. Student Assn., 1995. Mem.: ALA (life), Okla. Libr. Assn. (del. to Internat. Conv. Libr. and Assns. Bangkok 1999, del. to Internat. Conv. Libr. and Assns. Seoul 2006), Okla. Bibliographic Instrn. Coun. (pres. 1998—99), Assn. Coll. and Rsch. Libr. Democrat. United Methodist. Avocations: travel, reading, stamp collecting/philately, swimming. Office Phone: 405-208-5956. Business E-Mail: emwiles@peoplepc.com.

WILES, STEPHANIE, museum director; MA in Art History, Hunter Coll.; PhD, CUNY. Asst. drawing and prints dept. Pierpont Morgan Libr., NYC, 1981, curator drawings and prints; curator Davison Art Ctr., Wesleyan U., 1998; John G.W. Cowles dir. Allen Meml. Art Mus., Oberlin Coll., Ohio, 2004—, asst. prof. art Ohio. Office: Allen Meml Art Mus Oberlin Coll 87 N Main St Oberlin OH 44074 Office Phone: 440-775-8665. Office Fax: 440-775-6841. E-mail: stephanie.wiles@oberlin.edu.

WILES, WILLIAM WHARTON, retired federal government official; b. Knoxville, Tenn., June 9, 1931; s. James H. and Sally May (Wharton) W.; m. Lessley K. Decker, Aug., 1961; 1 child, Kenneth W. BA, Murray State U., 1953; MBA, U. Ky., 1959; PhD, U. Wis., 1973. Instr. U. Ky., 1959-61; with Fed. Res. Sys., Washington, 1964-98, sec. of bd., 1981-98. With U.S. Army, 1954-56. Home: 2635 Twin Ln York PA 17402 E-mail: Lessleyva@aol.com.

WILETS, LAWRENCE, physicist, educator; b. Oconomowoc, Wis., Jan. 4, 1927; s. Edward and Sophia (Finger) W.; m. Dulcy Elaine Margoles, Dec. 21, 1947; children: Ileen Sue, Edward E., James D.; m. Vivian C. Wolf, Feb. 8, 1976. BS, U. Wis., 1948; MA, Princeton U., 1950, PhD, 1952. Rsch. assoc. Project Matterhorn, Princeton, NJ, 1951-53, U. Calif. Radiation Lab., Livermore, 1953; NSF postdoctoral fellow Inst. Theoretical Physics, Copenhagen, 1953-55; staff mem. Los Alamos (N.Mex.) Sci. Lab., 1955-58; mem. Inst. Advanced Study, Princeton, 1957-58; mem. faculty U. Wash., Seattle, 1958—, prof. physics, 1962-95, prof. emeritus, 1995—. Cons. to pvt. and govt. labs.; vis. prof. Princeton U., 1969, Calif. Inst. Tech., 1971. Author: Theories of Nuclear Fission, 1964, Nontopological Solitons, 1989; contbr. over 180 articles to profl. jours. Del. Dem. Nat. Conv., 1968. NSF sr. fellow Weizmann Inst. Sci., Rehovot, Israel, 1961-62; Nordita prof. and Guggenheim fellow Lund (Sweden) U., Weizmann Inst., 1976—; Sir Thomas Lyle rsch. fellow U. Melbourne, Australia, 1989; recipient Alexander von Humboldt sr. U.S. scientist award, 1983. Fellow Am. Phys. Soc., AAAS; mem. Fedn. Am. Scientists, AAUP (pres. chpt. 1969-70, 73-75, pres. state conf. 1975-76), Explorers Club, Phi Beta Kappa (chpt. pres. 1996-97), Sigma Xi. Achievements include research on theory of nuclear structure and reactions, nuclear fission, atomic structure, atomic collisions, many body problems, subnuclear structure and elementary particles. Office: U Wash Dept Physics PO Box 351560 Seattle WA 98195-1560 Home Phone: 206-525-6769. Personal E-mail: wilets@comcast.net. Business E-Mail: wilets@u.washington.edu.

WILEY, CARL ROSS, timber company executive; b. Astoria, Oreg., Apr. 17, 1930; s. Hamilton Ross and Ada Ellen (Smith) W.; m. Dolores Eileen Brice, Dec. 19, 1953; children: Susan, Steven, Kenneth. BS in Indsl. Engring., Oreg. State U., 1958; grad. exec. tng. program, MIT, 1974. Quality control engr. Oreg. Metall. Corp., 1958-59; indsl. engr. Osborne Electronics Corp., Portland, Oreg., 1959-62; v.p. timber and mfg. Boise Cascade Corp., Idaho, 1962-80; exec. v.p. Roseburg (Oreg.) Lumber Co., 1980-85; chief exec. officer Puget Sound Plywood, Tacoma, 1986-93; pres., CEO Lane Plywood, Eugene, Oreg., 1993-96; retired, 1996. Bd. dirs. Boise YMCA, 1975-78. With AUS, 1951-53. Mem. Am. Plywood Assn. (trustee), Western Wood Products Assn. (bd. dirs., chmn. econ. svcs. 1974-80). Lutheran. E-mail: wileycd@juno.com.

WILEY, DAVID NATHAN, biologist, researcher; b. Buffalo, June 14, 1953; s. William B. and Audrey L. Wiley; m. Elizabeth J. Pomfret, July 5, 2002; children: Kaia Michelle, Luke Christopher, Nathan Quinn. PhD, Antioch U., Keene, NH, 2001. Sr. scientist Internat. Wildlife Coalition, East Falmouth, Mass., 1990—99; rsch. coord. NOAA, Office Nat. Marine Sanctuaries, Scituate, Mass., 2001—. Contbr. scientific papers. Recipient Environ. Leadership award, Switzer Found., 2001, Human Hero award, Mass. Soc. Prevention Cruelty Animals, 2007; named Team of Yr., Nat. Oceanic and Atmospheric Adminstrn., Office Nat. Marine Sanctuaries, 2008; named to Employee of Yr., Nat. Oceanic and Atmospheric Adminstrn., 2007. Office: Stellwagen Bank Nat Marine Sanctuar 175 Edward FosterRd Scituate MA 02066

WILEY, DAVID SHERMAN, sociologist, educator; s. Kenneth L. and Martha Louise Wiley; m. Christine Eppich Root, Aug. 25, 1985; children: Mark Alden Root-Wiley, Peter Kenneth Root-Wiley; m. Marylee Susan Crofts (div.); children: Stephen B., Thomas M. BA, Wabash Coll., Crawfordsville, 1957; MDiv, Yale U., New Haven, 1961; PhD, Princeton U., Sem., 1971. Cert. full prof. Dept. Sociology, Mich. State U., 1985. Race rels. worker World Student Christian Fedn., Salisbury, Southern Rhodesia, Zimbabwe, 1961—63; asst. prof & dir. African Studies Program U. Wis.-Madison, 1968—77; prof. sociology, dir. African Studies Ctr. Mich. State U., East Lansing, 1978—2008. Vice chairperson U.S. Nat. Commn. UNESCO, Wash., 1982—87; co-chairperson nat. Assn. Concerned Africa Scholars, East Lansing, 1991—94. Author: (book) Southern Africa: Society, Economy & Liber, The Third World Africa. Recipient Ralph Smuckler award, Mich. State U., 1997, Award, Coun. Nat. Resource Centers, 2008, Coalition Internat. Edn., 2007. Mem.: African Studies Assn. (past pres. 1998—99), United Ch. Christ. Mem. Christian Ch. Achievements include direction largest African Studies Center in the nation for 30 years; research in environment and development for 30 years in Zambia, Kenya, and South Africa. Office: Dept Sociology Mich State Univ Berkey Hall East Lansing MI 48824 Home Phone: 517-599-1858. Business E-Mail: wiley@msu.edu.

WILEY, EDWIN PACKARD, retired lawyer; b. Chgo., Dec. 10, 1929; s. Edwin Garnet and Marjorie Chastina (Packard) W.; m. Barbara Jean Miller, May 21, 1949; children: Edwin Miller, Clayton Alexander, Stephen Packard. BA, U. Chgo., 1949, JD, 1952. Bar: Wis. 1952, Ill. 1952, U.S. Dist. Ct. (ea. dist.) Wis. 1953, U.S. Supreme Ct. 1978. Assoc. Foley & Lardner, Milw., 1952-60, ptnr., 1960-98; ret. Bd. dirs. Genetic Testing Inst., Inc., other corps. and founds. Co-author: Bank Holding Companies: A Practical Guide to Bank Acquisitions and Mergers, 1988, Wisconsin Uniform Commercial Code Handbook, 1971; author: Promotional Arrangements: Discrimination in Advertising and Promotional Allowances, 1976; editor in chief U. Chgo. Law Rev., 1952. Bd. dirs. Blood Ctr. Southeastern Wis., pres., 1978-82; pres. Blood Ctr. Rsch. Found., Inc., 1983-87; v.p. Friends of Schlitz Audubon Ctr., Inc., 1975-87; pres. Wis. Conservatory ofMusic, 1968-73; pres. First Unitarian Soc. Milw., 1961-63; v.p. Mid-Am. Ballet Co., 1971-73, Milw. Ballet Co., 1973-74; pres. Florentine Opera Co., 1983-86; bd. dirs. Milw. Symphony Orch., pres., 1993-95; bd. dirs. Milw. Pub. Mus., Inc., sec., 1992-2005; bd. dirs. Wis. History Found., v.p., 1998-2005; bd. dirs. Preserve Our Parks, Inc., 1999—; mem. Wis. Gov.'s Commn. on Historic Sites, 2002-2003. Mem. ABA, State Bar of Wis., Milw. Bar Assn., Am. Law Inst., Order of Coif, Univ. Club, Phi Beta Kappa (pres. Greater Milw. assn. 1962-63). Home: 2505 E Bradford Ave #4307 Milwaukee WI 53211-4266 Office Phone: 414-297-5780. Personal E-mail: ewiley@mac.com. Business E-Mail: ewiley@foley.com.

WILEY, JAMES DEE, retired history and biology educator, national park service ranger; b. Douglas, Ariz., May 14, 1950; s. James David Wiley and Harriett D. Rattliff. BS in Edn., No. Ariz. U., 1972; MS in Edn., Corpus Christi State U., 1990; PhD, Kensington U., London, 1998. Cert. instr. Ariz. Assn. Cmty. Colls., 2000. Tchr./coach Douglas Pub. Schs., Ariz., 1985—2001; instr. Cochise C.C., Douglas, 1991—2001; pk. ranger Nat. Pk. Svc.-Independence NHP, Phila., 2003—07. Cons. Douglas Wild Life Zoo, 1990—2001. Contbr. articles to profl. jours. and pubs. Lobbyist Douglas Edn. Assn., 1991—2001, Douglas Pub. Schools, 1991—2001, Ariz. Edn. Assn., Phoenix, 1991—99. Mem.: NSTA (assoc.), NEA (life; polit. action com. 1991—95, Reach for the Stars award 1994), SW Herpalogical Assn. (assoc.), Ariz. Herpalogical Assn. (assoc.), Nat. Biology Teachers Assn. (assoc.), Douglas Edn. Assn. (life; pres. 1994—98), Ariz. Edn. Assn. (life; polit. action com. 1991—99), SCV (assoc.). Avocations: travel, reading, carving, photography. Home: PO Box 775 Reserve NM 87830 Personal E-mail: dr_jim_wiley@excite.com.

WILEY, JOHN D., academic administrator, educator; BS in Physics, Ind. U., 1964; MS in Physics, U. Wis., Madison, 1965, PhD in Physics, 1968. Tech. staff Bell Telephone Labs., Murray Hill, NJ, 1968—74; Alexander von Humboldt rsch. and tng. fellow Max Planck Inst., Stuttgart, Germany, 1974—75; mem. elec. and computer engring. faculty U. Wis., Madison, 1975—, co-founder Ctr. for X-Ray Lithography and Engring. Rsch. Ctr. for Plasma-Aided Mfg., chair Materials Sci. program, 1982—86, assoc. dean for rsch., Coll. Engring., 1986—89, dean, Grad. Sch., sr. rsch. officer, 1989—94, provost & vice chancellor for acad. affairs, 1994—2000, chancellor, 2001—08, chancellor emeritus, 2008—, prof. pub. affairs and ednl. leadership and policy analysis, sr. scholar Wis. Ctr. for Advancement of Postsecondary Edn.; interim dir. Wis. Inst. Discovery, 2008—. Chair Big Ten Coun. of Pres. and Chancellors, 2006; chmn. bd. Coun. for Higher Edn. Accreditation. Office: Wis Inst for Discovery U Wis-Madison 1500 Highland Ave Madison WI 53705 also: U Wis Lathrop Hall 1050 University Ave Madison WI 53706 Office Phone: 608-265-4927. E-mail: jdwiley@uwmad.wisc.edu.*

WILEY, RICHARD ARTHUR, lawyer; b. Bklyn., July 18, 1928; s. Arthur Ross and Anna Thorsen (Holder) W.; m. Carole Jean Smith, Aug. 13, 1955; children: Kendra Elizabeth, Stewart Alan, Garett Smith. AB, Bowdoin Coll., Brunswick, Maine, 1948, LLD, 1994; BCL, Oxford U., Eng., 1951; LLM, Harvard U., 1959. Bar: Mass. 1954, U.S. Ct. Mil. Appeals 1954, U.S. Dist. Ct. Mass. 1962, U. S. Supreme Ct. 1985. Atty. John Hancock Mut. Life Ins. Co., Boston, 1956-58; from atty. to mng. ptnr. Bingham, Dana & Gould, Boston, 1959-76; gen. counsel, asst. sec. Dept. Def., 1976-77; v.p., counsel First Nat. Bank Boston, 1977-78, exec. v.p., 1978-85, Bank of Boston Corp., 1985; ptnr. Csaplar & Bok, Boston, 1986-90, mem. exec. com., 1987-90, chmn., 1989-90, of counsel, 1990, Gaston & Snow, Boston, 1990-91; dir. Powers and Hall P.C., Boston, 1991-94, of counsel, 1994-95, Hill & Barlow, Boston, 1995—2002, Foley & Hoag LLP, Boston, 2002—. Bd. dirs., chmn. Mass. Higher Edn. Assistance Corp.; bd. dirs. Nomadic Structures, Inc., NP Med., Inc., Nypro, Inc; lectr. Boston U. Law Sch., 1961-64; past vice chmn. New Eng. Conf. on Doing Bus. Abroad; trustee New Eng. Legal Found., chmn., 1980-83; adj. prof. govt. and legal studies Bowdoin Coll., 1995-2002; adj. prof. law Boston Coll. Law Sch., 1998—. Author: Cases and Materials on Law of International Trade and Investment, 1961; contbr. articles to profl. jours. Bd. overseers Bowdoin Coll., 1966-81, pres., 1977-80, trustee, 1981-93, trustee emeritus, 1993—; mem. Mass. Edn. Financing Authority, 1986-91, chmn., 1987-91; mem. Wellesley (Mass.) Town Meeting, 1971-75, mem. fin. adv. com., 1972-74; chmn. Mass. Bd. Regents of Higher Edn., 1991; bd. regents Task Force on Student Fin. Aid, 1987; mem. Mass. Higher Edn. Coord. Coun., 1991-95, vice chmn., 1991-93, chmn., 1993-95; chmn. lawyers divsn. United Way Mass. Bay, 1975; mem. devel. com., trustees of donations Episcopal Diocese Mass., 1971-75; trustee, exec. com. North Conway Inst., mem., 1980-92, chmn., 1988-92; bd. trustees Internat. Coun. Trust, Boston; trustee, mem. exec. com., chmn. Mass. Taxpayers Found., 1989-92; chmn. bd. trustees World Peace Found., Boston, 1983-95; corporator Schepens Eye Rsch. Inst., 1991-95; dep. chmn. planning Mass. rep. state com., 1971, vice chmn. fin. com., 1971-72. Officer USAF, 1953-56. Decorated Air Force Commendation medal; recipient Dep. Def. Disting. Pub. Svc. medal, 1977; Rhodes scholar, 1949. Mem.: ABA (vice chmn. fgn. and internat. bus. law com. 1967—69), Boston Bar Assn. (exec. com., antitrust com. 1965—68), Boston Com. on Fgn. Rels. (chmn. 1980—83), Coun. on Fgn. Rels., Phi Beta Kappa.

WILEY, RICHARD EMERSON, lawyer; b. Peoria, Ill., July 20, 1934; s. Joseph Henry and Jean W. (Farrell) W.; m. Elizabeth J. Edwards, Aug. 6, 1960; children: Douglas S., Pamela L. BS with distinction, Northwestern U., 1955, JD, 1958; LLM, Georgetown U., 1962; LLD (hon.), Cath. U. of Am., 1998. Bar: Ill. 1958, DC 1972. Pvt. practice, Chgo., 1962—70; gen. counsel FCC, Washington, 1970—72, mem., 1972—74, chmn., 1974—77, chmn. FCC's adv. com. on advanced TV svc., 1987—96; mng. ptnr. Wiley Rein, LLC, Washington, 1983—; Nat. co-chmn. lawyers Bush-Quayle campaign, 1992, Bush-Cheney campaign, 2000. Prof. law John Marshall Law Sch., U. Chgo., 1963-70. Chmn. bd. Media Inst., 1999-, Inst. for Tele-Info., Columbia U., 1997—. Capt. AUS, 1959-62. Recipient Medal of Honor, Electronic Industries Am., 1996, Emmy award Nat. Acad. TV Arts & Sci. 1997, Disting. Svc. award Nat. Assn. Broadcasters, 2002, named one of 75 Best Lawyers,

Washingtonian mag., 2002, Internat. Achievement award N.Am. Broadcasters Assn., 2004; named Rep. Lawyer of Yr. by Rep. Nat. Lawyers Assn. 2004, named one of The 100 Most Influential Lawyers, Nat. Law Jour., 2006; named to The Consumer Electronics Hall of Fame, 2009 Fellow: Am. Bar Found.; mem.: ABA (chmn. Forum com. on comm. 1985—87, ho. of dels. 1969—71, 1977—84, chmn. young lawyers sect. 1977—84, chmn. bd. editors ABA Jour. 1984—89, chmn. com. on scope and correlation of work 1989, chmn. adminstrv. law & regulatory practice 1993—94, chmn. nat. law day 2003), Rep. Nat. Lawyers Assn. (bd. mem., co-chmn. judicial advocacy panel), Adminstrv. Conf. U.S. (coun., sr. fellow), Chgo. Bar Assn., Ill. Bar Assn., Fed. Comm. Bar Assn. (pres. 1987), Fed. Bar Assn. (pres. 1977), Phi Delta Kappa, Phi Delta Phi. Methodist. Office: Wiley Rein LLC 1776 K St NW Ste 1100 Washington DC 20006-2332 Office Phone: 202-719-7010. Business E-Mail: rwiley@wileyrein.com.

WILFERT, CATHERINE M., medical association administrator, pediatrician, epidemiologist, educator; b. LA, July 26, 1936; m. Samuel L. Katz; children: Rachel, Catherine stepchildren: John, David, William, Deborah, Susan, Penelope. BA with distinction, Stanford Coll., 1958; MD cum laude, Harvard U., 1962. Med. intern Boston City Hosp., 1962—63; resident in pediat. Children's Hosp., Boston, 1964—66, fellow in infectious diseases, 1966—68; asst. prof. pediat. and virology Duke U., 1969—73, assoc. prof. pediat., 1974—79, prof. pediat. and microbiology, chief pediatric infectious diseases, 1980—96, prof. emeritus; sci. dir. Elizabeth Glaser Pediat. AIDS Found., Santa Monica, Calif., 1997—. Chair Adv. Com. on Immunization Practices, 1980, Perinatal Working Group of Prevention Trials Network, NIH; mem. adv. com. Office of AIDS Rsch., 1999—2005. Recipient Christopher award, Am. Acad. Pediat., 2007. Mem.: NIH AIDS Coms., Inst. Medicine, Infectious Diseases Soc. Am. (pres. 2000). Office: Elizabeth Glaser Pediatric AIDS Found 1917 Wildcat Creek Rd Chapel Hill NC 27516-9786 Office Phone: 919-968-0008. Home Fax: 919-968-0447. Personal E-mail: wilfert@mindspring.com.

WILFORD, JOHN NOBLE, JR., science news correspondent; b. Murray, Ky., Oct. 4, 1933; s. John Noble and Pauline (Hendricks) W.; m. Nancy Everett Watts, Dec. 25, 1966; 1 child, Nona. Student, Lambuth Coll., 1951-52; BS, U. Tenn., 1955; MA, Syracuse U., 1956; Internat. Reporting fellow, Columbia, 1961-62; DHL (hon.), R.I. Coll., 1987; DSc (hon.), Middlebury Coll., 1991. Reporter Comml. Appeal, Memphis, summers 1954-55; reporter Wall St. Jour., NYC, 1956, 59-61; contbg. editor Time mag., NYC, 1962-65; sci. reporter N.Y. Times, 1965-73, asst. nat. editor, 1973-75, dir. sci. news, 1975-79, sci. corr., 1979—2008, sci. writer. Vis. journalist Duke U., 1984; McGraw lectr. Princeton U., 1985; Disting. prof. journalism, U. Tenn., Knoxville, 1989-90; mem. Am. Mus.-Mongolian Gobi Expdn., 1991, Dir.'s Visitor, Inst. for Advanced Study, 1995. Author: We Reach The Moon, 1969, The Mapmakers, 1981, The Riddle of the Dinosaur, 1985, Mars Beckons, 1990, The Mysterious History of Columbus, 1991; co-author: The New York Times Guide to the Return of Halley's Comet, 1985, (with William Stockton) Spaceliner, 1981, Israel: The Historical Atlas, 1997; editor: Scientists at Work, 1979, Cosmic Dispatches, 2000. With CIC AUS, 1957-59. Recipient Book award Aviation/Space Writers, 1970, Writing award Aviation/Space Writers, 1983, G.M. Loeb Achievement award U. Conn, 1972, Press award Nat. Space Club, 1974, AAAS-Westinghouse Sci. Writing award, 1983, Ralph Coats Roe medal ASME, 1995, Pulitzer prize, 1984, N.Y. Times Pulitzer Prize Winning Team, 1987, N.Y.C. Mayor's award, 2001, Am. Geol. Inst. award, 2001, Sagan award Coun. Sci. Soc. Pres., 2001, Outstanding Pub. Svc. award Archeol. Inst. America, 2009. Mem. Nat. Assn. Sci. Writers, Authors Guild, Soc. Profl. Journalists, Am. Geog. Soc. (councilor 1994-2000, sec. 2000—), Am. Acad. Arts and Scis., Century Assn., Sigma Chi, Phi Beta Kappa. Home: 232 W 10th St New York NY 10014-2976 Office: 620 8th Ave New York NY 10018-1405 Office Phone: 212-556-7485. Business E-Mail: wilford@nytimes.com.

WILHELM, CATHY S., elementary school educator; m. Larry Joseph Wilhelm, July 30, 1988; 1 child, Melanie Elaine; 1 child, Michael Eric Kyle. M, U. Akron, Ohio, 1979. Permanent Tchg. Cert. State of Ohio, 1979. Instr. English and Reading Highland Local Schs., Medina, Ohio, 1976—. Treas. Highland Edn. Assn., Medina, 1989—; mem. Strategic Planning Com. Highland Local Schs., Medina, 2005—06; mem. scholarship com. Highland Edn. Assn., Medina, past pres., 1979—88; mem. text com. Medina County Bd. Edn., 1979—98. Dir.(drama performance): Thespis Awards (Life Time Achievement Award, 2001). Chair exec. com. Highland Cmty. Support Network, Medina, 2004—06. Recipient Tchrs. Golden Apple award, Ashland Oil; named Who's Who Among Am. Tchrs.; fellow, Martha Holden Jennings Assn., 1983—84. Mem.: NOW, ACLU, LWV, AAUW, NEA (life), Ohio Edn. Assn., Nat. Campaign for Tolerance, Highland Found. for Ednl. Excellence, Phi Delta Kappa. Democrat-Npl. Office: Highland Local Schools 3880 Ridge Rd Wadsworth OH 44281 Office Fax: 330-239-7388.

WILHELM, DAVID C., venture capitalist; b. Ohio, Oct. 2, 1956; m. Degee Dodds; children: Luke, Logan. BA, Ohio U., 1977; MPP, Harvard U., 1990; PhD (hon.), U. Charleston; D in Pub. Svc. (hon.), Ohio U. Rsch. dir. pub. employee dept. AFL-CIO, 1981-83; campaign mgr. Senator Paul Simon, 1984, Senator Joseph Biden for Pres., Iowa, 1985-87, Richard M. Daley for Mayor, Chgo., 1989, 91, Gov. Bill Clinton for Pres., 1991-92; exec. dir. Citizens for Tax Justice, Washington, 1985-87; pres. The Strategy Group, Chgo., 1988-91; chmn. Dem. Nat. Com., 1993-94; sr. mng. dir. investment banking Kemper Securities, Inc. (now First Union), Chgo., 1995-97; founder, sr. v.p. Wilhelm & Conlon, Inc., Chgo., 1998—2004; founder, pres. Woodland Venture Mgmt., Chgo., 2002—; founder, ptnr. Adena Ventures, 2002—, Hopewell Ventures, 2004—; founder, pres. The Strategy Group. Lectr. U. Chgo.; bd. dirs. Christian Century Mag., League of Chgo. Treasures, Children's Meml. Hosp., Chgo., Ill. Venture Capital Assocs., Chicagoland Entrepreneurial Ctr., Ill. Ventures. Bd. dirs. Chgo. Project for Violence Prevention, Ctr. for Tax and Budget Accountability. Fellow Inst. of Politics, Harvard U., 1996 Democrat. Methodist. Office: Adena Ventures 20 E Circle Dr Ste 143 Athens OH 45701 also: Woodland Venture Mgmt 20 N Wacker Dr Ste 2200 Chicago IL 60606 E-mail: wilhelm@woodlandvc.com.*

WILHELM, GARY BRETZ, physician; s. Norman E. and Madeleine Bretz Wilhelm; m. Katherine Jean Kuhlman; 1 child, John Hunter. BA in Biology, Capital U., Columbus, Ohio, 1974; PhD in Human Anatomy and Neuroscis., U. Tex., Galveston, 1980; MD, U. Tex., San Antonio, 1986. Postdoctoral fellow dept. pathology U. Tex. Health Sci. Ctr., San Antonio, 1980—81, instr. in human anatomy, 1980—82; intern Brooke Army Med. Ctr., Fort Sam Houston, Tex., 1987; resident in orthop. William Beaumont Army Med. Ctr., Fort Bliss, Tex., 1991—96; commd. 2d lt. US Army, 1986, advanced through grades to col.; physician extender staff US Army Acad. Health Scis., San Antonio, 1990—91, resident physician Fort Bliss, 1991—96; chief, phys. exams clinics and aerospace medicine Munson Army Health Ctr., Ft. Leavenworth, Kans., 1996—; flight surgeon Mo. Army Nat. Guard, Jefferson City, 1996—; chif med. officer Cmty. Based Health Care Orgn., Ala., 2006—07; med. dir. Gentry Family Practice Clinic, 2007—. Orthopedic tech. course dir. Acad. Scis., Fort Sam Houston, 1990—91. Contbr. articles to profl. publs. Co-dir. Nat. Student Rsch. Forum, Galveston, 1978—79. Col. med. corps, flight surgeon Mo. Army NG. Decorated Meritourious Svc. medal US Army, Civilian Achievement award, Army Commendation Medal Cmty. Based Health Care Orgn., Nat. Def. Svc. medal, Global War Terrorism Medal; named Flight Surgeon of Yr., Soc. Army Flight Surgeons, 1988. Episcopalian. Avocations: flying, fox hunting, reading. Home: 9057 Hyland Creek Rd Bloomington MN 55437-1956

WILHELM, JOHN W., labor union administrator; m. Elizabeth B. Gilbertson, 1969; 2 children. B with high honors, Yale Coll., 1967. Organizer, bus. agent, Local 217 Hotel Employees & Restaurant Employees Union (HERE), New Haven, 1969—71, sec.-treas. Local 217, 1971—83, bus. mgr. Local 217, 1978—86, internat. v.p. HERE, 1982-1996, gen. sec.-treas., 1996-98, gen. pres., 1998—2004; merger with Union Needletrades, Indsl. &Textile Employees (UNITE) to form UNITE HERE, 2004, pres. hospitality industry Washington, 2004, pres. UNITE HERE, 2009—. Commr. Nat. Gambling Impact Study Commn., 1997—99; trustee HERE's Welfare/Pension Funds, So. Nev. Culinary & Bartenders Pension Fund. Named to Gaming Hall of Fame, Am. Gaming Assn, 2007. Mem.: Phi Beta Kappa. Office: UNITE HERE 1775 K St NW Ste 620 Washington DC 20006 Business E-Mail: jwilhelm@unitehere.org.*

WILHELM, KATE (KATY GERTRUDE), author; b. Toledo, June 8, 1928; d. Jesse Thomas and Ann (McDowell) Meredith; m. Joseph B. Wilhelm, May 24, 1947 (div. 1962); children: Douglas, Richard; m. Damon Knight, Feb. 23, 1963; 1 child, Jonathan. PhD in Humanities (hon.), Mich. State U., 1996. Writer, 1956—. Co-dir. Milford Sci. Fiction Writers Conf., 1963-76; lectr. Clarion Fantasy Workshop Mich. State U., 1968-94. Author: More Bitter Than Death, 1962; (with Theodore L. Thomas) The Clone, 1965, The Nevermore Affair, 1966, The Killer Thing, 1967, Let the Fire Fall, 1969, The Year of the Cloud, 1970, Abyss: Two Novellas, 1971, Margaret and I, 1971, City of Cain, 1971, The Clewiston Test, 1976, Where Late the Sweet Birds Sang, 1976, Fault Lines, 1976, Somerset Dreams and Other Fictions, 1978, Juniper Time, 1979; (with Damon Knight) Better Than One, 1980, A Sense of Shadow, 1981, Listen, Listen, 1981, Oh! Susannah, 1982, Welcome Chaos, 1983, Huysman's Pets, 1986; (with R. Wilhelm) The Hills Are Dancing, 1986, The Hamlet Trap, 1987, Crazy Time, 1988, Dark Door, 1988, Smart House, 1989, Children of the Wind: Five Novellas, 1989, Cambio Bay, 1990, Sweet, Sweet Poison, 1990, Death Qualified, 1991, And the Angels Sing, 1992, Seven Kinds of Death, 1992, Naming the Flowers, 1992, Justice for Some, 1993, The Best Defense, 1994, A Flush of Shadows, 1995, Malice Prepense, 1996, The Good Children, 1998, Defense for the Devil, 1999, No Defense, 2000, The Deepest Water, 2000, Desperate Measures, 2001, Skeletons, 2002, Clear and Convincing Proof, 2003, The Unhidden Truth, 2004, Storyteller, 2005, The Price of Silence, 2005, Sleight of Hand, 2006, 4 Wrongful Death, 2007, Cold Case, 2008; (multimedia space fantasy) Axoltl, U. Oreg. Art Mus., 1979, (radio play) The Hindenburg Effect, 1985; editor: Nebula Award Stories #9, 1974, Clarion SF, 1976; contbr. articles to popular mags., profl. jours. Mem. Nat. Writers Union, Mystery Writers Am., Authors Guild. Address: 1645 Horn Ln Eugene OR 97404-2957 E-mail: kate@katewilhelm.com.

WILHELM, ROBERT OSCAR, lawyer, civil engineer; b. Balt., July 7, 1918; s. Clarence Oscar and Agnes Virginia (Grimm) W.; m. Grace Sanborn Luckie, Apr. 4, 1959. BSCE, Ga. Tech. Inst., 1947, MSIM, 1948; JD, Stanford U., 1951. Bar: Calif. 1952, U.S. Supreme Ct. Mem. Wilhelm, Thompson, Redwood City, Calif., 1952—92; gen. cousnel Bay Counties Gen. Contractors; pvt. practice civil engring., Redwood City, 1952—. Pres. Bay Counties Builders Escrow, Inc., 1972-88. Author: The Manual of Procedures for the Construction Industry, 1971, Manual of Procedures and Form Book for Construction Industry, 9th edit., 1995, Construction Law for Contractors, Architects and Engineers; columnist Law and You in Daily Pacific Builder, 1955-2001. With C.E., AUS, 1942-46. Named to Wisdom Hall of Fame, 1999. Mem. Bay Counties Civil Engrs. (pres. 1957), Peninsula Builders Exch. (pres. 1958-71, dir.), Calif. State Builders Exch. (treas. 1971), Del Mesa Carmel Cmty. Assn. (bd. dirs. 1997-99), Masons, Odd Fellows, Eagles, Elks. Home: 134 Del Mesa Carmel Carmel CA 93923-7950 Office: 600 Allerton St Ste 202 Redwood City CA 94083 Home Phone: 831-625-5291.

WILHELM, WILLIAM JEAN, civil engineering educator; b. St. Louis, Oct. 5, 1935; s. Maurice Ferdinand and Winifred Eileen (McClintock) W.; m. Patricia Jane Zietz, Aug. 17, 1957; children: William, Robert, Andrew, Mary, David. BME, Auburn U., 1958, MS, 1963; PhD, N.C. State U., 1968. Lic. profl. engr., Kans. Structural engr. Palmer & Baker Engrs., Mobile, Ala., 1958-60; instr. engring. graphics Auburn U., 1960-64; asst. prof. civil engring. W.Va. U., Morgantown, 1967-72, assoc. prof., 1972-76, prof., 1976-79, chmn., 1974-79; dean engring., prof. Wichita State U., 1979-2000, dean, prof., emeritus, 2000—, dir. Ctr. for Productivity Enhancement, 1984-86, exec. dir. Ctr. for Tech. Application, 1988-91. Bd. dirs. Kans. Tech. Enterprise Corp., Orthopaedic Rsch. Inst. Via Christi Regional Med. Sys.; chair bd. dirs. Envision. Found.; mem. bldg. commn. Cath. Diocese of Wichita. Contbr. articles to profl. jours. Officer C.E. U.S. Army, 1959, 62. Recipient Recognition award Wichita State U. Alumni Assn., 1993, Engr. Svc. award Wichita Coun. Engring. Socs., 2000. Fellow NSPE, ASCE, Am. Soc. Engring. Edn. (George K. Wadlin award 1998, MidWest sect. Spl. Appreciation award 2001), Am. Concrete Inst. (Joe W. Kelley award 1986, Henry L. Kennedy award 1994); mem. Soc. Women Engrs. (sr., Rodney D. Chipp Meml. award 2000), Kans. Soc. Profl. Engrs. (pres. 1994-95, Outstanding Engr. of Yr. award 1989, Career Recognition award 2000), W.Va. Acad. Civil Engrs. (hon.), Order of the Engr., Sigma Xi, Phi Kappa Phi, Tau Beta Pi, Pi Tau Sigma, Chi Epsilon (chpt. hon. W.Va. U. 1979), Golden Key (hon.). Roman Catholic. Home: 7014 E 25th St N Wichita KS 67226-1734 Personal E-mail: billwilhelm1@cox.net.

WILHELMI, CYNTHIA JOY, business and information technology manager, information scientist executive consultant; Student, Iowa State U., Ames, 1964—66; BA in Art and Edn., U. Iowa, 1966; MA in Comm., U. Nebr., Omaha, 1996. Master Artist-in-Residence Nebr. Arts Coun., Omaha, 1985—91; grad. tchg. asst., tchg. fellow U. Nebr., Omaha, 1993—95; Family Friends of Eastern Nebr. program coord. Vis. Nurse Assn., Omaha, 1996—97; instr. Midland Luth. Coll., Fremont, Nebr., 1997—99; info. tech. cons., project mgr., test engr., bus. analyst Bass & Assocs., Omaha, 1999—2000; info. tech. cons. Robert Half Internat. Cons., 2000, Maxim Group/TEKSystems, 2000—02, Client Resources Inc., 2003; data mgr. TEKsystems, 2003; govt. bid proposal coord. NuGenSof cons. co., 2003—04; bus. sys. analyst Wells Fargo; data mgr. Raytheon, 2003, proposal coord., 2003—04; bus. sys. analyst Praxis Tech. Group, 2005; sr. quality assurance, testing engr. Acacia Tech. Svcs. Inc., 2006; sr. project mgr. and coord. Profl. Project Ptnrs., Inc., 2006; project mgr. MSI Solutions Integrators, 2006—07; ind. exec. cons., 2007—. Sr. project mgr., bus. analyst Alegent Health, Ameritrade, Omnium Worldwide, Lincoln Benefit Life, Raytheon, Wells Fargo, Praxis Tech. Group; IT data mgr., govt. info. tech. proposal coord.; sr. test engr. Ameritrade, Lincoln Benefit Life, Ameritas, Alegent Health, Nationwide Ins., 2006; project mgr. Alegent Health, Ameritrade, Lincoln Benefit Life, Wells Fargo; data mgr. Omnium Worldwide, Raytheon, Northrop Grumman Mission Sys., Ameritrade; 3d-party vendor mgr. Alegent Health, Lincoln Benefit Life; CD installation tester Lincoln Benefit Life; tech. documentor Alegent Health, Omnium Worldwide, Ameritrade, PerClick-dot-com, Ameritas, Raytheon Sys., Inacom; data mgr. Northrop Grumman Mission Sys.; bus. sys. cons. Wells Fargo, Nationwide Agribusiness Ins., Nationwide Insurance Agile Tech.; project mgr., enterprise field ops. release coord. Wells Fargo Corp. Offices; project mgr. MSI Sys. Integrators, Inc.; farm owner, mgr., 2001—. Editor, pub., contbg. author Salaam mag., 1985-86. Mem. adv. coun. Foster Grandparents, Omaha, 1999-2005; bd. dirs., pub. rels./publicity chair U. Nebr. Friends of Art, Omaha, 1997-99; bd. dirs. Nebr. SIDS Found., 2002-03; rsch bd. advisors Am. Biog. Inst., 2003, profl. women's adv. bd. mem., 2006, founding mem. internat. women's rev. bd., 2008, Internat. Biog. Ctr., Eminent Scientists Today, 2000. Named Outstanding Grad. Tchg. Asst., U. Nebr., Omaha, 1995, Adm. in the Gt. Navy of Nebr., 1990, Outstanding Intellectuals of 21st Century, Internat. Biog. Ctrs., 2000; named to Dictionary of Internat. Biography, Cambridge Blue Book, 1000 Gt. Scientists, 2000 Eminent Scientists of Today. Mem.: AAUW, Greater Des Moines Tennis Assn., Nebr. Adms. Assn., Soc. for Tech. Comm. (bd. dirs., chair pub. rels. 1999), Am. Meteor. Soc., Soc. for Collegiate Journalists (hon.), Am. Mensa (Nebr., Western Iowa exec. com. 2003—05, SIGHT coord. 2003—05, nat. nominating com. Nebr.-Western Iowa 2004—, nat. nominating com. Ctrl. Iowa 2006—09, local sec., CIM pres. 2008, asst. regional vice chair, Region 7 2008—), Ctrl. Hawkeye Gas Engine and Antique Tractor Assn., Phi Delta Gamma. Democrat. Office Phone: 515-707-4082. Personal E-mail: wilhelmi_c@yahoo.com. Business E-Mail: cwi813@mchsi.com.

WILHELMSEN, HAROLD JOHN, accountant; b. Kansas City, Mo., July 13, 1928; s. Karl John and Cora Irene (Reynolds) W.; m. Audrey Loraine Woodard, Oct. 14, 1950. BBA, U. Wis., 1950. CPA, Wis. With S.C. Johnson & Son Inc., Racine, Wis., 1953-90, dir. fin. South Pacific, 1970-72, mgr. overseas fin. svcs., 1972-76, contr. U.S. ops., 1976-78, v.p., contr. internat. ops., 1978-90, ret., 1990. Pres. Racine Symphony Orch. Assn., 1957-60; trustee Carthage Coll., Kenosha, Wis., 1984-91, dir., sec. Pinnacle Peak Country Club Estates, 1992-95; dir., 1993-97, pres. Pinnacle Peak Country Club, 1996-97; treas. Christ the Lord Luth. Ch. Served with U.S. Army, 1950-52. Mem.: Pinnacle Peak Country Club. Republican. Lutheran. Avocations: golf, bridge, reading, music. Personal E-mail: hjw-az@cox.net.

WILHITE, STEVE, automotive executive; married; 1 child. BA, Stanford U., 1974; MBA, U. Calif., Berkeley. Mktg. exec. Ford Motor Co.; sr. mktg. exec. Volkswagen of Am., 1990—99; v.p. worldwide mktg. comms. Apple Computer, Inc., 1999—2001; v.p. mktg. Nissan N.Am., Inc., 2001—04; sr. v.p. global mktg. Nissan Motor Co., Ltd., Tokyo, 2004—06; COO Hyundai Motor Am., Fountain Valley, Calif., 2006—. Office: Hyundai Motor Am 10550 Talbert Ave Fountain Valley CA 92708-6031 Office Phone: 714-965-3000. Office Fax: 714-965-3149.

WILHJELM, CHRISTIAN, conductor, artist; b. Long Branch, NJ, Nov. 6, 1949; s. Carl and Alice Wilhjelm; m. Jacqueline Sarracco; children: Carl, Hannah, Erik, Emma. BA in Music, New Eng. Conservatory, 1972; MA Edn., Coll. of NJ, 1978; EdD, Columbia U., 1998. Musician-French horn Richmond Symphony, Richmond, Va., 1972—76; band dir. North Brunswick Twp. HS, 1977—79, Ridgewood HS, NJ, 1979—82, Rye HS, NY, 1982—84, Pascack Hills HS, Montvale, NJ, 1984—, NYU Wind Ensemble, NYC, 2006—07; music dir. Ridgewood Concert Band, Ridgewood, 1983—; artist Montclair State U., NJ, 1996—2003; condr., music dir. The Goldman Band, NYC, 2000—05. Bd. dirs. Classical NJ, Westfield, NJ, 1998, Bergen Youth Orch., Engelwood, NJ, 2001—. Contbr. book Spotlight on Bands. Recipient Sudler Award of Merit, John Philip Sousa Found., 1998; fellow Paul Harris Fellowship, Rotary Internat., 1992. Mem.: Music Educator's Nat. Conf., Coll. Band Dir. Nat. Assn., Am. Fedn. of Musicians. Office Phone: 201-358-7020 2059. Personal E-mail: cwilhjelm@msn.com.

WILHOIT, GENE, educational association administrator; m. Rebecca Campbell Wilhoit; children: Christopher, Kara, Jason. BA in Hist. and Econs., Georgetown Coll.; M in Tchg., Polit. Sci. and Econs., Ind. U.; student in Edn. Adminstrn., W.Va. Coll. Grad. Studies. Social studies tchr., Ohio, Ind.; prog. dir. Ind. Dept. Pub. Instrn.; adminstr. Kanawha County, W.Va.; spl. asst. US Dept. Edn., 1979—83; exec. dir. Nat. Assn. State Bds. Edn., 1986—93; chair edn. commn. State Adv. Commn., 1989—91; dir., chief state sch. officer Ark. Dept. Edn., 1994—97; dep. commr. bur. learning support svcs. Ky. Dept. Edn., 1997—2000, commr. edn., 2000—06; exec. dir. Coun. Chief State Sch. Officers, Washington, 2006—. Spkr. in field. Office: Coun Chief State Sch Officers One Massachusetts Ave NW Ste 700 Washington DC 20001-1431 Office Phone: 202-336-7000. Office Fax: 202-408-8072.

WILINSKI, GRANT W., dean; s. Matthew W. and Irma P. Wilinski; m. Edwina M. Mraw, May 14, 2005. MS in Libr. Svc., Rutgers U., New Brunswick. Libr. Atlantic Cape CC, Mays Landing, NJ, 1988—2000, libr. dir., 2001—05, chair, social sci. dept., 2007—08, adj. faculty, 1993—, assoc. dean, academic support svc., 2005—. Pres. Coll. and Rsch. Libr. Sect., NJ. Libr. Assn. Contbr. articles to profl. jours., to conf. presenter. V.p. Literacy Volunteers Assn., Pleasantville, NJ, 2007—08. Mem.: ALA (assoc.). Avocations: classical music, travel. Home: 5981 Peach St Mays Landing NJ 08330 Office: Atlantic Cape CC 5100 Black Horse Pike Mays Landing NJ 08330 Office Fax: 609-343-4957. Business E-Mail: wilinski@atlantic.edu.

WILK, RONALD, physician; b. NYC, Nov. 27, 1944; BA, L.I. U., Bklyn., 1966; MD, U. Bologna, Italy, 1972. Diplomate Am. Acad. Neurology, 1980. Intern, resident Mt. Sinai Hosp., NYC, chief resident, 1977. Fellow: Am. Acad. Neurology.

WILKENING, LAUREL LYNN, academic administrator, aerospace scientist; b. Richland, Wash., Nov. 23, 1944; d. Marvin Hubert and Ruby Alma Wilkening; m. Godfrey Theodore Sill, May 18, 1974 BA, Reed Coll., Portland, Oreg., 1966; PhD, U. Calif., San Diego, 1970; DSc (hon.), U. Ariz., 1996. From asst. prof. to assoc. prof. U. Ariz., Tucson, 1973—80, dir. Lunar and Planetary Lab., head planetary scis., 1981—83, vice provost, prof. planetary scis., 1983—85, v.p. rsch., dean Grad. Coll., 1985—88; divsn. scientist NASA Hdqrs., Washington, 1980; prof. geol scis., adj. prof. astronomy, provost U. Washington, Seattle, 1988—93; prof. earth system sci., chancellor U. Calif., Irvine, 1993—98. Dir. Rsch. Corp., 1991-2003, Seagate Tech., Inc., 1993-2000, Empire Ranch Found., 1998-2003, 2005—2007; vice chmn. Nat. Commn. on Space, Washington, 1984-86, Adv. Com. on the Future of U.S. Space Program, 1990-91; chair Space Policy Adv. Bd., Nat. Space Coun., 1991-92; co-chmn. primitive bodies mission study team NASA/European Space Agy., 1984-85; chmn. com. rendezvous sci. working group NASA, 1983-85; mem. panel on internat. cooperation and competition in space Congl. Office Tech. Assessment, 1982-83; trustee NASULGC, 1994-97, UCAR, 1988-89, 97-98, Reed Coll., 1992-2002. Editor: Comets, 1982. Recipient trainee, NASA, 1967—70;

grantee fellow, U. Calif Regents, 1966—67. Fellow Meteoritical Soc. (councilor 1976-80), Am. Assn. Advanced Sci.; mem. Am. Astron. Soc. (chmn. div. planetary scis. 1984-85), Am. Geophys. Union, AAAS, Planetary Soc. (dir. 1994-2000, v.p. 1997-2000), Phi Beta Kappa. Democrat. Avocations: gardening, camping, swimming.

WILKENS, LENNY (LEONARD RANDOLPH WILKENS JR.), sportscaster, former professional sports team executive, retired professional basketball player; b. Bklyn., Oct. 28, 1937; s. Leonard Randolph Sr. and Henrietta (Cross) W.; m. Marilyn J. Reed, July 28, 1962; children: Leesha Marie, Leonard Randolph III, Jamée McGregor. BS in Econs., Providence Coll., 1960, HHD (hon.), 1980. Profl. basketball player St. Louis Hawks, 1960—68, Seattle SuperSonics, 1968—69, Cleve. Cavaliers, 1972—74; player/coach Seattle SuperSonics, 1969—72, head coach, 1977—85, gen. mgr., 1985—86; head coach Cleve. Cavaliers, 1986—93; vice chmn. Seattle SuperSonics, 2006—07, pres. basketball ops., 2007; counselor Jewish Employment Vocat. Svcs., 1962—63; salesman packaging divsn. Monsanto Co., 1966; player/coach Portland Trail Blazers, 1974—76; head coach Atlanta Hawks, 1993—2000, Toronto Raptors, 2000—03, NY Knicks, 2004—05; color analyst Pac-10 men's basketball FSN, 2004—05, NBA analyst, 2005—06, Seattle SuperSonics color analyst, 2006—. Head coach 4 NBA All-Star Teams, World Champion Basketball Team, 1979, Olympic Basketball Team, 1996, asst. coach, 92. Author: The Lenny Wilkens Story, 1974. Bd. regents Gonzaga U., Spokane; bd. dirs. Seattle Ctr., Big Bros. Seattle, Bellevue Boys Club, Wash., Seattle Opportunities Industrialization Ctr., Seattle U.; co-chmn. UN Internat. Yr. of Child prog., 1979; organizer Lenny Wilkens Celebrity Golf Tournament for Spl. Olympics. 2nd lt. US Army, 1961—62. Named to NBA All-Star Game, 1963-65, 67-71, 73, NIT-NIKE Hall of Fame, 1988, Naismith Meml. Basketball Hall of Fame, 1989 (as a player), 1998 (as a coach); named NBA All-Star Game MVP, 1971, Man of Yr., Boys High Alumni chpt. LA, 1979, Sportsman of Yr., Seattle chpt. City of Hope, 1979, Congl. Black Caucus Coach of Yr., 1979, Continental Basketball Assn. Coach of Yr., 1979, Coach of Yr., Black Pubs. Assn., 1979, NBA Coach of Yr., 1994; named one of NBA's 50 Greatest Players, NBA's Top Ten Coaches, 1997; recipient Whitney Young Jr. award NY Urban League, 1979, Disting. Citizens award Boy Scouts Am., 1980. Achievements include holding record for most career NBA wins. Office: FSN Northwest 3626 156th Ave SE Bellevue WA 98006 Office Phone: 425-641-0104. Office Fax: 425-641-9811.

WILKERSON, GERALD EUGENE, bishop; b. Des Moines, Oct. 21, 1939; Attended, Queen of Angels Sem., San Fernando, Calif., St. John Sem., Camarillo, Calif. Ordained priest, 1965; assoc. pastor Our Lady of Guadalupe, La Habra, Calif., 1965—71, St. Michael, LA, 1971—78, Am. Martyrs, Manhattan Beach, Calif., 1978—82; adminstr. Our Lady of Grace Ch., Encino, Calif., 1982—85, pastor, 1985—97; aux. bishop San Fernando Pastoral Region Archdiocese of LA, 1997—; ordained bishop, 1998. Roman Catholic. Office: 15101 San Fernando Mission Blvd Mission Hills CA 91345-1109

WILKERSON, LAWRENCE B., former federal official, retired military officer; b. Gaffney, SC, Jan. 28, 1945; m. Barbara Wilkerson; 2 children. Attended, Bucknell U., Lewisburg, Pa.; MA in Internat. Rels., US Naval War Coll., Newport, RI, MS in Nat. Security Studies; degree, Savina Regina U., Newport RI. Col. US Army, Vietnam, Korea, Japan and Hawaii, ret., 1997; exec. asst. US Navy Admiral Stewart A. Ring, Dir. Strategy and Policy, 1984—87; dep. exec. officer US Army Forces Command, Atlanta, 1989; spl. asst. to Gen. Colin Powell Chmn. the Joint Chiefs of Staff, 1989—93; dep. dir., and dir. USMC War Coll., Quantico, Va., 1993—97; cons. and advisor to Gen. Colin L. Powell, 1997—2000; mem. transition office US Dept. State, Washington, 2000—01, policy planning staff mem., East Asia and the Pacific and legis. and polit.-mil. affairs, 2001—02, assoc. dir. policy planning, 2002, chief of staff, 2002—05; from co-chmn. to chmn., US-Cuba Policy Initiative New America Found., Washington. Faculty mem. US Naval War Coll.; vis. Pamela C. Harriman prof. govt. and pub. policy College of William & Mary, Williamsburg, Va.; professorial lectr., honors program George Wash. U., Washington. Contbr. articles to profl. jours. including Proceedings, The Naval War Coll. Rev., Mil. Rev., Joint Force Quar. Office: Coll William & Mary Govt Dept Morton Hall Rm 10 100 Campus Dr Williamsburg VA 23185 also: George Wash U Honors Program 714 21st St NW Washington DC 20006

WILKERSON, MATT, biology professor; b. Morristown, Tenn., Aug. 1, 1977; s. Dennis and Alta Wilkerson; m. Karen Winn; 1 child, Abigail. MS, U. Tenn., Knoxville, 2003; attending, Northctrl. U., Prescott, Ariz. Instr. biology Walter State CC, Morristown, 2003—05, Carson Newman Coll., Jefferson City, Tenn., 2005—. Owner Pedal Shop, Morristown, 2003—. Contbr. articles to profl. jour. Youth pastor Liberty Hill United Meth. Ch., Morristown, 2001—04; dir. contemporary music First United Meth. Ch., Jefferson City, 2004—05. Methodist.

WILKERSON, PATRICIA HELEN, retired director; b. Victoria, Tex., Aug. 2, 1936; d. Milo Andrew and Gertrude H. (Nichols) Beeman; children: Cheryl Lynn, Susan Leigh, Debra Ann, Jon Craig. Student, U. Corpus Christi, Tex., 1954—56, Del Mar Coll., 1970—71, student, 1986—88. Tax clk. Nueces County Tax Assessor, Corpus Christi, Tex., 1956—57; corr. sec. Boy Scouts of Am. Gulf Coast Coun., Corpus Christi, 1957—58; elem. dir, nursery sch. coord. First Bapt. Ch., Corpus Christi, 1972—73, pre-K tchr., sec., 1975—85; dir. child devel. ctr. 2d Bapt. Ch., Corpus Christi, 1985—99, Northway Bapt. Ch., Dallas, 1999—2007; tchr. Mothers Day Out, 2008—09. ASSIST pre-sch. leader Corpus Christi Bapt. Assn., 1967—99; conf. leader, cons. Bapt. Gen. Conv., Dallas, 1967—2005; mem. early childhood adv. bd. Del Mar. Coll., Corpus Christi, 1981—86; mem. adv. com. Tex. Bapt. Weekday Assn., Dallas, 1995—98, Gulf Coast Tng. coalition. Writer Presch. Sunday Sch. Curriculum, 1992-99, Southern Bapt. Conv. Tchr. adult ESL Plymouth Pk. Baptist Ch., 2008—09, MOD tchr., 2008—09; Sunday sch. tchr. various Tex. Bapt. chs., 1959—2009; conf. leader Dallas Bapt. Assn., 2000—02. Mem. Bay Area Assn. Edn. Young Children (sec. 1981-82, co-chair conf. 1991, Week of the Young Child chair 1995-96). Avocations: reading, sewing, cats, nature study. Home: 2323 Anderson Irving TX 75062

WILKERSON, WILLIAM HOLTON, banker; b. Greenville, NC, Feb. 16, 1947; s. Edwin Cisco and Agnes Holton (Gaskins) W.; m. Ellen Logan Tomskey, Oct. 27, 1973; 1 child, William Holton Jr. AB in Econs., U. N.C., 1970. Asst. v.p. 1st Union Nat. Bank, Greensboro, NC, 1972-77; v.p. Peoples Bank & Trust Co., Rocky Mount, NC, 1977-79, exec. v.p., 1987-89, pres., 1989-90; sr. v.p. Hibernia Nat. Bank, New Orleans, 1979-86; group exec. officer, vice chmn. bd. dirs. Centura Banks, Inc., Rocky Mount, 1990-97, pres., 1998—2001, Wilkerson Co., Inc., Greenville, NC, 2001—. Bd. visitors U. N.C., Chapel Hill, 1999-2003; vice chmn., investment adv. com. City of Greenville; Pitt Memorial Hos. Found., bd. trustee. Mem. Greenville-Pitt Assn. Realtors, Rocky Mount C. of C. (bd. dirs. 1989-96, vice chmn. 1992-94, chmn. 1995), Omicron Delta Epsilon, Chi Beta Phi, Phi Sigma Pi. Republican. Home: 407 Rutledge Rd Greenville NC 27858 Office: PO Box 2095 Greenville NC 27836-0095

WILKES, BRENT AMES, management consultant; b. Melrose, Mass., Sept. 30, 1952; s. Gordon Borthwick and Frances (Ames) W.; 1 child, Erin; m. Linda Dadourian, Oct. 18, 1998. Bachelor, U. Mass., 1974; M of Pub. Affairs, U. Conn., 1977. Cert. assn. exec., 1998, assoc. risk mgmt., 1998, ins. cons., 2004. Adminstrv. asst. Town of Tolland, Conn., 1975-76; mgmt. specialist Mass. Dept. Community Affairs, Boston, 1976-79; adminstrv. asst. to mayor City of Gloucester, Mass., 1979-80; assoc. dir., dir. of field svcs. Mass. Mcpl. Assn., Boston, 1980-89; v.p., treas. Mass. Interlocal Ins. Assn., Boston, 1984-89; pres. MMA Consulting Group, Inc., Boston, 1989-94, MMA Mgmt. Svcs. Inc., Boston, 1995-98, N.E. Pub. Risk, Inc., Boston, 1998, Northeast Assn. Mgmt., Inc., Boston, 1999—; v.p., treas. Pub. Employer Risk Mgmt. Assn., Albany, NY, 1989—97, pres., 1997—; bd. dirs. NLC Mut. Ins. Co., 1994—2000. Bd. dirs. Assn. Govt. Risk Pools, 2000—07, pres., 2003—05; adj. prof. Suffolk U. Grad. Sch. Mgmt., Boston, 1980—82; lectr. numerous regional and nat. trade assns. Author and editor: Managing Small Towns, 1986; contbr. articles to profl. jours. Mem. fin. com. Town of Acton, Mass., 1977-79; mem. town meeting Town of Reading, Mass., 1987-89; pres. Unitarian Universalist Ch. of Reading, 1990-93, Unitarian Universalist Ch. of Saratoga Springs, 2008-. Mem. Am. Soc. Assn. Execs., Internat. City Mgmt. Assn. (cert. in mgmt.), NYC County Mgmt. Assn. Democrat. Unitarian Universalist. Avocations: golf, tennis, volleyball, reading, boating. Office: 9 Cornell Rd Latham NY 12110 Office Phone: 518-220-9760. Business E-Mail: bwilkes@neami.com.

WILKES, DELANO ANGUS, architect; b. Panama City, Fla., Jan. 25, 1935; s. Burnice Angus and Flora Mae (Scott) W.; m. Dona Jean Murren, June 25, 1960 (dec. Nov. 26, 2006). BArch, U. Fla., 1958. Cert. Nat. Coun. Archtl.; registration bds. cert. personal trainer, older adult specialty cert. Am. Coun. on Exercise. Designer Perkins & Will Partnership, Chgo., 1960-63; designer, job capt., project mgr. Harry Weese, Ltd., Chgo., 1963-66; project arch. Fitch Larocca Carrington, Chgo., 1967-69; arch. Mittelbusher & Tourtelot, Chgo., 1970-71; assoc. Bank Bldg. Corp., Chgo., 1972-75; sr. assoc. Charles Edward Stade & Assocs., Park Ridge, Ill., 1975-77; sr. arch. Consoer Morgan Arch., Chgo., 1977-83, mktg. coord., 1980-83; design cons. Chamlin & Assocs., Peru and Morris, Ill., 1969-82, dir. arch., 1983-86, v.p. arch., 1986-2000. Archtl. cons. Sweet's divsn. McGraw Hill, Inc., Chgo., 1984-90; ptnr. Deri Wilkes Assocs., 1990-95; trainer Fitness Barn, 1995-96, Q Sports Club, 1997-98, Alpha Fitness, 1999-2001; ptnr. River Town Properties, Comml. Devel., Palatka, Fla., 2004. Author: Colonel Ebenezer Folsom, 1778-1789, North Carolina Patriot and Tory Scourge, 1975, Shrangri-La's New Face, 2006; editor Folsom Bull., 1977-80; prodr. documentary film The Angry Minority, Menninger Found., 1978. Mem. coord. com. Dune Acres Plan Commn. (Ind.), 1983-91; bldg. commr. City of Dune Acres, 1984-89; chmn. Ind. party Dune Acres, 1987; elected trustee Dune Acres Town Bd., 1988-91, pres., 1988-89; mem. Dune Acres Civic Improvement Found., 1988-91 (leadership recognition for drive to restore Dune Acres Clubhouse); cons. Inst. of Crippled and Disabled, N.Y.C., 1978-83; guest lectr. field trip guide Coll. DuPage, Glen Ellyn, Ill., 1968-76; guest arch. med. adv. com. to Pres.'s Com. for Handicapped, 1977, 78; vice chmn. Westchester County Dem. Precinct, Porter County, Ind., 1986; chmn. selection com. Dem. Hdqrs., Porter County, 1986; treas. Com. to Elect Kovach to Coun., Porter County, 1986; vice chmn. Duneland Dems., 1988-92; pres. Ocean House Condominium Assn., St. Augustine, Fla., 1993-94; mem. Emil Maestre Music Assn. Concert Assn., 1000—. Mem.: AIA, Putnam County Hist. Soc., New Eng. Hist. Geneal. Soc. (councilor bd. trustees 2007—), Am. Soc. Interior Design (coord. info. fair 1979), Chgo. Assn. Commerce and Industry (display dir. 1979 mtg.), Art Inst. Chgo., Chgo. AIA (chmn. design awards display com. 1978-79, prodr. New Mem. Show 1979, chmn. pub. rels. com. 1980), Folsom Family Assn. Am. (pres. 1978-82, v.p. 1982-, nominating chmn. 1983, host ann. meeting, Chgo. 1981), Businessmen for Pub. Interest, Emanual Mastori Musical Assn., German Shorthaired Pointer Club North Fla., Gargoyle, Cook County Hist. Soc., Chgo. Lyric Opera Guild, Soc. Colonial Wars, Wilkes Family Rsch. Assn., Marsh Creek Country Club (mem. archtl. rev. bd. 1999—, chmn. Fla. landscape com. 2003). Democrat. Unitarian Universalist. Home: 332 Marsh Point Cir Saint Augustine FL 32080-5858 Office Phone: 904-471-6956. Personal E-mail: dawilkes@bellsouth.net.

WILKES, ELAINA B., psychologist; b. Metter, Ga., Aug. 4, 1962; d. Tommy Louis Beasley and Brenda M. Paige, Charles Paige (Stepfather); m. Johnny Charles Wilkes, May 27, 1989; 1 child, Skyler Elizabeth. Cert. edn. specialist Ga. Southern U., Statesboro; sch. psychology Ga. Profl. Stds. Commn., 1992. Sch. psychologist Tattnall County Bd. Edn., Reidsville, Ga., 1992—94, Emanuel County Bd. Edn., Swainsboro, Ga., 1994—. Mem. Family Connection, Swainsboro, 2007—08. Mem.: Ga. Assn. Sch. Psychologists. Baptist. Avocations: reading, travel. Office: Emanuel County Schs 258 Tiger Trail Swainsboro GA 30401

WILKES, JOHN MICHAEL, military officer, auditor; b. Pitts., Dec. 16, 1950; s. John Joseph Wukits and Anne Lebanik. BA in Econs. and Polit. Sci., U. Pitts., 1972; student, La Roche Coll., 1984—88, BS in Acctg. magna cum laude, 1991, MS in Human Resources Mgmt., 1995; AS in Math. and Physics with honors, C.C. Allegheny County, 1998; BS in Natural Scis., U. Pitts., 2004. Spl. accounts mgr. Dell Fastener Corp., Pitts., 1974—78; commd. ens. USN, 1980, advanced through grades to lt. comdr., 1990; auditor Office of Insp. Gen. US Dept. Agr., Hyattsville, Md., 1988—90; sales Sun Book Co., Pitts., 2000—04; asst. engring. dept. Destroyer squadron 10, USS STUMP, 1980—81; lt. missile sys. Destroyer Squadron 22, USS FAHRION, 1983—84, surface combatant with Task Group 60.4 Beirut, 1983—84; asst. tng. officer, staff duty officer Commander Naval Surface Group Mediterranean, 1985—89; pers. officer Naval Embarked Adv. Team, 1996—97. Asst. So Others Might Eat, Wash., DC, 1989—90. Decorated Naval Expeditionary Medal, Nat. Def. Svc. Medal, Sea Svc. Deployment Ribbon. Republican. Cath. Achievements include invention of Decorative Door Guard system; Illuminated Decorative Door Guard System. Avocations: golf, jogging. Home: 208 Lucille St Glenshaw PA 15116

WILKES, SIR MAURICE V., computer science emeritus professor, computer scientist; b. Dudley, Eng., June 26, 1913; BA, St. John's Coll., Cambridge, 1934, MA, 1936, PhD, 1937; Degrees (hon.), Newcastle-upon-Tyne, Hull, Kent City of London, Bath, Amsterdam, Munich, Linkoping, U. Pa., Phila.; Degree (hon.), Cambridge U., 1993. Rsch. in exptl. physics, Cavendish Lab. Cambridge U., 1934—37, univ. demonstrator in the math. lab., 1937, head computer lab (formerly called math. lab.), 1945—80, prof. computer tech., 1965—80, emeritus prof., 2002—; sr. consulting engr. Digital Equipment Corp., Maynard, Mass., 1980—86; adj. prof., elec. engring. and computer sci. MIT, 1981—85; mem. for rsch. strategy Olivetti Rsch. Bd., 1986—89; staff advisor on rsch. strategy Olivetti and Oracle Rsch. Lab., Cambridge, England, 1989—99; staff cons. AT&T Lab. (formerly Olivetti and Oracle Rsch. Lab.), Cambridge, England, 1999—2002. Author: Oscillations of the Earth's Atmosphere, 1949, Automatic Digital Computers, 1956, A Short Introduction to Numerical Analysis, 1966, Time-Sharing Computer Systems, 1968, Time-Sharing Computer Systems, 3rd edit., 1975, Memoirs of Computer Pioneer, 1985, Computing Perspectives, 1995; co-author: Preparation of Programs for an Electronic Digital Computer, 1951, Preparation of Programs for an Electronic Digital Computer, 2nd edit., 1958, The Cambridge CAP Computer and Its Operating System, 1979. War svc. in radar engring. and operational rsch., 1939—45, WWII. Recipient Harry Goode Meml. award, Am. Fedn. for Info. Processing Societies, 1968, Eckert-Mauchly award, Assn. for Computing Machinery and IEEE Computer Soc., 1980, IEEE Computer Soc. Pioneer award (Charter Recipient), 1980, McDowell award, IEEE Computer Soc., 1981, Faraday medal, IEE London, 1981, Pender award, U. Pa., 1982, C&C prize, Tokyo, 1988, ITALGAS prize for Computer Sci., Turin, 1991, Kyoto prize, Japan, 1992, Von Neumann medal, IEEE, 1997; co-recipient Mountbatten medal, Nat. Electronics Coun., London, 1997; named Fellow, Computer History Mus., 2001;, St. John's Coll., Cambridge, Eng., 1950—. Fellow: Royal Acad. Engring. (London), British Computer Soc. (first pres. 1957—60, disting. fellow 1973), Royal Soc., Assn. for Computing Machinery (coun. mem. 1991—94, Turning Lectr. 1967); mem.: Spanish Acad. Engring. (fgn. corresponding mem.), NAS, Royal Spanish Acad. Sciences (fgn. corresponding mem., fgn. assoc.), NAE (fgn. assoc.), Am. Acad. Arts & Sciences (fgn. hon. mem.), Worshipful Co. Scientific Instrument Makers (hon. freeman 2000). In 1946, attended the Moore School lectures on computers in Philadelphia, and began working on the EDSAC, which became operative in 1949. In 1951, along with two colleagues, published the first book on computer programming. Following this, proposed microprogramming, a system that became adopted throughout the computer industry. In 1965, published the first paper on cache memories, followed by the book on timesharing. In 1974, decided that local area networks could be more effective if based on computer rather than telecommunications technology, which led to the design study for what became known as the Cambridge Ring, published in 1975. This was the basis of a client server system that was defined as the Cambridge Model Distributed System in 1980. Office: Univ Cambridge Computer Lab William Gates Bldg Office SN03 15 JJ Thomson Ave Cambridge CB3 0FD England Office Phone: 441223 763699. Business E-Mail: maurice.wilkes@cl.cam.ac.uk.

WILKEY, MALCOLM RICHARD, retired ambassador, judge; b. Murfreesboro, Tenn., Dec. 6, 1918; s. Malcolm Newton and Elizabeth (Gilbert) W.; m. Emma Secul Depolo, Dec. 21, 1959. AB magna cum laude, Harvard U., 1940, LLB, 1948; LLD (hon.), Rose-Hulman Inst. Tech., 1984. Bar: Tex. 1948, NY 1963, US Supreme Ct. 1952, DC 1970. US atty. So. Dist. Tex., 1954-58; asst. atty. gen. US, 1958-61; ptnr. Butler Binion Rice & Cook, 1961-63; gen. counsel, sec. Kennecott Copper Corp., 1963-70; judge US Ct. Appeals DC Cir., 1970-85; US amb. to Uruguay, 1985-90. Ofcl. in charge fed. forces at Little Rock Sch. Crisis, Dept. Justice, 1958; mem. US-Chile Arbitration Commn., 1991-97; lectr. internat. constl. and adminstrv. law London Poly., 1979, 80; lectr. Tulane U. Law Summer Sch., Grenoble, France, 1981, 83, San Diego Law Summer Sch., Oxford, Eng., 1983, Brigham Young Law Sch., 1984, 93; vis. fellow Wolfson Coll., Cambridge U., 1985; chmn. Pres.'s Commn. on Revision Fed. Ethics Laws, 1989; spl. counsel to Atty. Gen. for inquiry into the House Banking Facility, 1992. Author: Is It Time For A Second Constitutional Convention, 1995, As the Twig is Bent, 2003. Del. Rep. Nat. Conv., 1960. Served from 2d lt. to lt. col. AUS, 1941-45. Named Am. mem., Fulbright Commn., 2002—; hon. fellow, Wolfson Coll., Cambridge. Fellow Am. Bar Found.; mem. Am. Law Inst. (adv. com. restatement fgn. rels. law of US), Jud. Conf. US (com. on standards for admission to fed. cts. 1976-79), Phi Beta Kappa, Delta Sigma Rho, Phi Delta Phi (hon.). Republican. Address: Av El Bosque 379 Providencia Santiago Chile E-mail: mrw@wilkey.us.

WILKIE, BARRY JAMES, manufacturing engineer; b. Oak Harbor, Wash., Dec. 12, 1956; s. Carrie Mae Wilkie; m. Carol Jean Warmuskerken, Nov. 18, 1983; children: Carrie Jean, William Barry, Gabrielle Cherilyn, Matthew James. MTech, U. Southern Miss., Hattiesburg, 2006. Chief prodn. engr. Northrop Grumman Ship Bldg., Pascagoula, Miss., 2003—07, quality mgmt. sys. mgr., 2007—. Home: 21239 Old Hwy 49 Saucier MS 39574-8423 Office: Northrop Grumman Corp PO Box 149 MS T500-01 Pascagoula MS 39568-0149 Office Fax: 228-933-6974. Personal E-mail: barrywilkie@bellsouth.net. Business E-Mail: barry.wilkie@ngc.com.

WILKIE, DONALD WALTER, retired biologist, aquarium administrator; b. Vancouver, BC, Can., June 20, 1931; s. Otway James Henry and Jessie Margaret (McLeod) W.; m. Patricia Ann Archer, May 18, 1958; children: Linda, Douglas, Susanne. BA, U. B.C., 1960, M.Sc., 1966. Curator Vancouver Pub. Aquarium, 1961-63, Phila. Aquarama, 1963-65; exec. dir. aquarium-mus. Scripps Instn. Oceanography, La Jolla, Calif., 1965-93, exec. dir. emeritus, 1993—; founding dir. Birch Aquarium of Scripps, 1992. Cons. aquarium design, rschg. exhibit content; sci. writer and editor naturalist-marine edn. programs. head coach, Scholastic Clay Targets Prog., 2003-08. Author books on aquaria and marine ednl. materials; contbr. numerous articles to profl. jours. Bd. mem. San Diego Shotgun Sports Assn., 2008; pres. UCSD Retirement Assn. 1999-02. Mem. San Diego (Calif.) Zool. Soc., Writingentstory Aquariums Scripps Instn. San Diego. Home: 4548 Cather Ave San Diego CA 92122-2632 Office: U Calif San Diego Scripps Instn Oceanography Libr 9500 Gilman Dr La Jolla CA 92093-0219 E-mail: dwilkie@ucsd.edu, donwilkie1@mac.com. *As a biologist and teacher my major goal has been to increase public interest in learning about our environment and promoting proper use of the earth's resources.*

WILKIE, ROBERT LEON, JR., former federal agency administrator; b. Frankfort, Germany, Aug. 6, 1962; s. Robert Leon and Joy Ann (Somerville) W.; m. Julia Cameron Bullard, May 19, 1990; children: Adam, Megan BA cum laude, Wake Forest U., 1985; JD, Loyola of the South, 1988; LLM in Internat. Law & Legis., Georgetown U., 1992; M in Strategic Studies, US Army War coll., 2002. Legis. counsel to Senator Jesse Helms US Senate, Washington, 1988-95; legis. dir. to Rep. David Funderburk US House Reps., 1995; dir. N.C. Republican Party, 1996-97; counsel & adv. to Senate Majority Leader Trent Lott US Senate, 1997—2003; sr. dir. NSC, Washington, 2003—05; spl. asst. to Pres. for nat. security affairs The White House, Washington, 2003—05; prin. dep. asst. sec for legis. affairs US Dept. Def., Washington, 2005—06, acting asst. sec. for legis. affairs, 2006, asst. sec. for legis. affairs, 2006—09. Mem. Loyola Moot Ct. Bd., 1988. Author newspaper polit. editorials, 1990-93. Staff mem. Rep. Nat. Conv., 1992. Intelligence officer USNR. Recipient Bustamonte award for outstanding achievement in internat. law The Soc. Jesus, New Orleans, 1987, Am. Jurisprudence awards for excellence in Latin Am. law Internat. Law and Legislation, 1987-88; named Jr. Intelligemce Officer (Res.) of the Yr., Office Naval Intelligence Mem. ABA, Rep. Nat. Lawyers Assn., The Federalist Soc. Republican. Roman Catholic. Avocations: English history, mil. history, So. history and lit., distance running.*

WILKIN, ALANA ZIMMER, elementary school educator; b. Danville, Pa., June 3, 1961; d. Albert Arthur and Alma Clara Zimmer; m. Timothy Vail Wilkin; children: Brandon Zimmer Madura, Albert Peyton Madura. BA, Thiel Coll., Greenville, Pa., 1983; MS, U. South Ala., Mobile, 1998. Cert. med. technologist Am. Soc. Clin. Pathologists, 1984, specialist in blood banking Am. Soc. Clin. Pathologists, 1984. Med. technologist Montefiore Hosp., Pitts., 1984—85, St. Elizabeth Hosp., West Lafayette, Ind., 1985—86; blood bank specialist St. Lukes

Episcopal Hosp., Houston, 1986—87; quality control technologist Gamma Biologicals, Houston, 1987—90; med. technologist - tng. specialist ARC, Mobile, 1990—97; quality control mgr./trainer Gamma Biologicals, Houston, 1997—2001; tchr. lang. arts Cypress-Fairbanks Ind. Sch. Dist., Houston, 2001—. Recipient Spotlight Tchr., Cypress-Fairbanks Ind. Sch. Dist., 2006. Mem.: Assn. Tex. Profl. Educators, Pi Lambda Theta, Kappa Delta Pi. Home: 13311 Blackbird Dr Cypress TX 77429 Office: Lowery Elem 15950 Ridge Park Houston TX 77095 Business E-Mail: alana.wilkin@cfisd.net.

WILKIN, RICHARD EDWIN, clergyman, religious organization administrator; b. nr. Paulding, Ohio, Nov. 3, 1930; s. Gaylord D. and Beulah E. (Tarlton) W.; m. Barbara A. Zehender, Aug. 10, 1952; children— Richard Edward, James Lee, Deborah Ann. Student, Giffin Jr. Coll., 1948-49; BS, Findlay Coll., 1952, D.D., 1975; postgrad., Ind. U., 1959-60. Ordained to ministry Churches of God Gen. Conf., 1953; pastor Neptune Ch. of God, Celina, Ohio, 1952-59, Wharton (Ohio) Ch. of God, 1959-64, Anthony Wayne Ch. of God, Ft. Wayne, Ind., 1964-70; adminstr., chief exec. Chs. of God Gen. Conf., Findlay, Ohio, 1970-87; supr. mission work India, Bangladesh, Haiti, 1970-85; dir. field edn. and Inst. for. Biblical Studies, faculty mem. Winebrenner Theol. Sem., Findlay, 1987-92, adj. facult O.T., 1993-97; interim sr. pastor Coll. 1st Ch. of God, Findlay, 1992-93. Dir. summer youth camps, sec., mem. exec. com. Ohio Conf., 1952-59, state clk., pres., 1959-64; chmn. Commn. on Edn., mem. exec. com. Ind. Conf., 1964-70; adv. com. Am. Bible Soc.; steering com. U.S. Ch. Leaders, 1979; pres. Ft. Wayne Ministerial Assn.; bd. dirs. Associated Chs. of Ft. Wayne and Allen County, 1966-70; tchr. Center Twp. Jr. High Sch., Celina, Mendon (Ohio) Union High Sch., Van Del High Sch., Van Wert, Ohio, 1954-59; interim pastor Shawnee First Ch. of God, Lima, Ohio, 1987-88, ch. cons., 1987-98. Vice pres. bd. trustees Winebrenner Haven, mem. adv. com. in race rels. regarding sch. reorgn. and busing, Ft. Wayne, 1967-69; trustee Winebrenner Theol. Sem., 1980-87, sec. bd. trustees; trustee U. Findlay, 1985-2008, chmn. com. trustees, elected trustee emeritus, 2008; sec. bd. of pensions Gen. Conf., Ch. of God, 1986-99; bd. dirs. Found. Great Lakes, Conf. Chs. of God, 1998-2006, chmn. adminstr.'s adv. com., 1998-2003; faculty chair, bd. trustees Coll. Liberal Arts, 2009. Recipient Outstanding Tchr. award, 1958; Disting. Alumnus award Findlay Coll., 1973, Outstanding Leadership award Ohio Conf. Chs. of God, 1986, Disting. Assoc. award U. Findlay, 1992; named Hon. Alumnus Winebrenner Theol. Sem., 1978.

WILKIN, RICHARD THOMAS, geochemist; b. Highland Park, Ill., July 11, 1965; s. James and Dorothy (Dvorak) W.; m. Melissa Marie Harreld, Mar. 3, 1990; children: Andrew, James. BA, U. Minn., 1988; MS, Mich. Technol. U., 1991; PhD, Pa. State U., 1995. Jr. scientist U. Minn., Mpls., 1987-89; rsch. asst. Mich. Technol. U., Houghton, 1989-90; from tchg. asst. to rsch. assoc. Pa. State U., University Park, 1991-99; environ. scientist U.S. EPA, Ada, Okla., 1999—. Mem. Am. Chem. Soc., Geochem. Soc., Geol. Soc. Am., Soc. Econ. Geologists, Min. Soc. Am. Home: 16730 County Road 3580 Ada OK 74820-1436 E-mail: wilkin.rick@epa.gov.

WILKINS, ADDI L., retired lay worker; b. Gleason, Tenn., June 9, 1933; d. Roy Thomas and Sendy Estelle Wilkins; children from previous marriage: Raybarn, Regina, Theresa, Roscoe, Anthony. At, Stowe Coll., St. Louis, 1953—55, St. Louis U., 1987, Valparaiso U., Ind., 1988. Consecrated Luth. Deaconess Assn., 1989. Adminstrv. asst. All Nation and Transfiguration Luth. Ch., St. Louis, coord. social ministry. Sec. no. zone women's group Luth. Women's Missionary League, St. Louis; sec. dist. bd. social ministry Luth. Family Svc. Luth. Ch. Mo. Synod; spkr. to ch. and youth groups. Chmn. bd. Pruitt Igo Devel. Housing Corp., St. Louis; bd. dir. United Ch. Christ Neighbor Houses, Friends of Moms; bd. mem. Luth. Family and Children Svcs. Recipient Cmty. Svc. award, Nat. Coun. Negro Women, 2004, Star Bethel Bapt. Ch., 2004; named Mother of Yr., Sigma Gamma Rho (St. Louis chpt.), 1989. Mem.: Luth. Deaconess Assn. Democrat. Lutheran. Avocations: gardening, reading, crafts, quilting. Home: 1905 E Warne Ave Saint Louis MO 63107-1017 Office Phone: 314-385-2653.

WILKINS, AMY P., publishing executive; BA, Holy Cross Coll., 1984. Assoc. pub., advt. dir. Health Mag. Time Inc., 1994—95, pub., 1995—97; pres. Petersen Youth Group1, 1997—98; pub. Biography Mag., 1998—2000, Smithsonian, Smithsonian Air & Space Mag., 2000; pub. Better Homes and Gardens mag. Meredith Corp., 2005, pub. Country Home, 2006—07; sr. v.p., pub. Martha Stewart Weddings, 2007—. Office: Martha Stewart Living Omnimedia Inc 11 W 42nd St New York NY 10036 Office Phone: 212-827-8000. Office Fax: 212-827-8204.

WILKINS, BARRATT (GEORGE WILKINS), librarian; b. Atlanta, Nov. 6, 1943; s. George Barratt and Mabel Blanche (Brooks) W. BA, Emory U., 1965; MA, Ga. State U., 1968, U. Wis., 1969. Reference libr. SC State Libr., Columbia, 1969-71; instl. libr. cons. Mo. State Libr., Jefferson City, 1971-73; asst. state libr. State Libr. Fla., Tallahassee, 1973-77, state libr., 1977—2003; dir. div. Libr. and Info. Svcs. State Fla., Tallahassee, 1986—2003; acting asst. sec. state Fla. Dept. of State, 1987. Abstractor Hist. Abstracts, 1967—71; dir. survey project Nat. Ctr. Edn. Stats., 1976—77, chmn. state libr. agys. survery steering coun., 2003—; bd. dirs. S.E. Libr. Network, Inc., 1979—82, treas., 1980—81, vice chmn., 1981—82; mem. adv. coun. US Pub. Printer, 1983—86, S.E. Atlantic Regional Med. Libr. Svcs., 1986—89; mem. planning com. Fla. Automated Edn. Commn., 1989—94; del The White House Conf., Libr., Info Svcs., 1991; mem. steering com. pub., state libr. surveys Nat. Ctr. Edn. Stats., 1992—; mem. adv. coun. Fla. State Bd. Ind. Colleges, Universities, 1995—98, Fla. State U. Sch. Info. Studies, 1999—2000; mem. pub. libr. surveys Nat. Ctr. Ednl. Stats., 1997—2003; mem. privacy, tech. task force State Fla., 2000—01; mem. Speakers Legis. Hist. Preservation Com., 2000—03; mem. libr. stats. revision com. Nat. Info. Stds. Orgn., 2001—03; del The White House Conf. Sch. Librs., 2002; bd. dirs. First Am. Found., Inc., Fla. Distance Learning Network, Inc.; mem. planning com. Fla. Gov.'s Conf. Libraries, Info. svcs.; cons. in field. Contbr. articles profl. jours. Mem. adv. com. statewide jail project Mo. Assn. Social Welfare, 1971-73, bd. dirs. ctrl. divsn., 1971-73; mem. State Univ. System Interinstl. Lib. Com., 1977-2003; bd. dirs. Fla. Ctr. Libr. Automation, 1984-2003, Fla. Ctr. for the Book, 1984—, Fla. Coll. Ctr. for Libr. Automation, 1990-2003, Coun. for Fla. Librs., 1981—; pres. Rose Hollow Homeowners Assn., 2004-; patron Atlanta Hist. Soc., Hist. Oakland Found. Recipient Leadership Achievement award Assn. Specialized and Coop. Libr. Agys., 1991, Outstanding Pub. Svc. award Gov. of Fla., 1991, Keppel award and Lorenz award Nat. Ctr. Edn. Stats., 1995—, Profl. Achievement award Assn. Specialized and Coop. Libr. Agencies, 2003, Disting. Alumni award U. Wis. Sch. Libr. and Info. Studies, 2003; U. Wis. fellow, 1969. Mem. ALA (coun. 1981-85, legis. com. 1982-86, com. on orgn. 1988-90, planning com., 1993-95, standards, 1996-98, legis. honor roll 1996), Assn. State Libr. Agys. (pres. 1976-77), Assn. Hosp. Instl. Librs. (bd. dirs. 1973-74), Am. Correctional Assn. (chair instn. libr. com. 1975-80), Southeastern Libr. Assn. (pres. 1982-84), Assn. Specialized and Coop. Libr. Agys. (bd. dirs. 1981-85, 87-89, stds. rev. 1997—2003, chair awards com., 2003-05, chair legis. com., 2005-), Fla. Libr. Assn. (hon. life mem.), Libr. Adminstrn. and Mgmt. Assn. (chair govt. affair com. 1984-86), Chief Officers of State Libr. Agys. (bd. dirs. 1980-82, pres. 1990-92, chair legis. com. 1992-96, chair rsch. & stats. com. 1998-2003), Univ. Club, Gov.'s Club, Beta Phi Mu, Phi Alpha Theta. Episcopalian. E-mail: barratt.wilkins@mac.com.

WILKINS, BURLEIGH TAYLOR, philosophy educator; b. Bridgetown, Va., July 1, 1932; s. Burleigh and Helen Marie (Taylor) W.; children: Brita Taylor, Carla Cowgill, Burleigh William. BA summa cum laude, Duke U., 1952; MA, Harvard U., 1954, Princeton U., 1963, PhD, 1965. Instr. MIT, Cambridge, 1957-60, Princeton U., 1960-61, 63; asst. prof. Rice U., Houston, 1965-66, assoc. prof., 1966-67, U. Calif., Santa Barbara, 1967-68, prof., 1968—. Author: Carl Becker, 1961, The Problem of Burke's Political Philosophy, 1967, Hegel's Philosophy of History, 1974, Has History Any Meaning?, 1978, Terrorism and Collective Responsibility, 1992; editor: The European Convention on Human Rights, 2008. Mem.: Phi Beta Kappa. Office: U Calif Dept Philosophy Santa Barbara CA 93106

WILKINS, CAROLINE HANKE, advocate, political organization worker; b. Corpus Christi, Tex., May 12, 1937; d. Louis Allen and Jean Guckian Hanke; m. B. Hughel Wilkins, 1957; 1 child, Brian Hughel. Student, Tex. Coll. Arts and Industries, 1956—57, Tex. Tech. U., 1957—58; BA, U. Tex., 1961; MA magna cum laude, U. Ams., 1964. Instr. history Oreg. State U., 1967-68; adminstr. Consumer Svcs. divsn. State of Oreg., 1977-80, Wilkins Assocs., 1980—. Mem. PFMC Salmon Adv. subpanel, 1982-86. Author: (with B. H. Wilkins) Implications of the U.S.-Mexican Water Treaty for Interregional Water Transfer, 1968. Mem. Kerr Libr. Bd., Oreg. State U., 1989—95, pres., 1994—95; mem. Corvallis-Benton County Libr. Found., 1991—2001, sec., 1993, v.p., 1994, pres., 1995, mission and goals com. chair, 2000—01; pres. Oreg. State-Corvallis chpt. UNIFEM, 1998—2002; mem. Women and Philanthropy, Oreg. State U. Giving Cir., 2003—07, Oreg. Jud. Fitness and Disability Commn., 2004—, vice chair, 2006, chair, 2007; Dem. precinct committeewoman Benton County, Oreg., 1964—90; publicity chmn. Benton County Gen. Election, 1964; chmn. Get-Out-the-Vote Com., Benton County, 1966; vice chmn. Benton County Dem. Ctrl. Com., 1966—70, 1st Congl. Dist., Oreg., 1966—67, chmn., 1967—68; vice chmn. Dem. Party of Oreg., 1968—69, chmn., 1969—74; mem. exec. com. Western States Dem. Conf., 1970—72; vice chmn. Dem. Nat. Com., 1972—77, mem. arrangements com., 1972, 1976, mem. Dem. Charter Commn., 1973—74, mem., 1972—77, 1985—89, mem. size and composition com., 1987—89, mem. rules com., 1988; mem. ethics commn. Oreg. Govt., 1974—76; del., mem. rules com. Dem. Nat. Conv., 1988; 1st v.p. Nat. Fedn. Dem. Women, 1983—85, pres., 1985—87, parliamentarian, 1993—95, 1999—2001, chair Pres.'s coun., 2001—03, chair by-laws com., 2003—05, parliamentarian, 2005—07, western regional dir., 2005—07; nominating com., 2008—09; pres. Oreg. Fedn. Dem. Women, 1997—2001; bd. dirs. Oreg. chpt. US Lighthouse Soc., pres., 1997—98; bd. dirs. Oreg. State U.-Corvallis Symphony, 1998—2001, v.p., 1999—2000, resources com., mem. endowment task force, 2007; bd. dirs. Oreg. State U. Acad. Lifelong Learning, 2003—08. Named Outstanding Mem. Nat. Fedn. Dem. Women, 1992, Woman of Achievement, Oreg. State U. Women's Ctr., 1998. Mem.: Soc. Consumer Affairs Profls., Nat. Assn. Consumer Agy. Adminstrs., Oreg. State U. Folk Club (pres. faculty wives 1989—90, scholarship chair 2000—01, grants com. 2002—03), Zonta Internat. (vice area bd. dirs. dist. 8 1992—94, bd. dist. 8 1994—96, by laws and resolutions chair 1997—98, internat. rels. coord. dist. chair 8 2000—02, mem. dist. 8 nominating com. 2003—06, chair 2005—06, parliamentarian 2006—08, Zonta Internat. Found. bd. dirs. 2007—08, chair devel. com. 2007—08). Office: 3311 NW Roosevelt Dr Corvallis OR 97330-1169

WILKINS, CHARLES L., chemist, educator; b. LA, Aug. 14, 1938; s. Richard and Lenore M. Wilkins; m. Ingrid Fritsch, 1997; children: Mark R., Connor W. Fritsch, Eric. BS, Chapman Coll., 1961; PhD, U. Oreg., 1966. Prof. chemistry U. Nebr., Lincoln, 1967-81; prof. U. Calif., Riverside, 1981-98; disting. prof. U. Ark., Fayetteville, 1998—. Recipient Frank H. Field and Joe L. Franklin award for Outstanding Achievement in mass spectrometry, Am. Chem. Soc., 1997, Eastern Analytical Symposium award in the fields of Analytical Chemistry, 2002, Alumni Disting. Achievement award, Ark. U., 2003, Alumni Achievement award, U. Oreg. Dept. Chemistry, 2004—05, Fulbright Coll. Master Rschr.; award, 2006. Fellow: Soc. Applied Spectroscopy (life). Office: U Ark Dept Chem & Biochem Fayetteville AR 72701 E-mail: cwilkins@uark.edu.

WILKINS, DAVID GEORGE, fine arts educator; b. Battle Creek, Mich., Sept. 12, 1939; s. George Henry and Marjorie Ewing (Pierce) Wilkins; m. Ann Thomas, June 25, 1966; children: Rebecca Louise, Katherine May. BA, Oberlin Coll., 1961; MA, U. Mich., 1963, PhD, 1969. Instr. U. N.H., Durham, 1963—64; prof. dept. history of art and arch. U. Pitts., 1967—2004, chair, 1989—92, 1998—2004, dir. univ. art gallery, 1976—92. Faculty mem summer sessions Sarah Lawrence Col-Univ Mich, Florence, Italy, 1975—81, Duquesne U., Rome, 2004, Rome, 07, Rome, 09. Author (with Bernard Schultz and Katheryn M Linduff): Art Past/Art Present, 2008; author: (with Bonnie Bennett) Donatello, 1984, Maso di Banco, 1985; author: (with K J Arbitman) The Illustrated Bartsch, Vol 53, Pre-Rembrandt Etchers, 1985, The Art of the Duquesne Club, 2002; author: (with Mark M Brown and Lu Donnelly) The History of the Duquesne Club, 1989; author: (with F. Hartt) History of Italian Renaissance Art, 6th edit., 2006; editor (with Rebecca L Wilkins): The Search for a Patron in the Middle Ages and the Renaissance, 1996; editor: (with Sheryl Reiss) Beyond Isabella: Secular Women Patrons of Art in the Italian Renaissance, 2001; editor: The Collins Big Book of Art, 2005, A Reflection of PA St. Paul Cathedral, Pitts., 1906-2006, 2007. Mem Humanities Coun, 1984—88; mus adv panel Pa Coun Arts, 1985—87; bd dirs Pittsburgh Ctr Arts, 1979—98; Mendelssohn Choir Pittsburgh, 1979—84. Recipient Chancellor's Disting. Tchg. award, U. Pitts., 1987; fellow William E. Suida, Kress Found, Kunsthistorisches Inst, Florence, 1966—67. Mem.: Renaissance Soc. Am., Italian Art Soc., Coll. Art Assn. (Disting. Tchg. Art History award 2005). Democrat. Home: 1005 East Shore Dr Silver Lake NH 03875 Business E-Mail: dgw2@pitt.edu.

WILKINS, DAVID HORTON, United States Ambassador to Canada, former state legislator; b. Greenville, SC, Oct. 12, 1946; m. Susan Clary; children: James, Robert. BA (hon.), Clemson U., 1968; JD, U. SC, 1971; degree (hon.), Med. U. SC, Citadel. Bar: SC. Mem. SC House Reps., 1980—2005, chmn. judiciary com., 1986—92, spkr. pro tempore, 1992-95, spkr., 1995—2005; US amb. to Can. US Dept. State, Ottawa, 2005—. Adj. prof. Greenville Tech. Coll., 1972—94; chmn. Greenville County Legis. Del., 1985—86; pres. Nat. Spkrs. Assn., 1998—2005; fellow Am. Acad. Matrimonial Lawyers. With US Army, 1971, with USAR, 1973—76. Recipient Friend of the Taxpayer award SC Assn. Taxpayers, others; named Outstanding Legislator of Yr. by SC C. of C., Dept. Probation of Parole, SC Sch. Bds. Assn., SC Troopers Assn., others, Nat. Rep. Legislator of Yr. Nat. Rep. Legis. Assn. Republican. Baptist. Office: DOS Amb 5480 Ottawa Pl Washington DC 20521-5480*

WILKINS, DOMINIQUE (JACQUES DOMINIQUE WILKINS), professional sports team executive, retired professional basketball player; b. Orléans, France, Jan. 12, 1960; came to US, 1964; s. John and Geraldine Wilkins; m. Nicole Berry, Sept. 26, 1992 (div.); m. Robin Wilkins; 6 children. BBA, U. Ga., 1982. Player Atlanta Hawks, 1982—94, LA Clippers, 1994, Boston Celtics, 1994—95, Panathinaikos-Athens, Greece, 1995—96, San Antonio Spurs, 1996—97, Teamsystem, Bologna, Italy, 1997—98, Orlando Magic, 1998—99, Anaheim Roadrunners, 2000; spl. asst. to the exec. v.p., player devel. asst. to v.p. basketball Atlanta Spirit, LLC (parent co. of NBA Atlanta Hawks, NHL Atlanta Thrashers and Philips Arena), 2000—04, v.p. basketball, 2004—, TV analyst. Named to NBA All-Rookie Team, 1983, NBA All-Star Team, 1986-94, All-NBA First Team, 1986, Ga. Sports Hall of Fame, 2004, Atlanta Sports Hall of Fame, 2005, Naismith Basketball Hall of Fame, 2006 Achievements include holding a single game record for most free throws without a miss (23), 1992; 9th all-time leading scorer in NBA history; NBA scoring leader, 1986; NBA slam dunk champion NBA, 1985, 90; won European Championship as a member of Panathinaikos-Athens, 1996. Office: Atlanta Spirit LLC 101 Marietta St NW Ste 1900 Atlanta GA 30303 Office Phone: 404-878-3800.*

WILKINS, FLOYD, JR., retired lawyer; b. Fowler, Calif., Sept. 8, 1925; s. Floyd and Kathryn (Springborg) W.; m. Holly Blee, June 18, 1949 (div. Jan. 1964); children: Douglas B., Janet H., Steven B., Kevin D.; m. Sybil Ann Perrault, Feb. 22, 1964. BS, U. Calif., Berkeley, 1946; LLB, Harvard U., 1952. Bar: N.Y. 1953, Calif. 1959. Assoc. Dwight, Royall, Harris, Koegel & Caskey, NYC, 1952-58; v.p., trust officer San Diego Trust & Savs. Bank, 1958-63; assoc., then ptnr., prin. Seltzer Caplan Wilkins & McMahon, P.C. and predecessors, San Diego, 1963-91. Lectr. U. So. Calif. Tax Inst., L.A., 1975, Title Ins. and Trust Co., L.A. and Santa Ana, Calif., 1973, 78, 83, Trust Svcs. of Am. Tax Forum, San Diego, U. Calif. Continuing Edn. of Bar, San Diego, 1977-91. Bd. dirs., pres. San Diego County Citizens Scholarship Found. Served with USNR, 1944-46. Mem. ABA, State Bar Calif., San Diego County Bar Assn. Republican. Avocations: travel, photography, wine, gardening. Home: 2005 Soledad Ave La Jolla CA 92037-3904 Personal E-mail: fwilkins@san.rr.com.

WILKINS, FRED CLAYTON, physician, educator, engineer; b. Barnwell, SC, Aug. 18, 1958; s. Fred C. Wilkins and Mary Josephine Erskine; m. Sharon Rawls Wilkins, Dec. 1, 1990 (dec. June 26, 2004); 1 child, Marshall Clayton. BS in Applied Sciences and Engring., US Mil. Acad., West Point, 1980; MS in Systems Mgmt., U. So. Calif., 1988; MD, U. Miss. Med. Ctr., 1997; M in Biomedical Sci., U. Miss., Jackson, 2004. Cert. flight instr. FAA, 1991. Airborne inf. officer Inf. Ctr., Fort Benning, Ga., 1980—81; flight instr. Army Aviation Ctr., Fort Rucker, Ala., 1982—84; aviation platoon leader Fourth Squadron, Seventh US Cav., Uijongbu, Republic of Korea, 1984—85; aviation maintenance co. comdr. Fifth Squadron, Seventeenth Air Cav., Fort Hood, Tex., 1986—88; sr. test program engr. USAF, Eglin, Fla., 1989—90; state aviation standardization officer Miss. Army N.G., Jackson, 1990—91; family practice resident Naval Hosp. Pensacola, Fla., 1997—98; dir. clin. services, sr. med. officer Naval Air Sta. Whiting Field, Pensacola, 1999—2002; naval aviator, flight surgeon dual designator Chief Naval Air Tng., Pensacola, 2003—. Adj. prof. Pensacola Jr. Coll., Fla., 2003—. Editor: (aviation textbook) Naval Helicopter Aerodynamics. Maj. US Army, 1980—93, Republic of Korea, lt. comdr. USN, 1997—2007. Recipient Proctor and Gamble Profl. Opportunity award, Am. Physiology Soc., 1993, Outstanding Student award, Miss. State Legislature and Bd. Higher Edn., 1997; fellow, Glaxo Rsch. Inst., 1993-1995; Hearin-Hess Scholarship, U. Miss., 1991-1992, Dean's Scholarship, 1992-1995, Health Profession Scholarship, USN, 1993-1997. Mem.: Am. Bd. Utilization Rev. and Quality Assurance (assoc.), US Naval Inst. (life), Army Aviation Assn. Am. (life; treas. 1982—83), Assn. Mil. Surgeons of the US (life). Christian. Avocations: flying, travel, sailing, scuba diving, tennis. Personal E-mail: clay.wilkins@navy.mil.

WILKINS, JAMES D., language educator; PhD, Ohio State U., Columbus, 1989. Assoc. prof., French Calvin Coll., Grand Rapids, Mich., 1989—97; prof., French Lee U., Cleve., Tenn., 1997—. Recipient Excellence Tchg. award, Lee U., 2003. Mem.: AATF, ACTFL (OPI tester trainer 1998—). Office: Lee Univ 1120 N Ocoee St Cleveland TN 37311 Office Fax: 423-614-8209. Business E-Mail: jwilkins@leeuniversity.edu.

WILKINS, MICHAEL JON, state supreme court justice; b. Murray, Utah, May 13, 1948; s. Jack L. and Mary June (Phillips) W.; m. Diane W. Wilkins, Nov. 9, 1967; children: Jennifer, Stephanie, Bradley J. BS, U. Utah, 1975, JD, 1976; LLM, U. Va., 2001. Bar: Utah 1977, U.S. Dist. Ct. Utah 1977, U.S. Ct. Appeals (10th cir.) 1987, U.S. Supreme Ct. 1986. Mng. ptnr. Wilkins, Oritt & Headman, Salt Lake City, 1989-94; judge Utah Ct. Appeals, 1994—2000; justice Utah Supreme Ct., 2000—, past assoc. chief justice. Mem. Gov.'s Adv. Com. on Corp., Salt Lake City, 1989-94; mem. Utah Supreme Ct. Complex Steering Com., 1993-94; mem. Judiciary Standing Com. on Tech., 1995-2000, chmn., 1995-2000; mem. Legis. Compensation Commn., 1994-95. Trustee Utah Law Related Edn. Project, Inc., Salt Lake City, 1991-95, chmn., 1992-94. 1st lt. U.S. Army, 1968-72. Mem. Lds Ch. Office: Utah Supreme Ct 450 S State St PO Box 140210 Salt Lake City UT 84114-0210*

WILKINS, RAYFORD, JR., telecommunications industry executive; b. Waco, Tex. m. Lorena Wilkins; 1 child. BBA, U. Tex., Austin, 1974. Comml. asst. Southwestern Bell Tel., Houston, 1974; with SBC Comm., 1983—2005, pres. Kans. & western Mo. area, pres. Pacific Bell Bus. Comm. Svcs., 1997, pres. SBC Comm. Svc., 1997—99, pres. CEO Southwestern Bell Tel., pres. SBC bus. comm. svcs., 1999—2000, pres., CEO Pacific Bell, 2000, grp. pres. SBC mktg. & sales, 2000, grp. pres., CEO SBC enterprise bus. svcs.; CEO diversified businesses AT&T Inc. (merger of SBC Comm. with AT&T Corp.), San Antonio, 2005—. Chmn. bd. Cingular Wireless; bd. mem. H&R Block, Telefonos de Mexico, Am. Movil. Bd. mem. AT&T Found., Tiger Woods Found., Tiger Woods Learning Ctr.; mem. adv. coun. U. Tex. McCombs Sch. Bus., Austin. Recipient Eagle award, Nat. Eagles Leadership Inst., 1997; named CEO of Yr., Minority Supplier Coun., 1997; named one of Top 50 African Ams., Black Enterprise mag., 1999, Nation's 50 Most Powerful Black Execs., Fortune mag., 2002, 50 Most Important African Ams. in Tech., eAccess Corp., 2002, 2005, 75 Most Powerful African Ams. in Corp. Am., Black Enterprise mag., 2005, 100 Most Important Blacks in Tech., US Black Engr. & Info. Tech. mag., 2006, Top 100 Blacks in Corp. Am., Black Profl. mag., 2006. Mailing: AT&T Inc 175 E Houston St PO Box 2933 San Antonio TX 78299-2933*

WILKINS, ROBERT HENRY, neurosurgeon, editor, educator; b. Pitts., Aug. 18, 1934; s. George H. and Mary M. (Lemon) W.; m. Gloria A. Kohl, Dec. 28, 1957; children: Michael I., Jeffrey K., Elizabeth A. BS, U. Pitts., 1955, MD, 1959. Diplomate Am. Bd. Neurol. Surgery. Intern, resident gen. surgery Duke U. Med. Ctr., Durham, NC, 1959-61, resident in neurosurgery, 1963-68, asst. prof. neurosurgery, 1968-72, prof. neurosurgery, 1976—2004, chief divsn. neurosurgery, 1976-96, emeritus prof. neurosurgery, 2005—; clin. assoc. surgery br. Nat. Cancer

Inst., Bethesda, Md., 1961-63; chmn. dept. neurosurgery Scott and White Clinic, Temple, Tex., 1972-75; assoc. prof. neurosurgery U. Pitts., 1975-76. Lectr. Cook County Grad. Sch. Medicine, Chgo., 1976-96; attending neurosurgeon Durham VA Hosp., 1968-72, 78-98; mem. Nat. Adv. Coun. Nat. Inst. Neurol. Disorders and Stroke, 1989-92. Co-editor: Neurosurgery, 2d edit., 3 vols., 1996, Neurosurgery Updates I and II, 1990, 91, Neurosurgical Operative Atlas, 1991-2000, Principles of Neurosurgery, 1994; editor Clin. Neurosurgery, 1972-75; assoc. editor Surg. Neurology, 1975-76; founding editor Neurosurgery, 1977-82, mem. editl. rev. bd., 1997-2001; mem. editl. bd. Jour. Neurosurgery, 1987-96, chmn., 1996-97, mem. adv. bd., 1997—; neurosurgery editor Key Neurology and Neurosurgery, 1993-96, Yr. Book of Neurology and Neurosurgery, 1994-97. Recipient Travel award Copenhagen, Nat. Inst. Neurol. Diseases and Blindness, 1965, Royal Australasian Coll. Surgeons, Found. lectr. Adelaide 1986. Fellow ACS (gov. 1996); mem. Congress Neurol. Surgeons (pres. 1979-80), Am. Assn. Neurol. Surgeons (treas. 1989-92), So. Neurosurg. Soc. (sec. 1988-91, pres. 1992-93), Soc. Neurol. Surgeons (v.p. 1995-96), Am. Bd. Neurol. Surgery (dir. 1991-97, chmn. 1996-97), Phi Beta Kappa, Alpha Omega Alpha. Democrat. Avocation: medical writing and editing. Office: Duke U Med Ctr PO Box 3807 Durham NC 27710-0001 Personal E-mail: rhwilkins@aol.com.

WILKINS, ROBERT PEARCE, writer, lawyer; b. Jesup, Ga., Sept. 10, 1933; s. Ransom Little and Sarah (Pearce) W.; m. Rose Truesdale, Jan. 7, 1956; children: Robert Pearce, Chisolm Wallace (dec.), Sarah Ruth Weiss, Rose Anne Brooks. BA, U. S.C., 1953, JD, 1954; LL.M., Georgetown U., 1957. Bar: S.C. 1954; cert. mediator and arbitrator, S.C. Atty. Office Gen. Counsel, Sec. Army, Washington, 1956; trust officer First Nat. Bank S.C., Columbia, 1957-60; practice law Columbia, 1960-64; ptnr. McLain, Sherrill & Wilkins, Columbia, 1964-68, McKay, Sherrill, Walker, Townsend & Wilkins, Columbia, 1969-75; sole practice law Columbia and Lexington, S.C., 1975-88; of counsel Nelson, Mullins, Riley & Scarborough, Lexington, 1988—. Pres. Sandlapper Press, Inc., 1967-72, pub. Sandlapper Mag. S.C., 1968-72; editor Sandlapper Mag. S.C., 1968-69, 89—; editor, pub. S.C. History Illustrated, 1970; pres. R.P.W. Pub. Corp.; mem., chmn. S.C. Splty. Adv. Bd. Estate Planning and Probate, 1982-85; lectr. in law U. S.C., 1971-78. Author: Draftin Wills and Trust Agreements in South Carolina, 1971, Drafting Wills and Trust Agreements in Michigan, 1978, Wills and Trust System (Arkansas), 1978, Drafting Wills and Trust Agreements: A Systems Approach, 1998, 3d edit., 1999, software edit., 50 Things to Do with the Rest of Your Life, 2003; (with others) Word Processing for a Law Office, 1979, also articles; editor: The Lawyer's Microcomputer, 1982-85, The Lawyer's PC, 1983-97, What a Lawyer Needs to Know to Buy and Use a Computer, 1984, The Perfect Lawyer, 1990-97, The Lawyers' Word, 1991, Shepard's Elder Care/Law Newsletter, 1991-95, Hot docs Toolbox, 1996-97, Drafting Wills and Trust Agreements Newsletter, 1997. Del., Spl. Liaison Tax Com. Southeastern Region, 1967-70; exec. com. Richland County Rep. Com., 1960-64; sec.-treas. Richland County Rep. Club, 1960; bd. dirs. Ctrl. Tb-RD Assn.; trustee Sch. Dist. 1, Lexington County, S.C., 1971-78, sec., 1972-75, chmn., 1975-78; mem. S.C. Commn. on Higher Edn., 1978-80, S.C. Commn. on Lawyer Competence, 1980-82; bd. dirs. Crime Stoppers of the Midlands, 1983-85, RPW Learning Ctr., 1987-94, Mt. Hope Cemetary, 1991—, also v.p., 1992—; v.p. 11th cir. Alumni Coun. U. S.C., 1993-95, mem. awards com., 1995-97; mem. commn. Riverbanks Zoo, 1986—, sec., 1991-95, chmn., 1995-96, 97—, vice-chmn., 1996-97. With AUS, 1954-55. Recipient Compleat Lawyer award Law Sch. U. S.C., 1997, Diamond Circle award U. S.C. Coll. Journalism and Mass Comms., 1998. Fellow Am. Bar Found., Am. Coll. Trust and Estate Counsel (publs. com. 1984-87, bd. regents 1986-87, mem. tech. com. 1989-98), Am. Coll. Tax Counsel, Coll. Law Practice Mgmt. (charter, trustee 1994-98), S.C. Bar (tax coordinating com. 1968-70, chmn. legal econs. com. 1973-75, ho. of dels. 1978-80, editor S.C. Lawyer 1989-91, mem. alternative dispute resolution sect. 1993—), S.C. Bar Found. (life, bd. dirs. 1984-88, v.p. 1986-87, pres. 1987-88); mem. ABA (ho. of dels. 1986-87, chmn. valuation subcom., estate and gift tax com., taxation sect. 1967-73, vice chmn. svc. and assistance to law student div. com. gen. practice sect. 1971-72, vice chmn. corp. counsel com. gen. practice sect. 1972-74, editor econs. of law practice sect. legal econs. 1974-78, sec. 1977-78, vice chmn. 1978-79, chmn. 1980-81, mem. standing com. assn. comm. 1981-84, real property, probate and trust law, mem. publs. com. 1985-89, editor Probate and Property, 1986-89), Richland County Bar Assn. (chmn. probate sect. 1973-74, unauthorized practice of law com. 1976), Lexington County Bar (chmn. mediation com. 1994—), Columbia Jaycees (sec.-treas. 1958-59), Columbia Estate Planning Coun. (pres. 1964-65), Am. Y-Flyer Yacht Racing Assn. (area v.p. 1971, internat. dir. 1972-73), Omicron Delta Kappa, Sigma Chi Clubs: Columbia Sailing (dir. 1968-71), Columbia Tip Off (dir. 1968-73), Columbia (pres. 1971-72). Home: 124 Lake Murray Ct Lexington SC 29072-9104 also: PO Box 729 Lexington SC 29071-0729 E-mail: rpw@50thingstodo.com.

WILKINS, SHARON KAY RAMSEY, music educator, director; d. James W. and Naomi Hicks Ramsey; m. Philip W. Wilkins, Aug. 29, 1964; children: Patrick Philip-Ramsey, Julie P. Buerke. BA in Music Edn., Evangel U., Springfield, Mo., 1965. Cert. in tchg. Education Mo., 1965. Tchr. USDESEA, Willard, Germany, 1967—84; ch. music dir. Evangel Temple, Springfield, 1973—2008. Dir. asst. prof. Evangel U., 2008—. Artistic dir. Mid Am. Singers, Springfield, 2008. Conservative. Avocations: travel, politics, sports. Home: 4224 S Kimbrough Springfield MO 65810

WILKINS, TERESA J., anthropologist, educator; d. Joseph Mtchell and Margaret McCallum Wilkins. BS in Art Mktg. and Prodn., Appalachian State U., Boone, NC, 1980; MA in Anthropology, U. Colo. Boulder, 1993, PhD in Anthropology, 1999. Asst, assoc prof. anthropology U. N.Mex, Gallup, 1997—2008, prof. anthropology, 2008—. Author (cultural anthropologist): (ethnography) Patterns of Exchange: Navajo Weavers and Traders (N.Mex Book award, 2008). Native Am. art judge Inter-Tribal Indian Ceremonial, Mus. Northern Ariz., Gallup, 1998—2008, SWAIA Santa Fe Indian Market. Mem.: Am. Anthrop. Assn. Achievements include research in navajo weavers & traders, navajo language study. Avocations: photography, art. Office: Univ N Mex Gallup 200 College Rd Gallup NM 87301 Business E-Mail: twilkins@unm.edu.

WILKINS, WALT (WILLIAM WALTER WILKINS III), prosecutor; b. Apr. 13, 1974; s. William Walter and Debra Ann (Dill) Wilkins; m. Donyelle Burton, 2003; 1 child, Mary Burton. Grad., Wofford Coll., 1996; JD, U. SC, 1999. Staff atty. Lockheed Martin Aircraft Argentina, 1999—2000; atty. Leatherwood, Walker, Todd & Mann, Greenville, SC, 2000—05; asst. US atty. US Dept. Justice, Greenville, 2005—08, US atty. Dist. SC Columbia, 2008—. Office: US Attys Office First Union Bldg 1441 Main St, Ste 500 Columbia SC 29201 Office Phone: 803-929-3000. Office Fax: 803-254-2912.*

WILKINS, WILLIAM J., lawyer; m. Gail Wilkins; 1 child, Sam. BA, Yale U., New Haven, 1974; JD, Harvard U., Mass., 1977. Assoc. King. & Spaulding, Atlanta; tax counsel US Senate Fin. Com., 1981—87, staff dir., chief counsel, 1987—88; ptnr. tax practice group Wilmer Cutler Pickering Hale and Dorr LLP, Washington, 1988; chief counsel IRS, Washington, 2009—; asst. gen. counsel US Dept. Treasury, Washington, 2009—. Past mem. governing bd. Am. Coll. Tax Counsel, Am. Tax Policy Inst. Mem.: ABA (chair taxation sect., vice chair govt. rels. Tax Sect., vice chair comm. Tax Sect.). Office: IRS 10th St and Pennsylvania Ave NW Washington DC 20004*

WILKINSON, ALAN HERBERT, nephrologist, educator; b. Johannesburg, July 11, 1948; came to U.S., 1985; s. Raymond C. and Nonie (Levick) W.; m. Angelika A. E. Adami, Dec. 22, 1973; one child: Rebecca Kate Adami. BS in Physiology, Biochemistry, Philosophy, U. Witwatersrand, South Africa, 1969, BS in Biochemistry with honors, 1970, MB, BCh, 1975; cert. health care mgmt., U. Calif., Irvine, 1998. Fellow Royal Coll. Physicians (U.K.), specialist in clin. hypertension. Vis. assoc. Dept. Internal Medicine U. Iowa, Iowa City, 1987-88; assoc. prof. of medicine UCLA Sch. Med., 1988-95, prof. med., 1995—; dir. clin. nephrology UCLA Dept. Med., 1988-93, dir. kidney and pancreas transplantation, 1993—. Contbr. articles to profl. jours. Mem. steering com. Nat. Kidney Found.; mem. U.S. Transplant Games, L.A., 1992; bd. dirs. So. Calif. Renal Disease Coun., 2002-04, pres., 2009-, med. adv., 2004—. Recipient Exceptional Svc. award Nat. Kidney Found., 1992; Nat. Kidney Found. fellow. Mem. Am. Soc. Transplantation, Internat. Nephrology Soc., Am. Soc. Nephrology. Avocations: ornithology, gardening. Office: UCLA Dept Med 200 Medical Plz Box 951693 Los Angeles CA 90095-1693

WILKINSON, ALBERT MIMS, JR., lawyer; b. Nashville, June 29, 1925; s. Albert Mims and Mary Nelle (Derryberry) W.; m. Edythe Bush, Mar. 27, 1953 (div.); children: William Terry, Elizabeth Ann, David Bush; m. Dolores Jean Attard, Oct. 22, 1971 (div.); 1 child, Mary Dolores. Student, Emory U., 1942-43; JD, U. Ga., 1949. Bar: Ga. 1948. Pvt. practice law, Atlanta, 1950-85; gen. counsel GEC-Marconi Avionics Inc., Atlanta, 1985-98; hon. legal adviser to Brit. Consul Gen. at Atlanta. Author: The Winning of the Revolutionary War in the South, 1976, The Rights of Unsecured Creditors-The Law in Ga., 1979; editor: Chronicles of the Old Guard of the Gate City Guard of Atlanta, 1858-2001 (3 vols.), 2002. Mem. DeKalb County Bd. Elections, 1966-72; chmn. 4th Congl. Dist. Republican Exec. Com., 1968-70, Ga. State Rep. Exec. Com., 1968-74; 1st vice chmn. Ga. Rep. Party, 1972-74, asst. gen. counsel, 1974-75; vice chmn., trustee Atlanta Counseling Center, Inc., 1960-83. Served with USCGR, 1943-46. Decorated Order Brit. Empire. Fellow Comml. Law Found.; mem. BA, Ga. Bar Assn., Atlanta Bar Assn., Ga. Soc. (pres. 1962-63), SAR, Southeastern Mem.'s Assn. (pres. 1960-61), Comml. Law League Am., Ga. Soc. Colonial Wars, Old Guard of Gate City Guard (comdt. 1986), N.C. Soc. of Cincinnati, Sphinx Club, Gridiron Club, Commerce Club, Civitan, Masons, Blue Key, Omicron Delta Kappa. Baptist. Home and Office: 66 Demorest Ln # 333 Sky Valley GA 30537-2581 Office Phone: 706-746-2374. Personal E-mail: amims@alltel.net. Business E-Mail: amims@windstream.net. *By precept and example my parents pointed out the upward way in life, on a foundation of religious faith. "To do justly, to love mercy, to walk humbly with thy God." Later a beloved teacher taught the lines from Ulysses as he prepared to set sail, "To strive, to seek, to find and never yield." Their inspiration has continued throughout my life.*

WILKINSON, ANN E., theater educator, actress; b. Atlantic, Iowa; BFA in Theatre, Knox Coll., Galesburg, Ill. Actress, LA, 1977—87; casting dir., owner operator Tepper-Gallegos Casting, LA, 1986—2000; casting dir. PMS Casting, Pella, Iowa, 2000—. Instr. theatre Ctrl. Coll. Pella, 2000—. Coun. mem. Iowa Casting Assn., Des Moines, 2008; bd. mem. Union St. Players, Pella, 2003—05; planning com. Cordova Project, Pella, 2003—08; bd. mem. Friends Ctrl. Arts, Pella, 2006—08, Pella Cultural and Heritage Dist., 2006—08; coun. mem. Chgo. Br. Screen Actors Guild Coun., 2008—; artistic dir., founder Pella Shakespeare Co., 2003—08; bd. mem., past v.p. Iowa Motion Picture Assn., Des Moines, 2003—08. Recipient Governor's Vol. award, State Iowa, 2007, Dr John Wesselink award, Ctrl. Coll., 2007—08. Mem.: Actor's Equity Assn., Am. Fedn. Radio and TV Artists, SAG. Avocations: travel, gardening, theater. Office Phone: 641-628-1798. Personal E-mail: pmscasting@aol.com. Business E-Mail: wilkinsona@central.edu.

WILKINSON, ANNE MARIE, mathematics professor; b. Boston, Apr. 4, 1968; d. Ruth Elaine VanDemark and Leland Wilkinson; m. Benson S. Farb, Dec. 28, 1996; children: Beatrice Henrietta Farb, Felix Paul Farb. AB in Math., Harvard Coll., Cambridge, Mass., 1989; PhD in Math., U. Calif., Berkeley, 1995. Benjamin peirce lectr. Harvard U., 1995—96; asst. prof. Northwestern U., Evanston, Ill., 1996—2002, assoc. prof., 2002—05, prof., 2005—. Postdoc. Rsch. fellowship, NSF, 1998—2001, Rsch. grant, 2002—. Office: Northwestern Univ Math Dept 2033 Sheridan Rd Evanston IL 60208-2730

WILKINSON, BARBARA J., pediatrician, educator; b. Mitcham, Surrey, Eng., June 5, 1946; came to U.S., 1954, naturalized, 1963. d. Arthur Frederick and Elizabeth (Law) Wilkinson. BA in Zoology with highest distinction, U. Maine, 1969; MD, Boston U., 1973. Diplomate Am. Bd. Pediatrics, 1981. Pediatric intern Boston City Hosp., 1973-74; fellow in neonatology U. Rochester/Strong Meml. Hosp., Rochester Gen. Hosp., Rochester, N.Y., 1976-78; resident in pediatrics Maine Med. Ctr., Portland, 1974-76, assoc. neonatologist, outreach educator, 1979-83; attending staff, courtesy staff, 1979—, lectr. for pediatric med. students, 1983—2003; clin. instr. pediatrics part time faculty U. Vt. Coll. Medicine/Maine Med. Ctr., Portland, 1980-83, clin. asst. prof. pediatrics part time faculty, 1983—2004. Participant at emergency and family practice grand rounds on bereavement Maine Med. Ctr., early 1990s, co-facilitator Sudden Infant Death Support Group, 1980-2004; adj. faculty in allied health scis. So. Maine Vocat. Tech. Inst., South Portland, 1984-86; adj. faculty pathophysiology courses So. Maine Tech. Coll., South Portland, 1998-2000. Mem., contact person Maine Children's Meml. Libr. Bereaved Parents; precinct ward clk. Elections, Portland, 1990s-01. Fellow Am. Acad. Pediatrics; mem. AAUW (life), Am. Acad. Pediat., Altrusa Internat., Nat. Honor Soc., Phi Beta Kappa, Phi Kappa Phi (life). Avocations: watercolor painting, silk screening, photography, reading. Home: 56 Garrison St Portland ME 04102-1933

WILKINSON, BETH ANN, lawyer, former mortgage company executive; b. 1962; d. Robert and Judith Wilkinson; m. David Michael Gregory, June 10, 2000; 3 children. BA cum laude, Princeton U., 1984; JD, U. Va., 1987. Bar: DC 1999, NY 1988. Asst. to gen. counsel for intelligence, spl. ops., & nat. security matters Dept, Army, US Dept. Def., 1987—91; asst. US atty. (ea. dist.) NY US Dept. Justice, 1991; ptnr., litig. dept. Latham & Watkins LLP, 1998—2006; exec. v.p., corp. sec., gen. counsel Fannie Mae (Fed. Nat. Mortgage Assn.), Washington, 2006—08; ptnr. litigation dept Paul, Weiss, Rifkind, Wharton & Garrison LLP, Washington, 2009—. Co-chair Latham and Watkins' White Collar Crime Practice Group. Author: "When Talk is Not Cheap: Communications With The Media, The Government, And Other Parties in High Profile White Collar Criminal Cases", Am. Criminal Law Review, 2002; featured on news programs such as NBC "Today" show, Nightline, NewsHour with Jim Lehrer, Face the Nation & Good Morning America, featured in National Law Journal, American Lawyer & Legal Times. Trustee Nat. Youth Leadership Forum; co-chmn. Constn. Project's Death Penalty Initiative. Recipient Exceptional Svc. award (2), US Dept. Justice; named one of 75 Best Lawyers in Washington, Washingtonian Mag., 2002. Achievements include prosecutor in Okla. City Bombings case; lead trial counsel for Gen. Electric; represented Ford Motor Co. during Firestone investigation. Office: Paul Weiss Rifkind Wharton & Garrison LLP 2001 K St NW Washington DC 20006 Office Phone: 202-223-7340. Office Fax: 202-204-7395. E-mail: bwilkinson@paulweiss.com.*

WILKINSON, BRUCE W., construction executive; b. Dallas, 1944; married. BA, U. Okla., 1966, JD, 1969; LLM, U. London, 1970. Gen. counsel Dresser Industries, Inc., Dallas, 1970-78; v.p., treas. CRS Sirrine, Inc. (now CRSS Inc.), Houston, 1978-79, sr. v.p., treas., 1979-82, pres., CEO, 1982—96, chmn. bd. dirs., CEO, 1989—96; interim pres., CEO Proler Internat., Inc., 1996; pres., CEO Tyler Corp., 1997; chmn., CEO Chem. Logistics Corp., 1998—99; prin. Pinnacle Equity Ptnrs., LLC, 1999—2000; pres., COO McDermott Internat., Inc., Houston, 2000, chmn. bd., CEO, 2000—, pres., COO J. Ray McDermott, S.A., 2002—03. Bd. dirs. Cameron Internat. Corp., 2002—. Office: McDermott Internat Inc 777 N Eldridge Pky Houston TX 77079-4425 Office Phone: 281-870-5901.

WILKINSON, DEANNA L., social sciences educator; d. Daniel J. and Marie K. Wilkinson; m. Keith Gooch; children: William Gooch, Benjamin Gooch. BA, Cornell Coll.; MA, U. Ill., Chgo.; PhD, Rutgers U., Newark, 1998. Asst. prof. Temple U., Phila., 1998—2005; assoc. prof. Ohio State U., Columbus, 2006—. Rsch. assoc. Harvard U., Boston, 1992—93, Columbia U., NYC, 1995—98. Author: (book) Guns, Violence and Identity, 2003; contbr. articles to profl. jours., chapters to books. Chair Ohio State U. Youth Violence Prevention Adv. Bd., Columbus, 2007—08; active Collective Action Youth Neighborhood Devel., Columbus, 2008, Strategies Against Violence Everywhere, Columbus, 2006—08. Recipient Soc. Rsch. Adolescene Young Investigator award, 2008. Mem.: Soc. Rsch. Adolescence, Am. Soc. Criminology. Office: Ohio State Univ 1787 Neil Ave CM 135 Columbus OH 43210 Office Fax: 614-292-4365. Business E-Mail: wilkinson.110@osu.edu.

WILKINSON, DENISE V., psychologist; b. Coral Gable, Fla., Apr. 17, 1953; d. John Edward Van Diver and Doris Helen Sandner; children: Melissa Brittany, Justin Bert. BA, Univ. S. Fla., Tampa, Fla., 1979, MA, 1981, Edn. Specialist, 1988. Cert. sch. psychologist 1987; lic. 1988. Mental health tech. Upper Pinellas Assn. for Retarded Citizens, Clearwater, Fla., 1974—76; psychometrist pvt. practice, Tampa, Fla., 1976—79, Devel. Ctr., Tampa, Fla., 1979; sch. psychologist Pasco County Sch. Bd., Land O'Lakes, Fla., 1982—. Sch. psychologist pvt. practice, Land O'Lakes, Fla., 1989—. Contbr. articles pub. to profl. jour. Recipient Student Svcs. Tchr. of the Yr., Pasco County Sch. Bd., 1996. Mem.: Nat. Assn. of Sch. Psychologist, Fla. Assn. of Sch. Psychologist. Independent. Unitarian Universalist. Avocations: photography, travel, beach, seashell collecting, collecting postcards. Office: Pasco County Sch Bd 7227 US Hwy 41 N Land O Lakes FL 34639 Home: 22846 Chesterview Loop Apt 101 Land O Lakes FL 34639-5343

WILKINSON, DORIS, medical sociology educator; b. Lexington, Ky., June 13, 1936; d. Howard Thomas and Regina Wilkinson. BA, U. Ky., 1958; MA, Case Western Res. U., 1960, PhD, 1968; MPH, Johns Hopkins U., 1985; postgrad., Harvard U., summer 1991. Asst. prof. U. Ky., Lexington, 1968-70; assoc. prof., then prof. Macalester Coll., St. Paul, 1970-77; exec. assoc. Am. Sociol. Assn., Washington, 1977-80; prof. med. sociology Howard U., Washington, 1980-84; vis. prof. U. Va., 1984-85; prof. sociology U. Ky., Lexington, 1985—. Chmn. panel women in sci. program NSF, Washington, 1976; rev. panelist Nat. Inst. Drug Abuse, Washington, 1978—79; mem. bd. sci. counselors Nat. Cancer Inst., Bethesda, Md., 1980—84; vis. scholar Harvard U., Cambridge, Mass., 1989—90, vis. prof. (summers), 1992, 93, 94, 97; Rapoport vis. prof. social theory (summers) Smith Coll., 1995, 96; bd. dirs. Nat. Conf. for Cmty. Justice, 1992—96; dir. Heritage Project, 2000—. Author: Workbook for Introductory Sociology, 1968; editor: Black Revolt: Strategies of Protest, 1969; editor: The Black Male in America, 1977, co-editor: Alternative Health Maintenance and Healing Systems, 1987, Race, Gender and the Life Cycle, 1991, Race, Class and Gender, 1996; social history photographic exhbn. "The African American Presence in Medicine" Harvard Med. Libr., 1991, Pearson Mus.-Southern Ill. U. Med. Sch., 1992, NJ Coll. Medicine and Dentistry, 1993, Louisville Mus. History and Sci., 1994, U. Cin. Med. Sch. Libr., 1994, Albert Einstein Coll. of Medicine, 1995, Midway Coll., 1996; contbr. articles to profl. jours. Bd. overseers Case Western Res. U., Cleve., 1982-87; apptd. Ky. Commn. on Women, 1993-96. Named to Hall of Disting. Alumni, U. Ky.,1989; recipient Pub. Humanities award U. Ky., 1990, Midway Coll. Women's History Month award, 1991, Gt. Tchr. award Nat. Alumni Assn. U. Ky., 1992, Disting. Scholar award Assn. Black Sociologists, 1993, Cmty. Svc. award Frankfort-Lexington Links, Inc., 2005-, Cmty. Svc. award Girl Scout Wilderness Road Coun., Lexington, Ky., 2005, Ida Lee Willis Mem. award Ky. Heritage Found., 2006 Coretta Scott King award Alpha Kappa Alpha, 2007; fellow Woodrow Wilson Found., 1959-61, Ford Found., 1989-90; grantee Social Sci. Rsch. Coun., 1975, Nat. Inst. Edn., 1978-80, Nat. Cancer Inst., 1986-88, Ky. Humanities Coun., 1988, 2001, 2008, Am. Coun. Learned Soc., 1989-90, NEH, 1991; Disting. Prof. in Coll. Arts and Scis., U. Ky., 1992-93, Coll. of Social Work Hall of Fame, U. Ky., 1999; Disting. Lectureship named in her honor African Am. Studies Rsch. Program, 2000; Endowed Professorship Created in the name of Doris Wilkinson, 2007, Lifetime Achievement award Women Leading Ky., 2004; grant, Ky. Humanities Coun., 2008-. Mem.: Ea. Sociol. Soc. (v.p. 1983—84, pres. 1992—93, I. Peter Gellman award 1987), Soc. Study Social Problems (v.p. 1984—85, pres. 1987—88), DC Sociol. Soc. (pres. 1982—83), So. Sociol. Soc. (honors com. 1993—94), Am. Sociol. Assn. (exec. assoc. 1977—80, budget com. 1985—88, v.p. 1991—92, mem. coun. 1994—97, elected History of Sociology sect. 2003, Dubois-Johnson-Frazier award 1988), Phi Beta Kappa.

WILKINSON, EDWARD ANDERSON, JR., retired military officer, manufacturing executive; b. Selma, Ala., Sept. 21, 1933; s. Edward Anderson and Alice Margaret (Moorer) W.; m. Barbara Anne Parker, June 4, 1955 (dec. June 1991); children: Daryl Edward, Daniel Bryan, Edward Anderson III, David Park; m. Sondra Marie Moore, Oct. 2, 1994. BS, U.S. Naval Acad., 1955; MS in Mech. Engring., 1964; grad., Nat. War Coll., 1972. Commd. ensign U.S. Navy, 1955, advanced through grades to rear adm., 1979; dir. Anti-Submarine Warfare Systems Program Office, Washington, 1978-79; dep. dir. Def. Mapping Agy., Washington, 1979-81; cmdr. Patrol Wings, U.S. Atlanta Fleet, Brunswick, Maine, 1981-83; dir. Def. Mapping Agy., Washington, 1983-85; ret., 1985; exec. v.p. Internat. Fed. Systems Intergraph Corp., Reston, Va. Recipient Decorated Legion of Merit, Dept. Def., Disting. Svc. medal. Methodist. Home and Office: 9680 Perdido Vista Dr Elberta AL 36530-6028 Home Phone: 251-961-1314. Business E-Mail: andson@gulftel.com.

WILKINSON, EUGENE PARKS, nuclear engineer, director; b. Long Beach, Calif., Aug. 10, 1918; s. Dennis William and Daisy Amelia (Parks) W.; m. Janice Edith Thuli, Mar. 28, 1942; children: Dennis Eugene, Stephen James, Marian Lynn, Rodney David. AB in Chemistry, San Diego State U., 1938. Instr. chemistry San Diego State U., 1938-39; commd. ensign U.S. Navy, 1940, advanced through grades to vice adm., 1970; served various locations including 1st comdg. officer USS Nautilus (1st nuclear-powered submarine), 1953-57; 1st comdg. officer USS Long Beach, 1959-63, 1st nuclear-powered surface ship; ret., 1974; exec. v.p. Data Design Labs., Cucamonga, Calif., 1977-80; pres., chief exec. officer Inst. Nuclear Power Ops., Atlanta, 1980-84, pres. emeritus, 1984—. Chmn. bd. dirs. MDM Svcs. Corp., Laguna Niguel, Calif. Decorated Legion of Merit, Silver Star, D.S.M. with three oak leaf clusters, others, Second Order Sacred Treasure Japan; recipient George Westinghouse Gold medal ASME, 1983, Oliver Townsend medal Atomic Indsl. Forum, 1984, Gold medal Uranium Inst., 1989. Mem. Am. Soc. Naval Engrs., Am. Nuclear Soc. (Henry DeWolf Smyth Nuclear Statesman medal 1994, Walter Zinn award 1998), Navy League, Submarine League, Nat. Acad. Engring. Avocations: tennis, bridge. Home: 1449 Crest Rd Del Mar CA 92014-2530

WILKINSON, HARRY EDWARD, management educator, consultant; b. Richmond Heights, Mo., June 30, 1930; s. Harry Edward and Virginia Flo (Shelton) W.; m. Sara Beth Kikendall, Aug. 30, 1958; children: Linda Beth, Cheryl Susan. BA in Physics, Princeton U., 1952; MBA, Washington U., St. Louis, 1957; DBA, Harvard U., 1960. Lic. psychologist, Mass. Staff engr. Southwestern Bell Tel. Co., St. Louis, 1954-57; traffic engr. New Eng. Tel. & Telegraph Co., Boston, 1957-60; sr. mgmt. cons. Harbridge House Inc., Boston, 1961-65; dean bus. adminstrn., dir. Mgmt. Inst., Northeastern U., Boston, 1965-67; pres., chmn. bd. Univ. Affiliates Inc., North Port, Fla., 1967-2000; vis. prof. mgmt. Rice U., Houston, 1990-94, 97-2000, dir. office of exec. devel., 1993-97. Cons. to various industries and govt., 1961—. Author: Influencing People in Organizations, 1993; contbr. articles to mgmt. jours. Lt. (j.g.) USNR, 1952-54, Korea. Mem. APA, Acad. Mgmt., N.Am. Case Rsch. Assn., Harvard Bus. Sch. Assn. Personal E-mail: hewilkinson@sbcglobal.net.

WILKINSON, JAMES ALLAN, lawyer, healthcare executive; b. Cumberland, Md., Feb. 10, 1945; s. John Robinson and Dorothy Jane (Kelley) W.; m. Elizabeth Susanne Quinlan, Apr. 14, 1973; 1 child, Kathryn Barrett. BS in Fgn. Svc., Georgetown U., Washington, DC, 1967; JD, Duquesne U., Pitts., 1978; MA, U Pitts., 2001. Bar: Pa. 1978, US Dist. Ct. (we. dist.) Pa. Legis. analyst Office of Mgmt. and Budget, Washington, 1972-73; dep. exec. sec. Cost of Living Coun., Washington, 1973-74; sr. fin. analyst US Steel Corp., Pitts., 1974-82; ptnr. Buchanan Ingersoll, Pitts., 1982-88; exec. v.p., gen. counsel Meritcare, Pitts., 1988—2006; sr. v.p. Culwell Health Inc., 1991—2001; exec. dir. Soc. for Contemporary Craft, 2007—09. Adj. prof. U. Pitts. Sch. Law, 1988-91. Author: Financing and Refinancing Under Prospective Payment, 1985, Family Caregivers' Guide Planning and Decision Making for the Elderly, 1998; contbr. articles to profl. jours. Chmn. Oversight Com. on Organ Transplantation, Pitts., 1986—; sec.-treas. bd. dirs. Pitts. Symphony Soc., 1986-98, exec. com. bd. dirs., 1999-2002, 03—, vice-chmn., 2003—; bd. dirs. We. Pa. Com. Prevention of Child Abuse, 1987-90, Comprehensive Safety Compliance, 1988-91, Buchanan Ingersoll Profl. Corp., 1988-90, Parental Stress Ctr., 1990-94; sec. Ross Mountain Club, 1995-98, 1999-2003, v.p., 1999-2001, pres., 2001-03; exec. com. bd. dirs. Carnegie Inst., 1997-2003, 05-07, sec., 2005-07, life trustee, 2002—; exec. com. bd. dirs. Carnegie Mus. Natural History, 1997-2003, Andy Warhol Mus., 1998—, vice chair, 2004-06, co-chair, 2006-07; exec. com. bd. dirs. Soc. for Contemporary Craft, 1999-05, treas., 2000-01, v.p., 2001-02, pres., 2002-04; bd. dirs. Craft Emergency Relief Fund, 2003—, treas., 2003-05, vice chair, 2006-08, chair, 2008-; sr 160 com. Alternative Dispute Resolution Pa. State Govt. Commn. Mem. Audubon Soc. Southwestern Pa. (treas. 1996-2000), Allegheny Land Trust (bd. mem. 2004-08), Greater Pitts. Arts Coun. (bd. dirs. 2008-), Duquesne Club. Republican. Episcopalian. Home: 1005 Elmhurst Rd Pittsburgh PA 15215-1819

WILKINSON, J(AMES) HARVIE, III, federal judge; b. NYC, Sept. 29, 1944; s. James Harvie and Letitia (Nelson) W.; m. Lossie Grist Noell, June 30, 1973; children: James Nelson, Porter Noell. BA, Yale U., 1963-67; JD, U. Va., 1972; JD (hon.), U. Richmond, 1997, U. SC, 1998; LLD (hon.), Christopher Newport U., 2003. Bar: Va. 1972. Law clk. to Hon. Lewis F. Powell, Jr. US Supreme Ct., Washington DC, 1972-73; asst. prof. law U. Va., 1973-75, assoc. prof., 1975-78, prof. law, 1981-82, 83-84; editor Norfolk Virginian-Pilot, 1978—81; dep. asst. atty. gen. Civil Rights divsn. US Dept. Justice, 1982-83; judge US Ct. Appeals (4th Cir.), 1984—, chief judge, 1996—2003. Author: Harry Byrd and the Changing Face of Virginia Politics, 1968, Serving Justice: A Supreme Court Clerk's View, 1974, From Brown to Bakke: The Supreme Court and School Integration, 1979, One Nation Indivisible: How Ethnic Separatism Threatens America, 1997. Bd. Visitors U. Va., 1970-73; Republican candidate for Congress from 3d Dist. Va., 1970; bd. dirs. Fed. Jud. Ctr., 1992-96, James Madison Meml. Found., 2003-. Served with US Army, 1968-69. Recipient Thomas Jefferson Found. medal Law, U. Va., 2004, Medal, Lawrenceville Sch., 2008. Mem. Va. State Bar, Va. Bar Assn., Am. Law Inst. Episcopalian. Office: US Ct Appeals 255 W Main St Ste 230 Charlottesville VA 22902-5058 Office Phone: 434-296-7063.*

WILKINSON, JOHN HART, lawyer; b. Newton, Mass., Dec. 31, 1940; s. Roger Melvin and Margaret (Carter) Wilkinson; children: Heather, Carter. BA, Williams Coll., 1962; LLB, Fordham U., 1965. Bar: NY 1965, US Dist. Ct. (so. and ea. dists.) NY 1968, US Ct. Appeals (2d cir.) 1981, US Ct. Appeals (11th cir.) 1982, US Ct. Appeals (3d cir.) 1984, US Ct. Appeals (5th cir.) 1987. Assoc. Donovan, Leisure, Newton & Irvine, NYC, 1965, 67-73, ptnr., 1973-98, editor, contbg. author firm's ADR Practice Book, 1990; law clk. presiding justice US Dist. Ct. (so. dist.) NY, 1967-68; of counsel Fulton, Rowe & Hart, NYC, 1998—. Spkr. field. Contbr. articles to profl. jours. Bd. dirs., pres. Childfind Am., Inc., 1993—94; vol. learning disabled children Chelsea Neighborhood, NYC, 1965—67; v.p. bd. dirs. Pelham (NY) Family Svc., 1982—85; bd. dirs. Catskill Ctr. Conservation Devel., 1993—. Recipient Am. Jurisprudence award, Fordham U. Mem.: ABA (alt. dispute resolution com. 1989—93), Assn. Bar City NY (profl. responsibility com. 1987—89, pub. assistance com. 1991—94), NY State Bar Assn. (alt. dispute resolution com. 1989—93). Avocations: woodworking, fly fishing, bicycling, camping. Office: Fulton Rowe & Hart One Rockefeller Plz New York NY 10020 Office Phone: 212-586-0700. Personal E-mail: johnhwilkinson@msn.com.

WILKINSON, KEITH D., biochemist, educator; BA in Chemistry cum laude, Albion Coll., 1972; MS, Univ. Mich., PhD in Biochemistry, 1977; postdoctoral study, Inst. Cancer Rsch., Fox Chase Cancer Ctr. Prof. biochemistry and dir., divsn. biol. & biomed. sci. Emory Univ., Atlanta. Vis. prof., doctoral programme in experimental biology and biomedicine Univ. Coimbra, Portugal. Recipient Albion Coll. Presidential award, Alfred P. Sloan Meml. Scholarship, NIH postdoctoral fellowship. Mem.: Am. Com. on Proteolysis, Am. Soc. Biol. Chemistry and Molecular Biol., Am. Chem. Soc. Office: Biol and Biomed Sci Emory Univ--Ste 314 1462 Clifton Rd Atlanta GA 30322 also: Biochem Dept--Emory Univ 4017 Rollins Rsch Bldg 1510 Clifton Rd Atlanta GA 30322 Office Phone: 404-727-2545, 404-727-5980. Business E-Mail: genekdw@emory.edu.

WILKINSON, LOUISE CHERRY, psychology professor, dean; b. Phila., May 15, 1948; BA magna cum laude, Oberlin Coll., 1970; EdM, EdD, Harvard U., 1974. Prof., chmn. dept. ednl. psychology U. Wis., Madison, 1976-85; prof., exec. officer Grad. Sch. PhD Program CUNY, NYC, 1984-86; disting. prof., dean Grad. Sch. Edn. Rutgers U., 1986—2003; dean Sch. Edn. Syracuse (NY) U., 2003—05, disting. prof. edn., psychology and comm. scis., 2003—. Chair ednl. strategic planning Rutgers U.; mem. nat. rev. bd. Nat. Inst. Edn., 1977, 85, 87; cons. Nat. Ctr. for Bilingual Rsch., 1982, 84, US Dept. Edn., 1995—96; adv. bd. Nat. Reading Rsch. Ctr., 1992—98; co-chair commn. on literacy leadership Internat. Reading Assn.; vis. prof. U. London, 2006—, East China Normal U., 2006—; hon. guest prof. Beijing Normal U., 2001—05. Co-author: Communicating for Learning, 1991; editor: Communicating in Classroom, 1982, Social Context of Instruction, 1984, Gender Influences in the Classroom, 2002; co-editor: Literacy and Language Learning, 2004, Improving Literacy Achievement in Urban Schs., 2008; contbr. articles to profl. jours.; mem. editl. bds. various publs.:. Fellow: APA, Am. Assn. for Applied and Preventive Psychology, Am. Psychol. Soc.; mem.: NJ Coun. Acad. Policy Advisors, Am. Ednl. Rsch. Assn. (v.p. 1990—92, program chair 1997). Home: 315 Riverside Dr #15A New York NY 10025

WILKINSON, RALPH RUSSELL, retired biochemistry educator, toxicologist; b. Portland, Oreg., Feb. 20, 1930; s. Tracy Chandler and Lavern (Russell) W.; m. Evelyn Marie Wickman, Aug. 5, 1956. BA, Reed Coll., 1953; PhD, U. Oreg., 1962; MBA, U. Mo., Kansas City, 1974. Rsch. chemist VA Hosp., Kansas City, Mo., 1973-74; sr. rsch. chemist Midwest Rsch. Inst., Kansas City, 1975-84; prof. Rockhurst Coll., Kansas City, 1985-86, Cleve. Chiropractic Coll., Kansas City, 1987-99, prof. emeritus, 1999—. Cons. in biochemistry, toxicology, environ. impact, tech. assessment, Kansas City, 1984—. Author: (book) Neurotoxins and Neurobiological Function, 1987; contbr. articles to profl. jours. Mem. Southtown Coun., Kansas City, Mo., 1989—, Spina Bifida Assn. Am., Kansas City, 1989—. NSF fellow, 1959-60. Mem. Am. Chem. Soc., Sigma Xi. Avocations: travel, history, biography, music, antiques. Home: 7911 Charlotte St Kansas City MO 64131-2175

WILKINSON, RICHARD H., archaeologist, educator; b. Apr. 26, 1951; s. Herbert and Mary Wilkinson; m. Anna L. Wagner, 1975; children: Ryan H., Mark W. PhD, U. Minn., Mpls., 1986. Regents prof., Egyptian archaeology U. Ariz., Tucson, 1989—, dir., Egyptian expdn., 1989—, editor in chief, jour. ancient Egyptian interconnections, 2008—. Editor and founder Directory N.Am. Egyptologists, 1988—; mem., nat. bd. dirs. Am. Rsch. Ctr. Egypt, 1994—2000; mem., editl. bd. KMT: Modern Jour. Ancient Egypt, 1994—, PalArch Jour. Egyptian Archaeology, Netherlands, 2008—; mem., bd. trustees Amarna Rsch. Found., 1996—. Author: (book) Egyptian Scarabs, Complete Gods and Goddesses of Ancient Egypt, Complete Temples of Ancient Egypt, Symbol and Magic in Egyptian Art, Reading Egyptian Art; co-author (with C. Nicholas Reeves): Complete Valley of the Kings; editor: Egyptology Today, Valley of the Sun Kings. Mem.: Internat. Assn. Egyptologists. Achievements include research in excavations around valley of kings, memorial temple of Tausert.

WILKINSON, ROBERT F., lawyer; s. William A. and Jessie F. Wilkinson; m. Barbara J. Avery, Aug. 12, 1978; children: William Jonathan, David Avery. AB, U. Mo., Columbia, 1977; MPH, MBA, Tulane U., New Orleans, 1980; JD, Loyola U., New Orleans, 1988. Bar: Mo. 1989, La. 1989, Ill. 1990. Environ. atty. Monsanto Co., St. Louis, 1990—96; ptnr. Thompson Coburn, St. Louis, 1996—2001, Husch Blackwell Sanders LLP, St. Louis, 2002—. Contbr. chapters to books. Bd. dirs. Westminster Christian Acad., St. Louis, 2000—. Mem.: La. State Bar Assn., The Mo. Bar, Air and Waste Mgmt. Assn., Environ. Law Inst., ABA. Office: Husch Blackwell Sanders LLP 190 Carondelet Plz Ste 600 Saint Louis MO 63105

WILKINSON, RONALD STERNE, science administrator, historian, environmentalist; b. Chgo., Feb. 16, 1934; s. Maurice Sterne and Florence Marie (Colby) W.; m. Mary Morgan Springer, May 18, 1963 (div. 1967); m. Karen Ensinger, June 14, 1969 (div. 1976). BA, Mich. State U., 1960, PhD, 1969. Chemist Berry Bros., Detroit, 1955-57; mem. faculty Mich. State U., East Lansing, 1960-70; sci. specialist Libr. of Congress, Washington, 1970-90, sr. sci. specialist, 1990—; assoc. in bibliography Am. Mus. Nat. History, NYC, 1976-82. Trustee William T. Hornaday Conservation Trust, La Jolla, Calif., 1989—; initiator 2d Nat. Forum on Biodiversity, Washington, 1997. Author: John Winthrop, Jr. and the Origins of American Chemistry, 1969, Benjamin Wilkes, The British Aurelian, 1982, Earth Decade Reading List series, 1990—, Aeronautical and Astronautical Resources of the Library of Congress, 2007; editor-in-chief The Mich. Entomologist (later The Great Lakes Entomologist), 1966-71; prodr., narrator ann. Earth Day environ. film festival, Washington, 1990—; contbr. more than 160 articles to sci. and history of sci. publs. Ryder scholar Mich. State U., U. London, 1960, Woodrow Wilson Found. fellow Harvard U., 1960-61, Fulbright scholar Univ. Coll., London, 1965-66. Fellow Linnean Soc. London, Geol. Soc. London, Royal Entomol. Soc. London; mem. Grolier Club (N.Y.C., asst. editor 1979-82). Democrat. Home: 228 9th St NE Washington DC 20002-6110 Office: Libr Of Congress Washington DC 20540-0001

WILKINSON, STANLEY RALPH, retired agronomist; b. West Amboy, NY, Mar. 28, 1931; s. Ralph Ward and Eva Goldie (Perkins) W.; m. Jean Saye; children: Rachael, Stanley Ralph., Augusta J. BS, Cornell U., 1954; MS, Purdue U., 1956, PhD, 1961. Soil scientist U.S. Regional Pasture Rsch. Lab., University Park, Pa., 1960-64, So. Piedmont Conservation Rsch. Ctr., Watkinsville, Ga., 1965-98, ret., 1998. Contbr. more than 22 chpts. to books, more than 145 articles to tech. jours. Past advance chmn. Boy Scouts Am. Served to capt. USAF, 1955-57. Recipient 3d prize Freedoms Found., 1956. Fellow Soil and Water Conservation Soc. Am., Am. Soc. Agronomy; mem. Agronomy Soc. Methodist. Personal E-mail: stanleywilkinson@att.net.

WILKINSON, TOM, actor; b. Leeds, West Yorkshire, Eng., Dec. 12, 1948; m. Diana Hardcastle, Jan. 5, 1988; children: Alice, Molly. Diploma in Eng. and Am. Lit., U. Kent; attended, Royal Acad. Dramatic Arts; LittD (hon.), U. Kent, 2001. Actor: (films) The Shadow Line, 1976, Bones, 1984, Sylvia, 1985, Wetherby, 1985, Sharma and Beyond, 1986, Paper Mask, 1990, In the Name of the Father, 1993, All Things Bright and Beautiful, 1994, Prince of Jutland, 1994, A Business Affair, 1994, Sense and Sensibility, 1995, The Ghost and the Darkness, 1996, The Full Monty, 1997, Wilde, 1997, Gillian Armstrong's Oscar and Lucinda, 1997, The Governess, 1998, Rush Hour, 1998, Shakespeare in Love, 1998, Ride with the Devil, 1999, The Patriot, 2000, Chain of Fools, 2000, In the Bedroom, 2001, Another Life, 2001, Black Knight, 2001, The Importance of Being Earnest, 2002, An Angel for May, 2002, Girl with a Pearl Earring, 2003, Eternal Sunshine of the Spotless Mind, 2004, A Good Woman, 2004, Ripley Under Ground, 2005, Batman Begins, 2005, The Exorcism of Emily Rose, 2005, Separate Lies, 2005, The Night of the White Pants, 2006, The Last Kiss, 2006, Dedication, 2007, Cassandra's Dream, 2007, Michael Clayton, 2007, RocknRolla, 2008, Valkyrie, 2008, Duplicity, 2009; (TV films) Squaring the Circle, 1984, Strangers and Brothers, 1984, A Pocket Full of Rye, 1985, The Woman He Loved, 1988, The Attic: The Hiding of Anne Frank, 1988, First and Last, 1989, Prime Suspect, 1991, Underbelly, 1992, An Exchange of Fire, 1993, Measure for Measure, 1994, Crossing the Floor, 1996, Cold Enough for Snow, 1997, The Gathering Storm, 2002, Normal, 2003, Recount, 2008; (TV miniseries) John Adams, 2008 (Primetime Emmy for Outstanding Supporting Actor in a Miniseries or a Movie, Acad. TV Arts and Scis., 2008, Best Performance by an Actor in Supporting Role in a Series, Mini-Series or Motion Picture Made for TV, Golden Globe award, Hollywood Fgn. Press Assn., 2009). Office: The Gersh Agy 232 N Canon Dr Ste 201 Beverly Hills CA 90210

WILKINSON, WARREN SCRIPPS, manufacturing executive; b. Detroit, Feb. 2, 1920; s. Almadus DeGrasse and Harriet Gertrude (Whitcomb) W.; m. Joan Todd, June 14, 1941; m. Mireille De Bary, Dec. 17, 1966. Grad., Hotchkiss Sch., Lakeville, Conn., 1937; BS in Math, Harvard U., 1941; student, Calif. Inst. Tech., 1941-42. With U.S. Rubber Co., Detroit, 1942-43, Hanson Van Winkle-Munning Co., Matawan, NJ, 1946-64, pres., 1961-64; v.p., gen. mgr. Hanson-Van Winkle-Munning div. M & Chems. Inc., 1964-66; chmn. RPI Designs, Marlette, Mich., 1966—. Overseer's com. on univ. resources Harvard U. With USN, 1943—46. John Harvard fellow, 1996. Home: 2 Woodland Pl Grosse Pointe MI 48230-1920

WILKINSON, WILLIAM SHERWOOD, lawyer; b. Williston, ND, Sept. 6, 1933; s. John Thomas and Evelyn (Landon) W.; m. Carol Ann Burns, Aug. 20, 1960; children— Leslie Ann, Richard Sherwood, Greta Diann. BS in Bus, U. Idaho, 1955; JD, U. Denver, 1960. Bar: Colo. 1960, Mich. 1966. Practiced in, Canon City, Colo., 1960-66; asst. dist. atty. 11th Jud. Dist., Colo., 1961-65; gen. counsel, sec. Mich. Farm Bur. Family Cos., Lansing, 1966-96. Lectr. Pre-Parole Release Center, Colo. State Penitentiary, 1961-65; instr. adult edn., Canon City, 1965; counsel Canon City Recreation Dist., 1964-65 Mem. lay adv. bd. St. Thomas More Hosp., Canon City, 1963-66; Del., county, dist. and congl. convs. Republican party, 1964. Served to capt. USAF, 1955-58. Recipient Cmty. Disting. Svc. award Canon City Jr. C. of C., 1964; named to Outstanding Young Men of Am., 1965. Mem. ABA, Colo. Bar Assn., Mich. Bar Assn., Am. Judicature Soc., Am. Corp. Counsel Assn., Nat. Coun. Farmer Coops. (legal, tax and acctg. com.), Phi Delta Phi, Tau Kappa Epsilon. Methodist (lay leader, mem. ch. ofcl. bd.). Home: 1707 Foxcroft Rd East Lansing MI 48823-2131 Personal E-mail: wwilca@aol.com.

WILKINSON, WINSTON, federal agency administrator, lawyer; b. Prince George's County, Md., 1944; m. Gloria Wilkinson; 4 children. BBA, Morgan State Univ., 1971; JD, Howard Univ., 1974. Atty. Nat. Ctr. for Cmty. Action; various positions through spl. asst. Office of Civil Rights & Office of Rehabilition Services US Dept. Edn., 1981—88; dep. dir. Office for Civil Rights US Dept. Health & Human Services, 1988—93; CEO Winston Wilkinson & Associates; dir. Office of Civil Rights US Dept. Health & Human Services, Washington, 2005—. Councilman Salt Lake County; legal counsel LDS Church. Served USN, 1972—76. Republican. Lds Ch. Office: Dept Health & Human Services 200 Independence Ave SW Washington DC 20201*

WIŁKOMIRSKI, JOSEF, conductor, writer, composer, educator, journalist; b. Kalisz, Poland, May 15, 1926; s. Alfred and Dorota (Temkina) W.; m. Margaret Zasińska, Aug. 16, 1980; 1 child, Wiosna. Magister of art, Music High Sch., Warsaw, 1950. Condr. State Philharmony, Cracow, Poland, 1950-51, Poznań, Poland, 1954-57, dir., chief condr. Szczecin, Poland, 1957-71; chief mgr., artistic dir. Sudettic Philharmony, Walbrzych, Poland, 1978—2005. Tchr. Music Sch., Szczecin, 1960-62; dir. Music Sch., Walbrzych, 1978-81; lectr. TV and radio. Compositions include Harp Concerto, Two Symphoniettas, Concerto for Violin and Cello, Symphonic Poems, Sonata for Violin, Sonata for Cello, Sonata for Double Bass, Songs, Trio, (ballet) The Fairy-Tale of Prince Fair, (symphonic suite) The Royal Castle in Warsaw; condr. concerts in 24 countries of Europe, America and Asia; recordings for broadcast in Poland, Ireland, Luxembourg, over 70 fairy tales for children; contbr. over 400 articles to profl. jours.; over 350 TV programs; autobiography, "80 Years of Life, 60 Years of Work", 2006. Mem. Town Coun., Walbrzych, 1990-98. Decorated knight's cross and comdr. cross with star Order Polonia Restituta: recipient Medal for Merit in Culture, Ministry of Culture, 1967, Prize for Pub. Cultivation of Music, Coun. of Province Szczecin, 1970, Medal of Nat. Edn., Ministry of Edn., 1989, Order of the Banner of Labour (1st class), State Coun., Warsaw, 1986, Cross of Warsaw Insurrection, 1986, Cross of Home Army, 1995, Medal of Vet. of War for Independence, 1995, Golden Medal of Merit for Children, 1998, Cultural award City of Wałbrzych, Key of Success prize Province of Lower Silesia, 2003, Reward of Merit for Walbrzych Region, 2005, Reward of Merit for Walbrzych City, 2006. Avocations: literature, history, psychology. Home Phone: 048-74-8413111. Personal E-mail: jotwu3@wp.pl.

WILKOW, BRIAN RICHARD, hospital administrator and clinician; b. Bklyn., June 3, 1964; s. Elliot and Marcia W. BS, Touro Coll., 1987. Lic. physician asst. Nat. Commn. on Cert. Physician Assts. Coord. physician assts. Luth. Med. Ctr., Bklyn., 1989—96; dir. physician asst. svcs. N.Y. Meth. Hosp., Bklyn., 1996—. Adj. lectr. Coll. Staten Is., N.Y., 1993—; EMT instr. coord. Staten Is. Emergency Med. Tng., 1993—; preceptor SUNY, Bklyn., 1996—. Pres. Shorefront Vol. Ambulance Corps, Bklyn., 1990-2000, Bklyn. Critical Incident Stress Mgmt. Team, 1999—; v.p. Temple Beth Ahavath Sholom, Bklyn., 1997-2001, pres. 2001—. Fellow Am. Acad. Physician Assts., Am. Assn. Surg. and Physician Assts., N.Y. State Soc. Physician Assts. Office: NY Meth Hosp 506 6th St Brooklyn NY 11215-3645 E-mail: brwpac@aol.com.

WILKS, DANA LYN, protective services official, writer; b. Long Beach, Calif., Dec. 27, 1964; d. Donald Lee and Helen Arlene Wilks; m. Kim Kreimeyer, Apr. 3, 2004. BA, Colo. State U., Fort Collins, 1988, MA, 1993. Ordained to ministry Universal Life Ch., Calif., 2004; cert. corrections mgr. Am. Correctional Assn., 2004. Cert. addicitons counselor New Beginnings, Fort Collins, Colo., 1988—91; grad. tchg. asst. Colo. State U., 1992—93; case mgr. supr. The Restitution Ctr., Greeley, 1993—96; free-lance rschr. Denver, 1995—2006; probation officer 19th Jud. Dist., Greeley, 1996—2001; probation supr. 18th Jud. Dist., Centennial, 2001—; instr. U. No. Colo., Greeley, 2004—05. Trainer Colo. Jud. Br., Denver, 1995—; presenter in field. Author short stories, of poems. Mem. So. Poverty Law Ctr., Montgomery, Ala., 2005—06; mem., vol. Human Rights Campaign, Washington, 2003—06; vol. Shambhala Meditation Centers, Red Feather Lakes, 2003—06; project dir. Trek for Hospice, 2006—. Recipient Outstanding Svc. award, Colo. Alcohol and Drug Driving Safety Program, 2004. Mem.: Colo. Probation Supr. Assn. (chairperson 2004—06), Am. Correctional Assn., Am. Probation and Parole Assn. Achievements include first to pass testing and be granted the American Correctional Association's Certified

Corrections Manager certification in Colorado. Avocations: travel, writing. Office: 18th Judicial Probation Dept 7305 S Potomac St 201 Centennial CO 80112-4041 Office Fax: 303-662-5900. E-mail: dana.wilks@judicial.state.co.us.

WILKS, DAVID M., energy executive; BS in Mech. Engring., Tex. A&M U., College Station; MS in Bus. Fin. Mgmt., George Washington U. Various positions in engring. and ops. Southwestern Pub. Svc. Co.; pres. Mktg. and Svcs. New Century Energies, 1997—98, pres. Delivery; pres. Energy Supply Xcel Energy (merger of No. States Power Co. and New Century Energies). Mem. Greater Golden C. of C.; mem. adv. bd. Tex. A&M Coll. Engring.; bd. dirs., bd. trustees Denver Area Coun. Boy Scouts Am. Recipient Ally award, Women's Vision Found., 2003. Office: Xcel Energy 414 Nicollet Mall Minneapolis MN 55401-1993

WILKS, JILL ANN, academic administrator, director; b. Passaic, NJ, Aug. 4, 1955; d. Edgar Lester and Doris Jean Schulte Wilks; m. William Michael Ransom, June 24, 2000; m. James Martin Aton, June 0, 1983 (div. June 0, 1996); 1 child, Jennifer Aton; 1 child, Hali Johnson. BA in Elem. Edn., Southern Utah U., Cedar City, 1978, BA in History, 1986; MA in Instrnl. Design, Utah State U., Logan, 2001. Ednl. dir. Discovery Sch., Cedar City, 1991—95; lang. and learning specialist Southern Utah U., 1980—2004, dir. experience and learning, 2004—. Owner Expanding Intelligence Prodns., Cedar City, 1990—, chief cons., 1990—. Author: (workbook) Your Expanding Intelligence. Mem.: Phi Kappa Phi. Non-Partisan. Avocations: cooking, carpentry, travel, skiing, running. Office: Southern Utah Univ 351 Univ Blvd Cedar City UT 84720 Personal E-mail: expanding.intelligence.prod@gmail.com. Business E-Mail: wilks@suu.edu.

WILKS, LARRY DEAN, lawyer; b. Columbia, SC, Jan. 8, 1955; s. Ray Dean and Jean (Garrett) W.; m. Jan Elizabeth McIllwain, May 2,1981; children: John Ray, Adam Garrett. BS, U. Tenn., 1977, JD, 1980. Bar: Tenn. 1981, U.S. Dist. Ct. (mid. dist.) Tenn. 1981, U.S. Supreme Ct. 1986, U.S. Ct. Appeals (6th cir.) 1993, U.S. Dist. Ct. (we. dist.) Tenn. 1996. Assoc. Mayo & Norris, Nashville, 1981-82; sole practice Springfield, Tenn., 1982-84; ptnr. Walton, Jones & Wilks, 1984, Jones & Wilks, 1984-89; pvt. practice Springfield, Tenn., 1989—. Chmn. Dem. Orgn. Robertson County Tenn., 1986-93. Fellow Tenn. Bar Found., Am. Bar Found., Nashville Bar Found.; mem. ABA, ATLA, Tenn. Bar Assn. (assoc. gen. counsel 1991-94, gen. counsel 1994-99, bd. profl. responsibility 1993-98, bd. govs. 1991—, young lawyers divsn. lifetime fellow, asst. treas. 1999-2000, treas. 2000—03, co-chair leadership law 2003-04, 2008-, v.p. 2004-2005, pres. elect 2005-06, pres. 2006-07, immediate past pres. 2007-08, co-chair leadership law 2008-), Tenn. Assn. Criminal Def. Lawyers, Tenn. Trial Lawyers Assn. (bd. govs. 2002—), Robertson County Bar Assn. (pres. 1993-96), Nat. Assn. Criminal Def. Laywers, Tenn. Young Lawyers Conf. (bd. dirs. 1987, editor quar. newsletter 1987-88, Mid. Tenn. v.p. 1988-89, v.p. 1989-90, pres.-elect 1990-91, pres. 1991-92), Robertson County U. Tenn. Alumni Assn. (pres. 2003-04).mem Methodist. Office: Atty at Law 509 W Court Sq Springfield TN 37172-2413 Office Phone: 615-384-8444.

WILL, CHRISTINA, school librarian; MS, Fla. State U., Tallahassee, 1995. Pub. svcs. libr. St. Johns River CC, St. Augustine, Fla., 1995—98, campus libr., 1998—. Mem. Coun. Instrnl. Affairs, Learning Resources Standing Com., Internet Course Task Force Writing Com., Fla., 1997—99, Info. and Referral Ctr. Oversight Com., St. Augustine, 1998—2001, Coll. Ctr. Libr. Automation, Info. Portal Com., Tallahassee, 1999—2002, chair, 2002—04; co-chair ALEPH Implementation Steering Com. OPAC Task Force, Fla., 2002—04; mem. dept. edn. Office of Articulation Statewide Course Numbering Sys. Faculty Discipline Com. Libr. & Info. Studies, Tallahassee, 2006—07. Campus capt. United Way St. Johns County, St. Augustine, 1998—2008. Mem.: Fla. Assn. Cmty. Colls.

WILL, CLARK BRADFORD, lawyer; b. Ft. Sam Houston, Tex., Sept. 17, 1955; s. Clement Herbert and Mary Louise (Cantu) W.; m. Donna Gail Fletcher, Oct. 14, 1978; children: Nathanael Aaron, Nicholas Andrew. BA with distinction, U. Tex., Austin, 1977; JD with distinction, St. Mary's U., San Antonio, 1980; diploma in Mil. Law, U. Va., Judge Advocate Gens. Sch., Charlottesville, 1981. Bar: Tex. 1980, U.S. Ct. Mil. Appeals 1981, U.S. Dist. Ct. (no., we., ea. dist.) Tex. 1986, U.S. Ct. Appeals (5th cir.) 1990, U.S. Ct. Fed. Claims, 2004. Legal asst. officer Ft. Sill, Okla., 1980-81, trial counsel Okla., 1981-84; assoc. Payne & Vendig, Dallas, 1986-88; mem. Payne & Vendig PC, Dallas, 1989-93, Brown, Herman, Scott Dean & Miles LLP, Ft. Worth, 1993—98; ptnr. Quilling, Selander, Cummiskey & Lownds, PC, 1998—. Elder Prince of Peace Luth. Ch., Carrollton, Tex., 1986-87, exec. elder, 1987-93; mem. Hillcrest Ch., Dallas, 1995-2004. Capt. U.S. Army, 1980-86. Army Commendation medal, 1984, Hon. Order Saint Barbara, 1984, Meritorious Svc. medal, 1986; Named one of Outstanding Young Men in Am., 1982. Mem. NRA, Dallas Bar Assn. (environ. law and litigation sect.), State Bar Tex. (litig. natural resources, and environ. law sect.), American Legion. Conservative. Lutheran. Avocations: golf, hunting, hockey, baseball. Home: 848 Aberdeen Ct Coppell TX 75019-2859 Office: Quilling Selander Cummiskey and Lownds PC 2001 Bryan St Ste 1800 Dallas TX 75201 Office Phone: 214-871-2100. Business E-Mail: cwill@qslpc.com.

WILL, CLIFFORD MARTIN, physicist, researcher, educator; b. Hamilton, Ont., Can., Nov. 13, 1946; m. Leslie Saxe Moser, June 26, 1970; children: Elizabeth Sue Torop, Rosalie Will Boxt. BS, McMaster U., Hamilton, 1968; PhD, Calif. Inst. Tech., 1971. Enrico Fermi fellow U. Chgo., 1972-74; asst. prof. physics Stanford U., Palo Alto, Calif., 1974-81; assoc. prof. physics Washington U., St. Louis, 1981—85, prof. physics, 1985—2005, James S. McDonnell prof. physics, 2005—, chmn. dept. physics, 1991—96, 1997—2002. Vis. assoc. physics Calif. Inst. Tech., 1976; chmn. com. on time transfer in satellite systems Air Force Studies Bd., Washington, 1984—86; rsch. assoc. Nat. Ctr. Sci. Rsch. Obs. Paris, Meudon, France, 1996; vis. prof. Hebrew U. Racah Inst. Physics, Jerusalem, 1997, U. Pierre and Marie Curie, Paris, 2006, Inst. Henri Poincare and U. Paris IX, 2006; chmn. sci. adv. com. NASA Gravity Probe B, 1998; rsch. assoc. Nat. Ctr. Sci. Rsch. Inst. Astrophysics, Paris, 2003—04, 2005, 06, 2007—. Assoc. editor Phys. Rev. Letters, 1989-92, Phys. Rev. D, 1999-2001; author: Theory and Experiment in Gravitational Physics, 1981, rev. edit., 1993, Was Einstein Right?, 1986, rev. edit., 1993. Alfred P. Sloan Found. fellow, 1975-79, McDonnell Ctr. Space Scis. fellow, 1981-, J.S. Guggenheim Found. fellow, 1996-97, J.W. Fulbright fellow, 1996-97, ; recipient Sci. Writing award Am. Inst. Physics, 1987, Disting. Alumni award, McMaster U., 1996, Fellows award St. Louis Acad. Scis., 2004. Fellow Am. Phys. Soc. (exec. com. astrophysics divsn. 1988-90, vice chair, chair elect, chair topical group on gravitation 1997-2001), Am. Acad. Arts and Scis.; mem. NAS, Am. Astron. Soc., Am. Assn. Physics Tchrs. (Richtmyer Meml. Lectr. 1987), Internat. Soc. Gen. Relativity and Gravitation (pres. 2004-07). Office: Washington U Dept Physics Campus Box 1105 1 Brookings Dr Saint Louis MO 63130-4899 Office Phone: 314-935-6244. Office Fax: 314-935-6219. Business E-Mail: cmw@wuphys.wustl.edu.

WILL, FRITZ G., physical chemist, consultant; b. Breslau, Germany, Jan. 12, 1931; came to U.S., 1959; s. Fritz and Adele M. Will; m. Hertha M. Will, May 24, 1958; children: Heike, Christian, Helen. BS in Physics, Tech. U., Munich, 1954, MS in Physics, 1956, PhD in Phys. Chemistry, 1959. Coord. fuel cell program Engring. R&D Labs., Ft. Belvoir, 1959-60; mem. rsch. staff GE R&D Ctr., Schenectady, N.Y., 1960-90, mgr. electrochemistry, 1969-73; dir. Cold Fusion Inst. U. Utah, Salt Lake City, 1990-91, rsch. prof., 1991-93; vis. scientist Electric Power Rsch. Inst., Palo Alto, Calif., 1993-94, mgr. electrochem. sci. and tech., 1994-98; pres., owner Battery Vision, Consulting, Santa Barbara, Calif., 1998—. Vis. prof. Nat. U. Singapore, 1997; chmn. internat. adv. panel Inst. Materials Sci. and Engring., 1997. Contbr. articles to profl. jours. Recipient Indsl. Rsch. award Indsl. Rsch. Inc., 1975, Citation Classic award Inst. Sci. Info., 1984. Mem. Electrochem. Soc. (divsn. editor of jour. 1974-84, chmn. phys. chemistry divsn. 1983-84, chmn. honors and awards com. 1984-85, pres. 1987-88, 4th Battery Rsch. award battery divsn. 1964) Achievements include original patent for nickel/metalhydride batteries employing AB5 compounds; research in advanced nickel-zinc batteries. Avocations: tennis, opera, classical music, photography.

WILL, GEORGE FREDERICK, editor, journalist, commentator; b. Champaign, Ill., May 4, 1941; s. Frederick L. and Louise (Hendrickson) Will; m. Madeleine Marion, 1967 (div.); children: Jonathan, Geoffrey, Victoria; m. Mari Maseng, Oct. 12, 1991; 1 child, David. BA, Trinity Coll., Hartford, Conn., 1962, Oxford U., Eng., 1964; MA, PhD in Politics, Princeton U., NJ, 1967; LLD (hon.), U. San Diego, 1977; LittD (hon.), Dickinson Coll., Georgetown U., 1978; degree (hon.), U. Ill., 1988. Prof. polit. philosophy Mich. State U., 1967-68, U. Toronto, 1968-70; mem. staff of Sen. Gordon Allott US Senate, Washington, 1970-72; Washington editor The Nat. Rev., 1973-76; syndicated columnist The Washington Post Writers Group, 1974—; contbg. editor, columnist Newsweek mag., 1976—; founding panel mem. This Week program (formerly This Week with David Brinkley), ABC, 1981—; contbg. analyst ABC News. Author: The Pursuit of Happiness and Other Sobering Thoughts, 1978, The Pursuit of Virtue and Other Tory Notions, 1982, Statecraft as Soulcraft, 1983, The Morning After: American Successes and Excesses 1981-86, 1986, The New Season: A Spectator's Guide to the 1988 Election, 1987, Men at Work: The Craft of Baseball, 1989, Suddenly: The American Idea Abroad and at Home 1986-1990, 1990, Restoration: Congress, Term Limits and the Recovery of Deliberative Democracy, 1992, The Leveling Wind: Politics, the Culture & Other News 1990-94, 1994, The Woven Figure: Conservatism and America's Fabric 1994-97, 1997, Bunts: Curt Flood, Camden Yards, Pete Rose, and Other Reflections on Baseball, 1998, With a Happy Eye But...America and the World 1997-2002, 2002, One Man's America: The Pleasures and Provocations of Our Singular Nation, 2008. Bd. governors Negro Leagues Baseball Mus. Recipient Pulitzer Prize for Commentary, 1977, Nat. Headliners Award, 1978, Silurian Award for Editl. Writing, 1980, 1991, Cronkite award, Ariz. State U., 1991, Madison Medal award, Princeton U., 1992, William Allen White award, William Allen White Sch. Journalism, U. Kans., 1993, Walter B. Wriston Lecture award, Manhattan Inst., 2003, Champion of Liberty Award, Goldwater Inst., 2006; named Young Leader Am., Time mag., 1974, Best Writer, Any Subject, Washington Journalism Rev., 1985; named one of 25 Most Influential Washington Journalists, Nat. Jour., 1997. Avocation: baseball. Address: ABC Pub Rels 77 W 66th St New York NY 10023-6201 Office: Washington Post Writers Group 1150 15th St NW Washington DC 20071*

WILL, KATHERINE HALEY, former academic administrator; b. Aug. 1952; m. Oscar Henry Will, III; 4 children. Student, Carleton Coll., 1970-73; BA in English, Tufts U., 1974; MA in English, U. Ill., Urbana, 1975, PhD in English, 1986. Instr. English Augustana Coll., Sioux Falls, S.D., 1977-86, asst. prof. English, 1986-90, faculty dir. new student seminar program, 1987-91, assoc. prof. English, 1990-96, dean grad. study, dir. gen. edn., 1991—96; provost, prof. English Kenyon Coll., Gambier, Ohio, 1996-99; pres. Whittier Coll., Calif., 1999—2004, Gettysburg Coll., Pa., 2004—08. Participant Mgmt. Devel. Seminar for Higher Edn. Adminstrs., Harvard U., summer 1992; cons. and presenter in field. Contbr. articles to profl. jours. Bd. dirs. United Way Great L.A. NEH fellow Summer Seminar in Romanticism and Gender, UCLA, 1989. Mem.: Annapolis Group (exec. com.), Coun. Ind. Colls. (bd. dirs.), Nat. Assn. Ind. Colls. and Univs. (bd. dirs.). Office Phone: 717-337-6011. Office Fax: 717-337-6008. E-mail: will@gettysburg.edu.

WILL, PETER MILNE, computer and robotics research executive; b. Peterhead, Scotland, Nov. 2, 1935; came to U.S., 1964; s. James and Margaret (Milne) W.; m. Angela Hay Giulianotti, Mar. 21, 1959; children: Christopher, Jonathan, Gabrielle. BS in Engring., Aberdeen U., 1958, PhD, 1960. Tchg. U. Conn., Stanford, 1966—71; mgr. automation systems Yorktown Heights Rsch. Ctr., IBM Corp., NY, 1965-78; industry tech. advisor, Advanced Mfg. Sys. IBM Corp., Boca Raton, Fla., 1978-80; dir. product. systems Schlumberger Well Services, Houston, 1980-83; dir. systems rsch. Schlumberger-Doll Rsch. Lab., Ridgefield, Conn., 1983-86; dir., VLSI Systems Rsch. Fairchild Semiconductor, Palo Alto, Calif., 1986-87; dir., mfg. rsch. ctr., Hewlett-Packard Lab. Hewlett-Packard Co., Palo Alto, Calif., 1987—88, dir. measurement & mfg. ctr., Hewlett-Packard Labs., 1988—90, dir. design strategy product generation, 1990-92; dir. high performance computing and communication Univ. So. Calif./Info. Scis. Inst., Marina del Rey, Calif., 1992—94, divsn. dir., 2000—02, dir., distributed scalable sys. divsn., 1994—2000, rsch. prof., dept. indsl. and sys. engring., 1997—, rsch. prof., dept. materials sci., 2000—, rsch. prof., astronautics and space tech. divsn., 2004—; fellow Info. Scis. Inst., 2002—; dir. Enterprise Integration Systems Divsn., 1994—; chief tech. officer Akroria Networks, 2000—01. Mem. computer sci. & tech. bd. NRC, Washington, 1982-85; mem. info. sci. & technology adv. group DARPA, Washington, 1988-94; adv. com. chmn. microelectronics info. processing com., chmn., design, mfg. and computer engring. com., mem. optics, comm. and systems com., NSF, 1978-86; mem. selections com. Sci. Rsch. Ctr. Grants, Canadian Sci. Coun., Ottawa, 1988-89; founder, operator MEMS Clearing House, 1994-2002; chmn., NRC Study on Info. Tech. in Mfg., 1993-94; founder, Laboratory for Molecular Robots, Univ. So. Calif., 1995; chmn. NIST Mfg. Systems Integration Divsn. Review Panel, 2001; mem. scientific adv. bd., Zyvex Corp., 2001-; mem. adv. bd. NASA MARS Tech., 2002-. Contbr. articles to profl. jours.; patentee in field. Recipient Joseph Engelberger medal in Robotics, Robotics Inst. of Am., 1990; Carnegie Fellowship 1958-60. Mem. IEEE, Assn. for Computing Machinery. Presbyterian. Avocations: sailing, gardening. Office: USC Information Sciences Inst 4676 Admiralty Way Ste 1001 Marina Del Rey CA 90292-6695 Office Phone: 310-822-1511. Business E-Mail: will@isi.edu.

WILL, ROLAND TRACY, II, writer, editor, journalist, publisher, television producer; b. Schenectady, NY, May 18, 1954; s. Albert Roland and Constance Mary (Headley) W.; m. Gay Adair Strandemo, July 1, 1989; children: Roland Leigh Leonard, Glenn Tracy. BA, U. Wis., 1988. Polit. sci. and comm. arts editor, pub., journalist Wis. Health Policy Report, Wis. Ind. News Svc., Madison, 1994—99. Author: (Compass Am. Guide) Wisconsin, 1994, 3d edit., 2001, History of Dane the Capital County, 2000; (plays) Packer Glory, 1984, Fatal Time to Final End, 1986; actor (plays) Bombs Away Enola Gay, 1983, Hans Brinker and Silver Skates: Rock Musical on Roller Skates, 1984, Light My Fire—Jim Morrison, 1985, The Cherry Orchard, 1985, The Hangwoman, 1986, The Phantom of Shoppko, 1987, Joe a Life: The Story of Joe McCarthy, 1988, Chain Reaction, 1996; series editor, contbr. Wisconsin: Buildings of America, 2009-; writer, prodr. (TV spl.) Spanish Spoken Here, 2005 (named Best Documentary, Wis. Broadcasters Assn.); author: Xiangjun Lu: Chinese Environmentalist; prodr., dir. WisOpinion: The Show Madison Capital Times, 2008, University Research Park: Origins and Collaboration, 2008. Bus. mem. Dane County Hist. Soc., Madison, 1995; sec. bd. dirs. Broom St. Theater, Madison, 1984-2005; curator photography exhibit Wis. Hist. Mus.; TV host/prodr. Wisconsin Stories, Wis. Pub. TV, 1999-2002; curriculum com. Waunakee Sch. Bd., 2005; vestry St. Dunstan's Episcopal Ch., Madison. Episcopalian. Avocations: history, architecture, travel. Office Phone: 608-235-1112. Personal E-mail: tracy.will@yahoo.com, will.video@gmail.com.

WILLAMOWSKI, MICHAEL, academic librarian; b. Brno, Czech Republic, Nov. 23, 1939; s. Reinhold Willamowski, Hanna Luise Willamowski; m. Sibylle Zwirner; children: Mathias, Mareike, Stefan; m. Ines Busekros (div. Dec. 23, 1976). Degree in physics, U. Hamburg, 1972, D rerum naturalium, 1975. Tchr., Hamburg, Germany, 1976—2004; acad. libr. Universitaet der Bundeswehr Hamburg, Germany, 1976—2004. Info. broker Universitaet der Bundeswehr, 1976—2004. Capt. Air Force, 1961—62, Germany. Mem.: Patriotische Gesellschaft von 1765. Evangelic-Lutheran. Achievements include invention of of semipermeable membranes for reverse osmosis. Home: Gruener Bogen 10 Oststeinbek 22113 Germany Home Phone: 0114914017136836. Personal E-mail: tuscade@hotmail.com.

WILLARD, ATOM (ADAM WILLARD), musician; b. San Diego, Aug. 15, 1973; Drummer Rocket from the Crypt, 1992—2000, Offspring, 2003—07; co-founder & drummer Angels & Airwaves, 2005—; co-founding mem. The Special Goodness. Musician: (albums) (with Rocket from the Crypt) Circa: Now!, 1992, Scream, Dracula, Scream!, 1995, RFTC, 1998, (with Angels & Airwaves) We Don't Need to Whisper, 2006, I-Empire, 2007. Co-recipient Woodie of Yr. award (with Angels & Airwaves), mtvU Woodie Awards, 2006. Office: c/o Geffen Records 2220 Colorado Ave Santa Monica CA 90404 also: c/o Modlife Inc 2251 Las Palmas Dr San Diego CA 92101

WILLARD, DAN EDWARD, computer scientist, educator; b. NYC, Sept. 19, 1948; s. Alfred and Ruth Willard; m. Irina Stern, June 1, 1997; 1 child, Robert Alfred. PhD, Harvard U., Cambridge, Mass., 1978. Rschr. ATT Bell Tel. Labs., Holmdel, NJ, 1979—83; prof. Albany State U., NY, 1983—. Contbr. articles to profl. jours. Achievements include patents for interactive telephone answering machine; research in mathematical logic has provided new interpretation for Goedel's famous Incompleteness Theorem; computational geometry. Office: SUNY 1400 Washington Ave Albany NY 12222

WILLARD, FRED, actor; b. Shaker Heights, Ohio, Sept. 18, 1939; m. Mary Willard, 1972; 1 child, Hope. Performer Second City, Chgo.; founding mem. Ace Trucking Co. Actor: (films) Teenage Mother, 1967, Model Shop, 1969, Hustle, 1975, Chesty Anderson, USN, 1976, Silver Streak, 1976, Fun with Dick and Jane, 1977, Cracking Up, 1977, Americathon, 1979, How to Beat the High Co$t of Living, 1980, First Family, 1980, National Lampoon Goes to the Movies, 1982, Moving Violations, 1985, Roxanne, 1987, Ray's Male Heterosexual Dance Hall, 1987, Portrait of a White Marriage, 1988, High Strung, 1991, Waiting for Guffman, 1996, Breast Men, 1997, Permanent Midnight, 1998, Can't Stop Dancing, 1999, Austin Powers: The Spy Who Shagged Me, 1999, Dropping Out, 2000, Chump Change, 2000, Best in Show, 2000, The Wedding Planner, 2001, How High, 2001, The Year That Trembled, 2002, Teddy Bears' Picnic, 2002, Nobody Knows Anything!, 2003, Killer Diller, 2004, 50 Ways to Leave Your Lover, 2004, Harold & Kumar Go to White Castle, 2004, Lovewrecked, 2005, (voice) Chicken Little, 2005, Date Movie, 2006, Church Ball, 2006, (voice) Monster House, 2006, Ira and Abby, 2006, For Your Consideration, 2006, I'll Believe You, 2006, Epic Movie, 2007, Fighting Words, 2007, I Could Never Be Your Woman, 2007, (voice) WALL-E, 2008, Harold, 2008; (TV films) Operation Greasepaint, 1968, How to Break Up a Happy Divorce, 1976, Escape from Bogen County, 1977, The Perfect Woman, 1981, Pen 'n' Inc., 1981, Lots of Luck, 1985, The History of White People in America: Volume II, 1986, Martin Mull Live from North Ridgeville, Ohio, 1988, Merrill Markoe's Guide to Glamorous Living, 1988, I, Martin Short, Goes Hollywood, 1989, Hart to Hart: Old Friends Never Die, 1994, Sodbusters, 1994, Back to Back, 1996, The Pooch and the Pauper, 2000, When Billie Beat Bobby, 2001, Spellbound, 2003, Wiener Park, 2005, Play Nice, 2006, Re-Animated, 2006; (TV series) This Is Tom Jones, 1969, Fernwood 2 Night, 1977, Mad About You, 1998—99, Maybe It's Me, 2001—02, A Minute with Stan Hooper, 2003—04, Everybody Loves Raymond, 2003—05, Saturday Night Live, 2004—05, Back to You, 2007—08. Office: c/o The Cast Theatre 5056 Woodley Ave Encino CA 91436

WILLARD, GARCIA LOU, artist; b. Huntington, W.Va., Apr. 15, 1943; d. Harry Lee and Laura Lillian (Riley) Hall; m. Victor Percy Young, Sept. 2, 1972 (dec. Mar. 1980); m. Roger Lee Willard, Aug. 22, 1988. Student, Marshall U., 1978—83, W.Va. U., 1993, U. N.D., 1994—95. Owner, pres. Young's Fine Art, Huntington, 1975-85, Dyna Line, Wheeling, W.Va., 1980-85; instr. pastel and drawing Oglebay Mus.'s Stifel Fine Art Ctr., Wheeling, 1984-87; instr. pastel and portraiture Ohio U., Athens, 1987; owner, operator Outlines, Phoenix, Ariz., 1988-91; contbg. artist Sonoran Gallery, Phoenix, 1993—. Mem. adv. bd. Profl. Art League, St. Clairsville, Ohio, 1984-85; lectr. and exhbn. juror various art orgns., Ohio, W.Va., Pa., 1987-88; art cons. Journey's End Designs, Wheeling, 1987. One woman shows include: Delf-Norona Mus., Moundsville, W. Va., Ariel Gallery, N.Y.C., Sonoran Gallery, Phoenix; Group shows include: Pen & Brush Club, N.Y.C., 1988, Hermitage Found. Mus., Va., 1988; contbr., illustrator: (book) Dr. Horton on African Art, 1985. Advisor Ariz. Fine Arts Commn., Phoenix, 1989-92. Recipient Best of Show award Delf-Norona Mus., 1985, Molly Guion award for graphics Catharine Lorillard Wolfe Art Club, 1988, Douglas Pickering Carnegie Mellon award, 1986. Fellow Am. Artists Profl. League (Pastel award 1988); mem. Pastel Soc. Am. (signature mem. artist mem., A & M design award, 1988), Acad. Artists Assn. (artist mem., award for pastel portrait 1989), Degas Pastel Soc. (artist mem., M. Grumbacher award for pastel excellence 1988), Nat. Drawing Assn., Art Assn. Harrisburg (artist mem.), Signature Mem. Pastel Soc. Am., N.Y.C. Republican. Avocations: archaeology, astronomy, papermaking, symphonies, travel. Office: Sonoran Gallery 8819 W Corrine Dr Peoria AZ 85381-8166 Home Phone: 623-594-1918; Office Phone: 623-773-1958. Personal E-mail: fleabite37@cox.net, rlwillard1@msn.com.

WILLARD, H(ARRISON) ROBERT, electrical engineer; b. Seattle, May 31, 1933; s. Harrison Eugene and Florence Linea (Chelquist) Willard. BSEE, U. Wash., 1955, MSEE, 1957, PhD, 1971. Lic. profl.

engr., Wash. Staff assoc. Boeing Sci. Rsch. Labs., Seattle, 1959-64; rsch. assoc. U. Wash., 1968-72, sr. engr., rsch. prof. applied physics lab., 1972-81; sr. engr. Boeing Aerospace Co., Seattle, 1981-84; dir. instrumentation and engring. MetriCor Inc. (formerly Tech. Dynamics, Inc.), Redmond, Wash., 1984-92; sr. engr. B.E. Meyers & Co., Inc., Redmond, 1992—. Contbr. articles to profl. jours. With US Army, 1957—59. Mem.: IEEE, Am. Geophys. Union, Sigma Xi, Phi Beta Kappa, Tau Beta Pi. Achievements include patents in field. Office: 14540 NE 91st St Redmond WA 98052-4939

WILLARD, HOWARD A., III, food products executive; With Salomon Brothers, Inc., Bain & Co.; various positions in fin., sales, info. services and corp. responsibility Philip Morris USA Altria Group, Inc., 1992—2008, exec. v.p. strategy and bus. devel., 2008—. Bd. mem. YMCA Greater Richmond, Va., Communities in Schools Va. Office: Altria Group Inc 6601 W Broad St Richmond VA 23230 Office Phone: 804-274-2200.*

WILLARD, JOHN GERARD, communications executive, consultant, writer, educator; b. Pitts., Nov. 20, 1952; s. Cornelius Merle and May E. (Hinds) W.; m. Lorraine L. Franze, Sept. 2, 1978; children: Mary Elizabeth, Kristen Anne, Lisa Lorraine, Jessica Kathleen. BA in Journalism, Duquesne U., 1974. Producer, dir. air talent Sta. WDUQ-FM, Pitts., 1971-73; master control tech. dir. Sta. KDKA-TV, Pitts., 1973; cons. comms. Better Bus. Bur., Pitts., 1974; asst. account exec. Marc & Co. Advt., Pitts., 1975; adminstr., employee benefit adminstrn. Rockwell Internat. Corp., Pitts., 1975-80, adminstr. relocation and corp. personnel procedures, 1980-81, mgr. corp. policy, 1981-82; pres. John G. Willard Cons., 1982—. Contbr. articles to profl. jours. Office: 360 Middlegate Dr Bethel Park PA 15102-1438 Home Phone: 412-831-8650; Office Phone: 412-831-5650. E-mail: jgw71@verizon.net.

WILLARD, LOUIS CHARLES, retired librarian; b. Tallahassee, Sept. 28, 1937; s. Bert and Rose (De Milly) W.; m. Nancy Booth, June 22, 1963. BA, U. Fla., 1959; BD, Yale, 1965, MA, 1967, PhD, 1970. Tchr. Tripoli (Lebanon) Boys' Sch., 1959-62; ordained to ministry Presbyn. Ch., 1965; acting librarian Princeton Theol. Sem., 1968-69, librarian, 1969-86; librarian, mem. faculty Harvard Div. Sch., 1986-99; dir. accreditation and instnl. evaluation Assn. Theol. Schs., 1999—2008. Mem. A.L.A., Theol. Library Assn., Soc. Bibl. Lit., Am. Acad. Religion, Phi Beta Kappa, Chi Phi. Home: 970 Villeroy Greens Dr PO Box 5040 Sun City Center FL 33571-5040 Office Phone: 813-634-7047. Business E-Mail: charles@willard.cc.

WILLARD, NANCY MARGARET, writer, educator; b. Ann Arbor, Mich. d. Hobart Hurd and Margaret (Sheppard) W.; m. Eric Lindbloom, Aug. 15, 1964; 1 child, James Anatole. BA, U. Mich., 1958, PhD, 1963; MA, Stanford U., 1960. Lectr. English Vassar Coll., Poughkeepsie, NY, 1965—. Author: (poems) In His Country: Poems, 1966; Skin of Grace, 1967; A New Herbal: Poems, 1968, Testimony of the Invisible Man: William Carlos Williams, Francis Ponge, Rainer Maria Rilke, Pablo Neruda, 1970, Nineteen Masks for the Naked Poet: Poems, 1971, The Carpenter of the Sun: Poems, 1974, A Visit to William Blake's Inn: Poems for Innocent and Experienced Travelers, 1981 (Newbery Medal 1982), Household Tales of Moon and Water, 1983, Water Walker, 1989, The Ballad of Biddy Early, 1989; (short stories) The Lively Anatomy of God, 1968, Childhood of the Magician, 1973; (juveniles) Sailing to Cythera and Other Anatole Stories, 1974, All on a May Morning, 1975, The Snow Rabbit, 1975, Shoes Without Leather, 1976, T0e Well-Mannered Balloon, 1976, Night Story, 1986, Simple Pictures are Best, 1977, Stranger's Bread, 1977, The Highest Hit, 1978, Papa's Panda, 1979, The Island of the Grass King, 1979, The Marzipan Moon 1981, Uncle Terrible, 1982, (adult) Angel in the Parlor: Five Stories and Eight Essays, 1983, The Nightgown of the Sullen Moon, 1983, Night Story, 1986, The Voyage of the Ludgate Hill, 1987, The Mountains of Quilt, 1987, Firebrat, 1988; (novel) Things Invisible To See, 1984, Sister Water, 1993, The Flying Bed, 2007; (play) East of the Sun, West of the Moon, 1989, The High Rise Glorious Skittle Skat Roarious Sky Pie Angel Food Cake, 1991, A Nancy Willard Reader, 1991, Pish Posh said Hieronymus Bosch, 1991, Beauty and the Beast, 1992; illustrator: The Letter of John to James, Another Letter of John to James, 1982, The Octopus Who Wanted to Juggle (Robert Pack), 1990, (novel) Sister Water, 1993, (essays) Telling Time, 1993, (juvenile) A Starlit Somersault Downhill, 1993, (juvenile) The Sorcerer's Apprentice, 1993; author, illustrator: An Alphabet of Angels, 1994; (juvenile) Gutenberg's Gift, 1995, The Good Night Blessing Book, 1996, Cracked Corn and Snow Ice Cream, 1997, The Tortilla Cat, 1998; (poems, with Jane Yolen) Among Angels, 1995, Swimming Lessons, 1996, The Magic Cornfield, 1997, The left Attended Story, 2008; editor: (anthology of poems) Step Lightly: Poems for the Journey, 1998, The Tale I Told Sasha, 1999, (juvenile) Shadow Story, 1999, (juvenile) The Moon and Riddles Diner and the Sunny Side Cafe, 2001, (juvenile) The Mouse, the Cat and Grandmother's Hat, 2003, Cinderella's Dress, 2003, (young adult) Paradise Lost, 2004, Sweep Dreams, 2005, The Flying Bed, 2007. Recipient Hopwood award, 1958, Devins Meml. award, 1967, John Newbery award, 1981, Empire State award, 1996; Woodrow Wilson fellow, 1960; NEA grantee, 1987. Mem. The Lewis Carroll Soc. Office: Vassar Coll Dept English Raymond Ave Poughkeepsie NY 12604-0001

WILLARD, RICHARD KENNON, lawyer, former pharmaceutical company executive; b. Houston, Sept. 1, 1948; s. Fair McDaniel Willard and Elsbeth Rowe (Kennon) Willard Armistead; m. Leslie Harral Hopkins, July 10, 1976; children: Stephen Hopkins, Lauren Suzanne. BA, Emory U., 1969; JD, Harvard U., 1975. Bar: D.C. 1988, Tex. 1978, Ga. 1975. Law clk. US Ct. Appeals, San Francisco, 1975-76, US Supreme Ct., Washington, 1976-77; atty. Baker & Botts, Houston, 1977-81; counsel for intelligence policy US Dept. Justice, Washington, 1981-82, dep. asst. atty. gen. civil divsn., 1982-83, asst. atty. gen., 1983-88; ptnr. Steptoe & Johnson, Washington, 1988-99; sr. v.p., gen. counsel The Gillette Co., Boston, 1999—2005; sr. v.p. gen. counsel Bristol-Myers Squibb Co., NYC, 2005—06. Adj. prof. Georgetown U. Law Ctr., 1991-96, Boston U. Law Sch., 2002-05. Note editor: Harvard U. Law Rev., 1974-75. Gen. counsel Republican Party of Tex., Austin, 1980-81. Served to 1st lt. U.S. Army, 1969-72. Mem. Met. Club. Episcopalian.

WILLARD, ROBERT F., career military officer; b. L.A., 1950; m. Donna J. Willard. Grad., U.S. Naval Acad., 1973; M in Engring. Mgmt., Old Dominion U. Advanced through grades to adm., 2005; F-14 naval aviator; served with Fighter Squadrons Two (VF-2), Twenty Four (VF-24), and One Twenty Four (VF-124) NAS Miramar; ops. and exec. officer, instr. Navy Fighter Weapons Sch. (Top Gun); exec. and commdg. officer Screaming Eagles; commdr. USS Tripoli, 1994, USS Abraham Lincoln, 1995—98; commdr. Carrier Group 5 USS Kitty Hawk, 2000—01; dep. chief of staff, comdr. US Pacific Fleet, 2001; comdr. 7th Fleet, 2002—04; vice chief naval ops. USN, 2005—07, comdr. US Pacific Fleet Honolulu, 2007—. Aerial coord. (films) Top Gun, 1986. Decorated Def. Disting. Svc. Medal, DSM, Legion of Merit (4), others; named Pacific Fleet Tailhooker of Yr., 1982. Office: Commander US Pacific Fleet 250 Makalapa Dr Pearl Harbor HI 96860 E-mail: bob.willard@navy.mil.

WILLARD-WOTRING, SHEILA DURAM, retired English language and humanities educator; b. Evanston, Ill., July 22, 1942; d. George Thomas and Eleanor Mae (Kent) Duram; m. Michael M. Gee Sr., 1964 (div. 1972); children: Dana Gee, Natalie Gee Sullivan, Michael M. Gee Jr.; m. John Morris Willard, 1985 (div. 2000), m. Blaine Colin Wotring, 2008. BA, U. Conn., 1964, MA, 1976, U. Mass., 1989; PhD, Somerset U., 1996. Cert. tchr. secondary edn., Conn. Asst. to dean St. Joseph's Coll. Women, West Hartford, Conn., 1976-77, Asnuntuck CC, Enfield, Conn., 1977-78; prof. Middlesex CC, Bedford and Lowell, Mass., 1978—2005; ret. prof. English humanities 2007. Adj. instr. Ea. Conn. State Coll., Willimantic, Conn., 1975-78, Springfield CC, Mass., 1977, U. Mass., Lowell, 1994, Commonwealth Honors Coll. U. Mass., Amherst, 1997-05, Salem State Coll., 2007; lectr. Humanities' Orgn., Conn. and Mass., 1980—. Editorial asst.: This Hallowed Ground, 1963, Seventeen from Everywhere, 1976, Sharing Literature with Children, 1977; contbr. poetry to anthologies, articles to jours. Vol. Unitarian Universalist Social and Ednl. Activist Roles, Conn. and Mass., 1972—. Mem. MLA (del. assembly), Nat. Coun. Tchrs. English, Conf. on Coll. Composition and Comm., New Eng. Regional Tchrs. English, C.C. Humanities Assn., Nat. Collegiate Hons. Coun., Phi Beta Kappa, Phi Kappa Phi. Democrat. Unitarian Universalist. Avocations: writing, painting, music. Home: 4 Walnut Hill Rd Derry NH 03038-5016 Personal E-mail: sdwotring@aol.com.

WILLAUER, GEORGE JACOB, American literature educator; b. Oct. 30, 1935; s. George Jacob and Mary Catherine (Eshleman) W.; m. Cynthia Cameron Thun, June 11, 1966; children: George Jacob III, Elizabeth Christian. BA, Wesleyan U., 1957; MA, U. Pa., 1959, PhD, 1965. Asst. instr. U. Pa., Phila., 1958-62; instr. Conn. Coll., New London, 1962-66, asst. prof., 1966-72, assoc. prof., 1972-78, prof., 1978—2002, chair dept. English, 1972—77, 1991—94, 2000—02. Charles J. MacCurdy prof. of Am. Studies, 1993-02; coll. marshal, 1989-02, dean of acad. programs, 1997-00; instr. Williams Coll.-Mystic Seaport Program in Maritime Studies, 1986-88; vis. prof. lit. U. Dar es Salaam, Tanzania, 1996. Author: A Lyme Miscellany: 1776-1976, 1977; editor: Original Discontent: Commentaries on the Creation of Connecticut's Constitution of 1818; contbr. articles to profl. jours. Trustee Cmty. Found. Southeastern Conn., 1996-02, pres. 2000-02; trustee Florence Griswold Mus., 1978-, pres. 1983-88, Lymes Youth Svc. Bur., 1978-83, Lyme Land Conservation Trust, 1996-02, Lyme Pub. Libr., 1988, Lyme Pub. Libr., Inc., 1955—, pres. 2004-, Lyman Allyn Art Mus., 1983-88, 96-04, Music Masterworks, 2001—, v.p., MacCurdy-Salisbury Ednl. Found., Conn. Humanities Coun., 2004—; deacon First Congl. Ch., Old Lyme. English-Speaking Union fellow, 1969, 72. Mem. MLA, Century Assn. Home: 55-1 Beaver Brook Rd Old Lyme CT 06371-3219

WILLAUER, WHITING RUSSELL, retired manufacturing executive, systems engineer; b. Boston, May 24, 1931; s. Whiting and Louise Knapp (Russell) Willauer-Jackson; m. Julie Mackie McConihe, Mar. 15, 2001 (div.); m. Julie Matheson Arnold, July 11, 1959 (div.); children: Whiting Russell, Jr., William Arnold. BS, Princeton U., 1955, MS, 1959; PhD, Georgetown U., 1964. Research assoc. joint research com. Dept. Def., 1951-52; ops. mgr. Civil Air Transport Airline Taiwan, 1952-53; scientist Analytic Services, Inc., 1958-61; asst. prof. astronomy Georgetown U., 1965-68; mgr. TRW Systems Group support to chief Naval ops., McLean, Va., 1968-73, TRW support to U.S. Navy Antisubmarine program, 1973-79, TRW Amphibious Ship Bldg. program, 1979-85; advanced systems mgr. TRW Systems Integration Group, 1985-90, cost estimating mgr., 1990-95, sr. cons., 1995-99; sr. v.p., chief strategist K12Nation.net, 1999-2000. Cons. Nat. Geog. Soc., 1961-65, U. Tex., 1962, NSF, 1963, Booz-Allen & Hamilton, 1966-67. Mng. editor: Jour. Astronautical Scis, 1969-71; Designer: Orrery Planetarium Nat. Geog. Soc. Asst. chief steward Alpine Venue XIII Olympic Winter Games, Lake Placid, 1980; mem. U.S. Olympic Com., bd. dirs., 1987-94, sec. nat. governing bodies, 1989-92, mem. membership svcs. com., 1988-92, mem. athletic devel. com., 1992-96; chef de mission Winter Pan Am. Games, Las Lenas, Argentina, 1990; asst. chief de mission XVI Winter Olympics, Albertville, France, 1992; U.S. Olympic Com. liaison to VI Paralympic Winter Games, Lillehammer, Norway, 1994. Research fellow Georgetown U., 1961-65. Fellow AAAS (coun.); mem. Am. Astronautical Soc. (v.p. fin.), Blue Ridge Ski Coun. (pres. 1976-78), U.S. Ski Assn. (pres. 1982-87, Julius Blegan award 1988, Mary and Bud Little award 1998), U.S. Ski and Snowboard Assn. (vice chmn. 1994-96, trustee emeritus 1997—), Internat. Ski Fedn. (chmn. U.S. del. 1983, 85, chmn. recreational skiing com. 1987-98, eligibility com. 1988-98), Ea. Ski Assn. (treas. 1980-82), Pan Am Sports Orgn. (winter games adv. com. 1988—), Sigma Xi, Chevy Chase Club (Md.), Nantucket Yacht Club (Mass.) (commodore 1981-83, bd. govs. 1957-59, 68—), Nantucket IOD Fleet Assn. (fleet capt. 2002-04), Arthur Knapp Prize 2003 IOD World Championship, USCG Aux. Flotilla 11-7 (sec. 2003—, Mem. of Yr. 2004), Nantucket Behavioral Health Svcs. (bd. dirs 2007-, pres. 2008-), Nantucket Alliance Substance Abuse Prevention (pres. 2004-05, sec. 2008-), Nantucket Island Bd. Selectman 2005-08, chmn. 2006-08), Nantucket Wharf Rat Club, Nantucket Shellfish Assn. (pres., 2008-). Personal E-mail: whitey@willauer.com.

WILLBANKS, T. SHAWN, educational association administrator; s. Steve and Carol Willbanks; children: Lynlee Howard, Andrew, Haley M. AAS in Drafting, U. Ark., Morrilton, 1986, BS in Edn., 2007; AAS in Electronic Sys. Tech., CC Air Force, 1990; AAS in Gen. Studies, Miss. County Coll., Blytheville, Ark., 1990. Lic. tchr., Ark., 1998; cert. in NICET engring., Ark., 1997. Owner, Conway, Ark., 1986—2008; cad, archtl., engring. Jefferson Area Vocat. Sch., Pine Bluff, Ark., 1999—2003; coll. instr. SEARK Coll., Pine Bluff, 2001—, nat. drafting cert. instr., 2003—08, mem., facility senitate, 2007—08, founder, marksman club, 2008—. Founder JAVC CAD and Drafting Scholarship Program, Pine Bluff. Author: (book) Blue Print to Life.

WILLBORN, STEVEN L., dean, law educator; BA magna cum laude, Northland Coll., 1974; MS in Counseling, U.Wis.-Madison, 1976; JD cum laude, U. Wis. Law Sch., 1976. Asst. prof. law U. Nebr.-Lincoln Coll. Law, 1979—82, assoc. prof., 1982—85, prof., 1985—99, Richard C. & Catherine Stuart Schmoker prof. law, 1999—, dean, 2001—. Pvt. practice, 1976—79; vis. prof. U. Mich. Law Sch., 1992. Co-author: Employment Law: Cases and Materials, The Statistics of Discrimination: Using Statistical Evidence in Discrimination Cases, 2002; contbr. articles to law jours. Grantee Lincoln Coll., Oxford U., 1993; vis. scholar Australian Nat. U., Canberra, 1988, U. Toronto, 1991; Fulbright Scholar, Inst. Advanced Legal Studies, U. London, 1985—86. Office: U Nebr-Lincoln Coll Law Ross McCollum Hall PO Box 830902 Lincoln NE 68583 E-mail: willborn@unl.edu.*

WILLCOX, RODERICK HARRISON, lawyer; b. Columbus, Ohio, Jan. 10, 1934; s. Richard V. and Marcella A. (Rehl) W.; m. Rita Kay Click, July 2, 1955; children: Sharon Marie Willcox Hazlewood, Kathy Lynn, Patricia Ann Willcox Hanna, Roderick Harrison Jr. BA, Williams Coll., 1955; LLB, U. Mich., 1958. Ptnr. Chester, Willcox & Saxbe, Columbus, Ohio, 1971—. Office: Chester Willcox & Saxbe LLP 65 East State St Ste 1000 Columbus OH 43215-3442 Office Phone: 614-221-4000. E-mail: rwillcox@cwslaw.com.

WILLE, LOIS JEAN, retired editor; b. Chgo., Sept. 19, 1931; d. Walter and Adele S. (Taege) Kroeber; m. Wayne M. Wille, June 6, 1954. BS, Northwestern U., 1953, MS, 1954; Litt.D. (hon.), Columbia Coll., Chgo., 1980, Northwestern U., 1990, Rosary Coll., 1990. Reporter Chgo. Daily News, 1958-74, nat. corr., 1975-76, assoc. editor charge editorial page, 1977; assoc. editor charge editorial and opinion pages Chgo. Sun-Times, 1978-83; assoc. editor editorial page Chgo. Tribune, 1984-87, editor editorial page, 1987-91, ret., 1991. Author: Forever Open, Clear and Free: the Historic Struggle for Chicago's Lakefront, 1972, At Home in the Loop: How Clout and Community Built Chicago's Dearborn Park, 1997. Recipient Pulitzer prize for public svc., 1963, Pulitzer prize for editorial writing, 1989, William Allen White Found. award for excellence in editorial writing, 1978, numerous awards Chgo. Newspaper Guild, numerous awards Chgo. Headline Club, numerous awards Nat. Assn. Edn. Writers, numerous awards Ill. AP, numerous awards Ill. UPI. Home: 1530 S State St Apt 1011 Chicago IL 60605 Personal E-mail: lowille@aol.com.

WILLE, ROSANNE LOUISE, educational consultant; b. Hackensack, NJ, Aug. 4, 1941; d. Albert Wille and Rose Marie (Rock) Eberhardt; m. George B. Jacobs, Mar. 12, 1980; children: Leigh, Steven, Alexander, Jeffrey. M Pub. Adminstrn., Rutgers U., 1986; PhD, N.Y.U., 1980. Dept. chair Rutgers U., Newark, 1978-84, Lehman Coll., Bronx, NY, 1984-87, dean, 1987-92, provost, sr. v.p., 1992—2002; cons. for higher edn., 2002—. Contbr. articles to profl. jours. Bd. dirs. Family Support Svcs., Bronx, N.Y., 1994-2002, bd. dirs. South Bronx Overall Economic Devel., Inc., Bronx, 1991-2002. Recipient Vision award Family Support Svcs., Bronx, 1996, Thousand Points of Light award Pres. George Bush, Washington, 1991. Mem. N.Y. Acad. Scis., N.Y. Acad. Medicine, Am. Assn. Higher Edn. Avocations: aviation, golf. Address: PO Box 799 Hampton Bays NY 11946 Personal E-mail: rlwille@earthlink.net.

WILLENBECHER, JOHN, artist; b. Macungie, Pa., May 5, 1936; s. John George and Geneva (Bacon) W. BA, Brown U., 1958; postgrad., N.Y. U., Inst. Fine Arts, 1958-61. Sculptor-mem. N.Y.C. Art Commn., 1980-92; mem. commn. for plaza and pavillion, Mpls. Inst. Arts, 1991. Exhibited in one-person shows including Hamilton Gallery Contemporary Art, N.Y.C., 1977, 80, 82, U. Mass. Art Gallery, Amherst, 1977, Wright State U. Art Gallery, Dayton, Ohio, 1977, Jaffe-Friede Gallery, Dartmouth Coll., Hanover, N.H., 1977, Fine Arts Ctr. U. R.I., Kingston, 1978, Neuberger Mus., SUNY at Purchase, 1979, Allentown (Pa.) Art Mus., 1979, Mpls. Inst. Arts, 1991, U. N.Mex. Art Gallery, Albuquerque, 1996, 5 Myles Gallery, Bklyn., 2003, CUNY Grad. Ctr., N.Y.C, 2003; exhibited in numerous group shows including Albright-Knox Art Gallery, Buffalo, 1963, Whitney Mus. Am. Art, N.Y.C., 1964-68; represented in permanent collections including Solomon R. Guggenheim Mus., N.Y.C., Met. Mus., N.Y.C., Whitney Mus. Am. Art, Albright-Knox Art Gallery, Phila. Mus. Art, Centre d'Art et Culture Georges Pompidou, Paris, Hirshhorn Mus. and Sculpture Garden, Washington, Art Inst. Chgo. Nat. Endowment for Arts grantee, 1977, Esther and Adolph Gottlieb Found. grantee, 1994. Achievements include being subject of profl. articles and catalogues.

WILLERSON, JAMES THORNTON, cardiologist, researcher, medical educator; b. Lampasas, Tex., Nov. 16, 1939; m. Nancy Beamer; 2 children. BS, U. Tex., Austin, 1961; MD, Baylor Coll. Medicine, 1965. Diplomate Internal Medicine 1972, Cardiovascular Disease 1974. Intern, internal medicine Mass. Gen Hosp., Boston, 1965—66, resident, cardiology, 1966—67, fellow, 1969—72; clin. assoc. NIH, Bethesda, Md.; former chief, cardiology St. Luke's Episcopal Hosp.; former chief, med. svcs. Meml. Hermann Hosp.; joined faculty, held positions including prof. medicine and dir., cardiovascular divsn. U. Tex. Southwestern Med. Sch., Dallas, 1972—89; chair, dept. medicine U. Tex. Med. Sch., Houston, 1989—2001, Edward Randall II Chair, dept. internal medicine, 1989—; prof. medicine U. Tex. Health Sci. Ctr., Houston, 1976—, Alkek/Williams Disting. Prof., 1989—, interim pres., 2000—01, pres., 2001—08; med. dir., chief cardiology rsch., co-dir. Cullen Cardiovascular Rsch. Lab. Tex. Heart Inst., St. Luke's Episcopal Hosp., 1993—, pres.-elect, 2004—07, pres., 2007—. Adj. prof. medicine Baylor Coll. Medicine, U. Tex. MD Anderson Cancer Ctr.; invited lectr. in field. Editor-in-chief Circulation, 1993—2004; contbr. several articles to profl. jours.; editl. bd. mem. of several peer-reviewed jours., author and co-author of several textbooks; co-editor: Cardiovascular Medicine, 3rd edit., 2007. Recipient James B. Herrick award, Am. Heart Assn., 1993, Disting. Svc. award, Coun. Clin. Cardiology, Am. Heart Assn., 2002, Merit medal, Internat. Acad. Cardiovascular Scis., 2004, Career Achievement award, Transcatheter Cardiovascular Therapeutics Mtg., 2005, Ignacio Chavez Medallion, Nat. Autonomous U. Mex., 2008; named Disting. Alumnus, U. Tex. Austin, 1999, Disting. Scientist, Am. Coll. Cardiology, 2000, Outstanding Cardiologist, Shanghai Internat. Symposium Cardiology, 2006, Lewis Katz Vis. Prof. in Cardiovascular Rsch. and Katz prize in Cardiovascular Rsch., Columbia U. Med. Ctr., 2007. Fellow: Royal Soc. Medicine; mem.: Nat. Am. Heart Assn. (former chmn. rsch. com. & NIH Cardiovascular & Renal Study Sect., bd. dirs. and steering com.), Inst. Med., Alpha Omega Alpha, Phi Beta Kappa. Achievements include creation of the Brown Foundation Institute of Molecular Medicine for the Prevention of Human Diseases; being honored as an international honorary member of the Japanese Circulation Soc. Among the first 7 physicians outside of Japan to be inducted & one of only 2 Americans to receive this honor in 2006. Office: U Tex Health Sci Ctr Dept Internal Medicine PO Box 20036 Houston TX 77225-1501 Home: 6601 Westchester Ave Houston TX 77005*

WILLERTON, BEVERLY KAY, mathematics educator; b. Borger, Tex., Apr. 23, 1951; d. Frank Quentin and Ozline M Ward; m. Donald L Willerton (div.); children: Justin, Joshua, Scott. BS, Midwestern State U., 1973. Math. tchr. Hirschi H.S., Wichita Falls, Tex., 1974—75; math. instr. U. N.Mex. at Los Alamos, 1987—, math. dept. chair, 1994—, divsn. chair, 2004—. Mem.: Nat. Assn. Devel. Edn., N.Mex. Assn. Two-Yr. Colls., Math. Assn. Am. Office: U NMex at Los Alamos 4000 University Dr Los Alamos NM 87544

WILLES, MARK HINCKLEY, media specialist; b. Salt Lake City, July 16, 1941; s. Joseph Simmons and Ruth (Hinckley) W.; m. Laura Fayone, June 7, 1961; children: Wendy Anne, Susan Kay, Keith Mark, Stephen Joseph, Matthew Bryant. AB, Columbia Coll., 1963, PhD, 1967. Staff banking and currency com. Ho. of Reps., Washington, 1966-67; asst. prof. fin. Wharton Sch. U. Pa., Phila., 1967-69; economist Fed. Res. Bank, Phila., 1967, sr. economist, 1969-70, dir. rsch., 1970-71, v.p., dir. rsch., 1971, 1st v.p., 1971-77; pres. Fed. Res. Bank of Mpls., 1977-80; exec. v.p., chief fin. officer Gen. Mills, Inc., Mpls., 1980-85, pres., COO, 1985-92, vice-chmn., 1992-95; chmn., pres., CEO Times Mirror Co., LA, 1995-2000; pub. L.A. Times, 1997-99; disting. prof. mgmt. Brigham Young U., Provo, Utah, 2000, 2004—; pres. Hawaii Honolulu Mission, Ch. of LDS, 2001—04. Office: Brigham Young Univ 3651 N 100 E Ste 300 Provo UT 84604 *My success is based on adherence to principles I learned in the home, which is the most basic and important organizational unit in the world. Three of those principles stand out in my mind: Be just, honest and moral—do things not only* *because they are required, but because they are right. Have mercy—care enough about others to be fair and kind. Be humble—you can get more done effectively with the help of others than you can do on your own.*

WILLET, E. CROSBY (EVERETT CROSBY WILLET), artist; b. Phila., Jan. 8, 1929; s. Henry Lee and Katharine Muriel (Crosby) W.; m. Augusta Winter, Nov. 27, 1954; children: William, Nancy Lee, Katharine Crosby, Henry Lee II. BA, Lafayette Coll., 1950; DFA (hon.), Orthodox Cath. Archdiocese, Phila., 1982. Apprentice Blenko Glass Co., Milton, W.Va., 1950; craftsman Willet Stained Glass Studio Inc., Phila., 1950-54, v.p., 1954-64, pres., 1964—. Works include: Portsmouth Priory, R.I., 1956, Folger Bay Washington Cathedral, 1973, Assocs. Dining Room, Smithsonian Instn., 1976, 2d Bapt. Ch., Houston, 1985-86, Gethsemane Cathedral, Fargo, N.D., 1992-95, Peachtree Road United Methodist Church, Atlanta, 2001, St. Martins Episcopal Ch., Houston, 2004. Recipient George Washington Kidd award Lafayette Coll., 1985, Elbert M. Conover award AIA/IFRAA, 2002, Lifetime Achievement award 2009. Fellow Stained Glass Assn. Am. (exec. bd. 1958-78, 81, pres. 1964-66); mem. InterFaith Forum, Religion, Art and Architecture (exec. bd. 1979-2001, Conover award, 2002), Am. Soc. Appraisers (sr. mem.), Appraisers Assn. Am., Nantucket Yacht Club, Moorings Club. Republican. Presbyn. Home and Office: Willet Hauser Archtl Glass 811 E Cayuga St Philadelphia PA 19124 Home Phone: 772-234-8824; Office Phone: 215-247-5721. E-mail: ecwillet@earthlink.net.

WILLETT, DON R., state supreme court justice; BBA, Baylor U.; JD, MA in Polit. Sci., Duke U. Law clk. to Honorable Jerre S. Williams US Ct. Appeals (5th cir.), Tex.; atty. Haynes and Boone, LLP, 1993—96; legal adv. to gov. Tex., 1996—2000; dep. atty. gen. for legal counsel Tex., 2000—04; justice Tex. Supreme Ct., 2005—. Served on Bush-Cheney 2000 Presidential Campaign and Transition Team; supreme ct. liaison Tex. Ctr. for Legal Ethics and Professionalism. Former mem. Tex. Commn. on Volunteerism & Cmty. Svc.; bd. mem. Nat. Fatherhood Initiative, Big Brothers Big Sisters Ctrl. Tex., SafePlace, Tex. Lyceum Assn. Recipient Austin Under 40 award for Govt./Polit. Affairs, 2006. Fellow: Tex. Bar Found.; mem.: Tex. Assn. for Ct. Administration (judicial adv. bd.), Am. Law Inst. Office: Tex Supreme Ct PO Box 12248 Austin TX 78711 Office Phone: 512-463-1312. Office Fax: 512-463-1365.*

WILLETT, DONALD, historian; s. Donald and Katherine Willett; m. Bernie Lee. PhD, Tex. A&M U. Assoc. prof. Tex. A&M U., Galveston, 1985—. Editor: (anthology) Invisible Texans: Women and Minorities in Texas. Recipient Ralph W. Steen award, East Tex. Hist. Assn., 2005, C. K. Chamberlain award, 1995. Mem.: Gulf South Hist. Assn. (pres. 2007—08), East Tex. Hist. Assn. (pres. 1998—99). Office: Texas A&M Univ at Galveston P O Box 1675 Galveston TX 77553 Business E-Mail: willettd@tamug.edu.

WILLETT, JOHN A., lawyer; b. NYC, Aug. 4, 1946; BA, Bucknell U., 1968; MBA, JD, Stanford U., 1972; LLM, NYU, 1976. Bar: Calif. 1972, N.Y. 1973. Ptnr., N.Y.C. office mgr. Arnold & Porter LLP, NYC. Fellow Am. Coll. Investment Counsel; mem. ABA, State Bar Calif., Assn. Bar City of N.Y. Office: Arnold & Porter LLP 399 Park Ave Fl 35 New York NY 10022-4690 Office Phone: 212-715-1001. Office Fax: 212-715-1399. Business E-Mail: john.willett@aporter.com.

WILLETT, ROSLYN LEONORE, public relations executive, food service consultant, writer, editor; d. Edward and Celia (Stickler) Sternberg; m. Edward Willett (div.); 1 child, Jonathan Stanley. BA, Hunter Coll., NYC; postgrad., Columbia U., CUNY, NYU, New Sch. Technologist in charge tech. svcs. and devel. Stein Hall & Co., NYC; editor McGraw-Hill, Inc., NYC, Harcourt Brace Jovanovich, Inc., NYC; pub. rels. writer Farley Manning Assocs., NYC; cons. pub. rels. and food svc. Roslyn Willett Assocs., Inc., NYC, 1959—. Adj. prof. Hunter Coll., Poly U., Columbia U. Sch. Pub. Health; dir. West End Writers Workshop, 1998—2002; seminar presenter in field. Author: The Woman Executive in Woman in Sexist Society, 1971, also short stories, novella and essays in mag. and on internet; assoc. editor Timber Creek Rev., Words of Wisdom, 2001-2007, Bulls Head Creek Rev., 2004-2005. V.p. North Shore Ams. for Dem. Action; ofcl. rapporteur Post-Assembly Tech. Sessions, WHO; juror Am. Film Festival, Arts and Scis., 1962—88; chmn. Women's Polit. Caucus, Inc. NY, NJ, Conn, 1971—73; v.p. Mid Hudson Arts and Sci. Ctr., Poughkeepsie, NY; apptd. to regional adv. coun. Fed. SBA, 1976—78; chmn. image of women com. NOW; bd. dirs. Small Bus. Task Force, Assn. for Small Bus. and Professions, 1981—85, Rhinebeck Chamber Music Soc., 1985—86, Will Inst., New Paltz, 1980—2001, Women Studies Abstracts, 1971—81; pres. Hunns Lake Assn., 1999—2001. Mem. Pub. Rels. Soc. Am. (accredited), Food Svc. Cons. Soc. Internat. (bd. dirs. 1978-80), NY Acad. Scis., Lyceum Soc., Inst. Food Technologists, Juilliard Assn., Assn. for Japanese Art in Am., Inc., Alliance Française, Paris Club, NY Print Club, Met. Mus. Art, Mus. Modern Art, Brlkn. Mus., Mus. Natural History, Phi Tau Sigma, Food Sci. Honors Soc. (electrd mem.). Avocations: dance, art collecting, hiking, swimming. Home: 97 W Hunns Lake Rd Stanfordville NY 12581-5606 Office: 441 West End Ave 15A New York NY 10024-5328 Personal E-mail: roslynwillett@yahoo.com.

WILLETT, THOMAS EDWARD, lawyer; b. NYC, Nov. 8, 1947; s. Oscar Edward and Alice (Fleming) W.; m. Marilyn Kenney, Dec. 28, 1969; children: Thomas Justin, Christopher Joseph. BS, USAF Acad., Colo., 1969; JD with distinction, Cornell U., 1972. Bar: N.Y. 1973, U.S. Ct. Claims 1973, U.S. Supreme Ct. 1977. Judge advocate USAF, Syracuse, NY, 1973-75, Kincheloe AFB, Mich., 1975-77, USAF Hdqs., Washington, 1977-79; assoc. Harris Beach LLP, Rochester, NY, 1979-84, ptnr., 1985—. Pres. Monroe County Legal Assistance Corp., Rochester, 1983-89. Capt. USAF, 1969-79. Mem. ABA, N.Y. State Bar Assn., Monroe County Bar Assn., Order of Coif. Office: Harris Beach LLP 99 Garnsey Rd Pittsford NY 14534 Home Phone: 585-586-1384; Office Phone: 585-419-8646. E-mail: twillett@harrisbeach.com.

WILLETT, WALTER CHURCHILL, epidemiologist, educator; b. Hart, Mich., June 20, 1945; s. Elwin Lintin and Lawain (Churchill) W.; m. Gail Valerae Pettiford, June 11, 1973; children: Amani, Kamali. Studied food sci., Mich. State U., 1963-66; MD, U. Mich., 1970; MPH, Harvard U., 1973, DPH, 1980. Diplomate Am. Bd. Internal Medicine. Lectr. in medicine U. Dar es Salaam, Tanzania, 1974-75, head community health dept., 1975-77; fellow clin. epidemiology Channing Lab. Med. Sch., Harvard U., Boston, 1977-80; asst. prof. epidemiology Sch. Pub. Health, Harvard U., Boston, 1980-84, assoc. prof. epidemiology, 1984-88, Fredrick John Stare prof. epidemiology and nutrition, 1987—, chmn. dept. nutrition, 1991—; prof. epidemiology and nutrition Harvard Med. Sch., 1992—. Statis. cons. New Eng. Jour. Medicine, Boston, 1987—; spkr. in field. Author: Nutritional Epidemiology, 1989, Eat, Drink and Be Healthy: The Harvard Medical School Guide to Healthy Eating, 2001, Nutritional Epidemiology, 2nd Edit.; contbr. over 900 articles to sci. publs. Recipient Charles S. Mott prize, GM Cancer Rsch. Found., 2001, Brinker award, Komen Found., 2003, Linus Pauling Inst. Prize Health Rsch., 2003, Rogers award, AAMC, 2003, Discovery Health Channel Med. Honors, 2004. Mem. Am. Epidemiol. Soc., Soc. for Epidemiol. Rsch., Am. Inst. Nutrition, Alpha Omega Alpha. Avocations: gardening, woodworking, skiing, bicycling, kayaking. Office: Harvard Sch Pub Health Dept Nutrition Bldg II Rm 311 651 Huntington Ave Boston MA 02115 Office Phone: 617-432-4680.*

WILLEY, CHARLES WAYNE, lawyer; b. Dillon, Mont., Oct. 7, 1932; s. Asa Charles and Elizabeth Ellen Willey; m. Helene D., July 21, 1962 (div.); children: Stephen Charles, Heather Helene, Brent David, Scott D.; m. Alexis W. Grant, Jan. 26, 1986. BS with honors, Mont. State U., 1954; JD with high honors, U. Mont., 1959. Bar: Mont. 1959, Calif. 1960, U.S. Ct. Claims 1975, U.S. Tax Ct. 1975, U.S. Ct. Appeals (9th cir.) 1959, U.S. Ct. Appeals (Fed. cir.) 1983, U.S. Supreme Ct. 1972. Law clk. to presiding judge U.S. Ct. Appeals (9th cir.), 1959-60; ptnr. Price, Postel & Parma, Santa Barbara, Calif., 1960-77; pvt. practice Santa Barbara, 1977-97; shareholder Hollister & Brace, Santa Barbara, 1998-2001. Prof. law corp.; instr. Santa Barbara City Coll., 1961—63, U. Calif., Santa Barbara, 1963—64; lectr. Mont. Tax Inst., 1990, 92, Am. Agr. Law Assn., 1993, 96; adj. prof. law U. Mont., 2005. Chief editor Mont. Law Rev., 1958—59. Pres. Legal Aid Found. Santa Barbara, 1970; mem. Laguna Blanca Sch. Bd., pres. 1980-81; v.p. Phoenix of Santa Barbara. Served to capt. USAF, 1954-56. Mem.: State Bar of Mont. (chair sect. bus., estates, tax, trusts and real estate 2004—05), State Bar of Calif., Santa Barbara County Bar Assn. (pres. 1972—73), Rotary, Kiwanis, Phi Delta Phi, Phi Eta Sigma, Phi Kappa Phi. Republican. Episcopalian. Avocations: reading, writing, travel. Office: 806 Parkview Way Missoula MT 59803 Home Phone: 406-549-3852.

WILLEY, FRIEDA ANDERS, adult education educator; b. Independence, VA, Aug. 17, 1936; d. David Alex Anders and Dixie Alice Snow; m. Edward Lake Willey, June 16, 1962; 1 child, Betsy Eden Hawthorne. AA, Bluefield Coll., 1958; BS in Elem. Edn., Salisburg U., 1977, MA, 1978. Elem. tchr. Cecil City Bd. of Edn., Elkton, Md., 1958—62, Dorchester City Bd. of Edn., Cambridge, Md., 1962—84; jr. high sch. tchr. Wythe City Bd. of Edn., Wytheville, Va., 1984—85, Harrington (Del.) Sch. Dist., 1985—86; secondary spl. edn. tchr. Orange County Bd. of Edn., Orange, Va., 1986—2003, adult educator, 1995—; interpreter Montpelier Found., Montpelier Station, Va., 1999—. Methodist. Avocation: reading, hist. places, writing fiction.

WILLHAM, RICHARD LEWIS, zoology educator; b. Hutchinson, Kans., May 4, 1932; s. Oliver S. and Susan E. (Hurt) W.; m. Esther B. Burkhart, June 1, 1954; children: Karen Nell, Oliver Lee. BS, Okla. State U., 1954; MS, Iowa State U., 1955, PhD, 1960. Asst. prof. Iowa State U., Ames, 1959-63, assoc. prof., 1966-71, prof. dept. animal sci., 1971-78, Disting. prof., 1978—; assoc. prof. Okla. State U., Stillwater, 1963-66. Cons. in field; tchr. livestock history; guest curator exhbn. Art About Livestock, 1990. Author: A Heritage of Leadership - The First 100 Years of Animal Science at Iowa State University, 1996;Portrait Hangs in S & S Club Gallery of Livestock Industry Leaders. Recipient Svc. award Beef Improvement Fedn., 1974, Edn. and Rsch. award Am. Polled Herefore Assn., 1979, Rsch. award Nat. Cattlemen's Assn., 1986, 91, Disting. Alumnus award Okla. State U., 1978, Regents Faculty Excellence award Iowa State U., 1993; named to Hall of Fame Am. Hereford Assn., 1982, Am. Angus Assn., 1988. Fellow Am. Soc. Animal Sci. (animal breeding and genetics award 1978, industry service award 1986). Home: 2316 Hamilton Dr Ames IA 50014-8201 Office: Iowa State U Dept Animal Sci Ames IA 50011-0001 Home Phone: 515-268-5216; Office Phone: 515-294-3533. E-mail: rwillham@iastate.edu.

WILLHITE, G. PAUL, chemical engineer, petroleum engineer, educator; BSChemE, Iowa State U., Ames, 1959; PhD in Chem. Engring., Northwestern U., 1962. Joined faculty U. Kans., 1969, co-founder, chair co-dir. Tertiary Oil Recovery Project, 1974, Ross H. Forney Disting. prof. Recipient John Franklin Carll Award, 2001, IOR Pioneer Award of Petroleum Engrs., 2004. Mem.: NAE, Am. Soc. Engring. Educators, Am. Inst. Chem. Engrs., Soc. Petroleum Engrs. Office: U Kans Sch Engring Eaton Hall 1520 W 15th St, Rm 1 Lawrence KS 66045 Office Phone: 785-864-2906. Office Fax: 785-864-4967. Business E-Mail: willhite@ku.edu.

WILLI, STEVEN MATTHEW, physician, educator, researcher; s. John Edward and Doris Mae (Smith) Willi; m. Maria Szpiech, July 27, 2002. BA cum laude, Johns Hopkins U., 1981, MD, 1985. Diplomate in pediatrics and pediatric endocrinology Am. Bd. Pediatrics. Resident in pediat. Children's Hosp. of Phila., 1985—88; fellow in pediatric endocrinology Children's Hosp. Phila., 1988—91; instr. pediat. U. Pa., Phila., 1991—92, assoc. prof. pediat., 2004—; asst. prof. pediat. Med. U. S.C., Charleston, 1992—98, assoc. prof., 1998—2004. Contbr. chpts. to books, articles to profl. jours. Med. dir. Camp Adam Fisher for Children with Diabetes, Summerton, S.C., 1995-2003; bd. dirs. Juvenile Diabetes Found., 1995-99; dir. Diabetes Ctr. for Children, Children's Hosp. of Phila., 2004—. Recipient Nat. Rsch. Svc. award NIH, 1990, Clin. Assoc. Physician award NIH, 1996; Healfman scholar, 1985. Fellow Am. Acad. Pediatrics; mem. Endocrine Soc., Lawson Wilkins Pediatric Endocrine Soc., Am. Diabetes Assn. Avocations: bicycling, photography. Office: Childrens Hosp of Phila Divsn Endocrinology/Diabetes 34th St Civic Ctr Blvd Philadelphia PA 19104-0001 Office Phone: 215-590-3174.

WILLIAM, DAVID, theater director, actor; b. London, Eng., June 24, 1926; arrived in Can., 1986; s. Eric Hugh and Olwen (Roose) W. BA, U. Coll., Oxford, Eng., 1950. Artistic dir. Glasgow Citizen's Theatre, The Nottingham Playhouse, The New Shakespeare Co., London, The National Theatre of Israel, Stratford Festival, Can., 1989-93. Vis. prof. theater dept. De Paul U., Chgo., 1985-88; founder, 1st artistic dir. Ludlow Festival. Profl. debut as Rosencrantz to Richard Burton's Hamlet, Old Vic Theatre, London, 1953; theatre directing credits include: Bacchae, The Importance of Being Earnest, The Tempest, Entertaining Mr. Sloane, Love Letters, Treasure Island, Hamlet, Love for Love, The Shoemaker's Holiday, Murder in the Cathedral, Troilus and Cressida, The Winter's Tale, She Stoops to Conquer, Antigone, Separate Tables, Romeo and Juliet, Othello, King Lear, Volpone, Albert Herring, The Merry Wives of Windsor, Twelfth Night; directing world premièrs of operas include: Therese, Royal Opera House Covent Garden, The Lighthouse, Edinburgh festival, Red Emma; other operas directed include Iphigenie en Tauride, The Fairy Queen, Lisbon, La Traviata, Scottish Opera, Il Re Pastore, Camden Festival, Albert Herring, Aldeburgh Festival, Cosl Fan Tutte, Opera St. Louis, Tosca, Can. Opera Co., Mrs. Mozart, Hartford Symphony Orch., 1999; appeared in Uncle Vanya as Serebryakov, As You Like It as Jaques, Twelfth Night as Malvolio; appeared in numerous TV prodns. most notably as Richard the Second in the BBC series An Age of Kings; compiled, directed and acted in My Shakespeare, Stratford Festival and CBC Radio; played A.E.H. in The Invention of Love, Guthrie Theatre, Mpls., 2000, Studio Theater, Washington, 2001, Boyet in Love's Labours Lost, Nat. Arts Ctr, Ottawa, 2005; played in Under Milk Wood, St. Mary's, Ont., 2004. Home: 194 Langarth St E London ON Canada N6C 1Z5 Personal E-mail: may.king@rogers.com.

WILLIAM, PAUL GRIFFIN, theology studies educator; b. Ft. Wayne, Ind., Apr. 12, 1957; married. PhD, Emory U., Atlanta, 1995. Assoc. prof. Old Testament and Hebrew Evangel U., Springfield, Mo., 1995—. Author: (textbook) Hebrew for Reading Comprehension. Mem.: Soc. Bibl. Lit. Avocations: bicycling, music. Home: 2215 E Livingston St Springfield MO 65803 Office: Evangel Univ 1111 N Glenstone Ave Springfield MO 65802 Business E-Mail: griffinw@evangel.edu.

WILLIAM, W. BRACKETT, dentist, educator; b. Akron, Ohio, Mar. 11, 1953; s. Theodore R. and Mildred Hammond Brackett; m. Martha Goel, July 18, 1998. DDS, Ohio State U., Columbus, 1977; MSD, Ind. U., Indpls., 1986. Asst. prof. dentistry Ind. U., 1981—87, Ohio State U., Columbus, 1987—93, U. Tenn., Memphis, 1993—98, U. Nebr., Lincoln, 1998—2003; prof. dentistry Med. Coll. Ga., Augusta, 2003—, dir. operative dentistry, Sch. Dentistry, 2008—. Dir. operative dentistry UNMC Coll. Dentistry, 1998—2003. Contbr. more than 60 dental rsch. articles to profl. jours. Mem.: Acad. Operative Dentistry. Office: Med Coll Ga Sch Dentistry Augusta GA 30912 Business E-Mail: wbrackett@mcg.edu.

WILL.I.AM, (WILLIAM JAMES ADAMS JR.), rap artist; b. Mar. 15, 1975; Founding mem. band Atban Klann, 1992—95, band Black Eyed Peas, 1998—. Co-founder i.am clothing, 2001—. Singer, prodr. (Black Eyed Peas albums) Behind the Front, 1998, Bridging the Gap, 2000, Elephunk, 2003, Monkey Business, 2005 (Favorite Rap/Hip-Hop Album, Am. Music Awards, 2006), Maximum Black Eyed Peas, 2005, Renegotiations: The Remixes, 2006, (solo albums) Lost Change, 2001, Must B 21, 2003, Songs About Girls, 2007; singer: (songs) Joints & Jams, 1998, Fallin' Up, 1998, Where is the Love? (feat. Justin Timberlake), 2003, Shut Up, 2003, Hey Mama, 2004 (MTV Video Music Award), Let's Get It Started, 2004 (Grammy, Best Rap Performance, 2005), Don't Phunk with My Heart, 2005 (Grammy award, Best Rap Group Performance, 2006), Don't Lie, 2005, My Humps, 2005 (MTV Video Music award for Best Hip-Hop Video, 2006, Grammy award, Best Group Pop Vocal Performance, 2007), (with Santana) I Am Somebody, 2005, (with Chrisette Michele) Be OK, 2007 (Grammy award, Best Urban/Alternative Performance, 2009), Yes We Can, 2008 (Webby award, Artist of Yr., Internat. Acad. Digital Arts and Scis., 2008, Outstanding Song, Outstanding Music Video, NAACP Image Awards, 2009). Co-founder Peapod Found., LA. Recipient MTV Europe award for Best Pop Act (with Black Eyed Peas), 2004, 2005, Favorite Pop Group & Rap Group, Am. Music Awards, 2005, Favorite Soul/Rhythm & Blues Grp., 2006, Favorite Rap/Hip-Hop Grp., 2006, Webby Artist of Yr., Internat. Acad. Digital Arts and Scis., 2008. Office: iam clothing PO Box 664 Hollywood CA 90078 Office Phone: 323-469-5181, 323-661-1524. Office Fax: 213-856-2712. E-mail: iamclothing@aol.com.*

WILLIAMS, AARON S., federal agency administrator; b. 1947; m. Rosa Williams; children: Michael, Steven. BS in Geography and Edn., Chgo. State U.; MBA in Mktg. and Internat. Bus., U. Wis., Madison. Coord. minority recruitment, project evaluation officer US Peace Corps, Chgo., 1970—71; exec. v.p. Internat. Youth Found.; various sr. level positions US Agy. for Internat. Devel. (USAID), 1982—2002, including mission dir. USAID South Africa, head L.Am. & Caribbean Bur., career min. US Sr. Fgn. Svc.; v.p. internat. bus. devel. RTI Internat., Rsch. Triangle Pk., NC, 2003—09; dir. US Peace Corps, Washington, 2009—. Vol. Peace Corps, Monte Plata, Dominican Republic, 1967—69, vol. prof. tchg. methods, Universidad Catolica Madre y Maestra Santiago, Chile, 1969—70; mem. adv. bd. Ron Brown Scholar Prog.; bd. dirs. CARE, Inst. Sustainable Communities, Pan Am. Devel. Found., Nat. Peace Corps Assn. Recipient Disting. Career Svc. award, USAID, Presdl. award for Disting. Svc. Mem.: Coun. Fgn. Rels. Office: US Peace Corps Hdqs 1111 20th St NW Washington DC 20526*

WILLIAMS, ALBERT NATHANIEL, writer, educator; s. Albert Nathaniel and Ann Williams. BA, Columbia Coll. Chgo., 1973. Writer, critic Chgo. Reader, 1985—; tchr. artist-in-residence Columbia Coll. Chgo., Chgo., 1985—. Activist, organizer Gay and Lesbian Town Meeting, Chgo., 1986—88. Recipient George Jean Nathan award, Chgo. Reader, 2000; named to Chgo. Gay and Lesbian Hall of Fame, 2003. Independent. Home Phone: 773-580-5556; Office Phone: 312-369-6141. Business E-Mail: awilliams@colum.edu, awilliams@chicagoreader.com.

WILLIAMS, ALFRED B., retired management educator; b. Oakland City, Ind., Sept. 17, 1940; s. Ross Merl and Jesse Adell (Helsley) W. BS cum laude, Oakland City U., 1963; MS, Ind. U., 1964; PhD, Ga. State U., 1974. Tchr. Arlington H.S., Indpls., 1964-65, Oakland City (Ind.) U., 1965-69; editor Southwestern Pub. Co., Cin., 1969-72, cons., 1981-93; adj. prof. Ga. State U., Atlanta, 1972-74; prof. mgmt. and bus. comm. U. La., Lafayette, 1975—2002, chmn. dept., 1986-96; prof. emeritus, 2002. Adj. prof. U. La., Lafayette, 2004-05; cons. John Wiley Pub. Co., NY, 1988-89, Irwin Pub., 1989. Author study guides; editor Info. Systems Bus. Comm. Jour., 1983, 93. Help One Student to Succeed reading mentor North Lewis Elem. Sch., New Iberia, La., 2003-07. Mem. AAUP, Assn. Bus. Communicators (bd. dirs. 1986-90, Francis W. Weeks Merit award 1984), La. Assn. Higher Edn., Sierra Club, Phi Delta Kappa, Phi Kappa Phi, Delta Pi Epsilon, Beta Gamma Sigma. Methodist. Personal E-mail: abwilliams917@aol.com.

WILLIAMS, ALICE NOEL TUCKERMAN, retired foundation administrator; b. Bethesda, Md., Dec. 21, 1918; d. Walter Rupert and Edith (Abercrombie-Miller) Tuckerman; m. Robert Hugh Williams, June 21, 1939 (dec. 1983); children: Sarah Fenno Williams Lord, Edith Tuckerman Williams Ward. Mem. ladies bd. St. John's Child Devel. Ctr., Washington, 1960—69; pres. ladies bd. St. John's Devel. Ctr., Washington, 1969-72, v.p., trustee, 1970-72. Bd. dirs. Recording For The Blind and Dyslectic, Washington, 1990—94. Mem. Colonial Dames Am. (pres. Washington chpt. 1970-74), Investment Group (co-founder, pres. 2004-06), Sulgrave Club. Episcopalian. Avocations: volunteer work, reading. Home: Fairhaven 7200 3rd Ave Sykesville MD 21784-5201

WILLIAMS, ALLEN W., JR., lawyer; b. Milw., Sept. 8, 1944; AB cum laude, Harvard U., 1966; JD cum laude, Columbia U., 1970, MBA, 1970. Bar: Wis. 1970. Legal counsel to Gov. Patrick J. Lucey State of Wis., 1971-72; ptnr. Foley & Lardner LLP, Milw. Chmn. legal com. Edison Electric Inst., 1981—. Mem. bd. editors Columbia Law Review, 1969-70. Bd. dirs. Planned Parenthood Wis., 1974-76; bd. dirs. Milw. Inst. Art and Design, 2005—, chmn., 2006. Mem. State Bar Wis., Milw. County Zool. Soc. (bd. dirs. 1977-89, pres. 1984-86), Med. Coll. Wis. (bd. dirs. 1977-97, chmn. 1984-1987). Office: Foley & Lardner LLP Firstar Ctr 777 E Wisc Ave Milwaukee WI 53202 Office Phone: 414-297-5808. Office Fax: 414-297-4900. Business E-Mail: awilliams@foley.com.

WILLIAMS, AMY MCDANIEL, lawyer; b. Birmingham, Ala., Sept. 7, 1962; BA cum laude, Duke U., 1985; JD magna cum laude, Cornell Univ., 1990. Bar: Va. 1990. Assoc. Hunton & Williams LLP, Richmond, Va., 1992—99, ptnr., bus. practice group, 1999—, chmn. ethics com., 2002—. Sr. note editor Cornell Law Rev., 1990. Mem.: ABA, Met. Richmond Women's Bar Assn., Nat. Assn. Women Lawyers. Office:

Hunton & Williams LLP Riverfront Plz East Tower 951 E Byrd St Richmond VA 23219-4074 Office Phone: 804-788-7388. Office Fax: 804-788-8218. Business E-Mail: awilliams@hunton.com.

WILLIAMS, ANN CLAIRE, federal judge; b. Detroit, Aug. 16, 1949; m. David J. Stewart. BS, Wayne State U., 1970; MA, U. Mich., 1972; JD, U. Notre Dame, 1975; degree (hon.), Lake Forest Coll., 1987, U. Portland, 1993, U. Notre Dame, 1997. Law clk. to Hon. Robert A. Sprecher, 1975-76; asst. US atty. US Dist. Ct. (no. dist.) Ill., Chgo., 1976-85; faculty Nat. Inst. for Trial Advocacy, 1979—, also bd. dirs.; adj. prof., lectr. Northwestern U. Law Sch., 1979—, John Marshall Law Sch., 1979—; judge US Dist. Ct. (no. dist.) Ill., 1985-99, US Ct. Appeals (7th cir.), Chgo., 1999—. Chief Organized Crime Drug Enforcement Task Force for North Ctrl. Region, 1983-85; mem. ct. adminstrn. and case mgmt. com. Jud. Conf. US, 1990-97, chair, 1993-97. Sec. bd. trustees U. Notre Dame; founder Minority Legal Resources, Inc. Recipient Earl Burns Dickerson award, Chgo. Bar Assn., 1997, Tradition of Excellence award, Minority Legal Resources, Inc., 1997, Thurgood Marshall Jurist of Year, Legal Ministry of Second Baptist Church, 1997, Alumni of Year, Black Law Students Assn, U. Notre Dame, 1997, Morton A. Brody Disting. Jud. Svc. award, Colby Coll., 2002. Mem. FBA, Fed. Judges Assn., Ill. State Bar Assn., Ill. Jud. Coun., Cook County Bar Asn., Women's Bar Assn. Ill., Black Women's Lawyers Assn. Greater Chgo. Office: US Ct Appeals 7th Circuit 219 S Dearborn St Ste 2612 Chicago IL 60604-1803*

WILLIAMS, ANN MEAGHER, retired hospital administrator; b. Hull, Mass., May 28, 1929; d. James Francis Meagher and Dorothy Frances (Meagher) Mullins; m. Joseph Arthur Williams, May 15, 1954; children: James G., Mara A., A. Scott (dec.), Gordon M., Mark J., Antoinette M., Andrea M. BS, Chestnut Hill Coll., Phila., 1950; MS, Boston Coll., Chestnut Hill, Newton, Mass., 1952; degree (hon.), Cape Cod CC, 2009. Radioisotope biologist Air Force Cambridge Rsch. Ctr., Bedford, Mass., 1952-55; asst. mgr. Roxbury Businessmen's Exch., Boston, 1956-66; owner, operator Chatterlane, Osterville, Mass., 1961-66; realtor James E. Murphy Inc., Hyannis, Mass., 1968-77, James E. Murphy, Inc., Osterville, 1995—2005; dir. cmty. affairs Cape Cod Hosp., Hyannis, 1977-95. Bd. dirs. YMCA Cape Cod, Inc., 2004-, Cmty. Coun., Mid Cape, Mass., 1977-88, Cape Cod Mental Health Assn., 1977-82, Ctr. for Individual and Family Svcs., Mid Cape, 1982-87, Am. Cancer Soc., Mid Cape, 1981-96, Cape Cod C.C. Ednl. Found., 1997—, exec. com., 1999—; mem. sch. com. Cape Cod Regional Tech. High Sch., 1978—, exec. com., 1983—; mem. United Way of Cape Cod, 1988-89; chmn. fin. com. City of Barnstable, Mass., 1969-77. Named Woman of Yr. Bus./Profl. Women's Club, 1982, YMCA Vol of Yr., 2008; recipient cert. of appreciation Am. Cancer Soc., 1983, 88, Pres. Recognition award United Way Cape Cod, 1989. Life Achievement award Mass. Assn. Sch. Cos., 2000. Mem.: Nat. Assn. Hosp. Devel., SE Mass. Hosp. Mktg. & Pub. Rels., New Eng. Hosp. Mktg. & Pub. Rels., Am. Soc. Hosp. Mktg. & Pub. Rels., Pure Water for World (bd. dir. 2006—), Chestnut Hill Coll. Alumnae Assn., Rotary Leadership Inst. (regional vice chmn. 2003—07, vice chmn. 2007—), Rotary Internat. (gov. 2002—03, Zone 31 membership coord. 2004—06, Zone 31 literacy coord. 2005—06), Rotary (bd. dir. Osterville 1993—98, pres. 1996—97, asst. gov. dist. 7950 1998—99, area rep. 1999—2000, gov. 2002—03), Hyannis Area C. of C. (bd. dir. 1993—98, ga 2002—03). Roman Catholic. Avocation: community theater. Home: 25 Wedgewood Dr Centerville MA 02632-3162

WILLIAMS, ANNA LASSITER, psychologist, researcher; d. Charles L. William and Jane W. (Williams) Metcalfe. BS, Coll. Charleston, SC, 2001; MA, Columbia U., NYC, 2004; postgrad., NYU; postgrad. semester at sea, U. Pitts. Rsch. asst. Columbia U., 2002; counselor alcohol & substance abuse, coord. early intervention program LI Coll. Hosp., NYC, 2003; case mgr. Urban Pathways, NYC, 2004—05; vocat. case mgr. FEGS, NYC, 2005; assoc. psychologist Austin State Hosp., Tex., 2006—. Rsch. assoc. Austin Neurol. Clinic, 2006—; chair patient satisfaction com. Austin State Hosp., 2006—. Mem. Greenpeace, Planned Parenthood Fedn. Am. Recipient Commonwealth award, Roanoke Coll., 1998, Loyal and Valuable Vol. Svc. award, Med. U. SC, 2000—02; grantee, Roanoke Coll., 1998. Mem.: APA, Am. Psychol. Soc., Internat. Neurol. Soc., Inst. Neurosci. and Consciousness Studies, Coll. Charleston Psychology Club, Kappa Delta Pi. Home: 4404 Barrow Ave Austin TX 78751-3914

WILLIAMS, ANTHONY, pharmaceutical executive; Undergrad. degree, Cambridge U. Trinity Coll., Eng.; MD, U. Coll. Hosp. Med. Sch., London. With Glaxo Group Rsch., Medeva Group Develop., Marion Merrell Dow, Dyax Corp.; v.p. med. affairs Aronex Pharmaceuticals, The Woodlands, Tex., 1998—2001; sr. v.p., head US clin. devel. Fresenius Biotech. N.Am., Lexington, Mass.; interim chief med. officer GenVec, Gaithersburg, Md.; v.p. clin. rsch. Synta Pharmaceuticals, Lexington, Mass., 2007—. Fellow: Royal Coll. Physicians, Royal Coll. Medicine; mem.: Am. Soc. Clin. Oncology. Achievements include development, design and direction of clinical trials in melanoma, pancreatic carcinoma, gastric carcinoma, sarcoma, leukemia, and lymphoma. Office: Synta Pharmaceuticals 45 Hartwell Ave Lexington MA 02421 Office Phone: 781-274-8200. Office Fax: 781-274-8228.

WILLIAMS, ANTHONY ALLAN (TONY WILLIAMS), lobbyist, former mayor; b. L.A., July 28, 1951; s. Lewis and Virginia W.; m. Diana Lynn Simmons; 1 child, Asantewa Foster. BA in Polit. Sci. magna cum laude, Yale U., 1982; JD, M of Pub. Policy, Harvard U., 1987. Law clk. to Hon. David Nelson US Dist. Ct., Boston, 1987-88; asst. dir. Boston Redevel. Authority, 1988-89; exec. dir. Cmty. Devel. Agy., St. Louis, 1989-91; dep. comptr. State of Conn., 1991-93; exec. dir. Cmty. Devel. Agy., St. Louis, 1989-91; dept. contr. State of Conn., 1991-93; CFO USDA, 1993—95, Washington, DC, 1995—98, mayor, 1999—2007; dir. state & mcpl. practice Arent Fox LLP, Washington, 2009—. Adj. prof. pub. affairs Columbia U., NYC, 1992-93. Pres. pro tempore, chmn. cmty. devel. com. Conn. Bd. Alderman, 1980-83; dir. comm. Conn. Spkr. House and Assembly Dem., 1983; second v.p., Washington, DC-based National League of Cities (NLC), 2002-. Served in USAF. Named Pub. Official of the Yr., Governing Magazine, 1997; named one of The 100 Most Influential Black Americans, Ebony mag., 2006; Kellogg Found. Nat. fellow, 1991. Democrat. Office: Arent Fox LLP 1050 Connecticut Ave NW Washington DC 20036 Office Phone: 202-857-6321. E-mail: williams.anthony@arentfox.com.*

WILLIAMS, ANTHONY ERVIN, music educator; b. Nashville, Aug. 25, 1960; s. Albert Osborne and Marion Ervin Williams. MusB in Organ Performance, U. Cin., 1982; MusM in Organ Performance, U. Mich., 1984; DMA in Organ Performance, Am. Conservatory Music, Hammond, Ind., 2006. Music dir., organist Good Shepherd United Meth. Ch., Dearborn, Mich., 1983—86; instr. music, univ. organist Fisk U., Nashville, 1986—90, assoc. prof. music, 2006—; asst. prof. music, univ. organist Dillard U., New Orleans, 1990—2005. Dir. Fisk Jubilee Singers Fisk U., Nashville, 1987—90, organist, 2006—; dir. music and arts First Presbyn. Ch., Hendersonville, Tenn., 2006—. Musician organ recitals. Bd. dirs. New Orleans Mission, 1992—2004, John Wesley Work III Meml. Found., Nashville, 2007—. Recipient Strader Organ scholarship, U. Cin., Coll. Conservatory of Music, 1978—82, Provost Extra Mile award, Dillard U. Mem.: Mus. Arts Soc. New Orleans (bd. dirs. 1992—2006), Am. Guild Organists (bd. dirs. New Orleans chpt. 1992—94, bd. dirs. Nashville chpt. 2006—). Avocations: cooking, travel, ballroom dancing. Home: 3603 Batavia St Nashville TN 37209-2530 Office: Fisk U 1000 17th Ave N Nashville TN 37208 Home Fax: 615-321-5645. Personal E-mail: awilli6034@aol.com.

WILLIAMS, ARMSTRONG, radio and television show host, political commentator; b. Marion, SC, Feb. 5, 1959; BA in Polit. Sci., SC State U., 1981. V.p. govtl./internat. affairs B&C Associations, High Point, NC; asst. to chmn. Clarence Thomas US Equal Employment Opportunity Commn., 1982—86; presdl. appointee US Dept. Agr.; legis. asst. to US Rep. Carrol Campbell; legis. aide/adv. to US senator Strom Thurmond; talk radio show host WOL Radio, 1450 AM, Washington, 1991, nationally syndicated, 1995—, XM Satellite Radio, 2008—; host nationally syndicated TV show The Right Side with Armstrong Williams, 1992—; host On Point with Armstrong Williams, TV One, 2002—05; co-host NY's Urban Talk, WWRL 1600 AM, NYC, 2005—07. Founder The Right Side Prodns., 2003—; co-founder, CEO Graham Williams Group; syndicated columnist Washington Times. Author: Beyond Blame: How We Can Succeed by Breaking the Dependency Barrier, 1995, Letters to a Young Victim: Hope and Healing in America's Inner Cities, 1996. Apptd. mem. Pres.'s Commn. White House Fellows, 2004; bd. dirs. Carson Scholars Fund, Inc., Youth Leadership Found. Named one of 100 Most Important Radio Talk-Show Hosts in the Country, Savoy mag., 2003; named to Vanity Fair's Hall of Fame, 1996. Mem.: Phi Beta Sigma. Republican. Office: 201 Massachusetts Ave Ste C1 Washington DC 20002 Office Phone: 202-546-5400.*

WILLIAMS, ARTHUR COZAD, retired broadcasting executive; b. Forty Fort, Pa., Feb. 12, 1926; s. John Bedford and Emily Irene (Poyck) W.; m. Ann Cale Bragan, Oct. 1, 1955; children: Emily Williams Van Hoorickx, Douglas, Craig. Student, Bucknell U., 1943-44; BA cum laude, U. So. Calif., 1949. Trainee Kaiser Aluminum, 1949; sales Sta. KPMC, 1950-51; v.p., mgr. KFBK and KFBK-FM Radio Stas., Sacramento, 1951-80; with public relations dept. Sacramento Bee, McClatchy Newspapers, 1981-86; ret., 1986. Dir.-treas. Norkal Opportunities, Inc.; pres. Sacramento Bee Credit Union. Served with AUS, 1944-46. Mem. Sigma Delta Chi. Clubs: Rotary, Sutter, Valley Hi Country, Masons, Shriners. Home: 1209 Nevis Ct Sacramento CA 95822-2532 Personal E-mail: artcwilliams@sbcglobal.net.

WILLIAMS, B. JOHN, JR., retired federal agency administrator, lawyer; b. Lancaster, Pa., Dec. 13, 1949; s. Bernard John and Sarah Elizabeth (Sykes) W.; m. Martha Caroline Roberts, Aug. 6, 1977; children: Robert, Sarah, Anne, Bernard. BA, George Washington U., 1971, JD, 1974. Bar: D.C., Pa., U.S. Tax Ct., U.S. Ct. Appeals (3rd, 9th and fed. cirs.), U.S. Supreme Ct. Law clk. to judge U.S. Tax Ct., Washington, 1974-76; assoc. Ballard, Spahr, Andrews & Ingersoll, Phila., 1976-81; spl. asst. to chief counsel IRS, Washington, 1981-83; dep. asst. atty. gen. Tax Div. Dept. Justice, Washington, 1983-84; ptnr. Morgan, Lewis & Bockius, Washington, 1984-85; judge U.S. Tax Ct., Washington, 1985-90; ptnr. Morgan, Lewis & Bockius, Washington, 1990-2000, Shearman & Sterling, Washington, 2000—02; chief counsel, IRS U.S. Dept. Treasury, Washington, 2002—03. Mem. adv. com. U.S. Ct. Appeals, Fed. Cir. Fellow Am. Coll. Tax Counsel; mem. ABA, Am. Law Inst., Phi Beta Kappa, Omicron Delta Kappa. Republican. Office: Skadden Arps, State Meagher and Flom LLP 1440 New York Ave Washington DC 20005 Office Phone: 202-371-7080.

WILLIAMS, BARBARA ANNE, retired academic administrator; b. Camden, NJ, Oct. 14, 1938; d. Frank and Laura Dorothy (Szweda) W. BA cum laude, Georgian Ct. U., 1963; MLS, Rutgers U., 1965; MA, Manhattan Coll., 1973; postgrad., NYU, 1976—81, postgrad., 1993—. Cert. English tchr., N.J.; joined Sisters of Mercy, 1957. Sec. Camden Cath. H.S., 1956-57; registrar Georgian Ct. U., Lakewood, NJ, 1960-66, dir. libr. svcs., 1966-74, dean acad. affairs, 1974-80, pres., 1980-2000, sci. and math. libr., 2000—04, pres. emerita, 2000—, archivist, 2003—. Mem. Mid-Atlantic Regional Archives Conf., 2003—, Soc. Am. Archivists, 2006—. Mem. editl. bd. N.J. Woman mag. Bd. dir., mem. ednl. adv. coun. Diocese of Trenton, N.J., 1983-90, NJ Natural Gas Co., 1986-91; mem. adv. bd. Ocean County Ctr. Arts, Lakewood, NJ, 1983-91; mem. Ocean County Pvt. Industry Coun., 1983-92; bd. dir. Monmouth/Ocean Devel. Coun., 1981-84; mem. State NJ Student Assistance Bd., 1995-99; mem. Ocean County School-to-Career Com., 1996-2000; mem. art adv. coun. Nat. Mus. Cath. Art and History, 2000—; trustee Camden Cath. H.S., 2005—. Named Outstanding Woman N.J. Assn. Women Bus. Owners, 1983; recipient Humanitarian award Monmouth/Ocean Devel. Coun., 1985, Salute to Policymakers award Exec. Women N.J., 1986, Woman in Leadership award Monmouth Coun. Girl Scouts, 1987, Citizen of Yr. Alcoholism & Drug Abuse Coun. Ocean County, 1993, Brotherhood/Sisterhood award Monmouth/Ocean County chpts. NCCJ, 1994, Friend of Scouting award Boy Scouts Am. Jersey Shore Coun., 1999, Leadership award Mercy Higher Edn. Colloquium, 2000. Mem. Assn. Mercy Colls. (pres. 1981-83, sec. 1996-98), Mercy Higher Edn. Colloquium (mem. exec. com. 1980-87), Ocean County Bus. Assn. (trustee 1982-84), Nat. Assn. Ind. Colls. and Univs. (secretariat 1981-83, 87-91), NAIA (coun. of pres. 1997-2000). Home and Office: Georgian Ct Univ 900 Lakewood Ave Lakewood NJ 08701-2600 Home Phone: 732-987-2511; Office Phone: 732-987-2441. E-mail: williamssb@georgian.edu.

WILLIAMS, BARBARA B., retired music educator; b. Roberta, Ga., Nov. 15, 1949; d. Charlie and Willie Etta Braswell; married; children: Vernon S., Jamie L. Blount, Todd J. MusB, Ft. Valley State Coll., Ga., 1971; MEd, Ga. Southwestern Coll., Americus, 1978; degree in Edn., Troy State U., Ala., 1991. Cert. tchr. Ga., 1971. Band dir. Dooly County Sch. Sys., Vienna, Ga., 1971—89, Ft. Valley Mid. Sch., Ga., 1989—97; adj. prof. music Ft. Valley State U., 2002—08. City coun. mem. City Ft. Valley, 1998—2008. Named Tchr. of Yr., Peach County Sch. Sys., 1991, Woman of Yr., Ctrl. Union Missionary Bapt. Ch., 1991. Mem.: Alpha Phi Alpha (Citizen of Yr. 2007), Alpha Kappa Alpha (Trailblazer award 2002). Democrat. Baptist. Avocations: fishing, bowling. Home: 705 Courtland Ave Fort Valley GA 31030 Personal E-mail: wms721@bellsouth.net.

WILLIAMS, BARBARA IVORY, retired educational researcher; b. Detroit, Apr. 28, 1936; d. Henry Oliver and Willa Mae (Frazier) I.; m. Alney Elliott Whitener, Jan. 1, 1987 (dec.). BS, Wayne State U., 1957, MEd, 1960; PhD, U. Washington, 1973. Tchr. Detroit Pub. Schs., 1957-68; program assoc. Mich.-Ohio Regional Lab., Detroit, 1968-70; lectr. predoctoral U. Wash., Seattle, 1970-73; sr. program assoc. Far West Lab. for Ednl. Research and Devel., San Francisco, 1973-76; sr. cons. E.H. White & Co., San Francisco, 1976-77; sr. program assoc. Northwest Regional Lab., Portland, Oreg., 1977-84; area coord. Ednl. Testing Service, Washington, 1984-85; edn. group dir. Research and Evaluation Assocs., Washington, 1985-87; ind. cons. Washington, 1987-89; assoc. dir. edn. studies Westat, Rockville, Md., 1989—2008. Mem. Am. Ednl. Research Assn., Am. Psychol. Assn., Nat. Assn. Black Sch. Educators, Phi Delta Kappa, Alpha Kappa Alpha (pres. Portland chpt. 1980-84). Democrat. Baptist. Avocation: needlecrafts. Home: 13601 Belle Chasse Blvd Unit 414 Laurel MD 20707-9433 E-mail: barbaraji@mac.com.

WILLIAMS, BARBARA KITTY, nursing educator; b. Kingsport, Tenn., July 14, 1944; d. Charles H. Penley and Ada Ruth Baldwin; m. Emerson Williams, Dec. 23, 1961. RN, Johnston Meml. Hosp. Sch. Nursing, Abingdon, Va., 1970; BS in Profl. Arts, St. Joseph's Coll., North Windom, Maine, 1981; BSN, East Tenn. State U., 1986; MSN, U. Va., 1991. RN Tenn., Va., clin. nurse specialist, Am. Nurses Credentialing Ctr., 1993. Critical care nurse Holston Valley Cmty. Hosp., Kingsport, 1971—74; faculty Kingsport Sch. Practical Nursing, 1974—76; asst. nursing dir. Johnson County Hosp., Mountain City, Tenn., 1976—78; dir. med. surg. svcs. Bristol (Tenn.) Regional Med. Ctr., 1978—85; assoc. prof. nursing Virginia Highlands CC, Abingdon, Va., 1988—2006. Adv. bd. YWCA, Bristol, Tenn., 1996—98; mem. bd. Shots for Tots, Rotary Club, Bristol, Tenn., 1995. Finalist Tribute to Women award, YWCA. Mem.: AAUP (award), Bristol Art Guild (pres. 1995—97), Pastel Soc. Am., Assn. Depot Artist, Bristol C. of C. (amb. 1995), Bristol Toastmasters (pres. 1982), Sigma Theta Tau. Methodist. Avocations: painting, travel.

WILLIAMS, BERNARD, Olympic athlete; b. Balt., Jan. 19, 1978; Student, Barton County C.C., Great Bend, Kans., U. Fla., 2000—. Co-winner Gold Medal 4X100 meter relay U.S.A. Track and Field Team, Sydney, 2000; gold medal 4x100m relay US World Outdoor Champions, 2001; bronze medal World Champion, 2001; gold medal 4x100m relay USA Champion, 2003; silver medal winner 200m Olympics, 2004. Office: Usa Track Field 132 E Washington St Ste 800 Indianapolis IN 46204-3674 Business E-Mail: olympic2@ufl.edu.

WILLIAMS, BETHIA, education educator; d. Charles and Ellen Scott; m. Kevin Williams, Oct. 22, 2005. BS in Edn. English, Theatre, and Speech, Mo. Southern State U., Joplin, 2000; MS in Edn. Integrating Tech., Walden U., 2005. Educator Neosho R-V SWAEC, Mo., 2000—, Upward Bound MSSU, Joplin, 2000—. Named Coll. Outstanding Instr., Upward Bound Students and Staff, 2002, Employee of Month, Neosho R-V Sch. Dist., 2007. Mem.: Profl. Devel. Com. (co-chair 2003—), Mo. State Tchrs.' Assn., Nat. Coun. Tchrs. of English. Office: SW Alternative Edn Ctr 115 W Brook St Neosho MO 64850 Personal E-mail: bethias@yahoo.com. Business E-Mail: williamsbethia@neosho.k12.mo.us.

WILLIAMS, BETHTINA QUBRÉ, minister; d. Cleophus Noble Marshall and Marilyn Etta Marshall-Pierce; m. Stanley Davis Williams, Feb. 28, 1986; children: Stanley II, Jonathan, Joshua. BA, Friends Internat. Christian U., Merced, Calif., 1990, MA, 1996, DMin, 2001. Ordained min. Living Word Christian Ctr., Inc., 1996. Adminstrv. asst. Tex. Tech. U., Lubbock, Tex., 1983—84; assoc. mgr. Paul Harris Store, Lubbock, 1987—89; libr. asst. Torreion (Spain) AFB, 1990—91; co-founder, co-pastor, exec. adminstr. Lighthouse of Faith Cmty. Ch., Ft. Walton Beach, Fla., 1997—; network pastor Life Cmty. Fellowship, 2001—. Adv. bd. West Navarre Elem. Sch., 2004—05; founder and CEO Kingdom Fashions, Inc., 2006—; exec. prodr. Lighthouse Live TV Broadcast, 2006—09; exec. dir. 5 Linx Enterprise Inc., 2009; guest Trinity Bd. Casting Network, 2009; founder 5 Te B Enterprises, 2009. Author: Women of Character and Destiny, 2005. Dir. outreach in humanitarian svc. Landstuhl (Germany) Base Chapel, 1993. Recipient Appreciation cert., Wayland Bapt. U., 1986, Commdr.'s Commendation medal, USAF, Ramstein, Germany, 1995, Appreciation cert., USAF, 2000, Commdr.'s medal, Hurlbut Field AFB, Fla., 2000, cert. of honor, King of Shai State, Ghana, 2004. Avocations: writing, exercise, singing, travel, motivational speaking. Office: Lighthouse of Faith Church Inc 755 Lovejoy Rd NW Fort Walton Beach FL 32548 Office Phone: 850-346-7044. Personal E-mail: wgodly@yahoo.com.

WILLIAMS, BILLY DEE, actor; b. NYC, Apr. 6, 1937; Student (Hallgarten scholar), Nat. Acad. Fine Arts and Design; student acting, Paul Mann, Sidney Poitier, Actor's Workshop in Harlem. Child actor; Broadway adult debut The Cool World, 1961; other stage appearances include A Taste of Honey, 1961, I Have a Dream, 1976, Hallelujah, Baby, Fences, 1988; films The Last Angry Man, 1959, The Out-of-Towners, 1970, The Final Comedown, Lady Sings the Blues, 1972, Hit!, 1973, Mahogany, 1975, The Bingo Long Travelling All-Stars and Motor Kings, 1976, Scott Joplin, 1977, The Empire Strikes Back, 1980, Nighthawks, 1981, Return of the Jedi, 1983, Marvin and Tige, 1983, Fear City, 1985, Number One with a Bullet, 1987, Batman, 1989, Driving Me Crazy, 1991, The Prince, 1996, Moving Targey, 1996, Mask of Death, 1996, Moving Target, 1997, The Contract, 1998, The Visit, 2000, The Ladies Man, 2000, Very Heavy Love, 2001, Good Neighbor, 2001, The Last Place on Earth, 2002, Undercover Brother, 2002, Today Will Be Yesterday Tomorrow, 2003, Constellation, 2005, Hood of Horror, 2006; TV films Carter's Army, 1970, Brian's Song, 1971, The Glass House (Emmy nomination), Scott Joplin: King of Ragtime, 1978, The Hostage Tower, 1980, Children of Divorce, 1980, Shooting Stars, 1983, Chiefs, 1983, Time Bomb, 1984, Dangerous Passion, 1990, The Jacksons: An American Dream, 1992, Marked for Murder, 1993, Triple Cross, 1995, Falling for You, 1995, The Fourth King, 1997, Hard Time, 1998, Epoch: Evolution, 2003, (TV series) General Hospital: Night Shift, 2007; guest appearances: TV series The Jeffersons, The Interns, The FBI, Mission Impossible, Mod Squad, Police Woman, Dynasty, In Living Color, The Hughleys, Gideon's Crossing,18 Wheels of Justice, Street Time, That 70's Show.

WILLIAMS, BOB, professional sports team executive; married; 2 children. Employee Omni Coliseum, Atlanta, pres., 1994—97; pres., Philips Arena and the in-house concert and entertainment promotions co. Atlanta Spirit, LLC. Bd. mem. Ga. Alliance Children, Atlanta Convention & Visitors Bur., Atlanta Sports Coun., Atlanta C. of C., Atlanta Tip-Off Club. Office: Atlanta Spirit LLC Philips Arena 1 Philips Dr Atlanta GA 30303*

WILLIAMS, BRADLEY BENNETT, historian; b. LA, Mar. 5, 1948; s. Robert E. and Helen L. Williams; m. Susan E. Poster, May 25, 1980. BA, U. So. Calif., 1972; MA, San Diego State U., 1977; PhD, U. Iowa, 1984. Cert. fundraising U. Calif., 1996. Dir. Heritage Mus., Coralville, Iowa, 1983—84; assoc. registrar LA County Mus. Art, 1984—85; registrar Skipball Mus., Hebrew Union Coll., LA, 1985—86; assoc. for alumni devel. Loyola Marymount U., LA, 1990—92; dir. Ninth Judicial Cir. Hist. Soc., Pasadena, 1992—. Editor: (scholarly jour.) Western Legal History, 1992—. Pres. Southwest Oral History Assn., 1997—98; mem. bd. dirs. Theodore Payne Found., LA, 1993; v.p. Pasadena Arts Council, 1987—90. Recipient Trustee's award, State Historical Soc. of Iowa, 1983, Svc. award, Southwest Oral History Assn., 1999; NEH Challenge Grant, Pasadena Hist. Soc., 1989. Mem.: Southwest Oral History Assn. (pres. 1997—98), Oral History Assn., Am. History Assn., Am. Assn. for State and Local History, Northwest Oral History Assn. (pres. 2005—). Home: 952 E Athens St Altadena CA 91001 Office: Ninth Judicial Cir Historical Soc 125 S Grand Ave Pasadena CA 91105 E-mail: historyconsultant@hotmail.com.

WILLIAMS, BRENT (BUZZ WILLIAMS), men's college basketball coach; b. Tex., Sept. 1, 1972; m. Corey Norman; children: Zera, Calvin, Mason. BS in Kinesiology, Okla. City U., 1994; MS in Kinesiology, Texas A&M U., Kingsville, 1999. Student asst. coach Navarro Coll. Bulldogs, 1990—92, Okla. City U. Stars, 1992—94; asst. coach U. Tex.-Arlington Mavericks, 1994—98, Tex. A&M-Kingsville Javelinas, 1998—99, Northwestern State U. Demons, 1999—2000, Colo. State U. Rams, 2000—03, assoc. head coach, 2003—04; asst. coach, recruiting coord. Tex. A&M U. Aggies, 2004—06; head coach U. New Orleans Privateers, 2006—07; asst. coach Marquette U. Golden Eagles, 2007—08, head coach, 2008—. Office: Marquette Univ c/o Dept Athletics Milwaukee WI 53201*

WILLIAMS, BRIAN, network news anchor; b. Middletown, NJ, May 5, 1959; m. Jane Stoddard, 1986; children: Allison, Douglas. Student, George Washington U., Cath. U. Am.; Doctorate (hon.), Elmira Coll., Providence Coll., Cath. U. Am., 2004; LLD (hon.), Villanova U., 2003; LHD (hon.), Bates Coll., 2005. Corr. various stas., Phila., Washington, Pittsburgh, Kans.; anchor, corr. Sta. WCBS-TV, NYC; anchor, mng. editor NBC Nightly News Sat., NYC, 1993—99; chief White House corr. NBC, Washington, 1994—96; anchor, mng. editor The News with Brian Williams MSNBC/CNBC, NYC, 1996—2004; anchor, mng. editor NBC Nightly News, NYC, 2004—. Fmr. vol. firefighter, NJ; mem. Coun. Fgn. Rels., NYC; bd. dirs. Congl. Medal of Honor Found. Recipient Emmy award, 1987, 1993, 2001, 2003, 2005, 4 Nat. Edward R. Murrow awards, 2005, George Foster Peabody award for Coverage of Hurricane Katrina, 2005, Sigma Delta Chi award, Soc. Profl. Journalists, 2006, Tulane President's Medal, Tulane U., 2006; named Father of Yr., Nat. Father's Day Com., 1996, Best Anchor, USA Today, Man of Yr., GQ Mag., 2001; named one of The World's Most Influential People, TIME mag., 2007. Office: NBC News 30 Rockefeller Plz Fl 3 New York NY 10112

WILLIAMS, BROWN F, media specialist; b. Evanston, Ill., Dec. 22, 1940; s. Jack Kermit Williams and Virginia Helen (Benjamin) Likar; m. Linda Francee Ludt, Sept. 1961 (div. 1968); 1 child, Eden Carol Williams McCarthy; m. Martha Amidon Powers, Sept. 1970 (div. 1974); m. Sandra Ann Matkowski, Jan. 1984 (dec. May 2000); 1 child, Bronwyn Emily. AB in Math. and Physics, U. Calif., Riverside, 1962, MA in Physics, 1964, PhD in Physics, 1966. Mgr. Electro-Optics Lab., Princeton, NJ, 1969-75; dir. RCA Labs., Princeton, 1976-82, v.p., 1982-87; pres. Williams Cons. Group, Princeton, 1988-90. CEO, chmn. Princeton Video Image, 1990—2004; v.p. R&D Evergreen Solar, 2004-Fellow IEEE; mem. AAAS, Am. Phys. Soc., Sigma Xi. Avocations: skiing, sailing, horseback riding. Home: 1 Devonshire Pl Boston MA 02109 Office Phone: 609-468-2652. E-mail: bfwilliams1@comcast.net.

WILLIAMS, CAROL H., advertising executive; b. Chgo. d. Clarence Earl Williams and Betty Jane Norment-Williams; m. Tipkins Hood; children: Tipkins Hood Jr., Carol Hood. Student, Northwestern U. Creative dir., sr. v.p. Leo Burnett Agy., Chgo., 1969—80, Foote-Cone & Belding, San Francisco, 1980—82; prin. owner Carol H. Williams Advt., Inc., Oakland, Calif., 1986—. Active US Dream Acad. Recipient Outstanding Women in Mktg. and Comm. award, Ebony Mag., 2001, Bus. Achievement award, Nat. Coalition 100 Black Women, Inc., 2003, Ad Agy. of Yr., Black Enterprise Mag., 2004; named a Woman to Watch, Advt. Age, 2002; named to Power 150, Ebony mag., 2008. Mem.: NAACP, TEC Internat., Rainbow/PUSH Coalition. Office: Carol H Williams Advertising Inc 555 12th St Ste 1700 Oakland CA 94607-4058

WILLIAMS, CAROLYN HASTINGS, lawyer; b. Oshkosh, Wis., Oct. 5, 1950; d. Russell Fisher and Jeannette Ellis Williams. BA, Lawrence U., Appleton, Wis., 1972, Smith Coll., Northampton, Mass., 1972, Cambridge U., England, 1975, MA, 1979; JD, Yale U., New Haven, Conn., 1978. Assoc. Williams & Connolly LLP, Washington, 1978—86, ptnr., 1987—. Mem. merit panel US Dist. Ct., Washington, 2005; bd. dirs. Ct. Appointed Spl. Advs., Talbot County, Md.; mem. Oxford-Cambridge Com., Washington, 1980—. Mem.: ABA (co-chmn. litig. sect. 2006—). Office: Williams & Connolly LLP 725 12th St NW Washington DC 20005

WILLIAMS, CAROLYN RUTH ARMSTRONG, university official; b. Birmingham, Ala., Feb. 17, 1944; d. Lonnie and Lois Adel America (Merriweather) Armstrong; m. James Alvin Williams Jr., Mar. 16, 1968. BS, Tenn. State U., 1966; cert., Hawaii U., 1970; MA, Northwestern U., 1972; MA, PhD, Cornell U., 1978; postgrad., Exeter U., Eng., 1985, MIT, 1990-93, Chinese U. of Hong Kong, 1992. Postdoctoral fellow Harvard U., 1982-83; spl. project asst. U.S. Senator Paul Tsongas, Boston, 1983; asst. vice chancellor N.C. Cen. U., Durham, 1983-87; asst. dean for minorities and women engring. programs Vanderbilt U. Sch. Engring., Nashville, 1987-97; cons. Stennis Rsch. Ctr. NASA, Nashville, 1997—. Assoc. dir. Cornell U. Career Ctr., Ithaca, N.Y., 1976-82, edn.cons. Youth Data, Ithaca, 1981—, LeMoyne Coll. Higher Edn. Preparation Program, 1977-83; cons. U.S. Dept. Edn. Rev. Bd.; judge Goodrich Collegiate Inventor Program; bd. dirs. Sta. WBGH TV, Boston; participant Nat. Scis. Resources Ctr. Conf. on pre-coll. edn. for scientists and engrs. Calif. Inst. Tech., 1992. Contbr. articles to profl. jours. Bd. dirs. So. Policies Ednl. Bd., 1983-87, Clean Commn. System of Durham Bd., 1982-87. Recipient Woman of Achievement and Recognition award YWCA, 1984-87, Affirmative Action award Vanderbilt U., 1989, 90. Mem. Nat. Assn. Women Deans and Adminstrv. Counselors (exec. bd. 1981—), Cornell Women Studies Program (exec. bd. 1981—), Nat. Soc. Black Engrs. (adv. bd., pres. region III 1990—, Black Engr. Leadership award 1988, Charles E. Tunstall award 1990, 91, Nat. Appreciation award 1997), Assn. Women in Sci. (exec. bd. 1990—, nat. sec. 1992—), Soc. Women Engrs. (tech. coord. 1988—, coord. tech. paper competition, chair adv. bd. 1990—), Nat. Assn. Minority Engring. Program Adminstrs. (sec., pres.-elect, chair region B 1990—, exec. bd., bd. dirs., nat. editor newsletter 1990—), Rotary, Phi Delta Kappa, Delta Sigma Theta, Omicron Delta (Vanderbilt chpt.), Phi Lambda Theta. Avocations: foreign travel, politics, playing piano, violin and harp, bowling, tennis. Office: Vanderbilt U Sch Engring PO Box 6006 Nashville TN 37235 Home: 1668 Southwood Trl Saint Cloud MN 56301-7500

WILLIAMS, CECIL, minister; b. San Angelo, Tex., Sept. 22, 1929; s. Earl Williams; m. Evelyn Robinson, 1982 (dec. 1981); children: Albert, Kim; m. Janice Mirikitani, 1982. BA, Huston-Tillotson U., Austin, 1952; BD, Southern Meth. U., 1955. Chaplain, tchr. Huston-Tillotson U., 1955—59; founder, minister Glide United Meml. Meth. Ch., San Francisco, 1963—. Co-creator Coun. on Religion and Homosexuality, 1964. Author: (Autobiography) I'm Alive, 1980; actor: (films) True Crime, 1999, America's Heart and Soul, 2004, The Pursuit of Happiness, 2006. Named to Power 150, Ebony mag., 2008. Office: Glide Meml United Meth Ch 330 Ellis St San Francisco CA 94102 Office Phone: 415-974-6000.

WILLIAMS, CECILIA LEE PURSEL, optometrist; b. Lewisburg, Pa., Nov. 15, 1948; d. Lee LaVerne and Geraldine May (Steininger) Pursel; m. Richard Lee Williams, May 17, 1975; 1 son, Kent Lee. Student, Lycoming Coll., 1966—68; BS, Pa. Coll. Optometry, 1970, OD, 1972. Lic. and/or cert. optometrist, D.C., Pa., N.Y., N.J., Va. Rsch. optometrist in soft lens materials Gumpelmayer Optik, Vienna, Austria, 1973; optometrist Sterling Optical Co. Contact Lens Ctr., Washington, 1974-79; pvt. practice optometry Springfield, Va., 1980—. Recipient Clin. Efficiency award Pa. Coll. Optometry, 1972; Women's Aux. of Pa. Optometrists scholar, 1968-70, 70-72; Pa. State grantee, 1968-70, 70-72. Mem. Optometric Ctr. of Nation's Capital (dir. 1977-80), Am. Optometric Assn., Va. Optometric Assn., No. Va. Optometric Soc., Nat. Honor Soc. for Optometry, Omega Delta. Home: 3600 Wilton Hall Ct Alexandria VA 22310-2176 Office: 7241 Commerce St Springfield VA 22150-3411 Office Phone: 703-866-9364.

WILLIAMS, CHARLES D., radiologist; b. Moultrie, Ga., Mar. 24, 1940; s. Ausburn Millard and Mary Savannah Williams; m. Patricia E. Williams, Oct. 20, 1986; 6 children. AB, Mercer U., 1962; MD, Med. Coll. Ga., 1966. Am. Bd. Radiology, 1974, lic. Ga., 1966, Fla., 1970, Tex., 1971. Rotating intern Med. Ctr. Ctrl. Ga., 1966—67, resident gen. practice, 1967—68; resident radiology Baylor Coll. Medicine, 1970—77, chief resident, 1973; fellow radiology Shands Tchg. Hosp. U. Fla. Coll. Med., 1973—74, instr. radiology, 1973—74; with Radiology Assoc. Tallahassee, P.A., 1974—. Mem. staff Tallahassee Meml. Hosp., Capital Regional Med. Ctr., Fla. State Hosp.; bd. dirs. Tallahassee Physician Assn., 1991—94; adv. bd. radiol. tech. program Thomas Technical Inst., 1988—2000; assoc. medicine in med. sci. Fla. State U., 1988; spkr., presenter in field. Contbr. articles to profl. jours. and pubs., chapters to books. Vol. Big Bend Hospice, Tree of Remberance, 2007; bd. dirs. Leon HS Band, 1986—88, Big Bend Comty. Orch., 1996—2000, Artist Series, Tallahassee, 1996—2000, chmn. fundraising com., 1998—2000, v.p., 1999—2000; adv. bd. Prime 55 Peoples Bank Tallahassee, 2002—. Capt. Fla. dept. pediats. USAF, 1968—70, Homestaed Air Force Base. Recipient Dir.'s award, TMRMC, 1985, Leadership Recognition award, 1987; named Hon. Texan, Gov. Tex., 2007; named one of Am.'s Top Physicians, Consumer's Rsch. Coun. Am., 2006. Fellow: Am. Acad. Pediats., Am. Coll. Radiology (councilor 1992—98, task force on teleradiology 1993—97, mem. com. on govt. rels. 1993—2000, mem. steering com. 1994—97, commn. on gen. and pediat. radiology 1994—97, liason of steering com. with commn. on gen. and pediat. radiology 1994—97, chmn. subcom. hepatic bilary std. 1995, chmn. subcom. revision of 1991 barium enema stds. 1995, chmn. subcom. thyroid std. 1995, mem. ref. com. 1996, task force on ethics 1997—98, task force on pub. affairs 1998—2001, mem. ethics com. 1998—2004, bd. chancellors 1998—2005, chmn. commn. on human resources 1998—2005, bd. dirs. Found. 1998—2005, bd. dirs. Inst. 1998—2005, mem. com. on fellowship credentials 1998—2005, bd. nom. com. 1999—2000, chair ad hoc com. for leadership devel. 2000, task force on workload shortages 2000—02, commn. on membership and chpt. programs 2003—06, alt. del. 2004—06, RADPAC bd. dirs. 2004—, mem. ethics com. 2005—, v.p. 2006—07, bd. chancellors 2006—07, exec. com. 2006—07, v.p. Inst. 2006—07, sect. coun. radiology 2006—07, del. AMA 2006—07, v.p. Found. 2006—07, bd. nom. com. 2006—07, com. on membership devel. 2006—, mem. branding com. 2007—08, intersoc. commn. on radiologist asst. 2007—08, mem. funding com. 2007—, Disting. Commn. Svc. award 1997, Disting. com. Svc. award 2000, Disting. Svc. award 2001, Disting. Com. Svc. award 2005); mem.: AMA (Physician's Recognition award 1977, 1980, 1983, 1986, 1989, 1992, 1995, 1998, 2001, 2004), Soc. Radiologists in Ultrasound, European Soc. Pediat. Radiology, Radiol. Soc. N.Am. (mem. assoc. scis. com. 2006—), Soc. Breat Imaging, Am. Inst. Ultrasound in Medicine, Southern Pediat. Radiol. Soc., Soc. Pediat. Radiology (liason ethics com. 1998—2005, mem. ad hoc com. for leadership 2000—04, mem. judiciary com. 2005—07, chair judiciary com. 2008), Am. Soc. Emergency Radiology, Am. Roentgen Ray Soc., Fla. Radiol. Soc. (ad hoc com. 1919—96, bd. dirs. 1986—2005, alt. councilor 1987—92, chmn. legislature com. 1990—92, councilor 1992—98, treas. 1993—94, sec. 1994—95, chmn. membership com. 1994—95, v.p. 1995—96, pres. elect 1996—97, chmn. pub. policy and legis. com. 1996—97, co-chmn. fin. com. 1996—97, pres. 1997—98, co-chmn. legis. com. 1997—99, mem. nom. com. 1998—2000, alt. councilor 1999—2000, chair stds. in radiol. practice 1999—2000, chair mem. in tng. 1999—2000, v.p. 2002, alt. councilor 2002—03, chair technologyst com. 2003—06, co-chair fellowship com. 2004—06, co-chair various award coms., Gold medalist 1999), Fla. Med. Assn. (editl. cons. 1985—86, Best Article award 1994, Pres. award 1997, Appreciation and REcognition cert. 2001), Capital Med. Soc. (mem. pubs. com. 1991—2007, mem. found. bd. 2008—). Republican. Avocations: writing, gardening. Office: 1600 Phillips Rd Tallahassee FL 32308 Mailing: O Box 12219 Tallahassee FL 32317-2219

WILLIAMS, CHARLES THEODORE, educational administrator; b. Boston, May 27, 1943; s. Charles Edward and Frances Mary (Schoonmaker) W.; m. Marsha L. Lichtman. AB, Boston Coll., 1967; MEd., Antioch Coll., 1975; postgrad. NYU; children— Scott, Devon. Tchr., Boston Pub. Schs., 1967-77; asst. prin. Huntington Union Free Sch. Dist., NY, 1977-79, asst. to supt., 1979-81, asst. supt. for curriculum and instrn., 1981-83, asst. supt. for adminstrn., 1984—94, English tchr., 1994—; mem. adj. faculty Dowling Coll.; cons. in field. Bd. dirs. Boston Area Planning and Action Com., 1975-77. Charles F. Kettering Found. fellow, 1980. Recipient Outanding Am. Tchr., Nat. Honor Roll, 2005-2006; named NY State Lottery Educator of Week, 2003. Mem. ASCD, Am. Assn. Sch. Adminstrs., Phi Delta Kappa. Office: PO Box PO Box 1500 Huntington NY 11743-0700

WILLIAMS, CHARLES WESLEY, retired engineering executive, consultant, researcher; b. Palestine, Ark. s. Fredrick Charles and Fannie Rochet (Southall) W.; m. Nancy Sue Rhea, Sept. 5, 1959; children: Brent L., Brian E. BSEE, U. Tenn., 1959, MS, 1963. Registered profl. engr., Ohio. Devel. engr. Mead Rsch. Lab., Chillicothe, Ohio, 1959-60, Oak Ridge (Tenn.) Nat. Lab., 1960-63; tech. mgr. EG & G Ortec, Oak Ridge, 1963-76, tech. dir. phys. and life sci., 1976-81, dir. positron emission tomograph sys., 1981—85; pvt. practice Oak Ridge, 1985—. Contbr. articles to profl. jours. Fellow: IEEE (life; v.p. NS 1979). Baptist.

WILLIAMS, CHRISTOPHER J., investment company executive; b. 1957; m. Janice Savin Williams. BArch, Howard U.; MBA, Dartmouth Coll., 1984. With Lehman Brothers, Inc., NYC, 1984—92; pres. Williams Fin. Markets; founder, chmn., CEO Williams Capital Group, L.P., 1994—, Williams Capital Mgmt., LLC, 2002—. Bd. dirs. Wal-Marts Stores, Inc., 2003—, Harrah's Entertainment, Inc., 2003—08, 2008—, Partnership for NYC. Bd. dirs. Nat. Dance Inst., Alvin Ailey Dance Found., WNYC Radio, Lincoln Ctr. Performing Arts; bd. trustees Teacher's Coll., Columbia U. Named a 40 Under 40, Crain's NY Bus., 1994. Mem.: Century Assoc., Young President's Org., Nat. Assoc. Securities Professionals (bd. dirs.), Securities Industry Assn. (bd. dirs. N.Y. dist.), Econ. Club N.Y. (bd. dirs.). Office: Williams Capital Management Llc 570 Fashion Ave Rm 504 New York NY 10018-1659 E-mail: Williams@willcap.com.

WILLIAMS, CHRISTOPHER T., history professor; b. Freetown, Sierra Leone, Dec. 21, 1944; s. John A. Williams and Kosonike M. Thompson; m. Judith O. Thomas; children: Ifetayoh A., Kayode O., Adeladi O. PhD, Kentt State U., Ohio, 1976. Prof. Kent State U., 1976—90, dean, 1990—2003, prof., 2003—. Contbr. articles to profl. jours. Vestry mem. Christ Episcopal Ch., Shaker Heights, Ohio, 2006—08. Recipient Most Disting. Prof. award, Kent State U., 1978, 1988—89. Mem.: Nat. Coun. Black Studies. Democrat. Episcopalian. Avocations: gardening, reading. Home: 17683 Plum Creek Tr Chagrin Falls OH 44023 Office: Kent State Univ Kent OH 44242 Office Phone: 330-672-2671. Business E-Mail: cwilliam@kent.edu.

WILLIAMS, CLARENCE, legislative staff member; Legis. dir. to congressman Kendrick Meek US House of Reps., Washington, 2003—08, legis. dir./chief of staff, 2008—. Democrat. Mailing: US House Reps 1039 Longworth House Office Bldg Washington DC 20515 Office Phone: 202-225-4506. Office Fax: 202-225-0777. Business E-Mail: clarence.williams@mail.house.gov.*

WILLIAMS, CLAUDIA BAXTER, retired media specialist, school librarian; b. Houston County, Ala., Mar. 12, 1930; d. L. J. and Ilene Chambers Baxter; m. Henry, Jr. Williams; children: Michael Duryea, Yul Karen. BS in Edn., Ala. State U., 1951; MEd in media, Auburn U., Ala., 1984. Librarian Shelby County Sch. Sys., Columbiana, Ala., 1951—52, Houston County Sch. Sys., Dothan, 1953—54; office clk. Hansberry Enterprises, Chgo., 1955—56; tchr., librarian Madison County Schs., Greenville, Fla., 1957—59; elem. sch. tchr. Houston County Schs., Dothan, Ala., 1962—64; media specialist Dothan (Ala.) City Schs., 1965—94. Textbook com. Dothan (Ala.) City Schs., 1978—89, English tchr. to Vietnamese students, 1989—92; yearbook advisor Carver Mid. Sch., Dothan, Ala., 1989—94. Contbr. articles Wiregras Roots-Genealogy Quarterly. Voter activation Ala. Dist. 85, Dothan, 1985; coord. Houston County Centennial Com., Dothan, 2003; bd. dirs. NBCAR Hist. Dist., Dothan, 2001—, Wiregrass Genealogy Soc., Dothan, 1999—. Recipient Disting. Svc. award, Ala. Hist. Commission, 2004, Centennial award, Houston County Bd. Comrs., 2003, Cmty. Svc. award, Zeta Phi Beta Sorority, 2006. Mem.: Southeast Ala. Genealogical Soc. (recording sec. 1998—99, Achievement of Excellence 1999), Ala. Assn. Women's Club (scholarship chair 1999—2003, Mabel S. Neely Individual Achievement award 1999, 2000, 2001), Ala. Edn. Assn., Nat. Ed. Assn. (life), Alpha Kappa Alpha. Democrat. Baptist. Achievements include the collection and compilation of various aspects of Southeast Alabama African American history. Avocations: reading, sewing, gardening, fabric artwork. Home: 2187 E Burdeshaw St Dothan AL 36303

WILLIAMS, CLAY C., energy executive; Engr. Shell Oil, 1985—92; assoc. SCF Partners, 1994—96; dir. corp. develop. Nat. Oilwell Varco, Houston, 1996—97, v.p. corp. develop., 1997—2000, 2001—02, v.p. pipeline services, 1999—2001, v.p. fin. & corp. develop., 2002—03, v.p., CFO, 2003—05, sr. v.p., CFO, 2005—. Office: Nat Oilwell Varco 10000 RIchmond Ave Houston TX 77042-4200

WILLIAMS, CLORETTA MAE, retired elementary school educator; b. St. Johns County, Fla., Apr. 17, 1932; d. Daniel and Flossie Evelana Cohen, Paul and Susie Green; married, Dec. 10, 1952; children: Janice Edmond, Audrey Jackson, Renee, Curtis. BS, Fla. Meml./Indsl. Coll., 1952; postgrad., numerous univs. Music and 3d grade tchr. Flagler County H.S., Bunnell, Fla., 1951—53; 1st grade tchr. Coleman Elem. Sch., Pompano, Fla., 1956—58; head start, 1st, 3d, 4th and 5th grade tchr. Charles Drew Elem. Sch., Pompano, Fla., 1958—86, ret., 1986. Sch. rep. Broward County North Area Advisory, Pompano, Fla., 1997; mem. adv. bd. Am.'s Choices Networking, Pompano, Fla., 2005. Recipient Tchr. of Yr. award, Charles Drew Sch.-Broward County Sch. Bd., 1964, Honored Pioneer of Broward County award, Broward County Hist. Com., 1999. Mem.: AARP, So. Poverty Law Ctr. (Plaque on Wall 2005), Heart Found. Democrat. Baptist. Home: 2738 NW Fourth Ct Pompano Beach FL 33069 Office: Mitchell/Moore Srs Program 910 NW Tenth St Pompano Beach FL 33060 also: E Pat Larkins Sr Program 520 Martin Luther King Jr Blvd Pompano Beach FL 33069

WILLIAMS, CONSTANCE, state legislator; b. June 27, 1944; m. Sankey V. Williams; 2 children. BA, Barnard Coll., 1966; MBA, U. Pa., 1980. Mem. Pa. House of Reps., Harrisburg, 1996—2001, Pa. State Senate, Harrisburg, 2001—. Democrat. Jewish. Office: 352 Main Capital Senate Box 203017 Harrisburg PA 17120-3017 Business E-Mail: chwilliams@pasenate.com.

WILLIAMS, CRAIG STEWART, organist, choirmaster, music educator, director; b. Lynwood, Calif., Sept. 17, 1962; s. Barry Edward and Malvina Louise Williams; m. Lee Nielsen Williams, July 8, 1990; children: Abigail Leigh, Stewart Thomas. MusB, U. So. Calif., 1984; MusM, Juilliard Sch., 1986, Rider U., 1997. Organist Peace Luth. Ch., Tustin, Calif., 1981—84; organist, dir. music Covenant Ch. LI, Floral Park, NY, 1986—87, 1st Presbyn. Ch., Jamaica, NY, 1987—94; organist JFK Internat. Airport Protestant Chapel, Jamaica, NY, 1987—95; organist, dir. music Calvary Bapt. Ch., NYC, 1995—2000, Cadet Chapel, US Mil. Acad., West Point, NY, 2000—. Commr. NYC Presbytery, 1992—95; demonstrator, recitalist Baldwin Organ Co., Babylon, NY, 1993—97; adj. faculty Rider U., 1999—, Nyack Coll., 2003—; cons. pipe organ project Calvary Bapt. Ch., NYC, 2001—03. Worship and workshop music leader Kiwanis Club, Middletown, NY, 2001—02; participant Mohonk Mountain House, Shawangunk, NY, 2003—09; vis. lectr. U. Redlands, Calif., 2003; recitalist AGO Regional Conv., 2005. Mem.: Hymn Soc. Am., Am. Guild Organists (dean 1990—92), Pi Kappa Lambda. Avocations: gardening, poetry. Office: Cadet Chapel US Mil Acad Bldg 722 West Point NY 10996 Office Phone: 845-938-7352. Business E-Mail: craig.williams@usma.edu.

WILLIAMS, CYNTHIA ANN, small business owner, pediatrics nurse, writer, model, mentor; b. Portsmouth, Va., Dec. 8, 1959; d. Kenneth Leroy and Connie Lee (Joyner) Miller; children: Sidney Lekenny Small, Joshua Tadarrell Small; children: Ebony Ashtone Shannon, Ashley Mahogany Smith;. Diploma in med. specialist, Acad. Health Sci., Fort Sam Houston, Tex., 1982, diploma for lic. practical nurse, 1986; AAS, U. Md., 1994; diploma in practical theology, Beacon U., 2004—. Cert. Basic Cardiac Life Support, 1982, Neonatal Advanced Life Support, 1986, lic. Practical Nurse, 1986, cert. Emergency Medical Technician Basic, 2001; Ordained Minister Victory New Testament Fellowship, 2000; foster parent Va. Enlisted US Army, 1981, advanced through ranks to staff sgt., ret., 2001; wardmaster mother baby unit Dewitt Army Cmty. Hosp., US Army, Fort Belvoir, Va., 1995—96; North Atlantic regional command retention Dewitt Army Cmty. Hosp., North Atlantic Regional Med. Command/US Army, Fort Belvoir, Va., 1996—98, in charge of ob-gyn clinic and well woman clinic, 1998—2000, in charge of ob-gyn clinic Seoul, Republic of Korea, 2000—01; in charge first replacement med. detachment,anthrax coord. 121st Gen. Hosp., 18th Med. Command, Seoul, Republic of Korea, 2001; owner, founder clothing line One of Those Women; owner NSE Enterprises; pvt. duty in- home pediat. nurse Continuum Pediatric Nursing, Virginia Beach, Va., 1998—; ind. distbr. Zija Internat.; ind. prof. Cash Flow Bus. Combat lifesaver instr. US Army, Taegu, 1987—2000, customer svc. sch. excellence instr., Seoul, 2000—01; EMT, 2001—02; CEO It's a New Day Prodns., Newport News, Va., 2004; ind. distbr. Zija Internat., New Face Model Prodns. Author: One Of Those Women, 2001, Marriage: Not Just A Simple "I Do", 2001, Prison Visit, 2007, Don't Anticipate, Just Participate, 2008, So You Call Yourself A Christian, 2008; host: blog, talk show One Of Those Women Speaks. Dir., founder FreeWill Fellowship Ministry, Richmond, 2000—; ptnr. in many ministries; mem. Organizing for America. Decorated Expert Field Med. Badge U.S. Army, Meritorious Svc. medal, 4 Commendation Medals; named Woman of Yr., 2007, Amb. of Poetry, 2007. Fellow: Am. Biog. Inst. (life), Internat. Biog. Assn. (life); mem.: VFW, Am. Biog. Inst. (mem. profl. internat. rsch. bd.), Potter's House Bishops Cir., Millionaire 300 Club, U.S. Official Presdnl. Prayer Team, Hampton Road's (Med. Reserve Corp), NonCommissioned Officer Assn., Mighty Warrior Intercessor Prayer Team, Boys Town Club (hon.). Achievements include Ambassador to the World Forum. Avocations: writing, gardening, art, crafts, mentoring young adults. Home and Office: Free-Will Fellowship Ministry 87 Deer Run Tr Newport News VA 23602-3880 Office Phone: 703-623-9981. Personal E-mail: oneofthosewomen@yahoo.com.

WILLIAMS, DANIECE H., biology professor; 1 child, Haley B. BS, Belhaven Coll., Jackson, Miss., 1989; MS, U. Southern Miss., Hattiesburg, 1992. MS mus. natural sci. lab Nature Conservancy, Jackson, 1990—90; biology lab. mgr. U. Southern Miss., 1992—93; biology instr. Hinds CC, Pearl, Miss., 1993—. Vol. Ducks Unlimited, Miss., 2002—07; with Garden Club, Brandon, Miss., 1999—2003; with worship com. Meth. Ch., Raymond, Miss., 2005—08. Recipient Life Star-Academic Faculty award, Hinds CC, 2002, Raymond Yard of Month award, Garden Club, 2004. Avocations: travel, horseback riding. Office: Hinds CC Hwy 80 E Pearl MS 39208

WILLIAMS, DANNA BETH, reading specialist, educator; b. Aurora, Ill., Apr. 13, 1956; d. Daniel Strango and Roberta Arlene Roberts; m. Norman Charles Williams, June 25, 1988; children: Scott, Samuel, Spencer. BSc, U. Nev., Reno, 1978; postgrad. in Curriculum and Instrn., Concordia U., Irvine, Calif., 2006—. Cert. TESOL Nev. Lic. of Edn., tchg.credential Calif. Reading specialist Job Corps, Stead, Nev., 1979; tchr. Churchill County Schools, Fallon, 1979—88; sub. tchr. Irvine Sch. Dist., Calif., 1988—90, Mission Viejo Sch. Dist., 1989—90; tchr. pvt. schools Orange County, 1990—96; tchr. Orange Unified Sch. Dist., 1996—2000, reading specialist, 2000—. Lang. arts mentor, tchr. Orange Unified Sch. Dist., 1999—2001, English lang. learner adv., 2005—, Consortium on Reading Excellence trainer fifth grade tchrs., 2003—04. Religious educator San Francisco Solano, 1988—91, 2002—04, Cath. Ch., 1983—88. Mem.: ASCD, Calif. Teachers Assn., Internat. Reading Assn. Roman Catholic. Home: 21022 Los Alisos Blvd Apt 614 Rancho Santa Margarita CA 92688 Office: Cambridge Elem Sch 425 N Cambridge Orange CA 92866 Office Phone: 714-997-6103. E-mail: dwilliam@orangeusd.k12.ca.us.

WILLIAMS, DARCEL PATRICE, writer, editor; b. Houston, Nov. 23, 1958; d. Leroy and Estelle Forch Williams; m. Jason LaRue Williams, Sr., May 26, 1979 (div. Sept. 0, 1985); 1 child, Jason LaRue II. Student, Tex. So. U., 1977—81, U. Houston, 1985—88. Lic. massage therapist City of Tulsa, 1993. Acctg. Taft Broadcasting, Houston, 1981—85; office mgr. DeColores Prodns., Houston, 1989—90; cmty. ctr. dir. Helping Hands - Riverview Pk., Tulsa, 1995; author Am. Book Pub. Group, Salt Lake City, 1999—, sr. editor, 1999—2003; CEO Accomplished Pub. LLC, mag. pub., 2008. Creative adviser/cons. Various Ind. Entrepreneurial Enterprises, Tulsa, 1989—2003; founder Pub. Orgn., 2008—. Author: (novel) Soaring On Clipped Wings (Book of Month, 2004), (screenplay) Fighting to Love; senior editor: novels Cryer's Valley, Have No Mercy, writer, dir.: Sadie's Soap Suds TV Show, 2004, author numerous poems; pub., editor-in-chief Accomplished Mag., 2009. Recipient Best New Writer of Yr. Disilgold Mag. award, Younity Reviewers Guild, 2004; named Humanitarian of Month, 2003. Mem.: Younity Revs. Guild Worldwide, Disilgold Lit. Network Assn., Nat. Writers Union, Authors Den Forum (life). Achievements include design of safety product for use in vehicular transportation of children; product for walking in hazardous environmental conditions. Avocations: singing, music, sewing and design, swimming, reading. Office Phone: 918-459-4613. Personal E-mail: eagledfly@yahoo.com, regaleagle1123@gmail.com.

WILLIAMS, DARLENE F., federal agency administrator; BA, Howard U.; MA, PhD, Stanford U.; MBA, Chgo. U. Asst. mgr., Pacific Bell Sr. mgr. Eastman Kodak; mgr. mktg., planning and rsch. Ryder Systems, Inc.; corp. policy mgr. TXU; gen. dep. asst. sec. policy devel. and rsch. HUD, Washington, 2003—05, gen. dep. asst. sec. adminstrn., 2005, asst. sec. policy devel. and rsch., 2005—09, gen. dep. asst. sec., adminstrn., 2009. Office: HUD 451 Seventh St SW Mail Code A Rm 6100 Washington DC 20410-6000 Office Fax: 202-619-8129.

WILLIAMS, DAVE HARRELL, investment company executive; b. Beaumont, Tex., Oct. 5, 1932; s. George Davis and Mary (Hardin) W.; m. Reba White, Mar. 15, 1975. BS in Chem. Engring, U. Tex., 1956; MBA (Baker scholar, Teagle fellow), Harvard U., 1961. Chartered fin. analyst. Chem. engr. Exxon Corp., Baton Rouge, 1959; security analyst deVegh & Co., NYC, 1961—64; dir. research Waddell & Reed, Kansas City, Mo., 1964—67; exec. v.p. Mitchell Hutchins, Inc., NYC, 1967—77; chmn. bd. Alliance Capital Mgmt. Corp., NYC, 1977—2001, chmn. emeritus, 2001—04. Contbr. articles to profl. jours. Trustee U.S.S. Intrepid Mus. Found. Served with USNR, 1956-59. Named one of Top 200 Collectors, ARTnews Mag., 2004—08. Mem. Fin. Analysts Fedn. (past officer, dir.), N.Y. Soc. Security Analysts (past pres.), Bond Club N.Y., Econ. Club N.Y., Knickerbocker Club, Grolier Club. Presbyterian. Avocation: Collector of Am. Prints. Office: White Williams Holdings 41 W 57th St 4th Fl New York NY 10019 Office Phone: 212-752-5480. Business E-Mail: dwilliams@white-williams.com.

WILLIAMS, DAVID ALFRED, elementary school music specialist; b. Jacksonville, Fla., May 24, 1961; s. Merle W. Long and John Alfred Williams, James Elbert Toby Long (Stepfather). A, Brewton Parker Coll., 1982; BFA in Music Edn., Tift Coll./Mercer U., Macon, Ga., 1984; M in Ednl. Adminstrn. and Leadership, Cambridge Coll., Mass., 2006, EdS in Ednl. Adminstrn. and Leadership, 2007. Profl. tchr. Ga., 2006, cert. Ga. Real Estate Bd., 2004. Music specialist Appling County Elem. Sch., Baxley, Ga., 1987—; owner, event cons. Seasonings, LLC; owner, cons. Seasonings, LLC- Catering & Events Planning Co.; owner, artist, instr. The Studio. Musician (pianist/vocalist): (albums) Reflections & Memories; musician: Remember When. Mem. First Bapt. Ch., Baxley, Ga., 2000—05. Mem.: Assn. Supr. & Curriculum Devel., Profl. Assn. Ga. Educators, Ga. Music Educators Assn. (assoc.), Nat. Music Educators Assn. (assoc.), Friends of Johnny Mercer (assoc.). Baptist. Avocations: swimming, travel, cake decorating, music, cooking, photography. Home: 556 Pineview Ave Baxley GA 31513 Office: Appling County Elem Sch 680 Blackshear Hwy Baxley GA 31513 Personal E-mail: david@thekeyboardkid.com. Business E-Mail: dwilliams@appling.k12.ga.us.

WILLIAMS, DAVID B., legislative staff member; Chief of staff to Rep. Michael Forbes US House of Reps., Washington, asst., appropriations com., profl. staff mem., govt. reform com., 2001—02, chief of staff to Rep. Steve Kagan, 2007—. Democrat. Office: 1232 Longworth House Office Bldg Washington DC 20515 Office Phone: 202-225-5665. Office Fax: 202-225-5729.*

WILLIAMS, DAVID M., theologian, educator; b. Morrisville, NY, May 14, 1966; s. Ellen L. and James Arthur Williams; m. Emily F. Robleto, June 28, 2008; children: David, David. PhD in Polit. Sci., Boston Coll., Chestnut Hill, Mass., 1993, PhD in Theology, 2001. Asst. prof. theology Belmont Abbey Coll., NC, 1999—2004, assoc. prof. theology, 2005—, dept. chair, 2005—. Mem.: Fellowship Cath. Scholars, Cath. Theol. Soc. Am. Roman Catholic. Avocations: surfing, computers, literature. Office: Belmont Abbey Coll 100 Belmont Mt Holly Rd Belmont NC 28012 Office Fax: 704-461-5051. Business E-Mail: davidwilliams@bac.edu.

WILLIAMS, DAVID OWEN, cardiologist; b. Phila., May 18, 1943; Graduate, Trinity Coll., Hartford, Conn., 1965; MD, Hahnemann Med. Coll., 1969. Cert. Nat. Bd. Med. Examiners, 1970, Am. Bd. Internal Medicine, 1972, Subspecialty Bd. Cardiovascular Disease, 1975, Interventional Cardiology 1999, lic. RI, 1976, Mass., 1996. Intern, resident, internal medicine Hahnemann Hosp., Phila., 1969—70, fellow in tchg., 1971—72; fellow in cardiology U. Calif. Sch. Medicine, Davis, 1972-74, asst. prof. med., 1974—76; asst. prof. medicine, divsn. biol., med. sci. Brown U., 1976—80, assoc. prof. medicine, divsn. biol., med. sci., 1980—85, prof., medicine, 1985—; asst. chief, dept. medicine Martinez Vet. Affairs Med. Ctr., Calif., chief, cardiology sect. Calif., 1974—76; cardiologist, divsn. cardiology RI Hosp., Providence, 1976—, physician in medicine, 1976—, assoc. physician in medicine, 1976—, physician-in-charge, 1989—91, dir., cardiac catheterization lab., 1976—, dir., interventional cardiology, 1992—. Adj. asst. prof. biomed. engring. U. RI, 1977—; consulting staff, dept. medicine Miriam Hosp., Providence, 1981—, Women and Infants Hosp. RI, 1982—, Roger Williams Gen. Hosp., Providence, 1987—; bd. mem. Interventional Cardiology Test Com. Am. Bd. Internal Med., 1997—. Serves on editl. bds. of several profl. jours. in medicine, serves as an editl. reviewer for several profl. jours.; contbr. articles to profl. jours.; editl. cons. Jour. Am. Coll. Cardiology, 1990—92, 2002—06, Med. Letter, 1990—. Cardiac care advisory com. RI Dept. Health, 1987—. Recipient Sci. & Tech. award, Gov. RI, 1991, Andreas R. Gruentzig award, Gruentzig Soc., 2006; named Alumnus of Year, Hahnemann U., 1990; named an Outstanding Med. Specialist Cardiology US, Town & Country mag., 1989; named one of Best Dr.'s America, 1992—93, 1993—94, Country's Best Heart Dr.'s, Good Housekeeping mag., 1996, Best Dr.'s America, American Health mag., 1996, Top Docs in RI, RI Monthly mag., 1994, 2002. Fellow: Soc. Cardiac Angiography (com. on interventional cardiology 1986), Am. Coll. Cardiology; mem.: Assn. U. Cardiologists, Am. Heart Assn., ACP, RI Med. Soc., Am. Fedn. Clinical Rsch., Am. Heart Assn. (exec. com., coun. cardiovascular radiology 1984—87, program com., scientific sessions 1989—91, clin. coun., com. on cardiac catheterization 1989—97, page award com., coun. on atherosclerosis 1993—95, coun. rep., coun. on clin. cardiology 1993—96, mem. cardiac catheterization and interventional cardiology com. 1995—97, coun. rep., coun. on clin. cardiology 1997—2000, fellow, coun. on arteriosclerosis, thrombosis and vascular biology 1997—, exec. com., coun. on clin. cardiology 1998, fellow, coun. on clin. cardiology 1998—, fellow, coun. cardiovascular radiology 2004—, bd. dirs., RI affiliate 1976—85). Office: RI Hosp Div Cardiology 593 Eddy St APC 814 Providence RI 02903-4971 Office Phone: 401-444-4581. E-mail: David_Williams@Brown.EDU.

WILLIAMS, DAVID R., sociologist, educator, senior research scientist; BTh hons., Carribean Union Coll.; MDiv cum laude, Andews U., 1979; MPH in Health Edn., Loma Linda U.; PhD; MA in Sociology, U. Mich., 1954, PhD in Sociology, 1986. Harold R. Cruse prof. sociology U. Mich, Ann Arbor; and dir. South Africa Initiatives Office U. Mich.; sr. scientist Survey Rsch. Ctr., U. Mich., Ann Arbor. Faculty assoc. African Am. Mental Health Rsch. Ctr., Ann Arbor, Mich.; mem. editl. bd: Contemporary Sociology, 1990—92, Social Psychology Quarterly, 1996—, Social Problems, 1996—; Mem. Nat. Acad. Scis. Panel on Needle Exchange and Bleach Distrbn. Programs, 1993—95, Nat. Sci. Found. Bd. Overseers for NORC's Gen. Social Survey, 1993—97; mem. rev. panel Nat. Inst. Mental Health Social and Group Processes Grants, 1996—99. Assoc. editor (sociological jour.) Ethnicity and Disease, 1993—; contbr. articles to profl. jours. Recipient Investigator award in Health Policy Rsch., Robert Wood Johnson found., 1995—96; fellow (Jr. faculty) in Social Scis., Yale U., 1990—91, (sr. faculty), 1992—93. Fellow: Am. Acad. Arts & Scis.; mem.: Internat. Soc. Hypertension in Blacks, Assn. Black Sociologists, Am. Psychol Assn., Am. Pub. Health Assn., Soc. Epedemiological Rsch., Am. Sociological Assn. (sec.-treas. med. sociology sect. 1995—97), Nat. Rsch. Coun., Nat. Acad Scis. Inst. Medicine. Office: Univ Mich Inst Social Rsch 426 Thompson St Rm 2230 Ann Arbor MI 48106-1248 E-mail: wildavid@umich.edu.

WILLIAMS, DAVID R. (DAFYDD RHYS WILLIAMS), research scientist, medical educator, retired astronaut; b. Saskatoon, Saskatchewan, Can., May 16, 1954; s. William and Isobel Williams; m. Cathy Fraser; 2 children. BSc in Biology, McGill U., 1976, MSc in Physiology, 1983, MD, CM, McGill U., 1983; LLD (hon.), U. Saskatchewan, 2004. Resident in family practice U. Ottawa Faculty Medicine, Canada, 1983—85; resident in emergency medicine U. Toronto, Canada, 1985—88; fellow in emergency medicine Royal Coll. Physicians & Surgeons, Canada, 1988; emergency physician Sunnybrook Health Sci. Ctr., 1988—89, med. dir., Advanced Cardiac Life Support Program, coord. postgraduate tng. in emergency medicine, 1990—92, dir., dept. emergency svcs.; emergency physician Emergency Assocs. Kitchener. Waterloo, Canada, 1988—90; med. dir. Westmount Urgent Care Clinic, 1989—90; with Can. Space Agy., 1992—95; astronaut NASA, Houston, 1995—2008, dir. Space and Life Scis. Directorate, Johnson Space Ctr., 1998—2002; dir. McMaster Centre for Med. Robotics at St. Joseph's Healthcare Hamilton, Hamilton, Ont., Canada, 2008—; prof. dept. surgery Michael G. DeGroote Sch. Medicine, McMaster U., 2008—. Lectr. dept. surgery U. Toronto, Canada, 1988, asst. prof. surgery, Canada, 1989—90, adj. prof. surgery, Canada; course dir. Can. Heart & Stroke Found., Am. Coll. Surgeons; asst. prof. surgery McGill U., adj. prof. surgery; mem. staff St. Mary's Hosp., Montreal Gen. Hosp.; mission specialist Neurolab, 1998; dir. space & life sci. directorate (first non-Am. to hold sr. mgmt. position with NASA) NASA, 1998—2002; first dep. associated adminstr. for crew health and safety, Office Space Flight NASA Hdqs., 2001; aquanaut, NEEMO 1 Mission (first Canadian to have lived and worked in space and in the ocean) NASA-NOAA, 2001, crew comdr., NEEMO 9, 06; mission specialist 3 STS-90 Mission (Columbia), 1998; mission specialist, spacewalker STS-118 Mission (Endeavour) to Internat. Space Station, 2007. Recipient Commonwealth cert. Thanks, 1973, Commonwealth Recognition award, 1975, A.S. Hill bursary, McGill U., 1980, Walter Hoare bursary, 1981, J.W. McConnell award, 1981—83, Psychiatry prize, Wood Gold Medal award, NASA Space Flight medal, 1998, Melbourne W. Boynton award, Am. Astronautical Soc., 1999, Bronze medal for contbn. to neuroscience during Mission STS-90, Ramon y Cajal Inst. Neurobiology, Spanish Coun. for Scientific Rsch., 1999, Rotary Nat. award for Space Achievement, 2000, NASA Outstanding Leadership medal, 2002, NASA Johnson Space Ctr. Space & Life Scis. Directorate Spl. Profl. Achievement award for implementation of Automatic External Defibrillator Program, 2003; named Patron of the Internat. Life Saving Fedn., 2002, Spokesperson for the Life Saving Soc. Cand. and Hon. Amb., SmartRisk Found. Fellow: Royal Coll. Physicians & Surgeons Can., Coll. Family Physicians Can.; mem.: Montreal Physiol. Soc., NY Acad. Sci., Soc. Neuroscience, Undersea and Hyperbaric Medicine Soc., Can. Aeronautics & Space Inst., Can. Soc. Aerospace Medicine, Aerospace Med. Assn., Can. Assn. Emergency Physicians, Ontario Med. Assn., Coll. Physicians & Surgeons Ontario. Avocations: flying, scuba diving, hiking, sailing, kayaking, canoeing, downhill and cross-country skiing. Office: McMaster Centre for Med Robotics St Joseph's Healthcare Hamilton 50 Charlton Ave E Hamilton ON Canada L8N 4A6

WILLIAMS, DAVID RUSSELL, retired music educator; b. Indpls., Oct. 21, 1932; s. H. Russell and Mary Dean (Whitmer) W.; m. Elsa Bühlmann, Jan. 30, 1960. AB, Columbia U., 1954, MA, 1956; PhD, U. Rochester, 1965. Dir. music Windham Coll., Putney, Vt., 1959-62; opera coach Eastman Sch. Music, Rochester, NY, 1962-65, assoc. prof. theory, adminstr. of MusM program, 1965-80; prof., chmn. dept. music U. Memphis (formerly Memphis State U.), 1980-87, prof. music, 1980-98, prof. emeritus, 1998—. Bd. dirs. Memphis Youth Symphony, Memphis Symphony, 1984-90; mem. exec. bd. Opera Memphis, 1980-87. Author: Bibliography of the History of Music Theory, 1971, Conversations with Howard Hanson, 1988, Music Theory from Zarlino to Schenker: A Bibliography and Guide, 1990, Music Theory from Boethius to Zarlino: A Bibliography and Guide, 2008; producer: Highwater Records album 8201 featuring John Stover, classical guitar, 1983; composer Suite for Oboe, Clarinet and Piano, 1968, Five States of Mind, 1970. Bd. dirs., sec. Rochester Philharm. Orch., 1976-78; v.p., bd. dirs. Rochester Chamber Orch., 1974-78; pres., bd. dirs. Opera Theatre of Rochester, 1973-74; bd. dirs., chmn. Am. Ritual Theatre, 1979-80; bd. sponsors Met. Opera Mid. South Region, Memphis, 1983—. Served as cpl. U.S. Army, 1957-59. Recipient Eastman Sch. Music Pub. award, 1970. Mem. NARAS (treas. Memphis chpt. 1984-86), Coll. Music Soc. (sec. 1973-83), Music Tchrs. Nat. Assn. Sci. (state chmn. 1971-74), Nat. Assn. Schs. of Music (chmn. region 8 1989-92), Tenn. Assn. Music Execs. in Colls. and Univs. (pres. 1986-87), Rochester Club, Univ. Club, Summit Club, Pi Kappa Lambda (pres. U. Memphis chpt. 1988-90), Phi Beta Kappa, Phi Mu Alpha, Sigma Alpha Iota. Avocations: language study, word puzzles. Home: 273 W Central Park St Apt 1 Memphis TN 38111-4570 *Having had a family background that was superior in so many ways has helped me to sharpen my purpose in life, in that it has made me realize to what an extent affirmative action is necessary in order to provide a milieu in which truly equal opportunity can exist. Many doors of opportunity have been held open for me; those of disadvantaged access are often not aware these doors exist. The more individuals I can lead to these portals, the more I will have achieved in my lifetime.*

WILLIAMS, DEANGELO, professional football player; b. Little Rock, Apr. 25, 1983; B in Mktg., U. Memphis, 2006. Running back Carolina Panthers, 2006—. Named Offensive Player of Yr., Conf. USA, 2003—05, First Team All-Conf., 2003—05. Achievements include leading the NFL in: rushing touchdowns (18), total touchdowns (20), 2008. Office: Carolina Panthers 800 S Mint St Charlotte NC 28202*

WILLIAMS, DERON MICHAEL, professional basketball player; b. Parkersburg, W.Va., June 26, 1984; married; 2 children. Student in sports mgmt., U. Ill., Urbana, 2002—05. Guard Utah Jazz, 2005—. Mem. US Men's Sr. Nat. Basketball Team, Beijing, 2008. Founder Point of Hope Found. Recipient Gold medal, men's basketball, Beijing Olympic Games, 2008; named to All-Star Rookie First Team, NBA, 2005—06. Office: Utah Jazz 301 W South Temple Salt Lake City UT 84101*

WILLIAMS, DOCIA SCHULTZ, small business owner; b. St. Louis, Sept. 12, 1930; d. John Frederick and Statira Jim (Thornton) Schultz; m. Stanley Good Southworth Jr. (div. 1983); 1 child, Sarah Elizabeth Southworth; m. Roy Donald Williams, Dec. 1, 1984. BA, Tex. Womans U., 1951. Fashion coordinator Ike Clark of Dallas, Dallas, 1951—53, Harveys Dept. Store, Nashville, Tex., 1953—55; model, coordinator Freelance, San Antonio, 1968; owner, boutique shop San Antonio, 1973—79; tour mgr. numerous travel co., 1979—89; owner, operator Mission City Tours, San Antonio, 1989—. With S.A. Writers Guild, San Antonio; writer C.S. Journal, San Antonio Conservation Soc., San Antonio, 2003—. Author: Spirits of San Antonio, 1992, When Darkness Falls, 1994, Ghosts Along The Texas Coast, 1993, Phantoms of the Plains, 1995, Best Tales of Texas Ghosts, 1998, Exploring San Antonio with Children, 2000, History and Mystery of the Menger Hotel, 2000; speaker (various profl. conventions). Nat. pres. Tex. Woman's U. Assn. of Former Students, 1982—84. Recipient Spirit of San Antonio award, San Antonio Hotel and Lodgings Assn., 2003, Disting. Alumni award, Garland HS Alumni Assn., 2007; named one of Ten Outstanding Women in San Antonio, Express News Pub. Co., 1973. Mem.: Nat. Assn. Women Bus. Owners (Entrepreneurial Spirit award 2004), Tour Guides Assn. of S.A. (charter mem., Disting. Svcs. award 2004), S.A. Coun. Presidents, San Antonio Hist. Soc., Nat. Soc. Arts and Letters. Methodist. Avocations: music, travel, creative writing, antiques. Home and Office: 1319 Vista Del Monte San Antonio TX 78216

WILLIAMS, DONALD JOHN, physicist, researcher; b. Fitchburg, Mass., Dec. 25, 1933; s. Toivo John and Ina (Kokkinen) Williams; m. Priscilla Mary Gagnon, July 4, 1953; children: Steven John, Craig Mitchell, Eino Stenroos. BS, Yale U., 1955, MS, 1958, PhD, 1962. Sr. staff physicist Johns Hopkins U. Applied Physics Lab., 1961-65; head particle physics br. Goddard Space Flight Center, NASA, 1965-70; dir. Space Environ. Lab., NOAA, Boulder, Colo., 1970-82; prin. investigator Energetic Particles expt. NASA Galileo Mission, 1977—2003; prin. staff physicist Johns Hopkins U. Applied Physics Lab., 1982-89, dir. Milton S. Eisenhower Rsch. Ctr., 1990-96, chief scientist rsch. ctr., 1996-99, ret., 1999. Mem. nat. and internat. sci. planning coms.; chmn. com. solar-terrestrial rsch. NAS, 1989—93; sci. adv. bd. USAF, 1993—97. Assoc. editor: Jour. Geophys. Rsch., 1967—69, Revs. Geophysics and Space Rsch., 1984—86; editor (with G. D. Mead): Physics of the Magnetosphere, 1969, Physics of Solar-Planetary Environments, 1976; mem. editl. bd. Space Sci. Revs., 1975—85; author (with L. R. Lyons): Quantitative Aspects of Magnetospheric Physics, 1983; contbr. articles to profl. jours. Lt. USAF, 1955—57. Recipient Sci. Rsch. award, NOAA, 1974, Disting. Authorship award, NOAA and Johns Hopkins Applied Physics Lab., 1976, 1985, 1997. Fellow: Am. Geophys. Union; mem.: Internat. Acad. Astronautics, Internat. Assn. Geomagnetism and Aeronomy (pres. 1991—95), Am. Phys. Soc., Sigma Xi. Home: 117 Tivoli Trace Ct Poinciana FL 34759 Personal E-mail: donaldwfl@verizon.net.

WILLIAMS, DONALD R., social sciences educator; b. Hamilton, Ohio, Feb. 11, 1956; BBA, U. Wis., Milw., 1977; PhD, Northwestern U., Evanston, Ill., 1984. Asst. prof. econs. Kent State U., Ohio, 1983—88, assoc. prof. econs., 1988—94, prof. econs., 1994—, assoc. dean grad. sch. of mgmt., 2003—06, assoc. dean Coll. Bus. Adminstrn., 2006—07;

dean Honors Coll., 2007—. Sr. rsch. assoc. CEPS/INSTEAD, Differdange, Luxembourg, 2002—; vis. prof. KU Leuven, Belgium, 2003—. Mem.: European Assn. Labour Economists, Soc. Labor Economists, Am. Econ. Assn. Office: Kent State Univ Coll Bus Administration Kent OH 44242 Business E-Mail: dwilliam@kent.edu.

WILLIAMS, DREW DAVIS, surgeon; b. San Augustine, Tex., Jan. 18, 1935; s. Floyd Everett and Villamae (Morehead) W.; m. Marilyn Raus, June 27, 1958; children: Leslie, Cynthia, Matthew, Jennifer, Amelia. BS, Tex. A&M Coll., 1957; MD, U. Tex., 1960; grad., naval flight surgeon, U.S. Naval Sch. Aviation Medicine, 1963. Diplomate Am. Bd. Surgery, Am. Bd. Quality Assurance and Utilization Rev. Physicians. Intern USPHS Hosp., Seattle, 1960-61; resident in gen. surgery U. Tex. Med. Br., Galveston, 1961-62, 64-68; resident in pulmonary svc. M.D. Anderson Hosp., Houston, 1968; pvt. practice Baytown, Tex., 1968—. Active staff San Jacinto (Tex.) Meth. Hosp., 1968-95, chief of surgery, 1972, 73, pres. med. staff, 1976; mem. courtesy staff Bay Coast Hosp., Baytown, 1968-95; cons. staff Baytown Med. Ctr. Hosp., 1972-95; 1st chmn. dept. surgery in devel. of family practice residency program affiliated with Tex. Med. Sch., Houston, 1977; mem. Tex. State Bd. Med. Examiners, 1983-89, sec.-treas., 1984-88, pres., 1988-89; unit med. dir., clin. instr. dept. preventive medicine and cmty. health U. Tex. Med. Br., Galveston, 1995-99. Contbr. chpt. to book and articles to profl. jours. Mem. Baytown Area Citizen's Adv. Panel. Flight surgeon USN, 1962—64, lt. comdr. USNR, ret., 1967. Clin. fellow, Am. Cancer Soc., 1966—67. Mem.: SAR (past pres. local chpt.), AMA (Physicians Recognition award), ACS, Ret. Physicians Orgn. (med. reserve com.), Houston Surg. Soc. (past pres.), Baytown Surg. Soc., East Harris County Med. Soc. (pres. 1982), Harris County Med. Soc. (exec. bd. 1994, chmn. coun. med. splty., co-chmn. disaster response com. of ret. physician orgn.), Singleton Surg. Soc. (past pres.), Tex. Surg. Soc., Tex. Med. Assn., Sovereign Colonial Soc.-Am. of Royal Descent, Colonial Order of the Crown, Soc. Descendents of Colonial Clergy, Sir William Osler Soc., Sons of Republic of Tex. (at large life), Magna Carta Barons, Am. Cancer Soc. (pres. Baytown chpt. 1970—71), Knights Templar, Shriners, Masons (32 degree). Democrat. Mem. Ch. of Christ. Avocations: hunting, fishing, genealogy, painting, gardening. Home and Office: 1217 Kilgore Rd Baytown TX 77520-3912 Office Phone: 281-422-7969. Business E-Mail: ddw@hal-pc.org.

WILLIAMS, E. FAYE, lawyer, political organization executive, health products executive; BS, Grambling State U., La.; MPA, U. So. Calif.; JD, Howard U.; PhD in Pub. Adminstrn., City U. LA; D of Ministry, Wesley Theol. Seminary. Former counsel US Congress; legis. counsel DC City Coun.; chief of staff to DC Coun. Mem. Marion Barry; pres., CEO Natural Health Options, Inc., Washington. Former prof. internat. law So. U. Law Ctr., Baton Rouge; pub. affairs dir. WWGB, Washington; commentator La. Radio Network. Bd. mem. Shundahia Network. Recipient Star Performer award, Asian Benevolent Soc., Humanitarian award, African Hebrew Israelites, Winnie Mandela Endurance with Dignity award, Support A Child Found., Inc., 2001, Cmty. Svc. award, Nation of Islam, Woman Entrepreneur of Yr. award, Indiana Black Expo; named one of Most Influential Black Americans, Ebony mag., 2006; named to Power 150, 2008. Mem.: Nat. Congress of Black Women (past gen. counsel, nat. chair 2006—). Office: Nat Congress Black Women Ste 200 1251 4th St SW Washington DC 20024-2307 Office Phone: 301-562-8000.

WILLIAMS, EARL PATRICK, JR., retired editor, freelance writer; b. Washington, May 14, 1950; s. Earl Patrick Sr. and Charlie Mae (Wright) W.; m. Susan Miller Day, July 20, 1985 (div. 2005). BA, U. Md., 1973; postgrad., Cath. U., Washington, DC, 1974. Duplication machine operator Applied Physics Lab. Johns Hopkins U., Silver Spring, Md., 1968—74; substitute tchr. Fairfax County Va. Schs., 1974—75; clk. U.S. Govt. Printing Office, Washington, 1975—76; editor U.S. GAO, Washington, 1976—2005, ret., 2005. Freelance writer, Washington, 1974—. Author: Amtrak's Washington-New York Corridor, 1977, What You Should Know About the American Flag, 1987, What You Should Know About Flags of the Confederacy, 1993; contbr. articles to mags. and newspapers. Active in efforts to achieve recognition of Francis Hopkinson, the designer of first ofcl. US flag; lectr. to sch. groups and civic orgns. on history of US flag; discussed history of US flag on radio and TV broadcasts nationwide. Recipient Cert. of Appreciation Mil. Order of World Wars, Bronze Good Citizenship medal Nat. Soc. SAR Mem.: N.Am. Vexillological Assn., Nat. Cathedral Assn., Star Spangled Banner Flag House Assn. Democrat. Methodist. Avocations: railroad buff, history, singing folk music. Home: 2323 40th Pl NW Apt 201 Washington DC 20007-1630

WILLIAMS, EDDIE NATHAN, retired think-tank executive; b. Memphis, Aug. 18, 1932; s. Ed and Georgia Lee (Barr) W.; m. Jearline F. Reddick, July 18, 1981; children: Traci Lynne (dec.), Edward Lawrence, Terence Reddick. BS, U. Ill., 1954; postgrad., Atlanta U., 1957, Howard U., 1960; LLD, U. D.C., 1986; DHL, Bowie State Coll., 1980, Chgo. State U., 1994, Dillard U., 2001; LLD, Benedict Coll., 2003, Clark-Atlanta U., 2005. Reporter Atlanta Daily World Newspaper, 1957-58; staff asst. U.S. Senate Com. on Fgn. Relations, Washington, 1959-60; fgn. service res. officer U.S. Dept. State, Washington, 1961-68; v.p. U. Chgo., 1968-72; pres., CEO Joint Ctr. for Polit. and Econ. Studies, Washington, 1972—2004, pres. emeritus, 2005—; pres., CEO Eddie Williams & Assocs., 2004—. Chmn. emeritus Nat. Coalition Black Civic Participation, 2005—. Editorial columnist: Chgo. Sun Times, 1970-72; contbr. articles to profl. jours. Am. Polit. Sci. Assn. fellow, 1958, MacArthur Found. fellow, 1988, Nat. Acad. Pub. Adminstrn. fellow, 1993, Am. Acad. Arts and Scis. fellow, 1998; recipient Adam Clayton Powell Award Congl. Black Caucus, 1981, Washingtonian of Yr. award Washingtonian Mag., 1991, Alumni of Yr. award U. Ill. Alumni Club of Greater Washington, 1994, Outstanding Leadership award Korean Am. Alliance, 1994. Mem. Kappa Tau Alpha, Omega Psi Phi, Sigma Pi Phi. Office: Eddie Williams & Assocs 1250 Connecticut Ave NW Ste 200 Washington DC 20036 Office Phone: 202-558-3521. Business E-Mail: ewilliams@eddiewilliamsllc.com.

WILLIAMS, EDNA ALETA THEADORA JOHNSTON, journalist; b. Halifax, NS, Can., Sept. 19, 1923; d. Clarence Harvey and Edna May (Lewis) Johnston; m. Albert Murray Williams, Apr. 16, 1949 (dec.); children: Murleta, Norma, Martin, Charla, Kerrick, Renwick, Julia. Student, Maritime Bus. Coll., 1943. Typist Dept. Treas. (Navy), Halifax, 1944-49; with Bedford (N.S.) Mag., Halifax br., 1954-55, Presbyn. Office, New Glasgow, N.S., 1965-67, Thompson and Sutherland, New Glasgow, 1967-69; family editor, columnist, reporter New Glasgow Evening News, 1969-88, ret., 1988; soc. corr. Evening News, 1997—. Mem. coun. Halifax YMCA; founding mem. Pictou County YM-YWCA, 1966—; ref. person media and religion Black History Month; New Glasgow Bapt. rep. Pictou County Coun. of Chs., 1978—82, sec., 1980—82; pres. ch. aux. 2d United Bapt. Ch., 1979—83; chorus dir. Men's Choir, 1980—, hon. mem. ch. aux., v.p., 1993—; treas. Ch.'s Men's Brotherhood, 1995—; organist St. James Anglican Ch., 1983—85, provincial organist, 1994—; organist St. Bee's Anglican Ch., 1996—2003; provincial pres. Women's Inst. of African United Bapt. Assn., 1983—86; bd. dirs. Pictou County YM-YWCA, 1967—77, corr. sec., v.p., 1974—75, 1975—77; past pres., past provincial dir., Home and Sch. provincial sec. African United Bapt. Assn. of N.S., 1988—90; sec. area IV Atlantic United Bapt. Conv., 1989—93; past officer local interracial com.; bd. dirs. Big Bros./Big Sisters, 1984—86, Pictou County United Way, 1983—96, Palliative Care Aberdeen Hosp., 1985—, Black United Front; chair Pictou County Srs. Festival, 1999—2001. Recipient Hon. award, United Way, 1993, Grot award, Black Cultural Ctr. N.S., 1999, honored by, Pictou County Music Festival, 1994, AUBA, 2008, award, 2d United Bapt. Ch., 1997, Cultural Heritage award, Town of New Glasgow, 2004, Palliative Care Vol. award, 2005, Honored over 50 yr. mem. and 20 yr. organist, African United Bapt. Assn. Women's Inst., 2005, Mentor award, BYZ (youth), 2008. Mem. N.S. Sr. Secretate, Can. Press Assn., Black Journalists Assn. N.S., Can. Bible Soc. (pres. 1998-2000, Certificate, 2004-), African United Baptist Assn. Women's Inst. Home: 230 Reservoir St New Glasgow NS Canada B2H 4K4 Office: Evening News 352 East River Rd Glasgow NS Canada B2H 5E2

WILLIAMS, EDWARD DAVID, information technology management consultant; b. Scranton, Pa., June 20, 1932; s. David Thomas and Mabel (Sims) W. m. Natalie Imnadze, Oct. 18, 1952; children: Denise, Claudia. BBA, Hofstra U., 1961; postgrad. in Bus. Adminstrn., Fairleigh Dickenson U., 1979. Cons. Cresap, McCormick and Paget, NYC, 1964—65; sr. mgmt. cons. Union Carbide Corp., NYC, 1965—67; asst. contr. data processing We. Union, NYC, 1967—69; v.p. mgmt. info. sys. ABC, Hackensack, NJ, 1970—86; v.p., chief info. officer Blue Cross Blue Shield of NJ, Newark, 1986—88; v.p. Chantico Pub. Co., Carrellton, Tex., 1989—90; pres. SMC-BIS Inc., Basking Ridge, NJ, 1990—93; pres., CEO Strategic Outsourcing Svcs. Inc., Mountain Lakes, NJ, 1993—97; sr. v.p. Computer Horizons Corp., Mountain Lakes, 1997—99; exec. v.p. PRT Group Inc., Windsor, Conn., 1999; pres. Ed. Williams Assoc. Ltd., Franklin Lakes, NJ, 1995—. Spkr. in field. With US Army, 1948-52. Decorated Silver Star with oak leaf cluster, Bronze Star with V; recipient Purple Heart with 2 oak leaf clusters, Combat Info. Badge. Mem. Soc. Mgmt. Info. Systems, NJ C. of C., Profit Oriented Systems Planning Bd. (bd. dirs.), Masons. Republican. Home and Office: Ed Williams Assoc Ltd 662 Cheyenne Dr Franklin Lakes NJ 07417 Office Phone: 201-847-9148. Personal E-mail: edward.d.williams@att.net.

WILLIAMS, EDWARD EARL, JR., entrepreneur, educator; b. Houston, Aug. 21, 1945; s. Edward Earl and Doris Jewel (Jones) W.; m. Susan M. Warren, June 28, 1983; children: Laura Michelle, David Brian. BS, U. Pa., 1966; PhD, U. Tex., 1968. Asst. prof. econs. Rutgers U., New Brunswick, NJ, 1968-70; assoc. prof. fin. McGill U., Montreal, Que., Canada, 1970-73; v.p. Svc. Corp. Internat., Houston, 1973-77; prof. adminstrv. sci. Rice U., Houston, 1978-82, Henry Gardiner Symonds prof., 1982—, prof. stats., 1995—. Chmn. bd. dirs. Edward E. Williams & Co., Houston, 1976-92; chmn. bd., pres. Tex. Capital Investment Co., 1979-95; chmn. bd. First Tex. Venture Capital Corp., 1983-92; mng. dir. First Tex. Venture Capital, LLC, 1992-2000, Svc. Corp. Internat., Simugram Sys., Inc.; adv. dir. Frost Nat. Bank Author: Prospects for the Savings and Loan Industry, 1968, An Integrated Analysis for Managerial Finance, 1970, Investment Analysis, 1974, Business Planning for the Entrepreneur, 1983, The Economics of Production and Productivity: A Modeling Approach, 1996, Entrepreneurship and Productivity, 1998, The N.Y. Times Pocket MBA Series: Business Planning, 1999, Models for Investors in Real World Markets, 2003, Preparing an Entrepreneurial Business Plan, 2004; contbr. articles to profl. jours. Benjamin Franklin scholar, Jesse Jones scholar U. Pa., 1966; fellow Tex. Savs. and Loan League, fellow NDEA U. Tex., 1968. Mem. So. Pacific Hist. and Tech. Soc., Santa Fe Rlwy. Hist. and Modeling Soc., Carlton Woods County Club, Jewish Comm. North, Beta Gamma Sigma, Alpha Kappa Psi. Republican. Office: Rice U Jesse H Jones Grad Sch Mgmt Houston TX 77251 Home: 51 N Lamerie Way The Woodlands TX 77382 Office Phone: 713-348-5381. Business E-Mail: jinkeynes@rice.edu.

WILLIAMS, EDWARD F(OSTER), III, retired environmental engineer; b. NYC, Jan. 3, 1935; s. E. Foster Jr. and Ida Frances (Richards) W.; m. Sue Carol Osenbaugh, June 5, 1960; children: Cecile Elizabeth, Alexander Harmon. BS in Engring., Auburn U., 1956; MA in History, U. Memphis, 1974. Registered profl. engr., Tenn. Engr. Buckeye Cellulose Corp. (subs. of Procter & Gamble), Memphis, 1957, process safety engr., 1960, resident constrn. engr. Perry, Fla., 1960-61, staff engr. Memphis, 1961-70; chief engr., v.p. Enviro-trol, Inc., Memphis, 1970-73; from v.p. to pres. Ramcon Environ. Corp., Memphis, 1973-80; pres. E.F. Williams & Assocs., Inc., Memphis, 1980-98; v.p. engring. Environ. Testing & Cons. of the Americas, Inc., 1998—2001, pres., 2001—06; ret., 2007. Chmn. bd. EFW Comml. Ventures, Inc., 1990—, Spiridon Press, Inc., 1998-99; bd. dirs. Mobile Process Tech. Inc., Memphis; v.p. Environ. Testing and Cons., Inc., Memphis, 1985-94; environ. coord. Shelby County, Tenn., 1995-96. Author: Fustest with the Mostest, 1968, Early Memphis and Its River Rivals, 1969, Great American Civil War Trivia Book, 1998; editor Environ. Control News for So. Industry, 1971-2001 Mem. N.B. Forrest Trail Com., 1964—, chmn., 1975—; mem. Shelby County Bd. Commrs., Memphis, 1978—94, chmn., 1987—88, 1990—92; mem. Shelby County Records Commn., 1978-, chmn., 1993-, Chickasaw Basin Authority, 1980-94, 98—, vice chmn., 1982-94; historian Shelby County, 1994—; environ. coord. Shelby County Mayor's staff, 1995—96; trustee Bolton Coll., 1982—, chmn., 1987—88, 1990—92; state chmn. Nat. Conf. Rep. County Ofcls., 1993—96; vice chmn. Shelby County Stormwater Steering Com., 1998—2002; vice-chmn. Memphis-Shelby local Emergency Planning Com., 1986—2003; vice chmn. Shelby County Courthouse Hist. Preservation Commn., 2000—, Mid-South Commn. on Aging, 2003—; bd. dirs. Better Bus. Bur., Memphis, 1995—; chmn. Shelby County Hist. Commn., 1997—98; bd. dirs. Southwest Tenn. C.C. Found., 2001—07; v.p. Memphis Belle War Meml. Found., 2000—05; adv. com. Boy Scouts of Am., Chickasaw Coun., 1980—2000; state rep. Tenn. Gen. Assembly, 1970—78; del. Rep. Nat. Conv., 1988, 1992, 1996, state exec. com., 1994—2002; vice chmn. Rep. Party of Shelby County, 2003—05; pres. Christ United Presbyn. Ch. Corp., 1995—98; trustee Faith Christian Acad., 2009—. Lt. USAF, 1957—60, capt. res. USAF, 1961—71, wing comdr. staff, 1958, Chem., Biol., & Radiol. Warfare. Named Tenn. Water Conservationist of Yr., Tenn. Conservation League, 1973, Tenn. Legis. Conservationist of Yr., Nat. Wildlife Fedn., 1974, Memphis Outstanding Engr., Memphis Joint Engrs. Coun., 1980; recipient Shelby County Environ. Improvement award, 1983, Tenn. Lifetime Environ. Stewardship award Tenn. Dept. Environ. and Conservation, 1995, Herff Honor award U. Memphis Coll. Engring., 2006. Mem. NSPE, ASME, Am. Acad. Environ. Engrs. (diplomate), Environ. Assesment Assn., TSPE, Water Environ. Fedn., Am. Indsl. Hygiene Assn. (chpt. pres.), Am. Soc. Safety Engrs. (Outstanding Achievement award 1995-96), Air and Waste Mgmt. Assn., Engrs. Club Memphis (bd. dirs. 1979-80, 98-2002, pres. 2000-01), Tenn. Water and Wastewater Assn., Rotary, C. of C. (environ. coun. chmn. 1988-2000, chmn. emeritus 2000—), Tenn. Hist. Soc. (v.p. 1972), Tenn. Hist. Commn. (vice-chmn. 1987-99), West Tenn. Hist. Soc. (pres. 1983-85), Am. Hist. Assn., Memphis Belle Meml. Assn. (bd. dirs. 2004-05) Memphis-Shelby County Tenn. Bicentennial Commn. (chmn. 1994-96), Davies Manor Assn. (pres. 1999-2000), Miss. Hist. Soc., Tau Beta Pi, Omicron Delta Kappa, Pi Tau Sigma, Phi Kappa Phi. Republican. Presbyterian. Avocation: history. Home: 2278 Holly Grove Dr Memphis TN 38119 also: PO Box 241813 Memphis TN 38124-1813 also: Shelby Co Office 150 Washington Ave Rm 210 Memphis TN 38103 Home Phone: 901-685-0365. *It has been my observation that history does not repeat itself, but human nature does. Knowledge of this principle can be put to use in politics, business, and other endeavors if one knows history.*

WILLIAMS, EDWARD JOSEPH, banker; b. Chgo., May 5, 1942; s. Joseph and Lillian (Watkins) W.; children: Elaine, Paul; m. Ana J. Ortiz, Apr. 20, 1996. BBA, Roosevelt U., 1973. Owner Mut. Home Delivery, Chgo., 1961-63; exec. v.p. Harris Trust and Savs. Bank, Chgo., 1964—. Mem. Consumer Adv. Council, Washington, 1986—. Trustee, treas. Adler Planetarium, Chgo., 1982; trustee Roosevelt U., Chgo., Art Inst. of Chgo.; bd. dirs. Chapin-May Found., Chgo. Botanic Garden, Chgo. Capital Fund; trustee, treas. Chgo. Low Income Housing Trust Fund; dir. Leadership Coun. for Met. Open Communities; dir., former pres. Neighborhood Housing Svcs. of Chgo.; chmn. Provident Med. Ctr., Chgo., 1986; bd. dirs. Voices for Ill. Children, Chgo. Coun. on Urban Affairs; pres. Neighborhood Housing Svcs. Recipient Disting. Alumni award Clark Coll., Atlanta, 1985. Mem. Nat. Bankers Assn., Urban Bankers Forum (Pioneer award 1986, 97), Econ. Club. Chgo. Clubs: Metropolitan, Plaza (Chgo.).

WILLIAMS, ELIZABETH, human services administrator; d. Sylvester and Lucinda Williams; m. Willie Alfred Oden (div.); 1 child, Robert Earl Oden (dec.). Student, Hammel Bus. Coll., Akron, Ohio, 1960—61, Washtenaw CC, Ann Arbor, Mich., 1962—63, Econ. Inst. Christian Edn., Stanford, Conn., 1968, Norwalk CC, Conn., 1969—70, Roosevelt U., Chgo., 1972, City Coll. NY, Manhattan, 1972—74. LCSW Mich., 1974. Founder, owner Al's Restaurant, Akron, 1964—68; head sports dept. Lord and Taylors, Stanford, 1968—70; supr., planner, bd. dirs. Washtenaw County Neighborhood Svcs., Ypsilanti, Mich., 1970—76; founder, exec. dir. New Bethel Cmty. Ctr., Ypsilanti, 1976—80, People's Choice Multi Purpose Ctr., Inc., Ypsilanti, 1976—80, founder, pres. LA, 1981—87; program dir. Watts Labor Com. Action, LA, 1980—81; founder, pres. EOW Enterprises, LA, 1987—94, SLW Fin. and Investment Corp., 1993—, EW Capital Sys. Enterprises, 2002—. Founder Sr. Citizens Edn. and Tutoring Program, 1970—76; program dir. campus svc. E. Mich. U., Ypsilanti, 1979—80; coord. youth tng. Mich. Tech. Inst., Ann Arbor, 1980; program coord. U. Mich. Dept. Continuing Edn. for Women. Founder Washtenaw County Lit. Coun., Ann Arbor, Mich., 1976—80; mem. Solid Front for Unity in Am., 1982—85, Nat. Orgn. Black Lawyers, Calif., Nat. Coun. Aging, Calif., Ypsilanti Orgn. Social Workers, Nat. and State Orgn. Social Workers, Calif., Ypsilanti area Coll. Life-Long Learning, Wayne State U., Detroit; rep. Bd. Licenses and Regulations, Mich.; spl. program dir. Mt. Zion Ch. of God in Christ, Ypsalanti, 1973—81; bd. mem. YWCA, Stanford, Conn.; state chair Conf. Black Women, Stanford; mem. Stanford Housing Project, MLK Birthday Commn., LA, 1982—85; program planner, program dir., recruiter, trustee Hong Kong Internat. Humanitarian Self Liquidating Loan Program, 1991—2005; mem., bd. dirs. Nat. Orgn. Social Workers; mem. exec. com. United Way, Calif.; mem. Mich. State Steering Com.; mem. bd. dirs. extended opportunity program Boy Scouts of Am., Ypsilanti. Recipient Pauline award, Ministers Alliance, LA, 1983—84, Entrepreneur award, Philanthropist Christian Club, LA, 1983—84, Agy. of Yr. award, Calif., 1983—84, Excellent Cmty. Svc. award, NAACP, 1984, Outstanding Svc. to LA Cmty. award, IRS, 1985, Humanitarian award, People's Choice bd. dirs., 1986, Keys to the City, Compton, 1987, Feeding the Hungry spl. award, 1987; named Exec. Adminstr. of Yr., Compton, Calif., 1983—84, Bus. Woman of Yr., CBS TV, 1984, Citizen of Week, KNX News, 1985, Bus. Woman of Yr., ACC News, 1986, Miss Christianity, ACC Churches and Cmty. News, 1987; Unique Partnership in Conservation award grant, So. Calif. Gas Co., 1986. Avocations: checkers, chess, cooking, dominoes, interior decorating.

WILLIAMS, ELIZABETH NUTT, psychologist, educator; BA in Psychology, Stanford U., 1989; MA in Counseling Psychology, U. Md., 1994, PhD in Counseling Psychology, 1997. Lic. psychologist Md. Asst. prof. psychology St. Mary's Coll. Md., St. Mary's City, 1997—2003, assoc. prof. psychology, 2003—, coord. women, gender and sexuality program, 2004—. Recipient Milton Dean Havron Social Scis. award, U. Md., 1996, Homer L. Dodge award for excellence in tchg., St. Mary's Coll. Md., 2003. Mem.: NOW, APA, Soc. Psychotherapy Rsch., Phi Beta Kappa (historian Zeta chpt. 1998—2001, pres. Zeta chpt. 2001—03). Office: St Mary's Coll Md Dept Psychology 18952 E Fisher Rd Saint Marys City MD 20686 Business E-Mail: enwilliams@smcm.edu.

WILLIAMS, ELIZABETH YAHN, poet, writer, educator, lawyer; b. Columbus, Ohio, July 20, 1942; d. Wilbert Henry and Elizabeth Dulson (Brophy) Yahn. BA cum laude, Loyola Marymount U., LA, 1964; secondary tchg. credential, UCLA, 1965; JD, Loyola U., 1971. Cert. tchr. h.s. and jr. coll. English and history. Writer, West Covina, Calif., 1964—; designer, 1966-68; tchr. jr./sr. h.s. LA City Schs., Santa Monica, Calif., 1964-65, La Puente H.S. Dist., Calif., 1965-67; legal intern, lawyer Garvey, Ingram, Baker & Uhler, Covina, Calif., 1969-72; lawyer, corp. counsel Avco Fin. Svcs., Inc., Newport Beach, Calif., 1972-74; pvt. practice Santa Ana, Calif., 1974—87; poetry project dir. Frank Craig Poetry Club of the Solana Beach Libr., 2005—06. Mem. faculty continuing edn. State Bar of Calif., 1979; adj. prof. Western State U. Sch. Law, Fullerton, Calif., 1980; mem. fed. cts. com. Calif. State Bar, San Francisco, 1977-80, Pubs. & Writers San Diego, Poets Inc. Author: (1-act plays) Acting-Out Acts, 1990, Grading Graciela, 1992, Boundaries in the Dirt, 1993; author: (lyricist) Peter and the Worry Wrens, 1995; author: (lyricist, narrator) Love in Our Midst, 2000; author: (poetry chapbooks) A Medley of Cherry, 2000, Verses for Violins, 2001, Joy: Moments for Reflection, 2002; co-author: Hither & Yahn II: Partners in Rhyme Take on the Holidays, 2006, Hither & Yahn I: Partners in Rhyme, 2006, Hither & Yahn III: Partners in Rhyme Spring Into Summer, 2007, Hither & Yahn IV: Partners in Rhyme UNCAGED, 2007; editor: The Music of Poetry, 1997, 1998, Pathways, 2009; co-editor: Seasonal Reflective, 2009; contbr. articles to profl. jours.; panelist (TV show) Action Now, 1971, interviewee Women, 1987; scriptwriter, dir.: TV show Four/Four, 1994; author: (3-act adaptation) Saved in Sedona, 1995; scriptwriter, prodr., host: TV show Guildelights to Success, 1996, Oceanside Pub. Libr's, National Author's Day, 2008—. Mem. alumni bd. Loyola-Marymount U., LA, 1980-84; mem. adv. bd. Rancho Santiago Coll., Santa Ana, 1983-84; spkr. Commn. on Status on Women, Santa Ana, 1979. Finalist San Diego Book & Writing awards, 2008; grantee, Ford Found., 1964—65, SLS, 2006, Va. Ctr. Creative Arts, France, 2008; scholar, Nat. Audio Theatre Found., 2004; Writer's grantee, Vt. Ctr. Studio, 2003, French scholar, Ohio State U., 1959, acad. scholar, Loyola-Marymount U., 1960—64, Book Expo 2000 scholar, Pubs. Mktg. Assn.-San Diego Pubs. Alliance Pub Mktg. U., 2000, Writing scholar, Episcopal Diocese of L.A., 1999. Mem.: Vista Village Idiots Literary Soc., Sunset Poets, Nat. League Am. Pen Women, Magee Park Poets, Calif. Women Lawyers (life; bd. dirs. 1975—76, co-founder), Phi Theta Kappa (life most disting. hon.). Avocation: art. Address: PO Box 233 San Luis Rey CA 92068-0233 Personal E-mail: dreywilliams@hotmail.com, joyinpoetry@yahoo.com.

WILLIAMS, ELLA, healthcare educator; b. Oct. 29, 1941; d. Gus and Velma Dukes Sr.; m. Charles B. Williams, Apr. 15, 1981; children: Beverly A. Jackson, Glynn D. Jackson, Donatus C. Mbaliri. BS in Edn., Southern U., Baton Rouge; postgrad., U. Houston. Unit mgr. Earl K. Long Hosp., Baton Rouge, 1963—72; tchr. Holy Child's Coll., Lagos, Nigeria, 1976—80; owner, mgr. Health Care Co., Houston, 1980—. Author: A Cultural Shock, 1984. Facility Home for Disabled and Mentally Challenger, Morgania, La., 2005—07. Grantee, U. Houston, 1980. Mem.: Houston Bd. Realtons. Avocations: travel, fishing, writing, history. Home: 7239 Mitchell Ln Morganza LA 70759-3109

WILLIAMS, ELLA MARILYN, mathematics educator; b. Raleigh, NC, Aug. 15, 1950; d. Thomas Harold and Ella W. BA, Bennett Coll., Greensboro, NC, 1972; MA, N.C. Ctrl. U., Durham, 1973. Cert. math. tchr., D.C. Tchr. D.C. Pub. Schs., Washington, 1973, Greensboro (N.C.) Pub. Schs., 1973-77; math. specialist U. D.C., Washington, 1977-80; tchr. DC Pub. Schs., Washington, 1980—. Participant in Honors Tchrs. Workshop, Mich. State U., East Lansing, 1987, St. John's Ins. Inst. for Educators, 2003, Nat. Security Agy. Summer Inst., 2005. Nominee for Presidential award, DC Pub. Schs. Math. Dept., Washington, 1987 Mem. Nat. Coun. Tchrs. of Math. (rep. standards implementation com., rep. 2000—, chmn. nominating com. 1989-2005, Rep., 1999—), D.C. Coun. Tchrs. of Math. (nominating com. 1989-2006). Home: 3715 Alabama Ave SE # B Washington DC 20020-2403 Office: DC Pub Schs Eastern High 1700 E Capitol St NE Washington DC 20003 Office Phone: 202-698-4500. Personal E-mail: emarilynw@aol.com.

WILLIAMS, ELLEN C., lobbyist, political organization worker; children: Sam, Joey. BA, U. Ky., 1980. Staff asst. Congressman Larry Hopkins, 1982; exec. dir. Young Rep. Fedn., 1983; staff Senator Bob Kasten, 1986—88; mem. Bush Quayle Campaign, 1988, Reagan Bush Campaign, 1984, Dole Kemp campaign, 1996, Bush Cheney campaign, 2000; staff Nat. Republican Senate Committee, 1988—89; regional polit. dir. Nat. Rep. Com.; exec. dir. Rep. Party of Ky., 1990—92, chmn., 1999—2004; vice chmn. Ky. Public Service Commission, 2004—05; commissioner for local devel. Gov. Kentucky, 2004—05; founder, lobbyist Capital Network LLC, Frankfort, Ky., 2006—; apptd. to Bd. Gov. by US Pres. George W. Bush USPS, 2006—. Cons. Lexington Bluegrass Bd. of Realtors; active Anderson County United Way Bd., Ch. of Lawrenceburg. Office: 519 Murray St Frankfort KY 40601 Office Phone: 502-227-1065.

WILLIAMS, ELLEN D., physics professor; BS in Chemistry, Mich. State U., 1976; PhD, Calif. Inst. Tech., 1981. Summer rschr. Miles Lab., Elkhart, Ind., 1974, Kodak Rsch. Lab., Rochester, NY, 1976; tchg. asst. Calif. Inst. Tech., 1976—79, grad. rsch. asst., 1977—81; rsch. assoc. Dept. Physics and Astronomy U. Md., 1981—83, asst. prof., 1983—87, assoc. prof., 1987—91, assoc. prof. Inst. Physical Sci. and Tech., 1990—91, dir. Chem. Physics Program, 1993—95, prof. Dept. Physics, Inst. Physical Sci. and Tech., 1991—, disting. prof., 2000—. Editl. bd. Nano Letters, 2003—. Recipient E.W. Mueller award, U. Wis., 1996, David Turnbull award, Materials Rsch. Soc., 2003; named Outstanding Woman of Yr., U. Md., 1996; Nat. Sci. Found. fellowship, 1976—79, IBM Grad. fellowship, 1979—80, Cottrell Rsch. Grant, 1983. Fellow: Japan Soc. for Promotion of Sci., Am. Vacuum Soc., Am. Physical Soc. (physics policy com. 2005—, David Adler Lectureship award 2001, Maria Goeppert-Mayer award 1990); mem.: Am. Acad. Arts & Sciences, NAS (bd. army svc. and tech. 2007—). Office: Dept Physics Univ Maryland John S Toll Physics Bldg College Park MD 20742-4111 Office Phone: 301-405-6156. E-mail: edw@physics.umd.edu.

WILLIAMS, ENID ROBERTA (ENID W. TROLL), psychologist, nurse; b. Long Beach, Calif., Mar. 1, 1923; d. Clarence Strong and Zita Marie (Stafford) Williams; m. John Hans Troll, Sept. 4, 1963. BSN, St. Louis U., 1945; MA in Voc. Guidance, Columbia U., Tchrs. Coll., 1958, profl. diploma in Rehab. counseling, 1958; postgrad., Rutgers U., 1961; MS in Psychiat. Nursing, Boston U., 1976, EdD in Human Svcs. and Counseling, 1982. Intern psychology Child Study Ctr., Phila., 1961-62; pre-doctoral fellow psychology NJ Dept. Insts. and Agys., 1962-63; school psychologist NYC and Conn. Pub. Schs., 1964-68; staff psychologist Harlem Valley State Hosp., Wingdale, N.Y., 1969-70; staff nurse, psychiat. The Arbour Hosp., Jamaica Plain, Mass., 1974—98; post-doctoral fellow geriatric mental health Harvard Med. Sch., Dept. Psychiatry, Boston, 1985-86, rsch. on effects of anesthesia on neuropsychological functioning; post-doctoral intern psychology Metrowest Youth Guidance Ctr., Framingham, Mass., 1988-89; cons. in psychology Boston, 1989—98. Recipient U.S. Pub. Health Nursing scholar, 1942-45,; grantee NIMH, Sch. Nursing, Boston U., 1973-74. Home: 1025 Chelwood Park Blvd NE Apt 134 Albuquerque NM 87112-5941 Personal E-mail: meadowlark411@aol.com.

WILLIAMS, ERIC S., cardiologist, educator; b. Louisville, 1946; MD, Ind. U., 1971. Diplomate Internal Medicine 1974, Cardiovascular Disease 1977. Intern, internal medicine Ind. U. Hosps., Indpls., 1971—72, resident, cardiology, 1972—73, fellow, 1973—75, resident, cardiology, 1975—76; prof. medicine, assoc. dir. Ind. U. Sch. Medicine, Dept. Medicine, Krannert Inst. Cardiology, Methodist Hosp., Indpls. Co-prog. dir., Clarian Cardiovascular Ctr. Ind. U. Sch. Medicine, Dept. Medicine, Krannert Inst. Cardiology, assoc. dean for Clarian Affairs. Mem.: Am. Coll. Cardiology (pres. Ind. chpt., chmn ECG com.), Am. Heart Assn., Nat. Bd. Governers. Office: Methodist Hosp Rm KI E480 1701 Senate Blvd Indianapolis IN 46202-1239 Office Phone: 317-962-0551. Business E-Mail: ewillia@iupui.edu.

WILLIAMS, ERVIN EUGENE, religious organization administrator; b. Corning, NY, Feb. 25, 1923; s. Douglas Lewis and Mina P. (Barnes) Williams; m. Ruth Evelyn Snyder, June 12, 1945; children: Roger Eugene, Virginia Ruth. Student, Toccoa Falls Coll., Ga., 1939, Cornell U., 1942; BA, Pa. State U., 1949; MA, Mich. State U., 1961, PhD in Communications, 1971. Ordained to ministry Ind. Bapt. Ch., 1950. Acad. dean Greensburg (Pa.) Bible Inst., 1949-51; min. Bapt. Ch., New Kensington, Pa., 1951-53; instr. Pa. State U., 1953-55; sr. min. East Lansing (Mich.) Trinity Ch., 1955-71; vis. prof. Trinity Evang. Div. Sch., Deerfield, Ill., 1968-71, prof. comm. and practical theology, 1971-77, dir. D Ministry program, 1975-76; gen. dir. Am. Missionary Fellowship, Villanova, Pa., 1977-92; exec. min. Ch. of the Apostles, Atlanta, 1993-95; ch. and instl. cons. Smyrna, Ga., 1995—; sr. pastor New Life Bible Ch., Man-O-War Cay, Abaco, The Bahamas, 1997—98; assoc. Mattocks & Assoc., Inc., Fairfax, Va., 2005—. Chaplain Mich. State U., East Lansing, 1955—71; cons. Haggai Inst. Advanced Leadership Tng., Atlanta, 1969—95; lectr. Calvary Bapt. Coll., Kansas City, Mo., 1962, Haggai Inst. Third World Leaders, Singapore, 1970—95; cons. to mission bds., 1967—76; assoc. dir. Camp of Woods, Speculator, NY, 1971—77; Staley lectr. Robert Wesleyan Coll., North Chili, NY, 1973, Judson Coll., Elgin, Ill., 1977—79. Author: What Say You?, 2007, Joy Where it Counts, 2007, Airplane Views of the Bible, 2007, A Second War on Terror, 2007, Divine Sovereignty and Human Responsibility, 2007; contbr. articles to profl. jours. Trustee Gospel Vols., Speculator, 1963—93, Dorothy H. Theis Meml. Found., Sierra Vista, Ariz., 1987—95; mem. bd. regents Owosso (Mich.) Coll., 1971—73. Pilot USAAF, 1942—45, prisoner of war, ETO. Decorated DFC, Air medal with 2 oak leaf clusters, POW medal, ETO Campaign medal with 6 clusters, Victory medal; recipient Presdl. citation. Mem.: Mich. Acad. Arts and Scis., Christian Assn. Psychol. Studies, Aircraft Owners and Pilots Assn., Nat. Sunday Sch. Assn., Phi Beta Kappa, Alpha Kappa Delta, Phi Kappa Phi, Pi Gamma Mu. E-mail: msupsu@bellsouth.net. *It is much more difficult to conceal ignorance and prejudice than it is to acquire knowledge and fairness.*

WILLIAMS, EVAN, Internet company executive; b. Nebr., Mar. 31, 1972; m. Sara Morishige; 1 child. Web application developer O'Reilly Media, Intel, Hewlett Packard; co-founder, CEO (and developer of Blogger) Pyra Labs (acquired by Google), 1998—2003; head, Blogger Google, 2003—04; co-founder Oden Inc. podcasting (acquired by Sonic Mountain in 2007), 2004, Obvious Corp. (spun off Twitter, Inc.), 2006, Twitter, Inc., San Francisco, 2007, chmn., 2007—08, CEO, 2008—. Named (with Paul Bausch and Meg Hourihan) People of Yr., PC Mag., 2004; named one of 50 Who Matter Now, Business 2.0, 2007, The World's Most Influential People, TIME mag., 2009. Office: Twitter Inc 539 Bryant St Ste 402 San Francisco CA 94107-1269 Office Phone: 866-924-2008.*

WILLIAMS, FRANK J., retired state supreme court chief justice, historian, writer; b. Providence, Aug. 24, 1940; s. Frank and Natalie L. (Corelli) W.; m. Virginia E. Miller, Aug. 24, 1966. BA, Boston U., 1962, JD, 1970; MS in Taxation, Bryant Coll., Smithfield, RI, 1986, LHD (hon.), 2004, Lincoln Coll., Ill., 1987; LLD (hon.), So. New England Sch. Law, 2001; LHD (hon.), Johnson & Wales U., 2002, Bridgewater Coll., Va.; Lincoln diploma of honor, Lincoln Meml. U., Harrogate, Tenn., 2002; LLD (hon.), Roger Williams U., Bristol, RI, 2004, Mass. Sch. Law, 2004, U. RI, Kingston, 2006, Okla. State U., 2007. Bar: RI 1970, US Dist. Ct. RI 1970, US Supreme Ct. 1976. Assoc. Tillinghast, Collins & Graham, Providence, 1970-75, Leonard Decof Ltd., Providence, 1976-78; law clk. Graham, Reid, Ewing & Stapleton, Providence, 1969; law clk., adminstrv. asst. RI Atty. Gen., Providence, 1967-68; pres. Frank J. Williams Ltd., attys.-at-law, Providence, 1978-95; assoc. justice RI Superior Ct., 1995-2001; chief justice RI Supreme Ct., 2001—08, ret., 2008. Judge of probate Town of Hopkinton, RI, 1978-82, 84-90, solicitor, 1978-82, 84-87; judge of probate Town of West Greenwich, RI, 1984-86, 92-95, solicitor, 1984-92, asst. solicitor, 1992-95; dep. judge of probate, 1987-92; solicitor Town of Coventry, RI, 1972-74, 76-78, Town of Barrington, RI, 1993-95, Town of Bristol, RI, 1995, Town of South Kingstown, RI, 1995; past spl. counsel Towns of Westerly, Bristol, Hopkinton, South Kingstown, City of Providence; atty. Town of Smithfield Sewer Authority, 1974-90; legis. counsel RI Retail Fedn., 1975-93, Credit Info. Bur., RI Mortgage Bankers Assn., 1992-95; adj. prof. Roger Williams U. Sch. of Law, 1997—, US Naval War Coll., 2003—; lectr. bus. and legal practice RI Sch. Design, Providence, 1976-80; panel of arbitrators Am. Arbitration Assn., panel of mediators RI Superior Ct., 1993-95; mem. RI Bd. Bar Examiners, 1987-95, chair, 1995; chair RI Housing and Mortgage Fin. Corp., 1995, Lincoln Forum, 1996—; apptd. to Mil. Commns. Rev. Panel for mil. tribunals, Guantanamo Bay, Cuba, 2004-06; chief judge, ct. milt. commission rev., 2007. Pres. Lincoln Group of Boston, 1976—88, Abraham Lincoln Assn., Springfield, Ill., 1986—95, Ulysses S. Grant Assn., 1990—; elected del. RI Constnl. Conv., 1986; elected town moderator Richmond, RI, 1992—95; dist. moderator Chariho Regional Sch. Dist., 1994; bd. dirs. John E. Fogarty Found. for Persons with Mental Retardation, 1975—, South County Hosp., 1995—2004, RI Coun. for the Humanities, 2001—07, Narragan-set Coun. Boy Scouts Am., 1969—80, 1998—2001. Capt. US Army, 1962—67, Germany and Vietnam. Decorated Bronze Star, Combat Infantryman's badge, Army Commendation medal, Air medal with 2 oak leaf clusters, Republic of Vietnam Gallantry Cross with silver star; recipient Disting. Eagle Scout award, 2005; named Hon. Brigadier Gen., R.I. Militia, 2003; named to RI Heritage Hall of Fame, 2004. Fellow: ATLA (jud.); mem.: RI Bar Assn. (chmn. new lawyers adv. com. 1976—87, ho. of dels. 1986—93, chmn. mcpl. law com. 1993), Conf. Chief Justices (bd. dirs. 2004—06), Am. Law Inst., Nat. Assn. for Ct. Mgmt., Am. Judges Assn., Am. Antiquarian Soc., Phi Alpha Delta, Alpha Phi Sigma, Phi Sigma Alpha. Roman Catholic. Office: 250 Benefit St Providence RI 02903 Office Phone: 401-222-3290. Business E-Mail: alincoln@courts.ri.us.*

WILLIAMS, FRANKLIN CADMUS, JR., bibliographer; b. Palestine, Tex., July 30, 1941; s. Franklin Cadmus and Cathryn Lucille (Pessoney) W. BA, Baylor U., 1963; MA, Stephen F. Austin State U., 1965; PhD, U. Wis., 1975. Cert. in secondary edn. English and History. Teaching fellow Stephen F. Austin State U., Nacogdoches, Tex., 1964-65, U. Wis., Madison, 1965-68; instr. English Austin Peay State U., Clarksville, Tenn., 1970-71; adj. asst. prof. East Tex. State U., Commerce, 1975; asst. prof. English Jarvis Christian Coll., Hawkins, Tex., 1976-78, 79-81; ind. scholar Palestine, Tex., 1981—; owner, bibliographer Goldsmith Archive, Palestine, 1981—. Cons. Diocese of Galveston-Houston, 1977-84, Tex. State Hist. Assn., Austin, 1988; speaker, editor Jarvis Christian Coll., Hawkins, Tex., 1976-78, 79-81; nat. teaching fellow Office Edn., Washington, 1976-77; del. to Baylor U., U. Wis. System, Madison, 1981. Author: Lone Star Bishops: The Roman Catholic Hierarchy in Texas, 1997; contbr. articles to profl. jours. Mem. Modern Lang. Assn., Tex. State Hist. Assn., Tex. Cath. Hist. Soc., Baylor Alumni Assn. (life), Wis. Alumni Assn. (life), Sigma Tau Delta. Avocations: reading, record collecting, historical genealogy, tennis, swimming. Office: PO Box 96 Palestine TX 75802-0096

WILLIAMS, FREDA VIDELL, speech pathology/audiology services professional; d. Norman Freeman Williams and Coreen Videlle Davis; children: Shannon O'Neal Otwell, Michael Scott Otwell. MS in Speech-Pathology and Audiology, Fla. State U., Tallahassee. Speech-lang. pathologist Sunland Tng. Ctr., Marianna, Fla., 1979, Jackson County Schs., 1979—79, Houston County Schs., Dothan, Ala., 1980—80, Sunland Tng. Ctr., Marianna, 1980—80, Wash. County Schs., Chipley, Fla., 1981—83, pvt. practice, 1983—87, Leon County Schs., Tallahassee, 1987—88, Programs Infants and Children, Anchorage, 1988—89, Lauderdale County Schs., Meridian, Miss., 1989—90, Dothan City Schs., Ala., 1990—97, Programs Infants and Children, Anchorage, 1997—99, Bay Dist. Schs., Panama City, Fla., 1999—2002, coord. speech-lang. pathology, 2002—. Coord. Emerald Coast Speech-Lang. Pathology Consortium, Panama City, 2004—. Builder Habitat Humanity, Panama City, 2005—06; councilwoman Dem. Exec. Com., Marianna, 1981—82; builder United Meth. Ch., Oaxaca, Mexico, 1983—83. Mem.: Am. Speech-Lang.-Hearing Assn. (assoc.). Conservative. Avocations: painting, swimming, walking, travel.

WILLIAMS, FREDERICK TYRONE, entrepreneur, pastor; b. Monroe, La., Mar. 27, 1982; s. Felix Anthony and Alberta Joyce Williams; m. Rakiyyah Nitaka Hart, July 27, 2005; children: Taylor Jerome Hart, Madisson Tiana Hope, Kennedy Caleb Aaron, Phoebe Laken McKenzie. BS in Bus. Mgmt., Kaplan U., Ft. Lauderdale, Fla., 2006. Microsoft Office Certified Olive Harvey Coll., Chgo., 2004; Church Planter North Am. Mission Bd., Ga., 2004; Area Youth Development Chgo. AYD, 2005; Television and Video Production DeKalb H.S. of Tech., Ga., 2000. Youth pastor Light of the World, Chgo., 2001—05, Christian Worship Ctr., Chgo., 2005—; case mgr. Riviera Manor Nursing Home, Chgo., 2002—06; CEO, chmn. Fred T. Williams Ministries, Chgo., 2006, Impact to Empower Comm., LLC, Chgo., 2006; CEO Nu Wine Graphics and Design, Chgo., 2006—. Singer, praise and worship leader: gospel choir workshop Nat. Black Coll. Choir Gospel Workshop of Am.; actor, composer, editor: (short film for television) Youth With A Purpose Motion Picture; musical recording, Undivided Attention by Out-World. Bd. mem. Christian Worship Ctr., Chgo., 2005. Democrat. Avocations: writing poetry / musical composition, public speaking, musical performances, travel. Office: Fred T Williams Ministries 1308 W 103rd St Suite 2 Chicago IL 60643 Office Fax: 773-881-8675; Home Fax: 773-881-8675. Personal E-mail: pastorfredwilliams@yahoo.com. Business E-Mail: contact@fredtwilliams.com.

WILLIAMS, GARY MURRAY, pathologist, educator; b. Regina, Sask., Can., May 7, 1940; s. Murray Austin and Selma Ruby (Domstad) W.; m. Julia Christine Lundberg; children: Walter, Jeffrey, Ingrid. BA, Washington and Jefferson Coll., 1963; MD, U. Pitts, 1967. Diplomate Am. Bd. Pathology, Am. Bd. Toxicology. Assoc. prof. pathology Temple U., Phila., 1971-75; mem. Fels Rsch. Inst., Phila., 1971-75; rsch. prof. N.Y. Med. Coll., Valhalla, 1975-98, prof. pathology, environ. pathology and toxicology, dir., 1999—. Mem. working group Internat. Agy. Rsch. on Cancer, Lyon, France, 1976, 80, 1982—83, 1985—87, 1989, 91, 1996—99; mem. subcom. on upper reference levels of nutrients NRC, 1999—2003, com. health effects dioxin, 2004—06; advisor joint expert com. on food additives WHO, 2001—08. Mem. editl. bd. Archives of Toxicology, 1988—, assoc. editor Food and Chem. Toxicology, 2005—; contbr. more than 510 articles to profl. jours.; editor or co-editor 8 books, —. Lt. comdr. USPHS, 1969-71. Recipient Sheard-Sanford award Am. Soc. Clin. Pathologists U. Pitts., 1967, Dean's Disting. Rsch. award NY Med. Coll., 2006, 50th Anniversary 5 Yr. Svc. medal WHO, 2006; named Disting. Scientist Am. Chem. Soc., 2005. Fellow Internat. Acad. Toxicol. Pathology (accreditation com. 2000), Royal Coll. Pathologists; mem. Soc. Toxicology (Arthur J. Lehman award 1982, Lectr. award 1996, Advancement Animal Welfare award 2002, Merit award, 2009), Soc. Toxicol. Pathology, Phi Beta Kappa, Alpha Omega Alpha. Home: 8 Elm Rd Scarsdale NY 10583-1410 Office: Dept Pathology NY Med Coll Valhalla NY 10595-1549 Home Phone: 914-723-8739; Office Phone: 914-594-4146. Business E-Mail: gary_williams@nymc.edu.

WILLIAMS, GEORGE ABIAH, physics educator; b. Bklyn., Apr. 1, 1931; s. George A. and Helen (Burchard) W.; divorced; children: Robin, Scott, Brian. BA, Colgate U., 1952; PhD, U. Ill., 1956. Research assoc. in physics Stanford U., 1956-59; mem. tech. staff Bell Tel. Labs., Murray Hill, N.J., 1959-63; vis. asst. prof. physics Cornell U., 1963-64; asso. prof. physics U. Utah, Salt Lake City, 1964-69, prof. physics, 1969—, asso. chmn. dept., 1975-82. Author: Elementary Physics: Atoms, Waves, Particles, 1969, 2d edit., 1976; (with R. Doerhoff and M. Bolen) Challenges to Science: Physical Science, 1973, (with Doerhoff, Bolen & R. Barnes) 2d edit., 1979. Mem. Am. Phys. Soc., Phi Beta Kappa. Home: 3415 Honeycut Rd # 7A Salt Lake City UT 84106-3811

WILLIAMS, GEORGE CHRISTOPHER, biologist, ecology and evolution educator; b. Charlotte, NC, May 12, 1926; s. George Felix and Margaret (Steuart) W.; m. Doris Lee Calhoun, Jan. 25, 1951; children: Jacques, Sibyl, Judith, Phoebe. AB, U. Calif., Berkeley, 1949; PhD in Biology, UCLA, 1955; ScD (hon.), Queen's U., Kingston, Ont., Can., 1995, SUNY, Stony Brook, 2000. Instr. and asst. prof. Mich. State U., East Lansing, 1955-60; assoc. prof. dept. ecology and evolution SUNY, Stony Brook, 1960-66, prof., 1966-90, emeritus prof. Adj. prof. Queens U., Kingston, Ont., Can., 1980-95. Author: Adaptation and Natural Selection, 1966, Sex and Evolution, 1975, Natural Selection: Domains, Levels and Challenges, 1992, The Pony Fish's Glow, 1997; co-author: (with R.M. Nesse) Why We Get Sick: The New Science of Darwinian Medicine, 1995; co-editor: (with James Paradis) Evolution and Ethics, 1989; editor: Quar. Rev. Biology, SUNY, 1965-98; contbr. article to profl. jours. With U.S. Army, 1944-46. Recipient Eminent Ecologist award Ecol. Soc. Am., 1989, Crafoord prize Royal Swedish Acad., 1999; fellow Ctr. Adv. Study Behavioral Sci., Stanford, 1981-82, Guggenheim Found., 1988-89. Fellow AAAS, NAS (Daniel Giraud Elliot medal 1992), Soc. Study Evolution (v.p. 1973, pres. 1989), Am. Soc. Ichthyologists and Herpetologists, Am. Soc. Naturalists (editor 1974-79), Icelandic Natural History Soc. Home Phone: 631-650-3122.

WILLIAMS, GEORGE LEO, historian, retired secondary school educator, landmark director; b. NYC, June 29, 1931; s. Leo Dominick and Cathryn Margaret (Schellderfer) W.; m. Adelia Gilda Musa, Feb. 26, 1958; children: Adelia, Marina, Gilda. BA, CUNY, 1953, MA, 1955; PhD, NYU, 1966. Tchr. Port Washington (N.Y.) Pub. Schs., 1953, chairperson integrated studies, 1960-65, coord. Amherst project, 1968-69, chairperson English dept., 1970-90; adminstrv. asst. secondary and higher edn. dept. NYU, NYC, 1965-66. Adj. prof. NYU, 1966-74, Adelphi U., Garden City, N.Y. 1967-69, Hofstra U., Hempstead, N.Y., 1967-74; chmn. profl. growth and devel. com. Port Washington Pub. Schs., 1973-90, chmn. bicentennial com. 1989-90, mem. policy bd. Port Washington Tchr. Ctr., 1987-90; mem. alumni bd. Queens Coll. History Dept., 1996-2000; dir., chmn., exhibit com. Sandminers Monument, Inc., 2004—. Co-author: (play) The Triumph of the Constitution, 1988, Secession: A Township Divided, 2005; author: Fascist Thought and Totalitarianism in Italy's Secondary Schools: Theory and Practice, 1922-1943, 1993, Port Washington in the Twentieth Century: Places and People, 1995, Papal Genealogy: The Families and Descendants of the Popes, 1998, (play) Remembrances of the First Colonial Settlement, 1993, A Family HIstory, Book I, 1990, Book II, 2006; contbg. author: Erziehungsstaaten, 1998; editor Port Arrow Community Newsletter, 1973-84, Cow Neck Peninsula Hist. Soc. Newsletter, 1974-77, Cow Neck Peninsula Hist. Soc. Jour., 2001—; contbg. editor L.I. Forum, 1985-2004; author, prodr. (video) Port Washington into the 21st Century, 1996. Chair landmarks com. Cow Neck Peninsula Hist. Soc., Port Washington, 1980—97, trustee, 1974—77, trustee emeritus, 2005—; commr. landmarks com. Village of Port Washington North, 1983—; pres. Hist. Soc. North Hempstead, 2001—04, pres. emeritus, 2005—; mem., chairperson Hist. Landmark Preservation Commn., North Hempstead, NY, 1984—, chmn., 1991—; chairperson 1701 Roslyn Grist Mil Com., 1997—; mem. Port Washington Continuing Edn. Adv. Coun., 1988—97; co-chair Roslyn Clock Tower Com., 1994—96; mem. Preservation League of N.Y., Bigelow Soc., N.Y. Pub. Libr., W.A.R. Goodwin Soc.; grant writer Dodge House Restoration Com.; mem. orgnl. com. Landmark on Main St., 1984—90; mem. Cow Neck Peninsula Hist. Soc. Dodge House Restoration Com.; adv. bd. records Town of North Hempstead, 1994—; mem. 1998 ann. com. L.I.R.R. to Port Washington; mem. Bay Walk Nautical Arts Com., 2006—; planning bd. mem. Long Island North Shore Heritage Area Bd., 2009; mem. North Shore Long Island Heritage Area Com., 2009—. Recipient environ. award Residents for a More Beautiful Port Washington, 1994, numerous Certs. of Appreciation, Civic award for Outstanding Cmty. Svc., Port Washington Rotary, 2001, Cert. of Appreciation, Port Washington Police Dist., 2001, Exec. Citation, Nassau County, 2001, citation N.Y. State Assembly, 2001, 07, Legis. citation Nassau County, 2001, Queens Coll. Dept. History Cert. Appreciation, 2002, Town of North Hempstead's Proclamation, 2002, 07, Cmty. Leadership award Cow Neck Peninsula Hist. Soc., 2007, State NY Office of Comptr. Proclamation, 2007. Mem.: Friends of the Arts, Friends of Planting Fields, Nat. Trust Hist. Preservation, N.Y. State Mus. Assocs., Fulbright Assn., Am. Hist. Assn. (cert. recognition 1988), Port Washington Tchrs. Assn. (v.p. 1963—64, bd. dirs. 1966—74, newsletter editor 1990—92, founder and 1st pres. ret. tchrs. chpt. 1991), Soc. for Preservation L.I. Antiquities, Assn. Pub. Historicans of N.Y. State, N.Y. State Hist. Assn., N.Y. Geneal./Biog. Soc., Residents for a More Beautiful Port Washington (Environ. Quality Recognition award 2003), Roslyn Landmark Soc., Pi Sigma Alpha, Phi Alpha Theta, Phi Beta Kappa. Home: 84 Radcliff Ave Port Washington NY 11050-1600 E-mail: geoleowms@aol.com.

WILLIAMS, GEORGE WALTON, language educator; b. Charleston, SC, Oct. 10, 1922; s. Ellison Adger and Elizabeth Simonton (Dillingham) W.; m. Harriet Porcher Simons, Nov. 28, 1953; children: George Walton Jr., Ellison Adger II, Harriet Porcher Stoney. BA, Yale U., 1947; MA, U. Va., 1949, PhD, 1957. Asst. cashier Carolina Savs. Bank, Charleston, 1949-54; asst. prof. English, Duke U., 1957-63, asso. prof., 1963-67, prof., 1967, chmn. dept. English, 1982-86, prof. emeritus, 1993—. Dir. summer inst. Commn. on English, Coll. Entrance Exam. Bd., 1962; pres. Durham Savoyards, Ltd., 1966-68, 81-82; sr. fellow Coop. Program in Humanities, Duke-U. N.C., 1969; Historiographer, Diocese of S.C., 1960-78; vis. prof. U.S. Mil. Acad., 1982-83 Author: St. Michael's, Charleston, 1751-1951, 1951, rev. edit., 2001, Image and Symbol in the Sacred Poetry of Richard Crashaw, 1963, The Craft of Printing and the Publication of Shakespeare's Plays, 1985, 5 children's books; editor: Romeo and Juliet, 1964, Complete Poetry of Richard Crashaw, 1970, Jacob Eckhard's Choirmaster's Book, 1971, Shakespeare's Speech-Headings, 1997; contbg. editor Dramatic Works of Beaumont and Fletcher, 1966-96; assoc. gen. editor Arden Shakespeare, 1996—. With US Army, 1943—45, ETO. Decorated Combat Inf. badge; recipient Outstanding Civilian Service medal Dept. Army, 1983; Guggenheim Found. fellow, 1977-78; Huntington Library fellow, 1981 Mem. MLA (com. on new variorum 1980-92, chmn. Shakespeare divsn. 1990), South Atlantic MLA (pres. 1980-81, J.H. Fisher award 2001), Southeastern Renaissance Conf. (editor 1960-70, 91-95, pres. 1973, hon. life 2002), SC Hist. Soc., Malone, Carolina Yacht Club (Charleston), St. Cecilia Soc. (Charleston), Elizabethan Club Yale U., N.Am. Guild Change Ringers, Phi Beta Kappa, Phi Kappa Phi. Home: 1 Tradd St Charleston SC 29401 Office: Duke U Dept English PO Box 90015 Durham NC 27708-0015 Office Phone: 919-684-5827.

WILLIAMS, GERALD ROSS, orthopedist, surgeon; b. Ft. Myers, Fla., Sept. 21, 1958; s. Gerald Ross Williams and Anna Boyce; m. Robin Kazanjian, June 10, 1984; children: Mark Edward, Alexis Anna. BS in Chemistry, Ursinius Coll., 1980; MD, Temple U., 1984. Diplomate Am. Bd. Orthop. Surgery, 1992. Intern, resident U. Tex. Health Sci. Ctr., San Antonio, 1984—89, fellow shoulder surgery; chief shoulder and elbow svc. U. Pa., Phila., 1999—. Editor: Shoulder Disorders- Diagnosis and Management, 1999, Shoulder and Elbow Arthroplasty, 2005. Office: Pa Orthop Inst 1 Cupp Pavilion 39th and Market Sts Philadelphia PA 19104 Business E-Mail: gerald.williams@uphs.upenn.edu.

WILLIAMS, H. THOMAS (TOM WILLIAMS), academic administrator, physicist, educator; b. Hampton, Va. BS in Physics, U. Va., 1965, PhD in Physics, 1967. NSF post-doctoral rsch. fellow Nat. Bur. Stds., 1967—69; rschr. Inst. for Theoretical Physics, U. Erlangen-Nuernberg, Germany, 1970—71; staff scientist Kaman Scis. Corp., Colorado Springs, Colo., 1971—73; mem. faculty Washington and Lee U., Lexington, Va., 1974—, assoc. dean, 1986—89, chair dept. physics, 1989—2000, physics prof., 2007—, Edwin A. Morris prof. physics, 1994—, chief acad. officer, provost, 2003—07. Cons. Nat. Bur. Stds., 1974—86, Los Alamos Sci. Lab., 1987—93. Office: Washington and Lee Univ Lexington VA 24450 Business E-Mail: williamsh@wlu.edu.

WILLIAMS, HAROLD MARVIN, lawyer, retired foundation, academic and federal agency administrator; b. Phila., Jan. 5, 1928; s. Louis W. and Sophie (Fox) W.; m. Nancy Englander; children: Ralph A., Susan J., Derek M. AB, UCLA, 1946; JD, Harvard Law Sch., 1949; postgrad. in law, U. So. Calif., 1955-59; DHL (hon.), Johns Hopkins U., 1987, Occidental Coll., 1997, Calif. State U., 1998. Bar: Calif. 1950. Pvt. practice, LA, 1950, 1953—55; with Hunt Food and Industries Inc., 1955-68, v.p., 1958-60, exec. v.p., 1960-68; gen. mgr. Hunt-Wesson Foods, 1964-66, pres., 1966-68, Hunt Food and Industries Inc., 1968; chmn. bd., fin. com. Norton Simon, 1968—70; prof. mgmt. UCLA, 1970-77; chmn. SEC, Washington, 1977-81; pres., CEO J. Paul Getty Trust, 1981-98, pres. emeritus; of counsel Skadden Arps et al, 1998—. Pres., dir. Special Investments Securities, Inc., 1961—66. Pub. mem. Nat. Advt. Review Bd., 1971—75; trustee Nat. Humanities Ctr., 1987—93; mem. Coun. Fgn. Rels., Com. Econ. Devel., Pres.' Com. Arts, Humanities, 1993—2001, Commn. Econ. Devel. State Calif., 1973—77; energy coord. City of LA, 1973—74; regent U. Calif., 1983—94; commn. rev. master plan higher edn. State Calif., Calif., 1985—87; co chair Calif. Citizens Commn. Higher Edn.; dir. Ethics Resource Ctr.; mem. Commn. Acad. Presidency; co-chmn. Pub. Comm. LA County Govt.; dir. Pub. Policy Inst. Calif., 1995—2003, Calif. Endowment, 1995—2004, Alliance for Coll. Ready Schs., Alliance for Excellent Edn.; chair bd. visitors UCLA Sch. Arts and Arch. 1st lt. AUS, 1951—53, Korea. Decorated Bronze Star. Mem.: State Bar Calif. Office: J Paul Getty Trust 1200 Getty Center Dr Ste 1100 Los Angeles CA 90049-1668 Office Phone: 310-440-6417. E-mail: hwilliams@getty.edu.

WILLIAMS, HELENA E., rail transportation executive; b. 1955; m. Paul R. Williams. BA with honors, SUNY, Oneonta; JD, St. John's U. Sch. Law, 1981. Bar: New York 1982. Labor counsel Met. Transp. Authority; assoc. counsel Office of Labor Rels., NYC; chief of staff Long Island Bus (formerly Met. Suburban Bus Authority), 1986—93, pres., 1993—98; atty. Schupbach, Williams & Pavone, 1999; dep. exec. Nassau County; sr. counsel Cablevision; pres. Long Island R.R. (LIRR), 2007—; interim pres., CEO Met. Transit Authority (MTA), 2009—. Bd. dirs. Long Island Assn. Named one of The 50 Most Influential Women on Long Island, Long Island Bus. News, 2009; named to The NY Pub. Transit Hall of Fame, 1999. Mem.: Tri-State CEO Rail Assn., Am. Pub. Transit Assn. Office: Met Transp Authority 2 Broadway 16th Fl New York NY 10004*

WILLIAMS, HENRY WARD, JR., lawyer, writer; b. Rochester, NY, Jan. 12, 1930; s. Henry Ward and Margaret Elizabeth (Simpson) W.; m. Barbara Dimmick; children: Edith Williams Linares, Margaret Williams Warren, Sarah Williams Farrand, Ann Williams Treacy, Elizabeth DeLancey Gandy, Victoria Maureen AB, Dartmouth Coll., 1952; LLB, U.Va., 1958. Bar: N.Y. 1959, U.S. Dist. Ct. (we. dist.) N.Y. 1959, U.S. Dist. Ct. (so. dist.) Mich. 1982, U.S. Ct. Appeals (2d cir.) 1963, U.S. Tax Ct. 1960, U.S. Supreme Ct. 1968, D.C. 1978. Ptnr. Harris, Beach & Wilcox, Rochester, 1958—78, Robinson, Williams, Angeloff & Frank, Rochester, 1979—80, Weidman, Williams, Jordon, Angeloff & Frank, Rochester, 1980—82, The Williams Law Office, Rochester, 1982—. Exec. editor Va. Law Rev., 1957-58 Chmn. Genesee Finger/Lakes Regional Planning Coun., 1973-89; majority leader Monroe County Legislature, 1967-73; councilman, dep. supr. Town of Wheatland, N.Y., 2002—; mem. alumni coun. Dartmouth Coll., 1995-99; mem. Nat. Ski Patrol Sys.; founding dir., chair Geva Theatre. Lt. (j.g.) USN, 1952-55. Mem. ABA, N.Y. State Bar Assn., Monroe County Bar Assn. (trustee 1982-85), Landmark Soc. Western NY, Rochester Yacht Club, Lake Yacht Racing Assn. (pres. 1985-87, hon. pres. 1988-90), Royal Ocean Racing Club, Royal Nfld. Yacht Club, Raven Soc., Order of Coif, Omicron Delta Kappa. Office: The Williams Law Office PO Box 8 Scottsville NY 14546-0008 Office Phone: 585-889-3000.

WILLIAMS, HOWARD WALTER, aerospace engineer, engineering executive; b. Evansville, Ind., Oct. 18, 1937; s. Walter Charles and Marie Louise (Bollinger) W.; m. Phyllis Ann Scofield, May 4, 1956 (div. Sept. 1970); m. Marilee Sharon Mulvane, Oct. 30, 1970; children: Deborah, Steven, Kevin, Glenn, Lori, Michele. AA, Pasadena City Coll., 1956; BSME, Calif. State U., Los Angeles, 1967; BSBA, U. San Francisco, 1978; PhD in Comml. Sci. (hon.), London Inst. Rsch., 1992. Turbojet, rocket engr. Aerojet-Gen. Corp., Azusa, Calif., 1956-59, infrared sensor engr., 1959-60, rocket, torpedo engr., 1960-66, power, propulsion mgr. propulsion divsn. Sacramento, 1967-73, high speed ship systems mgr., 1974-78, combustion, power mgr., rocket engine and energy mktg. mgr., 1979-89, dir. strategic planning, 1989-94; strategic analyst, program mgr. Pratt & Whitney Space Propulsion, West Palm Beach, Fla., 1995—2003. Mgmt. cons., 2004—. Author: (with others) Heat Exchangers, 1980, Industrial Heat Exchangers, 1985, History of Liquid Rocket Engine Development in the U.S., 1992, Aerojet: The Creative Company, 1997; co-inventor Closed Cycle Power System, 1969. Recipient Energy Innovation award U.S. Dept. Energy, 1985. Mem. AIAA (sr., Best Paper 1966), Am. Soc. Metals (organizing dir. indsl. heat exch. confs. 1985). Avocation: bicycling. *Personal philosophy: I hope to be as good a parent and grandparent as mine have been.*

WILLIAMS, HUGH ALEXANDER, JR., retired mechanical engineer, consultant; b. Spencer, NC, Aug. 18, 1926; s. Hugh Alexander and Mattie Blanche (Megginson) W.; m. Ruth Ann Gray, Feb. 21, 1950; children: David Gray, Martha Blanche Williams Heidengren. BS in Mech. Engring., NC State U., Raleigh, 1948, MS in Diesel Engring., 1950; postgrad. Inst. Mgmt., Benedictine U., Lisle, Ill., 1977. Registered profl. engr., Ill. Jr. engr.-field svc. engr. Baldwin-Lima Hamilton Corp., Ohio, 1950-52, project engr. Ohio, 1953-55, Electro-Motive divsn. Gen. Motors Corp., La Grange, Ill., 1955-58, sr. project engr., 1958-63, supr. product devel. engine design sect., 1963-86, staff engr. advanced mech. tech., 1986-87. Editor So. Engr., 1947-48; contbr. articles to profl. jours. Trustee Downers Grove San. Dist., Ill., 1965-92, pres., 1974-91, v.p., 1991-92; pres. Ill. Assn. San. Dists., 1976-77, bd. dirs., 1977-89; mem. statewide policy adv. com. Ill. EPA, 1977-79; mem. DuPage County Intergovtl. Task Force Com., 1988-92; elder Presbyn. Ch. Served with USAAC, 1945. Recipient Trustee Svc. award Ill. Assn. San. Dists., 1986, Citizens award Downers Grove Evening chpt. Kiwanis, 1991; Norfolk So. R.R. fellow, 1950. Fellow ASME (chmn. honors and awards com. 1993-96, Diesel and Gas Engine Power Divsn. Spkr. awards 1968, 84, Divsn. citation 1977, 97, Internal Combustion Engine award 1987, exec. com. Internal Combustion Engine divsn. 1981-87, 88-92, chmn. 1985-86, sec. 1988-92); mem. Soc. Automotive Engrs. (life), ASME (chmn. Soichiro Honda medal com. 1987-92, chmn. Internal Combustion Engine Award com. 1993-98), Ill. Assn. Wastewater Agys. (Outstanding Mem. award 1990, hon. mem. 1992), Raleigh Host Lions Club (pres. 1996-97), SAR (pres. Raleigh chpt. 2000-01), St. Andrew's Soc. NC, Jamestowne Soc. (1st NC Co. gov. 2008-09), Masons (32 degree), Sigma Pi. Republican. Achievements include patentee in field. Home: 2108 Weybridge Dr Raleigh NC 27615-5562 Personal E-mail: Hector26@aol.com.

WILLIAMS, IAN, English literature professor; BSc, U. Toronto, 2000, MA, 2001, PhD, 2005. Asst. prof. Fitchburg State Coll., Mass., 2005—. Grant, Kimmel Harding Nelson, 2007, fellowship, Cave Canem Found., Palazzo Rinaldi, Italy, 2009. Office: Fitchburg State Coll English Dept 160 Pearl St Fitchburg MA 01420 Business E-Mail: iwilliams@fsc.edu.

WILLIAMS, IAN GEORGE, writer; b. Liverpool, Eng., Sept. 21, 1949; s. Edward and Margaret (Cooper) W.; m. Anora Mahmudova, Nov. 30, 2002; children: Alexander James, Ian Anton Norbek, Owain Edward Davron. BA with honors, Liverpool U., 1973. Speechwriter for Neil Kinnock UK Labor Party, 1987, leader; pres. UN Corr. Assn., 1995—96, v.p., 1997—98. Author: The Alms Trade, 1989, The UN For Beginners, 1995, Deserter: Bush's War on Military Families, Veterans and His Own Past, 2004, Rum: A Social and Sociable History of the Real Spirit of 1776, 2005; contbr. chapters to books, numerous articles to mags. and profl. publs. Mem. Royal Inst. Internat. Affairs, London Press Club, Overseas Press Club (N.Y.C.). Avocations: theater, reading, bicycling, sailing. Home Phone: 917-362-1477; Office Phone: 212-686-8884. E-mail: uswarreport@igc.org.

WILLIAMS, IDA JONES, consumer and home economics educator, writer; b. Coatesville, Pa., Dec. 1, 1911; d. William Oscar and Ida Ella (Ruth) Jones; m. Charles Nathaniel Williams, Mar. 17, 1940 (dec. July 1971). BS, Hampton Inst., 1935; MA, U. Conn., Storrs, 1965. Cert. high sch. tchr., English, sci., home econs., Va., Pa. Tchr. sci. and home econs. Richmond County H.S., Ivondale, Va., 1935—36; tchr. English and home econs. Northampton County H.S., Chesapeake, Va., 1936—40, tchr. consumer and home econs. Machipongo, Va., 1940—70, Northampton Jr. H.S., Machipongo, 1970—76. Author: Starting Anew After Seventy, 1980 (plaque 1980), News and Views of Northampton County High Principals and Alumni, 1981, Great Grandmother, Leah's Legacy-Remember You're Free, 2000, History of Education for African Americans During the Segregation Period 1886 Through 1970 in Northampton County Virginia, 2007; co-author: The History of Virginia State Federation of Colored Women's Clubs, Inc., 1996; editor: Fifty Year Book 1935-1985 - Hampton Institute Class, 1985, Favorite Recipes of Ruth Family & Friends, 1986. V.p. Ea. Lit. Coun., Melfa, Va., 1987-89; active Ea. Shore Coll. Found., Inc., Melfa, 1988-2000, Gov.'s Adv. Bd. on Aging, Richmond, Va., 1992-94; instr. Ladies Cmty. Bible Class, 1976-80 (Plaque 1980); sec., treas., v.p. Hospice Support of Ea. Shore, 1980-94; mem. Northampton/Accomack Adv. Coun., 1992-94; marshall 28th anniv. commencement Ea. Shore CC, 1996; bd. dirs. Ea. Shore CC Found., 1998-2000; com. mem. Va. State Legis., 1995-2002 Recipient Jefferson award, Am. Inst. Pub. Svc., Wavy-TV-Bell Atlantic and Mattress Discounters, 1991, Nat. Sojourner Truth Meritorious Svc. award, Negro Bus. and Profl. Women's Clubs, Gavel Ea. Shore Ret. Tchrs. Assn., 1994, Gov.'s award for vol. excellence, 1994, Contribution to Edn. award, Ea. Shore Coll. Found., 1997, plaque, Southeastern Assn. Colored Women's Clubs, Inc., 2001, Leadership award, 2001, Dedicated Svc. award, Nat. Assn. Colored Women's Club, 1998, Exemplary Svc. award, 2001, Svc. award, E.S. C.C. Found., Inc., 2000, plaque 1st Black Northampton County, Ea. Shore Va. C. of C., 2002, Black Achievement award, Ebenezer A.M.E. Ch., 2003, Achievement award, Chester County Hist. Soc. of Pa., 2003, Ednl. Achievement award, Northampton County H.S. Alumni Assn., 2003, Dedicated Svc. award, S.E. Assn. Colored Women's Clubs Inc., 2003—05, Honored as Oldest Living Mem. of Ruth Family, 2006; named Home Econs. Tchr. of Yr., Am. Home Econs. Assn. and Family Cir., 1975, Woman of Yr., Prog. Women of E.S., 1997, Ida J. Williams scholarship in her honor, Keller Ch. Christ, 1999; Honored at Ceremony for Mother Ida Ella Ruth Jones at hist. road marker on Route 82, Pa., 2004, Honored at Ceremony for Uncle William Chester Ruth at historical road marker ceremony on Route 30, Pa. Hist. Mus., Salisbury Hist. Soc., 2006. Mem. AARP (Citation award 1996, Mem. of Yr. 1997, v.p. Northampton chpt. 1998-2000), Ida J. Williams Cultural Club (formerly Progressive Women of Ea. Shore. pres. 1985-93, Gold Necklace 1993, Woman of Yr. 1997), C. of C., Univ. Women (v.p. Portsmouth br. 1985-87), Ea. Shore Ret. Tchrs. (pres. 1977-84), Dist. L Ret. Tchrs. (pres. 1989-91, chmn. legis. com. 1998, 99, 2001, chmn. edn. and scholarship com. 2001-05, Dedicated and Outstanding Svc. award 2003), Va. State Fedn. Colored Women's Club (pres. 1990-94, editor history com. 1994-96) Mem. Ch. of Christ. Avocations: crafts, travel, writing, lecturing. Home and Office: PO Box 236 14213 Lankford Hwy Eastville VA 23347-0236

WILLIAMS, IFOR R., immunologist, director; b. Wallingford, England, June 10, 1960; s. Thomas Ffrancon and Astra Silvia Williams; m. Julie Sligh, Aug. 23, 1996 (div. Feb. 21, 2007); children: Grant Martin, Austin Heath. BS, Davidson Coll., NC, 1980; MD, PhD, Emory U., Atlanta, 1986. Cert. in anatomic pathology Am. Bd. Pathology, 1989, lic. Physician Ga., 1997. Pathology internship and residency Wash. U. Sch. Medicine, St. Louis, 1986—91, rsch. assoc., 1991—92; instr. dermatology Harvard Med. Sch., Boston, 1992—95, asst. prof. dermatology, 1995—97; asst. prof. pathology Emory U., 1997—2006, assoc. prof. pathology, 2006—. Assoc. dir., clin. immunology lab. Emory U. Hosp., Atlanta, 1997—2004, dir., clin. immunology lab., 2004—. Contbr. articles to profl. jours. Recipient Thomas B. Fitzpatrick Rsch. award, 1994, Career Devel. award, Dermatology Found., 1994, Janet and Elvin Price award, Crohn's and Colitis Found. Am., 2002. Fellow: Assn. Med. Lab. Immunologists, Coll. Am. Pathologists; mem.: Am. Soc. Investigative Pathology, Soc. Mucosal Immunology, Am. Gastroenterology Assn., Soc. Investigative Dermatology, Am. Assn. Immunologists, Pi Kappa Alpha, Davidson Coll. (sec. 1978—79). Methodist. Achievements include discovery of lymphotoxin and its receptor are required for the development of cryptopatches and isolated lymhoid follicles in the small intestine; that RANKL protein is critical for the development of specialized epithelial cells called M cells involved in antigen uptake into intestinal Peyer's patches. Avocations: running, skiing, racquetball. Office: Emory Univ 615 Michael St Whitehead 105D Atlanta GA 30322

WILLIAMS, J. VERNON, retired lawyer; b. Honolulu, Apr. 26, 1921; s. Urban and W. Amelia (Olson) W.; m. Malvina H. Hitchcock, Oct. 4, 1947 (dec. May 1970); children— Carl H. (dec.), Karin (dec.), Frances E., Scott S.; m. Mary McLellan, Sept. 6, 1980. Student, Phillips Andover Acad., 1937-39; BA cum laude, Amherst Coll., 1943; LL.B., Yale, 1948. Bar: Wash. 1948. Assoc. Riddell, Riddell & Hemphill, 1948-50, ptnr., 1950-95; sr. prin. emeritus Riddell Williams, P.S., Seattle, 1996—. Sec., dir. Airborne Freight Corp., 1968-79, gen. counsel, 1968-96. Chmn. March of Dimes, Seattle, 1954-55; Mem. Mayor's City Charter Rev. Com., 1968-69; chmn. Seattle Bd. Park Commrs., 1966-68; co-chmn. parks and open space com. Forward Thrust, 1966-69; dir. bd. and commrs. br. Nat. Recreation and Parks Assn., 1968-69; chmn. Gov.'s adv. com. Social and Health Services, 1972-75; Bd. dirs. Seattle Met. YMCA, 1965—, pres., 1976-79; trustee Lakeside Sch., 1971-79; mem. alumni council Phillps Andover Acad., 1970-73, Yale Law Sch., 1969-77; chancellor St. Mark's Cathedral, Seattle, 1964-2000. Served with USAAF, 1943-45. Mem. Univ. Club, Seattle Tennis Club, Birnam Wood Golf Club. Home: 2061 43rd Ave E #201 Seattle WA 98112 Office: 4500 1001 4th Ave Plz Seattle WA 98154-1065

WILLIAMS, JACK RAYMOND, retired civil engineer; b. Barberton, Ohio, Mar. 14, 1923; s. Charles Baird and Mary Williams; m. Mary Berneice Jones, Mar. 5, 1947 (dec.); children: Jacqueline Rae, Drew Alan; m. Betty Ruth Scholfield, Nov. 9, 1990 (dec.). Student, Colo. Sch. Mines, 1942—43, Purdue U., 1944—45; BS, U. Colo., 1946. Gravity and seismograph engr. Carter Oil Co., Western U.S. and Venezuela, 1946-50; with Rock Island R.R., Chgo., 1950-80, structural designer, asst. to engr. bridges, asst. engr., 1980-82, engr. bridges system, 1963-80; sr. bridge engr. thomas K. Dyer Inc., 1980-82; v.p. Alfred Benesch & Co., 1982-96. Served with USMCR, 1943-45. Fellow ASCE (life); mem. Am. Concrete Inst., Am. Ry. Bridge and Bldg. Assn. (past pres.), Am. Ry. Engring. Assn. (hon. mem., past chmn. com. 8, Concrete and Foundations, past chmn. com. 10 concrete ties). Home: 293 Minocqua St Park Forest IL 60466-1942

WILLIAMS, JAMES A., labor union administrator; b. 1951; m. Gerrie Williams; children: Aimee, Chrissy, Jimmy, Danny. Apprentice Local 252 Glaziers, Archtl. Metal & Glass Workers Union, Phila., 1968, apprentice, journeyman, 1971—75, pres., bus. mgr. Local 252, 1975; region gen. v.p. Internat. Union Painters & Allied Trade (IUPAT), 1994—95, gen. sec.-treas. elect, 1995—99, gen. sec.-treas., 1999—2002, gen. pres., 2003—. Apptd. exec. coun. AFL-CIO, 2003—, mem. bd. trustees Housing Investment Trust, 2005—, mem. adv. bd. Bldg. Investment Trust, 2005—. Contbr. articles to profl. jours. Apptd. commonwealth trustee Temple U., Phila., 1985—98. Infantryman US Army, 1969—71, Vietnam. Decorated 2 Bronze Stars, Army Accommodation medal, Air medal; recipient Labor Man of Yr. award, Israeli Bond Assoc., 1990, Vietnam Vets. Labor Leader of Yr. award, 1992. Office: IUPAT 1750 New York Ave NW Washington DC 20006 Office Phone: 202-637-0700.*

WILLIAMS, JAMES A., federal agency administrator; b. Nov. 24, 1954; B in Bus. Adminstrn., Va. Commonwealth U., 1979; M in Bus. Adminstrn., George Washington U., 1986. Exec. dir. FTC; dir. telecomm. procurement divsn. US Gen. Svcs. Adminstrn.; dep. asst. commr. procurement IRS, US Dept. Treasury, 1991—99, dir. procurement, 1999—2001, dep. assoc. commr. prog. mgmt., 2001—03; dir. US Visitor and Immigrant Status Indicator Tech. (US-VISIT) US Dept. Homeland Security, 2003—06; commr. fed. acquisition svc. US Gen. Svcs. Adminstrn., 2006—08, acting adminstr., 2008—. Mem. US Interagency Coun. on Homelessness, Nat. Capital Planning Commn. Mem. bus. industry coun. Radford U., Va.; mem. pres. com. Nat. Found. Arts & Humanities. Mem.: Sr. Execs. Assn. (bd. dirs.), Nat. Contract Mgmt. Assoc. (bd. advs.), Project Mgmt. Inst. Office: US Gen Svcs Adminstrn 1800 F St NW Rm 6137 Washington DC 20405 Office Phone: 202-501-0800. Business E-Mail: jim.williams@gsa.gov.*

WILLIAMS, JAMES ARTHUR, retired military officer, information technology executive; b. Paterson, NJ, Mar. 29, 1932; s. Charles M. and Elsie (Kretszchmar) W.; m. Barbara Widnall, June 26, 1959; children: Steven, Karen. BS, U.S. Mil. Acad.; MA in Latin Am. Studies, U. N.Mex. Commd. 2d lt. U.S. Army, 1954, advanced through grades to lt. gen.; asst. army attache U.S. Def. Attache Office, Caracas, Venezuela, 1966-72; exch. officer State-Def. Exch. Program Office of Sec. Def., Washington, 1972-74; comdr. 650th MI Group, Shape, 1974-76; dep. dir. estimates Def. Intelligence Agy., Washington, 1977-80; dep. chief staff for intelligence U.S. Army, Europe, 1980-81; dir. Def. Intelligence Agy., Washington, 1981-85; ret., 1985; v.p. PSC Corp., 1986; pres. Direct Info. Access Corp., Annandale, Va., 1987—2008; chmn. bd. dirs. Info. Ops. Inc., 2000—04; pres. Info Assure, Inc., Arnold, Md., 2004—. Sr. fellow Joint Forces Staff Coll., 1998; intelligence advisor Dept. Homeland Security, 2004; pres. Washington Inst. Foreign Affairs, 2007. Bd. visitors Joint Mil. Intelligence Coll., 1996. Decorated Legion of Merit, Bronze

Star with oak leaf cluster, Air medals, D.S.M., Nat. Intelligence D.S.M.; Legion of Honor (France); named Disting. Mem. Mil. Intelligence Hall of Fame. Mem. Assn. U.S. Army, Nat. Mil. Intelligence Assn. (chmn. bd. 1986—). Methodist. Office: Info Assure Inc 1997 Annapolis Exchange Pkwy Ste 210 Annapolis MD 21401

WILLIAMS, JAMES BUCHANAN, retired surgeon; b. El Paso, Tex., May 28, 1919; s. Jasper Buchanan and Clara Belle Williams; m. Willeen Agnes Brown, May 30, 1951; children: Brenda Joyce, James Buchanan II. BS, N.Mex. A&M, State College, 1947; MD, Creighton U. Sch. Medicine, Omaha, 1951; MS in Surgery, Creighton Med. Sch., Omaha, 1956. Cert. MD Nebr., 1956, Am. Bd. Surgery, 1957. Pres. Creighton U. Surg. Soc., Omaha, 1982—84, Cook County Physician, Chgo., 1982—84. Bd. dirs. N.Mex. State U., Las Cruces, 1985—90, Creighton Med. Planning Adv. Bd., Omaha, 1981—86. First lt. U.S. Air Corps, 1942—46. Recipient Alumni Merit award, N.Mex. A&M, 1961, Outstanding Alumni award, N.Mex. State U., 1967, Alumni Merit award, Creighton U. Sch. Medicine, 1999. Master: NAACP (life); fellow: Am. Coll. Surgeons; mem.: Alpha Omega Alpha Soc. Catholic. Achievements include establishing Clara B. Williams scholarship, N.Mex. A&M, 1985; street named in his honor (Williams Ave.), 1967. Avocations: fishing, hunting.

WILLIAMS, JAMES CASE, metallurgist; b. Salina, Kans., Dec. 7, 1938; s. Luther Owen and Clarice (Case) W.; m. Joanne Rufener, Sept. 17, 1960; children: Teresa A., Patrick J. BS in Metall. Engring, U. Wash., Seattle, 1962, MS, 1964, PhD, 1968. Rsch. engr., lead engr. Boeing Co., Seattle, 1961-67; tech. staff N.Am. Rockwell Corp., Thousand Oaks, Calif., 1968-74; mgr. interdivisional tech. program N.Am. Aerospace group, 1974, program devel. mgr. structural materials, 1974-75; prof. metallurgy, co-dir. Ctr. for Joining of Materials, Carnegie-Mellon U., Pitts., 1975-81; pres. Mellon Inst., Pitts., 1981-83; dean Carnegie Inst. Tech., Carnegie-Mellon U., Pitts., 1983-88; gen. mgr. materials dept. GE Aircraft Engines, 1988-99; prof., Honda chair Ohio State U., Columbus, 1999—, dean engring., 2001—04; lectr. RF Mehl Inst. Metals, 2008. Bd. dirs. com. on engring. and tech. systems NRC, 1996-2001; chmn. Nat. Materials Adv. Bd., 1988-95, materials and structures com. NASA Aero. Adv. Com. 1992-97; mem. NASA Propulsion Rsch. and Tech. Com., 1997-99; mem. Materials Sci. and Engring. Study, 1986-88; bd. govs. Inst. for Mechs. and Materials, U. Calif., San Diego, 1989-95; trustee Min. Math. Sci. and Engring., Cin., 1988-99; mem. sci. adv. bd. USAF, 1996-2001; mem. materials rsch. com. Def. Advanced Rsch. Projects Agy., 1981-2000; adv. com. Divsn. Engring. and Phys. Sci., NRC, 2001-04, chair Nanotechnology Assessment com., 2005-06. Co-author: Titanium, 2003, 2d edit., 2007; co-editor: Scientific and Technological Aspects of Titanium and Titanium Alloys, 1976; contbr. numerous articles to tech. jours. Trustee Oreg. Grad. Inst. Sci. and Tech., 1988-94; cons. Cubmaster Boy Scouts Am., 1976-77. Recipient Ladd award Carnegie Inst. Tech., Scott Tchg. award, OSU Engring. Coll., 2008; Adams award Am. Welding Soc.; Boeing doctoral fellow; named to GE Aircraft Engines Hall of Fame. Fellow: TMS-AIME, Am. Soc. Metals (Disting. lectr. on materials and soc. 1997, Campbell lectr. 1999, Gold medal 1992); mem.: AIME (Leadership award 1993, App to Pract award 2002), NAE, ASM, Internat. Ti Assn. (Achievement award 2003), Alpha Sigma Mu. Republican. Episcopalian. Home: 7711 Charlotte Hull Ct New Albany OH 43054-9680 Office: Ohio State U Dept Materials Soc and Engring 143 Fontana Labs 116 W 19th Ave Columbus OH 43210 Office Phone: 614-292-7251. Business E-Mail: williams.1726@osu.edu.

WILLIAMS, JAMES DALE, language educator, researcher; b. Phoenix, May 31, 1949; s. Elmer Don and Jessie Leona Williams; m. Ako Shimada, Oct. 13, 1973; children: Austin Ross, Sarah Elizabeth. BA in English, San Jose State U., Calif., 1971, MA in English, 1975; PhD in Rhetoric and Linguistics, U. So. Calif., LA, 1983. Vis. asst. prof. U. Calif., LA, 1981—84; dir. interdisciplinary writing program U. So. Calif., 1984—87; assoc. prof., dir. writing program U. NC, Chapel Hill, 1987—95; prof. rhetoric Governors State U., Chgo., 1995—98; prof., dir. faculty devel. Calif. Poly., Pomona, 1998—2000; prof. rhetoric & linguistics Soka U., Aliso Viejo, Calif., 2000—. Author: (books) The LEA Guide to Composition, 2001, Visions and Revisions: Continuity and Change in Rhetoric and Composition, 2002, Preparing to Teach Writing: Research, Theory and Practice, 3d edit., 2003, The Teacher's Grammar Book, 2d edit., 2005, An Introduction to Classical Rhetoric: Essential Readings, 2009; co-author (with Grace Snipper): Literacy and Bilingualism, 1990; co-author: (with David Huntley & Christine Hanks) The Interdisciplinary Reader, 1992; co-author: (with Jean Gillet & Charles Temple) Writing and Language Arts, Grades K—6, 2003; contbr. numerous articles to profl. jours. Co-founder Magnolia Charter Sch., Reseda, Calif., 1999—2002. Recipient Devel. award, IBM, 1991—92, Disting. Svc. award, Govs. State U., 1998; grantee Rsch. grant, U. So. Calif., 1980, U. Rsch. Coun., U. NC, 1988, Child Devel. grant, Frank Porter Graham Child Devel. Ctr., 1988, Innovative Tchg. grant, Lupton Found., 1989, Rsch. Devel. grant, Arts & Scis. Found., U. NC, 1990, Devel. grant, Ill. Bd. Higher Edn., 1997—98, DOE Title VII grant, US Dept. Edn., 2000; fellow, Stanford U. Ctr. Advanced Studies in Behavioral Scis., 1990. Mem.: Rhetoric Soc. of Am., Conf. Coll. Composition and Comm., Nat. Coun. Tchrs. English. Avocations: hiking, exercise, history. Office: Soka Univ 1 University Dr Aliso Viejo CA 92656 Business E-Mail: jwilliams@soka.edu.

WILLIAMS, JAMES EUGENE, management consultant; b. Macon, Ga., June 23, 1927; m. Linda K. Magnuson, June 23, 1984; children: Paul David, Lisa Jane Williams Robertson, Philip Alan, Gail Ellen Williams Feeney, Amanda Allen Thompson, Jason Douglas Allen, Joel Winston Allen BS in Aero. Engring., Iowa State Coll., 1950. Engr., Robins AFB, Ga., 1950-54, Hdqrs. USAF, Washington, 1954-61; dep. asst. sec. Office Asst. Sec. Air Force, Washington, 1961-85; dir. govt. bus. policy Northrop Corp., Washington, 1986-88; pvt. practice mgmt. cons. Chandler, Ariz., 1988—. Co-founder The Williams Inst. for Ethics and Mgmt., Tempe, 1993—. Recipient Presdl. Meritorious Exec. award, 1981, Presdl. Disting. Exec. award, 1982. Home: 955 E Knox Rd Unit 129 Chandler AZ 85225 Personal E-mail: LJWMS@aol.com.

WILLIAMS, JAMES FRANKLIN, II, dean, librarian; b. Montgomery, Ala., Jan. 22, 1944; s. James Franklin and Anne (Wester) Williams; m. Madeline McClellan, Jan. 1966 (div. May 1988); 1 child, Madeline Marie; m. Nancy Allen, Aug. 1989; 1 child, Audrey Grace. BA, Morehouse Coll., Atlanta, 1966; MLS, Atlanta U., 1967. Reference libr. Wayne State U. Sci. Libr., Detroit, 1968-69; document delivery libr. Wayne State U. Med. Libr., Detroit, 1969-70, head of reference, 1971-72, dir. med. libr. and regional med. libr. network, 1972-81, regional dir., 1975-82; assoc. dir. of librs. Wayne State U., 1981-88; dean librs. U. Colo., Boulder, 1988—. Bd. regents Nat. Libr. Medicine, Bethesda, Md., 1978—81; pres. Big Twelve Plus Libr. Consortium, 2000; bd. dirs. Coun. Librs. & Info. Resources, Ctr. Rsch. Librs., 1998—, Denver Art Mus., 1997—, pres., 1999—. Mem. editl. bd. Portal: Libraries and the Academy; contbr. articles to profl. jours., chapters to books. Bd. dirs. Educom, 1997—98, Boulder Cmty. Hosp., 2000—. Mem.: ALA (Visionary Leader award 1988, Melvil Dewey medal 2002), Boulder C. of C. (bd. dirs.), Assn. Rsch. Librs. (bd. dirs. 1994-96, 2000-03). Avocations: bicycling, travel, fishing. Office: U Colo Office Dean Librs PO Box 184 Boulder CO 80309-0184 Office Phone: 303-492-7511. Business E-Mail: james.williams@colorado.edu.

WILLIAMS, JAMES HENRY, JR., mechanical engineer, educator, consultant; b. Newport News, Va., Apr. 4, 1941; s. James H. Williams and Margaret L. (Holt) Mitchell; children: James Henry III, Mariella Louisa. Student, Newport News Apprentice Sch., 1965; BS, MIT, 1967, MS, 1968; PhD, Cambridge U., 1970. Sr. design engr. Newport News (Va.) Shipyard, 1960-70; asst. prof. mech. engring. MIT, 1970-74, assoc. prof., 1974-81, prof., 1981—2000, duPont prof., 1973, Edgarton prof., 1974-76, prof. writing and humanistic studies, 2000—. Cons. in field. Contbr. articles on stress analysis, materials and nondestructive testing to profl. jours. Recipient Charles F. Bailey Bronze medal, 1961, Silver medal, 1962, Gold medal, 1963, Baker award, 1976; named Prof. of Tchg. Excellence, Sch. Engring., 1991, C.F. Hopewell faculty fellow, 1993. Mem. ASME, Am. Soc. Nondestructive Testing, Nat. Tech. Assn. Office: MIT Room 3-360 77 Massachusetts Ave Rm 3-360 Cambridge MA 02139-4307 Office Phone: 617-253-2221. Business E-Mail: jhwill@mit.edu.

WILLIAMS, JAMES KENDRICK, bishop emeritus; b. Athertonville, Ky., Sept. 5, 1936; Student, St. Mary's Coll., Ky., St. Maur's Sch. Theology, South Union, Ky. Ordained priest Archdiocese of Louisville, 1963; pastor Holy Trinity Parish, Louisville, 1983—84; ordained bishop, 1984; aux. bishop Diocese of Covington, Ky., 1984—88; bishop Diocese of Lexington, Ky., 1988—2002, bishop emeritus Ky., 2002—08. Roman Catholic.

WILLIAMS, JAMES LEE, finance company executive; b. Tampa, Fla., Nov. 5, 1941; s. Donald Clark and Nell (Medlin) W.; m. Linda Taylor, Dec. 28, 1968; children: Donald Clark II, Taylor Lee. AA, St. Petersburg Jr. Coll., Fla., 1965; BS, Fla. State U., 1967. Mgmt. Ryder Truck Lines, Jacksonville, Fla., 1967—69; dist. mgr. underwriting divsn. U.S. Leasing Corp., Dallas, 1969—73; area v.p. Mfrs. Hanover Leasing Corp., Houston and London, 1973—79; v.p. corp. fin. Underwood Neuhause & Co. Inc., Houston, 1979—81; chmn., CEO 1st City Leasing Corp., Houston, 1981—85; mng. dir. capital markets 1st City Bancorp., Houston, 1985—89; mng. dir. fin. svcs. M.P.S.I. Sys. Inc., Dallas, 1989—90; pres., CEO Strategic Decisions Holdings Corp., Dallas, 1990—92; sr. mng. dir. Williams and Assocs., 1992; pres. Global Svcs. Capital Corp., Houston, 1993—96; v.p., dist. CFO Ikon Hou Adminstrv. Svc. Ctr., Houston, 1997—98; CFO Insync Internet Svcs., Houston, 1998—99, Walkabout Software, 1999—2001; pres. BancLeasing, Inc., 2001—03; mng. dir. Global Svcs., Houston, 2003—04; exec. dir. SIRE-Therapeutic Equestrian Ctrs., 2004—. Served with USN, 1959-62. Mem. Equipment Leasing Assn. (fed. govt. rels. com. 1984-88, 95—), Tex. Assn. Equipment Lessors (bd. dirs. 1985-89), Greater Houston Partnership (Arabian horse and Announcer's com. 1994-, chmn. Horse Show Announcers com. 2009-, Houston Livestock Show and Rodeo), Spcl. Commn. Harris Co. Ct., Houston Ctr. Club (bd. dirs. 1985-89), Lakeside Racquet Club (athletic com. 1986-89), Forum Club Houston. Republican. Presbyterian. Avocations: golf, jogging, swimming. Office: SIRE 24161 Spring Dr Hockley TX 77447

WILLIAMS, JAN R., dean, business educator; BS, Ga. Peabody Coll.; MBA, Baylor U.; PhD, U. Ark. CPA Tenn., Ark. Staff accountant Arthur Young & Co., Dallas; assoc. prof. U. Ga.; assoc. to full prof., assoc dean grad. programs Tex. Tech U., head Dept. Accounting and Info. Mgmt.; prof. U. Tenn., Knoxville, 1977—, head Dept. Accounting and Bus. Law, 1985—93, assoc. dean academic programs, 1995—98, Ernst & Young prof. Dept. Accounting and Bus. Law, dean Coll. Bus. Adminstrn., Stokely Found. leadership chair, 2008—. Faculty resident, ednl. cons. Ernst & Young Nat. Office, 1991—92. Mem.: Am. Accounting Assn. (pres. 1999—2000), Assn. to Advance Coll. Schs. of Bus. (AACSB) Internat. (bd. dirs.), Am. Inst. of CPAs, Tenn. Soc. of CPAs, Beta Alpha Psi. Office: U Tenn Coll Bus Adminstrn 463 James A Haslam II Bus Bldg 1000 Volunteer Blvd Knoxville TN 37996-4140 Office Phone: 865-974-4541. E-mail: jwilli13@utk.edu.*

WILLIAMS, JASON CHANDLER, professional basketball player; b. Belle, W.Va., Nov. 18, 1975; s. Terry Williams; m. Denika Williams; 2 children. Student, U. Fla. Guard Sacramento Kings, 1998—2001, Memphis Grizzlies, 2001—05, Miami Heat, 2005—08, LA Clippers, 2008, Orlando Magic, 2009—. Named to All-Rookie First Team, NBA, 1999. Office: Orlando Magic 600 W Amelia St Orlando FL 32801*

WILLIAMS, JATIKA, social worker, educator; b. LA, Apr. 23, 1975; d. Byron Eugene and Macomie Williams. B of Social Work, Calif. State U., LA; MSW, Calif. State U., Long Beach. Tchr. LA Unified Sch. Dist., 2000—07; social worker Jasmine Ctrs., Inc., Inglewood, Calif., 2004—07, LA County Dept. Children and Family Svcs., 2007—. Mem.: Phi Delta Gamma, Golden Key Honor Soc.

WILLIAMS, JEAN-PIERRE, research scientist; PhD in Geophysics & Space Physics, U. Calif., LA. O.K. earl postdoc. rschr., planetary sci. Calif. Inst. Tech., Pasadena, 2005—08, rsch. scientist, 2008—. Office Fax: 626-568-0935.

WILLIAMS, JEFFERY LYNN, secondary school educator, consultant, writer; b. Zanesville, Ohio, Sept. 17, 1965; s. Barbara June and Glenn Eugene Harris (Stepfather), Jeffrey James Williams; life ptnr. William Don LaRiccia. BS in Edn., Ohio State U., 1990; Med, John Carroll U., Ohio, 2003. Cert. Tchr. Ohio Dept. of Edn., 2006. Tchr. Whitehall (Ohio) City Schools, 1990—93, Chagrin Falls (Ohio) Exempted Village Sch. Dist., 1993—2000; K-12 dist. literacy tchr. leader and reading recovery tchr. Solon (Ohio) City Schs., 2000—; adj. prof. Ashland (Ohio) U., 2001—. Ednl. cons. Solon (Ohio) City Schs., 1998—. Siri adv. com. Ohio Dept. Edn., Columbus, 2001—04. Sgt. US Army, 1984—86. Recipient Tchr. of Yr., Chagrin Falls Schs., 1998, Tchr. of Month, Cuyahoga County Edn. Svc. Ctr., 1998. Mem.: Internat. Reading Assn., Reading Recovery Coun. of N.Am., Golden Key Nat. Honor Soc., Pi Lambda Theta Nat. Honor Soc. (Outstanding Excellence award 2007), Phi Kappa Phi, Phi Delta Kappa. Liberal. Roman Catholic. Achievements include development of Literacy Learning. Avocations: travel, writing, genealogy, cross country skiing, cooking. Home: 18844 Rivers Edge Dr Chagrin Falls OH 44023 Office: Solon City Schs 6795 Solon Blvd Solon OH 44139 Business E-Mail: jwilliams@solonboe.org.

WILLIAMS, JENNIFER ANN, public relations executive; b. Chgo., Jan. 15, 1965; children: Allen Pierre, Jason Austell, Jarvis Dominique. Cert. Office Automation Clk. U.S. Dept. Housing & Urban Devel., 1992; Office Asst. Ill. Dept. Human Svcs., 2002. Contracted hr profl. SPHERION, Chgo.; contracted adminstrv. profl. MANPOWER, Joliet, Genie Temp. Svcs., Joliet; pub. rels. mktg. profl. AFLAC, Joliet. Alumni Link Unlimited Scholarship Program, Chicago, Ill., —. Election judge Will County Clk.'s Office, Joliet. Recipient Grand Lady, Knights of St. Peter Claver, Jr. Daughters Divsn., 1980—81, Nat. Vice-Supreme Lady, Knights Of St. Peter Claver, Jr. Dau. Divsn., 1981—82; named to Nat. Dean of Students List, 2005; grantee scholarship, Knights of St. Peter Claver Orgn., 1982. Mem.: Knights of Columbus, Am. Turners, Knights of Peter Claver. Office: Will County Clerk's Office 302 N Chicago Joliet IL 60435 Home: PO Box 1112 Woodstock IL 60098 Office Phone: 312-576-9293. Personal E-mail: jenniferhasadream@yahoo.com.

WILLIAMS, JERRY RANDALL, radiation biologist; s. James Marshall and Hazel Arvella (Lands) W. BA in Physics and Math. magna cum laude, Tex. Christian U., 1957; BS, MS, Nat. U. Ireland, 1960; DSc, Harvard U., 1972. Guest worker Nat. Cancer Inst., Bethesda, Md., 1969-70; rsch. assoc. lab. radiobiology Harvard Sch. Pub. Health, Boston, 1972-73, asst. prof. radiobiology, 1973-78; sr. biologist, scientific advisor U.S. EPA, Washington, 1978-81; rsch. prof. radiology, pharmacology George Washington U., Washington, 1979-84, dir. environ. and radiol. hazards rsch., 1979-84; prof. oncology Johns Hopkins U., Balt., 1984—, dir. radiobiology lab., 1984—. Vis. prof. U. Tex., Arlington, 1976, 78, U. Ark. Med. Sch., 1989, Shanghai Second Med. U., 1989; Evan and Marion Helfaer Found. Disting. Lectr. Cancer Ctr. Med. Coll. Wis., Milw., 1993; cons. dept. dermatology Mass. Gen. Hosp., Boston, 1982-84; chmn. spl. study sect. Nat. Cancer Inst., 1992, 93, 94; mem. com. on possible biol. effects of electromagnetic fields Nat. Acad. Sci., 1993-94. Contbr. articles to profl. jours. Capt. U.S. Army, 1957-63. Decorated Commendation medal; Rotary Found. scholar, 1958-59. Mem. Radiation Rsch. Soc., AAAS, Am. Soc. Photobiology, Am. Soc. for Therapeutic Radiology and Oncology, Am. Assn. for Cancer Rsch., Alpha Chi, Kappa Mu Epsilon. Office: Johns Hopkins Oncology Ctr 600 N Wolfe St # 121 Baltimore MD 21287-0005

WILLIAMS, JEWELL, state legislator; b. Phila., Sept. 8, 1957; 3 children. Grad., Holy Family Coll., Phila., 1987, Phila. Police Acad., 1987. Mem. Dist. 197 Pa. House of Reps., Harrisburg, 2001—. Recipient Outstanding Polit. Contbn. award, Tuskegee U., 2002, Push Medallion award, Pa. Gov. Tom Ridge, 2000; named to Dobbins Wall of Fame, 2003. Mem.: NAACP, Masons (32 degree Lodge Hiram #5). Democrat. Office: 101 Irvis Office Bldg PO Box 202197 Harrisburg PA 17120-2004 also: Dist Office 2220 N Broad St Philadelphia PA 19132-4501 Office Phone: 717-772-2004, 215-763-2559. Office Fax: 717-787-7597, 215-763-2561.*

WILLIAMS, JIMMIE LEWIS, chemist, researcher; b. Indianola, Miss., June 3, 1953; s. West and Lorene (Mayfield) W.; m. Patricia Ann Rodgers; 2 children. BS in Chemistry, Jackson State U., Miss., 1975; MS in Chemistry, Yale U., 1977; PhD in Inorganic Chemistry, U. Calif., Riverside, 1983. From sr. rsch. scientist to sr. rsch. assoc. Corning (N.Y.) Inc., 1983-97, project mgr. environ. product devel., 1997—99; mgr. Materials Devel., Environ. Techs. Devel., Corning, NY, 2001—03; catalysis tech. leader crystalline materials rsch. dept., 2003—. Speaker and presenter in field. Contbr. articles to profl. jours. Coach sport programs, Corning, 1983—; vol. Big Bro. Program, Corning, 1983-85. Named one of Outstanding Young Men in Am., 1980, 83; recipient Percy L. Julian award Nat. Orgn. Profl. Advancement of Black Chemists and Chem. Engrs., 2006. Fellow Am. Inst. Chemists; mem. Am. Chem. Soc. (pres. Corning chpt. 1998, pres. Corning sect. 2002, Eugene S. Sullivan award), Nat. Org. Profl. Advancement Black Chemists and Chem. Engrs., (Percy L. Julian award, 2006) Am. Ceramic Soc., Air and Waste Mgmt. Assn., Soc. Automotive Engrs., Nat. Soc. Black Engrs. (Disting. Engr. of Yr. award 2001), NACCP (v.p. Elmira br. 1991—, President's award Elmira/Corning br. 1995), Sigma Xi (pres. local chpt. 1990-91). Achievements include patents in field; research on automotive and industrial emissions control. Office: Corning Inc SP-DV-02 Corning NY 14831 E-mail: williamsjl@corning.com.

WILLIAMS, JIMMY (JAMES F. M. WILLIAMS), lobbyist; Grad., The Citadel. With Fin. Svcs. Roundtable, Nat. Assn. Realtors; economic policy adviser to Senator Dick Durbin US Senate; v.p. fed. govt. affairs Wine and Spirits Wholesalers of America; sr. v.p. Ogilvy Govt. Rels. Office: Ogilvy Govt Rels 1111 19th St, NW, Ste 1100 Washington DC 20036 Office Phone: 202-729-4200. Office Fax: 202-530-9777.*

WILLIAMS, JOANNA POZZI, psychology professor; AB in Psychology, Brown U., Providence, 1955; MEd, Harvard U., Cambridge, Mass., 1956; MS in Exptl. Psychology, PhD in Exptl. Psychology, Yale U., New Haven, 1961. Prof. psychology and edn. Tchrs. Coll., Columbia U., NYC, 1975—; lectr. Grad. Sch. Edn. U. Pa., 1961—62, asst. prof., 1962—66, assoc. prof., 1966—74, prof. ednl. psychology, 1974—75; prof. Tchrs. Coll. Columbia U., 1975—. Editor: Jour. Ednl. Psychology, 1973—78; founding editor: Sci. Studies of Reading, 1997—2002. Recipient Lindback Disting. Tchg. award, U. Pa., 1963, Oscar Causey award, Nat. Reading Conf., 1983, Outstanding Tchr. award, Tchrs. Coll., Columbia U., 2006; named to Reading Hall of Fame, 1994; Guy Bond scholar, U. Minn., 1997. Fellow: APA (pres. divsn. 15 1977—78), Am. Ednl. Rsch. Assn. (v.p. divsn. C 1974—76); mem.: Internat. Reading Assn., Coun. for Exceptional Children, Soc. Sci. Study Reading (pres. 2004—05). Office: Columbia Univ Tchrs Coll Box 238 525 W 120 St New York NY 10027 Business E-Mail: jpw15@columbia.edu.

WILLIAMS, JOBETH, actress; b. Houston, Dec. 6, 1948; m. John Pasquin, Mar. 14, 1982; children: Nick, Will. Grad., Brown U. Appeared in plays A Coupla White Chicks Sitting Around Talking, 1980, Gardenia, 1982, Idiot's Delight, 1986, Cat on a Hot Tin Roof, 1993; films include Kramer vs. Kramer, 1979, The Dogs of War, 1980, Stir Crazy, 1980, Poltergeist, 1982, Endangered Species, 1982, The Big Chill, 1983, American Dreamer, 1984, Teachers, 1984, Desert Bloom, 1986, Poltergeist II, 1986, Memories of Me, 1988, Welcome Home, 1989, Switch, 1991, Dutch, 1991, Stop! Or My Mom Will Shoot, 1992, Me, Myself and I, 1993, Wyatt Earp, 1994, Parallel Lives, 1994, Little City, 1997, Just Write, 1997, Jungle 2 Jungle, 1997, When Danger Follows You Home, 1997, Justice, 1998, Repossessed, 2002, The Rose Technique, 2002, Into the Fire, 2004, Fever Pitch, 2005, Crazylove, 2005, In the Land of Women, 2007; TV films include Fun and Games, 1980, The Big Black Pill, 1981, Adam, 1983 (Emmy award nominee, Golden Globe award nominee), The Day After, 1983, Kids Don't Tell, 1985, Adam: His Song Continues, 1986, Murder Ordained, 1987, Baby M, 1988 (Emmy award nominee, Golden Globe award nominee), My Name is Bill W., 1989, Child in the Night, 1990, Victim of Love, 1991, Jonathan: The Boy Nobody Wanted, 1992, Sex, Love and Cold Hard Cash, 1993, Chantilly Lace, 1993, Voices from Within, 1994, Lemon Grove, 1994, Parallel Lives, 1994, Voices from Within, 1994, Season of Hope, 1994, Ruby Jean and Joe, 1996, Breaking Through, 1996, It Came From the Sky, 1998, A Chance of Snow, 1998, Justice, 1999, Jackie's Back!, 1999, Trapped in a Purple Haze, 2000, The Ponder Heart, 2001, Homeward Bound, 2002, 14 Hours, 2005, Into the Fire, 2005, Stroller Wars, 2006; TV series include The Guiding Light, 1977-81, Somerset, 1975-76, (voice) Fish Police, 1992, John Grisham's The Client, 1995-96, (voice) Stories from My Childhood, 1998, Payne, 1999; co-exec. prodr.: (TV movie) Bump in the Night, 1991; dir. (films): On Hope, 1994 (Acad. award nominee for Best Live Action Short Film 1995), Winona's Web, 2001.

WILLIAMS, JODY, political organization administrator; b. Rutland, Vt., Oct. 9, 1950; BA, U. Vt.; MA, Sch. Internat. Tng.; MA in Internat. Studies, Johns Hopkins U.; PhD (hon.), Briar Cliff Coll., Marlboro Coll.,

U. Vt., Williams Coll., Pa. State U., Royal Mil. Coll. Canada, Wesleyan U., Franklin Pierce Coll., Regis U., Shensu U., Rockhurst U., Gustaus Adolphus Coll., Lehman Coll., Smith Coll. Former coord. Nicaragua-Honduras Edn. Project, Washington; assoc. dir. Children's Project Med. Aid El Salvador, L.A./El Salvador, 1986—92; founder Internat. Campaign to Ban Landmines Vietnam Vet. Found. Am., Washington, 1991—; founding coord., amb. Internat. Campaign to Ban Landmines, Alexandria, Va., 1992—; founder Sponsor a Mine-Detection Dog program, 1998—. Patron Internat. Peace Found., Vienna, 1998—; adv. com., arms divsn. Human Rights Watch, 1998—; adv. com. Code of Conduct on the Arms Trade, Arias Found. for Peace and Human Progress, 1998—, Rep. Eddie Bernice Johnson's Women for World Peace Fund, 2003—; disting. vis. prof. social work and global justice Univ. Houston, Tex., 2004—. Contbr. articles to profl. jours, co-author: After the Guns Fall: The Enduring Legacy of Landmines, 1995. Founder Nobel Women's Initiative, 2006. Recipient Distinguished Peace Leadership award, Nuclear Age Peace Found., 1998, Fiat Lux award, Clark U., Hollywood Humanitarian award, 2002; co-recipient Nobel Peace Prize, 1997; named one of 100 Most Powerful Women in World, Forbes Mag., 2004. Address: ICBL 33 rue de Bruxelles 1470 Genappe Belgium E-mail: williams@icbl.org.*

WILLIAMS, JOHN, engineering educator; b. Pa. m. Kelly Williams. BS in Fundamentals Engring., Clarkson U., Potsdam, NY, 1991, MS, 1994, PhD, 1998. Asst. prof. Alfred U., NY, 1999—2002; assoc. prof., met dept. chair Alfred State, 2002—. Chair Mech. Engring. Tech. Dept. Heads Com., Washington, 2006—. Contbr. articles to profl. jours. Eucharistic min. St. Jude's Chapel, Alfred, 2008. Recipient Excellence Tchg. award, Alfred U., 2002. Mem.: ASME (chpt. chair 2001—08, vice chair 2001—08, com. chair 2001—08), NY State Engring. Tech. Assn. (mem. large 2007—), ASEE (vice chair comm. 2004—06, mem. engring. tech. divsn., sec. 2005—08, chair 2005—08), Tau Alpha Pi (hon.; faculty advisor 2003, bd. dirs. 2005—). Office: Alfred State Upper College Dr Alfred NY 14802 Office Fax: 607-587-4620. Business E-Mail: williajc@alfredstate.edu.

WILLIAMS, JOHN ALEXANDER, history professor; b. Chapel Hill, NC, Sept. 14, 1962; s. Max Ray and Sarah Johnson Williams; life ptnr. Olaf Friedrich Griese, June 12, 2003. PhD, U. Mich., Ann Arbor, 1996. Asst. prof. Bradley U., Peoria, Ill., 1998—2003, dir. Bradley Berlin seminar, 2000—, assoc. prof., 2003—. Author: (non-fiction book) Turning to Nature in Germany: Hiking, Nudism, and Conservation, 1900-1940; editor: Berlin Since the Walls End. Regents fellowship, U. Mich. History Dept., 1988—91. Mem.: German Studies Assn., Am. Hist. Assn., Phi Beta Kappa. Democrat. Avocations: travel, films. Office: Bradley Univ History Dept 1501 W Bradley Ave Peoria IL 61625 Office Fax: 309-677-3377. Business E-Mail: johnw@bradley.edu.

WILLIAMS, JOHN ALFRED, educator, author; b. Jackson, Miss., 1925; m. Lorrain Isaac; 1 son, Adam; children by previous marriage: Gregory, Dennis. Grad., Syracuse U., 1950, Nat. Inst. Arts and Letters, 1962; LLD, U. Mass., Dartmouth, 1978; LittD, Syracuse U., 1995, Southeastern U., SUNY, Old Westbury, 2001, U. Rochester, 2003. With Am. Com. on Africa, NYC; disting. prof. English La Guardia C.C., 1973-78, Rutgers U., 1979-93, Paul Robeson prof. English, 1990-93; Bard Ctr. fellow Bard Coll., 1994-95. Lectr. CCNY, 1968-69; guest writer Sarah Lawrence Coll., 1972-73; Regents lectr. U. Calif., Santa Barbara, 1972, U. Hawaii, 1974; vis. prof. Boston U., Hawaii, 1978-79, NYU, 1986-87. Started writing poetry during World War II, in Pacific; Author: The Angry Ones, 1960, Night Song, 1961, Sissie, 1963, The Man Who Cried I Am, 1967, Sons of Darkness, Sons of Light, 1969, Captain Blackman, 1972, Mothersill and the Foxes, 1975, The Junior Bachelor Society, 1976, (play) Last Flight from Ambo Ber, 1981, !Click Song, 1982 (Before Columbus Found. Am. Book award 1983), The Berhama Account, 1985, Jacob's Ladder, 1987, (poems) Safari West, 1998 (Am. Book award), Clifford's Blues, 1999, (opera) Vanqui, 1999, also 10 vols. of non-fiction, 7 anthologies. Recipient Centennial medal for outstanding achievement Syracuse U., 1970, award Nat. Endowment Arts, 1977, Lindback award for Disting. Tchg., Rutgers U., 1982; named to Nat. Lit. Hall of Fame, 1998. Home: 693 Forest Ave Teaneck NJ 07666-2042 *I've tried to adhere to the philosophies of W.E.B. DuBois. He never quit.*

WILLIAMS, JOHN ANDREW, physiology researcher, educator; b. Des Moines, Aug. 3, 1941; s. Harold Southall and Marjorie (Larsen) W.; m. Christa A. Smith, Dec. 26, 1965; children: Rachel Jo, Matthew Dallas. BA, Cen. Wash. State Coll., 1963; MD, PhD, U. Wash., Seattle, 1968. Staff fellow NIH, Bethesda, Md., 1969-71; research fellow U. Cambridge, Eng., 1971-72; from asst. to prof. physiology U. Calif., San Francisco, 1973-87; chair dept. physiology U. Mich., Ann Arbor, 1987—2008, prof. physiology & internal medicine, 1987—. Mem. gen. medicine study sect. NIH, Bethesda, 1985-88, NIDDK, DDK-C study sect., 1991-95. Contbr. numerous articles to profl. jours.; editor Am. Jour. Physiology: Gastrointestinal Physiology, 1985-91; assoc. editor Jour. Clin. Investigation, 1997-01; sect. editor Ann. Rev. Physiology, 2001-05. Trustee Friends Sch. in Detroit, 1992—2000. Grantee, NIH, 1973—. Fellow Am. Assn. Advancement Sci.; mem. Am. Physiol. Soc. (Hoffman LaRoche prize 1985, mem. coun. 1996-99, pres. 2003-04), Am. Soc. Cell Biology, Am. Soc. Clin. Investigation, Am. Gastroenterology Assn., Am. Pancreatic Assn. (pres. 1985-86), Assn. Am. Physicians. Democrat. Home: 1115 Woodlawn Ave Ann Arbor MI 48104-3956 Office: Dept Molecular & Intergrative Physiology Univ of Mich Med Sch Ann Arbor MI 48109 Office Phone: 734-647-2886. Business E-Mail: jawillms@umich.edu.

WILLIAMS, JOHN B., lobbyist, consultant; b. Toronto, Canada, June 29, 1982; s. Earnest B. Williams and Loretta A. Rymer-Williams. BA, U. Mass., Amherst, 2008. Staff John Kerry Pres., Boston, 2003—04, Samara Barend for US Congress, Corning, 2004—04; mng. ptnr. Williams & Mason Consulting Group, Fort Worth, Tex., 2008—, sr. cons. Dallas, 2008—. Mktg. & comm. com. U. Mass. Alumni Assn., Amherst, Mass., 2007—08. Mem.: Am. Assn. Polit. Cons., U. Mass. Alumni Assn. Liberal. Unitarian. Office: Williams & Mason Consulting Group 4004 OHare Court #501 Fort Worth TX 76155 Business E-Mail: john@williamsmason.com.

WILLIAMS, JOHN D., paper company executive; Grad., King's Coll. London Univ., England. Pres. SCA Packaging Europe, Brussels, 2005—08; pres., CEO Domtar Corp., Montreal, Quebec, Canada, 2009—. Office: Domtar Corp 395 de Maisonneuve Blvd W Montreal PQ H3A 1L6 Canada*

WILLIAMS, JOHN EDWARD, lawyer; b. Atlanta, May 21, 1946; s. Edward Carl and Mary E. (Griffin) W.; m. Kristin Forsberg, May 22, 1976; children: Alexandra, Courtney, Charles. BA, Yale U., 1968; JD, U. Va., 1974; LLM in Taxation, Georgetown U., 1977. Bar: Va. 1974, D.C. 1975, U.S. Dist. Ct. D.C. 1975, U.S. Tax Ct. 1975, U.S. Ct. Appeals (D.C. cir.) 1975, U.S. Supreme Ct. 1977. Law clk. to Judge Charles R. Richey U.S. Dist. Ct. (D.C. dist.), 1974-75; assoc. Patton, Boggs & Blow, Washington, 1975-78, Cadwalader, Wickersham & Taft, Washington, 1978-81; asst. to the commr. IRS, Washington, 1981-84; tax counsel Ropes & Gray, Washington, 1984-86; ptnr. David & Hagner, P.C., Washington, 1986-90, Winston & Strawn, Washington, 1990-2000; atty. Law Offices of John E. Williams, 2000—. Editl. bd. U. Va. Law Review, 1972-74; mem. Jud. Conf. of D.C. Cir., 1978, 82, 85, 87, 92. With USAR, 1968—74. Recipient IRS Commissioner's award, 1984. Mem. ABA (tax sect., chmn. tech. subcom., adminstrv. practice com. 1986-88), Met. Club, Yale Club N.Y.C., Heritage Hunt Club. Office: 3213 Duke St Ste 601 Alexandria VA 22314 Office Phone: 703-838-2939. Business E-Mail: johnedwardwilliams@earthlink.net.

WILLIAMS, JOHN HORTER, civil engineer, energy industry executive; b. Havana, Cuba, Aug. 17, 1918; s. Charles P. and Alice Magruder (Dyer) W.; m. Emily Alice Ijams, June 6, 1942 (dec.); children: John H., Burch I., S. Miller; m. Joanne Harwell Simpson., Feb. 1, 1975. BS, Yale U., 1940. Registered profl. engr., Okla., Minn. With The Williams Cos. Inc., Tulsa, 1940-42, 46-50, pres., dir., 1950-70, chmn., chief exec. officer, 1971-78, now hon. dir. Bd. dirs. Apco Argentina, Inc., Unit Corp.; hon. bd. dirs. Willbros Group, Inc. Served with USNR, 1942-46. Decorated Order of Condor of Andes (Bolivia); named Okla. Hall of Fame, 1977; recipient Outstanding Okla. Oil Man award Okla.-Kans. Oil and Gas Assn., 1982, Disting. Svc. award Nat. Petroleum Hall of Fame, 1985; inducted into Okla. Commerce and Industry Hall of Honor, 1986, Tulsa Hall of Fame, 1993. Mem. ASCE, Yale Engring. Assn. Office: The Williams Cos Inc Ste 4500 One Williams Ctr Tulsa OK 74172

WILLIAMS, JOHN JAMES, JR., architect; b. Denver, July 13, 1949; s. John James and Virginia Lee (Thompson) W.; m. Mary Serene Morck, July 29, 1972. BArch, U. Colo., 1974. Registered architect, Colo., Calif., Idaho, Va., Utah, N.Mex., Ind., Mo., Ga., Ariz., Tex. Project architect Gensler Assoc. Architects, Denver, 1976, Heinzman Assoc. Architects, Boulder, Colo., 1977, EZTH Architects, Boulder, 1978-79; prin. Knudson/Williams PC, Boulder, 1980-82, Faber, Williams & Brown, Boulder, 1982-86, John Williams & Assocs., Denver, 1986-97; John Williams Architecture P.C., 1997—. Panel chmn. U. Colo. World Affairs Conf.; vis. faculty U. Colo. Sch. Architecture and Planning, Coll. Environ. Design, 1986-91; dean's adv. bd. Coll. Arch. and Planning, 2000-04. Author (with others) State of Colorado architect licensing law, 1986. Commr. Downtown Boulder Mall Commn., 1985-88; bd. dirs. U. Colo. Fairway Club, 1986-88; mem. Gov's. Natural Hazard Mitigation Coun., State of Colo., 1990. Recipient Tchg. Honorarium, U. Colo. Coll. Architecture and Planning, 1977-80, 88, Excellence in Design and Planning award City of Boulder, 1981-82, Citation for Excellenc, WOOD Inc., 1982, 93, Disting. Profl. Svc. award Coll. Environ. Design U. Colo., 1988, James Sudler Svc. award AIA, Denver, 1998 Mem. AIA (sec. 1988, bd. dirs. Colo. North chpt. 1985-86, chair Colo. govtl. affairs com. 1995-98, Design award 1993, 2001, pres. 1990, sec. Colo. chpt. 1988, ednl. fund Fisher I traveling scholar 1988, state design conf. chair 1991, North chpt. Design award 1993, treas. Denver chpt. 1998, v.p. 1999, pres. edn. Colo. chpt. 2001, Disting. Svc. award Colo. chpt. 2001, Pres. Svc. award, 2004), Architects and Planners of Boulder (v.p. 1982), Nat. Coun. Architect Registration Bd., Nat. Golf Found. (sponsor), Kappa Sigma (chpt. pres. 1970). Avocations: golf, political history, fitness and health. Home: 1031 Turnberry Cir Louisville CO 80027-9594 Office: John Williams Architecture PC 350 Interlocken Blvd Ste 340 Broomfield CO 80021 Office Phone: 303-295-6190. Business E-Mail: johnw@jwarchitecture.com.

WILLIAMS, JOHN LEE, lawyer; b. Nashville, Dec. 23, 1942; s. Leslie Elwood and Gladys Mae (Ridings) W.; m. Norma Jean Givens, May 27, 1967; 1 child, Jacob Andrew. BA, Tenn. Technol. U., 1964; JD, U. Tenn., 1967. Bar: Tenn 1967. Ptnr. Porch, Peeler & Williams, Waverly, Tenn., 1967-78, Porch, Peeler, Williams & Thomason, Waverly, 1978—; asst. dist. atty. 23d Jud. Cir. Ct. Tenn., 1972-74; judge Ct. Gen. Sessions of Humphreys County, Tenn., 1978-82. County atty. Humphreys County, 1968—72, 1982—86, 1994—; city atty. City of Waverly, 1978—, City of McEwen, Tenn., 1978—, City of Lobelville, Tenn., 1985—89; gen. counsel Meriwether Lewis Elec. Coop., Centerville, Tenn., 1980—. State legal counsel Tenn. Jaycees, 1970; treas., sec. Humphreys County Dem. Exec. Com., 1978-2001; chmn. Humphreys County Election Commn., 1968-72. Col. U.S. Army ret. Mem.: Humphreys County Bar Assn. (pres. 1978—), Tenn. Bar Assn. (ho. of dels.), Masons (master 1985, 1999, 2005). Home: 1739 Ogden Rd Mc Ewen TN 37101 Home Phone: 931-296-1369; Office Phone: 931-296-7741. Business E-Mail: john.williams@porchpeeler.com.

WILLIAMS, JOHN LEICESTER, mechanical engineer, educator; b. Germiston, Transvaal, Republic of South Africa, July 22, 1952; came to U.S., 1971; s. Leicester Garnet and Drusilla Wallace (Pringle) W.; m. Lillian Yuriko Kubota, June 25, 1976; 1 child, Ian Nobuo. BS in Biology, U. Hawaii, 1975; MS, Northwestern U., 1979, PhD in Theoretical/Applied Mechanics, 1981. Asst. prof. mech. engring. Northeastern U., Boston, 1981-85, Syracuse (N.Y.) U., 1985-88, dir. univ. computer aided design and engring., 1986-88; asst. prof. orthopaedic surgery and bioengring. U. Pa., Phila., 1988-95; assoc. prof. orthopaedic surgery U. Mo., Kansas City, 1995—2005, assoc. prof. oral biology, 1999—2005; staff engr. De Puy Orthopaedics, Inc., Warsaw, Ind., 2005—. Referee Jour. Biomech. Engring., Jour. Biomechanics, Applied Mechanics Revs., J. Orthop. Rsch., Clin. Orthop. Rel. Res. Author: (with others) The Hip and Its Disorders, 1991; contbr. articles to profl.jours. Named Nat. Rsch. Svc. Tng. fellow NIH, 1976-80, grantee, 1984-86, NSF, 1985-86, Orthopaedic Rsch. and Edn. Found. Mem. ASME, Am. Soc. Biomechanics, Orthopaedic Rsch. Soc. Achievements include research in computer modeling of the spine for crash mechanics research, anisotropic mechanical and structural properties of bone and growth plate, ultrasonic characterization of bone tissue and composites and strain transduction by cells, shoulder and knee kinematics. Office Phone: 574-371-4718. Business E-Mail: jwilli58@depuys.jnj.com.

WILLIAMS, JOHN N., dean, dental educator; BA with honors, Transylvania U., Lexington, KY, 1974; DMD, U. Louisville, 1980, MBA, 1987. Asst. u. provost U. Louisville, 1988—91; dean U. Louisville Sch. Dentistry, 1999—2005; assoc. dean for ednl. programs U. of Louisville Sch. of Dentistry, 1991—98; prof. dept. periodontics, endontics and dental hygiene U. Louisville Sch. Dentistry; dean U. N.C. Sch. Dentistry, Chapel Hill, NC, 2005—. Mem. editl. bd. Jour. Contemporary Dental Practice. Mem.: Am. Acad. Devel. Medicine and Dentistry. Avocations: boating, classical & choral singing. Office: Sch Dentistry NC Univ CB #7450 1090 Old Dental Bldg Chapel Hill NC 27599-7450 Office Phone: 919-966-2731. Business E-Mail: john_williams@dentistry.unc.edu.

WILLIAMS, JOHN TOWNER, composer, conductor; b. LI, NY, Feb. 8, 1932; s. John and Esther Williams; m. Barbara Ruike, 1956 (dec. 1974); children: Jennifer, Mark, Joseph; m. Samantha Winslow, 1980. Student, UCLA; studied with Mario Castelnuovo-Tedesco, Los Angeles; student, Juilliard Sch.; studied with Madame Rosina Lhevinne, NYC; degree (hon.), Berklee Coll. Music, Boston, Northeastern U., Tufts U., U. So. Calif., Boston U., New Eng. Conservatory Music, Providence Coll. Pianist Columbia & Twentieth Century-Fox, 1956—; condr. Boston Pops Orch., 1980—93, laureate condr., 1993—; artist-in-residence Tanglewood Music Ctr., Boston, 1993—94. Guest condr. with orchestras including Cleveland Orch., Denver Symphony, Indianapolis Symphony, London Symphony Orch., Los Angeles Philharmonic, Montreal Orch., Philadelphia Orch., and Toronto Orch. Works include: composer (film scores) I Passed for White, 1960, Because They're Young, 1960, The Secret Ways, 1961, Bachelor Flat, 1962, Diamond Head, 1962, Gidget Goes to Rome, 1963, The Killers, 1964, John Goldfarb, Please Come Home, 1964, None But the Brave, 1965, How to Steal a Million, 1966, The Rare Breed, 1966, Not With My Wife, You Don't, 1966, The Plainsman, 1966, Penelope, 1966, A Guide for the Married Man, 1967, Valley of the Dolls, 1967 (Acad. award nominee), Fitzwilly, 1968, Sergeant Ryker, 1968, The Reivers, 1969 (Acad. award nominee), Daddy's Gone A-Hunting, 1969, Goodbye, Mr. Chips, 1969 (Acad. award nominee), The Story of A Woman, 1970, Fiddler on the Roof, 1971 (Acad. award for musical adaptation 1971), The Cowboys, 1972, The Poseidon Adventure, 1972 (Acad. award nominee), Images, 1972 (Acad. award nominee), Pete 'n' Tillie, 1972, The Paper Chase, 1973, The Long Goodbye, 1973, The Man Who Loved Cat Dancing, 1973, Cinderella Liberty, 1973 (Acad. award nominee), Tom Sawyer, 1973 (Acad. award nominee), Sugarland Express, 1974, Earthquake, 1974, The Towering Inferno, 1974 (Acad. award nominee), Conrack, 1974, Jaws, 1975 (Acad. award, Grammy award, Golden Globe award 1976), The Eiger Sanction, 1976, Family Plot, 1976, Midway, 1976, The Missouri Breaks, 1976, Raggedy Ann and Andy, 1977, Black Sunday, 1977, Star Wars, 1977 (Acad. award, 3 Grammy awards, Golden Globe award 1977), Close Encounters of the Third Kind, 1977 (2 Grammy awards, Acad. award nominee 1978), The Fury, 1978, Jaws II, 1978, Superman, 1978 (2 Grammy awards 1979), Meteor, 1979, Quintet, 1979, Dracula, 1979, "1941", 1979, The Empire Strikes Back, 1980 (2 Grammy awards, Acad. award nominee 1980), Raiders of the Lost Ark, 1981 (Grammy award, Acad. award nominee 1981), Heartbeeps, 1981, E.T., 1982 (Acad. award for best original score, 3 Grammy awards, Golden Globe award 1982), Monsignor, 1982, Yes, Giorgio, 1982 (Acad. award nominee), Superman III, 1983, Return of the Jedi, 1983 (Acad. award nominee), Indiana Jones and the Temple of Doom, 1984 (Acad. award nominee), The River, 1984 (Acad. award nominee), Space Camp, 1986, Emma's War, 1986, The Witches of Eastwick, 1987 (Acad. award nominee), Empire of the Sun, 1987 (Acad. award nominee), Jaws: The Revenge, 1987, Superman IV: The Quest for Peace, 1987, The Secret of My Success, 1987, The Accidental Tourist, 1988 (Acad. award nominee, Indiana Jones and the Last Crusade, 1989 (Acad. award nominee), Always, 1989, Born On The Fourth of July, 1989 (Acad. award nominee), Stanley and Iris, 1990, Presumed Innocent, 1990, Home Alone, 1990 (Acad. award nominee), Hook, 1991 (Acad. award nominee), JFK, 1991 (Acad. award nominee), Far and Away, 1992, Home Alone II, 1992, Jurassic Park, 1993, Schindler's List, 1993 (Acad. award 1993, Grammy award 1994), Sabrina, 1995 (Acad. award nominee for best original score 1996), Nixon, 1995 (Acad. award nominee 1996), Sleepers, 1996, Rosewood, 1997, The Lost World: Jurassic Park, 1997, Seven Years In Tibet, 1997 (Acad. award nominee), Amistad, 1997 (Acad. award nominee), Saving Private Ryan, 1998 (Acad. award nominee, Grammy award 1998), Stepmom, 1998, Star Wars Episode I: The Phantom Menace, 1999, Angela's Ashes, 1999 (Acad. award nominee, Grammy award 2000), The Patriot, 2000 (Acad. award nominee), Artificial Intelligence, 2001 (Acad. award nominee), Harry Potter and The Sorcerer's Stone, 2001 (Acad. award nominee), Minority Report, 2002, Star Wars Episode II: Attack Of The Clones, 2002, Harry Potter: The Chamber Of Secrets, 2002, Catch Me If You Can, 2002 (Acad. award nominee), Harry Potter: The Prisoner Of Azkaban, 2004, The Terminal, 2004, Star Wars Episode III: The Revenge of the Sith, 2005, War of the Worlds, 2005, Memoirs of a Geisha, 2005 (Broadcast Film Assn. award, 2006, Best Original Score-Motion Picture, Hollywood Fgn. Press Assn., Golden Globe award) 2006, Grammy award, 2007), Munich, 2005 (Grammy award, 2007), Indiana Jones and the Kingdom of the Crystal Skull, 2008 (Grammy award, 2009); composer music for songs including:(from Sabrina, lyrics by Alan and Marilyn Bergman) Moonlight, 1995 (Acad. award nominee 1996); composer:(TV programs) Heidi, 1969 (Emmy award), Jane Eyre, 1971 (Emmyaward), Masterpiece Theatre, 1971, Malcolm in the Middle, 2000, Smallville, 2001, (main theme) Jack & Bobby, 2004, others; composer numerous concert pieces and symphonies including Jubilee 350 Fanfare for the Boston Pops, 1980, theme to the 1984 Summer OlympicGames, Liberty Fanfare, 1987; recorded numerous albums with Boston Pops Orch. including Pops in Space, That's Entertainment (Pops on Broadway), Pops on the March, Pops Aroundthe World (Digital Overtures), Aisle Seat, Pops Out of This World, Boston Pops on Stage, America, the Dream Goes On; collaborator: (with Jessye Norman) With A Song in My Heart, Swing, Swing, Swing, Unforgettable; guest condr. major orchs. including London Symphony Orch., Cleve. Orch., Phila. Orch., Toronto Orch., Montreal Orch. Served with USAF, 1952-54. Recipient several gold and platinum records Rec. Industry Assn. Am., Kennedy Ctr. Honors, John F. Kennedy Ctr. Performing Arts, 2004. Fellow: Am. Acad. Arts and Sciences. Composer of over seventy-five film scores. Office: Boston Symphony Orch 301 Mass Ave Boston MA 02115 also: The Gorfaine Schwartz Agency Inc 4111 W Alameda Ave Ste 509 Burbank CA 91505-4171*

WILLIAMS, JOSEPH DALTON, pharmaceutical executive; b. Washington, Pa., Aug. 15, 1926; s. Joseph Dalton and Jane (Day) W.; m. Mildred E. Bellaire, June 28, 1973; children: Terri, Daniel. BS in Pharmacy, U. Nebr., 1950; DSc (hon.), Union U., 1991, U. Nebr., 1989; LHD (hon.), Albany Coll. Pharmacy, Union U., 1980, Rutgers U., 1987, Long Island U., 1988; DSc (hon.), Phila. Coll. Pharmacy and Sci., 1988, Long Island U., 1988, Albany Coll. Pharmacy of Union U., 1991; D Human Svcs. (hon.), Caldwell Coll., 1989; LLD (hon.), Bethune-Cookman Coll., 1990, Coll. St. Elizabeth, 1990, Seton Hall U., 1990, U. Md., 1991, St. Augustine Coll., 1992. Pres. Parke-Davis Co., Detroit, 1973-76; pres. pharm. group Warner-Lambert Co., Morris Plains, NJ, 1976-77; pres. Internat. Group, 1977-79; pres., dir. Warner-Lambert Corp., 1979-80, pres., chief operating officer, 1980-84, chmn., CEO, 1985-91, chmn. exec. com., 1991-97; retired, 1997. Bd. dirs. AT&T, 1984-1997, J.C. Penny & Co., 1985-1998, Exxon Corp., 1985-1997, Rockefeller Fin. Svcs. Inc., Rockefeller and Co., Inc., 1992-1999, Eckerd Corp., 1997-2000. Trustee emeritus Columbia U. With USNR, 1943—46. Mem. Am. Pharm. Assn., Links Club, Pine Valley Golf Club, Baltusrol Golf Club, Mid Ocean Club. Office: Warner-Lambert Co 55 Madison Ave Morristown NJ 07960-7397 Office Phone: 973-285-3277.

WILLIAMS, JOSEPH SCOTT, energy and natural resources company executive, former city commissioner; b. Chgo., Nov. 10, 1951; s. Hagle Eugene and Helen Elizabeth (Mellon) W.; m. Tamalou Mitchell, June 10, 1972 (dec. Apr. 2000); children: Troy Scott, Ari Layne; m. Terry Thompson, Aug. 26, 2006. Welding Cert., John A. Logan Coll., Carterville, Ill., 1971; Cert. in Mining Tech., Rend Lake Coll., Ina, Ill., 1975. Dealer S&S Motors, West Frankfort, Ill., 1970-74; coal mine laborer Peabody Coal Co., Freeburg, Ill., 1973; coal mine electrician Old Ben Coal Co., Sesser, Ill., 1973-76; alt. energy cons. Helios Devel. Co., West Frankfort, Ill., 1977-83; instr. Rend Lake Coll., Ina, 1979-82; coal mine repairman Freeman United Coal Co., Pittsburg, Ill., 1979-87; mgr. ops. Royal Talon Co., West Frankfort, 1989—, pres., 2000—, Egyptian Energies, Inc., West Frankfort, 1987—, Horn Dimond Coal Co., West Frankfort, 1991—. Mem. Ill. State Mining Bd., Springfield, 1993-2003, sec., 1996-2003; pres. United Mine Workers Labor Union 9878, West

Frankfort, 1990-2008. Precinct committeeman Rep. Party, Franklin County, 1988-94; reg. coord. Citizens for Sue Suter, 1990, Citizens for Jim Ryan, 1994; transition adv. com. mem. Jim Ryan Ill. Atty. Gen., Chgo., 1995; advisor, dir. Ill. YMCA Youth and Govt., 1992—; chaplain Racers for Christ, 2003—; commr. pub. health and safety City of West Frankfort, Ill., 1999-2003 Mem. Ill. Oil and Gas Assn. (dir. 1999-), West Frankfort C. of C. (dir. 1988-2003), Moose, Masons (32 deg.), Shriner (Krazy Klown unit dir. 1997-99), Lions (pres. 1992-93), Am. Assn. Profl. Landmen. Avocations: motorcycling, collecting automobiles and memorabilia. Office: Egyptian Energies Inc 107 S Van Buren St PO Box 127 West Frankfort IL 62896-0127 Personal E-mail: jsw127@gmail.com.

WILLIAMS, JOY, writer; b. Chelmsford, Mass., Feb. 11, 1944; d. William Lloyd and Elisabeth (Thomas) Williams; m. Rust Hills; 1 child, Caitlin. MA magna cum laude, Marietta Coll., Ohio, 1963; MFA, U. Iowa, 1965. Rschr., data analyst USN, Siesta Key, Fla., 1967-69; now writer. Vis. instr. U. Houston, 1982, U. Fla., 1983, U. Calif., Irvine, 1984, U. Iowa, 1984, U. Ariz., 1987. Author: State of Grace, 1973, The Changeling, 1978, Taking Care, 1982, Breaking and Entering, 1988, Escapes, 1990, The Quick and the Dead, 2000 (Pulitzer Prize finalist, 2000), Ill Nature: Rants and Reflections on Humanity and Other Animals, 2001 (Rez Short Story award, 2002), The Florida Keys: A History & Guide (10th edit.), 2003, Honored Guest, 2004; contbr. short stories to mags. Recipient Nat. Mag. award for fiction, 1980; NEA grantee, 1973, Guggenheim fellow, 1974. Mem.: AAAL (Harold and Mildred Strauss Livings award 1993), Phi Beta Kappa. Democrat. Office: 1425 E magee Rd Tucson AZ 85718 also: Amanda Urban ICM 40 W 57th St New York NY 10019-4001

WILLIAMS, JUAN, news correspondent; b. Colón, Panama, Apr. 1954; BA in Philosophy, Haverford Coll., Pa., 1976. Editl. writer, op-ed columnist, White House corr. Washington Post, 1976—99; host syndicated TV program America's Black Forum, 1996—; polit. contbr. FOX News Channel, 1997—; sr. nat. corr. Nat. Public Radio (NPR), 2000—, host, Talk of the Nation, 2000—01. Regular panelist Special Report with Bret Baier, Fox News Sunday with Chris Wallace. Author: Eyes on the Prize: America's Civil Rights Years, 1954-1965, 1988, Thurgood Marshall: American Revolutionary, 2000, My Soul Looks Back in Wonder: Voices of the Civil Rights Experience, 2004, Enough: The Phony Leaders, Dead-End Movements, and Culture of Failure That Are Undermining Black America — and What We Can Do about It, 2006; contbr. articles to Fortune, Atlantic Monthly, Ebony, GQ, New Republic; guest appearances Nightline, ABC, Washington Week in Review, PBS, Oprah. Office: FOX News Channel 400 N Capitol St NW Ste 550 Washington DC 20001*

WILLIAMS, JUANITA ROSALIE, artist; b. Zanesville, Ohio, Aug. 7, 1933; d. Joseph Russell and Gladys Lucille (Worden) Somers; m. Roy George Williams, Feb. 16, 1952 (div. 2002); children: Karin Sue Williams Brandi, Kenneth Roy. Grad. high sch., Zanesville. Juror Bexley (Ohio) Art Guild, Capital U., 1984. One-woman shows include Collector's Gallery Columbus Mus. Fine Art, Ohio, 1972, Pomerene Fine Arts Ctr., 1991, McDonough Gallery, Marietta Coll., 1991, Blue Sky Gallery, Columbus, 1992, exhibited in group shows at Zanesville Art Ctr., 1981, 1990, Franklin U., Columbus, Ohio, 1985, Marietta (Ohio) Coll., 1991, Pomerene Fine Arts Ctr., Coshocton, Ohio, 1991, No. Ariz. U., 1992, French Art Colony, Gallipolis, Ohio, 1992, Soc. Layerists in Multi-Media, San Miguel Allende, Mex., 1996, Albuquerque Mus., 2007, Marlborough, Eng., 1997, Sirius Gallery, Santa Fe, 2001, Giving Shelter Exhbn., 516 Arts Gallery, Albuquerque, 2008, Represented in permanent collections Zanesville Art Ctr., Ohio, Soc. Bank Cleve., Edward Cherry Corp., Columbus, Nat. WaterColor Soc. Bd. dirs. Zanesville Art Ctr., 1986-90. 92-95. Recipient 1st award Rocky Mountain Nat., 1984, Elsie and David Wu-Ject Key award Am. Watercolor Soc., 1989, 4th award San Diego Watercolor Soc., 1993. Mem. Nat. Watercolor Soc., Soc. Layerists in Multi-Media, Ohio Watercolor Soc. (silver Buckeye award 1986), Southeastern Ohio Watercolor Soc. (co-founder, 1st pres. 1978-79). Avocations: gardening, interior decorating, reading, metaphyics, travel. Mailing: 9908 Wild Turkey NW Albuquerque NM 87114 Office Phone: 505-792-7782. E-mail: juan1aran@aol.com.

WILLIAMS, KAREN HASTIE, lawyer; b. Washington, Sept. 30, 1944; d. William Henry and Beryl (Lockhart) Hastie; m. Wesley S. Williams, Jr.; children: Amanda Pedersen, Wesley Hastie, Bailey Lockhart. Cert., U. Neuchatel, Switzerland, 1965; BA, Bates Coll., 1966; MA, Tufts U., 1967; JD, Cath. U. Am., 1973. Bar: D.C. 1973. Staff asst. internat. gov. relations dept. Mobil Oil Corp., NYC, 1967-69; staff asst. com. Dist. Columbia U.S. Senate, 1970, chief counsel com. on the budget, 1977-80; law clk. to judge Spottswood Robinson III U.S. Ct. Appeals (D.C. Cir.), Washington, 1973-74; law clk. to assoc. justice Thurgood Marshall U.S. Supreme Ct., Washington, 1974-75; assoc. Fried, Frank, Harris, Shriver & Kampelman, Washington, 1975-77, 1975-77; adminstr. Office Mgmt. and Budget, Washington, 1980-81; of counsel Crowell & Moring, Washington, 1982, ptnr., 1982—2004; ret., 2005. Bd. dirs. Chubb Corp., Gannett Co., Inc., Sun Trust Bank, Inc., Washington Gas Light Co., Continental Airlines. Trustee, past chair Greater Washington Rsch. Ctr. Mem. ABA (pub. contract law sect., past chair), Nat. Bar Assn., Washington Bar Assn., Nat. Contract Mgmt. Assn., NAACP (legal def. fund, bd. dirs.). Office: Crowell & Moring 1001 Pennsylvania Ave NW Ste 1100 Washington DC 20004-2595

WILLIAMS, KENNETH SCOTT, entertainment and advertising company executive; b. Tulsa, Okla., Dec. 31, 1955; s. David Vorhees Williams and Mary Louise (Newell) Rose; m. Jann Catherine Wolfe, May 20, 1989; children: Catherine Eloise, Michael Holbrook. BA, Harvard Coll., 1978; MS, Columbia U., 1985. Bank officer Chase Manhattan Bank, NYC, 1978-82; asst. treas. Columbia Pictures Entertainment, NYC, 1982-84, v.p., treas., 1984-89, sr. v.p. fin. and adminstrn. Burbank, Calif., 1990-91; sr. v.p. corp. ops. Sony Pictures Entertainment, Culver City, Calif., 1991-95, exec. v.p., 1995-96; pres. Digital Studio divsn. Sony Pictures Entertainment, 1996-2000, Technicolor Digital Cinema, Burbank, Calif., 2002; pres., CEO Stan Lee Media, Inc., Encino, Calif., 2000—02; COO Ascent Media Group, Santa Monica, Calif., 2002—03, pres., CEO, 2003—06, investment adv. cons., 2007—; CEO Captive Media, Inc., 2007—. Past pres., bd. dirs. L.A. Conservancy; former chmn. Entertainment Tech. Ctr. U. So. Calif.; former trustee U. Calif., Riverside; bd. dirs. L.A. Music Ctr., L.A. Pub. Access TV Channel 36, chmn. bd.; bd. dirs. L.A. Master Chorale; mem. Blue Hill Troupe, NYC, 1979—. Mem. N.Y. Soc. Securities Analysts, Acad. Television Arts and Scis., Fin. Execs. Inst. (v.p.), Acad. Motion Picture Arts & Scis., Digital Coast Roundtable (bd. dirs.), Harvard Club So. Calif. (pres., bd. dirs.), Beta Gamma Sigma. Home: 457 Cuesta Way Los Angeles CA 90077-3434 Personal E-mail: kenneth_s_williams@hotmail.com. Business E-Mail: kwilliams@hcmn.com.

WILLIAMS, KEVIN, professional football player; b. Arkadelphia, Ark., Aug. 16, 1980; m. Tasha Williams, June 2005. BA in Gen. Studies, Okla. State U., Stillwater, 2003. Defensive tackle Minn. Vikings, 2003—. Named 1st Team All-Pro, AP, 2004, 2006—08; named to Nat. Football Conf. Pro Bowl Team, NFL, 2004, 2006—08. Office: Minn Vikings Football Club LLC 9520 Viking Dr Eden Prairie MN 55344*

WILLIAMS, KEVIN W., automotive executive; b. Lexington Park, Md., Sept. 27, 1961; B in Bus. Mgmt., Tenn. State U., 1983; MBA, Ctrl. Mich. U., 1989. Reliability analyst GM, Flint, Mich., 1983—89; gen. supr. prodn. Lansing Craft Ctr., 1989—91; program readiness mgr. GM EV1 electric vechicle program, 1991—93; reliability engr. North America Truck Group, 1993—95, asst. prodn. supr. Janesville, Wis., 1995—96, area mgr. gen. assembly, 1996; dir., supplier quality GM Europe, 1997—2000; exec. dir., supplier quality GM North America, 2000—03, v.p. quality, 2003—05, mem. North America Strategy Bd.; asst. mng. dir., mfg. mgr. GM de Mex., 2005—06, pres., mng. dir., 2006—. Bd. dirs. Motor Enterprises Inc. Mem.: Soc. Automotive Engineers (chmn. A World in Motion adv. com.). Office: GM Corp PO Box 33170 Detroit MI 48232-5170*

WILLIAMS, KIM ALLAN, cardiologist, educator; b. Chgo., Ill., Nov. 10, 1954; Attended, Coll. U. Chgo., 1971—75; MD, U. Chgo. Pritzker Sch. Med., 1979. Cert. Cardiology, Internal Medicine, 1982, Nuclear Medicine, 1986, Nuclear Cardiology. Intern, internal medicine Emory U., Atlanta, 1979—80, resident, cardiology, 1980—82; fellow, cardiology U. Chgo., 1982—85, fellow, clin. pharmacology Ill., 1984—85, fellow, nuclear medicine Ill., 1984—86; practicing, 1986—; assoc. prof. medicine U. Chgo. Pritzker Sch. Medicine, prof. medicine, radiology, dir., nuclear cardiology. Contbr. articles to profl. jours. Named one of Top Doctors, Chgo. Mag., 1996, 2000, 2004. Fellow: Assn. Black Cardiologists, Am. Heart Assn., Am. Soc. Nuclear Cardiology (chair, coalistion of cardiovascular organizations 2006—07, past pres.), Am. Coll. Cardiology (bd. trustee); mem.: AMA (chair, nuclear medicine sect. coun., AMA specialty svc. soc. 2006—07), Soc. Nuclear Medicine, Nat. Med. Assn., Assn. U. Radiologists, Am. Soc. Echocardiography. Office Phone: 312-702-6258. Office Fax: 773-702-4386, 773-702-3512. Business E-Mail: kwilliam@medicine.bsd.uchicago.edu.

WILLIAMS, LAWRENCE ERNEST, physicist; b. Youngstown, Ohio, Nov. 29, 1937; s. William Karapandza and Dorothy (Radulovich) Williams; m. Sonia Bell Bredmeyer; children: Erica, Beverley. BS in Physics, Carnegie-Mellon U., 1959; MS, U. Minn., 1962, PhD, 1965. Asst. prof. physics Western Ill. U., Macomb, 1968-70; asst. prof. radiology U. Minn., Mpls., 1973-78, NIH fellow, 1971-73, assoc. prof., 1978-80; imaging physicist City of Hope, Duarte, Calif., 1980—, prof., 2002—. Adj. assoc. prof. UCLA, 1982-92, adj. prof., 1992—; prof. Eurotech. Rsch. U., Palo Alto, Calif., 1983—; cons. Jet Propulsion Lab, Pasadena, Calif., 1981-84; mem. clin. oncology study sect. NIH, 2000-2003. Co-author: Biophysical Science, rev. 2d edit., 1979; editor Nuclear Medical Physics, 1987, assoc. editor, Med. Physics, 2005—; contbr. articles to med. jours.; patentee, inventor new method of abscess imaging; discoverer excited states in nuclear mass three system, mathematical model of tumor uptake of tracers; developer of a method to evaluate brake radiation doses; patentee, co-discoverer of tumor targeting by liposomes. Treas. United Meth. Ch., West Covina, Calif., 1982-83. Westinghouse Sci. Talent Search scholar, 1955, R.J. Wean scholar, 1957; NSF fellow U. Minn., 1961-62. Fellow Am. Coll. Angiology; mem. Soc. Nuclear Medicine (Gold medal exhibit 1983), Am. Assn. Physicists in Medicine, N.Y. Acad. Scis., Soc. for Computer Applications in Radiology, Sigma Xi. Methodist. Avocations: furniture refinishing, music, sketching. Office: City of Hope Med Ctr 1500 Duarte Rd Duarte CA 91010-3000 Office Phone: 626-359-8111 x 61488. E-mail: lwilliams@coh.org.

WILLIAMS, LAWRENCE SOPER, JR., photographer; b. Balt., July 8, 1917; s. Lawrence S. and Ida (Exall) W.; m. Avilda Leyshon Williams, Nov. 21, 1940; children: Jay Stephen, Wendy Lauren. Student, Md. Inst. Wirephoto operator AP, Balt., 1937—38; news photographer Balt. Sun Papers, 1938—40, Harris and Ewing News Photos, Washington, 1940—41; war corr., photographer Bur. Info. U.S. War Dept., Washington, 1941—45; picture editor Holiday mag., Phila., 1945—48; freelance photographer Havertown, Pa., 1949—59; pres. Lawrence S. Williams, Inc., Upper Darby, Pa., 1959—83, chmn., 1983—93. Pres. Archtl. Photographers Assn., N.Y.C., 1968-70, Paoli (Pa.) Woods Homeowner's Assn., 1985-86; chmn. archtl. landscape com. Robynwood Village, Hershey's Mill; vol., TV audio instr. West Chester Sch. Dist. Recipient Gold medal Artist Guild of Phila., 1965, Silver medal Artist Guild of Pa., 1964, George W. Berry trophy Soc. Comml. Photographers Del. Valley, 1961, 66, 78, 79, 82, Best of Show trophy Am. Mus. Photography, Phila., 1966, 71, 77, 79, 82, Best Comml. Print trophy Guild of Profl. Photographers Del. Valley, 1971, 70, Award of Excellence Am. Advtg. Assn. Pa., 1978, Pres.'s Cup Profl. Photographers Assn. Pa., 1971, Silver medal for Sixty Years World in Colour, Internat. Photo competition, Hague, Netherlands, 1973, numerous archtl., comml., indsl., pictorial awards. Fellow Am. Soc. Photographers; mem. Soc. Comml. Photographers Del. Valley (life), Profl. Photographers Assn. Pa. (life), Profl. Photographers Am., Inc. (life, master photography degree 1966, craftsman photography degree 1968), Shriners. Republican. Lutheran. Achievements include assembly of the largest collection of architectural photographs in U.S. consisting of over 250,000 negatives which are now in the archives of the Athenaeum of Philadelphia, Pa. Avocation: travel. Home: 14410 Shannondell Dr Audubon PA 19403-5609 Home Phone: 610-728-5427. Personal E-mail: larryvi1@gmail.com.

WILLIAMS, LENA ROSE, academic administrator; d. Tommie Lee Gibbs and Mable Johnson; m. Jimmie Lett Williams, Aug. 17, 1962; children: Michael Lee, Alfred Lee, Jimmie Lett Jr. BS, Lamar U., Beaumont, Tex., 1960; MA, U. San Francisco, 1982, EdD, 1986. Cert. Calif. Commn. Tchr. Credentialing. Tchr., adminstr. Vallejo City Unified Sch. Dist., Calif., 1067—2005. Office: Chapman Univ Coll 4820 Business Center Dr Ste 100 Fairfield CA 94534

WILLIAMS, LINDA DIANNE, retired music educator; d. James Melvin and Essie Mae Bowman; m. Fred Lee Williams (dec.); 1 child, Ryan Christopher Harley. B in Music Edn., Ohio State U., Columbus, 1972. Tchr. vocal music Arts Impact, Columbus, Ohio, 1972—77, Marion-Franklin HS, Columbus, Ohio, 1977—80, Beery Mid. Sch., Columbus, Ohio, 1980—2007; ret. Min. of music 1st Ch. of God, Columbus, Ohio, 1982—2000. Democrat. Avocations: music, travel, reading, shopping. Home: 2578 Anderley Ct Grove City OH 43123 Fax: 614-365-5412. E-mail: linda_williams124@hotmail.com.

WILLIAMS, LINDA FRANCES, public nutrition administrator; d. Junius and Frances Williams; children: Karl Junius, Kisha Marie DeMeyers. MSW, Western Mich. U., Kalamazoo, 2000; B, Calvin Coll., Grand Rapids, Mich., 1995. Specialty program in alcohol and drug abuse Western Mich. U., 2000. Fin. mgmt. specialist US HUD, Chgo., 1987—90; program specialist USDA Food Nutrition Svc., Grand Rapids, 1990—. Pres. Nat. Treasury Employees Union Chpt. 237, Chgo., 2007—. Composer: (songs) You Take the Cake (Chilites), 1983, Do What You Want (Chilites), 1984; author: It Ain't All About Eve and it Ain't Adam's Apple: Empowered to Break the Chains of the Past, 2008; contbr. to literary pubs. Fellow New Initiatives Grant, Prison Fellowship, 1996. Mem.: Alpha Kappa Mu. Achievements include design of software program for USDA; development of Exodus LifeChange Prisoner Reentry Program. Personal E-mail: lwilli8764@hotmail.com.

WILLIAMS, LINDA STALLWORTH, literature and language professor; b. Atlanta, Dec. 13, 1951; d. James Owen Stallworth and Pearl Bell Willis; m. Max Virgil Williams, Sept. 29, 1972; children: Laura LeAnne, Max Brenton. BA, U. W.Ga., Carrollton, 1972; MA, U. Ctrl. Okla., Edmond, 1986; PhD, U. Okla., Norman, 1990. Vis. lectr. U. Okla., Norman, 1988—91; prof. English Rose State Coll., Midwest City, Okla., 1991—94; acad. coord. faculty devel. Bd. Regents, U. Sys. Ga., Atlanta, 1996—98; assoc. prof. English N.Ga. Coll. and State U., Dahlonega, 1997—, prof. English, 2008. Recipient Dorothy Golden award for Excellence in Tchg. of Composition, Student Success in First-Year Composition Conf., 2001, Cert. of Appreciation for Patriotic Civilian Svc., Dept. of Army, 2005, 2007; named Ga. Prof. of Yr., Carnegie Found. Advancement Tchg., 2007. Mem.: Conf. Coll. Composition and Comm., Assn. Bus. Comm., Nat. Coun. Tchrs. of English. Home: 11000 Big Canoe Big Canoe GA 30143 Office: North Georgia Coll and State Univ 100 College Cir Dahlonega GA 30597 Office Phone: 706-864-1681. Business E-Mail: lswilliams@ngcsu.edu.

WILLIAMS, LISA A., music educator; d. Ida M. Williams. B in Music Edn., Howard U., Washington, 2000, M in Music Edn., 2003; MEd in Spl. Edn., U. San Diego, Calif., 2002; EdS in Spl. Edn., Fla. State U., Tallassee, 2005. Cert. tchr. Music K-12 Calif., Va., Fla., 2000, tchr. spl. edn. Fla., 2004. Tchr. spl. edn. San Diego City Schs., San Diego, 2000—02; tchr. music Fairfax County Schs., Fairfax, Va., 2002—03; tchr. spl. edn. Leon County Schs., Tallahassee, 2004—06, San Diego Unified Sch. Dist., 2006—07, dir. choral activities, 2007—. Acad. counselor Fla. State U., Tallahassee, 2003—04; site coord. Leon County Schs., Title I Program, Tallahassee, 2004; dir. children's choir Bethel AME Ch., San Diego, 2000—02. Named Riley Minority Educator of Yr., 2006; Spl. Edn. and Minority scholar, Howard U., Grad. asst., 2002—03, Childhood Edn., Reading and Disability Svcs. fellow, Fla. State U., 2005—06. Mem.: Nat. Assn. Music Educators, Phi Delta Kappa Internat. (Doctoral fellow 2003—04), Internat. Clarinet Assn., Nat. Assn. for Black Sch. Educators, NEA, Coun. for Exceptional Children, Tau Beta Sigma, Alpha Kappa Alpha (Ednl. Advancement Found. scholar 2005), Sigma Alpha Iota (life). Personal E-mail: pindrop26@aol.com.

WILLIAMS, LISA M., legislative staff member; Staff asst., Senator Joe Biden US Senate, Washington; legis. asst., Rep. Eni F. H. Faleomavaega US House of Reps., Washington, sr. policy dir., Rep. Eni F. H. Faleomavaega, 2001—02, legis. dir., Rep. Eni F. H. Faleomavaega, 2002—04, staff mem., fgn. affairs com., 2003—07, chief of staff to Rep. Eni F. H. Faleomavaega, 2004—, subcom. staff dir., fgn. affairs com., 2007—. Democrat. Office: 2422 Rayburn House Office Bldg Washington DC 20515 Office Phone: 202-225-8577. Office Fax: 202-225-8757. Business E-Mail: lisa.williams@mail.house.gov.*

WILLIAMS, LOUIS CLAIR, JR., public relations executive; b. Huntington, Ind., Nov. 7, 1940; s. Louis Clair and Marian Eileen W.; children— Terri Lynn, L. Bradley, Lisa C.; m. Mary Clare Moster. B.A., Eastern Mich. U., 1963. Copywriter, Rochester (N.Y.) Gas and Electric Co., 1963-65, editor RG&E News, 1965-66; employee info. specialist Gen. Ry. Signal Co., Rochester, 1966-67, supr. employment and employee rels., 1967-69; supr. pub. rels. Heublein, Inc., Hartford, Conn., 1969-70; dir. corp. communications Jewel Cos., Inc., Chgo., 1970-71; account exec. Ruder & Finn of Mid-Am., Chgo., 1971-73, v.p., 1973-76, sr. v.p., 1976-78; cons. Towers, Perrin, Forster & Crosby, Los Angeles, 1978-79; exec. v.p., gen. mgr. Harshe-Rotman & Druck, Inc., Chgo., 1979, pres. midwest region, 1979-80; v.p. Hill & Knowlton, Inc., Chgo., 1980-81, sr. v.p., 1981-83; pres. Savlin Williams Assocs., Evanston, Ill., 1983-85, L.C. Williams & Assocs., Chgo., 1985—. Mem. Internat. Assn. Bus. Communicators (chmn. found., pres., chmn. Chgo. chpt. 1979-80), Inst. Pub. Rels. (chmn. rsch. com. 2005), Pub. Rels. Soc. Am., Publicity Club Chgo. Personal E-mail: LCWA@att.net.

WILLIAMS, LOWELL CRAIG, lawyer, employee relations executive; b. Tehachapi, Calif., Dec. 3, 1947; s. Lyndon Williams and Gertrude (White) Sievert; m. Marsha Mendelssohn; children: John S., Jeffrey A. Bescheinigungeschichte, Georg August U., Germany, 1968; BA, U. Calif., Santa Barbara, 1969; JD, Columbia U., 1972. Bar: NY 1973, US Ct. Appeals (2nd cir.) 1974, US Supreme Ct. 1974. Assoc. Sullivan & Cromwell, NYC, 1972-75; sr. v.p. Elf Aquitaine, Inc., NYC, 1976-95; v.p. Compagnie des Machines Bull, NYC, 1995—, exec. v.p. group human resources, 1998-99; exec. dir. Exult Inc., NYC, 1999—2001; sr. advisor TPI Sourcing Inc., The Woodlands, Tex., 2002—03; v.p. global human resource svcs., gen. counsel EquaTerra, Inc., Houston, 2003—. Past pres. Scarsdale Synagogue. Mem. Internat. Bar Assn., German Law Assn. (past bd. dirs.), HROA (bd. trustee). Office: EquaTerra Inc Three Riverway No 1290 Houston TX 77056 Office Phone: 914-661-7904. Business E-Mail: lowell.williams@equaterra.com.

WILLIAMS, LUIDA K., retired elementary school educator; b. Valparaiso, Ind., May 15, 1942; d. Edgar Pricer and Velma (Cook) Williams. BS in Elem. Edn., Ind. U., Bloomington, 1965; MS in Elem. Edn., Butler U., Indpls., 1968. Cert. Tchr. William A. Bell Sch., 1965—2004; ret., 2004. Basketball coach William A. Bell Sch., 1968—90. Summer camp agent for at-risk children Englishton Camp, Lexington, Ind., 1970—2004; agent Jameson Camp, Indpls., 1966—2004. Recipient Tchr. of Yr. award, IPS Sch., 1991, Mary McClelland Vol. award, Jameson Camp, 1995, Tchr. of Yr. award, Soc. Intensified Edn. Mem.: NEA, Ind. Gen. Assembly (lobbyest 1970—90), Indpls. Edn. Assn. (rep. 1965—2004), Indpls. Edn. Assn., Ind. State Tchr. Assn. (ethics com. 1981—83). Avocation: tennis. Home: 7356 Mikesell Dr Indianapolis IN 46260 Home Phone: 317-255-2907.

WILLIAMS, LUTHER STEWARD, research scientist; b. Sawyerville, Ala., Aug. 19, 1940; s. Roosevelt and Mattie B. (Wallace) W.; m. Constance Marie Marion, Aug. 23, 1963; children: Mark Steward, Monique Marie. BA magna cum laude, Miles Coll., 1961; MS, Atlanta U., 1963; PhD, Purdue U., 1968, DSc (hon.), 1987, U. Louisville, 1992, Capitol Coll., 1996, Bowie State U., 1996, Tuskegee U., 1997, U. DC, 1999. NSF lab. asst. Spelman Coll., 1961-62, Atlanta U., 1962-63, instr. biology, faculty rsch. grantee, 1963-64, asst. prof. biology, 1969-70, prof. biology, 1984-87, pres., 1984-87; grad. tchg. asst. Purdue U., West Lafayette, Ind., 1964-65, grad. rsch. asst., 1965-66, asst. prof. biology, 1970-73, assoc. prof., 1973-79, prof., 1979-80, NIH Career Devel. awardee, 1971-75, asst. provost, 1976-80; dean Grad. Sch., prof. biology Washington U., St. Louis, 1980-83; v.p. acad. affairs, dean Grad. Sch. U. Colo., Boulder, 1983-84; Am. Cancer Soc. postdoctoral fellow SUNY-Stony Brook, 1968-69; assoc. prof. biology MIT, 1973-74; spl. asst. to dir. Nat. Inst. Gen. Med. Scis., NIH, Bethesda, Md., 1987-88; dep. dir. Nat. Inst. Gen. Med. Scis. NIH, Bethesda, 1988-89; sr. sci. advisor to dir. NSF, Washington, 1989-90, asst. dir. for edn. and human resources, 1990-99; visiting scholar Payson Ctr. Internat. Devel./Tech., Arlington, Va., 1999-2000; edn. cons., 2000—; provost, v.p. for acad. affairs Tuskegee U., Ala., 2006—. Educator, cons., 2000—; dir. edn., sr. advisor to dir. Mo. Bot. Garden, St. Louis, 2001-05; chmn. rev. com. MARC Program, Nat. Inst. Gen. Med. Scis., NIH, 1972-76; grant reviewer NIH, 1971-73, 76, NSF, 1973, 76-80, Med. Rsch. Coun. of N.Z., 1976; mem. life scis. sreening com. recombinant DNA adv. com. HEW, 1979-81; mem. nat. adv. gen. med. sci. council NIH, 1980-85; mem. adv. com. Office Tech. Assessment, Washington, 1984-87; chmn. fellowship adv. com. NRC Ford Found., 1984-85; mem.-at-large Grad. Record Exam. Bd., 1981-85, chmn. minority grad. edn. com., 1983-85; mem. health, safety and environ. affairs. com. Nat. Labs., U. Calif., 1981-87; mem. adv. panel Office Tech. Assessment, US Congress, 1985-86; mem. fed. task force on women, minorities and the handicapped in sci. and tech., 1987-91; mem. adv. panel to dir. sci. and tech. ctrs. devel. NSF, 1987-88; mem. nat. adv. com. White House Initiative on Historically Black Colls. and Univs. on Sci. and Tech., 1986-89; numerous other adv. bds. and coms. Contbr. sci. articles to profl. jours. Vice-chmn. bd. advisors Atlanta Neighborhood Justice Ctr., 1984-87; bd. dirs. Met. Atlanta United Way, 1986-87, Butler St. YMCA, Atlanta, 1985-87; trustee Atlanta Zool. Assn., 1985-87, Miles Coll., 1984-87, Atlanta U., 1984-87, 90-96; mem. nominating com. Dana Found; mem. St. Louis CC Found. Bd., 2004-06. NIH predoctoral fellow Purdue U., 1966-68; recipient William A. Hinton Rsch. Trng. award, Am. Soc. Microbiology, 1998, trustee award Acad. Scis. St. Louis, 2004; named to Black Coll. Hall of Fame, 2002. Fellow Am. Acad. Microbiology, Acad. Sci. St. Louis; mem. Am. Soc. Microbiology, Am. Chem. Soc., Am. Soc. Biol. Chemists (mem. ednl. affairs com. 1979-82, com. on equal opportunities for minorities 1972-84). Home and Office: 15286 Brightfield Manor Dr Chesterfield MO 63017 Office Phone: 314-577-5139. Business E-Mail: lswilliams1968@sbcglobal.net. E-mail: luther.williams@tuskegee.edu.

WILLIAMS, MAGGIE (MARGARET ANN WILLIAMS), political campaign manager, former federal official; b. Kans. City, Mo., Dec. 25, 1954; BA in Polit. Sci., Trinity Coll., 1977; MA in Comm., U. Pa., 1992. Aide to Congressman Morris K. Udall US Congress, 1977—78; dep. press sec. Dem. Nat. Convention, 1979—80, mgr. convention press office, 1980, convention staff mem. managing backstage & podium activities, 1984; dir. media rels. Ctr. on Budget & Policy Priorities; campaign press sec. for Congressman Robert Torricilli US Congress, 1982; comm. dir. Children's Def. Fund (CDF), 1984—89; mem. Clinton/Gore Presdl. Campaign, 1992; asst. to Pres., chief of staff to First Lady The White House, Washington, 1993-1997; pres. Fenton Communications, 2000—01; ptnr. GriffinWilliams LLC, 2005—; campaign mgr. Hillary Clinton 2008 Presdl. Campaign, 2008. Mem. adv. com. Harvard U. Inst. of Politics, 2007—. Democrat. Office: Hillary Clinton for President 4420 N Fairfax Dr Arlington VA 22203

WILLIAMS, MARC ADRIAN, medical educator, scientist, researcher; arrived in USA, 2000, permanent resident, 2008; s. Peter Henry and Ann Elizabeth Williams; m. Beverley Jayne Hunt, Oct. 3, 2003. BS in Molecular Biology, Applied Biology, U. Coventry, 1989; PhD in Exptl. Medicine & Hematology, U. London, 1999. Rsch. asst., scientist haematology and immunobiology U. London, St. Barts and Royal London Sch. Medicine, 1992—2000; post doc. fellowship in immunology U. Calif. San Diego, La Jolla, 2000—01; post doc. fellowship in immunology and autoimmunity Johns Hopkins U. Sch. Medicine, Balt., 2001—02, rsch. faculty assoc. in immunology, 2002—04, instr. medicine, 2004—06; asst. prof. environ. medicine U. Rochester Sch. Medicine, 2006—. Co-editor: Stem Cells and Devel. Jour., 2004—06; assoc. editor Stem Cells and Devel. Jour., New Rochelle, NY, 2006—, editl. bd. mem. Biomarker Insights Jour., Aukland, New Zealand, 2006—, Jour. of Innate Immunity, —, Jour. Receptor, Ligard and Channel Research, —; contbr. articles to profl. jours. Recipient Pres. prize, Royal Soc. Medicine, 1994. Mem.: Am. Thoracic Soc. (program com. mem. 2006—), Internat. Soc. Cellular Therapy, Gerson-Lehrman Group, Healthcare Coun., Austin (cons.), AAAAI (com. on air pollution, sub-committ on immunomodulation), Am. Acad. Allergy, Asthma and Immunology. Office: Univ Rochester Sch Med 601 Elmwood Ave Box 692 Rochester NY 14642-8692 Business E-Mail: marc_williams@urmc.rochester.edu.

WILLIAMS, MARIO, professional football player; b. Richlands, NC, Jan. 31, 1985; Student in profl. sports mgmt., NC State U., Raleigh, 2004—06. Defensive end Houston Texans, 2006—. Recipient Bob Warren award for integrity and sportsmanship; named First Team All-American, AP, 2005, Defensive Lineman of Yr., NFL Alumni, 2007; named to Am. Football Conf. Pro Bowl Team, NFL, 2008. Achievements include being the first overall selection in the NFL Draft, 2006. Office: Houston Texans Two Reliant Park Houston TX 77054*

WILLIAMS, MARK EDWARD, geriatrician; b. Charlottesville, Va., Feb. 2, 1950; s. William Lee and Merlyn (Carlton) W.; m. Jane Clark Williams, Aug. 11, 1973; children: John, James. AB, U. N.C., 1972, MD, 1976. Diplomate Am. Bd. Internal Medicine and Geriatric Medicine. Instr. medicine U. N.C. Sch. Medicine, Chapel Hill, 1979-80, med. dir., nurse practitioner evening clinic, 1979-80, asst. prof. medicine, 1985-88, assoc. prof., dir. program on aging, 1988—; fellow, instr. medicine (geriatrics) Monroe Community Hosp. U. Rochester (N.Y.) Sch. Medicine, 1980-81, sr. instr. medicine Monroe Community and Strong Meml. hosps., 1981-82, asst. prof., 1982-84, dir. Geriatric Consultative Svc. Monroe Community Hosp., 1983-84; co-dir. Geriatric Edn. Ctr. U. N.C. Sch. Pub. Health, Chapel Hill, 1986-88. Mem. study sects. and panels Nat. Inst. on Aging Monitoring Bd., 1983-89; mem. consensus devel. conf. panel NIH, 1991; mem. Adv. Panel for Office Tech. Assessment, Washington, 1987-89; cons. pvt. and govt. founds. Author: The American Geriatrics Society's Complete Guide to Aging and Health, 1995; assoc. editor Am. Geriatrics Soc. Geriatrics Rev. Syllabus, 1992; mem. bd. Am. Geriatrics Soc., 1987—; author comml. computer software biostats., music, children's edn.; contbr. chpts. to books and articles to profl. jours.; reviewer med. jours. John Motley Morehead scholar U. N.C., Chapel Hill, 1972-76, Robert Wood Johnson clin. scholar, 1978-80; fellow Salzburg (Austria) Seminar, 1983; grantee Robert Wood Johnson Found., U. Rochester, 1983-86, Nat. Int. Aging, U. Rochester, 1983-88, Bur. Health Professions, Health Resources and Svcs. Adminstrn., U. N.C., Chapel Hill, 1985-88, 88-92, John and Mary Markle Found., U. N.C., 1989, Robert Wood Johnson Found., U. N.C., Chapel Hill, 1987-91, Nat. Inst. Aging, U. N.C., Chapel Hill, 1990—. Mem. ACP, AAAS, Am. Geriatrics Soc. (bd. dirs. 1991—), Soc. Gen. Internal Medicine, Am. Assn. Pub. Health, Gerontol. Soc. Am., Am. Fedn. Clin. Rsch., Assn. Anthropology and Gerontology, N.C. Med. Soc. (mem. aging com. 1987—), Nat. Coun. on Aging, Inc., Royal Soc. Medicine, Sherlock Holmes Soc. London, Assn. Acad. Geriatric Medicine Programs. Achievements include creation of timed manual performance test-a well validated protocol that predicts future needs for care; first report of randomized clin. trial in ambulatory geriatric assessment. Office: U NC Sch Medicine Program On Aging Chapel Hill NC 27599-0001

WILLIAMS, MARNI DIANNE, pharmacist; PharmD, U. Fla., 2005. Asst. brand mgr. Procter & Gamble, Cin., 2005—08; dir., pharmacy student forum Am. Soc. Health Sys. Pharma, Bethesda, Md., 2008—. Office: Am Soc Health Sys Pharma 7272 Wisconsin Ave Bethesda MD 20814

WILLIAMS, MARSHA C., travel company executive; b. 1951; B in Econs., Wellesley Coll.; Masters, U. Chgo. Various positions Amoco Corp., 1989—93, treas., 1993—98, v.p., treas., 1997—98; chief adminstrv. officer Crate & Barrel, 1998—2002; exec. v.p., CFO Equity Office Properties, Chgo., 2002—07; sr. v.p., CFO Orbitz Worldwide, Inc., Chgo., 2007—. Bd. dirs. Davis Funds, Fifth 3rd Bancorp, Chgo. Bridge & Iron Co. N.V., Modine Mfg. Co., 1999. Office: Orbitz Worldwide Inc Ste 1000 500 W Madison St Chicago IL 60661 Office Phone: 312-894-5000. Office Fax: 312-894-5001.*

WILLIAMS, MARSHA RHEA, computer scientist, educator, researcher, consultant; b. Memphis, Aug. 4, 1948; d. James Edward and Velma Lee W. Cert., Schiller Coll., West Berlin, Germany, 1968; BS in Physics, Beloit Coll., 1969; MS in Physics, U. Mich., 1971; MS in Sys. and Info. Sci., Vanderbilt U., 1976, PhD in Computer Sci., 1982. Cert. data processor. Engrng. coop. student Lockheed Missiles & Space Co., Sunnyvale, Calif., 1967-68; asst. transmission engr. Ind. Bell Tel. Co., Indpls., 1971-72; sys. analyst, instr. physics Memphis State U., 1972-74; computer-assisted instrn. project programmer Fisk U., 1974-76; mem. tech. staff Hughes Rsch. Labs., Malibu, Calif., 1976-78; assoc. sys. engr. IBM, Nashville, 1978-80; rsch. and tchg. asst. Vanderbilt U., Nashville, 1980-82, spl. asst. to dean Grad. Sch., spring 1981, minority engr. advisor, 1975-76; cons. computer-assisted instrn. project Meharry Med. Coll., Nashville, summer 1982; assoc. prof. computer sci. Tenn. State U., Nashville, 1982-83, 84-90, full tenured prof., 1990—, univ. marshal, 1992-97. Assoc. prof. U. Miss., Oxford, 1983-84, faculty senator; assoc. program dir. Applications of Advanced Techs. Sci. and Engrng. Edn., NSF, 1987-88, apptd. USRA Sci. and Engrng. Edn. Coun., Advanced Design Program, 1992-94; cons. on minority scientists and engrs. Univ. Space Rsch. Assn., Washington, 1988; vis. scientist CSNET-Minority Instn. Networking Project Bolt, Beranek & Newman, Cambridge, Mass., 1989; mem. tech. staff Bell Comm. Rsch., Red Bank, N.J., 1990; prin. investigator NSF Computer Sci., Engrng. & Math. Scholarships Project, 2002-03; presenter papers profl. meetings. Editor-in-chief newspaper Pilgrim Emanuel Bapt. Ch., 1975-76. Advisr Chi Rho Youth Fellowship, Temple Bapt. Ch., 1975-81, adv. com. Golden Outreach Sr. Citizens Fellowship, 1979-80, 86-87, 89-93, Women's Day spkr., 1979-81, Ebenezer Missionary Bapt. Ch., 1993; adviser Nat. Soc. Black Engrng. Students, 1983-84; founder, coord. Tenn. State U. Assn. for Excellence in Computer Sci., Math. and Physics (AE-COMP), 1986-87, coord. Tech. Opportunities Fair, 1986, 87; dir. Tenn. State U. Minorities in Sci., Engrng. and Tech. Rsch. Project-MISET, 1989—; child sponsor World Vision, 1981—; mem., newsletter staff Lake Providence Missionary Bapt. Ch. Recipient Disting. Instr. award, 1984, Disting. Svc. citation Beloit Coll. Alumni Assn., 1994; grantee Digital Equipment Corp., 1989-92; rsch. grantee Tenn. State U., 1993, 94, NSF, 2002-03. Mem. NAACP (nat. judge ACT-SO sci. olympics 1992), Assn. Computing Machinery, Assn. Info. Tech. Profls. (edn. chmn., bd. dirs. 1986), Tenn. Acad. Sci., Info. Sys. Audit & Control Assn., Phi Kappa Phi. Home: PO Box 281946 Nashville TN 37228 Office: Tenn State U Dept Computer Sci PO Box 9604 Nashville TN 37209

WILLIAMS, MARY ELEANOR NICOLE, retired writer; b. Atlanta, May 14, 1938; d. Edward King Merrell and Bernice I. (Pitts) Smith; m. Charlie Lloyd Williams, July 25, 1993 (dec. June 1997); children: Mary Palmer, Susan Gober, Traci Bunch. Student, Fla. Jr. Coll., 1974. Lic. real estate broker, Fla. Editor, writer, former owner Southwestern Advt. and Pub., Carrollton, Ga., 1991-94; freelance writer children's stories. Author, editor: West Georgia Area Guide, 1991-93. Avocations: writing, music, travel, walking, art. Home: 103 Ferndale Rd Carrollton GA 30117

WILLIAMS, MARY ELLEN COSTER, federal judge; b. Flushing, NY, 1953; married; 2 children. BA summa cum laude in Latin and Greek, Cath. U., 1974, MA in Latin, 1974; JD, Duke U., 1977. Assoc. Fulbright and Jaworski, Washington, 1977—79, Schnader, Harrison, Segal and Lewis, Washington, 1979—83; asst. US atty. civil divsn. US Dept. Justice, Washington, 1983—87; ptnr. Janis, Schuelke and Wechsler Law Firm, Washington, 1987—89; adminstrv. judge GSA Bd. Contract Appeals, Washington, 1989—2003; judge US Ct. Fed. Claims, Washington, 2003—. Mem. editl. bd. Duke Law Jour. Fellow: American Bar Found. (life); mem.: DC Bar (sec.), DC Young Lawyers Sect. (chair), Bar Assn. of DC (found. pres., trustee, bd. dirs.), ABA (sect. rep. com. of ethics and professionalism 1998—2000, commn. on evaluation of rules of profl. conduct 1998—2000, presdl. task force on govt. lawyers 2000—01, chair sect. public contract law 2002—, sect. representative house delegates 2004—, chair elect, vice chair, sec.). Office: US Ct Fed Claims 717 Madison Pl NW Washington DC 20005*

WILLIAMS, MARY IRENE, business education educator; b. Hugo, Okla., June 30, 1944; d. Primer and Hylar B. (Tarkington) Jackson; m. Lee A. Williams (div. June 1981); 1 child, Monica Ariane. BS in Bus. Edn., Langston U., 1967; MS in Bus., Emporia State U., Kans., 1973; EdS, U. Nev., Las Vegas, 1977; DBA in Internat. Bus., Alliant U., 1992. Instr. Spokane (Wash.) C.C., 1967-70; tchr. bus. Topeka Pub. Schs., 1970-73; prof. C.C. So. Nev., Las Vegas, 1973—, assoc. dean of bus., 1978—93, dean acad. support svcs., 1993—95, prof. bus./mgmt., 1997—, chmn. bus. adminstrn. dept., 2006—; prof. bus./mgmt., asst. to assoc. v.p., asst. coord. bus. Langston U., Tulsa, 1995—97; prof. Coll. Southern Nev., 1997—2009, prof. emeritus. Adj. prof. So. Nazarene U., 1996-97; adj. prof. Tulsa Jr. Coll., 1997. Author: A Journey Upward, 2004. Recipient NISOD Leadership award Coll. Southern Nev., Outstanding Leader Nat. Inst. Staff Organizational Devel. award, Coll. Southern Nev., U. Texas, 2008; named Educator of Yr. Nucleus Plaza Assn., 1985, New Visions, Inc., 1986. Mem. AAUW, Nat. Bus. Edn. Assn., Alpha Kappa Alpha Avocations: exercising, studying languages, reading. Office: Coll So Nev 6375 W Charleston Blvd W2C Las Vegas NV 89146-1164 Personal E-mail: marywmslvnv@aol.com.

WILLIAMS, MARY PEARL, judge; b. Brownsville, Tex., Jan. 12, 1928; d. Marvin Redman and Theo Mae (Kethley) Hall; m. Jerre Stockton Williams, May 28, 1950; children: Jerre Stockton, Shelley Wiliams Austin, Stephanie Williams Laden. BA, U. Tex., 1948, JD, 1949. Bar: Tex. 1949, U.S. Supreme Ct. 1955, U.S. Dist. Ct. (we. dist.) Tex. 1987. Asst. atty. gen. State of Tex., Austin, 1949-50; relief judge Mcpl. Ct., Austin, 1964; asst. instr. dept. govt. U. Tex., Austin, 1966-67; atty. Office of Emergency Preparedness, Exec. Office of Pres., Washington, 1968-70; labor arbitrator, mem. arbitration panel Am. Arbitration Assn., 1972-73; judge County Ct. Law 2, Travis County, Tex., 1973-80, 53d Jud. Dist. Ct., Austin, 1981-2000, sr. judge, 2000—. Cons. HEW, 1966—67. Mem. adv. com. Juvenile Bd. Travis County, 1964—67; trustee United Way, 1974—78. Named Outstanding Woman, Austin Am.-Statesman, 1974, Austin Citizen, 1978, Woman of the Yr., Austin Dist. Bus. and Profl. Women, 1977; named to Austin HS Hall of Fame, 1996. Fellow: ABA, Am. Bar Found.; mem.: Inst. Jud. Adminstrn., Am. Judicature Soc., Am. Law Inst., Travis County Bar Assn., Coll. State Bar Tex., State Bar Tex., Jr. League Austin, Kappa Alpha Theta, Delta Kappa Gamma (hon.). Democrat. Methodist. Office: Travis County Courthouse PO Box 1748 Austin TX 78767-1748 Home: 3503 Mount Barker DR Austin TX 78731-5101 E-mail: greatimpy@aol.com.

WILLIAMS, MAURICE (MO WILLIAMS), professional basketball player; b. Jackson, Miss., Dec. 19, 1982; Student in criminal justice, U. Ala., Tuscaloosa, 2001—03. Guard Utah Jazz, 2003—04, Milw. Bucks, 2004—08, Cleve. Cavaliers, 2008—. Founder Mo Williams Found., 2005—; vol. Boys and Girls Club, YMCA. Named Nat. Freshman of Yr., The Sporting News, 2002, Freshman of Yr., Southeastern Conf., 2002; named to Eastern Conf. All-Star Team, NBA, 2009. Avocations: golf, video games. Office: Cleve Cavaliers One Center Court Cleveland OH 44115-4001*

WILLIAMS, MELVIN DONALD, anthropologist, educator; b. Pitts., Feb. 3, 1933; s. Aaron and Gladys Virginia (Barnes) W.; m. Faye Wanda Strawder, June 20, 1958; children: Aaron Ellsworth, Steven Rodney, Craig Haywood. AB, U. Pitts., 1955, MA, 1969, PhD, 1973. Cert. in secondary edn., social sci. Pa. Dept. Edn., 1974. Owner, operator Wholesale Periodical Distbn. Co., Pitts., 1955-66; instr. dept. sociology and anthropology Carlow Coll., 1969-71, asst. prof., 1971-75, chmn. dept. sociology and anthropology, 1973-75; assoc. prof. anthropology U. Pitts., 1976-79, adj. prof., 1979-82; prof. anthropology Purdue U., 1979-83, U. Md., College Park, 1983-88, U. Mich., Ann Arbor, 1988—. Olie B. O'Connor prof. Am. instns. Colgate U., 1976-77 Author: On the Street Where I Lived, Community in a Black Pentecostal Church, The Human Dilemma, The Black Middle Class, An Academic Village, Race for Theory; editor: Selected Readings in Afro-American Anthropology; contbr. articles to profl. publs. Co-chmn. project area com. Urban Redevel. Authority, Pitts., 1972—; co-dir. interdisciplinary family community project Western Psychiat. Inst. and Clinic, 1973-76; bd. dirs. Cath. Social Svc. of Allegheny County, Pa., 1973-76; coll. ombudsman, 1991-93, faculty senate, 1993-96. Career Svc. award U. Mich., 2004; fellow NSF, 1967, NDEA, 1969; grantee NSF, 1969-72, Cmty. Action Pitts., 1969-71, Social Sci. Rsch. Coun., 1974-75, Lilly Endowment, 1980-83, 85-86, Career Achievement award U. Mich., 2004, Lifetime Svc. award U. Mich., 2004. Fellow Am. Anthrop. Assn. (long range planning com. 2005—); mem. African Studies Assn., AAAS, AAUP, Am. Sociol. Assn., Assn. Study Afro-Am. Life and History, Soc. for Psychol. Anthropology, Am. Authors Assn. (long-range planning commn. 2005—). Home: 520 W Washington St Ann Arbor MI 48103-4232 Office: University of Michigan Dept Anthropology 101 West Hall 108 S University Ave Ann Arbor MI 48109-1107 Office Phone: 734-764-7274. Business E-Mail: mddoublu@umich.edu. *Personal philosophy: An abiding interest in people has stimulated me to discover more and more about humankind and has been an ever-present motivation to develop, grow and experience.*

WILLIAMS, MICHAEL ANTHONY, lawyer; b. Mandan, ND, Sept. 14, 1932; s. Melvin Douglas and Lucille Ann (Gavin) Williams; m. Marjorie Ann Harrer, Aug. 25, 1962 (div. 1989); children: Ann Margaret, Douglas Raymond, David Michael; m. Dorothy Ruth Hand, 1989. BA, Coll. of St. Thomas, 1954; LLB, Harvard U., 1959. Bar: Colo. 1959, N.D. 1959, U.S. Dist. Ct. Colo. 1959, U.S. Ct. Appeals (10th cir.) 1959, U.S. Supreme Ct. 1967. Assoc. Sherman & Howard and predecessor Dawson, Nagel, Sherman & Howard, Denver, 1959—65, ptnr., 1965—91; pres. Williams, Youle & Koenigs, P.C., Denver, 1991—2002; prin. Michael A. Williams LLC, Denver, 2002—. Served as 1st lt. USAF, 1955—57. Mem.: ABA, Coll. Commn. Arbitrators, Colo. Bar Assn., Am. Law Inst., Colo. Bar Found., Am. Bd. Trial Advs., Am. Coll. Trial Lawyers. Office: 950 17th St Ste 1800 Denver CO 80202-2811 Office Phone: 303-785-7999. Business E-Mail: mwilliams@wyk.com.

WILLIAMS, MICHAEL EDWARD, SR., dean; b. Mobile, Ala., July 30, 1960; s. Charles Edward and Ollie Jo (Hayes) Williams; m. Roberta Jean Norton, Nov. 28, 1987; children: Michael Edward Jr., Joshua Cody, Carey Alan. BS in Secondary Edn. Hist., Troy State U., 1982; MA in Hist., Auburn U., 1984; MDiv, Souwestern Bapt. Theological Sem., 1987, PhD in Ch. Hist., 1993. Grad. tchg. asst. Auburn (Ala.) U., 1982—84; pastor Trinity Hills Bapt. Ch., Benbrook, Tex., 1987—94; tchg. fellow ch. hist. Southwestern Bapt. Theological Sem., Fort Worth, Tex., 1991, adj. prof. ch. hist., 1994; adj. prof. hist. Dallas (Tex.) Bapt. U., 1991—94, asst. prof. hist., 1995—96, prof. hist., 1996—, dean coll. humanities and social scis., 1996—. Edtl. bd. Bap. Hist. Heritage Jour., 1997—, Jour. Tex. Bapt. Hist., Dallas, 1998—; editor Tex. Bapt. History Jour., 2008—; academic book review editor Bapt. Hist. Heritage Jour., Nashville, 2003—. Co-author: Presdl. Praise: Our Pres. & Their Hymns, 2008, co-editor Turning Points in Baptist History; author: Isaac Taylor Tichenor: The Creation of the Baptist New South, 2005, To God Be The Glory: The Centennial History of DBU, 1998 (Tex. Bapt. Hist. Soc. Ch. Hist. award, 1998), Victory Thru Faith: A History of the Rosen Heights Baptist Church, 1996 (Tex. Bapt. Hist. Soc. Ch. Hist. award, 1996); contbr. articles various profl. jours. Recipient Hon. Alumnus award, Decatur Bapt. Coll., 1999; named Prof. of Yr., Dallas Bapt. U., 1999—2000. Mem.: Tex. Baptist History Soc., So. Hist. Assn., Fellowship Bapt. Historians, Bapt. Hist. and Heritage Soc. (v.p. 2007—09, pres. 2009—). Independent. Bapt. Avocations: sports, jogging, bicycling, swimming, movies. Home: 169 Deer Creek Dr Aledo TX 76008 Office: Dallas Bapt U 3000 Mt Creek Pkwy Dallas TX 75211

WILLIAMS, MICHAEL J., philosopher, educator; b. July 7, 1947; m. Meredith Williams. BA, Oxford Univ.; PhD, Princeton Univ. Faculty Yale Univ., Univ. Md., Northwestern Univ.; Krieger-Eisenhower prof., chair of philosophy Johns Hopkins Univ., Balt. Author: Groundless Belief, 1977, Unnatural Doubts, 1992, Problems of Knowledge, 2001. Fellow: Am. Acad. Arts & Scis. Office: Dept Philosophy Gilman Hall 347 3400 N Charles St Baltimore MD 21218 Office Phone: 410-516-7030. Office Fax: 410-516-6848 410-516-6848. Business E-Mail: mwilliams@jhu.edu.

WILLIAMS, MICHAEL J., mortgage company executive; BS, Drexel U., 1980, MBA, 1983. Mgmt. positions DuPont; sr. mgr. KPMG Peat Marwick; various exec. positions Fannie Mae (Fed. Nat. Mortgage Assn.), Washington, 1991—99, sr. v.p. e-commerce, 1999—2000, pres. eBusiness, 2000—05, exec. v.p. regulatory agreements & restatement, 2005, exec. v.p., COO, 2005—09, pres., CEO, 2009—. Bd. dirs. Fannie Mae (Fed. Nat. Mortgage Assn.), 2009—. Office: Fannie Mae 3900 Wisconsin Ave NW Washington DC 20016-2892*

WILLIAMS, MICHAEL JAMES, lawyer; b. July 13, 1954; s. Robert L. and Carol J. (Edenborg) W.; m. Sherry L. Schnieder, Oct. 27, 1984; children: Taylor Michael, Tory Lyn. AA, N.D. State Coll. Sci., 1974; Bachelor's, U. N.D., Grand Forks, 1976, JD, 1979. Bar: N.D. 1979, U.S. Dist. Ct. N.D., 1982, U.S. Dist. Ct. Minn. 1982, U.S. Ct. Appeals (8th cir.) 1982, Minn. 1985. Atty. Kapsner & Kapsner, Bismarck, N.D., 1979-82; ptnr. Miller Norman Kenney & Williams, Moorhead, Minn., 1983-89; atty. Hagen Law Office, Fargo, N.D., 1989-92; ptnr. Maring Williams Law Office, Fargo, 1992—. Mem. N.D. Bar Assn. (pres. 2005), N.D. Trial Lawyers Assn. (prers. 2004), Minn. Trial Lawyers Assn., Minn. Bar Assn. Avocation: sports. Office: Maring Williams Law Office PC 1220 Main Ave Ste 105 Fargo ND 58107-2103

WILLIAMS, MICHAEL MAURICE RUDOLPH, nuclear engineering consultant; b. London, Dec. 1, 1935; s. Maurice Frederick Williams and Gwendoline M.A. Redington; m. Ann Doreen Betty, Dec. 13, 1958;

children: Nicholas C.M., Victoria L. BSc with honors, London U., 1958, PhD, 1961, DSc, 1968. Engr. Ctrl. Electricity Gen. Bd., London, 1962; rsch. assoc. Brookhaven Nat. Lab., Upton, NY, 1962-63; lectr. in physics U. Birmingham, England, 1963-65; reader in nuclear engring. Queen Mary Coll., London U., 1966-70, prof. nuclear engring., 1971-80, chmn. dept. nuclear engring., 1980-86; prof. nuclear engring U. Mich., Ann Arbor, 1987-89; cons. engr. Electrowatt Engring., Horsham, Sussex, England, 1989-98; pvt. practice, 1998—. Author: The Slowing Down and Thermalisation of Neutrons, 1966, Mathematical Methods in Particle Transport Theory, 1971, Random Processes in Nuclear Reactors, 1974, Aerosol Physics, 1991. Fellow Am. Nuclear Soc. (Arthur Holly Compton award 1994, Eugene P. Wigner award 2000), Inst. Physics, Instn. Nuclear Engrs. (v.p. 1972-75), Royal Soc. Arts & Scis. (Gotenburg, Sweden) (fgn. mem. 2008). Avocations: photography, movies of the 1930's and 1940's. E-mail: mmrw@nuclear-energy.demon.co.uk.

WILLIAMS, MICHAEL RICHARD, protective services official; b. Ypsilanti, Mich, Aug. 29, 1955; s. Jodie and Charlene (Walker) Williams; m. Karen Gayles Williams, Sept. 16, 1989. BBA, Western Mich. U., Kalamazoo, 1978; MDiv, Va. Union U., Richmond, Va., 2001. Auditor US Dept. Labor, Chgo., 1980—81, Mich. Dept. Treasury, Lansing, Mich., 1978—80; asst. mgr. corp. income tax Maccabess Mutual Life Ins. Co., Southfield, Mich., 1981—83; auditor US Dept. Labor OIG, Chgo., 1983—86; spl. agt. US Dept. Treasury IRS, Merrillville, Ind., 1986—90, US Dept Treasury OIG, Washington, 1990—. Pres. v.p. Genesis II Housing, Chgo., 1981—89. Author: (book poetry) Proverbs For The Heart, 1997, Mystseries In Human Nature, 1987. Vol. Detroit 300, 2003, Jamestown 400, Va., 2007; assoc. min. First Bapt. Ch., 1994—. Recipient Spl. Achievement award, Inspector Gen. Labor, 1983, Spl. award, Inspector Gen. Treas., 1993, Spl. Recognition award, Sec. Treasury, 2007. Independent. Baptist. Avocations: photography, music, writing, poetry.

WILLIAMS, MICHAEL SHADDEN, art director; s. Leland Shadden and Sheila Lane Williams; m. Lynn Bateman; children: Jessica Kaelyn, Alyssa Michelle children: Christopher Shadden. MusB in Vocal, U. Memphis, 1999; MS in Instrnl. Tech., Walden U., Baltimore, 2004; MusM, Boston U., 2009. Dir. choirs Snowden Mid. Sch., Memphis, 1999—2000, White Sta. Mid. Sch., Memphis, 2001—05; exec. Novus Canticus, Memphis, 2004—07; artistic dir. The Youth C, Memphis; dir. performing arts Crichton Coll., Memphis, 2005—; fine arts to exploratory coord. Collegiate Sch. Memphis, 2008—. Composer: (choral) There are around 70 working titles combined. Named Outstanding Music Educator of Yr., 2005. Conservative. Avocations: cooking, computers, recorder. Business E-Mail: mwilliams@crichton.edu.

WILLIAMS, MICHELLE, actress; b. Kalispell, Mont., Sept. 9, 1980; d. Larry and Carla; 1 child, Matilda Rose. Actor: (films) Lassie, 1994, Species, 1995, Timemaster, 1995, A Thousand Acres, 1997, Halloween H20: 20 Years Later, 1998, Dick, 1999, But I'm a Cheerleader, 1999, Perfume, 2001, Prozac Nation, 2001, Me Without You, 2001, The United States of Leland, 2003, The Station Agent, 2003, A Hole in One, 2004, Imaginary Heroes, 2004, Land of Plenty, 2004, The Baxter, 2005, Brokeback Mountain, 2005 (Critics Choice award, best supporting actress, Broadcast Film Critics Assn., 2006), The Hawk is Dying, 2006, I'm Not There, 2007, Incendiary, 2008, Deception, 2008, Synecdoche, New York, 2008, Wendy and Lucy, 2008; (TV series) Raising Caines, 1995, Dawson's Creek, 1998—2003; (TV films) My Son Is Innocent, 1996, Killing Mr. Griffin, 1997, If These Walls Could Talk 2, 2000. Named one of 21 Hottest Stars Under 21, Teen People mag., 1999. Avocations: reading, boxing. Office: Creative Artists Agency 2000 Avenue Of The Stars Los Angeles CA 90067-4700

WILLIAMS, MONTEL, television talk show host; m. Rochele See (div.); children: Ashley, Maressa; m. Grace Morley, 1992 (div. 2000); children: Montel, Wyntergrace. Host The Montel Williams Show, 1990—. Actor(TV films): Perry Mason: The Case of the Telltale Talk Show Host, 1993, Educating Matt Waters, 1996, (TV series): A Different World, The New Adventures of Robin Hood, JAG,: (films) War, Inc., 2008; co-author: Bodychange, 2001; author: A Dozen Ways to Sunday, 2001, Mountain Get Out of My Way; co-author: Climbing Higher, 2004. Recipient Daytime Emmy Award for Outstanding Talk Show Host, 1996. Office: 433 W 53rd St New York NY 10019-5603

WILLIAMS, NEIL, JR., retired lawyer; b. Charlotte, NC, Mar. 22, 1936; s. Lyman Neil and Thelma (Peterson) W.; m. Sue Sigmon, Aug. 23, 1958; children: Fred R., Susan S. AB, Duke U., 1958, JD, 1961. Bar: Ga. 1962, U.S. Dist. Ct. (no. dist.) Ga. 1977, U.S. Ct. Appeals (11th cir.) 1977. Assoc. Alston & Bird (and predecessor firm), Atlanta, 1961—65, ptnr., 1966—99, mng. ptnr., 1984-96; gen. counsel, global ptnr. Invesco (formerly Amvescap PLC), Atlanta, 1999—2002; ret., 2002. Bd. dir. Printpack, Inc., Atlanta, Acuity Brands, Inc., Atlanta, Inveso Mortgage Capital Inc., Atlanta. Chmn. bd. trustees Duke U., 1983—88, trustee, 1980—93; chmn. bd. trustees Vasser Woolley Found., Atlanta, 1975—, Leadership Atlanta, 1976—80; trustee Brevard Music Ctr., 1977—86, 1991—2001, Presbyn. Ch. USA Found., Jeffersonville, Ind., 1983—90, Research Triangle Inst., 1983—88, The Duke Endowment, Charlotte, NC, 1997—, Halle Found., Atlanta, 2005—; bd. dir. Atlanta Symphony Orch., 1970—76, 1984—93, 1995—98, pres., 1988—90; bd. dir. Woodruff Arts Ctr., 1987—98, 1999—, chmn., 2001—08; bd. counsellors The Carter Ctr., Atlanta, 1987—96, Ctrl. Atlanta Progress, 1984—96; bd. dir. Am. Symphony Orch. League, Washington, 1990—2000, chmn., 1995—99; vice chair The Duke Endowment, Charlotte, NC, 2008—. Recipient Disting. Alumni award Duke U., 1991, Rhyne award, 1996, Learned Hand award Am. Jewish Com., 2006. Mem. ABA, Am. Bar Found., State Bar Ga., Am. Law Inst., Atlanta C. of C. (bd. dirs. 1992-97, vice chmn. 1994-97), Piedmont Driving Club, Commerce Club (Atlanta), University Club (N.Y.C.), Phi Beta Kappa, Omicron Delta Kappa. Home: 3 Nacoochee Pl NW Atlanta GA 30305-4164 Office Phone: 404-881-7883. Business E-Mail: neil.williams@alston.com.

WILLIAMS, NEVILLE, solar power company executive; b. Muncie, Ind., Mar. 28, 1943; s. Donald Charles and Rose Eileen (Boughton) W. Student, U. Colo., 1964-66, U. Neuchatel, Switzerland, 1967. Freelance corr., Vietnam, 1968-69; freelance journalist Montreal, Que., Can., 1970-71, London, 1971-73; writer, prodr. Sta. WNBC-TV News, NYC, 1973-74; freelance writer Telluride, Colo., 1975-79; media liaison Office of Solar Energy U.S. Dept. Energy, Washington, 1979-80; dir. of mktg. Telluride Ski Resort, Inc., 1981-83; owner, operator Hist. Sheridan Opera House, Telluride, 1983-85; nat. media dir. Greenpeace USA, Washington, 1987-89; chmn. exec. dir., founder Solar Electric Light Fund, Washington, 1990—97. Chmn., CEO, founder Solar Electric Light Co., 1997-2003; chmn. SELCO-India, 1995-2005; founder, chmn. emeritus Standard Solar, Inc. Author: The New Exiles, 1971, Chasing the Sun, 2005; contbr. articles to NY Times mag., Outside, New Times, The Nation, The New Republic, Nature, Solar Today, others. Apptd. mem. Adv. Com. for Commerce and Devel., State of Colo., 1980-85, Gov.'s Motion Picture & TV Commn., 1981-85. Recipient Corp. Excellence award, U.S. Dept. of State, 2001. Fellow: Internat. Solar Energy Soc.; mem.: Clinton Global Initiative. Business E-Mail: neville@standardsolar.com.

WILLIAMS, NICOLE LEANN, human resources specialist, director; b. Flint, Mich., July 5, 1971; d. John L. Williams and Dr. Veronica M. Williams-Latnie; 1 child, Taylor Lee. BBA, Bradford Coll., Haverhill, Miss, 1999; MBA, Am. InterContinental U., Atlanta, 2002; PhD candidate, Capella U., Mpls., 2007. Human resources generalist Gen. Motors, Pontiac, Mich., 2000—03; sr. human resources rep. IPC Print Svc., Saint Joseph, Mich., 2003; dist. sr. human resources rep. FedEx Express, Novi, Mich., 2004—07; human resources mgr. Home Depot, Kalamazoo, 2004; regional dir. human resources CHRISTUS Schumpert Health Sys., Shreveport, La., 2007—; human resources cons. Soc. Indsl. Leaders & Vista Rsch., NYC, 2008—. Coord. Dem. Party, Shreveport, La., 2008. Mem.: Nat. Black MBA Assn., Soc. Human Resource Mgmt., Soc. Indsl. Orgnl. Psychology. Democrat-Npl. Avocations: travel, art, music. Office Phone: 318-681-4500. Personal E-mail: nicolewilliams_mba@yahoo.com. Business E-Mail: nl.williams@chistushealth.org.

WILLIAMS, NORMA JEAN, lawyer; b. NY, Sept. 19, 1952; d. Arthur Robert and Mildred (McDaniel) Williams; m. Bruce Ephraim Goldstein, Oct. 28, 1989. BA magna cum laude, Wesleyan U., Middletown, Conn., 1974; JD, U. Calif., Berkeley, 1977. Bar: Calif. 1977, US Dist. Ct. (no. dist. Calif.) 1977, US Dist. Ct. (so. dist. Calif.) 1991. Assoc. Crosby, Heafey, Roach & May, Oakland, Calif., 1977-81; assoc. counsel Crocker Nat. Bank, San Francisco, 1981-82; assoc. Berger, Kahn, Shafton & Moss, LA, 1983-84, Brown, Winfield & Canzoneri, LA, 1984-85; ptnr. Williams & Assocs, LA, 1985—98, 2003—; of counsel Arter & Hadden, 1999—2001, Reed Smith, 2001—03. Mem. Urban Land Inst., LA; mem. faculty Practicing Law Inst., NYC. Contbr. articles to profl. jours. Recipient Cert. Appreciation City of LA, 1987. Mem. State Bar Calif. (mem. exec. com. real property law sect. 1990-93, chair real property sect. 1993-96, so. Calif. co-chair fin. sub-sect. real property law sect. 1988-90), LA County Bar Assn. (exec. com. 1993-, chair real property sect., 2006-2007, bd. trustees, 2007-2009), Am. Coll. Real Estate Lawyers (hon.), Am. Coll. Mortgage Attys. (bd. regents 2004-, legis. com. chair, bus. devel. com. chair). Office: Williams & Assocs 555 W 5th St Ste 3100 Los Angeles CA 90013 Office Phone: 213-996-8464. Office Fax: 213-947-1799. E-mail: njwilliams@willassoc.com.

WILLIAMS, PAT, professional sports team executive; b. Phila., May 3, 1940; m. Ruth Williams; 19 children. B in Phys. Edn., Wake Forest U.; MS in Phys. Edn., Ind. U., 1964. Bus. mgr. Fla. State League Miami Marlins Class A Baseball Club, 1964—65; gen. mgr. West Carolina League Spartanburg Phillies, SC, 1965—67, pres., 1967—68, Orlando Double-A So. League Baseball Team, 1990—93; bus. mgr. Phila. 76ers, 1968—69, gen. mgr., v.p., 1974—86; gen. mgr. Chgo. Bulls, 1969—73, Atlanta Hawks, 1973—74; gen. mgr., COO Orlando Magic, 1986—96, sr. v.p., 1996—. Author: Making Magic, Coaching Your Kids to be Leaders: The Keys to Unlocking Their Potential, 2005, Who Wants to Be a Champion, How to Be Like Coach Wooden. Named Minor League Exec. of Yr., The Sporting News, 1967; named to Del. Sports Hall of Fame, 2001, Wake Forest Sports Hall of Fame. Mem.: Fellowship of Christian Athletes. Office: Orlando Magic 8701 Maitland Summit Blvd Orlando FL 32810-5915 Office Phone: 407-916-2401. Office Fax: 407-916-2986. E-mail: pwilliams@patwilliamsmotivate.com.*

WILLIAMS, PATRICIA BADIA, retired counselor, academic administrator, mathematics educator; d. Robert Murray Johnson and Orienta Badia Bozynski; m. Robert F. Williams, July 6, 1989; children: Kristin Marie Tyson, Aaron William Harrison stepchildren: Celeste Anderson, Lisa Hubbard, Thomas, Kyle, Jody, Beth Thayden, Megan Clark. BA in Psychology with distinction, U. Calif., San Jose, 1971; MA in Counseling Psychology, U. Santa Clara, Calif., 1976; postgrad., Kent State U., Ohio, U. Wash., Adams State Coll., U. N.Mex., U. Puget Sound, Youngstown State U., Ohio. Cert. master addictions counselor AODA Cert. Bd., nat. sch. counselor, nat. bd. counselor, tchr. Colo., secondary sch. tchr., tchr. Wash., Calif., lic. tchr., counselor Ohio, 2006, counselor Ariz., Wash. Jr. high math. tchr., 1971—74; math. tchr. Los Gatos Unified Sch. Dist., 1971—77, creative dance instr., 1971—74; instr. math Olympic Coll., Bremerton, Wash., 1978—79, instr. prevention of child sexual abuse, 1985; adj. prof. Seattle Pacific U., 1986; jr. high counselor, math. tchr. South Kitsap Sch. Dist. 402, Port Orchard, Wash., 1977—79; mid. sch. counselor Bainbridge Island Sch. Dist., Wash., 1979—89; jr. high counselor Marana Unified Sch. Dist., Ariz., 1989—93; mid. sch. counselor Fremont RE-1 Sch. Dist., Canon City, Colo., 1993—98; tchr. math. Canfield Village Sch. Dist., Ohio, 1999—2000; ret., 2000. Sch., cmty. trainer in prevention of child sexual abuse, 1985—87; tchr. talented and gifted program Canfield Village Mid. Sch., 2007. Active numerous civic orgns./founds.; vol. tchr. Ceasar Chavez Farmer Worker Assn., 1970—71; sec. Amici d'Italia Soc., Portland, Oreg., 2009; charter bd. dirs. Storybook Mus.; bd. dirs. Mid. Sch. Alternative Program, Canon City, 1996—97; bd. mem. Salem Hist. Hope Cemetery, 2006—08; charter mem. Kitsap County Human Rights Commn., 1989; trustee Salem Preservation Soc. Recipient Recognition Svc. to Youth, Kiwanis, 1998; named Outstanding Alumna of Yr., U. Santa Clara, 1999, Lifetime Hon. Rotarian Cmty. Svc., 1993. Mem.: Ohio Sch. Counselors Assn. (bd. dirs. 1999—2000, dist. 9 rep.), Nat. Assn. Forensic Counselors (Cert. clin. criminal justice specialist), Am. Sch. Counselors Assn., Am. Assn. Christian Counselors, Ohio Counselors Assn., Hope Historical (bd. dirs. 2006—08), Salem Preservation Soc. Achievements include development of peer mediation programs in Colorado and Arizona. Office Phone: 503-974-9844. Personal E-mail: p.badiaj8@comcast.net.

WILLIAMS, PATRICIA C., nursing educator; b. Winchester, Va., June 18, 1947; 1 child, Michael James. ADN, Shepherd U., Shepherdstown, W.Va., 1991; BSN, George Mason U., Fairfax, Va., 1996, MSN, 2003. Clin. educator, emergency dept. City Hosp. Inc., Martinsburg, W.Va., 2001—03; asst. prof. Hagerstown CC, Md., 2003—. Contbr. chapters to books. Recipient Cmty. Health award, George Mason U., 1996. Mem.: Emergency Nurses Assn. Office: Hagerstown CC 11400 Robinwood Dr Hagerstown MD 21742 Business E-Mail: williamsp@hagerstowncc.edu.

WILLIAMS, PATRICIA SUE, agricultural studies educator; b. Orange, Calif., Dec. 10, 1957; d. O. Dean and Cornelia Palmer Williams. B in Agrl. Sci., Calif. State Poly. U., San Luis Obispo, 1980; M in Agrl. Edn., Calif. Poly. State U., 1983. Clear single subject agr. sci. credential Calif., clear vocat. credential Calif. Agr. tchr. Hale Jr. High, Woodland Hills, Calif., 1981—82, Valencia HS, Placentia, Calif., 1982—85, Buena Pk. (Calif.) HS, 1985—94, Chino (Calif.) Unified Sch. Dist., 1994—98, Orange (Calif.) HS, 1998—. Dir. Mounted Assistance Unit, Silverado, Calif., 1999—2002; large animal rescue technician, Orange, 2001—; animal rescue US Humane Soc., 2005—; animal rescue technician LA Area B Emergency Animal Rescue Team, Redondo Beach, Calif., 2005—; pres., mem. Orange County Fair Auction Com., Costa Mesa, Calif.; mem., tchr. Calif. State Fairs and Shows Ethics Com., Sacramento; advisor FFA, Orange. Mem. choir First United Meth. Ch., Orange. Recipient Crystal Apple award, KNBC News, 1981, Outstanding Young Mem. award, Calif. Agr. Tchrs. Assn., 1987; named Outstanding FFA Advisor, 1982—. Master: ETI (v.p. 2000—04); mem.: MAU (pres.), Nat. Vocat. Agr. Tchrs. Assn., Calif. Teachers Assn., Calif. Agr. Tchrs. Assn. (Outstanding Young Mem. award 1987, Outstanding FFA Advisor 1982—), Am. Riding Club for the Handicapped. Avocations: horse camping, music, guitar, singing, travel. Home: 265 S Lime St Orange CA 92868 Office: Orange HS 525 N Shaffer St Orange CA 92867 Personal E-mail: appyonr@sbcglobal.net.

WILLIAMS, PAUL, retired federal agency administrator; b. Jacksonville, Ill., Aug. 6, 1929; s. Russell and Bernice (Wheeler) W.; m. Ora B. Mosby; 1 child, Reva Williams. BA, Ill. Coll., 1956, LHD, 1980. Dir. fin. City of Chgo., 1956-63; assoc. dir. fin. United Planning Orgn., Washington, 1964-65; internat. adminstrv. officer U.S. Dept. State, Washington, 1965-68; dir. office mgmt. U.S. HUD, Washington, 1968-93, gen. dep. dept. fair housing and equal opportunity, 1993-94, dep. ops. and mgmt., 1994-97, ret., 1997. Cons. S.E. Econ. Devel. Corp., Nat. Exec. Svc. Corp., 1998; Buzan learning instr. for mind mapping, 2000-2002. Author: Questionnaire on Execution of Urban Renewal Programs, 1959. Pres. Bel Pre Civic Assn., Wheaton, Md., 1978, bd. dirs., 1971, 79; pres. Bel Pre PTA, Wheaton, 1973, Rossmoor Kiwanis Club, 2002, Rossmore Kiwanis Found., 2004-05; bd. dirs. Rockville C. of C., African Am. C. of C. Sgt. U.S. Army, 1948-52. Recipient letter of recognition for 36 yrs. fed. svc. U.S. Pres., letter of recognition for 36 yrs. govt. svc. Senators of Md., citation for 36 yrs. dedicated govt. svc. Gov. of Md., cert. of recognition Nat. Assn. Black and Minority C. of C., 1987. Baptist. Avocations: reading, jogging, golf, tai chi. Home: Unit 306 2900 N LeisureWorld Blvd Silver Spring MD 20906-2321 Office Phone: 301-598-2899. Personal E-mail: owilli7738@aol.com.

WILLIAMS, PAUL ALLEN, biomedical engineer, researcher; b. Shreveport, La., Mar. 28, 1960; s. Duane Gene and Dorothy Ann (Morgan) W. BS BME, La. Tech. U., 1984, MSEE, 1993. Cert. engr.-in-tng. Rsch. assoc. Sch. Medicine La. State U., Shreveport, 1985-91; rsch. asst. Loma Linda (Calif.) U., 1991-94, rsch. instr., 1994—. Contbr. articles to profl. jours. Mem. IEEE, Internat. Neural Network Soc., N.Y. Acad. Scis., Biomed. Engring. Soc. Republican. Lutheran. Office: LLU Sch Medicine 11234 Anderson St Loma Linda CA 92354-2804 Home: 850 Prescott Way Apt B Riverside CA 92507-2971

WILLIAMS, PAUL STRATTON, executive recruiter; b. San Francisco, Oct. 9, 1959; s. Henry Stratton and Frances (Spurlock) W.; m. Laura Dawn Coleman, Sept. 15, 1984; children: Scott Coleman, Ryan Stratton. AB, Harvard Coll., 1981; JD, Yale U., 1984. Bar: Calif. 1984, Ohio 1987. Assoc. Gibson, Dunn & Crutcher, LA, 1984-87, Vorys, Sater, Seymour & Pease, Columbus, Ohio, 1987-90; gen. counsel Info. Dimensions, Inc., Dublin, Ohio, 1994-95; v.p., asst. gen. counsel Cardinal Health, Inc., 1995—99, sr. v.p., dep. gen. counsel, 2000—01, exec. v.p., chief legal off. and sec., 2001—05; ptnr. Major, Lindsey and Africa, 2005—. Bd. dir. State Auto Fin. Corp.; bd. dirs. Bob Evans Farms Restaurants, Compass Minerals. Mem. Harvard Club Central Ohio. Democrat. Avocation: fitness. Office Phone: 312-456-1848. Business E-Mail: pwilliams@mlaglobal.com.

WILLIAMS, PEDELAPHE, education educator; BA, Clark Atlanta U., MA, 1995; EdS, Troy State U., Phenix City, Ala, 1996. Cert. in edn. Ga.; ednl. leader Ga. Tchr. Atlanta City Schs., 1992—2004, Fulton County Schs., Atlanta, 2004—. Reading contact Bear Creek Mid. Sch., Fulton County Sch., Fairburn, Ga., 2008—, tchr. support specialist, 2009. Recipient Dewitt Wallace Reader's Digest, Clark Atlanta U., 1994. Mem.: Nat. Staff Devel. Coun., Internat. Reading Assn. Office: Bear Creek Middle Sch 7415 Herndon Rd Fairburn GA 30213

WILLIAMS, PEGGY RYAN, retired academic administrator; b. Montreal, Que., Can., May 27, 1947; d. Fred Smith and Carol (Kennedy) Ryan; m. David A. Williams, May 30, 1970. BA psychology, U. Toronto, St. Michael's Coll., 1968; MEd, U. Vt., 1976; EdD, Harvard U., 1983; LittD (hon.), Ithaca Coll., 2008. Caseworker, children's svcs. Monroe County Dept. Social Svcs., Rochester, NY, 1968-72; med. social worker Med. Ctr. Hosp. of Vt., Burlington, 1972; coord. instrn, academic advisor CC of Vt., Lamoille County, 1973—75, project dir. Northwestern Vt., 1975—76, regional dir. Montpelier, 1976-82; part-time instr. C.C. Vt., 1978—85; asst. to the pres. Johnson State Coll., Vt., summer 1981; tchg. fellow Harvard U., 1981; dir. ednl. and pers. svcs., office of chancellor Vt. State Colleges, Waterbury, 1982-85; assoc. prof. Trinity Coll., Burlington, 1985—89, chair, dept. bus & economics, 1985-88, assoc. acad. dean, 1988-89; pres. Lyndon State Coll., Lyndonville, Vt., 1989-97, Ithaca Coll., NY, 1997—2008, pres. emerita, 2008—. Adj. faculty Johnson State Coll., 1984—86. Active The Ithaca Downtown Partnership Cmty. Adv. Bd.; bd. mem. Sacred Heart Sch. Montreal, bd. chair, 1998—2001; bd. mem. Tompkins Trust Co., 1999—; com. mem. Cornell U. Johnson Mus. Art Cmty. Adv. Coun.; mem. adv. coun. Finger Lakes Land Trust, 2000—03. Recipient Jackie M. Gibbons Leadership award, Am. Coun. Edn./Nat. Identification Program, 1984, Margaret R. Williams Emerging Profl. award, Ale-Doma Shavlik award, Fla., 2009. Mem. Am. Assn. Higher Edn., 1973-, Am. Coun. on Edn., 1981- (bd. dirs., 2000-), Nat. Assn. Women in Edn., 1985-, Home: 83 Emery Hill Rd Johnson VT 05656 Business E-Mail: pwilliams@ithaca.edu.

WILLIAMS, PETER C., medical association administrator; b. Los Angeles, May 12, 1943; life ptnr. Karen E. Donegan; children: Elizabeth Greenwood, Alexis Coatney, Zanna. BA, Occidental Coll., Eagle Rock, Calif., 1965; JD, Harvard Law Sch., Cambridge, Mass, 1968; PhD, Harvard U., 1973. Vice dean academic affairs Sch. Medicine, Stony Brook, NY, 1998—. Ethics cons. U. Hosp., Stony Brook. Bd. mem. Human Svcs. Rsch. Inst., Somerville, Mass. Recipient Chancellors award, SUNY, 1980. Office: Sch Medicine Stony Brook NY 11794 Business E-Mail: peter.williams@stonybrook.edu.

WILLIAMS, PETER MACLELLAN, nuclear engineer; b. NYC, Aug. 30, 1931; s. Gilbert Harris and Evelyn (Buss) W.; m. Lois Crane, Oct. 6, 1956; children: Jane, Gilbert, Katherine, Anne, Louise, Robert. BChemE, Cornell U., 1954; MS in Nuclear Engring., MIT, 1957; PhD in Nuclear Engring., U. Md., 1971. Engr. DuPont Savannah River, Aiken, SC, 1954-55; task engr. AGN, San Ramon, Calif., 1957-60; project mgr. Am. Machine & Fdry., Greenwich, Conn., 1960-62; research staff Princeton U., NJ, 1962-67; sr. project mgr., specialist in high temperature gas cooled reactors U.S. Nuclear Regulatory Commn., Washington, 1967-91; dir. div. high temperature gas cooled reactors U.S. Dept. of Energy, Washington, 1991-94; cons. Internat. Atomic Energy Agy., Vienna, 1994—; cons. nuclear engr., 1995—. Mem. Chernobyl Tracking Team, 1986; U.S. del. to gas-cooled reactors working group, Internat. Atomic Energy Agy., 1991; steering com. mem. U.S.-Japan Implementing Agreement on gas-cooled reactors, 1991 Contbr. articles to profl. jours.; author various reports. Scoutmaster Boy Scouts Am., Potomac, Md., 1972, cubmaster, 1983-86; pres. PTA Winston Churchill High Sch., Potomac, 1981. Assoc. fellow AIAA; mem. Am. Nuclear Soc. (instr. workshhop gas coolent reactor 2001, instr. profl. devel. workshop 2005), Sigma Xi Democrat. Unitarian Universalist. Achievements include patent for liquid core nuclear rocket; patent pending for advanced helium turbine reactor. Home and Office: 9418 Thrush Ln Potomac MD 20854-3991 Office Phone: 301-299-7236. Personal E-mail: peterwill@starpower.net, peterw.l@verizon.net.

WILLIAMS, PHILIP COPELAIN, gynecologist, obstetrician; b. Vicksburg, Miss., Dec. 9, 1917; s. John Oliver and Eva (Copelain) W.; B.S. magna cum laude, Morehouse Coll., 1937; M.D., U. Ill., 1941; m. Constance Shielda Rhetta, May 29, 1943; children— Philip, Susan Carol, Paul Rhetta. Intern, Cook County Hosp., Chgo., 1942-43, resident in ob-gyn, 1946-48; resident in gynecology U. Ill., 1948-49; practice medicine specializing in ob-gyn, Chgo., 1949—; mem. staff St. Joseph Hosp., Ill. Masonic Hosp., Cook County Hosp., McGaw Hosp.; clin. prof. Med. Sch. Northwestern U., Chgo. Bd. dirs. Am. Cancer Soc. Chgo. unit and Ill. div. Served with U.S. Army, 1943-45. Recipient Civic award Loyola U., 1970; Edwin S. Hamilton Interstate Teaching award, 1984; diplomate Am. Bd. Ob-Gyn, Fellow ACS, Internat. Coll. Surgeons; mem. AMA, Chgo., Ill. med. socs., AMA, Chgo. Gynecol. Soc. (treas. 1975-78, pres. 1980-81), Am. Fertility Soc., Inst. Medicine, N.Y. Acad. Scis., AAAS. Presbyn. Clubs: Barclay, Carlton, Plaza. Contbr. articles to profl. jours. E-mail: pwill2oo@aol.com. Home: 1040 N Lake Shore Dr Chicago IL 60611 E-mail: pwill200@sbcglobal.net.

WILLIAMS, PHYLLIS CUTFORTH, retired realtor; b. Moreland, Idaho, June 6, 1917; d. William Claude and Kathleen Jessie (Jenkins) Cutforth; m. Joseph Marsden Williams, Jan. 21, 1938 (dec. 1986); children: Joseph Marlis, Bonnie Lou Williams Thompson, Nancy Kay Williams Stewart, Marjorie Williams Karren, Douglas Claude, Thomas Marsden, Wendy Kathleen Williams Clark, Shannon Irene Williams Ostler. Grad., Ricks Coll., 1935. Tchr. Grace (Idaho) Elem. Sch., 1935-38; realtor Williams Realty, Idaho Falls, Idaho, 1972-77; mem. Idaho Senate, Boise, 1977. Owner, mgr. river property. Compiler: Idaho Legisladies Cookbook, Cookin' Together, 1981. With MicroFilm Ctr., LDS Ch. Mission, Salt Lake City, 1989-90; former block chmn., vol. Cancer Drive; active Idaho State Legisladies Club, 1966-84, v.p., 1982-84; mem. Bonneville County (Idaho) Rep. Women. Recipient Cert. Appreciation to Phyllis Williams, The Ronald Reagan Presidential Found. award, 2003. Avocations: genealogy, music, politics, cooking, attending grandchildren's special events.

WILLIAMS, PHYLLIS ELEANOR, retired educator; b. Serene, Colo., Sept. 11, 1920; d. Thomas James and Rebecca Cecilia (Bruce) W. Diploma, Occupational Therapy Sch. U. Pa., 1948; BS in Occupational Therapy with honors, San Jose State U., Calif., 1959, MS in Sociology, 1963. RN, 1942. Dir. occupational therapy for cerebral palsied children St. Christopher's Hosp., Phila., 1948-50; occupational therapist Phila Easter Seal Soc., 1951-55; therapist Chandler Tripp Sch., San Jose, 1955-59; probation officer Santa Clara County Juvenile Probation Dept., San Jose, 1959-63; asst. supt. Juvenile Hall, San Jose, 1963-65; instr. sociology W. Valley Community Coll. Dist., Saratoga, Calif., 1965-78, chair dept. sociology, 1972-73, dir. human svcs., 1974-75, pres. acad. senate, 1975-76; provost Inst. Human Affairs West Valley and Mission Community Coll. Dists., Santa Clara, 1978-83, ret. Saratoga, 1983—. Trustee West Valley and Mission C.C. Dists., 1985-92; lectr. in field. Bd. mem. Saratoga Adult Day Care Ctr., Sr. Info. & Ref. Svcs. Bd., Women's Fund Adv. Bd. With Nurse Corps, USN, 1942-46, 50-51. Mem. LWV, AAUW, U. Calif. Alumni Assn. (life). Democrat. Episcopalian. Home: 505 Trail Dr Moss Landing CA 95039-9706 Home Phone: 831-633-5647. Personal E-mail: wilbart2@aol.com.

WILLIAMS, QUENTIN CHRISTOPHER, geophysicist, educator; b. Wilmington, Del., Jan. 1, 1964; s. Ferd Elton and Anne Katherine W.; m. Elise Barbara Knittle, Dec. 19, 1987; children: Byron Frederick, Alanna Katherine, Lynette Barbara, Benjamin Ferd. AB, Princeton U., 1983; PhD, U. Calif., Berkeley, 1988. Rsch. geophysicist Inst. of Tectonics, U. Calif., Santa Cruz, 1988-91; asst. prof. dept. earth sci. U. Calif., Santa Cruz, 1991-95, assoc. prof. dept. earth sci., 1995-99, prof. dept. earth sci., 1999—; chair Faculty Senate, U. Calif., Santa Cruz, 2007—09. Contbr. articles to profl. jours. Presdl. Faculty fellow, 1993-98. Fellow Am. Geophys. Union (Macelwane medal 2000), Mineral. Soc. Am. (award 2000); mem. Am. Phys. Soc. Office: U Calif Santa Cruz Dept Earth Sciences Santa Cruz CA 95064 Business E-Mail: qwilliams@pmc.ucsc.edu.

WILLIAMS, QUINN PATRICK, lawyer; b. Evergreen Park, Ill., May 6, 1951; s. William Albert and Jeanne Marie (Quinlan) Williams; children: Michael Ryan, Mark Reed, Kelly Elizabeth. BBA, U. Wis., 1972; JD, U. Ariz., 1974. Bar: Ariz. 1975, US Dist. Ct. Ariz. 1976, NY 1984. V.p., sec., gen. counsel Combined Comm. Corp., Phoenix, 1975-80; sr. v.p. legal and adminstrn. Swensen's Inc., Phoenix, 1980-86; ptnr. Winston & Strawn, Phoenix, 1985—89, Snell & Wilmer, Phoenix, 1989—2002; shareholder Greenberg Traurig, 2002—; pres. Enterprise network, 2001. Bd. dirs. Ariz. Venture Capital Conf., 1993—2000, Ariz. Tech. Coun., 2001—; co-chmn. Gov.'s Small Bus. Adv. Exec. Coun., 1996—2000; vice-chair Gov. Regulatory Coun., 1995—97; sec. GSPED High Tech. Cluster, 1993—; chair, bd. dirs. Greater Phoenix Econ. Coun., 1996—2000; mem. exec. com. A2Tech Coun., 2002—; mem. Gov.'s Coun. Innovation and Tech., 2003—. With USAR, 1967—73. Mem.: ABA, NY Bar Assn., Maricopa County Bar Assn., State Bar Ariz., Internat. Franchise Assn., Scotsdale C. of C. (bd. dirs. 2003—), Paradise Valley Country Club, Scottsdale Charros. Office: Greenberg Traurig 2375 E Camelback Rd Ste 700 Phoenix AZ 85016-9000 Office Phone: 602-445-8344. Business E-Mail: williamsq@gtlaw.com.

WILLIAMS, R. SETH, lawyer; BA, Pa. State U., 1989; JD with distinction, Georgetown U., 1992. Bar: Pa. 2003, US Dist. Ct. (ea. dist.) Pa. Asst. dist. atty. Dist. Atty.'s Office, Phila., 1992—2003, asst. chief Mcpl. Ct. Unit, chief Repeat Offenders Unit; assoc. Zarwin, Baum, DeVito, Kaplan, Schaer & Toddy, P.C., Phila. Tchr. adminstrn. of justice Pa. State U., Abington. Pres. Overbrook Park Civic Assn. Capt. JAG Corps. USAR. Mem.: Nat. Black Prosecutors Assn., Barristers Assn. Phila., Phila. Bar Assn. Office: Zarwin, Baum, DeVito, Kaplan, Schaer & Toddy 1515 Market St, Ste 1200 Philadelphia PA 19102 Office Phone: 215-569-2800. Office Fax: 215-569-1606. E-mail: rswilliams@zarwin.com.*

WILLIAMS, RACHEL D., literature and language professor; d. Alex C. and Sarah F. Hardy. MA in English Lit. and Lang., U. Mich., Ann Arbor. Lectr., english, ethnic studies, and women's studies Calif. State U. Sys.; ann. evening arts coord. West LA Coll. Culver City, Calif., academic senate sec., 2004—06, english prof., 2008—. GRE & GMAT reader Ednl. Testing Svc., Princeton, NJ.

WILLIAMS, RALPH CHESTER, JR., physician, educator; b. Washington, Feb. 17, 1928; s. Ralph Chester and Annie (Perry) W.; m. Mary Elizabeth Adams, June 23, 1951; children: Cathy, Frederick (dec.), John (dec.), Michael, Ann AB with distinction, Cornell U., 1950, MD, 1954; MD (hon.), U. Lund, Sweden, 1991. Diplomate Am. Bd. Internal Medicine. Intern Mass. Gen. Hosp., Boston, 1954-55, asst. resident in internal medicine, 1955-56; resident in internal medicine N.Y. Hosp., 1956-57; chief resident Mass. Gen. Hosp., Boston, 1959-60; guest investigator Rockefeller Inst., NYC, 1961-63; physician in internal medicine and rheumatology, 1963—; assoc. prof. U. Minn., Mpls., 1963-68, prof., 1968-69; prof., chmn. dept. medicine U. N.Mex., Albuquerque, 1969-88; Schott prof. rheumatology and medicine U. Fla., Gainesville, 1988-98; with rheumatology dept. U. N.Mex. Sch. Medicine, Albuquerque, 1998, emeritus prof. medicine, 1998—. Assoc. editor: Jour. Lab. and Clin. Medicine, 1966-69; mem. editl. bd.: Arthritis and Rheumatism, 1968—; contbr. articles to profl. jours. Capt. USAF, 1957—59. Recipient Regents' Meritorious Svc. award, U. N.Mex., 2003. Master Am. Coll. Rheumatology (Gold medal 2004); fellow ACP; mem. Am. Assn. Immunology, Assn. Am. Physicians, Am. Fedn. Clin. Rsch., Am. Soc. Clin. Investigation, Ctrl. Soc. Clin. Rsch., Western Soc. Clin. Investigation, Phi Beta Kappa, Alpha Omega Alpha. Achievements include research in immunologic processes and connective tissue diseases. Home: 624 E Alameda St Apt 13 Santa Fe NM 87501-2293 Office: Ste 400 1650 Hosp Dr Santa Fe NM 87505 Office Phone: 505-670-2232. Personal E-mail: coolypatch22@cybermesa.com.

WILLIAMS, REBA WHITE, corporate financial executive, writer, researcher; m. Dave H. Williams. BA in Enlgish, Duke U., Durham, NC; MBA, Harvard U., Cambridge, Mass.; MA in Art History, Hunter Coll., NYC; MA in Philosophy, CUNY, PhD in Art History. Former rschr. McKinsey & Co., Inc.; securities analyst Mitchell Hutchins, Inc. Dir. spl. projects, mem. bd. dir. Alliance Capital Mgmt.; vice chmn. White Williams Holdings, Ltd., 2001—. Mem. editl. bd. Print Quar.; contbr. articles to Am. Artist, Bus. and Soc., Instl. Investor Chgo. Daily News, Fin. Analysts Jour., others; author catalog essays. Mem. Manhattan Cmty. Bd. 8, 1999-2000; mem. Art Commn. City NY, 1995-98, pres., 1997-98; mem. NY State Coun. on the Arts, 1996-99, vice chmn., 1999; hon. keeper of Am. prints The Fitzwilliam Mus., Cambridge, Eng. Decorated Polish Order of Merit, cavalier of grand cross Order of Poland 1st class; recipient Pacesetter award NY City Coun., 1999, Disting. Cultural Leadership award NY Rep. County Com., 1999, Augustus Graham medal Bklyn. Mus., 1998; named one of Top 200 Collectors, ARTnews Mag., 2004-08, others. Mem. Cosmopolitan Club. Avocation: Collector of Am. Prints. Office: 41 W 57th St 4th Fl New York NY 10019 Office Phone: 212-752-1705. Business E-Mail: reba@rebawhitewilliams.com.

WILLIAMS, REDFORD BROWN, medical educator; b. Raleigh, NC, Dec. 14, 1940; s. Redford Brown Sr. and Annie Virginia (Betts) W.; m. Virginia Carter Parrott, August 9, 1940; children: Jennifer Betts, Lloyd Carter. AB, Harvard U., 1963; MD, Yale U., 1967. Diplomate Am. Bd. Internal Medicine. Intern, then resident Yale-New Haven Med. Ctr., 1967-70; sr. surgeon USPHS, Bethesda, Md., 1970-72; asst. prof. Duke U. Med. Ctr., Durham, NC, 1972, prof. psychiatry, 1977—, prof. psychology, 1990—, dir. behavioral medicine rsch. ctr., 1985—; CEO Williams LifeSkills, Inc., 1997—. Cons. NIH rev. coms., Bethesda, 1977—. Author: The Trusting Heart, 1989, Anger Kills, 1993, Lifeskills, 1998, In Control, 2006; contbr. articles to profl. jours. Dir. NC Heart Assn., Chapel Hill, 1980-83. Recipient Rsch. Scientist award NIMH, 1974—; NIH grantee, 1976—. Fellow Soc. Behavioral Medicine (pres. 1984-85, Upjohn Disting. Scientist award 1992), Acad. Behavioral Medicine Rsch. (pres. 1995—); mem. Am. Psychosomatic Soc. (bd. dirs. 1978-81, pres. 1992), Internat. Soc. Behavioral Medicine (pres.-elect 2004-06, pres. 2006-08). Unitarian Universalist. Avocation: tennis. Office: Duke U Med Ctr PO Box 3926 Durham NC 27710-0001 Home Phone: 919-383-2115; Office Phone: 919-684-3863. Business E-Mail: redfordw@duke.edu.

WILLIAMS, RICHARD DWAYNE, physician, educator, urologist; b. Wichita, Kans., Oct. 7, 1944; s. Errol Wayne and Roseanna Jane (Page) W.; m. Beverly Sue Ferguson, Aug. 29, 1964; 1 child, Wendy Elizabeth. BS, Abilene Christian U., 1966; MD, Kans. U., 1970. Diplomate Am. Bd. Urology, Nat. Bd. Med. Examiners. Intern, then resident in gen. surgery U. Minn., Mpls., 1970-72, resident in urology, 1972-76, asst. prof., 1976-79, U. Calif., San Francisco, 1979-84, assoc. prof., 1984; prof., chmn. dept. urology U. Iowa, Iowa City, 1984—. Chief urology VA Med. Ctr., San Francisco, 1979-84, VA Med. Ctr., Iowa City, 1984-88; mem. task force on bd. exams Am. Bd. Urology, 1981-85, guest examiner Oral exams, 1984-, trustee, 1994-2000; Rubin H. Flocks chair in urology U. Iowa, 1994, program com. chair Soc. Internat. Urology (SIU), 2007-09; mem. nat. adv. coun. NIDDK, NIH. Author: (with others) Advances in Urologic Oncology, 1987, Genitourinary Cancer: Basic and Clinical Aspects, 1987, Adult and Pediatric Urology, 1987, General Urology, 1988, Textbook of Medicine, 1988, also others; editor: Advances in Urologic Oncology, 1987; guest editor Seminars in Urology, 1985, Problems in Urology: Prostate Cancer, 1989; bd. editors Jour. Urology, 1980-88; mem. editorial bd. Urology, Jour. Urology; also articles. Bd. dirs. Iowa chpt. Nat. Kidney Found., bd. sci. advisors 1989-92; pres. Am. Found. Urologic Diseases, 2003-05. Maj. USAR, 1971-77. Bordeau scholar Kans. U. Med. Ctr., 1968-69; NIH, VA, Am. Cancer Soc. grantee. Fellow ACS (chmn. urology sect. No. Calif. chpt. 1980-82, chmn. ann. meeting programs 1988, mem. residency rev. com. urology 1993-99, vice chair 1995, chair 1997); mem. AAAS, Iowa Med. Soc., Iowa Urologic Soc., Am. Urologic Assn. (dir. seminar on residency evaluation 1987, bd. editors alt. 1988-, rep. North Ctrl. sect., prodr. slide presentations 1988, recipient prizes 1982, 87, com. mem. 1987-, bd. dirs. 1994, pres.-elect 1997, Hugh Hampion Young award, 2009), Am. Assn. for Cancer Rsch., Am. Soc. Clin. Oncology, Am. Assn. GU Surgeons, Clin. Soc. Genitourinary Surgeons (sec.-treas. 1997-2000), Soc. Internat. D'Urologie (pres. US sect. 2003-, program chair, 2007-), Soc. Univ. Urologists (chmn. com. on residency evaluation 1986-88, councillor 1987-, pres. 1993), Soc. Surg. Oncology, Soc. Urologic Oncology (chmn. membership com. 1987-90, sec. 1990-94, pres.-elect 1995, pres. 1996), Johnson County Med. Soc., Flock's Soc., Western Urologic Forum, Alpha Omega Alpha. Republican. Office: U Iowa Dept Urology 200 Hawkins Dr Iowa City IA 52242-1009 Office Phone: 319-356-0760.

WILLIAMS, RICHARD L., literature and language professor; b. Lewiston, Idaho, June 27, 1946; MA in ESL, U. Hawaii, Honolulu, 1972. Vol. Peace Corps, Thailand, 1969—71; efl lectr. & tchr. trainer Georgetown U. Program Spain, 1972—74; fulbright lectr. Fulbright Commn., Indonesia, 1974—75, 1977—97; English tchr. tng. program Biinational Fulbright Commn., Egypt, 1986—91; usia ea. european fellows program Office English Programs, US Dept. State, Liberec, Czech Republic, 1991—92; prof. internat. langs. Coll. Southern Nev., North Las Vegas, 2002—. Contbr. articles to profl. jours. Home: 3200 E Cheyenne Ave North Las Vegas NV 89030 Office: Coll Southern Nev 3200 E Cheyenne Ave North Las Vegas NV 89030 Office Fax: 702-651-4035. Business E-Mail: richard.williams@csn.edu.

WILLIAMS, RICHARD LEROY, federal judge; b. Morrisville, Va., Apr. 6, 1923; s. Wilcie Edward and Minnie Mae (Brinkley) W.; m. Eugenia Kellogg, Sept. 11, 1948; children: Nancy Williams Davies, R. Gregory, Walter L., Gwendolyn Mason. LLB, U. Va., 1951. Bar: Va. 1951. Ptnr. McGuire, Woods & Battle and predecessor firms, 1951-72; judge Cir. Ct. City of Richmond, 1972-76; ptnr. McGuire, Woods & Battle, 1976-80; dist. judge U.S. Dist. Ct., Richmond, Va., 1980—, sr. judge, 1992—. 2d lt. Air Corps., U.S. Army, 1940-45. Fellow Am. Coll. Trial Lawyers; mem. Va. State Bar, Va. Bar Assn., Richmond Bar Assn. Office: US Courthouse 701 E Broad St Ste 3000 Richmond VA 23219

WILLIAMS, RICHARD LUCAS, III, electronics executive, director, lawyer; b. Evanston, Ill., Oct. 30, 1940; s. Richard Lucas Jr. and Ellen Gene (Munster) W.; m. Karen Louise Carmody, Nov. 11, 1967 AB, Princeton U., 1962; LLB, U. Va., 1965. Bar: Ill. 1965, D.C. 1968, U.S. Supreme Ct. 1968. Assoc. Winston & Strawn, Chgo., 1968-74, ptnr., 1974-79; sr. v.p., gen. counsel Gould Inc., Rolling Meadows, Ill., 1979-81, sr. v.p., adminstrn., gen. counsel, 1981-90, also bd. dir., 1985-88; ptnr. Smith Williams and Lodge, Chgo., 1990-95, Vedder, Price, Kaufman & Kammholz, Chgo., 1995—2008; of counsel Williams Box & Saltzman, Chgo., 2009—. Bd. dirs. GNB Batteries, Inc., 1984-86, ULINE Inc., Waukegan, Ill. Bd. dirs., 1990—, Internat. Tennis Hall of Fame, Newport, R.I., 1993-97; v.p. Chgo. Dist. Tennis Assn., 1968-70; vice chmn. Am. Cancer Soc., Chgo., 1984; bd. dirs., pres. Lake Shore Found. for Animals, Chgo., 1990-94. With JAGC USNR, 1965-68. Mem. ABA, Ill. Bar Assn., Chgo. Bar Assn., Execs. Club Chgo. (co-chmn. Western Europe internat. com. 1990-97, 2003—), The Lawyers Club (Chgo., 1997—), Meadow Club (Rolling Meadows, gov. 1979-90, chmn. 1985-90), Club Internat. Home: 1200 N Lake Shore Dr Chicago IL 60610-2370 Office: Williams Box & Saltzman PC 20 M Walker Dr Ste 3230 Chicago IL 60606 Office Phone: 312-372-3311. Business E-Mail: rwilliams@wbs.law.com.

WILLIAMS, RICHARD THOMAS, lawyer; b. Evergreen Park, Ill., Jan. 14, 1945; s. Raymond Theodore and Elizabeth Dorothy (Williams) W. AB with honors, Stanford U., 1967, MBA, JD, Stanford U., 1972. Bar: Calif. 1972, U.S. Supreme Ct. 1977. Assoc.,then ptnr. Kadison Pfaelzer Woodard Quinn & Rossi, LA, 1972-87; ptnr. Whitman & Ransom, 1987-93, Whitman, Breed, Abbott & Morgan, LA, 1993-2000, Holland & Knight, LLP, LA, 2000—. Contbg. editor Oil and Gas Analyst, 1978-84. Mem. ABA, L.A. County Bar Assn. Office: Holland & Knight LLP 633 W 5th St Los Angeles CA 90071-2005 Office Phone: 213-896-2410. Business E-Mail: richard.williams@hklaw.com.

WILLIAMS, RICHMOND DEAN, library consultant and appraiser; b. Reading, Mass., Dec. 10, 1925; s. Theodore Ryder and Anabel Lee (Hutchison) W.; m. Eleanor Davidson Washbourne, Sept. 26, 1953; children— Richmond Lyttleton, Eleanor Davidson, Anne Ryder. AB cum laude, Williams Coll., 1950; MA, U. Pa., 1952, PhD, 1959. Instr., asst. dean Williams Coll., Williamstown, Mass., 1954-56; dir. Wyo. Hist. and Geol. Soc., Wilkes-Barre, Pa., 1956-60; asst. dir. Am. Assn. State and Local History, Madison, Wis., 1960-61; dir. libraries Eleutherian Mills-Hagley Found., Wilmington, Del., 1962-87. Instr. Acad. Lifelong Learning U. Del., 1996—; cons. archivist M.S. Hershey Found., Pa., 1981—, Md. Dept. Housing and Cmty. Devel., 1993—94; bd. dirs. Rhistoric Inc. Co-author: A Look at Ourselves, 1962; author: They Also Served, 1965; compiler: Directory of Historical Records in Delaware, 1995; (series) Writing Haiku—, 1997-06. Sec., U. Del. Library Assocs., Wilmington, 1972-86; mem. adv. bd. Del. Hist. Records, Dover, 1976-02; mem. Del. Humanities Forum, Wilmington, 1984-91; trustee Conservation Ctr. Phila., 1984-86. Served to 1st lt. AUS, 1943-47. Pennfield fellow U. Pa., 1953 Mem.: Am. Antiquarian Soc., Am. Assn. State and Local History (pres. 1974—76), Mid-Atlantic Regional Archives Com., Econ. History Assn. (sec.-treas. 1975—88), Phi Beta Kappa. Avocations: golf, book collecting. Home and Office: 202 Brecks Ln Wilmington DE 19807-3011 Business E-Mail: rdwms@udel.edu.

WILLIAMS, RICKY (ERRICK LYNNE WILLIAMS), professional football player; b. San Diego, May 21, 1977; s. Errick and Sandy Williams; children: Marley, Prince. Grad., U. Tex., Austin. Running back New Orleans Saints, 1999—2001, Miami Dolphins, 2002—03, 2005, 2007—, Toronto Argonauts, 2006. Actor: (films) Stuck On You, 2003. Founder Run Ricky Run Found. Recipient Heisman Trophy, 1998; named First Team All-Pro, NFL, 2002; named to Am. Football Conf. Pro Bowl Team, 2002. Achievements include leading the NFL in: rushing attempts, 2002, 2003, rushing yards, 2002, rushing yards per game, 2002, touches, 2003. Home: Miami Dolphins 15190 SW 16th St Weston FL 33326-2053*

WILLIAMS, RITA CARROLL, protective services official, language educator, poet, librarian; b. Norfolk, Va., Jan. 11, 1962; d. William Henry Carroll Jr. and Joyce Riddick Carroll; m. Stafford Clayton Williams Jr., Dec. 2, 1985; 1 child, Thaddeus Clayton. BA in English, BS in Geology, Elizabeth City State U., 1985; student in mid. grades lang. arts, 2002. Cert. English, lang. arts middle grades tchr. 2002. Libr. Rivers Correctional Instn. Author: (poetry) Daily Inspirations: Daily Living With God, 2002, Daily Inspirations: One More Day's Journey on the Way to Heaven, 2003, Book 2, 2003, (CD and cassette) The Sound of Poetry, numerous poems. Release preparation coord. Rivers Correctional Instn. Recipient Outstanding Achievement in Poetry award, Famous Poets Soc., 1999, Editor's Choice award, Internat. Libr. Poetry, 1999, 2003, Outstanding Poetry award, 2003, Spot award, Rivers Correctional Instn., 2004; named Employee of Month, 2005. Mem.: NEA, Internat. Soc. Poets, N.C. Assn. Educators, Alpha Kappa Mu (Cert. of Merit). Avocations: poetry, stamp collecting/philately, coin collecting/numismatics, sports card collecting. Home: 213 Linwood Dr Elizabeth City NC 27909-7022 Office Phone: 252-358-5200. Personal E-mail: praise1063@adelphia.net.

WILLIAMS, RITA TUCKER, lawyer; b. Atlanta, Jan. 26, 1950; d. Claude Edward and Lillian Bernice (Barber) Tucker; m. Raymond Williams, Jr., Jan. 1, 1973; children: Monet Danielle, Brandon Raynard, Blake Hassan. BA, Spelman Coll., 1972; MA, U. Mich., 1976; JD, Emory U., 1987. Bar: Ga. 1987. Tchr. pub. schs., Suisun, Calif., 1977-82; assoc. Alston & Bird, Atlanta, 1987-89, Bernard & Assocs., Decatur, Ga., 1989-90; prin. Williams & Assocs., Decatur, Ga., 1990—. Instr. seminar Nat. Inst. Trial Advocacy, Emory U., Atlanta, spring 1992-95, tutor 1st yr. law students, 1996. Named Outstanding Alumna, Emory U. Law Sch., 1996. Mem. ABA, State Bar Ga. Assn., Ga. Trial Lawyers Assn., Omicron Delta Kappa. Democrat. Office: 220 Church St Decatur GA 30030-3328 Office Phone: 404-370-3783. Personal E-mail: ritw@atlonline.com. Business E-Mail: rtwilliams@williamsandassoc.com.

WILLIAMS, ROBERT C., federal agency administrator; b. Boise, Idaho, June 1954; m. Karen Hassmann, Jan. 8, 1977. BCE, Tex. A&M U., 1976, MCE, 1979. Registered profl. engr., Tex. Officer, cons. sanitary engr. Army Med. Svc. Corps, Ft. McPherson, Ga., 1979—84; staff Office Health Assessment, Agy. Toxic Substances & Disease Registry, Atlanta, 1985—87, chief health scis. br., 1987—89, dir. divsn. health assessment & consultation, 1989—2003; chief of staff, Office Surgeon Gen., US Dept. Health & Human Services (HHS), Washington, 2003—07; acting dep. surgeon gen. HHS, 2007—. Environ. engr. spl. studies br., Ctr. Environ. Health, USPHS Commd. Corps, 1984, rank Rear Adm., 99, chief engr., asst. surgeon gen., 1999—2005, chief ops. officer, 2003, CEO, 2007—; adj. prof. Tex. A&M U. Sch. Rural Pub. Health; mem. academic adv. coun. Emory U., Atlanta. Contbr. numerous pubs. on environ. health issues. Recipient Disting. Svc. medal, USPHS, Meritorious Svc. medal, Surgeon Gen.'s medallion, Surgeon Gen.'s Exemplary Svc. medal (2), Outstanding Svc. medal (2), Commendation medal (3), Achievement medal, Crisis Response Svc. award, Unit Commendation medal (14), Gorgas medal, Assn. Mil. Surgeons; named Engr. of Yr., USPHS, Fed. Environ. Engr. of Yr., Calif. Found. Econ. Edn.; named a Top Ten Engr., Nat. Soc. Profl. Engrs. Fellow: ASCE (mem. gov. bd. Environ. & Water Resources Inst. 1999—2004, Govt. Engr. of Yr. 2003),

Soc. Am. Mil. Engrs. (nat. v.p.); mem.: Commd. Officers Assn., Water Environment Fedn., Am. Water Works Assn., Am. Acad. Environ. Engrs. (diplomat 1992—, bd. trustees, Stanley E. Kappe award 2004). Office: Office Surgeon Gen 5600 Fishers Ln Rm 18 66 Rockville MD 20857 Office Phone: 301-443-4000. Office Fax: 301-443-3574.*

WILLIAMS, ROBERT EUGENE, astronomer; b. Dunsmuir, Calif., Oct. 14, 1940; s. Francis Henry and Lois Evangeline (Youde) W.; m. Elaine Carolyn Eckwall, Dec. 29, 1961; 1 child, Scott Francis. AB, U. Calif., Berkeley, 1962; PhD, U. Wis., 1965. Rsch. asst. U. Calif., Berkeley, 1960-62; Wis. Alumni Rsch. Found. fellow U. Wis., 1962-65; from asst. prof. to assoc. prof. U. Ariz., Tucson, 1965-78, prof., 1978-83; vis. rsch. assoc. European So. Obs., Garching, 1983-84; NRC sr. rsch. fellow NASA-Ames Rsch. Ctr., 1984-85; dir. Cerro Tololo Inter-Am. Obs., La Serena, Chile, 1985-93, Space Telescope Sci. Inst., 1993—1998, principal investigator, 1999—. Mem. NASA space studies bd. NRC, 1995—; mem. exec. com. Aspen (Colo.) Ctr. for Physics, 1983-88, trustee/treas., 1982-88; adj. prof. Johns Hopkins U., 1993—; sr. Fulbright prof. Univ. Coll. London, 1972-73; mem. minority grad. fellowship panel NSF, 1982-85, CTIO Users Com., 1978-81, Kitt Peak Nat. Observatory Telescope Allocation Com., 1978-80, Cerro Tololo Inter-Am. Observatory Telescope Allocation Com., 1976-78; chmn. astronomy U.S. Nat. Fulbright Com., 1974-78; Walker-Ames disting. prof. U. Wash., Seattle, 1998; disting. lectr. U. Victoria, 1998. Author 100 profl. papers. Trustee Assoc. Univs., Inc., 1997—. Recipient Alexander von Humboldt award German Govt., 1991, Dorothy Klumpke Roberts prize, 1962; Fulbright prof. U. London, 1971-72; Heinz Pagels Meml. lectr., 1995, Stanford Bunyan lectr., 1995, Princeton U. Evnin lectr., 1997. Mem. Am. Acad. Arts and Scis., Internat. Astron. Union (U.S. nat. commn. 1990-92, pres.-elect 2006-), Am. Astron. Soc. (com. on astronomy and pub. policy 1994-96, edn. adv. bd. 1981-83, recipient Tinsley prize, 1998), Astron. Soc. of Pacific. Avocations: running, biking. Office: Space Telescope Science Institute 3700 San Martin Dr Baltimore MD 21218-2464

WILLIAMS, ROBERT JOSEPH, retired museum director, educator; b. Bennington, Vt., June 21, 1944; s. Joseph and Ruthe Allison (Moody) Williams. BS in Edn., U. Vt., 1970; MA in Interdisciplinary Social Sci., San Francisco State U., 1981. Tchr. adult edn. Mt. Anthony Union H.S., Bennington, Vt., 1972-74; columnist Bennington Banner, 1972-77; tchr. San Francisco State U., 1976-79; founder, dir. NORRAD Drug Rehab. Ctr., San Francisco, 1986-88; mus. curator Shaftsbury (Vt.) Hist. Soc., 1989—2005; ret., 2005. Founder, dir. Bennington Tutorial Ctr., 1971-74. Author: Toward Humanness in Education, 1981, Chalice of Leaves: Selected Essays and Poems, 1988, Modern Salvation: Guidelines from Cosmology, 1994, Superstring Displacement as a Common Factor in Gravity, Electromagnetic Radiation and Molecular Adhesion, 2004, Consolations on Seeing the Robin Go, 2009; author: (with others) Intimacy, 1985. Recipient Edmunds Essay medal Vt. Historical Soc., Montpelier, 1961, award League Vt. Writers, 1972, Golden Poet award World of Poetry, Sacramento, Calif., 1990. Democrat. Avocation: cosmology. Home: 102 Putnam St Bennington VT 05201-2348 *I sought the truth, and sought to live by it.*

WILLIAMS, ROBERT JOSEPH, behavioral health services executive, psychologist; b. Durango, Colo., Feb. 14, 1948; s. Owen C. and Florence K. Williams; m. Kay Lynn Williams, Mar. 24, 1973; children: Robin, Matthew, Nicholas. BA, U. Colo., 1970; MA, U. No. Colo., 1976; PhD, U. Minn., 1979. Diplomate Am. Bd. Psychol. Specialties. Tchr. math. Jefferson County Schs., Lakewood, Colo., 1970-76; psychologist Pikes Peak Mental Health Ctr., Colorado Springs, Colo., 1979-82, clin. dir., 1982-83; dir. Inst. for Family and Personal Devel., Colorado Springs, 1983-86; mng. ptnr. Marriage and Family Treatment Ctr., Colorado Springs, 1986-90; COO Quinco Behavioral Health Systems, Columbus, Ind., 1990-92, pres., CEO, 1992—2008; CEO Centerstone Ind., 2008—. Feedback cons. Ctr. for Creative Leadership, Colorado Springs and San Diego, 1986-96; facilitator Franklin Covey Ctr., Columbus, 1994-99; cons. Trustee Leadership Tng. Program, Indpls., 1991-98; adj. faculty U. Denver, U. Colo., Colorado Springs, 1981-90. Contbr. articles to profl. jours. Trustee Bartholomew Consol. Sch. Corp., Columbus, 1996-2001, pres., 1999-2000; past pres., moderator Leadership Bartholomew County; mem. Healthy Communities Coun. 1995—, co-chmn. 2004-05; bd. dirs. Columbus Ind. Philharmonic, 2001—07, pres. 2003-04; bd. mem. Rotary, 2004-05, Columbus Area C. of C., 2005—, pres. 2008-09. Sgt. USMCR, 1970—76. Boettcher Found. scholar, 1966-70; Regents scholar, 1966. Mem. Rotary Club, Masons., IUPUC (bd. adv., 2008-) Democrat. Presbyn. Avocations: hiking, reading, motorcycling, weight training. Office: Centerstone of Ind 720 North Marr Rd Columbus IN 47201 Business E-Mail: robert.williams@ccuterstone.org. E-mail: rjwilliams@quincoinc.com.

WILLIAMS, ROBERT LEON, retired psychiatrist, neurologist, educator; b. Buffalo, July 22, 1922; s. Leon R. and L. Paulyne (Ingraham) W.; m. Shirley Glynn Miller, Feb. 5, 1949; Karen, Kevin BA, Alfred U., 1944; MD, Albany Med. Coll., Union U., 1946. Chief neurology and psychiatry Lackland AFB Hosp., USAF, San Antonio, 1952-55; cons. neurology and psychiatry to USAF Surgeon Gen., 1955-58; faculty Coll. Medicine, U. Fla., Gainesville, 1958-72, prof., chmn. dept. psychiatry, 1964-72; prof. psychiatry Baylor Coll. Medicine, Houston, 1972-92, chmn. dept., 1972-90, prof. neurology, 1976-92, acting chmn. dept., 1976-77, prof. emeritus psychiatry and neurology, from 1992; ret. Mem. faculty various univs., part time 1949-58 including Albany Med. Coll. at Union U., Columbia Coll. Physisicans and Surgeons, Boston U., U. Tex., Georgetown U. Author: (with W.B. Webb) Sleep Therapy: A. Bibliography and Commentary, 1966, (with others) EEG of Human Sleep: Clinical Applications, 1974; editor: (with Ismet Karacan and Carolyn J. Hursch) Psychopharmacology of Sleep, 1976, Sleep Disorders: Diagnosis and Treatment, 1978, 2d edit., 1988; (with others) Phenomenology and Treatment of Anxiety, 1979, of Alcoholism, 1980, of Psychophysiological Disorders, 1982, of Psychosexual Disorders, 1983, of Psychiatric Emergencies, 1984 Served from 1st lt. to lt. col. USAF, 1949-58; col. Res., ret. Recipient Cert. Profl. Achievement USAF Surgeon Gen., 1967 Mem. Am. Psychiat. Assn., Am. Electroencephalographic Soc., Am. Coll. Psychiatrists (pres. 1982-83), Am. Acad. Neurology, AMA, Group for Advancement of Psychiatry, Benjamin Rush Soc. (pres. 1986-88), Accreditation Coun. for grad. Med. Edn. (residency rev. com. for psychiatry 1985-93), Alpha Omega Alpha. Achievements include research in basic psychophysiology of human sleep. Died Nov. 16, 2008.

WILLIAMS, ROBERTON CAPELL, III, economics professor; b. Keflavik, Iceland, Dec. 2, 1972; s. Roberton Capell Williams, Jr. and Jane Carlile Hilder. AB, Harvard Coll., 1990—94; PhD, Stanford U., 1994—99. Asst. prof. U. Tex., Austin, 1999—2007, assoc. prof., 2007—. Andrew W. Mellon fellow in econ. studies Brookings Instn., Washington, 2002—03; vis. rsch. scholar Stanford Inst. Econ. Policy Rsch., 2003—04; faculty rsch. fellow Nat. Bur. Econ. Rsch., Cambridge, Mass., 2000—08, rsch. assoc., 2008—. Co-editor: Jour. Environ. Econs. & Mgmt.; editor (assoc.): Jour. Pub. Econs.; mem. editl. coun.: Berkeley Electronic Jour. in Econ. Analysis & Policy; contbr. papers to profl. jours. and pubs. Grantee Grad. fellowship, NSF, 1994—97, STAR Grad. fellowship, EPA, 1997—99. Mem.: Assn. Environ. and Resource Economists, Nat. Tax Assn., Am. Econ. Assn., Austin Yacht Club. Avocations: sailboat racing, travel, landscape photography. Office: Dept Econs Univ Tex 1 University Sta #C3100 Austin TX 78712-0301 Business E-Mail: rwilliam@eco.utexas.edu.

WILLIAMS, ROBIN, actor, comedian; b. Chgo., July 21, 1951; s. Mr. and Mrs. Robert W.; m. Valerie Velardi, June 4, 1978 (div. 1988); 1 child, Zachary; m. Marsha Garces, Apr. 30, 1989 (separated Mar. 21, 2008); children: Zelda, Cody. Attended, Claremont Men's Coll., Marin Coll., Juilliard Sch., NYC. Started as stand-up comedian in San Francisco clubs, including Holy City Zoo, The Boardinghouse; actor: (TV series) Mork and Mindy, 1978-82; (films) Popeye, 1980, The World According to Garp, 1982, The Survivors, 1983, Moscow on the Hudson, 1984, The Best of Times, 1986, Club Paradise, 1986, Seize the Day, 1986, Good Morning Vietnam, 1987 (Golden Globe award 1988, Acad. Award nominee for best actor), The Adventures of Baron Munchausen, 1988, Dead Poets Society, 1989 (Best Actor nomination Golden Globe award, 1994, nominated best actor Acad. award), Cadillac Man, 1990, Awakenings, 1990, Dead Again, 1991, The Fisher King, 1991 (Golden Globe award, Acad. award nominee for best actor 1991), Dead Again, 1991, Hook, 1991, (voice only) Aladdin, 1992 (Spl. Achievement award Hollywood Fgn. Press, Nat. Bd. Rev. 1992), Toys, 1992, Mrs. Doubtfire, 1993 (Golden Globe award for Best Actor in a Musical or Comedy, 1994), Nine Months, 1995, Jumanji, 1995, The BirdCage, 1996, Jack, 1996, The Secret Agent, 1996, Hamlet, 1996, Deconstructing Harry, 1997, Father's Day, 1997, Flubber, 1997, Good Will Hunting, 1997 (Acad. award for Best Supporting Actor, SAG award for outstanding performance by a male actor in a supporting role), What Dreams May Come, 1998, Patch Adams, 1998, Bicentennial Man, 1999, Jakob the Liar, 1999, (voice only) A.I.: Artificial Intelligence, 2001, One Hour Photo, 2002, Death to Smoochy, 2002, Insomnia, 2002, The Final Cut, 2004, The House of D, 2004, Noel, 2004, (voice only) Robots, 2005, RV, 2006, The Night Listener, 2006, Man of the Year, 2006, (voice only) Happy Feet, 2006, Night at the Museum, 2006, License to Wed, 2007, August Rush, 2007, World's Greatest Dad, 2009, Shrink, 2009, Night at the Museum: Battle of the Smithsonian, 2009; (TV appearances) Laugh-In, 1977, Eight Is Enough, 1977, America 2-Night, 1978, Happy Days, 1978, '79, Out of the Blue, 1979, Homicide: Life on the Street, 1994, Friends, 1997, L.A. Doctors, 1999, Life with Bonnie, 2003, Law & Order: Special Victims Unit, 2008 (Favorite Scene-Stealing Guest Star, People's Choice Awards, 2009); theatre: Waiting for Godot, 1988; performer: (comedy albums) Reality, What a Concept, 1979 (Grammy award), Throbbing Python of Love, A Night at the Met (Grammy award); host Comic Relief, 1986; (comedy specials) ABC Presents a Royal Gala, 1988 (Emmy award, 1988), Carol, Carl, Whoopi & Robin, 1987 (Emmy award), Robin Williams: Live at the Met, 1986, Robin Williams Live, 1986, Comic Relief, 1986, Young Comedians All Star Reunion, 1988, Robin Williams: Live on Broadway, 2002 (Emmy nomination, Grammy award, 2003); host, Shakespeare: The Animated Tales, 1993 (CableAce Award, Best Entertainment Host) Recipient Golden Apple award Hollywood Women's Press Club, ACE award, Am. Comedy award, 1987, 88, Grammy award for best comedy rec., 1987, Man of Yr. award Hasty Pudding Theatricals, 1989, People's Choice award Favorite Comedy Motion Picture Actor, 1994, ShoWest Conv. award Male Star of Yr., 1994, Cecil B. DeMille award, Hollywood Fgn. Press, 2005, Hollywood Career Achievement award Hollywood Awards, 2006, Favorite Funny Male Star, People's Choice Award, 2007, 2008. Office: 1 Blackfield Dr Ste 409 Belvedere Tiburon CA 94920*

WILLIAMS, ROGER LAWRENCE, historian, educator; b. Boulder, Colo., June 22, 1923; s. Raymond Ustick and Mabel (Woolf) W. BA, Colo. Coll., 1947; MA, U. Mich., 1948, PhD, 1951. Asst. prof. Minn. State Coll., Mankato, 1950-52, MIT, Cambridge, 1952-55; vis. prof. Mich. State U., East Lansing, 1955-56; assoc. prof. Antioch Coll., Yellow Springs, Ohio, 1956-65; prof. U. Calif., Santa Barbara, 1965-71, U. Wyo., Laramie, 1971-78, Disting. prof., 1978-88. Author: French Revolution of 1870-71, 1969, The Mortal Napoleon III, 1971, The Horror of Life, 1980, Aven Nelson of Wyoming, 1984, Gérard and Jaume: Two Neglected Figures in the History of the Jussiaean Classification, 1988, Napoleon III and the Stoffel Affair, 1993, The Letters of Dominique Chaix, Botanist-Curé, 1997, Botanophilia in 18th Century France: The Spirit of the Enlightenment, 2001; co-author: How Modernity Came to a Provençal Town, 1988, Handbook of Rocky Mountain Plants, 1992, A Guide to Rocky Mountain Plants, 2002, French Botany in the Enlightenment: the Ill-fated Voyages of La Pérouse and His Rescuers, 2003, A Region of Astonishing Beauty, the Botanical Exploration of the Rocky Mountains, 2003, An Intellectual Biography of Elie-Abel Carrière, 2004, Revolution and Madness: Blanqui and Trelat, 2005, From Malesherbes to Tocqueville, The Legacy of Liberalism, 2006, Malesherbes: Botanist, Arborist, Agronome, 2007, French Connections: Cultivating American Trees in Revolutionary France, 2008; mem. editl. bd.: Antioch Rev., 1958—64; co-author: Botanists and Medical Herbalism in Montpellier, 2009. Vol. Rocky Mountain Nat. Park, Estes Park, Colo., 1986-87. Mem. French Hist. Studies (life), History Sci. Soc. (life), Hist. Soc., Nat. Coun. for History Edn., N.Y. Bot. Soc., Denver Bot. Soc. Home: 1701 S 17th St Laramie WY 82070-5406

WILLIAMS, RONALD A., health insurance company executive; b. Chgo., Nov. 11, 1949; m. Cynthia Williams; 1 child. BA in Psychology, Roosevelt U., 1970; MS in Mgmt., MIT, 1984; HHD (hon.), Howard U., 2009. Sr. v.p. mktg. and specialty products to exec. v.p. group and network svc. Blue Cross Calif., 1987—95, pres., 1995—99; sr. v.p. Vista Health Corp.; group mktg. exec. Control Data Corp.; pres., co-founder Integrative Sys.; pres. large group divsn. WellPoint Health Networks Inc., 1999—2001; exec. v.p., chief of health operations Aetna Inc., 2001—02, pres., 2002—06, chmn., pres., CEO, 2006—07, chmn., CEO, 2007—. Bd. dirs. Aetna Inc., 1992—, Lucent Technologies, 2003—06, Am. Express Co., 2007—; vice chmn. The Bus. Coun., 2008—; trustee The Conf. Bd. Named to Power 150, Ebony mag., 2008. Avocations: jazz, movies. Office: Aetna Inc 151 Farmington Ave Hartford CT 06156*

WILLIAMS, RONALD DEAN, minister, religious organization administrator; b. Decatur, Ill., Oct. 23, 1940; s. Henry Lawrence and Ella Loudica Williams; children: Scott Allan, Mark Lawrence, Derek James; m. Lorretta Ilene Williams, Sept. 1, 2007. BTh, LIFE Bible Coll., LA, 1965; DD, Internat. Ch. Foursquare Gospel, LA, 1992. Ordained to ministry Internat. Ch. Foursquare Gospel, 1966. Pastor Foursquare Gospel Ch., Surrey, Canada, 1965-69, missionary Hong Kong, China, 1969-85; prof. Life Bible Coll., 1985-95; mng. editor Fourquare World Advance, 1993—2002; comm. officer Internat. Ch. Foursquare Gospel, 1988-2000. Bd. dirs. Forsquare Gospel Ch., denominational historian, 2004—07; pres. exec. bd. Internat. Pentecostal Press Assn., Oklahoma City, 1990—98; comm. officer Pentecostal/Charismatic Ch. N.Am., Memphis, 1994—2005; coord. E. Coun. Foursquare Miss., 1979—82. Editor: The Vine and The Branches, 1992; mng. editor: Foursquare World Advance mag., 1985—2002. Coord. 19th Pentecostal World Conf., 2001, With USAF, 1958—61. Avocations: writing, golf, reading, music. Personal E-mail: ron@lifeshighest.com.

WILLIAMS, RONALD L., dentist; BS, U. Okla.; DDS, Baylor Coll. Dentistry. Resident St. Anthony's Hosp., Oklahoma City; cosmetic dentist Smile Solutions, Norman, Okla. Vol. dentist D-dent program, C.A.R.E. Mem.: Ctrl. Dist. Okla. Dental Assn., Okla. Dental Assn., Am. Dental Assn., Acad. Gen. Dentistry, Am. Acad. Cosmetic Dentistry, Cleve. County Dental Soc., Omicron Kappa Upsilon, Odontological Honor Soc. Office: Smile Solutions 550 24th Ave SW Norman OK 73069 Office Phone: 405-364-7385. Office Fax: 405-447-8888.

WILLIAMS, RONALD OSCAR, mathematician; b. Denver, May 10, 1940; s. Oscar H. and Evelyn J. (Johnson) Williams. BS in Applied Math., U. Colo., Coll. Engring., Boulder, 1964; postgrad., U. Colo., 1968—70, U. Denver, 1975; postgrad. Advanced Tech. Edn. Program, Hughes Aircraft Co., 1980—89; postgrad., George Washington U., DC, 1985; postgrad. Spl. Electronics Course, Lowry AFB, Denver; continuing edn. courses, Gen. Elec. Co., Control Data Corp., NASA, Boulder Police Dept. Computer programmer Apollo Sys. dept. Missile and Space div. Gen. Electric Co., Kennedy Space Ctr., Fla., 1965-67; computer programmer Apollo Sys. dept. Missile and Space divsn. Manned Spacecraft Ctr. (now Johnson Space Ctr.), Houston, 1967—68; computer programmer Grad. Sch. Computing Ctr. and Lab. Atmospheric and Space Physics U. Colo., Boulder, 1968-73; computer programmer analyst Def. Sys. divsn. Sys. Devel. Corp. at Ent AFB, Colorado Springs, Colo., 1974—75, NORAD Cheyenne Mountain Complex, Colorado Springs, 1974—75; engr. def. sys. and command-and-info. sys. Martin Marietta Aerospace (now Lockheed Martin), Denver, 1976—80; sys. engr., def. info. sys. divsn. space and comm. group Hughes Aircraft Co. at Aerospace Data Facility, Buckley AFB, Aurora, Colo., 1980—89; rsch. analyst Math. Rsch. Ctr., Littleton, Colo., 1990—, dir., sr. rsch. mathematician, 1996—. First chair trombonist Wash. Park Elem. Sch. Orch., All-City Elem. Sch. Orch., Merrill Jr. HS Concert Band, Merrill Jr. HS Concert Orch., Merrill Jr. HS German Band, Denver Jr. Police Band, Mile-High Boys' Band, Wells Music Dance Band. Vol. fireman Clear Lake City Fire Dept., Tex., 1968, Harris County Fire Fighters Assn., Tex., 1968; officer Boulder Emergency Squad, 1969-76, rescue squad officer, 1969-76, rescue SCUBA diver asst., liaison officer to cadets, 1971, pers. officer, 1971-76, exec. bd., 1971-76, Red Cross Std. First Aid to Injured, Advanced First Aid to Injured, Basic Life Support Cardiopulmonary Resuscitation, EMT, 1973—; charter mem. Am. Assn. Trauma Specialists, Am. Paramedic Assn., Nat. Assn. Trauma Specialists; res. dispatcher A-1 Ambulance, Boulder, 1973-74; spl. police officer Boulder Police Dept., 1970-75; spl. dep. sheriff Boulder County Sheriff's Dept., 1970-71; nat. adv. bd. Am. Security Coun., 1979-91, Coalition of Peace Through Strength, 1979-91. Non-commd. officer USMCR, San Diego, Camp Matthews, Camp Elliott, Camp Pendleton (Camp San Onofre), Twentynine Palms, Camp Wilson, Denver Fed. Ctr., 1958—66; mem. Emergency Med. Technician Assn. Colo. Decorated M1 Rifle Sharpshooter Badge, Basic US Marines Weapons Qualification Badge, Organized Res. medal, Marine Corps League medal, USMC Commemorative medal, Nat. Guard and Res. Commemorative medal, Am. Def. Commemorative medal, Hon. Svc. Commemorative medal, Hon. Discharge; recipient Award of Merit, Boulder Emergency Squad, 1971, 1972, Dedicated Svc. award, 1976, Top Cost Improvement Program award, Hughes Aircraft Co., 1982, Sys. Performance Improvement award, 1982, Spl. Recognition award, Grad. Sch. Georgetown U., DC, Nat. Securities Studies Program, Am. Security Coun., 1979; named to Paul R. Halmos Commemorative Walk, Carriage House Conf. Ctr., Math. Assn. America's Hdqs., Wash. Mem. AAAS, AIAA (sr.), Math. Assn. America, Am. Math Soc., Soc. Indsl. and Applied Math., Math. Study Unit of Am. Topical Assn., Armed Forces Comm. and Electronics Assn., Assn. Old Crows, Nat. Def. Indsl. Assn., Assn. For Intelligence Officers, Nat. Mil. Intelligence Assn., Nat. Cryptologic Mus. Found., Internat. Spy Mus. (Wash.), US Naval Cryptologic Vet. Assn., Friends of Bletchley Park, Marine Corps Assn., Marine Corps Heritage Found. (charter mem.), Marine Corps League, Nat. Mus. Marine Corps and Heritage Ctr. (campaign mem.), Air Force Assn., US Naval Inst., Nat. Geog. Soc., Smithsonian Inst., Nat. Space Soc., Soc. Amateur Radio Astronomers, Radio History Soc., Met. Opera Guild, Colo. Pub. Radio (classical music), Rocky Mountain PBS, Colo. Hist. Soc., Hist. Denver, Hist. Boulder, Colorado Railroad Hist. Found, Colorado Railroad Mus., Hawaiian Hist Soc., Nat. Audubon Soc., Audubon Soc. Greater Denver, Denver Bot. Gardens, Denver Mus. Nature and Sci., Denver Zool. Found., Pacific Aviation Mus. Pearl Harbor (founding mem.), Wings Over the Rockies Air & Space Mus., Alumni Assn. U. Colo. Boulder, South High Alumni and Friends Denver, Am. Mensa Ltd., Denver Mile-Hi Mensa, Acoustic Neuroma Assn., Nat. Brain Tumor Soc., Crystal Cathedral Ministries, Sparrows Club, Eagles Club, Summer Ptnr., Year End Ptnr., Swedish Club of Denver. Lutheran.

WILLIAMS, ROY, men's college basketball coach; b. Spruce Pine, NC, Aug. 1, 1950; m. Wanda; children: Scott, Kimberly. BA in Edn., U. NC, 1972, MAT, 1973. Basketball & golf coach Charles D. Owen HS, NC; asst. coach U. NC Tarheels, 1978—88, head coach, 2003—, U. Kans. Jayhawks, 1988—2003. Asst. coach U.S.A. Sr. Men's Nat. Basketball Team, 2003, US Olympic Men's Basketball Team, Athens, Greece, 2004. Named Nat. Rookie Coach of Yr., Basketball Times, 1989, Nat. Coach of Yr. 1990-92, 1997, 2006, Big 8 Coach of Yr. (7 times), Coach of Yr., AP, 1992, 2006, ACC Coach of Yr., 2006; recipient John R. Wooden Legends of Coaching award LA Athletic Club, 2003, Nat. Coach of Yr. award NY Athletic Club, 2005; named to Naismith Meml. Basketball Hall of Fame, 2007. Achievements include head coach of the NCAA Men's Basketball National Championship winning University of North Carolina Tarheels, 2005, 2009. Office: U NC Athletic Dept Men's Basketball PO Box 2126 Chapel Hill NC 27514 Office Phone: 919-962-6000. E-mail: williara@email.unc.edu.*

WILLIAMS, ROY EUGENE, JR., professional football player; b. Odessa, Tex., Dec. 20, 1981; Attended, U. Tex., Austin, 2000—03. Wide receiver Detroit Lions, 2004—08, Dallas Coyboys, 2008—. Vol. HAVEN Domestic Violence Shelter, 2004—, Boys and Girls Club, Detroit, 2004—. Actor: (films) Friday Night Lights, 2002. Named to All-Am. Dream Team, NFL Draft Report, 2004, Nat. Football Conf. Pro Bowl Team, 2006. Office: Dallas Cowboys Cowboys Ctr One Cowboys Pky Irving TX 75063*

WILLIAMS, RUBY JO, retired principal; b. Marshall, Tex., Sept. 26, 1936; d. Henry Clay and Luberta Smith; m. Q.D. Williams (dec. Apr. 1998). BA, Wiley Coll., Marshall, Tex., 1959; M in Edn., U. N. Tex., 1972; postgrad. in Mid-Mgmt., Tex. Woman's U., 1987. Cert. elem., secondary sch. educator, mid-mgr., Tex. Tchr. Gainesville (Tex.) Sch. Dist., 1962-69, Sherman (Tex.) Sch. Dist., 1969-86, appraiser, 1986-87, prin., 1987-96, Edison coord., 1996-98. Mem., past chmn. Grayson Coll. Trustees, Grayson County, 1992—, Comty. Block Grant, Sherman, Tex.; mem Hosp. Metraplex Bd., Sherman. Named Outstanding Citizen, City of Sherman, 1979. Mem. NAACP (life), AAUW (pres., v.p., Woman of Yr., Woman of Achievement, Outstanding Woman Educator 1978-79), Nat. Alliance of Black Sch. Educators, Tex. Elem. Prins. Assn., Goals for Sherman (multi-cultural chmn.) Mem. Ch. of Christ. Avocations: reading, traveling, cooking, sewing. Home: 2015 E Alma Ave Sherman TX 75090-4006

WILLIAMS, SANKEY VAUGHAN, health services researcher, internist; b. San Antonio, Apr. 15, 1944; s. James Sankey and Helen (Long) W.; m. Constance Hess, June 27, 1972; children: Elizabeth Helen, Jennifer Lee. AB, Princeton U., 1966; MD, Harvard U., 1970. Diplomate Am. Bd. Internal Medicine. Intern Hosp. of U. Pa., 1970-71, jr. resident, 1971-72, chief med. resident, 1974-75; assoc. dir. clin. rsch. Ctr. for Study of Aging, U. Pa., 1982-86; assoc. dir. for med. affairs Leonard Davis Inst. for Health Econs., U. Pa., 1978-90; dir. clin. scholars program U. Pa., Phila., 1988-96; prof. health care systems Wharton Sch., U. Pa., Phila., 1989—; prof. medicine U. Pa., Phila., 1989—, chief div. gen. internal medicine, 1992—, Sol Katz prof. medicine, 1992—. Commr. Prospective Payment Assessment Commn., U.S. Congress, Washington, 1988-91; chairman health svcs. rsch. devel. grants study sect. Agy. for Health Care Policy and Rsch., 1991-94; counselor for med. affiars to the pres. U. Pa., 1990-92. Co-editor: The Physician's Practice, 1980; author 35 revs, chpt. or editorials; contbr. 62 articles to various sci. jour., assoc. editor, annals of Internal Medicine, 2003-. Lt. comdr. USPHS, 1972-74. Recipient Career Devel. award Henry S. Kaiser Family Found., 1981-86. Mem. ACP (master, chmn. clin. privileges com. 1989-93, Soc. for Med. Decision Making (pres. 1985-86), Soc. for Gen. Internal Medicine (coun. 1979-84, editor Jour. Gen. Internal Medicine 1994-99, pres. 2000-01). Office: Hosp Univ of Pa Divsn Gen Internal Medicine 1220 Blockley Hall 423 Guardian Dr Philadelphia PA 19104-6021

WILLIAMS, SCOTT MATTHEW, science educator; s. Allen and Ann Williams; m. Mariola Elzbieta Drygas; children: Alexandra Drygas, Nicholas Drygas. AB, U. Chgo., Ill., 1976; PhD, Wash. U., St. Louis, 1981. Prof. Vanderbilt U., Nashville, 2002—. Mem.: AAAS.

WILLIAMS, SERENA, professional tennis player, apparel designer; b. Saginaw, Mich., Sept. 26, 1981; d. Richard and Oracene Williams. Prof. tennis player WTA Tour, 1995—; designer Aneres clothing line. TV appearances include: My Wife and Kids, 2002; Law and Order: Special Victims Unit, 2004; The Division, 2004; (voice) The Simpsons, 2001. Recipient Espy award for Best Female Athlete, ESPN, 2003, Espy award for Best Female Tennis Player, 2003, 2004; named WTA Most Improved Player, 1999, Player of the Year, TENNIS Mag., 1999, Female Athlete in the World, AP, 2002, WTA Tour Player of the Year, 2002, #1 most marketable female athlete, Sports Business Daily, 2003, Best Female Athlete, Black Entertainment TV (BET) Awards, 2007; named one of The 100 Most Powerful Celebrities, Forbes.com, 2008, Most Influential People in the World of Sports, Bus. Week, 2008. Achievements include winner of 34 career singles titles, 14 career doubles titles, and 2 mixed doubles titles, WTA tour; Grand Slam Championships: US Open, 1999, 2002, 2008, Wimbledon, 2002, 2003, 2009, Roland Garros, 2002, Austalian Open, 2003, 2005, 2007, 2009; Grand Slam Championships: (with Venus Williams) French Open, 1999, US Open, 1999, Wimbledon, 2000, 2002, 2008, 2009, Australian Open 2001, 2003, 2009; Mixed Doubles (w/ Max Mirnyi), Wimbledon, 1998; winner of doubles gold medal (with Venus Williams), Sydney Olympic games, 2000, Beijing Olympic games, 2008; winning 4 Grand Slam tournaments in a row, 2002-2003; signing largest endorsement deal to date by a female athlete with Nike, 2003; mem. US Fed Cup Team, 1999, 2003, 2007, US Women's Olympic Team, Sydney, 2000, Beijing, 2008. Office: c/o US Tennis Assn 70 W Red Oak Ln White Plains NY 10604-3602*

WILLIAMS, SHANNON RENEE, mental health services professional; d. Joyce Bromley Wright; m. Anthony Markell Williams, July 5, 1997; children: JaHarold, Justin, Jamilla. BS, Bowie State U., 1990, MA, 1993; PhD, Howard U., 2004. Lic. clin. profl. counselor Md. Mental health assoc. Regional Inst. for Children and Adolescents, Rockville, Md., 1990—94; correctional psychologist assoc. Dept. Pub. Safety and Correctional Svcs., Jessup, Md., 1994—2005; therapist Wash. Assessment and Therapy Svc., Lanham, Md., 2005—06; psychotherapist Bowie Counseling Svcs., 2006—08, All That's Therapeutic, 2006—; pvt. practice Upper Marlboro, 2007—. Coord. Diamonds in the Rough womanhood tng. program Paramount Bapt. Ch., Washington, 2000—. Mem.: APA. Avocations: reading, singing. Office Phone: 301-627-0568. Business E-Mail: docsrwilliams1@verizon.net.

WILLIAMS, SONIA KAY, retired secondary school educator; b. Duluth, Minn., Jan. 13, 1939; d. Allen Parke and Ruth Adelaide (Mitchell) Swayne; m. William Fedrick Williams, Mar. 26, 1960; children: Keith Douglass, Jennifer Gay. BMus, U. Tenn., Chattanooga, 1960; M in Secondary Tchg. of English, Statesboro U., 1975; edn. specialist, Valdosta State U., 1988. Tchr. North Chattanooga Jr. HS, 1960—61; music tchr. Savannah Country Day Sch., Ga., 1968—72; English tchr. Appling County Jr. HS, Baxley, Ga., 1972—74, Appling County Comprehensive HS, Baxley, 1974—2001; ret., 2001. Accompanist Appling Applause, Baxley, 1978-92; drama tchr. Appling County HS, 1990-92. Prodr. videotape Sonia's Signya's, 1991. Bd. dirs., Sunday sch. tchr. First United Meth. Ch., Baxley, 1980-94; pres. Friends of Libr., Baxley, 1990-92; charter mem. Appling Hist. Soc., Baxley, 1980—, bd. dirs., 1992-94; mem. Appling Heritage Com., Baxley, 1992-2009; vol. ARC, Am. Cancer Soc., Appling Co. Food Bank, 2003-09, CASA, 2002-09; ct.-apptd. spl. adv. for abused and neglected children. Named Star Tchr., Appling County C. of C., 1984, outstanding Retired Educator of Yr. Altamaha Tech. Coll., 2004; recipient Outstanding Educator award Ga. Retired Educators Assn., 2001, Cmty. Svc. award, 2003, 09 Cmty. Svc. award AARP, 2007. Mem. Nat. Coun. Tchrs. English, Ga. Assn. Educators (instrnl. and profl. devel. com. 1992-97, Dist. Tchr. of Yr. 1997-98), Lions Internat. (pres. Baxley Lions Club 2007), Delta Kappa Gamma (pres. Alpha Pi chpt. 1997-99). Avocations: reading, writing, swimming, drama. Home: 177 Torrance Rd Baxley GA 31513-6726

WILLIAMS, STEPHANIE F., oncologist; MD, U. Chicago, 1981. Cert. Internal Medicine, 1984, Med. Oncology, 1987. Residency in internal medicine Michael Reese Hosp., 1984; fellowship in hematology and oncology U. Chgo. Hosp., 1987; assoc. prof. clinical medicine, hematology/oncology Northwestern U., Ill.; med. dir. stem cell transplant program Hematology Oncology Associates Ill., LLC, Chgo. Editl. bd. mem. Leukemia and Lymphoma, Healthy Woman; reviewer Jour. Clin. Oncology, Bone Marrow Transplantation, Jour. Hematotherapy. Recipient U. Chgo. Cancer Rsch. Found. award. Mem.: Ill. Med. Oncology Soc. (pres. bd. dirs. 2007—09), Am. Cancer Soc. (Career Develop. award). Office: Hematology Oncology Associates Ill LLC 676 N St Clair Ste 2140 Chicago IL 60611*

WILLIAMS, STEPHEN, anthropologist, educator; b. Mpls., Aug. 28, 1926; s. Clyde Garfield and Lois (Simmons) Williams; m. Eunice Ford, Jan. 6, 1962; children: Stephen John, Timothy. BA, Yale U., 1949, PhD, 1954; MA, U. Mich., 1950; MA (hon.), Harvard U., 1962. Asst. anthropology dept. Peabody Mus., Yale U., 1950-52; mem. faculty Harvard U., Cambridge, Mass., 1958—, prof. anthropology, 1967-72, Peabody prof., 1972-93, prof. emeritus, 1993—, chmn. dept., 1967-69; rsch. fellow Peabody Mus., Harvard U., Cambridge, 1954-57, mem. staff, 1954—, dir. mus., 1967-77. Curator N.Am. Archaeology, 1962-93, hon. curator 1993—; dir. rsch. of Peabody Mus.'s Lower Miss. Survey, 1958-93. Author books and articles on N.Am. archaeology, "Fantastic" archaeology and the history of Am. anthropology. Home: 1017 Foothills Trail Santa Fe NM 87505-4537 Office: PO Box 22354 Santa Fe NM 87502-2354 Office Phone: 505-983-8836. Personal E-mail: williamsstephen@msn.com.

WILLIAMS, STEPHEN FAIN, federal judge; b. NYC, Sept. 23, 1936; s. Charles Dickerman and Virginia (Fain) Williams; m. Faith Morrow, June 11, 1966; children: Susan, Geoffrey Fain, Sarah Margot Nu, Timothy Dwight, Nicholas Morrow. BA, Yale U., 1958; JD, Harvard U., 1961. Bar: NY 1962, Colo. 1977. Assoc. Debevoise, Plimpton, Lyons & Gates, NYC, 1962—66; asst. atty. US Dist. Ct. (so. dist.), NY, 1966—69; asst. prof. law U. Colo., Boulder, 1969—77, prof., 1977—86; judge US Ct. Appeals (DC cir.), Washington, 1986—2001, sr. judge, 2001—. Vis. prof. UCLA, 1975—76; vis. prof., fellow in law and econs. U. Chgo., 1979—80; vis. William L. Hutchison prof. energy law So. Meth. U., 1983—84; cons. Adminstrv. Conf. US, 1974—76, FTC, 1983—85; mem. Boulder Area Growth Study Commn., 1972—73. Contbr. articles to profl. jours. and mags.; author: Liberal Reform in an Illiberal Regime: The Creation of Private Property in Russia, 1906-1915, 2006. With US Army, 1961—62. Mem.: ABA, Fed. Energy Bar Assn., Am. Law Inst. Office: US Courthouse 333 Constitution Ave NW Washington DC 20001 E-mail: SFWilliams@cadc.uscourts.gov.*

WILLIAMS, STEVEN A., JR., environmental services administrator, former federal agency administrator; b. Bellows Falls, Vt. m. Beth Williams; 2 children. B in Environ. Resource Mgmt., Pa. State U., D in Forest Resources; MS, U. N.D. Grad. tchg. asst. U. N.D., 1979—81, Pa. State U., 1981—85; wildlife biologist Mass. Divsn. Fisheries and Wildlife, 1985—89, asst. dir. for wildlife, 1989—92; dep. exec. dir. Pa. Game Commn., 1992—95; sec. Kans. Dept. Wildlife and Parks, 1995—2002; dir. US Fish & Wildlife Svc., US Dept. Interior, Washington, 2002—05; pres. Wildlife Mgmt. Inst., Washington, 2005—. Mem.: Wildlife Soc., Internat. Assn. Fish and Wildlife Agys. Office: Wildlife Management Institute PO Box 33819 Washington DC 20033-0819 E-mail: swilliams@wildlifemgt.org.

WILLIAMS, STEVEN L., theater educator, director; b. Albuquerque, N.Mex. s. Darlene and Rodger Williams; m. Nancy Eulberg; children: Nolan, Gavin. BFA in Theatrical Design, Ea. N.Mex U., Portales, 1992; MFA in Scenography, Ind. U., Bloomington, 1995. Dir. theatre U. Nebr., Omaha, 1995—, assoc. prof. theatre, 1995—. Freelance scenic and lighting designer, 1995—. Mem.: Am. Coll. Theatre Festival, Lighting Design Internat., US Inst. Theatre Tech. Office: Univ Nebraska Omaha Theatre 6001 Dodge St Omaha NE 68182 Office Fax: 402-554-3436. Business E-Mail: steven_williams@mail.unomaha.edu.

WILLIAMS, SUSAN L., educator; b. Santa Monica, Calif., Mar. 26, 1952; d. Wilkinson Albert and Harriet Ruth Stephens; children: Stephen L., Kate L. BSN, U. Mo., 1976; MBA with highest honors, N.Mex. State U., Las Cruces, 1986. RN, CRS. Head nurse Vets. Hosp., Columbia, Mo., 1977-78; head nurse-surg. side Parkland Hosp. Emergency Rm., Dallas, 1980-82; dir. Kimberly Quality Care, Las Cruces, 1986-88; owner, mgr. ERA Real Estate, Las Cruces, 1988-96; owner Phoenix Internat., Las Cruces, 1995—; asst. professor Dona Ana Br. C.C., Las Cruces, 1997—. Deans scholar U. MO., 1975-76. Mem. Nature Conservancy, OM Technical Rescue. Avocations: equestrian events, hiking, biking, geology, mountaineering. Office: Dona Ana Br CC PO Box 30001 Las Cruces NM 88003-8001 Office Phone: 505-527-7721. Business E-Mail: susawill@nmsu.edu.

WILLIAMS, SUSAN MICHELLE, veterinarian, educator; d. David Arthur and Ruth Alwine Mendes; m. Orlando C. Williams, Feb. 26, 1994; 1 child, Jonathan Cameron. BS, U. Calif., Davis, 1989; DVM, Tuskegee U., 1994; PhD, Mich. State U., East Lansing, 2001. Diplomate Am. Coll. Poultry Veterinarians, 2004. Anatomic pathology specialist Mich. State U., 2001—02; instr. U. Ga., Athens, 2002—05, asst. prof., 2005—. Troop com. leader Boy Scouts Am., Athens, 2005—; scholarship ministry chair Ebenezer Bapt. Ch. West, Athens, 2004—. Mem.: World Vet. Poultry Assn., Ga. Vet. Med. Assn., Am. Assn. Avian Pathologists (mem. chair 2002—06), AVMA, Phi Zeta (xi chpt. pres. 2009). Avocations: sewing, reading. Office: Univ Ga Coll Vet Me 953 Coll Sta Rd Athens GA 30602 Office Fax: 706-542-5630. Business E-Mail: smwillia@uga.edu.

WILLIAMS, SUSAN SHIDAL, literature and language professor; d. L. Neil and Sue (Sigmon) W. BA, Yale U., 1985, PhD, 1991. Asst. prof. English Ohio State U., Columbus, 1991-97, assoc. prof. English, 1997—2006, prof. English, 2006—, vice provost academic policy and faculty resources, 2009—. Author: Confounding Images: Photography and Portraiture in Antebellum American Fiction, 1997, Reclaiming Authorship: Literary Women in America 1850-1900, 2006; editor: The Scarlet Letter by Nathaniel Hawthorne, 2007; co-editor: Reciprocal Influences: Literary Production Distribution, and Consumption in America, 1999, American Periodicals; manuscript reviewer and contbr. articles to profl. jours. Mem. Columbus Symphony Orch. Chorus, 1992-98; Broad St. Presbyn. Ch. Columbus, 2001—, elder, 2006—09. Whiting fellow Yale Univ., New Haven, Conn., 1990-91, Steven Botein fellow Am. Antiquarian Soc., Worcester, Mass., 1997; Coca-Cola Crit. Difference for Women Rsch. grantee Ohio State U., 1996-97, NEH, 2006. Mem. MLA, Am. Studies Assn., Soc. History of Authorship, Reading & Pub., Rsch. Soc. Am. Periodicals (mem. adv. bd. 1997-2005), Nathaniel Hawthorne Soc. (mem. adv. bd. 2005—). Office: Office Academic Affairs Ohio State Univ 203 Bricker Hall 190 N Oval Mall Columbus OH 43210-1358 Office Phone: 614-292-5881. Office Fax: 614-292-3658. Business E-Mail: williams.488@osu.edu.

WILLIAMS, TERRANCE REYNOLDS, architecture educator; s. Frim Wetzel and Peggy Mae Williams; m. Christina Mcinerney, Dec. 28, 1975 (div. May 21, 1983); 1 child, Margaret Dawn. BArch, U. Oreg., Eugene, 1963; MArch, Cornell U., Ithaca, NY, 1969. Lic. profl., Calif., 1970, NY, 1972, NCARB, 1975, Conn., 1981, NJ, 1984, RI, 1983, Va., 1992, Tenn., 1995, Washington, 1998. Archtl. designer Hirshen & Van Der Ryn, Berkeley, Calif., 1965—67; arch. urban designer Levitich & Miller, Ithaca, 1967—68; sr. urban designer Mayors Office of Midtown Planning and Devel., NYC, 1969—70; dep. dir. Mayor's Office of Lower Manhattan Devel., NYC, 1970—74; dir. design Llewelyn-Davies Internat., Tehran, Iran, 1974—76, Thompson+Litton, Bristol, Tenn., 1995—98; dir. spl. projects I.M. Pei & Ptnrs., Kuwait, 1976—77; founding prin. Williams Group, NYC, 1977—92; arch. U. Va., Charlottesville, 1992—95; prof. arch. Cath. U. America, Washington, 1998—. Pres. Friends of Na-Bolom, NYC, 1971—74; assoc. dean, grad. studies CUA Sch. Arch., Washington, 1999—2004; fellow Inter-Am. Housing & Planning Ctr., Bogota, Colombia, 1963—64, Inst. Arch. & Urban Studies, NYC, 1968—69. Designer, Elmira State Mental Hosp. (Prog. Architecture Citation, 1970), a new city ctr. for Tehran, Shahestan Pahlavi (Prog. Architecture award, 1978). Vestryman Episcopal Ch. Epiphany, NYC, 1988—92. Recipient Prog. Architecture award, 1974, Spl. Recognition award, NYC Arts Commn., 1993. Fellow: AIA (pres. 1985—86, sec. 1978—84, AIA Chpt. award 1999). Liberal. Diest. Avocations: painting, cooking. Office: Cath Univ America Michigan Ave NE Washington DC 20064 Office Fax: 202-319-5728. Business E-Mail: williams@cua.edu.

WILLIAMS, TERRIE MICHELLE, public relations executive; b. Mt. Vernon, NY, May 12, 1954; MA, BA cum laude, Brandeis U., 1975; MS, Columbia U., 1977. Exec. dir. World Inst. of Black Community, NYC, 1982; dir. pub. rels. Essence Communications Inc., NYC, 1982-86, v.p., dir., 1986-88; pres. The Terrie Williams Agy., NYC, 1988—. Med. soc. worker N.Y. Hosp., NYC, 1977-80; program adminstr. Black Filmmaker Found., N.Y.C., 1980-81; exec. dir. Black Owned Communications Alliance, N.Y.C., 1981-82. Author: The Personal Touch, 1995. Recipient Entrepeneur of the Yr. award Nat. Assn. Market Developers, 1990, Flo Kennedy Media award, 1990, Matrix award N.Y. Women in Communications, 1991. Mem. Women in Communications, NOW, Brandeis U. Alumni Assn. (bd. dirs.), NY TV Acad. Arts and Scis., Pub. Rels. Soc. Am. (D. Parke Gibson award 1981). E-mail: tmwms@terriewilliams.com.

WILLIAMS, THELDA, Councilwoman; Div. comdr. Maricopa County Sheriff's Office Custody Support & Inmate Programs; councilwoman, Dist. 1 Phoenix City Coun., 1989—96, 2008—; interim mayor City of Phoenix, 1994. Chmn. Seniors, Families and Youth com.; mem. Econ., Commerce & Sustainability, Pub. Safety & Veterans coms. Former mem. Aviation Adv. Bd., Transit Commn., Block Watch Oversight Com., Deer Valley Planning Com., Phoenix Planning & Zoning Com., Govs. Commn. to Prevent Violence Against Women, Maricopa County Adult Probation Adv. Bd. Mem.: Women in Local Govt. Assn., Maricopa Assn. Govts. Bd. Office: 200 W Washington St 11th Fl Phoenix AZ 85003 Office Phone: 602-262-7444. Office Fax: 602-534-4793. Business E-Mail: council.district.1@phoenix.gov.*

WILLIAMS, THELMA B., retired principal; d. Joseph and Floria Bush; m. McDonald Williams, Oct. 9, 1955; children: Donald J., Patricia A. Johnson. BS in Edn., Paine Coll., 1963; EdM, U. Ga., 1974, EdS, 1981. Tchr. Levi White Elem., Augusta, Ga., 1963—72; reading specialist Richmond County Schs., Augusta, 1972—76; asst. prin. Glenn Hills High, Augusta, 1976—81; prin. W.S. Hornsby Elem., Augusta, 1981—99. Edn. vol. Richmond County Schs., 1999—2002; founder after-sch. tutorial program, 2005—. Past chair Hist. Commn.; mem. Augusta Richmond County Hist. Preservation Commn., 1995—2003, vice chair, 2006—; mem. several ministries Macedonia Bapt. Ch., organizer after school tutorial program, 2004; mem. Augusta Classic, 1998—, Alzheimer's Assn., Augusta, 1983—2003. Recipient Meritorious Svc. award, Richmond County Prin. Assn., 1999, Pres.'s award, Paine Coll., 2001, Disting. award of edn., Nat. Assn. Equal Opportunity in Higher Edn., 2002, United Negro Coll. Fund award, Tom Joyner Found., 2003, Yough Svc. award, Ga. Rep. Quincy Murphy, 2004, Outstanding Educators award, W.S. Hornsby and East Augusta Cmty. Neighborhood Assn. and PCS Nitrogen, 1998, Hon. Svc. award, Nat. Alumni Assn. Paine Coll., 2009. Mem.: Richmond County Ret. Tchrs. Assn., Art Factory for Creative Arts (sec. 1990—92), Loyal Christian Women Civic Group (v.p. 2006—, vice chair 2006—), Paine Coll. Alumni Assn. (chmn. ballot com. 1997—99, pres. Augusta chpt. 2001—09), Paine Coll. Platinum Club (pres. 1983—, lectr. Founder's Day 1994, nat. chairballots 1997—99, chmn. ballots com. 1997—99, local pres. 2001—09), Phi Delta Kappa, Zeta Phi Beta (Founder's Day Lectr. 1994). Avocations: travel, reading, baking, teaching. Personal E-mail: TBW51@comcast.net.

WILLIAMS, THEODORE JOSEPH, retired engineering educator; b. Black Lick, Pa., Sept. 2, 1923; s. Theodore Finley and Mary Ellen (Shields) W.; m. Isabel Annette McAnulty, July 18, 1946; children: Theodore Joseph, Mary Margaret, Charles Augustus, Elizabeth Ann. BSCh.E., Pa. State U., 1949, MSCh.E., 1950, PhD, 1955; MS in Elec. Engring., Ohio State U., 1956. Research fellow Pa. State U., University Park, 1947-51; asst. prof. Air Force Inst. Tech., 1953-56; technologist Monsanto Co., 1956-57, sr. engring. supr., 1957-65; prof. engring. Purdue U., Lafayette, Ind., 1965-94, ret., 1994, prof. emeritus, 1995—, dir. control and info. systems lab., 1965-66; dir. Purdue Lab. Applied Indsl. Control, 1966-94, dir. emeritus, 1995—; cons., 1964—2006. Vis. prof. Washington U., St. Louis, 1962-65; hon. prof. Inst. Automation, Academia Sinica, Shenyang, China, 1992. Author: Systems Engineering for the Process Industries, 1961, Automatic Control of Chemical and Petroleum Processes, 1961, Progress in Direct Digital Control, 1969, Interfaces with the Process Control Computer, 1971, Modeling and Control of Kraft Production Systems, 1975, Modelling, Estimation and Control of the Soaking Pit, 1983, The Use of Digital Computers in Process Control, 1983, Analysis and Design of Hierarchical Control Systems - With Special Reference to Steel Plant Operations, 1985, A Reference Model for Computer Integrated Manufacturing (CIM) - A Description from the Viewpoint of Industrial Automation, 1989, The Purdue Enterprise Reference Architecture, 1992; editor: Computer Applications in Shipping and Shipbuilding, 6 vols., 1973-79, Proceedings Advanced Control Confs., 19 vols., 1974-93, Architectures for Enterprise Integration, 1996. Served to 1st lt. USAAF, 1942-45; to capt. USAF, 1951-56. Decorated Air medal with 2 oak leaf clusters. Fellow AAAS, AIChE, Instrument Soc. Am. (hon. mem., pres. 1968-69, Albert F. Sperry gold medal 1990, Lifetime Achievement award 1995), Am. Inst. Chemists, Inst. Measurement and Control (London, Sr. Harold Hartley silver medal 1975), Indsl. Computing Soc.; mem. IEEE (sr.), Internat. Fedn. for Info. Processing (Silver Core award 1978), Soc. for Computer Simulation (hon.), Am. Chem. Soc., Am. Automatic Control Coun. (pres. 1965-67), Am. Fedn. Info. Processing Socs. (pres. 1976-78), Sigma Xi, Tau Beta Pi, Phi Kappa Phi, Phi Lambda Upsilon. Home: 208 Chippewa St West Lafayette IN 47906-2123 Home Phone: 765-463-7828.

WILLIAMS, THOMAS ALAN, high school guidance counselor, small business owner; b. Kingston, Pa., Dec. 15, 1961; s. Thomas Elwin and Lois Jean (Vanderhoff) Williams; m. Jeanne Ann Sweinberg, July 10, 1993; children: Lindsay Nicole, Thomas Lee. BS in Edn., Bloomsburg U., Pa., 1983; MS in Counselor Edn., U. Scranton, Pa., 1987. Cert. secondary counselor, elem. counselor. Tchr. N.W. Sch. Dist., Shickshinny, Pa., 1983-84; tchr. grades 4-6 Lake-Lehman (Pa.) Sch. Dist., 1984-88, tchr. social studies grades 7-8, 1988-93, tchr. social studies grades 10-12, 1993-99, tchr. grades 4-6, 1999—2008, HS Guidance Counselor, 2008, asst. athletic dir., 2001—04; pres. T&J Williams Enterprises Inc., 2001—; owner Curves, Lehman, 2001—, Plains, 2001—, Hanover, 2001—, Nanticoke, 2004—, Wilkes-Barre Twp., 2004—. Wrestling coach Lake-Lehman Sch. Dist., 1984—99; owner Curves for Women Exercise and Fitness Franchise, Plains, Pa., 2002—; pres. T&J Williams Enterprises, Inc., Dallas. Wrestling ofcl. Pa. Interscholastic Athletic Assn., Wilkes-Barre, 1981—. Recipient Pa. N.E. Regional Coach of the Yr., Regional Wrestling Com., 1995, Coach of the Yr., Times-Leader, 1990, 1991, 1992, 1994, 1995, 1996, 1997; named Pa. N.E. Regional Coach of the Yr., Regional Wrestling Com., 1991. Mem.: Wrestling Coaches Assn. (Coach of the Yr. 1992, 1995, Sportsmanship award 1995), Pa. Wrestling Coaches Assn., Pa. State Athletic Dirs. Assn., Nat. Wrestling Coaches Assn., Pa. Interscholastic Athletic

Assn. (chmn. dist. wrestling rep. 2007—, dist. 2 wrestling tournament dir. 2007—), Caldwell Consistory, Shriners, Masons. Republican. Methodist. Avocations: fishing, collectibles, photography, travel, gardening. Home: 1087 Mountain View Dr Dallas PA 18612-9539 Office: Lake-Lehman H S Lehman PA 18627 Personal E-mail: tnjwilly@aol.com.

WILLIAMS, THOMAS EUGENE, pediatric hematologist and oncologist, pharmaceutical executive; b. Texarkana, Ark., May 13, 1936; s. Thomas Earle and Frankie Jo (Garner) W.; m. Peggy Jane O'Neill, May 31, 1958; children: Thomas Eugene, Elizabeth Anne, James David. BA, Yale U., 1958; MD, U. Tex. Southwestern Med. Sch., 1962. Diplomate Am. Bd. Pediat., Am. Bd. Pediat. Hematology and Oncology. Rotating intern Hermann Hosp., Houston, 1962-63; pediat. resident Children's Med. Ctr., Dallas, 1963-65; fellow pediat. hematology U. Va. Sch. Medicine, Charlottesville, 1967-68; rsch. assoc. Cancer Rsch. Lab., U. Va., Charlottesville, 1968-69; asst. prof. pediat. and pathology U. Tex. Health Sci. Ctr., San Antonio, 1969-72, assoc. prof. pediat., asst. prof. pathology, 1972-73, assoc. prof. pediat. and pathology, 1973-79, assoc. prof. pediat., 1985-94; chief med. officer Amplimind Corp., Tucson, 2008; assoc. chief med. officer Ctr. DGD Rsch., San Antinio, Tex., 2008; sr. med. dir. ONYY Inc., 2009—. Med. dir. Santa Rosa Children's Hosp. Cancer Rsch. and Treatment Ctr., 1974—79, South Tex. Comprehensive Hemophilia Ctr., 1977—79, dir. pediat. bone marrow transplantation program, 1986—93; sr. clin. rsch. scientist Burroughs Wellcome Co., 1979—85; dir. new drug devel. Orphan Med., Inc., 1994—96; dir. med. affairs Ilex Oncology Svcs., Inc., 1997—98, ILEX Oncology Products, Inc., 1998—2002; clin. assoc. prof. pediat. U. N.C. Sch. Medicine, 1979—85; clin. fellow bone marrow transplantation program Johns Hopkins U. Sch. Medicine, Balt., 1985—94; sr. dir. Divsn. Oncology ICON Clin. Rsch., Inc., 2002—07; pres. and CEO Thistle Advisors Internat. Inc., 2008—; chief med. officer Amplimed Corp., 2008. Contbr. articles to profl. jours. Exec. dir. Episcopal Med. Missions Found., 1997—. Lt. cmmdr. USNR, 1965—67. Recipient travel award Am. Soc. Pharmacology and Exptl. Therapeutics, 1968; Am. Cancer Soc. advanced clin. fellow, 1968-69, 70-72. Mem. Am. Soc. Clin. Oncology, Am. Soc. Hematology, Am. Assn. for Cancer Rsch. Episcopalian. Office: Thistle Advisors Internat Inc 13300 Old Blanco Rd Ste 150 San Antonio TX 78216 Office Phone: 210-422-4779. Personal E-mail: twilliams@satx.rr.com. Business E-Mail: Ewilliams@thistleoncology.com.

WILLIAMS, THOMAS FRANKLIN, physician, educator; b. Belmont, NC, Nov. 26, 1921; s. T. F. and Mary L. (Deaton) Williams; m. Catharine Carter Catlett, Dec. 15, 1951; children: Mary Wright, Thomas Nelson. BS, U. N.C., 1942; MA, Columbia U., 1943; MD, Harvard U., 1950; DSc (hon.), Med. Coll. Ohio, 1987, U. N.C., 1992; DMS, Thomas Jefferson U., 2003. Intern Johns Hopkins, Balt., 1950—51, asst. resident physician, 1951—53; resident physician Boston VA Hosp., 1953—54; research fellow U. N.C., Chapel Hill, 1954—56, instr. dept. medicine and preventive medicine, 1956—57, asst. prof., 1957—61, assoc. prof., 1961—68, prof., 1968; attending physician Strong Meml. Hosp., Rochester, NY, 1968—; cons. physician Genesee Hosp., Rochester, NY, 1973—; prof. medicine, preventive medicine and cmty. health U. Rochester, 1968—92, prof. radiation biology and biophysics, 1968—91, on leave, 1983—91, prof. emeritus, 1992—; clin. prof. medicine U. Va., 1983—89; lectr. medicine Johns Hopkins U., 1983—89; clin. prof. depts. family medicine and medicine Georgetown U., 1983—89; dir. Nat. Inst. on Aging NIH, 1983—91; asst. surgeon gen. USPHS, 1983—91, ret., 1991; attending physician Monroe Cmty. Hosp., Rochester, 1991—, vice-chmn. cmty. coalition for long term care, 1991—; disting. physician VA Med. Ctr., Canandigua, NY, 1995—98. Adv. bd. U. Rochester Sch. Medicine and Dentistry, 1968—83; med. dir. Monroe Cmty. Hosp., Rochester, 1968—83; mem. rev. coms. Nat. Ctr. for Health Svcs. Rsch.; adv. bd. St. Ann's Home; mem. gov. bd. NRC, 1981—83; sci. dir. Am. Fedn. Aging Rsch., 1992—; cons. in field. Contbr. articles to profl. publs. With USNR, 1943—46. Recipient Civic award for health care, Rochester N.Y. C. of C., 1998; fellow, USPHS, 1966—67; scholar Markle scholar, 1957—61. Fellow: ACP, APHA; mem.: NAS (coun. 1980—83, governing bd. 1981—83, Gustav O. Lienhard award Inst. Medicine 1969), AAAS, Am. Clin. Climatol. Assn., N.C. Coun. for Human Rels. (chmn. 1963—66), Rochester Regional Diabetes Assn. (pres. 1977—79), Am. Gerontol. Soc., Am. Geriatrics Soc., Soc. Exptl. Biology and Medicine, Am. Fedn. Clin. Rsch., Am. Diabetes Assn. (bd. dirs. 1974—80), Monroe County Med. Soc., N.Y. State Med. Soc., Assn. Am. Physicians, Inst. Medicine. Episcopalian. Home: 287 Dartmouth St Rochester NY 14607-3202 Office: Monroe Cmty Hosp Office Med Dir Rochester NY 14620

WILLIAMS, THOMAS L., recreational facility executive; b. 1947; Degree, Calif. State U., Fresno, 1970. Various leading mgmt. roles MCA Recreation Svcs. Group, Hollywood, Calif., 1970-87; with Universal City Fla. Ptnr., Orlando, 1987—, pres., 1990; chmn., CEO Universal Parks and Resorts, Orlando, 1999—. Bd. dirs. NBC. Bd. dirs. Emeril Lagasse Found.; founding trustee World Class Schools, United Arts of Central Fla. Office: Universal City Fl Ptnr 1000 Universal Studios Plz Orlando FL 32819-7601*

WILLIAMS, THOMAS STAFFORD CARDINAL, cardinal, archbishop; b. Wellington, New Zealand, Mar. 20, 1930; s. Thomas Stafford and Lillian Maude (Kelly) Williams. STL, Pontifical U., Rome, 1960; B in Social Sci., Nat. U. Ireland, Dublin, 1962. Ordained priest Archdiocese of Wellington, New Zealand, 1959, archbishop, 1979—2005, archbishop emeritus, 2005—; parish priest, dir. of studies Cath. Enquiry Ctr., Wellington; missionary priest Archdiocese of Samoa-Apia; parish priest Porirua East, New Zealand, 1975—79; ordained bishop, 1979; elevated to cardinal, 1983; cardinal-priest Gesu Divin Maestro alla Pineta Sacchetti, 1983—; bishop New Zealand Mil., 1995—2005, bishop emeritus, 2005—. Mem. Congregation for Evangelization of Peoples. Roman Catholic. Office: 40 Walton Ave Waikanae 6010 New Zealand E-mail: t.williams@un.catholic.org.nz.

WILLIAMS, THOMAS W., electrical engineer; b. Rochester, NY, Aug. 3, 1943; s. Thomas Alfred and Mary Anne (Boryszewski) W.; m. Suzane Louise Sawyer, Dec. 26, 1964 (div. 1982); children: Megan Ren+245, David Thomas; m. Candace Merrill, Mar. 16, 1985. BSEE, Clarkson U., 1965; MA in Maths., Binghamton U., 1968; PhD in Elec. Engring., Colo. State U., 1971. From staff to sys. designer IBM, Endicott, NY, 1968-73, mem. LSI design rules and control group Boulder, Colo., 1973—77, from sr. engr., mgr. to sr. tech. staff, mgr. VLSI Design, 1977-1998; Synopsys fellow Test Technology, Synopsys, Inc. Guest prof., Robert Bosch fellow, U. Hannover, Germany, 1985, 1996-98; adj. prof. U. Calgary, Can. Contbr. articles to profl. jours. Grantee NSF. Fellow IEEE (W. Wallace McDowell award 1989); mem. IEEE (bd. govs. 1987-93, 95-, bd. dirs. 2001-02, 2007-), Phi Kappa Phi, Eta Kappa Nu. E-mail: t.williams@computer.org.

WILLIAMS, TIFFANI VIVIENNE, lawyer; b. Washington, Sept. 12, 1977; d. Desmond Ellis and Vivienne Valerie Williams. BS in Biology, Am. U., DC, 1999; MPH in Epidemiology Microbial Diseases, Yale U., New Haven, 2001; JD, U. Calif., Berkeley, 2004. Bar: DC 2005, NY 2006. Atty. Alston & Bird, LLP, DC, 2004—. Mem.: Am. Pub. Health Assn., Am. Health Lawyers Assn. Avocations: cooking, tennis, travel. Office: Alston & Bird LLP 950 F St NW Washington DC 20004 Business E-Mail: tiffani.williams@alston.com.

WILLIAMS, TOD CULPAN, architect, educator; b. Detroit, May 11, 1943; s. Richard Jamison and Bettina Joy (Culpan) Williams; m. Patricia Jones, June 21, 1966 (div. Mar. 1975); children: Rachel, Tod C.; m. Billie Tsien, Feb. 14, 1983; 1 child, Kai Tsien. BA, Princeton U., NJ, 1965; postgraduate student, U. Cambridge, Eng., 1966; MFA, Princeton U., NJ, 1967. Registered arch., NY, Conn., Mass., NJ, Mich., Tex. Assoc. Richard Meier & Assocs., NYC, 1967—74; owner, ptnr. Potters/Williams, NYC, 1975—78; prin. Tod Williams/Billie Tsien Archs., NYC, 1978—. Prof. architecture Coopen Union, NYC, 1974—89; advisor Princeton Sch. Architecture, 1983; Ruth Carter Stevenson chair U. Tex., Austin, 1995; Eliel Saarinen chair U. Mich., 2002; Louis I. Kahn chair Yale U., New Haven, 2003, New Haven, 05; Thomas Jefferson chair U. Va., 2004. Author, curator: book/exhbn. Window Room Furniture, 1982—83; contbr. articles to archtl. jours. Advanced fellow, Am. Acad. Rome (Graham Found.), 1983. Fellow: Am. Acad. Arts & Scis.; mem.: AIA (Disting. Architecture award 1982, 1986, 1987), Nat. Coll. Archs. Registration Bds. Office: Tod Williams/Billie Tsien 222 Central Park S New York NY 10019-1408 Office Phone: 212-582-2385.

WILLIAMS, TOM, college football coach; b. Ft. Worth, Tex., Dec. 22, 1969; m. Tonya Williams, 2000; children: Grace, Ana, Tre. BA in History, Stanford U., Calif., 1992, MA in Univ. Adminstrn., 1995. Practice squad San Francisco 49ers, 1993; grad. asst. Stanford U. Cardinal, 1993—94, linebackers coach, co-defensive coord., 2002—03, assoc. head coach, 2004; defensive coord. Fujitsu Frontiers, Japan, 1995; linebackers coach U. Hawaii Warriors, 1996—97, defensive coord., 1998; linebackers coach U. Wash. Huskies, 1999—2001; co-defensive coord., linebackers coach San Jose State U. Spartans, 2005—06; asst. spl. teams coach Jacksonville Jaguars, 2007, defensive asst., 2008; head football coach Yale U. Bulldogs, 2009—. Mailing: Yale Athletic Dept PO Box 208216 New Haven CT 06520-8216*

WILLIAMS, TONDA, entrepreneur, consultant; b. NYC, Nov. 21, 1949; d. William and Juanita (Rainey) W.; 1 child, Tywana. Student, Collegiate Inst., NYC, 1975—78, C.W. Post Coll., 1981—83; BA in Bus. Mgmt., Am. Nat. U., Phoenix, 1983; grad., LI Bus. Inst., 1996. Notary pub. NY. Asst. controller Acad. Ednl. Devel., NYC, 1971-81; mgr. office Chapman-Apex Constrn. Co., Bayshore, NY, 1982-84; specialist computer RGM Liquid Waste Removal, Deerpark, NY, 1985-87; contr. LaMar Lighting Co., Freeport, NY, 1987—; owner, pres. Omni-Star, Bklyn., 1981—; pres. Omni-Data Tech., Bayshore, NY, 1996—. Author: Tonda's Songs in Poetry, 1978, The Magic of Life, 1991; co-author: Computer Management of Liquid Waste Industry, 1986. Recipient Golden Poet award World of Poetry, 1992. Mem. Am. Mus. Natural History, Am. Soc. Notary Pubs. Avocations: bowling, chess, singing. Home: 74 Cedar Dr Bay Shore NY 11706-2419 Home Phone: 631-665-2152; Office Phone: 631-968-0016. Office Fax: 631-968-1016. Personal E-mail: odttax@aol.com. Business E-Mail: tonda@omnidatatech.com.

WILLIAMS, TONYA, legislative staff member, lawyer; BA in Polit. Sci., U. NC, Chapel Hill, 1995, JD, 1999. Assoc. Burford & Lewis, 2001—02; gen. counsel to pres. pro tempore of senate NC Gen. Assembly, 2002—07; dir. IP policy for N.Am. and S.Am. GlaxoSmith-Kline, 2007—08; chief of staff for Rep. G.K. Butterfield, US House of Reps., Washington, 2008—. Office: Office of Congressman GK Butterfield 413 Cannon House Office Bldg Washington DC 20515 Office Phone: 202-225-3101. Office Fax: 202-225-3354. Business E-Mail: tonya.n.williams@mail.house.gov.*

WILLIAMS, UNA JOYCE, retired psychiatric social worker; b. Youngstown, Ohio, June 24, 1934; d. Samuel Wilfred and Frances Josephine (Woods) Ellis; children: Wendy Louise, Christopher Ellis, Sharon Elizabeth. BA, U. Ala., 1957; MSW, Adelphi U., 1963. Diplomate in profl. counseling Internat. Acad. Behavioral Medicine, Counseling and Psychotherapy. Dir. Huntington Program Sr. Citizens, 1963—67; psychiat. social worker-supr. N.Y. State Dept. Mental Hygiene, Suffolk Psychiat. Hosp., Central Islip, 1969—72; info.-referral counselor Mental Health Assn. Nassau County, Hempstead, NY, 1993—; therapist Madonna Heights Family Clinic, Dix Hills, NY, 1994—99; med. and psychiat. social worker Northport VA Med. Ctr., NY, 1994—2005, psychiat. social worker acute psychiat. treatment svcs., 2005—08, med. social worker dialysis svcs., 2007—08. Cons. on programs for aging Luth. Social Svcs. Met. N.Y., 1959, sr. citizens programs, Bd. Edn. Port Jefferson, N.Y., 1961-63. Chmn. Huntington Twp. Com. Human Rels., 1970; sec. bd. trustess Unitarian Universalist Fellowship Huntington, 1984. Mem. NASW (diplomate in social work), Am. Assn. Family Counselors and Mediators,Germany Philatelic Soc. (pres. chpt. 30, 1990, Mem. of Yr. 1987). Avocations: painting, stamp collecting/philately, music (voice & piano), genealogy. Home: 316 Lenox Rd Huntington Station NY 11746-2640

WILLIAMS, VANESSA L. (VANESSA LYNN WILLIAMS), recording artist, actress; b. Millwood, NY, Mar. 18, 1963; d. Milton and Helen; m. Ramon Hervey II, 1988 (div. 1997); children: Melanie, Jillian, Devin; m. Rick Fox, 1999 (div.); 1 child, Sasha Gabriella Fox. Recording artist, 1988—. Stage appearances include: (Broadway) Kiss of the Spider Woman, 1993-95 (Theatre World award, 1995), Into the Woods, 2002 (nominee Drama Desk award for Outstanding Actress in a Musical, 2002, Tony award Best Actress in a Musical, 2002); film appearances include Pick-up Artist, 1987, Under the Gun, 1988, Another You, 1991, Harley Davidson and the Marlboro Man, 1991, Eraser, 1996, Hoodlum, 1997, Soul Food, 1997, Dance with Me, 1998, The Adventures of Elmo in Grouchland, 1999, Light It Up, 1999, Shaft, 2000, Johnson Family Vacation, 2004, Hannah Montana: The Movie, 2009; (TV films) Full Exposure: The Sex Tapes Scandal, 1989, The Kid Who Loved Christmas, 1990, Perry Mason: The Case of the Silenced Singer, 1990, Stompin' at the Savoy, 1992, Jacksons: An American Dream, 1992, Nothing Lasts Forever, 1995, Bye Bye Birdie, 1995, The Odyssey, 1997, Futuresport, 1998, Courage to Love, 2000 (also exec. prodr.), Don Quixote, 2000, A Diva's Christmas Carol, 2000, WW3, 2001, Keep the Faith, Baby, 2002, (TV mini series) Nothing Lasts Forever, 1995, (TV series) Ugly Betty 2006-(Outstanding Supporting Actress in a Comedy Series, NAACP Image award, 2007, 2008, Choice TV: Villain, Teen Choice Awards, 2007); guest appearances Partners in Crime, 1984, T.J. Hooker, 1986, The Love Boat, 1986, The Fresh Prince of Bel-Air, 1990, Between Brothers, 1997, Vanessa Williams and Friends: Christmas in N.Y., 1996, Star Trek: Deep Space Nine, 1996, L.A. Doctors, 1999, Ally McBeal, 2002, Boomtown, 2003, South Beach, 2006; albums: The Right Stuff, 1988, The Comfort Zone, 1991, The Sweetest Days, 1994, Star Bright, 1996, Next, 1997, Alfie, the Best of Vanessa, 1998; # 1 hit single Save the Best for Last; vocalist (soundtracks) Beverly Hills 90210, 1990, Harley Davidson and the Marlboro Man, 1991, Adventures of Priscilla, Queen of the Desert, 1994, The Mask, 1994, Pocahontas, 1995, Eraser, 1996, Dance with Me, 1998, The Adventures of Elmo in Grouchland, 1999, Isn't She Great, 2000; host Style World, 2000; spokesperson for Proactive Solution (Acne Medication); commercial appearances Radio Shack. Recipient 8 Grammy award nominations, received star on the Hollywood Walk of Fame, 2007; named one of 50 Most Beautiful People, People Mag., Top 25 Entertainers of Yr., Entertainment Weekly, 2007, The 100 Most Powerful Celebrities, Forbes.com, 2008 Achievements include being the first Black to be named Miss America, 1983 (resigned title 1983). Office: Mercury Records care Dawn Bridges 825 8th Ave New York NY 10019-7416 also: Mercury Records 11150 Santa Monica Blvd Los Angeles CA 90025-3380 Address: William Morris Agy 151 El Camino Dr Beverly Hills CA 90212

WILLIAMS, VENUS, professional tennis player; b. Lynwood, Calif., June 17, 1980; d. Richard and Oracene Williams. Prof. tennis player WTA tour, 1994—; owner V Starr Interiors; designer Venus Williams Collection Wilson's Leather Co.; designer EleVen fashion label, 2007—. Recipient ESPY award for outstanding women's tennis player, 2001, Espy award for Best Female Tennis Player, 2001, 2006, Espy award for Best Female Athlete, 2002; named Most Impressive Network Newcomer award, 1997, TENNIS Mag. Most Improved Player, WTA Tour, 1998 Mem.: WTA Tour Players' Coun. Jehovah'S Witness. Achievements include winner 41 career singles titles, 13 career doubles titles, WTA; winner 1 career doubles title, ITF; Grand Slam Championships: US Open, 2000, 2001, Wimbledon, 2000, 2001, 2005, 2007, 2008; Grand Slam Championships: (with Serena Williams) French Open, 1999, US Open, 1999, Wimbledon, 2000, 2002, 2008, 2009, Australian Open, 2001, 2003, 2009; mem. US Fed Cup Team, 1999, 2003-05, 2007, US Olympic Team, Sydney, 2000, Athens, 2004, Beijing, 2008; singles and doubles gold winner, Sydney Olympic games, 2000; doubles gold winner, Beijing Olympic games, 2008. Avocations: interior decorating, fashion design. Office: c/o US Tennis Assn 70 W Red Oak Ln White Plains NY 10604-3602*

WILLIAMS, VIRGINIA LEE, finance educator; d. John Thomas and Virginia Pearl Rendleman; m. Michael Lee Williams, May 28, 1994; children: Chad Michael Schuster, Mikala Lee. BS, So. Ill. U., Carbondale, 1993; MS, So. Ill. U., 2000. Lic. series 3 Chgo. Bd. Trade, 1987. Commody and futures comm. coord. A.G. Edwards and Sons, St. Louis, 1986—88; office sys. specialist So. Ill. U., 1988—95; bus. instr. Rend Lake Coll., Ina, Ill., 1995—98, Southeastern Ill. Coll., Harrisburg, Ill., 1996—97; asst. to chancellor So. Ill. U., 1997—2000; assoc. prof. Kaskaskia Coll., Centralia, Ill., 2000—. Adv. coun. office tech. dept. Kaskaskia Coll., 2000—, curriculum coun. mem., 2005—; spkr. in field. Editor: (allied health textbook review) From Patient to Payment. Heart walk team leader Am. Heart Assn., Centralia, 2004—05; adopt-a-family sponsor Bond, Clinton, Marion & Wash. County Cmty. Svcs., Centralia, 2005—08; parade participant Veterans Am., Centralia, 2006—07. Named Ill. Advisor of Yr., Future Bus. Leaders Am., 2006; grantee Rsch. grant, Regional Ctr. Distance Learning and Multimedia Devel., 2001, Ill. Cmty. Coll. Bd., 2002. Mem.: So. Ill. Bus. Edn. Assn., Nat. Bus. Edn. Assn., Phi Beta Lambda (advisor 2000—), Gamma Beta Phi, Delta Pi Epsilon. Avocations: singing, reading, walking. Office: Kaskaskia Coll 27210 College Rd Centralia IL 62801

WILLIAMS, W. CRAIG, prosecutor; m. Jennifer Williams; 3 children. BA in Pub. Policy Studies, Duke U., Durham, NC; 1987; JD with high honors, U. Fla. Coll. Law, 1997; grad., Naval Justice Sch.; LLM with high honors, Columbia U. Sch. Law, 2001. Chief prosecutor USMC; law clk. Hon. J.L. Edmondson, Chief Judge US Ct. Appeals (11th cir.); asst. US atty. gen. US Dept. Justice, Phila., Colo.; dep. legal counsel Chmn. the Joint Chiefs of Staff, Gen. Pete Pace. Mem. Critical Incident Response Team, Phila.; advisor US Solicitor Gen., Office of the Vice Pres. of the US, Nat. Security Coun., Dept. State Joint Terrorism Task Force, Dept. Justice. Weapons and sensor officer VMFA(AW)-121 Green Knights USMC, 1991, Gulf War, active svc. USMC Reserves. Decorated Air Medal (seven times), Joint Meritorious Svc. Medal; recipient ABA award, 1997; Harlan Fisk Stone Scholar, Columbia U. Republican. Mailing: 5035 Township Line Rd Drexel Hill PA 19026 Office Phone: 610-789-7077. Office Fax: 610-789-6757.

WILLIAMS, WALTER WAYLON, lawyer, agricultural products supplier; b. Gause, Tex., Nov. 12, 1933; s. Jesse Nathaniel and Lola Fay (Matthews) W.; m. Velmalene Von Gonten, Mar. 6, 1953; children—Diana Lee, Virginia Marie. BBA with honors, U. Tex., 1959, JD with honors, 1960. Bar: Tex. bar 1960. Since practiced in, Houston; mem. firm Fulbright, Crooker, Freeman, Bates & Jaworski, 1960-63, Bates & Brock, 1964-66, Brock, Williams & Boyd, 1966-79, Williams & Boyd, 1979-88; pres. Nat. Pecan Growers Coun., 1976-78, Tex. Pecan Growers Assn., 1976-78. Served with AUS, 1953-55. Named Outstanding Soldier of Second Army, 1955 Mem. ABA, Houston Bar Assn., State Bar Tex., Tex. Trial Lawyers Assn. (dir. 1972-76), Houston Trial Lawyers Assn. (dir. 1969), Assn. Trial Lawyers Am., Chancellors, Beta Gamma Sigma, Phi Delta Phi. Home: 545 Williams Rd Yoakum TX 77995-5320

WILLIAMS, WESLEY MONTGOMERY, medical researcher; BS in Biology, Norwich U., Northfield, Vermont, 1968; MA, SUNY, Plattsburgh, 1970; Ph.D., Univ. Rochester Sch. Medicine, NY, 1982. Postdoc. fellow dept. Neurology, U. Rochester Sch. Medicine, NY, 1983—86, am. heart assoc. postdoc. fellow dept. pharmacology, 1986—89; nrc assoc. Lab. Neurosciences,NIA,NIH, Washington, 1989—93; adj. assoc. prof. dept. anatomy & cell biology, Sch. Medicine, George Wash. U., 1993—2002; rsch. scientist Lab. Biochemistry, NHLBI, NIH, 1996—2002, Bethesda, Md., 1996—2002; sr. scientist McKesson Bio-Services, Rockville, 1994—2000; sr. instr. dept. medicine, Case Western Res. U., Cleveland, 2002—04, rsch. assoc. sch. dental medicine, 2006—, asst. prof. dept. pathology, sch. medicine, 2009—; ltc USAR, 1970—98. Cons. Alkermes, Cambridge, Mass., 1987; referee Biomedical Scis., 1986—. 18th and 19th century botanical art, Glohaven Peach (Selected artist award, 1998). Recipient Excellence in Rsch. award, AMA Edn. & Rsch. Found., 1983. Achievements include development of chronically implantable arterial catheter for use in small animal research. Home: 1757 Maywood Rd South Euclid OH 44121 Office: Case Western Reserve Univ 10900 Euclid Ave Cleveland OH 44106 Business E-Mail: wmw5@case.edu.

WILLIAMS, WESLEY SAMUEL, JR., lawyer; b. Phila., Nov. 13, 1942; s. Wesley Samuel and Bathrus Amanda (Bailey) W.; m. Karen Roberta Hastie, Aug. 17, 1968; children: Amanda Pedersen, Wesley Hastie, Bailey Lockhart. BA in French Lit. magna cum laude, Harvard U., 1963, JD, 1967; MA (Woodrow Wilson fellow), Fletcher Sch. Law and Diplomacy, 1964; LLM, Columbia U., 1969. Bar: D.C., U.S. Supreme Ct., N.Y. Spl. counsel D.C. City Council, 1967-69; assoc.-in-law Columbia U. Law Sch., 1968-69; legal counsel Com. on D.C. U.S. Senate, 1969-70; assoc. Covington & Burling, Washington, 1970-75, ptnr., 1975—. Trustee Penn Mut. Life Ins. Co., Phila., 1978—; bd. dirs. Broadcast Capital Cos., 1979-92, chmn., 1989-92, Carr Realty, Co., Inc., 1993—; mem. Pres.'s U.S. Circuit Judge Nominating Commn., 1977-80; gen. counsel D.C. Bar, 1979-81; adj. prof. Georgetown U. Law Sch., 1971-73; mem. exec. com. Washington Lawyers Com. Civil Rights Under Law, 1972—; mem. editorial bd. D.C. Real Estate Reporter; vice chmn., bd. dirs. Lockhart Cos., St. Thomas, U.S. Virgin Islands, 1987—, co-chief exec. officer, 1989—; vice chmn., bd. dirs. Blackstar Communications, Cos., 1987—. Author legal articles, texts. Pres. bd. trustee Nat. Child Rsch. Ctr., 1980-82; bd. overseers Harvard U., 1985-91, chmn. vis. com. Harvard U. Div. Sch., 1986-91; bd. dirs. World Affairs Coun. Washington, D.C., Inc., 1980—, Nat. Symphony Orch. Assn., 1977-92; bd. dirs. Family and Child Svcs. Washington, 1970—, pres., 1973-76; exec. com. community adv. com. Jr. League Washington, 1977-86; pres. standing com. Epsic. Diocese of Washington, 1983-88; sec. bd. trustees Protestant Episc. Cathedral Found., 1982-90; bd. regents Smithsonian Inst., 1993—. Fellow Am. Bar Found.; mem. ABA, Am. Law Inst., Nat. Bar Assn., Fed. Bar Assn., D.C. Bar Assn., Washington Bar Assn., Harvard Law Sch. Assn. (pres.), Order Hosp. St. John Jerusalem, Harvard Club, City Tavern Club, Met. Club, Chevy Chase Club, Univ. Club, Alpha Phi Alpha, Sigma Pi Phi.

WILLIAMS, WILLIAM COREY, theology educator, consultant; b. Wilkes-Barre, Pa., July 12, 1937; s. Edward Douglas and Elizabeth Irene (Schooley) W.; m. Alma Simmenroth Williams, June 27, 1959; 1 child, Linda. Diploma in Ministerial Studies, NE Bible Inst., 1962; BA in Bibl. Studies, Cen. Bible Coll., 1963, MA in Religion, 1964; MA in Hebrew and Near Ea. Studies, NYU, 1966, PhD in Hebrew Lang. and Lit., 1975; postgrad., Hebrew U., 1977-78, Inst. Holyland Studies, 1986. Ref. libr. Hebraic section Libr. Congress, Washington, 1967-69; prof. Old Testament So. Calif. Coll./Vanguard U., Costa Mesa, 1969—; adj. prof. Old Testament Melodyland Sch. Theology, Anaheim, Calif., 1975-77; vis. prof. Old Testament Fuller Theol. Sem., Pasadena, Calif., 1978-81, 84, Asian Theol. Ctr. Evangelism Missions, Singapore and Sabah, E. Malaysia, 1985, Continental Bible Coll., Saint Pieters-Leeuw, Belgium, 1985, 2000-01, Mattersey Bible Coll., England, 1985, Inst. Holy Land Studies, Jerusalem, 1986, Regent U., 1994. Transl. cons. reviser New Am. Std. Bible, 1969-94; transl. cons. New Internat. Version, 1975-76, New Century Version, 1991, The New Living Translation, 1992-95, New Internat. Version, Reader's Version, 1993-94; transl. cons. editor Internat. Children's Version, 1985-86. Author: (books, tapes) Hebrew I: A Study Guide, 1980, Hebrew II: A Study Guide, 1986, They Spoke From God, 2004; contbr. articles to International Standard Bible Encyclopedia, New International Dictionary of Old Testment Theology and Evangelical Dictionary of Biblical Theology; contbr. articles to profl. jours.; contbr. notes to Spirit Filled Life Study Bible; editor: They Spoke From God, 2004. Nat. Def. Fgn. Lang. fellow NYU, 1964-67; Alumni scholar N.E. Bible Inst., 1960-61; NEH fellow, summer 1992; recipient Disting. Educator's award Assemblies God, 1997. Mem. Soc. Bibl. Lit., Evang. Theol. Soc. (exec. office 1974-77), Inst. Bibl. Rsch., Lockman Found. (hon. mem. bd. dirs. 1992-94, mem. editl. bd. 1974-94). Home: 1817 Peninsula Pl Costa Mesa CA 92627-4591 Office: Vanguard U 55 Fair Dr Costa Mesa CA 92626-6520 Business E-Mail: wwilliams@vanguard.edu.

WILLIAMS, WILLIAM EARLE, artist, educator, curator; b. Vicksburg, Miss., Apr. 19, 1950; s. Willie and Estella (Steele) W.; m. Mary Katherine Meermans, Aug. 19, 1978; children: Emily Katherine, Daniel Earle. BA, Hamilton Coll., Clinton, NY, 1973; MFA, Yale U., 1978. Prof. art, curator photography Haverford (Pa.) Coll. Author: Party Pictures, 1985; author, editor: Photographers of Sculpture, 1988, Paul Strand: Prints in Ink, 2008; editor: Japanese Wood Block Prints, 1987, Gettysburg: Journey in Time, 1997, Unsung Heroes: African American Soldiers in the Civil War, 2007; one-man shows include Cleve. Mus. of Art, 1990, South East Mus., 2001, Bryn Mawr Coll., 2002, Canton-Fitzgerald Gallery, 2007, Mus. Fine Arts, Houston, 2008, exhibited in group shows at Allentown Mus. Art, 1995, Bardini Mus., Florence, Italy, 1990, Phila. Mus. Art, 2000, Princeton U. Mus., 2006, Represented in permanent collections Phila. Mus. Art, Met. Mus. Art, Cleve. Mus. Art, others. Fellow in photography, Pa. Coun. on the Arts, 1986, 1997, 2002, Pew fellow, 1997, Guggenheim fellow, 2003. Mem.: Soc. Photog. Edn. (bd. dirs. 1996—2003, vice chair 2000, treas. 2001), Phila. Athenaeum, Franklin Inn Club. Avocations: running, bicycling, walking. Home: 753 College Ave Haverford PA 19041-1301 Office: Haverford Coll 370 Lancaster Ave Haverford PA 19041-1336 Office Phone: 610-896-1259. Business E-Mail: wwilliam@haverford.edu.

WILLIAMS, WILLIAM HARRISON, retired librarian; b. Seattle, Apr. 18, 1924; s. William E. and Letah M. (Hollenback) W.; m. Mary Helen Sims, Apr. 19, 1945; children: Linda Lee, Dee Ann. BS, Brigham Young U., 1969, M.L.S., 1970. Dir. Provo Pub. Library, Utah, 1969-70; Wyo. State Librarian, 1970-78; dir. Wyo. state Archives and Hist. dept., 1971-78; exec. sec. Wyo. Hist. Soc., 1971-78; sr. research analyst Wyo. Taxpayers Assn., 1978-84. Served to lt. col. USAAF, 1943-64. Decorated USAF commendation with oak leaf cluster. Mem. Masonic Order, Order of the Ea. Star, Order of the Amaranth, Beta Phi Mu, Phi Alpha Theta. Home: 18616 N 99th Ave Apt 1028 Sun City AZ 85373 E-mail: weewilli@juno.com.

WILLIAMS, WILLIAM JOHN, JR., lawyer; b. New Rochelle, NY, Feb. 6, 1937; s. William John and Jane (Gormley) W.; m. Barbara Reuter. BA, Holy Cross Coll., Worcester, Mass., 1958; LLB, NYU, 1961. Bar: N.Y. 1961. With Sullivan & Cromwell LLP, NYC, 1962—68, ptnr., 1969—2004, of counsel, 2005—. Mem. legal adv. bd. NASD, 1988—94; mem. legal adv. com. NYSE, 1997—2000. Trustee NYU Law Sch. Found., 1977-2007, Holy Cross Coll., 1988-96; chmn. bd. Sofia Am. Sch. in Bulgaria; past gen. counsel, chmn. rules golf com., sec., v.p. and pres. US Golf Assn., 1974-88. Fellow Am. Bar Found.; mem. ABA, Am. Law Inst., N.Y. State Bar Assn., N.Y.C. Bar Assn. Democrat. Roman Catholic. Office: Sullivan & Cromwell LLP 125 Broad St Fl 32 New York NY 10004-2498

WILLIAMS, WILLIAM JOSEPH, retired hematologist, educator; b. Bridgeton, NJ, Dec. 8, 1926; s. Edward Carlaw and Mary Hood (English) W.; m. Margaret Myrick Lyman, Aug. 12, 1950 (dec. Aug., 1985); children: Susan Lyman, William Prescott, Sarah Robb; m. Karen A. Hughes, Feb. 18, 1989. Student, Bucknell U., 1943-45; MD, U. Pa., 1949. Diplomate: Am. Bd. Internal Medicine. (hematology com. 1976-80). From intern to assoc. prof. U. Pa., Phila., 1949—61, assoc. prof. to prof. medicine, chief hematology, 1961—69; sr. instr. microbiology Case We. Res. U., 1952; asst. prof. medicine Washington U., St. Louis, 1959—60; rsch. fellow Oxford U., England, 1960—61; mem. hematology tng. com. Nat. Inst. Arthritis and Metabolic Disease, 1964—68, mem. rsch. career program com., 1968—72; chmn. dept. medicine SUNY Health Sci. Ctr., Syracuse, 1969—92, prof. medicine, 1969—2006, interim dean Coll. Medicine, 1991—92, dean coll. medicine and v.p. biomed. scis., 2002—04, disting. svc. prof., 2002—06, disting. svc. prof.emeritus, 2006—, dean emeritus Coll. Medicine, 2004—. Vis. scientist Walter and Eliza Hall Inst., Melbourne, Australia, 1980; vis. prof. Monash U., Melbourne, 1980; mem. thrombosis adv. com. Nat. Heart and Lung Inst., 1969-73, chmn., 1971-73; adv. coun. Nat. Arthritis, Metabolism and Digestive Diseases, 1975-79; mem. residency rev. com. internal medicine Accreditation Coun. Grad. Med. Edn., 1983-89, mem. bd. appeals panel for internal medicine, 1989-2000; mem. NY State Coun. Grad. Med. Edn., 1987-89. Editor-in-chief: Hematology, 1972, 4th edit., 1989, Williams Hematology Companion Handbook, 1996; co-editor: Williams Manual of Hematology, 2003; contbr. articles to med. lit. Trustee Everson Mus. Art, 1975-81, 83-89. With USNR, 1944-46, 52-54. Recipient Research Career Devel. award Nat. Heart Inst., 1963-68; Daland fellow Am. Philos. Soc., 1955-57; Markle scholar, 1957-62 Mem. ACP (gov. Upstate N.Y. 1976-81), Am. Soc. Biochemistry and Molecular Biologists, Am. Soc. Clin. Investigation, Assn. Am. Physicians, Am. Clin. and Climatol. Assn., Am. Soc. Hematology, Interurban Clin. Club (sec. 1964-70), Alpha Omega Alpha. Mem. Soc. Friends. Home: 5160 Peck Hill Rd Jamesville NY 13078-9724 Office: 750 E Adams St Syracuse NY 13210-2306 Home Phone: 315-446-0546; Office Phone: 315-464-9788. Business E-Mail: williamw@upstate.edu.

WILLIAMS, WILLIAM MAGAVERN, headmaster; b. Niles, Mich., Dec. 22, 1931; s. Errol Edwin and Mary Elizabeth (Magavern) W.; m. Linda Carol Grush, June 15, 1958; children: Diana, William Jr., Sarah. BA, Williams Coll., 1953, LHD (hon.), 1984; postgrad. in Philosophy, Columbia U., 1954-58, MA in Ednl. Psychology, 1966. Tchr. elem. English, history, phys. edn. McTernan Sch., Waterbury, Conn., 1953-54; head guidance, boarding, and humanities depts., instr. English, coach varsity wrestling Riverdale Country Sch., Bronx, NY, 1955-66; headmaster Doane Acad., Burlington, NJ, 1966-70, Poly. Prep. Country Day Sch., Bklyn., 1970-00, headmaster emeritus, 2000—. Trustee Bklyn Inst. Arts and Scis., 1972-79, Bklyn. Ctrl. YMCA, 1974-78, Profl. Children's Sch., 1976-79, Bklyn. Children's Mus., 1979-82, Plymouth Ch. Pilgrims, 1979-86, NY State Assn. Ind. Schs., 1980-86, Northern Stage, 2003-2009; chmn. bd. dirs. Stafford Sch., Vt., 2002-03, United Ch. of Stafford, 2003-06. Mem. Headmasters' Assn., Country Day Sch. Headmasters' Assn. (v.p. 1998-99, pres. 1999-2000), Cum Laude Soc. (regent dist. III 1971-87, dep. pres. gen. 1981-87, pres. gen. 1987-96, regent-at-large 1996—), Guild Ind. Schs. N.Y. (pres. 1986-88). Avocations: sailing, skiing, chess, travel, civil war history. Home: 15 Beacon Hill Rd Strafford VT 05072 Personal E-mail: wmw232@aol.com.

WILLIAMS, WILLIAM PROCTOR, literature educator; b. Glade, Kans., Sept. 1, 1939; s. Joseph Earl and Mildred Bernice Williams; m. Antonia Forster, June 2, 1984; children: Elizabeth Anne Dewbray, William Proctor II. BA, Kans. State U., 1961, MA, 1964, PhD, 1968. Asst. prof. English No. Ill. U., DeKalb, 1967—70, assoc. prof. English, 1970—78, prof. English, 1978—99, assoc. dean rsch., grad. sch., 1982, dir. librs., 1982—83; vis. prof. English Mary Baldwin Coll., Staunton, 2004—07; sr. lectr. English U. of Akron, Ohio, 2000—. Editor Analytical and Enumerative Bibliography, DeKalb, 1976—2002. Author: An Introduction to Bibliographical and Textual Studies, 1985, A Bibliography of the Writings of Robert Graves, 1987; editor: Macbeth, 2006, Romeo and Juliet, 2007, Richard III, 2007; contbr. articles to profl. jours. Reader gen. ordination exam. Episcopal Ch., 1974—77. Fellow, Newberry Libr., 1974; sr. rsch. fellow, Fulbright Commn., 1983, Charlton Hinman fellow, Folger Shakespeare Libr., 2003—04, Rsch. grantee, Nat. Endowment for Humanities, 1978. Fellow: Bibliog. Soc. Am.; mem.: Malone Soc., Soc. Textual Scholarship, Midwest MLA (mem. exec. com. 1987—90), Shakespeare Assn. Am. Achievements include discovery of Castle Ashby manuscripts. Avocations: gardening, historic aircraft, cricket. Home: 2006 White Pond Dr Akron OH 44313 Office: U Akron Dept English Akron OH 44325 Business E-Mail: wpw@uakron.edu.

WILLIAMS, WILLIE, JR., physicist, researcher; b. Independence, La., Mar. 24, 1947; s. Willie Sr. and Lee Anner (Booker) W.; 1 child, Willie Williams III. BS, So. U., 1970; MS, Iowa State U., 1972, PhD, 1974. Mem. faculty Lincoln U., Lincoln University, Pa., 1974—, assoc. prof. physics, 1979-84, prof. physics, 1984—, chmn. dept., 1976-95, chmn. sci. and math. div., 1978-80, 83-88, founder, dir. Lincoln Advance Sci. and Engring. Reinforcement (LASER) Program, 1980-96, dir. pre-engring., 1976-96, dir., prin. investigator Early Alert-Young Scholars Program, 1992-96. Bd. dirs. women tech. program Lincoln U. Urban Ctr., Phila.; vis. prof. Ctr. for Teaching Innovation, Drexel U., 1975; liaison officer Nat. Assn. for Equal Opportunity in Higher Edn., Dept. Def. Program., 1987—; mem. steering com. NSF Comprehensive Ctr. for Minorities, Phila.; bd. dirs. Prime Inc., Phila. Contbr. articles to profl. jours. Chmn. Cheyney Lincoln Temple Cluster, 1974-78; pres. The Men Fedn., So. U., 1968-69. Recipient Lindback award for Outstanding Teaching, 1976, Outstanding Scientist award White House Initiative, 1988; named one of Outstanding Young Men of Am., 1979; fellow NASA, 1979, Mobil Oil Corp., 1977, Nat. Bur. Standards, 1979, Dept. Def., 1980-81, Navy fellow, 1982 Mem. AAAS, AAUP (pres. Lincoln U. chpt. 2001-03), Am. Assn. Physics, N.Y. Acad. Scis., Math. Assn. Am., Am. Phys. Soc., Nat. Soc. Black Physicists, Nat. Geog. Soc., Iowa State Alumna Assn., Sigma Xi, Sigma Pi Sigma. Baptist. Home: 448 W Baltimore Pike West Grove PA 19390-9201 Office: Lincoln U Dept Physics Lincoln University PA 19352 *Throughout my life I have always striven to achieve the very best and have held on to the belief that wherever possible improve upon today, so that everyone might have a better tomorrow! I have been guided by the principle of being selective in my endeavors, having specific objectives, followed by detailed analysis, concise actions, and intense work with continous review.*

WILLIAMS, WINFRED W., molecular biologist; MD, NYU. Resident Brigham & Women's Hosp.; program scientist dept. molecular biology Mass. Gen. Hosp. Co-chmn. Multicultural Affairs Office Adv. Bd. Mass. Gen. Hosp., adv. bd. Ctr. for Faculty Devel. Office: Massachusetts General Hospital 55 Fruit St BUL 123 Boston MA 02114-2696 Office Phone: 617-726-5050. Office Fax: 617-724-1122.*

WILLIAMS ADAMS, ANNETTE LYNN, emergency physician; d. Thomas F. and Karen Lou Adams; m. Justin Williams; children: Sean Barrett Williams, Shannon Fern Williams, Allison Fern Williams. MD, Tulane Sch. Medicine, New Orleans, 2002. Major airforce Lackland AFB, 1998—; flight physician U. AirCare, Cin., 2003—06; chief resident U. Cin., 2005—06; emergency physician Wilford Hall Med. Ctr., San Antonio, 2006—; emergency physician, dept. AEW, Balad, Iraq, 2008—. Curriculum dir. San Antonio Uniformed Svcs. Health Edn. Consortium, 2007—. Contbr. articles to profl. jours. Contbr. Soc. Prevention Cruelty Animals, People Ethical Treatment Animals; mem. St. Padre Pio Cath. Ch. Maj. USAF, 1998—, Lackland AFB. Mem.: Am. Coll. Emergency Physicians, Soc. Academic Emergency Medicine, Alpha Omega Alpha, Delta Delta Delta (intersorority coun. rep.). Home: 3511 Hilldale Point San Antonio TX 78261 Office Phone: 210-807-0011. Personal E-mail: annettelwilliams@gmail.com.

WILLIAMS-BOYD, DEBORAH KAY, finance educator; d. Jerry Carnell and Myrtle Virgus Williams; m. Sylvester Boyd, May 16, 1987; children: Kobie Dewayne Boyd, Debrasha Patrice Boyd, Sylvester Boyd. MBA, U. Tenn., Martin, 1980. Adj. instr. economics U. Tenn., Martin, 1984—2008, acct., 1980—. Author: (novels) From Then to Now (Martin Tenn. Cmty. Action award, 1999), You Don't Know Me (Martin Tenn. Unsung Hero, 2008). Omsbudsman NorthWest Tenn. Dist., Martin, 2006—08. Named Greek Advisor of Yr., Nat. Panhellenic Coun., 2007—08. Mem.: Delta Sigma Theta Sorority, Inc. (pres. 2007—, dir. 1999—, Lifetime Achievement award 2007). Democrat. Baptist. Avocations: travel, reading. Home: 754 Hawks Rd Martin TN 38237 Office: Univ Tenn University St Martin TN 38238 Office Fax: 731-881-7813. Business E-Mail: dboyd@utm.edu.

WILLIAMS-DE SILVA, LISA ANNETTE, small business owner, adult nurse practitioner; d. Joice Renee and Charles Braden (Stepfather); m. Lionel De Silva, June 12, 2003. BS in Bus., Ariz. State U., 1988, BSN, 2000, MSN, Nurse Practitioner, 2003. Cert. Achievement Cynosure Laser, Cert. Proficiency, Aesthetic Laser Sys. Sciton Aesthetic. Pres. Medical-Legal Support Svcs., Inc., Scottsdale, Ariz., 1998—. Owner and nurse practitioner Ultra Smooth Skin, Inc., Scottsdale, 2003—. Faculty Wives Club scholar, Ariz. State U., 1998—2000, STAR Program scholar, 1998—2000. Fellow: Am. Soc. Laser Medicine and Surgery (assoc.); mem.: Dermatology Nurses Assn., Internat. Acad. of Laser Medicine and Surgery (assoc.), Am. Assn. of Legal Nurse Consultants (assoc.), Am. Coll. of Phlebology (assoc.), Am. Acad. of Nurse Practitioners (assoc.). Avocations: hiking, travel, scuba diving. Office: Med-Legal Support Svcs Inc 14891 N Northside Scottsdale AZ 85260 Business E-Mail: lisa@ultrasmoothskin.com.

WILLIAMSEN, DANNYE SUE, personal development educator, publisher, ordained minister; b. Memphis, Mar. 26, 1949; d. Roy Fauntly and Arliss Wyleen Goodroe; m. Jon Charles Beckum, Dec. 23, 1969 (div. Mar. 1972); m. John Dean Williamsen, Dec. 24, 1986. BA cum laude, U. Memphis, 1995. Adminstr. Security Investments, Inc., Memphis, 1972—75; nightclub owner, investor Memphis, 1976—78; internat. tech. analyst ContiCommodity, Inc., Memphis, 1977—80; owner, tech. analyst Commodity Cons., Inc., Memphis, 1981; project mgr. B&P Devel. Co., Austin, Tex., 1982—84; asst. to pres. Memphis C. of C., 1984—86; owner, dental technician Williamsen Dental Lab., Memphis and Prophetstown, Ill., 1986—; ptnr., editor Personal Edn. Network, Prophetstown, Ill., 2001—; owner/pub. Networx Pub., Prophetstown, 2002—05, MindSlap! (formerly Williamsen Pubs.), Kennesaw, Ga., 2006—; life coach, 2006—; CFO Networking Entrepreneurs Inc, 2008. Bd. dirs. Heartland Equine Assisted Therapeutic Ctr., Rock Falls, Ill., 2000—01; show host Tips & Techniques for the Creative Entrepreneur, 2007, Express Yourself! Live Your Life Thoughtfully, 2008, Tweaking Your Life, 2009. Author: Illusions, 1998, It's Your Move! Transform Your Dreams from Wishful Thinking to Reality, 2004, Metaphysical Minute, 2006, MindSlap!, 2007, The Creative Matrix, 2007; editor: Creative Living-an Evolving Approach to Bus. Life, 2001—, (e-newsletter) Metaphysical Minute, 2003—04; columnist: Penwomanship Mag, 2003—05; editor: (newsletter) MindSlap!; editor: Tips & Techniques for the Creative Entrepreneur, 2007, Mindslap! Healing Your Self Esteem, 2008—, Tweaking Your Life!, 2009; prodr.: (show) Just a Taste..., 2007, (CD) Stop Wallowing & Start Winning, 2007; prodr.: (CD) Simplicity for the Soul, vol. I, 2007, The Church is a Living Organism, 2007. Mem. AAUW (pres. 1998-99), APA, NOW, NAFE, Am. Bus. Women's Assn., Assn. for Humanistic Psychology, Nat. Assn. Women Writers, Small Pubs. Assn. N.Am., Pubs. Mktg. Assn., Psi Chi, Chi Beta Phi., Atlanta Writer's Club. Avocations: reading, counseling, writing. Office: PO Box 2893 Kennesaw GA 30156-9115 Office Phone: 770-438-0889. Business E-Mail: dannyew@mindslaponline.com.

WILLIAMS-LATNIE, VERONICA MYRES, psychotherapist, social worker; b. Shreveport, La., May 11, 1947; d. McEura and Margie Virgina (Reagan) Myres; divorced; children: Nicole Leann, Jennifer Lyn, Erica Maria; m. Melvin Latnie Nov. 17, 2007 BA, La. Tech. U., Ruston, 1969; MSW, U. Mich., Ann Arbor, 1977; PhD, So. Calif. U., 2001. Diplomate Am. Bd. Clin. Social Workers, Am. Psychotherapy Assn.; cert. social worker, Mich. Probation counselor Citizens Probation Authority, Flint, Mich., 1970-72; unit dir., therapist Svcs. to Overcome Drug Abuse Among Teenagers, Flint, 1972-74; psychiat. therapist Psycho-Therapeutic Treatment Clin., P.C., Flint, 1974-77; psychiat. social worker Hurley Med. Ctr., Flint, 1977-79; field instr. Sch. Social Work U. Mich., Ann Arbor, 1978-79, 86—; psychiat. social worker Inst. Mental Health, Flint, 1979-81, Psychotherapeutic Treatment Clinic, 1981-83; clin. social worker Flint Bd. Edn., 1979-83; pupil apprasal spl. edn. Caddo Parish Sch. Bd., Shreveport, La., 1983—85; psychiat. therapist Mott Children's Health Ctr., 1986—92, Oakland Psychol. Clinic, P.C., 1991—92; owner and dir. V. Williams, PhD, MSW, ACSW, BCD, PC, Flint, Mich., 1992—. Developer dropout prevention program Flint Bd. Edn., 1986-98; Beecher Sch. Dist., 1998-2006. Bd. dirs. Boys & Girls Club. Mem. NASW, ACSW, NEA, Mich. Edn. Assn. Democrat. Office: Ste 110 225 E 5th St Flint MI 48502 Home Phone: 810-695-5610; Office Phone: 810-232-0018. E-mail: drvmwilliams@comcast.net.

WILLIAMSON, ALAN BACHER, literature educator, poet, writer; b. Chgo., Jan. 24, 1944; s. George and Jehanne (Bacher) W.; m. Anne Winters, Oct. 12, 1968 (div. Feb. 1988); 1 child, Elizabeth Kilner. BA, Haverford Coll., 1964; MA, Harvard U., 1965, PhD, 1969. Asst. prof. U. Va., Charlottesville, 1969-75; Briggs-Copeland lectr. Harvard U., Cambridge, Mass., 1977-80; Fannie Hurst lectr. Brandeis U., Waltham, Mass., 1980-82; prof. English, U. Calif., Davis, 1982—. Poetry panelist Nat. Endowment for Arts, 1989. Author: (criticism) Pity the Monsters, 1974, Introspection and Contemporary Poetry, 1984, Eloquence and Mere Life, 1994, Almost a Girl, 2001, Westerness: A Meditation, 2006, (poetry) Presence, 1983, The Muse of Distance, 1988, Love and the Soul, 1995, Res Publica, 1998, The Pattern More Complicated: New and Selected Poems, 2004. Poetry fellow Nat. Endowment for Arts, 1973; Guggenheim fellow, 1991. Mem. MLA (exec. com. div. on poetry 1987-91). Democrat. Buddhist. Office: U Calif Dept English Davis CA 95616 Business E-Mail: abwilliamson@ucdavis.edu.

WILLIAMSON, BARRY SCOTT, conductor, performing arts educator; b. Washburn, Wis., Dec. 13, 1955; s. Mortimer Leo and Esther Edna Williamson; 1 child, Caitlin Rose. MusB, Concordia Coll., Moorhead, Minn., 1978; MusM in Choral Conducting, U. of Ariz., 1982; Dr. of Mus. Arts in Choral Conducting, U. Tex., 1993. Vocal instr./coach Williamson Vocal Studio, Austin, Tex., 1986—; founding artistic dir. and condr. Tex. Choral Consort, Austin, 1997—; choir dir. and organist Koenig Ln. Christian Ch., Austin, 1998—. Dir. of music ministries St. John Neumann Cath. Ch., Austin, 1989—91; choir dir. Hyde Pk. Christian Ch., Austin, 1987—89; vocal music dir. Cholla H.S., Tucson, 1982—86; choirmaster and organist St. Alban's Episc. Ch., Tucson, 1984—86; condr., univ./cmty. chorus U. of Ariz., Tucson, 1981—82; asst. dir. Tucson Ariz. Boys Chorus, 1981—82; paid singer St. Phillip's On the Hill Episc. Ch., Tucson, 1981—82; vocal music dir. Rice Lake Sr. H.S., Rice Lake, Wis., 1980—81; choir dir. Bethany Luth. Ch., Rice Lake, 1980—81; vocal music dir., grades 7-12 Kasson-Mantorville Jr-Sr. H.S., Kasson, Minn., 1978—80; dir. of music ministries NW Hills United Meth. Ch., Austin, 1996—98; choir dir. St. John's Luth. Ch., Kasson, Minn., 1978—80; asst. dir.,Cconcordia choir Concordia Coll., Moorhead, Minn.; dir. of choral activities U. of Tex. at El Paso, 1993—96; choirmaster and organist St. Francis On the Hill Episc. Ch., El Paso, Tex., 1993—95; dir. of choral activities Trinity U., San Antonio, 1992—93; artistic dir. and condr. Austin Civic Chorus, Austin, 1987—91; condr. chorus U. of Tex. at Austin, 1986—88; asst. chorus dir., asst. to the condr. Austin Lyric Opera, Austin, 1986—88; dir. of music ministries Good Shepherd Episc. Ch., Austin, 1991—92. Mem.: Chorus Am., Tex. Choral Dirs. Assn., Am. Choral Dirs. Assn. Home: 134 Latham Ave Hopkinsville KY 42240-3687 Office: Texas Choral Consort Et Al PO Box 2022 Austin TX 78768-2022 E-mail: barry@txconsort.org.

WILLIAMSON, BRUCE A., gas industry executive; b. Great Falls, Mont., 1959; B in Fin., U. Mont., 1981; MBA, U. Houston, 1995. With Royal Dutch/Shell Group, 1981—95; sr. v.p. fin. bus. develop. and risk mgmt. PanEnergy Corp., v.p. fin., 1995—97; pres., CEO Duke Energy Internat., 1997—2001, Duke Energy Global Markets, 2001—02; CEO Dynegy Inc., Houston, 2002—04, chmn., CEO, 2004—07, chmn., pres., CEO, 2007—. Bd. dirs. Questar Corp., Dynegy, Inc., 2002—. Chancellor's nat. adv coun. U. Houston, Dean's adv. bd., C.T. Bauer Coll. Bus.; bd. dir. Greater Houston Partnership. Office: Dynegy Inc 1000 Louisiana Ste 5800 Houston TX 77002 Office Phone: 713-507-6400, 877-439-6349. Office Fax: 713-767-6652, 713-507-3871.

WILLIAMSON, CHARLES R., retired energy company executive; PhD in Geology, U. Tex., Austin, 1978. Rsch. assoc. Sci. and Tech. Divsn. Unocal Corp., Brea, Calif., 1977-83, chief exploration geologist U.K., 1983-86; exploration mgr., dir. Unocal Netherlands, The Hague, 1986-89; v.p. exploration Unocal Thailand, Bangkok, 1989-92; v.p. Energy Resources Divsn. Unocal, 1992-94, v.p. planning and info. svcs., 1994-95, v.p. corp. planning and econs., 1995-96, group v.p. internat. opers., 1996-97, group v.p. Asia Opers., 1997-99; exec. v.p. internat. energy ops. Unocal Corp., El Segundo, Calif., 1999—2001; CEO, chmn. Unocal (acquired by Chevron Corp.), 2001—05; exec. v.p., mem. exec. com. Chevron Corp., 2005; non-exec. chmn. Weyerhaeuser Co., 2009—. Mem. adv. bd. earth scis. dept. Stanford U.; bd. dir. Weyerhaeuser Co., 2004—, lead. dir., 2006—09; bd. dir. Talisman Energy Inc., 2006—, PACCAR Inc., 2006—. Mem. Am. Soc. Petroleum Geologists, Soc. Econ. Paleontologists and Mineralogists, Soc. Petroleum Engrs., Internat. Assn. Sedimentologists. Mailing: PACCAR Inc Bd Directors PO Box 1518 Bellevue WA 98009*

WILLIAMSON, CHARLES READY, III, lawyer; b. Boston, Jan. 2, 1944; s. Charles Ready, Jr. and Anne Margaret (Livingstone) Williamson; m. Julie Anne Williamson, Nov. 6, 1971; 1 child, Anne Lucinda. BA, Colgate U., 1965; LLB, Suffolk U., 1968. Bar: Mass. 1968, Oreg. 1970, US Supreme Ct. 1977. Law clk. to Judge Joseph B. Silverio Mass. Land Ct., Boston, 1968—69; VISTA atty., dep. dir. Multnomah county Legal Aid Svc., Portland, 1970—74; assoc. Kell, Alterman & Runstein, 1974—78, 1988—; pvt. practice Portland, 1978—88. Pres. Oreg. Legal Svc. Corp., 1976—77. Contbr. articles in field. Pres. Oreg. Consumer League, 1972—74; mem. Oreg. Bd. Psychologist Examiners, 1973—74; chmn. Oreg. Grad. Sch. Profl. Psychology, Pacific U.; councilor Met. Svc. Dist., 1978—84; treas. Dem. Bus. Forum, 1982—84. Mem.: ABA, Multnomah County Bar Assn., Oreg. Bar Assn. (pres.-elect 2002—03, pres. 2003—04), Portland City Club. Office: Kell Alterman & Runstein 520 SW Yamhill Ste 600 Portland OR 97204-1329

WILLIAMSON, CLINT (JOHN CLINT WILLIAMSON), ambassador; b. 1961; Asst. dist. atty., New Orleans; trial atty. organized crime sect. U.S. Dept. Justice; trial atty. Internat. Criminal Tribunal for Yugoslavia (ICTY) The Hague, Netherlands, 1994—2001; dir. Dept. Justice UN Mission Kosovo, 2001—02; sr. adv. Iraqi Ministry Justice, 2003; dir. stability ops. NSC, 2003—06, acting spl. asst. to Pres., sr. dir. relief, stabilization, and devel., 2006; US amb.-at-large for war crimes issues US Dept. State, 2006—. Office: US Dept State Office War Crimes Issues 2201 C St NW Washington DC 20520*

WILLIAMSON, DONALD ELLIS, state agency administrator, public health service officer; b. Louisville, Miss., June 17, 1955; m. Anita Hudspeth; 1 child, Jonathan Stuart. Student, East Miss. Jr. Coll., 1972-73, Miss. State U., 1973-75; MD cum laude, U. Miss., 1979. Diplomate Am. Bd. Internal Medicine. Intern, resident in internal medicine U. Va. Hosp., Charlottesville, 1979-82; with East Miss. State Hosp., Meridian, 1979; state TB control officer Miss. State Dept. Health, 1982-86; dir. divsn. disease control Ala. Dept. Pub. Health, 1986-88, dir. bur. preventive health svcs., 1988-92, state health officer, 1992—. Faculty mem. Injury Control Rsch. Ctr. U. Ala., Birmingham; clin. assoc. prof. dept. internal medicine U. South Ala.; presenter in field. Contbr. articles to profl. jours. Chmn. Ala. Pub. Health Care Authority, Ala. Radiation Adv. Bd. Health; mem. Ala. Commn. Aging, State Bldg. Commn., Statewide Health Coordinating Coun., Ala. Youth Svcs. Bd., Ala. Child Abuse & Neglect Prevention Bd., Ala. Resource Devel. Com., Ala. Anat. Bd., Planning and Adv. Coun. Devel. Disabilities, Ala. Bd. Med. Scholarship Awards, Pesticides Adv. Com., Gov.'s Interagy. Coordinating Coun., Ala. Juvenile Justice Coordinating Coun., Emergency Med. Svcs. Adv. Coun., 1986-92, Legis. Adv. Com. AIDS, 1988-90, Atty. Gen.'s Task Force Med.Waste, 1989, Water Resources Adv. Coun., exec. coun. Ala. Children's Svcs. Facilitation Team, 1993—; mem. med. adv. com. ARC. Recipient Mosby Book award, 1979, Dr. Robert Ramsey award, 1993; Pub. Health Leadership Inst. scholar, 1996. Mem. APHA, Assn. State and Territorial Health Ofcls. (exec. com. 1995-2000, pres. 1997-98), Am. Acad. of Pediatrics (Child Health Advocate of the Yr. award 1999), Pub. Health Found. (Theodore R. Ervin award 1999), Med. Assn. State Ala., Ala. Pub. Health Assn. (bd. dirs. 1991—, chmn. disease control and epidemiology sect. 1991-92, D.G. Gill award 1997), Pub. Health Found. (bd. dirs. 1995-99, treas. 1997—), Phi Theta Kappa, Phi Kappa Phi, Alpha Omega Alpha. Home: 8113 Lichfield Ct Montgomery AL 36117-5124 Office: Ala Dept Pub Health PO Box 303017 201 Monroe St Montgomery AL 36104-3735*

WILLIAMSON, DONALD RAY, retired military officer; b. Amarillo, Tex., Oct. 13, 1943; s. Floy Edwin and Dorothy Lorene (Orr) W.; m. Beverly Ann Howard, Aug. 31, 1963; children: Rebecca Ann, Catherine Paige. BS in Econs., W. Tex. State U., 1966; MA in Bus., Cen. Mich. U., 1977; degree, Dept. Def. Program Mgrs., 1982, U.S. Army Command and Gen. Staff Coll., 1980. Commd. 2d lt. U.S. Army, 1966, advanced through grades to lt. col., 1982, retired, 1986, comdg. officer combat support co. Ft. Hood, Tex., 1973-74, comdg. officer 2d aviation co., 1974-75, dep. insp. gen. Ft. Leavenworth, Kans., 1975-78, comdg. officer 213th aviation co. Rep. of Korea, 1978-79, asst. program mgr. advanced scout helicopter program, 1981-86; owner Witan Group, Chesterfield, Mo., 1986-88; pres., owner Sys. Test Evaluation Inc., Huntsville, Ala., 1988-99; gen. mgr. LESCO, Huntsville, Ala., 1999-2000. Contbr. articles to profl. jours. Decorated Bronze Star, 37 Air medals with "V" device, D.F.C. with oak leaf cluster, Legion of Merit. Mem. Army Aviation Assn. Am., Assn. U.S. Army, Lansing Jaycees (past pres.), Mensa. Avocations: flying, reading, tennis. Home: 2110 Greenslope Trl NE Huntsville AL 35811-2608

WILLIAMSON, DOUGLAS FRANKLIN, JR., lawyer; b. Anniston, Ala., Mar. 23, 1930; s. Douglas Franklin and Elizabeth Louise (Connor) W.; m. Barbara Tuerk, Dec. 28, 1957; children: Mary Leyden, Douglas Franklin III, Bruce Reynolds. AB summa cum laude, Amherst Coll., 1952; LLB, Yale U., 1955. Bar: NY 1958, Fla. 1976. Assoc. Breed, Abbott & Morgan, NYC, 1957-63, ptnr., 1963-72, Williamson & Hess and predecessor firm, NYC, 1972-79; of counsel Winthrop, Stimson, Putnam & Roberts, NYC, 1979-81, ptnr., 1982-95, sr. counsel, 1996-2000, Pillsbury Winthrop Shaw Pittman LLP and predessors, NYC, 2001—. Bd. dirs. World Wildlife Fund, Washington, 1979-88, treas., 1986-88, mem. nat. coun., 1988-2006; bd. dirs. Conservation Found., Washington, 1985-88, treas., 1986-88; bd. dirs. Ea. N.Y. chpt. Nature Conservancy, Mt. Kisco, N.Y., 1976-87, 93-97, sec., 1976-87, hon. dir., 1987—, chmn., 1993-94; bd. dirs. Oblong Land Conservancy, Pawling, N.Y., 1990-98, chmn. 1996-98; bd. dirs. Quaker Hill Civic Assn., Pawling, 1974-2000, past pres.; chmn. Pawling Assessment Rev. Bd., 1976-2001. With U.S. Army, 1955-57. Fellow: NY State Bar Found.; mem.: Assn. Bar City NY (life), Soc. Colonial Wars, Everglades Club, Quaker Hill Country Club (pres. 1980—81), Phi Beta Kappa, Phi Beta Kappa Soc. (sec. 1975—77, v.p. 1977—79).

WILLIAMSON, EDWIN DARGAN, lawyer, former federal official; b. Florence, SC, Sept. 23, 1939; s. Benjamin F. and Sara (Dargan) W.; m. Kathe Gates, July 12, 1969; children: Samuel Gates, Edwin Dargan Jr., Sara Elizabeth. BA cum laude, U. of the South, 1961, DCL (hon.), 1992; JD, NYU, 1964. Bar: NY 1965, DC 1988. Assoc. Sullivan & Cromwell LLP, NYC, 1964-70, ptnr., 1971-76, London, 1976-79, NYC, 1979-88, Washington, 1988—90, 1993—2006, sr. counsel, 2007—; legal adviser US Dept. State, Washington, 1990-93. Mem. Permanent Ct. Arbitration, 1991—2004; mem. U.S. adv. NTT DoCoMo, 2002—04. Regent U. of the South, Sewanee, Tenn., 1981-87, chmn., 1985-87, trustee, 1973-76, 1980-83, 2007-, coun. fgn. rels., 1995—; bd. dirs. Nat. Dance Inst., NYC, 1984-88, Episcopal Ch. Found., NYC, 1986-90; vestryman St. James Episcopal Ch., NYC, 1984-88; bd. mem. SC Govs. Sch. for Sci. and Math. Found., 2003-04. Mem. US Coun. Internat. Bus., Bus. and Industry Adv. Com. to OECD (vice chmn. com. on multinat. enterprise and investments 1993—2004, chmn. BIAC expert group on multilat agt. on investment 1996-99, vice-chmn. 1998-2004, mem. exec. com. USCIB 1999—2009, chmn. task force corp. govt. 2002-04), Met. Club. Republican. Office: Sullivan & Cromwell LLP 1701 Pennsylvania Ave NW Washington DC 20006-5805 Office Fax: 202-956-7081. Personal E-mail: edwinwilliamsonsr@msn.com. Business E-Mail: williamsone@sullcrom.com.

WILLIAMSON, (EULAH) ELAINE, elementary school educator; b. NYC, July 27, 1945; d. Eddie Lee and Eulah Genola (Hardie) Riley; m. George Leslie Williamson, Feb. 17, 1973 (div. 1999); children: George Todd, Michelle Elaine, Heather Dawn BA, Hampton U., 1967; MA in Urban Edn., Jersey City State Coll., 1998; postgrad., St. Peter's Coll., Jersey City. Cert. elem. tchr. K-8, supr., N.J. Tchr. elem. Englewood (N.J.) Pub. Schs., 1967-78, Irvington (N.J.) Pub. Schs., 1988-97; tchr. math. Hackensack (N.J.) Pub. Schs., 1997—. Mem. NEA, Nat. Mid. Sch. Assn., Nat. Coun. Tchrs. Math., Nat. Black Child Devel. Inst., N.J. Edn. Assn., Hackensack Edn. Assn., Profl. and Bus. Women NAACP, Phi Delta Kappa Democrat. Bapt. Avocations: photography, football, horseback riding. Office: Hackensack Mid Sch 360 Union St Hackensack NJ 07601-4394 also: 5/6 Sch 320 State St Hackensack NJ 07601 Office Phone: 201-646-8170. E-mail: blackie727@aol.com.

WILLIAMSON, IRVING A., federal official; m. Cheryl A. Parham; children: Patrick, Elizabeth. BA in History, Brown U., Providence, RI; MA in Internat. Rels., Johns Hopkins; JD, George Washington U. Fgn. svc. officer US Dept. State; mng. trade policy Port Authority of NY and NJ, 1985—93; dep. gen. counsel Office US Trade Rep., 1993—98; v.p. trade, investment, and econ. devel. Programs Africa America Inst.; pres. Williamson Internat. Trade Strategies, Inc.; commr. US Internat. Trade Commn., Washington, 2007—. Office: US Internat Trade Commn 500 E St NW Washington DC 20436*

WILLIAMSON, JOEL RUDOLPH, humanities educator, writer; b. Anderson County, SC, Oct. 27, 1929; s. James Henry and Carrie Mae (Swaney) W.; m. Marie Ahearn, Nov. 17, 1953 (div. May 1983); children: Joelle, William, Alethea; m. Anna Woodson, Oct. 18, 1986. AB, U. S.C., 1948, MA, 1951; PhD, U. Calif., 1964. Instr. dept. history U. N.C., Chapel Hill, 1960-64, asst. prof., 1964-66, assoc. prof., 1966-69, prof., 1969-85, Lineberger prof. in humanities, 1985—. Resident fellow Rockefeller Ctr., Bellagio, Italy, 1988; Eudora Welty prof. in so. studies Millsaps Coll., 1984; disting. vis. prof. Rhodes Coll., 1984; vis. prof. dept. history, assoc. Lowell House Harvard U., 1981-82. Author: After Slavery: The Negro in South Carolina During Reconstruction, 1861-1877, 1965, The Origins of Segregation, 1968, New People: Miscegenation and Mulattoes in the United States, 1980, The Crucible of Race, 1984 (Francis Parkman prize Soc. Am. Historians, Ralph Waldo Emerson award Phi Beta Kappa, Mayflower Cup, Frank L. and Harriet C. Owsley award 1985, Robert Francis Kennedy Book award, Pulitzer prize in History nomination 1985), A Rage for Order, 1986, William Faulkner and Southern History, 1993 (Pulitzer prize in History nomination 1994, Mayflower Cup), also articles. Lt. USN, 1951-55. Fellow Guggenheim Found., 1970-71, NEH, 1987-88, Ctr. for Advanced Study in Behavioral Scis., Stanford, Calif., 1977-78, summer 1979, 80, 81, So. fellow, 1961-62, Charles Warren Ctr., 1981-82. Mem. Soc. Am. Historians, Orgn. Am. Historians, Am. Hist. Assn., So. Hist. Assn., So. Assn. for Women Historians. Achievements include having two books (The Crucible of Race, 1984, William Faulkner and Southern History, 1993) that were among three finalists for the Pulitzer Prize in History. Avocation: travel. Home: 211 Hillsborough St Chapel Hill NC 27514-3522 Personal E-mail: annaleoww@aol.com.

WILLIAMSON, JOHN PRITCHARD, retired utilities executive; b. Cleve., Feb. 22, 1922; s. John and Jane (Pritchard) W.; m. Helen Morgan, Aug. 3, 1945; children: John Morgan, James Russell, Wayne Arthur. BBA, Kent State U., 1945; postgrad., U. Toledo, 1953-56, U. Mich., 1956. CPA, Ohio, ret. Sr. acct. Arthur Andersen & Co., Detroit and Cleve., 1945-51; dir. methods and procs. Toledo Edison Co., 1951-59, asst. treas., 1959-60, sec., 1960-62, sec.-treas., 1962-65, v.p. finance, 1965-68, sr. v.p., 1968-72, pres., chief exec. officer, 1972-79, chmn., chief exec. officer, 1979-86; founding chmn. Centerior Energy Corp. (now First Energy Corp.), 1985—86. Chmn. emeritus Toledo Edison Co.; dir. emeritus, chmn. 1st Nat. Bank of Toledo, 1974-75, Toledo Trust Co., 1976-79; chmn. N.Am. Electric Reliability Coun., 1984-87; founding chmn. Nat. Electric Security Com., 1987-88; guest lectr. U. Toledo, 1976-. Pres. Ohio Electric Utility Inst., 1972; chmn. East Cen. Area Power Coordination Pool, 1971-72, mem. exec. com. Edison Electric Inst., 1981-85; mem. Ohio Devel. Adv. Coun., 1973-79; exec. com. mem., trustee Assn. Edison Illuminating Cos., 1982-84; pres. Toledo C. of C., 1970; chmn. Ohio C. of C., 1979-81, life dir.; pres. Toledo Symphony Orch., 1985-86; hon. trustee Toledo Mus. Art, Toledo Hosp., Toledo Symphony; trustee U. Toledo Found., 1980-87; hon. trustee Kent State U. Found.; vice chmn. Greater Toledo Corp., 1984-86; trustee, treas. Rio Verde Cmty. Ch., 1989-92; founding elder Covenant Presbyn. Ch., Stephen minister, 1996; pres. Toledo Cmty. Chest, 1972; chmn. Greater Toledo Area United Way, 1971, Epworth Meth. Ch. Found.; dir. Rio Verde Comty. Assn., 1998-2003 Named Toledo Area Outstanding Citizen, 1976; recipient Kent State U. medallion, 1992; Williamson Alumni Ctr. named in his honor, 1991. Mem. Fin. Analysts Soc. Toledo (pres. 1968-69), Sys. and Procs. Assn. (internat. treas. 1960), Inst. Pub. Utilities (chmn. exec. com. 1969-70), Toledo Boys Club (Echo award 1974), Kent State U. Alumni Assn. (pres. 1971-72, Outstanding Alumnus 1974), Belmont Country Club, Rio Verde Country Club, Inverness Club (gov., treas. 1967-76, com. chair 1979 U.S. Open, 1986 PGA Championship, winner 1965 Amateur Invitational), Rio Verde Saddle Club (past pres.), Kiwanis (past pres. Toledo chpt., Disting. Svc. award 1977, 02, past internat. pres. award 2002), Ky. Cols. (hon.), Blue Key, Delta Sigma Pi, Beta Alpha Psi (hon.), Beta Gamma Sigma (hon.), Delta Upsilon. Republican. Home: 10661 Cardiff Rd Perrysburg OH 43551-3404 also: 18524 E Poco Vista Rio Verde AZ 85263-7125

WILLIAMSON, KEITH HARVEY, lawyer; b. St. Louis, May 16, 1952; s. Irving Alexander and Elizabeth Rebecca (Giddings) W.; 1 child. BA, Brown U., 1974; MBA, JD, Harvard U., 1978; LLM in Taxation, NYU, 1986. Bar: DC 1978, NY 1983. Assoc. Covington & Burling, Washington, 1978-81, Reavis & McGrath, NYC, 1981-88; dir. taxes Pitney Bowes Credit Corp., Shelton, Conn., 1988-94, asst. gen. counsel, 1993—94, v.p., sec., gen. counsel, 1994—98; sr. assoc. gen. counsel, mergers and acquisitions Pitney Bowes Inc., 1998—99, pres., capital svcs. divsn., 1999—2006; sr. v.p., sec., gen. counsel Centene Corp., St. Louis, 2006—. Bd. dirs. Clayton C.of C., Mathew-Dicky Boys & Girls Club; founder Minority Corp. Counsel Assn.; mem. Black Exec. Exch. Program, Urban League. Office: Centene Corp 7711 Carondelet Ave Saint Louis MO 63105 Home: 232 N Kings Hwy Blvd Unit 1208 Saint Louis MO 63108 Personal E-mail: keithwmson@aol.com. Business E-Mail: kwilliamson@centene.com.

WILLIAMSON, KENNETH LEE, chemistry professor; b. Tarentum, Pa., Apr. 13, 1934; s. James D. and Mary June (Becker) W.; m. Mary Louise Hoerner, Sept. 15, 1956; children: Christopher Lee, Tania Louise, Kevin Keith. BA cum laude (Nat. scholar), Harvard, 1956; PhD (Allied Chem. and Dye Co. fellow), U. Wis., 1960. Mem. faculty Mt. Holyoke Coll., 1961—, prof. chemistry, 1969—, Mary E. Woolley prof. chemistry, 1984-99, Mary E. Woolley prof. chemistry emeritus, 1999—. Mem. Grad. faculty U. Mass., 1965—; vis. prof. Cornell U., 1966, Dartmouth Coll., 1986-87, Harvard U., 1989-90, U. Trondheim, Norway, 1991, U. Louis Pasteur, Strasbourg, France, 1991, U. Amsterdam, Basel U., Switzerland, 1992, U. Canterbury, New Zealand and U. Auckland, New Zealand, 1994; vis. prof. MIT, 1996, 97, Calif. Inst. Tech., 2000. Author papers and books in field; patentee in field. Mem. South Hadley Hist. Commn., 1983—, South Hadley Cultural Coun., 2000-03; chair, Sycamores Com., South Hadley Hist. Soc., 1992-. NIH postdoctoral fellow Stanford, 1960-61; NSF sci. faculty fellow U. Liverpool, Eng.; also fellow of univ., 1968-69; Guggenheim fellow, 1975-76; Oxford (Eng.) U. fellow of univ., 1976, 1983; research assoc., Calif. Inst. Tech., 1975, 82. Mem. Am. Chem. Soc., AAAS, Sigma Xi. Congregationalist. Avocations: sailing, cabinetry. Home: 43 Woodbridge St South Hadley MA 01075-1138 E-mail: williamson98@comcast.net.

WILLIAMSON, MARILYN LAMMERT, literature educator, academic administrator; b. Chgo., Sept. 6, 1927; d. Raymond Ferdinand and Edith Louise (Eisenbies) Lammert; m. Robert M. Williamson, Oct. 28, 1950 (div. Apr. 1973); 1 child, Timothy L.; m. James H. McKay, Aug. 15, 1974. BA, Vassar Coll., 1949; MA, U. Wis., 1950; PhD, Duke U., 1956. Lectr. Duke U., Durham, NC, 1955-56, 58-59, N.C. State U., Raleigh, 1957-58, 61-62; asst. prof. Oakland U., Rochester, Mich., 1965-68, assoc. prof., 1968-72; prof. English Wayne State U., Detroit, 1972-90, Disting. prof. English, 1990-97, Disting. prof. emerita, 1997—, chmn. dept. English, 1972-74, 81-83, assoc. dean Coll. Liberal Arts, 1974-79, dir. women's studies, 1976-87, dep. provost, 1987-91, sr. v.p. for acad. affairs, provost, 1991-95, 98-200. Pres. Assn. Depts. English, 1976-77. Author: Infinite Variety, 1974, Patriarchy of Shakespeare's Comedies, 1986, British Women Writers 1650-1750, 1990, Tales of Two Dogs, 2005; editor: Renaissance Studies, 1972, Female Poets of Great Britain, 1981, Shakespeare Studies: Middle Comedies, 2003; contbr. articles to profl. jours. Pres. LWV, Rochester, 1963-65. Recipient Detroit Disting. Svc. award, 1986, Faculty Recognition award Bd. Govs., Wayne State U., 1991, 30 Yr. award Mich. Humanities Coun., 2004; Bunting Inst. fellow, 1969-70, AAUW fellow, 1982-83, J.N. Keal fellow, 1985-86. Mem.: MLA (exec. coun. 1977—80, mem. editl. bd. 1992—94), Fed. State Humanities Coun. (bd. dirs. 1994—2001, chair 1997—99), Mich. Coun. Humanities (bd. dirs. 1988—2001, chair 1991—93), Mich. Acad. (pres. 1978—79). Democrat. Home: 2275 Oakway Dr West Bloomfield MI 48324-1855

WILLIAMSON, MARK ADAM, science educator; b. Milton, Mass., Feb. 15, 1953; s. John Anthony and Patricia Ryan Williamson; m. Elizabeth Rogoff, Mar. 12, 1983; children: Benjamin Adam, Shira Patricia. PhD, Binghamton U., NY, 2000. Prof. Broome CC, Binghamton, 2000—, Tompkins-Cortland CC, Dryden, NY, 2003—, Onondaga CC, Syracuse, NY, 2005—08. Exhibitions include Chimera, The Village, Twoface, Ice On The River, Lascaux. Liberal. Home: 11 Woodside Rd E Apalachin NY 13732 Personal E-mail: mark13732@aol.com.

WILLIAMSON, MARVEL, dean, nursing administrator, sexologist, educator; b. Holton, Kans., Nov. 4, 1953; d. Thomas Arthur and Lois M. (Ihrig) Ansley; m. Paul Williamson, May 12, 1973; children: Marcus W., Sean W. BS in Nursing, Wichita State U., 1976; MS in Nursing, U. Ky., 1978; PhD, U. Iowa, 1987. Cert. sex educator, nurse educator. Fellow Acad. Nursing Edn. Prof. U. Iowa, Iowa City, 1980-89; dir. patient svcs. Ransom Meml. Hosp., Ottawa, Kans., 1989-91; dir. schs. nursing at Rolla, Sikeston and Kansas City Park Coll., Parkville, Mo., 1991-97; prof. Albany (Ga.) State U., 1997-99; sexologist Silver Spring, Md., 1999—2001; dean Kramer Sch. Nursing, Oklahoma City U., 2001—. Contbr. articles to profl. jours. Mem. ANA, Am. Assn. Sex Educators, Counselors and Therapists, Sigma Theta Tau. Home and Office: 3141 NW 18th St Oklahoma City OK 73107 Office: Oklahoma City U 2501 N Blackwelder Oklahoma City OK 73106 Office Phone: 405-208-5900.

WILLIAMSON, NANCY E, demographer; b. Cambridge, Mass., Mar. 22, 1945; d. Charles C and Betty Hook Thomas. BA, U. Mich., Ann Arbor, 1966; MS, Harvard Sch. Pub. Health, Boston, MA, 1969; PhD, Harvard U., Cambridge, MA, 1973; Post doc. fellowship, U. N. C., Chapel Hill, 1981. Asst. prof. Brown U., Providence, NC, 1971—76; assoc. Population Coun., Philippines, 1976—80; dir. Family Health Internat., Durham, 1981—2001, sr. scientist, 2004—, v.p. Arlington, Va., 2001—04. Cons. US AID, Washington, 1985—2000. Author: (book) Sons or Daughters: Cross Cultural Survey Parent Preferences. Mem. bd. dirs. Carolina Friends Sch., Durham, NC, 1990—94. Mem.: Internat. Union Sci. Study Population, Population Assn. Am. (bd. mem.). Office: Family Health Internat PO Box 13950 Durham NC 27709 Office Phone: 919-544-7040. Business E-Mail: nwilliamson@fhi.org.

WILLIAMSON, OLIVER EATON, business economics and law professor; m. Dolores Jean (Celeni); children: Scott, Tamara, Karen, Oliver, Dean. BS, Mass. Inst. Tech., 1955; MBA, Stanford U., 1960; PhD, Carnegie Mellon U., 1963; PhD (hon.), Norwegian Sch. Econ. and Bus. Adminstrn., 1986; PhD in Econ. sci. (hon.), Hochschule St. Gallen, Switzerland, 1987, Groningen U., 1989, Turku Sch. Econ. and Bus. Admin, St. Petersburg, Russia, 1996, HEC, Paris, 1997, Copenhagen Bus. Sch., 2000, U. Chile, 2000, Valencia U., 2004, Nice U., 2005. Project. engr. U.S. Govt., 1955-58; asst. prof. econ. U. Calif., Berkeley, Calif., 1963-65; assoc. prof. Pa. State U., Phila., 1965-68, prof., 1968-83, Charles and William L. Day prof. econ. and social sci., 1977-83; Gordon B. Tweedy prof. econ. law and orgn. Yale U., 1983-88; Transam. prof. of bus., econ. and law U. Calif., Berkeley, Calif., 1988-94, Edgar F. Kaiser prof. bus. adminstrn., prof. econ. and law, 1994—2008. Spl. econ. asst. to asst. atty. gen. for antitrust Dept. Justice,

1966—67; dir. Ctr. for Study of Orgnl. Innovation, U. Pa., 1976—83; cons. in field; Thomas Malthus lectr. Hertfordshire U., England, 2006. Author: The Economics of Discretionary Behavior, 1964; Corp. Control and Bus. Behavior, 1970; Markets and Hierarchies, 1975; The Econ. Instn. of Capitalism, 1985; Econ. Orgn., 1986, Antitrust Economics, 1987; The Mechanisms of Governance, 1996; assoc. editor, Bell. Jour. Econ., 1973-74; editor, 1975-82; co-editor Jour. Law, Econ. and Orgn., 1983—2003. Fellow Ctr. for Advanced Study in Behavioral Sci., 1977-78; Guggenheim fellow, 1977-78; Fulbright scholar, 1999; Am. Acad. Arts and Sci. fellow, 1983; recipient Alexander Henderson Award Carnegie-Mellon U., 1962, Alexander von Humboldt Rsch. prize, 1987, Irwin award Acad. Mgmt., 1988, John von Newmann lectr., 1999, H.C. Recktenwald prize in econs., 2004. Fellow Am. Acad. Polit. and Social Sci., Acad. Internat. Bus. (eminent scholar), Indsl. Orgn. Soc. (disting. fellow 2005), Am. Econ. Assn. (v.p. 2000-01, disting. fellow 2007); mem. NAS, Internat. Soc. for New Instnl. Econ. (pres. 1999-2001), Am. Law and Econ. Assn. (pres. 1997-98), Western Econ. Assn. (pres. 1999-2000). Office: Univ Calif Dept Econ Berkeley CA 94720-0001

WILLIAMSON, PETER DAVID, lawyer; b. Houston, Oct. 13, 1944; s. Sam and Sophie Ann (Kaplan) W.; m. Patricia Golemon; children: Heather, Amber, Asia, Ginger, Anna, Alison, Aaron. BA, U. Ill., 1966; JD, U. Tex., 1969. Bar: Tex. 1969, US Supreme Ct. 1974, US Ct. Appeals (4th, 5th, 6th, 8th, 9th, 10th, 11th and DC cirs.); lic. comml. pilot. Pvt. practice, Houston, 1971—. Founder IMMLAW, The Nat. Consortium of Immigration Law Firms. Mem. Am. Immigration Lawyers Assn. (pres. 1994-95). Home: 1522 Park St Houston TX 77019-5324 Office: Chamberlain Hrdlicka White Williams & Martin 2 Allen Ctr 1200 Smith St # 1400 Houston TX 77002 Home Phone: 281-236-6844; Office Phone: 713-658-2508. Business E-Mail: peter.williamson@chamberlainlaw.com. *I do not believe in the existence of national boundaries. The philosophy of my practice of the law is to help my clients achieve the ability to pass freely through such artificial political barriers.*

WILLIAMSON, R. MARK, lawyer; b. Pensacola, Fla., Oct. 7, 1960; MusB, La. State U., 1981; MusM, U. North Tex., 1983; JD with highest honors, Fla. State U., 1991. Bar: Wis. 1991, Ga. 1996. Assoc. Foley & Lardner Law Firm, Milw.; ptnr., co-leader, wealth planning group Alston & Bird LLP, Atlanta. Adj. prof. law Univ. Wis., Madison, Wis. Exec. editor Fla. Law Rev. Recipient Best Young Author award, Estates and Trusts Mag., 1997. Fellow: Am. Coll. Tax and Estate Counsel; mem.: Order of Coif. Office: Alston & Bird LLP One Atlantic Ctr 1201 W Peachtree St NW Atlanta GA 30309-3424 Office Phone: 404-881-7993. Office Fax: 404-881-7777. Business E-Mail: mwilliamson@alston.com.

WILLIAMSON, RICHARD HALL, federal agency administrator; b. Canton, NC, July 29, 1940; s. James Eustace and Gwendolyn (Nevada) H.; m. Julia Draper Brown, Nov. 7, 1965 (div. Jan. 1981); children: Shawn Nicol, Kevin Carson; m. Janie E. Shaheen, Nov. 18, 1998. BS in Physics, N.C. State U., 1962, MS in Nuclear Engring., 1970, postgrad., 1972. Instr. N.C. State U., Raleigh, 1968-72; chief, energy systems analysis AEC, Washington, 1972-75; asst. dir., energy analysis U.S. Energy R & D Adminstrn., Washington, 1975-77; dir., program analysis U.S. Dept. Energy, Washington, 1977-80, dir., policy devel., 1980-84, dep. asst. sec. for internat. affairs, 1984-94; dep. exec. dir. U.S. Energy Assn., Washington, 1995-99. Bd. dirs. Houston World Energy Congress Inc., 1994-99; chmn. Worth Assocs. Inc., Flint Hill, Va., 1998—2008. Author: A Group Strategy for Energy Research, Development and Demonstration, 1980; contbr. articles to jours. in field. Football ofcl. Atlantic Coast Conf., Greensboro, N.C., 1980-2002, Rose Bowl, Pasadena, Calif., 1995; treas. Sigma Alpha Mu Endowment Fund, 1994—, Sigma Alpha Mu Found., 1989—; treas. St. Simons Island Newcomers Club, 2001—03. 1st lt. U.S. Army, 1962-64; col. USAR, 1964-93. NSF fellow, 1964-65; AEC fellow, 1965-68; recipient Outstanding alumnus award IFC, N.C. State U., 1971, Presdl. Rank award U.S. Dept. Energy, 1990, Atlantic Coast Conf. Svc. to Football Officiating award, 2000. Mem. Atlantic Coast Conf. Ret. Football Ofcls. Assn. (ret. 2003—), Sigma Alpha Mu (nat. pres. 1984-86, Disting. Svc. award, 2007), Tau Beta Pi, Phi Kappa Phi, Omicron Delta Kappa, Sigma Pi Sigma, Pi Mu Epsilon. Republican. Methodist. Avocations: stamp collecting/philately, tennis, golf, skiing. Home: 906 Champney Saint Simons Island GA 31522-5464 Office Phone: 540-675-1250.

WILLIAMSON, RICHARD SALISBURY, lawyer, former ambassador; b. Evanston, Ill., May 9, 1949; s. Donald George Williamson and Marion (Salisbury) W.; m. Jane Thatcher, Aug. 25, 1973; children: Elizabeth Jean, Craig Salisbury, Richard Middleton. AB with honors, Princeton U., 1971; JD, U. Va., 1974. Bar: Ill., 1974, D.C., 1975. Legis. counsel, adminstrv. asst. to Rep. Philip M. Crane US Congress, 1974-76; assoc. Winston & Strawn LLP, Washington, 1977-80, ptnr., 1980, Chgo., 2007—; asst. to Pres. for intergovernmental affairs President's Task Force on Regulatory Relief, 1981-83; perm. rep. to UN US Dept. State, Vienna, 1983-85; sr. v.p., corp. & internat. relations Beatrice Cos., Inc., Chgo., 1985-86; ptnr. Mayer, Brown & Platt LLP, Chgo., 1986—2001; asst. sec. for internat. orgn. affairs US Dept. State, Washington, 1988-89, alt. rep. to UN for special polit. affairs, 2002—07, spl. envoy to Sudan, 2008—09. Chief US Delegation to US-USSR Bilateral Negotiations on Nuclear Nonproliferation, 1983—84, US Delegation, Fourth Gen. Conf. UN Indsl. Org., 1984, US Delegation to Nuclear Nonproliferation Treaty, 1984; mem. Ill. Econ. Bd., 1987—88, Pres. Gen. Adv. Com. on Arms Control & Disarmament, US Arms Control & Disarmament Agy., 1987—93, Nat. Leadership Network, Inst. Contemporary Studies, 1989—2001; bd. advisors Ctr. for Security Policy, 1989—98; mem. UN Assn. USA, 1989—2001, Adminstrv. Conf. US, 1989—92, vice chmn., 1981—83; mem. Fed. Home Loan Bank Bd., Chgo., 1991—94; chmn. Ill. Sec. State Merit Commn., 1993—99, Ill. Regulatory Relief Task Force, 1994—98; co-chmn. Enterprise Works Worldwide, 1996—2001; mem. Gov.-Elect George Ryan's Transition Team, 1998, Panel on Eminent Persons on Strengthening the Effectiveness of the Org. for Security & Cooperation in Europe, 2005, Coun. Fgn. Rels.; sr. adv. Nat. Bush for Pres. Campaign Com., 1987—88, Bush Adminstrn. Transition Team, 1988—89, US Delegation to UN Human Rights Commn., 1987, 89. Editor: Trade & Economic Growth, 1993, United States Foreign Policy and the United Nations System, 1996; co-editor: (with Paul Laxalt) A Changing America: Conservatives View the 80's From the United States Senate, 1980; author: Reagan's Federalism: His Efforts to Decentralize Government, 1990, The United Nations: A Place of Promise and of Mischief, 1991, Disorder in the New World, 1997, Seeking Firm Footing: America in the World in the New Century, 2001. Chmn. Ill. Rep. Party, 1999-2002. Recipient Fgn. Affairs award for Pub. Svc., US Dept. State, 1986, Superior Honor award, 1989, 2004, Award of Merit, Boy Scouts Am., 1996, Global Leadership award, Enterprise World Worldwide, 2001. Mem.: ABA, Washington DC Bar Assn., Ill. State Bar Assn. Republican. Office: Winston & Strawn LLP 35 W Wacker Dr Chicago IL 60601 E-mail: rwilliamson@winston.com.*

WILLIAMSON, SAMUEL RUTHVEN, JR., historian, educator; b. Bogalusa, La., Nov. 10, 1935; s. Samuel Ruthven and Frances Mitchell (Page) Williamson; m. Joan Chaffe Andress, Dec. 30, 1961; children: George Samuel, Treeby Andress, Thaddeus Miller. BA, Tulane U., 1958; AM, Harvard U., 1960, PhD, 1966, grad. in Advanced Mgmt., 1986; degree (hon.), Furman U., Va. Theol. Sem., Centre Coll., The U. of the South, 2006. Asst. prof. U.S. Mil. Acad., 1963—66; from instr. history to asst. dean Harvard U., 1966—69, asst. to dean of Harvard Coll., 1969—70; rsch. assoc. Inst. Politics, faculty assoc. Ctr. for Internat. Affairs, 1971—72; mem. faculty J.F. Kennedy Sch. Govt., 1971—72; from assoc. prof. history to provost U. N.C., Chapel Hill, 1972—84, provost univ., 1984—88; pres., vice chancellor U. of South, Sewanee, Tenn., 1988—2000, vice chancellor emeritus, prof. history, 2000—05, Robert M. Ayres Jr. disting. univ. prof., 2001—05; historiographer U. South, 2008. Cons. historian's office Office of Sec. Def., 1974—76; vis. fellow Churchill Coll., 1976—77; mem. vis. com. Harvard Coll., 1986—92; dir. Rsch. Triangle Inst., 1984—88; mem. bd. visitors Air U., 1994—2002. Author: The Politics of Grand Strategy: Britain and France Prepare for War 1904-1914, 1969, 1990; co-author: The Origins of U.S. Nuclear Strategy, 1945-53, 1993, July 1914: Soldiers, Statesmen, and the Coming of the Great War, 2003; editor: The Origins of a Tragedy, July 1914, 1981, War and Soc. Newsletter, 1973—88; co-editor: Essays on World War I: Origins and Prisoners of War, 1983, Austria-Hungary and the Origins of the First World War, 1991, Sewance Sesgivesentenniel History: In Making University south, 2008, Perspecture on the History of University South, 2009. Mem. cen. com. Morehead Found., 1978—93; vice chmn. bd. visitors Air U., 1996—98, chmn. bd. visitors, 1998—2000. Capt. US Army, 1963—66. Grantee, Ford Found., 1976; fellow, NEH, 1976—77, Nat. Humanities Ctr., 1983; Fulbright scholar, U. Edinburgh, 1958—59, Woodrow Wilson Ctr. scholar, Washington, 2002, Woodrow Wilson fellow, 1958—63, Danforth fellow, 1958—63. Mem.: Nat. Assn. Colls. and Univs. (vice chmn., chmn. bd. dirs. 1993—95), Internat. Inst. Strategic Studies, Am. Hist. Assn. (George Louis Beer prize 1970). Democrat. Episcopalian. Home: PO Box 837 Sewanee TN 37375-0837 Office: U of South duPont Libr Sewanee TN 37383-1000 Business E-Mail: swilliam@sewanee.edu.

WILLIAMSON, SANDRA KAYE, education educator; b. Greenville, Ohio, Aug. 28, 1951; d. James Sherman and Dortha Maria (Mikesell) Clapp; m. John Leslie Williamson, July 5, 1975; children: Bradley, Laura. BS, Ea. Ky. U., 1973, MEd, 1979; PhD, Kent State U., 1999. Cert. tchr., home economist. Educator West Clermont Schs., Amelia, Ohio, 1973—75, Fayette County Schs., Lexington, Ky., 1975—83, U. Akron, Ohio, 1990—93; tchg. fellow Kent State U., Ohio, 1993—95; instrl. technologist Neumann Coll., Aston, Pa., 1996—97; asst. prof. U. Del., Newark, 1997—99, Lincoln U., Pa., 2000—01, Wilmington U., Del., 2001—. Program coord. Tchg.-Learning Instruction: Gifted & Talented Learners, Applied Tech. Edn.; co-editor Interdisciplinary Jour. Problem-Based Learning. Editor: Am. Assn. Family & Consumer Sci., Districts, 1990—93; author: Orientation to Professional Studies: Home Economics, 1992, Nutrition for Healthy Living, 1997, (on-line chat rooms) Treehouses, 2000, Assesment & Evaluation, 2009; editl. cons.: Interdisiplinary Jour. Probelm Based Learning; editor (cons.): (journals) Interdisciplinary Journal of Problem Based Learning. Chmn. PTA, Medina, Ohio, 1986—89; mem. AHEA reaccreditation U. Akron, Akron, 1992—93. Mem.: TEPSIG, Am. Ednl. Rsch. Assn. (presenter Conf. 2005, 2006, session chair tchg. edn. 2007), AERA (editor), Kappa Delta Pi (counselor profl. devel., mem. data subcom.). Avocations: computer technology, emerging technologies. Home: 126 Soltner Dr Kennett Square PA 19348-1445 Office: 31 Read's Way New Castle DE 19720 Business E-Mail: sandra.c.williamson@wilmu.edu.

WILLIAMSON, THOMAS ARNOLD, publishing executive; b. Sagamore, Pa., Oct. 4, 1939; s. Thomas and Mabel (Kennedy) Williamson; m. Kathryn Steiner White, Mar. 1, 1980; 1 child, Thomas J. Grad., Phillips Exeter Acad., 1957; AB, Harvard U., 1961. From sales person to sr. v.p. Harcourt Brace & Co., NYC, 1962—88, sr. v.p., 1988—95; pres. Psychol. Corp., San Antonio, 1982—88; v.p. Holt Rinehart & Winston Harcourt Brace, 1989—95; pres. Harcourt Sch. Publishers, 1989—93, Learning Initiative, Austin, Tex., 1994—, T. Williamson Assocs., Inc., Austin, 1995—2005, Focused Learning, Ltd., Austin, 1998—2005; exec. v.p. Kathryn Williamson Real Estate Inc., Austin, 2003—. Bd. dirs. Lesson Lab, 2001—03, The Austin Project, 2000—08. Co-chmn. vis. com. to psychology dept. U. Tex., Austin, 1986—89, 1995—98; vol., chair chpt. 249 SCORE, 2003—04. Mem.: Hills Country Club, Town and Gown Club, Harvard Club N.Y.C. Office Phone: 512-731-4649, 512-261-0595. Personal E-mail: tawilliamson@austin.rr.com.

WILLIAMSON, THOMAS SAMUEL, JR., lawyer; b. Plainfield, NJ, July 14, 1946; s. Thomas Samuel and Winifred (Hall) W.; married; 2 children. BA, Harvard U., 1968; postgrad., Oxford U., Eng., 1968-69; JD, U. Calif., Berkeley, 1974. Bar: DC 1975, Calif. 1975, US Dist. Ct. (DC) 1977. Dir. tng. div. Alem Pub. Relations, Addis Ababa, Ethiopia, 1970-71; assoc. Covington & Burling, Washington, 1974-78, 81-82, ptnr., employment practice group, 1982—, mem. mgmt. com, 2005—08; dep. inspector gen. US Dept. Energy, Washington, 1978-81; solicitor US Dept. Labor, Washington. Mem. exec. com. Washington Lawyers Civil Rights Under Law, 1983—93, co-chmn., 1990—92; spl. advisor owners' workplace diversity com., gen. mgrs. working group NFL, 2002—. Mem. vis. com. Harvard U. Dept. Athletics, 1985—87; mem. Harvard U. Bd. Overseers, 1997—2003, pres., 2002—03. Recipient Wiley Branton award, Washington Lawyers' Com. Civil Rights and Urban Affairs, 2007; named one of 50 Most Influential Minority Lawyers in America, Nat. Law Jour., 2008; Rhodes scholar, 1968. Mem. ABA, Nat. Bar Assn., Coun. on Fgn. Rels., Washington Coun. Lawyers (bd. dirs. 1975-90). Avocations: camping, bicycling. Office: Covington and Burling LLP PO Box 7566 1201 Pennsylvania Ave NW Washington DC 20004-2401 Office Phone: 202-662-5438. Office Fax: 202-662-6291. Business E-Mail: twilliamson@cov.com.*

WILLIAMSON, WALTER BLAND, lawyer; b. Selma, Ala., Apr. 6, 1938; s. Walter Bland and Tina (Matheny) W.; children: Michael Davis, Amy Caroline; m. Dana Leigh Freiburger, Jan. 2, 1999. BS, Stetson U., 1959; JD, Emory U., 1963. Bar: Okla. 1969, Ga. 1963, U.S. Ct. Mil. Appeals 1963, U.S. Supreme Ct. 1969. Atty. Office Gen. Counsel Fed. Deposit Ins. Corp., Washington, 1967; atty. Office Std. Policy U.S. Dept. Commerce, 1968-69; shareholder Pray, Walker, Jackman, Williamson & Marlar and predecessors, Tulsa, 1969—2008, pres., 1993-98, of counsel, 2008—; sr. v.p. & gen. counsel Laredo Petroleum, 2008—. Steering com. conf. on nuclear power generation Nat. Energy Law and Policy Inst., 1981; adv. com. on natural gas allowables Okla. Corp. Commn., 1983, 88. Mem. Okla. Energy Resources Bd., 1992-95; trustee Grace and Franklin Bernsen Found., Philbrook Mus. Art; bd. dirs. Indian Nations Coun., Boy Scouts Am.; governing bd. Jasmine Moran Childrens Mus. Capt. U.S. Army, 1963-67. Mem. ABA (vice-chmn. natural gas mktg. and transp. com., natural resource sect. 1986-88, co-chmn. energy com. adminstrv. law and regulatory practice sect. 1998-2000), Okla. Bar Assn. (chmn. mineral law sect. 1982), Tulsa County Bar Assn. (chmn. mineral law sect. 1979), Ind. Petroleum Assn. Am. (regional v.p. 1991-95), Okla. Ind. Petroleum Assn. (chmn. legal com. 1979-83, gen. counsel 1983—, Mem. of Yr. 1987), Energy Advocates (coord. 1987-88, 91), Phi Delta Phi. Home: 1228 E 19th St Tulsa OK 74120-7419 Office: 15 W 6th St Ste 1800 Tulsa OK 74119 Home Phone: 918-566-0664; Office Phone: 918-513-4570. Business E-Mail: bwilliamson@laredopetro.com.

WILLIAMSON, WAYNE C., internist, geriatrician; b. Hammond, Ind., 1952; BA, Northwestern U., 1974; MD, U. Cin., 1978. Cert. Am. Bd. Internal Medicine, 1984, in Geriatric Medicine 1992. Intern Rush Presbyn., St. Luke's Med. Ctr., Chgo., 1978—79, resident, internal medicine, 1979—81, physician; asst. prof. Rush Med. Coll.; physician Northwestern Meml. Hosp., 1999—; mem. faculty Steinberg Sch. Medicine, 1999—. Office: Wayne C Williamson Md 17850 Kedzie Ave Ste 3000 Hazel Crest IL 60429-2086 Office Phone: 312-642-7493.

WILLIAMSON, WILLIAM PAUL, JR., journalist; b. Des Moines, Mar. 30, 1929; s. William Paul and Florence Alice (Dawson) W.; m. Vania Torres Nogueira, Nov. 27, 1959; children: Mary Liz, Jon Thadeus, Margaret Ann Student, Mexico City Coll., 1952, U. Havana, 1955; BA, U. No. Iowa, 1953; MA, U. Iowa, 1954. Editor Brazilian Bus., Rio de Janeiro, 1958-60; mng. ptnr. Editora Mory Ltd., Rio de Janeiro, 1960-79; editor Brazil Herald, Rio de Janeiro, 1960-80; exec. dir. Inter Am. Press Assn., Miami, Fla., 1981-94, hon. life mem., mem. adv. coun., 1994—, dir., 1966-80, chmn. awards com., 1975-80. Solo navigator 1st passage Madeira Island, Portugal-Madeira Island, Brazil, 1994-95. Editor for Brazil, Fodor's South America, 1970-79; contbr. articles to various newspapers and mags. Pres. Am. Soc., Rio de Janeiro, 1968; bd. dirs. Instituto Brasil-Estados Unidos, Rio de Janeiro, 1977-80, Am. C. of C. for Brazil, Rio de Janeiro, 1964-68; rear commodore Seven Seas Cruising Assn., 2000—. With USMC, 1946—48, with USMCR, 1948—51. Decorated Order of Rio Branco (Brazil); recipient Citizen of Rio de Janeiro award State Legislature, 1975; Hon. Carioca award O Globo Newspaper, Rio de Janeiro, 1972; Ralph Greenberg award Am. Soc. Rio de Janeiro, 1977; Outstanding Svc. to Freedom of Expression and Newspapers awards Internat. Fedn. of Newspaper Pubs. and Internat. Assn. of Broadcasting, 1994; Benemeritous Citizen award Mcpl. Legislature, Itaquai, Brazil, 1995. Mem. Am. Soc. Assn. Execs., South Fla. Soc. Assn. Execs. (pres. 1987), Soc. Profl. Journalists, Overseas Press Club Am., Brazil Fgn. Corr. Assn. (founder, mem. honor), Rio Yacht Club, Ilha da Madeira Yacht Club, Kappa Tau Alpha. Home: 3051 NE 47th Ct #204 Fort Lauderdale FL 33308-5304 Personal E-mail: billvania@yahoo.com.

WILLIAMS-PAISLEY, KIMBERLY, actress; b. Rye, NY, Sept. 14, 1971; d. Gurney and Linda Williams; m. Brad Paisley, Mar. 15, 2003; children: William Huckleberry, Jasper Warren. Grad., Northwestern U. Actress Creative Artists Agy., Beverly Hills, Calif. Actor: (films) Father of the Bride, 1991, Secret Games, 1992, Indian Summer, 1993, Samuel Beckett Is Coming Soon, 1993, Coldblooded, 1995, Father of the Bride Part II, 1995, The War At Home, 1996, Safe House, 1998, Elephant Juice, 1999, Simpatico, 1999, Ten Tiny Love Stories, 2001, How to Go Out on a Date in Queens, 2006, How to Eat Fried Worms, 2006, We Are Marshall, 2006, (TV films) Stood Up!, 1990, Jake's Women, 1996, Follow the Stars Home, 2001, The Christmas Shoes, 2002, (TV series) Relativity, 1996-97, According to Jim, 2001-09, (TV appearances) The MTV Movie Awards, 1992, Jake's Woman, 1996, The US Olympic Open Golf Championship, 1986; stage appearances: The Last Night of Ballyhoo, 1997, The Vagina Monologues, Speed the Plow; actor, dir., prodr.: (films) Shade, 2006; actor, co-prodr.: (TV films) Lucky 7, 2003, Identity Theft: The Michelle Brown Story, 2004. Spokesperson Elizabeth Glazer Pediatric AIDS Found.; bd. dirs. Earth Comm. Office. Office: c/o Creative Artists Agy 2000 Avenue Of The Stars Los Angeles CA 90067-4700*

WILLIAMS-PERRY, BRENDA LEE, pre-school educator; b. Colorado Springs, Colo., July 24, 1960; d. Arthur Lee and Rebecca Beard; m. Carl Eugene Perry, Jan. 11, 1991; 1 child, Kenneth Earl Williams Jr. AA in Child Devel., Almeda U., Boise, Idaho, 2006; BA in Early Childhood Edn., Almeda U., 2006; MA in Ednl. Adminstrn., Almeda U., Boise, 2006. Child Development Associate's Credential Coun. for Profl. Recognition, 2004, Directorship Certification Tex. Dept. of Protective & Regulatory Services, 2006, G-Tube Feeding Certification Gateway Child Devel. Ctr., 2004, Instructor CPR & First Aid Certified ARC, 2006, Infant Modules USAF, 2004. Dir. San Antonio Urban Ministries, 1999—2001; lead infant tchr. Jewish Cmty. Child Devel. Ctr., San Antonio, 2001—03; child devel. program technician Gateway Child Devel. Ctr., San Antonio, 2003—06; dir. St. Philip's Coll. Child Devel. Ctr., San Antonio, 2006—. Mem.: Nat. Black Child Devel. Inst. (assoc.). Home: 8021 W Military Dr Apt#807 San Antonio TX 78227-1861 Office: St Philip's College Child Dev Center 2207 Wyoming St San Antonio TX 78203 Personal E-mail: brendawilliamsperry@msn.com. E-mail: bwilliam@accd.edu.

WILLIAMS-RUDE, BEATRICE, editor; b. Phila., Apr. 21; d. Abraham and Sophie Walfish; m. Alan Rude, Apr. 17, 1998; 1 stepchild, A. James Rude; m. Robert Colburn Williams; 1 child, Mark Colburn Williams. BPS, Pace U., NYC, 1974; MALS, NYC, 1980. Rschr., reviewer, writer, 2002—; asst. Dale Wasserman's NYC. Mem.: NY Hist. Soc., Medici Archives Project, Nat. Arts Club. Avocation: opera. Home: 311 W 24 St New York NY 10011

WILLIAMS-THIERRY, ELIZABETH A., financial planner, consultant; b. San Francisco, Jan. 16, 1948; d. John and Myrtle Mary (Thierry) W.; children: Brian, Jonathan. Degree, U. Calif., 1979, MBA. Manpower coord., fed. programs U.S. Govt., San Francisco; patient svc. rep. Health Care Svc., Oakland, Calif.; ins. and real estate cons.; pres. Investments Unlimited, Oakland, EWJ & Assocs. Mktg. Firm; planning commr. City of Pitts.; CEO Ultimate Vacations Inc. Human rels. commr. Contra Costa County. Recipient Pub. Speaking award, Grand Juror award Contra Costa County; European Investment fellow. Mem. AAUW, NAFE, NAACP, Nat. Real Estate Owners Assn., Nat. Notary Assn., Order Ea. Star, Heroines Jericho, Daus. Isis, Soroptimist Inc., Toastmistress Club, Beta Phi Sigma. Home: PO Box 523 Pittsburg CA 94565-0052

WILLIE, CHARLES VERT, social sciences educator; b. Dallas, Oct. 8, 1927; s. Louis James and Carrie (Sykes) W.; m. Mary Susannah Conklin, Mar. 31, 1962; children: Sarah Susannah, Martin Charles, James Theodore. BA, Morehouse Coll., 1948, DHL (hon.), 1983; MA, Atlanta U., 1949; PhD, Syracuse U., 1957, DHL (hon.), 1992, Berkley Divinity Sch., Yale U., 1972, RI Coll., 1983, Johnson C. Smith U., Charlotte, NC, 1991, Franklin Pierce Coll., Rindge, NH, 1996, Haverford Coll., 2000; DD (hon.), Gen. Sem., 1974, Episcopal Div. Sch., 2004; MA (hon.), Harvard U., 1974; DL (hon.), Framingham State Coll., Mass., 1992; D of Engring. Tech. (hon.), Wentworth Inst. Tech., 1996; D of Canon Law (hon.), Seabury-Western Theol. Sem., 2005; DHL (hon.), Emerson Coll., 2008. Instr. to asst. prof. sociology Syracuse U., 1952-63, assoc. prof., 1964-67, prof., 1968-74, chmn. dept. sociology, 1967-71, v.p., 1972-74; prof. edn. and urban studies Grad. Sch. Edn. Harvard U., Cambridge, Mass., 1974-98, Charles William Eliot prof. edn. Grad. Sch. Edn., 1998-99, prof. emeritus Grad. Sch. Edn., 1999—. Instr. dept. preventive medicine SUNY Upstate Med. Ctr., Syracuse, 1955-60; rsch. dir. Washington Action for Youth delinquency prevention project, Pres.' Com. on Juvenile Delinquency and Youth Crime, Washington, 1962-64; vis. lectr. dept. psychiatry Harvard U. Med. Sch., Boston, 1966-67; vis. lectr. Episcopal Divsn. Sch., Cambridge, Mass., 1966-67; commr. Pres.'s Commn. on Mental Health, 1977-78; mem. tech. adv. bd. Maurice Falk Med. Fund, 1968-99; bd. dirs. Social Sci.

Rsch. Coun., 1969-75; master Boston Sch. Desegregation case, Fed. Dist. Ct., 1975; mem. nat. adv. com. Maxwell Sch. Syracuse U., 1992-2000, Hogg Found. Mental Health, 1998-02, Morehouse Rsch. Inst., 1997-02; bd. overseers Boston Sci. Mus., 1997-2001, overseer emeritus, 2002—; corporator Emerson Hosp., Concord, Mass., 1998-2006; chmn. bd. dirs. Judge Baker Children's Ctr., Boston, 2001-03; mem. nat. adv. com. The History-Makers, 2002-06. Author: Church Action in the World, 1969, The Family Life of Black People, 1970, (with A. McCord) Black Students at White Colleges, 1972, (with J. Beker-)Race Mixing in the Public Schools, 1973, (with B. Brown and B. Kramer) Racism and Mental Health, 1973, Black/Brown/White Relations, 1977, Oreo, 1975, (with R. Edmonds) Black Colleges in America, 1978, (with R. Reddick) A New Look at Black Families, 1976, 5th edit., 2003, The Sociology of Urban Education, 1978, The Caste and Class Controversy on Race and Poverty, 1979, 2d edit., 1989, The Ivory and Ebony Towers, 1981, (with S. Greenblatt) Community Politics and Educational Change, 1981, Race, Ethnicity and Socioeconomic Status, 1983, School Desegregation Plans That Work, 1984, Black and White Families, 1985, Five Black Scholars, 1986, (with Michael Grady) Metropolitan School Desegregation, 1986, Effective Education, 1987, (with Inabeth Miller) Social Goals and Educational Reforms, 1988, (with Michael Grady and Richard Hope) African-Americans and the Doctoral Experience, 1991, (with A. Garibaldi and W. Reed), The Education of African-Americans, 1991, Theories of Human Social Action, 1994, (with P. Rieker, B. Kramer and B. Brown) Mental Health, Racism and Sexism, 1995, (with Michael Alves) Controlled Choice, 1996, (with Ralph Edwards) Black Power/White Power in Public Education, 1998, (with Edwards and Alves) Student Diversity, Choice and School Improvement, 2002, (with R. Reddick and R. Brown) The Black College Mystique, 2006, (with S. Ridini and D. Willard) Grass Roots Social Action, 2008. Hon. trustee Episcopal Div. Sch., Cambridge; invited mem. United Negro Coll. Fund, pres. assembly, 1983-90; chair bd. dirs. Dana McLean Greeley Found. for Peace and Justice, 1989-92; mem. nat. exec. coun. Episcopal ch., 1967-74, v.p. gen. conv. House of Deps., 1970-74; host Inner City Beat nat. pub. affairs weekly TV program, monitor channel, 1991-92, metro ctr. exec. coun, NYU Sch. Edn., 2008-. Recipient Faculty Svc. award Nat. Univ. Ext. Assn., 1969, 50th Anniversary Disting. Alumnus award Syracuse U. Maxwell Sch., 1974, Spirit of Pub. Svc. award, 1994, Lee-Founders award Soc. for Study Social Problems, 1983, Family Scholar award, 1986, Disting. Career Contbn. award com. on role and status of minorities in edn. Am. Ednl. Rsch. Assn., 1990, Benjamin E. Mays Svc. award Morehouse Coll., 1994, Father John LaFarge, S.J. award Fairfield U., 1995, Disting. Career award Assn. Black Sociologists, 1996, Outstanding Book award for mental health, racism and sexism Myers Ctr. for Study of Human Rights, 1996, Arents Alumni award Syracuse U., 2000, Outstanding Tchr. award, Harvard U., 2005, US Spkr. and Specialist Grant award, US State Dept., The Bahamas, 2007. Fellow Am. Ednl. Rsch. Assn.; mem. Am. Sociol. Assn. (coun. 1980-83, 95-98, v.p. 1996-97, DuBois-Johnson-Frazier award 1994, William Foote Whyte award 2004, Career Disting. Scholarship award 2005), Ea. Sociol. Soc. (past pres., Robin M. Williams Disting. Lectureship award, 1994, Outstanding Contbn. award 2006, Merit award, 2006, Sorokin lectr. 2006), Am. Assn. Blacks Higher Edn. (Lifetime Achievement award, 2009), Phi Beta Kappa, Alpha Phi Alpha. Episcopalian. Home: 41 Hillcrest Rd Concord MA 01742-4615 Office: Harvard U Grad Sch Edn 410 Gutman Libr 6 Appian Way Cambridge MA 02138-3704 Office Phone: 978-369-2363. Home Fax: 978-371-1529. Personal E-mail: cvmswillie@comcast.net, cvmswillie@aol.com.

WILLIFORD, SANDRA SIMMONS, music educator; b. Anderson, SC, Nov. 6, 1972; d. Rocshell Simmons II; m. William Lamont Williford, June 22, 2006; children: Paris Monet, A'Lonzo Nygel. BA in Music, Ch., Charleston So. U., SC, 1995; B in Music Edn., Anderson U., SC, 1998; MEd, So. Wesleyan U., Central, SC, 2003. Cert. tchr. music S.C. Tchr. gen. music, choir dir. Parker Acad., Greenville, SC, 1998—99; tchr. gen. music, chorus Hughes Acad., Greenville, 1999—2000; tchr. gen. music, instr. performing arts, choir dir., coach step team Varennes Elem. Sch., Anderson, 2000—. Chairperson Parents and the Cmty. Varennes Elem. Sch., 2005—06. Vol. Adopt-A-Hwy., Anderson, 2004—. Recipient Golden Apple, Anderson Sch. Dist. #5, 2005—06; grantee, Donors Choose Grants, 2005—06. Mem.: Zeta Phi Beta. Avocations: singing, reading, movies. Home: 2504 McGaha Dr Anderson SC 29626 Office: Varennes Elem Sch 1820 Hwy 29 S Anderson SC 29626 Office Phone: 864-260-5215. E-mail: sandrawilliford@andersons.net.

WILLIG, BARBARA ADELE, music educator; b. Phila., Apr. 24, 1941; d. Paul and Jeanne Willig; 1 child, Julie Rose Braman. B Music Edn., Temple U., 1963, M Music Edn., 1976, supervision cert., 1982. Cert. music, vocal tchr., supr. Pa. Coord. music theater, accompanist Abington Mus. Theatre, Pa., 1984—87; co-dir. music theater workshop Bucks County CC, Richboro, Pa., 1990—98; mentor tchr. for student tchrs. Phila. Sch Dist.; supr. student tchrs. Drexel U., Phila.; cons., artist-in-residence Phila. Sch. Dist. Presenter, writer grants in field; leader arts groups, presenter Phila. Sch. Dist., 1988—96; devel. presch. music workshops Settlement Music Sch. Author curriculum materials; composer, condr.: sabbath svc. record and performance Chants for Peace, 1972; co-dir.: Pa. premier performance Alice in Wonderland. Vol. various election campaigns, 1990—; mem., sec., v.p. B'Nai B'Rith Educators Unit, Phila., 1992—. Recipient Svc. to Cmty. award, B'Nai B'Rith Educators Unit, 1993, Tchr. of Excellence award, Chapel of Four Chaplains. Mem.: LWV, Am. Choral Dirs. Assn., Nat. Orff Assn., Pa. Music Educators Assn., Music Educators Nat. Conf., Temple U. Boyer Coll. Music Alumni Assn. (pres.-elect 2005), Phi Delta Kappa. Avocations: fitness, tai chi, theater, travel, languages. Home: 813 Roslyn Ave Glenside PA 19038

WILLIG, ROBERT DANIEL, economics professor; b. Bklyn., Jan. 16, 1947; s. Jack David and Meg W.; m. Virginia Mason, July 8, 1973; children: Jared Mason, Scott Mason, Brent Mason, Alexandra Mason. BA, Harvard U., 1967; MS in Ops. Rsch., Stanford U., 1968, PhD in Econs, 1973. Lectr. Stanford U., Palo Alto, Calif., 1971-73; tech. staff Bell Labs., Holmdel, NJ, 1973-77, supr. dept. econs. rsch., 1977-78; prof. econs. and pub. affairs Princeton U., 1978—; task force on future of postal svc. Aspen Inst., 1978-80; dep. asst. atty. gen. U.S. Dept. Justice, Washington, 1989-91. Cons. in field; rsch. fellow U. Warwick, Eng., 1977; organizing com. Telecom Policy Rsch. Conf., 1977-78; rsch. adv. bd. Am. Enterprise Inst., 1980-88; mem. N.J. Gov.'s Task Force on Market-Based Pricing of Electricity, 1987; bd. dirs. Consultants in Industry Econs., Inc., 1992-2005, Competition Policy Assocs., Inc.; 2002-2005, mem. Def. Sci. Bd. Task Force on Antitrust for the Def. Industry, 1993-94, Transp. Rsch. Bd. Task Force, 1995-96; advisor Inter-Am. Devel. Bank, 1997-00; sr. cons. Compass, 2006—08; sr. cons., Compass Lexecon, 2008-. Author: Welfare Analysis of Policies Affecting Prices and Products, 1973, Contestable Markets and the Theory of Industry Structure, 1982; editor: Handbook of Industrial Organization, 1986, Can Privatization Deliver: Infrastructure for Latin America, 1999, Second Generation Reforms in Infrastructure Services, 2002; contbr. articles to profl. jours.; mem. editl. bd. MIT Press Series on Govt. Regulation, 1978-1989, Am. Econ. Rev., 1980-83, Jour. Indsl. Econs., 1985-89, Utility Policy, 1989-2001. Adv. bd. B'nai B'rith Hillel Found., Princeton U., 1978-89, Competition and Regulation Network Industries, 2009-. Grantee, NSF, 1979—85. Fellow Econometric Soc. (program com. 1978-81); mem. Am. Econ. Assn. (nominating com. 1980-81). Office: Princeton Univ Economics Dept Princeton NJ 08540

WILLINGHAM, CLARK SUTTLES, lawyer; b. Houston, Nov. 29, 1944; s. Paul Suttles and Elsie Dell (Clark) W.; m. Jane Joyce Hitch, Aug. 16, 1969; children: Meredith Moores, James Barrett. BBA, Tex. Tech U., 1967; JD, So. Meth. U., 1971, LLM, 1984. Bar: Tex. 1971. Ptnr. Kasmir, Willingham & Krage, Dallas, 1972—86, Finley, Kumble et al, Dallas, 1986—87, Brice & Mankoff, Dallas, 1988—98, Moseley Law PC, Dallas, 1999—2008, Barnes & Harrington PC, Dallas, 2008—. Contbr. articles to profl. jours. Bd. dirs. Dallas Summer Musicals, 1971—, exec. com., 1979-93, 97-2003, pres. 1994. Mem. ABA (chmn. agrl. com. tax sect. 1984-86), State Bar Tex. (chmn. agrl. tax com. 1985-87), Dallas Bar Assn., Am. Law Inst., Natl. Cattlemans Found.(trustee 2004-), Tex Ag Land Trust(trustee 2006-), Tex. Rangers Law Enforcement Assn.(bd. dirs.), Nat. Cattlemen's Beef Assn. (bd. dirs., pres. 1998), U.S. Meat Export Fedn. (exec. com. 1991-93), Beef Industry Coun. (exec. com. 1990-91, promotion chmn. 1992-94), Tex. Cattle Feeders Assn. (bd. dirs., pres. 1988), Tex. Bd. Vet. Med. Examiners (pres. 1994), Tex. Beef Coun. (bd. dirs., pres. 1989), Nat. Cattlemen's Found. (trustee 2004-), Tex. Agrl. Land Trust (trustee 2006-), Dallas Country Club. Republican. Episcopalian. Office: Barnes & Harrington PC 4515 Prentice Ste 201 Dallas TX 75206 Home: 3705 Haynie Ave Dallas TX 75205-1205 Home Phone: 214-526-7008; Office Phone: 214-525-3940. E-mail: clarkw@airmail.net.

WILLINGHAM, EDWARD BACON, JR., ecumenical minister, administrator; b. St. Louis, July 27, 1934; s. Edward and Harriet W.; m. Angeline Walton Pettit, June 14, 1957; children: Katie, Carol. BS in Physics, U. Richmond, 1956; postgrad., U. Rochester, 1958—59; MDiv., Colgate Rochester Div. Sch., 1960. Ordained to ministry Am. Bapt. Ch., 1960. Min. Christian edn. Delaware Ave. Bapt. Ch., Buffalo, 1960-62; dir. radio and TV Met. Detroit Coun. Chs., 1962-75; exec. dir. Christian Communication Coun. Met. Detroit Chs., 1976-98. Broadcast cons. Mich. Coun. Chs., 1965-75; guest cons. religious broadcasting Germany, 1968; coord. com. Mich. Ecumenical Forum, 1986, 90-92, chmn., 1991-92. Bd. mgrs. Broadcasting and Film Commn., Nat. Coun. Chs., 1965-73; mem. Muslim-Christian-Jewish Leadership Forum, 1987-98; bd. deacons 1st Bapt. Ch. Birmingham, chmn., 1994-95. Recipient Gabriel award Cath. Broadcasting Assn., 1972, 1st Ann. Ecumenical award Am. Bapt. Chs. Mich., 1992, Race Rels. award Booker T. Washington Bus. Assn. Detroit, 1983, Brotherhood award Bethel AME Ch., Detroit, 2000 Mem. Assn. Regional Religious Communicators (pres. 1969-71), World Assn. Christian Comm. (cen. com. 1973-78, chmn. N.Am. Broadcast sect. 1970-71, bus. mgr., 1972-98, Pioneer in Religious Comm. award 2004), Phi Gamma Delta. Office: 21440 Lathrup St Southfield MI 48075-4218

WILLINGHAM, JEANNE MAGGART, performing company executive, educator; b. Fresno, Calif., May 8, 1923; d. Harold F. and Gladys (Ellis) Maggart. Student, Tex. Woman's U., 1942; student profl. dancing schs. worldwide. Tchr. dance Beaux Arts Dance Studio, Pampa, Tex., 1948—; artistic dir. Pampa Civic Ballet, 1972—. Mem. Tex. Arts and Humanities Coun., Tex. Arts Alliance, Pampa C. of C. (fine arts com.), Pampa Fine Arts Assn. Office: Pampa Civic Ballet Beaux Arts Dance Studio 315 N Nelson St Pampa TX 79065-6013 Office Phone: 806-669-6361.

WILLINGHAM, MARY MAXINE, fashion retailer; b. Childress, Tex., Sept. 12, 1928; d. Charles Bryan and Mary (Bohannon) McCollum; m. Welborn Kiefer Willingham, Aug. 14, 1950; children: Sharon, Douglas, Sheila. BA, Tex. Tech U., 1949. Interviewer Univ. Placement Svc., Tex. Tech U., Lubbock, 1964-69; owner, mgr. buyer Maxine's Accent, Lubbock, 1969—. Speaker in field. Leader Campfire Girls, Lubbock, 1964-65; sec. Cmty. Theatre, Lubbock, 1962-64. Recipient Golden Sun award Dallas Market, 1985, Woman of Excellence award in Bus., YWCA, 2001; named Outstanding Mcht., Fashion Retailer Mag., 1971, also Outstanding Retailer. Mem. Federated Clubs (Temple, Tex.) Office Phone: 254-947-0933.

WILLINGHAM, TYRONE, college football coach; b. Kinston, NC, Dec. 30, 1953; m. Kim Willingham; children: Cassidy, Kelsey, Nathaniel. Degree in phys. edn., Mich. State U., East Lansing, 1977. Grad. asst. Mich. State U., 1977, secondary, spl. teams coach, 1980—82; secondary coach Ctrl. Mich. U., Mt. Pleasant, 1978—79; secondary, spl. teams coach NC State U., Raleigh, 1983—85; receivers, spl. teams coach Rice U., Houston; running backs coach Stanford U., Calif., 1989—91, head coach, 1995—2001; running backs coach Minn. Vikings, 1992—94; head coach U. Notre Dame, Ind., 2002—04, U. Wash., Seattle, 2005—. Pres. Am. Football Coaches Assn., 2008—. Former bd. mem. Opportunities Industrialization Ctr. West; former nat. adv. bd. mem. Stanford U. Haas Ctr. Pub. Svc. Recipient Medal of Honor, Big 10 Conf., 1977, Nat. Coach the Yr., Black Coaches Assn., 1995, 1996, Male Coach the Yr., 2002, Coach the Yr., Pac 10 Conf., 1995, 1999, Eddie Robinson Coach of Distinction award, State Farm, 2000, Nat. Coach the Yr., ESPN/Home Depot, 2002, Coll. Coach the Yr., Scripps, 2002, George Munger award, Coll. Coach the Yr., Maxwell Football Club, 2002, Sportsman the Yr. award, The Sporting News, 2002. Mem.: Am. Football Coaches Assn. (mem. rules com., child identification spokesman, pres. 2008, Region 5 Coach the Yr. 1999). Office: Dept Athletics Univ Wash Box 354070 Graves Bldg Seattle WA 98195 Office Phone: 206-543-2210.

WILLINGHAM, WARREN WILLCOX, psychologist; b. Rome, Ga., Mar. 1, 1930; s. Calder Baynard and Eleanor (Willcox) W.; m. Anna Michal, Mar. 17, 1954; children: Sherry, Judith, Daniel. Student, Ga. Inst. Tech., 1952; PhD, U. Tenn., 1955. Rsch. assoc. World Book Co., NYC, 1959-60; dir. evaluation studies Ga. Inst. Tech., Atlanta, 1960-64; dir. rsch. Coll. Bd., NYC, 1964-68, dir. access rsch. office Palo Alto, Calif., 1968-72; asst. v.p., disting. rsch. scientist Ednl. Testing Svc., Princeton, NJ, 1972—. Vis. prof. U. Minn., 1988; mem. adv. bd. on ednl. requirements on Sec. Navy, 1968; leader Psychometric Seminar, Nat. Inst. Testing and Evaluation, Jerusalem, 1999; cons. to numerous schs., colls. U.S. Office Edn. Author: Free Access Higher Education, 1970, Source Book for Higher Education, 1973, College Placement and Exemption, 1974, Assessing Experiential Learning, 1977, Selective Admissions in Higher Education, 1977, Personal Qualities and College Admissions, 1982, Success in College, 1985, Testing Handicapped People, 1988, Predicting College Grades, 1990; Gender and Fair Assessment, 1997; editor: Measurement in Education, 1969-72; mem. editl. bd. Jour. Ednl. Measurement, 1971-75, Alternate Higher Edn., 1976-80, Am. Ednl. Rsch. Jour., 1968-71; contbr. articles, tech. reports to profl. jours. Served to lt. USNR, 1955-59. Recipient Ann. award So. Soc. Philosophy and Psychology, 1958 Fellow Am. Psychol. Assn., AAAS; mem. Nat. Council on Measurement in Edn. (dir.), Am. Ednl. Research Assn., Am. Psychol. Soc., CAEL (hon. life mem.), Sigma Xi. Mailing: 131 Bertrand Dr Princeton NJ 08540

WILLIS, ARLENE M., legislative staff member; m. Jerry Lewis; 4 stepchildren; 3 children from previous marriage. Legal asst. for several San Bernardino and LA law firms; dist. office asst., Rep. Jerry Pettis US House of Reps., Calif., 1967—68, adminstrv. asst., chief of staff to Rep. Jerry Lewis Washington, 1978—; adminstrv. asst., Assemblyman Jerry Lewis Calif. State Assembly, Calif., 1968—78. Active Found. and Guilds for Loma Linda U. Children's Hosp., Boys and Girls Club, Found. Fighting Blindness, N St. Village. Recipient Pettis award, Loma Linda U. Children's Hosp., 2006. Republican. Office: 2112 Rayburn House Office Bldg Washington DC 20515 Office Phone: 202-225-5861. Office Fax: 202-225-6498.*

WILLIS, BEN, writer, artist; b. Racine, Wis., Dec. 4, 1930; s. Ben Sherlock Willis and Beryl Hester (Smith) Young; div. 1971. Attended, Phila. Coll. Art, 1953—54, Pa. Acad. Fine Arts, 1954—55, Academie Julian, Paris, 1955—57. Author: The Tao of Art, 1987, reprint edit., 2001; collaborator: The Art of Oriental Embroidery, 1980; exhibited in group shows Salmagundi Club, N.Y.C., 1971-75, 1980, Am. Watercolor Soc., Nat. Acad. Design, N.Y.C., 1978, Cicchinelli Galleries, N.Y.C., 1980, Nat. Arts Club, N.Y.C., 1980, Manasquan Group Artists, 1981, Pastel Soc., N.Y.C., 1982, Allied Artists Am., N.Y.C., 1982, Am. Artists Profl. League, N.Y.C., 1984; represented in numerous pvt. collections. Seaman 1st class, USN, 1948-52, Korea. Recipient 1st prize N.Y.C. Ctr., 1960, Manasquan Outdoor Art Show, 1981, Best in Show award Manasquan Group Artists, 1981, others. Fellow Alumni Fellowship Pa. Acad. Fine Art, Author's Guild. Episcopalian. Avocations: languages, music, reading, Judo. Home: 10 C Bennington Ln Whiting NJ 08759-1621

WILLIS, BEVERLY ANN, architect; d. Ralph William and Margaret Amanda (Porter) W. BFA, U. Hawaii, 1954; PhD in Fine Arts (hon.), Mt. Holyoke Coll., 1983. Registered architect, Calif. Prin. Willis Atelier, Honolulu, 1954-58, Willis & Assocs., Inc., San Francisco, 1958-88. Pres. Beverly Willis Architecture Found., 2002—; pres., dir. Architecture Rsch. Inst., Inc., NYC, 1993—2005; co-chair Rebuild Downtown Our Town Coalition, 2002; prof. Internat. Women's U., Kassel, Germany, 2000. Author: Invisible Images: The Silent Language of Architecture, 1997; contbg. author: City and Gender-International Discourse on Gender, Urbanism and Architecture, 2003, Creating Sustainable Urban Environments: Future Forms and Design for Sustainable Cities, 2005; prin. works include Union St. Stores (merit award San Francisco AIA, award of distinction State of Calif.), Nob Hill Cts. (merit award AIA), 1970, Margaret Hayward Park (grand and merit awards Pacific Coast Bldg. Con., Honor award Design Internat.), 1983, San Francisco Ballet Bldg., 1984, Manhattan Village Acad. H.S., N.Y.C., 1995; contbr. articles to profl. jours., chpts. to books. Founding trustee Nat. Bldg. Mus., Washington, 1976—, mem. bd. infrastructure and the constructed environ., 1971-79, chair fed. facility coun., 1976-79; pres. Beverly Willis Arch. Found., NYC, 2002—, Mus. Modern Art Program, 2007. Recipient Phoebe Hearst Gold Medal award, 1969. Fellow AIA (v.p. Calif. coun. 1979, pres. 1980); mem. Achievement Rewards for Coll. Scientists, Internat. Women's Forum, Lambda Alpha (pres. San Francisco chpt. 1981-82), Villa Taverna and Nat. Arts Club. Avocations: poetry, sketching, tennis. Office: 2 Columbus Ave New York NY 10023 Office Phone: 212-577-1200.

WILLIS, BRIAN G., chemistry professor; PhD, MIT, Cambridge, Mass. Mem. tech. staff Bell Laboratories, Lucent Techs., Murray Hill, NJ, 1999—2002; asst. prof. CHE Dept. U. Del., Newark; assoc. prof. CMBE Dept. UConn, Storrs, Conn., 2009—. Contbr. scientific papers. Recipient NSF Career award, NSF, 2003; grant, Office Naval Rsch., Dept. Energy, Intel Corp., U. Del. Rsch. Found. Mem.: AIChE. Achievements include patents pending for monolithic nanoscopic tunnel junctions. Office: CMBE Dept Univ Conn 191 Auditorium Rd Unit 3222 Storrs Mansfield CT 06269 Business E-Mail: bgwillis@engr.uconn.edu.

WILLIS, BRUCE, actor; b. Idar-Oberstein, Fed. Republic Germany, Mar. 19, 1955; came to U.S., 1957; s. David and Marlene Willis; m. Demi Moore, Nov. 21, 1987 (div. Oct. 18, 2000); children: Rumer Glenn, Scout Larue, Tallulah Belle; m. Emma Heming, March 22, 2009 Student, Montclair State Coll.; studied with Stella Adler. Mem. First Amendment Comedy Theatre. Actor: (off-Broadway prodns.) Heaven and Earth, 1977, Fool for Love, 1984, The Bullpen, The Bayside Boys, The Ballad of Railroad William; (films) The First Deadly Sin, 1980, The Verdict, 1982, Blind Date, 1987, Sunset, 1988, Die Hard, 1988, In Country, 1989, (voice only) Look Who's Talking, 1989, Die Hard 2: Die Harder, 1990, (voice only) Look Who's Talking Too, 1990, The Bonfire of the Vanities, 1990, Mortal Thoughts, 1991, Hudson Hawk, 1991, Billy Bathgate, 1991, The Last Boy Scout, 1991, Death Becomes Her, 1992, Striking Distance, 1993, Color of Night, 1994, North, 1994, Pulp Fiction, 1994, Nobody's Fool, 1994, Die Hard With a Vengeance, 1995, 12 Monkeys, 1995, Four Rooms, 1995, Last Man Standing, 1996, The Jackal, 1997, The Fifth Element, 1997, Mercury Rising, 1998, Armageddon, 1998, The Siege, 1998, Breakfast of Champions, 1999, The Sixth Sense, 1999, The Story of Us, 1999, The Kid, 2000, Unbreakable, 2000, Bandits, 2001, Hart's War, 2002, Grand Champion, 2002, True West, 2002, Tears of the Sun, 2003, (voice only) Rugrats Go Wild!, 2003, Charlie's Angels: Full Throttle, 2003, The Whole Ten Yards, 2004, Hostage, 2005, Sin City, 2005, Alpha Dog, 2006, Lucky Number Slevin, 2006, (voice only) Over the Hedge, 2006, Fast Food Nation, 2006, The Astronaut Farmer, 2007, Grindhouse (Planet Terror segment), 2007, Perfect Stranger, 2007, Live Free or Die Hard, 2007, Assassination of a High School President, 2008, What Just Happened, 2008; (TV appearances) Miami Vice, 1984, The Twilight Zone, 1985, Ally McBeal, 1999, Friends (3 episodes), 2000, That 70's Show, 2005; (TV series) Moonlighting, 1985-89 (People's Choice award 1986, Emmy award 1987, Golden Globe award 1987) actor, prodr.: (films) The Whole Nine Yards, 2000, 16 Blocks, 2006; exec. prodr.: Crocodile Hunter: The Collision Course, 2002, The Hip Hop Project, 2006; (TV movies) True West, 2002; (TV episodes) Touching Evil (12 episodes), 2004; singer (albums) The Return of Bruno, 1987, If It Don't Kill You, It Just Makes You Stronger, 1989; performer (concert film) The Return of Bruno, 1988 Named Internat. Broadcasting Man of Yr. Hollywood Radio and TV Soc.; recipient Star on Walk of Fame, 1998, People Choice award, 2000, Order of Arts & Letters, Govt. France, 2005; named one of The 100 Most Powerful Celebrities, Forbes.com, 2008*

WILLIS, BRUCE DONALD, retired judge; b. Mpls., Jan. 29, 1941; s. Donald Robert and Marie Evelyn (Edwards) W.; m. Elizabeth Ann Runsvold, July 17, 1971; children: Andrew John, Ellen Elizabeth. BA in English, Yale U., 1962; LLB, Harvard U., 1965. Bar: Minn., 1965, U.S. Dist. Ct. Minn. 1965, U.S. Ct. Fed. Claims 1989, U.S. Ct. Appeals (8th cir.) 1991, U.S. Supreme Ct. 1992. Assoc. Popham, Haik, Schnobrich & Kaufman, Ltd., Mpls., 1965-71, ptnr., 1971-95; judge Minn. Ct. Appeals, 1995—2008. Mem. jud. adv. bd. Law and Orgnl. Econs. Ctr., U. Kans., 1997—2001; adv. bd. Minn. Inst. Legal Edn., 1986—2003. Contbr. articles to profl. jours. Del. Rep. Nat. convs., 1976, 88; vice chmn. Ind.-Rep. Party Minn., 1979-81; mem. State Ethical Practices Bd., 1990-95, sec. 1990-91, vice chmn. 1991-92, chmn., 1992-93; mem. Minn. Commn. on Jud. Selection, 1991-94; mem. Minn. Bd. Jud. Stds., 1997—2005; mem. adv. com. on rules of civil appellate procedure Minn.

Supreme Ct., 1997—; mem. Evang. Luth. Ch. in America; mem. professionalism com. State Bar Assn., mem. judiciary com. Named one of 1990's Lawyers of Yr., Minn. Jour. Law and Politics, 1991, one of Minn.'s Best Trial Lawyers, Minn. Lawyer, 1991. Home: 2940 Walnut Grove Ln N Plymouth MN 55447-1567 Home Phone: 763-473-6845. Personal E-mail: willis.bruce@gmail.com.

WILLIS, CLAYTON, broadcaster, government official, educator, arts consultant; b. Washington, Aug. 11, 1933; s. William H. and Elizabeth Carl (Keferstein) W. Student, Sorbonne, Paris, 1953-54; BA, George Washington U., 1957; student, U. Oslo, 1953; grad., NY Inst. Fin., 1966, Assn. Commodities Exch. Firms Inc., 1966. Spl. assignment Am. Embassy, London, 1957; writer NBC Network radio show Tex and Jinx, 1958; spl. corr. NBC News, La Paz, Bolivia, 1959; spl. Washington corr. Fin. News TV Network (now CNBC), NYC, 1988; contbr., anchor, TV prodr., corr. Saudi Arabian TV, Newsweek mag., Phillips News Svc. Hope (Ark.) Star; contbr., corr. Christian Sci. Monitor, LA Times-Mirror Syndicate, Greenwich (Conn.) Time, Fin. News TV Network, New York, Mainichi, Tokyo, China Post, Taipei, Taiwan, Chattanooga Times, Nashville Tennesseean, Daily Nation of Kenya, Khartoum Echo, Sudan, The Washington Daily News, Washington Post, Cape Argus of Capetown, South Africa, Bangkok Post, Irish Times, Dublin; reporter, movie, art critic Albuquerque Tribune, 1959-61; asst. editor Newsweek Mag., NYC, 1961-62; TV broadcaster-writer UPI Newsfilm, NYC, 1962; White House corr., chief bur., anchor World Radio News, Houston; White House, Washington corr. WAVA Radio Sta., Washington, 1963-65; editorial writer, corr. Hearst Newspapers, NYC, 1965; press officer UN, NYC, 1965-66; spl. assignment Am. Embassy, Reykjavik, Iceland, 1967; editorial writer, critic, corr. NY Amsterdam News, NYC, 1967-68; cons. govt., law, and ethics programs Ford Found., NYC, 1968-69; dir. pub. affairs US EEOC, Washington, 1969-70; cons. OEO, Washington, 1970, Pres.'s Nat. Coun. on Indian Opportunity, Washington, 1970-71, Cmty. Rels. Svc., US Dept. Justice, Washington, 1970-73, Cabinet Com. on Opportunities for Spanish-Speaking People, 1971-72, Fed. Energy Adminstrn., Washington, 1973-74; dir. pub. affairs Office of Petroleum Allocation, U.S. Dept. Interior, 1973-74; dir. Congl. rels., dir. pub. affairs Pres.'s Nat. Commn. on Fire Prevention and Control, 1971-73; pub., editor, owner Four Corners Chieftain, Ignacio and Durango, Colo., 1972-73; lectr. Sch. of Bus., U. DC, Washington, 1973-74; owner, White House corr., photojournalist Willis News Svc., Washington, 1974—; pub. affairs dir. Inaugural Vets. Com., 1976-77. Adviser to Fernando E.C. de Baca, spl. asst. to the Pres., White House, 1974-76; lectr. nat., internat. affairs, Haiti, art, communications, energy; corr.-broadcaster Sta. KTEN-TV, Ada, Okla., 1985; mem. staff presdl. transition office US Pres. Bush, 1988-89, 90; dir. and curator L. Clayton Willis Art Collection, Palm Beach, Fla.; pres., White House corr., congressional corr., photojournalist, The Evening News Broadcasting Co., Willis News Service; prodr., anchor documentary programs Saudi Arabian TV, 1992—; exec. prodr., anchor Glimpses of the World documentaries, 1993; White House corr., photojournalist Hope Star, Ark., 1994—; dir., curator L. Clayton Willis Art Collection, Palm Beach; chmn. emeritus Haitian Art Mus., Delray Beach, Fla.; White House corr., exec. prod., host, commentator, critic The Clayton Willis Talk Show, WPBR, Palm Beach, Fla, 2000-. Co-author: Capital Fare, 1977, Lott-Willis Pictorial Digest of US Presidential Elections and Inaugurations, 1997; host/exec. prodr., commentator The Clayton Willis Talk Show, WPBR, 1998-; pres.'s White House corr. Evening News Broadcasting Co., Washington, 2000; contbr. articles to Daily Mail, London, London Sunday Express, Umtali Post, Zimbabwe, Gwelo (Zimbabwe) Times, To the Point news mag., Johannesburg, The Citizen, Johannesburg, Hartford Courant, Sacramento Union, Chattanooga Times, UPI Radio Networks, The Hope Star, Phillips News Svc. Broadcaster with Bush/Quayle Nat. Campaign Hdqrs., Washington, 1988; adviser Presdl. Transition Office of Pres. George Bush, 1988-89; loaned Haitian paintings for spl. exhbn. to Haitian Embassy, Washington, 1991, Milw. Art Mus., 1992, Hypoluxo Town Hall, Fla., 2005, Grace Gallery, Dania Beach, Fla. Recipient Outstanding Svc. award Harlem Prep. Sch., Johannes Gutenberg medal (Mainz, Germany), 1984, Letters of Cert. Appreciation Pres. of US, 1989. Covered Vietnam, Congo, Mid. East, Rhodesian and South African wars; covered Clarence Thomas and Robert Gates US Senate confirmation hearings, 1991; covered 2000 presdl. election and re-count, Palm Beach, Fla.; covered Haitian rebellion and fall of Pres. Aristide, Haiti, 2004; covered the 2004 Kerry-Bush Presidential Campaign, 2008 Obama-McCain Presidential Campaign. Office: 1711 6TH Ave S Lake Worth FL 33460-4333 Office Phone: 561-688-1777. Personal E-mail: lclaytonwillis@aol.com.

WILLIS, CRAIG DEAN, academic administrator; b. Cambridge, Ohio, Mar. 21, 1935; s. John Russell and Glenna (Stevens) W.; m. Marilyn Elaine Foster, June 9, 1956; Mark Craig, Bruce Dean, Todd Laine, Garth John. BA, Ohio Wesleyan U., Delaware, 1957; MA, Ohio State U., Columbus, 1960, PhD, 1969. Registrar Ohio Wesleyan U., 1964-69; dir. admissions Wright State U., 1970-72, dean, 1971-77; v.p. acad. affairs Concord Coll., 1977-82; pres. Lock Haven U. Pa., 1982—2004, Eastern Mich. U., Ypsilanti, 2004—05, Kans. Wesleyan U., 2009—. Chmn. internat. affairs com. Am. Assn. State Colls. and Univs.; A.C.E. pres.'s commn. on internat. edn.; vice chmn. Clinton region Mellon Bank Ctr., 1987, chmn., 88, also bd. dirs.; bd. dirs. Lock Haven U.; cons. Ellis Assocs., Princeton, W.Va., 1980—82. Chmn. bd. Kirkmont Preschool, Beavercreek, Ohio, 1974-77, Beavercreek Library, 1976-77, Regional Edn. Service Agy., Beckley, W.Va., 1978-82; mem. N.E.-Midwest leadership Coun., 1989—. Recipient Disting. Alumnus award dept. edn. Ohio Wesleyan U., 1991; scholar Sohio Oil, 1953, Govt. of France, Paris, 1964, Shell Oil Co, 1967. Mem. Commn. State Coll. and Univ. Pres., Assn. State Colls. and Univs., Clinton County C. of C. (pres.), Rotary (v.p., pres. elect, Citizen of Yr. award Lock Haven 1989), Ohio Wesleyan U. Alumni Assn. (Disting. Sesquicentennial Alumnus of the Edn. 1992), Phi Kappa Phi, Kappa Kappa Psi, Phi Delta Kappa, Kappa Delta Pi. Presbyterian. Office: Eastern Mich U 202 Welch Hall Ypsilanti MI 48197 Business E-Mail: cwillis@lhup.edu.

WILLIS, DONTRELLE (WAYNE), professional baseball player; b. Oakland, Calif., Jan. 12, 1982; m. Natalee Vitagliano, Dec. 8, 2006; 1 child, Adrianna Rose. Pitcher Fla. Marlins, Miami, 2003—07, Detroit Tigers, 2008—. Mem. Team USA, World Baseball Classic, 2006. Recipient Warren Spahn award, 2005; named Nat. League Rookie of Yr., 2003; named to, Nat. League All-Star Team, 2003, 2005. Achievements include being a member of the World Series Champion Florida Marlins, 2003. Mailing: c/o Detroit Tigers Comerica Pk 2100 Woodward Ave Detroit MI 48201

WILLIS, EDWARD OLIVER, management consultant, state agency administrator; b. St. Louis, Apr. 6, 1948; s. George Washington and Mary (Fantroy) W.; m. Jennifer Linnea Johnson, June 17, 1972 (div. Dec. 1991); children: Edward, Linnea, Eric; m. Linda Diane Clark, Aug. 8, 1992. AA, Am. River Coll., Sacramento, 1972; BS in BA, Calif. State U., Sacramento, 1974; MBA in Mgmt., Golden Gate U., San Francisco, 1978. Divsn. ops. supr., casualty claims investigator Allstate Ins. Co., Menlo Park, Sacramento, 1974-75; budget analyst Dept. Fin., State of Calif., Sacramento, 1975-77; assoc. govtl. program analyst Dept. Health, Medi-Cal Procurement Project, State of Calif., Sacramento, 1977-78; chief fiscal br. solid waste mgmt. bd. State of Calif., Sacramento, 1978-79, mgr. adminstrv. svcs. state lands commn., 1979-80, asst. to assoc. supt. pub. instrn. dept. edn., 1980-82, dep. dir. adminstrn. dept. fish and game, 1982-90, acting adminstr. office of oil spill prevention and response, 1990-92, dep. dir. adminstrn. dept. developmental svcs., 1992-93, dep. dir. adminstrv. svcs. program dept. toxic substances, 1993-94, asst. sec. policy devel. Calif. Environ. Protection Agy., 1994-95, chief dep. dir. Calif. Conservation Corps, 1995—98; owner, prin. cons. WW Assocs., 1994—; chief adminstrv. officer Santa Clara Valley Water Dist., San Jose, Calif., 1998—2002; interim exec. dir. Calif. Coun. Developmental Disabilities, Sacramento, 2005; prin. cons. CPS Human Resource, Sacramento, 2006. Part-time instr. Cosumnes River Coll., Sacramento, 1980-83. Author: Business Employment Equity Plan, 1994. Vol. United Way Campaign, United Negro Coll. Fund, Sacramento Children's Home, YMCA; 1st v.p. Nat. Black Child Devel. Inst., Sacramento, 1981-82; chmn. Black Adv. Com. to State Pers. Bd., 1984-85; mem. St. Francis of Assisi Sch. Bd., Sacrammento, 1996—, pres., 1991-93; bd. trustees Black Advocates in State Svc., 1992; bd. dirs. Nat. Forum for Black Pub. Adminstrs., Washington, 1993-04, 2d v.p., 2003-04, alternate del., GOP Nat. Convention, 2008; elected precinct committeeman, PeoVia, Ariz., 2008; Little League coach, 1996—. With USAF, 1966-70. Decorated Air medals (4). Mem. Nat. Forum for Black Pub. Adminstrs. (Sacramento chpt. bd. dirs. 1993—, 1st v.p. 1990-91, pres. 1991-93), Am. Soc. Pub. Adminstrn. (Pub. Adminstr. of Yr.). Avocations: golf, softball. Home: 27214 N Makena Pl Peoria AZ 85383 Office Phone: 602-574-1831. Personal E-mail: edwardowillis@msn.com.

WILLIS, FRANK EDWARD, retired air force officer; b. Clinton, Ill., June 19, 1939; s. William Edward and Bernardine (Saveley) W.; m. Clarice Marie Hull, June 7, 1961; children: Michael, Steven, William. BS in Engring., USAF Acad., Colorado Springs, Colo., 1961; MA in Bus. Mgmt., U. Nebr., Offutt AFB Ext. Campus, 1973. Commd. 2d lt. USAF, 1961, advanced through grades to maj. gen., 1989; dep. comdr. 314th Tactical Airlift Group, Little Rock AFB, 1978-79, comdr., 1979-80; vice comdr. 374th Tactical Airlift Wing, Clark Air Base, The Philippines, 1980-81, comdr., 1981-83, CMDR 317th Tactical Airlift Wing, Pope AFB, NC, 1983—84; vice comdr. Air Force Manpower and Pers. Ctr., Randolph AFB, Tex., 1984-85; comdt. Air Command and Staff Coll., Maxwell AFB, Ala., 1985-88; vice comdr. 22d Air Force, Travis AFB, Calif., 1988-89; dir. and dep. chief of staff for requirements Air Mobility and Mil. Airlift Command, Scott AFB, Ill., 1989-93; ret., 1993; co-owner retail hobby shop Tinker Town, Inc., St. Louis, 1994—2006; ret. Decorated D.S.M. (2), Legion of Merit (2), Air medal (7), Meritorious Svc. medal (2). Presbyterian. Avocations: electronics, computers, model building. Home: 14673 Air Garden Ln Colorado Springs CO 80921 Home Phone: 719-487-1907. Personal E-mail: frank@willis.net.

WILLIS, FRANK ROY, historian, educator; b. Prescot, Lancashire, Eng., July 25, 1930; s. Harry and Gladys Reid (Birchall) W.; children from previous marriage, Jane, Clare, Geoffrey. BA, Cambridge U., Eng., 1952, cert. in edn., 1955, diploma in devel. econs., 1974; PhD, Stanford U., Calif., 1959. Instr. Stanford U., 1959-60; from instr. to assoc. prof. history U. Wash., Seattle, 1960-64; assoc. prof. then prof. U. Calif., Davis, 1964—. Author: The French in Germany, 1962, France, Germany and the New Europe, 1945-1967, 1968, Europe in the Global Age, 1968, Italy Chooses Europe, 1971, Western Civilization: An Urban Perspective, 1973, World Civilizations, 1982, The French Paradox, 1982, Western Civilization: A Brief Introduction, 1987. Fellow, Rockefeller Found., Paris, 1962—63, Guggenheim Found., Rome, 1966—67, Social Scis. Rsch. Coun., Cambridge, 1973—74. Avocation: travel. Office: U Calif Dept History Davis CA 95616

WILLIS, GLADDEN WILLIAMS, retired pathologist, scientific photographer, tree farmer; b. Minden, La., Mar. 26, 1939; s. John Stillmon and Virgie Williams Willis; m. Lydia Hall, May 14, 1966; children: Charles Austin, Loye Stillmon. BS, Centenary Coll., 1960; MD, Tulane U., 1964. Intern La. State U. Med. Ctr., Shreveport, 1964-65, resident, 1965-69; fellow Meml. Sloan-Kettering Med. Ctr., NYC, 1969-71; pathologist St. Luke's Hosp., Houston, 1971-72, St. Mary's Hosp., Roswell, N.Mex., 1972-73, Ochsner Clinic Found., New Orleans, 1973—2005, dir. anat. pathology, 1976—2003, vice chmn. lab. medicine, 1996—2003. Contbr. articles to profl. jours., 2041 sci. photographs to encys. and books. Past pres. Jefferson Performing Arts Soc., Metarie, La. Capt. USAF, 1966—72. Recipient George Washington Honor medal, Valley Forge Found., 1996. Fellow Arthur Purdy Stout Soc., Royal Microscopical Soc.; mem. Assn. Dirs. of Anatomic Pathology, Internat. Acad. Pathology, Am. Soc. Media Photographers, NY Acad. Scis. Republican. Methodist. Avocation: photography. Home and Office: PO Box 719 Doyline LA 71023 Personal E-mail: gladdenwillis@hughes.net.

WILLIS, HAROLD WENDT, SR., real estate developer; b. Marion, Ala., Oct. 7, 1927; s. Robert James and Della (Wendt) W.; m. Patsy Gay Bacon, Aug. 2, 1947 (div. Jan. 1975); children: Harold Wendt II, Timothy Gay, April Ann, Brian Tad, Suzanne Gail; m. Vernette Jacobson Osborne, Mar. 30, 1980 (div. 1984); m. Ofelia Alvarez, Sept. 23, 1984; children: Ryan Robert, Samantha Ofelia. Student, Loma Linda U., 1950, San Bernardino Valley Coll. Ptnr. Victoria Guernsey, San Bernardino, Calif., 1950-63, co-pres., 1963-74, pres., 1974—. Pres. Energy Delivery Sys., Food and Fuel, Inc. San Bernardino City water commr., 1964-98, pres. bd. water commrs., 1964-98; bd. councillors Loma Linda U., Calif., 1968-85, pres., 1971-74; active So. Calif. Strider's Relay Team (set indoor Am. and World record in 4x800 1992, sec distance medley relay US and World record for 60 yr. old 1992); pres. So. Calif. Striders Track and Field Club, 2001-02. Ensign, US Mcht. Marine, 1945-46. Mem. Calif. Dairy Industries Assn. (pres. 1963, 64), Liga Internat. (2d v.p. 1978, pres. 1982, 83), Socal Striders Masters Track & Field Club (pres. 2001-02). Seventh-day Adventist (deacon 1950-67). Avocation: pvt. pilot. Office: PO Box 5607 San Bernardino CA 92412-5607 Office Phone: 909-889-0828 ext 303. Personal E-mail: foodnfuel@verizon.net. Business E-Mail: food.nfuel@vision.net.

WILLIS, JAKIE ARLETA, elementary and secondary educator; b. Richland, Ga. d. Jacob C.W. and Ardella (Alford) Williams; m. Frank A. Willis (dec.); children: Beverly Donita, Reginald Tyronne. BS, Albany State Coll., 1951; MA, NYU, 1957. Cert. elem. edn. Tchr. Stewart County, Lumpkin, Ga., 1951-63; tchr. Stratford Bd. Edn., Stratford, Conn., 1963-92; interim prin. Honeyspot Ho., Stratford Acad.; ret., 1992—. Named Outstanding Tchr. Am., Fuller & Dees, Washington, 1975. Mem. Assn. for Supervision and Curriculum Devel., NEA (life), Stratford Edn. Assn. (sec. 1965-67, pres. 1980-81), Conn. Edn. Assn. (life), Alpha Kappa Alpha (pres. Bridgeport, Conn. chpt. 1985-89, Albany chptr. 1998-2000), Semper Fidelis Club (sec. 1996—), Richland H&I Sch. Alumni Assn., Inc. (pres. 1995—), Alpha Kappa Alpha (life). Democrat. Methodist. Home: PO Box 71224 Albany GA 31708-1224

WILLIS, JOHN ALVIN, retired editor; b. Morristown, Tenn., Oct. 16, 1916; s. John Bradford and George Ann (Myers) W.; m. Claire Olivier, Sept. 25, 1960 (div.); m. Marina Sarda, Jan. 26, 1978 (div.) BA cum laude, Milligan Coll., 1938; MA, U. Tenn., 1941; postgrad., Ind U., Harvard U. Asst. editor Theatre World, NYC, 1945-65, editor, 1965—; asst. editor Screen World, NYC, 1948-65, editor, 1965—; tchr. pub. high schs., NYC, 1950-76; editor Dance World, 1966-80; asst. editor Opera World, 1952-54, Great Stars of Am. Stage, 1952, Pictorial History of Silent Screen, 1953, Pictorial History of Opera in America, 1959, Pictorial History of the American Theatre, 1950, 60, 70, 80, 85. Mem. Tony Theatre Awards Com. Nat. bd. dirs. U. Tenn. Theatre; mem. com. to select recipients for Mus. Theatre Hall of Fame, NYU. Lt. USNR, 1943-45. Recipient Lucille Lortel Lifetime Achievement award, 1993, Drama Desk Lifetime Achievement award, 1994, Nat. Bd. Rev. Lifetime Achievement Film History award, 1999, Profl. Excellence award Milligan Coll., 1999, Tony Award for Excellence in Theater, 2001; high sch. auditorium renamed John Willis Performing Arts Ctr. in his honor, Morristown, 1993. Mem. Actors Equity Assn., Broadway Theatre Inst. (Lifetime Achievement award 2003), Nat. Bd. Rev. Motion Pictures (past bd. dirs.). Home and Office: 190 Riverside Dr #1D New York NY 10024-1008

WILLIS, JOHN PATRICK, chemist; b. Albany, NY, Mar. 10, 1947; s. John James and Mary Catherine (Varden) W.; m. Tientje Jane Dirzuweit, July 22, 1972. BS, Iona Coll., 1969; MS, SUNY, Oswego, 1974; PhD, U. Conn., 1977. Assoc. prodn. chemist Winthrop Labs., Rensselaer, N.Y., 1970-72; rsch. chemist Uniroyal, Inc., Middlebury, Conn., 1977-79; postdoctoral rschr. U. Minn., Mpls., 1979-80; mgr. chem. rsch. Nova Biomed Corp., Newton, Mass., 1980-83; founder, chmn. Ilex Corp., Marlboro, Mass., 1983-87; med. cons., 1987-88; founder T.J. Assocs., Biomed. Cons., 1987-89; v.p., chief oper. officer Sharon Drive Corp., Westlake, Ohio, 1988-93; dir. rsch. Medisense, Inc., Waltham, Mass., 1993-97; pres., CEO Teknow Source Inc., Shirley, Mass., 1997—2004; chmn., CEO North Country Naturals, Inc., Shirley, Mass., 2000—05; tech. dir. biotech. Mohawk Innovative Tech, Inc., Albany, NY, 2001—04; rsch. prof. dept. chemistry and chem. biology Rensselaer Polytechnic Inst., Troy, NY, 2004—05; founder, chmn. Ultradian Diagnostics LLC, 2004—. Mem. adv. bd. Clin. Lab. Practice, Mass. Dept. Pub. Health, 1986-87, 128 Entrepreneurs' Ctr., Waltham, Mass., 1986-88; mem. tech. adv. coun. Edison Biotech. Ctr., Cleve., 1988-90. U. Conn. Rsch. Found. fellow, 1976. Fellow Am. Inst. Chemists; mem. Am. Chem. Soc., Electrochem. Soc., Am. Assn. Clin. Chemistry, N.Y. Acad. Scis., Sigma Xi, Phi Kappa Phi, Phi Lambda Upsilon. Achievements include research in bioelectrochemistry, organic electrochemistry and biosensors; patents in field. Office: Ultradian Diagnostics LLC 5 Univ Pl Ste A324 Rensselaer NY 12144 Office Phone: 518-618-0046. Personal E-mail: jwillis@tiac.net.

WILLIS, KATHLEEN A., librarian; b. Chgo., Jan. 8, 1962; d. Raymond George and Patricia Sue Bugielski; m. J. Thomas Willis, Aug. 14, 1982; children: Elyse Katherine, Heather Nicole, Victoria Lynn, John Thomas. BS in Human Svc. Adminstrn., Elmhurst Coll., Ill., 2000; MLIS, U. Ill., Urbana, 2004. Libr. assoc. AC Buehler Libr., Elmhurst Coll., 1994—2000, head access svcs., 2000—. Commn. chair Spl. Events Commn., Addison, 2005; bd. mem. Addison Sch. Dist. 4, Ill., 2000; v.p. Addison Dist. 4 Found. Ednl. Excellance, 2005. Mem.: AAUW (Elmhurst) (steering com. mem. 2008), Ill. Libr. Assn. Roman Catholic. Avocations: reading, swimming, gambling. Home: 611 Holly Ct Addison IL 60101 Office: Elmhurst Coll 190 Prospect Elmhurst IL 60126 Office Fax: 630-617-3332. Business E-Mail: kathyw@elmhurst.edu.

WILLIS, KEITH ALAN, energy scientist, engineer; b. Ferndale, Mich., Jan. 6, 1950; s. Frederick E. and Dora Ann (Moeller) W.; m. Valarie Sue Dennis, Dec. 1, 1975; children: Kimberly Christeen, Patricia Elené. BS in Aero. Engring., U.S. Naval Coll., San Diego, 1972; AAS in Climate Control, Oakland C. C., Auburn Hills, Mich., 1977; MS Engring Mgt., Kennedy Western U., 1998, PhD in Engring. Mgmt., 2000. Cert. Energy Mgr.; cert. Bus. Energy Profl.; Master's lic. in Refrigeration, Heating, and Elec. Work; Contractors lic. in Gas Heating, Hydronic, Warm Air, Sheet Metal, and Builders. Installation mgr. Hinson Heating and Air Conditioning, Inc., Royal Oak, Mich, 1973-82; project mgr. MPM Worldwide Corp., Tustin, Calif., 1983-84; mktg. application engr. Solidyne Corp., National City, Calif., 1984-85; consulting engr. TRIJ Power, Manila, 1985-86; automation systems engr. Verle A. Williams and Assocs., San Diego, 1986-87; ops. mgr. Staefa Control Systems, Chgo., 1987-92; sr. project mgr. Johnson Controls, Inc., Troy, Mich., 1993-97; dir. energy svcs. R.W. Mead Co, Fraser, Mich., 1997-99; bundled svcs. mgr. Limbach Co., 1999—2001; energy mgr. PES/DTE Energy, 2002—06; energy scientist Trane Inc., St. Paul, 2006—. Warrant officer USN, 1968-73, Viet Nam. Mem. Dispute Rev. Bd. Found. (charter mem.), Illuminating Engring. Soc. N. Am., Assn. Energy Engrs. (chartered life; cert. energy mgr., demand side mgmt. profl. soc., co-generation inst., plant mgrs. inst., environ. engrs. mgmt. inst., chpt. steering com. 1997—, sec. chpt. 1999—2008, pres. 2005-06, cert. energy mgr. rev. bd.). Avocations: boating, fishing, camping. Home: 130 Kangaroo Ridge Rd Byrdstown TN 38549 Office Phone: 931-864-3434. E-mail: doctorwillis@twlakes.net.

WILLIS, PATRICK L., professional football player; b. Bruceton, Tenn., Jan. 25, 1985; s. Ernest Willis; guardians Chris and Julie Finley. BA, U. Miss., 2006. Linebacker San Francisco 49ers, 2007—. Recipient Dick Butkus award, 2006, Conerly trophy, 2006, Chucky Mullins Courage award, 2006, Lambert trophy, 2006; named Southeastern Conf. Defensive Player of Yr., AP, 2006, NFL Defensive Rookie of Yr., 2007, NFL First Team All-Pro, 2007; named to Nat. Football Conf. Pro Bowl Team, NFL, 2007, 2008. Achievements include leading the NFL in: tackles (174), 2007. Mailing: c/o San Francisco 49ers 4949 Centennial Blvd Santa Clara CA 95054*

WILLIS, PAUL ALLEN, retired librarian, dean; b. Floyd County, Ind., Oct. 1, 1941; s. Clarence Charles and Dorothy Jane (Harritt) Willis; m. Barbara Marcum, June 15, 1963; children: Mark, Sally. AB, U. Ky., 1963, JD, 1969; MLS, U. Md., 1966. Cataloger Libr. Congress, Washington, 1963; head descriptive cataloging br. Sci. and Tech. Info. Facility NASA, College Park, Md., 1963-66; law libr., prof. law U. Ky., Lexington, 1966-73, dir. librs., 1973—2002, acting dean Coll. Libr. Sci., 1975-76, 88; dean librs. U. SC, Columbia, 2002—07; ret. Exec. sec. Ky. Jud. Retirement and Removal Commn., 1977-81; adv. com. Ctr. Jud. Conduct Orgns., Am. Judicature Soc., Chgo., 1979-81; chmn. Southeastern Libr. Network, Atlanta, 1998-99; exec. com. Ky. Hist. Soc., 1984-88; mem. Ky. Adv. Coun. on Librs., 1985-2002, adv. com. Online Computer Libr. Ctr., 1986-90; cons. SE Consortium Internat. Devel., U. Sriwijaya, Palembang, Sumatera, Indonesia, 1987-88, Hanoi U. Tech., 1999, 2001, Vietnam Nat. U., Ho Chi Minh City, 1999 Sr. fellow, UCLA, 1982. Mem. Assn. Southeastern Rsch. Librs. (chair 1986-88, bd. dirs. 2002-), Assn. Rsch. Librs. (bd. dirs. 2002—05). Personal E-mail: willis@sccoast.net.

WILLIS, RALPH WALKER, retired firefighter; b. Redondo Beach, Calif., Nov. 21, 1921; s. Achatius Walker and Elizabeth Margaret (Dehm) Willis; m. Helen Elizabeth Willis, May 18, 1946 (dec. June 2006). Grad. h.s., San Diego. Firefighter Richmond (Calif.) Fire Dept., 1946-67; pres. Firefighters Union IAFF AFL CIO, 1964—67. Author:

Sansei Banzai, 1986, War and Rememberance Revisted, 1988, The Eighth Regiment, 1995, My Life as a Jarhead, 1999 (The Ernie Pyle WWII Roundtable award). Sgt. USMC, 1941-45. Mem.: VFW (life), American's for Historical Accuracy (pres. emeritus), Iwo Jima Survivors Assn. American Independent Party. Avocations: travel, painting, writing. Home: 579 Camino Mercado # 218 Arroyo Grande CA 93420 Home Phone: 805-481-4614. Personal E-mail: jarheadrw@gmail.com.

WILLIS, RUTH, freelance/self-employed theater director, actress; b. Toledo, Nov. 7, 1932; d. Thomas LeRoy and Ruth Caroline (Ehmann) Ramsey; m. Charles Perrin Willis, Nov. 14, 1956; children: David, Laura. BE cum laude, U. Toledo, 1954. Grade sch. tchr. Toledo Pub. Schs., 1954—61; acting tchr. Cin. Children's Home, 1958—59, Contemporary Arts Mus., Houston, 1972, Jewish Cmty. Ctr., 1969—72; dir. Exptl. Wing Country Playhouse, 1968—72; mem. Actor's Studio Ariz. State U., Phoenix, 1980—81; dir. Plays for Living Family and Children's Svcs., Pitts., 1984—87; adult acting tchr. Point Park Coll. Conservatory, 1987—2001; artistic dir. Open Stage Theatre, 1991—. Dir.: (over 100 major prodns.); actor: (plays) The Women (named Best Actress, Assn. Cmty. Theatres, Cin.), The Sleeping Prince (named Best Actress, Country Playhouse, Houston), Sweet Bird of Youth (named Best Actress, Stagebrush Theatre, Scottsdale, Ariz.); dir.: Candida (named Best Dir.), Lucia Mad (Best Top Ten Evenings of Theatre, Pitts. Gazette, 1997). Gen. bd. mem. Mariemont Players, Cin., 1958—60, Phoenix Children's Theatre, 1978—81; exec. bd. mem., sec. Phoenix Theatre, 1978—79, exec. bd. mem., v.p., 1980—81; founder Open Stage Theatre, Pitts., 1991. Recipient Svc. award, Phoenix Little Theatre Bd. Dirs., 1981. Mem.: Charlevoix Garden Club, Nat. Soc. Arts and Letters, Pi Epsilon Delta. Avocations: piano, painting, yoga, gardening, decorating.

WILLIS, SELENE LOWE, electrical engineer, application developer, consultant, information technology manager; b. Birmingham, Ala., Mar. 4, 1958; d. Lewis Russell and Bernice (Wilson) Lowe; m. André Maurice Willis, June 12, 1987. BSEE, Tuskegee U., Ala., 1980; postgrad., UCLA, 1993—94, postgrad., 1996, postgrad., 1999. Component engr. Hughes Aircraft Corp., El Segundo, Calif., 1980—82; reliability and lead engr. Aero Jet Electro Sys. Corp., Azusa, Calif., 1982—84; sr. component engr. Rockwell Internat. Corp., Anaheim, Calif., 1984, Gen. Data Comm. Corp., Danbury, Conn., 1984—85; design engr. Lockheed Missile and Space Co., Sunnyvale, Calif., 1985—86; mgr. property Penmar Mgmt. Co., LA, 1987—88; aircraft mechanic McDonnell Douglas Corp., Long Beach, Calif., 1989—93; unix sys. adminstrn. Santa Cruz Ops., Calif., 1994; bus. ops. mgr., cons. New Start, Santa Monica, Calif., 1995; software developer Nat. Advancement Corp., Calif., 1996; entrepreneur Datatronics, Calif., 1996—; exec. v.p., owner LA Network Engr. Jet Propulsion Lab., 1996—2000; software engr., network engr., application engr., lead engr. Jet Propulsion Lab, Pasadena, Calif., 1996—2000, project mgr., 1999—2000, lead UNIX engr. LA, 1998—2000; mgmt. sys. engr. Tech. Jet Propulsion Lab., Pasadena, 1998—2000, mgr. project element, 1999—; cons., sr. project mgr. Amgen, Thousand Oaks, Calif., 1999—2000, sr. sys. engr., 2000—; mgr. project So. Calif. Edison, 2002—03, mgr., settlements, 2003—, mgr. energy supply and mgmt., 2003—05, mgr. structured contracts, 2005—. Cons., software designer Kern and Wooley, atty., Westwood, Calif., 1995; software developer Nat. Advancement Corp., Santa Ana, Calif., 1995—. Vol. Mercy Hosp. and Children's Hosp., Birmingham, Ala. 1972-74; mrm. LA Gospel Messengers, 1982-84, West Angeles Ch. of God and Christ, LA, 1990; cons., mgr. bus. ops. New Start, Santa Monica Bay Area Drug Abuse Coun., Calif., 1995; vol. Pres. Clinton's Going-To-Coll. Program through UCLA, 1997—; chair UCLA Transfer Coll. Scholarship Program, 1998-99. Scholar Bell Lab., 1976-80, UCLA, 1994, Gem Award, UTA, 1999, Outstanding Group Award, JPL, 1999. Mem. IEEE, ASME, Aerospace and Aircraft Engr., So. Calif. Profl. Engring. Assn., Tuskegee U. Alumni Assn., UCLA Alumni Assn. (scholarship and adv. com.), Eta Kappa Nu, Christian Ch. Avocations: piano, computers, softball, real estate.

WILLIS, SHARON J., music educator, director; d. Dorothy M. and Eldred Willis; m. Oliver R. Sueing, Sept. 16, 1978; children: Adrian Willis Sueing, Amarylis Jenee Sueing. PhD, U. Ga., Athens, 1988. Music chair, cons. Morris Brown Coll., Atlanta, 1995—2005; music dept. chair Clark Atlanta U., 2005—. Exec. dir. Americolor Opera, Atlanta, 1999—; black womanist rsch. scholar Interdenominational Theol. Ctr., Atlanta, 2008—. Author: (play) Unspoken; composer: (agora suite for organ) Solo Organ (Commd. by Am. Guild of Organist, 2006), (musical) Soriety, (mass) Celebration Mass honoring Dr. Martin Luther King, Jr., (organ suite) We Shall Overcome, Exodus, (mass) Solo Mass for William G. Revere, Mass in Memoria for Willie edwards Jackson, Requiem Mass for G. Johnson Hubert, (opera) Carmen J., The Seduction of King Solomon, The Opera Singer, 3kings and a PRINCE, Madam C. J. (Walker), The Great Divide, Pink Lady Opera, The Candlers of Callan, LaRoche, The Herndon Opera. Dir. music ministry Friendship Bapt. Ch., Atlanta, 2005—. Recipient Ga. Music Hall of Fame, 2003—08, Tchg. Excellence award, Vulcan Materials Co., 2004, Achievement Arts and Comm. award, Ga. Profl. Women's Inst., 2008; named Woman of Yr. in Fine Arts, Iota Phi Lambda, Inc., 1995. Mem.: Am. Composers Forum (Performance grant 2002), Am. Soc. Composers, Authors and Composers (mem.), Nu Lambda Omega, Alpha Kappa Alpha, Pi Kappa Lambda. Achievements include Teaching Excellence Award, Vulcan Materials Company, May 2004; Certificate of excellence, South Eastern African American Choral Festival, Composer; Honoree, Nu Lambda Omega, Foundation, Alpha Kappa Alpha, Inc., May 2008. Office: Clark Atlanta Univ 223 James P Brawley Dr Atlanta GA 30314 Business E-Mail: swillis@cau.edu.

WILLIS, SOLOMON LEE, mathematics educator; s. Eddie and Brenda Willis. BS in Math., Gardner Webb U., 1999; MA in Math. Edn., Appalachian State U., 2004. Cert. tchr. NC. HS math. tchr. Gaston Day Sch., Gastonia, NC, 2000—06; coll. math. tchr. Cleve. CC, Shelby, NC, 2002—. T-cubed regional instr. Tex. Instruments, Dallas, 2003—; AP calculus exam reader Coll. Bd., 2007—09. Dir., organizer talent show Gaston Day Sch.; educator adv. bd. Discovery Pl., Charlotte, NC, 2003—04. MELT scholar, Appalachian State U., 2002—04, Te@ch Tech. grantee, Best Buy, 2004. Mem.: Math. Assn. Am. (assoc.), Nat. Coun. Tchrs. Math. (assoc. Trust Fund scholar 2002—03). Personal E-mail: solomon.willis@yahoo.com.

WILLIS, TRICIA LEE, special education educator; d. Harold Lee and Belinda Lee Gibb; m. Don Edward Willis, Dec. 29, 2001; 1 child, Brandon Gibb. BA in History, Calif. State U., San Marcos, 1996; MBS, Southeastern U., 1999. Tchr. Atoka Coal Alt. Sch., Okla., 1997—98, Coalgate Pub. Schs., Okla., 1998—2005; literacy specialist Brinley Mid. Sch., Las Vegas, Nev., 2005—07, sec. tchr., 2007—08. Founding faculty Coalgate Alternative Sch., 2004—05. Grantee, Rural Okla. Cmty. Found., 2000, 2001, 2004—05, Okla. Arts Coun. Expressive Art, 2005. Mem.: Acad. Leadership and Curriculum Devel., Coun. for Exceptional Children. Achievements include development of program for emotionally disturbed students. Avocations: reading, travel, sports. Office: Brinley Mid Sch 2480 Maverick St Las Vegas NV 89108 Personal E-mail: tricia89134@cox.net.

WILLIS, WILLIAM DARRELL, JR., neuroscientist, educator; b. Dallas, July 19, 1934; s. William Darrell and Dorcas (Chamberlain) W.; m. Jean Colette Schini, May 28, 1960 (dec. Jan. 1, 2006); 1 child, Thomas Darrell. BS, BA, Tex. A&M U., 1956; MD, U. Tex. Southwestern Med. Sch., 1960; PhD, Australian Nat. U., 1963. Postdoctoral research fellow Nat. Inst. Neurol. Diseases and Blindness, Australian Nat. U., 1960-62, Istituto di Fisiologia, U. Pisa, Italy, 1962-63; from asst. prof. to prof. anatomy, chmn. dept. U. Tex. Southwestern Med. Sch., Dallas, 1963-70; chief lab. comparative neurobiology Marine Biomed. Inst., prof. anatomy and physiology U. Tex. Med. Br., Galveston, 1970—, dir. Marine Biomed. Inst., 1978—2004, chmn. dept. anatomy and neurosci., 1986—2004, Ashbel Smith prof., 1986-95, Cecil and Ida Green prof., 1995—. Mem. neurology B study sect. NIH, 1968-72, chmn., 1970-72, mem. neurol. disorders Program Project rev. com., 1972-76, Nat. Adv. Neurol. and Communicative Disorders and Stroke Coun., 1987-90; tng. grant com. Nat. Inst. of Neurol. Disorders and Stroke, 1994-98. Mem. editl. bd. Neurosci., Exptl. Neurology, 1970-90, Archives Italienne Biologie, Neurosci. Letters, 1976-92; chief editor Jour. Neurophysiology, 1978-83, Pain, 1986-89; assoc. editor Jour. Neurosci., 1986-89, editor-in-chief, 1993-94; sect. editor Exptl. Brain Rsch., 1990-92, 1995-2004. Mem. AAAS, Am. Assn. Anatomists (exec. com. 1980-86), Am. Pain Soc. (pres. 1982-83), Internat. Assn. Study Pain (coun. 1984-90), Am. Physiol. Soc., Soc. Exptl. Biol. Medicine, Soc. Neurosci. (pres. 1984-85), Internat. Brain Rsch. Orgn., Cajal Club, Sigma Xi, Alpha Omega Alpha. Office: U Tex Med Br 301 University Blvd Galveston TX 77555-1069 Home: 7312 Seawall Blvd Apt 109 Galveston TX 77551-1994 Office Phone: 409-772-2103. Business E-Mail: wdwillis@utmb.edu.

WILLIS, WILLIAM ERVIN, lawyer; b. Huntington, W.Va., Oct. 11, 1926; s. Asa Hannon and Mae (Davis) W.; m. Joyce Litteral, Sept. 1, 1949; children: Kathryn Cunningham, Anne Dresser, William. Student, Ind. U., 1944, NYU, 1945; AB, Marshall U., 1948; JD, Harvard, 1951; LHD (hon.), Marshall U., 1997. Bar: N.Y. 1952. Pvt. practice, NYC, 1951—; ptnr. Sullivan & Cromwell, 1960-94, sr. counsel, 1994—. Lectr. Practising Law Inst., 1963—; trustee Fed. Bar Council, 1968-72; mem. 2d Circuit Commn. on Reduction Burdens and Costs Civil Litigation, 1977-82. Co-author Doing Business in America; contbr. Edn. Civil Practice Law Rev. Forms and Guidance for Lawyers, also articles to legal jours. Mem. panel arbitrators Pub. Resources; trustee Tenafly (N.J.) Nature Ctr., 1994—2001, pres., 1997—2001; bd. dirs. Soc Yeager Scholars, Marshall U., Huntington, 1995—, v.p., 2001—04, pres., 2004—08. With AUS, 1944—46. Fellow Am. Coll. Trial Lawyers, Am. Bar Found.; mem. ABA (standing com. on fed. judiciary 1987-95, chair 1992-93, 94-95), N.Y. Bar Assn. (chmn. antitrust sect. 1976-77, exec. com. 1976-83), Assn. Bar City of N.Y. (chmn. profl. discipline com. 1983-86, chmn. ethics 2000 com. 1999—2003, judicial conduct 2000—05), Fed. Bar Coun. (trustee 1969-72), Am. Judicature Soc., Am. Arbitration Assn. (panel arbitrators), N.Y. Law Inst., N.Y. County Lawyers, Ins. Jud. Adminstrn., India House. Home: 190 Tekening Dr Tenafly NJ 07670-1219 Office: Sullivan & Cromwell 125 Broad St 28th Fl New York NY 10004-2498 Business E-Mail: wewillis@nysbar.com.

WILLISON, BRUCE GRAY, dean; b. Riverside, Calif., Oct. 16, 1948; s. Walter G. and Dorothy (Phillips) W.; m. Gretchen A. Illig; children: Patrick, Bruce G., Kristen, Jeffery, Geoffrey, Lea. BA in econs., UCLA, 1970; MBA, U. So. Calif., 1973. With Bank of Am., LA, 1973-79; joined First Interstate Bancorp, LA, 1979, dir. mktg., 1981, sr. v.p., mem. mng. com., 1981—82; sr. v.p. trust divsn. First Interstate Bank of Calif., LA, 1982—83, exec. v.p. world banking group, 1983-85; pres., CEO First Interstate Bank Ltd., LA, 1985-86; chmn., CEO First Interstate Bank Oreg., Portland, 1986-91; chmn., pres., CEO First Interstate Bank of Calif., LA, 1991—96; vice chmn. First Interstate Bancorp, LA, 1995—96; pres., COO H.F. Ahmanson and Co., Irwandale, Calif., 1996—99; dean UCLA Anderson Sch. Mgmt., 1999—2006, John E. Anderson chair in mgmt. Bd. dirs. IndyMac Bancorp., Inc., Sun America, Inc., Health Net Inc., 2000—, Homestore, Inc., 2002—. Bd. dirs. United Way of LA, Operation Hope Inc. Served to lt. USN, 1970—72.

WILLITS, TIM, computer game company executive; BS, U. Minn., 1995. Lead designer id Software, Mesquite, Tex., 1995—, co-owner, 2004—. Credited (computer games) The Ultimate Doom, Quake, Quake II, Quake III Arena, Quake III: Team Arena, lead designer Doom 3; exec. prodr.: (computer games) Quake 4. Office: id Software 3819 Towne Crossing 222 Mesquite TX 75150

WILLKE, THOMAS ALOYS, academic administrator, statistician, educator; b. Rome City, Ind., Apr. 22, 1932; s. Gerard Thomas and Marie Margaret (Wuennemann) W.; m. Geraldine Ann Page, Dec. 28, 1954; children: Richard, Susan, Donald, Jeanne, Mary, Kathleen. AB, Xavier U., 1954; MS, Ohio State U., 1956, PhD, 1960. Sr. engr. N.Am. Aviation, Columbus, Ohio, 1959-60; instr. math. Ohio State U., Columbus, 1960-61, assoc. prof., 1966-70, assoc. prof. stat., 1970-72, prof., 1972-73, dir. stats. lab., 1971-73, vice provost Arts and Scis., 1973-86, acting dean Univ. Coll., 1983-86, dean undergrad. studies Arts and Scis., 1986-87; prof. emeritus stat., under grad. dean Colls. Arts and Scis., 1987—; prof. math. scis. Otterbein coll., Westerville, Ohio, 1987-97, chmn. dept. math. scis., 1988-96; rsch. mathematician U.S. Nat. Bur. Standards, Washington, 1961-66; asst. prof. math. U. Md., College Park, 1963-66; prof. statistics, undergrad. dean Ohio State U., 1987—; prof. math. scis. emeritus Otterbein Coll., 1997—; pres. Ohio State Retirees Assn., 2008—09. Contbr. articles on statis. non parametric methods and robustness to profl. jours. Mem. Am. Statis. Assn., Math. Assn. Am. Roman Catholic. Home: 4375 Mumford Dr Columbus OH 43220-4438

WILLKIE, WENDELL LEWIS, II, lawyer; b. Indpls., Oct. 29, 1951; s. Philip Herman Willkie and Rosalie (Heffelfinger) Hall; m. Carlotta Fendig; children: Alexandra Elizabeth, Diana Fendig, Caroline Heffelfinger. AB, Harvard U., 1973; BA, Oxford U., Eng., 1975, MA, 1983; JD, U. Chgo., 1978. Bar: NY 1979. Assoc. Simpson, Thacher & Bartlett, NYC, 1978-82; gen. counsel NEH, Washington, 1982-84; assoc. counsel to Pres. The White House, Washington, 1984-85; chief of staff, counselor to Sec. US Dept. Edn., Washington, 1985, gen. counsel, 1985-88; counsel Office of the Pres.-elect, Washington, 1988-89; gen. counsel Dept. Commerce, Washington, 1989-93; v.p. Westvaco Corp., NYC, 1995-96, sr. v.p., gen. counsel, 1996—2002; sr. v.p., gen. counsel, sec. MeadWestvaco Corp. (formerly Westvaco Corp.), 2002—. Vis. fellow Am. Enterprise Inst., Washington, 1993-94. Co-author, editor: (with J.R. Lilley) Beyond MFN: Trade with China and American Interests, 1994. Harvard U. scholar, 1969-73, Rhodes scholar, 1973-75. Republican. Episcopalian. Office: Mead Westvaco 5 High Ridge Pk Stamford CT 06905 Business E-Mail: wlw2@meadwestvaco.com.

WILLMAN, DAVID, investigative journalist; BA in Journalism, San Jose U., Calif., 1978. Reporter Star-News, Pasadena, Calif., 1978—83; Metro staff reporter San Jose Mercury News, 1983—84, reporter Sacramento bur., 1984—86, reporter Washington bur., 1986—90; reporter Orange County edit. LA Times, 1990—92, fin. writer, 1992, Metro projects team, 1992—94, investigative team Washington bur., 1995—. Recipient Award for best coverage of a continuing story, Greater LA Press Club, 1993, Watchdog award, Orange County Press Club, 1993, Pulitzer Prize for local reporting, 1995, George Polk award, 1997, Consumer Journalism award, Nat. Press Club, 1999, Pulitzer prize for investigative reporting, 2001, Worth Bingham prize, 2004, David Nyhan prize for Polit. Journalism, Harvard U., 2005, Nat. Journalism award for Washington reporting, Scripps Howard Found., 2008. Office: LA Times DC Bur 1341 G St NW Ste 201 Washington DC 20005 Business E-Mail: david.willman@latimes.com.

WILLMORE, CATHERINE BERNADETTE, pharmacist professor, research scientist; d. William John and Theresa Ann Ferguson; m. John Powers Willmore, Sept. 3, 1982 (div. May 2004); children: Johnathon Ryan, Brandon Maurice, Darla Louisa, Daryl Christopher; m. Stephen Keith Fordham, Sept. 16, 2006 (div. June 5, 2008); 1 child, Danielle Elise Fordham. BS in Pharmacy, U. Conn., Storrs, 1984; PhD in Combined Disciplines Pharmacology & Toxicology, Med. Coll. Va. Commonwealth U., Richmond, 1999. Lic. Conn. Bd. Pharmacy, 1985, Va. Bd. Pharmacy, 1995, Md. Bd. Pharmacy, 1999, Ohilo Bd. Pharmacy, 2005, pharmacist Ark. Bd. Pharmacy, 2007. Pharmacist Brooks Drugs HSI Corp, Pawtucket, RI, 1985—95; relief pharmacist Rite Aid Corp., Harrisburg, 1995—2007, Walgreens Drug Stores Inc., Little Rock, 2007—; instr. U. Md. Sch. Pharmacy, Balt., 1999—2004; rsch. assoc. Walter Reed Army Rsch. Inst., Silver Springs, 2004—05; asst. prof. pharmacology Ohio Northern U., Ada, 2005—08; assoc. prof. pharmacology Harding U., Searcy, 2008—. Cons. Lafayette Instrument Co., Ind., 2000—; expert witness Various Legal Firms, 2004—. Contbr. articles to profl.jours., chapters to books. Vol. spkr concerned parents groups Various, vol. spkr. women's groups, 2005—08. Recipient Preceptor Yr., U. Conn., 1995, Winner, Med. Coll. Va., 1998, Dir's Travel award, Nat. Inst. Drug Abuse, 1998, award, Ctrl. Va. Chpt. Soc. Neuroscience, 1999. Mem.: Am. Assn. Colls. Pharmacy (assoc.; prof. 2005—08), Soc. Neuroscience (assoc.; scientist 1997—2008, Neuroscience Soc. Travel award 1999). Democrat. Achievements include development of drug library software: corrects polygraph readouts for drug impact(s). Avocations: running, travel, dance. Office: Harding Univ 915 E Market St Searcy AR 72149 Office Fax: 501-279-5202. Personal E-mail: profneurofarm@yahoo.com. Business E-Mail: cwillmor@harding.edu.

WILLNER, ALAN ELI, electrical engineer, educator; b. Bklyn, Nov. 16, 1962; s. Gerald and Sondra (Bernstein) W.; m. Michelle Frida Green, June 25, 1991. BA, Yeshiva U., 1982; MS, Columbia U., 1984, PhD, 1988. Summer tech. staff David Sarnoff Rsch. Ctr., Princeton, NJ, 1983, 84; grad. rsch. asst. dept. elec. engring. Columbia U., NYC, 1984-88; postdoctoral mem. tech. staff AT&T Bell Labs., Holmdel, NJ, 1988-90; mem. tech. staff Bell Comm. Rsch., Red Bank, NJ, 1990-91; prof. U. So. Calif., LA, 1992—, assoc. dir. Ctr. Photonic Tech., 1994—. Head del. Harvard Model UN Yeshiva U., 1982; instr. Columbia U., 1987; rev. panel mem. NSF, Washington, 1992, Washington, 93, Washington, 94, invited optical comm. workshop, 94; chair panel on optical info. and comm., 94; co-chair Conf. on Lasers and Electro-Optics; steering com. and tech. com. mem. Conf. Optical Fiber Comm. Author 1 book; contbr. articles to profl. jours.; editor-in-chief Jour. Lighwave Tech., IEEE Jour. Selected Topics in Quantum Electronics; assoc. editor Jour. Selected Areas in Comm. Mem. faculty adv. bd. U. So. Calif. Hillel Orgn., 1992. Recipient Disting. Lectr. award, IEEE Lasers and Electro-Optics Soc., Armstrong Found. prize, Columbia U., 1984, Best Engring. Tchr. award, USC/TRW, young investigator award, NSF, 1992, Eddy Paper Award, 2001, USL Assoc. Award for Univ. Wide Excellence in Tchg.; grantee NSF, Advanced Rsch. Projects Agy., Packard Found., Powell Found., Ballistic Missile Def. Orgn.; fellow, Semiconductor Rsch. Corp., 1986, Sci. and Engring., David and Lucile Packard Found., 1993, presdl. faculty, NSF, 1994, sr. scholar, Fulbright Found., 1997. Fellow: IEEE, Optical Soc. Am. (symposium organizer ann. mtg. 1992, panel organizer ann. mtg. 1993, symposium organizer ann. mtg. 1995, panel organizer ann. mtg. 1995, program com. for conf. on optical fiber commn. 1996, 1997, program co-chair ann. mtg. 2001, vice chair optical comm. group, tech. council chair-photonics divsn., co-chair sci. and engring. coun., bd. dirs., program co-chair of OSA Annual Mtg., tech. coun. chair photonics divsn.); mem.: IEEE (sr.; editor-in-chief IEEE/OSA Jour. Lightwave Tech.), Soc. Photo-Instrumentation Engring. (program chair telecomm. engring. photonics west 1995, chmn. conf. on emerging techs. for all-optical networks photonics west 1995, program com. for Conf. on Optical Fiber Comm. 1996, conf. program com. components for WDM), IEEE Lasers and Electro-Optics Soc. (chmn. optical comm. subcom. ann. mtg. 1994, bd. govs. 1998—2001, v.p. tech. affairs, mem. optical comm. tech. com., bd. govs., mem. optical networks tech. com., various awards coms., chmn. optical comm. tech. com., awards com. mem. Quantum Electronics, IEEE Fellow, pres.-elect, Disting. Lectr. award), Sigma Xi. Achievements include patents for localized photochemical etching of multilayered semiconductor body, optical star coupler utilizing fiber amplifier tech., and one-to-many simultaneous optical WDM 2-dim. plane interconnections. Home: 9326 Sawyer St Los Angeles CA 90035-4102 Office: U So Calif Dept Elec Engring Eeb 538 Los Angeles CA 90089-0001 Business E-Mail: willner@usc.edu.

WILLNER, ANN RUTH, political scientist, educator; b. NYC, Sept. 2, 1924; d. Norbert and Bella (Richman) W. BA cum laude, Hunter Coll., 1945; MA, Yale U., 1946; PhD, U. Chgo., 1961. Lectr. U. Chgo., 1946-47, rsch. assoc. Ctr. for Econ. Devel. and Cultural Change, 1954-56, 61-62; advisor on orgn. and tng. Indonesian Ministry for Fgn. Affairs, Jakarta, 1952-53; expert for small scale indsl. planning Indonesian Nat. Planning Bur., Jakarta, 1953-54; fgn. affairs analyst Congl. Reference Svc., Libr. of Congress, 1960; asst. prof. polit. sci. SUNY, Binghamton, 1962-63; postdoctoral fellow polit. sci. and Southeast Asian studies Yale U., New Haven, 1963-64; rsch. assoc. Ctr. Internat. Studies, Princeton U., 1964-69; assoc. prof. polit. sci. U. Kans., Lawrence, 1969-70, prof., 1970-98. Vis. prof. polit. sci. CUNY, 1975; cons. govt. agys. and pvt. industry Polit. sci. editor: Ency. of the Social Scis., 1961; mem. editl. bd. Econ. Devel. and Cultural Change, 1954-57, Jour. Comparative Adminstrn., 1969-74, Comparative Politics, 1977—; author: The Neotraditional Accomodation to Political Independence, 1966, Charismatic Political Leadership: A Theory, 1968, The Spellbinders, 1984, 2004; also monographs, jour. articles, book chpts., newspaper columns. Grantee Rockefeller Found., 1965, Social Sci. Rsch. and Am. Coun. Learned Socs., 1966. Mem. Am. Polit. Sci. Assn. (gov. coun. 1979-81), Nat. Press Club. Home: 560 N St SW # N405 Washington DC 20024-4605 Office Phone: 202-484-2092, 202-368-8143. Personal E-mail: arwill@earthlink.net.

WILLNER, DOROTHY, anthropologist, educator; b. NYC, Aug. 26, 1927; d. Norbert and Bella (Richman) W. Ph.B., U. Chgo., 1947, MA, 1953, PhD, 1961; postgrad., Ecole Pratique des Hautes Etudes, U. Paris, France, 1950—51. Anthropologist Jewish Agy., Israel, 1955-58; tech. asst., adminstrn. expert in community devel. UN, Mexico, 1958; asst. prof. dept. sociology and anthropology U. Iowa, Iowa City, 1959-60; research assoc. U. Chgo., 1961-62; asst. prof. dept. sociology and anthropology U. N.C., Chapel Hill, 1962-63, Hunter Coll., NYC, 1964-65; assoc. prof. dept. anthropology U. Kans., Lawrence, 1967-70, prof., 1970-90; professorial lectr. Johns Hopkins U. Sch. Advanced Internat. Studies, 1992. Cons. Washington Action for Youth, United

Planning Orgn., 1964; rsch. in field. Author: Community Leadership, 1960, Nation-Building and Community in Israel, 1969. Contbr. numerous articles to profl. publs. Fellow Am. Anthrop. Assn., Soc. Applied Anthropology, Royal Anthrop. Inst., Ctrl. States Anthrop. Soc. (past pres.), Assn. Polit. and Legal Anthropology (past pres.). Home: N 407 560 N St SW Washington DC 20024-4605

WILLNER, EUGENE BURTON, food and liquor company executive; b. Chgo., July 27, 1934; s. Fred and Mae (Goodhartz) W.; m. Karen Nell Kaye, Feb. 22, 1962; children: Tracy Fran, Kelly Kaye. BA, Northwestern U., 1956. Pres. World Wide Fisheries Inc., Chgo., 1956—60; merchandiser Edison Bros. Stores Inc., St. Louis, 1960—66; v.p. Mo. Supreme Life Ins. Co., St. Louis, 1966—67; exec. v.p. Exec. Agys., Inc., St. Louis, 1966—67; pres. Bluff Creek Industries, Inc., Ocean Springs, Miss., 1967—69, Purse String Stores, Inc., Miami, Fla., 1969—73, World Wide Fisheries, Miami, 1969—73, Renwill Seafoods, Inc., 1979—. Chmn. bd. Astral Liquors, Inc., Foxy Laidy Lounges, Prime Universal Seafood Corp., Miami, also Key West, Fla., Caracas, Venezuela, San Juan del Sur, Nicaragua, Quito, Ecuador; pres., chmn. bd. Common Markets, Inc., Miami, London and Moscow, 1980— Mem. Deering Bay Country Club, Turnberry Club, Grove Isle Club, Fisher Island Club, Palm Beach Country Club. Office: 29000 S Dixie Hwy Homestead FL 33033-2302 Address: PO Box 561944 Pinecrest FL 33256-1944 Office Phone: 305-251-0087. Personal E-mail: asiamoon@att.net.

WILLOCKS, KRISTIN, psychology educator; b. Dallas, Apr. 9, 1968; d. Milton Wilson and Jan Sheridan, Marsha Wilson (Stepmother); m. Keith Willocks, Aug. 8, 1992. MEd, U. Ga., Athens, 1991, EdS, 1992. Lic. Tenn. State Dept. Edn., 1993. Sch. psychologist Metro Nashville Pub. Sch., 1992—. Mem.: Nat. Assn. Sch. Psychologist.

WILLOCKS, ROBERT MAX, retired librarian; b. Maryville, Tenn., Oct. 1, 1924; s. Willis Lemuel and Hannah (Emert) W.; m. Neysa Nerene Ferguson, May 23, 1947; children— Margret Sharon, Samuel David, Mark Timothy, Robert Daniel, Kent Max. BA, Maryville Coll., 1949; B.D., Golden Gate Bapt. Theol. Sem., 1951, Th.M., 1962; MA in Library Sci, Peabody Coll., 1962. Ordained to ministry Bapt. Ch., 1950; pastor in Calif., 1950-56; missionary to Korea So. Bapt. Fgn. Mission Bd., Taejon, 1956- 65; asso. dir. library Heidelberg Coll., Tiffin, Ohio, 1965-67; dir. library Columbia Coll., SC, 1967-70; asst. dir. libraries Syracuse U., NY, 1970-76; assoc. dir. libraries U. Fla., Gainesville, 1976-83, acting dir. libraries, 1983-84, dep. dir. libraries, 1984-89, ret., 1989; pastor Northwood Bapt. Ch., Gainesville, 1981-92; libr. Bapt. Theol. Sem., Lusaka, Zambia, 1994-97, Ghana Bapt. Sem., Kumasi, 1998—2006. Acting dir. Fla. Ctr. for Libr. Automation, 1984; cons. Choong Chung Nam Province Library Assn., Republic of Korea, 1962—65; dir. Korea Bapt. Press, 1959—61; prof. ch. history Korea Bapt. Sem., 1957—65, acting pres., 1958—59, librarian, 1959—65; vice chmn. Korea Bapt. Mission, 1962—64; del. Fla. Gov.'s Conf. on Libraries, 1978. Editor: Korean translations Thus it is Written, 1963, The Progress of Worldwide Missions, 1965. Chmn. trustees Wallace Meml. Bapt. Hosp., Pusan, Korea, 1963-65; pres. bd. dirs. Phoenix Homeowners Assn., 1980-88; relief worker, Kenya, Turkey, Peru, 2007. With USNR, 1943-46. Mem. ALA (chmn. telefacsimile com. 1976-78, tech. com. 1980-84, chmn. standards com. 1985-88), Fla. Libr. Assn., Southeastern Library Assn., AAUP, Peabody Coll. Alumni Assn. (pres. S.C. 1968-69) Home: 1326 E Earll Dr Phoenix AZ 85014

WILLOUGHBY, SARAH-MARGARET C., retired chemist, educator, chemical engineer, consultant; b. Bowling Green, KY, Oct. 15, 1917; d. Austin Burrell Claypool and Minerva Dallas Renfrow-Claypool; m. John Richard Evans, II, Aug. 30, 1938 (dec. Dec. 1942); 1 child, Richard Claypool Evans; m. Olief Glenn Willoughby, June 18, 1948 (dec.); children: Sarah, Stephen(dec.). BS, Western Ky. U., 1938; PhD, Purdue U., 1950. Registered profl. engr., Ind., Tex. Chemist Devoe-Reynolds, Inc., Louisville, 1941—42; jr. engr. chem. lab. div. Curtiss-Wright Corp., Louisville, 1942—44; tech. asst. Purdue U., West Lafayette, Ind., 1944—46, fellow, 1946—50; rsch. chemist, coatings divsn. Monsanto Chem. Co., Boston, 1950—52; assoc. prof. of chemistry U. Tex., Arlington, 1954—84, co-dir. Ctr. for Microcrystalline Polymer Rsch. Studies, 1978—82, prof. emeritus chemistry, 1984. Cons. Albert H. Halff Assocs., Dallas, 1980—86. Co-edit., author Engineer-in-Training Manual, 1970. Recipient Outstanding Chem. Engr. award, Purdue U., 1996, Cmty. Growth Contbn. award, Arlington Hist. Soc., Tex.; named to Hall of Disting. Alumni, Western Ky. U., 1994, Am. Men and Women of Sci., Personalities of the South, 1974, Cmty. Leaders and Noteworthy Americans, 1978, Notable Women of Tex., 1984—85, Daughters of Guilds of Colonial Artisans and Tradesmen, 2005; nominee Dallas-Ft. Worth Trailblazer award, 1996. Fellow: Am. Inst. Chemists; mem.: Am. Chem. Soc. (emeritus mem.), Peyton Soc. Va. (life), Gold Star Wives Am. (life), NY Acad. Sci. (life), Soc. Women Engrs. (sr.), Nat. Soc. Daughters of Founders and Patriots (v.p. NE Tex. chpt. 1997—, pres. NE Tex. chpt. 2006—08), Plantagenet Soc., Colonial Dames Am., Nat. Soc. DAR (chpt. regent 1967—69, nat. bicentennial com. mem. 1975—76, Nat. Women's Issues essay award 2005), Nat. Soc. Children of Am. Revolution (Tex. sr. state pres. 1968—70), Nat. Soc. Colonial Dames of XVII Century (chpt. regent 1980—82), Magna Charta Dames and Barons (formerly Nat. Soc. Magna Charta Dames) (Tex. state pres. 1986—88, nat. chmn. edn.), Colonial Order of the Crown, Soc. Descendants of Knights of the Most Noble Order of the Garter, Sovereign Colonial Soc. Ams. of Royal Descent, Friends of St. George, Order Ky. Cols., Sigma Xi (pres. 1966—68, emeritus mem.), Alpha Chi Omega (Lambda Epsilon chapt.). Home: 1630 Pecan Park Dr Arlington TX 76012

WILLOUGHBY, STEPHEN SCHUYLER, mathematics professor; b. Madison, Wis., Sept. 27, 1932; s. Alfred and Elizabeth Frances (Cassell) W.; m. Helen Sali Shapiro, Aug. 29, 1954; children: Wendy Valentine (Mrs. Peter Gallen), Todd Alan. AB (scholar), Harvard U., 1953, AM in Teaching, 1955; EdD (Clifford Brewster Upton fellow), Columbia U., 1961. Tchr. Newton (Mass.) Pub. Schs., 1954-57, Greenwich (Conn.) Pub. Schs., 1957-59; instr. U. Wis., Madison, 1960-61, asst. prof. math. edn. and math., 1961-65; prof. math. edn. and math. NYU, 1965-87, dir. math. edn. dept., 1967-83, chmn. math., sci. and stats. edn. dept., 1970-80, 86-87, chmn. U. Faculty Coun., 1981-82; prof. math. U. Ariz., Tucson, 1987—2002; prof. emeritus math. and math. edn. NYU, 1987—; prof. emeritus math. U. Ariz., Tucson, 2002—. Mem. nat. bd. advisor Sq. One TV, 1983-94, U.S. Commn. on Math. Instrn., 1984-95, chmn., 1991-95; math. adv. com. Nat. Tchr. Exam. Successor (Praxis), 1989-94; edn. panel New Am. Schs. Devel. Corp., 1991-97; U.S. Nat. rep. Internat. Commn. on Math. Instrn., 1991-95. Author: Contemporary Teaching of Secondary School Mathematics, 1967, Probability and Statistics, 1968, Teaching Mathematics: What Is Basic, 1981, Mathematics Education for a Changing World, 1990, Real Math, 1981, 85, 87, 91, Math: Explorations and Applications, 1998, College Mathematics Through Applications, 1999, The Other End of the Log: Memoirs of an Education Rebel, 2002, SRA Real Math, K-6, 2007 2009; contbr. articles to profl. jours. and encys., chpts. to yearbooks and anthologies. Recipient Leadership in Math. Edn. Lifetime Achievement medal, 1995. Mem. Nat. Coun. Tchrs. Math. (dir. 1968-71, pres. 1982-84), Coun. Sci. Soc. Pres. (chmn. 1988). Home: 5435 E Gleneagles Dr Tucson AZ 85718-1805 Office: U Ariz Dept Math Tucson AZ 85721-0001 Personal E-mail: sswill@comcast.net.

WILLOUGHBY, WILLIAM FRANKLIN, II, retired physician, scientist, military officer; b. Washington, Feb. 4, 1936; s. William Westel and Patricia (De Zychlinska) W.; m. Mary Scott Fishburne, 1963 (div. 1974); children: Westel Woodbury, William Franklin III, Laura Fishburne, Mary Scott; m. Judith Eleanor Barbaras, Oct. 25, 1975; 1 child, Robert Alexander Willoughby. AB, Johns Hopkins U., 1957, MD, 1965, PhD in Microbiology, 1965; grad. with distinction, USAF War Coll., 1985. Diplomate Am. Bd. Pathology. Intern then resident in pathology Johns Hopkins Hosp., 1965—67; asst. prof. depts. pathology and microbiology Case Western Res. U., Cleve.; dir. Virginia Mason Rsch. Ctr., Seattle, 1972—75; assoc. prof. dept. pathology Sch. Medicine, Johns Hopkins U., Balt., 1975—87; prof., chmn. dept. pathology Sch. Medicine, U. S.C., Columbia, 1987-92; dir. labs. Cook County Hosp., Chgo., 1992-98, interim med. dir., 1994-96; ret., 1998. Cons. NIH, Bethesda, Md., 1979-98, mem. pathology A study sect., 1982-86; cons. NRC, Washington, 1981-84; mem. res. component med. coun., Dept. Def., Pentagon, 1991-93; maj. USAFR, 1975, advanced through ranks to maj. gen., 1993; dep. surgeon gen. for res. affairs, USAF, Bolling AFB, D.C., 1993-95; asst. surg. gen., Operation Desert Storm/Desert Shield, 1990-91, ret. 1995. Author: The Zychlinski Family: Their Polish Ancestors and American Descendants, 2007; mem. editorial bd. Am. Rev. Respiratory Disease, 1978-84; contbr. articles to profl. jours., reviewer numerous sci. manuscripts. Vestryman Trinity Episcopal Ch., Long Green, Md., 1984-87; bd. dirs. Ctrl. S.C. chpt. ARC, Columbia, 1989-92; bd. fellow Norwich U., 1992-95. Decorated D.S.M., Legion of Merit; recipient Edwin E. Osgood prize Va. Mason Rsch. Ctr., 1973; Arthritis Found. fellow Scripps Clinic and Rsch. Found., 1967-69; Poncine scholar Poncine Found., 1972-74; NIH rsch. grantee, 1976-91. Fellow Coll. Am. Pathologists; mem. AAAS, Am. Lung Assn. (nat. rsch. grant rev. com. 1978-82, chmn., 1981-82), Am. Soc. Investigative Pathology, Am. Assn. Immunologists, Am. Soc. Cell Biologists, Chgo. Coun. Fgn. Rels., Internat. Acad. Pathology, Assn. Pathology Chmns., Aerospace Med. Assn., Soc. USAF Flight Surgeons (bd. govs. 1993-96), Am. Thoracic Soc., Assn. Mil. Surgeons U.S., Soc. Med. Cons. to Armed Forces, Army Navy Club, Air Force Assn., Univ. Club Chgo., Silver Wings Assn., Johns Hopkins Club, City Club Chgo. Avocations: music, genealogy, antique automobiles, Chinese art. Home: 1416A S Federal St Chicago IL 60605-3057 Personal E-mail: wwilloughby@sbcglobal.net.

WILLS, DAVID WOOD, minister, educator; b. Portland, Ind., Jan. 25, 1942; s. Theodore Oscar Mitchell and Elizabeth Lochore (Wood) W.; m. Carolyn Reynolds Montgomery, Aug. 22, 1964; children: John Brookings, Theodore Worcester, Thomas Churchill. BA, Yale U., 1962; BD, Princeton Theol. Sem., 1966; PhD, Harvard U., 1975. Ordained to ministry Presbyn. Ch., 1970. Asst. prof. Sch. of Religion, U. So. Calif., 1970-72; asst. prof. dept. of religion Amherst Coll., Mass., 1972-78, assoc. prof., 1978-83, prof., 1983-90, prof. religion and Black studies, 1990-94, Winthrop H. Smith '16 prof. Am. history and Am. studies, dept. religion and Black studies, 1994—, also dir. Luce Program in Comparative Religious Ethics 1978-88. Author: Christianity in the United States, 2005; editor (with Richard Newman) Black Apostles at Home and Abroad, 1982, (with Albert Raboteau) Afro-American Religion: A Documentary History Project, 1987—. Kent fellow Danforth Found., 1966-70, 75, Ford Found. fellow, 1972, Inst. for Ecumenical and Cultural Rsch. fellow, 1972, Nat. Humanities Ctr. fellow, 1980-81, 94, NEH fellow for Coll. Tchrs., 1988-89, W. E. B. DuBois Inst. for Afro-Am. Rsch. fellow, 1989-91. Mem. Am. Acad. Religion (chair Afro-Am. religious history group 1975-78), Am. Hist. Assn., Am. Soc. Ch. History, Orgn. Am. Historians, Phi Beta Kappa. Home: 47 Stagecoach Rd Amherst MA 01002-3527 Office: Amherst Coll Dept Religion Amherst MA 01002 Office Phone: 413-542-2470. Business E-Mail: dwwills@amherst.edu.

WILLS, ELANA CUNNINGHAM, state supreme court justice; BS, Ark. State Univ., 1984; JD with honors, Univ. Ark., 1987. Bar: Ark. 1987. Assoc. Rose Law Firm, 1987—88; asst. atty. gen. State of Ark., 1988—93, dep. atty. gen., 1993—99, sr. asst. atty. gen., 1999—2003, dep. atty. gen., 2003—08; assoc. justice Ark. Supreme Ct., 2008—. Contbr. articles to law jours. Mem.: ABA, Ark. Bar Assn., Pulaski County Bar Assn. Office: Ark Supreme Ct Rm 1500 625 Marshall St Little Rock AR 72201 Office Phone: 501-682-6876, 501-682-6870.*

WILLS, GARRY, historian; b. Atlanta, May 22, 1934; s. John and Mayno (Collins) Wills; m. Natalie Cavallo, May 30, 1959; children: John, Garry, Lydia. BA, St. Louis U., 1957; MA, Xavier U., Cin., 1958, Yale U., 1959, PhD, 1961; LittD (hon.), Coll. Holy Cross, 1982, Columbia Coll., 1982, Beloit Coll., 1988, Xavier U., 1993, St. Xavier U., 1993, Union Coll., 1993, Macalester Coll., 1995, Bates Coll., 1995, St. Ambrose, 1997, George Wash. U., 1999, Spring Hill Coll., 2000, Siena Heights U., 2001, Gettysburg Coll., 2002, Am. U., 2003, Muhlenberg Coll., 2004, U. Conn., 2008; LittD, Bard Coll., 2009, Knox Coll., 2009. Fellow Ctr. Hellenic Studies, 1961—62; assoc. prof. classics Johns Hopkins U., 1962—67, adj. prof., 1968-80; Henry R. Luce prof. Am. culture and public policy Northwestern U., 1980—88, adj. prof., 1988—2005, prof. history emeritus, 2005—. Author: (book) Chesterton, 1961, Politics and Catholic Freedom, 1964, Roman Culture, 1966, Jack Ruby, 1967, Second Civil War, 1968, Nixon Agonistes, 1970, Bare Ruined Choirs, 1972, Inventing America, 1978, At Button's, 1979, Confessions of a Conservative, 1979, Explaining America, 1980, The Kennedy Imprisonment, 1982, Lead Time, 1983, Cincinnatus, 1984, Reagan's America, 1987, Under God, 1990, Lincoln at Gettysburg, 1992 (Pulitzer Prize for gen. non-fiction, 1993), Certain Trumpets: The Call of Leaders, 1994, Witches and Jesuits: Shakespeare's Macbeth, 1994, John Wayne's America, 1997, St. Augustine, 1999, A Necessary Evil, 1999, Papal Sin, 2000, Venice, Lion City, 2001, St. Augustine's Childhood, 2001, James Madison, 2002, Why Am I a Catholic, 2002, St. Augustine's Memory, 2002, Mr. Jefferson's University, 2002, St. Augustine's Sin, 2003, Negro President, 2003, St. Augustine's Conversion, 2004, The Rosary, 2005, Henry Adams and the Making of America, 2005, St. Augustine's Confessions, 2006, What Jesus Meant, 2006, What Paul Meant, 2006, Head and Heart, 2007, What the Gospels Meant, 2008, Epigrams of Martial. Recipient Merle Curti award, Orgn. Am. Historians, Nat. Book Critics Cir. award (2), Wilbur Cross medal, Yale U., Peabody award, NEH Presdl. medal, 1998, John Hope Franklin award, Chgo. Hist. Soc., First Freedom award, Coun. for the First Freedom, Lincoln Laureate, State of Ill., Lifetime Achievement award, English-Speaking Union. Mem.: AAAL, Am. Philos. Soc., Am. Antiquarian Soc., Am. Acad. Arts and Scis., Mass. Hist. Soc. Roman Catholic. Office: Northwestern U Dept History Evanston IL 60208 Business E-Mail: g-wills@northwestern.edu.

WILLS, J. ROBERT, retired academic administrator, theater educator, writer; b. Akron, Ohio, May 5, 1940; s. J. Robert and Helen Elizabeth (Lapham) W.; m. Barbara T. Salisbury, Aug. 4, 1984 (dec. 1998); m. Jeanne Hokin, June 2002. BA, Coll. of Wooster, 1962; MA, U. Ill., 1963; PhD, Case-Western Res. U., 1971; cert. in arts adminstrn, Harvard U., 1976. Instr. to asst. prof., dir. theatre Wittenberg U., Springfield, Ohio, 1963-72; assoc. prof., dir. grad. studies, chmn. dept. theatre U. Ky., Lexington, 1972-77, prof. theatre, dean Coll. Fine Arts, 1977-81; prof. drama, dean Coll. Fine Arts U. Tex., Austin, 1981-89, Effie Marie Cain Regents chair in Fine Arts, 1986-89; provost, prof. theatre Pacific Luth. U., Tacoma, 1989-94; prof. theatre, dean coll. fine arts Ariz. State U., Tempe, 1994—2006; ret. Cons. colls., univs., arts orgns., govt. agencies Author: The Director in a Changing Theatre, 1976, Directing in the Theatre: A Casebook, 1980, rev. edit., 1994; dir. 95 plays; contbr. articles to profl. jours. Bd. dirs. various art orgns., Ky., Tex., Wash., Ariz. Recipient grants public and pvt. agencies. Mem. Nat. Assn. State Univs. and Land-Grant Colls.(chmn. commn. on arts 1981-83), Coun. Fine Arts Deans (exec. com. 1984-89, sec./treas. 1986-89), Univ. and Coll. Theatre Assn. (pres. 1981-82), Assn. for Communication Adminstrn. (pres. 1986-87), Ky. Theatre Assn. (pres. 1976).

WILLS, JOHN ELLIOT, JR., retired historian, writer; b. Urbana, Ill., Aug. 8, 1936; s. John Elliot and George Anne (Hicks) W.; m. Carolin Connell, July 19, 1958; children: Catherine, Christopher John, Jeffrey David, Joanne, Lucinda. BA in Philosophy, U. Ill., 1956; MA in East Asian Studies, Harvard U., 1960, PhD in History and Far Ea. Langs., 1967. History instr. Stanford (Calif.) U., 1964-65, U. So. Calif., LA, 1965-67, asst. prof., 1967-72, assoc. prof., 1972-84, prof., 1984—2004, prof. emeritus, 2004—; acting chair East Asian Langs. and Cultures, 1987-89; dir. East Asian Studies Ctr. USC-UCLA Joint East Asian Studies Ctr., LA, 1990-94. Rsch. abroad in The Netherlands, Taiwan, China, Japan, Macao, Philippines, Indonesia, India, Italy, Spain, Portugal, Eng. Author: Pepper, Guns, and Parleys: The Dutch East India Company and China, 1662-1681, 1974, Embassies and Illusions: Dutch and Portuguese Envoys to K'ang-hsi, 1666-1687, 1984, Mountain of Fame: Portraits in Chinese History, 1994, 1688: A Global History, 2001; co-editor: (with Jonathan D. Spence) From Ming to Ch'ing: Conquest, Region, and Continuity in Seventeenth-Century China, 1979; editor: Eclipsed Entrepots of the Western Pacific: Taiwan and Central Vietnam, 1500-1800, 2002; contbr. articles to profl. jours. Grantee Nat. Acad. Scis., 1985, Am. Coun. Learned Soc., 1979-80; Younger Humanist fellow NEH, 1972-73. Mem. Assn. for Asian Studies, Am. Hist. Assn., Phi Beta Kappa, Phi Kappa Phi (recognition award 1986, 95). Avocation: travel. Home Phone: 626-755-6506. Business E-Mail: jwills@usc.edu.

WILLS, KATHERINE V. TSIOPOS, language educator; b. St. Louis, Sept. 30, 1957; d. Vasilios and Kalliope Stratos Tsiopos; m. Howard William Wills. BA in English and Anthropology, Washington U., St. Louis, 1979; MA in English and Writing, Ind. U., Bloomington, 1991; PhD in Composition and Rhetoric, U. Louisville, 2004. Cert. in Allied Health Technique in Histological Method St. Joseph's Hosp., 1990. Pres. Port of Nashville, Inc., Ind., 1986—90; asst. prof. English Ind. U.-Purdue U., Columbus, 1991—; v.p. Workplace Training Assocs., Inc., 1993—. Presenter in field. Contbr. over 60 articles in creative jours. Recipient essay award Scholastic Mag., Inc., 1973, award for acad. excellence and community svc. Am. Hellenic Progessive and Edn. Assn., poetry award Wednesday Club of St. Louis, Mo., 1977, Roger Conant Hatch hon. mention for writing, Washington U., 1977. Mem.: MLA, AAUP, Writing Program Adminstrs., TechRhet-Listserv, Conf. Coll. Composition and Communication, Nat. Conf. Tchrs. English, Multiethnic Lit., Assn. Bus. Communication, Phi Kappa Delta. Greek Orthodox. Avocations: scuba diving, motorcycling, fishing. Home: 7772 Bellsville Rd Nashville IN 47448-8995 Office Phone: 812-348-7215. Business E-Mail: kwills@iupui.edu.

WILLS, KIMBERLY KAY, legal association administrator, educator; d. Quentin F. and Donna M. Youngberg; m. Kirby A. Wills, May 11, 1996; children: Victoria M., Bailee M. BS, U. SD, Vermillion, 1997; MA, U. Phoenix, 2006. Coll. instr. Eastern N.Mex U., Ruidoso, 2006—, Pk. U., Holloman AFB, N.Mex., 2006—, Troy U., Holloman AFB, 2007—, asst. site dir., 2008—; bus. mgr. Wills Law Firm, P.C., Alamogordo, N.Mex., 2007—. Mem. P.E.O., Alamogordo, N.Mex., 2008. Recipient Rising Star award, U. SD, Dept. Mass Communication, 1995, Electronic Media award, 2001. Conservative. Avocations: skiing, boating, gardening, photography, travel. Office: Wills Law Firm PC 1208 New York Ave Alamogordo NM 88310 Office Fax: 866-626-4574. Business E-Mail: willslaw@tularosa.net.

WILLS, MICHAEL STEPHEN, nutritionist, quality assurance professional, photographer; b. Roslyn, NY, Mar. 10, 1953; s. Thomas Francis and Catherine Ann Wills; m. Svetlana Victorivna Shiryaeva, Jan. 26, 1994 (div. Aug. 2005); m. Barbara Ann Keegan, Jan. 15, 1979 (div. June 20, 1985); m. Pamela Jayne Sprinkle, Mar. 20, 2009; stepchildren: Charles Clancy, Kseniya Andreevna Shiryaeva 1 child, Sean Michael. BS with high honors, U. Ariz., 1975. Registered dietitian Am. Dietetics Assn., Ill., 1976. Newspaper carrier LI Newsday, Albertson, NY, 1966—69; dietetic technician Ariz. Med. Ctr., Tucson, 1972—73; dietetic practicum U.S. Army, San Francisco, 1973—73; dietetic technician Tucson Med. Ctr., 1973—75; dietetic internship U. Ariz., Tucson, 1975—76; dir. of food svc. Catskill (N.Y.) Meml. Hosp. and Nursing Home, 1976—77; food svc. dir. New Rochelle (N.Y.) Nursing Home, 1977—79; dir. of food svc. Grace Plz., Inc., Great Neck, NY, 1979—82; corp. dietitian Data Control Info., Inc., Hornell, NY, 1982—84, dir. software devel., 1984—86; quality assurance and customer support rep. The CBORD Group, Inc., Ithaca, NY, 1986—87, mgr. support and quality assurance, 1987—88, mgr. quality assurance, 1988—98, dir. quality assurance, 1998—2007, sr. adv. Analyst, 2007—; owner www-.MichaelStephenWills.com. Cons. ServiceMaster, Downers Grove, Ill., 1986—94, Abbot Labs., Chgo., 1987—88, Brown U., Providence, 1987—92, Hallmark Cards, Kansas City, Kans., 1987—94, 1988 Winter Olympics, Calgary, Alberta, Canada, 1987—88, Disneyland, Paris, 1993—93, The Walt Disney World Co., Orlando, Fla., 1993—, Cornell U., Ithaca, NY, 1995, Kaiser Permanente, LA, 2001—03, NSW Dept. Health, Sydney, 2002—04, Children's Hosp. Eastern Ontario, 2002—09, Disneyland, Anaheim, Calif., 2003, H.E.B. Markets, San Antonio, 2004—, Calif. Inst. of Tech., Pasadena, Calif., 2004—04, Gordon's Food Svc., Aramark, 2006—09; presenter in field. Contbr. articles to profl. jours. Alumni bd. dirs. U. Ariz. Coll. Agrl. & Life Scis., 2005—; mem. Unitarian Universalist Assn., Ithaca, 1992—2004. Recipient Photography awards, Photographic Soc. Am., 2005—07; scholar Promising Student, Herricks H.S. PTA, 1971, U. Ariz., 1973—74; NY State Regents scholar, N.Y. State Dept. Edn., 1971, Syntex Dietetic Internship scholar, Syntex Corp., 1975. Mem.: Am. Dietetic Assn. (licentiate), Amercian Soc. for Quality (assoc.; paper reviewer 2002—04), Photographic Soc. Am. (assoc.), Kappa Omicron Nu. Democrat. Roman Catholic. Achievements include development of functional reliability approach for software development; creation of an algorithm for calculating probability of concurrence for multi-user software applications; design of software application for measuring software performance benchmarks; creation of Olvera Valenzuela Memorial Scholarship for University of Arizona. Avocations: astronomy, writing, backpacking. Home: PO 258 20 West Malloryville Rd Freeville NY 13068 Office: The CBORD Group Inc 61 Brown Rd Ithaca NY 14850 Personal E-mail: mwills@twcny.rr.com. Business E-Mail: msw@cbord.com.

WILLS, RICHARD ANDREW, materials handling equipment company executive; b. York, Pa., Aug. 12, 1938; s. Richard Andrew Sr. and Romaine Louise (Gross) W. BS, George Washington U., 1960; MS, U. Colo., 1963, D of Bus. Adminstrn., 1972, PhD, 1973. Registered pharmacist, Pa., Colo., Mass., Washington. Pharmacist Shultz Drug Store, York, 1960—61; tchg. assoc. U. Colo., Boulder, 1961—66; asst. prof. mktg. Merrimack Coll., North Andover, Mass., 1966—67, Suffolk U., Boston, 1967—71; assoc. prof. Babson Coll., Wellesley, Mass., 1971—76; sales mgr., v.p. Wills Equipment Co., York, 1976—83, pres., CEO, 1983—. Adj. prof. pharmacy adminstrn. Mass. Coll. Pharmacy, Boston, 1970-73. Contbr. over 28 articles to profl. jours. Mem. York Symphony Chorus, 1981-96; condr. Symphony Orch. So. York County, 1988—; lead trombonist Brodbecks Band, Alecia Band. Mem. Rotary Club of York (com. mem. 1985—, chmn. music com., chmn. York Pride). Avocations: skiing, music, travel, boating, model railroading. Home: Wyndham Hills 875 Upland Rd York PA 17403 Office: Wills Equipment Co 705 Roosevelt Ave York PA 17404-2827 Home Phone: 717-852-7988; Office Phone: 717-845-3691.

WILLS, ROBERT HAMILTON, retired publishing executive; b. Colfax, Ill., June 21, 1926; s. Robert Orson and Ressie Mae (Hamilton) W.; m. Sherilyn Lou Nierstheimer, Jan. 16, 1949; children: Robert L., Michael H., Kendall J. BS, MS, Northwestern U., 1950. Reporter Duluth (Minn.) Herald & News-Tribune, 1950-51; reporter Milw. Jour., 1951-59, asst. city editor, 1959-62; city editor Milw. Sentinel, 1962-75, editor, 1975-91; exec. v.p. Jour./Sentinel, Inc., Milw., 1991-92, pres., 1992-93; vice-chmn., 1993; also bd. dirs. Jour./Sentinel, Inc., Milw.; pub. Milw. Jour. Sr. v.p., bd. dirs. Jour. Communications; pres. Wis. Freedom of Info. Council, 1979-86, charter mem., 1979; Pulitzer Prize juror, 1982, 83, 90. Mem. media-law rels. com. State Bar Wis., 1969-99; vice chmn. privacy coun. Wis. Pub. Svc. Commn., 1996-97; mem. Wis. Privacy Coun., 1994-95. Recipient Leadership award Women's Ct. and Civic Conf. Greater Milw., 1987; inducted into Journalism Hall of Achievement Medill Sch. Northwestern U., 1997, Wis. Newspaper Assn. Found. Hall of Fame, 2001. Mem. Wis. Newspaper Assn. (pres. 1985-86, Disting. Svc. award 1992), Wis. AP (pres. 1975-76, Dion Henderson award Svc. 1993), Am. Soc. Newspaper Editors, Internat. Press Inst., Milw. Press Club (Media Hall Fame 1993), Soc. Profl. Journalists (prs. Milw. chpt. 1979-80, nat. pres. 1986-87), Sigma Delta Chi Found. (bd. dirs. 1993-96, Wis. Newsman of Yr. 1973, Freedom of Info. award Milw. chpt. 1988). Home: 2064 Tiger Links Dr Henderson NV 89012-6111 E-mail: wills2064@juno.com.

WILLS, WILLIAM RIDLEY, II, retired insurance company executive, historian; b. Nashville, June 19, 1934; s. Jesse Ely and Ellen (Buckner) W.; m. Irene Weaver Jackson, July 21, 1962; children: William Ridley III, Morgan Jackson, Thomas Weaver. BA, Vanderbilt U., 1956. Agt., staff mgr. Nat. Life & Accident Ins. Co., Nashville, 1958-62, supr., 1962-64, asst. sec., 1964-67, asst. v.p., 1967-70, 2d v.p., 1970-75, v.p., 1975-81, sr. v.p., 1981-83, Am. General Services Co., 1982-83; dir. Nat. Life & Accident Ins. Co., Nashville, 1976-83; pres. Tenn. Hist. Soc., 1985-87; bd. dirs. Nat. Trust for Hist. Preservation, 1988-91. Author: History of Belle Meade: Mansion, Plantation and Stud, 1991, Old Enough to Die, 1996, Touring Tennessee: A Post Card Panorama, 1989-1955, 1996, Tennessee Governors at Home, 1999, Belle Meade Country Club: The First One Hundred Years, 2001, Gentleman, Scholar, Athlete: The History of Montgomery Bell Academy, 2005, Elizabeth and Matt: A Love Story, 2006, Yours to County On-A Nashville Banker Extraordinaire, Sam M. Fleming, Jr., 2007, (book) Jessie and Ridley: They Made a Difference, 2008. Nat. chmn. Living Endowment Drive Vanderbilt U., 1974; pres. Cumberland Mus. and Sci. Ctr., Nashville, 1977; gen. chmn. campaign United Way, Nashville, 1978; pres. YMCA of Met. Nashville, 1984; trustee Ladies Hermitage Assn., 1981—90; mem. Tenn. Hist. Commn.; chmn. YMCA Found. Mid. Tenn., 1998—99; chmn. bd. Montgomery Bell Acad., 1988—97, gen. chmn. $43 million capital campaign, 1999—2000; mem. adv. bd. Pub. Libr. Nashville and Davidson County, 2002—08; trustee Tenn. Hist. Soc., 2007—; pres. Monteagle Sundy Sch. Assembly, 2002—04; bd. dirs. Vanderbilt U., 1988—. Lt. USN, 1956—58. Recipient awards YMCA, 1977, 1983, United Way De Tocqueville award, 1989, Tenn. History Book award Tenn. Libr. Assn. and Tenn. Hist. Commn., 1991, Disting. Alumnus award Montgomery Bell Acad., 1996, H.G. Hill award YMCA of Mid. Tenn., 2003. Fellow Life Office Mgmt. Assn.; mem. Assn. Preservation Tenn. Antiquities (pres. Nashville chpt. 1987-89), Belle Meade Country Club, Coffee House Club, Round Table Literary Club. Presbyterian. Home Phone: 615-269-5429.

WILLSE, JAMES PATRICK, editor; b. NYC, Mar. 17, 1944; s. Sherman Stokes and Katherine (Mackey) W.; m. Sharon Margaret Stack, Sept. 15, 1973; 1 child, Elizabeth Ruth. BA, Hamilton Coll., 1967; MS, Columbia U., 1968. Nat. editor AP, NYC, 1969-74, news editor San Francisco, 1975-78; city editor San Francisco Examiner, 1978-82, mng. editor, 1982-84, NY Daily News, 1984-89, editor, 1989—93, pub., 1992—93; dir. news media Advance Publications, Inc., 1993—94; editor Star Ledger, Newark, 1995—. Named Beveridge Editor of Yr. Nat. Press Found., 1999, Breaking News Pullizer Prize, 2005; fellow Stanford U., 1975. Mem. Am. Soc. Newspaper Editors, AP Mng. Editors. Office: Star Ledger 1 Star Ledger Plz Newark NJ 07102-1291 Office Phone: 973-392-4127. E-mail: jwillse@starledger.com.*

WILLSIE, SANDRA KAY, internist, educator; BS in Med. Tech., Pittsburg State U., Kans., 1975; DO, Kansas City U. Medicine and Bioscis., Mo., 1983. Diplomate in internal medicine, pulmonary diseases and critical care medicine Am. Bd. Internal Medicine, Am. Bd. Osteo. Internists, 2000. Rotating intern Univ. Hosp., Kansas City, Mo., 1983-84; resident in internal medicine U. Mo.-Kansas City Affiliated Hosps., 1984-87; fellow in pulmonary diseases and critical care medicine Truman Med. Ctr.-West, Kansas City, Mo., 1987-89; instr. medicine U. Mo.-Kansas City Sch. Medicine, 1984-89; med. dir. pulmonary clinic Truman Med. Ctr., 1991-2000; asst. prof. medicine U. Mo. Kansas City Sch. Medicine, 1989-94, assoc. prof. medicine, 1994-99, dep. asst. dean, 1994—97, asst. dean, 1997-2000, prof. medicine, 1999-2000, Kansas City U. Medicine and Bioscis., 2000—02, vice dean acad. affairs, adminstrn., med. affairs, 2002—08, exec. v.p. acad. affairs, provost, dean, 2007—08, exec. v.p. rsch. & med. affairs, dean Coll. Osteo. Medicine, 2007—08, exec. dean; exec. v.p. rsch. & med. affairs, dean Coll. Osteo. Medicine Heartland Health Scis. U., 2008—. Invited bd. question author Am. Bd. Internal Medicine, 1995—2000, relevance reviewer for pulmonary disease bd. exam, 1996—2000; internal medicine subspecialty program pre-reviewer Accreditation Coun. for Grad. Med. Edn., 1997—2000; credentials com. Truman Med. Ctr., Inc., 1990—96, med. intensive care unit com., 1992—2000, intermediate care unit com., 1992—2000, exec. com. Truman Health Sys., 1998—2000, profl. standards com., 1998—2000. Contbr. articles to profl. jours. Bd. dirs. Girls to Women, 1995—2000, v.p. bd. dirs., 1996—2000. Fellow: Am. Coll. Physicians (state activities com. 1991—95, chair, state activities com. 1994, scientific presentations judge 1995—96, coun. mem. 1998—2004), Am. Coll. Osteo. Internists (program com. 2002—07, rsch. com. 2003—, Rschr. of Yr. 2004); mem.: Met. Med. Soc. (chair women in medicine com. 2002—08, pres. com. 1995—2000, bd. dirs. 1997—2000, exec. com. 1999—2000, chair women in medicine com. 2002—), Am. Osteo. Assn., Kans. City Pulmonary Roundtable (pres. 1995—2006), Soc. Critical Care Medicine, Am. Lung Assn. Mo. (bd. mem.), Jackson County Osteo. Assn., Mo. Assn. Osteo. Physicians and Surgeons, Am. Thoracic Soc., Am. Coll. Chest Physicians (chair, basic sci. com. 1995—98, scientific program com. 1995—2003, membership com. 1997—2001, gov. for Mo. 1997—2001, chair, scientific presentations and awards com. 1998—2000, vice chair, scientific program com. 1999—2000, chair, scientific program com. 2000—01, regent 2004—, Young Investigator award 1992). Office: Heartland Health Scis Univ Ste 110 14221 Metcaff Ave Overland Park KS 66223 Office Phone: 913-766-3114. Personal E-mail: sandra.willsie@gmail.com.

WILLSON, C. GRANT, chemical engineering and chemistry professor; b. Vallejo, Calif., Mar. 30, 1939; s. Carlton P. and Margaret Ann (Cosner) Willson; m. Deborah Jeanne Merritt, Dec. 13, 1975; children: William, Andrew. BS in Chemistry, U. Calif., Berkeley, 1962, PhD in Organic Chemistry, 1973; MS in Organic Chemistry, San Diego State U., 1969. With propellent rsch. Aeroject Gen. Corp., Sacramento, 1962-64; tchr., coach Fairfax H.S., LA, 1964-67; prof. Calif. State U., Long Beach, 1973-74, U. Calif., San Diego, 1974-78; mgr. polymer sci. and tech. IBM Almaden Rsch. Ctr., San Jose, Calif., 1978-93; prof. chemistry, chem. engring. U. Tex., Austin, 1993—. Contbr. articles to profl. jours.; patentee in field. Recipient Kosar award, Soc. Imaging Sci. and Tech., 1998, Aristotle award, Semicondr. Rsch. Corp., Photopolymer Sci. award, Japan, 2003, 2007 Nat. Medal Technology and Innovation. Fellow SPIE; m.Mem. NAE, AAAS, Soc. Photog. and Instrumentation Engrs., Am. Phys. Soc., Am. Chem. Soc. (Arthur K. Doolittle award 1986, ACS Chemistry of Materials 1991, Carothers award 1992, Coop. Rsch. award in Polymer Sci. 1993, Applied Polymer Sci. Award, 2004, Heroes of Chemistry award, Arthur Dehon Little award 2005, SEMI North America award), NAS (award for chem. in svc. to soc. 1999), Coun. for Chem. Rsch. (Malcom Pruitt award 1997), St. Francis Yacht Club, Sigma Xi. Avocations: sailing, skiing. Office: Univ Texas Dept Chem and Chem Engring Austin TX 78712 Business E-Mail: willson@che.utexas.edu.

WILLUMSTAD, ROBERT B. (BOB WILLUMSTAD), former insurance company executive, retired diversified financial services company executive; b. Bklyn., Aug. 22, 1945; m. Carol Willumstad; 2 children. Grad., Adelphi U., LLD (hon.), 2005. Various ops., retail banking and computer systems positions Chemical Bank, 1967—87; chmn., CEO consumer finance svcs. Travelers Group; chmn., CEO Global Consumer Group, Citigroup Inc., 2000—03; pres. Citigroup, Inc., 2002—05, COO, 2003—05; pres., CEO Citibank N.A., 2003—05; non-exec. chmn. Am. Internat. Group, Inc. (AIG), 2006—08, chmn., CEO, 2008; co-founder, mng. ptnr. Brysam Global Partners, LLC, 2007—08, sr. adv., 2008—. Bd. dirs. S.C. Johnson & Son Inc., Am. Internat. Group, Inc. (AIG), 2006—08. Bd. dirs. Habitat for Humanity Internat., 2001—; bd. trustees Am. Scandinavian Found., Adelphia U., 2005—. Recipient Frederick Douglass award, NYC Urban League, 2002. Mem.: Financial Services Roundtable (bd. dirs.). Office: Brysam Global Partners LLC 277 Park Ave 35th Fl New York NY 10172

WILLY, THOMAS RALPH, lawyer; b. Phila., Sept. 30, 1943; s. Albert Ralph and Dorothy Rose (Driver) W.; m. Kay Harris, Jan. 12, 1968; children: Elyn Alexandria, Jon Charles. BA in History, U. Mo., Kansas City, 1966, JD with distinction, 1974. Bar: Mo. 1974, Kans., 2007. Assoc. Deacy & Deacy, Kansas City, 1974-75, Logan, Hentzen, Haitbrink & Moore, Kansas City, 1975; ptnr. Hentzen, Haitbrink & Moore, Kansas City, 1976-78, Hentzen, Moore & Willy, Kansas City, 1978-80, Moore & Willy Profl. Corp., Kansas City, 1980-87, pres., dir., 1987-94; shareholder, dir., v.p. Van Osdol, Magruder, Erickson & Redmond, P.C., Kansas City, 1994—2007, Van Osdol & Magruder, PC, 2007—. Cons. Ctr. for Mgmt. Assistance, Kansas City, 1990-2000; presenter living will project, Midwest Bioethics Ctr., 1990-2000. Pres. Kansas City Swiss Soc., 1989-91, bd. dirs. 1993-96, 2004-07; bd. dirs. Greater Kansas City People to People, 1995-98, 2000-03, Friends of Art, Kansas City, Kansas City Consensus, Hist. Kansas City Found. Capt. USAF, 1966-70; sponsor US Army Internat. Officers Info. Program Cmmd and Gen. Staff Coll., Ft. Leavenworth, 1993—. Mem. ABA (sect. intellectual property law, sect. real property, trust & estate law, sect. bus. law), Mo. Bar Assn., Lions (bd. dirs. Leawood 1986-88, 90-92, 2008-, sec. 1988-90, v.p. 1996-97, pres. 2007-08). Home: 10314 Lee Blvd Shawnee Mission KS 66206-2629 Office: 2400 Commerce Tower 911 Main St Kansas City MO 64105-2009 Office Phone: 816-421-0644. E-mail: twilly@vomer.com.

WILMER, MARY CHARLES, artist; b. Atlanta, Aug. 25, 1930; d. William Knox and Harriott Creighton (Thomas) Fitzpatrick; m. John Grant Wilmer, Dec. 28, 1950; children: John Grant, Knox Randolph, Charles Inman, Mary Catherine; m. Olin Grigsby Shivers, May 18, 1982. Attended, Wellsley Coll., Mass., 1948—50, Agnes Scott Coll., Decatur, Ga., 1950—51, BA, 1970; BFA, Coll. of Art, 1974. Co-pres. St. Elizabeth's Guild, Cathedral of Saint Philip. Exhibited in one-woman shows at Image South Gallery, 1974, Aronson Gallery, 1977, 79, Heath Gallery, 1982-, Coach House Gallery, 1983, 89; two-person show (with daughter Catherine Wilmer) Swan Coach House Gallery, Atlanta, 2003; group shows include Colony Square, 1975, Coach House Gallery, 1999; portrait painter, 1974—. Bd. dirs. Hillside Cottages, 1963-65, Alliance Theatre Co., 1965-68, Atlanta Child Svcs., 1965-68, Atlanta Coll. Art, 1965-85, Atlanta Puppetry Arts, 1982-87, Atlanta Med. Heritage, 1999-2000; co-chmn. Ga. Commn. Nat. Mus. of Women in the Arts, (pres.) 1985-87; mem. Study Club, 1970-, Book Club, 2001-. Mem. Piedmont Driving Club, Jr. League, Piedmont Garden Club. Episcopalian. Address: 1 Vernon Rd NW Atlanta GA 30305-2964

WILMERDING, JOHN, art historian, educator, curator; b. Boston, Apr. 28, 1938; s. John Currie and Lila Vanderbilt (Webb) W. AB, Harvard U., 1960, AM, 1961, PhD, 1965. Asst. prof. art Dartmouth Coll., 1965-68, assoc. prof., 1968-73, Leon E. Williams prof., 1973-77, chmn. dept. art, 1968-72, chmn. humanities divsn., 1971-72; sr. curator Am. art Nat. Gallery of Art, 1977-83, dep. dir., 1983-88; Sarofim prof. Am. art Princeton U., 1988—2007, chmn. dept. art and archeology, 1992-99. Vis. lectr. history of art Yale U., 1972; vis. prof. fine arts Harvard U., 1976; vis. prof. art U. Md., 1979; vis. prof. art history U. Del., 1982; hon. curator painting Peabody Mus., Salem, Mass.; vis. curator Met. Mus., 1988-2007. Author: Fitz Hugh Lane, 1964, A History of American Marine Painting, 1968, Pittura Americana dell' Ottocento, 1969, Robert Salmon, Painter of Ship and Shore, 1971, Fitz Hugh Lane, 1971, Winslow Homer, 1972, The Genius of American Painting, 1973, American Art, 1976, American Light, The Luminist Movement, 1980, American Masterpieces from the National Gallery of Art, 1980, An American Perspective, 1981, Important Information Inside, 1982, Andrew Wyeth, The Helga Pictures, 1987, American Views: Essays on American Art, 1991, The Artist's Mount Desert: American Painters on the Maine Coast, 1994, Compass and Clock: Defining Moments in American Culture, 1999, Signs of the Artist: Signatures and Self-Expression in American Paintings, 2003, American Art in the Princeton University Art Museum, Vol. 1, 2004, Richard Estes, 2006, Tom Wesselmann, 2008. Trustee Nat. Gallery of Art, Washington, Solomon R. Guggenheim Mus., NYC, North East Harbor Libr., Maine, Wyeth Found. Am. Art, Crystal Bridges Mus. Am. Art. Guggenheim fellow, 1973-74. Fellow Phila. Atheneum (hon.); Mem. Coll. Art Assn., Am. Philos. Soc. Office: Princeton U Dept Art and Archaeology 105 McCormick Hall Princeton NJ 08544-1018 Home Phone: 609-497-1968; Office Phone: 609-258-3785. E-mail: wilmerdg@princeton.edu.

WILMERS, ROBERT GEORGE, bank executive; b. NYC, Apr. 20, 1934; s. Charles K. and Cecilia (Eitingon) W.; m. Elisabeth Roche de la Rigodiere; children: Robert G. Jr.(dec.), Christopher C.; stepchildren: Juliette Chevalier, Charlotte deCoupigny, Camille deWouters, Guilaume deWouters. BA, Harvard U., 1956; postgrad., Harvard Bus. Sch., 1958-59. Dep. fin. adminstr. City of N.Y., 1966-70; v.p. Morgan Guaranty Trust Co., NYC and Belgium, 1970-80; CEO M&T Bank Corp., Buffalo, 1983—88, pres., CEO, 1988—2000, chmn., pres., CEO, 2000—05, chmn., 2005—06, chmn., CEO, 2007—; chmn. Empire State Devel. Corp., NYC, 2008—. Bd. dirs. The Bus. Coun. N.Y. State, Fin. Svcs. Roundtable. Decorated officer de l'Ordre de la Couronne (Belgium), Chevalier de l'Ordre de la Legion d'honneur (France). also: 1 W 64th St New York NY 10023-6734 Office: M&T Bank 1 M&T Plz Buffalo NY 14203 Office Phone: 716-842-5425. Business E-Mail: rwilmers@mtb.com.

WILMETH, DON BURTON, theatre arts educator and historian, administrator, writer, editor, actor, director; b. Houston, Dec. 15, 1939; s. Perry Davis and Pauline W.; m. Judy Eslie Hansgen, June 10, 1963; 1 child, Michael Tyler. BA, Abilene Christian U., 1961; MA, U. Ark., 1962; PhD, U. Ill., 1964; MA ad Eundem (hon.), Brown U., 1970. Tchg. asst. U. Ark., Fayetteville, 1961-62, U. Ill., Urbana, 1962-64; asst. prof., head drama dept. Eastern N.Mex. U., Portales, 1964-67; from asst. to prof. theatre arts, dept. chmn. Brown U., Providence, 1967—2003, Asa Messer prof. emeritus, emeritus prof. theater and English, 2003—. Curator (hon.) H. Adrian Smith Collection of Conjuring Books and Magicana, 1988—95; cons. Internat. Exch. Scholars (Fulbright), Washington, 1982—84, Am. Memory Libr. Congress, 1992—95, Am. Theatre Series Sta. WNET-TV, NYC, Shaw Theatre Festival, Ont., 1993—2008; juror George Freedley Theater Book Award com., 1971—93, 1994—2005, 2008, Barnard Hewitt Book award com., 1985—89; mem. com. hist. figures Theatre Hall of Fame, 1993—; D.R. and Eva Mitchell vis. disting. prof. Trinity U., San Antonio, 1995; faculty Trintiy Repertory Theatre/Brown U. Consortium, 2001—; courtesy appt. Keene State Coll., 2006—; vis. prof. Smith Coll., 2000, Tuffs U., 2004; cons. Shakespear Am. Life NAt. Pub. Radio & Folger Shakespear Library, 2006—07. Dir.: numerous theatrical prodns. including (Brown U. Prodns.) Carousel (Rodgers and Hammerstein), 1968, The Devils, 1969, The Night of the Iguana (Tennessee Williams), 1970, Much Ado About Nothing (Shakespeare), Too True to Be Good, 1972, Dial "M" for Murder, 1972, The Beggar's Opera (John Gay), 1973, Company (Stephen Sondheim), 1974, Look Homeward, Angel, 1975, Secret Service, 1976, Romeo and Juliet (Shakespeare), 1977, The Hostage (Brendan Behan), 1978, The Seagull (Chekhov), 1979, The Importance of Being Ernest (Oscar Wilde), 1980, The Playboy of the Western World (J.M. Synge), 1982, The Rivals (Sheridan), 1983, Our Town (Thornton Wilder), 1985, Philadelphia Story, 1987, Mrs. Warren's Profession (Shaw), 1989, The Duchess of Malfi (John Webster), 1992, The Illusion, 1994, Sweeney Todd, 1998, Candide, 2002, also numerous prodns. at other venues; actor: Twelfth Night (Colo. Shakespeare Festival), 1960, The Tempest (Champlain Shakespeare Festival), 1962, The Passion of Dracula, 1979, The Runner Stumbles, 1984, Follies, 1991, A View from the Bridge, 2003, Carnival, 2004, Crucible, 2007, Annie Get Your Gun, 2008, Peter Pan, 2008; author: The American Stage to World War I, 1978, American and English Popular Entertainment, 1980, George Frederick Cooke, 1980 (Merritt award), The Language of American Popular Entertainment, 1981, Variety Entertainment and Outdoor Amusements, 1982; co-author: Theater in the United States: A Documentary History, Vol. I, 1750-1915, 1996; co-editor: Plays by Augustin Daly, 1984, Plays by William Hooker Gillette, 1983, Mud Show, American Tent Circus Life, 1988, Cambridge Guide to American Theatre, 1993, sole edit., 1996, 2007; series editor (book series) Cambridge Studies Am. Theatre and Drama, 1992—, Pagrave Studies in Theatre and Performance History, 2004—; co-editor: Cambridge History of Am. Theatre, 3 vols., 1998—2001 (Freedley and Barnard Hewitt awards, 1999), Cambridge Guide to World Theatre, 1988, Cambridge Guide to Theatre, 1995, Staging the Nation: Plays from the American Theatre, 1787-1909, 1998; cons., interviewe (documentaries) (PBS) Houdini, 2000, (PBS) Annie Oakley, 2006; contbr. articles, chapters to books; contbr. book revs., World Book Ency., Dictionary Am. Biography, Ency. N.Y.C., other ref. material, adv. editor several jours., curator an exhbn. drawn from theater collection, Franklin Pierce Coll., 2006, Cheshire County (NH) Hist. Soc., 2008. Trustee Historical Soc. Cheshire County, NH, 2009—; bd. dirs. Am. Inst. Am. Theatre Studies, Bloomington, Ind., 1981—84; corp. mem. Providence Pub. Libr., 1983—2004; bd. mgrs. Players of Providence, 1966—80; mem. adv. bd. East Lynne Theatre Co., Secaucus, NJ, 1981—, Langston Hughes Cultural Arts Ctr., Providence, 1982—92, Actors Theatre of Louisville, 1987—; bd.mem. Moco Arts Ctr. Keene, 2007—, sec., 2008—; grants panelist R.I. State Coun. Arts, Providence, 1981—2003. Recipient New Eng. Theatre award for theatre contbn. on nat. level, 1998, award, U. Ark., 1998, Anthony Denning award, Eng., 2001, Career Achievement award in Academic Theatre, Assn. Theatre in Higher Edn., 2001, Sustained Excellence in Editing award, 2003, William Williams award, Brown U., 2008; John Simon Guggenheim fellow, 1982. Mem.: Moco Arts Ctr. (bd. dirs. 2007—, 2008—), Nat. Theatre Conf., Coll. Fellows Am. Theatre (bd. dirs. 1995—96, dean 1996—98, dean emeritus), Soc. Advancement Edn. (bd. trustees 1977—91, N.Y.C.), Am. Soc. Theatre Rsch. (exec. com. 1976—78, 1980—83, 1985—88, pres. 1991—94, sec. 1995—2002, Disting. Scholarship award 2001), Am. Theatre and Drama Soc. (mem. exec. bd. 1995—99, Betty Jean Jones award 1999), Internat. Fed. Theatre Rsch. (exec. bd. 1995—97), Theatre Libr. Assn. (v.p. 1981—84, bd. dir. 2007—07, Disting. Svc. award 2004), Phi Beta Kappa. Avocations: reading, collecting theatre books and memorabilia, bookbinding. Office: Brown U Dept Theatre Speech and Dance PO Box 1897 Providence RI 02912-1897 Home: 228 Court St Keene NH 03431-3450 Personal E-mail: deebee.39@myfairpoint.net. Business E-Mail: don_wilmeth@brown.edu.

WILMOT, IRVIN GORSAGE, former hospital administrator, educator, consultant; b. Nanking, China, June 30, 1922; s. Frank Alonzo and Ethel (Ranney) W.; m. Dorothy Agnes Mohlfeld, Feb. 6, 1943; children: Marcia Beth, David Michael. BS, Northwestern U., 1955; MBA, U. Chgo., 1957. With Internat. Register Co., Chgo., 1946-47; buyer U. Chgo., 1947-49; adminstv. asst., then asst. supt. U. Chgo. Clinics, 1949-61; adminstr. NYU Med. Ctr.-Univ. Hosp., 1961-68, exec. v.p., 1968-81, Blue Cross-Blue Shield Greater N.Y., 1981-83, dir., 1977-81; exec. v.p., COO Montefiore Hosp. and Med. Ctr., NYC, 1984-85; healthcare cons., 1985—. Instr. then asst. prof. U. Chgo., 1957-61; assoc. prof. NYU, 1961-68; prof., 1968—; assoc. dir. U. Chgo. Grad. Program Hosp. Adminstrn., 1959-61; mem. hosp. rev. and planning coun. State of N.Y., 1979-87. Bd. dirs. N.Y. Blood Ctr., 1978-81. With USN, 1940-46. Fellow Am. Coll. Hosp. Adminstrs. (life, chmn. ctrl. com. insts. 1959-65, regent N.Y. State and P.R. 1974—); mem. Assn. U. Programs Hosp. Adminstrs. (exec. sec. 1959-61), Am. Hosp. Assn. (mem. coun.

rsch. and planning 1965-68, coun. on mgmt. 1979-80, coun. on fin. 1981-84, trustee 1979-81), Assn. Am. Med. Colls. (chmn. coun. tchg. hosps. 1970-71), Greater N.Y. Hosp. Assn. (bd. govs., pres. 1973-74), Hosp. Assn. N.Y. State (trustee, chmn. 1976-77). Home: 34 Helen Ave Rye NY 10580-2447

WILMOT, THOMAS RAY, medical entomologist, educator; b. Great Falls, Mont., Sept. 9, 1953; s. Donald D. and Jeanne M. W.; m. Gail A. Ballard, June 26, 1976; children: Lacey A., Eric T. BS in Entomology, Mont. State U., 1975; MS in Entomology, Oreg. State U., 1978; MPH, UCLA, 1984, PhD in Epidemiology, 1986. Inspector Cacade County Pesticide Program, Great Falls, Mont., 1970-75; mgr. Yakima County Mosquito Control, Wash., 1978-80; dir., entomologist Midland County Mosquito Control, Sanford, Mich., 1984—. Adj. instr. Saginaw Valley State U., University Center, Mich., 1988—; vector control cons., Midland, Mich., 1988—. Contbr. articles to profl. jours. Mem. Local Emergency Plan Com., Midland, Mich., 1990—; spkr. Dow Corning Spkrs. Bur., Midland, 1992-96. Pub. Health traineeship USPHS, 1980-84; recipient Achievement award Nat. Assn. Counties, 1994. Mem. Am. Mosquito Control Assn. (mem. editl. bd. 1989-92, regional dir., 2009-), Entomol. Soc. Am., Soc. for Vector Ecology (regional dir. 1990-99), Mich. Mosquito Control Assn. (pres. 1989, Disting. Svc. award 1994), Phi Kappa Phi. Avocation: coaching youth athletics. Office: Midland County Mosquito Control 2180 N Meridian Rd Sanford MI 48657-9200 Business E-Mail: twilmot@co.midland.ni. E-mail: wilmotg@mindnet.com.

WILMOTH, MARSHA H., elementary school educator; d. J.C. and T. Bearnease Bolden; children: Michele H., Sharon L., Leslie D. AA, Coffeyville Cmty. Jr. Coll., Kans., 1972; BS in Edn., Pittsburg State U., 1974; cert. reading specialist, Emporia State U., 1986. Mid. sch. English tchr. Wann (Okla.) Sch., 1974—75; Title 1 reading and math. tchr. K-9th grade, Indian edn. tutoring coord. and tchr. Lincoln Meml. Grade Sch., Caney, 1978—; Title 1 reading tchr. Caney (Kans.) HS, 1981—82; elem. tchr. Caney, 1982—83, Treasure Coordination, 2004—08; sutstitute tchr. Duncanville (Tex.) Schs., 1976—77. Sponsor youth activities Assemblies of God and Bapt. chs. Recipient recognition, Unified Sch. Dist. 436, Parent award; named High Qualified Tchr., Kans. State Dept. Edn. Mem.: NEA, Internat. Reading Assn., No. Cherokee Nation, Caney Valley Tchr. Assn., Kans. Edn. Assn., Ducks Unltd., Order Ea. Star, Alpha Upsilon Alpha, Kappa Delta Pi. Avocations: cooking, photography. Office: Caney Valley Unified Schs 201 E 1st Ave Caney KS 67333-1903 E-mail: mwilmoth@caney.com.

WILMOTT, TIMOTHY J., gaming company executive; m. Nancy Wilmott; 1 child, Meghan. BS magna cum laude in Indsl. Engring., MS magna cum laude in Indsl. Engring., Lehigh U.; MBA in Corp. Fin., U. Pa. From mem. staff to COO Harrah's Entertainment Inc., Las Vegas, 1987—2003, COO, 2003—07; pres., COO Penn National Gaming, Wyomissing, Pa., 2008—. Office: Penn National Gaming Ste 200 825 Berkshire Blvd Wyomissing PA 19610

WILMUT, IAN, biologist; b. Hampton Lucey, Eng., July 7, 1944; s. Jack and Eileen Mary (Dalgleish) W.; m. Vivienne Mary Craven, Sept. 9, 1967; children: Helen, Naomi, Dean. BSc in Agrl. Sci., Nottingham U., Eng., 1967, DS, 1998; PhD in Animal Genetic Engring., Cambridge U., Eng., 1971. Sr. scientist ABRO (Animal Rsch. Breeding Station, which is now known as the Roslin Inst.), Edinburgh, 1973-93; prin. investigator Roslin Inst., Midlothian, Scotland, 1993—, mem. sr. mgmt., joint head dept. gene expression and develop. Scientific advisor Geron Bio-Med, a wholly owned subsidiary of the Geron Corp., Menlo Park, Calif.; lectr. in field. Editor Jour. Reproduction Fertility, 1993—; co-author (with Colin Tudge and Keith Campbell) The Second Creation: Dolly and the Age of Biological Control, 2000, (with Roger Highfield) After Dolly: The Uses and Misuses of Cloning, 2006; contbr. articles to profl. jours. Hon. fellow U. Edinburgh, 1993; recipient Lord Lloyd of Kilgerran prize, Sir John Hammond Meml prize Soc. Study Fertility, Rsch. medal Royal Agrl. Soc. Eng., Sir William Young award Royal Highland & Agrl. Soc. Scotland; co-recipient Shaw prize in life sci. and medicine, 2008. Mem. Internat. Embryo Transfer Soc. (pres. 1994), NAS (fgn. assoc.), Order of the British Empire; fellow Royal Soc. Edinburgh, Acad. Med. Scis. Achievements include creating the first calf ever produced from a frozen embryo, named Frosty in 1973; with Keith Campbell, the birth of Megan and Morag, two Welsh mountain sheep cloned from differentiated embryo cells in 1995; with Keith Campbell, the production of a mammal cloned from adult cells, the lamb named Dolly in 1996; with Keith Campbell, creating Polly, a sheep cloned from fetal skin cells that had been genetically altered to contain a human gene in 1997; granted a license to clone human embryos for medical research in 2005. Avocations: hill walking, photography, curling, gardening. E-mail: ian.wilmut@bbsrc.ac.uk.

WILNER, ERIC MARK, radiologist; b. Tulsa, Okla., Dec. 5, 1949; s. Sol and Selma Wilner; m. Patricia. Harrison Wise, Aug. 10, 1997; children: Emily K., Allison A.; m. S. Scott, May 31, 1976 (div. July 17, 1996). BA, Northwestern U., Evanston, Ill., 1972; MD, Med. Coll. Wis., Milw., 1976. Diplomate Nat. Bd. Med. Examiners, 1977, in diagnostic radiology Am. Bd. Radiology, 1980, cert. fellowship in computed tomography & ultrasound Boston Va Med. Ctr., Mass., 1981, resident in diagnostic radiology New Eng. Med. Ctr. & Affiliated Hosps., 1980, flexible intern Cambridge Hosp., 1977. Ptnr. NE Radiology Associates, Mass., 1981—; staff radiologist Amesbury Health Ctr., Mass., 1981—, Health Diagnostics, Hallmark Health, Stoneham, Mass., 1999—, Metronorth MRI, Saugus, Mass., 2002—, Inmed Diagnostic Svcs. Ma, Stoneham, Mass., 2004—, Anna Jaques Hosp., Newburyport, Mass., 1981—, chief radiologist, 1985, 1988, 1991—92. Contbr. articles to profl. jours. Mem.: Radiol. Soc. N. Am., Am. Coll. Radiology. Office: 25 Highland Ave Newburyport MA 01950 Personal E-mail: emw125@comcast.net.

WILNER, MARION LEONARD, art educator; b. NYC, Sept. 27, 1929; d. Jack Frank and Madeline (Leff) Leonard; m. Myron Wilner, May 28, 1950; children: Andrew, Matthew, David. BS, NYU, 1950, MA, 1952. Prof. of art, coord. art transfer program Bristol CC, Fall River, Mass., 1966-89, prof. emerita, 1993. Advisor dean's adv. coun. coll. visual and performing arts U. Mass., Dartmouth, 1993; lectr. Sacred Hearts Convent, 1992, RI Jewish Hist. Soc., 1992, Brandeis U. Nat. Women's Com., 1991, 90, Universidade Nova, Lisbon, 1988, Universidade Dos Acores, 1987; vis. scholar U. Mass., Dartmouth, 1992; mem. Higher Edn. Nominating Coun., 1990; judge Ea. Edison Poster and Essay Contest, 1989, RI Regional Scholastic Art Awards, 1987, Ann. Regional Art Exhbn. Fall River Festival, 1985; writer art Fall River Herald News, 1994-, judge Portsmouth Arts Guild, 2007; lectr. Portsmouth Arts Guild, 2008. Prin. works exhibited in numerous one-woman and group shows including DeBlois Gallery, Newport, RI, 1992, 94, 2007, Bert Gallery, Providence, 1991, Dodge House Gallery, Providence, 1990, Fall River Hist. Soc., 1988, Newport Art Mus., 1987, Escola Superior de Belas Artes, Lisbon, 1986, Eastbourne Gallery, Newport, 1977, Facets Gallery, Fall River, 1993, New England Ctr. Gallery, U. NH, 1992, Fed. Res. Bank Boston, 1992, Deblois Gallery, Newport, RI, 2003, Perkins Gallery, Mass., 2004, Retropstctive at Bristol CC, Fall River, Mass., 2005, Bristol Art Mus., RI, 2006; group shows exhibited including Cotuit Center for the Arts, Mass., 2009, AS220, Providence; prin. works represented in numerous collections including Duro Industries, Inc., Bristol CC, Providence Art Club Mems. Show, Cianfarani award, 1998, RI Econ. Devel. Corp., 1999, Juried RI State Com., Nat. Mus. Women in Arts, 2000, Printable Views, Providence Art Club, 2009, Printmaking award, 2001, Deblois Gallery, Newport, RI, 2001, Newport Printmakers, 2009, Newport Art Mus., 2002, Juried Show, 2009, Krause Gallery, 2003, 2008. Trustee Swain Sch. Design, New Bedford, Mass., 1977-91, Fall River Pub. Libr., 1978-91; active Fall River Cultural Commn., 1988—, Fall River Arts Lottery Coun., 1989—; mem. adv. bd. SMU Ctr. for Jewish Culture, 1983; visual arts dir. Festival '82; graphic designer for various community orgns. Gulbenkian grantee Lisbon, Portugal, 1986, 88; recipient Outstanding Cmty. Svc. award Fall River Area C. of C. and Industry, 1996, Ruth Findley award Providence Art Club, 2002. Mem.: Deblois Gallery, 19 on Paper. Home: 786 Madison St Fall River MA 02720-5718

WILPON, FRED, professional sports team executive; b. Bklyn., Nov. 22, 1936; s. Nathan and Frances (Altman) W.; m. Judith Anne Kessler, Sept. 27, 1958; children: Jeffrey Scott, Robin Lynn, Bruce Nathan. BA, U. Mich., 1958. V.p. Hanover Equities Corp., NYC, 1959-69, Peter Sharp & Co., NYC, 1969-71; chmn. bd. Sterling Equities, Inc., Manhasset, NY, 1971—; pres. NY Mets, 1980—2002, CEO, 1980—; owner Brooklyn Cyclones, 2000—; chmn. NY Mets, 2003—. Mem. Vol. Urban Cons. Group, Mayor N.Y.C. Housing Task Force; trustee Jewish Inst. Geriatric Care, New Hyde Park, N.Y., 1976—, Green Vale Sch., Glen Head, N.Y., 1977—. Served with USAF, 1959. Mem. Young Pres. Orgn. Clubs: KP. Office: New York Mets 123-10 Roosevelt Ave Flushing NY 11368

WILSON, ADRIAN (ADRIAN LEMAR WILSON), professional football player; b. High Point, NC, Oct. 12, 1979; m. Alicia Wilson; children: Aubrei Reign, Adrian Jr. Student in parks, recreation and tourism mgmt., NC State U., Raleigh. Strong safety Ariz. Cardinals, 2001—; owner High Point Shoes, Scottsdale, Ariz. Founder Adrian Wilson Found., 2007—. Named to Nat. Football Conf. Pro Bowl Team, NFL, 2006, 2008. Mailing: Ariz Cardinals PO Box 888 Phoenix AZ 85001-0888*

WILSON, ALAN D., food products executive; Product supply, procurement, mfg. Procter & Gamble; dir. procurement for retail products McCormick & Co., Inc., Sparks, Md., 1993—94, v.p. corp. procurement, 1994—96; pres. McCormick Canada, 1998—2001; v.p., gen. mgr. sales and mktg. McCormick & Co., Inc., Sparks, 2001—02, pres. US consumer products divsn., 2003—05, pres. N.Am. consumer foods, US supply chain, 2005—06, pres., COO, 2007—08, pres., CEO, 2008—09, chmn., pres., CEO, 2009—. Dir. Williams Scotsman Internat. Inc., 2006—07; chmn.'s adv. coun. Grocery Mfrs. Assn. Office: McCormick & Co Inc 18 Loveton Cir Sparks MD 21152 Office Phone: 410-527-6966. Office Fax: 410-627-8289. Business E-Mail: alan_wilson@mccormick.com.*

WILSON, ANDREW MURRAY, religious studies educator; b. Syracuse, NY, Dec. 26, 1950; s. Richard Joseph and Susan Halpern Wilson; m. Lova Eng, July 1, 1982; children: Theodore Anlo, Lianne Sue, Samuel Jin Heung, Joonie Suann. BA, Harvard Coll., Cambridge, Mass., 1972; diploma, Unification Theol. Sem., Barrytown, NY, 1978; MTS, Harvard Div. Sch., Cambridge, 1980; PhD, Harvard U., Cambridge, 1985. Prof., scriptural studies Unification Theol. Sem., 1985—, academic dean, 2000—08. Chair, editl. rev. bd. New World Ency., St. Paul, 2006—. Contbg. editor anthology and jours.; contbr. articles to profl. jours. Organizer Grad. Students Better Presidency, NYC, 1980; organizer and spkr. Universal Peace Fedn., Tarrytown, NY, 1985—2008; spkr. and del. UPF Mideast Peace Initiative, Jerusalem, 2003—05. Mem.: Am. Acad. Religion. Home: 14 Thayer Ln Red Hook NY 12571 Office: Unification Theol Sem 30 Seminary Dr Barrytown NY 12507 Business E-Mail: wilson@uts.edu.

WILSON, ANNETTE SIGRID, retired elementary school educator; b. Harlan, Iowa, Jan. 30, 1953; d. Anker Christian and Ruth Edith Eastergard; m. John Roger Wilson, Dec. 21, 1974; children: Elicia Ruth, Elizabeth Annette. BS, Bob Jones U., 1975; diploma, Nancy Bounds Modeling and Finishing Sch., 1998; MAE, U. No. Iowa, 2001. Tchr. Arlington Bapt. Sch., Baltimore, Md., 1976—78, Calvary Bapt. Sch., Normal, Ill., 1978—80, Walnut Pub. Sch., Iowa, 1986—2000, Council Bluffs Cmty. Schs., 2000—04; trainer Area Edn. Agy., 1991—97; ret., 2004. Homebound spl. edn. instr., 1987. Contbg. author: Work on Creativity, 2004; co-author (with Benedicte Riis): Music Room, 2005. Recipient Optimist award for Youth Appreciation, 1992, 1996, Leadership award, Area XIII, 1998.

WILSON, ARTHUR THEODORE, education consultant; b. Newark, July 2, 1945; s. Elmer and Dorothy May (Outlaw-Sloan) W. BA in Humanities, New Sch., 1971, MA in Social Studies Edn., 1974; MA in Philosophy, U. London at Bedford Coll.; PhD in Program History, NYU, 1980. Cert. tchr., N.Y., N.J. Rschr. African Studies, NYC, 1972; tchr. Teaneck Alternative H.S., NJ, 1979—80, Hunter Coll., NYC, 1980—81; cons. gifted and talented program curriculum Bd. Coop. Ednl. Svcs. SUNY, Farmingdale, 1983—; artistic dir. VSA Theatre Co., New Brunswick, NJ, 2004—. Apptd. arts & edn. acad. artist N.J. Performing Arts Ctr., Newark, 1996—; advisor, tutor Master's Degree Program in Acting, New Actors Workshop, Antioch U., N.Y., 1995—; workshop leader Young Playwright's Festival, N.Y.C., 1981—; adj. prof. drama Drew U., Madison, N.J.; co-founder, workshop leader N.J. Young Playwrights Festival, 1983; project dir., playwright Am. Folk Theater Young Co.'s exch. program, London, 1984-85; theater workshop cons. Milneck Sch. for Deaf, L.I., 1984; lit. workshop cons. Orion Gifted and Talented Program, Lindenhurst, N.Y., 1984—; artistic dir. exch. program Manhattan Empire and Tukak Theater, Denmark; dir. playwriting in sch. project N.Y. Shakespeare Festival, 1986—; instr. N.Y. Lit. Assn., N.Y.C., 1984—; poetry reading and workshop with Poet Laureate Gwendolyn Brooks, Union Coll., 1985, guest poet for Mother Hale of Hale House, 1987; dir. playwriting in edn. dept. schs. N.Y. Shakespeare Festival, dir./prodr. Live! (radio edn. program), bd. dirs., cons. arts edn. New Dance Group Ctr., N.Y., 1987—; mem., Artist Collective Soc. Change, Inc., 2005-; resident artist, Young Audiences NJ, Princton, 2007-. Editor, writer, pub. Dance Giant Steps, Inc., Bklyn., 1981—; author: (play) The Extended Family, 1987, Peace By Peace, 2004; play and workshop: Words for the Journey; dir. Daddy Say, 1987, Children of Dahomey and Spirit Ensemble, 1986, Bound For Broadway, Broadway N.Y., 2004; dance editor; Feet Mag., 1969-72, Black Creations Mag., 1970-72; editor, pub.: Attitude: The Dancers' Monthly, 1982—; contbr. poetry to Open Mag., Other Countries, New Rain, A Taste of Salt; prodr.: (plays) Life Sea Treasures, 1989-90, Guns Like Candy, 1991, Red High Heels Snap Back, 1995; commns. include: A Tribute for All the Beautiful Black Men, N.Y.C., High Rise Snaps, Washington, D.C., Street Songs, N.Y., Trouble the Water, N.Y., Homeless Monologues, Baca, Bklyn., Hallelujah Roots, N.Y., choreo-poem for dancers, NYC, 2007, Dancing on Etarnityand, Spoken Word, Stories & Pictures, Albany Records, 2008, others.; Artist: Academy of Performing Arts, NY, 2008-09, Poet Resident Nai-Ni Chen Dance Co., 2008-09. Workshop leader N.J. Teen Program, 1983-84; advisor, workshop leader, founder N.J. Young Playwrights Festival, 1964-68; rsch. asst. Weeksville Project, Bjlyn., 1969-70; theater dir. local orgns. Recipient numerous scholars, 1970-79; grantee Bklyn. Art and Cultural Assn., 1983, N.Y. Dept. Cultural Affairs, 1983-84, N.Y. State Coun. on Arts, 1982-84, BECA Capezio Found., Heart grant Union County Bd. Freeholders, 1998-2004, N.J. Writers Project, N.J. State Coun. on the Arts, 1999-2005; N.J. State Coun. Arts fellow, 1985-86, Merit award for Poetry, Internat. Soc. Poets Conv., Phila., 2004. Mem. Black Writers Union, Dramatist Guild, Inc., ASSITEJ, Internat. Assn. Children's Theater Professionals, Am. Acad. Poets. Home: 919 Oak St Roselle NJ 07203-2001 Office Phone: 908-887-0782. Personal E-mail: adaddyblack@aol.com.

WILSON, BERTINA IOLIA, retired music educator; b. Southampton, Va., Aug. 17, 1938; d. Purcell Lee and Clarine Branch; m. Aug. 25, 1963 (div. May 1977); children: Brian Keith, Linda Elizabeth. BA, Newark State Coll., 1960; MA, Kean Coll., 1981. Cert. elem. edn. tchr., N.J. Tchr. Newark Bd. Edn., 1960-77, project coord., 1977—95; ch. organist, choir dir. Zion Hill Bapt. Ch., Newark, 1974—; vice prin. Newark Pub. Schs., 1995—97; ret., 1997. Mem. Newark Tchrs. Union, Project Coords. Assn. (exec. bd. Newark chpt. 1981—), Order of Eastern Star (Outstanding Ch. Musician 1986), Phi Delta Kappa (pub. rels. dir. 1987-89). Democrat. Avocations: singing, playing the organ. Home: 345 Mclean Pl Hillside NJ 07205-1748

WILSON, BLAKE SHAW, electrical engineer, researcher; b. Orlando, Fla., Mar. 7, 1948; s. Joseph Richard Hoyle and Jacqueline Lucy (Jones) W.; m. Doris Jane Rouse, Jan. 6, 1974; children: Nadia Jacqueline, Blair Elizabeth. BSEE, Duke U., 1974. Rsch. engr. Rsch. Triangle Inst., Research Triangle Park, N.C., 1974-78, sr. rsch. engr., 1978-83, sr. rsch. scientist, 1979-83, head neurosci. program, 1983-94, dir. Ctr. for Auditory Prosthesis Rsch., 1994—2002; sr. fellow, 2002—06; emeritus sr. fellow, 2007—. Guest scientist Coleman Meml. Lab., U. Calif., San Francisco, 1983-86; adj. asst. prof. otolaryngology Duke U. Med. Ctr., 1984-94, assoc. prof., 1994-2002, prof., 2002—; sci. adv. coun., Internat. Ctr. Hearing and Speech, Kajetany, Poland, 2003—; oversight com. cochlear implants Kresge Hearing Rsch. Inst., U. Mich., 1987—, U. Iowa, 1994—; sci. adv. coun. House Ear Inst., L.A., 1990; gen. chair Conf. Implantable Auditory Prostheses, Pacific Grove, Calif., 1991; co-chair Hearing Preservation Workshop, Indpls., 2002; spl. panel hearing aids NIDCD, 1992, ad hoc adv. com. hearing aid R & D, 1993—; guest of honor numerous internat. confs.; reviewer grant applications NIH, NSF, VA and Med. Rsch. Coun., Can.; cons. cochlear implants NIH; mem. faculty various continuing edn. courses; prin. investigator numerous projects, chief strategy advisor MED EL Med. Electronics GmbH, Innsbruck, Austria, 2007, co-dir. Duke Hearing Ctr., 2008-, chair Hearing Preservation Workshop, Res, Traingle Pk., 2005; presenter in field, expert Marie Curie Project, 2007-. Reviewer numerous jours. in field; contbr. numerous articles to profl. jours. Recipient Discover award for tech. innovation, 1996, Presdl. citation for major contbns. to restoration of hearing in profoundly deaf persons Am. Otologic Soc., Disting. Alumnus award Pratt Sch. Engring. Duke U., 2007, Neel Disting. Rsch. Leadership award Am. Acad. Otoloryngology-Head & Neel Surgery Found., 2008. Mem.: Brit. Cochlear Implant Group (hon.). Home: 2410 Wrightwood Ave Durham NC 27705-5802

WILSON, BONNIE JEAN, lawyer, educator, investor; b. Alameda County, Calif. d. August and Violet Adeline (Lockard) Ritzenthaler; m. Allan Nicholas Wilson (dec.); children: Albert Clyde, Bruce Allan. BA, U. Calif., Berkeley, cert. in elem. tchg.; JD, Thomas Jefferson SOL, 1981. Bar: Calif.; cert. tchr., Calif. Elem. sch. tchr. Contra Costa and San Diego Counties; intern San Diego County Dist. Atty. Office, 1981; pvt. practice La Jolla, Calif., 1982—. Mem. La Jolla Presbyn. Ch., San Diego Symphony Assn., Friends of the La Jolla Libr.; adv. dir. San Diego Opera Assn.; edn. activist, 1972-76. Mem. Calif. State Bar Assn., San Diego County Bar Assn., La Jolla Newcomer's Club (bd. dirs. 1968-69), U. Calif. Berkeley Alumni Club (bd. dirs. San Diego chpt. 1961-62), Am. Assn. Ind. Investors (bd. dirs. 1991-97), Pi Lambda Theta, La Jolla Beach and Tennis Club. Presbyterian. Home: 2235 Bahia Dr La Jolla CA 92037-7007

WILSON, BRENDA MARIE, secondary school educator; b. New Orleans, Feb. 4, 1951; d. Chester Simmons, Jr. and Lillie Mae Simmons; m. Eli Wilson, Jr., June 19, 1971; children: Eli III, LaVar Antoine. AS, So. U., 1972; BSc, Rochester Inst. Tech., NY, 1984; MSc, LI U., 1990. Adj. prof. L.I. (N.Y.) U., 1987—89, asst. dean, 1989—93; tchr. Bd. Edn., Bklyn., 1997—98; with accts. payable Chempiah Ministries, Queens, NY, 1998—2000; tchr. Orange County Pub. Schs., Orlando, Fla., 2001—. Mem. sch. adv. com. Orange County Pub. Schs., 2002—. V.p. Eli Wilson Ministries, Orlando, 2002—03. Named Tchr. of Yr., Orange County Pub. Schs., 2004. Mem.: Phi Gamma Nu, Alpha Kappa Alpha. Baptist. Office: Cerokee School 550 S Eola Dr Orlando FL 32801-3999 Home: 6503 Hawdsmoor Dr Orlando FL 32818

WILSON, BRENT LAWRENCE, lawyer, mediator; b. New Orleans, Jan. 9, 1952; s. Commodore Waddell and Mildred Louise (Quave) W.; m. Trojanell Theresa Bordenave, June 22, 1974. BA, Morehouse Coll., 1973; postgrad., U. Ga., 1973-74; JD, SUNY, Buffalo, 1976. Bar: La. 1976, Ga. 1979, U.S. Dist. Ct. (no. dist.) Ga. 1979, U.S. Ct. Appeals (5th and 11th cirs.) 1979, U.S. Ct. Appeals (3d cir.) 1982, U.S. Ct. Appeals (6th cir.) 1986. Field atty. NLRB, Atlanta, 1976-80; assoc. Elarbee, Thompson & Trapnell, Atlanta, 1980-87; ptnr. Elarbee, Thompson, Sapp & Wilson, Atlanta, 1987—. Lectr. Atlanta U., 1984; adj. prof. law Emory U., Atlanta, 1984-85; mem. Study Commn. on Employment Laws, 1997-98. Contbr. articles to profl. jours. Mem. Fulton County Bd. Ethics 1991, Homelessness Task Force United Way of Metropolitan Atlanta, 2005; exec. bd. dirs. Boys and Girls Clubs of Metro Atlanta, 1999—, exec. com., 2005; bd. dirs. St. Judes Recovery Ctr., Inc., 1989—, bd. chair, 2005; active Christ our Hope Cath. Ch. Recipient Am.'s Top Black Lawyers, Ga. Legal Elite, 2003, 2006, Best Lawyers for Bus., Chambers USA, 2005, 2006; named one of Top 100 Ga. Super Lawyers, 2004, 2005, 2006; named to Am.'s Top Black Lawyers, Black Enterprise Mag., 2003. Mem.: Labors and Employment Rels. Assn., ABA (mem. labor and employment law mgmt. com.), NAACP (life), Coll. Labor and Employment Lawyers, Atlanta Soc. African Am. Human Resources, Soc. Human Resource Mgmt. (legis. com. co-chmn. 1987—88, 1990—91), Nat. Employment Law Coun., Nat. Assn. Securities Dealers (arbitrator), State Bar Ga. (co-chair Ga. Diversity Prog. 1998—99), Nat. Bar Assn. (mem. comml., labor and arbitration sect.), Gate City Bar Assn., Atlanta Bar Assn. (sec., treas. labor and employment law sect. 1985, vice chmn. labor and employment law sect. 1986, chmn. labor and employment law sect. 1987), 100 Blackmen of Atlanta, Atlanta Morehouse, Lawyers Club Atlanta, 191 Club, Atlanta Bus. League, Am. Inns. Ct., Phi Alpha Delta, Omega Psi Phi. Avocations: spectator sports, racquetball, reading, travel. Office: Elarbee Thompson Sapp & Wilson LLP 800 Internat Tower 229 Peachtree St NE Atlanta GA 30303-1614 Office Phone: 404-659-6700, 404-582-8427. Business E-Mail: bwilson@elarbeethompson.com.

WILSON, BRIAN ANDREW, computing performance consultant, educator, writer, editor; b. Denver, July 10, 1967; s. Leonard Tom Jr. and Mary Ann (Slutz) W.; m. Amy Michelle Duncan, Apr. 28, 2001. BA in Music, Cleve. Inst. Music, 1990; BA, Case Western Reserve U., 1990; M in Info. Tech., Am. Intercontinental U., 2002. Cert. Mercury Cert. Product Cons., Mercury cert. instr. Software support, SQA engr. Borland Internat., Inc., Scotts Valley, Calif., 1990-92, software cons., 1992—94; pres., founder OnRamp Internet Svcs., Inc., Atlanta, 1995—96; founder Internet Gadsden, 1995—96, Internet Tuscaloosa, 1995—96; founder, sr. ptnr. TechSouth Consulting, Suwanee, Ga., 1996—. Vis. faculty Ga. Inst. Tech., Atlanta, 2005—. Author: Quattro Pro for Windows: Everything you Need, 1992; tech. editor: Using Quattro Pro 3, 1991, Using Quattro 4, 1992, Using Quattro Pro for Windows, 1992, Paradox for Windows: Programming, 1993, dBase IV 2.5: Quick Reference, 1993. Mem. Ga. Inst. Tech. Coll. Computing Ind. Ptnrs. Assn., Assn. Computing Machinery, Software Contractor's Guild, Aircraft Owners and Pilots Assn. Avocations: golf, sailing, music, flying, scuba. Office: 471 Henderson Lake Dr Canton GA 30115 Office Phone: 404-418-6401. Business E-Mail: bwilson@techsouth.com.

WILSON, BRUCE BRIGHTON, lawyer, retired transportation executive; b. Boston, Feb. 6, 1936; s. Robert Lee and Jane (Schlotterer) Wilson; m. Elizabeth Ann MacFarland, Dec. 31, 1958; children: Mabeth, Mary, Bruce Robert, Caroline Daly. AB, Princeton U., 1958; LLB, U. Pa., 1961. Bar: Pa. 1962. Assoc. Montgomery, McCracken, Walker & Rhoads, Phila., 1962-69; atty. US Dept. Justice, Washington, 1969-79, dep. asst. atty. gen. antitrust div., 1971-76; spl. counsel Consol. Rail Corp., Phila., 1979-81, gen. counsel litigation and antitrust, 1981-82, v.p., gen. counsel, 1982-84, v.p. law, 1984-87, sr. v.p. law, 1987-97, sr. v.p. merger, 1997. Bd. dirs. Carload Express, Inc., Phila. Indsl. Devel. Corp., Wayne Sr. Ctr., The Phila. Singers; mem. mgmt. com. Concord Resources Group, 1989-91. Chmn. Radnor Twp. Cabe Commn. Coun., 1993—2000, mem., 2002—, Radnor Twp. Ethics Commn., 2000—01, Radnor Twp. Civil Svc. Commn., 2008—; bd. trustees St. Mark's Sch., Southborough, Mass., 2008—; vestry St. Mary Episcopal Ch., Wayne, Pa., 2006—09. Fellow Salzburg Seminar in Am. Studies (Austria), 1965; fellow Felz Inst. State and Local Govt., 1967. Mem. ABA, Phila. Bar Assn., Corinthian Yacht Club, Merion Cricket Club, Beach Club Cape May. Republican. Episcopalian. Home: 224 Chamounix Rd Wayne PA 19087-3606 Personal E-mail: brucewilson224@comcast.net.

WILSON, BRUCE DUXBURY, lawyer; b. Charleston, SC, Feb. 12, 1948; BA, U. Vt., 1970; JD, Albany Law Sch., 1973. Bar: N.Y. 1974, U.S. Dist. Ct. (no. and we. dists.) N.Y. 1974, U.S. Supreme Ct. 1978. Clk. N.Y. State Atty. Gen., Albany, 1970; pvt. practice Ithaca, NY, 1974—; city prosecutor City of Ithaca, 1975-80; town atty. Town of Ulysses, Trumansburg, NY, 1993—2006; dep. county atty. Tompkins County, Ithaca, 1996—2005. Exam. counsel Ticor Title Ins. Corp.; mem. faculty Tompkins-Cortland CC, Ithaca, 1996. Bd. dirs. Greater Ithaca Activities Ctr., Inc., Drug Rehab. Ctr. Alpha House, Inc., Ctr. Arts at Ithaca, Inc., McGraw House, Hospicare, Ithaca Theatre Guild; mem. Cmty. Arts Task Force; chmn. Lansing Village Bd. Zoning Appeals. Capt. US Army. Mem.: U.S. Supreme Ct. Bar Assn., Tompkins County Bar Assn. (v.p., pres.-elect, pres. 1996—97), N.Y. State Bar Assn., Sertoma (bd. dirs. local club). Personal E-mail: brucedwilson@aol.com.

WILSON, BRUCE KEITH, consultant in men's health issues; b. Alton, Ill., Aug. 18, 1946; s. Lewis Philip and Ruth Caroline Wilson; children: Sarah Ann, Andrew James. BSN, U. Tex., San Antonio, 1975, MSN, 1977; PhD, North Tex. State U., Denton, 1987. Coord. Pan Am. U., Edinburg, Tex., 1982-83; house supr. HCA Rio Grande Regional Hosp., McAllen, Tex., 1986-87; program dir. Tex. Southmost Coll., Brownsville, 1983-86; prof. U. Tex.-Pan Am., Edinburg, 1986—2009; Cons. Mens Health Issues. Author: Logical Nursing Math., 1987; contbr. chpts. to books, numerous articles to profl. jours. With U.S. Army, 1966-68. Mem. Am. Assembly for Men in Nursing (bd. dirs. 1997-2001), Tex. League for Nursing (bd. dirs. 1993-97). Avocations: photography, computer. Home: 1702 Ivy Ln Edinburg TX 78539-5367 Office Phone: 956-381-3491. Personal E-mail: wilson@hiline.net.

WILSON, BRUCE MATTHEW, literature and language professor; b. DC, Mar. 22, 1948; s. George Matthew and Betty Jane Wilson; life ptnr. William Herbert Foskett; children: Peter Matthew, Crispin Andrew. PhD, U. Va., Charlottesville, 1976. Cert. shihan in Saga Goryu ikebana Daikakuji Temple, 2008. Prof. lit. and Asian studies St. Mary's Coll. Md., 1976—. Lectureship Fulbright, China, 1984—85, 1997—98. Translator (ikebana artist): (book) 100 Tang Poems. Attender Friends Meeting Washing, DC, 2001—08. Achievements include design of international Ikebana exhibits. Avocation: swimming. Home: PO Box 120 Dameron MD 20628 Office: St Mary's Coll Md Saint Marys City MD 20686 Office Phone: 240-895-0254. Personal E-mail: jadecicada@aol.com. Business E-Mail: bmwilson@smcm.edu.

WILSON, C. DANIEL, JR., library director; b. Middletown, Conn., Nov. 8, 1941; s. Clyde D. and Dorothy M. (Neal) W.; m. M. April Jackson, Apr. 1986; children: Christine, Cindy, Clyde, Ben. BA, Elmhurst Coll., 1967; MA, Dominican U., 1968; MPA, U. New Orleans, 1995. Trainee Chgo. Pub. Libr., 1967-68; instr. U. Ill., 1968-70; asst. dir. Perrot Meml. Libr., Greenwich, Conn., 1970-76; dir. Wilton Pub. Libr., Wilton, Conn., 1976-79; assoc. dir. Birmingham Pub. Libr., Birmingham, Ala., 1979-83; dir. Davenport (Iowa) Pub. Libr., 1983-85, New Orleans Pub. Libr., 1985-97, St. Louis County Libr., 1997—. With USMC, 1962-65. Mem. ALA, Internat. Assn. Met. Librs. (pres. 1998-2002), Mo. Libr. Assn., Am. Soc. Pub. Adminstrs., Rotary, Pi Gamma Mu. Episcopalian. Home: 511 W 4th St Hermann MO 65041 E-mail: dwilson@slcl.lib.mo.us.

WILSON, CARL WELDON, JR., construction company executive, civil engineer; b. Norfolk, Va., Sept. 4, 1933; s. Carl Weldon and Janie Marie (Ludford) W.; m. Jean Roberts, Feb. 13, 1960; children: Lisa Ann, Carl Weldon III. BCE, Tex. A&M U., 1954. Registered profl. engr., Tex. Engr. Magnolia Petroleum Co., Morgan City, La., 1954-55, Brown & Root, Houston, 1957-60; project mgr. Claude Everett Constrn. Co., Houston, 1960-62; pres. Falcon Constrn. Co., Houston, 1962-63; pres., owner Wilson Engring. and Constrn. Co., Houston, 1963-68; v.p. Divcon, Inc., Houston, 1968-71, Wilson Industries, Inc., Houston, 1971-81; pres., prin. owner BS&B Engring. Co., Inc., Houston, 1981-86; chmn., majority shareholder Task Internat., Inc., Houston, 1986—. Served to 1st lt. U.S. Army, 1955-57. Republican. Episcopalian. Avocations: tennis, running, painting. Home: 750 Bison Dr Houston TX 77079-4401 Office: Task Internat Inc PO Box 940121 Houston TX 77094-7121 Office Phone: 281-597-8650. Personal E-mail: taskintcww@aol.com. Business E-Mail: cwilson@silverfox.org.

WILSON, CAROLYN TAYLOR, librarian; b. Cookeville, Tenn., June 10, 1936; d. Herman Wilson and Flo (Donaldson) Taylor; m. Larry Kittrell Wilson, June 14, 1957 (dec.); children: Jennifer Wilson Rust, Elissa Anne Wilson. BA, David Lipscomb Coll., 1957; MLS, George Peabody Coll., 1976. Tchr. English Fulton County Sch. System, Atlanta, 1957-59; serials cataloger Vanderbilt U. Libr., Nashville, 1974-77; asst. libr. United Meth. Pub. House, Nashville, 1978-80; collection devel. libr. David Lipscomb U., Nashville, 1980—, acting dir. Beaman Libr., 1998, dir. Beaman Libr., 1999—. Cons. and rschr. in field; project dir. Tenn.'s Lit. Legacy for Tenn. Humanities Coun., 1994—, ALA grant, Frontier in Am. Culture, 1996-98; project dir. Tenn. Humanities Coun. grant, 1998—; rep. Tenn. Avd. Coun. Librs., Acad. Librs., 1999—. Rsch. asst. Handbook of Tennessee Labor History, 1987-89. Adv. bd. So. Festival of Books, Nashville, 1988-90, 90—, vol. coord., 1989, 90—; project dir. Women's Words (summer grant program) for Tenn. Humanities Coun., Tenn.'s Literary Legacy (summer grant program), 1994-96, Growing Up Southern (summer grant), 1996—, ALA grant The Frontier in Am. Culture, 1996—. Recipient Nat. Honor Soc. award Phi Alpha Theta, 1956, Internat. Honor Soc. award Beta Phi Mu, 1980, Frances Neel Cheney award Tenn. Libr. Assn., 1992, MIHOW award, Women Mentoring Women, 2008; nominee Athena award, 1992; Growing Up Southern summer grantee, 1996. Mem. ALA, Tenn. Hist. Soc., Tenn. Libr. Assn. (Frances Neel Cheney award 1992), Southeastern Libr. Assn. (chmn. outstanding S.E. author award com. 1991-92, chmn. So. Books competition 1992-94, sec. exec. bd. 1997—), Women's Nat. Book Assn. (pres., v.p., treas., awards chmn. 1980—), Disciples of Christ Hist. Soc. (bd. dirs. 2002—), Tenn. Writers Alliance (bd. dirs. 1995—). Democrat. Avocations: reading, cooking, jogging, sailing. Office: David Lipscomb U Beaman Libr # 310 Nashville TN 37204 Office Phone: 615-966-5837. Business E-Mail: carolyn.wilson@lipscomb.edu.

WILSON, CARRIE LEE STROUD, principal; b. Bellevue, La., Dec. 14, 1948; d. Jeffrie Edward Stroud and Mary Elizabeth Jones-Stroud; m. Victor George Wilson, Apr. 19, 1972; children: Geoffrey Victor, Kimberly Georgina Elizabeth, James Anderson Stuart. B.A, U. Redlands, 1971; MA in Edn., U. Calif.-Berkeley, 2003. Preliminary Adminstrv. Intern Servicing Credential Calif. Tchg. Credentialing Com., 2002, Preliminary Adminstrv. Servicing Credential Calif. Tchr. Credentialing, 2004, Emergency Tchg. Credential Calif. Tchg. Credentialing, 2001. Counselor Upward Bound/U. Redlands, Vallejo, Calif., 1967; asst. to teen post dir. Redlands City Recreation Dept., Redlands, Calif., 1968; recreation leader Redlands Recreation Dept., Calif., 1969—70, art instr., 1971; docent U. Calif., Berkeley, 1971—72; tchr./ drawing and composition-photography Vallejo City Unified Sch. Dist., 1998—99, asst. prin., 2002—03, vice prin., 2004—; tchr. Berkeley Unified Sch. Dist., Berkeley, Calif., 1973—74; real estate agt. Calif. Sch. Real Estate, Oakland, 1979—80; substitute tchr. Vallejo City Unified Sch. Dist., 1980—84, tchr., 1884—2000; art instr./exploratory art for young people Calif. Coll. Arts and Crafts, Oakland, 1985—86; tchr./summer sch. Vallejo City Unified Sch. Dist., 1999—2000, tchr./secondary/jr. high-middle sch., 1983—98, tchr./art-photography, 1998—99; academic dir. Jesse Bethel HS, Vallejo, 1999—2001, asst. prin., 2002—03, vice prin., 2003—. Chairperson/facilitator Springstowne Jr. HS, Vallejo, 1985—98, dept. head, 1991—98; state conf. presenter Calif. League of Mid. Schs., San Francisco, 1991—92; mentor-master-coach tchr. Springstowne Jr. HS, Vallejo, 1992—98; tchr. leader Jesse Bethel HS, Vallejo, 1998—2001, chairperson digital grant application to the state, 1999—2001, state standardized test coord., 2000—, chairperson com. for accreditation, 2001—02, state sch. intervention program for student achievement, 2001—03. Author: (poetry) What Time Is Fishin Time (pub. Famous Poets Soc., 1995), (essay) The Importance of Nature (pub. Nat. Essay Press, 1967); exhibitions include oil & acrylic painting thesis Journey of Self Expression, ceramics, Vase (Nat. Mus. of Arts- Wash., D.C., 1968), portraits on canvas/oil paintings (Patton State Hospital-Rehabilitation Ctr. For Young Women, 1969), Personal Expressions of African American Suburb Experience (Participant in Exhibit, 1968); contbr. (Cert./Black History Month, 1969); Compilation of Perspectives of an African American Woman (Cert. of Participation/Watts Summer Festival of Arts, L.A., 1965). Mem. ednl. reform programs for student achievement Vallejo City Unified Sch. Dist., 1995—2005; min. Jehovah's Witnesses, Vallejo, 1973—2005; mem. Vallejo Artist Guild, 1990—96; contbr. Continental Omega Boys and Girls Club, Vallejo, 2001—05; advisor Willie B. Atkins Tanner Project, Vallejo, 1998—2005. Recipient Tchr. of Yr., Elks B.P.O.E.; nominee, Calif. League Mid. Sch.; grantee Ednl. Opportunity Grant, Fed. Govt., 1967—71; Behring Scholar, U. Calif. Berkeley, Prin. Leadership Inst., 2001—03. Mem.: Vallejo Schs. Mgrs. Assn., ASCD, Assn. Calif. Sch. Adminstrs. Jehovah'S Witness. Achievements include recipient Phillip Harris Memorial Scholarship; missionary Ministry for Jehovah's Witnesses. Avocations: writing, art. Home: 119 Toni Ct Vallejo CA 94591-4272 Office: Jesse Bethel HS 1800 Ascot Pkwy Vallejo CA 94591-4272

WILSON, CASSANDRA, singer; b. Jackson, Miss., 1955; Albums include Point of View, 1986, Blue Skies, 1988, Days Aweigh, 1987, Jumpworld, 1990, She Who Weeps, 1991, Cassandra Wilson Live, 1992, Blue Light 'Till Dawn, 1993, Dance to the Drums Again, 1993, After the Beginning Again, 1994, New Moon Daughter, 1996 (Grammy award for Best Jazz Vocal Album), Travelling Miles, 1999, Belly of the Sun, 2002, Glamoured, 2003, Thunderbird, 2006, Loverly, 2008 (Grammy award for Best Jazz Vocal Album, 2009). Office: Blue Note NY 131 W 3rd St New York NY 10012 E-mail: adam@bluenote.com.*

WILSON, CECIL BRUCE, internist; b. Columbus, Ga., 1935; m. Betty Jane Wilson; 3 children. BA in History, Emory U., MD. Bd. cert. in internal medicine. Intern US Naval Hosp., Portsmouth, Va., 1961—62, resident in internal medicine San Diego, 1966—69; pvt. practice internal medicine Winter Park, Fla. Past pres. med. staffs Winter Park Meml. Hosp., Fla. Hosp. Med. Ctr., Orlando; past pres. Fla. Statewide Health Coun.; chair Local Health Coun. of East Cent. Fla. Flight surgeon USN, comdr. USN. Master: Am. Coll. Physicians (past chair bd. regents); mem.: AMA (mem. ho. del. 1992—, bd. trustees 2002—, chair bd. trustees 2006—07), Orange County Med. Soc. (past pres.), Fla. Med. Assn. (FMA) (pres., chair bd. gov. and exec. com.). Office: 1341 Orange Ave Winter Park FL 32789-4911 Office Phone: 407-647-2122. Office Fax: 407-647-6701.*

WILSON, CECILIA ANN, special education educator; b. Corning, NY, Feb. 8, 1959; d. Leroy Eugene and Helen Esther (Rodman) W. BA, Manhattanville Coll., Purchase, NY, 1981; M Spl. Edn., Mansfield U., Pa., 1986. Cert. tchr., tchr. asst., N.Y. Asst. tchr. mid. sch. Corning (N.Y.)-Painted Post Sch. Dist.; jr.-sr. high sch. tchr. spl. edn. Steuben-Allegany Bd. Coop. Ednl. Svcs., Bath, N.Y.; mid. sch. tchr. spl. edn. Penn Yan (N.Y.) Sch. Dist.; jr.-sr. high sch. resource room tchr., chmn. com. spl. edn. Avoca (N.Y.) Cen. Sch.; resource room tchr. Elmira (N.Y.) City Sch. Dist., varsity coach swimming, diving, cheerleading, softball, jr. varsity softball and volleyball. Mem. com. special edn. Resource Room, Cohocton (N.Y.) Ctrl. Sch. Dist.; coord. student affairs Empire State Speech & Hearing Clinic, Inc. Sec. N.Y. State area 15 Spl. Olympics; chairperson Relay for Life, 2004, youth chairperson. Mem. NEA. Home: 223 Pritchard Ave Corning NY 14830-1735

WILSON, CHANDRA DANETTE, actress; b. Houston, Aug. 27, 1969; children: Joy, Serena, Michael. BFA in Drama, NYU, 1991. Actor: (plays) The Good Times Are Killing Me (Outstanding Debut Performance, Theatre World award), Paper Moon: The Musical, The Family of Mann, Believing, Caroline, or Change (named one of Eight to Watch, Onstage and Behind the Scenes, NY Times, 2004); (Broadway plays) On the Town; (films) Philadelphia, 1993, Lone Star, 1996, Strangers with Candy, 2005; (TV series) Bob Patterson, 2001, Grey's Anatomy, 2005— (Outstanding Performance by a Female Actor in a Drama Series, SAG, 2007, 2007, Best Supporting Actress in Drama Series, NAACP Image awards, 2007, 2008, 2009). Named Favorite Scene Stealing Star, People's Choice Awards, 2008. Mailing: Grey's Anatomy Los Feliz Tower 4th Fl 4151 Prospect Ave Los Angeles CA 90027*

WILSON, CHARLES A., JR., United States Representative from Ohio, funeral director; b. Belmont, Ohio, Jan. 18, 1943; 4 children. BS, Ohio U., 1966; degree, Cin. Coll. Mortuary Sci. Mem. Ohio State Ho. Reps., Columbus, 1997—2004, Ohio State Senate, Columbus, Ohio, 2005—07, US Congress from 6th Ohio dist., 2007—, mem. sci. & tech. com., fin. svcs. com. Mem. banking, pensions and securities com. Ohio State Ho. Reps., mem. fin. and appropriations com., mem. agr. and devel. subcom., mem. rules and reference com.; vice chmn. Belmont (Ohio) Nat. Bank; bd. dirs. East Ohio Regional Hosp. Mem.: Bridgeport C. of C., St. Clairsville C. of C., Ohio Funeral Dirs. Assn., Blue Dog Coalition, Belmont Hills Country Club. Democrat. Roman Catholic. Office: US House Reps 226 Cannon House Office Bldg Washington DC 20515 also: 4137 Boardman Canfield Rd Canfield OH 44406-8087 Office Phone: 330-533-7250. Office Fax: 330-533-7136.*

WILSON, CHARLES BANKS, artist; b. Springdale, Ark., Aug. 6, 1918; s. Charles Bertram and Bertha Juanita (Banks) W.; children: Geoffrey Banks, Carrie Vee. Student, Art Inst. Chgo., 1936—41. Mag. and book illustrator, 1943-60; head art dept. N.E. Okla. A. & M. Coll., Miami, Okla., 1947-61; painter, printmaker. Executed murals, Okla. State Capitol, 1975; represented in permanent collections Met. Mus., NYC, Libr. of Congress, Washington, US Capitol Bldg., DC Corcoran Gallery, Smithsonian Inst., Will Rogers Meml. Mus., Philbrook Art Ctr., Tulsa, Nat. Cowbow Hall of Fame, Oklahoma City, Okla. State Capitol; retrospective exhbn. Gilcreae, 2007; illustrator numerous books; appeared on AETN-TV, Okla., 2006-07, AENBETN-TV, Ark., 2006; subject of profile Am. Artist (PBS), 2007, One Man Show, 5 Gallaries, Gilerea Mus. Bd. dirs. Thomas Gilcrease Mus. History and Art, Tulsa, 1957-61; chmn. Pub. Libr. Bd., Miami, Okla., 1954-59. Named to Okla. Hall of Fame, Okla. Historians Hall of Fame, 2001, named an Okla. Treasure, State of Okla. Arts Commn., 2001; named Charles Banks Wilson Bldg. in his honor Northeast Okla. A&M Coll.; recipient Western Heritage award Cowboy Hall of Fame, Disting. Svc. citation U. Okla., Lifetime Achievement award Ark. Art Coun., 2006; subject of books The Lithographs of Charles Banks Wilson, 1989, Search for the North American Purebloods, 2000, An Oklahoma Portrait, 1989. Mem. Internat. Inst. Arts and Letters (Geneva). Home and Office: 1611 E Mission Blvd Fayetteville AR 72703-3043 Office Phone: 479-442-9891. Personal E-mail: nag-pra-106-@earthlink.net. Business E-Mail: cvwilson@mail.uark.edu.

WILSON, CHARLES H. (CHARLES HARRISON WILSON), retired air force officer, financial planner, human resource development professional; b. Chgo., Sept. 6, 1941; s. Charles and Lorraine F. Wilson; m. Mona Dickerson, July 2, 1988; children: Audrey M., Angela M., Andrew M., Aaron M. BS, So. Ill. U., 1964; BA, U. Md., 1976; MBA, Webster U., 1979. Commd. 2d lt. USAF, 1964; def. logistics agy. Washington; advanced through grades to lt. col. USAF, 1986; exec. dir. exec. leadership program Dept. Def. (Pentagon), Washington, 1976-88. Mil. liaison Republic of China, 1977-80; adj. prof. Park Univ., St. Louis, 1977-80; mcpl. cons. City of Dayton, Ohio, 1980; pres. Advanced Ethonomics. Vice chmn. sch. bd. Alexandria Pub. Sch., Va., 2003—; bd. dir. Credit Union No. Va., Crises Link. Fellow D.C. Life Under Writers Tng. Coun.; Washington DC Area Sch. Bd. (chmn.), Am. Soc. Tng. and Devel., Internat. Pers. Mgmt. Assn. (human rights commn.), Omega Psi Phi, Toastmasters; elected to Alexandria City Sch. Bd, Queen St. Bus. Assoc. (bd. dirs.) Democrat. Methodist. Achievements include invention of microwave oven carousel. Avocation: flying. Home: 6101 Edsall Rd Apt 703 Alexandria VA 22304-6004 Office Phone: 202-429-4393, 703-587-8783.

WILSON, CHARLES NESBITT, lobbyist, former United States Representative from Texas; b. Trinity, Tex., June 1, 1933; s. Charles Edwin and Wilmuth (Nesbitt) Wilson; m. Jerry Wilson (div.); m. Barbara Livshin Alberstadt Zavacky, Feb. 2, 1999. Student, Sam Houston State U., Huntsville, Tex., 1951-52; BS, U.S. Naval Acad., 1956. Commd. ensign U.S. Navy, 1956, advanced through grades to lt.; ret., 1960; mem. Tex. Ho. of Reps., 1960-66, Tex. State Senate, 1966-72, US Congress from 2nd Tex. Dist., 1973—97; ranking minority mem. appropriations subcom. on fgn. ops., export financing & related programs; ptnr. Hooper, Owen, Gould & Winburn, 1996—. Mgr. lumber yard, 1962-72 Democrat. Methodist. Office: Hooper Owen Gould & Winburn Ste 730 801 Pennsylvania Ave NW Washington DC 20004-2687*

WILSON, CHARLES REGINALD, federal judge; b. Pensacola, Fla., 1954; BS, U. Notre Dame, 1976, JD, 1979. Bar: Fla. 1979. Law clk. to Hon. Joseph W. Hatchett US Ct. Appeals (11th cir.), 1979—80; asst. county atty. Hillsborough county, Fla., 1980—81; county judge 13th Jud. Cir. of Fla., 1986—90; pvt. practice Fla., 1981—86; US magistrate judge US Dist. Ct. (mid. dist.) Fla., 1990—94, US atty., 1994—99; judge US Ct. Appeals (11th cir.), Tampa, Fla., 1999—. Mem.: Ferguson-White Inn of Am. Inn of Ct., Fed. Bar Assn., Am. Law Inst. Office: 11th Cir Ct Appeals 801 N Florida Ave Ste 14B Tampa FL 33602-3849*

WILSON, CHARLES STEPHEN, cardiologist, educator; b. Geneva, Nebr., June 14, 1938; s. Robert Butler and Naoma Luella (Norgren) Wilson; m. Linda Stern Walt, Aug. 21, 1960; children: Michael Scott, Amy Lynn, Cynthia Lee. BA cum laude, U. Nebr., 1960; MD, Northwestern U., 1964. Diplomate Am. Bd. Internal Medicine subsplty. bd. cardiovascular disease, Nat. Bd. Med. Examiners. Intern Fitzsimons Gen. Hosp., Denver, 1964-65; fellow in internal medicine and cardiology Mayo Grad. Sch. Medicine, Rochester, Minn., 1968-72; practice medicine specializing in cardiology Lincoln, Nebr., 1972—; attending staff Bryan Meml. Hosp., 1972—, chmn. cardiology, 1976-79; clin. prof. medicine and cardiology U. Nebr. Med. Ctr., Omaha; med. dir. Bryan LGH Med. Ctr. Ultrafast CT Scanner, Lincoln, 2001—, Sch. Allied Health, Bryan LGH Coll. of Health Scis., 2002—. Mem. Mayor's Coun. on Emergency Med. Svcs., Lincoln, 1974-78; founder, chmn. Nebr. State Hypertension Screening Program; med. dir. Lincoln Mobile Heart Team, 1977-80, Lincoln Cardiac Rehab. Program, 1978-79; co-founder, pres. Nebr. Heart Inst., 1987; co-founder Lincoln Cardiac Transplant Program, 1987. Contbr. articles to profl. jours.; editorl. cons. Chest, 1975-76; assoc. editor Nebr. Med. Jour., 1981-88. Trustee U. Nebr. Found., 1983—, chmn. Nebr. Coordinating Commn. for Postsecondary Edn., 1984-88; mem. bd. regents U. Nebr., 1991—2009, chmn. 1994, 2001, 07. Served as maj. M.C., USAR, 1963-68. Gen. Motors Nat. scholar, 1956—60, Nat. Found. med. scholar, 1960—64, Mead Johnson scholar, ACP, 1968—71. Fellow ACP, Am. Coll. Cardiology (bd. govs. 1990-93, pres. Nebr. affiliate 1992-93), Am. Coll. Chest Physicans, Am. Heart Assn. (dir. Nebr. affilate 1973-80, pres. 1976-77); mem. Mayo Cardiovascular Soc., Nebr. Cardiovascular Soc. (pres. 1989-90), Nebr. Coun. on Pub. Higher Edn. (steering com. 1991—), Lincoln Heart Assn. (dir. 1972-75, pres. 1974-75), AMA, Nebr. Med. Assn. Lancaster County

Med. Soc., Am. Soc. Internal Medicine, Lincoln Found., U. Nebr. Chancellor's Club, Lincoln U. Club (dir. 1981-84), U. Nebr. Pres. Club, Phi Beta Kappa, Sigma Xi, Alpha Omega Alpha, Phi Delta Theta (pres. Nebr. Alpha chpt. 1959-60). Home: 7430 N Hampton Rd Lincoln NE 68506-1624 Office: Bryan LGH Ultrafast CT Scanner 1500 S 48th St Lincoln NE 68506

WILSON, CHESTER GOODWIN, electrical engineer, educator; s. Chester Goodwin and Patricia Susan Wilson; m. Chereis Francene Petrovich, May 24, 2002; children: Courtney Patricia, Chester Goodwin Jr. BS in Elec. Engring., Seattle U., Wash., 1991; MS in Applied Physics, U. Wash., Seattle, 1996; PhD in Elec. Engring., U. Wis., Madison, 2002. Product mgr. NW Mfg., Seattle, 1989—96; tchg. asst., physics dept. U. Wis., 1996—96, rsch. asst., engring. and physics dept., 1996—98, tchg. asst., 1998—2002, rsch. asst., rsch. fellow, elec. and computer engring. dept., 1998—2002; adj. faculty, rsch. fellow, elec. engring. and computer sci. dept. wims erc U. Mich., Ann Arbor, 2002—04; asst. prof., dept. elec. engring. & inst. micromanufacturing La. Tech U., Ruston, 2004—. Contbr. articles to profl. jours., scientific papers. Chief tech. officer Cyber Corps Interactive, Ruston, 2008, Carbon Capture Tech., Arcadia, La., 2008. Recipient Gerald Holdbridge Tchg. Excellence award, 2001; numerous grants, NASA, grant, Radiance Air Force, 2007—, Avoyelles, 2007—, ASEE, 2007—08, numerous grants, NSF. Mem.: IEEE. Achievements include invention of ion source for trimming IC circuits, integrated passives and MEMS devices; rechargeable cast microbatteries.

WILSON, CHRISTOPHER J., lawyer; b. Pensacola, Fla., May 25, 1965; BA cum laude, Thomas More Coll., 1988; JD cum laude, U. Notre Dame, 1991. Bar: Ohio 1991. Ptnr. Frost Brown Todd LLP; assoc. gen. counsel, asst. corp. sec. Cincinnati Bell, Inc. (formerly Broadwing, Inc.), Cincinnati, Ohio, 1999—2003, v.p., gen. counsel, 2003—. Mem. adv. coun. Nat. Assn. Minority and Women Owned Law Firms; mem. steering com. Gr. Cincinnati Minority Counsel Program. Mem.: Ohio State Bar Assn., Cincinnati Bar Assn. Office: Cincinnati Bell Inc 221 E Fourth St Cincinnati OH 45202 Business E-Mail: christopher.wilson@cinbell.com.

WILSON, CLARK R., geophysicist, educator; BA with high honors in Physics, U. Calif. San Diego Revelle Coll., 1970; MS in Earth Sci., U. Calif. San Diego Scripps Instn. Oceanography, 1973, PhD in Earth Sci., 1975. Asst. prof. to assoc. prof. U. Tex., Austin, 1976—89, prof., 1989—, Wallace Pratt prof. geophysics, 1992—. Chmn. dept. geol. scis. U. Tex., Austin, 1990—94, 2004—; geodynamics and geopotential fields prog. specialist NASA, Washington, 1996—99; head Geophys. Fluids Ctr. Hydrology, 1999—2004; mem. directing bd. Internat. Earth Rotation Svc., 2000—. Contbr. articles to sci. jours.; assoc. editor geodesy: Jour. Geophys. Rsch., 1993—99. Office: Geol Scis Dept U Tex 1 Univ Sta C1100 Austin TX 78712-0254 E-mail: crwilson@mail.utexas.edu.

WILSON, CLAUDE RAYMOND, JR., lawyer; b. Dallas, Feb. 22, 1933; s. Claude Raymond and Lottie (Watts) W.; m. Emilynn Wilson; children: Deidra Wilson Graves, Melissa Woodard Utley, Michele Woodard Dunn. BBA, So. Meth. U., Dallas, 1954, JD, 1956. Bar: Tex. 1956; CPA, Calif., Tex. With Cervin & Melton, Dallas, 1956-58, Tex. & Pacific R.R. Co., Dallas, 1958-60; atty. office regional counsel IRS, San Francisco, 1960-63, sr. trial atty. office chief counsel Washington, 1963-65; ptnr. Wilson & White, LLP, Dallas, 1965—98, Vial, Hamilton, Koch & Knox LLP, Dallas, 1998—2007, Looper Reed & McGraw, Dallas, 2007—. Chmn., Dallas dist. dir. IRS Adv. Commn., 1990-91. Chmn. Dallas Hist. Soc., 2000-01; mem. fin. com. Dallas Arboretum and Bot. Gardens, 2003-08, City of University Park, 2004-; bd. govs., mem. fin. com., mem. ethics com. Dallas Symphony Orch., 2004-08. Mem.: AICPA (coun. 1989—93, tax exec. com. 1998—2001), ABA, Tex. Soc. CPAs (pres. 1989—90, pres. Dallas chpt. 1983—84), Dallas Bar Assn. (pres. sect. taxation 1969—70), State Bar Tex., Greater Dallas C. of C. (chmn. appropriations and tax com. 1990—91), Dallas Petroleum Club, Masons, Delta Theta Phi., Delta Sigma Phi. Republican. Episcopalian. Office: Looper Reed & McGraw 4100 Thanksgiving Tower 1601 Elm St Dallas TX 75201 Office Phone: 214-237-6335. Business E-Mail: cwilson@lrmlaw.com.

WILSON, CLEALYN BULLOCK, elementary school educator; b. Phila., Mar. 25, 1950; d. Clinton Nathaniel Bullock and Odaris (Wilson) Jeter; s. Thomas A. Jeter Jr. (stepfather); m. Cecil Charles Wilson, Mar. 19, 1989. BS in Elem. Edn., Morgan State U., 1972; postgrad., We. Wash. U., 1976, Berry Coll., 1978; MEd in Early Childhood Edn., West Ga. Coll., 1980; postgrad., U. New Orleans, 1981, Wilmington Coll., 1991—. Cert. tchr. elem. and early childhood, Del.; cert. elem. tchr. La., Ga., Md. Tchr. 2nd grade Schaeffer Elem. Sch., Pitts., 1972-74; tchr. 1st grade Friends Lower Sch., Balt., 1974-75; follow through tchr. 1st grade Roosevelt Elem., Tacoma, Wash.; open space tchr. 2nd grade Boze. Elem Sch., Tacoma, 1976-77; title 1 tchr. reading resource North Heights Elem. Sch., Rome, Ga., 1977-80; tchr. 2nd grade Main Elem. Sch., Rome, 1980-81; tchr. 4th grade Nelson Elem. Sch., New Orleans, 1981; tchr. 1st and 3rd grades, resource tchr. lang. and early acad. program. Joseph A. Craig Elem. Sch., New Orleans, 1981-88; tchr. 1st grade, 1st and 2nd grade split Towne Point Elem. Sch., Dover, Del., 1988-90; tchr. first grade Willards (Md.) Elem. Sch., 1990-91, East Dover Elem. Sch., 1991-95, guidance counselor, 1995—. Tchr. homework Community Edn. Program, New Orleans, 1982, high potential tchr., 1983-84; team tchr. Capital Sch. Dist. Summer Reading Camp, Dover, 1992, coord., 1993; creator art projects The Edn. Ctr., Inc., 1992; cons. district-wide writing workshops; mem. district-wide English Lang. Arts Review and Selection Com.; chairperson Del. Tchrs. Forum. Youth coord., MYF co-leader, coun. on ministries, chancel choir, active aerobics programs, altar guild, tchr. Sunday sch. Whatcoat United Meth. Ch., chair Christian Edn., 1992—; layspeaker United Meth. Comm. Com.; active United Meth. Women.; counselor Camp Pe-Co-Meth, Centreville, Md., 1969, mgr. dining room, 1971; mem. choir, brownie leader, nominating com., chair Women's Day observance, instr. aerobics program Bethany United Meth. Ch., New Orleans; program aide Nat. Youth Sports Program; counselor Camp George. Recipient Tchr. of Yr. award State of Del., 1992-93, Capital Sch. Dist., Dover, 1992-93, Appreciation award Whatcoat United Meth. Ch. Winterim Summer Day Camp; named High Potential Tchr., Orleans Parish Cmty. Ctr., 1983-84. Mem. NEA, ASCD, Assn. for Childhood Learning Internat., Del. State Edn. Assn., Diamond State Reading Assn., Capital Educators Assn., Kent Coun. for Reading, Alpha Kappa Alpha (sub-debutantes, assist with youth awareness activities, project lead), Phi Delta Kappa, Kappa Delta Pi, Alpha Delta Kappa. Democrat. Avocations: aerobics, dance, cooking, doll collecting, poetry. Home: 130 Brandywine Dr Dover DE 19904-2287 Office: East Dover Elem Sch 852 S Little Creek Rd Dover DE 19901-4797

WILSON, COLIN HENRY, writer; b. Leicester, Eng., June 26, 1931; s. Arthur and Anetta Wilson; m. Joy Stewart; children: Sally, Damon, Rowan; 1 child from previous marriage, Roderick. Writer-in-residence Hollins (Va.) Coll., 1966—67; vis. prof. U. Wash., Seattle, 1967, Rutgers U., New Brunswick, NJ, 1974. Author: The Outsider, 1956, The Glass Cage, 1967, The Angry Years, 2007, Man Hunters, 2007, (novels) The Occult, 1971, The Black Room, 1971, The Space Vampires, 1975, Mysteries, 1978, others, (books) Access to Inner World, 1982, A Criminal History of Mankind, 1983, The Essential Colin Wilson, 1984, The Personality Surgeon, 1986, Spider World, 1987, The Misfits, 1988, Beyond the Occult, 1988, Written in Blood, 1989; author: (with Donald Seaman) Modern Encyclopedia of Murder, 1983, The Serial Killers, 1989; author: (with Damon Wilson) Encyclopedia of Unsolved Mysteries, 1987, Crimes of Passion, 2006; author: others, (plays) Mozart's Journey to Prague, 1991, Spider World: The Magician, 1992, The Strange Life of P. D. Ouspensky, 1993, From Atlantis to The Sphinx, 1996, Atlas of Holy Places and Sacred Sites, 1996, Alien Dawn, 1998, The Books in My Life, 1998, The Devil's Party, 2000, Spider World: The Magician, 2002, Spider World: Shadowland, 2003; author: (with Damon Wilson) Unsolved Mysteries Past and Present, 1993; author: (with Rand Fle'math) Atlantis Blueprint, 2000; author: (autobiography) Dreaming to Some Purpose, 2004, Atlantis and the Kingdom of the Neanderthals, 2006, The Angry Years, 2007, Super Consciousness, 2008. Mem.: Savage.

WILSON, COURTNEY B., military officer, museum administrator; b. Md. B in Am. History, Western Md. Coll.; M, Morgan State U.; grad., Fed. Law Enforcement Acad., 1976. With US Dept. Interior, Nat. Pk. Svc., 1975—82; chief of staff Md. Def. Force, spl. project officer, dep. chief of staff, commdg. gen., 2006—. Am. mil. cons. Nat. Firearms Mus., Md. Hist. Soc., Smithsonian Instn., Atlanta Hist. Soc., Va. Hist. Soc., Gettysburg Nat. Pk., Balt. Civil War Mus. and others. Exec. dir. B&O RR Mus. With US Army, Vietnam. Mem.: Mid-Atlantic Assn. Mus., Md. Mil. Hist. Soc., Greater Balt. History Alliance (pres.). Office: Md Def Force Pikesville Mil Reservation 610 Reisterstown Rd Pikesville MD 21208 also: B&O Railroad Mus 901 W Pratt St Baltimore MD 21223 Office Phone: 410-752-2490. Office Fax: 410-752-2499. Business E-Mail: cwilson@borail.org.

WILSON, D. EDWARD, JR., lawyer; b. New Orleans, Dec. 23, 1951; s. Donald Edward and Nellie (Courtney) W.; m. Lynn Whittlesey, Sept. 10, 1981; children: Robert Donald, Thomas Courtney, John Whittlesey. BA, U. Va., 1973; JD, Georgetown U., 1976. Law clk. to Judge R.L. Kunzig U.S. Ct. Appeals (fed. cir.), Washington, 1976-77; assoc. Morgan, Lewis & Bockius, Washington, 1977-81; assoc. counsel to the pres. The White House, Washington, 1981-84, gen. counsel Office of Adminstrn., 1984-85; prin. dep. asst. sec. for mgmt., Exec. Off. Pres. Dept. of the Treasury, Washington, 1985-86, acting gen. counsel, 1986-88; pvt. practice, 1988—; ptnr. Venable LLP, Washington, 2003—. Lectr. Nat. War Coll. Chmn. Goodwin House, Inc., 1996-2001, Goodwin House Found., 2005-06; mem. vestry St. Peter's Episcopal Ch., Arlington, Va., 1988-91. Recipient Disting. Svc. award Sec. Dept. Treasury, 1988, Gen. Counsel's award, 1988, Chief Counsel's award IRS, 1988. Mem. ABA, D.C. Bar, La. State Bar Assn., Washington Inst. for Foreign Affairs, So. Yacht Club (New Orleans), Met. Club (Washington). Republican. Episcopalian. Office: Venable LLP 575 7th St NW Washington DC 20004 Office Phone: 202-344-4000. Business E-Mail: dewilson@venable.com.

WILSON, DANIEL RICHARD, anthropologist, physician; b. Ft. Dodge, Iowa, Feb. 22, 1956; m. Sandra Lea Davis; 1 child, Victoria Elizabeth. BA Anthropology, Yale U., 1979; MD, U. Iowa, 1983; PhD Anthropology, Cambridge U., 1995; diploma mental health mgmt., Case Western Res. U., 1996. Cert. FABPN, 1989. Resident in psychiatry Harvard Med. Sch., 1987; neuropsychiatrist McLean Hosp. - Harvard Med. Sch., Belmont, Mass., 1987—92; assoc. prof. psychiatry U. Cin., 1993—98; med. dir. ODMH - Lewis Ctr., 1993—2000, ODMH - Statewide ISS, 1998—2000; prof. psychiatry U. Cin., 1998—2000; prof., chmn. psychiatry, prof. anthropology Creighton U., Omaha, 2000—. Recipient Huston award, U. Iowa Coll. Medicine, 1983, Nat. Exemplar Training Program award, Am. Psychiat. Assn., 1994; named Nat. Tng. Program of Yr., Nat. Alliance for Mentally Ill, 1995; vis. fellow, Clare Hall, Cambridge U., 1992—93, Slyster scholar, AMA, 1982—83, Burroughs-Wellcome fellow, Am. Psychiat. Assn., 1985—87, Overseas fellow, Royal Anthropol. Inst., 1997—, Rotary fellow, Cambridge U., England, 1992—93. Fellow: Am. Bd. Forensic Medicine (life); mem.: Am. Neuropsychiatric Assn. (pres. 2009—), World Psychiat. Assn. (chair Psychotherapy 2004—), Internat. Soc. Police Surgeons (life), Alpha Omega Alpha (life). Office: Creighton U Sch Med 3528 Dodge St Omaha NE 68131 Office Phone: 402-345-8828.

WILSON, DARCY BENOIT, science association director; b. Rhinebeck, NY, May 14, 1936; s. Darcy Wilson and Rosamonde Cyr; m. Dianne Haley, Dec. 24, 1973; children: Kathrine Josephine Cyr, Rebecca Louise Innes, Amy Louise Cosette Sanger, Jessica Grace Rosamonde, Jason Darcy Haley. BA, Harvard Coll., Cambridge, Mass., 1958; PhD, U. Pa., Phila., 1962. Asst. prof., med. genetics U. Pa. Sch. Medicine, Phila., 1966—69, assoc. prof., pathology & med. genetics, 1969—74, prof., dept. pathology, 1974—84, head, 1979—84; sci. dir. Med. Biology Inst., La Jolla, Calif., 1985—90, La Jolla Inst., 1990—92, Sidney Kimmel Cancer Ctr., San Diego, 1992—97, Torrey Pines Inst., San Diego, 1997—. Contbr. scientific papers to profl. jours. Numerous grants, NIH, 1961—. Mem.: Am. Assn. Immunologists. Home: 8669 La Jolla Scenic Dr N La Jolla CA 92037 Office: Torrey Pines Inst 8669 La Jolla Scenic Dr N San Diego CA 92121 Office Fax: 858-455-3804. Business E-Mail: dbwilson@tpims.org.

WILSON, DAVID GORDON, mechanical engineering educator; b. Sutton Coldfield, Warwick, Eng., Feb. 11, 1928; s. William and Florence Ida (Boulton) W.; m. Anne Ware Sears, July 18, 1963 (div. May 1988); children: John M.B., Erica Sears; m. Ellen Cecilia Warner, Dec. 30, 1988; 1 child, Susan Speck. Postgrad., MIT, Harvard U., 1955-57; BS with honors, U. Birmingham, UK, 1948; PhD, U. Nottingham, UK, 1953. Brush fellow, rsch. asst. Nottingham U., 1950-53; ship's 7th engr. officer Donaldson Line, Glasgow, UK, 1953; engr. Brush Elec. Engring. Co., Ltd., UK, 1953-55; sr. gas-turbine designer Ruston & Hornsby, Lincoln, UK, 1957-58; sr. lectr., mech. engring. U. Ibadan, Zaria, Nigeria, 1958-60; v.p., tech. dir. No. Rsch. and Engring. Corp., Cambridge, Mass., also U.K., 1960-66; assoc. prof. mech. engring. MIT, Cambridge, 1966-71, prof., 1971-94; prof. emeritus, 1994—; co-founder, chief sci. officer, pres. Wilson TurboPower, Inc., Woburn, Mass., 2001—09. Vis. engr., Boeing Airplane Co., 1956-57; vis. fellow MIT and Harvard U., 1955-56; cons., lectr. in field. Author: The Design of Gas-Turbine Engines, 1991, The Design of High-Efficiency Turbomachinery and Gas Turbines, 1984, (with T.P. Korakianitis), 2d edit., 1998; co-author: (with Frank Rowland Whitt) Bicycling Science, 1974, 2d edit., 1982, 3d edit., 2004, (with Richard Wilson et al) The Health Effects of Fossil-Fuel Burning, 1981, (with Douglas Stephen Beck) Gas-Turbine Regenerators, 1996; co-editor: (with Allan V. Abbott) Human-Powered Vehicles, 1995; editor: Solid-Waste-Management Handbook, 1977, The Treatment and Management of Urban Solid Waste, 1972; editor Human Power, 1984-2002. Recipient T. Bernard Hall prize Inst. Mech. Engrs., 1954, Lord Weir 1st prize Inst. Mech. Engrs., 1955, Indsl. Rsch. IR-100 award, 1974, Reclamation Industries Internat. prize, 1974; Power-Jets-Sch. scholar, 1954; Commonwealth Fund fellow MIT and Harvard U., 1955-57. Avocations: human power, biking, hiking, tennis, music. Office: MIT/Mech Engring Rm 3-137e Cambridge MA 02139 Personal E-mail: dgwilson@mit.edu.

WILSON, DAVID JAMES, chemistry researcher, educator; b. Ames, Iowa, June 25, 1930; s. James Calmar and Alice Winona (Olmsted) W.; m. Martha Carolyn Mayers, Sept. 6, 1952; children: John Wesley, Charles Steven, William David, Andrew Lyman, Joyce Ballin. BS in Chemistry, Stanford U., 1952; postgrad., 1952-53, 55-57; PhD, Calif. Inst. Tech., 1958. Mem. faculty U. Rochester, NY, 1957-69, assoc. prof. NY, 1963-67, prof. phys. chemistry NY, 1967-69; prof. Vanderbilt U., Nashville, 1969-95, prof. chemistry and environ. engring., 1977-95, prof. emeritus, 1995—, Alexander Heard disting. service prof., 1983-84; sr. rsch. assoc. Eckenfelder/Brown and Caldwell, Nashville, 1988-95, sr. rsch. fellow, 1995—. Vis. sr. lectr. chemistry U. Ife, Nigeria, 1964-65; vis. prof. U. Málaga, Spain, 1993-94; mem. Rochester Com. for Sci. Info., 1960-69, v.p., 1966-69; chmn. Nashville Com. for Sci. Info., 1971-74. Author: (book) Foam Flotation: Theory and Applications, Hazardous Waste Site Soil Remediation, Modeling of In Situ Techniques for Treatment of Contaminated Soils. Pres. Tenn. Environ. Coun., 1985-87. Sp-3 US Army, 1953—55, Army Chem. Ctr., Md. Recipient award Monroe County Conservation Coun., 1967, Tenn. Conservation League, 1971; Alfred P. Sloan Found. fellow, 1964-66. Mem. AAAS, Am. Chem. Soc., Tenn. Acad. Sci., Sigma Xi, Phi Beta Kappa. Avocations: ornithology, music, travel, hiking. Home: 11544 Quirk Rd Belleville MI 48111 Office Phone: 734-699-7623. Personal E-mail: djw1ls0n@sbcglobal.net.

WILSON, DAVID VANDIVER, II, lawyer; b. Houston, Jan. 9, 1968; s. David Vandiver and Emma Lee (Binion) W.; m. Susan Graham, Dec. 18, 1988; children: Katherine Elizabeth, Sarah Margaret, David Vandiver III. BS, Tex. A&M U., 1989; JD, South Tex. Coll. Law, Houston, 1993. Bar: Tex. 1993, Nev. 2007. Asst. dist. atty. Harris County, Houston, 1993-95; adj. prof. law South Tex. Coll. Law, 1994-95, 98—; asst. dist. atty. Angelina County, Lufkin, Tex., 1995-98; instr. Angelina Coll. Police Acad., Lufkin, 1995-98; shareholder Hays, McConn, Rice & Pickering, Houston, 1998—. Mem. editl. bd.: Houston Lawyer, 2002—, editor:, 2005—07, editor in chief:, 2007—08. Mem. exec. bd. Habitat for Humanity Angelina County, 1996-98; trustee First United Meth. Ch., Lufkin, 1996-98; bd. stewards Meml. Dr. United Meth. Ch., 2001-, bd. trustee Tex. Conf. United Meth. Ch., 2008-. Named Child Advocate of Yr. Black Adoption Coun. S.E. Tex., Beaumont, 1997; named to Houston's Top Lawyers List, Houston Tex. Mag., 2005-06; recipient 1st prize Bruno Bitker Essay Contest, 1992, Pres. award Houston Bar Assn., 2008, Disting. Alumnus award Duke U., 2008. Fellow Tex. Bar Found., Houston Bar Found.; mem. ABA (mem. ho. of dels. 1997-2000), Angelina County Bar Assn. (bd. dirs. 1996-98), Houston Bar Assn. Methodist. Avocations: hunting, fishing. Office: Hays Mcconn Rice Pickering 1233 West Loop S Ste 1000 Houston TX 77027-9100 Office Phone: 713-654-1111. Business E-Mail: dvw@haysmcconn.com.

WILSON, DENA SUZETTE, elementary school educator; b. Lubbock, Tex., Aug. 22, 1964; d. James Leroy and Rena Glyndell Louthan; m. Robert Hugh Wilson Jr., Dec. 16, 1989. BA in Family and Consumer Sci., U. Houston, 1986; M in Elem. Edn., Berry Coll., Mt. Berry, Ga., 2000. Cert. vocat. home econs. tchr. Tex., 1987, kindergarten tchr. Tex., 1988, self-contained elem. tchr. Tex., 2002, tchr. pre-kindergarten-8th grade Ga., Tex., tchr. 6-12 grade Ga., Tex. Tchr. pre-kindergarten Spring Ind. Sch. Dist., Tex., 1986—90; store mgr. Suzette's Cards & Gifts, 1990—97; tchr. grades 1 and 2 Bartow County Schs., Cartersville, Ga., 1997—2002; tchr. grade 3 Llano Ind. Sch. Dist., Tex., 2002—, Renaissance reading leadership team mem., 2006—08. Team leader site based leadership team Llano Elem. Sch., Tex., 2004—08; site based leadership team Llano Ind. Sch. Dist., Tex., 2004—. Sec. Child Welfare Bd., Llano, Tex., 2004—, Llano Corp. Children in Crisis, 2005—; dir. Awana 1st Bapt., 2003—08, dir. vacation bible sch., 2006—. Mem.: Assn. Tex. Profl. Educators, Internat. Reading Assn., Delta Kappa Gamma. Avocations: reading, antiques, cooking. Home: 407 W Sandstone Llano TX 78643 Office: Llano Elem Sch 1600 Oatman St Llano TX 78643 Mailing: PO Box 56 Llano TX 78643 Personal E-mail: robdena@yahoo.com.

WILSON, DONALD EDWARD, internist, educator, former dean; b. Worcester, Mass., Aug. 28, 1936; s. Rivers Rivo and Licine (Bradshaw) Wilson; m. Patricia C. Littell, Aug. 27, 1977; children: Jeffrey D.E., Sean D., Monique, Sheila L. AB, Harvard U., 1958; MD, Tufts U., 1962. Diplomate Am. Bd. Internal Medicine. Intern St. Elizabeth Hosp., Boston, 1962—63; resident in medicine, research fellow in gastroenterology VA Hosp. and Lemuel Shattuck Hosp., Boston, 1963—66; assoc. chief gastroenterology Bklyn. Hosp., 1968—71; instr. medicine SUNY Downstate Med. Center, Bklyn., 1968—71; asst. prof. medicine U. Ill., Chgo., 1971—73, asso. prof., 1973—75, prof., 1975—80, acting head dept. medicine, 1976—77; dir. divsn. gastroenterology U. Ill. Hosp., Chgo., 1971—78, chief of gastroenterology, 1973—80, physician-in-chief, 1976—77; prof., chmn. dept. medicine SUNY Downstate Med. Center, Bklyn., 1980—91; physician-in-chief State U. and Kings County Hosp., 1980—91; dean U. Md. Sch. Medicine, Balt., 1991—2006, v.p. of med. affairs, 1999—2006, dir. Program in Minority Health and Health Disparities Edn. and Rsch. Vis. prof. medicine U. London, Kings Coll. Med. Sch., 1977—78; mem. gastrointestingal drugs adv. bd. FDA, 1985—87, chmn., 1986—87; mem. Part II test com. Nat. Bd. Med. Examiners, 1985—88; mem. nat. digestive adv. bd. NIH, 1985—87, chmn., 1986—87, mem. gen. clin. rsch. ctrs. com., 1987—; mem. nat. adv. com. Agy. for Health Care Policy and Rsch., Dept. HHS, 1991—94, chmn., 1992—94; mem. residency rev. com. for internal medicine Acque, 1993—; mem. nat. com. fgn. med. edn. and accreditation U.S. Dept. Edn., 1994—; mem. nat. adv. rsch. resources com. NIH, 1997—2000; bd. dirs. Provident Bank Corp., 2002—. Contbr. articles to med. jours.; mem. editl. bd. Tufts Med. Alumni Bulletin, 1993—2002. Bd. vis. Harvard Sch. Pub. Health, 1992—94; bd. overseers Tufts U. Med. Sch., 2002—; bd. dirs. Balt. Symphony Orch., 1997—2004, Kernan Hosp., Balt., 1991—98, bd. dirs., Endowment Fund, 1996—; bd. dirs. Alliance to End Childhood Poisoning, 1992—95, The Baer Sch., Balt., 1992—, Mercy Med. Ctr., Balt., 1991—, U. Md. Med. Sys., 1991—. Capt. M.C. USAF, 1966—68. Recipient Rsch. award, HEW, 1971, 1974, John A. Hartford Found., Inc., 1972—79, Distilled Spirits Coun. U.S., 1972—74, VA, 1974. Master: ACP; mem.: AAAS, NAS, Inst. of Medicine, Assn. Profs. Medicine (sec.-treas. 1990—91), Am. Clin. and Climatol. Assn., Nat. Med. Assn., Assn. for Acad. Minority Physicians (sec./treas. 1986—), Assn. Am. Physicians, Chgo. Soc. Gastrointestinal Endoscopy (pres. 1979—80), N.Y. Soc. Gastroenterology, N.Y. Acad. Medicine, N.Y. Acad. Scis., Soc. Exptl. Biology and Medicine, Midwest Gut Club, Digestive Disease Found., Chgo. Soc. Gastroenterology (pres. 1978—79), Ctrl. Rsch. Club, Ctrl. Soc. Clin. Rsch., Accreditation Coun. Grad. Med. Edn. (rev. com. internal medicine), Am. Assn. Study Liver Disease, Am. Fedn. Clin. Rsch., Am. Gastroent. Assn., Md. Med Comprehensive Ins. Trust (mem. 1998—, chmn. 1998—2000, 2002—04), The Ctr. Club (Balt.), Med. Club Bklyn., 14 West Hamilton St. Club (Balt.), Harvard Club (Chgo., N.Y.C.), Sigma Pi Phi (grand boule). Office: U Md Sch Medicine 655 W Baltimore St Rm HSFII S441 Baltimore MD 21201-1509 Office Phone: 410-706-7410. Office Fax: 410-706-0235. E-mail: drwilson@som.umaryland.edu.*

WILSON, DONALD GREY, engineering management consultant; b. Bridgeport, Conn., Sept. 20, 1917; s. William Gray and Jeannetta McAvoy (Kerr) W.; m. Elizabeth Jean Lanning, Apr. 24, 1943 (div. Mar. 1971, dec. Mar. 2002); children: Kirk Lanning, Craig Gardner, William Grey. BSEE, Rensselaer Poly. Inst., 1938; SM, Harvard U., 1939, MES, 1947, PhD, 1948. Mgr. automatic fire alarm divsn. Sealand Corp., Bridgeport, Conn., 1939-40; instr. elec. engring. Rensselaer Poly. Inst., 1940-42; staff mem. Radiation Lab. MIT, 1942-45; prof. elec. engring. U. Kan., Lawrence, 1947-55, dept. head, 1948-55; dir. Phila. Brass & Bronze, 1962-64, Mallory-Xerox Corp., 1964-65. Cons. U.S. Naval Ordance Test Sta., China Lake, Calif., 1953-54; assoc. dir. rsch. dept. Stromberg-Carlson Co., San Diego, 1955-59, gen. mgr., 1959, asst. v.p., 1959-60; v.p. rsch. P.R. Mallory & Co., Indpls., 1960, v.p. rsch. and engring., 1961-71, v.p. rsch., engring. and environ. affairs, 1971-75; alt. dir. Mallory Metal. Products, Eng., 1967; pres. Contemporary Custom Cabinets, San Diego, 1975-76; v.p. Continental Resources and Minerals Corp., Dayton, Ohio, 1978-79; sr. v.p. Tanzi Mergers/Acquisitions, San Diego, 1983-86; mgmt. cons., 1976—; sr. lectr. U. Rochester, 1956-57; lectr. dept. elec. engring. San Diego State U., 1981-92, asst. dean coll. engring., 1987, prof. emeritus, 1992-96; mng. dir., exec. bd. Nat. Bur. Cert. Cons., 1988-94, sr. adv. counsel, 1994-2001; sr. advisor Nat. Bur. Energy Solutions, 2007—. Contbr. articles to profl. jours. Bd. dirs. Speech and Hearing Clinic, Indpls., 1960-66, Washington Twp. Sch. Dist., 1964-68, pres., 1966-67. Recipient Outstanding Acad. Advisor award San Diego State U., 1992. Fellow AAAS; mem. IEEE (sr. life, exec. com. San Diego sect. 1986-2003, 2004-07, chmn. S.W. area region 6 1999-2000, sec. region 6 2001-02, ethics and mem. conduct com. 2002-03, R&D policy com. 2000—, Third Millennium medal, Region 6 Outstanding Br. Counselor award 1992), Affiliation Profl. Cons. Orgns. (chmn. bd. govs. 1991-93 San Diego Engring. Coun. Outstanding Svc. award 2000), Intertel, Sigma Xi, Sigma Phi Epsilon, Tau Beta Pi, Eta Kappa Nu. Home: 1950 Silverleaf Cir #310 Carlsbad CA 92009 Home Phone: 760-704-1238. Personal E-mail: don.wilson@ieee.org.

WILSON, DORIS H., volunteer; b. Akron, Ohio, Jan. 26, 1921; d. Charles Peter and Emma Clara (Howald) Huff; m. Angus Francis Wilson, June 14, 1952; children: Ann Wilson Lambertus, Lea Wilson MacInnis. BS, U. Akron, 1945; postgrad., Framingham State Coll., 1965, Salem State Coll., 1968. Adminstrv. asst. divsn. comml. engr. Ohio Bell Tel. Co., Akron, 1941-52; adminstr. Framingham Ctr. Kindergarten and Nursery Sch., 1965-68. Author: (book) A History of Great Neck, Ipswich, 1984, 1996. Vol. nurse's aide ARC, Akron, 1940; active Gov.'s Coun. Civilian Def., Boston, 1960—66; co-founder, charter mem. Hospice at Home, Wayland, Weston, Natick, Sudbury, Mass., 1978; chmn. W. Suburban Area Boston Symphony Orch., 1978—81; docent Gt. Ho. at Castle Hill, Ipswich, Mass., 1984—2005, Whipple Ho., Ipswich, 1985—2002; treas. Nuc. Freeze Coun., Ipswich, 1986—87; charter mem., bd. dirs. Aplastic Anemia Found. Am. New Eng. region, Brookline, Mass., 1987—92; vol. office asst. Habitat for Humanity, St. Petersburg, Fla., 1988; mem. Ipswich Women's Club, 1981—2006. Recipient Election Poll Officer citation, Gov. of Mass., 1980, 1st pl. Ann. Short Story Contest, Gen. Fedn. Women's Club, 2002. Mem.: AAUW (Mass. state parliamentarian 1966—76, charter, pres. Framingham-Wellesley br., North Shore br., grantee 1974), Ipswich Citizens Advocating Renewable Energy, Friends Glen Magna (Danvers, Mass. dir. 1991—93), Ipswich Hist. Soc., Boston Symphony Assn. Vols., Peace Action, Ipswich Bay Yacht Club (dir. 1981—82), Wayland Women's Club (hon.; pres.). Democrat. Roman Catholic. Home: 8 Bowdoin Rd Ipswich MA 01938-2807

WILSON, DOUGLAS FREDERICK, professional sports team executive, retired professional hockey player; b. Ottawa, Ont., Can., July 5, 1957; s. Douglas and Verna Wilson; m. Katherine Ann Kivisto, July 11, 1981; children: Lacey Anne. Defenseman Chgo. Blackhawks, 1977—91, San Jose Sharks, 1991—93, dir. pro devel., 1997—2003, gen. mgr., 2003—; coord. player rels. and bus. devel. NHL Players Assn., 1993—97. Account exec. Coca-Cola, Chgo. Recipient James Norris Meml. Trophy for best NHL defenseman, 1981-82. Avocations: golf, travel. Office: San Jose Sharks 525 W Santa Clara St San Jose CA 95113

WILSON, DOUGLAS LEONARD, minister, educator; b. Lumberton, NC, June 8, 1964; s. James Martin and Ruby Wilson; m. Julia Kaye Roberts, May 19, 1983; children: Martin, Samuel. BS in Math. magna cum laude, N.C. State U., 1986; MRE, Foundations Bible Coll., Dunn, NC, 1990; DRE, Founds. Bible Coll., 1993. Ordained to ministry 1992. Tchr. Raleigh Christian Acad., NC, 1986-90; bookkeeper First Free Will Bapt. Ch., Raleigh, 1987-90; acct. Oscar N. Harris and Assocs., P.A., Dunn, 1990-93; dean Christian Edn. Founds. Bible Coll., Dunn, 1993—. Tchr. Founds. Christian Acad., Dunn, 1993—, prin., 1999—. Vol. Prisoners Hope Ministry, Lillington, NC, 1996—. Recipient Faculty Forum award, Founds. Bible Coll., 1995. Office: PO Box 1166 Dunn NC 28335-1166

WILSON, DUANE BUBBA REGAN, secondary school educator; b. Atlanta, Apr. 18, 1954; s. Ray and Evelyn Wilson; m. Kathi Groover, Sept. 24, 1977; children: Bryan Jordan, Victoria Marie. BS in Recreation, U. Ga., Athens, 1977. Cert. health/physical edn. tchr. U. Ga. Baseball coach Peachtree Ridge HS, Suwanee, Ga., 2003—, head softball coach, 2003—, summer baseball & softball camp dir., 2003—. Mem. ch. youth grp. Chapel Hill Harvester Ch., Decatur, Ga. Home: 5101 Cabot Creek Rd Buford GA 30518 Office: Peachtree Ridge HS 1555 Old Peachtree Rd Suwanee GA 30034 Business E-Mail: duane_wilson@gwinnett.k12.ga.us.

WILSON, E. B., manufacturing executive, consultant, writer; b. Albany, NY, May 13, 1931; s. Harold Edgar and Marie Elizabeth (Brush) W.; m. Mary Beth Weilbacher, Aug. 2, 1956. BA, St. Lawrence U., 1953, PhD (hon.), 2002; MBA, Harvard U., 1955. Mkt. dir. Richardson-Vicks, Inc., NYC, Paris, Manila, 1957-64; CEO Japan Kimberly-Clark Corp., Neenah, Wis., 1964-68, France, 1968-71; pres., CEO French ops. Kimberly-Clark, Corp., Neenah, Wis., 1968—73; v.p. internat. div., gen. mgr. Pillsbury Co., Mpls., 1971-76; exec. v.p. Shaklee Corp., San Francisco, 1976-79; pres., CEO Almay Cosmetics, Inc., NYC, 1979-84, Hathaway Group of Warnaco, NYC, 1984—89; chmn. Global Brands, Inc., NYC, 1989—; found., pres. EBI, Inc., Chatham, Mass., 1995—. Chmn., chief exec. officer Seco Co., Branford, Conn., Mortin Jonap, Ltd., Hauppauge, NY; bd. dirs. William Schneider, Inc., Miami, HMI, Inc., Norwood, Mass. Author: The Committee on Trustees, 2001; contbr. to columns Trusteeship jour. Trustee Chatham Hist. Soc., 2006-, St. Lawrence U., Canton, NY, 1986-2001, chmn. bd. trustees, 1995-2001, Boston Conservatory, 2000-, San Francisco Ballet, 1978, New Horizons Project, Cambridge, Mass., 2001-; devel. dir. Cen. Park Conservancy, NYC, 1983-89; mem. Pub. Edn. Nominating Coun., Commonwealth of Mass., 2007—. With USAR, 1955-57. Mem. Eastward Ho Club (v.p., gov., 1985-91), Harvard Club NY, Harvard Club Boston, Eagle Scout. Republican. Avocations: cooking, running, golf, reading, international travel. Home and Office: 1114 Orleans Rd North Chatham MA 02650 Personal E-mail: ebi@cape.com.

WILSON, ED, broadcast executive; BS in Fin., U. Ark., 1980. Sales trainee Viacom, NYC, 1980, mgr. Chgo.; sales mgr. KATV, Little Rock; mgr. southern region Paramount, Dallas, 1984, mgr. eastern region NYC; sr. v.p. Sony Pictures TV, LA, 1990; founder MaXaM Entertainment, 1994; pres. CBS Enterprises, NBC Enterprises, 2000—04, Fox TV Network, 2004—. Bd. mem. Univ. Tex. Comm. Bd. mem. Spine in Sports Found., Nat. Assn. TV Programming Executives Ednl. Found.; active mem. ReREAD. Mem.: Hollywood Radio and TV Soc. (bd. mem.), Nat. Assn. TV Programming Executives (bd. dirs., exec. com.). Office: Fox Broadcasting Co 10201 W Pico Blvd Los Angeles CA 90035

WILSON, EDWARD ALLYN, educational administrator; b. Gary, Ind., July 2, 1941; m. Elizabeth Ann Bonnette; children: Jennifer, Amy. BA in History, Olivet Nazarene U., 1963; MS in Ednl. Adminstrn., No. Ill. U., 1966; PhD in Ednl. Adminstrn. and Curriculum Devel., Ohio State U., 1973. Supt. Ontario (Ohio) Pub. Schs., 1973—75, Euclid (Ohio) Pub. Schs., 1975—86, Westerville (Ohio) Pub. Schs., 1986—2000, Carmel Clay Sch. Corp., 2000—01; ednl. specialist MS Cons., Inc. Past pres. Sch. Study Coun. Ohio; gd. govs. Westerville Fund; mem. adv. and distbn. com. Martha Holden Jennings Found.; pres. Westerville chpt. Am. Heart Assn.; past chmn. Franklin County Ednl. Coun.; past mem. alumni adv. coun. Ohio State U.; past pres. Euclid C. of C., Ohio. Named Ohio Supr. of Yr., 1994; named one of top 100 Edn. Adminstrs. N.Am., Exec. Educator, 1993. Mem.: ASCD, Hamilton-Boone County Ednl. Svc. Ctr. (chmn.), Franklin County Area Supt.'s Assn. (exec. com.), Ind. Assn. Pub. Sch. Supts., Ohio Assn. Supervision and Curriculum Devel., Ohio State U. Edliners (pres.), Sci. and Math. Achievement Required for Tomorrow, Ohio Math. and Sci. Coalition (exec. bd.), Buckeye Assn. Sch. Adminstrs. (bd. dirs., pres., Disting. Svc. award 2001), Am. Assn. Sch. Adminstrs., Olivet Nazarene U. Alumni Assn. (past mem. alumni bd. dirs.), Carmel C. of C., Westerville Area C. of C. (bd. dirs.), Rotary (pres. Westerville, Rotarian of Yr.), Sigma Tau Delta, Phi Delta Kappa (past chpt. pres.). Home and Office: 1029 Wood Glen Rd Westerville OH 43081-3240 Home Phone: 614-895-6949; Office Phone: 614-570-1659. E-mail: edwardh586@sbcglobal.net.

WILSON, EDWARD CONVERSE, JR., oil and natural gas production company executive; b. Cambridge, Mass., Jan. 1, 1928; s. Edward Converse and Jean (McLean) W.; m. Patricia Ann Cairns, Sept. 10, 1953; children— Amy Cairns, Sarah Converse. AB, Harvard U., 1949. Brokerage trainee Estabrook & Co., Boston, 1951; Midwest Stock Exch. clk. Paul H. Davis & Co., Chgo., 1951-52; mem. Chgo. Bd. Trade, 1952-78, dir., 1966-67, chmn., 1970-71; ptnr. Nolan & Wilson Co. (specialists on Midwest Stock Exchange), 1965-72; sr. ptnr. Wilson Prodn. Co., Ft. Smith, Ark., 1972-74. Mem. devel. com. Chgo. chpt. Nat. Multiple Sclerosis Soc., 1970; mem. vis. com. on univ. resources Harvard, 1971-74, 76-81; Bd. dirs. Franklin Blvd. Community Hosp., 1970-74. Served with USAAF, 1946-47. Mem. Racquet Club (Chgo.). Home: 11114 Wickwood Dr Houston TX 77024-7523

WILSON, EDWARD NATHAN, mathematician, educator; b. Warsaw, NY, Dec. 2, 1941; s. Hugh Monroe and Margaret Jane (Northrup) W.; m. Mary Katherine Schooling, Aug. 19, 1976; children: Nathan Edward, Emily Katherine. BA, Cornell U., 1963; MS, Stanford U., 1965; PhD, Washington U., St. Louis, 1971. Instr. Ft. Valley (Ga.) State Coll., 1965-67, Washington U., St. Louis, 1968-69, U. Calif., Irvine, 1970-71, Brandeis U., Waltham, Mass., 1971-73; asst. prof. Washington U., St. Louis, 1973-77, assoc. prof., 1977-87, dean grad. sch., 1983-93, dean univ. coll., 1986-88, prof., 1987—, chair dept. math., 1995-99. Mem. Grad. Record Exams. Bd., Princeton, N.J., 1986-90; sec.-treas. Assn. Grad. Schs. Contbr. articles to profl. jours. Mem. Brentwood Sch. Bd., Mo., 1984. Woodrow Wilson fellow, 1963; NSF fellow, 1963-65; NDEA fellow, 1967-70. Mem. Am. Math. Soc., Math. Assn. of Am. Democrat. Office: Washington U Campus Box 1146 1 Brookings Dr Saint Louis MO 63130-4899 Office Phone: 314-935-6729. Business E-Mail: enwilson@math.wustl.edu.

WILSON, EDWARD OSBORNE, biologist, educator, writer; b. Birmingham, Ala., June 10, 1929; s. Edward Osborne and Inez (Freeman) W.; m. Irene Kelley, Oct. 30, 1955; 1 child, Catherine Irene. BS, U. Ala., 1949, MS, 1950, LHD (hon.), 1980; PhD, Harvard U., 1955; DPhil, Uppsala U., Sweden; DSc (hon.), Duke U., 1978, Grinnell Coll., 1978, U. West Fla., 1979, Lawrence U., 1979, Fitchburg State Coll., 1989, Macalester Coll., 1990, U. Mass., 1990, Oxford U., 1993, Ripon Coll., 1994, U. Conn., 1995, Ohio U., 1996, Bates Coll., 1996, Coll. Wooster, 1997, U. Guelph, 1997, U. Portland, 1997, Kenyon Coll., 2002, U. of the South, 2002, Harvard U., 2004, Clark U., 2005; LHD (hon.), Hofstra U., 1986, Muhlenburg Coll., 1998, Yale U., 1998, Pa. State U., Bradford Coll., 1997, Conn. Coll., 2000, U. South Ala., 2003, Albion Coll., 2005, U. Puget Sound, 2006, Rockefeller U., 2007, Williams Coll., 2007; LLD, Simon Fraser U., Emory U., 2008, Grad. Theol. Found., 2008, U. Miss. Lavelle, 2008; DHC, U. Madrid Complutense, 1995, U. Montreal, 2004; DrRerNat, U. Würzburg, 2000. Jr. fellow Soc. Fellows, Harvard U., 1953—56, faculty, 1956—, Baird prof. sci., 1976—94, Pellegrino U. prof., 1994—97, rsch. prof., 1997—2002, curator entomology, 1971—97, hon. curator entomology, 1997—. Selection com. Guggenheim Found., 1982—89; bd. dirs. World Wildlife Fund, 1983—94, Orgn. Tropical Studies, 1984—91, N.Y. Bot. Garden, 1991—95, Am. Mus. Natural History, 1992—2002, Am. Acad. Liberal Edn., 1993—2004, Nature Conservancy, 1994—2002, Conservation Internat., 1997—. Author: The Insect Societies, 1971, Sociobiology: The New Synthesis, 1975, On Human Nature, 1978 (Pulitzer prize for non-fiction, 1979), Promethean Fire, 1983, Biophilia, 1984, Success and Dominance in Ecosystems, 1990, The Diversity of Life, 1992 (Nat. Wildlife Assn. award, Deutsche Umweltstiftung Book award, Sir Peter Kent Conservation prize), Naturalist, 1994 (L.A. Times Book prize sci., 1995), In Search of Nature, 1996, Consilience: The Unity of Knowledge, 1998 (Forkosch award Internat. Acad. Humanism, 2000), Biological Diversity: The Oldest Human Heritage, 1999, The Future of Life, 2002 (Natural World Book prize, U.K., 2002), Pheidole in the New World: A Dominant, Hyperdiverse Ant Genus, 2003 (Julia Ward Howe prize, 2003), From So Simple A Beginning, 2005, Nature Revealed, 2006, The Creation: An Appeal to Save Life on Earth, 2006; author: (with R.H. MacArthur) The Theory of Island Biogeography, 1967; author: (with C.J. Lumsden) Genes, Mind and Culture, 1981; author: (with Bert Holldobler) The Ants, 1990 (Pulitzer prize for non-fiction, 1991), Journey to the Ants, 1994 (Phi Beta Kappa prize sci., 1995), The Creation, 2006 (Green Book award, Stevens Inst. Tech. Ctr. Sci. Writings, 2007), The Superorganism, 2008; others. Recipient Cleve.-AAAS Rsch. prize, 1967, Mercer award, Ecol. Soc. Am., 1971, Nat. Medal Sci., 1976, Disting. Svc. award, Am. Inst. Biol. Scis., 1976, Archie Carr medal, U. Fla., 1978, Leidy medal, Acad. Natural Sci., Phila., 1979, Tyler Ecology prize, 1984, Silver medal, Nat. Zool. Park, 1987, German Ecol. Inst. prize, 1987, Weaver award scholarly letters, Ingersoll Found., 1989, Crafoord prize, Royal Swedish Acad. Scis., 1990, Prix d'Inst. de la Vie, Paris, 1990, Revelle medal, 1990, Gold medal, Worldwide Fund for Nature, 1990, Achievement award, Nat. Wildlife Fedn., 1992, Shaw medal, Mo. Bot. Garden, 1993, Internat. prize biology, Govt. of Japan, 1993, Eminent Ecologist award, 1994, Ecol. Soc. Am. Audubon medal, Audubon Soc., 1995, Pub. Understanding Sci. award, AAAS, 1995, John Hay award, Orion Soc., 1995, Schubert prize, Germany, 1996, Washburn medal, Mus. Sci., 1996, Hutchinson medal, Garden Club Am., 1997, Stone award, New Eng. Aquarium, 1999, Nonino prize, Letters and Sci., Italy, 2000, King Faisal Internat. prize for sci., 2000, Kistler prize, Found. for the Future, 2000, Phillips Meml. medal, World Conservation Union, 2000, Lewis Thomas prize, Rockefeller U., 2001, Nierenberg prize, Scripps Oceanographic Inst., 2001, Thoreau medal, Thoreau Soc., 2001, Lifetime Achievement award, Time, 2001, Global Environment Citizens award, Harvard U., 2001, Busk medal, Royal Geog. Soc., 2002, Presdl. medal, Republic of Italy, 2002, Silver Cross of Christopher Columbus, Dominican Republic, 2003, Lowell Thomas award, Explorers Club, 2004, Frances Hutchinson medal, Chgo. Bot. Garden, 2004, Gov.'s award, Island Alliance, Mass., 2004, Rachel Carson award, Internat. Soc. Ecotoxicology and Chemistry, 2004, Rungius medal, Am. Mus. Wildlife Art, 2005, Prince William of Orange medal, Leiden U., 2006, TED prize, Sampling Found., 2006, George B. Stibbitz Comms. Pioneer award, Am. Computer Mus., 2006, TED Biotech. Prize, 2007, Catalonia prize, Spain, 2007, Terceuteram Silver medal, Linnear Soc., 2007, Pirk award, Nat. PKC Assn., 2008; Guggenheim Found. fellow, 1978. Fellow: Deutsche Akad. Naturforsch, Am. Philos. Soc. (Franklin medal 1998), Am. Acad. Arts and Scis.; mem.: NAS, Royal Soc. Sci. Uppsala (Sweden), Russian Acad. Sci., Royal Entomol. Soc. (hon. life), Finnish Acad. Sci. and Letters, Royal Soc. London, Netherlands Entomol. Soc. (hon. life), Royal Soc. Edinburgh (life), Assn. Tropical Biology (hon. life), Acad. Humanism (hon. life), Am. Humanist Assn. (Disting. Svc. award 1982, hon. life, Humanist of Yr.), Zool. Soc. London (hon. life), Entomol. Soc. Am. (Founders Meml. award 1972, L.O. Howard award 1985, hon. life), Brit. Ecol. Soc. (hon. life), Am. Genetics Assn. (hon. life), Explorers Club (life, hon. life, medal). Home: Apt A-208 1010 Waltham St Lexington MA 02421 Office: Harvard U Mus Comparative Zoology Cambridge MA 02138 Office Phone: 617-495-2315. Business E-Mail: ewilson@oeb.harvard.edu.

WILSON, ELIZABETH M., medical association administrator; BS, So. Ill. U.; grad. mgmt. cert., Loyola U. Grad. Sch. Bus., Chgo. Positions of increasing responsibility Edelman Pub. Rels., Am. Hosp. Assn., Loyola U.; nat. dir. pub. rels. Alzheimer's Assn.; exec. dir., comm. and pub. affairs Nat. Safety Coun.; exec. dir. Am. Brain Tumor Assn., Des Plaines, Ill., 2008—. Office: Am Brain Tumor Assn 2720 River Rd Des Plaines IL 60018 Office Phone: 847-827-9910. Office Fax: 847-827-9918.*

WILSON, FLOYD, pathologist, educator; DVM, UC Davis, 1970. Assoc. prof. pathology Coll. Vet. Medicine, Starrkville, Miss., 2003—. Contbr. scientific papers to numerous profl. pubs. Mem.: AVMA. Home: 117 Formosa Dr Brandon MS 39047

WILSON, FLOYD C., oil industry executive; children: Christopher, Andrew. Founder, chmn., pres., CEO Hugoton Energy Corp., 1987—98; chmn., CEO 3TEC Energy Corp., 1999—2003; founder, pres., CEO Petrohawk Energy Corp., Houston, 2003—, chmn., 2004—; ptnr. Wilson Group Companies. Office: Petrohawk Energy Corp 1000 Louisiana St Ste 5600 Houston TX 77002-5038

WILSON, FRANCES C., career military officer; BS, Mich. State U.; MEd, Pepperdine U.; MA in Psychology, U. No. Colo.; MS in Bus. Mgmt., Salve Regina Coll.; PhD in Edn., U. So. Calif. Commd. 2d lt. USMC, 1972, advanced through grades to lt. gen., 2006; air traffic control officer Marine Corps Air Sta., Yuma, Ariz., Kaneohe, Hawaii, 1975; tchr. instrnl. mgmt. Marine Corps Devel. & Edn. Ctr., Quantico, Va.; staff sec. 3d Marine Divsn., Okinawa, Japan, 1980-81; asst. prof., co. officer brigade of midshipmen U.S. Naval Acad., Annapolis, Md.; mgmt. analyst HQ USMC, Washington; spl. asst. for gen. and flag officer matters Joint Staff, Pentagon, exec. asst. to vice dir., 1987; comdr. 4th Recruit Tng. Battalion, Parris Island, S.C., 1988-90, Camp H.M. Smith, Svc. Battalion Marine Corps Pacific; sec. Joint Staff, until 1997; commanding gen. Marine Corps Base, Quantico, 1997-99, Third Force Svc. Support Group, Okinawa, Japan, 1999—2001; dir. pers. mgmt. divsn. M&RA Hdqrs. USMC, 2001—03; comdt. Indsl. Coll. Armed Forces, Nat. Def. U., Ft. McNair, DC, 2003—06; pres. Nat. Def. U., Washington, 2006—. Decorated Def. Superior Svc. medal, Def. Meritorious Svc. medal, Meritorious Svc. medal, Navy Commendation medal, Navy Achievement medal; recipient Leadership award, USMC Women Officer Basic Sch. Office: Nat Def U Ft Lesley J McNair 300 Fifth Ave Marshall Hall Washington DC 20319

WILSON, FRANCES HELEN, retired occupational therapist; b. Pitts., Oct. 17, 1929; d. J. Vernon and Margaret Hassler (Prugh) Wilson. BA, Conn. Coll., 1951; advanced standing cert., Columbia Sch. Occupl. Therapy, 1953. Therapist Washington (Pa.) County Soc. Crippled Children and Adults, 1953-54; staff therapist Oakland VA Hosp., U. Pitts., 1955-66; supr. Occupl. Therapy Clinic, Aspinwall VA Hosp., Pitts., 1966-74, 81-85, Occupl. Therapy Clinic, Oakland VA Hosp., Pitts., 1974—85, ret., 1985. Active Jr. League Pitts., Inc.; vol. Pitts. (Pa.) Children's Mus. Mem. Western Pa. (treas. 1967-69), Am. Occupl. Therapy Assns., Presbyn. Univ. Hosp. Pitts. Vol. Assn., Pitts. (Pa.) Symphony Assn., Acad. Lifelong Learning, Conn. Coll. Club (treas. 1971-94), Twentieth Century Club (Pitts.). Republican. Presbyterian. Home: Washington Plz 1116 1420 Centre Ave Pittsburgh PA 15219

WILSON, FRANK CRANE, JR., orthopedist; b. Rome, Dec. 29, 1929; s. Frank crane and Cheyney Bryan Wilson; m. Ann Haebershan Irvin Wilson; children: Jennifar Wison, Ana, Robin Johnstar. BA in, Vanderbilt U., Nashville, Tenn., 1950; MD, Med. coll. Ga., Augusta, 1954. Lic. Am. Bd. Orthopaedic Surgery, NC, 1964. Instr. surgery UNC Sch. Medicine, Chapel Hill, 1964—65, asst. prof. surgery, 1965—68, assoc. prof. surgery, 1971—91, Kenan prof. orthopedic surgery, 1992—. Chief Divsn. Orthopedic, UNC Sch. Medicine, 1967—96; pres. Assn. Othopedic Chaimen, Chicago, 1978; chair coun. acad. socs. Assn. Am. Med. Coll., 1982—83; pres. Am. Orthopedic Assn., Chicago, 1986—87, Accreditation Coun. Grad. Med. Edn., 1986; chair president's coun. Assn. English- Speaking World, 1987—88; pres. Am. Bd. Orthopedic Surgery, Chicago, 1988—89. Contbr. articles to jours. Lectr. Retirement Cmtys. & Svc. Orgn., NC, 1964—. Recipient Thomas Jefferson award, U. NC, 1992, Distinguished Faculty Award, 1994. Mem.: Thomas Wolfe Soc., Interurban Orthopedic Soc., Southern Orthopedic Assn. (Distinguished Southern Orthopaedist award 1999), Am. Orthopedic Assn., Am. Acad. Orthopedic Surgeons, AMA, Alpha Omega Alpha (award 2007). Avocation: tennis. Home: Level Hill Rd Chapel Hill NC 27515 Office: Dept Orthpedic UNC Sch Medicine 3159A Bioinformatics Bldg 130 Mason Farm Rd Chapel Hill NC 27599

WILSON, GOLDER NORTH, medical educator; b. Frederick, Okla., Oct. 29, 1944; s. Harris Ward and Bobby Lark Wilson; m. Donna Margaret Tose; children: Benjamin Charles, Daniel Gold, Sarah Elizabeth, Shamus Robert. MD, Pritzker Sch. Medicine U. Chgo., PhD, 1972. Diplomate Am. Bd. Pediat., 1976. Assoc. prof. pediat. U. Mich., Ann Arbor, 1981—84; prof. pediat. UT Southwestern Med. Ctr., Dallas, 1988—2002; clin. prof. pediat. Tex. Tech U. Health Sci. Ctr., Amarillo, 2009—. Author: (book) Preventive Health Care for Children with Genetic Conditions (Commendation award, 2007). Lt. col. pub. health svc. Bethesda Army, 1973—75. Independent. Avocations: creative writing, golf. Home: 5347 W Mockingbird Dallas TX 75209 Office: Tex Tech Univ 1400 Coulter Amarillo TX 79106 Office Phone: 972-312-0440. Home Fax: 469-467-9343. Personal E-mail: theggnome@aol.com. Business E-Mail: golder.wilson@ttuhsc.edu.

WILSON, GRETCHEN, vocalist; b. Granite City, Ill., June 26, 1973; 1 child, Grace. Signed by Epic Records, 2003—. Singer: (singles) Redneck Woman, 2004 (Breakthrough Video of Yr., Country Music Television Music award, 2005), When I Think About Cheatin, 2004 (Female Video of Yr., Country Music Television Music award, 2005), (five singles) 5-Mo-Fo-Ya, 2005, (albums) Here for the Party, 2004, All Jacked Up, 2005; TV appearances include: In The Moment, 2004; co-author (with Allen Rucker): Redneck Women: Stories from My Life, 2006. Recipient Horizon award, Country Music Assn., 2004, Favorite New Artist, Am. Music Awards, 2004, Favorite Female Country Artist, 2005, Female Country Artist of Yr., Billboard Music Awards, 2004, New Country Artist of Yr., 2004, Top New Artist, Acad. Country Music Awards, 2005, Top Female Vocalist, 2005; named Female Vocalist of Yr., Country Music Assn., 2005. Achievements include first new artist to debut at #1 on Billboard's Country LP chart.

WILSON, GROVER GRAY, lawyer; b. Louisville, Apr. 1, 1951; BA, Davidson Coll., 1973; JD, Duke Univ., 1976. Bar: NC 1976. Fellow: Am. Coll. Trial Lawyers; mem.: Am. Bd. Trial Advocates, NC Assn. of Def. Attorneys, Forsyth County Bar Assn., NC Bar Assn. (pres. 2004), Phi Beta Kappa. Office: Wilson & Iseman LLP Ste 400 110 Oakwood Dr Winston Salem NC 27103

WILSON, HAROLD BATTING, retired treasurer; b. NYC, June 24, 1910; s. William Johnson and May LaForest Wilson; m. Edna Anita Helmling, Jan. 9, 1937 (dec. Apr. 1996). Cert. in acct. and bus. law, Fordham U., 1930—32. Registered pub. acct., N.Y., 1961; cert. Inst. Cert. Computing Profls.; data processor Data Processing Mgmt. Assn., 1963, computer technology Inst. Advanced Technology, 1967. Office boy Arthur Andersen & Co., NYC, 1929—32, acct./auditor, 1933—38; acct. Office of Comptr., NYC, 1938—40; prin. systems analyst Divsn. of Employment, NY State, Albany, 1941—70; investment adv. Registered with S.E.C., Naples, Fla., 1975—90; treas. Theatre '90 Inc., Syracuse, NY, 1990—2009. Corp. dir. Theatre '90 Inc., Syracuse, 1990—2009. Author: (book) How to Beat Wall St., 1991. Sgt. USAF, 1943—45, US. Recipient NY State cert. of merit, Gov. Nelson A. Rockefeller, 1971. Mem.: SAR Nat. Soc. Avocations: writing, sports. Home: 7235 Canton St Rd Baldwinsville NY 13027 Home Phone: 315-638-8448. Personal E-mail: holly@theatre90.com.

WILSON, H(AROLD) FRED(ERICK), chemist, research scientist; b. Columbiana, Ohio, Aug. 15, 1922; s. Lloyd Ralph and Erma Rebecca (Frederick) W.; m. Alice Marjorie Steer, Aug. 20, 1949; children: Janice, Deborah, James, Kathleen. BA, Oberlin Coll., 1947; PhD, U. Rochester, 1950. With Rohm & Haas Co., Phila., 1950-83, beginning as rsch. scientist, successively lab. head, rsch. supr., asst. dir., assoc. dir., dir. rsch., 1950-74, v.p., 1974-83, chief sci. officer, from 1981; now with Wilson Assocs., Cape May, N.J. Mem. U.S. nat. com. IUPAC, 1977-84, vice chmn., 1980-82, chmn., 1982-84, fin. com., 1979-89, chmn., 1981-89; chmn. I.R.I. Research Corp., 1980-82, dir., 1979-82 Patentee in field. Served to 1st lt. USAAF, 1942-46. Decorated Air Medal. Mem. Am. Chem. Soc., AAAS, Soc. Chem. Industry, Dirs. Indsl. Research. Home: 5203 Twin Silo Dr Blue Bell PA 19422 Personal E-mail: hfw44@verizon.net.

WILSON, HAROLD STACY, history professor, writer; b. Neva, Tenn., June 22, 1935; s. Joseph Hooker Wilson and Bertie Hazel Reece; m. Henrietta Sheppard Fair, June 21, 1968; children: Katherine McColl, Kyle Stacy. BA, King Coll., 1957; MA, Johns Hopkins U., 1959; PhD, Emory U., 1966. Asst. prof. Wesleyan Coll., Macon, Ga., 1962—66, Old Dominion U., Norfolk, Va., 1966—68, assoc. prof., 1968—2003, chair, history dept., 1991—98, mem. faculty senate, 1999—, vice-chair faculty senate, 2001—03, prof. history, 2003—09, dir., Rsch. Integrity Office, 2008—, emeritus history prof., 2009—. Fulbright prof. Fu Ren U., Taipei, Taiwan, 1971—72, Tamkang U., Taipei, 1971—72, Nat. U. Singapore, 1978—80; exch. prof. Kitakyushu U., Japan, 1995. Author: (history book) McClure's Magazine and the Muckrakers, 1970, Confederate Industry: Manufacturers and Quartermasters in the Civil War, 2002; editor: Textile History Rev., 1963—66; assoc. editor: Wesleyan Quar. Rev., 1964—66, editl. asst.: The Great American and The Blue and the Gray; contbr. scholarly articles and book revs. in field. Supporter Union Mission, Norfolk, Va., 1966—, Salvation Army, Norfolk, 1966—, Young Life, Norfolk, 1966—, Stas. WHRO-TV, WHRV-TV, Norfolk, 1966—, Norfolk Pub. Libr., 1966—; founder, Patrick scholarship King Coll., Bristol, Tenn., 1996—; short-term missioner South Am. Missionary Soc., Honduras, 2002—; founding mem. Christ the Redeemer Anglican Ch., Norfolk, 2005—. Nominee Peter Seaborg award, 2002; grantee Tech. and Tchg. grant, U. 21st Century, 1992; Rsch. grant, Nat. Found. Arts and Humanities, 1968, Faculty Field Rsch. grant, US Mil. Acad., 1987. Mem.: So. Hist. Assn. (chair arrangements com. 1987—88), Friends of Old Dominion U. Perry Libr. (life). Independent-Republican. Baptist. Avocations: hiking, swimming, travel. Home: 626 W Princess Anne Rd Norfolk VA 23517-1806 Office: Old Dominion Univ Hampton Blvd Norfolk VA 23529 Personal E-mail: hwilson@odu.org. Business E-Mail: hwilson@odu.edu.

WILSON, HEATHER ANN, former United States Representative from New Mexico; b. Keene, NH, Dec. 30, 1960; d. George Douglas and Martha Lou (Kernozicky) Wilson; m. Jay Hone; 3 children. BS in Internat. Politics, USAF Acad., Colo., 1982; MPhil in Internat. Rels., U. Oxford, Eng., 1984, PhD in Internat. Rels., 1985. US mission NATO, Brussels, 1987—89; dir. def. policy and arms control NSC, Washington, 1989—91; pres. Keystone Internat., Inc., Albuquerque, 1991—95; cabinet sec. N.Mex. Dept. Children, Youth and Families, Santa Fe, 1992—98; mem. US Congress from 1st N.Mex. dist., 1998—2009, mem. energy and commerce com., mem. permanent select com. on intelligence, ranking mem. tech. and tactical intelligence subcommittee. Adj. prof. U. N.Mex; mem. Def. Adv. Com. on Women in Svcs. Contbr. articles to profl. jours. Capt. USAF, 1982—89. Recipient Hero of the Taxpayer award, Ams. for Tax Reform, 1999, 2002, Spirit of Free Enterprise award, US C. of C., 2000, Guardian of Small Bus. award, Nat. Fedn. Ind. Bus., 2000, Golden Bulldog award, Watchdog of Treasury, 2000, Disting. Cmty. Health Superhero award, Nat. Assn. Cmty. Health Ctrs., Inc., 2005, Javits-Wagner-O'Day Champion award, 2005; named Rhodes scholar, 1982. Mem.: Kiwanis. Republican. Methodist. Avocations: hiking, skiing.*

WILSON, HEATHER MARIE, biologist; b. Eureka, Calif., May 29, 1976; d. Ron Richard and Edith Stanton Wilson; m. Paul L. Flint, May 26, 2008; 1 child, Coal Wiley Flint. PhD in Biol. Scis., U. Alaska, 2007. Wildlife biologist-airplane pilot U.S. Fish & Wildlife Svc., Office Migratory Bird Mgmt., Anchorage, 2003—. Mem.: The Wildlife Soc. Democrat. Buddhist. Achievements include research in Population ecology of migratory birds. Avocations: hunting, fishing, basketball. Office: US Fish & Wildlife Svc 1011 E Tudor Rd Anchorage AK 99503 Office Fax: 907-786-3641. Business E-Mail: heather_wilson@fws.gov.

WILSON, HOLLY LYN, social sciences educator, researcher; PhD, Pa. State U., State Coll., 1989. Asst. prof. philosophy Marquette U., Milwaukee, Wis., 1988—96; assoc. prof. philosophy U. La., Monroe, 1997—2008. Adj. prof. Greco Inst., Shreveport, La., 2004—. Tchr. Greco Inst., Shreveport, La., 2004—08. Recipient Course award, Ctr. Theology and Natural Scis., 2001; scholarship, Fulbright Commn., 2003—04. Mem.: North Am. Kant Soc., Am. Philos. Assn. Office: Univ LA Monroe 700 University Ave Monroe LA 71209 Business E-Mail: hwilson@ulm.edu.

WILSON, JACK, aeronautical engineer; b. Sheffield, Yorkshire, Jan. 5, 1933; arrived in US, 1956, naturalized, 1980; s. George and Nellie (Place) W.; m. Marjorie Reynolds, June 3, 1961 (div. Jan. 1991); children: Tanya Ruth, Cara; m. Carol Blixen, Jan. 3, 1997. BS in Aero. Engring., with 2d class hon., Imperial Coll., London, 1954; MS in Aero. Engring., Cornell U., Ithaca, NY, 1958, PhD in Aero. Engring., 1962. Cert. power pilot FAA. Sr. scientific officer Royal Aircraft Establishment, Farnborough, England, 1962-63; prin. rsch. sci. Avco-Everett Rsch. Lab., Everett, Mass., 1963-72; vis. prof. Inst. Mecanique des Fluides, Marseille, France, 1972-73; sr. scientist U. Rochester, NY, 1973-80; sr. rsch. assoc. Sohio/BP Am., Cleve., 1980-90; sr. engring. specialist Sverdrup Tech. Inc., Cleve., 1990-93, NYMA, Brook Park, 1994-98, DYNACS Engring. Co., Inc., Brook Park, 1998-2001, QSS Group Inc., Fairview Park, Ohio, 2001—06, ASRC Aerospace Corp., Fairview Park, Ohio, 2006—. Docent Cleve. Mus. Art, 2009—. Author: (chpt.) "Gas Lasers" of Applied Optics in Engineering VI, 1980, "Laser Sources" of Techniques in Chemistry XVII, 1982; contbr. articles to profl. jours. Glider pilot, instr. with Soaring Thunderbirds Gliding Club, Wadsworth, Ohio, 2007—. With U. London Air Squadron, 1952—54, pilot Royal Air Force Vol. Reserve, 1950—54. Recipient Soaring Gold Badge award, Fedn. Aero. Internat., Paris, 1998; co-recipient Manly award, Soc. Automotive Engrs., 1995. Fellow AIAA (assoc.; tech. com. 1991-92). Achievements include first to demonstrate gas-dynamic laser, measurements of air ionization rate at high speeds, wave rotor performance, and unsteady ejector thrust augmentation; patents in application of high speed flow to gas laser media, devel. of antimony dopant sources. Home: 13610 Shaker Blvd Apt 202 Cleveland OH 44120-1564 Office: ASRC Aerospace Corp 21000 Brookpark Rd Cleveland OH 44135-3127 Office Phone: 216-433-8573. Business E-Mail: jack.wilson-1@nasa.gov.

WILSON, JACK FREDRICK, retired federal government official; b. Salt Lake City, Apr. 2, 1920; s. John Lorimer and Mayme J. (James) W.; m. Gwendolyn Gwynn, Nov. 20, 1947; children— Wendy, Elaine, Barbara Ann, Laurel, John F. Jr., James C. BS, Brigham Young U., 1942; postgrad., Mont. State U., 1962, Pa. State U., 1965. Range conservationist Bur. Land Mgmt., Rawlins, Wyo., 1949-57, dist. mgr. Burley, Idaho, 1957-67, dist. and land office mgr. Riverside, Calif., 1967-72; dir. Boise Interagy. Fire Ctr., Idaho, 1972-81; dir. Office Aircraft Services U.S. Dept. Interior, Boise, 1981-87; dir. Boise Interagy. Fire Ctr., 1987-92; ret., 1992. Contbr. articles to profl. jours. Dir. county disaster com. ARC, 1982-88. Maj. USAF, 1942-47 Recipient Meritorious award U.S. Dept. Interior, 1976, Disting. Service award, 1981, EEO Performance award, 1985; Outstanding Contbn. to Fire Mgmt. award U.S. Dept. Agr. Forest Service, 1976, Pub. Lands Found. Life Time Svc. Award 2002. Mem. Soc. Am. Foresters (chmn. fire com. 1980-82), Am. Soc. Range Mgmt. (sec. pres. 1967), So. Calif. Assn. Foresters and Fire Wardens, Lions (sec. 1954-57). Mem. Ch. of Jesus Christ of Latter-day Saints. Avocations: long range weather forecasting, genealogy, reading, golf. Home: 1820 Sunrise Rim Rd Boise ID 83705-5138 Personal E-mail: jfwilson4@cableone.net.

WILSON, JACK MARTIN, academic administrator, science educator; b. Camp Atterbury, Ind., June 29, 1945; s. Jack Maurer and Ruth L. (Leiseder) Wilson; m. Judi Chang, Aug. 18, 1990; children: Gretchen, Erika, John, Jessica. AB, Thiel Coll., 1967; MA, Kent State U., 1970, PhD, 1972. Assoc. prof. physics Sam Houston State U., Huntsville, Tex., 1972-80, chmn. dept. physics 1980-81, chmn. div. chemistry and physics, 1981-82; prof. physics U. Md., College Park, 1984-90; dir. Anderson Ctr. for Innovation in Undergrad. Edn. Rensselaer Poly. Inst., Troy, NY, 1990-95, dean undergrad. and continuing edn., 1995-98, dean of faculty, 1997, interim provost, 1998, J. Erik Jonsson '22 Disting. prof. physics, engring. sci., info. tech., and mgmt.; v.p. academic affairs U. Mass., founding CEO UMassOnline, interim pres., 2003—04, pres., 2004—; prof. mgmt. U. Mass, Amherst. Mem. US Com. Internat. Union Pure and Applied Physics, Washington, 1984—90; IBM cons. scholar, 1992—95; founder, CEO, chmn. LearnLinc Corp., 1993; co-founder Paul Severino Ctr. for Technol. Entrepreneurship. Editor: Teacher Institutes and Workshops, 1984, The Education of the Physicist, 1985; also articles in field. Recipient Computers in Physics award, US Dept. Edn., 1985, Physics Teaching Resource Agents award, NSF, 1985, Developing Student Confidence award, Exxon Edn. Found., 1983, Theodore Hesburgh Award, Boeing Award, Pew Charitable Trust Prize, Outstanding Civilian Svc. Medal, US Army. Fellow: Am. Physical Soc.; mem.: AAAS, Am. Soc. for Engring. Edn., Am. Inst. Physics (governing bd. 1984—91), Am. Phys. Soc. (edn. com. 1982), Am. Assn. Physics Tchrs. (exec. officer 1982—90), Sigma Xi. Office: U Mass Office of Pres 225 Franklin St, 12th Fl Boston MA 02110 Office Phone: 617-287-7000.*

WILSON, JAMES CHARLES, JR., lawyer; b. Birmingham, Ala., Sept. 13, 1947; s. James C. and Angelina (Serio) W.; m. Ann Bullock, Mar. 1, 1975; children: Brent Trammell, Lucy Bullock. BA, Tulane U., New Orleans, 1969, JD, 1972; MBA, Samford U., Birmingham, Ala., 1995. Ptnr. Bradley, Arant, Rose & White, Birmingham, 1972-90, Lange, Simpson, Robinson & Somerville, Birmingham, 1990-93, Sirote & Permutt, P.C., Birmingham, 1993-96; v.p. and gen. counsel Shop-A-Snak Food Mart, Inc., Birmingham, 1996; pres. Lucent Holdings, Inc., Golden, Miss., 1997-98; ptnr. Baker, Johnston & Wilson LLP, Birmingham, Ala., 1999—2002; shareholder Baker Donelson, Bearman, Caldwell & Berkowitz, PC, Birmingham, 2003—. Adj. prof. internat. bus. transactions and internat. law U. Ala., Tuscaloosa, 1983-85, 89-96; internat. bus. transactions Cumberland Sch. Law, 1990-95, adj. prof. corp. fin., 2001—, adj. prof. securities regulation, 2003-08. Author: Alabama Business Corporation Law, 1980; co-author: Corporate Law for the Healthcare Provider: Organization, Operation, Merger and Bankruptcy, 1993, Alabama Business Corporation Law Guide, 1995, International Trade Settlements and Negotiations, 2006. Adv. bd. Jr. League of Birmingham, 1984; bd. dirs. Ala. chpt. Am. Liver Found., 1993-97, sec., 1994-95; trustee The Altamont Sch., 1995-2001, v.p., 1996-98, pres., 1998-2000. With U.S. Army, 1972-76. Mem.: ABA (sect. internat. law, tax and corp., banking and bus. law), Birmingham Bar Assn. (chmn. pub. rels. com. 1990, chmn. spl. projects com. 2002, chmn. membership benefits com. 2003), Ala. Law Inst., Ala. Bar Assn., Am. Law Inst., Birmingham Golf Assn. (pres., v.p., treas. 1982—84), Rotary (pres. Birmingham-Sunrise club 1986—87, bd. dirs. 2006—08). Office: 1600 Wachovia Tower 420 North 20th St Birmingham AL 35203 Office Phone: 205-244-3829. Business E-Mail: jwilson@bakerdonelson.com.

WILSON, JAMES HARGROVE, JR., lawyer; b. Oliver, Ga., Nov. 26, 1920; s. James Hargrove and Louise (Sealy) W.; m. Frances Audra Schaffer, Dec. 24, 1942 (dec. Nov. 1990); children: Susan Frances, James Hargrove. AB with honors, Emory U., 1940; LL.B. summa cum laude, Harvard U., 1947. Bar: Ga. 1947, D.C. 1951. Assoc. firm Sutherland, Tuttle & Brennan (now Sutherland, Asbill & Brennan LLP), Atlanta and Washington, 1947-53, ptnr., 1953—. Lectr. Emory U., 1959, chmn. bd. visitors, 1967-68; trustee The Northwestern Mut. Life Ins. Co., Milw., 1972-91; mem. advisory group Commr. of Internal Revenue, 1963-64 Pres.: Harvard Law Review, 1946-47. Chmn. bd. trustees Met. Atlanta Crime Commn., 1970-71; mem. Harvard U. Overseers Com. to Visit Law Sch., 1959-65; trustee Emory U., 1983-90, trustee emeritus, 1990—. Served to lt. comdr. USNR, 1942-46. Fellow Am. Bar Found., Am. Coll. Tax Counsel; mem. ABA, State Bar Ga., D.C. Bar, Atlanta Bar Assn., Am. Law Inst. (coun. 1974—), Lawyers Club Atlanta (pres. 1960-61), Am. Judicature Soc., Harvard Law Sch. Assn. (coun. 1981-85), Emory U. Alumni Assn. (pres. 1966-67), Capital City Club, Piedmont Driving Club, Peachtree Club, Phi Beta Kappa, Omicron Delta Kappa, Kappa Alpha. Methodist. Home: 3171 Marne Dr NW Atlanta GA 30305-1931 Office: Sutherland Asbill & Brennan LLP 999 Peachtree St NE Ste 2300 Atlanta GA 30309-3996

WILSON, JAMES LAWRENCE, retired chemical company executive; b. Rosedale, Miss., Mar. 2, 1936; s. James Lawrence and Mary Margaret (Klingman) W.; m. Barbara Louise Burroughs, Aug. 30, 1958; children: Lawrence Burroughs, Alexander Elliott. B.Mech. Engring., Vanderbilt U., 1958; MBA, Harvard, 1963. Vice pres. Nyala Properties, Inc., Phila., 1963-65; staff assoc. Rohm & Haas Co., Phila., 1965-67, exec. asst. to pres., 1971-72, treas., 1972-74, regional dir. Europe, 1974-77, group v.p., 1977-86, vice-chmn., 1986-88, chmn., CEO, 1988-99; ret., 1999. Treas. Warren-Teed Pharms., Inc., Columbus, Ohio, 1967-68, v.p., 1969; pres. Consol. Biomed. Labs., Inc., Dublin, Ohio, 1970-71; bd. dirs. Vanguard Group Investment Cos., Cummins Inc., AmeriSourceBergen Corp. Trustee Vanderbilt U., 1987—, Culver Ednl. Found., 1988—; chmn. Phila. High Sch. Acads., 1989-99. Mem. Chem. Mfrs. Assn. (bd. dirs. 1988-99, chmn. 1996).

WILSON, JAMES MILLER, IV, cardiovascular surgeon, educator; b. Atlanta, Mar. 11, 1946; s. James Miller Wilson III and Sara Sharp; m. Lisa VanLandingham; children: James Miller V, Robert Paul, Michael Simpson, Sara Ann. Student, Emory U.; MD, Duke U., 1971. Diplomate Am. Bd. Surgery, Am. Bd. Thoracic Surgery. Intern N.Y. Hosp., 1971-72; resident N.Y. Hosp.-Cornell Med. Ctr., 1972-73, U. Calif., San Francisco, 1975-80; attending staff Christ Hosp., Cin., 1980—, Bethesda Hosp., Cin., 1980—, Jewish Hosp., Cin., 1980—, Univ. Hosp., Cin., 1982—, Deaconess Hosp, Cin., 1982—, VA Med Ctr., Cin., 1983—, Children's Hosp., Cin., 1984—, Good Samaritan Hosp., Cin., 1994—; assoc. prof. clin. surgery U. Cin. Coll. Med., 1985—; chmn. dept. cardiovasc. surgery Deaconess Hosp., 1985—2001; dir. cardiac surgery Mercy Hosp., 2001—. Mem. open heart surgery adv. com., Ohio, 1995—; tech. adv. panel on cardiac surgery Nat. Quality Forum, chmn. Contbr. articles to profl. jours. Lt. Comdr. submarine svc. USN, 1973-75. Fellow ACS, Am. Coll. Cardiology, Am. Heart Assn. (cardiovasc. coun.), Am. Coll. Chest Physicians; mem. AMA, U.S. Naval Submarine League, UDT/SEAL Assn., U.S. Submarine Vets., Inc., Am. Assn. Thoracic Surgery, Thoracic Surgery Found., Assn. Acad. Surgery, Soc. Thoracic Surgeons, Ohio State Med. Assn., Cin. Acad. Medicine, Howard C. Nafziger Soc. Avocations: music, diving, hiking, skiing, horses. Home Phone: 513-271-9060; Office Phone: 513-603-8600. E-mail: jmwilson@alumni.duke.edu.

WILSON, JAMES QUINN, public policy professor; married; 2 children. AB, U. Redlands, 1952; PhD, U. Chgo., 1959; D (hon.), Harvard U., Cambridge, Mass. Henry Lee Shattuck prof. govt. Harvard U., 1961-86; James Collins prof. mgmt., UCLA, 1985-97; Ronald Reagan prof. pub. policy Pepperdine U., Malibu, Calif. Bd. dirs. Police Found., 1971-1993, Am. Enterprise Inst.; former dir. New Eng. Electric Sys., State Farm Ins, Protection One, RAND Corp., bd. trustees; chmn. coun. academic advisers Am. Enterprise Inst. Author: Negro Politics, 1960, Political Organizations, 1973, Varieties of Police Behavior, 1968, The Amateur Democrat, 1966, The Investigators, 1978, Thinking About Crime, 1983, (with R.J. Herrnstein) Crime and Human Nature, 1985, (with Roberta Wilson) Watching Fishes, 1985, Bureaucracy: What Government Agencies Do and Why They Do It., 1989, American Government: Institutions and Policies, 1991, The Moral Sense, 1993, On Character, 1991, Moral Judgment, 1997, The Marriage Problem: How Our Culture Has Weakened Families, 2002. Former chmn. Nat. Adv. Coun. Drug Abuse Prevention, Police Found.; chmn. com. law enforcement and the adminstrn. of justice NRC; former mem. Pres.'s Fgn. Intelligence Adv. Bd., US Atty. Gen.'s Task Force on Violent Crime, Commn. on Presdl. Scholars, Sloan Commn. on Cable Comms.; former dir. Joint Ctr. for Urban Studies MIT and Harvard. Recipient John Gaus award, 1994. Fellow Am. Acad. Arts and Scis.; mem. Am. Philos. Soc., Am. Polit. Sci. Assn. (pres., 1991-92, James Madison award, Lifetime Achievement award, 2001, Presdl. medal, 2003). Office: Pepperdine Univ Sch Pub Policy 24255 Pacific Coast Hwy Malibu CA 90263-7490

WILSON, JAMES ROSS, communications educator, broadcast executive; b. Petaluma, Calif., Nov. 25, 1939; s. Stanley Thomas and Billie (Ross) W.; m. Elizabeth Ann Buckleman, Dec. 29, 1964 (div. 1982); children: Greg, Tom. BA, Fresno State Coll., 1961; MA, Calif State U., Fresno, 1976. Radio and TV instr. Dept. Def. Info. Sch., Ft. Slocum, N.Y., 1962-65; news dir. Sta. KVON, Napa, Calif., 1965, Sta. KTIM, San Rafael, Calif., 1966; news reporter Sta. KMJ, Fresno, 1966-67, news dir., 1967-71; program dir. Sta. KMJ/KNAX-FM, Fresno, 1971-78, v.p., gen. mgr., 1978-82; news assignment editor Sta. KFSN-TV, Fresno, 1982-83; prof. mass comm., gen. mgr., faculty advisor KFSR-FM Calif. State U., Fresno, 1983—; jazz disk jockey Sta. KVPR, Valley Pub. Radio, Fresno, 1984-90; weekend news anchor KMPH-FM News Radio, 1994-96. Co-author: Mass Media/Mass Culture, 4th edit., 1997, 5th edit., 2000. Recipient Best Newscast award Calif. AP-TV-Radio Assn., 1971, Best News Documentary award Calif. AP-TV-Radio Assn., 1973-74, Broadcast Excellence award Billboard mag., 1976; Calif. State U. grantee, 1987. Mem. Broadcast Edn. Assn., Cen. Calif. Broadcasters Assn. (treas., bd. dirs. 1980-83), Assn. for Edn. in Journalism and Mass Communication, Soc. Profl. Journalists, Alpha Epsilon Rho, Phi Kappa Phi. Home: 4747 E Holland Ave Fresno CA 93726-2914 Office: Calif State U Dept Mass Comm Journalism Fresno CA 93740-0001 E-mail: james_wilson@csufresno.edu.

WILSON, JAMIA WELETHA, science educator; d. James Weldon and Virginia Wright Wilson. AS in Zoology, U. Fla., Gainesville, 1977; BS in Biology, No. Ariz. U., Flagstaff, 1980; MA in Edn. Adminstrn., Tex. So. U., Houston, 2006. Cert. pharmacy technician Tex., 1994. Second asst. mgr. Sav-On Drugs, Inc., Houston, 1980—84; secondary sci. tchr. Vanguard-Gifted Program HISD, Houston, 1984—90; life sci. tchr. Ft. Bend Ind. Sch. Dist., Houston, 1990—91; pharmacy technician

Walgreen's Drugs Inc, Houston, 1994—; project coord. TSU/HIV Prevention Ctr., Houston, 1995—96; h.s. physics tchr. Alief Ind. Sch. Dist., Houston, 2003—. Faculty advisor COSMO Sci. Math Club HNGC, Houston, 2005—; a+ challenge coach A+ Challenge, Houston, 2005—; sci. tutor Homework Assistance HNGC/AISD, Houston, 2005—; sci. dept. rep. Shared Decision Making Coun. HNGC/AISD, Houston, 2005—. Altar guild Kainos Cmty. Ch., Houston, 1998—2007; oboist Scott Joplin Chamber Orch., Houston, 1981—94. Mem.: NEA (corr.), Alpha Kappa Alpha (corr.). Democrat. Presbyterian. Avocations: music, sports. Home: 12011 Bob White Dr Houston TX 77035 Office: Hastings 9th Grade Ctr 6750 Cook Rd Houston TX 77072 Office Fax: 281-988-3419. Personal E-mail: cepiggy@aol.com. Business E-Mail: jwilson2@aliefisd.net, jamiawilson@ahefisd.net.

WILSON, JANE, artist; b. Seymour, Iowa, Apr. 29, 1924; d. Wayne and Cleone (Marquis) Wilson; m. John Gruen, Mar. 28, 1948; 1 child, Julia Gruen. BA, U. Iowa, 1945, MA, 1947. Mem. fine arts faculty Parsons Sch. Design, 1973-83, 89-90. Vis. artist U. Iowa, 1974; adj. assoc. prof. painting and drawing Columbia U., 1975—85, assoc. prof., 1985—86, prof., 1986—88, acting chair, 1986—88; Andrew Mellon vis. prof. painting Cooper Union, 1977—78. One-woman shows include Hansa Gallery, N.Y.C., 1953, 1955, 1957, Stuttman Gallery, 1958, 1959, Tibor de Nagy Gallery, 1960—66, Graham Gallery, 1968, 1969, 1971, 1973, 1975, Fischbach Gallery, 1978, 1981, 1984, 1988, 1990, 1991, 1993, 1995, 1997, Munson-Williams-Proctor Inst., Utica, N.Y., 1980, Cornell U., Ithaca, N.Y., 1982, Compass Rose Gallery, Chgo., 1988, Am. U., Washington, 1989, U. Richmond, Va., 1990, Earl McGrath Gallery, LA, 1990—91, 1993, Dartmouth Coll., Hanover, N.H., 1991, Amot Mus., Elmira, N.Y., 1993—94, Parrish Mus., Southampton, N.Y., 1996, Glenn Horowitz Gallery, East Hampton, N.Y., 1996, D. C. Moore Gallery, N.Y.C., 1999, 2001, 2003, 2004, 2007, Heckscher Mus., Huntington, N.Y., 2001, McKinney Ave. Contemporary, Dallas, 2003, Represented in permanent collections Met. Mus., Mus. Modern Art, Whitney Mus., Wadsworth Athenaeum, Heron Art Mus., NYU Rockefeller Inst., Vassar Coll., Pa. Acad. Fine Arts, Hirsch Horn Mus., Washington, Nelson-Atkins Mus., Kansas City, Mo., San Francisco Mus. Modern Art, Heckscher Mus., L.I. Mus., Stony Brook, others. Recipient Eloise Spaeth award, Guild Hall, East Hampton, N.Y., 1968, Lifetime Achievement award, 2001, Purchase prize, Childe Hassam Fund, 1971, 1973, 1981, Ranger Fund Purchase prize, 1977; Ingram-Merrill grantee, 1963, Louis Comfort Tiffany grantee, 1967. Mem.: Nat. Acad. Design (academician 1974—, pres. 1992—94), Am. Acad. Arts and Letters (award in Art 1985), Phi Beta Kappa. E-mail: jwi1010@aol.com.

WILSON, JEAN DONALD, endocrinologist, educator; b. Wellington, Tex., Aug. 26, 1932; s. J. D. and Maggie E. (Hill) Wilson. BA in Chemistry, U. Tex., 1951, MD, 1955. Diplomate Am. Bd. Internal Medicine. Intern, then resident in internal medicine Parkland Meml. Hosp., Dallas, 1955—58; clin. assoc. Nat. Heart Inst., Bethesda, Md., 1958—60; instr. internal medicine U. Tex. Southwestern Med. Sch., Dallas, 1960—61, prof., 1968—. Editor: Jour. Clin. Investigation, 1972—77. Sr. asst. surgeon USPHS, 1958—60. Recipient Fuller prize, Am. Urol. Assn., 1983, Lita Annenberg Hazen award, 1986, Dale medal, Soc. for Endocrinology, 1991, Pincus medal, Worchester Found., 1992. Fellow: Royal Coll. Physicians; mem.: NAS, Endocrine Soc. (Oppenheimer award 1972, Koch award 1993), Am. Soc. Biochemistry and Molecular Biology, Soc. Exptl. Biology and Medicine, Am. Philos. Soc., Assn. Am. Physicians (Kober medal 1999), Am. Soc. Clin. Investigation, Inst. Medicine, Am. Acad. Arts and Scis. (Amory prize 1977). Office: U Tex Southwestern Med Ctr Dept Internal Medicine 5323 Harry Hines Blvd Dallas TX 75390-8857 Home Phone: 214-351-1837; Office Phone: 214-648-3469. Office Fax: 214-648-8917. Business E-Mail: jwils1@mednet.swmed.edu.

WILSON, JEAN LOUISE, state legislator; b. Phila., June 13, 1928; d. Horace and Catherine (Lennox) Terry; m. Benjamin H. Wilson (dec.); children: Sheryl J. Gordon, Denise T. Munn. BS in Edn., Pa. State U., 1949. Tchr. Columbia Inst., Phila., 1949-50, Wilkes Coll., Wilkes Barre, Pa., 1950-51; office mgr., exec. sec. Camden Fibre Mills, Warminster, Pa., 1969-82; mem. Pa. Ho. of Reps., 1988-92. Legis. chmn. Doylestown V.I.A.; active Benj. H. Wilson Sr. Ctr., Ctr. for Learning in Retirement, Del. Valley Coll.; former mem. bd. Bucks County Opportunity Coun.; treas. Bucks County chpt. Fox Chase Cancer Ctr., 1997—2006. Avocations: duplicate bridge, golf. Home: 12 Far View Rd Chalfont PA 18914-2511

WILSON, JOANNE A.P., gastroenterologist, educator; b. Raleigh, NC, July 22, 1947; d. John H. and Conorah L. (Watson) Peebles; m. Kenneth H. Wilson, Aug. 15, 1969; children: Nora, Court, Sarah. BS in Chemistry, with highest honors, U. NC, Chapel Hill, 1969; MD, Duke U. Sch. Medicine, Durham, NC, 1973. Diplomate Am. Bd. Internal Medicine, cert. in Pediatric Gastroenterology. Intern, resident internal medicine Peter Bent Brigham Hosp., Harvard Med. Ctr., Boston, 1973-75; resident gastroenterology Georgetown Hosp., Washington, 1975—76; fellowship gastroenterology Vets. Affairs Med. Ctr., Washington, 1976-78; asst. prof. medicine U. Mich., Ann Arbor, 1978-86; assoc. prof., assoc. chief gastroenterology for outpatient svcs. Duke U. Med. Ctr., 1986-95, prof. gastroenterology, 1995—. Med. dir. Crohn's & Colitis Found., 1988—90; apptd. mem. Nat. Comm. on Digestive Diseases NIH, 2006. Contbr. articles to profl. jours. Bd. trustees Durham Acad. Recipient Trailblazer award, Duke Student Nat. Med. Assn., 2007. Fellow: ACP; mem.: Am. Soc. Gastrointestinal Endoscopy, Am. Gastroenterological Assn. (sec. 1997—2003, named one of Outstanding Women in Sci. 2008), Alpha Omega Alpha, Phi Beta Kappa. Achievements include being the first African American female to matriculate at Duke School of Medicine; first female secretary of the American Gastroenterological Association. Office: DUMC Dept Medicine PO Box 3858 Durham NC 27710-0001 Office Phone: 919-684-1817. Office Fax: 919-681-8147. Business E-Mail: joanne.wilson@duke.edu.*

WILSON, JOE (ADDISON WILSON), United States Representative from South Carolina, former senator, lawyer; b. Charleston, SC, July 31, 1947; s. Hugh deVeaux and Wray Smart (Graves) Wilson; m. Roxanne Dusenbury McCrory, Dec. 30, 1977; children: Michael Alan, Addison Graves, Julian Dusenbury, Hunter Taylor. BA, Washington & Lee U., Lexington, Va., 1969; JD, U. SC, Columbia, 1972. Bar: SC 1972. Staff mem. US Senator Strom Thurmond, Washington, 1967, US Rep. Floyd Spence, Columbia, SC, 1970-72; ptnr. Kirkland, Wilson, Moore, Taylor & Thomas, West Columbia, 1972—2001; mem. US Congress from 2nd SC dist., 2002—, mem. armed svcs. com., mem. edn. and labor com., mem. fgn. affairs com., asst. majority whip, ranking mem. subcommittee on workforce protections. Dep. gen. counsel US Energy Sec. Jim Edwards, Washington, 1981—82; presdl. appointee Intergovernmental Adv. Coun. Edn., 1990—91; bd. dirs. Bank of America, Lexington, SC; mem. SC State Senate, Columbia, 1984—2001. Vice chmn. SC Rep. Party, 1972—74; campaign mgr. Staff US Rep. Floyd Spence, 1974, 1978, 1980, 1982, 1998, Columbia; dist. campaign mgr. Staff Gov. Carroll Campbell, 1986. Served in USAR, 1972—75, positions to col. SC Army N.G., 1975—2003. Republican. Presbyterian. Office: US House Reps 212 Cannon House Office Bldg Washington DC 20515 Office Phone: 202-225-2452. Office Fax: 202-225-2455. E-mail: joe.wilson@mail.house.gov.*

WILSON, JOHN HUMAN, III, museum director, art historian; b. Fort Worth, Feb. 18, 1956; s. John Human Wilson II and Mary Ryan Wilson; m. Annasue McCleave, Sept. 4, 1982; children: John Human IV, Anna Sophia, Veronica Teresa. BA, So. Meth. U., Dallas, 1978; MA in History of Art, U. London, 1984, PhD in History of Art, 1992. Curator European and Am. art Spencer Mus. Art, U. Kans., Lawrence, 1988—90; curator painting and sculpture Cin. Art Mus., 1990—99; sr. curator collections Joslyn Art Mus., Omaha, 2005—08; exec. dir. Timken Museum Art, San Diego, 2008—. Cons., ind. scholar, Cin., 1999—2005. Author: (collection catalogue) American Paintings from Procter & Gamble: The Historic Cincinnati Collection; art cons. (film) Artworks. Mem.: Historians Brit. Art, Walpole Soc., Assn. Art Mus. Curators (mus. collections and exhibitions com. 2006), Turner Soc. (life), Athenaeum, Lit. Club Cin. (assoc.). Home: 4628 Narragansett Ave San Diego CA 92107 Office Fax: 402-342-2376.

WILSON, JOHN PASLEY, retired law educator; b. Newark, Apr. 7, 1933; s. Richard Henry and Susan Agnes (Pasley) Wilson; m. Elizabeth Ann Reed, Sept. 10, 1955 (div.); children: David Cables, John Pasley, Cicely Reed. AB, Princeton U., 1955; LLB, Harvard U., 1962. Bar: US Dist. Ct. NJ 1962, Mass. 1963, US Dist. Ct. Mass. 1963. Budget examiner Exec. Office of Pres., Bur. of Budget, Washington, 1955-56; assoc. Riker, Danzig, Scherer & Brown, Newark, 1962-63; asst. dean Harvard U. Law Sch., Cambridge, Mass., 1963-67; assoc. dean Boston U. Law Sch., 1968-82; dean Golden Gate U. Sch. Law, San Francisco, 1982-88, prof., 1988—2003, prof. emeritus, 2003—, dean emeritus, 2003—. Vis. prof. dept. health policy and mgmt. Harvard U., 1988; cons. Nat. Commn. Protection Human Subjects Biomedical and Behavioral Rsch.; mem. Mass. Gov.'s Commn. Civil and Legal Rights Developmentally disabled; former chmn. adv. com. Ctr. Cmty. Legal Edn., San Francisco. Author: (book) The Rights of Adolescents in the Mental Health System; contbr. chapters to books, articles to profl. jours. Bd. dirs. Greater Boston Legal Svcs., Chewonki Found.; mem. Health Facilities Appeals Bd., Mass.; assoc. mem. Dem. Town Com., Concord; chmn. Bd. Assessors, Concord; bd. overseers Boston Hosp. Women, past chmn. med. affairs com.; past mem. instl. rev. bd. Calif. Pacific Hosp., San Francisco. Served to lt. (j.g.) USNR, 1956—59. NIMH grantee, 1973. Mem.: Nat. Assn. Securities Dealers (arbitrator). Democrat. Personal E-mail: jwlsn7@comcast.net.

WILSON, JOHN SILVANUS, JR., federal agency administrator; BA, Morehouse Coll., 1979; MA in Theological Studies, Harvard U., MA, PhD in Ednl. Adminstrn., Planning and Social Policy. Prof. Afro-American Studies Dept. Harvard U.; dir. found. rels. and asst. provost MIT, Cambridge, Mass.; joined George Washington U., 2001, exec. dean Va. campus, 2002—06, assoc. prof. higher edn., 2006—09; exec. dir. White House's Initiative on Historically Black Colls. and Univs. US Dept. Edn., Washington, 2009—. Advocate, advisor Kresge Found., Mott Found., United Negro Coll. Fund; bd. mem. Spelman Coll., Atlanta, Independent Fed. Savings Bank, Washington. Office: US Dept Edn HBCU 1990 K St, NW, Ste 6114 Washington DC 20006 Office Phone: 205-502-7582. Office Fax: 205-502-7852. E-mail: john.wilson@ed.gov.*

WILSON, JOHN T., pediatrics and pharmacology educator; children from previous marriage: Mary Laurence, Anne Abigail, John Tyler. BS, Tulane U., 1960, MS, MD, Tulane U., 1963. Diplomate Am. Bd. Pediatrics, Am. Bd. Clin. Pharmacology (charter cert.). Pediatric intern Palo Alto (Calif.)-Stanford Med. Ctr., 1963-64, pediatric resident, 1964-65; rsch. assoc. dept. pharmacology U. Iowa, Iowa City, 1965-66; rsch. assoc. sect. on endocrinology Nat. Inst. Child Health Devel., Bethesda, Md., 1966-68; fellow in pediatrics, attending pediatrician and dir. Children's Hosp. of San Francisco, 1968-69, 69-70; rsch. assoc. George Peabody Coll. for Tchrs., Kennedy Ctr., Nashville, 1970-78; assoc. prof. pediatrics and pharmacology Vanderbilt U. Med. Ctr., Nashville, 1970-78; attending physician gen. pediatrics Vanderbilt Hosp. and Nashville Gen. Hosp., 1970-78; prof. pediatric medicine dir. La. State U. Med. Ctr., Child Clin. Rsch. Ctr., Shreveport, 1978—. Mem. editl. bd. Elsevier Sci. Pubs. Mem. editl. bd. Therapeutic Drug Monitoring, Jour. Clin. Pharmacology, Drugs in Breast Milk, Clin. Pharmacokinetics, Clin. Pharmacol Therapy; contbr. numerous articles to profl. jours. Lt. comdr. USPHS, 1965—68. Recipient The Paracelsus award U. Amsterdam, 1985, Pharm. Mfrs. Assn. Found. award for Clin. Pharmacology Units, 1979, NIH Rsch. Career Devel. award, 1969, 72, The John T. Halsey award Tulane U., 1963. Fellow: Am. Coll. Clin. Pharmacology, Am. Acad. Pediat.; mem.: Shreveport Med. Soc., Soc. Toxicology, Soc. Pediat. Rsch., N.Y. Acad. Scis., La. State Med. Soc., Am. Fedn. Clin. Rsch., Am. Pediat. Soc., Am. Soc. Clin. Pharmacology and Therapeutics, Stanford Med. Alumni Assn. Office: La State U Med Ctr 1501 Kings Hwy Shreveport LA 71103-4228 Office Phone: 318-675-5080.

WILSON, JONATHAN MICHAEL, literature educator, writer; b. London, Feb. 26, 1950; arrived in U.S., 1976; s. Lewis and Doris Wilson; m. Sharon Ann Kaitz, Aug. 30, 1980; children: Adam, Gabriel. BA with honors, U. Essex, Colchester, Eng., 1973; postgrad., Oxford U., Eng., 1974—77; PhD, Hebrew U., Jerusalem, 1980. Asst. prof. English Tufts U., Medford, Mass., 1984—91, assoc. prof. English, 1991—98, chair dept. English, 1998—2005, prof. English, 1998—, Fletcher prof. rhetoric and debate, 2001—, dir. ctr. humanities, 2007—. Vis. scholar Columbia U., NYC, 1976. Author: On Bellow's Planet, 1985, Herzog: The Limits of Ideas, 1990, Schoom, 1994, The Hiding Room, 1995, A Palestine Affair, 2003, An Ambulance Is on the Way, 2005, Marc Chagall, 2007. Simon Guggenheim fellow in fiction, 1994—95. Jewish. Avocation: soccer. Home: 44 Carver Rd Newton MA 02461 Office: Tufts U Dept English Medford MA 02115 Office Phone: 617-627-3364. Business E-Mail: jonathan.wilson@tufts.edu.

WILSON, JOSEPH CHARLES, IV, former ambassador; b. Bridgeport, Conn., Nov. 6, 1949; s. Joseph Charles III and Phyllis (Finnell) W.; m. Susan Dale Otchis, Apr. 27, 1973 (div. 1986); m. Valerie Elise Plame, Apr. 3, 1998; children: Sabrina Cecile, Joseph Charles, Trevor Rolph, Samantha Finnell Diana. BA in History, U. Calif., Santa Barbara, 1972; PhD in Human Letters, Nova Southeastern U., 2008. Fgn. svc. officer US Dept. State, Washington, 1976-98; congl. fellow Am. Polit. Sci. Assn., Washington, 1985-86; dep. chief of mission Am. Embassy, Bujumbura, Burundi, 1982-85, Brazzaville, Congo, 1986-88, Baghdad, Iraq, 1988-91; US amb. to Gabon, Sao Tome and Principe US Dept. State, 1992-95; polit. adv. to comdr. US Armed Forces Europe, 1995-97; spl. asst. to pres., sr. dir. for African affairs Nat. Security Coun., Washington, 1997-98; pres. JC Wilson Internat. Ventures, Washington, 1998—. Adj. scholar Mid. East Inst., 2002—04. Author: The Politics of Truth: Inside the Lies That Led to a War and Betrayed My Wife's CIA Identity--A Diplomat's Memoirs, 2004 (N.Y. Times Bestseller). Decorated comdr. Order of Equatorial Star (Gabon); recipient Disting. Alumni award U. Calif. Santa Barbara, 1991, 1995, Disting. Def. Dept. Civilian award, 1997; recipient Ron Ridenhour prize, 2003, Am. Patriot award Ams. for Informed Democracy, 2003, ACLL Nat. Civil Rights award, 2006, Peacemaker award, Physicians Social Responsibility, 2006. Mem. Am. Fgn. Svc. Assn. (William R. Rivkin award 1987), U. Calif. Santa Barbara Alumni Assn. Avocations: golf, bicycling, exercise, skiing. Office Phone: 505-629-9142.*

WILSON, JULIA ANN YOTHER, lawyer; b. Dallas, Sept. 6, 1958; d. Julian White and Mary Ann (Estes) Yother. BA, East Ctrl. U., Ada, Okla., 1980; JD, U. Okla., 1983. Bar: Okla. 1990, Calif. 1993, D.C. 1995; U.S. Ct. Appeals (9th cir.) Calif. 1993, U.S. Supreme Ct. 1993, U.S. Dist. Ct. (ctrl. dist.) Calif. 1993, U.S. Dist. Ct. (we. dist.) Okla., 1997. Assoc. Law Office of George Rodda Jr., Newport Beach, Calif., 1984-96; sole practice law Oklahoma City, 1996-97; assoc. Coldiron, Wilson & Assocs., Oklahoma City, 1997—2004; pvt. practice Oklahoma City, 2004—. Served to 1st lt. USAR, 1980-86. Mem. ABA, D.C. Bar Assn., Calif. Bar Assn., Oklahoma County Bar Assn., Okla. Bar Assn. (litigation sect.), Orange County Bar Assn. Office: 2500 S Broadway St Ste 116 Edmond OK 73013 Office Phone: 405-513-7318. Business E-Mail: julia.wilson@lawoklahoma.com.

WILSON, KAREN LEE, museum staff member, researcher; b. Somerville, NJ, Apr. 2, 1949; d. Jon Milton and Laura Virginia (Van Dyke) W.; m. Paul Ernest Walker, 1980; 1 child, Jeremy Nathaniel. AB, Harvard U., 1971; MA, NYU, 1973, PhD, 1985. Rsch. assoc., dir. excavation at Mendes, Egypt Inst. Fine Arts, NYU, 1979-81; coord. exhbn. The Jewish Mus., NYC, 1981-82, adminstrv. cataloguer, 1982-83, coord. curatorial affairs, 1984-86; curator Oriental Inst. Mus. U. Chgo., 1988-96, mus. dir., 1996—2003, rsch. assoc., 1988—; coord. Kish Project Field Mus. Natural History, Chgo., 2004—. Rsch. asso. Oriental Inst. U. Chgo. Author, editor: Mendes, 1982; contbr. articles to profl. jours. Mem.: Coll. Art Assn., Am. Oriental Soc. Office Phone: 312-665-7184, 773-702-9518. Business E-Mail: k-wilson@uchicago.edu.

WILSON, KAREN LYNN, esthetician; b. Hartford, Conn., Mar. 6, 1956; d. Derwood Alexander and Rita Harriet Briggs; m. Leo Franklin Wilson, Sept. 5, 2003; children: Jeffrey Thomas Haynes, Jason Brian Haynes. BS in Fin. (hon.), Williams Coll., Houston, 1999. Lic. Esthetician Conn. Cosmetology, 2004. Sales and mktg. dir. Bollitieri Tennis Acad., Bradenton, Fla., 1990—95; registrar Nortel Comm., Wethersfield, Conn., 1995—98; sr. fin. assoc. NextiraOne, Wethersfield, Conn., 1998—2002; mktg. staff Total Comm., East Hartford, Conn., 2001—04; esthetician Timeless Reflection @ Cutters' Edge, Rocky Hill, Conn., 2004—. Apptd. to employee counsel Williams Comm., Wethersfield, Conn., 1998—2000, AR task team, 2000—01. Team leader United Way, Wethersfield, Conn., 1998—2000; chairperson Diabetes Found., Wethersfield, 1998—2001; team leader disaster recovery Rebuilding After 911 Tragedy. Recipient Dedication to Customers during 911 Tragedy, NextiraOne, 2001, Tiffany award, Manpower Staffing Svcs., 1996, Cir. of Excellence award, Williams Comm., 2000, Superior Performance; Gold Level, 1996—97, Achieving Customer Excellence award, 2000. Mem.: Continuing Profl. Edn. (assoc.), ABMP (assoc.), Jr. Women's Club (assoc.). Office: Timeless Reflection @ Cutters' Edge 2162 Silas Deane Hwy Rocky Hill CT 06067 Home: 4 Carol Dr Uncasville CT 06382-2008 Personal E-mail: k_lunited@yahoo.com. E-mail: timeless@yahoo.com, skincarebykaren@sbcglobal.net.

WILSON, KENDRICK R., III, diversified financial services company executive; b. Morristown, NJ, 1947; s. Kendrick R. and Katharine Wilson. BA, Dartmouth Coll., Hanover, NH, 1972; MBA, Harvard Bus. Sch., Boston, 1975. Mng. dir. Salomon Bros.; sr. exec. v.p. E.F. Hutton & Co., 1987—88; co-founder, pres. Ranieri Wilson & Co., 1988—89; mng. dir., head investment banking, vice-chmn. Lazard Frres & Co. LLC, 1989—98; mng. dir. fin. institutions group The Goldman Sachs Group, Inc., 1998—; spl. adv. to sec. US Dept. Treasury, 2008—. Mem. supervisory bd. Celanese Corp., 1999—2004; bd. dirs. Meigher Comm., Inc., Am. Marine Holdings Corp., Bank United Corp. (and subs.), 1988—, Anthracite Capital Inc., 1998—. Trustee Hosp. Spl. Surgery, NYC, Middlebury Coll., Montana Land Reliance. Officer Special Forces US Army, Vietnam. Office: The Goldman Sachs Group Inc 85 Broad St 30th Fl New York NY 10004 Office Phone: 212-357-4111. Office Fax: 212-357-0926. Business E-Mail: ken.wilson@gs.com.*

WILSON, KENNETH GEDDES, physics research administrator; b. Waltham, Mass., June 8, 1936; s. E. Bright and Emily Fisher (Buckingham) Wilson; m. Alison Brown, 1982. AB, Harvard U., 1956, DSc (hon.), 1981; PhD, Calif. Tech. Inst., 1961; PhD (hon.), U. Chgo., 1976. From asst. prof. to prof. physics Cornell U., Ithaca, NY, 1963—74, James A. Weeks prof. in phys. sci., 1974—88; Hazel C. Youngberg Trustees Disting prof. Ohio State U., Columbus, 1988—. Co-author: Redesigning Education, 1974. Recipient Nobel prize in physics, 1982, Dannie Heinemann prize, 1973, Boltzmann medal, 1975, Wolf prize in physics, Wolf Found., Israel, 1980, Disting. Alumni award, Calif. Inst. Tech., 1981, A.C. Eringen medal, 1984, Franklin medal, 1982, Aneesur Rahman prize, 1993. Mem.: NAS, Am. Acad. Arts and Scis., Am. Phys. Soc., Am. Philos. Soc. Business E-Mail: wilson.9@osu.edu.*

WILSON, L. MICHELLE (MICHELLE WILSON), lawyer, information technology executive; b. Boise, Idaho, Jan. 20, 1963; d. Tom Martin and George Ann Wilson; m., 1 son. BA, Univ. Wash., Seattle, 1985; JD with honors, Univ. Chgo., 1988. Assoc. Perkins Coie, Seattle, 1988—94, ptnr., 1994—99; assoc. gen. counsel Amazon.com Inc., Seattle, 1999—99, v.p., gen. counsel, sec., 1999—2001; sr. v.p. HR, gen. counsel, sec. Amazon.com, Seattle, 2001—03, sr. v.p., gen. counsel, sec., 2003—. Recipient Dow Jones award Wall St. Jour., 1985. Mem. ABA, Washington State Bar Assn., Order of Coif, Phi Beta Kappa, Beta Gamma Sigma. Office: Amazon.com Inc 1200 12th Ave S Ste 1200 Seattle WA 98144-2734 Office Phone: 206-266-1000. Office Fax: 206-266-1821.*

WILSON, LANFORD, playwright; b. Lebanon, Mo., Apr. 13, 1937; s. Ralph E(ugene) and Violetta (Tate) W. Attended, San Diego State Coll., 1955-56; PhD in Humanities (hon.), U. Mo., 1985, Grinnell Coll., Iowa, 1994; PhD in Lit. (hon.), LI U., 1995. Playwright, 1962—; resident playwright, dir., co-founder Cir. Repertory Co., NYC, 1969-95. Instr. playwriting U. Houston, 2003—08. Author: (plays) So Long at the Fair, 1963, Home Free!, 1964, No Trespassing, 1964, The Sandcastle, 1964, The Madness of Lady Bright, 1964, Ludlow Fair, 1965, Balm in Gilead, 1965, This is the Rill Speaking, 1965, Days Ahead, 1965, Sex is Between Two People, 1965, The Gingham Dog, 1966, The Rimers of Eldritch, 1966, Wandering, 1966, Lemon Sky, 1969, Serenading Louie, 1970, The Great Nebula in Orion, 1970, The Hot L Baltimore, 1972, The Family Continues, 1972, The Mound Builders, 1975, Fifth of July, 1978, Brontasaurus, 1978, Talley's Folly, 1979, A Tale Told, 1981, Angels Fall, 1983, A Betrothal, 1984, Talley & Son, 1985, Burn This, 1987, A Poster of the Cosmos, 1987, The Moonshot Tape, 1990, Redwood Curtain, 1991, Trinity, 1993, I'm Not the Ocean, 1995, Sympathetic Magic, 1996, A Sense of Place (or Virgil is Still the Frogboy), 1997, Your Everyday Ghost Story, 1997, Book of Days, 1998, Rain Dance, 2003, (books) Balm in Gilead and Other Plays, 1966, The Rimers of Eldritch and Other

Plays, 1968, The Gingham Dog, 1969, Lemon Sky, 1970, The Hot L Baltimore, 1973, The Mound Builders, 1976, Fifth of July, 1979, Talley's Folly, 1980, Angels Fall, 1983, Serenading Louie, 1985, Talley & Son, 1986, Burn This, 1988, Redwood Curtain, 1992, 21 Short Plays, 1994, By the Sea, 1996, Collected Plays, Vol. I, 1997, Vol. II, 1999, Vol. III, 1999, Vol. IV, 2006, A Sense of Place, 1999, Sympathetic Magic, 1999, Book of Days, 2001, Rain Dance, 2005; translator: Three Sisters, 1984, Ghosts, 2002. ABC Yale fellow, 1969; Rockefeller grantee, 1967, 73, Guggenheim grantee, 1970, NEA grantee, 1990; recipient Vernon Rice award, 1966-67, Inst. Arts and Letters award, 1970, Obie award, 1972, 75, 84, 97, Outer Critics Circle award, 1973, Drama Critics Circle award, 1973, 80, Pulitzer prize, 1980, Brandeis award, 1981, John Steinbeck award, 1990, Edward Albee Last Frontier award, 1994, Am. Acad. of Achievement award, 1995, Am. Assn. Theatre Critics Best Play award, 1998, Guild Hall Lifetime Achievement award, 2000, William Inge Lifetime Achievement award, 2001; inducted into Theater Hall of Fame, 1996, Mo. Writers Hall of Fame, 1998; recipient Lucille Lortel's Edith Oliver award Sustained Excellence, 2001. Mem. Am. Acad. Arts and Letters, Dramatists Guild Am. Coun.

WILSON, LAWRENCE JOSEPH, chemist, researcher; s. James Lawrence Wilson and Lynn Diane WIlson; children: Shelby Lillian, Morgan Elizabeth. BSc, Furman U., Greenville, SC, 1985; PhD, Emory U., Atlanta, 1992. Sr. scientist Procter & Gamble Pharm., Mason, Ga., 1994—2000; prin. scientist Johnson & Johnson Pharm. R & D, Raritan, NJ, 2000—06; dir. medicinal chemistry NeurOP Inc., Atlanta, 2006—. Postdoc, assoc. Stanford U., Palo Alto, Calif., 1992—94; project mgr., cons. Emory U., Atlanta, 2006—. Contbr. articles to profl. pubs. Mem.: AAAS (life), Am. Chem. Soc. (life). Achievements include patents in field. Office: Neurop Inc 1256 Briarcliff Rd Atlanta GA 30329 Personal E-mail: wilsonlarr@gmail.com. Business E-Mail: lwilson@neuropinc.com.

WILSON, LEVON EDWARD, lawyer, educator; b. Charlotte, NC, Apr. 2, 1954; s. James A. and Thomasina Wilson. BSBA, Western Carolina U., 1976; JD, N.C. Ctrl. U., 1979; EdD, N.C. State U., 2001. Bar: NC 1981, US Dist. Ct. (mid. dist.) NC 1981, US Tax Ct. 1981, US Ct. Appeals (4th cir.) 1982, US Supreme Ct. 1984, Ga. 2007; lic. real estate broker NC, cert. mediator NC Alternative Dispute Resolution Commn., arbitrator BBB, registered mediator/arbitrator Ga. Office Dispute Resolution, 2008. Pvt. practice, Greensboro, NC, 1981-85; asst. county atty. Guilford County, Greensboro, 1985-88; asst. prof. N.C. Agrl. & Tech. State U., Greensboro, 1988-91, Western Carolina U., Cullowhee, NC, 1991-96, prof., 1996—, prof., head dept. bus. adminstrn., law and mktg., 1996—2002; pres. Integrated Mgmt. Resources, Inc., 2000—; prof. Sch. Acctg., Ga. So. U., Statesboro, 2005—. Pres. Trade Brokers Cons.; legal counsel, bd. dirs. Rhodes Assocs., Inc., Greensboro, 1982—; legal counsel Guilford County Sheriff's Dept., Greensboro, 1985-88; bd. dirs. Webster Enterprises, Inc. Contbr. articles to profl. jours. Bd. dirs. Post Advocacy Detention Program; active mem. Prison Litigation Study Task Force, Adminstrn. Justice Study Com. Recipient Svc. award Blacks in Mgmt., 1980, Excellence in Tchg. award Jay I. Kneedler Found. of Western Carolina U., 1994-95, 2003-2004; Student in Free Enterprise fellow, Bd of Govs. award for Excellence in Tchg. U. NC Sys, 2004-05. Mem. ABA, N.C. Bar Assn., Acad. Legal Studies in Bus., Southeastern Acad. Legal Studies in Bus. (former editor-in-chief Jour. of Legal Studies in Bus., mng. editor), N.C. Assn. Police Attys., N.C. Real Estate Educators Assn., So. Acad. Legal Studies in Bus., Phi Delta Phi, Beta Gamma Sigma. Democrat. Methodist. Office: Ga So U Sch Accountancy PO Box 8141 Statesboro GA 30460-8141 Home: PO Box 1414 Statesboro GA 30459-1414 Personal E-mail: levonwilson@msn.com. Business E-Mail: lwilson@georgiasouthern.edu.

WILSON, LINDA, librarian; b. Rochester, Minn., Nov. 17, 1945; d. Eunice Gloria Irene Wilson. BA, U. Minn., Morris, 1967; MA, U. Minn., 1968. Libr. rsch. svcs. U. Calif., Riverside, 1968-69, head dept. phys. scis. catalog, 1969-71; city libr. Belle Glade (Fla). Mcpl. Libr., 1972-74; instr. part-time Palm Beach Jr. Coll., Belle Glade, 1973; head adult-young adult ext. Kern County Libr. Sys., Bakersfield, Calif., 1974-80; dir. dist. libr. Lake Agassiz Regional Libr. System, Crookston, Minn., 1980-85; supervising libr. San Diego County Libr., 1985-87; county libr. Merced (Calif.) County Libr., 1987-93; learning network mgr. Merced Coll., 1994-95; city libr. Monterey Park (Calif.) Bruggemeyer Libr., 1995—2009. V.p. legis. Calif. Fedn. Bus., Profl. Women's Clubs, 2007-08; mem. Leadership Merced, 1987-88, East Site Based Coordinating Coun., Merced, 1990-92, Merced Gen. Plan Citizens Adv. Com., 1992-95, Sister City Com., Merced, 1992-95. Recipient Libr. award Eagles Aux., 1984, Woman of Achievement award Commn. on the Status of Women, 1990, Libr. award Calif. Libr. Trustees and Commrs., 1990, Woman of Yr. award Merced Bus. and Profl. Women, 1990, People Who Make a Difference award Monterey Pk. United Dems., 2003, Woman of Yr. award 29th Congl. Dist., 2004. Mem. ALA (sec. pub. libr. sys. sect. 1988-89), Met. Coop. Library Sys. (pres. 1999-2000), Calif. Libr. Assn. (sec. govt. rels. com. 1991-92, continuing edn. com. 1993-96, pub. rels. 1997-2000, nominations com. 2000-01, 2007-08, legislative com., 2008), Minn. Libr. Assn. (pres. pub. libr. divsn. 1985), Merced County Mgmt. Coun. (pres. 1989), Merced Bus. and Profl. Women (Woman of Yr. 1987, pres. 1988-89, 1st v.p. Sierra Mar dist., 2006-08, pres. elect 2008-09, pres., 2009-), East L.A.-Montebello Bus. and Profl. Women (v.p. 1998-2002, pres. 2002-05, 2007-09), Rotary (pres. Monterey Park chpt. 1999-2000), MERCI(bd. dirs., 2007) Democrat. Lutheran. Avocations: travel, walking, reading, swimming, stamp collecting/philately. Home: 1000 E Newmark Ave Apt 22 Monterey Park CA 91755-3129 E-mail: lindalwilson@juno.com.

WILSON, LINDA SMITH, retired academic administrator; b. Washington, Nov. 10, 1936; d. Fred M. and Virginia D. Smith; m. Malcolm C. Whatley, June 29, 1957 (div. 1969); 1 child, Helen K. Whatley; m. Paul A. Wilson, Jan. 22, 1970; 1 stepchild, Beth A. BA, Tulane U., 1957, HLD (hon.), 1993; PhD, U. Wis., 1962; DLitt (hon.), U. Md., 1993. Rsch. assoc. U. Md., College Park, 1962—64, rsch. asst. prof., 1964—67; vis. asst. prof. U. Mo., St. Louis, 1967—68; asst. to vice chancellor for rsch., asst. vice chancellor for rsch., assoc. vice chancellor for rsch. Washington U., St. Louis, 1968—75; assoc. vice chancellor for rsch. U. Ill., Urbana, 1975—85; assoc. dean U. Ill. Grad. Coll., Urbana, 1978—85; v.p. for rsch. U. Mich., Ann Arbor, 1985—89; pres. Radcliffe Coll., Cambridge, Mass., 1989—99, pres. emeritus, 1999; sr. lectr. Harvard Grad. Sch. Edn., 1989—2003; bd. dirs. Myriad Genetics, Tulane U., Tulane Murphy Found. Rsch. resources adv. coun. NIH, Bethesda, Md., 1978—82; mem. Nat. Commn. on Rsch., Washington, 1978—80; dir.'s adv. coun. NSF, Washington, 1980—89; com. on govt.-univ. relationships NAS, 1981—83, govt.-univ.-industry rsch. roundtable, 1984—89, coord. coun. for edn., 1991—93; energy rsch. adv. bd. Dept. of Energy, 1987—90; chmn. adv. com. office sci. and engring. pers. NRC, 1990—96; adv. com. edn. and human resources NSF, Washington, 1990—95; sci., tech. and states task force Carnegie Commn. on Sci., Tech. and Govt., 1991—92; overser Mus. Sci., Boston, 1992—2001; trustee Mass. Gen. Hosp., 1992—99, hon. trustee, 1999—2002; trustee Com. on Econ. Devel., 1995—; bd. dirs. Inacom, Inc., 1997—2003, Citizens Fin. Group, Inc., 1997—2000, Value Line, Inc., 1998—2000; bd. vis. Coll. Letters and Sci. U. Wis., 1999—2005; dean's adv. coun. Newcomb Coll., 1999—2006. Contbr. articles to profl. jours. and book chpts. Adv. bd. Nat. Coalition for Sci. and Tech., Washington, 1983—87; bd. govs. YMCA, Champaign, Ill., 1980—83. Recipient Centennial award, Newcomb Coll., 1986, Disting. Alumni award, U. Wis., 1997, Radcliffe medal, 1999; named One of 100 Emerging Leaders, Am. Coun. Edn. and Change Mag., 1978, Outstanding Alumna, Class of 1957, Tulane U., 2007. Fellow: AAAS (bd. dirs. 1984—88); mem.: Am. Coun. Edn. (commn. on women in higher edn. 1991—93, chair 1993), Inst. Medicine (coun. mem. 1986—89, com. on setting NIH priorities, com. on govt.-industry collaboration in biomed. edn. and rsch.), Assn. for Biomed. Rsch. (bd. dirs. 1983—86), Nat. Coun. Univ. Rsch. Adminstrs., Soc. Rsch. Adminstrs. (Disting. Contbn. to Rsch. Adminstrn. award 1984), Am. Chem. Soc. (bd. coun. com. on chemistry and pub. affairs 1978—80), Phi Kappa Phi, Phi Delta Kappa, Alpha Lambda Delta, Sigma Xi, Phi Beta Kappa. Home: 26 Honey Locust Dr Topsham ME 04086 Home Phone: 207-729-9129.

WILSON, LIZABETH ANNE (BETSY WILSON), dean, library director; b. Waterloo, Iowa, May 21, 1954; d. Martin Lucien and Joanne Hausser Wilson; m. Dean August Pollack, Sept. 1, 1983. BA, Northwestern U., 1972—77; MLS, U. of Ill., 1977—78. Asst. architecture and art libr. U. Ill., 1979—80, asst. undergrad. libr., 1980—86, asst. dir. librs. undergrad. and instrnl. svcs., 1986—92; assoc. dir. librs. for rsch. and instrnl. svcs. U. Wash., Seattle, 1992—2000, dean U. librs., 2001—. Chair of bd. of trustees OCLC, Inc., Dublin, 2003—07; exec. dir. Leopoldo Cicognara Program+, Urbana-Champaign, Ill., 1987—2004; co-founder UWired collaboration at the University of Washington, Digital Futures Alliance. Author (co-author): (journal article) The Bottom Line; contbr. chapters to books, articles. Recipient Margaret E. Monroe Libr. Adult Services award, RUSA/Am. Libr. Assn., 1995, Miriam Dudley Instrn. Libr. award, Assn. Coll. and Rsch. Libraries, 1995, EDUCAUSE Award for Systemic Progress in Tchg. and Learning, 2000. Mem.: Coun. on Libr. Resources (bd. mem. 2007—), Greater Western Libr. Alliance (pres. 2004), Digital Libr. Fedn. (mem. exec. com. 2004—07), OCLC Membs. Coun. (pres. 1999—2000), Assn. Rsch. Librs. (bd. dirs. 2003—06), Instrn. Sect. of ACRL (chair 1990—91), Assn. Coll. and Rsch. Librs. (pres. 2000—01, Excellence in Academic Libr. award 2004, Academic/Rsch. Libr. of Yr. 2007). Office: Dean of Libraries University Washington Box 352900 Seattle WA 98195-2900 Office Fax: 206-685-8727. Business E-Mail: betsyw@u.washington.edu.

WILSON, LLOYD LEE, registrar, educator; b. Elkton, Md., Sept. 14, 1947; s. Clifton Laws and Betty Raye (Bare) W.; m. Susan Sieg Wilson, 1992; children: Asa, Ryan, Morgan, Daniel. BS in Mgmt., MIT, 1969, MS in Mgmt., 1977; MA in Religion, Gorham Sch. Religion, 2009. Bus. mgr. med. clinics Mass. Gen. Hosp., Boston, 1970-73; ptnr. Willow Co., mgmt. cons., Cambridge, Mass., 1974-77; dir. community relations Wilson Neuropsychiat. Hosp., Charlottesville, Va., 1977-78; exec. dir. Jefferson Area United Transp. Inc., Charlottesville, Va., 1978-80, Va. Mountain Housing Inc., Blacksburg, 1980-82; gen. sec. Friends Gen. Conf. Religious Soc. Friends, Phila., 1982-85; dir. rsch. and devel. Va. Mountain Housing, Inc., Christiansburg, 1985-88, dir. multifamily housing, 1989-91, regional dir., 1991-92; pres. Friendly Mgmt. Svcs. Corp., Norfolk, Va., 1992-95, Not-for-Profit Mgmt., Inc., Norfolk, Va., 1995—2004; registrar Chowan U., Murfreesboro, NC, 2002—, asst. prof. religion, 2006—. Dir. instnl. rsch. Chowan U., Murfreesboro, N.C., 2000—; Asst. prof. of acctg., 2001—; pres., dir. Va. Housing Coalition, Inc., 1981-82; treas., bd. dirs., Cedar Grove Consulting, LLC, 2004—06, Fiddle Hill Farm, Inc., Barboursville, Va., 1982-89; bd. mgrs. Bible Assn. Friends in Am., Phila., 1983-85; mem. com. rec. ministers Balt. Yearly Meeting Friends, Sandy Spring, Md., 1984-86; asst. sec.-treas. Friends Meeting House Fund, Inc., Phila., 1984-85; asst. presiding clk. Comm. Commn. of Friends United Meeting, Richmond, Ind., 1987-88; recorded min. of gospel, Soc. of Friends, 1989— (presiding clk. Va. Beach monthly meeting 1990-92); dir. coordinating cabinet Va. Coun. Chs., 1988; presiding clk. N.C. Yearly Meeting of Friends, 1991-92. Author: Essays on the Quaker Vision of Gospel Order, 1993, Wrestling with one Faith Tradition, 2005, Holy Surrender, 2007; contbr. articles to profl. jours. Treas., bd. dirs. Norfolk (Va.) Quaker House, Inc., 1995-2000; bd. dirs. New Dominion Housing, Inc., Norfolk, 1992-94; vice chmn. Montgomery County Cmty. Svc. Commn., Christianburg, Va., 1980-82; mem. ednl. coun. MIT, 1977-89; bd. dirs. Am. Friends Svc. Com., Inc., Phila., 1980-83; bd. dirs. Interfaith Housing Corp. Cambridge, Inc., 1975-77, treas., 1976-77, also numerous others. Home: PO Box 647 Woodland NC 27897-0647 Office Phone: 252-398-6246. Business E-Mail: llwilson@alum.mit.edu, wilsol@chowan.edu.

WILSON, LOIS M., minister; b. Winnipeg, Man., Can., Apr. 8, 1927; d. Edwin Gardiner Dunn and Ada Minnie (Davis) Freeman; m. Roy F. Wilson, June 9, 1950; children: Ruth, Jean, Neil, Bruce BA, United Coll., Winnipeg, 1947, BDiv, 1969; Diploma in TV prodn., Ryerson Tech. Inst., 1974; DDiv (hon.), Victoria U., Toronto, 1978, United Theol. Coll., Montreal, 1978, Wycliff Coll., 1983, Queens U., Kingston, 1984, U. Winnipeg, 1986, Mt. Allison U., 1988; LLD (hon.), Trent U., Peterborough, 1984, Dalhousie U., 1989, Ripon Coll., Wis., 1992, U. Toronto, 2005, U. Manitoba, 2006; DCL, Acadia U., 1984; DHuml (hon.), Mt. St. Vincent, Halifax, 1984; DD, Regis Coll., U. Torento, 2009. Ordained to ministry United Church of Can., 1965. Minister, Thunder Bay, 1965-69, Hamilton, 1969-78, Kingston, 1978-80; moderator United Church of Can., Kingston, 1980-82, McGeachy sr. scholar, 1989-91; pres. Can. Council of Chs., Toronto, Ont., 1976-79; co-dir. Ecumenical Forum Can., Toronto, Ont., 1983-89; pres. World Council of Chs., Geneva, 1983-91; chancellor Lakehead U., Thurder Bay, Ont., 1990-2000; chmn. contemporary theology Lafayette-Orinda (Calif.) Presbyn. Ch., 1995; ind. senator Senate of Can., 1998—2002; apptd. ecumenist in residence Toronto Sch. Theology, 2006—09. Mem. adv. coun. internt. devel. studies U. Toronto, 1987-93, Fair Oto Can., Across Boundries Multifaith Inst., Mining Watch Can.; spokesperson Project Ploughshares, 1st and 2d UN Conf. on Disarmament, N.Y.C., 1978-82; officer Human Rights Commn., Ont., 1973; mem. bd. regents Victoria U., 1990—; chief Can. Fact finding Mission to Sri Lanka, 1992; team mem. Ctrl. Am. Monitoring Group to El Salvador and Guatemala, 1993; spl. envoy of Can. to The Sudan, 1999-02; lectr. in field; ecumenist in residence Queens Theol. Coll., Kingston, Ont., 2009. Author: Like a Mighty River, 1980, Turning the World Upside Down, 1989, Miriam, Mary and Me, 1992, Telling Her Story, 1992, Stories Seldom Told, 1997, Nuclear Waste, 2000, Streams of Faith, 2006, Transforming the Faith of Our Fathers; mem. adv. bd.: Can. Woman Studies Jour., York U., 1993—2004; contbr. articles to profl. publs. Apptd. Can. Senator, 1998; pres. Social Planning Coun., Thunder Bay, 1967—68, Can. Com. for Scientists and Scholars, Toronto, 1982; mem. Refugee Status Adv. Com., 1985—89; chmn. Urban Rural Mission, Can., 1990—96; mem. environ. assessment panel Can. Nuclear Fuel Waste Mgmt. and Disposal Concept, 1989—96; bd. dirs. Elizabeth Fry Soc., Hamilton, 1976—79, Amnesty Internat., 1978—90, Can. Inst. for Internat. Peace and Security, 1984—88, Energy Probe, 1981—86, Internat. Ctr. Human Rights and Dem. Devel., 1997—98, Can. Univ. Svc. Overseas, 1983—85; trustee Nelson Mandela Fund, 1990—92. Decorated Order of Can., Order of Ont., Companion of Order of Can.; sr. fellow Massey Coll. U. Toronto, 2005—; recipient Queens Jubilee medal, Commemorative medal for 125th Anniversary of Confederation of Can., 1992, World Federalist Peace award, 1985, Pearson Peace medal UN Assn. of Can., 1985; named hon. pres. Student Christian Movement of Can., Toronto, 1976. Mem. DPR Korea Assoc., Canada (chmn. 2002-09), Women, Peace and Security (co-chair 2001-03), CAW (pub. rev. bd. 1986—), Can. Assn. Adult Edn. (bd. dirs. 1986-90), Friends Can. Broadcasting (bd. dirs. 1986-94, v.p.), Civil Liberties Assn. (v.p. 1986—), UNIFEM (nat. v.p. 1993-95, mem. CCIC team to monitor El Salvador election 1994), World Federalists (pres. Can. chpt. 1996-2000, v.p. World Federalist Movement intern, 1998-, acting pres., 2004-09), Parliament of World's Religions (del. 1993), Christian-Jewish Dialogue Jerusalem (keynote speaker 1994). Mem. United Ch. Of Can. E-mail: royandlois.wilson@sympatico.ca.

WILSON, LYNN DEYO, radiation oncologist; b. Washington, May 26, 1962; BA, Denison U., 1984; MPH, Yale U., 1986; MD, George Washington U., 1990. Diplomate Am. Bd. Radiation Oncology. Intern Yale-New Haven Hosp., 1990-91, resident in therapeutic radiology, 1991-94, chief resident, 1993-94, radiation oncologist, 2006—; prof. therapeutic radiology, dermatology and surgery Yale U. Sch. Medicine, New Haven, asst. prof., 1994—2000, assoc. prof., 2000—06. Mem. AMA, Am. Soc. Therapeutic Radiology & Oncology, Am. Soc. Clin. Oncology, Am. Radium Soc. Office Phone: 203-737-1202.

WILSON, LYNTON RONALD, telecommunications industry executive, academic administrator; b. Port Colborne, Ont., Can., Apr. 3, 1940; s. Ronald Alfred and Blanche Evelyn (Matthews) W.; m. Brenda Jean (Black), Dec. 23, 1968; children: Edward Ronald, Margot Jean, Jennifer Lyn. BA, McMaster U., 1962, LLD, 1995; MA, Cornell U., 1967; D (hon.), U. Montreal, 1995; D in Civil Law, Bishop's U., Lennoxville, Que., Can., 1997; LLD, U. Cape Breton, 1998, Mount Allison U., 2000, Brock U., 2003. Dep. minister Ministry Industry and Tourism, Ont., Canada, 1978-81; pres., CEO Redpath Industries, Ltd., Toronto, Canada, 1981-88; mng. dir. N.Am. Tate and Lyle, PLC, 1986-89; chmn. bd. Redpath Industries, Ltd., Toronto, Canada, 1988-89; vice chmn. Bank of N.S., Toronto, Canada, 1989-90; pres., COO BCE, Inc., Montreal, Canada, 1990-92, pres., CEO, 1992-93, chmn., pres., CEO, 1993-96, chmn., CEO, 1996-98, chmn. bd. dir., 1998-2000; chancellor McMaster U., Hamilton, Ont., Canada. Chmn. bd. dir. CAE, Inc.; chmn. emeritus Nortel Networks Corp.; chmn. Daimler, Chrysler Can. Adv. Coun.; mem. supervisory bd. Daimler AG; mem. Prime Minister's adv. com. on public svc. Founding co-chmn. HISTORICA Found., Canada; chmn. Govt. Can. Competition Policy Rev. Panel. Decorated officer Order of Can. Mem. The Mount Royal Club of Montreal, York Club, Toronto Golf Club, Toronto Club, Rideau Club, Mount Bruno Country Club. Home: 2038 Lakeshore Rd E L6J 1M3 Oakville ON Canada Office: BCE Inc Oxford Tower 130 Adelaide St W Ste 2212 Toronto ON Canada M5H 3P5

WILSON, MAGGIE ISABELLE LOVELL, secondary school educator; b. Branchville, Ala., Jan. 26; d. Winston Porter and Ruth Kate (Buckner) Lovell. AB, Samford U., Birmingham, Ala., 1971; MA, EdS, U. Ala., 1978; MFA, Loyola U., 1979; PhD, Sussex U., Eng., 1981. Cert. elem./secondary tchr. Tchr. English Birmingham Pub. Schs., 1972-92; tchr. English secondary edn. Terrell County Schs., Dawson, Ga., 1992-93. Author, illustrator: Carousel of Creative Communication, 1976, Leeds, Her Story, 1979; author: Creative Expressions, 1980, Into Our Third Century, 1984, From Brush Arbor Days to the Twentieth Century, 1992. Historian Leeds (Ala.) First United Meth. Ch., 1990-99; docent Birmingham Mus. Art, 1970-80; pres. Sylacauga dist. United Meth. Women, 1981-84. Recipient numerous awards Ala. Watercolor Soc., Birmingham, 1970—, Pres. award Kappa Pi, Samford U., Birmingham, 1971, Art of Distinction Salon Des Nations, Paris, 1984. Mem. AAUW, Internat. Biog. Assn., Ala. Coun. Tchrs. English (bd. mem. 1976—), Leeds Art Coun., Leeds Hist. Soc., Birmingham Art Assn., Internat. Soc. Artists, Leeds Bus. and Profl. Women (pres. 1971-76, 86, 88—, Woman of Yr. 1996-97), Leeds United Meth. Women (pres. 1972-76, 84—, pres. Sylacauga dist. 1981-84), La. Watercolor Soc. (awards 1986-99), So. Watercolor Soc., Kappa Delta Epsilon, Phi Gamma Mu. Home: 1110 Montevallo Rd SW Leeds AL 35094-1926

WILSON, MALCOLM CAMPBELL, investment trust management executive; b. Phila., Dec. 9, 1942; s. James Murray and Janet (Haines) Wilson; m. Barbara Ann Bahmermann, June 10, 1989; children from previous marriage: Jennifer Marie, David Campbell, Andrew Russel. BS in Bus. Adminstrn., Drexel U., 1966, MBA in Fin., 1968. Chartered fin. analyst. Rsch. analyst Provident Nat. Bank, Phila., 1971—77, co-mgr. rsch. dept., 1977—78, dir. equity rsch., 1978—84, dir. econ. and investment rsch., 1984—88, chief investment officer PNC Fin. div., 1986—88, sr. v.p., mgr. personal svcs. group, 1989—92; exec. v.p., mgr. investment mgmt. and trust Phila. market PNC Bank, N.A., 1993—95; sr. v.p., mgr. Personal Svcs. Group, Mercantile-Safe Deposit and Trust Co., Balt., 1996—98, exec. v.p., mgr. investment mgmt. and trust, 1998—2003; mng. dir., ptnr. Davidson Capital Mgmt., Devon, Pa., 2003—. With USN, 1968—71. Fellow: Fin. Analysts Fedn.; mem.: N.Y. Soc. Security Analysts, Mayflower Soc., Pa. Soc. SAR. Republican. Episcopalian. Avocations: hunting, fishing, golf. Home: 103 Cawley Ct Chester Springs PA 19425 Office: Davidson Capital Mgmt 20 N Waterloo Rd Devon PA 19333 Office Phone: 610-254-2045. Business E-Mail: swilson@davidsoncapmgt.com.

WILSON, MARC FRASER, art museum director; b. Akron, Ohio, Sept. 12, 1941; s. Fraser Eugene and Pauline Christine (Hoff) W.; m. Elizabeth Marie Fulder, Aug. 2, 1975. BA in European History, Yale U., 1963, MA in History of Art, 1967. Translator, project cons. Nat. Palace Mus., Taipei, Taiwan, 1968-71; assoc. curator of Chinese art Nelson Gallery-Atkins Mus., Kansas City, Mo., 1971-73, curator, Oriental art, 1973—82; Menefee D. & Mary Louise Blackwell dir., CEO Nelson-Atkins Mus. Art, 1982—. Mem., rapporteur Indo-US Subcom. on Edn. and Culture, Washington, 1976-79; mem. adv. com. Asia Soc. Galleries, N.Y.C., 1984—, China Inst. in Am., 1985—. Mem. adv. com. Muni-Art Commn. on Urban Sculpture, Kansas City, 1984-87; com. mem. Kansas City-Xi'an, China, Sister City program, 1986—; mem. humanities coun. Johnson County Cmty. Coll., 1976-79; commr. Japan-U.S. Friendship Commn., Washington, 1986-88; panelist Japan-U.S. Cultural and Edn. Cooperation, Washington, 1986-88; mem. mayor's task force on race relations, 1996—; mem. indemnity adv. panel, 1995—; v.p. Brush Creek Ptnrs. 1995—. Recipient William Yates Medallion Civic Svc. award William Jewell Coll., 1995, Disting. Svc. award Baker U., 1997; grantee Ford Found., Japan, Hong Kong, Taiwan, 1969-71. Mem. Assn. Art Mus. Dirs. (treas., trustee 1988-90, chmn. works of art com. 1986-90), Mo. China Coun., Fed. Coun. Arts and Humanities (chmn. arts and artifacts indemnity adv. panel 1986-89, 1995-98). Avocations: farming, auto racing. Office: Nelson-Atkins Mus Art 4525 Oak St Kansas City MO 64111-1818 E-mail: mwilson@nelson-atkins.org.

WILSON, MAREN, anthropologist, educator; Prof. anthropology Ctrl. Ariz. Coll., Winkelman, 2000—, acting tutoring svcs. mgr., 2006—08. Recipient Excellence in Tchg. award, Nat. Inst. Staff and Orgnl. Devel., 2001, Exemplary Practice award, Nat. Coun. Student Devel., 2003; finalist Terry O'Bannion Shared Journeys award, League Innovation,

2003. Mem.: Delta Kappa Gamma, Soc. Anthropology Cmty. Colls. (co-pres. 2009—). Office: Ctrl Ariz Colls Aravaipa Campus 80440 E Aravaipa Rd Winkelman AZ 85292

WILSON, MARGARET SCARBROUGH, retail executive; b. Aug. 7, 1930; Student, Smith Coll., 1948-50; BA, U. Tex., 1952. Mem. staff Bayway Refinery Exxon Corp., NJ, 1960-61; mem. staff psychiat. ward VA Hosp., Houston, 1962; from mem. staff to chmn. Scarbroughs, Austin, Tex., 1952—74, chmn. bd., CEO, 1974—. Mem., bd. dirs. audit and contbns. coms. R.J. Reynolds Industries, 1978-85; hon. bd. dirs. Internat. Longevity Ctr., N.Y.C.; bd. dirs. Scarbrough Devel. Corp., Nat. Retail Fedn., 1991-2002, Am. Productivity & Quality Ctr., 1991-2002; chmn. San Antonio br. Fed. Res. Bank Dallas, 1975-76; trustee Nat. Policy Assn., 1997-98; pres., treas. Scarbrough Ventures LLC, 2001-, MSW-NSG Mgmt. LLC, 2000-, MSW-NSG Enterprises Ltd., 2000-, MSW-NSG Real Estate Ventures Ltd., 2001-. Trustee Com. Econ. Devel., 1973—, Cooper Inst. for Aerobics Rsch., Dallas, 1980-93, St. Stephen's Sch., Austin, 1979-83; mem. Nat. Com. U.S.-China Rels., 1976—, dir. 1980-94; mem. U.S. Coun. Internat. Bus., 1977—, mem. exec. com., 1978—, trustee, 1978—; bd. vistors Babcock Grad. Sch. Mgmt.-Wake Forest U., Winston-Salem, N.C., 1983-86; mem. bus. adv. coun. S.W. Tex. State U., 1983-86; mem. deptl. vis. com. dept. home econs. U. Tex.-Austin, 1983-84, pres.'s assocs., 1992—; mem. univ. coun. Rockefeller U., N.Y.C., 1982-86; mem. chancellor's coun. U. Tex. Sys., 1994—; mem. Tex. Rsch. League, 1977—, dir. audit com. 1986—, Friends of L.B.J. Libr., 1980—; assoc. mem. George Bush Presdl. Libr., 1995—; bd. dirs. World Bus. Coun., 1980-89; mem. adv. coun. Coll. Bus. Adminstrn., U. Tex.-Austin, 1964-68, Dean's Assocs. Coll. Fine Arts, 1985-87, Friends of Free Enterprise com. Coll. Engring., 1985-87; mem. India-U.S. Bus. Coun., 1976-82, dir., 1978-82; mem. Pres.'s Commn. on Pers. Interchange, 1972-73, UN Day Com., 1971-74; mem. Mayor's Bus. Roundtable, Austin, 1985-87; mem. Houston Com. Fgn. Rels., 1994—, Dallas Com. Fgn. Rels., 1997—, SRI Internat. Assocs. Program, 1998-99; mem. Conf. Bd. Mem. Alliance Francaise, Asia Soc. (adv. bd. Houston chpt., 1991-94, mem. N.Y. chpt.), Houston World Affairs Coun., Austin World Affairs Coun., English Speaking Union, Tex. Assn. Taxpayers, Retail Industry Trade Action Coalition (trustee 1984), Nat. Planning Assn. (trustee 1985-97), Am. Enterprise Inst. Am. Mgmt. Assn. (dir. 1969-72), Internat. C. of C., British Am. Bus. Inc., U.S. C. of C. (bd. dirs. 1980-82), Tex. Asian C. of C. (mem. adv. coun. 1997—), Tex. State Soc. Wash., World Econ. Devel. Congress (mem. adv. bd. 1993), Internat. Indsl. Conf. (mem. adv. coun. 1996-97), Coun. Fgn. Rels., World Econ. Forum, Bus. Coun. Internat. Understanding, Ctr. Strategic and Internat. Studies (Washington Round Table 1998—), Am. Enterprise Inst., Pacific Coun. on Internat. Policy, World Pres.'s Orgn. (internat. chpt., met. chpt., Dallas chpt., Houston chpt., Cen. Tex. chpt.), Pres.'s Cir. Nat. Acad. Scis., Inst. of Medicine and Inst. Engrs., Houston Forum, Brookings Instn., Bretton Woods Com., Brit.-N.A. Com., Tarry House, The University Club N.Y., Met. Club (Washington), Headliners Club, Tex. Breakfast Club of Washington, Kappa Kappa Gamma, numerous other local and nat. orgns. Office: 517 W 39th St Austin TX 78751-4904 E-mail: Margaret.Wilson@Scarbroughs.com.

WILSON, MARK LOWELL, philosopher, educator; Student, Reed Coll., 1965—67; BA, Univ. Wash., 1969; PhD, Harvard Univ., 1976. Asst. prof. Univ. Calif., San Diego, 1976—82, assoc. prof., 1982—84, Univ. Ill., Chgo., 1984—91; prof. Ohio State Univ., 1991—98, Univ. Pitts., 1998—. Fellow: Am. Acad. Arts & Scis. Office: Dept Philosophy Univ Pitts 1001 Cathedral of Learning Pittsburgh PA 15260 Office Phone: 412-624-5787. Business E-Mail: mlwilson@pitt.edu.

WILSON, MARK STEPHEN, research scientist; b. Newcastle upon Tyne, Eng., Jan. 28, 1978; s. Robert and Gloria Wilson; m. Laura Cari-Ann Bilenki, July 9, 2005. PhD, U. Edinburgh, Scotland, 2005. Vis. fellow rschr. Nat. Inst. Health, Bethesda, Md., 2005—. Vol. Charlies Pl., Washington. Mem.: NIAID, LPD, AAAI. Achievements include research in Discoveries in Allergy. Business E-Mail: wilsonmar@niaid.nih.gov.

WILSON, MARY ALICE, musician, educator; b. Nov. 2, 1939; MusB, Northwestern U., Evanston, Ill., 1961. Orch. band dir., pvt. tchr. Luth. Schs., Deerfield Pub. Schs., 1961-64; pvt. tchr. violin and piano Cleve., 1964-77; dir. Suzuki Program, violin tchr. W.Va. U., 1977—, chmn. music divsn., 2005; founder, leader Seneca String Quartet, Morgantown, W.Va., 1986—. Accompanist, Ch. vol. tchg. and music, Cleve., Chgo., Morgantown, 1960—. Recipient Outstanding Tchr. award, W.Va. U. Music Dept., 2005, outstanding leadership award, 2008; named Disting. Leader of Yr., 2008. Mem.: Am. String Tchrs. Assn. (co-developer, chmn. 5th yr. state solo competition, state sect. 2003—05, Studio Tchr. of Yr. 2008), W.Va. Music Tchrs. Assn. (dist. chmn. of strings 1977—, state officer pub. 1989—, State Outstanding Tchr. Yr. 1996), Music Tchrs. Nat. Assn. (state office of composition contest 1989—). Home: 237 Poplar Dr Morgantown WV 26505-2519 Personal E-mail: bigmacwil@hotmail.com. Business E-Mail: cbwilson@mail.wvu.edu.

WILSON, MARY ELIZABETH, epidemiologist, physician, educator; b. Indpls., Nov. 19, 1942; d. Ralph Richard and Catheryn Rebecca (Kurtz) Lausch; m. Harvey Vernon Fineberg, May 16, 1975. AB, Ind. U., 1963; MD, U. Wis., 1971. Diplomate Am. Bd. Internal Medicine, Am. Bd. Infectious Diseases. Tchr. of French and English Marquette Sch., Madison, Wis., 1963-66; intern in medicine Beth Israel Hosp., Boston, 1971-72, resident in medicine, 1972-73, fellow in infectious diseases, 1973-75; physician Albert Schweitzer Hosp., Deschapelles, Haiti, 1974-75, Harvard Health Svcs., Cambridge, Mass., 1974-75; asst. physician Cambridge Hosp., 1975-78; hosp. epidemiologist Mt. Auburn Hosp., Cambridge, 1975-79, chief of infectious diseases, 1978—2002, dir. Travel Resource Ctr., 1996—2002, mem. consulting staff, 2003—05. Mem. adv. com. immunization practices CDC, Atlanta, 1988—92; mem. acad. adv. com. Nat. Inst. Pub. Health, Mexico, 1989—91; cons. Ford Found., 1988; site dir. GeoSentinel Network, 1999—2002, spl. cons., 2002—; instr. medicine Harvard Med. Sch., Boston, 1975—93, asst. clin. prof., 1994—99, assoc. prof. medicine, 1999—2004, assoc. clin. prof., 2004—; assoc. Ctr. Health and Global Environment, 1996—2000; asst. prof. depts. epidemiology and population and internat. health Harvard Sch. Pub. Health, 1994—99, assoc. prof. population and internat. health, 1999—2008, assoc. prof. global health & population, 1999—; lectr. Sultan Qaboos U., Oman, 1991; chair Woods Hole Workshop, Emerging Infectious Diseases, 1993. Author: A World Guide to Infections: Diseases, Distribution, Diagnosis, 1991; editor (with Richard Levins and Andrew Spielman): Disease in Evolution: Global Changes and Emergence of Infectious Diseases, 1994; mem. editl. bd. Current Issues Pub. Health, 1999—2003, Emerging Infectious Diseases, Global Change and Human Health, 1999—2003; sect. editor travel medicine and tropical diseases: Infectious Diseases Clin. Practices; mem. editl. bd. Infectious Diseases Clin. Practices, 2006—; assoc. editor: Jour. Watch Infectious Diseases, 1997—; mem. editl. adv. bd. Clin. Infectious Diseases, 1999—2004, spl. sect. editor Emerging Infections, Clinical Infectious Diseases, 2006—. Mem. Cambridge Task Force AIDS, 1987—90; bd. dirs. Horizon Comm., West Cornwall, Conn., 1990—97; mem. Nat. Commn. on Indsl. Farm Animal Prodn., 2006—08; bd. mem. FXB USA, 2007—; bd. sci. counselors Ctr. Disease Ctrl. & Prevention, 2008—; bd. trustees Internat. Ctr. Diarrhea Disease Rsch., Bangladesh, 2009—. Recipient Lewis E. and Edith Phillips award, U. Wis. Med. Sch., 1969, Cora M. and Edward Van Liere award, 1971, Mosby Scholarship Book award, 1971, Leo Blacklow Tchg. award, 1999, Emanuel Wolinsky award, 2008; named to Northwestern Sch. Corp. Disting. Alumni Hall of Fame, 2007; fellow, Ctr. Advanced Study Behavioral Scis., Stanford, Calif., 2002; scholar-in-residence, Bellagio (Italy) Study Ctr., Rockefeller Found., 1996. Fellow: ACP, Royal Soc. Tropical Medicine and Hygiene, Infectious Diseases Soc. Am.; mem.: Am. Soc. Tropical Medicine Hygiene (councilor 2006—), Soc. for Epidemiol. Rsch., Internat. Union Against Tuberculosis and Lung Disease, Soc. for Vector Ecology, Wilderness Med. Soc., Internat. Soc. Travel Medicine, Peabody Soc., Mass. Infectious Diseases Soc., N.Y. Acad. Scis., Am. Soc. Microbiology, Aesculapian Club, Alpha Omega Alpha, Phi Sigma Iota, Sigma Sigma. Avocations: flute, hiking, reading, travel.

WILSON, MELINDA J., psychologist; b. Auburn, NY, Apr. 10, 1971; d. George M. and Linda J. Colburn; children: Matthew Kristopher, Ryan Gregory. AA in Social Scis., Jamestown CC, NY, 1991; BS in Ed. Elem. and Physically Handicapped Summa Cum Laude, Edinboro U. Pa., 1993, MEd in Ednl. Psychology, 2000, EdS in Sch. Psychology, 2003. Spl. edn. tchr. Gustavus Adolphus Learning Ctr., Jamestown, 1994—99, Jamestown Pub. Schs., 2000—01, Warren County Pub. Schs., Pa., 2001—03; sch. psychologist intern Westfield Acad. and Ctrl. Sch., NY, 2002—03; sch. psychologist Gilbert Pub. Schs., Ariz., 2003—, behavior cons., 2008—. Mem.: NASP, Kappa Delta Pi Edn. Honor Soc., Sorority Women Educators, Phi Sigma Pi Nat. Honor Frat. (treas. 1992—93). Avocations: travel, sports. Business E-Mail: mindy_wilson@gilbert.k12.az.us.

WILSON, MELVIN EDMOND, retired civil engineer; b. Bremerton, Wash., Aug. 3, 1935; s. Edmond Curt and Madeline Rose (Deal) W.; m. Deanna May Stevens, Nov. 22, 1957 (div. Mar. 1971); children: Kathleen, Debra Frank Baldwin. BSCE, U. Wash., 1957, MSCE, 1958. Registered profl. engr., Wash. Asst. civil engr. City of Seattle, 1958-60, assoc. civil engr., 1960-64, sr. civil engr., 1964-66, supervising civil engr., 1966-75, sr. civil engr., 1975-77, mgr. X, 1977-88; owner Wilson Cons. Svcs., Seattle, 1988-89; transp. sys. dir. City of Renton, Wash., 1989-96, ret., 1996. Owner Mel Wilson Photographer, Seattle, 1975-84. Contbr. reports to profl. jours. Rep. Renton transp. work group King County Growth Mgmt. Policy Com., Wash.; rep. Renton tech. adv. com. South County Area Transp. Bd., King County, 1992-96, developer svc. policy (adopted by Puget Sound Govtl. Conf.) to encourage travel by transit. successfuly led effort to make Renton first suburban city to receive direct transit svc. under Met. King County Plan, 1994; vol. personal trainer, 1988-2007; vol. trainer for medical patients, 1988—2007. Mem. ASCE, Am. Pub. Works Assn., Inst. Transp. Engrs., Tau Beta Pi, Sigma Xi. Avocations: physical fitness, art, psychology.

WILSON, MICHAEL MOUREAU, lawyer, physician; b. Cheverly, Md., Dec. 3, 1952; s. Kenneth Moureau and Helen (Rice) Smith. BS, MIT, 1974; JD, Georgetown U., 1977, MD, 1986. Bar: D.C. 1977, N.Y. 1980, U.S. Dist. Ct. D.C. 1980, U.S. Dist. Ct. Md. 1992, U.S. Ct. Appeals (D.C. cir.) 1980, U.S. Supreme Ct. 1981. Law clk. Hon. John B. Hannum U.S. Dist. Ct., Phila., 1977—78; assoc. Cravath Swaine & Moore, NYC, 1978—79; asst. to gen. counsel NSF, Washington, 1979—82; resident in psychiatry St. Elizabeth Hosp., 1986—89; pvt. practice med. malpractice litigation, 1989—. Notes editor Am. Criminal Law Rev., 1976-77. Mem. ABA, Assn. Trial Lawyers Am., D.C. Trial Lawyers Assn., Phi Beta Kappa. Office: 1120 19th St NW Ste LL-11 Washington DC 20036 Office Phone: 202-223-4488. E-mail: wilson@wilsonlaw.com.

WILSON, MICHAEL W., academic librarian, educator; b. Marion, NC, 1962; s. Louis D. and Carol Y. Wilson. BA in French, Ga. State U., Atlanta, 1986; MA in Libr. and Info. Sci., U. SC, Columbia, 1995. Cert. specialist in libr. and info. sci. U. SC, 2002. Reference libr. Ga. Perimeter Coll., Clarkston, 1995—98; libr. Dekalb County Pub. Libr., Decatur, Ga., 1997—98; off-campus libr., Livingston Libr. Shorter Coll., Atlanta, 1998—, adj. instr., info. literacy program, 2004—. Mem.: Atlanta Area Bibliographic Instrn. Group, Southeastern Libr. Assn. (chair, libr. instrn. round table (lirt) 2003—08), Ga. Libr. Assn. (chair, distance learning interest group 2003—08), Ga. Assn. Instrnl. Tech., Assn. Ednl. Comm. and Tech. Liberal. Office: Shorter Coll 6151 Powers Ferry Rd NW Ste 300 Atlanta GA 30339

WILSON, MIRIAM GEISENDORFER, retired physician, educator; b. Yakima, Wash., Dec. 3, 1922; d. Emil and Frances Geisendorfer; m. Howard G. Wilson, June 21, 1947; children— Claire, Paula, Geoffrey, Nicola, Marla. BS, U. Wash., Seattle, 1944, MS, 1945; MD, U. Calif., San Francisco, 1950. Mem. faculty U. So. Calif. Sch. Medicine, LA, 1965—, prof. pediatrics, 1969—2004, emeritus prof. pediatrics, 2004—. Office: U So Calif Med Ctr 1129 N State St Rm 1g24 Los Angeles CA 90033-1044 Personal E-mail: mfgwil@verizon.net.

WILSON, MIRIAM JANET WILLIAMS, publishing executive; b. London, Ont., Can., July 13, 1939; d. Ralph George and Lillian Conn Williams; m. Carson Winnette, Nov. 20, 1960 (div. 1971); children: Barrie Carson Winnette, Rebecca Lynn Winnette; m. Charles Lindsay Wilson, Dec. 14, 1973; 1 child, Charles William Wilson; stepchildren: Kenneth M., Carol Ann, Catherine S., Nancy L., Patrick L. Diploma in nursing, Glendale (Calif.) Sanitarium & Hosp., 1960. RN, Calif., Va., Ohio, Md., W.Va. Head nurse emergency and med. fls. Glendale Sanitarium and Hosp., 1960-65; psychometrist Harding Hosp., Worthington, Ohio, 1969-73; biofeedback specialist in assn. Dr. Randolph P. Johnston, Winchester, Va., 1980-84; dir. Stress Ctr. for Children and Adults, Shepherdstown, W.Va., 1985-87; pres. Rocky River Pubs. LLC, Shepherdstown, 1987—. Lectr. ednl., profl. and civic groups, 1984—. Author: Help For Children, 7 edits., 1987-2004, Stress Stoppers, 2 edits., 1987-89; contbr. articles to profl. publs. Mem. NAFE, Internat. Platform Assn., Am. Booksellers Assn., N.Y. Acad. Scis., Shepherdstown Women's Club. Avocations: gardening, music, reading. Office: Rocky River Pubs LLC PO Box 1679 Shepherdstown WV 25443-1679 Office Phone: 304-876-1868. E-mail: rockyriverpublishers@citlink.net.

WILSON, MYRON ROBERT, JR., retired psychiatrist; b. Helena, Mont., Sept. 21, 1932; s. Myron Robert, Sr. and Constance Ernestine (Bultman) Wilson. BA, Stanford U., 1954, MD, 1957. Diplomate Am. Bd. Psychiatry and Neurology. Dir. adolescent psychiatry Mayo Clinic, Rochester, Minn., 1965—71; pres., psychiatrist in chief Wilson Ctr., Faribault, Minn., 1971—86, chmn., 1986—90; ret., 1990. Assoc. clin. prof. UCLA, 1985—99. Contbr. articles to profl. jours. Chmn., CEO C. B. Wilson Found., LA, 1972—2006; bd. dirs. Pasadena (Calif.) Symphony Orch. Assn., 1987; vestryman, treas. St. Thomas' Parish, LA, 1993—96. Lt. comdr. USN, 1958—60. Fellow, Mayo Grad. Sch. Medicine, Rochester, 1960—65. Fellow: Internat. Soc. Adolescent Psychiatry (founder, treas. 1985—88, sec. 1985—88, treas. 1988—92), Am. Soc. Adolescent Psychiatry, Am. Psychiat. Assn.; mem.: Order St. John of Jerusalem, Sigma Xi (Mayo Found. chpt.). Episcopalian. Office Phone: 760-325-4956. Personal E-mail: mrobertwilson@aol.com.

WILSON, NANCY ESTHER, social worker; b. Ahoskie, N.C., June 15, 1915; d. Albert Raleigh and Hattie Bessie (Turner) L.; m. Robert E. Jackson (dec.); 1 child, Dwight E. Jackson-Wilson (dec.); m. James M. Wilson (dec.); children— Suzanne Wanda (dec.), James Albert (dec.). Student, Wycoff Heights Sch. Nursing, Bklyn., 1960. Supervising field monitor Dept. Social Services, N.Y.C., 1983—; mem. Social Services Employees Union Forum for Social Services. Mem. tng. program for social service employees Girl Scouts U.S.A. Recipient Appreciation award City N.Y. Human Resources Adminstrn.; Pub. Service award City N.Y. Dept. Welfare, 1983; Profl. Achievement award Bur. Spl. Services, 1963. Democrat. Roman Catholic. Clubs: Bowling Team (Bklyn., N.Y.); Bus. Women (Euclid, N.Y.), Holy Rosary Ch. Rosary Soc. Avocations: bowling; gardening; reading. Home: 3724 Polar St Brooklyn NY 11224-1245

WILSON, NORMAN GLENN, church administrator, writer; b. Rensselaer, NY, Nov. 3, 1936; s. Lawrence Wilbur and Wilhelmena Augusta (Knapp) W.; m. Nancy Ann Deyo, Nov. 17, 1956; children: Beth, Lawrence, Jonathan. BRE in Religious Edn., United Wesleyan Coll., 1958, DD (hon.), 1986; MA in Biblical Studies, Winona Lake Sch. Theology, 1968. Pastor The Wesleyan Ch., 1958-76, Gloversville, NY, 1963-66, North Lakeport, Mich., 1966-70, Owosso, Mich., 1970-76, dir. comm. Indpls., 1992—. Program prodr., speaker The Wesleyan Hour, Indpls., 1975—; mem. gen. adminstrn. coun. The Wesleyan Ch., Indpls., 1992—; disting. lectr. Staley Found., 1986. Author: How to Have a Happy Home, 1976, Christianity in Shoe Leather, 1978, The Constitution of the Kingdom, 1989, People Just Like Us, 1994, Follow the Leader, A Daily Spiritual Journey, 1996; editor, contbr.: Journey Into Holiness, 2000; The Call to Contentment, 2002; editor The Wesleyan Advocate, 1992-2004, Wesleyan Life, 2004-. Mem. Nat. Religious Broadcasters (bd. dirs. 1984-2005, Merit award 1984). Mem. Wesleyan Ch. Avocations: painting, antique cars. Home: 304 Scarborough Way Noblesville IN 46060-3881 Business E-Mail: wilsonn@wesleyan.org.

WILSON, OWEN, actor; b. Dallas, Nov. 18, 1968; s. Robert and Laura Wilson. BA in English, U. Tex., Austin, 1991. Actor: (films) The Cable Guy, 1996, Anaconda, 1997, Armageddon, 1998; Permanent Midnight, 1998, The Minus Man, 1999, Breakfast of Champions, 1999, The Haunting, 1999, Shanghai Noon, 2000, Meet the Parents, 2000, Zoolander, 2001, Behind Enemy Lines, 2001, I Spy, 2002, Shanghai Knights, 2003, The Big Bounce, 2004, Starsky & Hutch, 2004, The Life Aquatic with Steve Zissou, 2004, Meet the Fockers, 2004, The Wendell Baker Story, 2005, Wedding Crashers, 2005, (voice) Cars, 2006, Night at the Museum, 2006, The Darjeeling Limited, 2007, Drillbit Taylor, 2008, Marley & Me, 2008, Night at the Museum: Battle of the Smithsonian, 2009; actor, writer (films) Bottle Rocket, 1996, actor, exec. prodr. Rushmore, 1998, The Royal Tenenbaums, 2001, actor, prodr. You, Me and Dupree, 2006, (voice only) (TV series) King of the Hill, 1997; actor: (TV films) Heat Vision and Jack, 1999; assoc. prodr. (films) As Good as It Gets, 1997. Recipient Favorite On-Screen Match-Up (with Vince Vaughn), People's Choice Award, 2006, Best On-Screen Team (with Vince Vaughn), MTV Movie awards, 2006. Office: c/o United Talent Agy 9560 Wilshire Blvd Ste 500 Beverly Hills CA 90212*

WILSON, OWEN MEREDITH, JR., lawyer, mediator, arbitrator; b. Oakland, Calif., Dec. 22, 1939; s. O. Meredith and Marian Wilson; m. Sandra A. Wilson (div.); children: Ann, Melissa, Jennifer; m. Teddi Anne Wilson; children: Amanda, Lisa. Student, U. Utah, 1957-59; AB, Harvard U., 1961; LLB, U. Minn., 1965. Bar: Oreg. 1965. Ptnr. Lane Powell PC, Portland, Oreg., 1969—2005; prin. Wilson Dispute Resolution, Portland, 2005—. Mem. mediation panel U.S. Dist. Ct., 1986—. Mem. bd. visitors Law Sch. U. Minn., 1990-96. Mem. ABA, Oreg. State Bar Assn., Multnomah Bar Assn. Office: 202 NW 20th Ave Portland OR 97209 Home Phone: 503-292-6981; Office Phone: 503-972-5090. Business E-Mail: met@wilsonadr.com.

WILSON, PATRICIA POTTER, library and information science educator; b. Jennings, La., May 3, 1946; d. Ralph Harold and Wilda Ruth (Smith) Potter; m. Wendell Merlin Wilson, Aug. 24, 1968. BS, La. State U., 1967; MS, U. Houston-Clear Lake, 1979; EdD, U. Houston, 1985. Cert. tchr., learning resources specialist (libr.), Tex. Tchr. England AFB Elem. Sch., La., 1967-68, Edward White Elem. Sch./Clear Creek Ind. Schs., Seabrook, Tex., 1972-77; libr. C.D. Landolt Elem. Sch., Friendswood, Tex., 1979-81; instr./lectr. children's lit. U. Houston, 1983-86; with U. Houston/Clear Lake, 1984-87, asst. prof. libr. sci. and reading, 1988-94, assoc. prof. learning resources and reading edn., 1994—2001, assoc. prof. emerita, 2001—. Cons. Hermann Hosp., Baywood Hosp., 1986-87, Bedford Meadows Hosp., 1989-90, Wetcher Clinic, 1989; co-owner, v.p. Potter Farms, Inc.; pres. cabinet U. Houston Ctrl., Clear Lake. Author: Happenings: Developing Successful Programs for School Libraries, 1987, The Professional Collection for Elementary Educators, 1996, Premiere Events: Library Programs That Inspire Elementary Patrons, 2001, Leadership for Today's School Library, 2001, Igniting the Spark: Library Programs that Inspire High School Patrons, 2001, Center Stage: Library Programs That Inspire Middle School Patrons, 2002, Eagle on Ice: Eagle Scoute Paul Siple's Antaractic Adventures With Commender Byrd, 2008; editor: A Review Sampler, 1985—86, 1989—90; contbg. editor: Tex. Libr. Jour., 1988—94; contbr. articles to profl. jours. Trustee Freeman Meml. Libr., Houston, 1982—87, v.p., 1985—86, pres., 1986—87; trustee Evelyn Meador Libr., 1993—94, adv. bd., 1994—, Houston Symphony League-Bay Area, 1996—2005, bd., chair ann. fund campaign, 2005; founder Friends of Neumann Libr., 1998—2001; chmn. hospitality com. Lunar Rendevous Festival, 1998—2001; gen. chmn. Lunar Rendezvous Festival, 2002, mem. adv. bd., 2002—; mem. Assistance League of the Bay Area, 1997—; vol. Houston: A Visit from St. Nicholas Com., 2004—, co-chmn. kick-off event, 2005; mem. adv. bd. Bay Area Soc. Prevention Cruelty Animals, 1994—98, Bay Area Turning Point, 1998—; bd. dirs. Sta. KUHT-TV, 1984—87, Bay Area Houston Ballet and Theatre, 2001—04, vice chair bd. dirs., 2003—04, chmn. kickoff event, 2003; dir. Learning Resources Book Rev. Ctr., 1989—90; bd. dirs. Armand Bayou Nature Ctr., Houston, 1989—94; mem. Bay Area Houston Econ. Partnership, 2002—, mem. banquet com., 2002—; mem. Longhorn devel. bd. NASA and Clear Creek Ind. Sch. Dist., 2005—; mem. devel. and adv. coun. U. Houston Clear Lake, 2006—. Recipient Rsch. award, Tex. State Reading Assn., 1993, Pres. award, Tex. Coun. Tchrs. English, Disting. Tchg. award, Enron Corp., 1996, Disting. Alumni award, U. Houston-Clear Lake, 1998, Disting. Alumna award, U. Houston, Coll. Edn., 2002, Disting. Alumni award, U. Houston Ctrl., 2005, Bravo award, Bay Area Houston Ballet & Theater, 2006, Kay Burnett Outstanding Friend of the Arts Award, Arts Alliance Ctr. at Clear Lake, 2008, Philanthropy award, U. Houston-Clear Lake Pres.'s Cabinet, 2009; named Outstanding Vol. of Yr., Houston's Nat. Philanthropy Day, 1999; named one of 10 Men and Women of Heart, Bay Area Turning Point, 2001; grantee, Tex. Libr. Assn., 1993. Mem. Nat. Coun. Tchrs. English (Books for You rev. com. 1985-88, 97-98, Your Reading rev. com. 1993-96), Tex. Coun. Tchrs. English, Antarctican Soc., Clear Lake Panhellenic Assn., Lakewood Yacht Club, Travelers' Century Club, Bay Oaks Country Club, Phi Kappa Phi (sec. 1997-98, pres. 1998-99).

WILSON, PATRICK JOSEPH, actor; b. Norfolk, Va., July 3, 1973; m. Dagmara Dominczyk, June 18, 2005; 1 child. BFA in drama, Carnegie Mellon U., 1995. Actor: (Broadway plays) The Gershwins' Fascinating Rhythm, 1999, The Full Monty, 2000—01, Oklahoma!, 2002, Barefoot in the Park, 2006, All My Sons, 2008; (films) My Sister's Wedding, 2001, The Alamo, 2004, The Phantom of the Opera, 2004, Hard Candy, 2005, Little Children, 2006 (Young Hollywood award, 2006), Running with Scissors, 2006, Brothers Three: An American Gothic, 2007, Purple Violets, 2007, Evening, 2007, Life in Flight, 2008, Lakeview Terrace, 2008, Passengers, 2008, Watchmen, 2009; (TV miniseries) Angels in America, 2003. Office: c/o Tony Lipp Creative Artists Agency 2000 Avenue of the Stars Los Angeles CA 90067*

WILSON, PATTI L., psychologist, educator; b. Memphis, May 21, 1974; d. Charles W. and Linda Fay Wilson; life ptnr. Dustin T. Gault. BA, Christian Bros. U., 1995; MS, PhD, U. Memphis, 2000. Cert. psychologist, health svc. provider Tenn., Health Related Bds., Bd. of Examiners in Psychology, 2002, profl. spl. group State Tenn. Dept. Edn., 2006. Assoc. prof. Austin Peay State U., Clarksville, Tenn., 2000—03; sch. psychologist Houston County Schs., Erin, Tenn., 2001—04, Clarksville-Montgomery County Schs., 2004—. Contbr. articles to profl. jours. Mem.: NASP, Tenn. Assn. Sch. Psychologists (bd. mem. 2002—08, pres. elect 2005, past pres. 2008, pres. 2007), Phi Kappa Phi, Psi Chi, Alpha Chi. Home: 2830 Scenic Dr Clarksville TN 37043 Office: CMCSS 621 Gracey Ave Clarksville TN 37040 Business E-Mail: patti.wilson@cmcss.net.

WILSON, PAUL HOLLIDAY, JR., lawyer; b. Schenectady, NY, Sept. 4, 1942; s. Paul H. and Sarah Elizabeth (MacLean) W.; m. Elaine Hawley Griffin, May 30, 1964; children: Hollace, Paul, Kirsten, Katherine. AB, Brown U., 1964; LLB, MBA, Columbia U., 1967. Bar: N.Y. 1967, U.S. Dist. Ct. (so. dist.) 1968. Law clk. U.S. Dist. Ct. (so. dist.) N.Y., NYC, 1967-68; assoc. Debevoise & Plimpton LLP, NYC, 1968-75, ptnr., 1976—2008, fin. ptnr., 1980—88, 1991—93, 2001—08, dep. presiding ptnr., 1993-98; exec. v.p., gen. counsel sec. 1st Wind Holdings, LLC, Boston, 2009—. Vice-chmn., trustee St. Michael's Montessori Sch., N.Y.C., 1977-79, chmn. bd. trustees, 1979-81. Mem. ABA, Assn. Bar City N.Y. (mem. commn. on securities regulations 1985-88). Clubs: Vineyard Haven Yacht (Mass.) (vice-commodore 1985, commodore 1986-87). Avocations: sailing, reading, music. Office: First Wind Holdings LLC 85 Wells Ave Newtown MA 02549 Home Phone: 212-534-8744; Office Phone: 857-226-5144. Business E-Mail: phwilson@firstwind.com.

WILSON, PAUL LOWELL, mortgage company executive, lawyer; b. May 12, 1951; s. James Joseph and Edna Vivian (Halterman) W.; children: Meredith Elaine, Taylor Halterman; m. Abigail Mayer. AB, W.Va. U., 1973; JD, Coll. of William of Mary, 1976. Bar: W.Va., 1976, U.S. Dist. Ct. (so. dist.) W.Va. 1976, U.S. Dist. Ct. (ea. dist.) Va. 1991. Assoc. Brown & Peyton, Charleston, W.Va., 1976-78; title atty. Lawyers Title Ins. Corp., Williamsburg, Va., 1978-80; counsel edn. com. W.Va. Legislature, Charleston, 1977-78; gen. counsel A J & L Corp., Williamsburg, 1983-85, v.p., gen. counsel, 1985-91; mng. dir. 1st Capital Comml. Funding, Inc., 1997—. Bd. dirs. 503 Cert. Devel. Co., Richmond, Sta. WHRO-TV. Mem. York County Sch. Bd., 1986-94, chmn., 1992-94; pres. Nat. Housing Corp., 1986-93, The Preservation Group, Inc., 1991-97. Mem. W.Va. State Bar, Sigma Phi Epsilon. Presbyterian. Office Phone: 704-970-6067.

WILSON, PEGGY, state legislator; b. Anamosa, Iowa, Sept. 8, 1945; m. Woody Wilson; children: Iad, Gina, Chris. A in Registered Nursing, U. Alaska; AS, Kirkwood Cmty. Coll., 1969—73. Cert. Nationally Cert. Sch. Nurse. State rep. Dist. 2, Alaska, 2001—; EMT Tok Area Emergency Mgmt. Svc. Mem. Coun. State Govts., 1990—93; mem. fiscal policy com. Nat. Conf. State Legislatures, 2001—06, mem. women's legis. network, 2003—; mem. Pacific Northwest Econ. Region, 2001—09, Western Legis. Forestry Task Force, 2001—04, Wrangell/Petersburg Resource Adv. Com., 2002—09, Alaska Comprhensive Ctr. Adv. Bd., 2006, Alaska-Can. Electrical Intertie Steering Com., 2006. Mem. Tok Ambulance Squad. Mem.: Bus. and Profl. Women, Rotary Internat., Pilot Internat. (v.p.). Republican. Office: State Capitol Rm 408 Juneau AK 99801-1182 Office Phone: 907-465-3824, 907-874-3088. Office Fax: 907-465-3175. Business E-Mail: Rep_Peggy_Wilson@legis.state.ak.us.

WILSON, PEGGY MAYFIELD, retired chemist; d. Isaac Newton and Ella Lockwood Mayfield; m. Irving Ray Dunlap Jr. (dec.); m. William W. Wilson III, July 25, 1975 (dec.). BS in Chemistry, U. Tex., Austin, 1948, PhD in Chemistry, 1952. Spl. instr. U. Tex., Austin, 1952—53; from rsch. technologist to sr. rsch. technologist Mobil Rsch. Devel. Corp., Dallas, 1953—84, group mgr. dept. rsch., 1984—89; pres. Greater Duncanville Indsl. Corp., Tex., 1991—2000, Stone Gap Indsl. Corp., Duncanville, 1991—2000; ret., 2000. Regent East Tex. State U., Commerce, 1981—87. Founder, econ. devel. City of Cedar Hill, Tex., 1991—96; adv. bd. Cedar Valley Cmty. Coll.; chmn. bd. dirs. Cedar Hill Econ. Devel. Corp., 1994—96; chmn. Cedar Hill Comprehensive Plan Bd., 1997—99; coun. mem. City of Cedar Hill, 1996—98; active State Rep. Exec. Com., Tex., 1971—80; bd. dirs., treas. Internat. Mus. Cultures. Recipient Jean Harris award, Rotary, 1998, Golden Cedar Lifetime award, Cedar Hill C. of C., 2001; named Outstanding Rep. Woman, Tex. Fedn. Rep. Women, 1973. Mem.: Am. Chem. Soc., World Affairs Coun., Cedar Summit Book Club. Republican. Methodist. Achievements include patents in field. Avocation: gardening. Home: 1819 W Belt Line Rd Cedar Hill TX 75104

WILSON, PETER SCOTT, lawyer; b. Edinburgh, July 15, 1955; B in Commerce, McGill U., 1976; JD, Harvard U., 1979. Bar: N.Y. 1980. Assoc. Cravath Swaine and Moore LLP, NYC, 1979-87, ptnr., corp., 1987—. Mem. ABA, N.Y. State Bar Assn., Assn. Bar City of N.Y., Internat. Bar Assn. Democrat. Presbyterian. Office: Cravath Swaine & Moore LLP Worldwide Plaza 825 8th Ave New York NY 10019-7475 Office Phone: 212-474-1767. Office Fax: 212-474-3700. Business E-Mail: pwilson@cravath.com.

WILSON, R. DALE, marketing educator; b. Ironton, Ohio, July 16, 1949; s. Robert J. and Treva L. (Shively) Wilson; m. Emily J. Ray, June 19, 1971; 1 child, Travis Ray. BBA cum laude, Ohio U., 1971; MBA, U. Toledo, 1972; PhD, U. Iowa, Iowa City, 1977. Asst. prof. mktg. Pa. State U., University Park, 1976-80; v.p., dir. mktg. scis. Batten, Barton, Durstine & Osborn, Inc., NYC, 1980-83; vis. prof. Cornell U., Ithaca, NY, 1983-84; assoc. prof. Mich. State U., East Lansing, 1984-87, prof., 1987—. Cons. in field. Contbr. articles to profl. jours. Youth baseball and basketball coach, East Lansing, 1989—98. Grantee, Pa. State U., Mich. State U., IBM Corp. Mem.: Am. Soc. Competitiveness, Inst. Ops. Rsch. and Mgmt. Scis. (assoc. editor interfaces, cert. recognition 1983), Am. Mktg. Assn., Am. Acad. Advt., Beta Gamma Sigma. Office: Mich State U Eli Broad Grad Sch Mgmt Dept Mktg N322 N Business Complex East Lansing MI 48824-1122 Office Phone: 517-432-6403. Business E-Mail: wilsonrr@msu.edu.

WILSON, RACHEL I., neurobiologist, educator; b. Kansas City, Mo. AB in Chemistry, Harvard U., Cambridge, Mass., 1996; PhD, Calif. Inst Tech., San Francisco, 2001. Tng. neurophysiologist Heinrich-Heine-Universität, Düsseldor, Germany; postdoctoral fellow Calif. Inst. Tech., 2001—04; asst. prof. neurobiology Harvard Med. Sch., Boston, 2004—. Contbr. articles to profl. jours. Recipient Internat. Grand Prize in neurobiology, Eppendorf AG & Science jour., 2007; named a Pew Scholar, U. Calif., San Francisco, 2005, MacArthur Fellow, The John D. and Catherine T. MacArthur Found., 2008. Achievements include research in how sensory stimuli are encoded in patterns of electrical activity in the brain. Office: Harvard Med Sch Dept Neurobiology 220 Longwood Ave Boston MA 02115 Office Phone: 617-432-5571. Office Fax: 617-734-7557. Business E-Mail: rachel_wilson@hms.harvard.edu.*

WILSON, RAINN D. (RAINN DIETRICH WILSON), actor; b. Seattle, Washington, Jan. 20, 1966; m. Holiday Reinhorn, 1995; 1 child, Walter Mckenzie. Attended, Tufts U., U. Washington; studied acting, NYU grad. acting program; MFA in Acting, NYU, Tisch Sch. Arts, 1989. Writer, dir. The New Bozena, 2005; actor: (films) Galaxy Quest, 1999, Almost Famous, 2000, America's Sweethearts, 2001, Wheelmen, 2002, Full Frontal, 2002, Self Storage, 2002, House of 1000 Corpses, 2003, The Life Coach, 2005, Sahara, 2005, Blue in Green, 2005, Dominion, 2006, My Super Ex-Girlfriend, 2006, The Last Mimzy, 2007, Juno, 2007, The Rocker, 2008, (voice) Monsters vs. Aliens, 2009, Transformers: Revenge of the Fallen, 2009; (TV films) The Expendables, 1999, Slice o' Life, 2003; (TV series) Six Feet Under, 2003—05, The Office, 2005— (Outstanding Performance by an Ensemble in a Comedy Series, SAG, 2007, 2008); performer: (Broadway plays) London Assurance, The Tempest, —, (off-broadway) The New Bonzena, Plunge, Venus, Titus Andronicus, Twelfth Night; guest appearances One Life to Live, 1997, When Billie Beat Bobby, 2001, Dark Angel, 2001, CSI: Crime Scene Investigation, 2001, Law & Order: Special Victims Unit, 2002, MDs, 2002, Monk, 2003, Numb3rs, 2005, Entourage, 2005. Recipient Comedy/Variety — Music, Awards, Tributes — Specials, Writers Guild America, 2009. Avocations: tennis, chess, music.*

WILSON, RALPH COOKERLY, JR., professional football team executive; b. Columbus, Ohio, Oct. 17, 1918; s. Ralph Cookerly and Edith (Cole) W.; children: Christy Cole, Linda Brown, Edith Denise. AB, U. Va., 1940; postgrad., U. Mich., 1940-41. Pres. Ralph C. Wilson Jr. Enterprises (privately owned family bus.); engaged in profl. football, roadbuilding Detroit, 1946—; pres., owner Buffalo Bills Profl. Football Club, 1959—. With USNR, 1941-46. Decorated Commendation medal; named to Pro Football Hall of Fame, 2009. Mem. Ocean Club of Fla., Country Club of Detroit, Grosse Pointe (Mich.) Club, Buffalo Country Club, Shriners. Presbyterian. Office: Buffalo Bills Ralph Wilson Stadium and Main Office 1 Bills Dr Orchard Park NY 14127-2296*

WILSON, RALPH SLOAN, retinal surgeon; b. El Dorado, Ark., Nov. 12, 1937; s. George Evander and Lauree Eta (Doss) W.; AB, Davidson Coll., 1959; BS, U. Ark., 1963, MD (Research fellow), 1963; m. Sarah Mignon Ross, Dec. 27, 1958; m. Ann Jameson, 1987; children: Ralph Sloan, William Gregory, Steven Robert, John Matsek (stepson). Intern, U. Ark. Hosps., Little Rock, 1963-64; postgrad. ophthalmology Harvard Med. Sch., Boston, 1964-65; resident ophthalmology U. Ark. Hosps., 1965, U. Tex. Med. Br., Galveston, 1965-67; Heed fellow retinal pathology and surgery Mass. Eye and Ear Infirmary, Harvard Med. Sch., Boston, 1969: asst. prof. and dir. retina services dept. ophthalmology U. Ark. Med. Center, Little Rock, 1970-75, assoc. prof., 1975-81, prof., 1981—95, prof. emeritus, 1995-, acting chmn. ophthalmology dept., 1974-75; practice medicine specializing in retinal surgery Retinal Group, LTD., Little Rock, 1975-99; mem. Ark. State Bd. Dispensing Opticians; dir. Retina Service, US VA Hosp., Little Rock; chief staff, exec. com. Doctors Hosp.; dir. Ritchie Grocer Co., S.W. Trading Corp. Chmn. admissions com. U. Ark. Coll. Medicine; trustee Lyon Coll. (formerly Ark. Coll.), 1982-; pres., bd. dirs. Retinal Research Fund; bd. dirs. Ark. Eye & Kidney Bank, Ark. Soc. for Prevention of Blindness, 1971-73. Served to lt. comdr. USNR, 1967-69. Diplomate Am. Bd. Ophthalmology (examiner 1973-83); Hoffmann La Roche grantee, 1966-67; recipient AMA Physicians Recognition awards, 1969-99. Mem. Am. Acad. Ophthalmology (speakers bur., hon. award, sr. hon. award Pub. Info. Com.), Am. Acad. Retinal Surgeons (formerly Vitreous Soc., charter mem.), Assn. Rsch. and Vision in Ophthalmology, AMA, Ark., Pulaski County med. socs., Am., Ark. Assns. Ophthalmology, Am. Ophthal. Soc. (athletic chmn.), AAUP, Research to Prevent Blindness, So. Med. Assn., Pan Am. Soc. Ophthalmology, Société Française d'Ophthalmologie, Sociedad Boliviana de Oftalmologia, New Orleans Acad. Ophthalmology, Soc. Eye Surgeons, Internat. Eye Found., U. Tex. Med. Br. Ophthalmology Alumni Assn. (pres. 1970-72), Univ. Med. Group, Soc. Heed Fellows, Little Rock Acad. Surgery, Retina Soc., Ark. Acad. Ophthalmology (pres. 1975-76), Ark. Found. for Med. Care, Assn. VA Ophthalmologists, Ark. Ophthalmology sect. of Ark. Med. Soc. (pres. 1977-78), Assn. Mil. Surgeons, Alpha Omega Alpha, Alpha Tau Omega, Sigma Xi. Contbr. articles to profl. jours., Research in ocular melanomas, ocular fireworks injuries, mechanism of human accomodation and multiple ocular surgical techniques; holder patents in field. Home: 140 Washington Rd Rye NH 03870 Personal E-mail: cottagers@comcast.net. E-mail: cottagers@aol.com.

WILSON, REGGIE, artistic director, choreographer, dancer; b. Milw., 1967; BFA, Tisch Sch. Arts, NYU, 1988. Founder, dir. Reggie Wilson/Fist and Heel Performance Group, Bklyn., 1989—. Choreographer Either Side of the Mountain, Israel Mus., 1988, N/um, Dance Theater Workshop, NYC, 1989, Kaffir, 1990, A Black Burlesque, 1995, Wangena -- the birthday concerts, 2000, The Tail: Npinpee Nckutchie and the Tail of the Golden Dek, 2006, Shouting Rings, Movement Rsch., NYC, 1994, Fête Fuh So!, Bklyn. Acad. Music Majestic Theater, 1995, Love, Danspace Project, NYC, 1996, Africa in America, Tisch Auditorium, 1997, Rum and Salvation, Queen's Hall, Trinidad and Tobago, 1998, Qoqoda, Dance Place, Washington, 1999, The Tie-Tongued Goat and the Lightning Bug Who Tried to Put Her Foot Down, Danspace Project, 2002, Big Brick -- a man's piece, City Ctr., NYC, 2004, Left Moat-East, Governor's Island, NYC, 2006, We Ain't Going Home But We Gonna Get the Hell Up Outta Here, Victoria Theater, Dayton, Ohio, 2007, Accounting for Customs, Lower Manhattan Cultural Coun., 2007, Kwenda Vutuka, French Inst., NYC, 2008, The GOOD DANCE-dakar/brooklyn, Bklyn. Acad. Music Next Wave Festival, 2009. Recipient NY Dance and Performance (Bessie) award, 2002, Alpert award in the Arts for Dance, 2009; fellow Nat. Endowment for the Arts, 1992—96, NY Found. Arts, 1994, 1997, 2004, Guggenheim Found., 2002; McKnight Nat. fellow, Minn. Dance Alliance, 2000. Office: c/o Sopie Myrtil-McCounty Pentacle 246 W 38th St 8th Fl New York NY 10018 also: Fist & Heel Performance Group 476 Dean St #2 Brooklyn NY 11217 Office Phone: 718-636-9509, 212-278-8111 ext. 313. E-mail: fistandheel@verizon.net.*

WILSON, RHYS THADDEUS, lawyer; b. Albany, Ga., May 9, 1955; s. Joseph Farr Jr. and Betty Ann W.; m. Carolyn Reid Saffold, June 2, 1984. AB, Duke U., 1976; JD, U. Ga., 1979; LLM, Emory U., 1985. Bar: Ga. 1979. Pvt. practice law, Atlanta, 1979-89; sr. v.p., gen. counsel Monarch Capital Group, Inc., Atlanta, 1989-92, Jackson & Coker, Inc., Atlanta, 1992-93; pres. Jackson & Coker Locum Tenens, Inc., Atlanta, 1993-95; ptnr. Robins, Kaplan, Miller & Ciresi, Atlanta, 1995—2005, Nelson Mullins Riley & Scarborough LLP, 2006—. Spkr. CLE seminars. Contbr. articles to profl. jours. Bd. dirs. Atlanta Opera Co. Named Ga. Super Lawyer, Mergers & Acquisitions, 2004—. Mem. ABA, Ga. Bar Assn. (chmn. internat. law sect. 1987-88, exec. com. corp. and banking law sect. 1987-89, editl. bd. Ga. State Bar Jour. 1986-89), Atlanta Bar Assn. (editor newsletter 1984-86, Outstanding Svc. award 1986), Assn. for Corp. Growth, Atlanta Tech. Angels (bd. dirs. 2001-08), Visage Internat., Capital City Club. Episcopalian.

WILSON, RICHARD CHRISTIAN, engineering firm executive; b. Bethlehem, Pa., July 17, 1921; s. Christian and Laura Barrows (Langham) W.; m. Jean M. Avis, July 16, 1949; children— Richard A., Christy. BS, Carnegie-Mellon U., 1943; MS, Lehigh U., 1947; PhD, U. Mich., 1961. Mfg. engr. Westinghouse Electric Corp., East Pittsburgh, 1943; instr. mech. engring. Carnegie-Mellon U., Pitts., 1943-44; vacuum test engr. Kellex Corp., NYC, 1944; area supr. Carbide & Carbon Chem. Co., Oak Ridge, 1945-46; apparatus engr. Westinghouse Electric Corp., Jackson, Mich., 1947-55; instr. indsl. and operation engring. U. Mich., 1955-61, asst. prof., 1961-63, assoc. prof., 1963-66, prof., 1966-85, chmn. dept., 1973-77, assoc. dean Coll. Engring., 1968-72; pres. Techware, Inc., 1985-86, ret., 1986. Dir. Cascade Data Corp., 1969-72 Contbr. articles to profl. jours. Bd. dirs. Ecumenical Assn. Internat. Understanding, 1970-87, pres., 1975-76, 86-87; dir. Washtenaw Trombones and Jazzbones, 1995—. Mem. IEEE, Inst. Mgmt. Sci., Am. Inst. Indsl. Engrs., Ops. Research Soc. Am., Sigma Xi, Beta Theta Pi, Phi Kappa Phi. Clubs: Rotary. Home: 805 Mount Pleasant Ave Ann Arbor MI 48103-4776 Office: U Mich Dept Indsl Engring Ann Arbor MI 48109

WILSON, RICHARD EDWARD, composer, music educator, pianist; b. Cleve., May 15, 1941; s. James F. and Edith Ann (Zingler) Wilson; m. Adene Stevenson Green, May 15, 1971; children: Katherine Blanca, James Graham. AB magna cum laude, Harvard U., 1963; MA, Rutgers U., 1966. Asst. prof. music Vassar Coll., Poughkeepsie, NY, 1966-70, assoc. prof. music, 1970-76, prof. music, 1976—, chmn. dept. music, 1979-82, 85-88, 95-98, Mary Conover Mellon Chair, 1988—. Composer-in-residence Am. Symphony Orch., 1992—. Composer: Music for Violin and Violoncello, 1969; composer: (opera) Aethelred the Unready, 1994; composer: (four string quartets); composer: Eclogue for Piano Solo, 1974 (Burge prize, 1979), Figuration, 1980, Two Symphonies, 1984, 1987, Agitations, 1994, Pamietam, 1995, Five Love Songs, 1995, Transfigured Goat, 1996, A Child's London, 1997, Triple concerto for horn, bass clarinet, marimba and orch., 1998 (Koussevitzky commn.), Intimations for Piano and Orch., 2000, Revelry for Full Orchestra, 2002, Peregrinations for Viola and Orchestra, 2002, Organiety, 2003, Senza Furore, 2004, Diablerie, 2004, Timeshare, 2007, Gravitas, 2006, Chamisha Mizmorey Tehilim, 2006, String Quartet No 5, The Cells Has Many Secrets, 2008, Mnemonics, 2009, others. Recipient Walter Hinrichsen award, Am. Acad. Inst. Arts and Letters, 1986, Cleve. Arts prize, 1988, Exec.'s award Dutchess County, 1989, Stoeger prize, Chamber Music Soc. Lincoln Ctr., 1994, Acad. award in music, Am. Acad. Arts and Letters, 2004, Roger Session Memorial Boglizsco Fellowship, 2006—07;. Guggenheim fellow, 1992. Mem.: ASCAP, Am. Music Ctr., Century Assn., Harvard Club, Phi Beta Kappa. Home: 27 Vassar Lake Dr Poughkeepsie NY 12603-3120 Office: Vassar Coll Dept Music PO Box 18 Poughkeepsie NY 12604-0001

WILSON, RICHARD HARRY, JR., congressional chief of staff; b. Schnectady, NY, Aug. 19, 1957; s. Richard Harry and Phyllis JoAn Wilson; m. Leslie Jean Frazier, Dec. 5, 1987; children: Robert Dale Gordon, Stefanie Marie Gordon. BS summa cum laude, Martin U., Indpls., 2004; postgrad., Trinity Theol. Sem., Newburgh, Ind., 2007—. Dep. chief of staff Congressman Dan Burton, Indpls., 1993—. Mem. com. Dan Burton for Congress, 1992. Sgt. US Army, 1986—91. Recipient Pres.'s award, Martin U., 2005; named Ky. Col., Gov. of Ky., 1995, Sagamore of the Wabash, Gov. of Ind., 2001; named a Disting. Grad., Class of 1975, William Fremd HS, 2005. Mem.: VFW (life), DAV (life), Am. Polit. Sci. Assn., Acad. Polit. Sci., Am. Legion, Phi Kappa Tau. Republican. Lutheran. Office: Congressman Dan Burton 8900 Keystone Crossing Suite 1050 Indianapolis IN 46240 Office Fax: 317-846-7306. Personal E-mail: wilson_richard@comcast.net. Business E-Mail: rick.wilson@mail.house.gov.

WILSON, RICHARD K., microbiologist, researcher; AB in Microbiology, Miami U., 1981; PhD in Biochemistry, U. Okla., 1986. Rsch. fellow Calif. Inst. Technol., 1986—90; prof. genetics & microbiology Washington U. Sch. Medicine, 1990—, dir. Genome Sequencing Ctr., 1990—; founder & mng. dir. Orion Genomics, 1998—; researcher Siteman Cancer Ctr. Office: The Genome Center Washington University School of Medicine 4444 Forest Park Ave Campus Box 8501 Saint Louis MO 63108 Office Phone: 314-286-1800. Office Fax: 314-286-1810.*

WILSON, RICHARD LEE, political science professor; b. Worthington, Minn., Dec. 20, 1944; s. G. Roy and Dorothy Eileen (Johnson) W.; m. Carolyn Ann Dirks, Aug. 24, 1968 (div.); 1 child, Kevin Richard. BA, U. Chgo., 1966, postgrad., 1966-67; PhD, Johns Hopkins U., 1971; postgrad., Columbia U., 1988, Stanford U., 1992. Congl. aide 4th Congl. Dist. Md., 1971; asst. prof. polit. sci. U. Tenn., Chattanooga, 1971-76, assoc. prof., 1976-87, prof., 1988—. Registrar-at-large Hamilton County Election Commn., 1977-84; lectr. Robert A. Taft Inst. Govt., U. Tenn., Nashville, 1978, 79, 81; supr. state legis. and met. internship program U. Chattanooga, 1972-86; vis. prof. Govt. Fgn. Affairs Coll., Beijing, 1986-87; Fulbright prof. govt. Beijing U., 1988-89, Samford U., Birmingham, Ala., 1991-93. Author: Tennessee Politics, 1976, American Government, 1993, 2d edit., 1995, American Political Leaders, 2002 (Choice award 2003); editor: Encyclopedia of American Government, 2001, Historical Encyclopedia of Am. Bus., 2009; co-editor: Ready Reference: Censorship, 1997 (named Outstanding Ref. Source 1998 ALA), Encyclopedia of the Supreme Court, 2000 (named OUtstanding Ref. Scouce 2002 ALA); contbr. chpts. to books. Chmn. Hamilton County Health Planning Adv. Council, 1975-79; bd. dirs. Ga.-Tenn. Regional Health Commn., 1978-82; active Tenn. State Health Coordinating Council, 1977-81; exec. com. State Health Coordinating Council, 1979-81. Named Outstanding Educator of Yr., Signal Mountain (Tenn.) Jaycees, 1973, Outstanding Prof. of Yr., SGA, 1985-86, Outstanding Reference Source ALA, 2002; recipient Polit. Edn. award NAACP, 1980, Excellent Prof. award Fgn. Affairs Coll., Beijing, 1987, UTC Exceptional Merit award, 1990, 94; NEH grantee, 1988, 92. Mem. So. Polit. Sci. Assn., Midwest Polit. Sci. Assn., Am. Polit. Sci. Assn. (nat. rsch. grant 1995), Nat. Soc. Internships and Exptl. Edn., SAR, China People's Friendship Assn., Aircraft Owners and Pilots Assn. Methodist. Office: Univ of Tenn Dept Political Sci Fletcher Hall 414 Chattanooga TN 37403 Office Phone: 423-425-4226, 423-425-4281. Business E-Mail: richard-wilson@utc.edu.

WILSON, RICHARD RANDOLPH, lawyer; b. Pasadena, Calif., Apr. 14, 1950; s. Robert James and Phyllis Jean (Blackman) W.; m. Catherine Goodhugh Stevens, Oct. 11, 1980; children: Thomas Randolph, Charles Stevens. BA cum laude, Yale U., 1971; JD, U. Wash., 1976. Bar: Wash.

1976, U.S. Dist. Ct. (wc. dist.) Wash. 1976, U.S. Ct. Appeals (9th cir.) 1977. Assoc. Hillis, Phillips, Cairncross, Clark & Martin, Seattle, 1976-81, ptnr., 1981-84, Hillis, Cairncross, Clark & Martin, Seattle, 1984-87, Hillis Clark Martin & Peterson, Seattle, 1987—, mem. mgmt. com., 1991—2007, chmn. land use group, 2007—. Pres. Plymouth Housing Group, Seattle, 1998—2000, trustee, 1994—2001, bd. dirs., 2001—. Quality Child Care Svcs., Inc., Seattle; lectr. various bar assns., 1980—. Contbr. articles to profl. jours. Chmn. class agts. Yale U. Alumni Fund, New Haven, 1985—87, class agt., 1971—2001, mem. class coun., 1991—96, mem. Western Wash. exec. com. Yale capital campaign, 1992—97, vice chmn. leadership gifts com. Yale 25th reunion, 1995—96, 30th reunion, 2000—01; mem., vice chmn. Medina (Wash.) Planning Commn., 1990—92; trustee, performer Gilbert & Sullivan Soc., 1984—91; chmn. capital campaign Plymouth Congl. Ch., 1995, moderator, pres. ch. coun. Seattle, 1998—2000, pres. ch. corp., 2004—05. Mem. ABA, Wash. State Bar Assn. (dir. environ. and land use law sect. 1985-88), Seattle-King County Bar Assn., Kingsley Trust Assn. (trustee 2003-06, pres. 1996-98), Yale Assn. We. Wash. Congregationalist. Avocations: acting, singing, rare book collecting. Home: 2305 86th Ave NE Bellevue WA 98004-2416 Office: Hillis Clark Martin & Peterson 1221 2nd Ave Ste 500 Seattle WA 98101-2925 Office Phone: 206-623-1745, 206-470-7604. Business E-Mail: rrw@hcmp.com. *Notable cases include: Barrie vs. Kitsap County, 1980; Sore vs. Snohomish County, 1983; Conv. Ctr. Coalition vs. City of Seattle, 1986; Orion Corp. vs. State, 1987, Cougar Mountain Assocs. vs. King County, 1988; King County vs. Central Puget Sound Growth Management Hearings Board, 1998, 1999; Quadrant Corp. v. Central Puget Sound Growth Mgt. Hearings Bd., 2005.*

WILSON, ROBERT FOSTER, lawyer; b. Windsor, Colo., Apr. 6, 1926; s. Foster W. and Anne Lucille (Svedman) W.; m. Mary Elizabeth Clark, Mar. 4, 1951 (div. Feb. 1972); children: Robert F., Katharine A.; m. Sally Anne Nemec, June 8, 1982. BA in Econs., U. Iowa, 1950, JD, 1951. Bar: Iowa 1951, U.S. Dist. Ct. (no. and so. dists.) Iowa 1956, U.S. Ct. Appeals (8th cir.) 1967. Atty. FTC, Chgo., 1951-55; pvt. practice, Cedar Rapids, Iowa, 1955—. Pres. Lawyer Forms, Inc.; dir. Lawyers Forms, Inc.; mem. Iowa Reapportionment Com., 1968; del. to U.S. and Japan Bilateral Session on Legal and Econ. Rels. Conf., Tokyo, 1988, Moscow Conf. on Law and Bilateral Rels., Moscow, 1990; U.S. del. to Moscow Conf. on Legal and Econ. Rels., 1990. Mem. Iowa Ho. of Reps., 1959-60; pres. Linn County Day Care, Cedar Rapids, 1968-70. Sgt. U.S. Army, 1944-46. Mem. ATLA, Am. Arbitration Assn. (panel arbitrators), Iowa Bar Assn., Iowa Trial Lawyers Assn., Linn County Bar Assn., Am. Legion (judge adv. 1970-75, 87-93), Cedar View Country Club, Elks, Eagles, Delta Theta Phi. Democrat. Home: 2179 Blake Blvd SE Cedar Rapids IA 52403-1128 Office: 810 Dows Bldg Cedar Rapids IA 52403-7010 Home Phone: 319-364-4518; Office Phone: 319-364-1538. Personal E-mail: rwilsonlaw@aol.com.

WILSON, ROBERT WARNE, philanthropist; b. Detroit, Nov. 3, 1926; s. Clarence Warne Wilson and Margaret Ballantyne; m. Marillyn Buelow, Apr. 1957 (div. 1977). BA in Econs. magna cum laude, Amherst Coll., Mass., 1946; MA in Econs., U. Mich., 1947; postgrad., Mich. Law Sch., 1948-49. Trainee First Boston Corp., NYC, 1949-50, 52-53; securities analyst Nat. Bank of Detroit, 1953-58; securities analyst to v.p. Gen. Am. Inv., NYC, 1958-62; securities analyst A.G. Becker & Co., NYC, 1962-68; investor, 1968—86; philanthropist, 1987—. Bd. dirs. Bklyn. Mus., 1974-88, Bklyn. Botanic Garden, 1974-88, NYC Opera, 1977-98, chmn. 1981-93; adv. bd. Met. Opera, 1979-81; trustee Environtl. Def., 1986—, Lyric Opera of Chgo. Nat. Bd., 1995-01, Manhattan Inst., 1986-02, Whitney Mus. of Am. Art, 1978— v.p., World Monuments Fund, 1990— vice chmn., Deafness Rsch. Found., 1998-01. With US Army, 1951—52. Mem.: Phi Beta Kappa. Republican. Avocations: opera, museums, theater, movies, sightseeing. Office: 520 83rd St Brooklyn NY 11209-4520 Office Phone: 718-748-6113.

WILSON, ROBERT WOODROW, radio astronomer; b. Houston, Jan. 10, 1936; s. Ralph Woodrow and Fannie May (Willis) W.; m. Elizabeth Rhoads Sawin, Sept. 4, 1958; children: Philip Garrett, Suzanne Katherine, Randal Woodrow. BA with honors in Physics, Rice U., 1957; PhD, Calif. Inst. Tech., 1962. Research fellow Calif. Inst. Tech., Pasadena, 1962-63; mem. tech. staff AT&T Bell Labs., Holmdel, NJ, 1963—94, head wireless tech. rsch. dept., 1976-94; sr. sci. Harvard-Smithsonian Ctr. for Astrophysics, Cambridge, Mass., 1994—. Adj. prof. SUNY, 1978—. Discoverer 3 deg. k microwave background radiation, 1965, CO and other molecules in interstellar space using their millimeter wavelength radiation;. Recipient Henry Draper medal, Royal Astron. Soc., London, 1977, Nobel prize in physics, 1978, Herschel Medal, 1977; named Fairchild Disting. scholar, Caltech., 1987; fellow NSF fellow, 1958—61, Cole fellow, 1957—58. Mem.: AAAS, NAS (Herschel medal 1977), Internat. Sci. Radio Union, Am. Phys. Soc., Internat. Astron. Union, Am. Astron. Soc., Sigma Xi, Phi Beta Kappa. Office: Harvard-Smithsonian Ctr Astrophysics Rm M-309 MS 42 60 Garden St Cambridge MA 02138-2306 E-mail: rwilson@cfa.com.*

WILSON, ROBERTA BUSH, retired psychotherapist, accountant; b. Watertown, NY, Dec. 23, 1937; d. Robert King and Barbara P. (Wiggins) Banks; m. Marvin D. Bush, Feb. 28, 1959 (div. 1977); m. Asa A. Wilson, July 29, 2004. BA, Glenville State Coll., 1977; MS, W.Va. U., Morgantown, 1985. Lic. profl. therapist W.Va. Acct. GE Plastics, Parkensburg, W.Va., 1959—77; lit. vol. Parkensburg, 1977—89; outpatient site head Abraxas, Parkensburg, 1989—95; psychotherapist Westbrook Health Svc., Parkensburg, 1996—97; ret., 1997. Pres., bd. dirs. Lit. Vol. Program of Wood County, Parkersburg. Mem.: Profl. Women's Assn. (pres., bd. dirs., Hall of Fame 1995). Episcoplian. Avocations: gardening, travel, photography. Home: 111 Canterbury Dr Parkersburg WV 26104-8057

WILSON, ROBIN, interior designer; BA, U. Tex., Austin; MS in Real Estate Fin., NYU. Formerly with Mercer Mgmt. Consulting, Heidrick & Struggles; chmn., CEO Robin Wilson Home, 2000—. Commentator O at Home, MarketWatch, Wall Street Journ., CNN, ABC, NBC, CBS. Bd. mem. Boston Symphony Orch. Overseers, 1993—2003, YWCA, Austin, Boston & NYC, 1988—98, DoSomething, 2003—05, Public Allies, 2006—07. Named one of The 50 Most Powerful Women in NYC, NY Post, 2007. Mem.: Internat. Interior Design Assn. Office: Robin Wilson Home 230 Park Ave Ste 1000 New York NY 10169 Office Phone: 212-863-9197.

WILSON, ROBIN SCOTT, retired academic administrator, writer; b. Columbus, Ohio, Sept. 19, 1928; s. John Harold and Helen Louise (Walker) W.; m. Patricia Ann Van Kirk, Jan. 20, 1951; children: Kelpie, Leslie, Kari, Andrew. BA, Ohio State U., 1950; MA, U. Ill., 1951, PhD, 1959. Fgn. intelligence officer CIA, Washington, 1959-67; prof. English Clarion State Coll., Pa., 1967-70; assoc. dir. Com. Instnl. Cooperation, Evanston, Ill., 1970-77; assoc. provost instrn. Ohio State U., Columbus, 1977-80; univ. pres. Calif. State U., Chico, 1980-93, pres. emeritus, 1993—. Author: Those Who Can, 1973, Death By Degrees, 1995, Paragons, 1996; short stories, criticism, articles on edn. Lt. USN, 1953-57. Mem. AAAS, Phi Kappa Phi E-mail: robinwilson@comcast.net.

WILSON, ROBLEY CONANT, JR., language educator, editor, writer; b. Brunswick, Maine, June 15, 1930; s. Robley Conant and Dorothy May (Stimpson) W.; m. Charlotte A. Lehon, Aug. 20, 1955 (div. 1991); children: Stephen, Philip; m. Susan Hubbard, June 17, 1995. BA, Bowdoin Coll., 1957, D.Litt (hon.), 1987; M.F.A., U. Iowa, 1968. Reporter Raymondville Chronicle, Tex., 1950-1951; asst. publicity dir. N.Y. State Fair Syracuse, 1956; instr. Valparaiso U., Ind., 1958-63; asst. prof. English U. No. Iowa, Cedar Falls, 1963-69, assoc. prof., 1969-75, prof., 1975-2000, prof. emeritus, 2000—, editor N.Am. Rev. Cedar Falls, 1969-2000. Author: The Pleasures of Manhood, 1977, Living Alone, 1978, Dancing for Men, 1983 (Drue Heinz Lit. prize, 1982), Kingdoms of the Ordinary (Agnes Lynch Starrett award, 1986), Terrible Kisses, 1989, A Pleasure Tree, 1990 (Soc. Midland Authors Poetry award, 1990), The Victim's Daughter, 1991, A Walk Through the Human Heart, 1996, Everything Paid For, 1999, The Book of Lost Fathers, 2001, Splendid Omens, 2004, The World Still Melting, 2005; co-editor: 100% Pure Florida Fiction, 2000. Bd. dirs. Associated Writing Programs, Norfolk, Va., 1983-86; pres. Iowa Woman Endeavors, Inc., 1986-90. With USAF, 1951-55. Guggenheim fellow, 1983-84, Nicholl Screenwriting fellow, 1995-96. Mem.: PEN, Authors' Guild. Home: PO Box 4009 Winter Park FL 32793-4009

WILSON, RONALD A., judge; b. 1968; Presiding judge South Tucson City Ct., 2002—. Recipient Rosa Parks Living History Makers award, NAACP, 2006; named 40 Under 40 Tucson Bus. Edge Man of Yr., 2006. Personal E-mail: ronaldawilson@hotmail.com.

WILSON, RONALD LAWRENCE, professional hockey coach, former professional hockey player; b. Windsor, Ont., Can., May 28, 1955; BA in Econs., Providence Coll., 1977. Defenseman Toronto Maple Leafs, 1975—80, Minn. North Stars, 1985—88; asst. coach Moncton Hawks, 1988—90, Vancouver Canucks, 1990—93; head coach Anaheim Mighty Ducks, 1993—97, Washington Capitals, 1997—2002, San Jose Sharks, 2002—08, Toronto Maple Leafs, 2008—. Head coach Team USA, World Cup of Hockey, 1996, 2004, US Olympic Hockey Team, Nagano, Japan, 1998. Named to NCAA All-Am. East 1st Team, 1974—76, Providence Hall of Fame. Avocation: golf. Office: Toronto Maple Leafs Air Canada Ctr 40 Bay St Ste 300 Toronto ON M5J 2X2 Canada

WILSON, ROSS, former ambassador; b. Mpls., 1955; m. Margo Squire; 2 children. BA, U. Minn., 1977; MA, Columbia U., 1979; grad., Nat. War Coll., 1995. Intern Office of Soviet Union Affairs US Dept. State, Washington, 1978-80, econ. officer Office of Soviet Union Affairs, 1980-82, 87-90, polit. officer Office of Egyptian Affairs, 1982-84, econ.-comml. officer Prague, 1985-87, spl. asst. to under sec. for econ. & agrl. affairs Washington, 1990-92, dep. exec. sec., 1992-94, US Consul Gen. Melbourne, Australia, 1995-97, prin. dep. to amb.-at-Large, spl. adv. to sec. for new Ind. States of the former Soviet Union Washington, 1997—2000, US amb. to Azerbaijan Baku, 2000—03, exec. asst. & chief of staff for dep. sec. Washington, 2005, US amb. to Turkey Ankara, 2005—08; US sr. negotiator for the Free Trade Area of the Americas Office US Trade Rep., Exec. Office of the Pres., Washington, 2003—05. Recipient Presdl. Meritorious Svc. award, 2005, Azerbaijan Order of Honor.*

WILSON, RUSSELL EDWARD, music educator; b. Atlanta, Ga., Jan. 25, 1963; s. Thomas Edward and Vivian Heaton Wilson. M of Music Edn., VanderCook Coll. Music, 1994; MusB, Ga. State U., 1985. Cert. elem., secondary tchr. Ga. Band dir. Hapeville HS, 1987, North Clayton Mid. Sch., College Park, 1987—92, Riverdale Mid. Sch., 1992—98, Mundy's Mill Mid. Sch., Jonesboro, Ga., 1998—2006, Lee Mid. Sch., 2006—, Coweta County, 2006—. Lead tchr. Clayton County Pub. Schools, Jonesboro, Ga., 2001—06; pvt. studio instrn. Oboe Studio, McDonough, Ga., 1981—. Musician (prin. oboist): Tara Winds Concert Band, 1988—. Asst. orch. dir. First Bapt. Ch., Jonesboro, 2004—; comm. dir. Tara Winds Concert Band, Atlanta, 2005—06. Recipient Legion of Honor, John Philip Sousa Found., 2005. Mem.: Ga. Music Educators Assn. (dist. treas. 1990—92), Music Educators Nat. Conf., Internat. Double Reed Soc., Nat. Band Assn. Home: 366 Whitney Ln Mcdonough GA 30253 Personal E-mail: oboeman@aol.com. Business E-Mail: russell.wilson@cowetaschools.org.

WILSON, SAMUEL EARL, anesthesiologist; b. Ala. BS in Biology, Morehosue Coll., Altanta, 1981. Staff anesthesiologist Alfred I. duPont Hosp. Children, Wilmington, Del., 2005—. Mem.: Am. Soc. Anesthesiology. Office: Alfred I duPont Hosp Children 1600 Rockland Rd Wilmington DE 19803 Office Phone: 302-651-5340. Personal E-mail: samuel.wilson@mac.com.

WILSON, SARAH ELIZABETH, music educator; b. Lubbock, Tex., Sept. 4, 1981; d. C. Roy and Jane Ann Henry Wilson. BA in English, Oberlin Coll., Ohio, 2004; BM in Cello Performance, Oberlin Conservatory Music, 2005; MM in Cello Performance, Rice U., Houston, 2007. Cert. cello tchr. Suzuki Assn. Americas, 2007. Pvt. cello instr., Midland, Tex., 2003—; prin. cello Lubbock Symphony Orch., Tex., 2007—08, Midland-Odessa Symphony & Chorale, 2007—, cellist permian basin string quartet, 2007—; instr. cello & music appreciation U. Tex. Permian Basin, Odessa, 2008—; cellist Abilene Philharm. Orch., Tex., 2008—. Mem.: Suzuki Assn. Americas. Liberal. Roman Catholic. Avocations: cooking, gardening, tennis, travel. Home: 3416 75th St Lubbock TX 79423

WILSON, SCOTT THOMAS, psychologist, researcher; b. Bayonne, NJ, July 29, 1969; s. John Thomas and Patricia Jean Wilson; m. Denise Figlar, May 16, 1999; children: Liam Patrick, Ella Kinsey. BA in Psychology, Rutgers U., 1992; PhD in Clin. Psychology, Columbia U., 2003. Lic. clin. psychologist NY. Predoctoral fellow Columbia U., NYC, 1999—2000, postdoctoral rsch. fellow in psychiatry, 2005—; rsch. scientist NY State Psychiat. Inst., NYC, 2002—05; pvt. practice NYC, 2005—. Cons. Amador and Assocs., LLC, NYC, 2004—. Contbr. Suicide in Schizophrenia. Fellow Nat. Rsch. Svc. award, NIMH, 1999. Mem.: APA. Achievements include research in patients with severe mental illnesses, including schizophrenia and borderline personality disorder. Business E-Mail: stw16@columbia.edu.

WILSON, SHANDRA SHEPPARD, urologist; b. Wheatrige, Colo., Mar. 9, 1972; d. Sharon Marie and William David Sheppard; m. David Alliott Wilson; children: Amanda Nicole, Andrew Gabriel. BA, Denver U., 1993; BS; MD, Washington U., St. Louis, 1997. Resident U. Southern Calif., LA, 2000—03; fellow, urology, oncology U. Colo., 2003—04, asst. prof. Aurora, 2004—. Presenter in field. Contbr. articles to profl. jours. Local Bladder Cancer grant, U. Colo., 2006. Mem.: Am. Urologic Assn. Avocations: hiking, camping, running, snowboarding, travel. Home: 16 Mountain Willow Dr Littleton CO 80127 Office: Univ Colorado HSC 12631 E 17th Ave MS 319 Aurora CO 80045 Office Fax: 720-848-0170; Home Fax: 720-848-0180. Business E-Mail: shandra.wilson@uchsc.edu.

WILSON, STANLEY CHARLES, artist, educator, curator, art gallery director, consultant; b. LA, Feb. 2, 1947; s. Ernest Charles and Eleanor (Reid) W.; m. Jacquelyn Bellard, June 3, 1978; 1 child, Jendayi Asabi. BFA, Otis Art Inst., 1969, MFA, 1971. Asst. prof. Southwestern Coll., Chula Vista, Calif., 1972-73; prof. art Calif. Poly U., Pomona, 1973—; univ. gallery dir. Calif. Poly. U., Pomona, 1988—96; instr. Otis Parsons Watts Towers, LA, 1981-88; prof. emeritus Calif. State U., Pomona, 2002—. Bd. artists Brockman Gallery Prodns., LA, 1980-85; bd. dirs. Watt Towers Art Ctr., LA; vis. artist dept. art U. Nev., Las Vegas, 1990; vis. prof. sculpture Otis Art Inst., LA, 1991-92; bd. advisors The Armory Gallery, Pasadena, Calif.; apptd. Nat. Edn. Com., Princeton, NJ, 1996; chair Pasadena (Calif.) Arts Commn., 1997; co-chair sculpture panel Coll. Art Assn., LA, 1999; Disting. artist lecture Calif. State U., Northridge, 2001; grad. reviewer Memphis Coll. of Art and Design, Memphis, 2001; co-curator exhbn. Armony Ctr. for Arts, Pasadena, 2002; slide lectr., disting. artist series Calif. State U., Northridge, 2002; vis. artist, grad. reviewer Memphis Coll. Art and Design, 2001; art adv. com. Pasadena Ctr., 2006. One-man shows include Sol Del Rio Gallery, San Antonio, 1980, Brockman Gallery, 1982, Daniel Maher Gallery, 1983, Southwest Coll., 1984, Joyce Gordon Gallery, Oakland, Calif., 2009; 2 person exhbn. Calif. State U., Bakersfield, 2002; exhibited in group shows at Oranges/Sardines Gallery, 1984, Sparc Gallery, 1985, Mus. African Am. Art, 1985, L.A. Art Gallery, 1986, Muni Art Gallery Calif. State U. Dominguez Hills, Altars, Icons & Sacred Places, San Antonio Art Inst., 1992, Gallery 1078, Chico, Calif., Calif. State U., 2002, Calif. Poly. U., 2003, African AIDS Armory Ctr. for the Arts, Calif., 2004, Calif. African Am. Mus., 2005, Calif. AfroAm. Mus., L.A., 2005, U. Art Gallery Calif. Poly U., 2007; retrospective exhbn. at Kellogg U. Art Gallery, Calif. State Poly. U., Pomona, 2007; represented in permanent collections Calif. Mus. Afro-Am. History and Culture, Prairie View Coll., 1977, Tex. A&M U., 1977, Atlanta Life Ins. Co., 1984, Golden State Life Ins., 1985, Broadway Fed. Savs. & Loan Corp., L.A., 1986, LACTC Metro Rail Commn.; artist in residence Studio Mus. Harlem, N.Y., Spokane (Wash.) Coll., (vis.) Graduate Review Memphis Coll of Art and Design, 2001, Pasadena Art Alliance, 2005; contbr. articles to profl. jours. Chmn. Pasadena Arts Commn. NEA fellow, 1986; Visual Arts fellow Pasadena Art Commn., 1991; advanced placement, Studio Art Devel. Com.; Brody visual art fellow, L.A., 1998; recipient Gold Crown award in visual arts Pasadena Arts Coun., 1998; named emeritus prof. Calif. State Poly. U., Pomona, Calif., 2007. Progressive. Avocations: music, gardening, architecture, sports. Office Phone: 323-256-2997, 323-405-0976. Personal E-mail: scwilsonstudio@aol.com. Business E-Mail: scwilson@csupomona.edu, scwilsonstudio@ad.com.

WILSON, STEPHEN RAY, fertilizer manufacturing company executive; b. DuBois, Pa., Oct. 20, 1948; s. Richard C. and Marilyn J. (Stewart) W.; m. Susan K. Condon, Sept. 5, 1970; children: Jeffrey M., Elizabeth A. BA in Sociology, Northwestern U., 1970, MBA in Fin. and Acctg., 1974. CPA, Ill. Various positions Inland Steel Industries, Chgo., 1974-91, asst. treas., 1985-88; contr., treas. James T. Ryerson & Son, Chgo., 1988-89; v.p. info. mgmt. and fin. Joseph T. Ryerson & Son, Chgo., 1989-90; gen. mgr. corp. planning Inland Steel Industries, Inc., Chgo., 1990-91; sr. v.p., CFO, CF Industries, Inc., Deerfield, Ill., 1991—2003, pres., CEO, 2003—, chmn., 2005—. Bd. dirs. Northwestern Club Chgo., 1982-84; bd. trustees Chgo. Found. for Edn., 1993—. With U.S. Army, 1970-72. Mem. AICPA, Fin. Execs. Inst., Econ. Club Chgo. Avocations: running, golf, travel. Office: CF Industries Inc Ste 400 4 Parkway N Deerfield IL 60015-2590

WILSON, SYLVIA ALYCE, musician, educator; b. Mpls., June 19, 1950; d. Robert Leighton and Doris Mae (Seim) Butts; m. Dennis Charles Wilson, Sept. 12, 1970; children: Ryan Bradley, Virginia Anne Herzog. BS in Music Edn. with high distinction, U. Minn., Mpls., 1972, MA in Music Edn., 1987. Orch. tchr. Anoka-Hennepin Sch. Dist. No. 11, Coon Rapids, Minn., 1972—77, music tchr., 1986—89, 1992—; substitute music tchr. St. Louis Park (Minn.) Sch. Dist. No. 283, 1978—85; orch. tchr. Wayzata (Minn.) Sch. Dist. #284, 1985—86; orch./choir tchr. Roseville (Minn.) Area Pub. Schs. #623, 1989—90; talent devel. adv. Mid. Schs., 2005—. Musician Lake String Quartet, Mpls., 1982—85; piano tuner, pvt. music tchr., 1982—86; preschool music tchr. West Bank Sch. Music, Mpls., 1983—85; judge Minn. State HS League, St. Paul, 2003—07; presenter in field. Contbr. articles to profl. jours. Violinist, violist Cantati Evangelica, Mpls., 1995—2001, Mpls. Civic Orch., 1970—; mentor Minn. Music Edn. Assn., 2006—; VBS tchr. First Bapt. Ch. Mpls., 1990—94, choir dir., bell choir dir., 1992—2000. Recipient Meritorious Orch. Program award, Minn. String Tchrs. Assn., 1987, 2002; named Outstanding Sr., Am. Legion, 1968; grantee, Anoka-Hennepin Ednl. Found., 1999—2001; scholar, U. Minn., 1968. Mem.: NEA, Nat. Assn. Gifted Children (performer nat. convention 2007), Minn. Educators of the Gifted and Talented, Anoka-Hennepin Edn. Minn. (bldg. rep. 2000—05), Am. String Tchrs. Assn., Music Educators Nat. Conf., Pi Kappa Lambda, Sigma Alpha Iota (pres., v.p., treas., corr. sec. 1970—, co-chair benefit music scholarships, adv. U. MN Sigma Sigma chpt. 2005—, Music scholar 1970, Sword of Honor 1971, Svc. to Chpt. award 2005, Rose of Honor 2006). Home: 2700 Joppa Ave S Saint Louis Park MN 55416 Office: Northdale Mid Sch 11301 Dogwood St Coon Rapids MN 55448 Personal E-mail: swilsonusf@yahoo.com.

WILSON, TERILYN BARRETT, elementary school educator; b. Logan, W. Va., Aug. 17, 1950; d. Freeman J. and Marie P. Barrett; m. Kenneth Ray Wilson, Nov. 25, 1977; children: Melanie Brooke, Stephanie Marie. BA, Marshall U., 1972, M, 1973. Spl. edn. tchr. Putnam County Sch., Winfield, W.Va., 1972—73, Kanawha County Sch., Charleston, W.Va., 1973—74, Meade County Sch., Brandenburg, Ky., 1974—77, Logan County Sch., Logan, 1978, 1980—85, 2d grade tchr., 1985—90, spl. edn. tchr., 1998—2002, 5th grade tchr., 2003—. Chair, spl. edn. dept. Chapmanville Mid. Sch., Chapmanville, W.Va., 1990—2002, sec., faculty senate, 1994—98. Chief Logan State Pk. Found.; deacon, ch. bd. First Christian Ch., Logan, W.Va., 2003—05. Recipient Tchr. Yr., Logan County, 2008, Walmart, 2007, Arch Coal Tchr. Achievement award, 2008, award, Tchr. Leadership Inst., 2007. Mem.: Logan County (West Va. tchr. leadership inst. 2007), Assn. Supvision Curr. Devel., Internat. Reading Assn., Phi Delta Kappa, Delta Kappa Gamma, Internat. (v.p. 1992—96). Democrat. Avocations: reading, quilting, travel. Office: Chapmanville Mid Sch 300 Vance St Chapmanville WV 25508 Office Phone: 304-855-8378. Business E-Mail: twilson@access.k12.wv.us.

WILSON, TERRILYN LOUELLA, nursing educator; b. Lawrence, Kans., Mar. 1, 1952; d. Harry C. and Lola Elaine Crain; children: Juliet April Roberts, George John, Jennifer Lyn Sexton. Degree in Practical Nursing, Poplar Bluff Vocat. Sch., Mo., 1978; ADN, Ark. State U., 1990; BS, SouthEast Mo. State U., Cape Girardeau, 1995. RN Mo., 1990. Car hop A & W, Poplar Bluff, Mo., 1967—67; nurse's aid Doctors Regional Hosp., Poplar Bluff, 1967—70, RN or nurse, scrub, 1980—2003; nurse's aid Lucy Lee Hosp., Poplar Bluff, 1977—78; lpn Poplar Bluff Hosp., Poplar Bluff, 1978—80; nurse mgr. Golden Valley Meml. Hosp.,

Clinton, Mo., 2003—06; surg. tech. instr. Three Rivers CC, Polar Bluff, 1994—2003, nursing instr., evening program, 2006—. Office: Three Rivers CC 2080 Three Rivers Blvd Poplar Bluff MO 63901 Business E-Mail: twilson@trcc.edu.

WILSON, THEODORE HENRY, retired electronics executive, aerospace engineer; b. Eufaula, Okla., Apr. 23, 1940; s. Theodore V. and Maggie E. (Buie) W.; m. Barbara Ann Tassara, May 16, 1958 (div. 1982); children: Debbie Marie, Nita Leigh, Wilson Axten, Pamela Ann, Brenda Louise, Theodore Henry II, Thomas John, Margaret Mariana; m. Colleen Fagan, Jan. 1, 1983 (div. 1987); m. Karen L. Lerohl, Sept. 26, 1987 (div. 1997); m. Sandra Rivadeneira, Mar. 27, 1997. BSME, U. Calif., Berkeley, 1962; MSME, U. So. Calif., 1964, MBA, 1970, MSBA, 1971. Sr. rsch. engr. N.Am. Aviation Co. div. Rockwell Internat., Downey, Calif., 1962-65; propulsion analyst, supr. div. applied tech. TRW, Redondo Beach, Calif., 1965-67, mem. devel. staff systems group, 1967-71, sr. fin. analyst worldwide automotive dept. Cleve., 1971-72, contr. systems and energy group Redondo Beach, 1972-79, dir. fin. control equipment group Cleve., 1979-82, v.p. fin. control indsl. and energy group, 1982-85, mem. space and def. group Redondo Beach, 1985-93, ret., 1993. Lectr., mem. com. acctg. curriculum UCLA Extension, 1974-79. Mem. Fin. Execs. Inst. (com. govt. bus.), Machinery and Allied Products Inst. (govt. contracts coun.), Nat. Contract Mgmt. Assn. (bd. advisors), Aerospace Industries Assn. (procurement and fin. coun.), UCLA Chancellors Assocs., Tau Beta Pi, Beta Gamma Sigma, Pi Tau Sigma. Republican. Avocations: golf, bridge. Home: 3617 Via La Selva Palos Verdes Peninsula CA 90274-1115

WILSON, THOMAS BUCK, lawyer; b. Hartford, Conn., Nov. 25, 1939; s. Thomas S. and Mildred M. (Buck) W.; m. Gayle L. Davis, Aug. 26, 1967; children: Peter B., Jennifer D., Matthew T. BA, Trinity Coll., 1961; JD, U. Conn., 1967. Bar: Conn. 1967, US Dist. Ct. Conn. 1967, US Ct. Appeals (2nd cir.) 1975, US Supreme Ct. 1973. Atty. Suisman, Shapiro, Wool, Brennan & Gray, P.C., New London, Conn., 1967—2003, of counsel, 2003—. Town atty., Ledyard, Conn., 1971-79, 83-91, 95-2003; apptd. state atty. trial ref. State of Conn., 1988—; judge Mohegan Tribal Gaming Disputes Ct., 1996—. Author with other Conn. Lawyer's Basic Practice Manual Conn. Civil Procedure, 1972, rev. 1986. First lt. USAF, 1961-64. Mem. ABA, Conn. Bar Assn., New London County Bar Assn. (mem. standing com. recommendations bar admission 1996—), U. Conn. Law Sch. Alumni Assn. (pres. 1983-84). Democrat. Roman Catholic. Avocations: hiking, fishing.

WILSON, THOMAS H., museum director; BA in Anthropology, U. N.Mex, 1970; MA in Anthropology, U. Calif., Berkeley, 1972, PhD in Anthropology, 1976; JD, U. Md., 1989. Asst. prof. archaeology U. Nairobi, 1975—77; rsch. assoc. Internat. Louis Leakey Meml. Inst. African Prehistory, 1977—80; coast archaeologist Nat. Museums of Kenya, 1977—82, sr. rsch. assoc., 1982—83; vis. fellow The Johns Hopkins U., 1983—84; prog. officer Nat. Endowment for Humanities, 1985—90; dep. dir. Mus. African Art, NYC, 1990—92; exec. dir. Southwest Mus., LA, 1992—95; adj. prof. anthropology U. Southern Calif., 1992—95; atty., 1996—; dir. museums, dir. mus. studies Beloit Coll., 1997—99, adj. prof. anthropology, 1997—99; rsch. assoc. anthropology Field Mus. Natural Hist., 1997—2000; rsch. assoc. dept. anthropology Am. Mus. Natural Hist., 1997—2001; dir. Mus. N.Mex, 2000—03; adj. prof. anthropology U. N.Mex, 2000—03; dir. Ariz. Mus. Natural Hist. (formerly Mesa Southwest Mus.), Mesa, 2003—; instr. Mesa Cmty. Coll., 2004, 2005; faculty assoc. Ariz. State U., 2007. Pres. Coun. Mus. Anthropology, 1990—92; bd. mem. Ethnic Arts Coun. LA, 1992—95, N.Mex Commn. Pub. Records, 2000—03, Mesa Hist. Mus., 2005—, vice chair, 2007—08; bd. mem. Ariz. Humanities Coun., 2006—; mem. editl. bd. Native Peoples, 1992—95, Museum Anthropology, 1992—96, El Palacio, 2000—03, Southwest Quest, 2006—. Mem.: Ctrl. Ariz. Mus. Assn., Internat. Union Anthrop. & Ethnological Sciences, Mus. Assn. Ariz. (pres.-elect 2004—06, pres. 2006—08), Panafrican Assn. Prehistory and Related Studies, AAM, Am. Anthrop. Assn., Blue Key Nat. Honor Fraternity, Phi Kappa Phi, Phi Beta Kappa. Office: Ariz Mus Natural Hist 53 N Macdonald Mesa AZ 85201 Office Phone: 480-644-3418. Office Fax: 480-644-3424. Business E-Mail: tom.wilson@mesaaz.gov.

WILSON, THOMAS H., mathematics professor; b. Dayton, Ohio, July 6, 1947; MS, Stanford U., Palo Alto, Calif., 1975. Math. tchr. Miami Valley Sch., Dayton, 1975—81; curriculum devel. anaylst NCR Corp., Dayton, 1981—85. Chair Dayton Ministries Higher Edn., 2005—. Office: Sinclair CC 444 W 3rd St Dayton OH 45402 Business E-Mail: tom.wilson@sinclair.edu.

WILSON, THOMAS JOSEPH, insurance company executive; m. Jill Garling; 3 children. BSBA, U. Mich., 1979; M of Mgmt., Northwestern U., 1980. Various fin. positions Amoco Corp., Chgo., 1980-86; mng. dir. mergers and acquisitions Dean Witter Reynolds, Chgo., 1986-93; v.p. strategy and analysis Sears, Roebuck and Co., Chgo., 1993-95; sr. v.p., CFO The Allstate Corp., Northbrook, Ill., 1995-98; chmn., pres. Allstate Fin., 1999—2002; pres. Allstate Protection, 2003—05; pres., COO The Allstate Corp., Northbrook, Ill., 2005—06, pres., CEO, 2007—08, chmn., pres., CEO, 2008—. Bd. dirs. Rush-Presbyn.-St. Luke's Med. Ctr. and Fed. Res. Bank Chgo. Office: The Allstate Corp 2775 Sanders Rd Northbrook IL 60062-6110

WILSON, THOMAS LEON, physicist, researcher; b. Alpine, Tex., May 21, 1942; s. Homer Marvin and Ogarita Maude (Bailey) W.; m. Joyce Ann Krevosky, May 7, 1978; children: Kenneth Edward Byron, Bailey Elizabeth Victoria. BA, Rice U., 1964, BS, 1965, MA, 1974, PhD, 1976. With NASA, Houston, 1965—, astronaut instr., 1965-74, high-energy theoretical physicist, 1969—. Author 3 books; contbr. articles to profl. jours. Recipient Hugo Gernsback award, IEEE, 1964; fellow, NASA, 1969—76. Mem.: AAAS, Am. Nuc. Soc., Am. Assn. Physicists in Medicine, NY Acad. Scis., Am. Phys. Soc. Achievements include research on grand unified field theory, relativistic quantum field theory, quantum chromodynamics, quantum probability theory, supergravity, quantum cosmology, astrophysics, deep inelastic scattering, neutrino astronomy, neutrino tomography; discoverer classical uncertainty principle; subspeciality: relativity and gravitation; patentee in field; contributor to design of NASA's proposed lunar base; originator olive branch as symbol of man's 1st landing on moon (on Susan B. Anthony and Eisenhower dollars); and manual Saturn takeover for Apollo moon program. Home: 206 Woodcombe Dr Houston TX 77062-2538 Office: NASA Johnson Space Ctr Houston TX 77058 Home Phone: 281-480-2194; Office Phone: 281-483-2147. Business E-Mail: thomas.l.wilson@nasa.gov. E-mail: ThomasWilson@KickapooNovel.com.

WILSON, THOMAS MATTHEW, III, lawyer; b. Ware, Mass., Feb. 22, 1936; s. Thomas Matthew Jr. and Ann Veronica (Shea) W.; m. Deborah Ord Lockhart, Feb. 10, 1962; children: Deborah Veronica, Leslie Lockhart, Thomas Matthew IV. BA, Brown U., 1958; JD, U. Md., 1971. Bar: Md. 1972, U.S. Ct. Appeals (4th cir.) 1976, U.S. Supreme Ct. 1977. Sales mgr. Mid-Ea. Box Mfg. Co., Balt., 1966-74; asst. atty. gen., chief antitrust divsn. State of Md., Balt., 1974-79; ptnr. Tydings & Rosenberg, LLP, Balt., 1979—. Author: Defending an Antitrust Action Brought by a State Attorney General, 1987, The Spectre of Double Recovery in Antitrust Federalism, 1989; co-author: Reciprocity and the Private Plaintiff, 1972; mem. editl. adv. bd.: Bur. of Nat. Affairs Antitrust and Trade Regulation Report, 1979—. Fellow: Am. Bar Found. (coord. com. on legal edn. 1993-94), Md. Bar Assn. (antitrust subcom. 1975-78), Internat. Bar Assn. (sect. on bus. law, antitrust law and monopolies com. 1983—); mem. ABA (sect. on antitrust law 1974—, chmn. state antitrust enforcement com. 1986-89, antitrust sect. coun. 1990-93); Churchwarden's Chess Club, Annapolis Yacht Club. Republican. Achievements include patents for nail cartons. Home: Baobab Farm Hampstead MD 21074 Office: Tydings & Rosenberg LLP 100 E Pratt St Baltimore MD 21202-1009 Home Phone: 410-239-7950; Office Phone: 410-752-9708. Business E-Mail: twilson@tydingslaw.com.

WILSON, THOMAS S., professional sports team executive; m. Linda Wilson; 3 children. BBA, Wayne State U. Dir. mktg. NBA LA Lakers and NHL LA Kings, 1974—76; sales dir. NBA Detroit Pistons, 1977, exec. dir., 1979, pres., CEO, 1993—; CEO Palace Sports & Entertainment, Inc., pres., 1992—; CEO, gov. NHL Tampa Bay Lightning, 1999—, St. Pete Times Forum, Fla., 1999—. Bd. trustees William Beaumont Hosp. Recipient Disting. Citizen award, Boy Scouts Am., 1988, Ernst & Young Master Entrepreneur award for State of Mich., 2002, Gerald R. Sportsperson of Yr. award, Mich. Sports Hall of Fame, 2003; named Exec. of Yr., Oakland Execs. Assn., 1994. Office: Detroit Pistons 5 Championship Dr Auburn Hills MI 48326-1753 also: Tampa Bay Lightning St Pete Times Forum 401 Channelside Dr Tampa FL 33602*

WILSON, THOMAS STRONG, JR., (TAM WILSON), judge; b. Portland, Oreg., Aug. 13, 1944; s. Thomas Strong and Ruth (Isherwood) W. BA, Dickinson Coll., 1967; JD, U. Miami, 1971. Bar: Fla. 1971, D.C. 1972, U.S. Dist. Ct. (so. dist.) Fla., U.S. Ct. Appeals (5th cir.). Rsch. aide to Justice James Adkins Fla. Supreme Ct., Tallahassee, 1971-72; assoc. Preddy, Haddad, Kutner & Hardy, 1973, John R. Farrell, PA., 1973; asst. pub. defender Pub. Defender's Office, Dade County, Fla., 1974-77; sole practice Dade County, 1978-84; asst. state's atty. State's Atty.'s Office, Dade County, 1984-87, gen. master Family Divsn., 1987-90; judge Circuit Ct., Dade County, 1990. Served to ensign USNR, 1968-69. Recipient Steven Levine award, Dade County Bar Assn., 2003; named Judge of Yr., Am. Bd. Trial Advocates, Miami chpt., 1999, Dade County Trial Lawyers, 2003. Mem. Iron Arrow, Skull and Key. Roman Catholic. Office: 73 W Flagler St Ste 624 Miami FL 33130 Office Phone: 305-349-7161.

WILSON, TIMOTHY D., psychology professor; BA in Psychology, Hampshire Coll., Amherst, Mass., 1973; MA in Psychology, U. Mich., Ann Arbor, 1975, PhD in Psychology, 1977. Rsch. asst., Hwy. Safety Rsch. Inst. U. Mich., 1974, rsch. asst., Inst. Social Rsch., 1974—77, tchg. asst., 1975—76; asst. prof. Duke U., Durham, 1977—79, U. Va., Charlottesville, 1979—84, assoc. prof., 1984—93, assoc. chair dept. psychology, 1987—88, prof., 1993—2001, dir. grad. studies, 1995—97, 1998—99, chair dept. psychology, 2001—04, Sherrell J. Aston prof. psychology, 2001—. Co-author (with E. Aronson, R. Akert): Social Psychology: The Heart and the Mind, 1994, 2d edit., 1997, 3d edit., 1998, Can. edit., 2001, 4th edit., 2002, 5th edit., 2005, Can. 3d edit., 2007, 6th edit., 2007; author: Strangers to Ourselves: Discovering the Adaptive Unconscious, 2002; assoc. editor: Jour. Personality and Social Psychology: Attitudes and Social Cognition, 1999—2001; contbr. articles to profl. jours., ad hoc reviews to profl. jours. Grantee, NSF, 1986—, Nat. Inst. Mental Health, 1986—2007, Russell Sage Found., 2005—08; vis. scholar, U. Wash., 1986, Stanford U., 1992; vis. faculty mem., U. BC, 2008. Fellow: Am. Psychol. Soc., Soc. Personality and Social Psychology; mem.: APA, Am. Acad. Arts & Sciences, Soc. Exptl. Social Psychology, Internat. Soc. Self and Identity, Assn. the Scientific Study Consciousness, Phi Beta Kappa. Office: U Va Dept Psychology 102 Gilmer Hall PO Box 400400 Charlottesville VA 22904-4400 Office Phone: 434-924-0674. Office Fax: 434-982-4766. Business E-Mail: twilson@virginia.edu.*

WILSON, TOM, political organization administrator; m. Lysa Wilson; children: Alec, Abigail. Grad., U. Vt. Sr. cons., dir. Welch, Campbell & Pusateri, Ltd., NJ; exec. dir. Assembly Rep. Majority campaign com., 1990—91; comm. dir. Haytaian for US Senate campaign, 1994, Gov. Donald T DiFrancesco, 2001, NJ Bush-Cheney '04 campaign; exec. dir. Rep. State Com., 1995—96; campaign mgr. Gov. Christine Todd Whitman, 1997; chmn. NJ Rep. Party, 2004—. Mem. Rep. Nat. Com., 2004—. Republican. Office: NJ Rep Party 150 W State St Ste 230 Trenton NJ 08608 Office Phone: 609-989-8685.*

WILSON, TRACEY L., biology educator; d. Horace Clinton and Delores Wilson; 1 child, Horace J. BA in Biology, Fisk U., Nashville, 1991; PhD, Meharry Med. Coll., Nashville, 1998. Biology instr. Lawson State CC, Birmingham, Ala., 2000—. Office: Lawson State CC 3060 Wilson Road SW Birmingham AL 35221

WILSON, VAN RAY, secondary school educator; b. El Dorado, Ark., Mar. 19, 1947; s. Brooks Robert and Marjorie Audrey Wilson; m. Bonnie Young (div.); 1 child, William Brooks; m. Alice Ann McAteer, Sept. 28, 1979; 1 child, Clorinda Ann. BA in Edn., Kensington U., Glendale, Calif., 1992. Cert. tchr. automotive mechanics NY State Edn. Dept. Enlisted US Army, 1965, advanced through grades to SGE8, 1983, ret., 1986; automotive technician Staten Island, NY, 1987—90; HS tchr. NYC Dept. Edn., 1990—. Mem.: Am. Legion, Combat Infantrymen's Assn. (life), Golden Key. Avocations: auto restoration, sailing. Office: Ralph McKee Career-Tech HS 290 St Marks Pl Staten Island NY 10301 Office Phone: 718-420-2600 ext 528.

WILSON, WALTER CLINTON, retired oil and gas industry executive; b. Brownwood, Tex., Sept. 21, 1942; s. Henry Eliga and Lottie Mae (Palmore) Wilson; m. Debra M. Thompson, Aug. 26, 1965; children: Walter Scott, Aimée Renee. BS cum laude, Howard Payne U., 1965, HHD (hon.), 2009, PhD (hon.) in Humanities, 2009. CPA Tex. Fin. mgmt. Exxon Co. USA, Kingsville, Corpus Christi, Houston, Tex., 1965-81; asst. contr. Superior Oil Co., Houston, 1982-85, fin. cons., 1985-87; contr. EOG Resources, Inc. (formerly Enron Oil and Gas Co.), Houston, 1987-88, sr. v.p., CFO, 1988-2000; ret., 2000. Mem. adv. bd. H. S. Grace & Co., Houston, 2001—. Trustee Fin. Exec. Rsch. Found., 1998—2001; chmn. pers. com. 1st Bapt. Ch., Houston, 1985—87, chmn. deacons, 1994—96; trustee Howard Payne U., Brownwood, 1999—2008, chmn., 2002—04; bd. dirs. Lyric Performing Arts Co., Brownwood, 2004—, chmn., 2004—. Lt. USNR, 1966—69, Vietnam. Mem.: Kingwood Country Club, Club Corp. Am.-Houston Soc. Republican.

WILSON, WAYNE JEROME, psychology professor; b. Ft. Smith, Ark., Oct. 24, 1932; s. O. B. Wilson and Ora Lee (Luckey) Wilson Rogers. BA, So. Meth. U., Dallas, 1959, MA, 1961; PhD, Tex. Christian U., Ft. Worth, 1965. Prof. psychology Stephen F. Austin State U., Nacogdoches, Tex., 1964—2000; ret. prof. emeritus. Author: Good Murders and Bad Murders, 1991, 2d edit., 1996, Sexuality in the Land of Oz, 1994, The Psychopath in Film, 1999. With U.S. Army, 1953-55. Avocations: writing, jogging.

WILSON, WENDY MARIE, elementary school educator, consultant; b. Chgo., June 21, 1967; d. Richard John and Carol Lee (Orangias) Ziert; m. Chris Allan Wilson, June 17, 1989; children: Bailey Elizabeth, Grace Amelia Townley. BS in Edn., Loyola U., Chgo., 1991; MAT, Webster U., St. Louis, 1995. Cert. tchr. pre-K - 9 Ill., tchr. pre-K - 6 NY, tchr. gifted edn. ext. grades 5-9. Dir. Champlain Mill Presch., Winooski, Vt., 1990—91; tchr. Montessori K -2 and gifted grade 4 Savannah Chatham City Pub. Schs., Ga., 1991—94; coord. gifted students K - 8 Grant Mid. and Illini Elem. Schs., Fairview Heights, Ill., 1994—95; tchr. 3d grade Lexington Sch., Ky., 1999—2000; tchr. 4th grade Chesapeake Acad., Arnold, Md., 2000—01; tchr. gifted edn. and kindergarten Arlington Pub. Schs., Va., 2001—03; tchr. 1st grade Phelps and Clifton Springs Cen. Sch. Dist., NY, 2003—04; tchr. gifted edn. K-12 and social studies 8-12 Bloomfield Cen. Sch. Dist., NY, 2004—06; tchr. gifted and talented program grades 3-5 Canandaigua Elem/ Sch., NY, 2006—. Intern mus. edn. St. Louis Sci. Ctr., 1995; edn. cons. PBS Tchr. Source, Alexandria, Va., 2001—, mem. adv. bd., 2006—; Arlington County rep. No. Va. Coun. for Gifted/Talented Edn., Arlington, 2001—02. Mem. stained glass restoration com. Dundee Presbyn. Ch., NY, 2005—06. Recipient Canandaigua Nat. Bank Tchr. Recognition award, 2006. Fellow: Wayne-Finger Lakes Leadership Inst. (scholarship 2005—); mem.: ASCD, PEO. Democrat. Avocations: cooking, historic preservation, travel, opera, reading. Home: PO Box 100579 Arlington VA 22210-3579

WILSON, WENDY SCOTT, history educator; b. Litchfield, Ill., Jan. 21, 1946; d. John Denniston and Shirley Mansfield Wilson; m. Kenneth John Hilty, June 24, 2006; 1 child, Michaela Jane Thompson. BA, Wells Coll., Aurora, NY, 1968; M of Letters, U. Aberdeen, Scotland, 1970. Tchr. Lexington H.S., Mass., 1971—. Sr. lectr. Northeastern U., Boston, 1972—2006; presenter in field. Author: (textbook) American History on the Screen, 2d edit., 2002, World History on the Screen, 2d edit., 2003, Differentiated Instruction for Social Studies, 2006. Sr. warden Grace Episcopal Ch., Newton, Mass., 1998—2000. Recipient Julia Taylor Martin prize in History, Wells Coll., 1968. Mem.: Phi Alpha Theta (life). Episcopalian. Avocations: travel, writing, gardening, auto restoration. Office: Lexington Pub Sch 251 Waltham St Lexington MA 02421 Personal E-mail: wwhilty@yahoo.com.

WILSON, WILLIAM CAMPBELL MCFARLAND, gastroenterologist; b. Pitts., Pa., June 8, 1953; s. George Lincoln and Nancy Adair (Lytle) W.; m. Marlis Howland, June 25, 1977; children: Sarah, Stephen, Corrie. BS in Biology, Va. Tech, 1975; MD, Hahnemann U., 1979. Intern, residency R.I. Hosp., Providence, 1978-82; staff internist USAF Med. Ctr., Wright-Patterson AFB, Ohio, 1982-86; fellowship Hahnemann U., Phila., 1986-88; with Digestive Care, Dayton, Ohio, 1988—. Chmn. planning com. Dayton Gastroenterology Symposium, 1990—; com. patient edn. Miami Valley Hosp., Dayton, 1990—94, quality assurance com., 1992—, vice chmn. dept. medicine, 1994—96, chmn. dept. medicine, 1996—98, chief of staff-elect, 2002—04, bd. dirs., 2002—, chief of staff, 2004—06. Bd. dirs. Fairhaven Ch., Dayton, 1990—94, 2001—, Dayton Christian Schs., Inc., 1995—, physician, 1993—2003; bd. dirs. In His Name Ministries, 2000—02. Physician USAF, 1979—86. Fellow ACP; Mem. AMA, Am. Gastroenterological Assn., Am. Coll. Gastroenterology, Am. Soc. Gastrointestinal Endoscopy, Montgomery County Med. Assn., Alpha Omega Alpha. Avocations: tennis, woodworking, bicycling, photography, computers. Office: 75 Sylvania Dr Dayton OH 45440-3237 Office Phone: 937-320-5050. E-mail: wcmw@aol.com.

WILSON, WILLIAM HALL, JR., retired telecommunications executive; b. Jan. 25, 1942; s. William Hall and Mary Elizabeth (Wamsley) Wilson; m. Jeri Sue Ishida, Oct. 15, 1976; 1 child, Kauialoahaokalani Rae. BSEE, U. Tenn., Knoxville, 1964; MS in Systems Mgmt., U. So. Calif., LA, 1972. Registered: (patent agt.). Field engr. IBM, Atlanta, 1964—65; engr. Hawaiian Tel. Co., Honolulu, 1969—72, pers. adminstr., 1972—73; mgr. regulatory rels. Hawaiian Tel. Co./GTESC, Honolulu and Washington, 1973—78; dir. regulatory rels. Hawaiian Tel. Co., Honolulu and Washington, 1978—79; dir. systems and procedures GTE Service Co., Lexington, Ky., 1979—84; mgr. govt. comm. GTE Telecom, Inc., Washington, 1984—90; prin. cons. Telecoms. Assocs., McLean, Va., 1990—94; prin. engr. Performance Devel. Corp., Germantown, Md., 1991; patent examiner U.S. Patent and Trademark Office, Washington, 1994—99; electronics engr. FCC, Washington, 1999—2008. Capt. USAF, 1965—69. Mem.: Mensa. Achievements include Nationally rated tournament chess player. Home: 948 Waiakamilo Rd Honolulu HI 96817 Personal E-mail: whwilsonjr@earthlink.net.

WILSON, WILLIAM HARWELL, psychiatrist, educator; b. Memphis, Feb. 6, 1951; s. Joseph Harwell Wilson and Helen Wilson (Cobb) Carruthers; m. Paula Rea, Oct. 18, 1986; children: Rea Xan, Sanford Shepherd. BA, Brown U., 1973; MD, U. Pa., 1981. Diplomate Am. Bd. Psychiatry and Neurology, Nat. Bd. Med. Examiners. Resident in psychiatry U. Wis., Madison, 1981-85; asst. prof. psychiatry U. Pitts. Sch. Medicine, 1985-86, Med. Coll. Pa., Phila., 1986-89, Oreg. Health Scis. U., Portland, 1989—93, asst. dir. pub. psychiatry tng. program, 1989—94, assoc. prof. psychiatry, 1993—2003, prof. psychiatry, 2003—. Dir. prof. edn. unit Dammasch State Hosp., Wilsonville, Oreg., 1989-94; attending psychiatrist Oreg. Health Scis. U. Hosp., 1994—; dir. Inpatient Psychiatric Svc., 2002-. Contbr. numerous articles on treatment of schizophrenia to sci. jours. Grantee NIMH, 1989-93; Recipient of Mental Health award of Excellence, State Oreg. Disting. fellow Am. Psychiat. Assn.; mem. Soc. for Biol. Psychiatry, Psychiatry, World Fedn. Mental Health, Nat. Alliance for Mentally Ill (Exemplary Psychiatrist award 1992, 98), Am. Soc. Clin. Psychopharmacology. Office: Oreg Health Scis U Mail Code UHN-80 3181 SW Sam Jackson Park Rd Portland OR 97239-3011 Office Phone: 503-494-7353. Business E-Mail: wilsonw@ohsu.edu.

WILSON, WILLIAM J., language educator; b. Oxford, Ind., Sept. 18, 1932; s. William Woodward Wilson and Esta Ella (Burton) Dilley; m. Edith Lucille McElhaney, June 1, 1955 (dec. Mar. 1969); children: Susan Wilson Siener, Maura A., Kyle A. BS summa cum laude, Ill. State U., 1959; MA, Peabody-Vanderbilt U., Nashville, 1968; EdD, Nova U., Ft. Lauderdale, Fla., 1983. Tchr. Manteno (Ill.) High Sch., 1959-60; teaching asst. U. Ill., Urbana, 1960-61; tchr. Wheaton (Ill.) Central High Sch., 1961-67; editor Laidlaw Pubs., Chgo., 1968-69; asst. prof. Ball State U., Muncie, Ind., 1969-70; assoc. prof. English Palm Beach C.C., Lake Worth, Fla., 1970—. Test reader Ednl. Testing Svc., Princeton, N.J., 1965-96; pres. Am. Lang. Rsch. Found., Lake Worth, 1976—. Editor: New Approaches to Language and Composition, 1969; author children's mus. Winter Comes to Florida, 1974, children's mus. play A Cruise on the S.S. Eternal, 1975, Arnold's Answering Apparatus, 1976. Bd. dirs. Village Green Condominiums, Palm Springs, 1985-86. With USN, 1951-55. No. Ill. U. fellow in linguistics, DeKalb, 1965—66, humanities fellow, Peabody-Vanderbilt U., Nashville, 1967. Mem. VFW,

NEA, Am. Legion, Nat. Assn. Tchrs. English., Faculty Assn. Palm Beach C.C. (pres. emeritus 1999—), Kappa Delta Pi, Sigma Tau Delta. Democrat. Episcopalian. Avocations: kairos prison ministry, sports, square dancing, travel, collecting timepieces. Home: 2100 Springdale Blvd Apt 216Y Palm Springs FL 33461-6366 Office: Palm Beach C C 4200 Congress Ave Lake Worth FL 33461-6366 Office Phone: 561-967-7222. Personal E-mail: barktree@bellsouth.net. Business E-Mail: wilsonw@pbcc.edu.

WILSON, WILLIAM PRESTON, retired psychiatrist; b. Fayetteville, NC, Nov. 6, 1922; s. Preston Puckett and Rosa Mae (VanHook) W.; m. Dorothy Elizabeth Taylor, Aug. 21, 1950; children: William Preston, Benjamin V., Karen E., Tammy E., Robert E. BS, Duke U., 1943, MD, 1947. Diplomate Am. Bd. Psychiatry and Neurology (examiner). Intern Gorgas Hosp., Ancon, Panama; from resident psychiatry to prof. emeritus Duke U. Med. Ctr., Durham, NC, emeritus prof. psychiatry, 1985—; assoc. prof. psychiatry, dir. psychiat. rsch. U. Tex. Med. Br., Galveston, 1958-60; dir. Inst. Christian Growth, Burlington, NC, 1985—; dist. prof. counseling Carolina Evang. Divinity Sch., High Point, NC, 1996—2007; ret., 2007. Chief neurophysiol. labs. VA Hosp., Durham, N.C., 1961-76; sec. Am. Bd. Qualification in Electroencephalography, 1971-77; mem. N.C. Gov.'s Task force on Diagnosis and Treatment; mem. med. adv. com. N.C. Found. Mental Health Rsch.; bd. dirs. nat. divsn. Contact Teleminstry USA, also mem. internat. commn. healing; cons. numerous area hosps.; Finch lectr. Fuller Theol. Sem., Pasadena, Calif., 1974; vis. prof. psychiatry Marshall U. Sch. Medicine, Huntington, W.Va., 1985-89. Co-author: The Grace to Grow; editor: Applications of Electroencephalography in Psychiatry; co-editor: EEG and Evoked Potentials in Psychiatry and Behavioral Neurology; contbr. articles to med. jours.; Author: The Nuts and Bolts of discipleship. Mem. ofcl. bd. Asbury United Meth. Ch., Durham; mem. program and curriculum com. United Meth. Ch., 1973-81; trustee Meth. Retirement Home, Durham; pres. United Meth. Renewal Svcs., Inc., 1978-82. Served with AUS, 1943-46. Recipient Ephraim McDowell award Christian Med. Found., 1982, Pioneer in Christian Psychiatry award Congress on Christian Counseling, 1988; named Educator of Yr., Christian Med. and Dental Soc., 1996; EEG Montreal Neurol. Inst. fellow, 1954-55, postdoctoral fellow NIMH. Mem. Am. Psychiat. Assn., So. Psychiat. Assn. (pres. 1977-78), AMA, So. Med. Assn. (chmn. sect. neurology and psychiatry 1970), Med. Soc. N.C., Durham-Orange County Med. Soc. (chmn. student recruitment com. 1965), Soc. Biol. Psychiatry, Am. EEG Soc. (councillor), So. EEG Soc. (pres. 1964), Assn. Rsch. Nervous and Mental Diseases, Am. Epilepsy Soc., AAAS, Am. Acad. Neurology, Sigma Xi, Alpha Omega Alpha, U.S. Power Squadron Club (comdr. Durham 1971), AACC Republican. Home: 1209 Virginia Ave Durham NC 27705-3263 Office: PO Box 2347 Burlington NC 27216-2347 Office Phone: 919-812-3822. Personal E-mail: williamwilson@verizon.net.

WILSON, WILLIAM ROBERTS, JR., (BOB WILSON), lawyer; b. Rosedale, Miss., July 6, 1941; s. William Roberts Wilson Sr. and Mary Elizabeth (Boatner) W.; m. Elizabeth Ann Smith; children: William Roberts Wilson III, Elizabeth Ann, Augusta Elliott. Student, Vanderbilt U., Tenn., 1964; JD, U. Miss., 1969. Pvt. practice, Tuscaloosa, Ala. Chmn. bd., chmn. founder Charitable Food Bank, Miss. Sportsman Against Hunger; Am. Intertrade Group. Mem. NRA (life mem.), Ala. State Bar Assn., Miss. Bar Assn., Miss. Assn. Justice (life mem.), Assn. Trial Lawyers of Am. (sustaining mem.), Roscoe Pound Found. (fellow), Miss. State Bar Assn. (former commr.), Nat. Col. Advocacy, United Conservation Alliance (founding bd. mem.), Congressional Sportsmen Found. (bd. dirs.), Quail Unlimited (life mem., life sponsor), Miss. Wildlife Fedn. (life mem.), Ducks Unlimited (sponsoring mem.), Waterfowl, U.S.A., Delta Wildlife Found. (sponsoring founder), British Field Sport Soc. (life mem.), Catfish Point Hunting Club (gen. ptnr.), Athelstan Club, Delta Kappa Epsilon, Delta Theta Phi. Home: PO Box 2387 Tuscaloosa AL 35403-2387 Office Phone: 205-556-7313.

WILSON-SEGURA, CHANNELL MONIQUE, secondary school educator; b. Santa Fe, Oct. 26, 1979; d. Camille Montoya-Wilson; m. Channell Monique Segura, Aug. 4, 2001; children: Nevada Reese Bella Segura, Cole Mateo Calvin Segura. BA in English Lit. and Dance, U. N.Mex, Albuquerque, 2003, MA in Secondary Edn., 2006. Educator Capital HS, Santa Fe, 2004—. Avid tchr. & coord. Advancement Via Individual Determination. Recipient Tchr. Who Inspires, Ptnrs. in Edn., 2008. Office: Capital HS 4851 Paseo del Sol Santa Fe NM 87507

WILSON-WEBB, NANCY LOU, educational association administrator; b. Maypearl, Tex, Jan. 20, 1932; d. Madison Grady Wise and Mary Nancy Pearson-Bedford (Haney) Wilson; m. John Crawford Webb, July 29, 1972. BS magna cum laude, Abilene Christian U., Tex., 1953; EdM (hon.), Tex. Christian U., 1985. Cert. tchr., mid-mgmt., sch. adminstr., Tex. Tchr. elem. grades Ft. Worth Ind. Sch. Dist., 1953-67, adult edn. tchr., 1967-73; dir. adult edn. consortium for 38 sch. dists. Tex. Edn. Agy., 1973-2000. Pres. Nat. Commn. on Adult Basic Edn., "Most Outstanding adult ed. Admin. in US" by AAAC; 1994-95; pres. Tex. Adult Edn. Adminstrn., 1994; apptd. mem. Tex. State Literacy Coun., 1987-94, Tex. State Sch. Bd. Commn., 1994-99; exec. bd. Tex. Coun. Co-op Dir., 1989-2001, Bd. Nat. Assn. of AAACE, 1988; pres., 1994—; apptd. to Gov. Ann Richard's Task Force for Edn.; ranch owner, mgr., 1998-2003. Cons. to textbooks, 1994-98; editor textbooks, 1999. Pres. Jr. Womans Club, Ft. Worth, 1969, Fine Arts Guild, Tex. Christian U., Ft. Worth, 1970-72, Ft. Worth Womens Civic Club Coun., 1970, pres. Aquarius Women's Club; active Exec. Libr. Bd., Ft. Worth, 1990-2003, Jewel Charity Ball, 1988-2003; bd. dirs. Literacy Plus in North Tex., 1988-99, pres., 2001—; bd. dirs. Greater Ft. Worth Literacy Coun., 1976-88, 2002—, pres., 2001-03; commr. Ed-16 Task Forces Tex. Edn. Agy., 1985-94; literacy bd. dir. Friends of Libr., 1967-2002, Opera Guild Bd. Ft. Worth, 1965-85, Ft. Worth Ballet Guild, Johnson County (Tex.) Corr. Bd., 1990-2000; bd. dirs. Salvation Army, Ft. Worth, 1996-2003, Ft. Worth Libr.; active Tarrant County Bd. on Aging, 1997-98, Commn. Status of Women, Ft. Worth, 1973-99, Southside Ch. of Christ. Recipient Bevy award Jr. Womans Club, 1968, Proclamation Commr. Ct. Outstanding 43 Yr. Literacy Svc. to Tarrant County Com. Ctr., 1994, Tarrant County Woman of Yr. award, Fort Worth Star Telegram, 1995, Outstanding Leadership award Ft. Worth ISD Sch. Bd., 1985, 95, Mayor's Proclamation of Nancy Webb Week, 1996; named one of Most Outstanding Educators in U.S. Nat. Assn. Adult Edn., 1983, Most Outstanding Woman Edn., City of Ft. Worth, 1991, others; nominated to Tex. Hall of Fame for Women, 1991; named to Ft. Worth Hall of Fame, 1992; scholar Germany, 1983. Mem. NEA, DAR (Mary Isham Keith chpt. 1985-2002, Nat. Literacy award 1992, Leadership Literacy award 1985-87, 89, 94, Nat. Educators award 2003), AAUW, Am. Assn. Adult and Continuing Edn. (v.p. 1987-89, chair 1993 internat. conv. 1992, Nat. Adminstr. of Yr. in Adult Edn. 1998, Most Outstanding Adminstr. Adult Edn. in US 1999), Tex. Assn. Adult and Cont. Edn. (pres. 1985-86, Most Outstanding Adult Adminstr. in Tex. 1984), Tex. Coun. Adult Edn. Dirs. (pres. nat. com. on edn., Nat. Dept. Labor award 1992), Coun. World Affairs (bd. dir. 1980-2002), Am. Bus. Women's Assn., Ft. Worth C. of C., Lecture Found., Internat. Reading Assn. (Literacy Challenge award 1991), Ft. Worth Adminstrv. Assn., Southwest Cattle Raisers Assn., Ligon Assn., Zonta, Tanglewood Garden Club, Ft. Worth Garden Club (exec. bd. dirs. 2000-03), Woman's Club, Ft. Worth Petroleum Club, Carousel Dance Club, Met. Dinner Dance Club, Ridglea Country Club, Girls Svc. League, Aquarius (pres. 2001-02), Crescent Club (Dallas), Alpha Delta Kappa (Nat. Literacy award 1992), Greater Ft. Worth Literacy Coun. (pres. 2000-03), Phi Delta Kappa, Mary Isham Keith DAR (Nat. award 1993, Nat. Found. award 2003). Democrat. Mem. Lds Ch. Home: 3716 Fox Hollow St Fort Worth TX 76109-2616

WILT, FRED, biology professor; b. South Bend, Ind., Dec. 12, 1934; s. Lisle and Helen Freese Wilt; m. Diane Cravagan Wilt, July 27, 1987; children: Laura, Emily Gunning Cox Jason. AB summa cum laude, Ind. U., Bloomington, 1956; PhD, Johns Hopkins, Balt., 1959. Assoc. prof. Purdue U., West Lafayette, Ind., 1960—64; prof. molecular cell biology UC Berkeley, Calif., 1964—. Sci. advisor NSF, Washington, 1982—87; exec. head Miller Rsch. Inst. UC, Berkeley, 1987—93; vis. scientist & cons. Exploratorium, San Francisco, 2000—06; chmn. Gordon Conf. Biomineralization, New London, NH, 2002—04. Author: (textbook) Principles of Developmental Biology. Recipient Merit Rsch. award, NIH, 1989—99. Mem.: Am. Soc. Zoologists (chair, divsn. devel. biology 1975). Office: Univ Calif MCB Dept 142 Lsa Berkeley CA 94720-3200 Office Fax: 510-643-6791. Business E-Mail: wilt@berkeley.edu.

WILTENBURG, JOY, history professor; d. Robert Edward Wiltenburg and Florence Hope Fellows; m. Richard Berry Womer, Aug. 6, 1977; children: Ellen Wiltenburg Womer, James Wiltenburg Womer. BA, U. Rochester, NYC, 1976, MA, 1978; PhD, U. Va., Charlottesville, 1984. Assoc. editor Papers of William Penn, Hist. Soc. Pa., 1983—86; editor Biog. Dictionary Early Pa. Legislators, Hist. Soc. Pa., 1986—89; vis. lectr. U. Pa., 1989—91; asst. and assoc. prof., history dept. Rowan U., Glassboro, NJ, 1991—2004, prof. and chair, history dept., 2004—. Author: (book) Disorderly Women and Female Power in the Street Literature of Early Modern England and Germany; editor: Papers of William Penn: Volume Three, 1685-1700, Papers of William Penn: Volume Four, 1701-1718, Lawmakers and Lawmaking in Colonial Pennsylvania; translator: Women in Early Modern Germany: An Anthology of Popular Texts (Hon. Mention award Edit., Soc. Study Early Modern Women, 2004). Fellowship Coll. Tchr. and Ind. Scholars, Nat. Endowment Humanities, 1994—95, fellow, Am. Coun. Learned Soc., 1994—95, Rsch. grant, German Academic Exch. Svc. (DAAD), 1982. Mem.: Sixteenth Century Studies Assn., Am. Hist. Assn., Phi Beta Kappa. Avocations: flute, singing. Office: Rowan Univ 201 Mullica Hill Rd Glassboro NJ 08028

WILTON, MARILYN JEAN MUELLER, literature and language professor; d. Roy E. and Florence Kathlyn Samer Mueller; m. Larry Edward Wilton, June 25, 1971; children: Bruce Patrick, Krista Erin Wilton Antonuk. PhD, U. N.Mex, Albuquerque, 1994. Tchg. asst. U. N.Mex, 1989—91; English tchr. Cobre HS, Bayard, N.Mex., 1983—89, Highland HS & Youth Devel., Inc., Albuquerque, 1991—93, Cliff HS, N.Mex., 1994—96, Morenci HS, Ariz., 1996—97; English instr. Clovis CC, N.Mex., 1998—2001, Eastern Ariz. Coll., Thatcher, 2002—. Recipient Excellence award, Nat. Inst. Staff & Orgnl. Devel., 2001, Faculty Recognition award, Eastern Ariz. Coll. Alumni Assn., 2008. Office: Eastern Ariz Coll 615 N Stadium Ave Thatcher AZ 85552

WILTROUT, ROBERT H., federal agency administrator, medical researcher; b. Kutztown, Pa., Sept. 13, 1950; BA, Kutztown U., 1972; MS in microbiology, Pa. State U., U. Park, 1975; PhD in immunology, Wayne State U., Detroit, 1979; studied, Queens U., Kingston, Ontario, Can., 1981. Postdoctoral studies Lab. Immunodiagnosis NIH, Bethesda, Md.; staff fellow Biol. Response Modifiers Program Nat. Cancer Inst., NIH, Bethesda, Md., head exptl. therapeutics sect. of Lab. Expt. Immunology, 1986, prin. dep. dir. Ctr. for Cancer Rsch., 2002—05, dir., 2005—. Fellow USPHS, 1979. Mem.: Soc. Biol. Therapy, Soc. Leukocyte Biology, Am. Assn. Cancer Rsch., Am. Assn. Immunology. Office: Ctr for Cancer Rsch Nat Cancer Inst 31 Center Dr, Bldg 31, Rm 3A11 Bethesda MD 20892 Office Phone: 301-496-4345. E-mail: wiltrour@mail.nih.gov.*

WILTSCHKO, WOLFGANG, zoology educator; b. Aug. 21, 1938; s. Gottfried and Katharina (Woisetschlager) W.; m. Roswitha Brill, May 31, 1968; one child, Carsten. PhD, J.W. Goethe Univ., Germany, 1967, Habilitation, 1972. Scientific asst. J.W. Goethe Univ., Frankfurt, Germany, 1967-69, asst. prof., 1970-73; prof. zoology J.W. Goethe Univ, Frankfurt, Germany, 1975—. Vis. fellow Cornell Univ., Ithaca, NY, 1974-75. Co-author: Magnetic Orientation in Animals, 1995; contbr. articles. Recipient Elliot Coues award, Am. Ornithologists Union, 1994. Fellow: Am. Ornithologists Soc. (corr.); mem.: Deutsche Zoologen Gesellschaft, Deutsche Ornithol. Gesellschaft, Internat. Soc. Neuroethology, Internat. Ornithol. Congress. Achievements include research in orientation of animals in space and time and mechanisms of magnetoreception. Business E-Mail: wiltschko@bio.uni-frankfurt.de.

WILTSE, JAMES CLARK, civil engineer; b. Dearborn, Mich., Apr. 14, 1927; s. Cecil C. and Mary G. (Brashear) W.; m. Marlyn R. Glatus, Feb. 14, 1953; children: Richard, Mary, Michael. BSCE, U. Mich., 1953. Registered profl. engr., Mass. Civil engr. U.S. Army C.E., Detroit, 1954-67; project engr. USAF Civil Engring., London, 1968-72; civil engr. USN Facilities Engring. Command, Norfolk, Va., 1973-75; chief engr. USN Resident Office, Keflavik, Iceland, 1976-81; staff civil engr. USAF Electronic Systems Div., Kaiserslautern, Germany, 1982-91; spl. asst. ROICC Norfolk, Lantnavfac Eng Com, Norfolk, Va., 1992-93; quality assurance engr. HQ Lantnavfac, 1993-94; ret., 1994. Sgt. U.S. Army, 1946-47, Japan. Fellow ASCE (life); mem. Soc. Am. Mil. Engrs. Home: 8555 Lawson Ave Norfolk VA 23503-5220 Personal E-mail: JCWILTSE@aol.com.

WILTSE, JAMES CORNELIUS, retired electrical engineer; b. Tannersville, NY, Mar. 16, 1926; s. James Cornelius and Leah Ida Wiltse; m. Helen Citron Wiltse, June 20, 1986; m. Margaret Lucille John, Jan. 27, 1950 (div. May 15, 1986); 1 stepchild, David Citron; children: Linda Margaret, Paul James. BSEE, Rensselaer Poly. Inst., Troy, NY, 1946, MSEE, 1951; PhD, Johns Hopkins U., Balt., Md., 1959. Mgr. microwaves and antennas, 1959—63; dir. adv. tech. Electronic Comm., Inc., 1963—64; prin. rsch. scientist, lab chief Martin Marietta Corp., Orlando, Fla., 1964—68, mgr. dept. electromagnetics, 1968—72, dir. rsch. and tech., 1973—77, dir. Electronics Engring. Divsn., 1976; prin. rsch. engr. Ga. Inst. Tech., Atlanta, 1978—. Expert Dept. Electronics, New Delhi, 1993; assoc. dir. Ga. Tech Rsch. Inst., Atlanta, 1979—91. Contbr. articles to profl. jours.; editor, co-author: Millimeter Systems, 1981, Millimeter and Microwave Engineering for Communications and Radar, 1994. Lt. comdr. USNR, 1943—71. Named Author of Yr., Martin Marietta Corp, 1967, Engr. of Yr., Martin Marietta Corp., 1970, Govt. Engr. of Yr., Engrs. Greater Atlanta, 1984. Fellow: IEEE (Microwave Career award 2000), Soc. Photo-Optical Instrumentation Engrs. Independent. Achievements include research in Fresnel zone plate antennas; millimeter wave engineering; electromagnetic engineering; development of terahertz technology. Home: 11138 Big Canoe 9111 Shetland Trace Jasper GA 30143 Personal E-mail: james.wiltse@tds.net.

WILTSE, PETER CHRISTIAN, lawyer; b. Buffalo, Jan. 13, 1936; s. Harry Hersey and Sally K. (Lutzhoff) W. (div. 1988); m. Christine Wiltse, 1999; children: Lise Rene, Wende, Heather, Jessica. Student, Colgate U., 1953-56; JD, SUNY, Buffalo, 1960. Bar: N.Y., U.S. Dist. Ct. N.Y., U.S. Supreme Ct. Assoc. Saperston, Wiltse & Day, Buffalo, 1960-63; asst. trial atty. Erie County Dist. Atty., Buffalo, 1963; ptnr. Gross, Shuman & Wiltse, Buffalo, 1964-74; pvt. practice Hamburg, N.Y., 1974—. Avocations: marine aquaria, golf, boating. Office: 202 Main St Hamburg NY 14075-4917 Office Phone: 716-649-4423. Personal E-mail: petercwiltse@hotmail.com.

WILTZ, JAMES W., medical products executive; Sales & mgmt. positions Patterson Cos., St. Paul, 1969—80, v.p. midwest div., 1980—86, v.p. sales & dist., 1986—96, pres. dental supply unit, 1996—2003, pres., COO, 2003—05, pres., CEO, 2005—. Office: Patterson Cos 1031 Mendota Heights Rd Saint Paul MN 55120*

WILVER, PETER M., electronics executive, accountant; BBA in Acctg., Ohio State U. CPA. With Gen. Electric.; fin. dir. Grimes Aerospace Co., 1998—2000; v.p., CFO, internat. electronic materials divsn. Honeywell (formerly AlliedSignal), 2000; CFO, sr. v.p. Fisher Scientific Internat., Inc.; v.p. Thermo Fisher Scientific, Inc. (formerly known as Thermo Electron Corp.), 2004, v.p. fin. ops., 2000—04, v.p., 2004—06, CFO, 2004—, sr. v.p., 2006—. Office: Thermo Scientific Inc 81 Wyman St Waltham MA 02454-9046*

WIMBERGER, PETER HANS, museum director, educator; Student, Williams Coll., Mass., 1975—78; BA in Zoology and Botany with honors, U. Wash., Seattle, 1982; PhD in Ecology and Systematics, Cornell U., 1991. Postdoctoral rsch. fellow U. Mich., 1991—93; asst. prof., curator Ichthology U. Puget Sound, 1993—98, assoc. prof. biology, 1998—2001, dir., environ. studies, 2001—, dir., Slater Mus. of Natural History, 2004—. Vis. rsch. scholar, asst. prof. U. Wash., 1996—97; presenter in field. Contbr. articles to profl. publs. Office: Slater Mus of Natural History Univ Puget Sound 1500 N Warner St Tacoma WA 98416 Office Phone: 253-879-2784. Office Fax: 253-879-3352. Business E-Mail: wimbo@ups.edu.

WIMBERLY, CLARENCE RAY, retired engineering educator; b. Wichita Falls, Tex., Aug. 2, 1936; s. Clarence Buddy Wimberly and Addie Rae Richardson; m. Sandra Sue Erspamer, Aug. 29, 1959; children: Scott Alan, Susan Marie Richardson. BS in Aero. Engring., Tex. A&M U., Coll. Station, 1961, PhD in Mech. Engring., 1968; MME, U. Ala., Huntsville, 1965. Registered profl. engr., Bd. Tex., 1982, Bd. Miss., 1979, Bd. La., 1984; lic. pilot FAA, 1962. Project engr. NASA, Huntsville, 1962—67; sr. specialist LTV Aerospace Corp., Grand Prairie, Tex., 1967—70; assoc. prof. U. Miss., Oxford, 1970—79; prof. and dept. head Mont. State U., Bozeman, 1979—82; dean, engring. La. Tech U., Ruston, 1982—87, Memphis State U., 1987—92. Cons. NASA, Houston, 1971—72, US Army Missile Command, Huntsville, 1973—73, NOAA, Data Buoy Office, St. Louis, 1974—82; dir. U. Miss. Laser Labr. Contbr. scientific papers to profl. publs. (Army Rsch. grants, 1977). Airman USAF, 1954—57, Kans., Korea, Va. Grant, NSF. Achievements include research in DNRC on co-generation, state Montana. Home: 1408 Comanche Ct Arlington TX 76012 Office: Univ Tex Arlington 500 W First St Woolf Hall Arlington TX 76019 Home Fax: 917-543-0101. Personal E-mail: crsw@tx.rr.com. Business E-Mail: wimberly@uta.edu.

WIMBS, CASSANDRA M., musician, educator, writer; d. Brister R. and H. B. Wimbs. BS, Howard U., 1973, MS, 1977; cert. in Cinema Ethnographique, Sorbonne, Paris, 1986; MA, U. Calif., 1987. Host prodr. KPFA-FM, Berkeley, Calif., 1983—88; founding dir. R.O.O.T.S., Berkeley, 1984—; host/prodr. Paris Voice Newspaper, Paris, 1985—86; instr. ESL, Cairo, Paris. Registered organizer of 3 UN World Health Day, Jamaica, 2002—04; del. N.Y.C. area Nat. Dance Week, Jamaica, 2002—; former bd. dirs. African Am. Wax and History Mus., NYC; keynote black grad. spkr. U. Cal, Davis, 1990. Editor: (book/conf. procs.) Traditional Healing Systems of the African Diaspora, 1985 (Mayoral Proclamation from the City of Berkeley, 1985), 1988, Kwanzaa Function at the Junction; prodr.: (audio rec.) Blacks in Paris, 1986, (interviewer/prodr.) (live broadcast rec.) The Egyptian Woman, The Cairo Women's Club and the Friendship Force in Egypt, 1990. Citizen amb. Friendship Force Internat., Jamaica, 1997—; adv. bd. mem. Menshealthnetwork, Riverside Ch. Handbell Ringers Choir. Recipient Nat. Black Health and Fitness Month Proclamation Health award, Congress Meeks, 2008, Rosa Park Cert., Video of Mighty Times, Ops. Crossrds. Africa, Ghana, 1976, 1st Presdl. Champion Gold award. Mem.: UN Assn. Harlem Arts Alliance, Lambda Kappa Mu, Delta Sigma Theta. Liberal. Achievements include conducted 1st Bay Area Black History Bus Tour. Avocations: black heritage stamp collecting, health and fitness, travel, writing.

WIMETT, LYNN CATHY, educational association administrator, director; b. Racine, Wis., Dec. 9, 1949; d. Wallace and Mert Hoftiezer; m. William John Wimett, Sept. 14, 1973; children: Jeff, Cathy Sills, Mike, James. BSN, U. Md., Balt.; MS in Mgmt., Troy State U.; MS in Nursing, U. Md.; EdD, U. Mo. Cert. advance practice nurse, Am. Assn. NPs, 2007. Dir., graduate dept. Regis U., Aurora, Colo., 2008—, faculty, 1991—. Home: 14133 E Layton Dr Aurora CO 80015 Office: Regis Univ 3333 Regis Blvd Denver CO 80221

WIMMER, KATHRYN, retired elementary school educator; b. St. Louis, May 8, 1929; d. Arthur Jordan and Louise Clara Sykes; m. Harry William Wimmer, Aug. 4, 1951; children: Robert William, Richard Jordan. BS in Edn., U. Mo., 1951; postgrad., U. South Fla., 1971—72; PhD in Edn. (hon.), Yorker Internat. U., Milano, Italy, 2007. Cert. tchr. Mo., Fla. Tchr. Affton (Mo.) Sch., 1951—52, Heege Sch., Affton, 1965—67, Gulf Gate Sch., Sarasota, Fla., 1967—72; piano tchr. Crestwood, Mo., 1963—65. Artist, musician, tchr. music and art; tutor IQ, employment and aptitude testing. Oil paintings, watercolor paintings. V.p. Southgate Cmty., Sarasota, 1989—90; pres. bd. dirs. Assoc. Women's Club, Sarasota, 1990—91, bd. dirs., 1986—93; vol. Gulf Gate Libr., Sarasota, 1993—2007. Recipient tennis trophy, Bath and Racquet Tennis Club, Sarasota, 1979, swimming trophy, Southgate Cmty. Assn., 1987, 1988, Wall of Honor cert., Roosevelt H.S., St. Louis, 2003. Mem.: Roosevelt H.S. Alumni Assn., U. Mo. Alumni Assn., Mysterium High IQ Soc., Delta Gamma (scholarship chmn., treas., rush chmn., social chmn.). Democrat. Presbyterian. Achievements include thirteen of the tutored students who were tested successfully were sent to Pine View School for the gifted. Avocations: history, genealogy, interior decorating, piano, art. Personal E-mail: HarryKay@peoplepc.com, harrykay09@comcast.net.

WIMMER, KURT A., lawyer; b. Mar. 21, 1959; BJ, U. Mo., 1982; MA, Syracuse U., 1985, JD magna cum laude, 1985. Bar: Kans. 1987, Tex. 1988, DC 1993. Ptnr., Internet/Info. Tech. Practice Group Covington & Burling, Washington, mng. ptnr. London office, 2000—03, ptnr., media law & intellectual property, 1995—2006, 2009—; sr. v.p., gen. counsel Gannett Co., McLean, Va., 2006—09. Co-editor Communications Lawyer, ABA. Recipient Joseph A. Sprague Award, Nat. Press Photographers Assn., 2002. Mem.: ABA (bd. gov. ABA Forum on Comm. Law), Media Law Resources Ctr.-Defense Counsel Sect. (exec. com.), Media Inst. (chmn. First Amendment Com.). Office: Covington & Burling 1201 Pennsylvania Ave NW Washington DC 20004-2401 Office Phone: 202-662-5278. Business E-Mail: lwimmer@cov.com.*

WIMPFFEN, OTTO RUDOLPH, mathematics professor; b. Budapest, Hungary, June 21, 1938; arrived in U.S., 1952; s. John and Susan Wimpffen; m. Verlea Miller (div.); children: Steven, Suzanna Blanchard; m. Laurel Hetherington, Nov. 27, 1993. BS Mech. and Aerospace Engring., Ill. Inst. Tech., 1966; MBA, Loyola U., Chgo., 1972; postgrad., Chgo. State U., 1980—84. Mgr. engring. & prodn. Rep. Packaging, Chgo., 1963—68; engring. staff C. E. Niehoff & Co., Chgo., 1968—75; prof. math. Wilbur Wright Coll., Chgo., 1975—2006; ret., 2006. Bd. dirs. Am.-Spanish Inst., Chgo., 1976—80. 1st lt. N.G. US Army, 1962—63. Recipient Excellence in Tchg. award, Wilbur Wright Coll., 2004—05; Inherited European Title Count Otto Rudolph Wimpffen. Mem.: Math. Assn. Am., Chgo. Yacht Club (race com. 1993—), Little Current Yacht Club. Avocations: sailing, skiing, auto racing, travel.

WIMPRESS, GORDON DUNCAN, JR., management consultant, foundation administrator; b. Riverside, Calif., Apr. 10, 1922; s. Gordon Duncan and Maude A. (Waldo) Wimpress; m. Jean Margaret Skerry, Nov. 30, 1946; children: Wendy Jo, Victoria Jean, Gordon Duncan III. BA, U. Oreg., 1946, MA, 1951; PhD, U. Denver, 1958; LLD (hon.), Monmouth Coll., Ill., 1970; LHD (hon.), Tusculum Coll., Greenville, Tenn., 1971. Lic. comml. pilot. Dir. pub. rels., instr. journalism Whittier Coll., Calif., 1946-51; asst. to pres. Colo. Sch. Mines, Golden, 1951-59; pres. Monticello Coll., Alton, Ill., 1959-64, Monmouth Coll., Ill., 1964-70, Trinity U., San Antonio, 1970-77; vice chmn. S.W. Found. Biomed. Rsch., San Antonio, 1977-82, pres., 1982-92, also bd. govs.; pres. Duncan Wimpress & Assocs., Inc., San Antonio, 1992—. Chmn. scholarship commn. Valero Energy Corp.; bd. dirs. SW Rsch. Inst. Author: American Journalism Comes of Age, 1950. Mem. adv. bd. Alamo Area chpt. Am. Diabetes Assn.; ruling elder United Presbyn. Ch., U.S.A.; bd. dirs. ARC, Am. Heart Assn.; trustee San Antonio Med. Found. 1st lt. US Army, 1942—45, ETO. Decorated Bronze Star. Mem.: Pilots Internat. Assn., Nat. Pilots Assn., Am. Assn. Higher Edn., Am. Acad. Polit. and Social Sci., Newcomen Soc. N.Am., Assn. Former Intelligence Officers, Greater San Antonio C. of C., Mensa, North San Antonio C. of C., Confederate Air Force, Aircraft Owners and Pilots Assn., San Antonio Golf Assn., Ptz. Club, San Antonio Country Club, Argyle Club, Rotary (dist. gov. San Antonio club 1983—84), Quiet Birdmen, Sigma Upsilon, Sigma Phi Epsilon (trustee found.), Sigma Delta Pi, Sigma Delta Chi, Pi Gamma Mu. Presbyterian. Avocations: golf, skiing, flying. Home Phone: 210-492-2956; Office Phone: 210-492-8173. Personal E-mail: duncan.w@sbcglobal.net.

WINAND, RENÉ FERNAND PAUL, retired metallurgy educator; b. Ixelles, Belgium, Nov. 15, 1932; s. Fernand and Malvina (Lelievre) W.; m. Christiane Hauer, Mar. 25, 1961; children: Pascaline, Jean-Marc, Henri. BS, Free U. Brussels, 1951, MS in Electromech. Engring., 1954, PhD in Metallurgy, 1960. Engr. Ateliers de Constructions Electriques de Charleroi, Belgium, 1954-55, Brit. Petroleum Belgium, Antwerp, 1956-57; rsch. asst. Free U. Brussels, 1957-61, lectr., 1961-67, prof., 1967-98, head dept. metallurgy and electrochemistry, 1968-98, chmn. Faculty Applied Scis., 1977-80, chmn. Ctr. Indsl. Rsch., 1979-98, vice-rector, 1993-98, prof. emeritus, 1998—. Gollick lectr., U. Mo., Rolla, 1985. Patentee in field; contbr. articles to sci. jours. Decorated comdr. Order of Couronne, Belgium; recipient East Surface Treatment Sci. and Tech. award, 1995, Electrodeposition Sect. Electrochem. Soc. award, 1999. Mem. Minerals Metals and Materials Soc. U.S., Electrochem. Soc. U.S., Materials Rsch. Soc., Soc. for Info. Display, Belgian Acad. for Applied Scis., Royal Belgian Acad. for Overseas Scis., Royal Belgian Acad. Scis., Letters and Arts. Home Phone: 32-2-6533022. Personal E-mail: rch.winand@skynet.be.

WINANS, CECE, gospel vocalist; b. Detroit, Oct. 8, 1964; m. Alvin Love; children: Ashley, Alvin II. Albums with Bebe Winans include Lord Lift Us Up, 1985, Bebe and Cece Winans, 1987, Heaven, 1988, Different Lifestyles, 1991, Noel, 1993, Relationships, 1994, Bebe & Cece Winans Greatest Hits, 1996; solo albums include For Always (1987 Grammy award for Best Female Gospel Performance), Don't Cry (1989 Grammy award for Best Female Gospel Performance), Alone In His Presence, 1995 (Grammy award 1995), Everlasting Love, 1998, His Gift, 1998, Alabaster Box, 1999, CeCe Winans, 2001, Throne Room, 2001, Purified, 2005 (2 Grammy awards), Thy Kingdom Come, 2008 (Grammy award for Best Contemporary Gospel Album, 2009); appeared in films including White Men Can't Jump, 1992, Waiting to Exhale, 1995, The Prince of Egypt, 1998; appeared on TV shows including The Grammy Awards, Soul Train, Sesame Street, Martin, Living Single, Touched By an Angel, Christmas in Washington, Nat. Meml. Day Concert; host (TV program) Cece's Place, (radio program) On A Positive Note; author: Feel the Spirit, 1998. Recipient numerous Grammy, Stellar and NAACP Image awards. Office: CeCe Winans Ste 300-288 115 Penn Warren Dr Brentwood TN 37027*

WINANS, CHRISTOPHER D., insurance company executive; b. Phila., Dec. 15, 1950; s. Robert F. and Ellen (Harris) W.; m. Kathy Ann Finch, Apr. 10, 1980 (div. Aug. 1995); children: Benjamin C., Spencer R.; m. Laurie Ann English, Sept. 15, 1995. BA, Pa. State U., 1973. Reporter Doylestown Daily Intelligencer, Pa., 1977, The Trentonian, Trenton, NJ, 1978-79, Phila. Jour., 1979-80, UPI, Phila., 1980-81; cmty. news editor Del. County Daily Times, Primos, Pa., 1981-83; news editor Wall St. Jour., NYC, 1983-93; v.p. comms. A.M. Best Co., Oldwick, NJ, 1993-99; equity analyst PaineWebber Inc., NYC, Morgan Stanley; analyst Williams Capital Group; v.p. equity rsch. divsn. Lehman Brothers; v.p. media rels. Am. Internat. Group, 2005—08; sr. v.p. external affairs AXA Equitable Life Ins. Co., NYC, 2008—. Author: The Man Who Had Everything, 1990, The King of Cash, 1995. Office: AXA Equitable Life Ins Co 1290 Avenue of the Americas New York NY 10104*

WINAWER, SIDNEY J., physician, educator; b. NYC; s. Nathan and Sally Winawer; children: Daniel, Jonathan, Joanna. BA, NYU, 1952; MD, SUNY, 1956; DSc (hon.), SUNY Downstate Med. Ctr., 2005. Asst. in medicine Harvard Med. Sch., Boston, 1962—66; asst. physician Harvard Med. Svc. Boston City Hosp., 1964—66; with Meml. Sloan-Kettering Cancer Ctr., NYC, 1968—, chief gastroent. and nutrition svc., 1978—98, mem. with tenure of title, 1988—, Paul Sherlock chair, 1991—; prof. medicine Cornell U. Coll. Medicine, NYC, 1980—, dir. integrative oncology program, 1997—98. Head Ctr Prevention Cancer WHO, Geneva, 1985—2000; liaison rep Nat Cancer Adv Bd, Washington, 1984—89; mem adv comt cancer prevention Am Cancer Soc, 1988—90; mem sci adv bd ICRF; consult varios rev comts Nat Cancer Inst, Washington. Editor: (book) Prevention Colorectal Cancer, 1980, Basic and Clinical Perspectives of Colorectal Polyps and Cancer, 1988, Lar Bowel Cancers: Policy, Prevention, Research and Treatment, 1991, Management of Gastrointestinal Disease, 1992, Gastrointestinal Cancer, 1992, Cancer of the Colon, Rectum and Anus, 1994, Cancer Free, 1995, Healing Lessons, 1998; contbr. chapters to books, articles to profl jours. Capt USAF, 1959—61. Recipient Clin. Achievement award, Meml. Sloan Kettering Cancer Ctr., 1997, Alumni award, 1998, SUNY Downstate Med. Ctr., 2000, Disting. Gastroenterology award, SUNY, 2003, Constantine Medal, Italian Govt., 2002, Internat. Laurel award, Cancer Rsch. and Prevention Found., 2004, others; grantee Nat. Cancer Inst., 1974, 1977, 1980, 1985, 1988, 1990, 1993, 1999, 2003. Master: Am. Coll. Gastroenterology (pres. 1979—80, Baker Presdl. lectr. 1992, Disting. Sci. Achievement award 1982, Clin. Achievement award 1997); fellow: ACP; mem.: Internat. Digestive Cancer Alliance (co-chair), NY Soc Gastrointestinal Endoscopy (founder, pres. 1978—79, ann. lectr. 1985, Florence Lefcourt disting. svc. award 2006, Florence Lefcourt State of the Art award 2006), Am. Assn. Cancer Rsch., Am. Soc. Clin. Oncology (Am. Cancer Soc. award 2001), Am. Gastroentrol. Assn. (nat. chmn. cancer sect. 1989—91, U.S. multisoc. colorectal cancer task force, Joseph B. Kirsner award 1999), Am. Soc. Gastrointestinal Endoscopy (bd. dirs. 1974—78, disting. lectr. 1985, co-chair guidelines com. 1997—, Schindler award 1994). Jewish. Avocations: opera, cross country skiing, dance, swimming, bicycling. Office: Meml Sloan-Kettering Cancer Ctr 1275 York Ave New York NY 10021-6094 Office Phone: 212-639-7678. Business E-Mail: winawers@mskcc.org.

WINBLAD, ANN, investment company executive; BA in Math. and Bus. Adminstrn., U. St. Thomas, St. Paul, Minn., MA in Internat. Econs. and Edn.; LLD (hon.), U. St. Thomas. Systems programmer Fed. Reserve Bank; co-founder Open Systems, Inc., 1976-83; strategic planning cons., IBM, Microsoft, Price Waterhouse, and many start-ups; co-founding ptnr., mng. dir. Hummer Winblad Venture Ptnrs., San Francisco, 1989—. Bd. dirs. Dean & Deluca, Intacct, Market Wire, The Knot, Voltage Security, Arbor Software, Berkeley Systems, Net Perceptions; advisor The Software Forum, San Jose Ctr. for Software Develop., Stanford/MIT Venture Forum. Co-author: Object-Oriented Software, 1990; contbr. articles to profl. publs. Trustee U. St. Thomas, St. Paul, Mich. Office: Hummer Winblad Venture Partners 1 Lombard St Ste 300 San Francisco CA 94111-1130

WINBUSH, OLGA JOYCE, education educator, consultant; d. Harbart Theodore and Claudia Madeleine Tatum; m. Albert Steve Winbush, Oct. 19, 1976; children: LaKetta Denise, Albert Steve, Ari Solomon, Meko Meyatta. BA in Sociology, UCLA, 1976, PhD in Edn., 1999; MA in Human Devel., Pacific Oaks Coll., 1980. Multiple subject clear tchg. credential Commn. on Tchg. Credentialing, Calif., 1992. Tchg. asst. Westland Sch., LA, 1982—83; tchr. Children's Cmty. Sch., Van Nuys, Calif., 1983—93; adj. faculty Antelope Valley Coll., Lancaster, Calif., 1993—98; core faculty, prof. Pacific Oaks Coll., Pasadena, Calif., 1998—. Adj. faculty Chapman U., Lancaster, 1994—98; curriculum cons. Children's Cmty. Sch., Van Nuys, 1996—2003; literacy curriculum cons. First 5/Pacific Oaks Coll., Pasadena, 2003—; literacy cons. Bridging Resources in Tech. and Edn. Afterschool Program, Pasadena, 2003—, CORAL, Pasadena, 2004—05; presenter in field. Editor: (jour.) Pathways, 1992—96; contbr. articles to profl. jours. Mem. Found. for Excellence, Van Nuys, 1985—. Recipient Unsung Hero award, Bridging Resources in Tech. and Edn. Afterschool Prgram, 2004; grantee, First 5 Early Literacy Tng., 2003. Mem.: ND Study Group on Evaluation, Rschrs. of Color, Nat. Black Child Devel. Inst., Jack and Jill Am. (assoc.). Democrat. Avocations: travel, reading, photography. Office: Pacific Oaks College 5 Westmoreland Pl Pasadena CA 91103-3592 Office Phone: 626-397-1307. Personal E-mail: asojwin@msn.com. Business E-Mail: owinbush@pacificoaks.edu.

WINCHESKI, RUSSELL A., research scientist; b. Chgo., Mar. 6, 1967; s. Richard and Marlene Wincheski; m. Kathy D. Wincheski, Aug. 8, 1992; children: Clara, Louis. PhD, Coll. William and Mary, Williamsburg, Va., 1999. Rsch. scientist NASA, Hampton, Va., 1997—. Contbr. over 80 articles to profl. publs. Recipient Silver Snoop award, NASA, 2005, Exceptional Engring. Achievement medal, 2006; named to William and Mary Sports Hall of Fame, Coll. William and Mary, 2004. Mem.: Phi Beta Kappa. Achievements include development of material characterization and advanced material.

WINCHESTER, JAMES FRANK, medicine educator; b. Glasgow, Scotland, Mar. 24, 1944; came to U.S., 1976; s. Alexander Graham and Elizabeth Mary (McKillop) W.; m. Patricia Jane, May 16, 1968; children: J. Craig, Jane E. MB, ChB, Glasgow U., 1969, MD, 1981. Sr. registrar Royal Infirmary, Glasgow, 1974-76; asst. prof. medicine Georgetown U., Washington, 1976-82, assoc. prof., 1982-87, prof., 1987—, acting. dir. divsn. nephrology, 1988-94; chief Divsn. Nephrology and Hypertension Beth Israel Med. Ctr., NYC, 2004—. Attending physician Georgetown U. Med. Ctr., 1976—2000; chief med. officer Renol Tech Internat.; adj. prof. SUNY, Downstate Med. Ctr., NY; clin. prof. med. Albert Einstein Coll. of Medicine, 2000—; sr. lectr. Mailman Sch. of Pub. Health, Columbia Univ., 2001. Editor: Clinical Management of Poisoning and Drug Overdose, 1983, 1990, 97, Renal Dialysis, 1994; editor-in-chief Replacement of Renal Function by Dialysis, 1996, Advances in Renal Replacement Therapy, 1998—. Chmn. Nat. Kidney Found. of Nat. Capital Area, Washington, 1989. Fellow ACP, Royal Coll. Physicians; mem. Internat. Soc. Peritoneal Dialysis (sec.-treas. 1984-98, pres.-elect 1998—), Am. Soc. Artificial Internal Organs (pres. 1995-96), Nat. Kidney Found. (regional pres. 1991-93, bd. dirs. 1993—), Am. Fedn. Clin. Rsch., Am. Clin. Climatol. Assn., Am. Soc. Transplant Physicians, Am. Soc. Nephrology, Internat. Soc. Nephrology. Office: Beth Israel Med Ctr Divsn Nephrology and Hypertension New York NY 10003

WINCHESTER, JAMES R., state supreme court justice; b. Clinton, Okla., Mar. 23, 1952; m. Susan Winchester; 1 child, Davis. BA, U. Okla.; JD, Okla. City U. Pvt. practice, Weatherford, Okla., Hinton, Okla.; assoc. dist. judge Caddo County, Okla., 1983; dist. judge 6th Jud. Dist. Okla., 1983—97; U.S. adminstrv. law judge, 1997—2000; justice Okla. Supreme Ct., 2000—, vice chief justice, 2005—06, chief justice, 2007—08. Mem. exec. bd. Okla. Jud. Conf., 1992—96, pres., 1995. Named Outstanding State Trial Ct. Judge, Okla. Trial Lawyers Assn., 1986. Office: Oklahoma Supreme Ct Admin Office 1915 N Stiles Ste 305 Oklahoma City OK 73104-2861*

WINCHESTER, RICHARD LEE, JR., lawyer; b. Memphis, May 21, 1924; s. Cassius Lee and Harriet Haywood (Bond) Winchester; m. Bette Anne Thompson, July 15, 1944; children: Robin Ann, Richard Lee Jr., John Thompson. LLB, U. Tenn., 1949, JD, 1965. Bar: Tenn. 1949. Sr. ptnr. Winchester Law Firm, Memphis, 1972—; atty. Shelby County, 1961—64; city atty. City of Arlington, Tenn., 1966—. Gen. counsel, bd. chmn. Cmty. Bancshares, Inc.; sec. Beachfront Condos, Inc., N. Fla. Chmn. Germantown Planning Commn., 1958—61; pres., bd. dirs. Mid-South Fair Assn.; bd. dirs. ARC; mem. Gov.'s Commn. on Human Relations, 1962—68; vice chmn., treas. Memphis and Shelby County Dem. Exec. Com., 1958—72; state exec. com., pres. Tenn. Young Dems., 1960—61; del. state and nat. Dem. convs., 1964—68; nat. elector from Tenn., 1960—72; pres. Episc. Planning Commn.; trustee U. Tenn., 1975—84, Episc. Girls Home, Bowld Hosp. Capt. inf. US Army, 1942—46, PTO. Fellow: Tenn. Bar Found. (past pres. jr. sect.); mem.: Omicron Delta Kappa, Phi Kappa Phi, Nat. Assn. Legal Aid and Pub. Defenders, Am. Judicature Soc., Shelby County Bar Assn. (past pres. jr. sect.), Memphis Bar Assn. (past pres.), Tenn. Bar Assn., ABA (past del.), U. Tenn. Alumni Assn. (past bd. govs., 9th dist. rep.), Am. Legion (past post comdr., past state vice comdr.), Kiwanis, Tennessee, 40 and 8, Jesters, VFW (past post vice comdr.), Masons, Shriners, Phi Eta Sigma, Sigma Alpha Epsilon. Episcopalian. Office: Winchester Law Firm 6060 Poplar Ave Ste 38119 Memphis TN 38119 Office Phone: 901-685-9222.

WINCKLER, ALICIA JEAN, human resources vice president; b. Yankton, SD, Aug. 16, 1972; d. Myron Mark and Barbara Jean Winckler; 1 child, Lucas Hansen. BS in Psychology and Alcohol and Drug Abuse Studies, U. SD, 1994; MA in Indsl. Orgnl. Psychology, U. Colo., Denver, 1997. Project mgr. HR Avantis, Denver, 1996—98; compensation analyst Watson Wyatt Worldwide, Denver, 1997; assessment sys. cons. Sears, Roebuck & Co., Chgo., 1998—2000, mgr. testing and selection, 2000—01, mgr. orgnl. effectiveness, 2001—03, mgr. human resources, 2003—05; south ctrl. region human resource dir. Sears Holdings Corp., Chgo., 2005—06, western region human resources dir., 2006—07, human resources dir. market transformation team, 2007; group dir. orgn. effectiveness Coca Cola Enterprises, 2007—09; HR divisional. v.p. corp. functions Sears Holdings Corp., Hoffman Estates, Ill., 2009—. Adj. faculty mem. Chgo. Sch. Profl. Psychology, 2004. Mem.: APA (assoc.), Kappa Alpha Theta, Omicron Delta Kappa. Democrat. Roman Catholic. Avocations: music, travel. Office: Sears Holdings Corp 3333 Beverly Rd Hoffman Estates IL 60179 Home: 2020 W Pierce Ave Apt 4 Chicago IL 60622 Office Phone: 847-286-0674. Personal E-mail: aliciawinckler@msn.com.

WINCOR, MICHAEL Z., psychopharmacology educator, clinician, researcher, director; b. Chgo., Feb. 9, 1946; s. Emanuel and Rose (Kershner) Wincor; m. Emily E.M. Smythe; children: Meghan Heather, Katherine Rose. SB in Zoology, U. Chgo., 1966; PharmD, U. So. Calif., 1978. Rsch. project specialist U. Chgo. Sleep Lab., 1968-75; psychiat. pharmacist Brotman Med. Ctr., Culver City, Calif., 1979-83; asst. prof. U. So. Calif., LA, 1983-97, assoc. prof., 1997—, interim chair dept. pharmacy, 2001—02, assoc. dean external programs, 2003—06, dir. continuing pharmacy edn. and internat. programs, 2006—. Cons. Fed. Bur. Prisons Drug Abuse Program, Terminal Island, Calif., 1978—81, Nat. Inst. Drug Abuse, Bethesda, Md., 1981, The Upjohn Co., Kalamazoo, 1982—87, 1991—92, Area XXIV Profl. Stds. Rev. Orgn., LA, 1983, Brotman Med. Ctr., Culver City, Calif., 1983—88, SmithKline Beecham Pharms., Phila., 1990—93, Tokyo Coll. of Pharmacy, 1991, 2008, G.D. Searle & Co., Chgo., 1992—97, 1999—2001, Pfizer, NY, 1998—2004, Wyeth-Ayerst, Phila., 1999—2001, Novartis, East Hanover, NJ, 2002—04, AstraZeneca, Wilmington, Del., 2003—04, Nat. Assn. Bd. Pharmacy Continuing Profl. Devel. Com., 2003—04, Sanofi-Aventis, 2004—08, Takeda Pharms. N.Am., Inc., 2005—08, Meijo U., 2006, Showa Pharm U., 2007—08, U. Kebangsaan Malaysia, 2007. Contbr. more than 75 articles to profl. jours., chpts. to books, papers presented at nat. and internat. meetings and reviewer. Mem. adv. coun. Franklin Avenue Sch., 1986-89; bd. dirs. K.I. Children's Ctr., 1988-89; trustee Sequoyah Sch., 1992-93; mem. tech. com. Ivanhoe Sch., 1993-96; U. So. Calif. Amb., 2000—. Faculty scholar U. So. Calif. Sch. Pharmacy, 1978; recipient Cert. Appreciation Mayor of LA, 1981, Bristol Labs award, 1978, DuPont Pharma Innovative Pharmacy Practice award, 1995, Pharmacy Coun. Mental Health award, 1996, Outstanding Chpt. Advisor award Am. Pharm. Assn.-Acad. Students of Pharmacy, 2003. Mem. Am. Coll. Clin. Pharmacy (chmn. constn. and bylaws com. 1983-84, mem. credentials com. 1991-93, 95-97, ednl. affairs com. 1994, constn. and bylaws com. 1999-00), Am. Assn. Colls. Pharmacy (focus group on liberalization profl. curriculum 1990-92, mem. pharmacy practice planning commn. 1996-97, chmn. pharmacy practice awards com. 1998-00, mem. bylaws and policy devel. com. 2001-03, mem. computer tech. in edn. task force 2001-02, chmn. coun. of faculties strategic planning and resolutions com. 2001-03, mem. continuing pharmacy edn. ACPE liaison com., 2004-06, chair elect global pharmacy edn., 2008-), Am. Soc. Health-Sys. Pharmacists (chmn. edn. and tng. adv. working group 1985-88, chmn. com. on academia 1996-97), Am. Pharm. Assn. (del. ann. meeting ho. of dels. 1989, 1998), Sleep Rsch. Soc., Nat. Sleep Found., Am. Acad. Sleep Medicine, Calif. Pharmacists Assn. (trustee 1997-01, chmn. editl. rev. com. 1998-03), Hollywood-Wilshire Pharmacists Assn. (pres. 2006—07), U. So. Calif. Sch. Pharmacy Alumni Assn. (bd. dirs. 1979—, pres. 1998—2008), Coll. Psychiat. Neurol. Pharmacists (chmn. recertification com. 2003-06, chmn. program com. 2006-07, Judith J. Saklad Meml. Lecture award 2007), Rho Chi (Alumni award 2007), Phi Lambda Sigma. Avocation: photography. Office: 1985 Zonal Ave Los Angeles CA 90089-9121

WIND, ALAN MICHAEL, history educator; b. Little Falls, NY, Nov. 30, 1952; s. Joseph and Anne Wind; m. Patrice Wind, Oct. 26, 1985; 1 child, Zane. BA in Secondary Edn., Clemson U., SC, 1977; EdM, Ga. State U., Atlanta, 1988. Cert. educator Ga. Profl. Stds. Commn. Tchr. Beaufort High, SC, 1979—83, M.D. Collins High, Atlanta, 1984—87, Ridgeview Mid. Sch., Atlanta, 1987—88; tchr. Milton HS, Atlanta, 1988—91, Chattahoochee High, Alpharetta, Ga., 1991—. Cons. Fulton County, Atlanta, 2003, Prentice Hall, Atlanta, 2004; presenter in field. Named Chattahoochee High Tchr. of Month, 2004, Chattahoochee High Tchr. of Yr., 2004—05, Walmart Tchr. of Yr., Duluth, Ga., 2005—06; Barringer Rsch. fellowship, Thomas Jefferson Found., 2007. Mem.: Profl. Assn. Ga. Educators, Ga. Coun. for the Social Studies, Nat. Coun. for the Social Studies. Roman Catholic. Avocations: acting, softball, running, basketball, coaching. Home: 329 Fairbrook Cir Marietta GA 30067 Office: Chattahoochee High 5230 Taylor Rd Alpharetta GA 30022 Office Phone: 770-521-7600. Personal E-mail: alanmwind@yahoo.com.

WINDELS, PAUL, JR., lawyer; b. Bklyn., Nov. 13, 1921; s. Paul and Louise E. (Gross) W.; m. Patricia Ripley, Sept. 10, 1955 (dec. 1995); children: Paul III, Mary H., James H.R., Patrick D. AB, Princeton U., NJ, 1943; LLB, Harvard U., Cambridge, Mass., 1948. Bar: NY 1949. Spl. asst. counsel NY State Crime Commn., 1951; asst. U.S. atty. Ea. Dist. NY, 1953—56; NY regional adminstr. SEC, 1956—61, also spl. asst, U.S. atty. for prosecution securities frauds, 1956-58; lectr. law Am. Inst. Banking, 1950-57; mem. Windels, Marx, Lane & Mittendorf and predecessor firms, 1961—98, of counsel, 1998—. Author: Our Securities Markets-Some SEC Problems and Techniques, 1962. Trustee Bklyn. Law Sch.; trustee Lexington Sch. for the Deaf, Gerta Charitable Trust; past pres. Fed. Bar Coun. Capt. F.A., AUS, 1943-46, ETO; maj. USAR, ret. Recipient Flemming award for fed. svc.; decorated chevalier Order French Acad. Palms; officer Nat. Order Merit France. Fellow Am. Bar Found.; mem. ABA, NY State Bar Assn., Assn. of Bar of City of NY Republican. Presbyterian. Office: Windels Marx Lane & Mittendorf 156 W 56th St Fl 23 New York NY 10019-3867 Office Phone: 212-237-1210.

WINDER, CLARENCE LELAND, psychologist, educator; b. Osborne County, Kans., June 16, 1921; s. Clarence McKinley and Edna (Ikenberry) W.; m. Elizabeth Jane Jacobs, Aug. 14, 1943; children: David William, Christina Louise. Student, Santa Barbara State Coll 1941; AB with honors, U. Calif. at Los Angeles, 1943; MA, Stanford 1946, PhD, 1949. From instr. to assoc. prof. Stanford U., 1949-61; Psychol. Clinic, 1953-61; prof., dir. Psychol. Clinic, Mich. State 1961-62, prof. psychology, 1961-91, prof. emeritus, 1991—, ch dept., 1963-67; dean Coll. Social Sci. Mich. State U., 1967-74, assoc. provost, 1974-77, provost, 1977-86, provost emeritus, 1991—; prof., dir. Psychol. Svcs. Ctr., U. So. Calif., 1962-63. 1st lt. USAAF, 1943-45. Decorated Air medal with 7 clusters, D.F.C. Fellow APA, AAAS; mem. Sigma Xi. Achievements include research in psychol. aspects schizophrenia, parent-child rels., personality devel., and higher edn. adminstrn. Home: 1776 Hitching Post Rd East Lansing MI 48823-2144

WINDER, ROBERT OWEN, mathematician, computer engineer, geophysicist; b. Boston, Oct. 9, 1934; s. Claude V. and Harriet O. W.; m. Kathleen C. Winder; children by previous marriage: Katherine, Amy. AB, U. Chgo., 1954; BS, U. Mich., 1956; MS, Princeton U., 1958, PhD, 1962; MS, Ariz. State U., 2000. With RCA, 1957-78, group head Princeton and Somerville, NJ, 1969-75, dir. microprocessors, 1975-77, dir. systems, 1977-78; mgr. workstation devel. Exxon Enterprises, Inc., Princeton, 1978-85; v.p. Syntex Computer Systems Inc., Bordentown, NJ, 1985-88; mgr. product engring., Princeton Operation, Intel Corp., 1988-93; mgr. engring. ops. video products div., Intel, Chandler, Ariz., 1993-95. Vis. scholar dept. geol. scis. Ariz. State U., Tempe, 2001—06; active mem. gov. Acad. Village, Tucson, 2007—. Contbr. articles to profl. jours.; patentee in field. NSF fellow, 1956-57; Recipient David Sarnoff award RCA, 1975. Fellow IEEE.

WINDHAM, DONALD ERIC, bioinformatics analyst; b. Florence, SC, June 27, 1974; s. Donald Eugene Windham and Deborah Ann Robinson. BS in Zoology, NC State U., Raleigh, 1998, BS in Microbiology and Biology, 2002; MS in Info. Tech., Capelle U., 2008. Publs. staff NC State U. Computing Svcs., Raleigh, 1996—99; delivery lead IBM, Research Triangle Park, NC, 1999—2000, IT architecture specialist, 2000—02; bioinformatics specialist, sys. adminstr. NC State U. Fungal Genomics Lab., Raleigh, 2003—05; bioinformatics analyst NC State U. Ctr. Biology Nematode Parasitism, 2005—. Recipient One Team award, IBM, 2001. Mem.: Bioinformatics Orgn., Inc., Am. Soc. Microbiology. Office: NC State U Campus Box 7253 Raleigh NC 27603

WINDHAM, GAYLE C., epidemiologist; BA in Biology summa cum laude, U. Calif., San Diego, 1977; MS in Public Health, UCLA, 1980; PhD in Epidemiology, U. Calif., Berkeley, 1989. Epidemiologist Ctr. Disease Control, Ctr. Environ. Health, 1980—81, Inst. Preventive Medicine, U. Oslo, Nat. Inst. Pub. Health, Norway, 1982—83; EIS officer Ctr. Disease Control Calif. Dept. Health Svc., 1983—85; epidemiologist Calif. Dept. Health Svc., 1985—2006; rsch. scientist Calif. Health, 1986—; rsch. scientist supr. Calif. Dept. Pub. Health. Contbr. articles to jours. publs. Recipient Health Svc. Deans award, UCLA Sch. Pub. Health; Regents fellowship, UC Berkeley. Mem.: Internat. Soc. Environ. Epidemiology (sec., treas. citation), APHA, IEA, SER. Office: Calif Dept Pub Health 850 Marina Bay Pky Bldg P Richmond CA 94804 Business E-Mail: gayle.windham@cdph.ca.gov.

WINDHAM, JOHN FRANKLIN, lawyer, educator; b. Fayette, Ala., Jan. 21, 1948; s. Grover B. Windham Jr. and Nancy Katherine (McAdams) Haynie; 1 child, John Franklin Jr.; m. Denise Roche McNair, Apr. 6, 1999; 1 stepchild, Brittany Danielle McNair. BA, U. West Fla., 1970; JD, U. N.C., 1975. Bar: Fla. 1975, U.S. Dist. Ct. (no. dist.) Fla. 1976, U.S. Ct. Appeals (11th cir.) 1983, U.S. Supreme Ct. 1984. Acctg. supr. Monsanto Co., Research Triangle Park, N.C., 1970-72; law clk. to U.S. Atty Pensacola, Fla., 1974; assoc. Beggs & Lane, Pensacola, 1975-79, ptnr., 1979—. Adj. asst. prof. bus. law Troy State U., Pensacola, 1983-90. Mem. bd. dirs. Am. Cancer Soc., 1980-06, exec. com. Fla. divsn., 1982-93, 95-2000, chmn. legacies and planned giving, 1984-88, chmn. income devel., 1980-91, chmn. ad hoc adv. com., 1991-05, mem. risk adv. subcom., 1991-97, chmn. 1996-97, legal advisor, 1992—, vol. and staff devel. com., 1994-95, planning com., 1994-98, spokesperson tobacco media, 1995-96, mem. cause mktg. work group, 1995-96, mem. scholarship com., 1995-98, chmn. dist. VII steering com., 1995-96, v.p, 1996-97, mem. Winn Dixie adv. com., 1996-99, field ops. com. 1995-98, chmn. field ops. com., 1996-98, mem. task force volunteerism, 1996-97, call ctr. work group, 1996-98, mktg. and comms. com., 1997-2000, divsn. chartering com., 1997-98, chmn.-elect bd. 1997-98, chmn. bd. 1998-99, personnel subcom., 1998-99, patient svc. ctr. work group, 1998-99, audit com., 1999-00, nominating com., 1999—, evaluation adv. com., 2001-03, 05—08, bylaws com. chmn., 1990-96, triple 5 ad hoc com., 1995-95, cancer control com., 1994-96, stewardship com., 1996-02; mem. Nat. Assembly, 2002—, mem. budget and fin. com., nom. ad hoc com., bd. governance task force, 1990—2004, chmn. bylaws com., 2002—, stewardship com., 2006—, bd. governance com. 07-; chmn. bd. Escambia Christian Sch., Pensacola, 1976-86; deacon Ch. of Christ, 1985-95, 99-02; adminstrv. team First City Ch., 2002-04, mem. adv. bd.; elder First City Ch., 2004—; mem. adv. bd. Interim Healthcare, 1993-96, Panhandle Rehab. Injury Mgmt. and Evaluation, 1993-96; mem. found. bd. East Hill Christian Sch., 1995-97; bd. govs. Pensacola chpt. Order Granaderos e Dames de Galvez, 1990-98, pres. 1995-98; mem. U. West Fla. Found., 1983-85. Mem. Fla. Bar (workers compensation rules com. 1995-01, drafting subcom. 2000-01), Fla. Def. Lawyers Assn., Fla. Workers Compensation Inst., Southeastern Admiralty Law Inst. (bd. dirs. 1986-89), Northwest Fla. Blood Ctr. Found. (treas. 2002-04, pres. 2006-08), N.W. Fla. Blood Ctr. (bd. dirs. 2006—08), Fla. Blood Svc. (bd. dirs. 2008-), Northwest. Fla. Blood Svcs. Found. (pres. 2008-), U. West Fla. Nat. Alumni Assn. (bd. dirs.), Kiwanis (pres. Pensacola 1978-79, 88-89). Republican. Avocation: church activities. Office: Beggs & Lane PO Box 12950 Pensacola FL 32591-2950

WINDHAUSER, JOHN WILLIAM, retired journalism educator, consultant; b. Rochester, NY, Jan. 30, 1943; s. Milton Edward and Mary Ellen (McDonald) W.; m. Marlene Marie Most. BS, Tri-State U., 1966; MA, Ball State U., 1967; PhD, Ohio U., 1975. Editor, reporter, advt. and pub. rels. positions, 1964—77; asst. prof. journalism Colo. State U., Ft. Collins, 1971—77, Bradley U., Peoria, Ill., 1977—78; assoc. prof., dir. rsch. ctr. U. Miss., Oxford, 1979—82; prof. La. State U., Baton Rouge, 1982—2005, U. Memphis, 2005—; cons. Jomar Assocs. Cons. in field; rsch. judge Soc. Profl. Journalists; editl. bd. Journalism Quarterly, Newspaper Rsch. Jour. Author: The Editorial Process, 1978, 2d edit., 1985; co-editor, co-author: The Media in the 1984 and 1988 Presidential Campaigns, 1991; contbr. numerous articles to profl. jours.; editor Profl. Jour., Coll. Press Rev., 1972-81. Recipient Life Membership award Nat. Coun. Coll. Publs. Advisers, 1981, Presdl. award, 1973-81. Mem. Assn. Edn. in Journalism

WINDHORST, JOHN WILLIAM, JR., lawyer; b. Mpls., July 6, 1940; s. John William and Ardus Ruth (Bottge) W.; divorced; 1 child, Diana Elizabeth. AB, Harvard U., 1962; LLB, U. Minn., 1965. Bar: Minn. 1965, U.S. Tax Ct., U.S. Ct. Appeals (8th cir.) 1965, U.S. Dist. Ct. Minn. 1967, U.S. Supreme Ct. 1975. Law clk. to Hon. H.A. Blackmun U.S. Cir. Ct., Rochester, Minn., 1965-66; assoc. Dorsey & Whitney, Mpls., 1966-70; with office of Revisor of Statutes State of Minn., 1967, 69; ptnr. Dorsey & Whitney, 1971-96, of counsel, 1997—. Bd. dirs. St. Paul Chamber Orch., 1980-86, Harry A. Blackmun Scholarship Found., 1996—, Minn. Taxpayers Assn., 1999—. Mem. ABA, Minn. Bar Assn., Hennepin County Bar Assn., Harvard Club of Minn. (pres. 1977-78). Office: 50 S 6th St Ste 1500 Minneapolis MN 55402 Home: 6566 France Ave So Apt 204 Edina MN 55435 Office Phone: 612-340-2645. Business E-Mail: windhorst.john@dorsey.com.

WINDMAN, ARNOLD LEWIS, retired mechanical engineer; b. NYC, Oct. 17, 1926; s. Raphael and Anna (Wexler) W.; m. Patricia Foley, Dec. 13, 1967; children— Richard, Marjorie, Kevin, Colleen, Sean, JoAnn, Brian, William. B.M.E., Coll. City N.Y., 1947. Bar: registered profl. engr., N.Y., 13 other states. Project engr. F.E. Sutton, NYC, 1947-50; with Syska & Hennessy, Inc., NYC, 1950-90, pres., 1976-86, vice chmn., 1986-90, also bd. dirs. Pres. Am. Cons. Engrs. Coun., 1985-86; chmn. N.Y. State Bd. Engring. and Land Surveying, 1982-84; bd. dirs., v.p. Sea Pines Plantation, 1997-2000. Bd. dirs. Phelps Meml. Hosp., Tarrytown, N.Y., 1974-82; chmn. planning commn. Hilton Head Island, 2000. Mem. Am. Soc. Heating, Refrigerating and Air Conditioning Engrs., chpt. pres. (1965), N.Y. Assn. Cons. Engrs. (pres. 1981-82, dir. 1977), ASME, Tau Beta Pi, Pi Tau Sigma. Democrat. Jewish. Home: 1919 S Beach Club Vl Hilton Head Island SC 29928-4068 *Professional integrity, enthusiasm, and a continuing effort to train younger people for advancement are three key ingredients of a successful career.*

WINDRUM, KEN, communications educator; b. Burbank, Calif., Dec. 9, 1962; s. George Kenneth and Gloria Ann Windrum. PhD, UCLA, 2003. Adj. asst. prof. LA Pierce Coll., Media Arts, Woodland Hills, Calif., 1998—. Contbr. scientific papers. Office: LA Pierce Coll Media Arts 6201 Winnetka Ave Woodland Hills CA 91371 Personal E-mail: kwindrum@earthlink.net.

WINDSOR, ADRIAN SHARON, real estate broker, literature and language professor; b. Adrian, Mich., Oct. 19, 1938; d. LeRoy E. and Delores L. Wood; life ptnr. Ronald V. Knapp; children: Charles L. Proudfit, Kerren L. Bergman. BA, MA, U. Mich., Ann Arbor, PhD, 1967. Cert. internat. property specialist. Assoc. prof. English Colo. Women's Coll., Denver, 1968—77; dir. Sewall & Farrand acad. programs, assoc. prof. English U. Colo., Boulder, 1978—82; stock broker Dain Bosworth, 1982—85; real estate broker Adrian Windsor Broker, Irvine, Calif., 1988—; pres. Sovereign Holdings Internat. Corp. Dir. pub. rels. KGNU Pub. Radio, 1982—83; adj. prof. English Coastline CC, 1991—2006. Author: (book) Seven Tools to Transform Genius Into Practical Power. Bd. mem. Colo. Music Festival, 1978—84, v.p. devel., 1978—84; bd. dirs. LA Fund Raising Reconstruction of Biblioteque Alexendrina. Recipient Outstanding Adj. Faculty award, 1996. Mem.: Fedn. Internation Real Estate Brokers, Calif. Assn. Realtors, Nat. Assn. Realtors, Inside Edge Found. Edn. (bd. dirs. 2002—03, program dir. 2003—). Democrat. Avocations: spiritual counseling, motivation, educational leadership, philanthropic project development. Office: 14252 Culver Dr #205A Irvine CA 92604 Personal E-mail: arealwin@aol.com. E-mail: adrianwindsor@sbcglobal.net.

WINDSOR, HARRIET SMITH, former state official; b. June 30, 1940; children: James A. Smith Jr., Julia A. Smith-O'Hanlon. BA, Juniata Coll., 1962; PhD, MA, U. Del. Cert. lay spkr. Peninsula Conf. Former English tchr. Seaford Sr. HS; dean instrn., dept. English Chmn. Del. Tech. and Cmty. Coll. Owens Campus; mem., dir. State Personnel Gov. Thomas R. Carper's Cabinet, 1993—2001; sec. state State of Del., Dover, 2001—09. Writer, spkr. numerous local, state and nat. bds. Serves Dist. Com. Ordained Ministry; mem., choir dir., organist, ch. sch. tchr., supt., adminstrv. bd. chmn., chmn. Pastor Parish Rels. Com. Millsboro Grace United Meth. Ch., lay leader, 2002—. Recipient Millsboro's Woman of Year, 1989, Order of the First State, Governor Thomas R. Carper, Del., 2000; named Del. Mother of Yr., 1999, Woman of Yr., Sussex Ctrl. Jr. HS students; named to Del.'s Hall of Fame, 1997. Democrat. Methodist.*

WINDSOR, PATRICIA (KATONAH SUMMERTREE, PERRIN WINTERS, ANNA SEELING), author, educator, lecturer; b. NYC, Sept. 21, 1938; d. Bernhard Edward and Antoinette (Gaus) Seelinger; m. Laurence Charles Windsor, Jr., Apr. 3, 1959 (div. 1978); children: Patience Wells, Laurence Edward; m. Stephen E. Altman, Sept. 21, 1986 (div. 1989). Student, Bennington Coll., 1956—58, Westchester C.C.; AA, NYU. V.p. Windsor-Morehead Assoc., NYC, 1960—63; info. mgr. Family Planning Assn., London, 1974—76; faculty mem. Inst. Children's Lit., Redding Ridge, Conn., 1976—94, 1999—; editor-in-chief AT&T, Washington, 1978—80; instr. U. Md. Writers Inst., Open Univ., Washington, 1980—82; creative developer, faculty mem. Long Ridge Writer's Group, Danbury, Conn., 1988—2000, instr., 2006—; dir. Summertree Studios, Savannah, Ga., 1992—. Dir. Wordspring Lit. Cons., 1989—, Wordworks Writing Cons., 1999—, Born Author Lit. Cons., 2003-; dir. Devel. Writing Workshops, Katonah, NY, 1976-78; judge Internat. Assn. Bus. Communicators, Washington, 1979, 89; lectr. LI U., Jersey City State Coll., Skidmore Coll., others, 1987—; instr. Coastal Ga. Ctr. for Continuing Edn., 1996—, Armstrong Atlantic U. Continuing Edn., 1997-2000, Anne Arundel (Md.) C.C., 2000—, workshop coord., 2000—; dir., founder Born Author.com, 2002—; dir. Windsomethings Art & Crafts, 2004—; owner, designer Tiger Woman Crafts for Meditation, 2005-. Author: The Summer Before, 1973 (ALA Best Book award 1973, transl. 1980 Austrian State prize 1980, also Brit., Norwegian, German edits.), Something's Waiting for You, Baker D, 1974 (starred selection Libr. Jour., Brit., Japanese edits.), Home Is Where Your Feet Are Standing, 1975, Diving for Roses, 1976 (NY Times Outstanding Book for Young Adults award, starred selection Libr. Jour.), Mad Martin, 1976, Killing Time, 1980, Demon Tree, 1983 (pen name Colin Daniel), The Sandman's Eyes, 1985 (Edgar Allan Poe Best Juvenile Mystery award Mystery Writers Am.), How a Weirdo and a Ghost Can Change Your Life, 1986, The Hero, 1988 (highest rating Voice of Youth Advocate), Just Like the Movies, 1990, The Christmas Killer, 1991 (Edgar nominee, Brit., Danish, French edits.), Two Weirdos and a Ghost, 1991, A Weird and Moogly Christmas, 1991, The Blooding, 1996 (YALSA pick for reluctant readers), The House of Death, 1996, Nightwood (nominated Best Book 2006), 2006; columnist The Blood Rev., 1990-92, Savannah Parent, 1990-92; columnist Coastal Senior, 1997-99; also short stories in anthologies and mags.; actress: The Haunting of Hill House, City Lights Theatre Co., 1991; contr. articles Once Upon a Time Mag., 2003, 04, 05. Mem. City Lights Theatre Co., Savannah, Ga., 1991. Mem. Horror Writers Am., Internat. Women's Writing Guild, Children's Book Guild, Authors Guild, Poetry Soc. Ga., Savannah Storytellers. Avocations: skiing, painting, modern dance. Business E-Mail: info@bornauthor.com.

WINE, L. MARK, lawyer; b. Norfolk, Va., Apr. 16, 1945; s. Melvin Leon and Mildred Sylvia (Weiss) W.; m. Blanche Weintraub, June 8, 1969; children: Kim, Lara, Dana. BA with high honors, U. Va., 1967; JD, U. Chgo., 1970. Bar: D.C. 1970, U.S. Supreme Ct. 1977. Assoc. Kirkland & Ellis LLP, Washington, 1970-72, ptnr., 1978—2007, of counsel, 2008—; trial atty. land and natural resources divsn. Dept. of Justice, Washington, 1972-78. Mem. ABA. Office: Kirkland & Ellis LLP 655 15th St NW Ste 1200 Washington DC 20005-5793 Office Phone: 202-879-5024. Business E-Mail: mwine@kirkland.com.

WINE, MARK PHILIP, lawyer; b. Iowa City, Jan. 6, 1949; s. Donald Arthur and Mary Lepha Schneider; m. Carol Jean Sullivan; children: Nicholas Cox, Meredith Kathryn, Callie Ann, Cassidy Mae. AB, Princeton U., 1971; JD, U. Iowa, 1974. Bar: Iowa 1974, Minn. 1976, Calif. 1997, U.S. Dist. Ct. Minn. 1976, U.S. Ct. Appeals (8th cir.) 1976, U.S. Supreme Ct. 1984, U.S. Ct. Appeals (4th cir.) 1985, U.S. Ct. Appeals (7th and Fed. cirs.) 1992, U.S. Ct. Appeals (9th cir.) 1997, U.S. Dist. Ct. (so., no. and ctrl. dists.) Calif. 1997. Law clk. to judge U.S. Ct. Appeals (8th cir.), St. Louis, 1974-76; ptnr. Oppenheimer Wolff & Donnelly, 1976—2002, McDermott, Will & Emery, LA, 2002—08, Orrick Herrington and Sutcliffe, 2008—. Mem. ABA, Internat. Assn. Def. Counsel, Calif. Bar Assn., O.C. Bar Assn., Fed. Bar Assn.(O.C. chpt.), Princeton Club So. Calif. Democrat. Avocations: cooking, reading, golf. Home: 6220 E Fox Glen Dr Anaheim CA 92807 Office: Orrick Herrington & Sutcliffe LLP 4 Park Plz Ste 1600 Irvine CA 92614 Office Phone: 949-852-7704. Personal E-mail: mpwineca@sbcglobal.net. Business E-Mail: mwine@orrick.com.

WINE-BANKS, JILL SUSAN, lawyer; b. Chgo., May 5, 1943; d. Bert S. and Sylvia Dawn (Simon) Wine; m. Ian David Volner, Aug. 21, 1965; m. Michael A. Banks, Jan. 12, 1980. BS, U. Ill., Champaign, Urbana, 1964; JD, Columbia U., 1968; LLD (hon.), Hood Coll., 1975. Bar: N.Y. 1969, U.S. Ct. Appeals (2d, 4th, 5th, 6th, 7th and 9th cirs.), U.S. Supreme Ct. 1974, D.C. 1976, Ill. 1980. Asst. press. and pub. rels. dir. Assembly of Captive European Nations, NYC, 1965-66; trial atty. criminal divsn. organized crime & racketeering U.S. Dept. Justice, 1969-73; asst. spl. prosecutor Watergate Spl. Prosecutor's Office, 1973-75; lectr. law sem. in trial practice Columbia U. Sch. Law, NYC, 1975-77; assoc. Fried, Frank, Harris, Shriver & Kampelman, Washington, 1975-77; gen. counsel Dept. Army, Pentagon, Washington, 1977-79; ptnr. Jenner & Block, Chgo., 1980-84; solicitor gen. State of Ill. Office of Atty. Gen., 1984-86, dep. atty. gen., 1986-87; exec. v.p., chief oper., officer ABA, Chgo., 1987-90; atty. pvt. practice, 1990-92; v.p., dir. transaction and govt. rels. Motorola Internat. Network Ventures, 1992-97; dir. strategic alliances Motorola Cellular Infrastructure Group, 1997—99; v.p. alliance mgmt. Maytag Corp., 1999-2001; CEO Winning Workplaces, Evanston, Ill., 2001—03; chief officer Chgo. Pub. Schs. Edn. to Careers, 2003—08; mgmt. cons. F & H Solutions Group, 2008—. Mem. EEC disting. vis. program European Parliament, 1987; chmn. bd. dirs. St. Petersburg Telecom., Russia, 1994-97, Omni Capital Ptnrs., Inc., 1994-97. Trustee Roosevelt U., 2004—; mem. adv. bd. Project Lead the Way, UIC Econ. Edn. Recipient Spl. Achievement award U.S. Dept. Justice, 1972, Meritorious award, 1973, Cert. Outstanding Svc., 1975; decorated Disting. Civilian Svc. Dept. Army, 1979; named Disting. Vis. to European Econ. Cmty. Mem.: The Chgo. Network, Internat. Women's Forum, Exec. Club (bd. dirs. 1999—2001), Econ. Club. Office Phone: 312-960-6136. Business E-Mail: jwinebanks@fhsolutionsgroup.com.

WINEGAR, ALBERT LEE, computer company executive; b. Beloit, Wis., Apr. 23, 1931; s. Albert Richard and Theo Rayneta (Hubbell) W.; m. Phyllis M. Everill; June 21, 1953; children: Bradford, Steven, Kristine, Kathleen. BBA, U. Wis., 1954. With IBM Corp., 1956-79, div. dir. mgmt. services, 1977-79; v.p. corp. planning, then group v.p. field ops. Olivetti Corp., Tarrytown, NY, 1979-80, pres., 1980-81; v.p. field ops. NBI Inc., Boulder, Colo., 1981-84; pres., chief exec. officer Sensory, Inc., Santa Clara, Calif., 1984-85, VICOM Systems, Inc., Fremont, Calif., 1985-91, ret., 1991. Bd. dirs. JRL Sys., Inc., Advanced Sys. Integration Group, Acad. Software Inc., Adams Globalization, Inc.; pres. Barton Creek Water Supply Corp. V.p. bd. trustees Valley Hosp., Ridgewood, N.J., 1978-81; pres. NJ Bus. Arts Found., 1977-78, Estates of Barton Creek Homeowners Assn., 1992-94; elder Westlake Hills Presbyn. Ch., stewardship chmn., 2002, fin. chmn., 2003 Capt. AUS, 1954-56. Sloan Exec. fellow, Stanford U., 1970. Mem. Computer and Bus. Equipment Mfrs. Assn. (dir. 1980-81), Barton Creek Country Club, Beta Theta Pi. Republican. Home: 10015 Haynes Bridge Road 6 Alpharetta GA 30022-1909 Home Phone: 678-393-1511.

WINEKE, JOSEPH STEVEN, political organization administrator, former state legislator; b. Madison, Wis., Jan. 5, 1957; s. Edward and Jennie Lanigan Wineke; m. Debora Howe, 1980; children: Scott, Brian, Jessica. BA, U. Wis., 1980. Alderman, Verona, Wis., 1980-83; mem. Dist. 79 Wis. State Assembly, 1982—92; mem. Dist. 27 Wis. State Senate, 1993—98; chmn. Dem. Party of Wis., 2006—. Rsch. assoc. Pub. Expenditure Survey of Wis., Madison, 1980-83; real estate agt; lobbyist, pub. rels. coord., Intnat. Union Operating Engr., 1999-. Democrat. Office: Dem Party of Wis 222 W Washington St Ste 150 Madison WI 53703 Office Phone: 608-255-5172. Office Fax: 608-255-8919. Business E-Mail: joew@wisdems.org.*

WINELAND, DAVID J., physicist; BS in Physics, U. Calif., Berkeley, 1965; M in Physics, Harvard U., PhD in Physics, 1970. Postdoctoral rsch. assoc. U. Wash.; with Nat. Bur. of Standards (now the Nat. Inst. of Standards and Technology), Boulder, Colo., 1975—. Several published articles in Science and Nature. Recipient William F. Meggers award, Optical Soc. Am., 1990, Frederic Ives medal, 2004, Einstein medal for Laser Sci., Soc. Optical and Quantum Electronics, 1996, I. I. Rabi Award of the IEEE, IEEE, 1998, Dept. Commerce Silver and Gold medals, 2007 Nat. Medal Sci. Fellow: Am. Phys. Soc. (Davisson-Germer prize 1990, Arthur L. Schawlow prize 2001), Am. Optical Soc.; mem.: NAS. Office: Natl Inst Of Standards & Technoloy 100 Bureau Dr Stop 1070 Gaithersburg MD 20899-0001

WINER, DAVID M., computer software company executive, software developer, blogger; b. Bklyn., May 2, 1955; BA in Math., Tulane U., 1976; MS in Computer Sci., U. Wis., 1978. Lead developer Personal Software, Inc., 1979—81; founder, CEO Living Videotext, Inc. (acquired by Symantec 1987), 1981—88; founding mem. UserLand Software, Inc., 1988—, CEO, 1988—2002. Former mem. bd. advisors World Wide Web Consortium. Author: (computer software programs) OPML 1.0, 2000, RSS 0.92, 2001, RSS 2.0, 2002; co-author: Frontier, 1992—98, XML-RPC, 1998, RSS 0.91, 1999, Manila, 1999, SOAP 1.1, 2000, Radio UserLand, 2001—02; editor, blog writer: Scripting News, 1997—; contbg. editor: Wired, 1994—96; blog writer: DaveNet, 1994—2004. Named Tech Renegade, Wired, 2001; named one of Top 10 Tech. Innovators, InfoWorld, 2002, Most Important People on the Web, PC World, 2007; Seybold fellow, 1997, fellow, Berkman Ctr. for Internet & Soc., Harvard Law Sch., 2003. Office: UserLand Software 4115 Blackhawk Plz Cir Ste 100 Danville CA 94506 Office Phone: 925-465-1300.

WINER, EDWARD L., lawyer; BA, U. Minn., Phi Beta Kappa, 1965; JD cum laude, U. Minn., 1968. Bar: Minn. 1968, Minn. (US Dist. Ct.) 1969, (US Tax Ct.) 1976, diplomate: Am. Coll. Family Trial Lawyers, cert.: (Family Law Arbitrator). Fellow Am. Acad. Matrimonal Attys.; shareholder Moss & Barnett, PA, Mpls., 1968—. Law sch. mentor. Co-author: The Family Law Financial Deskbook: Financial Issues in Ante nuptial and Postnuptial Agreements, Minn. Continuing Legal Edu., 2008, Valuation Strategies in Divorce, 2nd edit., 1992; co-editor: Premarital and Marital Agreements, 1993; contbr. articles to profl. jours. Named one of Top 100 US Attys., Worth Mag., 2006, 2007—08, Top 10

Divorce Lawyers in US, Best Lawyers in Am., Minn. Top 25 Litigators, Minn. Lawyer, Top 100 Super Lawyers, Minn. Law and Politics, Top 40 Vote Getters, Top Appellate Lawyers, Best Lawyers in US, Town and Country Mag., Top 100 US Family Law Trial Lawyers; named to Leading Am. Attys. Fellow: Am. Acad. Matrimonial Lawyers (past pres. Minn. Chpt.); mem.: ABA (family law sect., faculty mem. 2008), Family Law Trial Advocacy Inst., Cardozo Soc. (steering com., CLE com.), Hennepin County Bar Assn. (family law sect.), Minn. State Bar Assn. (family law sect.), Phi Alpha Theta, History Hon. Soc. Avocations: physical fitness, photography, gardening. Office: Moss & Barnett Professional Association 4800 Wells Fargo Ctr 90 S 7th St Minneapolis MN 55402-4129 Office Phone: 612-877-5295. Business E-Mail: winere@moss-barnett.com.

WINER, ERIC P., hematologist, oncologist, educator; b. Boston, Dec. 8, 1956; s. Richard Shepherd and Rhoda Ruth (Woogmaster) W.; m. Nancy M. Borstelman, June 23, 1984; children: Jeffrey, Joel, Emily. BA magna cum laude, Yale U., 1978, MD, 1983. Diplomate Nat. Bd. Med. Examiners, Am. Bd. Internal Medicine, Med. Oncology; lic. N.C. Intern internal medicine Yale-New Haven Hosp., Conn., 1983-84, resident internal medicine, 1984-86, chief resident, internal medicine, 1986-87; instr. dept. medicine Yale U. Sch. of Medicine, New Haven, 1986-87; staff physician Yale New-Haven Hosp., 1986-87; fellow hematology/oncoolgy Duke U. Med. Ctr., Durham, N.C., 1987-89, assoc. in medicine, 1989-90, physician, 1989, asst. prof. medicine divsn. hematology-oncology, 1990-96, assoc. prof., 1996—97; dir. breast oncology ctr. Dana-Farber Cancer Inst., Boston, 1997—, chief divsn. women, 2007—; active staff mem., dept. medicine Brigham and Women's Hosp., 1997—; assoc. prof. Harvard Med. Sch., 1997—2008, prof. medicine, 2008—. Cadre mem. psycho-oncology com. Cancer and Leukemia Group B, 1989—, breast com., 1990—, co-chair, 2009-, GU working com., 1991-94, clin. econ. working group, 1995—; co-dir. multi-disciplinary breast oncology program, 1993—, mem. hematology-oncology fellowship com.; PI for Duke U. Nat. Surgical Adjuvant Breast Program, 1992—; reviewer Jour. Clin. Oncology, Jour. AMA, Archives of Internal Medicine, Cancer Chemotherapy and Pharmacology, Transplantation, New Eng. Jour. Medicine, Breast Diseases; assoc. prof. Harvard Med. Sch.; chief scientific adviser, Susan G. Komen for the Cure, 2007-. Contbr. numerous articles, abstracts to profl. jours., chpts. to books. Recipient Kushlan award for outstanding intern, jr. resident Yale U. Sch. Medicine, 1984, 85; Am. Cancer Soc. Career Devel. award, 1991-94, Wendell Rosse award, 1994, Claire W. and Richard P. Morse Rsch. award, 2002; grantee: A.W. Mellon Found., 1990-91, Glaxo, Inc. pharmacoecon. divsn., 1991-92, NIH, 1991—. Mem. Am. Soc. Clin. Oncology, Acad. Hospice Physicians, Alpha Omega Alpha. Office: Dana-Farber Cancer Inst Mayer 228 44 Binney St Boston MA 02115 Office Phone: 617-632-6876. Office Fax: 617-632-1930. Business E-Mail: ewiner@partners.org.

WINER, KAREN K., endocrinologist; d. Howard L. and Gloria B. Kantor; m. Samuel J. Winer, Sept. 14, 1986; children: Julia B., David J. MD, Sackler Sch. Medicine, Tel Aviv, 1984. Cert. endocrinologist Am. Bd. Pediat., 1998. Med. officer NIH, Bethesda, Md., 1998—.

WINER, WARD OTIS, mechanical engineer, educator; b. Grand Rapids, Mich., June 27, 1936; s. Mervin Augustus and Ina Katherine (Wood) W.; m. Mary Jo Wielinga, June 15, 1957; children: Mathew Owen, James Edward, Paul Andrew, Mary Margaret. Asso., Grand Rapids Jr. Coll., Mich., 1956; BS, U. Mich., Ann Arbor, 1958; MS, U. Mich., 1959, PhD, 1962; PhD (Cavendish Lab. fellow), Cambridge U., Eng., 1964. Asst. prof. dept. mech. engring. U. Mich., Ann Arbor, 1963-66, assoc. prof., 1966-69; assoc. prof. mech. engring. Ga. Inst. Tech., 1969-71, prof., 1971-84, regents' prof., 1984—2007, mem. exec. bd., 1983-88, chmn., 1984-86, dir. and chmn. Sch. Mech. Engring., 1988—2007, Eugene C. Gwaltney jr. chair George W. Woodruff Sch. Mech. Engring., 2001—07, Eugene C. Gwaltney jr. sch. chair emeritus, 2007—. Chmn. Gordon Research Conf. on Friction, Lubrication and Wear, 1980; mem. NRC, 1980-88; chmn. Com. on Recommendations for U.S. Army Basic Sci. Research, 1985-87; chair, Engring. Applied Sci. and Math. Pannel NCRA Assn. Program, 2007-08; mem. div. mech., structural, materials engring. adv. bd. NSF Engring. Directorate, 1984-89; bd. dirs. Taiho Tribology Rsch. Found. Co-editor: Wear Control Handbook, 1980; tech. editor: Jour. Lubrication Tech., 1980-84, Jour. of Tribology, 1984-87; contbr. articles to profl. jours. Democratic precinct chmn., 1967-68; Mem. exec. bd Horace H. Rackham Sch. Grad. Studies, U. Mich., 1968. Recipient Disting. Faculty Svc. award Coll. Engring. U. Mich., 1967, Alumni Merit award, 1998, Cert. Recognition, NASA, 1977, Clarence E. Earle Meml. award Nat. Grease Lubricating Inst., 1979, Disting. Prof. award Ga. Inst. Tech., 1987; named Hon. Alumni, Ga. Tech., 2003. Fellow AAAS, ASME (hon.; bd. comms. 1987-91, v.p. rsch. 1989-93, found. trustee 2006—, Melville medal 1975, Centennial medallion 1980, vice chair, 2009-, Mayor D. Hersey award 1986, Charles Russ Richards Meml. award 1988), Soc. Tribologists and Lubrication Engrs. (bd. dirs. 1983-86, Internat. award 1997), Brit. Tribology Trust (gold medal 1987), Am. Soc. Engring. Educators (Benjamin Garver Lamme award 1995, Donald Marlowe award 1996); mem. NAE, Metro Atlanta Engring. Soc. (Engr. of Yr. 1989), Rheology, Soc. Engring. Sci. (dir. 1980-84), AAUP (pres. Ga. Tech. chpt. 1972-74, v.p. state conf. 1973-75), Sigma Xi (chpt. pres. 1982-83, Sustained Rsch. in Engring. award 1975), Tau Beta Pi, Pi Tau Sigma, Phi Kappa Phi. Home: 1025 Mountain Creek Trl NW Atlanta GA 30328-3535 Business E-Mail: ward.winer@me.gatech.edu.

WINER, WARREN JAMES, insurance executive; b. Wichita, Kans., June 16, 1946; s. Henry Charles and Isabel (Ginsburg) W.; m. Mary Jean Kovacs, June 23, 1968 (div. Feb. 1973); m. Jo Lynn Sondag, May 3, 1975; children: Adam, Lauren. BS in Math., Stanford U., 1968. With Gen. Am. Life Ins. Co., St. Louis, 1968-73, dir. retirement plans, 1973-76, 2d v.p., 1976-80; v.p., sr. actuary Powers, Carpenter & Hall, St. Louis, 1980-84, sr. v.p., dir. pension div., 1984-85, pres., chief operating officer, 1985-86, lobbyist, commentator, 1985—. pres., chief exec. officer, 1986—; pres. W F Corroon, 1988-93; prin. William M. Mercer, 1993-94, mng. dir., 1994-95; exec. v.p. Gen. Am. Life Ins. Co., St. Louis, 1995—. Mem. Actuarial Exam. Com., Chgo., 1973-74. Contbr. articles to profl. jours. Bd. dirs. Lucky Lane Nursery Sch. Assn., St. Louis, 1978-93, pilot divsn. United Way, 1986-87; co-pres. Conway Sch. Parent Assn., 1986-87; bd. dirs. Paraquad, 1991—, chmn., 1994-99; bd. dirs. ATD, 1992—; chair triumph divsn. Unitd Way, 1996—. Fellow Soc. Actuaries; mem. Am. Acad. Actuaries, Enrollment of Actuaries (joint bd.), Am. Life Ins. Assn. (small case task force 1979-80), Life Office Mgmt. Assn. (ICPAC com. 1975-80), St. Louis Actuaries Club. Clubs: St. Louis, Clayton (St. Louis). Jewish. Avocations: bridge, wine tasting, swimming, weightlifting, bicycling. Office: Gen Am Benefits 13045 Tesson Ferry Rd Saint Louis MO 63128-3407

WINEY, KAREN I., engineering educator, researcher; b. Abington, Pa., Aug. 1, 1963; d. Donald A. and Patricia A. Winey; m. Russel J. Composto, July 11, 1987; children: Jordana, Rebecca. BS, Cornell U., 1985; MS, U. Mass., 1989, PhD, 1991. Postdoctoral fellow AT&T Bell Labs., Murray Hill, NJ, 1991-92; asst. prof. dept. materials sci. and engring. and dept. chem. and biomolecular engring. U. Pa., Phila., 1992-2000, assoc. prof., 2000—05, prof., 2005—. Cons. Dow Chem., Midland, Mich., 1999-2002, Rhodia, Inc., Cranberry, NJ, 2000—03, Colgate-Palmolive, Piscataway, NJ, 2003—05, Arkema, 2005-; presenter in field. Mem. editl. bd.: Macromolecules, 2001—05, Jour. Polymer Sci., 2000—; contbr. more than 90 articles to profl. jours. Recipient Young Investigator award, NSF, 1994—99, Cosslett award, Microscopy and Microanalysis Meeting, 2000; grantee, Office Naval Rsch., NSF, US Army, Petroleum Rsch. Found., Dow Chem. Mem.: Am. Chem. Soc., Materials Rsch. Soc., Am. Physics Soc. (mem.-at-large divsn. polymers 2001—04). Office: U Pa 3231 Walnut St Philadelphia PA 19104-6272 Office Phone: 215-898-0593. Business E-Mail: winey@seas.upenn.edu.

WINFIELD, DAVE (DAVID MARK WINFIELD), professional sports team executive, sportscaster, retired professional baseball player; b. St. Paul, Oct. 3, 1951; m. Tonya Winfield; children: Arielle Arline, David Mark II. Student, U. Minn.; LLD (hon.), Syracuse U., 1987. Outfielder San Diego Padres, 1973-80, NY Yankees, 1980-90, Calif. Angels, 1990-91, Toronto Blue Jays, 1991-92, Minn. Twins, 1992-94, Cleve. Indians, 1995; commentator Fox Broadcasting Co., Beverly Hills, Calif., 1996—2002; v.p., sr. adv. San Diego Padres, 2002—; analyst, Baseball Tonight ESPN, 2009—. Co-author (with Tom Parker) Winfield: A Player's Life, 1988. Founder David M. Winfield Found. for Underprivileged Youth, 1975—. Recipient Golden Glove award, 1979-80, 1982-85, 1987, Silver Slugger award, 1981-85, 1992, Babe Ruth award, 1992, Branch Rickey award, 1992, Roberto Clemente award, 1994; named Sporting News Am. League Comeback Player of Yr., 1990; named to the Nat. League All-Star Team, 1977-80, Am. League All-Star Team, 1981-88, Sporting News All-Star Team, 1979, 1982-84, 1992, Major League Baseball Hall of Fame, 2001, Coll. Baseball Hall of Fame, 2006. Achievements include member of Major League Baseball World Series Championship winning Toronto Blue Jays, 1992. Office: c/o San Diego Padres PETCO Pk 100 Park Blvd San Diego CA 92101*

WINFIELD, JOHN BUCKNER, rheumatologist, educator; b. Kentfield, Calif., Mar. 19, 1942; s. R. Buckner and Margaret G. (Katterfelt) Winfield; m. Patricia Nichols (div. 1968); 1 child, Ann Gibson; m. Teresa Lee McGrath, 1969 (div. 2000); children: John Buckner III, Virginia Lee; m. Leigh Fleming Callahan, 2001. BA, Williams Coll., 1964; MD, Cornell U., 1968. Diplomate Am. Bd. Internal Medicine. Intern in medicine N.Y. Hosp., NYC, 1968-69; staff assoc. LI/Nat. Inst. Allergy and Infectious Diseases NIH, Bethesda, Md., 1969-71; resident in medicine, fellow in rheumatology U. Va. Sch. Medicine, Charlottesville, 1971-73; fellow in immunology Rockefeller U., NYC, 1973-75; asst. prof. medicine U. Va. Sch. Medicine, Charlottesville, 1975-76, assoc. prof. medicine, 1976-78, U. N.C., Chapel Hill, 1978-81, prof. medicine, 1981—2006, chief div. rheumatology and immunology, 1978-99; dir. Thurston Arthritis Rsch. Ctr., U. N.C. Sch. Medicine, Chapel Hill, 1982—2001; dir Daughtridge Arthritis Ctr., Lenoir, NC, 2002—07; consulting rheumatologist Appalachian Regional Rheumatology, 2007—; Smith prof. medicine U. NC Sch. Med., Chapel Hill, 1987—2006, emeritus, 2006—, adj. prof. exercise sports physiology, 2003—; adj. prof. endodontics Neurosensory Disorders Ctr., UNC Sch. Dentistry, sr. mem.; owner Winfield Medical, L.L.C., 2004—. Adv. coun. Nat. Inst. Arthritis and Musculoskeletal and Skin Diseases, NIH, 1988-92; chmn. edn. com. Am. Rheumatism Assn., Atlanta, 1980-84; immunol. scis. study sect. NIH, 1979-83, Arthritis Musculoskeletal and Skin study sect., 1992-96; vice-chair fellowship com. Arthritis Found., 1982; med. coun. Lupus Found. Am., 1987-96. Author more than 130 med. and sci. articles in peer reviewed rheumatology and immunology jours.; mem. editl. bd. Arthritis and Rheumatism, Bull. Rheumatic Diseases, Rheumatology Internat., Clin. Exptl. Rheumatology, Am. Jour. Medicine, Clin. Immunology, Current Rev. Rheumatology. Sr. asst. surgeon with USPHS, NIH, Bethesda, Md., 1968-71. Recipient Borden prize Cornell U. Med. Coll., 1964, numerous rsch. grants NIH and Arthritis Found., 1975—, Sr. Investigator award Arthritis Found., 1976-79, Kenan award U. NC, 1985, NIH merit award, 1992. Fellow ACP; mem. Am. Assn. Immunologists, Am. Fedn. Clin. Rsch., Am. Soc. Clin. Investigation, Assn. Am. Physicians, Am. Clin. Climatol. Assn., Nat. Soc. Clin. Rheumatologists (treas. 1997-02), Henry Kunkel Soc. (councilor 2000-02), Chapel Hill Country Club; master, Am. Coll. Rheumatology. Republican. Episcopalian. Avocations: golf, on and off-road motorcycling, scuba diving instructor, skiing. Home: 102 Greenwood Ln Chapel Hill NC 27514-5957 Office Phone: 828-263-8370. Business E-Mail: john_winfield@med.unc.edu.

WINFIELD, MICHAEL D., engineering company executive; b. 1939; BSChemE, Ohio State U.; MBA, U. Chgo. Chem. engr. UOP, Des Plaines, Ill., 1962-74, mgr. refinery projects, 1974-76, asst. dir. tech. svcs., 1976-81, dir. bus. devel., 1981-83, v.p. tech. svcs., 1983-84, v.p. process svcs., 1984-92, pres., CEO, 1992—. Office: UOP 25 E Algonquin Rd Des Plaines IL 60016-6100

WINFIELD, RICHARD NEILL, lawyer; b. Chgo., Jan. 20, 1933; s. Richard Paul and Mary B. (Monaghan) Winfield; m. Deborah Mary Trainer, June 13, 1959; children: Richard Neill Jr., Pamela, Nicole. AB, Villanova U., 1955; LLB, Georgetown U., 1961. Bar: Va. 1961, N.Y. 1962, U.S. Dist. Ct. (so. dist.) N.Y. 1963. Assoc. Donovan, Leisure, Newton & Irvine, NYC, 1961-65; asst. counsel to Gov. Nelson A. Rockefeller Gov.'s Office, Albany, NY, 1965-67; assoc. Royall, Koegel, Rogers & Wells, NYC, 1967-69; ptnr. Clifford Chance US LLP (formerly known as Rogers & Wells), NYC, 1969—2002. Chmn. bd. consultors Sch. Law Villanova U., Pa., 1980—2004; faculty comm. law confs. Practising Law Inst., NYC, 1977—2001, chmn. libel litig. confs., 1979—2000; prof. Columbia Law Sch., Fordham Law Sch., 2002—. Editor: Libel Litigation, PLI, 1979, 1981, 1984, 1986, 1988, 1990, 1992, 1994, 1996, 1998, 2000; contbr. articles to profl. jours. Chmn. bd. trustees Convent Sacred Heart Sch., NYC, 1987—90; co-chmn. bd. dirs. Fund for Peace, 2000—; mem. bd. visitors Sch. Langs. and Linguistics, Georgetown U., Washington, 1987—93. Lt. USN, 1955—59. Recipient Alumni medallion, Coll. Liberal Arts & Scis. Villanova U., 1984, Loyalty award, Villanova U., 1986, First Amendment award, Deadline Club, 2002. Mem.: ABA (chmn. media law reform working group 1996—, Ctrl. Europe and Eurasian Law Initiative), Internat. Sr. Lawyers Project (co-founder, bd. dirs., treas.), Assn. Bar City of N.Y., N.Y. State Bar Assn., Century Assn. Republican. Roman Catholic. Avocations: travel, history. Home: 40 5th Ave New York NY 10011-8843 Office: Clifford Chance US LLP 31 West 52nd St New York NY 10019 Office Phone: 212-878-8233.

WINFREE, DANIEL EDWARD, state supreme court justice, lawyer; b. Fairbanks, Alaska, Feb. 12, 1953; s. James Richard and Betty Jane (Hering) W.; m. Cathleen Maureen Ringstad, July 16, 1983; children: Christina, James. BS in Fin., U. Oreg., 1977; MBA in Real Estate, U. Calif., Berkeley, 1981, JD, 1981. Bar: Alaska 1982, U.S. Dist. Ct. Alaska 1982, U.S. Ct. Appeals (9th cir.) 1982. Assoc. Perkins Cole, Anchorage, 1982-85; pvt. practice Valdez and Fairbanks, Alaska, 1985-90; shareholder Winfree & Hompesch, P.C., Fairbanks, 1990—2008; justice Alaska Supreme Ct., Anchorage, 2008—. Pres. Western States Bar Conf., 1997—98, ethics com., fee arbitration com. Chairperson Coll. of Fellows, U. Alaska Found., Fairbanks, 1995-96; pres. bd. trustees Alaska Bar Found. Mem. Alaska Bar Assn. (pres. 1994-95, mem. bd. govs. 1990-96, sec. 1990-91, treas. 1991-93, Disting. Svc. award, 2007), Rotary (bd. dirs. Fairbanks chpt. 1994-96). Office: Alaska Supreme Ct 303 K St Fl 5 Anchorage AK 99501-2013*

WINFREY, CAREY WELLS, journalist, editor; b. NYC, Aug. 1, 1941; s. William Colin and Mary (Robinson) Winfrey; m. Jane Elizabeth Keeney, Feb. 13, 1982; children: Graham William, Wells Millar. AB, Columbia U., 1963, MS in Journalism, 1967. Assoc. editor Time Inc., NYC, 1968-71; exec. producer Ednl. Broadcast Corp., NYC, 1971-77; reporter, fgn. corr. Africa NY Times, NYC, 1977-80; editor CBS Mags., NYC, 1981-90, editor Cuisine mag., 1983-84, v.p., editorial dir., 1985-87; founding editor-in-chief Memories mag. Diamandis Comm., Inc. (formerly mag. divsn. CBS), NYC, 1987-90; editor-in-chief Am. Health mag. Reader's Digest Publs., NYC, 1990-96; dir. Delacorte Ctr. for Mag. Journalism, Columbia U., NYC, 1996-98; asst. mng. editor People Mag. Time Inc., 1996—2001; editor-in-chief Smithsonian Mag., 2001—. Author: Starts and Finishes, 1975; exec. prodr.: (TV miniseries) Behind the Lines, 1971—75, Assignment America, 1975, WNET Reports, 1976—77; columnist Parenting mag., 1986—89. Lt. USMC, 1963—66. Recipient Meyer Berger award for Disting. Reporting, Columbia U., 1978. Office: Smithsonian Mag MRC 513 PO Box 37012 Washington DC 20013-7012 Office Phone: 202-633-6072. Business E-Mail: cwinfrey@si.edu.

WINFREY, JOHN CRAWFORD, economist, educator; b. Somerville, Tenn., July 2, 1935; s. Arthur Peter and Frances (Crawford) W.; m. Barbara Ann Strickland, July 20, 1957; 1 child, Mae Millicent. AB, Davidson Coll., 1957; PhD, Duke U., 1965. Asst. dir. data processing Hanes Hosiery, Winston Salem, NC, 1959-62; rsch. asst. in econs. Duke U., Durham, NC, 1963-64; asst. prof. econs. Washington and Lee U., Lexington, Va., 1965-68, assoc. prof., 1969-73, prof., 1974—. Vis. prof. Vanderbilt U., Nashville, 1966, Tufts U., Boston, 1975, UCLA, 1978, U. Ill., 1982, U. Va., 1986, Duke U., 1989, 95, U. Calif., Berkeley, 1993, U. Utrecht, Netherlands, 1995; adj. prof. Southern Va. U., 2009. Co-author: The Motion Commotion, 1972; author: Public Finance, Public Choice and the Public Sector, 1973, Social Issues, The Ethics and Economics of Taxes and Public Programs, 1997. Bd. dirs. Lexington Tennis Clinic, 1968-72, Rockbridge Area Conservation Coun., 1982-84, Rockbridge Area Social Svc., 2002—, Lexington Family Mentoring Program; mem. Rockbridge Area Behavioral Health Adv. Bd., 2001—, Nelson Fine Art Gallery, Lexington, Va.; pres. Rockbridge Arts Guild, 1986-88, 2001-02. Recipient Cmty. Svc. award Lexington Jaycees, 1971; NEH fellow, 1975, 78, 82, 86, 89, 93; vis. fellow U. Coll. Oxford U., Eng., 1979, 95. Fellow Soc. for Values in Higher Edn.; mem. Am. Econ. Assn., So. Econ. Assn., History of Econs. Soc., Eastern Econ. Assn., High Wheelers Club (Lexington), Sunrise Rotary Club. Democrat. Presbyterian. Home: 160 Kendal Dr #1035 Lexington VA 24450 Office: Washington and Lee U Dept Econs Lexington VA 24450 Business E-Mail: winfreyj@wlu.edu.

WINFREY, MARCELLENE S., music educator, church musician; b. Chgo., Dec. 4, 1949; d. Arthur S. and Nellye M. Winfrey; m. Darryl Jones, Nov. 27, 1988 (div. Sept. 0, 1994); 1 child, Troy L. B in Music Edn., Roosevelt U., 1980; MS in Elem. Edn., Xavier U., 1994; PhD in Christian Counseling, Ministry, Jacksonville Theol. Sem., 2008. Cert. music K-12 State of Ohio, 1989, elem. edn. K-8 State of Ohio, 1992, Orff-Schulwerk tchr. U. Cin., Coll. Conservatory Music, 2004. Distbn. clk. USPS, Chgo., 1969—74; instr. Chgo. City Wide Coll., 1980—82; educator Chgo. Pub. Schs., 1982—87; adminstr. So. Bapt. Day Care, Cin., 1988—88; min. music Union Bapt. Ch., 1988—93; music specialist Cin. Pub. Schs., 1988—; ch. organist Quinn Chapel AME, 1994—97; ch. musician Allen Temple AME, 1997—. Cooperating tchr. Coll. Conservatory Music; jr. achievement coord., 1992—94; United Way coord., 1993—97; mem. Local Sch. Dist. Mgmt. Com., Cin., 2004—; United Negro Coll. Fund coord., 2007—; facilitator Jacksonville Theol. Sem., 2008—; fine arts coord., 2008—. Musician (keyboardist): Metro City Band, 1995—98; musician: Helen Steiner Rice Project, 2002; musician: (prelude music) Nikki Giovonni, 2005; accompanist: Quarndera Battle-Ryan; soprano (women's chorus) Midsummer Night's Dream, 2005; chorus mem.: Porgy and Bess; conductor: Carmon DeLeone; singer: (choir) Carolfest, Music Hall Cin., 2007, Nat. Underground Freedom Mus., 2007. Vol. Race Rels. Com., 1989—93; mem., mentor Excel Club, Cin., 2004—05. Recipient Internat. Peace prize, United Cultural Conv., 2006. Mem.: ASCD (assoc.), Urban Music Leadership Com. (assoc.), Ohio Music Educators Assn. (assoc.; urban music leadership com.), Phi Delta Kappa (life). Avocations: travel, genealogy, gardening, walking, piano. Office: Western Hills HS 2144 Ferguson Rd Cincinnati OH 45238-3799 Office Fax: 513-363-8720.

WINFREY, OPRAH, television talk show host, actress, television producer; b. Kosciusko, Miss., Jan. 29, 1954; d. Vernon Winfrey and Vernita Lee. BA in Speech Comm. and Performing Arts, Tenn. State U., 1987; LHD (hon.), Duke U., 2009. News reporter Sta. WVOL Radio, Nashville, 1971-72; reporter, news anchorperson Sta. WTVF-TV, Nashville, 1973-76; news anchorperson Sta. WJZ-TV, Balt., 1976—78, host morning talk show People Are Talking, 1978—83; host talk show A.M. Chgo. Sta. WLS-TV, 1984; host The Oprah Winfrey Show, Chgo., 1985—, Oprah After the Show, Chgo., 2002—; nationally syndicated, 1986—; host series of celebrity interview spls. Oprah: Behind the Scenes; owner, prodr., chmn., CEO Harpo Prodns., 1986—. Ptnr., co-founder Oxygen Media, an Internet and cable TV co., 1998—; founder, editl. dir. O, The Oprah Magazine in conjunction with Hearst Mags., 2000; launched (mag.)first internat. edit., O, The Oprah Magazine in South Africa, 2002-, Oprah, After the Show, 2002-, O at Home, 2004-, Oprah & Friends, XM Satelite Radio Holdings, Inc., 2006-; online leader, Oprah.com, launched Live Your Best Life, 2003-; started Oprah Book Club; creator (TV series) Oprah's Big Give, 2007 Actress: (films) The Color Purple, 1985 (nominated Acad. award and Golden Globe award), Native Son, 1986, Beloved, 1998, (voice only) Charlotte's Web, 2006, (voice only) Bee Movie, 2007; (TV movies) There Are No Children Here, 1993, Before Women Had Wings, 1997;(TV appearances) Ellen, 1997, 30 Rock, 2008; actress, prodr. (TV miniseries) The Women of Brewster Place, 1989; prodr. (TV series) Dr. Phil, 2002—, Dr. Oz, 2009-; co-prodr. The Color Purple (Broadway), 2005; host, supervising prodr. celebrity interview series Oprah: Behind the Scenes, 1992, ABC Aftersch. Spls., 1991-93; host, exec. prodr. Michael Jackson Talks...to Oprah-90 Prime-Time Minutes with the King of Pop, 1993; exec. prodr. (TV movies) Overexposed, 1992, Nine, 1992, Oprah Winfrey Presents: Their Eyes Were Watching God, 2005; host Oprah Winfrey's Legends Ball (also exec. prodr.), 2006, Building a Dream: The Oprah Winfrey Leadership Acad. (also exec. prodr.), 2007, The Oprah Winfrey Oscar Special, 2007; exec. prodr. (TV miniseries) Oprah Winfrey Presents: The Wedding, 1998, David and Lisa, 1998, Tuesdays with Morrie, 1999, Amy and Isabelle, 2001, Their Eyes Were Watching God, 2005, A Dreary Date with Destiny, 2007; voice (video) Our Friend, Martin, 1999; guest appearances The Fresh Prince of Bel-Air, 1992, Ellen, 1997, Home Improvement, 1999, The Hughleys, 1999, Mad TV, 2002 and several others. Established Oprah Winfrey Found., 1987—, Oprah's Angel Network, 1997—, ChristmasKindness South Africa, 2002—, Oprah Winfrey Scholars Program, Oprah Winfrey Leadership

Academy for Girls, Henley-on-Klip, South Africa, 2006, Seven Fountains Primary Sch, South Africa, 2007. Recipient Woman of Achievement award NOW, 1986, Emmy award for Best Daytime Talk Show Host, 1987, 91, 92, 94, 95, 97, Hon. Nat. Book Award for influential contbn. to reading and books, 1999, Nat. Book Found's 50th Anniversary gold medal, 1999, America's Hope award, 1990, Industry Achievement award Broadcast Promotion Mktg. Execs./Broadcast Design Assn., 1991, Image awards NAACP, 1989, 91, 92, 94, Entertainer of Yr. award NAACP, 1989, CEBA awards, 1989, 90, 91, George Foster Peabody's 1995 Individual Achievement award, 1996, Gold Medal award IRTS, 1996, Lifetime Achievement award NATAS, 1998, People's Choice award, 1997, 98, Horatio Alger award, 1993, Bob Hope Humanitarian award, 54th Ann. Primetime Emmy Awards, 2002, Marian Anderson Award, Phila., 2003, AAP Honors award, Assn. Am. Publishers, 2003, Disting. Svc. award, Nat. Assn. Broadcasters, 2004, Global Humanitarian Action award, UN Assn. USA, 2004, Nat. Freedom award, Nat. Civil Rights Mus., 2005, Nat. Mag. award, Am. Soc. Mag. Editors, 2007, Humanitarian award, Elie Wiesel Found., 2007; ranked #1 Most Powerful In Industry, Entertainment Weekly, 1998, 200 Greatest Pop Culture Icons, VH1, 2003; named Broadcaster of Yr. Internat. Radio and TV Soc., 1988, TV Performer of Yr., TV Guide, 1997, Most Important Person in Books and Media, Newsweek, 1997; named one of The 50 Most Beautiful in the World, People, 1997, America's 25 Most Influential People of the 20th Century, TIME mag., 1998, The 100 Most Powerful Women in Entertainment, Hollywood Reporter, 2004, 06, 07, The 100 Most Influential People in the World, TIME Mag., 2004-09, The 100 Most Powerful Women, Forbes mag., 2005-09, 50 Women to Watch, Wall St. Jour., 2005, The 100 Most Influential Black Americans, Ebony mag., 2006, The 50 Most Powerful Women in Bus., Fortune mag., 1998-2008, 50 Who Matter Now, CNNMoney.com Bus. 2.0, 2006, The 100 Most Powerful Celebrities, Forbes.com, 2007-09; named to List Am. Billionaires, Fortune, 2003, 400 Richest Americans, 1999-, World's Richest People, 2003-, Power 150, Ebony mag. 2008, The Global Elite, Newsweek mag., 2008; inducted to Television Hall of Fame, 1994, Broadcasting and Cable Hall of Fame, 2002, NAACP Hall of Fame, 2005; elected to Nat. Women's Hall of Fame, Seneca Falls, NY. Initiated a campaign to establish a national database of convicted child abusers, and testified before U.S. Senate Judiciary Committee on behalf of National Child Protection Act in 1991, as a result, President Clinton signed the "Oprah Bill" into Law on December 20, 1993, establishing the national database used by law enforcement agencies around the world; third woman in American entertainment industry to own her own studio; first African-American woman to reach billionaire status; after receiving Lifetime Acheivement Award in 1998, permanently withdrew name from Daytime Emmy Award consideration; Oprah and Oprah Winfrey Show received a total of 39 Daytime Emmy awards: seven for Outstanding Host; nine for Outstanding Talk Show; twenty-one in the Creative Arts categories; and one for supervising producer of the ABC School Special, Shades of Single Protein; celebrated the 20th year anniversary of the Oprah Winfrey Show in November, 2005. Office: Oprah Winfrey Show Harpo Studios 1058 W Washington Blvd Chicago IL 60607 Address: Harpo Prodn PO Box 909715 Chicago IL 60607 Office Phone: 312-633-0808.*

WING, ADRIEN KATHERINE, law educator; b. Aug. 7, 1956; d. John Ellison and Katherine (Pruitt) Wing; children: Che-Cabral, Nolan Felipe. AB magna cum laude, Princeton U., 1978; MA, UCLA, 1979; JD, Stanford, 1982. Bar: N.Y. 1983, U.S. Dist. Ct. (so. and ea. dists.) N.Y. 1983, U.S. Ct. Appeals (5th and 9th cirs.). Assoc. Curtis, Mallet-Prevost, Colt & Mosle, NYC, 1982-86, Rabinowitz, Boudin, Standard, Krinsky & Lieberman, 1986-87; assoc. prof. law U. Iowa, Iowa City, 1987-93, prof., 1993—, disting. prof. law, 2001—, assoc. dean faculty R&D, 2006—09. Mem. alumni council Princeton U., 1983-85, 96-2000, mem. exec. com., 2002, trustee Class of '78 Alumni Found., 1984-87, 93—, v.p. Princeton Class of 1978 Alumni, 1993-98, trustee Princeton U. 1995; mem. bd. visitors Stanford Law Sch., 1993-96; vis. prof. U. Mich., 2002. Mem. bd. editors Am. J. Comp. Law, 1993—2001. Mem. Iowa Commn. on African Ams. in Prisons, 1999—. Recipient Disting. Alum award, Newark Acad., 2004, Gertrude Rush award, 2006, Ferguson award, AALS Clyde, 2009. Mem.: ABA (exec. com. young lawyers sect. 1985—87, law sch. site inspector 2002—), U.S. Assn. Constl. Law (bd. dir.), Am. Assn. of Law Schs. (minority sect. bd. 1996—, chair 2002), Am. Friends Svc. Com. (bd. dirs. Mid. East 1998—2004), Am. Soc. Internat. Law (exec. coun. 1986—89, exec. com. 1988—99, nominating com. 1991, 1993, group chair S. Africa 1993—95, membership com. 1994—95, exec. coun. 1996—99, v.p. 2007—09), Internat. Assn. Dem. Lawyers (UN rep. 1984—87), Nat. Conf. Black Lawyers (chmn. internat. affairs sect. 1982—95, UN rep.), Internat. Third World Legal Studies Assn. (bd. dirs. 1996—99, nominating trustee Princeton com. 1997—2000), Coun. on Fgn. Rels., Iowa Peace Inst. (bd. dirs. 1993—95), Iowa City Fgn. Rels. Coun. (bd. dirs. 1989—94), Transafrica Scholars Forum Coun. (bd. dirs. 1993—95), Black Alumni of Princeton U. (bd. dirs. 1982—87). Democrat. Avocations: photography, writing, poetry. Office: U Iowa Sch Law Boyd Law Bldg Iowa City IA 52242 Home Phone: 319-354-2849; Office Phone: 319-335-9129. E-mail: adrien-wing@uiowa.edu.

WING, EDWARD JOSEPH, biomedical researcher, educator, dean; b. Mineola, NY, June 19, 1945; s. Maurice John and Frances Elliott Wing; m. Rena Rimsky, Aug. 19, 1967; children: Jonathan Frederick, Kenneth Elliott. BA magna cum laude, Williams Coll., 1967; MD cum laude, Harvard U., 1971. Resident in medicine Peter Bent Brigham Hosp., Boston, 1971-73; asst. surgeon USPHS, Pitts., 1973-75; fellow infectious diseases Stanford U., Palo Alto, Calif., 1975-77; asst. prof. medicine U. Pitts., 1977-82, assoc. prof. medicine, 1982-88, prof. medicine, 1989—; physician-in-chief, dept. medicine Montefiore Univ. Hosp., Pitts., 1990, vice chmn. dept. medicine, 1991; physician-in-chief RI Hosp., Miriam Hosp.; exec. physician-in-chief Meml. Hosp. of RI, Vet. Affairs Med. Ctr., Women & Infants Hosp.; chair Dept. Medicine Brown U., Joukowsky Family prof. medicine; dean medicine and biological scis. Alpert Med. Sch., Brown U., 2008—. Jour. referee numerous med. and sci. jours.; grant reviewer NIH and VA. Contbr. numerous articles to profl. jours. NIH grantee, 1983, 84, 87, 91. Fellow Infectious Disease Soc. Am.; mem. Am. Assn. Immunologists, Am. Soc. for Microbiology, Am. Fedn. for Clin. Rsch., Reticuloendothelial Soc. Avocations: tennis, skiing, photography, windsurfing. Office: Brown U Med Sch Divsn of Biology and Medicine Box G-A Providence RI 02912 Office Phone: 401-863-3330. E-mail: Edward_Wing_MD@Brown.EDU.*

WING, ELIZABETH SCHWARZ, museum curator, educator; b. Cambridge, Mass., Mar. 5, 1932; d. Henry F. and Maria Lisa Schwarz; m. James E. Wing, Apr. 18, 1957; children: Mary Elizabeth Wing-Berman, Stephen R. BA, Mt. Holyoke Coll., 1955; MS, U. Fla., 1957, PhD, 1962. Interim asst. curator Fla. Mus. Natural History, U. Fla., Gainesville, 1961-69, asst. curator, 1969-73, assoc. curator, 1973-78, curator, 1978—2001, curator emeritus, 2001—; prof. anthropology dept. U. Fla., 1979—2001, prof. zoology dept., 1988—2001. US rep. Internat. Congress Archaeozoology, 1981—2001. Author: (with A.B. Brown) Paleonutrition, 1979, (with E.J. Reitz) Zooarcheology, 1999, 2nd edit., 2008, (with Lee A. Newsom) On Land and Sea, 2004; editor (with J.C. Wheeler) Economic Prehistory of the Central Andes, 1988; contbr. articles to profl. jours. Recipient Fryxell award Soc. Am. Archaeology, 1996; NSF grantee, 1961-64, 68-73, 79-80, 84-85, 89-91, 95-96. Mem. NAS, Soc. Ethnobiology (pres. 1989-91, trustee 1991-). Office: U Fla Dickinson Hall/Fla Mus Natural History PO Box 117800 Gainesville FL 32611-7800

WING, JAMES DAVID, lawyer; b. Milw., May 4, 1943; s. William H. and Elaine E. (Koehler) W.; children: Benjamin, Tracy, Nathaniel, John. BA, Beloit Coll., Wis., 1965; MA, U. Chgo., 1966, JD, 1969. Bar: Wis. 1969, Fla. 1975, U.S. Ct. Appeals (7th cir.) 1973, U.S. Dist. Ct. (mid. dist.) Fla. 1975, U.S. Ct. Appeals (5th cir.) 1978, U.S. Dist. Ct. (so. dist.) Fla. 1981, U.S. Ct. Appeals (11th cir.) 1981, U.S. Supreme Ct. 1979. Assoc. Whyte, Hirschboeck, Minahan, Harding & Harland, Milw., 1969-75, Carlton, Fields, Ward, Emmanuel, Smith & Cutler, Tampa, Fla., 1975-85, Myers, Kenin, Levinson, Frank & Richards/Shea & Gould, Miami, Fla., 1985-88, Fine, Jacobson, Schwartz, Nash, Block & England, Miami, 1988-94, Holland & Knight, Miami, 1994—. Fellow Ctr. for Internat. Legal Studies, Salzburg, Austria. Mem. Phi Beta Kappa, Phi Eta Sigma, Omicron Delta Kappa. Avocations: germanistics, tennis. Office: Holland & Knight LLP 701 Brickell Ave Ste 3000 Miami FL 33131 Office Phone: 305-374-8500, 305-789-7768. Fax: 305 789 7799. E-mail: james.wing@hklaw.com.

WING, JEANNETTE MARIE, computer science educator, consultant; b. Newark, Dec. 4, 1956; d. Omar and Camella Grace (Chien) W. SB and SM in Elec. Engring. and Computer Sci., MIT, 1979, PhD in Computer Sci., 1983. Asst. prof. U. So. Calif., LA, 1983-85, Carnegie Mellon U., Pitts., 1985-90, assoc. prof., 1990—. Cons. Digital Equipment Corp., Palo Alto, Calif., 1985—; lectr. Assn. for Computing Machinery, N.Y.C., 1991-92; examiner Ednl. Testing Svc., 1988-90. Author chpts. in books; assoc. editor Formal Aspects of Computing Jour., 1988—, Transactions on Software Engring. & Methodology, 1989—; contbr. articles to profl. jours. Mem. IEEE, Assn. for Computing Machinery, Coun. for Internat. Exch. of Scholars (disciplinary adv. com. 1991—). Avocations: ballet, martial arts, bicycling, reading. Office: Carnegie Mellon U Sch of Computer Sci 5000 Forbes Ave Pittsburgh PA 15213-3890

WING, KENNARD THOMPSON, educational organization official; b. Mobile, Ala., May 27, 1956; s. Kennard Loren and Phyllis Ellen (Thompson) W.; m. Cara Maureen McMenamin, Dec. 27, 1986; children: Thomas, Sara, James. BS, Brown U., 1978; MS, U. Pa., 1989. Cert. mgmt. acct. Statis. mgr. Gimbels, Phila., 1978-80; programmer, analyst Chase Econometrics, Bala Cynwyd, Pa., 1980-82; product mgr. Wharton Econometrics, Phila., 1982-84, acct. mgr., 1985-87; v.p. Thompson-Mayer, Phila., 1984-85; project dir. Interact, Bala Cynwyd, 1987-93; lectr. U. Pa., Phila., 1990-95; owner Kennard T. Wing & Co., Havertown, Pa., 1993-98, 2003—; project dir. OMG Ctr. for Collaborative Learning, Phila., 1998—2003. Adv. bd. Weston Inst., West Chester, Pa., 1988—89; adj. prof. Immaculata Coll., 2000; lead author Nonprofit Almanac, 2008. Contbr. articles to profl. jours. Co-founder Township Green, Haverford, Pa., 1990; vol. West Chester Small Bus. Devel. Ctr., Exton, Pa., 1991; pres. Haverford Twp. Adult Sch., 1994-95. Recipient Silver award, Soc. of Nat. Assn. Publs., 2003. Mem. Inst. Mgmt. Accts. Office: Kennard T Wing & Co 224 Kathmere Rd Havertown PA 19083

WING, THOMAS M., military officer, systems engineer; b. LA, Dec. 8, 1962; s. Wilbur Bill L. and Donna M. Wing; m. Elisa R. Martinez, Aug. 4, 1988; 1 child, Emily Rose. BS in Aerospace Engr., US Naval Acad., Annapolis, Md., 1984; MA, US Naval War Coll., 2008. Lic. USCG cert. master vessels to 1600 GT 1999, 2d mate, unlimited tonnage, all oceans 1999, cert. able seaman, unlimited tonnage, all oceans 1999. Commd. ensign USN, 1984, advanced through grades to CDR, 1999. Divsn. Officer USS Benjamin Stoddert Pearl Harbor, Hawaii, 1985—87, Navigator USS Lynde Mccormick San Diego, 1987—90, instr., curriculum developer Fleet Combat Tng. Ctr., 1990—92, Combat Sys. Officer USS Robert G. Bradley Charleston, SC, 1993—95, Weaps Off Comdesron 23 San Diego, 1995—97, C4 Everett, Wash., 2003—04, liaison officer Joint Theater Air and Ballistic Missile Def. Prince Sultan Air Base, Saudi Arabia, 2003, comusnavcent Manama, Bahrain, 2004—, br. head SPAWAR Sys. Ctr. Pacific, 2006—, CO CNRSW FP/LEPS, 1999—2000. Mem. vestry St. Timothy's Episc. Ch., San Diego, 2002—03. Decorated Combat Action ribbon USN, Civilian Meritorious Svc. award, Joint Svc. Commendation medal. Mem.: Naval war Coll. Fdn. (life), US Naval Acad. Alumni Assn. (life), US Naval Inst. (life), Wing Family Am. (assoc.). Episcopalian. Avocations: sailing, skiing, reading, writing. Office: Space and Naval Warfare Syst Ctr 53560 Hull St San Diego CA 92152-5001 Office Fax: 619-553-6307. Personal E-mail: tmwing@san.rr.com. Business E-Mail: tom.wing@navy.mil.

WINGARD, JOHN REID, medical educator; b. Charleston, SC, Jan. 30, 1947; m. Frances Diane Phillips, 1974; children: Ellen, Emily, Sally, Benjamin. BA in English, Yale U., 1969; MD, The Johns Hopkins U., 1973. Diplomate Am. Bd. Internal Medicine, subspecialty of Med. Oncology. Intern City of Memphis Hosp./U. Tenn. Ctr. for Health Scis., 1973-74, resident, 1974-76; chief resident V.A. Hosp., Memphis, 1976-77; instr. in medicine U. Tenn. Ctr. for Health Scis., Memphis, 1976-77; fellow in oncology and internal medicine The Johns Hopkins U. Sch. Medicine, Balt., 1977-79, various to asst. prof. oncology, 1977-87, assoc. prof. oncology, 1987-91, assoc. prof. medicine, 1990-91; prof. medicine Emory U. Sch. Medicine, Atlanta, 1991-96, prof. Winship Cancer Ctr., 1992-96; dir. bone marrow transplant program, prof. medicine U. Fla., Gainesville, 1996—; dep. dir. U. Fla. Shands Cancer Ctr., 2004—08. Dir. bone marrow transplant program Emory U. Sch. Medicine, 1991-96; dir. Bone Marrow Transplant Outpatient Clinic, Johns Hopkins Oncology Ctr., 1984-91; cons. Office of Disability Programs, Social Security Adminstrn., Balt., 1981-91; study group Nat. Inst. Allergy and Infectious Diseases, 1988—; adv. com. Internat. Bone Marrow Transplant Registry, 1989-91, 95—, sec.-treas., 1998—; chair, steering com. Blood and Marrow Transplant Clin. Trials Network, 2001—; bd. dirs. Found. Cellular Therapies, Nat. Marrow Donor Program. Contbr. articles to profl. jours.; contbr. chpts. to books; assoc. editor: Biology of Blood and Marrow Transplantation. Mem. Am. Soc. Microbiology, Am. Soc. Clin. Oncology, Am. Soc. Hematology, Internat. Soc. Exptl. Hematology, Am. Soc. Blood and Marrow Transplantation (pres. 2002-2003). Office: U Fla Coll Medicine PO Box 100277 Gainesville FL 32610-0277 Office Phone: 352-273-7760. Business E-Mail: wingajr@medicine.ufl.edu.

WINGATE, CONSTANCE BLANDY, retired librarian; b. Woodbury, NJ, Mar. 7, 1935; d. John Chase and Josephine Spond (Black) Blandy; m. Len B. Cooke Jr., 1978 (div. 1987); m. John B. Wingate, Mar. 12, 1999. BA, U. Pa., 1956; MA, U. Denver, 1957. Adult cons. Onondaga Library System, Syracuse, 1965-66; asst. dir. Mt. Vernon (N.Y.) Public Library, 1966-75; dep. dir. Queens Borough Public Library, Jamaica, NY, 1975-79, dir., 1980-94; ret., 1994. Founder pres. Literacy Vols. Mt. Vernon, 1972-74. Trustee METRO, 1980-91, v.p., 1985-88, pres., 1988-91; mem. N.Y. State Libr. Svcs. and Constrn. Act Adv. Coun., 1982-88, chmn., 1986-87; bd. dirs. Queens Coun. on the Arts, 1988-94, v.p., 1989-93; bd. dirs. Queens Mus. of Art, 1988-98, v.p., 1994-96, pres. 1996-98; bd. dirs. Queens Libr. Found., 1996-2003. Mem.: ALA, Circumnavigators Club (internat. sec. 2002—06, internat. bd. govs. 2006—08). Republican. Episcopalian. Home: 166-25 Powells Cove Blvd Whitestone NY 11357

WINGATE, MARTHA ANNE, writer, publishing executive; b. Savannah, Ga., Sept. 4, 1943; d. Linden Louis Guice and Stella Dee Turney; m. Thomas Russell Wingate, May 25, 1985; children: Alicia(dec.), Patrick, Faith, Elizabeth; m. Francis Hayden Webb, Dec. 31, 1962 (div. June 1983). BSSE, Tex. Coll. Arts Industries, Kingsville, Tex., 1967; MA, Tex. Womans U., Denton, 1982; PhD in English, Creative Writings, U. Utah, 1989. Cert. latent print examiner Internat. Assn. Identification, 1978. Staff writer Albany Jour., Ga., 1968—69; tchng. fellow Tex. Woman's U., 1980—81, U. Houston, 1984—85, 1986—89; communications cons. Southwestern Bell, 1981—83, AT & T, 1984; instr. Writer's Digest Sch., Cinn., Ohio, 1988—98; critic Writers Digest Criticism Svc., 1988—92; ptnr. Wingate & Wingate Writers, 1989—, Pink Tree Press, 1993—2002; asst. to CEO Project Gutenberg Literary Archive Foundation, Inc, 2001—; propr. Live Oak House, 2006—. Author: (non-fiction) Scene of the Crime: A Writer's Guide to Crime-Scene Investigation, 1992, Amateur Detectives: A Writer's Guide to How Private Citizens Solve Criminal Cases, 1996, (novels) Darling Corey's Dead, 1984, Too Sane A Murder, 1984, A White Male Running, 1985, Even Cops' Daughters, 1986, A Conspiracy of Strangers, 1986, Murder at the Blue Owl, 1988, Death Warmed Over, 1988, Hal's Own Murder Case, 1986, Death by Deception, 1988, The Eye of Anna, 1989, Deficit Ending, 1990, The Mensa Murders, 1990, The Buzzards Must Also Be Fed, 1991, Exception to Murder, 1992, Hacker, 1992, Yakuza, Go Home, 1993, The Day that Dusty Died, 1993, Inherited Murder, 1994, Bird in a Cage, 1995, Genealogy of Murder, 1996, The Thursday Club, 1997, Weaving Murder, 2006, Rentwing, 2006, Of Going Forth By Day, 2006, A Cop's Eye View in Poetry, 2006, First Swans, 2007, His Majesty, King Barba Negra, 2007, Montezumas Bride, 2007; editor: Dare the Mountain, 2006, Look to the Sky, 2006, The Bright Flame, 2006, High Justice, 2006, The Mark of Zorro, 2006, Swiss Family Robinson, 2006, Faith on Faith, 2006, The Tree House, 2006, The Blood Sun Comes, 2006. Mem.: Nat. Rifle Assn. (life). Avocations: reading, history. Home and Office: Live Oak House 809 North 1500 West Salt Lake City UT 84116 Personal E-mail: annewing2@aol.com.

WINGATE, THOMAS RUSSELL, writer; b. Corning, NY, Feb. 27, 1947; s. Paul Michael and Shirley Janet Smith; m. Martha Anne Guice, May 25, 1985; m. Naomi Loftus Wingate (div.); children: James, Rebecca. BA in History, U. Calif., LA, 1968; MA in History, U. Calif., Santa Barbara, 1970; MBA, U. Phoenix, 1989. Critic Writer's Digest Criticism Svc., Cin., 1992—98; sr. ptnr. Pink Tree Press, Salt Lake City, 1993—2002, Wingate & Wingate Writers, Salt Lake City, 1989—; CFO Project Gutenberg Literary Archive Found., Inc., Salt Lake City, 2001—. Mem.: NRA (life), Am. Mensa (life). Republican. Mem. Lds Ch. Avocations: reading, astronomy, history, poetry, movies. Home: 809 N 1500 W Salt Lake City UT 84116 Office Phone: 801-596-1887. Personal E-mail: utahpindar@aol.com.

WINGBLADE, LOREN CHARLES, social sciences educator; b. Chgo., Dec. 23, 1941; s. Loren Milton and Wanda S. Wingblade; m. Susan Leah Bozarth, Apr. 4, 1970. BS in Zoology, U. Wis., Madison, 1966; MA in Psychology, No. Ill. U., DeKalb, 1970; PhD in Psychology, Ind. U., Bloomington, 1977, MA in Sociology, 1988. Cert. bioethics Med. Coll. Wis.-Milw. Asst. prof. Westminster Coll., Fulton, Mo., 1977—83; vis. prof. Ind. U., 1983—89; prof. Jackson C.C., Mich., 1989—. Tchr. Ind. U., Purdue U.; adj. instr. Siena Heights U. Mem. bioethics com. Allegiance Health, Jackson, 2001—. Mem.: North Ctrl. Sociol. Assn., Midwest Sociol. Assn., Carnegie Coun. on Ethics and Internat. Affairs, NEA, Am. Assn. for the Advancement of Sci., Am. Soc. Bioethics and Humanities, Am. Sociol. Asn., APA. Democrat. Lutheran. Achievements include development of IBM-PC exercises for introductory psychology lab, assessment tool for introductory sociology course. Office: Jackson CC 2111 Emmons Rd Jackson MI 49201 Business E-Mail: loren_c_wingblade@jccmi.edu.

WINGER, ROGER ELSON, retired church administrator; b. Fisherville, Ont., Can., Dec. 25, 1933; s. Elson Clare and Bertha Caroline (Schweyer) W.; m. Della Bertha Lebien, June 7, 1958; children: Jeffrey, Karen Mohr, David, Thomas, Susan. AA, Concordia Jr. Coll., Ft. Wayne, Ind., 1953; BA, Concordia Sem., St. Louis, 1955, theol. diploma, 1958; DD (hon.), Concordia Luth. Sem., Edmonton, Alta., Can., 1991. Ordained to ministry, Luth. Ch., 1958. Pastor Holy Trinity Luth. Ch., London, 1958-64, Good Shepherd Luth. Ch., Coventry, Eng., 1964-69, Luth. Mission, Liverpool, Eng., 1969-72, Faith Luth. Ch., Dunnville, Ont., 1972-78, St. Matthew Luth. Ch., Smithville, Ont., 1972-78, St. Paul's Luth. Ch., Kitchener, Ont., 1978-91; pres. ea. dist. Luth. Ch.-Can., Kitchener, 1991-2000; ret., 2000. V.p. Ont. dist. Luth. Ch.-Can., 1982-88; sec. Luth. Ch.-Can., Winnipeg, Man., 1988-91; mem. bd. regents Concordia Luth. Sem., Edmonton, Alta., 1984-88, Concordia Luth. Sem., St. Catharines Ont., 1991-2000; bd. govs. Lutherwood; bd. dirs. Luth. Bible Translators Can. Lutheran. Avocations: photography, golf, woodworking. Home: 76 Deerwood Crescent Kitchener ON Canada N2N 1R3 E-mail: rogerdella@rogers.com.

WINGERT, HANNELORE CHRISTIANE, author, realtor, chemicals executive; b. Karlsbad, Czechoslavakia; came to US, 1962, naturalized, 1967; d. Andreas and Gisela Maria (Ciharz) Zwickel; m. Rudolf Wingert, Feb. 9, 1963; children: Angela Helene, Christopher Rudolf. I.BA, Stadt. Berufsschule, Germany, 1961; postgrad. in mgmt., Bergen C.C., 1983. Lic. real estate, NJ, Calif. Clk. various cos., NJ, 1963, bilingual sec. NJ, 1963-78; exec. sec., adminstrv. asst. Lurgi Corp., Hasbrouck Heights, NJ, 1978-81; sr. exec. sec. Degussa Corp., Teterboro, NJ, 1981-83, asst. product mgr. silica, 1983-85, asst. product mgr. H202, 1985-87, sales promotion coord., 1987; sales assoc. Schlott Realtors, Kinnelon, NJ, 1987-90, Coldwell Banker, 1990—2001, Hanson/McMillin Realty, Escondido, Calif., 2002—07, Windermere Exclusive Properties, Escondido, 2007. Author real estate newsletter, 1992—, cmty. newsletter, 1977-79, A Bucket Full of Love, A Bucket Full of Love for Mommy's Little Girl, 2008. Mem. Garden State Multiple Listing Svc.; chmn. master planning com. High Crest Lake, West Milford, NJ, 1974-75; advisor Jr. Woman's Club Kinnelon-Butler, NJ, 1973-74; techr. computer classes Bd. Realtors, Passaic County, 1989-92; vol. usher Ctr. of Arts, Escondido, 2006-. Mem. Nat. Assn. Realtors, Calif. Assn. Realtors, No. San Diego County Assn. Realtors, Sandicor Multiple Listing Svcs., Fed. Woman's Clubs (past pres.), High Crest Lake Woman's Club (West Milford, NJ, pres. 1972-73). Republican. Roman Catholic.

WINGET, JACK B., theater educator, director, actor; b. Lima, Ohio, Mar. 2, 1939; s. Richard Leroy and Edna Snider Winget; m. Toni Marie Nowak, Sept. 6, 1997; children: Ben Gill, Elizabeth Gill, Melissa McGuire-Hack, Shawn McGuire, Erin Murray, Kate Smith. PhD, Kent State U., Ohio, 1981. Prof. theatre Baldwin-Wallace Coll., Berea, Ohio, 1967—. Actor, dir. Beck Ctr., Lakewood, Ohio, 1975—96; dir. Clague Playhouse, Westlake, Ohio, 1976—96; actor, dir., artistic dir. Berea Grindstone Players, 2006—. Dir.: (writing and performance) A Nightmare of Crime (Bechberger Award, 2008). Mem. Rotary Club, Berea, Ohio, 2008—; bd. mem. Berea Sch. Employee's Credit Union, Ohio, 2006—. With USN, 1957—61. Recipient Faculty Excellence award, Baldwin-Wallace Coll., 1992, Outstanding Performance award, Karamu Actors Guild, 1999—2000; named Best Actor, Theta Alpha Phi, Baldwin-Wallace Coll., 2002; grant, Baldwin-Wallace Coll., 2006, Berea Arts Fest, 2006. Republican. Roman Catholic. Avocations: travel, photography, fishing. Home: 2012 Columbia Rd Valley City OH 44280 Office: Theatre and Dance Corner Beech and Bagley Berea OH 44017 Office Fax: 440-826-3380. Business E-Mail: jwinget@bw.edu.

WINGO, MARSHALL SCOTT, urologist; b. Atlanta, Ga., Sept. 9, 1974; married. BIE, Ga. Inst. Tech., Atlanta, 1997; MD, Emory U. Sch. Medicine, Atlanta, 2001. Diplomate Am. Bd. Urology, 2009. Urologist Lowcountry Urology Clinics, Charleston, SC, 2007—. Office: Lowcountry Urology Clinics 2687 Lake Pk Dr Charleston SC 29464

WINGO, WINSTON ALFONSO, art educator; b. Spartanburg, S.C., Nov. 7, 1952; s. Roy Lee and Mary Lue Wingo; m. Brenda Barksdale Wingo, Dec. 20, 1986; 1 child, Gina Barksdale. BA, Clatlin U., Orangeburg, S.C., 1976; MFA, Clemson U., S.C., 1980. Art instr. Clatlin U., 1980—82, Hughes Mid. Sch., Greenville, SC, 1982—92, Le Gable Mid. Sch., Roebuck, SC, 1992—, Ch. Jr. HS, Spartunburg, SC. Adj. prof. U. S.C., Spartanburg, 1988—89, Spartanburg, 2006, Converse Coll., Spartanburg, S.C. State U., Orangeburg, 1998; art tchr. MFA program Vt. Union U., Montpelier, 2005; adminstrv. asst. Hughes Mid. Sch., Greenville, 1988. Book, New American Painting, 2985, ArtSpeak, 1989, exhibitions include Camena di Commercio, Lucca, Italy, 1984, Morin Miller Gallery, NYC, 1990, Fxy Gold Gallery, Atlanta, 1990, Montreal Art Trader Gallery, Can., 1990, Museo del Bossetti, Pietrasanta, Italy, 1995, Lowe Gallery, Atlanta, 1995, Abney Gallery, 1996, SC State Mus., Columbia, 1996, La Napoule Art Found., France, 1999, Art Extended Gallery, Detroit, 2000, Greenville Mus. Art, SC, 2005, Ward-Nasse Gallery, NYC, 2006. Recipient Emulous award, Piedmont Assembly, 1995. Mem.: NEA, Nat. Art Edn. Assn., Spartanburg Art Mus. Assn. (bd. dirs. 1995—), S.C. Art Edn. Assn. (adviser 2006—), Artist Guild Spartanburg (chmn., pres. 1998—2002). Avocations: reading, collecting jazz music, Karate, Kung Fu. Home: 240 S Spring St Spartanburg SC 29306 Office: Wingo's Studios 240 S Spring St Spartanburg SC 29306 Business E-Mail: wingowa@spart2.org.

WINICK, BERNYCE ALPERT, artist, photographer; b. NYC; Student, Bklyn. Mus. Art Sch., 1938—41; BA in Fine Arts and Music, NYU; pvt. studies with, Mario Cooper, NA, AWS, 1969—86; student, Traphagen Sch. Fashion, 1958—61, Art Students League N.Y., 1961—64, Nat. Acad. Design Sch. Fine Arts, 1968—72. Artist, Woodmere, L.I., N.Y., 1969—. Designer, fashion artist, fashion con. in field. One-woman shows include Hewlett-Woodmere Pub. Libr., LI, 1969, Galerie Internat., NY, 1977, Thomas Moran (First prize Nat. Acad. Sch., 1972, Salmagundi Club 1981, 82, 87, 90, Nat. Arts Club, 1985, 2002, Nat. Acad. Sch., 1972 (First Prize Meml. award 2002), Gallery Internat. 57, NY, 1989, Discovery Art Gallery, Sea Cliff, LI, 1989, 96, 98, Glen Cove, NY, 1993-94, Chelsea Ctr., East Norwich, NY, 1993, 96, 98, 2000, 02, Z Gallery, SoHo, NY, 1994, County Exec. Bldg., 1997, Fine Arts Mus. LI, 1997, Town Hall, Hempstead, NY, 2000, Wisser Meml. Libr., 2003, Wiser Meml. Libr., NY Inst. Tech., 2004, 2007; exhibited in group shows at Discovery Art Gallery, Glen Cove, NY, 1988, 91-93, 1996, 2000, 02, Nat. Acad. Sch. Fine Arts, NY, 1972, Long Beach Mus., LI, 1979, 81-85, 89 (2d prize 1989), Chen Chung Gallery of St. John's U., NY, 1980, Salmagundi Club, NY, 1980-81, 2002 (Thomas Moran Meml. award, 1st prize), Am. Watercolor Soc., NY, 1982, 85, 88, 92, Fine Arts Mus. LI, 1983, 88-89, 91-92, 96 (2d prize), 97, Nat. Arts Club, NY, 1985-86, 88-89, 2002, Nassau County Mus., LI, 1985-86, 88, Nat. Assn. Women Artists, NY, 1986, 88, 91-93, C.W. Post Coll., LI, LI Arts Coun. Freeport, 1995-96, 1999 (First prize in black and white photography), 2006 (Fabian Adler Meml. award), Chelsea Cultural Ctr., NY, 1995, 2001, (Suburban Art League award), Rockville Ctr. Guild for the Arts, NY, 1995, 97 (Best in Show for photography), Chelsea Ctr. (Peacock Showcase award, First prize 2000, Merit award 2001), East Norwich, NY, Discovery Art Gallery, Sea Cliff, NY, 1998, Canton Art Inst. Ohio, Galerie Internat., Gallery Internat. 57, Z Gallery, Salle Augustin-Chenier, Quebec, Can., Town Hall, Town of Hempstead, NY, 2000, NY Inst. Tech., Wisser Meml. Libr., 2001, Nat. Arts Club (First prize 2002), Heckscher Mus., Huntington, NY, 2003, Mills Pond House, St. James, NY, 2002, 05 (1st prize watercolor), Nat. Arts Club, NY, 2001 (1st prize), NY Inst. Tech. Wissen Meml. Libr., Old Westbury Campus, 2004, 08, others; work included in US Dept. State Art in Embassies program, pvt. and corp. collections including Carnegie Hall; photographs in publs. including South Shore Record, 1995, Encyclopedia of Watercolour Landscape Techniques, 1996, Popular Photography, 1996-97, 99-00, 04, Photography on America Online, 1997, 99-2000, New York: Sterling Pub. Co., Inc., 1998, Watercolor Planning and Painting, 1998, Abstracts in Watercolor, 1996, NY Times, 1999, 2001, NY Inst. Tech., 2003, Wisser Meml. Libr., Old Westbury, NY, 2004, Mills Pond House (1st prize watercolor 2005), St. James, NY, 2005; photography in (books) Capturing the Seen and Unseen in Photographs, 2001, Thirty Nine Musical Photographs, 2003, Town and Country Mag.; photographs exhibited in Mill Pond House, Salmagundi Club, NYU, Nat. Assn. Women Artists, Artists Unlimited, Tampa, Fla., musical images to the Julliard Sch., 2003-07, Wisser Meml. Libr. NY Inst. Tech., 2008; Inuitational, author poetry; contbr. articles to profl. jours. Recipient award, Salmagundi Club, 2004, 2005, other awards, Fabian Adler Meml. award, L.I. Arts Coun., 2006, Wisser Meml. Libr. award, NY Inst. Tech., 2007, Casein and Acrylic prize, Nat. Soc. Painters, 2007, Peter Jones Meml. award, Audubon Artists Inc., 2007, First prize, Long Island Arts Coun., 2009. Fellow Royal Soc. Encouragment Arts Manufactures and Commerce; mem. Am. Watercolor Soc., Nat. Assn. Women Artists, Tri County Artists, Long Beach Art League, Art League of LI, Harvard Club, Arts Group, Poetry Group, Artist's Fellowship Inc. NY. Achievements include patents pending for my 2 face creams. Avocations: fashion design, piano, poetry. Home and Office: 923 Beth Ln Woodmere NY 11598-1507 Office Phone: 516-374-6415.

WINICK, HERMAN, physicist, educator; b. NYC, June 27, 1932; s. Benjamin and Yetta (Matles) W.; m. Renee Feldman, May 31, 1953; children: Alan Lee, Lisa Frances, Laura Joan. AB, Columbia Coll., 1953; PhD, Columbia U., 1957. Rsch. assoc., instr. U. Rochester, NY, 1957—59; from staff physicist to asst. dir. Cambridge Electron Accelerator Harvard U., Mass., 1959—73; dep. dir. Stanford Synchrotron Radiation Lab. Stanford Linear Accelerator Ctr., Calif., 1973—96. Rsch. prof. applied physics Stanford U., 1983-97, prof. emeritus, 1998—; chair tech. rev. com. Synchrotron Radiation Rsch. Ctr., Taiwan, 1984-93. Mem. editl. bd. Nuclear Instruments and Methods, 1982-2007; co-editor: Synchrotron Radiation Research, 1980; editor: Synchrotron Radiation Sources: A Primer, 1994. Recipient Humboldt Sr. Scientist award, 1986, Energy Related Tech. award U.S. Dept. Energy, 1987, U.S. Particle Accelerator Sch. prize, 1995, Disting. Assoc. award, U.S. Dept. Energy, 2000, Heinz R. Pagels Human Rights award N.Y. Acad. Scis., 2005. Fellow AAAS, Am. Phys. Soc. (chmn. com. on internat. freedom of scientist 1992, chair Forum on Internat. Physics 2007). Achievements include development of first wiggler and undulator magnets for synchotron radiation research. Home: 853 Tolman Dr Stanford CA 94305-1025 Office: SSRL SLAC 2575 Sand Hill Rd Menlo Park CA 94025-7015 Home Phone: 650-493-1900; Office Phone: 650-926-3155. E-mail: winick@slac.stanford.edu.

WINICK, MYRON, nutrition professor, physician; b. NYC, May 4, 1929; s. Charles B. and Ruth E. (Gesser) W.; m. Elaine L. Lasky, Sept. 19, 1964; children: Jonathan, Stephen. AB, Columbia U., 1951; MS, U. Ill., 1952; MD, SUNY, 1956. Intern U. Pa., Phila., 1956-57; asst. resident pediatrics Cornell U. Med. Coll., NYC, 1957-59, chief resident, 1959-60; attending pediatrician Stanford U. Hosp., 1963-64; asst. prof. pediatrics Cornell U. Med. Coll., NYC, 1964-68, assoc. prof. pediatrics and nutrition, 1968-70, prof., 1970-71; dir. Inst. Human Nutrition Columbia U. Inst. Human Nutrition, 1972-87, prof. pediatrics, 1972-89, R.R. Williams prof. nutrition, 1973-89, R.R. Williams prof. emeritus, 1990—; pres. U. Health Scis./Chgo. Med. Sch., North Chgo., Ill., 1990-93; dir. Ctr. for Nutrition, Genetics and Human Devel., 1975-87. Vis. prof. pediatrics U. Chile, Santiago, 1967; asst. attending pediatrician NY Hosp., NYC, 1964-68, assoc. attending pediatrician, 1968-70, attending pediatrician, 1970-71; attending pediatrician Presbyn. Hosp., NYC, 1972-89; cons. Pan Am. Health Orgn., 1966—; med. dir. Weight Watchers Internat., 1997—; sr. scientist Am. Health Found., 1999—. Author: Malnutrition and Brain Development, 1976; textbook Nutrition in Health and Disease, 1980; Growing Up Healthy; A Parent's Guide to Good Nutrition, 1982; For Mothers and Daughters: A Guide to Good Nutrition for Women, 1983; Your Personalized Health Profile: Choosing the Diet That's Right for You, 1985; Nutrition, Pregnancy and Early Infancy, 1989; The Fiber Prescription, 1992; editor: textbook Current Concepts in Nutrition, 1972—, Nutrition: Pre- and Postnatal Development, Vol. I, Human Nutrition: A Comprehensive Treatise, 1979, Columbia Ency. of Nutrition, 1988, (with Joan Lunden) Growing Up Healthy, 2004, Final Stamp: The Jewish Doctors in the Warsaw Ghetto, 2007; contbg. editor Nutrition Revs., 1969-76; mem. editl. bd. Jour. Nutrition, 1972-76, 82-86, The Year in Metabolism (now Contemporary Metabolism), 1975—; assoc. editor Growth, 1984—; nutrition editor Cancer Prevention, 1994—. Trustee Found. for Internat. Child Health; mem. nutrition interdisciplinary cluster Pres.' Biomed. Research Panel, 1975; mem. panel on infants and children Pres.' Commn. on Mental Health, 1977; cons. Office of Tech. Assessment, U.S. Congress, 1976-78; mem. Food and Nutrition Bd. NRC, 1982-88. With USNR, 1960-62. Bank of Am.-Gianini Found. fellow Stanford, 1962; NIH Spl. fellow, 1963; recipient NIH Career Devel. award, 1968-71; E. Mead Johnson award pediatric research, 1970; Osborne and Mendel award Am. Inst. Nutrition, 1976; Agnes Higgins award March of Dimes Found., 1983 Fellow Royal Soc. Health, Am. Soc. Nutritional Scis., Am. Acad. Pediatrics; mem. AAAS, Am. Soc. Cell Biology, Soc. Developmental Biology, Harvey Soc., Soc. Pediatric Rsch., Royal Soc. Medicine, Brit. Nutrition Soc., Am. Soc. Clin. Nutrition, NY Acad. Scis., NY Acad. Medicine, Soc. for Exptl. Biology and Medicine, Soc. for Neurosci., Internat. Soc. for Devel. Neurosci., Cosmos Club. Home: 165 West End Ave Apt 10K New York NY 10023 Business E-Mail: mw29@columbia.edu.

WININGER, MICHAEL T., research scientist; b. Hartford, Conn. BS, U. Conn., Storrs, 2003; PhD, Rutgers U., Piscataway, NJ, 2009. Engring. intern Adidas Am., Adidas Innovation Team, Portland, Oreg., 2004; vis. scientist Indsl. Tech. Rsch. Inst., Chutung, Hsinchu, Taiwan, 2007; postdoc. rsch. fellow Nat. Inst. Mental Health, Bethesda, Md. Home: 305 S 4th Ave Highland Park NJ 08904 Office: Rutgers Univ 599 Taylor Rd Piscataway NJ 08854 Personal E-mail: wininger@eden.rutgers.edu. Business E-Mail: wininger@rci.rutgers.edu.

WINK, AMY L., literature and language professor; d. Weldon E. and Winifred W. Wink. BA, Southwestern U., Georgetown, Tex., 1987; MA, Tex. A&M U., Coll. Sta., 1989, PhD, 1996. Vis. asst. prof. Stephen F. Austin State U., Nacogdoches, Tex., 1997—99, Emporia State U., Kans., 1999—2001; adj. prof. Austin CC, Tex., 2002—; part time asst. prof. Southwestern U., Georgetown, Tex., 2003—05. Author: (book) She Left Nothing in Particular: The Autobiographical Legacy of 19th Century Women's Diaries; editor: Tandem Lives: The Frontier Texas Diaries of Henrietta Baker Embree and Tennessee Keys Embree, 1856-1884. Mem.: Am. Driving Soc., Carriage Assn. America, Heart Tex. Morgan Horse Club, Houston Area Carriage Assn. (newsletter editor 2006—08). Avocation: photography. Office: Austin CC 5930 Middle Fiskville Rd Austin TX 78745 Business E-Mail: awink@austincc.edu.

WINKEL, RAYMOND NORMAN, aerospace scientist, consultant, retired military officer; b. Flint, Mich., Dec. 8, 1928; s. Norman Martin and Evelyn Matilda (Hylen) W.; m. Ellen Stefula, Dec. 29, 1955 (dec. Feb. 2006); children: Raymond Norman, Ann, Maryellen. *Moved to Muskegon, Michigan at age 1. Raised in Muskegon and graduated from Muskegon High School in 1946.* BS, U.S. Naval Postgrad. Sch., Monterey, Calif., 1964; MS, Villanova U., Pa., 1967; grad. advanced mgmt. program, Harvard U., 1973. Enlisted in USN, 1948, commd. ensign, designated naval aviator, 1951, advanced through grades to rear adm., 1979; service in Far East; comdg. officer Naval Electronics Systems Test and Evaluation Facility St. Inigoes, Md., 1969-71; dir. avionics U.S. Navy, 1973-76; project mgr. Navy/Marine Corps heavy lift helicopter, 1976-78; gen. mgr. Navy/industry team to develop new ship/aircraft weapon system for anti-submarine warfare LAMPS Mark III, 1978-81; ret. USN, 1981; v.p. Washington ops. Telephonics Corp., Huntington, NY, 1981-82; v.p. programs and contracts Astronautics Corp. Am., Milw., 1982-94; aerospace industry cons. Heathsville, Va., 1994-95. Decorated Legion of Merit, Air medal, Navy Achievement medal. Mem. Exptl. Aircraft Assn., U.S. Naval Inst., Assn. Naval Aviation, Mil. Officers Assn. Am., Kiwanis, Indian Creek Yacht and Country Club, U.S. Power Squadron. Republican. Roman Catholic. Home: 1860 Island Point Rd Heathsville VA 22473-3729

WINKELSTEIN, JERRY ALLEN, retired pediatrician; b. Syracuse, NY, Sept. 5, 1940; s. Warren W. and Lillian (Sirkin) Winkelstein; m. Marilyn Link, June 21, 1969; children: Beth, Amy. BA, Syracuse U., 1961; MD, Einstein Med. Sch., 1965. Diplomate Am. Bd. Pediatrics, 1972. Intern in pediatrics Johns Hopkins Hosp., Balt., 1965—66, resident in pediatrics, 1966—68, fellow in pediatrics, 1970—73, resident in immunology, 1971—72; asst. prof. pediat. Johns Hopkins U., Balt., 1973-76, assoc. prof., 1976-82, Eudowood prof. pediat., 1982—2005, prof. pathology, 1998—2005; dir. divsn. immunology dept. pediat. Johns Hopkins Hosp., Balt., 1980—2004. Contbr. articles to sci. jours. Trustee Immuno Deficiency Found., 1982—2009, Eudowood Bd., 2008—. Lt. comdr. USPHS, 1968—70. Recipient Mead-Johnson award, Am. Acad. Pediat., 1982, Lifetime Achievement award, Modell Found., 1996, Scientific Achievement award, Immune Deficiency Found., 2004. Mem.: Infectious Disease Soc., Am. Soc. Clin. Investigation, Soc. Pediatric Rsch., Am. Pediatric Soc. Home: 609 Stoney Spring Dr Baltimore MD 21210 Home Phone: 410-243-2766.

WINKELSTEIN, WARREN, JR., physician, educator; b. Syracuse, NY, July 1, 1922; s. Warren and Evelyn (Neiman) W.; children: Rebecca Winkelstein Yamin, Joshua, Shoshana; m. Veva Kerrigan, Feb. 14, 1976. BA, U. N.C., 1942; MD cum laude, Syracuse U., 1947; MPH, Columbia U., 1950. Diplomate Am. Bd. Preventive Medicine. Intern Charity Hosp., New Orleans, 1947-48; with ICA (Vietnam), 1951-53; from dir. div. communicable disease control to 1st dep. comdr. local, environ. health svcs. Erie County Health Dept., 1953-62; from assoc. prof. to prof. SUNY, Buffalo, 1962-68; prof. epidemiology, dean pub. health U. Calif., Berkeley, 1972-96, prof. emeritus, 1996. Dir. Internat. Environ. Epidemiology Inst., 1997. Author: Basic Readings in Epidemiology, 1972; contbr. articles profl. jours. With AUS, 1944-46. Mem. APHA, AAAS, Internat. Am. Epidemiol. Socs., Am. Heart Assn. Address: Dept Epidemiol Univ Calif Sch Pub Health Berkeley CA 94720-7360

WINKENWERDER, WILLIAM, JR., consulting firm executive, former federal agency administrator; b. Ashville, NC, Apr. 27, 1954; BS, Davidson Coll., 1976; MD, U. N.C., 1981; MBA, U. Pa., 1986; postgrad., Stanford U., 1991. Resident internal medicine N.C. Meml. Hosp. U. N.C., 1981-84; instr. dept. medicine Sch. Medicine U. Pa., 1984-87; spl. asst. to adminstr. Health Care Financing Adminstrn. US Dept. Health & Human Services, 1987-88; dir. quality assurance and utilization mgmt. Southeast Permanente Med. Group, Kaiser Permanente, Atlanta, 1988-90, assoc. med. dir., 1990-92; v.p. CMO so. ops. Prudential Health Care, Atlanta, 1992-95; v.p. primary care svcs. Emory Health Care, Atlanta, 1996-98; assoc. v.p. health affairs Robert Woodruff Health Scis. Ctr. Emory U., 1996-98; exec. v.p. health care svcs., vice chmn. Blue Cross Blue Shield Mass., Boston, 1998—2001; asst. sec. for health affairs US Dept. Def., Washington, 2001—07; founder, chmn. The Winkenwerder Co., LLC, Alexandria, Va., 2007—. Mem. exec. com. Emory Healthcare, Emory Clinic, 1996-98; chmn. CMO com. Prudential Healthcare, 1992-95; bd. dirs. Care Sci. Corp., Wharton Sch. Bus. Health Care Alumni, Fed. Employees Program-Blue Cross Blue Shield Assn., The Reed and Barton Co.; founder HCFA Effectiveness Initiative, U.S. Dept. Health and Human Svcs., participant Task Forces on Health and Human Svcs. AIDS and Minority Health, 1987-88, U.S. Pub. Health Risk Assessment and Quality Assurance, Sec.'s Minority Health, Sec.'s Catastophic Illness; rep. Prudential on Med. Dirs. Com. on Group Health Assn. Am.; spkr. in field. Contbr. articles to profl. jours. Kaiser Family Found. fellow, 1984-86, 87-88, Kellogg Pub. Health Policy fellow U. Pa., 1986, Wharton Washington fellow U. Pa., 1986. Mem.: AMA, Am. Soc. Internal Medicine, Health Care Forum's Physician Leader Network, Am. Assn. Health Plans (bd. dirs.), Am. Coll. Physician Execs., Am. Coll. Physicians, Davidson Coll. Alumni Assn. Office: The Winkenwerder Co LLC 330 John Carlyle St Ste 220 Alexandria VA 22314 Office Phone: 703-836-1035. Office Fax: 703-836-1743.*

WINKFIELD, TREVOR, painter; b. Leeds, England, 1944; Intermediate cert. art, Leeds Coll. Art, 1960—64; MFA, Royal Coll. Art, London, 1967. One-man shows include, Fishbach Gallery, NYC, 1977, Coracle Gallery, London, 1978, Blue Mountain Gallery, NYC, 1980, Inst. Contemporary Art, Boston, 1985, Edward Thorp Gallery, NYC, 1986, 1989, E.M. Donahue Gallery, NYC, 1995, 1996, Tibor de Nagy Gallery, NYC, 1997, 1999, 2002, 2004, 2006, Barbara Ann Levy Gallery, NYC, 1999, exhibited in group shows, Yale Ctr. Brit. Art, 1989, Washburn Gallery, NYC, 1992, Edward Thorp Gallery, NYC, 1990, Paula Cooper Gallery, NYC, 1991, Marlborough Gallery, NYC, 1992, Baxter Gallery, Portland, Maine, 1993, Phyllis Kind Gallery, Chgo., 1994, Bergamot Sta. Arts Ctr., Santa Monica, 1995, Whitney Mus. Am. Art at Champion, Stamford, Conn., 1997, Tibor de Nagy Gallery, NYC, 1999, 2001, AAAL, 2000 (Acad. award in Art, 2000), 2008 (Hassam, Speicher, Betts and Symons Purchase award, 2008), Geoffrey Young Gallery, Great Barrington, Mass., 2000, D.C. Moore Gallery, NYC, 2001, 2004, Brit. Consul-Gen.'s Residence, NYC, 2001, NAD, 2002, 2006, Westbeth Gallery, NYC, 2003, NY Acad. Sci., 2004, Painting Ctr., NYC, 2006. Recipient Engelhard award, 1986, Pollock-Krasner award, 1989, Chevalier, Ordre des Arts et des Lettres, 2003; fellow John Simon Guggenheim Meml. Found., 1990; Hillwood fellow, 1993. Office: c/o Tibor de Nagy Gallery 724 5th Ave New York NY 10019 Studio: 256 W 15th St Apt 5FE New York NY 10011 E-mail: trevorwink@aol.com.

WINKLE, WILLIAM ALLAN, music educator; b. Rapid City, SD, Oct. 10, 1940; s. Curis Powell and June Ada (Alexander) W.; m. Carola Kay Croll, June 16, 1968; children: Brenda, Rachelle. MusB, Huron U., 1962; MA, U. Vt., 1971; ArtsD, U. No. Colo., 1976; postgrad., North Tex. State U. Dir. choral and band Arlington H.S., SD, 1962—64; dir. band DeSmet H.S., SD, 1964—67; coord. music Huron Pub. Schs., SD, 1967—69; head instrumental music Huron Coll., 1969—71; dir. bands, prof. music Chadron State Coll., Nebr., 1971—. Instr. tuba music camp S.D. State U., Brooking, 1969-71, Internat. Music Camp, Dunseith, Nebr., 1977—, high sch. sessions U. Vt., Burlington, 1964-71; tubist, bassoonist Huron Symphony/Huron Mcpl., 1957-69, Nebr. Panhandle Symphony & Symphonia, Chadron, 1971—; tubist Blue Jean Philharmonic, Estes Park, Colo., 1960-64, Internat. Brass Quintet, 1985—; conductor, tour dir. Am. Youth Symphony and Chorus, European Tours, 1967-78; performing artist, clinician Yamaha Music Corp. USA, 1977—; adj. tuba tchr. Boise State U., 2007-08, tuba prof. 2007-. Author: List of Tuba/Euphonium Solos, 1984; co-author: Art of Tuba, 1992; contbr. articles to mags. Moderator, trustee, deacon, conf. bd. dir. United Ch. of Christ, 1974-90. Named to Omaha Bands Hall of Fame, U. Nebr., 2006, Nebr. Music Educators Assn. Hall of Fame, 2006; recipient Freedom Found. award, 1972, Chadron State Coll. Rsch. Inst. 5 awards, 1974-78; Paul Harris fellow, 2002. Mem. Chadron C. of C., Nebr. State Bandmasters (dist. VI and coll. rep. 1978-84, pres. 1998—), Internat. Music Camp (bd. dir. 1980-86, Disting. Svc. award 1987), Tubist Universal Brotherhood Assn. (internat. rep. 1971—, Nat. Sem. award 1975, 77), Music Educators Nat. Conf., Internat. Assn. Jazz Educators, Concert Bands Am., Nat. Band Assn. (chmn. Nebr. chpt. 1996—, citation of excellence 1999), Coll. Band Dirs. Nat. Assn., Nebr. Bandmasters Assn. (pres. 1999, Disting. Svc. award 2005), Phi Beta Mu (pres. Alpha Theta chpt. 1999—), Kappa Kappa Psi, Kappa Delta Pi. Democrat. Avocations: bicycling, swimming, walking. Office: Chadron State Coll 10th Main Chadron NE 69337 Home: 5596 S Impatiens Pl Boise ID 83714 Home Phone: 208-629-0192; Office Phone: 208-426-2647. Business E-Mail: winklewinds@cableone.net.

WINKLEBLACK, ARTHUR B., food products executive; BA in Bus. and Econs., UCLA; MBA, U. Pa. Exec. v.p., CFO C. Dean Metropoulos & Co., 1998—99; acting COO Perform.com, 1999—2001; CEO Freeride.com at Indigo Capital, 1999—2001; exec. v.p., CFO H.J. Heinz Co., Pitts., 2002—. Office: HJ Heinz Co 1 Ppg Pl Ste 3100 Pittsburgh PA 15222-5447

WINKLER, AGNIESZKA M., marketing executive; b. Rome, Feb. 22, 1946; came to U.S., 1953; naturalized, 1959; d. Wojciech A. and Halina Z. (Owsiany) W.; children from previous marriage: children: Renata G. Ritcheson, Dana C Sworakowski; m. Arthur K. Lund. BA, Coll. Holy Name, 1967; MA, San Jose State U., 1971; MBA, U. Santa Clara, 1981. Tchg. asst. San Jose State U., 1968-70; cons. to Ea. European bus. Palo Alto, Calif., 1970-72; pres./founder Commart Communications, Palo Alto, 1973-84; pres./founder, chmn. bd. Winkler Advt., Santa Clara, Calif., 1984—; chmn. bd. SuperCuts, Inc.; chmn., founder TeamToolz, 2000—04, The Winkler Group, 2004—. Bd. dirs. Reno Air, Lifeguard, Lifeguard Life Ins., IP Locks, C200, Inter-tel, Western Folklife Ctr., The

Cheesecake Factory Inc., 2007-; exec. com. C200. Author: Warp Speed Branding, 1999. Trustee Santa Clara U., 1991—; trustee O'Connor Found., 1987-93, mem. exec. com., 1988—, mem. Capital Campaign steering com., 1989; mem. nat. adv. bd. Comprehensive Health Enhancement Support System, 1991—; mem. mgmt. west com. A.A.A.A. Agy., 1991—, vice chair no. Calif. coun., 1996—; project dir. Poland Free Enterprise Plan, 1989-92; mem. adv. bd. Normandy France Bus. Devel., 1989-92; mem. bd. regents Holy Names Coll., 1987—; bd. dirs. San Jose Mus. Art, 1987; mem. San Jose Symphony, Gold Baton, 1986; mem. nat. adv. com. Chess, 1991—; dir. Bay Area Coun., 1994—. Recipient CLIO award in Advt., Addy award, others; named to 100 Best Women in Advt., Ad Age, 1988, Best Woman in Advt., AdWeek and McCall's Mag., 1993, one of 100 Best and Brightest Women in Mktg. & Advt., Nat. Assn. Women Bus. Owners, 1996. Mem. Family Svc. Assn. (trustee 1980-82), Am. Assn. Advt. Agys. (agy. mgmt. west com. 1991), Bus. Profl. Advt. Assn., Polish Am. Congress, San Jose Advt. Club, San Francisco Ad Club, Beta Gamma Sigma (hon.), Pi Gamma Mu, Pi Delta Phi (Lester-Tinneman award 1966, Bill Raskob Found. grantee 1965).

WINKLER, CHARLES HOWARD, investment company executive; b. NYC, Aug. 4, 1954; s. Joseph Conrad and Geraldine Miriam (Borok) W.; m. Darlene D.Hansen, March 28, 2009. BBA with highest distinction, Emory U., 1976; JD, Northwestern U., 1979. Bar: Ill. 1979, U.S. Dist. Ct (no. dist.) Ill. 1979. Assoc. Levenfeld & Kanter, Chgo., 1979-80, Kanter & Eisenberg, Chgo., 1980-84, ptnr., 1985-86, Neal Gerber & Eisenberg, Chgo., 1986-96; sr. mng. dir., COO Citadel Investment Group, LLC, Chgo., 1996—2001; sr. mng. dir. Citadel Trading Group, Chgo., 1996—2000, Aragon Investments Ltd., Chgo., 1996—2000; sr. mng. dir., COO Hudson Bay Capital Mgmt. LP, NYC, 2007—; bd. dir. Hudson Bay Internat Fund Ltd, 2007—08. Bd. dirs. Kensington Global Strategies Fund, Ltd., Antaeus Internat. Investments, Ltd., Jackson Investment Fund Ltd., Citadel Investment Group (Europe) Ltd., chief oper. officer, and sr. mng. dir. Amaranth Group Inc., 2001-07; hedge fund mgr. Author: (with others) Basic Tax Shelters, 1982, Limited Liability Companies: The Entity of Choice, 1995; mng. editor Northwestern Jour. Internat. Law and Bus., 1979. Mem. ABA (mem. sect. on taxation), Beta Gamma Sigma. Office: Hudson Bay Capital Mgmt LP 120 Broadway 40th Fl New York NY 10271 Home: 15 Ctrl Pk W A Apt New York NY 10023 Business E-Mail: cwinkler@hudsonbaycapital.com.

WINKLER, DANA JOHN, lawyer; b. Wichita, Kans., Jan. 2, 1944; s. Donald Emil and Hazel Claire (Schmitter) W.; m. Mary Ann Seiwert, Oct. 14, 1967; 1 child, Jonathan. BA, Wichita State U., 1967; JD, Washburn Law Sch., 1971. Staff writer Wichita Eagle & Beacon, 1961-67; ptnr. Davis, Bruce, Davis & Winkler, Wichita, 1972-77; asst. city atty. City of Wichita, 1977-99; dir. Wichita Mcpl. Fed. Credit Union, 1980—, pres., 1982, 99-2000, sec.-treas., 1994-98, v.p., 1998-99. Dir. Deaf and Hard of Hearing Counseling Svc., 1979-80. Vol. Sedgwick County United Way, Wichita, 1973-74; vice-chmn. Wichita Pub. Schs. Spl. Edn. Adv. Coun., 1987-89. 1st lt. U.S. Army, 1967-69. Mem. Kans. Bar Assn., Wichita Bar Assn. Republican. Roman Catholic. Home and Office: 1621 Harlan St Wichita KS 67212-1842 Personal E-mail: djwinkler@cox.net.

WINKLER, DOLORES EUGENIA, retired health facility administrator; b. Milw., Aug. 10, 1929; d. Charles Peter and Eugenia Anne (Zamka) Kowalski; m. Donald James Winkler, Aug. 18, 1951; 1 child, David John. Grad., Milw. Bus. Inst., 1949. Acct. Curative Rehab. Ctr., Milw., 1949-60; staff acct. West Allis (Wis.) Meml. Hosp., 1968-70, chief acct., 1970-78, reimbursement analyst, 1978-85, dir. budgets and reimbursement, 1985-95; ret., 1995. Mem. adv. coun., fin. com. Tau Home Health Care Agy., Milw., 1981—83. Mem.: Inst. Mgmt. Accts. (pres. 1983—84, nat. dir. 1986—88, pres. Mid Am. Regional Coun. 1988—89, award of excellence 1989), Healthcare Fin. Mgmt. Assn. (pres. 1989—90, Follmer Bronze award 1980, Reeves Silver award 1986, Muncie Gold award 1989, medal of honor 1993), Beta Chi Rho (pres. 1948). Avocations: travel, photography, golf. Home: 12805 W Honey Ln New Berlin WI 53151-2652

WINKLER, DONNY W., physics professor; s. Dennis L and Joanne N Winkler; m. Stephanie Livesay Winkler, Nov. 1, 2008. BS in Physics, Clemson U., SC, 1998, MS in Physics, 2001. Physics instr. Tri County Tech. Coll., Pendleton, SC, 2001—. Mem.: Am. Assn. Physics Tchrs., Sigma Pi Sigma. Business E-Mail: dwinkler@tctc.edu.

WINKLER, HEATHER STARR, music educator; b. Hopkinsville, Ky., Sept. 27, 1979; d. Barry and Penny Combs; m. William Edward Winkler, July 14, 2001; children: Morgan, William III, Kobe, Madison. BMME, U. Ky., Lexington, 2001. Cert. music tchr. k-12 EPSB Ky., 2001. Music educator Wilton Cmty. Schools, Iowa, 2002—04, Christian County Mid. Sch., Hopkinsville, Ky., 2005—. Asst. h.s. band dir. Christian County H.S., Hopkinsville, 2005—; sponsor Christian County Schools Winterguard, Hopkinsville, 2006—. V.p. girls softball Hopkinsville Christian County Youth League, Ky., 2007—08. Mem.: Ky. Music Educators Assn. Avocations: reading, arts and crafts, music, gaming. Business E-Mail: heather.winkler@christian.kyschools.us.

WINKLER, HENRY RALPH, retired academic administrator, historian; b. Waterbury, Conn., Oct. 27, 1916; s. Jacob and Ethel (Rieger) W.; m. Clare Sapadin, Aug. 18, 1940; children— Allan Michael, Karen Jean; m. Beatrice Ross, Jan. 28, 1973. AB, U. Cin., 1938, MA, 1940; PhD, U. Chgo., 1947; degree (hon.), Lehigh U., 1974, Rutgers U., 1977, No. Ky. U., 1978, St. Thomas Inst., 1979, Hebrew Union Coll., 1980, Xavier U., 1981, U. Akron, 1984, U. Cin., 1987, Thomas More Coll., 1989. Instr. U. Cin., 1939-40; asst. prof. Roosevelt Coll., 1946-47; mem. faculty Rutgers U., 1947-77, prof. history, 1958-77, chmn. dept., 1960-64; dean Faculty Liberal Arts, 1967, vice provost, 1968-70, acting provost, 1970, v.p. for acad. affairs, 1970-72, sr. v.p. for acad. affairs, 1972-76, exec. v.p., 1976-77, U. Cin., 1977, pres., 1977-84, pres. emeritus, 1984—, Univ. prof. history, 1977-86, prof. emeritus, 1986—. Mng. editor Am. Hist. Rev., 1964-68; vis. prof. Bryn Mawr Coll., 1959-60, Harvard, summer 1964, Columbia, summer 1967; faculty John Hay Fellows Inst. Humanities, 1960-65; bd. overseers Hebrew Union Coll., 1984—. Author: The League of Nations Movement in Great Britain, 1914-19, 1952, Great Britain in the Twentieth Century, 1960, 2d edit., 1966; editor: (with K.M. Setton) Great Problems in European Civilization, 1954, 2d edit., 1966, Twentieth-Century Britain, 1977, Paths Not Taken: British Labour and International Policy in the Nineteen Twenties, 1994, British Labour Seeks a Foreign Policy, 2004; mem. editorial bd. Historian, 1958-64, Liberal Edn., 1986—; mem. adv. bd. Partisan Rev., 1972-79; contbr. articles to jours., revs. Nat. chmn. European history advanced placement com. Coll. Entrance Exam. Bd., 1960-64; mem. Nat. Commn. on Humanities in Schs., 1967-68, Am. specialist Eastern Asia, 1968; exec. com. Conf. on Brit. Studies, 1968-75; chmn. bd. Nat. Humanities Faculty, 1970-73; chmn. adv. com. on history Coll. Entrance Exam. Bd., 1977-80; mem. council on acad. affairs, mem. bd. trustees, chmn., 1982-84; pres. Highland Park (N.J.). Bd. Edn., 1962-63; mem. exec. com. Nat. Assn. State Univs. and Land-Grant Colls., 1978-81, mem. Cin. Lit. Club, 1978—, pres., 1993—; bd. dirs. Am. Council on Edn., 1979-81; trustee Seasengood Good Govt. Found., 1979—, pres., 1991-93; trustee Thomas More Coll., 1986-93; mem. Ohio Indsl. Tech. and Enterprise Bd., 1983-89; bd. dirs. Nat. Civic League, 1986—, Planning Accreditation Bd., 1988—; mem. adv coun. U. Va.'s Coll at Wise, Ohio Humanities Coun., 1994—. With USNR, 1943-46. Recipient Lifetime Achievement award N.Am. Conf. on Brit. Studies, 1995, Bishop William Hughes award for disting. svc. to Cath. higher edn. Thomas More Coll., 1997, Leadership Medallion, Xavier U., 2003, Excellence award U. Cin., 2006. Mem. Am. Hist. Assn., Phi Beta Kappa, Tau Kappa Alpha, Phi Alpha Theta. Clubs: Comml., Bankers, Cin., Lit. Office: U Cin 571 Langsam Library Cincinnati OH 45221-0001 Business E-Mail: henry.winkler@uc.edu.

WINKLER, JONATHAN REED, historian, educator; b. Boston; PhD, Yale U., 2004; BA, Ohio U., 1997. Asst. prof. history Wright State U., Dayton, Ohio, 2005—, asoc. prof. history, 2029; adj. asst. prof. history U.S. Naval Acad., Annapolis, Md. Mem. Soc. for Historians of Am. Fgn. Rels. Recipient Roosevelt prize, Naval History, 2008. Mem.: Phi Beta Kappa. Office: Wright State University 3640 Col Glenn Hwy Dayton OH 45435 Personal E-mail: jonathan.winkler@aya.yale.edu.

WINKLER, MATTHEW ADAM, editor-in-chief, reporter; b. June 1, 1955; m. Lisa Winkler; 3 children. AB in History, Kenyon Coll., 1977, LLD. Reporter Mount Vernon News, Ohio, 1976—77; pub. rels. specialist Gehrung Assocs., Keene, NH, 1977—78; reporter, asst. editor Bond Buyer, 1978—80; with Dow Jones Capital Markets Reports, 1980; reporter Wall Street Jour., 1980—90; European Fin. corr. Wall Street Jour. Europe, Jour. London, 1982—87; with Bloomberg L.P., editor-in-chief Bloomberg News (formerly Bloomberg Bus. News) NYC, 1990—. Chmn. bd. trustees Kenyon Rev. Co-author: Bloomberg by Bloomberg, 1997. Trustee N.J. Symphony Orch., Overseas Press Club, 1998, Knight-Bagehot Fellowship Columbia U. Office: Bloomberg News 499 Park Ave New York NY 10022-1240*

WINKLER, PAUL FRANK, JR., astrophysicist, educator; b. Nashville, Nov. 10, 1942; s. Paul Frank and Estelle (Pye) W.; m. Geraldine Huck, Aug. 20, 1966 (div. 1979); children: Katharine Winkler Corcoran, Johanna Winkler Durrett; m. Janet Pippitt Beers, June 25, 1983; stepchildren: Sarah Creighton Beers, Nathan Pippitt Beers. BS, Calif. Inst. Tech., 1964; A.M., Harvard U., 1965, PhD, 1970. From instr. to prof. physics Middlebury Coll., Vt., 1969—84, William R. Kenan Jr. prof. physics, 1984-87, chmn. nat. scis. div., 1988-93, asst. to pres. for sci. planning, 1993-96, Gamaliel Painter Bicentennial prof. physics, 1997—. Vis. scientist MIT, Cambridge, 1973-74, 78-80; sr. vis. fellow Inst. Astronomy, U. Cambridge, 1985-86; vis. resident astronomer Cerro Tololo InterAm. Observatory, La Serena, Chile, 1990-91, 96-97; vis. fellow Joint Inst. for Laboratory Astrophysics, U. Colo., Boulder, 1991. Contbr. articles to profl. jours. NSF fellow, 1965-69, Alfred P. Sloan Found. fellow, 1976-80 Mem. Vt. Acad. Sci. and Engring., Am. Phys. Soc., Am. Astron. Soc., Internat. Astron. Union, Coun. on Undergrad. Rsch., Sigma Xi. Office: Middlebury Coll Dept Physics Middlebury VT 05753 Business E-Mail: winkler@middlebury.edu.

WINKLER, SHELDON, dentist, educator; b. NYC, Jan. 25, 1932; s. Ben and Lillian (Barsh) W.; m. Sandra M. Cohen, Aug. 13, 1961; children: Mitchell, Lori. BA, Washington Sq. Coll., 1953; DDS, NYU, 1956. Asst. prof. denture prosthesis NYU Coll. Dentistry, NYC, 1958-61, 66-68, rsch. asst. prof., 1962-63; dir. materials rsch. Consol. Metal Products Industries Inc., Albany, NY, 1963-65, cons. materials rsch., 1966-68; asst. prof. removable prosthodontics sch. dentistry SUNY, Buffalo, 1968-70, assoc. prof., 1970-79; prof., chmn. dept. prosthodontics Temple U. Sch. Dentistry, Phila., 1979-86, 94-96, asst. dean for advanced studies, continuing edn./rsch., 1987-89, acting asst. dean, 1993-95, prof. restorative dentistry, 1996—2006; prof. dentistry Ariz. Sch. Dentistry and Oral Health, Mesa, 2006—07, Midwestern U. Coll. Dental Medicine, Glendale, Ariz., 2007—. Asst. dir. dental dept. NYU Med. Ctr. Goldwater Meml. Hosp., NYC, 1966—68, vis. dentist dental dept., 1966—68; attending in prosthodontics E.J. Meyer Meml. Hosp., Buffalo, 1975—79; postgrad instr. First Dist. Dental Soc. NY, NYC, 1963—; cons. Coe Labs., Chgo., 1967—87, Harkness Ctr., Buffalo, Rosa Coplon Home & Infirmary, Buffalo, 1970—79, Erie C.C., Buffalo, 1979—, Lever Bros. Co., NYC, 1981—. VA Hosp., Phila., 1989—2005, Ivoclar N. Am., Amherst, NY, 2000—; lectr. dept. dental hygiene NYC C.C., 1967—68; hon. prof. Pierre Fauchard Sch. Dentistry, Asuncion, Paraguay, 1999—. Author: (with A. Davidoff and M.H.M. Lee) Dentistry for the Special Patient: The Aged, Chronically Ill and Handicapped, 1972, Essentials of Complete Denture Prosthodontics, 1979, 2d edit., 1988, 3rd edit., 2009; editor: Resins in Dentistry, 1975, Complete Dentures, 1977, Removable Prosthodontics, 1984, (with B.R. Lang, F.R. Lauciello and G.P. McGivney) Contemporary Complete Denture Occlusion, 2001; editor Jour. Implant Dentistry, 1990-97; sr. editor Jour. Oral Implantology, 2000—; contbr. articles to profl. lit.; co-designer McGowan-Winkler complete denture trays. Served as capt. AUS, 1956-58, 61-62. Recipient Outstanding Layman award Vocat. Tech. Alumni and Student Assn., SUNY, Buffalo, 1974, Internat. Edn. award Internat. Congress Oral Implantologists, 1992, journalism award Internat. Coll. Dentists, 1993, Academic Devotion award Chulalongkorn U., Bangkok, 1995. Fellow Am. Coll. Dentists, Greater N.Y. Acad. Prosthodontics; mem. ADA, Internat. Assn. Dental Rsch., Am. Assn. Dental Schs., Am. Acad. Implant Prosthodontics (Outstanding Personality Implant Prosthodontics award, 2002), Sci. Rsch. Soc. Am., Acad. Plastics Rsch., Am. Prosthodontic Soc., Am. Soc. Geriatric Dentistry, Internat. Congress of Oral Implantologists, Sigma Xi, Sigma Epsilon Delta, Omicron Kappa Upsilon. Home: 8672 E Eagle Claw Dr Scottsdale AZ 85266-1058 Office Phone: 480-588-8062. E-mail: swinkdent@cox.net.

WINLAND, THOMAS W., lawyer; b. Lancaster, Ohio, Mar. 18, 1949; BS, Ohio State U., 1971; JD, Duke U., 1974. Bar: Ohio 1974, D.C. 1982, US Patent and Trademark Office, US Ct. Customs and Patent Appeals 1980, US Claims Ct. 1982, US Ct. Appeals (Fed. Cir.) 1982. Ptnr. Finnegan, Henderson, Farabow, Garrett & Dunner, Washington DC. Named one of best lawyers in intellectual property law, Best Lawyers in Am., 2005—07. Mem. ABA (patent, trademark and copyright law sects., pub. contract law), Am. Intellectual Property Law Assn., D.C. Bar, Bar Assn. of D.C. Office: Finnegan Henderson Farabow Garrett & Dunner LLP 901 New York Ave NW Washington DC 20001-3315 Office Fax: 202-408-4400. Business E-Mail: tom.winland@finnegan.com.

WINN, ALBERT CURRY, clergyman; b. Ocala, Fla., Aug. 16, 1921; s. James Anderson and Elizabeth (Curry) W.; m. Grace Neely Walker, Aug. 29, 1944; children: Grace Walker (Mrs. Stewart E. Ellis), James Anderson, Albert Bruce Curry, Randolph Axson. AB, Davidson Coll., 1942, LLD, 1968; BD, Union Theol. Sem., Va., 1945, ThD, 1956; ThM, Princeton Theol. Sem., 1949; LLD, Stillman Coll., 1975. Ordained min. Presbyn. Ch., 1945. Asst. prof. Davidson Coll., 1946-47; pastor Potomac Rural Parish, Va., 1948-53; prof. Bible Stillman Coll., 1953-60; prof. theology Louisville Presbyn. Theol. Sem., 1960-73, pres., 1966-73; pastor 2d Presbyn. Ch., Richmond, Va., 1974-81, North Decatur Presbyn. Ch., Ga., 1981-86. Moderator Presbyn. Synod Ala., 1958, Presbyn. Synod Ky., 1969, Gen. Assembly, Presbyn. Ch. in U.S., 1979; vis. prof. Union Theol. Sem. in Va., 1987, Columbia Theol. Sem., 1987, Louisville Presbyn. Theol. Sem., 1988; interim pastor Cen. Presbyn. Ch., Atlanta, 1989-90, St. Andrews Presbyn. Ch., Tucker, Ga., 1993-94; parish assoc. Trinity Prebyn. Ch., Winston-Salem, NC, 1999-2007. Author: Layman's Bible Commentary on Acts, 1960, The Worry and Wonder of Being Human, 1966, Where Do I Go From Here, 1972, Proclamation Two: Epiphany, 1980, A Sense of Mission, 1981, Christ the Peacemaker, 1982, Plain Talk about the Apostles' Creed, 1985, The Christian Primer, 1990, Ain't Gonna Study War No More, 1993. Chmn. trustees Stillman Coll., 1965-70. Served as chaplain USNR, 1945-46. Mem. Phi Beta Kappa, Beta Theta Pi, Omicron Delta Kappa. Office: 421 Creekside Ter 3895 Old Vineyard Rd Winston Salem NC 27104 Office Phone: 336-786-3294.

WINN, CAROLYN PAUTKE, librarian, consultant; b. Detroit, June 5, 1927; d. Benno Edgar and Caroline Amelia (Milatz) Pautke; divorced; children: Eric, Gregory, Mathew. BS in Zoology, U. Mich., 1949, MA in Zoology, 1950; MLS, U. R.I., 1970. Cataloguer Mus. Zoology U. Mich., Ann Arbor, 1950-54; rsch. asst. U. Md., College Park, 1963-65, U. R.I., Kingston, 1965-67, cataloger, 1968-69, ast. ref. libr., 1969-70, instr. sci. ref. libr., 1970-73, asst. prof., sci. ref. libr., 1973-75; rsch. libr. Woods Hole (Mass.) Oceanographic Instn., 1975—94. Cons. Marine Biol. Lab./Woods Hole Oceanog. Instn. Libr., 1994—97. Contbr. articles to profl. jours. Observer, vol. White House Conf. Librs. and Info. Svcs., Washington, 1979; adv. com. N.E. Academic Sci. Info. Ctr., New Eng. Bd. Higher Edn., 1978. Grantee U. R.I., 1974-75, Woods Hole Oceanographic Instn., 1976-77, 80-81, 86-87, Bur. Land Mgmtm., 1982-84. Mem. ALA, Am. Geophys. Union. (subcom. electronic pub. 1983-87), Internat. Assn. Aquatic & Marine Sci. Librs. and Info. Ctrs. (founder, 1975, editor jour. 1989-90, pres. 1982-83), New Eng. On-Line Users Group (database com. 1979-86), New Eng. Libr. Assn., R.I. Libr. Assn., R.I. Health Scis. Librs. Consortium, Nat. Micrographics Assn., Soc. Scholarly Pub., New Eng. Microcomputer Users Group, Boston Libr. Consortium (collection mgmt. com. 1992-94), Cape Librs. Automated Materials Sharing, Inc. (pres. 1989-90, mem. coms.) E-mail: cpwinn90@hotmail.com.

WINN, H. RICHARD, surgeon; b. Chester, Pa., 1942; BA, Princeton U., 1964; MD, U. Pa., 1968. Diplomate Am Bd. Neurol. Surgeons. Intern U. Hosp., Cleve., 1968-69, resident surgery, 1969-70; resident neurolog. surgery U. Hosp. Va., Charlottesville, 1970-74; neurol. surgeon U. Wash. Hosp., Seattle, 1983—2002; prof., chmn. neurol. surgery U. Wash., Seattle, 1983—2002; prof. neurosurgery and neurosci. Mt. Sinai Med. Sch., NYC, 2003—. Bd. dirs. Am. Bd. Neurol. Surgery, 1995-2001, vice chmn., 2000-01. Founding editor Neurosurgical Clinics of North America; mem. editl. bd. Jour. Neurosurgery, 1995-2001, chair, 2001-2002; mem. editl. bd. Am. Physiology, 1995-2000, Am. Jour. Surgery. Recipient Disting. Alumnus, Haverford Sch., 2000. Fellow AAAS, Soc. Brit. Neurol. Surgeons (hon.); mem. AMA, Am. Assn. Neurol. Surgeons, Soc. Neurol. Surgeons (Grass prize 1999, Disting. Svc. award 2005), Congress Neurol. Surgeons. Office: Dept Neurosurgery Mount Sinai Sch Medicine One Gustave L Levy PO Box 1136 New York NY 10029 Office Phone: 212-241-9128. Business E-Mail: richard.winn@mountsinai.org.

WINN, JAMES JULIUS, JR., lawyer; b. Colon, Panama, Nov. 7, 1941; came to U.S., 1941; s. James Julius and Molly (Brown) W.; m. Elizabeth Kokernot Lacy, Aug. 15, 1970; children: Mary Ann W. Burns, E. Lacy W. Sakellaris, James Julius VI. AB, Princeton U., 1964; JD cum laude, Washington and Lee U., 1970. Bar: Md. 1970, U.S. Dist. Ct. Md. 1971, U.S. Dist. Ct. D.C. 1982. Assoc. Piper & Marbury, Balt., 1970-78; ptnr. Piper Rudnick LLP, Balt., 1978—2004; mem. Winn Group LLC, 2001—; gen. counsel Kokernot 06 Ranch, Inc., 2006—. Bd. dirs. The Columbia Bank. Assoc. editor, contbr. author Washington & Lee U. Law Rev., 1968-70. Counselor St. John's Ch., Western Run Parish, Glyndon, Md., 1974—; mem. com. on canons and other bus. Episc. Diocese Md., 1986—; dir. Ctr. for Ethics and Corp. Policy, 1988-95, chmn., 1991-95; dir. Ctr. Stage, 1986-2004; dir. Oldfields Sch., 1991-96; v.p., dir. Ruxton Country Sch., 1988-91; dir. The Jemicy Sch., 1999-2008, chmn. 2005-08. Mem. Md. State Bar Assn. (com. on corp. law of sect. of bus. law). Office: DLA Piper US LLP 6225 Smith Ave Baltimore MD 21209-3600 Office Phone: 410-580-4286.

WINN, JANICE GAIL, food products administrator; b. Springfield, Mass., Nov. 2, 1954; d. Rose Eleanor (Draskawich) W. BA, Western New Eng. Coll., 1976. Gen. mdse. mgr. Mott's Shop-Rite, East Hartford, Conn., 1979-84; sr. merchandiser Imperial Distbrs., Auburn, Mass., 1984-85; dir. of gen. mdse. Waldbaums Food Mart, Holyoke, Mass., 1985-91; dir. health, beauty care and gen. mdse. Big Y Foods, Inc., Springfield, 1991—. Republican. Avocations: travel, spending time with partner and family. Office: Big Y Foods Inc 2145 Roosevelt Ave Springfield MA 01104-1650 Home Phone: 413-525-3889; Office Phone: 413-504-4410. Personal E-mail: jan_winn1346@yahoo.com.

WINN, JOSEPH LAMPHER, retired electronics executive; b. Cambridge, Mass., Aug. 12, 1951; s. Joseph L. and Alicia M. (Muir) W.; m. Gail A. Cadogan, June 19, 1976; children: Kelly, Caroline, Joseph. BS in Fin., Boston Coll., 1973; MBA, Babson Coll., 1974. Fin. mgr. program Sanders Assocs. Inc., Nashua, N.H., 1974-78; fin. mgr. Digital Equipment Corp., Maynard, Mass., 1978-83; sr. v.p., controller Am. Cablesystems Corp., Beverly, Mass., 1983-88; exec. v.p., chief fin. officer Atlantic Radio Corp., Manchester, Mass., 1988—93; CFO & dir. Am. Radiosystems Corp., 1993—98; CFO Am. Tower Corp., Boston, 1998—2001, vice chmn., 2002—03. Bd. dirs. OnePIN, Westborough, Mass. Bd. trustees The Carroll Sch., 2002—03; trutee Babson Coll., 2001—. Roman Catholic. E-mail: joe.winn@americantower.com.

WINNEKER, RICHARD CRAIG, pharmacologist, researcher; b. Phila. BS in Animal Sci., Pa. State U., University Park, 1969; MS in Physiology, U. Ill., Champaign, 1976; PhD in Anatomy, U. Minn., Mpls., 1981. Principle rsch. scientist Sterling Rsch. Group, Rensselaer, NY, 1983—94; assitant v.p. Wyeth Rsch., Collegeville, Pa., 1994—2008. Contbr. articles to profl. jours. (Becaner Rsch. award, 1984). Mem.: Endocrine Soc. Achievements include patents for numerous awards. Personal E-mail: rwinneker@aol.com.

WINNEM, BJØRN MAGNE, anesthesiologist; b. Evenes, Norway, Sept. 21, 1947; s. Erling and Mary Irene (Burchard) W.; m. Dina Navjord, June 25, 1976; children: Marcus, Andreas. Student, U. Vienna, Austria, U. Bergen, Norway, 1967, MD, 1976. Cert. anesthesiologist. Resident in surgery SIA, Oslo, 1976; resident in medicine Torsby Hosp., Sweden, 1977, Narvik Hosp., Norway, 1977; physician Narvik Health Authority, 1977-78; clin. resident in anesthesiology U. Trondheim, Norway, 1978-79; resident in anesthesiology U. Tex. Health Sci. Ctr., San Antonio, 1979; resident anesthesiology and cardiology cardiovascular physiology U. Clin. Trondheim, 1980-83; rsch. fellow Inst. for Biomed. Tech., U. Trondheim, 1984-86; cons. Innherred Hosp., Levanger, Norway, 1986-87, Lillehammer Hosp., Norway, 1987-97; head anesthesia, intensive care Unprofor Normedcoy, Tuzla, 1994; mem. crictical care staff Ulleval Univ. Clinic, 1998-99; staff anesthesiologist Ullevål Univ. Clinic, 1999—; trauma anesthesiology expert Med. Readiness br. Hdqrs. Def. Command of Norway, 2002—. Contbr. articles to profl. jours. With UN Protection Force, Bosnia-Herzegovina,

1994, Internat. Security Assistance Force, Kabul, Afghanistan, 2003, Meymaneh, Afghanistan, 2006. Maj. M.C. Norwegian Mil., 1994. Recipient Golden Ball, Norwegian Football Assn., 1963; Nat. Rsch. Coun. grantee, 1984-86. Mem. Norwegian Med. Assn. (trustee 1996-98), Norwegian Anesthesiology Assn., Scandinavian Anesthesiology Assn., European Soc. Intensive Care Medicine, Internat. Trauma Anesthesiology and Critical Care Soc., Soc. of Critical Care Medicine. Avocations: soccer, scuba diving, skiing, mountain climbing, sailing. Home: Sigrid Undsetsvei 8 N 2615 Lillehammer Norway Office: Ullevaal Univ Clin Dept Anesthesiology Military Med Ops Ctr N 0407 Oslo Norway Business E-Mail: bmwinnem@mil.no. E-mail: bmw@winnem.com.

WINNER, GEORGE HENRY, lawyer, state legislator; b. Elmira, NY, July 31, 1949; s. George H. and Beverly S. (Sweet) W.; m. Lynn Hardman, Dec. 4, 1976; children: Catherine H., Elizabeth H., Meredith F. BA, St. Lawrence U., 1971. Bar: NY 1977, U.S. Dist. Ct. (no. and we. dists.) NY 1977. Ptnr., assoc. Winner, Sullivan & Delaney, Elmira, NY, 1977-84; counsel/legis. asst. Senate Dep. Majority Leader William T. Smith, Albany, NY, 1971—78; mem. Dist. 127 NY State Assembly, Albany, NY, 1979—2004; ptnr. Winner & Denton, Elmira, NY, 1984-94, Denton, Keyser, LaBreque & Moore, Elmira, 1995—2002, Keyser Maloney & Winner LLP, 2002—; adminstrv. asst. NY State Senate, Albany, NY, 1972-76, dep. minority leader, minority leader pro-tem, 1990—, mem. Dist. 57, 2004—. Dir. Peak Resorts, Inc., Virgil, NY, 1994—. Chemung County GOP exec. com., Elmira, 1980—. Mem. NY State Bar Assn., Chemung County Bar Assn. Republican. Avocations: skiing, golf, scuba diving. Home: 15 Abbey Rd Elmira NY 14905 Office: Capitol Office 415 Legislative Office Bldg Albany NY 12247 also: Dist Office 105 E Steuben St Bath NY 14810 also: Dist Office 228 Lake St PO Box 588 Elmira NY 14902 Office Phone: 607-732-2765, 607-776-3201, 518-455-2091. Office Fax: 607-732-2832, 607-776-5185, 518-426-6976. E-mail: winner@senate.state.ny.us.*

WINNER, KARIN E., editor; b. White Plains, NY, Dec. 27, 1945; BA in Journalism, U. So. Calif. West coast editor Women's Wear Daily, W mag.; features writer San Diego Union (merged with Evening Tribune to become San Diego Union-Tribune, 1991), 1976, asst. editor, 1980—83; exec. editor San Diego Union-Tribune, 1991—95, editor, 1995—. Mem.: Am. Soc. Newspaper Editors, Calif. Soc. Newspaper Editors (past pres.). Office: San Diego Union-Tribune 350 Camino De La Reina San Diego CA 92108 Mailing: San Diego Union-Tribune PO Box 120191 San Diego CA 92112-0191 Office Phone: 619-293-1201, 619-293-1354, 619-299-3131. E-mail: Karin.winner@uniontrib.com.*

WINNER, MICHAEL ROBERT, film director, producer, writer; b. London, Oct. 30, 1935; s. George Joseph and Helen (Zloty) W. Degree in law and econs. with honors, Cambridge U., Eng., 1956. Writer Fleet St. (newspapers), London, 1956-58. Columnist London Sunday Times, 1990, London News of the World, 1995. Engaged in film prodn., 1956; dir. films Play it Cool, 1962, West 11, 1963, The Mechanic, 1972, Death Wish II, 1981; dir., writer The Cool Mikado, 1962, You Must be Joking, 1965, The Wicked Lady, 1982; producer, dir. The System, 1963, I'll Never Forget What's 'isname, 1967, The Games, 1969, Lawman, 1970, The Nightcomers, 1971, Chato's Land, 1971, Scorpio, 1972, The Stone Killer, 1973, Death Wish, 1974, Won Ton Ton The Dog Who Saved Hollywood, 1975, Firepower, 1978, Scream for Help, 1983, Death Wish III, 1985; producer, writer, dir. films The Jokers, 1966, Hannibal Brooks, 1968, The Sentinel, 1976, The Big Sleep, 1977, Appointment With Death, 1987, A Chorus of Disapproval, 1988, Bullseye!, 1989, Dirty Weekend, 1992, Parting Shots, 1997; producer plays Nights at the Comedy, Comedy Theatre, London, 1960, The Silence of St. Juste, Gardner Centre, Brighton, 1971, The Tempest, Wyndhams Theatre, London, 1974, A Day in Hollywood, A Night in the Ukraine, Mayfair Theatre, London, 1978, (TV series London Weekend TV) Michael Winner's True Crimes, 1990, 91, 92, 93, 94; author: Winner's Dinners, 1999, rev. edit., 2000, Winner Guide to Whining and Dining, 2002, (autobiography) Winner Takes All, 2004, paperback edit., 2005, The Fat Pig Diet, 2007, Winners Dinners Book, 2009; actor: (BBC film) For the Greater Good, 1990, Decadence, 1993, The Flump, 2000, (TV series) Michael Winner's Dining Stars, 2009; actor and/or dir. commls. including Esure Ins., Kenco, Doritos, Books for Schs. Founder, chmn. Police Meml. Trust, 1984. Office: Scimitar Films Ltd 219 Kensington High St London W8 6BD England Home Phone: 0207 603 5510; Office Phone: 0207 603 4820. E-mail: winner@ftech.co.uk, mwinner@mistral.co.uk.

WINNER, PAUL KEVIN, medical educator, researcher; DO, NY Coll. Osteo. Medicine, NYC, 1981. Diplomate in neurology and child neurology Am. Bd. Neurosci., 1991. Dir., rschr. Premiere Rsch. Inst., West Palm Beach, Fla., 2000—; clin. prof. neurology Nova Southeastern U., Ft. Lauderdale, Fla., 2005—. Pres. Am. Headache Soc., Mt. Royal, NJ, 2006—08. Recipient John Graham award, Am. Headache Soc., 2008. Achievements include research in neuroscience on Migraine And Alzheimer's. Home: 4631 N Congress Ave West Palm Beach FL 33407 Office: Nova Southeastern Univ 3200 S University Dr Fort Lauderdale FL 33328

WINNOWSKI, THADDEUS RICHARD (TED WINNOWSKI), investment banker, consultant; b. Albany, NY, Feb. 20, 1942; s. Thaddeus Walter and Harriet Frances (Witko) W.; m. Sheila Margaret Neary, June 15, 1968; children: Dona, Paul. BS in Econs., Siena Coll., 1963; postgrad., Rensselaer Poly. Inst., 1968-72. Adminstrv. v.p. Key Bank N.A., Albany, N.Y., 1978-80; pres. Key Bank L.I., Sayville, N.Y., 1980-85; pres., CEO Key Bank Oreg., Woodburn, 1985-86, chmn., CEO Portland, 1986-95, chmn., 1995-97; exec. v.p., group exec. N.W. region Key Corp., Seattle, 1995-97, chmn., CEO, 1996-97; pres., CEO Centennial Bank, Eugene, Oreg., 1998—2002. Mem. adv. bd. Blue Cross/Blue Shield Oreg.; bd. regents U. Portland, 2002-. 1st lt. U.S. Army, 1964-66. Mem. Portland Bus. Alliance (hon. bd. dirs., former chmn.). Roman Catholic. Personal E-mail: twinnowski@yahoo.com.

WINOGRAD, AUDREY LESSER, retired advertising executive; b. NYC, Oct. 6, 1933; d. Jack J. and Theresa Lorraine (Elkind) Lesser; m. Melvin H. Winograd, Apr. 29, 1956; 1 child, Hope Elise. BA, U. Conn., 1953. Asst. advt. mgr. T. Baumritter Co., Inc., NYC, 1953-54; asst. dir. pub. rels. and creative merchandising Kirby, Block & Co., Inc., NYC, 1954-56; divsn. mdse. mgr., dir. advt. and sales promotion Winograd's Dept. Store, Inc., Point Pleasant, NJ, 1956-73, v.p., 1960-73, exec. v.p., 1973-86; pres., CEO AMW Assocs., Atlanta, 1976—2002, ret., 2002—. Editor: bus. newsletters. Active Alley Cat Allies, Fund for Animals; bd. dirs. Temple Beth Am, Lakewood, NJ, 1970—72, Temple Emanuel, Atlanta, 1999—2001. Mem.: LWV, NAFE, Noah's Lost Ark, Retail Advt. Conf., Am. Soc. Advt. and Promotion, NJ Assn. Women Bus. Owners, Monmouth County Bus. Assn. (bd. dirs. 1985—97, pres. 1988—90, Woman of the Yr. 1992—93, Person of the Yr. 1995), Monmouth Ocean Devel. Coun., Retail Advt. and Mktg. Assn. Internat., Jersey Pub. Rels. and Advt. Assn. (pres. 1982—83, bd. dirs.), Greenpeace (mem. physicians com., mem. Grey 2K), Environ. Defense, Wilderness Soc., Best Friends, Humane Soc. US, Delta Rescue, People Ethical Treatment Animals, In Defense of Animals, Ocean C. of C. (bd. dirs. 1994—97, Career Achievements and Contbns. to Soc. award 1993), Soc. Prevention Cruelty to Animals, Animal Protection Inst. Am., Humane Soc., Internat. Fund Animal Welfare, World Wildlife Fund, Friends of Animals, Defenders of Wildlife, Nat. Humane Edn. Soc., Atlanta Humane Soc., Natural Resources Def. Coun., Last Chance for Animals, United Animal Nat., Lifesavers Wild Horse Rescue, Audobon, Sierra Club. Avocations: collecting animal collectibles, gourmet cooking, environmental protection, exercise. Office: AMW Assocs 5304 Vernon Lake Dr Atlanta GA 30338-3527

WINOGRAD, BERNARD B., diversified financial services company executive; b. Detroit, Dec. 31, 1950; s. Daniel and Lillian (Walder) W.; m. Carol Leslie Snodgrass, Mar. 8, 1974; children: Simon James Bartholomew, Christina Lynn. BA, U. Chgo., 1970. Pub. affairs mgr. Bendix Corp., Southfield, Mich., 1975; exec. asst. to W.M. Blumenthal, 1975-77, dir. corp. communications, 1977-79, treas., 1979-83; exec. asst. to sec. US Dept. Treasury, Washington, 1977; exec. v.p. Taubman Investments, 1983-84; pres. Taubman Investment Co., 1984-96; exec. v.p., CFO Taubman Ctrs., Inc., 1996; CEO Prudential Real Estate Investors; pres., CEO Prudential Investment Mgmt. (PIM), 2002—; sr. v.p. Prudential Fin., Inc., 2002—08, exec. v.p., head US bus., 2008—. Mem. Urban Land Inst. (bd. dir.), Pension Real Estate Assn. (bd. dirs.). Office: Prudential Financial Inc 8 Campus Dr 4th Fl Parsippany NJ 07054*

WINOGRAD, NICHOLAS, chemist; b. New London, Conn., Dec. 27, 1945; s. Arthur Selig Winograd and Winifred (Schaefer) Winograd Mayes; m. Barbara J. Garrison. BS, Rensselaer Poly. Inst., 1967; PhD, Case We. Res. U., 1970. Asst. prof. chemistry Purdue U., West Lafayette, Ind., 1970-75, assoc. prof. chemistry, 1975-79; prof. chemistry Pa. State U., University Park, 1979-85, Evan Pugh prof. chemistry, 1985—. Cons. Lawrence Livermore Lab., 1997-2003; mem. chemistry adv. bd. NSF, Washington, 1987-90, analytical chemistry adv. bd., 1986-89. Contbr. articles to profl. jours. A.P. Sloan Found. fellow, 1974; Guggenheim Found. fellow, 1977; recipient Founder's prize Tex. Instruments Found., 1984, Faculty Scholar's Pa. State U., 1985, Bennedetti Pichler award Am. Microchem. Soc., 1991, Outstanding Alumnus award Case We. Res. U., 1991. Fellow AAAS (Sect. award); mem. Am. Chem. Soc. Avocation: running. Home: 138 Chemistry Ln Spring Mills PA 16875-9703 Office: Pa State U Dept of Chemistry 209 Chemistry Bldg University Park PA 16802-6300 Home Phone: 814-422-8069; Office Phone: 814-863-0001. Business E-Mail: nxw@psu.edu.

WINOKUR, MARISSA JARET, actress; b. NYC, Feb. 2, 1973; m. Judah Miller, Oct. 7, 2006; 1 child, Zev Isaac Miller. Studied at, Am. Musical and Dramatic Acad. Actor: (plays, Broadway) Grease, 1995, Hairspray, 2002 (Tony award for best actress, 2003), 2005; (plays) Guys and Dolls, Peter Pan, Little Shop of Horrors, Romeo and Juliet, Nunsense II, Grandma Sylvia's Funeral, Hair, Happy Days; (films) Demo Real, 1998, Why Love Doesn't Work, 1999, Never Been Kissed, 1999, American Beauty, 1999, Sleep Easy, Hutch Rimes, 2000, Scary Movie, 2000, Amy's Orgasm, 2001, On Edge, 2001, Now You Know, 2002, Fever Pitch, 2005; (TV films) Beautiful Girl, 2003; co-exec. prodr. (TV films) Beautiful Girl, 2003; actor: (TV films) Ultra, 2006, Fugly, 2007, Betrayals, 2007, (voice): (TV series) Shrek the Halls, 2007, (guest appearances) The Steve Harvey Show, 1998, Felicity, 1999, Dharma & Greg, 1999, 2000, Moesha, 2000, Curb Your Enthusiasm, 2000, Just Shoot Me, 2000, The Ellen Show, 2001, Boston Public, 2001, Stacked, 2005—06. Office Phone: 310-288-5888. Office Fax: 310-288-5868.

WINOLD, HELGA ULSAMER, retired music educator; m. Charles Allen Winold, Dec. 17, 1963; children: Bettina Julia Hoar, Claire Elisabeth, Hans Peter, Erika Marie Werdal. MusD D. Mus. Cello, Ind. U., Bloomington, IN, 1967. Vis. prof. music Freiburg Hochschule fuer Music, Germany, 1985—2007; prof. music Ind. U. Jacobs Sch. Music, Bloomington, 1964—2008; prof. Ind. U. Sch. Music, Bloomington, 1963—2008. Musician in fields. Achievements include research in motion studies and cello playing. Personal E-mail: winolds@gmail.com.

WINROTH, ANDERS, historian, educator; children: Hjalmar, Elsa. BA, Stockholm U., 1990; PhD, Columbia U., 1996. Rsch. fellow U. Newcastle upon Tyne, 1996—98; asst. prof. dept. history Yale U., 1998—2003, assoc. prof., 2003—04, prof., 2004—. Author: The Making of Gratian's Decretum, 2000; co-editor: Charters, Cartularies and Archives: The preservation and transmission of Documents in the Medieval West, 2002. Morse fellow, Yale U., 2001—02, MacArthur Found. fellow, 2003. Office: Yale Univ Dept of History PO Box 208324 New Haven CT 06520 Home Phone: 203-781-8429; Office Phone: 203-432-7657.

WINROW, BRIAN PAUL, law educator; b. Colo. m. Amanda Rene' Winrow. JD, MBA, U. SD, Vermillion. Asst. prof. Emporia State U., 2006—08, Winona State U., Minn., 2008—. Mem.: State Bar N.Mex. Business E-Mail: bwinrow@winona.edu.

WINSHIP, FREDERICK MOERY, journalist; b. Franklin, Ohio, Sept. 24, 1924; s. Wilbur William and Edna B. (Moery) W.; m. Joanne Tree Thompson, Aug. 29, 1967. AB, DePauw U., 1945; MS, Columbia, 1946. Corr. UPI, 1946—; assigned UN, 1947-49; editorial staff N.Y.C., 1950-60, cultural affairs editor, 1960-72, sr. editor, 1972-75, asst. mng. editor, 1975-80; sr. editor arts/theater NYC, 1980-98; Broadway critic, 1985-98; arts critic at large, 2000—. Contbr. articles mags. Pres. Letters Abroad, Inc., 1962-83; chmn. Easter Seal Soc., N.Y.C., 1964-73, Oratorio Soc. N.Y., 1965-75, N.Y. Conf. Patriotic Socs., 1967-72; Bd. dirs. Odell House-Rochambeau Hdgrs., 1965-75, N.Y. State Easter Seal Soc., 1969-72, Mus. of City of N.Y., 1974—, Am. Philharm. Orch., 1981-82, Friends of the Am. Theater Wing, 1990—. Recipient Am. Legion Journalism award, 1955; Whitelaw Reid Journalism fellow India, 1958; Creative Club Journalism award, 1962 Mem. S.A.R. (sec. N.Y. chpt. 1963-68), St. Nicholas, Founders and Patriots, Mayflower Descs., Soc. Colonial Wars (bd. dirs.), S.R., Soc. Cincinnati, Sigma Delta Chi. Republican. Episcopalian. Home: 419 E 57th St New York NY 10022-3060 Office Phone: 212-838-3095.

WINSHIP, MICHAEL P., history professor; s. Paul Michelini and Susan Reyburn Winship; m. Eleanor Fruchtman Fruchtman, June 13, 1983; children: Nathaniel Israel, Anna Dorothea. PhD, Cornell U., Ithaca, NY, 1991. E. merton coulter prof. history U. Ga., Athens, 2006—. Author: (history) Times and Trials of Anne Hutchinson; co-author (with Edward J. Lawson): The Constitutional Convention, Making Heretics, Seers of God. Office: Univ Georgia LeConte Hall Athens GA 30602 Business E-Mail: mwinship@uga.edu.

WINSLET, KATE, actress; b. Reading, Berkshire, Eng., Oct. 5, 1975; d. Roger and Sally Bridges Winslet; m. James Threapleton, Nov. 22, 1998 (div. Dec. 13, 2001); 1 child, Mia; m. Sam Mendes, May 24, 2003; 1 child, Joe Alfie. Actress (films) Heavenly Creatures, 1994 (Empire award for Best Brit. Actress, London Film Critics' Cir. award for Best Brit. Actress, New Zealand Film & TV awards Best Fgn. Actress), Sense and Sensibility, 1995 (BAFTA award for Best Actress in a supporting role, SAG award for outstanding performance by a female actor in a supporting role, Acad. award nominee, Golden Globe award nominee), A Kid in King Arthur's Court, 1995, Jude, 1996, Hamlet, 1996, Titanic, 1997 (Empire award for Best Brit. Actress, European Film award for Best Actress, Acad. award nominee, Golden Globe award nominee), Hideous Kinky, 1998, Holy Smoke, 1999, Faeries (voice only), 1999, Quills, 2000 (Las Vegas Film Critics Soc. Best Actress award), Enigma, 2001 (Brit. Ind. Film award for Best Actress), Christmas Carol: The Movie (voice only), 2001, Iris: A Memoir of Iris Murdoch, 2001 (Empire award for Best Brit. Actress, European Film award, LA Film Critics Assn. award for Best Supporting Actress, Acad. award nominee, Golden Globe award nominee), War Game, 2001, The Life of David Gale, 2003, Plunge: The Movie, 2003, Eternal Sunshine of the Spotless Mind, 2004 (Empire award for Best Brit. Actress, Internat. Cinephile Soc. award for Best Actress, Las Vegas Film Critics Soc. award for Best Actress, London Film Critics Cir. award for Brit. Actress of Yr., Online Film Critics Soc. award for Best Actress, Santa Barbara Internat. Film Festival Outstanding Performance of Yr. award, Acad. award nominee, Golden Globe award nominee), Finding Neverland, 2004, Romance & Cigarettes, 2005, All The King's Men, 2006, Little Children, 2006, Flushed Away (voice only), 2006, The Holiday, 2006, The Reader, 2008 (Acad. award for Best Actress, Golden Globe award for Best Supporting Actress, BAFTA award for Best Actress in a leading role, Broadcast Film Critics Asson. award for Best Supporting Actress, Chgo. Film Critics Asson. award for Best Supporting Actress, SAG award for outstanding performance by a female actor in a supporting role, Las Vegas Film Critics Soc. award for Best Actress, London Film Critics Cir. award for Best Actress, San Diego Film Critics Soc. award for Best Actress), Revolutionary Road, 2008 (Golden Globe award for Best Actress, Las Vegas Film Critics Soc. award for Best Actress, London Film Critics Cir. award for Best Actress, Alliance of Women Film Journalists Best Actress award, Detroit Film Critics Soc. Best Actress award, St. Louis Film Critics Assn. Best Actress award), (TV films) Anglo Saxon Attitudes, 1992, Pride (voice only), 2004, (TV series) Dark Season, 1991, Get Back, 1992, (theater performances include) Peter Pan, What the Butler Saw, A Game of Soldiers, Adrian Mole, (TV appearances) Casualty, 1993, (documentaries) Being Mick, 2001, co-creator (audio book) Listen to the Storyteller, 2000 (Grammy award for Best Spoken Word Album for Children). Recipient Gotham award, Independent Feature Projects, 2006, Desert Palm Achievement for Acting, Palm Springs Internat. Film Soc., 2007, Britannia award for British Artist of Yr., BAFTA/LA Cunard Britannia Awards, 2007; named one of The 50 Most Powerful Women in NYC, NY Post, 2007, The World's Most Influential People, TIME mag., 2009.*

WINSLETT, STONER, artistic director; b. Jacksonville, Fla., Aug. 17, 1958; m. Donald Paulding Irwin; children: Louise Gray Irwin, Elizabeth Irwin, Alexander Pankoff, Caroline Irwin. Student, Am. Ballet Theatre Sch., N.C. Sch. of the Arts; BFA summa cum laude, Smith Coll., 1980. Artistic dir. Richmond Ballet, 1980—. Cadmus leader-in-residence Jepson Sch. U. Richmond; pres. John Butler Found. Pres. John Butler Found. Recipient Gov.'s award for Arts, 2008; named Woman of Yr., YWCA; named one of 100 Most Influential Richmonders of 20th Century, Style mag. Mem.: Phi Beta Kappa. Office: Richmond Ballet 407 E Canal St Richmond VA 23219-3811

WINSLOW, DANIEL B., lawyer; b. 1958; BA magna cum laude, Tufts U., Medford, Mass., 1980; JD cum laude, Boston Coll. Law Sch., 1983. Bar: Mass. 1983, US Dist. Ct. (Mass.), US Ct. Appeals (1st cir.). Assoc., then ptnr. Sherin & Lodgen, 1983—95; assoc. justice, then presiding justice Mass. Dist. Ct., Wrentham, 1995—2002, civil mng. justice Southeast region, Cape & Islands, 1996—2002, assoc. justice So. Appellate Divsn., 2000—02; Gov.'s chief legal counsel Commonwealth Mass., 2002—04; ptnr. Duane Morris LLP, Boston, 2005—. Bd. editors (weekly newspaper) Mass. Lawyers, 1999—2002, Mass. Law Rev., 2000—03; contbr. articles to profl. jours. Named a SuperLawyer, Boston Mag., 2004; named one of Lawyers of Yr., Mass. Lawyers Weekly, 2003, 500 Leading Litigators, Lawdragon Inc., 2006. Mem.: Boston Bar Assn., Am. Judicature Soc., Fed. Bar Assn. (Mass. chpt.), Mass. Bar Assn., Am. Inns of Ct. (co-pres Boston Inn of Ct. 2000), Internat. Inst. Conflict Prevention & Resolution (apptd. Corp. Protocol Commn.). Office: Duane Morris LLP 470 Atlantic Ave Ste 500 Boston MA 02210 Office Phone: 857-488-4256. Office Fax: 857-401-3028. Business E-Mail: DBWinslow@duanemorris.com.*

WINSLOW, DAVID ALLEN, chaplain, retired military officer; b. Dexter, Iowa, July 12, 1944; s. Franklin E. and Inez Maude (McPherson) W.; m. Doribell Rivera Leclaire Winslow, Jan. 20, 2009; children: Frances, David. BA, So. Nazarene U., 1968; MDiv, Drew U., 1971, STM, 1974; cert. of achievement, Emergency Mgmt. Inst., FEMA, 1997. Ordained to ministry United Meth. Ch. Detroit Annual Conf., 1969; cert. FEMA instr. Clergyman, 1969—; assoc. min. All Sts. Episcopal. Ch., Millington, NJ, 1969-70; asst. min. Marble Collegiate Ch., NYC, 1970-71; min. No. NJ Conf. United Meth. Ch., 1971-75; joined chaplain corps USN, 1974, advanced through grades to lt. comdr., 1980, ret., 1995; chaplain Oak Knoll Naval Med. Ctr., Oakland, Calif., 1993-95; command chaplain USNS Mercy T-AH19, Oakland, 1993—95; disaster cons. Ch. World Svc., Cupertino, Calif., 1997—2001. Chaplain med. assistance team CA-6/nat. disaster med. sys. Contra/Costa County, Calif., 1997—2005; founding mem. Dept. Homeland Security, 2003; salesperson Dept. real estate State of Calif., 2000—. Author: The Utmost for the Highest, 1993, Epiphany: God Still Speaks, 1994, Be Thou My Vision, 1994, Evening Prayers At Sea, 1995, Wiseman Still Adore Him, 1995, God's Power At Work, 1996; (with Walsh) A Year of Promise: Meditations, 1995, editor: The Road to Bethlehem: Advent, 1993, Preparation for Resurrecton: Lent, 1994, God's Promise: Advent, 1994, The Way of the Cross: Lent, 1995; contbr. articles to profl. jours. Bd. dirs. disaster svcs. and family svcs. ARC, Santa Ana, Calif., 1988-91, Child Abuse Prevention Ctr., Orange, Calif., 1990-91; bd. dirs. Santa Clara County Coun. Chs., 1993-94, del., 1995-98; bd. dirs. Salvation Army Adult Rehab. Ctr. Adv. Coun., San Jose, Calif., 1995-2002; bd. dirs. emergency svcs. Santa Clara Valley chpt. ARC, San Jose, 1995-98; bd. dirs. disaster svcs. Interfaith Svc., Inc., San Jose Internat. Airport. Recipient Navy Achievement medal, Navy Commendation medal with Gold Star in lieu of 2nd award, Navy Expeditionary medal, Humanitarian Svc. medal, Battle "E" award, Nat. Def. Svc. medal, sea svc. deployment ribbon with silver star. Fellow Am. Acad. Experts in Traumatic Stress (cert. expert), USN League (hon.), Disabled Am. Vets. (life), Internat. Assn. Civil Aviation Chaplains, Sunrise Exch. Club (chaplain 1989-91), Dick Richards Breakfast Club (chaplain 1988-91), Kiwanis, Masons (life), Ancient Accepted Scottish Rite (32 Degree), Shriners. Avocations: golf, skiing, sailing. Office Phone: 408-858-5983.

WINSLOW, HELEN LITTELL, lawyer; b. Wilmington, Del., May 11, 1952; d. Julian Dallas and Jean (Littell) W.; m. Jonathan David Jaffe, Nov. 8, 1980; children: Kenan Winslow Jaffe, Nathaniel Harrington Jaffe, Saul Handler Jaffe. AB, Bryn Mawr Coll., 1974; JD, U. N.C., 1977. Bar: Del. 1977, U.S. Dist. Ct. Del. 1977, U.S. Ct. Appeals (3d cir.) 1980, U.S. Supreme Ct.1980. Law clk. to presiding judge U.S. Dist. Ct. Del., Wilmington, 1977-79; assoc. Richards, Layton & Finger, Wilmington, 1979—2001; asst. gen. counsel H.D. Lee Co., Inc., 2001—09, gen. counsel. Mem. ABA, Fed. Bar Assn. (v.p. Del. chpt. 1985-86, pres.

Del. chpt. 1987—89), Del. Bar Assn. (pres. 2005-06), Am. Judicature Soc. Democrat. Jewish. Avocation: singing. Office: HD Lee Co 3411 Silverside Rd Concord Pike Wilmington DE 19810

WINSLOW, JOHN FRANKLIN, lawyer; b. Houston, Nov. 15, 1933; s. Franklin Jarnigan and Jane (Shipley) W. BA, U. Tex., 1957, LLB, 1960. Bar: Tex. 1959, DC 1961. Atty., Hispanic law div. Libr. of Congress, Washington, 1965-68; counsel, com. on the judiciary House of Reps., 1968-71; atty., editor Matthew Bender & Co., Washington, 1973-79; atty. FERC, Washington, 1979-84; pvt. practice Washington, 1984—. Rschr. Hispanic Law Rsch., Washington, 1979—. Author: Conglomerates Unlimited: The Failure of Regulation, 1974, The Accurst Tower (Amazon), 2009; editor: Fed. Power Service, 1974-79; contbr. articles to Washington Monthly, Nation, 1975—. Mem. Tex. Bar Assn., D.C. Bar Assn. Office Phone: 202-338-4747. Personal E-mail: jfwinslow@aol.com.

WINSLOW, KELLEN BOSWELL, II, professional football player; b. San Diego, July 21, 1983; s. Kellen Winslow and Katrina Ramsey. Attended, U. Miami, Coral Gables, 2001—04. Tight end Cleve. Browns, 2004—09, Tampa Bay Buccaneers, 2009—. Recipient John Mackey award, Nassau County Sports Commn., 2003; named First Team All-Am., AP, 2003; named to Am. Football Conf. Pro Bowl Team, NFL, 2007. Office: Tampa Bay Buccaneers One Buccaneer Pl Tampa FL 33607*

WINSLOW, NORMAN ELDON, small business owner; b. Oakland, Calif., Apr. 4, 1938; s. Merton Conrad and Roberta Eilene (Drennen) W.; m. Betty June Cady, Jan. 14, 1962 (div. Aug. 1971); 1 child, Todd Kenelm; m. Ilene Ruth Jackson, Feb. 3, 1979. BS, Fresno State U., Calif., 1959. Asst. mgr. Proctors Jewelers, Fresno, 1959-62; from agt. to dist. mgr. Allstate Ins. Co., Fresno, 1962-69; ins. agt. Fidelity Union Life Ins., Dallas, 1969-71; dist. and zone mgr. 7-Eleven, Inc., Dallas, 1971-78; owner Ser-Vis-Etc. LLC, Fresno, Calif., 1978—. Expert witness, cons. Am. Arbitration/Calif. Superior Cts. Pub./editor Franchis-erviceNews; author: Hands in Your Pockets, 1992; contbr. numerous articles to profl. jours. With USAFNG, 1961-67. Mem. Nat. Coalition of Assn. of 7-11 Franchises (affiliate, mem. adv. bd. 1984-90), Sigma Chi Fraternity (Life). Republican. Methodist. Avocations: gardening, photography, travel, model railroading. Home: 1293 N Fancher Ave Fresno CA 93727 Office: Ser-Vis-Etc LLC PO Box 8444 Fresno CA 93747-8444 Personal E-mail: servisetc@aol.com.

WINSLOW, SANDRA EILEEN, financial manager, professor; b. Scotland, SD, May 18, 1947; d. Adolph and Olga Diede; m. David Christopher Winslow, Dec. 17, 1982; children: Dennis Ray Diltz, Patricia Rae Diltz. MBA, U. Phoenix, Albuquerque, 1998. Fin. mgr. Sci. Applications Internat. Corp., N.Mex., 2001—; adj. prof. Eastern N.Mex. U., Roswell, 2002—, instr., 2002—. Singer: (songs) Women's Barbershop. Treas. Lend-A-Hand, Roswell, 2007—08. Independent. Avocations: travel, singing, painting. Home: 706 W 4th St Roswell NM 88201 Office: SAIC 47 Gail Harris Roswell NM 88203 Office Fax: 575-347-3155. Personal E-mail: winslow_sandra@msn.com.

WINSTEAD, DWIGHT, medical products executive; BS in Med. Tech., Delta State U. Health care salesman Worthington Diagnostics, Johnson & Johnson; dir. materials mgmt., adminstrv. dir. clin. labs. Alton Ochsner Found. Hosp., New Orleans; exec. v.p. VHA, Inc.; pres. Owen Healthcare, 1997—2001; grp. pres. Clin. Svcs. and Consulting Cardinal Health, 2001, group pres. Automation and Info. Svcs., COO Clin. Technologies and Svcs., grp. pres. Clin. & Med. products, 2006—. Bd. dirs. Sonus Pharms., 1995—. Office: Cardinal Health 7000 Cardinal Pl Dublin OH 43017*

WINSTEAD, MELODY, science educator; d. Teryl Washington. BA, Coll. New Rochelle, NYC, 1980; MA, CCNY, NYC, 1993. Cert. secondary sci. edn. tchr. NY State, 1987. Staff developer sci. NYC Dept. Edn. Dist. 5, NYC, 1979—2004, tchr., 1997—99, NYC Dept. Edn., NYC, 1987—. Sci. inquiry specialist, New Rochelle, NY. Personal E-mail: melodywinstead@yahoo.com.

WINSTEIN, BRUCE DARRELL, physics professor; BS, UCLA; PhD, Calif. Inst. Tech., 1970. Samuel K. Allison disting. svc. prof. physics Univ. Chgo. Recipient W.K.H. Panofsky Prize in Experimental Particle Physics, Am. Phys. Soc., 2007. Fellow: Am. Acad. Arts & Scis.; mem.: NAS. Office: Physics Dept Univ Chgo 5640 S Ellis Ave Chicago IL 60637 Office Phone: 773-702-7594. Office Fax: 773-702-6645. Business E-Mail: bruce@hep.uchicago.edu.

WINSTEN, SAUL NATHAN, lawyer; b. Providence, Feb. 23, 1953; s. Harold H. and Anita E. Winsten; m. Patricia J. Miller, Aug. 7, 1977; children: David A., J. Benjamin, Jennifer M. BA, Beloit Coll., Wis., 1976; JD, Drake U., Des Moines, 1980. Shareholder DeWitt Ross & Stevens, Brookfield, Wis.; chmn. corp. counsel com. Wis. Mfrs. Commn., 2004—. Contbr. articles to profl. jours. Active Wis. Gov.'s Adv. Coun. on Internat. Trade, 1996-2003, co-chmn., 1999-2002; active Wis. Gov.'s Internat. Edn. Task Force, 1997-98; chmn. Wis. Mfrs. and Commerce Corp. Counsel Com., 2004-; adv. com. Great Lakes Area IRS Adv. Com. Tax Exempt Orgn./Govt. Entities Coun., 2005—. Mem. ABA (chmn. com. young lawyers divsn. 1989-90, governing coun., antitrust, bus. and internat. law sects.), Wis. Bar Assn. (chair tax exempt orgn. com. of bus law sect. 2005-06), Internat. Bar Assn., Japan-Am. Soc. Wis. (pres. 1993-94, co-founder 1990, sec. 1990-92), Nat. Assn. Japan-Am. Socs. (bd. dirs. 1991-97, exec. com. 1993-97), Order of Barristers, Hessen-Wisconsin, Inc. (bd. dirs.), Internat. Bar Assn. Office: DeWitt Ross & Stevens 13935 Bishops Dr Brookfield WI 53005-6605 Office Phone: 262-754-2852. Business E-Mail: snw@dewittross.com.

WINSTON, ARNOLD, psychiatrist, educator; b. NYC, May 1, 1935; s. Irving and Eva (Barban) W.; m. Beverly M. Winston, Oct. 21, 1938; children: Roy, Eric, Michael. AB, U. Chgo., 1956; MD, SUNY Med. Ctr., Bklyn., 1960. Med. intern Downstate Med. Ctr-Kings County Hosp., Bklyn., 1960-61, psychiatry resident, 1961-62, 63-65, chief psychiatry treatment unit, 1966-72; chief of svc. South Beach Psychiat. Ctr., SI, N.Y., 1972-74, dep. dir., 1974-75, dir., 1975-78; chmn. dept. psychiatry Beth Israel Med. Ctr., NYC, 1978—. Asst. prof. psychiatry SUNY, Bklyn., 1971-75, clin. assoc. prof. psychiatry, 1975-78; prof. psychiatry Mt. Sinai Coll. Medicine, N.Y.C., 1978-94; prof. psychiatry Albert Einstein Coll. Medicine, Bronx, N.Y., 1994—, vice chmn. dept., 1996; Ostmarka lectr. U. Trondheim, 1989; vis. prof. U. Vt., 1983. Author: Short-Term Psychotherapy, 2002; contbr. numerous chpts. to books, articles to profl. jours. Psychotherapy rsch. grantee NIMH, 1993-95. Fellow Am. Psychiat. Assn. (disting. life), N.Y. Acad. Medicine, Am. Coll. Psychiatrists, Am. Bd. Psychiatry and Neurology (diplomate). Avocations: tennis, skiing, gardening, golf. Office: Beth Israel Med Ctr 1st Ave & 16th St New York NY 10003 Home Phone: 212-593-0076; Office Phone: 212-420-2555. Business E-Mail: awinston@bethisraelny.org.

WINSTON, DAVID, political strategist, columnist; Former dir. planning for Speaker of House Newt Gingrich US House of Reps., Washington; sr. fellow Heritage Found.; columnist Roll Call. Election analyst CBS; spkr. in field. Republican. Office: The Winston Group Ste 710E 101 Constitution Ave, NW Washington DC 20001 Office Phone: 202-742-4580. Office Fax: 202-742-4650. E-mail: dwinston@winstongroup.net.*

WINSTON, HAROLD RONALD, lawyer; b. Atlantic, Iowa, Feb. 7, 1932; s. Louis D. and Leta B. (Carter) W.; m. Carol J. Sundeen, June 11, 1955; children: Leslie Winston Yannetti, Lisa Winston Shaw, Laura Winston Moritz. BA, U. Iowa, 1954, JD, 1958. Bar: Iowa 1958, U.S. Dist. Ct. (no. and so. dists.) Iowa 1962, U.S. Tax Ct. 1962, U.S. Ct. Appeals (8th cir.) 1970, U.S. Supreme Ct. 1969. Trust officer United Home Bank & Trust Co., Mason City, Iowa, 1958-59; mem. Breese & Cornwell, Mason City, 1960-62, Breese, Cornwell, Winston & Reuber, Mason City, 1963-73, Winston, Schroeder & Reuber, Mason City, 1974-79, Winston, Reuber, Swanson & Byrne, P.C., Mason City, 1980-92, Winston, Reuber & Byrne, Mason City, 1992-96, Winston & Byrne, P.C., Mason City, 1996—. Police judge, Mason City, 1961-73. Contbr. articles to profl. jours. Past pres. Family YMCA, Mason City, Cerro Gordo County Estate Planning Coun.; active local charitable orgns. Capt. USAF, 1955-57. Fellow Am. Coll. Trust and Estate Counsel, Am. Bar Found. (life), Iowa Bar Found. (life); mem. ABA, Iowa Bar Assn. (gov., lectr. ann. meeting 1977-79), 2d Jud. Dist. Bar Assn. (lectr. meeting 1981-82), Cerro Gordo County Bar Assn. (past pres.), Am. Judicature Soc., Mason City Country Club, Kiwanis, Masons. Republican. Presbyterian. Office: Winston & Byrne 119 2d St NW Mason City IA 50401-3105 Office Phone: 641-423-1913. Business E-Mail: hwinston@mchsi.com.

WINSTON, MICHAEL RUSSELL, historian; b. NYC, May 26, 1941; s. Charles Russell and Jocelyn Anita Prem Das Winston; m. Judith Ann Marianno, Aug. 10, 1963; children: Lisa Marie, Cynthia Eileen. BA magna cum laude, Howard U., 1962; MA, U. Calif.-Berkeley, 1964, PhD, 1974; DHL, Rollins Coll., 2008. Instr. dept. history Howard U., Washington, 1964-66, asst. dean Coll. Liberal Arts, 1968-69, asst. prof. dept. history, 1970-73, v.p. acad. affairs, 1983-90, prof. emeritus, 1990—; assoc. dir. Inst. Svc. to Edn., Washington, 1966; fellow Haus. Hof-und Staatsarchiv, Vienna, 1969; dir. Moorland Spingarn Rsch. Ctr., 1973-83; v.p., bd. dirs. Alfred Harcourt Found., Silver Spring, Md., 1992-93, pres., treas., 1993—2008. Cons. Smithsonian Instn., 1979—, nat. Inst. Edn., 1978-85, NSF, 1985—. Author: (with R.W. Logan) The Negro in the United States, 1970, The Howard Univ.Dept. of History, 1913-73, 1973; editor: (with R.W. Logan) Dictionary of Am. Negro Biography, 1982, (with G.R. McNeil) Hist. Judgements Reconsidered, 1988; mem. editl. bd. Washington History, 1993-97. Mem. exec. bd. Nat. Capital Area coun. Boy Scouts Am., 1988—90; trustee spl. contbn. fund NAACP, 1980—82; trustee D.C. Pub. Defender Svc., 1985—88; bd. trustees Woodrow Wilson Nat. Fellowship Found., 1997—2006; bd. mgrs. Hist. Soc. Washington; bd. dirs. Harcourt Brace Jovanovich, 1980—91, D.C. Pub. Libr. Found., 1994—2002, pres., 1995—99, Nat. Coun. for History Standards; mem. bd. overseers' com. to visit dept. history Harvard U., 1996—2008; mem. bd. gov. Folger Shakespear Lib., Washington, 2007—; mem. nat. adv. com. and coun. of scholars Libr. of Congress; nat. adv. bd. Protect Historic Am.; mem. Commn. on Coll. and Univ. Nonprofl. Studies ABA; mem. Nat. Ctr. for History in the Schs. UCLA/NEH. Moten fellow U. Edinburgh, 1962, Wilson fellow U. Calif., 1962, Ford fellow, 1969-70, Woodrow Wilson Internat. Ctr. Scholars fellow, 1979-80; sr. scholar, 2001—. Mem.: Nat. Coun. for History Standards, Coun. on Foreign Relations, Hist. Soc. Washington, Am. Antiquarian Soc., Orgn. Am. Historians, Am. Hist. Assn., Grolier Club, Cosmos Club (Washington), Phi Beta Kappa (Ralph Waldo Emerson prize com. 2000). Democrat. Episcopalian. Home: 1371 Kalmia Rd NW Washington DC 20012-1444 Home Phone: 202-829-4085. Personal E-mail: michaelrwinston@aol.com.

WINT, DENNIS MICHAEL, museum director; b. Macon, Ga., Mar. 17, 1943; s. Paul Kenneth and Mary (McClure) W. BS, U. Mich., 1965; tchr.'s cert., Lake Erie Coll., 1970; PhD, Case Western Res. U., 1977. Dir. environ. edn. Wiloughby Eastlake City Schs., 1968-70; dir. Ctr. Devel. Environment Curiculum, 1970-75; cons. Ohio Dept. Edn., 1975-77; dir. mus. and edn. Acad. Natural Scis., Phila., 1977-79, v.p., dir. natural history mus., 1979-82; dir. Cranbrook Inst. Sci., Bloomfield Hills, Mich., 1982-86; pres. St. Louis Sci. Ctr., 1986-95; pres., CEO The Franklin Inst., Phila., 1995—. Adj. asst. prof. Temple U.; past chmn. edn. and human resources adv. com. NSF, 1991-92; past pres. St. Louis Area Mus. Collaborative, 1991-92, mem. exec. com. Bd. govs. Greater Phila. 1st Partnership for Reform, 1995—98, mem. leadership com., 1995—98. Mem. Am. Assn. Mus. (bd. dirs. 2003-, vice chair 2006-), Assn. Sci.-Tech. Ctrs. (mem. nominating com., v.p. 1993-95, pres. 1995-97, chmn. internat. com. 2000-05, strategic planning com. 2002-05), Greater Phila. Cultural Alliance (bd. dirs. 1996-05, chmn. strategic planning com. 2000-05), Benjamin Franklin Fed. Tchg. Commn. (co-chair). Home: 222 N 20th St Philadelphia PA 19103

WINTER, AMY, art historian, critic; b. Conn., Oct. 13, 1948; d. Ezra Paul and Jennie (Strauss) W. BA, U. Iowa, 1974, MA, 1978; PhD, CUNY, 1995. Asst. to dir. Colgate U. Picker Art Gallery, Hamilton, NY, 1972-74; lectr. Parsons Sch. of Design, NYC, 1985-87; lectr., cons. Whitney Mus. of Am. Art, NYC, 1987—93; curator, educator Block Art Gallery, Northwestern U., 1997—98; asst. prof. Coll. SI, 1998—2000; dir., curator Godwin-Ternbach Mus., Queens Coll., CUNY, 2001—. Lectr. SUNY, Purchase, 1989; adj. asst. prof. SUNY, New Paltz, 1989-90, Queens Coll., CUNY, 2002; exec. asst. Met. Mus. Art, NYC, 1979-83; curatorial cons. Jewish Mus., NYC, 1981; lectr. sculpture series Storm King Art Ctr., Mountainville, NY, 1991-92. Author: Wolfgang Paalen, Artist and Theorist of the Avant-Garde, 2002; editor: Jour. Surrealism and the Americas, 2007—; contbr. numerous catalogues and essays in field. CUNY Grad. Ctr. fellow, 1986-90, Luce Found. dissertation fellow, 1990-91, Kress Found. rsch. travel fellow to Calif., Mex., Vienna, Paris, 1990-91, Smithsonian Instn. Pre-dissertation fellow, 1993-94; scholar-in-residence Pollock-Krasner House, 1994, Camargo Found., France, 1995. Mem. Internat. Assn. Art Critics, Assn. Am. Mus. Curators, Am. Assn. Mus., Coll. Art Assn., Queens Coun. on Arts. Avocation: photography. Office: Queens Coll 405 Klapper Hall 65-30 Kissena Blvd Flushing NY 11367 Office Phone: 718-997-4747. Office Fax: 718-997-4734. Business E-Mail: amy.winter@qc.cuny.edu.

WINTER, CHESTER CALDWELL, surgeon, educator, historian, writer; b. Cazenovia, NY, June 2, 1922; s. Chester Caldwell and Cora Evelyn (Martin) W.; m. Mary Antonia Merullo, Oct. 22, 1983; children by previous marriage: Paul, Ann, Jane. BA, U. Iowa, 1943, MD, 1946. Diplomate: Am. Bd. Urology. Intern Meth. Hosp., Indpls., 1946-47; med. resident St. Luke's Hosp., Cedar Rapids, Iowa, 1947; physician Calif., 1950-51; resident gen. surgery VA Hosp., Los Angeles, 1952-53; resident urology VA Hosp.-UCLA Med. Ctr., 1953-57; clin. asst. surgery UCLA, 1954-57, instr. surgery and urology, 1957-58, asst. prof. surgery and urology, 1958-59, asst. prof. Step II, 1959-60; prof. surgery and urology Ohio State U., 1960-88, prof. emeritus surgery and urology, 1988—, Louis Levy prof. urology, 1980-88. Dir. urology Ohio State U. Hosp., Columbus, 1960-78; cons. urology VA, Air Force hosps., Dayton, 1960-80. Author: Radioisotope Renography, 1963, Correctable Renal Hypertension, 1964, Nursing Care of Patients with Urologic Diseases, 4th edit, 1977, Practical Urology, 1969, Vesicoureteral Reflux, 1969, A Concise History of the U.S. and the State of Ohio, 2002, A Bicentennial History of the State of Ohio, 2003, Ohio Cities: Historical Descriptions, 2004, Concise Biographies of Notable Ohioans, 2005, A Concise History of Columbus Ohio and Franklin County, 2009; editl. cons. Exerpta Medica: Nuclear Medicine, Jour. AMA; mem. editl. bd. Andrology, Jour. Urology; contbr. articles to profl. jours. Served to capt. M.C. U.S. Army, 1943-46, 48-49. Fellow Am. Acad. Pediatricians, Am. Coll. Surgeons; mem. Am. Assn. Genitourinary Surgeons, Am. Urol. Assn., Soc. Univ. Surgeons, Soc. Pediatric Urology, Soc. Univ. Urologists, Internat. Soc. Urology, Urol. Investigators Forum, Ohio State Med. Assn., Columbus Surg. Soc., Central Ohio Urology Soc., Columbus Acad. Medicine, Ohio State U. Med. Soc. Home: 6425 Evening St Worthington OH 43085-3054 E-mail: cwinter3@ameritech.net.

WINTER, DAVID FERDINAND, electrical engineering educator, consultant; b. St. Louis, Nov. 9, 1920; s. Ferdinand Conrad and Annie (Schaffer) W.; m. Bettie Jeanne Turner; children: Suzanne, Sharie Winter Chappeau. BSEE, Washington U., St. Louis, 1942; MSEE, MIT, 1948. Registered profl. engr., Mo. Staff mem. radiation lab. MIT, Cambridge, 1942-45, rsch. assoc. electronics lab., 1945-48; prof. elec. engring. Washington U., St. Louis, 1948-55, affiliate prof. elec. engring., 1955-67; v.p. engring. and rsch. Moloney Elec. Co., St. Louis, 1955-74; v.p. rsch. and engring. Blackburn div. IT&T, St. Louis, 1974-82, dir. advanced tech. devel., 1982-86; pvt. practice cons. St. Louis, 1986—. Ct. recognized tech. expert on sources, mitigation, and effects of stray voltage on dairy cattle cons. Wis. Pub. Svc. Commn.; cons. Naval Ordanance Lab. of Ind., Indpls., 1950-53, other industries, St. Louis, 1979—. Contbr. articles to profl. jours.; holder 28 patents. Elder, pastor Maplewood Bible Chapel, St. Louis. Recipient Alumni Achievement award, Wash. U., Sch. Engring. & Applied Sci., St. Louis. Mo., 2003, Washington U., 2003. Fellow IEEE (life), Inst. Radio Engrs.; mem. NSPE, Am. Soc. Agrl. Engrs., Mo. Soc. Profl. Engrs., Sigma Xi, Tau Beta Pi, Eta Kappa Nu. Avocations: cabinet maker, photography, music instruments. Home and Office: 735 Harvard Ave University City MO 63130-3135 Office Phone: 314-727-4532. Personal E-mail: dfwinter@hotmail.com.

WINTER, DOUGLAS E., lawyer, writer; b. St. Louis, Oct. 30, 1950; s. William E. and Dorothy E. (Schuster) W.; m. Lynne G. Turner, July 9, 1977; step-children: Carl, John, Stephen. BS, U. Ill., 1971, MS, 1972; JD, Harvard U., 1975; postgrad., Judge Advocate Gen.'s Sch., 1977. Bar: Mo. 1975, Ill. 1976, DC 1976. Clk. to Hon. William H. Webster U.S. Ct. Appeals (8th cir.), St. Louis, 1975-76; assoc. Covington & Burling, Washington, 1976-84; ptnr. Bryan Cave LLP, Washington, 1985—. Vis. prof. U. Iowa, Iowa City, 1980-81. Author: Stephen King, 1982, Shadowings: The Reader's Guide to Horror Fiction, 1983, Stephen King: The Art of Darkness, 1984, Faces of Fear, 1985, Black Wine, 1986, Splatter: A Cautionary Tale, 1987, Prime Evil, 1988, Darkness Absolute, 1991, Black Sun, 1994, Millennium, 1997, Revelations, 1997, Run, 2000, Clive Barker: The Dark Fantastic, 2001, Introduction to Legal Writing, 2004, A Little Brass Book of Full Metal Fiction, 2006, American Zombie, 2009; contbr. articles to popular mags. and nat. newspapers. Capt. US Army, 1973-77. Recipient world fantasy award World Fantasy Conv., 1986, award Internat. Horror Guild, 1995, 96, 98; Named Book of Month, Best Suspense Novel of Yr. Run, 2000. Mem. Nat. Book Critics Circle, Horror Writers Assn. (chmn. grievance com. 1989—2006, trustee 1997—2006). Office: Bryan Cave LLP 1155 F St NW Washington DC 20004 Office Phone: 202-508-6000. Business E-Mail: dewinter@bryancave.com.

WINTER, JAY MURRAY, history professor; b. Hempstead, NY, May 28, 1945; s. Nathaniel and Bertha Winter; children: Anna, Jonathan. BA, Columbia U., NY, 1970; PhD, DLitt, U. Cambridge, Eng., 1970. Prof., history Columbia U., NYC; lectr., modern history Hebrew U. Jerusalem, 1970—73; lectr., social history Warwick U., England, 1973—79; lectr., history U. Cambridge, 1979—95, reader, modern history, 1995—2000; charles stille prof., history Yale U., New Haven, 2001—. Mem., bd. dirs. Rsch. Ctr. Hist. Grande Guerre, Peronne, Somme, 1992—. Dir.: (documentaries) The Great War and the Shaping of the Twentieth Century (Emmy award, 1997); author: (book) Sites of Memory, Sites of Mourning: The Great War in European Cultural History. Recipient Peabody award, 1997; fellowship, Guggenheim Found., 1996—97. Fellow: Royal Hist. Soc. Home: 490 Peddlers Rd Guilford CT 06437 Office: Yale Univ Dept History 320 York St New Haven CT 06520-8324

WINTER, JIMMY, entrepreneur, systems administrator; b. 1982; Web site designer Fastmusic Label, NYC, 1999; founder Music Arsenal, Omaha, 2003—. Named one of Best Entrepreneurs Under 25, BusinessWeek, 2006. Office: Music Arsenal 1909 S 61ST Ave Omaha NE 68106-2132 Office Phone: 800-231-9273. E-mail: info@musicarsenal.com.

WINTER, JUDY ELAINE, author, speaker; d. Lester App and Marie Pitcowicz; m. Richard Kent Winter, Aug. 7, 1976; children: Jenna Marie, Eric Richard(dec.). BA in Comm., Mich. State U., 1980. From advt. mgr. to corp. devel. assoc. WKAR-TV, East Lansing, Mich., 1985—88, corp. devel. assoc., 1988—92; freelance columnist DeWitt, Mich., 1996—. Cmty. adv. panel Lansing State Jour. Author: Breakthrough Parenting for Children with Special Needs: Raising the Bar of Expectations, 2006; contbr. articles to profl. jours. and periodicals, chapters to books. Co-chmn. Eric RicStar Winter Music Therapy Summer Camp, Mich. State U., 2003—. Recipient Cmty. Achievement award, Mich. Week, 2000, Disting. Achievement award, The Assn. Ednl. Pubs., 2000, 2002, Exceptional Parent award, Mich. Federated Chpts. Coun. Exceptional Children, 2002, Chief Everything Officer award, AOL and Dove, 2006, Outstanding Alumni award, Mich. State U. Coll. Com. Arts and Sci., 2007; named to Wall of Tolerance, Montgomery, Ala., 2003. Avocations: travel, gardening, walking, photography, community outreach. E-mail: jappwinter@aol.com.

WINTER, MELISSA E., federal official; b. Chgo., Nov. 16, 1967; Grad., Skidmore Coll., 1989. Staff asst. to Norman Mineta, exec. asst.; traveling aid to Senator Joseph Lieberman, 2000, senate exec. asst., dir. scheduling for presdl. campaign, 2004; traveling chief of staff to Michelle Obama Barack Obama Presdl. Campaign; dep. chief of staff to Michelle Obama Obama-Biden Transition Team, 2008—09; dep. chief of staff to First Lady Michelle Obama The White House, Washington, 2009—. Democrat. Office: The White House 1600 Pennsylvania Ave NW Washington DC 20500*

WINTER, MIRIAM THERESE (GLORIA FRANCES WINTER), nun, religious studies educator; b. Passaic, NJ, June 14, 1938; d. Mathias William and Irene Theresa (Marton) W. BMus, Cath. U. Am., Washington, DC, 1964; M in Religious Edn., McMaster Divinity Coll., Hamilton, Ont., Can., 1976; PhD in Liturgical Studies, Princeton Theol. Sem., NJ, 1983; LHD (hon.), Albertus Magnus Coll., New Haven, Conn., 1991, St. Joseph Coll., West Hartford, Conn., 1993, Mount St. Vincent U.,

Halifax, Nova Scotia, 2004. Joined Med. Mission Sisters, Roman Cath. Ch., 1955. Dir. liturgy and liturgical music Med. Mission Sisters, Phila., 1960-76, pub. rels. dir., coord., 1963-72; assoc. prof. liturgy, worship and spirituality Hartford (Conn.) Sem., 1980-85, prof., 1985—, prof. liturgy, worship, spirituality, and feminist studies, 1994—; founder, dir. Women's Leadership Inst., 1996—. Mem. faculty St. Therese's Inst., Phila., 1964-68, acad. dir., 1968-72, Immaculate Conception Sem. Summer Program, Mo., 1969, Cath. U. Summer Grad. Program, Washington, 1970, Hope Ecumenical Inst., Jerusalem, summer 1974, 75, 76, McMaster Divinity Coll. Grad. Program, 1976, Continuing Edn. Program, 1976, NY Archdiocesan Sch. Liturgical Music, summer 1980, 82, Vancouver Sch. Theology, summer 1982, USN Chaplains through Auburn Theol. Sem., 1990; mem. adj. faculty Union Inst., Cin., 1992-94, Sophia Ctr. Holy Names U., Oakland, Calif., 2002-; vis. faculty Islamic Religious Coun. of Singapore, 2007; with emergency relief work Internat. Rescue Com., Cambodia, 1979-80, Malteser-Hilfsdienst Auslandsdienst, Germany, 1984, Med. Mission Sisters, Ethiopia, 1985; lectr., instr., performer, worship leader, song leader for various groups by invitation, nat. and internat., 1967—. Author: Preparing the Way of the Lord, 1978, God-With-Us: Resources for Prayer and Praise, 1979, An Anthology of Scripture Songs, 1982, Why Sing? Toward a Theology of Catholic Church Music, 1984, WomanPrayer, Woman Song: Resources for Ritual, 1987, WomanWord: A Feminist Lectionary and Psalter, 1990, WomanWisdom: A Feminist Lectionary and Psalter, Women of the Hebrew Scriptures, Part I, 1992 (1st pl. award for books on liturgy Cath. Press Assn., 1992), WomanWitness: A Feminist Lectionary and Psalter, Women of the Hebrew Scriptures, Part II, 1992 (1st pl. award for books on liturgy Cath. Press Assn., 1993), The Gospel According to Mary: A New Testament for Women, 1993; co-author: Defecting in Place: Women Claiming Responsibility for Their Own Spiritual Lives, 1994 (2d pl. award for books on gender studies Cath. Press Assn., 1995), The Chronicles of Noah and Her Sisters: Genesis and Exodus According to Women, 1995 (2d pl. award for books on gender studies Cath. Press Assn., 1996), Songlines: Hymns, Songs, Rounds and Refrains, 1996, The Singer and the Song: An Autobiography of the Spirit, 1999, Out of the Depths, The Story of Ludmila Javorova, Ordained Roman Catholic Priest, 2001 (1st pl. award for books on popular presentation of the Cath. faith Cath. Press Assn., 2002), Eucharist with a small "e", 2005 (3d pl. award for books on liturgy, 2006), Paradoxology: Spirituality in a Quantum Universe, 2009; author: numerous songs including albums Keepsake, Hymns Re-Imagined, SpiritSong, EarthSong, WomanSong, Remember Me, Sandstone, Songs of Promise, RSVP: Let Us Pray, Gold, Incense and Myrrh, In Love, Seasons (Christian Oscar award Nat. Evang. Film Found., 1971), Knock, Knock, Praise the Lord in Many Voices (live rec. of Mass of a Pilgrim People premiered at Carnegie Hall), 1967, I Know the Secret, Joy is Like the Rain (Gold album in USA and Australia); contbr. articles to profl. jours. Bd. dirs. Capitol Region Conf. Chs., 1984-91, v.p., 1986-88. pres. bd. dirs., 1988-90, past pres., 1990-91, Archdiocesan Office Urban Affairs, 1986-95; mem. Christian Conf. ann. event WINFEST, 1986, 87; mem. small christian communities design team Archdiocese of Hartford, 1987-91; mem. major events design team RENEW, 1986; subcommn. chair Archdiocesan Office of Synod, 1991; mem. New Eng. team Ministry of Money, 1984-90, 93; mem. The New Century Hymnal editl. com. United Ch. of Christ, 1993-95; active Pediats. AIDS Unit Yale-New Haven Hosp., Covenant to Care, Voices of Joy Gospel Choir women imprisioned at Niantic. Grantee Lilly Endowment, 1989-90, 91-93; recipient Ho. of Reps. citation Commonwealth of Pa., 1968, Women in Leadership Edn. award YWCA Conn., 1989, Convenant to Care award for ministry to children, 1993; named to McMaster U. Alumni Gallery, 1982, Celebration of 120 Women in Leadership, 1987, Bayley-Ellard H.S. Hall of Fame, 1993, Conn. Women's Hall of Fame, 2002. Mem. ASCAP (Popular Awards list 1968—), AAUW (Excellence in Equity award Conn. chpt. 1995), N.Am. Acad. of Liturgy. Avocations: photography, calligraphy. Office: Hartford Sem 77 Sherman St Hartford CT 06105-2260 Home Phone: 860-233-0875; Office Phone: 860-509-9558.

WINTER, PETER MICHAEL, anesthesiologist, educator; b. Sverdlovsk, Russia, Aug. 5, 1934; arrived in U.S., 1938, naturalized, 1944; s. George and Anne Winter; m. Michelle Yakopec, Dec. 28, 1991; children: Karin Anne, Christopher George, Lia Lynn, Tori Anne. BA, Cornell U., 1958; MD, U. Rochester, 1962. Diplomate Am. Bd. Anesthesiology. Intern U. Utah, Salt Lake City, 1962-63; resident in anesthesiology, pharmacology and respiratory physiology Mass. Gen. Hosp., Boston, 1963-65; USPHS fellow Harvard U. Med. Sch., Mass., 1964-66; Buswell fellow dept. physiology, asst. prof. SUNY, Buffalo, 1966-69; assoc. prof. dept. anesthesiology Sch. Medicine, U. Wash., Seattle, 1969-74, prof., 1974-79; prof., chmn. dept. anesthesiology and critical care medicine U. Pitts. Sch. Medicine, 1979-96, Peter and Eva Safar prof. anesthesiology/critical care med., 1987—96, prof. emeritus, dir. faculty devel., 1996—. Anesthesiologist in chief Univ. Health Ctr. Hosps., Pitts., 1979—96. Editl. cons.: Anesthesiology CCMJ; contbr. chapters to books, papers and abstracts to publs. With US Army, 1953—56. Recipient Career Devel. award, NIH, 1971. Mem.: AMA, Assn. univ. Anesthetists, Internat. Anesthesia Rsch. Soc., Undersea Med. Soc., Soc. Critical Care Medicine, N.Y. Acad. Scis., Royal Soc. Medicine, Am. Soc. Anesthesiologists, Am. Coll. Chest Physicians, Morton Soc., Am. Alpine Club. Office: 3471 5th Ave Ste 910 Pittsburgh PA 15213-3221

WINTER, RALPH KARL, JR., federal judge; b. Waterbury, Conn., July 30, 1935; married. BA, Yale U., 1957, JD, 1960; JD (hon.), Bklyn. Law Sch., NY Law Sch. Bar: Conn. 1973. Rsch. assoc., lectr. Yale U., 1962—64, from asst. prof. assoc. prof. law, 1967—78, William K. Townsend prof. law, 1978—82, adj. prof. law, 1982—; spl. cons. subcom. on separation of powers US Senate Com. on Judiciary, 1968—72; sr. fellow Brookings Inst., 1968—70; adj. scholar Am. Enterprise Inst., 1972—82; judge US Ct. Appeals (2d Cir.), New Haven, 1982—97, chief judge, 1997—2000, sr. judge, 2000—; judge Fgn. Intelligence Surveillance Ct. (FISC), 2003—. Vis. prof. law U. Chgo., 1966; adv. com. civil rules Jud. Conf. US, 1987—92, chmn. adv. com. rules evidence, 1993—96, exec. com., 1998—2000, chmn. exec. com., 1999—2000. Contbr. articles to profl. jours. Recipient Conn. Law Rev. award, Learned Hand award, Fed. Bar Coun. Office: US Ct Appeals 2nd Cir US Courthouse 141 Church St New Haven CT 06510-2030*

WINTER, RICHARD LAWRENCE, diversified financial services company executive; b. St. Louis, Dec. 17, 1945; s. Melvin Lawrence and Kathleen Jane (O'Leary) Winter; m. Kathryn Ann Geppert, Dec. 4, 1993; children from previous marriage: Leigh Ellen, Jessica Marie, George Bradford. BS in Math., St. Louis U., 1967, MS in Math. (fellow), 1969; MBA, U. Mo., St. Louis, 1976. Rsch. analyst Mo. Pacific R.R., St. Louis, 1971-73; dir. fin. rels. Linclay Corp., St. Louis, 1973-74; asst. v.p. 1st Nat. Bank in St. Louis (now Centerre Bank, NA) subs. Boatmen's Nat. Bank, 1974-79; v.p. fin. UDE Corp., St. Louis, 1979-81; pres. Health Care Investments, Ltd., St. Louis, 1981—, Larus Corp., St. Louis, 1981—, Garden View Care Ctr., Inc., O'Fallon, Mo., 1987—, Garden View Care Ctr. of Chesterfield, Inc., 1990—, Garden View Care Ctr. of St. Louis, Inc., Valley Park, Mo., 1998—. Exec. bd. Duchesne Bank, St. Peters, Mo., 1989—97; lectr. math. U. Mo., St. Louis, 1972—74, St. Louis U., 1982—90. Chmn. Mo. State Coun. Arts, 2005—06; cmty. adv. bd. Coll. Fine Arts and Comm. U. Mo., St. Louis, 2003—; bd. dirs. Dance St. Louis, 1998—2004, 2006—, pres. bd. dirs., 2008—; bd. dirs. Mid-Am. Arts Alliance, 2005—06, Jazz St. Louis, 2006—; mem. fundraising staff St. Louis Symphony; exec. adv. bd. St. Louis U. Coll. Arts and Scis., 2000—; mem. fundraising staff Jr. Achievement; fundraising staff United Way St. Louis, Arts and Edn. Fund, St. Louis, 1974—79. With US Army, 1969—71. Mem.: Nat. Health Lawyers Assn., Mo. Athletic Club (St. Louis), Pi Mu Epsilon. Roman Catholic. Office: Ste 170 12444 Powerscourt Dr Saint Louis MO 63131-3659 Home: Ten Aragon Ave # 1208 Coral Gables FL 33134 Office Phone: 314-965-1991. Business E-Mail: richard-l-winter@gvcc.com.

WINTER, ROBIN OKNER, health facility administrator; b. Newark, Mar. 10, 1953; BA, Haverford Coll., Haverford, Pa., 1974; MD, Albert Einstein Coll. Medicine, 1978; M in Med. Mgmt., Carnegie Mellon U., 1999. Diplomate Am. Bd. Family Medicine (cert. in geriatric medicine). Dir. family medicine residency program JFK Med. Ctr., Edison, NJ, 1989—. Mem.: Assn. Family Medicine Residency Dirs. (pres. 2003—04). Office: JFK Med Ctr 65 James St Edison NJ 08818 Office Fax: 732-906-4986.

WINTER, ROGER JAY, artist; b. Ketchican, Alaska, June 30, 1957; s. Dennis Clifford and Margret Jane Winter; m. Lynn Laura Cutinha; children: Easton Cantwell, Mikaela Lurray. Degree, U. Md., Ausnbauch Germany, 1986. Owner Premium Wood Finishers and Art Ink, Fernandina, 1997—2003. Artist Endangered Arts, Fernandina, Fla., 1988—94. Exhibitions include Work on Display in Municipal Court House, Work on Display in Florida Community College (Library), one-man shows include Life Masks, Art Found in Unexpected Places, Winter Dream, Dream Masks Come Alive (Mus. Of Sci. and History). With Med. Germany, 1976—81, Nurenburg Germany. Personal E-mail: winterroger@rocketmail.com, godwal1216@yahoo.com.

WINTER, ROGER PAUL, former federal agency administrator; b. Hartford, Conn., July 13, 1942; s. Raymond Gustav and Marion Nellie (Stafford) W.; m. Delorise Allen, Aug. 22, 1966; children: Jonathan, Raymond Todd, Nicole. BA in Psychology, Wheaton Coll., 1964; LLD (hon.), Holy Family Coll., 1993. Asst. sec. Md. Dept. Human Resources, Balt., 1970-79, Md. Dept. Budget and Fiscal Planning, Annapolis, 1979-80; dir. Office of Refugee Resettlement, HHS, Washington, 1980-81, U.S. Com. for Refugees, Washington, 1981-2001; exec. dir. Immigration and Refugee Svcs. Am., Washington, 1994-2001; dir. Office U.S. Fgn. Disaster Assistance, Washington, 2001—02; asst. adminstr. Bur. Democracy Conflict & Humanitarian Response USAID, Washington, 2002—05; spl. rep. to Sudan US Dept. of State, 2005—06. Cons. on refugee affairs Women's Refugee Project, Washington, 1981-84; adv. bd. Refugee Policy Group, 1981-86; mem. bd. Refugee Voices, 1988-96; mem. exec. com. Coun. Washington Reps. on UN, 1989-91. Recipient Disting. Service Cambodian Assn. Am., 1982, Disting. Service award Indochina Resource Action Ctr., 1988. Mem. Nat. Ry. Hist. Soc.-Balt., Sudan Relief and Rehab. Assn. (bd. dirs., sec. 1991-93). Lodges: Eagles. Personal E-mail: rwinter4700@yahoo.com.

WINTER, RUTH GROSMAN (MRS. ARTHUR WINTER), journalist; b. Newark, May 29, 1930; d. Robert Delmas and Rose (Rich) Grosman; m. Arthur Winter, June 16, 1955; children: Robin, Craig, Grant. BA, Upsala Coll., 1951; MS, Pace U., 1989. With Houston Press, 1955-56; gen. assignment Newark Star Ledger, 1951-55, sci. editor, 1956-69; columnist L.A. Times Syndicate, 1973-78, Register and Tribune, syndicate, 1981-85, isyndicate.com, 1999-2001; co-owner Feed Your Family Right, 2007—. Columnist myskinMD.com, 2000-01; contbr. to consumer mags.; instr. St. Peters Coll., Jersey City.; vis. lectr. mag. writing Rutgers U. Author: Poisons in Your Food, rev. edits., 1971, 91, 99, 2004, How to Reduce Your Medical Bills, 1970, A Consumer's Dictionary of Food Additives, 1972, 3d rev. edit., 1994, 99, 2004, 7th edit. 2009, Vitamin E, The Miracle Worker, 1972, So You Have Sinus Trouble, 1973, Ageless Aging, 1973, So You Have a Pain in the Neck, 1974, rev. edit., 2000, A Consumer's Dictionary of Cosmetic Ingredients, 1974, 4th rev. edit., 1994, 6th rev. edit., 2005, 7th edit., 2009, Don't Panic, 1975, The Fragile Bond: Marriage in the 70's, 1976, Triumph Over Tension, 1976 (N.J. Press Women's Book award), Scent Talks Among Animals, 1977, Cancer Causing Agents: A Preventive Guide, 1979, The Great Self-Improvement Sourcebook, 1980, The Scientific Case Against Smoking, 1980, People's Guide to Allergies and Allergens, 1984, A Consumer's Guide to Medicines in Food, 1995, So What Can I Eat?, 2006; co-author: The Lean Line One Month Lighter Program, 1985, Thin Kids Program, 1985, Build Your Brain Power, 1986, Eat Right: Be Bright, 1988, A Consumer's Dictionary of Medicines: Prescription, Over-the-Counter and Herbal, 1994, 97, Super Soy,: The Miracle Bean, 1996, rev. edit., 2000, Pain in the Neck, 1997, rev. edit., 2000, Anti Aging Hormones, 1997, Brain Workout, 1997, 2003, Vitamin E: Your Protection Against Exercise Fatigue, Weakened Immunity, Heart Disease, Cancer, Aging, Diabetic Damage, Environmental Toxins, 1998, Smart Food, 1999, rev. edit., 2007, The Female Athlete's Body Book: Preventing and Treating Sports Injuries in Women and Girls, 2003, What Can I Eat? 2006, Feed Your Family Right, 2008, Fitness After 40, 2009. Recipient award of merit ADA, 1966, Cecil award Arthritis Found., 1967, Am. Soc. Anesthesiologists award, 1969, Arthritis Found. award, 1978; named Alumnus of Year Upsala Coll., 1971, Woman of Year N.J. Daily Newspaper Women, 1971, Woman of Achievement Millburn Short Hills Profl. and Bus. Women's Assn., 1991, Golden Triangle award Am. Dermatol. Assn., 1998. Mem. Soc. Mag. Writers, Authors League, Nat. Assn. Sci. Writers (Svc. award 2006, 07), Am. Med. Writers Assn. (Eric Martin Meml. award), N.J. Daily Newspaper Women (awards news series 1958, 70, named Woman of Achievement 1971, 83), Am. Soc. Journalists and Authors (pres. 1977-78, spl. service award 1983, Lifetime Achievement award 2004), N.J. Press Women (pres. 1982-84) Home and Office: 44 Holly Dr Short Hills NJ 07078-1318 Personal E-mail: writer@brainbody.com, ruthwriter@aol.com.

WINTER, STEVEN, internist, cardiologist; b. Bklyn., July 25, 1950; s. Nathan Harold and Magda (Markowitz) W.; m. Florence Stein, Aug. 20, 1972; children: Amy R., Daniel. BA, Yeshiva U., 1972; MD, U. Med./Dentistry of N.J., 1976. Diplomate Am. Bd. Internal Medicine with subspecialty in cardiovascular disease. Intern North Shore Univ. Hosp., Manhasset, N.Y., 1976-77; resident in medicine North Shore Univ. Hosp, Manhasset, N.Y., 1976-79, Meml. Sloan Kettering Cancer Ctr., Cornell Cooper Tng. Hosp., 1977-79; fellow in cardiology R.I. Hosp.-Brown U., Providence, 1979-81; pvt. practice SI, N.Y.; attending in medicine and cardiology S.I. U. Hosp., 1981—, St. Vincent's Med. Ctr., Richmond, 1985—; asst. clin. prof. SUNY, Bklyn., 1985—. Fellow ACP, Am. Coll. Cardiology; mem. AMA, Am. Heart Assn. Office: 2627B Hylan Blvd Staten Island NY 10306-4353

WINTER, TERENCE, writer, television producer; BA, NYU; JD, St. John's U. Sch. Law. Practiced law (2 years), NYC. Co-prodr., writer (TV series) Sister, Sister, 1994, Flipper, 1995, DiResta, 1998, The PJs, 1999, exec. prodr., writer Brooklyn Rules, 2006, The Sopranos, 2000— (co-recipient, Writers Guild award and Edgar Award for the episode, Pine Barrens, 2001, Emmy award for Best Writing in a Drama Series for the episode, Long Term Parking, 2004, Emmy award for Outstanding Writing for a Drama Series the episode, Members Only, 2006, Primetime Emmy for Outstanding Drama Series, Acad. TV Arts and Scis., 2007, Best Episodic Drama, Writers Guild Am., 2008), guest appearances (TV series), 2000, 2004; writer: TV series Diagnosis Murder, 1993; writer (TV series) The Cosby Mysteries, 1994, Charlie Grace, 1995, Xena: Warrior Princess (3 episodes: 1995, 1996, 1998), (TV episode) The Great Defender, 1995, Get Rich or Die Tryin', 2005, (video game) 50 Cent: Bulletproof. Mem.: Conn. Bar, NY Bar.

WINTER, THOMAS SWANSON, publishing executive; b. Teaneck, NJ, Dec. 28, 1937; s. Frank J. and Beulah (Swanson) W.; m. Dawne Cina, Mar. 28, 1978; children: Victoria Ruth, Abigail Swanson. AB, Harvard U., 1959, MBA, 1961. Asst. editor Human Events newspaper Human Events, Inc., Washington, 1961-64, editor, 1964—, co-owner, pres., 1966-99, pres., editor-in-chief, 1999—; pres. Fund for Objective News Reporting. Treas. Conservative Victory Fund, Washington, 1975—; 1st vice-chmn. Am. Conservative Union, 1972—. Mem.: Nat. Press, Capitol Hill. Lutheran. Home: 16 4th St SE Washington DC 20003-3804 Office: Human Events 1 Massachusetts Ave NW Washington DC 20001-1401 Office Phone: 202-216-0600. Business E-Mail: twinter@eaglepub.com.

WINTER, WILLIAM EARL, retired beverage company executive; b. Granite City, Ill., Sept. 21, 1920; s. William M. and Ada M. (Compton) W.; m. Dorothy E. Schuster, Feb. 20, 1944 (dec. 1976); children: William C., Douglas E.; m. Mildred E. Stiebel, Mar. 18, 1977. AB, U. Ill., 1942. With Seven-Up Co., St. Louis, 1946-81, v.p., dir. mktg., 1969-71, exec. v.p., 1971-74, pres., chief operating officer, 1974-76, pres., chief exec. officer, 1976-79, chmn. bd., 1979-81, also former dir., cons.; chmn. emeritus, 1996—; cons. Cadbury Beverages/Seven-Up, chmn. emeritus, 1996. Bd. dirs. YMCA Greater St. Louis, U. Ill. Found.; mem. exec. bd. St. Louis Area coun. Boy Scouts Am. Capt. U.S. Army, 1942-46. Named to Promotion Mktg. Hall of Fame, 1979, Beverage World Hall of Fame, 1986 Mem. Am. Mktg. Assn., Sales and Mktg. Execs. St. Louis, Promotion Mktg. Assn. Am. (chmn. bd. 1971-72), Phi Beta Kappa, Phi Eta Sigma, Omicron Delta Gamma. Home: 14112 Baywood Villages Dr Chesterfield MO 63017-3421 Home Phone: 314-878-9870.

WINTER, WILLIAM FORREST, Former Governor, Miss, lawyer; b. Grenada, Miss., Feb. 21, 1923; s. William Aylmer and Inez (Parker) W.; m. Elise Varner, Oct. 10, 1950; children: Anne, Elise, Eleanor. BA, U. Miss., 1943, LLB, 1949; LLD, William Carey Coll., 1980, Millsaps Coll., 1983, Troy State U., 1988, Davidson Coll., 1996, Miss. U. for Women, 2000, U. NC, 2004, Tougaloo Coll., 2004. Bar: Miss. 1949, DC 1973. Practice in Grenada, 1949-58; practice in Jackson, Miss., 1968—; ptnr. Watkins, Pyle, Ludlam, Winter and Stennis, 1968-80; sr. ptnr. Watkins Ludlam Winter & Stennis, 1985—; mem. Miss. Ho. of Reps., 1948-56; state tax collector, 1956-64; state treas., 1964-68; lt. gov. Miss., 1972-76; gov., 1980-84. Eudora Welty prof. So. studies Millsaps Coll., 1989; Jamie Whitten prof. law U. Miss., 1989; prof. pub. policy Miss. Valley State U., 2001—05; chmn. So. Growth Policies Bd., 1981, So. Regional Edn. Bd., 1982, MDC, Inc.; mem. Pres.'s Adv. Bd. on Race, 1997—99; chmn. Adv. Commn. on Intergovtl. Rels., 1993—97. Pres. bd. trustees Miss. Dept. Archives and History, 1969-2008; chmn. Kettering Found., 1990-93, Appalachian Regional Commn., 1983, Commn. on Future of South, 1986, Nat. Civic League, 1987-88, Nat. Commn. on State and Local Pub. Svc., Stennis Ctr. for Pub. Svc., Found. for the Mid South, 1990-92. With US Army, 1943—46, with US Army, 1951. Recipient Martin Luther King, Jr. Meml. award, NEA, 2001, Profile in Courage award, John F. Kennedy Libr., 2008; fellow Harvard U. Inst. Politics, 1985, Miss. Bar Found. Mem. ABA, Miss. Bar (Lifetime Achievement award, 1998), Hinds County Bar Assn., DC Bar, U. Miss. Alumni Assn. (pres. 1979), Phi Delta Phi, Omicron Delta Kappa, Phi Delta Theta, Univ. Club (Jackson). Democrat. Presbyterian. Office: Watkins Ludlam Winter & Stennis 190 E Capitol St PO Box 427 Jackson MS 39202-3306 Home Phone: 601-366-1741; Office Phone: 601-949-4800. Office Fax: 601-949-4804.

WINTER, WILLIAM JOSEPH, bishop emeritus; b. Pitts., May 20, 1930; Ordained priest Diocese of Pitts., 1955, aux. bishop, 1988—2005, aux. bishop emeritus, 2005—; ordained bishop, 1989. Roman Catholic. Office: Chancery Office 111 Blvd Of The Allies Pittsburgh PA 15222-1613

WINTER, WINTON ALLEN, JR., lawyer, state senator; b. Ft. Knox, Ky., Apr. 19, 1953; s. Winton A. and Nancy (Morsbach) W.; m. Mary Boyd, July 28, 1978; children: Katie, Molly, Elizabeth. BA, U. Kans., 1975, JD, 1978. Bar: Kans. 1978. Ptnr. law firm Stevens & Brand, LLP, Lawrence, Kans., 1978—; v.p., gen. counsel Peoples, Inc., 2000-02; pres., CEO Peoples Bank, 2002—; pres. Corp. for Change; mem. Kans. Senate, 1982-92. Bd. dirs. Lawrence United Fund, Boys Club of Lawrence. Mem. ABA, Kans. Bar Assn., Douglas County Bar Assn. Kans. U. Law Soc., Rotary. Republican. Roman Catholic. Note and comment editor Kans. Law Rev., 1977-78. Office: PO Box 1795 4831 W 6th St Lawrence KS 66049 Home Phone: 785-843-4479; Office Phone: 785-842-4004. Personal E-mail: wwinter@epeoples.com. Business E-Mail: wwinter@bankingunusual1.com.

WINTERER, PHILIP STEELE, lawyer; b. San Francisco, July 8, 1931; s. Steele Leland and Esther (Hardy) W.; m. Patricia Dowling, June 15, 1955; children: Edward J., Amey W. Marrella. BA, Amherst Coll., 1953; LLB with honors, Harvard U., 1956. Bar: N.Y. 1957, Republic of Korea 1958. Assoc., ptnr., head tax dept., dep. presiding ptnr. Debevoise & Plimpton, NYC, 1956—93, of counsel, 1994—96; ret., 1996. Treas. Harvard Law Rev. Contbr. articles to profl. jours. Past pres. Am. Italy Soc.; life trustee Amherst Coll.; chmn. emeritus Sch. of Am. Ballet; chmn. exec. com. Phipps Houses; trustee emeritus N.Y. State Bd. Nature Conservancy; past chmn. Austen Riggs Ctr.; past vice chmn. Adelphi U.; bd. govs. Emily Dickinson Mus.; past bd. govs. Folger Shakespeare Libr.; mem. adv. coun., past v.p. Adirondack Trail Improvement Soc. Recipient Amherst Coll. medal for Eminent Svc., 1980, Pres. medal Adelphi U., 2004. Mem.: Am. Coll. Tax Counsel, Tax Forum, Citizens Housing and Planning Coun. N.Y., Am. Law Inst., Coun. Fgn. Rels., Century Assn., Ausable Club (past pres.), Phi Beta Kappa (dir. fellows). Home: 57 Gulf Brook Way Keene NY 12942 also: 1165 5th Ave New York NY 10029-6931 Office: Debevoise & Plimpton 919 3rd Ave New York NY 10022 Personal E-mail: winterhill95@aol.com.

WINTERER-SCHULZ, BARBARA JEAN, graphics designer, writer; b. Manchester, NH, Apr. 1, 1938; d. John Edward and Elizabeth Virginia Grace; m. Allen George Winterer, Mar. 30, 1959 (div. 1977); children: Audrey Lyn Winterer-Chavez, Amy Jo Winterer DeNoble. AA, Mesa CC, Ariz., 1980; BS summa cum laude, U. Md., Heidelberg, Germany, 1996; postgrad. Sheriff's Tng. Acad., Montezuma County, Colo.; grad., U. Colo., 2004. Art designer Morningstar Art Design Studio, Dolores, Colo., 1988—. Interpreter Colo. State Pk.; US rail ranger Durango-Silverton RR; master gardener Colo. State U.; bd. dirs. S.W. Cmty. Resources; health care provider Archuleta County Sch. Dist., Pagosa Springs, Colo.; farm medic.; guest lectr. Northern Ariz. U., Mesa Verde Nat. Pk., UNESCO World Heritage Ctr. Contbr. articles to newspapers and jours. Del. People to People Amb. Program, 2007; asst. dir. Ariz. Myasthenia Gravis Found., 1977—80; ofcl. U.S. reporter World Eskimo Indian Olympics, Fairbanks, Alaska, 1994; mem. disaster response team ARC, Pagosa Springs, mem. Durango chpt. Durango; bd. dirs., chmn. pub. rels. com. Habitat for Humanity, Pagosa Springs; interpreter Chimney Rock Hist. Archeol. Site; interpretive docent, vol. Bur. Land Mgmt., Anasazi Heritage Ctr. Mus., 2004—; mem. Friends of Libr., Dolores, Colo.; appointed mem. sr. adv. bd. Monteruma County, Colo., 2007—. Recipient Humanitarian award, Phila. Inst. Human Potential, 1972, Chancellor of Germany award for Acad. Achievement, 1986, citation of Meritorious Achievement award in the Arts and Humanitarianism, Internat. Biog. Ctr., 1997, Gaming Lic., Colo.; scholar, Chancellor of Germany. Mem.: AAUW, Colo. Archeology Soc., Hihitsanom Archeol. Soc., Pub. Lands Interpretive Assn., Libr. of Congress (assoc.), Internat. Rotary Club, Nat. Fedn. Garden Clubs, Cortez Garden Club (pres.), Colo. Fedn. Garden Clubs, Phi Theta Kappa, Alpha Sigma Lambda. Avocations: gardening, gourmet cooking. Address: 2101 N Evergreen St PO Box 10295 Chandler AZ 85225 Office: Morningstar Art Design Studio PO Box 10295 Chandler AZ 85225 Office Phone: 480-699-0919.

WINTER-NEIGHBORS, GWEN CAROL, special education and art educator, consultant; b. Greenville, SC, July 14, 1938; d. James Edward (dec. 2002) and Evelyn (Lee) Walters (dec. 1998); m. David M. Winter Jr., Aug., 1963 (dec. Feb. 1980); children: Robin Carole Winter, Charles G. McCuen, Dustin Winter TeBrugge; m. Thomas Frederick Neighbors, Mar. 24, 1989. BA in Edn. and Art, Furman U., Greenville, SC, 1960, MA in Psychology, 1967; cert. in guidance/pers., Clemson U., SC, 1981; EdD in Youth and Mid. Childhood Edn., Nova Southeastern U., Ft. Lauderdale, Fla., 1988; postgrad., U. SC, Spartanburg, 1981-89; cert. clear specialist instrn. with honors, Calif. State U., Northridge, 1991; art edn. cert., Calif. State U., LA, 1991; JD, Glendale U., Calif., 1999. Cert. tchr. art, elem. edn., psychology, secondary guidance, SC. Tchr. 7th grade Greenville Jr. H.S., 1960—63; art tchr. Wade Hampton H.S., Greenville, 1963—67; prin. adult edn. Woodmont H.S., Piedmont, SC, 1983—85, Mauldin H.S., Greenville and Mauldin, SC, 1981; tchr. ednl. psychology edn. dept. Allen U., Columbia, SC, 1969; activity therapist edn. dept. SC Dept. of Corrections, Columbia, 1973—76; art specialist gifted edn. Westcliffe Elem. Sch., Greenville, 1976—89; tchr. self-contained spl. day class Elysian Heights Elem. Sch., Echo Park and L.A., Calif., 1989—91; art tchr. med. drawing Sch. Dist. Greenville County Blue Ridge Mid. Sch., Greer, 1991—95; tchr./asst. head edn. dept. N. Greenville Coll., 2001—02. Participant nat. conf. US Dept. Edn./So. Bell, Columbia, 1989; com. mem. nat. exec. com. Nova Southeastern U., 1988—89; asst. chmn., tchr. edn. dept. North Greenville Coll., 2001, adm., staff, 01, U. SC, Spartanburg, adj., student tchr., supr., 2002; adv. bd. SC Gov. Sch. for Arts and Humanities; parent/tchr. adv. bd. Spl. Edn.; adj. prof U. SC Univ. Ctr., Greenville, 2002—03; ind. rep. Primerica Fin. Svs., 2003—06; ind. agt. Robinson/Horace Mann Ins. Co. Mozart Book, 1988; author: Let's Sing a Song About America, 1988 (1st pl. Nat. Music award, 1990), numerous poems. Life mem. Rep. Presdl. Task Force, 1970—; mem. voter registration com. Lexington County Rep. Party, 1970—80; grand jury participant 13th Jud. Ct. Sys., Greenville, 1986—88, guardian ad litem, 1988—2005; mem. arts educators adv. task force SC Gov. Sch. Arts and Humanities, 2002—04; mem. spl. edn. parent adv. bd. representing Sue Cleveland Elem. Sch. Greenville Co. Sch. Dist., Spl. Edn. Topics and Trends, 2001—07; poll mgr. Greenville Co. Tchr. Incentive grantee Sch. Dist. Greenville County, 1986-88, Project Earth grantee Bell South, 1988-89, 94-95, Edn. Improvement Act/Nat. Dissimination Network grantee SC State Dept. Edn., 1987-88, Targett 2,000 Arts in Curricular grantee SC Dept. Edn., 1994-95, Alliance grantee Bus. Cmty. Greenville, 1992-95, Greer Art Rsch. grantee, 1993-94, SC Govs. Sch. Study grantee, 1994, Edn. Improvement Act Competitive Tchr. grantee SC Dept. Edn., 1994-95, Alliance Grand grant, 1995-96; recipient Am. Jurisprudence Bancroft-Whitney award Glendale U. Sch. Law, 1997, 98, Excellence Recognition in Real Property award Glendale Law Faculty, 1997, Excellence in Art of Appellate Advocacy, Glendale U. Sch. Law, 1998, Am. Jurisprudence Bancroft-Whitney award Constl. Law I, 1998. Mem.: AAUW, ABA, Rep. Party Piedmont Precinct SC (chmn. com.), Palmetto State Tchr. Assn., SC Art Edn. Assn., SC Arts Alliance, Nat. Mus. Women in Arts, Nat. Art Edn. Assn., Furman U. Singer Alumni, Phi Delta Kappa. Baptist Avocations: computers, art, writing, music. Office Phone: 864-845-3166. Personal E-mail: gwen.neighbors@gmail.com.

WINTEROWD, WALTER ROSS, language educator; b. Salt Lake City, Jan. 24, 1930; s. Harold Ross and Henrietta Ethel (Fike) W.; m. Norma Graham, Aug. 2, 1952; children: Geoffrey Ross, Anthony Gordon. BS, Utah State U., 1952; PhD, U. Utah, 1962. Asst. prof. U. Mont., Missoula, 1962-66; assoc. prof. U. So. Calif., Los Angeles, 1966-71, prof. English, 1971-79, McElderry prof. English, 1979-97, prof. emeritus, 1997—. Author: Rhetoric: A Synthesis, 1967, Contemporary Rhetoric, 1975, The Contemporary Writer, 1975, Composition/Rhetoric: A Synthesis, 1986, The Culture and Politics of Literacy, 1989, The Rhetoric of the "Other" Literature, 1990, (with Geoffrey Winterowd) The Critical Reader, Thinker, and Writer, 1992, The English Department: A Personal and Institutional History, 1998, Searching for Faith, 2005, (with Judith Rodby) the Uses of Grammar, 2005. Served with U.S. Army, 1953-55. Mem. Nat. Council Tchrs. English, AAUP Democrat. Home: 17551 San Roque Ln Huntington Beach CA 92647-6641 Personal E-mail: wrossw@msn.com.

WINTERS, BARBARA JO, musician; b. Salt Lake City; d. Louis McClain and Gwendolyn (Bradley) W. AB cum laude, UCLA, 1960, postgrad., 1961, Yale, 1960. Mem. oboe sect. L.A. Philharm., 1961-94, prin. oboist, 1972-94; ret. Clinician oboe, English horn, Oboe d'amore. Recs. movie, TV sound tracks. Avocations: painting, piano. Home: 3529 Coldwater Canyon Ave Studio City CA 91604-4060 Office: 151 S Grand Ave Los Angeles CA 90012-3013

WINTERS, DAVID DOUGLAS, lawyer; s. Frederick Douglas and Wanda Mae Hudson Winters; m. Debbie Elaine Tipton, Apr. 23, 1977; children: Charity, Patience, Ian. BS, US Naval Acad., Annapolis, Md., 1976; MS, U. So. Miss., Gulfport, 1987; diploma in Law, Oxford Brookes, UK, 1996; JD, So. Ill. U., Carbondale, 2002. Bar: US Patent Office 2001, Tenn. 2002, US Supreme Ct. 2003. With US Navy, 1971—94; internat. cons. group mng. dir. London, 1994—96; internat. bus. cons., negotiator Nagasaki, Japan, 1996—99; patent atty. Clarksville and Nashville, Tenn., 2002—. Standing city judge pro tem, Clarksville, 2004—. Author: The Boat Officer's Handbook, 1981, 1991. Founder Charles M. Hudson Grant for Excellence in Patent Law So. Ill. U., Sch. Law, 2005. Named Author of Yr., nashville Bar Jour., 2008. Mem.: Fed. Bar Assn., Tenn. Bar Assn. (del. 2007), Nashville Bar Assn., US Naval Inst., Brit. Spl. Forces Club, Mensa, Phi Delta Phi. Avocations: flying, yachting, scuba diving. Office: Winters Patent Law 2277-C Wilma Rudolph Blvd Ste 237 Clarksville TN 37040

WINTERS, JANE A., nurse, educator; MSN, Ohio State U., Columbus, 1990. RN staff Nationwide Children's Hosp., Columbus, 1976—; assoc. prof. nursing Columbus State CC, 2000—. Mem.: Sigma Theta Tau. Conservative. Avocations: reading, music, walking, cooking. Office: Columbus State CC 550 East Spring St Columbus OH 43216 Business E-Mail: jwinters@cscc.edu.

WINTERS, JILL MARY, nursing educator, director; b. Milw., June 30, 1955; d. John Paul Gabor and Ann Lorraine (Ladish) Gordy; m. Jack Mark Winters; children: David, Michael. BSN, U. Wis., Milw., 1978; MS in Nursing, Marquette U., 1991; PhD, U. Wis., 1996. Cert. CCRN. Nurse various hosps., Milw., 1978—85, Peck Foods Corp., Milw., 1985-88; asst. prof. U. Wis.-Milw., 1996—2001; assoc. prof., dir. rsch. Marquette U., Milw., 2001—. Contbr. numerous book chpts. and articles to profl. jours. Grantee, Nat. Inst. Nursing Rsch., Wis. Women's Health Found., Nat. Inst. Disability and Rehab. Rsch., Nat. Inst. Child Health and Human Devel., Children's Hosp. Wis. Mem. AACCN (grantee 1997), ANA, Midwest Nursing Rsch. Soc., Am. Nurses Found., Sigma Theta Tau (v.p. local chpt. 1997-99). Roman Catholic. Achievements include research in use of music to improve cardiac function and reduce anxiety after myocardial infarction, heart rate variability in infants with serious congenital heart defects and prematurity; heart rate variability with myocardial infarction and heart failure, accessibility of medical equipment for persons with disabilities, exercise and heart failure, and telehealth applications. Avocations: golf, running, cross country skiing. Home: 10320 N Provence Ct Mequon WI 53092-5228 Office: Marquette U Coll Nursing PO Box 1881 Milwaukee WI 53201-1881 Home Phone: 262-242-3922; Office Phone: 414-288-3848. Business E-Mail: jill.winters@marquette.edu.

WINTERS, MARTHA P., history and language educator; d. Charles LeRoy and Jacqueline Cleve Winters. BA in Letters, U. Okla., Norman, 1975, MA in Latin, 1978. Tchr. Latin, world history Ardmore H.S., Okla., 1978—85, Ctrl. Mid-H.S., Norman, Okla., 1985—97; tchr. world history Norman North H.S., Okla., 1997—2005, tchr. history, 1997—2008, tchr. Latin, world history, 2005—. Pres. Okla. Fgn. Lang. Tchrs. Assn., 1980—81; com. People to People-Social Studies, South Africa, 2004. Mem.: Am. Acad. Rome, Am. Sch. Classical Studies, Nat. Coun. for Social Studies, Am. Classical League. Republican. Office: Norman North HS 1809 Stubbeman Ave Norman OK 73069 Business E-Mail: mwinters@norman.k12.ok.us.

WINTERS, RICHARD ALLEN, mineral economist; b. Butte, Mont., Feb. 19, 1963; s. Allen S. and Doris Ellen Winters. BS in Fin. and Econs., U. Mont., 1986; MS in Mineral Econs., Colo. Sch. Mines, 1990, postgrad., 1991-93. Office engr. Morrison Knudsen Engrs., Richland, Wash., 1986-88, project acct., 1987-88; ops. analyst Echo Bay Mines, Denver, 1989; instr. Colo. Sch. Mines, Golden, Colo., 1991-92; cons. Coors Brewing Co., Golden, 1991-92; sr. rsch. engr. Phelps Dodge Mining Co., Morenci, Ariz., 1992-94; gold analyst Robertson, Stephens and Co., San Francisco, 1994-95; v.p. corp. devel. Golden Star Resources Ltd., Denver, 1995-99; v.p. RMB Resources, 2000—04, pres., 2005—. Pres. Mineral Econ. Grad. Student Assn., 1989-90. Mem. Soc. Mining, Metallurgy and Exploration, Assn. Environ. Resource Economists, Mineral, Econs. and Mgmt. Soc. Avocations: outdoors, jewelry craft. Office: 143 Union Blvd Ste 900 Lakewood CO 80228

WINTERS, ROBERT LOUIS, theater educator, consultant; b. Columbus, Ohio, Nov. 11, 1936; s. Robert Bernard and Freda Louise Winters; m. Connie Ann House, Dec. 29, 1974; children: Daniel Richard, Michael Robert, Jonathan Christopher. MA in Theater, Mich. State U., E. Lansing, 1962. Interim dir. Ohio U. Sch. Film, Athens; dir., faculty Ohio U. Sch. Theater, 1962—2008, prof. emeritus, 2004. Cons. theater programs schs. & communities Mich. Individual Arts Grants & West Va. Arts Orgns.; panel mem., panel chair Ohio Arts Coun.; bd. mem.- cons. Dir.'s Co., NYC, 1992—98. Prodr.(director): (touring group) The Appalachian Green Parks Project (Ohio Gov. award, 1974); dir.(prodr.): (plays, musicals, operas). V.p. City Athens Mcpl. Arts Commn., 2003—; artistic dir. emeritus Ohio Valley Summer Theater, Athens. Recipient Ohioana Citation inspiring tchg., disting. svc., Ohioana Libr. Assn., 1978, Citation Outstanding Contbn. Theater and Edn., Ohio Theatre Alliance, 1980; named Hon. Alumni, Ohio U.; named to Hall of Fame, Ohio Cmty. Theater Assn., 2000, Ohio Ednl. Theatre Assn., 2005. Avocations: photography, fishing. Home: 15019 Harmony Rd Athens OH 45701 Office: Ohio Univ Sch of Theater Kantner Hall Athens OH 45701 Business E-Mail: winters@ohio.edu.

WINTERS, SAM, lawyer; b. Tex. BA, U. Tex., 1944, JD, 1948. Bar: Tex. 1948. Shareholder Clark, Thomas & Winters, Austin, Tex.; bd. govs. U.S. Postal Svc., Washington, 1991—2000, vice chair, 1996-97, chmn. bd. govs., 1994-95, 98. Chmn. Tex. Rsch. League, 1990, 91; past mem. Nat. Hwy. Safety Adv. Com.; mem. devel. bd. U. Tex., Austin. With USN, World War II. Mem. ABA (past chair sect. pub. utilities, comm. and transp.), Am. Law Inst. (life), State Bar Tex. Office: Clark, Thomas & Winters PO Box 1148 Austin TX 78767

WINTERS, SHARON BETH, medical researcher, director; d. David Courtney and Rita Joyce (Hayes) Kinney; m. Brian J. Winters, May 9, 1992; children: Brendan David, Sean Patrick. BS, U. Pitts., 1988, MS, 1991. Trauma registrar Childrens Hosp. Pitts., 1987—88; mgr., data quality monitoring U. Pitts. Cancer Inst., 1988—93; adj. faculty U. Pitts., 1988—; cancer program coord. UPMC Presbyn., Montefiore, Eye & Ear Inst., 1989—97; program mgr., UPMC network registry U. Pitts. Med. Ctr. UPCI, 1997—2004; dir., registry info. svcs. UPMC Cancer Ctrs., 2004—. Edn. com. Nat. Cancer Registrars Assn., Chgo., 1999; bylaw com. chair Pa. Assn. Cancer Registrars, Harrisburg, 1999, program com. chair, 2006, pres., 2008—. Contbr. articles to profl. jours. (JH Rippey grant, 2007). Parent Hempfield PTO, Greensburg, Pa., 2001—09. Mem.: N. Am. Assn. Ctrl. Cancer Registries (PIP grant 2008), Pa. Cancer Control Consortium, Pa. Assn. Cancer Registrars (pres. 2008—), Nat. Cancer Registrars Assn. Democrat. Avocations: family activities, travel, outdoor life. Office: UPMC Cancer Ctrs 5150 Ctr Ave Pittsburgh PA 15232 Personal E-mail: sharon_winters@hotmail.com. Business E-Mail: winterssb@upmc.edu.

WINTERS, STANLEY B., history professor, consultant, writer; b. NYC, June 5, 1924; m. Helen Plavner, Sept. 12, 1948 (div. Dec. 1969); children: Jenifer O'Neill, Neal Winters; m. Zdenka Müllerová, Jan. 9, 1970. AB, NYU, 1948; AM, Columbia U., 1950; PhD, Rutgers U., 1966. Cert. secondary social studies educator, N.J. Artist, draftsman Art Glass Co., NYC, 1942-43; instr. history NYU, 1949-50; dir., co-propr. Clinton Hill Day Sch., Newark, 1950-56; tchr. social studies Livingston (N.J.) H.S., 1956-57; disting. prof. history Newark Coll. Engring./N.J. Inst. Tech., 1957-91; disting. prof. emeritus history N.J. Inst. Tech., Newark, 1991—. Adj. prof. history Rutgers U., Newark, 1980-91, rsch. assoc. Urban Studies Ctr., New Brunswick, 1961-62; cons., columnist Office of Info., Newark, 1972-80. Author: Karel Kramář's Early Political Career, 1966, From Riot to Recovery: Newark After Ten Years, 1979, T.G. Masaryk, 1850-1937: Thinker and Politician, 1990; co-author, editor: Intellectual and Social Developments in the Habsburg Empire, 1975, Great Britain, the USA and the Bohemian Lands 1848-1938 1991; editor: Dynasty, Politics and Culture, 1991, East Ctrl. Europe jour., 1975-91; mem. editl. bd. Bohemia-Zeitschrift, Munich, 1985-2003; columnist (pseudonymous weekly) NJ Afro-Am. newspaper, 1958-64; contbr. over 200 articles to profl. jours. and publs. Pres., co-founder Clinton Hill Neighborhood Coun., Newark, 1955-61; chmn. edn. com. br. NAACP, Newark, 1960-64; candidate city coun., Newark, 1962; candidate Essex County Freeholder, 1965; trustee Preservation and Landmarks Com., Newark, 1980-93; pres. Czechoslovak History Conf., Chapel Hill, N.C., 1988-90. Staff sgt. U.S. Army, 1943-46, ETO. Recipient Szendzimir award, Polish Inst. Arts and Scis., N.Y.C., 1971, N.J. Inst. Tech. Pub. Svc. award, 1982, Josef Hlávka Meml. medal, Czechoslovak Acad. Scis., Prague, 1991, Disting. Svc. award, Czechoslovak History Conf., 1995, František Palacky Hon. medal, Acad. Scis. Czech Republic, 2003; grantee, NEH, 1967, N.J. Com. Humanities, 1976—77, 1985. Mem. Am. Hist. Assn. (life, nominated first Czech historian as hon. fgn. mem.), Organization Am. Historians, Am. Assn. Advancement Slavic Studies, Collegium Carolinum, Josef Pekař Hist. Soc. (hon.), Hist. Assn. of Czech Republic (hon.), Phi Beta Kappa. Avocations: chess, travel, walking, correspondence, pre-contemporary music. Home: 463 MacArthur Dr Port Charlotte FL 33954-3432

WINTERS, THOMAS ANDREW, microbiologist; b. Chgo., Jan. 26, 1960; s. Jack Arthur and Cynthia Lee (Hanna) W.; m. Mary Elizabeth Hull, Oct. 26, 1985; children: Elizabeth Marie, Michelle Lee. BS, Mich. State U., 1983; PhD, Ohio State U., 1990. Instr., lectr. Bay de Noc C.C., Escabana, Mich., 1984; grad. rsch. assoc. dept. med. microbiology and immunology Ohio State U. Coll. Medicine, Columbus, 1985-90, asst. lab. instr., 1985-87, lab. instr., lectr., 1987-90; rsch. fellow dept. radiation medicine Georgetown U., Washington, 1990-96, Am. Cancer Soc. fellow, 1992-95; postdoctoral fellow radiation oncology br. NIH, Bethesda, Md., 1996-97, staff scientist dept. nuclear medicine, 1997—. Contbr. articles to profl. jours. Mem. Radiation Rsch. Soc. (Travel award 1994), AAAS, Planetary Soc. Achievements include identification, differential inhibition and purification of herpes simplex virus (type 2) uracil-DNA glycosylase DNA repair enzyme, identification, purification and characterization of human enzymes responsible for repair of ionizing radiation induced DNA single-strand breaks. Home: 18801 Sunset Hills Ct Gaithersburg MD 20879-1734 Office: NIH Clin Ctr Dept Nuclear Medicine 9000 Rockville Pike Dept Nuclear Bethesda MD 20892-0003

WINTERS, VERNON MICHAEL, lawyer; b. Syracuse, NY, Sept. 15, 1961; s. Robert C. Winters, Jr. and Anne C. Kopf; m. Kathleen M. Wardlaw, May 24, 1997; children: Mitchell William, Elizabeth Shannon. BA in Econ., U. Calif., Berkeley, 1983; JD, U. Calif. Hastings Coll. the Law, 1987. Extern law clerk, Justice Stanley Mosk Ca. Supreme Ct., San Francisco, 1987; assoc. Landels, Ripley & Diamond, LLP, San Francisco, 1987—88; fed. law clk. US Dist. Ct., Ctrl. Dist. Calif., Hon. Robert C. Bonner, 1988—89; ptnr. Cooley Godward, LLP, Palo Alto, Calif., 1990—98, Day, Casebeer, Madrid, Winters & Batchelder, LLP, Cupertino, Calif., 1998—99, Latham & Watkins, LLP, Menlo Park, Calif., 1999—2002, Weil, Gotshal & Manges, LLP, Redwood Shores, Calif., 2002—. Adv. com. Ctr. Advanced Study & Rsch. Intellectual Property, Seattle, 2001—; adj. prof. U. Calif., Berkeley Sch. Law, 2003—; commr. Commn. Jud. Nominees Evaluation, LA, 2007—08. Author: (treatise) Modern Patent Litigation: Strategies for Turning Losing Cases Into Winning Ones; editor: Hastings Constitutional Law Quarterly, San Francisco, 1986—87; mem. nat. editl. bd. The Fed. Lawyer, DC, 2001—; contbr. articles to profl. jours. Bd. mem. Jr. Achievement, Bay Area, Inc., San Francisco, 1999—2000. Recipient Am. Jurisprudice award, Thompson West Pub. Co., 1987. Office: Weil Gotshal & Manges LLP 201 Redwood Shores Pky Redwood City CA 94065 Office Phone: 650-802-3000. Office Fax: 650-802-3100. Business E-Mail: vern.winters@weil.com.

WINTERS, WILLIAM THOMAS (BILL WINTERS), diversified financial services company executive; b. NYC, Sept. 27, 1961; s. William Thomas and Ann Wilson (Vickey) W.; m. Adriane Besonc, Sept. 19, 1984. BA, Colgate U., 1983; MBA, Wharton Bus. Sch., 1988. V.p., head global commodity swop group J.P. Morgan & Co. Inc., NYC, 1988-91; dep. head investment bank, head credit & rate markets J.P. Morgan Chase & Co., co-CEO investment Bank, 2004—. Bd. dirs. JPMorgan Cazenove. Office: JP Morgan Chase & Co 125 London Wall EC2Y 5AJ London England also: 270 Park Ave New York NY 10017*

WINTERSHEIMER, DONALD CARL, retired state supreme court justice; b. Covington, Ky., Apr. 21, 1931; s. Carl E. and Marie A. (Kohl) W.; m. Alice T. Rabe, June 24, 1961; children: Mark D., Lisa Ann, Craig P., Amy T., Blaise Q. BA, Thomas More Coll., 1953; MA, Xavier U., 1956; JD, U. Cin., 1959; LHD (hon.), No. Ky. U., 1999. Pvt. practice, Covington, 1960-76; city solicitor City of Covington, 1962-76; judge Ky. Ct. Appeals, Frankfort, 1976-83; justice Ky. Supreme Ct., Frankfort, 1983—2007. Chmn. Ky. Supreme Ct. Criminal Rules Com., 1988-94, Continuing Jud. Edn. Com., 1983—2007, Rules Com., 1994—2007; del. Foster Parent Rev. Bd., 1985-2002; mem. adv. bd. Sta. WNKU-FM, 1984-94, Am. Soc. Writers on Legal Subjects. Published articles in Law Jour. of Nat. Legal Ctr. for Medically Disabled, Issues in Law & Medicine, Albany Law Review, Quinnipiac Law Review, Temple Law Review, No. Ky. U. Chase Law Rev., NYU Annual Survey of Am. Law. Trustee Sta. WNKU-FM. Recipient Cmty. Svc. award Thomas More Coll., 1968, Disting. Alumnus award, 1982, Monsignor Murphy award, 2007, Disting. Alumni award Coll. Law/U.Cin., 1998, Lincoln award No. Ky. U., 2007; named Disting. Jurist Chase Coll. Law, 1983, Outstanding Jurist Phi Alpha Delta Law Frat., 1990, Murphy award, Thomas More Coll., 2006, Lincoln award Northern Ky. U., 2007. Mem. ABA, Am. Judicature Soc., Ky. Bar Assn., Ohio Bar Assn., Cin. Bar Assn., Inst. Jud. Adminstrn., Am. Inns of Ct. (founder Chase chpt.). Democrat. Roman Catholic. Home Phone: 859-581-8781.

WINTERSTEIN, JAMES FREDRICK, academic administrator; b. Copperas Cove, Tex., Apr. 8, 1943; s. Arno Fredrick Herman and Ada Amanda Johanna (Wagnr) W.; m. Diane Marie Bochmann, July 13, 1963; children: Russell, Lisa, Steven, Amy. Student, U. N.M., 1962; D of Chiropractic cum laude, Nat. Coll. Chiropractic, 1968; cert., Harvard Inst. for Ednl. Mgmt., 1988. Diplomate Am. Chiropractic Bd. Radiology; lic. chiropractic, Ill., Fla., S.D., Md. Night supr. x-ray dept. DuPage Meml. Hosp., Elmhurst, Ill., 1964-66; x-ray technologist Lombard (Ill.) Chiropractic Clinic, 1966-68, asst. dir., 1968-71; chmn. dept. diagnostic imaging Nat. Coll. Chiropractic, Lombard, Ill., 1971-73, chief of staff, 1985-86; pres. Nat. U. Health Scis., Lombard, Ill., 1986—; pvt. practice West Chicago, Ill., 1968-73, Fla., 1973-85. Faculty Nat. Lincoln Coll. Post-Profl., Grad. and Continuing Edn., 1967—; chmn. x-ray test com. Nat. Bd. Chiropractic Examiners, 1971-73; govs. adv. panel on coal worker's pneumoconiosis and chiropractic State of Pa., 1979; v.p. Am. Chiropractic Coll. Radiology, 1981-83; mem. adv. coun. on radiation protection Dept. Health and Rehabilitative Svcs. State of Fla., 1984-85; cons. to bd. examiners State of S.C., 1983-84, State of Fla., 1980-85; cons. to peer review bd. State of Fla., 1980-84; trustee Chiropractic Centennial Found., 1989-90; mem. adv. com. Aids Alternative Health Ptnrs., 1996-2000, Consortial Ctr. for Chiropractic Rsch., 1998—; bd. dirs. Fedn. Ill. Ind. Colls. and Univs., 1995—; bd. dirs. Alternative

Medicine, Inc., 1999—; spkr. in field. Pub. Outreach (Nat. Univ. Health Scis. monthly); author numerous monographs on chiropractic edn. and practice; co-inventor composite shielding and mounting means for x-ray machines; contbr. articles to profl. jours. Chmn., bd. dirs. Trinity Luth. Ch., West Chgo., 1970-72, Luth. High Sch., Pinellas County, Fla., 1979-82, St. John Luth. Ch., Lombard, 1988; chmn. bd. edn. First Luth. Sch., 1975-79; chmn. First Luth. Congregation, Clearwater, Fla., 1979-82; chmn. bldg. planning com. Grace Luth. Ch. and Sch., St. Petersburg, Fla., 1984-85; bldg. planning com. ch. expansion, new elem. sch., First Luth. Sch., 1975-79; stewardship adv. coun. Fla./Ga. dist. Luth. Ch. Mo. Synod, 1983-85; trustee West Suburban Regional Acad. Consortium, 1993-99. With U.S. Army, 1961-64. Recipient Cert. Meritorious Svc. Am. Chiropractic Registry of Radiologic Technologists, Cert. Recognition for Inspiration, Guidance, and Support Delta Tau Alpha, 1989, Cert. Appreciation Chiropractic Assn. South Africa, 1988, 1st pl. Fund Raiser Ride for Kids award Pediat. Brain Tumor Found. U.S., 1997, Cert. Appreciation Ill. Chiropractic Soc., 1997, Hope and Support award Alternative Health Ptnrs., 1998, Chiropractor of Yr., Ill. Chiropractic Soc., 2000, Person of the Yr., Alternative Medicine, Inc., 2001, NUHS Bd. Trustees Disting. Svc. award, 2002, President's citation award Maryland Chiropractic Assn., 2003. Mem. APHA, Am. Chiropractic Assn., Am. Chiropractic Coll. Radiology (pres. 1983-85, exec. com. 1985-86), Am. Chiropractic Coun. on Diagnostic Imaging, Am. Chiropractic Coun. on Diagnosis and Internal Disorders, Am. Chiropractic Coun. on Nutrition, Nat. Univ. Alumni Assn., Am. Acad. Chiropractic Physicians (sec.), Assn. Chiropractic Colls. (sec.-treas. 1986-91), Coun. Chiropractic Edn. (sec.-treas. 1988-90, v.p. 1990-92, pres. 1992-94, immediate past pres. 1994-96), Fla. Chiropractic Assn. (chmn. radiol. health com. 1977-85, Disting. Svc. award 1999). Republican. Lutheran. Avocations: reading, automobile rehabilitation, harley-davidson motorcycles, fishing.

WINTHROP, JOHN, wines and spirits company executive; b. Salt Lake City, Apr. 20, 1947; children: Grant Gordon, Clayton Hanford. AB cum laude, Yale U., 1969; JD magna cum laude, U. Tex., 1972. Bar: Calif. 1972. Law clk. 9th cir. U.S. Ct. Appeals, LA, 1972-73; conseil juridique Coudert Freres, Paris, 1973-75; v.p. gen. counsel MacDonald Group, Ltd., LA, 1976-82; pres., CEO MacDonald Mgmt. Corp. and MacDonald Group Ltd., LA, 1982-86; pres., chief exec. officer MacDonald Corp. (gen. contractors), LA, 1982-86; chmn., CEO Comstock Mgmt. Co., LA, 1986—; pres., CEO Winthrop Investment Properties, Los Angeles, 1986—; CEO Veritas Imports, LA, 1995—. Bd. dirs. Plus Prods., Tiger's Milk Prods., Irvine, Calif., 1977-80. Contbr. articles to profl. jours. Bd. dirs., sec. L.A. Sheriff's Dept. Found.; bd. dirs. L.A. Opera. Mem. Nat. Eagle Scout Assn. (life), French-Am. C. of C. (bd. dirs. 1982-87), Urban Land Inst., Yale Club N.Y., Calif. Club, The Beach Club, Elizabethan Club, Order of the Coif, Beta Theta Pi. Office: Veritas Imports Penthouse 9460 Wilshire Blvd Beverly Hills CA 90212-2720 E-mail: jwinthrop@veritaswine.com.

WINTHROP, LAWRENCE FREDRICK, judge; b. Apr. 18, 1952; s. Murray and Vauneta (Cardwell) W. BA with honors, Whittier Coll., 1974; JD magna cum laude, Calif. Western Sch., 1977. Bar: Ariz. 1977, Calif. 1977, U.S. Dist. Ct. Ariz. 1977, U.S. Dist. Ct. (so. dist.) Calif. 1981, U.S. Ct. Appeals (9th cir.) 1981, U.S. Dist. Ct. (cen. dist.) Calif. 1983, U.S. Supreme Ct. 1983. Assoc. Snell and Wilmer, Phoenix, 1977—83, ptnr., 1984—93, Doyle, Winthrop, P.C., Phoenix, 1993—2002; judge divsn. one Ariz. Ct. Appeals, Phoenix, 2002—. Judge pro tem Maricopa County Superior Ct., 1987-97; lectr. Ariz. personal injury law and practice and state and local tax law Tax Exec. Inst., Nat. Bus. Inst., Profl. Edn. Systems, Inc., Ariz. Trial Lawyers Assn., Maricopa County Bar. Editor-in-chief: Calif. Western Law Rev., 1976-77. Fellow, Ariz. Found. Legal Svcs. and Edn.(bd. dir. 2005-, pres. 2009-); Charter benefactor, Maricopa County Bar Found.; mem. Ariz. Supreme Ct. Com. on Examinations, 1995-2002; bd. dir. Ariz. Tax Rsch. Assn., 1989-93; bd. dir. Ariz. Assn. Defense Counsel, past. pres. 1988-89; chmn. Valley of Sun Sch. & Habilitation Ctr., 1994-96, bd. dir. 1989-97; mem. Vol. Lawyers' Program, 1980-2002, mem. Bd. Certified Ct. Reporters, Commn. Judicial Conduct, 2009- Mem. Calif. Bar Assn., Ariz. Bar Assn., Am. Bd. Trial Advs., Aspen Valley Golf Club, Lorna Lockwood Inn Ct. (co-pres. 2005-06). Republican. Methodist. Avocations: music, golf. Home: 83 W Cypress St Phoenix AZ 85003 Office: 1501 W Washington St Phoenix AZ 85007 Office Phone: 602-542-1430. Business E-Mail: lwinthrop@appeals.az.gov.

WINTLE, SUZANNE, elementary school educator; BA in Elem. Edn., Univ. Omaha, Nebr. Tchr., Nebr., 1970—71, Westchester, Ill., 1971—76, Florence Sawyer Sch., Bolton, Mass., 1976—. Facilitator Sawyer Sch. Study Group. Named Mass. Tchr. of Yr., 2006. Office: Florence Sawyer Sch 100 Mechanic St Bolton MA 01740 Office Phone: 718-338-3635. Business E-Mail: swintle@nrsd.net.

WINTON, CALHOUN, literature educator; b. Ft. Benning, Ga., Jan. 21, 1927; s. George Peterson and Dorothy (Calhoun) Winton; m. Elizabeth Jefferys Myers, June 30, 1948; children: Jefferys Hobart, William Calhoun. Student, Ga. Inst. Tech., 1944-46; BA, U. of the South, 1948; MA, Vanderbilt U., 1950, Princeton U., 1954, PhD, 1955. Instr. Dartmouth Coll., Hanover, NH, 1954-57; asst. prof. U. Va., Charlottesville, 1957-60; asst. prof. then assoc. prof., asst. dean Grad. Sch. U. Del., 1960-67; prof. dept. English U. S.C., Columbia, 1967-75, chmn. dept., 1970-73; prof. U. Md., College Park, 1975-97, dir. Rsch. Ctr. for Humanities, 1988-90, prof. emeritus, 1997—; capt. USN, 1944—67. Del. Joint Nat. Com. Langs., Washington, 1986—90, Washington, 1995—99. Author: (biography) Captain Steele, 1964, Sir Richard Steele, 1970; author: (with others) Colonial Book in the Atlantic World, 2000, Agent of Change, 2007; editor: Plays of Aaron Hill, 1981, John Gay and the London Theatre, 1993; contbr. Oxford Dictionary of National Biography, 2004. Bd. dirs. Md. Fedn. Tchrs., Balt., 1986—89; pres. faculty guild U. Md., 1986—89. Am. Philos. Soc. grantee, 1960, Guggenheim Found. fellow, 1965—66, Folger Shakespeare Libr. fellow, Washington, 1970, John Carter Brown Libr. fellow, Providence, 1995, 2003, Fulbright Commn. Lecture grantee, Ankara, Turkey, 1979—80. Mem.: MLA (mem. exec. com. South Atlantic chpt. 1977—80), Literary Soc. Washington, Am. Antiquarian Soc., E. Ctrl. Soc. 18th Century Studies (pres. 1987), Am. Soc. 18th Century Studies (founder 1970—), Assn. Princeton Grad. Alumni (exec. bd. 1986—90), Princeton Club (NY, Washington), Cosmos Club Washington. Democrat. Episcopalian. Avocations: swimming, book collecting. Office: The Univ of the South PO Box 3128 Sewanee TN 37375-3128 Business E-Mail: cwinton@mail.umd.edu.

WINTOUR, ANNA, editor-in-chief; b. London, Nov. 3, 1949; arrived in US, 1976; d. Charles and Elinor Wintour; m. David Shaffer, Sept. 1984 (div. 2001); children: Charles, Katherine;. Student, Queens Coll. Dep. fashion editor Harper's/Queen mags., London, 1970—76; fashion editor Harper's Bazaar Hearst Corp., NY, 1976—77; fashion and beauty editor Viva Mag., NY, 1977—78; contbg. fashion/style editor Savvy Mag., NY, 1980—81; sr. editor NY mag., 1981—83; creative dir. US Vogue Condé Nast Publs., NY, 1983—86, editor-in-chief British Vogue London, 1986—87, editor-in-chief House and Garden mag. NY, 1987—88, editor-in-chief Vogue NY, 1988—. Appeared in (documentaries) Catwalk, 1996, Seamless, 2005, The September Issue, 2009. Trustee Met. Mus. Art, NYC. Named an Officer of the Order of Brit. Empire (OBE), 2008; named one of The 10 Most Fascinating People of 2006, Barbara Walters, The 100 Most Influential Women in NYC Bus., Crain's NY Bus., 2007, The 50 Most Powerful Women in NYC, NY Post, 2007, 2008. Office: Vogue 4 Times Sq New York NY 10036

WINTROB, JAY S., insurance company executive; b. Anaheim, Calif., 1958; married; 2 children. BA in Polit. Sci., summa cum laude, U. Calif., Berkeley, 1979; JD, U. Calif., 1982. Corp. securities lawyer O'Melveny & Myers LLP, L.A.; asst. to chmn. Kaufman & Broad, 1987, corp. v.p., 1987—89; sr. v.p. AIG SunAmerica Life Assurance Co., 1989—91, exec. v.p., 1991—95, vice chmn., 1995—98, CEO, 1998—2000, chmn., CEO, 2001—; pres., CEO AIG Retirement Services, Inc. Am. Internat. Group, Inc. (AIG), 2001—09, CEO Domestic Life & Retirement Services, 2009—; pres., CEO First SunAmerica Life Insurance Co., 2001—. Bd. dirs. AIG Sun Am., AIG; mem. adv. bd. Thomas Weisel Ptnrs. Group, Inc. Bd. mem. Bet Tzedek Legal Services, Cedars-Sinai Med. Ctr., KCET Pub. TV, LA World Affairs Coun., Skirball Cultural Ctr.; bd. trustees J. Paul Getty Trust, 2004—. Recipient Ecumenical Coun. Leadership award, Archdiocese LA, 2001, Luis Lainer Founder's award, Bet Tzedel Legal Services, 2002. Mem.: Order of Coif. Office: American International Group Inc (AIG) 70 Pine St New York NY 10270*

WINTRODE, RALPH CHARLES, lawyer; b. Hollywood, Calif., Dec. 21, 1942; s. Ralph Osborne and Maureen (Kavanagh) W.; m. Leslie Ann O'Rourke, July 2, 1966 (div. Feb. 1994); children: R. Christopher, Patrick L., Ryan B.; m. Denise A. Beetham, Aug. 24, 1999. BS in Acctg., U. So. Calif., 1966, JD, 1967. Bar: Calif. 1967, N.Y. 1984, Japan 1989. From assoc. to ptnr. to of counsel Gibson, Dunn & Crutcher, Tokyo, L.A., Newport Beach and Irvine, Calif., 1967—. Sec. Music Ctr. Los Angeles County, 1986-88; bd. dirs. Coro Found., L.A. County, 1986-87. Mem. Newport Harbor Club, Am. Club Tokyo. Avocations: sailboat racing, auto racing, flying. also: 333 S Grand Ave Ste 4400 Los Angeles CA 90071-1548 Office: Gibson Dunn And Crutcher Llp 3161 Michelson Dr Ste 1200 Irvine CA 92612-4412 E-mail: wintrode@cox.net.

WINTROL, JOHN PATRICK, lawyer; b. Wichita, Kans., Feb. 13, 1941; s. Clarence Joseph and Margaret (Gill) W.; m. Janet Lee Mitchell; children: John Howard, Joanna Lee. BA cum laude, Rockhurst Coll., 1963; JD, Georgetown U., 1969. Bar: DC 1969, U.S. Ct. Appeals (4th, 5th, 11th and DC cirs.) 1981, U.S. Dist. Ct. Md. 1984. Law clk. to Hon. Howard Corcoran U.S. Dist. Ct., Washington, 1969-71; assoc. Howrey & Simon, Washington, 1971-77; mng. ptnr. Perito, Duerk & Pinco, Washington, 1978-85; ptnr. Finley Kumble, Washington, 1985-87, Laxalt, Washington, Perito & Dubuc, Washington, 1988-91, McDermott, Will & Emery, Washington, 1991—2002, John P. Wintrol L.L.C., Washington, 2003—. Mem. jud. conf. U.S. Ct. Appeals (D.C. cir.); adj. prof. George Washington Sch. Law, 2007—. Vol. Peace Corps, Turkey, 1963-65; pres. bd. trustees Holton Arms Sch. Mem.: ABA. Roman Catholic. Office: 2000 M St NW Ste 700 Washington DC 20036 Home Phone: 301-229-6208; Office Phone: 202-261-1056. Business E-Mail: jwintrol@jpwlaw.net.

WINWOOD, STEPHEN LAWRENCE, musician, composer; b. Birmingham, Eng., May 12, 1948; s. Lawrence Samuel and Lillian Mary (Saunders) W.; m. Eugenia Crafton, Jan. 17, 1987; children: Mary Clare, Elizabeth Dawn, Stephen Calhoun, Lillian Eugenia. Rec. artist Spencer Davis Group, 1964-67, Blind Faith, 1970, Traffic, 1967-74; solo artist N.Y.C. and in England, 1974—. Dir. F.S. Ltd. Albums include: Arc of a Diver, 1980, Talking Back to the Night, 1982, Back in the High Life, 1986, Roll With It, 1988 (Grammy 1989), Chronicles, Refugees of the Heart, 1991, Traffic: Far From Home, 1994, Junction 7, 1997, About Time, 2003, 9 Lives, 2008. Recipient 14 Gold Record awards, 4 Platinum Record awards, 2 Grammy awards, Lifetime Achievement award Ivor Novello's, 2002; inductee (with band Traffic) Rock 'N Roll Hall of Fame, 2004. Address: 41 Rodney Rd Cheltenham GL50 1HX England

WINZER, PETER J., telecommunications industry executive, researcher; b. Vienna, Jan. 15, 1973; s. Johannes Winzet and Brigitte Winzer; m. Andrea Winzer, Sept. 6, 1998. Dr. techn., Vienna U. Tech., 1998. Rsch. asst. Vienna U. Tech., 1996—2000; mem. tech. staff Bell Labs., Lucent Techs., Holmdel, NJ, 2000—06; disting. mem. tech. staff Bell Labs, Alcatel-Lucent, 2007—. Recipient Internal prizes, Bell Labs. Office: Alcatel-Lucent 791 Holmdel-Keyport Rd Holmdel NJ 07733 Business E-Mail: peter.winzer@ieee.org.

WIORKOWSKI, JOHN JAMES, mathematics professor; b. Chgo., Sept. 30, 1943; BS, U. Chgo., 1965, MS, 1966, PhD, 1972. Rsch. assoc. U. Chgo., 1972; asst. prof. Pa. State U., University Park, 1973-74; assoc. prof. U. Tex. at Dallas, Richardson, 1975, assoc. prof. and program head Math. Scis. Program, 1979-81, prof., 1981—, asst. to v.p. acad. affairs, 1980-85, asst. v.p. acad. affairs, 1985-94, assoc. provost, 1994-2001, vice-provost, 2001—, head math. scis. program, 1996-98. Cons. to Fed. Energy Adminstrn., 1975, Tex. Instruments, 1977, Frito-Lay Inc., 1977-78, Republic Nat. Bank, 1979; mem. panel studying 55 mile per hour speed limit Nat. Acad. Sci. Contbr. articles to profl. jours. Served to capt. U.S. Army, 1968-71. Decorated Army Commendation medal, NSF grantee, 1975—; Am. Coun. Edn. fellow, 1981-82. Mem. Am. Statis. Assn. (chpt. pres. 1974, v.p 1977, chpt. pres. 1978), AAAS, Inst. Math. Stats., Biometric Soc., Sigma Xi. Unitarian Universalist. Home: 9922 Lincolnshire Ct Rockwall TX 75087-4509 Office: U Tex at Dallas PO Box 830688 Richardson TX 75083-0688 Office Phone: 972-883-2274. Personal E-mail: wiorkow@msn.com. Business E-Mail: wiorkow@utdallas.edu.

WIOT, JEROME FRANCIS, radiologist; b. Cin., Aug. 24, 1927; s. Daniel and Elvera (Weisgerber) W.; m. Andrea Kockritz, July 29, 1972; children— J. Geoffrey, Jason. MD, U. Cin., 1953. Diplomate: Am. Bd. Radiology (trustee, pres.). Intern Cin. Gen. Hosp., 1953-54, resident, 1954-55, 58-59; gen. practice medicine Wyoming, Ohio, 1955-57; mem. faculty U. Cin., 1959-67, 68—, prof., chmn. radiology, 1973-93, acting sr. v.p., provost for med. affairs, 1985-86, prof. emeritus, 1998—; practice medicine specializing in radiology Tampa, Fla., 1967-68. Contbr. articles to med. jours. Bd. dirs. Ruth Lyons Fund, U. Cin. Found., 1997—2003, U. Cin. Hosp., 2005—. Served with USN, 1945-46. Fellow Am. Coll. Radiology (pres. 1983-84, chmn. commn. on diagnostic radiology); mem. Radiol. Soc. N.Am., Am. Roentgen Ray Soc. (pres. 1986-87), Am. Bd. Radiology (pres. 1982-84), Ohio Med. Assn., Cin. Acad. Medicine, Radiol. Soc. Greater Cin., Ohio Radiol. Soc. Office: U Cin Med Ctr Dept Radiology 234 Goodman St Cincinnati OH 45267-1000 Office Phone: 513-475-8755. E-mail: jfwiot@hotmail.com.

WIPF, PETER, chemist; b. Aarau, Switzerland, Sept. 5, 1959; came to U.S., 1988; s. Max and Lina (Furter) W.; m. Salla Kaarina Valtanen, July 16, 1987; children: Peter Charles, Heidi Maija-Lina. Diploma in Chemistry, U. Zurich, 1984, PhD, 1987. Rsch. assoc. U. Va., Charlottesville, 1988-90; asst. prof. U. Pitts., 1990—. Contbr. articles to profl. jours.; author book chpts. in field. Recipient Swiss NSF fellowship, 1988-90. Mem. Am. Chem. Soc., Swiss Chem. Soc., AAAS, Pitts. Cancer Inst. Achievements include rsch. in transmetalation reactions and their applications in organic synthesis; devel. of methodology for peptide analogs and total synthesis of biol. activ. products. Office: U Pitts Dept Chemistry Pittsburgh PA 15260

WIPKE, W. TODD, chemistry professor; b. Dec. 16, 1940; BS, U. Mo., Columbia, 1962; PhD, U. Calif., Berkeley, 1965. Rsch. chemist Esso Rsch. and Engring. Co., Baton Rouge, 1962; postdoctoral rsch. fellow Harvard U., 1967-69; asst. prof. Princeton U., 1969-75; assoc. prof. chemistry U. Calif., Santa Cruz, 1975-81, prof. chemistry, 1981—2004, rsch. prof. chemistry, 2004—. Founder, sr. v.p. Molecular Design Ltd., San Leandro, Calif., 1978-91; founder, chmn. bd. GluMetrics Inc., 2002-04, dir. 2005-; founder, dir. Leptogen, Inc., 2006—; cons. Ciba-Geigy, Basle, Switzerland, 1978-82, BASF, Ludwigshafen, Fed. Republic Germany, 1974-78, Squibb, Princeton, N.J., 1976-81; adv. EPA, 1984—; mem. sci. adv. bd. Pharmix, Scitegic, Tosk; co-founder Leptogen, 2006. Editor: Computer Representation and Manipulation of Chemical Information, 1973, Computer-Assisted Organic Synthesis, 1977; editor-in-chief: (jour.) Tetrahedron Computer Methodology, 1987-92; editor: Tetrahedron and Tetrahedron Letters, 1987-92; contbr. articles to profl. jours. Capt. US Army, 1966—67. Recipient Eastman Kodak Rsch. award, 1964, Texaco Outstanding Rsch. award, 1962, Alexander von Humboldt Sr. Scientist award, 1987; Merck Career Devel. grantee, 1970; NIH fellow, 1964-65. Mem. Am. Chem. Soc. (assoc., Computers in Chemistry award 1987, St. Charles Found. Alumni award 1996), Assn. Computing Machinery, Chem. Soc., Am. Assn. Artificial Intelligence (charter), Chem. Structure Assn. (charter), Internat. Soc. Study Xenobiotics. Office: U Calif Dept Chemistry Santa Cruz CA 95064

WIPPMAN, DAVID, dean, law educator; BA summa cum laude, Princeton U., 1976; MA, Yale U., 1978, JD, 1982. Law clk. for Hon. Wilfred Feinberg US Ct. Appeals (2nd cir.); prof., assoc. dean Cornell Law Sch.; vice provost internat. rels. Cornell U.; dean, William S. Pattee prof. law U. Minn. Law Sch., 2008—. Dir. Office Multilateral and Humanitarian Affairs, Nat. Security Coun., 1998—99; vis. scholar U. Ulster, Northern Ireland. Co-author: International Law, Norms, Actors, Process: A Problem-Oriented Approach, Can Might Make Rights? Building the Rule of Law After Military. Office: U Minn Law Sch Walter F Mondale Hall, Office 381 229-19th Ave S Minneapolis MN 55455 Office Phone: 612-625-4841. E-mail: dwippman@umn.edu.*

WIRA, CHARLES RYAN, physician, educator; b. Hanover, NH, Jan. 4, 1970; s. Charles Robert and Madelyn Ryan Wira; m. Christina Marie Fontecchio, June 17, 2000; children: Gabriella Ruth, Charles Fontecchio. BS in Biochemistry, English, U. NH, Durham, 1993. Cert. med. dr. Dartmouth Med. Sch., 2000. Dir. New Hope Family Ctr., Pahokee, Fla., 1993—95; asst. prof. Yale Sch. Medicine, New Haven, 2005—. Pastoral coun. mem. Aquinas House, Hanover, 1997—2000. Mem.: Soc. Academic Emergency Med. Independent. Roman Catholic. Achievements include research in managment of accidental hypothermia; myocardial dysfunction in stroke. Avocation: family activities. Business E-Mail: charles.wira@yale.edu.

WIRASINHA, HEMAMALI ANUSHKA, computer scientist, researcher; b. Colombo, Sri Lanka, Mar. 1, 1972; d. Armyne Edwin and Hemamali Cornelia Wirasinha. Diploma in econ., London U., 1991; BS in Econ. with honors, U. London, 1994; postgrad., Harvard U., 1996; PhD in Computers and Info. Sci. (hon.), Cosmopolitan U., Miami, Fla., 2004. Jr. mgmt. exec. Ceylon Shipping Lines Ltd., Colombo, Sri Lanka, 1994—95; assisting lectr. in micro computers and info. tech. Harvard U., Cambridge, Mass., 1996—98. Dir. Ceylon Shipping Lines Ltd., Colombo, Sri Lanka, 1998—; author Prentice Hall India, Delhi, India, 2002—, Publish Am., Frederick, Md.; advanced level GCE AS/A2 examiner and moderator in computing U. London Edexcel; Sigma Xi ambassador Packard Internat. Sci. Networking Initiative, Sri Lanka, India, Maldives. Author: (book) Spread the Word Around: MS Word, 2001, Cyber Ethics, 2001, Study Buddy, 2001, Digital Art, 2001, Computer Tutor, 2001, Java Essence, 2002, PC Private Eye, 2002, Doctor PC, 2002, I Want to Teach the World to Click!: Computing for the Visually Impaired, 2002, Office Essentials: MS Office XP, 2002, Visually Learn PC (India Times Bestseller 2003), 2002, On Your Marks Net Set Go! Surviving in an E-World (India Times Bestseller 2003), 2002, Flash in a Flash: Web Development, 2002, Computing for the Asian Woman and the Curious Man, 2003, Microchip Militant, 2004. Establishing chpt. Young Politicians of Am., Cambridge, Mass.; contributory America's first responders alliance, Cambridge, Mass., 2004. Recipient Excellence award, Internat. Modeling and Talent Assn., 1997. Mem.: IEEE, AAAS, Brit. Computer Soc., Women in Tech. Internat., Assn. for Women in Computing, Am. Assn. for Artificial Intelligence, Harvard Faculty Club, Sigma Xi, Outstanding Student Honor Soc. Achievements include research in computer security; viability and usability of microchip implantations and advanced tech. to aid the visually impaired. Avocations: writing, travel, fashion, sports, swimming. Address: 6 Charles Way Colombo 3 Sri Lanka Home: PMB 324 1770 Massachusetts Ave Cambridge MA 02140-2808 Fax: 011 941 12575065; Home Fax: 617-864-1094. Personal E-mail: anushkawirasinha@post.harvard.edu. E-mail: anushka1@sigmaxi.org.

WIRE, GARY LEE, retired metallurgist; b. Freeport, Ill., May 29, 1943; s. John Raymond and Grace Florence W.; m. Janet Marie, Jun. 10, 1967; children: Cynthia, Jacqueline. BS in Engring., Northwestern U., 1966; PhD in Physics, U. Ill., 1972. Mgr. mech. rsch. Westinghouse Hanford, Richland, Wash., 1973-82; mgr. materials properties rsch. IIT Rsch. Inst., Chgo., 1982-85; mgr. materials Bettis Atomic Power Lab., West Mifflin, Pa., 1985-96, adv. engr., 1996—2006; ret., 2006. Contbr. articles to profl. jours. Mem. ASME (Robert J. McGrattan award 1997). Avocations: woodwork, bridge. Home: 123 Barrington Oakdale PA 15071 Personal E-mail: jangary2@comcast.net.

WIRE, WILLIAM SHIDAKER, II, retired apparel and footwear manufacturing company executive; b. Cin., Jan. 5, 1932; s. William Shidaker and Gladys (Buckmaster) W.; m. Alice Dumas Jones, Aug. 31, 1957 (dec.); children: Alice Wire Freeman (dec.), Deborah Wire Suber; m. Cheryl C Yates, Sept. 25, 2004. Student, U. of South, 1950; AB, U. Ala., 1954, JD, 1956; LLM, NYU, 1957. Bar: Ala. 1956. Atty. Hamilton, Denniston, Butler & Riddick, Mobile, 1959-60; with Talladega Ins. Agy., Ala., 1961-62, Genesco, Inc., Nashville, 1962-94, former chmn. and CEO. Bd. dirs. Genesco Inc., Dollar Gen. Corp., Am. Endoscopy Svcs., Inc., Nashville Bank & Trust Co. Mem.: Burnt Pine Golf Club (Destin, Fla.), Golf Club Tenn., Univ. Club (NY), Belle Meade Country Club (Nashville), Kappa Alpha. Presbyterian. Home: 706 Overton Park Nashville TN 37215-2452

WIREBAUGH, AMY, physical therapist, educator; b. Mpls., Apr. 08; d. James and Judy Wirebaugh. D in Phys. Therapy, Duke Med., Durham, 2006. Phys. therapist Carilion Clinic, Roanoke, Va., 2006—; adjunct prof. Jefferson Coll. Health Scis., Roanoke, Va., 2007—. Mem.: APTA.

WIRKEN, CHARLES WILLIAM, lawyer; b. Moline, Ill., Aug. 29, 1951; s. Walter William and Elizabeth Claire Wirken; children: Nicole, Michelle. BS, U. Ariz., 1972, JD, 1975. Bar: Ariz. 1975, U.S. Dist. Ct. Ariz. 1976, U.S. Ct. Appeals (9th cir.) 1980, U.S. Ct. Appeals (Fed. cir.) 1985, U.S. Ct. Appeals (10th cir.) 2004, U.S. Supreme Ct. 1980. Assoc. Killian, Legg & Nicholas, Mesa, Ariz., 1975-79; ptnr. Killian, Nicholas, Fischer, Wirken, Cook & Pew, Mesa, 1980-97, Gust Rosenfeld P.L.C., 1997—. Pres. Vol. Lawyers Project, Phoenix, 1981-83; judge pro tem Ariz. Ct. Appeals, 1985-99, Maricopa County Superior Ct., 1986—; mem. civil study com. Maricopa County Superior Ct., 1984—; bd. dirs. Cmty. Legal Svcs., Phoenix, 1979-82. Exec. v.p. East Valley Partnership, Mesa, 1984; pres. Tri-City Cath. Social Svc., Mesa, 1983, 84; bd. dirs. East Valley Cultural Alliance, Mesa, 1984. Mem. State Bar Ariz. (bd. govs. 1995-06, pres. 2004-05, chair trial practice sect. 2001-02, chair civil practice and procedure com. 2006-07, bd. trustees, client protection fund), Maricopa County Bar Assn. (bd. dirs. 1983-91, pres. 1989-90), East Valley Bar Assn. (pres. 1979-80), Mesa C. of C. (dir. 1980-83, v.p. 1982-83), Rotary (bd. dirs. 1988-90, pres. 1987-88). Democrat. Roman Catholic. Home: 1708 E Knoll St Mesa AZ 85203-2171 Office: Gust Rosenfeld PLC 201 E Washington Ste 800 Phoenix AZ 85004-2327 Home Phone: 480-644-9657; Office Phone: 602-257-7959. Business E-Mail: cwirken@gustlaw.com.

WIRKEN, JAMES CHARLES, lawyer; b. Lansing, Mich., July 3, 1944; s. Frank and Mary (Brosnahan) W.; m. Mary Morse, June 12, 1971; children: Christopher, Erika, Kurt, Gretchen, Jeffrey, Matthew. BA in English, Rockhurst Coll., 1967; JD, St. Louis U., 1970. Bar: Mo. 1970, U.S. Dist. Ct. (we. dist.) Mo. 1970. Asst. prosecuter Jackson County, Kansas City, Mo., 1970-72; assoc. Morris, Larson, King, Stamper & Bold, Kansas City, 1972-75; dir. Spradley, Wirken, Reismeyer & King, Kansas City, 1976-88, Wirken & King, Kansas City, 1988-93; CEO The Wirken Law Group, Kansas City, 1993—. Adj. prof. U. Mo., Kansas City, 1984—89, 2001—; columnist Wirken Tips: Law Office Mktg., Mgmt. and Econ. The Daily Record, 2006, Wirkens Quips Quotes, Wit and Wisdom The Daily Record, 2003—06. Author: (books) Managing a Practice and Avoiding Malpractice, 1983; co-author: Missouri Civil Procedure Form Book, 1984; mem. editl. bd.: jours. Emerging Trends and Theories of Lender Liability, 1991, host: Wirken on the Law KMBZ-FM, 1998—2007, Kans. City Morning News Sunday Edit. KMBZ-FM, 2007—08. Named Best the Bar, Kans. City Bus. Jour., 2005—07, Mo. Super Lawyer, 2006—08. Mem. ABA (exec. coun.), Nat. Conf. Bar Pres. (coun. 1992-96), Nat. Caucus of Met. Bar Leaders (exec. coun., pres. 1988-94), Am. Trial Lawyers Assn., L.P. Gas Group (founder, chair 1986-90, founder, chair lender liability group 1987-96), Mo. Bar Assn. (bd. govs. 1977-78, 2004—, chmn. econs. and methods practice com. 1982-84, quality and methods of practice com. 1989-91, vice chmn. young lawyers sect. 1976-78), Mo. Assn. Trial Attys. (bd. govs. 1983-85), Kansas City Met. Bar Assn. (pres. young lawyers sect. 1975, chair legal assistance com. 1977-78, chair tort law com. 1982, pres. 1990). Home: 47 W 53rd Kansas City MO 64112 Office: The Wirken Law Group PC 4740 Grand Blvd Ste 200 Kansas City MO 64112 Office Phone: 816-471-0330. Business E-Mail: jwirken@wirkenlaw.com.

WIRT, FREDERICK MARSHALL, retired political scientist, educator; b. Radford, Va., July 27, 1924; s. Harry Johnson, Sr. and Goldie (Turpin) W.; m. Elizabeth Cook, Sept. 6, 1947; children: Leslie Lee, Sandra Sue, Wendy Ann. BA, DePauw U., 1948; MA, Ohio State U., 1949, PhD, 1956. Instr. to prof. polit. sci. Denison U., Granville, Ohio, 1952-66; vis. prof., lectr. U. Calif., Berkeley, 1966-68, 69-72; dir. policy scis. grad. program U. Md. Balt. County, 1972-75; prof. polit. sci. U. Ill., Urbana, 1975-2000; ret., 2000. Dir. Inst. for Desegregation Problems, U. Calif.-Berkeley, 1970-72; cons. Motion Picture Assn. Am., Rand Corp., Nat. Inst. Edn., SUNY Sch. Edn. Albany; vis. prof. U. Rochester, Nova U., U. Melbourne; acad. visitor London Sch. Econs. Author: Politics of Southern Equality, 1970 (honorable mention for best book 1972), Power in the City, 1974; (with others) School Desegregation in the North, 1967, The Polity of the School, 1975, Political Science and School Politics, 1977, Education, Recession, and the World Village, 1986, (with others) Culture and Education Policy in the American States, 1992, Ain't What We Was: Civil Rights in the New South, 1997 (Best Book on So. Politics award So. Polit. Sci. Assn., 1998), The Political Dynamics of American Education, 3d edit., 2005. Mem. Granville City Charter Commn., 1964. Grantee Am. Philos. Soc., Denison Rsch. Assn., U. Ill. Rsch. Bd., NEH, Ford Found., Ctr. Advanced Studies; fellow U. Ill., Dept. Edn., Spencer Found.; recipient Lifetime Achievement award Am. Ednl. Rsch. Assn., 1995, Am. Polit. Sci. Assn., 1994. Mem. Am. Polit. Sci. Assn. (nat. council), Midwestern Polit. Sci. Assn., Am. Ednl. Rsch. Assn., Policy Studies Orgn. Office: U Ill Dept of Polit Sci Urbana IL 61801 Home: 2340 W Seltice Way Apt 146A Coeur D' Alene ID 83814 E-mail: fmwirt@verizon.net.

WIRT, MICHAEL JAMES, library director; b. Sault Sainte Marie, Mich., Mar. 21, 1947; s. Arthur James and Blanche Marian (Carruth) W.; m. Barbara Ann Hallesy, Aug. 12, 1972; 1 child, Brendan. BA, Mich. State U., 1969; MLS, U. Mich., 1971; postgrad., U. Wash., 1990. Cert. libr., Wash. Acting libr. U. Mich. Ctr. for Rsch. on Econ. Devel., Ann Arbor, 1971-72; instnl. svcs. libr. Spokane County (Wash.) Libr. Dist., 1972-76, asst. dir., 1976-79, acting dir., 1979, dir., 1980—. Mem. adv. com. Partnership for Rural Improvement, Spokane, 1982-85, Wash. State Libr. Planning and Devel. Com., 1984-85, Ea. Wash. U. Young Writers Project Adv. Bd., 1988-89; mem. issues selection com. Citizens League of Greater Spokane, 1991-93, City of Spokane Indian Trail Specific Plan Task force, 1992-95; mem. comm. com. United Way Spokane County, 1994, campaign chair local govt. divsn., 1996. Mem. Wash. Libr. Assn. (2d v.p. 1984-86, dir. 1989-91, pub. rels. com. 1993-2001, chair legis. planning com. 2003—, conf. coord. 2003-05, Merit award 1984, Pres. award 1998), Wash. Libr. Network (rep. Computer Svc. Coun. 1983-86, v.p., treas. State Users Group 1986-87), Am. Libr. Assn. (Pub. Libr. Affiliates Network 1990-93, PLA Bus. Coun. 1990-94, chmn. 1991-94), Spokane Valley C. of C. (local govt. affairs com. 1987-2000, co-chair 1996-98, pub. policy com. 2000-2005, mem. local governance com. 2003-2005, governence com. 2005—), Spokane Regional C. of C. (local govt. com. 1990-94, human svcs. com. 1990-92, chmn. 1991-92, govt. reorgn. task force 1995), Spokane Civic Theatre (bd. dirs. 1996-2001, v.p. 1997-98, 2000, sec. 1998-2000), Inland N.W. Legis. Coalition, Momentum (local govt. strategy com. 1992-94), New Century (govt. collaboration com. 1997-98), Inland N.W. Coun. Librs. (bd. dirs. 1979—, chmn. 1997-98). Office: Spokane County Libr Dist 4322 N Argonne Rd Spokane WA 99212-1853 Office Phone: 509-924-4122. Business E-Mail: mwirt@scld.org.

WIRTH, GARRETT ANDREW, plastic surgeon; s. Carl and Caroline Wirth; m. Christine Wirth; children: Kerilee Powers, Ryan Powers, Quinn children: Hannah, Garrett. BS, Muhlenberg Coll., Allentown, Pa., 1992; MS, Albany Med. Coll., NY, 1995, MD, 1998. Diplomate Am. Bd. Plastic Surgery, 2006. Assoc. clin. prof. plastic surgery U. Calif., Irvine Med. Ctr., Orange, 2005—. Fellow: ACS. Office: Aesthetic and Plastic Surgery Inst 200 S Manchester Ste 650 Orange CA 92868 Office Fax: 1-714-456-7718.

WIRTH, GERALD, conductor, composer; Student, Bruckner Konservatorium, Linz, Austria. Mem. Wiener Sängerknaben, choirmaster, 1986—89; chorus master Landestheater Salzburg, 1989—91; artistic dir. Calgary (Can.) Boys' Chorus, 1991—98; music dir. Calgary Civic Symphony and Sangita, 1994—98; assoc. condr. Calgary Philharmonic Orch., 1997—98; artistic dir. Vienna (Austria) Boys Choir; co-founder Wirth Music Acad., 2004. Guest condr., Australia, Hong Kong, China, Russia, United States. Achievements include development of Wirth-method for elementary music education in the choral setting. Office: Vienna Boys Choir Augarten Palais A-1020 Wien Austria Home: Tradigist 4 A-3203 Rabenstein Austria Home Phone: 43 2722 67814; Office Phone: 43 1 216 39 42. Business E-Mail: gerald@baeckerhof.at.

WIRTH, MICHAEL K. (MIKE WIRTH), oil company executive; b. Oct. 1960; m. Julie Wirth; 4 children. BS, U. Colo. With Chevron Corp., 1982—, design engr., 1982, sr. retail mgr. mktg. Western Ops., 1998—99, gen. mgr. retail mktg., 1999—2000; pres. mktg. Caltex Corp., Singapore, 2000—01; pres. mktg. Asia/Middle East/Africa Chevron-Texaco Corp, 2001—04, pres. Global Supply and Trading, 2004—06, exec. v.p. Global Downstream, 2006—. Office: Chevron Hdqs 6001 Bollinger Canyon Rd San Ramon CA 94583*

WIRTH, PETER, lawyer; b. Halgehausen, Germany, July 17, 1950; U.S., 1956; BA, U. Wis., 1972; JD, Harvard U., 1975. Bar: Mass. 1975. Assoc. Palmer & Dodge, Boston, 1975-81, ptnr., 1982-96, of counsel, 1996—; exec. v.p. legal and corp. devel., chief legal officer, sec. Genzyme Corp., Cambridge, 1996—. Lectr. grad. tax program Boston U., 1982-85. Mem. ABA, Mass. Bar Assn., Phi Beta Kappa. Office: Genzyme Corporation 500 Kendall St Cambridge MA 02142 Office Phone: 617-768-6882, 617-252-7600.

WIRTH, RUSSELL D. L., JR., investment and merchant banker; b. Milw., June 30, 1930; s. Russell and Mary (McMahon) W.; m. Alice Guion Ardrey, Jan. 4, 1958 (div. Jan. 1971); children: Mary Elizabeth, Russell III. BA summa cum laude, Yale U., 1951; MA honors with distinction, Sch. Advanced Internat. Studies, Johns Hopkins U., 1954; postgrad., NY U., 1957—59; grad. with honors, Airborne Sch. and Spl. Forces Officers Sch., 1980. Staff student comdt. US Senate Fgn. Relations Com., Washington; personal aide to chmn. Senate Fgn. Rels. Com. Alexander Wiley, Washington, 1954—55; coord. with Pres. Eisenhower, White House, Washington; personal asst. to mng. ptnr. corp. underwriting dept. Blyth & Co., Inc., Wall Street, 1957-59; U.S. loan officer for Latin Am., US Devel. Loan Fund, Washington, 1960-61; co-founder, pres. Saint-Phalle, Spalding & Wirth, Inc., Buenos Aires, 1962-63; exec. v.p. Internat. Investment Co., Washington, 1963-64; investment officer Chase Internat. Investment Co., 1965-67; asst. to pres. David Rockefeller, Chase Manhattan Bank, 1965-67; co-founder, pres. Puerto Rican Fin. Group (PRFG), San Juan, 1968-92; co-founder, dir., stockholder jointly with Sun Oil Co. Hemisphere Oil Co., San Juan, 1978—93, bd. exec. com., 1978—93; founder and ltd. ptnr. in devel. with Tishman Realty and Constrn. Co., Concord Centre Complex, Concord, Calif., 1980-84; founder, mng. dir. Wirth and Co. Internat. Investment Bankers, 1989—; asst. to chmn. Chase Internat. Investment Corp. Rep. candidate Congress 5th dist. Milw., 1956. 2d lt.-capt. USMCR, Korea, 1951-53; maj. US Army Spl. Forces (Airborne), Res. and N.G., 1977-84. Decorated Silver Star, Bronze Star, Purple Heart, UN Korean War medal with 3 battle stars, Disting. Svc. medal Gov. US VI, US and Korean presdl. unit citations; named Scholar of the House, Yale U. Mem. Phi Beta Kappa., Yale U. Episcopalian. Achievements include World and US ranked amateur athlete, 1985-95: US Nat. champion, sprint triathlon; 2x US All-Am. in US Triathlon; 4x Fla. State champion, sprint triathlon; Fla. State half-marathon champion; 4th in world in Iron Man World Triathlon Championship; qualified and completed Boston, NYC, San Francisco, Miami marathons; mem. U.S. Nat. Triathlon Team USA, which won World Triathlon Championship, Cancun, Mex., 1995.

WIRTSCHAFTER, DAVID, talent agency executive; Agent William Morris Motion Picture Divsn., Beverly Hills, Calif.; pres. William Morris Agy. (WMA), Beverly Hills, Calif., 2005—09; co-CEO William Morris Endeavor Entertainment (WME), 2009—.*

WIRTZ, ROCKY (W. ROCKWELL WIRTZ), professional sports team executive, beverage company executive; b. Oct. 5, 1952; s. William and Joan (Roney) Wirtz; 3 children. Grad., Northwestern U., 1975. Former v.p. Wirtz Corp., pres., 2007—, Wirtz Beverage Group, Judge & Dolph Ltd.; chmn. Chgo. Blackhawks, 2007—. Pres. First Security Trust & Savings Bank. Former trustee Northwestern U., Loyola Acad.; trustee North Shore County Day Sch., Winnetka, Ill. Mem.: Econ. Club of Chgo. Office: Wirtz Corp 680 N Lakeshore Dr, 19th Fl Chicago IL 60611 also: Judge & Dolph, Ltd 1501 Michael Dr Wood Dale IL 60191

WIRZ, GEORGE OTTO, bishop emeritus; b. Monroe, Wis., Jan. 17, 1929; Student, St. Francis Sem., Milw., Marquette U., Cath. U. Ordained priest Diocese of Madison, Wis., 1952, aux. bishop Madison, Wis., 1977—2004; ordained bishop, 1978. Office: Diocese of Madison 3577 High Point Rd PO Box 44983 Madison WI 53744-4983

WISBAR, REBECCA KITTOK, lawyer; b. New Orleans, May 31, 1960; d. C. D. Kittok and Joan M. Desemar; m. Frederick William Wisbar; children: Taylor, Ashley. BA, U. Va., Charlottesville, 1982; JD, La. State U., Baton Rouge, 1986. Bar: La. 1986, US Dist. Ct. (ea, we. and mid. dists.) La., Tex. 2006. Ptnr. Akers & Wisbar LLC, Baton Rouge. Lectr. in field; judge oral arguments. Mem.: Baton Rouge Bar Assn., La. Bar Assn., La. Bankers Assn., La. Assn. Def. Counsel, Dsylexia Assn. Greater Baton Rouge (bd. dirs. 2006—). Office: Akers & Wisbar LLC 8280 YMCA Plz Dr Bldg 8-C Baton Rouge LA 70820 Office Phone: 225-767-1003. Office Fax: 225-767-2280.

WISBAUM, WAYNE DAVID, lawyer; b. Niagara Falls, NY, May 29, 1935; s. Franklin C. and Elizabeth (Boff) W.; m. Janet Katz, July 3, 1960; children: Karen, Wendy, Deborah. BA, Cornell U., 1956; LL.B., Harvard U., 1959. Bar: N.Y. 1960. Assoc. Kavinoky & Cook, Buffalo, 1960-66, sr. ptnr., 1966—. Pres., chmn. bd. dirs. Kleinhans Music Hall Mgmt. Inc., 1990-2000, life emeritus, 2003-. Pres. Buffalo Coun. on World Affairs, 1968-70; mem. Young Leadership Cabinet Nat. United Jewish Appeal, 1967-73; mem. com. on leadership devel. Nat. Coun. Jewish Fedn. and Welfare Funds, 1967—; mem. Mayor's Com. on Youth Opportunity; bd. dirs. Anti-Defamation League; mem. Coun. Internat. Studies, SUNY, Buffalo; chmn. Buffalo chpt. Am. Jewish Com.; pres., chmn. bd. dirs. Buffalo Found. Jewish Philanthropies, 2001-07; bd. govs. United Jewish Fedn., Buffalo; chmn. bd. dirs. Buffalo Philharm. Orch. Soc., 1985-87; bd. dirs., mem. exec. com. Burchfield Art Ctr.; bd. dirs., pres. Jewish Family Svc. of Erie County; vice chmn., bd. dirs. Artpark, Irish Classical Theatre; trustee Buffalo and Erie County Park Libr., Daemen Coll., 2004—; dir. emeritus Zool. Soc. Buffalo and Erie County, 2005—. Served to capt. U.S. Army, 1964. Recipient United Jewish Fedn. Buffalo Leadership award, 1967, Cmty. Rels. award Am. Jewish Com., 1985, Abram Pugash award Jewish Family Service, 1985, Cmty. Leadership award Israel Bonds, 2001, honoree Citation banquet Nat. Conf. for Cmty. and Justice, 2004, Citizen of Yr. award Buffalo News, 2003; named Harvard Alumnus of Yr., 1990. Mem. ABA, N.Y. State Bar Assn. (chmn. com. lawyers title guaranty funds, Root/Stimson award 2003), Erie County Bar Assn., Am. Law Inst., Harvard Law Sch. Assn. Western N.Y. (sec.), Harvard Club (pres. Buffalo chpt., mem. N.Y.C. chpt.), Buffalo Club, Cornell Club (N.Y.C. chpt.), Zeta Beta Tau. Home: 180 Greenaway Rd Buffalo NY 14226-4166 Office: Kavinoky & Cook 120 Delaware Ave Rm 600 Buffalo NY 14202-2793 Office Phone: 716-845-6000. Business E-Mail: wwisbaum@kavinokybook.com.

WISCHGOLL, THOMAS, engineering educator; s. Burkhard Michael and Maria Elisabeth Wischgoll. PhD, U. Kaiserslautern, Germany, 2002. Postdoc. rschr. U. Calif., Irvine, 2003—05; asst. prof. Wright State U., Dayton, Ohio, 2005—. Mem.: IEEE. Office: Wright State Univ Col Glenn Hwy Dayton OH 45435 Office Fax: 937-775-5133. Business E-Mail: thomas.wischgoll@wright.edu.

WISDOM, EMMA NELL JACKSON, writer, educator; b. Somerville, Tex., Dec. 19, 1942; d. Herbert R.B. and Linnell Ruth (Malone) Jackson; m. Edward Henry Wisdom Jr., May 27, 1962; children: Rolanda Michelle, Edward H. III. AS, U. Tenn., 1979; BAS cum laude, Tenn. State U., 1991, MA in Edn., 1995. Lic. cosmetologist, Tenn.; cert. profl. sec., pre-purchase home-ownership trainer. Program coord. Meharry Med. Coll., Nashville, 1980, asst. to pres., 1980-84; exec. asst. Meharry Med. Group, P.C., Nashville, 1984-86, exec. dir., 1986-89; features editor Met. Times Newspaper, Nashville, 1990; instnl. aide Tenn. State U., Nashville, 1990-93; instr. Nashville Urban League, 1997-99; writer-cons. Nashville Pride Newspaper, 1996—. Mem. nat. adv. bd. Today's Sec., N.Y.C., 1981-82; mem. adv. bd. U.S. Postal Svc., Nashville, 1994-96. Author: A Practical Guide to Planning a Family Reunion, 1988, 2d edit., 1997, Family Reunion Organizer, 1992, So You Want to Write a Book?, 1997, Dreammaker, 2006; editor: Invisible Scars and Other Writing About Relationships, 1997, Lady and the Champ, 2003, Echoes of Love, 2006, A Place Called Nickel Stop Station, 2008, The Biggest Cop-Out I've Ever Heard, 2008. Bd. dirs. Nashville Symphony Guild, 1985-89, ARC, Nashville, 1989-95; ctr. dir. Sr. Ctr. Inc. at Hadley Pk. Sr. Ctr., 2004-06. Recipient Philanthropist award in edn. The Time is Now, 1991. Mem. Wordshop Writers Group (co-founder, pres., treas. 1990-93), Tenn. Writers Alliance (founding, chmn. 1995-98, bd. dirs.), Phi Kappa Phi. Avocations: reading, crossword puzzles. Office: Post Oak Publs PO Box 70455 Nashville TN 37207-0455 Fax: 615-228-8073. E-mail: ewisdom@aol.com.

WISDOM, RITA PARKER, literature and language professor; d. Troy H. and Mary Justine Pearse Parker; m. Jack Neil Wisdom, May 30, 1968; children: Jennifer Wisdom Schepers, M.D., Cynthia Wisdom Boggan, Christina Wisdom Cloud, Katherine Wisdom Reichling, Jonathan Jack. BA, Tex. Woman's U., Denton, 1995; M in English, U. Dallas, Irving, Tex., 2004. Writing ctr. coord. Tarrant County Coll. NE, Hurst, Tex., 2001—05, instr., 2005—. Mem.: Nat. Coun. Tchrs. English. Avocations: reading, music. Office: Tarrant County Coll NE 828 Harwood Rd Hurst TX 76054

WISE, AARON NOAH, lawyer; b. Hartford, Conn., Feb. 14, 1940; s. Joseph J. and Ethel (Sklar) W.; m. Genevieve Ehrlich, Dec. 17. 1966; children: Haywood Martin, Paul Russell, Renee Alicia AB, Boston U., 1962; JD, Boston Coll., 1965; LLM in Comparative/Internat. Law, NYU, 1971; certificat de Doctorat, d' Université en Droit U. Paris, 1970. Bar: NY 1965, US Dist. Ct. (so. dist.) NY 1965. Internat. atty. Schering-Plough, Kenilworth, NJ, 1969-74; ptnr. Conboy Hewitt O'Brien & Boardman, NYC, 1974-80, Wise Lerman & Katz PC (formerly Rosenbaum Wise Lerman & Katz), NYC, 1981-95, Klepner & Cayea, NYC, 1995-98, Brand, Cayea & Brand, LLC, 1998-2000, Siller Wilk LLP, NYC, 2000—02, Gallet Dreyer & Berkey, LLP, NYC, 2002—. Author: International Sports Law and Business (Kluwer Law Internat., 1997, 3 vols.), Foreign Businessman's Guide to U.S. Law-Practice-Taxation, 2009; contbr. articles to pubs. in U.S. and Europe. Mem.: ABA, NY State Bar Assn. Avocation: multi-lingual including French, German, Spanish, Portuguese, Italian, Russian and Japanese. Home: 38 Cummings Cir West Orange NJ 07052-2264 Office: Gallet Dreyer & Berkey LLP 845 Third Ave New York NY 10022-6601 Office Phone: 212-935-3131. Business E-Mail: anw@gdblaw.com.

WISE, ALLEN F., health care company executive; b. Wichita, Kans., Aug. 20, 1942; BS, Wichita State U. Exec. v.p. of operations Health Care Systems Inc., 1985—90; pres., CEO Keystone Health Plan, 1991-94; COO Independence Blue Cross, Phila., 1991—94; exec. v.p. Metra Health Co., 1994—95; pres., CEO Wise Health System, 1994; exec. v.p. United HealthCare Corp., 1995—96; pres., CEO Coventry Health Care, Inc., Bethesda, Md., 1996—2004, non-exec. chmn., 2004—08, exec. chmn., 2008—09, exec. chmn., CEO, 2009—. Bd. dir., chmn. Health-Markets Inc.; bd. dir. Magellan Health Services Inc., NCP Group Inc. Office: 6705 Rockledge Dr Ste 900 Bethesda MD 20817-1814*

WISE, BOB (ROBERT ELLSWORTH WISE JR.), educational association administrator, former governor, congressman; b. Washington, Jan. 6, 1948; m. Sandy Casber; children: Robert, Alexandra. BA, Duke U., 1970; JD, Tulane U., 1975. Bar: W.Va. 1985. Sole practice, Charleston, W.Va., 1975—80; atty., legis. coun. for judiciary com. W.Va. Ho. of Dels., 1977—78; mem. W.Va. State Senate, 1980—82, US Congress from 2nd W.Va. dist., Washington, 1983—2001, whip at large, 1986—2001, mem. govt. reform and oversight com., transp. and infrastructure com.; gov. State of W.Va., 2001—05; pres. Alliance for Excellent Edn., 2005—. Bd. dirs. Pub. Edn. Network, C-Change; bd. trustees America's Promise; adv. com. mem. Campaign for Educational Equity, Editorial Projects in Edn., Nat. HS Ctr. Dir. West Virginians for Fair and Equitable Assessment of Taxes, Inc. Mem.: ABA, W.Va. State Bar Assn. Democrat. Avocations: bluegrass music, Tae Kwon Do. Office: Alliance for Excellent Edn 1201 Connecticut Ave NW Ste 901 Washington DC 20036 Office Phone: 202-828-0828. Office Fax: 202-828-0821. E-mail: wise@all4ed.org.*

WISE, BRET W., chemical company executive; m. June Wise; 3 children. BS, Ind. U. CPA. Ptnr. KPMG; v.p., CFO WCI Steel, Inc., Warren, Ohio; sr. v.p., CFO Ferro Corp., Cleve., 1999—2002; CFO, sr. v.p. DENTSPLY Internat. Inc., York, Pa., 2002—05, exec. v.p., 2005—06, pres., COO, 2006, chmn., pres., CEO, 2006—. Bd. dir. Dental Trade Alliance. Mem. AICPA, Fin. Execs. Inst. Office: DENTSPLY Internat Inc Susquehanna Commerce Ctr 221 W Philadelphia St York PA 17405*

WISE, CHARLES DAVIDSON, science educator; b. Huntington, W. Va., June 13, 1926; s. Fred Eugene Wise and Maggie M. Harshbarger; m. Juanita Irene Meadows, Mar. 22, 1947; 1 child, Sandra. AB, MS, W. Va. U., 1950; PhD, U. N.Mex., 1962. Cert. tchr. N.Mex., W. Va., Tex. Tchr. St. Albans (W. Va.) High Sch., 1951-53; lab. assst. Marshall U., 1950-51; grad. fellow U. N.Mex., Albuquerque, 1953-55, grad. asst., 1960-61; rsch. scientist U. Tex., Port Aransas, Tex., 1958-60; prof. Ball State U., Muncie, Ind., 1961-91; rep. Ind. State Legislature, Indpls., 1967-69; senator Ind. State Senate, Indpls., 1969-73. Contbr. articles to profl. jours., 1958—. Bd. dirs. Mental Health Svc. East Cen. Ind., 1974-77;

pres. Muncie Bicentennial Festival Com., 1975-77. With U.S. Army, 1944-46. Recipient fellowship U. Ind., 1957, U. Tex., 1957-58, Marshall U. Alumni Community Achievement award, 1993; named Alumnus of Yr., East Bank High Sch., W.Va., 1977. Fellow Ind. Acad. Sci.; mem. Nat. Assn. State Legislators (life mem.), Nat. Audubon Soc., Ind. Audubon Soc. (past pres., conservation award 1977), E. Cen. Ind. Audubon Soc. (pres. 1988-90, conservation award 1984), Sigma Xi Rsch. Soc. (pres. Ball State U. chpt., bd. dir. Hoosier Environ. coun. 1990-93). Republican. Presbyterian. Avocations: birdwatching, travel, languages, genealogy, history. Home: 1032 Brickyard Ave Milton WV 25541 Office: Ball State Univ Muncie IN 47306-0001 Office Phone: 765-285-8820.

WISE, GEORGE EDWARD, lawyer; b. Chgo., Feb. 26, 1924; s. George E. and Helen L. (Gray) W.; m. Patricia E. Finn, Aug. 3, 1945; children: Erich, Peter, Abbe, Raoul, John. JD, U. Chgo. Bar: Calif. 1949, U.S. Dist. Ct. (no. dist.) Calif. 1948, U.S. Ct. Appeals (9th cir.) 1948, U.S. Dist. Ct. (cen. dist.) 1950, U.S. Supreme CT. 1955. Law clk. Calif. Supreme Ct., 1948-49; sr. ptnr. Wise, Wiezorek, Timmons & Wise, Long Beach, 1949—; of counsel Wise Pearce Yocis & Smith, Long Beach. With USNR, 1943-45. Fellow Am. Coll. Trial Lawyers; mem. ABA, Los Angeles County Bar Assn., Long Beach Bar Assn. (pres. 1970, Atty. of Yr. 1990), Calif. State Bar. Home: 5401 E El Cedral St Long Beach CA 90815-4112 Personal E-mail: georgewise@yahoo.com.

WISE, JEFFREY BRUCE, plastic surgeon, educator; s. Jonathan Franklin and Lesly Spitzer Wise; m. Allison Nicole Miller, Sept. 4, 2005; 1 child, Kate Dylan. BA, Yale U., New Haven, 1997; MD, Cornell U., NYC, 2001, 2003; degree in Otolaryngology, U. Pa., Phila., 2006; degree in Facial Plastic and Reconstructive Surgery, NY U., 2007. Clin. asst. prof. NY U. Sch. Medicine, 2008—. Office: Jeffrey B Wise MD LLC 1680 Route 23 Ste 100 Wayne NJ 07470 Office Fax: 973-684-5580. Personal E-mail: jeffreywisemd@gmail.com.

WISE, JOHN AUGUSTUS, lawyer, director; b. Detroit, Mar. 30, 1938; s. John Augustus and Mary Blanche (Parent) W.; m. Helga M. Bessin, Nov. 27, 1965; children: Monique Elizabeth, John Eric. Student, U. Vienna, 1957—58; AB honors cum laude, Coll. Holy Cross, 1959; JD, U. Mich., 1962; postgrad., U. Munich Law Faculty, 1962—63. Bar: Mich. 1963, D.C. 1966. Assoc. Dykema, Gossett, Detroit, 1962-64; asst. to pres. Internat. Econ. Policy Assn., Washington, 1964-66; assoc. Parsons, Tennent, Hammond, Hardig & Ziegelman, Detroit, 1967-70; pres. Wise & Marsac P.C., Detroit, 1970-2001; sr. ptnr. Williams, Mullen, Clark & Dobbins, PLLC, Detroit, 2001—04; of counsel, ptnr. Howard & Howard, P.C., Detroit, 2004—. Dir. Peltzer & Ehlers Am. Corp., 1975-80, Colombian Am. Friends Inc., 1974-89. Dir. Hyde Park Coop., 1974-77; trustee Friends Sch., Detroit, 1977-81, Brighton Health Svcs. Corp., 1991-94, Providence Hosp., 2001-, chair fin. com., 2009—; chmn. bd. dirs. Brighton Hosp., 1995—2009. Ford Found. grantee U. Munich, 1962-63. Mem. ABA, Mich. Bar Assn., Internat. Bar Assn., Detroit Athletic Club, Detroit Econ. Club. Roman Catholic. Home: 1221 Yorkshire Rd Grosse Pointe Park MI 48230-1105 Office: 450 W Fourth St Royal Oak MI 48067 Office Phone: 248-723-0435. E-mail: jwise@howardandhoward.com.

WISE, JOYCE KATHRYN, nursing educator; b. Inglewood, Calif., Apr. 14, 1954; d. George Walter and Lillian Myrtle Beauchamp; m. Albert L. Wise; children: Jennifer Renee, Matthew Brian Garrett. AA, Citrus CC, Azusa, Calif., 1975; BSN, Azusa Pacific U., 1979; MSN, U. Phoenix, 2002. Cert. sex-addiction counselor, Am. Assn. Christian Counselors, 2008. Nursing instr. El Camino Coll., Torrance, Calif., 1998—, Santa Monica Coll., Calif., 2003—. Cons. Duhaney Home Care, El Segundo, Calif., 2004—05; life coach personal & profl. Contbr. articles to profl. jours. Recipient Shero Assemblyman Curen prize, 51st Assembly Dist., 2007. Mem.: Pediat. Nursing Soc., Nursing Honor Soc. Avocations: swimming, scuba diving, snorkeling, travel. Office: El Camino CC 16007 Crenshaw Blvd Torrance CA 90505 Personal E-mail: joyce_kwise@gmail.com.

WISE, L. DAVID, toxicologist; b. Powell, Wyo., Apr. 7, 1952; s. Eldon O. and Phyllis J. Wise; m. Diane A. Soifer, Aug. 1, 2006; children: Grady Brent, Melea Elizabeth. BA, U. Colo., Boulder, 1974; PhD, U. Cin., 1981. Postdoc. fellow U. Calif., Irvine, 1981—82; sr. scientist Warner-Lambert/Parke-Davis Co., Ann Arbor, 1983—85; disting. sr. investigator Merck Rsch. Labs., West Point, 1985—. Mem.: Teratology Soc. Office: Merck Rsch Labs Safety Assessment W45-115 West Point PA 19486

WISE, LORRAINE E., educational consultant; d. Alonza Jerome and Elsie Virginia Beulah; 1 child, Hillary Lauren Beulah. BA, Fed. City Coll., 1974; MSW, Howard U., 1977. From program asst. to sr. policy specialist US Dept. Edn., 1974—94, sr. policy specialist student achievement and sch. accountability programs, 1994—. Nat. parental involvement expert US Dept. Edn., Office Elem. and Secondary Edn., Student Achievement ans Sch. Accountability, Washington, 1994—. Contbg. author Reaching All Families: Creating Family-Friendly Schools, Family Involvement in Children's Education:Successful Local Approaches, discussant (various profl. symposiums), expert (various parental involvement programs); contbr. chapters to books. Recipient Plaque for Continued Support, Nat. Coalition Title I Chpt. 1 Parents Bd. Dirs., 2001, VIP award, Nat. Coalition Title I Parents, 2003, Plaque, NJ Assn. Parent Coord., Commitment and Dedication to Parents, 2003, Nat. Coalition of ESEA Title I Parents, 2005. Mem.: Am. Ednl. Rsch. Assn. Office: US Dept Edn 400 Md Ave SW Washington DC 20202 Business E-Mail: lorraine.wise@ed.gov.

WISE, PATRICIA, opera singer, educator; b. Wichita, Kans. d. Melvin R. and Genevieve F. (Dotson) W.; 1 child, Jennifer. B. Music Edn., U. Kans., Lawrence, 1966. Prof. voice Ind. U. Sch. Music, Bloomington, 1995—; tchr. master classes San Francisco, Vienna Conservatory, Salzburg (Austria) Mozarteum; voice tchr. Domingo Young Artist program Washington Opera. Debut as Susanna in Marriage of Figaro, Kansas City, 1966; over 40 prin. roles include Lucia, Gilda, Micaela, Juliette, Zerbinetta, Pamina, Musetta, Lulu, Violetta, Nedda, others; appeared with leading Am. opera cos. including, Chgo., Santa Fe, N.Y.C., San Francisco, Houston, San Diego, Miami, Balt., Phila., Pitts.; European appearances, 1971-76, London Royal Opera, Glyndebourne Festival, Vienna Volksoper, Geneva Opera; guest artist with Vienna, Hamburg, Munich, Cologne, Frankfurt, and Berlin State Operas; guest appearances in Madrid, Barcelona, Rome, La Scala Milan, Nice, Paris Chatelet, Zurich, Dresden, Salzburg Festival, Theatro Colon, Buenos Aires; appeared with orchs. including, Chgo. Symphony Orch., Los Angeles Symphony Orch., N.Y. Handel Soc., Israel Philharm. Orch., Vienna Philharm. Orch., N.Y. Philharm., Cleve. Orch., Berlin Symphonic Orch., BBC Orch., Nat. Orch. France; Angel Recordings; internat. TV, film appearances. Recipient Morton Baum award N.Y.C. Ctr., 1971, Dealey Meml. award Dallas Symphony, 1966, Naftzger young Artist award Wichita Symphony, 1966, Midland Young Artist award Midland (Tex.) Symphony Orch., 1966; M.B. Rockefeller Fund grantee, 1967-70; Sullivan Found. grantee, 1967-68; named Kammersänger Vienna Staatsoper, 1989. E-mail: patwise@indiana.edu.

WISE, PENELOPE M., librarian; b. Glens Falls, NY, Nov. 6, 1953; d. Robert J. Murray and Elaine Winifred Maynard; m. Gregory A. Wise, June 4, 1977; children: Ryan L., Samantha J., Christopher J. BA, Coll. St. Joseph, Rutland, Vt., 2000; MLS, U. Albany, NY, 2003. Serials, electronic resources libr. Mercyhurst Coll., Erie, Pa., 2004—. Home: 2633 Prospect Ave Erie PA 16510 Office: Mercyhurst Coll 501 E 38th St Erie PA 16546 Personal E-mail: wisepennym@hotmail.com. Business E-Mail: pwise@mercyhurst.edu.

WISE, PHYLLIS M., physiologist, educator; BA, Swarthmore Coll., 1967; MA, U. Mich., 1969, PhD, 1972; DSc (hon.), Swarthmore Coll., 2008. Postdoctoral fellow U. Mich., 1972—74; rsch. assoc. physiology U. N.Mex., 1974—75, adj. asst. prof. physiology, lectr. biology, 1975—76; asst. prof. physiology U. Md., Balt., 1976—82, assoc. prof. physiology, 1982—87, prof. physiology, 1987—93; prof. and chair physiology U. Ky., Lexington, 1993—2001; disting. prof. neurobiology, physiology, behavior and membrane biology U. Calif., Davis, 2002—05, dean divsn. biol. sciences, 2002—05; prof. physiology, biophysics, ob-gyn. and biology U. Wash., Seattle, 2005—, provost, 2005—, v.p. academic affairs, 2005—07, exec. v.p., 2007—. Vis. sci. ob-gyn. U. Goettingen, Germany, 1985—86. Recipient Rsch. Career Devel. award, NIH, 1982—87, Merit award, 1986—96, 2001—10, Nathan W. Shock award, 1991, Burroughs-Wellcome professorship, 1997, Robert W. Kellemeier award, Gerontol. Soc. Am., 1999, Albert D. and Elizabeth H. Kirwan Meml. prize, 2000, Excellence in Sci. award, Fedn. Am. Societies for Exptl. Biology, 2002, Women in Endocrinology Mentor award, 2003, Roy O. Greep award, 2004, Women of Influence award, Puget Sound Bus. Jour., 2008; fellow Ford Found., 1972—74. Fellow: AAAS; mem.: Inst. Medicine, Am. Physiol. Soc. (Solomon Berson award 1998), Endocrine Soc., Soc. for Neuroscience (Presdl. Speaker 1997), Soc. for the Study of Reproduction. Office: U Wash 301 Geberding Hall Box 351237 Seattle WA 98195-1230 Office Phone: 206-543-7632. E-mail: pmwise@u.washington.edu.*

WISE, RONNIE W., retired library director; b. Memphis, Tenn., Apr. 26, 1951; s. Mabern W. and Wilma Faye Wise; m. Michele S. Teper, July 18, 2006. BA in Art Edn., Delta State U., Cleve., 1973, MLS, 1979, U. Southern Miss., Hattiesburg, 1987. Profl. libr. Bolivar County Libr. Sys., Cleve., Miss., 1976—86, libr. sys. dir., 1986—2006; founder, chmn., dir. Bolivar County Literacy Coun., Cleve., 1990—2006. Mem. legislative com. Miss. Libr. Assn., Jackson, Miss., 1989—94; vice-chair, intellectual freedom com. Southeastern Libr. Assn., 1990—92. Contbr. articles to profl. jours.; author: (book) The Wise Family Chronicles, (comic book) Archie and Friends Raise Literacy Awareness in Mississippi (Governor's award, 1994). Recipient Partnership award, Miss. Arts Commn., 1997, Outstanding Achievement award, Miss. Libr. Assn., 1993—94. Mem.: Libr. Guild. Liberal. Jewish. Avocations: reading, music, movies.

WISE, SHARON, political organization administrator; Dir. cmty. rels. for Rep. Dave Camp US House of Reps.; co-chmn. Mich. Rep. Party, 2009—. V.p. bd. dirs. Nat. Charter Sch. Inst.; owner Sassy Sandwich. Bd. dirs. Traverse City Area C. of C.; Rep. nat. committeewoman women for Mich., 1997—2004. Republican. Office: Mich Rep Party Secchia-Weiser Mich Rep Ctr 520 Seymour St Lansing MI 48933 Office Phone: 517-487-5413. Office Fax: 517-487-0090.*

WISE, THERESA, air transportation executive; BA in Math. and Chemistry, St. Olaf Coll., Northfield, Minn.; MS in Ops. Rsch. and Applied Math., PhD in Ops. Rsch. and Applied Math., Cornell U., Ithaca, NY. With NW Airlines Corp., Minn., 1993—, mng. dir. info. svcs., v.p. Info. Svcs. Group, 2001—07, sr. v.p., chief info. officer, 2007—. Office: NW Airlines Corp 2700 Lone Oak Pky Eagan MN 55121 Office Phone: 612-726-2111.

WISE, WILLIAM JERRARD, lawyer; b. Chgo., May 27, 1934; s. Gerald Paul and Harriet Muriel (Rosenblum) Wise; m. Peggy Spero, Sept. 3, 1959; children: Deborah, Stephen, Betsy, Lynne. BBA, U. Mich., 1955, MBA, 1958, JD with distinction, 1958. Bar: Ill. 1959. Spl. atty. Office Regional Counsel, IRS, Milw., 1959-63; with McDermott, Will & Emery, Chgo., 1963-70, Coles & Wise, Ltd., Chgo., 1971—80, Wise & Stacks, Ltd., Chgo., 1980—2000, Querrey & Harrow, Chgo., 2000—. Lectr., contbr. Ill. Inst. Continuing Legal Edn.; arbitrator Cir. Ct. Cook County Ill., 1990—. Bd. dirs. Blind Svc. Assn., Chgo., 1964—74; active Village of Winnetka, Ill., 1974—75; dir., treas. Suzuki Orff Sch. Young Musicians, Chgo., 1981—91. With US Army, 1958—59. Mem.: Chgo. Bar Assn. Home: 1401 Tower Rd Winnetka IL 60093-1628 Office: Querrey & Harrow 175 W Jackson Blvd Ste 1600 Chicago IL 60604-2827 Home Phone: 847-446-2079; Office Phone: 312-540-7104. Personal E-mail: dididoe@yahoo.com. *I believe that one succeeds best in our society if one gives as little thought as possible to one's personal well being.*

WISEHART, MARY RUTH, retired religious organization administrator; b. Myrtle, Mo., Nov. 2, 1932; d. William Henry and Ora (Harbison) W. BA, Free Will Bapt. Bible Coll., 1955, George Peabody Coll. Tchrs., 1959, MA, 1960, PhD, 1976. Tchr. Free Will Bapt. Bible Coll., Nashville, 1956-60, chmn. English dept., 1961-85; exec. sec.-treas. Free Will Bapt. Women Nat. Active for Christ, 1985-98. Author: Sparks Into Flame, 1985, Beyond the Gate, 1998; contbr. poetry to jours. Mem. Scribbler's Club. Free Will Baptist. Avocations: photography, music, drama. Personal E-mail: wisemrw@aol.com.

WISELY, DONNA, secondary school educator, athletic trainer; d. Donald and Theresa Keller; m. John Wisely, Mar. 25, 1995; children: Alexander children: Caroline. BS, So. Ill. U., Carbondale, 1990; MA, Northeastern Ill. U., Chgo., 2002. Cert. athletic trainer 1991, lic. Ill., 1991. Athletic trainer Twp. H.S. Dist., Hoffman Estates, Ill., 1991—2005, tchg. asst., 1992—2005; tchr. Larkin Ctr., Elgin, Ill., 2004—05; vocat. coord. Cmty. Unit Sch. Dist., St. Charles, Ill., 2005—. Athletic trainer Mike Glenn Camp, Decatur, Ga., 1989—99, World U. Games, Buffalo, 1993—93, Am. Hearing Impaired Hockey Assoc., Chgo. area, 1995—99, Atlanta Com. for Olympic Games, 1996—96, Prairie State Games, Various, Ill. Vol. Women In Need Growing Stronger, Chgo. area, 2000. Dr. John Jevitz Continuing Edn. scholar, Ill. Athletic Trainers Assn., Inc., 2000—01, Grad. Merit scholar, Northeastern Ill. U., 2000—02. Mem.: NEA, Ill. Edn. Assn., Nat. Athletic Trainers Assn., Gt. Lakes Athletic Trainers Assn., Ill. Athletic Trainers Assn. (sec., v.p. 1995—2005, mem. Hall of Fame 2006). Avocation: travel.

WISEMAN, ALAN M(ITCHELL), lawyer; b. Long Branch, NJ, July 6, 1944; s. Lincoln B. and Gertrude (Gorcey) W.; m. Paula Wiseman, July 8, 1965; children: Steven, David, Julie. BA, Johns Hopkins U., 1965; JD, Georgetown U., 1968. Bar: Md. 1968, Ill. 1970, DC 1973. Law clk. Hon. William J. McWilliams, Md. Ct. Appeals, 1968-69; assoc. Schiff, Hardin & Waite, Chgo., 1970-74; ptnr. Howrey Simon Arnold White, LLP, Washington, 1976—, co-chair antitrust practice group, chmn. pro bono and charitable activities com. Editor Georgetown Law Jour., 1967-68. Mem. US C. of C. (coun. antitrust policy 1983-2001).

WISEMAN, DENNIS R., science educator; b. Jeffersonville, Ind., Apr. 21, 1952; s. Helen P. Wiseman. BS in Elem. Edn., Ind. U., New Albany, 1970—80; MEd, U. Louisville, Ky., 1984—87. Tchr. Jefferson County Pub. Schs., Louisville, 1984—2006, sci. consulting tchr., 2006—. Mem.: NEA. Home: 4525 Estate Dr Louisville KY 40216 Office: 4309 Bishop Ln Louisville KY 40218

WISEMAN, DONNA L., dean, education educator; BS in Elementary Edn., Okla. State U.; MS in Edn., Ark. State U.; PhD, U. Mo.-Columbia. Tchr. E.M. Trout Elem. Sch. Ponca City Pub. Schs., Okla., 1968—71; grad. asst. reading dept. Ark. State U., 1975—76; supr. of student tchrs. Office of Ednl. Field Experiences, U. Mo., Columbia, 1976—79, asst. dir. student tchg., 1978—79; asst. prof. reading, ednl. curriculum and instruction Tex. A&M U., 1979—84, assoc. prof., 1984—90, program chair Divsn. Elem. Edn., Coll. Edn., 1984—90, prof., 1990—96, assoc. dean Coll. Edn., 1991—96, interim dept. head Dept. Edn. Curriculum and Insturction, 1993—95, sr. assoc. Ctr. for Study and Implementation of Collaborative Learning Cmtys., 1995—96; LD and Ruth Morgridge endowed chair for tchr. edn. No. Ill. U., 1997—2001; assoc. dean, prof. Coll. Edn., U. Md., College Park, 2001—07, interim dean, prof., 2007—08, dean, prof., 2008—. Author: Learning to Read With Literature, 1992; co-author: Becoming a Teacher in a Field Based Setting: An Introduction to Education and the Classroom, 1998, Learning to Teach Language Arts in a Field Based Setting, 2005; contbr. articles to profl. jours. Mem.: Nat. Reading Conf., Nat. Coun. for Tchrs. of English, Internat. Reading Assn., Assn. Tchr. Edn., Am. Assn. Colls. for Tchr. Edn., Am. Edn. Rsch. Assn., Kappa Delta Pi, Phi Delta Kappa. Office: Coll Edn U Md at College Park College Park MD 20742 Office Phone: 301-405-0866. E-mail: dlwise@umd.edu.

WISEMAN, DOUGLAS CARL, education educator, department chairman, dean; b. Nashua, NH, Feb. 28, 1935; s. Howard W. and Ruth D. (Aiken) W.; m. Donna Wiseman; children: Mark, Cynthia, Lori, Alan, Kathleen, Steve. BEd, Plymouth State Coll., NH, 1961; MS, Ind. U., 1962, PED, 1970. Cert. tchr. health, math., phys. edn., sci. Tchr., track coach Nashua (N.H.) Pub. Schs., 1960-61, tchr., baseball coach, 1962-63; tchg. asst. Ind. U., Bloomington, 1961-62; tchr. high sch., wrestling coach Portage (Mich.) High Sch., 1963-64; instr., asst. prof., soccer, wrestling and tennis coach Plymouth (N.H.) State Coll., 1964-69; asst. prof. Northeastern U., Boston, 1969-71; dir. athletics, chmn. phys. edn. dept. Plymouth State Coll., 1971-80, assoc. dean, dir. undergrad. studies, 1993-96, prof., accreditation coord., 1996-98, ret., 1998, prof. emeritus, 1998—; prof., chair dept. edn. Univ. Sys. of N.H., 1980—. Aquatics cons. Am./Nat. Red Cross, Laconia, N.H., 1971-98, State Dept. Edn., Concord, 1980-98. Author, contbg. editor: Adapted Physical Education, 1982, Practical Research, 1989, Quantitative Research, 1992, Physical Education for Exceptional Students, 1994, Introduction to Educational Research, 1995, Educational Research, 1996, Research Strategies for Education, 1999; contbr. more than 50 articles to profl. jours. Cert. police officer Ashland, N.H., 1992-98; chair sch. bd. Plymouth Regional Sch. Dist., 1989-91; divsn. staff officer-pub. edn., flotilla career counseling officer USCG Aux., 2001-2002; deacon Superstition Foothills Baptist Ch., 2007-, chaplain North Am. Mission bd, 2008-; lt. Pinal County Sheriffs office, Chaplain Lt. 2008-, bd. dirs. Pinal County Justice Found. with US Army, 1953-56, US Paratroopers, 1954--56; hon. discharge 1956. AAHPERD Ea. Dist. scholar, 1990-91. Republican. Avocations: reading, hiking, boating, Tae Kwon Do. Personal E-mail: seaquest05@msn.com.

WISEMAN, ERIC C., apparel executive; b. 1955; BS, Wake Forest U., 1977, MBA, 1988. Exec. v.p. JanSport VF Corp., Greensboro, NC, 1995—98, pres. Bestform Intimates, 1998—2000, v.p. & chmn. global intimate apparel, 2000—03, v.p. & chmn. sportswear coalition, 2003—04, v.p. & chmn. outdoor & sportswear coalitions, 2004—05, exec. v.p. global brands, 2005—06, pres., COO, 2006—07, pres., CEO, 2008, chmn., pres., CEO, 2008—. Bd. dirs. V.F. Corp., 2006—, Cigna Corp., 2007—. Bd. visitors Babcock Grad. Sch. Mgmt., Wake Forest U. Office: VF Corp 105 Corporate Ctr Blvd Greensboro NC 27408 Mailing: VF Corp PO Box 21488 Greensboro NC 27420-1488 E-mail: eric_wiseman@vfc.com.*

WISEMAN, FRANK L., JR., chemistry professor; Prof., chair chemistry dept. Georgetown Coll., Ky. Recipient US Prof. of Yr. award, Carnegie Found. for Advancement of Tchg. and Coun. for Advancement and Support of Edn., 2006. Avocations: painting, hunting. Office: Chemistry Dept Georgetown Coll 400 E College St Georgetown KY 40324 Office Phone: 502-863-8103. E-mail: Frank_Wiseman@georgetowncollege.edu.

WISEMAN, MELISSA S., economics professor; PhD, Tex. Tech U., Lubbock, 1999. Assoc. prof. economics Houston Bapt. U., 1999—. Mem. dept. chair acct. econ. & Fin., El Paso, Tex., 2009. Recipient Opal Goolsby Outstanding Tchg. award, Houston Bapt. U., 2003; named Cert. of Merit, Nat. Academic Advising Assn., 2005. Office: Houston Baptist Univ 7502 Fondren Houston TX 77074

WISEMAN, PATRYCE AVSHARIAN, ecologist; BS, U. Mich., Ann Arbor, 1994; MS, U. Vt., Burlington, 1998; PhD, U. Idaho, Moscow, 2008. Contbr. scientific papers to numerous profl. jours. Mem.: Am. Soc. Mammalogists, Internat. Soc. Study Behavioural Ecology, Animal Behaviour Soc. Personal E-mail: pwiseman@vandals.uidaho.edu.

WISEMAN, THOMAS ANDERTON, JR., federal judge; b. Tullahoma, Tenn., Nov. 3, 1930; s. Thomas Anderton and Vera Seleta (Poe) W.; m. Emily Barbara Matlack, Mar. 30, 1957; children: Thomas Anderton III, Mary Alice, Sarah Emily. BA, Vanderbilt U., 1952, LL.B., 1954; LLM, U. Va., 1990. Bar: Tenn. Pvt. practice, Tullahoma, 1956-63; ptnr. Haynes, Wiseman & Hull, Tullahoma and Winchester, Tenn., 1963-71; treas. Tenn., 1971-74; ptnr. Chambers & Wiseman, 1974-78; judge U.S. Dist. Ct. (mid. dist.) Tenn., Nashville, 1978—, chief judge, 1984-91, sr. judge, 1995—; 6th cir. rep. Jud. Conf. of the U.S., 1996—2001, chair dist. judges conf., 1998-99. Mem. Tenn. Ho. of Reps., 1964-68; adj. prof. law Vanderbilt U. Sch. Law; cons. to judiciary of Brcko, Bosnia, 2002; mem. pattern jury instrn. com. 6th cir., 1988—. Asso. editor: Vanderbilt Law Rev, 1953-54. Democratic candidate for gov., Tenn., 1974; Chmn. Tenn. Heart Fund, 1973, Middle Tenn. Heart Fund, 1972. Served with U.S. Army, 1954-56. Fellow Tenn. Bar Found.; mem. Fed. Judges Assn. (bd. dirs. 1982-87, v.p. 1982-91, 87-91), Masons (33 deg.), Shriners, Amateur Chefs Soc. Presbyterian. Office: US Dist Ct 777 US Courthouse 801 Broadway Nashville TN 37203-3816 Office Phone: 615-736-7013.

WISER, RYAN, research scientist; b. Portland, Oreg., Aug. 13, 1971; s. John and Jo Ann Wiser; m. Maureen Wiser, Dec. 30, 1995; 1 child, Lindsey. BS, Stanford U.; MS, U. Calif., Berkeley, PhD, 2002. Staff scientist Lawrence Berkeley Nat. Lab., 1995—. Office: Lawrence Berkeley Nat Lab 1 Cyclotron Rd Berkeley CA 94720

WISER, VERA ROUBICEK, psychologist; d. Richard and Eva Mandlova Roubicek; m. Berton Jay Wiser, Dec. 26, 1980; children: Danielle Roubicek Jacobs, Justin Allen. Law, Charles U. Law Sch., Prague, 1968; MA, Montclair State Coll., Upper Montclair, NJ, 1979. Cert. sch. psychologist NJ Dept. Edn., 1979. Sch. psychologist Westwood Schs., NJ, 1980—83, NE Ind. Sch. Dist., San Antonio, 1984—87, Columbus City Schs., 1987—. Liberal. Avocations: travel, reading, films, theater. Home: 4881 Powderhorn Ln Westerville OH 43081 Office: Columbus City Schs 2571 Neil Ave Columbus OH 43202 Office Fax: 614-365-6718. Personal E-mail: verapsych@post.com. Business E-Mail: vwiser@columbus.k12.oh.us.

WISH, JAY BARRY, nephrologist, specialist; b. Hartford, Mar. 30, 1950; s. Martin and Evelyn Lillian (Lassman) W.; m. Linda Kristina Hansen, June 29, 1971; (div. 1980); children: Allen Jeremy, Robin Lindsey; m. Diane Elizabeth Perkins, June 5, 1983 (div. 2006); children: Jeffrey Bryan, David Phillip. BA, Wesleyan U., 1970; MD, Tufts U., 1974. Diplomate Am. Bd. Internal Medicine, Am. Bd. Nephrology. Resident in medicine New England Med. Ctr., Boston, 1974-79; instr. in medicine Tufts U., Boston, 1978-79; lectr. in health sci. Northeastern U., Boston, 1978-79; asst. prof. of medicine Case Western Res. U., Cleve., 1979-85, assoc. prof. of medicine, 1985-96, prof. medicine, 1996—; dir. hemodialysis U. Hosps. of Cleve., 1980—, dir. continuing edn., 1987-95. Chmn. Med. Adv. Bd. Kidney Found. of Ohio, Cleve., 1985-88. Author: Renal Disease and Hypertension, 1982, Disorders of Potassium, 1984, Metabolic Diseases, 1986, Rheumatic Diseases of the Kidney, 1993, Acid-Base and Electrolyte Disorders in the Critically Ill Patient, 1993, Assuring Quality of Care in Dialysis Patients, 1994, Algorithms and Care Paths for Quality Improvement, 2000, Adequacy of Hemodialysis, 2008, Quality, Safety and Accountability in Dialysis, 2008; contbr. articles to med. jours. Chmn. med. rev. bd. End-Stage Renal Disease Network #22, Pitts., 1982-87, End-State Renal Disease Network #9, Indpls., 1992-2000, pres., 2001-06; mem. exec. com. Forum of End-Stage Renal Disease Networks, 1992-2006, v.p., 1996-98, pres., 1998-2001; bd. dirs. Renal Phys. Assn., 1993-99, sec. 1996-97, treas., 1997-98; mem. Nat. Kidney Found. Fellow Am. Coll. of Physicians; mem. Cleve. Restoration Soc., Am. Soc. of Nephrology, Internat. Soc. of Nephrology, Alpha Omega Alpha. Democrat. Jewish. Avocation: performing arts. Office: U Hosps Cleve 11100 Euclid Ave Cleveland OH 44106-1736 Home Phone: 216-849-3950; Office Phone: 216-844-3163. Personal E-mail: jaywish@earthlink.net.

WISH, LESLIEBETH BERGER, psychotherapist, writer, management consultant; d. Irving L. and Miriam Solomon Berger; m. Peter A. Wish, Nov. 16, 1984; 1 stepchild, Carly Sidra. AB in History & English, Carnegie Mellon U., 1970; MA in English, Ohio U., 1971; MA in Social Svc. Mgmt., Byrn Mawr Coll., 1976; EdD in Human Devel., U. Mass., 1996. Lic. clin. social worker Md., 1980, Mass., 1982, Fla., 2003, diplomate clin. social work Bd. Examiners, 1988; cert. aquatics fitness instr. 2005. Post doctoral tng. in marriage & family therapy sys. Georgetown U. Med. Sch., DC, 1979—82; dir. social work & families The Linwood Sch., Ellicott City, Md., 1980—81; dir. human resource devel. & clin. svcs. The New England Inst. Family Rels., Framingham, Mass., 1982—94; faculty coord., admissions acad. advisor Grad. Ctr. Bus. & Counseling Webster U., Sarasota, 2001—04; v.p. Gulfcoast Healthstyle, Sarasota, Fla., 1994—. Girls' career workshop developer Girls, Inc., Sarasota, Fla., 2006—07; lectr., cons. in field; founder lovevictory.com; adv. bd. mem. & feature writer, expert Qualityhealth-.com; mem. med. adv. bd., columnist Relationship Realities, 2009—. Author: Incest, Women & Work, 1998; author, contbg. editor: Trafalgar Publs., 2001—06; contbr. articles to popular mags., websites;, author numerous poems. Chair Sarasota Women's Advisory Commn., 1994—2001; pres. coun. Easter Seals, 2002—; co-coord. counseling network, spl. ops. Warrior Found., 2006—; co-coord. counselor network Spl. Ops. Warrior Found.; co-coord. Child Abuse Task Force, Sarasota, 2006—07; program and workshop devel. The Women's Resource Ctr., Sarasota, 2007—, bd. mem., 2009—; active bd. mem. Womens Resource, Sarasota, Fla., 2009, U. South Fla., Acad. Lifelong Learning Faculty, 2008—; adv. bd. mem. & writer qualityhealth.com, 2009—; columnist Rels. Realities, www.qualityhealth.com, Rels. & Sexual Health Newsletter Online. Recipient Md.'s Best Small Press award, Md. Arts Commn., 1981. Mem.: Am. Biog. Inst. (Woman Yr. 2006), Women's Leadership & Acad. Honor Society (mortar bd. 1970), Phi Kappa Phi. Achievements include first to expand sex education and awareness of sexual issues at work and home for The New England Institute of Family Relations; research in the connection between childhood sexual abuse and its impact on work and career in women; on career-family history inventory. Avocations: travel, opera, writing, painting.

WISHARD, DELLA MAE, former newspaper editor; b. Bison, SD, Oct. 21, 1934; d. Ervin E. and Alma J. (Albertson) Preszler; m. Glenn L. Wishard, Oct. 18, 1953; children: Glenda Lee, Pamela A., Glen Evin. Grad. HS, Bison. Mem. SD Ho. of Reps., Pierre, 1984-96; pub., editor Bison Courier, SD, 1996-2000; owner Wishards Rentals, Rapid City, SD, 2004—. Colunist: County Farm Bur., 1970—96. State comitteewoman Rep. Ctrl. Com., Perkins County, SD, 1980—84, SD, 1998—2001; Rep. precinct comitteewoman Pennington County, 2006—; chmn. Perkins County Rep., 2000—03. Mem.: SD Farm Bur. (state officer 1982), Am. Legis. Exch. Coun. (state coord. 1985—91, state chmn. 1991—96), Fed. Rep. Women (chmn. Perkins County chpt. 1978—84). Lutheran. Avocations: writing, gardening. Home and Office: 3900 S Valley Dr Rapid City SD 57703

WISHARD, GORDON DAVIS, SR., lawyer; b. Indpls., Jan. 7, 1945; s. William Niles Jr. and Caroline (Davis) W.; m. Anne Emison; children: Claire Wishard Hoppenworth, Gordon Davis Jr. BA, Williams Coll., 1966; JD, Ind. U., 1969. Bar: Ind. 1969, US Dist. Ct. (so. dist.) Ind. 1969, US Ct. Appeals (7th cir.) 1976, US Supreme Ct. 1980, US Tax Ct. 1983. Ptnr. Ice Miller, Indpls. Mem. Am. Coll. Trust and Estate Coun. (Ind. chmn. 1990-95). Avocations: hunting, fishing. Office: Ice Miller 1 American Sq Indianapolis IN 46282-0020 Office Phone: 317-236-2476.

WISHART, GEORGE, marketing and media information company executive; Grad., U. Western Ont. Various positions including sr. bus. dir. to pres. Jacobs Suchard Internat., Inc. Kraft Foods Inc., 1987—99; v.p. retail svcs. grp. Spectra Mktg. Inc. VNU, 1999, pres. MediaPlan; global mng. dir. Nielsen In-Store Nielsen Co. (formerly VNU), 2006—. Office: Nielsen Co Corp Hdqs 770 Broadway New York NY 10003 Office Phone: 646-654-5000.*

WISHART, RONALD SINCLAIR, retired chemical company executive; b. Bklyn., Mar. 1, 1925; s. Ronald Sinclair and Elizabeth Lathrop (Phillips) W.; m. Betty B. Burnup, Sept. 14, 1951 (dec. Dec. 1973); children: Michael Sinclair, James Ronald; m. Eleanor Dorothy Parrish Dooley, Jan. 11, 1975; stepchildren: Donna Dooley Willix, Arthur D. Dooley. BChemE, Rensselaer Poly. Inst., Troy, NY, 1948. Engr., chemist Linde air divsn. Union Carbide Corp., Tonawanda, NY, 1948-51; sales rep. Chgo., Cleve., 1951-56; region mgr. Chgo., 1956-57; product mgr., mktg. mgr. Silicones divsn. NYC, 1957-64; gen. mgr., pres., 1964-66; pres. devel. and coating materials divsns., 1966-71; corp. dir. energy and transp. policy, 1972-82; v.p. fed. govt. rels., 1983-85; v.p. pub. affairs Danbury, Conn., 1985-90; chief of staff to chmn. of corp. Union Carbide, NYC, 1984-85. Mem. adv. coun. Gas Rsch. Inst., Energy Modeling Ctr., Stanford U., 1979-83, Environ. and Energy Policy Ctr., John F. Kennedy Sch. Pub. Policy, Harvard U., 1980-87; energy com. Aspen Inst., 1976-88; chmn., exec. dir. Electricity Consumers Resource Coun., Washington, 1976-79. Author: The Marketing Factor, 1966; contbr. chpts. to books and articles to profl. jours.; patentee silicone formulas. Vol. Am. Field Svc., Burma, 1944-45; pres., trustee, elder White Plains Presbyn. Ch., NY, 1987-90; elder Palm City Presbyn. Ch., 1996-2002; treas., bd. dirs. St. Christopher's Jenni Clarkson Home, 1968-91; mem. exec. bd. Westchester Putnam coun. Boy Scouts Am., White Plains, 1985-91; v.p. Carbide Retiree Corps.; v.p. Hospice Martin and St. Lucie, Inc., 1994-99, pres. 2000-02; pres. Lancewood Assn., 1997. Mem. NAM (mem. energy com.), Am. Mgmt. Assn. (v.p. 1966-69), Chem. Mfrs. Assn. (chmn. energy com. 1974-78), Nat. Petroleum Refiners Assn. (v.p. 1972-76, chmn. issues com. 1985-89), Internat. Fedn. Ind. Energy Users (chmn. 1978), Am. Chem. Soc., Soc. Chem. Industry, US C. of C. (mem. energy com.), Harbor Ridge Yacht and Country Club. Republican. Presbyterian. Avocations: golf, reading, bridge. Home: 1329 Lancewood Ter Palm City FL 34990

WISHENGRAD, MARCIA H., lawyer; b. Hudson, NY, Feb. 10, 1936; d. Joseph and Jessie (Diamond) W.; m. Robert J. Metzger, Sept. 3, 1961; 1 child, Jocelyn M. BA, Cornell U., 1957, JD, 1960. Bar: N.Y. 1960, U.S. Dist. Ct. (so. and ea. dists.) N.Y. 1962, U.S. Supreme Ct. 1964. Atty. Monroe County Family Court, Rochester, N.Y., 1963-65, Monroe County Legal Aid Soc., Rochester, 1965-67; sr. urban renewal atty. City of Rochester, 1971-74; dep. county atty. Monroe County, Rochester, 1974-93; pvt. practice Rochester, 1963—. Bd. visitors State Sch. Industry, Rochester, 1983-98, pres., 1991-98; bd. dirs. ARC, Monroe County, 1983-2000, pres. 1991-93; v.p. Arc Found. of Monroe, 1990-99. Mem. N.Y. State Bar Assn., Monroe County Bar Assn., Greater Rochester Assn. of Women Attys. (judiciary com.), Rochester-Monroe County Domestic Violence Consortium. Republican. Jewish. Avocations: boating, tennis, reading. Office Phone: 585-325-3427. Business E-Mail: attycpa@juno.com.

WISHNER, MAYNARD IRA, retired finance company executive, lawyer; b. Chgo., Sept. 17, 1923; s. Hyman L. and Frances (Fisher) W.; m. Elaine Loewenberg, July 4, 1954; children: Ellen Kenemore, Jane Wishner, Miriam Segel. BA, U. Chgo., 1944, JD, 1947; LHD (hon.), Spertus Inst., 1998, Hebrew Union Coll., 2001, Spertus Coll. Judaica, 2001. Bar: Ill. 1947. Staff Chgo. Commn. on Human Relations, 1947-52, exec. dir., 1954—55; chief ordinance enforcement div. Law Dept., City of Chgo., 1952-55; mem. law firm Cole, Wishner, Epstein & Manilow, Chgo., 1955-63; with Walter E. Heller & Co., Chgo., 1963-86, pres., 1974-86; of counsel Rosenthal and Schanfield, Chgo., 1986-95, ret., 1995—. Dir. Walter E. Heller Internat. Corp., Am. Nat. Bank & Trust Co., and br. cos., Chgo. Pres. Jewish Fedn. Met. Chgo., 1987-89; chair Nat. Jewish Community Rels., 1992-94, pres. Coun. Jewish Fedn., 1993-96; chmn. bd. govs. Am. Jewish Com., 1977-80, nat. pres. 1980-83, hon. pres., recipient Human Rights medallion, 1975; bd. dirs. Nat. Found. for Jewish Culture; chmn. Ill. Humanities Coun.; commr. Nat. Hillel Found.; mem. vis. com. U. Chgo. Sch. Social Svc. Adminstrn. and Divsn. of the Humanities; chair Ill. Humanities Coun., 1991-93; bd. govs. Jewish Agy. for Israel. Recipient Rosenwald award Jewish Fedn. Met. Chgo., Officers Merit medal Republic of Poland, United Hellenic Leadership Coun. Frisis award, Civic Achievement award U. Chgo. Home: 1410 Sheridan Rd Wilmette IL 60091-1895 Home Phone: 847-256-5015. E-mail: maynwish@aol.com.

WISHNICK, MARCIA MARGOLIS, pediatrician, geneticist, educator; b. NYC, Oct. 10, 1938; d. Hyman and Tillie (Stoller) Margolis; m. Stanley Wishnick, June 12, 1960; 1 child, Elizabeth Anne. BA, Barnard Coll., 1960; PhD, NYU, 1970, MD, 1974. Diplomate Am. Bd. Pediatrics, Nat. Bd. Med. Examiners. Rsch. technician Lederle Labs./Am. Cyanamid, Pearl River, NY, 1960-66; postdoctoral fellow N.Y. Pub. Health Lab., NYC, 1970-71; resident in pediatrics NYU-Bellevue Med. Ctr., NYC, 1974-77, asst. prof. pediatrics, 1977-82; clin. assoc. prof. pediatrics Bellevue Med. Ctr. NYU Med. Ctr., NYC, 1982-87; clin. prof. pediatrics NYU-Bellevue Med. Ctr., NYC, 1987—2003; pvt. practice, NYC, 1977—2003. Contbr. articles to profl. jours. Fellow Am. Acad. Pediatrics; mem. AMA, N.Y. Pediatric Soc., N.Y. Med. Soc.

WISMER, PATRICIA ANN, retired secondary school educator; b. York, Pa., Mar. 23, 1936; d. John Bernhardt and Frances Elizabeth Loreen Marie (Fry) Feiser; m. Lawrence Howard Wismer, Aug. 4, 1961. BA in English, Mt. Holyoke Coll., 1958; MA in Speech/Drama, U. Wis., 1960; postgrad., U. Oreg., 1962, Calif. State U., Chico, 1963-64, U. So. Calif., 1973-74. Tchr., co-dir. drama program William Penn Sr. High Sch., York, 1960-61; instr. English, dir. drama York Jr. Coll., 1961-62; assoc. church editor San Francisco Examiner, 1962-63; reporter, publicist News Bur. Calif. State U., Chico, 1963-64; chmn. English Dept. Chico Sr. H.S., 1966-96; mentor tchr. Chico Sr. High Sch., Chico Unified Sch. Dist., 1983-93. Judge writing awards Nat. Coun. Tchr. English, 1970—; cons. No. Calif. Writing Project, 1977—; curriculum cons., freelance writer and photographer, 1996—. Author: My Life with Vanessa: A Journal of the Plagued Years, 1998, 40 Year Photo Retrospective, 2002; newsletter editor Chico Cat Coalition, 1999-2004; (poetry/ photo book project) Ambient Light and Shadow, 2005. Mem. Educators for Social Responsibility, Planetary Soc., Upper Calif. Coun. Tchrs. English (bd. dirs. 1966-85, pres. 1970-71), Calif. Assn. Tchrs. English, Nat. Coun. Tchrs. English, NEA, Calif. Tchrs. Assn., Chico Unified Tchrs. Assn. Democrat. Lutheran. Avocations: photography, play production, video production. Home: 623 Arcadian Ave Chico CA 95926-4504 Office: PO Box 1235 Cannon Beach OR 97110-1235 Personal E-mail: pwismer@aol.com.

WISNER, FRANK GEORGE, insurance company executive, former ambassador; b. NYC, July 2, 1938; s. Frank Gardiner W. and Mary Knowles (Fritchey) W.; m. Genevieve de Virel, July, 1969 (dec. 1974); 1 dau., Sabrina; m. Christine de Ganay, June, 1976; 1 son, David; stepchildren: Caroline Sarkozy, Olivier Sarkozy. BA, Princeton U., 1961. With Fgn. Svc. Dept. U.S. Dept. State, Algiers, Morocco, 1962-64; from dep. amabassador's staff aide to sr. advisor Vietnamese province Tuyen Duc Agy. Internat. Devel., Vietnam, 1964-68; officer-in-charge Tunisian affairs U.S. Dept. State, Washington, 1968-71; chief econ.-comml. sect. Am. Embassy, Tunis, Tunisia, 1971-73, chief polit. sect. Dacca, Bangladesh, 1973-74; dir. plans and mgmt. Bur. Pub. Affairs, Washington, 1974-75; spl. asst. to dir., then dep. dir. Pres.' Interagy. Task Force Refugee Resettlement, Washington, 1975; spl. asst. to undersec. polit. affairs, 1975-76; dir. office So. African affairs U.S. Dept. State, Washington, 1976-77, dep. exec. sec., 1977-79; U.S. amb. to Zambia Lusaka, 1977-82; dep. asst. sec. African affairs U.S. Dept. State, Washington, 1982-86; U.S. amb. to Egypt Cairo, 1986-91; U.S. amb. to Philippines Manila, 1991-92; under sec. of state for internat. security affairs Washington, 1992-93; under sec. of def. for policy Dept. Def., Washington, 1993-94; U.S. amb. to India U.S. Dept. State, 1994-97; vice chmn. external affairs Am. Internat. Group Inc., NYC, 1997—. Bd. dirs. EOG Resources; trustee Am. U. of Beirut, Am. U. Cairo; mem. bd. bus. Coun. Internat. Understanding; bd. U.S.-India Bus. Coun.; bd. refugees Internat., United Svcs. Orgn. Decorated Legion of Honor (Romania); recipient meritorious honor award Dept. State, 1973, superior honor award, 1992, disting. svc. award, 1997; recipient Mil. Medal of Honor Govt. Vietnam, 1968, Social Welfare medal of honor, 1968. Mem. Coun. on Fgn. Relations, Metropolitan Club (Washington), Ivy Club (Princeton, N.J.), Knickerbocker Club (N.Y.), Brook Club (N.Y.). Episcopalian. Office: Am Internat Group Inc 18th Fl 70 Pine St New York NY 10270-0002

WISNER, GAIL ANN, media specialist; b. Cedar Rapids, Iowa, Jan. 6, 1955; d. John Frederick and Darlene Doris Wipperman; m. Arthur Steven Wisner, Mar. 20, 1982; children: Melissa Joi, Steven Herbert, Melissa Joi, Steven Herbert, Brian John. BA, Buena Vista Coll., Storm Lake, Iowa, 1977; MA, McDaniel Coll., Westminster, Md., 1995. Media specialist Thurmont Elem. Sch., Md., 1995—98; media specialist NW Mid. Sch., Taneytown, Md., 1998—. Pres. SMACC, Carroll County, Md., 2002—04. Mem.: CCEA. Home: 1504 Brown Rd Westminster MD 21158 Office: NW Mid Sch 99 Kings Dr Taneytown MD 21787

WISNER, PAMELA L., social worker; b. Stevensville, Newfoundland, Can., Dec. 4, 1958; d. John R. Wisner, Leslie S. Wisner. BA in Psychology and Sociology, U. Mobile, 1980; M in Counseling, La. Bapt. U., 1998. LCSW Ala. Bd. Social Work Examiners, 1995, cert. Cognitive Behavioral Therapist 1999, Forensic Counselor 1999, Addictions specialist, Domestic Violence Counselor endorsement 1999. Dir. cmty. svc. RAPHA, Mobile, Ala., 1995—96; coord., counselor Charter of Mobile, 1996—2000; therapist, family cons. Gulf Coast Therapeutic Program, Inc., Mobile, 2000—. Mem.: Nat. Bd. Cognitive Behavioral Therapists, Am. Psychotherapy Assn. (diplomate 1999). Avocation: Avocations: travel, reading, cats, crafts, cooking. Office: Therapeutic Programs 601 Bel Air Blvd Ste 200 Mobile AL 36606-3524 Home: 6213 Burnt Wood Dr S Mobile AL 36695

WISNICKI, JEFFREY LEONARD, plastic surgeon; b. NYC, May 15, 1957; s. Joseph and Lorraine (Justman) Wisnicki; m. Rebecca Lynn O'Shields, Feb. 2, 1997; children: Justin Robert, Brandon Lawrence. BS summa cum laude, Rensselaer Poly. Inst., 1976; MD cum laude with honors, Union U., 1980. Diplomate Am. Bd. Plastic Surgery. Intern in surgery Stanford (Calif.) U. Med. Ctr., 1980-81, resident in gen., plastic and reconstructive surgery, 1981-84, chief resident in plastic and reconstructive surgery, 1985-86; fellow in plastic and reconstructive surgery Dartmouth-Hitchcock Med. Ctr., Hanover, NH, 1984; active staff Good Samaritan Hosp., West Palm Beach, Fla., 1986—, Wellington Regional Hosp., West Palm Beach, 1986—; chief divsn. plastic surgery John F. Kennedy Meml. Hosp., West Palm Beach, 1990-93; chmn. dept. surgery Palms West Hosp., West Palm Beach, 1991-93, chief med. staff, 1994-97, chmn. bd. trustees, 1997—2002, trustee, 2002—03; chief divsn. plastic surgery Good Samaritan and St. Mary's Hosp., West Palm Beach, 1997—2001, Good Samaritan Hosp., 2001—04. Clin. instr. surgery U. Calif., San Francisco, 1985; bd. dirs. Interplast, 1985-86, clin. faculty, 1986—90; presenter in field. Contbr. chpts. to books and articles to profl. jours. Named Best Plastic Surgeon, Palm Beach Mag., 1998. Fellow ACS; mem. Am. Soc. Plastic & Reconstructive Surgeons, Alpha Omega Alpha. Office: 13005 Southern Blvd Ste 133 Loxahatchee FL 33470 Office Phone: 561-798-1400. Business E-Mail: info@drwisnicki.com.

WISNIEWSKI, P. MICHELLE, retired obstetrician, gynecologist; b. Oneida, NY, June 26, 1945; d. Henry Francis Wisniewski and Kathryn Starr Holloway; m. Anna Cebula Costello, Sept. 20, 1998; m. Louise Marie Benyovszky, Sept. 22, 1984 (div.); children: Ladislaus Michael, Alexander Paul. BS, Georgetown U., 1967; MD, Universidad Autonoma de Guadalajara, Mexico, 1975. Bd. Cert. Am. Bd. of Ob/Gyn, 1983, lic. Physican and Surgeon NJ, Pa., 1977, Residency in Ob/Gyn Hahnemann U., 1980. Chairperson, dept of ob/gyn Health Care Plan of NJ., Cherry Hill, NJ, 1980—82; attending physician ob/gyn NE Hosp., Phila., 1882—1987, Nazareth Hosp., Phila., 1984—90, Pa. Hosp., Phila., 1987—91; chairperson, dept. of ob/gyn Mercy Hosp., Wilkes-Barre, Pa., 1991—92. Author: (medical research) Journal of Reproductive Medicine (Fellowship, Internat. Soc. for the Study of Vulvovaginal Disease, 1987), (photographic exibit) The Natural and Scenic Beauty of the Florida Keys, 2003, Butterflies & Warblers in the Florida Keys, 2008—, Key West Bottanical Garden & Tropical Forest, Butterflies of the Everglades, 2009. Chmn. Fla. Keys Coun. People with Disabilities, Key West, Fla., 2002—08; sr. dir. Disability and Disaster: Surviving the Fla. Keys, Serving People Who are Deaf or Hard of Hearing, 2007; lobbyist Key West City Coun., Monroe County Commn., Key West, Fla., 2001—07; active plaintiff Assn. for Disabled Am., Miami, Fla., 2001—, pres., 2006—. 1st lt. US Army, 1967—70, Rep. Vietnam. Decorated Bronze Star Medal, Air Medal for Valor, Mil. Medal of Honor & Gallantry Cross Rep. Vietnam; recipient Hon. Conch Cert., Monroe Fla. County Mayor, 2002. Fellow: Am. Coll. Ob-Gyn. (life). Achievements include led the struggle to make the Florida Keys accessible for people with disabilities; aided passage of transgender civil rights legislation. Personal E-mail: kwimages@bellsouth.net.

WISNIEWSKI, THOMAS MARK, neuroscientist, neurologist, psychology professor; b. Gdanzig, Poland, Oct. 21, 1960; s. Henryk and Krystyna Wisniewski; m. Sarah Anne Rawstron-Wisniewski, Nov. 6, 1982; children: Anna Rebecca, George Henry John, Amy Alexandra. MBBS, King's Coll. Sch. Medicine, London, 1983. Diplomate in neurology Am. Bd. Psychiatry and Neurology, 1989, in neuropathology Am. Bd. Pathology, 1990, registered Brit. Med. Assn., 1983, lic. med. NY State, 1985. Chief resident neurology NY U. Sch. Medicine, NYC, 1987—88, dir. conformational disorders lab., 1997—, dir. neuropathology core, 2002—, dir. pearl barlow ctr. memory evaluation and treatment, 2007—, prof. neurology, pathology and psychiatry, 2005—; chief resident pathology Columbia-Presbyn. Med. Ctr., NYC, 1989—90. Contbr. articles to numerous rsch. jours. (Zenith award, Alzheimer's Disease Assn., 1999, Alzheimer's Disease award, Jour. Alzheimer's Disease, 2002). Mem.: Am. Assn. Neuropathology, Am. Acad. Neurology, Brit. Med. Assn. Achievements include patents for synthetic immunogenic but non-amyloidogenic peptides homologous to amyloid ß for induction of an immune response to amyloid ß; mucosal immunization to prevent prion infection; inhibition of amyloid ß deposition in Alzheimer's disease patients by blocking the binding between amyloid ß and pathological chaperones; invention of detection of Alzheimer's Amyloid by magnetic resonance imaging; patents for method for treating amyloid disease; induction of Toll-like receptor 9 signaling as a method for preventing or ameliorating Alzheimer's disease; fluorescent compounds based on a styrl scaffold and their use as amyloid imaging agents. Office: NY Univ Sch Medicine Millhauser Lab HN419 550 1st Ave New York NY 10016 Business E-Mail: thomas.wisniewski@nyumc.org.

WISSE, RUTH R., religious educator; b. Czernowitz, Romania, May 13, 1936; arrived in US, 1993; d. Leo and Masha (Welczer) Roskies; m. Leonard Herschel Wisse, Mar. 17, 1957; children: William R., Jacob E., Abigail E. PhD, McGill U., Montreal, 1969. Prof. McGill U., 1978-92, Harvard U., Cambridge, Mass., 1993—. Chmn. dept. Jewish studies

McGill U., 1976—79; dir. Ctr. for Jewish Studies Harvard U., 1993—96. Author: (books) The Schlemiel as Modern Hero, 1971, A Little Love in Big Manhattan: Two Yiddish Poets, 1988, If I Am Not For Myself: The Liberal Betrayal of the Jews, 1992, The Modern Jewish Canon: A Journey through Language and Culture, 2000; co-editor: The Penguin Book Of Modern Yiddish Verse, 1988; editor: Shtetl, a and Other Yiddish Novellas, 1986, The Best Of Sholem Aleichem, 1991, The I.L. Peretz Reader, 2002. Recipient Itsik Manger prize, Tel-Aviv Municipality, 1989, I.J. Segal Prize for Lit., Jewish Pub. Libr., Montreal, 1971, 1989, Nat. Humanities medal for Yiddish in America, NEH, 2007; Killam fellow, 1975—76. Fellow: Am. Acad. for Jewish Rsch.; mem.: Assn. for Jewish Studies (bd. dirs., pres. 1985—89). Office: Harvard Univ 6 Divinity Ave Cambridge MA 02138-2020

WISWALL, DOROTHY ROLLER, language educator; b. Alpirsbach, Germany, Aug. 6, 1947; d. Albert and Else Roller; m. Thomas S. Wiswall, June 5, 1976; children: James, Karen. AB, Cornell Univ., 1971; AM, Univ. Mich., 1972, PhD, 1979. Instr. Sch. for Internat. Tng., Brattleboro, Vt., 1971; tchg. fellow Univ. Mich., Ann Arbor, 1971—75; adj. prof. Niagara Univ., 1981—91, Canisius Coll., Buffalo, 1991—2003, Buffalo State Coll., 2001—. Workshop presenter BOCES, Buffalo, 1998—99; v.p. Am. Assn. Tchrs. German, Buffalo, 1998—2002; docent Buffalo Mus. Sci., 2004—; tutor Lit. Vols. Buffalo, 2004—. Author: A Comparison of Selected Poetic and Scientific Works of Albrecht von Haller, 1981, (poetry) In the Seasons of My Mind, 2007. Treas. Grand Island Cmty. Chorus, 2006—; mem. coun. St. Timothy Luth. Ch., Grand Island, 1999—2005, deacon, 2004—; pres. bd. dirs. STLCC Child Care Ctr., Grand Island, NY, 1995—99. Recipient 2d prize, Faculty divsn. Martin Luther King Poetry Contest at Canisius Coll., 2003; Travel grantee, U., Bern, Switzerland, 1977. Mem.: Am. Assn. Tchrs. German (v.p. 1998—2002), Zonta Internat. Club Buffalo (bd. dirs. 2004—06, sec. 2006—08, pres. 2008—), Phi Sigma Iota. Lutheran. Avocations: swimming, sewing, violin, poetry. Personal E-mail: twiswall@roadrunner.com.

WISWALL, FRANK LAWRENCE, JR., lawyer, educator; b. Albany, NY, Sept. 21, 1939; s. Frank Lawrence and Clara Elizabeth (Chapman) W.; m. Elizabeth Curtiss Nelson, Aug. 9, 1975; children by previous marriage: Anne W. Kowalski, Frank Lawrence III. BA, Colby Coll., 1962; JD, Cornell U., 1965; PhD in Law, Cambridge U., 1967. Bar: Maine 1965, NY 1968, Va. 1974, US Supreme Ct. 1968; lic. master near coastal steam and motor vessels, 1960—. Assoc. Burlingham, Underwood, NYC, 1967-73; maritime legal adviser Rep. of Liberia, 1968-88; prof. (ad honorem) Internat. Maritime Law Inst., 1999; vice-capt. coxswain and divsn. US Coast Guard Aux., 2006—; writer, cons. in field internat. maritime law, 1988—. Legal com. Internat. Maritime Orgn., London, 1972-74, vice-chmn. 1974-79, chmn., 1980-84; tutorial supr. internat. law Clare Coll., Cambridge, Eng., 1966-67; vis. lectr. Cornell Law Sch., 1969-76, 82; lectr. U. Va. Law Sch. and Ctr. Oceans Law and Policy, 1978-82; prof. law Cornell U., 1984; Johnsen prof. maritime law Tulane U., 1985; vis. prof. law World Maritime U., Malmo, Sweden, 1986-2003; prof.,fellow Internat. Maritime Law Inst., Malta, 1991—, governing bd., 1992—; del. Internat. Conf. Marine Pollution, London, 1973; del., chmn. drafting com. Internat. Conf. Carriage of Passengers and Luggage by Sea, Athens, 1974; del. Internat. Conf. Safety of Life at Sea, London, 1974, UN Conf. Carriage of Goods by Sea, Hamburg, 1978, XIII Diplomatic Conf. Maritime Law, Brussels, 1979, UN Conf. Law of Sea, Caracas, Venezuela, 1974, NY, 1980; del., chmn. com. final clauses Internat. Conf. Limitation of Liability for Maritime Claims, London, 1976; chmn. com. of whole Internat. Conf. Carriage Hazardous Substances by Sea, 1984; del. internat. conf. Maritime Terrorism, Rome, 1988; counsel various marine casualty bds. investigation, 1970-90, harbormaster, Port of Castine, 1960-62; chmn. joint internat. working group acts piracy and maritime violence, 1998-2001, joint internat. working group criminal offenses on high seas, various orgns., 2004-07. Author: The Development of Admiralty Jurisdiction and Practice Since 1800, 1970; editor-in-chief Benedict on Admiralty, Vols. 6, 6A-6F (Internat. Maritime Law), 1992—, Com. Maritime Internat. Handbook of Maritime Convs., 1997, 2001, 04; mem. editl. bd. Jour. Maritime Law and Commerce, 1993—, Benedict's Maritime Law Bull., 2002—, World Maritime U. Jour. Maritime Affairs; contbr. articles to profl. jours. Ofcl. prin. Diocese Mid-Atlantic States, 1988—, Diocese UK, 1997—, Anglican Cath. Ch.; chancellor Missionary Diocese NE, 1993—, Diocese Australia, 1998—; spkr. assembly laity Anglican Cath. Ch., 1995—2007; chmn. Am. Maritime Law Found., 2002—. Recipient Yorke prize U. Cambridge, 1968-69. Fellow Royal Hist. Soc.; mem. Nat. Lawyers Assn., Comité Maritime Internat. (titulary mem., exec. councillor 1989-96, v.p. 1997-2005, v.p. honoris causa 2005-), Maritime Law Assn. US (chmn. com. intergovtl. orgns. 1983-87, chmn. com. CMI 1987-95), Ecclesiastical Law Soc., Selden Soc., Am. Soc. Legal History, US Navy League (pres. Penobscot coun. 1997), Oxford and Cambridge Club (London), Century Assn., Alpha Delta Phi, Phi Delta Phi. Office: PO Box 201 Castine ME 04421-0201

WISWALL, THOMAS S., lawyer; b. Port Jefferson, NY, Dec. 9, 1949; s. Richard H. and Ann Swartz Wiswall; m. Dorothy Roller Wiswall, June 5, 1976; children: James, Karen. BA, Trinity Coll., Hartford, Conn., 1971; JD, U. Mich., Ann Arbor, 1974. Assoc. Phillips Lytle LLP, Buffalo, 1974—81, ptnr., 1982—. Chair, comm. profl. ethics Bar Assoc. Erie County, Buffalo, 2007—; fed. ct. mediator US Dist. Ct., Buffalo, 2009—. Treas. Grand Island Cmty. Chrus, Inc., NY, 2006—; deacon St. Timothy Lutheran Ch., Grand Island, NY, 2003—. Recipient Cmty. Resource of Yr. award, Buffalo/Niagara WorldConnect, 2001; named Best Lawyers in America, 2008. Mem.: German Am. Lawyers Assn., Bar Assn. Erie County, NY State Bar Assn., Am. Bar Assn., Pi Gamma Mu, Phi Beta Kappa. Avocations: music, running, drawing, German. Office: Phillips Lytle LLP 3400 HSBC Ctr Buffalo NY 14203 Business E-Mail: twiswall@phillipslytle.com.

WIT, HAROLD MAURICE, retired investment banker, lawyer; b. Boston, Sept. 6, 1928; s. Maurice and Martha (Bassist) W.; children from previous marriage: David Edmund, Hannah Edna (dec.); 1 stepchild, Simon; m. Susan King, Sept. 16, 1999. AB magna cum laude, Harvard, 1949; JD (editor law jour.), Yale, 1954. Bar: N.Y. 1954. Assoc. Cravath, Swaine & Moore, NYC, 1954-58; asst. sec. One William St. Fund, Inc., NYC, 1958-59, v.p., sec., 1959-60; assoc. Allen & Co., 1960-70; assoc Allen & Co., Inc., 1965—, v.p., 1965-70, exec. v.p., 1970-98, mng. dir., mem. exec. com.; ret. Mgr. Allen Investments II LLC. Former trustee South Folk-Shelter Island chpt. Nature Conservancy, 1993-2000; cofounder Group for South Fork; pres. South Fork Watchdogs, Inc.; mem. Panel on Future of Govt. in N.Y., 1979-80; mem. vis. com. Harvard U. Div. Sch., 1990-97. With Mass. N.G., 1947-50; lt. (j.g.) USNR, 1951-53, Korea. Mem. VFW, Am. Legion, Korean War Vets. Assn., University Club (N.Y.C.), Harvard Club (N.Y.C.), Phi Beta Kappa, Phi Delta Phi. Home: 150 E 69th St New York NY 10021-5704 also: 57 Cross Hwy East Hampton NY 11937-0348 Office: Allen & Co Inc 711 5th Ave New York NY 10022-3111 Office Phone: 212-832-8000.

WITBRODT, JANE ANN, medical researcher; d. Leo Evert and Norma Leona Klender; life ptnr. Howard R. Weeks; children: Bethany Joy Schwerdtfeger, Barbara Kay Matiska, Scott Allan. MPH, U. Calif., Berkeley, 1995; PhD student, Karolinska Inst., Stockholm, 2008—. Youth devel. worker Bay County Juvenile Home, Essexville, Mich., 1982—83; caseworker Big Brothers-Big Sisters Saginaw Bay Area, Mich., 1984—85; substance abuse counselor Bay Haven, Bay Med. Ctr., Bay City, Mich., 1985—88; children's program coord. Bay County Women's Ctr., Bay City, 1988—90; dir. Bay Haven Outpatient Clinic, Essexville, 1988—90; rsch. asst. Clew Assocs., Berkeley, 1990, Marin Inst., San Rafael, Calif., 1990—92; rsch. assoc. Pub. Health Inst., Berkeley, 1992—96; rsch. assoc., sr. analyst Alcohol Rsch. Group, Emeryville, Calif., 1996—. Office: Alcohol Rsch Group 6475 Christie Ave Ste 400 Emeryville CA 94608-1010 Office Fax: 510-985-6459. Business E-Mail: jwitbrodt@arg.org.

WITCHER, MICHAEL H., homeland and national security expert; b. Birmingham, Ala., Apr. 27, 1970; s. Pam Grass and James S. Witcher. BS in Bus. Adminstrn., Birmingham-Southern Coll., Ala., 1993. Bus. account exec. GTE Wireless, Birmingham, Ala., 1998—99; dir. sales, mktg. and pub. rels. Vazda Studios, Birmingham, 1999—2001; west coast IT/control systems sales mgr. Prophet Systems Innovations, Denver, 2001—02; homeland security dir. BSI2000, Washington, DC, 2002—04, Praetorian Sys., Birmingham, Ala., 2006—; homeland and nat. security dir. Omega Force, 2004—. Capt. Mountain Brook Police Dept., Explorers, Mountain Brook, Ala., 1985—88; co-chairman Pub. Rels. Com., Operation New Birmingham, Ala., 1995—97; fundraiser Ala. Symphonic Assn., Birmingham, 1995—97; govtl. affairs com. Chamber of Commerce, Birmingham, 1997—, law enforcement com., 1997—; fin. com. mem. Colo. State Rep. Party, Denver, 2002—05; program mem. Infraguard, Washington, 2006—; citizen's acad. class mem. FBI, Birmingham, 2006—, steering com., P.U.S.H. Homeland Sec. Program, 2006—. Author: (poetry) Over 300 poems, 6 published poems (Top 50 Poetic Works award, 2006); dir.: (wrote, directed, and edited video) Rebuilding a City Center;, author multiple marketing pieces and op-eds. Eagle scout; campaign mgr. multiple polit. campaigns, Birmingham, 1996—2000; founder, chmn. Omega Polit. Action Com., Birmingham, 1996—2004; bd. mem., treas. Birmingham Advt. Fedn., Birmingham, 1999—2001; bd. mem., exec. com. Ala. Zool. Soc., Birmingham Zoo, Ala., 1999—2005; bd. mem. Rocky Mountain Butterfly Consortium, Denver, 2002—03. Mem.: Birmingham Mus. of Art (assoc.), Alpha Tau Omega (life). Achievements include listing in Top 40 Under 40, Birmingham Business Journal. Avocations: horseback riding, soccer, Karate, sailing, travel. Home Phone: 205-967-0323; Office Phone: 205-910-0866. E-mail: mhwitcher@gmail.com.

WITCOFF, SHELDON WILLIAM, lawyer; b. Washington, July 10, 1925; s. Joseph and Zina (Ceppos) W.; m. Margot Gail Hoffner, Sept. 6, 1953; children: Lauren Jill, David Lawrence, Lisa Ann, Julie Beth. BS in Elec. Engring, U. Md., 1949; JD, George Washington U., 1953. Bar: D.C. 1953, N.Y. 1955, Ill. 1956. Patent examiner Patent Office, Dept. Commerce, 1949-53; patent lawyer Bell Telephone Labs., Murray Hill, NJ, 1953-55; ptnr. Bair, Freeman & Molinare, Chgo., 1955-69, Allegretti, Newitt, Witcoff & McAndrews, Chgo., 1970-88, Allegretti & Witcoff, LTD, Chgo., 1988-95, Banner & Witcoff Ltd., Chgo., 1995—. V.p., dir. Art Splty. Co., Chgo., 1967-84; v.p. Caspian Fur Trading Co., N.Y.C.; co-founder Child Abuse Unit for Studies, Edn. and Svcs., Chgo. Fire and police commr., Skokie, Ill., 1960-63. Served with USNR, 1943-46. Mem. Am. Bar Assn., Intellectual Property Assn. of Chgo., Order of Coif, Tau Epsilon Phi, Phi Delta Phi., B'nai B'rith. Office: 10 S Wacker Dr Chicago IL 60606-7407 Office Phone: 312-463-5000. Personal E-mail: witcoff@hotmail.com, switcoff@gmail.com. Business E-Mail: switcoff@bannerwitcoff.com.

WITCOVER, JULES JOSEPH, columnist, writer; b. Union City, NJ, July 16, 1927; s. Samuel and Sarah (Carpenter) W.; m. Marian Laverty, June 14, 1952 (div. Oct. 1990); children: Paul, Amy, Julie, Peter; m. Marion Elizabeth Rodgers, June 21, 1997. AB, Columbia Coll., 1949; MS, Columbia Grad Sch. Journalism, 1951. Reporter Hackensack (NJ) Star-Telegram, 1949-50, Providence Jour., 1951-52, Newark Star-Ledger, 1953, Washington Bur. Newhouse Newspapers, 1954-69, LA Times, Washington, 1970-72, Washington Post, 1973-76; columnist Washington Star, 1977—81, Balt. Sun, Washington, 1981—2005, Tribune Media Svcs., 1977—. Author: 85 Days: The Last Campaign of Robert Kennedy, 1969, The Resurrection of Richard Nixon, 1970, White Knight: The Rise of Spiro Agnew, 1972, (with Richard M. Cohen) A Heartbeat Away: The Investigation and Resignation of Vice President Spiro T. Agnew, 1974, Marathon: The Pursuit of the Presidency, 1972-76, 1977, (novel) The Main Chance, 1978, (with Jack W. Germond) Blue Smoke and Mirrors: How Reagan Won and Why Carter Lost the Election of 1980, 1981, (with Germond) Wake Us When It's Over: Presidential Politics of 1984, 1985, (with Germond) Whose Broad Stripes and Bright Stars?: The Trivial Pursuit of the Presidency 1988, 1989, Sabotage at Black Tom: Imperial Germany's Secret War in America, 1914-1917, 1989, Crapshoot: Rolling the Dice on the Vice Presidency, 1992, (with Germond) Mad as Hell: Revolt at the Ballot Box 1992, 1993, The Year the Dream Died: Revisiting 1968 in America, 1997, No Way to Pick a President: How Money and Hired Guns Have Debased American Elections, 1999, Party of the People: A History of the Democrats, 2003, The Making of an Ink Stained Wretch: Half a Century Pounding the Political Beat, 2005, Very Strange Bedfellows: The Short and Unhappy Marriage of Richard Nixon and Spiro Agnew, 2007. With USN, 1945-46. Recipient Washington Corr. award Sigma Delta Chi, 1963, Alumni award Columbia Grad. Sch. Journalism, 1972; Reid Found. fellow, Europe, 1958. Roman Catholic.

WITEK, JAMES EUGENE, retired public relations executive; b. LaPorte, Ind., Sept. 14, 1932; s. Stanley and Victoria (Peret) W.; m. Mary Carolyn Hood, June 18, 1955; children: James Jay, Janet Marie, Jeffrey Patrick, Jean Theresa. AB, Ind. U., 1954; MA, U. Mo., 1970. Joined U.S. Army, 1954, commd. 2d lt., 1954, advanced through grades to lt. col., 1968; editor, pub. Infantry Mag., Fort Benning, Ga., 1968-70; advisor to Vietnamese Mil. Region IV Ranger Comdr., 1970-71; plans officer CINCPAC, Hawaii, 1971-75; exec. editor Soldiers, Washington, 1975-77, editor in chief, 1977-79; dir. public affairs Nat. Com. for Employer Support Guard and Res., Arlington, Va., 1979-82, ret., 1982; dep. dir. pub. relations Am. Legion, Washington, 1982-86; mgr. pub. rels. Dowty Aerospace, Sterling, Va., 1986-99; ret. Decorated Legion of Merit, Bronze Star, Air Medal, Purple Heart, Vietnamese Cross of Gallantry with Silver Star. Mem. Am. Legion, Ret. Officers Assn., Disabled Am. Vets., Phi Beta Kappa, Tau Kappa Alpha, Pi Kappa Phi. Roman Catholic. Home: 3240 Atlanta St Fairfax VA 22030-2128

WITHEE, DIANA KEERAN, art historian, art dealer, educator; d. Royal Victor and Johanna Polterock Keeran; m. Gregory Wallace Withee, June 8, 1968 (div. 2007); children: Christopher Edward, Jeffrey Wallace, Brett Andrew. BA in Art History cum laude, Pomona Coll., Claremont, CA, 1969; MA in Art History, Tulane U., 1976; ABD in Art History, U. Md., College Park, 1994. Rsch. & prodn. asst., art documentaries Nat. Mus. of Am. Art, Washington, 1980—83; art history instr. Montgomery Coll., Rockville, Md., 1984—85; art history instr. & cons. Montgomery County Pub. Schs., Rockville, Md., 1986—87; curatorial asst., manuscripts and rare books Walters Art Gallery, Baltimore, Md., 1988—90; mus. educator Nat. Gallery of Art, Washington, 1990—93; guide supr., mus. educator Hillwood Mus., Washington, 1993—98; art dealer Sumner and Dene Gallery, San Diego, 1999—2002, Whitt-Krauss Objects of Fine Art, San Diego, 1999; art instr. Ctrl. Tex. Coll., San Diego, 2001—04; art dealer Susan St. Fine Art Gallery, Solana Beach, Calif., 2002—; co-owner Keeran Properties, Helendale, Calif., 2004—. Cons. Time-Life Books, Alexandria, Va., 1992; bd. dirs. San Diego State U. Arts Coun.; panelist, art critic San Diego Inst. The Living Artist, 2002—05. Prodn. asst. (videotape) Anni Albers, William H. Johnson, Reuben Nakian, Jacob Kainen:Five Decades as an Artist, asst. prodr. Americans in Brittany and Normandy, curator (art exhibition) More than a Miniature: Works of Art in Medieval Manuscripts, (exhibition) The Power of the Press: Revolution & Communications 1450-1600; author: (mag. articles) The Walters Art Gallery Bulletin, (contributing author) Culture et Revolution: The French Revolution and Its Aftermath, (instructor's manual) The Inquiring Eye: The European Renaissance, (book) Teacher Programs in Art Museums: A Directory; contributing author (magazine) The Post, presenter (symposium paper) Intimate Portrayals of Napoleon's Family, (scholarly conference paper) Anatomical Observations of Women's Life Stages in the Frescoes of Thera, (scholarly conference presentation) An Altar in the Miniature Fresco at Thera and Its Implications, lecturer (scholarly lecture) Timeless Cycles: Youth, Beauty and Ag in the Bronze Age Frescoes of Thera, scholarly presenter (scholarly conference presentation) The Boxing Boys and Fishermen Frescoes at Thera: An Analysis of their Physical Ages and Its Implications, Physical Growth and Aging Characteristics Depicted in the Theran Frescoes at Thera, conference presenter (conference presentations) Developing Good Relationships Between Guides and Security, lecturer (museum lecture series) C.W.Post and the Breakfast Cereal Revolution, The Gilded Age: The Newport Mansions; editor: (newsletter) COVA Newsletter. Recipient Letter of Commendation, Nat. Gallery of Art, 1991, Cash Bonus award, 1992; scholar Grad. assistantship, U. Md., 1986-1988; Mus. fellowship, U. of Md., 1988-89, Travel fellowship, Wash. Chpt., Am. Inst. of Archaeology, 1991. Mem.: Phi Kappa Phi. Achievements include development of new methodology of deciphering Aegean Bronze Age art; ran numerous national programs in museum education for National Gallery of Art; re-organization of entire Hillwood guide program; volunteered to teach Navy & Marine personnel aboard the aircraft carrier John C. Stennis on its deployment to participate in war in Afghanistan two months after 9/11. Home: 850 State St #128 San Diego CA 92101

WITHERELL, BRUCE M., mortgage company executive; b. 1959; BSBA, Carnegie Mellon U., Pitts., 1982. With Household Fin. Corp., Hicksville, NY; positions to v.p. mortgage capital markets First Boston Corp., NYC, 1983—91; head residential and comml. contract fin. Lehman Brothers Holdings, Inc., 1991—95, head derivative and fin., 1995—96, global head trans. mgmt. & documentation, 1996—99, co-COO corp. adv. divsn., 1999—2000, chief adminstrv. officer, mem. exec. com. of wealth & asset mgmt. and fixed income divsns., 2000—03, CEO Lehman Bros. Bank & Aurora Loan Services, 2003—06; mng. dir., co-head residential mortgage bus. Morgan Stanley, 2006; COO Freddie Mac (Fed. Home Loan Mortgage Corp.), 2009—. Office: Freddie Mac 8200 Jones Branch Dr Mc Lean VA 22102-3110 Office Phone: 703-903-2000.*

WITHERELL, DENNIS PATRICK, lawyer; b. Dec. 15, 1951; s. Thomas William and Kathryn Marie (Savage) Witherell; m. Suzanne Witherell; children: Natalie, Jay stepchildren: Jodi Brouilette, Shelby Watson, Shane Allen. AB with highest honors, U. Mich., Ann Arbor, 1973; JD summa cum laude, Ohio State U., Columbus, 1977. Bar: Ohio, US Dist. Ct. (no. dist.) Ohio, US Ct. Appeals (6th cir.). Law clk. U.S. Ct. Appeals (6th cir.), Cin., 1977—78; assoc. Shumaker, Loop & Kendrick LLP, Toledo, 1978—83, ptnr., 1983—. Exec. bd. NW Ohio chpt. March of Dimes Birth Defects Found., Toledo, 1978—91; chmn. March of Dimes Birth Defects Found., N.W. Ohio chpt., 1982—84; trustee Kidney Found. of Northwest Ohio, 1988—94, pres., 1992—93; trustee Life Connection of Ohio, 1991—2004, 2006—, Vis. Nurse-Extra Care, 1994—99. Mem.: ABA, Nat. Multiple Sclerosis Soc. (bd. trustees Northwest Ohio chpt. 1999—, chmn. 2004—06), Soc. of Ohio Hosp. Attys., Toledo Bar Assn, Ohio State Bar Assn. (chmn. health care law com. 1988—92), Am. Health Lawyers Assn. Roman Catholic. Home: 3218 Stonegate Dr Maumee OH 43537-9476 Office Phone: 419-321-1221.

WITHERELL, MICHAEL S., physicist, educator; b. Toledo, Sept. 22, 1949; s. Thomas W. and Marie (Savage) W.; m. Elizabeth Hall. BS in Physics, U. Mich., 1968; MS, U. Wis., 1970; PhD in Physics, U. Wis., Madison, 1973. Instr. Princeton (N.J.) U., 1973-75, asst. prof., 1975-81, U. Calif., Santa Barbara, 1981-83, assoc. prof., 1983-86, prof., 1986-99, prof. physics, 2005—, vice chancellor for rsch., 2005—; dir. Fermi Nat. Accelerator Lab. (Fermilab), Batavia, Ill., 1999—2005. Guggenheim fellow John S. Guggenheim Found., 1989-90; recipient Gold award US Sec. Energy, 2004 Fellow AAAS, Am. Physical Soc. (W.K.H. Panofsky prize 1990); mem. NAS Achievements include research in application of technologies to study particle physics: silicon vertex detectors and high-speed data acquisition sys. Office: U Calif Santa Barbara Office of Rsch 3227 Cheadle Hall Santa Barbara CA 93106-2050 Office Phone: 805-893-8270. Business E-Mail: witherell@research.ucsb.edu.

WITHERS, HUBERT RODNEY, radiotherapist, radiobiologist, educator; b. Queensland, Australia, Sept. 21, 1932; arrived in U.S., 1966; s. Hubert and Gertrude Ethel (Tremayne) W.; m. Janet Macfie, Oct. 9, 1959; 1 child, Genevieve. MB BS, U. Queensland, Brisbane, Australia, 1956; PhD, U. London, 1965, DSc, 1982. Bd. cert. Ednl. Coun. Fgn. Med. Grads. Intern Royal Brisbane and Associated Hosps., 1957; resident in radiotherapy and pathology Queensland Radium Inst. and Royal Brisbane Hosp., 1958-63; U. Queensland Gaggin fellow Gray Lab., Mt. Vernon Hosp., Northwood, Middlesex, England, 1963—65, Royal Brisbane Hosp., 1966; radiotherapist Prince of Wales Hosp., Randwick, Sydney, Australia, 1966; vis. rsch. scientist lab. physiology Nat. Cancer Inst., Bethesda, Md., 1966-68; assoc. prof. radiotherapy sect. exptl. radiotherapy U. Tex. Sys. Cancer Ctr. M.D. Anderson Hosp. & Tumor Inst., Houston, 1968-71, prof. radiotherapy, chief sect. sect. exptl. radiotherapy, 1971-80; prof. dir. exptl. radiation oncology dept. radiation oncology UCLA, 1980-89, 1991—94, prof. vice chair, dir. exptl. radiation oncology dept. radiation oncology, 1991—94, Am. Cancer Soc. Clin. Rsch. prof. dept. radiation oncology, 1992—94, interim dir. Jonsson Comprehensive Cancer Ctr., 1994—95, chmn. radiation oncology, 1994—2005. Assoc. grad. faculty U. Tex., Grad. Sch. Biomed. Scis, Houston, 1969-73, mem. grad. faculty, 1973-80; prof. dept. radiotherapy Med. Sch., U. Tex. Health Sci. Ctr., Houston, U. Tex. Med. Sch., Houston, 1975-80; prof., dir. Inst. Oncology, The Prince of Wales Hosp., U. NSW, Sydney, Australia, 1989-91; mem. com. mortality mil. pers. present-at-atmosphere tests of nuc. weapons Inst. Medicine, 1993-94; mem. radiation effects rsch. bd. NRC, 1993-99; mem. com. neutron dose reporting Internat. Commn. Radiation Units and Measurements, 1982-93, mem. report com. clin. dosimetry for neutrons, 1993-98; mem. task force non-stochastic effects radiation Internat. Com. Radiation Protection, 1980-84, mem. com. 1, 1992-00; mem. radiobiology com. Radiation Therapy Oncology Group, 1979-89, mem. dose-time com., 1980-89, mem. gastroenterology com., 1982-89;

fellow Royal Australian Coll. Radiologists Edn. Bd., 1989-91; trustee Am. Bd. Radiology, 1995-04; mem. cancer rsch. coord. com. U. Calif., 1991-97, mem. standing curriculum com. UCLA biomed. physics grad. program, 1993-2007; cons. exptl. radiotherapy U. Tex. Sys. Cancer Ctr., 1980—. Mem. Am. editl. bd.: Internat. Jour. Radiat. Oncol. Biol. Phys., 1982-89, 1991-2007, internat. editl. bd., 1989-91; cons. editor: The European Jour. Cancer, 1990-95; editl. bd. dirs.: Endocurietherapy/Hyperthermia Oncology, 1991—2001, Radiation Oncology Investigations, 1992-2002; assoc. editor: Cancer Rsch., 1993-94, editl. bd. 1995-97. Mem. Kettering selection com. Gen. Motors Cancer Rsch. Found., 1988-89, chmn., 1984, 1989, 1990-94, 2002-04, awards assembly, 1990-94, 2002-04, adv. coun., 1994-2006. Decorated officer Order of Australia, 1998; Named Gilbert H. Fletcher lectr. U. Tex. Sys. Cancer Ctr., 1989, Clifford Ash lectr. Ont. Cancer Inst., Princess Margaret Hosp., 1987, Erskine lectr. Radiol. Soc. N.Am., 1988, Ruvelson lectr. U. Minn., 1988, Milford Schultz lectr. Mass. Gen. Hosp., 1989, Del Regato Found. lectr. Hahnemann U., 1990, Bruce Cain Meml. lectr. New Zealand Soc. Oncology, 1990; recipient Medicine prize Polish Acad. Sci., 1989, Second HS Kaplan Disting. Scientist award Internat. Assn. Radiation Rsch., 1991, Gray medal Internat. Commn. Radiation Units, 1995, U.S. Dept. Energy Fermi award 1997, Radiation Rsch. Soc. Failla award, 1988, Gold medal Royal Australian and N.Z. Coll. Radiologists, 1997, Charles F. Kettering prize GM Cancer Rsch. Found., 1998; Emmanuel van der Schueren medal Belgian Rad One Soc., 2004, Gold medal Gilbert H. Fletcher Soc., 2005, Gold medal Radiol. Soc. N.Am., 2005. Fellow Am. Coll. Radiology, ACS Oncology Group (ethics com. oncology 2002—), Royal Australasian Coll. Radiologists (bd. cert., Gold medal 1997), Am. Bd. Radiology (bd. cert. therapeutic radiology 1977, Am. Coll. Radiology adv. com. patterns of care study 1988-93, radiation oncology adv. group 1993-98, others, Gold medal 2004), Am. Radium Soc. (credential com. 1986-89, 93-94, treas. 1993-94, pres. 1996-97, others, Janeway medal 1994), Am. Soc. Therapeutic Radiology and Oncology (Gold Medal awards com. 1982, 93, 00, publs. com. 1993-97, vice-chair publs. com., 1996-97, keynote address 1990, Gold medal 1991, Fellow 2006), Nat. Cancer Inst. (ad-hoc rev. coms. 1970—, radiation sudy sect. 1971-75, cons. U.S.-Japan Coop. Study high LET Radiotherapy 1975-77, cancer rsch. emphasis grant rev. com. 1976, clin. cancer ctr. rev. com. 1976-79, toxicology working group 1977-78, reviewer outstanding investigator grants 1984-93, bd. sci. counselors, 1986-88), Nat. Cancer Inst. Can. (adv. com. rsch. 1992-95), Pacific N.W. Radiol. Soc. (hon.), Tex. Radiol. Soc. (hon.), So. Calif. Radiation Oncology Soc. (sec., treas., 1992-94, pres. 1997-98), European Soc. Therapeutic Radiology and Oncology (hon.; Regaud lectr. 2000), Polish Oncology Soc. (hon., Gold medal 2002), Austrian Radiation Oncology Soc. (hon.), Phila. Roentgen Ray Soc. (hon.), Radiation Rsch. Soc. (pres. 1982-83, honors and awards com. 1984-88, ad hoc com. funds utilization 1987-89, adv. com. Radiation Rsch. Jour. 1988-96, Failla awardm 1988). Office: David Geffen Sch Medicine UCLA 10833 Le Conte Ave Los Angeles CA 90095-1714 Office Phone: 310-825-8278. Business E-Mail: hwithers@mednet.ucla.edu.

WITHERS, JOHN LOVELLE, II, United States Ambassador to Albania; s. John L. Sr. and Daisy P. Withers; m. Maryruth Coleman. BA in Hist., Harvard U., Cambridge, Mass.; MA in East Asian Studies, McGill U., Montreal, Que., Can.; PhD in Modern Chinese Hist., Yale U., New Haven; student, Nanjing U., China. Joined US Dept. State, 1984, polit. officer US Embassy The Hague, Netherlands, 1985—86, Lagos, Nigeria, 1988—90, Moscow, 1991—93, desk officer, Office Chinese Affairs, 1986—88, Office of No. European Affairs Ireland, Iceland, 1993, spl. asst. Office Dep. Sec., 1993—96, dep. chief of mission US Embassy Riga, Latvia, 1997—2000, dir. Office North Ctrl. European Affairs, 2001—02, dir. ops. ctr., 2003—05, US amb. to Albania, 2007—. Office: DOS Amb 9510 Tirana Pl Washington DC 20521-9510*

WITHERS, W. RUSSELL, JR., broadcast executive; b. Cape Girardeau, Mo., Dec. 10, 1936; s. Waldo Russell Sr. and Dorothy Ruth (Harrelson) W.; 1 child, Dana Ruth. BA, S.E. Mo. State U., 1958. Disc jockey Sta. KGMO Radio, Cape Girardeau, 1955-58; account exec. Sta. WGGH Radio, Marion, Ill., 1961-62; v.p. LIN Broadcasting Corp., Nashville, 1962-69; exec. v.p., dir. Laser Link Corp., Woodbury, NY, 1970-72; owner Withers Broadcasting of Hawaii, 1975-79, Withers Broadcasting of Minn., 1974-79, Withers Broadcasting Cos., Iowa, 1981—, Mood Music Ill., Mt. Vernon, 1973—, Mood Music, Inc., Cape Girardeau, 1972—, Royal Hawaiian Radio Co., Inc., others, WROY - WRUL, 2006, WYNG, 2007. Owner various radio and TV stas. including KREX-TV, Grand Junction, Colo., KREY-TV, Montrose, Colo., KREG-TV, Glenwood Springs, Colo., Page Ins. and Real Estate, Mt. Vernon, Ill.; chmn. bd., CEO Withers Beverage Corp., Mobile, Ala., 1973—79; chmn. adv. bd. Mut. Network; bd. dirs. Theatrevision, Inc., Turneffe Island Lodge, Ltd., Belize, Sta. WDTV, Clarksburg, W.Va., WMIX-AM-TV, Mt. Vernon, KGMO-KAPE, Cape Girardeau, KOKX AM-FM, Keokuk, Iowa, KTRC, Santa Fe, KRHW and KBXB, Sikeston, Mo., WKIB Anna, Cape Girardeau, WMOK, WREZ and WZZL, Paducah, Ky., WSDR-WSSQ, WZZL, Sterling Rock Falls, Ill., WILY, WRXX (FM), Centralia, Ill., WEBQ and WEBQ-FM, Harrisburg, Ill.; pres. Ill. Pub. Airports Assn.; co-chmn. TARPAC; chair NAB Radio Bd., 2007—08. Bd. dir., chmn. bd. Mt. Vernon Tourism and Conv. Bur.; chmn. Mt. Vernon Airport Authority; bd. regents Lincoln Acad.; past pres. IPAA; past chmn. Conv. & Visitors, Airport Authority; bd. dir. No. Colo. C.C., Libr. Am. Broadcasters, Radio Bd., AP. With U.S. Army, 1957-58. Recipient Alumni Achievement award, SEMO State U., 2007; named Broadcaster of Yr., Ill., 2006, W.Va, 2007. Mem. Mt. Vernon C. of C. (bd. dir.), Nat. Assn. Broadcasters (bd. dir., exec. com.), Ill. Broadcasters Assn., Stadium Club, Mo. Athletic Club, Elks, Moose, AmVets, Masons, Shriners, Sigma Chi. Christian Scientist. Home: 16074 Hawthorne Rd Mount Vernon IL 62864-2852 Office: PO Box 1508 Mount Vernon IL 62864-0030 Home Phone: 618-244-4300; Office Phone: 618-242-3500. Personal E-mail: wrwithers@mvn.net.

WITHERSPOON, CAROLYN BRACK, lawyer; b. Little Rock, Mar. 29, 1950; d. Gordon Paisley and Mildred Louise (Lemon) Brack; m. Joseph Roger Armbrust, July 25, 1970 (div. 1976); 1 child, Catherine Paisley Armbrust; m. John Leslie Witherspoon, June 15, 1979. Student, So. Meth. U., 1970; BA, U. Ark., 1974, JD with honors, 1978. Bar: Ark. 1978, U.S. Dist. Ct. (ea. and we. dists.) Ark. 1978, U.S. Ct. Appeals (8th cir.) 1979, U.S. Supreme Ct. 1981. Asst. atty. City of Little Rock, 1978, chief dep. atty., acting city atty., 1984—85; assoc. House, Wallace & Jewell, Little Rock, 1985—87, ptnr., 1987—90; dir. McGlinchey Stafford Lang, Little Rock, 1990—97, Cross, Gunter, Witherspoon & Galchus, Little Rock, 1997—. Mem. com. Fed. Ct. Practice, 1988—91; mem. civil practice com. Ark. Supreme Ct., 1989—97, mem. continuing legal edn. bd., 1998—2001; chair adv. com. Civil Justice Reform Act, 1993—95; chair State Bd. Bar Examiners, 2001—05. Contbr. articles to profl. jours. Commr. Ark. Real Estate Commn., 1978—81; past chmn. Little Rock Housing Authority Bd. Commn.; past pres., bd. dirs. Advs. for Battered Women; past pres. Women's Found. Ark., Ark. Women's History Inst. Recipient Labor Law award, Am. Jurisprudence, 1977. Fellow: Coll. Labor and Employment Lawyers, Am. Bar Found. (Ark. Fellows Past chair); mem.: ABA (ho. dels. 1997—, equal employment opportunity com.), Am. Employment Law Coun., William R. Overton Inn of Ct. (pres. 1992—93), Nat. Inst. Mcpl. Law Officers (state chmn. 1985—87, v.p. 1987—89), Pulaski County Bar Assn. (pres. 1989—90), Ark. Assn. Women Lawyers (pres. 1982—83), Ark. Bar Assn. (pres. 1995—96, Golden Gavel award 1989, Ark. Inst. Cont. Legal Edn. award 1991, Golden Gavel award 1993, Charles L. Carpenter award 2005), Transp. Lawyers Assn. (mem. exec. com. 1997—99), Nat. Conf. Bar Pres. (mem. exec. coun. 1996—99), Am. Jur Soc., Am. Law Inst. Avocations: hunting, fishing, reading, travel. Office: Cross Gunter Witherspoon and Galchus 500 President Clinton Ave Ste 200 Little Rock AR 72201-1747 Office Phone: 501-371-9999. Business E-Mail: cspoon@cgwg.com.

WITHERSPOON, KEVIN B., history professor; b. Bethesda, Md., Dec. 14, 1970; s. Lynn Ralph Witherspoon and Valerie Wilson Stephenson; m. Jacqueline Fernandez Witherspoon, Dec. 9, 2000; children: Alexis, Andrew. MA, U. Maine, Orono, 1996; BA, Fla. State U., Tallahassee, 1993, PhD, 2003. Lectr. Fla. State U., Tallahassee, 2004—06; asst. prof. Lander U., Greenwood, SC, 2006—. Master scholar Tchg. Am. History SC., Columbia, 2007—. Author: (book) Before the Eyes of the World: Mexico and the 1968 Olympic Games. Mem.: SC Hist. Assn., South East World History Assn., Am. Hist. Assn. Office: Lander Univ 320 Stanley Ave Greenwood SC 29649 Business E-Mail: kwitherspoon@lander.edu.

WITHERSPOON, MARIA BERNARDA PENA, principal; b. San Cristobal, Dominican Republic, Dec. 20, 1955; came to U.S., 1969; d. Benjamin de Jesus and Belen Pena; m. James Howard Witherspoon, Aug. 6, 1977 (div. Feb. 1991). AA in Social Svcs., Pima CC, Ariz., 1980; BS in Child Devel. and Family, U. Ariz., 1981, MEd in Bilingual Edn., 1986, ednl. adminstrn. cert., 1989. Cert. basic elem. tchr. with bilingual endorsement Ariz., prin. Ariz., bilingual elem. edn. NY, sch. adminstr., supr. NY. Family counselor El Rio Neighborhood Ctr., Tucson, 1979; pre-sch. tchr. Project Head Start, Tucson, 1980; data collector U. Ariz., Tucson, 1982; bilingual educator Tucson Unified Sch. Dist., 1984-88; bilingual curriculum specialist Stafford Engring. and Tech. Magnet Sch., Tucson, 1988—; asst. prin. Leonardo da Vinci Intermediate Sch., 1999—2002; prin. Roberto Clemente Pub. Sch., 2002—. Mem. Spanish Lang. Arts Adoption com. Tucson Unified Sch. Dist. Mem. Task Force on Native Am. Studies, Tucson, 1986. Mem. AAUW, NEA, Tucson Edn. Assn. (alt. state del., assembly rep.), Nat. Assn. Bilingual Edn., Assn. for Supervision and Curriculum Devel., Am. Home Econs. Assn., Nat. Assn. Female Execs, N.Y.C. Elem. Sch. Prin.'s Assn., Assn. Family and Consumer Svc, ADASA (mem. & sec.). Republican. Roman Catholic. Home: 9550 113th St South Richmond Hill NY 11419-1111 Office: Roberto Clemente Primary Sch PS19K 325 S 3d St Brooklyn NY 11211 Office Phone: 718-387-8554. Personal E-mail: mariawith@aol.com.

WITHERSPOON, REESE (LAURA JEAN REESE WITHERSPOON), actress; b. New Orleans, Mar. 22, 1976; d. John and Betty Witherspoon; m. Ryan Phillippe, June 5, 1999 (div. Oct. 5, 2007); children: Ava Elizabeth, Deacon. Co-owner prodn. co. Type A Films; global amb. Avon cosmetics, 2007—. Actress (films) The Man in the Moon, 1991, A Far Off Place, 1993, Jack the Bear, 1993, S.F.W., 1994, Freeway, 1996, Fear, 1996, Twilight, 1998, Overnight Delivery, 1998, Pleasantville, 1998, Cruel Intentions, 1999, Election, 1999, Best Laid Plans, 1999, American Psycho, 2000, Little Nicky, 2000, The Trumpet of the Swan (voice only), 2001, Legally Blonde, 2001, The Importance of Being Earnest, 2002, Sweet Home Alabama, 2002, Vanity Fair, 2004, Just Like Heaven, 2005, Walk the Line, 2005 (Acad. award for Best Actress, Golden Globe award for Best Actress, SAG award for Best Actress in a motion picture, BAFTA award for Best Actress in a leading role, Teen Choice award), Rendition, 2007, Four Christmases, 2008, Monsters vs. Aliens (voice only), 2009, actress, exec. prodr. Legally Blonde 2: Red, White & Blonde, 2003, actress, prodr. Penelope, 2006, actress (TV films) Wildflower, 1991, Desperate Choices: To Save My Child, 1992, (TV miniseries) Return to Lonsome Dove, 1993, (TV appearances) Friends, 2000, King of the Hill, 2000, The Simpsons, 2002. Recipient Movieline Young Hollywood award for breakthrough female performance, 1999, People's Choice Awards, Favorite Leading Lady, 2006, Favorite Female Movie Star, 2008, 2009; named Best Actress, Catalan Internat. Film Festival awards, 1997, Favorite Female Film Star, People Mag., 2004, Best Actress (for Election), Nat. Soc. Film Critics, Kansas City Film Critics Cir., Online Film Critics Soc., Best Actress (for Walk the Line), Austin Film Critics Assn., Boston Soc. Film Critics, Broadcast Film Critics Assn., Fla. Film Critics Cir., Kansas City Film Critics Cir., Las Vegas Film Critics Soc., Nat. Soc. Film Critics, NY Film Critics Cir., Online Film Critics Soc., Washington D.C. Area Film Critics Assn., San Francisco Film Critics Cir.; named one of 25 Most Intriguing People, People Mag., 2001, 50 Most Beautiful People, 2002, 100 Most Influential People, TIME mag., 2006, 50 Most Powerful People in Hollywood, Premiere mag., 2006, The 100 Most Powerful Celebrities, Forbes.com, 2008; named to Hollywood Reporter's Women in Entertainment: Power 100, 2007. Office: Creative Artists Agy 2000 Ave of the Stars Los Angeles CA 90067*

WITHERSPOON, WALTER PENNINGTON, JR., orthodontist; b. Sept. 3, 1938; s. Walter P. and Florence Evelyn (Jones) W.; m. Joyce Ann Smith, Sept. 6, 1970; 1 child, Annie Melissa. BS, U. S.C., 1960; DDS, U. N.C., 1964, MSO, 1969. Pvt. practice, Columbia, 1969—. Med. staff Bapt. Med. Ctr., Columbia, 1970—, Lexington County Hosp., West Columbia, 1974—. Host Nite Line Broadcasting Co. Adv. bd. 1st Palmetto Bank and Trust, West Columbia, 1982; mem. adv. bd. 1st Citizens Bank; candidate S.C. Ho. of Reps., 1994; del. S.C. Rep. Com., 1989—; mem. platform com. S.C. Rep. Party Conv., poll com., 1992; del. Rep. Nat. Conv., Houston, 1992, rules com., task force on edn.; Rep. nat. committeeman, 1996-2008, rules com., rep. nat. com.; pres. Rep. Electoral Coll., 1996, 2000; bd. dirs. Southeastern Coll. Assemblies of God, Lakeland, Fla., 1984, Brookland Plantation Home for Boys, Orangeburg, S.C.; pres. Friends of Irmo Libr.; chmn. Lexington County Rep. Party; commr. Richland/Lexington Counties Commn. for Tech. Edn., S.C. Commn. on Alcohol and Drug Abuse; bd. dirs. Centerplace for Homeless; mem. Presdl. Visit-Ticket Com.; amb. Irmo C. of C.; vol. lockup telethon Muscular Dystrophy Assn. Lt. USN, 1964-66; candidate US Senate, 2006-08; treas. Fin. Devel. Champions For Life, Columbia, SC. Recipient Century Mem. award Boy Scouts Am., 1984. Mem. ADA, Greater Columbia Dental Assn. (pres. 1975-76), U. NC Dental Alumni Assn. (bd. dirs.), SC Dental Assn. (ho. of dels. 1971-73, 91-96, legis. com. 1993), SC Orthodontic Assn. (ctrl. dist. dir., state rep.), Am. Assn. Orthodontists, (polit. action com.), Sertoma (pres. 1975-76), Am. Legion (mem. baseball com.), So. Assn. Orthodontists (SC rep. Am. Assn. Orthodontists polit. action com.), Cen. Dist. Dental Soc. Home: 250 Lancer Dr Columbia SC 29212-1216

WITHEY, JEFFREY HOWARD, molecular biologist, researcher; b. Canton, NY, Sept. 7, 1968; s. Howard Greene Withey, Jr. and Ruth Frame Withey; m. JoAnne Rupert, July 8, 1995; 1 child, Theodore John. BS, Johns Hopkins U., 1990; PhD, U. Mich., 2000. Sr. lab technician Johns Hopkins U., Balt., 1990—94; rsch. fellow Med. Sch. U. Mich., Ann Arbor, 2000—. Grantee Nat. Rsch. Svc. award, Nat. Inst. Allergy and Infectious Disease, 2002—. Mem.: AAAS, Am. Soc. Microbiology. Liberal. Roman Catholic. Achievements include studies in E. coli that showed that directed proteolysis is not the major function of tmRNA, an unusual RNA having qualities of both tRNA and mRNA. Avocations: tennis, music. Office: U Mich Med Sch Unit for Lab Animal Medicine 104 ARF Ann Arbor MI 48109-0614 Business E-Mail: jwithey@umich.edu.

WITHROW, JAMES A., music educator; b. Harrisburg, Pa., Nov. 24, 1964; s. James L. and Joyce M. (Yeckley) Withrow. BS in Edn., Clarion U. of Pa., Pa., 1987. Instructional II Pa., 1993. Music educator South Ea. Sch. Dist., Fawn Grove, Pa., 1988—; vol. Leo Enterprises/Red Lion Fire Co., Red Lion, Pa., 2005—. Yearbook adv. Delta-Peach Bottom Elem. Sch., Delta, Pa., 2001—. Vol. Leo Enterprises/Red Lion Fire Dept., Red Lion, Pa., 2005. Mem.: Pa. Music Educators Assn. (assoc.), Nat. Assn. for Music Edn. (assoc.). Office: Delta-Peach Bottom Elem Sch 1081 Atom Rd Delta PA 17314

WITHROW, LUCILLE MONNOT, nursing home administrator; b. Alliance, Ohio, July 28, 1923; d. Charles Edward Monnot and Freda Aldine (Guy) Monnot Cameron; m. Alvin Robert Withrow, June 6, 1945 (dec. 1984); children: Cindi Withrow Johnson, Nancy Withrow Townley, Sharon Withrow Hodgkins (dec.), Wendel Alvin. AA in Health Adminstrn., Eastfield Coll., Mesquite, Tex., 1976. Lic. nursing home adminstr., Tex.; cert. nursing home ombudsman. Held various clerical positions, Dallas, 1950-72; office mgr., asst. adminstr. Christian Care Ctr. Nursing Home, Mesquite, Tex., 1972-76; head adminstr. Christian Care Ctr. Nursing Home and Retirement Complex, Mesquite, 1976-91; nursing home ombudsman Tex. Dept. Aging and Tex. Dept. Health, Dallas, 1991-93; legal asst. Law Offices of Wendel A. Withrow, Carrollton, Tex., 1993—. Com. on geriatric curriculum devel. Eastfield Coll., Mesquite, 1979, 87; ombudsman adv. com. Sr. Citizens Greater Dallas; cons. in field. Vol. Dallas Arboretum and Bot. Soc.; mem. Ombudsman adv. com. Sr. Citizens of Greater Dallas; charter mem. Stage Show Prodns. Recipient Volunteerism award, Tex. Atty. Gen., 1987, Tex. Gov., 1992. Mem. Tex. Assn. Homes for Aging, Am. Assn. Homes for Aging, Health Svcs. Speakers Bur., White Rock Kiwanis. Mem. Ch. Of Christ. Avocations: reading, travel, theater. Home: 11344 Lippitt Ave Dallas TX 75218-1922 Office: Law Office of W A Withrow 1120 Metrocrest Dr Ste 200 Carrollton TX 75006-5872

WITHY, KELLEY, medical educator; MD, U. Calif., San Diego, 1991; PhD, U. Hawaii, Honolulu, 2007. Cert. in family medicine Long Beach Meml., 1994. Assoc. prof. U. Hawaii, 1996—. Office: John A Burns Sch Medicine 651 Ilalo St MEB 401J Honolulu HI 96813 Office Fax: 808-692-1258.

WITKE, DAVID RODNEY, retired newspaper editor, consultant; b. Council Bluffs, Iowa, Mar. 24, 1937; s. Arnold and Rosamond Louise (Storer) W.; m. Priscilla Bill Smith, Oct. 8, 1960; 1 son, Carl. BS in Journalism, Northwestern U., 1959. Reporter, editor The Courier, Champaign-Urbana, Ill., 1962-66; copy editor The Register, Des Moines, 1966-70, city editor, 1970-73, asst. mng. editor adminstrn., 1973-74, asst. mng. editor electronics, 1974-75, mng. editor, 1975-83, dir. ops., 1983-85, dep. editor, omsbudsman, 1985-87, exec. sports editor, 1987-98, sr. editor, 1998—2002, ret., 2002; freelance cons., 2002—. Rep. Iowa Freedom of Info. Coun., Des Moines, 1973—, pres., 1986-88; vis. lectr. Drake U., 1986—, Iowa State U., 1990—; adj. faculty Simpson Coll., 2003—, adv. bd., 2007—; juror Pulitzer Prize, 1989-91; tng. cons. The Register, Des Moines, 2003—; lectr. in field. Bd. dirs. Des Moines Pastoral Counseling Ctr., 2005—. Served to lt. (j.g.) USN, 1959-62, PTO. Mem. Assoc. Press Mng. Editors Assn., Mid-Am. Newspaper Assn., AP Sports Editors Assn., Iowa Newspaper Found., The Prairie Club, Sigma Delta Chi. Unitarian Universalist. Home and Office: 2521 48th Pl Des Moines IA 50310-2506 Office Phone: 515-274-0578.

WITKIN, ERIC DOUGLAS, lawyer; b. Trenton, NJ, May 14, 1948; s. Nathan and Norma Shirley (Stein) W.; m. Regina Ann Bilotta, June 8, 1980; children: Daniel Robert, Sarah Ann. AB magna cum laude, Columbia U., 1969; JD, Harvard U., 1972. Bar: N.Y. 1973, D.C. 1989, U.S. Dist. Ct. (so. and ea. dists.) N.Y. 1974, U.S. Dist. Ct. (we. dist.) N.Y. 2001, U.S. Ct. Appeals (2d and D.C. cirs.) 1974, U.S. Supreme Ct. 1977, U.S. Dist. Ct. D.C. 1989. Assoc. Poletti, Freidin, Prashker & Gartner, NYC, 1972-80, ptnr., 1980-85; sr. atty. labor Kaye, Scholer, Fierman, Hays & Handler, NYC, 1985-88; of counsel Akin, Gump, Strauss, Hauer & Feld, Washington, 1988-90; counsel Benetar, Bernstein, Schair & Stein, NYC, 1990-99; ptnr. Roberts & Finger, LLP, NYC, 1999-2001, Greble & Finger, LLP, NYC, 2001; counsel Brown, Raysman, Millstein, Felder & Steiner LLP, NYC, 2001—06, Thelen Reid Brown Raysman Steiner, LLP, NYC, 2006—08; spl. counsel Littler Mendelson PC, NYC, 2008—. Treas., founder Property Owners Against Unfair Taxation, NYC, 1983-90, Park Ridge Neighborhood Assn., Harrison, NY, 2000-; trustee Congregation Emanu-El of Westchester, 1996-2007, pres., 2002-04. Lawrence Chamberlain scholar Columbia U., NYC, 1968; recipient Alumni medal Alumni Fedn. Columbia U., 1982 Mem. ABA (labor and employment law sect.), N.Y. State Bar Assn. (labor and employment law sect., com. on equal employment opportunity law), Assn. of Bar of City of NY (spl. com. on sex and law 1975-82, com. on labor and employment law 1982-85, 92-94), Westchester County Bar Assn., Columbia Coll. Alumni Assn. (pres. 1988-90, bd. dirs. 1974—, Robert Lincoln Carey prize, Alumni prize 1969, Lions award 1990), Alumni Fedn. Columbia U. (alumni trustee nominating com. 1990-97, pres. 1997-99), Am. Soc. Pers. Adminstrn. (contbr. monthly newsletter 1986-88), Soc. Human Resource Mgmt., Soc. Columbia Grads. (bd. dirs. 1994-97), Human Resources Assn. NY, Phi Beta Kappa. Clubs: Harvard (NYC), Am. Yacht (Rye, NY) Avocations: piano, sailing. Home: 103 Wendover Rd Rye NY 10580-1939 Office: Littler Mendelson PC 900 3rd Ave New York NY 10022 Office Phone: 212-497-8487. Business E-Mail: ewitkin@thelen.com.

WITKIN, EVELYN MAISEL, retired geneticist; b. NYC, Mar. 9, 1921; d. Joseph and Mary (Levin) Maisel; m. Herman A. Witkin, July 9, 1943 (dec. July 1979); children— Joseph, Andrew. AB, NYU, 1941; MA, Columbia U., 1943, PhD, 1947; DSc honoris causa, N.Y. Med. Coll., 1978, Rutgers U., 1995. Mem. staff genetics dept. Carnegie Inst., Washington, 1950-55; mem. faculty State U. N.Y. Downstate Med. Center, Bklyn., 1955-71, prof. medicine, 1968-71; prof. biol. scis. Douglass Coll., Rutgers U., 1971-79, Barbara McClintock prof. genetics, 1979-83, Waksman Inst. Microbiology, 1983-91; Barbara McClintock prof. emerita Waksman Inst. Microbiology, Rutgers U., 1991—. Author articles; mem. editorial bds. profl. jours. Postdoctoral fellow Am. Cancer Soc., 1947-49; fellow Carnegie Instn., 1957; Selman A. Waksman lectr., 1960; Phi Beta Kappa vis. scholar, 1980-81; grantee NIH, 1956-89; recipient Prix Charles Leopold Mayer French Acad. Scis., 1977, Lindback award, 1979, Nat. Medal of Science award, 2002. Fellow AAAS, Am. Acad. Microbiology; mem. NAS, Am. Acad. Arts and Scis., Environ. Mutagen Soc., Am. Genetics Soc. (Thomas Hunt Morgan medal, 2000), Am. Soc. Microbiology. Home: 1 Firestone Ct Princeton NJ 08540-5220 E-mail: ewitkin@aol.com.

WITKIN, JOEL-PETER, photographer, poet; b. Bklyn., Sept. 13, 1939; s. Max and Mary (Pellegrino) W.; 1 child, Kersen Ahanu; m. Barbara Anne Gilbert, 2005. B.F.A., Cooper Union, 1974; M.F.A., U.

N.Mex., 1986; student (fellow), Columbia U., 1973-74. Artist in residence Zerybthia Rome, Italy, summer 1996; represented by Galerie Baudoin Lebon, Paris, Catherine Edelman Gallery, Chgo., Silverstein Photography, NYC; artist in residence Berlin, fall 1998, Paris, winter 1998. Lectr. Am. Acad. Rome, 1996, Princeton U., 1997, Camera Work, Berlin, El Escorial, Spain, 1998, Yale U., 2001, Internat. Ctr. Photography, 1999, Moscow Ho. Photography, 2001, Ecole Beaux Arts Superior, Paris, 2005, The Academia, Milano, 2007. Exhibited in Projects Studio One, NYC, 1980, Galerie Texbraun, Paris, 1982, Baudoin Lebon, Paris, 1982, 86, 90, 94, 97, 2000, 02, 04, Kansas Ctiy Art Inst., 1983, Stedelijk Mus., Amsterdam, 1983, Fraenkel Gallery, 1983-84, 87, 91, 93, 95, 97, Pace WildenStein MacGill Gallery, NYC, 1983, 84, 87, 89, 91, 93, 95, 97, San Francisco Mus. Modern Art, 1985, Bklyn. Mus., 1986, Galerie Baudoin Lebon, Paris, 1987, 89, 91, 95, 97, 2000, 02, 04, 07, 08 Centro de Arte Reina Sofia Mus., Madrid, 1988, Palais de Tokyo, Paris, 1989, Fahey/Klein Gallery, LA, 1987, 89, 91, 97, 98, 2005, Mus. Modern Art, Haifa, Israel, 1991, Photo Picture Space Gallery, Osaka, Japan, 1993, 95, 2001, Guggenheim Mus., NYC, 1995, Interkamera, Prague, 1995, Il Castello de Rivoli Mus., Turin, 1995, Encontros de Fotografia, Cuembra, Portugal, 1996, 98, Rencontres de la Photographie, Arles, France, 1996, Taipei Photo Gallery, Taiwan, 1994, 96, 98, Mus. of Fine Arts, Santa Fe, 1998, Wildenstein Gallery, Tokyo, 1998, Pace Wildenstein, LA, 1998, Sternburg Mus., Prauge, 1999, Mesiac Fotographie, Slovakia, 1999, Hotel De Sully, Paris, 2000, Catherine Edelman Gallery, Chgo., 2000, 05, 09, Ricco/Maresca Gallery, NYC, 1997, 99, Athens Sch. Fine Art, 2000, Ctr. Contemporary Art, Honolulu, 2000, Hasted/Hunt Gallery, NYC, 2001, 04, Etherton Gallery, Tucson, 2001, 05, Linda Durham Gallery, Santa Fe, 2005, Stadt Mus., Jena, 2002, Picture Photo Space, Osaka, 2002, Infinito Gallery, Turin, 2002, Galeria Juana de Aizpuru, Madrid, 2003, Photoes Pana, Madrid, 2003, Le Garage Galerie, Toulouse, 2003, ARCO, Madrid, 2004, Gary Tatintsian Gallery, Moscow, 2005, Moscow House Photography, 2005, Witkin Vintage, Hasted/Hunt, NYC, 2006, Café Françoise, Brussels, Paris-Photo, 2006, Chgo. Art Fair, 2007, Cite2000 Internat. des Arts, Paris, 2006, Medici Palace, Seravezza, Italy, 2007, Galleria Ca Di Fra, Milano, 2007, Maison de la Culture de Namur, Belgium, 2007, Luz Bienal de las Artes, Zaragoza, 2007, Paris Photo, 2007, Palazzo Reale, Milano, 2008, Edelman Gallery Chgo., 2008, Silverstein Photography. NYC, 2009, Festival of Nordic Art, Norway, 2009; group shows: Mus. Modern Art, NYC, 1959, San Francisco Mus. Moder Art, 1981, Whitney Biennial, 1985, Palais de Tokyo, Paris, 1986, La Photographie Contemporaine en France, 1996, Foto Masson, Goteberg, Sweden, 1997, Hanlin Museum, So. Korea, 1997, Bogardenkapel, Bruges, 1998, Hayward Gallery, London, 1997, Strasborg Mus. d'Art Moderne et Contemporaine, 1998, The Ansel Adams Ctr., San Francisco, 1999, Camera Work, San Francisco, 1999, The Louvre, Paris, 2000, Museé Bourdelle, Paris, 2000, John Gibson Gallery, NYC, 2000, The High Mus. Art, Ga., 2000, Fotografie Forum, Frankfort, 2001, Nat. Gallery of Can., 2002, Hotel de Sully, Paris, 2002, The Israel Mus., Jerusalem, 2002, The Whitney Mus., NYC, 2002, H. Lunn Collection, Lille, 2003, Photology, Milan, 2003, Akira Ikeda Gallery, Berlin, 2003, Aperture: Photography Past/Forward, NYC, 2003, Nat. Gallery Can., Ottawa, 2004, Yancey Richardson Gallery, NYC, 2004, Ideal And Reality, Museo Morandi, Bologna, Italy, 2004, 08, Guggenheim, Bilbao, 2005, Bruce Silverstein, NYC, 2005, Ctr. D'Art Del'Yonne, 2005, Wessel and O'Connor Fine Art, NYC, 2005, Mus. Contemporary Photography, Chgo., 2005, Cité Internat., Cite International Paris, 2008: "The Book", Paris, 2006, Houston Ctr. for Photography, Silver Retrospective, 2006, "Eye of the Beholder", Richard Avedon collection, 2006, "The Invisible Landscape", Nat. Gallery Can., 2007, Miami Mus., Charles Cowles collection, 2007, Mus. Photography, Bogota, Columbia, 2007, Photo London, Silverstein-Photography, 2007, Terry Etherton Gallery, Tucson, Ariz., 2007, Dalton Gallery, Agnes Scott Coll., Decatur, Ga., (Group Shows) Art & Basel, Miami, 2007, Getty Mus., La., The Nude, 2007, 2nd St. Gallery, Charlottesville, Va., 2008, Bologna Art Fair, 2008, Picasso Mus., Barcelona, 2008, Las Meninas, 2008, Art Basel (Silverstein) 2008, Extraordinary Bodies, The Mutter Mus., Pa., 2008,others; represented in permanent collections, Mus. Modern Art, NYC, San Francisco Mus. Modern Art, 1980, Nat. Gallery Art, Washington, Victoria and Albert Mus., London, George Eastman House, NY, Getty Collection, Moder Museet,Stockholm, Sweden, Whitney Mus., NYC, Guggenheim Mus., NYC, Met. Mus., NYC, Tokyo Met.Mus. Photography, 2008, Nat. Gallery Can., Metropolitan Mus. Art, NYC, Phila. Mus. Art, Trouble in Paradise, TVcon Mus. Art, 2009, Aboukrat Gallery, Paris, French Nat. Ctr. Spatial Rsch., 2009, Bestiare Imaginaire, Galleries Baudoin Lebon, Paris, 2009; UBS Bank, Basel, Gianfrknco Composti Collection, Milano; (perm collections): The Hassalblad Found, Sweden, Art Concern, Kortrijk.subject of monographs: Joel-Peter Witkin, 1985, 88-89, 91, 93, 95-96, 98-2003, 06-08, 09; editor: Masterpieces of Medical Photography, 1987, Harms Way, 1994; visual editor: Songs of Experience, 2002, Songs of Innocence, 2003, Songs of Experience and Songs of Innocence, 2004-05, 21st Edits., The Jour. Joel-Peter Witkin 21 edits, 2009, Bourgeoisie-in-de-Nile, 2006, The History of Hats in Art, NY Times, 2006, Maestro Witkin, Delpire Editeuyr, 2009, Portfolio of Etchings: Landfall Press, Santa Fe, 2007; artist in residence: Paris, 1994, 98, 2000, Rome, 1996, Berlin, 1998, Buenos Aires, 2003, Moscow, 2005., La Photographie Americaine Bibliothe que Nationale de France, 2008, Maccarone Gallery Curaned by Alison Gingas, NYC, Gallerie Hotel La Marcheau-Bastille Paris, 2008, Marietime, Contemporary Art Gallery U. Scnn., 2008; contbr. articles to profl. jours. Served with U.S. Army, 1961-64, Photographer. Decorated Commandeur des Arts et de Lettres (France), 2000; recipient The Augustus Saint Gaudens medal The Cooper Union, 1996, Disting. Alumni award The Cooper Union, 1986, Internat. Ctr. Photography award, 1988, award for N.Y. Times "The Plague Yr.," Soc. Publ. Designers, 2000; Ford Found. grantee, 1977, 78, Nat. Endowment in Photography grantee, 1980, 81, 86, 92; Smithsonian Archives Am. Art award, 2009, Named The Cooper Union Alumni Hall of Fame, 2009 Address: 1707 Five Points Rd SW Albuquerque NM 87105-3017 Home Phone: 505-842-6511; Office Phone: 505-843-6682. Business E-Mail: jwitkin1@comcast.net. *My work is based on the nature of man and his relation to the divine. In the work I attempt to establish: A creative and intellectual standrad for still photography in a society in moral freefall.*

WITKOP, BERNHARD, chemist; b. Freiburg, Baden, Germany, May 9, 1917; came to U.S., 1947, naturalized, 1953; s. Philipp W. and Hedwig M. (Hirschhorn) W.; m. Marlene Prinz, Aug. 8, 1945; children: Cornelia Johanna, Phyllis, Thomas. Diploma, U. Munich, 1938, PhD, 1940, Golden Dr. Diploma, 1990; ScD, Privat-Dozent, 1947. Matthew T. Mellon research fellow Harvard U., 1947-48, mem. faculty, 1948-50; spl. USPHS fellow Nat. Heart Inst., NIH, 1950-52; vis. scientist Nat. Inst. Arthritis and Metabolic Diseases, 1953, chemist, 1954-55, chief sect. metabolites, 1956-87, chief lab. chemistry, 1957-87, scholar, 1987-92, hon. scholar emeritus, 1993; vis. prof. U. Kyoto, Japan, 1961, U. Freiburg, Fed. Repubic Germany, 1962; adj. prof. U. Md. Med. Sch., Balt.; Nobel symposium lectr. Stockholm-Karlskoga, 1981. Mem. bd. Internat. Sci. Exchange, 1974; exec. com. NRC, 1975; mem. Com. Internat. Exchange, 1977, Paul Ehrlich Award Com., Frankfurt, 1980-97; bd. dirs. Leo Baeck Inst., NY. Editor: Fedn. European Biochem. Soc. Letters, 1979-90. Recipient Superior Svc. award USPHS, 1967; Paul Karrer Gold medal U. Zurich, 1971; Kun-ni-to (medal of sci. and culture 2d class) Emperor of Japan, 1975; Alexander von Humboldt award for sr. U.S. scientists, 1978 Mem. NAS, Am. Chem. Soc. (Hillebrand award 1958, Golden Membership 1997), Am. Acad. Arts and Sci., Am. Philos. Soc., Acad. Leopoldina (fgn.), Pharm. Soc. Japan (hon.), Chem. Soc. Japan (hon.), Japanese Biochem. Soc. (hon.), Acad. Scientiarum et Artium Europaea, Rheinisch-Westfälische Akademie der Wissenschaften. Office: NIH-Dept Health Edn & Welfare 2A 04 Bldg 8 Bethesda MD 20892-0001 *A career between two worlds and two wars, spanning 50 years of research aims changing from structural to dynamic aspects, may be considered epigonal in the sense that my teacher H. Wieland (Nobel Prize 1928) always considered biochemistry as a neglected area of organic chemistry. In a small way I tried to follow his example and interests, such as oxidation mechanisms, natural products and highly active toxins.*

WITMER, CAREY, publishing executive; BA in Liberal Arts, U. Iowa. Group sr. v.p. Fox Associates; joined Meredith Corp., 1998, advertising dir. Midwest Living mag., publisher Country Home mag., assoc. publisher Better Homes and Gardens, 2006—08, publisher Family Circle, 2008—. Office: Meredith Corp 125 Park Ave New York NY 10017 Office Phone: 212-557-6600.*

WITMER, JOHN RICHARD, librarian; b. Dallas, Dec. 26, 1949; s. John Albert and Doris May (Ferry) W.; m. Joyce Ann Pelzl, Nov. 25, 1972; 1 child, Katherine Anne. Student, Wheaton Coll., Ill., 1967-70; BS, West Tex. State U., 1971; MSLS, East Tex. State U., 1974; postgrad., Dallas Theol. Sem., 1978-81. Cert. secondary tchr., driving instr., learning resources specialist, Tex. Learning resources specialist Sherman (Tex.) Ind. Sch. Dist., 1974-76, Ector County Ind. Sch. Dist., Odessa, Tex., 1978-80; acting head libr. Calvary Bible Coll., Kansas City, Mo., 1976-77; head libr. Am. Christian Coll., Tulsa, 1977-78; tech. svcs. libr. Odessa Coll., 1980-82; tchr. county youth ctr. Ector County Ind. Sch. Dist., Odessa, Tex., 1985; reader svcs. libr. Wayland Bapt. U., Plainview, Tex., 1986-87; vis. tchr. Lubbock (Tex.) Ind. Sch. Dist., 1987-88; learning resources specialist Dallas Ind. Sch. Dist., 1988-90, 94-99; head libr. San Elizario Ind. Sch. Dist., El Paso, Tex., 1991-94; audio visual libr. Klein Ind. Sch. Dist., Houston, 1999—2003; literary cafe libr. Alief Ind. Sch. Dist., Houtson, 2003—. Deacon Scofield Meml. Ch., Dallas, 1971-74, Odessa Bible Ch., 1981-86; mem. cast, crew Permian Playhouse, Odessa, 1979-82. Capt. U.S. Army, 1972-85. Mem. Tex. Libr. Assn. (life), Classroom Tchrs. Dallas (bldg. rep. 1989-90), Odessa Profl. Educators (sec., v.p., pres. state dist. rep. 1978-81), Odessa Univ. Kiwanis (v.p., pres. 1984-85). Republican. Avocations: collecting books and trivia, church work, contests, travel. Home: 15114 Runbell Pl Houston TX 77095-3228 Home Phone: 281-345-4590. E-mail: johnwitmer@juno.com.

WITMEYER, JOHN JACOB, III, lawyer; b. New Orleans, Dec. 18, 1946; s. John J. and Thais Audrey (Dolese) W. BS, Tulane U., 1968; JD with distinction, Duke U., 1971. Bar: NY. Assoc. Mudge Rose Guthrie & Alexander, NYC, 1971-76; ptnr. Ford Marrin Esposito & Witmeyer (now Ford, Marrin, Esposito, Witmeyer & Gleser LLP), NYC, 1976—. Bd. trustees Gregorian U. Found., 1999—; adv. coun. Paul Tulane Coll., Tulane U., 1998—2006, Sch. Liberal Arts Tulane U., 2006—; bd. dirs. Tulane Assocs., Tulane U., 2001—. Ret. col. US Army. Mem.: Order of the Holy Sepulchre (knight comdr. with star). Office: Ford Marrin Esposito Witmeyer & Gleser LLP Wall St Plz New York NY 10005-1875 Business E-Mail: jjwitmeyer@fmew.com.

WITOLD, KACZANOWSKI, painter, sculptor; b. Warsaw, May 15, 1932; arrived in US, 1968; s. Feliks and Zofia Kaczanowski; divorced; children: Paul Kaczanowski, Paulina Kaczanowski, Wit Kaczanowski. Grad., Fine Art Acad., Warsaw, 1956. Exhibitions include Otis Art Inst., LA, 1973, Represented in permanent collections Conoco Oil Co., Houston, United Calif. Bank, Beverly Hills. Achievements include Co-designer Auschwitz Cultural Ctr. Home: 329 Detroit St Denver CO 80206 Studio: Zwirki 1 Wigury 53a m15 02-091 Warsaw Poland

WITONSKY, SHARON, veterinarian, educator; b. Dallas; BA, Earham Coll., Richmond, Ind., 1989; DVM, U. Minn., St. Paul, 1993; PhD, U. Tenn., Knoxville, 1997. Cert. D ACVIM, 2003. Asst. prof. VM-RCVM, Blacksburg, Va., 2000—06, assoc. prof., 2006—. Contbr. chapters to books to profl. jours. Recipient, Earlahm Coll., 2005, Pfizer award, VMRCVM, 2006. Mem.: AVMA, EPM Soc., ACVIM (chair), Phi Beta Kappa. Office: VMRCVM Va Tech Phase II Duck Pond Dr Blacksburg VA 24061-0442 Office Fax: 540-231-1676. Business E-Mail: switonsk@vt.edu.

WITORSCH, PHILIP, internist, educator; b. NYC, July 11, 1937; s. Benjamin and Sarah (Etkin) Witorsch; m. Joan Linda Pellman, June 7, 1959; children: Beth Joy, Jeffrey Lee. BA, NYU, 1958, MD, 1962. Diplomate Am. Bd. Internal Medicine, Am. Bd. Pulmonary Disease. Intern, resident internal medicine Yale U., New Haven Hosp., 1962—64; clin. assoc., clin. investigator Nat. Inst. Allergy and Infectious Diseases NIH, Bethesda, Md., 1964—67; resident, chief resident in internal medicine, fellow pulmonary diseases VA. Hosp., Washington, 1967—69; chmn. pulmonary and critical care medicine, dir. med. intensive care unit, med. dir. respiratory therapy Washington Hosp. Ctr., 1969—82, sr. attending in medicine, 1969—2005; prof. medicine and physiology, dir. sect. environ. medicine and toxicology, divsn. pulmonary diseases and allergy, med. dir. for respiratory care George Washington U., 1983—95; prof. medicine and pharmacology Georgetown U. Med. Ctr. and Hosp., 1995—, dir. environ. occupl. toxicology assessment program, 1995—; attending physician medicine Georgetown U. Hosp., 1995—; dir. clin. cons. svc. clin. pharmacology divsn. Georgetown U. Med. Ctr. and Georgetown U. Hosp., 1995—; med. dir. occupl. health program Georgetown U. Med. Ctr., 2005—. Cons. pulmonary disease VA Hosp. NIH, Dept. State, Andrews AFB, Dept. Justice, Dept. Labor. Contbr. articles to profl. jours. With USPHS, 1964—67. Fellow: ACP, Royal Soc. Medicine, Am. Geriatric Soc., Am. Coll. Chest Physicians (gov. Washington chpt. 1995—97); mem.: AMA (Physicians Recognition award 1972, 1975, 1978, 1981, 1984, 1987, 1990, 1993, 1996, 1999), Montgomery County Med. Soc., Am. Coll. Occupl. and Environ. Medicine, Am. Coll. Toxicology, Am. Soc. Internal Medicine, Am. Heart Assn., Am. Assn. Respiratory Therapy, Am. Fedn. Clin. Rsch., Med. Chirurgical Faculty Md., Med. Soc. DC, DC Thoracic Soc., Am. Thoracic Soc., Soc. Critical Care Medicine, Phi Beta Kappa, Alpha Omega Alpha. Office: Dept Pharmacology Georgetown Univ Med Ctr MED-DENT SE 402 Box 571443 3900 Reservoir Rd NW Washington DC 20057-1443 Home Phone: 301-983-0758; Office Phone: 202-687-0398. Business E-Mail: Witorscp@georgetown.edu.

WITSCHEY, WALTER ROBERT THURMOND, anthropologist, educator, former museum director; b. Charleston, W.Va., June 19, 1941; s. Robert E. and Sarah Elizabeth (Thurmond) W.; m. Joan DuRelle Vincent, July 19, 1980; children: Anne Elizabeth, Schon Roberts Parris, Sarah C. Brauner, Walter Robert Thurmond II, Benjamin Hart Vincent. BA in Physics, Princeton U., 1963; MBA in Ops. Rsch., U. Va., 1965; MA in Anthropology-Maya Archaeology, Tulane U., 1989, PhD in Anthropology-Maya Archaeology, 1993. Systems engr. IBM Corp., Richmond, Va., 1965-67, mktg. rep., 1967-69; v.p. The Computer Co., Richmond, Va., 1969-70, pres., CEO, 1970-84; cons., pub., proprietorship Gatewood Co., Richmond, Va., 1978—; dir., CEO Sci. Mus. Va., Richmond, Va., 1992—2007, dir. emeritus, 2007—; prof. anthropology and sci. edn. Cook-Cole Coll. Arts and Scis., Longwood U., Farmville, Va., 2007—. Bd. dirs. Highland Data Svcs., 1982-85; vis. instr. computer systems U. Va., 1985-86; instr. word processing, Delgado Community Coll., 1989; lectr. microcomputer applications, Our Lady Of Holy Cross Coll., 1989-92; lectr. dept. Anthropology, Tulane U., 1987-92, asst. to the dir., 1987-88, lectr., curriculum cons., 1988-92, adj. instr. A.B. Freeman Sch., 1991; adj. faculty dept. Sociology, Anthropology and Mathematical Scis., Va. Commonwealth U., 1992—. Contbr. articles to profl. jours. Dir. Assn. Sci.-Tech. Ctrs., 1995—, Sci. Mus. Va. Found., Richmond, 1981-90, La. Sci. Ctr., New Orleans, 1985-90; pres., dir. Richmond-on-the-James, 1984-85; sec., dir. Richmond Cmty. H.S. Policy Bd.; cons. Federated Arts Coun., Richmond; pres. Va. Rail Policy Inst., 2008-. Tinker Found. archaeol. rsch. grantee (3), Middle Am. Rsch. Inst. archaeol. grantee, Mesoam. Ecology Inst. archaeol. rsch. grantee (3), Middle Am. Rsch. Inst. archaeol. rsch. grantee (3), pvt. archaeol. rsch. grantee. Mem. AAAS, Am. Assn. Mus., Soc. Am. Archaeology, Va. Acad. Sci. (pres. 2003-04), Sigma Xi. Presbyterian. Avocation: field archaeology. Office: Longwood U 201 High St Farmville VA 23909

WITT, ALICIA, actress; b. Worcester, Mass., Aug. 21, 1975; d. Robert and Diane W. Home edn. Actress Internat. Creative Mgmt., Beverly Hills, Calif. TV appearances: Cybill, 1995-98, The Disappearance of Vonnie, 1994, Blackout, 1993, Twin Peaks, 1991, Hotel Room, Ally McBeal, 2000, Ring of the Nibelungs, 2004; film appearances: Dune, 1984, Liebestraum, 1991, Bodies, Rest and Motion, 1993, Fun, 1994 (Spl. Jury Recognition award Sundance Film Festival 1994), Four Rooms, 1995, Mr. Holland's Opus, 1995, Citizen Ruth, 1996, The Reef, 1997, Bongwater, 1998, Urban Legend, 1998, (voice) Gen 13, 1998, Cecil B. DeMented, 2000, Playing with Mona Lisa, 2000 (Best Actress award U.S. Comedy Arts Festival 2000), Vanilla Sky, 2001, Ten Tiny Love Stories, 2001, American Girl, 2002, Two Weeks Notice, 2002, The Upside of Anger, 2005, 88 Minutes, 2007; prodr. On the Wise, 2005; actor, prodr. Girls' Lunch, 2004; TV film appearances Ring of the Nibelungs, 2004, Blue Smoke, 2007; TV guest appearances Twin Peaks, 1990, Hotel Room, 1993, The Sopranos, 2000, Ally McBeal, 2000, The Twilight Zone, 2003, (mus. theater) The Gift, 2000; stage appearances Dissonance, 2007. Recipient Spl. Jury Recognition for acting, Sundance Film Festival, 1994, Ind. Spirit Award nomination, 1995. Avocations: listening to big-band recordings, chess, backgammon, bowling. Office: Brillstein-Grey Entertainment 9150 Wilshire Blvd Ste 350 Beverly Hills CA 90212

WITT, BETSY, criminologist, educator; PhD, Sam Houston State U., Huntsville, 2004. Author: (textbook) Briefs of Leading Cases in Corrections. Mem.: Acad. Criminal Justice Scis. (sec., treas. juvenile justice sect. 2008—). Office: Limestone Coll 1115 Coll Dr Gaffney SC 29340 Business E-Mail: bwitt@limestone.edu.

WITT, DAVID L., curator, writer; b. Kansas City, Mo., Nov. 3, 1951; s. Lloyd Vernon and Dean Witt. BS in Polit. Sci., Kans. State U., 1974; M Liberal Studies, U. Okla., 2000. Naturalist Naish Nature Ctr., Edwardsville, Kans., summers 1967-70; asst. curator Seton Mus., Cimarron, N.Mex., summers 1972-74; curatorial asst. Riley County Hist. Mus., Manhattan, Kans., 1973-74; mus. asst. Millicent Rogers Mus., Taos, N.Mex., 1976-77; curator The Gaspard House Mus., Taos, N.Mex., 1978-79, The Harwood Found., Taos, N.Mex., 1979—2005, Acad. for Love of Learning, Santa Fe, 2005—. Author: The Taos Artists, 1984, Taos Moderns: Art of the New, 1992 (Southwest Book award Border Regional Libr. Assn. 1993), Modernists in Taos from Martin to Dasburg, 2002 (S.W. Book award Border Regional Libr. Assn. 2003, Ralph Emerson Twitchell award N.Mex. Hist. Soc. 2003); co-author: Spirit Ascendant: The Art and Life of Patrociño Barela, 1996 (S.W. Book award Border Regional Libr. Assn. 1997); contbr. Taos Artists and Their Patrons, 1898-1950; contbr. articles to profl. jour. Organizer first N.Mex. Art History Conf., 1986; founder S.W. Art Hist. Coun., 1990. Mem. PEN, Am. Assn. Mus., N.Mex. Assn. Mus. (pres. 1986-88). Home: PO Box 317 Taos NM 87571-0317 Personal E-mail: davidlwitt@cybermesa.com.

WITT, DENNIS RUPPERT, mathematics educator; b. Buffalo, Apr. 25, 1954; s. Carlton Albert and Elinor Marie W.; m. Donna Violet Endres, July 9, 1983. BS in Math., SUNY, Fredonia, 1976; cert. in Cobol programming, Erie C.C., 1979; MS in Edn., Canisius Coll., 1981, MS in Ednl. Adminstrn., 1993. Cert. math. tchr. and sch. dist. adminstr., N.Y. Tchr. jr. high math. Frontier Ctrl. Sch. Dist., Hamburg, NY, 1977—90, tchr. sr. high math., 1988—2001, tchr. mid. sch. math, 2001—. Cons. spl. computer projects Goldome Realty Credit Corp., Amherst, N.Y., 1985-87, Chevrolet/GMC Saginaw divsn., Buffalo, 1988, Faulring's Cabinet Making, North Collins, N.Y., 1989, Avanti Corp., 1987, Gen. Mills, 1975-77; adminstrv. asst, prin. Frontier Summer Sch., 1993-96; curriculum cons. in field. Mem.planning com., chair bike ride Am. Diabetes Assn., 2008—, mem. exec. Tour de Cure, 2009—. Named Girls Cross-Country Coach of Yr., Channel 7 TV, Buffalo, 1987. Mem.: Am. Diabets Assn. (exec. planning com. mem. 2009—), Frontier Ctrl. Tchrs.' Assn. (rep. coun. 1995—, chmn. membership com. 2002—07, mem. exec. com. 2002—, trustee benefit fund 2002—, mem. negotiation team 2005—, treas. 2006—, co-chair negotiation 2007—08). Avocations: weight training, bicycling. Office: Frontier Ctrl Sch 2751 Amsdell Rd Hamburg NY 14075-1335 Office Phone: 716-926-1730 ext. 3480.

WITT, HUGH ERNEST, manufacturing executive, consultant; b. Winchester, Ky., Nov. 18, 1921; s. Hugh E. and Louella (Milliken) W.; m. Janie Bryan (dec. Oct. 1990); m. Evelyn Chapman, Apr. 22, 1993. Student, Transylvania U., 1941-43; BS, U. Ky., 1945; MS, MIT, 1957. Asst. to dep. asst. sec. Dept. of Air Force, Washington, 1954-61, dep. asst. sec., 1961-70, Dept. of Navy, Washington, 1970-73; prin. dep. asst. Sec. of Def., Washington, 1973-74; fed. procurement policy adminstr. Office Mgmt. and Budget, Washington, 1974-77; dir., govt. liaison United Techs. Corp., Washington, 1977-81, v.p., govt. liaison, 1981-87, cons. to United Techs. Corp., 1987—. Pres. Old Town Civic Assn., Alexandria, Va., 1961-63; bd. dirs. Alexandria Hist. Found.; mem. Alexandria Bd. Archtl. Rev., 1964-77; trustee Alexandria Hosp. Found., 1992-94. Alfred P. Sloan fellow MIT, Cambridge, Mass., 1956-57. Fellow Nat. Contract Mgmt. Assn.; mem. Aerospace Industries Assn., Nat. Security Indsl. Assn., MIT Alumni Assn., Soc. Sloan Fellows, Kappa Alpha.

WITT, JAMES LEE, management consultant, former federal agency administrator; b. Paris, Ark., Jan. 6, 1944; m. Lea Ellen; children: Jimmy, Michael. Ph.D (hon.), Ark. Tech U., 2007. Founder, owner Witt Constrn. Co., 1968—78; county judge Yell County, Ark., 1978—88; dir. Office Emergency Services Ark. Office Emergency Services, Little Rock, 1988—93; dir. Fed. Emergency Mgmt. Agy. (FEMA), Washington, 1993—2001; chmn., CEO James Lee Witt Assoc., LLC, Washington, 2002—; CEO Internat. Code Coun., 2003—06; CEO, Crisis Mgmt. & Preparedness Services Global Options Group, LLC, 2006—; nat. co-chmn. ProtectingAmerica.org, Washington, 2006—. Co-author (with James Morgan): Stronger in the Broken Places: Nine Lessons for Turning Crisis into Triumph, 2002. Chmn. bd. Child Devel., Inc., charter; Gov.'s rep. state disasters, Presdl. disasters Recognized for reinvention efforts Nat. Assn. Counties; recipient Clara Barton Disting. Humanitarian award, ARC Greater Ark., 2007 Office: James Lee Witt Associates 1501 M St NW Washington DC 20005*

WITT, JIM, executive editor; Grad., Tex. State U., San Marcos, 1974. Asst. mng. editor, news Star-Telegram Arlington, 1986—92, editor, 1992—95; pub. Star Telegram Northeast Tarrant County Ed., 1995—95; sr. v.p. & exec. editor Ft. Worth Star-Telegram, 1996—. Named to University Star Hall of Fame, Tex. State U.-San Marcos, 2007. Fellow: Transforming News Orgns. for the Digital Now Knight Media Ctr.; mem.: Tex. AP Mng. Editors, Am. Soc. Newspaper Editors. Office: Ft Worth Star-Telegram 400 W 7th St Fort Worth TX 76102-4793 Office Phone: 817-390-7704. E-mail: jwitt@star-telegram.com.

WITT, MELVIN SYLVAN, periodical editor, publisher; b. Stockton, Calif., Dec. 25, 1925; s. Arnold and Sarah (Peletz) W.; m. Dorothy Halling, June 17, 1949; children: Ann, Mallory. BS, U. Calif., Berkeley, 1948; JD, U. Calif., San Francisco, 1951. Bar: Calif. 1952. Trial atty. State Compensation Ins. Fund, LA, 1954-57; appellate atty. Calif. Indsl. Accident Commn., San Francisco, 1957-60, trial referee, 1961-64; pvt. practice Berkeley, 1966-68; rsch. atty. Calif. Continuing Edn. of Bar, Berkeley, 1969-75; sec., dep. commr. Calif. Workers' Compensation Appeals Bd., San Francisco, 1964-66, chmn., 1975-80, Calif. Workers' Compensation Adv. Commn. to Calif. State Bar, 1974-75; founder, editor, pub. Calif. Workers' Compensation Reporter, Berkeley, 1973—2007. Adj. prof. law Golden Gate U. Law Sch., San Francisco, 1971—75, 1981, McGeorge Law Sch., U. of Pacific, Sacramento, 1973—75; lectr. U. Calif. Ext., Berkeley, 1961—75. Editor, co-author: California Workers' Compensation Practice, 2nd edit., (Calif. CEB) 1973. With inf., U.S. Army, 1944-46, ETO. Named Pub. Ofcl. of Yr., Calif. Applicants' Attys. Assn., Sacramento, 1980; recipient commendation by resolution Calif. State Legislature, Sacramento, 1981; CAAA scholar, 1999, Lifetime Achievement award, State Bar Calif. Workers' Compensation Sect., 2006. Mem. 78th Inf. Divsn. Vets. Assn. Democrat. Avocation: military history.

WITT, ROBERT E., academic administrator; b. Sept. 16, 1940; m. Anne Witt; children: Peter, Karen. BA in Econs., Bates Coll., 1962; MBA, Dartmouth Coll., 1964; PhD in Bus. Adminstrn., Pa. State U., 1968. Rsch. asst. Amos Tuck Sch., Dartmouth Coll., Hanover, N.H., 1964-65; instr. mktg. Pa. State U., 1967-68; asst. prof. Coll. and Grad. Sch. Bus., U. Tex., Austin, 1968-71, assoc. prof., 1971-75, chmn. dept. mktg., 1973-83, prof., 1975-83, Zale Corp. centennial prof. bus., 1983-85, Betty and Glenn Mortimer centennial prof. bus., 1985-95, centennial chairperson bus. edn. leadership, 1986-95, acting dean, then dean, 1985—95; interim pres. U. Tex., Arlington, 1995-96, pres., 1996—2003, U. Ala., 2003—. Mem. budget coun. dept. mktg. adminstrn. U. Tex., Austin, 1969-85, mem. faculty exec. devel. program 1969—, mem. dean's coun., 1986—; mem. athletes adv. com. NCAA, 1986—; mem. acad. adv. bd. World Mgmt. Coun., 1988; mem. future directions coun. U. Tex. Ex-Students Assn., 1978-88, mem. exec. coun., 1981-83, 87-89; mem. adv. bd. dirs. Post Oak Bank, 1993—, Frost Nat. Bank, 1993—; mem. Acctg. Edn. Change Commn., 1992—; bd. dirs. Life Ptnrs. Group. Assoc. editor Social Sci. Quar., 1970-72; mem. editl. rev. bd. Jour. Mktg., 1971-73, 82-85; contbr. articles to profl. jours. Bd. dirs. Austin Symphony, 1991—, Univ. Coop. Soc., 1978-82. Recipient Top Hand award U. Tex. Ex-Students Assn., 1988. Mem. Am. Mktg. Assn. (fellow doctoral consortium 1967, progran chmn. doctoral consortium 1972, reviewer, presenter), Assn. for Consumer Rsch. (treas. 1976, mem. exec. com. 1975-76, reviewer, conf. session chmn.), Am. Assembly Collegiate Schs. of Bus. (bd. dirs. 1991—, mem. visitation com. 1991, mem. govtl. rels. com. 1986-89, chmn. govtl. rels. com. 1987-89), So. Mktg. Assn. (conf. trach chmn., presenter), Beta Gamma Sigma (v.p. U. Tex. chpt. 1973-74, pres. chpt. 1974-75), Phi Kappa Phi. Office: Office of Pres PO Box 870100 203 Rose Administration Tuscaloosa AL 35487-0100 Office Phone: 205-348-5100. Office Fax: 205-348-8377. E-mail: witt@pres.ua.edu.*

WITT, RUTH HUTT, management consultant; b. Columbus, Aug. 8, 1957; d. Thomas Micijah and Mary Barnes; children: Jeffrey Tyler Sheppar, William Fisher III. B of Elec. Engring. Tech., Ohio Inst. Tech., Columbus, 1979. Metallurgical tech. Reynolds Metal, Richmond, Va.; bus. analyst Va. Power, Lavisa; mng. prin. Oracle, Reston. Home: 15255 Brazil Cir Dale City VA 22193 Office: Oracle 1910 Oracle Way Reston VA 20190

WITT, STUART O., aerospace transportation executive; b. Bakersfield, Calif. m. Susan Etoch; 3 children. Grad., Calif. State U., Northridge, 1974, Naval Fighter Weapons Sch. (TOPGUN), 1980, U. Md. Ctr. Creative Leadership, 1996, Naval Aviation Schs. Command, 1997. Engring. test pilot B-1B, F-16C and F-23 Westinghouse Electric Corp. (now Northrop Grumman), 1985—93; program mgr. CTA, 1993, v.p., Western Region dir., exec. v.p., dir. State and Comml. practice; gen. mgr., bd. dirs. Mojave Air and Space Port, Calif. Trustee area 2 Kern Cmty. Coll. Bd. Trustees. F-14 Tomcat pilot VF-14 USN, FA-18A project pilot USN, Naval Air Warfare Ctr., China Lake, Calif. Mem.: Soc. Exptl. Test Pilots, Calif. Space Authority (hon.; life). Office: Mojave Air and Space Port 1434 Flightline St Mojave CA 93501 Office Phone: 661-824-2433. Office Fax: 661-824-2914. E-mail: stuart@mojaveairport.com.

WITT, TOM, economics researcher, educator; b. Borger, Tex., Apr. 22, 1944; s. Eugene Thomason and Helen C. (Hathaway) W.; m. Grethe A. Myles, Mar. 4, 1976. BA, Okla. State U., Stillwater, 1966; MA, Washington U., St. Louis, 1968, PhD, 1974. Asst. prof. dept. econs. W.Va. U., Morgantown, 1970-75, assoc. prof. dept. econs., 1975-80, acting asst. dean Grad. Sch., 1977-78, exec. dir. Bur. Bus. Rsch., 1985—, dir. Ctr. Econs. Rsch., 1985—, acting assoc. dean Coll. Bus. and Econs., 1985-86, assoc. dean rsch. and outreach Coll. Bus. and Econs., 1994—2006. Cons. Nat. Regulatory Rsch. Inst., Columbia, Ohio, 1980-81, Am. Electric Power, 1995—, Allegheny Power, 1997—, exec. legis. br. Govt. W.Va., 1985—; cons., expert witness W.Va. Human Rights Commn., Charleston, 1984; expert witness W.Va. Atty. Gen., 1987-88, Ashland Oil, 1992-93. Author: Power from the Appalachians, 1989, also monographs; co-editor: West Virginia in the Nineties: Policies for Econ. Progress; econs. columnist The State Jour., Charleston; contbr. articles to profl. jours. Pres. Cheat Canyon Park Homeowners, Morgantown, 1979-87, Monongalia Arts Ctr., 1980-81; bd. dirs., treas. Friends of W.Va. Pub. Radio, Charleston, 1985-93, chmn., 1989-91; sec.-treas. Cheat Neck Pub. Svc. Dist., 1989-95; mem. Monongalia County Econ. Devel. Authority, 1994—. Mem. Am. Econ. Assn., Regional Sci. Assn., Assn. for Univ. Bus. and Econ. Rsch. (pres. 2000-2001). Home: 3202 Deerfield Ct Morgantown WV 26508-8612 Office: Bureau of Bus & Econ Rsch WV U PO Box 6025 Morgantown WV 26506-6025 Business E-Mail: twitt@wvu.edu.

WITT, WALTER FRANCIS, JR., lawyer; b. Richmond, Va., Feb. 18, 1933; s. Walter Francis and Evelyn Virginia (Riggleman) W.; m. Rosemary Winter, Sept. 5, 1964; children: Leslie Anne Millman, Walter Francis III. BS, U. Richmond, 1954, JD, 1966. Bar: Va. 1966, DC 1974. Assoc. Hunton and Williams, Richmond, 1966-74, ptnr., 1974—. Contbr. articles to profl. jours. 1st lt. US Army, 1955-57. Mem. ABA (chmn. real property com. sect. gen. practice 1995-2000, Va. Bar Assn., Richmond Bar Assn., DC Bar Assn., Phi Beta Kappa, Phi Delta Phi. Home: 8901 Tresco Rd Richmond VA 23229-7725 Home Phone: 804-740-8420; Office Phone: 804-788-8391. Personal E-mail: wittwf@aol.com.

WITTBRODT, EDWIN STANLEY, financial planner, consultant, retired military officer; b. Flint, Mich., Aug. 13, 1918; s. Stanley Frank and Marie (Ross) W.; m. Joan Helen Miller, Apr. 22, 1950; children: Stephanie Rita, Candace Lee, Edwin Stanley. Student, Gen. Motors Inst. Tech., 1936-38, Grad. Sch. Dept. Agr., 1950-51, Indsl. Coll. Defense U., 1961-62, George Washington U., 1962, U. So. Calif., 1963-64, Defense Computer Inst., 1967, U. NH, 1976. Joined U.S. Army, 1941, commd. 2d lt., 1942; advanced through grades to brig. gen. USAF, 1968; various assignments, 1941-49; budget officer Hdqrs. USAF, 1949-53, 56-61; dir. budget and acctg. Hdqrs. N.E. Air Command, Nfld., 1953-56; comptroller space systems div. Los Angeles, 1962-64; comptroller aero., systems div. Wright-Patterson AFB, 1964-66; asst. comptroller USAF, 1966-67; dir. acctg. and fin. Hdqrs. USAF, 1967-68; asst. comptroller air force for acctg. and fin., comdr. Air Force Acctg. and Fin. Ctr., Denver, 1968-71; v.p. systems Cen. Bank Denver, 1971-81, v.p. info. resources mgmt., 1981-84. Bd. dirs. Computer Congenerics Corp. Colo., Hasa Corp. Co-chmn. Combined Fed. Campaign, Denver, 1968-87; Hon. dir. USO, Denver, 1968-71, mem. council, 1971-87. Decorated D.S.M., Legion of Merit, Soldier's medal, Commendation medal with oak leaf cluster; recipient Gen. Jimmy Doolittle Disting. Fellow award, Flint No. Alumni Assn. Disting. Fellow award, 1990, Treas. Dept. Pioneer in Elec. Commerce award, 1995. Mem. Am. Soc. Mil. Comptrollers (past pres. Washington chpt., nat. v.p. 1968-70, pres. Denver chpt. 1971-72), Assn. Govt. Accountants, Assn. Mil. Banks (dir. 1974-84), Am. Inst. Banking, Denver C. of C. (chmn. mil. affairs com. 1979-82), Aurora C. of C. (def. coun. 1987—), Air Force Assn. (v.p. N. Colo. 1971-72, pres. Silver and Gold chpt. 1972-73, state treas. 1976-83, pres. Mile High chpt. 1987-88) Clubs: Columbine Country. *I have adopted two attitudes that I believe assisted me in all of my undertakings: (1)— that of being what I call a "responsible non-conformist" and (2)— "no problems— just opportunities.".*

WITTCOFF, HAROLD AARON, chemist; b. Marion, Ind., July 3, 1918; s. Morris and Bessie (Pruss) W.; m. Dorothy Brochin, 1946; 2 sons AB magna cum laude, DePauw U., Greencastle, Ind., 1940; PhD, Northwestern U., Evanston, Ill., 1943; grad., Advanced Mgmt. Program, Harvard U., Cambridge, Mass., 1964. From mem. staff to v.p., dir. chem. R&D Gen. Mills, Inc., Mpls., 1943—79; v.p., dir. corp. rsch. Gen. Mills Chemicals, Inc., 1969—79; dir. R & D Koor Chems., Beer Sheva, Israel, 1979-82; dir. process evaluation and rsch. planning Chem Systems, Tarrytown, N.Y., 1982-85; sci. adviser NEXANT/Chem Systems, White Plains, NY, 1985—; adj. prof. chemistry U. Minn., 1973-82. Vis. prof. Chulalongkorn U., Thailand, 1995-2005; adj. prof. chemistry Weizmann Inst., Israel, 1979-2005. Author: The Phosphatides, 1951, Industrial Organic Chemistry: A Perspective 2 vols. 1980; Pharmaceutical Chemicals in Perspective, 1989, Industrial Organic Chemicals, 1996, 2nd edit., 2004, Organic Chemistry Principles and Industrial Practice, 2003; patentee in field. Recipient Minn. award Am. Chem. Soc., 1976 Mem. Phi Beta Kappa, Sigma Xi, Phi Eta Sigma. Home: 12700 Sherwood Pl Apt 207 Minnetonka MN 55305 Personal E-mail: hawittcoff@yahoo.com. Business E-Mail: hwittcoff@nexant.com.

WITTE, ANN DRYDEN, economics educator; b. Oceanside, NY, Aug. 28, 1942; d. Harry Clifford and Frances Elizabeth (Ferguson) Dryden; 1 child, Jeffrey Dryden. BA in Polit. Sci. and History with highest honors, U. Fla., 1963; MA in Econs., Columbia U., 1965; PhD in Econs. and Oceanography, N.C. State U., 1971. Econ. analyst U.S. Govt., Washington, 1963-66, systems analyst, 1966-67; instr. econs. Tougaloo (Miss.) Coll., 1967-68, N.C. State U., Raleigh, 1970-72; vis. asst. prof. U. N.C., Chapel Hill, 1972-74, asst. prof. econs., 1974-79, assoc. prof., 1979-83, prof., 1984—85; rsch. assoc. Nat. Bur. Econ. Rsch., 1984—; prof. Wellesley (Mass.) Coll., 1985—, Fla. Internat. U., Miami, 1992—2000. Cons. to subcom. on oversight House Ways and Means Com., 1979; Fulbright lectr. Fed. U. Pernumburo, Recife, Brazil, 1981, Fed. U. Ceará, Fortaleza, Brazil, 1984 Cen. Sch. of Planning and Statis., Warsaw, 1987, Victoria U., Wellington, N.Z., 1988; lectr. testimony joint econ. com. U.S. Congress, Washington, 1980, coms. U.S. Ho. of Reps., Washington, 1982; resident scholar Rockefeller Found. Study and Conf. Ctr., Bellagio, Italy, 1983; mem. adv. group Internal Revenue, 1989; mem. com. on status of women in econs. profession, 1993-96; spkr., presenter in field. Author: Work Release in North Carolina: The Program and the Process, 1973, Work Release in North Carolina: An Evaluation of Its Post Release Effects, 1975, (with others) Basic Issue in Corrections Performance, 1982, (with Carl Simon) Beating the System; The Underground Economy, 1982, (with Peter Schmidt) An Economic Analysis of Crime and Justice: Theory, Methods and Applications, 1984; editor: (with V. Kerry Smith) Advances in Applied Micro-Economics, Vol. 3, 1984; (with Peter Schmidt) Predicting Recidivism Using Survival Models, 1988, (with Jeffrey Roth and John Scholz) Tax Compliance: An Agenda for Research; adv. editor Evaluation Rev., 1982—; mem. adv. bd. Criminological Research: Advances In Quantitative Method and Application, 1983-84; mem. editorial bd. Rev. Regional Studies, 1976-79, Law and Soc. Rev., 1985-89, Jour. Quantitative Criminology, 1988-2001, Policy Studies Rev., 1988-94; referee Am. Econ. Rev., Demography, Econometrica, Land Econs., Jour. Polit. Econ., Quar. Jour. Econs., numerous others; contbr. numerous articles to profl. jours. Rsch. and adv. com. N.C. Dept. Correction, 1974-76; advisor criminal justice planning N.C. Gov.'s Office, 1977; spl. com. correctional programs N.C. Employment and Tng. Coun., 1982-85, spl. com. on social expts. MacArthur Found., 1984; bd. dirs. Police Found., Washington, 1984-91; mem. committee on Fgn. Tax Matters, 1991-95 tech. expert group Nat. Evaluation Project Pregnant & Substance Abusing Women & Infants HHS, 1991-95; econs. adv. panel NSF, 1992-94. Rsch. grantee Nat. Inst. Justice, Washington, 1978-92, Nat. Inst. Child Health and Devel., Washington, 1981-83, NIMH, Washington, 1981-85, NSF, Washington, 1982-90, 93-96, U.S. Dept. HHS, 1995-; Woodrow Wilson fellow, Harvard Law Sch. fellow, Cambridge, 1987-88. Fellow Am. Soc. Criminology, Am. Statis. Assn., Royal Statis. Soc.; mem. Am. Tax Policy Inst. (bd. trustees 1990—95, subcom. on internat. taxation), Nat. Acad. Scis. (panel on research and rehabilitative techniques 1977-80, ad hoc com. future of justice research 1982, com. on research on law enforcement and adminstrn. of justice 1980-84, ex-officio mem. 1984-88, chair panel for research on taxpayer compliance 1984-88), Am. Econ. Assn. (census adv. com. 1979-85, chair 1981, com. status of women in econs. profession 1993-95), Am. Statis. Assn. (com. on law and justice statistics 1982-84, cons. 1981), Law and Soc. Assn. (trustee 1981-82, 87-90, program com. 1984, Kalven prize com. 1990-91), Nat. Tax Assn./Tax Inst. Am. (program com. 1985, 91, bd. dirs. 1990-94), Ea. Econ. Assn. (program com. 1985-86), Inst. Law and Social Policy (adv. com. on criminal justice 1983-86), Phi Beta Kappa. Avocations: swimming, hiking, modern chamber music, travel, reading.

WITTE, ARNOLD STEWART, neurologist; b. NYC, Dec. 14, 1952; s. Henry Dennis Witte and Shirley Block; m. Debra J. DeLuca, Apr. 29, 1984; children: Samantha, Russell, Daniel, Larissa. BS, SUNY, Stony Brook, 1973; MD, Tufts U., 1977. Diplomate Am. Bd. Internal Medicine, Am. Bd. Neurology & Psychiatry, Am. Bd. Electrodiagnostic Medicine, lic. NJ, Pa. Intern U. Hosps. Cleve., Cleve., 1977—78, resident, 1978—79; resident in neurology Hosp. of U. Pa., Phila., 1980—81, fellow, 1982—83; asst. prof. neurology Thomas Jefferson U. Hosp., 1983—86; mem. staff Capital Health Sys. at Mercer, 1986—, chief dept. neurology, 1989—96, 1999, vice chief dept. neurology, 2000—. Cons. Trenton Psychiat. Hosp., 1987—, Forensic Psychiat. Hosp., 1987—; courtesy staff St. Francis Med. Ctr., 1993—; active staff Robert Wood U. Hosp., Hamilton. Contbr. articles to profl. jours. Mem.: AMA, Mercer County Med. Soc., Am. Acad. Neurology, Alpha Omega Alpha. Office: 2 Princess Rd Lawrenceville NJ 08648 Office Phone: 609-895-9000.

WITTE, ERIC, legislative staff member; Legis. asst., Rep. Leonard Boswell US House of Reps., Washington, sr. legis. asst., Rep. Leonard Boswell, 2001—02, comm. dir., Rep. Leonard Boswell, 2002—05, legis. dir., Rep. Leonard Boswell, 2003—05, chief of staff to Rep. David Loebsack, 2007—. Democrat. Office: 1221 Longworth House Office Bldg Washington DC 20515 Office Phone: 202-225-6576. Office Fax: 202-225-0757.*

WITTE, OWEN NEIL, microbiologist, molecular biologist, educator; b. Bklyn., May 17, 1949; BS, Cornell U., 1971; MD, Stanford U., 1976. Predoctoral fellow Stanford U. Med. Sch., Palo Alto, Calif., 1971-76, MIT Ctr. Cancer Rsch., Cambridge, Mass., 1976-80; asst. prof., Dept. Microbiology, Molecular Genetics UCLA, 1980-82, assoc. prof., Dept. Microbiology, Molecular Genetics, 1982-86, prof., Dept. Microbiology, Molecular Genetics, 1986—, pres.'s chair in devel. immunology, Dept. Microbiology, Molecular Genetics, 1989—, founding dir., Inst. for Stem Cell Biology and Medicine, 2005—; investigator UCLA Howard Hughes Med. Inst., 1986—; prof., microbiology, immunology & molecular genetics UCLA David Geffen Sch. Medicine, 1996—, prof. molecular and med. pharmacology. Adv. bd. mem. Pew Scholars in Biomedical Sci., Damon Runyon Scholars Bd., Lasker Prize Award Jury. Contbr. articles to profl. jours. Am. Cancer Soc. faculty scholar, 1982-87; recipient Faculty award UCLA, 1990, award in basic cancer rsch. Milken Family Med. Found., 1990, Richard and Hinda Rosenthal Found. award Am. Assn. Cancer Rsch., 1991, William Dameshek prize Am. Soc. Hematology, 1993; Outstanding Investigator grantee Nat. Cancer Inst., 50th Anniversary Commemorative award, Leukemia Soc. of Amer., 1999, Warren Alpert Found. prize, 2000, de Villiers Internat. Achievement award, Leukemia and Lymphoma Soc., 2003 Fellow Am. Acad. Arts and Scis., 1996, Am. Acad. Microbiology, 1997; mem. NAS, Inst. Medicine. Office Phone: 310-206-0386. E-mail: owenw@microbio.ucla.edu.

WITTE, ROBERT JAY, lawyer; b. Oklahoma City, May 16, 1968; s. Richard Owen and Janice (Hester) W.; m. Deborah Lynn Hammond, June 15, 1991; children, Brandon Ryan, Courtney Nicole. BA with highest honors, U. Okla, 1990; JD cum laude, So. Meth. U., Dallas, 1993. Bar: Tex. 1993, US Dist. Ct. 1994, US Ct. Appeals (5th cir.) 1994, US Supreme Ct., 1999, US Ct. Appeals (10th cir.) 2002. Atty. Strasburger and Price LLP, Dallas, 1993—. Bd. dirs. Tex. Young Lawyers Assn., 2000—05. Bd. dirs. Dallas Summer Musicals, 2005-, DSM Gala co-chair, 2008; bd. dirs. Dallas Arts Dist. Alliance, 2005-, Am. Heart Assn., 1997-2001; bd. dirs., pres. U. Okla. Club of Dallas, 2002—; bd. dirs., chair. Make-A-Wish Found. of North Tex., 1996—; founding chair Muscular Dystrophy Assn. Dallas Legal Leaders: Hot Hundred Who Care. Recipient Dallas Heart Ball Debra Sue Payne award, Nat. Philanthropy Day award, 2001; named a Tex. Super Lawyer, Tex. Monthly, 2003—07; named one of Best Dallas Lawyers Under 40, D Mag., 2002, 2004, 2006, Best Lawyers in Dallas, 2005, 2007, 2008, Top 40 Bus. Leaders Under 40, Dallas Bus. Jour., 2002, 2005, 2006. Mem. Dallas Bar Assn., Dallas Assn. Young Lawyers (Com. chair leadership devel. 1997—, bd. dirs. 1999-2005, trustee), ABA, Tex. Bar Found., Dallas Bar Found., Leadership Dallas Alumni Assn. Republican. Methodist. Avocations: golf, softball, following college and professional sports, politics. Office: Strasburger and Price LLP 901 Main St Ste 4400 Dallas TX 75202 Office Phone: 214-651-4612. Office Fax: 214-659-4089. Business E-Mail: robert.witte@strasburger.com.

WITTELS, BARNABY CAESAR, lawyer, writer; b. Phila., Mar. 28, 1948; s. David G. and Beatrice Tanya (Graitcer) Wittels; m. Heidi Jo Linsk, Sept. 8, 1974 (div. Aug. 1997); children: Kate Sophie, William David; m. Mary M. Labaree, Sept. 20, 1998. BA cum laude, Temple U., 1970; MA in Pol. Sci., Boston U., 1972, JD, 1975. Bar: Pa. 1975, U.S. Dist. Ct. (ea. dist.) Pa. 1985, U.S. Dist. Ct. Appeals (2d, 3d and 4th cirs.) 1986. Asst. defender Defender Assn. Phila., 1975-80; law clk. to Hon. Stanley Kubacki Ct. Common Pleas Phila. County, 1980-84; ptnr. Wittels, Newman & Bomstein, Phila., 1980-82; assoc. LaCheen & Alva, Phila., 1982-86; ptnr. LaCheen & Assoc., Phila., 1986—2003, LaCheen, Dixon, Wittels & Greenburg, Phila., 2003—. Advisor Temple U. Parliamentary Debate Team, 2004—; mem. lawyers assistance com. Pa. Supreme Ct. Contbr. columns in newspapers. Chair N.W. Victim Svcs., Phila., 1981—84, mem. counsel, 1984—90, bd. dirs., 1983—90, chair, 1997—2003, founding mem., mem. bd. dirs. counsel, 2003—; baseball coach Chestnut Hill Fathers Club, 1985—98, commr., 1991—93, 1992—98; vol. Lawyers Concerned for Lawyers, 2003—; committeeman 21st divsn. Dems., Phila., 1985—90; active various polit. and jud. campaigns, 1980—; mem. exec. com. N.W. Interfaith Movement, 1985—86. Mem.: ABA, NACDL, Phila. Bar Found. (Apothaker award 1983), Pa. Bar Assn., Phila. Bar Assn. (mem. fee dispute com. 1996—, mem. com. to elect good judges 1987—88, mem. lawyers assistance com. 2003—), Pa. Assn. Criminal Def. Lawyers, Germantown Cricket Club. Jewish. Avocations: writing, baseball, football, reading, woodworking. Office: LaCheen Wittels & Greenberg 1429 Walnut St 13th Fl Philadelphia PA 19102 Office Phone: 215-735-5900. Office Fax: 215-735-4649. Personal E-mail: barnabyw@aol.com.

WITTEN, EDWARD, mathematical physicist, educator; b. Balt., Aug. 26, 1951; s. Louis Witten; m. Chiara Nappi; 3 children. BA in history, Brandeis U., 1971; MA, Princeton U., 1974, PhD, 1976; PhD (hon.), Brandeis U., 1988, Hebrew U. of Jerusalem, 1993, Columbia U., 1996, U. Southern Calif., 2004. Postdoctoral fellow Harvard U., 1976—77, jr. fellow, 1977—80; prof. physics Princeton U., NJ, 1980—87; prof. Sch. Natural Scis, Inst. for Advanced Study, Princeton, NJ, 1987—; Charles Simonyi prof. Princeton U., NJ, 1997—. Vis. prof. Calif. Inst. Tech., 1999—2001. Contbr. articles to maps. and profl. jours.; co-author (with M.B. Green and J.H. Schwarz): Supersting Theory, Vol. 1 and 2, Cambridge Univ. Press. Bd. dirs. Americans for Peace Now, 1992—. MacArthur Fellow, 1982; recipient Einstein medal Einstein Soc. Berne, Switzerland, 1985, Phys. and Math. Sci. award N.Y. Acad. Sci., 1985, Dirac medal Internat. Ctr. Theoretical Physics, 1985, Alan Waterman award NSF 1986, Fields Medal, Internat. Union of Mathematicians, 1990, Madison medal, Princeton Univ., 1992, NJ Pride award, 1996, Award of the Golden Plate, Am. Acad. of Achievement, 1997, Klein medal, Stockholm U., 1998, Dannie Heineman prize, Am. Inst. of

Physics, 1998, Nemmers prize in Math., Northwestern U., 2000, Clay Rsch. award, Clay Math. Inst., 2001, Shalom award, Americans for Peace Now, 2002, Nat. Medal of Science, 2002; co-recipient Crafoord prize in Math., Royal Swedish Acad. Scis., 2008. Fellow: Am. Philosophical Soc., Am. Phys. Soc., Am. Acad. Arts & Scis., NAS; mem.: Acad. Scis. Paris (assoc.), Pontifical Acad. Scis. Office: Inst for Advanced Study Sch Natural Scis 1 Einstein Dr Princeton NJ 08540-4920 Office Phone: 609-734-8000, 609-258-2055. Office Fax: 609-258-1124. E-mail: ewitten@princeton.edu.

WITTEN, JASON (CHRISTOPHER JASON WITTEN), professional football player; b. Elizabethton, Tenn., May 6, 1982; Attended, U. Tenn., 2000—02. TE Dallas Cowboys, 2003—. Founder Jason Witten SCORE Found. Named First Team All-Pro, AP, 2007; named to Nat. Football Conf. Pro-Bowl Team, NFL, 2004—08. Achievements include tying the NFL record for receptions by a tight end in a single game (15), 2007. Office: Dallas Cowboys One Cowboys Pkwy Irving TX 75063-4999*

WITTEN, LOUIS, physics professor; b. Balt., Apr. 13, 1921; s. Abraham and Bessie (Perman) W.; m. Lorraine Wollach, Mar. 27, 1949 (dec. 1987); children: Edward, Celia, Matthew, Jesse; m. Francis L. White, Jan. 2, 1992. BE, Johns Hopkins U., Balt., 1941, PhD, 1951; BS, NYU, 1944. Research assoc. Princeton U., NJ, 1951-53; research assoc. U. Md., College Park, 1953-54; staff scientist Lincoln Lab., MIT, 1954-55; assoc. dir. Martin Marietta Research Lab., Balt., 1955-68; prof. physics U. Cin., 1968-91, prof. emeritus, 1991—. Trustee Gravity Research Found. Editor: Gravitation: An Introduction to Current Research, 1962, Relativity: Procs. of Relative Conf. in Midwest of 1969, Symposium on Asymptotic Structure of Space-Time, 1976; patentee in field; contbr. numerous articles to sci. jours. First lt. Air Corps US Army, 1942—46. Fulbright lectr. Weitzmann Inst. Scis., Rehovot, Israel, 1963-64 Fellow Am. Phys. Soc.; mem. Am. Math. Soc., Internat. Astron. Union, AAAS. Office: Univ Cincinnati Dept Physics Cincinnati OH 45221-0011 Home Phone: 513-631-8442; Office Phone: 513-556-0532. Personal E-mail: lwittenw@gmail.com. Business E-Mail: louis.witten@uc.edu.

WITTENBERG, HENRY TAYLOR, JR., physician, surgeon; b. Kansas City, July 5, 1933; s. Henry Taylor and Ruby Lena (Pratt) Wittenberg; m. Helen Marie Marlar, Sept. 7, 1963; children: Heather Melanee, Henry Taylor III. BS in Pharmacy, U. Kans., Lawrence, 1956; DO, Kansas City U. Medicine and Bioscis., 1960. Lic. Mo., 1960, Okla., 1962, cert. Am. med. dir. 1998. Intern Lakeside Hosp., Kansas City, 1960—61; preceptor Claremore Health Ctr., Okla., 1962—64; physician pvt. practice, Independence, Mo., 1961—62, Blue Star Clinic, Claremore, 1962—, Claremore Regional Hosp., 1962—; interim home health med. dir., 2004—. Chief staff Claremore Regional Hosp., 1962—; founder, bd. mem. First Bank of Okla., 1977, v.p. bd., 1977—87; founding mem. Okla. chpt. Am. Med. Dirs., 1991, v.p. bd., 1991—95; med. dir. Wood Manor Nursing Home, 1987—, Claremore Nursing Home, 1989—, Trinity Hospice, 2000—, Colonial Care Nursing Home, 2002—; mem. gov.'s com. Emergency Med. Svc., 1995—2000; mem. adv. bd. Unicare Welfare HMO, 2002—04. Editor-in-chief: U. Kans. Jayhawker U. Kans. Yearbook, 1956. Founding mem., pres. Claremore Jaycees; chmn. Rogers County March of Dimes, 1965—67; Jaycee founder group, original cast mem. Claremore Gridiron, 1966—; lay reader St. Paul's Episcopal Ch., jr. warden, 1998, sr. warden, 1999. Recipient Omicron Delta Kappa Scholastic award, Kans. U., Otto Schnellbacjer award Outstanding Contbr. Campus L:ife, Nat. Leadership award, Nat. Rep. Congressional Com., cert. for contbns. to ambulatory care and pub. health, CDC; named Physician of Yr., Claremore, Okla., 1996, Rep. of Yr., Nat. Rep. Congressional Com. and Bus. Adv. Coun., 2001; named one of Am.'s Top Family Doctors, Consumer Rsch. Coun. Am., 2004, 2007. Mem.: Rogers County Med. Soc. (v.p. 1996, program dir. 1986—97), Okla. Osteo. Assn. (life), U. Kans. Gold Medal Club, Shrine (Potentate's Honor award 2003), Scottish Rite, Masons, Rho Sigma Chi, Sigma Sigma Phi, Psi Sigma Alpha, Kappa Psi (pres.), Delta Chi. Episcopalian. Achievements include delivery over 3000 babies. Office: Blue Star Clinic 206 E Blue Star Dr Claremore OK 74017 Home Phone: 918-341-4278; Office Phone: 918-341-4040.

WITTENBORG, KARIN, university librarian; m. Michael B. Sullivan. BA, Brown U., 1969; MLS, SUNY Buffalo, 1976. Various positions SUNY Buffalo, 1976—79; libr. mgmt. intern MIT, 1981—82; chief gen. reference dept. and curator social sci. collections Stanford U., 1979—85; assoc. univ. libr. collections UCLA, 1985—93; univ. libr. U. Va., 1993—. Adv. coun. Academic Computing and Libr. Stanford U.; mem. com. info. resources Brown U.; exec. com. Digital Libr. Fedn. Recipient Zintl Leadership award, U. Va., 2005. Avocations: cooking, running, gardening. Office: Univ Virginia Library PO Box 400113 Charlottesville VA 22904 Office Phone: 434-924-7849. Fax: 434-924-1431. E-mail: kw7g@virginia.edu.

WITTENBRAKER, RICK L., lawyer, waste management executive; b. New Castle, Ind., Mar. 25, 1948; BBA cum laude, Tex. Christian U., Ft. Worth, 1970; JD, U. Tex., Austin, 1973. Bar: Tex. 1973. Ptnr. Bracewell & Patterson, LLP, Houston, 1983—2003; sr. v.p., gen. counsel, chief compliance officer Waste Mgmt. Inc., Houston, 2003—. Mem. exec. com. bd. dirs. Spring Branch Edn. Found., Houston; bd. trustees Tex. Christian U.; bd. dirs. Assn. Cmty. Broadcasting (Houston Pub. Broadcasting). Mem.: Beta Gamma Sigma. Office: Waste Mgmt Inc 1001 Fannin St Ste 4000 Houston TX 77002 Office Phone: 713-512-6361. E-mail: rwittenbraker@wm.com.

WITTENBRINK, BONIFACE LEO, priest; b. Evansville, Ill., June 30, 1914; s. Max C. and Catherine Rose (Pautler) W. PhL, Gregorian U., Rome, 1939; STL, Ottawa U., Can., 1943; MA, Cath. U. Am., 1947. Ordained priest Oblates of Mary Immaculate, Roman Cath. Ch., 1941. Instr. Latin, logic, history and religion St. Henry's Coll., Belleville, Ill., 1943-48; instr., registrar, prin. high sch. dept. Coll. of Our Lady of the Ozarks, Carthage, Mo., 1948-52; founding dir. King's House of Retreats, Buffalo, Minn., 1952-53; mission procurator Roman Cath. Ch., St. Paul, 1955-56, 59-62; prin. Alemany High Sch. for Boys, Oblate Western Province, San Fernando, Calif., 1956-59; permanent sec. Conf. Maj. Superiors of Men, Washington, 1963-69; exec. dir., sec. Found. for Community Creativity, Washington, 1970-71; founder, dir., then dir. devel. Radio Info. Svc. for Blind and Handicapped, Belleville, 1972-84; pres., then local dir. Friends of Eye Rsch., Boston, 1983-87; exec. v.p. Citizens for Eye Rsch., Belleville, 1987—. Pres. Oblate Ednl. Assn., St. Paul, 1961-62; sci. adv. bd. Nat. Acad. Child Devel., 1984-86; mem. com. Eye Experience St. Louis, 1984; adv. bd. Welfare of the Blind, Inc., 1984—; adv. coun. svcs. for print-handicapped Nat. Pub. Radio, 1976-77; active Internat. Christian Leadership, 1968-72; bd. dirs. LOGOS Translators; ptnr. CBMI. Bd. dirs. Technoserve, 1968-72, Internat. Book Svc., 1969-72; vol. Ill. Literacy Project, 1989-90; founding charter mem., bd. dirs. Washington Workshops Found.; mem. Vision Awards Dinner Com., 1998—. Recipient RPI Internat. Vision award, 27th Annual Vision Awards, Agrama Harmony Gold and Light award, 2000, Beverly Hills, Calif. Mem. Madison County Assn. Blind, Mo. Coun. Blind, Am. Coun. of Blind (ednl. radio com. 1974-76), Am. Found. for Blind (radio talking book com. 1973-76), Inst. for Study of Econ. Systems (bd. dirs. 1971-72), Ednl. Communications Assn., Coun. for Dept. of Peace, Wycliffe Bible Translators Assn., Vols. for Internat. Tech. Assistance, Ill. Radio Info. Svc., Soc. Internat. Devel., UN Assn., Rotary Internat. (Paul Harris fellow), Belleville Econ. Progress, Eagles, KC, Press Club St. Louis, Am. Assn. Ret. Persons. Avocations: reading, travel. Home: 200 N 60th St Belleville IL 62223-3951

WITTENBURG, MICHAEL SHANE, concert pianist, music educator; b. Saarbrücken, Germany, Nov. 26, 1973; s. John Steven and Margaret Wittenburg; 1 child, Karl Frederick. MusB in Performance-Piano, Eastman Sch. Music, 1996, MusM in Performance and Lit.-Piano, 1998; MusM in Performance-Orchestral Conducting, U. Tenn., Chattanooga, 2001. Instr. music Lee U., Cleveland, Tenn., 2001—04, asst. prof. music, 2004—07; organist Christ United Meth. Ch., Chattanooga, 1999—; sect. violin Chattanooga Symphony and Opera, 1999—. Recipient Performer's cert. in Piano, Eastman Sch. Music, 1996; named Oustanding Grad. Student in Music: Performance, U. Tenn., Chattanooga, 2000; fellow Opera Coaching, Eastman Sch. Music, 1996—98. Mem.: Am. Fedn. Musicians (mem. local 80), Pi Kappa Lambda (Faculty Inductee 2005). Conservative. Avocations: tennis, travel. Home: 4500 Holly Tree Ct Apt 212 Orlando FL 32811-7114 Personal E-mail: deliusfan@aol.com.

WITTENSTEIN, GEORGE JUERGEN, retired surgeon, retired educator; b. Tubingen, Germany, Apr. 26, 1919; s. Oskar Juergen and Elisabeth (Vollmoeller) W.; m. Elisabeth Hartert, Apr. 26, 1947 (dec. Jan. 1966); m. Christel J. Bejenke, July 1, 1966; children: E. Deirdre, Nemone E., W. Andreas, Catharina J. MD, U. Munich, 1944; MSc in Surgery, U. Colo., 1956, MD, 1956. Diplomate Am. Bd. Surgery and Thoracic Surgery. Instr. U. Colo. Sch. Medicine, Denver, 1953-60; instr., clin. asst., then prof. UCLA Sch. Medicine, 1964-73; prof., chair dept. surgery Olive View UCLA Med. Ctr., Sylmar, 1974—91; ret. Vis. prof. at various European med. schs., 1991-98; cons. numerous univs.; clin. expert cons. med. jours. Contbr. sci. articles to profl. publs. Bd. dirs. Friends of U. Calif.-Santa Barbara Libr., 1965-75; trustee Santa Barbara Mus. Art, 1968-75. Boettcher Found. scholar, 1955; recipient honor German and Bavarian Govts., Large Medal of Honor Fed. Rep. Germany, 1995, Order of Merit Govt. of State of Bavaria, 2003. Home: 4004 Cuervo Ave Santa Barbara CA 93110-2412 Personal E-mail: cbejenke@aol.com.

WITTER, JONATHAN W., bank executive; b. 1969; MBA, Wharton Sch. Bus. U. Pa., 1995. Economist Agy. for Healthcare Policy & Rsch., Washington, 1991—93; assoc. cons. Deloitte & Touche, Phila. & London; v.p. customer delivery Applied Predictive Technologies, Washington; assoc. prin. McKinsey & Co., 1998—2004; exec. v.p., head of distbn. Wachovia Corp., 2004—08; COO retail banking group Morgan Stanley, NYC, 2008—. Office: Morgan Stanley 1585 Broadway New York NY 10036*

WITTES, JANET TURK, statistician; d. Amos and Regina Wallace Turk; m. Robert Wittes, June 14, 1964; children: Naomi Haia Reichstein, Benjamin, Jeremy. BA in Math., Radcliffe Coll., Cambridge, Mass., 1964; MA in Stats., Harvard U., Cambridge, Mass., 1965, PhD in Stats., 1970. Assoc. prof. Hunter Coll., NYC, 1974—82; chief biostats. rsch. br. Nat. Heart, Lung, and Blood Inst., Bethesda, Md., 1983—89; pres. Stats. Collaborative Inc., Washington, 1990—. Editor in chief Controlled Clin. Trials, Balt., 1990—95. Contbr. scientific papers in field. Trustee Studio Theatre, Washington, 2007—. Fellow: AAAS, Soc. Clin. Trials (pres. 1996), Am. Statis. Assn.; mem.: Internat. Biometric Soc. (pres. 1988—88). Office: Stats Collaborative Inc 1625 Massachusetts Ave NW Ste 600 Washington DC 20036 Business E-Mail: janet@statcollab.com.

WITTHUHN, BURTON ORRIN, retired university official; b. Allentown, Pa., Aug. 22, 1934; s. Ray Arthur and Mae Marcella (Kline) W.; m. Patricia King, June 24, 1961; children: Jonathan, Andrew. BS, Kutztown U., Pa., 1956; MEd, Pa. State U., 1962, PhD, 1968. Tchr. Allentown (Pa.) Pub. Schs., 1956-63; teaching asst., assoc. Pa. State U., University Park, 1963-66, rsch. asst., 1965-66; asst. prof. Ohio State U., Columbus, 1967-70; prof., chmn. dept. geography Edinboro (Pa.) State Coll., 1970-79, assoc. v.p. acad. affairs, 1980-83; provost, v.p. acad. affairs Edinboro Univ. of Pa., 1984-88, Western Ill. U., Macomb, 1988-93, acting pres., 1993, provost, v.p. acad. affairs, prof. geography, 1994—2002, ret., 2002. Vis. rsch. prof. Nat. Taiwan Normal U., 1978; cons. Project Africa/Carnegie-Mellon U., Pitts., 1967-70, 92, 87, 95; mem. mid. states periodic rev. team, Phila., 1986—; mem. mid. states evaluation team in conjunction with Am. Optometric Assn., 1987; mem. evaluation team Pa. Dept. Edn., 1988; mem. accreditation team Am. Optometric, 1990—; evaluator Higher Learning Commn. North Cen. Assn., 1994—; examiner Lincoln Found. for Bus. Excellence, 1996-2000; vice-chmn. Quad Cities Grad. Ctr., 1991-2000; mem. nat. screening com. for Africa, Inst. of Internat. Edn., 1994-96. Co-author: Discovery in Geography, 1976; co-author: So You Want to Go to College: 50 Questions to Ponder, Strategies for Timely Degree Completion: Connecting the Parts, Strategies for Timely Degree Completion: Myths and Realities, Technology: Bridge or Barrier To More Timely Degree Completion?, 1998; mem. editl. bd. Pa. Geographer, Chronicle of CQI; contbr. chpts. to books. Mem. Edinboro Planning & Zoning Commn., 1973-77, McDonough County Tuberculosis Sanitorium Bd., 2003-; vol. Habitat Humanity, Loaves and Fishes, McDonough Dist. Hosp. Recipient Disting. Alumnus award Kutztown U., 1990; Fulbright Hays fellow, Ethiopia, Kenya, Uganda, 1965. Mem. Nat. Coun. Geog. Edn. (exec. bd. 1977-80, mem. award com. for region IV 1981), Pa. Coun. Geog. Edn. (exec. sec. 1976-79, pres. 1975-76, Outstanding Prof. award 1978), Rotary (pres. Macomb club 1998-99, Edinboro club 1972-73), State Univ. Annutants Assn. (pres. Macomb Chptr. 2003—). Methodist. Avocations: reading, golf, photography, volunteering. Home: 24 Heritage Green Hudson WI 54016 Personal E-mail: 13jose22@msn.com.

WITTICH, JOHN JACOB, retired academic administrator, finance company executive; b. Huntley, Ill., Nov. 13, 1921; s. John and Eva (Karl) W.; m. Leah Elliott, Apr. 2, 1944; children: Karen Ann Zvonar, Jane Ellen Tock, John Elliott. BA, DePauw U., 1943, LLD (hon.), 1971; MA, U. N.Mex., 1949; PhD, Stanford U., 1952; LHD (hon.), Ill. Coll., 1979; DPS (hon.), MacMurray Coll., 1980. Tchr. Albuquerque H.S., 1948-49; tchg. asst. Stanford, 1949-51; asst. prof. psychology Coll. of Pacific, Stockton, Calif., 1951-52; dean of admissions and fin. aid, assoc. prof. DePauw U., Greencastle, Ind., 1952-61; exec. dir. Coll. Center of Finger Lakes, Corning, NY, 1961-63, Coll. Student Personnel Inst., Claremont, Calif., 1963-68; adj. prof., dir. grad. studies in student pers. Claremont Grad. Sch., 1963-68; pres. MacMurray Coll., Jacksonville, Ill., 1968-80; dir. Fla. Assn. Colls. and Univs., 1980-84; dir. higher edn. program Stetson U., 1981-88; v.p. Capital Formation Counselors, Inc., Belleair Bluffs, Fla., 1983—2005. Contbr. articles to profl. jours. Exec. com. Divsn. Higher Edn., Ctrl. Ill. Conf. of United Meth. Ch., 1968-80; exec. com. Fedn. Independent Ill. Colls. and Univs. and Assoc. Colls. Ill.; non-pub. adv. com. Ill. Bd. Higher Edn., 1972-78; mem. Nat. Merit Scholarship Selection Com., 1956, 61; cons. Calif. Gov.'s Conf. on Edn., 1965, on Youth, 1966; trustee Fla. Endowment for Humanities, 1982-85; presdl. counsellor Stetson U., 1987—2008; bd. dirs. DeLand House Next Door, 1990-94; citizens adv. com. West Volusia Hosp. Authority, 1992-2002, vice-chmn., 2001-02; rsch. project evaluator for human subjects regional office U.S. FDA, 2003-07, sr. odyssey rsch. programs U. Ill., 2008. With USMC, 1943-46, PTO. Recipient DePauw Achievement award, 1969, Alumni citation DePauw U., 1994; Rockefeller fellow Aspen Inst. for Humanistic Studies, 1979. Mem. APA, Am. Coll. Pers. Assn. (commn. chmn.), Nat. Assn. Coll. Admissions Counselors (exec. bd. 1955-58), Cen. States Coll. Assn. (exec. com. 1969-77, sec.-treas. 1970-77), 4th Marine Divsn. Assn. WW II, Sigma Chi. Home Phone: 217-607-0732.

WITTIG, CAROL HILL, special education educator; d. C.B. and Nell M. Hill; 1 child, Karen. BA, Wayne State U., Detroit, 1973; MA, Oakland U., Rochester, Mich., 1999; MA in Spl. Edn., U. Mich., Dearborn, 2001. Mktg. rep. Ameritech Pub., Troy, Mich., 1973—93; tchr. spl. edn. Detroit Pub. Sch., 2000—. Mem.: DAR, Paint Creek Ctr., Detroit Inst. Arts, Am. Mensa, Learning Disabilities Assn. Am., Internat. Reading Assn., Pi Lambda Theta (Internat. Honor Soc.). Home: PO Box 432 Saint Clair MI 48079

WITTIG, DON, judge; b. San Antonio, Sept. 18, 1941; s. Don A. and Miriam (Moon) W.; children: Jeffrey A., Marie C., Sarah Elizabeth. Student, US Naval Acad., Annapolis, Md., 1960-61; BA in Govt., St. Mary's U., 1963, JD, 1965. Bar: Tex. 1965, US Dist. Ct. (so. dist.) Tex. 1970, US Ct. Claims 1965, US Tax Ct. 1965, US Ct. Customs and Patent Appeals 1965, US Ct. Mil. Appeals 1965, US Ct. Appeals (5th cir.) 1965. Ptnr. Lorance, Thompson & Wittig, Houston, 1972-80, Ellis, Wittig & Smith, Houston, 1984-85; pvt. practice Houston, 1985-88; judge 125th Dist. Ct., Houston, 1988—99; judge, sr. justice 14th Ct. Appeals, 1999—2001. Author: New Local Rules, 1988, A Practical Guide to Ct's. Charge, 1989, Streamlining Trial and Pretrial Practice, 1991. Mem. Internat. Com. Houston Livestock and Rodeo. Fellow Tex. Bar Found. (cert. arbitrator and mediator, double bd. cert. trial atty.), Nat. Arbitration Assn., State Bar Tex., Tex. Bar Found., Cameron County Bar Assn. (dir.). Avocations: writing, reading, golf. Office Phone: 956-233-9094. Personal E-mail: donwittig@gmail.com.

WITTIG, RAYMOND SHAFFER, lawyer, intellectual property technology manager; b. Allentown, Pa., Dec. 13, 1944; s. Raymond Battie and Alice (Shaffer) Wittig; m. Beth Glover, June 21, 1975; children: Meaghan G., Allison G. BA, Pa. State U., 1966, MEd, 1968; JD, Dickinson Sch. Law, 1974. Bar: U.S. Ct. Appeals (DC cir.) 1978. Rsch. psychologist Intext Corp., Scranton, Pa., 1968; minority counsel Small Bus. Com., US House of Reps., Washington, 1975-84; pvt. practice Washington, 1984-92; tech. mgmt. group leader Geo-Ctrs., Inc., Newton, Mass., 1992—2005; prin. Sci. Apps. Internat. Corp. Tech. Mgmt. Advisors, 2005—. Capt. US Army, 1969—71. Mem.: ABA, AAAS, Assn. Univ. Tech. Mgrs., Am. Intellectual Property Law Assn., Fed. Lab. Consortium, Nat. Order Barristers, Licensing Execs. Soc.

WITTIG, SIGMAR, academic administrator, researcher, retired aerospace transportation executive; b. Nimptsch, Germany, Feb. 25, 1940; MS in Engring., Technical U., Aachen, Germany, 1964, DSc, 1967; Dr (hon.), U. Thessaloniki, Greece, 1998, U. Ufa, Russia, 1999; Dr-Ing E.h, U. Darmstadt, Germany, 2000; Dr (hon.), Purdue U.; Dr (hon.), Tech. U., Budapest, Hungary, 2003. Asst. Univ. Aachen, Germany, 1964-67; asst. prof. Purdue U., West LaFayette, Ind., 1967-71; assoc. prof., 1971-76; rsch. engr. part time Westinghouse Elec. Corp., 1971-76; dir., prof. U. Karlruhe, 1976—; v.p., 1989-94; pres., 1994—2002; CEO, chmn. German Aerospace Center, Cologne, Germany, 2002—07. V.p. German Rsch. Assn., 1989-95. Author, co-author of more than 200 articles to profl. jours. Recipient Isromac award Hawaii, 1990, Karl-Heinz Beckurts award large Rsch. Ctr., 1992, Korean Soc. Mech. Engrs. award, 1995. Mem. Acad. Scis. Heidelberg, Leopoldina. Avocation: sports.

WITTKOPP, GREGORY MARK, museum director; m. Dora Apel; 1 child, Rachel Apel. BS in Architecture, U. Mich., Ann Arbor, 1982; MA in Art History, Wayne State U., Detroit, 1994. Asst. to curator Hist. Mus. of Bay County, Bay City, Mich., 1982—83; exhbns. curator Saginaw Art Mus., Mich., 1983—85; asst. curator Cranbrook Art Mus., Bloomfield Hills, Mich., 1985—86, assoc. curator, 1986—89, collections curator, 1989—91, collections curator, mus. adminstr., 1991—94, dir., 1994—. Archtl. intern William O. Prine, Saginaw, 1981, Wigen, Tincknell and Meyer, Saginaw, 1983; mem. dir.'s search com. Mus. Contemporary Art Detroit, 2007—09. Author: (book) Saarinen House and Garden: A Total Work of Art, 1995; editor: A Life Without Beauty is Only Half Lived: A Brief History of Cranbrook, 1999. Recipient Pres.' award for excellence, Cranbrook Ednl. Cmty., 1994. Mem.: Soc. Archtl. Historians, Coll. Art Assn., Midwest Mus. Assn., Mich. Assn. Mus. (bd. dirs. 1998—2006, v.p. programs 2001—03, pres. 2003—05, co-chair ann. Southeast conf. 2005, pres. 2005—06), Am. Assn. Mus. Office: Cranbrook Art Mus 39221 Woodward Ave Bloomfield Hills MI 48303 Office Phone: 248-645-3315. Office Fax: 248-645-3324. Business E-Mail: gwittkopp@cranbrook.edu.

WITTLINGER, TIMOTHY DAVID, lawyer; b. Dayton, Ohio, Oct. 12, 1940; s. Charles Frederick and Dorothy Elizabeth (Golden) W.; m. Diane Cleo Dominy, May 20, 1967; children: Kristine Elizabeth, David Matthew. BS in Math., Purdue U., 1962; JD with distinction, U. Mich., 1965. Bar: Mich. 1966, U.S. Dist. Ct. (ea. dist.) Mich. 1966, U.S. Ct. Appeals (6th cir.) 1968, U.S. Supreme Ct. 1971. Assoc. Clark Hill (formerly Hill Lewis), Detroit, 1965-72, ptnr., 1973—2007, head litigation dept., 1976-91, gen. counsel, 1997—2007, chief legal officer, 1997—2007, of counsel, 2008—. Profl. assistance com. U.S. Dist. Ct. (ea. dist.) Mich., 1981-82; mem. Mich. Supreme Ct. Com. to Evaluate Mediation Ct. Rule, 1997-98; author, lectr. Ctr. for Internat. Legal Studies, 1999—; mem. coll. fellows Ctr. Internat. Legal Studies, Salzburg, Austria. Mem. ho. of deps. Episc. Ch., NYC, 1979-2003; vice chmn. Robert Whitaker Sch. Theology, 1983-87; sec. bd. trustees Episc. Ch., Diocese of Mich., Detroit, 1983—, sec. conv. Episc. Diocese of Mich., 1990—, ch. atty., 1997—, sec. Episc. nat. econ. justice implementation com., 1988-95, Episc. nat. exec. coun., 1991-97, nat. audit com., 2000-03; mem. nat. Standing Commn. on Ministry Devel., 2000-06; ministry com. Nat. Episc. Jubilee, Nat. Episc. Coalition for Social Witness and Justice, Fifth Province Episc. Ecclesiastical Ct. Appeal, 1997-2000; treas. Episcopal Ch. Province V, 2006-; bd. dirs. Episc. Student Found., U. Mich., 1990-93, 2000-02, 2007-; dir. Grubb Inst. Behavioral Studies Ltd., Washington, 1986—, London, 1986—; bd. dirs., treas., Birmingham Village Playhouse, 2000—; bd. trustees, Michigan Interfaith Trust Fund, 2007-. Mem. ABA, Engring. Soc. Detroit, Assn. Profl. Responsibility Lawyers. Home: 736 N Glenhurst Dr Birmingham MI 48009-1143 Office: Clark Hill 500 Woodward Ave Ste 3500 Detroit MI 48226-3435

WITTMAN, RANDY SCOTT, professional basketball coach; b. Indpls., Oct. 28, 1959; m. Kathy Wittman; children: Ryan, Lauren. BS, Ind. U., 1983. Draft pick Washington Bullets, 1983; player Atlanta Hawks, 1983—88, Sacramento Kings, 1988—89, Ind. Pacers, 1989—92, asst. coach, 1992—93, Dallas Mavericks, 1993—94, Minn. Timberwolves, 1994—99, 2001—05, 2006—07, head coach, 2007—08; asst. coach

Orlando Magic, 2005—06; head coach Cleve. Cavaliers, 1999—2001; asst. coach Washington Wizards, 2009—. Named to Ind. U. Hall of Fame, 1995. Office: Washington Wizards 601 F St NW Washington DC 20004*

WITTMAN, ROBERT J., United States Representative from Virginia, former state legislator; b. Washington, Feb. 3, 1959; m. Kathryn Jane Sisson; children: Devon W. Gooch, Josh. BS, Va. Poly. Inst., 1981; MPH in Health Policy/Adminstrn., U. NC, 1990; PhD in Pub. Policy/Adminstrn., Va. Commonwealth U., 2002. Mem. town coun. Town of Montross, Va., 1986—96, mayor Va., 1992—96; mem. bd. suprs. County of Westmoreland, Va., 1996—2005, chmn. bd. suprs. Va., 2004—05; mem. Va. State Ho. Dels. from 99th dist., 2006—07, mem. Agrl., Chesapeake and Natural Resources, Transp. and Militia Police and Public Safety Coms., 2006—07; mem. US Congress from 1st Va. dist., 2007—. Field dir. Divsn. Shellfish Sanitation, Va. Health Dept. Mem. Montross Fall and Spring Festival Com., 1992—, No. Neck Planning Dist. Commn., 2003; chmn. Montross-Westmoreland Sewer Authority, 2000—, Rappahannock River Basin Commn., 2001—, Interstate Shellfish Sanitation Conf., 2002—. Mem.: No. Neck Christian Men's Group, Boy Scouts of Am., Pi Alpha Alpha. Republican. Episcopalian. Office: US Congress 1123 Longworth House Office Bldg Washington DC 20515 also: 4500 Plank Rd Ste 105-A Fredericksburg VA 22407

WITTMAN, THOMAS A., stock exchange executive; Attended, Slippery Rock U., Pa., 1983—86. Sr. v.p. Phila. Stock Exch., exec. v.p., chief tech. officer; pres. NASDAQ OMX PHLX, Inc., 2008—. Office: NASDAQ OMX Group Inc One LIberty Plz 165 Broadway 50th Fl New York NY 10006*

WITTMAN, VANESSA AMES, insurance company executive; b. New London, Conn., Apr. 16, 1967; m. Drew M. Wittman; children: Parker, Mason. BS, U. N.C., 1989; MBA, U. Va., 1993. Assoc. Anderson Consulting, 1989—91; investment banker Morgan Stanley, 1993—96; ptnr. Sterling Payot, 1996—97; CFO Metricom, Inc., 1997—99; sr. dir. corp. devel. Microsoft Corp., 1999—2000; v.p., corp. devel. 360networks, 2000—02, CFO broadband network svcs., 2002—03; exec. v.p., CFO Adelphia Comm. Corp., 2003—08, Marsh & McLennan Companies, Inc., 2008—. Bd. dirs. InfoSpace, Inc., Bellevue, Wash. Avocations: tennis, skiing. Office: Marsh & McLennan Companies Inc 1166 Ave of Americas New York NY 10036*

WITTMER, JAMES FREDERICK, preventive medicine physician, educator; b. Carlinville, Ill., Dec. 30, 1932; s. Franklin Benjamin and Eva Caroline (Zihlman) W.; m. Juanita Lou Wilkey, June 29, 1962; children: Ellen, Carol, Nancy. MD, Washington U., St. Louis, 1957; MPH, Harvard U., 1961. Diplomate Am. Bd. Preventive Medicine. Intern U. Va. Hosp., Charlottesville, 1857-58; commd. capt. USAF, 1958, advanced through grades to col., 1971; ret., 1979; dean allied health U. Tex. Health Sci. Ctr., San Antonio, 1979-80; asst. med. dir. Conoco Oil Co., Ponca City, Okla., 1980-81; assoc. med. dir. Mobil Oil Corp., NYC, 1981-83; dir. health, environ. and safety ITT, NYC, 1983-95, corp. v.p., 1990-95. Clin. prof. medicine Cornell U. Med. Coll., NYC, 1984—; lectr. environ. medicine NYU, NYC, 1984—; adj. prof. U. Tex. Sch. Pub. Health, Houston, 1987—, prof. occupl. health, 1996—97; nat. coord. com. on clin. preventive svcs. USPHS, 1994—97; cons. office hearings and appeals U.S. Social Security Adminstrn., 1997—2003; cons. Met. Health Dist., San Antonio, 2002—08. Mem. Pres.'s Com. on Employment People with Disabilities, Washington, 1986-2000, chmn. med. and ins. com., 1986-90. Fellow ACP, Am. Coll. Occupational and Environ. Medicine (bd. dirs. 1990-97, sec. 1992-94), Am. Coll. Preventive Medicine, Aerospace Med. Assn., N.Y. Acad. Medicine; mem. AMA. Home and Office: 159 Sabine Rd Boerne TX 78006-6217 Home Phone: 830-537-4782; Office Phone: 830-537-4782. Business E-Mail: wittmer@gvtc.com.

WITTPENN, JOHN RYDER, ophthalmologist, consultant; b. Glen Ridge, Nj, Mar. 4, 1955; s. John Ryder and Shirley Kline Wittpenn; m. Denise Taneyhill Wittpenn, May 26, 1984; children: John Nicholas, James Daniel, Joseph Andrew. MD, Johns Hopkins U., Balt., 1982. Lic. NY, 1988. Resident Wilmer Inst. Ophthalmology, Balt., 1983—86; fellow Mass. Eye and Ear Infirmary, Boston, 1986—87; chief resident ophthalmology U. Southern Calif., LA, 1987—88; asst. prof. ophthalmology SUNY, Stony Brook, NY, 1988—2000; ptnr. Ophthalmic Cons. LI, Stony Brook, 2000—. Pres. Bd. Edn., Mt. Sinai, NY, 1996. Office: Ophthalmic Cons Long Island 2500 Rt 347 24A Stony Brook NY 11790

WITTS, SIMON, computer software company executive; m. Karen Witts; children: Peter, Daniel, Hannah. B in math & physics, M in info. tech., Univ. London. Sales mgmt. positions IBM UK Ltd.; enterprise sales mgmt. positions Microsoft Corp., Redmond, Wash., 1993—2003, pres. Microsoft Canada, v.p. sales & mktg. EMEA, corp. v.p. enterprise & ptnr. group, 2003—. Bd. dir. Avanade Inc. Office: Microsoft Corp 1 Microsoft Way Redmond WA 98052-6399

WITTSTEIN, EDWIN FRANK, theater director, set designer; b. Mt. Vernon, NY, Apr. 7, 1929; s. Nathan Harry and Miriam (Goldman) W. Student, Parsons Sch. Design, 1946-50; BS, NYU, 1950; postgrad., Cooper Union, 1950-52. Stage designer Dramatic Workshop prodn. The Inspector General, 1947; set designer Gertrude Stein's Yes Is for a Very Young Man; set and costume designer Ounga Opera, Phila., 1950, (opera) The Celebrated Jumping Frog of Calaveras County, Venice, Italy, 1953, The Transposed Heads, 1958, The Fantasticks, 1960-2002; designer Broadway prodn. Kean, 1961; set and costume designer The Gondoliers, N.Y.C. Opera, 1963, The Knack (directed by Mike Nichols), 1964, The Marriage of Figaro, N.Y.C. Opera, 1965, The Amen Corner, 1965, Happy Birthday Wanda June, Enter Laughing, 1965, The Room, A Slight Ache, 1965, The Yearling, 1965, Serjeant Musgrave's Dance, 1966 (Obie award 1966), You Know I Can't Hear You When the Water's Running, 1967, set designer Merchant of Venice, Shakespeare Festival Conn., 1967, As You Like It, Richard II, Shakespeare Festival Conn., 1968, The Man in the Glass Booth, 1968, The Basement, The Tea Party, Celebration, 1969, (for Cin. Playhouse) The Miser, Volpone, The Good Woman of Setzuan, Angel Street, He Who Gets Slapped, 1968-70, The Country Wife, Shakespeare Theatre, Conn., 1973, Ulysses in Nightown, 1974 (Tony award nomination 1974, Maharam award 1974), The Torchbearers, 1978, The Aspern Papers, 1978, Love's Labors Lost, 1983, Berkshire Theatre Festival, 1988, Tusitala, 1988, Tete a Tete, 1989, The Hasty Heart, 1990, Trains, 1991, (sets, costumes 30th anniversary tour) The Fantasticks, 1990, Sarah, Plain and Tall, 1991 (Emmy nomination 1991), Colette Collage, 1991, March of the Falsettos, 1991, Falsettoland, 1991, (prodn. designer Hallmark Hall of Fame TV) An American Story, 1992, (prodn. designer Hallmark Hall of Fame TV) Skylark, 1993, (prodn. designer Hallmark Hall of Fame TV) A Place for Annie, 1993, (set designer off-Broadway) I Do! I Do!, 1996, The Fantasticks, 2006; designer TV shows Armstrong Circle Theatre, The Tonight Show with Steve Allen, NBC operas Cosi Fan Tutte, La Traviata, La Boheme, Boris Godounov, Cavalleria Rusticana, Blithe Spirit, The Diary of Anne Frank, Camino Real, The Royal Family, The Prince of Homburg; prodn. designer TV series The Adams Chronicles (Emmy nomination 1975); designer TV films A Memory of Two Mondays, 1971, For Ladies Only, 1982, Legs, 1982, Samson and Delilah, 1983, Heartsounds, 1984; designer TV spl. Echoes in the Darkness, 1987; designer films Bananas, 1971, Play It Again Sam, 1971, The Seven-Ups, 1972; art dir. films Smile, 1975, Fame, 1979; prodn. designer film Endless Love, 1981; set and costume designer (ballet) Coppelia, 1992; one-man show (painting) Hammond Museum, N. Salem, N.Y., 1999; drawer, writer Positano Sketch Book, 2000; designer sets and costumes for new revival of The Fantasticks, Broadway, 2006. Home: 339 E 87th St New York NY 10128-4801

WITTY, ANDREW, pharmaceutical executive; BA in Economics, Nottingham U., 1985. Joined Glaxo UK, 1985; dir. pharmacy & distribution Glaxo Pharms. UK; dir. bus. devel. Biocompatibles Ltd.; internat. product mgr. Glaxo Holdings plc; mng. dir. Glaxo South Africa, area dir. South & East Africa; v.p., gen. mgr. mktg. Glaxo Wellcome Inc.; sr. v.p. Asia Pacific, Pharms. Internat. GlaxoSmithKline plc, Singapore, 2001—03, pres. Pharmaceuticals Europe Brentford, England, 2003—08, CEO, 2008—. Mem. working group Pharma Futures; econ. adviser Gov. of Guangzhou, China, 2000—02; bd. mem. Singapore Econ. Devel. Bd., Singapore Land Authority Bd., Min. of Law, 2002—03; bd. dirs. GlaxoSmithKline plc, 2008—; non-exec. dir. Office Strategic Coordination Health Rsch. Mem. Imperial Coll. Commercialization Adv. Bd., Health Innovation Coun., INSEAD UK Coun. Recipient Pub. Svc. medal, Govt. of Singapore, 2003. Office: GlaxoSmithKline plc One Franklin Plaza PO Box 7929 Philadelphia PA 19101 also: 980 Great W Rd Brentford TW8 9GS England*

WITTY, THOMAS EZEKIEL, III, psychologist, researcher; b. Greensboro, NC, Oct. 11, 1955; s. Thomas Ezekiel, Jr. and Peggy (Coggins) Witty; m. Ginger Lynell Kissee, June 28, 1997; children: Ezekiel Thomas, Zoe Anne. BA in English, U. N.C., Greensboro, 1980; MS, Va. Commonwealth U., 1989; PhD, U. Mo., 1995. Lic. psychologist Miss., cert. in rehab. Am. Bd. Profl. Psychology, 2008. Tchr. secondary English, debate and cross-country coach Henry County Pub. Schs., Collinsville, Va., 1981-87; fin. aid. counselor asst. Va. Commonwealth U., Richmond, 1987-89; substance abuse counselor Dist. 19 Alcoholism Svcs., Petersburg, Va., 1990; grad. rsch. asst. U. Mo., Columbia, 1990-94, grad. instr., 1992-94; postdoctoral fellow Rusk Rehab. Ctr., Columbia, 1995-98; chief psychology Mo. Rehab. Ctr., Mt. Vernon, 1998-2001; psychologist North Miss. Med. Ctr., Tupelo, 2001—. Rsch. cons. Coun. on Rehab. Edn., Inc., Champaign, Ill., 1991; ad hoc reviewer Jour. Rehab. Psychology, 1995—98; internship selection com. U. Mo. Health Svcs. Consortium, Columbia, 1996—98; faculty Family Medicine Residency Ctr., Tupelo, Miss., 2001—; alt. mem. instl. rev. bd. N. Miss. Med. Ctr., 2002—. Contbr. articles to profl. jours. Walter Scott Monroe Rsch. fellow, U. Mo., 1992—95, Postdoctoral fellow, NIH, 1995—98, Rsch. grantee, U. Mo. Rsch. Bd., 1997. Mem.: APA (divsn. 17, 22, 38, 50), Miss. Psychol. Assn., Sierra Club, KC, Kappa Delta Pi. Democrat. Roman Catholic. Avocations: running, swimming, bicycling, hiking, camping. Office: North Miss Med Ctr Dept Behavioral Health 830 S Gloster St Tupelo MS 38801 Office Phone: 662-377-3812, 662-377-3161. Business E-Mail: twitty@nmhs.net.

WITZ, GISELA, research scientist, educator; b. Breslau, Federal Republic of Germany, Mar. 16, 1939; came to U.S., 1955. d. Gerhardt Witz and Hildegard (Sufeida) Minzak. BA, NYU, 1962, MS, 1965, PhD, 1969. Assoc. rsch. scientist NYU Med. Ctr., NYC, 1970-73, rsch. scientist, 1973-77, asst. prof., 1977-80, U. Medicine and Dentistry of N.J.-Robert Wood Johnson Med. Sch., Piscataway, NJ, 1980-86, 1986—93, prof., 1993—2000, prof. emeritus, 2001—. Dep. dir. Joint Grad. Program in Toxicology, Rutgers U./Univ. Medicine and Dentistry of N.J.-Robert Wood Johnson Med. Sch., 1988, assoc. dir. 1992-2000; cons. Nat. Rsch. Coun., Washington, 1982-83, 85-86. Recipient Dupont Teaching award, NYU, 1966, Univ. Scholar, Founders Day award, N.Y. U., 1969, Student Appreciation award Rutgers Assn. Toxicology Grad. Students, 1996; honoree 3d Ann. Women in Sci. Symposium, 2000. Fellow Oxygen Soc.; mem. Am. Assn. Cancer Rsch., Am. Chem. Soc., Soc. Toxicology, N.Y. Acad. Sci., Sigma Xi. Avocations: gardening, painting. Office: U Medicine and Dentistry NJ Robert Wood Johnson Med Sch Piscataway NJ 08854 E-mail: witz@eohsi.rutgers.edu.

WIXEN, JOAN SAUNDERS, journalist; b. Boston, Dec. 26, 1931; d. Harry Hyman and Sadye (Ginsburg) Saunders; m. Burton N. Wixen, Aug. 9, 1953; children: Randall, Warren, Bradford. BA, U. So. Calif., LA, 1952; MS, UCLA, 1953. West coast corr. Sunday Mag., Detroit News, 1972—78; journalist LA Times, Christian Sci. Monitor, Chgo. Sun Times, Miami Herald, Fla., San Francisco Chronicle, Washington Star, Buffalo Evening News, LA Daily News, Parade. Contbr. articles to mags. including Family Cir., New Woman, Pageant, Modern Maturity, Eve, to syndicates including United Features, LA Times-Washington Post, N.Am. Newspaper Alliance, Universal Press Syndicate, others. Personal E-mail: saunderswixen@earthlink.net.

WIXOM, WILLIAM DAVID, art historian, museum administrator, educator; b. Phila., July 17, 1929; s. Clinton Wood and Beatrice Rachel (Hunt) W.; m. Nancy Coe, Aug. 8, 1959; 3 children. BA, Haverford Coll., Pa., 1951; MA, Inst. Fine Arts NYU, 1963. Asst. curator to curator medieval and renaissance decorative arts Cleve. Mus. Art, 1958-78, chief curator early western art, 1979; chmn. dept. medieval art and The Cloisters Met. Mus. Art, NYC, 1979-98, curator emeritus. Lectr. Barnes Found., Merion, Pa., 1951—52, curatorial cons. for medieval art, mem. curatorial adv. com., 2002—05; adj. assoc. prof. history of art Case Western Res. U., Cleve., 1967—78, adj. prof., 1978, NYU, 1981—82; mem. adv. coun. Snite Mus. Art Notre Dame U., 1974—95. Author: Treasures from Medieval France, 1967, Renaissance Bronzes from Ohio Collections, 1975, Picturing the Apocalypse: Illustrated Leaves from a Medieval Spanish Manuscript, 2002, A Glimpse at the Fountains of the Middle Ages, 2003, Medieval Sculptures at the Metropolitan, 800 to 1400, 2005, Late Medieval Sculpture at the Metropolitan, 1400 to 1530, 2007; contbg. author The Royal Abbey of Saint Denis in the Time of Abbot suger, 1981, The Treasury of San Marco, 1985, Gothic and Renaissance Art in Nuremberg, 1986, Festschrift Gerhard Bott, 1987, Hommage a Hubert Landais, 1987, The Cloisters, Studies in Honor of the Fiftieth Anniversary, 1992, Festschrift Gerhard Schmidt, 1994, Enamels of Limoges 1100-1350, 1996, Studies in Honor of Kurt Weitzmann, 1995, The Dictionary of Art, 1996, The Glory of Byzantium, Art and Culture of the Middle Byzantine Era, AD-843-1261, 1997, Sculptures hors contexte, Louvre conférences et colloques, 1997, Mirror of the Medieval World, 1999, Romanesque Sculpture in American Collections, 1999, Tilman Riemenschneider, Master Sculptor of the Late Middle Ages, 1999; contbr. articles to profl. jours. Bd. dirs. Internat. Ctr. Medieval Art, N.Y.C., 1971-82, pres., 1971-74. Belgium-Am. Ednl. Found. fellow, 1962; Nat. Endowment Arts grantee, 1973; fellow Pierpont Morgan Libr., 1979-2001; J. Paul Getty Mus. Guest Scholar, 1996. Fellow Soc. of Antiquaries of London; mem. Coll. Art Assn. (dir. 1979-83), Medieval Acad. Am., Internat. Ctr. Medieval Art. Mem. Soc. Of Friends. Office: Dept Medieval Art Met Mus Art New York NY 10028

WIXON, HENRY N., lawyer; b. 1954; BS, U. Md., 1976, MS, 1980; JD, George Washington U., 1986. Bar: Md. 1986, DC 1989, US Patent & Trademark Office, US Supreme Ct. 1990. Ptnr., vice chmn. Intellectual Property dept. Wilmer Cutler Pickering Hale & Dorr, Washington. Mem.: Fed. Bar Assn. (past chmn. Comm. & IP Law sect., Patent, Trademark & Copyright com.), Am. Intellectual Property Law Assn. (charter mem. Biotechnology Practice com.), ABA, Md. Bar Assn. (mem. Com. on Representing Emerging Companies), DC Bar Assn., Biotechnology Ind. Assn. (mem. Intellectual Property Com.), Internat. Fedn. Advancement of Genetic Engring. & Biotechnology, No. Va. Biotechnology Council, Va. Biotechnology Assn. Office: Wilmer Cutler Pickering Hale & Dorr Willard Office Bldg 1455 Pennsylvania Ave NW Washington DC 20004 Office Fax: 202-942-8459, 202-942-8484. Business E-Mail: henry.wixon@wilmerhale.com.

WIXTROM, DONALD JOSEPH, translator; b. Republic, Mich., Oct. 14, 1928; s. Joseph Albert and Edith (Johnson) W.; m. Marilyn Jean Sjoquist, Oct. 14, 1961; children: Joe Alan, Lorna Jean, Aaron Matthew. Free lance translator, Republic, 1966—. Mem.: Am. Translators Assn. Baptist. Home and Office: 6035 Dogwood Rd Republic MI 49879-9214 Home Phone: 906-376-2613.

WIZDA, CHRISTINE ANNE, history professor; b. Flemington, NJ, Sept. 21, 1977; d. Thomas Steven and Elaine Ann Wizda. BA, Rider U., 1999; MA, U. Houston, 2003, M in Applied Med. Anthropology, 2004, PhD, 2004—. Tutor Rider U., Lawrenceville, NJ, 1996—99; tchg. asst. U. Houston, 1999—2006. Recipient The Chancellor's List, 2003; named to, 2006; grantee scholarship, U. Coll., Cork, Ireland, 1998; Murry Miller scholar, U. Houston, 2002, conf. grantee, 2003, scholar for field work in Belize, Office Internat. Studies, 2003. Mem.: Soc. Mil. History, Orgn. Am. Historians, Am. Hist. Assn., Phi Beta Delta, Phi Alpha Theta, Pi Gamma Mu.

WLASCHIN, KEN, cultural organization administrator, writer; b. Bradish, Nebr., July 12, 1934; s. Bernard A. and Lucy M. (Stevens) W.; m. Maureen N. Kennedy Martin, Mar. 22, 1961; 1 child, Scott Martin. BA, Dartmouth Coll., 1956; MA, U. Coll., Dublin, Ireland, 1957; postgrad., U. Poitiers, France, 1960. Program dir. Nat. Film Theater, London, 1969-83, London Film Festival, 1970-83; artistic dir. LA Film Expn., 1984-86; dir. exhbn. Am. Film Inst., LA, 1986-97, dir. creative affairs and preservation, 1998—; dir. Beachwood Press, 1995—. Theater critic Rome Daily Am. & Daily Sketch, Rome and London, 1962-67; art critic Art Voices Mag., Rome, 1962-68; film critic Films and Filming Mag., London, 1973-82; story editor London Weekend TV, 1968. Author: (TV play) Ticket to Trieste, 1961, (novel), The Italian Job, 1964, Rome A City, 1964, Guide to Cinema, 1970, Encyclopedia of Movie Stars, 1979, Faber Book of Movie Verse, 1994, Opera on Screen, 1997, Gian Carlo Menotti on Screen, 1999, Encyclopedia of Opera on Screen, 2004, Encyclopedia of American Opera, 2005, Songs of the Silent Cinema, 2008, Silent Mystery and Detective Movies, 2009. With US Army, 1958-61, ETO. Mem. Brit. Film Inst., Brit. Film Acad. Avocation: opera. Home: 1050 E Ramon Rd #35 Palm Springs CA 92264

WLEUGEL, JOHN PETER, manufacturing executive; b. Hoyanger, Sogn, Norway, July 1, 1929; s. Johan and Helga (Faye) W.; m. Leonor Abaroa, Dec. 1959; children— Jan Andrew, Cecilia Maria. BA, U. Copenhagen, 1953; MBA, U. Toronto, 1957. With Belgium Machine Tool Assn., 1953-54, Massey-Ferguson Ltd., Toronto, 1954-71, treas., 1968-71; sr. v.p. Bata Shoe Orgn., Bata Ltd., Toronto, Ont., Canada, dir., officer several subsidiaries, 1972—89; dir., officer several TSX listed companies, 1991—2005; prof., exec.-in-residence, internat. adv. bd. Schulich Sch. Bus., York U., North York, Canada, 1990—. Mem.: Financial Execs. Inst., Tarpon Cove Yacht and Racquet Club (Naples, Fla.), Caledon Ski Club (Ont.), U. Club Toronto. Home: 5 Campbell Crescent Toronto ON Canada M2P 1P1 Office: Schulich Sch Bus York U 4700 Keele St Toronto ON Canada M3J 1P3

WLODAWER, ALEXANDER, medical researcher; b. Poland; PhD, UCLA, 1974; Doctor Honoris Causa, Tech. U., Lodz, Poland, 2004. Postdoctoral training Stanford U.; joined Nat. Bur. Standards, 1976; joined ABL Basic Rsch. Program, Ctr. Cancer Rsch., Nat. Cancer Inst., NIH, Frederick, Md., 1987, chief Macromolecular Crystallography Lab., 1999—, also head Protein Structure Sect. Vis. fellow Sidney Sussex Coll., U. Cambridge, 1998—99; adj. prof. biochemistry and molecular biology George Washington U., assoc. mem. Inst. Biomedical Sciences; editor FEBS Jour.; mem. editl. bd. Protein Sci., Acta Biochimica Polonica. Mem.: Polish Acad. Sciences (fgn. mem.), Protein Soc., Am. Crystallographic Assn. Office: Macromolecular Crystallography Lab NCI Frederick Bldg 536 Rm 5 PO Box B Frederick MD 21702-1201 Office Phone: 301-846-5036. Office Fax: 301-846-6322. E-mail: wlodawer@nih.gov, wlodawer@ncifcrf.gov.

WOBUS, REINHARD ARTHUR, geologist, educator; b. Norfolk, Va., Jan. 11, 1941; s. Reinhard Schaffer and Oral (Phares) W.; m. Sheridan Whitcher, Mar. 18, 1967; children: Erik Reinhard, Cameron Wright. BA, Washington U., St. Louis, 1962; MA, Harvard U., 1963; PhD, Stanford U., 1966. Asst. prof. geology Williams Coll., Williamstown, Mass., 1966-72, assoc. prof., 1972-78, prof., 1978-85, Edna McConnell Clark prof. geology, 1985—, dept. chmn., 1988-96. Geologist U.S. Geol. Survey, Denver, 1967-86; vis. prof. Colo. Coll., Colorado Springs, 1976, 82-83, Colo. State U., Ft. Collins, summers 1977-84; bd. dirs. Colo. Outdoor Edn. Ct., Florissant, Williamstown Rural Lands Found.; cofounder Keck Twelve-Coll. Geol. Consortium, mem. governing bd., 1986—, exec. com., 2005—08. Contbr. maps and articles on Precambrian geology of So. Rocky Mountains to profl. jours. Danforth fellow, 1962, Woodrow Wilson fellow, 1962, NSF fellow, 1962-66. Fellow Geol. Soc. Am.; mem. Am. Geophys. Union, Nat. Assn. Geosci. Tchrs., Coun. on Undergrad. Rsch., Colo. Sci. Soc., Mineral Soc. Am., Phi Beta Kappa, Sigma Xi. Current work includes petrology and geochronology of Precambrian igneous and metamorphic rocks and mid-Tertiary volcanic rocks, so. Rocky Mountains, Silurian volcanic rocks, coastal Maine. Home: 20 Grandview Dr Williamstown MA 01267-2528 Office: Williams Coll Dept Geoscis Williamstown MA 01267 Office Phone: 413-597-2470. Business E-Mail: rwobus@williams.edu.

WODLINGER, MARK LOUIS, broadcast executive; b. Jacksonville, Fla., July 13, 1922; s. Mark H. and Beatrice Mae (Boney) W.; m. Marilyn Stone-Birk; children: Kevin, Michael, Stephen, Mark. BS, U. Fla., 1943. Salesman Sta. WQUA, Moline, Ill., 1948; mgr. Sta. WOC-AM-FM-TV, Davenport, Iowa, 1949-58; v.p. Sta. WMBD-TV, Peoria, Ill., 1959-61; v.p., gen. mgr. Sta. WZZM-TV, Grand Rapids, Mich., 1962-63, Sta. KMBC-TV, Kansas City, Mo., 1963-69; pres. Intermedia, Kansas City, 1969-73; builder, owner comml. radio stas. Swaziland, Africa; operator Radio Malawi, Blantyre, and Marknews TV and Radio News Bur., Nairobe, Kenya, 1971-74; owner, pres. Sta. KBEQ, Kansas City, 1973-77; owner Sta. WCJX-FM, Miami, 1985-86, Sta. WPWR WIXI-FM, Naples and Ft. Myers, Fla., 1986-95, Sta. KKLO-AM, Leavenworth, Kans., 1982-92, Sta. KCWV, Kansas City, Mo., 1982-90, TV-5, Hit Video USA, Satellite Music Network, Houston, 1985-88, SMR-2-way radio/telephone, Naples, Fla., 1993—95, San Francisco, 1993—; mng. dir. Radio Hirszolgalat; owner Roxy Radio, Budapest,

Hungary, 2007—08, Roxy Advt. Network, 2007—08. Mem. Wodlinger Broadcasting Co., Naples, 1978—; ptnr. Wireless Cable, Naples, 1990—; owner, ptnr. KABELTEL KFT (Hungary), Budapest, Sopron, Nagykanizsa, Szombathely, 1991-96; comml. FM Radio Ikva, Sopron, 1993—2008, FM Radio Zalaegerszeg, 1995—, comml. FM Reflex Radio 99.2 MHz, Szekesfehervar, Hungary, 1996—2001, FM Love Radio 97.8, Tallinn, Paide, Rakvere, Tartu, Sindi, Viliandi and marjamaa, Estonia, 1993—2007; ptnr., chmn. bd. dirs. wireless cable TV Ukrainian-Am. Broadcasting, Kiev, Ukraine, 1990—95, comml. TV Channel 7, 1990—95, comml. FM Radio 69.89, Kiev, 1992—95; owner, ptnr. comml. FM Radiocentras, Vilnius, Lithuania, 1992-96; owner, ptnr. comml. FM Radiola 99.70 MHz, 1996—, European HiT Radio; ptnr. joint mktg. AT&T Paradyne, Largo, Fla., 1992-94; owner, ptnr., chmn. bd. dirs. real estate devel., Croatia, 1991—95; owner outdoor advt. billboards, Tallinn, Estonia, 1993-95; owner, ptnr. real estate devel., Hungary, 1991—. Bd. dirs. Kansas City Philharm., Kansas City Civic Coun., Naples YMCA, Budapest Festival Orch., 2000; mem. Conservancy, Naples Civic Assn. Served to lt. USN, Air 1941-45. Mem. Nat. Assn. Broadcasters, Mo. Assn. Broadcasters, Broadcast Pioneers. Clubs: Kansas City, Univ., Vanguard, Carriage, Port Royal, Naples Yacht, Houston Yacht, White Lake Yacht (Whitehall, Mich.), Haile Plantation Country Club. Lodges: Rotary, Reynolds Plantation Country Club, Lake Oconee, Ga. Republican. Episcopalian. Business E-Mail: wodlinger@mmsales.eu.

WODNICKI, ADAM JULIUSZ, pianist, educator; b. Przemysl, Poland, Dec. 22, 1951; arrived in US, 1977, naturalized, 1986; s. Bronislaw Wodnicki and Malwina Wodnicka; m. Marta Janina Hoffman-Wodnicka, Nov. 15, 1973; children: Maya Andrea Wodnicka, Natalia Eva Wodnicka. MusM, Acad. of Music, Cracow, Poland, 1974. Faculty mem. Acad. of Music, Cracow, Poland, 1973—77; asst. prof. U. of Tex. at Austin, 1979—80; regents prof. piano U. North Tex. Coll. Music, 1980—. Artistic co-dir. Internat. Piano Masterclasses, Varna, Bulgaria, 2000—08; mem. bd. of artistic advisors Internat. Piano Festival and Course, Aveiro, Portugal, 2001—04. Performance editor (music) I.J. Paderewski: Complete Works; performer: (albums) CDCM Computer Music Series, vol.1, Computer Music Compositions, K. Szymanowski: 12 Studies op.33 (nominated Fryderyk award, Poland, 09), R. Muczynski: Piano Trios, I.J.Paderewski: Piano works, vol.1, I.J.Paderewski: Piano works, vol.2, D.Dzubay, R.Muczynski, D. Shostakovich:Sonatas for Cello and Piano, CDCM Computer Music Series, vol.27, J.Schwantner:and the Mountains Rising Nowhere, CDCM Computer Music Series, vol.14, Computer Music Currents 8; performer: (with Joseph Banowetz and Vladimir Ashkenazy) Sergey Taneyev: The Composer's Birthday, for narrator and piano four hands; co-prodr.: (piano music CD) Balakirev (nominated Grammy award);, editor piano concerts. Recipient 3 prizes, VIII Festival of Polish Pianists, 1974, nat. competition prize, Chopin Soc., Warsaw, Poland, 1969—71, Worldwide Steinway Artists Roster, Steinway&Sons, NY, 1997—; Touring Artists Roster, Tex. Commn. on the Arts, 1996—. Mem.: Music Teachers Nat. Assn., Am. Liszt Soc. Office: Univ of North Tex Coll of Mus PO Box 311367 Denton TX 76203-1367 Personal E-mail: mnawod@juno.com.

WOEBER, KENNETH ALOIS, physician; b. Feb. 2, 1935; MB, BChir, MD, U. Witwatersrand, Johannesburg, South Africa, 1957. Intern Johannesburg Hosp., 1958-59; rsch. fellow Harvard Med. Sch., 1962-64, instr. medicine, 1965-68, asst. prof. medicine, 1968-70, assoc. prof. medicine, 1970-72; prof. clin. medicine U. Calif., San Francisco, 1975—, vice-chmn. medicine, 1981-2000, chief clin. endocrinology, 2000—. Chmn. subsplty. bd. endocrinology and metabolism Am. Bd. Internal Medicine, 1985-87. Contbr. articles to profl. jours. Recipient Van Meter prize Am. Thyroid Assn. Fellow Royal Coll. Physicians of Edinburgh. Home: 6 Bartel Ct Belvedere Tiburon CA 94920-1656 Office: U Calif San Francisco at Mt Zion PO Box 1640 San Francisco CA 94143-1640 Office Phone: 415-885-7574. Business E-Mail: ken.woeber@ucsf.edu.

WOELFEL, JAMES WARREN, philosophy and humanities educator; b. Galveston, Tex., Aug. 16, 1937; s. Warren Charles and Mary Frances (Washinka) W.; m. Sarah Chappell Trulove, Nov. 24, 1982; children by previous marriages: Skye Caitlin, Allegra Eve, Sarah Judith; stepchildren: Ann Marie and Paul Trulove. BA, U. Okla., 1959; MDiv, Episcopal Div. Sch., Cambridge, Mass., 1962; MA, Yale U., 1964; PhD, U. St. Andrews, Scotland, 1967. Asst. prof. philosophy and religion U. Kans., Lawrence, 1966-70, asst. prof. philosophy, 1970-71, assoc. prof. philosophy and religion, 1971-75, prof. philosophy and religious studies, 1975-88, prof. philosophy, 1988—, acting chmn. dept. religious studies, 1983-84, dir. Humanities and Western civilization program, 1985—. Manuscript reader for various presses, jours. Author: Bonhoeffer's Theology, 1970, Borderland Christianity, 1973, Camus: A Theological Perspective (republished as Albert Camus on the Sacred and the Secular, 1987), 1975, Augustinian Humanism, 1979, The Agnostic Spirit as a Common Motif in Liberal Theology and Liberal Scepticism, 1990, Portraits in Victorian Religious Thought, 1997, The Existentialist Legacy and Other Essays on Philosophy and Religion, 2006; co-editor (with Sarah Chappell Trulove): Patterns in Western Civilization, 1991, 4th edit., 2006; contbr. essays, revs. to profl. jours.; contbr. articles to profl. jours. Danforth grad. fellow Episcopal Div. Sch., Cambridge, Mass., 1959-62, U. St. Andrews, 1962-63, 65-66, Yale U., New Haven, 1963-65; Fulbright scholar U. St. Andrews, 1962-63, Pub. Scholar award Kans. Humanities Coun., 1997; grantee NEH, Exxon Found., Mellon Found., Menninger Found., Inst. for Ecumenical and Cultural Rsch., Oxford Round Table. Mem. Assn. Core Texts and Courses, Phi Beta Kappa. Democrat. Avocations: piano, walking. Home: 808 Alabama St Lawrence KS 66044-3942 Office: U Kans Humanities & Western Civilization Program Bailey Hall 1440 Jayhawk Blvd Rm 308 Lawrence KS 66045-7574 Office Phone: 785-864-3011. E-mail: woelfel@ku.edu.

WOERNER, ALFRED IRA, medical device manufacturer, educator; b. Jersey City, Sept. 21, 1935; s. Theodore and Miriam (Mann) W.; m. Margaret R. Martin, Nov. 27, 1958; children: John, Michael, Judith. DME, Stevens Inst., 1956; MS, Stevens, 1961; MBA, NYU, 1965; LLB, LaSalle U., 1963; PhD, Calif. State U., 1990; diploma for motorcycle tech., Thomson-Direct Edn. U., 2002. Gen. program mgr. Becton Dickenson & Co., Ruthuferd, N.J., 1959-63; group v.p., asst. to pres. Howmet Corp., NYC, 1963-69; gen. mgr., v.p. Wide Range Industries, NYC, 1969-72; pres., owner New World Market Ltd., Westwood, N.J., 1972—, Fairfield Surg. Corp., Stanford, Conn., 1972—. Cons. Woerner Assocs., Westwood; prof. Fairleigh Dickinson U., Teaneck, N.J., 1969-96. Author: Program Management, 1988. Pres. Bd. Edn., Westwood, 1978-86; adv. Stevens Inst. Tech., Hoboken, N.J., 1972-80; commodore Bay Island Marina, 2002—; musician Fla. Sun Coast Jazz Band, 2002—. Mem. AMA, ASME, Am. Acad. Cons., Am. Statistical Assn., Fla. Condo Assn. (dir. 2002—). Achievements include five patents in Medical Industry; development of new process in orthopedic surgery industry. Home: 7560 Bay Island Dr S South Pasadena FL 33707-4562 Office: Fairleigh Dickinson U 1000 River Rd Teaneck NJ 07666-1996 Personal E-mail: mrwaiw@aol.com. Business E-Mail: mrwaiw@wmconnect.com.

WOERTZ, PATRICIA ANN, agricultural company executive, retired oil company executive; b. Pitts., Mar. 17, 1953; married; 3 children. BS in Acctg., Pa. State U., 1974; grad. Internat. Exec. Devel. Program, Columbia U., 1994. Acct. Ernst & Young, Pitts., 1974—77; with Gulf Oil Corp., Pitts., 1977-81, Houston, 1981-85; with debt. reduction process, merger of Gulf and Chevron, 1985-87; fin. mgr. Chevron Info. Tech. Co., 1989-91, strategic planning mgr., 1991-93; pres. Chevron Can. Ltd., Vancouver, B.C., 1993-96, Chevron Internat. Oil Co., 1996-98; v.p. logistics and trading Chevron Products Co., Chevron Corp., 1996-98, v.p., 1998—2001; pres. Chevron Products Co., 1998—2001; exec. v.p. Global Downstream ChevronTexaco Corp, San Francisco, 2001—06; pres., CEO Archer Daniels Midland Co., Decatur, Ill., 2006—07, chmn., pres., CEO, 2007—. Bd. dirs. Archer Daniels Midland Co., 2006—, The Proctor & Gamble Co., 2008—. Bd. trustees U. San Diego; bd. visitors Pa. State U.; vice chmn. Kennedy Ctr. Corp. Fund. Recipient Alumni Fellow award, 2002; named a Disting. Alumna, Pa. State U., 2005; named one of Most Powerful Women in Bus., Fortune mag., 2005, 50 Most Powerful Women in Bus., 2006, 2007, 2008, 100 Most Powerful Women, Forbes mag., 2006—09, 50 Who Matter Now, CNNMoney.com Bus. 2.0, 2006, 50 Women to Watch, The Wall St. Jour., 2006, 2008. Mem.: World Econ. Forum, Internat. Bus. Coun., U.S. C. of C., Nat. Petroleum Coun. Office: Archer Daniels Midland Co 4666 Faries Pkwy Decatur IL 62526*

WOESE, CARL R., biophysicist, microbiology educator; b. Syracuse, NY, July 15, 1928; AB in Math. and Physics, Amherst Coll., 1950, DSc (hon.), 1985; PhD in Biophysics, Yale U., 1953; postgrad., U. Rochester, 1953-55; DSc (hon.), Syracuse U., 1994. Rsch. assoc. biophysics Yale U., New Haven, 1955-60; biophysicist GE Rsch. Lab., 1960-63; prof. microbiology U. Ill., Urbana-Champaign, 1964—. Stanley O. Ikenberry chair U. Ill., 1996—. Contbr. articles to profl. jours. Recipient Bergey award Bergey's Manual Trust, 1983, John D. and Catherine T. MacArthur award, 1984, Leeuwenhoek medal 1990, 1992, 23d Brown-Hazen Lctrs. award, 1992, Roger W. Stanier Meml. Lctr. award U. Calif., Berkeley, 1993, Nat. Medal Sci., 2000, Crafoord prize, 2003; Univ. Sr. scholar U. Ill., 1986. Fellow Explorer's Club, Indian NAS, Am. Acad. Arts and Scis., Am. Acad. Microbiology; mem. Deutsche Gesellschaft fur Hygiene und Mikrobiologie (corr.), Deutsche Akademie Der Naturforscher Leopoldina, Bayerische Akademie der Wissenschaften (corr.), Max-Planck Soc., NAS (Selman A. Waksman award 1997), Ctr. Advanced Study U. Ill. Office: U Ill Chem & Life Scis Lab 131 Burrill Hall 601 S Goodwin Ave Urbana IL 61801-3709

WOFFORD, CHLOE ARDELIA See MORRISON, TONI

WOFFORD, GARRY, music educator; s. General Vernon Wofford; m. Karen Writer; children: James, Benjamin. B of Music Edn., Hardin-Simmons U., Abilene, Texas, 1972; M of Music Edn., Tex. Tech U., Lubbock, 1991. Cert. music edn. Tex., 1967. Band dir. Childress H.S., Tex., 1982—87, Smyer H.S., Tex., 1987—92, Vernon H.S., Tex., 1992—2000; adj. instr. music, applied guitar and piano instr. Vernon Coll., Tex., 1998—. Organist First Bapt. Ch., Vernon, 1992—; musician, mem. Country Praise Revival. Mem.: Tex. Band Masters Assn., Tex. Music Educators Assn., Phi Mu Alpha (life). Home: 8554 Cr 128w Vernon TX 76384 Office: Vernon College 4400 College Dr Vernon TX 76384 Personal E-mail: gwofford@vernoncollege.edu.

WOFSY, STEVEN CHARLES, astrophysicist, researcher; b. NYC, June 24, 1946; BS in Chemistry with honors, U. Chgo., 1966; MA in Chemistry, Harvard U., 1967, PhD in Chemistry, 1971. Rsch. assoc. Smithsonian Astrophysical Obs., Cambridge, Mass., 1971-73; lectr. on atmosphere Harvard Univ., Div. Applied Scis., Cambridge, 1973-77, chemistry and rsch. fellow, assoc. prof., 1977-82, sr. rsch. fellow, 1982—. Contbr. numerous articles to profl. jours. Mem. AAAS, Am. Geophysical Union (James B. MacIlwane award 1982), Am. Soc. Limnology and Oceanography.

WOGAMAN, GEORGE ELSWORTH, insurance company executive, financial consultant; b. Mikado, Mich., May 29, 1937; s. Edgar R. and Leah Katherine (McGuire) W.; m. Sandra Lee Jensen, Apr. 10, 1965; children: Jennifer, Christopher. Grad. various ins. courses. CLU, registered rep.; cert. ChFc. With Blair Transit Co., Dun & Bradstreet, Chrysler Engring. Co., 1955-61; exec. chef Westward Ho!, 1961-68; owner, mgr. George Wogaman Ins. Agy., Grand Forks, N.D., 1969—. Mem. pres. coun. Farmers Ins. Group, 1988—98, 1999—2004; alderman East Grand Forks (Minn.) City Coun., 1979—2000, v.p., 1982—2000. Mem. Red River Valley Estate Planning Coun.; mem. Wesley United Meth. Ch., Grand Forks; pres. bd. dirs. Econ. Devel. and Housing Authority, East Grand Forks, Minn., 2009. Recipient Pub. Svc. award East Grand Forks City Coun., 1979. Mem. Am. Soc. CLU's, North Valley Life Underwriters Assn. (Life Underwriter of Yr. 1988), Famers Financial Solutions. Home: 1818 19 h St NW East Grand Forks MN 56721-1013 Office: 2612 Gateway Dr Grand Forks ND 58203-1406 Office Phone: 701-772-7108. Business E-Mail: gwogaman@farmersagent.com.

WOGAMAN, JOHN PHILIP, retired minister and educator; b. Toledo, Mar. 18, 1932; s. Donald Ford and Ella Louise (Kilbury) W.; m. Carolyn Jane Gattis, Aug. 4, 1956; children: Stephen Neil, Donald George, Paul Joseph, Jean Ann. BA, U. Pacific, 1954; STB, Boston U., 1957, PhD, 1960. Ordained to ministry United Meth. Ch., 1957. Pastor First Meth. Ch., Marlborough, Mass., 1956-58; staff asst. divsn. world missions United Meth. Ch., 1960-61; asst. prof., then assoc. prof. U. Pacific, 1961-66; prof. Christian social ethics Wesley Theol. Sem., Washington, 1966—2002, dean, 1972-83, prof. emeritus, 2002; interim pres. ILIFF Sch. Theology, Denver, 2004—06. Sr. pastor Foundry United Meth. Ch., Washington, 1992-2002, interim sr. pastor St. Luke UMC, Omaha, Nebr., 2008-09; mem. com. religious and civil liberties Nat. Coun. Chs., 1966-2003; chairperson United Meth. Infant Formula Task Force, 1980-84, Muskie Com., 1982-91, World Meth. Coun., 1986-91, United Meth. Gen. Conf., 1988, 92, 96, 2000; pres. Interfaith Alliance, 1997-99; chmn. bd. dirs. Interfaith Conf. of Met. Washington, 2002-03. Author: Methodism's Challenge in Race Relations, 1960, Protestant Faith and Religious Liberty, 1967; Guaranteed Annual Income: The Moral Issues, 1968, A Christian Method of Moral Judgement, 1976, Christians and the Great Economic Debate, 1977, Faith and Fragmentation, 1985, revised 2004, Economics and Ethics, 1986, Christian Perspectives on Politics, 1988, rev. edit., 2000, Christian Moral Judgement, 1989, Making Moral Decisions, 1990, Christian Ethics, 1993, To Serve the Present Age, 1995, Speaking the Truth in Love, 1999, From the Eye of the Storm: A Pastor to the President Speaks Out, 1999, An Unexpected Journey: Reflections on Pastoral Ministry, 2004, Moral Dilemmas, 2009; editor: The Population Crisis and Moral Responsibility, 1973, Readings in Christian Ethics, 1996, Communitarian Ethics, 2007 Pres. Stockton (Calif.) Fair Housing Com., 1963-64, Suburban Md. Fair Housing, 1970; mem. Calif. Dem. Ctrl. Com., 1964-66. Lilly fellow, 1959-60; recipient Rsch. award Assn. Theol. Schs., 1975. Mem.: Phi Beta Kappa, Am. Theol. Soc. (pres. 2004—05), Soc. Christian Ethics (pres. 1976—77), Cosmos Club (Washington). Home: 4620 45th St NW Washington DC 20016-4479

WOHL, FRANK HAROLD, lawyer; b. Richmond, Va., June 5, 1942; AB, Dartmouth Coll., 1963; JD, U. Chgo. Law, 1966. Bar: NY 1967. Asst. U.S. atty. So. Dist. NY, NYC, 1971—79; ptnr. Rosenman & Colin, NYC, 1979—84, Lankler Siffert & Wohl, LLP, NYC, 1984—. Chair NYC Civilian Complaint Rev. Bd., 1999—2002. Fed. RICO adminstr. Fulton Fish Market, NYC, 1988—92; dir. Broodwood Child Care, Bklyn., 1992—99. Lt. comdr. JAGC USNR, 1967—71. Fellow: Am. Coll. Trial Lawyers (Access to Justice award 2000); mem.: Fed. Bar Coun. (trustee 2004—), NY Coun. Def. Lawyers (bd. mem. 1998—2002), Fed. Bar Found. (dir. 1996—2002), Bar Assn. City of NY. Office: Lankler Siffert & Wohl LLP 500 Fifth Ave New York NY 10110-3398 Home Phone: 718-834-9583; Office Phone: 212-921-8399.

WOHLCKE, ANNE ELIZABETH, historian, educator; d. Charles Edward Wohlcke and Jane Janzen Zeok; m. David Sheridan, June 24, 2000; children: Maia Elizabeth Sheridan, Cian Alexander Sheridan. BA, Loyola Marymount U., LA; MA, Va. Tech. U., Blacksburg, 1996; PhD, U. Calif., Irvine, 2004. Asst. prof. history Eastern Ky. U., Richmond, 2004—06, Calif. State Poly. U., Pomona, 2006—. Contbr. articles to profl. jours. (James Soltow award, 2006). Mem.: Am. Soc. Eighteenth Century Studies, World History Assn., Am. Hist. Assn. Office: Cal Poly Pomona History Dept 3801 West Temple Ave Pomona CA 91768 Office Fax: 909-869-4724. Business E-Mail: aewohlcke@csupomona.edu.

WOHLEBER, LYNNE FARR, archivist, librarian; b. Pitts., Mar. 16, 1939; d. Donald Elmer and Helen Rose (Lula) F.; m. David Louis Wohleber, Oct. 14, 1972 (div. Sept. 1989); 1 child, Jeffrey David. AB, Allegheny Coll., 1961; MLS, U. Pitts., 1991. Sec. comm. Aluminum Co. Am., Pitts., 1968—73; shop mgr. The Thread Shed, Pitts., 1986—90; libr. Coun. Am. Embroiderer's Libr., Carnegie, Pa., 1985—93; archivist Episcopal Diocese Pitts., 1989—2009; ret. Cons. Calvary Episcopal Ch. Archives, Pitts., 1992—93, Bapt. Home Libr., Mt. Lebanon, Pa., 1994, First United Meth. Ch. Archives, Pitts., 1995, Episcopal Diocese of Albany, 2000; archival cons. Christ Ch., New Brighton, 2001, Old St. Luke's, Scott Twp., 2002, Grace Ch., Pitts., 2005, Ascension, Oakland, 2008; bldg. archives workshop instr., 1995, 2000—07; 250th anniversary comm. com. Episcopal Diocese of Pitts., 2007—08; presenter in field. Libr. com., bd. deacons, rec. sec. Bower Hill Cmty. Ch., 1996-99, nominating com. 1998-99, elder, 2003-06, 09; contemporary svc. task force, 2002-04; coord. presch. program Am. Lung Assn., Pitts., 1977-87; capt., ward chair Am. Cancer Soc., Pitts., 1978-84; newsletter editor Mendelssohn Choir of Pitts., 1973-87; den leader Boy Scouts Am., Mt. Lebanon, Pa., 1983-84. Mem. Soc. Am. Archivists (planning com. 1999 Pitts. conf.), Mid-Atlantic Regional Archives Conf. (co-chair spl. events 1992, publs. com. 1996-2001, panelist 1999 spring conf., conf. local arrangements publicity com. 2003—04), Nat. Episcopal Historians and Archivists (Pitts. coord. for 1997 Episcopal Tri-History Conf., bd. dirs. 1996-2004, treas. 1999-2004, membership sec. 2005—), Hist. Soc. Episcopal Ch., Curators, Archivists and Record Profls. We. Pa. (co-chair Archives Week 1999 com.), Women's Episcopal History Project, Episcopal Archivists Network, Beta Phi Mu. Republican. Presbyterian and Episcopalian. Home: 110 Skylark Cir Pittsburgh PA 15234-1018 Personal E-mail: gingercat65@hotmail.com.

WOHLGENANT, RICHARD GLEN, lawyer, director; b. Porterville, Calif., Dec. 2, 1930; s. Carl Ferdinand and Sara Alice (Moore) W.; m. Teresa Joan Bristow, Dec. 27, 1959; children: Mark Thomas, Tracy Patrice, Timothy James. BA, U. Mont., Missoula, 1952; LL.B., Harvard U., Cambridge, Mass., 1957. Bar: Colo. 1957, U.S. Dist. Ct. Colo. 1957. Assoc. Holme Roberts & Owen LLP, Denver, 1957-62; ptnr./mem. Holme Roberts & Owen, Denver, 1962-99, of counsel, 2000—. Bd. dirs. Adopt-A-Sch., Denver, 1976-80, St. Joseph Found., Denver, 1990-93, Denver Com. Coun. Fgn. Rels., 1988-98, Japanese-Am. Soc. Colo., 1993-98, Rocky Mountain chpt. U.S. Mex. C. of C., 1993-00; bi-nat. bd. U.S./Mex. C. of C., 2000—01; mem. Chamber of the Americas, 2001—03; adv. bd. Human Med. Genetics Prgm., U. Colo. H.S.C., 2000—03; trustee Helen K.and Arthur E. Johnson Found., 2003—, dir. Cordillerm Found, 2002- Mem. ABA, Colo. Bar Assn., Denver Bar Assn., Am. Coll. Real Estate Lawyers, Univ. Club, Law Club, City Club, Cactus Club, Denver Press Club, Mile High Club. Republican. Roman Catholic. Home: 300 Ivy St Denver CO 80220-5855 Office: Holme Roberts & Owen LLP 1700 Lincoln St Denver CO 80203-4500

WOJAHN, R. LORRAINE, retired state senator; b. Tacoma, Sept. 17, 1920; m. Gilbert M. Wojahn (dec.); children: Mark C., Gilbert M. Jr. (dec.). Student, U. Washington, 1938—39. Mem. Wash. State Ho. of Reps., Olympia, 1969-76, Wash. State Senate, Olympia, 1977—2001, ret., 2001. Pres. pro tempore; vice chmn. rules, health and human svcs. com.; mem. labor and commerce, ways and means coms. Bd. dirs. Allenmore Hosp.; trustee Consumer Credit Counseling Svcs., Inc., Tacoma-Pierce County; active, past pres. Eastside Boys and Girls Club, Tacoma-Pierce County; active Wash. State Hist. Soc. Mem.: Alpha Chpt. (hon.), Delta Kappa Gamma (hon.). Democrat.

WOJCICKI, ANDREW ADALBERT, chemist, educator; b. Warsaw, May 5, 1935; s. Franciszek Wojcicki and Janina (Kozlow) Hoskins; m. Marba L. Hart, Dec. 21, 1968; children: Katherine, Christina. BS, Brown U., 1956; PhD, Northwestern U., 1960; postdoctoral fellow, U. Nottingham, Eng., 1960-61. Asst. prof. chemistry Ohio State U., Columbus, 1961-66, assoc. prof., 1966-69, prof., 1969-2000, prof. emeritus, 2001—, acting chmn., 1981-82, assoc. chmn., 1982-83, 84-86. Vis. prof. Academia Sinica, Taipei, Taiwan, 2002-03, Case Western Res. U., 1967, U. Bologna, Italy, 1988, Nat. Sci. Council Chemistry Rsch. Promotion Ctr., Taiwan, 1994, U. Sydney, Australia, 1998; vis. researcher U. Coll. London, 1969; sr. U.S. scientist Alexander von Humboldt Found., Mulheim/Ruhr, Germany, 1975-76; vis. scholar U. Calif.-Berkeley, 1984; assoc. dean Coll. of Math. and Phys. Scis., Ohio State U., 1996-98. Contbr. articles to profl. jours. Guggenheim fellow U. Cambridge (Eng.), 1976; recipient Disting. Teaching award Ohio State U., 1968, Humboldt Sr. award Humboldt Found., 1975-76, Casimir Funk Natural Sci. award, Polish Inst. of Arts and Scis. in Am., 2001. Mem.: Am. Chem. Soc. (Columbus sect. award 1992), Phi Lambda Upsilon, Sigma Xi. Home: 825 Greenridge Rd Columbus OH 43235-3411 Office: Ohio State U 100 W 18th Ave Columbus OH 43210-1185 Office Phone: 614-292-3500. Business E-Mail: wojcicki.1@osu.edu.

WOJCICKI, ESTHER DENISE, journalist, educator; d. Philip and Rebecca Hochman; m. Stanley G Wojcicki, Nov. 17, 1961; children: Susan, Janet, Anne. BA, U. of Calif., 1958—61; MJ, U. Calif., 1962—63; Gen. Secondary, U. of Calif., 1961—62; Advanced Degree, Sorbonne, 1964—66; M.A., San Jose State U., 1988—90, Ednl. Adminstrn. Credential, 1988—89. Cert. Nat. Bd. for Profl. Tchg. Stds. Secondary tchr. Pacific HS, San Leandro, Calif., 1962—63; English-journalism tchr. San Carlos HS, Calif., 1966—68; reporter LA Times, 1956—58; stringer, writer Time Mag., New York, 1961—63; journalism dept. chair, tchr. Palo Alto HS, Calif., 1984—, instrnl. supr., 1988—94. Ednl. cons. Stanford Learning Systems, Calif., 1990—, Google, 2006—; adviser Campanile HS Category; health ednl. cons. Google Edn. Outreach Page, 2006; mem. bd. curriki Sun Microsys., 2007—; online edn. writer Huffington Post, 2007—. Editor: Using Technology in the Classroom, Writing Center; contbr. booklet & video Assignment Rescue.

Dir. of edn. Varian Fry Found., Menlo Park, Calif., 1998—2003; chair of evaluation com. Mid-Peninsula Gideon Hausner Day Sch., Palo Alto, Calif., 1999—2003; chair Stanford Campus Homeowners, Stanford, Calif., 1969—73; pres. Stanford Campus Recreation Assn., Stanford, Calif., 1978—80. Recipient Excellence in Scholastic Journalism, Soc. of Profl. Journalists, 2001, 1st Pl. Gen. Excellence award, Calif. Newspaper Pub.'s Assn., 2005, Gold Key award, Columbia U., 2009; named First Pl. Coach, Thinkquest Internat., 2000, Tchr. of Yr., Calif. Credential Commn., 2002; Carnegie Found. scholar, Carnegie Found., 2000—02. Mem.: Friends Lurdes Mutola Found. (pres. 2007—), VIP Tone Com. (bd. dirs. 2008), Classwish Com. (adv. bd. 2008), Creative Commons (bd. dirs. 2008—), Calif. Teachers Assn. (assoc.), Journalism Educators of Am. (assoc.). Avocations: travel, jogging, hiking. Office: Palo Alto High School 50 Embarcadero Rd Palo Alto CA 94301 Home Phone: 650-493-0919; Office Phone: 650-329-3831, 650-329-3863. Personal E-mail: ewojcicki@gmail.com, estherwoj@gmail.com. Business E-Mail: ewojcicki@pausd.org, esther@creativecommons.org.

WOJCICKI, STANLEY GEORGE, physicist, researcher; b. Warsaw, Mar. 30, 1937; came to U.S., 1950; s. Franciszek and Janina (Kozlow) W.; m. Esther Denise Hochman, Nov. 17, 1961; children: Susan Diane, Janet Maia, Anne Elizabeth. AB, Harvard U., 1957; PhD, U. Calif., Berkeley, 1961. Physicist Lawrence Radiation Lab., Berkeley, 1961-66; asst. prof. physics Stanford U., 1966-68, assoc. prof., 1968-74, prof., 1974—, chmn. dept., 1982-85, 2004—07, dep. dir. Superconducting Supercollider Central Design Group, 1984-89; chmn. Stanford Linear Accelerator Center Exptl. Program Adv. Com., 1979-81. Chmn. High Energy Physics Adv. Panel, 1990-96; spokesperson FermiLab Main Injector Neutrine Oscillation Search expt. Assoc. editor Phys. Rev. Letters for Exptl. High Energy Physics, 1978-80. Recipient Alexander von Humboldt Sr. Am. Scientist award, 1981; NSF fellow, 1964-65; Sloan Found. fellow, 1968-72; Guggenheim fellow, 1973-74 Fellow Am. Phys. Soc. Office: Stanford U Varian Physics Bldg 382 Via Pueblo Mall Stanford CA 94305-4060 Office Phone: 650-926-2806. Personal E-mail: sgwojcicki@gmail.com. Business E-Mail: sgweg@slac.stanford.edu.

WOJCIECHOWSKI, SHEILA, zoological park administrator; b. Spring Valley, Ill., May 26, 1973; d. Donald and Joyce Wojciechowski. BS, U. Ill., Urbana, 1995, MS, 1996. Sr. zookeeper Brookfield Zoo, Ill., 1997—. Contbr. articles to profl. jours. Mem.: Am. Assn. Zookeepers, Girl Scouts. Office: Brookfield Zoo 3300 Golf Rd Brookfield IL 60513 Business E-Mail: sheilawoj@sbcglobal.net.

WOJCIESZAK, MAGDALENA ELZBIETA, communications educator, researcher; b. Warsaw, July 17, 1978; d. Wlodzimierz Wojcieszak and Joanna Anna Konieczna-Wojcieszak. MA, Doctorate, U. Pa., Phila., 2008. Cert. in sociology U. degli Studi di Urbino, Italy, 2001. Freelance journalist, Warsaw, 2002—03; intern Stefan Batory Found., Warsaw, 2002; rschr. Grade News, Stanford U., Palo Alto, Calif., 2003; media planner OMD, Warsaw, 2003; rsch. intern dept. program analysis Polish Pub. TV, Warsaw, 2003; media planner Zenith Optimedia, Warsaw, 2004; rsch. fellow to tchg. asst. Annenberg Sch. Communication, U. Pa., 2004—08, prin. investigator, 2005—06, Warsaw Sch. Social Psychology, Warsaw, 2007, U. Pa; assoc. prof. polit. communication IE Sch. Communication, IE U., Segovia, Spain, 2009—; evaluation methods specialist Ctr. Global Communication Studies, U. Pa., 2009—; rsch. team mem. Ctr. Global Communication Studies and Ctr., Comm. Policy Rsch., U. Pa., 2009—. Contbr. articles to numerous profl. jours. (Ann. prize Excellence, 2005). Recipient James D. Woods award, U. Pa., 2006; European Union Socrates Erasmus fellowship, 2001. Mem.: Nat. Communication Assn., Midwest Assn. Pub. Opinion Rsch., Am. Assn. Pub. Opinion Rsch., Internat. Assn. Media and Communication Rsch., Mid-Western Polit. Sci. Assn., Am. Polit. Sci. Assn., Internat. Communication Assn., East Bound Jour. (assoc. editor 2005), Assn. Edn. Journalism and Mass Communication, Jour. Communication (editl. bd. mem. 2009—). Office: IE Univ IE Sch Communication C/ Cardenal Zúñiga 12 Segovia 40003 Spain Office Phone: 34633134922. Office Fax: 34 921 4493. Business E-Mail: magdalena.wojcieszak@ie.edu.

WOJCIK, BARBARA ELZBIETA, statistician, researcher; arrived in US, 1987; d. Stanislaw and Stanislawa Marciniak; m. Zbigniew M. Wojcik, 1974; children: Martin R., Paulina M. BSEE, MSEE, Tech. U. Warsaw, 1973; PhD, Polish Acad. Scis., 1979. From asst. to assoc. prof. Sys. Rsch. Inst., Polish Acad. Scis., Warsaw, 1975—89; instr. Wichita State U., Kans., 1988; engr., data analyst Beech Aircraft, Fort Sam Houston, 1988—90; vis. asst. prof. U. Tex., San Antonio, 1990—91; supervisory statistician Ctr. for Healthcare Edn. and Studies, Fort Sam Houston, Tex., 1993—2001; dep. dir. Ctr. for AMEDD Strategic Studies, Fort Sam Houston, 2001—. Adj. prof. Webster U., Fort Sam Houston, Tex., 1992—94; asst. prof. US Army, Baylor U., 1993—2001. Contbr. numerous papers and articles to profl. jours. and pubs. Recipient Rschr. of Yr. award, US Army, Baylor U., 1996, 1999; named one of the Top 25 Cancer Rschrs. in the U.S., Am. Cancer Soc., 1998. Mem.: APHA. Achievements include research in healthcare, epidemiology, statistics, rough sets. Office: Ctr for AMEDD Strategic Studies 1608 Stanley Rd Bldg 2268 Fort Sam Houston TX 78234 Business E-Mail: barbara.wojcik@amedd.army.mil.

WOJCIK, CASS, decorative supply company executive, retired municipal official; b. Rochester, NY, Dec. 1920; s. Emit M. and Casimira C. (Krawiecz) Wojcik; m. Lillian Leocadia Lendzion, Sept. 25, 1948 (dec. Jan. 2007); 1 child, Robert Cass. Student, Lawrence Inst. Tech., 1941—43, Yale U., 1943—44, US Sch. for European Pers., Czech Republic, 1945. Owner Nat. Florists Supply Co., Detroit, 1948—88, Nat. Decorative, Detroit, 1950—89; co-owner Creaton Ctr., Detroit, 1955—60, Wojcik Family Collection Collectqables Mktg., 1995—. Cons.-contr. hort-bot. design auto show displqays, TV prodrs., designers and decorators; with S.E. Mich Coun. Bouts Exec. Comm. Nen, Regional Planning and Evaluation Coun., 1969—75; city-wide mem. Detroit Bd. Edn., 1970—75; commr. Detroit Pub. Schs. Employees Retirement Commn., 1975; mem. Area Occupl. Ednl. Commn., Ednl. Task Force; chmn., grand marshal Ann. Gen. Pulaski Day Parade, Detroit, 1970—71; mem. Friends of Belle iSLE; mem. pastoral coun. Archdiocese of Detroit, ', 1983—86, 1988—92; v.p. rsch. Bama Coll., Ft. Lauderdale, Fla., 1989—94; vice chmn. '13th Congl. Dist. Rep. Party Mich., 1987—91; elected Electoral Coll., 1988. With US Army, 1944—46. Decorated Bronze Star; recipient citation, Polish-Am. Congress, 1971, 3d prize Art in Park, City of Oakiland Park, Fla. Mem.: Mich. Heritage Coun., Internat. Platform Assn., Nat. Coun. Tchr. Retirement, Mcpl. Fin. Officers Assn. US, Nat. Coun. Great Cities Schs., Big Cities Sch. Bd. Com., Nat. Sch. Bd. Assn., Mich. Sch. Bd. Assn., SE Mich. Coun. Govts., Nat. Geog. Soc., Polish Century Club. Office Phone: 561-750-9033.

WOJCIK, MARTIN HENRY, not-for-profit executive; b. Chgo., May 10, 1948; s. Henry Martin and Mary Lorraine (Naughton) W. BS, Ill. Inst. Tech., 1970; M. in Humanities, Bonn U., W. Ger., 1975. Cert. fundraising exec. 2007. Price adminstr. R.R. Donnelley & Sons., Chgo., 1970-72; dir. devel. Citizens for a Better Environment, Milw., 1976-79, pres. Chgo., 1979-85; dir. found. rels. Northwestern U., Evanston, Ill., 1987-89; dir. corp. and found. rels. Mayo Found., Rochester, Minn., 1989—2002; sr. v.p., COO, Scripps Health Found., La Jolla, Calif., 2002—04; dir. devel. The Biodesign Inst., Ariz. State U., Tempe, 2005—07; capital campaign dir. Calif. divsn. Am. Cancer Soc., 2008—. Bd. dir. Citizens for Better Environment, Chgo., chmn. bd. dir., 1990—91, 1999—2001; mem. policy adv. com. Ill. EPA, Springfield, Ill., 1980—82. Bd. dirs. Rochester Civic Theatre, 1991-97, pres. bd. dirs. 1994-95; bd. dirs. Wasie Found., 2003-07; mem. adv. panel Minn. State Arts Bd., 1995, 97, 99, 2001; adv. coun. KSDS Pub. Radio, San Diego, 2003-; panelist, Ariz. Commn. on the Arts, 2007, 08, Arizona Planned Giving Inst., 2007—. Mem. Ill. Inst. Tech. Alumni Assn., Planned Giving Roundtable Ariz., Assn. Fundraising Profls. Roman Catholic. Home: 8507 N 84th Pl Scottsdale AZ 85258-2401 Office Phone: 858-354-8245.

WOLANER, ROBIN PEGGY, Internet and magazine publisher; b. Queens, NY, May 6, 1954; d. David H. and Harriet (Radlow) W.; children: Terry David, Bonnie Lee. BS in Indsl. and Labor Rels., Cornell U., 1975. Sr. editor Viva Mag., NYC, 1975-76; editor Impact Mag., NYC, 1976-77; circulation mgr. Runner's World Mag., Mountain View, Calif., 1977-79; cons. Ladd Assocs., San Francisco, 1979-80; gen. mgr. Mother Jones Mag., San Francisco, 1980-81, pub., 1981-85; founder, pub. Parenting Mag., San Francisco, 1985-91, pres., 1991-92; v.p. Time Pub. Ventures, 1990-96; pres., CEO Sunset Pub. Corp., 1992-95; exec. v.p. CNET, 1997—2002; founder, CEO Tee Bee Del.com, 2006—. Bd. dirs. Working Assets, Tides Found. Author: Naked in the Boardroom: A CEO Bares Her Secrets So You Can Transform Your Career, 2005. Jewish. Home: 124 Jordan Ave San Francisco CA 94118 Personal E-mail: robin_wolaner@yahoo.com.

WOLANIN, THOMAS RICHARD, federal agency administrator, educator; b. Detroit, Dec. 1, 1942; s. Chester Richard and Helen Theresa (Luszki) W.; m. Donna M. Christian; children: Peter, Andrew. BA magna cum laude, Oberlin Coll., 1965; MA, Harvard U., 1970, PhD, 1972. Staff dir. subcom. on labor-mgmt. rels. House Edn. and Labor Com., 1975-77, dep. staff dir. subcom. on select edn., 1977-78; exec. asst. to pres. NYU, 1981-82; analyst Senate Budget Com., 1982-83; staff dir. subcom. on investigations House P.O. and Civil Svc. Com., 1983-85, 87-91; staff dir. subcom. on postsecondary edn. House Edn. and Labor Com., 1978-81, 85-87;, 91-93; dep. asst. sec. legis. and congl. affairs U.S. Dept. Edn., Washington, 1993-96; sr. assoc. The Inst. for Higher Edn. Policy, Washington, 1996—. Instr. govt. Oberlin Coll., 1967-69; asst. prof. polit. sci. U. Wis., Madison, 1971-78; rsch. prof. edn. policy and polit. sci. George Washington U., Washington, 1997-00. Author: Presidential Advisory Commissions: Truman to Nixon, 1975; co-author: Congress and the Colleges: Higher Education in National Politics, 1976; contbr. articles to profl. jours. Bd. dirs. Am. Youth Policy Forum. Woodrow Wilson fellow, 1965-66, fellow Harvard U., 1965-67, 69-71, Congl. fellow, 1971-72, Spencer fellow Nat. Acad. Edn., 1975-81, Fulbright Found., 2005; grantee Ford Found., 1972-73, 73-74, USIA, 1990; scholar The Brookings Instn., 1970 Mem. Polish Am. Arts Assn. Washington, Congl. Fellowship Alumni Assn., Phi Beta Kappa. Democrat. Avocations: military history, polish history, literature. Office: Inst Higher Edn Policy 1320 19th St NW Ste 400 Washington DC 20036-1635 Office Phone: 202-861-8223 Ext. 214. Business E-Mail: twolanin@ihep.org.

WOLANSKYJ, ALEXANDRA, hematologist; d. Bohdan Markian Wolanskyj and Urania Wolanskyj nee Vassalakis; m. Robert Jay Spinner, Dec. 3, 2000; children: Maxwell Alexander Spinner, Noah Daniel Spinner. BSc with honors, Concordia U., Montreal, Que., 1987; MD, U. Montreal, 1992; MS in Internal Medicine, Mayo Grad. Sch. Medicine, Rochester, Minn., 1995, MS in Hematology-Oncology, 1998. Registered Am. Bd. Internal Medicine, 1995, in hematology Am. Bd. Internal Medicine, 1998, in oncology Am. Bd. Internal Medicine, 1998. Asst. prof. medicine Mayo Clinic, Rochester, 2004—, chair edn., divsn. hematology, 2006—. Chair, hematology course Mayo Clinic Coll. Medicine, Med. Sch., 2006—. Prodr.: (musical album) Lesya (Winner Best Original Song, 1987, Album of Yr., 1987); contbr. articles to profl. med. jours. Named Tchr. of Yr., Med. Coll. Ohio, 2001, Mayo Grad. Sch. Medicine, 2006; grantee Edn. Innovation, Mayo Coll. Medicine, 2004. Fellow: Royal Coll. Surgeons and Physicians Can.; mem.: ACP, Am. Soc. Clin. Oncology, Am. Soc. Hematology.

WOLCHUK, ROMAN, engineering educator; b. Lancut, Poland, Feb. 22, 1922; s. Philip and Josephine Macewych Wolchuk; m. Martha D. Shyprykevich, Apr. 27, 1987; 1 child, Martha Ihor. Student Engr., Tech. U. Lviv, Ukraine; Degree, Tech. U., Vienna, Austria; Diploma in Civil Engring., Tech. U. Graz, Austria, 1946. Cert. prof. engr., NY, PA. Engr. Ammann & Whitney, NYC, 1950—51, F.R. Harris, NYC, 1952—54, D.B. Steinman, NYC, 1954—56; pvt. cons. practice Wolchuk & Mayrbauri, NYC, 1959—66; Prin. Weidlinyer Assocs., 1982—88; prin. pvt. cons. practice Jersey City, 1988—. Contbr. articles to profl jours. Mem. Republican Party, 1985; Ukrainian Scouting Orgn., 1946. Recipient Creative Contrbn. award, US Steel Design Competition, 1959, Merit prize, Bridge Competition, Am. Inst. Steel Constrn., 1972, Congressional medal, NRCC, 2006. Fellow: Ukranian Engrs. Soc. (pres. 1956), Am. Soc. City Engrs.; mem.: Internat. Assn. Bridge & St. Engring. Avocations: tennis, skiing. Office: 921 Bergen Ave Ste 637 Jersey City NJ 07306 Office Phone: 201-659-7128. Office Fax: 201-659-6370. Business E-Mail: wolchuk@bellatlantic.net.

WÖLCK, WOLFGANG HANS-JOACHIM, linguist, educator; b. Koenigsberg, Germany, Sept. 19, 1932; came to U.S., 1963; s. Walter Erich and Margarete (Brettschneider) W.; m. Carolyn Ann Burch, June 18, 1966. Student, Birkbeck Coll., London, 1956; Staatsexamen, Christian Albrecht U., Kiel, Germany, 1960; PhD, J.W. Goethe U., Frankfurt, Germany, 1963. Instr. German and Latin Liverpool (Eng.) Inst., 1957-58; instr. Albert Ludwig U., Freiburg, Germany, 1964-65; asst. prof. Ind. U., Bloomington, 1966-69; assoc. prof. linguistics SUNY-Buffalo, 1970-74, prof., 1975-97; disting. svc. prof. SUNY, Buffalo, 1997—; chmn. dept. SUNY-Buffalo, 1977-87, 89-91, dir. Latin Am. Studies program, 1972-76; research fellow Instituto de Estudios Peruanos, Lima, Peru, 1976-77; advisor Ministry of Edn., Lima, 1972, 82-83; advisor, E.U. rsch. project linguistic diversity LINEE, 2007—; rsch. prof. Belgian Nat. Sc. Found., 1991—93. Cons. Fischer-Price Toys, Inc., East Aurora, N.Y., 1980—; hon. prof. San Marcos Nat. U., Lima, 1972; mem. Fulbright Nat. Screening Com., 1993-96, E.C. Scientific Com. Linguistic Minorities, EUROMOSAIC, 1996-2004, hon. mem. Rsch. Ctr. for Multilingualism, Brussels, rsch. amb. German Academic Exchange Svc. DAAD, 2009- Founding mem. Peru Earthquake Relief Com., Washington, 1972; field rep. United Way Campaign, Buffalo, 1977-81. Recipient Bronze medal Mazaryk U., Brno, Czech Republic, 1971; Fulbright grantee, 1963-64. Mem. Am. Dialect Soc., Linguistic Soc. Am., Societas Linguistica Europea, Linguistic Assn. Can. and U.S., Am. Assn. Applied Linguistics, Ctr. for Cognitive Sci., Centre for Multilingual Rsch., Sociedad Boliviana de Linguistica (hon.), Internat. Inst. Buffalo (bd. dirs. 1996—, pres. 1999-2002), Ellicottville Ski Club (bd. dirs. 1988-94); mem. deans adv. coun. U. Buffalo, 2005—. Home: 611H Skinnersville Rd Buffalo NY 14228-2503 Office Phone: 716-645-0128. Business E-Mail: wwolck@buffalo.edu.

WOLCOTT, HUGH DIXON, obstetrics and gynecology educator; b. NYC, Jan. 12, 1946; s. Charles Edmund and Joan Degrau (Loveland) W.; m. Jane Jarrell Smith; children: Allison, James. BS, U.S. Naval Acad., 1967; MSE, Princeton U., 1969; MD, Northwestern U., 1979. Diplomate Am. Bd. Ob-Gyn, Am. Bd. Med. Examiners. Commd. ensign USN, 1967, advanced through grades to capt., 1990; aviator, Fighter Squadron 14 Naval Air Station, Oceana, Va., 1971-74; test pilot Naval Air Test Ctr., Patuxent River, Md., 1974-76; staff physician Naval Hosp., Portsmouth, Va., 1984, Jacksonville, Fla., 1984-86, dir. colposcopy and laser clins. Portsmouth, Va., 1986-89, dir. ob-gyn. residency program, 1989-91, acting chmn. dept. ob-gyn., 1990-91; ret., 1991; asst. prof. Med. Coll. Hampton Roads, Norfolk, Va., 1991—. Chmn. dept. ob-gyn. Sentara Hosps, Norfolk, 1996—2001; ob-gyn. splty. advisor Sentara Health Mgmt. Corp., 2000—; chmn. bd. mgr.s Mid-Atlantic Women's Care, LLC, 2005—; mem. Congl. Adv. Com. for Healthcare, 2006—. Contbr. articles profl. jours. Mem. steering com. Sentara ObRight Patient Safety Initiative, 2005—. Awarded 1st prize scientific paper by resident physician Am. Coll. Obstetricans and Gynecologists; recipient Guggenheim fellowship Princeton U., 1967-68; Trident scholar U.S. Naval Acad., 1966-67. Fellow Am. Coll. Ob.-Gyns. (chmn. Navy sect. armed forces dist. 1989-91), Assn. Profs. Ob.-Gyns. (assoc.); mem. Am. Assn. Gynecol. Laparoscopists. Episcopalian. Home: 835 Botetourt Gdns Norfolk VA 23507-1814 Office: Woman Care Ctrs 100 Kingsley Ln Ste 400 Norfolk VA 23505 Home Phone: 757-627-1290.

WOLCOTT, JOHN WINTHROP, III, retired manufacturing executive; b. Balt., Dec. 3, 1924; s. John Winthrop, Jr. and Dorothy C. (Fraser) W.; m. Elizabeth Thelin Hooper, Apr. 24, 1948 (div. 1985); children: John Winthrop IV (dec.), Elizabeth T., Katherine C.; m. Karen E. Jones, Oct. 1, 1985; 1 child, Oliver Lund. B.Indsl. Engring., Gen. Motors Inst., 1951. Registered profl. engr., Ohio. With Gen. Motors Corp., 1946-53, Weatherhead Co., Cleve., 1957-60; v.p. H.K. Porter Co., Inc., Pitts., 1960-64; pres., dir., CEO Ametek, Inc., NYC, 1964-66; v.p. Am. Machine & Foundry Co., 1966-77, group exec. process equipment group, 1967-70; exec. v.p. ops., dir. AMF, Inc., 1970-77; pres., chief exec. officer, dir. Transway Internat. Corp., NYC, 1978-86, chmn. bd., 1982-86. Served with USCGR, 1943-46. Mem. Soc. Colonial Wars. Episcopalian. Home: 210 Carrsbrook Dr Charlottesville VA 22901-1004

WOLD, JOHN SCHILLER, geologist, former congressman; b. East Orange, NJ, Aug. 31, 1916; s. Peter Irving and Mary (Helff) W.; m. Jane Adele Pearson, Sept. 28, 1946; children: Peter Irving, Priscilla Adele, John Pearson. AB, St. Andrews U., Scotland and Union Coll., Schenectady, 1938; MS, Cornell U., 1939; LLD (hon.), U. Wyo., 1991; DSc with honors, Union Coll., 2008. Dir. Fedn. Rocky Mountain States, 1966-68; v.p. Rocky Mountain Oil and Gas Assn., 1967, 68; mem. Wyo. Ho. of Reps., 1957-59; Wyo. Republican candidate for U.S. Senate, 1964, 70; mem. 91st Congress at large from Wyo.; chmn., CEO Wold Trona Co., Inc.; pres., chmn. Wold Talc Co.; ret. Wold Nuclear Co., Wold Mineral Exploration Co., Casper, Wyo.; founding pres. Wyo. Heritage Soc.; founder Central Wyo. Ski Corp. Chmn. Wyo. Natural Gas Pipeline Authority, 1987-91; chmn. bd. Nuclear Exploration and Devel. Corp., Mineral Engring. Co., chmn., CEO Gastech, 2005—. Chmn. Wyo. Rep. Com., 1960-64, Western State Rep. Chmns. Assn., 1963-64; mem. exec. com. Rep. Nat. Com., 1962-64; chmn. Wyo. Rep. State Fin. Com.; Active Little League Baseball, Boy Scouts Am., United Fund, YMCA, Boys Clubs Am.; former pres. bd. trustees Casper Coll.; trustee Union Coll. Served to lt. USNR, World War II. Named Wyo. Man of Yr. AP-UPI, 1968; Wyo. Mineral Man of Yr., 1979, Wyo. Heritage award, 1992, Wyo. Oil/Gas and Mineral Man of 20th Century, Am. Heritage Ctr. of U. Wyo., 1999; named Benefactor of Yr., Nat. Coun. for Resource Devel., 1993. Mem. Wyo. Geol. Assn. (hon. life, pres. 1956), Am. Assn. Petroleum Geologists, Ind. Petroleum Assn. Am., AAAS, Wyo. Mining Assn., Sigma Xi, Alpha Delta Phi. Episcopalian (past vestryman, warden). Home: 1231 W 30th St Casper WY 82601-5372 Office: Mineral Resource Ctr 139 W 2nd St Casper WY 82601-2473 Office Phone: 307-265-7252. Business E-Mail: gastech@woldoil.com.

WOLDE GIORGIS, GIRMA, President of Ethiopia; b. Addis Ababa, Ethiopia, Dec. 1924; 5 children. Grad. sub-lt., Guenet Mil. Sch., 1944; student, Sch. Social Sci., The Netherlands. Cert. in Air Traffic Mgmt. Sweden, in Air Traffic Control Can. Dir. gen. Ministry of Commerce, Industry and Planning, Ethiopia, 1959, mem., 2000—, mem. econs. subcommittee; pres. Ethiopia, 2001—. Asst. instr. air navigation & air traffic control tng., 1947; head tech. svc. Civil Aviation Authority, 1947; head civil aviation Federated Govt. Eritrea, 1955, dir. gen. civil aviation, 58; bd. mem. Ethiopian Airlines, 1958; mem. Civil Adv. Coun. to Mil. Govt., 1974; mgr. Import & Export Enterprise; first vice commr. Peace Commn., 1976; head logistics, Demobilization of X-Army Persons Internat. Com. Red Cross, Ethiopia, 1990; founder Environment & Devel. Soc. Ethiopia (LEM), 1992, v.p. Bd. mem. Ethiopian C. of C., 1967; mem. Coun. of People's Reps., Ethiopia; bd. dirs. Ethiopian Red Cross Soc., 1982. Enlisted as soldier Ethiopian Army, 1941, transferred to Ethiopian Air Force, 1946. Speaks Amharic, English, French, Italian and Tigrinya. Office: Office of the Pres PO Box 1031 Addis Ababa Ethiopia

WOLDEN, SUZANNE LEESA, pediatric radiation oncologist; b. West Covina, Calif., June 30, 1969; MD, U. Calif. San Francisco Sch. Medicine, 1994. Cert. Radiation Oncology. Intern Cornell Med. Ctr., NY, 1994—95; resident Stanford U. Med. Ctr., Calif., 1995—98; asst. attending Meml. Sloan-Kettering Cancer Ctr., NY, 1998—. Contbr. articles to profl. jours. Named one of Medical Marvel, NY Mag., 2006. Office: Meml Sloan-Kettering Cancer Ctr 1275 York Ave New York NY 10021 Office Phone: 212-639-5148.

WOLDMAN, SHERMAN, pediatrician; b. Buffalo, Apr. 1, 1932; s. Joseph Harry and Sadie (Weinstein) W. m. Fern Marlene Weinstein, Dec. 28, 1952; children: Deborah Janine Case, Scott Alan, Sabina Heide Muller. BS in Pharmacy magna cum laude, U. Buffalo, 1953, MD with high honors, 1957. Diplomate Am. Bd. Pediat. Intern Millard Fillmore Hosp., Buffalo, 1957-58; resident in pediat. Womens & Children's Hosp., Buffalo, 1958—60, active staff, 1961—2004, emeritus, 2005; pvt. practice Buffalo, 1961-66, Cheektowaga, NY, 1962—2004; mem. active staff Millard Fillmore Hosp., Buffalo, 1961—2004, chmn. dept. pediat., 1985-91, emeritus, 2005; pediatrician pvt. practice, 2005, Clermont, 2006. Clin. asst. pediat. SUNY Sch. Medicine, Buffalo, 1962, clin. assoc. 1970, clin. asst. prof., 1973, clin. assoc. prof., 2001, preceptor Sch. Nursing, 1976-82; attending pediatrician Booth Meml. Hosp., Buffalo, 1969-72; sch. physician Williamsville Ctrl. Schs., NY, 1962-94, chmn. of physicians, 1970-94; courtesy staff St. Joseph Intercmty. Hosp., Cheektowaga, 1963-80, Kenmore Mercy Hosp., NY, 1963-70, 1974-82, Sisters of Charity Hosp., Buffalo, 1991-2003, Erie County Med. Ctr., Buffalo, 1979-83, Buffalo Gen. Hosp., 1987-95; provisional staff Mercy Hosp., Buffalo, 1982-83, courtesy staff, 2000-03; sch. physician LTES, Cape May, NJ, 2005-07, med. advisor, 2007-. Vol. Leukemia and Lymphoma Soc., 1975, bd. trustees Western NY and Finger Lakes chpt. 1975-2005, pres. 1977-79, v.p. 1979-81, profl. edn. com. 1975-2005, Vol. So. NJ/Shorechapter 2005-, nat. bd. trustees 1978-87, vice chmn. patient aid com., 1980-87; task force on sch. health Erie County Health Dept., NY; trustee Temple Beth David Ner-Israel, Buffalo, 1964-65; vol.

staff pediatrician, vol. medicine Clinic Cape May County House, NJ, 2006—07. Co-recipient recognition cert. Cheektowaga NY C. of C., 1982; Myron L. Woldman Vol. of Yr. award Western NY chpt. Leukemia Soc. Lymphoma, 1987, nat. chmn.'s citation 1999; Disting. Physician award Millard Fillmore Health Sys., 1995. Mem.: Maimonides Med. Soc. (pres. Buffalo chpt. 1982—83), Med. Soc. County of Erie, N.Y. (chmn. pub. health com. 1978—79), Buffalo Pediat. Soc. (pres. 1969—70), Med. Soc. State of N.Y., Am. Acad. Pediat. (PREP fellow 1979—85, 1992—94, 1994—96, 1997—99, 2000—02), Gibson Anat. Soc. (hon.), Phi Lambda Kappa (alumni pres. 1965, v.p. alumni 1980—81), Rho Chi, Alpha Omega Alpha. Avocations: gardening, computers. Personal E-mail: swoldman@comcast.net.

WOLDT, HAROLD FREDERICK, JR., newspaper publishing executive; b. Atlanta, July 4, 1947; s. Harold Frederick and Dorothy Rose (Lansdowne) W.; m. Lisa Diane Neves; children: Lauren Rae, Katherine Neves, Caroline Neves. BS in Journalism, So. Ill. U., 1969. Classified advt. rep. Chgo. Tribune, 1969-70, classified automobile staff mgr., 1970-72; nat. advt. sales rep. Chgo. Tribune newspapers, NYC, 1972-74, city circulation mgr., 1974-77; nat. circulation mgr. Chgo. Tribune, 1977-80, circulation mgr., 1980-84; v.p., circulation News & Sun Sentinel Co., Ft. Lauderdale, Fla., 1985; circulation dir. Newsday, Inc., Melville, NY, 1986-88, v.p., circulation LI, NY, 1988-94; sr. v.p. circulation Newsday, pres. Distbn. Systems. Am. subs. of Newsday, Inc., 1994-98; v.p. sales circulation mktg. The N.Y. Times, NYC, 1998—2000; dir. circulation Omaha World-Herald; v.p. circulation San Jose Mercury News, Calif., 2001—04, 2006—; sr. v.p. circulation LA Newspaper Group, 2007—, dir. circulation LA Daily News, 2007—. Speaker, participant Am. Press Inst.; bd. dirs. Abilities Health and Rehab. Svcs. (Nat. Ctr. for Disability Svcs.), Albertson, LI, N.Y., 1992-94. Bd. dirs. Robert R. McCormick Boys Club, Chgo., 1980-81; chmn. United Way campaign, Chgo. Tribune, 1980, Omaha World-Herald United Way Campaign, 1999-2000, bd. dir. San Jose Children's Discovery Mus. Calif., Ronald McDonald House Charities of the Bay Area, San Francisco, 2002—. Mem. Am. Pubs. Newspaper Assn. (circulation and readership com. 1988-93), Internat. Circulation Mgrs. Assn. (pres. 1991-92), Alpha Delta Sigma, Tau Kappa Epsilon. Personal E-mail: hfwoldt@aol.com.

WOLEVER, RUTH Q., psychologist, researcher; BA in Spanish, U. Va.; PhD in Clinical Psychology, U. Miami, 1994. Lic. clinical psychologist, cert. health svcs. provider. Intern U. NC Chapel Hill Sch. Medicine, 1994; rsch. dir. Duke Integrative Medicine; asst. clinical prof. dept. psychiatry & behavioral sciences Duke U. Sch. Medicine. Former instr. Dade County Pub. High Sch.; former dir. South Fla. Youth Program. Office: Duke Center for Living Campus 3475 Erwin Rd Durham NC 27705 Office Phone: 919-660-6610.*

WOLF, AIZIK LOFT, neurosurgeon; b. Bogota, Colombia, Jan. 17, 1956; came to U.S., 1963; s. Jose Wolf and Judy Grimberg Loft. AB, U. Chgo., 1977; MD, Yale U., 1981. Diplomate Am. Bd. Neurol. Surgery. Asst. prof. neurosurgery, chief epilepsy surgery U. Md. Hosp., Balt., 1987-93, asst. prof. neurology, chief Gamma knife skull base surgery, 1990-93; dir. Miami Neurosci. Ctr. Doctors Hosp., Coral Gables, Fla., 1993—. Office: Doctors Hosp 5000 University Dr Coral Gables FL 33146-2094 Office Phone: 786-308-3700. E-mail: drwolf@miamineurosciencecenter.com.

WOLF, ALFRED A., physicist, educator; b. Phila., July 21, 1925; s. Jacob Wolf, Anna Wolf; m. Enid G. Wolf, Nov. 24, 1957 (div. Dec. 1981); children: Marcus M., Laurence J. BSEE, Drexel U., Phila., 1948; MSEE, U. Pa., Phila., 1954, PhD, 1958; ScD, U. Juarez, Mexico, 1977, MD, 1978. Engr.-in-charge Naval Air Devel., Johnsville, Pa., 1949—56; chief scientist Gen. Dynamics, Rochester, NY, 1957—60; dir. rsch. Litton Industries, Silver Spring, Md., 1960—63; disting. prof. elec. engring. Drexel U., Phila., 1963—65; tech. dir. RCA, Burlington, Mass., 1965—67; assoc. tech. dir. Naval Ship R&D Ctr., Annapolis, Md., 1967—78; pres. Prime Rsch. Found., Annapolis, 1978—. Asst. prof. elec. engring. U. Pa., Phila., 1949—59; Pa. scholar, 1952—54; sr. sci. advisor USN, 1971—76; adj. assoc. prof. U. Rochester, 1960—62; adj. prof. U. Md., Annapolis, 1967—69, George Washington U., Washington, 1969—99. Author (prize winning): Biophysics of Wound Healing, 1989; contbr. 105 articles to profl. jours. (14 awards). Cpl. US Army, 1943—46. Recipient Citation of Honor, Drexel U., 1961, Honor citations (8), USN, 1972—83; named Notable Am. of Bicentennial Era, Am. Biog. Inst., 1976; nominee Nobel Prize in Physics, 1972; grantee, NSF, 1956—59; Pa. scholar, 1952—54. Mem.: IEEE (life), Engring. in Medicine and Biology Soc. (chmn. Balt. sect. 1990—95), Sigma Xi. Democrat. Jewish. Achievements include discovery of first high temperature superconductor; 24 patents for electronics devices and systems. Avocation: writing. Home and Office: Prime Rsch Found 562 Ferry Point Rd Annapolis MD 21403-1308

WOLF, ALICE KOERNER, state legislator, former mayor; b. Vienna, Dec. 24, 1933; d. Frederick Koerner and Renee (Engel) K.; m. Robert A. Wolf, 1955; children: Eric Jeffrey, Adam Nathaniel. BS, Simmons Coll., 1955; MPA, Harvard U., 1978; EdD (hon.), Wheelock Coll., 2001. Residence staff MIT, Lincoln Lab, 1955-62, Computer Corp Am., 1967-71, pers. dir., 1971-76; mem. Cambridge Sch. Com., 1974-81, vicechairwoman, 1976—77, 1980—81; mem. Cambridge City Coun., 1984—93; vice mayor Cambridge, Mass., 1986—89, mayor Mass., 1990—91; mem. 25th Middlesex Mass. House of Reps., Boston, 1997—. Del. Dem. Nat. Conv., 1980, 84, 88, 92, 2008, State Conv. Mem. NOW, Mass. Women's Polit. Caucas Cambridge Mental Health Assn., Am. for Dem. Action, Nat. Orgn. Women Am. Civil Liberties Union, Nat. Democrat. Office: State House Rm 167 Boston MA 02133 Home: 48 Huron Ave Cambridge MA 02138-6706 Office Phone: 617-722-2810, 617-497-7284. Personal E-mail: alicewolf@alicewolf.org. Business E-mail: rep.alicewolf@hou.state.ma.us.

WOLF, BARRY, geneticist, pediatric educator; b. Chgo., June 19, 1947; s. Bert D. and Toby E. W.; children: Michael Loren, Bryan Phillip. BS, U. Ill., 1969; MD, U. Ill. Coll. Medicine, 1974; PhD, U. Ill., 1974. Diplomate Am. Bd. Pediatrics, Med. and Biochem. Genetics. Intern, resident in pediatrics Childrens Meml. Hosp., Northwestern U., Chgo., 1974-76; fellow Yale U. Sch. Medicine, New Haven, 1976-78; prof. human genetics Med. Coll. Va., Richmond, 1978-2001, vice chair for rsch. dept. pediatrics, 1996-2000; dir. rsch. Conn. Children's Med. Ctr., 2001—05; assoc. chmn., dir. rsch. Dept. Pediats. Sch. Medicine U. Conn., 2001—01; chmn. Dept. Med. Genetics Henry Ford Hosp., Detroit, 2005—. Author over 175 jour. articles and book chpts. dealing with inherited disorders of metabolism and biochem. genetics, specifically disorders of biotin metabolism. Recipient E. Mead Johnson award for pediatric rsch. Am. Acad. Pediatrics, 1988, Borden award in nutrition Am. Inst. Nutrition, 1987, Outstanding Scientist of Va. award Va. Sci. Mus., 1986, Ounce of Prevention award Action for Prevention of Va., 1985. Mem. Am. Soc. Clin. Investigation, Am. Pediat. Soc., Soc. Pediatric Rsch., Soc. Inherited Metabolic Diseases, Soc. Study Inborn Errors of Metabolism, Am. Soc. Human Genetics. Avocation: japanese cloisonne. Office: Henry Ford Hosp Dept Med Genetics 3031 W Grand Blvd Suite 700 Detroit MI 48202 Home Phone: 248-433-9003; Office Phone: 313-916-3116. Business E-Mail: bwolf1@hfhs.org.

WOLF, BARRY M., lawyer; b. NYC, Nov. 14, 1959; BS summa cum laude, SUNY, Albany, 1981; JD cum laude, U. Mich., 1984; LLM, NYU, 1989. Bar: N.Y. 1985. Ptnr. Weil, Gotshal & Manges LLP, NYC, co-head global corp. dept., 2000—. Mem.: ABA, Private Investment Fund Forum, N.Y. State Bar Assn. Office: Weil, Gotshal & Manges LLP 767 Fifth Ave New York NY 10153 Office Phone: 212-310-8209. E-mail: barry.wolf@weil.com.

WOLF, BARTH JOEL, lawyer, energy executive; BA, Univ. Wis., Green Bay; JD, Univ. Wis., Madison. Bar: Wis. 1984. Sec., mgr. legal svcs. Integrys Energy Group, Green Bay, Wis., 1999—2007; v.p. legal services, chief compliance officer Integrys Bus. Support LLC, Green Bay, Wis., 2007; v.p., chief legal officer, sec. Integrys Energy Group, Green Bay, Wis., 2007—. Office: Integrys Energy Group 700 N Adams St PO Box 19001 Green Bay WI 54307-9001 Office Phone: 920-433-4901. Office Fax: 920-433-1526.*

WOLF, BRANA, editor-at-large; b. Eboli, Italy; Fact checker women's mag., freelance fashion editor; worked with photographer Steven Meisel Italian Vogue; editor-at-large Harper's Bazaar US; cons. Louis Vuitton, Versace, Michael Kors, Zac Posen; ad campaign stylist Valentino, D&G. Named one of Eight Most Powerful Fashion Editors in Am., Forbes-.com. Office: Harper's Bazaar Mag 300 W 57th St New York NY 10019

WOLF, BRIAN R., orthopedist, educator; married. MD, Loyola U. Stritch Sch. Medicine, Maywood, Ill., 1997. Asst. prof., dept. orthopaedics U. Iowa Hosps., 2003—. Head team physician U. Iowa Athletics, 2003—; dir. U. Iowa Sports Medicine Fellowship, 2008—. Fellow: Am. Acad. Orthopaedic Surgeons; mem.: Iowa Orthopaedic Soc., Mid-America Orthopaedic Assn., Am. Orthopaedic Soc. Sports Medicine, Alpha Omega Alpha. Home: Dept Orthopaedics Univ Iowa Hosp Iowa City IA 52242 Office: Univ Iowa Hosps 66 Crabapple Ct Iowa City IA 52246

WOLF, CARL F.W., retired pathologist, consultant; b. New Hyde Park, NY, Feb. 4, 1933; s. Fritz J.C. and Bertha E. (Heidemann) W. BSChemE, MIT, 1953; MS in Chem. Engring. Practice, MIT, Cambridge, 1954; MD, Hahnemann Med. Coll., Phila., 1968. Diplomate Am. Bd. Pathology in Anatomic & Clin. Pathology; cert. med. blood banking transfusion medicine, 1974, pathology, 1997. Intern in pathology N.Y. Hosp., NYC, 1968-69, asst. pathologist II, 1969-71, provisional asst. pathologist, 1971-72, asst. dir. blood bank, 1971-76, asst. attending pathologist, 1972-79, assoc. attending pathologist, 1979-87, attending pathologist, 1987—2006; ret., 2006. Fellow in pathology Cornell U. Med. Coll., 1969-72, instr. in pathology, 1972-73, asst. prof. pathology, 1973-79, assoc. clin. prof. pathology, 1979-83, assoc. prof. clin. pathology, 1983-87, prof. clin. pathology, 1987-2002, prof. clin. pathology and lab. medicine, 2002-06, prof. emeritus clin. pathology and lab medicine, 2006-; vis. fellow dept. pathology Meml. Hosp. for Cancer and Allied Diseases, NY, 1970; USPHS trainee in exptl. pathology Cornell U. Med. Coll., 1969-71; rsch. assoc. NY Blood Ctr., 1969-75; attending pathologist, dir. clin. lab. Burke Rehab. Ctr., White Plains, NY, 1974-1996; assoc. investigator Lindsley F. Kimball Rsch. Inst.-NY Blood Ctr., 1975-83, 84-87; dir. Blood Bank and Transfusion Svc. NY Hosp., NYC, 1976-2004; cons. in clin. pathology NY Hosp. Westchester divsn., 1976-1994; vol. cons. on info. tech. Dept. Pathology and Lab. Medicine Weill Cornell Med. Coll., Cornell U., 2006—; lectr. in field. Contbr. numerous articles to profl. jours., chpts. to books. Fellow Am. Soc. Clin. Pathologists, N.Y. Acad. Medicine; mem. AMA, AIChE, Am. Assn. Blood Banks, Coun. Hosp. Blood Bank Dirs. Greater N.Y. Region (bd. dirs., chmn.), Soc. for Study of Blood, Blood Banks Assn. N.Y. State, Am. Chem. Soc., Acad. Clin. Lab. Physicians and Scientists, Internat. Soc. Cellular Therapy, Alpha Omega Alpha, Phi Lambda Upsilon, Tau Beta Pi. Home: 435 E 70th St Apt 21-j New York NY 10021-5347 Office Phone: 212-249-2180. Business E-Mail: cwolf@med.cornell.edu.

WOLF, CHARLES, JR., economist, educator; b. NYC, Aug. 1, 1924; s. Charles and Rosalie W.; m. Theresa van de Wint, Mar. 1, 1947; children: Charles Theodore, Timothy van de Wint. BS, Harvard U., Cambridge, Mass., 1943, M.P.A., 1948, PhD in Econs., 1949. Economist, fgn. service officer U.S. Dept. State, 1945-47, 49-53; mem. faculty Cornell U., 1953-54, U. Calif., Berkeley, 1954-55; sr. economist The Rand Corp., Santa Monica, Calif., 1955-67, head econs. dept., 1967-81; dean The Rand Grad. Sch., 1970-97, prof. pub. policy, 1997—, sr. econ. advisor, 1981—, corp. fellow in internat. econs., 1996—; sr. fellow Hoover Inst., 1988—. Bd. dirs. Capital Income Builder Fund, Capital World Growth Fund; lectr. econs. UCLA, 1960-72; mem. adv. bd. ctr. internat. bus. and edn. rsch., UCLA Anderson Grad. Sch. Bus., 1996—. Author: The Costs and Benefits of the Soviet Empire, 1986, Markets or Governments: Choosing Between Imperfect Alternatives, 1989, 2d edit., 1993, Linking Economic Policy and Foreign Policy, 1991, Long-Term Economic and Military Trends: The United States and Asia, 1994-2015, 1995, The Economic Pivot in a Political Context, 1997; co-author: Economic Openness: Many Facets, Many Metrics, 1999, Asian Economic Trends and Their Security Implications, 2000, European Military Prospects, Economic Constraints and the Rapid Reaction Force, 2001, Straddling Economics and Politics: Cross-Cutting Issues, in Asia, the United States and the Global Economy, 2002, Fault Lines in China's Economic Terrain, 2003, North Korean Paradoxes, 2005, The Russian Economy: Progress and Retreat on the Transitional Road, 2006, Modernizing the North Korean System, 2008, Looking Backward and Forward: Policy Issues in the Twenty-first Century, 2008; contbr. articles to profl. jours. Mem. Assn. for Public Policy Analysis and Mgmt. (pres. 1980-81), Am. Econs. Assn., Econometric Soc., Coun. on Fgn. Rels., Pacific Coun. Internat. Policy, Internat. Inst. Strategic Studies London. Clubs: Cosmos (Washington); Riviera Tennis (Los Angeles); Harvard (N.Y.). Office: The Rand Corp 1776 Main St Santa Monica CA 90407-2138 Office Phone: 310-451-6926. Business E-Mail: wolf@rand.org.

WOLF, CHARLES BENNO, lawyer; b. Chgo., Apr. 16, 1950; s. Ludwig and Hilde (Mandelbaum) W.; m. Sarah Lloyd, Sept. 1, 1973; children: Walter Ludwig, Peter Barton. AB, Brown U., 1972; JD, U. Chgo., 1975. Bar: Ill. 1975, U.S. Dist. Ct. (no. dist.) Ill. 1975, U.S. Ct. Appeals (3rd, 4th, 5th, 6th, 7th, 8th, 9th, 10th, and 11th cirs.) 1985, U.S. Supreme Ct. 1985. Ptnr. Vedder, Price, P.C., Chgo., 1975—; exec. com. Vedder, Price, Kaufman & Kammholz, Chgo., 1999—2008. Co-author: ERISA Claims and Litigation, 10th edit., 1995; sr. editor: Employee Benefit Law, 2007-; contbr. articles to profl. jours. Fellow Am. Coll. Employee Benefits Counsel; mem. ABA (co-chair labor sect. subcom. on collective bargaining and employee benefits, past co-chair subcom. on multi-employer plans), Internat. Found. Employee Benefit Plans. Office: Vedder Price Kaufman & Kammholz 222 N La Salle St Ste 2600 Chicago IL 60601-1100 Office Phone: 312-609-7888. Business E-Mail: cwolf@vedderprice.com.

WOLF, DALE B., former health care company executive; BA, Univ. Colorado; MBA, Univ. Denver. V.p. specialty ops. The Travelers, 1988—94; sr. v.p. bus. devel. MetraHealth Cos., Inc., 1995; exec. v.p. SpectraScan Health Svcs., Inc., 1995—96; sr. v.p. Coventry Health Care, Bethesda, Md., 1996—98, CFO, 1996—2004, treas., 1996—2004, exec. v.p., 1998—2004, CEO, 2004—09, pres., 2008—09. Bd. dir. HealthExtras Inc. Mem.: Soc. of Actuaries.*

WOLF, DALE EDWARD, former Governor of Delaware; b. Kearney, Nebr., Sept. 6, 1924; m. Clarice Wolf; 4 children. BSc, U. Nebr., 1945; PhD in Agronomy and Weed Control, Rutgers U., 1949. With Dept. Agr., 1946; assoc. prof. agronomy Rutgers U., 1949; with E.I. duPont de Nemours & Co., Inc., from 1950, dir. agrichem. mktg., then gen. mgr. biochem. dept., 1972-79; v.p. biochems., also chmn. bd. subs. Endo Labs., Inc., Wilmington, Del., from 1979; group v.p. Agrl. Products, Wilmington, Del., from 1983; dir. Del. Devel. Office, Dover, 1987-89; lt. gov. State of Del., Dover, 1989-93, gov., 1992—93. Vice chmn. WSFS Bank, 1998-2005; trustee Christiana Care Health Svcs., 2002-. Co-author: Principles of Weed Control, 1951. Bd. dirs. Del. chpt. ARC, 1975; gen. campaign chmn. United Way Del., 1978, also bd. dirs.; gen. campaign chmn. Girls Club Del., 1987; chmn. Del. Found. for Literacy, 1993-98; mem. adv. bd. U. Del. Hotel, Restaurant Mgmt. Sch., 1993-; chmn. Stand Up for What is Right and Just, 2003-07, vice chmn., 2000—. 1st lt. AUS, 1943-46. Decorated Bronze Star, Purple Heart; recipient Josiah Marvel award, Del. State C. of C., 2005, Liberty Bell award, Del. Bar Assn., 2007. Mem. Nat. Agrl. Chem. Assn. (chmn. 1981-83), Pharm. Mfrs. Assn. (dir.), Masons, Farmhouse Fraternity, Sigma Xi, Alpha Zeta. Republican.

WOLF, DAN C., real estate company executive, broker; b. Palmer, Alaska, Mar. 23, 1957; s. Daniel Frederick and Sylvia Ann Wolf; m. Kristi Wolf; children: Corene Danielle, Ryan Daniel, Cody. Cert. Coun. Residential Specialists, GRI Alaska State Assn. Realtors. Assoc. broker Vista Real Estate, Anchorage, 1983, RE/MAX Properties, Inc., Anchorage, 1985—; co-owner Keller Williams Realty Alaska Grp. Co-owner Powerhouse Gym, Anchorage. Avocations: weightlifting, skiing. Office: Keller Williams Realty Alaska Grp 101 W Benson Blvd #503 Anchorage AK 99503 Office Phone: 907-865-6510. Office Fax: 907-865-6515.*

WOLF, DICK (RICHARD A. WOLF), television producer; b. NYC, Dec. 20, 1946; m. Susan Scranton, 1970 (div. 1981); m. Christine Marburg, 1983; 3 children. Student, U. Pa. Exec. producer, pres. Wolf Films, Inc. Copywriter, producer over a dozen campaigns and 100 TV commls., 1969-76; producer, writer (screenplay) Skateboard, 1978, School Ties, 1992; writer, script cons. (TV series) Hill Street Blues, 1985 (Emmy award, Writer's Guild nominations for episode What are Friends For); writer, producer (film) No Man's Land, 1987; writer, producer and actor (film) Masquerade, 1988; writer, exec. producer 4 installments (series TV movies) Gideon Oliver, 1989; writer, creator, exec. producer (series TV movies) Christine Cromwell, 1989-90, (TV series) Nasty Boys, 1990, H.E.L.P., Law & Order, 1990, (Producers Guild Am. shared award Episodic TV 1996, Emmy award Outstanding Drama Series, 1996/97), Mann & Machine, 1992, The Human Factor, 1992, Crime and Punishment, 1993, South Beach, 1993, New York Undercover, 1994, Swift Justice, 1996, Arrest and Trial, 2000, Dragnet, 2003-04; creator, exec. producer (TV series) Feds, 1997, Players; exec. producer (TV series) Law & Order: Special Victims Unit, 1999—, D.C., 2000, Deadline, 2000-01, Law & Order Crime & Punishment, 2002—; exec. prodr., writer Law & Order Criminal Intent, 2001—; prodr. (TV documentary) Twin Towers, 2003; exec. prodr. (TV specials) Tony Bennett: An American Classic, 2006 (Primetime Emmy for Outstanding Variety, Music or Comedy Spl., Acad. TV Arts and Scis., 2007). Recipient Norman Lear Achievement award in TV, Producers Guild Am., 2008. Office: Wolf Films Inc c/o Universal TV 100 Universal City Plz Universal City CA 91608-1002

WOLF, EDWARD LINCOLN, physicist, educator; b. Cocoa, Fla., Nov. 22, 1936; s. Norman Lincoln and Harriet (Burgess) W.; m. Carol Joyce Euwema, June 15, 1958; children: Douglas Wakefield, David Lincoln. BA, Swarthmore Coll., 1958; PhD, Cornell U., 1964. Postdoctoral fellow U. Ill. Dept. Physics, Urbana, 1964-66; research assoc. Eastman Kodak Co., Rochester, NY, 1967-75; prof. physics Iowa State U., Ames, 1975-85; head dept. physics, prof. Polytechnic U., Bklyn., 1986—95, prof. physics, 1986—. Sr. vis. fellow Cavendish Lab. U. Cambridge, U.K., 1973-74; vis. prof. U. Pa., Phila., 1982; program dir. condensed matter physics NSF, 1996-98. Author: Principles of Electron Tunneling Spectroscopy, 1985; editor: Materials and Mechanisms of Superconductivity, 1985, Nanophysics and Nanotechnology, 2004, 2d edit., 2006, Quantum Nanoelectronics Wiley-VCH, 2009. Fellow Am. Phys. Soc.; mem. AAAS, Materials Rsch. Soc., Phi Beta Kappa, Sigma Xi. Presbyterian. Avocations: jogging, bicycling, music. Office: Poly Inst NYU Dept Physics Six Metrotech Ctr Brooklyn NY 11201-3850 Office Phone: 718-260-3629. E-mail: ewolf@poly.edu.

WOLF, FRANK RUDOLPH, United States Representative from Virginia, lawyer; b. Phila., Jan. 30, 1939; m. Carolyn Stover; children: Frank, Virginia, Anne, Brenda, Rebecca. Student, U. Miss., Oxford, 1957—58; BA, Pa. State U., 1961; LLB, Georgetown U. Sch. Law, 1965. Bar: Va., Washington, DC. Lawyer pvt. practice; legis. asst. Staff of US Rep. Edward G. Biester, Jr. of Pa., 1968-71; asst. Staff of US Sec. Interior Rogers C.B. Morton, 1971-74; dep. asst. sec. Congl. and Legis. Affairs US Dept. Interior, 1974-75; mem. US Congress from 10th Va. dist., 1981—; mem. appropriations com.; mem. depts. of state, justice, commerce, and related agencies subcommittee. Served in US Army, 1962—63, served in USAR, 1963—67. Republican. Presbyterian. Office: US House Reps 241 Cannon Ho Office Bldg Washington DC 20515-4610 Office Phone: 202-225-5136.*

WOLF, G. VAN VELSOR, JR., lawyer; b. Balt., Feb. 19, 1944; s. G. Van Velsor (dec.) and Alice Roberts (Kimberly) W. (dec.); m. Ann Holmes Kavanagh, May 19, 1984; children: George Van Velsor III, Timothy Kavanagh (dec.), Christopher Kavanagh, Elisabeth Huxley. BA, Yale U., 1966; JD, Vanderbilt U., 1973. Bar: N.Y. 1974, U.S. Dist. Ct. (so. dist.) N.Y. 1974, U.S. Ct. Appeals (2d cir.) 1974, Ariz. 1982, U.S. Dist. Ct. Ariz. 1982, U.S. Ct. Appeals (9th cir.) 1982. Agrl. advisor U.S. Peace Corps., 1966-70; assoc. Milbank, Tweed, Hadley & McCloy, NYC, 1973-75; vis. lectr. law Airlangga U., Surabaya, Indonesia, 1975-76; editor-in-chief Environ. Law Reporter, Washington, 1976-81; assoc. Lewis & Roca, Phoenix, 1981-84, ptnr., 1984-91, Snell & Wilmer, Phoenix, 1991—. Vis. lectr. law U. Ariz., 1990, Vanderbilt U., 1991, U. Md., 1994, Ariz. State U., 1995; cons. Nat. Trust Hist. Preservation, Washington, 1981. Editor: Toxic Substances Control, 1980; editor in chief Environ. Law Reporter 1976-81; contbr. articles to profl. jours. Bd. dirs. Ariz. divsn. Am. Cancer Soc., 1985—96, sec. Ariz. divsn., 1990—92, vice-chmn. Ariz. divsn., 1992—94, chmn. Ariz. divsn., 1994—96, bd. dirs. S.W. divsn., 1996—2003, chmn., 1996—98, nat. bd. dirs., 1999—, bd. dirs. Gt. West divsn., 2003—, bd. dirs., Cancer Action Network, 2002—05, pres. Cancer Action Network, 2003—04, nat. treas., 2004—06, nat. vice chair, 2006—07, chair-elect, 2007—08, nat. chair, 2008—; bd. dirs. Herberger Theatre Ctr., 1998—2006, sec., 2001—03, vice chmn., 2003—04; bd. dirs. Phoenix Little Theatre,

1983—89, chmn., 1985—87. Recipient St. George medal Am. Cancer Soc., 1998 Mem. ABA (vice-chmn. SONREEL commn. state and regional environ. coop. 1995-98, co-chmn. 1998-2000, vice-chmn. environ. audits task force 1998-99, vice-chmn. SONREEL ann. meeting planning com. 1998-99), Assn. of Bar of City of N.Y., Ariz. State Bar Assn. (coun. environ. & nat. res. law sect. 1988-93, chmn. 1991-92, CLE com. 1992-98, chmn. 1997-98), Maricopa County Bar Assn., Ariz. Acad., U. Club Phoenix. Office: Snell & Wilmer 400 E Van Buren Phoenix AZ 85004-2202 Office Phone: 602-382-6201. Business E-Mail: vwolf@swlaw.com.

WOLF, GARY WICKERT, retired lawyer; b. Slinger, Wis., Apr. 19, 1938; s. Leonard A. and Cleo C. (Wickert) W.; m. Jacqueline Weltzin, Dec. 17, 1960; children: Gary, Jonathan. BBA, U. Minn., 1960, JD cum laude, 1963. Bar: N.Y. 1964, U.S. Ct. Appeals (2d cir.) 1969, U.S. Dist. Ct. (so. dist.) N.Y. 1969, U.S. Supreme Ct. 1971. Assoc. Cahill, Gordon & Reindel, NYC, 1963—70, ptnr., 1970—2003, counsel, 2004—. Bd. dirs. N.J. Resources Corp., 1995—2008, N.J. Natural Gas Co., 1995—2007. Mem. N.Y. State Bar Assn. (com. on securities regulation), Anglers Club (N.Y.C.), Henryville Conservation Club, Mashomack Fish and Game Club. E-mail: garywwolf@msn.com.

WOLF, HAROLD HERBERT, pharmacy educator; b. Quincy, Mass., Dec. 19, 1934; s. John I. and Bertha F. (Sussman) W.; m. Joan Z. Silverman, Aug. 11, 1957; children: Gary Isaac, David Neal. BS, Mass. Coll. Pharmacy, 1956; PhD, U. Utah, 1961; LLD (hon.), U. Md., 1994. Asst. prof. pharmacology Coll. Pharmacy Ohio State U., 1961-64, assoc. prof., 1964-69, prof., 1969-76, Kimberly prof., 1975-76, chmn. divsn. pharmacology, 1973-76; dean Coll. of Pharmacy, U. Utah, Salt Lake City, 1976-89, prof. pharmacology, 1976—2005, dir. Anticonvulsant Drug Devel. Program, 1989—2002, prof. emeritus, 2005—. Vis. prof. U. Sains Malaysia, 1973-74; mem. Nat. Joint Commn. on Prescription Drug Use, 1976-80; mem. NIH rev. com. Biomed. Rsch. Devel. Grant Program, 1978-79; external examiner U. Malaya, 1978, 92, 96, U. Sains Malaysia, 1980. Contbr. articles in field of ctrl. nervous sys. pharmacology and field of pharm. edn. Recipient Alumni Achievement award Mass. Coll. Pharmacy, 1978, Disting. Faculty award U. Utah, 1989, Rosenblatt prize, 1989, Disting. Alumnus award Coll. Pharmacy, U. Utah, 1991, Weaver prize, 2000. Fellow AAAS, Acad. Pharm. Scis.; mem. Am. Soc. Pharmacology and Exptl. Therapeutics, Am. Pharm. Assn. (task force on edn. 1982-84), Am. Assn. Colls. of Pharmacy (pres. 1977, Disting. Pharmacy Educator award 1988, scholar in residence 1989, chmn. commn. on implementing change in pharmacy edn. 1989-92, 95-96), Am. Soc. Hosp. Pharmacists (commn. on goals 1982-84), Am. Coun. on Pharm. Edn. (bd. dirs. 1985-88), Soc. Neurosci. Jewish. Office: Univ Utah Coll Pharmacy Salt Lake City UT 84112 Business E-Mail: hwolf@hsc.utah.edu.

WOLF, HEATHER, library director; Grad. in Bus. Adminstrn., U. Pacific, Stockton, Calif.; MLS, U. Ariz. Br. mgr., regional br. coord. Maricopa County Libr. Dist., Ariz.; br. mgr., supervisory reference libr. and supervisory libr. collection support svcs. City of Mesa Libr., Ariz., acting dir., 2006, dir., 2006—. Office: City of Mesa Libr 64 E First St Mesa AZ 85201 Office Phone: 480-644-2712. E-mail: heather.wolf@cityofmesa.org.

WOLF, JEFFREY STEPHEN, physician; b. Hartford, Conn., July 30, 1946; s. Abraham and Norma Wolf; m. Nina Loving Lockridge; children: Sarah Loving, Lawren Hiley. BS, McGill U., 1968; MD, Med. Coll. Va., 1972, MS, 1973. Diplomate Am. Bd. Colon and Rectal Surgery. Intern in surgery Mt. Sinai Hosp., NYC, 1972-73, resident, 1973-75, N.Y. Med. Coll.-Met. Hosp., NYC, 1975-77; chief resident in surgery Met. Hosp., NYC, 1977-78; fellow colon-rectal surgery Grtr. Balt. Med. Ctr., 1978-79; colon-rectal surgeon Portsmouth, Va., 1979—. Fellow ACS, Am. Soc. Colon and Rectal Surgery; mem. AMA, Portsmouth Acad. Medicine, Med. Soc. Va., Am. Soc. Colon and Rectal Surgeons, So. Med. Assn., Chesapeake Colon-Rectal Soc., S.E. Va. Soc. Colon-Rectal Surgeons. Office: 3235 Academy Ave Ste 200 Portsmouth VA 23703-3200 Office Phone: 757-484-9653.

WOLF, JEROME L., lawyer; BA, George Washington U., 1970; JD, Duquesne U. Sch. Law, 1973. Bar: NY 1974, Fla. 1984, cert.: Fla. Bd. Legal Specialization and Edn. (wills, trusts and estates). Ptnr. Berger Singerman, Boca Raton, Fla., Duane Morris LLP, Boca Raton. Contbr. articles to law jours. Named one of Top 100 Attys., Worth mag., 2005—06, Top South Fla. Lawyers in Tax and Estate Law, South Fla. Legal Guide, 2007. Mem.: ABA, South Palm Beach County Bar Assn., Fla. Bar (mem. real property and probate and trust law sects., chmn. trust law com. 1991—95, chmn., lectr. bi-ann. will and trust drafting seminar, recipient Ann. Svc. award from real property, probate and trust law sect. 1993), NY State Bar Assn. (mem. trusts and estates sect., mem. com. on estate planning, chmn. subcommittee on fin. planning 1983—84, chmn. subcommittee on cmty. property 1979—82, mem. com. on estate planning for the disabled), Palm Beach County Bar Assn. (mem. estate and probate continuing legal edn. com. 1986—, lectr. ann. probate and guardianship law seminar 1987—89, 1993). Office: Duane Morris LLP Ste 300 2700 N Military Trail Boca Raton FL 33431-1808 Office Phone: 561-962-2111. Office Fax: 561-516-6317. E-mail: jwolf@duanemorris.com.*

WOLF, JOHN M. JACK, adult education seminar consultant; b. Upper Darby, Pa., Aug. 21, 1946; s. Herbert Michael and Elizabeth (Collins) W.; m. Gloria Ann Pettinati, Feb. 1, 1969 (div. 1978); m. Diane Elaine Batterson, Sept. 10, 1983 (div. 1994); children: John Michael Jr., Jessica Diane. BS, Drexel U., 1969; MBA, Temple U., 1972; PhD, Walden U., 1990. Salesman Lit Bros., Upper Darby, 1961-63, Cousins Shoes, Upper Darby, 1963-69; purchasing agt. Philco-Ford Co., Phila., 1969-70; sales rep. Conn. Gen. Life Ins. Co., Phila., 1970-75, Provident Life & Accident Ins. Co., Cherry Hill, NJ, 1975-78; pres. Associated Cons., Haddonfield, NJ, 1978-96; sr. ptnr. Lifelong Learning Ptnrs., Bradenton, Fla., 1996—. Cons. in field. Chmn. U.S. Jaycees, Haddonfield, 1979; co-chmn. March of Dimes, Haddonfield, 1983. Mem. Am. Mgmt. Assn., Soc. for Accelerative Learning & Tchg., Internat. Alliance Learning Creative Edn. Found., Statue of Liberty Found., Tau Kappa Epsilon. Avocations: soccer, music, travel, skiing. Office: Lifelong Learning Ptnrs 4115 Pinar Dr Bradenton FL 34210 Office Phone: 941-758-1800. Personal E-mail: wolfman73@aol.com.

WOLF, JOSEPH ALBERT, mathematician, educator; b. Chgo., Oct. 18, 1936; s. Albert M. and Goldie (Wikoff) W. BS, U. Chgo., 1956, MS, 1957, PhD, 1959. Mem. Inst. for Advanced Study, Princeton, 1960-62, 65-66; asst. prof. U. Calif., Berkeley, 1962-64, assoc. prof., 1964-66, prof., 1966—94, Miller research prof., 1972-73, 83-84, prof. grad. sch., 1994—; prof. honorario Universidad Nacional de Cordoba, Argentina, 1989. Vis. prof. Rutgers U., 1969-70, Hebrew U., Jerusalem, 1974-76, Tel Aviv U., 1974-76, Harvard U., 1979-80, 86 Author: Spaces of Constant Curvature, 1967, 5th edit., 1984, Unitary Representations on Partially Holomorphic Cohomology Spaces, 1974, Unitary Representations of Maximal Parabolic Subgroups of the Classical Groups, 1976, Classification and Fourier Inversion for Parabolic Subgroups with Square Integrable Nilradical, 1979; (with G. Fels, A.T. Huckleberry) Cycle Spaces of Flag Domains: A Complex Geometric Approach, 2005; Harmonic Analysis on Commutative Spaces, 2007; co-editor, author: Harmonic Analysis and Representations of Semisimple Lie Groups, 1980, The Penrose Transform and Analytic Cohomology in Representation Theory, 1993, Geometry and Representation Theory of Real and P-Adic Grps., 1997, Global Differential Geometry: The Mathematical Legacy of Alfred Gray, 2000; editor Letters in Math. Physics, Jour. of Group Theory in Physics; contbr. articles to profl. jours. Alfred P. Sloan rsch. fellow, 1965-67, NSF fellow, 1959-62; recipient Médaille de l'Université de Liège, 1977, Humboldt prize, 1995. Mem. Am., Swiss Math. Socs. Office: U Calif Dept Math Berkeley CA 94720-3840 Business E-Mail: jawolf@math.berkeley.edu.

WOLF, MARTIN EUGENE, lawyer, educator; b. Balt., Sept. 9, 1958; s. Eugene Bernard and Mary Anna (O'Neil) W.; m. Nancy Ann Reinsfelder, May 9, 1980; children: Matthew Adam, Allison Maria, Emily Elizabeth. BA, Johns Hopkins U., 1980; JD, U. Md., 1991. Bar: Md. 1991, US Dist. Ct. Md. 1992, US Ct. Appeals (4th cir.) 1992, US Ct. Appeals (2nd cir.) 1993, US Ct. Appeals (3rd cir.) 1998, US Ct. Appeals (11th cir.) 2000, US Ct. Fed. Claims 2001, US Ct. Appeals (Fed. cir.) 2003, US Supreme Ct. 2006, US Ct. Appeals (6th cir.) 2007. Mgmt. trainee Giant Foods, Inc., Landover, Md., 1980-82, dept. mgr., 1982-83, ops. analyst, 1983-86, fin. coord., 1986-89; law clk. Piper & Marbury, LLP, Balt., 1989—91, assoc., 1991—96; prin. Law Office of Martin E. Wolf, Abingdon, Md., 1996—99; ptnr. Quinn, Gordon & Wolf Chartered, Towson, Md., 2000—, Best Lawyers in Am., 2008. Pres. bd. dirs. Chesapeake Search & Rescue Dog Assn., Inc., 2000—02. Named one of Trial Lawyer of Yr., Md. Assn. Justice, 2009. Mem. ABA, Md. State Bar Assn., Harford County Bar Assn., Harford County Bar Found. (Vol. Svc. award 1992, 94), Assn. Am. Justice(pub. justice), Maryland Consumer Rights Coalition(bd. dir.) Democrat. Roman Catholic. Avocations: lacrosse, hockey. Home: 801 Renard Court Forest Hill MD 21050 Office Phone: 410-825-2300. Business E-Mail: mwolf@quinnlaw.com.

WOLF, NAOMI, writer; b. San Francisco, Nov. 12, 1962; d. Leonard and Deborah W.; m. David Shipley, Sept. 1993. BA, Yale U., 1984. Author: The Beauty Myth: How Images of Beauty Are Used Against Women, 1990, Fire With Fire: The New Female Power and How It Will Change the 21st Century, 1993, The Treehouse: Eccentric Wisdom from My Father on How to Live, Love and See, 2005, The End of America: A Letter of Warning To A Young Patriot, 2007; contbr. to periodicals including New Republic, N.Y. Times, Wall Street Journal. Rhodes scholar, 1986. Office: c/o John Brockman Inc 5 E 59th St New York NY 10022

WOLF, NEAL LLOYD, lawyer; b. Chgo., Feb. 8, 1949; s. Ira and Bettye (Brainin) W.; m. Caren Ellen Mirsky, June 11, 1972 (div. Apr., 1995); children: Michael Elliot, Brian Martin. AB magna cum laude, Princeton U., 1970; JD, U. Chgo., 1974. Bar: Ariz. 1974, U.S. Dist. Ct. Ariz. 1974, U.S. Ct. Appeals (9th cir.) 1975, Ill. 1983, U.S. Dist. Ct. (no. dist.) Ill. 1983, U.S. Ct. Appeals (7th cir.) 1983, U.S. Ct. Appeals (8th cir.) 1985, U.S. Supreme Ct., 1985, U.S. Dist. Ct. (no. dist.) Tex., 1990. Ptnr. Lewis and Roca, Phoenix, 1974-83, Winston & Strawn, Chgo., 1983-86, 89—, Ross & Hardies, Chgo., 1986-89, Orrick, Herrington & Sutcliff, LA; ptnr., chmn. litig. dept. LeBoeuf, Lamb, Greene & MacRae LLP, San Francisco, now ptnr. Chgo. Mem. ABA. Avocations: golf, reading, movies, tennis. Office: LeBoeuf Lamb Green & MacRae LLP 180 N Statson Ave Ste 3700 Chicago IL 60615-6710 Office Phone: 312-794-8010. Office Fax: 312-794-8000. Business E-Mail: nwolf@llgm.com.

WOLF, PETER MICHAEL, investment manager, consultant, writer; b. New Orleans, Dec. 6, 1935; s. Morris and Ruth (New) W.; m. Alessandra Cantey, July 3, 1967; children: Phelan Godchaux, Alexis Ambler. BA, Yale U., 1957; MA, Tulane U., 1963; PhD, NYU, 1968. Ptnr. Wolf and Co., New Orleans, 1958-62; assoc. Wilbur Smith & Assocs., NYC, 1968-70; faculty mem. NYU, 1966-67, Pratt Inst., NYC, 1968-70; adj. prof. Cooper Union, NYC, 1971-87; chmn. bd. fellows, mem. faculty Inst. Arch. and Urban Studies, NYC, 1972-82; prin. Peter Wolf Assocs., NYC, 1970—. Participant, advisor Investment Policy com. Fiduciary Counsel Inc., 2000-04; organizer of exhbns. Mus. Modern Art, NYC, 1969; writer exhbns. Whitney Mus. Art, NYC, 1970; contbr. exhbns. Mus. Modern Art, NYC, 1973, Albany Inst Art, 1975; vis. scholar/artist Am. Acad. in Rome, 2001 Author: Hot Towns: The Future of the Fastest Growing Communities in America, 1999; Land in America: Its Value, Use and Control, 1981; On Streets, 1979; The Future of the City: New Directions in Urban Planning, 1974; The Evolving City, Urban Design Proposals by Ulrich Franzen and Paul Rudolph, 1974, Another Chance for Cities, 1970, Eugene Hénard and the Beginning of Urbanism in France 1900-1914, 1969. Trustee Guild Hall, East Hampton, NY, 1981-86, 99—, Van Allen Inst., 1995-2008, Godchaux Res. Plantation Fund, pres., 1994—; chmn. bd. trustees Van Allen Inst., NY, 1999-2000; adv. bd. Nat. Acad. Design, 1999—; dir. Franklin Realty Co., 2005—; trustee Village Preservation Soc. 2005—; founder, trustee, chmn. Thomas Moran Trust, 2006—. NEA fellow, 1979; Graham Found. fellow, 1967-68, 94-95; Fulbright fellow, 1965-66; Ford Found. grantee, 1971-74; recipient Charles P. Shattuck award Nat. Rsch. Ednl. Trust Fund, 1983. Mem.: Inst. Pvt. Investors. Avocation: tennis. Home: 325 West End Ave New York NY 10023-8135 Office: 19 W 44th St Ste 812 New York NY 10036 Home Phone: 212-874-2489; Office Phone: 212-302-4240.

WOLF, ROBERT, diversified financial services company executive; b. Mar. 8, 1962; married; 2 children. BS in Economics, U. Pa. Wharton Sch., 1984. Formerly with Salomon Bros., 1984—94; joined UBS AG, 1994, global head credit trading, rsch. & distbn., 1998—2001, global head fixed income, 2002—04, COO UBS Investment Bank, 2004—07, pres., COO, 2007—, chmn., CEO UBS Group Americas, 2007—, mem. exec. bd., 2008—. Mem. President's Econ. Recovery Advisory Bd., 2009—. Mem. athletics bd. overseers U. Pa.; mem. undergrad. exec bd. Wharton Sch.; bd. trustees Children's Aid Soc.; mem. exec. leadership coun. Multiple Myeloma Rsch. Found., Norwalk, Conn.; bd. dirs. Partnership NYC, Nat. Sports Mus. Mem.: Fin. Services Round Table, Coun. Fgn. Rels. Office: UBS 1285 Ave Americas New York NY 10019*

WOLF, SHARON ANN, psychotherapist; b. Dallas, May 13, 1951; d. Frank Allan and Ursula (Mohnblatt) W.; 1 child, Allan. BA in Psychology, New Eng. Coll., 1973; MA in Counseling Psychology, Antioch Grad. Sch., 1976; PhD in Clin. Psychology, Union Grad. Sch., 1989. Cert. Mental Health Counselor, 1997. Behavioral spl. ednl. planner Philbrook Children's Learning Ctr., Concord, N.H., 1972; asst. to spl. edn. cons. N.H. Hosp., Concord, 1972-73; spl. edn. planner Rochester (N.H.) Child Devel. Ctr., 1973; counseling practicum Morrill Sch., Concord, N.H., 1973, Contoocook Valley Mental Health Ctr., Henniker, N.H., 1973-74, counseling psychology intern, 1974-76; lab. instr. New Eng. Coll., Henniker, 1973; ednl. and guidance counselor asst. Hillsboro (N.H.)-Deering Sch. Dist., 1973-74; pediatric psychology intern parent-infant devel. program Ctrl. N.H. C.M.H. Ctr., Concord, 1986-87; assoc. psychologist Easter Seal Rehab. Ctr., Manchester, N.H., 1976-80, Ctrl. N.H. Community Mental Health Svcs., Concord, 1980-88; intern forensic psychology Concord Dist. Ct., 1987-88; pvt. practice Northfield, N.H., 1988—. Psychol. cons. children and youth program Twin Rivers Counseling Ctr., Franklin, N.H. 1980-83, therapist, 1984-86; therapist Ctrl. N.H. Comm. Mental Health Ctr., 1980-83, Parent-Infant Devel. Program, Concord, N.H., 1983-88. Fellow Am. Orthopsychiat. Assn.; mem. Am. Assn. Suicidology, Am. Assn. Counseling and Devel., New England Coun. on Crime and Delinquency, N.H. Assn. of the Deaf, N.H. Registry of Interpreters for the Deaf. Avocations: rug hooking, music. Office: PO Box 253 Tilton NH 03276-0253

WOLF, STEPHEN M., consumer products company executive, former air transportation executive; b. Oakland, Calif., Aug. 7, 1941; BA, San Francisco State U., 1965. Various positions Am. Airlines, Los Angeles, 1965-79, v.p. western div., 1979-81; sr. v.p. mktg. Pan Am. World Airlines, NYC, 1981-82; pres., COO Continental Airlines, Houston, 1982-83; pres. Republic Airlines, Mpls., 1984-85, pres., CEO, 1985-86; chmn., pres., CEO Tiger Internat., Los Angeles, 1986-87; chmn., pres., chief exec. officer UAL Corp. and United Airlines, Chgo., 1987-92, chmn., CEO, 1992-94, former pres., dir.; sr. adv. Lazard Frères & Co. LLC, 1994—; adv. Air France, 1994-96; chmn., CEO USAIR Inc, Arlington, Va., 1996-98; chmn. US Airways Group, Inc., Arlington, 1998—2001, non exec. chmn., 2002—03; mng. ptnr. Alpilles LLC, 2003—; chmn. R.R. Donnelley & Sons Co., 2004—, Lehman Brothers Pvt. Equity Advisory Bd., 2005—08. Bd. dirs. Altria Group, Inc., 1993-2008, Philip Morris Internat., Inc., 2008-, R.R. Donnelley & Sons Co., 1995-, Chrysler Group LLC, 2009- Bd. dirs. Alzheimer's Disease and Related Disorders Assn., Chgo., Art Inst., Chgo., Chgo. Symphony Orch., Muscular Dystrophy Assn., Rush-Presbyn.-St. Luke's Med. Ctr., Chgo., J.L. Kellogg Sch. Bus. Adv. Coun., Northwestern U. Trustee, The Brookings Instn., Northwestern U., mem. bus. adv. com. Transportation Ctr. Office: RR Donnelley and Sons 111 S Wacker Dr Chicago IL 60606*

WOLF, STEVEN E., surgeon, educator; b. Balt., Oct. 16, 1964; s. Gerald Wayne and Margaret Louise (Melcher) W.; m. Kristin Steele, Dec. 2, 1989; children: Travis O., Hailey E. BS in Zoology cum laude, U. Tex., 1986; MD, U. Tex. Med. Br., Galveston, 1990. Diplomate Am. Bd. Surgery, Tex. State Bd. Med. Examiners, Mo. State Bd. Healing Arts. Resident in surgery U. Mo., Kansas City, 1990-95; rsch. fellow in trauma and burns Shriners Hosp. for Children, Galveston, 1995-96, staff surgeon, 1996, clin. fellow in critical care and burns, 1996—97; asst. prof. surgery U. Tex., Galveston, 1996; vice-chair for rsch., dept. surgery U. Tex. Health Sci. Ctr., San Antonio, Betty and Bob Kelso Disting. Chair in Burn and Trauma Surgery, 2007—; dir., US Army Inst. Surgical Rsch. Burn Ctr. Brooke Army Med. Ctr., Fort Sam Houston, Tex. Chmn. info. sys. steering Shriners Burns Inst., 1996-97; mem. pharmacy and therapeutics com. U. Tex., 1997; mem. burn adv. bd. Beiersdorf-Jobst Internat., 1997. Co-author (chpt.) Baillere's Clinical Endocrinology, 1996; contbr. several articles to profl. jours. Mem. ACS (assoc.), Soc. Parenteral & Enteral Nutrition, Am. Burn Assn., Assn. Acad. Surgery, AMA, Am. Soc. for Parenteral and Enteral Nutrition, Assn.for Academic Surgery, AAAS, J. Bradley Aust Surgical Soc., Shock Soc., Singleton Surgical Soc., Soc. for Critical Care Medicine; elected to Am. Assn. for the Surgery of Trauma, Eastern Assn. for the Surgery of Trauma, Soc. U. Surgeons, So. Surgical Assn., Surgical Infection Soc., Tex. Surgical Soc. Republican. Methodist. Achievements include work with mortality determinants in massive pediatric burns; team member that developed an adaptable arm sling for military burn patients. Office: U Tex Health Sci Ctr Dept Surgery 7703 Floyd Curl Dr San Antonio TX 78229-3900 Business E-Mail: wolfs@uthscsa.edu.

WOLF, TIMOTHY VAN DE WINT, food products executive; b. Apr. 27, 1953; s. Charles and Theresa Wolf; m. Mary Therese Merritt. BA in Econs. cum laude, Harvard U., 1974; MBA in Fin., U. Chgo., 1976. Fin. analyst to sr. fin. analyst Tennant Co., Mpls., 1976-79; mgr. mktg. planning and analysis Electrolux div. Consolidated Food Corp., Stamford, Conn., 1979-80; mgr. bus. planning Pepsi USA, Purchase, NY, 1980-81, mgr. bus. devel. and competitive analysis, 1981-82, dir. bus. planning fountain beverage div., 1982-84; sr. dir. bus. planning Taco Bell Corp., Irvine, Calif., 1984-86; v.p., controller Taco Bell & other sr. fin. mgmt. positions Pepsico, Purchase, NY, 1986—95; CFO Adolph Coors Co. & Coors Brewing Co., 1995—2005; global CFO Molson Coors Brewing Co., Denver, 2005—08; chief integration officer MillerCoors (joint venture), Chgo., 2008—; exec. leadership positions Taco Bell Corp.; various of fin. leadership positions, including sr. v.p., Adminstrn., Euro Disney Walt Disney Co.; sr. v.p., Human Resources Hyatt Hotels Corp.; CFO Coors Brewing Co.; contr. PepsiCo, Inc., 1980—89; Chief Integration Officer MillerCoors LLC, 2008—. Bd. dirs. Irvine Med. Ctr., Xcel Energy, Inc., Borders Group, Inc. Harvard Coll. scholar, Cambridge, Mass. Mem.: Harvard of So. Calif., U. Calif. Chancellor's (Irvine). Avocations: tennis, skiing, golf, German history, international relations. Office: Borders Group Inc 100 Phoenix Dr Ann Arbor MI 48108 Office Phone: 734-477-1100. Office Fax: 734-477-4538.*

WOLF, WERNER PAUL, physicist, researcher; b. Vienna, Apr. 22, 1930; arrived in U.S., 1963, naturalized, 1977; s. Paul and Wilhelmina Wolf; m. Elizabeth Eliot, Sept. 23, 1954; children: Peter Paul, Mary-Anne Githa. BA, Oxford U., Eng., 1951, DPhil, MA, Oxford U., Eng., 1954; MA (hon.), Yale U., 1965. Rsch. fellow Harvard U., 1956-57; Fulbright travelling fellow, 1956-57; Imperial Chem. Industries rsch. fellow Oxford U., 1957-59, univ. demonstrator, lectr., 1959-62; lectr. New Coll., 1957-62; faculty Yale U., 1963—2001, prof. physics and applied sci., 1965-76, dir. grad. studies dept. engring. and applied sci., 1973-76, Becton prof., 1976-84, chmn. dept. engring. and applied sci., 1976-81, chmn. council engring., 1981-84, Raymond J. Wean prof. engring. and applied sci., prof. physics, 1984—2001, prof. emeritus, 2002—, dir. undergrad. studies dept. applied physics, 1987-94, dir. grad. studies coun. engring., 1989, chmn. dept. applied physics, 1990-97, chair commn. on econ. status of faculty, 1990-92, dir. ednl. affairs for engring., 1994-99. Cons. Dupont Exptl. Sta., Wilmington, Del., 1957, Hughes Aircraft, Culver City, Calif., 1957, GE Rsch. Lab., Schenectady, N.Y., 1960, Mullard Rsch. Labs., Salfords, England, 1961, IBM, Yorktown Heights, N.Y., 1962-66, Brookhaven Nat. Lab., 1966-80, GE R & D Ctr., Schenectady, 1966-93, U. Bridgeport, 1995-96, Nat. U. Singapore, 1994-96; vis. prof. Technische Hochschule, Munich, Germany, 1969; Sci. Research Council sr. vis. fellow Oxford U., 1980, 84; vis. fellow Corpus Christi Coll., 1984, 87; mem. program com. Conf. Magnetism and Magnetic Materials, 1963, 65, 86, chmn., 1968, mem. adv. com., 1964-65, 70-76, 85-88, chmn., 1972, steering com., 1970-71, conf. gen. chmn., 1971; mem. organizing, program coms. Internat. Congress on Magnetism, 1967, internat. program com., 1978-79, planning com., 1979-85; vis. physicist Brookhaven Nat. Lab., 1966, 68, vis. sr. physicist, 1970, research collaborator, 1972, 74, 75, 77, 80; mem. vis. com. dept. phys./sci. U. Del., 1980, 84, 86; mem. NATO Advanced Study Inst. Program Com., 1983, 85, internat. adv. bd. Yamada Conf. XXV on Magnetic Phase Transitions, 1990; mem. bd. visitors Fairfield U. Sch. Engring., 1996-2005. Editor: CASE Reports, 1988-90; contbr. articles to profl. jours. Recipient sr. U.S. scientist award, Alexander von Humboldt Found, 1983, Sheffield Disting. Tchg. award, Yale U. Faculty Engring., 2000; named vis. guest fellow, Royal Soc. London, 1987. Fellow IEEE (life), Am. Phys. Soc. (edn. com. 1977-80, program dir. Indsl. Grad. Intern Program 1978-79, chmn. fellowship com., Div.

Condensed Matter Physics 1981-83); mem. Conn. Acad. Sci. and Engring., Yale Sci. and Engring. Assn. (Meritorious Svc. award 1985). Home: 37 Apple Tree Ln Woodbridge CT 06525-1258 Office: Yale U Dept Applied Physics PO Box 208284 New Haven CT 06520-8284

WOLFARD, JASON, basketball coach, educator; b. Norman, Okla., Jan. 19, 1976; s. Dave and Kay Wolfard; m. Kate Evans, July 24, 1999; children: Anabel, Ella, Lucas. BA in Biology, Webster U., MO, 1999; MS in Computer Edn., Fontbonne U., St. Louis, MO, 2001; MA in Athletic Adminstrn., William Woods U., Columbia, MO, 2006. Tchr. Kirkwood Sch. Dist., Mo., 1999—2003, Lindbergh Sch. Dist., Saint Louis, Mo., 2004—; basketball coach Lindbergh HS, Saint Louis, 1996—. Innovative Grant, NEA, 2002. Mem.: Mo. Basketball Coaches Assn. (assoc. newsletter editor / com. mem. 2007), NEA. Office: Lindbergh HS 4900 S Lindbergh Blvd Saint Louis MO 63126

WOLFBERG, MELVIN DONALD, optometrist, educational association administrator, consultant; b. Altoona, Pa., June 24, 1926; s. Max Alex and Claire (Schiffman) Wolfberg; m. Audrey Iris Koch, Apr. 26, 1952; children: Debra Lynn, Michael Alex, Daniel Ben; m. Linda Diane Machesic, Dec. 4, 1979. OD, Pa. Coll. Optometry, Phila., 1951; D of Ocular Sci. (hon.), New England Coll. Optometry, 1989, Ill. Coll. Optometry, 1990; LHD (hon.), Pa. Coll. Optometry, 1998. Lic. optometrist, Pa. Pvt. practice and ptnr. optometric practice, Selinsgrove, Pa., 1951-79; pres. Pa. Coll. Optometry, Phila., 1979-89, chmn. bd., 1976-79; v.p. profl. rels. Bausch and Lomb, Rochester, NY, 1991-95; pres. In Vision Inst., Boston, 1991-95; ptnr./dir. Sylvan Learning Ctr., Vero Beach, Fla., 1996—. Cons. to sec. HEW, Washington, 1970-77; dir. Better Vision Inst., N.Y.C., 1960-80. Mem. Selinsgrove City Coun., 1961-62; pres. Selinsgrove Community Chest, 1957; chmn. Optometrists Rep. Nat. Com., 1972, 76; chmn. Nat. Inter-Profl. Health Coun., Washington, 1972-77; dir. Univ. City Sci. Ctr., Phila., 1980-87; adv. com. Coun. Higher Edn., Commonwealth Pa., 1980-89. Served with U.S. Army, 1944-46, ETO. Decorated Purple Heart, Bronze Star, Silver Star; named Man of Yr. Central Pa. Optometric Soc., 1964, Alumnus of Yr. Pa. Coll. Optometry, 1970; recipient Carel C. Koch Meml. medal, 1989. Fellow Am. Acad. Optometry (pres. 1985-86, Eminent Svc. award, 2005); mem. Pa. Assn. Colls. and Univs. (exec. com. 1982-89, sec.-treas. 1985-88, vice chmn. 1988-89), Pa. Optometric Assn. (pres. 1959-61, Optometrist of Yr., Ewalt Meritorious Svc. award 2003), Am. Optometric Assn. (pres. 1969-70, Disting. Svc. award 1994, named to Nat. Optometry Hall Fame 2004), Pa. Coll. Optometry Alumni Assn. (pres. 1957), Beta Sigma Kappa. Office Phone: 772-299-0502. Business E-Mail: ilovesylvan@bellsouth.net.

WOLFE, BARBARA L., economics professor, researcher; b. Phila., Feb. 15, 1943; d. Manfred and Edith (Heimann) Kingshoff; m. Stanley R. Wolfe, Mar. 20, 1965 (div. Mar. 1978); m. Robert H. Haveman, July 29, 1983; children: Jennifer Ann Wolfe, Ari Michael Wolfe. BA, Cornell U., Ithaca, NY, 1965; MA, U. Pa., 1971; PhD, U Pa., 1973. Asst. prof. Bryn Mawr (Pa.) Coll., 1973-76; rsch. assoc. Inst. Rsch. on Poverty, Madison, Wis., 1976-77, dir., 1994—2000; from asst. prof. to assoc. prof. U. Wis., Madison, 1977-88, prof., 1988—, dir., LaFollette Sch. Pub. Affairs, 2006—. Adj. prof. Australian Nat. U., 2002-; resident scholar NIAS, Wassenear, Netherlands, 1984-85, 96-97, 2007; vis. scholar Russell Sage Found., N.Y., 1991-92. Co-author: Succeeding Generations, 1994; editor: (book) Role of Budgetary Policy in Demographic Transitions, 1994, contbr. articles to profl. jours. Mem. Commn. on Children with Disabilities, Washington 1994-95, Tech. Adv. Panel Social Security, Washington, 1994-95; vice chair bd. on children, youth and families Inst. Medicine, 2005—, Nat. Acad. Social Ins., 1990—; mem. adv. comm. dir., NIH, 2006-. Recipient Fulbright award, Coun. Internat. Exch. of Scholars, 1984, Best Article of Yr. award, Rev. Income and Wealth, 1992; Guggenheim fellow, 2008. Mem.: Population Assn. Am., Am. Soc. for Health Econ., Internat. Health Econ. Assn., Inst. Medicine, Assn. Pub. Policy Mgmt. (policy coun. 2001—04), Internat. Inst. Pub. Fin. (bd. mgmt. 1994—2000, v.p. 2000—03), Am. Econ. Assn. (bd. CSWEP com. 1989—92, exec. bd. 1996—99). Office: U Wis Inst Rsch on Poverty 1180 Observatory Dr Madison WI 53706-1320 Office Phone: 608-262-3581. Business E-Mail: wolfe@lafollette.wisc.edu, bwolfe@wisc.edu.

WOLFE, BRIAN THOMAS, music educator; b. Fayetteville, Ark., Aug. 30, 1979; s. Thomas E. and Carol J. Wolfe; m. Erin J. Johnson, July 10, 2006. MusB in Edn., U. Ark., Fayetteville, 2002; MusM, U. Ariz., Tucson, 2004. Grad. asst. U. Ariz., Tucson, 2002—04; dir. bands Rincon U. HS, Tucson, 2004—. Clinician George N. Parks Drum Maj. Acad., Amherst, Mass., 1998—; dir. SunCon Marching Festivals, Tucson, 2006—. Mem.: Ariz. Ambs. Music Staff, Am. Music Educators Assn. (assoc.), Am. Band Assn. (assoc.), Coll. Band Dirs. Nat. Assn. (assoc.), Tau Beta Sigma (hon.), Kappa Kappa Psi (life; sgt. at arms alumni coord. 2002—03). Avocation: travel. Office: Rincon U HS 421 N Arcadia Tucson AZ 85711 Personal E-mail: dmhorn179@yahoo.com.

WOLFE, DAVID LOUIS, lawyer; b. Kankakee, Ill., July 24, 1951; s. August Christian and Irma Marie (Nordmeyer) Wolfe; m. Gail Lauret Fritz, Aug. 25, 1972; children: Laura Beth, Brian David, Kaitlin Ann. BS, U. Ill., 1973; JD, U. Mich., 1976. Bar: Ill. 1976, US Dist. Ct. (no. dist.) Ill. 1976. Assoc. Gardner, Carton & Douglas, Chgo., 1976—82, ptnr., 1983—, mem. mgmt. com., 1980—84, Ill. Inst. Continuing Legal Edn., Employee Benefits Sec. Coun., Chgo. Bar Assn., Lake Shore Nat. Bank, Ill. State Bar Assn., Daughters Charity Nat. Health Sys., Lutheran Health Sys., AM. Assn. Homes & Svcs. Aging, Mich. Assn. Cert. Pub. Accts., Diversified Investment Advisors, Decalogue Soc., Conf Cons. Actuaries, Ind. Pension Conf., Inst Internat. Rsch., Lake Shore Bank Chgo. Contbr. articles to legal publs. Co-founder, mem. steering com. adv. bd. HR Hosp.; bd. dirs. World Law Group, 2006—08. Recipient Recognition award, Ill. Inst. Continuing Legal Edn., 1981—84; named Leader in Field, Chambers USA, 2006—; named to Best Lawyers America, 1993—. Mem.: NCAA (cert. contract advisor), ABA (sects. on taxation, corp. banking and bus. law 1981—90), Ill. State Bar Assn. (employee benefits sect. coun. 1986—95, past chmn., Recognition award 1983), NFL Players Assn. (cert. contract advisor 1983—88), Phi Eta Sigma, Sigma Iota Lambda, Beta Gamma Sigma, Beta Alpha Psi, Phi Kappa Phi. Office: Drinker Biddle 8 Reath 191 N Wacker Dr Ste 3700 Chicago IL 60606 Office Phone: 312-569-1313. Personal E-mail: dwolfe@gcd.com. Business E-Mail: david.wolfe@dbr.com.

WOLFE, DEBORAH ANN, lawyer; b. Detroit, May 4, 1955; d. Adam and Mary A. (Smyth) Wolfe; m. Lester D. McDonald, May 23, 1987; children: Molly, Thomas. Student, Ariz. State U., Tempe, 1973-76; BA in Polit. Sci., Bus., Tex. Christian U., Ft. Worth, 1977; postgrad., So. Meth. U., Dallas, 1977-78; JD, U. San Diego, 1980; grad., Gerry Spence's Trial Lawyers Coll., 1999. Bar: Calif. 1981, Ariz. 1982; cert. civil litig. specialist NBTA, 1999. Pvt. practice, San Diego, 1981—83, 1989-91; ptnr. Kremer & Wolfe, San Diego, 1983-86; assoc. D. Dwight Worden, Solana Beach, Calif., 1986-89; owner Wolfe & McDonald, 1991-96; shareholder Nugent & Newnham, San Diego, 1996—2003, Nugent Weinman Abbene Alcock & Wolfe, San Diego, 2004—06; owner Wolfe Legal Group, PC, San Diego, 2006—. Adj. faculty U. San Diego School Law. Floutist San Diego City Guard Band, 1981-93, Grossmont Sinfonia, La Mesa, 1982-83, Classical/Chamber Music Quartet, San Diego, 1983-87, Foothills United Meth. Ch. band, 1997—; leader Girl Scouts. Named one of Lawyers of the Yr. Calif. Lawyer Mag., 1996, one of top ten plaintiff legal malpractice lawyers in Calif., 2001, Outstanding Trial Lawyers award San Diego Trial Lawyers Assn. 1987, Trial Lawyer of Yr. award 1996, 2005. Mem. Am. Assn. Justice, Consumer Attys. Calif., Consumer Attys. San Diego (pres. 1996, Outstanding Trial Lawyer award 1996, 2000, 02, Trial Lawyer of Yr. award 1996, 2005), Am. Bd. Trial Advocates, Lawyers Club (San Diego), San Diego Inns of Ct. (master), Nat. Bd. Trial Advocates. Democrat. Methodist. Office: Wolfe Legal Group PC 401 W A St Ste 2230 San Diego CA 92101-3536 Office Phone: 619-234-3363. Business E-Mail: info@wolfelegalgroup.com.

WOLFE, ERIC ANDREW, literature and language professor; b. Englewood, NJ, Apr. 9, 1963; s. James Snow and Susan May Kalbfus Wolfe; m. Lori Ann Robison, May 27, 1995; children: Juliet Helena Robison, Oliver Duncan Robison. AB, Stanford U., Calif., 1984; PhD, Ind. U., Bloomington, 1997. Vis. asst. prof. U. SC., Lancaster, 1998—2001; assoc. prof. & dir. grad. studies Dept. English, U North Dakota, Grand Forks, 2001—. Democrat. Office: Dept English Univ N Dakota 276 Centennial Dr Stop 7209 Grand Forks ND 58202-7209 Business E-Mail: eric.wolfe@und.edu.

WOLFE, ETHYLE RENEE, academic administrator; b. Burlington, Vt., Mar. 14, 1919; d. Max M. and Rose (Saiger) Wolfe; m. Coleman Hamilton Benedict, Dec. 4, 1954. BA, U. Vt., 1940, MA, 1942; postgrad., Bryn Mawr Coll., 1942—43; PhD, NYU, 1950; LHD (hon.), CUNY, 1989; LittD (hon.), Iona Coll., 1989. Tchg. fellow U. Vt., 1940—42; rsch. fellow Latin Bryn Mawr (Pa.) Coll., 1942—43; instr. classics Bklyn. Coll., 1947—49, instr. classical langs., 1949—54, asst. prof., 1954—59, assoc. prof., 1960—68, prof., 1968—, acting chmn. dept. classics and comparative lit., 1962—63, chmn. dept., 1967—72; dean Bklyn. Coll. Sch. Humanities, 1971—78; exec. officer Bklyn. Coll. Humanities Inst., 1980—89; provost and v.p. for acad. affairs Bklyn. Coll., 1982—88, provost emeritus, 1989. Exec. com., chmn. com. on undergrad. affairs, com. on univ.-wide programs CUNY; study group AAAS, 1987—89, pub., 1987—89; dir. Nat. Core Visitors Programs, 1985—89, Fund for Improvement of Postsecondary Edn.-funded Ctr. for Core Studies, 1987—88; co-chair senate report Chancellor's Coll. Prep. Initiative, 1991; exec. com The Liberal Art of Sci.: Agenda for Action. Mem. editl. bd.: Classical World, 1965—71; co-editor: The Am. Classical Rev., 1971—76; contbr. articles to profl. jours. Recipient Kirby Flower Smith award, 1939, Goethe prize, U. Vt., 1940, Alumni Achievement award, 1985, Nat. Presdl. medal, NEH, Charles Frankel prize, 1990; named Ethyle R. Wolfe Inst. for the Humanities Bklyn. Coll. in her honor, 1989; named to Hall of Honor, U. Vt., 1991, Disting. U. Faculty Sen. Emeritus, CUNY, 1992; grantee, NEH, 1971, 1982—84, Mellon Found., 1982—85, 1986—89, Exxon, 1986—89, Josiah Macy, 1986—90. Mem.: Am. Soc. Papyrologists, Classical Assn. Atlantic States (exec. com.), Vergilian Soc. Am., Archeol. Inst. Am., Am. Philol. Assn., N.Y. Classical Club (past pres., exec. com.), Phi Beta Kappa (pres. 1988—90, past pres. Rho of N.Y. chpt., Spl. Citation of Honor on Sesquicentennial U. Vt. 1998). Home: 360 W 22nd St New York NY 10011-2600 Office: care Ethyle R Wolfe Inst Humanities Bklyn Coll Bedford Ave # H Brooklyn NY 11222 Personal E-mail: ethylewolfe@gmail.com.

WOLFE, GARY DONALD, commissioner, retired librarian; b. Altoona, Pa., Mar. 19, 1941; s. Donald George and Norma Rosmond (Cooper) W.; m. Mary Susan Olex, Aug. 5, 1967; children: Mark Douglas, Michelle Marie. BS in Elem. Edn., St. Francis Coll., Loretto, Pa., 1970; MLS, U. Pitts., Pa., 1972. Libr. clk. Altoona Pub. Libr., 1959-61; acting children's libr. Coyle Free Libr., Chambersburg, Pa., 1961-63; asst. prof. librarianship St. Francis Coll., 1963-75; adminstr. Centre County Libr., Bellefonte, Pa., 1975-89; dir. libr. devel. State Libr. Pa., Harrisburg, Pa., 1989-95; dep. sec. edn., commr. for libs. State of Pa., Harrisburg, Pa., 1995—. Editor: Automated Circulation: A Study, 1981. Vol. driver Am. Cancer Soc., Lower Paxton Twp. Sr. Vol. Van Svc. Sgt. USAR, 1963—69. Recipient Disting. Alumni award St. Francis Coll., 1997, Cert. of Commendation, Am. Assn. Sch. Librs., 2003. Mem. Pa. Libr. Assn. (treas. 1983-85, cert. of merit 1986, Disting. Svc. award 1997), Pa. Citizens for Better Librs. (bd. mem. 2003-, Lifetime Achievement award 2003). Republican. Avocation: reading. Home: 2407 Wicklow Dr Harrisburg PA 17112-9620 Personal E-mail: garydwolfe@comcast.net.

WOLFE, GEORGE C., theater director, producer, playwright; b. Frankfurt, Ky., Sept. 23, 1954; s. Costello and Anna Wolfe. BA, Pomona Coll., 1976; MFA, NYU, 1983. With Inner City Cultural Center, Los Angeles, Calif., 1975—78; teacher City Coll. of N.Y. & Richard Allen Ctr. for Cultural Art; resident dir. Public Theatre, NYC, 1990—93; prodr. N.Y. Shakespeare Festival, NYC, 1993—; head prodr. Public Theatre, NYC, 1992—2004. Works include: writer, lyricist (plays) Paradise!, 1985; writer, dir. The Colored Museum, 1986 (Elizabeth Hull-Kate Warriner award, Dramatists Guild, 1986), Jelly's Last Jam, 1992 (Drama Desk award, 1992, Joe A. Callaway award, Stage Dirs. and Choreographers Found., 1993); writer Queenie Pie, 1987, The Wild Party, 2000; scene contbr. Urban Blight, 1988; curator Festival of New Voices, 1990, 92; adaptor, dir. Spunk, 1990 (Obie award best dir., 1990); dir., prodr. (Broadway shows) Angels in America: Millennium Approaches, 1992, (Tony award best dir., 1993), Angels in America: Perestroika, 1993 (Tony award nominee best dir., 1994), Twilight: Los Angeles, 1994, The Tempest, 1995, On the Town, 1998, Elaine Stritch At Liberty, 2002, Topdog/Underdog, 2002, Caroline, or Change, 2004 (Tony nom. best dir. of a musical, 2004); dir. (NY theater) Mother Courage and Her Children, 2006; prodr., lyrics, Bring in Da Noise, Bring in Da Funk, 1996 (Tony award for best dir., 1996); prodr. Golden Child, 1998, Take Me Out, 2003; dir. (TV movie), Lackawanna Blues, 2005 (Outstanding Directorial Achievement in Movies for TV, Director's Guild Am., 2005); actor: A Delicate Balance, 1996 (Tony award best leading actor, 1996); dir (films) Nights in Rodanthe, 2008. Grantee Rockefeller Found., Nat. Endowment for Arts, Nat. Inst. Musical Theatre; recipient Hull-Warriner award, 2 Audleco awards, The George Oppenheimer/Newsday award, CBS-FDG New Play award, NYU Disting. Alumni award, HBO/USA Playwrights award, Person of Yr. award Nat. Theatre Conf., Spl. Achievement award Audleco, Spirit of the City award, LAMBDA award, Career Achievement award, New Dramatists, 2005; named A Living Landmark, N.Y. Landmarks Conservancy. Mem. Dramatists Guild (mem. exec. bd.), Dir. Guild of Amer., Writers Guild of Amer., bd. dirs. Young Playwrights Festival, N.Y.C. Office: Joseph Papp Pub Theater 425 Lafayette St New York NY 10003-7087

WOLFE, GEORGE CROPPER, retired private school educator, artist, writer; b. New Orleans, Sept. 6, 1933; s. Howard Edward and Amaryllis (Brannen) Wolfe; m. Catherine Vasterling, June 2, 1955; children: David, Michael, Philip. BFA, La. State U., 1956; MEd, U. New Orleans, 1972, MS in Urban Planning, 1975; postgrad., Tex. Tech U., Junction, 1986-93; MA in Art, Northwestern State U., Natchitoches, La., 2007. Cert. tchr. art, social studies La. Elem. tchr. Live Oak Manor Sch., Waggaman, La., 1962-65; tchr. art Isidore Newman Sch., New Orleans, 1965-96; adj. prof. art Northwestern State U., Natchitoches, La., 1997-99; co-owner design studio Wolf Patrol Prodns. Author: (book) 3D-Wizardry: Design in Papier Mache Plaster and Foam, 1995, (video) Sculpture in Motion, 2000 (Silver Telly award, 2001), 3-D Wizardry (Telly award, 1996), Papier Maché Plaster and Foam; one-man shows include Hanchley Gallery, Northwestern U., 1999, Dragons of the Mind, Northwestern State U., 2006, 50 Yr. Retrospective Art Show, Hauchley Gallery, 2006, exhibited in group shows at New Alexandria (La.) Mus. Art, commn. sculpture, Echo Totem, Alexandria Mus. Art, 1998, Alex the Red, 1998, Hands Supporting Hands, Wesley Found., 1999, commn. life size puppets, Two by Two, Northwestern State U. Summer Theatre, 1999, commn. sculpture, Rhino, Northwestern State U., 2004; contbr. articles to profl. jours.; author: Don Quixote Mancha Sculpture Home of Dr. & Mrs. David Holcombe, Alexandria, 2008. With USCG, 1956—58. Mem.: La. Art Edn. Assn. (pres. 1978—79, coord. conf. 2005), Nat. Art Edn. Assn. (La. Art Educator of the Yr. 1990, Ret. Art Educator of the Yr. 2000—01, Victor Lowenfeld award 2002), Phi Delta Kappa (v.p., Rsch. award 1996), Kappa Delta Pi. Home: 342 Jefferson St Natchitoches LA 71457-4382

WOLFE, GREGORY BAKER, international relations educator; b. LA, Jan. 27, 1922; s. Harry Norton and Laura May (Baker) W.; m. Mary Ann Nelson, June 15, 1946; children: Gregory Nelson, Laura Ann, Melissa Helene. AB, Reed Coll., 1943; MA, Fletcher Sch. Law and Diplomacy, 1947, PhD, 1961; Dr. honoris causa, U. Autonoma de Guadalajara, Mex., 1984; DHL, S.E. Coll. Osteo. Medicine, Miami, Fla., 1985, U. Tecnologica Equinoccial, Quito, Ecuador, 2000, U. Tecnologica de Santiago, Dominican Republic, 2001, Fla. Internat. U., 2008. With internat. div. Arthur D. Little, Inc., Cambridge, Mass., 1951-57; dir. Greater Boston Econ. Study Com., 1957-61; dir. Latin Am. program Com. Econ. Devel., 1961-64; dir. intelligence and rsch. for Am. republics State Dept., 1964-68; pres. Portland State U., 1968-74; dean Sch. Internat. Svc. Am. U., Washington, 1975-79; pres. Fla. Internat. U., Miami, 1979-86, prof. internat. rels., 1979—83, emeritus pres. and prof., 1983—; vis. scholar Cambridge U., Eng., 1986-87; chmn. Ednl. Facility Authority, Dade County, Fla., 1998—2009. Fed. negotiator Joint Transp. Com. Washington 1962-66 Contbr. articles to profl. jours. Chmn. bd. trustees Internat. Fine Arts Coll., 1993—2004, U. de Palermo Found., Buenos Aires, 1998-2006; bd. dirs. Chopin Found. U.S., Inc., 1988-96, Concert Assn. Fla., Inc., 1988—; founding chmn. Brickell Ave. Lit. Soc., 1 988-96. Recipient Fla. Internat. Ctr. award, 1980, Leonard Abess award, 1984, Orden del Merito Civil, King of Spain, 1986, Fulbright lectr., Ecuador, 1989. Home Phone: 305-466-4412. Personal E-mail: gbwaloe@hotmail.com.

WOLFE, JAMES RONALD, retired lawyer; b. Pitts., Dec. 10, 1932; s. James Thaddeus and Helen Matilda (Corey) W.; m. Anne Lisbeth Dahle Eriksen, May 28, 1960 (dec. 1996); children: Ronald, Christopher, Geoffrey; m. Patricia D. Yoder, Oct. 30, 1999. BA summa cum laude, Duquesne U., 1954, DHL (hon.), 1997; LLB cum laude, NYU, 1959. Bar: N.Y. 1959. Assoc. Simpson Thacher & Bartlett, NYC, 1959-69, ptnr., 1969-95, counsel, 1996-99, ret., 1999—. Co-editor: West's McKinney's Forms, Uniform Commercial Code, 1965. Served to 1st lt. U.S. Army, 1955-57. Mem. Assn. Bar City N.Y. Roman Catholic. Home: 500 SE 5th Ave Apt 601 Boca Raton FL 33432-5510 Office: Simpson Thacher & Bartlett 425 Lexington Ave New York NY 10017-3954

WOLFE, JOHN F., publishing executive; BS in Commerce, Washington and Lee U., 1965; PhD (hon.), Ohio State U., 1999. V.p. Dispatch Printing Co., 1969, pres., 1973—99, chmn., CEO, 1994—; pub. The Columbus Dispatch, 1975—. Trustee COSI Building Devel. and Fin. Resources Corp.; minority owner Columbus Blue Jackets. Bd. mem. Columbus C. of C.; trustee Franklin County Bd. Parks and Rec. Recipient Disting. Svc. Award, Soc. Profl. Journalists, 1981, C. of C. Columbus Award, 1993; named to Am. Acad. Achievement, 1987. Office: Dispatch Printing Co 34 S 3rd St Columbus OH 43215 Office Phone: 614-461-5000. Office Fax: 614-461-6087.*

WOLFE, JOHN LESLIE, lawyer; b. Cuyahoga Falls, Ohio, Dec. 6, 1926; s. Leslie George and Phyllis (Bond) W.; m. Barbara Lou Carle, Dec. 27, 1950 (div.); children: David, Karla. AB, U. Akron, 1950; JD, U. Mich., 1953. Bar: Ohio 1953, U.S. Dist. Ct. (no. dist.) Ohio 1955, U.S. Ct. Appeals (6th cir.) 1966, U.S. Supreme Ct. 1970. Sole practice, Akron, 1953—56; asst. pros. atty. Summit County, Akron, 1956—57; assoc. Hershey & Browne, Akron, 1957—61, ptnr., 1961—85, Wolfe, Williams & Abdenour, Akron, 1986—90; sole practice Akron, 1991—. Asst. atty. gen. State of Ohio, 1971-74; adj. prof. trial practice U. Akron, 1975-80; counsel Tri County Regional Planning Commn. of Portage, Summit and Medina Counties, 1960-74. Trustee Akron Law Libr., 1961—; past pres. Progress Through Preservation. Served with U.S. Army, 1945-47. Recipient Ohio Legal Ctr. Inst. award of merit, 1966. Mem.: ATLA, ABA, Nat. Employment Lawyers Assn., Ohio Acad. Trial Lawyers, Akron Bar Assn., Ohio State Bar Assn. Home: 45 Mayfield Ave Akron OH 44313-6827 Office Phone: 330-535-2441. Personal E-mail: wolfe81@sbcglobal.net.

WOLFE, JONATHAN W., lawyer; BA with distinction, Cornell U., Ithaca, NY; JD, NYU. Bar: NJ, NY, US Dist. Ct. NJ, US Dist. Ct. NY (so. dist.), US Tax Ct. Mem. litig. dept. Milbank, Tweed, Hadley, and McCloy, NYC; ptnr. Skoloff & Wolfe PC, Livingston, NJ, 2003—. Author, lectr. NJ Inst. Continuing Legal Edn. Fellow: Am. Bar Found.; mem.: ABA (bd. govs. 2008—, house dels., chair family law com. Gen. Practice, Solo, and Small Firm Sect., mem. Nat. Conf. Team of Young Lawyers Divsn.), NJ Family Law Am. Inn Ct., NJ State Bar Assn. (co-chair membership com.). Office: Skoloff & Wolfe PC 293 Eisenhower Pky Livingston NJ 07039 Office Phone: 973-992-0900. Office Fax: 973-992-0301.

WOLFE, MARGARET RIPLEY, historian, educator, consultant; b. Kingsport, Tenn., Feb. 3, 1947; d. Clarence Estill and Gertrude Blessing Ripley; m. David Earley Wolfe, Dec. 17, 1966; 1 child, Stephanie Ripley. BS magna cum laude, East Tenn. State U., 1967, MA, 1969; PhD, U. Ky., 1974. Instr. history East Tenn. State U., 1969-73, asst. prof., 1973-77, assoc. prof., 1977-80, prof., 1980—, prof. history emerita, 2004—, sr. rsch. prof. history, 1999—2004, prof. history emerita, sr. faculty affiliate, 2004—06. Disting. vis. prof. in history Washington and Lee U., 2006. Author: Lucius Polk Brown and Progressive Food and Drug Control, Tennessee and New York City, 1908-1920, 1978, An Industrial History of Hawkins County, Tennessee, 1983, Kingsport, Tennessee: A Planned American City, 1987, Daughters of Canaan: A Saga of Southern Women, 1995; gen. editor: Women in Southern Culture Series, 1995-2004; contbg. author to books, also introductions to books; contbr. articles to profl. jours. Mem. Tenn. Com. for Humanities, 1985-85, exec. coun. mem., 1984-85; mem. Women's Symphony Com., Kingsport, 1990-95; exec. com. Tenn. Commemorative Woman's Suffrage Commn., 1994-95; mem. state rev. bd. Tenn. Hist. Commn., 1995—2005. Haggin fellow U. Ky., 1972-73; recipient Disting. Faculty award East Tenn. State U., 1977, East Tenn. State U. Found. rsch. award, 1979, Alumni cert. merit, 1984. Mem. AAUP, ACLU (exec. com. Tenn. 1991-92), NOW, Tenn. State Employees Assn., Am. Studies Assn. (John Hope Franklin Prize com. 1992), Am. Hist.

Assn., Orgn. Am. Historians, So. Assn. Women Historians (pres. 1983-84, exec. com. 1984-86), So. Hist. Assn. (com. on status of women 1987, program com. 1988, interim chair program com. 1988, mem. com. 1993, 94, 95, nominating com. 1994, chair nominating com. 1995, chmn. mem. com. 1997, exec. coun. 1998-2000), Smithsonian Assocs, Tenn. Hist Commn. (state rev. bd. 1995-2005), Tenn. Hist. Soc. (editl. bd. 1995—2004), Coordinating Com. for Women in History, East Tenn. Hist. Soc. (mem. editl. bd. Jour. East Tenn. History 1995-2004), Phi Kappa Phi. E-mail: mrwolfe47@embarqmail.com.

WOLFE, MAURICE RAYMOND, retired museum director, educator; b. Paris (Neuilly), France, Oct. 13, 1924; s. Guy Ellsworth and Genevieve (Plion) W.; m. Warwick Ellen Griffin, Nov. 4, 1955; 1 child, Shavaun. BA, U. Calif. in Sociology, Berkeley, 1948; MA in Sociology, U. Calif., Berkeley, 1952; postgrad. study, U. Paris Sorbonne, 1951; Cert. of Completion Sch. of Edn., U. Calif., Berkeley, 1954, postgrad., 1955. Rsch. asst. dept. of edn. U. Calif., Berkeley, 1949; tchr. of English and history Castlemont H.S., Oakland, Calif., 1954; lectr. in anthropology, philosophy, sociology and edn. U. Md. Overseas, 1956-59; lectr., instr. in philosophy and sociology U. Md., Munich, 1960-62; faculty mem. Merritt Coll., Oakland, Calif., 1962-88, chmn. dept. behavioral scis., 1967-87; dir. and founder Merritt Coll. Anthropology Mus., Oakland, 1973-88; rsch. assoc. U. Calif. Lowie Mus. of Anthropology, 1985-89. Lectr. Pers. Mgmt. for Execs., U.S. Govt. Sponsored, Berkeley, Calif. 1966-67, San Francisco State U., 1967-68, Calif. State U., Hayward, Dept. Sociology, 1970-71; adj. instr. Monterey Peninsula Coll., 1990, 91, Hartnell Coll., Salinas, Calif., Chapman U., 1992-95, Golden Gate U., 1995-98; adj. prof. Golden Gate U., 1997—. Editor: (jour.) Socioloqus, 1952. Recipient French Govt fellowship, Sorbonne, Paris, 1956; named to list of Great Teachers of Calif., Calif. Assn. Comty. Colls., Santa Barbara, 1984. Home: 33751 E Carmel Valley Rd Carmel Valley CA 93924-9303 Personal E-mail: warwickwolfe@aol.com.

WOLFE, PETER J., retired performing arts educator; s. Paul H. and Frances Anderson Wolfe. BA, Allegheny Coll., Meadville, 1965; JD, UB Law Sch., Buffal, 1968. Tchr. english and drama West Seneca Ctrl. Sch., NY, 1968—2000; adj. prof. Hilbert Coll., Hamburg, NY, 2000—. Dir.: (plays). Bd. mem., sec., benefit chair Young Audiences Western NY, Buffalo, 2000—07; bd. mem. Burchfield Nature and Art Ctr., West Seneca, 2005—08. Home: 135 Oakland Pl Buffalo NY 14222 Office: Hilbert Coll 520 S Park Ave Hamburg NY 14075 Office Fax: 716-649-0702. Business E-Mail: p.wolfe@hilbert.edu.

WOLFE, RALPH STONER, microbiology educator; b. New Windsor, Md., July 18, 1921; s. Marshall Richard and Jennie Naomi (Weybright) W.; m. Gretka Margaret Young, Sept. 9, 1950; children: Daniel Binns, Jon Marshall, Sylvia Suzanne. Mem. faculty U. Ill., Urbana, 1953—, prof. microbiology, 1961—. Cons. USPHS, Nat. Inst. Gen. Med. Scis. Contbr. microbial physiology rsch. papers to profl. jours. Guggenheim fellow, 1961, 75, USPHS spl. postdoctoral fellow, 1967; recipient Pasteur award Ill. Soc. for Microbiology, 1974, Selman A Waksman Award in Microbiology Nat. Acad. of Sciences, 1995, Applied Environ. Microbiology award Procter & Gamble, 1999. Mem. NAS (Selman Waksman award in microbiology 1995), Am. Acad. Arts and Scis., Am. Soc. Microbiology (Carski Disting. Teaching award 1971, Abbott Lifetime Achievement award 1996, Procter & Gamble award in Applied and Environ. Microbiology, 1999, hon. mem.), Am. Soc. Biol. Chemists. Office: U Ill Dept Microbiology B103 Chem & Life Scis Bldg 601 S Goodwin Ave Urbana IL 61801-3709 Office Phone: 217-333-0065.

WOLFE, REGINA WENTZEL, business ethics educator; b. Washington, Oct. 1, 1946; d. Wilfred H. and Marie Radice Wentzel; m. Stephen M. Wolfe, June 15, 1968; children: Cathleen Anne, S. Michael. BS in Bus. Adminstrn., Georgetown U., Washington, 1968; M in Theology and Ministry, Loyola U., Chgo., 1981; PhD, U. London, 1993. Fin. adviser bd. govs. Our Lady Maryknoll Hosp., Hong Kong, 1974—76; rsch. assoc., spl. projects mgr. Bus. Internat. Asia/Pacific Ltd, Hong Kong, 1976—78; religious edn. coord. St. Jospeh's Ch., Hong Kong, 1978—79; asst. editor, prodn. editor The Tablet, London, 1987—88; vis. asst. prof. Loyola U., Chgo., 1992—94; assoc. prof. theology Sch. Theology-Seminary St. John's U., Collegeville, Minn., 1994—2004; Christopher chair, bus. ethic, sch. of bus. Dominican U., River Forest, Ill., 2004—. Editor: (book) Ethics and World Religions: Cross-Cultural Case Studies, 1999; contbr. chapters to books. Mem.: Internat. Assn. Bus. & Soc., Acad. of Mgmt., Am. Acad. Religion, Cath. Theol. Soc. Am., European Bus. Ethics Network, Soc. for Bus. Ethics (newsletter editor 2005—), Soc. Christian Ethics (exec. dir. 2001—06, vice chair U.S. Cath. China bur. bd. 2005—). Avocation: travel. Office: Brennan Sch of Bus Dominican Univ 7900 W Division St River Forest IL 60305 Business E-Mail: rwolfe@dom.edu.

WOLFE, RICHARD PEEL, lawyer; b. Brookhaven, Miss., May 31, 1937; s. Hubert Heuck and Nell (Peel) W.; m. Ann Perkins Terrell, Aug. 20, 1960; children: Susan W. Huppman, Emily W. Leigh. AB magna cum laude, Princeton U., 1959; JD, Harvard U., 1962; M in Civil Law, Tulane U., 1965. Bar: La. 1963, U.S. Dist. Ct. (ea. dist.) La. 1963, U.S. Ct. Appeals (5th cir.) 1963. Assoc. Monroe & Lemann, Attys., New Orleans, 1963—68, ptnr., 1968—96, sect. head, corp. sect., 1974—96, mgmt. com., 1989—93; ptnr. Jones, Walker, Waechter, Poitevent, Carrère & Denègre, Attys., New Orleans, 1997—2005, of counsel, 2006—. Mem. IRS-Tax Lawyers S.W. Regional Liaison Com., 1976-77; presenter in field. Mem. Bd. Liquidation, City Debt for City of New Orleans, 2004—; bd. deacons St. Charles Ave. Presbyn. Ch., 1967—70, 1972—75, chmn., 1970; bd. dirs. New Orleans Opera Assn., 2005—09; mem. planning com. Tulane Corp. Law Inst., Tulane Law Sch., 1988—2000; bd. dirs. Met. Crime Commn. of New Orleans, 1997—2001, Bur. Govtl. Rsch., 1984—90; trustee La. Nature and Sci. Ctr., 1980—84; chmn. Gallier Ho. Mus. Coun., Tulane U., 1986—88, trustee, 1978—86; mem. com. to nominate alumni trustees Princeton U., 1979—81, chmn., 1981; mem. Audubon Pk. Commn., New Orleans, 1971—77; trustee Metairie Pk. Country Day Sch., 1973—77; mem. agy. rels. com. United Way of Greater New Orleans, 1973—75; bd. dirs. La. Mus. Found., 2006—. Mem.: ABA (corp. stockholder relationships com. 1967—77, sect. of taxation 1967—97), La. State Law Inst. (mem. corps. com. 2008—), La. State Bar Assn. (liaison com. with dist. dir. IRS 1974—80, chmn. sect. on taxation 1975—76, task force on legal practice designation and specialization 1981—83, cert. tax law specialist 1986—96), Soc. of War of 1812, Cap and Gown Club (Princeton U.), New Orleans Lawn Tennis Club, La. Club, Boston Club, New Orleans Country Club, Harvard Club (N.Y.C.), Phi Beta Kappa. Republican. Presbyterian. Home: 7916 Plum St New Orleans LA 70118 Office: Jones Walker 201 St Charles Ave Ste 5100 New Orleans LA 70170 Office Phone: 504-582-8182.

WOLFE, ROBERT KENNETH, engineering educator; b. Chattanooga, Sept. 5, 1929; s. Robert Earl and Mae Bell (Hicks) W.; m. Mary Chacharonis, 1959; children: Robert Kenneth Jr., Ann Marie. BSChemE, Ga. Inst. of Tech., 1952, PhD, 1956. Chem. engr. Mallinckrodt Chem. Works, St. Louis, 1955-60; mgr. systems engring. IBM, Chgo., 1960-68; ops. rsch. mgr. Owens Ill., Toledo, 1968-73; prof. engring. U. Toledo, 1973-96, prof. emeritus, 1997—. Chair sys. engring PhD program U. Toledo, 1978-80. Contbr. articles to profl. jours. Recipient Outstanding Tchg. award, The U. Toledo, 1994. Mem. AIChE, Inst. Indsl. Engrs., Ops. Rsch. Soc. Am., Inst. Mgmt. Sci., Sigma Xi, Alpha Pi Mu (advisor 1987), Tau Beta Pi (Outstanding Undergrad. Prof. award 1995). Avocations: walking, swimming, decision education. Home: 8627 Augusta Ln Holland OH 43528-9244 Office: U Toledo 2801 W Bancroft St Toledo OH 43606-3328 Office Phone: 419-861-3478. Personal E-mail: kwolfe2029@sbcglobal.net.

WOLFE, SARAH CATHARINE, curator; b. Washington, Nov. 21, 1976; d. David Richard and Ann Furr Wolfe. B in History and Anthropology, Colo. State U., Fort Collins, 1998; M of Maritime History and Underwater Archaeology, East Carolina U., Greenville, NC, 2001. Conservation technician East Carolina U. Maritime Conservation Lab./Joyner Libr., 1999—2001; archaeological rschr. Md. Archaeological Conservation Lab., Prince Frederick, 2001—02; curator of collections and exhibits Mus. Aviation Flight and Tech. Ctr., Robins AFB, Ga., 2002—. Author: (publication) Anglo-American Naval Edged Weapons in the Age of Fighting Sail: Historiographical and Cultural Analysis of the Axe, Pike and Sword as Weapons and Symbols, 1775 — 1865; exhibitions include Total Force: The Workers Behind Robins Air Force Base. Roy N. Lokken Meml. scholar, East Carolina U., 2000. Mem.: Am. Assn. Museums (project head Mus. Aviation 2005), Soc. Hist. Archaeology, Golden Key Nat. Honor Soc., Phi Alpha Theta (v.p. 1997—98), Phi Theta Kappa. Liberal. Avocations: history, underwater archaeology, animals, travel. Office: Mus Aviation Flight and Tech Ctr 1942 Heritage Blvd Robins AFB GA 31098-2442 Home: 6800 Meteor Pl Apt 203 Springfield VA 22150-1997

WOLFE, SIDNEY MANUEL, physician; b. June 12, 1937; s. Fred and Sophia Esther (Marks) W.; m. Suzanne M. Goldberg; children: Hannah, Leah, Rachel, Sarah. BS, Western Res. U., 1960, MD, 1965. Intern. Cleve. Met. Gen. Hosp., 1965-66, resident internal medicine, 1969-70; staff assoc. NIH, 1966-72; dir. Pub. Citizens Health Research Group, Washington, 1972—. Contbr. articles to med. jours. Served with USPHS, 1966-69. McArthur fellowship, 1990—. Office: Pub Citizen Health Rsch Group 1600 20th St NW Washington DC 20009

WOLFE, TOM (THOMAS KENNERLY WOLFE JR.), writer, journalist; b. Richmond, Va., Mar. 2, 1931; s. Thomas Kennerly and Helen (Hughes) W.; m. Sheila Berger; children: Alexandra, Thomas AB, Washington and Lee U., 1951, DLitt (hon.), 1974; PhD in Am. Studies, Yale U., 1957; DFA (hon.), Mpls. Coll. Art, 1971, Sch. of Visual Arts, 1987; LHD (hon.), Va. Commonwealth U., 1983, Southampton Coll., NY, 1984, Randolph-Macon Coll., 1988, Manhattanville Coll., 1988, Longwood Coll., 1989; DLitt (hon.), St. Andrews Presbyn. Coll., 1990, Johns Hopkins U., 1990, U. Richmond, 1993. Reporter Springfield (Mass.) Union, 1956-59; reporter, Latin Am. corr. Washington Post, 1959-62; city reporter N.Y. Herald Tribune, 1962-66; mag. writer N.Y. World Jour. Tribune, 1966-67; contbg. editor New York mag., 1968-76, Esquire Mag., NYC, from 1977. Writer N.Y. Sunday Mag., 1962-66; contbg. artist Harper's Mag., NYC, 1978-81. One-man show of drawings include Maynard Walker Gallery, NYC, 1965, Tunnel Gallery, NYC, 1974; author: The Kandy-Kolored Tangerine-Flake Streamline Baby, 1965, The Electric Kool-Aid Acid Test, 1968, The Pump House Gang, 1968, Radical Chic and Mau-mauing the Flak Catchers, 1970, The Painted Word, 1975, Mauve Gloves and Madmen, Clutter and Vine, 1976, The Right Stuff, 1979 (Am. Book award 1980), In Our Time, 1980, From Bauhaus to Our House, 1981, The Purple Decades: A Reader, 1982, The Bonfire of the Vanities, 1987, A Man in Full, 1998, Ambush at Fort Bragg (audio), 1997, Hooking Up, 2000, I Am Charlotte Simmons, 2004; editor, contbr. The New Journalism, 1973; contbr. articles to Esquire Mag., others. Recipient Front Page awards for humor and fgn. news reporting Washington Newspaper Guild, 1961, Soc. Mag. Writers award for excellence, 1970, Frank Luther Mott Rsch. award, 1973, Harold D. Vursell Meml. award Am. Acad. and Inst. Arts and Letters, 1980, Columbia Journalism award, 1980, Nat. Sculpture Soc. citation for art history, 1980, John Dos Passos award, 1984, Gari Melchers medal, 1986, Benjamin Pierce Cheney medal Ea. Wash. U., 1986, Washington Irving medal St. Nicholas Soc., 1986, Theodore Roosevelt medal Theodore Roosevelt Assn., 1990, Wilbur Cross medal Yale Grad. Sch. Alumni Assn., 1990, St. Louis Literary award, 1990, Quinnipiac Coll. Pres. award, 1993, Golden Plate award, Acad. Achievement, 2005; named Va. Laureate for Lit., 1977; Chicago Tribune Literary Prize for Lifetime Achievement, 2003. Office: Little Brown and Co Hachette Book Group USA 237 Park Ave New York NY 10017*

WOLFEN, WERNER F., lawyer; b. Berlin, May 15, 1930; came to U.S., 1939; s. Martin and Ruth Eva (Hamburger) W.; m. Mary Glasier, July 1, 1956; children: Richard, James, Lawrence (dec.). BS, U. Calif., Berkeley, 1950, JD, 1953. Bar: Calif. 1953. Assoc. Irell & Manella, LA, 1953-57, ptnr., 1957-98, sr. ptnr. emeritus, 1999—2008, Broadcom Corp., 1994—2008; pres. Capri Investment Co. LLC, 1999—2008. Bd. dirs. Calhoun Vision, Inc., Pre-Cash Corp., Broadcom Corp., 1994-08; bd. visitors UCLA Sch. Arts and Arch., 1995—. Bd. dirs. UCLA Found., 1992-2003; bd. dirs. L.A. Goal, 1994-, pres., 1994-99. Mem. ABA. Democrat. Jewish. Office Phone: 310-203-7521.

WOLFENSBERGER, DONALD, political scientist, columnist; BA in English, North Ctrl. Coll.; MA in Polit. Sci., U. Iowa. Vol. Peace Corps, Tanzania; legis. dir. to Rep. John B. Anderson US House of Reps., min. staff dir. Subcommittee on Rules and Organ., 1979—80, min. staff dir. Subcommittee on Legis. Process, 1981—90, min. staff dir. House Rules Com., 1991—94, chief of staff House Rules Com., 1995—96; guest scholar Woodrow Wilson Internat. Ctr. for Scholars, 1997—98, dir. Congress Project; reporter, author Procedural Politics column Roll Call, 2006—. Author: Congress and the People: Deliberative Democracy on Trial, 2000. Office: Woodrow Wilson Ctr One Woodrow Wilson Plaza 1300 Pennsylvania Ave, NW Washington DC 20004-3027 Office Phone: 202-691-4128. E-mail: don.wolfensberger@wilsoncenter.org.*

WOLFENSOHN, JAMES DAVID, former President of the World Bank, diplomat; b. Sydney, Dec. 1, 1933; naturalized U.S. citizen, 1980, s. Hyman and Dora (Weinbaum) W.; m. Elaine Ruth Botwinick, Nov. 26, 1961; children: Sara, Naomi, Adam. BA, U. Sydney, 1954, LLB, 1957; MBA, Harvard U., 1959; DSc (hon.), U. New South Wales, 2006. Bar: Supreme Ct. of Australia 1957. Lawyer Allen Allen & Hemsley, Australia; ptnr. Ord Minnett (brokers), Australia, 1963-65; mng. dir. Darling & Co. (investment bankers), Australia, 1965-67, J. Henry Schroder Wagg, London, 1968-70; pres. J. Henry Schroder Banking Corp., NYC, 1970-76; exec. dep. chmn., dir. Schroders Ltd., London; prin. exec. officer Schroder Group, London, 1974-77; exec. ptnr. Salomon Bros., NYC, 1977-81; chmn. Salomon Bros. Internat., London, 1977-81; pres., CEO James D. Wolfensohn, Inc., 1981-95; pres. The World Bank Group, Washington, 1995—2005; spl. Mid. East envoy for Gaza Strip withdrawal US Dept. State, Washington, 2005—06; sr. adv. Citigroup, Inc., 2005—, chmn. internat. adv. bd., 2005—; founder, chmn. Wolfensohn & Co., LLC, 2005—. Vis. lectr. fin. U. New South Wales, 1963-66; bd. dir., Rockefeller Univ.; mem. Coun. on Fgn. Rels., Century Assn. Contbr. articles to profl. jours. Mem. Australian Olympic Team, 1956; chmn. bd. dirs. John F. Kennedy Ctr. for the Performing Arts, Washington, 1990-95, chmn. emeritus, 1995—; bd. dirs. Met. Opera Assn., 1977-93, Joint Ctr. for Polit. Studies, 1978-88, mem. emeritus, 1988—; trustee Rockefeller Found., 1979-85, Population Coun., 1977-84; trustee Inst. for Advanced Study, Princeton, N.J., 1979—, chmn., 1986-2007, chmn. emeritus, 2007-; trustee Brookings Inst., 1983-90, hon., 1990—; trustee Rockefeller U., 1985-94, Howard Hughes Med. Inst., 1987-96; steering com. Bilderberg mtgs., treas. Am. Friends of Bilderberg, Inc., 1985—; pres. Internat. Fedn. Multiple Sclerosis Socs., 1977-83, Carnegie Hall, 1972—, bd. dirs., chmn., 1980-91, chmn. emeritus, 1991-; bd. dirs. Nat. Multiple Sclerosis Soc., 1977-82. With Royal Australian Air Force, 1952-57. Recipient Business Com. for the Arts Leadership award, 1994, David Rockefeller prixe from Mus. of Modern Art, NYC; decorated by govts. of Australia, Germany, France, Norway and Russia; honored by HM Queen Elizabeth of Eng. with KBE and HM, King of Morocco, 1995. Mem. Australian Olympic Fencing Team, 1956; Fellow Am. Acad. Arts and Scis.; mem. Coun. on Fgn. Rels., Century Assn., Harvard Club (NYC), Australian Club (Sydney). E-mail: ccase@worldbank.org.

WOLFENSON, AZI U., electrical, mechanical and industrial engineer, consultant; b. Rumania, Aug. 1, 1933; arrived in Peru, 1937; s. Samuel G. and Polea S. (Ulanowski) Wolfenson; m. Rebeca Sterental, Jan. 10, 1983; 1 child, Michael Ben;children from previous marriage: Ida, Jeannette, Ruth, Moises, Alex. Mech., Elec. Engr., U. Nacional de Ingenieria, Peru, 1955; Indsl. Engr., U. Nacional de Ingenieria, 1967; MSc in Indsl. Engring., U. Mich., 1966; PhD in Engring. Mgmt., Pacific Western U., 1983; PhD in Engring. Energy, Century U., 1985; D in Philosophy of Engring. (hon.), World U. Roundtable, Ariz., 1987. Power engr. Peruvian Trading Co., 1956-57; gen. mgr. AMSA ingenieros S.A., 1957-60; prof. U. Nacional de Ingenieria, Peru, 1956-72, dean mech. and elec. engring., 1964-66, dean indsl. engring., 1967-72; dir. SWSA Automotive Parts, Peru, 1954-77; project mgr. Nat. Fin. Corp., Cofide, 1971-73; Peruvian dir. Corporacion Andina de Fomento, CAF, 1971-73; rep. in Peru CAF, 1973-74; pres. DESPRO cons. firm, 1973-76; exec. pres. Electroperu, 1976-80. Cons. engr., 1964—; dir. Tech. Transference Studies, 1971—72. Author: (book) Work Communications, 1966, Programmed Learning, 1966, Production Planning and Control, 1968, Transfer of Technology, 1971, National Electrical Development, 1977, Energy and Development, 1979, El Gran Desafio, 1981, Hacia una politica economica alternativa, 1982, The Power of Communications: The Media, 1987; contbr. articles to newspapers and jours. Mem. Nat. Coun. Fgn. Investment and Tech. Transfer, 1972—73, Superior Coun. Electricity, 1964—66; metal mech. expert for andean group, 1970—71; promoter, co-founder, gen. mgr. La Republica Newspaper, Peru, 1981; pres. PROA Project promotion AG, Switzerland, 1982—; chmn. Inst. for the Devel. of the Ams., Inc., Fla., 1993—; co-founder El Popular, 1983, El Nacional, 1985, Todo Sport, 1993, El Chino, 1994, La Reforma, 1997, El Men, 1999, La Razon, 2001; pres. bd. dirs., newspapers; v.p. bd. dirs. Island Way Cmty. Assn., 1995—97; mem. exec. bd. dirs. Miami State Israel Bonds, 1997; mem. consultative coun. Instituto Peruano de Deportes, 1999; mem. consultive coun. Min. Econ. and Fin., 1973—74; councilman at the Concejo Provincial De Lima, 1969—75; pres. Peruvian Jewish Cmty., 1966—70, Peruvian Hebrew Sch., 1976—78. Recipient Recognition award, Israel Govt., 1967, Disting. Contbn. award, City of Lima, 1970, 1971, Disting. award, Trujillo, 1978, Huaral, 1979, City Coun. Huancayo, 1980, Piura, 1980, Disting. Contbn. to Elec. Devel. in Peru, 1979, Disting. Svc. awards, Order Merit, Peru, 1980, Disting. Comision Integracion Electrica Regional medal, CIER, 1984, El Sol Radiante, City Hall of Magdalena, Peru, 1995, Medal of Honor, Electrical Engring. Colegio de Ingenieros del Peru, 2003, Spl. award, Gente mag., 2006; named Exec., Gente Mag., 1979. Fellow: Brit. Inst. Mgmt., Inst. Prodn. Engrs.; mem.: J.C.C. Fla., FCL, AIIE (sr.), ASME, MTM Assn., AAAS, World Assn. Newspapers (exec. mem. 2003), Asociacion Periodistas Peru, Circulo Periodistas Peru, Swiss sect. PEN Club INternat., Swiss Soc. Writers, United Writers Assn., Assn. Energy Engrs., Am. Nuc. Soc. (vice chmn. 1988, 1990, chmn. Swiss sect. 1991—93, Significant Contbn. to Advancement of Nuc. Sci. award 1995), Inst. Adminstrv. Mgmt., Asociacion Peruana Avance Ciencia, Assn. Mgmt. Sci. (dir. 1968), Am. Inst. Mgmt. Sci., Am. Soc. Engring. Edn., Asociacion Electrotechnica del Peru, Inst. Peruano Ingenieros Mecanicos (pres. 1965—66, v.p. 1967, dir. 1969, 1970, 1976), Colegio Ingenieros Peru (medal of honor award 2003), Alumni Assn. Mich., Pacific Western and Century U., Hebraica Club, Club dr 2000. Home: 3781 NE 208th Ter Miami FL 33180-3835 Office: 3601 NE 207th St Ste 1205 Aventura FL 33180 Personal E-mail: aziwolfenson@aol.com.

WOLFER, DALE, retired music educator; b. Denver, June 2, 1928; s. George Earl and Hazel Grace Wolfer; m. Annette Baldwin, June 26, 1931; children: Chrisann, Suzanne, Michael Shane, Eric Jon. B in music edn., Colo. A&M, 1951; M in music edn., Denver U., 1958. Music dir. Olathe HS, Colo., 1953—54; choral dir. Grand Junction HS, Colo., 1954—58, Littleton HS, Colo., 1958—72, Lanier HS, U. Tex, Austin, Tex., 1972—88; music dir. Hillcrest Sch., Jos, Nigeria, 1988—90; prof. Lutheran Ch. HS, Bratislava, Slovakia, 1990—91; ret., 1991. Ch. worker Lutheran Hour Ministries, Istebna, Poland, 1998, Tikhovitsy, Russia, 99, Wittenberg, Germany, 2000. Summer music studies Western State Coll., Gunnison, Colo., 1948—50, U. Salzburg, Salzburg, Austria, 1968, Fred Waring Workshop, Paul Christiansen Workshop, 1968; mem. nat. com. Nat. Intercollegiate Band, Denver, 1951; host/docent Cherokee Ranch Castle, Sedalia, 2007; ch. choir dir. various denominations, 1983—90, ch. handbell dir., 1994—2003. 1st lt. US Army, 1951—53, Korea. Decorated Purple Heart US Army, Korea, Air medal. Mem.: Am. Choral Dir. (life). Lutheran. Avocations: travel, fishing, hiking, handbells, stained glass art. Home: 1447 Pineridge Ln Castle Rock CO 80108-0213

WOLFERSTEIG, ELOISE SMITH, retired music educator; b. Bklyn., Oct. 7, 1930; d. George Francis and Louise C. (Becker) Smith; m. Robert Frederick Wolfersteig; 1 child, Patricia Lynn Albritton. MusB, West Minster Choir Coll., Princeton, NJ, 1953; MusM, Jamestown Coll., ND, 1958; MEd, Ga. Coll., 1973. Choir dir. St. Francis Assisi Cath. Ch.; tchr. Jacob Tome Inst., Md., 1953—54, Bainbridge (Md.) Elem. Sch., 1954—55; dir. Officers' Wives Nursery Sch., Bermuda, 1955—56; music tchr. Baldwin City Schs., Milledgesville, Ga., 1965—75; gifted edn. tchr. Bibb City Sch., Macon, Ga., 1975—90; music tchr. Cherokee City Sch., Andrews, NC, 1990—91; gifted edn. tchr. Clay City Schs., Hayesville, NC, 1991—95; tech. cons. Andrews, NC, 1995—99; dir. sch. age choirs Blairsville, Ga., 1998—. Recipient District Star Tchr., Macon, Ga., 1985, Tchr. of Yr., Spl. Edn., Macon, Ga., 1988; finalist Excellence in Singing, Met. Opera, 1958. Mem.: DAR (pres., regent), Delta Kappa Gamma, Phi Delta Kappa, Sigma Alpha Iota. Avocations: poetry, art, writing, drawing. Home: 5316 Pine Crest Rd Young Harris GA 30582 Personal E-mail: rfwolfer@windstream.net.

WOLFERSTEIG, JEAN LOIS, retired medical association administrator; b. Kingston, NY, July 13, 1950; d. Evelyn Anna Schupp and John Raymond Wolfersteig; m. William Edward Miller. AS in Liberal Arts, Ulster County CC, 1970; BA in Secondary Edn., State U. Coll., 1972; MS in Pub. Svc. Adminstrn., Russell Sage Coll., Albany, New York, 1983. Unit mgr. Wassaic Devel. Ctr., Wingdale, NY, 1972—75, staff devel. specialist, 1976—79; dir. of staff devel. and tng. Westchester

Devel. Disabilities Svcs. Office, Tarrytown, NY, 1979—84, Hudson River Psychiat. Ctr., Poughkeepsie, NY, 1984—92, quality mgmt. dir., 1992—98, dir. for facility admin. svcs., 1998—2002, CEO, 2002—07. Bd. mem. Cmty. Adv. Bd. for Marist Coll., Poughkeepsie, 1985—90; adj. faculty Westchester CC, Valhalla, 1981—84; bd. mem. Adv. Bd. for Orange County CC. Forensic Mental Health Program, Middletown, NY, 1985—85. Co-author: (international presentations) Balanced Scorecard and Performance Improvement. Chairperson of selection com. Herman B. Snow Scholarship Fund, Poughkeepsie, 1991—2001. Recipient Salute to Women in Industry, Dutchess County YWCA, 1992, Leadership and Svc. award, Nat. Alliance for Mentally Ill (Mid-Hudson), 2006, NY State Legis. Resolution, Hudson River Pyschiat. Ctr., 2007, Disting. Svc. award, Eliot Spitzer, Gov. NY State, 2007, Mental Health Cert. of Appreciation, 2007. Mem.: Nat. Alliance Mentally Ill (Leadership award 2006), Nat. Assn. of State Mental Health Dirs., Phi Kappa Phi. Avocations: writing, sailing, travel, gardening.

WOLFERSTEIG, ROBERT FREDERICK, retired musician; b. Kingston, NY, Mar. 31, 1929; m. Eloise Smith; 1 child, Patricia Lynn Albritton. MusB, Coll. Conservatory Music, Cin., 1950; MusM, Westminster Choir Coll., Princeton, NJ, 1952; MusD, Ind. U., Bloomington, 1963; studied with Michael Schneider, studied with Parvin Titus, 1950, studied with Alexarder McCurdy, 1952, studied with Oswald Ragatz, 1961, studied with Karl Schuke, studied organ building with Karl Schuke, harpsichood with Sylvia Kind, studied with Sylvia Kind. Singer, asst. organist St. John's Episcopal Ch., Kingston, NY, 1943—46; organist, choir master Terrace Pk. Episcopal Ch., Cin., 1946—50; organist Wayne Presbyn. Ch., Pa., 1950—52; organist, choir dir. USNTC Dependents' Chapel, Bainbridge, Md., 1952—54, USNB Chapel of Peace, Bermuda, 1954—56; coll. organist First Presbyn., Jamestown, ND, 1956—59; choir dir. Irvington Presbyn., Indpls., 1959—61; organist USACP, Berlin, 1961—62; organist, choir dir. First Presbyn., Winston-Salem, NC, 1962—65; organist Temple Emanuel, Winston-Salem, 1962—65; coll. organist Ga. Coll., 1965—91; organist, choir dir. First Presbyn., 1965—68; organist, choir master St. Stephen's Episcopal, Milledgeville, Ga., 1968—70; organist, choir dir. First Presbyn., Macon, Ga., 1970—72, Hope Luth., Milledgeville, 1972—74; supply musician to numerous chs. worldwide, 1974—80, 1982—88, 1994—98; organist, choir dir. First Christian Ch., Macon, 1980—82; cellist Macon Symphony Orch., 1982—85; organ soloist Macon GA Symphony Orch., 1984; organist St. Andrew in Mountains, Andrews, NC, 1988—93; organist, choir master St. Francis of Assisi Cath. Ch., Blairsville, Ga., 1998—2007; organist St. James Episcopal, Clayton, Ga., 2007—; joint recitals with wife in New Zealand, Hong Kong, Germany, US; retired, 1990. Recipient Ft. Wayne; named Winner Nat. Organ-Playing Contest, Ist Pres Ch., Wayne, Ind., 1961; grantee Fulbright, Berlin's Hochschule fur Musik, 1961—62. Mem.: SAR, Order Ky. Colonels, Am. Theater Organ Soc., Am. Guild Organists, Pi Kappa Lambda, Phi Mu Alpha Sinfonia. Home: 5316 Pine Crest Rd Young Harris GA 30582 E-mail: rfwolfer@windstream.net.

WOLFF, ALEJANDRO DANIEL, ambassador; b. 1956; d. Gerard and Toni Wolff; m. Alexandra Wolff; children: Philip, Michael. Grad. magna cum laude, UCLA, 1978. Fgn. svc. officer US Dept. State, 1979—, mem. policy planning staff Washington, 1981—82; amb. Am. Embassy, Rabat, 1983—85, Brussels, 1985—88; with Office of Soviet Union Affairs US Dept. State, Washington, 1988—89, with Office Under Sec. Polit. Affairs, 1989—91; amb. Am. Embassy, Santiago, Chile, 1991—94, dep. chief of mission to Cyprus Nicosia, 1994—96; dep. exec. sec. US Dept. State, Washington, 1996—98, exec. asst. to Sec. of State Madeleine Albright and Colin Powell, 1998—2001; dep. chief of mission US Mission to UN, Paris, 2001—05; dep. US rep. to UN US Dept. State, NYC, 2005—, acting permanent US rep. to UN, 2006—07. Office: UN 140 E 45th St 7th Fl New York NY 10017*

WOLFF, CANDIDA (CANDI WOLFF), lawyer, former federal official; b. Sharon, Conn., June 9, 1964; m. Mark Roger Wolff; 2 children. BA in Math & Polit. Sci., Mount Holyoke Coll., 1986; JD, George Washington U., 1989. Pub. policy lobbyist Akin, Gump, Strauss, Hauer & Feld, LLP, 1989—93; tax counsel to Senator Malcolm Wallop US Senate, 1993—95; legis. counsel US Senate Steering Com., 1995—96, dep. staff dir. Senate Rep. Policy Com., 1997—2000; dep. asst. to v.p. for legis. affairs The White House, 2001—02, asst. to v.p. for legis. affairs., 2002—04, asst. to pres., dir. legis. affairs, 2005—07; ptnr. Washington Coun. Ernst & Young, 2004, Hogan & Hartson LLP, Washington, 2008—. Office: Hogan & Hartson LLP 555 Thirteenth St NW Washington DC 20004 Office Phone: 202-456-2230, 202-637-6404. Office Fax: 202-456-0200, 202-637-5910. E-mail: cpwolff@hhlaw.com.*

WOLFF, CATHERINE ELIZABETH, opera company executive; b. Evanston, Ill., June 11, 1957; AB with honors, Vassar Coll., 1979; MA in Performing Arts Mgmt., Am. U., 1982. Cert. exec. program for non-profits arts leaders Stanford Graduate Sch. Bus., Ctr. for Social Innovation/Nat. Arts Strategies, 2007. Adminstrv. asst. Opera Am., 1982-85; artistic adminstr. Pitts. Opera, 1985-94; exec. dir. Del. Symphony Orch., Wilmington, 1994-95; gen. dir. Syracuse (N.Y.) Opera Co., 1996—2007; gen. and artistic dir. Syracuse Opera Co., 2007—. Music panelist NYS Coun. Arts, 2000—02, co-chair music panel, 2003, auditor, 2004—. Mem. steering com. Arts and Culture Leadership Alliance Ctrl. NY, 2004—07, founding pres., 2005—06. McGuire fellow Vassar Coll., 1979. Mem. Opera Am.(Career Svc. award 2006), Am. Symphony Orch. League, Phi Beta Kappa. Office: Syracuse Opera Co PO Box 1223 Syracuse NY 13201-1223 Business E-Mail: cwolff@syracuseopera.com.

WOLFF, DEBORAH H(OROWITZ), lawyer; b. Phila., Apr. 6, 1940; d. Samuel and Anne (Manstein) Horowitz; m. Morris H. Wolff, May 15, 1966 (div.); children: Michelle Lynn, Lesley Anne; m. Walter Allan Levy, June 7, 1987. BS, U. Pa., 1962, MS, 1966; postgrad., Sophia U., Tokyo, 1968; JD, Villanova U., 1979, LLM, 1988. Tchr. Overbrook H.S., Phila., 1962-68; homebound tchr. Lower Merior Twp., Mongomery County, 1968-71; asst. dean U. Pa., Phila., 1975-76; law clk. Stassen, Kostos and Mason, Phila., 1977-78; assoc. Spencer, Sherr, Moses and Zuckerman, Norristown, Pa., 1980-81; ptnr. Wolff Assocs., Phila., 1981—. Lectr. law and estate planning, Phila., 1980—. Founder Take a Brother Program; bd. dirs. Germantown Jewish Ctr.; h.s. sponsor World Affairs Club, Phila., 1962-68; mem. exec. com., sec. bd. Crime Prevention Assn., Phila., treas., bd. dirs., 1965—; v.p. bd. dirs. U. Pa. Alumnae Bd., Phila., 1965—, pres. bd. dirs., 1993—, v.p. organized classes, bd. crime prevention; chmn. urban conf. Boys Club Am., 1987, treas., 1999; active Hahnaman Brain Tumor Rsch. Bd.; v.p., bd. dirs. Crime Prevention; treas. Assn. of Alumnae ds.; mem. Alumni Class Leadership Counsel bd. U. Pa., 2001—, sec., 2006-. Recipient 3d Ann. Cmty. Svc. award Phila. Mayor's Com. for Women, 1984; named Pa. Heroine of Month, Ladies Home Jour., 1984. Mem.: Lions (pres. Germantown Club 1997—). Avocations: bridge, tennis. Home and Office: 422 W Mermaid Ln Philadelphia PA 19118-4204 Personal E-mail: debbyw@comcast.net.

WOLFF, DERISH MICHAEL, economist; b. Boston, May 14, 1935; s. Nathan and Ruth Mae (Derish) W.; m. Maureen Robinson; children: Jeffrey Scott, Hayley Beth. BA, U. Pa., Phila., 1957; MBA, Harvard U., Cambridge, Mass., 1959. Fin. analyst Sigmund Werner, Inc., Belleville, NJ, 1959-61; devel. economist Louis Berger, Inc., East Orange, NJ, 1961-65, chief economist, 1965-67, v.p., 1968-75, exec. v.p., 1976-82, pres., CEO, 1982—2002, chmn., 2002—. Dir. Berger Group Holdings, CHELBI, Ammann & Whitney, ABAM, Klohn-Crippen, Berger Devine Yaeger, RBA Group, guest lectr. UN Fgn. Svc. Dist., EA Engring., Sci. & Tech., UN Fgn. Svc. Inst., Newark Inst. Tech., U. Nev., Ga. Inst. Tech., The New Sch., Harvard U., Rutgers U., U. Denver, Tsinghua U.; vis. lectr. MIT, 2001—; mem. industry adv. panel Dept. of State, 2001-05; mem. Bretton Woods Com., 1987—. Mem. editl. bd. Modern Engring. Tech, 1978-80, Nat. Devel.-Modern Govt., 1972-79, Constrn. Bus. Review, 1991-95. Mem. adv. com. NJ Inst. Tech., 1995-, bd. overseers 2006-; class chmn. U. Pa. Ann. Giving, 1975-82; mem. adv. bd. Huntsman Program U. Pa., 1997—; U.S. presdl. trade del. to Japan, 1986; indsl. sector adv. com. Dept. of Commerce, 1988-92; adv. com. US Trade and Devel. Program, 1989-92. Recipient Pres.'s medal for lifetime achievement, N.J. Inst. Tech., 2003. Mem. Am. Cons. Engrs. Coun. (chair internat. engring. com. 1983-85, vice chair 1986-93), Internat. Engring. and Constrn. Industries Coun. (del. 1986, 87, chmn. 1988-90), Bldg. Futures Coun. (co-chmn. 1994-2006), Ctr. Strategic and Internat. Studies (steering group/GATT negotiations 1989), Phi Beta Kappa. Clubs: Harvard, Penn. Jewish. Office: Berger Group Holdings Inc PO Box 1946 412 Mt Kemble Ave Morristown NJ 07962-1946 Office Phone: 973-407-1001. Business E-Mail: dwolff@bergergroup.com.

WOLFF, EDWARD, physician; b. NYC, Apr. 15, 1941; s. Julius and Molly W.; m. Marilyn Alice Pels; children: Shanna, Loryn, Kimberly. BS, Muhlenberg Coll., 1962; MD, Georgetown U., 1966. Intern U. Ala. Hosp., Brimingham, 1966-67; resident N.Y. Med. Coll., NYC, 1967-71; physician pvt. practice, Great Neck, NY, 1976—. Attending physician North Shore U. Hosp., Manhasset, NY, St. Francis Hosp. Heart Ctr., Roslyn, NY. Fellow Am. Coll. Physicians; mem. AMA, N.Y. State Med. Soc., Nassau County Med. Soc. Office: Ste 404 107 Northern Blvd Great Neck NY 11021 Office Phone: 516-498-1818.

WOLFF, EDWARD ALVIN, electronics engineer; b. Chgo., Oct. 31, 1929; s. Samuel S. and Lillian P. Wolff; m. Anna Lee Tishk, June 19, 1951; children: David Steven, Eliot Marvin, Susan Toby. BSEE, U. Ill., 1951, MS, 1953; PhD, U. Md., 1961. Electronic scientist Naval Research Lab., Washington, 1951-54; project engr. Md. Electronic Mfg. Corp., Litton Industries, College Park, Md., 1956-59, Electromagnetic Research Corp., College Park, Md., 1959-61; engring. mgr. Aero Geo Astro-Keltec Industries/Aiken Industries, Alexandria, Va., 1961-67; v.p. Geotronics, Inc., Falls Church, Va., 1967-71; supervisory electronics engr. NASA Goddard Space Flight Ctr., Greenbelt, Md., 1971—; system mgr. Network TDRS System, 1981-89, MRJ, Inc., Oakton, Va., 1989-98; cons. in field, 1998—. Instr. Tex. A&M U., 1962. Author: Spacecraft Technology, 1962, Antenna Analysis, 1966, 2d edit., 1988, Geoscience Instrumentation, 1974, Urban Alternatives, 1975, Microwave Engineering and Systems Applications, 1988. Mem. Md. Gov.'s Sci. Resources Adv. Bd., 1963—67; pres. U.S. Environment and Resources Coun., 1972—75; treas. World Environment and Resources Coun., 1975—81. With US Army, 1954—56. Fellow: IEEE (life; bd. dirs. 1971—72), Washington Acad. Scis.; mem.: NSPE, AIAA, Phi Eta Sigma, Sigma Tau, Eta Kappa Nu. Home: 16870 Island Cove Dr Apt 130 Jupiter FL 33477-2356 Personal E-mail: ewolff@bigfoot.com. *Everything I have done has been with the help of others. In return, as I have acquired management responsibilities, a primary objective has been to help others achieve their goals.*

WOLFF, EDWARD NATHAN, economist, educator; b. Long Branch, NJ, Apr. 10, 1946; s. Arthur Seymour and Ethel (Kalmenoff) Wolff; m. Jane Zandra Forman, Nov. 27, 1977; children: Spencer, Ashley. BA, Harvard U., 1968; PhD, Yale U., 1974. Rsch. assoc. Nat. Bur. Econ. Rsch., NYC, 1974-77, 2001—; asst. prof. NYU, NYC, 1974-79, assoc. prof., 1979-84, prof., 1984—; mng. editor Rev. Income and Wealth, 1987—2004; sr. scholar Levy Econs. Inst., 1999—. Cons. Aspen Inst., 1993, World Bank, 1994—97, Jerome Levy Econs. Inst., 1995—96, Century Found., 1999—2002, UN, 2000—02, 2005—06, Math. Policy Rsch., 2002—03, Econ. Policy Inst., 2000—06; others; vis. scholar Russell Sage Found., 2003—04. Author: Growth, Accumulation and Unproductive Activity, 1987, Top Heavy: A Study of Increasing Unequality of Wealth in America, 1995, Economics of Poverty, Inequality, and Discrimination, 1997, Retirement Insecurity, 2002, Does Education Really Help? Skill, Work and Inequality, 2006, Poverty and Income Distribution, 2009; editor: International Comparisons of Household Wealth Distribution, 1987, Research in Economic Inequality, Vol. 4, 1993, The Economics of Productivity, 1997, Quality of Life in Advanced Industrialized Nations, 2004, International Perspectives on Household Wealth, 2006; co-author: Productivity and American Leadership: The Long View, 1989, Competitiveness, Convergence, and International Specialization, 1993, Downsizing in America, 2003, Retirement Income: The Crucial Role of Social Security, 2005; co-editor: International Perspectives on Profitability and Accumulation, 1992, Poverty and Prosperity in the USA in the Late Twentieth Century, 1993, Convergence of Productivity, 1994, Assets for the Poor, 2001; contbr. articles to profl. jours. Grantee, NSF, 1984—90, Exxon Found., 1984—88, Fishman-Davidson Ctr. U. Pa., 1987—89, Sloan Found., 1990—98, 2006—, Mellon Found., 1991—95, Russell Sage Found., 1997—2003, 2008—, Ford Found., 1997—2005, Kauffman Found., 2004—07, Sloan Found., 2006—, W.E. Upjohn Inst., 2008—. Mem.: Eastern Econs. Assn. (pres. 2002—03), Internat. Input-Output Assn. (coun. 1995—2003), Internat. Assn. Rsch. Income and Wealth (coun. mem. 1987—), Am. Econ. Assn. Avocations: tennis, skiing. Office: NYU Dept Econs 269 Mercer St Rm 700 New York NY 10003-6633 Home Phone: 212-924-4386; Office Phone: 212-998-8917. Office Fax: 212-995-4186. Business E-Mail: ew1@nyu.edu.

WOLFF, ELEANOR BLUNK, actress; b. Bklyn., July 10, 1931; d. Sol and Bessie (Schultz) Blunk; m. William Howard Wolff, June 19, 1955; children: Ellen Jill, Rebecca Louise. BA in Edn., Speech and Theatre, Bklyn. Coll., 1972, MS in Spl. Edn., 1975; postgrad., Adelphi U., Garden City, NY, 1980-81. Cert. tchr., N.Y. Fashion model Garment Ctr., NYC, 1949—50; sec. to v.p. out-of-town/export sales Liebmann Breweries Inc., Bklyn., 1950—58; tchr. N.Y.C. Bd. Edn., Bklyn., 1971-76; sec. to dir. environ. programs, pub. affairs officers, speakers bur. project leader Power Authority State of N.Y., NYC, 1976-85; tchr. Hewlett-Woodmere (N.Y.) Sch. Dist., 1986-89; instr. adult edn. County of Nassau, NY, 1986-97. Actress/model, N.Y.C., 1992—; mem. Love Creek Prodns. V.p. program devel. for youth ctr. Wavecrest Gardens Cmty. Assn., Far Rockaway, NY, 1959-63; teen leader Far Rockaway Jewish Ctr. Youth Coun., 1965-68; pres. Parents Assn. P.S. 215Q, Far Rockaway, 1966-67; tutor NYC Bd. Edn. Sch. Vol. Program, Far Rockaway, 1969-71, New Ground Inc., Mineola, NY, 2004—; chair civic affairs Dem. Club, Far Rockaway, 1961-63; committeewoman Dem. Ctrl. Com., Queens County, NY, 1963-64, Nassau County Dem. Party, 1998-; v.p. membership, constn. com. Nassau County Dem. Women's Caucus, 1988, 89; awards com. Bklyn. Coll., 1993-97, chair theatre arts affiliate, 1990-94, 2001-; comm. adv. com. Hewlett-Woodmere Sch. Dist. 14, 1996-97, zone leader, 2007—; press/media steward vol. Goodwill Games, 1998; vol. program presenter Child Abuse Prevention Svcs., Roslyn, NY, 2003-05; vol. income tax assistance IRS, 2004-. Named Mother of Yr. Congregation Shaaray Tefila, Far Rockaway, 1968; recipient Merit award Wavecrest Gardens Cmty. Assn., 1960, Theater Arts Trophy for disting. svc. Bklyn. Coll. Alumni, 1992. Mem.: SAG (awards nominating com. 2000—01, 2006—07), AFTRA, Actors Equity Assn., Alumni Assn. Bklyn. Coll. (life), Cmty. Garden Club of North Woodmere Park (corr. sec. 2001—03, rec. sec. 2006—). Avocations: painting, piano, gardening. Home Phone: 516-295-1649. Personal E-mail: eleanorwolff@cs.com.

WOLFF, ELROY HARRIS, lawyer; b. NYC, May 20, 1935; s. Samuel and Rose Marian (Katz) W.; children: Ethan, Anna Louise. AB, Columbia U., 1957, LL.B., 1963. Bar: N.Y. 1963, D.C. 1969. Assoc. Kaye, Scholer, Fierman, Hays & Handler, NYC, 1963-65; atty.-adviser to commr. FTC, Washington, 1965-67; sr. trial atty. Dept. Transp., 1967-69; assoc. Leibman, Williams, Bennett, Baird & Minow, Washington, 1969-70, ptnr., 1970-72, Sidley & Austin, Washington, 1972-99; sr. counsel Sidley Austin Brown & Wood, Washington, 2000—04. Mem. adv. com. on practice and procedure FTC, 1969-71; chmn. adv. com. on procedural reform CAB, 1975 Served to 1st lt. USAF, 1957-60. Mem. ABA (chmn. spring meeting program 1992-94, coun. 1995-98), Union Internationale des advocats (chmn. competition law com. 1994-98), Army and Navy Club. Office: 1629 K St NW Ste 300 Washington DC 20036 Home: 321 Aegean Rd Palm Beach Gardens FL 33410 Home Phone: 302-539-7311; Office Phone: 202-257-4035. Business E-Mail: e.wolff@mchsi.com.

WOLFF, FRANK PIERCE, JR., lawyer; b. St. Louis, Feb. 27, 1946; s. Frank P. and Beatrice (Stein) W.; m. Susan Scallet, May 11, 1984; children: Elizabeth McLane, Victoria Hancox. BA, Middlebury Coll., 1968; JD, U. Va., 1971. Bar: Mo. 1971, U.S. Ct. Appeals (5th cir.) 1974, U.S. Ct. Appeals (8th cir.) 1975, U.S. Supreme Ct. 1975. Ptnr. Lewis, Rice & Fingersh, St. Louis, 1971—90; leader Bosnoss Sec., 1996—2007; ptnr., ops. ptnr., mgmt. com. Bryan Cave LLP, St. Louis, 1990—. Bd. dirs. Misco Shawnee, Inc. Bd. dirs. Leadership St. Louis, 1985-88, Washington U. Child Guidance Clinic, St. Louis, 1976-79, Jewish Family and Children's Svc., St. Louis, 1981-83, John Burroughs Sch., 1995-2000, BJC Health Sys., Inc., 1998-2001, The Butterfly House, 2001—; gen. counsel Mo. Bot. Garden, St. Louis, 1981—, Mo. Hist. Soc., St. Louis, 1997—, spcc counsel Opera Theatre St. Louis, 2005-, St. Louis Sci. Ctr., 2000-, Webster U., 2006-; trustee St. Louis Children's Hosp., 1995-2001, chairperson mission vision and values com., 1996-2001, mem. exec. com., 1997-99; co-chmn. Parks Task Force, 2004 Inc. Capt. USAR, 1968-76. Mem. ABA, Mo. Bar Assn., Bar Assn. Met. St. Louis (chmn. corp. sect. 1984-85), Noonday Club, Westwood County Club (chmn. fin. com. 1989-91, treas. 1989-91, v.p. 1991-93, pres. 1994-95, exec. com. 1989-95). Office: Bryan Cave LLP One Metropolitan Square 211 N Broadway Ste 3600 Saint Louis MO 63105 Home: 30 Brighton Way Unit 2 S Saint Louis MO 63124 Office Phone: 314-259-2330. Business E-Mail: fpwolff@bryancave.com.

WOLFF, GEORGE LOUIS, biomedical researcher; b. Hamburg, Germany, Aug. 24, 1928; came to U.S., 1940; s. Adolf and Eva (Nathan) W.; m. Eleanor Herstein, Aug. 30, 1953; children: David Bernard, Adrienne Ann. BS cum laude, Ohio State U., 1950; PhD, U. Chgo., 1954. Postdoctoral fellow Nat. Cancer Inst., Bethesda, Md., 1954-56, biologist, 1956-58; rsch. assoc. Inst. for Cancer Rsch., Phila., 1958-63, asst. mem., 1963-72; rsch. biologist Nat. Ctr. for Toxicol. Rsch.-FDA, Jefferson, Ark., 1972-74, chief divsn. mutagenesis rsch., 1974-79, sr. sci. coord. for genetics, 1979-88, sr. rsch. biologist, 1988-99, guest worker, 1999—. Adj. prof. biochemistry U. Ark. for Med. Scis., Little Rock, 1973—, adj. prof. pharmacology and toxicology, 1981-; cons. Ark. Children's Hosp. Nutrition Ctr., 2002- Contbr. more than 100 articles to profl. jours. Pres., v.p., treas. Jewish Fedn. Ark., Little Rock, 1983-92; bd. dirs., officer Nat. Conf. for Com. and Justice, vice chair, 1995-2000 Office: NCTR 3900 Nctr Rd Jefferson AR 72079-9501 E-mail: gwolffar@prodigy.net.

WOLFF, L. THOMAS, physician, educator; b. Suffern, NY, 1942; MD, Albany Med. Coll., 1968. Dir. emeritus rural med. edn. program Upstate Med. U., Syracuse, NY; co-founder N.Y. State Area Health Edn. Sys.; disting. teaching prof. emeritus family medicine SUNY Upstate Med. U., NY. Co-investigator IDEATEL. Mem.: ABFP (pres. 1998—2003). Office: SUNY Upstate Med U Div Family Medicine 200 Madison Irving Med Ctr Syracuse NY 13210

WOLFF, MANFRED ERNST, chemist, pharmaceutical executive; b. Berlin, Feb. 14, 1930; came to U.S., 1933; s. Adolph Abraham and Kate (Fraenkel) W.; m. Helen S. Scandalis, Aug. 1, 1953 (div. 1971); children: Stephen Andrew, David James, Edward Allen; m. Susan E. Hurbert, Jan. 19, 1973 (div. 1975); m. A. Gloria Johnson, Dec. 25, 1982. BS, U. Calif., Berkeley, 1951, MS, 1953, PhD, 1955. Registered U.S. patent agt. Rsch. fellow U. Va., 1955-57; sr. medicinal chemist Smith, Kline & French Labs., Phila., 1957-60; mem. faculty U. Calif., San Francisco, 1960-82, prof. medicinal chemistry, 1965-82, chmn. dept. pharm. chemistry, 1970-82; dir. discovery rsch. Allergan Labs, Irvine, Calif., 1982-84; v.p. discovery rsch. Allergan Pharms., Irvine, 1984-89; v.p. R & D Immunopharmaceutics Inc., San Diego, 1989-91, sr. v.p. R & D, 1991-95; pres. Intellepharm., Inc., Laguna Beach, Calif., 1997—. Adj. prof. medicinal chemistry U. So. Calif., 1982—2002; elected mem. U.S. Pharm. Conv. Com. of Revision, 1990—; lectr. Sch. Med. Chemistry Drew U., NJ, 1998-2008. Editor: Burger's Medicinal Chemistry and Drug Discovery, Vol. 1-5, 5th edit., 1995-97; asst. editor Jour. Medicinal Chemistry, 1968-71; mem. editl. bd. Medicinal Chemistry Rsch., 1991-95, PharmSci., 1999-2004; contbr. articles to profl. jours.; patentee in field. Fellow AAAS, Am Assn. Pharm. Scientists; mem. Am. Chem. Soc. Achievements include discovery of Alphagan and Lumigan medicines for glaucoma, Tazorac medicine for psoriasis, and Thelin medicine for pulmonary arterial hypertension. Office Phone: 949-494-5458. Personal E-mail: drwolff@aol.com.

WOLFF, MICHAEL A., state supreme court judge; Grad., Dartmouth Coll., 1967; JD, U. Minn., 1970. Lawyer Legal Svcs.; mem. faculty St. Louis U. Sch. Law, 1975-98; judge Mo. Supreme Ct., 1998—, chief justice, 2005—07. Chief counsel to gov., 1993-94, spl. counsel, 1994-98. Co-author: Federal Jury Practice and Instructions, 4th edit; author monthly column Law Matters: Reflections of Chief Justice Michael A. Wolff, 2005. Chief counsel to Gov. St. Louis, 1993-94, spl. counsel, 1994-98. Office: Supreme Ct Mo PO Box 150 Jefferson City MO 65102-0150*

WOLFF, MITCH, engineering educator, researcher; b. Newcomerstown, Ohio, Oct. 30, 1960; s. James Henry Wolff; married. PhD, Purdue U., West Lafayette, 1995. Prof. Wright State U., Dayton, Ohio, 1995—. Home: 5061 Lincrest Pl Huber Heights OH 45424 Office: Wright State Univ 3640 Colonel Glenn Hwy Dayton OH 45435 Office Fax: 937-775-5009. Business E-Mail: mitch.wolff@wrighte.edu.

WOLFF, OTTO J., federal agency administrator; b. 1942; BS in Fin., Pa. State U. Profl. staff mem. com. on house adminstrn. U.S. Ho. Reps.; dep. asst. sec. for adminstrn. US Dept. Commerce, 1981—93, asst. sec. for adminstrn., CFO Washington, 2001—. Office: US Dept Commerce 1401 Constitution Ave NW Washington DC 20230*

WOLFF, PHILLIP MARK, psychology professor; b. Phila., May 14, 1964; s. Wallace Walter Wolff and Marjorie Erics Horton; m. Grace Unhie Song, July 12, 1998; children: Nathaniel Max, Alison Young. PhD, Northwestern U., Chgo., 1999. Asst. prof. U. Memphis, 2001—04, Emory U., Atlanta, 2004—. Faculty Summer Inst. Linguistics Stanford U., 2007. Editor: (book) Words and the World: How Words Capture Human Experience, Categorization Inside and Outside the Laboratory; author: Instructional Design: Implications from Cognitive Science; contbr. articles to profl. jours. Grantee, Office Naval Rsch., 2001—02; Conf. grant, NSF, 2005. Mem.: Cognitive Sci. Soc., Psychonomic Soc. Liberal. Achievements include research in representation of causation and causal reasoning. Office: Emory Univ 532 Kilgo Cir Atlanta GA 30322 Business E-Mail: pwolff@emory.edu.

WOLFF, RICHARD JOSEPH, public relations executive, consultant, historian; b. Hackensack, NJ, Oct. 13, 1952; s. Richard Hamilton and Irene Marie (Ciruzzi) W. AB, Georgetown U., 1974; MA, Columbia U., 1976, PhD, 1979. Asst. dean, prof. St. John's U., Queens, NY, 1980-85; ptnr. pub. rels. Kekst & Co., Inc., NYC, 1985-97; mng. dir. Eastern region and L.Am. Golin/Harris Internat., NYC, 1997—2002, worldwide mng. divsn. G/H Fin., 1997—2002; CEO, The Global Cons. Group, NYC, 2002—. Mem. Columbia U. Seminar Modern Italy, NYC, 1983—; founding mem. St. John's U. Seminar Vatican Studies, Queens, 1994—. Author: Between Pope and Duce, 1990, Dorothy Day, 1994; contbr. articles to profl. jours.; editor Catholics, the State and the European Radical Right, 1987. Chmn., commr. North Hudson Sewerage Authority, Hudson County, NJ, 1988—; mem. adv. com. Senator Robert Menendez, NJ, 1994—. Recipient Howard Marraro prize Am. Cath. Hist. Assn., 1982, Internat. fellow Columbia U., 1977; named to Order of Malta, Knight of Magistral Grace. Mem. Order of Malta, Phi Beta Kappa. Roman Catholic. Avocations: golf, reading, travel, politics. Office: The Global Consulting Group 22 Cortlandt St 14th Fl New York NY 10007

WOLFF, ROBERT D., professional society administrator; m. Phyllis Wolff; 2 children. Grad., US Mil. Acad., West Point, NY; PhD in Civil Engring., Stanford U., Calif. Registered profl. engr., DC. Civil engr. US Army; sr. civilian civil engr. Sr. Exec. Svc. US Air Force, 1994—97, dir. logistics plans, 1997, ret., 1998; v.p. CH2M Hill, 1998—2002; exec. dir. Soc. Am. Mil. Engrs. (SAME), Alexandria, Va., 2002—. Engr. officer US Army, Vietnam, Cambodia. Fellow: Soc. Am. Mil. Engrs. (Goethals Medal for Engring. Achievement 1992); mem.: ASCE, Air Force Assn., Assn. of US Army, Army Engr. Assn., Internat. Facility Mgmt. Assn. Office: Soc Am Mil Engrs 607 Prince St Alexandria VA 22314-3117 Office Phone: 703-549-3800 ext. 110. Office Fax: 703-684-0231. E-mail: rwolff@same.org.

WOLFF, STUART, online real estate executive; BSEE, Brown U.; MSEE, Princeton U., D in Elec. Engring. Former founder and CEO CareNet Am., others.; former v.p. And Interactive; former v.p. bus. svcs. TCI Interactive (subs. Telecomms. Inc.); chmn., pres. Real Select, Inc. (subs. Homestore.com., Inc.), Thousand Oaks, Calif. Recipient MONBUSHO fellowship, Japanese Min. of Edn., Tokyo Inst. Technology, 1986. Office: Homestore-com Inc 225 W Hillcrest Dr Ste 100 Thousand Oaks CA 91360-7884

WOLFF, TOBIAS (TOBIAS JONATHAN ANSELL WOLFF), writer, English professor; b. Birmingham, Ala., June 19, 1945; s. Arthur Saunders and Rosemary (Loftus) Wolff; m. Catherine Dolores Spohn, 1975; children: Michael, Patrick, Mary Elizabeth. BA in English, Hertford Coll., Oxford, Eng., 1972; MA, Stanford U., Calif., 1978; LHD (hon.), Santa Clara U., Calif., 1996. Faculty Goddard Coll., Plainfield, Vt., Ariz. State U., Tempe; prof. Syracuse U., NY, 1980—97; English/creative writing tchr. Stanford U., 1997—, dir. creative writing prog., 2000—02; Ward W. & Priscilla B. Woods prof. Stanford U. Sch. Humanities & Scis. Author: (novels) Ugly Rumours, 1975, The Barracks Thief, 1984 (PEN/Faulkner award for fiction, 1985), Old School, 2003, (short story collections) In the Garden of the North American Martyrs, 1981 (St. Lawrence award for fiction, 1982), Back in the World, 1985, The Night in Question, 1997, Our Story Begins: New and Selected Stories, 2008 (LA Times Book prize, 1989, The Story Prize, 2009), (memoirs) This Boy's Life, 1989, In Pharaoh's Army, 1994 (Esquire-Volvo-Winterstone's award, 1994); editor: Matters of Life and Death: New American Stories, 1983, Best American Short Stories, 1994, The Vintage Book of Contemporary American Short Stories, 1994. Recipient O. Henry award, 1981, 1982, 1985, Rea award for Short Story, 1989, Whiting Writer's award, 1989, Fairfax prize for lit., George Mason U., 2001; grantee Wallace Stegner Fellowship in Creative Writing, Stanford U., 1975, NEA, 1978, 1985, Ariz. Coun. Arts & Humanities, 1980, Guggenheim Found., 1982. Office: Stanford U Dept English Stanford CA 94305-2087 Office Phone: 650-723-0504.

WOLFF, VIRGINIA EUWER, writer; b. Portland, Oreg., Aug. 25, 1937; d. Eugene Courtney and Florence Evelyn (Craven) Euwer; m. Art Wolff, July 19, 1959 (div. July 1976); children: Anthony Richard, Juliet Dianne. AB, Smith Coll., 1959; postgrad., Goddard Coll., Warren Wilson Coll., L.I. U., Portland State U., Lewis & Clark Coll. Cert. tchr., Oreg. Tchr. The Miquon Sch., Phila., 1968-72, The Fiedel Sch., Glen Cove, NY, 1972-75, Hood River Valley (Oreg.) H.S., 1976-86, Mt. Hood Acad., Govt. Camp, Oreg., 1986-98. 2d violinist Quartet con brio, Portland, 1989-94, Parnassius Quintet, Portland, 1996—. Author: Probably Still Nick Swansen, 1988, The Mozart Season, 1991, Make Lemonade, 1993, Bat 6, 1998, True Believer (Nat. Book award, Michael L. Printz honor, Pacific N.W. Booksellers Assn. award, Jane Addams Book honor, 2002), 2001, represented US, honor book, Internat. Board on Books for Young People, 2004, book, This Full House, 2009. Violinist Mid-Columbia Sinfonietta, Hood River, 1976—92, Oreg. Sinfonietta, Portland, 1988—, Parnassius Chamber Ensemble, 2000-. Recipient Young Adult Book award Internat. Reading Assn., 1989, PEN U.S.A. Ctr. West, 1989, Best Young Adult Book of Yr. award Mich. Libr. Assn., 1993, Child Study Children's Book award Bank Street Coll., 1994, Oreg. Book award Oreg. Lit. Arts, 1994, 2001, Jane Addams Children's Book award Jane Addams Peace Assn. and the Women's Internat. League for Peace and Freedom, 1999, Nat. Book award, 2001, Printz Honor Book award, 2002, Jane Addams Honor Plaque, 2002, Evelyn Sibley Lampman award for svc. to the children of Oreg., Oreg. Libr. Assn., 2005, Disting. NW Writer award, Willamette Writers, 2008; named to Carnegie medal Shortlist, ALA, 2002. Mem. Soc. Children's Book Writers/Illustrators (Golden Kite 1994, 2002), Chamber Music Soc. Oreg. Avocations: chamber music, swimming, hiking, playing violin, gardening. Office: Curtis Brown Ltd care Elizabeth Harding 10 Astor Pl Fl 3 New York NY 10003-6982

WOLFF, WILLIAM F., III, investment banker; b. NYC, Apr. 12, 1945; s. William F., Jr. and Nancy (Wimpfheimer) Wolff; m. Phyllis Fox, June 1, 1969; children: Kenneth, Laura, Jonathan, Gillian. BA, U. Mich., 1967; JD, Columbia U., 1970, MBA, 1971. Bar: N.Y. 1970. V.p. Salomon Bros., Inc., NYC, 1971-78; prin. Morgan Stanley & Co., NYC, 1978-83; mng. dir. Lehman Bros., NYC, 1983-2000, UBS Warburg, NYC, 2000—02, Endurance Capital, NYC, 2002—03; mng. ptnr. Lykos Capital Mgmt., 2003—07. Trustee St. David's Sch., NYC, 1985—2004; dir. City Harvest, 1999—2005. Mem.: Ocean Beach Club (Elberon, N.J.) (trustee 1985—89, treas. 2007—). Office: 40 W 57th St New York NY 10019 Personal E-mail: rwolff3@yahoo.com.

WOLFGRAM, KENNETH CHARLES, retired agricultural engineer; b. Rochester, Minn., Dec. 6, 1944; s. Ellsworth Stanley and Helen Edith (Ranfranz) W.; m. Janet Caroline Waldron, Dec. 30, 1966; Derek Edwin, Sarah Caroline. BS in Agrl. Engring., U. Minn., 1966. Design engr. Allis Chalmers, Milw., 1965-69, project engr. Topeka, 1969-72, Omsteel Industries, Omaha, 1972-73; design engr. Caterpillar Inc., Aurora, Ill., 1973-75, sr. design engr., 1975-84, project engr., 1984-87, sr. project engr. Decatur, Ill., 1987-95, engring. supr. Joliet, Ill., 1995-98; tech. mgr. Claas Caterpillar Europe, Harsewinkel, Germany, 1998-2000, Caterpillar Agrl. Products, Dekalb, Ill., 2001—03; chief engr.-Challenger, AGCO, Jackson, Minn., 2003—04; staff engr. BELCAN ENGRG, Jackson, Minn., 2004—06; ret., 2006. Patentee in field. Mem. SAE (bd. dirs. 1995-98), Am. Soc. Agrl. Engring. Home: 414 E Kings Rd Fairmont MN 56031

WOLFINGER, NICHOLAS H., educator; b. Palo Alto, Calif., May 2, 1966; s. Raymond E. and Barbara Kaye Wolfinger. AB, U. Calif., Berkeley, 1990; MA, UCLA, LA, 1992, PhD, 1998. Assoc. prof. U. Utah, Salt Lake City, 2005—. Author: (research monograph) Understanding the Divorce Cycle. Liberal. Office: Univ Utah 225 S 1400 East AEB 228 Salt Lake City UT 84112 Office Fax: 801-581-5156. Personal E-mail: nick.wolfinger@fcs.utah.edu.

WOLFINGER, RAYMOND EDWIN, retired political science professor; b. San Francisco, June 29, 1931; s. Raymond Edwin and Hilda (Holm) W.; m. Barbara Kaye, Aug. 7, 1960; 1 son, Nicholas Holm. AB, U. Calif.-Berkeley, 1951; MA, U. Ill., 1955; PhD, Yale U., 1961. Asst. prof. polit. sci. Stanford U., Calif., 1961—66, assoc. prof., 1966-70, prof., 1970-71, U. Calif., Berkeley, 1971—, Heller prof. polit. sci., 1995—2006; ret., 2006. Dir. U. Calif. Data Archive and Tech. Assistance, 1980-92; chmn. bd. overseers Nat. Election Studies, Ann Arbor, Mich., 1982-86 Author: The Politics of Progress, 1974, (with others) Dynamics of American Politics, 1976, 80, (with Steven J. Rosenstone) Who Votes, 1980, (with others) The Myth of the Independent Voter, 1992; mem. editorial bd. Brit. Jour. Polit. Sci., 1980-84, Am. Polit. Sci. Rev., 1985-88. Bd. dirs. S.W. Voter Rsch. Inst., San Antonio, 1988-96, Consortium of Social Sci. Assns., 1987-93, pres. 1988-90. 1st lt. U.S. Army, 1951-53. Fellow Ctr. for Advanced Study in Behavioral Scis., 1960-61; Guggenheim fellow, 1965; Ford Found. faculty research fellow, 1970-71 Fellow Am. Acad. Arts and Scis. (chair Class III membership com. 1998-99); mem. Am. Polit. Sci. Assn. (sec. 1981-82), AAUP (council 1981-84), Western Polit. Sci. Assn. (v.p. 1988-89, pres. 1989-90). Democrat. Office: Univ Calif Dept Polit Sci Berkeley CA 94720-1950 Business E-Mail: vturnout@berkeley.edu.

WOLFMAN, BERNARD, lawyer, educator; b. Phila., July 8, 1924; s. Nathan and Elizabeth (Coff) W.; m. Zelda Bernstein, Dec. 25, 1948 (dec. Oct. 1973); children: Jonathan L., Brian S., Dina A.; m. Toni A. Grotta, June 12, 1977. AB, U. Pa., 1946, JD, 1948; LLD (hon.), Jewish Theol. Sem., 1971, Capital U., 1990. Bar: Pa. 1949, Mass. 1976. Mem. law firm Wolf, Block, Schorr & Solis-Cohen, Phila., 1948-63; prof. law U. Pa. Law Sch., 1963-76, dean, 1970-75, Kenneth W. Gemmill prof. tax law and tax policy, 1973-76, chmn. Faculty Senate, 1969-70; Fessenden prof. law Harvard U., 1976—2007, Fessenden prof. emeritus, 2007—. Vis. prof. Stanford U. Law Sch., 1982, NYU Law Sch., 1987-88; Irvine lectr. Cornell U. Law Sch., 1980; Halle lectr. Case Western Res. U. Law Sch., 1983; Cleve. State U. Sch. Law; Sugarman lectr., 1989; Altheimer lectr. U. Ark. Sch. Law, Little Rock, 1994; Polisher lectr. Dickinson Coll. Law, 1998; mem. editl. bds. law divsn. Aspen Law & Bus. (formerly Little Brown & Co.), Jour. Corp. Taxation; gen. counsel AAUP, 1966-68, mem. coun., 1979-82; prof.-in-residence tax divsn. Dept. Justice, 2003; cons. to ind. counsel Lawrence E. Walsh (Iran-Contra prosecution), 1987-89; adv. group to commr. internal revenue, 1966-67; cons. tax policy U.S. Treasury Dept., 1963-68, 77-80; chmn. Task Force Univ. Governance, U. Pa., 1968-70; steering com. IRS project Adminstrv. Conf. US, 1974-80; vice chmn. bd. advs. NYU-IRS Continuing Profl. Edn. Project, 1981-85; mem. legal activities policy bd. Tax Analysts, 1974—; exec. com. Fed. Tax Inst. New Eng., 1976—; pres. Fed. Tax Inst. New Eng., 2004—. Author: (with Diane K. Ring) Federal Income Taxation of Corporate Enterprise, 1971, 4th edit., 2008; (with D. Schenk) Ethical Problems in Federal Tax Practice, 1981, 4th edit., 2008, (with D. Schenk and K. Harris) Standards of Tax Practice; supp, 2006; sr. author: Dissent Without Opinion: The Behavior of Justice William O. Douglas in Federal Tax Cases, 1975; contbr. articles to profl. jours. Adv. com. Commn. Philanthropy and Pub. Needs, 1973-75; mem. Phila. regional council Pa. Gov.'s Justice Commn., 1973-75; trustee Found. Center, NYC, 1970-76, Fedn. Jewish Agys. Greater Phila., 1968-74; bd. dirs. Phila. Lawyers Com. Civil Rights Under Law, 1970-74, Phila. Defender Assn., 1955-69; mem. Nat. Lawyers Adv. Council of Earl Warren Legal Tng. Program. Served with AUS, 1943-45. Fellow Am. Bar Found., Am. Coll. Tax Counsel (past regent 1st cir.); mem. ABA (coun. sect. individual rights and responsibilities 1978-82, coun. sect. taxation 1982-85), Am. Law Inst., ACLU (nat. dir. 1973-75), Order of Coif (exec. com. 1982-91, v.p. 1986-89, pres. 1989-91), Phi Beta Kappa. Home: 229 Brattle St Cambridge MA 02138-4623 Office: Harvard Law Sch 1545 Mass Ave Cambridge MA 02138 Office Phone: 617-495-4623. E-mail: wolfman@law.harvard.edu.

WOLFMAN, BRUNETTA REID, education educator; b. Clarksdale, Miss., Sept. 4, 1931; d. Willie Orlando and Belle Victoria (Allen) Reid Griffin; m. Burton Wolfman, Oct. 4, 1952; children: Andrea, Jeffrey. BA, U. Calif., Berkeley, 1957, MA, 1968, PhD, 1971; DHL (hon.), Boston U., 1983; DP (hon.), Northeastern U., 1983; DL (hon.), Regis Coll., 1984, Stonehill Coll., 1985; DHL, Suffolk U., 1985; DET (hon.), Wentworth Inst., 1987; AA (hon.), Roxbury Community Coll., 1988. Asst. dean faculty Dartmouth Coll., Hanover, N.H., 1972-74; asst. v.p. acad. affairs U. Mass., Boston, 1974-76; acad. dean Wheelock Coll., Boston, 1976-78; cons. Arthur D. Little, Cambridge, Mass., 1978; dir. policy planning Dept. Edn., Boston, 1978-82; pres. Roxbury C.C., Boston, 1983-88, ACE sr. assoc., 1988-94, NAWE sr. assoc., 1994-98; assoc. v.p. acad. affairs George Washington U., Washington, 1989-92, prof. edn., 1992-96, prof. edn. emeritus, 1996—. Mem. Accrediting Commn. on Edn. on Health Svcs. Adminstrn.; pres. bd. dirs. Literacy Vols. of Capitol Region; mem. comm. com. bd., pub. rels. com. LVA, Inc.; bd. dirs. Am. Coun. Edn., Harvard Cmty. Health Plan. Author: Roles, 1983; contbr. articles to profl. jours. Mem. bd. overseers Wellesley Coll., 1981, Boston Symphony Orch.; trustee Mus. Fine Arts, Boston; mem. Coun. on Edn. for Pub. Health; chair Provincetown bd. Coun. on Aging, 1999—2005; mem. Holocaust meml. com. NCCJ; bd. dirs. Boston-Fenway Program, 1977, Freedom House, Boston, 1983, Boston Pvt. Industry Coun., 1983; bd. dirs., co-chmn. NCCJ, Boston, 1983; bd. dirs. Elder Svcs. Cape Cod and the Islands, 2003, adv. coun. mem., 2009; mem. Cape Cod Outer Cape Interfaith Group on Holocaust, Genocide and Human Rights. Recipient Freedom award, NAACP No.Calif., 1971, Amelia Earhart award, Women's Edn. and Indsl. Union, Boston, 1983, Provincetown Sr. Citizen of Yr., 2004; named Wolfman Courtyard in their honor, Evergreen Ctr., 2000; scholar Nat. Assn. Women in Edn. Mem. AAUW, Am. Sociol. Assn., Assn. Black Women in Higher Edn., Greater Boston C. of C. (edn. com. 1982), Sierra Club, Mass. Audubon Soc., Cosmos Club (Washington), Provincetown Art Assn. (sec. bd. trustees, mus. sch. com., nominating com.), Alpha Kappa Alpha (Humanitarian award 1984), Phi Delta Kappa, Cape Cod Found. (bd. dir. 2008). Home: 657 Commercial St Provincetown MA 02657-1759 Personal E-mail: bruburt2@comcast.net.

WOLFMAN, EARL FRANK, JR., surgeon, educator; b. Buffalo, Sept. 14, 1926; s. Earl Frank and Alfreda (Peterson) W.; m. Lois Jeannette Walker, Dec. 28, 1946; children— Nancy Jeannette, David Earl, Carol Anne. BS cum laude, Harvard U., Cambridge, Mass., 1946; MD cum laude, U. Mich., 1950. Diplomate Am. Bd. Surgery. Intern U. Mich., Ann Arbor, 1950-51, asst. resident in surgery, 1951-52, resident in surgery, 1954-55, from jr. clin. instr. surgery to assoc. prof., 1955-66, asst. to dean, 1960-61, asst. dean, 1961-64; practice medicine specializing in surgery, 1957—, Sacramento, 1966—; prof. surgery Sch. Medicine, U. Calif., Davis, 1966—, founding chmn. dept. surgery, 1966-78, founding assoc. dean, 1966-76, mem. staff, chief surg. svcs. Med. Ctr., 1966-78, founding chmn. div. surg. scis., 1966-78. Contbr. articles to profl. jours. Served to lt. M.C. USNR, 1952-54. Fellow ACS; mem. AMA (del. 1987-99), Ctrl. Surg. Soc., Western Surg. Soc., Sacramento Surg. Soc., Pacific Coast Surg. Soc., Frederick A. Coller Surg. Soc., Soc. Surgery Alimentary Tract, Am. Assn. Endocrine Surgeons, Sierra Sacramento Valley Med. Soc., Calif. Med. Assn. (trustee 1991-2000), Am. Soc. Gen. Surgeons. Office: U Calif Davis Sch Medicine Dept Surgery 2221 Stockton Blvd Fl 3 Sacramento CA 95817-2214 Business E-Mail: efwolfman@ucdavis.edu.

WOLFORD, JOANNE M., academic administrator, director; d. William Lester and A. Virginia Vandervort Morton; m. Robert L. Wolford, Aug. 29, 1959; children: Christine L. Thomas, Stephen L. BS in Edn., Ohio U., Athens, 1958; MS in Libr. Sci., Western Res. U., Cleve., 1959. Dir. youth svcs State Libr. Ohio, Columbus, 1964—68; dir. lib. tech. Ohio U., Lancaster, 1970—92. Membership chairperson Friends Fairfield Co. Dist. Lib., Lancaster, Ohio, 1998—. Mem.: Assn. Christian Librs. Office: Ohio Christian Univ 1476 Lancaster Pike Circleville OH 43113

WOLFORD, LARRY M., surgeon; s. Donald Ralph and Wilma Irene Wolford; m. Denise Hazel LeBlanc, June 11, 1983; children: Dax Patrick, Dallas Danielle, Demi Denise, Dylan Dion, Dash Larry. BS, U. Pitts., 1965; DMD, Temple U., Phila., 1969; cert. in Oral Surgery, U.Tex. Southwestern Med. Sch., Dallas, 1973; diploma of Hon. Merit (hon.), U. São Paulo, Brazil, 1995. Diplomate Am. Bd. Oral and Maxillofacial Surgery. Asst. dir. dept oral and maxillofacial surgery and ctr. for correction dentofacial deformities John Peter Smith Hosp., Fort Worth, 1973—83, coord. Ft. Worth cleft palate program, 1973—83; prof. oral and maxillofacial surgery Baylor Coll. Dentistry, Dallas, 1983—87, dir. of oral and maxillofacial surgery grad. program, 1984—86, clin. prof. of oral and maxillofacial surgery, 1987—; dir. oral and maxillofacial surgery fellowship program Baylor Coll. Dentistry Tex. A&M U. Sys. and Baylor U. Med. Ctr., Dallas, 1985—. Mem. adv. com. Am. Bd. Oral and Maxillofacial Surgery, 1985—91. Co-author: Dentofacial Deformities: Surgical Orthodontic Correction, 1980, Surgical Treatment Objective: A Systematic Approach to the Prediction Tracing, 1985; co-editor: Cleft / Craniofacial / Cosmetic Surgery, 2000; contbr. 22 chapters to books;, author 170 manuscripts. Recipient 1st William F. Harrigan award, William F. Harrigan Soc., 1982, Diplomat Am. Coll. Dentists award, Am. Coll. Dentistry, 1987, William J. Gies Found. Oral and Maxillofacial award for major contributions, 1990. Mem.: ADA, Am. Soc. Tempormandibular Joint Surgeons, Am. Assn. Oral and Maxillofacial Surgeons (mem. com. ann. sci. sessions 1977—83, chmn. planning com. combined meeting AAO/AAOMS 1980, chmn. com. annual sci. sessions 1980—82, spl. cons. com. annual sci. sessions 1982—83, mem. planning com. combined meeting AAO/AAOMS 1983). Achievements include development of many surgical procedures and instruments; research in over 100 clin. and lab. studies; porous block hydroxyapatite (Interpore 200) for bone grafting in the craniofacial area; tempormandibular joint concepts for total joint prostheses for reconstruction; mitek mini anchors for disc repositioning in tempormandibular joint surgery. Avocation: sports cars. Office: 3409 Worth St Ste 400 Dallas TX 75246 Office Phone: 214-828-9115.

WOLFORD, RICHARD G., food products executive; With Dole Foods, 1967—87, pres. packaged foods, 1982—87; CEO HK Acquisition Corp., 1988—96, Del Monte Foods Co., San Francisco, 1997—98, pres., CEO, 1998—2000, chmn., pres., CEO, 2000—. Office: Del Monte Foods Co One Market The Landmark San Francisco CA 94105

WOLFOWITZ, PAUL DUNDES, former President of the World Bank; b. NYC, Dec. 22, 1943; s. Jacob and Lillian (Dundes) W.; m. Clare Selgin, Nov. 25, 1968 (div. 2002); children: Sara Elizabeth, David Samuel, Rachel Dahlia. BA in Math. and Chemistry, Cornell U., 1965; MA, U. Chgo., 1967, PhD in Polit. Sci., 1972. Lectr., asst. prof. Yale U., 1970-73; with US Arms Control & Disarmament Agy., 1973-77, spl. asst. to dir., 1974-75, dep. asst. dir., 1976, spl. asst. for Strategic Arms Limitation Talks (SALT), 1976-77; dep. asst. sec. for regional progs., prog. analysis & evaluation US Dept. Def., Washington, 1977-80; vis. assoc. prof. Paul H. Nitze Sch. Advanced Internat. Studies, Johns Hopkins U., 1980-81, dean, prof internat. rels., 1994—2001; dir. policy planning staff US Dept. State, Washington, 1981-82, asst. sec. for East Asian & Pacific affairs, 1982-86, US amb. to Indonesia Jakarta, 1986-89; under sec. for policy US Dept. Def., Washington, 1989—93, dep. sec., 2001—05; pres. The World Bank Group, Washington, 2005—07; vis. scholar Am. Enterprise Inst., Washington, 2007—; chmn. Internat. Security Adv. Bd. US Dept. State, Washington, 2008—09. Chmn. US-Taiwan Bus. Coun., 2008—. Recipient Presdl. Citizens medal. Office: American Enterprise Institute 1150 Seventeenth St NW Washington DC 20036*

WOLFRAM, CHARLES WILLIAM, law educator; b. Cleve., Feb. 28, 1937; s. Carl P. and Dona M. (Minich) W.; m. Nancy Russell Bass, Dec. 18, 1965; children: Catherine Dana, Peter Russell. AB, Notre Dame U., 1959; LLB, U. Tex., 1962. Bar: D.C. 1962, Minn. 1974. Assoc. Covington & Burling, Washington, 1962-64; mem. FAA Contract Appeals Panel, Washington, 1964-65; asst. prof. law U. Minn., 1965-67, assoc. prof., 1967-70, prof., 1970-81; prof. law Cornell U., Ithaca, N.Y., 1982-84, Charles Frank Reavis Sr. prof. law, 1984-99, Charles Frank Reavis Sr. prof. emeritus, 1999—. Assoc. dean acad. affairs Cornell U., Ithaca, 1986-90, interim dean, 1998-99; vis. prof. U. So. Calif. Law Center, 1976-77. Author: (with J. Morris Clark) Professional Responsibilty: Issues for Minnesota Attorneys, 1976, Modern Legal Ethics, 1986;

contbr. chpts. to books, articles to profl. jours. Mem. Am. Law Inst. (chief reporter Restatement of Law Governing Lawyers, 1986- 2000), Order of Coif. Democrat. Office: 2887 College Ave #148 Berkeley CA 94705 Office Phone: 510-841-5542. E-mail: charlesw.wolfram@yahoo.com.

WOLFRAM, DAVID ANTHONY, information technology executive; s. Hans Gerhard (dec.) and Bettine Rosalind (Kauffmann) W. BSc with honors, U. Melbourne, 1984, MSc, 1986; PhD, Cambridge U., Eng., 1990, Oxford U., 1991; Exec. MBA, Australian Grad. Sch. Mgmt. U. NSW, 2003. Cert. european engr., chartered IT profl., PMP; chartered engr. Rsch. asst. U. Oxford, 1990; jr. rsch. fellow Christ Ch., Oxford, 1990-94, BT fellow, 1994; lectr. in computer sci. Australian Nat. U., Canberra, 1995-2000, vis. fellow Rsch. Sch. Info. Sci. and Engring., 2000; with Microsoft Corp., USA, Redmond, Wash., 2000—02; project mgr. Expert Info. Svc. (now Infosys Tech. Australia), Melbourne, 2003—07; sr. mgr. Infosys Tech., Australia, 2007—08, Accenture, 2008—. Program chair Computing: The Australasian Theory Symposium, 2000, mem. steering com., 2000—. Author: The Clausal Theory of Types, 1993 (reprinted 2009); contbr. articles to profl. jours.; guest editor: Electronic Notes in Theoretical Computer Science, Vol. 31, 2000; guest editor spl. issue Theoretical Computer Science, 2003. Mem. Trinity Coll., Cambridge, England, Christ Ch., Oxford, England. Recipient Commonwealth Postgraduate Rsch. award, Australian Govt., 1984—85; grantee Lockey Fund Travel Grant, U. Oxford, 1993; recipient, Rae & Edith Bennett Travelling Scholarship, U. Melbourne, 1988—90, Rouse Ball Fund Travel Grant, Trinity Coll., Cambridge, 1990. Fellow: Royal Soc. Arts, Brit. Computer Soc., Cambridge Philos. Soc. (life); mem.: IEEE (sr.), Project Mgmt. Inst. (bd. dirs. Melbourne chpt. 2006—09), Assn. Computing Machinery (sr.), London Math. Soc., Internat. Soc. for Philos. Enquiry (diplomate), Melbourne Cricket Club, Am. Australian Assn., Ordre du Tastevin (chevalier). Avocations: photography, tennis, chess. Office: Accenture Australia GPO Box 5176 Melbourne VIC 3001 Australia

WOLFRAM, DIETMAR, Information Scientist Educator; PhD, U. Western Ont., London, 1990. Prof. Sch. Info. Studies, U. Wis.-Milw., 1990—.

WOLFRAM, STEPHEN, physicist, computer company executive; b. London, Aug. 29, 1959; came to U.S., 1978; Degree, Eton Coll., 1976, Oxford U., 1978; PhD in Theoretical Physics, Calif. Inst. Tech., 1979. With Calif. Inst. Tech., Pasadena, 1979-82, Inst. for Advanced Study, Princeton, NJ, 1983-86; prof. physics, math, computer sci. U. Ill., Champaign, 1986-90; founder, dir. Ctr. for Complex Sys. Rsch., 1996—98; pres., CEO Wolfram Rsch. Inc., Champaign, 1987—. Author: Theory and Applications of Cellular Automata, 1986, Mathematica: A System for Doing Mathematics by Computer, 1998, 2d edit., 1991, Mathematica Reference Guide, 1992, Mathematica: The Student Book, 1994, The Mathematica Book, 3rd edit., 1996, 5th edit., 2003, Cellular Automata and Complexity, 1994, A New Kind of Science, 2002; editor jour. Complex Systems, 1986— Fellow MacArthur Found., 1981; recipient World Leadrers of Tomorrow award, World Economic Forum, 1999; named Scientist of Yr., R&D Mag., 2002. Office: Wolfram Rsch Inc 100 Trade Centre Dr Champaign IL 61820-7237 Business E-Mail: s.wolfram@wolfram.com.

WOLFRAM, THOMAS, physicist, educator; b. St. Louis, July 27, 1936; s. Ferdinand I. and Audrey H. (Calvert) W.; m. Eleanor Elaine Burger, May 22, 1965; children: Michael, Gregory, Melanie, Susan, Steven. BA, U. Calif., Riverside, 1959, PhD in Physics, 1963; MA in Physics, UCLA, 1960. Engr. Atomics Internat., Canoga Park, Calif., 1960-63; mem. tech. staff N.Am. Aviation Corp. Sci. Ctr., Thousand Oaks, Calif., 1963-68; group leader in solid state physics Rockwell Internat. Sci. Ctr., Thousand Oaks, 1968-72, dir. div. physics and chemistry, 1972-74; prof. physics, chmn. dept. physics and astronomy U. Mo., Columbia, 1974-83; dir. phys. tech. divsn. AMOCO Corp., 1983-87; v.p., gen. mgr. AMOCO Laser Co., 1987-95; bus. cons., 1995—. Cons. in field. Author: The Venture, The Dragon Tamers, Electronic and Optical Properties of d-Band Perovskites; editor: Inelastic Electron Tunneling Spectroscopy, 1978; contbr. articles to profl. jours. Recipient Disting. Prof. award Argonne Univs. Assn., 1977 Fellow: Am. Phys. Soc. Home and Office: 228 Trafalgar Ln San Clemente CA 92672 Personal E-mail: ewolfram@cox.net. *Crisis is the catalyst for constructive change.*

WOLFSON, AARON HOWARD, radiation oncologist, educator; b. Nashville, May 13, 1955; s. Sorrell Louis and Jacqueline Adele (Falis) W.; m. Adrienne Sue Mates, Dec. 16, 1979; children: Alexis Ellyn, Andrew Lane. BA, U. Fla., 1978, MD, 1982. Diplomate Am. Bd. Radiology. Intern internal medicine Jackson Meml. Hosp., Miami, Fla., 1982—83; staff physician Pub. Health Svc., Miami, 1983—85; pvt. practice Palm Beach Gardens, Fla., 1985—86; resident in radiation oncology Med. Coll. Va., Richmond, 1986—89; from instr. to assoc. prof. radiation oncology U. Miami, Miller Sch. Medicine, 1989—2003, prof., 2003—, vice chair dept. radiation oncology, 2005—. Co-dir. Gynecology Site dis. group Sylvester Cancer Ctr., 2001—. Contbr. articles to profl. jours. Bd. dirs. Children's Home Soc., Ft. Lauderdale, Fla., 1993—, Temple Beth Israel, Sunrise, Fla., 1994—; mem. spkrs. bur. U. Miami, 1993—; vol. spkr. Broward County Schs., 1990—; exec. v.p. Temple Beth Israel, 1996-98, pres., 1998-99. Sylvester Cancer Ctr. grantee, 1992. Mem. Gynecologic Oncology Group (bd. dir. 2007-), Radiation Therapy Oncology Group, Am. Soc. Therapeutic Radiology and Oncology. Jewish. Achievements include research on malignant tumors of the female genital tract; patent for radiation implant for gynecologic cancer. Office: Univ Miami 1475 NW 12th Ave # D-31 Miami FL 33136-1002 Home Phone: 954-370-8038; Office Phone: 305-243-4210. Business E-Mail: awolfson@med.miami.edu.

WOLFSON, HOWARD L., corporate communications specialist, political analyst; b. Middletown, NY, 1967; m. Terri McCullough; 1 child, Sarah. BA, U. Chgo., 1989; MA in Am. History, Duke U., 1991. Reporter local politics northern Va. newspaper; chief of staff and press sec. US Rep. Nita M. Lowey, 1993; comm. dir., spokeperson Charles Shumer campaign for US Senate, 1998; comm. dir. Hillary Rodham Clinton campaign for US Senate, 1999—2000, 2005—06; campaign dir. NYC Comptroller Bill Thompson, US Rep. Kirsten Gillibrand, US Rep. Michael Arcuri; ptnr. The Glover Park Group, NYC. Commentator Meet the Press, This Week with George Stephanopoulis, Larry King Live, Hardball with Chris Matthews, The Inside Hall. Exec. dir. Dem. Congl. Campaign Com., 2001—02. Named to 35 Under 35, NY Mag., 50 Under 42, Details mag., 40 Under 40, Crain's NY, 2005. Democrat. Office: The Glover Park Group 121 E 24th St 10th Fl New York NY 10010 Office Phone: 646-495-2700. Office Fax: 646-495-2710.*

WOLFSON, JAY, medical educator, consultant, lawyer; b. Chgo., July 13, 1952; s. Max Joseph and Ida (Kolender) W.; m. Maxine Loren Coplan, May 4, 1988; children: Alan H., Marc J., Joel L. AB, U. Ill., 1973; MA, NYU, 1974; MPH, Ind. U., 1975; DPH, U. Tex., 1981; JD, Stetson Coll., 1993. Asst. prof. health adminstrn. Sch. Pub. Health U. S.C., Columbia, 1978-80; assoc. prof. health adminstrn. Coll. of Pub. Health U. Okla., Oklahoma City, 1981-84; v.p. Health Cost Mgmt., Inc., Tampa, Fla., 1984—; assoc. prof. healthcare, fin. & poicy Coll. Pub. Health, U. South Fla., Tampa, 1991-95; prof. health law and fin. U. South Fla. Coll. Pub. Health, Tampa, 1995—; prof. medicine U. South Fla., Tampa, 1997—, chmn. dept. pub. health policy and mgmt. Coll. Pub. Health, dir. Fla. Pub. Health Info. Ctr., 1991—; trustee Tampa Gen. Hosp., 1988—99; prof. medicine Fla. State U., 2003, disting. svc. prof. pub. health and medicine, 2005; assoc. v.p. health law, policy and safety USP Health, 2005—. Co-dir. Stetson-U. South Fla. Ctr. for Law and Medicine, 2000—; spl. guardian ad litem for Theresa Marie Schiavo, 2002-04; dir. Fla. Pub. Health Info. Ctr., 1990—; vis. prof. Tokyo U. Coll. Medicine, 1985; sr. fin. cons. Fla. Office Pub. Counsel, Tallahassee, 1986—; cons. Fla. Dept. Ins., Tallahassee, 1987—, Fla. Dept. Health and Rehab. Svcs., Tallahassee, 1987—, Dun & Bradstreet Co., N.Y.C., 1987—; mem. medicare competitive pricing review com., 1998-2004; gen. counsel Am. Bd. Healthcare Risk Mgmt., 1994—. Author: Managing Employee Health Benefits, 1985; contbr. articles to profl. jours. Trustee Hillsborough County Hosp. Authority, Tampa, 1988-1999, Fla. Health Scis. Ctr., Inc., 1998-1999; pres. Kids Health Care Found., Inc., 1997—. Marcus and Teresa Levi scholar NYU, 1974; W.K. Kellogg Found. fellow, 1983; Sr. Fulbright scholar to Japan, 1985, Faculty scholar US Ctr Disease Control and Prevention, 1998-1999. Mem. Am. Pub. Health Assn., Health Care Fin. Mgmt. Assn., Am. Coll. Healthcare Execs. Jewish. Avocation: writing. Office: U South Fla Coll Pub Health 13301 N 30th St Tampa FL 33612-3807 E-mail: jwolfson@hsc.usf.edu.

WOLFSON, MARLA R., medical educator; m. Fred H Wolfson, May 5, 1974. PhD, Temple U. Sch. Medicine, Phila., 1985. Cert. in phys. therapy Pa., 1975. Assoc. prof. Temple U. Sch. Medicine, 1997—2007, prof. physiology, medicine & pediat., 2008—. Cons., Phila. Contbr. scientific papers to profl. jours. Home and Office: Temple Univ Sch Medicine 3420 N Broad St Philadelphia PA 19140 Office Fax: 215-707-4003. Business E-Mail: marla.wolfson@temple.edu.

WOLFSON, MICHAEL GEORGE, retired lawyer; b. Chgo., Sept. 1, 1938; s. A. Lincoln M. Weingarten and Brina (Nelson) W.; m. Rita Sue Parsont, Sept. 11, 1966; children: Bethany Lynne, Sara Wynne, Deborah Kay. Student, MIT, 1956-58; BA, U. Chgo., 1961, JD, 1964, postdoctoral, 1964-65. Bar: Ill. 1964, N.Y. 1969. Assoc. Cravath, Swaine & Moore, NYC, 1965-71, Brown, Wood, Fuller, Caldwell & Ivey, NYC, 1971-73; ptnr. Sidley Austin LLP, NYC, 1974—2002, sr. counsel, 2003—06, ret., 2006. Mediator, specializing in comml. and internat. disputes. Woodrow Wilson fellow, 1961; Ford Found. fellow in internat. trade and devel., 1965. Fellow Am. Bar Found. (life); mem. ABA. Avocations: reading, photography, fly fishing, bicycling. Home Phone: 212-517-7759; Office Phone: 212-839-5321. Business E-Mail: mwolfson@sidley.com.

WOLFSON, OURI, computer scientist; b. Bucharest, Romania, Mar. 18, 1951; came to U.S., 1975; s. Munish and Paula (Simon) W.; children: Daniel, Maya, Natalie. BA, Tel Aviv U., 1976; PhD, NYU, 1984. From software specialist to project leader Am. Broadcasting Co., 1979-81; tech. staff AT&T Bell Labs., 1981-85; asst. prof. computer sci. The Technion, Israel, 1985-90; rsch. scientist Columbia U., NYC, 1989-91; assoc. prof. U. Ill., Chgo., 1991—. Cons. in field. Grantee NSF, USAF, Hughes Aircraft Co., NATO, others, 1988—. Avocations: skiing, tennis, reading, movies, classical music. Home: 781 Highland Pl Highland Park IL 60035-4844 Office Phone: 312-996-6770. Business E-Mail: wolfson@uic.edu.

WOLFSON, SARAH ELIZABETH, singer, educator, physical education educator; BM, Juilliard Sch., NYC, 1999, MM, 2001. Cert. yoga tchr. Yoga Alliance, 2008. Adj. prof. Columbia U., NYC, 2007—. Singer: Concert Artists Guild Competition (1st Place, 2007), (chamber music) Love Past Cure - Monteverdi, Despina, Cosi fan tutte, Bacchis, La belle Hélène, Micaela, La tragédie de Carmen, Am. Symphony Orch., (chautauqua chamber music) Recital - Brazil Guitar Duo, (opera north) Poppea, L'incoronazione di Poppea, Cin. Chamber Orch., Ravinia Festival, Brevard Music Festival, (apprentice) Santa Fe Opera, (young artist) Fla. Grand Opera, Wolf Trap Opera, (performer) Rubin Mus. Himalayan Art, numerous operas and festivals. Mem. Sing for Hope, NYC, 2006—; fundraiser Bent on Learning, NYC, 2006. Recipient 1St Place, Vocal Arts Soc. Discovery Series, 2004, William Schuman award, Juillard Sch., 2001; Lucrezia Bori grant, 1998—99.

WOLFSON, WARREN D., dean, law educator, former judge; BA in Journalism, U. Ill., Chgo., 1955; JD, U. Ill., Urbana-Champaign, 1957. Pvt. practice atty.; judge Cir. Ct. of Cook County, Ill., 1975—2006, Ill. Appellate Ct. (1st. dist.), 1994; interim dean DePaul U. Coll. Law, Chgo., 2009—. Adj. prof. U. Chgo.; instr. and lectr. IIT Chgo.-Kent Coll. Law, 1971—. Co-author: Materials in Trial Advocacy: Problems and Cases, 2007, Trial Evidence, 2009. Recipient Ill. Pub. Defender Assn. Award of Meritorious Svc., 1989, Chgo. Coun. Lawyers Commitment to Justice Award, 1993, Disting. Svc. Award, Nat. Inst. Trial Advocacy, 1999, Recognition for Dedication and Commitment to Legal Edn., Chgo.-Kent Coll. Law, 2003, Lifetime Achievement Award for Excellence in Advocacy, Stetson Coll. Law, 2009. Office: DePaul U Coll Law 25 E Jackson Bldv Chicago IL 60604 Office Phone: 312-362-8701.*

WOLGEMUTH, RICHARD LEE, pharmaceutical executive; b. Lebanon, Pa., June 29, 1945; s. Clyde Hess and Mary Grace (Longenecker) W.; m. Cheryl Ann Hamman, May 1968; children: Richard Brent, Erryl Clyde, Christina Jo, Travis Grant. BSc in Biology and Chemistry, Ashland Coll., Ohio, 1968; MS in Gastrointestinal Physiology, Ohio State U., PhD in Gastrointestinal Physiology, 1975. Jr. pharmacologist Warren Teed Pharms., Columbus, Ohio, 1969-75; scientist I Rohm & Haas Co., Phila., 1975-77; sr. rsch. scientist Adria Labs., Columbus, Ohio, 1977-83, mgr. pharms. and med. chems., 1984-85, dir., project coord., 1985-87, dir. regulatory affairs, 1987-92; group dir. to v.p. global regulatory affairs GlaxoSmithKline, 1992—2003; sr. v.p. global regulatory scis. Bristol-Myers Squibb, 2003—. Cons. Nat. Inst. Occupl. Safety and Health, Cin., 1975-77. Author: Drug Design & Delivery, 1990; contbr. articles to Jour. Med. Chemistry, Jour. Organic Chemistry, Biochemical Medicine. Pres. Kimberly Woods Assn., Plain City, Ohio, 1987; co-chmn. Johnathan Alder Tax Levy Com., Plain City, 1982; bd. trustees Plain City Libr., 1985. Mem. Am. Soc. Cancer Chemotherapy, NY Acad. Scis., Soc. Exptl. Biology and Medicine, Regulatory Affairs Profl. Soc. Republican. Mem. Ch. of the Brethren. Achievements include patents for Anthracycline anti-cancer antibiotics, anti-convulsants, diagnostics; methods for treating kidney stones. Office: Bristol Myers Squibb 345 Park Ave New York NY 10154-0037

WOLIN, NEAL STEVEN, federal agency administrator; b. Chgo., Dec. 9, 1961; m. Nicole Elkon; children: Ethan, Oliver. BA summa cum laude in Hist., Yale U., 1983; MS in Devel. Economics, U. Oxford, Eng., 1985; JD, Yale U., 1988. Bar: Ill. 1989, DC 1989, Conn. 2002, US Supreme Ct. 1995. Law clk. to Eugene H. Nickerson US Dist. Ct. (ea. dist.) NY, Bklyn., 1988-89; adj. asst. prof. law Bklyn. Law Sch., 1989; assoc. Wilmer, Cutler & Pickering, Washington, 1989-90; spl. asst. to dir. ctrl. intelligence CIA, 1990-93; dep. legal adv. NSC The White House, 1993-94, exec. asst. to the nat. security adv., 1994-95; dep. gen. counsel US Dept. Treasury, 1995-99, gen. counsel, 1999-2001; exec. v.p., gen. counsel Hartford Fin. Svcs. Grp., Inc., 2001—07, pres., COO property-casualty ops., 2007—09; dep. asst. to Pres. Barack Obama & dep. counsel for econ. policy The White House, Washington, 2009; dep. sec. US Dept. Treasury, Washington, 2009—. Vis. fellow Brookings Instn., Washington, 2001; adj. lectr. in pub. policy JFK Sch. Govt., Harvard U., 2001; bd. dir. Coun. Foreign Relations, appeased mem. Bd. overseers RAND Corp. Inst. Civil Justice; mem. bd. regents U. Hartford; mem. Presdl. Adv. Commn. on Holocaust Assets in US, 1999—2000. Recipient Alexander Hamilton award, Sec. Treasury, 2001; named one of 100 People to Watch, Washingtonian mag., 1999; Charles and Julia Henry Fellow, Henry Trust, Oxford U., 1983—84, Coker Tchg. Fellow, Yale Law Sch., 1987—88. Mem.: Coun. Fgn. Rels., Phi Beta Kappa. Office: US Dept Treasury 1500 Pennsylvania Ave NW Rm 3000 Washington DC 20220 Business E-Mail: neal.wolin@do.treas.gov.

WOLIN, ROBERT EVERETT, lawyer; BA, Lafayette Coll., 1969; JD, NYU, 1973. Bar: NY 1974, Pa. 1979, Tex. 1983, US Dist. Ct. (so. NY, ea. Pa., No. Tex. dist.). Law clk. Judge James A. Coolahan, US Dist. Ct. N.J., 1973—75; adminstrv. ptnr. & mem. mgmt. com. Kirkpatrick & Lockhart Nicholson Graham LLP, Dallas. Mem.: ABA, N.Y. State Bar Assn., Tex. Bar Assn., Dallas Bar Assn., Phi Beta Kappa. Office: Kirkpatrick & Lockhart Nicholson Graham LLP Suite 1800 2828 N Harwood St Dallas TX 75201-6966 Office Phone: 214-939-4909. Office Fax: 214-939-4949. Business E-Mail: rwolin@klng.com.

WOLINSKY, EMANUEL, internist, educator; b. NYC, Sept. 23, 1917; s. Jacob and Bertha (Siegel) W.; m. Marjorie Claster, Nov. 15, 1946; children: Douglas, Peter. BA, Cornell U., 1938, MD, 1941. Diplomate Am. Bd. Med. Microbiology. Intern, resident medicine N.Y. Hosp., 1943-45; bacteriologist Trudeau Lab., Saranac Lake, NY, 1947-56; mem. faculty Case Western Res. U. Sch. Medicine, 1956-98, prof. medicine, 1968-88, prof. pathology, 1981-88, prof. emeritus, 1988-98, ret., 1998. Dir. microbiology Cleve. Met. Gen. Hosp., 1959-91, acting dir. dept. pathology, 1980-86, chief div. infectious diseases, 1961-83. Co-editor Textbook of Pulmonary Diseases, 5th edit., 1993; Asso. editor: Am. Rev. Respiratory Diseases, 1973-79; Contbr. articles to profl. jours., textbooks. Mem. Tb panel U.S.-Japan Co-op. Med. Sci. Program, 1969-75. Recipient Crystal Cross award Ohio Thoracic Soc., 1995, Louis Weinstein award Clin. Infectious Diseases, 1995, Maurice Saltzman award Mt. Sinai Healthcare Found., 1999; named to Med. Hall of Fame, Cleve. Mag., 1998. Mem. Am. Soc. Microbiology (Gardner Middlebrook award 1998), Am. Thoracic Soc. (Trudeau medal 1986), Infectious Diseases Soc. Am. (Soc. Citation award, 2004), Phi Beta Kappa, Alpha Omega Alpha. Home: 24761 S Woodland Rd Cleveland OH 44122-3327

WOLINTZ, ARTHUR HARRY, neurologist, ophthalmologist; b. Bklyn., May 30, 1937; s. Louis and Celia (Ragofsky) W.; m. Carol Sue Bergstein, Nov. 28, 1963; children: Robyn Joy, Ellen Sharon. Student, NYU, 1955-58; MD summa cum laude, SUNY, Bklyn., 1962; postgrad., Columbia U., 1967-68. Diplomate Am. Bd. Psychiatry and Neurology, Am. Bd. Ophthalmology; licensee Nat. Bd. Med. Examiners, U. State of N.Y. Intern Maimonides Hosp., Bklyn., 1962-63, jr. resident in medicine, 1963-64; resident Nat. Inst. Neurol. Diseases and Blindness, Bethesda, Md., 1964-66; chief resident Mt. Sinai Hosp., NYC, 1966-67; clin. asst. prof. neurology Downstate Med. Ctr. SUNY, Bklyn., 1968-69, resident in ophthalmology, 1969-71, from asst. prof. to prof., 1971—, prof. clin. ophthalmology and clin. neurology, 1977—, interim chief ophthalmology, 1983, acting regional chmn. dept. ophthalmology, 1984, prof. ophthalmology, 1987—, chmn. dept. ophthalmology, 1987-96; Disting. tchg. prof., chair emeritus dept. ophthalmology SUNY-Health Sci. Ctr. Bklyn., 1995, 96—; asst. neurologist Presbyn. Hosp., NYC, 1967-68; instr. neuropathology Coll. Physicians and Surgeons Columbia U., NYC, 1967-68; instr. neurology Mt. Sinai Sch. Medicine, NYC, 1967-68; assoc. dir. neurology Maimonides Med. Ctr., Bklyn., 1968-69; asst. neurologist Coney Island Hosp., Bklyn., 1968-69. Vis. neurologist Kings County Hosp. Ctr., Bklyn, 1968-69; chief divsn. ophthalmology and neuro-ophthalmology Kingsbrook Jewish Med. Ctr., Bklyn., 1971, sec. med. and dental staff 1976-77, v.p. 1978-79, pres. 1980-81, dir. ophthalmology 1981; attending physician State Univ. Hosp., Bklyn., 1971, Kings County Hosp. Ctr., Bklyn., 1971; cons. Luth. Med. Ctr., Beth Israel Med. Ctr., Brookdale Hosp. Med. Ctr., Bklyn., L.I. Coll. Hosp., Bklyn., Maimonides Med. Ctr., Cath. Med. Ctr. Bklyn. and Queens, Bklyn. VA Hosp. Author: Essentials of Clinical Neuro-Ophthalmology, 1976; contbr. chpts. to sci. textbooks and handbooks, articles to profl. jours. Pres. Flatbush Jewish Ctr., Bklyn. With USPHS 1964-66. Recipient J. Eugene Chalfin Meml. Lectr. award Alumni Assn. State Univ.-Kings County, 1981, Tchr. of Yr. award dept. ophthalmology Interfaith Med. Ctr., 1988, Greats in Ophthalmology in Bklyn. award SUNY Downstate Med. Ctr. Dept. Ophthalmology, 2004, Alumni Svc. award SUNY Downstate Med. Ctr. Coll. Medicine, 2007. Fellow ACP, ACS, Am. Acad. Ophthalmology and Otolaryngology, Am. Acad. Neurology; mem. AMA, AAAS, Med. Soc. County Kings, Med. Soc. State N.Y., Bklyn. Ophthal. Soc., N.Y. Acad. Medicine, Am. Acad. Neurology, Alumni Assn. SUNY (pres.-elect 1989, pres. 1990-91, Richard C. Troutman M.D. Master Tchr. award in ophthalmology 1987, Disting. Alumni Achievement award 1997, Frank L. Babbott M.D. Meml. award 2002, Clarence and Mary Dennis Dedicated Svc. award 2004, Kingbrook Pres.'s award 2004), Oddfellows, Alpha Omega Alpha. Avocations: Torah reader, cantor. Home and Office: 100 Ocean Pky Apt 4H Brooklyn NY 11218-1755 Office Phone: 718-854-7360. Personal E-mail: ahwolintz@aol.com.

WOLITZER, PHILIP, accountant, educator; b. Podkamien, Poland, Dec. 14, 1920; came to US, 1928, naturalized, 1928; BBA cum laude, CCNY, 1941; MBA with honors, NYU, 1961; cert. CPA, NY. m. Regina Wurm, Nov. 21, 1942; children: Diana, Peggy, Steven. Fin. and bus. cons., Bklyn., 1946—; prof. LI U., Bklyn., 1947—, chmn. dept. acctg., taxation, and law, 1964-82, dir. acad. div. Sch. Bus., 1980-82; dir. Bus. Game, 1970-82, Venture Capital Game, 1973-82, Friendship Dairies Inc., 6HW Capital Corp.; cons. NY State Edn. Dept., 1988—. Chmn., United Hosp. Fund, Leukemia Fund, Greater NY Fund, United Jewish Appeal Drives; mem. Regents External Degree Program, NY State, 1972—; mem. exec. com. Parents Assn. of Pub. Sch., 206, 1951-64, Sheepshead Bay HS, 1962-69; treas.-guardian Benevolent Assn., 1947-83; bd. dirs. Jewish Ctr. Nachlath Zion, 1970—, v.p., 1973-76. Served with AUS, 1943-46. Editor: Bus. Game Manual, 1970-83, Venture Capital Game Manual, 1973-83, Course Handbook for Analysis of Financial Statements, 1968—; co-author Ethics and the CPA, 1999; contbr. articles to profl. jours. Recipient Alumni Assn. award LI U., 1982; named one of Outstanding Young Men of Am. Outstanding Discussion Leader Found. for Acctg. Edn., 1988-89. Mem. AICPA, AAUP (vice chmn. 1969-71), Am. Acctg. Assn., Am. Econ. Assn., Accts. Club Am. (bd. govs. 1970—, v.p. 1981-84, pres. 1984-86), NY State Soc. CPAs (com. chmn. 1960-86, dir., 1967-73, 81-84, exec. com. 1970-73, sec. 1970-72, v.p. 1973-74, dir. tech. svcs. 1983-86, Outstanding CPA Educator award 1985, Disting. Svc. award 1990, Hall of Fame 2004-), Common Cause, Beta Gamma Sigma, Accountas Club America (Lifetime Profl. Achievement award 2007-, Chancellors award 2008-) KP.

Democrat. Home: 2348 E 21st St Brooklyn NY 11229-4802 Office: LI U University Plz Brooklyn NY 11201 Office Phone: 718-488-1152. Business E-Mail: pwolitzer@nysscpa.org.

WOLK, MICHAEL JAY, cardiologist, educator; b. NYC, Nov. 21, 1938; BA, Colgate U., Hamilton, NY, 1960; MD, Columbia U. Coll. Physicians & Surgeons, 1964. Diplomate Am. Bd. Internal Medicine, 1971, Am. Bd. Cardiovascular Disease, 1973. Intern, internal medicine SUNY Downstate Med. Ctr., Bklyn., 1964-65, resident, internal medicine, 1965-67, chief resident, 1966—67; resident cardiology New Eng. Med. Ctr., Boston, 1967-69; fellow cardiology Cornell U. Med. Ctr., NYC, 1969-70; mem. staff NY Hosp., 1969—; assoc. clin. prof. Weill Med. Coll., Cornell U., 1969—98, clin. prof. medicine, 1998—; pvt. practice NYC, 1969—. Contbr. several articles to profl. jours. Named a Med. Honoree, 12th Ann. Heart of the Hamptons Gala, 2008. Fellow: ACP, Am. Coll. Cardiology (past pres., exec. com., chair, budget, fin. and investment com.). Office: 425 E 61st St New York NY 10065 also: Michael Wolk Md 425 E 61st St Fl 6 New York NY 10065-8795 Office Phone: 212-752-2000.

WOLK, SCOTT JOSEPH, astrophysicist; b. Cleve., May 23, 1966; s. Alan M. and Phyllis G. Wolk; m. Nancy Ruth Adams, June 15, 1997; children: Sylvia, Leah. PhD, Stony Brook, NY, 1996. Astrophysicist Smithsonian Astrophys. Obs., Cambridge, Mass., 1996—. Mem.: Am. Astron. Soc. Office: Smithsonian Astrophys Obs 60 Garden St Cambridge MA 01730

WOLKEN, MATTHEW J., mechanical engineer, educator; BSME, U. Calif., Irvine, 1997. Engr. Masimo, Irvine, 1997—99; design engr. Sensorex, Garden Grove, Calif., 1999—2003; instr. ITT Tech. Inst., Henderson, Calif., 2003—08, Anaheim, Calif., 2003—08, Irvine Valley Coll., 2006—. Co-owner NVDMapping, Anaheim, 2007—08. Office: Irvine Valley Coll 5500 Irvine Center Dr Irvine CA 92618 Business E-Mail: mwolken@ivc.edu.

WOLKOFF, EUGENE ARNOLD, lawyer; b. NYC, June 9, 1932; s. Oscar and Jean (Zablow) W.; m. Judith Gail Edwards, Oct. 15, 1967; children: Mandy, Elana, Alexa, Justine. AB, Bklyn. Coll., 1953; LLB, St. John's U., 1961. Bar: NY 1962, N.Mex. 1994. Practiced in, NYC and Santa Fe; mem. Callahan & Wolkoff, NYC, 1965—; gen. counsel BGK Group of Cos. Served to lt. col. USAFR, 1953-75. Mem. ABA, NY State Bar Assn., N.Mex. Bar Assn., Pi Beta Gamma. Office: 330 Garfield St Santa Fe NM 87501-2640 also: 88 Pine St 21st Fl New York NY 10005 Office Phone: 505-992-5100. Business E-Mail: gene@bgkgroup.com.

WOLKOFF, NEAL LAWRENCE, stock exchange executive; b. 1955; s. Martin and Evelyn Wolkoff; m. Janet Lynn Armuth, May 30, 1983; 3 children. BA, Columbia U., 1977; JD, Boston U., 1980. Bar: NY, US Dist. Ct. (so. dist.) NY. Trial atty. Divsn. Enforcement Commodity Futures Trading Commn.; atty. NY Mercantile Exch., Inc., NYC, 1981—93, exec. v.p., 1993—2002, acting pres., 2000—01, exec. v.p., COO, 2002—03; cons. Am. Stock Exchange LLC, acting CEO, 2005, chmn., CEO, 2005—08; CEO ELX Electronic Liquidity Exch., 2009—. Guest lectr. Columbia U. Sch. Internat. and Pub. Affairs; spkr. in field.

WOLKOV, HARVEY BRIAN, oncologist, researcher; b. Cleve., Feb. 8, 1953; s. Sidney and Norma Wolkov; m. Lauren Cronin, Jan. 9, 1993; 1 child, Nicole. BSc, Purdue U., West Lafayette, Ind., 1975, MSc, 1977; MD, Med. Coll. Ohio, Toledo, 1979. Diplomate Am. Bd. Radiology. Intern U. Calif., San Francisco, 1979-80; resident Stanford Med. Ctr., Calif., 1980-83, chief resident, 1982; rsch. asst. Stanford U., 1982; from asst. clin. prof. to assoc. clin. prof. U. Calif., Davis, 1983-97, assoc. clin. prof., 1997—; med. dir. Mercy Hosps., Sacramento, 1987-90, Sutter Cancer Ctr. Dept. Radiation Oncology, Sacramento, 1990—. Mem. adv. bd. Nat. Graves Disease Found., Jacksonville, Fla., 1993—; dir. Sutter Gamma Knife Ctr., 1997—; co-prin. investigator radiation oncology Children's Oncology Group, 2001—. Author (with others): (book) Intraoperative Radiation, 1989, Frontiers in Radiation, 1991, Textbook Radiation Oncology, 2004; contbr. articles to profl. jours. Bd. dirs. Sutter Hosps. Found., Sacramento. Mem.: Calif. Radiol. Soc. (exec. com. 2001—), Sutter Inst. Med. Rsch. (chair rsch. com. 1996—, hosp. chair oncology com. 2003—, neuroscience inst. leadership com. 2003—), Calif. Radiation Oncology Soc. (pres.-elect 1999, pres. 2000—01), Am. Soc. Therapeutic Radiology and Oncology (bd. dirs. 2000—03, vice chair outcome rsch., fin. com., corp. rels., workforce, comm., coronary artery radiation therapy coms., Internat. Travel award 1987, inaugural fellow 2006), Radiation Therapy Oncology Group (com. chair 1986—90, publ. com. 1990—, mem. com. 1990—, lung and brain com. 1990—), No. Calif. Radiation Oncology Soc. (pres. 1999—2001), Coun. Affiliated Radiation Oncology Soc. (pres. 1999—2000), Assn. Residents Radiation Oncology (exec. com. 1997—2000, advisor emeritus 2000—, faculty advisor 1997—2000), Am. Cancer Soc. (reviewer 1990—, fellow 1978, 1983), Am. Coll. Radiology (chmn. stds. accreditation com. 1997—2003, councilor at large 1999, alt. councilor 2000—03, councillor 2003—, mem. expert panels, credentials com., fellow 1997). Avocations: painting, sculpture, travel, cello. Office: Sutter Cancer Ctr 2800 L St Ste 10 Sacramento CA 95816-5616 Personal E-mail: hbwolkov@comcast.net. Business E-Mail: wolkovh@radiological.com.

WOLL, HARRY J., electrical engineer; b. Farmington, Minn., Aug. 25, 1920; s. Henry L. and Clara M. (Fredrickson) W.; m. Mary V. Cowan, Feb. 15, 1947; children: Daniel, Alice. BSE.E., N.D. State U., 1940; postgrad., Ill. Inst. Tech., 1940-41; PhD, U. Pa., 1953. With RCA Corp., 1941-85, chief engr. aerospace systems div. Burlington, Mass., 1963-69, div. v.p. govt. engring. Moorestown, NJ, 1969-75; div. v.p., gen. mgr. RCA Automated Systems, Burlington, 1975-81; staff v.p., chief engr. RCA Electronic Products and Labs., Princeton, NJ, 1981-85. Patentee in field. Chmn. bd. trustees Moore Sch. Elec. Engring., U. Pa. 1976-90; trustee U. Pa., 1989-91. Recipient 50th Anniversary gold medal Moore Sch. Elec. Engring., U. Pa., 1973 Fellow AAAS, IEEE (past chmn. Phila. sect., past chmn. fellow com.), Aerospace Industries Tech. Council (past chmn.); mem. KC, Sigma Phi Delta, Phi Kappa Phi, Madison West Rotary Club. Roman Catholic. Home Phone: 608-230-3725. Personal E-mail: hjwoll@cs.com.

WOLLAM, JEAN FARR, retired diplomat; b. Holyoke, Mass., Oct. 5, 1917; d. Howard George and Nettie Hillman Farr; m. Park Fields Wollam, July 7, 1982 (dec.). Sec. pvt. industry, Holyoke, 1935—40; civil servant US Govt., Washington, 1941—46; passport clk. US Consulate, Berlin and Frankfurt, Germany, 1946—49; econ. asst. US Embassy, Bogota, Colombia, 1949—51, US Consulate, Monterrey, Mexico, 1952—54; adminstrv. asst. US Dept. State L.Am. Affairs, Washington, 1954—58; pers. officer US Embassy, Saigon, Vietnam, 1958—59, Phnom Penh, Cambodia, 1959—61, Beirut, 1964—66, Athens, Greece, 1966—70, Lagos, Nigeria, 1971—73, Rome, 1973—76; placement officer Dept. State, Washington, 1961—64. Mem.: Gen. Soc. Mayflower Descs. Episcopalian. Avocations: bridge, writing. Home: 201 Grand Ave Carlsbad CA 92008 Personal E-mail: jfwollam@roadrunner.com.

WOLLE, CHARLES ROBERT, judge; b. Sioux City, Iowa, Oct. 16, 1935; s. William Carl and Vivian (Down) W.; m. Kerstin Birgitta Wennerstrom, June 26, 1961; children: Karl Johan Knut, Erik Vernon, Thomas Dag, Aaron Charles. AB, Harvard U., 1959; JD, Iowa Law Sch., 1961. Bar: Iowa 1961. Assoc. Shull, Marshall & Marks, Sioux City, 1961-67, ptnr., 1968-80; judge Dist. Ct. Iowa, Sioux City, 1981-83; justice Iowa Supreme Ct., Sioux City and Des Moines, 1983-87; judge U.S. Dist. Ct. (so. dist.) Iowa, Des Moines, 1987-92, chief judge, 1992-99, sr. U.S. dist. judge, 2001—. Faculty Nat. Jud. Coll., Reno, 1983-2004 Editor Iowa Law Rev., 1960-61. V.p. bd. dirs. Sioux City Symphony, 1972-77; bd. dirs. Morningside Coll., Sioux City, 1977-81. Fellow Am. Coll. Trial Lawyers; mem. Sioux City C. of C. (bd. dirs. 1977-78); Iowa State Bar Assn. Avocations: sports, art, music, literature, skiing. Office: Sr US Dist Judge US Dist Ct SD IA 110 E Ct St Des Moines IA 50309 Business E-Mail: charles_wolle@iasd.uscourts.gov.

WOLLENBERG, BRUCE FREDERICK, electrical engineering educator, consultant; b. Buffalo, June 14, 1942; s. Henry William and Louise Viola (Swanson) W.; m. Ruth Elsie Kunz, June 5, 1965; children: Anne Louise, Allen Louis, Amy Lynn, Aaron Lee BEE, Rensselaer Poly. Inst., 1964, M Engring., 1966; PhD, U. Pa., 1974. Sr. engr. Leeds & Northrup Co., North Wales, Pa., 1966—74, Power Techs. Inc., Schenectady, 1974—84; prin. cons. Control Data Corp., Plymouth, Minn., 1984—89; prof. elec. engring. U. Minn., Mpls., 1989—, dir. grad. studies, dir. Ctr. for Electric Energy. Adj. prof. Rensselaer Poly. Inst., Troy, N.Y., 1979-84; cons. Empros Systems Internat., Plymouth, 1989—, No. States Power Co., Mpls., 1990—, Energy Control Cons., Fairfax, Va., 1990—; cons. on electric utility engring Author: Power Generation Operation and Control, 1984, 1996; also articles Chmn. bd. dirs. Loudonville (N.Y.) Christian Sch., 1978-83; chmn. Colonie (N.Y.) Zoning Bd., 1979-84; bd. dirs. Minn. Youth Symphony, Mpls., 1985-87 Recipient Tech. Excellence award, Control Data Corp., 1987; named Outstanding Tchg. Prof., HKN, 2002—03. Fellow IEEE (Power Engring. Soc., Third Millenium medal 2000, Outstanding Power Engring. Educator award 2002); mem. Nat. Acad. Engring., U. Minn. Acad. Disting. Prof., Tau Beta Pi, Eta Kappa Nu, Sigma Xi. Republican. Avocation: collecting records and cds. Home: 5100 Prescott Dr Minnetonka MN 55345-4847 Office: Univ of Minn Elec Engring Dept 200 Union St SE Minneapolis MN 55455-0154 Home Phone: 952-933-7456; Office Phone: 612-626-7192. E-mail: wollenbe@umn.edu.

WOLLER, JAMES ALAN, lawyer; b. Adrian, Mich., Dec. 27, 1946; s. Robert Arthur and Florence Emma (Jacob) W.; m. Jill Ann Samis, Aug. 18, 1968 (div. Aug. 1978); 1 child, Emily Erin; m. Elizabeth Julia Frey, May 22, 1982 (div. Apr. 1999); m. Carol Pierini, Oct. 29, 1999. BA, U. Mich., 1969; JD, Columbia U., 1974. Bar: N.J. 1974, U.S. Dist. Ct. N.J. 1974, U.S. Tax Ct. 1976, U.S. Supreme Ct. 1995. Assoc. McCarter & English, Newark, 1974-79; v.p. Pfaltz & Woller, PA, Summit, NJ, 1979-86, pres., 1987—. Editor Columbia U. Human Rights Law Rev., 1973-74; author New Jersey Real Property Statutes Annotated Deskbook, 2007. Mem.: ABA, Perth Amboy Libr. Bd. Trustees, Summit Bar Assn. (pres. 1987—88), Union County Bar Assn., NJ Bar Assn., Columbia Law Sch. Assn. NJ (trustee 1992—97, v.p. 1997—2001, pres. 2001—03), Raritan Yacht Club (Perth Amboy, NJ) (commodore 1994—95, fin. sec. 1988—89, treas. 1989—92, 2006—), Downtown Assn. (trustee 1997—99, treas. 1999, v.p. 2000, pres. 2001). Republican. Episcopalian. Avocations: sailing, skiing. Home: 187 High St Perth Amboy NJ 08861 Office: Pfaltz & Woller PA 382 Springfield Ave Ste 217 Summit NJ 07901-2780 Home Phone: 732-324-8460; Office Phone: 908-273-1974. Personal E-mail: jimwoller@aol.com.

WOLLERT, GERALD DALE, retired food products executive, securities trader; b. LaPorte, Ind., Jan. 21, 1935; s. Delmar Everette and Esther Mae W.; m. Carol Jean Burchby, Jan. 26, 1957; children— Karen Lynn, Edwin Del. BS, Purdue U., 1957. With Gen. Foods Corp., 1959-89, dir. consumer affairs White Plains, N.Y., 1973-74, mng. dir. Cottee Foods div. Sydney, Australia, 1974-76, gen. mgr. Mexico div. Mexico City, 1978-79, pres. Asia/Pacific ops. Honolulu; corp. v.p. worldwide coffee and internat. div. Kraft Gen. Foods Corp., Honolulu, 1979—89; ret., 1989; pres. GDW Investment Systems LLC, 2004—. Dir. Gen. Foods cos., Japan, Peoples Republic China, Korea, India, Taiwan, Singapore, Philippines. Webelos leader Boy Scouts Am., Mexico City, 1978-79; co. gen. chmn. United Fund campaign, Battle Creek, Mich., 1964-65, White Plains, N.Y., 1972-73. Served with U.S. Army, 1958. Mem. Asian-U.S. Bus. Coun., Oahu Country Club (Hawaii), Venice Golf and Country Club (Fla.), Legacy Hills (Ind.) Club.

WOLLMAN, GLENN DAVID, physician, medical guide; b. Brooklyn, Ny, June 24, 1946; s. Leonard and June. MD, U. Miami, Coral Gables, 1972. Med. dir. integrative medicine program St. Francis Med. Ctr., Santa Barbara, Calif., 1998—2002; chief med. officer EmCare, Santa Barbara, Calif., 1999—2003; prof. Santa Barbara Coll. of Oriental Medicine, Santa Barbara, Calif., 2003—. Cmty. lectr. Santa Barbara City Coll., Santa Barbara, Calif., 1998. Fellow: Am. Coll. Emergency Physicians (life); mem.: St Ynez Valley Cottage Hosp. (hon.), Lompoc Healthcare Dist. (hon.), Cottage Hosp. Med. Staff (hon.). Achievements include Medical Guide (a new field in medicine), hospital based integrative medicine program. Avocations: meditation, music, painting, martial arts. Home and Office: Living Suite 1543 Portesuello Ave Santa Barbara CA 93105 Office Fax: 805-687-3070. Personal E-mail: gdwed@aol.com.

WOLLMAN, NATHANIEL, retired economics professor; b. Phila., May 15, 1915; s. Leon and Rose (Schimmel) Wollman; m. Lenora Levin, Dec. 25, 1939 (dec. Dec. 1994); children: Stephen, Eric. AB, Pa. State U., 1936; PhD, Princeton U., 1940; LLD, Colo. Coll., 1972. From instr. to asst. prof. Colo. Coll., 1939-48; from assoc. prof. to prof. econs. U. N.Mex., 1948-81, prof. emeritus, 1981—, chmn. dept. econs., 1960-69, dean Coll. Arts and Scis., 1969-81. Economist Resources for Future, 1959—60, 1964—65; chmn. Internat. Environ. Programs Com., 1976—79. Author (with others): Water Supply and Demand, 1960, Value of Water in Alternative Uses, 1962, Water Resources of Chile, 1968, Man, Materials and Environment, 1973, The Outlook for Water Revisited, 2000, Water Resources Update, 2000; author: (with Gilbert Bonem) The Outlook for Water: Quality, Quantity and National Growth, 1971. With USNR, WWII. Mem.: Am. Econs. Assn. Home: 25 Delcliffe Ln Lewiston ME 04240

WOLLMAN, ROGER LELAND, federal judge; b. Frankfort, SD, May 29, 1934; s. Edwin and Katherine Wollman; m. Diane Marie Schroeder, June 21, 1959; children: Steven James, John Mark, Thomas Roger. BA, Tabor Coll., Hillsboro, Kans., 1957; JD magna cum laude, U. S.D., 1962; LLM, Harvard U., 1964. Bar: S.D. 1964. Law clerk Hon. George T. Mickleson US Dist. Ct (So. Dist, SC), 1962—63; sole practice Aberdeen, 1964—71; states atty. Brown County, Aberdeen, 1967—71; justice S.D. Supreme Ct., 1971—85, chief justice, 1978—82; judge US Ct. Appeals (8th cir.), 1985—, chief judge, 1999—2002. Mem. Jud. Conference of US, 1999—2002. With US Army, 1957—59. Mem.: Am. Jud. Soc. Office: US Ct Appeals US Courthouse & Fed Bldg 400 S Phillips Ave Rm 315 Sioux Falls SD 57104-6851*

WOLMAN, JONATHAN PALEY, newspaper editor, journalist; b. Madison, Wis., Aug. 1, 1950; s. Joseph Martin and Anne (Paley) W.; m. Deborah Eve Lamm, Sept. 24, 1978; children: Jacob, Emma, Sophia. BA, U. Wis., 1972. Reporter AP, Detroit, 1973-74, Madison, 1973, news editor Mich. news, 1975, Urban Affairs Team Washington, 1976-77, news editor Wash. (D.C.) news, 1978-80, news editor, 1980-84, asst. bur. chief Washington (D.C.) Divsn., 1984-88, bur. chief Washington, 1989-98, mng. editor New York, 1998-2000, exec. editor, 2000—02, sr. v.p., 2002—04; editl. page editor The Denver Post, 2004—07; editor, pub. The Detroit News, 2007—; bd. drs. U. Wis. Sch. Journalism & Mass Communication. Bd. drs. UNN Wis. Sch. Journalism & Mass Comm. Mem. Am. Soc. Newspaper Editors, 1994—, Detroit Econ. Club (bd. mem., 2009-). Office: The Detroit News 615 W Lafayette Blvd Detroit MI 48226 Home Phone: 313-222-2300; Office Phone: 313-222-2110. Business E-Mail: jon.wolman@detnews.com.

WOLMAN, M. GORDON, geography educator; b. Balt., Aug. 16, 1924; s. Abel and Anna (Gordon) W.; m. Elaine Mielke, June 20, 1951; children: Elsa Anne, Abel Gordon, Abby Lucille, Fredericka Jeannette. Student, Haverford Coll.; AB in Geology, Johns Hopkins U., 1949; MA in Geology, Harvard U., 1951, PhD in Geology, 1953. Geologist U.S. Geol. Survey, 1951-58, part-time, 1958—; assoc. prof. geography Johns Hopkins U., Balt., 1958-62, B. Howell Griswold, Jr. prof., geography and internat. affairs, 1962—. Prof. Johns Hopkins U., 1962—, chmn. dept. geography and environ. engring., 1958—90, interim provost, 1987, 90, prof. environ. health sci., 1998—; adv. com. geography U.S. Office Naval Rsch., Oak Ridge Nat. Lab.; exec. com. divsn. earth sci. NRC; internat. environ. programs com., environ. studies bd., com. water, com. mineral resources and environ., chmn. nat. commn. water quality policy NAS; chmn. NRC Com. Adv. U.S. Geol. Survey; chmn. NAS Commn. Geoscis., Environment and Resources, NRC Bd. Sustainability, 1995—2000; chmn. study land use and populationNRC Tri-Acad., China, India; environ. adv. com. Savannah River Tech. ctr.; chmn. U.S. Com. for IIASA, 1999—2003; chmn. adv. com. mgmt. and protection of water resources State. of Md., 2004—08. Author: Fluvial Processes in Geomorphology, 1964; editl. bd.: Science mag. Pres. bd. trustees Park Sch., Balt.; pres. bd. dirs. Sinai Hosp., Balt., Resources for Future, 1980-87; adv. com. Inst. Nuc. Power Ops., 1982-85; active Balt. City Charter Revision Commn., Cmty. Action Com., Balt. With USNR, 1943-46. Recipient Meritorious Contbn. award Assn. Am. Geographers, 1972, Disting. Career award Geomorphology, 1993, D.L. Linton award Brit. Geomorphological Rsch. Group, 1994, Rachel Carson award Chesapeake Appreciation Inc., Ian Campbell medal Am. Geol. Inst., 1997, Nev. Med. Desert Rsch. Inst., Abel Wolman award Chesapeake sect. AWWA, 2003, Lifetime Achievement award Nat. Coun. for Sci. and the Environment, 2004, Outstanding Contbn. to Water Environment award Water Environment Fedn., 2004, Eisenhower medal Johns Hopkins U., 2005, Benjamin Franklin medal in Earth and Environ. Sci., Franklin Inst., 2006, Inaugural Kerk Bryan Lectr. award, Boston, 2007, Olivia Irvine Dodge Conservation award, Irvine Nature Ctr., 2008. Fellow Am. Acad. Arts and Scis., AAAS; mem. ASCE, NAS, NAE, Am. Geophys. Union (chmn. subcom. sedimentation, pres. hydrol. sect., Robert Horton medal 2000), Geol. Soc. Am. (v.p. 1983, pres. 1984, Penrose medal 1999), Am. Philos. Soc., Am. Geog. Soc. (councillor 1965-70, Cullum Geog. medal 1989), Washington Geol. Soc., Agrl. Hist. Soc., Md. Acad. Scis. (exec. com. 1970-75), Am. Geophysical Union, Phi Beta Kappa, Sigma Xi. Home: 2104 W Rogers Ave Baltimore MD 21209-4553 Office: Johns Hopkins U Dept Geography/Environ Engr Baltimore MD 21218 Home Phone: 410-664-2816; Office Phone: 410-516-7090. Business E-Mail: wolman@jhu.edu.

WOLMAN, MARTIN, lawyer; b. Albany, NY, Feb. 2, 1937; s. Benjamin S. and Sonya W.; children: Koren M. Wolman-Tardy, Barton T., William B., Brandon S. AB, Brown U., 1958; LLB, U. Calif., Berkeley, 1964. Bar: Calif., 1964, Conn., 1965. Atty. Conn. Bank & Trust Co., Hartford, 1964-67; assoc. Day Pitney (formerly Day, Berry & Howard), Hartford, 1967-72, ptnr., 1972—2007, of counsel, 2008—. Mem. Conn. Law Revision Commn., 1985-2002. Trustee Russell-Sage Coll., Troy, NY, 1990-96, Wadsworth Atheneum, 1994-2002, Lyme Acad. Coll. Fine Arts, 2003—, Chmn., 2008-; trustee Kingswood-Oxford Sch., West Hartford, Conn., 1980-93, chmn., 1986-89; bd. dirs. Hartford Hosp., 1991—2008, chmn., 2003-2007; bd. dirs. Inst. Living, 1994, Hartford Health Care Corp., 1996—; bd. govs. Hill-Stead Mus., Farmington, Conn., 1990-94. Lt. (j.g.) USN, 1958-61. Fellow Am. Coll. Trust and Estate Counsel (chmn. Conn. chpt. 1981-86); mem. Conn. Bar Assn. (chmn. exec. com. probate sect. 1979-82). Office: Day Pitney Blue Back Sq 75 Isham Rd Ste 300 West Hartford CT 06107-2237 Business E-Mail: mwolman@daypitney.com.

WOLMAN, WILLIAM, economist, journalist, broadcaster; b. Montreal, Que., Can. s. Nathan and Toba (Wexler) W.; m. Ann Livia Colamosca, Jan. 7, 1982; children: John, Flora. BA, McGill U., 1948; PhD, Stanford U., 1957. Asst. prof. econs. Wash. State U., Pullman, 1954-60; v.p. Citicorp, NYC, 1969-71, Argus Rsch. Corp., NYC, 1971-74; chief economist CNBC, Ft. Lee, N.J., 1989—; econs. editor Bus. Week, NYC, 1960-69, sr. editor, 1974-83, editor, 1984-89, exec. editor, 1983-84, chief economist, 1989—. Author: The Judas Economy: The Triumph of Capital and the Betrayal of Work, 1997, The Great 401K Hoax, 2002. Avocations: skiing, photography.

WOLNY, WITOLD PAUL, social studies educator, consultant; b. Chorzow, Upper Silesia, Poland, Jan. 12, 1962; s. Teodor and Krystyna Wolny. PhD in Philosophy, U. Seville, Spain; MD STD, U. Salamanca, Spain. Prof. religion and philosophy U. Coll. Cardenal Spinola, U. Seville, Spain, 1993—2002, head, human scis. divsn., 1995—96; dir. internat. office CEU Andalusia, Seville, 1996—2002; cons. internat. programs U. Va. Coll., Wise, Va., 1996—; assoc. prof. religion U. Va. Coll. Wise, 2006—. Bd. mem. Western Va. Internat. Educators, 2006—08. Office: Univ Va Wise 1 College Ave Wise VA 24293 Business E-Mail: ww4p@uvawise.edu.

WOLOCH, ISSER, history educator; b. NYC, 1937; m. Nancy S. Woloch; children: David, Alex. AB, Columbia Coll., 1959; PhD, Princeton U., 1965. From lectr. to asst. prof. history Ind. U., Bloomington, 1963-66; asst. prof. history UCLA, 1966-69; assoc. prof. history Columbia U., NYC, 1969-75, prof., 1975-98, Moore collegiate prof., 1998—2007, prof. emeritus, 2007—. Mem. adv. bd. Ctr. History of Freedom, 1995-99; mem. Inst. for Advanced Study, Princeton, 1973-74, 88; fellow NEH, 1980-81. Author: Jacobin Legacy, 1970, The French Veteran from the Revolution to the Restoration, 1979, Eighteenth-Century Europe, 1982, The New Regime, 1789-1820s, 1994 (Leo Gershoy award Am. Hist. Assn. 1995); editor: Revolution and the Meanings of Freedom in the Nineteenth Century, 1996, Napoleon and His Collaborators, 2001 (Literary award, Napoleonic Soc. of Am. 2002); mem. editl. bd. Jour. Modern History, 1992-94. Guggenheim fellow, 1981-82.

WOLOSHIN, DOUGLAS, lawyer; b. NYC, Feb. 19, 1948; BA in Acctg., Villanova U., Pa.; JD, Georgetown U. Law Ctr., Washington, 1973. Bar: DC 1973, US Dist. Ct. (DC), US Tax. Ct. Ptnr. Fisher Wayland Cooper Leader LLP, 1986—2000, Shaw Pittman LLP, Washington, 2000—01, Duane Morris LLP, 2001—, mng. ptnr. Washington office, mem. ptnrs. bd., head Project Fin. Practice Group (Singapore). Bd. dirs. Vienna Baseball Found., Inc., Va. Mem.: ABA, DC Bar Assn. Office: Duane Morris LLP 505 9th St NW Ste 1000 Washington DC 20004 also: 5 Shenton Way 10 01 UIC Bldg Singapore 068808 Office Phone: 202-776-7831. Fax: 202-403-3913. Business E-Mail: DWoloshin@duanemorris.com.*

WOLOSOFF, BRUCE GERMONT, composer; adopted s. Alvin B. and s. Jeanette Germont Wolosoff; m. Margaret Julia Garrett, Sept. 16, 1989; children: Juliet Garrett, Katya Garrett. BA, Bard Coll., Annandale-on-Hudson, NY, 1977; MusM, New Eng. Conservatory, Boston, 1980. Vis. artist Hayground Sch., Bridgehampton, NY, 2004—. Composer: (string quartet) Songs without Words (18 divertimenti for string quartet), (chamber opera) Madimi, (orchestral work) Sinfonia, (ballet) The Passions. Mem.: ASCAP. Home: PO Box 392 Shelter Island Heights NY 11965 Business E-Mail: bwolosoff@yahoo.com.

WOLPE, HOWARD ELIOT, former Congressman, political scientist; b. LA, Nov. 2, 1939; s. Leon Zacharias and Zelda Harriet (Shapiro) W.; c. Michael Stevenson, Robert Hollister, Todd Hollister, Jerry Hollister. BA, Reed Coll., 1960; PhD, MIT, 1967. Cons. Peace Corps, 1966-67, Fgn. Service Inst., Dept. State, 1967-72; assoc. prof. polit. sci. Western Mich. U., Kalamazoo, 1967-72; mem. Kalamazoo City Commn., 1969-72, Mich. State Legislature, 1973-76; regional rep. of US Senator Donald Riegle of Mich., 1977-78; mem. US Congress from 3d Dist. Mich., 1979—93; spl. envoy of Pres. Clinton to Great Lakes region of Africa; dir. Africa Program & Project on Leadership & Building State Capacity Woodrow Wilson Ctr., Washington. Dem. candidate for Gov. of Mich., 1994; mem. House sci., space and tech. com., chmn. subcom. on investigations and oversight, mem. fgn. affairs com., Africa subcom.; chmn. Dem. Caucus Task Force on Environment and Energy, Africa subcom.; prof. Inst. Public Policy Studies Univ. Mich.; vis fellow Brookings Inst; Public Policy Scholar Woodrow Wilson Ctr. Author: Urban Politics in Nigeria: A Study of Port Harcourt, 1974, (with Robert Melson) Nigeria: Modernization and the Politics of Communalism, 1974, numerous articles in profl. jours. Recipient Star Crystal award for excellence, African-Am. Inst., Legislator of the Yr. award, Mich. Audubon Soc., Lifetime Achievement award, Sierra Club. Mem.: Council on Fgn. Rels., Nat. Endowment for Democracy (bd. mem.), Africare. Democrat. Office: Woodrow Wilson Ctr 1 Woodrow Wilson Plz 1300 Pennsylvania Ave NW Washington DC 20004-3027 Office Phone: 202-691-4046. Business E-Mail: howard.wolpe@wilsoncenter.org.

WOLPER, DAVID LLOYD, motion picture and television executive; b. NYC, Jan. 11, 1928; s. Irving S. and Anna (Fass) W.; m. Margaret Dawn Richard, May 11, 1958 (div.); children: Mark, Michael, Leslie; m. Gloria Diane Hill, July 11, 1974. Student, Drake U., 1946, U. So. Calif., 1948. V.p., treas. Flamingo Films, TV sales co., 1948-50, v.p. West Coast Ops., 1954-58; chmn., pres. Wolper Prodns., LA, 1958—. Cons., exec. producer Warner Bros., Inc., 1976—. TV prodns. include Race for Space, Making of the President 1960, 64, Biography series, Story of... series, The Yanks are Coming, Berlin: Kaiser to Khrushchev, December 7: Day of Infamy, The American Woman in the 20th Century, Hollywood and The Stars, March of Time Specials, The Rise and Fall of the Third Reich, The Legend of Marilyn Monroe, Four Days in November, Krebiozen and Cancer, National Geographic, Undersea World of Jacques Cousteau, China: Roots of Madness, The Journey of Robert F. Kennedy, Say Goodbye, George Plimpton, Appointment With Destiny, American Heritage, Smithsonian, They've Killed President Lincoln, Sandburg's Lincoln, Primal Man, The First Woman President, Chico and the Man, Get Christie Love, Welcome Back, Kotter!, Collison Course, Roots, Victory at Entebbe, Roots: The Next Generations, Moviola, The Thorn Birds, North and South Books I, II, III, Napoleon and Josephine, Alex Haley's Queen, Men Of The Dragon, Unwed Father, The Morning After; feature films include The Hellstrom Chronicle, Devil's Brigade, The Bridge at Remagen, If It's Tuesday, This Must Be Belgium, Willy Wonka and The Chocolate Factory, Visions of Eight, This is Elvis, Murder in the First, Surviving Picasso, L.A. Confidential; live spl. events include Opening and Closing Ceremonies 1984 Olympic Games, Liberty Weekend July 3-6, 1986. Trustee L.A. County Mus. Art, Am. Film Inst., L.A. Thoracic and Cardiovascular Found., Boys and Girls Clubs Am., U.S. Golf Assn. Found.; bd. dirs. Amateur Athletic Assn. L.A., L.A. Heart Inst., Acad. TV Arts and Scis. Found., So. Calif. Com. for Olympic Games, U. So. Calif. Cinema/TV Dept.; bd. govs. Cedars Sinai Med. Ctr.; com. mem. U.S. Olympic Team Benefit; mem. adv. com. Nat. Ctr. Jewish Film. Recipient award for documentaries, San Francisco Internat. Film Festival, 1960, 7 Golden Globe awards, 5 George Foster Peabody awards, Disting. Svc. award, US Jr. C. of C., award, Monte Carlo Internat. Film Festival, 1964, Grand Prix for TV Programs, Cannes Film Festival, 1964, medal of Chevalier, French Nat. Legion of Honor, 1990, Disting. Svc. award, Nat. Assn. Broadcasters, 2007, David L. Wolper Student Documentary Achievement award named in his honor, Internat. Documentary Assn., David L. Wolper Ctr. for Study of Documentary named in his honor, U. So. Calif.; named to TV Hall of Fame, 1988. Mem.: NATAS (50 Emmy awards, 145 Emmy nominations), Caucus for Prodrs., Writers and Dirs., Prodrs. Guild Am. (David L. Wolper Prodr. of Yr. award named in his honor), Acad. Motion Picture Arts and Scis. (Oscar award, 11 Oscar nominations). Office: The David L Wolper Co Inc 617 N Rodeo Dr Beverly Hills CA 90210 Business E-Mail: thewolperletter@msn.com.

WOLPERT, ANN J., library director; BA, Boston U.; MLS, Simmons Coll., Boston. Libr. Boston Redevelopment Authority, 1967—76; with Arthur D. Little Inc., 1976—92, from tech. info. specialist, to mgr. Rsch. Libr., to dir. Cambridge Info. Ctr.; dir. Rsch. and Info. Svc. Harvard Bus. Sch., 1992—93, exec. dir. Libr. and Info. Svcs., 1993—95; dir. Mass. Inst. Tech. Librs., 1996—. Mem. Strategic Planning Com. Mass. Bd. Libr. Commr., 1992—; cons. U. N.Mex., Cornell U., Adelphi U., NYC, INCAE campuses, Costa Rica, Nicaragua, League European Rsch. Librs., Amsterdam, Nat. Libr. China, Malaysia U. Sci. and Tech.; spkr. in field; chmn. mgmt. bd. Mass. Inst. Tech. Press; bd. dirs. Tech. Rev., Inc. Mem. edtl. bd. Libr. and Info. Sci. Rsch., The Jour. Libr. Adminstrn., mem. adv. com. Sci. and Engring. Indicators; contbr. libr. papers to various publs.; reviewer Tech. Rev. Advisor Publ. Com. Mass. Med. Soc.; bd. dir. Boston Libr. Consortium; hon. bd. trustees Simmons Coll.; mem. bd. dirs. Boston Libr. Consortium, NIH's Pub. Access Working Group, Steering Coms. Coalition Networked Info., Digital Libr. Fedn.; mem. Nat. Network Women Leaders Higher Edn. Am. Coun. Edn., Dean's Com., Pres.'s Acad. Coun., OpenCourseWare Faculty. Named to Nat. Network for Women Leaders in Higher Edn., Am. Coun. Edn. Mem.: Info. Tech. Strategic Planning and Resources Coordinating Coun., Coun. Edtl. Tech., Com. Intellectual Property, Assn. Rsch. Libr. (past pres. 2004—05, v.p. to pres., mem. intellectual property and copyright com.). Office: Building 14S-216 MIT 77 Massachusetts Ave Cambridge MA 02139-4307 Office Phone: 617-253-5297. Office Fax: 617-253-8894. E-mail: awolpert@mit.edu.

WOLPERT RICHARD, CHAVA, artist; b. Frankfurt, Germany, Feb. 26, 1933; arrived in Palestine, 1934, arrived in U.S., 1958; d. Ludwig Y. and Else (Ahrens) Wolpert; m. Henry A. Richard, 1959 (dec. 1971). Student, Bezalel Acad. Arts and Design, Jerusalem, 1954—56. Artist-in-residence The Jewish Mus., NYC, 1958—88. Painter, designer/creator of contemporary style ceremonial Judaica such as candelabra, Passover sets, Torah ornaments, decorative Judaica in enamel, silver, other metals, glass, porcelain, wood, acrylics, fabrics and oil painting; represented in 11 mus. collections in U.S., Australia, Europe, Israel. Pvt. Israeli Army, 1951—53. Recipient 2 Merit awards Interfaith Forum on Religion, Art and Arch., 1980, 83, Jurors' Choice award Liturgical Art Guild, 1991, Best in Judaica award Liturgical Art Guild, 1997. Mem. Judaic Art Guild, Defunct As of Spring. Avocations: reflexology, healing with herbs. Office Phone: 718-896-4451.

WOLRAICH, MARK LEE, pediatrician, educator; BA, SUNY, Binghamton, 1966; MD, SUNY, Syracuse, 1970. Diplomate Am. Bd. Pediat. Pediatric intern SUNY, Syracuse, 1970-71; pediatric resident U. Okla. Health Scis. Ctr., Oklahoma City, 1973-74; pediatric fellowship U. Oreg. Health Scis. Ctr., 1974-76; asst. prof. U. Iowa, 1976-81, assoc. prof., 1981-86, prof., 1986-90, Vanderbilt U., 1990-2001, dir. divsn. child devel., dir. child devel. ctr., 1990-99, dir. ctr. for chronic illnesses and disabilities in children, 1990-2000; investigator J.F. Kennedy Ctr. for Rsch. on Edn. and Human Devel., 1990-2001; prof. pediat., dir. Child Study Ctr. Okla. U. Health Scis. Ctr., 2001—. Med. supr. U. Iowa Divsn. of Devel. Disabilities, 1980-90; vis. prof. Great Ormond St. Hosp. for Sick Children, London, 1983, U. Cape Town, Rondebosch Cape, South Africa, 1986, Columbus Children's Hosp., Ohio State U., Dept. Pediat., 1988; mem. Iowa State Foster Care Rev. Bd. Co-editor Advances in Developmental and Behavioral Pediatrics, 1981-92; cons. editor Am. Jour. on Mental Deficiency; editl. adv. bd. A Guide to Parent Counseling; editor The Classification of Child and Adolescent Mental Disorders in Primary Care-Diagnostic and Statistical Manual for Mental Disorders in Primary Care Child and Adolescent Version, 1996; cons. reviewer Developmental Medicine and Child Neurology, Pediatrics, Nutrition and Behavior, Jour. Pediatrics, Jour. of Social and Personal Relationships, Applied Rsch. in Mental Retardation, Jour. of Clin. Psychology, Jour. Developmental and Behavioral Pediatrics, Clin. Pediatrics, others; contbr. numerous articles to profl. publs. Recipient Disting. and Dedicated Svc. award Spina Bifida Assn. Iowa, 1979, Lou Holloway award Health Scis. Edn.; grantee NIMH, 1987-90, 98-2001, Nat. Inst. on Disability and Rehab. Rsch., 1987-89, NIH, 1988-91, Iowa Dept. Human Svcs., 1986-89, U. Iowa, 1979-87, United Cerebral Palsy Rsch. and Endl. Found., Inc., 1978-87, Iowa March of Dimes, 1980, Sugar Assn., Inc., 1983, Internat. Life Scis. Inst., 1988-91, W.T. Grant Found., 1989; MCH Lend grant, 1999—, CDC grant, 2002; named to Children and Adults with Attention-Deficit/Hyperactivity Disorder Hall of Fame, 2003. Fellow Am. Acad. Pediat. (com. 1992-2000, chair com. on psychosocial aspects child and family health 1997-2000, chair child and adolescent health action group 2000-04, chair-elect mgmt. com., 2004-, chmn. mgmt. com. 2006—), Am. Acad. Cerebral Palsy and Devel. Medicine; mem. Soc. for Devel. and Behavioral Pediat. (pres. 1994-95, program dir. 1990-93), Soc. Pediatric Psychology Assn. (assoc., Lee Salk award for disting. svc.), Soc. for Pediatric Rsch. (sr.), Am. Acad. on Comm. in Healthcare (charter), Am. Pediatric Soc., Ctr. Diseases Control & Prevention (mem. bd. sci. counsellors). Office: Okla U Health Scis Ctr 1100 NE 13th St Oklahoma City OK 73117

WOLSKI, VICTOR J., federal judge, lawyer; m. Lisa Wolski. BA in Hist., U. Pa., 1984, BS in Econs., 1984; JD, U. Va., 1991. Bar: Calif., DC, Oreg., Wash., US Ct. Fed. Claims, US Ct. Appeals, 9th & Fed. circuit, US Supreme Ct. Asst. to sec. USDA, 1988; asst. to gen. counsel US Dept. Energy; law clerk US Dist. Ct. (northern dist. Calif.), 1991—92; atty. Pacific Legal Found., 1992—97; tax counsel to Senator Connie Mack US Senate, Washington, 1997—2000; gen. counsel & chief tax adviser Joint Econ. Com., US Congress, 1999—2000; atty. Cooper & Kirk, Washington, 2000—03; judge US Ct. Fed. Claims, Washington, 2003—. Office: US Ct Fed Claims 717 Madison Pl NW Washington DC 20005 Home Phone: 703-920-8740.*

WOLSKY, JACK, retired art educator; b. Rochester, NY, Aug. 5, 1930; s. Benjamin and Mary Wolsky; m. Gladys Mindlin Wolsky, Dec. 20, 1953; children: Bonnie, Sharon, Marsha. AS, Rochester Inst. Tech., 1951; BS, SUNY, Buffalo, 1955, MS, 1957. Prof. art SUNY, Brockport, NY, 1959—85, prof. emeritus, 1985—; ret., 1985. Mem. adv. bd. Jewish Cultural Arts Commn., Rochester, NY, Modern Arts Adv. Evaluation Com., Rochester and Monroe County, NY, Rochester Inst. Tech. Alumni Assn. Exec. Coun.; juror Western Gateway project N.Y. State Dept. Transp.; juror Monroe County-Greater Rochester Internat. Airport Competition, 2001—. Represented in permanent collections Meml. Art Gallery, Rochester, Munson-Williams-Proctor Inst., Utica, N.Y., State Univ. Coll. at Brockport, New Britain (Conn.) Mus. Am. Art, Rochester Inst. Tech. Adviser, vol. Rochester chpt. ARC, 1993—; bd. dirs. Temple B'rith Kodesh, Rochester, Friends of Sch. of Arts, Rochester. Recipient Kosciuszko Found. award, 1963, Juror's award, Rochester Finger Lakes Show, 1962, Harry Hoffman Meml. award, Albright Art Gallery, 1964, Rochester C. of C. Civic award in culture and arts, 1999, Chancellor's award for excellence in tchg., SUNY, 1979, SUNY Faculty Rsch. fellowship, 1968, 1970, 1973, Visual Arts award, Arts and Cultural Coun. Greater Rochester, 2002, Lillian Fairchild award, U. Rochester, Faculty Exch. scholarship, SUNY. Avocations: tennis, gardening. Home: 80 St Paul St Apt 3B Rochester NY 14604 Personal E-mail: gwolsky823@aol.com.

WOLSON, CRAIG ALAN, lawyer; b. Toledo, Feb. 20, 1949; s. Max A. and Elaine B. (Cohn) Wolson; m. Ellen Carol Schulgasser, Oct. 26, 1986; children: Lindsey, Michael, Geoffrey. BA, U. Mich., 1971, JD, 1974. Bar: NY 1975, US Dist. Ct. (so. and ea. dists.) NY 1975, US Ct. Appeals (2d cir.) 1975, US Supreme Ct. 1978. Assoc. Shearman & Sterling, NYC, 1974—81; v.p., asst. gen. counsel Thomson McKinnon Securities Inc., NYC, 1981—85; v.p., sec., gen. counsel J.D. Mattus Co., Inc., Greenwich, Conn., 1985—88; also bd. dirs. J.D. Mattus Co., Inc. and affiliated cos., Greenwich, Conn.; v.p., asst. gen. counsel Chem. Bank, NYC, 1988—95; of counsel Williams & Harris, NYC, 1995-96; ptnr. Williams & Harris LLP, NYC, 1996-97; counsel Brown & Wood L.L.P., NYC, 1997-98, Mayer, Brown & Platt, NYC, 1999-2001; spl. counsel Schulte Roth & Zabel LLP, NYC, 2001—03; ptnr. Duane Morris, LLP, NYC, 2003—06; spl. counsel Cadwalader, Wickersham & Taft LLP, Charlotte, NC, 2006—08; expert witness & cons. structured fin. & derivatives, 2008—. Dep. clk. Lucas County Courthouse, Toledo, 1968-69, 71-72 Articles and administrv. editor U. Mich. Law Rev., 1973-74. Named a NY Super Lawyer, Law and Politics, 2006. Mem.: ABA, Assn. of Bar of City of N.Y. (securities regulation com. 1994—97, corp. law com. 1997—2000, project fin. com. 2000—03, corp. law com. 2003—05, chmn. 2004—08, mem. structured fin. com. 2008—), N.Y. State Bar Assn., Pi Sigma Alpha, Phi Eta Sigma, Phi Beta Kappa. Avocations: reading, theater. Home: 29 Punch Bowl Dr Westport CT 06880-2130 Home Phone: 203-222-8687; Office Phone: 203-858-4804. Personal E-mail: cwolson01@aol.com.

WOLTER, JOHN AMADEUS, librarian, federal official; b. St. Paul, July 25, 1925; s. Amadeus Frank and Marjorie (Wears) W.; m. Joan Patricia Venard, July 6, 1956; children: Mark, Thomas, Matthew, David. Student, Coll. of St. Thomas, 1950; BA, U. Minn., 1956, MA, 1965, PhD, 1975; postgrad., Georgetown U., 1957. Officer, seaman Isthmian Lines Inc., NYC, 1943-50, 57-60; marine transp. officer Mil. Sea Transp. Ser., Washington, 1956-57; instr., map libr. U. Minn., 1961-64, asst. to dir. univ. librs., 1964-65, research fellow, 1965-66; asst. prof. Wis. State U., River Falls, 1966-68; asst. chief geography and map. div. Libr. of Congress, Washington, 1968-78, chief, 1978-91, acting dir. pub. svc. and collections MGMT I, 1989-90; cons. in geography, 1991-93. Mem. U.S. Bd. Geog. Names, 1969-83, vice chmn., 1980-81, chmn., 1981-83. Editor: Progress of Discovery: Johann Georg Kohl, 1993, Images of the World: The Atlas Through History, 1996, The Napoleonic War in the Dutch East Indies. The Minto Collection: Essay and Bibliography, 1999; rev. editor cartography divsn. Surveying and Mapping, 1971-72; mem. editl. bd. Cartographica, 1971-80, Am. Cartographer, 1974-79, Terrae Incognitae, 1973-75, ACSM Bull., 1974-80, Surveying and Mapping, 1972-80; editl. advisor The Portolan, 1986—; contbg. editor Imago Mundi, 1979-91; contbr. articles to profl. jours. Served with U.S. Army, 1950-56. Libr. of Congress Disting. Svc. award, 1992, Smithsonian Inst. Cert. of award, 1986. Mem. Internat. Geog. Union (U.S. nat. com. 1972-80, 84-88), Internat. Cartographic Assn. (U.S. mem. commn. on history of cartography 1972-76, corr. 1976-92, Assn. Am. Geographers (editorial bd. Annals 1988-92), Spl. Librs. Assn. (sec.-treas. geog.and map div. 1965), Soc. History Discoveries (sec.-treas. 1972-75, coun. 1976-78, v.p. 1983-85, pres. 1985-87), Am. Congress Surveying and Mapping (chmn. publs. com. 1978-80, Presdl. citation 1985), N.Am. Soc. Oceanic History, Soc. for History of Discoveries, Washington Map Soc., Soc. Nautical Rsch., U.S. Naval Hist. Found., Philip Lee Phillips Soc. (bd. dirs. ex officio), DAV, Am. Mcht. Marine Vets., Theta Delta Chi. Home: 901 Moonstone Cir Salisbury MD 21804 Home Phone: 410-860-2675. Personal E-mail: jawjo@comcast.net.

WOLTERS, CURT CORNELIS FREDERIK, economic consultant, retired foreign service officer; b. Nymegen, The Netherlands, Mar. 13, 1938; came to U.S., 1957; s. Frederik and Cornelia Johanna (Jansen) W.; m. Sara J. Daughters, June 10, 1962 (div. 1980); children: Gwyneth, Chad; m. Charlotte Cooper, Sept. 22, 1980 (div. 1988); children: Lottena, Cicely; m. Sylvana K. Perry, Apr. 1989 (div. 2003); 1 child, Roger, m. Salome Kebede, Apr. 29, 2004; 1 child, Mariam. Student, Wash. State U., 1958-61, U. Bonn, Fed. Republic Germany, 1962-63; BA, U. Oreg., 1964, MA, 1966; MBA, U. Washington, 1976; PhD, Pacific Western U., 1989. Asst. sec. Rep. Botswana Govt., Gaborone, 1966-68; program advisor The Ford Found., NYC, 1968-74; sr. rsch. analyst & economist Seattle C. of C., 1974—76; sr. assoc. Inst. Pub. Adminstrn. N.Y., NYC, 1976-78; freelance economist Africa, 1978-79; supv. program officer, economist, diplomat (AID) Dept. State, Washington, 1979—2002; sr. mem Raven Assocs. LLC; mgr. & owner CWEDAS LLC; chief economist Lummi Indian Bus. Coun., 2003—07, sr. economic advisor., 2008—. Cons. Inst. for Puget Sound Needs, Seattle, 1975-76, Pacific Cons., Washington, 1976; chair Am. Cmty. Assoc., U.S. Embassy, Lusaka, Zambia, 1998—2001. Contbr. numerous articles to profl. jours. publs.; author project evaluations. Mem. civic action com. Congress of Racial Equality, Eugene, Oreg., 1965-66; vol. campaign Dixie Lee Ray Gubernatorial Campaign, Seattle, 1976; sch. bd. treas., chmn. fin. com. Internat. Sch. Islamabad, 1989-93. Carnegie Found. fellow, 1964-65, Africa-Asia pub. svc. fellow Maxwell Sch., 1966-68, DAAD fellow German Govt., U. Bonn, 1962-63; recipient Air Def. Command Outstanding Achievement award USAF, 1960,Meritorious Svc. award, 1992-93, Superior Svc. award, US Embassy, Islamabad, 93-94, Meml. Order of Tin Hats, Kabaw Valley Shellhole chpt. Lusaka, Zambia, 1997—2001. Mem. Am. Econ. Assn., Air Force Assn., Wilson Ctr. (assoc. of Smithsonian Instn.), Am. Fgn. Svc. Assn., Holland Am. Club (treas. Greater Seattle area 1975-76), Am. Legion., wash. Coun. Econ. Edn.(bd. mem., 2005-), Wash. Consular Assoc. 2005-, Civil Air Patrol(sr. officer), Bellingham Composite Squadron, Vets. Fgn. Wars. Office: Raven Assocs LLC PO Box 28113 Bellingham WA 98228

WOLTERS, PAUL JOHN, medical educator; b. St. Paul, July 31, 1964; s. Paul J. Wolters and Amy J. Schnert; life ptnr. Paul Wolters; children: Lauren A., Rachel M. MD, U. Minn., Mpls., 1992. Asst. prof. medicine UCSF, San Francisco, 1995—2007, assoc. prof. medicine, 2008—. Contbr. articles to profl. jours. Rsch. grant, NIH, 2000—09. Mem.: Am. Thoracic Soc. Achievements include research in response of mast cells to severe bacterial infections. Office: UCSF HSE Rm 201 box 0111 San Francisco CA 94143

WOLTERS, RAYMOND, historian, educator; b. Kansas City, Mo., July 25, 1938; s. Raymond M. and Margaret G. (Reilly) W.; m. Mary McCullough, June 23, 1962; children: Jeffrey, Kevin, Thomas. BA, Stanford U., 1960; MA, U. Calif.-Berkeley, 1962, PhD, 1967. Instr. dept. history U. Del., Newark, 1965-67, asst. prof., 1967-70, assoc. prof., 1970-75, prof., 1975-96, Thomas Muncy Keith prof., 1996—. Mem. editl. adv. bd. Acad. Am. Ency.; author: The New Negro on Campus, 1975, The Burden of Brown, 1984, Right Turn, 1996, Du Bois and His Rivals, 2002, (book) Race and Education, 2008. Fellow NEH, 1971-72, Am. Coun. Learned Socs., 1978-79, Earhart Found., 1989-90; recipient Silver Gavel award ABA. Mem. Am. Hist. Assn., Orgn. Am. Historians, So. Hist. Assn. Home: 20 Bridlebrook Ln Newark DE 19711-2061 Office: U Del History Dept Newark DE 19716 Home Phone: 302-731-4181; Office Phone: 302-831-2378. Business E-Mail: wolters@udel.edu.

WOLTZ, HOWARD OSLER, JR., retired metal products executive; b. Mt. Airy, NC, Apr. 2, 1925; s. Howard Osler and Louise (Elliott) W.; m. Joan Elizabeth Moore, Dec. 29, 1949 (dec., June 14, 2007); children: Louise, Joan Woltz Robins, Howard O. III, Edwin Moore. LLB, U. Va., 1948. Bar: N.C., 1948. Ptnr. law firm, Mt. Airy, 1948-54; pres., founder Dixie Concrete Products, Inc., Mt. Airy, 1953-69; founder Dixie Exposaic, Inc., Mt. Airy, 1963; pres., chmn. bd. Insteel Industries (formerly Exposaic Industries, Inc.), Mt. Airy, 1969-89, chmn., CEO, 1989-91, non-exec. chmn., 2005—; ret., 2005. Mem. N.C. Ho. of Reps., 1951-53; chmn. Mt. Airy-Surry County Airport Authority, 1987-93; former pres. Greater Mt. Airy United Fund. Mem. Nat. Concrete Masonry Assn. (pres. 1965), N.C. Concrete Masonry Assn. (pres. 1959), Wire Reinforcement Inst. (chmn. 1982), Am. Wire Producers Assn. (bd. dirs. 1987-91), N.C. State Bar Assn., Mt. Airy C. of C. (Citizen of Yr. 1991). Rotary (past pres. Mt. Airy). Republican. Home: 3103 Summit Hills Mount Airy NC 27030 E-mail: howardwoltz@embarqmail.com.

WOLVEN, ANN REED, literature and language professor, journalist; b. Washington, May 12, 1959; d. William Thomas III and Winifred Vycital Reed; m. Gregory Allen Wolven, Nov. 6, 1982; children: Christopher James, Katherine Erienne. BA in English, Mary Baldwin Coll., Staunton, Va., 1981; MS in Journalism, Northwestern U., Evanston, Ill., 1982; M in Secondary English Edn., Lynchburg Coll., Va., 1989. Gen. assignment reporter The Potomac News, Md., 1978—80; corr. Lerner Newspapers, Washington, 1982; gen. assignment reporter Amherst-Nelson Pub. Coll., Va., 1983—86; journalism educator Lynchburg Coll., Va., 1986—89; English educator Mecklenburg County Pub. Schs., Skipwith, Va., 1992—97; English/Reading/ESL educator Vincennes U., Ind., 1998—2001; English educator Lincoln Trail Coll., Robinson, Ill., 2001—. Freelance journalist, Vincennes, 1992—. Mem. Lincoln HS Athletic Assn., Vincennes, 1993—2006; girl scout leader Shagbark Girl Scout Coun., Vincennes, 1998—2001; leader Jr. Achievement, Vincennes, 1999—2000; pres. Riley Elem. PTO, Vincennes, 2000—01; seedling grants chair Clark Academic Boosters, Vincennes, 2000—05, pres., 2004—05; mem. Lincoln HS Football Parents, Vincennes, 2003—06, Lincoln HS Volleyball Parents, Vincennes, 2004—06, Lincoln HS Girls Basketball Parents, Vincennes, 2005—06. Recipient Gen. Assignment Reporting award, Va. Press Assn., 1984, 1985, First Pl. Yearbook, Am. Scholastic Press Assn., 1995, 1996, 1997; grantee, Eisenhower Profl. Devel. Program, 2000—01. Mem.: IEA, NEA, NCTE, MLA, Tri-State U. Football Assn., Tri-State U. Parents Assn. Achievements include design of online composition and analysis course; online introduction to literature course; online English literature since 1800 course. Avocations: fossil hunting, gardening, reading, computers, travel. Home: 1403 Old Orchard Rd Vincennes IN 47591 Office: Lincoln Trail Coll 11220 State Hwy 1 Robinson IL 62454 Business E-Mail: wolvena@iecc.edu.

WOLYNES, PETER GUY, chemistry researcher, educator; b. Chgo., Apr. 21, 1953; s. Peter and Evelyn Eleanor (Etter) W.; m. Jane Lee Fox, Nov. 26, 1976 (div. 1980); m. Kathleen Cull Bucher, Dec. 22, 1984; children: Margrethe Cull, Eve Cordelia, Julia Jean. AB with highest distinction, Ind. U., 1971; AM, Harvard U., 1972, PhD in Chem. Physics, 1976; DSc (hon.), Ind. U., 1988. Rsch. assoc. MIT, Cambridge, 1975-76; asst. prof., assoc. prof. Harvard U., Cambridge, 1976-80; vis. scientist Max Planck Inst. für Biophysikalische Chemie, Gottingen, Fed. Republic Germany, 1977; assoc. prof. chemistry U. Ill., Urbana, 1980-83, prof. chemistry, 1983-2000, prof. physics, 1985-2000, prof. physics and biophysics, 1989-2000, mem. Ctr. for Advanced Study, 1989-2000; William H. and Janet LyCan prof. chemistry Ctr. for Advanced Study U. Ill., Urbana, 1993-96, Robert Eiszner prof., 1996-2000; prof. chemistry and biochemistry U. Calif., San Diego, 2000—, Francis H.C. Crick prof., 2001—, prof. physics, 2003—. Vis. prof. Inst. for Molecular Sci., Okazaki, Japan, 1982, 87; vis. scientist Inst. for Theoretical Physics, Santa Barbara, Calif., 1987, Ecole normale Supérieure, Paris, 1992; Merski lectr. U. Nebr., 1986; Denkewalter lectr. Loyola U., 1986; Hinshelwood lectr. Oxford U., 1997; Harkins lectr. U. Chgo., 1997; FMC lectr. Princeton U., 1998; Matsen lectr. U. Tex., 2002; Rice lectr. U. NC, 2005; lifson lectr. Weizmann Internat., 2009. Contbr. numerous articles to profl. jours. Sloan fellow, 1981-83, J.S. Guggenheim fellow, 1986-87; Beckman assoc. Ctr. for Advanced Study, Urbana, 1984-85; Fogarty scholar NIH, 1994-98; recipient Hirschfelder prize U. Wis., 2009-. Fellow AAAS, Am. Phys. Soc. (Biol. Physics prize 2004), Am. Acad. Arts and Scis., The Biophys. Soc.; mem. NAS, Am. Chem. Soc. (Pure Chemistry award 1986, Peter Debye award 2000, Edgar Fahs Smith award Phila. sect. 2005), Royal Soc. London(fgn.), German Acad. Sci. Leopoldina, Isreal Chem. Soc. (hon. life mem.), Phi Beta Kappa, Sigma Xi, Phi Lambda Upsilon (Fresenius award 1988), Sigma Pi Sigma, Alpha Chi Sigma. Home: 12737 Sandy Crest Ct San Diego CA 92130-2795 Office: U Calif San Diego Dept Chem and Biochemistry 9500 Gilman Dr MC 0371 La Jolla CA 92093-0371 Home Phone: 858-509-2730; Office Phone: 858-822-4825. Business E-Mail: pwolynes@ucsd.edu.

WOLYNEZ, ALLEN LAWRENCE, psychology professor; b. Bklyn., Oct. 24, 1968; s. Ruby and Eileen Sherry Wolynez; m. Leony Achacoso. B in Bus., Bklyn Coll.; MEd in Sch. Psychology, LI U., Bklyn. Cert. sch. psychologist NY. Sch. psychologist Dept. Edn., Bklyn., 1991—. Business E-Mail: awolyne@schoools.nyc.gov.

WOMACK, BOBBY (ROBERT DWAYNE WOMACK), musician, songwriter; b. Cleve., Mar. 4, 1944; Co-founding mem. of gospel group The Valentinos. Writer, singer: songs Looking for a Love, 1962, It's All Over Now, 1964, How I Miss You Baby, 1969, That's the Way I Feel About Cha, 1971, Woman's Gotta Have It, 1972, Harry Hippie, 1972, Nobody Wants You When You're Down and Out, 1973, Check It Out, 1975, Daylight, 1976, How Could You Break My Heart, 1979, Love Has Finally Come at Last, 1984, I Wish He Didn't Trust Me So Much, 1985, albums The Womack Live, 1967, Fly Me to the Moon, 1969, My Prescription, 1970, Communication, 1971, Understanding, 1972, Across 110th Street, 1972, The Facts of Life, 1973, Lookin' for a Love Again, 1974, I Don't Know What the World is Coming To, 1975, Safety Zone, 1975, I Can Understand It, 1975, BW Goes C&W, 1976, Home Is Where the Heart Is, 1976, Pieces, 1977, Roads of Life, 1979, The Poet, 1981, The Poet II, 1984, So Many Rivers, 1985, Someday We'll All Be Free, 1985, Womagic, 1986, Last Soul Man, 1987, Save the Children, 1989, I Still Love You, 1993, I Wanna Make Love to You, 1993, Soul Seduction Supreme, 1994, Resurrection, 1994, Back to My Roots, 1999, Traditions, 1999, Christmas Album, 2000. Recipient Pioneer award, Rhythm & Blues Found., 1996; named to Rock & Roll Hall of Fame, 2009. E-mail: info@bobbywomack.com.*

WOMACK, CHRISTOPHER C., utilities executive; b. Greenville, Ala, 1958; Attended Exec. Program, 2001—01; B, Western Mich. U.; M in Pub. Adminstrn., American U. Sr. v.p., sr. prodn. officer Southern Co. (Southern Co. Generation); legis. aide to Leon Panetta US House of Reps., staff dir., subcommittee on pers. & police (com. house on adminstr.); govtl. affairs rep. (Alabama Power) Southern Co., 1988, chief people officer, sr. v.p., human resources, 1998, exec. v.p., external affairs (Georgia Power), dir., cmty. rels. & sr. v.p., pub. rels. & corp. svcs. (Alabama Power), exec. v.p., pres., external affairs, 2009—. Office: Southern Co 30 Ivan Allen Jr Blvd NW Atlanta GA 30308 Office Phone: 404-506-5000. Office Fax: 404-506-0455.

WOMACK, DESTINY MARY LOUISE, artist; b. Tacoma, Wash., Nov. 18, 1980; d. Betty Mae and Moriss Charles; m. Jeremy James Womack, Oct. 10, 2003; 1 child, Trinity Morissa Mae. Artist Womack Original Art, Guthrie, Okla., 2005—. Original abstract paintings. Achievements include development of a unique acrylic painting technique. Office: Womack Original Art Po Box 1142 Guthrie OK 73044 Personal E-mail: info@destinywomack.com.

WOMACK, GUY LEE, lawyer, military officer; b. Atlanta, Jan. 23, 1953; s. Ivey Lee and Mary Jane (Jenkins) W.; m. Gilda Ann Garza, Mar. 26, 2005; children from previous marriage: Paige Ann, Geoffrey Lee, Amy Elizabeth. BA in Polit. Sci., U. Ga., 1977; JD, Woodrow Wilson Coll. Law, 1980. Bar: Ga. 1980, U.S. Ct. Mil. Appeals 1981, U.S. Supreme Ct. 1989, U.S. Ct. Appeals (5th cir.) 1993, (11th cir.) 1997, U.S. Dist. Ct. (so. dist.) Tex. 1990, (so. dist.) Tex. 1994, Ala. 1997, U.S. Ct. Appeals (4th cir.) 1997, U.S. Dist. Ct. Colo. 2001, U.S. Dist. Ct. Ariz. 2001, U.S.Ct. Appeals (10th cir.) 2003, U.S. Dist. Ct. (no. dist.) Ind. 2004, U.S. Dist. Ct. (no. and cen. dists.) Ill. 2005, U.S. Ct. Appeals (7th cir.) 2005. Commd. 2d lt. USMC, 1980, advanced through grades to lt. col., 1995, exec. officer Co. I 2d Bn. Camp LeJeune, N.C., 1981-82, def. counsel 2d div., 1982-83, prosecutor, dep. staff judge advocate 2d Marine div., 1983-84, prosecutor Guantanamo Bay, Cuba, 1984-86, student amphibious warfare sch. Quantico, Va., 1986-87, house counsel/prosecutor Naval Investigative Service Legal Services Support Sect. Camp LeJeune, 1987—; asst. U.S. atty. U.S. Dist. Ct. (so. dist.) Tex., 1990-96; pvt. practice, 1997—. Chmn. Law Day Observance Naval Legal Service Office, Guantanano Bay, 1986. Mem. ABA (Pub. Service award 1986), Assn. Trial Lawyers Am., State Bar Tex., State Bar Ga., Tex. Criminal Def. Lawyers Assn., Ga. Assn. Criminal Def. Lawyers, Marine Corps Assn. (life), Nat. Assn. Chiefs Police, Nat. Rifle Assn. (life), Profl. Assn. Diving Instrs. (pres. scuba instr. council Guantanamo 1984-86). Republican. Baptist. Avocations: scuba diving, running, tae kwan do, shooting sports, reading. Home: 3730 Brookvale Ct Kingwood TX 77345-1229 Office: 402 Main St Ste 6-N Houston TX 77002 Office Phone: 713-224-8815, 716-224-8812. Fax: (713) 224-2815. E-mail: guy.womack@usa.net.

WOMACK, TODD, legislative staff member; m. Katie Womack; 3 children. Spokesperson Erlanger Med. Ctr., Chattanooga; dir. pub. rels. UnumProvident Corp., Chattanooga; comm. dir. Mayor Bob Corker, Chattanooga; polit. dir., comm. dir. Bob Corker for US Senate, 2006; transition dir. Senator Bob Corker, Washington, 2006, chief of staff, 2007—. Baptist. Office: Office of Senator Bob Corker 185 SDOB Washington DC 20510-4207 Office Phone: 202-224-3344. E-mail: todd_womack@corker.senate.gov.*

WOMBLE, WILLIAM FLETCHER, lawyer; b. Winston-Salem, NC, Oct. 29, 1916; s. Bunyan Snipes and Edith (Willingham) Womble; m. Jane Payne Gilbert, Oct. 11, 1941; children: William Fletcher, Jr., Jane Womble Haver, Russell G., Ann Womble Strader. Student, U. NC Law Sch., Chapel hill, Summer Sch., 1938; AB, Duke U., 1937, JD, 1939; LHT (hon.), High Point U., 2000. Bar: NC 1939, US Supreme Ct. 1950. Assoc. Womble Carlyle Sandridge & Rice P.L.L.C. and predecessors, Winston-Salem, 1939-47, mem., 1947—. Permanent mem. 4th Cir. Jud. Conf. Campaign chmn. Forsyth County Cmty. Chest, 1949; mem. NC Gen. Statutes Commn., 1953—55, NC Bd. Higher Edn., 1955—57, 1960—63, NC Adv. Budget Commn., 1957—58; trustee, past chmn., life trustee High Point U., 1950—; trustee Winston-Salem State U., 1953—55, Children's Home, 1959—75, pres., 1969—75, Winston Salem C. of C., 1960—61; bd. dirs. Triad United Meth. Home (now Arbor Acres United Meth. Retirement Cmty.), 1976—87, 1989—97, treas., 1975—79, pres., 1979—85; hon. chair United Way, Forsyth County, 1998; mem. People-to-People Citizen Amb. Program, 1981, 1986, NC Ho. of Reps., 1953—58, chmn. com. higher edn., vice chmn. fin. com., 1957; chmn. adminstrv. bd. Centenary United Meth. Ch., 1961—63, chmn. bd. trustees, 1983—85; trustee Sr. Svcs., Inc., 1998—2005, chair ann. fund., 2004—05; bd. dirs. Children's Ctr. Assn.for the Physically Handicapped, Inc., 1952—56, pres., 1952—53, hon. bd. mem., 1998—; bd. dirs., pres. Experiment in Self-Reliance, Inc., 1964—65. Served to maj. USAF, 1941—46. Recipient Fifty Yr. award, Fellows Am. Bar Found., ABA, 1995; named Trustee of the Yr., Gen. Bd. Global Mins. of United Meth. Ch., Health and Wlfare Minst. Dept., 1989. Fellow: Am. Bar Found. (life; state chmn. 1984—89); mem.: ABA (ho. dels. 1978—87, bd. govs. 1982—85, exec. coun. Nat. Conf. Bar Pres. 1985—88, ethics com. 1985—91, chmn. jud. code subcom. 1988—91, chair affiliate outreach com. 1994—97, coun. mem. sr. lawyers divsn. 1995—97), Forsyth County Bar Assn. (pres. 1962), Am. Judicature Soc., NC State Bar (trustee Interest on Lawyers Trust Accounts 1983—91, vice chmn. 1989—91, Chief Justice's Professionalism award 2001), NC Bar Assn. (pres. 1966—67, chmn. endowment founders campaign 1986—87, chair sr. lawyers divsn. 1994—95, Judge John J. Parker award 1984), Soc. Cin., Old Town Club, Rotary (local pres. 1964). Democrat. Methodist. Home: 1244 Arbor Rd 441 Winston Salem NC 27104-1139 Office: Womble Carlyle Sandridge & Rice One W 4th St Winston Salem NC 27101 Office Phone: 336-721-3603. Office Fax: 336-733-8369. Business E-Mail: wwomble@wcsr.com.

WON, CHANG-HEE, science educator; b. Seoul, Republic Of Korea; s. Yongchol and Bokkyu Won; married. PhD, U. Notre Dame, 1995. Asst. prof. Temple U., Phila., 2005—. Achievements include patents for modular navigation system. Office: Temple Univ 1947 N 14th St Philadelphia PA 19122 Office Fax: 215-204-5960. Business E-Mail: cwon@temple.edu.

WON, DONGHO, communications engineer, educator; b. Seoul, Republic of Korea, Sept. 23, 1949; s. Jaeyoun Won and Joja Lee; m. Yoonsook Han, Nov. 28, 1978; children: Sooseob, Hayoung. Bs in Electronic Engring., Sungkyunkwan U., Suwon, Republic of Korea, 1976, MS in Electronic Engring., 1978, PhD in Electronic Engring., 1988. Rsch. scientist Electronics & Telecom. Rsch. Inst., Seoul, 1978—80; rsch. scientist, dept. electronic engring. Tokyo Inst. Tech., 1985—86; dir. computer ctr. Sungkyunkwan U., Suwon, 1992—94, dean divsn. student and acad. affairs, 1995—97, dir. info. and comm. tech. rsch. lab., 1997—99, dean grad. sch. info. and comm., 1999—2001, dean divsn. r&d affairs, 2002—04, dir. authentication tech. rsch. ctr., 2004—, prof. sch. info. and comm. engring., 1982—. Info. tech. adv. bd. mem. Office Prime Min. Korea, Seoul, 1996—98; program com. chair 3rd Internat. Conf. Info. Security and Cryptology, Seoul, 2000; gen. chair 5th Internat. Conf. Info. Security and Cryptology, Seoul, 2002—02; info. tech. adv. bd. mem. Bd. Audit and Inspection of Korea, Seoul, Republic of Korea, 2002—03; dir. Korea Info. Security Agy., Seoul, Republic of Korea, 2005—; vis. prof., dept. computer sci. U. Calif., Irvine, 2004—05. Author: (book) Information and Coding Theory, 1993, Computer Science, 2000, Introduction to Information Engineering, 2000, Modern Cryptography and its Application, 2002, Modern Cryptography, 2003 (Outstanding Acad. Book award, NAS, Republic of Korea, 2005); contbr. articles to profl. jours. Recipient Outstand Achievement Honor award, Korean Min. Info. and Comm., 2001, Outstanding Achievement Honor award, Nat. Intelligence Svc., Republic of Korea, 2000. Mem.: IEEE, Inst. Electronics, Info., and Comm. Engrs., Korea Inst. of Electronics Engrs. (life; dir. 2004—05, Outstanding Contbn. award 1999), Korea Inst. Info. Security & Cryptology (life; hon. pres. 2003—, pres. 2002—03, Outstanding Contbn. award 2006). Achievements include patents for method for electronically signing on the basis of personal identifying information having self-certified characteristic; self-certified ID-based key exchange scheme; method for key distribution using proxy server; method for generating session key for group communication in mobile environment; authorization method in radio frequency identification system. Home: 903 Sinbanpo 17th Apt 334 Jamwon-dong Seoul 137-951 Republic of Korea Office: Sungkyunkwan Univer Dept Computer Engring 300 Cheoncheon-dong Jangan-gu Gyeonggi-do Suwon 440-746 Republic of Korea Office Fax: 82-31-290-5696; Home Fax: 82-31-290-5696. Business E-Mail: dhwon@security.re.kr.

WON, KWANG WOONG, chemical engineer; b. Seoul, Korea, Dec. 24, 1940; came to U.S., 1965; s. Dong Shick and Dal Mak (Yoon) W.; m. Christina C. Kim, May 31, 1969; children: Alvina J., Erik J. BS, Seoul Nat. U., 1964; MS, Wayne State U., 1967; PhD, U. Calif., Berkeley, 1974. Registered profl. engr., Calif.; lic. chem. engr. Rsch. and teaching asst. U. Calif., Berkeley, 1970-74; prin. process engr. Fluor Corp., Irvine, Calif., 1974-83; prin. tech. specialist Advanced Tech. div. Fluor Daniel Inc., Irvine, Calif., 1983—. Lectr., adj. prof. U. So. Calif., 1977—. Author: Chemical Engineering of Supercritical Fluids, 1985; contbr. articles to profl. jours.; patentee infinite dilution volatilities of polar organic solutes in hydrocarbons, a gel layer effect on ultrafiltration mass flux, phase equilibria of waxes, fats, oils and gas. Served with Army, Republic of Korea, 1964-65. Mem. AAAS, Am. Inst. of Chem. Engrs. (prof. devel. cert.1985, referee Jour. 1979—), Am. Chem. Soc., Toastmasters, Irvine Club. Republican. Roman Catholic. Avocations: tennis, skiing, marine water study. Home: 703 Corte Topacio San Clemente CA 92673-5620 Office: Fluor TechInc 3333 Michelson Dr Irvine CA 92612-0625

WON, YONG SUN, electronics engineer; s. Jung Sook Choi; m. Kyung Hee Lee, Oct. 5, 1997; 1 child, Da Young. BS, Sogang U., Seoul, Republic of Korea; MS, Pohang U. of Sci. and Tech., Republic Of Korea, 1995; PhD, U. Fla., 2006. Rsch. fellow Samsung Petrochemical Co. Ltd., Ulsan, 1995—99; sr. engr. Samsung Electro-Mechanics Co. Ltd., Suwon, 1999—2001, 2007—; vis. rschr. Nat. Inst. Standards and Tech., Gaithersburg, Md., 2006—07. Office: Samsung Electro-Mechanics Co Ltd 314 Maetan3-Dong Yeongtong-Gu Suwon 443-743 Republic of Korea Office Phone: 82-31-210-5621. Office Fax: 82-31-300-7900 (#9695). Personal E-mail: highhababin@hotmail.com. Business E-Mail: yongsun.won@samsung.com.

WONDER, JOHN WALDER, classicist, educator; b. Palo Alto, Calif. s. John Paul and Jane Walder Wonder; m. Brigid Vianest Wonder; children: David Michael, Jennifer Katherine, Christopher John. PhD, U. Calif., Berkeley. Faculty, classics dept. San Francisco State U., 1994—. Cons. in field. Contbr. articles to profl. jours. Mem.: Calif. Classical Assn., Am. Inst. Archaeology, Virgilian Soc. (dir., trustee 2005—). Home: 36 Corliss Dr Moraga CA 94556 Office: San Francisco State Univ 1600 Holloway Ave San Francisco CA 94132

WONDER, STEVIE (STEVELAND HARDAWAY JUDKINS, STEVELAND MORRIS), musician; b. Saginaw, Mich., May 13, 1950; m. Syreeta Wright, 1971 (div. 1972); m. Kai Milla Wonder, 2001; children: Kailand, Mandla Kadjaly Carl Stevland Morris; children: Aisha, Keita, Mumtaz. Student pub. schs. in Detroit until age 12; then transferred to, Mich. Sch. for Blind. Recording artist Motown Records, Detroit, 1963—70; founder, pres. music pub. co. Black Bull Music, Inc., 1970—, Wondirection Records, Inc., 1982—. (singles) Fingertips, 1963, Uptight/Purple Raindrops, 1965, Someday At Christmas/The Miracles of Christmas, I'm Wondering/Everytime I See You I Go Wild, 1966, I Was Made To Love Her/Hold Me, 1967, Shoo-Be-Doo-Be-Doo-Da-Day/Why Don't You Lead Me To Love, You Met Your Match/My Girl, 1968, For Once In My Life, I Don't Know Why, My Cherie Amour, Yester-Me, Yester-You, Yesterday, Never Had a Dream Come True, Signed, Sealed, Delivered I'm Yours, Heaven Help Us All, I Wish (Grammy award, 1977), Don't You Worry 'Bout a Thing, You Haven't Done Nothin', Boogie on Reggae Woman (Grammy award, 1975), Isn't She Lovely, Sir Duke, Another Star, As, You Are the Sunshine of My Life (Grammy award, 1974), Superstition (Grammy award, 1974), Higher Ground, Living For the City (Grammy award, 1975), I Just Called to Say I Love You; singer: (albums) Tribute to Uncle Ray, 1962, With a Song In My Heart, 1963, The Jazz Soul of Little Stevie, 1963, The Twelve-Year Old-Genius, 1963, Stevie At The Beach, 1964, Down to Earth, 1966, Uptight, 1966, Someday at Christmas, 1967, I Was Made To Love Her, Someday At Christmas, 1967, Eivets Rednow (Featuring Alfie), 1968, For Once in My Life, 1968, Stevie Wonder's Greatest Hits, 1968, My Cherie Amour, Talk of The Town, 1969, Live at the Talk of the Town, 1970, Signed, Sealed and Delivered, 1970, Live In Person, 1970, Steve Wonder's Greatest Hits Vol. 2, 1971, Where I'm Coming From, 1971, Talking Book, 1972, Music of My Mind, Stevie Wonder Live, Where I'm Coming From, Talking Book, 1972, Portrait, 1976, Innervisions, 1973 (Grammy award, 1974), Fulfillingness' First Finale, 1974 (Grammy award, 1975), Songs In the Key of Life, 1976 (Grammy award, 1977), Looking Back, 1977, Stevie Wonder's Journey Through the Secret Life of Plants, 1979, Hotter than July, 1980, Stevie Wonder's Original Musiquarium, 1982, Woman in Red, 1984, In Square Circle, 1985 (best soul/R&B album of yr., Down Beat mag. Readers' poll, 1986), I Just Called to Say I love You, 1984 (Acad. award, Golden Globe award for single, 1984), Characters, 1987, Jungle Fever, 1991, Inner Peace, Motown Legends, 1995, Natural Wonders, 1995, Conversation Peace, 1996, Song Review, 1996, At the Close of a Century, 1999, The Definitive Collection, 2002, A Time to Love, 2005 (Grammy for Best Male Pop Vocal Performance, 2006), (Soundtrack) Bamboozled; actor: (films) Bikini Beach, Muscle Beach Party, 1964; frequent appearances (TV series) Mike Douglas Show, guest host Saturday Night Live. Recipient Nelson Mandela Courage award, 1991, numerous Grammy awards, numerous awards for best singer/songwriter, Rock Music award, 1977, Am. Music award, 1978, Am. Video award for best rhythm and blues video for Ebony and Ivory, 1982, Century award, Billboard Music Awards, 2004, Grammy Award (with Beyoncé) for Best R&B Performance by Duo, 2006, Grammy Award (with Tony Bennett) for Best Pop Collaboriation with Vocals, 2007, Lifetime Achievement award, Nat. Civil Rights Mus., 2006, George Gershwin prize for Popular Song, Libr. of Congress, 2009; named Musician of Year, Down Beat mag. Rock/Blues Poll, 1973—75, 1977—78, Best Selling Male Soul Artist of Year, Nat. Assn. Rec. Merchandisers, 1974; named to Songwriters Hall of Fame, 1982, Rock and Roll Hall of Fame, 1989, NAACP Image Awards Hall of Fame, 2008. Office: 4616 W Magnolia Blvd Burbank CA 91505-2731*

WONDERS, WILLIAM CLARE, geography educator; b. Toronto, Apr. 22, 1924; s. George Clarence and Ann Mary (Bell) W.; m. Lillian Paradise Johnson, June 2, 1951; children: Karen Elizabeth, Jennifer Anne, Glen William. BA with honors, Victoria Coll., U. Toronto, 1946; MA, Syracuse U., 1948; PhD, U. Toronto, 1951; Fil. Dr. h.c., Uppsala U., 1981. Teaching asst. dept. geography Syracuse U., 1946-48; lectr. dept. geography U. Toronto, 1948-53; asst. prof. geography dept. polit. economy U. Alta., 1953-55, assoc. prof. geography, 1955-57, prof., head dept. geography, 1957-67, prof. dept. geography, 1967-87, Univ. prof., 1983—, prof. emeritus, 1987—. Vis. prof. geography U. B.C., 1954, U. Okla., 1965-66, St. Mary's U., 1977, U. Victoria, 1989, J.F. Kennedy Inst., Free U. Berlin, 1990; guest prof. Inst. Geography, Uppsala (Sweden) U., 1962-63; rsch. fellow in Geography U. Aberdeen, Scotland, 1970-71, 78; vis. fellow in Can. Studies, U. Edinburgh, Scotland, 1987. Author: Looking at Maps, 1960, The Sawdust Fusiliers, 1991, Norden and Canada-A Geographer's Perspective, 1992, Alaska Highway Explorer, 1994; author: (with T. Drinkwater et al.) Junior Atlas of Alberta, 1979; contbr., editor: Canada's Changing North, 1971, rev. edit., 2003, The North, 1972, The Arctic Circle, 1976, Knowing the North, 1988, Geographica's Pocket World Reference, 2000, Frontiersmen & Settlers, 2002, Geordies, Yankees and Canucks, 2006; contbr. articles to jours. and encys., chapters to books. Active Nat. Adv. Com. on Geog. Rsch., 1965-69; chmn. Boreal Inst. No. Studies (Can. Circumpolar Inst.), 1960-62; mem. Can. Permanent Com. on Geog. Names, 1981-94, Alta. Hist. Sites Bd., 1978-83, vice-chmn., 1982-83; policy bd. Can. Plains Rsch. Centre, U. Regina (Sask.), 1975-86; adv. bd. Royal Tyrrell Mus. Paleontology, 1984-89; bd. dirs. Muttart Found., 1986-93, 95-98, v.p., 1991-93. Decorated Order of Can., Can. Forces Decoration; recipient Queen's Jubilee medal; NSF sr. fgn. scientist fellow, 1965-66; Can. Coun. leave fellow, 1969-70, 77-78; Nuffield Found. fellow, 1970-71. Fellow Arctic Inst. N.Am., Royal Soc. Can., Royal Can. Geog. Soc. (Massey medalist 1998); mem. Can. Assn. Geographers (past pres.), Can. Assn. Scottish Studies (councillor 1974-77), Scottish Soc. No. Studies, Champlain Soc. (councillor 1981-86), Sigma Xi, Gamma Theta Upsilon. E-mail: wwonders@shaw.ca.

WONES, SUZANNE L., academic librarian; b. Cambridge, Mass., Mar. 21, 1969; d. David Robert and Constance G. Wones; m. Scott A. Lozier, June 12, 1999; 1 child, Henry David Lozier. BA cum laude, U. Mass., Amherst, 1991; MA, U. NH, Durham, 1997; MS in Info. Sci., U. Mich., Ann Arbor, 2000. Head access and rsch. svcs. John F. Kennedy Sch. Govt. Libr., Cambridge, 2004—07; head access svcs. Harvard Law Sch. Libr., Cambridge, 2007—. Recipient Dean's award for Academic Excellence, John F. Kennedy Sch. Govt., 2004. Mem.: Am. Assn. Law Librs., Assn. Coll. and Rsch. Librs. (legis. network coord., New Eng. chpt. 2002—06). Liberal. Episcopalian. Office: Harvard Law Sch Libr 1545 Massachusetts Ave Cambridge MA 02138

WONG, AH-SAN, planetary scientist, musician, writer; d. Chuen Wong and Mei Leung; m. Michael T. Elliott, Oct. 3, 2005; 1 child, Logan Tian-Yang. BS in Physics, Calif. State U., Fresno, 1992; MS in Physics, Calif. Inst. Tech., Pasadena, 1995, PhD in Physics, 2002. Sr. rsch. fellow U. Mich., Ann Arbor, 2002—06; rsch. fellow Calif. Inst. Tech., Calif., 2006—. Mem.: Am. Astron. Soc. (mem. divsn. planetary sci.), Am. Geophys. Union.

WONG, ALBERT J., medical educator; BA, Johns Hopkins U., Balt., 1980; MD, Johns Hopkins U., 1983. Lic. Md., 1983. Prof. cancer biology and neurosurgery Stanford U., Calif., 2005—. Founder, pres., CEO Alteris Therapeutics, Inc., Phila., 2002—05. Grantee Rsch. grant, NIH, 1989—. Mem.: Am. Soc. Clin. Oncology, Soc. Neuro-Oncology, Am. Assn. Cancer Rsch. Achievements include development of anti-cancer vaccine based on EGFRvIII; therapy for human brain tumors; tumor specific alternative splice forms as basis for anti-cancer vaccines; discovery of EGFRvIII; alternative splice forms in biologic samples; and properties of Gab1; and properties of mLEEK. Home Fax: 866-465-4505. Business E-Mail: ajwong@stanford.edu.

WONG, ALBERT WING KUEN, finance educator; b. Hong Kong, June 17, 1951; s. Bee Wong and Woon Lee; m. Titania Wong, Nov. 10, 1975; children: Betty, Chapmun. PhD in Bus. Adminstrn., Sussex Coll. Tech., Eng., 1982; PhD in Banking and Fin., Wis. Internat. U., 2003. Mng. dir., CEO Charise Fin. Planning Ltd., Hong Kong, 1994—; prof. dept. banking and fin. Shenzhen U., China, 2001—. Hon. advisor Inst. Crisis and Risk Mgmt., Hong Kong, 2003; coun. mem. China Reform Coun., Beijing, 2006—; advisor Qing Yuan Tak Ednl. Bur., China. Hon. advisor Hong Kong Wushu Coach Assn., 2004. Named Hon. Assoc., Hong Kong Bapt. U. Sch. Bus., 2005. Fellow: Hong Kong Soc. Economists (founder pres.), Chartered Inst. Secs., Soc. Registered Fin. Planners (founder fellow); mem.: Tung Koon Wong Clansmen's Assn. Hong Kong (chmn. 2007—), Hong Kong Soc. Doctorate (founder pres.), Rotary Internat. (chpt. pres. 2003—04). Liberal. Avocations: golf, swimming, bowling. Office: Charise Fin Planning Ltd 4-6 Hennessy Rd Wanchai Hong Kong Home Phone: (852) 90905703, (852) 6011 6766; Office Phone: (852) 2866 7451, (852) 2866 9198. Office Fax: (852) 24097672. Personal E-mail: professor.albertwong@gmail.com.

WONG, ANDREA J., broadcast executive; b. 1966; BS in Elec. Engring., MIT, 1988; MBA, Stanford U., 1993. Rschr. ABC News PrimeTime Live, 1993—94; exec. asst. pres. ABC TV Network, 1994—95; exec. asst. to pres. ABC, Inc., 1995—97, v.p., exec. asst. pres., 1997—98; v.p. alt. series & specials. ABC Entertainment, 1998—2000, sr. v.p. alt. series & specials., 2000—04, exec. v.p. alt. programming, specials & late night, 2004—07; pres., CEO Lifetime Entertainment Svcs., 2007—. Named a Woman to Watch, Fortune mag., 2008; named one of The 100 Most Powerful Women in Entertainment, Hollywood Reporter, 2006, 2007. Office: Lifetime Entertainment Services World Wide Plz 309 W 49th St New York NY 10019

WONG, ANDREW L., rheumatologist, educator; b. San Francisco, Mar. 3, 1958; s. Nguey A. and Choy H. Wong; m. Lydia C. Lo, May 19, 1985; children: Aaron P., Adam T. MD, Loma Linda U. Sch. Medicine, Calif., 1983. Cert. physician and surgeon Med. Bd. Calif., 1984. Chief rheumatology Olive View-UCLA Med. Ctr., Sylmar, 1990—, dir. rheumatology program, 2007—; prof. clin. medicine David Geffen Sch. Medicine UCLA, 2003—. Contbr. articles to profl. jour. Bd. mem. Calif. Dept. Health Sevcs. Med., Sacramento, 2001—; mem. inservice tng. exam com. Am. Bd. Internal Medicine, 2006—08; rsch. steering com. Arthritis Found., SCC, LA, 2008—; mem. academic senate faculty welfare com. UCLA, 2005—08. Recipient award, Olive View Edn. & Rsch. Inst., 2007; named one of America's Top Physicians, 2008, Southern Calif. Super Doctors, LA Mag., 2008; grant, Arthritis Found., SCC, 2007. Fellow: ACP, Am. Coll. Rheumatology; mem.: Loma Linda U. Adventist Health Scis. Ctr. Couns. Avocation: skiing. Home: 20824 Campania Ln Porter Ranch CA 91326 Office: Olive View-UCLA Med Ctr 14445 Olive View Dr 2B182 Sylmar CA 91342 Office Fax: 818-364-4573. Business E-Mail: alunwong@ucla.edu.

WONG, BRIAN JET-FEI, surgeon; b. LA, Sept. 23, 1963; s. Richard Toy and Hazel F. (Lue) W. BS, U. So. Calif., 1985; postgrad., Oxford U., 1985-86; MD, Johns Hopkins U., 1990; PhD, U. Amsterdam, 2001. Resident U. Calif., Irvine, 1990-96, clin. instr., 1997-98, asst. prof., 1998—2001, assoc. prof., 2001—06, prof., 2006—07, vice chmn. Rsch. assoc. Beckman Laser Inst., Irvine, 1994—. Recipient Physician Excellence, Orange County Med. Assn.; named one of Best Dr. in USA. Mem. ACS, Biomed. Optical Soc., SPIE, Am. Acad. Facial Plastic Surgery. Avocation: surfing. Office: Univ Calif Irvine Beckman Laster Inst 1002 Health Scis Rd Irvine CA 92612 Office Phone: 714-456-5753.

WONG, CARSON, surgeon, educator; married. MD, U. Western Ont., London, 1995. Diplomate Am. Bd. Urology, Inc., 2003. Asst. prof. U. Okla., Dept. Urology, 2003—08, chief minimally invasive and robotic surgery, 2003—, assoc. prof., 2008—. Contbr. articles to profl. jours. Fellow: RCS (Can.), ACS; mem.: Can. Urol. Assn., Endourological Soc., Am. Urol. Assn. Office: Univ Okla Dept Urology 920 Stanton L Young Blvd WP3150 Oklahoma City OK 73104 Office Fax: 405-271-3118.

WONG, CHI-HUEY, chemistry professor; b. Taiwan, Aug. 13, 1948; came to US, 1979; m. Yieng-Lii, Mar. 26, 1975; children: Heather, Andrew. BS in Chem. and Biochemical Sci., Nat. Taiwan U., 1970, MS in Biochemical Sci., 1977; PhD in Organic Chemistry, MIT, 1982. Asst. rsch. fellow Inst. Biol. Chemistry Academia Sinica, Taipei, Taiwan, 1974-79; postdoctoral fellow Harvard U., 1982—83; asst. prof. chemistry Tex. A&M U., 1983—86, assoc. prof., 1986—87, prof. biochemistry and biophysics Inst. Biosciences and Tech., 1987—89; prof., Ernest W. Hahn chair chemistry Scripps Rsch. Inst., La Jolla, Calif., 1989—, mem. Skaggs Inst. Chem. Biology, 1996—; dir. Genomics Rsch. Ctr. Academia Sinica, Taipei, Taiwan, 2003—. Cons. Dow Chem., 1983—88, W.R. Grace, 1984—87, Miles Lab., 1985—88, G.D. Searle, 1988—90, Amgen, 1991—93, Abbott Labs., 1991—94, Lilly Rsch. Labs., 1991—93, Dow Corning, 1992—94, Mitsubishi Chem. Grp. Sci. and Tech. Rsch. Ctr., Japan, 2005—; sci. adv. Amylin, San Diego, 1989—93, Cytel, 1991—97, Inst. Chemistry, Academia Sinia, 1992—2000, chmn. bd., 1994—2000; sci. adv. Osi Pharm., 1992—98, Affymax, 1992—95, Oncogene Sci., 1993—98, RedCell, 1993—97, ArQule, 1994—95, Inst. Biol. Chemistry, Academia Sinica, 1994—2002, Inst. Molecular and Cell Biology, Nat. U. Singapore, 1994—97, Medinox, Inc., 1996—, Advanced Medicine, Inc., 1997—2000, Kosan Biosciences, 1997—2002, Pharmanex, 1997—, Max-Planck-Inst., Dortmund, Germany, 2000—, Momenta, 2001—03, Diversa, 2001—, Serenex, 2001—, Devel. Ctr. Biotechnology, Taiwan, 2004—; sci. adv., bd. dirs. Indsl. Tech. Rsch. Inst., Taiwan, 2004—; head frontier rsch. prog. glycotechnology Inst. Phys. and Chem. Rsch. (RIKEN), Japan, 1991—99; founder, sci. adv. Combichem, Inc., San Diego, 1994—98; vis. prof. Chem. Ctr. U. Lund, Sweden, 1995—98; corr. rsch. fellow Inst. Biol. Chemistry Academia Sinica, 1996—2002, disting. vis. scholar Inst. Chemistry, 1999—2002; founder, bd. mem., chmn. sci. adv. bd. Optimer Pharms., Inc., San Diego, 1999—; hon. prof. Shanghai Inst. Organic Chemistry, Chinese Acad. Scis., 1999—. Contbr. articles to sci. jours.; mem. editl. bd.: Biocatalysis, 1991—, Carbohydrate Letters, 1995—, Drug Discovery Today, 1996—99, Current Opinion in Chem. Biology, 1998—, Advanced Synthesis and Catalysis, 2000—, editor-in-chief: Bioorganic and Medicinal Chemistry, 1993—, mem. exec. bd. editors: Tetrahedron Publs., 1993—, mem. adv. bd.: Jour. Organic Chemistry, 1993—97, Jour. Chem. Soc., Perkin Trans. 1, 1993—2002, Jour. Am. Chem. Soc., 2005—, Chemistry: An Asian Jour., 2006—; co-author: Enzymes in Synthetic Organic Chemistry, 1994, Combinatorial Chemistry in Biology, 1999, Catalysis from A to Z: A Concise Ency., 1999; author: Carbohydrate-based Drug Discovery, Vols. 1 and 2, 2003. Lt. Taiwan Army, 1970-71. Recipient Searle Scholar award in Biomedical Scis., 1985—88, Presdl. Young Investigator in Chemistry award, NSF, Washington, 1986—91, Arthur C. Cope Scholar award, Am. Chem. Soc., 1993, Divsn. Carbohydrate Chemistry Melville L. Wolfrom award, 1995, Harrison Howe award in Chemistry, 1998, Claude S. Hudson award in Carbohydrate Chemistry, 1999, San Diego Sect. Outstanding Scientist award, 1999, Award for Creative Work in Synthetic Organic Chemistry, 2005, Roy Whistler award, Internat. Carbohydrate Orgn., 1994, Disting. Rsch. Achievement award, Chinese Am. Chem. Soc., 1994, Taiwanese Am. Found. prize in Sci. and Engring., 1997, Internat. Enzyme Engring. award, 1999, Presdl. Green Chemistry Challenge award, 2000. Fellow: AAAS; mem.: NAS, Am. Acad. Arts and Scis., Academia Sinica. Achievements include patents in field. Office: Scripps Rsch Inst Dept Chemistry 10550 N Torrey Pines Rd La Jolla CA 92037-1000 E-mail: wong@scripps.edu.

WONG, DAVID T., biochemist, researcher; b. Hong Kong, Nov. 6, 1935; arrived in US, 1957; s. Chi-Keung and Pui-King Wong; m. Christina Lee, Dec. 28, 1963; children: Conrad, Melvin, Vincent. Student, Nat. Taiwan U., 1955—56; BS, Seattle Pacific U., 1961; MS, Oreg. State U., 1964; PhD, Oreg. Health Sci. U., 1966. Post doctoral fellow U. Pa., Phila, 1966—67; sr. biochemist Lilly Rsch. Labs., Indpls., 1968-72, rsch. biochemist, 1973-77, sr. rsch. scientist, 1978-89, rsch. advisor, 1990-97, Lilly rsch. fellow, 1997-99, cons., 2000—. Adj. prof. biochemistry and molecular biology Ind. U. Sch. Medicine, 1986—96, adj. prof. neurobiology, 1991—2008, adj. prof. emeritus, 2009—. Mem. editl. bd.: Chinese Jour. Physiology, 1996—2000; contbr. articles to sci. jours. Recipient Scientist of Yr. Pres.' award, Chinese Neurosci. Soc., 1991, Discoverers award, Pharm. Mfr. Assn., 1993, Lifetime Rsch. award, Mental Health Assn. Ind., 1996, World Difference award, Ind. Health Industry Forum, 1996, Pharm. Discoverer's award Prozac, Nat. Alliance Rsch. Schizophrenia and Depression, 1996, Outstanding Achievement in Neurosci. Rsch. award, Lilly Neuroscience Eli Lilly and Co., 2000, Cornerstone award, Am. Drugstore Mus. Indpls., 2000, Excellence award, Asian Am. Alliance, Inc., 2002, Pioneer Recognition award, Com. 100, 2002, Excellence award, U.S. Pan Asian Am. C. of C., 2002, Hon. Ga. Citizen, mem. Goodwill Amb. Corp., State of Ga., 2003, Ind. living Legend award, Ind. Hist. Soc., 2008; named Alumnus of Growing Vision, Seattle Pacific U., 1991, Alumnus of Yr., 1998, Disting. Alumni Scientist award, Oreg. Health and Sci. U., 2004; Alumni fellow, Oreg. State U., 2003. Mem.: Ind. Chinese-Am. Profls. Assn. (pres. 2000), Soc. Chinese Bioscientists Am. (Disting. Scientist award for drug discovery 2004), Soc. Neurosci. (pres. Indpls. chpt. 1987, 1988), Am. Soc. Pharmacology and Exptl. Therapeutics, Am. Coll. Neuropsychopharamcology, Indpls. Assn. Chinese Ams. (pres. 1987). Achievements include patents in field; development of drugs, Prozac (fluoxetine serotonin uptake inhibitor) Cymbalta (Duloxetine, a serotonin and norepinephrine uptake inhibitor), Strattera (atomoxetive a norepinephrine uptake inhibitor) for attention deficit hyperactivity disorder and priligy dapoxetine; research in biochemistry and pharmacology of neurotransmission; potentially useful substances which enhance transmission of norepinephrine, dopamine, serotonin, acetylcholine, and GABA-neurons; natural products led to the discovery of caboxylic ionophores: Narasin and A204, which increase transport of cations across biomembranes. Home: 5812 E Fall Creek Parkway N D Indianapolis IN 46226-1051 Home Fax: 317-254-8288. Personal E-mail: dtwongindy@iquest.net.

WONG, DEAN, radiologist, educator; m. Susan Resnick. MD, U. Toronto, 1977; PhD, Johns Hopkins U.Sch. Hygiene & Pub. Health, Balt., 1990. Diplomate abnm 1982. Prof. radiology Johns Hopkins U. Sch. Medicine, Balt., prof. psychiatry, prof. neuroscience & environmental health sci., 1993—, vice chair radiology, 2008. Dir. Sect. High Resolution Brainpet Imaging; fellow Am. Coll. Neuropsychopharmacology, 2001—; cons. Mind-Lundbeck Found. Rsch. Ctr., Lundbeck, Aarhus, Denmark, 2005—. Researcher (brain imaging) Acad. Molecular Imaging (Best Abstract award, 2005); contbr. scientific papers. Fellow: ACNP; mem.: Soc. Nuc. Imaging Drug Devel., NY Acad. Sciences, Soc. Neuroscience, Soc. Nuc. Medicine (Kuhl Lassen award 2003). Office: Johns Hopkins Univ School Medicine 601 N Caroline St JHOC 3245 Baltimore MD 21287

WONG, EDWARD VINCENT, investment company executive; b. Houston, Nov. 12, 1927; s. Samuel Bark and Mary Eng-Shee Wong; m. Ernestine Elizabeth Kobl (dec.). BS, Stewart Inst., NJ; BA, Inst. Culinary Arts, New Haven, 1956; MBA, Hartford Grad. Ctr., Conn., 1978; D, Pace U., NYC, 1980. Investment exec. Far East Asian Group, Hong Kong. Mem. US Trade Commn.; sr. fellow Overseas Devel. Coun. Far East. Author: International Monetary. Mentor Holy Name Soc., Hartford, Conn., St. Joseph Catheral, Hartford, Conn. Col. US Army. Named Knight of St. Gregory, Vatican, Pope Pius XII, 1952. Fellow: Les Amis Escoffer Soc., Soc. Culinaire Philanthropique. Democrat. Roman Catholic. Avocations: piano, poetry, chess, art.

WONG, ELIZABETH HUNG, organist, choirmaster; m. James Wong, Jan. 5, 2002. MusM, Performer's Cert., Northwestern U., Evanston, Ill., 1995. Asst. organist, choirmaster Christ Ch., Bronxville, NY, 2001—02; organist, choirmaster Ch. of the Epiphany, N.Y.C., 2004—. Mem.: Assn. Anglican Musicians, Am. Guild Organists (sec. 2004). Office: Church of the Epiphany 1393 York Ave at 74th St New York NY 10708 Business E-Mail: wongehyh@gmail.com.

WONG, GUANG WILLIAM, physiologist, educator; s. Hai-Lum Wong and Pook-Sooi Goh; m. Injoo Chung, May 23, 1999; 1 child, Alycia M. PhD, Harvard U., Boston, Mass., 2000. Postdoc. fellow Whitehead Inst. Biomed. Rsch., M.I.T., Boston, 2001—07; asst. prof. Johns Hopkins U., Baltimore, Md., 2008—. Area leader SGI-USA (Buddhist Orgn.), Baltimore, 2008. Recipient Pharmacia Allergy Rsch. award, Pharmacia Inc. (Sweden), 2000; fellowship, Nat. Inst. Health, 2004—07. Achievements include research in treatment of diabetes and obesity. Office: Johns Hopkins Univ 855 N Wolfe St Baltimore MD 21205

WONG, HENRY KEUNG, dermatologist, educator; s. Cheun and Leung Wong; m. Barbara Aufierio, Oct. 26, 1996; 1 child, Harrison Kiam-Aufiero. B, Johns Hopkins U., 1985; MS, NYU, 1990, MD, PhD, NYU, 1992. Cert. Am. Bd. Dermatology, Am. Bd. Med. Specialties. Tchg. asst. internal medicine Washington U., St. Louis, 1992—93; tchg. asst. dermatology NYU Med. Ctr., NYC, 1993—96; sr. investigator Walter Reed Army Inst., Silver Spring, Md., 1996—2000; asst. prof. Uniformed Svc. Univ., Bethesda, Md., 1997—2000; sr. staff physician Henry Ford Health Sys., Detroit, 2000—; asst. prof. microbiology and immunology Wayne State U., Detroit, 2004—. Maj. US Army. Recipient Jack F. Mahon award, Uniform Svc. U., Bethesda, Md., 2000, Career Devel. award, Dermatology Found., 2001—02. Fellow: Am. Assn. Immunology, Soc. Investigative Dermatology, Am. Acad. Dermatology. Office: Henry Ford Hosp One Ford Pl 4D Detroit MI 48202 Office Phone: 313-874-9171. Office Fax: 313-874-4851. Business E-Mail: hwong1@hfhs.org.

WONG, JAMES BOK, economist, chemical engineer, technologist, consultant; b. Canton, China, Dec. 9, 1922; came to U.S., 1938, naturalized, 1962; s. Gen Ham and Chen (Yee) W.; m. Wai Ping Lim, Aug. 3, 1946, (dec.); children: John, Jane Doris, Julia Ann; m. Betty KC Yeow, May 25, 2002. BS summa cum laude in Agr., U. Md., 1949, BS summa cum laude in Chem. Engring., 1950; MS, U. Ill., 1951, PhD, 1954. Rsch. asst. U. Ill., Champaign-Urbana, 1950-53; chem. engr. Std. Oil of Ind., Whiting, 1953-55; process design engr., rsch. engr. Shell Devel. Co., Emeryville, Calif., 1955-61; sr. planning engr., prin. planning engr. Chem. Plastics Group, Dart Industries, Inc. (formerly Rexall Drug & Chem. Co.), LA, 1961-66, supr. planning and econs., 1966-67, mgr. long range planning and econs., 1967, chief economist, 1967-72, dir. econs. and ops. analysis, 1972-78, dir. internat. techs., 1978-81; pres. James B. Wong Assocs., LA, 1981—. Chmn. bd. dirs. United Pacific Bank, 1988—; tech. cons. various corps. Author: Jade Eagle, 2000, Silk Tiger, 2008; contbr. articles to profl. jours. Bd. dirs., pres. Chinese Am. Citizens Alliance Found.; mem. Asian Am. Edn. Commn., 1971-81; grand marshal Chinese Am. Citizens Alliance. Served with USAF, 1943—46. Recipient L.A. Outstanding Vol. Svc. award, 1977. Mem. Am. Chem. Soc., Am. Inst. Chem. Engrs., VFW (vice comdr. 1959), Commodores (named to exec. order 1982), Sigma Xi, Tau Beta Pi, Phi Kappa Phi, Pi Mu Epsilon, Phi Lambda Upsilon, Phi Eta Sigma. Home: 2460 Venus Dr Los Angeles CA 90046-1646 Office Phone: 323-876-4083. Personal E-mail: wjaeagle@aol.com. *Personal philisophy: A man's reputation is his most prized possession.*

WONG, JOSEPH WING PING, Hong Kong government official; b. Hong Kong, 1948; Grad., U. Hong Kong, 1969; one-year post-graduate course, Oxford U., 1975; eight-week Exec. Program, Stanford U., 1989. Asst., dep. dir. Trade, 1984—87; dep. sec. Civil Service, 1988—89, Trade and Industry, 1989—91; Hong Kong's Permanent Rep. to WTO (GATT at the time), 1991—94; dir. Home Affairs, 1994—95; sec. Edn. and Manpower, 1995—2000, Civil Service, 2006—. Office: Sec for Commerce Industry and Tech Level 29 One Pacific Pl 88 Queensway Hong Kong Hong Kong Office Phone: (852) 2918 7500. Office Fax: (852) 2840 1621. E-mail: citbenq@cedb.gov.hk.

WONG, KAU-FUI VINCENT, engineering educator, educator; b. Segamat, Johore, Malaysia, Nov. 22, 1949; came to U.S., 1979; s. Kee-Lim Charles and Min-Moy Mary (Leong) W. BE with honors, U. Malaya, Kuala Lumpur, Malaysia, 1973; MS, Case Western Res. U., 1975, PhD, 1977. Profl. Engr., Fla. Asst. engr. Nat. Electricity Bd., Kuala Lumpur, 1973, rsch. engr., 1976-79; asst. prof. U. Miami, Fla., 1979-83, assoc. prof. Fla., 1983-95, dir. grad. studies Fla., 1990-93, prof. Fla., 1996—, acting dept. assoc. chmn., 1997—98. Dir. Fla. Ctr. Solid & Hazardous Wastes, 1990-95; grad. councilor Coll. of Engring. U. Miami, Coral Gables, 1991—1999, evaluator Abet Mech. Engring., 2000-2007 Editor: Waste-To-Energy Plants, 1991; co-editor: Resource Recovery, 1982, Municipal & Hazardous Wastes, 1984; contbr. numerous articles to profl. jours. Faculty advisor Malaysian Student Assn., U. Miami, 1980—2000, Pi Tau Sigma, 1987—; pres. bd. dirs. Castle Condo Inc., Miami, 1982-83. Recipient ASME Curriculum Innovation Honorable Mention award, 1990. Fellow ASME(chmn., 2009-)(Best Paper award U. ASME, 2006), AIAA (assoc. fellow, life), Am. Geophys. Union, Water Pollution Control Fedn. (Canham runner up 1990), Fla. A.I. Researchers Soc., Sigma Xi, Tau Beta Pi. Office: U Miami Mech Engring Dept Coral Gables FL 33124

WONG, KON MAX, electrical engineer educator; b. Macau, China, June 11, 1945; arrived in Can., 1976; s. Ho Ting and Sin Hung (Yung) Wong; m. Margaret Ellen Rumsey, Aug. 25, 1984; children: An Zhong Alexander, Hui Zhong Richard. BSc in Engring., U. London, 1969; DIC, Imperial Coll., London, 1972; PhD, U. London, 1974, DSc, 1995. Rsch. engr. Plessey Telecom Rsch., Taplow, 1969-76; assoc. prof. Tech. U. Nova Scotia, Halifax, Can., 1976-81; prof. McMaster U., Hamilton, Canada, 1981—, Mitel Prof. signal processing, 1999—, chmn. dept. elec. engring., 1985—86, 1988—94, 2003—; hon. prof. South East U., Nanjing, China, 1995—; vis. prof. Chinese U. Hong Kong, Hong Kong, 1997—. Cons. Defence Rsch. Establishments, Can., 1986—, Mitel Corp., Ottawa, Can., 1993—, Lockheed-Martin, Ottawa, 1993-94, Canadian Marconi, Ottawa, 1995-97, Spotwave wireless, 2000—; assoc. editor IEEE Transaction on Signal Processing, 1997-99. Contbr. articles to textbooks, to profl. jours. Recipient Outstanding Achievement medal, IBC, 2000, Plato award, 2006, Best Rsch. Paper award, Informationstechnische Gesellschaft, 2003. Fellow: IEEE (Best Rsch. Paper award 2006, 2008), Royal Soc. Can., Canadian Acad. Engring., Royal Statistics Soc., Inst. Physics, Inst. Elec. Engrs. (Best Rsch. Paper award 1989). Avocations: piano, painting, philosophy, swimming, table tennis. Office: Dept Elec & Computer Engring McMaster U Hamilton ON Canada

WONG, KUAN YEW, engineering educator, researcher; m. Huey Chin Ch'ng. B in Indsl. Engring. with 1st class honors, Tech. U. Malaysia, 1999, M in Engring. Mgmt., 2001; PhD in Mech. and Mfg. Engring., U. Birmingham, Eng., 2005. Environ. engineering; diploma in music, cert. chartered IT profl. Design engr. Hitachi Cable, Senai, Johor, Malaysia, 1999—2000, environ. mgmt. sys. com., 1999—2000; lectr. Tech. U. Malaysia, Skudai, 2000—06, sr. lectr., 2007—, head metrology lab, 2001—02, head indsl. engring. lab, 2008—, mem. e-learning com., 2005—07, mem. academic pub. com., 2006—, head mfg. sys. area for advanced materials and mfg. rsch. cluster, 2007—09, com. mem. instl. repository, 2007—. Regional editor: Internat. Jour. Knowledge Mgmt. Studies, 2005—, assoc. editor: VINE: Jour. Info. and Knowledge Mgmt. Sys., 2005—, mem. editl. rev. bd.: Interdisciplinary Jour. Info., Knowledge, and Mgmt., 2005—, Internat. Jour. Doctoral Studies, 2006—, mem. editl. adv. bd.: Libr. Rev. Jour., 2006—, Internat. Jour. Applied Systemic Studies, 2006—, mem. editl. bd.: Internat. Jour. Legal Info. Design, 2006—, Internat. Jour. Mechatronics and Mfg. Sys., 2007—, Internat. Jour. Design Engring., 2007—; mem. editl. bd. Internat. Jour. Applied Decision Scis., 2007—; program com.: 2nd Knowledge Mgmt. in Orgns. Conf., 2007; contbr. articles to profl. jours. and confs., chapters to books. Recipient Best Student award in indsl. engring., Tech. U. Malaysia, 2000, Excellent Svc. award, 2006, Best Internat. Jour. Paper award, 2007; grantee, Intel Corp., 2006, Min. Higher Edn., Malaysia, 2006, Min. Sci., Tech. and Innovation, Malaysia, 2006, Intel Tech. Pte., Ltd., 2007, Emerald Group Pub. Ltd., 2007, Latin Am. Coun Mgmt. Schs., 2007, Nat. Sci. and Tech. Coun. State of Mex. Govt., 2008; rsch. scholar, Malaysian Govt., 2002. Mem.: Brit. Computer Soc., Malaysian Scientific Assn., Instn. Engring. and Tech., Soc. Environ. Auditors Malaysia (assoc.), U. Birmingham Alumni Assn., Old Paulians Assn. Achievements include research in knowledge management systems; layout optimization using metaheuristics; the best practices of world class manufacturing; development of framework for knowledge management implementation in small and medium enterprises; one US copyright for a structured automated database for quadratic assignment problem instances. Avocations: piano, hiking, travel. Office: Tech U Malaysia Faculty of Mech Engring Skudai Johor 81310 Malaysia Business E-Mail: wongky@fkm.utm.my.

WONG, KWONG-KWOK, medical educator; b. Hong Kong, Nov. 13, 1960; s. Yuet Wong and Ying Peng; m. Rita Siu-Fee Cheng; children: Man-Wai Ophelia, Isabel See-Wai. BSc, Chinese U. Hong Kong, 1984, PhD, 1990, MPhil, 1987. Sr. rsch. scientist Pacific NW Nat. Lab., Richland, Wash., 1995—2001; asst. prof. Baylor Coll. Medicine, Houston, 2001—06; assoc. prof. UT MD Anderson Cancer Ctr., Houston, 2005—. Adj. assoc. prof. Chinese U. Hong Kong, 2004—. Youth ministry Ft. Bend Cmty. Ch., Mo. City, Tex., 2007. Recipient EHSD Outstanding Performance award, Pacific NW Nat. Lab., 2000, Young Investigator award, Children Oncology Group, 2003; grantee, Nat. Cancer Inst., 2006. Mem.: Soc. Neuro-Oncology, Am. Assn. Cancer Rsch. Achievements include patents for method of detection of salmonella based on DNA sequences derived from Salmonella pathogenicity island; method for producing partially digested DNA restriction fragments; methods of detecting cancer based on prostatin; storing data encoded DNA in living organisms; visualization of information with an established order; methods of detecting cancer based on osteopontin. Home: 5443 Emberwood Way Sugar Land TX 77479 Office: UT MD Anderson Cancer Ctr Unit 1362 1515 Holcombe Blvd Houston TX 77030 Personal E-mail: kkwong5443@gmail.com. Business E-Mail: kkwong@mdanderson.org.

WONG, MARGARET WAI, lawyer; b. Hong Kong, July 27, 1950; d. Mien Lin and Kuan Kuo (Kwan) Hwang; m. Kam M. Chan, Jan. 3, 1983. AA, Ottumwa Heights Coll. (Iowa), 1971; BSc in Chemistry-Biology, Western Ill. U., 1973; JD, SUNY-Buffalo, 1976. Bar: Ohio 1977, N.Y. 1977, D.C. 1980, U.S. Dist. Ct. 1980, U.S. Ct. Appeals (6th cir.) 1983. Instr. bus. law SUNY-Fredonia, 1977; mgmt. trainee Cen. Nat. Bank, Cleve., 1977-78; chief legal and fin. officer Buffalo City Govt., 1979-80; assoc. Berger & Kirchenbaum, Cleve., 1980-81; prin. Margaret W. Wong & Assocs., Cleve., 1981—; co-founder, co-owner Pearl of the Orient Restaurant, Cleve., 1978—; co-founder, cons. Richmond Apothe-Care, Inc. Pharmcy, Cleve., 1982-95, Cleve. Apothe-Care, Inc. Pharmacy, 1986—. Contbr. articles to legal jours. Trustee, Women Space, Cleve., 1982—, Fedn. Community Planning, Cleve., 1983-84, Women City Club, Cleve., 1983—, Orgn. Chinese Ams., Cleve., 1983—, Cleve. Coun. Human Relations, 1983—; sec., trustee Chinese Assn. Greater Cleve., 1980—; bd. dirs. Greater Cleve. Growth Assn., Inter-Mus. Conservation Assn., Notre Dame Coll., Greater Cleve. Roundtable, NCCJ. Named one of Top Ten Outstanding Young Women, Glamour mag., 1983; YWCA Career Woman of Yr., 1984. Mem. ABA (vice chmn. immigration, naturalization and aliens sect. 1993-94), Fed. Bar Assn. (pres.-elect 1993, pres. 1994), N.Y. State Bar Assn., D.C. Bar Assn., Cuyahoga County Bar Assn., Cleve. Bar Assn., Ohio Bar Assn., Cleve. Trial Lawyers Assn., Am. Assn. Immigration Lawyers. Club: Zonta (trustee 1983-84) (Cleve.). Office: Margaret W Wong & Assoc 3150 Chester Ave Cleveland OH 44114 Office Phone: 216-566-9908. Business E-Mail: wong@imwong.com.

WONG, NATHAN DONALD, medicine and epidemiology researcher, educator; b. Downey, Calif., Apr. 18, 1961; s. Donald Wah and Mew Lun (Hee) W.; m. Mia K. Park, July 21, 1996; 1 child, David. BA, Pomona Coll., Claremont, Calif., 1983; MPH, Yale U., New Haven, Conn., 1985, PhD, 1987. Lectr. medicine Yale U., New Haven, 1987; asst. prof. U. Calif., Irvine, 1988—94, assoc. prof., 1994—2002, dir. heart disease prevention program, dept. medicine, 1991—, prof., 2003—; prof. dept. epidemiology UCLA, 2003—. Prin. investigator Antihypertensive Lipid-Lowering to Prevent Heart Attack Trial and other lipid and cardiovasc. prevention trials, 1994—; co-prin. investigator Women's Health Initiative, 1995—; investigator NIH Multiethnic Study of Atherosclerosis (MESA), Coronary Artery Risk Development in Young Adults, Cardiovascular Health Study, and Epidemiology of Diabetes Interventions and Complications Studies; interviewed for various publs. and programs, including ABC Eyewitness News, L.A. Times, Orange County Register, CBS News, USA Today, N.Y. Times, others; profl. cons. Cedars-Sinai Med. Ctr., 2002—; editor-in-chief textbook Preventive Cardiology, Mcgraw-Hill, 2000, 2d edit, 2005; co-editor (textbook) Metabolic Syndrome and Cardiovascular Disease, 2007. Mem. editl. bd.: Preventive Cardiology, Jour. Cardiovascular Drugs, Jour. Cardiometabolic Risk; contbr. chapters to books, over 150 articles to profl. jours. Mem. Calif. Senate Hearing Panel on Youth Phys. Edn. and Fitness, 1991; chair Calif. Cardiovasc. Disease Prevention Coalition, 1998-99; spkr. numerous internat., nat. and local confs., hosps., and med. spkrs. burs. Rsch. grantee, Bristol Myers-Squibb, Pfizer, Merck. Fellow Am. Coll. Cardiology (membership and credentialing com. 2003—09, prevention of cardiovasc. disease com. 2003-04, taskforce 4, 34th Bethesda Conf. 2003), Am. Heart Assn. Coun. on Epidemiology and Prevention, Am. Soc. Preventive Cardiology (pres. elec. 2009-). Achievements include research in computed tomography, metabolic syndrome, diabetes, lipids, hypertension, preventive cardiology, coronary and aortic calcium. Avocations: running, hiking, skiing, photography. Office: Heart Disease Prevention Program Sprague Hall 112 Univ Calif Irvine CA 92697-4101 Home Phone: 949-240-2840. Business E-Mail: ndwong@uci.edu.

WONG, PATRICIA M.Y., library director; BA, Univ. Calif., Berkeley, 1983, MLIS, 1984. Cataloger Oakland Unified Sch. Dist., 1984—85; children's libr. Oakland Pub. Libr., 1984—87, Berkeley Pub. Libr., 1989, supervising libr., 1989—99, prog. dir. Partnerships for Change, 1990—95; libr. prog. mgr. Oakland Pub. Libr., 1999—2001; dep. dir. libr. services Stockton-San Joaquin County Pub. Libr., 2001—07, interim dir. libr. services, 2005; county libr. Yolo County Libr., Woodland, Calif., 2008—. Trainer, various programs Calif. State Libr., 2001—04; trainer, cons. Calif. Cultural Crossroads, Calif. State Libr., 2004—; lectr. Sch. Libr. & Info. Sci., San Jose State Univ., 2006—. Contbr. chapters to books, articles to profl. jours. Named one of the Movers & Shakers, Libr. Jour., 2007. Mem.: ALA (councilor-at-large 1996—2007, mem. exec. bd. 2001—05, chair budget & rev. com. 2005—), U.S. Bd. on Books for Young People (bd. dir. 1995—96), Asian/Pacific Am. Libr. Assn. (pres. 1999, Advocacy award 2006), Chinese Am. Libr. Assn. (bd. dir. 1991—93, pres. Calif. chapt. 1993). Office: Stockton-San Joaquin County Pub Libr 605 N El Dorado St Stockton CA 95202 also: Yolo County Library 226 Buckeye St Woodland CA 95695-2600 E-mail: pattywong61@comcast.net.

WONG, RAY L., lawyer; BA, U. Utah, 1975; JD, Harvard U., 1978. Bar: Idaho, Calif. Assoc. Hancock Rothert & Bunshoft LLP, 1981—85, ptnr., 1985—2005, chmn., 2000—04. Sr. warden, chancellor St. Aidan's Episc. Ch. Named to Northern Calif. Super Lawyers, 2004—09, America's Leading Bus. Lawyers, Chambers USA, 2006—09, Best Lawyers in America, 2008—10, Best Lawyers in the Bay Area, 2009, Best Lawyers in San Francisco, 2009. Mem.: Fedn. Def. and Corp. Counsel, Bar Assn. San Francisco (chair judiciary com.), ABA (co-vice chair ann. meeting 2007, co-chair ann. meeting 2008), Bay Area Asian American Bar Assn., San Francisco Legal Aid Soc. (mem. bd. dirs.). Office: Duane Morris LLP Ste 2000 One Market Spear Tower San Francisco CA 94105 Office Phone: 415-957-3149. Office Fax: 415-520-6907. Business E-Mail: RLWong@duanemorris.com.*

WONG, RICHARD CHI KIT, gastroenterology; b. Hong Kong, Sept. 28, 1961; s. Pak Hung and Ching Wan (Tsui) W.; m. Victoria Mai Ling Wong, Sept. 4, 1989; 1 child, Stephanie Ka Yee. BSc, U. London, 1983, MB, BChir, 1986. Diplomate Am. Bd. Internal Medicine. Intern in medicine St. George's Hosp., London, 1986-87; intern in surgery Epsom Dist. Hosp., Surrey, Eng., 1987; rsch. fellow The Children's Hosp., Boston, 1987-88; resident in medicine Northwestern Meml. Hosp., Chgo., 1988-91, chief medical resident, 1991-92; gastroenterology fellow Brigham and Women's Hosp., Boston, 1992—. Contbr. articles to profl. jours. Recipient Elek prize Rsch. award St. George's Hosp., 1983, Sir Theo Crawford prize in Pathology, 1985, Rambach award Intern of Yr. Northwestern Meml. Hosp., 1988-89. Mem. Am. Coll. Physicians (assoc., co-chmn. assocs. com. 1991-92), Am. Gastroent. Assn. (trainee). Avocations: horticulture, photography. Office: Brigham & Women's Hosp Div of Gastroenterology 75 Francis St Boston MA 02115-6106

WONG, RICHARD YUE-CHIM, academic administrator, economics professor; b. Shanghai, June 20, 1952; s. Lu Au and Yan Pao (Tsai) W.; m. Jane Chun-Kwong Chan, Dec. 30, 1982; c. Michael Bo-Lin, Christina Hsi-Lin. AB, AM, U. Chgo., 1974, PhD, 1981. Asst. lectr. Chinese U. Hong Kong, 1976-80, lectr., 1981-86, sr. lectr., 1987—92; reader U. Hong Kong, 1992—95, prof., 1995—, dep. vice-chancellor. Dir. Hong Kong Ctr. Econ. Rsch., 1987—; vis. scholar Econ. Rsch. Ctr., NORC, U. Chgo., 1985, Hoover Instn., Stanford (Calif.) U., 1989. Part time mem. cen. policy unit, 1991-1992; mem. econ. adv. com., 1992-2001, Hong Kong com. Pacific econ. coop. coun., 1992-2000, dental coun. Hong Kong, 1991-1994, industry tech. devel. com., 1993-1996, U. grants com., 1993-, housing authority, 1998-, chief execs. commn. innovation tech., 1998-1999, exch. fund adv. com., 1999-, hosp. authority, 2001-2003, coun. adv. innovative tech., 2002-; founding trustee Chinese U. Shaw Coll., 1986-99. Mem. Am. Econ. Assn., Econometric Soc., Hong Kong Econ. Assn., Royal Econ. Soc., East Asian Econ. Assn. (sec. gen.), Hong Kong Inst. Econ. Sci. (vice chmn.), Mont Pelerin Soc. (v.p.). Office: U Hong Kong Vice-Chancellor's Office Pokfulam Rd Hong Kong Hong Kong Office Phone: (852) 2859 1122. Office Fax: (852) 2858 1082. E-mail: rycwong@hku.hk.

WONG, SANDRA LYNN, oncologist, educator; MD, Northwestern U., Chgo., 1997. Diplomate in gen. surgery Am. Bd. Surgery, 2004. Asst. prof., surgery U. Mich., Ann Arbor, 2005—. Contbr. articles to jours. Fellow: ACS; mem.: Am. Soc. Clin. Oncology (chair-elect health svcs. com. 2008—). Office: Univ Mich 1500 E Med Ctr Dr 3310 CCC Ann Arbor MI 48109-5932

WONG, SIMON S., environmental health scientist, educator; arrived in U.S., 1992; m. Nina Ning Sun, May 17, 1999; children: Toby, Michael. MD, China Med. U., Shenyang, 1982, MPH, 1988. Cons. U. Ariz., Tucson, 1992—93, rsch. assoc., 1994—96, asst. rsch. scientist, 1997—2002, asst. prof., 2003—07, assoc. prof., 2008—. Contbr. articles to profl. jours. Grantee, USAF, 2000—, Am. Lung Assn., 2001—03, Health Effects Inst., 2005—. Mem.: Am. Thoracic Soc., Soc. Toxicology. Office: Univ Ariz 1501 N Campbell Ave Tucson AZ 85724-5073

WONG, THOMAS TANG YUM, engineering educator; b. Hong Kong, July 27, 1952; arrived in U.S., 1976; s. Kwai Sun and Yee Yuen (Fung) W.; m. Min-I Lee, June 9, 1984; children: Clara Joyce, Lillian Denise. BSc in Engring., U. Hong Kong, 1975; MS, Northwestern U., Evanston, Ill., 1978, PhD, 1981. Product engr. Motorola Semiconductor, Inc., Hong Kong, 1975-76; teaching asst. Northwestern U., 1976-78, rsch. asst., 1978-80, postdoctoral fellow, 1980-81; asst. prof. Ill. Inst. Tech., Chgo., 1981-86, assoc. prof., 1986-96, prof., 1996—, dir. grad. program dept. elec. engring., 1987-95, chmn. dept. elec. and computer engring., 2001—05; dir. rsch. and devel. Telecomm. Equipment Corp., Chgo., 1994—2001; chief sci. authority Quintech Electronics & Comms., Inc., Indiana, Pa., 1997-99. Cons. to pvt. industry, 1981—; chmn. Chicagoland Microwave Symposium, 1988. Author: Fundamentals of Distributed Amplification, 1993; co-author: Electromagnetic Fields and Waves, 2006; contbr. articles to profl. jours.; book reviewer tech. publs.:. Trustee Sch. Dist. 73.5, Ill., 1995—2001. GE fellow, 1983; rsch. grantee NASA, 1989-91, U.S. Dept. Energy, 1992—, pvt. industry, 1993—. Mem. IEEE (chmn. joint Chgo. chpt. Antenna Propagation and Microwave Theory Techniques Soc. 1987-88, mem. steering com. joint symposium Antennas Propagation Soc./Internat. Union of Radio Sci./Nuclear Electromagnetic Pulse 1992), AAUP, Am. Soc. Engring. Edn., Am. Phys. Soc., Tau Beta Pi, Eta Kappa Nu. Achievements include patents for microwave electronics and communications. Office: Ill Inst Tech Dept Elec/Computer Engring Chicago IL 60616 Business E-Mail: twong@ece.iit.edu.

WONG, WANDA YUK-WA, graphics designer, educator; d. Nung and Fung-Mei Cheng; m. Kenneth K. Wong, Apr. 7, 1985; children: Norman James, Simon Jimmy, Cynthia Janice. BA, U. Calif., Berkeley, 1987; MBA, Calif. State U., Hayward, 1998. Academic award evaluator IBM Corp., Berkeley, Calif., 1985—87; ptnr. Photo Type, Oakland, Calif., 1988—; instr. Chabot Coll., Hayward, 2000—; lectr. Calif. State U., Hayward, 2000—01. Alumni scholar, U. Calif., Berkeley, 1981—82. Avocations: travel, reading, crafts. Office: Chabot Coll 25555 Hesperian Blvd Hayward CA 94545 E-mail: wwong@chabotcollege.edu.

WONG, Y(ING) WOOD, real estate investment company executive, real estate development company executive, venture capital investment company executive; b. Hong Kong, Apr. 28, 1950; came to U.S., 1969; s. Loyee K.H. and Margaret M.C.L. Wong; m. Leslie K.P. Chan, Dec. 18, 1977; children: Joshua H., Jonathan H. AA in Biology, Menlo Coll., Atherton, Calif., 1971, BS in Bus. Adminstrn., 1974; BA in Zoology, U. Calif., Berkeley, 1972; MBA, Northwestern U., Evanston, Ill., 1976. Auditor Touche Ross & Co., CPAs, San Francisco, 1976-78; founder, mng. dir. Wong Properties, Palo Alto, Calif., 1976—; founder, venture capital ptnr. Wongfratris Investment Co., Palo Alto, 1986—; founder, ptnr. Corona Main Devel., L.L.C., Palo Alto, 2003—, Sweet Orchid LLC(Frozen Desserts), Palo Alto, 2009—. Instr. Golden Gate U., 1977. Trustee Crystal Springs Uplands Sch., Hillsborough, Calif., 1993-98; advisor The Pei Ying Mid. Sch., Guangzhou, China, The Pui Ying Christian Svcs. Soc., Vancouver, Can.; bd. dirs. Peninsula Symphony, Los Altos, Calif., 2002-03. Named Hon. Citizen of Taishan City, China; established Wood Wong Fgn. Students Exch. Grant, Menlo Coll., 1997—, established Margaret Wong Meml. Music award endowment, Taishan (China) Pei Ying Mid. Sch., 2004—. Mem. Internat. Platform Assn., Commonwealth Club Calif., Beta Alpha Psi. Office: 51 Jordan Pl Palo Alto CA 94303-2903 E-mail: wood.wong@wongfratris.com.

WONG-DIAZ, FRANCISCO RAIMUNDO, lawyer, educator; b. Havana, Cuba, Oct. 29, 1944; came to U.S., 1961; s. Juan and Teresa (Diaz de Villegas) Wong; 1 child, Richard Alan. BA with honors, No. Mich. U., 1965; MA with highest honors, U. Detroit, 1967; PhD, MA, U. Mich., 1974; JD, U. Calif., Berkeley, 1976. Bar: Calif. 1980, Fla. 1987, U.S. Dist. Ct. (no. dist.) Calif. 1990. Prof. City Coll. San Francisco, 1975—, dept. chmn., 1978-85; rsch. atty. Marin Superior Ct., 1980-81; ct. arbitrator Marin Mcpl. Ct., 1985; atty. pvt. practice, Kentfield, Calif., 1980—; academic fellow FDD, 2007—. Adj. asst. prof. San Francisco State U., 1977; assoc. dean Miami-Dade Coll., 1986; dir. Cutcliffe Cons., Inc., Hawthorne, LaFamila Ctr., Inc., San Rafael, Calif., 1980-85, Small Bus. Inst., Kentfield, 1982-86; cons. ICC Internat., San Francisco, 1980-82; polit. commentator Univision KDTV, 1980—; bd. dirs. Pedro Pan Group, Inc.; prostate cancer devel. rsch. com. U. Calif. San Francisco Cancer Ctr. Author: American Politics in a Changing World, 1999, 2d edit., 2004; bd. editors Indsl. Rels. Law Jour., 1975-76; mem. editl. bd. Calif. Lawyer, 1991-93. Lector St. Sebastian's Ch., 1984—, parish coun., 1995; bd. dir. Am. Cancer Soc., 1999—; mem. devel. rsch. program, fellowship com. U. Calif.-San Francisco, 2002—; mem. adv. bd. Redes en Accion, 2002—; mem. Com. on the Present Danger, 2005—; mem. World Assn. Internat. Studies. Vis. scholar U. Calif. Berkeley Sch. Bus., 1983-84, US Dept. State scholar, Washington, 1976; Horace C. Rackham fellow U. Mich., 1970, summer fellow U. Calif. Berkeley, 1995, Nat. Security Law Ctr. U. Va., 1996, Acad. fellow Found. for the Def. Democracies, 2007—; recipient Patient Courage award, ACS, 2004; named Best New Vol. of Yr., Am. Cancer Soc., 2000, One of One Hundred Most Influential Hispanics in the Nation, Hispanic Bus. Mag., 2000. Mem. ABA, Am. Polit. Sci. assn., Latino Ednl. Assn. (co-founder, treas. 1985), Cuban Am. Nat. Coun., World Affairs Coun. (sem. leader San Francisco 1980), World Assn. Internat. Studies, Pacific Coun. Internat. Policy, U. Calif. San Francisco PC Advocates, Commonwealth Club, Proteus USA. Roman Catholic. Business E-Mail: fwong@ccsf.edu.

WONHAM, WALTER MURRAY, electrical engineer, educator; b. Montreal, Que., Can., Nov. 1, 1934; m. Vera Anne Hale; children: Marjorie Jane, Cynthia Margaret. B of Engring., McGill U., Montreal, 1956; PhD, U. Cambridge, Eng., 1961. Asst. prof. elec. engring. Purdue U., Lafayette, Ind., 1961-62; rsch. scientist Rsch. Inst. for Advanced Studies, Balt., 1962-64; assoc. prof. Brown U., Providence, 1964-69; rsch. assoc. NASA, Cambridge, Mass., 1967-69, cons., 1969; prof. elec. engring. U. Toronto, Ont., Canada, 1970—, J. Roy Cockburn prof., 1991-96, Cockburn chair, 1991, univ. prof., 1996—2000, univ. prof. emeritus, 2000—. Author: Linear Multivariable Control: A Geometric Approach, 1974, 3d edit., 1985 (Russian transl. 1980, Chinese transl. 1984); assoc. editor Soc. for Indsl. and Applied Math., Jour. on Control and Optimization, 1965-79, Sys. Control Letter, 1981-85. Recipient Brouwer medal Netherlands Math Soc., 1990; Athlone fellow, Gt. Britain, 1956-58; spl. scholar Nat. Rsch. Coun. Can., 1958-60; sr. postdoctoral resident rsch. assoc. NAS USA, 1967-69. Fellow: IEEE (life control sys. sci. and engring. award 1987), Royal Soc. Can.; mem.: U.S. NAE (fgn. assoc.). Office: U Toronto Dept Elec Engring 35 St George St Toronto ON Canada M5S 3G4 Personal E-mail: wonham@control.utoronto.ca.

WONNACOTT, PAUL, retired economics professor; b. London, Ont., Can., Mar. 16, 1933; s. Gordon Elliott and Muriel Johnston Wonnacott; m. Donna Elizabeth Cochrane, July 2, 1960; children: David, Ann, Alan, Bruce. BA, U. Western Ont., 1955; MA, Princeton U., 1957, PhD, 1959. Instr., asst. prof. econs. Columbia U., NYC, 1958-62; assoc. prof., prof. econs. U. Md., College Park, 1962—91, prof. emeritus, 1992. Rsch. staff Royal Commn. Banking and Fin., Toronto, 1962; sr. staff economist Coun. Econ. Advisers, Washington, 1968-70; assoc. dir. divsn. internat. fin. Fed. Res. Bd., Washington, 1974-75; vis. scholar Office Internat. Monetary Rsch., U.S. Treasury, 1980; econ. adviser to Under Sec. of State, 1990-91; mem. Pres.'s Coun. Econ. Advisers, 1991-93; Alan Holmes prof. econs. Middlebury Coll., 1994-2000, ret., 2000, 38th pres., 2008. Author: The Canadian Dollar, 1960, 2d rev. edit., 1965, (with R.J. Wonnacott) Free Trade between the United States and Canada: The Potential Economic Effects, 1967, (with H.G. Johnson and H. Shibata) Harmonization of National Economic Policies under Free Trade, 1968, Macroeconomics, 1974, 3d rev. edit., 1984, (with R.J. Wonnacott) Economics, 1979, 4th rev. edit. 1990, Spanish edit., 1981, 3d rev. edit., 1987, (with Y. and C. Crusius) Portuguese edit., 1982, 2d rev. edit., 1985, (with A. Blomquist) Can. edit., 1983, 4th rev. edit., 1994, Lithuanian edit., 1998, The United States and Canada: The Quest for Free Trade, 1987, The Last Good War: A Novel, 2007; contbr. articles to profl. jours. Fellow Brooking Inst., 1957-58, Ford Found., 1963-64; vis. fellow Inst. Internat. Econs., 1986, 93-94. Home: 10100 Bevern Ln Potomac MD 20854 Personal E-mail: paulwon@refraction.org.

WONNACOTT, RONALD JOHNSTON, retired economics professor; b. London, Ont., Can., Sept. 11, 1930; s. Gordon and Muriel (Johnston) W.; m. Eloise Howlett, Sept. 11, 1954; children: Douglas, Robert, Cathy Anne. BA, U. We. Ont., 1955; AM, Harvard U., 1957, PhD, 1959. Mem. faculty U. We. Ont., London, 1958—96, prof. econs., 1964—96, chmn. dept., 1969—72, prof. emeritus, 1996—. Vis. assoc. prof. U. Minn., Mpls., 1961-62; cons. Resources for the Future, Econ. Council Can., Can.-Am. Com., C.D. Howe Inst. Author: Canadian-American Dependence: An Interindustry Analysis of Production and Prices, 1961, Canada's Trade Options, 1975, Selected New Developments in International Trade Theory, 1984, The Economics of Overlapping Free Trade Areas and the Mexican Challenge, 1991, (with G.L. Reuber) The Cost of Capital in Canada, 1961, (with Paul Wonnacott) Free Trade Between the U.S. and Canada, 1967, Economics, 1979, 4th edit., 1990, (with Thomas H. Wonnacott) Introductory Statistics, 1969, 5th edit., 1990, Econometrics, 1970, 2d edit., 1979, Regression, 1981 Fellow Royal Soc. Can.; mem. Am. Econ. Assn., Can. Econ. Assn. (pres. 1981), London Hunt Club, Sunningdale Golf Club (Eng.), Hon. Co. Edinburgh Golfers, Craigleith Ski Club. Home: 171 Wychwood Pk London ON Canada N6G 1S1 Personal E-mail: wonnacot@uwo.ca.

WOO, ALEX, jewelry designer; BA, Cornell Univ. Owner and designer Alex Woo Jewelry, NYC, 1999—. Recipient Design Award, Women's Jewelry Assn., 1998; named NY's Rising Star, Crain's Bus. 40 Under

40, 2005, Rising Star, JCK Show, Design Ctr., 2006; named to Elite Women, Hispanic Bus. Mag., 2005. Office: Alex Woo Inc 48 W 48TH St Ste 601 New York NY 10036-1703 Office Phone: 212-226-1352. Office Fax: 212-226-5533.

WOO, CAROLYN YAUYAN, dean; b. Hong Kong, Apr. 19, 1954; arrived in US, 1972; m. David E. Bartkus; children: Ryan, Justin. BS in Economics, with honors and highest distinction, Purdue U., 1975, MS in Indsl. Adminstrn., 1976, PhD in Strategic Mgmt., 1979. Asst. prof. mgmt. Purdue U., 1981—85, assoc. to full prof., 1985—93, assoc. exec. v.p. acad. affairs, 1995—97; dir. profl. master's programs Purdue U. Krannert Sch. Mgmt., 1993—95; Martin J. Gillen dean Mendoza Sch. Bus., Notre Dame U., 1997—, Ray and Milann Siegfried chair entrepreneurial studies, 1997—. Bd. dirs. Aon Corp., 1998—, Nisource Industries Inc., 1998—, Circuit City Stores Inc., 2001—. Bd. dirs. Catholic Relief Services, 2004—; bd. regents U. Portland, 2004—. Recipient TIEM Found. Disting. Scholar award, Internat. Coun. Small Bus., 1987, Excellence award for edn., Asian Am. Alliance, 2002, John S. Day alumni academic svc. award, Krannert Sch. Mgmt., Purdue U., 2003. Mem.: Com. of 100, Assn. to Advance Collegiate Schools Bus. Internat. (bd. dirs. 1999—, vice chair 2002—03, chair 2003—04). Office: Notre Dame Univ 204 Mendoza College Business Notre Dame IN 46556-5646 Office Phone: 574-631-7992. Business E-Mail: Carolyn.Y.Woo.5@nd.edu.

WOO, CHIA-WEI, physicist, educator; came to US, 1955, naturalized, 1972; s. Chih-Ming and Janet (Hsia) W.; m. Yvonne Lo, Jan. 23, 1960; children: Dekai, Deyi, Dehwei, Detian. BS, Georgetown Coll., Ky., 1956; MA, Washington U., 1961, PhD, 1966; DLitt, Georgetown Coll., 1995; DSc, Washington U., 1996. Applied mathematician Monsanto Co., St. Louis, 1959—62; asst. rsch. physicist U. Calif.-San Diego, La Jolla, 1966—68; asst. prof. physics Northwestern U., Evanston, Ill., 1968—70, assoc. prof., 1971—73, prof., 1973—79, chmn. dept. physics and astronomy, 1974—79; provost, prof. physics U. Calif.-San Diego, 1979—83; pres. San Francisco State U., 1983—88; founding pres. Hong Kong U. Sci. and Tech., 1988—2001; sr. advisor Shui On Group, 2001, The Coll. Bd., 2005—. Vis. assoc. prof. U. Ill., Urbana, 1970-71; hon. prof. Inst. Physics, Chinese Acad. Scis., Beijing, 1978—, Fudan U., Shanghai, 1978—, Shenzhen U., 1986—, Peking U., 1996—; sr. advisor, Shenzhen Mcpl. Govt., 1995-; convenor, Shenzhen-Hong Kong Devel. Rsch. Inst., 2006-. Alfred P. Sloan Rsch. fellow, 1971-73; decorated Cmdr. of Most Excellent Order of British Empire, 1996-; Gold Bauhinia Star, Hong Kong, 2000-; Chevalier de la Legion d'Honneur, France, 2001-. Fellow Am. Phys. Soc. Office: Hong Kong U Sci and Tech SSQ T6/8B Clear Water Bay Kowloon Hong Kong Business E-Mail: woo@ust.hk.

WOO, DEREK, electrical and computer engineer; s. Charles and Shirley Woo; m. Yvonne Fennema, Mar. 9, 1996; children: Gabriel, Julian. BScEE, U. Western Ont., London, 1991. Design engr. Ont. Power Generation (Ont. Hydro), Toronto, 1989—93; cons. Siemens AG, Toronto, 1993—94, Accenture (formerly Andersen Consulting), Toronto, NYC, Chgo., 1994—96; pres. Eidetic Sys. Inc., NYC, 1996—; v.p., firmwide tech. Fortune 100 Fin. Firm, NYC, 2004—. Grantee, Govt. of China, 1987; scholar, Imperial Oil (Esso), 1987—91. Mem.: IEEE, IEEE Stds. Assn.

WOO, DONG HYUK, graduate research assistant; b. Seoul, Republic of Korea, Apr. 9, 1979; s. Sang Kyu Woo and Young Hee Shin; m. Jung In Sung, June 18, 2005; 1 child, Nolan Hyunjae. BS, Seoul Nat. U., Republic of Korea, 2005; MS, Ga. Inst. Tech., Atlanta, 2007. Grad. rsch. asst. Ga. Inst. Tech., Atlanta, 2005—; grad. intern tech. Intel, Santa Clara, Calif., 2006; architecture intern NVIDIA, Santa Clara, 2008. Achievements include research in multi & many core processors. Home: 2000 Monroe PL NE 6110 Atlanta GA 30324 Personal E-mail: donghyuk.woo@gmail.com.

WOO, HONGUK, research scientist; b. Seoul, Republic Of Korea, May 8, 1972; m. You Jin Seo, June 19, 1999; children: Erin, Jayden. BS, Korea U., 1995; MSCS, U. Tex., Austin, 2002, PHD, 2008. Engr. KCC med., Seoul, 1994—98; rsch. intern IBM, Austin, 2001—02; cons. Samsung SDS, Seoul, 2002—03; rsch. asst. U. Tex., Austin, 2003—08; rschr. Samsung Electronics, Suwon, Kyungki-Do, Republic of Korea, 2008—. Korea Info. & Telecom. IT scholarship, Korea Govt., 2003—05. Mem.: IEEE. Achievements include first to developing the real-time event monitor for sensor-based systems; invention of prototyping the model-based cyber-physical system; development of implementing the next-generation e-brokerage system.

WOO, JANICE, librarian; d. Kenneth and Patricia Woo. BA, U. Calif., Berkeley, 1975; MLIS, 1980, ABD, 1999. Prints & photographs intern Libr. Congress, Washington, 1980; archivist Pacifica Radio, Los Angeles, 1981—83; libr. NY Pub. Libr., NYC, 1983—84, Columbia U., NYC, 1984—88; head cataloging & tech. svcs. Bklyn. Mus., 1988—89; assoc. U. libr. dir. New Sch. Parsons Sch. Design, NYC, 1989—91; instr. U. Calif., Berkeley, 1991—94; spl. collections libr. Calif. Coll. Arts & Crafts, San Francisco, 2000—02; dir. librs. Calif. Coll. Arts, Oakland, Calif., 2003—. Bd. dir. Statewide Calif. Electronic Libr. Consortium, Los Angeles, 2004—, BayNet, San Francisco, 2006—08. Musician: (performer) Punk Rock Orchestra; contbr. articles to profl. jours. Bd. dir. Kensington Symphony Orch., Calif., 2008. Doctoral fellowships, U. Calif, 1991—97. Office: Calif Coll Arts 5212 Broadway Oakland CA 94618 Business E-Mail: jwoo@cca.edu.

WOO, KENNETH ROGER, urologist; b. LA, July 27, 1969; s. Roger and Julie Woo; m. Christine H. Sohn, May 16, 1998. BS in Molecular Biology magna cum laude, UCLA, 1992; MD with distinction, Mt. Sinai Sch. Medicine, NYC, 1996. Resident urology NYU Med. Ctr., 1996—2002. Contbr. articles to profl. jours. Grantee Yamanouchi USA Rsch., 1999. Fellow: Am. Coll. Surgeons; mem.: AMA, Endourol. Soc., Am. Assn. Clin. Urologists, Am. Urol. Assn., Golden Key, Phi Beta Kappa. Avocations: tennis, hiking. Office Phone: 410-879-4879. Personal E-mail: kennethwoo@comcast.net.

WOO, KYU SUNG, architect; b. Seoul, Korea; arrived in US, 1967; BS in archtl. engring., MS in archtl. engring., Seoul Nat. U.; MArch, Columbia U., 1968; MArch in urban design, Harvard U., 1970. With Sert, Jackson & Associates, 1970—74; urban design cons. Harbison New Town, SC, 1973—80; sr. urban designer Mayor's Office of Midtown Planning and Devel., NYC, 1975; founder Woo Associates, Cambridge, Mass., 1978; prin. Woo and Williams, Cambridge, Mass., 1979—90, Kyu Sung Woo Architects, Inc., Cambridge, Mass., 1990—. Lectr. MIT, Harvard U. Recipient Ho Am prize in the Arts, Samsung Corp., 2008. Fellow: Am. Inst. Architects. Office: Kyu Sung Woo Architects 488 Green St Cambridge MA 02139 Office Phone: 617-547-0128. E-mail: kswa@kswa.com.*

WOO, S. B. (SHIEN-BIAU WOO), retired state official, physicist, educator; b. Shanghai, Aug. 13, 1937; came to US, 1955; s. C.K. and Kuo-Ying (Chang) W.; m. Katy K.N. Wu, July 20, 1963; children: Chih-I, Chih-Lan. BS in Physics and Math. summa cum laude, Georgetown Coll., Ky., 1956; MS in Physics, Washington U., St. Louis, 1962, PhD in Physics, 1964. Prof. physics U. Del., Newark, 1966—2002; lt. gov. State of Del., Dover, 1985-89. Pres. Del. State Senate; chmn. Bd. Pardons; cons. E.I. DuPont Co., Wilmington, Del., 1968, Del. State Coll., Dover, 1980—81; steering com. 80-20 initiative, 1998—2001; pres. 80-20 PAC, 2001—06, 80-20 Ednl. Found., 2005—; vis. prof. Internat. Relations,Tsinghua U., Beijing, 2008. Contbr. articles to profl. jours. Chmn. bd., chief exec. officer Chinese Am. Community Ctr., Hockessin, Del., 1982-83; sec. Asian-Am. caucus Democratic Nat. Conv., 1983-84; pres., co-chmn. Gov.'s Internat. Trade Council, 1985-89; chmn. Gov.'s task force on High Tech., 1985-89. Recipient Highest Achievement award Asian Am. High Tech. Conv., 1985; Army Rsch. grantee, 1972-87, NSF grantee, 1978-81; Inst. fellow Kennedy Sch., Harvard U. Mem. Am. Phys. Soc., AAAS, AAUP (exec. com. nat. council 1974-77), Orgn. Chinese Ams. (bd. dirs. 1977-79, nat. pres. 1990-91), Sigma Xi. Independent. Home: 5 Farm House Rd Newark DE 19711-7458 Office Phone: 866-367-8020. Business E-Mail: sbw@udel.ed.

WOO, SAVIO LAU-YUEN, bioengineering educator; b. Shanghai, June 3, 1942; naturalized; s. Kwok Chong and Fung Sing Woo; m. Patricia Tak-kit Cheong, Sept. 6, 1969; children: Kirstin Wei-Chi, Jonathan I-Huei. BSME, Chico State U., 1965; MS, U. Wash., 1966, PhD, 1971; DSc (hon.), Calif. State U., 1998. Rsch. assoc. U. Wash., Seattle, 1965—70; asst. research prof. U. Calif.-San Diego, La Jolla, 1970—74, assoc. rsch. prof., 1974—75, assoc. prof., 1975—80, prof. surgery and bioengring., 1980—90; vice chmn. for rsch., dir. Musculoskeletal Rsch. Ctr., U. Pitts., 1990—; prof. ortho surgery U. Pitts., 1990—93, prof. mech. engring., 1990—, Albert B. Ferguson Jr. prof. orthopaedic surgery, 1993—2004, prof. civil and environ. engring., 1994—2000, prof. rehab. sci. and tech., 1994—, W.K. Whiteford prof. bioengring., 1998—2007, Carnegie centenary prof., 2002, prof. bioengring., 2007—. Prin. investigator VA Med. Ctr., San Diego, 1972—90, Pitts., 1990—; cons. bioengr. Children's Hosp., San Diego, 1973—80; cons. med. implant cos., 1978—85; vis. prof. biomechanics Kobe (Japan) U., 1981—82; dir., CEO M&D Coutts Inst. for Joint Reconstrn. and Rsch., 1984—90; sci. adv. com. Whitaker Found., 1986—95, Steadman-Hawkins Sports Medicine Found., 1990—, Aircast Found., 1998—2004, OsteoArthritis Scis. Inc., 1992—95; adv. bd. Coll. Engring., Computer Sci. and Tech. Calif. State U., Chico, 1994—; adv. com. coord. grad. program in biomed. engring. U. Edmunton, U. Calgary, 1997—99; bioengring. adv. com. Nat. Health Rsch. Inst., Taiwan, 1996—; biomed. engr. dept. adv. bd. Wayne State U., 1996—; bioengring. dept. adv. bd. Med. Coll. Ohio, 2004—. Assoc. editor Jour. Biomech. Engring., 1979—87, Jour. Biomechanics, 1978—, Jour. Orthopedic Rsch., 1983—2001, Materials Sci. Reports, 1990—97, Jour. Inst. Mech. Engrs., 1990—94, mem. internat. adv. bd. Jour. Knee Surgery, Sports Tramuatology, Arthroscopy, 1993—, mem. editl. bd. Jour. Ortho. Sci., 1995—, Jour. Ortho. Surgery, 1998—2002, Jour. Musculoskeletal Rsch., 1998—, Am. Jour. Sports Medicine, 1995, Am. Acad. Ortho. Surgery, 1995—2000, Healthcare Eng., 1999—, Tech. and Health Care, 2000—05, Jour. Mechanics in Medicine and Biology, 2001—, Frontiers in Bioscience Jour., 2001—, Acta Clinica, 2002—, Jour. Biomed. Engring., 2006—, Jour. Molecular and Cellular Biomechanics, 2005—, Jour. Biomed. Engring., 2006—, Jour. Ortho. Surgery and Rsch., 2006—. Recipient Rsch. Career Devel. award, NIH, 1977—82, Elizabeth Winston Lanier Kappa Delta award, 1983, awards for excellence in basic sci. rsch., Orthopaedic Rsch. Soc. and Am. Acad. Orthopaedic Surgeons, 1983, 1986, 1990, 1993, 2002, Wartenweiler Meml. Lectureship, 1987, Citation award, Am. Coll. Sports Medicine, 1988, O'Donoghue award, Am. Orthopaedic Soc. Sports Medicine, 1990, 1997, H.R. Lissner award, 1991, Giovanni Borelli award, 1993, Muybridge medal, Internat. Soc. Internat. Biomechanics, 1995, GOTS-Beiersdorf AG Res. award, 1996, Olympic Gold Medalist and prize, 1998, Cabaud Meml. award, AOSSM, 1999, Albert Trillat Young Inventors award, ISAKOS, 1999, Chancellor's Disting. Res. award, U. Pitts., 1999. Fellow: ASME (chmn. honors com. bioengring. divsn. 1978—83, mem. exec. com. 1984—89, chmn. bioengring. divsn. 1986—87, sec., chmn. biomechanics com., Robert Henry Thurston award 2005), Biomed. Engring. Soc. (bd. dirs. 1984—86, 2005—07, Disting. Lectr. 2005), Am. Inst. Med. and Biol. Engring. (founding chmn. coll. fellows 1992—94, bd. dirs. 1992—94); mem.: NAS, NAE, Internat. Soc. Arthroscopy, Knee Surgery and Orthop. Sports Medicine (chmn. scientific com. 2007—), World Assn. Chinese Biomed. Engring. (founding pres. 2002—), US Nat. Commn. Biomechanics (exec. com. 1988—2000, chmn. 1994—97), Chinese Speaking Ortho Soc. (chmn. edn. com. 1997—2000, bd. dirs. 1997—2003), Internat. Soc. Fractures Repair (bd. dirs. 1986—94, v.p. 1987—90, pres. 1990—92), Am. Soc. Biomechanics (bd. dirs. 1977—87, pres. 1985—86), Soc. for Tennis Medicine and Sci. (hon.; bd. dir. 1997—2005), We. Orthopaedic Assn. (hon.), Can. Orthopedic Rsch Soc. (hon.), Arthroscopy Assn. N. Am. (hon.), Herodicus Soc. (hon.), Orthopaedic Rsch. Soc. (chmn. program com. 1983—84, bd. dirs. 1983—87, pres. 1985—86), Am. Acad. Orthopedic Surgeons, World Coun. for Biomechanics (chmn. 1998—2002), Internat. Olympic Com. Olympic Acad. of Scis., Acad. Sinica, Inst. Medicine (chmn. sect. I 1996—98). Office: U Pitts 300 Tech Dr 405 Ctr for Bioengring Pittsburgh PA 15219

WOO, VERNON YING-TSAI, lawyer, real estate developer; b. Honolulu, Aug. 7, 1942; s. William Shu-Bin and Hilda Woo; children: Christopher Shu-Bin, Lia Gay. BA, U. Hawaii, 1964, MA, 1966; JD, Harvard U., 1969. Pres. Woo Kessner Duca & Maki, Honolulu, 1972-87; pvt. practice law Honolulu, 1987—. Judge per diem Honolulu Dist. Family Ct., 1978-84, 1995-2002. Bd. dirs. Boys and Girls Club of Honolulu,. 1985-95, pres., 1990-92. Mem.: ABA, Honolulu Bd. Realtors, Hawaii Bar Assn. Home: 2859 Pahoehoe Place Honolulu HI 96817 Office: 201 Merchant St Ste 2302 Honolulu HI 96813 Home Phone: 808-595-3344; Office Phone: 808-529-8822. Personal E-mail: vwoo@hawaii.rr.com.

WOOD, ANDELYS, literature and language professor; b. Randolph, Vt., Jan. 10, 1947; d. Robert and Lyndell Wood. AB, Middlebury Coll.; PhD, Ind. U. Prof. English Union Coll., Barbourville, Ky., 1977—. Recipient Exemplary Tchr. award, Gen. Bd. Higher Edn. and Ministry United Meth. Ch., 1997, 2007—08, Excellence Tchg. award, Union Coll., 1998, Excellence Rsch. award, 1994, 1996, 2000, 2005. Mem.: MLA, Children's Lit. Assn., Ky. Philol. Assn. (v.p. to pres. 1989—91). Office: Union Coll CPO 809 310 College St Barbourville KY 40906 Business E-Mail: acwood@unionky.edu.

WOOD, BETTY JEAN, conceptual artist, educator; b. Pitts., Ind., Mar. 2, 1942; d. Ralph Alphas and Mary Cordis Blanton; m. John E. Ayers, Aug. 25, 1963 (div. May 1987); children: Mark Ayers, Kristin Ayers Torres; m. Frederick Harrison Wood, Jr., Nov. 28, 1987 (dec. Jan. 2002); children: Andrew, Christopher. BA with honors, Pa. State U., 1984; MFA, U. Okla., 1992. Artist-in-residence Okla. Arts Coun., 1993—2003; asst. instr. Okla. Arts Inst., Okla. State U., Stillwater, 1998; guest lectr. Southwestern State U., Weatherford, Okla., 2001; instr. Oklahoma City Mus. of Art., 2002—; guest lectr. Goddard Art Ctr., Ardmore, Okla., 2003. Spl. project asst. ConservArt Assoc., Culver City, Calif., 1991—93; asst. preparator Fred Jones, Jr. Mus. of Art, U. Okla., 1992—2005, installation asst., 1992; co-coord. SummerWind Arts Festival, Norman, 1994—96; coord. SummerWind Arts Festival, Children's Events, 1995—; art cons. Dept. Edn., San Juan, 1986; bd. dirs. Children's Art Network, Norman, 1996—2001; coord./curator spl. exhbn. Ctrl. Pa. Festival of the Arts, State College, 1973—87; adj. prof. U. Okla., Norman, Okla., 1997—98, 2004—06, Okla. City U., 2009—; artist in residence, Costa Rica, 2006, Vt. Studio Ctr., Johnson, 2007. Author: (book reviews) Museologist, 1986—87, Community Based Art Education, 1995; one-woman shows include Bricktown Fin. Inst., Okla., numerous others, exhibited in group shows at 50th Anniversary Nat. Art Exhibit, Wind River Valley Artist's Guild, Wyo., Leslie Powell Gallery, Okla., IAO Gallery, Okla., Gallery on the Sq., Ky., Period Gallery, Nebr., Suite 2 Portfolio, Okla., Kirkpatrick Galleries of Omniplex, Okla., Goddard Art Ctr., Ardmore, Okla., East Ctrl. U., Ada, Okla., Purdue U., West Lafayette, Ind., Lamar U., Beaumont, Tex., Mus. Great Plains, Lawton, Okla., Soho Art Dist., NYC, Murray State Coll., Tishomingo, Okla., Mainsite Art Gallery, Norman, Okla., A Dogi Print Exhbn., Spain, France, Eng., 2009, Internat. Print Exhbn., Taiwan, Ponca City Gallery, Okla., Pass Gallery, Norman, 2007, U. Okla., 2007, Southwestern State U., Okla., 2007, Oklahoma City U. Gallery, 2007, Am. Print Alliance, Peachtree City, Ga., 2007, Internat. Print Exhbn., Spain, Eng. and France, 2007, Internat. Visions Exhbn., Oklahoma City, 2007, Redlands CC, El Reno, Eng., 2008, others, Represented in permanent collections Okla. Visual Arts Coalition, Oklahoma City, Sch. of Art, U. Okla., Okla., exhibited in group shows at others, over 375 exhbns., Represented in permanent collections Fred Jones, Jr. Mus. of Art, Norman, Okla., Okla. Sch. of Arts and Scis., Chickasha, Okla., Sch. of Visual Arts, Pa. State U., University Pk., Pa., Okla. City Art Mus., pvt. collections U.S. and abroad, exhibitions include Lawton, Enid, Ponca City, Okla., 2008, Internat. Print Exhbn., Spain, 2008, Eng., 2008, France, 2008, Tulsa Art Ctr., Okla., 2008, Redlands Cmty. Coll., El Reno, Okla., 2008, Firehouse Art Ctr., Norman, Okla., 2007—08, Lachen Meyer Art Ctr., Cushing, Okla., 2007—08, Invit. Salon Exhbn. Small Works, Kutztown, Pa., 2007—08, Invit. Exhbn., Okla. City, 2007—08, Leslie Powell Gallery, Lawtown, Okla., 2007, Los Milagros, Okla. City, 2007, Okla. State U., Coll. Medicine, Tulsa, Okla., 2008, ADOGI Internat. Print Exhbn., Spain, 2008—09, Eng., 2008, France, 2008, Leslie Powell Gallery, Lawton, 2009, IAO Gallery, Okla. City, 2009, APW Gallery, NYC, 2009, 20th, 21st Small Works Exhbn., Kutztown, Pa., 2009, 28th INTL Print Exhbn., Spain, Eng., France, 2009, Okla. Ctr. Fold, Lawtown, 2009, Okla. Arts Coun., Okla. City, 2009, Okla. Arts Inst., 2009, Okla. Visual Arts Coalition, 2009, Governor's Gallery, Okla. City, 2009. Recipient numerous awards for art. Mem.: Southern Graphics Coun., Okla. Visual Arts Coalition, Fred Jones Jr. Mus. Art, Oklahoma City Mus. Art, Mus. Women in Art, Nat. Mus. for Women in Art, Five to Nine Artists, Jacobson House Found., U. Okla. Art Alumni Assn. (pres. 1993), Pa. State U. Alumni Assn., Beta Sigma Phi Sorority (pres. 1983—84). Democrat. Avocations: children's/adult's workshops, reading, antiques, art, music. Home: 3316 Riviera Dr Norman OK 73072-7613 Office Phone: 405-850-2051. Business E-Mail: fredwood@ou.edu.

WOOD, BRENDA JEAN, pastor, evangelist; b. Patrick AFB, Fla., Sept. 24, 1961; d. Terry Robert Hubbard and Cherry Ann Redwine, James William Redwine (Stepfather); m. Ross Landan Wood, Apr. 11, 1981; adopted children: Dwight Adam Myers, Christopher Wayne Pitts children: Jared Ross, Leslie Anne. AA, Weatherford Coll., Weatherford, Texas, 1981; BA Psychology, Calif. State U., San Bernardino, Calif., 1995; MS Marriage & Family Therapy, Fuller Theol. Sem., Pasadena, Calif., 1999, MA in Theology, 2002. Ordained min. Bethel Christian Ctr., 2004, lic. min. Assemblies of God, Calif., 1999. Youth pastor Full Gospel Assembly of God, Norco, Calif., 1995—97; intern counselor Turning Point Counseling, Diamond Bar, Calif., 1997—99; christian edn. dir. New Life Christian Fellowship, Riverside, Calif., 1998—98, youth pastor, 1998—98, sr. pastor, 1998—2004; pastor, founder Word of Life Ministries Internat., 2004—; evangelist Word of Life Ministries in Nigeria and India. Spkr. Religious and Civic Functions, 1995—; evangelist New Life Christian Fellowship, Mexico, 2002—, Nigeria, 2003, pastoral counselor, Calif., 1995—; parenting educator Safe Haven Program, Riverside, Calif., 2002—03. Chaplain Calif. Dept. of Forestry, Riverside, Calif., 2001—04; bd. mem. Cops and Clergy, Riverside, Calif., 2002, mem., 2002, Jurupa C. of C., Riverside, Calif., 2003, Riverside C. of C., 2007—, Pastors Prayer Fellowship, Riverside, Calif., 2001. Scholar Music, Weatherford Coll., 1979. Avocations: gardening, travel. Home: 1804 Noah Dr Corona CA 92880 Personal E-mail: pastorbrenda@theword.us.

WOOD, CORINNE GIESEKE, former lieutenant governor; b. Barrington, Ill., May 28, 1954; m. Paul R. Wood; children: Ashley, Brandon, Courtney. BS, U. Ill., 1976; JD, Loyola U., 1979. Bar: Ill. 1979. Pvt. practice; counsel Ill. Savs. and Residential Fin. Bd.; atty. Hopkins & Sutter, Chgo.; gen. counsel Ill. Commr. of Banks and trusts; state rep. 59th dist. 90th Ill. Gen. Assembly, Springfield; rep. State of Ill., 1997—99, former lt. gov. Springfield, 1999—2003. Appointed spec. asst., Ill. Atty. Gen. Former co-capt. Shields Twp. Rep. Precinct; Lake Forest chmn. John E. Porter for Congress, 1994, 96; adv. mem. Coun. of Women Advisors to U.S. Congress; past 1st v.p., bd. dirs. Women's Rep. Club, past pres., bd. mem. 10th Congl. Dist. of Lake Forest/Lake Bluff chpt.; past pres. (fin. chmn.), mem. bd. govs. Lake County Rep. Fedn.; bd. dirs. Allendale Shelter Club, Allendale Assn.; adv. bd. A Safe Place; transition bd. dirs. Anne M. Kiley Ctr. for the Developmentally Disabled; mem. LWV of Lake Forest/Lake Bluff; mem. Lake Forest Open Lands Assn.; former Lake Forest chmn., sustaining mem. Jr. League of Chgo.; former new mems. chair, membership com., Sunday sch. tchr. First Presbyn. Ch. of Lake Forest; den leader Pack 43, Boy Scouts Am.; plan commr. City of Lake Forest, 1993-97, sr. housing commr., 1993-97, ad hoc com. on sr. housing bd. mem. Recipient City of Lake Forest Spl. Recognition of Pub. Svc. award. Mem. ABA, Ill. Bar Assn., Lake County Bar Assn., Chgo. Bar Assn., House Financial Insts. Comm., Comm. on Aging, Edn. Appropriations Comm., Labor and Commerce Comm., appointed mem., Legislative Rsch. Bureau, bd. mem. Republican.

WOOD, CYNTHIA WILDER, elementary school educator; b. West Point, NY, July 4, 1952; d. Robert Morse and Cynthia Rich Wood. AA in Early Childhood Edn., Centenary Coll., 1974; BS in Health Edn., U. Conn., 1984; MAT in Elem. Edn., U. Portland, 1989. Med. assoc. pvt. med. office, Greenwich, Conn., 1974—80; radiol. tech. United Hosp., Port Chester, NY, 1980—84, Providence Milw. Hosp., Clackamas, Oreg., 1985—88, Williamette Falls Hosp., Oregon City, 1988—90; tchr. elem. sch. Portland Pub. Schs., 1990—2003, mentor reading coach, 2003—08, tchr., 1st grade, 2008—. Mem. Consortium Ednl. Advancement and Devel., Portland, 1994—2007; presenter in field. Mem. Alameda Tuesday Club, Portland, 1992—2000. Mem.: ASCD, Alpha Delta Kappa. Democrat. Episcopalian. Avocations: reading, needlepoint, gardening. Home: 5022 NE Sumner St Portland OR 97218 Office: Whitman Elem Sch 7326 SE Flavel St Portland OR 97206 Office Phone: 503-916-6370. Business E-Mail: cwood@pps.k12.or.us.

WOOD, DAVID M., oil industry executive; B in Geology, Nottingham U., Eng. Mgr. frontier exploration Murphy Oil Corp., 1994—95, gen. mgr. frontier exploration, 1995—97, v.p. frontier exploration & prodn., 1997—99, sr. v.p. frontier exploration & prodn., 1999—2003, pres. Murphy Exploration & Prodn. Co.-Internat., 2003—06, exec. v.p., 2007—08, pres., CEO, 2008—. Office: Murphy Oil Corp PO Box 7000 El Dorado AR 71731-7000 Office Phone: 870-862-6411.*

WOOD, DIANE PAMELA, federal judge; b. Plainfield, NJ, July 4, 1950; d. Kenneth Reed and Lucille (Padmore) Wood; children: Kathryn Hutchinson, David Hutchinson, Jane Hutchinson; m. Robert L. Sufit, 2006. BA, U. Tex., 1971, JD, 1975; JD (hon.), Georgetown U., 2003, Ill. Inst. Tech., 2004. Bar: Tex. 1975, DC 1978, Ill. 1993. Law clk. US Ct. Appeals (5th cir.), 1975—76, US Supreme Ct., 1976—77; atty.-adv. US Dept. State, Washington, 1977—78; assoc. Covington & Burling, Washington, 1978—80; asst. prof. law Georgetown U. Law Ctr., Washington, 1980—81, U. Chgo., 1981—88, prof. law, 1988—95, assoc. dean, 1989—92, Harold J. and Marion F. Green prof. internat. legal studies, 1990—95, sr. lectr. law, 1995—; spl. cons. antitrust divsn. internat. guide US Dept. Justice, 1986—87, dep. asst. atty. gen. antitrust divsn., 1993—95; judge US Ct. Appeals (7th cir.), 1995—. Contbr. articles to profl. jours.; bd. editors: Am. Jour. Internat. Law. Bd. dirs. Hyde Park-Kenwood Cmty. Health Ctr., 1983—85. Fellow: Am. Acad. Arts and Scis.; mem.: Am. Law Inst. (elected coun. mem. 2003), Am. Soc. Internat. Law, Phi Alpha Delta. Democrat. Office: US Courthouse Rm 2602 219 S Dearborn St Chicago IL 60604-1803*

WOOD, DONALD EURIAH, retired lawyer; b. Guymon, Okla., May 27, 1935; s. Theodore and Lula Elizabeth (Rider) W.; m. Lynda Sharon Harris, Sept. 30, 1960; children: Donald Craig, Tana Dawn, Kristen Lynn. BA, Panhandle A&M Coll., 1958; LLB, Okla. U., 1964, JD, 1970. Bar: Okla. 1964. Asst. county atty., Texas County, 1964; county atty., 1965-67; dist. atty. Okla. 1st Jud. Dist., Guymon, 1967—2003; ret., 2003. Adv. com. Okla. Commn. Criminal and Traffic Enforcement Systems, 1972; active Gov.'s Commn. Cmty. Affairs and Planning, 1972-75; faculty Panhandle State Coll., 1974-92; mem. Okla. Dist. Atty. Tng. Coun., 1976-2003; active Okla. Bur. Narcotics and Dangerous Drugs Commn., 1992-98. Served with inf. AUS, 1958-60. Named Okla. Prosecutor of Yr., Assn. Okla. Narcotic Enforcers, 1994-95. Mem. Okla. Bar Assn. (legal ethics com. 1971-72), Texas County Bar Assn. (pres. 1966, 1970-71), Nat. Dist. Attys. Assn., Okla. Dist. Attys. Assn. (pres. 1972, exec. com. 1971-2001), Elks Club, Rotarian Club, Phi Alpha Delta. Presbyterian. Home: Chesterfield Villas 14901 N Outer Forty Dr Apt 319 Chesterfield MO 63017 Business E-Mail: donewood@gm.com.

WOOD, DONALD F., lawyer; b. Bonne Terre, Mo., July 25, 1944; BSBA, Washington U., 1966; JD, Harvard U., 1969. Bar: Tex. 1970. Adminstrv. ptnr. Vinson & Elkins, L.L.P., Austin. Fellow Houston Bar Found. (chmn. 1991); mem. Beta Gamma Sigma, Omicron Delta Kappa. Office: Vinson & Elkins LLP 2801 Via Fortuna Ste 100 Austin TX 78746 Business E-Mail: dwood@velaw.com.

WOOD, DOUGLAS LYNN, medical educator; b. Columbia, Mo., June 24, 1951; s. Cecil Vernon and Wilda Fay (Palmer) W.; m. Julia Ann Sandbothe, May 28, 1977; children: Ethan, Amanda, Paul, Benjamin. BA cum laude with distinction in Biology, Carleton Coll., 1973; MD magna cum laude, U. Mo., 1977. Diplomate Am. Bd. Internal Medicine, Am. Bd. Cardiovasc. Diseases. Asst. prof. medicine Mayo Grad. Sch. Medicine, Rochester, Minn., 1983—91, assoc. prof. medicine, 1991—2003, vice chmn. dept. medicine, 1993—2008, prof. medicine, 2003—. Cons. cardiovasc. diseases Mayo Clinic, Rochester, 1983-2008, vice-chair dept. medicine, 1993—, chair divsn. health care policy and rsch., 2007—; pres., CEO, chmn. bd. dirs. Immanuel-St. Joseph's Mayo Health Sys., Mankato, Minn.; chair Sec.'s Adv. Com. on Regulatory Reform, Dept. HHS, 2001-02, mem. practicing physicians adv. com., 2000-04. Contbr. articles to profl. jours. Mem. coun. on performance measurement Joint Commn. on Accreditation of Healthcare Orgns., Oakbrook Terrace, Ill., 1995-2007; mem. CPT editl. panel AMA, Chgo., 1994-97; chair fin. coun. St. Pius X Ch., Rochester, 1993-97; mem. Minn. Citizens Forum on Health Care Costs, 2003-04; mem. Gov.'s Quality Control Coun., 2006—; trustee Minn. Med. Assn., 2008-. Fellow ACP, Am. Coll. Cardiology; mem. Am. Coll. Physician Execs., Alpha Omega Alpha, Sigma Xi. Office: Mayo Clinic 200 1st St SW Rochester MN 55905-0002 Home Phone: 507-285-1624; Office Phone: 507-284-3725, 507-284-1446, 504-284-2511. Business E-Mail: wood.douglas@mayo.edu.

WOOD, ELIZABETH ANN, special education educator; b. Pittsfield, Mass., Aug. 2, 1979; d. Dennis Roy Luczynski and Tami Lee Daley; m. Jason Richard Wood, Aug. 31, 2000; 1 child, Haley Elizabeth. BA in Sociology, BA in Early Childhood Edn., Mass. Coll. Liberal Arts, 2001, MEd in Spl. Needs, 2003. Cert. early childhood and moderate disability tcur. Mass. Mgr. Subway, North Adams, Mass., 1996—2002; lead pre-kindergarten tchr. North Berkshire YMCA, North Adams, 2001—03; spl. needs tchr. Hillcrest Edn. Ctrs., Pittsfield, Mass., 2003—. Mem.: Nat. Honor Soc. Roman Catholic. Avocations: sewing, exercise, scrapbooks. Home: 2 Daniels Ct Adams MA 01220 Office: Hillcrest Edni Ctrs 1450 W Housatanic St Pittsfield MA 01201 Business E-Mail: lwood@hillcrestec.org.

WOOD, ERIC FRANKLIN, earth and environmental sciences educator; b. Vancouver, BC, Can., Oct. 22, 1947; s. Lorne George and Olga Eugena (Hryvnak) Wood; children: Eric Alexander, Emily Holding. BASc with hons., U. B.C., 1970; SM, MIT, 1972, MSCE, 1973, ScD, 1974. Rsch. asst. MIT, Cambridge, 1970-73; rsch. scholar Internat. Inst. for Applied Systems Analysis, Vienna, 1974-76; prof. civil engring. and environ. Princeton (N.J.) U., 1976—. EOS sci. steering com. NASA, 1984-87, sci. adv. working group, 1992, land surface processes adv. com., 1985-90, Landsat sci. working group, 1992-93, MTPE Biennial Rev. Panel, 1997; mem. Continental Internat. Project sci. steering com. World Climate Rsch. Program, 1993-95; chair hydrologic applications project, Global Energy & Water Experiment, World Climate Rsch. Program; mem. policy adv. panel Continental Water-Energy Climate Project, NOAA, Office of Global Programs, 1996-97, Climate Working Group, Climate Program Office, 2007-, co-chair sci. adv. group, 2003—. Co-author: An Introduction to Groundwater Contamination from Hazardous Wastes, 1984; assoc. editor: Water Resources Research, 1977-82, Applied Math. and Computation, 1983—, Jour. of Forecasting, 1984-2000, Rev. in Geophysics, 1988-93; editor (books) Recent Developments in Real-Time Forecasting/Control of Water Resources Systems, 1980, Scale Effects in Hyrology, 1986, Land Surface-Atmospheric Interactions for Climate Models: Observations, Modeling and Analysis, 1990; contbr. numerous articles to profl. jours. Recipient Rheinstein award Princton U., 1980. Fellow Am. Geophys. Union (mem. editl. bd. Water Resources Monographs, 1980-85, exec. mem. hydrology sect. 1984-85, 88-92, 94-95, union fellows com. 1994-98, chair 1998-2000, Fall meeting com., 2001-03, Horton Medal Com. 2002-04, union meeting com. 1988-90, chmn. remot sensing com., 1988-92, Horton rsch. com. 1992-95, Robert E. Horton award 1988), Am. Meteorol. Soc. (coun. 1999-2002, Atm awards 2003-, hydrology com. 1987-90, chair 1997—, Robert E. Horton Lctr., 2001); mem. NAS (com. on flood levee policy, water sci. technology bd. 1997-2000, bd. atmospheric sci. and climatology 1999-2002, com. on hydrologic sci. 1999—, chair 2002-09, vice-chair com. integrated ohs 2005-08), NSF (mem. com. of flood hazard mitigation 1979-80, panel on engring. and global climate change 1991), European Geosci. Union (Dalton medal, 2007). Avocations: squash, sailing, skiing. Office: Princeton U Dept Of Civil Engring Princeton NJ 08544-0001

WOOD, EVAN RACHEL, actress; b. Raleigh, NC, Sept. 7, 1987; d. Ira David Wood and Sara Lynn Moore. Actor: (films) Digging to China, 1998, Practical Magic, 1998, Detour, 1999, Little Secrets, 2001, S1m0ne, 2002, Thirteen, 2003, The Missing, 2003, Down in the Valley, 2005, Pretty Persuasion, 2005, The Upside of Anger, 2005, (voice only) Asterix and the Vikings, 2006, Shark Bait, 2006, Running with Scissors, 2006, King of California, 2007, In Bloom, 2007, (voice only) Terra, 2007, Across the Universe, 2007, The Life Before Her Eyes, 2007, The Wrestler, 2008, Whatever Works, 2009; (TV films) In the Best of Families: Marriage, Pride & Madness, 1994, Search for Grace, 1994, A Father for Charlie, 1995, Death in Small Doses, 1995, Get to the Heart: The Barbara Mandrell Story, 1997, Down Will Come Baby, 1999; (TV series) Profiler, 1998—99, Once and Again, 1999—2002, (TV appearances) American Gothic, 1995—98, Touched by an Angel, 2000, The West Wing, 2002, CSI: Crime Scene Investigation, 2003. Office: c/o Toni Howard Internat Creative Mgmt 10250 Constellation Blvd Los Angeles CA 90067*

WOOD, FRANK MAXWELL, former prosecutor, lawyer; b. Forest Park, Ga. m. Suzanne Brunson; children: Frank, Sydney, James. BA, LaGrange Coll., 1981; JD, U. Ga., 1985. Law clk. Floyd County Superior Ct., 1985—87; staff atty. Pros. Attys.' Coun. Ga., 1992—94; asst. dist. atty. Ocmulgee Dist. Atty.'s Office, 1994—97; pvt. practice Macon, Ga.; US atty. (mid. dist.) Ga. US Dept. Justice, 2001—09. Mem. Martha Bowman Meml. United Meth. Ch. With USAF, col. Ga. Air Nat. Guard.

WOOD, GEORGIANNA ADELINE, primary school and language educator; b. Miami, Fla., Oct. 1, 1951; d. Hayes Stearns Wood Sr. and Georgina Gomez Wood. BA, Fla. State U., Tallahassee, 1973; MA, U. South Fla., Tampa, 1977; ESL endorsement, Tex. Woman's U., Denton, 1987. Kindergarten tchr. Manatee County Sch. Sys., Bradenton, Fla., 1974—79, Pinellas County Sch. Sys., Clearwater, Fla., 1979—80; 1st, 2d and 3d grade tchr. Pulaski County Sch. Dist., Little Rock, 1980—83; kindergarten/ESL tchr. Dallas Ind. Sch. Dist., 1983—, grade level chmn., early childhood facilitator, supervising/mentor tchr., 1990—. Sec. bd. dirs. Arts for People, Dallas, 1986—88. Named ESL Tchr. of Year, Lorenzo Dezavala Elem. Sch., Dallas, 1989, Tchr. of Yr., Preston Hollow Elem. Sch., Dallas, 1995; finalist K-3 Dallas. Mem.: Kindergarten Tchrs. Tex., Nat. Assn. Edn. Young Children, Assn. Childhood Edn. Internat., Assn. Tex. Profl. Educators. Office: Preston Hollow Elem Sch 6423 Walnut Hill Ln Dallas TX 75230 Personal E-mail: gewood@academicplanet.com.

WOOD, GORDON STEWART, historian, educator, writer; b. Concord, Mass., Nov. 27, 1933; s. Herbert G. and Marion (Friberg) W.; m. Louise Goss, Apr. 30, 1956; children: Christopher, Elizabeth, Amy. AB, Tufts U., 1955; AM, Harvard, 1959; PhD, Harvard U., 1964. Fellow Inst. Early Am. History and Culture, Williamsburg, Va., 1964-66; asst. prof. Harvard U., Cambridge, Mass., 1966-67; assoc. prof. U. Mich., Ann Arbor, 1967-69; prof. history Brown U., Providence, 1969—; Pitt. prof. Cambridge U., 1982-83. Bancroft lectr. U.S. Naval Acad., 1986; Anson G. Phelps lectr. NYU, 1986; Charles Edmundson lectr. Baylor U., 1987; Samuel Paley lectr. Hebrew U., Jerusalem, 1987; presdl. lecture series on presidency, 1991; trustee, visiting prof. history & law Northwestern U., 2003; bd. trustees Tufts U. Author: The Creation of the American Republic, 1776-1787, 1969, The Rising Glory of America, 1760-1820, 1971; co-author: The Great Republic, 1977, The Radicalism of the American Revolution, 1992 (Pulitzer Prize for history 1993); co-editor: Imagined Histories: American Historians Interpret the Past, 1998, The American Revolution: A History, 2002, The Americanization of Benjamin Franklin, 2004, Revolutionary Characters: What Made the Founders Different, 2006, The Purpose of the Dast: Reflections on the uses of History, 2008. Mem. coun. Inst. Early Am. History and Culture, 1980-83; bd. trustees Colonial Williamsburg. With USAF, 1955-58. Recipient Bancroft prize Columbia U., 1970, Disting. Visitor award Australian-Am. Ednl. Found., 1976, Douglass Adair prize, 1984, Emerson prize Phi Beta Kappa, 1992, Kidger award New Eng. Tchrs. Assn., 2001, Boston Authors Club prize, 2005; Sunderland fellow U. Mich. Law Sch., 1990, All Souls Coll. fellow, 1991, Fletcher Jones Found. Disting. fellow The Huntington, 1997-98; Woodrow Wilson Ctr. guest-scholar, 1993-94; named to Rhode Island Heritage Hall of Fame, 2000; Dr. of Letters, La Trobe Univ., Austrailia, Dr. of Law, Providence Coll. Mem. Am. Hist. Assn. (John Dunning prize), Orgn. Am. Historians, Soc. Am. Historians, Nat. Hist. Soc. (chmn. bd. advisors), Soc. Historians of the Early Am. Republic (pres.), Am. Acad. Arts and Scis., Am. Philos. Soc. Office: Brown Univ Dept of History Box N Providence RI 02912-9040

WOOD, HOUSTON G., engineering educator, researcher; b. Tupelo, Miss., Oct. 4, 1944; s. Houston G. and Jane Poe Wood; m. Kathryn Diane Franzen; children: Andrea Wood Grattan, Heather Wood Harrison. BA, Miss. State U., Starkville, 1965, MS, 1967; PhD, U. Va., Charlottesville, 1977. Prof. U. Va., 2004—, assoc. prof. Home: 5040 Clearfields Ct Crozet VA 22932 Office: Univ Virginia 122 Engineers' Way Charlottesville VA 22904

WOOD, H(OWARD) JOHN, III, astrophysicist, astronomer; b. Balt., July 19, 1938; s. Howard John Jr. and Cara (Loss) W.; m. Austine Barton Read, June 10, 1961 (div. Jan. 1975); children: Cara Loss, Erika Barton; m. Maria Ilona Kovacs, May 22, 1977; 1 child, Andreas M. BA in Astronomy, Swarthmore Coll., 1960; MA, Ind. U., 1962, PhD, 1965. Lectr., asst. prof. then assoc. prof. U. Va., Charlottesville, 1964-70; staff astronomer European So. Obs., Santiago, Chile, 1970-75; Fulbright Rsch. fellow U. Vienna Obs., 1976-78; rsch. assoc. Ind. U., Bloomington, 1978-81; asst. to the dir. Cerro Tololo Inter-Am. Obs., La Serena, Chile, 1982-83; physicist, astronomer NASA/Goddard Space Flight Ctr., Greenbelt, Md., 1984—, mgr. instrument synthesis and analysis lab., 2000—08, optics lead engr., Advanced Topographic Laser Altimeter System, 2008—. Optics lead engr. Mars Observer Laser Altimeter, 1989-90, GFC Hubble Space Telescope, Greenbelt, 1990—; GFC advisor optics and outreach James Webb Space Telescope, Greenbelt, 1996—; GFC advisor, participant Hubble Space Telescope Allen Comm., NASA, Danbury, Conn., 1990, Greenbelt; co-chmn. Hubble Space Telescope Ind. Optical Rev. Panel, Columbia, Md., 1990-91; mem. panel The Townes/SAGE Panel-Jet Propulsion Lab., Pasadena, 1991-92 Co-author: (Book) Physics of Ap Stars, 1976; contbr. articles to profl. jours. Grantee NSF (10), 1965-82, Am. Astron. Soc., 1978. Mem. Internat. Astron. Union (Commn. 29 1962—), Optical Soc. Am. (chair optical tech. divsn. 1999-2001, co-chair ann. meeting 2002), Am. Astronomical Soc., Sigma Xi. Achievements include discovery of Balmer-Line variability of Ap stars; discovery of magnetic fields in southern Ap stars; alignment testing and delivery of the DIRBE photometric cryogenic telescope on the COBE spacecraft; alignment and optical prescription for Hubble Space Telescope while in orbit. Office: NASA/Goddard Space Flight Ctr Code # 551 Greenbelt MD 20771-0001 Office Phone: 301-286-8278. Business E-Mail: howard.j.wood@nasa.gov.

WOOD, JACKIE DALE, physiologist, educator, researcher; b. Picher, Okla., Feb. 16, 1937; s. Aubrey T. Wood and Wilma J. (Coleman) Wood Patterson. BS, Kans. State U., 1964, MS, 1966; PhD, U. Ill., 1969. Asst. prof. physiology Williams Coll., Williamstown, Mass., 1969-71; asst. prof. U. Kans. Med. Ctr., Kansas City, 1971-74, assoc. prof., 1974-78, prof., 1978-79; prof., chmn. dept. physiology Sch. Medicine, U. Nev., Reno, 1979-85; chmn. dept. physiology coll. medicine Ohio State U., Columbus, 1985-97, prof. physiology and internal medicine, 1997—. Cons. NIH, Bethesda, Md., 1982-88. Editor: (book) Physiology of the Digestive Tract. Adv. bd. Internat. Found. Functional Gastrointestinal Disorders, Milw., 1997—2008. Recipient Rsch. Career Devel. award NIH, 1974; named Hon. Citizen City of Atzugi Japan, 1987; Alexander von Humboldt fellow, W.Ger., 1976, grantee NIH, 1971—. Fellow Am. Gastroent. Assn.; mem. AAAS, Am. Physiol. Soc. (assoc. editor 1984-96, rsch. award 1986), Soc. Neuroscience. Office: Ohio State U Dept Physiology and Cell Biology 304 Hamilton Hall 1645 Neil Ave Columbus OH 43210-1218 Home Phone: 614-457-2820; Office Phone: 614-292-5449. Business E-Mail: wood.13@osu.edu.

WOOD, JAMES, magazine editor, literary critic; b. Durham, Eng., 1965; m. Claire Messud; 2 children. Chief lit. critic The Guardian, London, 1990—; sr. editor The New Republic, Washington, 1996—; also editor-at-large Kenyon Rev.; prof., practice lit. criticism Harvard Univ., 2003—. Author: The Broken Estate, 2000, The Book Against God, 2003, The Irresponsible Self, 2004. Recipient British Press Young Journalist of Yr. award, 1990. Fellow: Am. Acad. Arts & Scis. Office: New Republic 1331 H St NW Suite 700 Washington DC 20005 Office Phone: 202-508-4444.

WOOD, JAMES EDWARD, JR., religion educator, author; b. Portsmouth, Va., July 29, 1922; s. James E. and Elsie Elizabeth (Bryant) W.; m. Alma Leacy McKenzie, Aug. 12, 1943 (dec. Oct. 2000); 1 son, James Edward III BA, Carson-Newman Coll., 1943; BD, So. Bapt. Theol. Sem., 1947, ThM, 1948; MA, Columbia U., 1949; postgrad., U. Tenn., 1943-44; cert. in Chinese, Yale U., 1949-50; Japanese diploma, Naganuma Sch. Japanese Studies, Tokyo, 1950-51; PhD., So. Bapt. Theol. Sem., 1957; LLD, Seinan Gakuin U., Japan, 1983; LLD (hon.), Capital U., 1996; DHC (hon.), Bucharest U., Romania, 1998. Ordained to ministry So. Bapt. Ch., 1942. Pastor Bapt. chs., Tenn. and Ky., 1942-48; Bapt. missionary to Japan, 1950-55; prof. religion and lit. Seinan Gakuin U., Japan, 1951-55; assoc. prof. history of religions Baylor U., Waco, Tex., 1955-58, prof. hist. religion, dir. J. M. Dawson Inst. Ch. State Studies, 1958—73, 1980—99, 1st dir. honors program, 1959-64, founder chmn. interdeptl. grad. degree program in ch.-state studies, 1962-73, 80-95, founder Baylor Univ. Ch. State Rsch. Ctr., 1968, founder, chmn. faculty-student Far Eastern exch. program, 1970-72, Simon and Ethel Bunn Disting. prof. ch.-state studies, 1980-99, Simon and Ethel Bunn Disting. prof. emeritus, 1999—. Exec. dir. Bapt. Joint Com. on Pub. Affairs, Washington, 1972—80; mem. ctrl. panel Bapt. World Alliance Commn. on Religious Liberty and Human Rights, 1965—75, 1980—2000, Commn. on Freedom, Justice and Peace, 1975—80; chmn. Bapt. Com. on USA Bicentennial, 1973—76; mem. So. Bapt. Inter-Agy. Coun., 1972—80, vice chmn., 1975—76, sec., 1976—77; fellow Internat. Acad. for Freedom of Religion and Belief, 1985—, pres., 1990—2000, hon. pres., 2000—; vis. prof. So. Bapt. Theol. Sem., 1974, N.Am. Bapt. Theol. Sem., Sioux Falls, SD, 1974, SD, 79, Okla. Bapt. U., Shawnee, 1977; vis. scholar Christ Coll. Oxford U., 1983; vis. prof. Bulgarian Bapt. Theol. Sem., Sofia, Bulgaria, 1998; vis. prof. Faculty of Canon Law Cath. U., Leuven, Belgium, 1999; vis. prof. others; vis. lectr. Tex. A&M U., 1962, 65, 68, Ashland Theol. Sem., Ohio, 1971; lectr. Union Theol. Sem., NYC, 1974, Va., 89; Vernon Richardson lectr. U. Bapt. Ch., Balt., 1975; lectr. Ea. Bapt. Theol. Sem., Phila., 1975, Duquesne U., 1976, Wake Forest U., 1978, U. Richmond, 1979, First World Congress on Religious Liberty, Amsterdam, 1977, Rice U., 1977, 84, Notre Dame Law Sch., 1980, U. Kans., 1982, U. So. Calif., 1983, 2d World Congress on Religious Liberty, Rome, 1984, U. Faculty of Law, Warsaw, 1984, Loyola U., 1985, Chinese Inst. Religion, Beijing, 1986, Brigham Young U. Law Sch., 1986, Naval Coll. Chaplains, Providence, 1988—95, faculty law U. Oviedo, Spain, 1989, Austin Coll., 1989, 95, U. Kans. Law Sch., 1990, U. Tirana, Albania, 1992, U. Malta, 1994, Brigham Young U. Law Sch., 1995, 97, 2005, U. Pitts. Law Sch., 1997, U. Kiev, 1998; chair Internat. Consultation on Religious Rights and Ethnic Identity, Budapest, 1992; mem. internat. adv. bd. World Report on Freedom Conscience 2nd. Human Rights Ctr. U. Sussex, England; co-chair consultation on Freedom of Conscience Human Rights and Belief, Moscow, 1993; chair Internat. Consultation Religious Liberty and Social Peace, Malta, 1994; Carver-Barnes lectr. Southeastern Bapt. Theol. Sem., 1981; Asian Found. lectr. Seinan Gakuin U., Japan, 1983; ecumenical consultation on edn. Nat. Coun. Chs., 1974; spkr. in field. Co-author: Church and State in Scripture, History and Constitutional Law, 1958; author: A History of American Literature: An Anthology, 1952, The Problem of Nationalism, 1969, Nationhood and the Kingdom, 1977, Secular Humanism and the Public Schools, 1986, Reflections on Church and State, 1995; (edited by Derek H. Davis) The Separation of Church and State Defended: Selected Writings of James E. Wood, Jr., 1995, Church-State Relations in the Modern World, 1999, Church and State In Historical Perspective, vol. 1, 2005, Church and State In The Modern World, vol. 2, 2005, and numerous others; editor: Markham Press Fund, Baylor U. Press, 1970-72; editor, contr.: Jewish-Christian Relations in Today's World, 1971, Baptists and the American Experience, 1976, Religion and Politics, 1983, Religion, the State, and Education, 1984, Religion and the State: Essays in Honor of Leo Pfeffer, 1985, Ecumenical Perspectives on Church and State, Protestant, Catholic and Jewish, 1988, Readings on Church and State, 1989, The First Freedom: Religion and the Bill of Rights, 1990, contr. co-editor: The Role of Religion in the Making of Public Policy, 1991, The Role of Government in Monitoring and Regulating Religion in Public Life, 1993, Problems and Conflicts Between Law and Morality in a Free Society, 1994, founding editor Jour. Ch. and State, 1959-73, 80-93, mem. editl. coun., 1973-80, mem. editl. bd., 1993-99; mem. editl. bd. Religion and Public Edn., Religious Freedom Reporter; area editor, contbr. Ency. So. Bapts., 1982, Church and State in Am. History, 1987; contbr. Changing Trends in Education, 1992, Law, Religion and Human Rights in Global Perspective, 1995, Dialogue of Democracy: An American Politics Reader, 1996, United Nations' Contributions to the Prevention and Settlement of Conflicts, 2003, The New Inquisitors, 2004, many others; contbr. over 300 articles to profl. jours. Sponsor Ams. for Pub. Schs., 1963-68; bd. dirs. Waco (Tex.) Planned Parenthood, 1966-72, pres., 1971-72; sponsor Christians Concerned for Israel, 1968—, Tex. Conf. Chs. Consultation on Religion and Public Edn., 1971, Nat. Christian Leadership Conf. for Israel, 1978—; pres. Waco area ACLU, bd. dirs. Tex. unit, 1968-72; pres. Nat. Coun. Religion and Pub. Edn., 1979-83, exec. com., 1975-90, bd. dirs., 1972-90; chmn. exec. com. Coun. Washington Reps. on UN, 1977-80, mem. council exec. com., 1973-80; exec. com. Nat. Coalition on Pub.

Edn. and Religious Liberty, 1973-95; mem. religious liberty com. Nat. Coun. Chs. U.S.A., 1972—, mem. com. internat. concerns on human rights, 1973-80; Am. rep. Chs. Montreux Colloquium on Helsinki Final Act, 1977; v.p. Waco Conf. Christians and Jews, 1983-86, Internat. Acad. for Freedom of Religion and Belief, 1985-90, pres., 1990-2000, hon. pres., 2000—; mem. internat. adv. bd. World Report on Freedom of Conscience, Human Rights Ctr., U. Sussex, Eng.; trustee Internat. Devel. Conf., 1974-80; nat. coun. Am.-Israel Friendship League, 1977—; founder, chmn. Waco Human Rights Week, 1981-86; mem. ch. rels. com., U.S. Holocaust Meml. Coun., 1990-97; adv. com. on religious freedom abroad U.S. State Dept., 1998-2004. Recipient Disting. Alumnus award, Carson-Newman Coll., 1974, Religious Liberty award, Alliance for Preservation of Religious Liberty, 1980, Henrietta Szold award, Tex. region Hadassah, 1981, Human Rights award, Waco Conf. Christians and Jews, 1986, Cir. of Achievement award, Baylor U. Mortar Bd., 1991, Religious Freedom Lifetime award, Ams. United Ctrl. Tex., 1993, W.R. White Meritorious Svc. award, 1996, Human Rights Leadership award, Freedom mag., 1998, Herbert H. Reynolds Exemplary award, 2004, Alma M. and James E. Wood, Jr. endowed scholarship, Baylor U., 2004—, Disting. Svc. in Promoting Religious Freedom award, Brigham Young U. Internat. Ctr. for Religious Studies, 2005. Mem. Am. Soc. Ch. History, Am. Acad. Religion, Am. Soc. Internat. Law, Am. Soc. Sci. Study of Religion, N. Am. Soc. Ecumenists, NCCJ (ad. com. on ch. state and taxation 1979-85), ACLU, Supreme Court Hist. Soc., Soc. for Scholarly Publishing, Va. Hist. Soc., Phi Eta Sigma, Pi Kappa Delta, Alpha Psi Omega. Democrat. Home: 203 Barrington Ln Yorktown VA 23693-5622 Business E-Mail: james_wood@baylor.edu.

WOOD, JAMES JERRY, lawyer; b. Rockford, Ala., Aug. 13, 1940; s. James Ronald and Ada Love Wood; m. Earline Luckie, Aug. 9, 1959; children: James Jerry, William Gregory, Diana Lynn. AB, Samford U., 1964, JD, 1969. Bar: Ala. 1969, U.S. Supreme Ct. 1976. Dir. legal affairs Med. Assn. State of Ala., Montgomery, 1969-70; asst. atty. gen. State of Ala., Montgomery, 1970-72; asst. U.S. atty. Middle Dist. Ala., Montgomery, 1972-76; pvt. practice, 1977-78; pres. Wood & Parnell, P.A., Montgomery, Ala., 1979-89; pvt. practice Montgomery, 1990—. Gen. counsel Ala. Builders Self-Insurers Fund, Home Builders Assn. of Ala.; chmn. character and fitness com. Ala. State Bar, 1981-84, 86-89, chair task force on quality of life, 1990-92, chair task force on mem. svcs., 1994-96. Capt. USAR, 1974-79. Fellow: Ala. Law Found., Am. Bar Found.; mem.: FBA (pres. Montgomery chpt. 1974—75), ABA (ho. of dels. 1990—98), Def. Rsch. Inst., Ala. Coun. Assn. Execs. (pres. 2001), Ala. Bar Assn., Ala. Assn. Workers Compensation Group Self-Insured Funds (chmn.), Am. Soc. Assn. Execs., Am. Nat. Inns of Ct., Rotary (pres. Montgomery Capital chpt. 1986—87, 1996—97). Republican. Baptist. Office: PO Box 241206 Montgomery AL 36124-1206 Home Phone: 334-356-0573; Office Phone: 334-834-3006. E-mail: jerrywood@hbaa.org.

WOOD, JAMES MICHAEL, lawyer; b. Oakland, Calif., Mar. 22, 1948; s. Donald James and Helen Winifred (Reimann) Wood; m. Cynthia Ahart Wood; children from previous marriage: Nathan, Sarah, Ruth 1 stepchild, Alexandra. BA, St. Mary's Coll., 1970; JD, U. San Francisco, 1973. Bar: Calif. 1973, U.S. Dist. Ct. (no., ctrl. and so. dists.) Calif. 1973. Rsch. atty. Alameda County Superior Ct., Oakland, 1973—76; ptnr. Reed Smith LLP, Oakland, 1976—. Presenter profl. confs. Contbr. articles to profl. jours. Chair of bd. dirs. Food and Drug Law Inst., Washington, DC. Recipient Disting. Pro Bono Svc. award, Reed Smith Sean Halpin; named Atty. of Yr., Aids Legal Referral Panel, 2006. Mem.: ABA (litig. sect., health litig. com., litig. products liability com.), Food Drug Law Inst. (bd. dirs., adv. com. 1999—2008), Nat. Health Lawyers Assn., Am. Acad. Hosp. Attys., Def. Rsch. Inst., Alameda County Bar Assn., No. Calif. Assn. Def. Counsel, State Bar Calif. Office: Reed Smith LLP 1999 Harrison St Ste 2200 Oakland CA 94612-3572 Home Phone: 510-883-0323; Office Phone: 510-466-6758. Business E-Mail: jmwood@reedsmith.com.

WOOD, JAMES NOWELL, foundation administrator, retired museum director; b. Boston, Mar. 20, 1941; s. Charles H. and Helen N. (Nowell) Wood; m. Emese Forizs, Dec. 30, 1966; children: Lenke Hancock, Rebecca Nowell. Diploma, Universita per Stranieri, Perugia, Italy, 1962; BA, Williams Coll., Williamstown, Mass., 1963; MA (Ford Mus. Tng. fellow), NYU, 1966. Asst. to dir. Met. Mus., NYC, 1967-68, asst. curator dept. 20th century art, 1968-70; curator Albright-Knox Art Gallery, Buffalo, 1970-73, assoc. dir., 1973-75; dir. St. Louis Art Mus., 1975-80; pres., dir. Art Inst. Chgo., 1980—2004; pres., CEO J. Paul Getty Trust, LA, 2007—. Vis. com. visual arts U. Chgo., 1980—94; bd. dirs. Pulitzer Found. Arts, 2005—, Sterling & Francine Clark Art Inst., NYU Inst. Fine Arts. Mem.: Assn. Art Mus. Dirs., Intermuseum Conservation Assn. (past pres.). Office: J Paul Getty Trust 1200 Getty Ctr Dr Los Angeles CA 90049 Office Phone: 310-440-7600. Business E-Mail: jwood@getty.edu.*

WOOD, JANIS LOUISE, retired assistant principal; b. Wichita Falls, Tex., June 26, 1947; d. J. D. Richmond and Sarah Helena Stevens; m. Tommy Joe Kennedy (div.); children: Pamela Kathleen Leidy, John David; m. Jack Kelsey Wood, Aug. 7, 1970. AA, Eastfield Coll., Dallas, 1973; BA cum laude, U. Tex., Dallas, 1976; MEd, E. Tex. U., Commerce, 1997. Cert. tchr. Tex. Tchr. Plano Ind. Sch., Tex., 1978—82; owner, designer Wood Studios, Plano, 1984—90; tchr. Garland Ind. Sch. Dist., Tex., 1992—97, asst. prin., 1997—98, HS asst. prin., 1998—2001; ret., 2001. Instr. writing Collin County CC, Plano, 1992—94, Richland CC, Richardson, Tex., 1992—94; cons. human resources Millennium Cirs., Dallas, 2004—06. Bd. dirs. Garland Sports Hall of Fame, 2004—06. Recipient Super Tchr. award, Naaman Forest HS, 1992, Life Saving award, Garland Police, 2000. Mem.: Phi Theta Kappa. Republican. Avocations: gardening, reading.

WOOD, JEAN CAROL, poet, lyricist; b. Oklahoma City, Apr. 6, 1940; d. Howard Melvin and Ethel Matillda (Carroll) Sage; m. Harold David Wood; children: Howard David, Troy Don, Kevin Dale, L'lana Cayé. Freelance writer, 1976—. Contbr. poems in collections; lyricist: songs As It Should Be, 2001—02, As It Should Be III, 2005, Glory, 2006; author: (poem) Rest On His Thumb, 2003, The Transport Of a Winged Being, Are You Ready for the Conflict, 2007, The Adventure (Best Poem, 2007), (book) Glory Land, 2006, (poems) Are You Ready For the Conflict, The Adventure. Recipient trophy, Internat. Soc. Poets, 2003. Mem.: Internat. Soc. Poets. Avocations: writing, gardening, reading. Home: 1047 W Windsor Way Mustang OK 73064

WOOD, JERRY (JEROME C. WOOD), diversified financial services company executive; b. Seattle, 1953; m. Monica R. Wood. BS in Acctg., Manhattan Coll., 1975; MBA, NYU, 1980. Trader fixed income divsn. Morgan Stanley, 1978—85, v.p., 1985—87, prin., 1987—92, mng. dir., 1992—2003, 2006—, co-head instl. clients and svcs., 2007—; global co-head, fixed income Credit Suisse First Boston, 2003—05. Bd. dirs. Companions in Courage Found., 2007—. Office: Morgan Stanley 1585 Broadway New York NY 10036

WOOD, JIM, mayor, Oceanside, California; b. Manchester, NH, Jan. 31, 1948; s. Dwight and Harriet Wood; m. Pam Wood; 3 children. Grad., Mira Costa Coll. Police officer City of Oceanside, Calif., 1971—2002, mayor Calif., 2004—; councilman Oceanside City Coun., Calif., 2002—04. Sr. investigator FBI, NCIS, Secret Service. Mailing: City of Oceanside 300 N Coast Hwy Oceanside CA 92054 Office Phone: 760-435-3029, 760-966-4401. E-mail: jwood@ci.oceanside.ca.us.*

WOOD, JOHN ARMSTEAD, planetary scientist, geological sciences educator, artist; b. Roanoke, Va., July 28, 1932; s. John Armstead and Lillian Cary (Hall) W.; m. Elisabeth Mathilde Heuser, June 12, 1958 (div.); children: Crispin S., Georgia K.; m. Julie Marie Nason, Sept. 9, 1989. BS in Geology, Va. Polytech. Inst., 1954; PhD in Geology, Mass. Inst. Tech., 1958; post-doctoral study, U. Cambridge, Eng., 1959-60. Staff scientist Smithsonian Astrophys. Obs., Cambridge, Mass., 1959, 1961—62, 1965—2004, ret., 2004; research asso. Enrico Fermi Inst. U. Chgo., 1962-65; prof. Harvard U., Geol. Scis. Dept., 1976-95; assoc. dir. Harvard-Smithsonian Center for Astrophysics, 1981—86. Vice chmn. Lunar Sample Analysis Planning Team, 1971—72; mem. NRC, Space Studies Bd., 1998—2001; chair Com. on Lunar and Planetary Exploration, 1999—2001. Author: Meteorites and the Origin of Planets, 1968, The Solar System, 1979, 2d edit., 2000. Recipient NASA medal for exceptional sci. achievement, 1973, J.L. Smith medal NAS, 1976, G.K. Gilbert award Geol. Soc. Am., 1992. Fellow AAAS, Am. Geophys. Union (F.L. Whipple award 2004), Meteoritical Soc. (pres. 1971-72, Leonard medal 1980); mem. NAS, Am. Acad. Arts and Scis., Cambridge Art Assn., Cosmos Club. Achievements include having asteroid no. 4736 named in his honor Johnwood. Home: 71 Langdon St Cambridge MA 02138-2501 Personal E-mail: JAWood@alum.mit.edu.

WOOD, JOHN F., lawyer, former prosecutor; m. Julie Myers, 2005. Grad., U. Va.; JD, Harvard Law Sch. Staff mem. to Senator John C. Danforth US Senate, Washington DC; law clk. to Hon. J. Michael Luttig, US Ct. Appeals (4th Cir.), 1996—97; law clk. to Justice Clarence Thomas US Supreme Ct., 1997—98; assoc. Kirkland & Ellis LLP, 1998—2001; dep. assoc. atty. gen., counsel to assoc. atty. gen. US Dept. Justice, 2001—02; dep. gen. counsel, Office Mgmt. & Budget Exec. Office of the Pres., 2002—03; counselor to US atty. gen. US Dept. Justice, 2003—05; chief of staff to sec. US Dept. Homeland Security, 2005—07; US atty. (we. dist.) Mo. US Dept. Justice, Kansas City, 2007—09; ptnr. Hughes Hubbard & Reed LLP, Washington, 2009—. Office: Hughes Hubbard & Reed LLP 1775 I St, NW Washington DC 20006-2401 Office Phone: 202-721-4600. Office Fax: 202-721-4646. E-mail: woodj@hugheshubbard.com.

WOOD, JOHN LOUIS, chemistry professor; b. Keokuk, Iowa, Dec. 4, 1961; PhD, U. Pa., Phila., 1991. Postdoc. fellow Harvard U., Cambridge, Mass., 1991—93; prof. chemistry Yale U., New Haven, 1993—2006; A. I. Meyers prof. Colo. State U., Ft. Collins, 2006—. Office: Colo State Univ Campus Delivery 1872 Fort Collins CO 80523

WOOD, JOHN MARTIN, lawyer; b. Detroit, Mar. 29, 1944; s. John Francis and Margaret Kathleen (Lynch) Wood; m. Judith Anne Messer; children: Timothy Peter, Meagan Anne. BA, Boston Coll., 1966; JD, Cath. U. Am., 1969. Bar: D.C. 1970, Va. 2001, U.S. Dist. Ct. D.C. 1970, U.S. Dist. Ct. Va. 2001, U.S. Ct. Appeals (D.C. cir.) 1973, U.S. Ct. Appeals (3d cir.) 1973, U.S. Ct. Appeals (4th cir.) 1973, U.S. Supreme Ct. 1973. Trial atty, tax divsn. Dept. Justice, Washington, 1969-73; assoc. Reed Smith LLP, Washington, 1973-80, ptnr., 1980—, mng. ptnr., 1989-95, dir. legal pers., 1995-98. Dir. adv. bd. Salvation Army, Va. and Met. Washington, Leadership Washington, 1993—. Mem.: Fairfax Bar Assn., The Currituck Club N.C., River Bend Golf and Country Club, Barristers Club Washington, Delta Sigma Pi, Phi Alpha Delta. Home: 9490 Oak Falls Ct Great Falls VA 22066-4143 Office: Reed Smith LLP 3110 Fairview Park Dr Ste 1400 Falls Church VA 22042 Office Phone: 703-641-4248. Business E-Mail: jwood@reedsmith.com.

WOOD, JONATHAN STUART, economist, educator; b. New Orleans, Nov. 14, 1944; s. John Joseph and Linelle Marie (Waguespack) W.; m. Ann M., Apr. 7, 1973; children: Elizabeth, Christopher, Julie, Jonathan. Grad., NASA Summer Inst. in Space and Engring., 1965; BS in Mech. Engring., Tulane U., 1966; MS in Aerospace Engring., Princeton U., 1970; MBA in Econs., NYU, 1975, MPhil in Econs. and Fin., 1978, PhD in Econs. and Fin., 1980. Rschr. on bio-engring study of neck whiplashes Tulane Med. Sch. and Tulane Sch. Engring. (for US Dept Health, Edn. and Welfare), 1963; materials tester and lab. analyst Svc. Foundry, New Orleans, 1964; ops. rsch. & econ. analyst Grumman Aerospace Corp., Bethpage, NY, 1969-74; sr. investment analyst, cons. to common stock dept. Prudential Ins. Co., Newark, 1974-76; instr. fin. & acctg. Sch. Bus. U. Conn., Storrs, 1976-78; Liberty Fund Rsch. fellow Stanford U. Inst. Humane Studies Rsch. Seminar in Econs., Palo Alto, Calif., 1977; asst. prof. econs. & fin. Tulane U., New Orleans, 1978-84; assoc. prof. econs. & fin. Coll. Bus. Adminstrn. Loyola U., New Orleans, 1984—. Prof. econs. and fin. Pace U. Grad. Sch. Bus. Adminstrn., N.Y.C., 1975-76; vis. prof. fin. Grad. Sch. Bus. Adminstrn. NYU, 1980; vis. prof. fin. Grad. Sch. Bus. Tulane U., 1985, 91, lectr., 1990; presenter in field.; cons. economist; expert in bus. valuation; adj. prof. in econ. and fin. Pace U. Grad. Sch. Bus. Adminstrn., N.Y., 1975-76; appeared on WWL-TV discussing current econ. and fin. events focusing on La. econ. matters; rschr., lectr. in field; conducted interviews and seminars in field. Author: Chemical Kinetic Influences, 1968, Chemical Kinetic Influences in Liquid Propellant Rocket Combustion Instability, 1969, 70, Effectiveness Evaluation of Orbital Observatories (with Joseph R. Fragola), 1975, Heterogeneous Expectations and Security Price Distributions, 1978, Entrepreneurship and the Co-Ordination of Expectations in the Stock Market, 1980, 82, Some Refinements in the Austrian Trade-Cycle Theory, 1984, Capital Formation Problems in the United States and the Question of a Capital Shortage, 1984, Methodologies for Valuation of Closely-Held Companies (with Dr. Michael A. Dalton and Robert I. Glover), 1989, Valuation of Closely-Held Companies & Professional Practices by Experts (with Dr. Michael A. Dalton and Dr. Robert I. Glover), 1989, Real Value of Damage Caps for Medical Malpractice in Louisiana (with Michael A. Dalton), 1997; referee Quarterly Rev. Econs. and Bus., 1982, Rev. Austrian Econs., 1989; contbr. chpts., reviews to books. Chmn. fin. com., mem. exec. bd. Short-Fern St. Neighborhood Assn., 1984-85; lectro, Eucharistic min., mem. com. Univ. Parish St. Thomas More Tulane U.; dir. Operation New Start, Inc.; softball coach Carrollton Boosters; elected to u. senate, 1986—; U. Senate Parking Com., 1986-87; faculty acad. affairs budget com., 1986-89, 89-92; Blue Ribbon Task Force for libr.'s acad. future, 1986-87; u. senate designatee to Fin. Com. of bd. trustees, 1991-92, 92-93; advisor to Endowment Com. of Bd. Trustees, 1991-93. Recipient MBA Top Gun award as Outstanding Tchr., Loyola U., 1993. Mem. Am. Econ. Assn., Am. Fin. Assn., We. Econ. Assn., We. Fin. Assn., So. Econ. Assn., So. Fin. Assn., Ea. Fin. Assn., Southwestern Social Scis. Assn., Opers. Rsch. Soc. Am./Inst. Mgmt. Sci., Pontchartrain Astronomy Soc., Student Recruitment Team, Grad. Edn. Task Force, Entrepreneurship Task Force, Curriculum Com., Advising Com. (chmn. 1986-87), MBA Curriculum Task Force. Avocations: astronomy, music. Home and Office: 500 Arlington Dr Metairie LA 70001-5516 Office Phone: 504-866-7200. Personal E-mail: stuartwood13@msn.com.

WOOD, JOSEPH S., academic administrator; b. 1947; m. Diane Wood. AB, Middlebury Coll., 1968; MA, U. Vt., 1974; PhD, Pa. State U., 1978. Ops. asst. Interlake Steamship Co., Cleve., 1968—69; mem. faculty U. Nebr., Omaha, 1977—87; assoc. prof. geography George Mason U., Fairfax, Va., 1987—97, chmn. geography & earth systems sci. dept., 1990—95, course leader integrative studies, New Century Coll., 1995—97, vice provost academic affairs, prof. geography, 1997—2000, interim provost, 1999; prof. geography U. So. Maine, Portland, Maine, 2000—, provost & v.p. academic affairs, 2000—07, interim pres., 2007—. Vis. prof. S. China Normal U., Guangzhou, China, 1984; project assoc. Assn. Am. Geographers, Washington, 1987—88. Mem. Creative Econ. Steering Com. City of Portland, Maine; mem. bd. dirs. Maine Philanthropy Ctr.; pres. bd. dirs. Ctr. Prevention of Hate Violence, Maine. Combat engr. US Army, 1969—71, Vietnam.

WOOD, J(OSHUA) WARREN, III, lawyer, arbitrator, mediator; b. Portsmouth, Va., Aug. 31, 1941; s. Joshua Warren and Mary Evelyn (Carter) Wood; m. Marcia Neal Ramsey, Feb. 29, 1964; children: Lauren Elaine Yeh, Joshua Warren IV. AB, Princeton U., 1963; JD, U. Va., 1971. Bar: Va. 1971, NJ 1976, US Supreme Ct. 1977, NY 1982. Comml. banking asst. Bankers Trust Co., NYC, 1967-68; assoc. McGuire, Woods & Battle, Richmond, Va., 1971-75; v.p., gen. counsel, sec. Robert Wood Johnson Found., Princeton, NJ, 1975—2003; pres., gen. counsel Global Ctr. Dispute Resolution Rsch., NYC, 2004—05; of counsel Greenbaum, Rowe, Smith & Davis LLP, Woodbridge, NJ, 2005—07, The Legato Law Firm LLC, Bridgewater, NJ, 2007—. Mem. AAA/ABA/AMA Commn. Alternative Dispute Resolution Health Care; master Marie L. Garbaldi Am. Inn Ct. Alternative Dispute Resolution; internat. and domestic US mediator Exec. Mediator Svc., Morristown, NJ, 2008—. Mem. editl. bd. Va. Law Rev., 1969—71. Mem. coun. internat. advisors Internat. Ctr. for Corp. Accountability, NYC. Capt. arty. US Army, 1963—67. Decorated Army Commendation medal. Mem.: ABA, Internat. Ctr. Dispute Resolution, Roster of Arbitrators, Nat. Rostar Arbitrators, Internat. Bar Assn. (mem. arbitration com.), Am. Arbitration Assn. (bd. dirs., mem. panel arbitrators, task force mass torts and alternative dispute resolution), NJ Bar Assn., Va. Bar Assn., NY Bar Assn., Princeton Club, Order of Coif. Office: 757 Route 202/206 N Bridgewater NJ 08807 Home Phone: 609-921-2890; Office Phone: 908-725-9800. Office Fax: 908-725-9890. Business E-Mail: jw.wood3@verizon.net.

WOOD, KERRY (LEE), professional baseball player; b. Irving, Tex., June 17, 1977; s. Garry and Terry Wood; m. Sarah Pates. Pitcher Chgo. Cubs, 1998—2008; relief pitcher Cleve. Indians, 2008—. Named Nat. League Rookie of Yr., 1998; named to Nat. League All-Star Team, 2003, 2008. Achievements include most strikeouts in a 9 inning game (20); led Nat. League in strikeouts (266), 2003; more than 3,000 career strikeouts; fastest to reach 1000 strikeouts in MLB history, both in appearances (134 games) and innings pitched (853). Avocation: fishing. Office: Cleve Indians 2401 Ontario St Cleveland OH 44115*

WOOD, KIMBA MAUREEN, federal judge; b. Port Townsend, Wash., Jan. 2, 1944; BA cum laude, Conn. Coll., 1965; MSc, London Sch. Econs., 1966; JD, Harvard U., 1969. Bar: US Dist. Ct. DC 1969, US Ct. Appeals (DC cir.) 1969, NY 1972, US Dist. Ct. (ea. and so. dists.) NY 1974, US Ct. Appeals (2d cir.) 1975, US Supreme Ct. 1980, US Dist. Ct. (we. dist.) NY 1981. Assoc. Steptoe & Johnson LLP, Washington, 1969—70; with Office Spl. Counsel OEO Legal Svcs., 1970—71; assoc. to ptnr. LeBoeuf, Lamb, Leiby & MacRae, NYC, 1971—88; judge US Dist. Ct. (so. dist.) NY, 1988—, chief judge, 2006—. Mem.: ABA (chmn. civil practice, procedure com. 1982—85, mem. coun. 1985—88, jud. rep. 1989—91), Fed. Bar. Coun. (trustee 1978—, v.p. 1984—85), Am. Law Inst., NY State Bar Assn. (chmn. antitrust sect. 1983—84). Office: US Dist Ct US Courthouse 500 Pearl St Rm 1610 New York NY 10007-1316

WOOD, L. LIN, JR., lawyer; b. Raleigh, NC, Oct. 19, 1952; s. Lucian Lincoln and Josephien (Currin) Wood; m. Deborah Anne Jamison, July 25, 1987; children: Elizabeth, Ashley, Matthew Carlton. BA cum laude, Mercer U., 1974, JD cum laude, 1977. Bar: Ga. 1977, US Dist. Ct. (No. Dist.) Ga. 1977, US Dist. Ct. (Mid. Dist.) Ga. 1977, US Dist. Ct. (Dist. Colo.), US Ct. Appeals (5th Cir.) 1977, US Ct. Appeals (11th Cir.) 1981, US Supreme Ct. Assoc. Jones, Cork, Miller & Benton, Macon, Ga., 1977—80, Freeman & Hawkins, Atlanta, 1980—83; ptnr. Wood & Grant, Atlanta, 1983, Powell Goldstein LLP (now Bryan Cave LLP), Atlanta. Staff mem. Mercer Law Rev., 1975—77; numerous appearances on various TV networks including NBC, CBS, ABC, CNN, MSNBC, Court TV; spkr. in field. Recipient Am. Jurisprudence award, 1976, 1977, US Law Week award, 1977; named Ga. Super Lawyer, 2008, 2009; named one of Top 100 Ga. Super Lawyers, Law and Politics mag., 2006, 2007, 2008, Georgia's Elite Lawyers, 2008. Mem.: Atlanta City Club, Ga. Trial Lawyers Assn., Lawyers Club Atlanta, Atlanta Bar Assn., State Bar Ga., Assn. Trial Lawyers Am., ABA (vice-chmn. media law & defamation torts com.). Republican. Methodist. Office: Bryan Cave LLP One Atlanta Ctr 14th Floor 1201 W Peachtree St NW Atlanta GA 30309 Office Phone: 404-572-6633. Office Fax: 404-572-0633. E-mail: lin.wood@bryancave.com.*

WOOD, LARRY (MARY LAIRD), journalist, writer, public relations executive, educator, environmental consultant; b. Sandpoint, Idaho; d. Edward Hayes and Alice (McNeel) Small; children: Mary, Marcia, Barry. BA summa cum laude, U. Wash., 1939, MA summa cum laude, 1940; postgrad., Stanford U., 1940—43, U. Calif., Berkeley, 1946—47, U. Wis., 1971—72, U. Minn., 1971—72, U. Ga., 1972—73, U. Calif., Santa Cruz, 1974—76, Stanford Hopkins Marine Sta., 1977—80. Cert. secondary and jr. coll. tchr., Wash., Calif. Feature writer and columnist Oakland Tribune and San Francisco Chronicle, Calif., 1939—; archtl. and environ. feature and travel writer and columnist San Jose Mercury News (Knight Ridder), Calif., 1972-90; tchg. fellow Stanford U., 1940-43; dir. pub. rels. 2-counties, 65-park 100,000 acre East Bay Regional Park Dist., No. Calif., 1948-68; pres. Larry Wood Pub. Rels., 1946—; pub. rels. dir. Calif. Children's Home Soc., 1947-58. Prof. pub. rels., mag. writing, journalism, investigative reporting San Diego State U., 1974-75; disting. vis. prof. journalism San Jose State U., 1976; assoc. prof. journalism Calif. State U., Hayward, 1978; prof. sci. and environ. journalism U. Calif. Berkeley Ext. grad. divsn., 1979—; press del. nat. convs. Am. Geophys. Union Internat. Conf., 1986—, AAAS, 1989—, Nat. Park Svc. VIP Press Tour, Yellowstone after the fire, 1989—, Nat. Assn. Sci. Writers, 1989—, George Washington U./Am. Assn. Neurol. Surgeons Sci. Writers Conf., 1990, Am. Inst. Biol. Scis. Conf., 1990, Nat. Conf. Sci. Writers, Am. Heart Assn., 1995, Internat. Cardiologists Symposium for Med./Sci. Writers, 1995, Annenberg Program Electronic Media Symposium, Washington, 1995; EPA del. to USSR and Ea. Europe; expert witness on edn., pub. rels., journalism and copyright; spl. media guest Sigma Xi, 1990—; mem. numerous spl. press corps; selected White House Spl. Media, 1993—; selected mem. Duke U. 14th Ann. Sci. Reporters Conf., 1995; internat. press guest Can. Consulate Gen. Dateline Can., 1995—, French Govt. Tourist Office, 1996—, Ministerio delle Risorse Agricole Alimentarie Forestali and Assocs. Conf., 1995; appeared in TV documentary Larry Wood Covers Visit of Queen Elizabeth II; cons. in field. Contbr. articles to newspapers and mags. including LA Times-Mirror Syndicate, Knight-Ridder Syndicate,

Washington Post, Phila. Inquirer, Chgo. Tribune, Miami Herald, Oakland Tribune, Seattle Times, San Francisco Chronicle, 36 Million Circulation Parade, San Jose Mercury News, LA Time/Monitor Worldwide News Syndicate (4 Nat. Headliner awards), Monterey Peninsula Herald, Calif., Washington Post, Phila. Inquirer, Hawaiian Airlines In Paradise, MonitoRadio, Donnelly Pubs., Sports Illus., Life, Mechanix Illus., Popular Mechanics, Parents (contbg. editor), House Beautiful, Am. Home (awards 1988-89), Travelday, Better Homes and Gardens, Sunset, Archtl. Digest, National Geographic World, Travel & Leisure, Chevron USA/Odyssey (Calif. Pub.'s award 1984), Xerox Edn. Publs., Europe's Linguapress, PSA Mag., Off Duty, Oceans, Sea Frontiers, AAA Westways, AAA Via, Travelin', others; home and garden columnist, editor, 5-part series Pacific Coast Ports, 5-part series Railroads of the West, series Immigration, Youth Gangs, Endangered Species, Calif. Lighthouse Chain, Lighthouses of the World, Pacific Coast Wetlands, Elkhorn Slough Nat. Estuarine Res., Ebey's Landing Nat. Hist. Island Res., Calif. Water Wars, BLM's Adopt a Horse Program, Mt. St. Helen's Eruption, Oreg's Covered Bridges, Loma Prieta Earthquake, Oakland Firestorm, Missing Children, Calif. Prison Reform, Columbia-Alaska's Receding Glacier, Calif. Underwater Parks, others; author: Wonderful U.S.A.: A State-by-State Guide to Its Natural Resources, 1989; co-author: McGraw-Hill English for Social Living, 1944, Fawcett Boating Books, 1956-66, Fodor's San Francisco, Fodor's California, 1982-89, Bell and Howell/Charles Merrill Focus on Life Science, Focus on Physical Science, Focus on Earth Science, 1983, 2d edit, 1987, State of California's Golden State Travel Guide, 1998; contbr. Earth Science 1987; author: (with others) anthology West Winds, 1989; reviewer Charles Merrill texts, 1983-84; book reviewer Profl. Communicator, 1987—; selected writings in permanent collections Oakland Pub. Libr., U. Wash. Main Libr.; contbr., author Journalism Quar.; author script PBS/AAA America series, 1992; contbg. editor: Parents, Fashion Showcase, Spokane Mag.; contbr. chpt. to books. Nat. chmn. travel writing contest Assn. for Edn. in Journalism and Mass Comm. Soc. Am. Travel Writers, 1979-83; judge writing contest for Nat. Assn. Real Estate Editors, 1982—; invited Nat. Park Svc. Nat. Conf. Sci. Writers, 1985, Postmaster Gen.'s 1992 Stamps, 1991, Internat. Geophys. Union Conf., 1982—, The Conf. Bd., 1995—, Corp. Comm. Conf., Calif. Inst. Tech. Media and Sci. Seminar, 1995—, Med. Writers Delegation to Russia and Estonia, 1997, NY Times Opinion Rsch. Co. Corp. Image Conf., 1999, EPA and Dept. Energy Tech. Conf., 1992, Am. Soc. Photogrammetry and Remote Sensing Internat. Conv. Mapping Global Change, 1992-, US Conf. on Oceans, 1998, NY Mus. Modern Art Matisse Retrospective Press Rev. and all media previews, 1992—, celebration 150th anniversary Oreg. Trail, 1993, Nat. Coun. Advancement Sci. Writing, 1977-2003, Sigma Xi Nat. Conf., 1988-2003, Nat. Sci. Writers Confs., 1977-2003, PRSA Travel and Tourism Conf., 1993—, Internat. Conf. Environment, 1994-95, Quality Life Europe, Prague, 1994, Calif. Sesquicentennial, 1996, 14th Ann. Sci. Writers Conf., 1996, Picasso Retrospective, 1996, others; mem. Gov.'s Conf. Tourism NC, 1993-2008, Calif., 1976—, Fla., 1987—, NC Govs. conf. on tourism and film, 2000-, U.C. Irvine Calif. Computer Sci. Symposium, 2000, Sea Grant's conf. on sci. in the news, 2000, NY conf. bd. conf. on environ. journalism, 2000, on economics, 2001; press guest 14 US states and 12 fgn. countries' Depts. Tourism, 1986—; chmn. New Com. for Sci./Journalism Curricula U. Wash., 2006-. Named to Broadway Hall of Fame, U. Wash., 1984; recipient Broadway Disting. Alumnus award, 1995; citations for environ. writing Nat. Park Svc., US Forest Svc., Bur. Land Mgmt., Oakland Mus. Assn., Oakland C. of C., Chevron USA, USN plaque and citation, Best Mag. articles citation Calif. Pubs. Assn., 1984, US Treasury award, 1946; co-recipient award for best Sunday newspaper mag. Nat. Headliners, citation for archtl. features Oakland Mus., 1983; honoree for achievements in journalism Nat. Mortar Bd., 1988-89; named one of 10 V.I.P. press 1989; named one of Calif.'s top 40 Contemporary Authors, 1989; nat. honoree Social Issues Resources Series, 1987; recipient, Gov.'s Calif. Women of Achievement award, 1988-90. Mem.: AAAS, Calif. Acad. Scis., Am. Bd. Forensic Examiners, Pub. Rels. Soc. Am. (charter mem. travel, tourism, environment and edn. divsns.), Nat. Sch. Pub. Rels. Assn., Environ. Cons. N.Am., Am. Assn. Edn. in Journalism and Comm. (exec. bd. nat. mag. divsn. 1978, panel chmn. 1979—80, author Journalism Quart. jour.), Women in Comm. (nat. bd. officer 1975—77, book reviewer Prof. Communicator), Soc. Profl. Journalists (nat. bd. for hist. sites 1980—), Nat. Press Photographers Assn. (Bay area internet project 1989—, hon. life, honoree 1995), Investigative Reporters and Editors (charter), Nat. Assn. Sci. Writers, Bay Area Advt. and Mktg. Assn., Internat. Assn. Bus. Communicators, Am. Assn. Med. Writers, Soc. Am. Travel Writers, Am. Film Inst., Soc. Environ. Journalists (charter), Calif. Acad. Environ. News Writers, Am. Mgmt. Assn., Nat. Soc. Environ. Journalists (charter), Calif. Environ. Leadership Roundtable, Am. Heritage Found. (citation 1986—88), Fine Arts Mus., San Francisco, Calif. State Parks Found., Purple and Gold Soc., Mortar Board Alumnae Assn. (life honoree 1988—89), Stanford Alumni (life), U. Calif., Berkeley Alumni (life; v.p., scholarship chmn. 1975—81), U. Wash. Com. (life; charter mem. ocean scis. alumni, dept. adv. sci. journalism, disting. alumni 1987), Nat. Parks and Conservation Assn., Calif. Environ. Leadership Roundtable (trustee), Nat. Wildlife Fedn., Oceanic Soc., Nature Conservancy, Smithsonian Audubon Soc., Internat. Oceanog. Found., Calif. Writers Club (state bd., Berkeley bd. 1989—, honoree ann. conv. Asilomar, Calif. 1990), Nat. Press Club, San Francisco Press Club, Seattle Advt. and Sales Club (former officer), Seattle Jr. Advt. Club (charter), Phi Beta Kappa (statewide chmn. scholarship awards 1975—81, v.p., bd. dirs. Calif. Alumni Assn.), Pi Lambda Theta (charter 1995—, planning com.), Theta Sigma Phi. Home and Office: Piedmont Pines 6161 Castle Dr Oakland CA 94611-2737 *A creed I follow is Ralph Waldo Emerson's statement: "Nothing great was ever achieved without enthusiasm".*

WOOD, LINCOLN JACKSON, aerospace engineer; b. Lyons, NY, Sept. 30, 1947; s. William Hulbert and Sarah Brock (Strumsky) Wood. BS with distinction, Cornell U., 1968; MS in Aeronautics and Astronautics, Stanford U., 1969, PhD, 1972. Staff engr. Hughes Aircraft Co., El Segundo, Calif., 1974-77; tech. staff Jet Propulsion Lab. Calif. Inst. Tech., Pasadena, 1977-81, tech. group supr. Jet Propulsion Lab., 1981-89, tech. mgr., 1989-91, dep. tech. sect. mgr., 1991-99, dep. leader Ctr. of Excellence for Deep Space Comm./Nav. Sys., 2000—03, tracking and nav. svc. sys. mgr., deep space mission sys. engring. and ops. programs, 2003—04, program mgr., 2004—. Bechtel instr. engring. Calif. Inst. Tech., Pasadena, 1972—74, lectr. in sys. engring., 1975—76, vis. asst. prof., 1976—78, vis. assoc. prof., 1978—84; cons. in field. Contbr. articles to profl. jours. Bd. dirs. Boys Republic, Chino Hills, Calif., 1991, 1997—2007. Fellow: AIAA (assoc.; assoc. editor Jour. Guidance, Control and Dynamics 1983—89, tech. com. astrodynamics 1985—86, chmn. 1986—88); mem.: AAAS, IEEE (sr.), Am. Astron. Soc. (sr.; assoc. editor Jour. Astron. Scis. 1980—83, space flight mechanics com. 1980—97, gen. chmn. AAS/AIAA Space Flight Mechanics Meeting 1993, chmn. space flight mechanics com. 1993—95), Los Solteros (pres. 1991, 1997—2005), Sigma Xi. Office: Jet Propulsion Lab 4800 Oak Grove Dr Mail Stop 301-150 Pasadena CA 91109 Business E-Mail: lincoln.j.wood@jpl.nasa.gov.

WOOD, LISA GODBEY, federal judge, former prosecutor; b. Lexington, Ky., Jan. 28, 1963; married; 2 children. BA summa cum laude, U. Ga., 1985, JD summa cum laude, 1990. Bar: Ga. 1990. Law clk. to Hon. Anthony A. Alaimo US Dist. Ct. (so. dist.) Ga., 1990; assoc. Gilbert, Harrell, Summerford & Martin, Brunswick, Ga., 1991—2004, ptnr., 1995—2004; US atty. (so. dist.) Ga. US Dept. Justice, Savannah, Ga., 2004—07; judge US Dist. Ct. (so. dist.) Ga., 2007—. Adv. com. US Dist. Ct.; disciplinary review panel State Bar Ga.; mem. Ga. Bd. Pub. Safety. Mem.: ABA, Def. Rsch. Inst. Office: Fed Justice Ctr 600 James Brown Blvd Augusta GA 30901

WOOD, MALISSA J., cardiologist, educator; b. Maryville, Mo., Apr. 9, 1963; d. Robert and Malissa (James) Wood; m. David F. Lawlor, June 18, 1997; children: Seamus, Caitlin. MD, U. Mo. Sch. Med., Kansas City, 1987. Diplomate Am. Bd. Internal Medicine, cert. in Cardiovascular Disease. Intern, resident internal medicine Beth Israel Hosp., Boston, 1987-90, chief resident internal medicine, 1990-91, cardiovasc. fellow, 1991-94; fellow interventional medicine U. Tex. Health Scis. Ctr., San Antonio, 1994-95; pvt. practice South Tex. Cardiovasc. Consultants, San Antonio, 1995; now clin. cardiologist, staff physician Cardiac Ultrasound Lab. Mass. Gen. Hosp., Boston. Asst. prof. medicine Harvard Med. Sch., Boston; co-dir. women's health prog. Mass. Gen. Hosp. Heart Ctr. Contbr. articles to profl. jours., chapters to books; spkr. in field. Recipient Vice Chancellors award, U. Mo., 1987. Fellow: Am. Coll. Cariology; mem.: Am. Soc. Echocardiography (bd. dirs. 2006—), Am. Heart Assn. (chair Women in Heart Disease prog. 1997—98), Back Bay Echo Soc. Boston (pres.). Achievements include research in using echocardiography to better understand cardiac adaptations to changing loading conditions, particularly the cardiac response to conditions such as pregnancy, strenuous exercise and exposure to altitude. Avocations: running, bicycling, swimming, kayaking, piano. Office: Mass Gen Hosp Dept Cardiac Ultrasound 55 Fruit St YAW 5 Boston MA 02114 Office Phone: 617-724-1986.*

WOOD, MARCUS ANDREW, lawyer; b. Mobile, Ala., Jan. 18, 1947; s. George Franklin and Helen Eugenia (Fletcher) W.; m. Sandra Lee Pellonari, July 25, 1971; children: Edward Alan, Melinda Janel. BA cum laude, Vanderbilt U., 1969; JD, Yale U., 1974. Bar: Oreg. 1974, U.S. Dist. Ct. Oreg. 1974, U.S. Ct. Appeals (9th cir.) 1982. Assoc., then ptnr. Rives, Bonihadi & Smith, Portland, Oreg., 1974-78; ptnr. Stoel Rives LLP and predecessor firms, Portland, 1974—. Pres., bd. dirs. Indochinese Refugee Ctr., Portland, 1980, Pacific Ballet Theatre, Portland, 1986-87; bd. dirs. Outside In, Portland, 1989-2006. Lt. USNR, 1969—71. Mem.: ABA, Phi Beta Kappa. Home: 9300 NW Finzer Ct Portland OR 97229-8035 Office: Stoel Rives 900 SW 5th Ave Ste 2300 Portland OR 97204-1229 Home Phone: 503-203-1359. Business E-Mail: mwood@stoel.com.

WOOD, MARK D., lawyer; b. Chgo., Jan. 8, 1966; BS with high honors, U. Ill., 1987; JD cum laude, U. Mich., 1990. CPA Ill., 1987; bar: Ill. 1990, US Dist. Ct., No. Dist. Ill. Ptnr., co-chair securities practice Katten Muchin Rosenman LLP, Chgo. Mem.: ABA, Am. Bar Assn. Office: Katten Muchin Rosenman LLP 525 W Monroe St Chicago IL 60661 Office Phone: 312-902-5493. Office Fax: 312-577-8858. E-mail: mark.wood@kattenlaw.com.

WOOD, MARY ELIZABETH, retired secondary school educator, church musician; b. Berwyn, Ill., Apr. 15, 1929; d. Ralph Jerome Compton and Dora Mary Langlois; m. Harvey Eugene Wood, Aug. 21, 1954 (dec.); children: Joseph, Ann, Kim, Lynn, Christopher, Curtis, Carol, John, Nicole. BA in English and Edn., Marycrest U., Davenport, Iowa, 1951; MA in English and Edn., Mich. State U., East Lansing, 1958; AA in Music summa cum laude, Lansing C.C., Mich., 1980. Cert. permanent tchr. Mich. Tchr. H.S. Oxford (Iowa) Schs., 1951—52; tchr. jr. and sr. H.S. Gobles (Mich.) Schs., 1952—55; tchr. Cement City H.S., 1957—58, Portland H.S., 1958—60, Dimondale H.S., 1960—62; tchr. H.S. completion adults Holt Pub. Schs., 1965—95. Cantor Immaculate Heart Mary Ch., Lansing, Mich., 1970—84; dir. music Holy Cross Ch., Lansing, 1983—88, St. Peter Cath. Ch., Eaton Rapids, Mich., 1989—91, St. Jude Cath. Ch., DeWitt, Mich., 1992—2002; painter religious iconography; musician Ch. Resurrection, Lansing. Singer: (albums) Jesus Lives by Fr. Lucien Deiss; composer: (children's operettas) The Country Cousin, 1984, The Touch, 1994, (liturgical music) Dedication Mass of St. Peter, 1992. Mem.: Nat. Assn. Pastoral Musicians (co-chmn. Lansing chpt. 1995—). Roman Catholic. Avocations: sewing, reading, singing, music, writing. Home: 5102 Killarney Dr Holt MI 48842 Home Phone: 517-694-0303. Personal E-mail: tinlizzy1929@aim.com.

WOOD, MAURICE, medical educator; b. Pelton, Eng., June 28, 1922; came to U.S., 1971; s. Joseph and Eugenie (Lumley) W.; m. Erica Joan Noble, May 1, 1948; children: Roger Lumley, Ashley Michael, Frances Jane. MB BS, U. Durham, Eng., 1945. Diplomate Am. Bd. Family Practice. Sr. ptnr. med. practice South Shields County, Durham, 1950-71; gen. practice teaching group U. Newcastle, Newcastle-on-Tyne, Eng., 1969-71; gen. clin. asst. dept. psychology-medicine South Shields Gen. Hosp., 1966-71; assoc. prof., dir. rsch. in family practice Med. Coll. Va.-Va. Commonwealth U., Richmond, 1971-73, prof., dir. rsch. in family practice, 1973-87, prof. emeritus, 1987—. Cons. advisor WHO, Geneva, 1979-90, chmn. working party to develop a classification for primary care, 1979-90; founding mem. exec. dir. N.Am. Primary Care Rsch. Group, Richmond, 1972-92, past pres., pres. emeritus, 1993—; chmn. com. on cmty. oriented primary care Insts. of Medicine, 1982-84. Assoc. editor Jour. Family Practice, 1976-83. Recipient award for meritorious svc. Va. Acad. Family Physicians, 1976; Maurice Wood award for career achievement in primary care rsch. founded in his honor, 1995. Fellow Royal Coll. Gen. Practitioners, Am. Acad. Family Physicians, World Orgn. Famaly Drs. (WONCA); mem. Inst. Medicine-Nat. Acad. Sci., Soc. Tchrs. Family Medicine (Curtis Hames Career Research award 1984), Ambulatory Sentinel Practice Network, Internat. Primary Care Network (treas., bd. dirs.), N.Am. Primary Care Rsch. Group (treas., bd. dirs., exec. dir., 1982-92), Rotary. Episcopalian. Personal E-mail: wood150w@verizon.net.

WOOD, MICHAEL B., principal; b. Texarkana, Tex., Dec. 27, 1960; s. Donald R. and Emma Frances (Pope) W.; m. Rhonda Lee Fry, June 4, 1988. BA, Harding U., 1984, MEd, 1987. Cert. spl. edn. K-12, elem. edn. 1-6, elem. adminstrn. K-6. Asst. elem. prin. Bald Knob (Ark.) Pub. Schs.; spl. edn. tchr. Searcy (Ark.) Pub. Schs.; elem. prin. Bald Knob (Ark.) Pub. Schs. Developer of phys. edn. program grades 1-5. Mem. Ark. Assn. Elem. Sch. Prins., Searcy Edn. Assn. (pres.), Prins. Task Force for Ark. Renewal Consortium, Phi Delta Kappa. Office: Harding Univ 915 E Market, Box 12254 Searcy AR 72149-2254

WOOD, MICHAEL M., United States Ambassador to Sweden; married; 2 children. Co-founder, CEO Hanley Wood, LLC, 1976—2005; mem. bd. advisors Weronis Suhler Stevenson, 2005; founder Redwood Investments, LLC, 2005; U.S. amb. to Sweden, 2006—. Former mem. Harvard Joint Ctr. for Housing Studies, long range planning com. Nat. Assn. Home Builders. Recipient Top Exec. of Yr. award, Media Bus. mag., 2005. Office: US Embassy 5750 Stockholm Pl Washington DC 20521*

WOOD, MICHAEL W., lawyer; b. Austin, Tex. B, Rice Univ., Houston, 1967; JD, Univ. Tex., 1970. Bar: Tex. 1971, US Supreme Ct., US Ct. of Appeals (5th cir.), US Tax Ct. Co-founder Wood Campbell Moody & Gibbs, 1971; ptnr. Nathan Wood Sommers & Lippman; sr. v.p. and CEO Azurix Water Resources; co-ptnr. in charge of Houston office Akin Gump Strauss Hauer & Feld LLP, Houston, 2002—. Bd. trustees Houston Grand Opera; former bd. dir. Houston Ballet Found. and Wortham Theater Ctr. Mem.: ABA, Houston Bar Assn. Office: Akin Gump Strauss Hauer & Feld LLP 44th Fl 1111 Louisiana St Houston TX 77002-5200 Office Phone: 713-220-8111. Office Fax: 713-236-0822. Business E-Mail: mwood@akingump.com.

WOOD, MICHELLE GAFFNER, language educator; married. MS, Wright State U., Dayton, Ohilo, 1997. Assoc. prof. English Cedarville U., Cedarville, Ohio, 1995—. Office: Cedarville Univ 251 N Main St Cedarville OH 45314

WOOD, NANCY ELIZABETH, psychologist, educator; d. Donald Sterret and Orne Louise (Erwin) W. BS, Ohio U., 1943, MA, 1947; PhD, Northwestern U., 1952. Prof. Case We. Res. U., Cleve., 1952—60; specialist, expert HEW, Washington, 1960—62; chief rschr. USPHS, Washington, 1962—64; prof. U. So. Calif., LA, 1965—. Learning disabilities cons., 1960-70; assoc. dir. Cleve. Hearing and Speech Ctr., 1952-60; dir. licensing program Brit. Nat. Trust, London. Author: Language Disorders, 1964, Language Development, 1970, Verbal Learning, 1975 (monograph) Auditory Disorders, 1978, Levity, 1980, Stoneskipping, 1989, Bird Cage, 1994, Out of Control, 1999. Pres. faculty senate U. So. Calif., 1987—88. Recipient Outstanding Faculty award, Trojan Fourth Estate, 1982, Pres.' Svc. award, U. So. Calif., 1992. Fellow APA (cert.), AAAS, Am. Speech and Hearing Assn. (legis. coun. 1965-68); mem. Internat. Assn. Scientists. Republican. Methodist. Office: U So Calif University Park Los Angeles CA 90089-0001

WOOD, NANCY J., secondary school educator; b. Washington, Iowa, Feb. 4, 1956; d. Joseph E. and Mabel A. Wood. BA in Music, Cen. Coll., Pella, Iowa, 1978. Cert. tchr. Iowa, 1978, Fla., 1994. Choral dir. K-12 Fonda (Iowa) Cmty. Schs., 1978—80; choral dir. 6-12 Sigourney (Iowa) Cmty. Schs., 1980—81; choral dir. West Liberty (Iowa) Cmty. Schs., 1981—84, Taft MS/Cedar Rapids Schs., Cedar Rapids, Iowa, 1984—94, Robinswood MS/Orange County Pub. Schs., Orlando, Fla., 1994—99, Conway MS/Orange County Pub. Schs., Orlando, 1999—. Home: 3006 E Grant St Orlando FL 32806-3315 Office Phone: 407-249-6420 230. E-mail: woodn@ocps.net.

WOOD, PAMELA SHARON, music educator, soprano; b. San Francisco, Mar. 29, 1944; d. Clinton Barford and Pearl (Henderson) Wood; m. Eric Scott Fraley, Dec. 28, 1968 (div. 1981); children: Ayanna Fraley Moore, Amara Fraley; m. Stephen B. Ambush, July 25, 1982 (div. 1996). B in Music Edn. summa cum laude, Howard U., Washington, 1967; MusM in Vocal Performance, U. Mass., 1980. Cert. in Music Divsn. Yale Summer Sch. Mus. Art, 1968, in tchg. and musicianship Kodaly Musical Tng. Inst. Inc., 1976, assoc. cert. Kodaly Ctr. Am., Wellesley, Mass., 2000. Music instr. and choral dir. Baccus and Hamilton Jr. High Schs., Wash., DC, 1967—69; music instr. and choral dir., elem. and jr. high sch. music specialist pub. schs., Stoneham, Mass., 1969—70; chmn. dept. music theory and edn. Elma Lewis Sch. of Fine Arts, Nat. Ctr. of Afro-American Artists, Inc., Boston, 1970—76; music tchr. Boston Pub. Schs. and Kodaly Ctr. of Am., 1981—82; voice tchr. Tufts U., Medford, Mass., 1982—87; music instr. Wheelock Coll., Boston, 1983—87, Roxbury CC, Boston, 1986—87; lectr. music MIT Sch. Humanities, Arts and Social Scis., Cambridge, Mass., 1987—96, sr. lectr. music, 1996—. Condr. Women's Inn at Pine St., Boston, 1995—2001, Sisters St. Joseph Cmty. Chorus, Brighton, Mass., 1996—2004, Pine Manor Coll., Chestnut Hill, Mass., 2004—05, voice tchr., 2002—05; faculty Kodály Music Inst., Boston, 1999—; devel. Solfege course Mass. Inst. Tech., 2000; presenter in field, 1971—. Singer (soprano soloist): Steve Reich & Musicians, 1974—88, NY and Israel Philharm., London, Boston, Chgo., San Francisco Symphonies, 1974—96; clinician, artist-in-residece, soloist, arranger Buckingham, Brown & Nichols Sch., Rhode Island Coll., Kodaly Music Inst., Nat. Film Preservation Found., Ravinia Festival, U. Conn. Storrs, 2004, Buckingham, Brown & Nichols Sch., RI Coll., Nat. Film Preservation Found., Conn. Elem. Gen. Music Conf. Alice Parker's Sing! Kodaly Music Inst., 2005, Pine Manor Coll., Nat. Film Preservation Found., Kodaly Music Inst., 2006, Kodaly Music Inst., Nat. Film Preservation Found., 2007, Kodaly Music Inst., North Andover Pub. Schs., Boston Pub. Schs. Vocal Music Tchrs., Summer Inst. Contemporary Performance Practice, Northern Calif. Assn. Kodaly Educators, Boston Area Kodaly Educators, 2008, Summer Inst. Contemporary Performance Practice, Kodaly Music Inst., Camp Cadenza, 2009. Bd. overseers New Eng. Conservatory of Music, Boston, 1996—2004; assoc. bd. mem. Kodaly Ctr. America, Wellesley, Mass., 1996—; panelist Mass. Coun. Arts Humanities, 1982—83; bd. dirs. Boston Orchestra & Chorale, 1991—94, Boston Orch. & Chorale, 1991—94; convener, chair adv. com. New Eng. Conservatory Music, Boston, 1992—95; adjudicator Nat. Assn. Negro Bus. Profl. Women's Clubs, 1995, 1997, 2001, 2002; search com. Boston Children's Chorus, 2003, bd. mem., 2006—09; nat. conf. program team Orgn. Am. Kodaly Educators, 2004—05, Conservatory Lab Charter sch. Learning Through Music Think Tank, 2006, New Eng. Spiritual Ensemble, 2007—08. Recipient Sponsors and Patrons award, Met. Opera Co., 1972, Nat. Assn. Tchrs. of Singing, 1981, Black Achiever, Greater Boston YMCA, 1994; honoree, Oberlin Black Musicians' Guild, Oberlin Conservatory of Music, 2003. Mem.: Internat. Kodaly Soc., Orgn. Am. Kodaly Educators (nat. conf. team 2004—05), Nat. Assn. Study and Performance of African-Am. Music, Ctr. Black Music Rsch., Boston Area Kodaly Educators, Pi Kappa Lambda. Office: Mass Inst of Tech 77 Massachusetts Ave Cambridge MA 02139 Home Phone: 508-879-1145. Office Fax: 617-253-4523. Business E-Mail: psw@mit.edu.

WOOD, PATRICK HENRY, III, former commissioner; b. Port Arthur, Tex., July 4, 1962; m. Kathleen Ryder; 4 children. BS in Civil Engring., Tex. A&M U.; JD, Harvard Law Sch. Atty. Baker & Botts LLP, Washington; engr. Arco Indonesia; legal counsel to chmn. Tex. Railroad Commn.; advisor to Commr. Jerry Langdon Fed. Energy Regulatory Commn. (FERC), Washington, staff mem., 1991—93, chmn., 2001—05, Pub. Utility Commn. Tex., 1995—2001. Bd. dirs. SunPower Corp., 2005—; chmn. advisory bd. Airtricity N. Am., Chgo., 2006—. Office: Airtricity Inc 401 N Michigan Ave Ste 3020 Chicago IL 60611

WOOD, QUENTIN EUGENE, oil industry executive; b. Mechanicsburg, Pa., Mar. 5, 1923; s. Lloyd Paul and Greta (Myers) W.; m. Louise Lowe, Apr. 14, 1958. BS, Pa. State U., 1948. Petroleum engr. Quaker State Oil Refining Corp., Parkersburg, W.Va., 1948-52, chief engr. Bradford, Pa., 1952-55, mgr. prodn., 1955-68, v.p. prodn. Oil City, Pa., 1968-70, exec. v.p., 1970-73, pres., chief ops. officer, 1973-75, pres., chief exec. officer, 1975-82, chmn., chief executive officer, 1982-88, chmn. bd., 1988-90, dir., 1990-93. Bd. dirs. Pa. Mfrs. Ins. Co.; chmn. industry tech. adv. com. U.S. Bur. Mines, 1960-70, Penn Grade Tech. Adv. Com., 1955-69, Pa. Oil and Gas Conservation Commn., 1961-71. Trustee Pa. State U., 1976-94, pres., 1979-87. 1st lt. USAAF, 1943-46. Mem. Am. Inst. Metall. Engrs., Pa. Grade Crude Oil Assn. (dir.), Pa. Oil

Producers Assn. (past pres., dir. Bradford dist.), Am. Petroleum Inst. (dir.), Nat. Petroleum Refiners Assn. (dir.). Home: 1000 Vicars Landing Way Apt B201 Ponte Vedra FL 32082-3139

WOOD, R. STEWART, JR., retired bishop; b. Detroit, June 25, 1934; s. Raymond and Marjorie Wood; m. Kristin Lie Miller, June 25, 1955; children: Lisa, Raymond, Michael. AB, Dartmouth Coll., 1956; MDiv, Va. Theol. Sem., 1959; MA in Counseling and Sociology, Ball State U., 1973; postgrad., Va. Seminary. Ordained to diaconate and priesthood Episc. Ch., 1959. Assoc. rector St. Paul's, Columbus, Ind., 1959—60; vicar Episc. Ch., Seymour and Bean Blossom, Ind., 1960—63; assoc. rector Grace Ch., Muncie, Ind., 1963—66, rector, 1966—70; exec. dir. Episc. Cmty. Svcs., Indpls., 1970—76; rector All Saint's Episc. Ch., Indpls., 1973—76, Christ Ch., Glendale, Ohio, 1976—84, St. John's Ch., Memphis, 1984—88; elected Bishop Coadjutor Diocese Mich., Detroit, 1988—89, diocesan bishop, 1990—2000; ret., 2000. Dir. summer camps, conf. ctr.; dep. Gen. Conv. 1970, 73, 76, 82; exec. coun. 1972-76, Coalition for Ordination of Women, bd. dirs. Episcopalian. Avocations: camping, golf, tennis, photography. Office: Box 968 255 Robert Frost Ln Quechee VT 05059-0968 Office Phone: 802-295-8912. E-mail: stewwood@aol.com.

WOOD, RICHARD ROBINSON, real estate company executive; b. Salem, Mass., Nov. 8, 1922; s. Reginald and Irene Margaret (Robinson) Wood; m. Pamela Vander Wiele, Mar. 8, 1951 (div. Apr. 1969); children: Christopher Robinson, Bryant Cornelius, Marcella Wood Mackenzie; m. Jane Philbin, Sept. 19, 1970. AB, Harvard Coll., 1944; postgrad., Mass. Inst. Tech., 1947-48. V.p. Hunneman & Co., Boston, 1959-72; trustee, sec. Mass. Real Estate Investment Trust, Boston, 1967-69; trustee Suffolk Franklin Savings Bank, 1967-74; pres., chmn. Continential Real Estate Equity, Boston, 1972-74; exec. v.p. ITEL Real Estate Corp., San Francisco, 1974-75; v.p. Baird & Warner, Chgo., 1976-80; pres., chmn. Renwood Properties, Inc., Cambridge, Mass., 1981—. Founder Real Estate Securities 2d Syndication Inst., 1972, pres., 1976—78; pres., chmn. ILCO Properties, Chgo., 1981—87; v.p., dir. Common Goal Capitol Group, Balt., 1986—; gen. ptnr. Common Goal Mortgage Fund, Balt., 1986—; mem. Coun. Rural Housing and Devel., 1988—; v.p., bd. dirs. St. Katherines Care Ctrs., 1990—; chmn. Inst. Responsible Housing Preservation, 1994—99, 19 Chauncy St. Trust, 1995—. Mem. Mayor's Citizen Adv. Bd., Boston, 1965—67, Coun. Rural Housing and Devel., 1988—; committeeman, treas. Mass. Rep. State Com., Boston, 1964—72; pres. Boston Rep. City Com., 1965—67. With M.C. US Army, 1943—44. Mem.: Nat. Leased Housing Assn., White Mountain Ski Runners, Badminton and Tennis Club, Harvard Club N.Y., Longwood Cricket Club, Harvard Club Boston. Avocations: tennis, skiing. Home: 280 Rollins Rd Contoocook NH 03229-2658 Home Phone: 617-354-5182; Office Phone: 617-876-4455. Personal E-mail: renwoodprops@aol.com.

WOOD, ROBERT A., pediatrician, allergist, educator; b. Clifton Springs, NY, Jan. 17, 1956; s. I. Robert and Carol Ann W.; m. Renee M. Wood, May 29, 1982. BA with honors, SUNY, Buffalo, 1978; MD, U. Rochester, 1982. Diplomate Am. Bd. Pediatrics, Am. Bd. Allergy and Immunology. Intern pediat. Johns Hopkins Children's Ctr., Balt., 1982—83, resident allergy and immunology, 1983—85, fellowship, 1986—88; assoc. prof. to prof. pediatrics Johns Hopkins U. Sch. Medicine, Balt., 1988—, dir. Pediat. Allergy Clinics and Pediat. Allergy Consultation Svc., dir. Divsn. Pediatric Allergy and Immunology, 2005—. Dep. editor Pediatric Asthma and Allergy and Immunology, assoc. editor Annals of Allergy and Asthma, editor Pediatric Allergy; contbr. articles to med. jours.; author: Food Allergies for Dummies, 2007. Fellow: Am. Coll. Allergy and Immunology, Am. Acad. Allergy and Immunology, Am. Acad. Pediat. Office: Johns Hopkins Hosp CMSC 1102 600 N Wolfe St Baltimore MD 21287 Office Phone: 410-955-5883. Office Fax: 410-955-0229. E-mail: rwood@jhmi.edu.

WOOD, ROBERT CHARLES, lawyer, real estate developer; b. Chgo., Apr. 8, 1956; s. Roy Edward and Mildred Lucille (Jones) W.; m. Jennifer Jo Briggs, Oct. 1984; children: Jacqueline Jones, Reagan Keith. BA in History, So. Meth. U., 1979, BBA in Real Estate, 1979, JD, 1982. Bar: Tex. 1983. Appraiser McClellan-Massey, Dallas, 1977—79; rschr., acquisitions officer Amstar Fin. Corp., Dallas, 1979—80; prin. Robert Wood Cons., Dallas, 1981—98; ptnr. Welch & Wood Attys. and Y2K Cons., Dallas, 1998—2000; pvt. practice Dallas, 1995—; real estate investor and developer, 1998—. Cons. Plan Mktg. Cos., 1983-84; pvt. practice law, Dallas, 1983-84; gen. counsel Diversified Benefits, Inc., Dallas, 1984-86; nat. accts. mgr. Lomas & Nettleton Real Estate Group, Dallas, 1987-88; sr. pension cons., prin. Eppler, Guerin &Turner, 1988-93; chmn. adv. coun. on devel. Medisend, 1991; nat. consulting coord. fin. advisors coun., v.p. Callan Assocs., San Francisco, 1994-95; atty. at law, 1995—; exec. v.p., gen. counsel, Rushmore Investment Advisors, Plano, Tex., 2002-06. Author: Electionomics: How the Money Managers View the Election, 1992, After the Congress Vote: How the Managers See Things Now, 1993, Y2K--The Year 2000 Issue: How Y2K Affects the Markets, 1998; mem. So. Meth. U. Law Rev., 1981-82; contbr. articles to profl. publs. Bd. dirs. Dallas unit Am. Cancer Soc., 1982-87, mem. spl. events com., 1986-87, mem. crusade com., 1987-88, mem. medisend adv. com., 1988-94, chmn. corp. devel. bd., 1989-95. Mem. Tex. Bar Assn., Phila. Bar Assn., Phi Gamma Delta. Avocations: skiing, tennis, bicycling. Office Phone: 214-369-3209. E-mail: rccwood@aol.com.

WOOD, ROBERT WARREN, lawyer; b. Des Moines, July 5, 1955; s. Merle Warren and Cecily Ann (Sherk) W.; m. Beatrice Wood, Aug. 4, 1979; 1 child, Bryce Mercedes. Student, U. Sheffield, Eng., 1975-76; AB, Humboldt State U., 1976; JD, U. Chgo., 1979. Bar: Ariz. 1979, Calif. 1980, Wyo. 2000, NY 1989, DC 1993, Mont. 1998, US Tax Ct. 1980, Roll of Solicitors of Eng. and Wales, 1998. 1998. Assoc. Jennings, Strouss, Phoenix, 1979-80, McCutchen, Doyle, San Francisco, 1980-82, Broad, Khourie, 1982-85, Steefel, Levitt & Weiss, 1985-87, ptnr., 1987-91, Bancroft & McAlister, 1991-93; prin. Robert W. Wood, P.C., 1993—2005; ptnr. Wood & Porter, 2006—. Instr. in law U. Calif., San Francisco, 1981—82. Author: Taxation of Corporate Liquidations: A Complete Planning Guide, 1987, 2nd edit., 1994, The Executive's Complete Guide to Business Taxes, 1989, Corporate Taxation: Complete Planning and Practice Guide, 1989, S Corporations, 1990, The Ultimate Tax Planning Guide for Growing Companies, 1991, Taxation of Damage Awards and Settlement Payments, 1991, 3d edit., 2005, Office Tax Guide, 1991; co-author: (with others) California Closely Held Corporations: Tax Planning and Practice Guide, 1987, Legal Guide to Independent Contractor Status, 3d edit., 2000; editor: California Small Busines Guide, 4 vols., 1998, Home Office Money & Tax Guide, 1992, Tax Aspects of Settlements and Judgements, 1993, 2d edit., 1998, 3d edit., 2005, 4th edit. 2008, Qualified Settlement Funds & Section 468B, 2009; editor-in-chief The M & A Tax Report; editor: Limited Liability Companies: Formation, Operation and Conversion, 1994, 2d edit., 2001, Limited Liability Partnerships: Formation, Operation and Taxation, 1996; mem. editl. bd. Real Estate Tax Digest, The Practical Accountant, Jour. Real Estate Taxation. Fellow: Am. Coll. Tax Counsel; mem.: Calif. Bd. Legal Specialization (cert. specialist taxation), Can. Bar Assn., Law Coun. Australia, Bohemian Club. Republican. Office: Wood & Porter 333 Sacramento St San Francisco CA 94111 Office Phone: 415-834-1800. Business E-Mail: wood@woodporter.com.

WOOD, ROGER CONANT, biology professor, researcher; b. Binghamton, NY, May 20, 1941; s. Frances Wright and Albert Elmer Wood; m. Gary Leigh Whitehurst, June 29, 1974; children: Seth Hand, Nathaniel Wiley. BA, Princeton U., NJ, 1962; PhD, Harvard U., Cambridge, Mass., 1971. Prof. zoology Richard Stockton Coll., Pomona, NJ, 1971—; dir. rsch. Wetlands Inst., Stone Harbor, NJ, 1993—. Commr. Cape May County Mcpl. Utilities Authority, Middle Township, NJ, 1991—94; mem. NJ Coun. Humanities, Trenton, NJ, 1993—96; chmn. bd. trustees Wetlands Inst., Stone Harbor, NJ, 1983—93, pres. 1st lt. US Army, 1963—65, Bavaria, Germany. Recipient Outstanding Marine Rsch. Edn., NJ Marine Edn. Assn., 2006; fellow, NSF, 1974—75, 1980—81. Achievements include invention of terrapin excluder device and discovery of the world's largest turtle fossil from Venezuela. Avocation: gardening. Office: Richard Stockton Coll NJ PO Box 195 Pomona NJ 08240-0195 Business E-Mail: roger.wood@stockton.edu.

WOOD, SAMUEL H., science company executive, physician, scientist; MA in Psychology, U. Richmond; MD in Biochemistry and Molecular Biophysics; PhD in Biochemistry and Molecular Biophysics, MCV-VCU; MBA, San Diego State U. Bd. cert. Ob-Gyn., Reproductive Endocrinology and Infertility. Clin. faculty U. Calif., San Diego; founder, CEO Stemagen Corp., La Jolla, Calif.; founder, pres. Reproductive Scis. Ctr.-a Fertility Ctr. Featured on Frontline, Good Morning America, Discovery Channel, BBC, Today, New York Times, others; contbr. articles to profl. jours. Achievements include being the donor of DNA in the creation of the first mature cloned human embryos using DNA from adult skin cells in a somatic cell nuclear transfer. Office: Stemagen Corp 4150 Regents Park Row Ste 275 La Jolla CA 92037 Office Phone: 858-453-2305. Office Fax: 858-225-0376. Business E-Mail: info@stemagen.com.

WOOD, SHELTON EUGENE, JR., education educator, minister, consultant; b. Douglas, Ga., May 20, 1938; s. Shelton and Mae Lillie (Pheil) Wood; m. Edna Louise Wood, Aug. 25, 1961; children: Shelton John, Deirdre Louise. AA, St. John's U., 1958; BA, U. Nebr., 1959; MEd, Coll. William and Mary, Williamsburg, Va., 1971; PhD, Sussex U., 1973; EdD, Southeastern U., Washington, DC, 1975; MBA, Ctrl. Mich. U., Mount Pleasant, 1977; MA, U. Okla., Norman, 1980; D in Ministry, Wesleyan Bible Coll., 1999; Cert. in Internt. Rels., Fgn. Svc. Inst., 1971; Cert. in Mgmt., Indsl. Coll. Armed Forces, 1970. Area mgr. Marshall Fields Corp., Fla., 1957-58; transp. supr. Greyhound Corp., Jacksonville, Fla., 1959-62; officer US Army, 1963, advanced through grades to inf. col., 1996; with Redstone Readiness Group, 1977-80; chief studies and analysis divsn. Korean Inst. for Def. Analysis, 1981-83; faculty St. John River C.C., 1984-90; nat. and internat. bus. and mgmt. cons., 1995—; sr. pastor Fellowship Wesleyan Ch., Spring Hill, Fla., 1998—2005, asst. dist. supt. Fla., 2005—. Faculty Wesleyan Bible U., 1997—; pres. Georgetown Wesleyan U. of the Americas, 2005-. Author: Strategic for Implementing A Family Life Ministry Ctr., 1997; contbr. articles to profl. jours. Active Boy Scouts Am., 1977—90; lay leader United Meth. Ch., Falls Ch., Va., 1977—79, St. James United Meth. Ch., 1986—90; mem. dist. bd. ministerial develop. Fla. Dist. of Wesleyan Ch., 1999, chair evangelism and ch. growth com., 1999—; bd. dirs. Baby Love. Decorated Bronze Star with 2 oak leaf clusters, Air medal with 3 oak leaf clusters, Purple Heart with 2 oak leaf clusters; Sussex Coll. fellow, 1969-70. Mem. NEA, Am. Soc. Trainers and Developers (pres. S.E. chpt. 1974-75), Am. Def. Preparedness Assn., Putnam County C. of C. (pres. 1990-91), Toastmasters Internat. (Disting. Toastmaster 1989), Kiwanis (pres. 1989-90), Rotary (pres. 2009-), Phi Kappa Delta, Phi Delta Kappa. Address: 8485 Chatsworth St Spring Hill FL 34608 Office Phone: 352-346-1730. Personal E-mail: ewood11@tampabay.rr.com.

WOOD, STEPHEN WRAY, minister, educator, legislator; b. Winston Salem, NC, Oct. 6, 1948; s. D.W. and Annie Lee (Harris) W.; m. Starr Smith, June 18, 1978; children: Allyson, Joshua. BTh., John Wesley Coll., 1970; BA, Asbury Coll., 1973; MA, U. NC, Greensboro, 1979; DMin, Luther Rice U., Ga., 1980; MDiv, Houston Grad. Sch. Theology, 1990. Asst. dean, asst. prof. John Wesley Coll., High Point, NC, 1975-81; min. Soc. of Friends, 1980—. Adj. prof. Luther Rice U.; assoc. prof. Houston Grad. Sch. Theology; pres. Triad Christian Counseling, Greensboro, 1979. Contbr. articles to hist., ednl. and religious jours., Dictionary of NC Biography, Oxford Internat. Roundtable, 1997—; composer, singer religious music. Trustee John Wesley Coll., High Point, 1981—; bd. dirs. Friends Ctr.-Guilford Coll., Greensboro, 1982-89; vice chmn. Guilford County Rep. Party, NC, 1981-85; mem. NC State Ho. Reps., 1985-86, 89-90, 91-92, 93-94, 95-96, 97-98, 99-2000, 2003-05, spkr. pro tem, 1997—; apptd. mem. Selective Svc. Commn., 2001—; chaplain High Point Jaycees. With US Army, 1970-71; capt. NC State Militia. Mem. BMI (affiliate songwriter 1978—). Avocations: golf, book collecting, reading, cowboy boots. Office: 8098 Reynolda Rd Pfafftown NC 27040 Personal E-mail: repstevewood@juno.com. *I often reflect upon the maternal advice proffered me as a child, "Steve, if at first you don't succeed, try, try again." We may be down but not out. There is no such thing as the good old days because the future is just as bright as the promises of God. We conquer by continuing. Life is not a problem to be solved, it is a gift to be enjoyed.*

WOOD, TERRI LYNN, secondary school educator; b. Covina, Calif., Aug. 22, 1959; d. Karolyn Anne and Arthur Daniel Bast; m. Peter Joseph Wood, Oct. 22, 1983; children: Austin Pierce, Amber Leigh. Degree in Comm. Arts & Broadcast, Calif. Poly. U., Pomona, 1986. Cert. single subject clear tchg. Calif. Commn. Tchr. Credentialing, 1982, SB 395 ESL 2001. Lang. arts tchr. Canyon Hills Jr. HS, Chino Hills, Calif., 1983—, drama tchr., 1994—, dept. chair, 1997—2003, activities dir., 2006—. Mem. recuit leader Assistance League Pomona Valley, 1994—96. Mem.: Calif. Activities Dirs. Assn., Assn. Chino Tchrs., Nat. Educators Assn., Calif. Tchr. Assn. Conservative. Avocations: reading, travel, photography, gardening, dance. Home: 2286 N Euclid Ave Upland CA 91784 Office: Canyon Hills Jr HS 2500 Madrugada Dr Chino Hills CA 91709 Personal E-mail: terriwood22@yahoo.com. Business E-Mail: terri_wood@chino.k12.ca.us.

WOOD, TERRY LEE, mathematics educator; BA, Mich. State U., 1964, MA, 1968, PhD, 1976. Cert. tchr., Mich. Elem. tchr. Lansing (Mich.) Pub. Schs., 1964-65, 66-68; tchr., researcher The Lab. Schs., Chgo., 1979-80; vis. asst. prof. Purdue U., West Lafayette, Ind., 1985-88, asst. prof. math. edn., 1988-93, assoc. prof., 1993-98, prof., 1998—. Co-editor: Transforming Children's Mathematics Education, 1990, Recreating Elementary Mathematics Education: Insights and Issues, 1993, Mathematics Teacher Education International Perspectives, 1999, Beyond Classical Pedagogy: Teaching Elementary School Mathematics, 2001, editor International Handbook of Mathematics Teacher Education, 2008; mem. editl. bd. Ednl. Studies in Math., Jour. Tchr. Edn., Brit. Soc. Learning Math., Math. Tchr. Edn. and Devel. Robert L. Snodgrass scholar. Mem. AAAS, APA, Am. Ednl. Rsch. Assn., Nat. Coun. Tchrs. Math., Psychology Math. Edn. Internat., Psychology Math. Edn. N.Am., Soc. Rsch. in Child Devel. Home Phone: 765-337-1681. Business E-Mail: twood@purdue.edu.

WOOD, THOMAS WILLARD, retired health industry executive, retired military officer; b. Logan, Utah, Jan. 21, 1939; s. Elmer Raymond and Leola (Pitkin) W.; m. Blanche Loila Dowdle, Sept. 11, 1959 (div.); children: Dianna Wood Perry, Jeffery Thomas (dec.); m. Charlene Taulbee, Oct. 5, 1974; children: Douglas Winston Remington, Angela Christine Douglas, Thomas Willard II, Michael Joseph, Matthew David. BA, Utah State U., 1962; MS, Cen. Mich. U., 1975; postgrad., Indsl. Coll. Armed Forces, 1975, Armed Forces Staff Coll., 1976. Commd. 2d lt. USAF, 1962, advanced through grades to col., 1983; chief protocol Hdqrs. Air Force Logistics Command, Wright-Patterson AFB, Ohio, 1972-75; chief spl. project div. Hdqrs. 21st Air Force, McGuire AFB, N.J., 1977-78; chief inquiries br. Office Legis. Liaison, The Pentagon, Washington, 1978-82; dep. dir. Directorate Competition Advocacy Ogden Air Logistics Ctr., Hill AFB, Utah, 1982-85; air attache U.S. Def. Attache Office, Am. Embassy, Wellington, New Zealand, 1985-88; ret. dean New Zealand Mil. Attache Corps, 1986—88; chief protocol, dep. dir. pub. and govtl. affairs Hdqrs. U.S. Comdr.-in-Chief Pacific, Camp Smith, Hawaii, 1988-89; ret., 1989; adminstrv. asst. to v.p. mktg. Hawaii Med. Svc. Assn., Honolulu, 1989-91; sr. account exec. client rels. Baxter Internat. Inc., San Antonio, 1991-92; sr. account exec. prescription svc. divsn. Caremark, Inc., San Antonio, 1992-95; with corp. accts. prescription svc. divsn. Caremark Inc., San Antonio, 1996-97; sr. account exec. field ops. Caremark Pharm. Svcs., Medpartners Inc., San Antonio, 1997-99; sr. acct. mgr. field ops. CaremarkRx Inc., San Antonio, 1999-2000. Sr. nat. acct. mgr. Caremark Inc., San Antonio, 2000-02, assoc. nat. acct. exec., 2003-04, strategic acct. exec., 2007-09, ret. High priest LDS Ch., also ch. organist, pianist, tchr.; music chmn., high coun. San Antonio North Stake, 2006-; mem. groundbreaking and dedication com. San Antonio Tex. Temple, 2002-05. Decorated DFC, Air medal with nine oak leaf clusters; Gallantry Cross with palm (Vietnam); named hon. Royal New Zealand Air Force Navigator, 1988. Mem. Disting. Flying Cross Soc. (pres. Alamo chpt. 2003-07). Avocation: walking. Home: 1351 Grey Oak Dr San Antonio TX 78213-1602

WOOD, VIRCHEL EDGAR, orthopedist, surgeon, educator; s. Virchel Edgar and Gladys Brome Wood; m. Esther June Wood, Aug. 15, 1958; children: Tamarin, Laurel, Garry, Darrell, Victoria. BA in Chemistry, Atlantic Union Coll., Lancaster, Mass., 1956; MD, Loma Linda U., Calif., 1960. Diplomate Am. Bd. Orthop. Surgery, 1969. Rotating internship Wash. Sanitarium & Hosp., Takoma Park, Md., 1960—61; resident gen. surgery Harbor Gen. Hosp., Torrance, Calif., 1961—63; resident orthop. surgery U. Mass., Worcester, 1963—66; chief, orthop. svc. US Army Hosp., Fort Leonard Wood, Mo., 1967—69; fellow hand surgery Columbia-Presbyn. Hosp., NYC, 1970, U. Iowa, Iowa City, 1970; orthopaedic hand surgeon Loma Linda U. Med. Ctr., 1971—. Chief hand surgery svc. Loma Linda U., 1971—2000, prof. orthop. surgery, 1986—, dir. microsurgery lab., 1989—92, consulting chief hand surgery svc., 2000—06, vice-chair dept. orthop., 2000—. Contbr. chapters to books, scientific papers. With MC US Army, 1967—69. Recipient U. Disting. Svc. award, Loma Linda U. Sch. of Medicine, 2004, Editor's Choice award, Nat. Libr. of Poetry, 1998, Centennial Vanguard award, Loma Linda U. Allied Health Sci. Ctrs., 2006; named Outstanding Tchr. of Yr., Loma Linda U. Sch. Medicine, 1973, Outstanding Faculty Rschr., Walter E. Macpherson Soc. Loma Linda U., 1994, 1995, Alumnus of Yr., Neufeld Soc. Loma Linda U., 1996, Honored Alumnus, President's Coun. Loma Linda U. Alumni Assn., 1999. Mem.: AAUP, ACS, AMA, Academic Orthop. Soc., Am. Orthop. Assn., Am. Soc. Surgery of Hand (Most Frequently Cited Author in Congenital Hand Lit. Past 50 Years 1995), Am. Acad. Orthop. Surgeons, Inland Orthop. Soc., Calif. Med. Assn., Internat. Congenital Hand Anomalies Study Group, Internat. Soc. Poets (assoc.), Alpha Omega Alpha. Seventh-Day Adventist. Avocations: travel, museums, gemology, archaeology, poetry. Office: Loma Linda Univ Orthopaedics Ste 218 11406 Loma Linda Dr Loma Linda CA 92354 Office Fax: 909-558-6118.

WOOD, VIVIAN POATES, mezzo soprano, educator, author; b. Washington, Aug. 19, 1923; d. Harold Poates and Mildred Georgette (Patterson) W. Studies with Walter Anderson, Antioch Coll., 1953-55; studies with Denise Restout, Saint-Leu-A-Forêt, France and Lakeville, Conn., 1960—62, studies with Denise Restout, 1964—70; studies with Paul A. Pisk, 1968—71; studies with Paul Ulanowsky, NYC, 1958—68; Elemer Nagy, 1965-68, Vyautas Marijosius, 1967-68; MusB, Hartt Coll. Music, 1968; postgrad. (fellow), Yale U., 1968; MusM (fellow), Washington U., St. Louis, 1971, PhD (fellow), 1973. Debut in recital series Internat. Jeunesse Musicals Arts Festival, 1953; solo fellowship Boston Symphony Orch., Berkshire Music Ctr., Tanglewood, 1964, St. Louis Symphony Orch., 1969, Washington Orch., 1949, Bach Cantata Series Berkshire Chamber Orch., 1964, Yale Symphony Orch., 1968. Appearances in U.S. and European recitals, oratorios, operas, radio and TV, 1953-68; soloist Landowska Ctr., Lakeville, 1969, Internat. Harpsichord Festival, Westminister Choir Coll., Princeton, N.J., 1973; prof. voice, head voice area Sch. of Music, U. So. Miss., Hattiesburg, 1971-2000, ret. 2000, prof. emerita, 2000—; asst. dean Coll. Fine Arts, 1974-76, acting dean, 1976-77; guest prof. Hochschüle für Musik, Munich, 1978-79; prof. Italian Internat. Studies Program, Rome, 1986; Miss. coord. Alliance for Arts Edn., Kennedy Ctr. Performing Arts, 1974—; mem. Miss. Gov.'s Adv. Panel for Gifted and Talented Children, 1974—, 1st Miss. Gov.'s Conf. on the Arts, 1974—. Author: Polenc's Songs: An Analysis of Style, 1971. Recipient Young Am. Artists Concert award N.Y.C., 1955; Wanda Landowska fellow 1961-68. Mem. Miss. Music Tchrs. Assn., Nat. Assn. Tchrs. of Singing, Music Tchrs. Nat. Assn., Am. Musicology Soc., Golden Key, Mu Phi Epsilon, Delta Kappa Gamma, Tau Beta Kappa (hon.), Pi Kappa Lambda. Democrat. Episcopalian.

WOOD, WENDY DEBORAH, filmmaker; b. NYC, Oct. 4, 1940; d. John Meyer and Marion Emily (Peters) W.; m. William Dismore Chapple, Dec. 7, 1963; 1 child, Samuel Eliot. BA cum laude, Vassar Coll., 1962; MA, Stanford U., 1964. Tchg. asst. Stanford U., 1962-64; photographer, film editor Bristol (Eng.) U., 1964-66, asst. dir. Internat. Conf. Film Schs., 1966; rsch. asst. biology dept. U. Conn., Storrs, 1970-72; sr. media specialist Aetna Life & Casualty Co., Hartford, Conn., 1972-89; media writer, prodr., dir. U. Conn. Ctr. for Media and Tech., Storrs, 1989—2006. Pres. Chapple Films, Inc., 1972—. Films include: Yankee Craftsman, 1972, Alcoholism, Industry's Costly Hangover, 1974, Draggerman's Haul, 1975, Flight Without Wings, 1977, Auto Insurance Affordability, 1981 (2 awards), Where Rivers Run to the Sea, 1981 (award), Our Town is Burning Down, 1982 (6 awards), Wellness at the Worksite, 1984 (4 awards), Aenhance, 1989 (3 awards), Tiffany: Magician in Glass. Mem. jury N.Y. Internat. Video and Film Festival; bd. dirs. Windham Regional Arts Coun., 1987, 88, 89; mem. peer rev. com. Conn. Commn. Higher Edn., 1992-96. Recipient CINE Golden Eagle award Coun. on Internat. Non-Theatrical Events, 1972, 76, 84, 1st Place award Indls. Photography, 1974, cert. Outstanding Creativity U.S. TV Commls. Festival, 1974, EFLA award Am. Film Festival, 1974, 76, Dir's. Choice award Sinking Creek Film Festival, 1975, award Columbus Film Festival, 1975, award Excellence Life Ins. Advts. Assn., 1975, Silver Screen award U.S. Indsl. Film Festival, 1976,

81, 1st place award Conn. Film Festival, 1977, 1st prize Nat. Outdoor Travel Film Festival, 1978, 1st pl. Houston Film Festival, 1982, CINE Golden Eagle, 1982, 84, award Am. Film Festival, 1982, N.Y. Film Festival, 1982, 83, Silver CINDY award Assn. Visual Communicators, 1985, Conn. Film/Video Festival 1st pl. award, 1997, Gold award Conn. Film Festival, 1997, others. Mem. Info. Film Prodrs. Am. (nat. dir., pres. chpt. 1981-82, Cindy award 1971, 72, 81, 82, 85, 87), Internat. Quorum Motion Picture Prodrs., Audio Visual Communicators (pres. Conn. chpt. 1985, treas. 1988). Democrat. Mem. Soc. Of Friends. Home: 604 Phoenixville Rd Chaplin CT 06235-2211 E-mail: woodwendy@earthlink.net.

WOOD, WILLIAM MCBRAYER, lawyer; b. Greenville, SC, Jan. 27, 1942; s. Oliver Gillan and Grace (McBrayer) W.; m. Nancy Cooper, 1973 (dec. 1993); children: Walter, Lewis; m. Jeanette Dobson Haney, June 25, 1994. BS in Acctg., U. S.C., Columbia, 1964, JD cum laude, 1972; LLM in Estate Planning (scholar), U. Miami, 1980. Bar: S.C. 1972, Fla. 1979, D.C. 1973, U.S. Tax Ct. 1972, U.S. Ct. Claims 1972, U.S. Supreme Ct. 1977; cert. mediator, SC, 2006. Intern ct. of claims sect., tax divsn. U.S. Dept. Justice, 1971; law clk. to chief judge U.S. Ct. Claims, Washington, 1972-74; ptnr. firm Edwards Wood, Duggan & Reese, Greer and Greenville, 1974-78; asst. prof. law Cumberland Law Sch., Samford U., Birmingham, Ala., 1978-79; faculty Nat. Inst. Trial Advocacy: N.E. Regional Inst., 1979, 83-90, 95-97, Fla. Regional Inst., 1989; teaching team 5th intensive trial techniques course Hofstra U., 1983; assoc. then capital ptnr. firm Shutts & Bowen, Miami, 1980-85; sole practice Miami, 1985—; also Rock Hill, SC, 1994—2004; of counsel Griffin, Smith, Caldwell, Helder & Helms, Monroe, NC, 2001—07. Lectr. Nat. Bus. Inst. Seminars, 2003—07. Contbg. editor: The Lawyers PC; Fla. editor: Drafting Wills and Trust Agreements; substantive com. editor ABA: The Tax Lawyer, 1983-2007. Pres. Piedmont Heritage Found., Inc. 1975-78; del. State Rep. Conv., 1985, 87, 90, Fla. State Rep. Conv., 1986, 88, 90, SC State Conv., 1978; exec. committeeman Miami-Dade County Republicans, 1985-94, Mecklenberg County NC Rep. Party, 2005—2008; co-legal counsel, Mecklenberg County, NC, 1990-92; apptd. Miami-Dade County Indsl. Devel. Authority, 1990-94; mem. vestry Episc. Ch., 1993-94; committeeman, former cubmaster, Boy Scouts Am., Coral Gables, Fla.; With USAF, 1965-69, Vietnam. Decorated Air Force Commendation medal; recipient Am. Jurisprudence award in real property and tax I, 1971; winner Grand prize So. Living Mag. travel photo contest, 1968. Mem. ABA (taxation sect., tchg. law com., 1994-2000), Greer C. of C. (pres. 1977, Outstanding leadership award 1976), Greater Greenville C. of C. (dir. 1977), Order Wig and Robe, Estate Planning Council South Fla., Omicron Delta Kappa, Recording Acad. (Grammys), Club: Bankers (bd. govs. 1989-94). Lodge: Masons, Scottish Rite, Rotary, Recording Acad-.(Grammy). Office: 5345 Wilgrove Mint Hill Rd Charlotte NC 28227-3467 Office Phone: 305-374-4441. E-mail: wmwood@bellsouth.net.

WOOD, WILLIS BOWNE, JR., retired utilities executive; b. Kansas City, Mo., Sept. 15, 1934; s. Willis Bowne Sr. and Mina (Henderson) W.; m. Dixie Gravel, Aug. 31, 1955; children: Bradley, William, Josh. BS in Petroleum Engring., U. Tulsa, 1957; grad. advanced mgmt. prog., Harvard U., 1983. With So. Calif. Gas Co., LA, 1960-74, from v.p. to sr. v.p., 1975-80, exec. v.p., 1983-84; pres., CEO Pacific Lighting Gas Supply Co., LA, 1981-83; from sr. v.p. to chmn., pres., CEO, Pacific Enterprises, LA, 1984-93, chmn., CEO, 1993-98; ret., 1998. Bd. dirs. Automobile Club So. Calif., chmn. bd. dirs., 2005—07, vice chmn., 2007—. Past bd. dirs. LA World Affairs Coun.; past dir., past chmn. bus coun. for Sustainable Energy Future, 1994—; past dir. Pacific Coun. Internat. Affairs; trustee U. So. Calif.; past trustee, past vice-chmn. Harvey Mudd Coll., Claremont, Calif., 1984—2005; trustee emeritus, past chmn. Calif. Med. Ctr. Found., LA, 1983—2002; past trustee, past pres. SW Mus., LA; trustee John and Dora Haynes Found., 1998—. Recipient Disting. Alumni U. Tulsa, 1995; inductee U. Tulsa Engring. Hall of Fame, 2001. Mem. Soc. Petroleum Engrs., Calif. State C. of C. (past bd. dirs.), Am. Automobile Assn. (dir. 1999-2007, chmn. 2002-05), NAM (past bd. dirs.), Calif. Club, Shady Canyon Golf Club. Republican.

WOODALL, DAVID MONROE, engineer, researcher, dean; b. Perryville, Ark., Aug. 2, 1945; m. Linda Carol Page, June 6, 1966; 1 child, Zachary Page. BA, Hendrix Coll., 1967; MS, Columbia U., 1968; PhD, Cornell U., 1976. Registered profl. engr., Idaho. Nuc. engr. Westinghouse Corp., Pitts., 1968-70; asst. prof. U. Rochester, NY, 1974-77, U. N.Mex., Albuquerque, 1977-79, assoc. prof., 1979-83, chair dept., 1980-83, prof., 1984-86; group physics mgr. Idaho Nat. Engring. Lab., Idaho Falls, 1986-92; assoc. dean, dir. rsch. U. Idaho, Moscow, 1992-99, acting dean, 1999; dean coll. sci., engring., math. U. Alaska, Fairbanks, 1999—2003; dir. Ctr. for Nanosensor Tech., 2001—03. Provost & v.p. for academic affairs, Oregon Inst. of Tech., 2003—07, interim pres., 2007-, EAC comm. Accreditation Bd. Engring. Tech., 1990-95, bd. dir., 1997-2003; cons. in field. Contbr. articles to profl. jours. Grantee NSF, DOE, AFOSR, Office Naval Rsch., DMEA, others. Mem. Am. Nuc. Soc. (chpt. chair 1982-83), Am. Soc. Engring. Edn. (divsn. chair 1993, 95, chair engring. rsch. coun., v.p.). Office: Oregon Institute of Technology 3201 Campus Drive Klamath Falls OR 97601 Business E-Mail: david.woodall@oit.edu.

WOODALL, PEGGY KEATON, special education educator; b. Hot Springs, Ark., Dec. 15, 1946; d. Harry Craig and Jo Mitchell Keaton; m. Robert L. Keaton, Nov. 7, 1998; children: Leslie Suzanne Overton, Russell Craig Foster. PhD, U. Santa Barbara, Calif., 2002. Dir. spl. edn. Arkadelphia Pub. Sch., Ark., 2006—08; asst. prof. Henderson State U., Arkadelphia, Ark., 2008—. Mem.: Phi Kappa Phi, Delta Kappa Gama. Home: 284 Tanglewood Rd Hot Springs AR 71913 Office: Henderson State Univ Box 7860 Arkadelphia AR 71999-001 Office Fax: 870-230-5459; Home Fax: 870-230-5459. Personal E-mail: pwoodall@cablelynx.com. Business E-Mail: woodalp@hsu.edu.

WOODALL, SAMUEL ROY, JR., lawyer; b. July 8, 1936; s. Samuel Roy Woodall; m. Jane Marvin Brock, Aug. 5, 1958; children: Samuel Roy III, Lawrence B., Claiborne A., George G. BA, U. Ky., 1958, LLB, 1962; postgrad., Yale U., 1959. Bar: Ky. 1962. Atty. Ky. Dept. Ins., 1962-64, gen. counsel, 1965-66; commr. ins. Commonwealth Ky., 1966-68; assoc. firm Wyatt, Grafton and Sloss, Louisville, 1968-69, ptnr., 1969-72; pres. Western Pioneer Life Ins. Co. (and predecessors), Louisville, 1972-76; asst. to pres. Am. Life & Accident Ins. Co., Louisville, 1976-80; pres. Nat. Assn. Life Cos., Washington, 1980-93; v.p. and chief counsel state rels. Am. Coun. Life Ins., Washington, 1993-98; with Morris, Manning & Martin (Atlanta-based firm), Washington, 1998—2001; ins. cons. Congl. Rsch. Svc., Libr. of Congres, Washington, 2001—; sr. ins. policy analyst U.S. Treasury Dept., 2002—. Guest instr. ins. law U. Louisville, 1968—69. Note editor: U. Ky. Law Rev., 1961—62. Pres. Citizen's Met. Planning coun., Louisville, 1970—71; chmn. City of Louisville Riverfront Commn., 1970—75, Ky. Heritage Commn., 1964—77; bd. dirs. Bingham Child Guidance Clinic, Louisville, 1969—76, Youth Performing Arts Coun., 1979—80. Recipient Sullivan medallion, U. Ky., 1958; named one of Ky.'s 3 Outstanding Young Men, Ky. Jr. C. of C., 1968; fellow Woodrow Wilson, Yale U., 1959. Mem.: ABA, Fedn. Ins. Counsel, D.C. Bar Assn., Ky. Bar Assn., Phi Beta Kappa, Phi Alpha Delta (pres. chpt. 1961—62). Home: 2851 29th St NW Washington DC 20008-4111 Office: US Dept Treasury 15th and Pennsylvania Ave NW Washington DC 20220

WOODALL, THOMAS A., state supreme court justice; b. Meridian, Miss., July 14, 1950; m. Debbie Bogan, 1972; children: Scott, Matthew, Claire. BA in History, Millsaps Coll., 1972; JD, U. Va., 1975. Former legal editor Michie Co.; with Rives and Peterson, Birmingham, Ala., 1975—91; ptnr. Woodall and Maddox, Birmingham, 1991—96; circuit judge Jefferson County, 1996—2001; assoc. justice Ala. Supreme Ct., 2001—. Mem. Ala. Pattern Jury Instrn.-Civil Com., 1985—2001, vice chmn., 1992—2001. Mem.: Birmingham Bar Assn. (chair com. on grievance, civil ct. procedures and membership). Republican. Methodist. Office: Ala State Supreme Ct 300 Dexter Ave Montgomery AL 36104-3741*

WOODALL, WILLIAM ROBERT, legislative staff member; Staff dir., rules com. US House of Reps., Washington, chief of staff to Rep. John Linder. Co-author (with N. Boortz and J. Linder): Fairtax: The Truth: Answering the Critics. Republican. Office: 1026 Longwood House Office Bldg Washington DC 20515 Office Phone: 202-225-4272. Office Fax: 202-225-4696.*

WOODARD, CAROL JANE, educational consultant; b. Buffalo, Jan. 19, 1929; d. Harold August and Violet Maybelle (Landsittel) Young; m. Ralph Arthur Woodard, Aug. 19, 1950; children: Camaron Jane, Carsen Jane, Cooper Ralph. BA, Hartwick Coll., 1950; MA, Syracuse U., 1952; PhD, SUNY, Buffalo, 1972; LHD (hon.), Hartwick Coll., 1991; postgrad., Bank St. Coll., Harvard U. Cert. tchr., NY State. Tchr., Orchard Park, NY, 1950-51, Danville, Ind., 1951-52, Akron, NY, 1952-54; dir. Garden Nursery Sch., Williamsville, NY, 1955-65; tchr. Amherst Coop. Nursery Sch., NY, 1967-69; asst. prof. early childhood edn. SUNY, Buffalo, 1969-72, lab. demonstration tchr. and student teaching supr., 1969-76, assoc. prof., 1972-79, prof., 1979-88, prof. emeritus, 1988—; dir. Consultants in Early Childhood, 1988—. Cons. Lutheran Ch. Am., Villa Maria Coll., Buffalo Pub. Sch., Buffalo Mus. Sci., Headstart Tng. Programs, Erie Cmty. Coll., NY State Dept. Edn., numerous workshops.; cons. sch. systems, indsl. firms, pub., civic orgns. in child devel.; vis. prof. The Netherlands and East China Univ., Shanghai, People's Republic of China; sci. trainer The Wright Group, 1995. Author 7 books for young children, 2 textbooks in field; co-author: Physical Science in Early Childhood, 1987; co-author nat. curriculum for ch. sch. for 3-yr.-olds; author: (booklet) You Can Help Your Baby Learn; author/coord. TAKE CARE child protection project, 1987; contbr. chpt. to books, articles to profl. jour. Trustee Hartwick Coll., Oneonta, NY, 1978-87, trustee emeritus, 2004-; cons. EPIC Birth to Three Program, 1992; design cons. indoor playground Noah's Ark Jewish Ctr., Buffalo, 1992; Sites Project coord., cons. Let's Talk project Buffalo Pub. Sch., 1994—2005; student tchg. supr. SUNY, Fredonia, 1994-2004. Mem. Nat. Assn. Edn. Young Children, Early Childhood Edn. Council Western NY, Assn. Childhood Edn. Internat., Phi Delta Kappa, Pi Lambda Theta. Home: 85 Ruskin Road East Aurora NY 14052-3028 Office Phone: 716-655-1925.

WOODARD, DIANE E., music educator; d. Harry Moore and Mary Purdy Woodard; m. Bruce N. Wardrep, Sept. 12, 1998. B in Music Edn., Ga. Coll., 1970; MusM, Ga. State U., 1975, cert. in edn. specialist, 1985, PhD, 1994. Cert. tchg. Ga. Choral dir. Babb Jr. HS, Forest Park, Ga., 1970—79, Jonesboro HS, Ga., 1979—2001, chair music dept., 1981—91; asst. choral dir. Woodward Acad., College Park, Ga., 2001—02; choral dir. Galloway Sch., Atlanta, 2002—. Music tchr. Fountain Jr. H.S., Forest Park, 1971—72. Organist, choir dir. St. Timothy's Luth. Ch., Forest Park, 1983—87; mem. Atlanta Symphony Orch. Chorus, 1983—. Mem.: MENC (so. divsn. bd. dirs. 1995—97, nat. assembly state pres. 1995—97), Am. Choral Dirs. Assn. (treas. Ga. chpt. 1977—80), Ga. Music Educators Assn. (organizing chair all-state chorus event 1978, 1979, chair choral divsn. 1979—81, organizing chair all-state chorus event 1982, 1983, 1985, region chair all-state chorus auditions 1994, pres. 1995—97, so. divsn. bd. nat. conf. 1995—98, nat. assembly state pres. 1997, exec. com. 1997—98, bd. dirs. 1997—98, region chair all-state chorus auditions 1998, 1999, 2000, 2002—05, dist. chair all-state chorus auditions 1990, coun. 1975—87, Music Educator of Yr. 2004). Office: Galloway Sch 215 W Wieuca Rd NW Atlanta GA 30342

WOODARD, JOSEPH LAMAR, law librarian, emeritus professor; b. Auburndale, Fla., Dec. 28, 1937; s. Wilbur Allen and Florence Virginia (Ladd) Woodard; m. Eleanor Eugenia Cummings, Aug. 7, 1964; children: Robert Edward, James Frederick. BA, U. Fla., 1959, JD, 1962; MLS, Columbia U., 1964. Bar: Fla. 1962, U.S. Dist. Ct. (mid. dist.) Fla. 1970. Asst. reference libr. Columbia U., NYC, 1962—64; asst. libr. Cahill, Gordon, Reindel and Ohl, NYC, 1964—65; law libr. Tulane U., 1965—69; ptnr. Schuh, Schuh and Woodard, St. Petersburg, Fla., 1969—71; law libr. Stetson U., 1971—2001, prof. law, 1979—2001, law libr., prof. emeritus, 2001—. Pres. Tampa Bay Libr. Consortium, 1981, 1988—89. Stated clk. Presbytery Tampa Bay, 2005—06. With USAR, 1957—63. Named to Hall of Fame, Stetson U. Coll. Law, 2006. Mem.: ABA, Pinellas Pub. Libr. Coop. (sec.-treas. 1993—94, pres. 1994—95), Am. Assn. Law Librs. (sec.-treas. SE chpt. 1975—78), Fla. Bar Assn. Republican. Personal E-mail: lamar@woodardfamily.org.

WOODBURN, RALPH ROBERT, JR., lawyer; b. Haverhill, Mass., Nov. 3, 1946; s. Ralph Robert and Josephine Marie (McClure) W.; m. Janet M. Smith, Sept. 15, 1985. BA, Mich. State U., 1967; JD, Harvard U., 1972; LLM, Boston U., 1981. Bar: Mass. 1972, U.S. Tax Ct. 1987. Assoc. Bowers, Fortier & Lakin, Boston, 1972-76; from assoc. to ptnr. Haussermann, Davison & Shattuck, Boston, 1976-83; ptnr. Palmer & Dodge, Boston, 1983—2005, Edwards Angell Palmer & Dodge, Boston, 2005—. Tchr. Harvard Ctr. for Lifelong Learning, Cambridge, Mass., 1986-89; chmn. Wellesley Cable Access Bd., 1993-95, dir. Keokuk Area Cmty. Found., 2009-. Contbr. articles to Boston Bar Jour. and Estate Planning. Treas. Exeter Assn. of New Eng., Boston, 1985-89, v.p., 1989-91, pres., 1991-93. Fellow Am. Coll. Trust and Estate Counsel; mem. ABA, Boston Bar Assn. (chmn. probate legislation 1983-93), Brae Burn Country Club (Newton, Mass.), Keokuk Country Club (Iowa), Harvard Club of Boston, Boston Probate and Estate Planning Forum (program chair 1996-97, moderator 1997-98), Harvard Travellers Club, Boston Com. Fgn. Rels. Home: 25 Cypress Rd Wellesley MA 02481-2918 Office: Edwards Angell Palmer & Dodge LLP 111 Huntington Ave Boston MA 02199-7613 Office Phone: 617-239-0123. Business E-Mail: rwoodburn@eapdlaw.com.

WOODBURY, RICHARD BENJAMIN, anthropologist, educator; b. West Lafayette, Ind., May 16, 1917; s. Charles Goodrich and Marion (Benjamin) W.; m. Nathalie Ferris Sampson, Sept. 18, 1948. Student, Oberlin Coll., 1934-36; BS in Anthropology cum laude, Harvard U., 1939, MA, 1942, PhD, 1949; postgrad., Columbia U., 1939-40. Archeol. research, Ariz., 1938, 39, Fla., 1940, Guatemala, 1947-49, El Morro Nat. Monument, N.Mex., 1953-56, Tehuacan, Mex., 1964; archaeologist United Fruit Co. Zaculeu Project, Guatemala, 1947-50; assoc. prof. anthropology U. Ky., 1950-52, Columbia U., 1952-58; rsch. assoc. prof. anthropology interdisciplinary arid lands program U. Ariz., 1959-63; curator archeology and anthropology U.S. Nat. Mus., Smithsonian Instn., Washington, 1963-69, acting. head office anthropology, 1965-66, chmn. office anthropology, 1966-67; prof., chmn. dept. anthropology U. Mass., Amherst, 1969-73, prof., 1973-81, prof. emeritus, 1981—, acting assoc. provost, dean grad. sch., 1973-74. Mem. divsn. anthropology and psychology NRC, 1954-57; bd. dirs. Archaeol. Conservancy, 1979-84, Valley Health Plan, Amherst, 1981-84, Mus. of No. Ariz., 1983-90; liason rep. for Smithsonian Instn., Com. for Recovery of Archeol. Remains, 1965-69; assoc. seminar on ecol. systems and cultural evolution Columbia U., 1964-73; mem. exec. com. bd. dirs. Human Relations Area Files, Inc., New Haven, Conn., 1968-70; cons. Conn. Hist. Commn., 1970-72. Author (with A.S. Trik) The Ruins of Zaculeu, Guatemala, 2 vols., 1953, Prehistoric Stone Implements of Northeastern Arizona, 1954, Alfred V. Kidder, 1973, Sixty Years of Southwestern Archaeology, 1993, (chpt.) (with James A. Neely) The Prehistory of the Tehuacan Valley, Vol. 4, 1972; editor: (with I.A. Sanders) Societies Around the World (2 vols.), 1953, (with others) The Excavation of Hawikuh, 1966, Am. Antiquity, 1954-58, Abstracts of New World Archaeology; editor-in-chief: Am. Anthropologist, 1975-78; mem. editorial bd.: Am. Jour. Archeology, 1957-72. Mem. sch. com., Shutesbury, Mass., 1979—82; chmn. fin. com. Friends of Amherst Stray Animals (Dakin Animal Shelter), 1983—85, trustee, 1991—; mem. Shutesbury Hist. Commn., 1998—2006, sec., 1999—2004. With USAF, 1942—45. Fellow, Mus. No. Ariz., 1985. Fellow AAAS (coun. rep. Am. Anthrop. Assn. 1961-63, com. on desert and arid zones rsch. Southwest and Rocky Mountains divsn. 1958-64, vice-chair 1962-64, com. arid lands 1969-74, sec. 1970-72), Am. Anthrop. Assn. (exec. bd. 1963-66, A.V. Kidder award 1989), Archeol. Inst. Am. (exec. com. 1965-67); mem. Soc. Am. Archeology (treas. 1953-54, pres. 1958-59, chmn. fin. com. 1987-89, Fiftieth Anniversary award 1985, Disting. Svc. award 1988), Ariz. Archeol. and Hist. Soc., Nature Conservancy, Archeol. Conservancy (life). Office: Univ Mass Dept Anthropology Machmer Hall Amherst MA 01003

WOODCOCK, DAVID GEOFFREY, architect, educator; b. Manchester, Eng., May 28, 1937; s. Herbert Edwin and Constance Mary (Bristol) Woodcock; m. Kathleen Mary Bishop, Oct. 1, 1960 (dec. 1964); 1 child, Jonathan Alfred; m. Valerie Frances Gubbins, July 4, 1964; children: Frances Mary, Penelope Jane. BA in Architecture with 1st class honors, U. Manchester, 1960, D in Town Planning, 1966. Arch. emeritus, Tex. Lectr. U. Manchester, 1961; asst. prof. Tex. A&M U., College Station, 1962-66; sr. lectr. Kent. Inst. Art & Design, Canterbury, England, 1966—70; assoc. prof. Tex. A&M U., College Station, 1970—76, prof., 1976—; dir. Ctr. Heritage Conservation, 1991—2007. Pvt. practice, Canterbury, 1966—70, College Station, 1980—. Bd. dirs. Opera and Performing Arts Soc., Tex. A&M U., 1980—83, 1988—91, pres., 1993—94; peer reviewer U.S. Gen. Svc. Adminstrn., 2004—; active Episc. Diocese Tex. Archtl. Commn., 1987—95; mem. adv. bd. Hammons Sch. Architecture Drury Coll., Mo., 1990—93, Savannah (Ga.) Coll. Arts and Design/Architecture, 1987—93. Recipient Rsch. Excellence award, Tex. Hist. Commn., 1991, Romieniec award for Archtl. Edn., Tex. Soc. Archs., 1995, Truett Latimer Profl. award, Preservation Tex., Inc., 1998. Fellow: AIA (hist. resource com. adv. group 2005—09, chair 2009), Assn. Collegiate Schs. Architecture (regional dir. 1981—84, Disting. prof. 1991), Nat. Coun. Preservation Edn., Assn. Preservation Tech. Internat. (bd. dirs. 1990—, v.p. 1998—99, pres. 1999—2001, Harley J. McKee award 2003), Soc. Antiquaries London. Avocations: drawing, cross disciplinary education. Office: Tex A&M U Dept Architecture College Station TX 77843-3137 Office Phone: 979-845-7850. Business E-Mail: d-woodcock@tamu.edu.

WOODCOCK, JANET, federal agency administrator; b. Washington, Pa., Aug. 29, 1948; d. John and Frances (Crocker) W.; m. Roger Henry Miller, Nov. 16, 1981; children: Kathleen Miller, Susanne Miller. BS cum laude, Bucknell U., 1970; MD, Northwestern U., Chgo., 1977. Diplomate Am. Bd. Internal Medicine. Intern Hershey Med. Ctr./Pa. State U., 1977-78, resident in internal medicine, 1978-80, chief resident in medicine, 1980-81; fellow in rheumatology U. Calif./VA Med. Ctr., San Francisco, 1982-84; instr. medicine divsn. rheumatology and immunology VA Med. Ctr., San Francisco, 1984-85; med. officer divsn. biol. investigational new drugs Ctr. for Biologics Evaluation and Rsch./FDA, Rockville, Md., 1986-87, group leader divsn. biol. investigational new drugs, 1987-88, dep. dir. divsn. biol. investigational new drugs, 1988, dir. divsn. biol. investigational new drugs, 1988-90; dir. office of therapeutics rsch. and rev. Ctr. for Biologics Evaluation and Rsch., FDA, Rockville, Md., 1992-94, acting dep. dir., 1990-92; dir. Ctr. for Drug Evaluation and Rsch., FDA, Rockville, Md., 1994—2005, 2008—, acting dir., 2007—08; dep. commr. ops., chief med. officer FDA, Rockville, Md., 2005—08. Instr. medicine, asst. prof. divsn. gen. internal medicine Hershey Med. Ctr./Pa. State U., 1981; analytical chemist rsch. divsn. A.B. Dick Co., Niles, Ill., 1971-73. Nat. Merit scholar Bucknell U., 1966, Pa. State scholar, 1966; Rsch. fellow Am. Rheumatism Assn.; VA Investigator grantee, 1985; recipient Presdl. Rank Meritorious Exac. award, Nathan Davis award, AMA, Pub. Svc. award, Am. Assn. Cancer Rsch., Pub. Health Leadership award, Nat. Org. Rare Disorders, VIDA award, Nat. Alliance Hispanic Health, Award for Leadership in Personalized Medicine, Personalized Medicine Coalition, 2005 Mem. Alpha Omega Alpha, Alpha Lambda Delta. Office: Ctr Drug Evaluation & Rsch US Food & Drug Admin 5600 Fishers Lane Rockville MD 20857*

WOODEN, JOHN ROBERT, retired college basketball coach; b. Martinsville, Ind., Oct. 14, 1910; s. Joshua Hugh and Roxie (Rothrock) W.; m. Nellie C. Riley, Aug. 8, 1932; children: Nancy Anne, James Hugh. BS, Purdue U., 1932; MS, Ind. State U., 1947. Athletic dir., basketball and baseball coach Ind. State Tchrs. Coll., 1946-48; head basketball coach UCLA, 1948-75. Lectr. to colls., coaches, business. Author: Practical Modern Basketball, 1966, They Call Me Coach, 1972; co-author: Wooden--a Lifetime of Reflections and Observations On and Off the Court, 1997, Inch and Miles--Pyramid to Success for Kids, 2004, One on One, 2004; contbr. articles to profl. jours. Served to lt. USNR, 1943-46. Named All-Am. basketball player Purdue U., 1930-32, Coll. Basketball Player Yr., 1932, to All-Time All-Am. Team Helms Athletic Found., 1943, Nat. Basketball Hall of Fame, Springfield (Mass.) Coll., as player, 1960, as coach, 1970, Ind. State Basketball Hall of Fame, 1962, Calif. Father of Yr., 1964, 75, Coach of Yr. U.S. Basketball Writers Assn., 1964, 67, 69, 70, 72, 73, Sportsman of Yr. Sports Illustrated, 1973, GTE Acad. All-Am., 1994, Nat. Collegiate Backetball Hall of Fame, 2006; recipient Whitney Young award Urban League, 1973, 1st ann. Velvet Covered Brick award Layman's Leadership Inst., 1974, 1st ann. Dr. James Naismith Peachbasket award, 1974, Medal of Excellence Bellarmine Coll., 1985, Sportslike Pathfinder award to Hoosier with extraordinary svc. on behalf of Am. youth, 1993, 40 for the Age award Sports Illustrated, 1994, the 1st Frank G. Wells Disney award for role model to youth, 1995, Disting. Am. award Pres. Reagan, 1995, Svc. to Mankind award Lexington Theol. Sem., 1995, NCAA Theodore Roosevelt Sportsman award, 1995, Vince Lombardi award for excellence, 2000, Ind. Legend award, 2000, Presdl. Medal of Freedom, 2003, Pres. Ford award NCAA, 2006; named Basketball Coach of Century, 2000. *I have tried to live the philosophy of my personal definition of* *success which I formulated in the middle thirties shortly after I entered the teaching profession. Not being satisfied that success was merely the accumulation of material possessions or the attainment of a position of power or prestige, I chose to define success as "peace of mind which can be attained only through the self-satisfaction that comes from knowing you did your best to become the best that you are capable of becoming.".**

WOODFIN, CAROL GALE, history professor; b. Waco, Tex., July 2, 1956; d. Yandall Clark and Leta Frances Beene Woodfin. BA, Hardin-Simmons U., Abilene, 1978; MA, Wake Forest U., Winston-Salem, 1987; PhD, Vanderbilt, Nashville, 1997. Cert. Internat. Bapt. Theol. Sem., 1986. Assoc. editor European Bapt. Press Svc., Rueschlikon, Switzerland, 1980—87; publs. and archives specialist So. Bapt. Hist. Commn., Nashville, 1991—93; assoc. prof. history Palm Beach Atlantic U., West Palm Beach, Fla., 1993—2007, Hardin-Simmons U., Tex., 2007—. Translator: (book) Zwingli: 1484-1984: Reformation in Zurich; contbr. articles to profl. jours. Sabbatical study grant, Palm Beach Atlantic U., 2003—04, grant, 2007, Libr. study grant, St. Deiniol's Libr., Wales, 2004. Mem.: Conf. Faith and History (bd. dir. 2000—06), Bapt. History and Heritage Soc., Phi Alpha Theta. Office: Hardin-Simmons Univ 2200 Hickory St P O Box 16125 Abilene TX 79698 Business E-Mail: cwoodfin@hsutx.edu.

WOODFORD, ARTHUR MACKINNON, library director, historian; b. Detroit, Nov. 23, 1940; s. Frank Bury and Mary-Kirk (MacKinnon) W.; m. Mary R. Woodford; children: Mark, Cristopher, Amy, Joyce, Kathleen, Lindsey. Student, U. Wis., 1958-60; BA in History, Wayne State U., 1963; AM in LS, U. Mich., 1964. Libr. Detroit Pub. Libr., 1964-74; asst. dir. Grosse Pointe (Mich.) Pub. Libr., 1974-77; dir. St. Clair Shores (Mich.) Pub. Libr., 1977—2005, Suburburn Libr. Coop., 2007—. Author: All Our Yesterdays, 1969, Detroit and Its Banks, 1974, Detroit: American Urban Renaissance, 1979, Charting The Inland Seas, 1991, Tonnancour, 1994, vol. 2, 1996, This Is Detroit: 1701-2001, 2001. With USNR, 1958-64. Mem. Mich. Libr. Assn. (v.p. 1988-89), Gt. Lakes Maritime Inst., Prismatic Club Detroit (pres. 1982), Algonquin Club of Detroit and Windsor (treas. 1983-93). Avocations: tennis, bridge, reading, model ship building. Home: 3284 S Channel Dr Harsens Island MI 48028

WOODFORD, PETER C., lawyer; BA, Dartmouth Coll., 1971; JD with honors, George Washington U., 1978. Bar: Ill. 1978, US Ct. Appeals (3rd, 5th, 7th cir.), US Dist. Ct. (no. dist.) Ill., US Dist. Ct. (ea. dist.) Mich., US Tax Ct. Ptnr., gen. counsel Seyfarth Shaw LLP, Chgo. Mem.: ABA. Office: Seyfarth Shaw LLP 131 S Dearborn Ste 2400 Chicago IL 60603-5577 Office Phone: 312-460-5908. Office Fax: 312-460-7908. Business E-Mail: pwoodford@seyfarth.com.

WOODHOUSE, GAY VANDERPOEL, former state attorney general, lawyer; b. Torrington, Wyo., Jan. 8, 1950; d. Wayne Gaylord and Sally (Rouse) Vanderpoel; m. Randy Woodhouse, Nov. 26, 1983; children: Dustin, Houston. BA with honors, U. Wyo., 1972, JD, 1977. Bar: Wyo. 1978, U.S. Dist. Ct. Wyo., U.S. Supreme Ct. Dir. student Legal Svcs., Laramie, Wyo., 1976—77; assoc. Donald Jones Law Offices, Torrington, 1977—78; asst. atty. gen. State of Wyo., Cheyenne, 1978—84, sr. asst. atty. gen., 1984—89, spl. U.S. atty., 1987—89, asst. U.S. atty., 1990—95, chief dept. atty. gen., 1995—98, atty. gen., 1998—2000. Chmn. Wyo. Tel. Consumer Panel, Casper, 1982—86; advisor Cheyenne Halfway House, 1984—93; chmn. Wyo. Silent Witness Initiative Zero Domestic Violence by 2010, 1997, Wyo. Domestic Violence Elimination Coun., 1999—2001; mem. State Bar Commn. First Dist., 2002—05; spl. projects cons. N.Am. Securities Adminstrs. Assn., 1987—89; Chmn. bd. Pathfinder, 1987; S.E. Wyo. Mental Health. Mem.: Wyo. State Bar (pres.-elect 2006—07, pres. 2007—08), Federalist Soc. for Law and Pub.Policy Studies (v.p., Wyo. chpt. 2003—04), Prevent Child Abuse Wyo. (pres. 2004—05), Laramie County Bar Assn., Cheyenne (Wyo.) C. of C., Cheyenne Rotary (bd. dirs.), Toastmasters, Rotary. Republican. Avocations: inline speed skating, stained glass. Office: 123 Capitol Bldg Cheyenne WY 82002-0001 Mailing: PO Box 1888 Cheyenne WY 82003 Office Phone: 307-432-9399. Fax: 307-638-1975. Personal E-mail: gaywoodhouselaw@aol.com. Business E-Mail: Gay@gaywoodhouselaw.com.

WOODHOUSE, JOHN FREDERICK, retired wholesale distribution executive; b. Wilmington, Del., Nov. 30, 1930; s. John Crawford and Anna (Houth) W.; m. Marilyn Ruth Morrow, June 18, 1955; children: John Crawford II, Marjorie Ann Woodhouse Purdy. BA, Wesleyan U., 1953, DHL, 1997; MBA, Harvard U., 1955. Bus. devel. officer Can. Imperial Bank of Commerce, Toronto, Ont., Canada, 1955—59; various fin. positions Ford Motor Co., Dearborn, Mich., 1959—64, Cooper Industries, Inc., Mount Vernon, Ohio, 1964—67, treas. Houston, 1967—69, Crescent-Niagara Corp., Buffalo, 1968—69; exec. v.p., CFO Sysco Corp., Houston, 1969—71, pres., COO, 1972—83, pres., CEO, 1983—85, chmn., CEO, 1985—96, mem. exec. and fin. coms., 1996—98, chmn. bd. dirs., chmn. exec. com., 1998—2000, sr. chmn., 2000—01; ret. Bd. dirs., men. exec. com. Shell Oil Co., 1991-2002; bd. dirs. Harvard Bus. Sch. Assocs., 1995-2001. Chmn. Mich. 16th dist. rep. Club, 1962-64; treas. Cooper Industries Found., 1967-69; trustee Wesleyan U., 1976-92, vice-chmn., 1986-92, chmn. comprehensive capital campaign, 1998-05; ruling elder Presbyn. Ch.; trustee, chmn. audit com., mem. exec. com. Mt. Holyoke Coll., South Hadley, Mass., 1996-2006; bd. dirs. Winrock Internat. Inst. Agrl. Devel., 1993-2000, mem. fin. com., mem. exec. com., chmn. investment com.; bd. advisors The Retail Food Industry Ctr., U. Minn., 1998-2002; trustee The Am. Inst. Food Distbn., Elmwood Pk., N.J., 2001-07, The Food Inst., 2001-07, Presbyn. Mo-Ranch Assembly, Hunt, Tex., 2002—, Meml. Park Conservancy, Houston, 2004—. Diplomate recognition Nat. Restaurant Assn., 2001, Hall of Fame award Nat. Frozen Foods Assn., 2002, Raymond Baldwin award Wesleyan U., 2005. Mem. Nat. Am. Wholesale Grocers Assn. (bd. dirs. 1990-2002, vice chmn. 1992, chmn. 1994-96), Internat. Foodservice Distbrs. Assn. (Herbert Hoover award 2000), Fin. Execs. Inst., Harvard Bus. Sch. Club, Sigma Chi (Significant Sig 1992). Avocations: backpacking, canoeing, tennis. Office: CLW Group 11111 Katy Freeway Ste 870 Houston TX 77079 Home Phone: 281-497-6127; Office Phone: 832-358-1700. E-mail: john.f.woodhouse@sbcglobal.net.

WOODHOUSE, MICHAEL A., restaurant holdings company executive; BS in Natural Scis., MS in Natural Scis., Queen's Coll., Cambridge, Eng. Exec. v.p., CFO S&A Restaurant Corp.; pres., internat. divsn. Pearle Health Svcs., Inc.; exec. v.p., CFO T.G.I. Friday's Inc., 1987; CFO Tia's Inc., Dallas; v.p., fin. Daka Internat. Inc., 1993—94, sr. v.p., CFO, 1994—95; sr. v.p., fin., CFO CBRL Group, 1995—99, exec. v.p., COO, 1999—2000, pres., COO, 2000—01, pres., CEO, 2001—04, chmn., pres., CEO, 2004—. Bd. dirs. CBRL Group, 1999—. Office: CBRL Group 305 Hartmann Dr Lebanon TN 37088

WOODHOUSE, THOMAS EDWIN, lawyer, trust company administrator; b. Cedar Rapids, Iowa, Apr. 30, 1940; s. Keith Wallace and Elinor Julia (Cherny) W.; m. Kiyoko Fujiie, May 29, 1965; children: Miya, Keith, Leighton. AB cum laude, Amherst Coll., 1962; JD, Harvard U., 1965. Bar: N.Y. 1966, U.S. Supreme Ct. 1969, Calif. 1975. Assoc. Chadbourne, Parke, Whiteside & Wolff, NYC, 1965-68; atty./adviser AID, Washington, 1968-69; counsel Pvt. Investment Co. for Asia S.A., Tokyo, 1969-72; ptnr. Woodhouse Lee & Davis, Singapore, 1972-74; assoc. Graham & James, San Francisco, 1974-75; asst. gen. counsel Natomas Co., San Francisco, 1975-81; mem. Lasky, Haas, Cohler & Munter, San Francisco, 1982-90; trust adminstr. Ronald Family Trust A, 1989—2008, co-trustee, 2009—; trust adminstr. Gordon P. Getty Family Trust, 1994—2008; sole practice Berkeley, 1990—2001. Of counsel Wilson, Sonsini, Goodrich & Rosati, Palo Alto, Calif., 1992-95; instr. law faculty U. Singapore, 1972-74; CEO, Vallejo Investments, 1997—. chmn. Police Rev. Com. of Berkeley (Calif.), 1980-84; mem. Berkeley Police Res., 1986—; bd. dirs. Friends Assn. of Svcs. for Elderly, 1979-84; clk. fin. com. Am. Friends Svc. Com. of No. Calif., 1979-83; pres. Zyzzyva Inc., lit. quar., 1985-87. Trustee Freedom from Hunger, 1989-99, Coun. of Friends Bancroft Libr., 1997-2002, chmn. 2002-2003, Coun. of Friends Amherst Coll. Libr., 1990-97, 2005-, Mark Twain Luncheon Club, 2002—, Dominican Sch. of Philosophy and Theology, 1998-2003; treas. Book Club Calif., 2008-. With U.S. Army, 1958. Fellow Am. Bar Found. (life); mem. Calif. Bar Assn., Assn. Internat. de Bibliophilie, Harvard Club, Univ. Club, Book Club Calif., Roxburghe Club, Grolier Club, Faculty Club U. Calif.-Berkeley, Mira Vista Golf and Country Club. Republican. Roman Catholic. Home and Office: 1800 San Antonio Ave Berkeley CA 94707-1618 Personal E-mail: robert606@earthlink.net.

WOODHURST, ROBERT STANFORD, JR., architect; b. Abbeville, SC, July 12, 1921; s. Robert Stanford and Eva (Ferguson) W.; m. Dorothy Ann Carwile, Aug. 4, 1945; 1 son: Robert Stanford III. BS in Architecture, Clemson U., 1942. Registered arch., S.C., Ga., NCARB. Designer Harold Woodward, Arch., Spartanburg, SC, 1946-47; assoc. arch. F. Arthur Hazard, Arch., Augusta, Ga., 1947-54; ptnr. Woodhurst & O'Brien, Architects, Augusta, Ga., 1954-83, Woodhurst Partnership, Augusta, Ga., 1983—. V.p. Southeastern Architects and Engrs., Inc., Augusta, 1964-83; lectr. history architecture N. Augusta Community Coll.; mem. nat. exam. com. Nat. Council Arch tl. Regis. Bds.; pres. Ga. State Bd. Archs. Chmn. Augusta-richmond County Planning Commn., 1966-68; trustee Hist. Augusta, Inc., active Mayor's Adv. Com., 1965-68; mem. Augusta Bldg. Code Bd. Appeals, 1955-58. Served to capt. U.S. Army, 1942-45. Decorated Air medal with 7 oak leaf clusters; Croix de Guerre avec palms (France); prisoner of war, Germany. Fellow AIA (Bronze medal 1942); mem. Ga. Assn. AIA (pres. 1977, Bronze medal 1977, Rothchild Silver Medal 1987), Soc. Archtl. Historians, Nat. Coun. Archtl. Registration Bds., Augusta Country Club, Pinnacle Club. Democrat. Baptist. Achievements include designed and built: 1st Bapt. Ch., Augusta, Univ. Hosp. Med Ctr., Augusta, Peabody Apts. and Irvin Towers, Augusta, W. Lake Country Club, Augusta, Med. Libr., Med. Coll. Ga., Libr. Voorhees Coll., Denmark, S.C., Ambulatory Care Ctr. Univ. Hosp. Augusta, Married Students Apts., Med. Coll. Ga., Covenant Presbyn. Ch., Augusta, Student Ctr. Voorhees Coll., Pres.' Home Voorhees Coll., others. Home: 810 Dogwood Ln Augusta GA 30909-2704 Office: Woodhurst Partnership 607 15th St Augusta GA 30901-2601 Office Phone: 706-724-4343. Personal E-mail: twparch@aol.com.

WOODLAND, N. JOSEPH, retired optical engineer, retired mechanical engineer; b. Atlantic City, Sept. 6, 1921; BSME, Drexel U., 1947, DEng (hon.), 1998; MME, Syracuse U., 1956. Tech. asst. to unit chief, liquid thermal diffusion project for separating uranium isotopes Manhattan Project, Oak Ridge, Tenn., 1943—46; mech. designer Burlington Industries, 1947; lectr. in mech. engring. Drexel U., 1948—49, cons., 1987; cons. in aircraft hydraulics design, 1950; various positions at staff and sr. levels IBM Corp., 1951—87; cons., 1987—88. Recipient Nat. Medal Tech. for invention of bar code, 1992; named one of Drexel U.'s 100 Most Outstanding Alumni, 1992. Mem.: Anthony J. Drexel Soc. Achievements include patents in field.

WOODLEY, DAVID TIMOTHY, dermatology educator; b. Aug. 11, 1948; s. Raoul Ramos-Mimosa and Marian (Schlueter) W.; m. Christina Paschall Prentice, May 4, 1974; children; David Thatcher, Thomas Colgate, Peter Paschall. AB, Washington U., St. Louis, 1968; MD, U. Mo., 1973. Diplomate Am. Bd. Internal Medicine, Am. Bd. Dermatology, Nat. Bd. Internal Medicine. Intern Beth Israel Med. Ctr., Mt. Sinai Sch. Medicine, N.Y. Hosp., Cornell U. Sch. Medicine, NYC, 1973-74; resident in internal medicine U. Nebr., Omaha, 1974-76; resident in dermatology U. N.C., Chapel Hill, 1976-78, asst. prof. dermatology, 1983-85, assoc. prof. dermatology, 1985-88; prof. medicine, co-chief divsn. dermatology Cornell U. Med. Ctr., NYC, 1988-89; prof., vice chair dept. dermatology Stanford (Calif.) U., 1989-93; prof., chair dept. dermatology Northwestern U., Chgo., 1993-99. Research fellow U. Paris, 1978-80; expert NIH, Bethesda, Md., 1983-89; prof., assoc. chmn. dermatology Stanford U Sch. Medicine, 1989-93; chmn. dermatology Sch. Medicine Northwestern U., 1993-99; prof., chmn. dermatology U. So. Calif., 1999—; mem. study sect. NIH. Contbr. chpts. to books and articles in field to profl. jours. Mem. Potomac Albicore Fleet, Washington, 1982-83, Chapel Hill, 1983—, Jungian Soc. Triangle Area, Chapel Hill, 1983—. Fellow Am. Acad. Dermatology; mem. ACS (assoc.), Dermatology Found., Am. Soc. for Clin. Rsch., Soc. Investigative Dermatology, Assn. Physician Poets, Am. Soc. for Clin. Investigation. Office: U So Calif Keck Sch Medicine Dept Dermatology UC Norris Cancer Ctr Topping Tower 3905 1441 Eastlake Ave Los Angeles CA 90033 Office Phone: 323-865-0983.

WOODLEY, JOHN PAUL, JR., consulting firm executive, former civilian military employee; b. Shreveport, La., Sept. 28, 1953; s. John Paul and Hazel Eugenia (Iles) W.; m. Priscilla Anne Ingersoll, June 6, 1981; children: Elizabeth Ingersoll, Cornelia Ingersoll. BA, Washington & Lee U., 1974, JD, 1977. Bar: Va. 1977, U.S. Ct. Appeals (4th cir.) 1978, U.S. Dist. Ct. (ea. dist.) Va. 1979, U.S. Ct. Mil. Appeals 1979, U.S. Supreme Ct. 1982, U.S. Ct. Appeals (5th cir.) 1984, U.S. Ct. Appeals (11th and fed. cirs.) 1985. Law clk. to judge US Dist. Ct., Richmond, Va., 1977-79; pvt. practice Richmond, 1985-86; ptnr. Woodley Simon & Woodley, Richmond, 1986—90; asst. commonwealth atty. Henrico county State of Va., 1990—94, dep. atty. gen. (govt. ops) Richmond, 1994—98, sec. nat. resources, 1998—2001; asst. dep. under sec. for environment US Dept. Def., Washington, 2001—03; prin. dep. asst. sec. (civil works) Dept. Army, US Dept. Def., 2004—05, asst. sec. (civil works), 2003—04, 2005—09; consulting dir. Advantus Strategies, LLC, 2009—. Treas. Richmond Rep. Com., 1988. Capt. JAGC, U.S. Army, 1979-85, maj. Res., 1986. Decorated Legion of Merit, Meritorious Svc. medal with 2 oak leaf clusters, Army Commendation medal with 1 oak leaf cluster, Army Achievement medal; recipient Sec. Def. medal for Outstanding Pub. Svc. Mem. ABA, Rep. Nat. Lawyers Assn. (bd. govs. 1988), Va. State Bar, Richmond Bar Assn., Assn. Trial Lawyers Am., Phi Beta Kappa, Assn. Va. Hearing Officers, Va. Trial Lawyers Assn., Va. Rep. Lawyers Assn. (chmn. 1987—), Richmond First Club. Roman Catholic. Avocation: skiing. Office: Advantus Strategies LLC 1011 E Main St Ste 400 Richmond VA 23219 Office Phone: 804-228-4500. Office Fax: 804-228-4501.*

WOODLEY, SHAILENE DIANN, actress; b. Simi Valley, Calif., Nov. 15, 1991; d. Loni and Lori Woodley. Actress (TV films) Replacing Dad, 1999, A Place Called Home, 2004, Felicity: An American Girl Adventure, 2005, Once Upon a Mattress, 2005, Final Approach, 2007, (TV series) Crossing Jordan, 2001—04, The O.C., 2003—04, The Secret Life of the American Teenager, 2008, actress (guest appearance) The District, 2001—02, Without a Trace, 2003, Everybody Loves Raymond, 2004, Jack & Bobby, 2004—05, My Name Is Earl, 2006, Close to Home, 2007, CSI: NY, 2007, Cold Case, 2007. Office: c/o Elements Entertainment 1635 North Cahuenga Blvd, 5th Fl Los Angeles CA 90028*

WOODLOCK, DOUGLAS PRESTON, judge; b. Hartford, Conn., Feb. 27, 1947; s. Preston and Kathryn (Ropp) W.; m. Patricia Mathilde Powers, Aug. 30, 1969; children: Pamela, Benjamin. BA, Yale U., 1969; JD, Georgetown U., 1975. Bar: Mass. 1975. Reporter Chgo. Sun-Times, 1969-73; staff mem. SEC, Washington, 1973-75; law clk. to Judge F.J. Murray U.S. Dist. Ct. Mass., Boston, 1975-76; assoc. Goodwin, Procter & Hoar, Boston, 1976-79, 83-84, ptnr., 1984-86; asst. U.S. atty. Boston, 1979-83; judge U.S. Dist. Ct., Boston, 1986—. Instr. Harvard U. Law Sch., 1981, 82; mem. U.S. Jud. Conf. Com. on Security Space and Facilities, 1987-95; chmn. New Boston Fed. Courthouse Bldg. Com., 1987-98. Articles editor Georgetown Law Jour., 1973-75; contbr. articles to profl. jours. Chmn. Commonwealth of Mass. Com. for Pub. Counsel Svcs., 1984-86, Town of Hamilton Bd. Appeals, 1978-79. Recipient Dir.'s award U.S. Dept. Justice, 1983, Thomas Jefferson award for Pub. Architecture, AIA, 1996. Mem. ABA, Mass. Bar Assn., Boston Bar Assn. (Citation award of judicial excellence 2005), Am. Law Inst., Am. Judicature Soc., Am. Bar Found., Fed. Judges Assn. (bd. dirs. 1996-2001), Mass. Hist. Soc. Office: US Courthouse 1 Courthouse Way Ste 4110 Boston MA 02210-3006

WOODMAN, GREY MUSGRAVE, psychiatrist; b. Birmingham, England, Jan. 26, 1922; came to U.S., 1959, naturalized 1963; s. Edward Musgrave and Ida (Cullen) W.; m. Irene Woodman; children: Sheila, Shonagh. BA, Oxford U., Eng., 1943, MA, BM, BChir, 1945; grad., Clinton Citizens Police Acad., 2001. Ship's surgeon Brit. Merchant Marines, 1946-48; intern Whipps Cross Hosp., London, 1949-50, med. registrar, 1951-53, Gen. Hosp., Newcastle-on-Tyne, England, 1953-54; gen. practice London, 1954-56; physician USAF Hosp., 1956-59; resident in psychiatry U. Okla. Med. Ctr., 1959-62; staff psychiatrist Western Mo. Mental Health Ctr., Kansas City, 1962-76; med. dir. Mental Health Ctr. Clinton County, Clinton, Iowa, 1976-87; pvt. practice Clinton, 1976—; founder, dir. Lincolnshire Clinic, The London Psychiat. Clinic, 1997—. Mem. staff Jane Lamb Health Ctr., Mercy Hosp., Comphealth; psychiat. cons. Mufon. Mem. Prevent Child Abuse Coun. Recipient Internat. Order of Merit, 1999, Claire Behr Meml. award, Pathway Living Ctr., 2006. Fellow Royal Soc. Medicine (London, life); mem. AMA (life), Am. Psychiat. Assn. (life), Am. Acad. Med. Hypoanalysts (clin.), Brit. Med. Assn., World Fedn. Mental Health, Iowa Med. Soc. (past chmn. hospice com.), Internat. Assn. Social Psychiatry, Clinton Co. Prevent Child Abuse Coun., Am. Red Cross (mental health specialist 1996—), Oxford Club (life), Moose. Republican. Episcopalian. Home: East Park Care Centre Jeffreyston Kilgetty Wales SA68 0RE Personal E-mail: greyufowales@googlemail.com.

WOODMAN, HAROLD DAVID, historian, educator; b. Chgo., Apr. 21, 1928; s. Joseph Benjamin and Helen Ruth (Sollo) W.; m. Leonora Becker; children— Allan James, David Edward. BA, Roosevelt U., 1957; MA, U. Chgo., 1959, PhD, 1964. Lectr. Roosevelt U., 1962-63; asst. prof. history U. Mo., Columbia, 1963-66, assoc. prof., 1966-69, prof., 1969-71, Purdue U., West Lafayette, Ind., 1971-97, Louis Martin Sears disting. prof., 1990-97, prof. emeritus, 1997—; chmn. Com. on Am. Studies, 1981-94. Author: Conflict and Consensus in American History, 1966, 9th rev. edit., 1996, Slavery and the Southern Economy, 1966, King Cotton and His Retainers, 1968, Legacy of the American Civil War, 1973, New South-New Law, 1995; mem. editl. bd. Jour. So. History, 1972-75, Wis. Hist. Soc., 1972-76, Bus. History Rev., 1971-77, Agrl. History, 1976-82, Am. Hist. Rev., 1981-84, Jour. Am. History, 1985-88. Served with U.S. Army, 1950-52. Recipient Otto Wirth award Roosevelt U., 1990; Woodrow Wilson Internat. Center for Scholars fellow, 1977; Faculty grant Social Sci. Rsch. Coun., 1969-70; Nat. Humanities Ctr. fellow, 1983-84 Mem. Am. Hist. Assn., Orgn. Am. Historians, Econ. History Assn., Agrl. History Soc. (pres. 1983-84, Everett E. Edwards award 1963), Soc. Am. Historians, Bus. History Conf. (pres. 1981-82), Ind. Assn. Historians (pres. 1983-84), So. Hist. Assn. (exec. coun. 1982-85, Ramsdell award 1965, pres. 1995-96). Office: Purdue U Dept History West Lafayette IN 47907 Home: 2737 Westminster Ct West Lafayette IN 47906 Business E-Mail: hwoodman@purdue.edu.

WOODMAN, RONALD F., aerospace scientist; b. Piura, Peru, 1934; m. Gladys Woodman; children: Karma, Randy, Pauline, Suzette, Christian, Elgin. BS in Engring., Nat. Univ. Engring., Peru; PhD, Harvard, 1967. Exec. pres. Geophysical Inst. Peru, Mayorazgo. Recipient Appleton Prize, Royal Soc., 1999. Mem.: NAS (fgn. assoc.), Internat. Assn. Geomagnetism and Aeronomy. Achievements include creating the entire field of mesosphere, stratosphere, and troposphere wind profile measurements with VHF radars. Office: Geophysical Inst Peru Apartado 13-0207 Lima 13 Peru Business E-Mail: ronw@geo.igp.gob.pe.

WOODMAN, STEWART, chef; b. Pa., 1974; m. Heidi Woodman; 1 child. Apprentice The Fairmont Banff Springs hotel, Alberta, Canada; sous chef Essex House, NYC, Le Bernardin, NYC; chef Mercer Kitchen, NYC, Jean Georges, NYC, Zoe, NYC, Restaurant Levain, Mpls.; co-owner, exec. chef Five Restaurant & Street Lounge, Mpls., 2005—06, Heidi's, Mpls., 2007—. Recipient Best New Chef award, Food and Wine Mag., 2006. Office: Heidis 819 W 50th St Minneapolis MN 55419 Office Phone: 612-354-3512.*

WOODRESS, JAMES LESLIE, JR., language educator; b. Webster Groves, Mo., July 7, 1916; s. James Leslie and Jessie (Smith) W.; m. Roberta Wilson, Sept. 28, 1940. AB, Amherst Coll., 1938; A.M., NYU, 1943; PhD, Duke U., 1950; LittD, U. Nebr., 1995. News editor Sta. KWK, St. Louis, 1939-40; rewriteman, editor UPI, NYC, 1940-43; instr. English, Grinnell (Iowa) Coll., 1949-50; asst. prof. English, Butler U., Indpls., 1950-53, asso. prof., 1953-58; asso. prof. English, San Fernando Valley (Calif.) State Coll., 1958-61, prof., 1961-66, chmn. dept., 1959-63, dean letters and scis., 1963-65; prof. English, U. Calif.-Davis, 1966-87, chmn. dept., 1970-74; vis. prof. Sorbonne, Paris, 1974-75, 83. Author: Howells and Italy, 1952, Booth Tarkington: Gentleman from Indiana, 1955, A Yankee's Odyssey: The Life of Joel Barlow, 1958, Dissertations in American Literature, 1957, 3rd edit., 1968, Willa Cather: Her Life and Art, 1970, 3rd edit., 1981, American Fiction 1900-50, 1974, Willa Cather: A Literary Life, 1987; editor: Eight American Authors, 1971, American Literary Scholarship: An Annual, 1965-69, 75-77, 79, 81, 87, Critical Essays on Walt Whitman, 1983, Cather's The Troll Garden, 1983, (with Richard Morris) Voices from America's Past, anthology, 1961-62, 75. Served to lt. AUS, 1943-46. Ford Fund for Advancement Edn. fellow, 1952-53; Guggenheim fellow, 1957-58; Fulbright lectr. France, 1962-63; Fulbright lectr. Italy, 1965-66; recipient Hubbell medal, 1985 Mem. MLA (sec. Am. Lit. group 1962-63), AAUP, Phi Beta Kappa. Address: 892 Harrison Ave Claremont CA 91711-4128

WOODRING, CARL, English language educator; b. Terrell, Tex., Aug. 29, 1919; s. Felix Jessie and Naomi (Cole) W.; m. Mary Frances Ellis, Dec. 24, 1942 (dec. March 2, 2003). BA, Rice U., 1940, MA, 1942; AM, Harvard U., 1947, PhD, 1949. Instr. English U. Wis., 1948-51, asst. prof., 1951-54, assoc. prof., 1954-58, prof., 1958-61, Columbia U., NYC, 1961—, chmn. dept. English, 1968-71, George Edward Woodberry prof. lit., 1976-88, George Edward Woodberry prof. lit. emeritus, 1988—, chmn., co-chmn. Columbia Soc. Fellows in the Humanities, 1975-78. English dissertation selection com. Woodrow Wilson Nat. Fellowship Found., 1962-66; Phi Beta Kappa vis. scholar, 1974-75 Author: Victorian Samplers—William and Mary Howitt, 1952, Politics in the Poetry of Coleridge, 1961, Wordsworth, 1965, Virginia Woolf, 1966, Politics in English Romantic Poetry, 1970 (Van Am award, Christian Gauss prize 1971), Nature into Art: Cultural Transformations in Nineteenth-Century Britain, 1989, Literature: An Embattled Profession, 1999 (Violet Crown award); editor: Prose of the Romantic Period, 1961, Table Talk of Samuel Taylor Coleridge, 1990, The Columbia History of British Poetry, 1993; co-editor: The Columbia Anthology of British Poetry, 1995; mem. editl. bd. Studies in English Literature, 1961—; editl. adviser: Wordsworth Circle, 1970—, Essays in Literature, 1973—. With USNR, 1942-45. Fellow Fund Advancement Edn., 1955, Guggenheim Found., 1955, Am. Coun. Learned Socs., 1965, Nat. Humanities Ctr., 1987; Dexter scholar Harvard Coll., 1948; recipient Bowdoin prize, 1947, Disting. Alumnu award Rice U., 1986. Mem. MLA (mem. exec. coun. 1965-68), Internat. Assn. Univ. Profs. of English, Keats-Shelley Assn. Am. (bd. dirs., Disting. Scholar award 1982), Am. Acad. Arts and Scis., Acad. Lit. Studies, Assn. Depts. English (pres. 1971), Grolier Club. Personal E-mail: carlwoodring@sbcglobal.net.

WOODRING, DEWAYNE STANLEY, religious organization administrator; b. Gary, Ind., Nov. 10, 1931; s. J. Stanley and Vera Luella (Brown) Woodring; m. Donna Jean Wishart, June 15, 1957; children: Judith Lynn Bigelow, Beth Ellen Carey. BS in Speech with distinction, Northwestern U., Evanston, Ill., 1954; postgrad., Northwestern U., 1954—57; MDiv, Garrett Theol. Sem., 1957; LHD, Mt. Union Coll., 1967; DD, Salem Coll., 1970. Ordained to ministry Meth. Ch., 1955. Assoc. dir. youth Gary YMCA, 1950—55; min. edn. Griffith Meth. Ch., Ind., 1955—57; min. adminstrn. and program 1st Meth. Ch., Eugene, Oreg., 1957—59; dir. pub. rels. Dakotas area Meth. Ch., 1959—60, dir. pub. rels. Ohio area, 1960—64; adminstrv. exec. to bishop Ohio East area United Meth. Ch., Canton, 1964—77, asst. gen. sec. Gen. Coun. Fin. and Adminstr. Evanston, Ill., 1977—79, assoc. gen. sec., 1979—84; exec. dir., CEO Religious Conf. Mgmt. Assn., Indpls., 1982—. Staff dept. radio svcs. 2d Assembly World Coun. Chs., Evanston, 1954; chmn. comm. commn. Ohio Coun. Chs., 1961—65; v.p. Ohio East Area United Meth. Found., 1967—76; exec. com. Nat. Assn. United Meth. Found., 1968—72, World Meth. Coun., 1986—2001; vice-chmn. commn. entertainment and program North Ctrl. Jurisdictional Conf., 1968—72, chmn., 1972—76; mem. divsn. interpretation United Meth. Ch., 1969—72, mem. commn. gen. conf., 1972—93, mgr., exec. dir., 1976—93; chmn. bd. mgrs. United Meth. Bldg., Evanston, 1977—84; mem. adv. bd. Nassau/Paradise Island, 1997—99, Red Lion Hotels and Inns, PR Conv. Ctr.; lectr., cons. in field; del. White House Travel and Tourism Conf., 1995. Creator (radio series) The Word and Music, prodr., dir. (TV series) Parables in Miniature, 1957—59. Adviser East Ohio Conf. Comm. Commn., 1968—76; bd. dirs. First Internat. Summit Edn., 1989; trustee, 1st v.p. Copeland Oaks Retirement Ctr., Sebring, Ohio, 1969—76; pres. Guild Assocs., 1971—. Recipient Cert. Meeting Profl. award, 1985, Cert. Expt. Mgr. award, 1988, Sagamore of Wabash award, State Ind., 2007; named one of 25 Leaders Who Shaped The Industry, Convention South Mag., 2008; named to, Ky. Cols., 1989, Hall of Leaders, Conv. Liaison Coun., 1994. Mem.: ISAE (Meeting Planner of the Yr. award 1990), Marriott Customer Leadership Forum (mem. customer adv. bd.), Found. Internat. Meetings (bd. dirs.), Cert. Meeting Profls. (bd. dirs. 1983—92), Ind. Conv. Visitors Assn. (bd. dirs. 1996—2000, bd. advisors), Def. Orientation Conf. Assn. (chaplain), Conv. Industry Coun. (bd. dirs., past chmn.), Meeting Profl. Internat., Am. Soc. Assn. Execs. Home: 7224 Chablis Ct Indianapolis IN 46278-1540 Office: 7702 Woodland Dr Ste 120 Indianapolis IN 46278 Office Phone: 317-632-1888.

WOODRING, JOHN HOWELL, radiologist; b. Louisville, Sept. 10, 1951; s. Franklyn Howell and Dorothy Moore Woodring; m. Catherine Anne Martin, Aug. 27, 1977; children: Paul Martin, Mark Reynolds. BS, U. of Louisville, 1972; MD, U. of Ky., 1976. Lic. diagnostic radiology Am. Bd. of Radiology. Intern Louisville Gen. Hosp., 1976—77; resident physician U. of Ky. Med. Ctr., Lexington, 1977—80; asst. prof. of diagnostic radiology U. of Ky., Lexington, 1980—84, assoc. prof. of diagnostic radiology, 1984—92, prof. of diagnostic radiology, 1992—98; staff radiologist Lexington VA Med. Ctr., Lexington, 1999—. Chief of radiology svc. Lexington VA Med. Ctr., 2000—02. Contbr. articles to sci. jours. (Cert. of Merit Am. Roentgen Ray Soc., 1994). Asst. scoutmaster Boy Scouts of Am., Louisville, 1968—77; senior-high counselor 1st United Meth. Ch., Lexington, 1984—87, Sunday sch. tchr., 1992—2000. Fellow: Am. Coll. of Chest Physicians (hon.), Am. Coll. of Radiology (hon.); mem.: Soc. of Thoracic Radiology, Radiol. Soc. of N.Am. (life), So. Med. Assn. Liberal. Presbyterian. Achievements include first to demonstrate role of computed tomography in evaluation of coronary artery disease, and evaluation of cervical spine fractures; propose the use of endobronchial stents in the treatment of right pneumonectomy syndrome; role of computed tomography in the evaluation of congenital lobar emphysema; identify risk factors for the development of salicylate-induced pulmonary edema; demonstrate that there is no statistically significant difference in the distribution of pleural effusion between the right and left hemithorax in congestive heart failure; development of pulmonary artery-bronchus ratio as a means of diagnosing congestive heart failure. Avocations: model trains, antique cars, music, literature. Home: 336 Arcadia Park Lexington KY 40503 Office: Radiology Svc Lexington VA Med Ctr CDD-114 1101 Veterans Dr Lexington KY 40502

WOODROOFE, MICHAEL BARRETT, mathematics and statistics professor; b. Corvallis, Oreg., Mar. 17, 1940; s. Robin Russell and Helen Barrett Woodroofe; m. Fran Smock; children: Russell, Carolyn Hitko, Blake. BS in Math., Stanford U., Calif., 1962; PhD in Math., U. Oreg., Eugene, 1965. Rsch. assoc. Stanford U., 1965—66; asst. prof. stats. Carnegie Mellon U., Pitts., 1966—68; prof. math. and stats. U. Mich., Ann Arbor, 1968—2008, chair stats., 1977—83; vis. assoc. prof. math. Columbia U., NYC, 1970—71; vis. prof. math. MIT, Cambridge, 1976—77; prof. II stats. Rutgers U., New Brunswick, NJ, 1983—84. Assoc. editor Annals Probability, 1980—2008, Jour. Statis. Planning and Inference, 1980—2008, Sequential Analysis, 1980—2008. Contbr. over 100 rsch. articles to profl. jour. Collegiate chair U. Mich., 1994. Recipient Mentoring award, U. Mich., 2007, Lockwood award, 1992; grants, NSF, 1977—2008. Fellow: Inst. Math. Stats. (mem. coun., editor annals stats. 1992—94); mem.: Internat. Statis. Inst. Office: Univ Mich 1085 S Univ Ann Arbor MI 48109-1107

WOODRUFF, BOB (ROBERT WARREN WOODRUFF), newscaster; b. Bloomfield Hills, Mich., Aug. 18, 1961; m. Lee Woodruff, Sept. 11, 1988; children: Mack, Cathryn, Nora, Claire. BA, Colgate U., 1983; JD, U. Mich., 1987. Atty.; law tchr. Beijing; translator during Tiananmen Sq. uprising CBS News, Beijing, 1989; corr., Justice Dept. ABC News, Washington, fgn. corr. Belgrade, Kosovo, Europe, Middle East, London bur. corr., corr. NYC, 2002; interim anchor ABC World News Tonight, NYC, 2005, co-anchor, 2006. Co-author (with Lee Woodruff): In an Instant: A Family's Journey of Love and Healing, 2007. Recipient Alfred I. Dupont award for 9/11 reporting, George Foster Peabody award for 9/11 reporting, David Bloom award for excellence in enterprise reporting, Radio & TV Corr. Assn., 2006, Christopher Reeve Spirit of Courage award, Christopher and Dana Reeve Found., 2007, Peabody award, 2008, Daniel Pearl award, 2008. Fluent in Mandarin Chinese. Office: ABC News Press Rels Fl 2 47 W 66th St New York NY 10023-6201

WOODRUFF, C(HARLES) ROY, retired professional association executive, consultant; b. Anniston, Ala., Sept. 27, 1938; m. Kay Carolyn Jernigan, June 26, 1962; children: Charles R. Jr., Earl David. BA, U. Ala., 1960; BD, So. Bapt. Theol. Sem., 1963, PhD in Psychology of Religion and Pastoral Care, 1966. Diplomate Am. Assn. Pastoral Counselors; lic. profl. counselor, Va. Asst. pastor Ft. Mitchell Bapt. Ch., South Ft. Mitchell, Ky., 1960-63; Protestant chaplain Silvercrest Hosp., New Albany, Ind., 1963-66; dir. dept. pastoral care and edn. Bryce State Hosp., Tuscaloosa, Ala., 1966-71; assoc. prof., chaplain supr. dept. patient counseling Med. Coll. Va., Richmond, 1971-76; assoc. prof., chmn. dept. psychology of religion and pastoral care Midwestern Bapt. Theol. Sem., Kansas City, Mo., 1976-78; exec. dir. Peninsula Pastoral Counseling Ctr., Newport News, Va., 1978-88, Am. Assn. Pastoral Counselors, Washington, 1988—2003; interim pastor Vienna (Va.) Bapt. Ch., 2004—06. Lecturing fellow Interpreter's House, Lake Junaluska, N.C., 1968-78; pastoral counselor, clin. supr. Psychol. Clinic, U. Ala., Tuscaloosa, 1969-71; adj. staff mem. The Counseling Inst., Kansas City, 1976-78, adj. prof., John Leland Ctr. for Theol. Studies, Fairfax, Va., vis. prof., Korea Profl. Inst. of Psychotherapy and Spiritualty, Seoul, Korea. Author: Alcoholism and Christian Experience, 1968, Spiritual Care for Addicted Persons and Families, 2006; (with others) Alcohol, In and Out of the Church, 1968, Work Adjustment: The Goal of Rehabilitation, 1973, Pastoral Theology and Ministry, Key Resources, 1983, The Dictionary of Pastoral Care and Counseling, 1990; also articles. Apptd. by Gov. of Va. to Bd. Profl. Counselors, Commonwealth of Va., 1987-95 (chmn. 1993-95); mem. Nat. Mental Health Leadership Forum, 1990-93; pres. Coalition on Ministry in Specialized Settings, 1996-2000. Recipient Disting. Svc. award Va. Inst. Pastor Care, 2002, Disting. Contbns. award Am. Assn. Pastoral Counselors, 2003, award Wayne E. Oates Inst., 2004; United Meth. Ch. Gen. Bd. Christian Social Concerns grantee, 1965; So. Bapt. Theol. Sem. teaching fellow, 1965-66. Fellow Coll. Chaplains of Am. Protestant Hosp. Assn.; mem. Assn. for Clin. Pastoral Edn. (cert. supr.), Assn. Couples for Marriage Enrichment (cert.). Home: 10827 Burr Oak Way Burke VA 22015-2416

WOODRUFF, FAY, paleoceanographer, geological researcher; b. Boston, Jan. 23, 1944; d. Lorande Mitchell and Anne (Fay) W.; m. Alexander Whitehill Clowes, May 20, 1972 (div. Oct. 1974); m. Robert G. Douglas, Jan. 27, 1980; children: Ellen, Katerina. RN, Mass. Gen. Hosp. Sch. Nursing, Boston, 1966; BA, Boston U., 1971; MS, U. So. Calif., 1979. Rsch. assoc. U. So. Calif., LA, 1978-81, rsch. faculty, 1981-96. Keynote spkr. 4th Internat. Symposium on Benthic Foraminifera, Sendai, Japan, 1990. Contbg. author: Geological Society of America Memoir, 1985; contbr. articles to profl. jours. Life mem. The Nature Conservancy, Washington, 1992; bd. dirs. Friends of Friendship Park, Inc., 1995-2001; co-founder, v.p. Resources Families Adopted Ea. European Children, Inc., LA, 1996-2000. NSF grantee, 1986-94. Mem. Am. Geophys. Union, Geol. Soc. Am., Internat. Union Geol. Scis. (internat. commn. on stratigraphy, subcommn. on Neogene stratigraphy 1991-99), Soc. Woman Geographers (sec. So. Calif. chpt. 1990-96), Soc. Econ. Paleontologists and Mineralogists (sec., editor N.Am. Micropaleontology sect. 1988-90), Sigma Xi. Office: Univ So Calif Earth Scis Los Angeles CA 90089-0001

WOODRUFF, JUDY CARLINE, broadcast journalist; b. Tulsa, Nov. 20, 1946; d. William Henry and Anna Lee (Payne) W.; m. Albert R. Hunt, Jr., Apr. 5, 1980; children: Jeffrey Woodruff, Benjamin Woodruff, Lauren Ann Lee. Student, Meredith Coll., 1964-66; BA, Duke U., 1968. News announcer, reporter Sta. WAGA-TV, Atlanta, 1970-75; news corr. NBC News, Atlanta, 1975-76, White House corr. Washington, 1977-83; anchor Frontline, PBS documentary series, 1984—90; corr. MacNeil-Lehrer News Hour, PBS, Washington, 1983-93; anchor, sr. corr. CNN, Washington, 1993—2005; moderator Vice Presidential Debate, 1988, America Votes, 2003, 2004; sr. corr., polit. editor The News Hour With Jim Lehrer, 2007—. Bd. advisors Henry Grady Sch. Journalism, U. Ga., 1979-82, Benton Fellowship in Broadcast Journalism, U. Chgo., 1984-90, Knight Fellowship in Journalism, Stanford U., 1985-99; bd. visitors Wake Forest U., 1982-89; trustee Duke U., 1985-97, emerita; founding bd. dirs. Internat. Women's Media Found.; vis. fellow, Joan Shorenstein Ctr.on the Press, Politics and Pub. Policy, Harvard U., 2005—; vis. prof. media and politics Duke U., 2006. Author: This is Judy Woodruff at the White House, 1982; corr: PBS Special Generation Next, 2006. Active Commn. on Women's Health, The Commonwealth Fund.; bd. trustee Freedom Forum, Urban Inst.; trustee Nat. Mus. Am. History, 2006—. Recipient award Leadership Atlanta, Class of 1974, Atlanta chpt. Women in Comms., 1975, Edward Weintal award for excellence in fgn. policy reporting, 1987, Joan Shorenstein Barone award for series on def. issues, 1987, Helen Bernstein award for excellence in journalism N.Y. Pub. Libr., 1989, Pres.'s 21st Century award Nat. Women's Hall of Fame, 1994, CableAce award for best newscaster, 1995, CableAce Best Anchor Team award, 1996, Allen H. Neuharth award for excellence in journalism, 1995, News and Documentary Emmy award, 1997, Internat. Matrix award, Assn. for Women in Comm., 2003, Leonard Zeidenberg First Amendment award, Radio-Television News Directors Assn. and Found., 2003; named to Ga. Assn. of Broadcasters Hall of Fame, 2003; grantee Pew Charitable Trusts, 2006—. Mem. NATAS (Atlanta chpt. Emmy award 1975), White House Corrs. Assn.

WOODRUFF, MARY BRENNAN, elementary school educator; d. John L. and Josephine Brennan; m. Paul R. Woodruff; children: Christopher, Jeffery. BS, SUNY, Brockport; MS, SUNY, Buffalo, 1987. Cert. elem. tchr. N.Y., 1968. Third grade tchr. Middleport (N.Y.) Elem., fifth grade tchr., 1979—2003, math specialist K-6, 2003—05, math specialist 5-8, 2005—. Sch. improvement presenter, mem., dist. curriculum guide, facilitator Social Studies curriculum, Royalton-Hartland Cen. Sch., Middleport, NY, 1989, co-author mentor program for Royalton-Hartland District, Project "Deep" Elem. Econ. faciliator Contributing author Royalton-Hartland Curriculum Guide 1989; designer of spelling program 5th grade. Campaign mgr. Rep. Legislator, Orleans County, 1979-87. Recipient Roualton-Hartland Tchr. of Yr. award, Royalton, 1999. Mem.: ASCD, Royalton-Hartford Tchrs. Assn. (pres. 1998—, v.p., chmn. grievance com.), N.Y State United Tchrs. (Leadership award 1997, 2004), Delta Kappa Gamma, Delta Xi. Avocations: political action, writing, reading. Office Phone: 716-735-3722.

WOODRUFF, THEODORE SHERMAN, economics professor; b. NYC, Apr. 23, 1948; s. Paul Bernard and Gertrude Theodora Woodruff. PhD, Columbia U., NYC, 1976. Asst. prof. economics Mt. Holyoke Coll., South Hadley, Mass., 1976—78, St. Bonaventure U., Allegany, NY, 1978—94; prof. economics St. Ambrose U., Davenport, Iowa, 1995—. Mem.: Phi Beta Kappa. Home: 2207 Scott St Davenport IA 52803 Office: St Ambrose Univ 518 W Locust St Davenport IA 52803 Office Fax: 563-333-6268. Business E-Mail: woodrufftheodores@sau.edu.

WOODRUFF, THOMAS ELLIS, electronics consulting executive; b. Stockton, Calif., Feb. 8, 1921; s. Ennis Casselberry and Gracella (Scotford) W.; m. Doris Elaine Walters, Jan. 14, 1947 (div. Aug. 1962); children: Mary Ann Woodruff Mahaffy, Patricia Lee; m. Ruth Elizabeth Craik, Feb. 25, 1964; 1 child, Robert Peter; stepchildren: Gordon Lee Vickers, Barbara Ann Vickers, Mary Jean Vickers. AA, Stockton Jr. Coll., 1941; BSEE, U. Calif., Berkeley, 1943. Registered profl. engr., Calif. Engr. GE, Syracuse, N.Y., 1944-47; staff engr. Hughes Aircraft Co., Culver City, Calif., 1947-56; mgr. electronics design Sanders Assocs., Nashua, N.H., 1956-58, chief engr. preliminary design, 1958-60, mgr. spl. programs div., 1960-62, corp. dir. systems, 1962-65, v.p., gen. mgr. corp. systems group, 1965-73, v.p. antisubmarine weapons and communications, 1966-72, dir., 1968-70, sr. dir., 1970-76, v.p. gen. mgr. ocean systems group, 1972-76, v.p. sci. and tech., 1976-88, corp. cons., 1989—; v.p. Sanders Nuclear Corp., Nashua, 1966-71. Mem. adv. com. Def. Intelligence Agy., Washington, 1978-83; joint adv. com. MIT Lincoln Lab., Bedford, Mass., 1988-89; cons. Superconductor Tech., Inc., Santa Barbara, Calif., 1988—, Oryx, Inc., Paramus, N.J., 1989—, Sanders/Lockheed, 1988-91, ret. 1992. Patentee, co-patentee 14 inventions in electronics for computers, control systems, video displays, submarine detection devices, others. Mem. IEEE (sr.). Republican. Avocations: skiing, photography, motorcycling, swimming. Home: 532 Lower Georges Valley Rd Spring Mills PA 16875-8200 Home Phone: 814-422-0234. E-mail: twuff@ieee.org.

WOODRUFF, VIRGINIA, broadcast journalist, writer; b. Morrisville, Pa. d. Edwin Nichols and Louise (Meredith) W.; m. Raymond F. Beagle Jr. (div.); m. Albert Plaut II (div.); 1 child, Elise Meredith. Student, Rutgers U. News corr. Sta. WNEW-TV Metromedia, NYC, 1967; nat., internat. critic-at-large Mut. Broadcasting System, 1968-75; lectr. Leigh Bur., 1969-71; byline columnist NY Daily Mirror, NYC, 1970-71; first Arts critic Teleprompter and Group W Cable TV, 1977-84; host/producer The First Nighter NY Times primetime cable highlight program, 1977-84; pres., chief exec. officer Starpower, Inc., 1984-91; affiliate news corr. ABC Radio Network, NYC, 1984-86; pres. Promarket People Inc., 1991-93; S.W. contbg. corr. Am. in the Morning, First Light, Mut. Broadcasting System, 1992; S.W. freelance corr. Voice of Am., USIA, 1992—. Perennial critic Off-Off Broadway Short Play Festival, NYC, 1984—; was 1st Woman on 10 O'Clock News, WNEW-TV, 1967. Contbg. feature writer Vis a Vis mag., 1988-91. Celebrity panel Arthritis Telethon, NYC, 1976. Selected episodes of First Nighter program in archives NY Pub. Libr., Billy Rose Theatre Collection, Rodgers and Hammerstein Collection, Performing Arts Rsch.Ctr. Mem. Drama Desk. Clubs: National Arts, Dutch Treat. Presbyterian. Personal E-mail: vwoodruff50@yahoo.com.

WOODRUM, PATRICIA ANN, librarian; b. Hutchinson, Kans., Oct. 11, 1941; d. Donald Jewell and Ruby Pauline (Shuman) Hoffman; m. Clayton Eugene Woodrum, Mar. 31, 1962; 1 child, Clayton Eugene, II. BA, Kans. State Coll., Pittsburg, 1963; MLS, U. Okla., 1966. Br. libr. Tulsa City-County Libr. System, 1964-65, head brs., 1965-66, head reference dept., 1966-67, chief extension, chief pub. svc., 1967-73, asst. dir., 1973-76, exec. dir., 1976-96. Active Leadership Tulsa Alumni; exec. dir. Bot. Garden/Edn. and Rsch. Ctr. Recipient Disting. Libr. award Okla. Libr. Assn., 1982, Leadership Tulsa Paragon award, 1987, Women in Comm. Newsmaker award, 1989, Outstanding Alumnus award U. Okla. Sch. Libr. Info. Studies, 1989, Headliner award Tulsa Press Club, 1996, Disting. Alumnus Coll. Arts and Scis., U. Okla., 2000; inducted into Tulsa City-County Libr. Hall of Fame, 1989, Okla. Womens Hall of Fame, 1993. Mem. ALA, Pub. Libr. Assn. (pres. 1993-94), Okla. Libr. Assn. (pres. 1978-79, Disting. Libr. award 1982, Meritorious Svc. award 1996), Tulsa Press Club. Democrat. Episcopalian. Avocations: swimming, gardening. Office Phone: 918-728-2700. Business E-Mail: pwoodrum@tulsaconnect.com.

WOODS, CAROL SMITH, private school educator; d. David E. and Margaret (Ballinger) Smith; m. William Kent Woods, Apr. 1, 1980; children: Stephen, Todd. BA, U. Iowa, Iowa City, 1967; MEd, Xavier U., 1997. Tchg. coord. Montessori Ctr. Rm., Cin., 1975—2006; dir. Cin. Masonic Children's Learning Ctr., 2006—. Cons. Am. Montessori Soc., Cin., 1982—99; adj. prof. Xavier U., Cin., 1992—2000; presenter in field. Author: Wood's Words, 2002, Early Literacy Handbook, 2003, Woods' Words Advanced, 2006; contbr. articles to profl. jours. Fellow: Acad. Orton-Gillingham Practitioners and Educators; mem.: ASCD, Am. Montessori Soc., Internat. Dyslexia Assn. Avocations: reading, exercise, crossword puzzles. Home: 3750 Broadview Dr Cincinnati OH 45208

WOODS, DAN, information technology manager, consultant; BA in Computer Sci., U. Mich., 1982; MS in Journalism, Columbia U., 1989. Database editor The News and Observer/Nando.net, 1992—95; info. tech. cons. Time Inc. New Media, 1995—99, TheStreet.com, 1998—99; CTO CapitalThinking, 1999—2002. Mem. CTO adv. coun. InfoWorld; bd. mem. Big Star Entertainment; mem. policy adv. bd. on pub. key infrastructure Am. Bankers Assn. Author: The Education of a CTO, 2003; co-author: Developers Guide to the Java Web Server, 1999; contbr. articles to profl. jours.

WOODS, DAVID G., dean; MusB, Washburn U.; MusM, Northwestern U., PhD in Music; student, Aspen Inst., Copenhagen Conservatory Music. Dir. music Colo. Acad., 1966—73; chmn. div. music. edn. Iowa State U., Ames, 1974—84; dir. Sch. Music U. Ariz., 1985—91; dean Coll. Fine Arts U. Okla., 1991—97; dean Sch. Music. Ind. U., 1997—99; dean Sch. Fine Arts U. Conn., 2000—. Author: Phoebe in Her Petticoat, Congotay; co-author: Teaching Music in 21st Century, Jump Right In!; contbr. chapters to books, Handbook for Rsch. in Music Teaching & Learning, Second Handbook for Rsch. in Music Teaching & Learning. Fulbright scholar to Iceland, 1979, Fulbright scholar to Australia, 1986. Office: Office of the Dean U Conn Sch Fine Arts 830 Bolton Rd Rm 202 Unit 1128 Storrs Mansfield CT 06269 Home Phone: 860-429-5809; Office Phone: 860-486-3016. E-mail: david.woods@uconn.edu.

WOODS, DONALD E., healthcare executive; b. Memphis, Nov. 1, 1946; s. John Thomas and Hazel O. (Perry) W.; m. Shirlene M. Durutta, 1978 (div. 1992); children: Donald E. Jr., Lori Ann, Ryan Christopher; m. Joan M. Turley, 1995 (div. 2000); children: Kathryn Ashley, Lauren Rose. BS in Acctg., U. So. Calif., 1972, MBA, 1976. CPA, Calif. Audit supr. Ernst and Young, LA, 1972-76; asst. v.p. Am. Med. Internat., Beverly Hills, Calif., 1976-80; corp. contr. Safeco Title Ins. Co., Panorama City, Calif., 1980-82; sr. v.p. fin. Heritage divsn. Beverly

Enterprises, Md., 1982-84; co-founder, CFO Hannover Health Care, Inc., Md., 1984-85; founder, pres., CEO Oakwood Living Ctrs., Inc., McLean, Va., 1985-91; owner, pres. HMS of Newport (R.I.), Inc., 1992—; owner, gen. mgr. Lizzie Borden Bed and Breakfast, LLC, Fall River, Mass. Sgt. USMC, 1964-68. Mem. AICPA, Newport C. of C. Avocations: sailing, skiing. Home: 173 Gideon Lawton Ln Portsmouth RI 02871 Office: HMS of Newport Inc PO Box 610 Newport RI 02840-0011

WOODS, DUANE C., waste management executive; b. Spokane, Wash., 1951; BA, U. Wash., Seattle, 1973; JD, U. Puget Sound, Tacoma, Wash., 1980. Bar: Wash. 1980. Asst. sec. State of Wash.; local and state policy and mgmt. positions City of Seattle; ptnr. Heller, Erhman White & McAuliffe and Summit Law Group; v.p., gen. counsel Western Group Waste Mgmt., Inc., Houston, sr. v.p. Western Group. Mem.: Phi Beta Kappa. Office: Waste Mgmt Inc 7025 N Scottsdale Rd Ste 200 Scottsdale AZ 85253 Office Fax: 480-624-8400, 866-863-7960.

WOODS, ELEANOR C., music educator; b. Stamford, Conn., Oct. 30, 1939; d. Richard and Anna Marie (Feldtmose) Cunliffe; m. David R. Woods, Aug. 18, 1962; children: Richard, Laurie. BA, Smith Coll., 1961; MAT, Yale U., 1962. String tchr., music tchr. Kariat Jr. High Sch., Spring Valley, N.Y., 1962-65; musich tchr. Flint Hill Sch., Fairfax, Va., 1966-68; violin tchr. Am. U. Prep, Washington, 1972; pvt. instr. Washington, 1972—; violin tchr. Nat. Cathedral Sch., St. Albans, Washington, 1988—. Chmn. Washington Internat. Competition, 2001—. Named Tchr. of Yr., Am. String Tchrs. Assn. of Md., 1993. Mem. Md. State Music Tchrs. Assn. (chmn., judge of competitions 1976—), Wash. Music Tchrs. Assn. (judge of competitions 1976—), Suzuki Assn. Am., Suzuki Assn. Greater Washington Area.

WOODS, HARRY ARTHUR, JR., lawyer; b. Hartford, Ark., Feb. 15, 1941; s. Harry Arthur and Viada (Young) W.; m. Carol Ann (Meschter), Jan. 21, 1967; children: Harry Arthur III, Elizabeth Ann. BA in Econs., Okla. State U., 1963; JD, NYU, 1966. Bar: Okla., 1970. Assoc. White and Case, NYC, 1966—67, Crowe and Dunlevy, Oklahoma City, 1971—75, ptnr., 1976—, dir. Councilman City of Edmond, 1975-79; mayor pro tem, 1977-79. Capt. JAGC, U.S. Army, 1967-71. Fellow Am. Bar Found.; mem. ABA (ho. of dels. 2003-05, interim state del. 2004-05), Am. Law Inst., Internat. Assn. Def. Counsel, Okla. Bar Assn. (pres. 2004, bd. govs. 2001-05, profl. responsibility tribunal 1999-02; Outstanding Svc. award 1982, Golden Gavel award 1998, Neil Bogan Professionalism award 1998), Ruth Bader Ginsburg Inn of Ct. (pres. 1998-00), Okla. County Bar Assn. (bd. dirs. 2001-03). Democrat. Methodist. Avocations: rock climbing, flying, jogging, bicycling, photography. Office: Crowe and Dunlevy PC Ste 1800 20 N Broadway Oklahoma City OK 73102-8273 Office Phone: 405-235-7754. Office Fax: 405-272-5236. Business E-Mail: harry.woods@crowedunlevy.com.

WOODS, JAMES, actor; b. Vernal, Utah, Apr. 18, 1947; m. Kathryn Morrison-Pahoa, 1980 (div. 1983); m. Sarah Owen, June 2, 1989 (div. 1990). Student, MIT, 1965-69. Performances include (Broadway prodns.) Borstal Boy, Trial of the Catonsville 9, Finishing Touches, Moonchildren (Theatre World award), off-Broadway prodn. Saved (Obie award, Clarence Derwent award); actor (films) The Visitors, 1971, Hickey and Boggs, 1972, The Way We Were, 1973, The Gambler, 1974, Night Moves, 1975, Distance, 1975, Alex & the Gypsy, 1976, The Choirboys, 1977, The Onion Field, 1979 (Golden Globe award nomination), The Black Marble, 1980, Eyewitness, 1981, Split Image, 1982, Fast-Walking, 1982, Videodrome, 1983, Against All Odds, 1984, Once Upon a Time in America, 1984, Cat's Eye, 1985, Joshua Then and Now, 1985, Salvador, 1986 (Acad. award nomination, 1987), Best Seller, 1987, Cop, 1988, The Boost, 1988, True Believer, 1989, Immediate Family, 1989, The Hard Way, 1991, Straight Talk, 1992, Diggstown, 1992, Chaplin, 1992, The Getaway, 1994, The Specialist, 1994, Curse of the Starving Class, 1994, Nixon, 1995, Casino, 1995, Ghosts of Mississippi, 1996 (Acad. award nomination, Golden Globe nomination), For Better or Worse, 1996, Killer: A Journal of Murder, 1996, (voice) Hercules, 1997, Contact, 1997, Vampires, 1998, Kicked in the Head, 1998, Another Day in Paradise, 1998, True Crime, 1999, The General's Daughter, 1998, Any Given Sunday, 1999, The Virgin Suicides, 2000, Race to Space, 2001, Scary Movie 2, 2001, Riding in Cars with Boys, 2001, John Q, 2002, (voice only) Stuart Little 2, 2002, Northfork, 2003, This Girl's Life, 2003, Ark, 2005, Pretty Persuasion, 2005, Be Cool, 2005, End Game, 2006; (TV films) All the Way Home, 1971, Footsteps, 1972, A Great American Tragedy, 1972, Foster and Laurie, 1975, F. Scott Fitzgerald in Hollywood, 1976, The Disappearance of Aimee, 1976, Raid on Entebbe, 1977, The Gift of Love, 1978, And Your Name is Jonah, 1979, The Incredible Journey of Doctor Meg Laurel, 1979, Badge of the Assassin, 1985, Promise, 1986 (Emmy award, Golden Apple award, Golden Globe award), In Love and War, 1987 (Golden Globe award nomination), My Name Is Bill W. (Emmy award 1989), Women & Men: Stories of Seduction, 1990, The Boys, 1991, Citizen Cohn, HBO, 1992 (Emmy nomination, Lead Actor - Miniseries, 1993), Jane's House, 1994, Indictment: The McMartin Trial, 1995 (Emmy nomination, Cable Ace nomination), The Summer of Ben Tyler, 1996 (Golden Globe nomination), Dirty Pictures, 2000, Showtime, 2000 (Best Actor in Mini-Series of Motion Picture Made for TV award Golden Satellite 2000), (voice only) Legend of the Lost Tribe, 2002, Rudy: The Rudy Giuliani Story, 2003; (TV miniseries) Holocaust, 1978; (TV series) Shark, 2006-; (TV appearances) Kojak, 1974, The Rockford Files, 1974, Welcome Back, Kotter, 1975, The Streets of San Francisco, 1975, The Rookies, 1975, Barnaby Jones, 1976, Police Story, 1976, Young Maverick, 1979, 80, (voice) The Simpsons, 1994, Fallen Angels, 1995, Clerks, 2002, Celebrity Poker Showdown 2004, 2005, (voice only) Family Guy, 2005, ER, 2005; dir., writer (films) Falling In Love in Pongo Ponga, 2002 Recipient Daytime Emmy for Outstanding Performer Animated Program for Disney's Hercules, 2000. Mem. Acad. Motion Picture Arts and Scis., Internat. Platform Assn., Players Club, Mountaingate Country Club. Avocations: golf, photography, cooking. Office: Guttman Assocs 118 S Beverly Dr Ste 201 Beverly Hills CA 90212-3016

WOODS, JAMES STERRETT, toxicologist; b. Lewistown, Pa., Feb. 26, 1940; s. James Sterrett and Jane Smith (Parker) W.; m. Nancy Fugate, Dec. 20, 1969; 1 dau., Erin Elizabeth. AB, Princeton U., 1962; MS, U. Wash., 1968, PhD, 1970; MPH, U. N.C., 1978. Diplomate Am. Bd. Toxicology. Rsch. assoc. dept. pharmacology Yale U. Sch. Medicine, New Haven, 1970-72; staff fellow environ. toxicology. Nat. Inst. Environ. Health Scis. br. NIH, Research Triangle Park, NC, 1972-75, head biochem. toxicology sect., 1975-77; sr. rsch. leader environ. occupl. health risk evaluation Battelle Ctrs. for Pub. Health Rsch. and Evaluation, Seattle, 1978—2006; prof. U. Wash., Seattle, 1979—. Pres. Am. Bd. Toxicology, 1997-98. Contbr. articles to profl. jours. With USN, 1962-66. Scholar USPHS, 1966-70; Fellow Am. Cancer Soc., 1970-72. Mem. AAAS, Am. Assn. Cancer Rsch., Am. Soc. Pharmacology and Exptl. Therapeutics, Pacific NW Assn. Toxicologists (founding pres.), Soc. Epidemiology Rsch., Soc. Toxicology, Am. Coll. of Epidemiology, Am. Bd. Toxicology (pres. 1997-98). Home: 4525 E Laurel Dr NE Seattle WA 98105-3838 Office: Univ Wash Ste 100 4225 Roosevelt Way NE Seattle WA 98105 Office Phone: 206-685-3443. Business E-Mail: jwoods@u.washington.edu.

WOODS, JASON C., medical educator; s. H. Clay and Sherrill B. Woods; m. Ann T. Rohrer. BS, Rhodes Coll., Memphis, Tenn., 1997; PhD, Wash. U., Saint Louis, Mo., 2002. Asst. dean Wash. U., 2004—, sr. rsch. scientist, 2004—08, asst. prof., 2008—. Sci. and bus. cons. Multiple Orgns., 2002—. Contbr. scientific papers to jours. Maj. Rsch. grant, NIH, 2008. Mem.: Am. Phys. Soc., Am. Physiol. Soc., Internat. Soc. Magnetic Resonance in Medicine (sec., hyperpolarized media study group 2008—09). Achievements include research in significant contributions in validating 3He MRI as a noninvasive morphometric measure of lung.

WOODS, JEAN FRAHM, science educator; b. Boise, Idaho, Oct. 24, 1931; d. Theodore Roosevelt and Bonnie Mae (Gross) Frahm; m. Lonnie Lee Woods, June 24, 1951 (dec. May 7, 1977); children: Jeffrey Lee, Nicholaus Lon, Karl Eugene. BS in Sci. Edn., Home Econs., U. Idaho, Moscow, 1954; MS in Zoology, U. Wis., 1960. Tchr. 4th grade Rapid City Schs., SD, 1954-55; tchr. 7th and 8th grades Lovelock Schs., Nev., 1956-57; tchr. biology, chemistry, home econs. Richfield HS, Idaho, 1957-59; dietitian U. Idaho, Moscow, 1961-62; tchr. sci., home econs. Eagle Jr. HS, Idaho, 1962-63; sci. tchr. 7th grade Meridian Schs., Idaho, 1981-97. Tchr. of Yr. Meridian Schs., 1987. Mem. AAUW, Nat. Sci. Tchrs. Assn., Idaho Sci. Tchrs. Assn., Boise Home Economists (treas. 1968, pres. 1969), Native Daus. of Idaho, Ret. Educators Assn., Delta Kappa Gamma (1st v.p.) 2001-03. Avocations: reading, birdwatching. Home: 3518 Catalina Rd Boise ID 83705-4604

WOODS, JEFFREY GEORGE, economist, researcher; s. George Theodore and Helen Louise Woods. AA in Bus., Parkland Coll., 1978; BS in Bus., Eastern Ill. U., 1980, MA in Econ., 1982; PhD in Econ., So. Ill. U., Carbondale, 1993. Rsch. economist Calif. Dept. Ind. Rels., San Francisco, 2000—08; econ. lectr. Calif. State U., Hayward, 2001—08; vis. assoc. prof., economics Sch. Bus. U. Indpls., 2009—. Editor review bd. Sci. Jours. Internat. Contbr. scientific papers. Mem.: Am. Econ. Assn. Office: Univ Indpls 1400 E Hanna Ave Indianapolis IN 46227 Home: 945 Norwick Cir Greenwood IN 46143 Business E-Mail: woodsjg@uindy.edu.

WOODS, JOHN ELMER, plastic surgeon; b. Battle Creek, Mich., July 5, 1929; m. Janet Ruth; children: Sheryl, Mark, Jeffrey, Jennifer, Judson. BA, Asbury Coll., 1949, DHL, 1999; MD, Western Res. U., 1955; PhD, U. Minn., 1966. Intern Gorgas Hosp., Panama Canal Zone, 1955-56, resident in gen. surgery, 1956-57, Mayo Grad. Sch., Rochester, Minn., 1960-65, resident in plastic surgery, 1966-67, Brigham Hosp., Boston, Mass., 1968; fellow, transplant cons. Harvard Med. Sch., Cambridge, Mass., 1969; cons. in gen. and plastic surgery Mayo Clinic, Rochester, 1969-93, vice chmn. Dept. Surgery; asst. prof. Mayo Med. Sch., Rochester, 1973-76, assoc. prof., 1976-80, prof. plastic surgery, 1980-93, Stuart W. Harrington prof. surgery. Vis. prof. Yale Sch. Medicine, New Haven, 1984, Harvard Sch. Medicine, Cambridge, 1984. Contbr. over 200 articles to profl. jours.; also 26 book chpts. and 1 film. Recipient Disting. Mayo Clinician award, 1991, Disting. Mayo Alumnus award, 1999. Mem. AMA (coun. on sci. affairs 1985-87), ACS (grad edn. com. 1985-87), Am. Bd. Med. Specialties, Am. Bd. Plastic Surgery (sec.-treas. 1985-88, chmn. 1988-89), Am. Soc. Plastic Surgeons Ednl. Fedn. (pres. 1984-85). Avocations: skiing, sailing, reading, the arts. Office: Mayo Clinic Plummer N-10 Rochester MN 55905-0001 Business E-Mail: woods.john@mayo.edu.

WOODS, JOHN MAYNARD, lawyer; b. New Canaan, Conn., Jan. 14, 1955; s. John Eric and Margery (Maynard) W.; m. Elizabeth Anne Duff, Apr. 9, 1983; children: Avery Carson, Katherine McKercher, Abigail Elizabeth. AB, Middlebury Coll., 1976; JD with honors, Tulane U., 1980. Bar: N.Y. 1981, U.S. Dist. Ct. (ea. and so. dists.) N.Y. 1981, U.S. Ct. Appeals (5th cir.) 1984, U.S. Ct. Appeals (2d cir.) 1988, U.S. Ct. Appeals (4th cir.) 1992, U.S. Supreme Ct. 1998, U.S. Ct. Appeals (1st cir.) 2001, U.S. Ct. Appeals (11th cir.) 1999. Assoc. Thacher, Proffitt & Wood LLP, NYC, 1980-87, ptnr., maritime, admiralty internat. litig., ins., environ. law, 1987—, and head, litig., maritime and ins. practice group. Contbg. editor Bus. Ins. Guide, 1989, Recreational Boating Law, 1992. Mem. ABA, Maritime Law Assn. U.S. (bd. dirs.), Assn. Bar City N.Y., Average Adjuster Assn. U.S. (chmn. 2006-07). Office: Thacher Proffitt & Wood 2 World FinancialCtr New York NY 10281 Office Phone: 212-912-7672. Office Fax: 212-912-7751. Business E-Mail: jwoods@tpw.com.

WOODS, JOHN WILLIAM, electrical, computer and systems engineering educator, consultant; b. Washington, Dec. 5, 1943; s. John Gill and Margaret (McHugh) W.; m. Harriet Hemmerich, June 17, 1972; children: Anne, Christopher. BSEE, MIT, 1965, MSEE, 1967, PhD, 1970. Sr. rsch. engr. Lawrence Livermore (Calif.) Nat. Lab., 1973-76; asst. prof. Rensselaer Poly. Inst., Troy, NY, 1976-78, assoc. prof., 1978-84, prof., 1985—. Vis. prof. Delft Tech. U., The Netherlands, 1985, Heinrich-Hertz Inst., Berlin, 2000; program dir. NSF, Washington, 1987-88; assoc. dir. Ctr. for Image Processing Rsch., 1992—; cons. Kodak, Rochester, N.Y., 1985-86, Johns Hopkins Applied Physics Lab., Laurel, Md., 1987, Calian Comms. Ltd., 1990-91, Thomson Electronics, 2005, Alcatel Lucent, 2007; co-founder Focus Interactive Tech., Inc., 1993; assoc. dir. NSF I/U Ctr. for Next Generation Video, 1998-2001, dir. 2002-05; mem. compression com. Digital Cinema Initiatives, 2003-04. Author: Multidimensional Signal, Image, and Video Processing and Coding, 2006; co-author: Probability and Random Processes for Engineers, 1986, 3d edit., 2002; editor: Subband Image Coding, 1991; co-editor: Handbook of Visual Communications, 1995; mem. editl. bd. Graphical Models and Image Processing, 1989-93; contbg. author book chpts., articles to profl. jours. Mem. Com. Acad. Excellence, Clifton Park, N.Y., 1984. Capt. USAF, 1969-73. Grantee NSF, Army Rsch. Office, Advanced Rsch. Projects Agy., Ctr. Advanced TV Studies, 1978-2007. Fellow: IEEE (editl. bd. Trans. on Video Tech. 1990—2002, Third Millennium medal 2000); mem.: SPIE, Visual Comm. and Image Process (co-chair 2008), Nat. Com. for Info. Tech. Stds., Internat. Stds. Orgn. (mem. motion pictures expert group 2001—), IEEE Signal Processing Soc. (assoc. editor jour. 1979—82, com. chmn. 1983—85, ad. com. 1986—88, ednl. com. chmn. 1987—93, 1st IEEE Internat. Conf. on Image Processing 1994, co-chmn. tech. program com., Best Paper awards 1977, 1986, Meritorious Svc. award 1989, Tech. Achievement award 1993). Roman Catholic. Home: 43 Longview Dr Clifton Park NY 12065-2318 Office: Rensselaer Poly Inst ECSE Dept Troy NY 12180-3590 Home Phone: 518-383-3703; Office Phone: 518-276-6079. E-mail: woods@ecse.rpi.edu.

WOODS, KRYSTYNA JANINA, artist, pharmacist; b. Warwick, Queensland, Australia, Jan. 28, 1961; arrived in U.S., 1998; d. Jan and Janina Dzierzanowski; m. Ross Maxwell Woods, Aug. 28, 1993; children: Harrison George Maxwell, Jack Henry Alexander. BPharm, U. Queensland, Brisbane, 1980. Registered pharmacist Pharmacy Bd. Queensland. Pre-registration pharmacist, asst. mgr. Payless Chemists, Brisbane, Queensland, 1980—81; pharmacist, mgr. Benowa Pharmacy, Gold Coast, Australia, 1981—83; chief pharmacist, asst. mgr. Sorrento Pharmacy, Gold Coast, Australia, 1983—85; chief pharmacist, mgr. Moses Edward St. Pharmacy, Brisbane, 1986—88; chief pharmacist, part-time mgr. Aspley Day & Night Pharmacy, Brisbane, 1988—93; locum pharmacist mgr. Auchenflower Pharmacy, Brisbane, 1993—95, Terry White Pharmacy, Brisbane, 1993—95, Transit Ctr. Pharmacy, Brisbane, 1993—95; owner, mgr., chief pharmacist Indooroopilly Day & Night Pharmacy, Brisbane, 1995—2000. Model, actress Viviens Model Agy., Brisbane and Sydney, 1985—93; actress, model print, TV, radio and stage Margo Mott/Buckinghams, Gold Coast, 1985—93, Queensland Theatre Co., Brisbane, 1985—93, Javeenbah Little Theatre, Gold Coast, 1985—93, Gold Coast Little Theatre, 1982—84; mentor Young Australian Profls. in Am., NYC, 2003; represented Queensland, Australia in Miss World Pageant, 1985; lectr. Mt. Gravatt Tech. Coll. Further Edn., Brisbane, 1989; interviewed by mags. N.J. Monthly, 2001, Australian House and Garden Mag., 1999, Sunday Mail Mag., 1998, Matters Mag., 2005. One-woman shows include Natura Gallery, Heritage Hotel, Brisbane, 1995—97, Brisbane Herbsfest, 1995—97, Wentworth Gallery, Palm Beach, 1995—96, White Plains, 1995—96, Boston, 1995—96, Chgo., 1995—96, Madison Studio Gallery, 2001, The Show Gallery, Chatham, 2002—03, Internat. Art Expo, N.Y.C., 2003, Solange Rabello Art Gallery, Miami, 2003—04, Australian Consulate, N.Y.C., 2003, Arts Coun. of Morris Area, 2004, Happy Dog Gallery, Piermont, N.Y., 2004—08, Maplewood Open Studio Exhbn., 2005, South Orange, exhibitions include Village Gallery, Laguna Beach, 2003, Maplewood/South Orange Artist Studio Tours, 2004—, executed murals, S. Orange/Maplewood, NJ, 2005, exhibitions include NJ Ctr. for Visual Arts Blank Canvas Exhbn., 2006—08, Maplewood/South Orange Two Towns in Harmony Mural, NJ Ctr. for Visual Arts Blank Canvas, 2006—08. Rep. city for state visit by Queen Elizabeth II; asst. to pres. in presentation to MP regarding protection of pharmacy ownership Queensland Pharmacy Guild, Brisbane, 1997; mentor, Australian profl. NYC, 2003. Recipient Award of Merit for Outstanding Achievement, Manhattan Arts Internat., 1999, Art Show awards, city couns. and art assns., 1977—89, Adjudicator's Choice award, Warana Drama Festival and Arts, 1982. Mem.: Australian Am. Assn., Arts Coun. of Morris Area (invited spkr. art promotion 2002), Nat. Mus. Women in Arts, Maplewood Club, Internat. Friends Club, Catharine Lorillard Wolfe Art Club (assoc.). Episcopalian. Avocations: tennis, golf, interior decorating, reading, travel. Office: Krysia D Designs 422 Walton Rd Maplewood NJ 07040 Personal E-mail: krysiadart@aol.com.

WOODS, LAWRENCE MILTON, airline company executive; b. Manderson, Wyo., Apr. 14, 1932; s. Ben Ray and Katherine (Youngman) Woods; m. Joan Frances Van Patten, June 10, 1952; 1 child, Laurie. B.Sc. with honors, U. Wyo., 1953; MA, N.Y. U., 1973, PhD, 1975; LL.D., Wagner Coll., 1973. CPA Colo., Mont.; bar: Mont. 1957. Acct. Peat, Marwick, Mitchell & Co. (C.P.A.'s), Billings, Mont., 1953; supervisory auditor Army Audit Agy., Denver, 1954-56; acct. Mobil Producing Co., Billings, Mont., 1956-59; planning analyst Socony Mobil Oil Co., NYC, 1959-63, planning mgr., 1963-65; v.p. N.Am. divsn. Mobil Oil Corp., NYC, 1966-67, gen. mgr. planning and econs. N.Am. divsn., 1967-69, v.p. N.Am. divsn., 1969-77, exec. v.p. N.Am. divsn., 1977-85, also dir. N.Am. divsn.; pres., CEO, dir. Centennial Airlines, Inc., 1985-87. Bd. dirs., chmn. The Heartland Funds, 2005. Author: Accounting for Capital, Construction and Maintenance Expeditures, 1967, The Wyoming Country Before Statehood, 1971, Sometimes the Books Froze, 1985, Moreton Frewen's Western Adventures, 1986, British Gentlemen in the Wild West, 1989; co-author: Takeover, 1980; editor: Wyoming Biographies, 1991, Wyoming's Big Horn Basin, 1996, Agent R, 2000, John Clay, Jr., 2001, Asa Shinn Mercer, 2003, A Material Witness, 2003, Alex Swan, 2006; contbr. Accountants' Encyclopedia, 1962; editor: Edward Shelley's Journal, 2005. With US Army, 1953—55. Mem.: AICPA, ABA, Mont. Bar Assn. Republican. Lutheran. Office: High Plains Pub Co PO Box 1860 Worland WY 82401-1860

WOODS, NANCY FUGATE, nursing educator; BS, Wis. State U., 1968; MSN, U. Wash., 1969; PhD, U. NC, 1978; D (hon.), U. Pa., Phila., U. Haifa, Israel, Chiang Mai U., Thailand. Staff nurse Sacred Heart Hosp., Wis., 1968, Univ. Hosp., Wis., 1969-70, St. Francis Cabrini Hosp., 1970; nurse clinician Yale-New Haven Hosp., 1970-71; instr. nursing Duke U., Durham, N.C., 1971-72, from instr. to assoc. prof., 1972-78; assoc. prof. physiology U. Wash., Seattle, 1978-82, prof. physiology, 1982-84, chairperson, dept. parent and child nursing, 1984-90, dir., ctr. women's health rsch., 1989—, prof., dept. family and child nursing, 1990—, dean, sch. nursing, 1998—2008. Pres. scholar U. Calif., San Francisco, 1985-86. Contbr. articles to profl. jours. Named Reid Endowed Dean in Nursing, 2007. Fellow ANA, Am. Acad. Nursing, Inst. Medicare, N.A.S.; mem. AAUP, APHA, Am. Coll. Epidemiology, Soc. Menstrual Cycle Rsch. (v.p. 1981-82, pres. 1983-85), Soc. Advancement Women's Health Rsch. Office: U Wash Sch Nursing PO Box 357260 Seattle WA 98195-7260*

WOODS, PENDLETON, college director, author; b. Ft. Smith, Ark., Dec. 18, 1923; s. John Powell and Mabel (Hon) W.; m. Lois Robin Freeman, Apr. 3, 1948; children: Margaret, Paul Pendleton, Nancy Cox. BA in Journalism, U. Ark., 1948; D (hon.), Okla. Christian U., Oklahoma City, 2005. Editor, asst. pub. mgr. Okla. Gas & Electric Co., Oklahoma City, 1948—69; dir. Living Legends of Okla., Okla. Christian U., Oklahoma City, 1969—82; dir. project, promotion Enterprise Sq. and Am. Citizenship Ctr., 1982—92, dir. Nat. Edn. Program and Am. Citizenship Ctr., 1992. Arbitrator BBB; leader youth seminars in field; state pub. affairs officer Employer Support Guard and Res. Author: You and Your Company Magazine, 1950, Church of Tomorrow, 1964, Myriad of Sports, 1971, This Was Oklahoma, 1979; recorded Sounds of Scouting, 1969, Born Grown, 1974 (We. Heritage award Nat. Cowboy Hall of Fame), One of a Kind, 1977, Countdown to Statehood, 1982, The Thunderbird Tradition, 1989, A Glimpse at Oklahoma, 1990, Historic Oklahoma County, 2002; editor Libertas. Vol. reader Okla. Libr. for the Blind; past pres. Okla. Assn. Epilepsy, Keep Okla. Beautiful, Okla. City Mental Health Clin.; past pres., hon. lifetime dir. Variety Health Ctr.; pub. rels. chmn. Okla. County chpt. ARC; past chmn. We. Heritage award Nat. Cowboy Hall of Fame; Am. Freedom Coun.; charter dir. Okla. Vets. Med. Rsch. Found.; cons. Exec. Svc. Corps.; ex-state comdr. Am. ex-Prisoners of War; vol. Okla. City VA Hosp.; state historian Okla. N.G.; chmn. Okla. City Independence Day Parade; exec. dir. Okla. City Bicentennial Commn.; v.p. Okla. City chpt. Freedom Found.; v.p. & bd. dirs. Campfire Girls Coun.; bd. dirs. Okla. Jr. Symphony, past pres.; bd. dirs. Zoo Amphitheater of Okla. City, Will Rogers Centennial Commn., Greater Okla. City Tree Bank Found., Boy Scout Am. (life); bd. dirs., co-founder Ctrl. Pk. Neighborhood Assn.; dir. Okla. for Resource Preservation; chmn. State Directional Signage Task Force. With US Army, WWII and Korean War, ret. col. Named Outstanding Young Man of Yr., Oklahoma City Jr. C. of C., 1953; recipient Silver Beaver award Boy Scouts Am., 1963, Wokan award Oklahoma City Coun. Camp Fire Girls, 1968, Silver medal Advt. Fedn. Am., Disting. Cmty. Svc. award Neighborhood Devel. and Conservation Ctr., 2 Commendation awards Am. Assn. for State and Local History, 4 honor medals Freedoms Found., Jefferson Davis medal United Daus. of Confederacy, Okla. Disting. Svc. medal (2), Outstanding Contbn. to Okla. Mus., Okla. Mus.

Assn., 1987, Outstanding Contbn. to Okla. Tourism award Okla. Dept. Tourism, 1989, Cmty. Svc. award U. Ark. Alumni Assn., 1992, Citizenship and Patriot awards SAR, 1992, 5 Who Care award KOCO-TV, 1993, Jefferson award Am. Inst. for Pub. Svc., 1993, Mayor's award in Beautification, 1994, George Washington award Youth Leadership Found., St. Augustine, Fla., 1993, Golden Rule award J.C. Penney Found., 1999, Lifetime Achievement award Keep Okla. Beautiful, Pres.'s Vol. Svc. award, 2005; inducted into Okla. Journalism Hall of Fame, 2001, Okla. Mil. Hall of Fame, 2002, Okla. Historians Hall of Fame, 2007, Okla. Outstanding Older Worker award, Washington, DC, 2007. Mem.: DAR (Medal of Honor 2005, Nation's Most Outstanding Ex-prisoner of War 2005, Outstanding Older Worker award for Okla. 2007), VFW, DAV, Okla. Distributive Edn., Okla. Jr. C. of C. (hon. life, past internat. dir.), Ctrl. Okla. Bus. Communicators (past pres., hon. life), Advt. Fedn. Am. (past dist. dir.), Soc. Assoc. Indsl. Editors (past v.p.), Okla. Vets. Coun. (chmn.), Okla. Heritage Assn., Okla. City Beautiful (publ. editor), Okla. Safety Coun. (publ. editor), Okla. County Hist. Soc. (dir., past pres.), 45th Inf. Divsn. Assn. (past pres.), Korean War Vets. Assn., Am. Legion, Mus. Unassigned Lands (chmn.), Mil. Order World Wars (regional comdr., Oklahoma City comdr., Okla. State comdr., nat. staff, Gold and Silver Patrick Henry Patriotism medals), Okla. Hist. Soc. (life; publ. editor,), Words of Jesus Found. (pres.), Okla. Zool. Soc. (past pres.), Okla. Geneal. Soc., Okla. County Sr. Nutrition Found. (sec., bd. dirs.), Freedom's Found. (v.p.), Nat. Eagle Scout Assn. (Okla. chmn.), U. Ark. Alumni Assn. (charter pres. Oklahoma City chpt.), Okla. Lung Assn. (pub. rels. com.), Am. Cancer Soc. (dir. Okla. County chpt.), Okla. Travel Industries Assn., Am. Ex-Prisoners of War (state comdr.), Okla. City Hist. Preservation Commn., Okla. City Clean and Green Coalition, Lincoln Park Country (pres.), Oklahoma City Advt. Club (past pres., hon. life), Kappa Sigma (nat. commr. publs.), Sigma Delta Chi. Home: 541 NW 31st St Oklahoma City OK 73118-7334 Office Phone: 405-425-5032. Personal E-mail: penwoods@cox.net.

WOODS, R. CLIVE, electrical engineer, educator; b. Leicester, Eng. arrived in US, 2002; MA, DPhil, Oxford U., 1980, DSc, 2005. Postdoctoral rsch. asst. U. Oxford, England, 1980—82; sr. scientist Plessey Rsch. Ltd., Towcester, England, 1982—83; lectr. electronic engring. U. Sheffield, England, 1983—87, lectr. (Grade B) electronic engring., 1987—92, sr. lectr. electronic engring., 1993—2001; prof. elec. engring. Iowa State U., Ames, 2001—06; dept. chair, Voorhies disting. prof. La. State U., Baton Rouge, 2006—. Invited prof. Nat. Inst. Applied Sci., Lyon, France, 1995; Marie Curie fellowship com. EU, Brussels. Author: Digital Logic Design, 2002; musician: (albums) Martyr of Antioch, 2000, A tenor, all singers above?, 2001; accompanist, repetiteur Internat. Gilbert & Sullivan Festival, Buxton, Eng., 1994—2006; contbr. articles to profl. jours. Mem. Am. Soc. Engring. Edn., 2003—07. Media fellow, Brit. Assn., 1989. Fellow: Inst. Engring. Tech.; mem.: IEEE (sr.), Instn. Elec. Engrs. (mem. profl. group com., assoc. editor Electronics and Comm. Jour. 1999—2002). Achievements include patents in field. Avocations: piano, photography, fencing, gliding. Office: Louisiana State U Dept Elec and Computer Engring Baton Rouge LA 70803-5901

WOODS, REGINALD FOSTER, management consulting executive; b. Charleston, W.Va., Sept. 25, 1939; s. Reginald Foster and Jean Lee (Hill) W.; m. Katharine Terry Norden, May 11, 1963; children: Eric Arthur, Elizabeth Terry, Tracy Lee. BME, Cornell U., 1961, MME, 1962, MBA, 1963. Mktg. specialist Gen. Electric Co., NYC, 1963-64; dir. flight equipment and facilities planning Eastern Airlines, NYC, 1964-70; v.p. planning Butler Internat., Inc., Montvale, NJ, 1970, sr. v.p. fin., 1971-80, exec. v.p., 1980-86, pres., 1986-87; chmn. Mgmt. Resources Group, Inc., Saddle River, NJ, 1987-96; pres., CEO The Advantage Ptnrs., Chatham, NJ, 1992-94; pres. DCG Corp., 1994—2004; chmn. Dynamic Literacy LLC, Charlottesville, Va., 2006—. Bd. dirs. DCG Corp., Roseville, Calif., The Greenleaf Co., Cranford, NJ, Scitent, Inc., Charlottesville, Va., Hemoshear LLC, Charlottesville. Mem. Keswick Club, Keswick Hunt Club. Home and Office: Fox Ridge Farm 4822 Bann Field Dr Duxbury MA 02332

WOODS, RICHARD DALE, lawyer; b. Kans. City, Mo., May 20, 1950; s. Willard Dale and Betty Sue (Duncan) W.; m. Cecelia Ann Thompson, Aug. 11, 1973 (div. July 1996); children: Duncan Warren, Shannon Cecelia; m. Mary Linna Lash, June 6, 1999. BA with distinction, U. Kans., Lawrence, 1972; JD, U. Mo., 1975. Bar: Mo. 1975, Kans. 2000, US Dist. Ct. (we. dist.) Mo. 1975, US Tax Ct. 1999. Assoc. Shook, Hardy & Bacon L.L.P., Kansas City, Mo., 1975-79, ptnr., 1980-2000; shareholder Kirkland & Woods, P.C., Overland Park, Kans., 2001—. Gen. chmn. Estate Planning Symposium, Kansas City, 1985-86; chair Northland Coalition, 1993. Chmn. fin. com. North Woods Ch., Kansas City, 1986-88, 93-96; mem. sch. bd. N. Kansas City Sch. Dist., 1990-97, treas., 1992-97; mem. North Kansas City Ednl. Found., 1998-2002, pres., 1999-2002; mem. devel. com. Truman Med. Ctr., 1992—, chmn., 1992-98; mem. Clay County Tax Increment Fin. Commn., 1990-99; bd. dir. Heart of Am. Family Svcs., 1998-2004, sec., 2000-01, v.p. 2003-04, The Family Conservancy, 2005-07, v.p., 2005, chmn., 2006-07, Gilda's Club Kans. City, 2003—, sec., 2005-07. Named to Best Lawyers in Am., Trusts and Estates, 1993—. Fellow Am. Coll. Trust and Estate Counsel (Kans. state chair 2006-); mem. ABA, Mo. Bar Assn., Kans. Bar Assn., Johnson County Bar Assn., Kansas City Met. Bar Assn., Lawyers Assn. Kans. City (sec., v.p., pres. young lawyers sect. 1981-84), Kans. City Estate Planning Soc. (bd. dirs. 1985-88, 93-95), Ea. Kans. Estate Planning Coun. Democrat. Office: Kirkland & Woods PC 6201 College Blvd Ste 250 Overland Park KS 66211 Office Phone: 913-469-0900. E-mail: rwoods@kcnet.com.

WOODS, ROBERT EDWARD, lawyer; b. Albert Lea, Minn., Mar. 27, 1952; s. William Fabian and Maxine Elizabeth (Schmit) W.; m. Cynthia Anne Pratt, Dec. 26, 1975; children: Laura Marie Woods, Amy Elizabeth Woods. BA, U. Minn., 1974, JD, 1977; MBA, U. Pa., 1983. Bar: Minn. 1977, US Dist. Ct. Minn. 1980, US Ct. Appeals (8th cir.) 1980, Calif. 2000, US Ct. Appeals (9th cir.) 2000. Assoc. Moriarty & Janzen, Mpls., 1977-81, Berger & Montague, Phila., 1982-83, Briggs and Morgan, St. Paul and Mpls., 1983-84, ptnr., 1984-99; exec. v.p., gen. counsel InsWeb Corp., Redwood City, Calif., 1999-2000; gen. counsel BORN Info. Svcs., Inc., Mpls., 2000—04; pvt. practice Mpls., 2004—07; sr. v.p. gen. counsel Sec. Analysts Internat. Corp., Mpls., 2008—. Adj. prof. William Mitchell Coll. Law, St. Paul, 1985; exec. com., bd. dirs. LEX MUNDI, Ltd., Houston, 1989-93, chmn. bd. 1991-92; bd. dirs. Midwest Asia Ctr., 1993-95, chmn. bd., 1994-95. Co-author: (with others) Business Torts, 1989, (Carter G. Bishop) CCH Tax Research Consultant, Business Stages from Start-Up to Termination, 2005; sr. contbg. editor: Evidence in America: The Federal Rules in the States, 1987. Mem. ABA, Minn. State Bar Assn., State Bar of Calif., Hennepin County Bar Assn., Ramsey County Bar Assn. (chmn. corp., banking and bus. law sect. 1985-87), Assn. Trial Lawyers Am., Wharton Club of Minn., Phi Beta Kappa. Home: 28 N Deep Lake Rd North Oaks MN 55127-6506 Office: 110 Cheshire Ln Ste 300 Minneapolis MN 55305 Office Phone: 952-838-2883. Business E-Mail: rwoods@robertewoodspa.com.

WOODS, RYAN JOHN, education director; s. Robin Lee Woods-Brisson and Timothy John Brisson (Stepfather); m. Karen Kristine Hoffmann. BS in Social Sci. Edn., Boston U., EdM in Curriculum & Tchg. Cert. history tchr. Mass. Dept. Edn. Spl. programs coord. John F. Kennedy Presdl. Libr., Boston, 2002—05; edn. coord. Mary Baker Eddy Libr., Boston, 2005—07; dir. edn. New Eng. Hist. Geneal. Soc., 2007—. Co-chair pub. programs com. Mary Baker Eddy Libr., 2006—07; spkr. in field. Contbr. articles to profl. jours. Planning com. mem. Civic Edn. Project, Boston, 2004; First Night Boston cultural ptnr. liasion, 2006—; cmty. outreach com. mem. Fenway Alliance, Boston, 2006—; mem. Dem. Nat. Com., DC, 2006—; pub. rels. com. mem. Boston U., Sch. Edn., 2006; pres. Boston U., Sch. Edn. Alumni Assn., 2008—; career adv. com. chair Boston U., Sch. Edn., Boston, 2006—; councillor Boston U. Coun., 2008—; exe. com. Boston U. Adv. Coun., 2008—; trustee Partnership Historic Bostons, 2009—; bd. dirs. Am. Friends Boston Stump, 2009—. Recipient Excellence In Svc. award, Nat. Archives & Records Adminstrn., US Govt., 2004, Letter of Recognition Svc., Dem. Leader, US Ho. Reps., 2004, Chmn. Dem. Nat. Com., 2004, Office Treas. & Receiver Gen., Commonwealth Mass., 2004. Mem.: Soc. Colonial Wars, Lafayette Soc., Am. Assn. Museums, Student & Youth Travel Assn. (assoc.), Mus. Educators Roundtable (assoc.), Greater Boston Conv. & Visitor Bur. (assoc.), Nat. Coun. Social Studies (assoc.), Assn. Supervision & Curriculum Devel. (assoc.), New Eng. League Mid. Schs. (assoc.). Home: 86 Hooker Ave West Somerville MA 02144 Office: New Eng Hist Geneal Soc 101 Newbury St Boston MA 02116 Office Fax: 617-536-7307. Personal E-mail: ryjwoods@gmail.com. Business E-Mail: rwoods@nehgs.org.

WOODS, SANDRA KAY, real estate executive; b. Loveland, Colo., Oct. 11, 1944; d. Ivan H. and florence L. (Betz) Harris; m. Gary A. Woods, June 11, 1967; children: Stephanie Michelle, Michael Harris. BA, U. Colo., 1966, MA, 1967. Personnel mgmt. specialist CSC, Denver, 1967; asst. to regional dir. HEW, Denver, 1968-69; urban renewal rep. HUD, Denver, 1970-73, dir. program analysis, 1974-75, asst. regional dir. cmty. planning and devel., 1976-77, regional dir. fair housing, 1978-79; mgr. ea. facility project Adolph Coors Co., Golden, Colo., 1980, dir. real estate, 1981, v.p. chief environ. health and safety officer, 1982-96, v.p. strategic selling initiatives, 1996—2000; pres. Woods Properties LLP, Golden, 2000—. Mem. Exec. Exch., The White House, 1980. Bd. dirs. Golden Local Devel. Corp., 1981-82; fundraising dir. Coll. Arts and Scis., U. Colo., boulder, 1982-89, U. Colo.found.; mem. exec. bd. NCCJ, Denver, 1982-94; v.p. women in bus. Inc., Denver, 1982-83; mem. steering com. 1984 Yr. for All Denver Women, 1983-84; mem. 10th dist. Denver br. Fed. Res. Bd., 1990-96, chmn. bd., 1995-96; bd. dirs. Nat. Jewish Hosp., 1994—; chmn. Greater Denver Corp., 1991—. Named one of Outstanding Young Women Am., U.S. Jaycees, 1974, 78, Fifty Women to Watch, Businessweek, 1987, 92, Woman of Achievement YWCA, 1988. Mem. Indsl. Devel. Resources Coun. (bd. dirs. 1986-89), Am. Mgmt. Assn., Denver C. of C. (bd. dirs. 1988-96, Disting. Young Exec. award 1974, mem. Leadership Denver, 1976-77), Colo. Women's Forum, Nat. Assn. Office and Indsl. Park Developers (sec. 1988, treas. 1989), Committee of 200 (v.p. 1994-95), Phi Beta Kappa, Pi Alpha Alpha, PEO Club (Loveland). Republican. Presbyterian. E-mail: sandrawoods@qwest.net.

WOODS, STUART, writer; b. Manchester, Ga., Jan. 9, 1938; s. Stuart Franklin Lee and Dorothy Callaway Woods. BA in Sociology, U. Ga., 1959. Writer, creative dir. various advt. agys., NYC and London, 1960-73; freelance writer, 1973—. Author: (novels) Under the Lake, 1987, White Cargo, 1988, Palindrome, 1991, LA Times, 1993, Dead Eyes, 1994, Heat, 1994, Imperfect Strangers, 1995 (Grand Prix de Litérature Policière, 1997), Choke, 1995, (non-fiction) Blue Water, Green Skipper, 1977, A Romantic's Guide to the Country Inns of Britain and Ireland, 1979, (Will Lee novels) Chiefs, 1981 (Edgar Allan Poe award, 1982), Run Before the Wind, 1983, Deep Lie, 1986, Grass Roots, 1989, The Run, 2000, Capital Crimes, 2003, Mounting Fears, 2009 (Publishers Weekly bestseller), (Stone Barrington novels) New York Dead, 1991, Dirt, 1996, Dead in the Water, 1997, Swimming to Catalina, 1998, LA Dead, 2000, Cold Paradise, 2001, The Short Forever, 2002, Dirty Work, 2003, Reckless Abandon, 2004, Two Dollar Bill, 2005, Dark Harbor, 2006, Fresh Disasters, 2007, Shoot Him If He Runs, 2007, Hot Mahogany, 2008 (Publishers Weekly bestseller), Loitering With Intent, 2009 (Publishers Weekly bestseller), (Holly Barker novels) Orchid Beach, 1998, Orchid Blues, 2001, Blood Orchid, 2002, Iron Orchid, 2005, (Ed Eagle novels) Santa Fe Rules, 1992, Short Straw, 2006, Santa Fe Dead, 2008, (Rick Barron novels) The Prince of Beverly Hills, 2004, Beverly Hills Dead, 2008; contbr. articles to numerous publs. including Yachting, TV Guide, NY Times Op-Ed Page. Airman USNG, 1961—62. Mem.: Authors Guild, Writers Guild America, Royal Yacht Squadron Eng., Century Assn. NYC, NY Yacht Club. Democrat. Avocations: yachting, aviation. Address: 88 Parker Farm Rd Mount Desert ME 04660 Office: Janklow & Nesbit c/o Anne Sibbald 445 Park Ave New York NY 10022 Business E-Mail: stuart@stuartwoods.com.*

WOODS, TIGER (ELDRICK WOODS), professional golfer; b. Cypress, Calif., Dec. 30, 1975; s. Earl Dennison Woods (died May 5, 2006) and Kultida W., m. Elin Nordegren, Oct. 5, 2004; children: Sam Alexis Woods, Charlie Axel Woods. Student, Stanford U., Calif., 1994—96. Profl. golfer, 1996—; winner Optimist Internat. Jr. World Championship, 1984, 1985, 1988, 1989, 1990, 1991, Ins. Youth Golf Classic (youngest ever to win), 1990, Ins. Youth Golf Classic, 1992, CIF-So. Calif. HS Invitational Championship, 1991, So. Calif. Jr. Championship, 1991, PING/Phoenix Jr. Championship, 1991, 1992, Edgewood Tahoe Jr. Classic, 1991, LA City Jr. Championship, 1991, Orange Bowl Jr. Internat. Championship, 1991, US Jr. Amateur Championship (youngest ever to win), 1991, US Jr. Amateur Championship, 1992, US Jr. Amateur Championship (only golfer to win three times), 1993, Nabisco Mission Hills Desert Jr. Championship, 1992, Pro Gear San Antonio Shootout, 1992, So. Calif. Jr. Best Ball Championship, 1993, US Amateur Championship (youngest ever to win, largest comeback ever), 1994, US Amateur Championship, 1995, 1996, Western Amateur Championship, 1994, So. Calif. Golf Assn. Amateur Championship, 1994, Pacific N.W. Amateur Championship, 1994, William Tucker Invitational, 1994, Jerry Pate Invitational, 1994, Stanford Invitational, 1995, Walt Disney World/Oldsmobile Classic, 1996, Las Vegas Invitational, 1996, NCAA Championship, 1996, John A. Burns Invitational, 1996, Cleve. Golf Championship, 1996, Tri-Match Championship (Stanford U., Ariz. State U., U. Ariz.), 1996, Cougar Classic, 1996, Pac-10 Championship (shot course record 61), 1996, NCAA West Regional, 1996, Masters Tournament, 1997, 2001, 2002, 2005, Mercedes Championships, 1997, 2000, Asian Honda Classic, 1997, GTE Byron Nelson Classic, 1997, Motorola Western Open, 1997, 1999, Johnnie Walker Classic, 1998, 2000, BellSouth Classic, 1998, PGA Grand Slam, 1998, 1999, 2000, 2001, 2002, 2005, 2006, Meml. Tournament, 1999, 2000, 2001, 2009, PGA Championship, 1999, 2000, 2006, 2007, Buick Invitational, 1999, 2003, 2005, 2006, 2007, 2008, Deutsche Bank-SAP Open, 1999, 2001, 2002, WGC NEC Invitational, 1999, 2000, 2001, 2005, Nat. Car Rental Classic, 1999, Tour Championship, 1999, WGC Am. Express Championship, 1999, 2002, 2003, 2005, 2006, WGC Am. CA Championship (formerly WGC Am. Express Championship), 2007, World Cup individual and team titles (with Mark O'Meara), 1999, AT&T Pebble Beach Pro-Am, 2000, Bay Hill Invitational, 2000, 2001, 2002, 2003, Arnold Palmer Invitational, 2008, 2009, US Open Championship, 2000, 2002, 2008, Brit. Open Championship, 2000, 2005, 2006, Bell Can. Open, 2000, World Cup (with David Duval), 2000, The Players Championship, 2001, Williams World Challenge, 2001, Buick Open, 2002, 2006, 2009, WGC Accenture Match Play Championship, 2003, 2004, 2008, Western Open, 2003, Ford Championship, 2005, 2006, WGC Bridgestone Invitational, 2006, 2007, 2009, Deutsche Bank Championship, 2006, Target World Challenge, 2006, 2007, Wachovia Championship, 2007, BMW Championship, 2007, Dubai Desert Classic, 2008. Mem. US Team World Amateur Team Championships, Versailles, France, 1994, Walker Cup Match, Porthcawl, Wales, 1995, Ryder Cup, 1997, 99, 2002, 04, 06, Dunhill Cup, 1998, President's Cup, 1998, 2000, 03, 05; founder, chmn. Tiger Woods Design, 2006—. Co-founder (with father, Earl) Tiger Woods Found. 1996-; With the Tiger Woods Foundation, initiated and supported community-based programs that promote the health, education and welfare to America's children (programs include: Tiger Woods Learning Center, Southern California, started in 2006, Start Something (partners with Target Corporation), started in 2000, Tiger Woods Foundation National Junior Golf Team, Target World Challenge (also host), Tiger Jam (AT&T-sponsored event) (also host) and various grant/scholarship programs). Recipient Dial award, 1993, Jack Nicklaus Trophy, PGA Am., Golf Writers Assn. Am., 1997, 1999, 2000, 2001, 2002, 2003, 2005, 2006, ESPY award, Best Male Athlete, ESPN, 1998, 2000, 2001, 2002, 2008, ESPY award, Best Golfer, 2005, 2006, 2007, 2008, ESPY award, Best Championship Performance, 2008, Mark H. McCormack award as No. 1 player on world ranking, 1998—, Byron Nelson award, PGA Tour, 1999—2003, 2005—07, Golf Digest, 2008, Vardon Trophy, PGA of Am., 1999, 2000, 2001, 2002, 2003, Charlie Bartlett award, Golf Writers Assn. Am., 2007; named Player of Yr., Am. Jr. Golf Assn., 1991, Golf Digest, 1991, 1992, Golf World, 1993, 1994, LA Times, 1994, Orange County, 1994, PGA Tour Player of Yr., 1997, 1999, 2000, 2001, 2002, 2003, 2005, 2006, 2007, Player of Yr., Golf Writers Assn. Am., 2006, So. Calif. Player of Yr., 1991, 1992, 1993, Nat. Amateur of Yr., Titleist-Golfweek, 1991, 1992, Orange County League MVP, 1994, Pac-10 Player of Yr., 1995, 1996, First Team All-Am., 1995, 1996, Sportsman of Yr., Sports Illustrated, 1996, 2000, Reuters, 2000, PGA Tour Rookie of Yr., 1996, Fred Haskins Coll. Player of Yr., 1996, Jack Nicklaus Coll. Player of Yr., 1996, Male Athlete of Yr., AP, 1997, 1999, 2000, 2006, World Sportsman of Yr., World Sports Acad., 1999, Most Powerful Person in Sports, Sporting News, 2000, World Champion of Champions, L'Equipe, France, 2000; named one of Most Influential People in the World of Sports, Bus. Week, 2007, 2008, The 100 Most Powerful Celebrities, Forbes.com, 2008, The World's Most Influential People, TIME mag., 2009; named to First Team Rolex Jr. All Am., 1991, 1992, The Calif. Hall of Fame, 2007, Power 150, Ebony mag., 2008. Achievements include winning 14 major PGA Tour events including Masters Tournament, 1997, 2001, 2002, 2005, PGA Championship, 1999, 2000, 2006, 2007; US Open Championship, 2000, 2002, 2008, Brit. Open Championship, 2000, 2005, 2006; youngest player, first African Am., first Asian Am., and having largest margin of victory (12 strokes) to win Masters Tournament, 1997; first player ever to win US Open, Brit. Open and PGA Championship in same yr., 2000; first player ever to hold all 4 major golf championships at the same time, 2001; ranked number 1 player in world for a record 264 consecutive weeks, 1999-2004; youngest to win 50 PGA Tour titles with victory at Buick Open, 2006; winner of the inaugural FedEx Cup, 2007; tied with Ben Hogan for third place all-time on career PGA Tour wins list. Office: PGA PO Box 109601 100 Avenue Of Champions Palm Beach Gardens FL 33418-3665*

WOODSIDE, DENNIS, information technology executive; BS in Indsl. Rels., Cornell U., NYC, 1991; JD, Stanford Law Sch., Calif., 1995. Law clk. to Dennis G. Jacobs US Ct. Appeals (2nd cir.) NY; mergers & acquisitions atty. Munger, Tolles & Olson LLP, 1996—98; assoc. ptnr. McKinsey & Co., 1998—2003; dir. bus. ops. Google Inc., 2003—05, mng. dir. emerging markets, 2005—06, v.p., mng. dir. UK, Benelux & Ireland Dublin, 2006—09, v.p. Americas NYC, 2009—. Office: Google Inc Hdqs 1600 Amphitheatre Pkwy Mountain View CA 94043 Office Phone: 650-253-0000. Office Fax: 650-253-0001.

WOODSIDE, FRANK C., III, lawyer, educator, physician; b. Glen Ridge, NJ, Apr. 18, 1944; s. Frank C. and Dorothea (Poulin) W.; m. Julia K. Moses, Nov. 15, 1974; children: Patrick Michael, Christopher Ryan. BS, Ohio State U., Columbus, 1966, JD, 1969; MD, U. Cin., 1973. Diplomate Am. Bd. Legal Medicine, Am. Bd. Forensic Medicine. Mem. Dinsmore & Shohl, Cin.; clin. prof. pediats. emeritus U. Cin., 1992—. Adj. prof. law U. Cin., 1973—. Editor: Drug Product Liability, 1985—. Fellow Am. Coll. Legal Medicine, Am. Coll. Forensic Examiners, Am. Soc. Hosp. Attys., Soc. Ohio Hosp. Attys.; mem. ABA, FBA, Ohio Bar Assn., Internat. Assn. Def. Counsel, Def. Rsch. Inst. (chmn. drug and med. svc. com. 1988-91), Cin. Bar Assn. Office: Dinsmore & Shohl 1900 Chemed Ctr 255 E 5th St Cincinnati OH 45202-4700 Home Phone: 513-821-7889; Office Phone: 513-977-8266. Business E-Mail: frank.woodside@dinslaw.com.

WOODSIDE, LISA NICOLE, retired humanities educator; b. Portland, Oreg., Sept. 7, 1944; d. Lee and Emma (Wenstrom) W. Student, Reed Coll., Portland, Oreg., 1962—65; MA, U. Chgo., 1968; PhD, Bryn Mawr Coll., Pa., 1972; cert. Inst. Ednl. Mgmt., Harvard U., Cambridge, Mass., 1979; MA, West Chester U., Pa., 1994. Cert. tchr. ecstatic trance postures Cuyamungue Inst., N.Mex., 2003, wellness counseling, creative energy options. Mem. dean's staff Bryn Mawr Coll., 1970-72; asst. prof. Widener U., Chester, Pa., 1972-77, assoc. prof. humanities, 1978-83, asst. dean student svcs., 1972-76, assoc. dean, 1976-79, dean, 1979-83; acad. dean, prof. humanities Holy Family Coll., Phila., 1983—2008, v.p., dean acad. affairs, prof. humanities, 1990-98, prof. humanities, 1998—2008, prof. emeritus, 2008—. Cons. State NJ Edn. Dept., 1990, Houghton-Mifflin for English reader, 2000; cons., reader Test of Spoken English Ednl. Testing Svc., 2002—04; accreditor Commn. on Higher Edn., Mid. States Assn., 1977—83, 1994. Co-author: New Age Spirituality: An Assessment. City commr. for cmty. rels., Chester, 1980-83; mem. Adult Edn. Coun. Phila. Recipient Crasilneck award for best paper Am. Soc. Clin. Hypnosis; Am. Assn. Papyrology grantee Bryn Mawr Coll., S. Maude Kaemmerling fellow. Mem.: MLA, AAUW (univ. rep. 1975—83), APA, Pa. Coll. Tchrs. Assn., Mid. States Classics Assn., Audubon Soc., Psi Chi, Alpha Sigma Lambda, Phi Eta Sigma. Personal E-mail: liswoodside@comcast.net.

WOOD-SMITH, DONALD, plastic surgeon; b. Sydney, June 30, 1937; s. William Frederick and Vera Mary; children: Christina Margaret, Donald William, Phillip Raynor. MB, BChir, Sydney U., 1954. Diplomate Am. Bd. Plastic Surgery. Surg. resident Lewisham Hosp., Sydney, 1954—57, Royal Marsden Hosp., 1957-58; resident plastic surgery NYU Hosp. Med. Ctr., 1960-64, asst., assoc. and attending surgeon, 1964-92; prof. plastic surgery Columbia Presbyn. Med. Ctr., 1991—. Vis. surgeon Bellevue Hosp., 1964-92, London Ind. Hosp., 1999-2005; chmn. plastic surgery Manhattan Eye Ear and Throat Hosp., 1975-77; assoc. prof. plastic surgery NYU, 1977-84, prof., 1984-92; surgeon, dir. plastic surgery Manhattan Eye Ear and Throat Hosp., 1977-84; cons.

plastic surgeon NY Eye and Ear Infirmary, chmn. dept. plastic and reconstructive surgery, 1984— Author: Nursing Care of the Plastic Surgery Patient, 1967, Cosmetic Facial Surgery, 1973; contbr. articles to med. jours. Fellow ACS, Royal Coll. Surgeons of Edinburgh; mem. Am. Assn. Plastic Surgeons, Am. Soc. Plastic Surgeons, Am. Soc. Maxillofacial Surgeons, NY Acad. Medicine, Brit. Assn. Plastic, Reconstructive & Aesthetic Surgeons. Office: 830 Park Ave New York NY 10021-2757 Address: 56 Hanley St London WIG 9QA England Home Phone: 212-744-2225; Office Phone: 212-744-2224. Personal E-mail: dw830@aol.com.

WOODSOME, EDWIN VALENTINE, JR., lawyer; AB summa cum laude, Holy Cross Coll., 1968; JD magna cum laude, Harvard U., 1971. Bar: Mass. 1972, Calif. 1973, D.C. 1973. Law clk. to Hon. James R. Browning US Ct. Appeals (9th cir.), 1971—72; ptnr. Orrick, Herrington & Sutcliffe LLP, LA, 2003—. Mem.: State Bar Calif., D.C. Bar, ABA (litig. sect., environ. sect., employment sect.), L.A. County Bar Assn. Office: Orrick Herrington & Sutcliffe LLP 777 S Figueroa St Ste 3200 Los Angeles CA 90017 Office Phone: 213-612-2398. Business E-Mail: ewoodsome@orrick.com.

WOODSON, CHARLES C., professional football player; b. Fremont, Ohio, Oct. 7, 1976; Attended, U. Mich., Ann Arbor, 1995—98. Cornerback Oakland Raiders, 1998—2005, Green Bay Packers, 2006—. Recipient Jim Thorpe award, 1997, Bronko Nagurski award, 1997, Heisman Meml. Trophy, 1997; named Freshman of Yr., Big 10 Conf., 1995, First Team All-Conf., 1995—97, Defensive Player of Yr., 1997, Chevrolet, 1996, 1997, Walter Camp Player of Yr., 1997, Player of Yr., Sporting News, 1997, Defensive Rookie of Yr., AP, Pro Football Weekly, Football Digest, 1998, First Team All-Pro, AP, 1999; named to Am. Football Conf. Pro Bowl Team, NFL, 1998—2001, Nat. Football Conf. Pro Bowl Team, 2008. Avocations: bowling, reading. Office: Green Bay Packers Lambeau Field Atrium 1265 Lombardi Ave Green Bay WI 54304*

WOODSON, GAYLE ELLEN, otolaryngologist; b. Galveston, Tex., June 9, 1950; d. Clinton Eldon and Nancy Jean (Stephens) W.; m. Kevin Thomas Robbins; children: Nicholas, Gregory, Sarah. BA, Rice U., 1972; MD, Baylor Coll. Medicine, 1975. Diplomate Am. Bd. Otolaryngology (bd. dirs., residency rev. com. for otolaryngology, exam. chair). Fellow Baylor Coll. Medicine, Houston, 1976, Inst. Laryngology & Otology, London, 1981-82; asst. prof. Baylor Coll. Medicine, 1982-87; asst. attending Harris County Hosp. Dist., Houston, 1982-86; with courtesy staff Saint Luke's Episcopal Hosp., Houston, 1982-87; assoc. attending The Methodist Hosp., Houston, 1982-87; asst. prof. U. Calif. Med. Sch., San Diego, 1987-89; chief otolaryngology VA Med. Ctr., San Diego, 1987-92; assoc. prof. U. Calif. Sch. Med., San Diego, 1989-92; prof. otolaryngology U. Tenn., Memphis, 1993—2000, So. Ill. U., 2003—. Numerous presentations and lectures in field. Contbr. numerous articles and abstracts to med. jours., also videotapes. Recipient deRoldes award, Am. Layrngol. Assn., 2003. Fellow ACS (bd. govs.), Royal Coll. Surgeons, Soc. Univ. Otolaryngologists (past pres.), Am. Soc. Head and Neck Surgery, Am. Laryngol. Assn. (pres.-elect de Roaldes award, 2003), Triological Soc.; mem. AMA, Am. Acad. Otolaryngology-Head and Neck Surgery (bd. dirs. 1993-96), Am. Med. Women's Assn. (past pres. Memphis br.), Soc. Head and Neck Oncologists Eng., Am. Physiol. Soc., Assn. Women Surgeons, Am. Soc. Head and Neck Surgeons, Johns Hopkins Soc. Scholars, Collegium OtoRhinolaryngolicum Amicus Sacrum. Office: Southern Illinois Univ PO Box 19662 Springfield IL 62794-9662 Home Phone: 217-726-0026. Business E-Mail: gwoodson@siumed.edu.

WOODSON, MIKE, professional basketball coach; b. Indpls., Mar. 24, 1958; m. Terri Woodson; children: Alexis, Mariah. Grad., Ind. U., 1980. Profl. basketball player NY Knicks, 1981—82, NJ Nets, 1982, Kans. City Kings (now Sacramento Kings), 1982—86, LA Clippers, 1986—88, Houston Rockets, 1988—91, Cleve. Cavaliers, 1991, asst. coach, 1999—2001, Milw. Bucks, 1996—99, Phila. 76ers, 2001—03, Detroit Pistons, 2003—04; head coach Atlanta Hawks, 2004—. Office: Atlanta Hawks Centennial Tower 101 Marietta St NW Ste 1900 Atlanta GA 30303*

WOODSON, RILEY DONALD, thoracic and cardiovascular surgeon, lawyer; b. Winfield, Kans., Dec. 24, 1931; s. Riley Delma and Virginia Marie Woodson (Stepmother), Ruth Benedict Woodson; married; children: Riley David, Wade Clinton. BA, U. Kans., 1953, MD, 1956; JD, U. Toledo, 1984. Bar: Ohio 1984, US Dist. Ct. (no. dist. Ohio) 1985; Med. Licensure Kans., 1956, Calif., 1961, Ariz., 1962, Ohio, 1968, diplomate Am. Bd. Surgery, 1964, Am. Bd. Thoracic Surgery, 1968, Am. Bd. Cardiothoracic Surgery, 1978. Intern Parkland Meml. Hosp., Southwestern Med. Sch., Dallas, 1956—57; resident in gen. surgery U. Minn. Hosps., Mpls., 1957—63; resident in thoracic and cardiovasc. surgery U. Oreg. Med. Sch., Portland, 1965—67; asst. prof. surgery, asst. chief, thoracic and cardiovasc. surgery U. Ill. Sch. Medicine, Chgo., 1967—69; assoc. prof. surgery, chief, thoracic and cardiovasc. surgery Med. U. Ohio, Toledo, 1969—78, clin. assoc. prof. surgery, 1979—; pvt. practice Toledo, 1978—92, Palm Springs, Calif., 1993—96; contract med. malpractice case analyst Jacobson, Maynard, Tuschman & Kalur, LLC, Toledo, 1997—98; ptnr. Sodeman, Kirkhope & Woodson, LLP, Toledo, 2001—. Pres. Ohio Coll. Chest Physicians, Columbus, 1971—72; medicolegal case cons., Toledo, Port Clinton, Ohio, 1975—2006; mem. jud. and profl. rels. Ohio State Med. Assn., Columbus, 1986—90; bd. dirs. Palm Springs Acad. Medicine, 1994—96. Author 29 works in nat. and internat. med. and legal publs. Nat. basic and advanced CPR faculty Am. Heart Assn., 1976—83; exec. com. mem., bd. trustees sec., med. dir. Regional Emergency Med. Svcs. NW Ohio, Toledo, 1975—79; trustee NW Ohio Heart Assn., Toledo, 1976—80. Capt. USNR, 1963—88. Recipient Owl Soc., U. Kans., 1952, Sachem Cir., Omicron Delta Kappa (Pres.), 1953, Russell Hayden Outstanding Med. Student Rsch. medal, 1956, Outstanding Resident Rsch. award, Portland Surg. Soc., 1967, Ann. Outstanding Med. Writing award, NW Medicine, 1967, Golden Apple for Tchg. Excellence, Med. U. Ohio, 1972, Outstanding Physician Vol., NW Ohio Heart Assn., 1980; Summerfield scholar, U. Kans., 1949, Nat. Honor Soc. scholar, 1949, Athletic scholarship Basketball and Track, 1949. Fellow: ACS (sr.), Soc. Vascular Surgery (disting. fellow), Am. Coll. Legal Medicine (sr.), Am. Coll. Angiology (sr.), Am. Coll. Chest Physicians (sr.; gov. 1972—78), Am. Coll. Cardiology (sr.); mem.: AMA, AAUP (sr.), ABA, Am. Soc. Law and Medicine, Soc. Internat. Surgery, Undersea Med. Soc., Assn. Academic Surgery, Assn. Mil. Surgeons of US, Toledo Surg. Soc. (founding mem.), Am. Thoracic Soc. (sr.), Soc. Thoracic Surgeons (sr.), Am. Assn. Surgery of Trauma (sr.), Am. Assn. Vascular Surgery (sr.), Toledo Acad. Med., Ohio Med. Assn., Ottawa County Bar Assn., Toledo Bar Assn. (mem. JD/MD and continuing legal edn. commns. 1985—), Ohio Bar Assn., U. Kans. Varsity K Club, Shrine, Scottish Rite, Knights Templar, Phi Kappa Phi, MENSA, Beta Theta Pi (U. Kans. chpt. pres. 1953). Office: 4445-E Marin Pines Port Clinton OH 43452 Office Phone: 419-797-7311. Office Fax: 419-797-7311. Personal E-mail: rd_woodson2@hotmail.com.

WOODSON, RODERICK KEVIN, sportscaster, football coach, retired professional football player; b. Fort Wayne, Ind., Mar. 10, 1965; Attended, Purdue U., West Lafayette, Ind. Cornerback Pitts. Steelers, 1987—96, San Francisco 49ers, 1997, Balt. Ravens, 1998—2002, Oakland Raiders, 2002—04; ret.; defensive secondary coach Valley Christian Sr. High, Dublin, Calif.; analyst, NFL Total Access NFL Network. Named 1st Team All-Pro, AP, 1989, 1990, 1992—94, 2002, Defensive Player of Yr., 1993; named to Am. Football Conf. Pro Bowl Team, NFL, 1989—94, 1996, 1999—2002, NFL 75th Anniversary All-Time Team, 1994, Pro Football Hall of Fame, 2009. Achievements include leading the NFL in: yards per kick return, 1989; kick off returns, 1991; interceptions, 1999, 2002; member of Super Bowl XXXV winning Baltimore Ravens, 2001. Office: Valley Christian Sr High 7500 Inspiration Dr Dublin CA 94568*

WOODS-TAYLOR, CLEORA LYNESIA, mathematics educator, consultant; d. Ray Clayton and Clara Lynn Woods; children: Lynesia Raychelle Taylor, Christa Lanetria Taylor. BS, Prairie View A&M U., Tex., 1991; MA, U. Mo., Kansas City, 2003, EdS in Sch. Adminstrn., 2008. Cert. tchr. Mo., 2003. Adj. instr. algebra Houston C.C. (NW Campus), 1992; instr. algebra Houston Ind. Sch. Dist., 1992—93, Faith Acad., Kansas City, Mo., 1995—99, Lincoln Coll. Prep. Acad., Kansas City, Mo., 2001—06; dir. math. Kansas City Sch. Dist., Mo., 2006—. Math cons. Mo. Math Acad. Dir. of performing arts dept. Harvest Ch., Kansas City, Mo., 1995—2001. Mem.: Alpha Kappa Alpha. Office: Bd Edn 1211 McGee Ste 905A Kansas City MO 64109 Office Phone: 816-418-7478. Office Fax: 816-418-7539. Business E-Mail: ctaylor@kcmsd.net.

WOODSWORTH, ANNE, retired academic administrator, librarian; came to U.S., 1983; d. Thorvald Ernst and Roma Yrsa Lindner; 1 child, Yrsa Anne. BFA, U. Man., 1962; BLS, U. Toronto, 1964, MLS, 1969; PhD, U. Pitts., 1987. Edn. libr. U. Man., 1964—65; reference libr. Winnipeg Pub. Libr., 1965—67; reference libr. sci. and medicine dept. U. Toronto, 1967—68; med. libr. Toronto We. Hosp., 1969—70; rsch. asst. to chief libr. U. Toronto, 1970—71, head reference dept., 1971—74; pers. dir. Toronto Pub. Libr., 1975—78; dir. librs. York U., Toronto, 1978—83; assoc. provost for librs. U. Pitts., 1983—88, assoc. prof., 1988—91; dean Palmer Sch. Libr. and Info. Sci., L.I. U., 1991—98; dean Sch. Edn. Dowling Coll., Oakdale, NY, 1999—2000; dean sch. info. and libr. sci. Pratt Inst., Bklyn., 2000—02, acting provost, 2002—03; provost Katherine Gibbs Sch., Melville, NY, 2003; learning sys. advisor Bklyn. Pub. Libr., 2003—06. Pres. Anne Lindner Ltd., 1974—83; rsch. libraries adv. coun. OCLC, 1984—87. Author: The Alternative Press in Canada, 1972, Leadership and Research Libraries, 1988, Patterns and Options for Managing Information Technology on Campus, 1990, Library Cooperation and Networks, 1991, Managing the Economics of Leasing and Contracting Out Information Services, 1993, Reinvesting in the Information Job Family, 1993, The Future of Education for Librarianship: Looking Forward from the Past, 1994. Sec., mem. bd. trustees Katharine Gibbs Sch., L.I., 2003-04; dir. Sr. Fellows Inst., 1995-98; trustee L.I. Librs. Resources Coun., 1993-96; bd. dirs. Population Rsch. Found., Toronto, 1980-83. Grantee Can. Coun., 1974, Ont. Arts Coun., 1974, Coun. on Libr. Resources, 1986, 88, 91, 93; UCLA sr. fellow, 1985. Mem. ALA (com. on accreditation 1990-94, councillor 1993-97), Can. Assn. Rsch. Librs. (pres. 1981-83), Assn. Rsch. Librs. (bd. dirs. 1981-84, v.p. 1984-85, pres. 1985-86), Assn. Coll. and Rsch. Librs. (chair K.G. Saur award com. 1991-93), Assn. for Libr. and Info. Sci. Edn. (chair honors and awards com. 1995, bd. dirs. 1998-99, v.p. 1998-99), Am. Soc. Higher Edn., Internet Soc., Am. Soc. Info. Sci. (convenor 1999-2000), Archons of Colophon. Personal E-mail: alwoods@intergate.com.

WOODWARD, BOB (ROBERT UPSHUR WOODWARD), editor, writer; b. Geneva, Ill., Mar. 26, 1943; s. Alfred E. and Jane (Upshur) Woodward; m. Elsa Walsh, Nov. 25, 1989; children: Tali, Diana. BA, Yale U., 1965. Reporter Montgomery County Sentinel, Md., 1970-71, The Washington Post, 1971-78, met. editor, 1979-81, asst. mng. editor, 1981—2008, assoc. editor, 2008—. Author: Wired: The Short Life and Fast Times of John Belushi, 1984, Veil: The Secret Wars of the CIA, 1981-1987, 1987, The Commanders: The Pentagon and the First Gulf War, 1989-1991, 1991, The Agenda: Inside the Clinton White House, 1994, The Choice: How Bill Clinton Won, 1996, Shadow: Five Presidents and the Legacy of Watergate, 1974-1999, 1999, Maestro: Greenspan's Fed and the American Boom, 2000, Bush At War: Inside the Bush White House, 2002, Plan of Attack, 2004, The Secret Man: The Story of Watergate's Deep Throat, 2005, State of Denial: Bush at War, Part III, 2006, The War Within: A Secret White House History 2006-2008, 2008; co-author: (with Carl Bernstein) All the President's Men, 1974, The Final Days, 1976, (with Scott Armstrong) The Brethren: Inside the Supreme Court, 1979. Served with USN, 1965—70. Office: Washington Post Co 1150 15th St NW Washington DC 20071-0002

WOODWARD, CLINTON BENJAMIN, JR., civil engineer, educator; b. El Paso, Tex., Mar. 4, 1943; s. Clinton Benjamin and Iris Elizabeth (Zant) Woodward; m. Willie Ann Shollenbarger, June 14, 1969 (div. June 1976); m. Deon Bennett Speir, Nov. 22, 1979; 1 child, Clinton Benjamin III. BSET, N.Mex. State U., 1976, MSCE, 1984, PhD, 1986; MS, Colo. State U., Ft. Collins, 1978. Registered profl. engr., N.Mex. From asst. mgr. to pres. Woodward Enterprises Co., Inc., Las Cruces, N.Mex., 1968-82; prof., program dir. structural engring. N.Mex. State U. Las Cruces Campus, 1987—2007; emiretus prof., cons., 2008—. Contbr. articles to profl. jours. With USN, 1962-66. Mem. ASCE, Am. Soc. for Engring. Edn., Forest Products Soc., Soc. Wood Sci. and Tech., Tau Beta Phi, Chi Epsilon, Phi Kappa Phi, Sigma Xi. Avocations: camping, fly fishing. Business E-Mail: cwoodwar@nmsu.edu.

WOODWARD, DAVID REID, retired history professor; b. Clarksville, Tenn., Oct. 9, 1939; s. Felix Grundy Woodward and Laura Henrietta Miller; m. Martha Vera Cobb, Feb. 26, 1966; 1 child, Catherine Cobb Irving. BA, Austin Peay U., Clarksville, 1961; MA, U. Ga., Athens, 1963, PhD, 1965. Instr., history Converse Coll., Spartansburg, SC, 1965; asst. prof. history Tex. A & M U., College Station, 1965—70; assoc. prof. Marshall U., Huntington, W.Va., 1970—73, prof., 1973—2006. Author: (book) Lloyd George and the Generals, Military Correspondence of Field-Marshall Sir William Robertson; co-author: (with dr. robert maddox) America and World War I: A Selected Annotated Bibliography of English-Language Sources; author: (book) Hell in the Holy Land: World War I in the Middle East, and numerous others; contbr. articles to profl. jours., chapters to books. Recipient COLA award for Outstanding Tchg., Coll. Liberal Arts, Marshall U., 1999, Disting. Svc. award, Marshall U., 2004—05. Home: 1802 Wiltshire Blvd Huntington WV 25701

WOODWARD, JACKIE, marketing professional; B in Journalism, U. Mo., Columbia, 1987. Acct. supr. GolinHarris (subs. Interpublic Grp.), 1983—87; gen. mgr. consumer products UltimateBid.com, 2000—01; v.p. global mktg. McDonald's Corp., 2001—06; v.p. media/mktg. svcs. Miller Brewing Co., 2006—08, MillerCoors LLC (merger of Miller and Coors Brewing Cos.), 2008—. Mem.: Media & Entertainment Profls. Office: MillerCoors LLC Hdqs 1225 17th St Denver CO 80202 Office Phone: 303-279-6565. Office Fax: 303-277-5415.*

WOODWARD, JAMES FRANKLIN, science educator; b. Boston, Dec. 22, 1941; s. William Redin and Edith Jones Woodward; life ptnr. Carole Schulze. BA, Middlebury Coll., 1964; MS, NYU, 1969; PhD, U. Denver, 1972. Prof. Calif. State U., Fullerton, 1972—2005, prof. emeritus, 2005—. Contbr. articles to profl. jours. Mem.: AIAA, NY Acad. Scis., History Sci. Soc., Internat. Soc. Gen. Relativity and Gravitation (life). Independent. Achievements include patents for propulsion based on transient inertial effects (Mach effects). Avocations: hiking, flamenco guitar. Office Fax: 657-278-5810. Business E-Mail: jwoodward@fullerton.edu.

WOODWARD, JAMES HOYT, academic administrator, engineering educator; b. Sanford, Fla., Nov. 24, 1939; s. James Hoyt and Edith Pearl (Breeden) Woodward; m. Martha Ruth Hill, Oct. 13, 1956; children: Connie, Tracey, Wade. BS in Aero. Engring. with honors, Ga. Tech. Inst., 1962, MS in Aero. Engring., 1963, PhD in Engring. Mechanics, 1967; MBA, U. Ala.-Birmingham, 1973. Asst. prof. engring. mechanics USAF Acad., Colo., 1965-67, assoc. prof. Colo., 1967-68; asst. prof. NC State U., 1968-69; assoc. prof. engring. U. Ala., Birmingham, 1969-70, assoc. prof., 1973-77, prof. civil engring., 1977-89, asst. v.p., 1973-78, dean engring., 1978-84, acad. v.p., 1984-89; chancellor U. NC, Charlotte, 1989—2005, chancellor emeritus, prof. engring., 2005—; interim chancellor NC State U., Raleigh, 2009—. Dir. tech. devel. Rust Engring. Co., Birmingham, 1970—73; cons. in field. Contbr. articles to profl. jours. With USAF, 1965—68. Mem.: Am. Soc. Engring. Edn., Sigma Xi. Methodist. Office: U NC Charlotte Chancellors Emeriti Office 9201 Univ City Blvd Charlotte NC 28223-0002 also: NC State U Office of Chancellor Raleigh NC 27695 Office Phone: 704-687-2484, 919-515-2191. Business E-Mail: etdeese@uncc.edu. E-mail: chancellor@ncsu.edu.*

WOODWARD, JANET CLAIRE, school librarian, educator; b. LA, June 2, 1953; d. Donald and Nancy Woodward; m. David Sokal; children: Jacob, Ira. BA, Antioch Coll., Yellow Springs, Ohio; MA, U. Wash., Seattle, 1993. Cert. tchr. Wash. State, 1983, media libr. Nat. Bd., 2005. Tchr. Seattle Sch. Dist., 1986—; sch. libr. Garfield HS, Seattle, 1998—. Instr. U. Wash., 2006—. Com. mem. Garfield HS Found., Seattle, 2002—08. Mem.: ACLU (students advisor 2004—09). Democrat. Office: Garfield HS 400 23rd Ave Seattle WA 98122 Business E-Mail: jwoodward@seattleschools.org.

WOODWARD, JASON E., plant pathologist, educator; s. Hugh and Carrie Woodward; m. Jennifer Woodward; children: Jacob, Jack. BS, Southwestern Okla. State U., Weatherford, 1999; MS, Okla. State U., Stillwater, 2002; PhD, U. Ga., Athens, 2006. Asst. prof., ext. plant pathologist Tex. AgriLIFE Ext., Lubbock, 2006—; asst. prof. Tex. Tech U., Lubbock, 2006—. Office: Tex Agri Life Ext Svc 1102 E Fm 1294 Lubbock TX 79403

WOODWARD, JOANNE GIGNILLIAT, actress; b. Thomasville, Ga., Feb. 27, 1930; d. Wade and Elinor (Trimmier) W.; m. Paul Newman, Jan. 29, 1958; children: Elinor Terese, Melissa Stewart, Clea Olivia. Student, La. State U., 1947-49; grad., Neighborhood Playhouse Dramatic Sch., NYC. First TV appearance in Penny, Robert Montgomery Presents, 1952; understudy broadway play Picnic, 1953; appeared in plays Baby Want a Kiss, 1964, Candida, 1982, The Glass Menagerie, Williamstown Theatré Festival, 1985, Sweet Bird of Youth, Toronto, 1988; motion pictures include Three Faces of Eve, 1957 (Acad. award Best Actress, Nat. Bd. Rev. award, Fgn. Press award), Count Three and Pray, 1955, Long Hot Summer, 1958, No Down Payment, 1957, Sound and the Fury, 1959, A Kiss Before Dying, 1956, Rally Round the Flag Boys, 1958, The Fugitive Kind, 1960, Paris Blues, 1961, The Stripper, 1963, A New Kind of Love, 1963, A Big Hand for the Little Lady, 1965, A Fine Madness, 1965, Rachel, Rachel, 1968, Winning, 1969, WUSA, 1970, They Might Be Giants, 1971, The Effect of Gamma Rays on Man-in-the-Moon Marigolds, 1972 (Cannes Film Festival award), Summer Wishes, Winter Dreams, 1973 (N.Y. Film Critics award), The Drowning Pool, 1975, The End, 1978, Harry and Son, 1984, Glass Menagerie, 1987, Mr. & Mrs. Bridge, 1990, Philadelphia, 1993, The Age of Innocence (voice), 1993, My Knees Were Jumping: Remembering the Kindertransports, (voice) 1998; TV appearances include All the Way Home; TV-film appearances in Sybil, 1976, Come Back, Little Sheba, 1977, See How She Runs, 1978 (Emmy award), Streets of L.A., 1979, The Shadow Box, 1980, Crisis at Central High, 1981, Do You Remember Love?, 1985 (Emmy award), Blind Spot, 1993 (Emmy nomination, Lead Actress - Miniseries, 1993), Breathing Lessons, 1994 (Emmy nomination, Lead Actress - Special, 1994, Golden Globe award, Best Actress), James Dean: A Portrait, 1996; narrator film documentary Angel Dust, TV documentary on Group Theatre, 1989. Co-recipient (with Paul Newman) Kennedy Ctr. Honors for Lifetime Achievement in the Performing Arts. Democrat. Episcopalian. Office: Icm Artists 470 Park Ave S New York NY 10016-6819*

WOODWARD, KIRK, theater director; b. Louisville, Nov. 22, 1947; s. Ernest and Mary Hardin (Morris) W.; m. Patricia Ann Woodward, June 23, 1984; children: Erin, Heather, Craig. BA, Washington and Lee U., 1969; MBA in Health Care Adminstrn., U. Phoenix, 2008. Cert. project mgmt. profl. 2009. Acting instr. NYC Housing Authority, 1975; dir. acting studies Pushcart Players, Verona, NJ, 1979-82; dir. New Scripts Project, NYC, 1986; pres. The Attic Ensemble, Jersey City, 1982-85; programmer analyst Time Warner Inc., NYC, 1985—2001; mng. dir. Stage Left, Inc., NYC, 1986-95; instr. Adult Sch. Montclair, 1998—. Tech. writer Vis. Nurse Svc., NYC, 2001—; artistic dir. Troupe of Vagabonds Theatre, Bloomfield, NJ, 2002—; instr. Performers Theater Workshop, 1989—2004. Author: (play) Who's Who in Murder, 1990 (1st pl. award Hardin County Playwriting Competition), The Art of Writing Reviews, 2009. Elder Presbyn. Ch. Upper Montclair. 1st lt. USAR, 1970-72, Korea. Lt. US Army, 1970—73. Mem. Soc. for Tech. Comm., Dramatists Guild Am., Delta Upsilon. Presbyterian. Avocation: piano. Home: 25 Melrose Pl Montclair NJ 07042-2531 Office: VNSNY 5 Penn Plz New York NY 10001 Home Phone: 973-744-5755; Office Phone: 212-609-5509. Personal E-mail: kwdwd@aim.com.

WOODWARD, LAWRENCE H., lawyer; b. Radford, Va., May 29, 1957; married; 2 children. BA, Hampden-Sydney Coll., Va., 1979; JD, U. Richmond, Va., 1982. Bar: Va. 1982, US Ct. Mil. Appeals and US Dist. Ct. 1984, Ea. Dist. Va., US Supreme Ct., US Ct. Claims. Shareholder Shuttleworth, Ruloff, Swain, Haddad & Morecock, PC, Va. Beach, Va. Certified agent NFL, NBA; specialist entertainment law, sports law. Mem.: ABA, Va. State Bar, Portsmouth Bar Assn. Achievements include obtaining multi-million dollar negligence and malpractice jury verdicts; aquittals in criminal defense cases ranging from murder, fraud, conspiracy and drug offenses; sucessfully negotiating multimillion dollar endorsement deals and team contracts for NFL and NBA players. Office: Shuttleworth Ruloff Swain Haddad & Morecock PC 4525 S Blvd Suite 300 Virginia Beach VA 23452

WOODWARD, LESTER RAY, lawyer; b. Lincoln, Nebr., May 24, 1932; s. Wendell Smith and Mary Elizabeth (Theobald) W.; m. Marianne Martinson, Dec. 27, 1958; children: Victoria L. Woodward Eisele, Richard T., David M., Andrew E. BSBA, U. Nebr., 1953; LLB, Harvard U., 1957; LLD (hon.), Bethany Coll., 1974. Bar: Colo., 1957. Assoc. Davis, Graham & Stubbs, Denver, 1957-59, 60-62, ptnr., 1962—2004, sr. counsel, 2004—. Teaching fellow Sch. Law Harvard U., 1959-60, mem., bd. dirs. Internat. Devel. Buterprises, 2006- Bd. dirs. Bethany Coll., Lindsborg, Kans., 1966-74, 87-95, chmn., 1989-92; bd. dirs. Pub. Edn. Coalition, Denver, 1985-92, chmn., 1988-89; mem. Colo. Commn. Higher Edn., Denver, 1977-86, chmn., 1979-81; mem. bd. edn. Denver Pub. Schs., 1999-2005, pres., 2003-05. Mem. ABA, Colo. Bar Assn., Am. Law Inst. Republican. Lutheran. Home: 680 Bellaire St Denver CO 80220-4935 Home Phone: 303-322-8758; Office Phone: 303-892-7392. Business E-Mail: les.woodward@dgslaw.com.

WOODWARD, PATRICIA, theater director, educator; d. James and Rose Conway; m. Kirk Woodward, June 23, 1984; children: Erin, Heather, Craig. BA in Dramatic Arts, Pace U., NYC, 1976. Artistic dir. Prep. Repertory, NYC, 1977—79; recruitment/activities coord. dept. performing arts Pace U., NYC, 1978—. Artistic dir. Stage Left, Inc., NYC, 1979—87; adj. lectr. performing arts Pace U., 1990—; dir., choreographer Clifton HS, NJ, 1995—2005, Montclair HS, NJ, 1999—; instr. Performers Theater Workshop, West Orange, NJ, 1997—2003, NJ Sch. Dramatic Arts, Bloomfield, NJ, 2006—. Dir., choreographer: (musical) Sweet Charity, 1999 (Nominee Outstanding Choreography, 1999, Paper Mill Playhouse Rising Star award, 1999). Stephen's min. Presbyn. Ch. Upper Montclair, 1998—2001; pres. Showstoppers, Montclair, 1999—2001. Mem.: Am. Fedn. Radio and TV Artists. Avocation: singing. Office: Pace Univ Dept Performing Arts 1 Pace Plz New York NY 10038

WOODWARD, RALPH LEE, JR., retired historian, educator; b. New London, Conn., Dec. 2, 1934; s. Ralph Lee and Beulah Mae (Suter) W.; m. Sue Dawn McGrady, Dec. 30, 1958; children: Mark Lee, Laura Lynn, Matthew McGrady; m. Janice Chatelain, Aug. 8, 1996. AB cum laude, Central Coll., Mo., 1955; MA, Tulane U., 1959, PhD, 1962. Asst. prof. history Wichita U., Kans., 1961-62, U. S.W. La., Lafayette, 1962-63, U. NC, Chapel Hill, 1963-67, assoc. prof., 1967-70; prof. history Tulane U., New Orleans, 1970-99, head dept. history, 1973-75, chmn. dept. history, 1986-88; dir. Tulane Summer in C. Am., 1975-78; prof. in charge Tulane Jr. Year Abroad, Paris, 1975-76; Penrose prof. L.Am. studies Tex. Christian U., Ft. Worth, 1999—2003; ret., 2003. Fulbright lectr. U. Chile, U. Catolica de Valparaiso, Chile, 1965-66, U. del Salvador, Universidad Nacional, Buenos Aires, 1968; vis. prof. US Mil. Acad., West Point, NY, 1989; regional liaison officer Emergency Com. to Aid Latin Am. Scholars, 1974; Joe & Teresa Long prof. social studies Tarleton State U., Stephenville, Tex., 2007. Author: Class Privilege and Economic Development, 1966, Robinson Crusoe's Island, 1969, Positivism in Latin America, 1850-1900, 1971, Central America: A Nation Divided, 1976, 3d edit., 1999, Tribute to Don Bernardo de Galvez, 1979, Belize, 1980, Nicaragua, 1983, 2d edit., 1994, El Salvador, 1988, Guatemala, 1992, Rafael Carrera and the Emergence of the Republic of Guatemala, 1993 (Alfred B. Thomas Book award), A Short History of Guatemala, 2008, Reflections on Central American History, 2008; editor: Central America: Historical Perspectives on the Contemporary Crises, 1988, Here and There in Mexico: The Travel Writings of Mary Ashley Townsend, 2001; assoc. editor: Revista del Pensamiento Centroamericano, 1975, Research Guide to Central America and the Caribbean, 1985, Encyclopedia of Latin American History and Culture, 1996; contbg. editor: Handbook of Latin American Studies, 1987-90; series editor: World Bibliographical Series, 1987-2000; contbr. articles to profl. jours. Bd. dirs. Common Cause Miss., 2004—05. Capt. USMC, 1955—58. Recipient Alfred B. Thomas Book award Southeastern Coun. L.Am. Studies, 1994; Henry L. and Grace Doherty Found. fellow Tulane U., 1962; named La. Humanist of Yr. La. Endowment for Humanities, 1995, Disting. Svc. award, Conf. Latin Am. History, 2002. Mem. Am. Hist. Assn. (mem. Conf. L.Am. History, pres. 1989, mem. gen. com. 1974-76, com. on Andean studies 1972-77, chmn. com. on Ctrl. Am. studies 1996-98, Disting. Svc. award 2002), Southeastern Conf. L.Am. Studies (program chmn. 1975, pres. 1975-76), Geography and History Acad. Guatemala, Southern Hist. Assn. (mem. L.Am. and Caribben sect.). Democrat. Episcopalian. Home Phone: 660-248-9891. Personal E-mail: clioclio@sbcglobal.net.

WOODWARD, SANDRA S., literature and language educator; b. San Diego, Jan. 4, 1948; d. Harold Herbert Woodward and Grace LaVerne Woodward (Usher). BA in English, Brigham Young U., Provo, Utah, 1969; MEd, U. Utah, Salt Lake City. Tchr. English Kennedy Jr. High, Salt Lake City, 1969—75; tchr. English, Latin Granger H.S., West Valley City, 1976—. Mem. nat. Latin exam adv. com. Am. Classical League, 1998—; chair world langs. dept. Granger H.S., West Valley City, Utah, 2000—, advisor nat. honor soc., Granger chpt., 2000—. Recipient Utah Lang. Arts Tchr. Yr., Utah Coun. Tchrs., 1980, Nat. Merit Tchg. award, Nat. Merit Scholarship Orgn., 1988, Excel Educator Yr., Granite Sch. Dist., 1999. Mem.: Utah Classical Assn. (acl liaison), Am. Classical League (nat. latin exam adv. com., coun. mem.). Office: Granger High School 3690 S 3600 W West Valley City UT 84119 Office Fax: 1-801-646-5336. Personal E-mail: sandra.woodward@granite.k12.ut.us.

WOODWARD, TIMOTHY ANDRE, gastroenterologist; b. Jackson, Tenn., Nov. 20, 1957; s. Solon Wellington and Rubye Maye Woodward; m. Evelyn Daran Dawson; children: Mckenzie, Britt, Daran Abigail, Miriam. BA, Harvard U., Cambridge, Mass, 1979; MD, Mayo Coll. Medicine, Rochester, Minn., 1983. Diplomate Fla., 1994. Gastroenterologist Mayo Clinic, Jacksonville, Fla., 1994—. Author: (novels) Cadillac Orpheus. Mem., bd. dirs. Fla. State Coll., Jacksonville, 2007—09; dir. mem. Am. Cancer Soc., Jacksonville, 2007—09. Mem.: Am. Gastroenterologic Assn. Office: Mayo Clinic 4500 San Pablo Rd Jacksonville FL 32224 Business E-Mail: woodward.timothy@mayo.edu.

WOODWARD, WENDY ANN, radiation oncologist; BA in Chemistry, Mt. Holyoke Coll., S. Hadley, Mass., 1993; MD, PhD in Molecular Biology, Thomas Jefferson U., Phila., Pa., 2000. Cert. Am. Bd. Radiology, 2006. Med. intern Albert Einstein Med. Ctr., Phila., 2000—01; resident, radiation oncology U. Tex., MD Anderson Cancer Ctr., Houston, 2001—05; rsch. fellow Baylor Coll. Medicine, Houston, 2003—04; asst. prof., breast radiation oncology U. Tex. MD Anderson Cancer Ctr., Houston, 2005—. Contbr. several articles to profl. jours. Recipient Eleanor Montague prize, Resident Manuscript Contest, 2003, Roentgen Rsch. award, Radiological Soc. N.Am., 2004, Fletcher award, 1st pl. Resident Rsch. award, U. Tex. MD Anderson Cancer Ctr., 2005; named Intern of Yr., Albert Einstein Med. Ctr., 2001; Gibbon Scholar, Thomas Jefferson U., 1993—2000, Foerderer Fellowship, 1993, Fellowship, Clin. Epidemiology Workshop, Cancer Edn. Consortium, 2002, ASTRO travel grant, Gordon Conf. on Radiation, 2004, ASTRO Travel grant, Translational Rsch. Symposium, 2006, K12 grant, Ctr. for Clin. and Translational Scis., U. Tex. Health Scis. Ctr., 2006—09. Mem.: Am. Assn. Women in Radiology (mem. exec. com. 2004, mem.-in-tng.-at-large 2004—05), Am. Soc. Therapeutic Radiology and Oncology (mem. rsch. evaluation com. 2005—), Am. Radium Soc. (Young Oncologist Essay award 2003, Travel award, Barcelona, Spain 2005), Am. Soc. Clin. Oncology (Merit award 2003), Gilbert H. Fletcher Soc., Alpha Omega Alpha, Sigma Xi. Office: Univ Tex MD Anderson Cancer Ctr MDA ACB p1-2855 Unit 1202 1515 Holcombe Blvd MDA ACB P1-2855 Unit Houston TX 77030 Office Phone: 713-563-8481. Business E-Mail: wwoodward@mdanderson.org.

WOODWELL, GEORGE MASTERS, ecologist, conservationist; b. Cambridge, Mass., Oct. 23, 1928; s. Philip McIntire and Virginia (Sellers) W.; m. Alice Katharine Rondthaler, June 23, 1955; children: Caroline Alice, Marjorie Virginia, Jane Katharine, John Christopher. AB, Dartmouth Coll., 1950; AM, Duke U., 1956, PhD, 1958; DSc (hon.), Williams Coll., 1977, Miami U., 1984, Carleton Coll., 1988, Muhlenberg Coll., 1990, Duke U., 1994, Dartmouth Coll., 1996. Mem. faculty U. Maine, 1957-61, assoc. prof. botany, 1960-61; vis. asst. ecologist, biology dept. Brookhaven Nat. Lab., Upton, NY, 1961-62, ecologist, 1965-67, sr. ecologist, 1967-75; founder, dir. Ecosystems Center, 1975-85; dep. and asst. dir. Marine Biol. Lab., Woods Hole, Mass., 1975-76; founder, pres. and dir. Woods Hole Research Ctr., 1985—2005, dir. emeritus, 2005—. Founder, chmn. Conf. on Long Term Biol. Consequences of Nuclear War, 1982-83. Editor: Ecological Effects of Nuclear War, 1965, Diversity and Stability in Ecological Systems, 1969, (with E.V. Pecan) Carbon and the Biosphere, 1973, The Role of Terrestrial Vegetation in the Global Carbon Cycle: Measurement by Remote Sensing, 1984, The Earth in Transition: Patterns and Processes of Biotic Impoverishment, 1990, (with K. Ramakrishna) Forests for the Future, 1993, (with F.T. Mackenzie) Biotic Feedbacks in the Warming of the Earth, 1995, Forests In A Full World, 2001, The Nature of a House: Building a World that Works, 2009. Founding trustee Environ. Def. Fund, 1967, Natural Resources Def. Coun., 1970, vice chmn., 1974-04, World Resources Inst., 1982-96, Woods Hole Rsch. Ctr., 1985-; bd. dirs. Conservation Found., 1975-77, Ctr. for Marine Conservation, 1990-98, The Ocean Conservancy, 1999-2006, World Wildlife Fund, 1970-84, chmn., 1980-84, Ruth Mott Fund, 1984-91, chmn., 1989-91; bd. trustees Inst. Environ. Rsch. in Amazon, 1996—; adv. com. TMI Pub. Health Fund, 1980-94; bd. trustees World Media Found., 1998-, Grand Canyon Nat. Pk. Found., 1999-2008, chmn., 2007-08. Recipient Joseph Priestley award Dickinson Coll., 1993, Hutchinson medal Garden Club of Am., 1993, Disting. Svc. award Am. Inst. Biol. Scis., 1982, Heinz Environ. prize, 1996, Volvo Environ. prize, 2001; Fellowship Montgomery fellow, Dartmouth Coll. Fellow AAAS, Am. Acad. Arts and Scis.; mem. NAS, Brit. Ecol. Soc., Ecol. Soc. Am. (v.p. 1966-67, pres. 1977-78), Sea Edn. Assn. (bd. dirs. 1980-85), World Comm. on Forests and Sustainable Development, 1994-98, Sigma Xi. Achievements include rsch., pub. on structure and function of natural communities, biotic impoverishment, especially ecological effects of ionizing radiation, effects of persistent toxins, world carbon cycle and global climatic disruption, sci. and internat. environ. affairs. Office: Woods Hole Rsch Ctr PO Box 296 Woods Hole MA 02543 Home Phone: 508-548-0680; Office Phone: 508-540-9900 x104. Business E-Mail: gmwoodwell@whrc.org.

WOODY, CAROL CLAYMAN, data processing executive; b. Bristol, Va., May 20, 1949; d. George Neal and Ida Mae Clayman; m. Robert William Woody, Aug. 19, 1972. BS in Math., Coll. William and Mary, Williamsburg, Va., 1971; MBA with distinction, Wake Forest U., 1979; PhD in Info. Sys., Nova Southeastern U., 2004. Programmer trainee GSA, 1971-72; systems engr. Citizens Fidelity Bank & Trust Co., Louisville, 1972-75; programmer/analyst-tng. coord. Blue Bell, Inc., Greensboro, N.C., 1975-79; supr. programming and tech. svcs. J.E. Baker Co., York, Pa., 1979-82; fin. design supr. bus. systems Lycoming divsn. AVCO, Stratford, Conn., 1982-83; project mgr. Yale U., New Haven, 1984-97; cons. ImageWork Technologies Corp., 1998-2001; co-owner Sign of the Sycamore, antiques; sr. mem. tech staff Software Engrng. Inst. Carnegie Mellon U., 2001—. Mem. Data Processing Standards Bd., 1977, CICS/VS Adv. Council, 1975; speaker Nat. Fuse Conf., 1989, Aion expert systems nat. conf., 1990, bus. sch. Coll. William & Mary, 1994. Author various manuals; contbr. articles to profl. jours. Recipient Outstanding Alumni award Nova Southeastern U., 2008. IBM Corp. fellow, 1978; Stephen Bufton Meml. Ednl. Found. grantee, 1978-79. Mem. IEEE (section editor, 2003-06, disting. spkr., 2005-07), Am. Bus. Woman's Assn. (chpt. v.p. 1978-79, Merit award 1978), NAFE (founder shoreline network 1993), Assn. for System Mgmt., Assn. for Image Info. Mgmt., Project Mgmt. Inst., Delta Omicron (alumni pres. 1973-75, regional chmn. 1979-82, 2006-). Republican. Presbyterian. Home: PO Box 344 Sewickley PA 15143-0344

WOODY, MARY FLORENCE, nursing educator, academic administrator; b. Chambers County, Ala., Mar. 31, 1926; d. Hugh Ernest and May Lillie (Gilliland) W. Diploma, Charity Hosp. Sch. Nursing, 1947; BS, Columbia U., 1953, MA, 1955. Staff nurse Wheeler Hosp., Lafayette, Ala., 1947-48; polio nurse Willard Parker Hosp., NYC, 1949; staff nurse, supr. VA Hosp., Montgomery, Ala., 1950-53; faculty, field supr. nursing dept. Columbia U. Tchrs. Coll., NYC, 1955-56; asst. dir. nursing Emory U. Hosp., Atlanta, assoc. dir., DON, 1984-93; clin. asst. prof. Emory U. Sch. Nursing, Atlanta, 1956-68, interim dean, 1992-93; asst. dir., DON Grady Meml. Hosp., Atlanta, 1968-79; founding dean, prof. Auburn U. Sch. Nursing, Ala., 1979-84; disting. emeritus prof. Emory U., 2003—. Chair Ga. Statewide Master Planning Com. for Nursing and Nursing Edn., 1971-75; faculty preceptor patient care adminstrn. Sch. Public Health, U. Minn., 1977-79; bd. dirs. Wesley Woods Found. & Long Term Hosp.; chair bd. dirs. Am. Jour. Nursing Co., 1978-83. Recipent Spl. Recognition award 5th Dist. and Ga. Nurses Assn., 1978, 93, Disting. Achievement in Nursing Svc. award Columbia U. Tchrs. Coll. Alumni Assn., 1992, Jane Van de Vrede Outstanding Svc. to Citizens Ga. award Ga. League Nursing, Cert. Spl. Recognition award Ga. Nurses Assn., 1993, Internat. Founders award Sigma Theta Tau, 1999, The Marie Hippensteel award, 1999, Disting. Prof. award Emeritus Coll. Emory U., 2003; named Ga. Women Pioneer in Health Care, Ga. Commn. on Women and Ga. Womens History Month Com., 1998, Hall of Fame Nursing, Tchrs. Coll., Columbia, U., N.Y Fellow Am. Acad. Nursing (charter, Living Legend 1997); mem. Am. Nurses Assn., Nat. League Nursing, Am. Heart Assn., Emory U. Nell Hodgson Woodruff Sch. Nursing Alumni Assn. (hon.), Sigma Theta Tau (Marie Hippensteel Lingemald award for excellence in nursing 1999); mem. Nursing Tchr.'s Coll. Columbia U. of Hall of Fame (charter). Democrat. Address: 19488 Veterans Memorial Pkwy Lafayette AL 36862

WOODY, TERESA ANN, lawyer; b. Littlefield, Tex., Jan. 8, 1960; d. Ronald L. and Shirley A. (Yates) Woody; m. Rik N. Siro, Aug. 9, 1980; children: Alexander L. Siro, Lia A. Siro. BA with high distinction, U. Calif., Berkeley, 1982; JD magna cum laude, U. Calif., Hastings, 1985. Bar: Mo. 1985, Calif. 1986, Kans. 1995, U.S. Ct. Internat. Trade 1998. Law clk. Hon. Ross T. Roberts, U.S. Dist. Ct. (we. dist.) Mo., Kansas City, 1985-86; assoc. Spencer Fane Britt & Browne, Kansas City, 1986-92; ptnr. Spencer Fane Britt & Browne, LLP, Kansas City, 1993—2004, chair litig. dept., 2001—04; ptnr. Stueve Siegel Hanson Woody LLP, Kansas City, 2004—07, Woody Law Firm PC, Kansas City, 2007—. Pres., bd. dirs. Westport Ballet Theatre, Kansas City, 1988—89, Mattie Rhodes Counseling and Arts Ctr., Kansas City, 1994—95; mem. steering com. Centurions Leadership Program, Kansas City, 1992—94. Mem.: ABA (chair com. environ. litig. techs. 1996—97), Assn. Women Lawyers Greater Kansas City (pres. 1992—93), Midwest Regional Conf. Women Law (co-chair 1997—98), Nat. Conf. Women's Bar Assns. (bd. dirs. 1994—97). Office: Woody Law Firm PC 1044 Main St Ste 500 Kansas City MO 64105 Office Phone: 816-421-4246. Business E-Mail: teresa@woodylawfirm.com.

WOOFTER, VIVIEN PERRINE, interior designer, consultant; d. Orie Ray and Hazel Lucille (Bostic) Perrine; m. Perry Wilson Woofter, Oct. 5, 1952; children: James Perry, Lori Evan Hugh. BS in Home Econ., W.Va. U., 1952, LHD (hon.), 1998. Lic. interior designer Va., 2003. Interior designer GSA, Washington, 1968—76; head interior design The White Ho., 1976—77, U.S. Dept. Health & Human Services, 1977—81; sr. interior designer U.S. Dept. of State, 1981—88; dir. interiors & furnishings divsn. Overseas Buildings Ops., U.S. Dept. of State, 1988—. Mem. W.Va. U. Alumni Bd., Morgantown, 1994—; vol. mem. designer renovation W.Va. U. President's Ho. Com., 1996—2003; mem. W.Va. U. Found. Bd., 1999—; pres. Coll. Creative Arts Vis. Com., 2001—. Author: Develop. Furniture Standards- Phys. Handicap (Written up in Congl. Record, 1977); interior design Interior Design Hdqs. Bldg. for HHS (Fed. Design Coun. of Excellence, 1979), Riyadh Embassy, Paris, Buenos Aires - (Meritorius Honor & Superior Honor, 1988). Restoration work Met. Theater, Morgantown, 2003. Mem.: Internat. Interior Design Assoc. Achievements include development of Art Programs for all new embassies; Culturally Significan Program for US State Dept. Overseas Ident; a Maintenance Manual for US State Dept. Culturally Significant Buildingsofp; Featured in Articles, in Architectural Digest, Southern Accents, Paris Match, Chicago Tribune, other newspapersnchi. Home: 4856 N 35th Rd Arlington VA 22207 Office: Interiors & Furnishings Div Overseas Buildings Ops US Dept State Washington DC 20520 Personal E-mail: vivienwoofter@erols.com. E-mail: woofterv@state.gov.

WOO HO, DOREEN WOO, bank executive; b. Australia, 1946; m. James Ho; 3 children. BA in East Asian Studies, Smith Coll., 1968; MA in East Asian Studies & Chinese History, Columbia U. Corr. TIME mag., Phnom Penh, Cambodia, 1972—73; with Citibank, 1974—98; pres. consumer credit group Wells Fargo & Co., San Francisco, 1998—, pres. corp. trust services, 2004—. Mem. exec. com. Wells Fargo Diversity Coun. Bd. dirs. San Francisco Opera Assn., 2001—, v.p. treas., exec. com. mem., chair audit com., vice chair dir. & officers com., fin. adv. com.; co-founder Asian Pacific Islander Am. Scholarship Fund; mem. Com. of 100, 2005—. Recipient Fin. Woman of Yr., San Francisco Fin. Women's Assn., 2004; named one of The Bay Area's 100 Most Influential Women, The San Francisco Bus. Times, 2005, The 25 Most Powerful Women in Banking, US Banker mag., 2005—07. Avocation: opera. Office: Wells Fargo & Co 420 Montgomery St San Francisco CA 94163 Mailing: San Francisco Opera Assn 301 Van Ness Ave San Francisco CA 94102

WOOLDREDGE, WILLIAM DUNBAR, health facility administrator; b. Salem, Mass., Oct. 27, 1937; s. John and Louise (Sigourney) W.; m. Johanna Marie; children: John, Rebecca Wistar. BA, Colby Coll., 1961; MBA, Harvard U., 1964. Staff assoc. Sun Oil Co., Phila., 1964-67; treas. Ins. Co. N.Am., Phila., 1967-72, B.F. Goodrich Co., Akron, Ohio, 1972-84, sr. v.p., 1979, exec. v.p., chief fin. officer, mem. mgmt. com., 1979-84; chief fin. officer, exec. v.p., dir. Belden & Blake Corp., North Canton, Ohio, 1984-89; sr. v.p., chief fin. officer, dir. Belden & Blake Oil Prodn., Inc., 1984-89; prin. dir. Carleton Group, Cleve., 1989-92; CFO, COO, v.p. King's Med. Co., Hudson, Ohio, 1993—, also bd. dirs. Pres. Hudson Econ. Devel. Corp. Bd. dirs. Salvation Army, North Park Coll. and Seminary; trustee Children's Hosp. Med. Ctr., Akron. With U.S. Army, 1956-58. Mem. Fin. Execs. Inst. Clubs: Country of Hudson. Episcopalian. Home: 100 College St Hudson OH 44236-2925 Office: King's Med Co 1920 Georgetown Rd Hudson OH 44236-4060 E-mail: wdwooldred@aol.com.

WOOLDRIDGE, WILLIAM CHARLES, lawyer; b. Miami, Fla., Feb. 24, 1943; s. Clarence Edward and Easter Marguerite (Souders) W.; m. Joyce L. Norton, June 15, 1968; children: William Charles, John Michael. BA, Harvard U., 1965; LLB, U. Va., 1969. Bar: Va. 1969. Atty. Norfolk and Western Ry. Co., 1973-82; with Norfolk So. Corp., 1982-2000, v.p. dept. law, 1996-2000. Author: The Wooldridge Family, 2002. Pres. John Marshall Found., Richmond, Va., 1992-94; pres. Norfolk Hist. Soc., 1995-96; chair Friends of Chrysler Mus. Hist. Houses, 1997-99; bd. dirs. Sta. WHRO (FM and TV), 1997-00, WHRO Found., 2003-05, Libr. Va. Found.2002-08, Capt. JAGC, US Army, 1969-73. Republican.

WOOLEY, GERALDINE HAMILTON, poet, writer; b. Idlewild, Mich., Feb. 15, 1942; d. Charles Loren and Alice (Smith) Hamilton; m. David Wooley, June 11, 1961 (div. 1983); children: Vickie Wooley Houston, Monica Wooley Roberts, Deborah Wooley Williams. GED, Flint, Mich. Cosmetologist pvt. practice, Flint, Mich., 1967-70; tchr's. aide Flint Comty. Schs., 1969-71; nurse's aide Clara Barton Home, Flint, 1972; factory worker GM AC Plant, Flint, 1973-76; child care worker Beecher Cmty. Schs., Flint, 1987-89; poet, songwriter Flint, 1994—. Songwriter Hilltop Records, Hollywood, Calif., 1996—. Author: (poems) Between The Raindrops, 1995 (Editor's Choice 1995), At Water's Edge, 1995 (Editor's Choice 1995), Tapestry, 1996 (Editor's Choice 1996), Memories of Tomorrow, 1996 (Editor's Choice 1996), (poems) A Treasury of Famous Poets, 1997 (Editor's Choice award 1997). Mem. PTA Flint Sch. Dist., 1969-70. Named to Internat. Poetry Hall of Fame, 1996. Mem. Internat. Soc. Of Poets, Nat. Writers Assn., Internat. Black Writers. Democrat. Avocations: camping, playing organ, exploring old houses, writing. Home: 723 E Lansing Apt 611E Idlewild MI 49642 Office Phone: 810-423-2053.

WOOLF, ALAN, pediatrician; MD, U. Chgo., 1976. Diplomate Bd. Med. Examiners, 1977. Pediatrician Children's Hosp., Boston, 1983—2008. Achievements include research in toxicology and poisoning prevention. Home: 300 Longwood Ave Boston MA 02115 Office: Children's Hosp 300 Longwood Ave Boston MA

WOOLF, KENNETH HOWARD, architect; b. NYC, Aug. 19, 1938; s. Howard Walter and Elizabeth Ann (Levy) W.; m. Elizabeth Adair Rainwater, July 3, 1965; children: Robert Gregg, Susan Adair, Jennifer Adair. BArch, Cornell U., 1961. Staff arch. Look & Morrison, Archs., Pensacola, Fla., 1965-72; pvt. practice arch. Pensacola, Fla., 1972—. Instr. architecture Pensacola Jr. Coll., part-time 1967-76; chmn. Pensacola Archtl. Rev. Bd., 1970-81; mem. Gulf Breeze Planning Bd., 1976-78; chmn. Pensacola City Bd. Adjustment and Appeals, 1995—. Prin. works include Coca-Cola Bottling Co. Plant, Pensacola, 1974, 3 profl. office bldgs. towers, Pensacola, 1976, 1984, 1992, Bapt. Hosp. addition, 1977, The Village, Housing for Elderly, 1978, 1981, 1998, 2006, 09, Azalea Trace Ret. Cmty. Complex, 1980, 1999, Northview Cmty., 1981, Coca-Cola Bottling Plant, Beaumont, Tex., 1983, Episcopal Day Sch., Pensacola, 1993, 6 oncology ctrs., 1990, 1994, 1996, 1999, 2002, 2003, 2005. With USN, 1961-65. Named Jaycee of Yr., 1970. Mem. AIA (sec. N.W. Fla. chpt. 1976-77, 77-78, pres. 1979-81, Comml.

Design Hon. award 1975), Rotary. Episcopalian. Home: 15 N Sunset Blvd Gulf Breeze FL 32561-4051 Office: 100 W Gadsden St Pensacola FL 32501-3910 Office Phone: 850-438-3653. Business E-Mail: khwarch@caytel.net.

WOOLF, NANCY JEAN, neuroscientist, educator; b. Ft. Sill, Okla., July 27, 1954; d. Lee Allen and Rachel Christine (Sedjo) W.; m. Larry Lee Butcher, Dec. 24, 1983; children: Lawson Frederick, Ashley Ellen. BS, UCLA, 1978, PhD, 1983. Grad. researcher UCLA, 1979-83, asst. rsch. neuroscientist, 1984-92, adj. assoc. prof., 1992—2003, adj. prof., 2003—. Contbr. 50 articles to various sci. publs. Recipient Colby prize Sigma Kappa Found., Indpls, 1990; named Woman of Yr. Coll. of the Desert, Palm Desert, Calif., 1976. Mem. AAAS, Assn. Acad. Women (Grad. Woman of Yr. UCLA 1983), Soc. for Neurosci. Achievements include compilation of complete map of central nervous system neurons that utilize the neurotransmitter acetylcholine; MAP-2 alterations with classical conditioning, model of dendtritic transduction site for the conscious memory trace. Office: U Calif Dept Psychology 405 Hilgard Ave Los Angeles CA 90095-9000 Business E-Mail: rwoolf@ucla.edu.

WOOLF, STEVEN MICHAEL, artistic director; b. Milw., Dec. 23, 1947; s. Raleigh and Lenore (Shurman) W. BA in Theatre, U. Wis., 1968, MFA, 1971; D of Fine Arts (hon.), U. Mo., 1993. Prodn. stage mgr. The Juilliard Sch. Drama, NYC, 1973-75; project prodr. Musical Theatre Lab., NYC, 1974-75; prodn. stage mgr. Barter Theatre, Abingdon, Va., 1976-79, Stagewest, Springfield, Mass., 1976-79; prodn. mgr. Repertory Theatre of St. Louis, 1980-83, acting artistic dir., mng. dir., 1983-85, mng. dir., 1985-86, artistic dir., 1986—. Adj. faculty Webster U., St. Louis, 1982—; mem. nat. negotiating coms. League of Resident Theatres, N.Y.C., 1986—; on-site evaluator Nat. Endowment for the Arts, 1985. Dir. plays A Life in the Theatre, 1982, the Crucible, 1986, Company, 1987, The Voice of the Prairie, 1988, 90, The Boys Next Door, 1989, Dog Logic, 1990, Born Yesterday, 1990, Terra Nova, 1991, The Diary of Anne Frank, 1991, Other Peoples Money, 1991, Six Degrees of Separation, 1992, Sight Unseen, 1993, Lion in Winter, 1993, Death and the Maiden, 1993, The Living, 1994, Wait Until Dark, 1994, The Caine Mutiny Court Martial, 1994. The Life of Galileo, 1995, Death of a Salesman, 1995, Betrayal, 1996, As Bees in Honey Drown, 1997, Who's Afraid of Virginia Woolf, 1998, Closer, 1998, Dinner With Friends, 2000, The Dresser, 2001, The Shape of Things, 2002, Copenhagen, 2003, Two Rockin' Gents, 2003, The Goat, Or Who is Sylvia, 2003, Blue/Orange, 2004, The Crucible, 2004, The Retreat From Moscow, 2004, Henry IV & Humble Boy, 2006, The History Boys, 2007, Angels in America, 2008, Frost Nixon, 2008, others. Mem. ad hoc coms. for funding Mo. Arts Coun., St. Louis, 1988; chair citizen rev. panel Reg. Arts Commn., St. Louis, 1986; bd. dirs. Mo. Citizens for the Arts, 1990—; exec. com. League of Resident Theatres, 1990—. Recipient award Mo. Citizens for the Arts, 1992, Women's Polit. Caucus, 1993, award for Individual Excellence in the Arts, Arts Edn. Coun., 1993. Mem. AFTRA, Soc. of Stage Dirs. and Choreographers, Actors Equity Assn. Office: Repertory Theatre St Louis 130 Edgar Rd Saint Louis MO 63119-3228 Home Phone: 314-367-4401; Office Phone: 314-968-7340. Personal E-mail: swoolf@repstl.org.

WOOLF, WILLIAM BLAUVELT, retired association executive; b. New Rochelle, NY, Sept. 18, 1932; s. Douglas Gordon and Katharine Hutton (Blauvelt) W. AA, John Muir Jr. Coll., 1951; student, U. Calif., Berkeley, 1995; BA, Pomona Coll., 1953; MA, Claremont Grad. Sch., Calif., 1955; PhD, U. Mich., 1960. Instr., asst. prof., asso. prof. U. Wash., Seattle, 1959-68; assoc. sec., dir. adminstrn. AAUP, Washington, 1968-79; mng. editor Math. Revs., Am. Math. Soc., Ann Arbor, Mich., 1979-90, acting exec. editor, 1984-85; assoc. exec. dir. Am. Math. Soc., Providence, 1990-96. Bd. dirs. Nat. Child Rsch. Ctr., Washington, 1975-77; trustee Friends Sch., Detroit, 1985-90, treas., 1986-90; mem. Law and Justice Coun., Jefferson County, Wash., 1998—, chmn., 2001; mem. Wash. State U. Jefferson County Adv. Team, 1999-2003, chmn., 2002-2003, Jefferson County Edn. Com., 1998-2003, chmn., 1999-2001; bd. dirs. Jefferson County Farmers Market Assn., 2002-03. Fulbright Research fellow U. Helsinki, Finland, 1963-64 Fellow AAAS; mem. ACLU (life, treas. Washington 1966-68, bd. dirs. Washtenaw County and Mich. State 1989-90, bd. dirs. R.I. State 1993-95, treas. 1994-95, chmn. Jefferson County chpt. 2003-2005), Am. Math. Soc., Math. Assn. Am. Mem. Soc. Of Friends.

WOOLFENDEN, JAMES MANNING, nuclear medicine physician, educator; b. LA, Nov. 8, 1942; BA with distinction, Stanford U., 1964; MD, U. Wash., 1968. Diplomate Am. Bd. Nuclear Medicine (chmn. credentials com. 1993-94, vice chmn. exams. com. 1993-95, chmn. exam. com. 1995-96, sec. 1994-96, chmn. 1996-97, life mem.), Nat. Bd. Med. Examiners. Med. intern L.A. County-U. So. Calif. Med. Ctr., 1968-69; med. resident West L.A. VA Med. Ctr., 1969-70; nuclear medicine resident L.A. County-U. So. Calif. Med. Ctr., 1972-74; from asst. prof. radiology to assoc. prof. radiology U. Ariz., Tucson, 1974-84, prof. radiology, 1984—2007, prof. emeritus. Med. staff Univ. Med. Ctr., Tucson, 1974-2007; cons. VA Med. Ctr., 1974-2007; cons. med. staff Tucson Med. Ctr., 1975-2004, Carondelet St. Joseph's Hosp., 1974-98, St. Mary's Hosp., Tucson, 1976-90; mem. Nat. Cancer Inst. site visit team NIH, 1976, mem. NHLB Inst. site visit team NIH, 1976, mem. diagnostic radiology study sect., 1989-97, chmn., 1995-97; med. liaison officer network EPA, 1983-85; cons.-tchg. med. staff Kino Cmty. Hosp., 1984-94; med. officer Clin. Ctr., NIH, Bethesda, 1984-85; mem. Ariz. Cancer Ctr., U. Ariz., 1988—, sr. clin. scientist Univ. Heart Ctr., 1990—; Ariz. bd. regents U. Ariz. Presdl. Search Com., 1990-91; chmn. Ariz. Atomic Energy Commn., 1979-80, Ariz. Radiation Regulatory Hearing Bd., 1981—; bd. dirs. Calif. Radioactive Materials Mgmt. Forum, chmn., 1994-95, Western Forum Edn. in Safe Disposal of Low-Level Radioactive Waste, 1990-2000, vice chmn., 1991-92, chmn., 1992-94. Manuscript reviewer: Noninvasive Med. Imaging, 1983-84, Jour. Nuclear Medicine, 1985—, Investigative Radiology, 1989-94, Archives of Internal Medicine, 1990—; contbr. book chpts.: Diagnostic Nuclear Medicine, 2d edit., 1988, Adjuvant Therapy of Cancer, 1977, Fundamentals of Nuclear Medicine, 1988, others; contbr. articles to profl. jours. Mem. Am. Heart Assn. Coun. on Cardiovasc. Radiology. Maj. U.S. Army, 1970-72, Vietnam. Fellow Am. Coll. Nuc. Physicians (long range planning com. 1981-83, govt. affairs com. 1984-94, exec. com. 1987-91, sec. 1989-91, parliamentarian 1991-95, treas. 1996-98, publs. com. 1993-98, chmn. publs. com. 1993-94, pres.-elect 1998-99, pres. 1999-2000, others); mem. AMA (diagnostic and therapeutic tech. assessment reference panel 1982-98), Am. Nuc. Soc., Soc. Nuc. Medicine (com. on audit 1992-99, trustee 1992-96, ho. dels. 1996-2003, fin. com. 1996-99, bd. dirs. 1997-99, bronze medal for sci. exhibit 1984, bd. dirs., sec.-treas. So. Calif. chpt. 1993-95, pres.-elect 1995-96, pres. 1996-99), Assn. Univ. Radiologists, Ariz. Med. Assn., European Assn. Nuc. Medicine, Pima County Med. Soc., Radiol. Soc. N.Am., Soc. for Molecular Imaging. Office: Ariz Health Scis Ctr Radiology Rsch 1501 N Campbell Ave Tucson AZ 85724-5067

WOOLF-WADE, SARAH JANE, retired elementary school educator, writer; d. Robert Alden Proctor and Ethelyn Winifred Haslam; m. Gregory Buxton Woolf, Sept. 8, 1956 (div.); 1 child, Bradford Robert Woolf; m. Stanley Wade, 1982. AB with honors, Am. U., 1957; MA, Boston U., 1967, EdD, 1980. Contbr. poems, travel articles to profl. jours.; author: (poems) Nightsong, 2003, Down the Bristol Road, 2008. Vol. literacy specialist Bristol (Maine) Sch., 1999—. Grantee, Tchrs. as Travelers; tchr. as scholar grantee, Harvard U., Marion Thomas grant for advanced study in India, Brookline Found. Mem.: Brookline Tchrs. Assn. (v.p., rep.), New England Reading Assn., Mass. Reading Assn., Internat. Reading Assn., Pemaquid Poets and Live Poets Soc., Pi Lambda Theta. Avocation: travel. Home: 251 Pemaquid Tr New Harbor ME 04554 Personal E-mail: sallyjww@gmail.com.

WOOLLAM, JOHN ARTHUR, electrical engineering educator, physics professor; b. Kalamazoo, Mich., Aug. 10, 1939; s. Arthur Edward and Mildred Edith (Hakes) W.; children: Catherine Jane, Susan June. BA in Physics, Kenyon Coll., 1961, Doctorate (hon.) in Sci., 2008; MS in Physics, Mich. State U., 1963, PhD in Solid State Physics, 1967; MSEE, Case Western Res. U., 1978; Doctorate (hon.), Linköping (Sweden) U., 2004. Rsch. scientist NASA Lewis Rsch. Ctr., Cleve., 1967-80; prof. U. Nebr., Lincoln, 1979—, dir. Ctr. Microelectronic and Optical Materials Rsch., 1988—2000; pres. J.A. Woollam Co., Inc., Lincoln, 1987—. Editor Jour. Applied Physics Com., 1979-94. Trustee J.A. Woollam Found. Grantee NASA, NSF, USAF, Advanced Rsch. Projects Agy. Fellow Am. Phys. Soc., Am. Vacuum Soc. (chmn. thin film divsn. 1989-91). Office: U Nebr Dept Elec Engring 209NWSEC Lincoln NE 68588-0511

WOOLLEY, BRIAN N., lawyer; s. Stuart W. and Shirley S. Woolley; m. Patricia L. Martin, Oct. 26, 1985; children: Meredith, Philip. BS, Iowa State U., 1978; JD, Northwestern U., Chgo., 1982. Bar: Mo. 1982, U.S. Dist. Ct. Western Dist. Mo. 1982, Ill. 1984, No. Dist. Ill. 1984, U.S. Cts. Appeal for 7th, 8th and 10th Circuits. Assoc. Lathrop, Koontz, Kansas City, Mo., 1982—84, D'Ancona & Pflaum, Chgo., 1984—86; mem. Lathrop & Gage LLP, Kansas City, Mo., 1986—. Guest lectr. U. Mo., Kansas City, 2001—07. Contbg. editor: The Developing Labor Law, 2003—09. Bd. dirs., pres. Wonderscope Children's Mus., Shawnee, Kans., 1996—2004; chmn., legal counsel com. Farmhouse Fraternity Bd. Dirs., Kansas City, Mo., 2000—; bd. dirs. Arthritis Found. of Greater Kansas City (Mo.), 2004—09, Arthritis Found. Heartland Regional Coun., 2007—09. Mem.: ABA, Am. Health Lawyers Assn., Soc. Human Resource Mgmt. Office: Lathrop & Gage LLP 2345 Grand #2800 Kansas City MO 64108

WOOLLEY, DONNA PEARL, lumber company executive; b. Drain, Oreg., Jan. 3, 1926; d. Chester A. and Mona B. (Cheever) Rydell; m. Harold Woolley, Dec. 27, 1952 (dec. Sept. 1970); children: Daniel, Debra, Donald. Diploma, Drain High Sch. Sec. No. Life Ins. Co., Eugene, Oreg., 1943—44; sec., bookkeeper D & W Lumber Co., Sutherlin, Oreg., 1944, Woolley Logging Co. & Earl Harris Lumber Co., Drain, 1944—70; pres. Woolley Logging Co., 1970—, Smith River Lumber Co., 1970—, Mt. Baldy Mill, 1970—81, Drain Plywood Co., 1970—81, Woolley Enterprises, Inc., Drain, 1973—, Eagle's View Mgmt. Co., Inc., Eugene, 1981—. Bd. dirs. Wildlife Safari, Winston, 1991, Oreg. Cmty. Found., Portland, 1990-99, chair, 1997-99; bd. trustees Linfield Coll., McMinnville, U. Oreg. Found., Eugene, Oreg. Trl. coun. Boy Scouts Am., 1980—, World Forestry Ctr., Portland, 1990, Umpqua C.C. Fedn., 2001. Recipient Pioneer award, U. Oreg., 1982, Pres.'s medal, 2005, Econ. and Social Devel. award, Soroptimist Club, 1991, First Citizen of Eugene award, 2000, Aubrey Watzek award, Lewis & Clark Coll., 2001, Howard Vollum award, Associated Fund Raisers in Philanthropy Oreg. chpt., 2001, Pioneer award, Umpqua C.C., 2003, Hart Pioneer award, Wildlife Safari, 2003, Pres. medal, U. Oreg., 2005, Paul Harris fellow, Rotary, 2006. Mem. Oreg. Women's Forum, Pacific Internat. Trapshooting Assn., Amateur Trapshooting Assn., Eugene C. of C. (bd. dirs. 1989-92), Arlington Club, Town Club (bd. dirs., pres.), Sunnydale Grange, Cottage Grove/Eugene Rod & Gun Club. Republican. Avocations: golf, travel. Office: Eagle's View Mgmt Co Inc 1399 Franklin Blvd Eugene OR 97403-1979

WOOLLEY, LESLIE ANN, legislative staff member; b. Ada, Okla., Apr. 7, 1953; d. William Walter and Lois Ann (Drummond) W.; m. Doyle Cameron Bartlett. BA, Okla. State U., 1975, MBA, 1976. Legis. asst. for Rep. Wes Watkins, US House of Reps., Washington, 1977-81, Rep. Bill McCollum, Washington, 1981-84, Rep. Norm Shumway, Washington, 1986-87; asst. v.p. Chemical NY, Inc., Washington, 1984-86; legis. dir. for Senator Bob Graham, Washington, 1987; banking legis. asst. for Senator Zell Miller, Washington; dep. to chmn. for policy Fed. Deposit Insurance Corp., 1994—97; dir. bus. & pub. liaison US Dept. Treasury, 2000—01; profl. staff mem. US Senate Com. on Homeland Security and Govt. Affairs; v.p. internat. and congl. rels. Conf. of State Bank Supervisors (CSBS), 2005—08; chief of staff for Rep. Emanuel Cleaver, US House of Reps., 2008—. Mem. Women in Housing and Fin. (pres. 1984-85), Women as Leaders Seminar (bd. dirs. 1985-91), Okla. State Soc. (pres. 1990-91), Okla. Cattlemens Assn., Fla. State Soc. Home: 609 Oakley Pl Alexandria VA 22302-3611 Office: Office of Congressman Emanuel Cleaver 1641 Longworth House Office Bldg Washington DC 20515-2505 Office Phone: 202-225-4535. Office Fax: 202-225-4403. E-mail: lesile.woolley@mail.house.gov.*

WOOLLEY, ROGER SWIRE, lawyer; b. Chgo., Nov. 18, 1924; s/ Anthony Walter and Agnes Louise (MacMurray) W.; m. Patricia Ann Jundt, 1951 (dec. 1978), Susan Naomi Pignolet, 2006; children: Elliott Payne, Merrit Ann. BA, Coll. William & Mary, 1947; student, Exeter Coll., London, 1947-48; LLB, Columbia U., 1951. Bar: Calif., US Supreme Ct., 1952. Legal counsel Solar Aircraft, San Diego, 1952-54; prin. Law Offices of Roger S. Woolley, Rancho Santa Fe, Calif., 1954—. Active Automobile Club So. Calif., L.A., dir. 1974-98, chmn. 1988-90; active Am. Automobile Assn., Falls Church, Va., Orlando, Fla., dir., 1986-97, chmn., 1991-93; founding dir., sec. Bank La Jolla, 1962-68; founding dir., sec. Rancho Santa Fe Savs. & Loan, 1972-78; founding dir., sec. Torrey Pines Bank, 1979-84; dir. Scripps Meml. Hosp. Found., La Jolla, Calif. 1984—; trustee emeritus The Endowment Assn. of Coll. William & Mary, Williamsburg, Va.; chmn., mem. Calif. State Hwy. Commn., 1958-67. Lt. jr. U.S. Navy, 1942-46, WW II. Mem. ABA, State Bar Calif., San Diego County Bar Assn., Rotary Club Rancho Santa Fe. Office: Law Offices of Roger S Woolley PO Box R Rancho Santa Fe CA 92067

WOOLLING, KENNETH RAU, vascular internist; b. Indpls., Mar. 6, 1918; m. Catherine Margaret McColl, Mar. 20, 1948; 2 children. BA magna cum laude, Butler U., 1939; postgrad., Harvard U., 1939-40; MD, Ind. U., 1943; MS in Medicine, U. Minn., 1951. Diplomate Nat. Bd. Med. Examiners, Am. Bd. Internal Medicine, Am. Bd. Cardiovascular Disease. Intern Indpls. City Hosp. (now Wishard Meml.), Indpls., 1943-44; resident in internal medicine Marion County Gen. Hosp., Indpls., 1947; fellow, first asst. internal medicine Mayo Found., Rochester, Minn., 1948-52; mem. med. staff, mem. tchg. staff postgrad. med. edn. Marion County Gen. Hosp. (name now Wishard Meml. Hosp.), Indpls., 1952—; founder, dir., peripheral vascular diseases clinic Indpls City & Marion County Gen. Hosp. (now Wishard Meml.), Indpls., 1952-68; pvt. practice internal medicine and cardiovascular diseases Indpls, 1952—; founder, dir. peripheral vascular diseases clinic Meth. Hosp., Indpls., 1967-72, founder, dir. vascular lab., 1970-73, mem. med. staff, tchr. staff postgrad. med. edn., 1952—. Mem. med. staff St. Vincent Hosp., St. Francis Hosp. and Winona Meml. Hosp., Indpls., 1952—; charter mem. med. staff Cmty. Hosp., Indpls., 1952—; charter mem. med. adv. com. Butler U., Indpls, 1956—. Contbr. articles to profl. jours., 1950—. Capt. Med. Corps U.S. Army, 1944-46. Fellow ACP, Am. Coll. Chest Physicians, Coun. on Cardiology Am. Heart Assn., Am. Coll. Angiology (gov. state of Ind. 1979-80); mem. AMA (50 Yr. award 1993), SAR, Internat. Union Angiology, Am. Soc. Internal Medicine, Am. Diabetes Assn., Ind. State Med. Soc., Ind. Diabetes Assn., Am. Fedn. for Clin. Rsch., N.Y. Acad. Med. Scis., North Ctrl. Clin. Soc., Mayo Cardiovascular Soc., Ind. Hist. Soc., Res. Officers Assn., Indpls. Med. Soc., Am. Legion, Shriners, Masons (Scottish Rite and Mystic Tie Lodge, 50 yr. award 1989), Contemporary Club of Indpls., Indpls. Athletic Club, Columbia Club, Highland Golf and Country Club, Phi Delta Theta (50 yr. award 1985), Phi Kappa Phi, Phi Chi. Presbyterian. Office: PO Box 80192 Indianapolis IN 46280-0192

WOOLLISCROFT, JAMES O., dean, medical educator; BS summa cum laude, U. Minn., 1972, MD, 1976. Resident internal medicine U. Mich., Ann Arbor, faculty Dept. Internal Medicine, 1980, prof. internal medicine, 1993—, prof. Dept. Med. Edn., Josiah Macy, Jr. prof. med. edn., 1996, Lyle C. Roll prof. medicine, 2001, assoc. chair Dept. Internal Medicine; chief of staff U. Mich. Hosps. and Health Ctrs., Ann Arbor; assoc. dean, dir. grad. med. edn. U. Mich. Med. Sch., Ann Arbor, exec. assoc. dean, 1999—2006, interim dean, 2006—07, dean, 2007—. Recipient Career Achievement in Med. Edn. Award, Soc. Gen. Med. Edn., 2004. Office: U Mich Med Sch Office of Dean 1301 Catherine Rd Ann Arbor MI 48109 Office Phone: 734-763-9600.*

WOOLSEY, LYNN C., United States Representative from California; b. Seattle, Nov. 3, 1937; 4 children. Student, U. Wash.; BS, U. San Francisco, 1981. Mgr. human resources Harris Digital Telephone, 1969—80; owner Woolsey Personnel Svs., 1980—92; mem. US Congress from 6th Calif. dist., 1993—, asst. whip, 1993—, mem. edn. & labor com., fgn. affairs com., internat. affairs com., sci. & tech. com. Mem. Petaluma City Coun., 1984—92, vice mayor, 1986, 91; founding mem. Missing & Exploited Children's Caucus; mem. Afterschool Caucus, Child Care Caucus, Congl. Friends of Animals, Congl. Human Rights Caucus, Congl. Task Force Internat. HIV/AIDS, Internat. Workers Rights Caucus, Intelligent Transp. Sys. Caucus, Livable Cmyts. Task Force, Sonoma County Commn. Status of Women; co-chair Congl. Progressive Caucus, Dem. Caucus Task Force Welfare Reform, Edn. Task Force Calif. Delegation Bipartisan Caucus; chair Dem. Caucus Task Force Children & Families. Mem.: NOW, LWV, Sierra Club. Democrat. Office: US Ho Reps 2263 Rayburn Ho Office Bldg Washington DC 20515-0506 Address: Santa Rosa Dist Office Ste 200 1101 Coll Ave Santa Rosa CA 95404 also: San Rafael Dist Office Ste 354 1050 Northgate Dr San Rafael CA 94903 Office Phone: 202-225-5161.*

WOOLSEY, R. JAMES (ROBERT JAMES WOOLSEY), lawyer, former CIA director; b. Tulsa, Sept. 21, 1941; s. Robert James and Clyde (Kirby) W.; m. Suzanne Haley, Aug. 15, 1965; children: Robert Nathaniel, Daniel James, Benjamin Haley. BA with great distinction, Stanford U., 1963; MA (Rhodes scholar), Oxford U., Eng., 1965; LLB, Yale U., 1968. Bar: Calif. bar 1969, D.C. bar 1970. Program analyst Office Sec. Def., Washington, 1968-70, NSC, Washington, 1970; gen. counsel US Senate Armed Services Com., 1970-73; assoc. firm Shea & Gardner, Washington, 1973-77, ptnr., 1979-89, 1991-93; under sec. Dept. Navy US Dept. Def., 1977—79; amb. & US rep. to negotiation on conventional armed forces in Europe US Dept. State, 1989-91; dir. CIA, Washington, 1993-95; ptnr. Shea & Gardner, 1995—2002; v.p. Global Strategic Security Booz Allen Hamilton, McLean, Va., 2002—08, sr. exec. adv., 2008—; of counsel Goodwin Procter LLP, Washington, 2008—. Adv. U.S. del. SALT, Helsinki and Vienna, 1969-70 Mem. Pres.'s Commn. on Strategic Forces, 1983-84, Fed. Ethics Law Reform, 1989; Blue Ribbon Commn. on Defense Mgmt., 1985-86; del.-at-large Soviet Arms Talks, Geneva, 1983-86; mem. Rumsfeld Commn. to Assess Ballistic Missile Threat, 1998; mem. Nat. Commn. on Terrorism 1999-2000; trustee Stanford U., 1972-74, Regent Smithsonian Instution, 1989-93; bd. chmn. Freedom House; adv. bd. chmn. Clean Fuels Found., New Uses Council; vice-chmn. adv. bd. Global Options LLC; trustee Ctr. for Strategic & Internat. Studies; past mem. bd. gov. Phila. Stock Exch.; dir. Info. Sys. Lab., Linsang Ptnrs., Fibersense Tech. Corp., Invicta Networks, DIANA LLC, Agorics Inc.; mem. bd. adv. BioDefense Corp.; past bd. dir. Martin Marietta, British Aerospace, Fairchild Industries, Titan Corp., DynCorp, USF&G, Sun Healthcare Group, Inc., Yurie Systems, Inc. Served with U.S. Army, 1968-70. Mem. Council Fgn. Relations, Phi Beta Kappa. Presbyterian. Office: Goodwin Procter LLP 901 NY Ave NW Washington DC 20001 E-mail: jwoolsey@goodwinprocter.com.

WOOLSEY, ROBERT PAUL, church musician; s. Ralph Alzore and June Virginia (Hanneman) Woolsey. Student, Calif. Inst. Arts, Valencia, 1973—74. Assoc. musician St. Paul's Cathedral, LA, 1975—76; audio cons., engr. Skyline Recording, LA, 1979—80; co-founder, tech. dir. Woolsey Green Prodn., LA, 1981—93; freelance sound editor LA, 1994—98; prin. organist St. Andrew & St. Charles Episcopal Ch., LA, 1999—2006, St. James Episcopal Ch., S. Pasadena, Calif., 2006—; aux. organist Cathedral Our Lady Angels, LA, 2005—. Prodr.(dir.): (DVD) Ven Creator Spiritus, 2005;, composer musical arrangements; featured guest performer with condr. Paul Salamanovich:; one-man shows include Royce Hall, UCLA, 2008—09. Recipient Grammy Nomination Best Jazz Vocal Group, Nat. Acad. Recording Arts and Scis., 1984. Mem.: Am. Guild Organists. Avocations: video photographer, scuba diving. Personal E-mail: woolsey.robert@gmail.com.

WOOLSON, GLORIA JEAN, education educator; b. Syracuse, NJ, Nov. 7, 1941; d. Glen James Manuel and Mattie Florence Turner. BA, SUNY, Oswego, 1965, MA in Curriculum Devel., 1985. 5th grade tchr. Auburn City Sch. Dist., NY, 1965—66; 6th grade tchr. Jordan-Elbridge Ctrl. Sch. Dist., Jordan, NY, 1966—70, 3d grade tchr., 1970—2002; adj. tchr. Cayuga CC, Auburn, 2004—, Onondaga CC, NY, 2007. Dir. one-rm. sch. program Spafford Hist. Soc.; deacon, mem. choir, clk. trustee, moderator Plainville United Ch. of Christ, NY. Recipient Excellence in Tchg. award, Syracuse U. Sch. Edn., 1996, Spl. Svc. award, Onondaga County Tchrs. Assn., 1997. Mem.: NY State Ret. Tchrs., Jordan-Elbridge Edn. Assn. (sec., bldg. rep., social dir.). Avocations: antiques, exercise, reading, travel. Home: 7688 Tater Rd Memphis NY 13112-8755 Personal E-mail: gmw7688@localnet.com.

WOOLSTON-CATLIN, MARIAN, retired psychiatrist; b. Seattle, Jan. 20, 1931; d. Howard Brown and Katharine Nichols (Dally) Woolston; m. Randolph Catlin Jr., July 5, 1959; children: Laura Louise, Jennifer Woolston, Randolph III. BA cum laude, Vassar Coll., 1951; MD, Harvard U., 1955. Diplomate Nat. Bd. Med. Examiners. Intern in pediatric medicine Children's Hosp., Boston, 1956, asst. resident in pediatric medicine, 1956; resident in psychiatry Mass. Mental Health Ctr., Boston, 1957-59; fellow in child psychiatry Tavistock Clin., London, 1960; spkr. Rhodes House, U. Oxford, 1961; Commonwealth fellow in child psychiatry Harvard U. at Gaebler Children's Unit, Waltham, Mass., 1975-78, clin. instr. psychiatry, 1978-79; pvt. practice

Wellesley Hills, Mass., 1978-91, Medfield, Mass., 1991—2006; ret., 2006. Clin. instr. psychiatry Harvard U. at Mass. Mental Health Ctr., Boston, 1957-59, 78-82, Tufts U. at Mass. Mental Health Ctr., 1957-59; mem. exec. bd. Parents' and Children's Svcs., Boston, 1983-86. Designer H.H. Hunnewell Meml. Garden for New Eng. Flower Show Mass. Hort. Soc., 1975 (Ames Cup award). Exec. bd. Ext. Divsn. New Eng. Conservatory Music, 1972-75; charter mem. reuse com. Medfield State Hosp., 1992—; charter mem. Nat. Women's History Mus., 2004; corporator Schepens Eye Rsch. Inst., 2005—, adv. bd., rsch. com. 2006—; adv. bd. Women's Eye Health Task Force, 2005—. Fellow Am. Acad. Child and Adolescent Psychiatry; mem. AMA, Am. Psychiat. Assn. (life), Mass. Psychiat. Assn., Mass. Med. Soc., New Eng. Coun. Child and Adolescent Psychiatry (hon.), Boston Vassar Club (exec. bd. 1963-75), Hills Garden Club Wellesley (exec. bd. and design chief 1973-75). Episcopalian. Avocations: landscape design, sculpting. Office Phone: 508-359-8046.

WOOLVERTON, DIANE MARIE, literature language and education professor; d. Robert Paton, Jr. Marshall and Delores Mildred Merkling; m. Thomas Roy Woolverton, July 8, 2000; 1 child, Shawn Kirean Copeland. BS in Philosophy, Buffalo State Coll., NY, 1989; BS in Secondary Edn. English, Buffalo State Coll., 1999, MS in English Edn., 2003. Cert. Tchr. U. the State NY, 2004, Written English and English Vocabulary Brainbench, 2004, Content Editor/Proofreader Grammatika, 2004. English and reading tchr. St. Benedict's RC Sch., Amherst, NY, 1999—2005; owner, pres. ReadWrite Resources, Buffalo, 2004—; adj. prof. Medaille Coll., Buffalo, 2004—, Buffalo State Coll., D'Youville Coll., 2007—; educator Williamsville Ctrl. Sch. Dist., NY, 2006—. Writer ReadWrite Resources, Buffalo, 2004—. Actor: (semi-profl. drama/theatre) Lend Me a Tenor (Kay award, 1993). Dir. St. Benedict Ann. Sch. Musicals; mem. Rep. Nat. Com., Buffalo, 2006—, NYS English Coun., Albany; vol. Project Flight: Books for Kids, Buffalo, 1997—98. Mem.: Nat. Coun. Tchrs. English (assoc.). Conservative. Avocations: painting, travel, reading. Office: ReadWrite Resources 1749 Hertel Ave Buffalo NY 14216-3001

WOOLWORTH, ERIC S., professional sports team executive; m. Jocelyn Woolworth; 1 child, Cassidy. Grad. cum laude, Georgetown U.; JD cum laude, Georgetown U. Law Ctr. Gen. counsel Miami Heat, Fla., 1995—2001, interim pres., 2000—01, pres. bus. ops., 2001—. Bd. mem. Big Bros. Big Sisters, Children's Craniofacial Assn. Office: Miami Heat AmericanAirlines Arena 601 Biscayne Blvd Miami FL 33132*

WOOSLEY, STANFORD EARL, astrophysicist; b. Texarkana, Tex., Dec. 8, 1944; s. Homer Earl and Wanda Faye (Fisher) W.; m. Petra Berkemeyer; children William D., Amanda Faye. BA in Physics, Rice U., 1966, PhD in Astrophysics, 1971. Rsch. assoc. Rice U., Houston, 1971-73; rsch. fellow in physics Kellogg Radiation Lab. Calif. Inst. Tech., Pasadena, 1973-75; asst. prof. astronomy U. Calif., Santa Cruz, 1975-78, assoc. prof., 1978-83, prof. astronomy and astrophysics, 1983—. Cons. Lawrence Livermore Nat. Lab., 1974-; chair dept. astronomy and astrophysics, U. Calif. Santa Cruz, 1983-1987, 1989-1991, 1998-2003, 2006; dir. DOE-SciDAC Computational Astrophysics Consortium, 2006-. Editor: High Energy Transients, 1984, Supernova, 1991, Nuclear Astrophysics, 1993, Internat. Jour. Modern Physics, 1994-, New Astronomy, 1996-; contbr. over 400 articles to profl. jours. Named A. V. Humboldt Prof. 1995-97; Outstanding Faculty, Divsn. Biological and Phys. Sci., U. Calif. Santa Cruz, 2004, faculty rsch. lectr., 2007. Fellow Am. Phys. Soc. (H. A. Bethe prize 2005); mem. Am. Astron. Soc. (Bruno Rossi prize 2005), Internat. Astronomical Union, Am. Acad. Arts and Sci., Nat. Acad. Sci. (Physics Divsn.). Achievements include research into the lives and deaths of massive stars and supernova, nucleosynthesis and x-ray and gamma ray bursts. Home: 115 Auburn Ave Santa Cruz CA 95060-6231 Office: U Calif Dept Astronomy and Astrophysics Santa Cruz CA 95064

WOOSNAM, RICHARD EDWARD, venture capitalist, lawyer; b. Anderson, Ind., June 27, 1942; s. Richard Wendell and Ruth (Cleveland) W.; m. Diane Dalto; children: Cynthia S., Elizabeth C. BS, Ind. U., 1964, JD, 1967, MBA, 1968. Bar: Ind. 1967, US Dist. Ct. (so. dist.) Ind. 1967. Instr. bus. law Ind. U., Bloomington, 1966-68; assoc. Ferguson, Ferguson & Lloyd, Bloomington, 1967-68; dep. pros. Monroe County, Bloomington, 1967-68; tax acct. Price Waterhouse, Phila., 1968-69; v.p., treas. Innovest Group, Inc., Phila., 1969-82, chmn., pres., 1983—. Bd. dirs. Innovest Talent Svcs., Inc., Ind. U. Found., Phila. Hospitality, Inc., Phila. Zoo, Pa. Acad. Fine Arts, Arts and Bus. Coun. Greater Phila.; vice chmn. World Affairs Coun. Phila.; chmn. Walnut St. Theatre. Mem. ABA, Ind. Bar Assn., Union League Phila., Sunday Breakfast Club, Pa Soc. Office: 1528 Walnut St Ste 1701 Philadelphia PA 19102 Business E-Mail: rwoosnam@innovestgrp.com.

WOOSTER, JOHN T., JR., insurance company executive; Pres. Hannaford Co., Washington; founder, pres. Wooster Comm., NYC, 1988—89; v.p. comm. Am. Internat. Group, Inc., 1989—2001, spl. advisor, comm., 2001—05, 2006—, sr. v.p. comm., 2005—06. Office: Am Internat Group Inc 70 Pine St New York NY 10270*

WOOSTER, ROBERT, history professor; b. Beaumont, Tex., Aug. 27, 1956; s. Ralph Ancil and Edna Lee (Jones) W.; m. Catherine Cox, 1992. BA, Lamar U., 1977, MA, 1979; PhD, U. Tex., 1985. Scholar in residence Tex. State Hist. Assn., Liberty, 1985-86; asst. prof. Tex. A&M U., Corpus Christi, 1986-90, assoc. prof., 1990-95, prof., 1995—, chmn. dept. humanities, 1997—2000, Piper prof., 1998, Frantz prof. history, 2001—04, regent's prof., 2008. Author: Soldiers, Sutlers and Settlers (Bates award 1987), U.S. Military and Indian Policy, 1988, History of Fort Davis, 1990, Nelson A. Miles and The Twilight of the Frontier Army, 1993, The Civil War 100, 1998, The Civil War Bookshelf, 2001, Frontier Crossroads: Fort Davis and the West, 2006; editor: Soldier, Surgeon, Scholar: The Memoirs of William Henry Corbusier, 2003; co-editor: (with William Kessel) Encyclopedia of Native American Wars & Warfare, 2005; editl. adv. bd. Southwestern Hist. Quar., Austin, Tex., 1989—, Military History of the West, 1995—, Jour. of the West, 1996-2000. Dep. dir. U.S. Mil. Acad./ROTC fellowship U.S. Mil. Acad., West Point, N.Y., 1990. Fellow Tex. State Hist. Assn. (pres. 2005—06); mem. Orgn. Am. Historians. Democrat. Home: 4600 Ocean Dr Apt 708 Corpus Christi TX 78412-2543 Office: Texas A&M Univ 6300 Ocean Dr Corpus Christi TX 78412-5599 Office Phone: 361-825-2402. Business E-Mail: robert.wooster@tamucc.edu.

WOOSTER, ROSSITZA BOUNEVA, economics professor; m. Michael Robert Wooster. PhD, U. Oreg., Eugene, 2002. Asst. prof. Portland State U., Oreg., 2008—. Contbr. articles to profl. pubs. Recipient Phi Beta Kappa, St. Lawrence U., 1995, Omicron Delta Epsilon, 1995. Office: Dept Economics Portland State Univ PO Box 751 Portland OR 97207 Office Fax: 503-725-3945.

WOOSTER, STEPHANIE LYNNE, art historian, artist; b. Livonia, Mich., Dec. 7, 1975; d. Ronald J. and Patricia Lynne Wooster. BA magna cum laude, Kalamazoo Coll., Mich., 1998; MFA with distinction in Painting, Pratt Inst., Bklyn., 2003, MS with distinction in Art History, 2003. Tchr. English Sch. No. 160 Advanced English Study, St. Petersburg, Russia, 1996—97; grading asst. Pratt Inst., Art History Dept., Bklyn., 2000—02; instr. sch. art history U. St. Andrews, Scotland, 2004—05; adj. prof., Art History Hope Coll., Art Dept., Holland, Mich., 2007; vis. asst. prof., Art History Founds. Grand Valley State U., Allendale, 2007—. Co-editor: INFERNO: Jour. Art History; exhibitions include Gov.'s Residence, Lansing, Mich., Pratt Inst., Bklyn., Internat. Mus.Horse, Lexington, KY, Muskegon Museum Art, Mich., Mt. Pleasant, Mich., Kalamazoo Coll., Mich., Fla. State U. Mus.Fine Arts, Tallahassee, Fla., Hammerstein Ballroom, Manhattan Ctr., NY, Grand Rapids, Mich., Michican Equine Artists Founders Exhbn., Grand Rapids, Mich. (First Pl. award, 1998), ARC Gallery, Chgo., Studio 23/The ARTS Ctr., Bay City, Mich., Preservation Trust Mus., St. Andrews, Scotland, Williamsburg Art and Hist. Ctr., Bklyn., Stephen F. Austin State U., Nacogdoches, 2007, Lowell Area Arts Coun., Mich., 2007, Festival of the Arts Regional Arts Competition, Grand Rapids Art Mus., 2007, 36th Ann. Juried Spiritual Art Competition, First United Meth. Ch., Grand Rapids, Mich., 2009. Recipient Brian Gougeon Art prize, Art Dept., Kalamazoo Coll., 1995, Michael Waskowsky Art prize, 1997, Sr. Exhbn. Paintings award, 1998, Cert. of Excellence award for outstanding merit in grad. fine arts, Fine Art Dept., Pratt Inst., 2003, Pratt Cir. Outstanding Academic Achievement award, Pratt Inst., 2003, Art prize, Arts Coun. Greater Rapids, MIch., 2009; scholar, Art Dept., Kalamazoo Coll., 1994—98, 1998; Beatrice Cox Pratt in Venice scholarship, Art History Dept., Pratt Inst., 2001, Pratt Alumni Venice scholarship, 2001, scholarship, U. Pitts. Ctr. for Russian and East European Studies, Summer Lang. Inst., 2007. Mem.: Am. Assn. Advancement Slavic Studies, Assn. of the Historians of Nineteenth-Century Art, Coll. Art Assn., Am. Acad. Equine Art (assoc.), Urban Inst. Contemporary Arts (visual arts com.), Equine Art Guild, Alpha Lambda Delta, Phi Beta Kappa (Southwestern Assn.). Home: 7700 Riverview Dr Apt 204 Jenison MI 49428 Office Phone: 616-331-3724. Personal E-mail: wooster.stephanie@gmail.com.

WOOTEN, CECIL AARON, retired religious organization administrator; b. Laurel, Miss., June 3, 1924; s. Cecil A. and Alice (Cox) W.; m. Helen Moss, Apr. 4, 1947; children: Michael, Margaret, Martin, Marsha, Mark. BS in Mech. Engring, U. Ala., 1949. With CBI Industries, 1941—83, bd. dirs., 1965-83, mng. dir. CBI Constructors Ltd., London, 1957-62, mgr. Houston sales dist., 1962-64, v.p. engring., 1964—68, v.p., mgr. corp. svcs. Oak Brook, Ill., 1968-69, sr. v.p.-gen. sales mgr., 1969-78; sr. v.p. comml. devel. Chgo. Bridge & Iron Co. (subs. CBI Industries), 1978-79; sr. v.p. corp. adminstrn. CBI Industries, Oak Brook, 1980-83; dir. devel. Christian Family Services, Gainesville, Fla., 1983-86, Denver Ch. of Christ, 1986-88, Boston Ch. of Christ, 1988-92; pres. Internat. Chs. of Christ, Inc., LA, 1994-99; chair Internat. Chs. Christ, LA, 1999—2000, retired, 2002. Bd. dirs. Oak Brook (Ill.) Bank. Former trustee Elmhurst (Ill.) Coll.; former bd. sponsors Good Samaritan Hosp., Downers Grove, Ill. Served to 1st lt. AUS, 1943-46. Mem. ASME, NSPE, Rotary. Personal E-mail: cecilwooten@hotmail.com.

WOOTEN, JAMES H., JR., lawyer, engineering executive; BA in Criminal Justice, U. Ill., 1978; JD, U. Chgo., 1982. Assoc. Gardner, Carton & Douglas, Chgo., 1982—88; assoc. gen. counsel, asst. sec. Ill. Tool Works Inc., Glenview, Ill., 1988—2005, v.p., gen. counsel, 2005, sr. v.p., gen. counsel, corp. sec., 2005—. Mem.: ABA, Cook County Bar Assn., Exec. Leadership Coun., Minority Corp. Counsel Assn., Soc. Corp. Secs. and Governance Profls., Am. Corp. Counsel Assn., Chgo. Bar Assn., Phi Delta Phi. Office: Illinois Tool Works 3600 W Lake Ave Glenview IL 60026 E-mail: jwooten@itw.com.*

WOOTEN, JOEL ORBA, JR., lawyer; b. Hazlehurst, Ga., June 4, 1950; s. Joel Orba and Mary Eleanor (Whitlock) W.; m. Sybrina G. Franklin; children: Joel III, Katherine, Frank. BBA, U. Ga., 1972, JD, 1975. Bar: Ga. 1975, U.S. Dist. Ct. (mid. dist.) Ga. 1976, U.S. Ct. Appeals (11th cir.) 1981. Ptnr. Kelly, Denney, Pease & Allison, Columbus, Ga., 1975-88, Butler, Wooten, Overby & Cheeley, Columbus, Ga., 1988—. Bd. regents Univ. Sys. of Ga., 1999-2006, chair, 2004-05. With U.S. Army, 1972. Mem. Am. Bar Assn., Fed. Bar Assn., Ga. Trial Lawyers Assn., State Bar Ga. (chmn. gen. practice & trial sect. 1990-91), Columbus Lawyers Club (pres 1988-89), Columbus Younger Lawyers (pres. 1983-84), Assn. Trial Lawyers Am., U. Ga. Alumni Soc. (bd. dirs. 1981-83, 89-91). Office: Butler, Wooten, & Fryhofer, LLP 105 Thirteenth St Columbus GA 31901 Office Phone: 706-322-1990.

WOOTEN, KATHY A., finance educator, accountant; b. Jackson, Miss. 1 child, Robbie Swindle. MBA, Millsaps Coll., Jackson, 2001. Med. billing coding instr. Copiah Lincoln CC, Natchez, Miss., 2002—05; asst. prof. acctg. Belhaven Coll., Jackson, 2005—. Advisor Belhaven Acctg. Club, Jackson, 2005—. Vol. Natchez Adams Ch. Am. Red Cross. Mem.: Krewe Phoenix, Natchez Festival Music Guild. Conservative. Avocations: travel, cooking, gardening. Office: Belhaven Coll 1500 Peachtree St Box 757 Jackson MS 39202 Business E-Mail: kwooten@belhaven.edu.

WOOTEN-BLANKS, LESLIE, biologist; b. Chattanooga, Apr. 16, 1971; d. Charles L. and Sharon Mitchell Wooten; m. Cheyene Blanks, Sept. 30, 2006; children: Lesley-Anne Hardesty, Jared Blanks. PhD, Med. U. SC., Charleston, 2007. Cancer biologist Med. U. SC., 2000—; adj. prof. biology Coll. Charleston, 2003. Contbr. articles to profl. jours. Postdoc. fellowship, NIH. Office: Med Univ SC 173 Ashley Ave Charleston SC 29425 Business E-Mail: wootenl@musc.edu.

WOOTON, DAVID L., chemist, consultant; b. Plainfield, NJ, June 23, 1948; s. Donald T. and Ruth E. Wooton; m. Lynda W. Wiedegreen, Sept. 6, 1969; children: Mark E., Tim A., Jennifer M. BS, Western Ky. U., BowlingGreen, 1970, MS, 1972; PhD, Va. Poly. Inst., Blacksburg, 1976. Postdoc. Va. Poly. Inst., 1976—77; rsch. scientist Ashland Petroleum-R&D Dept., Catlettsburg, Ky., 1977—79; advisor analytical chemistry Petroleum Additive Divsn. Ethyl Corp., Richmond, Va., 1979—2001; prin. cons. Wooton-Consulting, Beaverdam, Va. Contbr. articles to profl. jours. Achievements include development of in-service lubricant fluid FTIR anlayses methods currently used extensively; research in large frame gas turbines; root cause identification of lubricant problems.

WOOTTON, DAVID MACMULLEN, mechanical engineer, educator; BS, Cornell U., Ithaca, NY, 1987; MS, MIT, Cambridge, Mass., 1990; PhD, Ga. Inst. Tech., Atlanta, Ga., 1998. Violin repair and restoration Reuning and Son Violins, Ithaca, NY, 1980—87; project engr., safety and crashworthiness GM, Warren, Mich., 1987—90; noise and vibration cons. Harris Miller and Hanson Inc, Lexington, Mass., 1987—2000; postdoctoral fellow, biomedical engring. Johns Hopkins U., Baltimore, 1998—2000; asst. prof. mech. engring. Drexel U., Philadelphia, 2000—06; assoc. prof. mech. engring. Cooper Union Advancement Sci. and Art, NYC, 2006—. Achievements include patents for poly (vinyl alcohol) cryogel for bioengineering applications. Office: Cooper Union 51 Astor Place New York NY 10003

WOOTTON, JOHN FRANCIS, physiology educator; b. Penn Yan, NY, May 31, 1929; s. John Edenden and Margaret Eliza (Smith) W.; m. Joyce Albertine Mac Mullen, Aug. 28, 1959; children: J. Timothy, David M., Barbara H., Bruce C. BS, Cornell U., 1951, MS, 1953, PhD, 1960. Grad. rsch. asst. Cornell U., Ithaca, NY, 1956-60, from asst. prof. to prof. emeritus, 1962—2004, prof. emeritus, 2004—, assoc. dean Grad. Sch., 1980-83; post doctoral fellow U. Coll., London, 1960-62. Grad. faculty rep. field of physiology Cornell U., 1990-92, 93-97, chmn. dept. physiology, 1997-98, co-chmn. dept. biomed. scis., 1998-99, chmn. 1999-2000; vis. scientist MRC Molecular Biology, Cambridge, Eng., 1969-70, Nat. Inst. Med. Rsch., London, 1985-86, 92-93, 2002; temporary sr. rsch. assoc. Stanford (Calif.) U., 1977-78. Contbr. articles to profl. jours. 1st lt. USAR, 1954-56. Rsch. and Travel grantee NIH, USDA Burroughs Wellcom Fund, Med. Rsch. Coun., Cornell Biotech. Program. Mem. AAAS, Am. Soc. Biochemistry and Molecular Biology, Am. Chem. Soc., Biophys. Soc., Protein Soc., Sigma Xi (v.p., pres. Cornell chpt.). Avocations: travel, choral singing, gardening, art, fishing. Office: Cornell U Dept Biomed Scis T8-008A Vet Rsch Tower Ithaca NY 14853-5908 Business E-Mail: jfw1@cornell.edu.

WOPAT, TOM, actor, singer; b. Lodi, Wis., Sept. 9, 1951; Actor: (Broadway plays) I Love My Wife, 1977—79, City of Angels, 1989—92, Guys and Dolls, 1992, Annie Get Your Gun, 2001, 42nd Street, 2002—03, Chicago, 2004—05, 2007, Glengarry Glen Ross, 2005, A Catered Affair, 2008; (TV series) The Dukes of Hazzard, 1979—85, Fantasy, 1982, The Dukes, 1983, Blue Skies, 1988, A Peaceable Kingdom, 1989; (TV films) Burning Rage, 1984, Christmas Comes to Willow Creek, 1987, Just My Imagination, 1992, Contagious, 1997, The Dukes of Hazzard: Reunion!, 1997, Meteorites!, 1998, The Dukes of Hazzard: Hazzard in Hollywood, 2000, The Hive, 2008; (films) Story, Songs and Stars, 1984, Bonneville, 2006; singer: (albums) Tom Wopat, 1983, Don't Look Back, 1990, Learning to Love, 1995, Hands On, 1995, The Still of the Night, 2000, Dissertation on the State of Bliss, 2005.

WORAM, BRIAN J., lawyer, construction executive; b. Perth Amboy, NJ, July 24, 1960; m. Allison M. Woram. BS in Mech. Engring., Tex. A&M U., College Station, 1981; JD, U. Tex., Austin, 1986. Bar: Tex. 1986. Reservoir engr. Exxon Co.; assoc. to shareholder Locke, Liddell & Sapp; regional gen. counsel Centex Homes (subs. of Centex Corp.), 1995—97, v.p., gen. counsel, 1997—98, sr. v.p., gen. counsel, 1998—2005; sr. v.p., chief legal officer Centex Corp., 2005—. Contbr. articles to profl. jours. Recipient Tex. Supper Lawyer, Best Lawyer in Dallas. Mem.: ABA, High Production Homebuilder Gen. Counsel Forum (chmn.), Tau Beta Pi, Pi Tau Sigma, Phi Delta Phi. Mailing: Centex Corp PO Box 199000 Dallas TX 75219-9000

WORBOYS, ROGER DICK, retired communications executive; b. Syracuse, NY, Sept. 1, 1947; s. Carl Stape and Dorothy Elsa (Dick) W.; m. Mary Lee Tasker, Nov. 27, 1971; children: Thomas, Elizabeth. Bachelors degree, Alfred U., 1969; M in Bus., U. N.H., 1971. Mgr.-regional mgr. Continental Cablevision, Boston, 1974-86; v.p. ops. Simmons Comm., Stamford, Conn., 1986-88, Insight Comm., Glasgow, Scotland, NYC, 1988-95, Bresnan Comms., White Plains, N.Y., 1996-98, sr. v.p., 1999-2000; ret., 2001. Adv. bd. ctr. venture rsch. U. NH. Bd. trustees Alfred U.; bd. dirs. Cross Roads House, N.H. Chpt. Nature Conservancy; adv. bd. Newport Computer Svcs. Mem.: Rotary Internat., Portsmouth N.H. C. of C. (pres. 1983), Mechanics Fre Soc. Roman Catholic.

WORCESTER, HOWARD LESTER, internist; b. Kansas City, Mo., Jan. 3, 1945; s. Howard Elmer and Alma Jane (Evans) W. div.; m. Tammy Worcester; children: Tiffany, Chase. BS, U. Oregon, 1967, MD, 1971. Diplomate Am. Bd. Internal Medicine, Am. Bd. Forensic Pathology. Intern Harbor Gen. Hosp. UCLA, 1971-72; med. officer U.S. Army, West Germany, 1972-75; resident U. Calif., Irvine, 1975-77, chief med. resident, 1977-78; pvt. practice internal medicine Meml. Hosp., Long Beach, Calif., 1978—. Dir. utilization rev. Long Beach Meml. Hosp., 1983—, trustee, 1983—, also bd. dirs.; cons. Sultanate of Oman, Muscat, Oman, 1984—. Patron L.A. County Mus. Major U.S. Army, 1972-75. Recipient Merck scholarship U. Oreg. Med. Sch., 1969 Mem. Long Beach Meml. Hosp. Med. Group (pres. 1983—), Long Beach Meml. Med. Svc. Orgn. (pres. 1993-96), Phi Beta Kappa, Alpha Omega Alpha. Episcopalian. Avocations: cooking, wine collecting, travel, sports. Home: 11042 Skyline Dr Santa Ana CA 92705-2473 Office: Meml Med Group 2650 Elm Ave Ste 309 Long Beach CA 90806-1600 Office Phone: 562-595-8549. Personal E-mail: lesworcester@hotmail.com.

WORDEN, KATHARINE COLE, sculptor; b. NYC, May 4, 1925; d. Philip Gillette and Katharine (Pyle) Cole; m. Frederic G. Worden, Jan. 8, 1944; children: Fred, Dwight, Philip, Barbara, Katharine. Student, Potters Ch., Tucson, 1940-42, Sarah Lawrence Coll., 1942-44. Exhibited in group shows at Royce Galleries, Galerie Francoise Besnard, Paris, Cooling Gallery, London, Galerie Schumacher, Munich, Selected Artists Gallery, N.Y.C., Art Inst. Boston, Reid Gallery, Nashville, Weiner Gallery, N.Y.C., Boston Athanaeum, House of Humor and Satire, Gabrovo, Bulgaria, 1983, Newport Bay Club, 1984; pvt. collections Grand Palais, Paris, Dakar and Bathurst, Africa. Occupl. therapist psychopathic ward L.A. County Gen. Hosp., 1953-57; Headstart vol., Watts, Calif., 1965-67; tchr. sculpture Watts Towers Art Ctr., 1967-69; participant White House Women Doers Luncheon meeting, 1968; dir. Cambridgeport Problem Ctr., Cambridge, Mass., 1969-71; mem. Jud. Nominating Commn., 1976-79; bd. overseers Boston Mus. Fine Arts, 1980-83; bd. govs. Newport Seamens Ch. Inst., 1989-91; tustee Comm. Rsch., Miami, Fla., 1960-69, chmn. bd., 1966-69; trustee Newport Art Mus., 1984-86, 92-94, Jamestown Cmty. Theatre, 1994-97, 99-2005, 06-08, Newport Health Found., 1986-91, Hawthorne Sea Fund, 1990-93; bd. dirs. Boston Ctr. for Arts, 1976-80, Child and Family Svcs. Newport County, 1983-97, 99-2005, 06—; mem. Nat. Com. for the Performing Arts, 2006-07. Mem. Common Cause (Mass adv. bd. 1971-72, dir. 1974-75), Mass. Civil Liberties Union (exec. bd. 1973-74, dir. 1976-77). Home: 9 Meadow Ln Jamestown RI 02835

WORDEN, MARK K., multimedia designer, educator; s. Reese Jr. E. and Mary Worden; 1 child, Natalie L. BS in Info. Tech., U. Phoenix, Costa Mesa, Calif., 2004; attending in Instrnl. Design and Tech., Calif. State U., Fullerton, 2007—. Cert. internet webmaster 2001. Tech. coord. CCS, Orange, Calif., 2000—04; web multimedia instrnl. designer Coastline Coll., Fountain Valley, Calif., 2004—, career edn. instr., 2007—. Internet cons. Internet Promotion Group, Villa Pk., Calif., 1999—. Mem.: Toastmasters Club (area gov. 1997—98). Conservative. Office: Coastline Coll 11460 Warner Ave Fountain Valley CA 92708 Personal E-mail: mnedrow@aol.com. Business E-Mail: mworden@coastline.edu.

WORDEN, SIMON PETE, science administrator, career military officer; b. Mich., 1949; m. Nancy Worden. BS, U. Mich., 1971; PhD in Astronomy, U. Ariz., 1975; attended, Nat. War Coll., 1987; Nat. Security Studies, Maxwell Sch. Citizenship and Pub. Affairs, Syracuse U., NY, 1997. 2d. lt. USAF, 1971, advanced through grades to brig. gen., 2000, ret., 2004; astrophysicist Air Force Geophysics Lab., Nat. Solar Observatory, Sunspot, N.Mex., 1975—79; chief advanced tech. divsn. Air Force Space Sys. Divsn., LA AFB, Calif., 1979—83; spl. asst. to dir. Strategic Defense Initiative Orgn., Dept. Defense, 1983—86; sr. policy analyst Office Sci. and Tech. Policy, Exec. Office of Pres., 1986—87; sr. rsch. fellow Nat. Defense U. Fort Lesley J. McNair, Washington, 1986—87; crew comdr. Space Defense Ops. Ctr., chief spl. ops. branch US Space Command, Cheyenne Mountain AFB, Colo., 1987—89; dir. advanced concepts, sci. and tech. Nat. Space Coun., Exec. Office of Pres., Washington, 1989—91; dep. tech. Ballistic Missile Defense Orgn., Washington, 1991—93; technical adviser to spl. asst. for theater air defense USAF Hdqs., Washington, 1993—94, dep. Battlespace Dominance, Directorate of Operational Requirements, Dep. Chief Staff for Air and Space Ops., 1997—98, dep. dir. operational requirements, 1998—99, dep. dir. command and control, 2000; dir. analysis and engring. Space Warfare Ctr., Air Force Space Command, Falcon AFB, Colo., 1994, comdr. 50th Space Win Colo., 1994—96; dep. dir. requirements Air Force Space Command, Peterson AFB, Colo., 1996—97; vice dir. ops. US Space Command, Peterson AFB, Colo., 2000—02; dir. devel. and transformation Space and Missile Sys. Ctr., Air Force Space Command, LA AFB, Calif., 2002—04; rsch. prof. astronomy U. Ariz., Tucson, 2004—05, rsch. prof. planetary scis. and rsch. prof. optical scis., 2005—06; dir. NASA Ames Rsch. Ctr., Moffett Field, Calif., 2006—. Sci. co-investigator NASA; cons. Defense Advanced Rsch. Projects Agency (DARPA); Congl. fellow, chief advisor on NASA space issues Office of Senator Sam Brownback, 2004; guest tchr. Internat. Space Univ. Contbr. articles to profl. jours. Decorated Defense Superior Svc. Medal with oak leaf cluster, Legion of Merit with oak leaf cluster, Defense Meritorious Svc. Medal with three oak leaf clusters, Meritorious Svc. Medal; recipient NASA Outstanding Leadership Medal, Air Force Outstanding Rsch. and Devel. Medal. Office: NASA Ames Rsch Ctr Moffett Field CA 94035

WORDEN, SKIP, writer; MBA, Ind. U., Bloomington, 1988; MA, U. Pitts., Penn., PhD, 1994; MDiv, Yale U., New Haven, 1998. Contbr. articles to profl. jours. Founder Mgt. and Religion Area Acad. Mgmt. Mem.: Beta Gamma Sigma. Personal E-mail: skipworden2004@yahoo.com.

WORELL, JUDITH P., psychologist, educator; b. NYC; d. Moses and Dorothy Goldfarb; m. Leonard Worell, Aug. 11, 1947 (div.); children: Amy, Beth, Wendy; m. H.A. Smith, Mar. 23, 1985 BS magna cum laude, Queens Coll., 1950; MA, Ohio State U., 1952, PhD in Clin. Psychology, 1954; DHL (hon.), Colby-Sawyer Coll., 1993. Research assoc. Iowa Psychopathic Hosp., Iowa City, 1957-59; research assoc. Okla. State U., 1960-66; asst. prof. U. Ky., Lexington, 1969-71, assoc. prof., 1971-75, prof. ednl. and counseling psychology, 1976—, dir. counseling psychology tng. program, 1980-93, chairperson dept. ednl. and counseling psychology, 1993-97, prof. emerita, 1999—. Author: (with C.M. Nelson) Managing Instructional Problems, 1974; (with W.E. Stilwell) Psychology for Teachers and Students, 1981; Psychological Development in the Elementary Years, 1982; (with Fred Danner) The Adolescent as Decision-maker: Applications to Development and Education, 1989; (with Pam Remer) Feminist Perspectives in Therapy: An Empowerment Model for Women, 1992; (with N. Johnson) Shaping the Future of Feminist Psychology: Education, Research, and Practice, 1997, (with Norine Johnson & Michael Roberts) Beyond Appearance: A New Look at Adolescent Girls, 1999, Encyclopedia of Women and Gender: Sex Similarities and Differences and the Impact of Society on Gender, 2001, (with Pam Remer) Feminist Perspectives in Therapy: Empowering Diverse Women, 2003, (with Carol Goodheart) Oxford Handbook of Girls' and Women's Psychological Health, 2006; assoc. editor Jour. Cons. and Clin. Psychology, 1976-79, mem. editl. bd., 1984-89; assoc. editor Psychol. Women Quar., 1984-89, editor, 1989-95; mem. editorial bd. Sex Roles, 1984-2000, Psychol. Assessment, 1991-97, Clin. Psychology Rev., 1991-97, Women and Therapy, 1992-2000; cons., reviewer 10 jours.; contbr. articles to profl. jours. Named U. Ky. Campus Woman of Yr., 1976, Outstanding Univ. Grad. prof., 1991, Disting. Ky. psychologist, 1990; USPHS fellow, 1953; NIMH rsch. grantee, 1962-69. Fellow APA (pres. Clin. Psychology of Women 1986-88, chmn. com. state assn. rels. 1982-83, fellow selection divsn. 35 com. 1983-84, policy and planning bd. 1989-92, publs. and comm. bd. 1992-99, chair 1996-98, chair jours. com., pres. divsn. psychology of women 1997-98, Disting. Leader for Women in Psychology 1990, Carolyn Wood Sherif award, 2001, Psychology of Women Heritage award 2004, coun. rep. 2000-02, chair women's caucus 2002) Soc. Psychol. Study of Social Issues (chmn. fellow com. 2005-), Ky. Psychol. Assn. (pres. 1981-82, rep. at large 1995-97), Southeastern Psychol. Assn. (exec. coun. mem.-at-large, pres.-elect 1993-94 pres. 1994-95), Am. Women in Psychology, Phi Beta Kappa. Home: 3892 Gloucester Dr Lexington KY 40510-9729 Office: U Ky Dept Ednl and Counseling Psychology 245 Dickey Hl Lexington KY 40506-0017 E-mail: jworell@insightbb.com.

WORENKLEIN, JACOB JOSHUA, lawyer; b. NYC, Oct. 1, 1948; s. Abraham and Cela (Zyskind) W.; divorced; children: David, Daniel, Laura; m. Cindy Sternkler, Feb. 26, 1995; 1 child, Sasha Anne. BA, Columbia U., 1969; MBA, JD, NYU, 1973. Bar: N.Y. 1974. From assoc. to ptnr. Milbank, Tweed, Hadley & McCloy, NYC, 1973-93, chmn. firm planning com., 1988-90, exec. com., 1990-93, sr. advisor to exec. com., 1993-94; mng. dir., group head of global project fin. group Lehman Bros., NYC, 1993-96; mng. dir., head project fin, commodity fin., export fin. Soc. Gen., NYC, 1996-98, mng. dir., global head project and sector fin. Paris and NYC, 1998—2003; chmn., CEO U.S. Power Generating Co., NYC, 2003—08, Astoria Generating Co., 2006—08. Mem. investment banking mgmt. com. Lehman Bros., 1993-96; mem. adv. coun. Amoco Power Resources Corp., 1995-97; adj. prof. fin. NYU Stern Sch. of Bus.; bd. dirs., mem. audit com. CDC Globeleq, 2004—, Ormat Techs., Inc., 2004—. Mem. editl. bd. Jour. Structured and Project Fin., 1996—; contbr. articles to profl. jours. Chmn. bd. Old Broadway Synagogue, N.Y.C., 2001-, pres. 1978-2001; trustee Fedn. Jewish Philanthropies, N.Y.C., 1984-86; bd. overseers United Jewish Appeal-Fedn. Jewish Philanthropies, 1987, chmn. lawyers divsn. major gifts, 1989-91, chmn. lawyers divsn., 1991-93, bd. dirs., 1991-97; trustee Jewish Cmty. Rels. Coun. N.Y., 1995-98, Com. for Econ. Devel., 2001-. Mem. Coun. on Fgn. Rels. Office Phone: 212-792-0180. E-mail: jworenklein@gmail.com.

WORK, BRUCE VAN SYOC, small business owner, consultant; b. Monmouth, Ill., Mar. 20, 1942; s. Robert M. and Evelyn (Ruskin) W.; m. Janet Kay Brown, Nov. 12, 1966; children: Bruce, Terra. BA, Monmouth Coll., 1964; BS, U. Mo.-Rolla, 1966; postgrad., U. Chgo., 1978-79. Registered profl. engr., Ill. Various mgmt. positions Midcon Corp. (and subs.), 1966-79; pres. Indsl. Fuels Corp., Troy, Mich., 1979-85, Costain Coal Inc., Troy, Mich., 1985-89; pvt. practice small bus. cons., 1989-92; bus. cons. Wallis Oil Co., 1992-2000; small bus. cons., 2000—. Mem. various coms. Cuba United Meth. Ch.; bd. mem. Mo. Petroleum Storage Tank Ins. Fund, IDA-Cuba, Mo. Mem. Detroit Athletic Club, Blue Key. Office: 2280 Hwy DD Cuba MO 65453-9684 Office Phone: 573-885-4724. *People are the key to our success. Treat each individual as you would like to be treated.*

WORK, CHARLES ROBERT, lawyer; b. Glendale, Calif., June 21, 1940; s. Raymond P. and Minna M. (Fricke) W.; m. Linda S. Smith, Oct. 4, 1965 (div.); children: Matthew Keehn, Mary Lucila Landis, Benjamin Reed; m. Veronica A. Haggart, Apr., 1985, 1 child, Andrew Haggart. BA, Wesleyan U., 1962; JD, U. Chgo., 1965; LLM, Georgetown U., 1966. Bar: D.C. 1965, Utah 1965. Asst. U.S. atty. D.C., 1966-73; dep. adminstr. law enforcement assistance adminstrn., U.S. Dept. Justice, 1973-75; ptnr. Peabody, Lambert & Meyers, Washington, 1975-82, McDermott, Will & Emery, Washington, 1982—. Recipient Rockefeller Pub. Service award 1978. Mem. D.C. Bar (pres. 1976-77). Office: McDermott Will & Emery 600 13th St NW Fl 12-8 Washington DC 20005-3005 Office Phone: 202-756-8030. E-mail: cwork@mwe.com.

WORK, ROBERT O., civilian military employee, retired military officer; b. 1953; BS in Biology, U. Ill.; MS in Sys. Mgmt., U. So. Calif.; MS in Space Sys. Ops., Naval Postgrad. Sch., Monterey, Calif.; MS in Internat. Pub. Policy, Johns Hopkins Sch. Advanced Internat. Studies. Dinsting. grad. Naval Reserve Officers Training Course, U. Ill. Commd. 2nd lt. USMC, 1974, various positions including comdr. artillery battery/artillery battalion, dir. Strategic Initiatives Group, base comdr. Camp Fuji, Japan, mil. asst. & sr. aide to sec. of Navy Richard J. Danzig, ret. as col., 2001; sr. fellow maritime affairs, then v.p. strategic studies Ctr. Strategic & Budgetary Assessments, Washington; under sec. Dept Navy US Dept. Def., Washington, 2009—. Adj. prof. George Washington U. Office: US Dept Navy Office of Undersec 1000 Navy Pentagon Washington DC 20350*

WORKMAN, CHARLES THOMAS, language educator; s. Vane V. and Mattie Ruth Workman; m. Edna Smith Walker, Aug. 8, 1964; 1 child, Charley Edward. PhD, Tulane U., New Orleans, 1967. Instr. English and German Va. Tech, Blacksburg, 1962—64; prof. English dept. Samford U., Birmingham, 1967—, chmn., English dept., 1982—93. Question writer State High Sch. Academic Competition. Contbr. articles to profl. jours. Judge Home Sch. Regional Consortium, Birmingham, 2004—07; pres. Ala. Creative Writers Conclave, Birmingham, 1969—71. Recipient Outstanding Tchr. award, Sch. Arts and Scis., Samford U., 2005. Baptist. Office: Samford Univ 800 Lakeshore Dr Birmingham AL 35229 Business E-Mail: ctworkma@samford.edu.

WORKMAN, DARIN D., music educator; s. Lyle Workman and Ruth Bramman; m. Jennifer Augustin, May 27, 1988; children: Caitlin, Kristopher. MusB, Hastings Coll., Nebr., 1987. Instrumental music instr. Seward County CC, Liberal, Kans., 1995—. Office: Seward County CC 1801 N Kansas Liberal KS 67901 Business E-Mail: darin.workman@sccc.edu.

WORKMAN, DEBORAH S., literature and language professor, director; d. Edward L. and Hazel M. Workman. PhD, Kent State U., Ohio, 1986. Instr., tchg. fellow Kent State U., 1975—89; assoc. prof. English Chancellor U., Cleve., 1989—. Editor (photographer): (poetry book) Toward Solomon's Mountain; contbr. columns in newspapers. Founder & exec. dir. Sanctuary Sr. Dogs, Cleve., 1999—. Named Humanitarian of Yr., Geauga County Humane Soc., 2001. Mem.: Ohio Assn. Nonprofit Orgns., Nat. Coun. Tchrs. English. Democrat. Office: Chancellor Univ 3921 Chester Ave Cleveland OH 44114 Business E-Mail: workman@chancelloru.edu.

WORKMAN, JEROME JAMES, JR., chemist; b. Northfield, Minn., Aug. 6, 1952; s. Jerome James and Louise Mae (Sladek) W.; m. Rebecca Marie Zittel, Aug. 3, 1974; children: Cristina Louise, Stephannie Michelle, Daniel Jerome, Sara Marie, Michael Timothy. BA with honors, St. Mary's U., Winona, Minn., 1976, MA with distinction, 1980; PhD in Biol. Chemistry with high commendation, Columbia Pacific U., San Rafael, Calif., 1984; exec. cert. in Strategy & Innovation, Mass. Inst. Tech., Cambridge, 2009; CSEP in Sr. Exec. Program, Columbia U., NYC, 2004, CED in Exec. Devel., 2004, CBE in Bus., 2006. Cert. in bus. excellence Columbia U., 2006. Prin. Workman & Assocs., Mankato, Minn., 1980-82; pres. Biochem. Cons., Mankato, Minn., 1982-84; sr. chemist Technicon Instruments, Tarrytown, NY, 1984-87; sr. scientist Hitachi Instruments, Danbury, Conn., 1987-89; supervising scientist Bran & Luebbe/Technicon, Tarrytown, 1987; mgr. tech. support NIR Systems/Perstorp Analytical, Silver Spring, Md., 1989-90, mgr. mktg., 1990-92, dir. mktg., 1992-93; assoc. advisor Inst. Textile Tech., Charlottesville, Va., 1992—; prin. scientist Perkin Elmer Corp., Norwalk, Conn., 1993-96; sr. rsch. fellow Kimberly-Clark Corp., Analytical and Measurement Tech., Neenah, Wis., 1996—2002; chief tech. officer, v.p. rsch. and engring. Argose, Inc., Waltham, Mass., 2002—04; dir. rsch. and tech. Thermo Fisher Sci., Inc. (formerly Thermo Electron Corp.), Madison, Wis., 2004—07; dir. measurement sys. Luminous Med. Inc., Carlsbad, Calif., 2007—09; v.p. tech. rsch. Masimo Corp., Irvine, Calif., 2009—. Instr. Fedn. Analytical Chemistry and Spectroscopy Socs.; external examiner U. Guelph, Ont., Can., 1993-94, chair rep. indsl. adv. bd. Ctr. for Process Analytical Chemistry 1993—2002; apptd. mem. subcom. on process analytical techs. U.S. FDA, 2002, vis. prof., 2002; mem. Nat. Acads. nat. rsch. panel on assessment of NIST programs, 2003—; mem. NRC panel U.S. Nat. Acads., 2003—. Author: Handbook of Organic Compounds: NIR, IR, Raman, and UV-Vis Spectra Featuring Polymers and Surfactants, 3 vols., 2000; co-author: Statistics in Spectroscopy, 1991, 2003, (jour. series) UV-Vis Spectroscopy, 1993, Near-Infrared Spectroscopy in Agr., 2003, FTIR Analysis of Polymers, 2006, FTIR Analysis of Gemstones, 2006, Chemometrics in Spectroscopy, 2007, Practical Guide to Interpretive Near-Infrared Spectroscopy, 2007; editor: The Process Pages for NIRnews, Internat. Com. for Near Infrared Spectroscopy, 1993—97; co-editor: Applied Spectroscopy: A Compact Reference for Practitioners, 1998, Near-Infrared Reflectance Spectroscopy in Analysis of Agricultural Products, 2003, Spectroscopy Letters 1996-2002, 2003; contbg. editor: Spectroscopy Mag.; assoc. editor Wiley-Intersci. Series in Lab. Automation, 1993, Applied Spectroscopy Reviews, 1995—2000, Lab. Robotics and Automation, 1995—98, process editor Jour. Near Infrared Spectroscopy, 1995—97, mem. adv. editl. bd. Spectroscopy, 1995—; contbr. articles. Recipient Heart of Gold award Minn. affiliate Am. Heart Assn., 1984, Ea. Analytical Symposium award, 2002, Award of Appreciation US Dept. Commerce, 2007; named Scientist of Yr. IBC, 2002; Am. Heart Assn. H.N. and H.B. Shapira scholar, 1971-72; NSF grantee, 1977-78. Fellow: ASTM (exec. com., chair main com. on molecular spectroscopy, Appreciation award 2000, Award of Merit 2002, Appreciation award 2005, 2006), Am. Inst. Chemists, Royal Soc. Chemistry U.K. (chartered chemist, chartered scientist); mem.: Coblentz Soc. (bd. mgrs. 2002—06, Williams-Wright Award for Spectroscopy 2009), Joint Com. Atomic and Molecular Phys. Data (chmn. UV-VIS, exec. coun.), Coun. Near-Infrared Spectroscopy (pres.), Soc. for Applied Spectroscopy (Nat. Tour spkr. 2006), Am. Chem. Soc. (instr. course on Practical Near-IR Analysis), Nat. Honor Soc., Sigma Xi, Delta Epsilon Sigma. Achievements include research in molecular spectroscopy, statistics and chemometrics; development and applications of spectroscopic methods and sensors to consumer and medical products and processes; US and international patents for analytical systems. Office: Masimo Corp Forty Parker Irvine CA 92618 Business E-Mail: jworkman04@gsb.columbia.edu.

WORKMAN, JOHN MITCHELL, chemist; b. Uniontown, Pa., Oct. 25, 1949; s. Hugh Lawrence and Mary Louise (Mitchell) W.; m. Gayle Sue Zappin, Nov. 20, 1987. BA in Psychology, Miami U., Oxford, Ohio, 1971; MS in Edn., Kans. State U., 1976; MS in Chemistry, U. Cin., 1985, PhD in Chemistry, 1987; MBA in Fin., Wright State U., 1995. Tchg. and rsch. asst. dept. chemistry Wright State U., Dayton, Ohio, 1977—81; grad. tchg. asst. U. Cin., 1982—83, grad. rsch. asst., 1983—86; sr. scientist Chemsys Inc., Beavercreek, Ohio, 1986—89, dir. elemental analysis, 1989—93, lab. dir., 1993—. Contbr. articles to jours. Analytical Chemistry, Applied Spectroscopy. With 1st Inf. Divsn., Health Services Command US Army, 1972—74. Mem.: Materials Info. Soc., Air Force Assn., Soc. for Applied Spectroscopy, Am. Phys. Soc., Am. Chem. Soc., Sigma Iota Epsilon, Sigma Pi Sigma, Sigma Xi. Personal E-mail: tacitfalcon@woh.rr.com.

WORKMAN, JOHN P., JR., marketing professor; b. Wilmington, NC, Sept. 26, 1958; s. John P. and Elinor A. Workman; m. Jeanne Marie Bertch, June 19, 1993; children: Justina Suzanne, Juliana Leigh. BS, NC State U., 1980; MBA, U. Va., 1984; PhD, MIT, 1991. Product mktg. engr. Tex. Instruments, Johnson City, Tenn., 1980—82, field sales engr. Fairfax, Va., 1984—85; asst. prof. mktg. U. NC, Chapel Hill, 1991—98; assoc. prof. mktg. Creighton U., Omaha, 1998—2002, prof. mktg., 2003—. Expert witness Kutak Rock, Omaha, 2000—02; vis. fellow Jesuit Inst. at Boston Coll., 2005—06. Music min. St. Stephen the Martyr Ch., Omaha, 1998—; bd. dirs. Colleagues in Jesuit Bus. Edn., 2002—04; dir. Ignatian Commons Initiative. Recipient Best Paper award in mktg. strategy track, Am. Mktg. Assn., 1997, Best Paper of Yr. award, Jour. of Acad. Sci., 2000, Teacher of Yr., Creighton U. Coll. Bus., 2002, Outstanding Faculty award, 2003; Rsch. grant, Mktg. Sci. Inst., 1995, 1998. Mem.: Acad. Mgmt., Acad. Mktg. Sci., Am. Mktg. Assn. (mem. academic coun. 2000—02). Roman Catholic. Avocations: piano, jogging, ice skating, Web surfing. Office Fax: 402-280-5565. Business E-Mail: workman@creighton.edu.

WORKMAN, MARGARET LEE, state supreme court justice, lawyer; b. May 22, 1947; d. Frank Eugene and Mary Emma (Thomas) W.; m. Edward T. Gardner III; children: Lindsay Elizabeth, Christopher Workman, Edward Earnshaw. AB in Polit. Sci., W.Va. U., 1969, JD, 1974. Bar: W.Va. 1974. Asst. counsel to majority, pub. works com. U.S. Senate, Washington, 1974-75; law clk. 13th jud. cir., W.Va. Ct., Charleston, 1975-76, judge, 1981-88; pvt. practice Charleston, 1976—81, 1999—2009; justice W.Va. Supreme Ct. of Appeals, Charleston, 1989-99, 2009—, chief justice, 1993, 97. Advance person for Rosalyn Carter, Carter Presdl. Campaign, Atlanta, 1976. Democrat. Episcopalian. Office: WVa Supreme Ct Appeals Capitol Complex Bldg 1 Rm E-302 Charleston WV 25305*

WORKMAN, SHARON JOY, journalist; b. Louisa, Ky., May 20, 1930; d. Charlie B. Workman and Jessie Virginia Beaire; children: Patrick Corsiglia, Joan Brecn, James Corsiglia, Cynthia Corsiglia. BA, Marshall Coll., 1952; MA in Lit., Oxford U., Eng., 1990; MA in Creative Writing, Dartmouth Coll., 1992; studied French at, U. Laval, Quebec, U. Lyon, France, Villefranche-sur-Mer and MonfLarquin, France, Spa, Belgium. Feature writer The Herald-Advertiser, Huntington, W.Va., 1951—52; mil. intelligence analyst Hdqrs. US Armed Forces Far East, Psychol. Warfare Sect., Japan, 1952—54; reporter Life Mag., NYC, 1954—59, People Mag., NYC, 1974—88. Mem.: DAR, TIME-LIFE Alumni Assn., Dartmouth Club, Overseas Press Club, The Coll. Club of Boston, The Tokeneke Club. Republican. Methodist. Avocations: travel, swimming, opera, museums, concerts. Home: 9 Hale Ln Darien CT 06820 Personal E-mail: sharonworkman@aol.com.

WORKMAN, WILLIAM DOUGLAS, III, town manager; retired mayor, gas industry executive; b. Charleston, SC, July 3, 1940; s. William Douglas Jr. and Rhea (Thomas) W.; m. Marcia Mae Moorhead, Apr. 23, 1966 (div. Dec. 1995); children: William Douglas IV, Frank Moorhead; m. Patti Gage Fishburne Marks, June 22, 1996; stepchildren: Gage Russell Marks, Barnwell Johnson Marks, Kemp Fishburne Marks. BA, The Citadel, 1961; grad., U. S.C., 1962. Reporter Charleston News & Courier, 1965-66, Greenville (S.C.) News, 1966-70; tchr., adminstr., dean allied health scis. Greenville Tech. Coll., 1967-75; exec. asst. to gov. State of S.C., Columbia, 1975-78; mktg. exec. Daniel Internat. Corp., Greenville, 1978-90, dir. facilities Fluor Daniel, 1991-93; v.p. S.C. ops. Piedmont Natural Gas, Greenville, 1994—2004; pres., bd. dirs. Greenville County Rsch. & Tech. Devel. Corp., 1999—2006; mayor City of Greenville, 1983-95. Chmn. bd. dirs. Greenville Area Devel. Corp., 2002—05. Chmn. Greenville County Rep. Conv., 1980, 82, 87, 89, 91, S.C. 4th Congl. Dist. Rep. Conv., 1980, 82, 84; chmn. S.C. Rep. Conv., 1984, 89, vice chmn., 1982, 87; Rep. nominee for U.S. Ho. of Reps. from 4th Dist. S.C., 1986; mem. S.C. Adv. Commn. on Intergovtl. Rels., 1990-96; bd. dirs. S.C. Appalachian Coun. Govts., 1991-95, Mcpl. Assn. S.C., 1990-95, pres., 1993-94; trustee Sch. Dist. Greenville County, 1969-75, vice-chmn.; bd. dirs. YMCA Camp Greenville, 1973-83, 90-95, chmn., 1975; chmn. S.C. Health Coordinating Coun., 1976-78; founder S.C. Literacy Assn., treas., 1969-73; bd. dirs.; Greenville City Coun., 1981-83, So. Growth Policies Bd., 1992-95. With U.S. Army, 1962-64; ret. lt. col. USAR. Named Outstanding State Chmn., S.C. Jaycees, 1969, Order of Palmetto, 1978; named 2000 Bus. Person of Yr., Greenville Mag., Vol. of Yr., S.C. Econ. Devel. Assn., 2000, Disting. Svc. award, SC Econ. Devel. Assn., 2003, Wiseman Vision award, Devel. Dists. Appalachia Assn., 2004. Mem. Savanna River Maritime Commn., 2009, Greater Island Coun., Res. Officers Assn., Assn. U.S. Army, Am. Legion, Nat. Mgmt. Assn. (Mgr. of Yr. award Greenville chpt. 1985), SC Downtown Devel. Assn. (bd. dirs., 1985-1995), Beaufort Citadel Club, Dogwood Hills Cmty. Club, Carolina Yacht Club, VFW. Home: 3985 Charleston Hwy Walterboro SC 29188 Office Phone: 843-368-1010. Personal E-mail: bill@billworkman.com.

WORLEY, JAMES GLENN, theater educator; b. Dallas, Jan. 20, 1961; s. Billy Doyen and Norma Jo Worley; children: Madelaine MacKenzie, Maxwell Russell. BA in Drama, Angelo State U., Tex., 1983, MA in Theatre Mgmt., 1985; MFA in Directing, U. Tex., Austin, 1997. Prodn. state mgr. Okla. Shakespeare Festival, Durant, 1985—85; asst. prof. Angelo State U., Tex., 1998—2004, assoc. prof., 2006—; lighting designer New Fed. Theatre, NY, 1985, tech. dir., 1985; stage carpenter Juilliard Sch. Drama, 1985—86; shop carpenter Roundabout Theatre Co., 1986—87; tour stage mgr. Daedalus Theatrical Tours, 1987—88; designer Angelo Civic Theatre, Tex., 1988—90, guest lighting designer, 2004, tech. dir., 1988—90, artistic dir., 1990—91, actor, guest dir., 2006, guest sound designer, 2008, stage mgr., 2008; shop foreman SW Studios Inc., Dallas, 1991—92, tech. dir., 1992—93. Tech. dir. Zilker Pk. Summer Musicals, Austin, Tex., 1997—97. Dir.(designer): (theatrical production) Godspell, (set and sound designer) My Three Angels, Blithe Spirit, The Taming of the Shrew, XSR: Die! (Cross Stage Right and Die!), Pippin, Necessary Targets, (set and lighting designer) The Laramie Project, (lighting designer) Jesus Christ Superstar, (set designer) A Midsummer Night's Dream, (sound designer) A Lie of the Mind, Absent Friends, (set/lighting and sound designer) Terra Nova. Occasional guest artist Angelo Civic Theatre, 1998—2008.

Recipient Excellence award, Kennedy Ctr./Am. Coll. Theatre, 2004. Mem.: Tex. Ednl. Theatre Assn. (assoc.). Democrat. Home: 2216 Liveoak San Angelo TX 76901 Office: Angelo State Univ 2801 W Ave N San Angelo TX 76901

WORLEY, ROBERT BRUCE, JR., lawyer; b. Mobile, Ala., Mar. 9, 1960; s. Robert Bruce and Linda (Knight) Worley; m. Catherine Anna Steck, Nov. 14, 1987; children: Nancy Jane, Catherine Turner. BBA with honors and distinction, U. Ky., 1982; JD, Tulane U., 1985. Bar: La. 1985, Tex. 2003, US Dist. Ct. (ea. dist. La.) 1985, US Dist. Ct. (mid. dist. La.) 1986, US Dist. Ct. (we. dist. La.) 1988, US Dist. Ct. (ea. dist. Ark.) 1996, US Dist. Ct. (we. dist. Ark.) 1996, US Dist. Ct. (cen. dist. Ill.) 1997, US Dist. Ct. (so. dist. Tex.) 2001, US Dist. Ct. (ea. dist. Tex.) 2001, US Ct. Appeals (5th cir.) 1990, US Ct. Appeals (4th cir.) 1990, US Ct. Appeals (6th cir.) 1996, US Ct. Appeals (7th cir.) 1997, US Ct. Appeals (11th cir.) 1998, US Ct. Appeals (8th cir.) 1999, US Supreme Ct. 1999. Assoc. Gelpi, Sullivan, Carroll and Laborde, New Orleans, 1985—88; ptnr. Kullman Firm, New Orleans, 1988—99, Jones, Walker, Waechter, Poitevent, Carrere & Denegre, New Orleans, 1999—. Chmn. profl. employment com. Jones Walker et al, New Orleans, 2001—04, chmn. United Way, 2000—, mem. bd. dirs., 2009—. Mem., pres. New Orleans Area Habitat for Humanity Bd., 2006—08; chair lawyers com. New Orleans United Way Campaign, 2003; v.p., chmn. La. Jr. Tennis Coun.; v.p. La. Tennis Assn.; former pres. ch. coun. Rayne Meml. United Meth. Ch.; vice chmn. Southern Tennis Assn. Collegiate Com. Recipient Leadership in Law award, City Business, 2006; named One of Best Labor and Employment Lawyers, New Orleans Mag., 2005, 2006, 2007, 2008. Mem.: ABA, Am. Inns Ct., Coll. Master Adv. and Barristers, New Orleans Bar Assn., La. State Bar Assn. Avocations: tennis, swimming, fishing. Office: Jones Walker et al 201 St Charles Ave New Orleans LA 70170-5100 Office Phone: 504-582-8192. Business E-Mail: rworley@joneswalker.com.

WORMAN, HOWARD JAY, internist, educator; b. Paterson, NJ, May 21, 1959; s. Louis and Dora (Rubin) W. BA, Cornell U., 1981; MD, U. Chgo., 1985. Diplomate Am. Bd. Internal Medicine. Intern NY Hosp., NYC, 1985—86, resident, 1986—87; guest investigator Rockefeller U., NYC, 1987—90; asst. prof. Mt. Sinai Sch. Medicine, NYC, 1990—94; asst. attending physician Mt. Sinai Hosp., NYC, 1990—94; asst. prof. Columbia U. Coll. Physicians and Surgeons, NYC, 1995—98, assoc. prof., 1998—2007, prof., 2007—; asst. attending physician NY Presbyn. Hosp., Columbia-U. Med. Ctr., NYC, 1995—98, assoc. attending physician, 1998—2007, attending physician, 2007—; dir. divsn. digestive and liver diseases NY Presbyn. Hosp., NYC, 1999—2002. Mem. med. adv. com. Muscular Dystrophy Assn., 2000—05. Mem. editl. bd. Hepatology, Frontiers in Biosci., World Jour. Gastroenterology; assoc. editor Biomed. Ctrl. Cell Biology, The Open Jour. Gastroenterology; mem. bd. reviewing editors Molecular Biology of the Cell; contbr. articles to profl. jours. Recipient Physician-Scientist award NIH, 1987-92; Charles E. Culpeper scholar in Med. Scis., 1994-95, Irma T. Hirschl scholar, 1997-2002. Mem. AAAS, ACP, Am. Chem. Soc., Am. Fedn. Med. Rsch. (Trainee award in clin. rsch. 1989, Henry Christian award 1990), Am. Soc. Cell Biology, Am. Assn. Study of Liver Diseases, Am. Gastroent. Assn., Am. Soc. Clin. Investigation, N.Y. Acad. Scis. (vice chmn. biol. scis. sect. 1992-93, chmn. 1993-94), Am. Diabetes Assn., Hon. Order Ky. Cols., Phi Beta Kappa. Democrat. Jewish. Avocations: music, reading. Office: Columbia U Coll Physicians-Surgeons 630 W 168th St New York NY 10032-3795 Office Phone: 212-305-8156. Business E-Mail: hjwl4@columbia.edu.

WORMER, THOMAS ANDREW, surgeon; b. Buffalo, Dec. 3, 1956; s. Donald Andrew and Elinor Ann (Bliss) W.; m. Melissa Jane Ertell, Apr. 11, 1988; children: Matthew Thomas, Margaret Elizabeth, Samuel James, Sarah Jane. BS, Allegheny Coll., 1978; MD, Albany Med. Coll., 1984. Diplomate Am. Bd. Surgery. Intern Millard Fillmore Hosp., Buffalo, 1984—85, resident in gen. surgery, 1985—89; attending surgeon F.F. Thompson Hosp., Canandaigua, NY, 1989—95, chief surgery, 1994—99. Fellow ACS; mem. Canandaigua Med. Soc. (pres. 1994), N.Y. State Med. Soc. Presbyterian. Office: Canandaigua Medical Group 335 Parrish St Canandaigua NY 14424-1794 E-mail: twormer@rochester.rr.com.

WORMLEY, DAVID NEAL, engineering educator; BSME, MIT, 1962, MSME, 1964, PhD in Mech. Engring., 1968. Mem. faculty MIT, 1967—92, head dept. mech. engring., 1982—91, assoc. dean engring., 1991—92; dean Coll. Engring., prof. mech. engring. Pa. State U., University Park, 1992—. Past chmn. exec. com. NRC Transp. Rsch. Bd.; past chair adv. com. NSF Engring. Directorate. Fellow: ASEE (pres. 2005), ASME (Lewis Moody award, Dynamic Sys. and Control Divsn. Edn. award 1997); mem.: Am. Soc. Engring. Edn., Pi Tau Sigma, Sigma Xi. Achievements include research in dynamic systems and control with application to transportation, energy production and conversion and fluid actuation systems. Office: Pa State U 101 Hammond Bldg University Park PA 16802

WORMMEESTER, JUSTIN T., legislative staff member; BA in Bus. Adminstrn. and Polit. Sci., Hope Coll., Holland, Mich., 1999; student, Cath. U. America, Washington. Legis. asst. to congressman Pete Hoekstra US House of Reps., 1999—2001, sr. legis. asst., 2002—04, legis. dir., 2005, dep. chief of staff, 2005—08, chief of staff, 2008—. Republican. Mailing: US House Reps 2234 Rayburn House Office Bldg Washington DC 20515 Office Phone: 202-225-4401. Office Fax: 202-225-0779. Business E-Mail: justin.wormmeester@mail.house.gov.*

WORNALL, ILAH RUTH (RUTHIE WORNALL), publishing executive, educator; b. Harrison, Ark., Dec. 29, 1941; d. William Curtis and Velora Delia (Copeland) Davis; m. James Frederick Wornall, Nov. 23, 1974; children: Desirée Blythe, John Bristow V. BS in Edn., U. Ctrl Mo., 1963, MS in Edn., 1971. Cert. edn.specialist U. Ctrl. Mo., 1976. Tchr. Consolidated Sch. Dist #2, Raytown, Mo., 1963—80; owner Wornall Publ. Co., Overland Park, Kans., 1988—. ESOL tchr. Emmanuel Bapt. Ch., 1999—2000, 2002—03, tchr. Spanish, 2003. Author: Three Ingredient Cookbook, Vol. I, 1988, Three Ingredient Cookbook, Vol. II, 1990; columnist: Weston Chronicle News, 1991—; author: Three Ingredient Cookbook, Vol. III, 1991, Three Ingredient Low Cholesterol Cookbook, 1991, Three Ingredient Party Cookbook, 1992, Three Ingredient Main Dish Cookbook, 1993, Two Ingredient Cookbook, 1994, Three Ingredient Low Fat Cookbook, 1995, Three Ingredient Low Sugar Cookbook, 1996, Best of the Three Ingredient Cookbooks, 1996, The Three Ingredient Dieters Cookbook, 1997, (novels) Murder in San Miguel, 1998, Murder in Guanajuato, 1998, Murder at the University of Guanajuato, 1999, Microwave Three Ingredient Cookbook, 2001, The Best of Cooking with 3 Ingredients, 2002, 3 - Ingredient Recipes for College Students, 2005, 3 - Ingredient Recipes for Reluctant Chefs, 2007, 3 - Ingredient Vegetable Recipes, 2008; contbr. articles to profl. jours., local newspapers. Vol. at nursing homes, 1986—2006; vol. Ciudad de Los Ninos Orphanage Salamanca, Guanajuato, Mexico; former mem. AAUW; involved in bldg. ch. in Guanajuato, 2000—07. Mem.: DAR, Help With Bible Sch., Teach Sunday Sch., Sing in Choir, Friends of Animales, Amigos de Animales, Republic Party Club, Ret. Raytown Tchrs. Club, Rainbow Connection. Republican. Baptist. Avocations: horseback riding, reading, writing, singing, interior decorating. Office: Wornall Publ Co 9800 W 104th St Overland Park KS 66212 Home Phone: 913-888-1530.

WORNER, THERESA MARIE, internist, educator; b. Breckenridge, Minn., Feb. 19, 1948; d. William Daniel and Elizabeth (Stelten) W.; m. Martin Herbst, Mar. 24, 1979. AB, St. Theresa Coll., 1970; MD, U. Minn., 1974. Diplomate Am. Bd. Internal Medicine. Rotating intern Kings County Hosp., Bklyn., 1974-75, resident medicine, 1975-77; fellow VA Med. Ctr., Bronx, NY, 1977-78, chief med. sect. Alcoholism treatment program, 1978-87; asst. prof. medicine Mt. Sinai Sch. Medicine, NYC, 1984-87; mem. faculty Postgrad. Ctr., 1985-90; physician in charge alcoholism svcs. L.I. Coll. Hosp., Bkyn., 1987-92; assoc. prof. clin. medicine SUNY, Health Sci. Ctr., Bkyn., 1988—; dir. rsch. 32BJ Health Fund, 1992-99; clin. assoc. prof. Pub. Health Cornell U. Med. Coll., 1996—; pres. Menachem Publ., Bethlehem, NH, 1999—. Pres./founder Alcohol. Info, 1995-97; advisor Patient Care Mag., 1984—; cons. REA, 1996—. Referee Hepatology, 1986, Jour. Study Alcohol, 1984—, Substance Abuse, 1992—, Alcoholism: Clinical and Exptl. Rsch., 1992—, Drug and Alcohol Dependence, 1993—, Drug Therapy, 1994—, Addiction, 1996—; contbr. numerous articles to profl. jours. Active Israel Mus., Israeli Opera, Israel Symphony. Grantee Child Welfare Adminstrn., 1991, 92, 93; recipient Physicians Recognition award AMA, 1984, 89, 91, 96, Cert. of Merit Govt. Employees Ins. Co., 1986, PACT Intern Site award, 1991, 92. Fellow ACP, N.Y. Acad. Medicine; mem. AAAS, Am. Med. Soc. on Alcoholism and Other Drug Dependence, Am. Soc. Internal Medicine, Am. Assn. for Study Liver Diseases (Travel award 1978), N.Y. Acad. Scis., Rsch. Soc. on Alcoholism, Internat. Soc. Biologic Rsch. in Alcoholism.

WORRALL, JOHN DENNIS, economics professor, consultant, writer; b. Wildwood, NJ, July 29, 1942; s. John and Adele Veronica (McKenna) W.; m. Suzanne Elizabeth Hopkins; children: Heather, John; m. Janet Priscilla Moran; 1 child, Kevin. BA, Rutgers U., 1969, MA, 1972, PhD, 1976. Asst. dir. Rutgers Bur. Econ. Rsch., New Brunswick, NJ, 1974-77; dir. rsch. Nat. Ctr. for Employment Handicapped-Human Resources Ctr., LI, NY, 1977-78; v.p., dir. econ. rsch. NCCI, NYC, 1979-83; prof. econs. Rutgers U., Camden, NJ, 1983—, asst. dir. Bur. Econ. Rsch. New Brunswick, NJ, 1983—. Advisor Courier Post newspaper, Camden, 1994-97; John R. Commons lectr. U. Wis. Bus. Sch., Madison, 1991. Co-author: An Evaluation of Policy Related Rehabilitation Research, 1975; co-editor: Placement in Rehabilitation, 1979, Benefit Issues in Workers' Compensation, 1985; editor: Safety and the Workforce, 1983; assoc. editor Jour. Ins.: Math. and Econs., 1990-2000, Jour. Risk and Ins., 1992—. Del. White House Conf. on Handicapped, Washington, 1977; pres. South Jersey Irish Am. Unity Conf., Fedn. Irish Am. Socs., Phila., 1996-98; bd. dirs. St. Patrick's Day Observance Com., Phila., 1996-98, Phila. Immigration Resource Ctr., 1999-2001. Sgt. U.S. Army, 1960-66. Named Outstanding Faculty Mem. Rutgers U. Alumni Assn., 1991; honoree Gaelic Ball, Ladies Ancient Order Hibernians, Phila., 1998. Fellow Risk Theory Soc. (sec. 1990, pres. 1991); mem. Nat. Acad. Social Ins., Am. Econs. Assn., Am. Risk and Ins. Assn. (Robert I. Mehr award 2001), Commodore John Barry Soc. (pres. 1996-98). Roman Catholic. Avocations: golf, fishing. Office: Rutgers U Armitage Hall Camden NJ 08102 Office Phone: 856-225-6290. Business E-Mail: jworrall@crab.rutgers.edu.

WORRALL, ROBERT, information technology executive; MBA, Calif. State U., Hayward. Head info. tech. orgn. Worlds of Wonder; v.p. worldwide info. tech. ops. Sun Microsystems, Inc., v.p. applications Global Sales and E-Commerce orgns., v.p. info. tech., chief info. officer, 2006—. Named one of Ones to Watch, CIO Mag., 2006. Office: Sun Microsystems Inc 4150 Network Cir Santa Clara CA 95054 Office Phone: 650-960-1300.

WORRELL, ANNE EVERETTE ROWELL, newspaper publisher; b. Surry, Va., Mar. 7, 1920; d. Charles Gray and Ethel (Roache) Rowell; m. Thomas Eugene Worrell, Sept. 12, 1941; 1 child, Thomas Eugene. Student, Va. Intermont Coll., 1939, LittD (hon.), 1991; student, U. Richmond, 1965. Founding stockholder Worrell Newspapers Inc., 1949, v.p., dir., 1969-73; v.p., sec. Worrell Investment Co., Charlottesville, Va.; pres. The Genan Co. (formerly Bristol Newspapers). Pres. Bristol Jr. League, 1959; bd. dirs. The Corp. for Thomas Jefferson's Poplar Forest Found., Va. Hist. Soc., Va. Intermont Coll., Antiquities; active Monticello Cabinet. Named Outstanding Alumna, Va. Intermont Coll., 1981. Mem.: Nat. Trust for Hist. Preservation, Greencroft Club, Farmington Country Club, Contemporary Club. Episcopalian. Office: Pantops PO Box 5386 Charlottesville VA 22905-5386

WORRELL, BRIAN, manufacturing executive; m. Kate Worrell; 3 children. B in Economics, U. North Carolina, Chapel Hill, 1992. Mem. fin. mgmt. program GE, Louisville, 1992, mem. corp. audit staff, product line and supply chain fin. mgr., global fin. planning and analysis leader, GE Healthcare, 1997, CFO healthcare monitoring and info. tech., 2000—03, CFO oil & gas bus. Florence, Italy, 2003—06, v.p. corp. audit staff, 2006—. Office: GE 3135 Easton Turnpike Fairfield CT 06828*

WORRELL, FRANK CLAYTON, psychology professor; b. Port of Spain, Trinidad and Tobago, Oct. 29, 1960; s. Eli Cleophous and Rita Mary Worrell. BA with honors, U. Western Ont., London, Can., 1985, MA, 1987; PhD, U. Calif., Berkeley, 1994. Cert. in pupil pers. svcs. Calif. Commn. Tchr. Credentialling, 1991, sch. psychologist 1993, lic. psychologist Pa. Bd. Psychology, 1996. Tchr. St. Mary's Coll., Port of Spain, 1980—81, tchr., counselor, 1986—87; prin. Daniell Ednl. Cmty. HS, Port of Spain, 1987—88; asst.-assoc. prof. Pa. State U., State Coll., 1994—2003; assoc. prof. U. Calif., Berkeley, 2002—07, prof., 2007—. Mem. AIDS Project, State Coll., 1996—2001, East Bay Ctr. Performing Arts, Richmond, Calif., 2005, Calif. Found. Gifted Edn., 2006. Commonwealth scholarship, Govts. Can. and Trinidad and Tobago, 1983—85. Fellow: APA (pres., divsn. 16 2007); mem.: Soc. Study Sch. Psychology. Office: Univ Calif Berkeley 4511 Tolman Hall Berkeley CA 94720-1670

WORRELL, RICHARD VERNON, orthopedic surgeon, dean; b. Bklyn., June 4, 1931; s. John Elmer and Elaine (Callender) Worrell; m. Audrey Frances Martiny, June 14, 1958; children: Philip Vernon, Amy Elizabeth. BA, NYU, 1952; MD, Meharry Med. Coll., 1958. Diplomate Am. Bd. Orthop. Surgery, Nat. Bd. Med. Examiners. Intern Meharry Med. Coll., Nashville, 1958—59; resident in gen. surgery Mercy-Douglass Hosp., Phila., 1960—61; resident in orthop. surgery State U. N.Y. Buffalo Sch. Medicine Affiliated Hosps., 1961—64; resident in orthop. pathology Temple U. Med. Ctr., Phila., 1966—67; pvt. practice orthop. surgery Phila., 1967—68; asst. prof. acting head divsn. orthop. surgery U. Conn. Sch. Medicine, 1968—70; attending orthop. surgeon E.J. Meyer Meml. Hosp., Buffalo, Millard Fillmore Hosp., Buffalo, VA Hosp., Buffalo, Buffalo State Hosp.; clin. instr. orthop. surgery SUNY, Buffalo, 1970—74; chief orthop. surgery VA Hosp., Newington, Conn., 1974—80; asst. prof. surgery (orthop.) U. Conn. Sch. Medicine, 1974—77, assoc. prof., 1977—83, asst. dean student affairs, 1980—83; prof. clin. surgery SUNY Downstate Med. Ctr., Bklyn., 1983—86; dir. orthop. surgery Brookdale Hosp. Med. Ctr., Bklyn., 1983—86; prof. orthop. U. N.Mex. Sch. Medicine, 1986—97, prof., vice chmn. dept. orthop., 1997—99, prof. emeritus, 1999—; dir. orthop. oncology U. N.Mex. Health Scis. Ctr., 1987—99; mem. med. staff U. N.Mex. Cancer Ctr., 1987—99; chief orthop. surgery VA Med. Ctr., Albuquerque, 1987—97. Cons. in orthop. surgery Newington (Conn.) Children's Hosp., 1968—70; mem. sickle cell disease adv. com. NIH, 1982—86. Bd. dirs. Big Bros. Greater Hartford. Served to capt. M.C. USAR, 1962—69. Fellow: ACS, Royal Soc. Medicine, London, Am. Acad. Orthop. Surgeons; mem.: AMA, N.Mex. Soc. Clin. Oncology, Internat. Soc. Orthop. Surgery and Traumatology, Orthop. Rsch. Soc., Internat. Fedn. Surg. Colls. (assoc.), Am. Soc. Clin. Oncology, Am. Soc. Clin. Pathologists, Am. Orthop. Assn., Alpha Omega Alpha. Personal E-mail: rworrellmd@aol.com. Business E-Mail: rworrell@salud.unm.edu.

WORRELL, SHARYN DIANNE KELLEY, volunteer, retired flight attendant; b. Lynn, Mass., Feb. 23, 1948; d. Richard Allen Kelley and Norma Lovett (Gregory); m. Blaine Patten Worrell, Feb. 15, 1979 (div. Dec. 20, 1985); 1 child, Ryan Richard. Flight attendant United Airlines, 1966—2002. Spkr. and co-founder Speakers' Bur. LA-based Flight Attendants; spkr. in field. Co-founder Young Women's League for Muscular Dystrophy Assn., LA, 1975; asst. supt. of Sunday sch.; summer Sunday sch. supt.; sch. bd. Immanuel Luth. Ch. and Sch., Palatine, Ill., 1990—93, pub. rels. chair, 1992—2002, bd. of human care ministry com. mem., 1999—2001, pres's. vol. svc. award chmn., 2000—04, bd. of trustees, sec. of congregation, 2001—03; bd. mem. Aux. Good Shepherd Hosp., Barrington, Ill., 2000—, hon. pres., mem. chair, 2000—02, chef fest bd. mem., founder sch. artwork project, 2003—06; founding mem. Immanuel Luth. Sch. Edn. Found., Palatine, 1998—2003; program chair Art in the Barn, bd. mem.; reach for the stars event chairperson Immanuel Luth. Sch. Edn. Found., Palatine, Ill., 1998—2003. Recipient Vol. Recognition, YMCA, 1988, Servant of Youth award, Boy Scouts Am., Merit awards, United Air Lines, Pres.'s Vol. Svc. Lifetime award, George W. Bush, 2006. Mem.: DAR, Colonial Daughters Seveteenth Century, Clipped Wings, Winthrop Soc. (life), Hereditary Order Families Pres. 1st Ladies America (life), Order of Three Crusades (life), Order Desc. Ancient Hon. Artillery Co. (life), Natl. Soc. Old Plymouth Col. Desc. (life), Military Order Crusades (life), Baronial Order Magna Charta (life), Plymouth Hereditary Soc. (life; marshall gen.), Nat. Guild St. Margaret of Scotland (life), Nat. Order Blue & Gray (life; 1st vice comdr.), Desc. Ill. Sons & Dau. Kings Britain (life), Towne Family Assns., Swift River Valley Hist. Soc., Isaac Cummings Family Assn., Nat. Soc. Colonial Daus. Seventeenth Century, Ill. State Soc. Dames Ct. of Honor (3d v.p.), Nat. Soc. Magna Carta Dames and Barons, Daus. Am. Colonists (state v.p.), Order First Families R.I. and Providence Plantations, Nat. Soc. Sons and Daus. Pilgrims (Ill. br. organizing gov. historian gen.), Nat. Soc. U.S. Daus. 1812, Continental Soc. Daus. Indian Wars (charter mem., cradle roll), Soc. Desc. Washington's Army at Valley Forge (organizing Ill. brigade comdr.), Soc. Dau. Colonial Wars, Daus. Union Vets. of Civil War 1861-1865 (life; chaplain), Nat. Sons and Daus. Antebellum Planters (life), Presdl. Families Am. (life), Order Crown of Charlemagne in U.S.A. (life), Order Descs. Colonial Physicians and Chirugiens (life), Order First Families of Maine (life; corr. sec. gen., charter mem., 2d v.p.), Family of Bruce Soc. Am. (life), Guild Colonial Artists and Tradesmen (life; charter mem.), Sons and Daus. Colonial and Antebellum Bench and Bar (life), Soc. Mayflower Descs. State of Ill. (life; chmn. jr. membership, elder), Soc. Descs. of Colonial Clergy (life), Nat. Soc. Women Descs. Ancient and Hon. Arty. Co. (life; first v.p., treas., state chaplain, hospitality chmn.), Assn. Daus. Early Am. Witches (life; nat. corr. sec. gen., guest spkr., v.p. gen.), Hereditary Order Descs. Loyalists and Patriots Am. Revolution (life; organizing sec. gen.), Order First Families Conn. (life; founding mem.), Nat. Soc. Descs. Early Quakers (life), Nat. Soc. Daus. of Union (life; chaplain, historian gen., chpt. regent), Hereditary Order First Families Mass. (life; primary), Her. Ord. Desc. Colonial Govs. (life), Nat. Soc. Colonial Dames XVII Century (charter mem., chpt. historian, state chaplain, hon. chpt. pres., chpt. libr., state chair heraldry and coat arms, chpt. chaplain, guest spkr., state 2d v.p.), Huguenot Soc. Ill. (registrar, dir.), Barrington Hist. Soc., New Eng. Historic Geneal. Soc., Am. Genealogist, Topsfield Hist. Soc., N.H. Hist. Soc., Essex Soc. Genealogists, New Eng. Historic Geneal. Soc., Order Merovingian Dynasty (life; adv. coun.), Order Ams. Armorial Ancestry (life), Flagon and Trencher (life), Nat. Soc. New Eng. Women (life; colony pres., nat. yearbook chmn., guest spkr., Vol. Cmty. Svc. award 1995), Ill. Cameo Soc. (life), Piscataqua Pioneers (life). Lutheran. Achievements include Lobbied 3 years for exoneration of 6 women executed in 1692 as Salem witches during the Witch Hysteria. Acting Gov. Jane Swift signed the Bill on October 31, 2001 exonerating all 6. Avocations: genealogy, volunteering. Home: 269 Bluff Ct Lake Barrington IL 60010-7312 Personal E-mail: sdworrell@aol.com, shariworrell@aol.com.

WORRELL, STEWART PHILLIP, lawyer, diversified financial services company executive; b. Montreal, Apr. 13, 1956; s. Arthur Agustus and Sybil Agatha (Jones) Worrell. Chmn. The Libr. Trust, Montreal, 1999—. Charter mem. Mbanx, Toronto, 1998—. Author: (poetry) Children Dressed in Black, 1999. Mem. Fed. Bar Assn., InterAm. Bar Assn., Conseil de Roi, US Ski Assn., Beaconsfield Yacht Club, Univ. Club. Avocations: skiing, sailing, chess, golf, photography.

WORSFOLD, VICTOR LEONARD, retired social sciences educator; b. Glasgow, Scotland; s. Victor Leonard Worsfold and Mary MacMillan Thomson. MA, U. St. Andrews, Scotland, 1966; diploma in edn., U. Oxford, Eng., 1967; MA, U. Toronto, Can., 1970; PhD, Harvard U., Cambridge, Mass., 1975. Asst. prof. Antioch Grad. Sch. Edn., Cambridge, 1973—75; asst. to assoc. prof. U. Tex., Richardson, 1975—2001; ret., 2001; cons. U. Tex., Dallas, 2001—07. Contbr. articles to profl. jours. Founding mem. Dallas Symphony Chorus, 1970—86; bd. dirs. Suicide in Crisis Ctr., Dallas, 1975—82. Named Outstanding Tchr. award, Chancellor of U. Tex. Sys., 1988—89. Home: 2424 Winterstone Dr Plano TX 75023

WORSLEY, JAMES RANDOLPH, JR., lawyer; b. Rocky Mount, NC, July 28, 1924; s. James Randolph and Helen Marie (Killian) W.; m. Cornelia Cheston, Feb. 11, 1956; children: Cornelia Worsley Newell, Julia Worsley Neilson, Charlotte Cheston Worsley. BS, E. Carolina U., 1944; postgrad., Harvard U., 1944-45, LLB, 1949. Bar: N.C. 1949, D.C. 1949. Assoc. Klagsbrunn, Hanes & Irwin, Washington, 1949-54; ptnr. Ober, Kaler, Grimes & Shriver (and predecessor firm), Washington, 1955-94, coun., 1995—. Chmn. Md. Potomac Water Authority, 1969-71, Montgomery County (Md.) Charter Revision Commn., 1967; mem. pastoral coun. Archdiocese of Washington, 1975-78; bd. dirs. Madeira Sch., McLean, Va., 1975-81. Fellow Am. Bar Found.; mem. Chevy Chase Club, Met. Club, Knights of Malta. Democrat. Roman Catholic. Avocations: sailing, tennis. Home: 11 Quincy St Chevy Chase MD 20815-4226 Office: Ober Kaler Grimes & Shriver 1401 H St NW Ste 500 Washington DC 20005-2175 Office Phone: 202-408-8400.

WORTEL, GARY G., publishing executive; b. Ottawa, Can., 1956; m. Patti C. Wortel; children: Erin, Garrett, Elise, Patrick. BA, San Jose State U., Calif. With San Jose Mercury News, Calif., 1978—93, Tennessean,

Nashville, 1993—2001, display advt. mgr., advt. dir.; v.p. advt. & mktg. St. Paul Pioneer Press, 2001—05; pres., pub. Sun News, Myrtle Beach, SC, 2005—07, Ft. Worth Star-Telegram, 2007—. Office: Ft Worth Star-Telegram 400 W 7th St Fort Worth TX 76102-4793 Office Phone: 817-390-7454. E-mail: gwortel@star-telegram.com.

WORTEY, ELIZABETH NORMAN, librarian, associate director; b. Nuremberg, Bavaria, Germany, Aug. 27, 1967; d. Richard Norman and Emme Norman Grigsby. MS, U. North Tex., Denton, 1990; BEd, Hardin Simmons U., Abilene, Tex., 1989, MEd, 2001. Head pub. svcs. Okla. Bapt. U. Mabee Learning Ctr., Shawnee, 1990—95; assoc. dir. pub. svcs. Hardin Simmons U. Libr., 1995—, prof., 1995—. Vol. Paramount Theatre, Abilene. Mem.: Tex. Libr. Assn., Assn. Coll. and Rsch. Librs., ALA. Office: Hardin Simmons Univ 2200 Hickory St Abilene TX 79698 Office Fax: 325-677-8351. Business E-Mail: enorman@hsutx.edu.

WORTH, GEORGE JOHN, retired English literature educator; b. Vienna, June 11, 1929; arrived in U.S., 1940, naturalized, 1945; s. Adolph and Theresa (Schmerzler) W.; m. Carol Laverne Dinsdale, Mar. 17, 1951; children: Theresa Jean (Wilkinson), Paul Dinsdale. AB, U. Chgo., 1948, MA, 1951; PhD, U. Ill., 1954. Instr. English U. Ill., Urbana, 1954-55; faculty U. Kans., Lawrence, 1955—, assoc. prof., 1962-65, prof. English lit., 1965-95; prof. emeritus English, 1995—; asst. chmn. dept. U. Kans., Lawrence, 1961-62, assoc. chmn., 1962-63, acting chmn., 1963-64, chmn., 1964-79. Author: James Hannay: His Life and Work, 1964, William Harrison Ainsworth, 1972, Dickensian Melodrama, 1978, Thomas Hughes, 1984, Great Expectations: An Annotated Bibliography, 1986, (book) Macmillan's Magazine, 1859-1907, 2003; editor: (with Harold Orel) Six Studies in Nineteenth Century English Literature and Thought, 1962, The Nineteenth Century Writer and His Audience, 1969, (with Edwin Eigner) Victorian Criticism of the Novel, 1985. Mem. MLA, Dickens Fellowship, Dickens Soc., Midwest Victorian Studies Assn., Rsch. Soc. for Victorian Periodicals. Office: U Kans Dept English Wescoe Hall Lawrence KS 66045-7590 E-mail: GJWorth@aol.com.

WORTH, JOHN EUGENE, anthropologist, educator; s. Roy Eugene Worth and Dorothy Janis Williamson; m. Concha Rodriguez Garcia; children: Christopher, Henry. BA, MA, U. Ga., Athens, 1988; PhD, U. Fla., Gainesville, 1992. Registered profl. archaeologist Register Profl. Archaeologists, 2008. Anthropologist Fernbank Mus. Natural History, Atlanta, 1992—98; program dir. Coosawattee Found., Calhoun, Ga., 1998—2001; asst. dir. Randell Rsch. Ctr., FLMNH, Pineland, Fla., 2001—07; asst. prof. U. West Fla., Pensacola, 2007—. Author: (book) The Struggle for the Georgia Coast, The Timucuan Chiefdoms of Spanish Florida (Rembert Patrick Book award, 1999). Bd. mem. Ga. Nat. Hist. Register Rev. Bd., Atlanta, 1998—2001; coun. mem. Ga. Coun. Am. Indian Concerns, Atlanta, 2000—02. Recipient C.B. Moore Excellence Archaeology award, Lower Miss. Survey, 1998. Mem.: Fla. Archeol. Coun.

WORTH, LYNN HARRIS, writer; b. Flushing, Sept. 21, 1934; d. Andrew Lamar Harris and Jean Hofmann; m. Chauncey Merrill Smith, Jr., June 20, 1992. AA in Journalism, Vt. Coll., 1954; degree in Interior Design, NY Sch. Interior Design, 1971. Editl. asst. Time Mag., NYC, 1954—56; pub. rels. asst. Silver Hill Found., New Canaan, Conn., 1958—61. Ptnr. Chameleon Interiors, Westport, Conn., 1972—84. Editor and pub.: Va. Hunting Preserve Jour., editor, pub.: Magyar Vizsla News, mem. editl. staff: AKC Perspectives; contbr. articles to mags.; editor: Clarksville About Town, 2004—05. Publicity dir. Westport Young Woman's League, 1967—68; publicity/pub. rels. dist 2 Girl Scouts Am., Fairfield County, 1967—69; publicity/pub. rels. LWV, Westport; founding mem. Lake Country SPCA; pres. Vizsla Club of Am. Welfare Found.; co-chmn. Revitalization com. Town of Clarksville, Va., 2004—09; publicity/pub. rels. polit. campaign for Gov. Tom Meskill, Conn. Mem.: Magyar Vizsla Soc. (founding mem.), numerous regional dog clubs, Vizsla Club of Am. (Am. Kennel Club del., v.p., sec. 1980—). Home: PO Box 1755 Clarksville VA 23927 Personal E-mail: lynhar@aol.com.

WORTHAM, JOYCELYN FOY, education specialist; b. Columbia, SC, Sept. 12, 1953; d. James and Betty Jean (Pierce) Foy; 1 child, Danzi Elizabeth. BS, Tuskegee U., 1975; MA, U. Ala., 1976, EdD, 1993; MEd, Tuskegee U., 1983. Support tchr. Brewer-Porch Remedial Ctr., Tuscaloosa, Ala., 1975-76; team leader Lurleen B. Wallace Devel. Ctr., Decatur, Ala., 1976-78; hosp. tchr. U. Va. Hosp., Charlottesville, Va., 1978-80; spl. educator Prattville (Ala.) Elem., 1980-90; project coord. U. Ala., Tuscaloosa, 1990—. Adj. instr. Ala. State U., 2006; specialist Ala. Dept. Edn.; cons. in field. Troop leader Girl Scout Am., Montgomery, Ala., 1988. Recipient Outstanding Emotional Conflict Tchr. award, 1987, Tommy Russell award for Excellence in Grad. Study, 1989, Outstanding Women in Am. award, 1983; named co-writer tchr. edn. grant U.S. Dept. Edn., 1990. Mem. Coun. for Exceptional Children (pres. 1981-82), Coun. for Children with Behavior Disorders. Roman Catholic. Avocations: tennis, dance. Office: Gordon Persons Aersow Bldg PO Box 302101 50 N Ripley St Montgomery AL 36130-2101 Office Phone: 334-353-5552. Personal E-mail: jwortham@bellsouth.net.

WORTHEN, DENNIS BRENT, researcher, educator; b. Wilmington, Del., June 3, 1943; s. Charles Stanley and Mary Katherine (Gruler) W.; m. Patricia Lynn Urban, May 1, 1965; children: David Brian, Daniel Bret. BA, U. Mich., Ann Arbor, 1964; ABA in Liberal Arts, North ctrl. Mich. Coll., Petoskey; MS, Case Western Res. U., Cleve., 1973, MLS, 1976, PhD, 1972—76. Mgr. Kroger Co., Detroit, 1965—66; profl. sales rep. E.R. Squibb & Sons, Cadillac, Mich., 1966—72; instr. libr. sci. Case Western Res. U., Cleve., 1974—76; chief, info. svcs. Norwich Eaton Pharms., Norwich, NY, 1976—85, mgr. formularies and reimbursement, 1986—88, dir. pharmacy and govt. rels., 1988—92; dir. pharmacy affairs Procter & Gamble Pharms., Cin., 1992—99; dir. Lloyd Libr. and Mus., Cin., 1999—2001, rsch. scholar, 2001—. Adj. prof. U. Miss., Oxford, 1987—, U. Cin., 1999-; vis. prof. Queen's U., Belfast, No. Ireland, 1986—. Co-author: Enteral Hyperalimentation with Chemical Defined Elemental Diets, The Millis Study Commission on Pharmacy, Pharmacy in World War II, Heroes of Pharmacy, 2008; series editor: Jour. Clin. Pharmacy and Therapeutics; contbg. editor Pharmacy Times; contbr. numerous articles to profl. jours. Mem. vis. com. Bd. of Overseers Case Western Res. U., Cleve., 1976-82, Mcpl. Planning Commn., Norwich, 1986-88; exec. dir. Lloyd Libr. and Mus., Cin., 1999-2001, Lloyd rsch. scholar, 2001-. Grantee Nat. Libr. Medicine, Washington, 1984-86. Mem. Am. Assn. Colls. Pharmacy, Am. Assn. History Medicine, Am. Inst. History Pharmacy, Am. Pharmacists Assn., Internat. Acad. History Pharmacy, Drug Info. Assn. (various offices 1975-80), Pharm. Mfrs. Assn. (vis. scientist 1986—), Am. Assn. Pharm. Scientists (various offices 1988—99), Beta Phi Mu. Home: 1723 Old Farm Dr Loveland OH 45140 Office: Lloyd Libr and Mus 917 Plum St Cincinnati OH 45202 Business E-Mail: dbworthen@lloydlibrary.org.

WORTHEN, KEVIN, academic administrator, law educator; AS, Coll. Ea. Utah, 1978; BA summa cum laude, Brigham Young U., 1979, JD summa cum laude, 1982. Law clerk for Judge Malcolm R. Wilkey U.S. Ct. Appeals, Columbia Cir., 1982—83; Judge Byron R. White U.S. Supreme Ct., 1984; atty. Jennings, Strouss & Salmon, Phoenix, 1984—87; Fulbright scholar U. Chile Law Sch., 1994; prof. law Brigham Young U., J. Ruben Clark Law Sch., 1987—, assoc. dean, 1999—2004, dean, 2004—08, BYU advancement v.p., 2008—. Chmn. Utah State Constl. Revision Commn. Contbr. articles to law jours. Order of Coif. Mem.: Ariz. State Bar Assn. Office: Brigham Young U J Reuben Clark Sch Law D 364 ASB Provo UT 84602 Office Phone: 801-422-2640. Business E-Mail: kevin_worthen@byu.edu.*

WORTHING, CAROL MARIE, retired minister; b. Duluth, Minn., Dec. 27, 1934; d. Truman James and Helga Maria (Bolander) W.; children: Gregory Alan Beatty, Graydon Ernest Beatty. BS, U. Minn., 1965; MDiv, Northwestern Theol. Seminary, 1982; DMin, Grad. Theol. Found., Notre Dame, Ind., 1988; MBA in Ch. Mgmt., Grad. Theol. Found., Donaldson, Ind., 1993; cert., Austin Presbyn. Theol. Sem., 2001; PhD, Grad. Theol. Found., 2002. Cert. Episcopal Diocese of Tex., 2003. Secondary educator Ind. (Minn.) Sch. Dist., 1965-78; teaching fellow U. Minn., 1968-70; contract counselor Luth. Social Svc., Duluth, 1976-78; media cons. Luth. Media Svcs., St. Paul, 1978-80; asst. pastor Messiah Luth. Ch., Fargo, ND, 1982-83, vice pastor, 1983-84; assoc. editor Luth. Ch. Am. Ptnrs., Phila., 1982-84; editorial assoc. Luth. Ptnrs. Evang. Luth. Ch. Am., Phila. and Mpls., 1984—2004; parish pastor Resurrection Luth. Ch., Pierre, SD, 1984-89; assoc. pastor Bethlehem Luth. Ch., Cedar Falls, Iowa, 1989-90; exec. dir. Ill. Conf. Chs., Springfield, 1990-96, Tex. Conf. of Chs., 1996—2003; ret., 2003. Mem. pub. rels. and interpretation com. Red River Valley Synod, Fargo, 1984-86, mem. ch. devel., Pierre, 1986-87; mem. mgmt. com. office comm. Luth. Ch. in Am., N.Y.C., Phila., 1984-88; mem. mission ptnrs. S.D. Synod, 1988, chmn. assembly resolutions com., 1988; mem. pre-assembly planning com., ecumenics com., chmn. resolutions com. N.E. Iowa Synod, 1989-90; mem. ch. and society com., 1990-96; ecumenical com., 1995-96; Luth. Ecumenical Rep. Network, 1995—2003; mem. Cen. and So. Ill. Synod, 1996; mem. S.W. Tex. Synod, 1996—2003, mem. ecumenical com., 1998-2001; mem. ecumenical com. Mpls. Area synod and St. Paul Area synod ELCA, 2004-06; nat. edn. cons. Am. Film Inst., Washington, 1967-70; chaplain state legis. bodies, Pierre, 1984-89; mem. exec. bd. Luth. Ecumenical Rep. Network for Region 4, Evang. Luth. Ch. in Am., 2002-03; preacher Nat. Cathedral, Washington, 2002. Author: Cinematics and English, 1967, Peer Counseling, 1977, Tischrede Lexegete, 1986, 88, 90, Way of the Cross, Way of Justice Walk, 1987, Introducing Collaboration as a Leadership Stance and Style in an Established Statewide Conference of Churches, 1993, The Anointing of Jesus--A, Christological Necessity, 2001, The Portrait on the Wall, Dust & Fire, Vol XXII, 2008 Co-facilitator Parents of Retarded Children, 1985; bd. dirs. Countryside Hospice, 1985; cons. to adminstrv. bd. Mo. Shores Women's Ctr., 1986, Journey into Prayer Com., 2007-08, co-chair Spiritual Form Com., 2008-, ret. leader, 2009-, leader McCabe Renewal Ctr., 2009- Named John Macquarrie fellow, Grad. Theol. Found., 2002, homilist, Tex. Day, Washington Nat. Cathedral, 2002. Mem. NAFE, Nat. Assn. Ecumenical Staff (chair of site selection com. 1991-92, chair of scholarship com. 1993-94, mem. profl. devel. com. 1993-94, chair program planning com. 1996, bd. dirs. 1995-96), Pierre-Ft. Pierre Ministerium (v.p. 1986-87, pres. 1987-88). Democrat. Avocations: writing prose and poetry, concerts, theater, art, photography. Home: 3800 London Rd Apt 601 Duluth MN 55804-2226 *Ecumenism is, I believe, about full coherence between our ecclesiology and our ethics. The Spirit of God calls the church to come together for a compassionate purpose: to respond to all who suffer, so that the world might be transformed into God's own vision of peace, justice, and love.*

WORTHINGTON, BRUCE R., lawyer, energy executive; b. 1949; BA in Econs. cum laude, Claremont McKenna Coll.; JD, U. Calif., Davis. Bar: Calif. 1974. Joined law dept. Pacific Gas and Electric Co., 1974, sr. counsel, chief counsel corp., 1991—94, v.p., gen. counsel, 1994—95, sr. v.p., gen. counsel, 1995—97, PG&E Corp., San Francisco, 1997—. Corp. rep. Calif. Minority Counsel Prog. Mem.: ABA (vice chair Sect. Pub. Utility, Comm., and Transp. Law), Calif. Bar Assn., San Francisco Bar Assn.

WORTHINGTON, JOHN M., retail executive; With Famous-Barr divsn. May Dept. Stores; with Kohl's Corp., Menomonee Falls, Wis., 1993—, sr. v.p., territory dir. NE region, exec. v.p., dir. stores, 2005—07, sr. exec. v.p. store ops., 2007—. Mem. retail adv. bd. Inst. Mktg. Brigham Young U. Marriott Sch. Mgmt. Office: Kohls Corp N56 W17000 Ridgewood Dr Menomonee Falls WI 53051-5660 Office Phone: 262-703-7000.

WORTHINGTON, MELVIN LEROY, minister, writer; b. Greenville, NC, June 17, 1937; s. Wilbur Leroy and Alma Lee (Braxton) W.; m. Anne Katherine Wilson, Sept. 12, 1959; children: Daniel Edward, Lydia Anne. Diploma, Imperial Detective Acad., Cin., 1965; B.Bibl.Edn., Columbia Bible Coll., SC, 1959; B.Th., Luther Rice Sem., Jacksonville, Fla., 1967, B.Div., 1969, M.Th., 1970, D.Th., 1974; M.Ed., Ga. State U.-Atlanta, 1979; EdD, Vanderbilt U., 1998. Ordained to ministry, Central Conf. Free Will Baptists, 1957. Pastor Union Chapel Free Will Bapt. Ch., Chocowinity, NC, 1959-62, Palmetto Free Will Bapt. Ch., Vanceboro, NC, 1959-62, First Free Will Bapt. Ch., Darlington, SC, 1962-66, Wesconnett Free Will Bapt. Ch., Jacksonville, Fla., 1967, First Free Will Bapt. Ch., Amory, Miss., 1967-72, Albany, Ga., 1972-79; exec. sec. Nat. Assn. Free Will Bapt., Inc., Antioch, 1979—2002, chmn. Sunday Sch. bd., 1975-77, asst. moderator, 1977-79, chmn. grad. study com., 1976-77, exec. sec. emeritus, 2002—; pastor Liberty Free Will Bapt. Ch., Ayden, NC, 2003—. Clk. S.C. State Assn. Free Will Bapt., Florence, 1966-67; asst. moderator Ga. State Assn. Free Will Bapt., Moultrie, 1973-74, moderator, 1975-79; pres. Ga. Bible Inst., Albany, 1978 Editor in chief: Contact mag., 1979—2002, author editorial, 1980—2002; contbr. articles to profl. jours. Adv. bd. Nat. Fedn. Decency, 1985; nat. bd. dirs. Christian Leaders for Responsible TV, 1986 Mem. Evang. Press Assn., Religious Conf. Mgmt. Assn. (dir. 1983, v.p. 1986, pres. 1989-92, 2009-), Nashville C. of C., Future Farmers Am. (N.C. Farmer degree 1955, Am. Farmer degree 1957). Democrat. Mem. Free Will Baptist Ch. Office: Nat Assn Free Will Bapt Inc 5233 Mount View Rd Antioch TN 37013-2306 Office Phone: 252-746-3132. *The basic principle which has guided, governed and guarded my life has been a burning desire to find, follow and finish the will of God.*

WORTHINGTON, ROBERT FLETCHER, JR., lawyer; b. Knoxville, Tenn., July 17, 1931; s. Robert Fletcher Worthington and Rachel Ann Boggs; m. Julia McCrary (dec.); children: Julia Elizabeth Worthington Farry, Katherine Louisa Worthington Kinnard; m. Carole Lynch Worthington; 1 child, Cassandra Lynch. LLD, U. Tenn., 1957. Bar: Tenn. 1957, DC 1977. Assoc. Baker & Baker, Knoxville, 1957—59; ptnr. Baker, Young, Young & Baker, Knoxville, 1959—63, Baker Worthington, Knoxville, 1963—94; of counsel Baker, Donelsen, Bearman, Caldwell & Berkowitz, Knoxville, 1994—. Gen. counsel Tenn. Valley indsl. com. Tenn. Gas Assn. and NeWire, Inc. Mem. past pres. coun. Tenn. Bus. Roundtable; past vice chmn. Tenn. Higher Edn. Commn.; gen. counsel World's Fair, Knoxville, 1982; mem. adv. bd. conf. Cumberland Trail; mem. adv. bd. Florence Crittenton Agy., Inc. Devel. Coun., Cmty. Sch. Arts; chmn. bd. govs. Club LeConte; bd. dirs. Boathouse Benevolent Soc., Inc., Knoxville Zool. Soc., East Tenn. Hist. Soc. 1st lt. inf. US Army, 1953—60. Named to Dean's Cir., U. Tenn. Coll. Law-, Best Lawyers in Am., 1991—. Mem.: ABA, D.C. Bar Assn., Knoxville Bar Assn., Tenn. Bar Assn., Phi Delta Phi. Office: Baker Donelson Bearman Caldwell & Berkowitz 265 Brookview Ctr Way Ste 600 Knoxville TN 37919 Office Phone: 865-549-7000. Office Fax: 865-633-7200. Business E-Mail: rworthington@bakerdonelson.com.

WORTHINGTON, TRACY, retired operations research analyst; b. Wichita, Kans., Mar. 6, 1939; s. Maurice Glenn Worthington and Thelma Evelyn Mendenhall; m. Margaret Eloise Ward, May 20, 1961; 1 child, Kimberly Marie. BS, Wichita State U., 1972; M in Engring., Tex. A & M U., College Station, 1976. EIT Kans. State Bd., 1972. Pvt. sector, 1956—74; machinist, toolmaker, insp., draftsman, planner, engr., further light aircraft and off-set printer mfg. and design Pub. sector, 1974—95; engr., analyst, advance devel. and testing of precision guided munitions, electronic counter measure devices; ret. Fed. Govt., 1995. With USAF, 1961—65. Mem.: Air Force Assn. (life). Personal E-mail: tmew@frontiernet.net.

WORTHINGTON, WILLIAM ALBERT, III, lawyer; b. June 26, 1950; s. William Albert Jr. and Patricia Lou (Reynolds) W.; children: Elizabeth Clark, Emily Robin, Katherine Anne, William Jackson. BS, U. Utah, 1972; JD, Washington and Lee U., 1976. Bar: Tex. 1976, U.S. Dist. Ct. (so. dist.) Tex. 1977, U.S. Ct. Appeals (5th cir.) 1977, U.S. Ct. Appeals (11th cir.) 1981, U.S. Supreme Ct. 1981, U.S. Dist. Ct. (we. dist.) Tex. 1982, U.S. Dist. Ct. (ea. dist.) Tex. 1986, U.S. Dist. Ct. (no. dist.) Tex. 1993. Assoc. Sewell & Riggs, Houston, 1976—82, ptnr., 1982—89, shareholder, 1990—94; ptnr. Strasburger & Price, LLP, Houston, 1994—. Exec. editor Washington and Lee Law Rev., 1976; contbr. articles to law jours. Active Houston YMCA, Amnesty Internat. U.S.A., ARC; del. state bar of Tex. to Rep. Cuba, 2001. Mem. Am. Law Inst., Def. Rsch. Inst., Product Liability Adv. Coun., Houston Bar Found., Tex. Bd. Legal Specialization (cert. civil trial lawyer, personal injury trial lawyer), Tex. Bar Found., U.S. Cycling Fedn., Sierra Club. Office: Strasburger & Price LLP 1401 Mckinney Ste 2200 Houston TX 77010-3033 Home Phone: 713-661-2977; Office Phone: 713-951-5600. Business E-Mail: william.worthington@strasburger.com.

WORTHLEY, HAROLD FIELD, retired minister, educator; b. Brewer, Maine, Nov. 3, 1928; s. Herbert Morrison and Aline May (Field) W.; m. Barbara Louise Bent, June 25, 1955; children: Susan Louise Field, Laura May, David Bruce. AB, Boston U., 1950, MA, 1951; STB, Harvard Div. Sch., 1954, STM, 1956, ThD, 1970. Ordained to ministry United Ch. of Christ, 1954. Min. Congl. chs., Maine, N.H. and Mass., 1952-62; assoc. prof. religion, chaplain Wheaton Coll., Norton, Mass., 1963-77; exec. sec., archivist Congl. Christian Hist. Soc., Boston, 1971—2004; exec. dir. Am. Congl. Assn., 1999—2004; libr. Congl. Libr., Boston, 1977—2004, libr. emeritus, 2004—. Editor Bull. of Congl. Library, 1976—2004, Hist. Intelligencer, 1980-86. Author: Inventory of the Records of the Particular Churches of Massachusetts, 1620-1805, 1970; contbr. articles to profl. jours. Fellow Pilgrim Soc., Congl. Christian Hist. Soc. Home: 14 Mansfield Ave Norton MA 02766-2212 E-mail: blwhfw@msn.com.

WORTHY, GRAHAM ANTHONY JAMES, biology professor, researcher; m. Tamara Ann Worthy; children: Colin, Kelsey. BSc, U. Guelph, Ont., Can., 1979, MSc, 1982, PhD, 1986. Prof. marine biology Tex. A&M U., Galveston, 1990—2001; prof. marine mammalogy U. Ctrl. Fla., Orlando, 2001—. Dir. Tex. Marine Mammal Stranding Network, Galveston, 1991—2001. Office: Univ Central Florida 4000 Central Florida Blvd Orlando FL 32816-2368 Office Fax: 407-823-5769. Business E-Mail: gworthy@mail.ucf.edu.

WORTHY, K(ENNETH) MARTIN, retired lawyer; b. Dawson, Ga., Sept. 24, 1920; s. Kenneth Spencer and Jeffrie Pruett (Martin) W.; m. Eleanor Vreeland (Blewett), Feb. 15, 1947 (dec. July 26, 1981); children: Jeffrie Martin (dec.), William Blewett; m. Katherine Teasley (Jackson), June 17, 1983. Attended, The Citadel, 1937-39; PhB, Emory U., 1941; MBA cum laude, Harvard U., 1943; JD cum laude, Emory U., 1947. Bar: Ga., 1947; D.C., 1948. Assoc. Foley and Lardner (formerly Hopkins, Sutter, Hamel, and Park), Washington, 1948-51, ptnr., 1952-69, 72-90, sr. counsel, 1991—2001, ret. ptnr., 2001—; of counsel Gilbert, Harrell, Sumerford & Martin, Brunswick, Ga., 2008—; chief counsel IRS, 1969—72; asst. gen. counsel Treasury Dept., 1969—72. Mem. Nat. Coun. Organized Crime, 1970-72; cons. Justice Dept., 1972-74. Co-author: (with John M. Appleman) Basic Estate Planning, 1957; contbg. articles to profl. jour. Del. Montgomery County Civic Fedn., 1951—61, D.C. Area Health and Welfare Coun., 1960—61; pres. Sea Island Property Owners Assn., 2004—05; chmn. dept. fin., mem. diocesan coun. Episc. Diocese, Washington, 1969—70; trustee Associated Marine Inst. Found., 1999—2002, Ga. Wilderness Inst., 1997—2003, emeritus, 2003—; trustee St. Simons Island Libr. Found., 2000—, chmn., 2001—05; fellow Aspen Inst., 1982—92; trustee St. John's Coll., Annapolis, Santa Fe, 1987—93, 1995—2001, Sherman Found., Newport Beach, Calif., 1991—, Barker Found., Washington, 1958—62, pres., 1960—61; mem. coun. Emory U. Law Sch., 1976—2001, chmn., 1993—95, emeritus, 2001—; bd. dirs. Assn. Citadel Men, 1964—68; trustee Chelsea Sch., 1981—2001, trustee emeritus, 2001—. Capt. US Army, 1943—46, 1951—52. Recipient Army Commendation Ribbon, 1945; Treasury Exceptional Svc. Award and medal, 1972; IRS Commr. Award, 1972; Disting. Alumnus Award, Emory U., 1992. Fellow Am. Bar Found., Am. Coll. Tax Counsel (bd. regents 1980-88, chmn. 1985-87), Atlantic Coun. (counselor 1989-99); mem. ABA (coun. taxation sect. 1965-69, 72-75, chmn. 1973-74, del. Nat. Conf. Lawyers and CPAs 1981-87, ho. of dels. 1983-89, chmn. audit com. 1985-90; Disting. Svc. award taxation sect. 2004), Fed. Bar Assn. (nat. coun. 1969-74, 77-79), Ga. Bar Assn., D.C. Bar, Am. Law Inst., Am. Tax Policy Inst. (trustee 1989-98), Rotary, Chevy Chase Club, Met. Club, Sea Island Club, Ivy League Club (pres. 2002-03), Harvard Club N.Y.C., Phi Delta Theta, Phi Delta Phi, Omicron Delta Kappa. Office: Foley and Lardner 3000 K St NW Ste 500 Washington DC 20007-5143 also: Gilbert Harrell Sumerford & Martin PO Box 190 Brunswick GA 31521-0190 Personal E-mail: kmartinworthy@aol.com. Business E-Mail: kworthy@foley.com.

WORTLEY, GEORGE CORNELIUS, lobbyist, former United States Representative from New York; b. Syracuse, NY, Dec. 8, 1926; s. George C. and Arlene (Hirsh) W.; m. Barbara Jane Hennessy, May 13, 1950; children: George C. IV, Ann Wortley Lavin, Elizabeth Wortley Ring. BS, Syracuse U., 1948. Newspaper pub., pres. Manlius Pub. Corp., Fayetteville, NY, 1950-92; pres. Nat. Editorial Found., 1968-73; mem. US Congress from 27th N.Y. Dist., 1981—89, US House Banking, Fin. & Urban Affairs Com., US House Select Com. on Aging, Select Com. on Children, Youth & Family; prin. Dierman, Wortley, Zola & Associates, Inc. (DWZ), Washington, 1989—. Pres. Am. Newspapers Reps., 1966—68; bd. dirs. Dierman, Wortley, Zola & Assocs., Washington Solutions. Pres. Hiawatha coun. Boy Scouts Am., 1972-75; mem. Nat. Commn. on Hist. Publs. and Records, 1977-80, Fayetteville Sr. Citizen Housing Commn., 1977-80; mem. allocations com. United Way of Ctrl. N.Y., 1979-81; mem. pub. rels. com. St. Camillus Health Care Ctr., 1971-78; mem. fed. legis. com. Am. Lung Assn., 1974-77; bd. dirs.

Crouse-Irving Meml. Hosp. Found., 1975-87, pres. 1979-81; bd. dirs. Am. Heart Assn., Upstate N.Y., 1960-80, chmn. pub. rels. com., 1970-74, chmn. legis. com. 1977, mem. fund raising adv. com., 1974-79; trustee Cazenovia Coll., 1981-94; bd. dirs. Onondaga Hist. Assn., 1980-90; dir. Global Leadership Inst., 1987-2001. Served with MMR, USNR, WWII. Recipient Silver Beaver award Boy Scouts Am., 1973, Silver Antelope award, 1981 Mem. Nat. Newspaper Assn. (legis. com. 1976-80), Greater Syracuse C. of C. (dir. 1979-81), Upstate Coun. Indsl. Editors, LeMoyne Coll. Pres.'s Assocs., Syracuse U. Alumni Asn. (nat. treas. 1973-77), Former Mems. of U.S. Congress Assn., Navy League of U.S., Cosmos Club, Georgetown Club, Coral Ridge Yacht Club, Lions, KC, Kappa Sigma (pres. 1957-59). Republican. Roman Catholic. Office: Dierman Wortley Zola & Associates 1710 Rhode Island Ave NW Ste 200 Washington DC 20036 Office Phone: 202-296-4442. Office Fax: 202-429-2882. E-mail: wortley@dwz-dc.com.*

WORTLEY, MICAHEL D., lawyer; b. Tulsa, June 9, 1947; BA with highest honors, So. Meth. U., 1970, JD with honors, 1978; MRP, U. NC, 1973. Bar: Tex. 1978. Shareholder Johnson & Wortley PC, 1985—93, mng. dir., 1993—93; ptnr., co-head Corp. Fin. & Securities Sect. Vinson & Elkins LLP, Dallas, 1993—. Mem.: ABA, Dallas Bar Assn. Office: Vinson & Elkins LLP Trammell Crow Center 2001 Ross Ave, Ste 3700 Dallas TX 75201 Office Phone: 214-220-7732. E-mail: mwortley@velaw.com.

WORTMAN, MARLENE STEIN, historian; b. Vienna; d. Leon and Pauline (Lindenbuam) Stein; m. Richard S. Wortman, June 14, 1960; 1 child, Leonie. AB, Syracuse U., 1958; PhD, U. Chgo., 1966; postgrad. in law, Bklyn. Law Sch., 1988-92. Asst. prof. in Am. history Ill. Inst. Tech., Chgo., 1969-77; ind. scholar Inst. for Rsch. in History, NYC, 1977-81, Princeton (N.J.) Rsch. Forum, 1981-87. Pres., v.p. Princeton Rsch. Forum, 1981-85; grants officer Inst. for Rsch. in History, N.Y.C., 1980; coord. Chgo. Met. Area Women's History Group, 1974-76. Editor: (book) Women in American Law, 1985; co-author: The Roads They Made: Women in Illinois History, 1977; contbr. articles to profl. jours; editor: (newsletter) Conf. Group in Women's History, 1975-77. Vice pres. ACLU, N.J., 1982-84, co-chair Women's Rights Com., 1983-87. Conf. grantee on housing N.J. Com. for Humanities, Princeton, 1983; grantee NEH, 1979-81; recipient travel fellowship Am. Philos. Soc., 1975, rsch. fellowship Ill. Inst. Tech., 1974. Mem. NOW, Planned Parenthood. Avocation: hiking. Home: 410 Riverside Dr Apt 91 New York NY 10025-7924

WORTMAN, RICHARD S., historian, educator; b. NYC, Mar. 24, 1938; s. Joseph R. and Ruth (Nacht) W.; m. Marlene Stein, June 14, 1960; 1 child, Leonie. BA, Cornell U., 1958; MA, U. Chgo., 1960, PhD, 1964. Instr. history U. Chgo., 1963-64, asst. prof., 1964-69, asso. prof., 1969-76, prof., 1976-77; prof. history Princeton U., 1977-88, dir. Russian studies, 1982-88; prof. history Columbia U., 1988—; Bryce prof. history, 2001—; prof. emeritus, 2009—. Trustee Nat. Coun. for Soviet and Ea. European Rsch., 1983-89; sr. fellow Harriman Inst., 1985-86; bd. dirs. Soc. Ct. Studies, London, 2002—; mem. adv. bd. Kennan Inst., 2005—, Soc.Court Studies, Washington, 2002—. Author: The Crisis of Russian Populism, 1967, The Development of a Russian Legal Consciousness, 1976, (with Leopold Haimson and Ziva Gallili) The Making of Three Russian Revolutionaries: Voices from the Menshevik Past, 1987, Scenarios of Power: Myth and Ceremony in Russian Monarchy, vol. I, 1995, vol. II (George L. Mosse prize Am. Hist. Assn., Efim Etkind prize), 2000, Scenario's of Power, 2006. Social Sci. Rsch. Coun. grantee, 1975-76; Guggenheim fellow. Mem. Am. Assn. Advancement Slavic Studies (pres. Mid-Atlantic Slavic Conf. 1982-83, Disting. Contbn. Slavic Studies award, 2007), AAUP., Am. Hist. Assn., Am. Assn. Advancement, Soc. for Court Studies. Home: 410 Riverside Dr Apt 91 New York NY 10025-7924 Business E-Mail: rsw3@columbia.edu.

WOS, PAUL M., music educator, infosystems specialist, educator; b. Buffalo, Feb. 19, 1957; s. Iggy J. and Angeline W. (Kotas) W. MusB, E Astman Sch. Music, NYC, 1978; postgrad, E Astman Sch. Music, 1987—; MusM, U. Ky., 1980. Cert. elem., secondary music tchr., N.Y. Dir. instrumental music Gaskill Jr. High Sch., Niagara Falls, N.Y., 1981-85; chmn. music dept. Niagara Falls High Sch., 1985—. Regional site dir. Nat. Computer Tng. Inst., Fremont, Calif., 1984-85; instr. computers Niagara Falls City Schs., 1983-97, North Tonawanda (N.Y.) City Schs., 1985-88; ednl. tech. cons. Niagara Falls Tchr. Resource Ctr., 1988—; tchr. trainer music and tech. N.Y. State Edn. Dept., 1988—. Author: Computer Basics Vol. 1, 1984, Computer Basics Vol. 2, 1984, How to Use Your Microcomputer, 1985, Comprehensive Musicianship: Text and Worksheets, 2005, Music Theory AP Text & Worksheets, 2007; patentee compute software Applecreek Downs, 1983. Named Tchr. of Yr., Niagara Falls City Schs., 2005. Mem. Music Educators Nat. Conf., Phi Mu Alpha Sinfonia, Nat. Band Assn., NY State Band Dirs. Assn. Roman Catholic. Home: 2923 North Ave Niagara Falls NY 14305-3334 Office: Niagara Falls High Sch 4455 Porter Rd Niagara Falls NY 14305 Business E-Mail: pwos@nfschools.net.

WOSMAN, BRIAN D., physical education educator, director; s. James J. and Brenda Wosman; m. Amanda U. Amanda Miller; children: Haleigh M., Nolan J. BS in Phys. Edn., Culver Stockton Coll., Canton, Mo., 1996. Phys. edn. tchr. health tchr. Palmyra R-I, Mo., 2001—08, dir. transp. athletic dir., 2008. Named Coach of Yr., 2001, 2007. Home: 306 Breckenridge Palmyra MO 63461 Office: Palmyra R-I Sch Dist 1723 S Main Palmyra MO 63461 Office Fax: 573-769-1013. Business E-Mail: wosmanb@palmyra.k12.mo.us.

WOSTAL, HOLLY ANN, music educator; b. New Braunfels, Tex., Dec. 22, 1960; d. Samuel Joseph and June Marie Wostal; 1 child, Richard Ross. BA in Music Edn., Houston Bapt. U., 1986; M.Applied Music in Conducting, U. of Houston, 1990; attending in Bus. Acctg., Mo. Southern State U., Joplin, BSBA in Acctg. Cert. all level music tchr. Tex., 1986, Mo., 2005. Asst. h.s. dir. Alief Ind. Sch. Dist., Alief, Tex., 1986—88; asst. choral condr. Houston Symphony, 1988—90; cmty. choral/symphonic dir. Lee Coll., Baytown, Tex., 1990—93; elem. music tchr. Sheldon Ind. Sch. Dist., Houston, 1991—92, Pasadena Ind. Sch. Dist., Pasadena, Tex., 1992—93; head h.s. choral dir. Bastrop Ind. Sch. Dist., Bastrop, Tex., 1998—2004; jr./sr. h.s. choral dir. Carl Junction R-1 Sch. Dist., Carl Junction, Mo., 2004—06; dean's first Mo. Southern State U., 2008. Music coord. and condr. City of Baytown, Tex., 1992—93; choir dir. First United Meth., Bastrop, 2001—02, First Christian Ch., Ruidoso, N.Mex., 1997—98, St. John's United Meth., Baytown, 1992—93. Scholar Grad. scholar, MD Anderson, 1988, Dept. of Music scholar, Houston Bapt. U., 1984—86. Mem.: Mo. Choral Dirs. Assn. Avocations: travel, hiking, crossword puzzles, cooking. Home: 1709 Dogwood Dr Joplin MO 64801

WOTEKI, CATHERINE ELLEN, nutritionist; b. Ft. Leavenworth, Kans., Oct. 7, 1947; d. Joseph Jeremiah and Catherine (Costello) O'Connor; m. Thomas Henry Woteki, June 7, 1969. BS, Mary Washington Coll., 1969; MS, Va. Poly. Inst. and State U., 1971, PhD, 1973. Registered dietitian. Asst. prof. Drexel U., Phila., 1975-77; project dir. Congl. Office of Tech. Assessment, Washington, 1977-80; group leader USDA, Washington, 1980-83; dep. dir. Nat. Ctr. for Health Statis., Washington, 1983-90; dir. Food and Nutrition Bd., Washington, 1990-93; dep. assoc. dir. for sci. Office of Sci. and Tech. Policy, Washington, 1994-95; undersec. food safety USDA Office of Food Safety, Washington, 1996—2001; dean agrl. Iowa State U., 2002—05; global dir. sci. affairs Macs, Inc., 2005—. Contbr. articles to profl. jours. Named Outstanding alumna Va. Poly. Inst. and State U., 1987; recipient Elijah White award Nat. Ctr. for Health Statis., 1987, Spl. Recognition award USPHS, 1987, Staff Achievement award Inst. of Medicine, 1991. Mem. Am. Inst. Nutrition, Am. Dietetic Assn. Coun. on Rsch., Inst. Food Technologists, Am. Pub. Health Assn., Inst. Medicine Office Phone: 703-821-4900.

WOTT, JOHN ARTHUR, retired arboretum and botanical garden executive, horticulture educator; b. Fremont, Ohio, Apr. 10, 1939; s. Arthur Otto Louis and Esther Wilhelmina (Werth) W.; children: Christopher, Timothy, Holly. BS, Ohio State U., 1961; MS, Cornell U., 1966, PhD, 1968. Mem. staff Ohio State Coop. Extension Svc., Bowling Green, 1961-64; rsch. asst. Cornell U., Ithaca, NY, 1964-68; prof. Purdue U., West Lafayette, Ind., 1968-81; prof. Ctr. Urban Horticulture U. Wash., Seattle, 1981—2006, prof. emeritus, 2006—; assoc. dir. Ctr. Urban Horticulture U. Wash., Seattle, 1990-93, acting dir., 2004—05; dir. arboreta Washington Park Arboretum, Seattle, 1993—2005. Writer columns for Nursery Mgmt. Profession, Balls and Burlap, Am. Nurseryman, The Arboretum Found.; contbr. articles to profl. jours. and papers including Nursery Mgr. Profl., Balls and Burlap, Arboreteum Found. Bull., Am. Nurseryman. Mem. Am. Soc. Hort. Sci. (com. chmn. 1967-82), Am. Assn. Bot. Gardens and Arboreta, Internat. Plant Propagators Soc. (internat. pres. 1984, internat. sec.-treas. 1985—2006). Avocations: music, antiques. Office Phone: 206-543-8602. Personal E-mail: jwott10623@aol.com. Business E-Mail: jwott@u.washington.edu.

WOUK, HERMAN, writer; b. NYC, May 27, 1915; s. Abraham Isaac and Esther (Levine) W.; m. Betty Sarah Brown, Dec. 9, 1945; children: Abraham Isaac (dec.), Nathaniel, Joseph. AB with gen. honors, Columbia U., 1934; LHD (hon.), Yeshiva U., 1954; LLD (hon.), Clark U., 1960; LittD (hon.), Am. Internat. Coll., 1979; PhD (hon.), Bar-Ilan U., 1990, Hebrew U., 1997; DLitt (hon), George Washington U., 2001, Trinity Coll., 1998. Writer radio programs for various comedians, NYC, 1935; asst. writer weekly radio scripts comedian Fred Allen, 1936-41. Presdl. cons. to U.S. Treasury, 1941; vis. prof. English Yeshiva U., 1952-57; scholar-in-residence Aspen Inst. Humanistic Studies, 1973-74 Author: (novels) Aurora Dawn, 1947, The City Boy, 1948, Slattery's Hurricane, 1949, The Caine Mutiny, 1951 (Pulitzer Prize award for fiction, 1952), Marjorie Morningstar, 1955, Youngblood Hawke, 1962, Don't Stop the Carnival, 1965, The Winds of War, 1971, War and Remembrance, 1978, Inside, Outside, 1985 (Washingtonian Book award, 1986), The Hope, 1993, The Glory, 1994, A Hole in Texas, 2004, (dramas) The Traitor, 1949, The Caine Mutiny Court-Martial, 1953, (comedy) Nature's Way, 1957, (non-fiction) This is My God, 1959, The Will to Live On, 2000, (screenplays for TV serials) The Winds of War, 1983, War and Remembrance, 1986. Trustee Coll. of V.I., 1961-69; bd. dirs. Washington Nat. Symphony, 1969-71, Kennedy Ctr. Prodns., 1974-75. Exec. officer U.S.S. Southard USNR, 1942-46, PTO. Recipient Richard H. Fox prize, 1934, Columbia U. medal for Excellence, 1952, Alexander Hamilton medal, 1980, U. Calif.-Berkeley medal, 1984, Golden Plate award Am. Acad. Achievement, 1986, USN Meml. Found. 'Lone Sailor' award, 1987, Yad Vashem KaZetnik award, 1990, Bar Ilan U. Guardian of Zion award, 1998, USCD medal U. Calif.-San Diego, 1998. Mem. Naval Res. Assn., Dramatists Guild, Authors Guild, Internat. Platform Assn. (Ralph Waldo Emerson award 1981), PEN Clubs: Bohemian (San Francisco); Cosmos, Metropolitan (Washington); Century Assn. (N.Y.C.). Jewish. Office: care BSW Literary Agy 303 Crestview Dr Palm Springs CA 92264

WOYS, JAMES E., health and medical products executive; B in Acctg., Ariz. State U., Tempe; MBA, Golden Gate U., San Francisco. Cons. Arthur Andersen, 1980—82, Price Waterhouse, 1982—86; dir. corp. fin. & tax Found. Health Corp., 1986—90, v.p., CFO govt. div., 1990—95, sr. v.p. federal services, 1995—98, COO, sr. v.p. Federal services, 1998—99; COO Federal services Health Net, Inc., Woodland Hills, 1999—2001, pres. Federal services, 2001—05, pres. govt. and specialty services, mem. exec. oper. team, 2005—07, interim CFO, 2006—07, exec. v.p., COO, 2007—. Office: Health Net Inc 21650 Oxnard St Woodland Hills CA 91367 Office Phone: 818-676-6000.*

WOYSKI, MARGARET SKILLMAN, retired geology educator; b. West Chester, Pa., July 26, 1921; d. Willis Rowland and Clara Louise (Howson) Skillman; m. Mark M. Woyski, June 19, 1948; children: Nancy Elizabeth, William Bruno, Ronald David, Wendelin Jane. BA in Chemistry, Wellesley Coll., Mass., 1943; MS in Geology, U. Minn., Mpls., 1945, PhD in Geology, 1946. Geologist Mo. Geol. Survey and Water Resources, Rolla, 1946-48; instr. U. Wis., Madison, 1948-52; lectr. Calif. State U., Long Beach, 1963-67, lectr. to prof. Fullerton, 1966-91, assoc. dean Sch. Natural Sci. and Math., 1981-91, emeritus prof., 1991—. Contbr. articles to profl. jours.; author lab. manuals; editor guidebooks. Fellow Geol. Soc. Am. (program chmn. 1982); mem. South Coast Geol. Soc. (hon. pres. 1974), Mineral Soc. Am. Home: 2525 Brea Blvd # 119 Fullerton CA 92835-2787

WOZNEY, JOHN M., research scientist; b. Lynn, Mass., July 3, 1954; s. Gilbert P. and Norma-Jeanne Thomas Wozney. AB, Harvard U., Cambridge, Mass., 1975, PhD, 1981. Postdoc. fellow MIT, 1981—83; staff scientist Genetics Inst., 1983—85, sr. scientist, 1985—91, dir., bone & connective tissue rsch., 1991—93, sr. dir., bone biology & applications, Wyeth Rsch. Andover, Mass., 1993—2000; asst. v.p., musculoskeletal therapeutics Wyeth Rsch., Cambridge, 2001—. Contbr. articles to profl. sci. jours. Named one of Top 20 Rsch. Scientists, R&D Directions, 2007. Mem.: Am. Soc. Bone & Mineral Rsch., Orthop. Rsch. Soc. Achievements include discovery of molecular cloning of the Bone Morphogenetic Protein (BMP) family. One of these is the bone-inductive protein BMP-2, which is the active ingredient in the INFUSE product. Avocations: travel, gardening. Office: Wyeth Rsch 87 Cambridge Park Dr Cambridge MA 02140 Office Fax: 617-665-5250. Business E-Mail: jwozney@wyeth.com.

WOZNIAK, A. RACHEL, educator; d. Flotkoetter L. Jerome and Linda Meeker Flotkoetter, Dianne Thomas Flotkoetter (Stepmother); m. Scott E. Wozniak, May 29, 2004; children: Abigail Madelyn, Lily Katherine. MA, Regent U., Virginia Beach, Va., 2005. Cert. Blackboard, Va., 2004, in online instrnl. design Va., 2005. Adj. instr. Regent U., 2005—07; faculty Tidewater Bible Coll., Virginia Beach, 2005—06. Group leader Atlanta City Ch., Peachtree City, Ga., 2008—08.

WOZNIAK, JANET, psychiatrist; b. Edison, NJ, July 15, 1961; married. AB, Harvard U., Cambridge, Mass., 1983; MD, Cornell Med. Coll., NYC, 1987. Cert. gen. adult psychiatist Am. Bd. Psychiatry and Neurology, 1992, in child and adolecent psychiatry 1994. Author: (book) Is Your Child Bipolar?. Office: Mass Gen Hosp Yawkey 6900 Boston MA 02114 Home Fax: 617 503-1038.

WOZNIAK, ROBERT ANDREW, architectural technology professor; s. Robert Andrew Wozniak and Edythe Edna Wozniak-DeMarco; m. Mary Elizabeth Parks, Aug. 27, 1988; children: Robert (Bobby) Andrew III, Stephen Barnes, Joseph Michael. BPS, SUNY, Buffalo, 1984; postgrad., Ind. State U., Terre Haute, 1991—95; profl. devel. courses, Rio Salado CC, Phoenix, Mesa CC, Ariz., Vincennes U., Ind., 1986—99. TJ/MacMillan cert. Weyerhaeuser, 1999, AutoCAD Level 1 cert. AutoDesk, 2000; cert. permanent tchr. Ariz. CC Bd., 1988. Designer, drafter Father & Son/Bainbridge Constrn., Buffalo, 1984; contractor, draftsman and modelbuilder Profl. Solar, Inc., North Tonawanda, NY, 1984; project coord. Schneider Design Assoc., Archs., Engrs. & Planners, P.C., Buffalo, 1985; asst. project mgr. Wallace & Watson, Archs. & Planners, P.C., Tempe, Ariz., 1985—86; scale modelbuilder Environ. Archtl. Modelbuilders, Tempe, 1986—87; instr. Phoenix Inst. Tech., 1987—88; part-time instr. Mesa CC, Ariz., 1988—90; engrng. technician Symons Corp., Phoenix, 1990; asst. prof. Vincennes U., Ind., 1990—95, assoc. prof., 1995—97, archtl. program coord., 1997—2000; archtl. designer, project mgr. Harrington Sandberg Architecture & Engrng., P.C., Jamestown, NY, 2000—05; assoc. prof. Pa. Coll. Tech., Williamsport, 2005—. Pvt. practice Wozniak Svcs., Buffalo, Phoenix, Vincennes, Williamsport, 1984—. Designer numerous mcpl. and pvt. projects. Percussionist various Christian venues including Continental Singers, 1982—. Mem.: AutoDesk User's Group Internat. Achievements include designed, crafted and patented sculptural block sets. Avocations: travel, family and church-based mission projects. Office: Pa Coll Tech One College Ave Williamsport PA 17701 Business E-Mail: rwozniak@pct.edu.

WOZNIAK, STEVE (STEPHEN GARY WOZNIAK), computer scientist, philanthropist; b. San Jose, Calif., Aug. 11, 1950; s. Jerry; m. Alice Robertson, 1980 (div.); m. Candice Clark, 1987 (div.); 3 children; m. Suzanne Mulkern, 1990. BS in computer sci. and elec. engrng., U. Calif., Berkeley, 1987; DSc (hon.), NC State U., 2004. Designer calculator chips Hewlett-Packard Co., 1976; co-founder Apple Computer, Inc., 1976, v.p. R&D, 1976—81, designer, 1979—81, re-joined as principal, v.p. engrng., 1983—85, cons., 1985—; co-founder CL9 - Remote Control Co., pres., 1985—89; founder US Festivals, San Bernardino, Calif., 1983; co-chmn. Axlon, Inc., Sunnyvale, Calif., 1986—; co-founder Wheels of Zeus (wOz), Los Gatos, Calif., 2002, chmn., CEO, 2002—04, chief tech. officer, pres., 2004—06; co-founder, exec. v.p., chief tech. officer Jazz Technologies, Inc. (formerly Acquicor Tech. Inc.), Irvine, Calif., 2006—09; chief scientist Fusion-io, Salt Lake City, 2009—. Bd. dirs. Jacent, Danger, Inc., Acquicor Tech. Inc., 2005—, en2go International Inc., 2008—; Dem. convention del. (Hart), 1984; former tchr. Co-author (with Gina Smith): iWoz: Computer Geek to Cult Icon: how I invented the personal computer, co-founded Apple, and had fun doing it, 2006; performer: Dancing with the Stars, 2009. Founder Elec. Frontier Found.; founding sponsor Tech Museum, Silicon Valley Ballet, Children's Discovery Museum, San Jose, Calif. Recipient Grace Murray Hopper award, Assn. Computing Machinery, 1979, Nat. Medal Tech., presented by Pres. Ronald Reagan, 1985, Fellow award, Computer History Mus., 1997, Heinz Award for Tech., 2000, numerous awards from tech. and cmty. groups; named to Nat. Inventor's Hall of Fame, 2000, Consumer Electronics Hall of Fame, 2004. Mem.: Fremason, Charity Lodge (life). Achievements include invention of the first line of Apple products - the Apple I and II computers; influenced the popular Macintosh computer; supports the Los Gatos School Dist., providing students and teachers with hands-on teaching and donations of state-of-the-art tech. equip; sponsored computers for schs. in USSR through US/USSR Iniative, 1990; youngest Fortune 500 man in 1982 at age 27; involved in charitable activities in field of education. Office: Fusion-io 6350 S 3000 E 6th Fl Salt Lake City UT 84121 Office Phone: 408-358-6030.*

WRAGE, WILLIAM, retired language educator; b. Lincoln, Ill., Jan. 10, 1936; s. Henry William and Emelia Wrage; m. Marie-Claire Connes, Aug. 26, 1959; children: David William, Eric Andrew. BA, Wash. U., St. Louis, 1957; PhD, U. Wis., Madison, 1963. Asst. prof. French Miami U., Oxford, Ohio, 1963—69; assoc. prof. Ohio U., Athens, 1969—72, prof. French, 1972—2006. Recipient Numerous awards, Ohio U.; Numerous Tchg. grants. Avocations: painting, photography, gardening, travel. Home: 6955 Cornell Rd Athens OH 45701

WRANCHER, ELIZABETH ANN, retired music educator, opera singer; b. Indpls., Oct. 19, 1930; d. Charles Edwin and Evelyn Louise (Helck) W. MusB, Ind. U., 1955. Opera singer, Europe, 1955-68; asst. prof. music U. South Fla., Tampa, 1968-74; pvt. practice Winter Park, Fla., 1974—; assoc. prof. music U. Ctrl. Fla., Orlando, 1974—2003; ret., 2003. Cons. Disney World, Orlando, 1987—; summer tchr. Music Theatre Bavaria, Oberandorf, Germany, 2001. Actress in 3 German movies, 1963-67; opera concert singer, 1968-91; recorded music of Thomas Beversdorf. Past bd. dirs., adv. bd. Orlando Opera Co. Recipient Life Achievement award, 1993, T.I.P. award U. Ctrl. Fla., 1996; Fulbright scholar, Germany, 1955; U. Ctrl. Fla. grantee, 1987. Mem.: Fla. State Music Tchrs. Assn., Fla. Vocal Assn., Nat. Assn. Tchrs. Singing (pres. Ctrl. Fla. chpt. 1996—), Nat. Arts and Letters, Nat. Federated Music Clubs (life), Wed. Music Club (1st v.p. 2004—05, pres. 2005—06, bd. dirs. 2007), Phi Kappa Lambda, Mu Phi Epsilon (life). Republican. Baptist. Achievements include concert recordings in Mozartdeum Archives, Salzburg, Austria, Augsburg Germany Archives. Avocations: art, pastels, philosophy, religions. Home: 2630 Amsden Rd Winter Park FL 32792-3513 Home Phone: 407-678-1916. Personal E-mail: ewrancher@yahoo.com.

WRATE, GLENN THOMAS, engineering educator; b. Ishpeming, Mich., June 1, 1962; s. Victor and Marion Wrate; m. Sylvia Anne Paull; children: Rebecca Anne, Stephanie Anne. BSEE, Mich. Technol. U., Houghton, 1984; MSEE, 1986, PhD, 1997, EE. Cert. pe, Calif. Asst. engr., spl. studies & hvdc stations LA Dept. Water & Power, 1986—88, assoc. engr., standards & procedures, 1988—90, asst. group leader,spl. studies & hvdc stations, 1990—92; asst prof. Milw. Sch. Engrng., prof, 2008—, assc prof. Rschr. No. States Power, Mpls., 1993—97. Recipient Falk Engrng. Educator award, Milw. Sch. Engrng., 2001, Karl O. Werwath Engrng. Rsch. award, 2003. Mem.: IEEE (milw. sect. chair 2006—07, Extraordinary Svc. award 2000). Home: 2439 N 73rd St Milwaukee WI 53213-1211 Office: Milwaukee School Engring 1025 N Broadway Milwaukee WI 53202 Personal E-mail: glenn.wrate@sbcglobal.net. Business E-Mail: wrate@msoe.edu.

WRAY, BETTY BEASLEY, allergist, immunologist, pediatrician; b. Ga., 1935; MD, Med Coll. Ga., 1960. Diplomate Am. Bd. Allergy and Immunology, Am. Bd. Clin. Lab. Immunology. Intern Talmadge Meml. Hosp., Augusta, Ga., 1960-61, resident in pediatrics, 1962, 64-65, fellow in pediatric allergy, 1966-68; staff mem. Med. Coll. Ga., Augusta, 1979—, prof. pediat. medicine, interim dean Sch. Medicine, v.p. clin. activities, 2000—02, prof. emeritus, 2002—. Mem.: Am. Coll. Allergy, Asthma and Immunology, Am. Acad. Pediat., Am. Acad. Allergy and Immunology, Am. Pediatric Soc. Office: Med Coll Georgia BG 1009 Augusta GA 30912

WRAY, FRANCIS, biology professor; b. Rockford, Ill. married; children: Aj Kool, Maya Kool. Assoc. prof. Dept. Biology, Cin., 1995—. Office: Raymond Walters Coll 9555 Plainfield Rd Cincinnati OH 45236

WRAY, MATT, healthcare educator; married. PhD, U. Calif., Berkeley, 2000. Scholar, Robert Wood Johnson Found. Health & Soc. Harvard U., Cambridge, 2006—08; asst. prof. Temple U., Phila., 2008—. Mem.: Am. Sociol. Assn. Office: Temple Univ 1115 W Berks St 751 Gladfelter Hall Philadelphia PA 19119 Office Phone: 215-204-1445. Business E-Mail: mwray@temple.edu.

WRAY, THOMAS JEFFERSON, lawyer; b. Nashville, July 17, 1949; s. William Esker and Imogene (Cushman) W.; m. Susan Elizabeth Wells, Aug. 19, 1972; children: William Clark, Caroline Kell. BA, Emory U., 1971; JD, U. Va., 1974. Bar: Tex. 1974, U.S. Dist. Ct. (so., no. and ea. dists.) Tex. 1976, U.S. Ct. Appeals (5th and 11th cirs.) 1976, U.S. Supreme Ct. 1987. Assoc. Fulbright & Jaworski, L.L.P., Houston, 1974-82; ptnr. Fulbright & Jaworski, Houston, 1982—. Editor (assoc.): Tex. Employment Law Handbook, 2005—09; contbr. chapters to books. Mem. ABA, Coll. Labor and Employment Lawyers, Houston Bar Assn., Houston Mgmt. Lawyers Forum (chmn. 1981-82), Briar Club, Phi Beta Kappa. Republican. Episcopalian. Home: 3662 Ella Lee Ln Houston TX 77027-4105 Office: Fulbright & Jaworski 1301 Mckinney St Ste 5100 Houston TX 77010-3095 Office Phone: 713-651-5585. Business E-Mail: tjwray@fulbright.com.

WRBICAN, SUE, art educator; MFA, RISD, Providence, 1996. Streaming media prodn. mgr. Morgan Stanley, Maslow Media, NYC, 2000—05; asst. prof. photography George Mason U., Fairfax, Va., 2005—. Collaborative public art installation, The Frozen Car (Mathy fellowship, 2008), progressive art project, Tire Fire (Mid Atlantic Arts Found., 1999), video, The Dog Poem, Back Roof (NAP Video Festival, Kutztown, PA, 1997), installation, The Impala Diaries, collaborative community project, Dream Houses in Miniature. Pac mem. Md. Art Pl., Baltimore. Chevrolet Collegiate scholarship, Chevrolet, Rsch. grant, GMU. Mem.: Soc. for Photographic Edn. Office: George Mason Univ 4400 Uniiversity Dr Fairfax VA 22030

WREDE, ROBERT CLINTON, JR., mathematician, educator; b. Cin., Oct. 19, 1926; s. Robert Clinton and Ruth Ann (Ramsdell) W.; m. Jeanne Snedden, Jan. 29, 1948; children: Scott, Brian, James Clayton. BS, Miami U., Oxford, Ohio, 1949, MA, 1950; postgrad., U. Cin., 1950-51; PhD, Ind. U., 1956. Instr. Miami U., 1950-51; teaching fellow Ind. U., Bloomington, 1951-55; from instr. to assoc. prof. San Jose (Calif.) State U., 1955-63, prof. math., 1963-89, prof. emeritus, 1989—. Cons. rsch. div. IBM, San Jose, 1957-58, Hunter's Point Radiation Lab., San Francisco, 1959. Author: Intro To Vector & Tensor Analysis, 1963, rev. edit., 1972, Schaum's Outlines Advanced Calculus, 2d edit., 2002, Insights into Calculus, 2008, Algebra, 2008, Geometry, 2008, Outlines Advanced 3rd edit., 2009; manuscript cons. John Wiley & Sons, 1961—. Div. leader Urban Coalition, San Jose, 1969—. Pfc. USMC, 1944-45. Mem. AAUP, Math. Assn. Am., Am. Math. Soc., Tensor Soc. (Japan). Home: 132 Wingfoot Ct Aptos CA 95003-5428 Office: Math & Computer Sci Dept San Jose State U 1 Washington Sq San Jose CA 95112-3613 Personal E-mail: robertrio@aol.com.

WREN, CASEY LEIGH, broadcast technician, department chairman; b. Grand Junction, Colo., Sept. 23, 1974; s. Charlotte Marie Wren; m. Tonya NP Parkerson, June 3, 2000. BS in Radio & TV Broadcasting, Bob Jones U., Greenville, SC, 1998, MS in Radio & TV Broadcasting, 2000. Broadcast engr. Bloomberg L.P., NYC, 2000—03; ops. mgr. KKCO-TV, Grand Junction, 2003—06, mng. cons., 2007; radio & tv dept. chair Bob Jones U., 2006—. Mem.: Broadcast Educators Assn., Nat. Religious Broadcasters.

WREN, FRANK, professional baseball team executive; b. Hamilton, Ohio; m. Teri Wren; children: Kyle, Colby, Jordan. Outfielder Montreal (Can.) Expos minor league sys., 1976-81, coach, 1981-84; gen. mgr. Montreal Expos Class A affiliate, Jamestown, N.Y., 1985-86; asst. dir. scouting Montreal Expos, 1986-91, dir. L.Am. scouting and ops., 1989-91; asst. gen. mgr. Fla. Marlins, 1991-97; gen. mgr. Balt. Orioles, 1998-99; asst. gen. mgr. Atlanta Braves, 1999—2007, exec. v.p., gen. mgr., 2007—. Office: Atlanta Braves PO Box 4064 Atlanta GA 30302

WREN, GAYDEN, playwright, theater director; b. NYC, May 24, 1961; s. Gayden and Mary Alice Wren; m. Sara Holliday, July 7, 2001. BA, Oberlin Coll., 1983. Entertainment editor NY Times Syndicate, NYC, 1995—. Author: (book) A Most Ingenious Paradox: The Art of Gilbert & Sullivan, 2002, (theater) As If, 1985, Baseball, Sex and Other Facts of Life, 1995, Ernest, 1984, An Evening with Gilbert & Sullivan, 1994, A Gilbert & Sullivan Christmas Carol, 1995, ID, 1986, Moonlight and Midnight, 1983, A Night on the Tomb, 1983, Swords & Frenchmen, 1982, Tales from the Bible, 1983, Two for the Show, 1982, Very Truly Yours, Gilbert & Sullivan, 1996, The World According to Gilbert & Sullivan, 1990; dir.: (Operas) The Sorcerer, 1983—84, HMS Pinafore, 1996, The Pirates of Penzance, 1981, Patience, 1981, 1988, 1999, 2000, Iolanthe, 1982, 1986, 1993, 2005, Princess Ida, The Mikado, 2004, Ruddigore, 1981, 1984, 2002, The Gondoliers, 1982, 2006, Utopia, Limited, 2002. Dir. The Gilbert & Sullivan Light Opera Co. of LI, Merrick, NY, 1984—; artistic dir. The New Punctuation Army Inc., NYC, 1984—; chmn. Citizens for Classic Movies, NYC, 1992—; artistic dir. Troupers Light Opera, New Canaan, Conn., 2002—03. Home: 19-92 78th St East Elmhurst NY 11370 Office: New York Times Syndicate 500 Seventh Ave 8th Fl New York NY 10018 Business E-Mail: wreng@nytimes.com.

WREN, JOHN D., advertising executive; b. July 22, 1952; m. Diane Wren; 2 children. BA, MBA, Adelphi U., 1975. Mgmt. cons. Arthur Anderson & Co., 1975—81; with Norton Simon Inc., 1981—84, Needham Harper Worldwide, 1984—86; CFO Diversified Agency Services (subs. Omnicom Group, Inc.), 1986—90, pres., 1990—93, chmn., CEO, 1993—95; pres. Omnicom Group, Inc., NYC, 1995—97, pres., CEO, 1997—. Bd. dirs. Omnicom Group, Inc., 1993—. Named Agy. Exec. of the Yr., Advertising Age, 2006. Republican. Office: Omnicom Group Inc 437 Madison Ave Fl 9 New York NY 10022-7001*

WREN, STEPHEN COREY, mathematician, inventor; b. St. Louis, Sept. 4, 1956; s. Donald W and Jo V (Mask) Wren; 1 child, Corey. BA in Math./Computer Sci., Washington U., St. Louis, 1979. Actuary William Mercer, St. Louis, 1980-83; pres. CIM, St. Louis, 1983—2000; managing mem Variant USA, St Louis, 2000—. Instr St Louis Univ, 1986—87, Webster Univ, 1985—86. Achievements include invention of computerized marketing networks.

WRENN, CHRISTOPHER JAY, physician; b. Margarita, Panama Canal Zone, July 16, 1947; s. Earl Walton and Maxine Elizabeth (Luther) Wrenn; m. Nancy Margaret Bowie, June 27, 1970; children: Kristina Elizabeth, Courtney Bowie. BS, Baylor U., 1969; MD, U. Nebr., 1973. Diplomate Am. Bd. Pediatrics, Am. Bd. Allergy and Immunology. Intern pediatrics Children's Med. Ctr., Dallas, 1973-74, resident pediatrics, 1974-76, chief resident pediatrics, 1976-77; staff pediatrician Los Barrios Unidos Community Clinic, Dallas, 1977-78; fellow allergy and immunology Med. Br. U. Tex., Galveston, Tex., 1978-80; practice medicine specializing in allergy Graves-Gilbert Clinic, Bowling Green, Ky., 1980-83, Wichita Clinic, 1983-84, Allergy Clinic, Tyler, Tex., 1984—. Staff pediatrician Dallas County Juvenile Detention Ctr., 1975—78, Buckner Bapt. Children's Home, 1977—78. Co-author: Pediatrics by Self Instruction, 1982. Fellow: Am. Coll. Allergists, Am. Acad. Pediat.; mem.: Am. Acad. Allergy and Immunology. Presbyterian. Avocation: writing fiction and poetry. Office: Allergy Clinic PA 1128 Medical Dr Tyler TX 75701

WRIGHT, ALAN, lawyer; b. Ft. Worth, May 17, 1956; BA with high honors, U. Tex., 1978, MPA, 1982, JD with honors, 1982. Bar: N.Mex. 1982, Tex. 1985, admitted to practice: US Ct. Appeals (10th Cir.) 1982, US Dist. Ct. (Dist. N.Mex.) 1983, US Dist. Ct. (No. Dist.) Tex. 1984, US Ct. Appeals (5th Cir.) 1984, US Dist. Ct. (We. Dist.) Tex. 1986, US Supreme Ct. 1987, US Dist. Ct. (So. Dist.) Tex. 1992, US Dist. Ct. (Ea. Dist.) Tex. 1992, US Ct. Appeals (3rd Cir.) 1992, US Ct. Appeals (11rd Cir.) 1992, US Ct. Appeals (6th Cir.) 1993, US Ct. Appeals (8th Cir.) 1995, US Ct. Appeals (Fed. Cir.) 2005. Ptnr., appellate law Haynes and Boone LLP, Dallas. Mem.: Dallas Bar Found., Dallas Bar Assn., ABA, State Bar N. Mex., Phi Beta Kappa. Office: Haynes and Boone LLP 2323 Victory Ave Dallas TX 75219-7657 Office Phone: 214-651-5575. Office Fax: 214-200-0614. Business E-Mail: alan.wright@haynesboone.com.

WRIGHT, ANDREW, English literature educator; b. Columbus, Ohio, June 28, 1923; s. Francis Joseph and Katharine (Timberman) W.; m. Virginia Rosemary Banks, June 27, 1952; children: Matthew Leslie Francis, Emma Stanbery. AB, Harvard U., 1947; MA, Ohio State U., 1948, PhD, 1951. Prof. English lit. U. Calif., San Diego, 1963—, chmn. dept. lit., 1971-74; dir. U. Calif. Study Center, U.K. and Ireland, 1980-82. Vis. prof. U. Queensland, Australia, 1984, Colegio de la Frontera Norte, San Antonio del Mar, Baja, Calif., 1991-92. Author: Jane Austen's Novels: A Study In Structure, 1953, Joyce Cary: A Preface to His Novels, 1958, Henry Fielding: Mask and Feast, 1965, Blake's Job: A Commentary, 1972, Anthony Trollope: Dream and Art, 1983; Fictional Discourse and Historical Space, 1987; contbg. author numerous books, articles to profl. jours., numerous short stories to lit. mags.; editorial bd. Nineteenth Century Fiction, 1964-86. Bd. dirs. Calif. Coun. Humanities, 1983-87. Guggenheim fellow, 1960, 70; Fulbright Sr. Research fellow, 1960-61 Fellow Royal Soc. Lit.; mem. MLA, Jane Austen Soc., Athenaeum (London), Trollope Soc., Santayana Soc., Phi Beta Kappa. Home: 7227 Olivetas Ave La Jolla CA 92037-5335 Office: U Calif San Diego Dept Lit La Jolla CA 92093-0410 Business E-Mail: ahwright@ucsd.edu.

WRIGHT, BAGLEY, venture capitalist, entrepreneur, art collector; m. Virginia Bloedel; children: Merrill, Charles, Robin, Bing. BA, Princeton U., 1946. With Daily Mirror, Newsweek; real estate developer Pentagram Corp., Harbor Properties; chmn Physio Control Corp., 1968—80. Developer Space Needle, Seattle. Named one of Top 200 Collectors, ARTnews Mag., 2004, 2006. Avocation: Collector of Contemporary Art; Japanese Art. Office: 407 Dexter Ave Seattle WA 98109

WRIGHT, BETTY REN, children's book writer; b. Wakefield, Mich., June 15, 1927; d. William and Revena Evelyn (Trezise) W.; m. George Albert Frederiksen, Oct. 9, 1976. BA, Milw.-Downer Coll., 1949. With Western Pub. Co., Inc., 1949-78, mng. editor Racine Editl., 1967-78. Author: The Doll House Murders, 1983, Christina's Ghost, 1985, The Summer of Mrs. MacGregor, 1986, A Ghost in the Window, 1987, The Pike River Phantom, 1988, Rosie and the Dance of the Dinosaurs, 1989, The Ghost of Ernie P., 1990, A Ghost in the House, 1991, The Scariest Night, 1991, The Ghosts of Mercy Manor, The Ghost of Popcorn Hill, 1993, The Ghost Witch, 1993, A Ghost Comes Calling, 1994, Out of the Dark, 1995, Haunted Summer, 1996, Too Many Secrets, 1997, The Ghost in Room 11, 1998, A Ghost in the Family, 1998, Pet Detectives, 1999, The Moonlight Man, 2000, The Wish Master, 2000, Crandalls' Castle, 2003, The Blizzard, 2003, Princess for a Week, 2006; contbr. articles to mags. Recipient Alumni Svc. award Lawrence U., 1973, Lynde and Harry Bradley Maj. Achievement award, 1997, numerous awards for books including Mo. Mark Twain award, 1986, 96, Tex. Bluebonnet award, 1986, 88, Young Readers award Pacific N.W. Libr. Assn., 1986, Reviewer's Choice Booklist, Ala. Young Readers award, 1987, Ga. Children's Choice award, 1988, Ind. Young Hoosier Book award, 1989, 96, Children's Choice Book/Internat. Reading Assn.—CBC, 1984, S.C. Children's Choice award, 1995, Okla. Sequoyah Children's Choice award, 1988, 95, award Fla. Sunshine State, 2001, Notable Wis. Author for Youth Lit. award, 2006. Mem.: Coun. Wis. Authors (Juvenile Book award 1985, 1996), Allied Authors, Phi Beta Kappa. Avocations: reading, travel. Home and Office: 6223 Hilltop Dr Racine WI 53406-3479

WRIGHT, BLANDIN JAMES, lawyer; b. Detroit, Nov. 29, 1947; s. Robert Thomas and Jane Ellen (Blandin) Wright; m. Kay Heideman, 1969 (div. 2000); children: Steven Blandin, Martha Kay; m. Gina Almonte, 2002; children: Oliver Stefan, Elliot Sebastian. BA, U. Mich., 1969; JD, Dickinson Law Sch., Pa. State U., 1972; LLM in Taxation, NYU, 1973; MS in Taxation with honors, Am. U., 1992. Bar: Pa. 1973, Fla. 1976, U.S. Tax Ct. 1977, DC 1978, U.S. Supreme Ct. 1977, Va. 1984, NY 1991; CPA, Tex., 1978, Va., 1983. Atty. Office Internat. Ops. Nat. Office IRS, Washington, 1973-76; tax dir. Intairdril Ltd., London, 1976-78; tax atty. Allied Chem. Corp., Houston, 1978-79; v.p., gen. counsel Assoc. Oiltools, Inc., London, 1979-82; v.p. taxes, gen. counsel J. Lauritzen, Inc., Charlottesville, Va., 1982-85; sole practice Charlottesville, Va., 1985-88; ptnr. Richmond & Fishburne, Charlottesville, Va., 1988—89, of counsel, 1990-91; tax counsel Mobil Oil Corp., NYC, 1990, Fairfax, Va., 1990-95; vice chmn., gen. counsel Cruise Holdings, Ltd., Miami, 1996—98; pres. Maritime Capital Group, Inc., Miami, 1998—2004; chmn. Internat. Hospitality, Inc., 1999—2004; tax counsel Internat. Tax Advisors, 2004—; tax chair Becker & Poliakoff, 2005—06; ptnr. Rothstein Rosenfeldt Adler, Fort Lauderdale, Fla., 2006—. Officer Pamaco Partnership Mgmt. Corp., Va., 1986-91, CRW Energy Corp., 1986-90, Transp. & Tourism Internat., Inc., 1986—, Hotsprings Assocs., Inc., 1989-91, MDM Hotels, Inc., 1992-95, Internat. Shipping & Resorts, Inc., 1992—, United Holdings Ltd., 1993-96, Cruise and Resorts Internat., Inc., 1994—; bd. dirs. Blandin J. Wright, P.C., Internat. Hospitality, Inc., CRS Holdings, Inc, Maritime Capital Group, Silversea Cruises, Ltd., Jewel River Cruises, Ocean Star Cruises. Contbr. articles to profl. jours. Coach Charlottesville Youth Soccer, Baseball and Basketball, 1984-89; coach London Youth Baseball, 1982. Recipient Who's Who in the World, Who's Who in America, Who's Who in American Law, Who's Who in Finance and Industry. Mem. ABA, AICPA, Am. Arbitration Assn. (arbitrator 1985-90), Tex. Soc. CPAs, Va. Soc. CPAs, Fairfax County Bar Assn., Broward County Bar Assn., Farmington Country Club, Deering Bay Yacht and Country Club, Saucon Valley Country Club, Gerrards Cross Golf Club, Gerrards Cross Lawn Tennis Club, Mensa, Beta Gamma Sigma. Roman Catholic. Office: Rothstein Rosenfeldt Adler Ste 1650 401 E Las Olas Blvd Fort Lauderdale FL 33301 Office Phone: 954-315-7249, 954-522-3456. Office Fax: 954-527-8663. Business E-Mail: bwright@rra-law.com. E-mail: blandin@earthlink.net.

WRIGHT, BONNIE H., middle school educator; b. Raleigh, NC, Sept. 30, 1960; d. William T. and Secunda P. Huxster; m. Tony T. Wright, Aug. 8, 1989 (dec.); 1 child, Josh Gordon. BA in Early Childhood Edn., U. NC, Charlotte, 1982, BA in Intermediate Edn., 1984, BA in Intermediate Edn., 2002; MA in Math., Nova Southeastern U., 2008. Cert. mentor N.C., 1989. Mid. sch. math tchr. Scotland County Schs., Laurinburg, NC, 1984—88; 5th grade tchr. Charlotte-Mecklenburg Schs., NC, 1988—89, 6th grade tchr., 1989—90, elem. and mid. sch. math tchr., 1992—2000; mid. sch. math tchr. Wake County Pub. Schs., Raleigh, NC, 1991—92; 7th and 8th grade sci. tchr. Charlotte Christian Sch., NC, 2000—07; 7th and 8th grade tchr. Providence Day Sch., NC, 2007—. Migrant edn. instr. Scotland County Schs., Laurinburg, NC, 1984—85; math tutor Charlotte Christian Sch., 2000—07. Vol. Operation Christmas Child Charlotte Christian Schs., 2000—07; Sunday sch. tchr. U. City United Meth. Ch., Charlotte, 1994—98; Bible svc. project Charlotte Christian Schs., 2002—07. Recipient Tchr. of Yr. award, Sycamore Ln. Mid. Sch. in Scotland County, 1987, Unsung Am. Heroes award, ING, 2005; named to Nat. Honor Roll Outstanding Tchrs., 2006. Fellow: N.C. Assn. Educators (assoc.), Internat. Reading Assn. (assoc.), Assn. Christian Schs. (assoc.), PTO (assoc.); mem.: Parent Tchr. Fellowship (assoc.), N.C. Coun. Tchrs. Math. (assoc.), N.C. Sci. Tchrs. Assn. (assoc.), Delta Zeta (life). Dc Statehood Party. Methodist. Avocations: travel, coin collector, piano, cross-stitching, scrapbooking. Office: Providence Day Sch 5800 Sardis Rd Charlotte NC 28270 Office Fax: 704-887-7042. Business E-Mail: bonnie.wright@providenceday.org.

WRIGHT, BONNIE SHANKLE, assistant principal, choir director; b. Jan. 16, 1960; d. Preston and Adeline Luttrell Shankle; m. James Barry Wright, June 9, 1984; children: Preston, David. B in Music Edn., Ind. U., 1983; MA in Tchg., Bethel Coll., 1990. Cert. ednl. specialist Union U., 2005. Tchr. Covington Elem., Tenn., 1986—99; chorus, drama tchr. Covington HS, 1999—2003; asst. prin. Covington Integrated Arts Acad., 2003—05. Instr. Red Cross, 1983—2004; pianist, bell choir dir. First United Methodist Ch., Covington, 1997—2005, choir dir., 2003—05. Mem.: Alpha Delta Kappa (pres. 2003). Republican. Methodist. Office: Covington Integrated Arts Acad 760 Bert Johnston Covington TN 38019

WRIGHT, BURTON, sociologist; b. Detroit, Jan. 31, 1917; s. Burton and Hazel Marie (Thomas) Wright; m. Marie Fidelis Gallivan, Jan. 26, 1942; children: Burton III(dec.), Catherine Margaret(dec.). AA, C.Z. Coll., 1944; BA, U. Wash., 1947, MA, 1949; PhD, Fla. State U., 1972. Enlisted USN, 1937, commd. and advanced through grades to comdr., 1957; dir. Naval Res. Recruiting, 1960-64; ret., 1964; mem. faculty U. Wash., 1947-49, George Washington U., Washington, 1954-60, Rollins Coll., Winter Park, Fla., 1966-69; prof. dept. sociology U. Ctrl. Fla., Orlando, 1972-82, prof. emeritus, 1982-89; ret., 1989; prof. sociology Troy State U., 1991—. Cons. Ford Found., 1951, Dept. Air Force, 1955, U.S. Army Chem. Corps, 1956; mem. faculty Northwestern U., summers 1956-59; vis. prof. sociology Troy U., Dothon; dir. Am. Sociol. Assn. Nat. Honors Program, 1981-89. Author: (with J.P. Weiss and C.M. Unkovic) Perspective: An Introduction to Sociology, 1975, (with V. Fox) Criminal Justice and the Social Sciences, 1978, (with J.P. Weiss) Social Problems, 1980; contbr. articles to publs. Decorated Navy Commendation medal. Fellow Am. Anthrop. Assn.; mem. AAUP, Am. Sociol. Assn. (membership com. 1983-86), Soc. Psychol. Study Social Problems, Am. Acad. Arts and Scis., Soc. Study Social Problems, So. Sociol. Soc., North Ctrl. Sociol. Soc., Univ. Club (Winter Park). Roman Catholic. Home: 502 Dunleith Blvd Dothan AL 36303-2936 Personal E-mail: bw7626@ala.net.

WRIGHT, BYRON T., physicist, researcher; b. Waco, Tex., Oct. 19, 1917; s. Wilbur and Dora (Thompson) W.; m. Lorna Doone Bloemers, Oct. 21, 1944 (dec. 1964); children— Carol Ann, Susan Lee, Gail Elizabeth. BA, Rice U., 1938; PhD, U. Calif., Berkeley, 1941. Physicist Naval Electronics Lab., 1941-42, Manhattan Project, 1942-46; mem. faculty UCLA, 1946—, prof. physics, 1956—, asso. dean grad. div., 1972-80. Ford Found. vis. scientist CERN, 1963-64 Fulbright research scholar, 1956-57; Guggenheim fellow, 1963-64 Fellow Am. Phys. Soc. Spl. research accelerator devel., nuclear structure physics. Home: 1225 Chickory Ln Los Angeles CA 90049-1403

WRIGHT, C. T. ENUS, former academic administrator; b. Social Circle, Ga., Oct. 4, 1942; s. George and Carrie Mae (Enus) W.; m. Mary Stephens, Aug. 9, 1974. BS, Fort Valley State U., Ga., 1964; MA, Atlanta U., 1967; PhD, Boston U., 1977; LHD, Mary Holmes Coll., 2000. Tchr. Ga. Pub. Schs., Social Circle, 1965-67; mem. faculty Morris Brown Coll., Atlanta, 1967-73, divsn. chmn., 1973-77; program dir., asst. provost Eastern Wash. U., Cheney, 1977-81; v.p. acad. affairs Talladega Coll. (Ala.), 1981-82; pres. Cheyney U. Pa., Cheyney, 1982-85; v.p. and provost Fla. Meml. Coll., 1985-89; pres. Internat. Found. and Coord. African-African Am. Summit, 1989-2001; chmn., founder The Light of Hope Inst., 2000—; pres., CEO IFESH, 2001—04; pres. AZ Africa, 2004—. Cons. and lectr. in field; bd. dirs. Internat. Found. Edn. and Self Help, England, Leon Sullivan Trust, South Africa, People's Investment Fund for Africa, Fountain Hills Kiwanis Club, 2006—; chmn. adv. com. AMI Consultants, 2002—. Author: (booklet) The History of Black Historical Mythology, 1980; contbr. articles to profl. jours. Commr. Wash. Pub. Broadcasting, Olympia, 1980—84; exec. com. Boy Scouts Am., Phila., 1982—; Goodwill Amb. State of Ga., 1997—; chmn. com. World Children Relief, 2002—; bd. mem. Fountain Hills Sch., 2007—. Human Rels. scholar, 1969, Nat. Tchg. fellow, Boston U., 1971. Mem. NEA (coms. 1965—), Am. Assn. Colls. and Univs. (coms. 1982—), Am. Hist. Assn. (coms. 1970—), Assn. Study Afro-Am. Life and History (coms. 1965—), Nat. Assn. Equal Opportunity in Higher Edn. (coms. 1982—), Kiwanis Club Fountain Hills (bd. dirs. 2006—), Lions Club, Tuscan Club. Baptist. Address: 17420 E Dull Knife Dr Fountain Hills AZ 85268 Office Phone: 480-837-5534. E-mail: ctwright31@cox.net.

WRIGHT, CAROLYN D., poet, literature and language professor; b. Mountain Home, Ark., 1949; d. Ernie E. Wright and Alyce E. Collins; m. Forrest Gander, 1983; 1 child, Brecht. BA in French, Memphis State U., 1971; MFA, U. Ark., Fayetteville, 1976. Lectr. poetry San Francisco State U., 1979—81; prof. English Brown U., Providence, 1983—, Israel J. Kapstein prof. English. Co-editor Lost Roads Pubs., 1978—2005; vis. faculty Burren Sch. Art., Ireland, 1996, U. Iowa., 1997, U. Cin., 2004. Author: (poetry) Terrorism, 1979, Translations of the Gospel Back into Tongues, 1981, Further Adventures With You, 1986, String Light, 1991 (Poetry Ctr. Book award), Just Whistle, 1993, Tremble, 1996, Deepstep Come Shining, 1998, Steal Away: Selected and New Poems, 2002, One Big Self: Prisoners of Louisiana, 2003, Cooling Time: An American Poetry Vigil, 2005, Rising, Falling, Hovering, 2008 (Internat. Griffin Poetry prize, 2009), (lit. maps) The Lost Roads Project: A Walk-in Book of Arkansas, 1994, The Reader's Map of Arkansas, 1994. Recipient Witter Bynner prize for poetry, AAAL, 1986, Whiting Writers award, 1989, Gov.'s award for arts, RI, 1990, Disting. Alumni award, U. Ark.,

1998, Lannan Lit. award, 1999; named Poet Laureate of RI, 1994—99; fellow, Nat. Endowment Arts, 1981, 1988, John Simon Guggenheim Meml. Found., 1987, Lila Wallace-Reader's Digest Found., 1992, John D. & Catherine T. MacArthur Found., 2004. Fellow: Am. Acad. Arts & Scis. Office: Brown U 68 1/2 Brown St Rm 201 Providence RI 02912 Office Phone: 401-863-9405. Business E-Mail: Carolyn_Wright@Brown.edu.*

WRIGHT, CATHY L., museum director; Studied, U. Colo. Boulder; M, U. Denver. Hist. tchr. U. Colo., Colo. Springs; tchr. southwest studies Colo. Coll.; dir., chief cur. Taylor Mus., Colo. Springs Fine Arts Ctr.; dir. Albuquerque Mus. Art and Hist., 2006—. Juror N.Mex State U. Art Gallery Student Exhbn., 2007, Colo. State Fair Fine Arts Exhbn., Pueblo, 2007. Office: Albuquerque Mus Art & Hist 2000 Mountain Rd NW Albuquerque NM 87104 Business E-Mail: clwright@cabq.gov.

WRIGHT, CECILIA POWERS, gifted and talented educator; b. Phila., Sept. 30, 1946; d. Robert Francis and Rosemary (Redditt) Powers. BS, West Chester U., Pa., 1968; MS, Pa. State U., 1972; MA, Gratz Coll., Melrose Park, Pa., 1996; EdD, Immaculate U., 2006. Tchr. Haverford Twp. Sch. Dist., Havertown, Pa., 1968—73; author/editor and instr. McGraw Hill, Paoli, Pa., 1973—78; tchr. Lower Merion Sch. Dist., Wynnewood, Pa., 1987—90; gifted tchr. West Chester Area Sch. Dist., 1990—, tchr., 1999—2007; instr. Neumann Coll., Aston, Pa., 2006—. Assoc. prof., cons. Regional Tng. Ctr., Gratz Coll., Randolph, NJ, 1996—; seminar presenter Coll. NJ, Trenton, 1998—2000; adj. prof. Neumann Coll., 2006—. Author (and editor): Careers: A Multicultural View, 1977 (Excellence award, 1977). Leader Girl Scouts U.S., Havertown, 1983—87; chairperson good citizens DAR, Chester County, Pa., 1996—. Recipient award, Nat. Band Assn., 2000—01; named to Leaders in Am. Elem. Edn., Haverford Twp. Sch. Dist., 1971. Mem.: NEA, Band and Orch. Assn. (pres. 2000), Pa. State Edn. Assn. (rep. 1998—). Avocations: painting, travel, bicycling. Home: 15 E Wilmot Ave Havertown PA 19083 Business E-Mail: cwright@wcasd.net.

WRIGHT, CHARLES PENZEL, JR., writer, educator; b. Pickwick Dam, Tenn., Aug. 25, 1935; s. Charles Penzel and Mary Castleman (Winter) Wright; m. Holly McIntire, Apr. 6, 1969; 1 child, Luke Savin Herrick. BA, Davidson Coll., 1957; MFA, U. Iowa, 1963; postgrad., U. Rome, 1963—64. Mem. faculty U. Calif., Irvine, Calif., 1966—83, prof. English, 1976—83; Souder Family Prof. Poetry U. Va., Charlottesville, 1983—. Vis. prof. N.Am. Lit. U., Padua, Italy, 1968—69; disting. vis. prof. U. Degli Studi, Florence, Italy, 1992. Translator: The Storm and Other Poems (Eugenio Montale), 1978 (PEN Translation prize, 1979), Orphic Songs (Dino Campana), 1984; author: (books) The Grave of the Right Hand, 1970, Hard Freight, 1973, Bloodlines, 1975, China Trace, 1977, The Southern Cross, 1981, Country Music - Selected Early Poems, 1982, The Other Side of the River, 1984, Halflife, 1988, Zone Journals, 1988, Xionia, 1990, The World of the Ten Thousand Things, 1990, Quarter Notes, 1995, Chickamauga, 1995 (Lenore Marshall Poetry prize Acad. Am. Poets, 1996), Black Zodiac, 1997 (Pulitzer prize poetry, 1998), Appalachia, 1998, North American Bear, 1999, Negative Blue, 2000, A Short History of the Shadow, 2002, Buffalo Yoga, 2004, Scar Tissue, 2006 (Griffin Poetry prize (internat.), 2007), Littlefoot, 2007, Sestets, 2009. With AUS, 1957—61. Recipient Nat Book award for Poetry, 1983, citation in poetry, Brandeis U. Creative Arts Awards, 1987, L.A. Times Book prize, 1997, award, Nat. Book Critics Circle, 1997, Amb. Book award, 1998, Preano AnTicho Fattore, Italy, 1999, Poetry prize, Griffen Internat., Can., 2007, Bobbitt Nat. Poetry prize, Libr. Congress, 2008, Premio Internat. Mario Luzi, Italy, 2008; fellow Guggeheim fellow, 1976, Ingram Merrill fellow, 1980, 1993; scholar, Fulbright Found., 1963—65. Mem.: Acad. Am. Poets (chancellor), Am. Acad. Arts and Sci., Am. Acad. Arts and Letters, Fellowship of So. Writers. Home: 940 Locust Ave Charlottesville VA 22901-4030 Office: English Dept Univ Va Charlottesville VA 22901

WRIGHT, CHRIS, professional sports team executive; b. Eng. arrived in US, 1978; m. Walla Wright; children: Christy, Jeff, Ned. Grad., Carnegie Coll. Phys. Edn., Headingly Leeds, Yorkshire, Eng. Gen. mgr. Maj. Indoor Soccer League Pitts. Spirit, 1981—86, Maj. Indoor Soccer League Minn. Strikers, 1986—87; cons. State of Minn.; pres. Minn. Timberwolves, 2005—. Office: Minn Timberwolves 600 First Ave N Minneapolis MN 55403*

WRIGHT, CLARK PHILLIPS, computer systems specialist; b. Orange, Tex., Aug. 30, 1942; s. Madison Brown and Mary Elizabeth (Phillips) W.; m. Stacy Charlotte Klutz, June 5, 1965 (div. Oct. 1979); m. Cora Lou Alexandria Schelling, Oct. 31, 1979; 1 child, Isaac Schelling. BA, U. Tex., 1965. Computer programmer Lockheed Electronics Co., Houston, 1965-67; prin. analyst Control Data Corp., St. Paul, 1967-76; computer scientist DBA Systems, Inc., Lanham, Md., 1976-79; engring. specialist Ford Aerospace Corp., Houston, 1979-90, Loral Aerospace Corp., 1990-97, Lockheed Martin Space Mission, 1997—. Precinct chmn. Rep. Party of Tex., 1982-86. Mem. IEEE, Math. Assn. Am., Assn. Computing Machinery, SAR (chartered, sec., treas.), Sons Republic Tex., Info. Sys. Security Assn., Masons, Rotary. Avocations: travel, photography. Home: 5000 Park Ave Dickinson TX 77539-7013 Office: Lockheed Martin Space Ops PO Box 58487 Houston TX 77258-8487 Home Phone: 281-337-1736; Office Phone: 281-853-3186. Personal E-mail: cpwright2@verizon.net. Business E-Mail: clark.p.wright@lmco.com.

WRIGHT, CLELL E., music educator; MusB, Samford U., Birmingham, 1983; MusM in Choral Conducting, Southwestern Bapt. Theol. Sem., Fort Worth, Texas, 1987; MusD, U. Mo., Kan. City, 2001. Dir. music ministries Bonhomme Presbyn. Ch., St. Louis, 1995—2001; dir. choral activities and logsdon prof. ch. music Hardin-Simmons U., Abilene, Tex., 2001—. Mem.: Tex. Music Educators Assoc., Am. Choral Dirs. Assn., Pi Kappa Lambda, Phi Mu Alpha Sinfonia. Avocations: horseback riding, travel, winemaking. Office: Hardin-Simmons Univ HSU Box 16230 Abilene TX 79698 Business E-Mail: cwright@hsutx.edu.

WRIGHT, DANA JACE, retired emergency nurse practitioner; b. Cleve., Apr. 20, 1952; d. William James and Murl Jean (White) Ewing; m. David Alan Samball, June 22, 1968 (div. Apr. 1971); 1 child, David; m. David M. Wright, July 11, 1981; children: William James, Karen Marie. A in Nursing, Valencia C.C., 1973, AA, 1973; BS in Respiratory Therapy, U. Cen. Fla., 1975; MEd, Auburn U., 1979; D in Nursing, Case Western Res. U., 1982. RN, Fla., Ohio, N.Y., Ga.; cert. emergency med. technician; cert. and registered respiratory therapist; cert. med.-surg. nurse; lic. real estate agt., N.Y. Nursing asst. Holiday Hosp., Orlando, Fla., 1970-71, staff nurse critical care unit, intensive care unit, 1973; pvt. duty nurse Med. Personnel Pool, Orlando, 1973-74; nurse critical care burn team Upjohn, Inc., Augusta, Ga., 1976-77; ednl. dir. dept. respiratory therapy U. Hosp., Augusta, 1975-76; mem. staff respiratory therapy VA Hosp., Augusta, 1976-77; clin. instr. respiratory therapy Med. Coll. Ga., Augusta, 1976-77, Columbus Coll., 1977-78; ednl. dir. respiratory therapy Med. Ctr. Hosp., Columbus, 1977-79; staff nurse, relief supr. Kelly Health Care, Beachwood, Ohio, 1979-81; staff nurse Med. Staff, Inc., Cleve., 1981-83; dir. nursing S.R.T. Med. Staff Inc., Cleve., 1983; pres. Wright Properties, Buffalo, 1987-94, Med. Ctr. Vending, 1994-97; ret. nurse, 1994. Part-time nurse Millard Fillmore Suburban Hosp., 1990-91. Treas. Ch. Women's Assn., Snyder, N.Y., 1985-86, Clerk Ch. Coun., 2008-; mem. nursing resources panel North Ohio Lung Assn., 1981-82; mem. Profl. Parent Network, Buffalo, 1987—, Erie Co. Commn. on the Status of Women, 2000-08, vol. Food Shuttle, 1996-; rep. of McLain found. to grantmakers, 2000-; com. reviewer Internat. Charity Project Grants, 2004-09; bd. dirs. Virginia Guildersleeve Internat. Fund., 2008-09, v.p. Mem. ANA (alt. del. 1993-94), Am. Assn. Nurses Practicing Independently (assoc.), Nat. Nurses Bus., N.Y. State Nurses Assn. (nurse rsch. cons. 1991-92, 94, chair nurse entrepreneurs 1992-94, WNY regional review team 1992-94), Women's Dental Guild, Internat. FEdn. of u. Woman, AAUW (mem. at large 2003-08). Republican. Home and Office: 49 Colony Ct Buffalo NY 14226-3507 Personal E-mail: dwright394@aol.com.

WRIGHT, DARRELL DEAN, educator; b. Topeka, July 8, 1954; m. Phyllis Thomas Bosch. MS, U. Ala., Tuscaloosa, 1989. Divsn. chair, faculty Shelton State CC, Tuscaloosa, Ala., 1985—2008. Home: 1614 Harmony Ln Tuscaloosa AL 35406 Office: Shelton State CC 9500 Old Greensboro Rd Tuscaloosa AL 35405 Business E-Mail: dwright@sheltonstate.edu.

WRIGHT, DAVID ALLEN, professional baseball player; b. Norfolk, Va., Dec. 20, 1982; Draft pick NY Mets, 2001, third baseman, 2004—. Mem. US nat. team World Baseball Classic, 2009. Founder David Wright Found., 2005—. Recipient Gold Glove award, 2007, 2008, Silver Slugger award, 2007, 2008, Joan Payson award, Baseball Writers Assn. America, NY Chpt., 2009; named Nat. League Rookie of Yr., NJ Sports Writers, 2004; named to Nat. League All-Star Team, Maj. League Baseball, 2006—09. Office: NY Mets Citi Field 126th St & Roosevelt Ave Flushing NY 11368*

WRIGHT, DAVID BURTON, retired newspaper publishing company executive; b. Fowler, Ind., Aug. 29, 1933; s. Claude Matthew and Rose Ellen (Lavelle) Wright; m. Geraldine F. Gray, May 9, 1964; children: David Andrew, Anne Kathleen. AB, Wabash Coll., 1955. CPA Ind. Audit staff George S. Olive Co. C.P.A.s, Indpls., 1958-63, mgmt. cons., 1963-65; controller Herff Jones Co., 1965-69, corp. controller, asst. sec., 1970-71; asst. bus. mgr. Indpls. Newspapers Inc., 1971-77; asst. sec., treas. Central Newspapers Inc., 1975-79, Muncie Newspapers Inc., 1975-93, Indpls. Newspapers Inc., 1975-93, bus. mgr., 1977-93; sec., treas. Central Newspapers Inc., 1979-89; v.p. Indpls. Newspapers Inc., 1982-93. Mem. St. Francis Hosp. Adv. Bd., Indpls., 1983—99. Sec. St. Francis Hosp. adv. Bd., Indpls., 1986—87, v.p., 1987—91, pres., 1991—93. Served US Army, 1956—58. Mem.: Ind. Assn. CPAs, Knights Columbus, Indpls. Econ. Club. Roman Cath. Home: 6713 Forrest Commons Blvd Indianapolis IN 46227-2396 E-mail: daviddavegerry@aol.com.

WRIGHT, DAVID JOHN, telecommunications systems specialist, educator; b. London, June 20, 1947; arrived in Canada, 1981; m. Mina Wright; 2 children. BA with honors, Cambridge U., 1968, PhD, 1972. Sr. scientific officer Dept. Environment, London, 1972-76; lectr. Ahmadu Bello U., Zaria, Nigeria, 1976-78, Sussex U., Brighton, United Kingdom, 1978-81; assoc. prof. U. Ottawa, Canada, 1981-87, prof., 1987—. Vis. rschr. Nortel Networks, Ottawa, 1988-89; provider cons. and tng. for the telecomms. industry on bus. opportunities arising from controlling climate change, environ., sustainability corporate social responsibility and Wireless Networking. Author: Broadband: Business Services, Technologies and Strategic Impact, 1993 (translated into Japanese, 1994), Telelearning via the Internet, 1999, The Business Case for the Web Based Training, 2000, Voice Over Packet Networks, 2001; contbr. articles to profl. jours. and chpts. to books. Mem. IEEE. Avocation: piano.

WRIGHT, DAVID L., food and beverage company executive; b. Wenatchee, Wash., Mar. 12, 1949; s. Franklin Sven and Mary Elizabeth (Collins) W.; m. Karen Sue Rice, Mar. 28, 1981; children: Kara, Erin, Jonathan, Anna Catherine. BA, U. Calif., Davis, 1971; MA, Columbia U., 2008. Chief of rsch. dept. of benefit payments State of Calif., Sacramento, 1972-75; profl. staff mem. com. on agr. U.S. Ho. Reps., Washington, 1975-77; adminstrv. asst., chief of staff Rep. William C. Wampler, Washington, 1977-81; spl. asst. for legis. affairs to Pres. The White House, Washington, 1981-84; dir. govt. affairs PepsiCo Inc., Purchase, NY, 1984-87, v.p. worldwide govt. affairs, 1987—2005; ret. Mem. exec. com. US Coun. Internat. Bus., 1997-2005; bd. dirs. US C. of C., 2003-05, Green Mountain Valley Sch., 2007-; vice chair Harvard Ctr. on Media and Child Health, 2004-06. Capt. USAR, 1971-79. Mem Capitol Hill Club, Columbia Univ. Club. Personal E-mail: davidwright37@aol.com.

WRIGHT, DEBORAH C., bank executive; b. Bennetsville, SC, Jan. 30, 1958; BA, Radcliffe, 1979; MBA, JD, Harvard U., 1984. Assoc. corp. fin. First Boston Bank, 1984; dir. mktg. NYC Partnership, Harlem, 1987; apptd. Housing Authority Bd. NYC, 1992, commr., 1994—96; dir. Upper Manhattan Zone Devel. Corp., 1996—99; pres, CEO Carver Bancorp, Harlem, 1999—, chmn., 2005—. Bd. dirs. Carver Bancorp, Inc., Kraft Foods, Time Warner, 2005—. Bd. dirs. Harvard U., Meml. Sloan-Kettering Cancer Ctr., Partnership NYC, Ministers and Missionaries Benefit Bd. Am. Baptist Churches; founding mem. Lower Manhattan Develop. Corp. Named Community Banker of the Year, The Am. Banker, 2003; named one of The 100 Most Influential Women in NYC Bus., Crain's NY Bus., 2007. Office: Carver Bancorp 75 W 125th St New York NY 10027

WRIGHT, DELL, residential care and treatment facility executive; b. Greenville, SC, Aug. 29, 1944; s. Thomas C. and Marie (Tate) W.; m. Ines R. Teran, Oct 22, 1977; children: Anthony, Andre, Fionna, Al-Jonn. Diploma in computer tech., Control Data Inst., 1969. Electronic tester RCA, Marlboro, Mass., 1970-71; customer svc. rep. Honeywell Info. Systems, Inc., Waltham, Mass., 1971-75; computer technician Bendix Field Engring., Columbia, Md., 1975-78; sr. field engr. Ford Aerospace and Comm. Corp., Palo Alto, Calif., 1978-79; systems integration engr. Kentron Internat./NASA/JPL, Pasadena, Calif., 1979-83; sr. fabrication technician Rockwell Internat., Anaheim, Calif., 1983-84; computer engr. Al-Johi Internat., Dhahran, Saudi Arabia, 1984-85; sr. test engr. Gen. Dynamics, San Diego, 1985-88; owner Wrights Food Vending Svc., 1988—90; pres., founder Residential Care and Treatment Facility for Youth, 1991—. Author: Inspirational, 1995, My Life's Journey, 2005; inventor mechanical multiple picture frame. Chair, utilities commr. City of Colton, Calif., 1996—. With U.S. Army, 1962-65. Democrat. Avocations: rv camping, fishing, motorcycling.

WRIGHT, DONALD P., retail executive; Sr. v.p. real estate and engring. Safeway, Inc. Office: Safeway Inc 5918 Stoneridge Mall Rd Pleasanton CA 94588 Office Phone: 925-467-3000. Office Fax: 925-467-3323.*

WRIGHT, DOUGLAS TYNDALL, former university administrator; b. Toronto, Ont., Can., Oct. 4, 1927; s. George C. and Etta (Tyndall) W. BASc. with honors in Civil Engring, U. Toronto, 1949; MS in Structural Engring, U. Ill., 1952; PhD in Engring, U. Cambridge, 1954; D.Eng. (hon.), Carleton U., 1967; LLD (hon.), Brock U., 1967, Concordia U., 1982; DSc (hon.), Meml. U. Nfld., 1969; DHL (hon.), Northeastern U., 1985; LLD (hon.), U. Waterloo, 1995; DUniv (hon.), Strathclyde U., Glasgow, 1989; D de L'Université (hon.), Compiegne U., France, 1991; D Univ. (hon.), Université de Sherbrooke, 1992; DSc, McMaster U., 1993, Queen's U., 1993; LLD (hon.), U. Waterloo, 1995; LLD, U. Toronto, Can., 2005. Lectr. dept. civil engring. Queen's U., 1954-55, asst. prof., 1955-58, assoc. prof., 1958; prof. civil engring. U. Waterloo, 1958-67, chmn. dept. civil engring., 1958-63, dean engring., 1959-66; chmn. Ont. Com. on Univ. Affairs Govt. of Ont., 1967-72, Ont. Commn. Post-Secondary Edn., Toronto, 1969-72, dep. provincial sec. for social devel., 1972-79; dep. minister culture and recreation, 1979-80; pres. U. Waterloo, Ont., 1981-93, prof. engring. Ont., 1981—, pres. emeritus Ont., 1995—. Vis. prof. U. Autónoma Mex., 1964, 66, U. Sherbrooke, 1966—67; cons. engr. Netherlands and Mexican Pavillions Expo, 1967, Olympic Sports Palace, Mexico City, 1968, Ont. Place Dome and Forum, 1971; tech. advisor Toronto Skydome, 1984—92; bd. dirs. Bell Can., 1984—99, Rsch. in Motion, 1998—2007, Com Dev Ltd., Geometrica Inc., Perimeter Inst. for Theoretical Physics; mem. Premier's Coun. on Sci. and Tech., Ont., 1985—91; Can. rep. Coun. Internat. Inst. Applied Sys. Analysis, Laxenburg, Austria, 1986—97; prime min.'s personal rep. to Coun. Misn. of Edn., 1990—91. Contbr. articles to profl. jours. Bd. govs. Stratford Shakespearean Festival, 1984—86, mem. senate, 1987; bd. dirs. African Students Found., Toronto, 1961—66, Ont. Curriculum Inst., 1964—67, Ont. R&D Challenge Fund, 1998—2004, NB Innovation Found., 2001—05. Decorated Officer Order of Can., chevalier Ordre National du Mérite (France); recipient Gold medal Ont. Profl. Engrs., 1990, Gold Medal award Can. Coun. Profl. Engrs., 1992, Sir. John Kennedy Medal award Engring. Inst. Can., 1995, Can. Entrepreneur of Yr. award, 1997; Athlone fellow, 1952-54. Fellow ASCE, Can. Acad. Engring., Engring. Inst. Can. (del. Engrs. Coun. Profl. Devel., N.Y.C. 1961-70); mem. Assn. Profl. Engrs. Province Ont., Internat. Assn. Bridge and Structural Engring., Internat. Assn. Shell Structures, Royal Can. Yacht Club, Univ. Club (Toronto).

WRIGHT, DOUGLASS BROWNELL, retired judge, lawyer; b. Hartford, Conn., May 30, 1912; s. Arthur Brownell and Sylvia (Stephens) W.; m. Jane Hamersley, Sept. 24, 1938 (dec. Feb. 1997); children: Jane C., Douglass B., Hamersley S., Elizabeth B., Arthur W.; m. Ann Hallowell Ferguson, Nov., 1999. AB, Yale U., 1933; LL.B., Hartford Coll. Law, 1937. Bar: Conn. 1937. Legal dept. Aetna Life Ins. Co., 1937-39; partner Davis, Lee, Howard & Wright, Hartford, 1939—; lectr. law U. Conn., 1946—; asst. state's atty. Conn., 1952-59; judge Conn. Circuit Court, 1959-65, Conn. Superior Ct., 1965—98; ret., 1998. Leader orch. Judge Wright and the Four Wrongs Author: Connecticut Law of Torts, 1956, Connecticut Legal Forms, 5 vols., 1958, Connecticut Jury Instructions, 3 vols., 1960, 76. Sec., dir. Captioned Films for the Deaf, Inc.; bd. dirs., pres. Am. Sch. for Deaf, 1942—; trustee Hartt Mus. Found., 1949—, Good Will Boys Club Hartford, 1950—; regent U. Hartford; bd. dirs. Vis. Nurse Assn., Newington Home for Crippled Children, Hartford Times Farm, Loomis Sch.; incorporator Conn. Inst. for Blind. Served as lt. USNR, 1942-45. Mem. Phi Beta Kappa, Psi Upsilon. Clubs: University (Hartford), Hartford Golf (Hartford), Hartford Tennis (Hartford), 20th Century (Hartford); Coral Beach and Tennis (Bermuda); Hillsboro (Pompano Beach, Fla.). Congregationalist. Home: 20 Loeffler Rd Apt T519 Bloomfield CT 06002-2273 Office: 95 Washington St Hartford CT 06106-4431 Home Phone: 860-726-2217.

WRIGHT, EDWARD LEONARD, astronomy educator; b. Washington, Aug. 25, 1947; s. Rufus William and Gertrude (Leonard) W.; m. Patricia Jaskun, Mar. 18, 1978; children: William, Diana. AB summa cum laude, Harvard U., 1969, PhD, 1976. Asst. prof. physics MIT, Cambridge, 1976-80, assoc. prof., 1980-81; prof. astronomy UCLA, 1981—. Recipient Jr. Fellowship Harvard U. Soc. Fellows, 1973-76. Fellow Am. Acad. Arts & Scis. Achievements include co-investigation of the Cosmic Background Explorer (COBE); research on the Space Infra Red Telescope Facility (SIRTF). Office: UCLA Dept of Astronomy 405 Hilgard Ave Los Angeles CA 90095-9000

WRIGHT, ELEASE, insurance company executive; BS in Edn., U. Conn. Sr. v.p. human resources Aetna Inc., Hartford, Conn., 1999—. Mem.: advisory bd., Cornell Univ. Center for Advanced Human Resource Studies, bd. of advisors, Univ. Conn. School of Bus., Exec. Leadership Council. Office: 151 Farmington Ave Hartford CT 06156-0001

WRIGHT, ETHEL, secondary school educator; b. Apr. 5, 1947; m. James A. Wright, Sept. 26, 1969; children: Cassandra, Hannibal, Omari. BS in English, Alcorn State U., Lorman, Miss., 1970; MS in Edn., Butler U., Indpls., 1975. Tchr. Simmons H.S., Arcola, Miss., 1970-71; tchr. English Indpls. Pub. Schs., 1971—. Mem. textbook adoption com. Indpls. Pub. Schs., 1979, liaison for Tchrs. Ctr., mem. film preview com. Clk., Dem. Com., Indpls. Recipient ABCD award Indpls. Pub. Schs., 1985, 92; Gregg and Reed scholar Indpls. Pub. Schs. Mem. NEA, Indpls. Edn. Assn. Avocations: reading, gardening, sewing, growing houseplants, travel.

WRIGHT, FAITH-DORIAN, artist; b. Bklyn., Feb. 9, 1934; d. Abraham and Molly (Janoff) J.; children: Jordan Merritt, Igrid-beth. BS, NYU, 1955, MA, 1958; postgrad., Pratt and Parsons Sch. of Design. Works exhibited in Kathryn Markel Gallery, N.Y.C., 1981, 92, Cumberland Gallery, Nashville, 1981, 92, Barbara Gillman Gallery, Miami, 1982, Hand and Hand Gallery, 1985, 86, Suzanne Gross, Phila., 1986, 87, Gallery Four, Alexandria, Va., 1986, 87, 88, Henri Gallery, Washington, 1986, 87, 88, 89. 90. 91. 92. 93. 94, Benton Gallery, Southampton, 1986-, King Stephen Mus., Hungary, 1987, Nat. Gallery Women in the Arts, 1987, 88, 90, 91, 92, Ruth Volid Gallery, Chgo., 1990, James Gallery, Pitts., 1990, Aart Vark Gallery, Phila., 1990, Merrill Chase Gallery, Chgo., 1990, 91, 92, Guild Hall Mus., East Hampton, N.Y., 1991, Joy Berman Gallery, Phila., 1992, Ctr. for Book Arts, N.Y.C., 1992, Barnard-Biederman Fine Arts, N.Y.C., 1994, Arlene Bujese Gallery, East Hampton, 1994, 95, 96, Stoney Brook U., 1994, Harper Collins Exhbn. Space, 1995, Ctr. for Book Arts, 1996, arlene bujese, 1997, Galerie Cargo, Paris, 1997, N.Y. State Mus., Albany, 1997, U. Mont., Missoula, 2002, Nat. Mus. Women in Arts, Washington, 2002, Arlene Bujese, East Hampton, N.Y., 1997-03, Seton Hall U., NJ, 2003, Arlene Bujese Gallery, East Hampton, N.Y. 2003—, Gayle Wilson Gallery, Southampton, N.Y., 2004-2005, Brunswick Gallery Southampton, 2007; permanent collections Nat. Postal Art Mus., Ottawa, Can., Nat. Inst. Design, Ahmedabad, India, Fine Arts Acad., New Delhi, India, Mus. Modern Art, N.Y.C., Nat. Mus. Women in the Arts, Washington, D.C., Israel Mus., Jerusalem, Brenau Coll., Grainsville, Ga. Blue Cross, Blue Shield, Phila., Mc Donald's, Oakbrook, Ill., The Hyatt Collection, Chgo., Guild Hall Mus., Saul, Ewing, Reineck & Saul, Phila., Shevick, Ravich, Koster, Tobin, Clark, N.J., Sidley & Austin, L.A., Catalano & Sparber, N.Y., Islip (N.Y.) Mus. of Art, NY Pet Rescue Orgn., Larchmont, Islip (NY) Mus.; contbr. critical essays to various periodicals. Mem. Women in Arts, Women's Caucus for Arts, Artists Equity, Visitation Bd. of Met. Mus.-Rockefeller Connection. Address: 300 E 74th St New York NY 10021-3712

WRIGHT, FRANCES JANE, educational psychologist; b. LA, Dec. 22, 1943; d. step-father John David and Evelyn Jane (Dale) Brinegar. BA, Long Beach State U., 1965; MA, Brigham Young U., 1968, EdD, 1980; postgrad., U. Nev., 1970, U. Utah, 1972-73; postdoctoral, Utah State U., 1985-86. Cert. secondary tchr., adminstr., Utah. Asst. dir. Teenpost Project, San Pedro, Calif., 1966; caseworker Los Angeles County, 1966-67; self-care inservice dir. Utah State Tng. Sch., American Fork, Utah, 1968, vocat. project designer, 1968; tchr. mentally handicapped Santa Ana Unified Schs., Calif., 1968-69; state specialist intellectually handicapped State Office Edn., Salt Lake City, 1969-70; vocat. counselor Manpower, Salt Lake City, 1970-71; tchr. severely handicapped Davis County Schs., Farmington, Utah, 1971-73, diagnostician, 1973-74, resource elem. tchr., 1974-78; instr. Brigham Young U., Salt Lake City, 1976-83; resource tchr. jr. high Davis County Schs., Farmington, 1978-90; ednl. cons. Murray, Utah, 1973-90; chief ednl. diagnostician Ctr. for Evaluation of Learning and Devel., Layton, Utah, 1989-90. Clin. dir. assessment and observation program Idaho Youth Ranch, 1990-95, clin. dir. intake program, 1992-94, supr. family preservation svc./aftercare teams, 1993-95, co-ranch treatment dir. and placement officer, 1995; cons. juvenile correctional dist. 5, 1996-2000; cons., counselor address issues with youth and families, 2001-06; program mgr. Libery Care Svcs. Mental Health Clinic, 2006—; clinician Region 5 Behavioral Health, 2006—; clin. cons. Magic Hot Springs Youth Camp, 1996-97; mem. cmty. accountability bd. McNeil Assn., 1996-2000, Dist. 5 Juvenile Justice Coun., 1997—, parent project facilitator, 1998-2000; trainer Detour prison prevention programfor adolescents, 1997-2000; cons. Northstar Family Preservation, 1997-2001; mem. Juvenile Justice Coun., 1996—; acting chmn. Dist. 5 Juvenile Justice Coun., 1998-99, chmn. 1999-2001; mem. Idaho Juvenile Justice Commn., 1999-2001; adv. bd. So. Central Learning Ctr., 1999-2001; mem. oversight bd., evaluator Status Offender prog. 1997-2000; program dir. Liberty Care Svc.; clin. program mgr. Liberty Care Svcs., 2002-06; clinician Adult Behavior Health Dept. Health/Welfare, 2006—; lectr. in field; pvt. cons./counselor lic. in juvenile justice, youth, edn. and other related concerns. Named Profl. of Yr. Utah Assn. for Children with Learning Disabilities, 1985, Prol. of the Yr., Idaho Youth Ranch Treatment Ctrs., 1992, 1993. Mem. Assn. Children/Adults with Learning Disabilities (del. 1979-85, 87, nat. nominating com., 1985-86, nat. bd. dirs. 1988-91), Am. Counseling Assn., Idaho Mental Health Counselors Assn., Utah Assn. Children/Adults with Learning Disabilities (exec. bd. 1978-84, profl. adv. bd. 1985-90, coord. LDA orgn. Idaho 1991-2000), Coun. Learning Disabilities, ASCD (regional adv.), Nat. Wildlife Found., World Wildlife Fedn., Best Friends Animal Sanctuary, Job's Daughters. Democrat. Mem. Lds Ch. Avocations: genealogy, horseback riding, sketching, crafts, reading. Home: 2176 Julie Ln Twin Falls ID 83301-8361 Office: Liberty Care Svc Pvt Mental Health Clin 460 Main Ave S Ste C Twin Falls ID 83301-7972 Office Phone: 208-736-2177. Business E-Mail: libertycare@onewest.net. *Personal philosophy: I dream of the day when man will value man and his surrounding world for their intrinsic value instead of what they can or could do for a specific person.*

WRIGHT, FRANK, artist, educator; b. Washington, Oct. 10, 1932; s. John Franklin and Margaret (Young) W.; m. Mary Eleanor Dow, May 31, 1957; 1 child, Suzanne Elizabeth. BA, Am. U., 1954; MA in Art History, U. Ill., 1960. Instr. Am. U., Washington, 1958-59; Paul J. Sachs fellow Nat. Gallery of Art, Washington, 1959-60, Harvard U., Cambridge, Mass., 1960-61; printmaking fellow Atelier 17, Paris, 1961—64; instr. Corcoran Sch. Art, Washington, 1966-70; asst. prof. to prof. fine arts George Wash. U., Washington, 1970—. NASA guest artist Columbia Space Launch STS-5, 1982. Exhibited in shows at Corcoran Gallery of Art, Washington, 1981, Kennedy Galleries, N.Y, 1981, Johnson Space Ctr., Houston, 1983, Allentown (Pa.) Art Mus., 1983, Md. Hall, Annapolis, 1998, Strathmore Hall, Bethesda, Md., 1998. Mem. Hist. Soc. D.C. Fellow Leopold Schepp Found., 1956, Print Coun. Am., 1959. Mem. Nat. Soc. Arts and Letters (advisor 1992—), Cosmos Club (art com. 1993), Omicron Delta Kappa (Beta Cir.). Avocation: Collecting Washingtonianamaterial. Home: 3520 Bradley Ln Chevy Chase MD 20815-3260 Office: 2301 E St NW Apt 1019 Washington DC 20037 Home Phone: 301-652-6777; Office Phone: 202-822-4989. Business E-Mail: fwright@gwu.edu.

WRIGHT, FREDERICK LEWIS, II, lawyer; b. Roanoke, Va., Sept. 17, 1951; s. Frederick Lewis and Dorothy Marie (Trent) W.; m. Margaret Suzanne Rey, Oct. 16, 1982; children: Lauren Elizabeth, Emily Trent. BA, Ga. State U., 1978; JD, U. Ga., 1981. Bar: Ga. 1982, US Dist. Ct. (no. dist.) Ga. 1984, US Ct. Appeals (11th, 8th and 4th cirs.) 1984, US Supreme Ct. 1990. Law clk. to presiding justice US Ct. Appeals, Atlanta, 1981-82; ptnr. Smith, Currie and Hancock, Atlanta, 1982-96, Vaughn, Wright and Boyer, Atlanta, 1997—. Articles editor Ga. Law Rev., 1980—81. Mem.: ABA (forum com. constrn. industry), Ga. Def. Lawyers Assn., Fed. Bar Assn., Def. Rsch. Inst., Order of Coif. Methodist. Office Phone: 770-805-9889. Personal E-mail: fwright@mindspring.com.

WRIGHT, GEORGE THADDEUS, humanities educator; b. S.I., NY, Dec. 17, 1925; s. George Thaddeus and Tekla Alida (Anderson) W.; m. Jerry Honeywell, Apr. 28, 1955 (dec. 2006). AB, Columbia, 1946, MA, 1947; student, U. Geneva, Switzerland, 1947-48; PhD (Dr. Benjamin P. Wall meml. fellow 1955-56), U. Calif., Berkeley, 1957. Lectr. English U. Calif. at Berkeley, 1956-57; instr., then asst. prof. U. Ky., 1957-60; asst. prof. San Francisco State Coll., 1960-61; assoc. prof. U. Tenn., 1961-68; prof. English U. Minn., Mpls., 1968-89, Regents' prof., 1989-93, prof. emeritus, 1993—, chmn. dept. English, 1974-77. Fulbright lectr. Am. lit. U. d'Aix Marseille, France, 1964-66, U. Thessaloniki, Greece, 1977-78 Author: The Poet in the Poem: The Personae of Eliot, Yeats and Pound, 1960, W.H. Auden, 1969, rev. edit., 1981, Shakespeare's Metrical Art, 1988, paperback edit., 1991, Aimless Life: Poems, 1961-1995, 1999, Hearing the Measures: Shakespearean and Other Inflections, 2002; author of poems; editor: Seven American Literary Stylists from Poe to Mailer, 1973; contbr. articles to profl. jours. Served with U.S. Army, 1944-46. Recipient Robert Fitzgerald Prosody Lifetime Achievement award, 2003; Guggenheim fellow, 1981-82; NEH fellow, 1984-85. Mem. Shakespeare Assn. Am., MLA (William Riley Parker prize 1974, 81), Phi Kappa Phi. Home: 2617 W Crown King Dr Tucson AZ 85741-2569

WRIGHT, GINA A., voice educator; d. Joseph and Helen Inguagiato; m. Darren L. Wright, Aug. 13, 1983; children: Sabrina, Ashley. MusB in Vocal Performance, Bradley U., Peoria, Ill., 1980, MusM, 1982. Vocal instr. Bradley U., Peoria, 1995—. Mem.: Nat. Assn. Tchrs. Singing (Vocal Pedagogy & Voice Sci. grant 2008). Home: 5727 N Sheridan Rd Peoria IL 61614 Office: Bradley Univ 1501 N Bradley Ave Peoria IL 61625 Business E-Mail: ginaw@bradley.edu.

WRIGHT, GLADYS STONE, music educator, writer, composer; b. Wasco, Oreg., Mar. 8, 1925; d. Murvel Stuart and Daisy Violet (Warren) Stone; m. Alfred George Wright, June 28, 1953. BS, U. Oreg., 1948, MS, 1953. Dir. bands Elmira (Oreg.) U-4 H.S., 1948-53, Otterbein (Ind.) H.S., 1954-61, Klondike H.S., West Lafayette, Ind., 1962-70, Harrison H.S., West Lafayette, 1970-84. Organizer, condr. Musical Friendship Tours, Ctrl. Am., 1967-79; v.p., condr. U.S. Collegiate Wind Band, 1975—; bd. dirs. John Philip Sousa Found., 1984—; chmn. Sudler Cup, 1986—, Sudler Flag, 1982; pres. Internat. Music Tours, 1984—, Key to the City, Taxco, Mex., 1975. Editor: Woman Conductor, 1986—; composer: marches Big Bowl and Trumpets and Tabards, 1987; contbg. editor: Informusica (Spain). Recipient Medal of the order John Philip Sousa Found., 1988, Star of Order, 1991, Internat. Contbrn. to Music award Phi Beta Mu, 2000; 1st woman guest condr. U.S. Navy Band, Washington, 1961, Goldman Band, NYC, 1958, Kneller Hall Band, London, 1975, Tri-State Music Festival Massed Orch., Band, Choir, 1985; elected to Women Bd. Dirs. Hall of Fame of Disting. Women Condrs., 1994; inductee Hall of Fame Disting. Condrs., Nat. Band Assn., 1999; named Ind.'s Sagamore of the Wabash, 2004. Mem. Am. Bandmasters Assn. (bd. dirs. 1993, 1st woman mem.), Women Band Dirs. Nat. Assn. (founding pres. 1967, sec. 1985, recipient Silver Baton 1974, Golden Rose 1990, Hall of Fame 1995), Am. Sch. Band Dirs. Assn., Nat. Band Assn. (Citation excellence 1970), Tippecanoe Arts Fedn. (bd. dirs. 1986-90), Tippecanoe Fife and Drum Corps. (bd. dirs. 1984), DAR, Col. Dames-Pre Quitanen Chpt., New Eng. Women, Tau Beta Sigma (Outstanding Svc. to Music award 1970), Phi Beta Mu (1st hon. woman mem. 1972), N.Am. Wildlife Park (Battleground, Ind., bd dirs. 1985, 1990—). Avocation: history.

WRIGHT, GREGORY A., oil industry executive; BBA, Ohio State U., 1971; MBA, U. Del., 1979. With Columbia Gas Systems Inc., 1972—81; positions through v.p. Valero Energy Corp., 1981—95; v.p. corp. comm. Tesoro Corp., San Antonio, 1995—2001, sr. v.p., CFO, 2001—03, exec. v.p., CFO, 2003—07, 2008—, exec. v.p., Chief Adminstrv. Officer, 2007—08. Office: Tesoro Petroleum 300 Concord Plz San Antonio TX 78216-6999

WRIGHT, HARRISON MORRIS, historian, educator; b. Phila., Oct. 6, 1928; s. Sydney L. and Catharine W. (Morris) W.; m. Josephine Stearns Cole, July 20, 1957; children— Rebecca H., J. Rodman, Thomas F., Daniel H., James L. BA, Harvard U., Cambridge, Mass., 1950, MA, 1953, PhD, 1957. Teaching fellow Harvard, 1955-57; mem. faculty Swarthmore Coll., 1957—, prof. history, 1968-87, Isaac H. Clothier prof. history and internat. relations, 1987-93, chmn. dept., 1968-79, provost, 1979-84, Clothier prof. and provost emeritus, 1993—, acting pres., 1982. Bd. dirs. Paul Cuffee Sch., 2001—07. Author: New Zealand, 1769-1840: Early Years of Western Contact, 1959, The Burden of the Present: Liberal-Radical Controversy over Southern African History, 1977; Editor: The New Imperialism— Analysis of Late Nineteenth-Century Expansion, 1961, 2d edit., 1976, Sir James Rose Innes: Selected Correspondence (1884-1902), 1972. Mem. Jamestown Harbor Commn., RI, 2000—03. Fulbright scholar New Zealand, 1950-51; Ford Found. fgn. areas fellow Eng. and Ghana, 1961-62; grantee Am. Philos. Soc., S. Africa, 1966-67; grantee Old Dominion Fund, S. Africa, 1971 Mem.: Jamestown Hist. Soc. (bd. dirs. 1997—2003, 2004—, v.p. 2005—), RI Hist. Soc. (bd. dirs. 1998—2005), Hist. Soc. Pa. (coun. 1984—91, v.p. 1986—88, chmn. 1989—91, coun. emeritus 1992—), Sailing Inst. (bd. dirs. 1998—2007), Humanities Forum R.I. (bd. dirs. 1995—2000), Newport Hist. Soc. (bd. dirs. 1973—88, 2006—), Phi Beta Kappa. Home: PO Box 209 Jamestown RI 02835-0209

WRIGHT, HARRY HERCULES, psychiatrist; b. Charleston, SC, Jan. 4, 1948; s. Harry Vernon and Agnes Lucile (Simmons) W. BS, U. S.C., 1970; MD, MBA, U. Pa., 1976. Resident in psychiatry Wm. S. Hall Psychiat. Inst., Columbia, SC, 1977—79; adminstrv. fellow in psychiatry NIMH, Rockville, Md., 1979; fellow in child psychiatry William S. Hall Psychiat. Inst., 1979—81, instr. child psychiatrist, 1981—; instr. dept. neuropsychiatry and behavioral sci. U. S.C. Sch. Medicine, 1981—82, asst. prof., 1982—86, assoc. prof., 1986—90, prof., 1990—. Contbr. articles to profl. jours. Bd. dirs. Carolina Children's Home, 1992—, Zero to Three, 1997—; bd. trustees, First Steps to Sch. Readiness, 1999-2003; mem. landmarks commn. City of Columbia, 1986-98. Recipient Freed award, Hall Psychiat. Inst., 1978, Outstanding Svc. award, Sickle Cell Found., Clin. Sci. Rsch. award, 1998, Am.'s Top Doctors award, 2001—08, Rsch. Advancement award, U. SC, 2002, 2004, 2006, 2008; grantee Falk fellow, 1977—79, Laughlin fellow, 1979. Mem.: Am. Coll. Psychiatrists, Am. Soc. Human Genetics, Soc. Study Psychiatry and Culture, Acad. Orgnl. and Occupl. Psychiatry, So. Med. Assn., Am. Soc. Adolescent Psychiatry, World Assn. Infant Mental Health, World Psychiat. Assn., Am. Acad. Child Psychiatry, Am. Physiatry Assn., Autism Soc. Am., Riverbank Zool. Soc., Sigma Xi, Omicron Delta Kappa. Methodist. Home: PO Box 12474 Columbia SC 29211-2474 Office: 3555 Harden St Ext Ste 301 Columbia SC 29203-6894 Office Phone: 803-434-4250. Business E-Mail: harry.wright@uscmed.sc.edu.

WRIGHT, HERBERT E(DGAR), JR., geologist; b. Malden, Mass., Sept. 13, 1917; s. Herbert E. and Annie M. (Richardson) W.; m. Rhea Jane Hahn, June 21, 1943; children: Richard, Jonathan, Stephen, Andrew, Jeffrey. AB, Harvard U., 1939, MA, 1941, PhD, 1943; DSc (hon.), Trinity Coll., Dublin, Ireland, 1966, U. Minn., 1996; PhD (hon.), Lund U., Sweden, 1987. Instr. Brown U., 1946-47; asst. prof. geology U. Minn., Mpls., 1947-51, asso. prof., 1951-59, prof., 1959-74, Regents' prof. geology, ecology and botany, 1974-88, Regents' prof. geology, ecology & botany emeritus, 1988—; dir. Limnological Research Center, 1963-90. Served to maj. USAAF, 1942-45. Decorated D.F.C., Air medal with 6 oak leaf clusters; recipient Pomerance award Archeol. Inst. Am., 1985, Ann. award Sci. Mus. Minn., 1990; Guggenheim fellow, 1954-55, Wenner-Gren fellow, 1954-55. Fellow AAAS, Geol. Soc. Am. (Ann. award archeol. divsn. 1989, Disting. Career award geology and geomorphology divsn. 1992), Soc. Am. Archeology (Fryxell award 1993); mem. NAS, Ecol. Soc. Am., Internat. Quaternary Assn. (hon. pres. 16th Congress 2003), Am. Quaternary Assn. (Career award 1996). Achievements include research on Quaternary geology, paleoecology, paleolimnology and environ. archaeology in Minn., Wyo., Sweden, Yukon, Labrador, Peru, eastern Mediterranean. Home: 1426 Hythe St Saint Paul MN 55108-1423 Office: U of Minn 310 Pillsbury Dr SE Minneapolis MN 55455-0219 Business E-Mail: hew@umn.edu.

WRIGHT, IAN M., automotive executive, electrical engineer; arrived in US, 1993; married; 2 children. Student, NSW Inst. Tech. (now U. Tech.), Sydney. With Scitec, Australia; sr. dir. engring. Network Equipment Techs. Inc., Fremont, Calif., 1993—98; dir. engring. at optical internetworking unit Cisco Systems, 1998—2000; sr. v.p. engring. for optical networking products Ditech Comm. Corp., 2000; v.p. vehicle devel. Tesla Motors Inc., San Carlos, Calif., 2003—04; founder, CEO Wrightspeed Inc., Burlingame, Calif., 2005—. Office: Wrightspeed Inc 1400 Rollins Rd Ste B Burlingame CA 94010 Office Phone: 650-787-8729. Office Fax: 650-343-8905. E-mail: ian@wrightspeed.com.

WRIGHT, JAMEELAH R., pre-school educator; BA in Sociology, Rutgers U., New Brunswick, NJ, 2003; degree in Early Childhood Edn., Montclair State U., NJ, 2005; student in Reading, Kean U., Union, NJ, 2006—. Lead tchr. Three Stages Learning Ctr., East Orange, NJ, 2004—, Urban Flower Project, East Orange, 2004—. Named Most Positive Personality, Three Stages Learning Ctr., 2004, Most Profl. Staff Mem., 2006—08, Outstanding Lead Tchr., 2006—08. Mem.: Internat. Reading Assn., Nat. Coun. Tchrs. English, Nat. Assn. Edn. Young Children. Avocations: writing, poetry. Office: Three Stages Learning Ctr 91 South Harrison St East Orange NJ 07017

WRIGHT, JAMES EDWARD, historian, educator, former academic administrator; b. Madison, Wis., Aug. 16, 1939; s. Donald J. and Myrtle (Hendricks) Wright; m. Joan Bussan, Sept. 3, 1962 (div.); children: James J., Ann Marie, Michael J.; m. Susan DeBevoise, Aug. 18, 1984. BS, Wis. State U., 1964; MS, U. Wis., 1966, PhD, 1969; MA (hon.), Dartmouth Coll., 1980. From asst. prof. to assoc. prof. history Dartmouth Coll., Hanover, NH, 1969—80, prof. history, 1980—, assoc. dean faculty, 1981—85, dean faculty, 1989—97, acting pres., 1995, provost, 1997—98, pres., 1998—2009, pres. emeritus & Eleazar Wheelock prof., 2009—. Sr. historian U. Mid Am., Lincoln, Nebr., 1976—77; humanist-in-residence Colo. Humanities Coun., Georgetown, 1975. Author: Galena Lead District, 1966, Politics of Populism, 1974, Progressive Yankees, 1987; author: (co-editor) Great Plains Experience, 1978. Trustee Kimball Union Acad., Meriden, NH, 1990—94; dir. Sherman Fairchild Found., Greenwich, Conn., 1991—; chair Hanover Dem. Town Com., 1970—74; bd. dirs. Divsn. 1 NCAA, 2001—03. Cpl. USMC, 1957—60. Recipient New Englander of Yr., New England Coun., 2007, Semper Fidelis award, Marine Corps. Scholarship Found., 2008, Comdr. in Chief's Gold medal, VFW; Danforth fellow, 1964—69, Guggenheim fellow, 1973—74, Charles Warren fellow, Harvard U., 1980—81. Fellow: Am. Acad. Arts and Scis.; mem.: Western History Assn. (chair Caughey prize 1986—87), The Century Assn., Orgn. Am. Historians (chair film, media com. 1983—85), Phi Beta Kappa. Office: 2 Dorrance Pl Ste A Hanover NH 03755 Home: 138 Browns Hill Sunapee NH 03782 Office Phone: 603-646-0016. Business E-Mail: james.wright@dartmouth.edu.

WRIGHT, JAMES F., agricultural products executive; Sr. level positions K-Mart Corp., 1974—88, Western Auto Supply Co., 1988—96; pres., CEO Tire Kingdom, 1997—2000; pres., COO Tractor Supply Co., Brentwood, Tenn., 2000—, pres., CEO, 2004—07, chmn., pres., CEO, 2007—09, chmn., CEO, 2009—. Bd. dir. Spartan Stores Inc. Mem.: Automotive Parts and Accessories Assn. (past chmn.). Office: Tractor Supply Co 200 Powell Pl Brentwood TN 37027*

WRIGHT, JAMES RALPH, retired lawyer; b. Pitts., Jan. 18, 1944; s. Paul J. and Gertrude M. (Stienecker) W.; m. Harriett Ann Howard, Sept. 7, 1968; children: Karen, Cathy. BS, Ohio State U., 1966; JD, George Washington U., 1969. Bar: D.C. 1973, U.S. Dist. Ct. D.C. 1975, U.S. Ct. Appeals (D.C. cir.) 1981. Dir. legal affairs Airport Operators Coun., Internat., Washington, 1969-70; with NAS, Washington, 1970—2006, staff officer, counsel com. on motor vehicles, 1973-74, staff counsel, 1974-80, gen. counsel, 1980—2006; ret. Exec. dir. Nat. Academies' Corp., a Calif. nonprofit pub. benefit corp., 1986—. Editor, pub. newsletter, 1985-90. Mem. ABA.

WRIGHT, JANE COOKE, oncologist, educator, consultant; b. NYC, Nov. 30, 1919; d. Louis T. and Corinne (Cooke) W.; m. David D. Jones. AB, Smith Coll., 1942; MD with honors, N.Y. Med. Coll., 1945; D in Med. Scis., Women's Med. Coll. Pa., 1965; ScD, Denison U., 1971. Intern Bellevue Hosp., NYC, 1945-46, resident, 1946, mem. staff, 1955-67; resident Harlem Hosp., 1947, chief resident, 1948; clin. Cancer Rsch. Found., Harlem Hosp., 1949-52; dir., 1952-55; mem. staff Harlem Hosp., 1949-55; practice medicine specializing in clin. cancer chemotherapy NYC; mem. faculty dept. surgery Med. Ctr., N.Y. U., NYC, 1955-67, adj. assoc. prof., 1961-67, also dir. cancer chemotherapy services research, 1955-67; prof. surgery N.Y. Med. Coll., NYC, 1967-87, prof. surgery emeritus, 1987—, assoc. dean, 1967-75; mem. staff Manhattan VA Hosp., 1955-67, Midtown, Met., Bird S. Color, Flower-Fifth Ave. Hosps., all NYC, 1967-79, Westchester County Med. Center, Valhalla, NY, 1971-87, Lincoln Hosp., Bronx, NY, 1979-87. Cons. Health Ins. Plan of Greater N.Y., 1962—94, Blvd. Hosp., 1963—, St. Luke's Hosp., Newburgh, NY, 1964—; pelvic malignancy rev. com. N.Y. Gynecol. Soc., 1965—66, St. Vincent's Hosp., NYC, 1966—, Dept. Health, Edn. and Welfare, 1968—70, Wyckoff Heights Hosp., NYC, 1969—, NIH, 1971—, others; adv. bd. Skin Cancer Found. Contbr. articles to profl. jours. Mem. Manhattan coun. State Commn. Human Rights, 1949—, Pres.'s Commn. Heart Disease, Cancer and Stroke, 1964-65, Nat. Adv. Cancer Coun. NIH, 1966-70, N.Y. State Women's Coun., 1970-72; bd. dirs. Medico-CARE, Health Svcs. Improvement Fund Inc.; trustee Smith Coll., Northampton, Mass., 1970-80. Recipient numerous awards, including; Mademoiselle mag. award, 1952; Lady Year award Harriet Beecher Stowe Jr. High Sch., 1958; Spirit Achievement award Albert Einstein Sch. Medicine, 1965; certificate Honor award George Gershwin Jr. High Sch., 1967; Myrtle Wreath award Hadassah, 1967; Smith medal Smith Coll., 1968; Outstanding Am. Women award Am. Mothers Com. Inc., 1970; honored as one of 150 Am. Women Physicians at exhbn. Changing the Face of Medicine at the Nat. Libr. Medicine, NIH, 2003; Golden Plate award Am. Acad. Achievement, 1971; Exceptional Black Scientists Poster Ciba Geigy, 1980. Fellow N.Y. Acad. Medicine; mem. Nat. Med. Assn. (edit. bd. jours.), Manhattan Ctrl. Med. Soc., N.Y. County Med. Soc. (nominating com.), AMA, AAAS, Am. Assn. Cancer Rsch. (dir. Rsch. Salute 1971-74, Appreciation award for 50 Yr.of service, 2004, established Jane Cooke Wright lectureship 2006), N.Y. Acad. Scis., N.Y. Cancer Soc., Internat. Med. and Rsch. Found. (v.p.), Am. Cancer Soc. (dir. div.), N.Y. Cancer Soc. (pres. 1970-71), Am. Soc. Clin. Oncology (sec. treas. 1964-67, Spl. Appreciation award as a founding mem. 2004), Contin Soc., Sigma Xi, Lambda Kappa Mu, Alpha Omega Alpha. Clubs: The 400 (N.Y. Med. Coll.). Achievements include AACR and AACR minorities in Cancer Research (MICR) council has selected to name a lectureship in my honour. Address: 7002 Kennedy Blvd East Apt 9C Guttenberg NJ 07093 Home Phone: 201-662-8922.

WRIGHT, JANE LANIER, school librarian; b. Springfield, Mo. d. Berry Gene and Lanier Davis Payne, Jeannie Payne (Stepmother); m. Raymond Albert Wright; 1 child, Randle Bernard. BA, U. Ctrl. Fla., Daytona Beach, 1997; MA in Libr. Sci., U. South Fla., Tampa, 1998. Libr. head children's and audio visual sects. County Volusia DeLand Libr., Fla., 2002—; br. head holly hill libr. County Volusia, Holly Hill, Fla., 1998—2002. Actor: (ednl and entertaining performance). Com mem. Samsula Woman's Club, New Smyrna Beach, Fla., 2004—08. Mem.: ALA. Democrat. Baptist. Office: County Volusia DeLand Pub Libr 130 E Howry Ave Deland FL 32724

WRIGHT, JASON HOWARD SEBASTIAN, private equity company executive; b. Waterbury, Conn., Nov. 2, 1960; s. Joseph Thomas and Lyda (Hawkins) W. AB, Georgetown U., 1982. With Aetna Life & Casualty Co., Hartford, Conn., 1982—87, mgr. corp. pub. rels., 1987-88, dir. corp. comms., 1988—90; v.p. comm. RJR Nabisco, 1990—93; sr.

v.p. Nabisco Group Holdings Corp. (formerly RJR Nabisco), 1993—2000; prin. Geer Mountain Holdings, LLC, 2000—; sr. v.p. comm. & pub. affairs Merrill Lynch & Co. Inc., 2003—07. Bd. dirs. CCW Holdings Corp. Trustee Mus. for African Art, NYC, Cooper Union for the Advancement of Sci. and Art, James Beard Found., Internat. Ctr. for Journalists. Democrat. Avocation: tennis. Office: 1 West St Ste 3601 New York NY 10004 Office Phone: 212-243-1670. Business E-Mail: jasonwright@geermountain.com.

WRIGHT, JAY, men's college basketball coach; b. Churchville, Pa., Dec. 24, 1961; m. Patricia Reilly; children: Taylor, Colin, Reilly. B in Economics, Sociology, Bucknell U., Lewisburg, Pa., 1983. Adminstrv. asst. Phila. Stars, US Football League, 1983; asst. coach U. Rochester Yellowjackets, 1984—86; aide Drexel U. Dragons, 1986—87; asst. coach Villanova U. Wildcats, 1987—92, head coach, 2001—; asst. coach U. Nevada Las Vegas Runnin' Rebels, 1992—94; head coach Hofstra U. Pride, 1994—2001. Asst. coach, World Championship for Young Men Qualifying Team USA Basketball, 2000, head coach, World Univ. Games, 05, head coach, Pan Am. Games, 07. Active Coaches vs. Cancer, Phila. Chpt. Recipient Harry Litwack award, Herb Good Club, Phila., 2006; named Eastern Basketball Coach of Yr., 2000, Coach of Yr., America East Conf., 2000, 2001, Phila. Big Five Eastern Coll. Coach of Yr., 2005, Co-Developmental Coach of Yr., USA Basketball, 2005, Nat. Coach of Yr., CBS/Chevrolet, Naismith Awards, Nat. Assn. Basketball Coaches, 2006, Coach of Yr., Big East Conf., 2006, 2009. Office: Villanova Univ Dept Athletics 800 Lancaster Ln Villanova PA 19085-1603*

WRIGHT, JEANNE ELIZABETH JASON, retired advertising executive; b. Washington, June 24, 1934; d. Robert Stewart and Elizabeth (Gaddis) Jason; m. Benjamin Hickman Wright, Oct. 30, 1965; stepchildren: Benjamin (dec.), Deborah, David, Patricia. BA, Radcliffe Coll., 1956; MA, U. Chgo., 1958. Psychiat. social worker Lake County Mental Health Clinic, Gary, Ind., Psychiat. and Psychosomatic Inst., Michael Reese Hosp., Chgo., Jewish Child Care Assn., NYC, 1958-70; gen. mgr. Black Media, Inc. (advt. rep. co.), NYC, 1970-74, pres., 1974-75; pres., exec. editor, syndicator weekly editorial features Black Resources, Inc., NYC, 1975-99; ret., 1999. Mem. planning com. First Black Power Conf., Newark, 1966, Second Black Power Conf., Phila., 1967, First Internat. Black Cultural & Bus. Expn., N.Y.C., 1971; nat. bd. dirs. Afro-Am. Family & Community Svcs., Inc., Chgo., 1971-75; founding coun. mem. Nat. Assault on Illiteracy Program, 1980-99; pres. Metro-N.Y. chpt. Nat. Assn. Media Women, Inc., 1986-89. Recipient Pres.' award Nat. Assn. Black Women Attys., 1977, 2d ann. Freedom's Jour. award Journalism Students and Faculty of U. D.C. Dept. Communicative and Performing Arts, 1979, Communication award Harlem Svc. Ctr., ARC, 1988, Spl. award Beta Omicron chpt. Phi Delta Kappa, 1982; named Disting. Black Woman in Industry, Nat. Coun. Negro Women, 1981. Mem. AAAS, Nat. Assn. Social Workers, Acad. Cert. Social Workers, Nat. Assn. Media Women (pres. Met. N.Y. chpt. 1986-89, Nat. Media Woman of Yr. award l984, 86, Founders award l986), Newswomen's Club N.Y., U. Chgo. Alumni Assn., NAACP, Radcliffe Club, Harvard Club, Alpha Kappa Alpha Sorority Inc. (Gamma Zeta Omega Chpt.). Democrat.

WRIGHT, JEFFREY A., biology, physics educator; BA, Bellarmine Univ.; MA, Univ. Louisville. Cert. Nat. Bd. Tchg. Standards. Tchr. Trinity H.S., 1990—98; physics, biol. tchr. Louisville Male Traditional H.S., 1998—. Chmn. Physics Alliance; mentor tchr. Nat. Bd. Certification. Recipient Disney Tchr. award, 2005, Amgen Sci. Tchr. award, Ky. Sci. Tchrs. Assn., 2006, Presdl. award, 2008; named Ky. H.S. Tchr. of Yr., 2005, Ky. Tchr. of Yr., 2006. Mem.: LATTICE Tech. Alliance, Louisville Area Chemistry and Physics Alliances, Ky. Assn. Physics Tchrs., NEA, Ky. Edn. Assn., Nat. Sci. Tchr. Assn., Louisville Area Amateur Astronomers. Office: Louisville Male HS 4409 Preston Hwy Louisville KY 40213 Office Phone: 502-485-8292. Office Fax: 502-485-8770. Business E-Mail: JWright4@Jefferson.k12.ky.us. E-mail: jeffery.wright1@jefferson.kysci.us.

WRIGHT, JEREMIAH ALVESTA, JR., retired minister; b. Phila., Sept. 22, 1941; s. Jeremiah A. and Mary Elizabeth (Henderson) W.; m. Ramah E. Bratton, Oct. 22, 1989; 1 child, Jamila; children from previous marriage: Janet Marie Wright Hall, Jeri Lynn Wright Haynes, Nikol Reed, Nathan Reed. AB, Howard U., 1968, MA, 1969; MA in Religion, U. Chgo., 1974; D Ministry, United Theol. Sem., Dayton, Ohio, 1990. Ordained to ministry Am. Bapt. Ch., 1967. Asst. pastor Mt. Calvary Bapt. Ch., Rockville, Md., 1967-69; interim pastor Zion Bapt. Ch., Hagerstown, Md., 1969; asst. pastor Beth Eden Bapt. Ch., Chgo., 1969-71; pastor Trinity United Ch. of Christ, Chgo., 1972—2008. Rsch. asst. Am. Assn. Theol. Schs., Chgo., 1970-72; exec. dir. Chgo. Ctr. for Black Religious Studies, 1974-75; adj. prof. Chgo. Theol. Sem., 1974-75, Cath. Theol. Union, 1975; lectr. Chgo. Cluster of Theol. Schs., 1975—; mem. com. for racial justice United Ch. of Christ, 1976-80, ecumenical strategy com. Ill. Conf., 1975-76, resolutions com., 1973-74, urban mins. com. task force, 1975-76. Co-author: (with Jini Kilgore Ross) God Will Answer Prayer, 1974, What Makes You So Strong?: Sermons of Joy and Strength from Jeremiah A. Wright, Jr., 1993, Good News!: Sermons of Hope for Today's Families, 1995, (with Colleen Birchett) Africans Who Shaped Our Faith, 1995, (with Jawanza Kunjufu) Adam! Where Are You?: Why Most Black Men Don't Go to Church, 1997, (with Frank Madison Reid, III & Colleen Birchett) When Black Men Stand Up for God: Reflections on the Million Man March, 1997; author: What Can Happen When We Pray: A Daily Devotional, 2002, From One Brother To Another, Volume 2: Voices of African American Men, 2003; composer: (songs) Jesus Is His Name, 1975; contbr. articles to profl. jours. Dir. Creative Writing Workshop, Chgo., 1969-70; proposal writer, editor Dropout Prevention Program Chgo. Bd. Edn., 1971-72; bd. dirs. Malcolm X Sch. Nursing, 1974-84, Office of Ch. in Soc., United Ch. Christ, 1974-76. Recipient commendations Pres. of U.S., 1965-66; Howard U. grad. fellow, 1968-69, Rockefeller fellow, 1970-72, Carver medal, Simpson Coll, 2008 Mem. Ch. Fedn. Greater Chgo., Emergency Sch. Aid Act, Urban Ministerial Alliance, Ill. Conf. Chs., Mins. for Racial and Social Justice, United Black Christians, Omega Psi Phi, Alpha Kappa Mu. Home: 9167 S Pleasant Ave Chicago IL 60620-5512 Office: Trinity United Ch of Christ 400 W 95th St Chicago IL 60628-1120 *If there is one thing in this world that God's children need to learn, it is that being different does not mean that one is deficient!.**

WRIGHT, JESSE HARTZELL, psychiatrist, educator; b. Altoona, Pa., Sept. 21, 1943; s. Jesse H. and Marion (Stone) W.; m. Susanne Judy Wright, July 9, 1967; children: Andrew, Laura. BS, Juniata Coll., 1965; MD, Jefferson Med. Coll., 1969; PhD, U. Louisville, 1976. Diplomate Am. Bd. Psychiatry and Neurology, Am. Bd. Med. Examiners; lic. psychiatrist, Ky. Asst. prof. U. Louisville, 1975-79, assoc. prof., 1979-87, prof., 1987—; clin. dir. Norton Psychiat. Clinic, Louisville, 1975-83, med. dir., 1983—; chief adult psychiatry U. Louisville, 2000—09, vice-chmn academic affairs, dir. depression ctr., dept. psychiat., 2009—; resident in psychiatry U. Mich., Ann Arbor, 1970-73. Author: first multimedia computer program for psychotherapy, Good Days Ahead, chpts. to books; contbr. articles to prof. jours; author: (self help book for depression) Getting Your Life Back, (textbook with DVD) Learning Cognitive-Behavior Therapy, others. Fellow Am.Psychiat. Assn., Am. Coll. Psychiatrists; mem. Ky. Psychiat. Assn. (sec. 1979-80, v.p. 1980-81, pres. 1982-83), Acad. Cognitive Therapy (founding pres.), Alpha Omega Alpha. Avocations: gardening, running, theater, skiing. Home: 15 Indian Hills Trl Louisville KY 40207-1532 Office: Univ Psychiatric Group 401 E Chestnut St Louisville KY 40202

WRIGHT, JOAN L., artist; d. William Henry and Elsie Christina (Motzer) Harrison; m. Barry Duane Wright; children: Stephen Craig, Michael Alan, Jeffrey Lynn. Student, Art League LA, 1964-68, Valley Coll., 1966-69. Designer, sculpture, glazer Al Hardy, Burbank, Calif., 1951-53; budget coord. Los Angeles County, North Hollywood, Calif., 1953; writer Intermountain Contractor, Salt Lake City, 1954-56; artist, instr. Art League LA, Van Nuys, Calif., 1966—, Sylmar, Calif., 1966—; jewelry designer, artist, 1968—. Rep. for State of Calif. Presdl. Arts Program, Washington. Contbr. articles to art publs.; films, children's books, album covers; featured in many books and publs. western art; collector plates, Danbury Mint, Norwalk, Conn., 1995—, other pub. cos., installations of murals worldwide, exhibitions include Gene Autry Western Heritage Mus., LA, Lancaster Mus. Art, Ronald Reagan Libr., Simi, Calif., Las Vegas (Nev.) Art Mus., Chas Russell Mus., China, Learnin' Tree, Boulder, Colo., Scafa, other cos. Mem.: Wildlife Waystation, Oil Painters Am., Internat. Art and Culture Assn., Women Artists of West (bd. dirs. 1971—73, pres. 1974—77, v.p. 1978—), Audubon Soc. Avocations: birdwatching, environmental activities, sports, stained glass, stamp collecting/philately. Office Phone: 818-419-0483. Personal E-mail: jwartist1@aol.com.

WRIGHT, JOHM W., social studies educator; b. Atlanta, July 23, 1969; m. Mona May Wright, Feb. 14, 2003. BA, Berry Coll., Rome, GA, 1991; MFA, U. Ga., Athens, 1995; PhD, La. State U., Baton Rouge, 2006. Asst. prof. comm. & theatre U. Wisconsin-Manitowoc, 2004—; tchr. tech. dir. Westridge Sch., Pasadena, Calif., 1995—98. Contbr. chapters to books. Campaign mgr. Com. Elect Steve Farrow GA State Senate, Dalton, Ga., 1992. Mem.: Assn. Theatre Higher Edn. Avocations: writing, acting.

WRIGHT, JOHN, classics educator; b. NYC, Mar. 9, 1941; s. Henry and Dorothy (Chaya) W.; m. Ellen Faber, June 16, 1962; children: Jennifer, Emily. BA, Swarthmore Coll., 1962; MA, Ind. U., 1964, PhD, 1971. Instr. classics U. Rochester, NY, 1968—72, asst. prof., 1972—75; assoc. prof. Northwestern U., Evanston, Ill., 1975-77, prof., 1977—83, dept. chmn., 1978—97, 2000—01, John Evans prof. Latin lang. and lit., 1983—2001, prof. emeritus in svc., 2002—05, prof. emeritus, 2005—. Author: The Play of Antichrist, 1967, Dancing in Chains: The Stylistic Unity of the Comoedia Palliata, 1974, The Life of Cola de Rienzo, 1975, Essays on the Iliad: Selected Modern Criticism, 1978, Plautus: Curculio, Introduction and Notes, 1981, rev. edit., 1993, Ralph Stanley and the Clinch Mountain Boys: A Discography, 1983, The Five-String Banjo Stanley Style, 1984, rev. edit. (Clyde Pharr) Homeric Greek: A Book for Beginners, 1985, It's the Hardest Music in the World to Play: The Ralph Stanley Story in His Own Words, 1987, Traveling the High Way Home: Ralph Stanley and the World of Traditional Bluegrass Music, 1993; albums Everything She Asks For, 1993, Traveling the High Way Home, 1995, Promises, 1996, Ellen and John Wright 1, Ellen and John Wright 2, 1998, I Shook Hands with Eleanor Roosevelt, 2004; contbr. articles to profl. jours. Fellow Am. Acad. Rome, 1966-68; Nat. Endowment Humanities Younger humanist fellow, 1973-74; named to Honorable Order of Ky. Colonels; recipient songwriting prize Santa Fe Bluegrass and Old Time Music Festival, 1996. Mem.: Am. Fedn. of Musicians, Local 1000, BMI, Nat. Acad. Recording Arts and Scis., Am. Acad. in Rome Soc. of Fellows, Internat. Bluegrass Music Assn. (Print Media Personality of Yr. 1994), Chgo. Area Bluegrass Assn. Home: 1137 Noyes St Evanston IL 60201-2633 Personal E-mail: jhwright@northwestern.edu.

WRIGHT, JOHN COLLINS, retired chemistry professor; b. Oak Hill, W.Va., Aug. 5, 1927; s. John C. and Irene (Collins) W.; m. Margaret Ann Cyphers, Sept. 11, 1949; children: Jeffrey Cyphers, John Timothy, Curtis Scott, Keith Alexander. BS, W.Va. Wesleyan Coll., 1948, LLD, 1974; PhD, U. Ill., 1951; DSc (hon.), U. Ala., 1979, W.Va. Inst. Tech., 1979. Research chemist Hercules, Inc., 1951-57; mem. faculty W.Va. Wesleyan Coll., 1957-64; asst. program dir. NSF, 1964-65; dean Coll. Arts and Scis., No. Ariz. U., 1966-70, W.Va. U., Morgantown, 1970-74; vice chancellor W.Va. Bd. Regents, Charleston, 1974-78; pres. U. Ala., Huntsville, 1978-88, prof. chemistry, 1988-95, prof. emeritus, 1995—; interim pres. W.Va. Coll. Grad. Studies, Institute, 1975-76. Hon. rsch. assoc. Univ. Coll., London, 1962-63; cons. NSF, 1965—, Army Sci. Bd., U.S. Army, 1979-82, Nat. Sci. Resources Ctr. Served with USNR, 1945-46. Mich. fellow Center Study Higher Edn., U. Mich., 1965-66 Mem. AAAS, NSTA. Office: 2312 Clubhouse Ave Huntsville AL 35802 Office Phone: 256-883-2272. E-mail: johnhasp@aol.com.

WRIGHT, JOHN COTTON, archivist, consultant; b. Sharon, Mass., July 27, 1928; s. George Carroll and Dorothy (Cotton) Wright; m. VerlieAnn Kapule Malina, May 23, 1978. Degree in philosophy, U. Hawaii, Manoa, 1955, MLS, 1987. Cert. archivist Acad. Archivists. Editl. asst. U. Hawaii Press, Honolulu, 1953—55; self employed Kona, Hawaii, 1956—57; adminstrv. asst. Oahu Rwy. and Land Co., Honolulu, 1958—61; asst. to chmn. Dillingham Corp., Honolulu, 1962—66; historian, archivist Bernice Pauahi Bishop Mus., Honolulu, 1966—81; pres. Wright Cons., Kailua, Hawaii, 1982—; prodn. editor Mechas Press, LLC, Honolulu, 1998—. Cons. Mariners Mus., Newport News, Va., 1967, JDR 3rd Fund, NYC, 1975, NYC, 77, Asia Found., San Francisco, 1979, San Francisco, 81. Mem.: Internat. Coun. Archives (hon.). Office: Wright Cons 361 Kaimake Loop Kailua HI 96734-2018 Office Phone: 808-261-3714.

WRIGHT, JOHN DANIEL, minister; b. Middletown, Ohio, July 30, 1984; s. Hargie and Ilene Wright. LittD (hon.), Christian Ministry Inst. Tex.; DD (hon.), St. Luke Evang. Sch. Bibl. Studies. Ordained minister 2001, lic. to preach 2003, evangelist 2003. Pres., CEO, Johnsboro Online, Richmond, Ky.; founder Am. Assoc. Wedding Officiants. Recipient Ky. Col., The Hon. Paul E. Patton, Gov. Ky., 2002. Mem.: Masons. Republican. Home: PO Box 236 Richmond KY 40476-0236 Personal E-mail: jdw@jdwright.us.

WRIGHT, JOHN F., state supreme court justice; BS, U. Nebr., 1967, JD, 1970. Atty. Wright & Simmons, 1970-84, Wright, Sorensen & Brower, 1984-91; mem., coord. Commn. on Post Secondary Edn., 1991-92; judge Nebr. Ct. Appeals, 1992-94; assoc. justice Nebr. Supreme Ct., 1994—. Chmn. bd. dirs. Panhandle Legal Svcs., 1970. Mem. Scottsbluff Bd. Edn., 1980-87, pres., 1984, 86. Served with U.S. Army, 1970, Nebr. N.G., 1970-76. Recipient Friend of Edn. award Scottsbluff Edn. Assn., 1992. Office: Nebr Supreme Ct 2207 State Capitol PO Box 98910 Lincoln NE 68509-8910*

WRIGHT, JOSEPH ROBERT, JR., corporate executive; b. Tulsa, Sept. 24, 1938; s. Joe Robert and Ann Helen (Cech) W. BS, Colo. Sch. Mines, 1961; M.I.A., Yale U., 1964. V.p. Booz, Allen & Hamilton, 1965-71; dep. dir. Bur. Census, Dept. Commerce, 1971-72; dep. adminstr. Social and Econ. Statis. Adminstrn., 1972-73, acting asst. sec. econ. affairs, 1973; asst. sec. adminstr. Dept. Agr., 1973-76; pres. Citicorp Retail Inc. and Retail Consumer Svcs. Inc., NYC, Citicorp, Inc., NYC, 1976—81; dep. sec. Dept. Commerce, Washington, 1981—82; dep. dir. Office Mgmt. and Budget, Washington, 1982-88; chmn. Pres.'s Coun. on Integrity and Efficiency, 1982-89, Pres.'s Coun. on Mgmt. Improvement, 1984-89; dir. Office Mgmt. and Budget, 1988-89; exec. v.p., vice chmn., bd. dirs. W.R. Grace & Co., NYC, 1989-94; chmn. Grace Energy, Inc., 1989—94, Grace Environ,. Inc., 1989—94; chmn., CEO, dir. AmTec, Inc., NYC, 1994—2000, Chron. GRC, Internat., 1997—2000, Co-Chron. Baker & Taylor, 1996—2002; vice chmn. Terremark Worldwide, 2000—. Fed. co-chmn. Coastal Plains Regional Commn., 1981-82, Four Corners Regional Commn., 1981-82, New Eng. Regional Commn., 1981-82, Old West Regional Commn., 1981-82, Pacific N.W. Regional Commn., 1981-82, S.W. Border Regional Commn., 1981-82; co-chmn. Baker & Taylor, 1996-2002; chmn. GRC Internat., 1997-2000; vice chmn. Jefferson Consulting, 1998-2004; pres., CEO, dir. PanAmSat Inc., 2001-06; bd. dirs. Travelers, 1990-99, Harcourt Bruce Janovich, 1990-92, GRC Internat., 1994-99, Baker & Taylor, 1995-2002, PanAmSat Inc., 1995-2006, VersoTech, 1998-2004, Titan Corp., 2000-05, AT&T Govt. Markets, 2000-05, Terremark Worldwide, 2000—, Sci. Games Inc., 2004—, Intelsat Ltd., 2006-08; chmn., dir. Intelsat, Ltd., Bermuda, NYC, 2006—; vice chmn. Sci. Games 2008-09, pres., CEO 2009. Mem. Pres. Export Coun., 1989-93, adv. bd. Coun. for Excellence in Govt., 1988-96; trustee Hampton U., 1990-98; mem. Pres.'s Commn. on Postal Reform, 2004-05; mem. Pres.'s Nat. Security Telecomm. Adv. Coun., 2005-09; mem. FCC Network Reliability and Interoperability Coun., FCC Media Security and Reliability Coun.; mem. Def. Bus. Bd., 2007—. 1st lt. AUS, 1963—65. Recipient Disting. Achievement medal Colo. Sch. Mines, 1985, Pres.'s Citizens award and medal, 1989; named Govt. Exec. of Yr. Govt. Computer News Mag., 1988. Mem. Nat. Acad. Pub. Adminstrn. (mem. com. for responsible fed. budget), Colo. Sch. Mines Alumni Assn., Chief Execs. Orgn., World Bus. Coun., Coun. on Fgn. Rels., Reagan Alumni Assn., NY Econ. Club, Bridge Golf Club (NY), Lost Tree Country Club (Fla.). Home: 10 Gracie Sq Apt 7G New York NY 10028-8031 Office: Scientific Games 750 Lexington Ave 25th Fl New York NY 10022 Office Phone: 212-318-9173.

WRIGHT, JOSEPHINE ROSA BEATRICE, musicologist; b. Detroit, Sept. 5, 1942; d. Joseph Le Vander and Eva Lee Garrison W.; Mus.B., U. Mo., Columbia, 1963, M.A., 1967; Mus.M., Pius XII Acad., Florence, Italy, 1964; Ph.D., N.Y.U., 1975. Instr. music York Coll., CUNY, 1972-75, asst. prof., 1975; asst. prof. Afro-Am. studies in musicology Harvard U., Cambridge, Mass., 1976-81; assoc. dir. integration of Afro-Am. folk arts with music project, Nat. Endowment Humanities, 1979-82; assoc. prof. music and Black studies Coll. of Wooster, 1981-90, prof. music and Black studies, 1991-2000, prof. Music and The Josephine Lincoln Morris prof. Black studies, 2000-, chair Africana studies, 2002—; panelist, cons. on music Mass. Coun. of Arts and Humanities, 1978-80; cons. Nat. Endowment Humanities, 1982-83, 87, 89, 90, Ohio Humanities Coun., 1986; apptd. mem. Nat. Artistic Directorate, Am. Classical Music Hall of Fame, Cin. Author: Ignatius Sancho (1729-1780), An Early African Composer in England: The Collected Edition of His Music in Facsimile, 1981; editor: Am. Music, 1993-97, Music in African Am. Culture series, 1995—2000; editor of new music: The Black Perspective in Music, 1979-91, (with Sam Floyd) New Perspectives on Music: Essays in Honor of Eileen Southern, 1992; co-editor: The Bicentennial Issue of The Black Perspective in Music, 1976, (with Eileen Southern) African-American Traditions in Song, Sermon, Tale and Dance, 1991, (with Eileen Southern) Images: Iconography of Music in African-American Culture, 2000; mem. editl. bd. Jour. Am. Musicol. Soc., 2003, Am. Music, 2004, Jour. Soc. for Am. Music, 2006—; contbr. articles to profl. jours. Sr. advisor Oxford U. Press. Mem. Am. Musicol. Soc. (dir.-at-large 1998-2000), Soc. Am. Music (bd. dirs.), Nat. Coun. for black studies, U. Mo. Faculty of Arts and Sci. Alumni Assn. (trustee 1982-85), Pi Kappa Lambda. Democrat. Anglican. Office Phone: 330-263-2044. Business E-Mail: jwright@wooster.edu.

WRIGHT, JUDITH MARGARET, law librarian, educator, dean; b. Jackson, Tenn., Aug. 16, 1944; d. Joseph Clarence and Mary Catherine (Key) Wright; m. Mark A. Johnson, Apr. 17, 1976; children: Paul, Michael. BS, U. Memphis, 1966; MA, U. Chgo., 1971; JD, DePaul U., 1980. Bar: Ill. 1980. Librarian Oceanway Sch., Jacksonville, Fla., 1966-67; program dir. ARC, South Vietnam, 1967-68; documents and reference librarian D'Angelo Law Library, U. Chgo., 1970-74, reference librarian, 1974-77, dir., lectr. in law, 1980—2000, law libr., assoc. dean for libr. and info. svcs., lectr. in law, 2000—. Mem. adv. bd. Legal Reference Svcs. Quar., 1981—. Mem.: Chgo. Assn. Law Libraries, Am. Assn. Law Libraries, ABA. Democrat. Methodist. Office: U Chgo Law Sch D'Angelo Law Libr 1111 E 60th St Chicago IL 60637-2745 Home Phone: 773-947-0282; Office Phone: 773-702-9616. Office Fax: 773-702-2889. Business E-Mail: jm-wright@uchicago.edu.

WRIGHT, JUDITH RAE, retired accountant; b. Paoli, Ind., Feb. 16, 1929; d. Samuel Earl and Bernice Louise (Lomax) Hudelson; m. James Edward Walters, July 11, 1947 (div. June 1971); children: Jamie Jo, Jennifer Rae; m. George Ralph Wright, Feb. 20, 1972 (dec. Apr. 1977). Student, Northwood Inst., West Baden, Ind., 1968-69, Ind. U.-Purdue U., Indpls., 1972-77. Acct. Ind. Hwy. Commn., Indpls., 1969—75, Ind. Dept. Correction, Indpls., 1975—76, Ind. Dept. Pub. Welfare, Indpls., 1976-78, Ind. Office Social Svcs., Indpls., 1978-79; acct. supr. Ind. Dept. Pub. Welfare, Indpls., 1979-92; ret., 1992. Mem. First Christian Ch. Recipient Gov.'s Spl. Achievement award, 1992. Mem. Assn. Govt. Accts., Am. Legion Aux., Order of Eastern Star, Kappa Kappa Kappa. Home Phone: 765-349-9252.

WRIGHT, JUDY A., science educator; MEd, U. Phoenix. Educator Calhoun Christian Sch., Battle Creek, Mich., 1989—2008. Pride grant, Kellogg Found., 2002, 2006. Office: Calhoun Christian Sch 20 S Woodrow Battle Creek MI 49015

WRIGHT, KATHLEEN M., literature and language professor; MS in English, SUNY, Buffalo, 1973. Cert. tchr. NY. Prof. English Peace Corps, Seoul, Republic of Korea, 1973—75; prof. lit. & English SUNY Orange, Middletown, NY, 1977—. Recipient SUNY Chancellor's award, 1992, Human Rights award, Orange County, 1999, Tchr. Appreciation award, SUNY Orange Student Senate, 2000, Fulbright Scholar awards; grants, NEH, 2005. Mem.: Asian Studies Devel. Program, Hawaii, CC Humanities Assn. Achievements include development of courses in L.Am. Literature and Internat. Lit.: Non-European. Office: SUNY Orange 115 South St Middletown NY 10940 Business E-Mail: kathleen.wright@sunyorange.edu.

WRIGHT, KATIE HARPER, educational administrator, journalist; b. Crawfordsville, Ark., Oct. 5, 1923; d. James Hale and Connie Mary (Locke) Harper; m. Marvin Wright, Mar. 21, 1952; 1 child, Virginia K. Jordan. BA, U. Ill., 1944, MEd, 1959; EdD, St. Louis U., 1979. Elem.

and spl. edn. tchr. East St. Louis (Ill.) Pub. Schs., 1944-65, dir. Dist. 189 Instrnl. Materials Program, 1965-71, dir. spl. edn. Dists. 188, 189, 1971-77, asst. supt. programs, 1977-79; interim supt. East St. Louis Sch. Dist. 189, 1993-94. Adj. faculty Harris/Stowe State Coll., 1980, adj. prof. edn. emeritus; mem. staff St. Louis U., 1989—; interim supt. Dist. 189 Schs., 1994—; mem. Pres.'s Commn. on Excellence in Spl. Edn. Author: Delta Sigma Theta/East St. Louis Chapter History, 1992; contbr. articles to profl. jours.; feature writer St. Louis Argus Newspaper, 1979—. Mem. Ill. Commn. on Children, 1973-85, East St. Louis Bd. Election Comms., East St. Louis Fin. Adv. Authority, 1999—; pres. bd. dirs. St. Clair County Mental Health Ctr., 1970-72, 87—; bd. dirs. River Bluff coun. Girl Scouts USA, 1979—, nat. bd. dirs., 1981-84; bd. dirs. Jackie Joyner-Kersee Youth Ctr. Found., 1991—, United Way, 1979—, Urban League, 1979—, Provident Counseling Ctr., 1995-98; pres. bd. trustees East St. Louis Pub. Libr., 1972-77; pres., bd. dirs. St. Clair County Mental Health Ctrs., 1987; mem. adv. bd. Magna Bank; charter mem. Coalition of 100 Black Women; mem. coord. coun. ethnic affairs Synod of Mid-Am., Presbyn. Ch. U.S.A.; mem. Ill. Dept. Corrections Sch. Bd., 1995—; charter mem. Metro East Links Group, Gateway chpt. The Links, Inc.; mem. Ill. Minority/Female Bus. Coun., 1991—; mem. Pres.'s Commn. on Excellence in Spl. Edn., 2001--. Recipient of more than 150 awards including Lamp of Learning award East St. Louis Jr. Wednesday Club, 1965, Outstanding Working Woman award Downtown St. Louis, Inc., 1967, Ill. State citation for ednl. document Love is Not Enough, 1974, Delta Sigma Theta citation for document Good Works, 1979, Girl Scout Thanks badge, 1982, award Nat. Coun. Negro Women, 1983, Cmty. Svc. award Met. East Bar Assn., 1983, Journalist award Sigma Gamma Rho, Spelman Coll. Alumni award, 1990, A World of Difference award, 1990, 92, Edn. award St. Louis, YWCA, 1991, SIU-E-Kimmel award, 1991, St. Clair County Mental Health award, 1992, Gateway East Met. Ministry Dr. M.L. King award, 1993, Nat. Coun. Negro Women Black Leader of Yr., 1995, Disting. Alumni award U. Ill., 1996, Pioneer award Mosque 28B, 2000, Tri Del Globe award, 2001, Urban League Merit award, 2002, Ill. Office of Edn. award, 2002, Eugene B. Redmond Writers Club award, 2002, NFPW Quest award, 2004, Liberty Bell award St. Clair County Bar Assocs., 2005, St. Clair County Bar Assn. award, 2005, Remarkable St. Louisian award, 2007, United Way award, 2008; named Woman of Achievement, St. Louis Globe Democrat, 1974, Outstanding Adminstr. So. Region III Office Edn., 1975, Woman of Yr. in Edn. St. Clair County YWCA, 1987, Nat. Top Lady of Yr., 1988, Disting. Alumnus U. Ill., 1996, Citizen Amb., South Africa, 1996, sch. named after her East St. Louis Sch., 2005; named to Vashon H.S. Hall of Fame, 1989, Sr. Illinoisan Hall of Fame, 1997; East St. Louis Elem. Sch. named for Dr. Katie Harper Wright, 2005, St. Andrews Ageless-Remarkable St. Louisans award, 2007, First Place prize Nat. Fedn. Press Women, 2007. Mem. Am. Librs. Trustees Assn. (regional v.p. 1978-79, 92, nat. sec. 1979-80), Ill. Commn. on Children, Mensa, Coun. for Exceptional Children (mem. pres.'s commn. excellence spl. edn.), Top Ladies of Distinction (pres. 1987-91, nat. editor 1991—, Journalism award 1992, Media award 1992), Delta Sigma Theta (chpt. pres. 1960-62, Letters award 2000), Kappa Delta Pi (pres. So. Ill. U. chpt. 1973-74), Phi Delta Kappa (Svc. Key award 1984, chpt. pres. 1984-85), Iota Phi Lambda, Phi Lambda Theta (chpt. pres. 1985-87), East St. Louis Women's Club (pres. 1973-75). Republican. Home: 733 N 40th St East Saint Louis IL 62205-2138

WRIGHT, KENNETH BROOKS, lawyer; b. Whittier, Calif., June 5, 1934; s. Albert Harold and Marian (Schwey) W.; m. Sandra Beryl Smith, June 20, 1959; children: Margo Teresa, Daniel Brooks, John Waugh. BA cum laude, Pomona Coll., 1956; JD, Stanford U., 1960. Bar: Calif. 1961, U.S. Supreme Ct. 1979. Assoc., then ptnr. Lawler, Felix & Hall, 1961—77; ptnr. Morgan, Lewis & Bockius, LA, 1978—99, counsel, 1999—2003, ret. ptnr., 2004. Tchg. team leader Nat. Inst. Trial Advocacy, 1978-80; governing com. Calif. Continuing Edn. Bar, 1973-77, chmn., 1975-76; nat. panel arbitrators Am. Arbitration Assn., 1970-91; lectr. ABA Sect. Litig. Nat. Inst., 1979-86; bd. dirs. L.A. Internat. Comml. Arbitration Ctr. Chmn. bd. editors: Am. Bar Jour, 1977-81. Pres. Pomona Coll. Alumni Assn., 1970-71; pres. parent tchr. coun. Campbell Hall Sch., 1973-74, bd. dirs., vice chmn., 1994—; counsel Vol. League San Fernando Valley, 1979-81; chmn. sect. adminstrn. justice Town Hall of Calif., 1970-71; sr. warden Episcopal Ch., 1973-74. Served with U.S. Army, 1956-57. Mem. ABA (dir. programs litig. sect. 1977-81, coun. 1982-88, standing com on comm. 1978-88, chmn. 1987-88, chmn. sect. book pub. com. 1986-89, pres. fellows young lawyers 1985-86, bd. dirs. 1980-89), Internat. Bar Assn., Assn. Bus. Trial Lawyers (chair com. alt. dispute resolution 1991-93, bd. dirs. 1993-96), Am. Law Inst., Am. Bar Found., State Bar Calif. (gov. com. continuing edn. bar 1972-77, chmn. 1975-76), Conf. Barristers (exec. com. 1966-69, 1st v.p. 1969), L.A. County Bar Assn. (com. judiciary 1981-83, chmn. CLE adv. com. 1989-91, vice-chmn. CLE com. 1991-93, bd. dirs. L.A. Lawyers 1989-94), L.A. County Bar Found. (bd. dirs., trustee 1993-99, exec. com. internat. sect. 1996-99), Jonathan Club, Phi Beta Kappa. Republican. Avocations: skiing, tennis. Home: 824 Foothill Ln Ojai CA 93023 Office: Morgan Lewis & Bockius 300 S Grand Ave Los Angeles CA 90071-3109

WRIGHT, KIRBY MICHAEL, writer, editor; b. Honolulu, Sept. 1, 1955; s. Harold Stanley and June Gertrude (McCormack) W.; m. Darcy Laureen Mobraaten, Dec. 28, 1991. BA, U. Calif., San Diego, 1983; MFA, San Francisco State U., 1994. Pub. rels. dir. Winners Circle Resorts, Carlsbad, Calif., 1987-90; instr. Palo Alto (Calif.) Adult Sch., 1994-95; writer GT Prodn. Co., Palo Alto, 1995-96, editor, 1997—. Author: The Rainbow Warrior, 1998; (screenplay) Gordon & Al, 1996; (dramatic monologue) Blue Mesa Review, 1994 (1st pl. award Browning Soc. 1993, 94); (play) Houdini, 1999; (novel) Ulua Lines, 2000, Punahou Blues, 2005, Molokai Nui Ahina, 2007; (poetry) Before the City, 2003. Rschr. Ctr. for Auto Safety, Washington, 1980; advisor SAT Success, Palo Alto, 1998. Recipient Poetry prize Ann Fields Trust, San Francisco, 1993, 1st pl. Poets award Acad. Am. Poets, San Francisco, 1993, 1st pl. San Diego Book awards, 2002. Fellow Arts Coun. Santa Clara County, Arts Coun. Silicon Valley. Democrat. Roman Catholic. Avocations: boxing, surfing, gourmet cooking. Home: 1604 Marbella Dr Vista CA 92081 Home Phone: 760-727-2850. Personal E-mail: kibs33@yahoo.com.

WRIGHT, LARRY JAN, epidemiologist; s. J. Evan and Mary Bluemel Wright; m. LaVonda Eddington, June 17, 1960; children: Deborah Hamilton, Karl Larry, Tana Lynn. BS, U. Utah, Salt Lake City, 1960, MD, 1964. Diplomate Am. Bd. Internal Medicine, 1972. Intern, resident on ward medicine Barnes Hosp. Wash. U., St. Louis, 1964—66; clin. assoc. Nat. Inst. Allergy and Infectious Diseases, Bethesda, Md., 1966—68; sr. med. resident U. Wash. Hosps., Seattle, 1968—69; clin. infectious disease fellow U. Wash., Seattle, 1969—71; pvt. practice Inter-Mountain Clinic, Salt Lake City, 1971—89; clin. dir. microbiology, virology, and molecular laboratories LDS Hosp. and Urban Ctrl. Region, Salt Lake City, 1989—2000, infectious disease cons., epidemiology rschr., 1989—. Pres. InterMountain Clinic, Inc, Salt Lake City, 1981—86; vice chmn. dept. medicine LDS Hosp., Salt Lake City, 1988—89, pres. med. staff, 1989—90; bd. govs. IHC Corp., Salt Lake City, 1989—91. Contbr. articles to profl. jours. Governing bd. Work Activity Ctr. for Adults with Disabilities, Salt Lake City, 1992—98. Lt. comdr. USPHS, 1966—68. Nat. Found. scholar, March of Dimes, 1960—64. Fellow: ACP, Infectious Disease Soc. Am.; mem.: Am. Soc. for Internal Medicine, Am. Soc. for Microbiology, Alpha Omega Alpha, Phi Beta Kappa. Achievements include research in infectious diseases. Avocations: sailing, skiing, golf, hiking, travel. Office: LDS Hosp 370 9th Ave Salt Lake City UT 84103

WRIGHT, LAURA H., corporate financial executive, air transportation executive; m. Randy Wright; children: Lindsay, Jeffrey. BS in Accounting, U. North Tex., MS in Accounting, 1982. CPA. Tax mgr. Arthur Young & Co., Dallas; dir. corp. taxation SW Airlines Co., 1988—90, dir. corp. fin., 1990—95, asst. treas., 1995—98, treas., 1998—2004, v.p., fin., 2001—04, sr. v.p., fin., CFO, 2004—. Office: Southwest Airlines Co 2702 Love Field Dr Dallas TX 75235 Office Phone: 214-792-4000. Office Fax: 214-792-5015.*

WRIGHT, LILYAN BOYD, physical education educator; b. Upland, Pa., May 11, 1920; d. Albert Verlenden and Mabel (Warburton) Boyd; m. Richard P. Wright, Oct. 23, 1942; 1 child, Nicki Wright Vanek. BS, Temple U., 1942, MEd, 1946; EdD, Rutgers U., 1972. Tchr. health and phys. edn. Woodbury (N.J.) High Sch., 1942-43, Glen-Nor High Sch., Glenolden, Pa., 1944-46, Chester (Pa.) High Sch., 1946-54; chmn. women's dept. health and phys. edn. Union (N.J.) High Sch., 1954-61; with Trenton State Coll., 1961-90, head women's program health and phys. edn., 1967-77, chmn. dept. health, phys. edn. and recreation, 1977-86, adj. faculty mem., 1990-92, prof. emeritus, 1991—. Mem. N.J. State Com. Div. Girls and Women's Sports, 1958-80; chmn. New Atlantic Field Hockey Sectional Umpiring, 1981-85; chmn. New Atlantic Field Hockey Assn., 1985-90; with recreation after sch. program Newport Counseling Ctrl., 1992-93; vol. coach field hockey Goshen-Lempster Coop. Sch., 1995-2007. Vol. tchr. exercise Woodlawn Nursing Home, Newport, NH, 2000—; vol. tchr. NH strong living program Newport Sr. Ctr., 1999—; vol. tchr. aerobics Newport Rec. Ctr., 1993—; trustee Olive Pettis Libr., Goshen, NH, 1992—; mem. budget com. City Goshen, 1999—; mem. vestry Ch. Epiphany, Newport, 1992—2007, sr. warden, 1995—99, 2002—05; vestry St. Luke's Episc. Ch., 1988—91, clk. vestry, 2000—02; mem. dist. ednl. improvement team Goshen-Lempster Sch. Dist., 1995—2000, mem. sch. bd., 2001—06; chmn. trustees Olive Pettis Libr., 1998—. Recipient U.S. Field Hockey Assn. award, 1989, Joseph D. Vaughan award NH Com. Aging, 2001, Rosabel Koss Honor award Nat. Com. Aging and Adult Devel., 2003, Vol. Lifetime award Newport Recreation Assn., 2005; ARC Scholarship in her honor N.J. Athletic Assn. Girls, 1971; named to Hall of Fame, Temple U., 1976, Trenton State Coll., NJ, 2000, John H. Clark's Officials Hall Fame, NH, 2004; named Nat. Honorary and Emeritus Field Hockey Umpire Mem. AAHPERD (chmn. Ea. Dist. Assn. Div. Girls and Women's Sports, sec. to coun. for svcs. Ea. Dist. Assn. 1979-80, chmn. 1980-81, chair com. on Aging and Adult Devel. of Ea. Dist. 1993-97, 2001-05, NJ rep. to council for svcs. 1984-85, Honor Fellow award 1986), N.J. AHPER (pres. 1974-75, past pres. 1975-76, v.p. phys. edn. div., parliamentarian 1990-2005, Disting. Svc. and Leadership award 1969, 93, Honor Fellow award 1977, Presdl. Citation award 1993, 95-99, 2002-04, Disting. Leadership award 1994), NJ Women's Lacrosse Assn. (umpiring chmn. 1972-76), Nat. Assn. Phys. Edn. in Higher Edn., Ea. Assn. Phys. Edn. Coll. Women, North Jersey, Ctrl. Jersey Bds. Women's Ofcls., Chester Am. Federation of tchrs.(pres. 1949-54), U.S. Field Hockey Assn. (exec. com., chair honorary umpire award com. 1992), North Jersey Field Hockey Assn. (past pres.), NH Field Hockey Umpires' Assn., No. NH Lacrosse Officials Bd., US Women's Lacrosse Assn. (Honorary and Emeritus Umpiring Rating award), Kappa Delta Epsilon, Delta Psi Kappa (past pres. Phila. alumni chpt.), Kappa Delta Pi. Home: PO Box 239 Goshen NH 03752-0239

WRIGHT, LORI DUNKLE, musician, educator; b. Kettering, Ohio, Sept. 17, 1967; d. Robert Kean and Elaine Mary Dunkle; m. Douglas Allan Wright, Aug. 1, 1992; 1 child, Rebecca Ann. MusB in Edn., Ohio State U., 1989, MA, 2001. Tchg. Cert., K12 Music Ohio Dept. of Edn., 1989. Orch. dir. Kent City Schs., Ohio, 1990—91, Worthington City Schs., Columbus, Ohio, 1991—. Clinician Ministry of Edn., Santiago, Chile, 2002; cellist, asst. prin. Springfield Symphony Orch., Ohio, 1991—; state treas. Ohio Music Edn. Assn., 2004—. Mem.: NEA (assoc.), Am. Fedn. of Musicians (assoc.), Music Edn. Nat. Conf. (assoc.; treas., state of ohio 2004—), Am. String Tchrs. Assn. (assoc.), Ohio State U. Alumni Assn. (life), Phi Kappa Phi (life), Delta Omicron (life). Conservative-R. Christian. Avocations: travel, golf, camping, hiking, backpacking.

WRIGHT, MADELEINE ELAINE PATE, humanities educator; d. Julian Everette and Mermize Sanders Pate; m. Booker Taliaferro Wright, May 17, 1969; children: Kijana Kamal, Nyala Ayanna. PhD, U. Mich., Ann Arbor, 1975. Lectr. U. Mich. Sch. Pub. Health, 1970—75; instr. Houston CC, 1978—. Bd. mem. CG Jung Ctr., Houston, 1985—90. Author: (non fiction) Sisters Helping Sisters; dir.: (African Dance Soc.) Created Comm. Cmty. African Dance Workshops, (girl's rites of passage mentoring prog.) (Impact Award, 1998). Active mem. and officer The Links Inc., Houston, 1988—2008. Recipient Outstanding Tchr., Houston CC, 1991. Mem.: APA. Baptist. Avocations: dance, yoga, travel. Office: Houston CC 1300 Holman Houston TX 77004 Office Phone: 713-718-6245. Personal E-mail: dearmadeleine@me.com. Business E-Mail: madeleine.wright@hccs.edu.

WRIGHT, MARGARET HAGEN, computer scientist, administrator; b. San Francisco, Feb. 18, 1944; m. 1965; 1 child. BS in Math. with distinction, Stanford U., 1964, MS in Computer Sci., 1965, PhD in Computer Sci., 1976; D in Math. (hon.), U. Waterloo, 2003. Rsch. assoc., dept. ops. rsch. Stanford U., 1976—81, sr. rsch. assoc., dept. ops. rsch., 1981—88; mem. tech. staff Bell Lab., Lucent Tech., 1988—93, disting. mem. tech. staff, 1993—2001, head, sci. computing rsch. dept., 1997—2000; Silver prof. computer sci., Courant Inst. Math. Sci. NYU, 2001—, chair, dept. computer sci., Courant Inst. Math. Sci., 2005—. Adv. com. Directorate Math. and Physical Sci., Nat. Sci. Found., 1994—98, chair., 1997—98; sci. adv. com. Math. Sciences Rsch. Inst., Berkeley, Calif.; lectr. in field. Assoc. editor Jour. Sci. Stats. Computer Programming, Math. Programming, Soc. Indsl. and Applied Math. Jour. on Sci. Computing, editor-in-chief Soc. Indsl. and Applied Math. Rev., Soc. Indsl. and Applied Math. Jour. on Optmization. Fellow Inst. Ops. Rsch. and Mgmt. Scis.; mem. Am. Acad. Arts and Scis., NAE (vice chair mem. com. 2004, chair mem. com. 2005), NAS, Assn. Computing Machinery (bd. dirs. numerical analysis assn. spl. interest group), Soc. Indsl. and Applied Math. (pres. 1995-96, Disting. Svc. to Profession award 2000), Math. Programming Soc., Am. Math. Soc. (Disting. Pub. Svc. award 2001). Achievements include research contributing to enlarged knowledge of methods for nonlinear programming, particularly unconstrained; linearly constrained and nonlinearly constrained optimization; mathematical software, numerical linear algebra; software library development. Office: NYU Courant Inst Math Scis 251 Mercer St New York NY 10012 Office Phone: 212-998-3056. Office Fax: 212-995-3883. Business E-Mail: mhw@cs.nyu.edu.

WRIGHT, MARSHALL, manufacturing executive, diplomat; b. El Dorado, Ark., July 14, 1926; s. John Harvey and Helen Vaughan (Williams) W.; m. Mable Olean Johnson, Sept. 12, 1950 (dec. June 1989); children: William Marshall, Jefferson Vaughan; m. Lind Grose-close Vaughan, Mar. 31, 1990. Student, U. Ark., 1946-48, Cornell U., 1957-58; BS in Fgn. Service, Georgetown U., 1951. Joined U.S. Fgn. Service, 1953; vice consul Egypt, 1953-55; adminstrv. officer Can., 1956; econ. officer Burma, 1958-60; polit. officer Thailand, 1966-67; spokesman for State Dept., 1964-66; country dir. for Philippines, 1969; sr. mem. NSC, 1967-68, dir. long range planning, 1970-72; asst. sec. state for congl. relations, 1972-74; sr. fellow Nat. War Coll., 1969-70; v.p. govt. affairs Eaton Corp., 1974-76, v.p. pub. affairs, 1976-80, v.p. corp. affairs, 1980-91. Chmn. Cleve. ARC; trustee Cleve. Orch., Cleve. Inst. Music; chmn. Cleve. Com. Fgn. Rels.; vice chmn. Govtl. Rsch. Inst.; mem. Conf. Bd. Pub. Affairs Rsch. Coun., MAPI, Pub. Affairs Coun.; bd. dirs. Cleveland Town Hall, Bus. Industry Polit. action Com. With USMC, 1944-46. Recipient Meritorious Service award State Dept., 1966, Distinguished Service award, 1972 Mem. Am. Fgn. Svc. Assn., Met. Club, Dacor, Mayfield Country, Union, Moss Creek Golf Club, Berkeley Hall Golf Club. Home: 22 Cedar Ln Hilton Head Island SC 29926-1025 Home Phone: 843-837-7474; Office Phone: 843-837-7474. Personal E-mail: wmmwright@gmail.com.

WRIGHT, MARY ANN, automotive components company executive; b. Dearborn, Mich. B in Econs. and Internat. Bus., U. Mich., Ann Arbor; MS in Engring., U. Mich.; MBA, Wayne State U., Detroit. Various positions in fin., product and bus. planning, and engring. Ford Motor Co., Dearborn, Mich., 1988—2005, lead engr. Ford Taurus and Mercury Sable redesign and the Lincoln LS, 2000, chief engr. Ford Escape Hybrid, 2005, dir. sustainable mobility techs. and hybrid vehicle programs; exec. v.p. engring., product devel., comml., and program mgmt. Collins & Aikman Corp., Southfield, Mich., 2006—07; v.p., gen. mgr. hybrid sys. Johnson Controls Power Solutions, 2007—; CEO Johnson Controls-Saft Advanced Power Solutions, 2007—. Mem. bd. govs. Argonne Nat. Lab. UChicago Argonne; mem. bd. dirs. Electric Drive Transp. Assn., Washington. Coach, mentor FIRST Robotics; mem. exec. bd. Greater Milw. YMCA. Named one of Leading 100 Women in the Automotive Industry, Automotive News, 50 Women to Watch, The Wall St. Jour., 2008. Office: Johnson Controls Power Solutions 5757 N Green Bay Ave Glendale WI 53204*

WRIGHT, MARY ELLEN, theater educator; b. Commerce, Tex. d. Joseph Perry and Ora Berniece Gentry; m. James Hatfield; children: Christopher Collin, Sarah Allison Wright Metzger. BA summa cum laude, U. Tex., Tyler, 1988, MAIS, 1991—91; PhD, Tex. Tech U., Lubbock, 2001. Lectr. U. Tex. at Tyler, 1994—95, 1996—2001, asst. prof., 2002—. Adjudicator Tex. U. Interscholastic League, 1993—, St. Gregory's Sch., Tyler, 1999—; conf. planner Assn. for Theatre in Higher Edn., 1994—98; presenter in field. Costume designer (musical) Annie, (play) The Mandrake; dir.: (play) A Small Family Business, Eleemosynary; costume designer (play) Oleanna (Citation for Excellence in Costume Design, 1992); author: (play) Maggie and Mac; author: (presenter) (workshop) Creative Drama in the Classroom; costume designer (play) Othello; dir.: (play) The King Stag; costume designer (musical) The Fantasticks; dir.: (play) Art; costume designer (musical) Sound of Music, (play) Comic Potential (Citation of Excellence for Costume Design, 2001); dir.: (play) Beauty Queen of Leenane, Pygmalion; contbr. articles to profl. publs. Recipient award, Assn. for Theatre in Higher Edn., 2002, Citation of Excellence for Festival Hosting, Kennedy Ctr./Am. Coll. Theatre Festival, 1999—2000; grantee Adrian Hall Del. Project, Tex. Commn. on the Arts, 2003. Mem.: Tex. Ednl. Theatre Assn., Assn. for Theatre in Higher Edn. (conf. planner 1994—98), Alpha Chi, Phi Kappa Phi, Alpha Psi Omega (advisor 1996—2003), Gamma Phi Beta (life). Home: 556 S Fair Oaks Ave Ste # 101-411 Pasadena CA 91105 Office: Calif State LA 5151 State Univ Dr Los Angeles CA 90032 Business E-Mail: mary.wright3@calstatela.edu, ladygentry@mac.com.

WRIGHT, MARYLYN RILEY, music educator; b. Paris, Tex., Aug. 9, 1944; d. Lewis E. and EvaMae Hooten Riley; m. Bill F. Wright, Aug. 9, 1980; children: Holly Dee Jenkins, Frankie Lynn Nichols, Julie Ann Black, Caroline Kay Sellers. AA, Henderson Co. Jr. Coll., Athens, Tex., 1980; BFA, U. Tex., Tyler, 1982; MusM, East Tex. State U., Commerce, Tex., 1984; EdD, Tex. A&M U., Commerce, 2007. Cert. in lifetime tchg. Tex. State Coordinating Bd., 1982. Dir., choral music Mabank ISD, Tex., 1984—91; music dept. coord. Trinity Vally CC, Athens, Tex., 1991—. Chair, commn. rsch. and publ. Tex. Assn. Music Schs., 2008—. Composer: (songs) Fields of Life (1st Pl. award, 2007). Innovative Tchg. grant, TVCC, 1999—2000. Mem.: Tex. CC Tchrs. Assn., Tex. Music Educators Assn., Tex. Assn. Music Schs. (commn. cooperation higher edn. 2005—07), Athens Music Study Club (pres. 1995—97, treas. 1998—99). Office: Trinity Valley CC 100 Cardinal Dr Athens TX 75751 Office Fax: 903-675-6280. Business E-Mail: mwright@tvcc.edu.

WRIGHT, MINTURN TATUM, III, retired lawyer; b. Phila., Aug. 7, 1925; s. Minturn T. and Anna (Moss) Wright; m. Nonya R. Stevens, May 11, 1957; children: Minturn T., Richard S., Robert M., Marian F. BA, Yale U., 1949; LLB, U. Pa., 1952. Bar: Pa. 1953, U.S. Ct. Appeals (3d cir.) 1953, U.S. Supreme Ct. 1962. Law clk. US Ct. Appeals (3d cir.), 1952-53; assoc. Dechert LLP, Phila., 1953-61, ptnr., 1961-95, chmn., 1982-84; ret. Vis. prof. U. Pa. Law Sch., 1965—69, 1993—97; bd. dirs. Cotiga Devel. Co. Contbr. articles to profl. jours. Trustee Acad. Natural Scis., Phila., 1958—, chmn., 1976—81; trustee Marshall-Reynolds Found., Hawk Mountain Sanctuary Assn., chmn. bd. dirs., 1992—97. With US Army, 1943—46. Mem.: ABA, Phila. Bar Assn., Pa. Bar Assn., Milldam Club. Episcopalian. Office: Dechert LLP Cira Ctr 2929 Arch St Philadelphia PA 19104-2808 Office Phone: 215-994-2689.

WRIGHT, PAMELA ANN, surgeon; b. Silver Spring, Md., Mar. 6, 1964; d. Harold Bell and Geogeann Wright; m. John George Menkart, Oct. 8, 1994; children: Nicole, Matthew, Danielle. BS, U. Md., Coll. Pk., Md., 1985; MS, U. Md., Balt., 1988, MD, 1992. Diplomate Am. Bd. Surgery. Intern U. Md. Med. Ctr., Balt., 1992—93, resident, 1993—99; trauma rsch. fellow NIH, 1994—96; surgeon Horizon Surg. Group, Rockville, Md., 1999—2003, Pamela Wright MD, LLC, Bethesda, Md., 2003—. Assoc. med. dir. breast programs Suburban Hosp., Bethesda, 2006—. Fellow: ACS; mem.: Am. Soc. Breast Surgeons, Alpha Omega Alpha. Office: 6420 Rockledge Dr Ste 3700 Bethesda MD 20817 Office Phone: 301-530-5151.

WRIGHT, PATRICIA I., state official, school system administrator; BA, James Madison U.; MEd, Va. Commonwealth U.; PhD in Math. Edn., U. Va. Math. tchr. Chesterfield County Pub. Schs., Sussex County Pub. Schs.; state math. specialist Va. Dept. Edn., assoc. dir. secondary instrn., dir. secondary instrn., asst. supt. instruction, dep. supt., acting supt., chief dep. supt., supt. pub. instrn., 2008—. Office: Va Dept Edn PO Box 2120 Richmond VA 23218 Office Phone: 804-225-2023.*

WRIGHT, PETER MELDRIM, lawyer; b. Charlottesville, Va., Apr. 10, 1946; s. David McCord and Caroline Wallace (Jones) W.; m. Astrid Gabriella Mercedes Sandberg, June 4, 1972; children: David Habersham, Christian Langdon. AB, U. Ga., 1967, JD, 1972. Bar: Ga. 1972, US Dist. Ct. (no. dist.) Ga. 1972. Assoc. Jones, Bird & Howell, Atlanta, 1972-77, ptnr., 1977-82, Alston & Bird, Atlanta, 1982-2001; gen. counsel Resource Healthcare of Am., Inc., 2001—. Sec. Atlanta coun. Soc. Colonial Wars in Ga., 1985-88, dep. gov., 1989-91, mem. coun., 2003-06; mem. Soc. Cin. Ga., Savannah, historian, 1996—, v.p., 1998-2004, pres., 2004-07, v.p., 2007-. Mem. Ga. Bar Assn., Ga. Hist. Soc. (bd. curators 1993-2000, sec. 1994-98; v.p. Atlanta chpt. 1998-2000), Skidway Health and Living Svs., Inc. (chmn., dir. 2008-,dir., 2003-, pres., 2003-08), Oglethorpe Club (Savannah, Ga.), St. Andrew's Soc. Savannah. Office: Resource Healthcare Am One Buckhead Plz Ste 900 3060 Peachtree Rd NW Atlanta GA 30305

WRIGHT, RICHARD NEWPORT, III, retired engineering executive, engineering educator; b. Syracuse, NY, May 17, 1932; s. Richard Newport and Carolyn (Baker) Wright; m. Teresa Rios, Aug. 23, 1959; children: John Stannard, Carolyn Maria, Maria, Elizabeth Rebecca, Edward Newport. BCE, Syracuse U., 1953, MCE (Parcel fellow), 1955; PhD, U. Ill., 1962. Jr. engr. Pa. R.R., Phila., 1953-55; instr. civil engring. U. Ill., Urbana, 1957-62, asst. prof., 1962-65, assoc. prof., 1965-70, prof., 1970-74, adj. prof., 1974-79; chief structures sect. Bldg. Rsch. divsn. U.S. Bur. Stds., Washington, 1971—72; dep. dir. Ctr. Bldg. Tech., 1972—73, dir., 1974—91; dir. Bldg. and Fire Rsch. Lab. Nat. Inst. Stds. and Tech., 1991—99; chmn. Bd. Infrastructure and Constructed Environment, 1999—2002; ret., 2002. Pres. Internat. Coun. Bldg. Rsch., Studies and Documentation, 1983—86, dir. pratice, edn., and rsch. sustainable infrastructure, 2007—. Contbr. articles to profl. jours. Govt. ofcl., Gaithersburg, Md., 1971—99; pres. Montgomery Village Found., 1989—90, 2001—03, bd. dirs., 1985—. With AUS, 1955—57. Recipient Henry L. Michel award Industry Advancement Rsch., Civil Engring. Rsch. Found., 1999, Internat. Award, Japan Soc. Civil Engrs., 2003; named Fed. Engr. of the Yr., Nat. Soc. Profl. Engrs. Fellow: AAAS; mem.: NAE (sec. civil engring. section 2006—), ASCE (hon.). Home: 20081 Doolittle St Montgomery Village MD 20886-1354 Office: Dept of Commerce Nat Inst Standards & Tech Bldg And Fire Research Labs Gaithersburg MD 20899-0001 Personal E-mail: richard.n.wright@verizon.net.

WRIGHT, RICHARD OSCAR, III, pathologist, educator, clinical ethicist; b. La Junta, Colo., Aug. 9, 1944; s. Richard O. Jr. and Frances R. (Curtiss) W.; m. Bernale Trout, May 31, 1969; children: Lauren Diane, Richard O. IV. BS in Biology, Midwestern State U., 1966; MS in Biology, U. Houston, 1968; DO, Kans. City U., Medicine and Biosci., 1972; MA in Bioethics, Midwestern U., 2001. Cert. anatomic pathology and lab. medicine Am. Osteo. Bd. Pathology. Sr. attending pathologist Normandy Met. Hosps., St. Louis, 1977-81, Phoenix (Ariz.) Gen. Hosps., 1981-97, dir. med. edn., 1989-92, 96—; clin. asst. prof. pathology Coll. Osteo. Medicine, Western U., Pomona, Calif., 1985—; dir. labs., chmn. dept. John C. Lincoln Hosp., Deer Valley, 1997—, dir. med. edn., 1997—; v.p. Osteo. Postdoctoral Tng. Inst., Kirksville, Mo., 1998—2000. Clin. instr. pathology Ohio U. Coll. Osteo. Medicine, Athens, 1976—77; clin. prof. pathology Kirksville Coll. Osteo. Medicine, 1985—; vis. lectr. pathology New Eng. Coll. Osteo. Medicine, Biddeford, Maine, 1989—92; clin. asst. prof. pathology Midwestern U. Ariz. Coll. Osteo. Medicine, 1997—; cons. pathologist Phoenix Indian Med. Ctr., 1992—94; adv. bd. Inter Soc. Coun. Pathology, Chgo., 1992—98; sec. med. staff John C. Lincoln Hosp.-Deer Valley, 1997—99, v.p. med. staff, 2000—03, pres. med. staff, 2004—07; dir. John C. Lincoln Health Network Bd., 2001—. Active Ariz. Rep. Party, Phoenix, Rep. Nat. Coun., Washington; precinctman Dist. 18 Maricopa County, Ariz., 1996-98, Madison Heights Precinct, 1996-98; dir. John C. Lincoln Healthcare Network, 2001—; chmn. bd. trustees Phoenix (Ariz.) Gen. Hosp., 1994-95; ex-officio, trustee, 1995-97; dir. John C. Lincoln Health Network Guild, 1997—; dir., v.p. found. adv. coun. Lincoln Health Found.-Phoenix Gen. Hosp. Osteo. Endowment Fund, 1997-2008, emeritus dir. 2008-. Recipient Mead-Johnson award, Nat. Osteo. Assn., 1975. Fellow Am. Osteo. Coll. Pathologists (disting., pres. 1989-90, bd. govs. 1984-91), Coll. Pathologists, Coll. Am. Pathologists, Am. Soc. Clin. Pathologists; mem. Ariz. Osteo. Med. Assn. (del. dist. 2 ho. of dels. 1998, 2000), Century Club Alumni Assn., AAAS, Alpha Phi Omega, Rho Sigma Chi, Psi Sigma Alpha. Presbyterian. Office: Anatomic Pathology Assoc 19829 N 27th Ave Phoenix AZ 85027-4001 Home Phone: 602-944-3086; Office Phone: 623-879-5500. E-mail: richard.wrightd.o@jcl.com.

WRIGHT, ROBERT C. (ROBERT CHARLES WRIGHT), investment company executive, former media and entertainment company executive; b. Rockville Center, NY, Apr. 23, 1943; m. Suzanne Werner, Aug. 26, 1967; children: Kate, Christopher, Maggie. AB in Hist., Coll. Holy Cross, Worcester, Mass., 1965; LLB, U. Va., 1968. Bar: NY 1968, Va. 1968, Mass. 1970, NJ 1971. Law sec. to chief judge US Dist. Ct., NY, 1970—73; various positions GE, 1973—78, gen. mgr. plastics sales dept., 1978—80, v.p., gen. mgr. housewares, audio and cable TV ops., 1983—84, pres., CEO GE Fin. Svcs. Inc., 1984—86, vice chmn., 2000—08; pres. Cox Cable Comm., Atlanta, 1980—83; exec. v.p. Cox Comm., 1980—83; pres., CEO NBC, NYC, 1986—2001, chmn., CEO, 2001—04, NBC Universal, 2004—07; sr. adv. Lee Equity Ptnrs., LLC, 2008—. Bd. dirs. GE, 2000—08, Motion Picture & TV Fund Corp., Damon Runyon Cancer Res. Found.; bd. trustees Am. Film Inst.; hon. trustee Found. Am. Women in Radio & TV; bd. governors NY - Presbyn. Hosp.; trustee Coll. Holy Cross. Co-founder, chmn. Autism Speaks, 2005—. Recipient Steven J. Ross Humanitarian of Yr. award, UJA Fedn. NY; named one of The 100 Most Influential People in the World, TIME mag., 2008; named to Advt. Hall of Fame, Am. Advt. Fedn., 2009. Office: Lee Equity Partners LLC 767 5th Ave 6th Fl New York NY 10153 Office Phone: 212-888-1500.*

WRIGHT, ROBERT JOSEPH, lawyer; b. Rome, Ga., Dec. 13, 1949; s. Arthur Arley and Maude T. (Lacey) W.; m. Donna Ruth Bishop, Feb. 18, 1972; children: Cynthia Ashley, Laura Christine. BA cum laude, Ga. State U., 1979; JD cum laude, U. Ga., 1983. Bar: Ga. 1983, U.S. Dist. Ct. (no. dist.) Ga. 1983, U.S. Dist. Ct. (mid. dist.) Ga. 1985. Assoc. Craig & Gainer, Covington, Ga., 1983-84, Heard, Leverett & Adams, Elberton, 1984-86; gen. counsel Group Underwriters, Inc., 1987—2002; legal cons. Health Plan Select, Athens, 2001—. Mem. editl. staff Ga. Jour. Internat. and Comparative Law, 1981-82. Mem. State Bar Ga. (sec. legal econs. sect. 1987-88, chmn. legal econs. sect. 1988-90), Order of Coif, Masons, Phi Alpha Delta. Baptist. Home: 1030 E Canyon Creek Ct Watkinsville GA 30677-1500 Personal E-mail: rjw30677@bellsouth.net.

WRIGHT, ROBERT PAYTON, lawyer; b. Beaumont, Tex., Feb. 15, 1951; s. Vernon Gerald and Huberta Read (Nunn) W.; m. Sallie Chesnutt Smith, July 16, 1977; children: Payton Cullen, Elizabeth Risher. AB, Princeton U., 1972; JD, Columbia U., 1975. Bar: Tex. 1975. Ptnr. Baker Botts L.L.P., Houston, 1975—. Author: The Texas Homebuyer's Manual, 1986. Mem. Am. Coll. Real Estate Lawyers (bd. govs. 2002-05), State Bar Tex. (chmn. coun. real estate, probate, trust law sect. 1994-95), Houston Bar Assn. (chmn. real estate sect. 1989-90), Tex. Coll. Real Estate Lawyers, Houston Real Estate Lawyers Coun., Houston Club. Episcopalian. Office Phone: 713-229-1237.

WRIGHT, RON, legislative staff member; Coun. mem., Arlington, Tex., 2000—08; mayor pro tem, 2004—08; dist. mgr. for Rep. Joe Narton, US House of Reps., 2000—08, chief of staff Washington, 2008—. Office: Office of Congressman Joe Barton 2109 Rayburn House Office Bldg Washington DC 20515 Office Phone: 202-225-2002. Office Fax: 202-225-3052. E-mail: ron.wright@mail.house.gov.*

WRIGHT, SABRA DELL, music educator; b. Abilene, Tex., Nov. 4, 1953; d. Clead Elman Stark and Dettie Dell Quickel Stark; m. Richard Patrick Wright, Nov. 13, 1987; children: Richard Steven, Jerrod Sterling. B in Music Edn., Tarleton State U., Stephenville, Tex., 1975; M in Elem. Edn., Ariz. State U., Flagstaff, 1993. Cert. all-level music edn. Tex. Bd. Edn., 1975, K-12 music edn. Ariz. State Bd. Edn., 1992. Owner/tchr. Pirouette Dancers Studio, Stephenville, Tex., 1971—75; elem. music tchr. Irving Ind. Sch. Dist., Tex., 1975—80; mgr., horse trainer Bar Nothing Quarter Horse and Thoroughbred Ranch, Arthur City, Tex., 1980—85; mgr. brood mare farm Karho Arabians, Scottsdale, Ariz., 1985—86; elem. music tchr. Paradise Valley Ind. Sch. Dist., Phoenix, 1986—96; jr. high choral dir. Wichita Falls Ind. Sch. Dist., Tex., 1996—97; elem. music tchr. Iowa Pk. Consol. Ind. Sch. Dist., Tex., 1997—. Dance, choreography cons. U.S. Bi-Centennial Celebration, Irving, Tex., 1975—76; adult leader/ mgr. Wichita Count 4-H Horse Club, Iowa Park, Tex., 1998—2004; horse trainer, riding instr. Ridin' Right Tng. Facility, Iowa Park, 1998—. Student aide Teens Aid the Retarded, Irving, 1968—71, STARS: Teens Aid the Retarded, Stephenville, Tex., 1971—75; adult den leader Boy Scouts Am., Wichita Falls, 1996—97, Iowa Park, Tex., 1997—2004; instr. Whispers of Hope Riding Facility, Wichita Falls, 1998—2004. Recipient Outstanding Leadership award, Wichita Coty 4-H Orgn., 2000—01; scholar, Tarleton State U., 1971—75, Tex. State Teens Aid the Retarded, 1975. Mem.: Ariz. State Tchrs. Assn. (site rep., tchr. adv. 1993—96), Tex. Assn.Choral Dir. (assoc.), Tex. Music Educators Assn. (assoc.), Assn. Tex. Profl. Educators (assoc.), Am. Quarter Horse Assn. (assoc.), Am. Paint Horse Assn. (assoc.). Non-Partisan. Christian. Avocations: reading, community theater, horseback riding. Office: Bradford Elem 809 Texowa Rd Iowa Park TX 76367 Business E-Mail: swright@ipcisd.net.

WRIGHT, SALLY COPELAND, musician, educator; b. Portsmouth, Va., July 18, 1965; d. Emmet O and Betty Anne Copeland; m. Robert Charles Wright, June 9, 1990. MusB, East Carolina U., Greenville, NC, 1987; MusM, Fla. State U., Tallahassee, 1989. Adj. prof. piano & ear tng. sight singing Old Dominion U., Norfolk, Va., 1989—, dir. cmty. music divsn., 2003—; ch. pianist Corolla Chapel, NC, 2004—. Chmn. founder, (ODU & Norfolk acad.) guild ctrs. Nat. Piano Guild, Va., 1990—. Musician: (soloist) Whalehead Concerts Svc. 1903 Steinway, 2008. Vol. Garden Joy Sch.; bd. mem. property chmn. Tidewater Wesley Ctr., Norfolk, 2005—08; bd. mem. Portsmouth Cmty. Concert Assn., Inc, Va., 2000—; vol. firefighter Sta. 7- Carova Beach, Carova, NC; sanctuary patrol officer, vol. Corolla Wild Horses, NC, 2007—. Named Hall of Fame, Amer Coll. Musicians, 1990; grantee, Presbyn. Women Thank Offering, USA, 2003. Mem.: Music Tchrs. Nat. Assn. (nat. cert. mem.). Avocation: gardening. Office: Old Dominion Univ Music Dept 244 Diehn Fine & Performing Arts Norfolk VA 23529

WRIGHT, SCOTT OLIN, federal judge; b. Haigler, Nebr., Jan. 15, 1923; s. Jesse H. and Martha I. Wright; m. Shirley Frances Young, Aug. 25, 1972. Student, Central Coll., Fayette, Mo., 1940-42; LLB, U. Mo., Columbia, 1950. Bar: Mo. 1950. City atty., Columbia, 1951-53; pros. atty. Boone County, Mo., 1954-58; practice of law Columbia, 1958-79; U.S. dist. judge Western Dist. Mo., Kansas City, from 1979. Pres. Young Democrats Boone County, 1950, United Fund Columbia, 1965. Served with USN, 1942-43; as aviator USMC, 1943-46. Decorated Air medal. Mem. ABA, Am. Trial Lawyers Assn., Mo. Bar Assn., Mo. Trial Lawyers Assn., Boone County Bar Assn. Clubs: Rockhill Tennis, Woodside Racquet. Lodges: Rotary (pres. Columbia 1965). Unitarian Universalist. Office: Charles E Whitaker Courthouse 400 E 9th St Ste 8662 Kansas City MO 64106-2684 Office Phone: 816-512-5700.

WRIGHT, SHANE M., corporate financial executive; married; 2 children. B in Econ., Whitman Coll., 1986. Joined, fin. mgmt. program GE Co., 1988, exec., corporate audit staff; fin. mgr., Asia Pacific GE Transp.; fin. mgr., Asia, Europe & Africa GE Energy; mgr., fin. planning & analysis GE Oil & Gas; CFO, property & casualty ins. solutions GE Transp., CFO, GE Healthcare Internat.; v.p., CFO GE Aviation, 2008—. Office: GE Aviation 1 Neumann Way Cincinnati OH 45215 Office Phone: 513-243-2000.*

WRIGHT, STEVEN JAY, environmental engineering educator, consultant; b. Spokane, Wash., June 23, 1949; s. Bennie J. and Margaret Jean (Wiker) W.; m. Dayle Kathleen Wilson, Dec. 26, 1971; children: Glenn, Daniel. BS in Agrl. Engring., Wash. State U., 1971, MS in Hydraulic Engring., 1973; PhD in Civil Engring., Calif. Inst. Tech., 1977. Registered profl. engr., Mich. Rsch. engr. Calif. Inst. Tech., Pasadena, 1977; prof. civil and environ. engring. U. Mich., Ann Arbor, 1977—. Mem. tech. adv. bd. Mich. Great Lakes Protection Fund, Lansing, 1990—; vis. Erskine fellow U. Canterbury, New Zealand, 1992. Author: Essentials of Engineering Fluid Mechanics, 1990; contbr. articles to profl. jours. Leader Boy Scouts Am., Chelsea, Mich., 1985—. Recipient Lorenz Straub award U. Minn., 1978, James R. Rumsey award Mich. Water Pollution Control Fedn., 1983; postdoctoral fellow Swiss Nat. Sci. Found., 1984-85. Mem. ASCE (J.C. Stevens award 1986), Am. Geophys. Union, Internat. Assn. for Hydraulic Rsch., Assn. Ground Water Scientists and Engrs. Achievements include research in mixing of contaminant discharges in rivers and lakes, density intrusions, groundwater contaminant transport, and water infiltration through clay land fill liners. Home: 126 South St Chelsea MI 48118-1236 Office: U Mich 113 EWRE Ann Arbor MI 48109

WRIGHT, SUSAN WEBBER, federal judge; b. Texarkana, Ark., Aug. 22, 1948; d. Thomas Edward and Betty Jane (Gary) Webber; m. Robert Ross Wright, III, May 21, 1983; 1 child, Robin Elizabeth. BA, Randolph-Macon Woman's Coll., 1970; MPA, U. Ark., 1972, JD with high honors, 1975. Bar: Ark. 1975. Law clk. U.S. Ct. Appeals (8th Cir.), 1975-76; from asst. prof. to assoc. prof. law U. Ark., Little Rock, 1976—83, prof., 1983-90, asst. dean, 1976-78; dist. judge U.S. Dist. Ct. (ea. dist.) Ark., Little Rock, 1990—, chief judge, 1998—2005; judge Fgn. Intelligence Surveillance Ct. (FISC), Washington, 2009—. Vis. assoc. prof. Ohio State U., Columbus, 1981, La. State U., Baton Rouge, 1982—83; mem. adv. com. U.S. Ct. Appeals (8th cir.), St. Louis, 1983—88. Author (with R. Wright): Land Use in a Nutshell, 1978, Land Use in a Nutshell, 2d edit., 1985; editor-in-chief: Ark. Law Rev., 1975; contbr. articles to profl. jours. Mem.: Am. Law Inst., Pulaski County Bar Assn., Ark. Bar Assn., Am. Judicature Soc., Ark. Women's Forum. Anglican. Office: US District Court 600 W Capitol Ave Ste 522 Little Rock AR 72201-3329 Office Phone: 501-604-5100. Business E-Mail: susan_wright@ared.uscourts.gov.*

WRIGHT, SUZANNE WERNER, foundation administrator, volunteer; m. Bob Wright, Aug. 26, 1967; children: Kate, Christopher, Maggie. BA, Sarah Lawrence Coll., 1998. Co-founder, bd. mem. Autism Speaks, 2005—. Bd. mem. Make-A-Wish Found. of Metro NY, 2004—, Laura Pels Found., Inner-City Found. for Charity and Edn., Champions of Caring Project; bd. trustees Sarah Lawrence Coll. Named one of The 100 Most Influential People in the World, TIME mag., 2008. Office: Autism Speaks 2 Park Ave, 11 Fl New York NY 10016 Office Phone: 212-252-8584. Office Fax: 212-252-8676.

WRIGHT, THEODORE PAUL, JR., political science professor; b. Pt. Washington, NY, Apr. 12, 1926; s. Theodore Paul and Margaret (McCarl) W.; m. Susan Jane Standfast, Feb. 18, 1967; 1 child: Henry Sewall; m. Kim Rivers; children Margaret Standfast, Catherine Berrian (Mrs. Matthew H. Smith). BA magna cum laude, Swarthmore Coll., 1949; MA, Yale U., 1951, PhD, 1957. Instr. govt. Bates Coll., Lewiston, Maine, 1955-57; asst. prof., 1957-64; assoc. prof., 1964-65; assoc. prof. polit. sci. Grad. Sch. Public Affairs, SUNY, Albany, 1965-71, prof., 1971-95; prof. emeritus SUNY, Albany, 1995—. Mem. Columbia U. Faculty seminar on South Asia, 1967—. Author: American Support of Free Elections Abroad, 1964; contbr. chapters to books, articles to profl. jours. Trustee Am. Inst. Pakistan Studies, 1973-82; bd. dirs. Am. Coun. Study of Islamic Societies, 1998—, European Conf. on Modern South Asian Studies, 1974-. Served with USNR, 1944-46. Carnegie intern Indian civilization U. Chgo., 1961-62; Fulbright rsch. prof. India, 1963-64; Am. Inst. Indian Studies rsch. fellow India, 1969-70; Am. Coun. Learned Socs. grantee on South Asia in London, 1974-75; Am. Inst. Pakistan Studies/Fulbright rsch. fellow, Pakistan, 1983-84, Fulbright lectr., 1990-91. Mem. South Asian Muslim Studies Assn. (pres. 1988-2000, newsletter editor 2000—), Assn. Asian Studies (chmn. NY Conf. on Asian Studies 1988-89), Coun. for Study of Islam and Democracy, Dutch Settlers Soc. of Albany (pres. 1988-90, 98-2001, 1st v.p. 2002-), The New Netherland Inst. (bd. dirs. 2000—, sec. 2007—), Adirondack Mountain Club, Phi Beta Kappa (chpt. pres. 1992-93), Phi Delta Theta. Unitarian Universalist. Home: 17 Wellington Way Niskayuna NY 12309 Personal E-mail: wright15@juno.com.

WRIGHT, THEODORE ROBERT FAIRBANK, biologist, educator; b. Kodaikanal, Tamil Nadu, India, Apr. 10, 1928; s. Horace Kepler and Adelaide Caskey (Fairbank) Wright; m. Eileen Marie Yongen, Jan. 6, 1951 (dec. Jan. 2002). AB in Biology, Princeton U., 1949; MA in Biology, Wesleyan U., 1954; PhD in Zoology, Yale U., 1959. Asst. professor biology Johns Hopkins U., Balt., 1959-65; assoc. prof. biology U. Va., Charlottesville, 1965-75, prof. biology, 1975-95; prof. emeritus, 1995—. Vis. scientist Max Planck Inst. for Biology, Tubingen, 1975-76, Devel. Biology Ctr., U. Calif., Irvine, 1982. Editor: The Genetics and Biology of Drosophila, vol. 2a-c, 1978, vol. 2d, 1980, Genetic Regulatory Hierarchies in Development, 1990; co-editor: Advances in Genetics, 1988-92. With U.S. Army, 1950-52. NIH postdoctoral fellow Max Planck Inst. for Biology, Tubingen, Fed. Republic Germany, 1958-59; NSF grantee, 1967-72, 90-93; NIH grantee, 1972-93; Am. Cancer Soc. grantee, 1988-90. Fellow AAAS; mem. AAUP, Genetics Soc. Am., Soc. for Devel. Biology, Va. Acad. Sci., Sigma Xi.

WRIGHT, THOMAS PARKER, artist; b. Springfield, Mo., July 3, 1924; s. James Lewis and Vesta Marie (Parker) Wright; m. Elizabeth Jane Smith; children from previous marriage: Jeffrey, Kathleen, Thomas, Ramona, Karen. BA in Math., Henderson State U., 1948; MA in Math., La. State U., 1962; postgraduate studies in Higher Edn. Adminstrn., UCLA, Westwood, 1976. Math., sci. tchr. Hondo (N.Mex.) Union H.S., 1950-53; prin. Westridge (Ark.) H.S., 1954-55; math. tchr. Santa Ana (Calif.) Unified Sch. Dist., 1955-63; math., computer instr. Santa Ana Coll., 1963-71; adminstrv. dean Rancho Santiago CC., Santa Ana, 1971-79; art gallery mgr. Lahaina (Hawaii) Galleries, Inc., 1979-80; pres. Maui Fine Arts, Inc., Kihei, 1981—2006; computer sci. instr. Maui C.C., Kahului, Hawaii, 1983-94; software developer Nat. Ctr. Excellence High Performance Computing NSF, Kihei, Hawaii, 1994—2006. Multi-media and internet software developer NSF. One-man shows include Maui C.C., 1989, exhibited in group shows at Art Maui, 1984, 1986, 1989; contbr. chapters to books; developer (ednl. software) Quizcenter, 2000—05. Pres. Santa Ana Tchrs. Assn., 1960, Santa Ana Coll. Faculty Assn., 1965. 2d lt. USMCR, 1944—46, 1st lt. USMCR, 1950—52. Mem.: NEA, U. Hawaii Profl. Assembly. Republican. Presbyterian. Avocations: painting, computer art, ocean fishing, photography. Home: 902 Wilshire Ct Mc Kinney TX 75070 Home Phone: 972-547-0295. Business E-Mail: wrightt@hawaii.edu. E-mail: liztomw@netscape.net.

WRIGHT, TONY, advertising executive; b. London; Student, U. Sorbonne, Paris, Free U. Berlin. With Saatchi & Saatchi, London, Chiat/Day, LA & Toronto; co-founder McElligott Wright Morrison White (sold to Omnicom), Mpls., 1989; founding ptnr. (with Omnicom) Berlin Wright Cameron, NYC; worldwide chief strategy & planning officer Ogilvy & Mather, 1995—2004; CEO, pres. Lowe Worldwide (divsn. Interpublic), NYC, 2004—06, chmn., 2006—. Named to Advt. Hall of Achievement, Am. Advt. Fedn., 2001. Office Phone: 212-605-8000. Business E-Mail: tony.wright@loweworldwide.com.*

WRIGHT, WAYNE KENNETH, retired federal agency statistician; b. Chelsea, Mass., Jan. 26, 1944; s. Wayne K. and Louise Annette (Olson) W.; m. Sharon Kay Brown, Aug. 30, 1964 (div. 1974); 1 child, Trent Edward; m. Linda Susan Berkel, Mar. 15, 1975 (div. 1979); 1 child, Stacey Danielle; m. Bonnie Sue Oberhelman, Apr. 3, 1982; 1 child, Forrest Kenneth. BS in Sociology, U. Iowa, 1971; postgrad., U. North Iowa, 1971-72; cert. in marketing, Atlanta U., 1988. Survey asst. Shive-Hall-Hattery Engring., Cedar Rapids, Iowa, 1962-66; chem. lab technician Wilson Packing Plant, Cedar Rapids, 1966-71; grad. rsch. asst. U. No. Iowa, Cedar Falls, 1971-72, grad. tchg. asst., demographic and econ. stats., 1972-73; survey statistician U.S. Bur. Census, Kansas City, Kans., 1973-74, info. specialist, 1974-83, Charlotte, NC, 1983—2009; data specialist U.S. Bur. of Census, Charlotte, NC, 1991—2009. Named Ky. Col., 1987; named Hon. Citizen, City of Beloit (Wis.), 1974. Fellow Alpha Kappa Delta. Lutheran. Avocations: fishing, camping, hiking, alpine skiing and racing. Home: 1417 Morrocroft Trl Gastonia NC 28054-6499 Personal E-mail: wrghtgmp@aol.com.

WRIGHT, WILEY REED, JR., lawyer, retired judge, mediator; b. Seattle, Jan. 31, 1932; s. Wiley Reed and Gertrude Ellen (Datson) W.; m. Sally Harrison Clarke, 1955 (div. 1963); children: Wiley III, Margaret, Andrew; m. Roberta Hostinsky, Oct. 18, 1963; children: Cathryn, Amy, Susan. BS in Commerce, Washington and Lee U., 1954, LLB, 1956. Bar: Va. 1956, U.S. Dist. Ct. (ea. dist.) Va. 1956, U.S. Ct. Appeals (4th cir.) 1956, U.S. Supreme Ct. 1993. Law clk. to hon. judge U.S. Dist. Ct., Alexandria, Va., 1958-59; ptnr. Clarke, Richard, Moncure & Whitehead, Alexandria, 1959-68; judge corp. and cir. cts. Alexandria, 1968-79; chief judge cir. ct., 1979-84; ptnr. Hazel & Thomas P.C., Alexandria, 1984-96; mediator McCammon Mediation Group Ltd., Richmond, Va., 1996—. Mem. at large Va. State Bar Coun., 1984-90; mem. Jud. Coun. Va., 1982-84, vice chmn. jud. conf. Va., 1980-82. Assoc. editor: Virginia Circuit Judges Benchbook, 1987. Legal counsel to Alexandria C. of C., 1984-88. 1st lt. U.S. Army, 1956-58. Fellow: Va. Law Found., Am. Bar Found.; mem.: Va. Bar Assn., Omicron Delta Kappa, Phi Delta Phi.

Avocations: boating, fishing. Home: 579 Lovers Ln Lancaster VA 22503 Office: McCammon Group Bank of Am Ctr 6641 W Broad St Ste 400 Richmond VA 23230-1728 Office Phone: 804-343-0922. Business E-Mail: bwright@kaballero.com.

WRIGHT, WILLIAM COOK, archivist, director; b. Jersey City, July 11, 1939; s. Harry Cook and Edna Marguerite Tompkins) W. BA, Gettysburg Coll., 1961; MA, U. Del., 1965, PhD, 1971. Tchr. Salem (N.J.) High Sch., 1961-65; adj. instr. U. Del., Newark, 1968-70; assoc. dir. N.J. Hist. Commn., Trenton, 1970-76; head Bur. Archives and History N.J. State Libr., Trenton, 1976-83; dir. Div. Archives and Records Mgmt., N.J. State Dept., Trenton, 1983-85; chief Bur. Records Mgmt., Trenton, 1985-89, ret., 1989. Coord. state hist. records adv. bd. Nat. Hist. Publs. and Records Commn. 1976-87; mem. adv. com. for papers of William Livingston; sec. N.J. State Records Com., 1976-85, chmn., 1985; mem. adv. bd. dirs. N.J. Archives Series, 1971-86; mem. region 2 adv. coun. Nat. Archives and Records Svc., 1976-77; mem. adv. com. N.J. Newspaper Project, 1983-85, state rev. com. for hist. sites, 1976-79; mem. implementation and planning com. N.J. Supreme Ct., 1982 Author monograph: The Secession Movement in the Middle Atlantic States, 1972; compiler Directory of N.J. Newspapers, 1765-1970; contbr. articles and book revs to profl. jours. Mem. Lawrence Twp. Cultural and Heritage Adv. Com., 1989-92, chmn., 1991. Recipient Award of Recognition N.J. Hist. Commn., 1992. Mem. Acad. Cert. Achivists (cert.). Home: 7 Redwood Ct Glassboro NJ 08028-2934 Personal E-mail: wcwright@comcast.net.

WRIGHT, WILLIAM EVAN, physician, consultant; b. NYC, Aug. 1, 1946; s. Samuel and Frances Elnora (Perpente) W.; m. Diana Claire Dryer, Aug. 15, 1970; children: Jason William, Elizabeth Garland, Edwin Samuel. BA in Music, U. Rochester, 1968; MD, U. Pa., 1972; MSPH, U. Utah, 1979; MS in Physiology, Harvard U., 1980. Diplomate Am. Bd Internal Medicine, Am. Bd. Preventive Medicine, Occupl. Medicine, Am. Bd. Ind. Med. Examiners; ACOEM cert. med. rev. officer; cert. FAA med. examiner. Intern LDS Hosp., Salt Lake City, 1972-73, resident, 1973-75, U. Utah Med. Ctr., Salt Lake City, 1978-79, Harvard Sch. Pub. Health, Boston, 1979-80; asst. prof. U. So. Calif., LA, 1980-86; med. dir. U.S. DEA, Arlington, Va., 1986-96; program mgr., site med. dir. DynCorp, Reston, Va., 1991-96; med. dir. Md. Office, CORE, Inc., Irvine, Calif., 1996—2003; cons. Office of Worker Advocacy, U.S. Dept. Energy, Washington, 2003—05; pres. WorkWright, Inc., 2005—. Cons. Westwood Group, 2003—05; dist. med. cons. U.S. Dept. Labor, 2006—; med. dir. Reliable Review Svcs., Boca Raton, Fla., 2007—. Author, editor: (med. textbook) Couturier's Occupational and Environmental Infectious Diseases, 2009; Contbr. articles to profl. jours. Maj. M.C., U.S. Army, 1975-77. Fellow ACP, Am. Coll. Occupl. and Environ. Medicine, mem. Cosmos Club (Washington), Alpha Omega Alpha. Avocation: music. Home: 6801 Wemberly Way Mc Lean VA 22101-1532 Office Phone: 703-556-0092. E-mail: ww4ohs@cox.net.

WRIGHT, WILLIAM GRANDFIELD, biology professor; b. Pasadena, Calif., Aug. 8, 1951; s. Howard Walter Wright, Jr. and Jane Caroline Wright; m. Deborah Jean Bird, Sept. 14, 1996; m. Eva Lisa Ostling, Apr. 27, 1975 (div.); children: Sara Emily, Thomas Walter. PhD, UC San Diego, Scripps Instn. Oceanography, La Jolla, Calif., 1985. Postdoc. fellow U. Wash., Friday Harbor Labs, 1985—86, Yale U., New Haven, 1986—90; asst. prof., assoc. prof. Biology Colo. State U., Fort Collins, 1990—2000; assoc. prof. Biol. Scis. Chapman U., Orange, Calif., 2000—. Contbr. to rsch. papers. Office: Biol Scis Chapman Univ One Univ Dr Orange CA 92866

WRIGHTMAN, CAROLINE ANNE MCGHEE, nursing educator; b. Mar. 14, 1942; d. William Hanen and Lola Jeanette (Oberg) McGhee; m. Larry Keith Wrightman, Mar. 24, 1974. BSN, Loma Linda U., 1965; MNursing in Psychiatry, UCLA, 1975. Clin. instr. pediat. Pacific Union Coll., Glendale, Calif., 1970—72; clin. instr. psychiat. nursing LA County Sch. Nursing, 1972—73; crisis unit dir., mental health counselor LA County Mental Health, Arcadia, 1976—79; adminstrv. dir. psychiatry Fla. Hosp., Orlando, 1979—84; dir. inpatient svcs. Battle Creek (Mich.) Adventist Hosp., 1984—86; asst. prof. Walla Walla Coll., Portland, Oreg., 1988—91, 1999—2006; case mgr. Pacificare Behavioral Health, 1996—98; county designated mental health profl. Columbia River Mental Health, Vancouver, Wash., 1991—96, nurse care coord., 2006—07; dir. nursing edn. Concorde Career Inst., Portland, Oreg., 2008—. Adventist. Home: 11528 SE Tyler Rd Portland OR 97086-6844 Office: Concorde Career Inst 1425 NE Irving St Portland OR 97232 Office Phone: 503-281-4181. Personal E-mail: wrightmanc@juno.com. Business E-Mail: cwrightman@concorde.edu.

WRIGHTON, MARK STEPHEN, academic administrator, chemistry professor; b. Jacksonville, Fla., June 11, 1949; s. Robert D. and Doris (Cutler) Wrighton; children: James Joseph, Rebecca Ann. BS, Fla. State U., 1969; PhD, Calif. Inst. Tech., 1972; DSc (hon.), U. West Fla., 1983. From asst. prof. chemistry to provost MIT, Cambridge, 1972—90, Frederick G. Keys prof in chemistry, 1981, head dept. chemistry, 1987—90, provost, 1990—95; chancellor, prof. Washington U., St. Louis, 1995—. Mem. Nat. Sci. Bd., 2000—06; bd. dirs. Brooks Automation, Consortium Fin. Higher Edn., Danforth Plant Sci. Ctr., Nidus Ctr. for Sci. Enterprise, Barnes Jewish Hosp., BJC HealthCare, St. Louis Regional Chamber and Growth Assn., Cabot Corp., Corning Inc. Author: Organometallic Photochemistry, 1979. Trustee Mo. Bot. Garden, Innovate St. Louis, Symphony Orch.; mem. Civic Progress; bd. dirs. United Way Greater St. Louis; trustee St. Louis Sci. Ctr. Recipient Herbert Newby McCoy award, Calif. Inst. Tech., 1972, Disting. Alumni award, 1992, E.O. Lawrence award, Dept. Energy, 1983, Halpern award in photochemistry, N.Y. Acad. Scis., 1983, Fresenius award, Phi Lambda Upsilon, 1984, Dreyfus tchr.-scholar, 1975—80; fellow, Alfred P. Sloan, 1974—76, MacArthur fellow, 1983—88. Fellow: AAAS; mem.: Acad. of Sci. of St. Louis, Electrochem. Soc., Am. Chem. Soc. (award in pure chemistry 1981, award in inorganic chemistry 1988), Am. Philos. Soc., Am. Acad. Arts and Scis., Sigma Xi. Office: Washington Univ Office of Chancellor One Brookings Dr Campus Box 1192 Saint Louis MO 63130-4899 Office Phone: 314-935-5100. Business E-Mail: wrighton@wustl.edu.

WRIGHT PENN, ROBIN, actress; b. Dallas, Apr. 8, 1966; d. Fred Wright; m. Sean Penn, Apr. 27, 1996; children: Dylan Frances, Hopper Jack. Actress: (TV series) The Yellow Rose, 1983-84, Santa Barbara, 1984-87 (Emmy awards Best Ingenue in a Daytime Drama series 1985-87); (films) Hollywood Vice Squad, 1986, The Princess Bride, 1987, State of Grace, 1990, Denial, 1991, The Playboys, 1992, Toys, 1992, Forrest Gump, 1994, The Crossing Guard, 1995, Moll Flanders, 1995, Loved, 1996, She's so Lovely, 1997, Loved, 1997 (Seattle Film Festival Award for best actress, 1997), Hurly-Burly, 1998, Just to Be Together, 1999, Message in a Bottle, 1999, Unbreakable, 2000, The Pledge, 2001, The Last Castle, 2001, White Oleander, 2002, The Singing Detective, 2003, A Home at the End of the World, 2004, Nine Lives, 2005, Sorry Haters, 2005, Max, 2005, Breaking and Entering, 2006, Room 10, 2006, Hounddog, 2007, (voice only) Beowulf, 2007, What Just Happened?, 2008, State of Play, 2009; actor, exec. prodr. (films) Virgin, 2003; (TV miniseries) Empire Falls, 2005. Office: c/o ID Pub Rels 8409 Santa Monica Blvd West Hollywood CA 90069

WRIGLEY, DREW H., prosecutor, lawyer; b. Fargo, ND, Oct. 1965; BA, U. N.D., 1988; JD, Am. U., 1991. Pros. atty. City of Fargo, 1992—93; asst. dist. atty. Phila. Dist. Atty.'s Office, 1993—98; gen. counsel for pub. policy N.D. Workers Compensation Bur., 1998—99; exec. dir., legal counsel ND Rep. Party, 1999—2000; dep. chief of staff Office of Gov. of ND, 2000—01; US atty. Dist. ND US Dept. Justice, 2001—. Office: US Attys Office Quentin N Burdick US Courthouse 655 First Ave N Ste 250 Fargo ND 58102-4932 Office Phone: 701-297-7400. Office Fax: 701-297-7405.*

WRIGLEY, WILLIAM, JR., (BILL WRIGLEY JR.), candy company executive; b. 1964; s. William and Alison (Hunter) Wrigley; m. Kandis Wrigley (div.); 3 children; m. Heather Ann Rosbeck, Aug. 22, 2007. Asst. to pres. William Wrigley Jr. Co., Chgo., 1985—92, v.p., 1991—98, sr. v.p., 1999, pres., CEO, 1999—2006, exec. chmn., 2006—. Bd. dirs. William Wrigley Jr. Co., 1988—. Recipient Hunt-Scanlon Human Capitol Advantage award, 2003, Golden Plate award, Acad. Achievement, 2006; named one of Forbes' Richest Americans, 2006. Office: William Wrigley Jr Inc 410 N Michigan Ave Chicago IL 60611

WRINKLE, JOHN NEWTON, lawyer; b. Chattanooga, July 31, 1929; s. John Stuart and Anne (Ownbey) W.; m. Louise Rucker Agee, Feb. 1, 1958; children: Anne Blair, Margaret Rucker. BA, Vanderbilt U., 1951; LLB, Yale U., 1955. Bar: Ala. 1955, U.S. Dist. Ct. (no. dist.) Ala. 1956, U.S. Ct. Appeals (5th cir.) 1958, U.S. Ct. Appeals (11th cir.) 1981, U.S. Tax Ct. 1957. Assoc. White, Bradley, Arant, All & Rose, Birmingham, Ala., 1955-63; ptnr. Bradley Arant Rose & White LLP, 1963-92, counsel, 1993—. Coord. pre-law students Birmingham So. Coll., 1989—. Trustee Birmingham Symphony Assn., 1970-79, 80-83, Episcopal Found. Jefferson County, 1994-2000; mem. bd. advisors St. Andrew's Sewanee Sch., 1985—; bd. dirs. Yale Law Sch. Fund, 2005—. With USAF, 1951-52. Disting. fellow Birmingham-Southern Coll., 1995—. Fellow Am. Coll. Trust and Estate Counsel; mem. ABA, So. Employee Benefits Conf. (steering com. 1970-73), Birmingham Bar Assn., Assn. of Bar of City of N.Y., Birmingham Com. Fgn. Rels., Redstone Club, Mountain Brook Club, Knickerbocker Club (N.Y.C.), Yale Club (N.Y.C.), Phi Beta Kappa, Phi Alpha Delta. Episcopalian. Home: 2 Beechwood Rd Birmingham AL 35213-3914 Office: Bradley Arant Boult Cummings LLP 1819 5th Ave N Birmingham AL 35203 Office Phone: 205-521-8000. Business E-Mail: jwrinkle@babc.com.

WROBBEL, KAREN, education educator, consultant; b. Phila., Nov. 14, 1956; d. Raymond and Lillian Sauter; m. Paul H Wrobbel, Aug. 20, 1977; children: Elizabeth Gorden, Rebekah Stathakis. BA, Biola U., 1981; MA, Wheaton Coll., 1988; EdD, U. Minn., 2005. Cert. elem. tchr. Assn. Christian Schs. Internat., 2003, Bible specialist Assn. Christian Schs. Internat., 2003. Tchr. Christiansen Acad., Rubio, Venezuela, 1982—83; asst. head and tchr. Evang. Christian Acad., Madrid, 1983—97; children's edn. coord. Evang. Alliance Mission, Wheaton, Ill., 1997—2003; assoc. prof. Trinity Internat. U., Deerfield, Ill., 2003—, dir. Sch. Edn., 2006—. Children's edn. cons. Evang. Alliance Mission, Wheaton, Ill., 2003—; sch. bd. mem. Hinkson Christian Acad., Moscow; co-chair Intermission Missionary Kid Edn. Consultation, Colorado Springs, Colo., 1999—2001. Contbg. editor (newsletter) World Pulse, 2002—04; contbr. articles to profl. jours. Recipient Mary LeBar award in Christian Edn., Wheaton Coll., 1988. Mem.: ASCD, Nat. Coun. Tchrs. Math., Am. Ednl. Rsch. Assn., Phi Delta Kappa. Evangelical Christian. Office: Trinity Internat Univ 2065 Half Day Rd Deerfield IL 60015 Office Phone: 847-317-7178. Office Fax: 847-317-4786. Business E-Mail: kwrobbel@tiu.edu.

WROBEL, BRUCE J., energy and utilities company executive; Degree in Econs. and Mgmt. Sci., MIT, 1980. Co-founder US power co. (acquired by Sithe Energies Inc., 1986), 1981; exec. v.p. worldwide bus. devel. and fin. Sithe Energies Inc., 1986—99; founder EnCom, Japan, 1999, Guinea Aluminum Products Corp. (GAPCO); CEO, pres. Herakles Capital Corp., NYC; CEO Sithe Energies Inc., NYC, 2003—.

WROBLE, ARTHUR GERARD, judge; s. Arthur Stanley and Sophia P. Wroble; m. Mary Ellen Sheehan, Nov. 19, 1977; children: Sophia Ann, Sarah Jean, Stacey Margaret. BSBA with honors, U. Fla., Gainesville, 1970, MBA, 1971, JD, 1973. Bar: Fla. 1973, US Ct. Appeals (5th cir.) 1974, US Dist. Ct. (so. dist.) Fla. 1974, US Supreme Ct. 1976, US Ct. Appeals (11th cir.) 1981, US Dist. Ct. (mid. dist.) 1982, US Dist. Ct. (no. dist.) Fla. 1986, US Army Ct. Mil. Rev. 1989, US Ct. Mil. Appeals 1990, Fla. Supreme Ct. Cir./County Mediator 2007. Ptnr. Burns, Middleton, Farrell & Faust, Palm Beach, Fla., 1973—80, Steel, Hector, Davis, Burns, Middleton, et al (merger), Palm Beach, 1980—82, Wolf, Block, Schorr & Solis-Cohen, Phila. & West Palm Beach, 1982-87, Scott, Royce, Harris & Bryan, PA, Palm Beach, Fla., 1987-89, Grantham and Wroble, PA, Lake Worth, Fla., 1989-92; prin. Arthur G. Wroble, PA, West Palm Beach, 1992-2000; cir. judge 15th Jud. Ct. Fla., Palm Beach, 2001—07. Mem. 15th Jud. Cir. Ct. Nominating Commn., 1979-83; mem. U. Fla. Law Ctr. Coun., 1981-84, 99—, US Magistrate Merit Selection Panel, so. dist. Fla., 1987; adv. bd. alternative sentencing program Palm Beach County Pub. Defender's Office; adj. instr. bus. law Coll. Boca Raton (now Lynn U.), 1988; 16th dist. screening com. US Svc. Acad., Fla., 2001-07. Contbr. articles to profl. jours. Bd. dirs. Palm Glades Girl Scout Coun., 1996—2006, 2006—08; co-chmn. profl. devel. United Way, 1984—85; dir. Leadership Palm Beach County, 1990—92. Served to lt. col. JAG, USAR. Named Eagle Scout, Boy Scouts Am., 1962; named to Athletic Hall Fame, Bishop Moore HS, Orlando, 1997. Mem. ABA, Fla. Bar (bd. govs. young lawyers sect. 1979-83, bd. govs. 1985-89), Palm Beach County Bar Assn. (pres. young lawyers sect. 1978-79, bd. dirs. 1979-81, sec.-treas. 1981-83, pres. 1984-85), Fla. Bar Found. (bd. dirs. 1990-93), Fla. Assn. Women Lawyers, Fla. Coun. Bar Assn. Pres. (bd. dirs. 1986-92), Hispanic Bar Assn. of Palm Beach County, F.M. Cunningham Bar Assn., Guild Cath. Lawyers Diocese Palm Beach, Inc. (pres. 1980-81, bd. dirs. 1981-2001, Monsignor Jeremiah P. O'Mahoney Outstanding Lawyer award 1993), Legal Aid Soc. Palm Beach County, Inc. (bd. dirs. 1981-2000), Univ. Fla. Alumni Assn., Palm Beach County Club (pres. 1983-84), Kiwanis (pres. 1980-81, pres. West Palm Beach found. 1989-2000, dir. 1991-2007, Citizen of Yr. 1994, George F. Hixon fellowship 1999), KC (grand knight 1978-79), Am. Inns of Ct. LIV (West Palm Beach chpt. pres. 1999-2000, bd. dirs. 1995-2000), Am. Legion. Roman Catholic. Achievements include 87% of decisions reviewed on appeal were affirmed.

WROBLEY, RALPH, lawyer; b. Denver, Sept. 19, 1935; s. Matthew B. and Hedvig (Lyon) W.; m. Madeline C. Kearney, June 13, 1959; children: Kirk Lyon, Eric Lyon, Ann Lyon. BA, Yale U., 1957; JD, U. Chgo., 1962. Bar: Mo. 1962. With Bell Tel. Co., Phila., 1957-59; assoc. Stinson Morrison Hecker LLP, Kansas City, Mo., 1962-65, mem. mng. com., 1982—86; ptnr. Bryan, Cave, LLP, Kansas City, 1988-92, Husch, Blackwell, Sanders LLP, Kans. City, 1992—2007, mem. exec. com., 1992—2000, of counsel, 2008—. Bd. dirs. Human Resources Corp., 1971; mem. Civic Coun. Kansas City, 1986-2001; chmn. Pub. Housing Authority of Kansas City, 1971-74; vice chmn. Mayor's Adv. Commn. on Housing, Kansas City, 1971-74; bd. govs. Citizens Assn., 1965—, vice chmn., 1971-75, chmn., 1978-79; bd. dirs. Coun. on Edn., 1975-81, v.p., 1977-79; bd. dirs., pres. Sam E. and Mary F. Roberts Found., 1974-96; trustee Clearinghouse for Mid Continent Founds., 1977-96, chmn. 1987-89; bd. dirs. Bus. Innovation Ctr., 1984-91, vice-chmn. 1987-91, adv. bd. dirs., 1993-99, Midwest Regional Adv. Bd. Inst. Internat. Edn., 1989-93, Internat. Trade Assn., 1989-92, v.p., 1990; vice chmn., bd. dirs. Mid-Am. Coalition on Healthcare, 1991-2003, Helzberg Entrepreneurial Mentoring Program, 2006-, chmn. elect 2009. Mem. Mo. Bar Assn., Yale Club (pres. 1969-71, outstanding mem. award 1967, White House fellowship semi-finalist, 1972). Republican. Presbyn. (elder) Home: 1015 W 67th Ter Kansas City MO 64113-1942 Office: 4801 Main St Kansas City MO 64112 Office Phone: 816-983-8111, 816-983-8000. Business E-Mail: ralph.wrobley@huschblackwell.com. E-mail: ralphwrobley@gmail.com.

WRONG, DENNIS HUME, retired sociologist, educator; b. Toronto, Nov. 22, 1923; s. Humphrey Hume and Mary Joyce (Hutton) W.; m. Elaine L. Gale, Nov. 24, 1949 (div. Oct. 1965); 1 child, Terence Hume; m. Jacqueline Conrath, Mar. 26, 1966; stepchildren: Jaya, Sheila Mehta. BA, U. Toronto, 1945; PhD, Columbia U., 1956. Tchr. Princeton U., 1949-50, Rutgers U., 1950-51, U. Toronto, 1954-56, Brown U., 1956-61; mem. grad. faculty New Sch. Social Research, 1961-63; prof. sociology, chmn. dept. Univ. Coll., NYU, 1963-65; prof. sociology NYU, 1966-94, prof. emeritus, 1994—. Rsch. asst. George F. Kennan and Robert Strunsky, Inst. Advanced Study, 1951-53; vis. prof. U. Nev., 1965-66; vis. fellow Oxford (Eng.) U., 1978, European U. Inst., 1996-97; Simon vis. prof. U. Manchester, Eng., 1978. Author: American and Canadian Viewpoints, 1955, Population, 1956, 2d edit., 1959, Population and Society, 1961, 3rd edit., 1977, Skeptical Sociology, 1976, Power: Its Forms, Bases and Uses, 1979, 3rd edit., 1995, Class Fertility Trends in Western Nations, 1980, The Problem of Order: What Unites and Divides Society, 1994, 2d edit., 1995, The Modern Condition: Essays at Century's End, 1998, The Oversocialized Conception of Man (reissue of Skeptical Sociology), 1999, Reflections on a Politically Skeptical Era, 2003, 2d edit. 2005, The Persistence of the Particular, 2005-06; editor: Social Research, 1961-64, (with Harry L. Gracey) Readings in Introductory Sociology, 1967, 3rd edit., 1977, Contemporary Sociology: A Journal of Reviews, 1972-74, Max Weber, 1970; mem. editl. bd. Dissent, 1966—; contbg. editor Partisan Rev., 1981-87. Predoc. fellow, Canadian Social Sci. Rsch. Found., 1953-54, Guggenheim fellow, 1984-85, Woodrow Wilson Internat. Ctr. for Scholars fellow, 1991-92. Mem.: Soc. for Advancement of Socio-Econs., Eastern Sociol. Soc., Am. Sociol. Assn. Personal E-mail: dhwrong@voicenet.com.

WRONKA, JOSEPH MICHAEL, social policy analyst, human rights activist, educator; b. Bklyn., Dec. 20, 1948; s. Chester Philip and Mary Elizabeth (Falcickio) W.; children: Christopher, Carolyn. BA, Bklyn. Coll., 1970; MA, Duquesne U., 1972; postgrad., U. Nice, France, 1974-76; PhD in Social Policy, Brandeis U., 1992. Instr. West Ga. Coll., Carrollton, 1972-74; assoc. staff psychologist Bklyn. Psychiat. Ctrs., 1976-80; instr. human svcs. Kotzebue (Alaska) Tech. Ctr., 1981-83; counselor alcoholism and drug Fairbanks (Alaska) Native Assn., 1983-84; employment securities specialist Job Svc. Dept. Labor, Fairbanks, 1984-85; instr. U. Alaska, Fairbanks, 1984-87; dir. humans svcs. Copper River Native Assn., Glenallen, Alaska, 1985-86; acad. coord., instr. Alaska Native Studies Honors Inst., Fairbanks, 1987; asst. prof. Mass. Coll. Pharmacy, Boston, 1989; prof. social work Springfield (Mass) Coll., 1992—. Vis. instr. Framingham (Mass.) State Coll., 1988—; adj. NYU, Caldwell Coll., St. Francis Coll., Rampo Coll., 1976-81, Franklin Pierce Coll., New Hampshire, 1991, Sch. Social Work, Sankt Poelten, Austria, 2000, Berne, Switzerland, 2007, Hannover, Germany, 2008, Simmons Coll., 2003-04, U. Zurich, 2008; prin. investigator Universal Declaration Human Rights Project; vis. scholar Heller Sch. Ctr. Social Change Brandeis U., Waltham, Mass., 2000-03; vis. scholar Heller Sch., Brandeis U., 2002-2004; permanent rep. United Nations Geneva, Internat. Assn. Schs. Social Work, 2009. Author: (books) Creating a Human Rights Culture, 1995, A Little Humility Please: Human Rights and Social Policy in the United States, 1998, Human Rights and Social Policy in the 21st Century, 1998, The Dr. Ambedkar Lectures on Creating A Human Rights Culture, 2002, Global Distributive Justice as a Solidarity Right, 2007, Human Rights and Social Justice: Social Action and Service for the Helping and Health Professions, 2008; prodr., dir. (play): Everyday-A Play in One Act, 1974. Group coord. Amnesty Internat, Fairbanks, 1985. Grantee State of Alaska, 1986. Mem. Coun. Social Work Edn., Internat. Fedn. Social Work, Human Rights Action Internat. (pres.). Roman Catholic. Avocations: musician, swimming, writing. Office: Springfield Coll Sch Social Work 263 Alden St Springfield MA 01109-3707 Office Phone: 413-748-3067. Business E-Mail: joseph_wronka@spfldcol.edu, jwronka@spfldcol.edu.

WROTH, JAMES MELVIN, retired military officer; b. Lincoln, Nebr., Feb. 2, 1929; s. Charles M. and Reba (Sharp) Wroth; m. Donna Mae Benson, June 4, 1951 (dec.); children: Mark, David S., Mary E. Bannon; m. Molly B. Mullan, June 15, 1975; stepchildren: Edward H. Mullan-(dec.), Philip C. Mullan. BS, U. Nebr., 1951; postgrad., F.A. Sch., 1955—56, Command and Gen. Staff Coll., 1962—63; MBA, Syracuse U., 1963; with, Armed Forces Staff Coll., 1967; postgrad., Army War Coll., 1968, Harvard U., 1972. Commd. 2d lt. US Army, 1951, advanced through grades to brig. gen., 1973, U.S. Army, Republic of Korea, 1952-53; instr. A.A.A. Sch., Ft. Bliss, Tex., 1954-56; with 3d Inf. Div., Ft. Benning, Ga., also Germany, 1957-61; with Office Chief of Staff US Army, 1963-66; comdg. officer 1st Bn. 31st Arty., Republic of Korea, 1967; exec. asst. to asst. sec. US Army, 1968-70; exec. officer I Field Force Vietnam Arty., 1970; comdg. officer 52d Arty. Group, Vietnam, 1971; with Office Dep. Chief Staff for Personnel, Dept. Army, 1972-75; comdg. gen. VII Corps Arty. and Augsburg Germany Mil. Community, 1975-77; comdr. 2d ROTC region, Ft. Knox, Ky., 1977-79; ret., 1979; v.p., dir. mgmt. scis. ops. Gen. Research Corp., McLean, Va., 1979-82; group v.p Info. Systems & Network Corp., Bethesda, Md., 1982-93; pres. J-Tech, Inc., 1993—96. Trustee Washington Adventist Hosp. Found., 1989—93. Decorated D.S.M., Legion of Merit, Bronze Star, Air Medal with V device, Army Commendation medal, Vietnamese Gallantry Cross with palm; recipient F. A. Assn. award, 1950, John J. Pershing award, 1951, 40 and 8 award, 1951, Presdl. Unit Citation, US Coast Guard, 2005. Mem.: U.S. Coast Guard Aux. (past flotilla comdr.), Ret. Officers Assn. (past chpt. pres.), Nat Soc. Pershing Rifles (past nat. comdr.), Indian Creek Yacht and Country Club (dir. 2000—03), Indian Creek Yacht Club (past commodore), Beta Gamma Sigma, Alpha Kappa Psi. Personal E-mail: jim.wroth@us.army.mil.

WROTH, L(AWRENCE) KINVIN, law educator; b. Providence, July 9, 1932; s. Lawrence Counselman and Barbara (Pease) W.; m. Susan Collins, May 2, 1958 (div. 1972); children: Ann K., Caroline D., Eliza H.; m. Deborah Bethell, Aug. 10, 1972; 1 dau., Katharine L.; stepchildren—Thomas Colder, John H., David H., Elizabeth T. and Sarah B. Zobel. BA, Yale U., 1954; LLB, Harvard U., 1960. Bar: Mass. 1960, Maine 1974. Teaching fellow, asst. prof. law Dickinson Sch. Law, 1960-62; rsch. assoc. Harvard U., 1962-64; assoc. prof. law U. Maine

Sch. Law, Portland, 1964-66, prof., 1966-96; assoc. dean Sch. Law U. Maine, 1977-78, acting dean, 1978-80, dean, 1980-90; prof. Vt. Law Sch., 1996—, dean, 1996—2004, pres., 2003—04; dir. Land Use Inst. Vt. Law Sch., Royalton, 2005—. Rsch. fellow Charles Warren Center Studies in Am. History, Harvard U., 1968-74; cons. civil and probate procedure, profl. and jud. responsibility, and ct.-bar rels. Maine Supreme Jud. Ct., 1967-96; cons. civil, probate, family ct. and criminal procedure and evidence Vt. Supreme Ct., 1969— Author: (with R.H. Field and V.L. McKusick) Maine Civil Practice, 2d edit., 1970; editor-in-chief: Province in Rebellion, 1975; editor: (with H.B. Zobel) Legal papers of John Adams, 1965; reporter: Vermont Rules of Civil Procedure, 1971, Vermont Rules of Criminal Procedure, 1974, Maine Rules of Probate Procedure, 1980, (with J. Dooley) Vermont Rules of Evidence, 1982, Maine Code of Judicial Conduct, 1993, Vermont Code of Judicial Conduct, 1994. Pres. Greater Portland Landmarks, Inc., 1966—69, adv. trustee, 1969—85; adv. coun. Nat. Trust Hist. Preservation, 1967—70; mem. Maine Commn. on Legal Needs, 1989—90, Commn. to Study Future of Maine's Cts., 1991—93, Commn. on Future of Vt.'s Judiciary, 1998—99, Vt. Bus. Roundtable, 1998—2004; bd. dirs. Maine Bar Found., 1983—89, sec., 1983—86, v.p., 1987, pres., 1988, fellow, 1991; bd. dirs. Pine Tree Legal Assistance Inc., 1985—96, Nat. Assn. IOLTA Programs, Inc., 1988—90, Portland Symphony Orch., 1990—98, v.p. ops. and resources, 1991—95, pres., 1995—96. Recipient Littleton-Griswold prize Am. Hist. Assn., 1966, Howard H. Dana award Maine Bar Found., 1991, Justice Louis Scolnik award Maine Civil Liberties Union, 1992, Herbert Harley award Am. Judicature Soc., 1994. Fellow Am. Bar Found.; mem. ABA, Maine Bar Assn. (Disting. Svc. award 1990), Am. Law Inst., Vermont Bar Assn., Colonial Soc. Mass., Mass. Hist. Soc. Office: Vt Law Sch PO Box 96 South Royalton VT 05068-0096 Office Phone: 802-831-1268. E-mail: kwroth@vermontlaw.edu.

WROTTEN, MARYLEAN, medical coordinator, counselor; d. Evelyn Saxton and Perry Elmore; 1 child, Evelyn DeShawn Wroten. Student, Audrey Cohn Coll., 1984. Approved med. authorized pers. Fedn. Puerto Rican Orgns., 1991; strategist crisis intervention pers. Fedn. Puerto Rican Orgns., 1991, cert. CPR-First Aid Fedn. Puerto Rican Orgns., 2004. Resident therapist Audrey Cohen Coll., 1991—; med. coord. Agy. Fedn. Multicultural Orgns., NY, 1991—. Author: (poetry) I Love God (Editor's Choice award, 2004), Hope, 2004. Youth coord. Jackson Dem. Club, Bronx, 1995—99; Sunday sch. tchr. Praying Band of Faith, Bronx, 1985—89; proposal rev. com. Neighborhood Adv. Bd., Bronx, 1995—96; del. 1199 Nat. Health & Human Employees Union, NYC, 1996—2004. Mem.: Internat. Soc. Poets (disting.). Democrat. Pentecostal. Avocations: hiking, reading, volunteering, singing. Office: Federation Multicultural Organization 2 VanSinderen Ave Brooklyn NY 11207 Personal E-mail: Lynnmary10@yahoo.com.

WRUBLE, BERNHARDT KARP, lawyer; b. Wilkes-Barre, Pa., Mar. 21, 1942; s. Maurice and Ruth Yvonne (Karp) W.; m. Judith Marilyn (Eyges), Nov. 16, 1968 (div. 1987); children: Justine, Vanessa, Alexis; m. Jill (Diamond), Nov. 24, 1990; children: Mattia, Austin. BA in Polit. Sci., Williams Coll., Williamstown, Mass., 1963; JD, U. Pa., 1966; postgrad., N.Y. Univ., 1972—74, Harvard U., 1978. Bar: Conn. 2003, Minn. 2000, DC 1981, NY 1968, US Supreme Ct. 1972, U.S. Dist. Ct. (so. dist.) N.Y., 1969, U.S. Dist. Ct. (ea. dist.) N.Y., 1972, U.S. Ct. Appeals (2d cir.), 1972, U.S. Supreme Ct., 1972, U.S. Ct. Appeals (7th cir.), 1974, U.S. Ct. Appeals (D.C. and 4th cir.), 1984, U.S. Ct. Appeals (5th cir.), 1985, U.S. Ct. Appeals (11th cir.) 1986. Law clk. to presiding judge U.S. Ct. Appeals (3d cir.), 1966—67; assoc. Simpson, Thacher, and Bartlet, NYC, 1968—73, ptnr., 1974—77; prin. dep. gen. counsel U.S. Dept. Army, Washington, 1977—79; dir. Office Govt. Ethics, Washington, 1979; exec. asst. to sec. and dep. sec. U.S. Dept. Energy, Washington, 1979—81; dir. President's Interagy. Coal Export Task Force, Washington, 1980—81; ptnr. Verner, Liipfert, Bernhard, McPherson, and Hand, Washington, 1981—99; sr. v.p. legal affairs N.W. Airlines, St. Paul, 1999—2001. Pres. Bridges Resort and Tennis Club, Warren, Vt., 2007—09. Bd. dir. Epilepsy Found. Am., 1983, chmn., 1991. Hartford County Pro Bono Award, 2004. Mem. ABA, D.C. Bar Assn., N.Y. State Bar Assn., Williams Coll. Alumni Assn. (pres. Washington chpt. 1986-91), Williams Coll. Soc. Alumni Assn. (exec. com. 1988-91). Democrat. Office Phone: 860-521-3543. Personal E-mail: bkwruble@yahoo.com.

WRUBLE, BRIAN FREDERICK, investor; b. Kalamazoo, Apr. 18, 1943; s. Milton and Rose Muriel (Nathanson) W.; m. Susan Roberta Shifrin, June 23, 1968 (div. Oct. 1984); children: Amy Carolyn, Jordan Todd; m. Kathleen Wilson Bratton, Apr. 20, 1985; 1 child, Henrietta Zane Bratton. BEE, Cornell U., 1965, MEE, 1966; MBA with distinction, NYU, 1976. Field engr. Sperry Gyroscope Corp., Lake Success, NY, 1966—70; v.p. Alliance One Instl. Svcs., Inc., NYC, 1970—76, H. C. Wainwright and Co., Inc., NYC, 1976-77, Wainwright Securities, Inc., NYC, 1977; v.p., co-mgr. fundamental equities rsch. Smith Barney, Harris Upham & Co., NYC, 1977-79; exec. v.p. chief fin. ops. Equitable Life Assurance Soc. U.S., NYC, 1979-92; chmn., pres., CEO Equitable Capital Mgmt. Corp., NYC, 1985-92; chief investment officer Equitable Life Assurance Soc. U.S., NYC, 1991-92; pres., COO, dir. Delaware Mgmt. Holdings, Inc., 1992-95; pres., CEO The Delaware Group, 1992-95; pres., COO Delaware Mgmt. Co., 1992-95; chmn. Delaware Distributors, Inc., 1992-95; chmn., CEO Delaware Svc. Co., Inc., 1992—95; gen. ptnr. Odyssey Ptnrs., L.P., NYC, 1995—2007; mng. prin. Odyssey Investment Ptnrs., LLC, NYC, 1997—98, spl. ltd. ptnr., 1999—2004; pvt. investor, 2004—. Chmn., pres. Equitable Realty Assets Corp., Atlanta, 1983—92; v.p., dir. TELMARI, Inc., NYC, 1982—83, Equitable Variable Life Ins. Co., 1987—92; chmn. Equico Capital Corp., NYC, 1984—92; CEO Equitable Gen. of Okla., Oklahoma City, 1985—86; trustee Equitable Retirement Plans, NYC, 1980—86; trustee bd. III Oppenheimer Funds, 2001—, trustee bd. I, 2005—, chmn. bd. I, 2006—; pres. Hudson River Trust, 1991—92, Equitable Funds, 1991—92, The Jackson Lab., 1999—2007, chmn., 2007—; mem. investment adv. bd. Zurich Fin. Svc. Group, 2004—07, mem. investment mgmt. adv. coun., 2008—; dir. Spl. Value Opportunities Fund LLC, 2004—. Vice-chmn. Boys Choir of Harlem, NYC, 1984—92; vice chmn. Corp. Ptnrs. Phila. Art Mus., 1993—95; bd. govs. Jerome Levy Econ. Inst., 1990—2001; bd. dirs. Harlem Youth Devel. Found., 1989—92, Corp. Ptnrs. Phila. Art Mus., 1992—95, The Jackson Lab. Corp., 1991—99, Inst. for Advanced Study, 1992—, treas., 2006—. Recipient Heroes award Boys Choir Harlem, 1990, Founders award, 1993. Mem.: IEEE, Phila. C. of C. (bd. dirs. 1992—95, mem. exec. com. 1993—95), Inst. CFAs (CFA, bd. trustees 1992—98, vice chmn. 1993—94, chmn. 1994—95, bd. trustees rsch. found. 1994—95, 2000—02, assoc. editor CFA Digest 1983—), N.Y. Soc. Security Analysts, Assn. Investment Mgmt. and Rsch. (gov. 1992—98, C. Steward Sheppard award 2000). Republican. Jewish. Avocations: skiing, amateur radio.

WU, CARL, medical researcher; PhD, Harvard U., 1979. Postdoctoral fellow Harvard U., 1979—82; joined Lab. Biochemistry Nat. Cancer Inst., NIH, 1982, chief Lab. Molecular Cell Biology, Ctr. Cancer Rsch., 1996—, also head Chromosome Structure and Gene Regulation Sect., Lab. Molecular Cell Biology. Contbr. articles to sci. jours. Recipient Outstanding Young Scientist Award, Md. Acad. Sciences, 1987, Young Investigator Award, Am. Soc. Biochemistry and Molecular Biology, 1992. Mem.: NAS, Am. Acad. Arts and Sciences. Office: Lab Molecular Cell Biology Nat Cancer Inst Ctr Cancer Rsch 37 Convent Dr Bldg 37 Rm 6068 Bethesda MD 20892-4255 Office Phone: 301-496-3029. Office Fax: 301-435-3697. E-mail: carlwu@helix.nih.gov.*

WU, CHANGXU, researcher, consultant; PhD, U. Mich., Ann Arbor, 2007. Human factors scientists, cons. Xing Xing Inc., Hu Zhou, 1995—2002; rschr. State U. NY, Buffalo, 2009—. Mem.: Human Factors & Ergonomics Soc. Office: State Univ NY Buffalo 414 Bell Hall Buffalo NY 14260 Business E-Mail: changxu.buffalo@gmail.com.

WU, CHENG-HUNG, engineering educator, researcher; b. Taipei, Taiwan, Oct. 2, 1976; s. Chin-Kuang Wu and Yueh-Ching Wu Liao; m. Mei-I Wu, June 29, 2002. PhD, U. Mich., Ann Arbor, 2006. Enterprise resource planning system consultant Taiwan, 2001. Cons. ARES Internat. Corp., Taipei, 2000—02; asst. prof. Dept. Indsl. Engring. and Engring. Mgmt., Nat. Tsing Hua U., Hsinchu, Taiwan, 2006—07, Inst. Indsl. Engring., Nat. Taiwan U., Taipei, 2007—. Exec. editor Internat. Jour. Electronic Bus. Mgmt., Hsinchu, 2006—. 2nd lt. Taiwan Army, 2000—00, Taipei. Grant, Nat. Sci. Coun., Taiwan, 2006—, 2008—, fellowship, U. Mich. - Ann Arbor. Mem.: INFORMS. Achievements include research in resource allocation in complex processing networks with reliability considerations; development of decision support system for flexible resource allocation; research in capacity portfolio planning in high tech industry. Office: Inst of Indsl Engring NTU 1 Sec 4 Roosevelt Rd Taipei 106 Taiwan Office Fax: +886-2-23625856. Business E-Mail: taiwan.wu@gmail.com.

WU, DAVID, United States Representative from Oregon; b. Taiwan, Apr. 8, 1955; arrived in US, 1961; m. Michelle Wu; children: Matthew, Sarah. BS, Stanford U., Calif., 1977; student, Harvard Med. Sch.; JD, Yale U., New Haven, 1982. Clk. to fed. judge, Portland, Oreg.; ptnr. Cohen & Wu, Oreg., 1988-98; mem. US Congress from 1st Oreg. dist., 1999—, mem. edn. and labor com., mem. sci. & tech. com., mem. fgn. affairs com., chmn. subcommittee on tech. and innovation, mem. exec. bd. Congl. Asian Pacific Am. Caucus, mem. New Dem. Coalition. Democrat. Office: 620 SW Main Ste 606 Portland OR 97205 Office Phone: 202-225-0855, 503-326-2901. Office Fax: 503-326-5066.*

WU, DE TING, mathematics professor, researcher, writer; b. Shanghai, Jan. 9, 1938; came to U.S., 1981; s. Bing Huo and Wei Fen (Zhang) W.; m. Pei Hua Zhang, July 16, 1974; 1 child, Yin. BA, Peking U., China, 1962; MA, U. Ga., 1983, PhD, 1988. Instr. Shanghai Textile Coll., 1963-71; worker Shanghai # 12 Textile Factory, 1971-78; sr. lectr. Shanghai Textile Coll., 1978-81; tchg. asst. U. Ga., Athens, 1981-88; assoc. prof. Morehouse Coll., Atlanta, 1989—. Editor: Selected Problems from Theoretical Mechanics, 1981. Bd. dirs. Orgn. Chinese Ams., 1992-96, Asian-Pacific Ams. of Coun. of Ga., 1994. Mem. AAUP, Shanghai Mechanics Assn., Am. Math. Soc., Math. Assn. Am. Avocations: photography, travel, playing contract bridge. Office: Morehouse Coll Dept Math 830 Westview Dr SW Dept Math Atlanta GA 30314-3773

WU, FA YUEH, retired physics professor; b. China, Jan. 5, 1932; m. Jane Ching-Tsu Chang, Apr. 6, 1963; children: Yvonne, Yolanda. PhD, Wash. U., St. Louis, 1963. Asst. prof. Va. Poly. Inst., Blacksburg, 1963—67; prof. Northeastern U., Boston, 1967—2006. Program dir. NSF, Washington, 1983—84. Author: (book) Exactly Solved Models: A Journey in Statistical Mechanics, Selected Papers (1963-2008). Rsch. grants, NSF, 1968—2007. Office: Northeastern Univ Dept Physics Boston MA 02115

WU, FENGTAO, language educator; m. Xiufang Ling; 1 child, Miaomiao. MA, Ind. U., Bloomington, 1987. Lic. oral proficiency interview tester Americnan Coun. Tchg. Fgn. Lang., 2002. Lead tchr. Middlebury Coll. Summer Sch., Vt.; lang. dir. Duke-Washington U. Overseas Program, Beijing, 2000, Hangzhou, Zhejiang, China, 2002—04; sr. lectr. Wash. U., St. Louis, 2005—, coord. Chinese lang., 2009. Author: (book) Grammar Made Easy. Recipient award, Dept. State, 1981. Mem.: Chinese Lang. Tchrs. Assn.

WU, FRANK H., law educator, journalist; b. Cleve., Aug. 20, 1967; s. Hai and Grace (Ma) Wu. BA, Johns Hopkins U., 1988; JD, U. Mich., 1991. Bar: Calif. 1992, DC 1995. Law clerk to Honorable Frank Battisti, Cleve., 1991—92; assoc. Morrison & Foerster, San Francisco, 1992-94; fellow Stanford U. Law Sch., Palo Alto, Calif., 1994-95; asst. prof. Howard U. Law Sch., Washington, 1995—98, assoc. prof., 1998—2001, prof., 2002—04, 2009—, clinic dir., 2000—02; dean, prof. law Wayne State U. Law Sch., Detroit, 2004—08. Scholar-in-residence Deep Springs Coll., 2001—03; vis. prof. U. Mich., 2002—03, U. Md., George Washington U., Peking U.; adj. prof. Columbia U., 2002—04. Co-author: (book) Beyond Self Interest, 1996, Race, Rights and Reparation: Law and the Japanese American Internment, 2001; contbg. author: book The Affirmative Action Debate, 1996, Illegal Immigration Viewpoints, 1996; author: Yellow: Race in America Beyond Black and White, 2001. Chmn. DC Human Rights Commn., 2001—03, DC Ct. Appeals Bd. Profl. Responsibility, 2003—04; bd. dirs. Leadership Conf. on Civil Rights Edn. Fund, 2004—; trustee Gallaudet U., 2000—. Recipient Chang-Lin Tien Edn. Leadership award, 200 Trailblazer, Nat. Asian Pacific Am. Bar Assn., 2007. Fellow: Am. Bar Found.; mem.: Com. of 100, Am. Law Inst., Asian Pacific ABA (dir. edn1. fund 1995—98). Office: 5160 Linnean Ter NW Washington DC 20008 Office Phone: 202-487-5775. Business E-Mail: frankhwu@mac.com.

WU, GEORGE H., federal judge; b. NYC, 1950; BA, Pomona Coll., 1972; JD, U. Chgo. Law Sch., 1975. Bar: Calif. 1975. Assoc. Latham & Watkins, 1975—79, LeBoeuf, Lamb, Leiby & MacRae, 1989—91; law clk. Hon. Stanley N. Barnes, US Ct. Appeals (9th cir.), 1976—77, 1979; asst. US atty. US Atty's Office (Ctrl. dist.) Calif., 1982—89, 1991—93; judge LA Mcpl. Ct., 1993—96, LA Superior Ct., 1996—2007, US Dist. Ct. (Ctrl. dist.) Calif., 2007—. Asst. prof. law U. Tenn. Coll. Law, 1979—82. Office: US Dist Ct 312 N Spring St Los Angeles CA 90012

WU, GUOYAO, animal scientist, nutritionist, educator; b. China, July 28, 1962; s. Fanjiu Wu and Meixiao Huang; m. Yan Chen, Aug. 7, 1995; 1 child, Neil David. BS in Animal Sci., South China Agrl. U., 1982; MS in Animal Nutrition, Beijing Agrl. U., 1984; MS in Animal Biochemistry, U. Alta., Can., 1986, PhD in Animal Biochemistry, 1989; postgrad. in metabolism/diabetes, McGill U., Mont., Can., 1989-91; postgrad. in biochemistry, Meml. U. Nfld., Can., 1991. Grad. tchg. asst. U. Alta., 1985-88; postdoctoral rschr. Royal Victoria Hosp., McGill U., 1989-91, Meml. U. Nfld., 1991; asst. prof. dept. animal sci. and faculty nutrition Tex. A&M U., College Station, 1991-96, assoc. prof., 1996—. Reviewer Amino Acids, Am. Jour. Clin. Nutrition, Am. Jour. Physiology, Analytical Biochemistry, Biochimica et Biophysica Acta, Can. Jour. Physiology and Pharmacology, Diabetes, Diabetologia, Gastroenterology, Gene, Hormone and Metabolic Rsch., Jour. Animal Sci., Jour. Nutrition, Jour. Nutritional Biochemistry, Jour. Cellular Physiology, Metabolism, Poultry Sci., Reproduction-Nutrition-Devel., Can. Diabetes Assn., Med. Rsch. Coun. Can., U. Toronto Banting and Best Ctr., Can.; editl. advisor Biochem. Jour., 1993—; mem. editl. bd. Jour. Nutrition, 1997—; contbr. articles to profl. jours. Grantee Tex. A&M U., 1992—, Ajinomoto Inc., Japan, 1992, USDA, 1992—, Houston Livestock Show and Rodeo, 1992-95, Am. Heart Assn., 1995—; nat. scholarship for grad. studies abroad Ministry Edn. China, 1984-86, grad. tchg. assistantship U. Alta., 1985-88, dissertation fellowship, 1989, Ctr. Rsch. Fund award, 1988, Andrew Stewart Grad. prize, 1989, U. Alberta, Can. Rsch. Inst. fellowship Royal Victoria Hosp., 1988, fellowship Can. Diabetes Assn., 1989, Med. Rsch. Coun. Can. fellow, 1989-91; established investigator Am. Heart Assn., 1998—. Mem. AAAS, Am. Diabetes Assn., Am. Heart Assn., Am. Soc. for Nutritional Scis., Am. Heart Assn., Am. Physiol. Soc., Am. Soc. Animal Sci., Biochem. Soc. U.K., Can. Soc. Nutritional Scis., Juv. Diabetes Found. Internat. (grantee 1992-94), Soc. for the Study of Reproduction. Home: 4707 Shoal Creek Dr College Station TX 77845-4410 Office: Tex A&M Univ Dept Animal Sci College Station TX 77843-0001

WU, HARRY PAO-TUNG, retired librarian; b. Jinan, Shandong, China, May 1, 1932; arrived in U.S., 1960; s. James Ching-Mei and Elizabeth Hsiao (Lu) Wu; m. Irene I-Len Sun, June 23, 1961; children: Eva Pei-Chen, Walter Pei-Liang. BA, Nat. Taiwan U., Taipei, 1959; postgrad., Ohio State U., 1962; MLS, Kent State U., 1966. Archive and libr. asst. Taiwan Handicraft Promotion Ctr., Taipei, 1959-60; student asst. Kent State U. Libr., 1960-61; reference libr. Massillon (Ohio) Pub. Libr., 1964-65, acting asst. dir., 1965, asst. dir., head adult svcs., 1966; dir. Flesh Pub. Libr., Piqua, Ohio, 1966-68, St. Clair County Libr. Sys., Port Huron, Mich., 1968-96; founder, dir. Blue Water Libr. Fedn., Port Huron, 1974-96; ret., 1996. Pres. Mich. Libr. Film Cir., Lansing, 1977—79; mem. St. Clair County Literacy Project Com., 1986—96. Cmty. mem. editl. bd. Times Herald, 1998—99. Bd. dirs. Mich. Waterways Coun. Girl Scouts U.S., Port Huron, 1985—86, Blue Water Reading Coun., 1987—88, United Way St. Clair County, Mich., 1990—91; trustee Libr. Mich., 1992—95; mem. sister city com. City of Port Huron, 2002—04. Mem.: ALA, Chinese-Am. Librs. Assn., Detroit Suburban Librs. Roundtable, Assn. Ednl. Comm. and Tech., Am. Mgmt. Assn., Mich. Libr. Assn., Port Huron Internat. Club (pres. 1988), Rotary (dir. 1972—74, 1988—90, grand marshall Internat. Day Parade 2005, Paul Harris fellow 1988). Home: 1518 Holland Ave Port Huron MI 48060-1511

WU, HEKUN ANDRE, music educator, director; s. Shijia Wu and Xidi Zheng; m. Elise Hae-Ryung Yun, June 24, 2000. MusD, U. Minn. Sch. Music, Mpls. Prof. violoncello Shanghai Conservatory Music, 1983—87; vis. prof. violoncello &conducting Wellesley Coll., Mass., 1996—2005; prof. violoncello & conducting U. Del., Newark, 1999—2002, Willamette U., Salem, Oreg., 2005—. Artist faculty L'Academie Internat. d'Ete de Nice, France; guest prof. Shanghai Conservatory Music; music dir. conductor Salem Chamber Orch., Oreg., 2005—08. Musician: (concerts) Concerto Soloist, Conductor & Recitalist. Mem.: US Coll. Music Soc. Achievements include research in recitals & recording. Office: Willamette Univ 900 State St Salem OR 97301 Business E-Mail: hwu@willamette.edu.

WU, HONG, pathologist; arrived in U.S., 1988; d. Xing-Yu Wu and Xu-Zhi Xu; m. Lance Mark Wiseman, Nov. 24, 1999. MD, Peking Union Med. Coll., Beijing, 1986; PhD, U. Va., 1992. Diplomate in surg. and clin. pathology and in dermatopathology Am. Bd. Pathology. Rsch. asst. dept. med. genetics Inst. Basic Med. Scis., Chinese Acad. Med. Scis., Beijing, 1987—88; rsch. assoc. dept. microbiology U. Va. Sch. Medicine, Charlottesville, 1993—94; resident dept. pathology and lab. medicne U. Pa., 1994—99, fellow dept. dermatology, 1999—2000; mem., staff pathologist dept. pathology Fox Chase Cancer Ctr., Phila., 2000—. Contbr. articles to profl. jours. Mem.: Am. Soc. Clin. Pathologists, Coll. Am. Pathologists, Am. Soc. Dermatopathology. Office: Fox Chase Cancer Ctr 7701 Burholme Ave Philadelphia PA 19111 E-mail: hong.wu@fccc.edu.

WU, HONG, economics professor; d. Baocheng Wu and Yanhua Sun; m. Xuan Wang; children: Richard Wang, Alexander Wang, Christopher Wang. PhD, West Va. U., Morgantown, 2002. Asst. prof. economics Ripon Coll., Wis., 2003—06, U. St. Thomas, 2006—. Contbr. articles to profl. jour. Mem.: Midwest Econ. Assn., Am. Econ. Assn.

WU, HSIU KWANG, economist, educator; b. Hankow, China, Dec. 14, 1935; came to U.S., 1952, naturalized, 1963; s. Kao Cheng and Edith (Huang) W.; m. Kathleen Gibbs Johnson, Aug. 17, 1968. Grad., Lawrenceville Sch., 1954; AB, Princeton U., 1958; MBA, U. Pa., 1960, PhD, 1963. Prof., group coordinator fin., econs. and internat. bus. Boston U., 1968-72; prof., chmn. fin., econs. and legal studies faculty U. Ala., 1972-81, Lee Bidgood prof. fin. and econs., 1978-97, Ala. Banker Edn. Found. Banking Chair prof., 1973-78, prof. emeritus fin., 1997—; econ. adviser Office of Comptroller of Currency, U.S. Treasury, 1966-69, 75-80; dir. Ala. Fed., 1984-88, SECOR Bank FSB, 1988-93, chmn. bd., 1992-93. Cons. instl. investor study SEC, 1969-70; mem. com. examiners undergrad. program for counseling and evaluation test in bus. Ednl. Testing Service, 1971, 77 Co-editor: Elements of Investments, 2d rev. edit, 1972; Contbr. articles to law and econ. jours. Sloan Faculty fellow Sloan Sch. Mgmt., Mass. Inst. Tech., 1965-66 Mem. Am. Fin. Assn., Fin. Mgmt. Assn. Home: 3201 Old Barn Ct Ponte Vedra Beach FL 32082-3713

WU, HUIQUAN, chemical engineer; s. Shichang Wu and JingNan Tong; m. Meiyu Shen; children: David Xing, Angela Yue. BSc, Wuhan Inst. Tech., Hubei, China, 1985; MSc, Chengdu U. Sci. and Tech., Sichuan, China, 1988; PhD, Iowa State U., Ames, 2001. Sr. process devel. engr. ACM Rsch., Inc., Freemeont, Calif., 2001—02; chem. engr. FDA, Silver Spring, Md., 2002—. Sr. process devel. engr. LSI R & D Ctr., Santa Clara, Calif., 2001. Recipient Outstanding Interctr. Sci. Collaboration award, FDA, 2005, Commrs. Spl. Citation award, 2006, CDER Excellence Analytical Sci. award, 2006. Mem.: Sigma Xi. Achievements include patents for electroplishing method; pharmaceutical research in the area of quality-by-design and process analytical technology.

WU, JAMES CHEN-YUAN, aerospace engineering educator; b. Nanking, China, Oct. 5, 1931; came to U.S., 1953, naturalized, 1963; s. Chien Lieh and Cheng-Ling Wu; m. Mei-Ying Chang, Sept. 7, 1957; children— Alberta Yee-Hwa, Norbert Mao-Hwa. Student, Nat. Taiwan U., 1949-52; BS, Gonzaga U., 1954; postgrad., Columbia U., 1954; MS (univ. fellow), U. Ill., 1955, PhD, 1957. Engr. Wah Chang Corp., NYC, 1954; researcher Mass. Inst. Tech. at Cambridge, 1957; asst. prof. Gonzaga U., Spokane, Wash., 1957-59; research specialist Douglas Aircraft Co., 1959-65, group leader, 1960-61, supr., 1961-62, br. chief, 1963-65; prof. aerospace engring. Ga. Inst. Tech., 1965-96; pres. Applied Aero, LLC, 1996—. Cons. N.Am. Aviation Co., Geophys. Tech. Corp., European Atomic Energy Commn., Ispra, Italy, European Atomic Energy Commn. (research center), U.S. Army Research Office, Durham, S.C. Contbr. articles to profl. jours. Chmn. bd. dirs. Chinese-Am. Inst. Recipient profl. achievement award Douglas Aricraft Co., 1963, Outstanding Tchrs. award Gonzaga U., 1959; Asso. fellow Am. Inst. Aeros. and Astronautics Mem. Am. Soc. Engring. Sci. (founding), Soc. Indsl. and Applied Math. (vice-chmn. Pacific N.W. 1958-59), Am. Astron. Soc. (sr.), Am. Phys. Soc., Nat. Assn. Chinese Ams. (pres. Atlanta chpt.), Sigma Xi, Tau Beta Pi, Sigma Alpha Nu. Office: Sch Aerospace Engring Georgia Inst Tech 48365 Avalon Heights Ter Fremont CA 94539-8005

WU, JANE JIAJING, history professor, consultant; d. Wenqi Wen Wu and Grace En Hu; m. John Yongqiang Lu, Mar. 8, 1968; 1 child, Jia Grace Lu. Degree in History, Mich. State U., East Lansing, 1989. Asst. prof. SW Mo. State U., Springfield, 1989—92; prof. history and chinese lang. Coll. DuPage, Glen Ellyn, Ill., 1992—. Bd. mem. Girl Scouts DuPage County, 1994—2000. Named Woman of the Yr. in Edn., YWCA, DuPage County, 2002, Outstanding faculty of Yr., Ill. Cmty. Coll. Assn., 2007. Mem.: CC Humanities Assn. Home: 1919 Greensboro Dr Wheaton IL 60189 Office: Coll DuPage 425 Fawell Blvd Glen Ellyn IL 60137 Business E-Mail: wujane@cod.edu.

WU, JASON, apparel executive; b. Taipei, Rep. of China; Grad., Parsons Sch. Design, NYC. Freelance designer Integrity Toys Inc., Chesapeake City, Md., 1998—2000, creative dir., 2000, ptnr., designer Fashion Royalty line; intern Narciso Rodriguez; designer Jason Wu Collection, 2006—. Recipient Rising Star award for Women's Apparel, Fashion Group Internat., 2008; finalist Coun. Fashion Designers of America/Vogue Fashion Fund, 2008. Achievements include designing the gown worn by the First Lady for the 2009 Presdl. Inaugural Balls. Office: c/o Anne Fahey C&M Media 307 Seventh Ave Ste 1802 New York NY 10001*

WU, JENQ-LANG, engineering educator; b. Yunlin, Taiwan, Nov. 10, 1968; s. Yi-Min Wu and Chun-Mei Cheng; m. Hang-Yi Ho, Apr. 20, 2002; children: Shang-Hui, Shang-Chia. BS in Electrical Engring., Nat. Taiwan Inst. Tech., Taipei, 1991, PhD in Electrical Engring., 1996. Asst. prof. dept. electronic engring., Hwa-Hsia Coll. Tech. & Commerce, Chung-Ho, Taiwan, 1998—2002, assoc. prof., 2003—05, dept. elec. engring., Nat. Taiwan Ocean U., Keelung, Taiwan, 2006—. Contbr. articles to profl. jours. Mem.: Chinese Automatic Control Soc. Office: Nat Taiwan Ocean Univ Elec Engring Dept No 2 Pei-Ning Rd Keelung 202 Taiwan Office Fax: 886 2 24635408. Business E-Mail: wujl@mail.ntou.edu.tw.

WU, JIAN YOUNG, science educator; married. PhD, Peking U., Beijing, 1986. Prof. Georgetown U., Washington, 1995—.

WU, JIM S., radiologist; married. MD, Baylor Coll. Medicine, Houston, 1999. Diplomate am. bd. radiology ABR, 2004. Staff radiologist Beth Israel Deaconess Med. Ctr., Boston, 2005—. Office: Beth Israel Deaconess Med Center 330 Brookline Ave Boston MA 02215

WU, JOHN GUOQIANG, literature and language professor; PhD, U. North Tex., Denton, 1999. Tchr. English Renaissance Charter Sch., Irving, Tex., 1999—2000; instr. Richland Coll., Dallas, 2001—. Contbr. CND. Org, 2008—09. Liberal. Office: Richland Coll 12800 Abram Rd Dallas TX 75243

WU, JULIAN K., neurosurgeon; b. China, Mar. 9, 1956; ScB, Brown U., Providence, 1977; MD, U. Conn., Farmington, 1981. Diplomate Am. Bd. Neurol. Sugery, 1990. Intern Boston City Hosp., 1981—82; resident Tufts New Eng. Med. Ctr., Boston, 1982—87; chief neurosurgery Beth Israel Deconess Med. Ctr., Boston, 1997—2005; assoc. prof. neurosurgery Harvard U. Med. Sch., Boston, 2000—05; assoc. chmn. neurosurgery Tufts Med. Ctr., 2005—, prof. neurosurgery, 2007—. Bd. mem. Brain Tumor Soc., 1994—. Contbg. author (books) The Practice of Neurosurgery, 1996, Cancer Of The Nervous System, 2004. Recipient Charlton Fund award, Tufts U. Med. Sch., Boston, 1991. Master: Sigma Xi; fellow: Am. Coll. Surgeons; mem.: Neursurgeons Soc. Am., Am. Assn. Neurol. Surgeons. Office: Tufts Med Ctr 800 Washington St Boston MA 02111

WU, JUNRU, physics educator; b. Shanghai, Apr. 5, 1944; came to U.S., 1980; s. Xien Zhon and Meizhen (Li) W.; m. Yiying Lin, Jan. 28, 1976; children: Kathy H., Jane. MS in Physics, UCLA, 1981, PhD in Physics, 1985. Tchg. asst. UCLA, 1980-85, adj. asst. prof., 1985-87; asst. prof. physics U. Vt., Burlington, 1987-93, assoc. prof., 1993-96, prof., 1996—, chmn. physics dept., 1998—. Contbr. more than 80 articles to Jour. Acoustics Soc. Am., Ultrasound in Medicine and Biology. Rsch. grantee NIH, 1990—. Fellow Acoustical Soc. Am., Am. Inst. Ultrasound in Medicine (mem. bioeffect com. 1992-95, mem. tech. standards com. 1996—). Office: U Vt Dept Physics Burlington VT 05405-0001 Home Phone: 802-862-7791. Business E-Mail: jwu@zoo.uvm.edu.

WU, LIN, cardiologist, researcher; s. Zhuofu Wu and Guilan Li; married; 1 child, Yueming. MD, Henan Med. U., Zhengzhou, China, 1985. Diplomate Beijing Med. U., 1990. Vice-chief physician cardiology First Hosp. Beijing Med. U., 1987—98; sr. scientist CV Therapeutics, Palo Alto, Calif., 1992—. Postdoc. rsch. fellow U. Fla., Gainesville, 1999—2001. Contbr. articles to numerous profl. jours. Recipient Sci. and Tech. Advance awards, China Ministry Health, 1996, Sci. Advancement award, China Ministry Edn., 1999. Achievements include patents for reduction of cardiovascular symptoms. Home: 1921 Nobili Ave Santa Clara CA 95051 Office: CV Therapeutics 3172 Porter Dr Palo Alto CA 94304

WU, LIN L., retired botanist, ecologist, educator; b. Beijing, Mar. 18, 1939; arrived in US, 1973; s. Jan-nan Lee and Wen-in Wiu; m. Li-Chun Lin (div.); children: Michael Y., George Z.; m. Frances F. Wu, June 1989. BS, Nat. Taiwan U., Taiwan, 1968; PhD, U. Liverpool, Eng., 1973. Rsch. asst. Inst. Botany Academia Sinica, Taipei, Taiwan, 1968—69, asst. rsch. fellow, 1969—70, assoc. rsch. fellow, 1975—78; rsch. assoc. Duke U., Durham, NC, 1973—75, U. Calif., Davis, Calif., 1978—79, asst. prof., 1979—83, assoc. prof., 1983—91, prof., 1991—2006, prof. emeritus, 2006—. Mem.: Internat. Soc. Eco. Toxicology and Chemistry, Am. Soc. Agronomy, Am. Soc. for Horticulture Sci. Avocations: reading, gardening, photography. Home: 2734 Brandywine Pl Davis CA 95616 Office: U Calif Dept Plant Scis Davis CA 95616 Personal E-mail: linlwu@sbcglobal.net. Business E-Mail: llwu@ucdavis.edu.

WU, MAN, musician; b. Hangzhou, China, 1963; arrived in US, 1990; Master's, Ctrl. Conservatory Music, Beijing. Pipa virtuoso; prin. mem. Silk Road Project; frequent collaborator with Kronos Quartet. Musician: (albums) An Anthology of the Classic Pipa Pieces, 1989, The Overlord Removed of His Armour, 1991, The Wedding Banquet: Original Motion Picture Soundtrack, 1993, Wu Man: Chinese Music for the Pipa, 1993, Eat Drink Man Woman: Original Motion Picture Soundtrack, 1994, World Music Sampler II, 1994, Nature and Spirit: Pipa & 14 Players, 1994, Blues in the East: Work by Sola Liu, 1994, Carry the Day: Work by Henry Threadgill, 1995, China Collage: Sola & Wu Man, 1996, Wu Man & Ensemble: Chinese Traditional & Contemporary Music, 1996, Music for the Motherless Child, 1997, Ghost Opera with Kronos Quartet: Work by Tan Dunn, 1997, Early Music/Kronos Quartet: Work by John Dowland, 1997, The Child God-Music by Bun-Ching Lam, 1998, Music for Airports/Bang on a Can All Star, 1998, China: Time to Listen, 1998, In C: Terry Riley, 2000, Spring Snowfall, 2000, Wu Man: Chinese Traditional & Contemporary Music for Pipa & Ensemble, 2000, Aki No Yugure/Autumn Dusk, 2001, The Silk Road: A Music Caravan, 2002, Silk Road Journeys: When Strangers Meet, 2002, Wu Man/Tastu Aoki: Posture of Reality, 2003, Wu Man Pipa: From a Distance, 2003, Lou Harrison: For Strings, Silk Road Journeys: Beyond the Horizon, 2005, Wu Man and Friends, 2005. Recipient First prize, First Nat. Music Performance Competition, 1989, Glenn Gould Protégé prize in Music and Communication, 1999; Bunting fellow, Radcliffe Inst. Advanced Study, US Artists Broad fellow, 2008. Achievements include first artist from China to perform at the White House. Office: c/o Earl Blackburn Opus 3 Artists 470 Park Ave S 9th Fl N New York NY 10016*

WU, MAN-LI C., research scientist; m. Spencer T. Wu, Sept. 28, 1968. PhD, U. Chgo., Ill., 1976. Rsch. scientist NASA Goddard Space Flight Ctr., Greenbelt, Md., 1979—. Recipient Incentive award, NASA GSFC, 1994, award, 1995, Sci. Achievement award, 1998, Spl. Act award, 1999, Performance award, 2000, 2002, Gen. Recognition award, 2001, Spl. Act award, 2001; Rsch. grant, NASA, 2009—. Mem.: Sigma XI.

WU, MARGARET, research scientist; Sr. scientific advisor ExxonMobil Rsch. & Engring. Co. Recipient Thomas Alva Edison Patent award, 2005. Mem.: Am. Chem. Soc. (award in indsl. chemistry 2007), Chinese Am. Chem. Soc. Office: ExxonMobil Rsch & Engring Co Rt 22 East Annandale NJ 08801 Office Phone: 908-730-2157. Office Fax: 908-730-3314. Business E-Mail: margaret.m.wu@exxonmobil.com.

WU, MICHELLE M., dean, law educator; BA, U. Calif., San Diego, 1991; JD, Calif. Western Sch. Law, San Diego, 1994; MS in Librarianship, U. Wash., Seattle, 1995. With George Washington U. Sch. Law, Washington, 1995—2001; interim dir. law libr. U. Houston, 2001—04; dir. law libr. Hofstra U. Sch. Law, Hempstead, NY, 2004—, interim sr. vice dean academic affairs, 2007—08, assoc. dean info. svcs. & prof. law, 2008—. Editor: (book) Beyond the Books: People, Politics, and Librarianship; contbr. articles to profl. jour. Office: Hofstra Univ Sch Law 122 Hofstra Univ Hempstead NY 11549-1220

WU, MIN, cell biologist, researcher, educator; b. Qixian, China, Oct. 4, 1958; s. Han Zhang Wu and Su Bi Cheng; m. Yun Zeng, July 12, 1985; 1 child, Lu-shen. BSc in Medicine, Luzhou (China) Med. U., 1983; MD, Shanghai Second Med. U., 1988; PhD, Leeds U., Eng., 1997. Lectr. Luzhou (China) Med. Sch., 1988-91, assoc. prof., 1992—, rsch. asst., 1993-94; rsch. officer Leeds (Eng.) U., 1994-97; rsch. assoc. pulmonary divsn. Ind. U./Purdue U., Indpls., 1998-2001, asst. scientist, 2001—. Sr. scientist Synvirion, Ltd., Leeds, 1988—; hon. prof. Tsinghua U., Beijing, 1988—; vis. scientist Peking U., Beijing, 1994-95, Tohoku U., Sendai, Japan, 1991-92; mem adv. coun., GM Cancer Rsch. Found. Author: Medical Microbiology, 1990; contbr. articles to profl. jours. Mem. Life Sci. Soc. for Chinese Bioscientists in U.K. (v.p. 1995-96, pres. 1996-97), Drug Delivery System Soc., chinese Immunology Soc., Biochem. Soc., Chinese Scholars Assn. (exec. mem. 1993-94), Leeds Chinese Scholars Assn. (pres. 1994-95). Avocations: football, painting, singing. Office: Res Asso Pulmonary Divsn IUPU 1 1001 W 10th St #425 Indianapolis IN 46202-2859

WU, MING-CHENG, research scientist; b. Shanghai, Sept. 19, 1961; s. Yucai Wu and Quifeng Shen; m. Yuqin Zhao, Oct. 6, 1996; children: Lawrence J., Claire L. BS, Fudan U., Shanghai, China, 1983; PhD, Copenhagen U., Denmark, 1990. Staff rsch. engr. Delphi Powertrain, Auburn Hills, Mich., 2007—; staff rsch. scientist Delphi Rsch. Labs, Shelby Township, 1999—2006, Gen. Motor Corp., Warren. Chair AVS-Mich. Chpt., Warren, 1999—2000. Mem.: SAE. Achievements include patents for exhaust emission control, exhaust systems and exhaust sensors. Office: Delphi Corp 3000 Univ Dr Auburn Hills MI 48326 Business E-Mail: michael.wu@delphi.com.

WU, NAIJUN, senior fellow; married. PhD, Brigham Young U., Provo, UT, 2000. Asst. prof. Nanjing U. Tech., Nanjing, Jiangsu, China, 1990—96; sr. rsch. fellow Merck Co., Inc., Rahway, NJ, 2000—. Contbr. scientific papers, chapters to books. Recipient award, Merck Rsch. Lab., 2007; Grad. Rsch. fellowship, Brigham Young U., 1997—2000. Mem.: Am. Chem. Soc. Achievements include research in ultra-high pressure liquid chromatography; fast gas chromatography; supercritical fluid chromatography. Business E-Mail: naijun_wu@merck.com.

WU, QIANHONG, engineering educator, researcher; s. Jiantao Wu and Xiane Ma; m. Yuejuan Ma, Aug. 14, 2006. BS in Engring., Huazhong U. Sci. and Tech., Wuhan, China, 1993; MEE, Chinese Acad. Scis., Beijing, 1999; MS in Mech. Engring., CUNY, 2004, PhD in Mech. and Biomed. Engring., 2005. Mech. engr. Beijing Shougang Ctrl. Design Inst., Capital Steel & Iron Corp., P. R. China, 1993—96; rsch. asst. Chinese Acad. Scis., 1996—99, CUNY, 1999—2005; asst. prof. Villanova U., Pa., 2005—. Contbr. articles to profl. jours. Recipient Exceptional Student prize, Huazhong U. Sci. and Tech., 1989—93, Outstanding Graduation Thesis award, 1993, Biomedical Engring. award, Harold Shames and NY Ctr., 2004, TUM Acad. Challenge award, ISPO, 2006, 3d Pl. Acad. Challenge award, 2006; Guanghua fellowship, Huazhong U. Sci. and Tech., 1992, Mario Capelloni Dissertation fellowship, CUNY, 2004—05. Mem.: ASME, Am. Soc. Engring. Edn., Am. Phys. Soc., Internat. Sports Engring. Assn., Biomedical Engring. Soc. Achievements include development of a new experimental and theoretical approach to study lift generation in porous media; discovery of the reason for the longevity of red cells in microcirculation and the lift, the enhanced lift mechanism for human skiing or snowboarding; design of a new type of high speed train model. Avocations: travel, reading, sports. Office: Villanova Univ 800 Lancaster Ave Villanova PA 19085 Business E-Mail: qianhong.wu@villanova.edu.

WU, S. DAVID, dean, industrial and systems engineering educator; PhD, Pa. State U., University Park. Co-founder Ctr. Value Chain Rsch. Lehigh U., Bethlehem, Pa., 2002, chmn. indsl. and systems engring. dept., Lee A. Iacocca prof., dean P.C. Rossin Coll. Engring. and Applied Sci., 2004—. Co-editor: Handbook of Quantitative Supply Chain Analysis: Modeling in the E-Business Era, 2004. Fellow: Inst. Indsl. Engrs. Office: PC Rossin Coll Engring and Applied Sci Lehigh U 19 Memorial Dr W Bethlehem PA 18015-3045 Office Phone: 610-758-5308. Office Fax: 610-758-5623. E-mail: sdw1@lehigh.edu, david.wu@lehigh.edu.

WU, SHUNING, statistician; m. Danni Wang, May 30, 2004. PhD, Iowa State U., Ames, 2007. Rsch. asst. Iowa State U., 2004—07; sr. statis. analyst ISO Innovative Analytics, San Francisco, 2007—. Contbr. articles to profl. jours. Recipient Tchg. Excellence award, Iowa State U., 2007, Premium Acad. Excellence award, 2004, Excellent Leader award, Tsinghua U., 2002. Mem.: IEEE, IIE, INFORMS. Home: 1419 Sherman St Apt D Alameda CA 94501

WU, SING-YUNG, physician, researcher; b. China, 1939; MB, Nat. Taiwan U., 1963; PhD, U. Wash., 1969; MD, Johns Hopkins U., 1971. Staff physician VA Med. Ctr., Long Beach, Calif., 1977—; asst. prof. U. Calif., Irvine, 1977—84, assoc. prof., 1985—90, prof. dept. radiol. scis. and medicine, 1990—. Editor: Thyroid Hormone Metabolism, 1991, 1994; author: Gold File-The Transfer of Nationalist China's Gold Reserve from Shanghai to Taiwan in 1949, 2007. Office: Thyroid Rsch Lab 5901 E 7th St Long Beach CA 90822 Office Phone: 562-826-5808. Business E-Mail: sing.wu@va.gov.

WU, TAI TE, biological sciences and engineering educator; b. Shanghai, Aug. 2, 1935; m. Anna Fang, Apr. 16, 1966; 1 child, Richard. MB, BS, U. Hong Kong, 1956; BSMechE, U. Ill., Urbana, 1958; SM in Applied Physics, Harvard U., Cambridge, Mass., 1959; PhD in Engring. (Gordon McKay fellow), Harvard U., 1961. Rsch. fellow in structural mechanics Harvard U., 1961-63; rsch. fellow in biol. chemistry Harvard U. (Med. Sch.), 1964, rsch. assoc., 1965-66; rsch. scientist Hydronautics, Inc., Rockville, Md., 1962; asst. prof. engring. Brown U., Providence, 1963-65; asst. prof. biomath. Grad. Sch. Med. Scis., Cornell U. Med. Coll., NYC, 1967-68, assoc. prof., 1968-70; assoc. prof. physics and engring. scis. Northwestern U., Evanston, Ill., 1970-73, prof., 1973-74, prof. biochemistry and molecular biology and engring. scis., 1973-85, acting chmn. dept. engring. scis., 1974, prof. biochem., molecular biology, cell biology and biomed. engring., engring. scis., applied math., 1985-94, prof. biochemistry, molecular biology, cell biology, biomed. engring., 1994—. Author (with E.A. Kabat and others): Variable Regions of Immunoglobulin Chains, 1976, Sequences of Immunoglobulin Chains, 1979, Sequences of Proteins of Immunological Importance, 1983, Sequences of Proteins of Immunological Interest, 1987, 5th edit., 1991; editor: New Methodologies in Studies of Protein Configuration, 1985, Analytical Molecular Biology, 2001, Best Scientific Discovery or Worst Scientific Fraud of the 20th Century, 2006; contbr. articles to profl. jours. Recipient Progress award Chinese Engrs. and Scientists Assn. So. Calif., LA, 1971, Rsch. Career Devel. award NIH, 1974-79; C.T. Loo scholar, 1959-60. Mem. Am. Soc. Biochem. and Molecular Biology, Sigma Xi, Tau Beta Pi, Pi Mu Epsilon Office: Northwestern U Dept Biochem Molecular and Cell Biology Evanston IL 60208-3500 Office Phone: 847-491-7849. Business E-Mail: t-wu@northwestern.edu.

WU, TIEN-SHUENN, engineer, researcher, consultant; b. Fung-San, Taiwan, Republic of China, Mar. 7, 1955; s. Kai-Kuen and Li-Fun (Lee) W.; m. Shu-Lin Hsu, Dec. 24, 1980; children: Chi-Valry, Chi-Ray. BS, Nat. Taiwan U., 1977; MS, N.C. State U., 1982, PhD, 1987. Registered profl. engr., Fla., Ga. Tchg. and rsch. asst. N.C. State U., Raleigh, 1981-86; postdoctoral assoc. U. Fla., Gainesville, 1987-89; hydrologist N.W. Fla. Water Mgmt. Dist., Tallahassee, 1989-93; sr. rsch. assoc. NRC, Athens, Ga., 1993-96; sr. environ. engr. HydroGeologic Inc., Herndon, Va., 1996-97; water resources engr. N.W. Fla. Mgmt. Dist., Havana, Fla., 1997-98; environ. specialist III Fla. Dept. Environ. Protection, Tallahassee, 1998—2002, environ. mgr., 2002—07, profl. engr. III, 2007—. Vis. scientist EPA, Athens, 1997; adj. prof. FAMC Engring. Sch., 1992, 98, 2000; v.p. Chinese Am. Water Resource Assn., 2007-. Contbr. articles to profl. jours. Prin. Tallahassee Chinese Sch., 2005-06, prin. 2d lt. China Corps Engrs., 1977—79. Mem. ASCE (v.p. N.E. Ga. chpt. 1994-95, pres. 1995-96, dir. 1996-97, Outstanding Pres. award 1996). Home: 932 Alachua Ave Tallahassee FL 32308-6918 Office: Fla Dept Corrections 2601 Blair Stone Rd Tallahassee FL 32399-2500 Home Phone: 850-577-3058; Office Phone: 850-410-4095. Business E-Mail: tien-shuenn.wu@dep.state.fl.us.

WU, TUNG, curator, artist, art historian, educator; b. Fuzhou, Fukien, China, Dec. 10, 1940; came to U.S., 1965; s. Chin-Wen and Jingrong (Chen) W.; m. Ying Chin, July 16, 1974. BA, Normal U., Taipei, Taiwan, 1962; postgrad., U. Mich., 1967-70, Harvard U., 1979—. Rsch. asst. Nat. Palace Mus., Taichung, Taiwan, 1962-65; with visual art archive U. Mich., 1966-68; rsch. asst. Cleve. Mus. Art, 1968; Ford Found. curatorial intern Nelson-Atkins Mus. Art, Kansas City, Mo., 1969; rsch. fellow Mus. Fine Arts, Boston, 1971-79, asst. curator, 1980-84, assoc. curator, 1984—85, curator Asian art, 1985—91, Matsutaro Shoriki curator Asian art, 1992—2004, emeritus Matsutaro Shoriki curator Asian art, 2005—, head dept. art of Asia, Oceania and Africa, 1999—2004. Guest rsch. fellow The Palace Mus., Beijing; tchg. asst. U. Kans., Lawrence, 1969, Harvard U., 1978, vis. lectr., 75, Emmanuel Coll., Boston, 1992, Seoul Nat. U., 2006; assoc. prof. Simmons Coll., Boston, 1993; advisor Chinese Inst. Am., NYC, 1985—, Chinese Cultural Found., San Francisco, 1985—87, Nat. Mus. History, Taipei, 1984—; cons. Project Emperor-One, Boston, 1983—86; panelist mus. program NEA, 1995; panelist Korea Found. Workshop on Korean painting, Seoul, 2000, Workshop Korean Buddhist art, Gyoengju, Republic of Korea, 2002, Workshop Korean crafts, 2003, Workshop Korean archaeology, 2004, Korean architecture, Gyoengju, 2005; vis prof. archaeology, art history Korea U., Republic of Korea, 2007—. Mem. Nat. Com. on U.S.-China Rels., Washington, 1985—, Nat. Devel. Seminar Taipei, 1989, 92, Nat. Edn. Reform, Taipei, 1994; The Ink Soc. of Hong Kong (advisor 2003—), dept. Asian trade art Peabody Mus., Salem. Mass., 1991—; trustee W.A. Compton Found. Oriental Arts, 1988-2004 Grantee Freer Found. U. Mich., 1968, Ford Found., Kansas City, 1969, Smithsonian Instn., Washington, 1978; recipient Outstanding Alumnus award Taiwan Normal U., 1997, Best Exhibition Catalogue, Independent Publ. Assn, 1997 Mem. Taoist Soc. Japan, Soc. Chinese Kunqu Opera, Soc. Chinese Calligraphy. Office: Mus Fine Arts Asiatic Dept 465 Huntington Ave Boston MA 02115-5597 Office Phone: 010-390-1210. Personal E-mail: wutungart@yahoo.com, wutung@hotmail.com.

WU, VIVIAN Y., finance educator; married. PhD, Harvard U., Cambridge, Mass. Asst. prof. U. Southern Calif., LA, 2005—. Achievements include research in health economics and policy. Office: Univ Southern Calif 650 Childs Way Los Angeles CA 90089-0626

WU, WAYNE WEN-YAU, artist; b. Tachia, Taiwan, Republic of China, Oct. 5, 1935; s. K. C. Kau and Chin-Fong (Chen) Wu; m. Amy Hsueh, Dec. 25, 1961; children: Ingrid, Judy, David. BA in Fine Arts, Taiwan Normal U., 1959. Supr. art edn. ctr. Taichung (Taiwan) Libr., 1970-74; instr. fine arts dept. Taiwan Normal U., Taipei, 1973-74; instr. paintings Hunter Mus. of Art, Chatanooga, Tenn., 1980-92; artist, painting instr. Wayne Wu's Art Studio, Atlanta, 1994-2000, San Jose, Calif., 2000, Salinas, Calif., 2000—04, Gilroy, Calif., 2004—. One-man shows include Taiwan Mus. Art, 1995, Hunter Mus. Am. Art, 1980, 1998, Taipei Internat. Art Fair, 2001, 2004, Korea Internat. Art Fair, 2004, Taichung Seaport Art Ctr., 2006, Nat. Gallery, Nat. History Mus., Taipei, Taiwan, 2009—, others, over 100 group shows. Mem.: Am. Watercolor Soc. Home: 7440 Carnoustie Ct Gilroy CA 95020

WU, WEI, research scientist; s. Zhen Wu and YaYuan Song; m. Yan Jin, July 8, 2008. PhD, Israel Inst. Tech., Haifa, 2007. Rsch. assoc. UCF, Orlando, Fla., 2007—. Contbr. scientific papers to profl. jours. Lady Davis Fellowship, Israel Inst. Tech, 2003—07. Home Phone: 407-925-7005; Office Phone: 407-823-0599. Personal E-mail: wuwei98@gmail.com. Business E-Mail: weiwu@mail.ucf.edu.

WU, XIANREN, telecommunications industry executive, researcher; m. Lin Wu, June 26, 2002; 1 child, Shuangying Sherri. PhD in Elec. Engring., U. Calif. Santa Cruz, 2008. Rschr. U. Calif. Santa Cruz, 2002—. Contbr. numerous articles to profl. jours., confs., chapters to books. Recipient Best Paper award, Internat. Symposium on Performance Evaluation of Computer and Telecomm. Sys. Conf., 2007; Chancellor's fellowship, U. Calif. Santa Cruz, 2007. Master: AAAS; mem.: IEEE.

WU, XIN, electrical engineer, researcher, educator; s. Jizhou Wu and Lingling Liu. B of Engring., Tsinghua U., Beijing, 1996; MS, Chinese Acad. Scis., Beijing, 1999; M of Engring., Johns Hopkins U., Balt., 2001; PhD, U. Md., College Park, 2004. Rsch. asst Johns Hopkins, Balt., 1999—2001, U. Md., College Park, 2001—03; rsch. engr. Etenna Corp, Laurel, Md., 2003—04; spl. operation engr. Ansys/Fluent Inc., Austin, Tex., 2004—05; product mgr. Fluent Inc., 2005—. Contbr. articles to profl. jours. Scholarship, Tsinghua U., 1998, Chinese Acad. Scis., 1998, Johns Hopkins U., 1999, U. Md., 2001—03. Mem.: IEEE. Independent Thinkers. Achievements include patents pending for mesh fencing technique for PCB edge radiated emission suppression; research in computational electromagnetics, radiated EMI noise reduction technologies, electromagnetic bandgap materials, high-speed eletronic packaging performance and signal integrity analysis, electromagnetic modeling and EMC. Avocations: travel, soccer, reading, photography, history.

WU, XINGRU, petroleum engineer; PhD, U. Tex., Austin, 2006. Rsch. asst. U. Tex., Austin, 2002—06; reservoir engr. BP, Houston, 2005—. Mem.: Soc. Petroleum Engrs. Personal E-mail: wuxru@yahoo.com. Business E-Mail: xingru.wu@bp.com.

WU, XU, communications educator; b. Beijing, Aug. 3, 1969; s. Jilu Wu and Jiamin Guo; m. Wei Liu, Aug. 8, 2000. LLB, Renmin U. China, Beijing, 1992; MA in Mass Communication, U. Fla., Gainesville, 2002, PhD, 2005. Nat. corr. & editor Xinhua News Agy., Beijing, 1992—97; ptnr., chief editor Unicorn Communication Consulting Co. Ltd., Beijing, 1997—99; sr. editor, account mgr. Brand Times, Econ. Daily Newspaper Group, Beijing, 1999—2000; asst. prof. Ariz. State U., Phoenix, 2005—. Adj. prof. Johns Hopkins U., Washington. Author: (book) Chinese Cyber Nationalism, 2007 (Chiang Ching-Kuo Found. Jr. award, 2007), On China's Neo-nationalism, Student Time of 50 Chinese Intellectuals; contbr. columns in newspapers. Cons. China State Coun. Info. Office, Beijing, 2007—08; pres. Assn. Asian Communicators, Gainesville, 2003—05; editor newsletter Chinese Communication Assn., Singapore, 2008. Alumni fellowship, U. Fla., 2002—05, Dean's Rsch. grant, Cronkite Sch. Journalism, Ariz. State U., 2006—08. Mem.: Internat. Studies Assn., Chinese Communication Assn. (mem. steering com. 2008—), Assn. Edn. Journalism and Mass Communication, Internat. Communication Assn. Achievements include research in Chinese cyber nationalism and its implications; soft power PR & Beijing olympics; stakeholder identifying & positioning models; China's online media order and it's implications. Avocations: swimming, yoga, music, reading. Office: Arizona State Univ 555 N Central Ave Phoenix AZ 85004-1248 Office Fax: 602-496-7041. Personal E-mail: xuwu992000@yahoo.com. Business E-Mail: xu.wu@asu.edu.

WU, XUANHUI, electrical engineer; s. Rongren Wu and Guiyuan Pan. BS in Engring., Zhejiang U., Hangzhou, 2001; MS in Engring., Nat. U. Singapore, 2004; PhD student, U. Miss., University, 2004—. Rsch. asst. Inst. Infocomm Rsch., Singapore, 2002—04, U. Miss., 2004—08; antenna r&d engr. Radiowaves Inc., Billerica, Mass., 2008—. Contbr. scientific papers to profl. jours. Mem.: IEEE, Phi Kappa Phi, Sigma Xi. Achievements include research in computational electromagnetics and antenna design. Home: 33 Beech St Billerica MA 01821

WU, YIDER, research scientist; b. Taipei, Taiwan, Jan. 11, 1968; arrived in US, 1992, permanent resident; s. Jui-han and Hsiu-yu Wu. BS, Nat. Tsing-Hua U., Taiwan, 1990; MS, U. Mass., Lowell, 1994; PhD, N.C. State, Raleigh, 1999. Rsch. asst. NC State, Raleigh, 1994—99; mem. of tech. staff Advanced Micro Devices, Sunnyvale, Calif., 1999—2004; dept. mgr. Macronix, 2004—; dir. Eon Silicon Solution Inc., Taiwan, 2005—. Patent adv. Advanced Micro Devices, Sunnyvale, Calif., 2000—04; presenter at profl. confs. Contbr. scientific papers, articles to profl. jours. (introductory invited paper, 2000). Mem. Taiwanese Assn. of N.C., Raleigh, 1995—98; v.p. Taiwanese Student Assn., N.C. State, Raleigh, 1995—96. With Taiwan Army, 1990—92. Scholar Outstanding Rschr., Semiconductor Rsch. Corp., 1998. Mem.: IEEE, Semiconductor Rsch. Corp. Buddhist. Achievements include patents in field. Avocations: jogging, swimming, travel, hiking. Personal E-mail: yider_wu@yahoo.com.

WU, YONGJUN, application developer; b. Yiwu, Zhejiang, China, Oct. 8, 1978; married. PhD, Rensselaer Poly. Inst., NY, 2005. Software engr. Microsoft, Redmond, Wash., 2005—. Contbr. chapters to books, scientific papers. Mem.: IEEE.

WU, YU-CHIEN, medical researcher; d. Min-Hsiung Wu and Dai; m. Yi-Min Hunang, Nov. 25, 2008. MD, Kaohsiung Med. U., Taiwan, 2000; PhD, U. Wis., Madison, 2006. Med. intern Chung-Ho Meml. Hosp., Kaohsiung, 1999—2000; med. resident, radiology dept. Chang-Gung Meml. Med. Ctr., Linkou, Taiwan, 2000—01; rsch. asst., med. physics dept. and Waisman lab. brain imaging & behavior U. Wis., 2001—06, rsch. assoc., radiology and med. physics dept., 2006—07, asst. scientist, radiology dept. and Waisman lab. brian imaging and behavior, 2007—. Jour. reviewer Magnetic Resonance Medicine, 2006—. Dr. Samuel Ting's fellowship, 1990, 1992—93, Vilas Travel fellowship, 2006. Mem.: Nat. Multiple Sclerosis Soc., Orgn. Human Brain Mapping, Internat. Soc. Magnetic Resonance Medicine.

WUBBENA, JAN HELMUT, music professor; b. Dover, Del., July 11, 1947; s. Wyatt Jan and Erika Luise Wubbena; m. Teresa Lee Roper, May 17, 1980; children: Robert, Mary. BA, Lebanon Valley Coll., Annville, Pa., 1969; MusM, U. Colo., Boulder, 1970, D of Mus. Arts, 1975. Asst. prof. music Ferrum Coll., Va., 1975—77; prof. music John Brown U., Siloam Springs, Ark., 1977—. Organist, choirmaster Grace Episcopal Ch., Siloam Springs, 1977—. Composer: (choral work) With Every Power for Good, 1980, There is a Land of Pure Delight, 1999, Guide Us Waking Lord, 2002. Fellow: Am. Guild Organists (assoc.; chpt. dean 1982—84, coord. for edn. in Region VII 1984—88, chair nat. com. on ednl. resources 1988—90, dist. convenor for Ark. 2006—); mem.: Assn. Anglican Musicians. Episcopalian. Home: 410 E Jefferson St Siloam Springs AR 72761 Office: John Brown Univ 2000 W University Ave Siloam Springs AR 72761 Office Phone: 479-524-7159. Personal E-mail: wubbenark@cox.net. Business E-Mail: jwubbena@jbu.edu.

WUEBBLES, DONALD JAMES, atmospheric scientist, educator; b. Breese, Ill., Jan. 28, 1948; s. James Edward and Helen (Isaac) W.; m. Barbara J. Yaley, June 13, 1970; children: Ryan, Kevin, Alan. BS, U. Ill., 1970, MS, 1972; PhD, U. Calif. Davis, 1983. Atmospheric scientist Nat. Oceanic and Atmospheric Adminstrn., Boulder, Colo., 1972-73, Lawrence Livermore (Calif.) Nat. Lab., 1973-94, group leader, 1987-94; prof. dept. atmospheric scis. U. Ill., 1994—, head dept. atmospheric scis. Urbana, 1994—2006, dir. sch. earth, society, and environment, 2006—08, Henry E. Preble Endowed prof., 2009—. Dir. The Environ. Coun., 1997-99. Author: Primer on Greenhouse Gases, 1991 (Spl. Achievement award 1991); co-author: Scientific Assessment of Ozone Depletion, 1994, Climate Change 1994: Radiative Forcing of Climate Change, 1994, Climate Change 1995: The Science of Climate Change, 1995; contbr. articles to profl. jours. Chairperson, mem. sch. site coun., Livermore, 1985-90. Recipient Stratosphere Ozone award, EPA, 2005, Nobel prize, IPCC, 2007. Fellow AAAS, AGU; mem. Am. Geophys. Union, Am. Meteorol. Soc., Am. Chem. Soc., Sigma Xi. Home: 3405 S Persimmon Cir Urbana IL 61802-7128 Office: U Ill Dept Atmospheric Scis 105 S Gregory St Urbana IL 61801-3070 Office Phone: 217-244-1568. Business E-Mail: wuebbles@illinois.edu. E-mail: wuebbles@atmos.uiuc.edu.

WUEBBLING, DONALD J., lawyer, insurance company executive; b. Nov. 29, 1945; m. Carol Wuebbling; children: Matthew, Monica. Sr. v.p. & gen. counsel Western & Southern Fin. Group, Cin. Bd. mem. ServerVault Corp. Former pres. Assn. of Life Insurance Counsel; bd. dirs. Cin. Symphony Orchestra, 2006—, Investment Advisors, Eagle Realty Group, Integrity and Nat. Integrity Life Insurance Counsel; bd. trustees May Festival. Office: Western and Southern Fin Group 400 Broadway Cincinnati OH 45202 Office Phone: 513-629-1469.

WUENSCH, BERNHARDT JOHN, ceramic engineering educator; b. Paterson, NJ, Sept. 17, 1933; s. Bernhardt and Ruth Hannah (Slack) W.; m. Mary Jane Harriman, June 4, 1960; children: Stefan Raymond, Katrina Ruth. SB in Physics, MIT, 1955, SM in Physics, 1957, PhD in Crystallography, 1963; DEng (hon.), Hanyang U., Seoul, 2003. Rsch. fellow U. Bern, Switzerland, 1963-64; asst. prof. ceramics MIT, Cambridge, 1964-69, assoc. prof. ceramics, 1969-74, prof., 1974—, TDK chair materials sci. and engring., 1985-90, dir. Ctr. Materials Sci. and Engring., 1988-93, acting dept. head dept. materials sci. and engring., 1980. Vis. prof. Crystallographic Inst., U. Saarland, Fed. Republic Germany, 1973; physicist Max Planck Institut für Festkorperforschung, Stuttgart, Fed. Republic Germany, 1981; mem. US nat. com. for crystallography NRC, NAS, 1980-82, 89-94; mem. NE regional com. for selection of Marshall Scholars, 1970-73, chmn., 1974-80. Co-editor: Modulated Structures, 1979, Neutron Scattering in Materials Science, 1995; adv. editor: Physics and Chemistry of Minerals, 1976—85; assoc. editor Can. Mineralogist, 1978—80; editor: Zeitschrift fuer Kristallographie, 1981—88, Jour. Ceramic Processing Rsch., 2000—. Ford Found. postdoctoral fellow, 1964-66. Fellow Am. Ceramic Soc. (Outstanding Educator award 1987), Mineral. Soc. Am.; mem. AAAS, Am. Crystallographic Assn., Mineral. Assn. Can., Materials Rsch. Soc. Episcopalian. Home: 190 Southfield Rd Concord MA 01742-3432 Office: MIT 77 Massachusetts Ave Rm 13-4037 Cambridge MA 02139-4307 Office Phone: 617-253-6889. Business E-Mail: wuensch@mit.edu.

WUERL, DONALD WILLIAM, archbishop; b. Pitts., Nov. 12, 1940; s. Francis J. and Mary A. (Schiffhauer) W. BA, Cath. U. Am., 1962; MA, Cath. U. Am., Rome, 1963; ThM, Pontifical Gregorian U., Rome, 1967; ThD, Pontifical U. St. Thomas, Rome, 1974; DD (hon.), Duquesne U., 1989, Washington and Jefferson Coll., 1990; HLD (hon.), La Roche Coll., 1990; LHD (hon.), St. Vincent Coll., 1992. Ordained priest Diocese of Pitts., Pa., 1966; asst. pastor, parochial vicar St. Rosalia Ch., Pitts., 1967-69; sec. to Cardinal John Wright Congregation for Clergy, Rome, 1969-79; vice-rector St. Paul Sem., Pitts., 1980-81, rector, 1981-85; ordained bishop, 1986; aux. bishop Archdiocese of Seattle, Wash., 1986—87; bishop Diocese of Pitts., Pa., 1988—2006; archbishop Archdiocese of Washington, 2006—. Sec. to Bishop of Pitts., 1967-69; lectr. Duquesne U., Pitts., 1968-69, 80-85, Pontifical U. St. Thomas, 1975-79; lectr. adult theology program Diocese of Pitts., 1967-69, dir. Inst. Continuing Edn. for Priests, 1982-84, assoc. gen. sec., 1985; ofcl. Congregation for Clergy, Rome, 1969-79; mem. alumni bd. govs. Cath. U. Am., 1977-84, vice-pres. for religious, 1981-82; exec. sec. to Papal rep. for Study of Sems. in U.S., 1982-85. Author: The Forty Martyrs, 1971, Fathers of the Church, 1975, The Catholic Priesthood Today, 1976, A Visit to the Vatican, 1981, The Church and Her Sacraments: Making Christ Visible, 1990; co-author: The Teaching of Christ: A Catholic Catechism for Adults, 1976, rev., 1984, 91, abridged, 1979, study guide, 1977, A Catholic Catechism, 1986; contbg. author: New Catholic Ency.; contbr. articles to religion publs.; author religious cassette programs. Recipient Disting. Pennsylvanian award Gannon U., 1989, Brotherhood award NCCJ, 1991, Tree of Life award Jewish Nat. Fund, 1992, Disting. Alumni award Cath. U. Am., 1992; named Vectors/Pitts. Man of Yr. in religion, 1988. Mem. Am. Cath. Hist. Assn., Cath. Theol. Soc. Am., Fellowship Cath. Scholars, Acad. Romana Universale, Phi Kappa Theta (Man of Achievement award 1988). Roman Catholic. Office: Archdiocesan Pastoral Ctr 5001 Eastern Ave Hyattsville MD 20782-3447 Mailing: PO Box 29260 Washington DC 20017-0260

WUETHRICH, MARCEL, research scientist; m. Christine Otth, Feb. 27, 1997; children: Lea Elaine, Lars Andrew. PhD, U. Bern, Switzerland, 1995. Sr. scientist U. Wis., Madison, 1997—. Office: Univ Wis 1550 Linden Dr Madison WI 53706

WUHL, CHARLES MICHAEL, psychiatrist; b. N.Y.C., Sept. 24, 1943; s. Isadore and Sali (Ackner) W.; m. Gail; children— Elise, Amy. M.D., U. Bologna, 1973. Diplomate Am. Bd. Psychiatry and Neurology. Intern, N.Y. Med. Coll., 1975-76, resident in psychiatry, 1976-77; fellow in child psychiatry Columbia Presbyn. Med. Center, 1977-78; practice medicine specializing in psychiatry and child psychiatry, Englewood, N.J., 1978—; attending staff, mem. faculty N.Y. Med. Coll.; psychiatrist NYU, also asst. clin. prof. psychiatry NYU Sch. Medicine. Contbr. to Psychosocial Aspects of Pediatric Care, 1978, World Book Ency., 1980—. Mem. Am. Psychiat Assn., AMA, Am. Acad. Child Psychiatry. Office: 163 Engle St Englewood NJ 07631-2530 Office Phone: 201-569-2228. Business E-Mail: cw3@nyu.edu.

WULBERT, DANIEL ELIOT, mathematician, educator; s. Morris and Anna (Greenberg) W.; children: Kera, Noah. BA, Knox Coll., 1963; MA, U. Tex., Austin, 1964, PhD, 1966. Rsch. assoc. U. Lund, Sweden, 1966-67; asst. prof. U. Wash., Seattle, 1967-73; prof. U. Calif.-San Diego, La Jolla, 1973—, provost Revelle Coll., 2003—. Vis. prof. Northwestern U., Evanston, Ill., 1977. Contbr. articles in field. Office: Provost Bldg Revelle Coll 0321 U Calif San Diego La Jolla CA 92093-0321 Business E-Mail: dwulbert@ucsd.edu.

WULF, WILLIAM ALLAN, engineering educator; b. Chgo., Dec. 8, 1939; s. Otto H. and Helen W. (Westermeier) Wulf; m. Anita K. Jones, July 1, 1977; children: Karin, Ellen. BS, U. Ill., 1961, MSEE, 1963; PhD in Computer Sci., U. Va., 1968. Prof. computer sci. Carnegie-Mellon Univ., Pitts., 1968—81; chmn., CEO Tartan Labs., Pitts., 1981—87; univ. prof., AT&T prof. engring. U. Va., Charlottesville, Va., 1988—. Bd. dir. Inst. Women; asst. dir. NSF, Washington, 1988—90; cons. various computer mfrs. Author: Fundamental Structures of Computer Science, 1981. Bd. dirs. Pitts. High Tech. Coun., 1982—88. Recipient Kenneth Andrew Roe award, Am. Assn. Engring. Socs., 2001, Chair's award, 2007. Fellow: AAAS, Assn. Women in Sci., Assn. Computing Machinery, Venezuelan Acad. Engring., Am. Philos. Soc.; mem.: NAE (pres. 1996—2007, councillor), Chinese Acad. Engring., Japanese Acad. Engring., Russian Acad. Sci., Spanish Acad. Engring., Am. Acad. Arts and Scis. Avocations: woodworking, photography. Office: Dept Computer Sci Univ Va Thornton Hall Charlottesville VA 22901

WULKER, LAURENCE JOSEPH, portfolio manager, educator, financial planner; b. Cin., Apr. 6, 1945; s. Joseph Laurence and Dorothea Clare (Link) W. BS, Xavier U., Cin., 1967, MA, 1971; cert. fin. planner, Coll. Fin. Planner, 1985. Instr. Lloyd HS, Erlanger, Ky., 1967-68, Elder HS, Cin., 1968-73, Peoples HS, Cin., 1973-74, Regina HS, Cin. Tech. U., Cin., 1974-75; stockbroker Harrison-Bache, Cin., 1976-78; portfolio mgr., fin. planner, v.p. investments UBS, Cin., 1978—2009; instr. U. Cin., 1981-98, Nat. Inst. Fin., South Plainfield, NJ, 1986-88; sys. operator investor forum Compuserve, Ohio, 1985—86; sys. operator fin. planning forum Tristate Online, Cin., 1991—93; dir. Omega portfolio mgr. Oppenheimer & Co., 2009—. Spkr. numerous seminars 1984-. Author column Japanese-Am. League Newsletter, 1985-96; contbr. articles to Cin. Enquirer, Cin. Post, Cin. Bus. Courier. Bd. dirs., v.p., pres. No. Ky. Symphony, 1993-99; treas. Friends of Findlay Market, Findlay Market Assn., 1999—; bd. dirs. Riverwinds Condo Assn., Behringer- Crawford Mus., 2003—. Named one of the best stockbrokers in the country Money Mag., 1987; Fulbright scholar HEW, 1972. Mem. Internat. Assn. Fin. Planners (bd. dirs. Cin. chpt. 1980-87), Fulbright Soc., Order Ky. Cols. Roman Catholic. Avocations: computers, tennis, golf, volleyball, reading. Home: Riverwinds Condos 558 Davenport Ave No 11 Cincinnati OH 45204-1362 Home Phone: 513-921-2966; Office Phone: 513-723-9200. Office Fax: 513-723-9224. Business E-Mail: laurence.wulker@opco.com.

WUN, TED, medical educator; MD, Albany Med. Coll., NY, 1984. Diplomate in hematology Am. Bd. Internal Medicine, 1990, in med.oncology Am. Bd. Internal Medicine, 1991. Prof. medicine UC Davis Sch. Medicine, Sacramento, 2003—08. Office: UC Davis Cancer Ctr 4501 X St Sacramento CA 95817 Office Fax: 916-734-7946.

WUNDER, CHARLES C(OOPER), physiologist, biophysicist, educator; b. Pitts., Oct. 2, 1928; s. Edgar Douglas and Annabel (Cooper) W.; m. Marcia Lynn Barnes, Apr. 4, 1962; children: E(dgar) Douglas, David Barnes, Donald Charles. AB in Biology, Washington and Jefferson Coll., 1949; MS in Biophysics, U. Pitts., 1952, PhD in Biophysics, 1954. Assoc. U. Iowa, Iowa City, 1954-56, asst. prof. physiology and biophysics, 1956-63, assoc. prof. physiology and biophysics, 1963-71, prof. physiology and biophysics, 1971-98, prof. emeritus, 1998—. Cons. for biol. simulation of weightlessness U.S. Air Force, 1964; vis. scientist Mayo Found., Rochester, Minn., 1966-67. Author: Life into Space: An Introduction to Space Biology, 1966; also chpts., numerous articles, abstracts Recipient Research Career Devel. award NIH, 1961-66; AEC predoctoral fellow U. Pitts., 1951-53; NIH spl. fellow, 1966-67; grantee NIH, NASA Mem. Am. Physiol. Soc., The Biophys. Soc. (charter), Aerospace Med. Assn., Iowa Acad. Sci. (chmn. physiology sect. 1971-72, 83-84, 96-97), Am. Soc. Biomechanics (founding), Aerospace Physiologist Soc., Iowa Physiol. Soc. (pres. 1996-97), Am. Soc. for Gravitational and Space Biology (Founders award 2000). Presbyterian. Achievements include the establishment of chronic centrifugation as an approach for investigating gravity's role as a biological determinant. Home: 702 W Park Rd Iowa City IA 52246-2425 Office: U Iowa BSB Iowa City IA 52242

WUNDERER, CORNELIA BEATRIX, aerospace scientist; b. Germany; MS, U. NH, Durham, 1997; PhD, Tech. U. Munich, Germany, 2003. Rsch. asst. Space Sci. Rsch. Ctr., U. NH., Durham, 1997—98; rschr. Max Planck Inst. Extraterrestrial Physics, Garching, Germany, 1998—2001, 2001—03; Charles H. Townes post doc. fellow Space Sciences Lab., UC Berkeley, Calif., 2003—06, sr. fellow, 2006—. Fellowship, U. Calif., Berkeley, 2003—06. Mem.: Am. Astrophysy. Soc., Deutsche Physikalische Gesellschaft. Office: Space Sci Laboratory UC Berkeley 7 Gauss Way Berkeley CA 94720

WUNDERLICH, BERNHARD, retired physical chemistry professor; b. Brandenburg, Germany, May 28, 1931; came to U.S., 1954, naturalized, 1960; s. Richard O. and Johanne (Wohlgefahrt) W.; m. Adelheid Felix, Dec. 28, 1953; children: Caryn Cornelia, Brent Bernhard. Student, Humboldt U., Berlin, Germany, 1949-53, Goethe U., Frankfurt, Germany, 1953-54, Hastings Coll., 1954-55; PhD, Northwestern U., 1957. Instr. chemistry Northwestern U., Evanston, Ill., 1957-58, Cornell U., Ithaca, NY, 1958-60, asst. prof., 1960-63; assoc. prof. phys. chemistry Rensselaer Poly. Inst., Troy, NY, 1963-65, prof. phys. chemistry, 1965-88, prof. emeritus, 1988—; prof. chemistry U. Tenn., Knoxville, 1988-2001, prof. emeritus, 2001—; Disting. scientist div. chemistry Oak Ridge Nat. Lab., 1988-2001. Cons. E.I. duPont de Nemours Co., 1963-88; dir. Lab. for Advanced Thermal Analysis; rsch. in solid state of linear high polymers and thermal analysis, 1980-2001. Author: Macromolecular Physics, Vol. 1, 1973, Vol. 2, 1976, Vol. 3, 1980, Thermal Analysis, 1990, Thermal Analysis of Polymeric Materials, 2005; author computer and audio courses on Crystals of Linear Macromolecules, and Thermal Analysis of Materials; contbr. over 575 articles to profl. jours.; mem. editl. bd. Chemistry, 1965-68, Makromolekulare Chemie, 1966-96; mem. editl. bd. Jour. Thermal Analysis and Calorimetry, 1963-2001, mem. hon. bd., 2004—; mem. adv. bd. Jour. Polymer Sci., 1963-2001, Macromolecules, 1984-88, Polymers for Advanced Tech., 1988-2001, Macromolecular Sci. and Physics, 1995-2001, Thermochim. Acta, 1996-2001. Recipient Humboldt award, 1987-88, award for applied chem. thermodynamics Swiss Soc. for Thermal Analysis and Calorimetry, 1993, TA Instruments award Internat. Conf. Thermal Analysis and Calorimetry, 1996. Fellow Am. Phys. Soc., N.Am., Thermal Analysis Soc. (Mettler award in thermal analysis 1971, Disting. Svc. award 2002); mem. Am. Chem. Soc. Home: 200 Baltusrol Rd Knoxville TN 37934-3707 Home Phone: 865-675-4532. Personal E-mail: wunderlich@chartertn.net.

WUNDERMAN, JAN DARCOURT, artist; b. Winnipeg, Man., Can., Jan. 22, 1921; d. Rene Paul and Georgette Marie (Guionet) Darcourt; m. Frank Joseph Malina, 1938 (div. 1945); m. Lester Wunderman (div. 1967); children: Marc, Geroge, Karen Renee. BFA, Otis Art Inst., LA, 1942. One man shows include Easthampton Guild Hall, LI, 1977, Denise Bibro Fine Art Gallery, NYC, 1992-94, 1996-2002, 04, 06-08, Roko Gallery, 1963, 66, 68, 71, 73, 76, Bibro Show: Painting Survey, 1950-2006, 2006-07; represented in numerous permanent pub., corp. and pvt. collections including Zimmerli Mus., NYU Loeb Collection, Norfolk Mus., Health and Sci. Ctr., Salt Lake City, Alfred Kouri Collection, Skidmore Coll. Print Collection, Nat. Assn. of Women Artists, Rutgers U., 1994, Albright Knox Mus., 1998-99, Daimler Chrysler Coll., Germany, 2002, Northwest Airlines, Detroit, 2003, Bibro Gallery: Invitational, 2008, abstract-nonrepresentational. Recipient Ohashi award Pan Pacific Exhbn., Tokyo and Osaka, 1962, Emily Lowe award 1965, J.J. Akston Found. prize, 1965, Canaday Meml. prize, 1979, Marian De Solo Mendes prize, 1981, Charles Horman Meml. prize, 1983, Amelia Peabody award Nat. Assn. Women, 1991, Grumbacher Gold medal of honor, 1992, Doris Kreindler award 1992; named Am. Soc. Contemporary Artists, 2008. Mem. Nat. Assn. Women Artists (medal of honor 1966, Marcia Brady Tucker award 1965, E. Holzinger prize 1966, Jane C. Stanley prize 1977, Marge Greenblatt award 1990, Amelia Peabody award 1991, Solveig Stomsoe Palmer prize 1997), Am. Soc. Contemporary Artists (corr. sec. 1977-78, Bocour award 1980, Elizabeth Erlanger Meml. award 1990, Kreindler award 1992, N. Ransom award 2002), Contemporary Artists Guild (Irwin Zlowe Meml. award 1998). Avocations: history, travel. Address: Denise Bibro Fine Art Gallery 529 West 20th St New York NY 10011 Office Phone: 212-673-1452.

WUNNICKE, BROOKE, lawyer; b. Dallas, May 9, 1918; d. Rudolph von Falkenstein and Lulu Lenore Brooke; m. James M. Wunnicke, Apr. 11, 1940; (dec. 1977); 1 child, Diane B. BA, Stanford U., 1939; JD, U. Colo., 1945. Bar: Wyo. 1946, Colo. 1969, U.S. Dist. Ct. Wyo. 1947, U.S. Dist. Ct. Colo. 1970, U.S. Supreme Ct. 1958, U.S. Ct. Appeals (10th cir.) 1958. Pvt. practice law, 1946—69; ptnr. Williams & Wunnicke, Cheyenne, Wyo., 1956—69; counsel Calkins, Kramer, Grimshaw & Harring, Denver, 1969—73; chief appellate dep. atty. Dist. Atty's Office, Denver, 1973—86; counsel Hall & Evans L.L.C., Denver, 1986—. Adj. prof. law U. Denver Coll. Law, 1978-97, 1st Frank H. Ricketson Jr. adj. prof., 2003; lectr. Internat. Practicum Inst. Denver, 1976-2003. Author: Ethics Compliance for Business Lawyers, 1987; co-author: Standby Letters of Credit, 1989, Corporate Financial Risk Management, 1992, UCP 500 and Standby Letters of Credit-Special Report, 1994, Standby and Commercial Letters of Credit, 2000, 2009, Annual Supt., Legal Opinion Letters Formbook, 2002, 2009, Annual Supt.; contbr. articles to profl. jours. Pres. Laramie County Bar Assn., Cheyenne, 1967-68; Dir. Cheyenne C. of C., 1965-68 Recipient Outstanding Svc. award, Colo. Dist. Attys. Coun., 1979, 1982, 1986, Disting. Alumni awards, U. Colo. Sch. Law, 1986, 1993, William Lee Knous award, 1997, Lathrop Trailblazer award, Colo. Women's Bar Assn., 1992, Eleanor P. Williams award for Disting. Svc. to Legal Profession, 1997, Potter Lifetime Profl. Svc. award, 1999, Nat. award, Def. Rsch. Inst., 1999, Law Star award, Denver Coll. Law, 2003. Fellow Colo. Bar Found., Am. Bar Found.; mem. ABA, Wyo. State Bar, Denver Bar Assn. (hon. life; trustee 1977-80, award of Merit 2004), Colo. Bar Assn. (hon., life, Award of Merit 1999), Am. Arbitration Assn. (comml. panel), William E. Doyle Inn of Ct. (hon.), Order of Coif, Phi Beta Kappa. Independent. Avocations: reading, writing. Office: Hall & Evans LLC 1125 17th St Ste 600 Denver CO 80202-2037 Office Phone: 303-628-3363. Business E-Mail: wunnickeb@hallevans.com.

WUNNING, STEVEN H., manufacturing executive; B engring., Univ. Mo.; MBA, Univ. Ill. Mfg. mgmt. positions Caterpillar Inc., Peoria, Ill., 1973—87; mgmt. positions Caterpillar Logistics Services Inc., 1987—90, v.p., 1990—94, pres., 1994—98; corp. v.p. logistics & prod. services Caterpillar Inc., Peoria, Ill., 1998—2000, corp. v.p. logistics div., 2000—04, group pres., 2004—. Bd. dir. Black & Veatch Holding Co. Chmn. Ctrl. Ill. chpt. Am. Red Cross; trustee Proctor Hosp., Peoria, Ill., Manufacturers Alliance MAPI, Arlington, Va. Office: Caterpillar Inc 100 NE Adams St Peoria IL 61629*

WUNSCH, CHARLES ROBERT, lawyer; b. Murfreesboro, Tenn., Feb. 10, 1956; s. Billy Dean and Sally Jane (Mayer) W.; m. Amy Sloan Cooley, July 29, 1978; children: Benjamin Hardy, Evan Dean. BA in History, Stanford U., Calif., 1978; JD cum laude, Cornell U., 1981. Bar: Mo. 1981, U.S. Dist. Ct. (we. dist.) Mo. 1981, U.S. Ct. Claims 1985, U.S. Tax Ct. 1986. Assoc. Watson, Ess, Marshall & Enggas, Kansas City, Mo., 1981-87, ptnr., 1988-90; atty. Sprint Corp., Westwood, Kans., 1990-92; sr. atty. through assoc. gen. counsel Sprint PCS Sprint Nextel Corp., Overland Park, Kans., 1992—2002, v.p. corp. transactions, 2002—08, gen. counsel, corp. sec., 2008—. Contbr. articles to profl. jours. Cubmaster Pack 3399 Heart of Am. coun. Boy Scouts Am., Mission, Kans., 1988-90, asst. cubmaster Pack 3428, 1990, 92, asst. scoutmaster troop 428, 1992—; cubmaster Pack 3428, 1993—; trustee Countryside Christian Ch., Mission, 1989, deacon, 1989-92, elder, 1992-94; bd. dirs. Kaw Valley Habitat for Humanity, 1991—, v.p., 1992—. Recipient Mo. Bar Pres.'s award, 1990. Mem. Mo. Bar Assn. (legal edn. com. 1987-90, chmn. bus. law com. 1988-90). Republican. Avocations: reading, genealogy, stamp collecting/philately. Office: Sprint Nextel Corp 6391 Sprint Pkwy Overland Park KS 66251-6100*

WUNSCH, JAMES STEVENSON, political science professor; b. Detroit, Sept. 27, 1946; s. Richard Ellis and Jane Rolston (Kershaw) W.; m. Lillian C. Hedlund, Mar. 29, 1969 (div. Feb. 1983), 1 child, Kathryn; m. Mary Gayle Gundlach, Aug. 19, 1983; children: Hallie, Hannah. BA, Duke U., 1968; MA, Ind. U., 1971, PhD, 1974. Rsch. fellow U. Ghana, Accra, 1971-72; asst. prof. Creighton U., Omaha, 1974-78, assoc. prof., 1978-86, prof. polit. sci., 1986—, chmn. dept., 1983-93, 96—, dir. African studies program, 1998—. Social sci. analyst and cons., Ghana, Liberia, Kenya, Sudan, Thailand, Philippines, Joint African Inst., African Devel. Bank, UNDP, USAID, Washington, 1978-80; vis. assoc. prof. Ind. U., Bloomington, 1985-86; sr. project mgr. Assocs. in Rural Devel., Burlington, Vt., 1987-88, cons., Bangladesh, Zambia, Nigeria, South Africa, Swaziland, Botswana, Liberia, Uganda, 1985—; USIA Disting. lectr., South Africa, 1993. Author: The Failure of the Centralized State, 1990, Local Governance in Africa, 2004 (monograph) Rural Development, Decentralization and Administrative Reform, 1988; mem. bd. editors Pub. Adminstrn. and Devel., 1998—; contbr. more than 40 articles to profl. jours., chpts. to books. Bd. dirs. Omaha Symphony Chorus, 1977-78, Nebr. Choral Arts Soc., 1982-96, Voices of Omaha, 1982-85, Trinity Cathedral, Omaha, 1980-83; participant Leadership Omaha, 1982-83; mem. Omaha Com. Fgn. Rels., 1975-95; mem. govt. affairs com. Greater Omaha C. of C., 1980-85; mem. issues and interests com. Nebr. Rep. party, 1984-88. Recipient R.F. Kennedy Quality Tchg. award Creighton U., 1985, Burlington No. award, 1992, Dean's award for excellence in tchg., 1994, Dean's award for excellence in scholarship, 2000, Dean's award for excellence insvc., 2006, Student Senate award for excellence in advising, 1989; rsch. award NSF, NEH, USAID, Am. Philos. Soc., Dean's Spl. award, 2007; Fulbright-Hays fellow in Ghana, 1971-72, Internat. Affairs fellow N.Y. Coun. Fgn. Rels., 1978-79. Mem. Am. Polit. Sci. Assn., Midwest Polit. Sci. Assn., African Studies Assn., Internat. Studies Assn., Phi Beta Kappa, Pi Sigma Alpha, Phi Beta Delta. Presbyterian. Avocations: vocal music, camping, cross country skiing, bicycling. Home: 1631 N 53rd St Omaha NE 68104-4947 Office: Creighton U Dept Polit Sci 30th And California Omaha NE 68178-0001 Office Phone: 402-280-2568. Business E-Mail: jwunsch@creighton.edu.

WUNSCH, JOHN D., former bank executive, financial consultant; BA, U. Minn., 1971. Pres. Perrybell Investments Inc., 1990—97; CEO, pres. Family Fin. Strategies Inc., 1997—2002; exec. positions Bank of Montreal (Harris myCFO Inc.), 2002—06, Bank of Montreal (Harris Bank N.A.), 2002—06. Bd. dirs. ADC Telecom. Inc., 1991—, Med. Graphics Corp., 1997—, Telident, Inc., 1997; mng. mem. Immersive Video Solutions LLC, 2007—; independent cons. in fin. svcs., 2001—02. Avocations: fishing, flying, skiing, motorcycling, hunting. Office: ADC Telecommunications Inc 13625 Technology Drive Minneapolis MN 55440 Office Phone: 952-938-8080. Office Fax: 952-917-1717.

WUORI, STEPHEN J., energy executive; BS in Civil Engring., Mich. Technol. U., Houghton. Pres. Enbridge Pipelines Inc. and Enbridge Energy Ptnrs., L.P. Enbridge, Inc., 1997—2000, group v.p. planning and devel., 2001—03, group v.p., CFO, 2003—06, exec. v.p., CFO & corp. devel., 2006—08. Office: Enbridge Energy Ptnrs LP 1100 Louisiana Ste 3300 Houston TX 77002 Office Phone: 713-821-2000.*

WURDEMAN, LEW EDWARD, Internet company executive, consultant; b. Colorado Springs, Colo., Oct. 31, 1949; s. Robert Martin and Shirley Gladys (Reetz) W. Student, U. Tex., 1967-69, U. Minn., 1969-72. Adminstr. Control Data Corp., Bloomington, Minn., 1969-81; product splst., 1981-83; sys. mgr., 1983-84; cons., 1984-89; mgr. The Roach Orgn., Inc., Mpls., 1989-90; computer cons. Wurdeman Enterprises, Inc., Farmington, Minn., 1991-93; sr. cons. Norstan Consulting, Minnetonka, Minn., 1993-2001; photographer Vividere Glamour Photography, 1996—; tree farm owner Golden Pond Farm, 2003—. Freelance photographer; virtual tour photographer 360 Minn., 2003—. Commr. Parks and Recreation Dept., City of Farmington, Minn., 2001-03. Mem. Internat. Freelance Photographers Orgn., Internat. Glamour Photographers Assn., Photog. Soc. Am. Profl. Photographers Am. Republican. Lutheran. Avocations: computers, photography. Office: Link Up Hosting PO Box 332 Farmington MN 55024-0332 Office Phone: 612-327-6178. Business E-Mail: lew@wurdeman.org. E-mail: lew@linkuphosting.com.

WURM, ALEXANDER, physics professor; b. Muenster, Germany, June 4, 1971; s. Klaus E. and Christa R. Wurm; m. Kathleen Anne Decker, July 19, 1996; children: Katja Tennessee, Thomas Austin. MA in Physics, U. Tex., Austin, 1995, PhD, 2002; diploma in Physics, Julius Maximilians U., Würzburg, Germany, 1997. Postdoc. rschr. Inst. Fusion Studies, U. Tex., Austin, Tex., 2002—05; asst. prof. physics Western New Eng. Coll., Springfield, Mass., 2005—. Fellowship, US Dept. Energy Fusion Energy Postdoc. Rsch. Program, 2002—04. Mem.: Am. Phys. Soc., Gamma Beta Phi. Office: Western New Eng Coll 1215 Wilbraham Rd Box H-5180 Springfield MA 01119 Business E-Mail: awurm@wnec.edu.

WURMFELD, SANFORD, artist, educator; b. NYC, Dec. 6, 1942; s. Charles Jacob and Esther W.; m. Rella Stuart-Hunt, Dec. 11, 1971; children: Jeremy Philip, Treva. BA in Art with honors, Dartmouth Coll., 1964; ind. study, Rome, 1964—65. Lectr. Hunter Coll., NYC, 1967—72, asst. prof., 1972—77, assoc. prof., 1977—80, chmn. dept. art, 1978—2006, prof. art, 1980—, Caroff prof., 2000—. Vis. artist lectr. Calif. State Coll., Hayward, Cooper Union, NY, Bard Coll., Anondale-on-Hudson, NY, Drexel U., Phila., 1970, SUNY, Fredonia, 1971, Livingston Coll., New Brunswick, NJ, 1973, Whitney Mus., 1982, Met. Mus. Art, 1987, Princeton U., 1990, The Slade Sch. U. Coll., London, 1991, Chelsea Coll. Art, London, 1991, Whitney Mus., 1992, Hochschule der Kurst, Berlin, 1995, Simon Fraser U., Vancouver, 1996, U. Victoria, B.C., 1996, Acad. Minerva, The Netherlands, Glasgow Sch. of Art, Scotland, 1997, external examiner, 1999—2003. One-man shows include E-Cyclorama, Edinburgh Coll. Art, 2008, Neuberger Mus., Purchase, NY, 2009, "Cyclorama 2000" Talbot Rice Gallery, Edinburgh, 2004, Altötting, Germany, 2003, Cyclorama, 2000, Karl Ernst Osthaus Mus., Hagen, Germany, 2000, Susan Caldwell Gallery, Inc., N.Y., 1978, Bard Coll. Invitational Exhibit, 1977, Susan Caldwell Gallery, 1976-77, Galarie Denise Rene, 1974, Rockefeller Meml. Gallery, Fredonia, N.Y., 1971, Tibor de Nagy Gallery, 1968, Bryant Park, N.Y., Fischbach Gallery, 1969; group shows include Mus. Modern Art, N.Y., 1968, Grank Palais, Paris, 1968, Kunsthaus, Zurich, 1968, Tate Gallery, London, 1968, Ft. Worth Art Ctr., 1969, Galerie de Gestlo, Kunstfair, Basel Switzerland, 1970, 72, Columbia Film Festival, 1973, Galerie Denise Rene, 1974, Hopkins Ctr. Galleries, 1974, Lehigh U., 1976, Susan Caldwell Gallery, 1977-79, Toni Birckhard Gallery, Cin., 1980, Carnegie Internat., 1983, Shanghai Exhbn. Hall Shanghai, China, 1986, Long Beach Mus. of Art, Calif., 1989, William Paterson Coll. of N.J., 1990, Hallwells Contemporary Arts Ctr., Buffalo, 1991, Louis Stern Fine Arts, L.A., 1995, Andre Zarre Gallery, N.Y., 1996, 2003, Condeso-Lawcer Gallery, N.Y., 1997, Karl Ost Haus-Mus., Hagen, Germany, Mucsarnok, Budapest, 1999, 02, Am. Acad. Arts and Letters, 2000, Hunter Coll. Times Sq. Gallery, 2003, 04, Concordia Coll., Ann Arbor, 2006, Panorama Mesdag, The Hague, 2006, Pratt Manhattan Gallery, 2007, Wooster Art Space, 2007; represented in permanent collections at Espace de l'Art Conret, Mouans-Sartoux, France, Karl Ernst Osthaus Mus., Hagen, Germany, Met. Mus. Art, N.Y., Guggenheim Mus., N.Y., SUNY, Fredonia, Ctrl. Trust Co., Cin., AT&T, N.Y., Baxter Travenol Labs., Deerfield, Ill., GE Corp., Fairfield, Conn., Sprengler Mus., Hannover, Germany, City of Hannover, Shreve, Lamb & Harmon Corp., N.Y., Silkscreeners Guild, Germany, Warner Nat. Corp., Cin., U. N.C., William Hayes Ackland Meml. Art Ctr., Chapel Hill, others; contbr. articles to profl. jour. Recipient Ames award Dartmouth Coll., 1964; fellow Guggenheim Found., 1974, Nat. Endowments for the Arts Individual Artist's, 1987-88; CUNY faculty rsch. grantee. Home: 18 Warren St New York NY 10007-1066 Office: Hunter Coll Dept Art 695 Park Ave New York NY 10021-5024 Office Phone: 212-233-1570. Business E-Mail: swurmfel@hunter.cuny.edu.

WURN, KATHLEEN MARIE, English educator; b. San Antonio, June 8, 1950; d. Maurice and Irene Aelvoet DeCock; m. Thomas Arnold Wurn, May 6, 1972; children: Lisa S. Latham, Jeffrey T. BA, St. Mary's U., San Antonio, 1972. Secondary tchr. cert. Tex. English tchr. Medina Valley HS, Castroville, Tex., 1982—. Student coun. advisor Medina Valley HS, 1992—. Entertainment chmn. Am. Cancer Soc. Relay for Life, Devine, Tex., 1999—2006. Named Excel Tchr. of Yr., Medina Valley HS, 2001, Tchr. Amb., MetLife, 2003, Tchr. of Yr., VFW, 2005; grantee, Tex. Learn and Serve, 1999—2002, State Farm Ins., 2005—06. Mem.: ATPE, Alamo Assn. Student Couns. (dist. advisor 2006—, Advisor of Yr. 2006—), Tex. Assn. English Tchrs., Tex. Assn. Student Couns. Home: 13802 French Park Helotes TX 78023 Office: Medina Valley HS 8365 FM 471 S Castroville TX 78009

WÜRSIG, BERND GERHARD, marine biology educator; b. Barsinghausen, Germany, Nov. 9, 1948; s. Gerhard Paul and Charlotte Annemarie (Yorkowski) Würsig; m. Melany Anne Carballeira, Nov. 19, 1969; children: Kim Wuersig, Paul Wuersig. BS, Ohio State U., 1971; PhD, SUNY, Stony Brook, 1978. Postdoct. rschr. U. Calif., Santa Cruz, 1978-81; prof. Moss Landing (Calif.) Marine Labs., 1981-89; prof. marine biology, dir. Marine Mammal Lab. Tex. A&M U., Galveston, 1989—. Regents prof., 2006—, dir. The Inst. of Marine Life Scis., 1996—, chair, inter disciplinary program grad. studies marine biology, 2008—. Govt. cons. Minerals Mgmt. Svc., Washington, 1980—. Contbr. articles to profl. jours., 7-part miniseries to TV on lives of dolphins, dolphin problems induced by humans, also Discovery Channel show on Life of B Würsig; co-author: The Hawaiian Spinner Dolphin, 1994, Whales, Dolphins and Porpoises, 1995; sr. advisor (IMAX film) Dolphins, 2000 (nominee Acad. award best spl. category nature movie), sr. author The Marine Mammals of the Gulf of Mexico, 2000; co-editor: The Encyclopedia of Marine Mammals, 2002, 2nd edit., 2009. Recipient Chmn.'s award for rsch. and exploration, Nat. Geog. Soc., 1998, Alban-Heiser award for excellence in Tex. conservation rsch., Zool. Soc. Houston, 1991, Regents Professorship award, Tex. A&M U., 2006, Disting. Achievement award, 2008; Fulbright Found. scholar, 2001—03. Mem. Marine Mammal Soc. (pres. 1991-93), N.Y. Acad. Scis., Soc. Cryptozoology, Am. Behavior Soc., Am. Mus. Natural History, Soc. Archimedes. Clubs: Explorers (N.Y.C.) (fellow of research). Avocations: photography, diving, airplane piloting, skiing, hiking. Home: 2402 Creekridge Dr Pearland TX 77581-5728 Office Phone: 409-740-4413. Business E-Mail: wursigb@tamug.edu.

WURSTER, CHARLES FREDERICK, environmental scientist, educator; b. Phila., Aug. 1, 1930; s. Charles Frederick and Helen B. Wurster; children: Steven Hadley, Nina F., Erik Frederick. SB, Haverford Coll., 1952; MS, U. Del., 1954; PhD, Stanford U., 1957; DSc (hon.), SUNY, 2009. Rsch. asst. Stanford U., 1954-57; Fulbright fellow Innsbruck, Austria, 1957-58; rsch. chemist Monsanto Rsch. Corp., 1959-62; rsch. assoc. biol. scis. Dartmouth Coll., 1962-65; asst. prof. biol. scis. SUNY, Stony Brook, 1965-70; assoc. prof. environ. scis. Marine Scis. Rsch. Ctr., 1970-94, prof. emeritus, 1994—. Founding trustee, sec., mem. exec. com. Environ. Def. Fund, 1967—; vis. prof. Macquarie U., Sydney, 1988; mem. adminstr.'s pesticide policy adv. com. EPA, 1975—78; leader ecol. tours worldwide. Contbr. articles to profl. publs. Scholar, U. Wash., Seattle. Fellow: AAAS; mem.: Environ. Def. Soc. (New Zealand) (bd. dirs. 1980—), Nat. Pks. Conservation Assn. (trustee 1970—79), Defenders Wildlife (dir. 1975—84, 1987—96). Achievements include research on DDT, PCBs, other chlorinated hydrocarbon effects on phytoplankton, birds; relationship between environmental sciences and public policy; seabird protection; instrumental in banning several insecticides, including DDT, Dieldrin and Aldrin. Address: 644 Hillside Dr E Seattle WA 98112 Office Phone: 206-325-3665. Personal E-mail: cfwurster@yahoo.com.

WURSTER, DONALD C., career military officer; b. Washington, 1951; BS, USAF Acad., Colo. Springs, 1973; disting. grad., Squadron Officer Sch., Maxwell AFB, Ala., 1982; MA, Webster U., St. Louis, 1983; disting. grad., Air Command Staff Coll., Maxwell AFB, 1987; grad., Air War Coll., 1994, Indsl. Coll. Armed Forces, Ft. Lesley J. McNair, Washington DC, 1997. Commd. 2nd lt. USAF, 1973, advanced through ranks to lt. gen., 2007—; pilot Rescue Weather Reconnaissance Wing, Osan Air Base, Republic of Korea, 1975—76; instr. pilot Air Rescue Recovery Squad., Elmendorf AFB, Alaska, 1976—79; evaluator pilot Aircrew Tng. Test Wing, Kirtland AFB, N.Mex., 1979—80; weapon sys. program mgr. Hdqs. Milt. Airlift Command, Scott AFB, Ill., 1983—86; asst. ops. officer Spl. Ops. Squad., Eglin AFB, Fla., 1987—89; program element monitor for rescue spl. ops. forces Office Sec. Air Force for Acquisition, DC, 1989—91; ops. officer, comdr. Spl. Ops. Squad., RAF Woodbridge, RAF Alconbury, England, 1991—94; asst. electronics, comm., spl. programs Office Asst. Sec. Def. Spl. Ops. Low-Intensity Conflict, Forces Resources, DC, 1994—96; comdr. Ops. Group, Herbert Field, Fla., 1997—98, Spl. Ops. Wing, Herbert Field, 1998—99; inspector gen. US Transp. Command, Hdqs. Air Mobility Command, Scott AFB, 1999—2000; comdr. Spl. Ops. Command Pacific, Camp H.M. Smith, Hawaii, 2000—03; spl. asst. to comdr. US Spl. Ops. Command (USSOCOM), MacDill AFB, Fla., 2003—04, dir. Ctr. Intelligence Info. Ops., 2003—04, dep. dir. Ctr. Spl. Ops., 2004—06; vice comdr. Air Force Spl. Ops. Command (AFSOC), Hurlburt Field, 2006—07, comdr., 2007—. Decorated Def. Suprior Svc. medal with two oak leaf clusters, Legion Merit with oak leaf cluster, Def. Meritorious Svc. medal, Meritorious Svc. medal with four oak leaf clusters, Air medal, Aerial Achievement medal with oak leaf cluster, Air Force Commendation medal with oak leaf cluster, Air Force Achievement medal, Humanitarian Svc. medal with bronze star. Office: Air Force Spl Ops Command Hdq Hurlburt Field FL 32544

WURTELE, CHRISTOPHER ANGUS, paint and coatings company executive; b. Mpls., Aug. 25, 1934; Valentine and Charlotte (Lindley) W.; m. Heather Campbell (div. Feb. 1977); children: Christopher, Andrew, Heidi; m. Margaret Von Blon, Aug. 21, 1977. BA, Yale U., 1956; MBA, Stanford U., 1961. V.p. Minn. Paints, Inc., Mpls., 1962—65; exec. v.p. Minn. Paints, Inc. (merged with Valspar Corp. 1970), Mpls., 1965—73, pres., CEO, 1973-96, chmn., 1973-98. With USN, 1956—59. Mem.: Mpls. Club. Episcopalian. Home: 2970 Gale Rd Wayzata MN 55391 Office: 4900 IDS Ctr 80 S 8th St Minneapolis MN 55402

WÜRTH, REINHOLD, manufacturing executive; b. Ohringen, Apr. 20, 1935; m. Carmen Wurth; 3 children. Dr., senator, U. Tubingen. Lic. profl. pilot Harley-Davidson motorcycles. First apprentice screw trade Wurth Group, Kunzelsau, 1949, head bus. and mgmt., 1954, chmn. adv. bd., 1994—. Head Interfacultative Inst. Entrepreneurship U. Karlsruhe, 1999—2003; mem. supervisory bd. IKB Deutsche Industriebank AG, Dusseldorf; shareholder, mem. bd. trustees Robert-Bosch Found.; chmn. adv. bd. Entrepreneurs Soc. Internat. Cooperation Baden-Wurttemberg. Decorated Disting. Svc. Cross, 1st class, Order of Merit Rep. Germany; recipient Medal Econ. Merits, Baden-Wurttemberg, Chevalier dans l'Ordre des Arts et des Letters, French Ministry Culture, 2000, Ludwig-Erhard Medal, Ludwig-Erhard Found., 2004; named one of World's Richest People, Forbes Mag., 1999—2007, Top 200 Collectors, ARTnews Mag., 2004—08. Avocation: Collector of Modern and Contemporary Art. Office: A Wurth GmbH & Co KG Reinhold-Wurth Str 12-17 Kunzelsau Germany

WURTMAN, RICHARD JAY, neuroscientist, educator, inventor; b. Phila., Mar. 9, 1936; s. Samuel Richard and Hilda (Schreiber) W.; m. Judith Joy Hirschhorn, Nov. 15, 1959; children: Rachael Elisabeth, David Franklin. AB, U. Pa., 1956; MD, Harvard U., 1960. Intern Mass. Gen. Hosp., 1960-61, resident, 1961-62, fellow medicine, 1965-66, clin. assoc. in medicine, 1985—; research assoc., med. research officer NIMH, 1962-67; mem. faculty MIT, Cambridge, 1967—, prof. endocrinology and metabolism, 1970-80, prof. neuroendocrine regulation, 1980-94, Cecil H. Green disting. prof., 1994—; dir. Clin. Rsch. Ctr., MIT, Cambridge, 1985—2005; prof. neurosci. MIT, 1984-94. Lectr. medicine Harvard Med. Sch., 1969—; prof. Harvard-MIT Divsn. Health Scis. and Tech., 1978—; Smithies lectr. Oxford U., 2002; sci. dir. Ctr. for Brain Scis. and Metabolism Charitable Trust, 1981—; invited prof. U. Geneva, 1981; Sterling vis. prof. Boston U., 1981; vis. fellow Balliol Coll., Oxford U., 1997; mem. small grants study sect. NIMH, 1967-69, preclin. psychopharmacology study sect., 1971-75; behavioral biology adv. panel NASA, 1969-72; coun. basic sci. Am. Heart Assn., 1969-74; rsch. adv. bd. Parkinson's Disease Found., 1972-80, Am. Parkinson's Disease Assn., 1978—; com. phototherapy in newborns NRC-Nat. Acad. Scis., 1972-74, com. nutrition, brain devel. and behavior, 1976, mem. space applications bd., 1976-82; mem. task force on drug devel. Muscular Dystrophy Assn., 1980-87; chmn. life scis. adv. com. NASA, 1979-82; chmn. adv. bd. Alzheimer's Disease Assn., 1981-84; assoc. neurosci. rsch. program MIT, 1974-82; chmn. life scis. adv. bd. USAF, 1985—94; founder, chmn. sci. adv. bd. Interneuron Pharms., Inc., 1989-99; co-founder Wurtco, 1999, Back Bay Sci., 1999. Author: Catecholamines, 1966; (with others) The Pineal, 1968; editor: (with Judith Wurtman) Nutrition and the Brain, Vols. I and II, 1977, Vols. III, IV, V., 1979, Vol. VI, 1983, Vol. VII, 1986, Vol. VIII, 1990, contbr. articles to profl. jours.; chpts. to books. Mem. bd. overseers Boston Symphony Orch., 1997—; trustee New World, Symphony, 2007—; bd.

dirs. Fenway Cmty. Health Ctr., Boston, 1998—2003, Provincetown Art Assn. and Mus., 2000—, pres., 2005—. Recipient various awards and lectureships. Mem. Endocrine Soc. (Ernst Oppenheim award 1972), Am. Physiol. Soc., Am. Soc. Biol. Chemists, Am. Soc. Pharmacology and Exptl. Therapeutics (John Jacob Abel award 1968), Am. Soc. Neurochemistry, Soc. Neurosci., Am. Soc. Clin. Nutrition, Am. Inst. Nutrition (Osborne & Mendel award 1982), Porcellati Lecture ESN, Lanas Lecture U. Mich. Achievements include some 80 U.S. patents on new treatments for diseases and conditions; invention of melatonin for promoting sleep, of dexfenfluramine for treating obesity, of citicoline for treating stroke and of Sarafem for the treatment of premenstrual syndrome, and of pyrimidine fatty acid mixtures for enhancing brain synapse formation in neurodegenerative diseases. Home: 300 Boylston St Boston MA 02116-3923 Office: Mass Inst Tech 77 Massachusetts Ave, 46-5023 Cambridge MA 02139-1323 Office Phone: 617-253-6731. Business E-Mail: dick@mit.edu.

WURZBACH, LINDA, educational consultant; b. San Antonio, Jan. 21, 1954; d. Delmar Earl Wurzbach, Dorothy Lang Wurzbach; m. Mark Allison Tatom. BS, U. Tex., 1975, MEd, 1978. Lic. tchr. Tex. Tchr. Austin Ind. Sch. Dist., Tex., 1976—81; project mgr. Tex. Sch. for the Blind and Visually Impaired, Austin, 1981—82, tchr., 1982—89; project dir. The Psychol. Corp., San Antonio, 1989—90; planner Tex. Edn. Agy., Austin, 1990—96; sr. project assoc. Coun. Chief State Sch. Officers, Washington, 1996—98; pres. Resources for Learning, LLC, Austin, 1998—. Cons. in field. Editor: TxBESS Toolkit, 2005, TxBESS Activity Profile, 2001, Fine Arts Curriculum Frameworks, 2000; author: Works in Progress, 1997, Portfolio Assessment for Beginning Teachers, 1999, Performance Assessment System, 2000; prodr.: (video) If You Love It, Teach It, 2000, Express Yourself, 2001, Fine Arts for All Students, 2003, Beginning Teacher Induction Toolkit: A Systems Approach, 2004; contbr. articles to profl. jours. Mem.: ASCD, Women Pres.' Orgn., U.S. Women's C. of C., Nat. Coun. Measurement in Edn., Am. Ednl. Rsch. Assn., Nat. Staff Devel. Coun. Home: 4504 Moose Dr Austin TX 78749 Home Phone: 512-282-7882. Personal E-mail: lindaw@resourcesforlearning.net.

WURZEL, LEONARD, retired candy manufacturing company executive; b. Phila., Feb. 4, 1918; s. Maurice L. and Dora (Goldberg) W.; m. Elaine Cohen, Aug. 18, 1949; children— Mark L., Lawrence J. BS, Washington and Jefferson Coll., 1939; MBA, Harvard, 1941. With Loft Candy Corp., Long Island City, NY, 1946-64, v.p., 1949-56, exec. v.p., 1956-57, pres., 1957-64, dir., 1949-64; chmn., dir. Calico Cottage Candies, Inc., 1964-94; ret., 1994; mayor Village of Sands Point, NY, 1989—; elected mayor, 2009. Capt. US Army, 1941—46. Decorated Bronze Star. Mem. Assn. Mfrs. Confectionery and Chocolate (bd. dirs., past pres., chmn.), Candy Chocolate and Confectionery Inst. (bd. dirs., treas.), Retail Confectioners Internat. (bd. dirs., past pres.) Home: 25 Woodland Dr Sands Point NY 11050-1136 Office: 26 Tibbits Ln Sands Point NY 11050-1135

WUSINICH, JOSEPH F., III, lawyer, educator; b. Phila., Pa., Oct. 30, 1946; s. Joseph F. Wusinich Jr. and Mary M. (Madden) Wusinich; m. Catherine T. Consalvi, Sept. 7, 1968; children: Nicole, Lisa, Dana, Maria, Christa, Joanna, Catherine. BSc in Mgmt. Mktg., St. Joseph's U., Phila., 1968; JD, DePaul U., Chgo., 1974; LLM in Trial Advocacy, Temple U., Phila., 1995. Bar: Pa. 1974, U.S. Dist. Ct. (ea. dist.) Pa. 1976, U.S. Circuit Ct. Appeals Third Circuit 1976, U.S. Supreme Ct. 1984. Assoc. house counsel Liberty Mut. Ins. Co., Phila., 1974—76; law ptnr. Landis & Wusinich, West Chester, Pa., 1976—80, Wusinich & McCarthy, West Chester, Pa., 1980—85, Wusinich & Brogan, West Chester, Pa., 1993—2000, Wusinich, Brogan & Stanzione, Downington, Pa., 2000—; sr., mng. atty. Law Offices Joseph F. Wusinich, III, West Chester, Pa., 1985—93. Pres. coun., bd. trustees Immaculata U., Pa., 1997—; chair, vice chair med. health related issues PA. Bar Assn., Harrisburg, 2000—. Contbr. bull. and articles in field. Lt., chief tng. ops. officer, combat engr. US Army, 1968—71, Vietnam. Decorated Army Commendation medal US Army, Bronze Star medal; recipient Defender of Life award, Pro-Life of Chester County, West Chester, Pa., 1998, St. Thomas More award, Pro-Life Union of S.E. Pa., Phila., 2002. Master: Hon. John E. Stively, Jr. Am. Inn Ct. (pres. elect 2002—03, pres. 2003—06); mem.: KC, Downington Pa. chpt. (3rd degree Knight 1987—). Republican. Roman Catholic. Avocation: basketball. Office: Wusinich Brogan Stanzione 537 W Uwchlan Ave Ste 200 Downingtown PA 19335 Office Phone: 610-594-1600. Office Fax: 610-594-6518. Business E-Mail: info@wusinichbrogan.com.

WUSSLER, ROBERT JOSEPH, broadcast executive, media consultant; b. Newark, Sept. 8, 1936; s. William and Anna (MacDonald) Wussler; children: Robert Joseph, Rosemary, Sally, Stefanie, Christopher, Jeanne. BA in Comm. Arts, Seton Hall U., South Orange, NJ, 1957, LLD (hon.), 1976, Emerson Coll., Boston, 1976. With CBS News, NYC, 1957-72; v.p., gen. mgr. Sta. WBBM-TV, Chgo., 1972-74; v.p. CBS Sports, NYC, 1974-76, pres., 1977-78, Sta. CBS-TV, NYC, 1976-77, Pyramid Enterprises Ltd., NYC, 1979—80; exec. v.p. Turner Broadcasting System Inc., Atlanta, 1979—89, sr. exec. v.p., from 1987, bd. dirs.; pres. Atlanta Sports Teams, Inc., 1981-87; pres., chief exec. officer COMSAT Video Enterprises, Inc., Washington, 1989-92; pres. Wussler Group, 1992—. Chmn. bd. dirs. NATAS, 1980—84, 1986—90; co-owner Denver Nuggets, 1989—92; bd. dirs. Atlanta Hawks Ltd., Atlanta Braves Nat. League Baseball Club, Inc. Trustee Marymount Manhattan Coll., 1977—81; bd. regents Seton Hall U., 1978—84. Recipient Emmy awards, numerous other nat. and internat. news and sports awards. Mem.: European Broadcasting Union, Nat. Cable TV Assn. (mem. satellite network com.), Cable Advt. Bur., Ariz. Heart Inst., Internat. Radio and TV Soc., Dirs. Guild Am. Roman Catholic. Home and Office: 222 North Ave Westport CT 06880-2233 Personal E-mail: rjwtv@aol.com.

WÜTHRICH, KURT, molecular biologist, biophysicist, educator; b. Oct. 4, 1938; MS in Chemistry, Physics and Maths., U. Bern, Switzerland, 1962; Eidgenössisches Turn-und Sportlehrerdiplom, U. Basel, Switzerland, 1964, PhD in Chemistry, 1964; D in Chemistry (hon.), U. Siena, Italy, 1997; PhD (hon.), U. Zürich, Switzerland, 1997, Ecole Polytechnique Fédérale, Lausanne, Switzerland, 2001, U. Sheffield, Eng., 2004, U. Valencia, Spain, 2004, King George's Med. U., Lucknow, India, 2005, U. Pecs, Hungary, 2005, Lomonosov State U., Russia, 2006; PhD, U. Del Norte Asuncion Paraguay, 2007, U. Verona, Italy, 2007, U. Rene Descartes, Paris France, 2007. Postdoctoral tng. U. Basel, U. Calif., Berkeley, Bell Telephone Labs., Murray Hill, N.J., 1964-69; prof. biophysics ETH Zurich, Zürich, Switzerland, 1972—, chmn. dept. biology, 1995-2000; prof. structural biology The Scripps Rsch Inst., La Jolla, 2001—. Mem. coun. Internat. Union Pure and Applied Biophysics, 1975-78, 87-90, sec. gen., 1978-84, v.p., 1984-87; mem. gen. com. Internat. Coun. Sci. Unions, 1980-86, standing com. on free circulation of scientists, 1982-90. Editor Jour. Biomolecular NMR, Quar. Rev. Biophysics, Macromolecular Structures; contbr. articles to profl. jours. Recipient Friedrich Miescher prize Schweizerische Biochemische Gesellschaft, 1974, shield of faculty of medicine Tokyo U., 1983, P. Bruylants medal Cath. U. Louvain, 1986, Stein and Moore award Protein Soc., U.S., 1990, Louisa Gross Horwitz prize Columbia U., 1991, Gilbert N. Lewis medal U. Calif., Berkeley, 1991, Marcel Benoist prize Swiss Confederation, 1992, Disting. Svc. award Miami Winter Symposia, 1993, Prix Louis Jeantet de Médecine, Geneva, 1993, Kaj Linderstrøm-Lang prize Kaj Linderstrøm-Lang Found., Copenhagen, 1996, Eminent Scientist of RIKEN (Tokyo), 1997, Kyoto prize in Advanced Tech., 1998, Guenther Laukien prize Exptl. Nuclear Magnetic Resonance Conf., 1999, Otto Warburg medal Soc. for Biochemistry and Molecular Biology, Germany, 1999, World award M. Gorbatschow Found., 2002, Nobel Prize in Chemistry, 2002, Bijvoet medal, Utrecht U., 2008, Paul Walden Medal, Riga Tech. U., 2008, Jabir Ibn Hyyan medal, Saudi Chem. Soc., 2009; Swiss award, 2002; Fgn. fellow Indian Nat. Sci. Acad.; hon. fellow NAS India. Fellow: AAAS; mem.: Latvian Inst. Org. Sys. ISMAR, U.S. Nat. Acad., World Innovation Found., Schweizerische Akademie der Medizinischen Wissenschaften, Schweizerische Akademie der Technischen Wissenschaften, Acad. Scis. Inst. France, Academia Europea, European Molecular Biology Orgn., Deutsche Akad. der Naturforscher Leopoldina, Korean Magnetic Resonance Soc. (hon.), Korean Acad. Sci. Technol. (hon.), Indian Biophys. Soc. (hon.), Nuc. Magnetic Resonance Soc. Japan (hon.), Groupement Ampère (hon.), Latvian Acad. Sci. (hon.), European Acad. Arts and Humanities (hon.), Hungarian Acad. Sci. (hon.), Internat. Soc. Magnetic Resonance in Medicine (hon.), Royal Soc. Edinburgh (hon.), Royal Soc. Chemistry (hon.), Swiss Chem. Soc. (hon.), Nat. Magnetic Resonance Soc. India (hon.), Japanese Biochem. Soc. (hon.), Am. Acad. Arts and Scis. (hon.). Office: ETH Zurich Inst Molecular Biology Biophysics 8093 Zurich Switzerland also: Scripps Rsch Inst Dept Molecular Biology 10550 N Torrey Pines Rd La Jolla CA 92037 Office Phone: +41-44-633-2475.

WVOLLMANN, WILLIAM TANNER, writer; b. LA, July 28, 1959; married; 1 child. Student, Deep Springs Coll., Calif.; BA in Comparative Lit., summa cum laude, Cornell U.; grad. student, U. Calif., Berkeley. Author: You Bright and Risen Angels, 1987, The Rainbow Stories, 1989, The Ice-Shirt, 1990, Whores for Gloria, 1991, 13 Stories and 13 Epitaphs, 1991, An Afghanistan Picture Show, 1992, Fathers and Crows, 1992, Butterfly Stories, 1993, The Rifles, 1994, The Atlas, 1996, The Royal Family, 2000, Argall: The True Story of Pocahontas and Captain John Smith, 2001, Rising Up and Rising Down: Some Thoughts on Violence, Freedom and Urgent Means, 2004, Expelled from Eden: A William T. Vollmann Reader, 2004, Europe Central, 2005 (Nat. Book award for Fiction, 2005), Poor People, 2007, Riding Toward Everywhere, 2008; contbr. articles to mags., NY Times Book Review. Recipient PEN Center USA West award for fiction, Whiting Writers award, 1988, Mildred and Harold Strauss Livings award, AAAL, 2008. Mailing: Viking Publicity 375 Hudson St New York NY 10014

WWHEATON, ELIZABETH M., finance company executive, educator; d. Edward James and Ila Jean Schauer. BBA, Sam Houston State U., Huntsville, Tex., 1992; MS, Grambling State U., LA, 1994; MA, PhD, Temple U., Phila., 2007. Desktop pub. Jefferies & Co., Houston, 1997—99; rsch. asst. Temple U., 2000—05, adj. prof., 1999—2003, South Meth. U., Dallas, 2006—07, economics lectr., 2007—; founder & chief exec. officer Equip the Saints, Prairie View, Tex., 2007—. Eligibility examiner I & II Louisianan Dept. Social Svcs., Monroe, La., 1996—97. Elder Presbyn. Ch. USA, 1994—2008. Achievements include research in area of the economics of human trafficking; child labor. Office: Equip the Saints PO Box 2879 Prairie View TX 77446 Business E-Mail: ewheaton@equipthesaints.net.

WWRUPP, MICHAEL RICHARD, immunologist; s. Richard Lynn and Louise Fletcher Rupp; m. Naomi Nakano Rupp, July 27, 1996. BS, U. Calif., Davis, 1996; MD, U. Southern Calif., LA, 2000. Diplomate Am. Bd. Internal Medicine, 2005, Am. Bd. Allergy & Immunology, 2006. Intern-resident, internal medicine & pediat. U. Tex. Med. Sch., Houston, 2001—04; fellow, clin. immunology & allergy U. Miss. Med. Ctr., Jackson, 2004—06; staff allergist & immunologist Allergy & Asthma Clinic Southern N.Mex, Las Cruces, 2006—. Spkrs. bur. Meda Pharms., El Paso, Tex., 2007—. Named Eagle Scout, Boy Scouts America, 1987; named one of Top Consult Svc., U. Miss. Med. Ctr., 2005—06, Americas Top Drs., Castle Connoly, 2007; named to Dean's Honor List, U. Calif., 1993—96, Nat. Dean's List, 1996. Mem.: N.Mex Allergy Soc., Am. Coll. Allergy, Asthma, and Immunology, Am. Acad. Allergy, Asthma and Immunology (com. mem. 2005—08). Mem. Lds Ch. Achievements include developed and established the first combined MD, MBA program at the University of Southern California; research in studied the relationship between treatment of sleep disorders and rhinitis. Avocations: cooking, travel, computers, camping, woodworking. Office: Allergy & Asthma Clinic Southern N Mex 3800 E Lohman Ave Ste A Las Cruces NM 88011

WYANT, CLYDE W., JR., manufacturing executive; b. Ada, Okla., Sept. 20, 1938; s. Clyde W. and Geneva Pauline (George) W.; m. Anne L. Edgerton, Nov. 23, 1984; children: Lynn, John, James, Markham, Carolyn BA in History, Stanford U., 1960; MBA, Harvard U., 1965. Asst. to pres. Helmerich & Payne, Inc., Tulsa, 1965-68, fin. v.p., 1968-85; exec. v.p., chief fin. officer Purolator Products Co. (formerly Facet Enterprises, Inc.), Tulsa, 1985-90; exec. v.p., CFO, treas. Lennox Internat., Inc., 1990-2001. Dir. Am. Nursery Products, Tahlequah, Okla., Hawkins Energy Co., Tulsa. Vice pres., trustee Holland Hall Sch., Tulsa, 1978-86; trustee Hillcrest Med. Ctr., Tulsa; vice chmn. admissions com. Tulsa Area United Way, 1979-86, chmn. allocations com., 1987, pres.-elect 1989, pres., 1990; fin. com. chmn. Community Network for Public Edn., Tulsa, 1983-85, Okla. Profl. Affairs Tribunal, 1989—; pres., treas., dir. Jr. Achievement of Greater Tulsa, 1978-86; community advisor Jr. League of Tulsa, 1979-82. Served to lt. U.S. Army, 1960-62 Recipient Bronze Leadership award Jr. Achievement, 1983 Mem. Fin. Execs. Inst. (pres. 1979-80), Am. Petroleum Inst., Mid-Continent Harvard Bus. Sch. Assn. (pres. 1980-82) Clubs: Tulsa Tennis (pres. 1985). Avocations: fishing, cooking, tennis. also: Two Warren Pl E 61st St Ste 1100 Tulsa OK 74136-0523 Home: 2140 Lake Park Blvd Richardson TX 75080-2252

WYATT, ADRIAN FREDERICK, physicist, researcher; b. Bristol, England, Oct. 1, 1938; s. Frederick and Kitty Wyatt; m. Anne Elizabeth Meredith, Dec. 28, 1961; children: Katrina, Amanda. BSc, U. Bristol, 1960; PhD, U. Oxford, 1963. Tech. staff Bell Labs., Murray Hill, NJ, 1963-64; lectr. U. Nottingham, England, 1964-76; prof. physics U. Exeter, England, 1976—. Chmn. Low Temperature Group Inst. Physics, London, 1979-82. Mem. editl. bd. Jour. Low Temperature Physics, 1992—; contbr. articles to profl. jours. Fellow: Royal Soc.; mem.: Inst. Physics (Holweck medal and prize 2004). Office: U Exeter Dept Physics Stocker Rd Exeter EX4 4QL England Office Phone: 44 1392 264181. Office Fax: 44 1392 264111. Business E-Mail: A.F.G.Wyatt@exeter.ac.uk.

WYATT, DEBRA SUE, speech educator; b. Harlingen, Tex., Feb. 24, 1954; d. Howard Louis and Martha Etta Tutt; m. Larry W. Wyatt, Sept. 19, 1980; 1 child, Kristopher Nolan. MA in Speech Comm., U. Tex. Pan Am., Edinburg, 1997. Speech comm. instr. South Tex. Coll., Weslaco, 1999—. Recipient E-Instr of Yr., Distance Edn., 2007—08. Libertarian. Christian. Achievements include development of web course and speech communication. Avocation: farming. Home: 7222 Mile 2 East Mercedes TX 78570 Office: South Texas Coll 400 N Border Ave Weslaco TX 78596 Business E-Mail: dwyatt@southtexascollege.edu.

WYATT, GERARD ROBERT, biology professor, researcher; b. Palo Alto, Calif., Sept. 3, 1925; came to Can., 1935; s. Horace Graham and Mary Aimee (Strickland) W.; m. Sarah Silver Morton, Dec. 19, 1951 (dec. Mar. 1981); children— Eve Morton, Graham Strickland, Diana Silver; m. Mary Evelyn Rogers, Mar. 16, 1985 BA, U. B.C., Can., 1945; postgrad., U. Calif.-Berkeley, 1946-47; PhD, Cambridge U., 1950. Research scientist Can. Dept. Agr., Sault Ste. Marie, Ont., 1950-54; asst. prof. biochemistry Yale U., New Haven, 1954-60, assoc. prof., prof. biology, 1960-73; prof. biology Queen's U., Kingston, Ont., 1973-94, prof. emeritus, 1994—; sci. dir. Insect Biotech Can., 1990-93. Contbr. articles to profl. jours. Guggenheim fellow, 1956; Killam Research fellow, 1985 Fellow Royal Soc. Can. Avocation: natural history. Home: 114 Earl St Kingston ON Canada K7L 2H1 E-mail: meandj@kos.net.

WYATT, HELEN J., special education educator; b. Fayette, Miss., Jan. 1, 1948; d. Milton Louis and Hazel James; m. Dewitt Wyatt, Aug. 26, 1973; children: Derrick Dewayne, Carla Amaris. BS in Bus. Edn., Alcorn A & M Coll., Lorman, Miss., 1969; MS in Spl. Edn., Alcorn State U., Miss., 1979, MEd in Adminstrn and Supervision, 1994; EdD in Spl. Svcs. and Exceptional Edn., Nova Southeastern U., 2000. Lic. bus. edn. tchr. Miss. State Dept. Edn., spl. edn. tchr. La. Dept. Edn., child search coord. La. Dept. Edn., parish or city sch. supr. instrn. La. Dept. Edn., parish or city sch. supr.dir. spl. edn. La. Dept. Edn., supr. student tchg. La. Dept. Edn. Tchr. St. Joachim Cath. Elem. Sch., Chgo., 1970—71; counselor, employment and tng. instr. Fayette Pub. Svc. Careers Program, 1971—74; exec. sec. Alcorn State Admission Office, Lorman, 1975—78; spl. edn. tchr. Tensas Parish Sch. Dist., St. Joseph, La., 1978—86, Concordia Parish Sch. Dist., Vidalia, La., 1987—89, facilitator individual edn. plan, 1989—2000; assoc. prof., dir. Am. Reads-Miss. Alcorn State U., 2000—. Parish monitor Concordia Parish Spl. Edn. Dept., Vidalia, 1989—2000; state monitor La. State Dept. of Edn., Baton Rouge, 1995—2000; cons. automated individual edn. plan Region 6 parishes, Alexandria, La., 1998—2000; presenter for spl. edn. tngs. Concordia Spl. Edn. Dept., Vidalia, 1989—2000; adminstr. Alcorn State U., 2000—; trainer Americorps members Am. Reads-Miss., Alcorn State, 2000—; workshop presenter Multi-State Cross Program Tng. Conf., Nashville, 2005. Author: (practicum) Assisting Newly Hired Special Education Teachers to Function More Effectively Through Inservice Training and Mentoring; contbr., workshop presenter: 10th Nat. Svc. Orientation Life After AmeriCorps (Commendation, Gov. of Miss., 2003); writer (handbook) Guidebook for New Special Education Teachers (Commendation, Spl. Edn. Supr., 2000). Mentor for youth Zion Hill #1 Bapt. Ch., Natchez, Miss., 1995—2005. Recipient Cmty.-Based Tutorial Program grant, La. Dept. of Edn., 2000—07, Conf. commendations, Miss. Commn. Vol. Svc., 2000—07, sci. fair judge commendations, Natchez-Adams Sch. Dist., 2001—04, Cert. of Excellence, SW Miss. Ctr. Ednl. Tech., 2003, Read Across Am. Appreciation cert., NEA, 2006. Mem.: NAACP, CEC (assoc.), Alcorn Alumni Assn. (life), Phi Delta Kappa (assoc.; historian 1996—97, Cert. Appreciation 1997), Delta Sigma Theta (pres., v.p., treas. Vidalia Alumnae chpt. 1966—2007, Pres.'s award Vidalia Alumnae chpt. 2006). Democrat. Baptist. Avocations: travel, reading, completing puzzles, playing computer games. Home: 401 S Spruce St Vidalia LA 71373 Office: Alcorn State U 1000 ASU Dr 480 Alcorn State MS 39096 Office Fax: 601-877-6213. Personal E-mail: hjwyatt@bellsouth.net. E-mail: hwyatt@alcorn.edu.

WYATT, JAMES ALEXANDER, III, lawyer; b. Winter Pk., Fla., Jan. 5, 1974; m. Megan Wyatt. BS, Spring Hill Coll., Mobile, Ala., 1996; JD, U. Ala., Tuscaloosa, 1999. Bar: Ala. 2000, US Dist. Ct. (so., no., & mid. dists.) Ala. 2000, US Ct. Appeals (5th cir.) 2000. Law clk. to Justice Gorman Houston Ala. Supreme Ct., Montgomery, 1999—2000; atty. Carr Allison, Mobile, Ala., 2000—01, Parsons, Lee & Juliano, PC, Birmingham, Ala., 2001—. Coord. mediation project Jefferson County Dist. Ct., Birmingham, Ala., 2004—05. Mem.: ABA, Ala. State Bar, Def. Rsch. Inst. Office: Parsons Lee & Juliano PC PO Box 530630 Birmingham AL 35253 Office Fax: 205-324-7097. Business E-Mail: awyatt@pljpc.com.

WYATT, JAMES FRANK, JR., lawyer; b. Talladega, Ala., Dec. 1, 1922; s. James Frank and Nannie Lee (Heaslett) W.; m. Rosemary Barbara Slone, Dec. 21, 1951; children: Martha Lee, James Frank III. BS, Auburn U., 1943; JD, Georgetown U., 1949, postgrad., 1950. Bar: D.C. 1949, Ala. 1950, Ill. 1953, U.S. Supreme Ct 1953. Atty. Office Chief Counsel, IRS, 1949-51; tax counsel Universal Oil Products Co., Des Plaines, Ill., 1951-63, asst. treas., 1963-66, v.p. fin., treas., 1966-75; treas. CF Industries, Inc., Long Grove, Ill., 1976-78, v.p. fin., treas., 1978-82; assoc. Tenney & Bentley, 1983-85, Arnstein, Gluck, Lehr, Barron & Milligan, 1985-88; pvt. practice, 1989—. Dir. 1st Nat. Bank, Des Plaines. Village trustee, Barrington, Ill., 1963-75; bd. dirs. Buehler YMCA, Barrington Twp. Republican Orgn., 1963—; pres. Barrington Area Rep. Workshops, 1962-63. Served to capt., Judge Adv. Gen. Corps AUS, 1944-47. Mem. Tax Execs. Inst. (v.p. 1965-66, chpt. pres. 1961-62), Fed., Am., Chgo. bar assns., Barrington Home Owners Assn. (pres. 1960-61), Newcomen Soc., Assn. U.S. Army, Scabbard and Blade, Phi Delta Phi, Sigma Chi. Clubs: Barrington Hills Country; Economics, University (Chgo.). Episcopalian. Office: 200 Applebee St Barrington IL 60010-3060 Home Phone: 704-896-1131.

WYATT, JOE BILLY, academic administrator; b. Tyler, Tex., July 21, 1935; s. Joe and Fay (Pinkerton) Wyatt; m. Faye Hocutt, July 21, 1956; children: Joseph, Sandra Faye. BA, U. Tex., 1956; MA, Tex. Christian U., 1960. Systems engr. Gen. Dynamics Corp., 1956—65; mgr. Digital Computer Lab., 1961—65; dir. computer ctr., assoc. prof. computer sci. U. Houston, 1965—72; dir. Office Info. Tech. Harvard U., 1972—76, sr. lectr. computer sci., 1972—82, v.p. adminstrn., 1976—82; chancellor Vanderbilt U., Nashville, 1982—2000, chancellor emeritus, 2000. Faculty Harvard U. Kennedy Sch., 1976—82; bd. dirs., chmn. com. on math/sci. Am. Coun. of Edn.; bd. dirs. El Paso Energy, Inc., Ingram Micro., Inc., Advanced Networking and Sys. Corp., Hercules Corp., Aerostructures Corp.; prin. Washington Adv. Group. Author (with others): Financial Planning Models for Colleges and Universities, 1979; editor-in-chief: Jour. Applied Mgmt. Sys., 1983; contbr. articles to profl. jours.; patentee in field. Trustee EDUCOM, Princeton, NJ, 1973—81, Harvard U. Press, 1976—83, pres., 1975—76, chmn. bd., 1976—79; trustee Leadership Nashville, 1983—93; active Coun. Competitiveness; bd. dirs. Nashville Inst. Arts, 1982—83, Ingram Industries, 1990—96; chmn. adv. com. IST, NSF, 1978—85; vice-chmn. bd. Mass. Tech. Devel. Corp., Boston, 1977—83; alumni bd. dirs. Harvard Bus. Sch., 1982—92; chmn. New Am. Schs., 2002—, Edn. Quality Inst., 2002—. Recipient award for exemplary leadership, CAUSE, 1982, Nat. Tree of Life award, Jewish Nat. Fund, 1988; named Outstanding Tennessean, Gov. of Tenn., 1986; fellow, Gallaudet Coll., 1981—83. Fellow: AAAS; mem.: IEEE, Bus. Higher Edn. Forum (exec. com. 1990—93), So. U. Rsch. Assn., Inc. (chmn. coun. pres. 1988—89), U. Rsch. Assn. (bd. trustees 1988—, chmn. 1997—), Assn. Computing Machinery (pres. Dallas and Ft. Worth chpt. 1963—65), Am. Coun. Edn. (chmn. adv. com.

on tech. edn. 1980—81, bd. dirs. 1990—92), Nat. Assn. Ind. Colls. and Univs. (policy bd. 1980—82), Hosp. Corp. Am. (bd. dirs. 1984—89), Assn. Am. Univs. (chmn. exec. com. 1990—91), Govt. Univ. Industry Rsch. Roundtable (chmn. 1998—), Nashville C. of C. (bd. dirs. 1983—86, pres. 1996—97), Experimental Aircraft Assn. (pres. adv. com., found. bd. 1997—), Aircraft Owners and Pilots Assn., Harvard Club, Beta Gamma Sigma, Sigma Xi, Phi Beta Kappa (hon.). Methodist. Office: Vanderbilt U 2525 West End Ave Ste 1430 Nashville TN 37203 E-mail: joe.b.wyatt@vanderbilt.edu.

WYATT, JOHN, legislative staff member; Grad., Duke U., Durham, NC. Staff asst., fgn. rels. com. US Senate, Washington, spl. asst. state projects, Senator Phil Gramm, staff mem., judiciary com., 2003—05, dir. state projects, Senator John Cornyn, 2003—07, sr. legis. asst., Senator John Cornyn, 2007—08; chief of staff to Rep. Pete Olson US House of Reps., Washington, 2009—. Republican. Roman Catholic. Office: 514 Cannon House Office Bldg Washington DC 20515 Office Phone: 202-225-5951. Office Fax: 202-225-5241.*

WYATT, JOSEPH LUCIAN, JR., lawyer, writer; b. Chgo., Feb. 21, 1924; s. Joseph Lucian and Cecile Gertrude (Zadico) W.; m. Marjorie Kathryn Simmons, Apr. 9, 1954; children: Daniel, Linn, Jonathan. AB in English Lit. with honors, Northwestern U., 1947; LLB, Harvard U., 1949. Bar: Calif. 1950, U.S. Dist. Ct. (cen. dist.) Calif. 1950, U.S. Ct. Appeals (9th cir.) 1950, U.S. Tax Ct., U.S. Supreme Ct. 1965. Assoc. firm Brady, Nossaman & Walker, Los Angeles, 1950-58, ptnr. LA, 1958-61; pvt. practice LA, 1961-71; sr. mem. Cooper, Wyatt, Tepper & Plant, P.C., LA, 1971-79; of counsel Beardsley, Hufstedler & Kemble, LA, 1979-81; ptnr. Hufstedler & Kaus, LA, 1981-95; sr. of counsel Morrison & Foerster, LA, 1995—. Mem. faculty Pacific Coast Banking Sch., Seattle, 1963-92, Southwestern Grad. Sch. Banking, 1988-89; advisor Restatement, Trusts 3d, 1988—. Author: Trust Administration and Taxation, 4 vols., 1964—; editor: Trusts and Estates, 1962-74. Lectr. continuing legal edn. programs, Calif. and Tex.; trustee Pacific Oaks Coll. and Children's Sch., 1969-97; counsel, parliamentarian Calif. Democratic party and presdl. conv. dels., 1971—; mem. Calif. State Personnel Bd., 1961-71, v.p., 1963-65, pres., 1965-67; bd trustees Calif. Pub. Employees Retirement System, 1963-71. 1st sgt. USAAF, 1942-45. Fellow Am. Coll. of Trust and Estate Counsel; mem. ABA, Internat. Acad. Estate and Trust Law (treas. 1990-96), Am. Law Inst., Calif. State Bar Assn. (del. state conf. 1956, 62-67), L.A. Bar Assn. (trustee 1956). Democrat. Christian Scientist. Avocations: fishing, composing doggerel. Home: 1119 Armada Dr Pasadena CA 91103-2805 Office Phone: 213-892-5200. E-mail: jwyatt@mofo.com, jwyatt3@charter.net.

WYATT, JUSTIN K., chemistry professor; s. Gary and Ellen Wyatt. PhD, U. Calif., Davis, 1999. Assoc. prof. dept. chemistry Coll. Charleston, SC, 2001—. Ruth L. Kirschstein fellowship, NIH, 2007—08. Mem.: Am. Chem. Soc. Office: Coll Charleston 66 George St Charleston SC 29424 Business E-Mail: wyattj@cofc.edu.

WYATT, MARCIA JEAN, fine arts and speech educator, administrative assistant; b. Petersburg, Va., Nov. 2, 1959; d. Andrew Ezekiel and Lillian (Bonner) Wyatt; m. Nicholas Charles Cooper-Lewter, Nov. 29, 1986 (div. 1998). BS in Elem. Edn., Va. State U., Ettrick, 1984; MEd in Spl. Edn., Bethel Coll. & Seminary, 1993; Degree in Adminstrv. Ednl. Leadership, St. Mary's U., Mpls., 2000; MS in Theology, Andersonville Theol. Sem., 2008. Lic. minister, 1987; ordained to clergy, 1990. Tchr. Marion Cmty. Schs., Ind., 1985-86, Inglewood Unified Schs., Calif., 1986-87; office mgr. C.R.A.V.E. Christ Counseling, Tustin, Calif., 1986—; asst. minister New Garden of Gethsemane B.C., LA, 1987-90; assoc. minister New Hope Bapt. Ch., St. Paul, 1990—; assoc. pastor New Garden of Gethsemane B.C., La., 1990—; assoc. minister New Hope Bapt. Ch., 1990—, pulpit coord., 2002; pres. C.R.A.V.E. Christ Singers, LA, 1987-90; adminstr. asst. Eldorado Bank, Orange, Calif., 1988-90; tchr. fine arts Broadway Cmty. Sch., Mpls., 1996—, Mpls. Sch. Dist., 1990—; assessment coord. Broadway Cmty. Sch., Mpls., 1999—; with Wyatt Consulting, Shoreview, Minn., 1986—; 4th grade tchr. Hall Cmty. Sch., Mpls. Founder, dir. Diversity in Motion program for A.A. students, 1992—; stage dir. Babu's Magic with dancer Chuck Davis, 1994; cons. Everyday Learning Corp., 1996—; assessment coord., curriculum writer Mpls. Pub. Schs., 1999—; 4th/5th grade curriculum instrn. assessment team lead Elizabeth Hall Elem. Sch., extended day coord., 2003; tchr. intermediate Spl. Program Emotional Needs Elizabeth Hall Sch., 2004-05. Nominated to Pres.'s Commn. White House Fellowships, 1993; mem. C.R.A.V.E. Christ Ministries (Relax in Christ, Affirm with Christ, Visualize Christ, Experience Christ); pulpit coord. New Hope Bapt. Ch.; 1st v.p. Minn. State Bapt. Conv. Women's Aux., 2006—. Finalist Minn. Tchr. of Yr., Edn. Minn., 2005; grantee, Star Tribune, 1994—96, African Studies, U. Wis., 1995—96, FASSE, U. Minn., 1996, Namibia, Fulbright (US Govt.), 1996. Mem. NAFE, Alpha Kappa Alpha. Avocations: reading, music, fish breeding, travel. Office Phone: 612-668-2650. Personal E-mail: mwyattprs@yahoo.com. Business E-Mail: marcia.wyatt@mpls.k12.mn.us.

WYATT, PAIGE A., mechanical engineer, educator; b. Longview, Tex., May 14, 1968; d. Raymond F. and Catherine A. Neathery; m. David M. Wyatt, Mar. 27, 1993; children: Katie A., Payton A. BS in Mech. Design Engring. Tech., Okla. State U., Stillwater, 1991; MS in Engring. Mgmt., Wash. State U., Tri-Cities, 1996. Mfg. engr. Rubbermaid, Winfield, Kans., 1988—90; mech. engr. Kaiser Engrs. Hanford, Richland, Wash., 1991—95, Parsons Engring., Richland, 1995—96; assoc. prof. Columbia Basin Coll., Pasco, Wash., 1996—. Coord. Design Camp, Pasco, 1999—. Recipient Cmty. Leadership award, Wash. Assn. Sch. Adminstrs., 2006. Home: 2201 S Cleveland St Kennewick WA 99338 Office: Columbia Basin Coll 2600 N 20th Ave Pasco WA 99301 Business E-Mail: pwyatt@columbiabasin.edu.

WYATT, ROBERT ODELL, journalism educator; b. Jackson, Tenn., Feb. 7, 1946; s. Odell and Sera Mae (Mebane) Wyatt. BA, U. of the South, 1968; MA, Northwestern U., Evanston, Ill., 1970, PhD, 1973; MS, U. Tenn., 1977; Cert. in Theology, Seabury-Western Theol. Sem., 2002; MTS, Vanderbilt U., Nashville, 2004. Ordained priest Episcopal Ch., 2004. From asst. to assoc. prof. U. Tenn., Nashville, 1973-79; assoc. prof. Mid. Tenn. State U., Murfreesboro, 1979-84, prof., 1984—, dir. Office Comm. Rsch., 1989—. Vis. prof. comm. U. Caen, France, 1994; cons. in comm.; mem. Pulitzer Prize Jury, 1980, 85, 91, 93, 99, chair jury, 1985, 91, 93, 99; bd. trustees Seabury-Western Theol. Sem., Evanston, Ill., 1996-2001, St. Augustine Coll., Chgo., 2008-, Episcopal Charities, Chgo., 2008-. Author: Free Expression and the American Public, 1991 (Sigma Delta Chi award for rsch. on journalism 1992); co-author, Free Expression in 5 Cultures, 2004; editor book sect. The Nashville Tennessean, 1978-93; contbr. articles to profl. jours. Worcester prize World Assn. for Pub. Opinion Rsch., 1996, Vanderbilt U. Founder's medal, 2004. Mem. Assn. for Edn. in Journalism and Mass Comm., Internat. Comm. Assn., Am. Assn. Pub. Opinion Rsch. Democrat. Episcopalian. Office: St Helena's Episcopal Ch Burr Ridge IL 60527

WYATT, TODD A., medical educator; m. Stephanie M. Ahlschwede, Feb. 21. PhD, U. NC, Chapel Hill, 1992. Prof. U. Nebr. Med. Ctr., Omaha, 1995—. R01 grant, NIH, 2008—. Office: UNMC Coll Pub Health 985300 Nebr Med Ctr Omaha NE 68198-5300 Office Fax: 402-559-6584. Business E-Mail: twyatt@unmc.edu.

WYATT, TOM (JOHN THOMAS WYATT), apparel executive; b. 1955; m. Cheryl F. Wyatt; 2 children. Specialty account sales rep. Vanity Fair Corp., pres. Vanity Fair Intimates, Vanity Fair Coalition, 1995—97; pres. Warnaco Intimate Apparel, NYC, 1997; chmn., CEO Parisian, 1998; pres., CEO Cutter & Buck, Seattle, 2004—06; pres. GapBody Gap Inc., San Francisco, 2006—07, pres. Outlet divsn., 2007—08, pres. Old Navy divsn., 2008—. Bd. mem. Gap Found. Office: Gap Inc 2 Folsom St San Francisco CA 94105

WYATT, WILSON WATKINS, JR., public relations executive, writer; b. Louisville, Dec. 3, 1943; s. Wilson Watkins Sr. and Anne (Duncan) W.; m. Jane Clay, Aug. 15, 1964 (dec. 1975); children: Carol, Wilson III, Sarah Wyatt; m. Kathleen Valonis, June 14, 1998. Student, U. of the South, 1961-65. Reporter The Courier-Jour., Louisville, 1965-67; pub. rels. account exec. Doe-Anderson Advt., Louisville, 1967-68; account exec. Zimmer-McClaskey-Lewis (McCann-Ericksn Advtsg.), Louisville, 1968-70; ptnr. Bennett & Wyatt Pub. Rels., Louisville, 1970-71; state rep., vice chair appropriations and revenue com. Ky. Gen. Assembly, Frankfort, 1969-71; exec. dir. Louisville Cen. Area Inc., 1971-77; dir. corp. affairs and communications Brown & Williamson Tobacco Corp., Louisville, 1977-82; v.p. pub. policy BATUS Inc., Washington, 1982-86, v.p. corp. affairs Louisville, 1986-90; sr. v.p. corp. affairs PNC Fin. Corp., Pitts., 1990-92; sr. v.p. corp. comm. and govt. rels. The Travelers Cos., Hartford, 1992-94; exec. dir., CEO Am. Acad. of Actuaries, Washington, 1995-98; CEO Wyatt Comm. Cons., 1998—. Lead U.S. def. pub. rels. activities against hostile takeover for B.A.T. Industries, U.K., 1989-90; chmn. Travelers Found., 1991-94; moderator Working Writers Forum, Md., 2006-. Mem. youth adv. com. Atlantic Inst., 1967-68; del. North Atlantic Treaty Assn. Young Leaders Conf., 1967; chmn. Leadership Effort for All Dems., Ky., 1967-68; regional campaign coord. for Robert F. Kennedy, Ky.-Ind., 1968; mem. Pres.'s Forum, Washington, 1988-91; trustee Conn. Policy Econ. Commn., 1992-95; mem. exec. com. Hartford Downtown Coun., 1992-94; mem. Am. Savings Edn. Campaign US Dept. Labor, 1996. Named one of Outstanding Young Men in Am., Ky. Jaycees, 1973. Mem. The Pres.'s Forum, Pub. Affairs Rsch. Coun. (conf. bd. 1986-95), Forum I, Assn. Chief Execs. Coun., Pub. Affairs Coun. (bd. dirs. 1982—, exec. com. 1982-86), Speakers Club (Washington), Greater Hartford C. of C. (exec. com. 1992-94), Hartford Stage (bd. dirs. 1993-95), St. Michaels Food & Wine Festival (adv. com.), Md. Writers Assn., Working Writers Forum, Bay to Ocean Writers Conf. (steering com.), Delmarva Rev. (bd. chmn.), Eastern Shore Writers Assn. (pres. 2007-). Avocations: boating, photography, writing. Home and Office: PO Box 298 Bozman MD 21612 Personal E-mail: wwwtwo@earthlink.net.

WYBENSINGER, NETONIS (TONNIE WYBENSINGER), legislative staff member; Staff asst., Rep. Pat Toomey US House of Reps., Washington, 2003, legis. correspondent, Rep. Pat Toomey, 2003—04, legis. asst., Rep. Pat Toomey, 2004, legis. asst., Rep. Tom Feeney, 2004—06, legis. dir., Rep. Tom Feeney, 2006—07, chief of staff to Rep. Tom Feeney, 2007—08, chief of staff to Rep. Blaine Luetkemeyer, 2009—. Republican. Office: 1118 Longworth House Office Bldg Washington DC 20515 Office Phone: 202-225-2956. Office Fax: 202-225-5712.*

WYCHE, CYRIL THOMAS, lawyer; b. Greenville, SC, Jan. 28, 1926; C. Granville and Mary (Wheeler) W.; m. Harriet Smith, June 19, 1948; children: Sara McCall, Bradford Wheeler, Mary Frances. BE, Yale U., 1946; LLB, U. Va., 1949; LLD (hon.), Clemson U., 1997, Furman U., 1997; HLD (hon.), Wofford Coll. Bar: S.C. 1948, U.S. Dist. Ct. S.C. 1950, U.S. Ct. Appeals (4th cir.) 1952, U.S. Ct. Claims 1964, U.S. Supreme Ct. 1970. Ptnr. Wyche, Burgess, Freeman & Parham, P.A., Greenville, SC, 1948—. Pres., bd. dirs. YMCA, Greenville, 1960; pres. Greenville Little Theatre, 1965, Arts Festival Assn., Greenville, 1970, Greenville Community Corp., 1976—; bd. dirs. Greater Greenville C. of C., 1980. Served with USN, 1943-46. Named Environmentalist of Yr., State of S.C., 1979; recipient Conservation award Gulf Oil Corp., 1983, Alexander Calder award, 1996, Garden Clubs Am., 1999, Oak Leaf award The Nature Conservancy, 1996, Order of the Palmetto award S.C. Gov., 1996. Mem. ABA (Environ. award 2002), S.C. Bar Assn., Greenville County Bar Assn., Am. Judicature Soc., Nat. Wildlife Fedn. (Spl. Conservation Achievement award 2003). Presbyterian. Avocations: skiing, scuba diving, piano, tennis, white water canoeing. Office: Wyche Burgess Freeman & Parham 44 E Camperdown Way PO Box 728 Greenville SC 29602-0728 Home Phone: 864-288-6049; Office Phone: 864-242-8213. E-mail: twyche@wyche.com.

WYCHE, JAMES RAMAGE, lawyer; s. Madison Baker Wyche III and Marguerite Ramage Wyche; m. Sally B. Hubbard. BS magna cum laude in Fin., Clemson U., 2000; JD cum laude, Duke U., 2003. Bar: NC 2003, US Dist. Ct. (mid. dist.) NC 2003. Intern Sen. J. Strom Thurmond, 1997; atty. Kennedy Covington Lobdell & Hickman, Charlotte, NC, 2003—08, K & L Gates LLP, 2008—. Bd. dirs. young leaders United Way, Charlotte; bd. dirs. Camp Sea Gull, Camp Seafarer. Scholar, Wachovia Bank Nat. Assn., 1998—2000. Mem.: Phi Kappa Phi, Beta Gamma Sigma, Omicron Delta Kappa. Office: K & L Gates LLP 214 N Tryon St 47th Flr Charlotte NC 28202

WYCHE, MADISON BAKER, III, lawyer; b. Albany, Ga., Aug. 11, 1947; s. Madison Baker Jr. and Merle (McKemie) W.; m. Marguerite Jernigan Ramage, Aug. 7, 1971; children: Madison Baker IV, James Ramage. BA, Vanderbilt U., 1969, JD, 1972. Bar: Ga. 1972, U.S. Dist. Ct. (mid. dist.) Ga. 1972, U.S. Ct. Appeals (5th cir.) 1973, S.C. 1976, U.S. Dist. Ct. S.C. 1977, U.S. Ct. Appeals (4th cir.) 1977, U.S. Supreme Ct. 1980, U.S. Ct. Appeals (11th cir.) 1981, U.S. Dist. Ct. (no. dist.) Ga. 1995. Assoc. Perry, Walters, Lippitt & Custer, Albany, 1972-76, Thompson, Ogletree & Deakins, Greenville, SC, 1976-77, Ogletree, Deakins, Smoak & Stewart, Greenville, 1977-80; shareholder Ogletree, Deakins, Nash, Smoak & Stewart P.C., Greenville, 1980—. Bd. dirs. Happy Ho., Inc., Albany, 1975. Co-editor Labor and Employment Law for South Carolina Lawyers, 1999, 3d edit., 2004. Co-incorporator, sec. Tenn. Intercollegiate State Legislature, Nashville, 1967-69; mem. employer and employee rels. com., legal issues & workplace policy com. N.C. Citizens for Bus. and Industry, Raleigh, 1984—; mem. Greenville C. of C., gen. counsel, 2003-06, bd. dirs., 2003-06; mem. Advantage Greenville, Greenville Chamber Found., 2003-06; United Way Greenville; bd. dirs. Palmetto Soc. of the United Way, 1992-2004; mem. vestry Christ Episcopal Ch., Greenville, 1981-85; treas. All Saints Episcopal Ch., Linville, NC 2001-05; mem. bd. visitors Clemson U., 1998-2001, mem. profl. advancement and continuing edn. bd., 2003—; bd. dirs. Blue Ridge coun. Boy Scouts Am., 1999-2000; bd. dirs. Internat. Arts Festival, ARTISPHERE, Greenville, 2003—, gen. counsel, 2006—. Capt. US Army, 1969—77. Recipient Eagle Scouts award Boy Scouts Am., 1961, God and Country award, 1961, named One Hundred Most Powerful Employment Lawyers in America, 2009, named one of Best Lawyers in America, 2008-09, SC Super Lawyers, 2008-09. Mem. ABA, Coll. Labor and Employment Lawyers, SC Bar Assn. (unauthorized practice of law com. 1977-95, chmn. 1982-92, ho. of dels. 1991-98, 2004—, nominating com. 1992-95, CLE divsn., chmn., 1997-98, exec. com. 1995-99, chmn. seminars subcom. 1995-97), Ga. Bar Assn., Atlanta Bar Assn., S.C. Def. Trial Lawyers Assn., St. Andrews Soc. Upper S.C. (bd. dirs. 1979-81, v.p. 1986-87, pres. 1988-90, scholarship chmn. 1998—), Vanderbilt U. Alumni Assn. (pres. S.C. chpt. 1990-95, bd. dirs. 1994—), The Poinsett Club (v.p., bd. dirs., 2000-02, 08-) (Greenville, S.C.), Rotary (bd. dirs. 1982-84, Paul Harris fellow 1986), Commerce Club of Greenville (bd. dirs. 1990-2007), Phi Delta Phi. Office: Ogletree Deakins Nash Smoak & Stewart PO Box 2757 Greenville SC 29602-2757 Office Phone: 864-271-1300.

WYCHE, SAM DAVID, county official, former professional football coach; b. Atlanta, Jan. 5, 1945; m. Jane Wyche; children: Zak, Kerry BA, Furman U., 1966; MBA, U. S.C., 1969. Profl. football player Continental Football League, Wheeling Ironmen, 1966, Cin. Bengals, 1968-70, Washington Redskins, 1971-73, Detroit Lions, 1974-75, St. Louis Cardinals, 1976, Buffalo Bills, 1976; owner sporting goods store, Greenville, SC, 1974-92; asst. coach San Francisco 49ers, 1979-82; head coach Ind. U., Bloomington, 1983, Cin. Bengals, 1984-91, Tampa Bay Buccaneers, 1992-95; sports analyst NBC Sports, 1996-97, former co-host NFL on NBC Pre-Game Show NYC, 1998—99; sports analyst NFL on CBS, NYC, 1999—2000; quarterbacks coach Buffalo Bills, 2004—05. Vol. football asst. Pickens HS, SC. Rep., dist. 3 Pickens County Coun., 2008—. Named Coach of Yr. NFL, 1988. Republican. Office: Pickens County Coun Adminstrn Facility 222 McDaniel Ave Pickens SC 29671 Office Phone: 864-898-0023.

WYCKOFF, E. LISK, JR., lawyer; b. Middletown, NJ, Jan. 29, 1934; m. Elizabeth Ann Kuphal; children: Jenny Adele, Edward Lisk III, Elizabeth Hannah Longstreet. BA, Duke U., 1955; JD, U. Mich., 1960. Bar: N.Y. 1961, U.S. Dist. Ct. (so. and ea. dists.) N.Y. 1962, U.S. Ct. Appeals (2d cir. 1963), U.S. Tax Ct. 1974. Ptnr. Trubin Sillcocks, 1975—79, Kelley Drye & Warren, 1979—93, Kramer, Levin, NYC, 1993—2001. Lectr. Practising Law Inst., 1970—, various profl. and bus. orgns. in U.S. and abroad; spl. counsel N.Y. Bankers Assn., 1974-98; counsel N.Y. State Senate Com. Housing and Urban Renewal, 1969-71, N.Y. State Senate Com. Judiciary, 1963-64, Com. Affairs of the City of N.Y., 1962; mem. N.Y.C. Mayor's Taxi Study Commn., 1967 Directing editor, author West's McKinney's Forms on Estates and Trusts, 1974—; commentator McKinney's Not-For-Profit Corp. law, 1995—; contbr. articles to profl. jours. Trustee Inner-City Scholarship Fund., Inc., 1993—2004; chmn., bd. dirs. 1652 Wyckoff House and Assn., Inc., 1982—; trustee Goodspeed Opera Co., 1996—, Florence Griswold Mus., 1997—; trustee emeritus Wildlife Conservation Soc., 1993—; elector Wadsworth Atheneum; trustee, pres. Homeland Found., 1988—; mem. Concilium Socalium to Vatican Mus., 1991—; trustee emeritus NY Geneal. and Biographic Soc., 2002—. Recipient Star, Order of St. Gregory the Great, 2002; named papal hon. Knight Commdr., 1998. Fellow: Am. Bar Found., Am. Coll. Trust and Estate Counsel; mem.: ABA, St. Nicholas Soc., Holland Soc., Assn. of Bar of City of N.Y., N.Y. State Bar Assn., Internat. Bar Assn., Internat. Fiscal Assn., Old Lyme Country Club, N.Y. Yacht Club, Essex Yacht Club (Conn.), Mashomack Fish and Game Preserve Club (Pine Plains, N.Y.), Racquet and Tennis Club (N.Y.C.), Knickerbocker Club. Avocations: tennis, sailing.

WYCKOFF, SYLVIA SPENCER, art educator, artist; b. Pitts., Nov. 14, 1915; d. Lynn Boyd Wyckoff and Bess Jeannette Hohes. BFA, Syracuse U., NY, 1937, MFA, 1944. Cert. art tchr. NY, 1987. Art tchr. various pub. schs., Homer and Cobleskill, NY, 1937—42; instr. Coll. Visual Arts, Syracuse U., 1942—81, asst. to full prof., chmn. freshman core program, 1971—72, chmn. London art program; ret., 1981. Adj. art instr. Cazenovia Coll.; judge arts recognition and talent search Nat. Found. Arts, Princeton, NJ, 1983. Exhibited in group shows, Cortland, NY, 1938, Syracuse Regional Show, 1942—45 (1st prize for watercolor, 1943), with Rick Wolff, Oneida, NY, exhibitions include Nat. League Am. Pen Women, NYC and Washington, DC, 1968 (1st prize for watercolor, 1945), Chancellor's Office, Syracuse U., 1976, St. Lawrence U., Munson William Proctor Mus. Art, Utica, NY, 1980—81, Cazenovia Watercolor Soc., 1981—95, Core Faculty-Wells Coll., one-woman shows include Coleman Hall, Cazenovia, NY, 1975, New Coll. Art Bldg., Cazenovia Coll., 2004. Dispatcher CAVAC (Cazenovia Area Vol. Corps., NY, 1974—91; vol. Stone Quarry Art Pk. Recipient 1st prize for watercolor, Onondaga Hist. Soc., 1945, Gordon Steele award for painting, Assoc. Artists of Syracuse, 1968, spl. award, NY State Tchrs. Assn., 1981. Mem.: Nat. Mus. Women in Arts (charter mem.), Stone Quarry Art Pk., Manson Williams Proctor Mus., Cazenovia Watercolor Soc. (founder 1976, first recipient Priscilla Hancock award 1992), Sigma Chi Alpha, Eta Phi Upsilon (hon.), Alpha Xi Delta (award to 10% Top Alumnae 1967). Presbyterian. Achievements include first woman on athletic bd., Syracuse U., 1974; named in honor of Spl. Sylvia Wyckoff Book award, Alpha Sigma Lambda, U. Coll. Syracuse, NY, 1981. Avocations: painting, drawing, bridge, knitting. Home: 4 Liberty St Cazenovia NY 13035

WYCKOFF, THERI LYNNE, education educator; d. Karen Lee Forey; m. Mark A. Wyckoff, Sept. 4, 2000. BS in Elem. Edn., U. Nebr., Omaha, 1982, MS in Elem. Edn., 1992. Lic. profl. tchr. Nev. Supr., facilitator Omaha Children's Mus., 1981—83; tchr. Omaha Pub. Schs., 1983—2001; tech. learning strategist Clark County Sch. Dist., Las Vegas, Nev., 2001—02; tchr. St. Elizabeth Ann Seton Sch., Las Vegas, 2002—03; edn. prof. Coll. Southern Nev., Las Vegas, 2003—, faculty senator, 2006—08. Mem.: AAUP. Office: Coll Southern Nev 3200 E Cheyenne Ave S2A North Las Vegas NV 89030 Office Fax: 702-651-4908. Business E-Mail: theri.wyckoff@csn.edu.

WYCOFF, CHARLES COLEMAN, writer, retired anesthesiologist; b. Glazier, Tex., Sept. 2, 1918; s. James Garfield and Ada Sharpe (Braden) W.; m. Gene Marie Henry, May 16, 1942 (dec.); children: Michelle, Geoffrey, Brian, Roger, Daniel, Norman, Irene, Teresa. AB, U. Calif., Berkeley, 1941; MD, U. Calif., San Francisco, 1943; postgrad., U. London, 1954-55. Diplomate Am. Bd. Anesthesiology. Intern San Francisco County Hosp., 1943-44; resident in anesthesiology U. Calif. Hosp., San Francisco, 1944-45; tng. in anesthesiology Walter Reed Gen. Hosp., 1945; founder The Wycoff Group of Anesthesiology, San Francisco, 1947-53; chief of anesthesia St. Joseph's Hosp., San Francisco, 1947-52, organizer residency tng. program in anesthesiology, 1950, San Francisco County Hosp., 1954, chief anesthesia, 1953-54; tchr. practice anesthesiology Presbyn. Med. Ctr., NYC, 1955-63; asst. prof. anesthesiology Columbia U., NYC, 1955-63; clin. practice anesthesiology St. Francis Meml. Hosp., San Francisco, 1963-84. Prodr., dir. films on regional anesthesia; contbr. articles to sci. jours. Scoutmaster Boy Scouts Am., San Francisco, 1953-55. Capt. MC, US Army, 1945-47. Mem. Alumni Faculty Assn. Sch. Medicine U. Calif.-San Francisco (councilor-at-large 1979-80). Democrat. Avocations: researching origins of human behavior, writing, gardening. Home: 3875 Castro Valley Blvd Spc 55 Castro Valley CA 94546-4584

WYDEN, RON(ALD) (LEE), United States Senator from Oregon; b. Wichita, Kans., May 3, 1949; s. Peter and Edith W.; m. Laurie Oseran, Sept. 5, 1978 (div. 1999); 2 children; m. Nancy Bass, Sept. 2005. Student, U. Santa Barbara, 1967-69; AB in Polit. Sci., with distinction, Stanford U., 1971; JD, U. Oreg., 1974. Bar: Oreg. 1975. Campaign aide Senator Wayne Morse, 1972, 74; co-founder, co-dir. Oreg. Gray Panthers, 1974-80; dir. Oreg. Legal Services for Elderly, 1977-79; instr. gerontology U. Oreg., 1976, U. Portland, 1980, Portland State U., 1979; mem. 97th-104th Congresses from 3d Oreg. dist., Washington, 1981-96; US Senator form Oreg., 1996—. Mem. com. fin. US Senate, com. intelligence, com. energy and natural resources, com. budget, spl. com. on aging. Contbr. articles to profl. journals. Mem. Oreg. Environmental Coun. Recipient Service to Oreg. Consumers award Oreg. Consumers League, 1978, Citizen of Yr. award Oreg. Assn. Social Workers, 1979, Significant Service award Multnomah County Area Agy. on Aging, 1980, Philip A. Hart Pubilc Svc. award Consumer Fedn. Am., 1999, Champion of Sci. award, U. Oreg./The Sci. Coalition, 2003; named Young Man of Yr. Oreg. Jr. C. of C., 1980, Senator of Yr. Nat. Assn. Police Orgn., 1997, People of Yr (with Rep. Christopher Cox) PC Computing mag., 1999, Legis. of Yr. Info. Tech. Coun., 2000; named one of 50 Most Important People on the Web, PC World, 2007; named to Legis. Hall of Fame Am. Electronics Assn. Mem. ABA, Iowa Bar Assn., Oreg. Bar Assn. Democrat. Jewish. Office: US Senate 230 Dirksen Senate Office Bldg Washington DC 20510-0001 also: District Office Ste 585 1220 SW 3rd Ave Portland OR 97204 Office Phone: 202-224-5244, 503-326-7525. Office Fax: 202-228-2717. E-mail: senator@wyden.senate.gov.*

WYDICK, RICHARD CREWS, lawyer, educator; b. Pueblo, Colo., Nov. 1, 1937; s. Charles Richard and Alice Wydick; m. Judith Brandli James, 1961; children: William Bruce, Derrick Cameron. BA, Williams Coll., 1959; LL.B., Stanford U., 1962. Bar: Calif. bar 1962. Asso. firm Brobeck, Phleger & Harrison, San Francisco, 1966-71; mem. faculty U. Calif. Law Sch., Davis, 1971—, prof. law, 1975—2003, dean, 1978-80, prof. emeritus, 2003—. Author: Plain English for Lawyers, 5th edit., 2005 Served to capt. USAR, 1962-66. Office: Sch Law U Calif Davis CA 95616

WYGANT, FOSTER LAURANCE, art educator; b. Dayton, Ohio, Oct. 30, 1920; s. Harold F. and M. Esther (Weber) W.; m. Rae E. Hoyt, 1 child, Nancy Laura Profl. diploma, Juilliard Sch. Music, 1942; BA, Columbia U., 1949, MA, 1956, Ed.D., 1959; postgrad., Am. Art Sch., Art Students League, 1951-53. Clarinetist Dallas Symphony and free-lance clarinetist, NYC, 1945-47; publicity, fund-raising positions, and free-lance artist, 1952-56; tchr. art, pub. schs., 1956-59; asst. prof. Montclair State Coll., NJ, 1959-63, assoc. prof., 1963-68; prof. art edn. U. Cin., 1968-87, chmn. dept., 1968-84, dir. Sch. Art Edn. and Art History, 1984-86, emeritus prof., 1987—. Pub., owner Interwood Press, 1987—; vis. sr. lectr. Leeds Coll. Art, Eng., 1966; regional chmn. Scholastic Awards Program, 1968-84; chmn. Action for Arts in Ohio Schs., 1974-75. Author: Art in American Schools in the Nineteenth Century, 1983, School Art in American Culture 1820-1970, 1993, School Art in American Culture Supplement: 1900-1915, 1997; editor, prin. author: Standards for Art Teacher Preparation Programs, 1979, Principles, Purposes and Standards for School Art Programs, 1982; contbr. numerous articles to profl. jours. Pres. Tri-State Chamber Players, Inc., 2002—. With US Army, 1941—45. N.Y. State and Juilliard Sch. Music scholar, 1939-41; Kellogg Found. fellow Columbia U., 1955-56 Nat. Art Edn. Assn. (V. Pres., nat. dir. higher edn. divsn. 1975-79, Recognition award 1980, Disting. Svc. award 1982, Disting. fellow 1995), Ohio Art Edn. Assn. (pres. 1972-74, Disting. fellow 2000), Seminar for Rsch. in Art Edn., Coun. for Policy Studies in Art Edn., Am. Fedn. Musicians, Phi Beta Kappa. Home: 3562 Interwood Ave Cincinnati OH 45220-1824 Office Phone: 513-751-5239. Business E-Mail: wygantfl@ucmail.uc.edu.

WYKA, TOM, information technology manager; b. Passaic, NJ, Apr. 11, 1966; married; 2 children. B in Bus., Bucknell U., Lewisburg, Pa.; MBA, Seton Hall U., South Orange, NJ. Cert. project mgr. IT industry. Democrat. Roman Catholic. Mailing: PO Box 350 Lake Hiawatha NJ 07034

WYKLE, MAY L., dean, educator, researcher; BSN, Case Western Res. U., 1956, MSN Psychiat. Nursing, PhD Edn. Dean and Florence Cellar prof. gerontol. nursing, Frances Payne Bolton Sch. Nursing Case Western Res. U., Cleve., 1988—, faculty assoc., Univ. Ctr. Aging and Health. Established ednl. programs, Europe, Africa, Asia; vis. prof. U. Mich., U. Tex.-Houston, U. Zimbabwe-Africa; del., served on planning com. White House Conf. on Aging, 1993. Contbr. articles, chapters to books; author: Decision Making in Long-Term Care, Practicing Rehabilitation with Geriatric Clients, Stress and Health Among the Elderly, Family Caregiving Across the Lifespan, Service Minority Elders in the 21st Century (AJN Book of Yr. award, 2000). Dir. Robert Wood Johnson Tchg. Nursing Home Project; project dir. several tng. grants; cons. nursing homes, psychiat. hosps.; mem. bd. dirs. numerous cmty. orgns., nursing homes, profl. assns. Recipient Humanitarian award, Outstanding Contbns. to Nursing Profession, 1999, Acad. award, NIMH Geriatric Mental Health, Merit award, Cleve. Coun. Black Nurses, Belle Sherwin award, Cleve. Vis. Nurse Assn., Leadership award excellence in geriatric care, Midwest Alliance in Nursing, Disting. nurse-scholar lectr. award, Nat. Coun. Nursing Rsch., Nursing Educator award, New Cleve. Woman mag.; named first Pope Eminent scholar, Rosalynn Carter Inst. Human Devel. Southwestern State U., Americus, Ga., Outstanding Rschr. in State of Ohio, Ohio Rsch. Coun. on Aging, Ohio Network Edn. Cons. in field of Aging, 1992. Fellow: Gerontol. Soc. Am. (Gerontol. Doris Schwartz Nursing Rsch. award), Am. Acad. Nursing; mem.: NIA, NIMH, NINR, Vets Adminstrn. (geriatric/gerontology adv. com.), Sigma Theta Tau Internat. (pres.-elect 1999). Office: Frances Payne Bolton Sch Nursing 10900 Euclid Ave Cleveland OH 44106*

WYKOFF, GARY LEE, writer; b. Erie, Pa., Apr. 27, 1953; s. Donald Lloyd Wykoff and Thelma Jean Anderson. BA, Pa. State U., State College, 1976. Founder, editor, pub., writer, artist Ind. Press, Erie, 1991—2006. Founder, educator, editor Word Factory, Erie. Contbr. articles to publs.; author: Sounding the Madness, 2005, Street #4, 2006, Hit Singles, 2007. Recipient Stairways Outstanding Cmty. Svc. award, Student Achievement award, Pa. State U. Mem.: Mensa, Pax Christyi. Avocation: poetry.

WYLAND, MARK, state legislator; b. Escondido, Calif. 1 child, Nicole. BA in Internat. Rels., Pomona Coll.; MA in Polit. Sci., Columbia U. Former vice chmn. Election Com.; state assembly, Dist. 74 Calif., 2000—06; vice chmn. Vets. Affairs Subcom., Edn. Com.; mem., trustee Escondido Union Sch. Bd.; mem. Edn. Com., Govt. Orgn. Com., Budget Com., Revenue & Taxation Com., Utilities Com., Commerce Com., San Diego Children & Families First Commn.; trustee Pomona Coll.; state senator, Dist. 38 Calif., 2006—. Republican. Mailing: 27126-A Paseo Espada ! 1621 San Juan Capistrano CA 92675 Office Phone: 949-489-9838. Office Fax: 949-489-8354. Business E-Mail: Senator.Wyland@senate.ca.gov.*

WYLDE, KATHRYN S., business organization executive; BA, St. Olaf Coll., 1968. With Lutheran Med. Ctr., 1968—79; pres., CEO, NYC Housing Partnership, 1982—96; founding pres., CEO NYC Investment Fund, 1996—; pres., CEO Partnership for NYC, 2000—. Bd. dirs. Fed. Res. Bank NY, 2009—, NYC Econ. Devel. Corp., Luth. Med. Ctr., Bklyn., Biomed. Rsch. Alliance NY, NYC Leadership Acad., Manhattan Inst. Policy Rsch. Recipient HBSCNY Bus. Statesman award; named one of The 100 Most Influential Women in NYC Bus., Crain's NY Bus., 2007. Office: Partnership for NYC One Battery Pk Plz 5th Fl New York NY 10004 Business E-Mail: kwylde@nycp.org.

WYLE, FREDERICK S., lawyer; b. Berlin, May 9, 1928; came to U.S., 1939, naturalized, 1944; s. Norbert and Malwina (Mauer) W.; m. Katinka Franz, June 29, 1969; children: Susan Kim, Christopher Anthony, Katherine Anne. BA magna cum laude, Harvard U., 1951, LL.B., 1954. Bar: Mass. 1954, Calif. 1955, N.Y. 1958. Teaching fellow Harvard Law Sch., 1954-55; law clk. U.S. Dist. Ct., No. Dist. Calif., 1955-57; assoc. firm Paul, Weiss, Rifkind, Wharton & Garrison, NYC, 1957-58; pvt. practice San Francisco, 1958-62; spl. asst. def. rep. U.S. del. to NATO, Paris, 1962-63; mem. Policy Planning Council, Dept. State, Washington, 1963-65; dep. asst. sec. def. for European and NATO affairs Dept. Def., Washington, 1966-69; v.p. devel., gen. counsel Schroders, Inc., NYC, 1969-71, atty., cons., 1971-72; chief exec. officer Saturday Rev. Industries, Inc., San Francisco, 1972-76; individual practice law San Francisco, 1976—82. Internat. counsel to Fed. States Micronesia, 1974-82; cons. Rand Corp., Dept. Def., Nuclear Regulatory Commn. Contbr. to: Ency. Brit, 1972, also articles in profl. publs., newspapers. Trustee US Interest Bicycle Club Casino, 1996-99; trustee in bankruptcy Garden City, Inc., 2000-07; liquidating trustee Synthetic Industries, 2000—, Biosurg. Industries, 2000-08: Chpt. 11 trustee Winchester Convalescence Hosp., San Jose, 2008-; negotiator for Gov. of Calif. with Indian tribes re gambling, 2003. With AUS, 1946-47. Mem. Internat. Inst. Strategic Studies, Phi Beta Kappa. Office: 3 Embarcadero Ctr Fl 7 San Francisco CA 94111-4065 Office Phone: 415-788-0781.

WYLE, NOAH, actor; b. Hollywood, Calif., June 4, 1971; m. Tracy Warbin, 2000; children: Owen Strausser, Auden. Artistic prodr. The Blank Theatre Co., LA. Actor: (films) Crooked Hearts, 1991, A Few Good Men, 1992, Swing Kids, 1993, There Goes My Baby, 1994, The Myth of Fingerprints, 1997, Can't Stop Dancing, 1999, Scenes of the Crime, 2001, Enough, 2002, White Oleander, 2002, The Californians, 2004, W., 2008; (TV films) Blind Faith, 1990, Guinevere, 1994, Pirates of Silicon Valley, 1999, Fail Safe, 2000, The Librarian: Quest for the Spear, 2004; (TV series) ER, 1994—2006 (SAG award for outstanding performance by ensemble in drama series, 1998, 1999, TV Guide award for supporting actor of yr. in drama series, 2001), 2009; assoc. prodr. Myth of Fingerprints, 1997. Office: The Blank Theatre Co 1301 Lucile Ave Los Angeles CA 90026

WYLIE, CHRISTOPHER CRAIG, biologist, educator; b. Cardigan, Wales, U.K., Sept. 15, 1945; s. Joseph Watson Craig and Edna Millicent (Greenside) W.; m. Janet Heasman, Dec. 1976; children: Matthew, Sara, Michael, Jake. BSc, U. Coll. London, 1966, PhD, 1971; MA (hon.), Cambridge U., 1992. Lectr. anatomy U. Coll. London, 1970-75; sr. lectr. anatomy St. George's Hosp. Med. Sch., London, 1976-82, reader in developmental biology, 1983-85, prof. anatomy and embryology, 1985-88; F.J. Quick prof. biology Cambridge U., 1988-94; Martin Lenz Harrison chair of developmental biology and genetics U. Minn. Sch. Medicine, Mpls., 1994—2000, dir. Ctr. Developmental Biology, 1994—2000; William Schubert prof. pedait. & dir., divsn. developmental biology Cin. Childrens Hosp. Med. Ctr., 2000—. Founder mem. Wellcome/CRC Inst. Devel. and Cancer, Cambridge, 1991. Editor 8 books; editor-in-chief Devel., 1987—; contbr. articles to profl. jours.; appearances U.K. radio, TV. Avocations: racquet sports, hiking, cross country skiing, theater. Office: Children's Hosp Rsrch Fdn 3333 Burnet Ave Cincinnati OH 45229 Home: 411 Bishopsbridge Dr Cincinnati OH 45255 Personal E-mail: xenopus1@netscape.net. Business E-Mail: christopher.wylie@cchmc.org.

WYLIE, GLENN RICHARD, research scientist, educator; s. Allan and Janice Wylie; m. Amber Wylie; 1 child, Justin. PhD, U. Oxford, Eng., 1999. Postdoc. rsch. scientist U. Oxford, 1999—2000, Nathan Kline Inst. Psychiat. Rsch., Orangeburg, NY, 2000—02, rsch. scientist, 2002—05; clin. rsch. scientist Kessler Med. Rehab. Rsch. and Edn. Ctr., West Orange, NJ, 2005—; asst. prof. U. Medicine and Dentistry NJ, Newark, 2005—. Achievements include research in human brain function. Office: Kessler Med Rehab Rsch 300 Executive Dr West Orange NJ 07052 Business E-Mail: gwylie@kmrrec.org.

WYLIE, GUY STEPHEN, psychologist, educator; s. Henry John and Shirley Elizabeth Wylie; m. Janiese Arends, May 17, 1981. BA, Bucknell U., Lewisburg, Pa., 1973; MS, Kans. State Coll. at Pittsburg, 1976; PhD in Counseling, Kans. State U., 1989. Cert. counselor Nat. Bd. for Cert. Counselors, Inc., 1983. Human svc. program coord./psychology instr. Western Nebr. C.C., Scottsbluff, Nebr., 1977—. Bd. mem. Panhandle Partnership for Health and Human Svcs., Panhandle of Nebraska, Nebr., 1997—2003; chmn. region i behavioral health adv. bd. Panhandle Mental Health Ctr., Scottsbluff, Nebr., 1985—; co-chairperson State of Nebr. Substance Abuse Adv. Bd., Lincoln, Nebr., 1994—96; bd. mem. Nebr. State Mental Health Adv. Bd., Lincoln, 1986—90. Pottery and sculpture. Pres. and dir. Scottsbluff-Gering Duplicate Bridge Club, Scottsbluff, Nebr., 1990—2009. Recipient Excellence in Tchg. award, WNCC Phi Theta Kappa, 1999—2000, Outstanding Faculty Mem. award, 1981—82, UNMC Coll. of Nursing Tchr. award, U. of Nebr. Med. Ctr. Coll. of Nursing, 1991. Mem.: Nat. Orgn. for Human Svcs., APA, ACA, Am. Contract Bridge League (unit bd. mem. 1990—2009, Bronze Life Master 2003), Elks (scholarship com. chmn. 1988—2009, Elk of the Yr. 2001-2002). Avocations: potter, bridge. Office: Western Nebraska Community College 1601 East 27th St Scottsbluff NE 69361 Office Fax: 308-635-6100. Personal E-mail: gwylie@wncc.net.

WYLIE, JAMES MALCOLM, adult education educator; b. NYC, Mar. 16, 1938; s. James M. and Nancy Beatrice (Worthy) Wylie. BS, Boston U., 1960. Columnist Mexico City Times, 1964; prof. Cooper Union Coll., NYC, 1986—. Author: The Lost Rebellion, 1971, The Homestead Grays, 1977, The Sign of Dawn, 1981; participant Spoleto Festival U.S.A., 2001.

WYLIE-ROSETT, JUDITH, dietician, educator; BS, U. Ark., Fayetteville, 1966; MEd, Teacher's Coll., Columbia U., NYC, 1971, EdD, 1980. Registered Dietitian. Dietetic internship NY Hosp.-Cornell Med. Ctr., NYC, 1967, dietitian, metabolic rsch. unit, 1967—69; assoc. in medicine, dept. medicine Albert Einstein Coll. Medicine, Bronx, NY, 1971—79, head, divsn. nutrition, dept. cmty. health, 1980—84, asst. prof., dept. cmty. health, 1980—84, asst. prof., dept. epidemiology and social medicine, 1984—88, assoc. prof., dept. epidemiology and social medicine, 1988—95, prof., dept. epidemiology and population health, 1995—, head, divsn. health, behavior and nutrition, 1998—. Cons. for NIH clin. trials and studies. Ad Hoc Reviewer Demonstration and Edn. grants Nat. Heart, Lung and Blood Inst., 1985—, mem. of several editl. bds., reviewer for several profl. jours. Coord., nutrition svcs. Door Multi-Svc. Youth Ctr., 1973—78. Fellow: NY Acad. Medicine; mem.: Am. Assn. Diabetes Educators, Am. Dietetic Assn. (award for excellence in the practice of clin. nutrition 1990, Mary P. Huddleson award 1995), Am. Heart Assn., Am. Diabetes Assn. (bd. dirs. 1981—84, award for outstanding profl. educator in the field of diabetes 1991, Woman of Valor award by Bronx Diabetes Coalition 1996), Phi Upsilon Omicron. Office: 1308 Belfer Bldg Albert Einstein Coll Medicine 1300 Morris Park Ave Bronx NY 10461 Office Phone: 718-430-3345. Office Fax: 718-430-8634. E-mail: jwrosett@aecom.yu.edu.*

WYLLY, BARBARA BENTLEY, volunteer; b. Bala-Cynwyd, Pa., June 10, 1924; d. William Henry and Virginia (Barclay) Bentley; m. William Beck Wylly, Apr. 26, 1947; children: Virginia Wylly Johnson, Barbara Wylly Klausman, Thomas C. II. A, Briarcliff Jr. Coll., 1943. Pres. bd. dirs. Hillside Hosp. Inc., Atlanta, 1982, mem. adv. coun., 1982—; pres. Atlanta Symphony Assocs., 1975—76, mem. adv. bd., 1976—; chmn. bd. dirs. Ctr. Puppetry Arts, Atlanta, 1988—2004, mem. exec. com., 1988—. Bd. dirs. Mountain Conservation Trust, 1996—2008, mem., adv. coun., 2008—; bd. dirs. Atlanta Opera Guild, 1999—; mem. bd. sponsors Georgian Chamber Players, 2000—. Republican. Episcopalian. Avocations: walking, reading, music. Office: Ctr Puppetry Arts 1404 Spring St NW Atlanta GA 30309-2820 Home: 1223 Lenbrook 3747 Peachtree Rd Atlanta GA 30319

WYLY, CHARLES JOSEPH, JR., entrepreneur; b. Lake Providence, La., Oct. 13, 1933; s. Charles Joseph and Flora (Evans) W.; m. Caroline Denmon; children: Martha, Charles Joseph III, Emily, Jennifer. BS, La. Tech. U., 1956. Sales rep. IBM Service Bur. Corp., 1956-64; v.p. Wyly Corp., Dallas, 1964-65, exec. v.p., 1965-69, pres., 1969-73, chmn. exec. com., 1973-76, dir., 1964-76; chmn. bd. Earth Resources Co., 1968-80. Vice chmn. bd. dirs. USACafes, Inc. (Bonanza Internat., Inc.), 1968-89, Sterling Software, Inc.; chmn. Tex. High-Speed Rail Authority, 1990-91, Maverick Capital, 1990-96; ret. chmn. Michaels Stores, Inc. Mem. Pres.'s Advisory Council on Mgmt. Improvement, 1970-73; vice-chmn. Devel. Council So. Methodist U. Found. Sci. and Engring., 1970-71; Mem. Republican Nat. Fin. Com., 1970—; Bd. dirs. Dallas County United Way Fund; pres. Dallas Theater Center., 1972-79. Mem. Am. Mgmt. Assn., Pi Kappa Alpha, Omicron Delta Kappa, Delta Sigma Pi, Beta Gamma Sigma. Clubs: City, Crescent, Park City, Brookhollow (Dallas). Office: Ste 1000 300 Crescent Ct Dallas TX 75201-7852

WYMAN, CHARLES ELY, biotechnologist, research director, chemical engineer; b. Greenfield, Mass., Oct. 23, 1944; s. Ely Warren and Ruth Harriett (Aschenbach) W.; m. Carol Joy Wroblewski, Feb. 17, 1968; children: Marc Ely, Kristin Lee. BS Chem. Engring. summa cum laude, U. Mass., 1967; MA Chem. Engring., Princeton U., 1969, PhD in Chem. Engring., 1971; MBA, U. Denver, 1988. Sr. chem. engr. Monsanto Co., Springfield, Mass., 1971-74; asst. prof. U. N.H., Durham, 1974-78; sr. engr. Solar Energy Research Inst., Golden, Colo., 1978-79, group mgr., 1979-81, dep. div. mgr., 1981, biotech. research br. mgr., 1984-91; mgr. process devel. Badger Co., Inc., Cambridge, Mass., 1981-84; alternative fuels div. dir Nat. Renewable Energy Lab. formerly Solar Energy Rsch. Inst., Golden, 1991—. Adj. prof. Colo. Sch. Mines, 1986; mem. thesis com. U. Mass., Amherst, 1973-74; spl. mem. grad. faculty U. Colo., Boulder, 1986-87; mem. adv. bd. dept. biology U. Colo., Denver, 1987-89; vis. fellow Colo. State U., Ft. Collins, 1986-87, affiliate prof., 1986—; mem. organizing com. 8th, 9th, 10th symposia on biotech. for fuels and chems., co-chmn. 11th, 12th and 14th, chmn. 13th and 15th; bd. dirs. Colo. Inst. for Rsch. in Biotech., 1987—; moblzn. analyst U.S. Army, Charlottesville, Va., 1974-78. Co-editor Proc. 10th-15th Symposia on Biotech. for Fuels and Chems.; mem. internat. editorial bd. Biomass and Bioenergy, 1991—; assoc. editor Jour. Solar Energy Engring., 1989—; mem. editorial bd. Process Biochemistry, 1993—; contbr. numerous articles to profl. jours. Coach Cohasset (Mass.) Boys Soccer Team, 1982-83, Lakewood (Colo.) Advanced Soccer Team, 1986-89. Capt. U.S. Army, 1970-78. Mem. ASME, Am. Inst. Chem. Engrs., Am. Chem. Soc., Am. Sect. Internat. Solar Energy Soc., ACS div. Biochem. Tech., Colo. Biotech. and Med. Tech. Roundtable, Sigma Xi, Phi Kappa Phi, Tau Beta Pi, Beta Gamma Sigma. Congregationalist. Achievements include patents in field. Office: Nat Renewable Energy Lab 1617 Cole Blvd Golden CO 80401-3305

WYMAN, DAVID SWORD, retired historian, educator; b. Weymouth, Mass., Mar. 6, 1929; s. Hollis Judson and Ruth (Sword) W.; m. Mildred Louise Smith, Sept. 13, 1950; children: James Nayler, Teresa Carol. AB, Boston U., 1951; EdM, Plymouth State Coll., 1961; AM, Harvard U., 1962, PhD, 1966; DHL (hon.), Hebrew Union Coll. Jewish Inst. Religion, 1986, Yeshiva U., 1988. Various positions, 1951-57; tchr. pub. schs. Tilton, NH, 1957-60; tchr. pub. high sch. Penacook, NH, 1960-61; prof. history U. Mass., Amherst, 1966-91, Josiah DuBois prof. history, 1986-91, Josiah DuBois prof. emeritus, 1991—, chmn. Judaic Studies Program, 1977-78, 82-84, chmn. David S. Wyman Inst. for Holocaust Studies, 2003—. Acad. advisor Simon Wiesenthal Ctr., L.A., 1983—; nat. coun. Nat. Christian Leadership Conf. for Israel, 1986, numerous radio and TV appearances; historian advisor to films. Author: Paper Walls: America and the Refugee Crisis, l938-4l, l968, The Abandonment of the Jews: America and the Holocaust, l94l-45, l984 (Anisfield-Wolf award l984, Stuart Bernath award l984, Theodore Saloutos book award l984, Present Tense Lit. award 1984, Boston Hadassah Myrtle Wreath award l985, Nat. Jewish Book award l985), new edit., 2007; co-author: A Race Against Death: Peter Bergson, America, and the Holocaust, 2002; editor: America and the Holocaust, l3 vols. documents, l989-90, The World Reacts to the Holocaust, 1996; contbr. articles to profl. jours., chpts. to books. Recipient Chancellor's medal, U. Mass., 1986, Achievement award Isaac M. Wise Temple, Cin. 1986, Humanitarian award Bklyn. Holocaust Meml. Com., 1986, Herbert Katzki award Am. Jewish Joint Distbn. Com., 1999; elected to Boston U. Collegium Disting. Alumni, 1986; Woodrow Wilson fellow, 1961-62, 65-66; grantee Social Sci. Rsch. Coun., 1969-70, Am. Coun. Learned Socs., 1969-70, Charles Warren Ctr. at Harvard U., 1969-70. Mem. Soc. for Am. Baseball Rsch., N.H. Hist. Soc., Friends Hist. Assn., Phi Beta Kappa. Avocations: baseball, local history. Home: 61 Columbia Dr Amherst MA 01002-3105

WYMAN, MILTON, ophthalmologist; b. Cleve., Oct. 1, 1930; s. Sam and Elsie Wyman; m. Marlyn Percer Wyman, Aug. 10, 1952; children: Karen D. Myers, James B. DVM, Ohio State U., Columbus, 1963, MS, 1964. Rsch. fellow Mark Morris, Kans., 1963—65; trustee Ohio State U. Vet. Med., Columbus, 1965—69, assoc. prof., 1970—75, prof., 1975—92, assoc. dean, 1984—92, clin. prof., 1989—92; specialty practice ophthalmology Med. Vet. Columbus, 1992—. Cons. NIH, Bethesda, Md., 1972—92; clin. cons. Grady Animal Hosp., Cin., 1970—88, Wilmington Animal Hosp., Wilmington, NC, 1972—89. Recipient Disting. Tchg. award, Ohio State U., 1970; named Veterinarian of Yr., Ohio, 1973. Fellow: Am. Acad. Ophthalmology; mem.: Coll. Vet. Medicine Alumni Soc., Assn. Rsch. Vision & Ophthalmology, Am. Coll. Vet. Ophthalmologists, Am. Assn. Vet. Clinicians, Am. Soc. Vet. Medicine, Ohio Vet. Med. Assn., Am. Vet. Med. Assn., Am. Animal Hosp. Assn., Phi Kappa Phi, Gamma Sigma Delta. Episcopalian. Business E-Mail: mwyaman1@columbus.rr.com.

WYMAN, RALPH MARK, multifamily office firm executive; b. Usti, Czechoslovakia, Feb. 7, 1926; arrived in U.S., 1941, naturalized, 1946; s. Hans and Stella (Parnas) Wyman; m. Lotte Ann Novak, Oct. 25, 1947; 1 child, Leslie Andrea Wyman Cooper. Student, Upper Can. Coll., 1942, Bucknell U., 1942-43; BSBA, NYU, 1945; postgrad., Columbia U., 1945-46. Asst. mgr. export dept. Liebermann Waelchi & Co., Inc., NYC, 1946-47; trainee White Weld Co., 1947-48; v.p. H. O. Canfield Co., 1948-65, vice chmn. bd. dirs., 1965-79, bd. dirs., 1953-79, Pantasote Inc., 1960-89, vice chmn. bd. dirs., 1967-89; mng. partner United Eagle Mgmt. Co., Eagle Mgmt. Co., 1960-95; pres. Veritas, Inc., 1960—2005; bd. dirs., chmn. Eagle Capital Internat. LLC, 1985—; bd. dirs., vice chmn. Affiliate Artists, Inc., 1971-88; chmn. New Eng. Genspring Family Offices, 2003—. Pres. Panwy Found.; bd. dirs. United Way Greenwich, Conn., 1980—86, Kids in Crisis, Greenwich, 1993—2001, sec., 1995—2001; trustee Greenwich Acad., 1963—71, chmn., 1968—70; elder, trustee Synod New Eng., 1974—76; trustee Princeton Theol. Sem., 1976—2001, vice chmn., 1997—2001, trustee emeritus, 2001—; trustee Ctr. Theol. Inquiry, 1997—2008. Mem.: Indian Harbor Yacht Club, Lambda Chi Alpha. Home: 34 Baldwin Farms N Greenwich CT 06831-3307 Office: # 4 Greenwich Office Park IV Greenwich CT 06831-5246 Home Phone: 203-869-1821; Office Phone: 203-661-6616. Business E-Mail: ralph.wyman@gemspring.com.

WYMAN, RICHARD THOMAS, information technology manager, researcher; b. Wilmington, Del., June 4, 1951; s. William Harper and Marian Kathryn (Bode) W., Pa. State U., 1969-71, Def. Language Inst., 1974-75, Control Data Inst., Dallas, 1979. Enlisted U.S. Army, 1971, served to staff sgt., 1979; data ctr. mgr. thrift svcs. divsn. ADP Inc., Dallas, 1979-80; support mgr. Electronic Data Sys., Inc., Dallas, 1980-85, info. modeling analyst, 1985-90; pres. Strategic InfoSource, Plano, Tex., 1991-93; sr. cons. The SABRE Group, Ft. Worth, 1993-97; assoc. Perot Sys. Corp., Richardson, Tex., 1997-98; info. architect The Technical Resource Connection, Inc., Tampa, Fla., 1998—2005; enterprise architect Perot Sys. Corp., Plano, Tex., 2005—. Rep. 101st Airborne Divsn. Nat. Conf. Skill Maintenance, Ft. Meade, Md., 1977. Author: (spl. course) U.S. Army Intelligence, 1978-79. Co-chmn. sub-com. City Bond Referendum Com., Plano, 1990; mem. City of Plano Historic Landmark Com., 1993-97, vice chmn. 1996, chmn. 1996-97. Recipient Army Commendation medal, 1978, 79, Vol. Svc. award, Office of Mayor, Plano, 1990. Achievements include patents pending for computer system and process for aiding in an outsourcing environment. Home: 3608 Trailview Dr Plano TX 75074 Office: Perot Systems Corp 2300 W Plano Pkwy Plano TX 75075

WYMAN, RICHARD VAUGHN, engineering educator, company executive; b. Painesville, Ohio, Feb. 22, 1927; s. Vaughn Ely and Melinda (Ward) W.; m. Anne Fenton, Dec. 27, 1947; 1 son, William Fenton. BS, Case Western Res. U., 1948; MS, U. Mich., 1949; PhD, U. Ariz., 1974. Registered profl. engr., Nev., Ariz.; registered geologist, Ariz., Calif.; lic. water right surveyor, Nev., cert. minerals appraisor, 1991-. Geologist N.J. Zinc Co., 1949, 52-53, Cerro de Pasco Corp., 1950-52; chief geologist Western Gold & Uranium, Inc., St. George, Utah, 1953-55, gen. supt., 1955-57, v.p., 1957-59; pres. Intermountain Exploration Co., Boulder City, Nev., 1959-93; tunnel supt. Reynolds Electric & Engring. Co., 1961-63, mining engr., 1965-67; asst. mgr. ops. Reynolds Electric and & Engring. Co., 1967-69; constrn. supt. engr. Sunshine Mining Co., 1963-65; lectr. U. Nev., Las Vegas, 1969-73, assoc. prof., 1973-80, dept. chmn., 1976-80, prof., 1980-92, prof. emeritus, 1992—, chmn. dept. civil and mech. engring., 1984-90, chmn. dept. civil and environ. engring., 1990-91. Mineral rep. Ariz. Strip Adv. Bd., 1976-80, U.S.B.L.M.; mem. peer rev. com. Nuclear Waste Site, Dept. Energy, Las Vegas, 1978-82; pres. Ariz. Juno Resources, Boulder City, 1980-87, v.p., 1990-97; pres. Wyman Engring. Cons., 1987—2009; cons. Corp. Andina de Fomento, Caracas, Venezuela, 1977-78; v.p. Comstock Gold, Inc., 1984-93; program evaluator Accreditation Bd. for Engring. and Tech., 1995-2001. Contbr. articles to profl. jours. Sec. Washington County Republican Party, Utah, 1958-60; del. Utah Rep. Conv., 1958-60; scoutmaster Boy Scouts Am., 1959-69; mem. citizens adv. com., tech. adv. com. Clark County Regional Flood Control Dist., 1998-2004. Served with USN, 1944-46. Recipient Order of Engr. award, 2000. Fellow ASCE (life; edn. divsn. 1990, local rep. nat. conv. Las Vegas), Soc. Econ. Geologists (life); mem. AIME/SME (life, chmn. So. Nev. sect. 1971-72, dir. 1968-2002, sec.-treas. 1974-92, chmn. Pacific S.W. Minerals Conf. 1972, gen. chmn. nat. conv. 1980, Disting. Mem. award 1989, Legion of Honor 1999), Assn. Engring. Geologists (dir. S.W. sect. 1989-91), Am. Inst. Minerals Appraisers, Am. Water Works Assn., Nev. Mining Assn. (assoc.), Northwest Mining Assn., Geological Soc. Nev., Assn. Ground Water Scientists and Engrs., Arctic Inst. N.Am. (life), Am. Soc. Engring. Edn., Soc. for History of Discoveries, Am. Philatelic Soc., SAR, Am. Legion, Sigma Xi (pres. Las Vegas sect. 1986-91), Phi Kappa Phi (pres. U. Nev. Las Vegas chpt. 100 1982-83), Sigma Gamma Epsilon, Tau Beta Pi. Congregationalist. Home: 610 Bryant Ct Boulder City NV 89005-3017 Office: Wyman Engring PO Box 60473 Boulder City NV 89006-0473 Home Phone: 702-293-4178. Business E-Mail: rwyman02@cox.net.

WYNAR, BOHDAN STEPHEN, retired librarian, writer, editor; b. Lviv, Ukraine, Sept. 7, 1926; came to U.S., 1950, naturalized, 1957; s. John I. and Euphrosina (Doryk) W.; children: Taras, Michael, Roxolana. Diplom-Volkswirt Econs., U. Munich, Germany, 1949, PhD, 1950; MA, U. Denver, 1958. Methods analyst, statistician Tramco Corp., Cleve., 1951-53; freelance journalist Soviet Econs., Cleve., 1954-56; adminstrv. asst. U. Denver Librs., 1958-59, head tech. svcs. div., 1959-62; assoc. prof. Sch. Librarianship, U. Denver, 1962-66; dir. div. libr. edn. State U. Coll., Geneseo, NY, 1966-67, dean Sch. Libr. Sci., prof., 1967-69; pres. Libraries Unlimited Inc., 1969—2002. Author: Soviet Light Industry, 1956, Economic Colonialism, 1958, Ukrainian Industry, 1964, Introduction to Bibliography and Reference Work, 4th edit, 1967, Introduction to Cataloging and Classification, 8th edit, 1992, Major Writings on Soviet Economy, 1966, Library Acquisitions, 2d edit, 1971, Research Methods in Library Science, 1971, Economic Thought in Kievan Rus', 1974; co-author: Comprehensive Bibliography of Cataloging and Classification, 2 vols., 1973, Ukraine: A Bibliographic Guide to English Language Publications, 1990, Independent Ukraine: A Bibliographic Guide to English Language Publications, 1989-99, 2000, Wynar's Introduction to Cataloging and Classification, 2000; editor Ukrainian Quar., 1953-58, Preliminary Checklist of Colorado Bibliography, 1963, Studies in Librarianship, 1963-66, Research Studies in Library Science, 1970—, Best Reference Books, 3d edit., 1985, 4th edit., 1992, Colorado Bibliography, 1980; gen. editor: American Reference Books Ann., 1969-2001; editor: ARBA Guide to Subject Encyclopedias and Dictionaries, 1985, ARBA Guide To Biographical Dictionaries, Reference Books in Paperback, An Annotated Guide, 2d edit., 1976, 3rd edit., 1991, Dictionary of Am. Library Biography, 1978, Ukraine-A Bibliographic Guide to English-Language Publications, 1990, 99, International Writings of Bohdan S. Wynar 1949-1992, 1993, Independent Ukraine, Bibliographic Guide, 2000, My Life-Memoirs-, 2003, Recommended Reference Books for Medium-Sized and Small Libraries, 1981-2001; co-editor, contbr. Ency. Ukraine, 1955—; editor Library Sci. Ann., 1984-90, 98, Libr. Info. Sci. Annual 1984-90, 98—. Bd. dirs., mem. exec. bd. ZAREVO, Inc. Mem. ALA (pres. Ukrainian Congress com. br., Denver 1976), Colo. Library Assn., N.Y. Library Assn., Am. Assn. Advancement Slavic Studies (pres. Ukrainian Research Found. 1976-90), AAUP, Ukranian Hist. Assn. (exec. bd.), Sevčenko Societe Scientifique (Paris), Ukrainian Acad. Arts and Scis. (N.Y.C.). Home Phone: 303-798-9083.

WYND, CHRISTINE ANNE, nursing service administration; b. Cleve., Aug. 12, 1952; d. John Martin and Jean Marie (Long) Doman; m. Robert S. Wynd, Mar. 24, 1975 (div. July 1985); 1 child, Nathan Robert; m. Charles Frederick Santose, July 25, 1987; 1 child, Rachel Amelia. BSN, St. John Coll., 1974; MSN, Ohio State U., 1978; PhD in Nursing, Case Western Res. U., 1989. Cert. community health nursing ANA. Staff nurse USN Nurse Corps, San Diego, 1974-77, staff nursing educator, 1976-77; grad. asst. Ohio State U., Columbus, 1977-78; assoc. project dir. Ohio Commn. on Nursing, Columbus, 1978-80; instr. Ohio State U., Columbus, 1980-83, Case Western Res. U., Cleve., 1983-87; asst. prof. U. Akron, Ohio, 1987-91; dir. dept. nursing rsch. Cleve. (Ohio) Clinic Found., 1991—, chmn. nursing rsch. com., 1992. Cons. JS Consumer Products, Fort Collins, Colo., 1992. Contbr. articles to profl. jours. Disaster svcs. nurse ARC, Cleve., 1980. Lt. col. USAR, 1972-92. Decorated Army Achievement medal U.S. Army Nurse Corps, Washington, 1990, 9A Specialty Designator, U.S. Army Nurse Corps, Washington, 1991. Mem. Sigma Theta Tau (chmn. rsch. grants and awards com. 1991-92, mem. heritage com. 1992). Episcopalian. Avocation: sailing. Home: 1190 Hunters Trl Broadview Heights OH 44147-1930 Office: Cleve Clinic Found 9500 Euclid Ave # P37 Cleveland OH 44195-0001

WYNDEWICKE, KIONNE ANNETTE (ANNETTE JOHNSON MOORER), retired secondary school educator; b. Preston, Miss. d. Clifton Thomas and Missouria (Jackson) Johnson; m. Eugene C. Moorer, 1961 (div.). BS, Ill. State U., 1961; postgrad., Williams Coll., 1972, Columbia Coll., 1972; MEd, Nat. Coll. Edn., 1982. Social worker Cook County Dept. Pub. Aid, 1961; reading tchr. grades 3-8 Chgo. Bd. Edn., 1961—89; asst. to news dir. Sta. WCIU-TV, 1972-74; asst. women's editor Chgo. Defender, 1970-72; social sec. Dr. William R. Clarke, 1972—77; ret., 1992. Part-time photog. model; fashion commentator; pub. rels. cons.; pub. spkr. Contbr. articles to local newspapers. Co-chmn. installation Profl. Women's Aux., Provident Hosp., 1961, corr. sec., 1969, publicity chmn., 1969—72, 1974—77. Recipient Outstanding Cmty. Svc. award, Beatrice Caffrey Youth Svc., Inc., 1978, 1983, 1985; named Woman of the Day, Sta. WAIT Radio, 1978; named one of 13 persons in US to attend Inoovative Tchr. Tng. Seminar, Williams Coll., 1972, 25 Black Women of Chgo. to receive Kizzy award, 1977. Lutheran. Home: 2901 S King Dr Apt 1514 Chicago IL 60616-3314

WYNDRUM, RALPH WILLIAM, JR., communications consultant; b. NYC, Apr. 20, 1937; s. Ralph W. and Virginia M. (Woolley) W.; m. Meta Schmidt, Apr. 23, 1960; children: Dorothy, Jeanne, Ralph, Joan BS, Columbia U., 1959, MSEE, 1960, MS Bus. Adminstrn., 1978; DSc, NYU, 1963. Mem. tech. staff Bell Labs., Murray Hill, NJ, 1963—65, supr. exploratory circuit design, 1965—69, head loop transmission tech. dept. Holmdel and Whippany, NJ, 1969—79, head advanced loop transmission sys. dept. Whippany, 1979—87, head internat. loop sys. dept., 1987, dir. sys. analysis ctr., 1987—90, dir. quality process ctr., 1990—92, dir. quality, engring., software and techs., 1993—94; v.p. AT&T World Svcs., 1994—, dir. process engr. ctr., 1995—96; tech. v.p. AT&T Labs., 1996—99, v.p. program mgmt., 1999—2000, exec. cons., 2000—; CEO Exec. Engring. Cons., 2000—; staff exec. SmartOrg, Inc., Menlo Park, Calif., 2001—04. Adj. prof. N.J. Inst. Tech., 1965, Rutgers U., 2004—, Stevens Inst. Tech., 1980—88, mem. industry adv. bd., 2000—07; pres. The Innovation Inst., Washington, 2007—. Contbr. articles to profl. jours.; patentee in field Fellow: IEEE (bd. dirs. 1988—90, v.p. publs. 1990—91, bd. dirs. 2000—01, 2003—04, v.p. tech. activities 2003—04, exec. com. 2004, bd. dirs. 2006, Pres.'s Leadership award 1991); mem.: IEEE-USA (v.p. tech. policy 2002—03, bd. dirs. 2002—, pres. 2006, CEO, Innovation Inst. 2006—), Am. Assn. Engring. Socs., Washington, D.C. (bd. chair 2009), IEEE Components, Packaging and Mfg. Tech. Soc. (pres. 1992—95), IEEE Comm. Soc. (chmn. conf. bd. 1981—87), Shrewsbury River Yacht Club, Sigma Xi, Beta Gamma Sigma, Eta Kappa Nu. Republican. Roman Catholic. Office: 35 Cooney Ter Fair Haven NJ 07704-3001 Office Phone: 732-219-0005. Business E-Mail: r.wyndrum@ieee.org, rww@monmouth.com. E-mail: rwyndrum@comcast.net.

WYNER, YEHUDI, composer, pianist, conductor, educator; b. Calgary, Alta., Can., June 1, 1929; s. Lazar and Sarah Naomi (Shumiatcher) Weiner; m. Nancy Joan Braverman, Sept. 16, 1951 (div. 1967); children: Isaiah, Adam, Cassia; m. Susan M. Davenny, June 15, 1967. Diploma, Juilliard Sch. Music, 1946; AB, Yale U., 1950, B.Mus., 1951, M.Mus., 1953; MA, Harvard U., 1952. Vis. assoc. prof. Hofstra Coll., 1959; lectr. Queens Coll., NYC, 1959-60; instr. Hebrew Union Coll., NYC, 1957-59; music dir. Westchester Reform Temple, NYC, 1959-68; asst. prof. theory Yale U., 1963-69, assoc. prof. theory, 1969-77, chmn. composition dept., 1969-73; prof. music SUNY, Purchase, 1978-89, dean music, 1978-82. Faculty Tanglewood Music Ctr. (formerly Berkshire Music Ctr.), 1975-97; vis. prof. composition Cornell U., 1987, Ziskind vis. prof. composition Brandeis U., 1987-88, Walter Naumburg prof. composition, dir. contemporary ensemble, 1989-2005, prof. emeritus, 2005-; vis. prof. Harvard U., 1991-93, 96-98, 2003-04, 07-08; Mary Duke Biddle Disting. composer Duke U., 1995; master composer Atlantic Ctr. for the Arts, 2005.; Howard Harison vis.prof. Eastman Sch. Music, 2008; guest prof. resident, Vanderbilt U. 2008; faculty artist Sarasota Music Festival, 2009. Mus. dir. Turnau Opera Assn., 1961—64, New Haven Opera Soc., 1968—77, mem. Bach Aria group, 1968—, composer, condr. Tanglewood, 1961, composer-in-residence Santa Fe Chamber Music Festival, 1982, Am. Acad. Rome, 1991; composer-in-residence: Atlantic Ctr. Arts, 2005; composer: Easy Suite for Piano, 1949, Songs, 1950—2004, Two Chorale Preludes for Organ, 1951, Partita for piano, 1952, Dance Variations for wind octet, 1953, rev., 1959, Psalm 143, chorus, 1952, Sonata for piano, 1954, Concert Duo for violin and piano, 1955—57, Dedication Anthem, 1957, Serenade for Seven Instruments, 1958, Passover Offering for Flute, Clarinet, Cello and Trombone, 1959, Three Informal Pieces for violin and piano, 1961, Friday Evening Service for Cantor, Chorus, Organ, 1963, orchestrated, 1972, (incidental music for play) The Old Glory, 1964, Torah Service with Instruments, 1966, Da Camera for piano and orch., 1967, Cadenza! for clarinet and harpsichord (or piano), 1969, De Novo for cello and small ensemble, 1971, Liturgical Fragments for the High Holidays, 1971, Three Short Fantasies for piano, 1963—71, Canto Cantabile for soprano and concert band, 1972, (music for the play) The Mirror, 1972—73, Memorial Music for soprano and 3 flutes, 1971—73, Intermedio for soprano and string orchestra, 1974, Wedding Music, 1976, Dances of Atonement for violin and piano, 1976, Fragments from Antiquity: 5 songs for soprano and symphony orch., 1978, Romances for Piano Quartet, 1980, All the Rage for flute and piano, 1980, Processionals and Marches, 1979, 1980, Tanz and Maissele for clarinet, violin, cello, piano, 1981, On This Most Voluptuous Night for soprano and 7 instruments, 1982, Wind Quintet, 1984, String Quartet, 1985, Composition for Viola and piano, 1987, Toward the Center for piano, 1988, Sweet Consort for flute and piano, 1988, Leonardo Vincitore for 2 sopranos, string bass and piano, 1988, O To Be a Dragon, four songs for women's chorus and piano, 1989, Trapunto Junction for brass trio and percussion, 1991, Changing Time for small ensemble, 1991, New Fantasies for piano, 1991, Amadeus' Billiard for small ensemble, 1991, II Cane Minore for 2 clarinets and bassoon, 1992, Wedding Dances: From the Notebook of Suzanne de Venné, 1993, Post Fantasies for piano, 1993, Prologue and Narrative for cello and orch., 1994, Song Cycle for soprano, baritone and piano: Restaurants, Wines-Bistros, Shrines, 1994, More Fantasies for piano, 1994—2002, Lyric Harmony for orch., 1995, Praise Ye the Lord for soprano and ensemble, 1996, Brandeis Sunday for string quartet, 1996, A Mad Tea Party for soprano, tenor, baritones, flute, violin, cello and piano, 1996, Epilogue for orch., 1996, Horntrio, 1997, Madrigal for string quartet, 1999, The Second Madrigal: Voices of Women for soprano and eleven players, 1999, Quartet for oboe and string trio, 1999, Commedia for clarinet and piano, 2002, Tuscan Triptych: Echoes of Hannibal (string orch. version of String Quartet 1985), 2002, (piano concerto) Chiavi in mano, 2004 (Pulitzer Prize for music, 2006), (commns.) Yale U., 1958, Mich. U., 1959, Fromm Found., 1960, Koussevitzky Found. at Lib. Congress, 1960, 1991, Ford Found., 1971, Yale Band, Yale Repertory Theater, Cantilena Chamber Players, Aeolian Chamber Players, Santa Fe Chamber Music Festival, Collage of Boston, N.Y. Woodwind Quintet, Frank Taplin project, NEA Consortium, Boston Symphony Chamber Players, Atlantic Symphonietta, Carnegie Hall Am. Composers Orch., RNCM Mancester Internat. Cello Festival, Boston Symphony, The Cantata Singers; pub. Associated Music Pub., Inc.; recs.: Bridge, New World, Albany, Naxos, Pro Arte & Columbia Records. Recipient Elise Stoeger prize, Lincoln Ctr. Chamber Music Soc., 1998; Rome Prize fellow, 1953—56, Alfred E. Hertz fellow, U. Calif., 1953—54, Guggenheim fellow, 1960, 1977, Rockefeller Found. fellow, Bellagio, 1998, Inst. Arts and Letters grant, 1961, grantee, NEA, 1976. Mem. Am. Music Ctr., Am. Acad. Arts and Letters (elected); fellow Am. Acad. Arts & Scis.

WYNGAARDEN, JAMES BARNES, retired physician; b. East Grand Rapids, Mich., Oct. 19, 1924; s. Martin Jacob and Johanna (Kempers) W.; m. Ethel Vredevoogd, June 20, 1946 (div. 1977); children: Patricia Wyngaarden Fitzpatrick, Joanna Wyngaarden Gandy, Martha Wyngaarden Krauss, Lisa Wyngaarden, James Barnes Jr. Student, Calvin Coll., 1942—43, Western Mich. U., 1943—44; MD, U. Mich., 1948; DSc (hon.), U. Mich., Med. Coll. of Ohio, 1984, U. Ill., 1985, George Washington U., 1986, U. SC, West Mich. U., 1989, Duke U., 2006; PhD (hon.), Tel Aviv U., 1987. Diplomate Am. Bd. Internal Medicine. Intern Mass. Gen. Hosp., Boston, 1948-49, resident, 1949-51; vis. investigator Pub. Health Rsch. Inst., NYC, 1952-53; investigator NIH, USPHS, Bethesda, Md., 1953-56; asso. prof. medicine and biochemistry Duke U. Med. Sch., 1956-61, prof., 1961-65; vis. scientist Inst. Biologie-Physiochemique, Paris, 1963-64; prof., chmn. U. Pa. Med. Sch., 1965-67; physician-in-chief Med. Svc. Hosp. U. PA., Phila., 1965-67; Frederic M. Hanes prof., chmn. dept. medicine Duke U. Sch. of Medicine, Durham, NC, 1967-82; physician-in-chief Med. Svc. Duke U. Hosp., Durham, 1967-82; chief of staff Duke U. Hosp., Durham, 1981-82; dir. NIH, Bethesda, MD, 1982-89; assoc. dir. life scis. Office of Sci. and Tech. Policy, Exec. Office of Pres., The White House, 1989-90; dir. Human Genome Orgn., 1990-91; fgn. sec. NAS, 1990-94; prof. medicine, assoc. vice chancellor for health affairs Duke U., Durham, NC, 1990-94, ret., 1994; mem. staff VA, Durham County Hosps.; sr. assoc. dean internat. med. programs U. Pa., Phila., 1995-97. Cons. Office Sci. and Tech. Exec. Office of Pres., 1966-72; Mem. Pres.'s Sci. Adv. Com., 1972-73; mem. Pres.'s Com. for Nat. Medal of Sci., 1977-80; mem. adv. com. biology and medicine AEC, 1966-68; mem. bd. sci. counselors NIH, 1971-74; mem. adv. bd. Howard Hughes Med. Inst., 1969-82; mem. adv. council Life Ins. Med. Research Fund, 1967-70; adv. bd. Sci. Yr., 1977-81; vice-chmn. Com. on Study Nat. Needs for Biomed. and Behavioral Rsch. Personnel, NRC, 1977-81; bd. dirs. Idera Pharm., prin. Wash. Adv. Group, 1995-02. Author: (with W.N. Kelley) Gout and Hyperuricemia, 1976; mem. editorial bd. Jour. Biol. Chemistry, 1971-74, Arthritis and Rheumatism, 1959-66, Jour. Clin. Investigation, 1962-66, Ann. Internal Medicine, 1964-74, Medicine, 1963-90; editor: (with J.B. Stanbury, D.S. Fredrickson) The Metabolic Basis of Inherited Disease, 1960, 66, 72, 78, 83, (with O. Sperling and A. DeVries) Purine Metabolism in Man, 1974, (with L.H. Smith, Jr.) Cecil Textbook of Medicine, 16th edit., 1982, 19th edit., 1992. Bd. dirs. Royal Soc. Medicine Found., 1971-76, The Robert Wood Johnson Found. Clin. Scholar Program, 1973-78. Ensign USNR, 1943-46; sr. surgeon USPHS, 1951-56, rear adm. USPHS, 1982-90. Recipient Borden Undergrad. Research award, U. Mich., 1948, NC Gov.'s award for sci., 1974, Disting. Alumnus award We. Mich. U., 1984, Robert Williams award Assn. Profs. Medicine, 1985, Dalton scholar in medicine, Mass. Gen. Hosp., 1950, Richard Schweiker Excellence in Govt. award, 1985, Fedn. of Am. Socs. of Exptl. Biology Pub. Svc. award, 1989, Humanitarian award Nat. Orgn. for Rare Diseases, 1990; Royal Coll. Physicians fellow, 1984. Mem. Am. Rheumatism Assn., Am. Fedn. Clin. Rsch., So. Soc. Clin. Investigation (pres. 1974, founder's medal 1978), ACP (John Phillips Meml. award 1980), Am. Soc. Clin. Investigation, AAAS, Am. Soc. Biol. Chemists, Assn. Am. Physicians (councillor 1973-77, pres. 1978, Kober medal 1991), Endocrine Soc., Nat. Acad. Scis., Royal Acad. Scis. Sweden, Am. Acad. Arts and Sci., Inst. Medicine, Sigma Xi. Clubs: Interurban Clinical (Balt.). Democrat. Presbyterian. Avocations: tennis, skiing, painting. Home Phone: 919-383-0921. Personal E-mail: jwyngaarden@nc.rr.com.

WYNIA, STEVEN, industrial technical educator; MS, SD State U., Brookings, 1988. Program coord. SD State U., 1989—94; asst. prof. Black Hills State U., Spearfish, SD, 2001—. Office: Black Hills State Univ 515 W Blvd Rapid City SD 57701 Personal E-mail: s51677w@yahoo.com. Business E-Mail: stevewynia@bhsu.edu.

WYN-JONES, ALUN (WILLIAM WYN-JONES), software developer, mathematician; b. Tremadoc, Gwynedd, Wales, Aug. 15, 1946; arrived in U.S., 1976; s. Goronwy Wyn and Mai Jones; m. Jocelyn Ripley, July 29, 1977; 1 stepchild, Electra Truman BSc honors, U. Manchester, UK, 1968; MSc, U. Coll. London, 1970. Rsch. engr. Marconi-Elliott Computer Labs., Borehamwood, England, 1970—71; asst. tutor math. Poly. North London, 1971—72; programmer CRC Info. Sys., Ltd., London, 1972—76; mgr. devel. Warner Computer (now Warner Ins.), NYC, 1976—80; pres., owner, developer Wallsoft Sys., Inc., NYC, 1982—92, Integrity Sys. Corp., NYC, 1980—94. Cons. investment banking divsn. Goldman, Sachs & Co., N.Y.C., 1994-2000, FirstRain, Inc., N.Y.C., 2000-02, Thomson Fin., 2002-04, XL2Web, 2005—08, KPMG Credit Portfolio Mgmt., 2008-; invited spkr. profl. confs Author, co-author computer software Recipient Byte Award Distinction Byte Editors and Columnists, 1988, Readers Choice award Data Based Advisor Readers, 1990, 91 Mem. AAAS, Am. Math. Soc., Math. Assn. Am Achievements include development of template programming in automatic code generation. Home: 4 Aspect Ct 521 Manchester Rd London E143NX England Office Phone: 4402073115225. Personal E-mail: awynjones@comcast.net, awynjones@verizon.net. Business E-Mail: alun.wgn-jones@lepmg.co.uk.

WYNN, ALBERT RUSSELL, lobbyist, former United States Representative from Maryland; b. Phila., Sept. 10, 1951; m. Jessie Jackson, Jan. 14, 1994 (sep.); 1 child, Gabrielle; m. Gaines Clore Wynn. BS, U. Pitts., 1973; student, Howard U.; JD, Georgetown U., 1977. Intern African Regional Affairs, U.S. State Dept., 1972-73; exec. dir. consumer protection divsn. Prince George's County, 1977-81; mem. Md. Ho. of Dels., 1983-86; lawyer Albert R. Wynn & Assocs., 1982-86; mem. Md. State Senate from Dist. 25, 1987-92, US Congress from 4th Md. Dist., Washington, 1993—2008; dep. Dem. whip; mem. commerce com.; ptnr. pub. policy & law practice Dickstein Shapiro LLP, Washington, 2008—. Mem. banking & fin. svcs com., internat. rels. com., Patuxent Inst. reform task force, 1988-92, joint com. econ. devel. strategy, 1989-92; del. Dem. Nat. Conv. 1984, 88,96; pres. Metro. Washington coun. consumer agencies. Mem. NAACP legal assistance program, coalition on black affairs, voter registration, edn. coalition, gov.'s task force drunk & drugged driving; 1st vice chmn. legis. black caucus; chmn. Prince George's County black elected officials alliance. Named one of The 100 Most Influential Black Americans, Ebony mag., 2006—08; named to Power 150, 2008. Mem. J. Franklin Bourne Bar Assn., Kappa Alpha Psi (past pres.). Democrat. Baptist. Office: Dickstein Shapiro LLP 1825 Eye St NW Washington DC 20006-5403 Office Phone: 202-225-8699.*

WYNN, JOHN THOMAS, retired academic administrator, farming executive, economic consultant, oil and gas producer; b. Corsicana, Tex., May 4, 1938; s. Sam Grady and Marjorie (Reese) W.; m. Sally Ruth Adams, Mar. 19, 1958 (div. 1975); children: Martha Maria, Catherine Clarissa, Lorraine Lemae; m. Myra Louise Alexander, Oct. 30, 1976; 1 child, John Thomas. AA, Wharton County Jr. Coll., 1960; BBA in Gen. Bus., Agrl. and Mech. Coll. Tex., 1962; MBA, Tex. A&M U., 1965; PhD in Higher Edn. Mgmt., U. So. Miss., 1973. Asst. registrar, then. instr. Tex. A&M U., College Station, 1962—67; exec. dean Delgado C.C., New Orleans, 1967—74, program dir., 1977—78; asst. exec. sec. So. Assn. Colls and Schs., Atlanta, 1974—77; pres. emeritus Williamsburg Tech. Coll., Kingstree, SC, 1978—94; pres., CEO econ. cons. M&W Farm & Ranch, Egypt, Tex., 1994—. Cons. AID, Dominican Republic, 1966; bd. govs. Coastal Edn. Consortium, Conway, S.C., 1982-90; mem. exec. com. pres.'s coun. S.C. Tech. Edn. Coll., Columbia, 1985-86. Vestryman St. Thomas Episc. Ch., College Station, 1962-67, St. George Episc. Ch., New Orleans, 1969-72; vestryman St. Thomas' Episc. Ch., Wharton, Tex., 1998-2001, 06—, sr. warden, 1999-2000; Rep. precinct 2 chmn., Wharton County, Tex., 1998-2000, 2008-. Served as sgt. USAR, 1955-62. Recipient Order of the Palmetto S.C. Gen. Assembly, 1994; named Hon. Order of Ky. Cols.; col. Aide-de-Camp, La., col. Aide-de-Camp, Ala.; col. Aide-de-Camp, N.Mex. Mem. Future Farmers Assn. (hon.), S.C. Tech. Edn. Assn. (bd. dirs. 1985-88), Kingstree C. of C. (bd. dirs. 1981-84), Kiwanis, Masons (32 degree), Shriners (hon.), Phi Delta Kappa, Kappa Delta Pi. Avocations: chess, camping, music composition, reading. Home and Office: PO Box 307 Egypt TX 77436 Office Phone: 979-677-3572. Personal E-mail: johnwynn@agristar.net. Business E-Mail: egypttexas@agristar.net.

WYNN, STEVE ALAN (STEPHEN A. WYNN), hotel and gaming company executive; b. New Haven, Conn., Jan. 27, 1942; m. Elaine Paschal, 1963; children: Kevyn, Gillian. BA, U. Pa, 1963. Pres., CEO Best Brands, Inc., 1969-72; chmn., pres., CEO Mirage Resorts Inc. (formerly Golden Nugget Inc.), 1973—2000; mng. mem. Valvino Lamore, LLC, 2000—02; chmn., CEO Wynn Resorts Ltd., 2002—; owner Wynn Las Vegas Resort, 2005—, Wynn Macau, 2006—. Bd. trustees John F. Kennedy Ctr. for Performing Arts, 2006—. Named one of Top 200 Collectors, ARTnews Mag., 2004—08, 100 Most Influential People, Time Mag., 2006, Forbes' Richest Americans, 2003—, World's Richest People, Forbes mag., 2004—, People to Watch in 2007, Sunday Star Ledger. Jewish. Avocation: Collector of French Impressionism; Modern and Contemporary Art. Office: Wynn Resorts Ltd 3145 Las Vegas Blvd S Las Vegas NV 89109

WYNN, THOMAS GRANT, anthropologist, educator; b. Akron, Ohio, Oct. 6, 1949; s. Donald Dewey Wynn and Mary Eleanor Smith; m. Elizabeth Nielson Nielson, Sept. 18, 1982; children: Donald Scott, Emily Kathryn, Rachel Mary. AB, Occidental Coll., LA, 1971; PhD, U. Ill., Urbana, 1976. Prof. anthropology U. Colo., Colo. Springs, 1977—. Author: (book) The Evolution of Spatial Competence; co-author: The Rise of Homo sapiens: The evolution of modern thinking; contbr. articles to profl. jours. Recipient Viking Fund medal, Wenner-Gren Found., 2008. Office: Dept Anthropology Univ Colo Colorado Springs CO 80933-7150 Office Fax: 719-262-3364. Business E-Mail: twynn@uccs.edu.

WYNN, WILL, Mayor, Austin, Texas; b. Beaumont, Tex. m. Anne Elizabeth Wynn, 1992; 2 children. B in Environ. Design cum laude, Tex. A&M U., 1984. Founder CIVITAS Investments, Inc., 1997; mayor City of Austin, Tex., 2003—. With Hill Country Conservancy, St. David's Found., Women and their Work, KLRU, Blanton Mus., Austin Poetry Slam, Austin Film Soc.; chmn. Downtown Austin Alliance; dir. Children's Mus. and Heritage Soc. Recipient Scenic Hero award, Scenic Austin; named Austinite of Yr., Austin Under Forty. Mem.: Urban Land Inst. Avocations: listening to music, canoeing, bicycling. Mailing: PO Box 1088 Austin TX 78767 Address: City Hall 301 W 2nd St 2nd Fl Austin TX 78701 Office Phone: 512-974-2250. Office Fax: 512-974-2337. Business E-Mail: will.wynn@ci.austin.tx.us.*

WYNNE, BRIAN JAMES, retired professional society administrator; b. NYC, Dec. 2, 1950; s. Bernard and Dolores (Doyle) W. Student, Institute des Sciences Politiques, Paris, 1970-71; BA, Coll. Holy Cross, 1972; MA, U. So. Calif., 1974. Staff Exec. Cons., Inc., McLean, Va., 1974-76; prin., 1976-78; exec. dir. Indsl. Designers Soc. Am., Washington, 1978-88. Cons. to various non-profit orgns.; dir. Worldesign 85, founder Worldesign Found. Mem. Am. Soc. Assn. Execs., Indsl. Designers Soc. Am. (hon.), Phi Sigma Iota. Home: 5200 N Ocean Blvd Apt 1004 Lauderdale By The Sea FL 33308-3019

WYNNE, JAMES J., research scientist; b. Bklyn., Mar. 19, 1943; AB in Physics, Harvard U., 1964, MA in Physics, 1965, PhD in Physics, 1969. Mgr. Laser Physics and Chemistry Group IBM T.J. Watson Rsch. Ctr.; rsch. scientist IBM Watson Rsch. Ctr., 1971—. Contbr. articles, scientific papers. Co-recipient R.W. Wood prize, Optical Soc. Am., 2004; named one of Inventors of the Yr., Ea. NY Intellectual Property Law Assn., 2001; named to National Inventors Hall of Fame, 2002. Achievements include patents in field; development of Lasik eye surgery. Office: Watson Rsch Ctr 1101 Kithawan Rd Ste 134 Yorktown Heights NY 10598*

WYNNE, MARTHA ELLEN, psychology professor; d. Robert Owen Wynne and Betty Breece Purdy; children: Meredith Elizabeth Wynne-Morton, Noah Evan Wynne-Morton. BA, Smith Coll., Northampton, Mass., 1970; MA, U. Iowa, 1972; PhD, U. Mich., Ann Arbor, 1979. Cert. sch. adminstr. Ill. State Bd. Edn., Springfield, 1990. Dir. spl. edn. Western MO Mental Health Ctr., Kans. City, Mo., 1978—79; assoc. prof. Loyola U., Chgo., 1979—. Due process hearing officer Ill. State Bd. Edn., 1985—95; parent adv., Chgo. Area, 1999—. Founding mem. Child Internat., Chgo. Area, 1985—2000. Mem.: NASP. Liberal. Avocations: reading, travel. Office: Loyola Univ Chgo 820 N Mich Ave Chicago IL 60611 Office Fax: 312-915-6660. Business E-Mail: mwynne@luc.edu.

WYNNE, PATRICIA M, finance company executive; PhD, U. Mass. Med. Sch., Worcester; MBA, Isenberg Sch. Mgmt, Amherst, 2008. Bar: US Patent and Trademark Office (agent) 2008. Licensing assoc. U. Mass. Med. Sch., Shrewsbury, 2004—08; licensing officer MassBiologics, Jamaica Plain, Mass., 2008—. Mem. Audio Jour., Worcester, 2003—06. Postdoc. fellowship, NIAAA, 2005—08. Mem.: Licensing Execs Soc.

WYNNE, WILLIAM FRANCIS, lawyer; b. NYC, Sept. 21, 1952; s. William F. and Catherine Wynne; m. Barbara Brizzi Wynne; children: William, Andrew, Emily. AB in Econs., Rutgers U., 1973; JD, U. Pa., 1976. Bar: N.Y. 1977. From assoc. to ptnr. White & Case LLP, NYC, 1976—. Office: White & Case LLP 1155 Avenue of the Americas New York NY 10036-2787 Business E-Mail: wwynne@whitecase.com.

WYNNE-EDWARDS, HUGH ROBERT, geologist, educator, entrepreneur; b. Montreal, Que., Can., Jan. 19, 1934; s. Vero Copner and Jeannie Campbell (Morris) W.-E.; married Janet Elizabeth McGregor; children from previous marriages: Robin Alexander, Katherine Elizabeth, Renée Elizabeth Lortie, Krista Smyth, Jeannie Elizabeth, Alexander Vernon. BSc with 1st class honors, U. Aberdeen, Scotland, 1955; MA, Queen's U., Kingston, Ont., Can., 1957, PhD, 1959; DSc (hon.), Meml. U., 1975. Registered profl. engr., B.C., 1995. With Geol. Survey Can., 1958-59; lectr. Queen's U., 1959-61, 1961-72, asst. prof., then assoc. prof., 1961-68, prof., head dept. geol. scis., 1968-72; prof., then Cominco prof., head dept. geol. scis. U. B.C., Vancouver, Canada, 1972-77; asst. sec. univ. br. Ministry of State for Sci. and Tech., Ottawa, Canada, 1977-79; sci. dir. Alcan Internat. Ltd., Montreal, 1979-80, v.p. R & D, chief sci. officer, 1980-89; CEO Moli Energy Ltd., Vancouver, 1989-90; pres. Terracy Inc., Vancouver, 1989—; sci. advisor Teck Corp., Vancouver, 1989-91; pres., CEO B.C. Rsch. Inc., Vancouver, 1993-97, exec. chmn., pres., 1997-2000. Chmn. Silvagen Inc., 1996-99; advisor Directorate Mining and Geology, Uttar Pradesh, India, 1964, Grenville project Que. Dept. Natural Resources, 1968-72; vis. prof. U. Aberdeen, 1965-66, U. Witwatersrand, Johannesburg, South Africa, 1972; UN cons., India, 1974; pres. SCITEC, 1977-78; mem. sci. adv. com. CBC, 1980-84; mem. Sci. Coun. Can., 1983-89, Nat. Adv. Bd. on Sci. and Tech., 1987-90 indsl. liaison com. UN Ctr. for Sci. and Tech. in Devel., 1982-84; vice chmn. tech. adv. group Bus. Coun. for Sustainable Devel., Geneva, 1991; mem. Nat. Biotech. Adv. Coun., 1995-98; chmn. Neurosci. Can. Partnership, 1999-2003, Azure Dynamics Inc., 2000-01; pres. Silvagen Holdings Inc., 1999-2000; bd. dirs. Welichem Biotech Inc., chmn., 2000-; bd. dirs. Photon Control Inc. Bd. dirs. Royal Victoria Hosp., Montreal, 1984-89. Decorated officer Order of Can., 1991; recipient Spendiarov prize 24th Internat. Geol. Congress, Montreal, 1972. Fellow Can. Acad. Engring., Royal Soc. Can., World Acad. Arts and Scis.; mem. Can. Rsch. Mgmt. Assn. (vice chmn. 1982-84, chmn. 1984-85, Assn. medal 1987), Univ. Club (Montreal). Mem. United Ch. Canada. Avocations: tennis, skiing, carpentry. Office: Terracy Inc 2030 27th St West Vancouver BC Canada V7V 4L4 Office Phone: 604-926-1191. Business E-Mail: hughwynn@terracy.com.

WYRICK, CHARLES LLOYD, JR., editor, writer; b. Greensboro, NC, May 5, 1939; s. Charles Lloyd and Edythe Ellen (Ellis) W.; m. Constance Michelle Hooper, Aug. 22, 1964; 1 child, Charles Lloyd, III; m. Katherine Harrison, Apr. 26, 1997; 1 child, Christopher Conrad. BA, Davidson Coll., NC, 1961; MFA, U. NC, 1967. Instr. Stephens Coll., Columbia, Mo., 1964—66; asst. head programs div. Va. Museum, Richmond, 1966-68; exec. dir. Assn. Preservation Va. Antiquities, Richmond, 1968-70; pres. Research & Restoration, Inc., Richmond, 1970-73; dir. Del. Art Mus., Wilmington, 1973-79, Gibbes Mus. Art, Charleston, S.C., 1980-86; pres. Wyrick & Co., Charleston, 1986—, Dixie Media, Inc., Charleston, 1989—; sr. editor Gibbs Smith, Pub., 2005—09; editor, pub. "Omnibus", 1989-94. Mem. Richmond Commn. Archt. Rev., 1969-72, New Castle County Hist. Rev. Bd., Del., 1975-88, also vice chmn.; mem. Bd. Archtl. Rev. City of Charleston, 1988-94, chmn., 1992-94; mem. Charleston Consortium on Higher Edn.; cons. in field. Author: "The 17th Street Market", 1972; contbr. articles to profl. jours. Bd. visitors Davison Coll., 1974-77; chmn. Econs. of Amenities City of Charleston, 1978; chmn. bd. dirs. SC Coastal Conservation League, 1989-94, Charleston Area Arts Coun., 1989-91, Friends of Charleston County Courthouse, 1989-94, Pub. Art Trust, 1988-90; adv. com. SC Dept. Natural Resources, 1992-2004, Arts History Comm. City Charleston, 2007-. 1st lt. US Army, 1961—63. Recipient 1st award spl. column writing Va. Press Assn., 1973 Mem. Assn. Am. Pubs., Pubs. Assn. of South (bd. dirs. 1990-92, pres. 1991-92), SC Acad. Authors (bd. dirs. 1990-92), Carolina Yacht Club, Yeamans Hall Club, Cedar Creek Racquet Club. Office: PO Box 89 Charleston SC 29402-0089 Home: 3 Chisolm St Unit 201 Charleston SC 29401-1838 Office Phone: 843-795-9946.

WYRICK, JERMAINE ALBERT, lawyer; b. Detroit, Oct. 19, 1971; s. Albert and Loretta Wyrick. BA in Polit. Sci., U. Mich., 1993; JD, Wayne State U., 1996. Bar: Mich., US Dist. Ct. (ea. dist.) Mich., 1997, US Ct. Appeals (6th cir.), 1997, US Supreme Ct., 2001. Pvt. practice, Detroit, 1997—. Bd. dirs. Coalition Affirmative Action Preservation NAACP, Legal Redress, Detroit; lectr. in field. Bd. dirs. Coleman A. Young Scholarship Found.; with Angels Night Wayne County Juvenile Ct., 1998. Coun. on Legal Edu. Opportunity fellow, Ohio, 1993; recipient Achievement award Coleman A. Young Found., 1989-92, Disting. Grad. award, 1993, Pro Bono Project award FBA ea. dist. Mich., 1997, Fed Bar Assn. award, 1997, 2001, Trailblazer award Jordan Ednl. Svcs., 2004, Civil Rights and Edn. award U.S. Attys. Office, 2005, Five Under Ten award U. Mich. African Am. Alumni Coun. Mem. ABA, ATLA, Nat. Bar Assn. (region IV bd. dirs.), Mich. Trial Lawyers Assn., Wolverine Bar Assn.(bd. dirs.). Democrat. Mem. Hartford Meml. Bapt. Ch. Avocations: basketball, golf. Office: Law Offices Jermaine A Wyrick P L C Ste 1610 615 Griswold Detroit MI 48226-3319 Home: 615 Griswold St Ste 1610 Detroit MI 48226-3991 Home Phone: 313-850-6647; Office Phone: 313-964-8950. E-mail: attyjaw1@ameritech.net.

WYRICK, STEPHEN VON, religion educator, minister; b. Dallas, Mar. 1, 1952; s. Floyd A. and Maxine (Clark) W.; m. Janet Lynn Matthews, Aug. 2, 1974; children: Bradley, Paul. BA, Dallas Bapt. U., 1973; MDiv, Southwestern Bapt. Theol. Sem., Fort Worth, 1976; PhD, Southwestern Bapt. Theol. Sem., 1981. Ordained to ministry So. Bapt. Ch., 1976. Pastor Northrich Bapt. Ch., Richardson, Tex., 1982-86; chmn. divsn. of religion, prof. Calif. Bapt. Coll., Riverside, 1986—. Adjunct prof. Golden Gate Bapt. Theol. Sem., Brea, Calif., 1987-94; chmn. divsn. religion, prof. U. Mary Hardin Baylor, 1994—. Recipient NEH grants, 1988, '89. Mem. Soc. Bibl. Lit., Am. Schs. of Oriental Rsch., Israel Exploration Soc., Glaser Archaeol. Found. (bd. dirs.). Office: U Mary Hardin Baylor 900 College UMHB Station Belton TX 76513

WYRSCH, JAMES ROBERT, lawyer, educator, writer; b. Springfield, Mo., Feb. 23, 1942; s. Louis Joseph and Jane Elizabeth (Welsh) W.; m. B. Darlene Wyrsch, Oct. 18, 1975; children: Scott, Keith, Mark, Brian, Marcia. BA, U. Notre Dame, Ind., 1963; JD, Georgetown U., Washington, DC, 1966; LLM, U. Mo., Kansas City, 1972. Bar: Mo. 1966, US Ct. Appeals (8th cir.) 1971, US Ct. Appeals (10th cir.) 1974, US Ct. Appeals (5th cir.) 1974, US Ct. Appeals (6th cir.) 1982, US Ct. Appeals (11th cir.) 1984, US Ct. Appeals (7th cir.) 1986, US Ct. Appeals (4th cir.) 1990, US Ct. Appeals (9th cir.) 1998, US Ct. Mil. Appeals 1978, US Tax Ct. 1983, US Supreme Ct. 1972, US Ct. Appeals (2nd cir.) 2009. Assoc. Wyrsch, Hobbs & Mirakian P.C., Kansas City, Mo., 1970-71, of counsel, 1972-77, ptnr., 1978—, pres., shareholder, 1988—. Adj. prof. U. Mo., Kansas City, 1981—; mem. Mo. Supreme Ct. Procedures Com., 1983—; mem. adv. coun. legal assts. program U. Mo. at Kansas City, 1985-88; mem. cir. ct. adv. com. Jackson County, Mo., 1998—; mem. jud. selection com. U.S. Magistrate US Dist. Ct. Mo., 1985; mem. fed. practice com. US Dist. Ct. Mo., 1985-88; mem. subcom. to draft model criminal instrns.for dist. cts. of 8th cir., 1986—; bd. dirs. Kansas City Bar Found.; Mo. membership chmn. US Supreme Ct. Hist. Soc., 2002-06, nat. membership vice chair, 2006-07, nat. membership chair, 2007-08. Contbr. articles to profl. jours.; co-author: Missouri Criminal Trial Practice, 1994. Capt. US Army, 1966—69. Recipient Joint Svcs. Commendation medal, 1969, U. Mo. Kansas City Svc. award Law Found., 1991-92, Lawyer of Yr. award Mo. Lawyers Weekly, 2001, Practitioner of Yr. award U. Mo. Kans. City Law Sch. Alumni Assn., 2002, Liberty & Justice award KC Bar Assn., 2007; named Best of the Bar, Kansas City Bus. Jour., 2002-06, Dean of Trial Bar award Kans. City Met. Bar Assn., 2002, Lifetime Achievement award Kansas City Bar Assn., 2004, Charles Shaw Trial Advocacy award Mo. Assn. Crminal Def. Lawyers, 2004; named a KC Legal Leader of Yr., Daily Record, 2005. Fellow: Internat. Acad. Trial Lawyers, Mo. Bar Found., Am. Bar Found. (life), Am. Coll. Trial Lawyers (Mo. state chair 2004—06); mem.: ATLA, ABA, ACTL Access to Justice Comm. (nat. vice chair 2007—08, nat. chair 2008—09), Nat. Lawyers Assn. (chmn. criminal law com. 2003), Coll. Master Advs. and Barristers (sr. counsel), Mo. Assn. Criminal Def. Attys. (dir. 1978, sec. 1982), Nat. Assn. Criminal Def. Attys., Am. Bd. Trial Advs. (adv.), Kansas City Met. Bar Assn. (chmn. anti-trust com. 1981, chmn. bus. tort, anti-trust, franchise com. 1998), Mo. Bar Assn. (vice chmn. criminal law com. 1978—79), Am. Arbitration Assn. (panel arbitrators 1976—2000), Country Club of Blue Springs, Kansas City Club, Phi Delta Phi. Democrat. Roman Catholic. Home: 1501 NE Sunny Creek Ln Blue Springs MO 64014-2044 Office: Wyrsch Hobbs & Mirakian PC 1000 Walnut St Ste 1600 Kansas City MO 64106-2140 Office Phone: 816-221-0080. Business E-Mail: jimwyrsch@whmlaw.net.

WYRTKI, KLAUS, oceanography educator; b. Tarnowitz, Germany, Feb. 7, 1925; came to U.S., 1961; s. Wilhelm and Margarete (Pacharzina) W.; m. Helga Kocher, June 6, 1954 (div. 1970); children: Undine, Oliver; m. Erika Maassen. PhD magna cum laude, U. Kiel, Germany, 1950. With German Hydrographic Inst., Hamburg, 1950-51; German Rsch. Coun. postdoctoral rsch. fellow U. Kiel, 1951-54; head Inst. Marine Rsch., Djakarta, Indonesia, 1954-57; sr. rsch. officer, then prin. rsch. officer div. fisheries and oceanography Commonwealth Sci. and Indsl. Rsch. Orgn., Sydney, Australia, 1958-61; assoc. rsch. oceanographer, then rsch. oceanographer Scripps Instn. Oceanography, U. Calif., 1961-64; prof. oceanography U. Hawaii, Honolulu, 1964—, prof. emeritus, 1993. Chmn. North Pacific Expt., 1974-80, com. on climate changes and ocean Internat. Assn. Phys. Scis. of the Oceans; mem. Spl. Com. on Ocean Rsch. Working Group on Prediction of El Nino, Sci. Working Group on Topography Expt., panel on climate and global change NOAA. Author: El Nino—The Dynamic Response of the Equatorial Pacific Ocean to Atmospheric Forcing, 1975; editor: Oceanographic Atlas of the International Indian Ocean Expedition, 1971; mem. editl. bd. Jour. Phys. Oceanography, 1971-79. Recipient Excellence in Rsch. award U. Hawaii, 1980, Rosenstiel award U. Miami, 1981, Prince Albert I medal Internat. Assn. Phys. Scis. Ocean, 2003, Alexander Agassiz medal NAS, 2004 Fellow Am. Geophys. Union (Maurice Ewing medal 1989), Am. Meteorol. Soc. (Harald Ulrick Sverdrup Gold medal 1991), Deutsche Meteorologische Gesellschaft (Albert Defant medal 1992), Am. Acad. Arts & Scis. E-mail: wyrtki@aloha.net.

WYSCHOGROD, EDITH, philosophy educator; b. NYC; d. Morris and Selma Shurer; m. Michael Wyschogrod, Mar. 6, 1955; children: Daniel, Tamar. AB, Hunter Coll., 1957; PhD, Columbia U., 1970. Prof. philosophy Queens Coll., Flushing, NY, 1967-92; J. Newton Rayzor prof. philosophy and religious thought Rice U., Houston, 1992—2003, emerita, 2003—. Vis. prof. philosophy Villanova U. 2003; Croghan vis. prof. religion Williams Coll. 2004. Author: Emmanuel Levinas: The Problem of Ethical Metaphysics, 1974, 2d edit., 2000, Spirit in Ashes, 1985, Saints and Postmodernism, 1990, An Ethics of Remembering: History, Heterology and the Nameless Others; co-editor: Lacan and Theological Discourse, 1989, The Enigma of Gift and Sacrifice, 2002, The Ethical, 2003, Crossover Queries: Dwelling with Negatives, Embodying Philosophy's Others, 2006. Nat. Humanities Ctr. fellow, 1981, Woodrow Wilson Ctr. fellow, 1987-88, Guggenheim fellow, 1995-96. Fellow Am. Acad. Arts and Scis.; mem. Am. Acad. Religion (pres. 1992-93). Home: Apt 9C 522 West End Ave New York NY 10024 Home Phone: 212-873-3511. E-mail: stedith@rice.edu.

WYSHNER, DAVID B., travel company executive; BA magna cum laude, Yale U.; MBA, U. Pa. With investment banking divsn. Merrill Lynch & Co., 1991—99; with Cendant Corp., 1999—2004, exec. v.p. fin., planning and devel., exec. v.p., treas., 2004—06, vice chmn., CFO travel content divisn., 2005; treas. Avis Budget Group, Parsippany, NJ, 2006—07, CFO, 2006—. Office: Avis Budget Group Inc 6 Sylvan Way Parsippany NJ 07054 Office Phone: 973-496-4700. Office Fax: 212-413-1924.*

WYSIN, GARY MATTHEW, physics professor; b. Port Clinton, Ohio, Oct. 21, 1956; s. Norbert Aloysious Wysin and Rosemary Evelyn Darr; m. Marcilene Sousa, Nov. 4, 2005; 1 child, Nayara Winona Sousa Wysin. BSEE, U. Toledo, Ohio, 1978, MS in Physics, 1980; MS, Cornell U., Ithaca, NY, 1984, PhD, 1985. Prof. Kans. State U., Manhattan, 1988—. Vis. rsch. prof. Fed. U. Minas Gerais, Belo Horizonte, Brazil, 1989—2000. Contbr. articles to profl. jours. Rsch. grant, NSF. Achievements include research in magnetic vortices. Avocations: hiking, running, winemaking, bicycling. Office: Dept Physics Kans State Univ 309 Cardwell Hall Manhattan KS 66506-2601 Office Fax: 785-532-6806.

WYSOCKI, CHARLES JOSEPH, neuroscientist; b. Utica, NY, May 4, 1947; s. Charles C. and Helen T. (Szczesna) W.; m. Linda Lorraine Moore, Dec. 21, 1968; children: Tracy Lynn, Theresa Marie, Alexandra Charlene. BA, SUNY, Oswego, 1973; MS, Fla. State U., 1976, PhD in Psychobiology, 1978. Grass Found. fellow The Jackson Lab., Bar Harbor, Maine, 1973; postdoctoral tng. Monell Chem. Senses Ctr., Phila., 1978-81, asst. mem., 1980-83, assoc. mem., 1983-90, mem., 1990--; adj. prof. anatomy U. Pa., Phila., 1985--. Sci. advisor Olfactory Rsch. Fund, N.Y.C., 1989—; chmn. of tng. Monell Chem. Senses Ctr., Phila., 1989—; project officer, coord. U.S. Russia Sci. Esch. Program in the Chem. Senses, Washington, 1990—. Editor: Chemical Senses Vol. 3: Genetics of Perception and Communication, 1991; contbr. editor: (newsletter) The Armoa-Chology Rev., 1986--; contbr. articles to profl. jours. With U.S. Army, 1968-70, Vietnam. NIH grantee 1985--; recipient

Kenji Nakanishi Rsch. award Takasago Internat. Corp., 1988. Mem. Assn. for Chemoreception Scis. (membership chmn. 1989-91), N.Y. Acad. Scis., Soc. Neurosci., Internat. Brain Rsch. Orgn., Sigma Xi (Best Student Rsch. award 1976). Office: Monell Chem Senses Ctr 3500 Market St Philadelphia PA 19104-3308 Office Fax: 215-573-0909. Business E-Mail: wysocki@monell.org.

WYSONG, EARL EDWARD, sociologist, educator; b. Kokomo, Ind., June 25, 1944; s. Earl Wysong and June Maxine Talbert; m. Janet Sue Myers, Aug. 30, 1966; children: Kristi Lynn, Heather Sue. BS in Edn., Ind. U., 1968; MA in Sociology, Ball State U., Muncie, Ind., 1971; PhD in Sociology, Purdue U., 1990. Cert. secondary edn. Ind. Dept. Pub. Instrn., 1968. Asst. prof. sociology Ind. U., Kokomo, 1991—95, assoc. prof. sociology, 1995—98, prof. sociology, 1998—. Author: (books) High Risk and High Stakes: Health Professionals, Politics, and Policy, 1992; co-author: The New Class Society, 1999, The New Class Society: Goodbye American Dream, 2d edit., 2003, 3rd edit., 2008; mem. editl. bd.: Jour. Contemporary Sociology, 2001—05; contbr. chapters to books, articles to profl. jours. Doctoral Dissertation Improvement grantee, NSF, 1990, Faculty Fellowship Rsch. grantee, Ind. U. Kokomo, 1992, 2006. Mem.: Am. Fedn. Tchrs., Am. Sociol. Assn., Ind. Acad. Social Scis. (dir. sociology and anthropology 1993—96, exec. v.p. 1997—98, pres. 1998—99, dir. sociology and anthropology 2008—), North Ctrl. Sociol. Assn., Midwest Sociol. Soc., Soc. for the Study Social Problems (program co-chair 1999—2000). Home: 2850 East Southway Blvd Kokomo IN 46902 Office: Ind Univ Kokomo 2300 South Washington St Kokomo IN 46904-9003 Office Phone: 765-455-9394. Business E-Mail: ewysong@iuk.edu.

WYSOPAL, CHRIS, software company executive; m. Debra Kavaler, Apr. 2008. BS in Computer Sys. and Engring., Rensselaer Polytech. Inst., Troy, NY. Prin. software engr. Lotus Devel. Corp.; co-founder L0pht Heavy Industries, webmaster, graphic designer, Hacker News Network; mgr. rsch. group Symantec (formerly @stake), v.p. rsch. devel., dir. devel.; founder VulnWatch, 2001, moderator, 2001—; co-founder, CTO Veracode, 2006—. Founder Orgn. for Internet Safety; spkr. in field. Co-author: (book) The Art of Software Security Testing, 2006; contbr. articles to profl. publs. Named one of 100 Most Influential People in IT, eWeek, 2008; named to InfoWorld CTO 25, 2008. Office: Veracode 15 New England Exec Pk Burlington MA 01803 Office Phone: 781-425-6040. Office Fax: 781-425-6039.

WYSS, JOHN BENEDICT, lawyer; b. Evanston, Ill., Nov. 23, 1947; s. Walther Erwin and Caroline Nettie (Benedict) W.; m. Joanne P. Comstock, Oct. 22, 1994; children: John Christian, Kirsten Dunlop. BS in Physics summa cum laude, Stanford U., 1969; JD, Yale U., 1972. Bar: Calif. 1972, D.C. 1974, U.S. Supreme Ct. 1976. Trial atty. antitrust div. U.S. Dept. Justice, Washington, 1972-74; assoc. Kirkland & Ellis, Washington, 1974-78, ptnr., 1978-83, Wiley Rein LLP, Washington, 1983—. Mem. ABA, Phi Beta Kappa. Office: Wiley Rein LLP 1776 K St NW Washington DC 20006-2304 Office Phone: 202-719-7038. Business E-Mail: jwyss@wileyrein.com.

WYZIK, SUSAN ALDRICH, history professor; b. Barton, Vt., Apr. 5, 1948; d. Edwin John Aldrich and Marilyn Edith Aldrich-Meleleu; m. Ronald Walter Wyzik, July 4, 1969; children: Laurie, Kimberly, Ryan. Student, Springfield Tech. C.C., Mass., 1988; BA, Mount Holyoke Coll., South Hadley, Mass., 1991. History instr. Springfield Tech. C.C., 1992—. Advisor paraprofessionals update program Springfield Tech. C.C., 2000—02. Chairperson various fundraisers Springfield Tech. C.C., 1993—. Recipient Rosemarie Becker award, Springfield Tech. C.C., 2001. Mem.: Phi Theta Kappa. Avocations: martial arts, kayaking, reading, writing. Office: Springfield Tech CC One Armory Sq Springfield MA 01101 Business E-Mail: swyzik@stcc.edu.

WYZNER, EUGENIUSZ, diplomat; s. Henryk and Janina Wyzner; m. Elzbieta Laudanska, June 27, 1961; 1 child, Jaroslaw. LLM, U. Warsaw, 1954; postgrad., Hague Acad. Internat. Law, Netherlands, 1958. Mem. staff Ministry Fgn. Affairs, 1956—71, dir. legal dept., 1971—73; ambassador to Geneva, 1973-78; dir. dept. internat. orgns. Ministry Fgn. Affairs, Warsaw, 1978-81; chmn. UN Disarmament Commn., 1982; undersec. gen. conf. services and spl. assignments UN, NYC, 1982-92, undersec. gen. pub. info., 1992-94; dep. min. for fgn. affairs Republic of Poland, Warsaw, 1994-95, 1st dep. min. for fgn. affairs, sec. of state, 1996-97; permanent rep. amb. to UN NYC, 1998-99; mem., chmn. permanent com. Internat. Civil Svc. Commn., NYC, 1999—. Vice-chmn. preparatory com. Internat. Conf. on Human Rights, chmn. com. on periodic reports on human rights, 1965-68; chmn. sub-com. of UN Com. on Peaceful Uses of Outer Space, 1967-82; pres. Rev. Conf. of Parties to Treaty on Prohibition of Nuclear Weapons, 1977; mem. Polish del. of UN Gen. Assembly, UN Programme Planing and Budgeting Bd., 1984-93; chmn. UN Publs. Bd., 1982-93; chmn. com. for 2000 review conf. of the parties to the treaty on the non-proliferation of nuclear weapons, 1998-99. Decorated Cross of Polonia Restituta Polish Council of State, 1969, 77, Golden Cross of Merit, 1964, Comdr.'s Cross with a star Order of Polonia Restituta, 1996, Comdr. of the Legion d'Honneur, Pres. of France and Grand Comdr.'s Cross of the Order of the Phoenix, Pres. of Greece, 1996. Mem. Internat. Inst. Outer Space Law (bd. dirs. 1974—, Citation 1977), Internat. Peace Acad. (bd. dirs. 1983-91), Internat. Congress Inst. (bd. dirs. 1987-90), Internat. Congress Acad. (mem. senate 1990-95). Office: Internat Civil Svc Commn Rm 1050 2 United Nations Plz New York NY 10017-4403 Business E-Mail: wyzner@un.org.

XANDERS, BRIAN, professional sports team executive; m. Amy Xanders; children: Reid, Mary Claire. B in Bus. Mgmt., Fla. State U., Tallahassee, MBA; attended NFL managers program, Stanford U., Calif., 2005. Various football ops. positions, mem. defensive coaching staff Atlanta Falcons, 1994—2007; asst. gen. mgr. Denver Broncos, 2008—09, gen. mgr., 2009—. Spkr. on labor economics and player pers. issues. Office: Denver Broncos Football Club 13655 Broncos Pky Englewood CO 80112*

XANTHEAS, SOTIRIS STAVROS, chemist, researcher; b. Athens, Greece, June 20, 1961; came to U.S., 1984; s. Stavros S. and Effie (Beneas) X.; m. Maria A. Hadjos, July 7, 1990; children: Effie, Christina Stavroula. Diploma in chem. engring., Nat. Tech. U. of Athens, 1984; PhD in Phys. Chemistry, Iowa State U., 1990. Nat. coll. and univ. assn. for sci. postdoctoral fellow Pacific N.W. Lab., U.S. Dept. Energy, Richland, Wash., 1990-92; sr. rsch. scientist Pacific N.W. Nat. Lab., Richland, 1992-97; chief scientist Batelle Pacific N.W. Nat. Lab., Richland, 1998—2004, lab. fellow, 2004—. Adj. mem. Inst. Elec. Structure and Laser, Found. Rsch. and Tech., Hellas, Crete, Greece. Contbr. articles to sci. jours. Sci. and Rsch. scholar Austrian Fed. Ministry, 1984. Mem. Am. Chem. Soc., fellow: Am. Phys. Soc., Alpha Chi Sigma. Christian Orthodox. Avocations: skiing, soccer, volleyball. Office: Chem Materials Scis Divsn Pacific NW Lab PO Box 999 MS K1-83 Richland WA 99352-0999 Office Phone: 509-375-3684.

XI, JINXIANG, engineering educator, researcher; s. Xianchao Xi and Xiuyu Huang; m. Xiuhua April Si; 1 child, Jensen Siyuan. BS, Shanghai Jiaotong U., China, 1999; MS, Xi'an Jiaotong U., China, 2000; PhD, Tex. A&M U., Coll. Sta., 2005. Rsch. asst. Xi'an Jiaotong U., 1996—99, U. Calif., Irvine, 2000—01, Tex. A&M U., Coll. Sta., 2001—05; postdoc. rsch. assoc. Va. Commonwealth U., Richmond, 2005—07, rsch. asst. prof., 2007—08; asst. prof. sys. engring. U. Ark., Little Rock, 2008—. Instr. U. Ark., Little Rock, 2008—. Contbr. articles to profl. jours. Nominee STLE award for Excellence in Tech. Pub., Soc. Tribologists and Lubrication Engrs., 2006. Mem.: ASME. Baptist. Achievements include invention of enhanced delivery of nanoparticle and micron sized pharmaceutical aerosols to the lung through hygroscopic growth; research in modeling aerosol transport and deposition in pediatric nasal airways, optimizing inhaler devices of nasal drug delivery for infants and toddlers; investigated effects of geometric simplification; development of an effective lagrangian method; a technique for automated localized detection of early stage lung cancer. Office: Univ Ark Little Rock 2801 S University Ave ETAS 300J Little Rock AR 72204 Office Fax: 501-569-8698. Personal E-mail: xjinxiang@gmail.com. Business E-Mail: jxxi@ualr.edu.

XI, YUTAO, medical researcher; m. Geru Wu. PhD, Xi'an Jiaotong U., 2005. Rsch. fellow Tex. Heart Inst., Houston, 2006—08, rsch. assoc., 2008; reviewer Internat. Jour. Cardiology, 2009—. Mem.: Biophysics Soc. Achievements include patents for new device on cell strength.

XIA, GUOHUA, scientist, psychiatrist, psychologist; married; 1 child, M-Y. MB in Clin. Medicine, Beijing Med. U., 1986; MA in Marriage and Family Therapy, U. Nebr., Lincoln, 1998, PhD in Psychology, 2002. Lic. Calif., Ohio, 2007. Physician The 2nd Hosp. of Hebei Med. U., Shijiazhuang, China, 1986—93; counselor Counseling and Psychotherapy Ctr. Peking U., Beijing, 1993—95; tchr. ZhongGuanCun Software Coll., Beijing, 1993—95; database analyst, info. specialist and grad. asst. U. Nebr., Lincoln, 1995—2001; physician U. Texas, Houston, 2001—02, U. Tex. Southwestern Med. Ctr., Dallas, 2002—05; asst. prof. Case Western Reserve U., 2005—07, head, Transcranial Magnetic Stimulation program, 2005—07; asst. clin. prof. U. Calif., Davis, 2007—. Sec. Hebei Mental Health Orgn., Shijiazhuang, 1990—93. Contbr. articles to profl. jours., chapters to books. Recipient Young Investigator award, Nat. Alliance for Rsch. on Schizophrenia and Depression, 2005, NCDEU New Investigator award, NIMH, 2006. Mem.: Am. Psychology Assn., Psychol. Assn. China, Chinese Med. Assn. (Excellent Acad. Paper award 1993), Chinese Mental Health Assn., Am. Psychiatry Assn., Kappa Omicron Nu.

XIA, JESSIE QING, research scientist; b. Nantong, Jiangsu, China, Dec. 26, 1977; d. Shenghuai Xia and Jianping Zhu; m. Liang Zhai; children: Eric R. Zhai, Stephanie L. Zhai. BE, Tsinghua U., Beijing, 2000; MS, Duke U., Durham, NC, 2006, PhD, 2007. Rsch. asst. Duke U., 2001—07; postdoctoral rsch. assoc. Nat. Inst. Statis. Scis., Durham, 2007—. Recipient award, Twenty First Southern Biomed. Engring. Conf., 2002, Predoctoral award, Dept. Def., Breast Cancer Rsch. Program, 2004. Mem.: IEEE, Am. Statis. Assn., SPIE, Biomed. Engring. Soc., Sigma Xi. Office: NISS 19 T W Alexander Dr Rsch Triangle Pk Durham NC 27709 Office Fax: 919-685-9310. Business E-Mail: qing.xia@duke.edu.

XIA, MING, political science professor; b. Chengdu, Sichuan, China, May 20, 1965; naturalized, US, 1996; s. Chenglu Xia and Xuewen Zhang; m. Leslie Lei Xu, Nov. 14, 1989; 1 child, Julia C. BA in Internat. Politics, Fudan, Shanghai, 1985; LLM in Internat. Politics, Fudan U., Shanghai, 1988; PhD in Polit. Sci., Temple U., Phila., 1997. Asst. prof. Fudan U., Shanghai, 1988—91; tchg. asst. Temple U., 1991—97; from asst. to assoc. prof. CUNY, SI, 1997—2006, prof., 2007—; residential fellow George Wash. U. and Woodrow Wilson Internat. Ctr. Scholars, DC, 2003—04; vis. rsch. fellow East Asian Inst., Nat. U. Singapore, Singapore, 2004. Seminar assoc. Columbia U., NYC, 2002—; vis. prof. Jishou U., Hunan, China, 2007, Fudan U., Shanghai, 2007; guest prof. Contemporary China Rsch. Ctr., Shanghai Social Scis. Acad., Shanghai, 2005—. Author: (books) The Dual Developmental State, The People's Congresses and Governance in China; prodr.: (documentary movie) China's Unnatural Disaster, The Tears of Sichuan Province, 2009; columnist: electronic jour. China in Perspective. Friend NY Philharm. Recipient Travel grant, Ctr. East Asian Studies, Temple U., 1994—96, Am. Polit. Sci. Assn., 1995—96, Travel award, U. Chgo., 1996, Dolphin Outstanding Scholarly Achievement award, CUNY, 2002—03, Salute to Scholar Cert. of Honor award, 2003; grantee Rsch. Found. award, PSC-CUNY Rsch. Found., 1998—2006; fellow Rsch. fellowship, East Asian Inst., Nat. U. Singapore, 2004;, Woodrow Wilson Ctr. Internat. Scholars, 2003—04, Scholarly Incentive fellowship, CUNY, 2004, Presdl. fellowship, 2003, fellowship, US China Law Soc., 2005—06, Tchg. fellowship, Overseas Young Chinese Forum, 2007. Mem.: Internat. Network Social Network Analysis, Assn. Asian Studies, Am. Polit. Sci. Assn. Avocations: music, violin. Home: 40 Larrison Loop Staten Island NY 10314 Office: CUNY Coll SI 2800 Victory Blvd Staten Island NY 10314 Office Phone: 718-982-3197. Office Fax: 718-982-2888. Personal E-mail: fudanxia@aol.com. Business E-Mail: xia@mail.csi.cuny.edu.

XIA, YUAN-QING, research scientist; s. Henghai Xia and Shuren Shang; m. Xiao M. Wang, Jan. 10, 1983; 1 child, John. MB, Shandong Med. U., 1982; MS, U. NC, Charlotte, 1995. Scientist Food & Drug Adminstrn., Jinan, Shandong, 1982—92, adminstr., 1982—92; tchg. asst. U. NC, 1992—95; assoc. rsch. scientist Bristol Myers Squibb Co., Princeton, NJ, 1995—2000, sr. rsch. scientist, 2005—; sr. rsch. chemist Merck & Co. Inc., Rahway, NJ, 2000—05. Contbr. articles to profl. jours. Mem.: Am. Soc. Advanced Sci., Am. Assn. Pharm. Scientists, Am. Chem. Soc., Am. Soc. Mass Spectrometry, Phi Beta Delta Honor Soc. (hon.). Achievements include development of automated bio analytical techniques in quantification of drugs in biological fluids via on-line purification and analysis of biological samples with liquid chromatography mass spectrometry; research in separation of in source collision-induced dissociation metabolites interference from drug molecules in bioanalysis.

XIANG, SHU, civil engineer, researcher; married. PhD, U. Tenn., Knoxville, 2007. Grad. rsch. asst. U. Tenn., Knoxville, 2004—07, postdoc. rsch. assoc., 2007—. Contbr. articles to profl. jours. Mem.: Assn. Asphalt Paving Techs. Achievements include patents for a rubber modified cementitious substance and method of making the same. Office: Univ Tenn Knoxville 223 Perkins Hall Knoxville TN 37996 Office Fax: 865-974-2669. Business E-Mail: xshu@utk.edu.

XIAO, DONG, research scientist; s. Jianguo Xiao and Lin Zhu; m. Yi Ren. PhD, NC State U., Raleigh, 2006. Rsch. asst. NC State U., 2001—06; rsch. assoc. U. Ill. Urbana-Champaign, 2006—. Contbr. articles to profl. jours. Achievements include design of non-metallic structure. Home: 1650 Logan Dr Apt 1 Carbondale IL 62901 Personal E-mail: xiaodongmail@yahoo.com.

XIAO, JING, science educator, researcher; PhD, U. Mich., Ann Arbor. Prof. U. NC, Charlotte, 2002—, assoc. dean rsch., coll. computing and informatics, 2008—. Program dir. Nat. Sci. Found., Arlington, Va., 1998—2000.

XIAO, ZHIJIE, economics educator; b. Changsha, China; s. Ruqing Xiao and Guangwei Li. BSc, MSc, People's U. of China, Beijing, 1991; MA, Yale U., 1995, MPh, 1996, PhD, 1997. Prof. U. Ill., Champaign, 1997—. Mem. Am. Statis. Assn., Econometric Soc., Inst. Math. Stats. Office: U Ill 1206 S 6th St Champaign IL 61820-6978

XIAO, ZHOUSHENG, pharmacologist, bone biologist; permanent resident, 2005; m. Changhong Jiang; 1 child, Zheng. MD, Nanhua U., Hengyang, China, 1987; PhD in Molecular Pharmacology, Ctrl. S. Univ., Changsha, China, 2003. Postdoctoral staff human metabolic sect. NIEHS, 1995—96; rsch. assoc. nephrology and medicine Duke U. Med. Ctr., 1996—99; rsch. asst. prof. nephrology and medicine Duke U. Med. Ctr., 2001—04; assoc. prof. pharmacology Clin. Pharmacology Inst. Ctrl. S. Univ., Changsha, 1999—2001, prof. pharmacology Clin. Pharmacology Inst., 2003—07; rsch. asst. prof. Kidney Inst./Internal Medicine U. Kans. Med. Ctr., Kansas City, 2004—. Vice-dir. molecular pharmacology lab., Xiangya Sch. Medicine Ctrl. S. Univ., Changsha, 1999—2001, PhD mentor Clin. Pharmacology Inst., 2003—07. Recipient Young Investigator award, Nature Sci. Found. Commn. Hunan, 1996, Excellent Young Tchr. & Rschr. award, Edn. Commn. China, 1999, 1st Prize of Sci. & Tech. Progress award, U. Commn. China, 2001, Young Investigator award of 25th ASBMR, Am. Soc. Bone & Mineral Rsch., 2003, 3d Prize of Sci. & Tech. Progress award, State Edn. Commn. China, 1999; Rsch. grant for Runx2 isoforms function in osteoblastic differentiation of Bone marrow derived mesenchymal stem cells, 1999, Rsch. grant for phytoestrogens regulating osteoblastic differentiation in bone marrow-derived mesenchymal stem cells, Nat. Nature Sci. Found. China, 2001, Rsch. grant. for differential function & regulation of Runx2 isoforms, NIH & Nat. Inst. Arthritis & Musculoskeletal & Skin Diseases, 2003, Rsch. grant for P&F Project, NIH & Nat. Inst. Diabetes, 2006. Mem.: Chinese Pharmacological Soc., Am. Soc. Bone & Mineral Rsch. Achievements include discovery of how phytoestrogens regulate osteoblastic differentiation in bone marrow-derived mesenchymal stem cells; how runx2 isoforms play a different role in bone formation; how primary cilia and polycystin -1 have an important role in bone development and bone formation; a new mutation of CYP2C19 gene in Chinese bai population. Home: 12761 Mackey St Overland Park KS 66213 Office: Kidney Inst/Univ Kans Med Ctr 3901 Rainbow Blvd Kansas City KS 66160 Office Fax: 913-588-9251. Business E-Mail: zxiao@kumc.edu.

XIE, CHI, transportation engineer, researcher; b. Leng Shui Jiang, China, Oct. 16, 1975; arrived in US, 2000; s. Yisheng Xie and Ping Yang; m. Li Sheng, June 27, 2007. B in Engring., Tsinghua U., Beijing, China, 1998; M in Engring., Nat. U. Singapore, 2000; MS, U. Mass., Amerst, 2005; PhD, Cornell U., Ithaca, NY, 2007. Rsch. scholar Nat. U. Singapore, 1998—2000; rsch. asst. U. Mass., Amherst, 2001—03; tchg. asst. Cornell U., Ithaca, 2003—06; vis. scholar U. Tex., Austin, 2006—07, Rsch. fellow, 2008—. Contbr. articles to profl. jours. Recipient Student Competition winner, Mil. Ops. Rsch. Soc., 2004, John E. Perry Tchg. award, Cornell U., 2005; grantee, 2004, 2007; scholar, Nat. U. Singapore, 1998. Mem.: ASCE, IEEE, Inst. Transp. Engrs., Transp. Rsch. Bd., Inst. Ops. Rsch. and Mgmt. Scis. Achievements include addressed and solved an evacuation network optimization problem integrating roadway contraflow and intersection control in his PhD dissertation. Avocations: swimming, skiing, golf. Office: Univ Tex 1 University Station C1761 Austin TX 78712-0278 Office Phone: 512-471-4622. Office Fax: 512-475-8744. Business E-Mail: chi.xie@mail.utexas.edu.

XIE, HAIYONG, computer scientist; m. Yang Gao. PhD, Yale U., New Haven, 2007. Contbr. scientific papers. Mem.: Sigma Xi. Achievements include research in the theory of P4P: proactive provider participation in Internet resource optimization; invention of the P4P algorithms to optimize Internet resources for providers and P2P applications; development of the first P4P network system to demonstrate its effectiveness in optimizing Internet resources; design of the complete P4P architecture.

XIE, JIANG, engineering educator; arrived in US, 1999, permanent resident, 2007; d. Minggan Xie and Chunze Jiang; m. Zhong Chen. BS in Engring., Tsinghua U., Beijing, 1997; MPhil in Elec. and Electronic Engring., Hong Kong U. Sci. and Tech., 1999; MSEE, Ga. Inst. Tech., Atlanta, 2002; PhD in Elec. Engring., Ga. Inst. Tech., 2004. Grad. tchg. asst. Hong Kong U. Sci. and Tech., 1997—99; grad. rsch. asst. Ga. Inst. Tech., 1999—2004; asst. prof. elec. and computer engring. U. NC, Charlotte, 2004—. Symposium co-chair IEEE Global Comm. Conf., 2009—, 16th Internat. Conf. on Computer Comm. and Networks, 2007, 17th Internat. Conf. on Computer Comm. and Networks, 2008, 3d Internat. Conf. on Comm. and Networking, China, 2008; vice co-chmn. tech. program IEEE Internat. Symposium on Multimedia, 2007; gen. co-chair 1st Internat. Conf. on Mobile Wireless Middleware, Oper. Systems and Applications, 2008, 2nd Internat. Conf. on Mobile Wireless Middleware, Operating Systems, and Applications, 2009; co-chmn. tech. program 4th Internat. Wireless Internet Conf., 2008; chair publicity 1st Internat. Workshop on Convergence of Heterogeneous Wireless Networks, 2005, 3d Internat. Wireless Internet Conf., 2007, 2d Internat. Conf. on Nano-Networks, 2007, Internat. Workshop on Intelligent Sys. and Smart Home, 2007, 4th IEEE Internati. Conf. on Ubiquitous Intelligence and Computing, 2007, IFIP Internat. Conf. on Networking, 2007, 6th Internat. Conf. Ubiquitous Intelligence and Computing, 2009. Assoc. guest editor Jour. Computer Sci., 2006; editor: Computer Networks Jour., 2007—, Jour. of Network and Computer Applications, 2008—, Jour. of Comm., 2008—; contbr. chapters to books, articles to profl. jours. Recipient Grad. Tchg. Excellence award, William States Lee Coll. Engring., U. NC-Charlotte, 2007; Bonnie Cone fellow, U. NC-Charlotte ADVANCE Program, 2007. Mem.: IEEE, IEEE Women in Engring., Assn. Computing Machinery, Eta Kappa Nu. Office: Univ NC-Charlotte Dept Elec and Computer Engring 9201 University City Blvd Charlotte NC 28223

XIE, KAI JI, aeronautical engineering educator; b. Shaoxing, Zhejiang, China, July 22, 1935; s. Lizheng and Zhongwan (Ma) X.; m. Yuqin Zhu, July 18, 1966; children: Weina, Zhen. BS, Nanjing U. Aero., Astronautics, China. Asst. prof. Nanjing (China) Aero.-Astro. U., 1978-83, dir. radio office, 1975-89, assoc. prof., 1984-92; vice chief engr. Inst. of Unmanned Air Vehicle, Nanjing, 1990—; prof. Nanjing Aero-Astro U., 1993—. Recipient First Sci. and Technique award Com. Sic. and Technique of China, 1985, 2d Sci. and Technique award Aviation Industry Dept. China, 1987, 89, 1st Sci. and Technique award, 1997, 3d Sci. and Technique Progress of China award, Com. of Edn. China, 1993; named Specialist of Spl. Contribution, State Coun. of China, 1993. Mem. Elec. Inst. China, Aviation Inst. China. Avocations: painting, travel, fishing. Office: Nanjing Aero Astro U 29 Yudao St Jiangsu Nanjing 210016 China Home: 9866 S Houston Oak Dr Germantown TN 38139 Home Phone: 901-373-3832. Business E-Mail: kjxie@nuaa.edu.cn.

XIE, LEXING, computer scientist; d. Dingchuan Xie and Zhaoling Ye. BS, Tsinghua U., Beijing, 2000; PhD, Columbia U., NYC, 2005. Rsch. staff mem. IBM T J Watson Rsch. Ctr., Hawthorne, NY, 2005—; adj. faculty Columbia U., 2007—. Mem.: IEEE, ACM. Personal E-mail: elodiexie@hotmail.com.

XIE, LIANG, application developer; PhD in Computer Engring., Pa. State U., Univ. Pk., 2008. Cert. in engring., Broadcom Inc., 2008. Mgr. Huawei Tech., Shanghai, 1998—2003; scientist, sr. staff engr. Broadcom Inc., Sunnyvale, Calif., 2008—. Contbr. articles to rsch. paper. Recipient Gold Medal award, Huawei Tech., 2001, Best Student Paper award, ACNS, 2008. Mem.: ACM, Sigma Xi. Achievements include patents for 3 patents with Samsung Information Systems in USA. Office: Broadcom Inc 190 Mathilda Pl Sunnyvale CA 94086 Business E-Mail: lxie@cse.psu.edu, lxie@broadcom.com.

XIE, XIANG-QUN SEAN, pharmacist, educator; PhD, U. Conn., Sch. Pharmacy, Storrs, 1993; MBA, Sch. Bus. Administrn., U. Conn., 2003. Dir. ims nmr lab. and assoc. prof. U. Conn., 1995—2003; prof. medicinal chemistry U. Houston, Coll. Pharmacy, 2003—06; prof. pharm. scis. U. Pitts., Sch. Pharmacy, 2006—. Achievements include research in structure-based drug Design, NMR, GPCRs. Office: Univ Pitts 3501 5th Ave 10016 BST3 Pittsburgh PA 15260 Office Fax: 412-383-5298. Personal E-mail: xxie678@hotmail.com.

XIE, YANG, medical educator; m. Guanghua Xiao; 1 child, Olivia Yueran Xiao. MD; PhD, U. Minn., Mpls., 2006. Asst. prof. U. Tex. Southwestern Med. Ctr., Dallas, 2006—. Mem.: Am. Statis. Assn. Office: UT Southwesternedu 5323 Harry Hines Blvd Dallas TX 75390-8551

XIE, ZHIXIAO, research scientist, educator; PhD, SUNY, Buffalo, 2002. Asst. prof. FAU, Boca Raton, Fla., 2003—. Office: Florida Atlantic Univ Geoscis Dept 777 Glades Rd Boca Raton FL 33431

XIE, ZHONGCONG, anesthesiologist, educator; s. Liqiong Xie and Jirong Xue; m. Yin Wu; 1 child, Julie Yin. MD, Xuzhou Med. Coll., P.R. China, 1985; PhD, Wayne State U., Detroit, 1994. Instr. anesthesia Harvard Med. Sch., Boston, 2000—05, asst. prof., 2005—. Office: MA General Hos 55 Fruit St Boston MA 02114 Office Fax: 617-726-4176. Business E-Mail: zxie@partners.org.

XIN, WANG, researcher; BS in Electronic Engring., Tsinghua U., Beijing, 2002, MS Electronic Engring., 2005; Ph student in Computer Engring., U. of Calif., Santa Cruz, 2005—. Rsch. asst. China Edn. & Rsch. Network R & D Ctr., Beijing, 2003—04; rsch. intern Microsoft Rsch. Asia, Beijing, 2004—05, Bosch Rsch. and Tech. Ctr., Palo Alto, Calif., 2008—. Contbr. articles to profl. sci. jours., chapters to books. Chancellor fellowship, UC Santa Cruz, 2005. Mem.: IEEE, ACM. Office: Univ Calif E2-315 1156 High St Santa Cruz CA 95064 Business E-Mail: wangxin@soe.ucsc.edu.

XING, JUN, academic administrator, educator; PhD, U. Minn., Twin Cities, 1993. Dir. Oreg. State U., Corvallis, 2002—06; v.p. United Bd. Christian Higher Edn. Asia, Hong Kong, 2006—07. Author: (books) Teaching for Change. Personal E-mail: jameshsing@hotmail.com.

XING, MICHAEL MINGZHAO, endocrinologist, educator; Diplomate in endocrinology and internal medicine Am. Bd. Internal Medicine. Assoc. prof. medicine and oncology Johns Hopkins U. Sch. Medicine, Balt., 2003—, cons. clin. endocrinologist, assoc. dir. thyroid tumor ctr., physician scientist. Contbr. articles to med. and sci. publs. Grantee, NIH, Am. Cancer Soc. Mem.: Endocrine Soc. (com. mem.), Am. Thyroid Assn. Achievements include research in biomedical and clinical practice. Office: Johns Hopkins Sch Medicine 1830 East Monument St Ste 333 Baltimore MD 21287

XING, YIPING, electrical engineer, researcher; PhD, Stevens Inst. Tech., Hoboken, NJ, 2006. Sys. engr. China Unicom, Chengdu, 2001—02; rsch. asst. dept. elec. and computer engring. Stevens Inst. Tech., 2002—. Contbr. articles to profl. jours. Recipient Grad. Fellowship award Sch. Engring., Stevens Inst. Tech., 2005, Best Ph.D thesis award in elec. engring., 2006; named Outstanding Rsch. Asst. dept. elec. and computer engring., 2005. Mem.: IEEE (CCNC Best Student Paper award 2006, DySPAN Student Travel Grant award 2005). Achievements include research in next generation wireless communication networks. Office: Stevens Inst Tech Dept Elec and Computer Engring 1 Castle Point Hoboken NJ 07030 Personal E-mail: yipingxing@gmail.com. E-mail: yxing@stevens.edu.

XINGGUO, XIONG, engineering educator; m. Hongli Lu, July 10, 1999. BS in Physics, Wuhan U., China, 1994; PhD in Computer Engring., U. Cin., 2005; PhD in Elec. Engring., Shanghai Inst. Microsys. and Info. Tech., 1999. Asst. prof. U. Bridgeport, Conn., 2005—. Contbr. chapters to books, articles to numerous engring. jours., scientific papers. Grantee, Ohio Bd. Regents, 2003. Mem.: IEEE. Achievements include patents for micromachined comb interdigitated capacitive accelerometer; integration and fabrication sequence of movable silicon microstructure with glass substrate; research in conceived dual-mode built-in self-test for capacitive MEMS devicecs; first to developed self-repairable MEMS comb accelerometer.

XINGJIAN, GAO, writer; b. Ganzhou, China, Jan. 4, 1940; naturalized, France; Degree in French and Lit., Beijing Fgn. Langs. Inst., 1962. Translator Chinese Writers Assn. Resident playwright People's Art Theatre, Beijing. Author: (books) A Preliminary Discussion of the Art of Modern Fiction, 1981, A Pigeon Called Red Beak, 1985, Collected Plays, 1985, In Search of a Modern Form of Dramatic Representation, 1987, Soul Mountain, 1999 (Nobel prize for literature, 2000), One Man's Bible, 2002, (plays) Signal Alarm, 1982, Bus Stop, 1983, Wild Man, 1985, The Other Shore, 1986, Fugitives, 1989, Summer Rain in Peking; contbr. articles to profl. literary jours. Recipient Chevalier de l'Ordre des Arts et des Lettres, French Govt., 1992, Prix Communauté Française de Belgique, 1994, Prix du Nouvel An chinois, 1997. Fluent in French and Chinese. Office: c/o Author Mail Editions de l Aube 13 Pl Andre Masson 84240 La Tour d Aigues France

XIONG, HUI, finance educator; PhD, U. Minn., Twin Cities, 2000. Asst. prof. Rutgers Bus. Sch., Newark, 2005—. Editor: (book) Encyclopedia of GIS. Recipient ESA Innovation award, IBM, 2008. Office: Rutgers Univ Ackerson Hall 200K 180 Univ Ave Newark NJ 07102 Business E-Mail: hxiong@rutgers.edu.

XIONG, NING, computer scientist; b. Shanghai, Nov. 11, 1964; arrived in Sweden, 2000; s. Dezheng and Guiling (Li) Xiong; m. Xiaoyu Wang, Oct. 10, 1968. BS, Dong Hua U., Shanghai, 1986, MS, 1989; PhD with Excellent Distinction, U. Kaiserslautern, Germany, 2000. Asst. lectr. Dong Hua U., Shanghai, 1989—92, lectr., 1992—95; rsch. asst. U. Kaiserlautern, Germany, 1996—2000; guest rschr. Swedish Defence Rsch. Agy., Stockholm, 2000—01; rschr. Royal Inst. Tech., Stockholm, 2001—02; sr. lectr. Mid Sweden U., 2003—04; sr. lectr. dept. computer sci. and electronics Mälardalen U., 2004—. Project leader in intelligent robotics Dong Hua U., Shanghai, 1990—95; key rschr. in fuzzy systems U. Kaiserslautern, Kaiserslautern, Germany, 1996—2000; cons. feature selection Schott Glass Co., Mainz, Germany, 2000; prin. investigator in sensor management Swedish Defence Rsch. Agy., Stockholm, 2000—01; co-chair Swedish Artificial Intelligence and Learning Sys. Conf., 2005. Author: (book) Designing Compact and Comprehensible Fuzzy Controllers Usng Genetic Algorithms., 2001; mem. editl. bd.: Internat. Jour. Hybrid Intelligent Sys., 2007—; contbr. articles to profl. jours, papers to sci. confs. and convs., 2000, chapters to books. Recipient Outstanding Paper award, Sci. and Tech. Com., Shanghai, 1995; named an Outstanding Young Tchr., Dong Hua U., 1993; grantee Doctoral Fellowship, German Academic Exchange Service, 1995-2000. Mem.: IEEE. Avocations: travel, ping pong/table tennis. Office: Mälardalen U Dept Computer Science and Electronics SE-721 23 Västerås Sweden Office Phone: 0046 21 151716. Personal E-mail: n.xiong@ieee.org. Business E-Mail: ning.xiong@mdh.se.

XIONG, RENQIANG, mechanical engineer, researcher; s. Guangqun Xiong and Sane Zhang; m. Xiaoxing Feng, July 28, 2006. BS, Zhejiang U., Hangzhou, China, 1999; MS, Zhejiang U., 2002; PhD, U. Fla., Gainesville, 2007; MS, U. Fla., 2007. Rsch. asst. Zhejiang U., 1999—2002, U. Fla., 2003—07; postdoc. fellow Ga. Inst. Tech., Atlanta, 2007—08; sr. rsch. engr. Microfluidics Corp., Newton, Mass., 2008—. Contbr. scientific papers to profl. pubs. Recipient Award, U. Fla., 2004. Mem.: ASME, Sigma XI. Achievements include research in fuel cell science, engineering and technology; multiphase flow, heat and mass transfer, thermophysics and heat transfer. Office: Microfluidics Corp 30 Ossipee Rd Newton MA 02464

XIONG, TOUSU SAYDANGNMVANG, minister, theology studies educator; b. Hmong Long Cheng, June 23, 1966; arrived in U.S., 1976, naturalized, 1996; s. Nhialue Saydang and May (Vang) X.; m. Zoua Pahoua Moua, Sept. 14, 1993; children: Chivkeeb Genesis Toupa, Naamonunas Ruth, Nujsimloob Hebrews, Nkaujzuapaaj Esther. BA in Bibl. Studies, Simpson Coll., San Francisco, 1989; MA in Theology, Mennonite Brethren Bibl. Sem., Fresno, Calif., 1991; AS in Computerized Acctg., Phillips Jr. Coll., Fresno, Calif., 1993. Ordained to ministry Christian and Missionary Alliance, 1991. Assoc. min. Hmong San Raphael (Calif.) Bapt. Ch., 1986-88; youth min. Hmong Alliance Ch. of Santa Barbara, Goleta, Calif., 1984-85, Hmong Alliance Ch. of Fresno, 1989—; med. record acct. Dr. Suchat Jariangprasert Med. Clinic, Fresno, Calif., 1993—96; assoc., shareholder Wal-Mart Stores, Inc., Bentonville, Ark., 1998—. Mission coun., Santa Barbara, Calif.; scoutmaster Boy Scouts Am., 1984—85. Avocations: hiking, camping, computers. Office: Hmong Alliance Ch Fresno 8234 E Belmont Ave Fresno CA 93727-9725 Mailing: PO Box 8764 Fresno CA 93747 Personal E-mail: xteagle76@yahoo.com. *In my life as I have experienced both the world of the Hmong Animistic Religion in the East and the Christian faith from the West, I have come to realize that Jesus Christ is superior, for Jesus is the way, the truth and the life pointing us towards the Supreme and Creator Being.*

XIUZI, YE, engineering educator; b. Guangfeng, Jiangxi, China, Feb. 16, 1966; s. Xinhai Ye and Ximei Zheng; m. Ruisheng Yu; children: William Ye, Jessica Ye. PhD in Engring., Tech. U. Berlin, 1994. Prin. scientist Solid Works Corp., Concord, Mass., 1995—2007; cheung kong chair prof. Zhejiang U., Hangzhou, China, 2001—; chmn. New Dimension Sys. Co. Ltd., Hangzhou, 2003—; postdoc. rsch. scientist MIT, Cambridge. Contbr. articles to profl. jours. Office: Zhejiang Univ Hangzhou Zhejiang 310027 China Business E-Mail: yxz@cs.zju.edu.cn, yexz@newdimchina.com.

XU, BIN, civil engineering researcher, educator; s. Tianming Xu and Chunjiao Chen; m. Hairong Zheng; 1 child, Xinzhe. PhD, Ibaraki U., Japan, 2001. Postdoctoral fellow of Japan soc. for promotion of sci. Ibaraki U., Hitachi, Ibaraki, Japan, 2001—03; vis. scholar U. Missouri, Rolla, Mo., 2003—; furong prof. Hunan U., Changsha, Hunan, China, 2005—. Pres. Chinese Students and Scholars Assn., Hitachi, Ibaraki, Japan, 2000—01. Recipient Grant-In-Aid for Sci. Rsch., Japan Soc. for the Promotion of Sci. (JSPS), Furong Scholar Award, Hunan Provincial Govt., China, Excellent Grad., Huazhong U. Sci. and Technology, 1992, 1994; fellow Postdoctoral Fellowship, Japan Soc. for the Promotion of Sci.; scholar Monbusyo Scholarship, Ministry of Edn., Culture, Sports, Sci. and Tech. (MEXT), Guanghua Scholarship, Huazhong U. Sci. and Technology, 1994, Huazhong U. of Sci. and Tech. (HUST), 1991, 1990. Mem.: Asian Com. for Exptl. Mechanics, Rsch. subcommittee on Health Monitoring for Concrete Structures, Concrete Com., Rsch. subcommittee on Monitoring of Bridge Vibration and its Standardization, Structural Engring. Com., JSCE, Internat. Assn. for Bridge Maintenance and Safety, Japan Soc. Civil Engrs. Achievements include research on intelligent structures, structural health monitoring, soft identification algorithms, advanced sensing techniques. Office: Univ Missouri-Rolla 1870 Miner Circle Rolla MO 65409-0030

XU, CAILIN, research scientist; PhD, Lanzhou U., 2003. Rsch. scientist Nature Conservancy, Conn. Chpt., Mass.; postdoc. assoc. U. Alta., Edmonton, Canada. Recipient Sci. and Tech. Progress award, 2004, 2005; Killam Postdoc. fellowship, 2005—07. Mem.: Am. Fisheries Soc., Wildlife Soc., Soc. Conservation Biology, Sigma Xi.

XU, DONG, physicist, researcher; b. Shanghai, Nov. 25, 1965; s. Zhao-Zhuo Xu and Bai-Fan Hu; m. Zhao-Jing Tong; 1 child, Tong. BEng, Tsinghua U., China', 1989; MS in sci., Chinese Acad. Scis., 1992; PhD, Tech. U. Munich, 1997. Vis. scientist Fraunhofer Inst. Applied Solid-State Physics, Germany, 1996, Walter Schottky Inst., Garching, Germany, 1997; rsch. engr. Nippon Telegraph and Telephone Corp., Atsugi, Japan, 1997—. Contbr. articles to profl. jours. Recipient Prize of Dir. Shanghai Inst. Metallurgy, 1990, 91; Volkswagen Found. fellow, 1993-96. Mem. IEEE, Nat. Geog. Soc.

XU, DONGMEI, molecular biologist, director; d. Yufang Yang; m. Zengyu Du, Dec. 18, 1984; 1 child, Frank Xiaofeng Du. PhD, U. Ky., Lexington, 1996. Program dir. USSTC, Winchester, Ky., 2006—; adj. faculty U. Ky., 2006—. Sr. scientist USSTC, 1996—2006. Vol. Natural Resources, Lexington, 2006—. Master: CORESTA; mem.: ASPB, AAAS.

XU, FENG, research scientist, educator; b. Xiaoshan, Zhejiang, China, Feb. 20, 1964; s. Rupeng Xu and Aiqing Chai; m. Ling Ying, Oct. 6, 1963; 1 child, Duo. PhD, Dalian Inst. Chem. Physics, China, 1999. Assoc. prof. Dalian Inst. of Chem. Physics, Dalian, Liaoning, China, 1999—2001; postdoctoral rschr. analytical instruments divsn. Shimadzu Corp, Kyoto, 2001—03; postdoctoral rschr. U. Tokushima Dept Medicinal Chemistry, Tokushima, Japan, 2003—05; rsch. assoc. La. State U. Chemistry Dept., Baton Rouge, 2005—. Mem. internat. adv. bd. analytical abstracts Royal Soc. of Chemistry, London, 2004—. Author: Electrophoresis, Analytical Chemistry; contbr. articles to profl. jours. Office: La State U 8000 GSRI Rd Bldg 3100 Baton Rouge LA 70820 Office Phone: 225-578-5248. E-mail: fengxu22@gmail.com.

XU, GUANGYAO, research scientist; PhD, U. Md., Balt., 2007. Contbr. scientific papers. Mem.: ASME, Sigma Xi, Sci. Rsch. Soc. Achievements include first to nonlinear and time-varying dynamic analysis of high-dimensional models; improve the efficiency and accuracy of the dynamic relaxation method for nonlinear structures analysis. Personal E-mail: xuguangyao@gmail.com.

XU, JAY JIE, museum director; m. Jennifer Chen. MA, Princeton U., 1993. Asst. cur. Shanghai Mus., 1988—90; fellow Asian art dept. Met. Mus. Art, 1994—96; dir. Asian art dept., cur. Chinese art Seattle Art Mus., 1996—2003; Pritzker cur. Asian art Art Inst. Chgo., 2003—06, Pritzker chmn. Asian & ancient art dept., 2006—08; dir. Asian Art Mus. San Francisco, 2008—. Mem. selection com. Mellon Prog. Chinese Mus. Professionals, 2003—, mng. dir., 2007—. Co-author: Art of the Houma Foundry, 1996 (Shimada prize, 1997). Recipient Outstanding Merit award, Shanghai Mus., 1989; fellow Smithsonian Inst., 1996; Hon. Marc Haas '29 Meml. fellowship, Princeton U. Dept. Art & Arch., 1993, Jane & Morgan Whitney fellowship, Met. Mus. Art, 1994, Ittleson fellowship, Nat. Gallery Art Ctr. for Advanced Study, 1996, Patterson Sims fellowship, Seattle Art Mus., 2001. Office: Asian Art Mus 200 Larkin St San Francisco CA 94102

XU, JINGHAI J. (JIM XU), toxicologist, researcher; s. Liang Xu and Shaoying Ye; m. Li Julia Yu, Aug. 24, 1996; children: Enya Jane, Elisa Mei. PhD, MIT, 1998. Lab. head Pfizer Ctrl. Rsch., Groton, Conn., 1998—2005; head predictive toxicology Pfizer Rsch. Tech. Ctr., Cambridge, Mass., 2005—. Co-editor Wiley & Sons, NYC, 2007—; com. chair Applied Pharm. Toxicology, Boston, 2007—; lectr. MIT, Cambridge, 2007—. Editor: (book) Emerging Technologies Impacting Drug Discovery and Development. Sci. amb. Pfizer Global R & D, New London, Conn.; campaigner United Way, Groton, Conn. Recipient W. C. Ebaugh award, Denison U., 1992, Achievement award, Pfizer Ctrl. Rsch., 2001, Team award, Pfizer Global Rsch. & Devel., 2007; fellow, MIT, 1996—97; Presdl. Scholarship, Denison U., 1992. Mem.: Soc. Toxicology, Am. Chem. Soc., Internat. Soc. Study of Xenobiotics. Independent. Achievements include patents pending for BSEP polypeptide variants and uses thereof; automated in vitro cellular imaging assays for micronuclei and other target objects; research in systems biology; systems toxicology; high content screening and analysis; drug induced liver injury; drug drug interactions; predictive toxicology. Avocations: travel, hiking, reading, theater. Personal E-mail: jimxu2@gmail.com.

XU, JINGYE, research scientist; married. Attending, U. Ill., Chgo., 2005—. Tchg. rsch. asst. U. Ill., 2005—; internship Motorola Inc., Schaumburg, Ill., 2007. Contbr. numerous sci. papers. V.p. Chinese Student and Scholar Assn. UIC, Chgo., 2006—07. Recipient 2nd Pl. Robot Soccer Competition, Chinese Automation Assn., 2003, Championship Robot Soccer Competition, 2004, Travel award, U. Ill., 2008. Mem.: IEEE. Achievements include development of waveform based timing analyzer; wireless communication system for soccer robots; research in noise separation in digital circuits; optimization technique for interconnect pipelining. Avocations: swimming, basketball, travel.

XU, JINHUI, engineering educator; b. Yuanjiang, China, Jan. 7, 1970; arrived in US, 1995; s. Changlin Xu and Shuzhen Yang; m. Binhin Wang, July 1, 1995; 1 child, Nicole Wang. BS, U. Sci. Tech. China, Hefei, 1992, MS, 1995; PhD, U. Notre Dame, South Bend, Ind., 2000. Rsch. asst. Fla. Internat. U., Miami, 1995—96; tchg. asst., rsch. asst. U. Notre Dame, South Bend, Ind., 1996—99, grad. fellow, 1999—2000; asst. prof. U. Buffalo SUNY, 2000—06, assoc. prof., 2006—. Cons. Brilliant Optical Network LLC, Buffalo, 2002; spkr. in field. Contbr. scientific papers to profl. jours. Recipient Faculty Partnership award, IBM, 2001, Faculty Early Career Devel. award, NSF, 2005. Mem.: Spl. Interest Group Automata and Computability Theory, Am. Soc. Engring. Edn., Assn. Computing Machinery. Office: Dept Computer Sci Engring SUNY Buffalo Buffalo NY 14260

XU, JINYOU, medical researcher; b. Shanghai, May 20, 1966; s. Fushen Xu and Xiuying Shang; m. Xin Gu; children: Andy, Alexandra. PhD, U. Pitts., 1997. Postdoc. rsch. fellow Scripps Rsch. Inst., La Jolla, Calif., 1997—2000; rsch. fellow Merck & Co., Inc., Rahway, NJ, 2000—. Contbr. scientific papers (Thomas Edison Patent award, 2007). Recipient Bioorganic & Medicinal Chemistry Letters Most Cited Paper award, 2005—08. Achievements include discovery of Januvia medicine for the Type II diabetes. Office: Merck & Co Inc 126 E Lincoln Ave Rahway NJ 07065-4607 Business E-Mail: jinyou_xu@merck.com.

XU, J.M. (JIMMY XU), physicist, educator, engineer; PhD, U. Minn., Mpls. Prof. U. of Toronto, Toronto, Ontario, Canada, 1987—99; prof. engring., prof. physics Brown U., Providence, 1999—. Dir. Nortel Inst. of Telecomm., Toronto, Ontario, Canada; invited spkr. in field. Contbr. articles to profl. jours. Recipient 1995 Steacie prize of Can., 1995, 6 other internat. and Can. prizes and awards for rsch. achievements; two endowed chair professorships, JPLdistinguished vis. scientist, IEEE, NASA, others, 1987—2000, Guggenheim fellowship, 2005, Charles C. Tillinghast Jr. '32 U. Prof. award, Brown U., 2005—; fellow, Inst. Physics, AAAS. Achievements include patents in field.

XU, JUAN, medical researcher; PhD, Nanyang Technol. U., Singapore, 2006. Software engr. Stratech Sys. Ltd., Singapore, 2005—06; rsch. assoc. UPMC Eye Ctr., Pitts., 2006—. Mem.: IEEE. Achievements include patents pending for glaucoma imaging. Office: Univ Pitts 203 Lothrop St EEI-835 Pittsburgh PA 15213

XU, JUNCHENG, engineer, researcher; b. Beijing, 1975; B, Tsinghua U., Beijing, 1998, M, 2000; PhD, Va. Tech. U., Blacksburg, 2005. Rschr. Va. Tech., Blacksburg, 2000—05; sr. sensor scientist Luxtron, Santa Clara, Calif., 2006—. Grantee Grad. Student Travel award, Va. Tech., 2005; scholar, Ctr. Photonics Tech., Va. Tech., 2000—05. Mem.: IEEE, Optical Soc. Am., Sigma Xi. Achievements include development of fiber optic pressure and temperature sensors for oil wells; patents for optical fiber sensors for harsh environments; optical fiber pressure and acceleration sensor fabricated on a fiber endface; dual-frequency He-Ne lazer; patents pending for intrinsic fabry-perot structure with micrometric tip; miniature fiber optic pressure and temperature sensors; fiber optic sensor for gas sensing. Avocations: tennis, badminton, travel, chess, guitar. Personal E-mail: jcthu@gmail.com.

XU, LE, engineer; s. Guoliang Xu and Qinchan Zhu. BS in Engring., Tsinghua U., Beijing, 2001; MS, NC State U., Raleigh, 2003, PhD, 2006. Analyst KEMA Consulting, Raleigh, 2006; prin. engr. Quanta Tech., Raleigh, 2007—. Mem.: IEEE (eastern. NC sect. computational intelligent soc. chair 2007). Office: Quanta Technology 4020 Westchase Blvd Ste 300 Raleigh NC 27607 Business E-Mail: lxu@quanta-technology.com.

XU, LUOYU ROY, engineering educator; PhD in Aeronautics and Materials Sci., Calif. Inst. Tech., Pasadena, 2001. Asst. prof. civil and environ. engring. Vanderbilt U., Nashville, 2001—. Recipient Young Investigator award, Office of Naval Rsch., 2003. Mem.: AIAA, ASME. Home: 9526 Grand Haven Dr Brentwood TN 37027

XU, MIN, research associate; b. Shaoyang, Hunan, China, Oct. 24, 1973; PhD, East China U. Sci. and Tech., Shanghai, 2002, Iowa State U., Ames, 2008. Cert. in radiation producing device user, Ames Lab., USDOE, in neutron and X-ray scattering, Office Sci., USDOE. Rsch. asst. Ames Lab., USDOE, 2003—08, rsch. assoc., 2008—; adj. instr. Des Moines Area CC. Chief editor Jour. Metall. Engring., Internat., Jour. Materials Sci. and Engring., New Delhi; guest editor Jour. Nanomaterials, Nasr City, Cairo; invited reviewer, profl. jours. Contbr. articles to profl. jours. Recipient Top prize, 9Th Internat. Conf. Quasicrystal, 2005. Mem.: Sci. Rsch. Soc., Minerals, the Metals and Materials Soc., Am. Chem. Soc., Materials Rsch. Soc., Sigma Xi. Achievements include research in significant contribution in materials science and engineering and related fields. Office: Iowa State Univ Ames Lab 37 Wilhelm Hall Ames IA 50011 Office Phone: 515-294-7901. Business E-Mail: minxu@iastate.edu, minxu@ameslab.gov.

XU, PEI, agriculturist, educator; PhD, Purdue U., West Lafayette, NY, 2007. Rsch. asst. Purdue U., 2004—07; asst. prof. SUNY, Morrisville, NY, 2007—. Contbr. articles to profl. jours. Tchg. grant, SUNY Morrisville, 2007. Mem.: China Agrl. Economics Rev., Am. Agrl. Economics Assn. (agribusiness group mem. 2006—08). Office: SUNY Morrisville St Coll Morrisville NY 13408 Business E-Mail: xup@morrisville.edu.

XU, PING, chemist; b. Shanghai, Apr. 29, 1957; came to U.S., 1985; s. Yuan Xu and Changfu Zhu; m. Shuhong Wang, Feb. 17, 1987; children: Helen W., Olivia W. BS, East China U. Chem. Tech., Shanghai, 1982, MS, 1984, U. Cin., 1987, PhD, 1991. Asst. prof. East China U. Chem. Tech., 1984-85; Paul J. Flory meml. fellow U. Cin., 1990-92; sr. rsch. chemist Quantum Chem. Corp., Cin., 1991-94; polymer scientist W.L. Gore & Assocs., Inc., Elkton, Md., 1994—. Vis. scientist Oak Ridge (Tenn.) Nat. Lab., 1998—; vis. scientist Nat. Inst. Stds. and Tech., Gaithersburg, Md., 1999—. Contbr. numerous articles to sci. jours. Mem. AAAS, Am. Chem. Soc., Material Rsch. Soc. Achievements include research in engineering, rubber elasticity, polymer morphology and polymer physics. Home: 22 Piersons Rdg Hockessin DE 19707-9291 Office: WL Gore & Assocs Inc 2401 Singerly Rd Elkton MD 21921-2733 E-mail: pxu@aol.com.

XU, RENMEI, engineering educator; d. Zigen Xu and Shuying Huang; m. Weijiang Ding. MS, Western Mich. U., Kalamazoo, 2001, PhD, 2006. Grad. asst. Western Mich. U., 1999—2001, 2003—06; asst. prof. Ball State U., Muncie, Ind., 2006—. Contbr. articles to profl. jours. Mem.: Tech. Assn. Graphic Arts, Phi Kappa Phi. Achievements include research in study of the effects of paper physical properties on print gloss and ink mileage; flexo platemaking using rapid prototyping; study of print quality of dry-toner color electrophotography for production printing. Office: Ball State Univ Dept Tech Muncie IN 47306 Business E-Mail: rxu@bsu.edu.

XU, SHANG-ZHI, toxicologist, director; married. BA, Anhui Med. U., Hefei city, 1989; MS, China Pharm. U., Nan Jing city, 1994; PhD, Peking Union Med. Coll, Beijing, 1999. Sr. scientist Mayo Clinic, Rochester, Minn., 2005—07; dir. Wuxi AppTech, Inc., St Paul, Minn., 2007—. Contbr. to publs. Rsch. grant, NIH, 2003, T32 fellowship, 2006—07. Mem.: Sigma Xi, Soc. Toxicology. Home: 4415 7th St NW Rochester MN 55901

XU, XIANGYUAN, academic administrator, educator; b. Sept. 1946; Grad., Tsinghua U., 1970, MSC, 1982. Prof. Tsinghua U., dep. dean Postgraduate Sch.; pres. Hainan U.; now pres. Capital Normal U., Beijing, advisor Internat. Resonance Ionization Spectroscopy, mem. Internat. Com. of Physics on Elec. and Atomic Collisions. Vis. scholar Stanford U., 1985—87; mem. standing com. Beijing People's Congress, dep. dir. ESC Commn. Office: Capital Normal U 105 Xi San Huan Beijing 100037 China Office Phone: (10) 68902214. Office Fax: (10) 68415011. Business E-Mail: xyxu-dmp@mail.tsinghua.edu.cn.

XU, YANG, engineering educator; s. Guanliang Xu and Xiujing Shu; m. Sharon Zhang. PhD, Carnegie Mellon U., Pitts., 2004. Sr. rschr. Qualcomm Inc., San Diego, 2005—07. Cons. Barcelona Design, Fremont, Calif., 2002. Recipient QualStar, Qualcomm, 2006—07. Mem.: ACM, IEEE. Achievements include 5 patents. Home: 3510 N PineGrove St #504 Chicago IL 60657 Office: Ill Inst Tech 3301 S Dearborn St Chicago IL 60616 Office Fax: 312-567-8976. Business E-Mail: yxu@ece.iit.edu.

XU, YAO L, marketing professional, consultant; b. Guangzhou, China, Sept. 2, 1963; s. Yong C. Xu and Xiao T. He. B in Econs., Fgn. Trade Inst. of Guangzhou, 1985. Staff Fgn. Econ. Rels. and Trade Commn. of Guangdong Province, China, 1985—89; sales mgr. Sinomart Internat. Inc., NYC, 1989—91; sales dir. Charles Jacquin Inc., Phila., 1991—96; self-employed Yulex Enterprises Inc., Yardley, Pa., 1996—98; founder Panda We Save Org., 1997—; mktg. cons. Charles Jacquin Inc., Phila., 1998—2002. New product devel., mktg. and consulting in china Charles Jacquin Inc., Phila., 1998—2002. Mem. Nat. Rep. Com., Washington, 1994—2002, Rep. Presdl. Roundtable, Washington, 1997—98. Avocations: reading, swimming, singing. Office: Charles Jacquin Inc 2633 Trenton Ave Philadelphia PA 19125 Home Phone: 215-321-7965; Office Phone: 215-425-9300. Office Fax: 215-425-9438; Home Fax: 011-86-20-8454-2371. Business E-Mail: ALECYAOXU@AOL.COM.

XU, ZHI-HUI, research scientist; PhD, Royal Inst. Tech., Stockholm, 2004. Rsch. asst. Royal Inst. Tech., 1999—2004; postdoc. rschr. U. SC, Columbia, 2004—. Office: Univ SC 300 Main St Columbia SC 29208

XU, ZHIJIE, research scientist; s. Congyou Xu and Ping Ding; m. Heng Wang, July 30, 2004; children: Sean Jixiang, Audrey Zijin, Alice Zipei. BS in Engring., Zhejiang U., Hangzhou, China, 1997; MS, Nat. U. Singapore, 2001; PhD, Rensselaer Poly. Inst., Troy, NY, 2006. Structural engr. Beijing Ins. Nuc. Engring., 1997—99; rsch. assoc. Idaho Nat. Lab., Idaho Falls, Idaho, 2007—, rsch. scientist, 2009—. Mem.: Inst. Physics, Materials Rsch. Soc., Am. Phys. Soc., Sigma Xi. Achievements include research in computational mechanics, computational materials, multiscale modelling & computational fluid dynamics, modelling of reactive fluid flow biofilm growth dislocation dynamics in dynamics strain aging; patents pending for copy detection system using correlations.

XUAN, JIANHUA JASON, engineering educator; s. Gan Xuan and Meiying Zhang; m. Bing Yang; children: Kenneth Ming, Maxwell Wei. PhD, U. Md., Balt., 1997. Asst. prof. Cath. U. Am., Washington, 2001—06; assoc. prof. Va. Tech, Arlington, 2006—. Contbr. articles to jour. publs. Grant, NIH, 2002, 2005, NASA, 2003, DoD, 2004. Mem.: IEEE. Achievements include bioinformatics for cancer research. Office: Virginia Tech 4300 Wilson Blvd Ste 750 Arlington VA 22203 Office Fax: 703-528-5543. Business E-Mail: xuan@vt.edu.

XUAN, XIANGCHUN, engineering educator; b. Feidong, Anhui, China, Feb. 15, 1973; s. Guifang Wang; m. Ping Hong; children: Lefan, Allen Hong. PhD, U. Toronto, Canada, 2006. Asst. prof. Clemson U., SC, 2006—. Office: Clemson Univ ME Dept 239 Fluor Daniel Engring Bldg Clemson SC 29634-0921 Office Fax: 864-656-7299. Business E-Mail: xcxuan@clemson.edu.

XUE, FEI, epidemiologist; MB, Nanjing Med. U., Jiangsu, China, 1999; MS, Mich. State U., East Lansing, 2003; DSc, Harvard Sch. Pub. Health, Boston, 2007. Diplomate Min. Health China, 2001. Rsch. assoc. Harvard Sch. Pub. Health, 2003—06; epidemiologist i3 Drug Safety, Boston, 2007—. Intern gen. medicine Nanjing Gulou Hosp., 1998—99; resident physician ob-gyn. Nanjing Women's and Children's Hosp., 1999—2001; grad. rsch. asst. Mich. State U., 2001—03. Contbr. articles to profl. sci. jours. Recipient Competitive award, Nat. Inst. Child Health & Human Devel. and CIHR's Inst. Human Devel. and Child and Youth Health, 2006; Presdl. scholarship, Harvard U., 2003—07, MacMahon Travel grant, 2005. Mem.: Red Cross Soc. China, Soc. Epidemiologic Rsch. (Competitive award 2006), Internat. Soc. Pharmacoepidemiology. Office: i3 Drug Safety 950 Winter St Ste 3800 Waltham MA 02451 Office Fax: 781-472-8464. Personal E-mail: n2fei@channing.harvard.edu. Business E-Mail: fei.xue@i3drugsafety.com.

XUE, FEI, communications educator; BA, Huazhong U. Sci. & Tech., MA, 2000; PhD, U. Ala. Asst. prof. Sch. Mass Comm. & Journalism, U. Southern Miss., Hattiesburg, 2004—, grad. coord., 2008—. Contbr. articles to profl. jours. Grantee Vis. Prof. Program, Advt. Ednl. Found., 2007, Lucas Endowment Faculty Excellence, U. Southern Miss., 2008. Mem.: Chinese Communication Assn., Assn. Edn. Journalism & Mass Communication, Am. Acad. Advt. Office: Univ Southern Miss 118 College Dr 5121 Hattiesburg MS 39402 Office Phone: 601-266-5652. Business E-Mail: fei.xue@usm.edu.

XUE, JINYU, physicist, medical specialist; b. Kunming, Yunnan, China, June 7, 1965; s. Jianzhu Xue and Faying Chen; 1 child, Peisen. PhD, LaTrobe U., Melbourne, Australia, 1998. Diplomate ABR/NJ, 2008. Rsch. assoc. Boston U., 1998—2000; asst. prof. Robert Wood Johnson Med. Sch.-UMDNJ, 2007—. Grantee, C.R.Bard, Inc., 2004. Mem.: Am. Bd. Radiology, Am. Assn. Physicists in Medicine, Am. Soc. Therapeutic and Radiology Oncology. Achievements include the Gamma Knife project. Home: 42 Fairhaven Dr Cherry Hill NJ 08003 Office: Cooper U Hosp One Cooper Plaza Camden NJ 08076 Personal E-mail: yn66us@yahoo.com. E-mail: xue-jinyu@cooperhealth.edu.

XUE, YONG, columnist, educator; b. Beijing, Oct. 30, 1961; s. Shuguang Xue and Shiguan Yang; m. Wei Zhuang; 1 child, Eva Sicun. PhD, Yale U., New Haven, 2004. Asst. prof. Suffolk U., Boston, 2005—. Columnist variety Chinese newspapers, 2003—. Home: 61 Mystic St Arlington MA 02474 Office: Suffolk Univ 8 Ashburton Pl Boston MA 02108 Business E-Mail: yxue@suffolk.edu.

XUE, YUAN, engineering educator; d. Li Xue and Xiuying Sun; m. Yi Cui. BS, Harbin Inst. Tech., 1998; MS, U. Ill., Urbana-Champaign, 2002, PhD, 2005. Rsch. asst. U. Ill., Urbana-Champaign, 2000—05; asst. prof. Vanderbilt U., Nashville, 2005—. Contbr. articles to profl. jours. Vodafone fellow, Vodafone-U.S. Found., 2003, 2004. Achievements include research in resource management in wireless networks.

YABLON, JEFFERY LEE, lawyer; b. Chgo., June 28, 1948; s. Robert R. and Faye I. (Goldberg) Y.; m. Jean C. LaPrade, Apr. 17, 1983. BA with honors, U. Wis., 1970; JD, Stanford U., 1973. Bar: Calif. 1974, D.C. 1975. Law clk. to Judge Cynthia Holcomb Hall U.S. Tax Ct., Washington, 1973-75; Fulbright scholar U. Florence, Italy, 1975-76; assoc. Covington & Burling, Washington, 1976-80, Lee, Toomey & Kent, Washington, 1980-82, Pillsbury Winthrop Shaw Pittman LLP, Washington, 1982-84, ptnr., 1984—. Mem. bd. advisors Taxation of Exempts Jour., 1998—. Contbr. articles to legal jours.; editl. adv. bd. Moment Mag., 2000—. Mem. ABA, State Bar Calif., D.C. Bar, Cosmos Club. Jewish. Office: Pillsbury Winthrop Shaw Pittman LLP 2300 N St NW Washington DC 20037-1172 Office Phone: 202-663-8441. Business E-Mail: jeffery.yablon@pillsburylaw.com.

YABUKI, JEFFREY W., data processing company executive, former accounting company executive; BBA, Calif. State U. Cert. CPA Calif., Minn., lic. Nat. Assn. Securities Dealers. With Am. Express Co., 1987—99; v.p., mergers & acquisitions Am. Express Tax Bus. Svcs., Mpls., 1996—98, pres., CEO NYC, 1998—99; pres. H&R Block Internat., 1999—2002; exec. v.p., COO H&R Block Inc., Kans. City, 2002—05; pres., CEO Fiserv, Inc., Brookfield, Wis., 2005—. Bd. dir. PetSmart, Inc., 2004—, Fiserv Inc., 2005—, MBIA. Former mem. Minn. Bd. Accountancy. Recipient Innovator award, Bank Technology News, 2007. Office: Fiserv Inc 255 Fiserv Dr Brookfield WI 53045

YACANTE, MARIA LUCY, music educator, researcher; b. San Juan, Argentina, July 4, 1941; arrived in U.S., 1978; d. Carlos Alberto Yacante and Maria Elena Cuello. Maestra Normal Nacional, Sarmiento Normal Sch., San Juan, Argentina, 1966; MusB in piano, Tex. Wesleyan U., Ft. Worth, 1982; MusM in piano pedagogy, Tex. Christian U., Ft. Worth, 1984, post grad., 1989. Prof. of music Sarmiento Normal Sch., San Juan, Argentina, 1975—76, Nat. U. of San Juan, Argentina, 1975—78; piano accompanist Tex. Wesleyan U., 1978—82; piano instr. piano prep. divsn. Tex. Christian U., 1983—88; piano tchr. Our Lady of Victory, Ft. Worth, 1985—86, Ft. Worth Music and Arts Sch., 1986—87, independent piano studio, Ft. Worth, 1983—2006, Ray Rich Music Edn., Ft. Worth, 2006—07, Independent Piano Studio, Fort Worth, 2008—. Piano tchr. Inst. Superior de Artes, San Juan, Argentina, 1963—64; adjudicator piano festivals, 1989, 92, 2000; spkr. Reflections on Learning and Tchng., 2001—; adjudicator Ft. Worth Piano Tchrs. Forum, 2002, 04, 07; student in tchrs. program Plano Tex. Internat. Acad. and Festival (formerly Tex. Christian U./Cliburn Piano Inst.), 1989—94, 2004—07. Performer solo recitals. Mem.: Ind. Piano Tchrs. Forum (chair 2002—), Tex. Fedn. of Music Clubs, Tex. Music Tchrs. Assn., Music Tchrs. Nat. Assn., Ft. Worth Piano Tchrs. Forum (first v.p., piano recitals 2004—), Ft. Worth Music Tchrs. Assn. Forum (chair 2002—06), Pi Kappa Lambda. Avocations: reading, writing, drawing. Home: PO Box 100912 Fort Worth TX 76185-0912 Personal E-mail: lucy_yacante@att.net.

YACCARINO, LINDA, telecommunications industry executive, marketing professional; m. Claude Yaccarino; children: Matthew, Christian. B in Telecomm., Pa. State U., 1985. V.p. advt./prog. sales Select Media Comm., 1988—93; with syndication divsn. Turner Broadcasting Sys., Inc., 1993—96, mgr., v.p. sales Turner Entertainment, 1997—99, sr. v.p., 1999—2004, exec. v.p., gen. mgr. ad sales/mktg., 2004—09, exec. v.p., COO ad sales/mktg., 2009—; v.p. sales CNBC, 1996—97. Active Adults & Children with Learning & Devel. Disabilities; bd. dirs. Young Audiences of NY. Named Advt. Working Mother of Yr., Advt. Women of NY/Working Mother Mag., 2006; named a Woman to Watch, Advt. Age mag., 2007; named one of Women Who Rule in Sales & Mktg., Assn. Women in Radio & TV, 2006, Top 25 Women in TV, TV Week, 2008, Top Women in Cable, CableFax Mag., 2008; named to Wonder Women roster, Multichannel News, 2005. Mem.: Women in Cable & Telecomm. Office: Turner Entertainment 1 CNN Ctr Atlanta GA 30348 Office Phone: 404-827-1700. Business E-Mail: linda.yaccarino@turner.com.*

YACH, DEREK, epidemiologist, health policy analyst; b. Cape Town, South Africa, Nov. 21, 1955; s. Solm and Estelle (Mauerberger) Y.; m. Yasmin Elizabeth Van Schirnding, Mar. 29, 1987. MB, ChB, U. Cape Town, 1979; BSc with honours in Epidemiology, U. Stellenbosch, South Africa, 1983; MPH, Johns Hopkins U., 1985. Intern depts. medicine and surgery Groote Schuur Hosp., Cape Town, South Africa, 1980; rsch. officer Inst. for Biostats., Med. Rsch. Coun., Johannesburg, South Africa, 1981, sr. chief rsch. officer, 1986-89, dir. Epidemiology Ctr., 1992-95; chief policy action coordination WHO, Geneva, 1995—. Project supr. cmty. health dept., rsch. officer dept. medicine U. Cape Town, 1984, hon. sr. lectr., 1986—; hon. cons. epidemiologist Johannesburg City Health Dept., 1987-95; pub. health advisor, cons. Devel. Bank So. Africa, Johannesburg, 1992-95; hon. sr. lectr. Witwatersrand U. Med. Sch., Johannesburg, 1993-95; adj. assoc. prof. internat. health and devel. Tulane U. Sch. pub. Health, New Orleans, 1993-95; alt. dir. Mauerberger Found. Fund, 1984-95; mem. adv. com. Internat. Exec. Health Care Confs., 1995; vis. fellow Johns Hopkins U. Sch. Pub. Health, 1992; Heath Clark lectr. London Sch. Hygiene and Tropical Medicine, 1995; mem. adv. bd. program for health policy in econs. under stress Ben Gurion U. Negev Faculty Health Scis. and Monaster Ctr. for Econ. Rsch., 1995—; founder, pres. Tobacco Control Commn. for Africa, 1994-96; convenor confs. in health; condr., presenter numerous confs., seminars and workshops in field, including Internat. Assn. for Study Lung Cancer Workshop, Cape Town, 1993, World Bank Human Resource Devel. Seminar, Washington, 1996; mem. ad hoc commn. on future WHO, 1994-96; pub. health advisor World Bank, Lesotho, 1993-95; program mgr. tobacco free initiative, WHO, 1998-2000; exec. dir. noncommunicable diseases and mental health, 2000—; reviewer numerous sci. jours. Mem. editl. bd. Internat. Jour. Health Promotion, 1993—, Paediatric and Perinatal Epidemiology, 1990—, Cmty. Health Assn. South Africa Jour. Comprehensive Health, 1990, Tobacco Alarm, 1986—, Urbanisation and Health, 1989—, South African Jour. Sports Medicine, 1990—, Devel. So. Africa, 1993—, Tobacco Control: Internat. Jour., 1994—, South African Jour. Pub. Health, 1995—; contbr. over 100 articles and revs. to sci. jours., chpts. to books Bd. dirs. Coun. Against Smoking/Heart Found., South Africa, 1991-95; coun. mem. Child Accident Prevention Found., South Africa, 1989-92. Lt. South Africa Med. Svcs., 1990-91. Recipient Norhistan prize for best non-specialist article South African Med. Jour., 1982, silver medal Cmty. Health Asn. So. Africa, 1994; post-intern scholar South Africa Med. Rsch. Coun., 1981, postdoctoral scholar, 1984-85; Guy Elliot med. fellow U. Cape Town, 1983-84, Kellogg Found. travel fellow, U.S. and Brazil, 1991, Henry J. Kaiser Family Found. travel fellow APHA Conf., Washington, 1992, Com. on Health in So. Africa travel felow to APHA Conf., San Francisco, 1993. Fellow Royal Geog. Soc.; mem. Epidemiol. Soc. So. Africa (exec. com. 1985, 87, 90, conf. convenor 1987, 91, chmn. 1987-88, 90-92), Internat. Epidemiol. Assn., Nat. Med. and Dental Assn., Royal Soc. South Africa, South African Assn. for Conflict Intervention, N.Y. Acad. Scis., Inst. de Vie. Jewish. Avocation: long-distance sea swimming. Home: 205 Wakeman Ln Southport CT 06890 Personal E-mail: derek.yach@pepsico.com.

YACKIRA, MICHAEL WILLIAM, electric power industry executive; b. NYC, Aug. 14, 1951; s. Alan Israel and Lillian (Landau) Y.; m. Roberta Guido, July 24, 1977; 3 children BS in Acctg., Herbert H. Lehman Coll., CUNY, 1972. CPA. Sr. acct. Arthur Andersen, NYC, 1972-75; v.p. St. Joe Petroleum, Houston, 1975-83; mgr. fin. analysis U.S. Industries, Stamford, Conn., 1983-84; dir. bus. analysis and research GTE Svc. Corp., Stamford, 1984-85, dir. bus. devel. and analysis, 1985-86, asst. controller budget planning and analysis, 1986-87; v.p. fin. and revenues GTE Fla., Tampa, 1987-88; v.p. fin. and info. mgmt. GTE Info. Svcs., Tampa, 1988-89; v.p. corp. devel. and planning FPL Group, Inc., Juno Beach, Fla., 1989-91; chief planning officer Fla. Power and Light Co., 1990-91; sr. v.p. market and regulatory services, then sr. v.p. CFO Fla. Power & Light Co., Juno Beach, 1991—98; pres. FPL Energy Inc., 1998—2000; v.p., CFO Mars Inc., 2001—02; exec. v.p. strategy & policy NV Energy Inc. (was Sierra Pacific Resources), Las Vegas, Nev., 2003; corp. exec. v.p., CFO NV Energy Inc., Las Vegas, Nev., 2003—07, pres., COO, 2007, pres., CEO, 2007—. Bd. dir. Am. Heart Assn., United Way So. Nev. Office: NV Energy Inc 6226 W Sahara Ave Las Vegas NV 89146 Mailing: NV Energy Inc PO Box 98910 Las Vegas NV 89151-0001*

YADAV, ANAND KRISHNA, biotechnologist, educator; s. Chhabi Lal and Jaldevi Yadav; m. Maya Govind Yadav, May 14, 1970; children: Niraj Kumarmangalam, Nalini Vishakha Sakhi. Ph.D., U. Ill., Urbana-Champaign, 1972. Assoc. prof. hort. Ft. Valley State U., 1984—90, prof. medicinal plants biotech. Ga., 1990—. Mem. bd dirs. World Assn. Vedic Studies, Atlanta, 2004—07. Grants, USDA, 1993—2008. Mem.: Internat. Soc. Hort. Sci. (vice chair, medicinal plants sect. 2006—). Hindu. Achievements include research in medicinal & nutraceutical plants biotechnology in vitro plant culture & genetic transformation for value-added bioactive traits on several medicinal and nutraceutical plant species. Avocations: music, travel. Office: Ft Valley State Univ 1005 State Univ Dr Fort Valley GA 31030-4313

YADAV, MADHAV P., chemist; married. PhD, Southern Ill. U., Carbondale, 1988. Rsch. scientist Purdus U., W. Lafayette, Ind., 1988—92; reseach assoc. U. of Calif., Riverside, Calif., 1992—2004; rsch. chemist USDA-ARS, Ea. Reg. Res. Ctr., Wyndmoor, Pa., 2004—. Office: USDA ARS Eastern Reg Res Ctr 600 E Mermaid Ln Wyndmoor PA 19038 Office Fax: 215-233-6406. Business E-Mail: madhav.yadav@ars.usda.gov.

YADAV, PRASHANT, economics educator; arrived in Spain, 2004, permanent resident; s. Surendra and Usha Yadav. BS in Chemical Engring., Indian Inst. Tech., Roorkee, 1995; PhD, U. Ala., Tuscaloosa, 2004. Prof. supply chain mgmt. MIT, Spain, 2004—. Office: MIT-Zaragoza International Logistics Pro Avenida Gomez Laguna 25 Zaragoza 50009 Spain

YADAVALLI, GOPALA KRISHNA, medical educator; BS, Penn. State U., U. Pk., 1991; MD, Jefferson Med. Coll., Phila., 1995. Cert. Am. Bd. Internal Medicine, 2000, in infectious diseases Am. Bd. Internal Medicine, 2002. Chief, infectious diseases clinic, Veterans Affairs Med. Ctr. Louis Stokes Cleve., 2003—; assoc. program dir., internal medicine U. Hosps. Case Med. Ctr., Cleve., 2004—; asst. prof. medicine Case Western Res. U., Cleve., 2005—. Mem. Sivananda Ctr., Columbia, SC, 2008—08.

YADAVALLI, KAMESHWAR, electronics engineer; BTech, Indian Inst. Tech. Madras, Tamil Nadu; MS, PhD, U. Notre Dame, Ind. Postdoc. scholar U. Notre Dame, 2005, UCLA, 2005—08. Nat. Talent Search scholarship, Govt. of India, 1994—2000. Mem.: IEEE. Achievements include research in single electron memory devices, quantum-dot cellular automate logic devices, III-V compound semiconductor integration on silicon.

YADEKA, THEOPHILUS ADENIYI, hospital administrator; b. Ibadan, Nigeria, Apr. 16, 1939; came to U.S., 1971; s. Joshua A. and Alice (Opawole) Y.; m. Julianah M., Aug. 23, 1965; children: Olatunde, Mofoluke, Ayoola, Mobolaji, Adedoja. Diploma, S.D.A. Nursing Sch., 1965, SUNY, 1972; BS in Healthcare Adminstrn., St. Francis Coll., 1976; MS in Healthcare & Hosp. Adminstrn., L.I. U., 1977. Lic. pvt. sch. tchr. clin. instr. Charge and staff nurse Met. City Hosp., NYC, 1971—74, Barnabas Hosps., NYC, 1974—77; prin. hosp. adminstr. Ministry of Health/State Hosp. Mgmt. Bd., Ibadan, Nigeria, 1978-85; asst. chief hosp. adminstr. State Hosps. Mgmt. Bd., Ibadan, Nigeria, 1985-89; asst. DON Lincoln Hosp., Bronx, NY, 1977—78, 1989-90; asst. dir. Bronx Lebanon Hosp. Ctr., 1990—95; clin. instr., healthcare cons., 1999—. Fellow Internat. Biog. Ctr. Eng.; mem. Am. Coll. Hosp. Adminstrs., Am. Coll. Nursing Home Adminstrs., Inst. Health Svc. Adminstrs. Nigeria. Home: PO BOX 151 Centerport NY 11721-0151 Office Phone: 212-564-0500.

YADRICK, ROBERT MARTIN, operations analyst; b. Kansas City, Mo., Oct. 24, 1949; s. John George and Joanne Jean Yadrick; m. Patricia Eileen (Koelzer), May 30, 1986 (div. 2004); children: Lauren Nicole, John Nicholas; m. Virginia Sitz, July 29, 2009. BA, Rockhurst Coll., 1971; MA, U. Mo., 1973, PhD, 1975. Cert. profl. ergonomist Bd. Certification in Profl. Ergonomics, Inc. Asst. prof. psychology Columbia (Mo.) Coll., 1975-78; rsch. assoc. U. Mo., Columbia, 1978-79; sr. rsch. assoc. Ctrl.-N.E. Colo. Health Sys. Agy., Inc., Denver, 1979-82; sr. human factors engr. McDonnell Douglas Corp., St. Louis, 1982-90; rsch. scientist Metrica, Inc., San Antonio, 1991; pers. rsch. psychologist USAF Rsch. Lab., Brooks AFB, Tex., 1991-99; occupl. analyst USAF, Randolph AFB, Tex., 1999—, quality assurance mgr., 2001—09, ops. rsch. analyst, 2009—. Adj. lectr. U. Tex. San Antonio, Our Lady of the Lake U., St. Mary's U., Wayland Bapt. Univ.; editor newsletter Insight, Human Factors and Ergonomics Soc., Santa Monica, Calif., 1994-96, reviewer visual performance tech. group, 1995-97; reviewer jour. Behavior Rsch. Methods, Instruments and Computers, 1996. Contbr. articles to profl. jours. Recipient Lab. Dir.'s award Armstrong Lab., 1996. Mem.: Sigma Xi. Avocations: flying, hiking, water sports. Personal E-mail: sloper52@aol.com. Business E-Mail: robert.yadrick@randolph.af.mil.

YAEGER, DOUGLAS HARRISON, gas industry executive; b. St. Louis, Mar. 3, 1949; s. Walter Earl and Mary Eloise (Drinkwater) Y.; m. Lynn Mary Halloran, June 24, 1951; children: Lauren Harrison, Drew Halloran. BS, Miami U., Oxford, Ohio, 1971; MBA, St. Louis U., 1976. Sales asst. Miss. River Transmission Corp., St. Louis, 1974-75, coordinator mktg. and regulatory supply, 1975-78, coordinator mktg. and supply, 1978, mgr. mktg. and supply coordination, 1978-81, asst. v.p. mktg., 1981-82, v.p. mktg., 1982-86, sr. v.p. mktg., 1986-88, exec. v.p., 1988-90; v.p. Laclede Gas Co., St. Louis, 1990—97, pres., 1997—2000, chmn., CEO, 1999—2000; chmn., pres., CEO Laclede Group Inc., St. Louis, 2000—. Bd. dir. Am. Gas Assn., First Banks Inc., St. Louis. Dir. Barnes Jewish Hosp., St. Louis; bd. commr. St. Louis Sci. Ctr. Mem. Am. Gas Assn., So. Gass Assn., Interstate Natural Gas Assn., Assn. Corp. Growth, Sunset Country, Media, Strathalbyn Farm, The Planning Forum, St. Louis Club. Avocations: golf, fishing, hunting. Office: LACLEDE GAS COMPANY 720 Olive St Saint Louis MO 63101

YAES, ROBERT JOEL, radiologist, educator; b. NYC, July 11, 1942; s. Michael and Etta (Schwartz) Y.; m. Joyce Idelson, Nov. 17, 1986. BS, MIT, 1963, DSc, 1967; MB, Meml. U. Newfoundland, St. Johns, Can., 1978, MD, 1980. Diplomate Am. Bd. Radiology. Rsch. assoc. U. Helsinki, Finland, 1967-68; faculty assoc. U. Tex., Austin, 1968-70; Humbolt fellow U. Mainz, Fe. Republic of Germany, 1970-72; asst. prof. Meml. U. Newfoundland, St. Johns, 1972-76; resident Meml. Sloan Kettering Care Ctr., NYC, 1980-82, SUNY, Bklyn., 1982-85, fellow Stoneybrook, 1985-86; asst. prof. radiation medicine U. Ky. Med. Ctr., Lexington, 1988-92; asst. prof. radiation therapy U. Md. Med. Ctr., Balt., 1992—. Mem. AMA, Ky. Med. Soc., Am. Soc. Therapeutic Radiology and Oncology, Radiol. Soc. North Am., Am. Phys. Soc., Radiation Rsch. Soc. Achievements include research in applications of mathematical models to clinical radiation therapy, tumor heterogeneity, intrinsic radioresistance, altered fractionation schedules, Californium Neutron Brachytherapy. Office: FDA Divsn Med Imaging and Radiopharm Drug Products 5600 Fishers Ln Rockville MD 20857 Business E-Mail: robert.yaes@fda.hhs.gov. E-mail: yaes@cder.fda.gov.

YAFFE, BARBARA MARLENE, journalist; b. Montreal, Que., Can., Mar. 4, 1953; d. Allan and Anne (Freedman) Yaffe. Student, McGill U., 1970-73; BA, U. Toronto, 1974; B of Journalism, Carleton U., 1975. Reporter Montreal Gazette, 1975-76, Toronto Globe and Mail, 1976-79, reporter, columnist Halifax, N.S., 1979-81; chief nat. TV news bur. CBC, St. Johns, Nfld., Canada, 1981-84, Edmonton, Alta., Canada, 1983; reporter Toronto Globe and Mail, St. John's, 1984-86; editor Sunday Express, St. John's, 1987-88, Vancouver Sun, 1988-93, columnist, edit. bd. adv., 1993—. Recipient Gov. Gen.'s award, Roland Michener Found., 1977, Commentary award, Jack Webster Found., 2004, Animal Action award, Internat. Fund for Animal Welfare, 2004. Office: c/o Vancouver Sun Ste 1 200 Granville St Vancouver BC Canada V6C 3N3 Office Phone: 604-605-2189. Business E-Mail: byaffe@uancouversun.com.

YAFFE, JAMES, writer; b. Chgo., Mar. 31, 1927; s. Samuel and Florence (Scheinman) Y.; m. Elaine Gordon, Mar. 1, 1964; children: Deborah Ann, Rebecca Elizabeth, Gideon Daniel. Grad., Fieldston Sch., 1944; BA summa cum laude, Yale U., 1948. Prof. Colo. Coll., Colo. Springs, 1968—2002, prof. emeritus, 2002—. Author: Poor Cousin Evelyn, 1951, The Good-for-Nothing, 1953, What's the Big Hurry?, 1954, Nothing But the Night, 1959, Mister Margolies, 1962, Nobody Does You Any Favors, 1966, The American Jews, 1968, The Voyage of the Franz Joseph, 1970, So Sue Me!, 1972, Saul and Morris, Worlds Apart, 1982, A Nice Murder for Mom, 1988, Mom Meets Her Maker, 1990, Mom Doth Murder Sleep, 1991, Mom Among the Liars, 1992, My Mother the Detective, 1997; play The Deadly Game, 1960, (with Jerome Weidman) Ivory Tower, 1967, Cliffhanger, 2007; also TV plays, stories, essays, revs. Served with USNR, 1945-46. Recipient Nat. Arts Found award, 1968 Mem. P.E.N., Authors League, Writers Guild of Am., Dramatists Guild, A.A.U.P., Mystery Writers of Am., Phi Beta Kappa. Clubs: Elizabethan (Yale). Jewish. Avocations: music, bridge, movies. Home: 12 W 72 St New York NY 10023

YAFFE, STUART ALLEN, physician; b. Springfield, Ill., July 6, 1927; m. Natalie, 1952; children: Scott, Kim Yaffe Schoenburg. BS cum laude, U. Alaska, 1951; MD, St. Louis U., 1956. Diplomate Am. Bd. Family Practice. Intern St. Louis CIty Hosp., 1956-57, resident, 1957-58; physician pvt. practice, 1958—; clin. assoc. prof. So. Ill. U. Sch. Medicine., Springfield, 1971—; ptnr. Springfield Clinic, 1989—. With U.S. Army, 1945-47. Mem. AMA, Am. Acad. Family Physicians, Ill. Acad. Family Physicians, Ill. State Med. Soc., Sangamon County Med. Soc. Office: 1100 Centre West Dr Springfield IL 62704-2100 Home Phone: 217-546-3604; Office Phone: 217-793-9960.

YAGAMI, KAZUO, historian; s. Iko and Tomeko Yagami; m. Frances Tay; children: Michelle, Michael. BA in English, Daito Bunka U., Tokyo, 1981; PhD, Fla. State U., Tallahassee, 2002. Vis. asst. prof. U. North Fla., Jacksonville, 2002—03; lectr. U. No. Colo., Greeley, 2004—06; asst. prof. Savannah State U., Ga., 2006—. Author: Konoe Fumimaro and the Failure of Peace in Japan, 1931-1941: A Critical Appraisal of Three-time Prime Minister. Faculty and Rsch. and Publ. grantee, U. No. Colo., 2004, Japan-United States Friendship Commn. grantee, NE Asia Coun., Assn. Asian Studies, Inc., 2000, dissertation rsch. grantee, Fla. State U. Mem.: Am. Hist. Assn. (assoc.). Office: Savannah State Univ 3219 College St Savannah GA 31404 Home: 7845 Preservation Rd Tallahassee FL 32312 Personal E-mail: kazuoyagami@yahoo.com. Business E-Mail: yagamik@savstate.edu.

YAGDJIAN, KAREN, mathematics professor; PhD in Phys. & Math. Sciences, Moscow State U. Assoc. prof. U. Texas Pan Am., Edinburg, 2004. Author: (book) The Cauchy Problem for Hyperbolic Operators. Multiple Characteristics. Office: Univ TX-Pan Am 1201 W Univ Drive Edinburg TX 78541-2999 Business E-Mail: yagdjian@utpa.edu.

YAGGI, W. TIMOTHY, manufacturing executive; B, Princeton U., NJ; MBA in Mktg., Mich. State U. Direct mktg. position J. Crew, NYC; various sales and mktg. positions including mktg. mgr. personal care divsn. Norelco Consumer Products Co., Stamford, Conn.; with Whirlpool Corp., 1994—, various positions including v.p. global growth and brand mktg., gen. mgr. brand merchandising, gen. mgr. laundry mktg. strategy, various positions including gen. mgr. Roper and Estate, dir. mktg. Whirlpool cooking products, dir. mktg. Whirlpool brand dishwashers and compactors, v.p. ops. and strategy, 2000, v.p. KitchenAid, 2001—02, v.p. Whirlpool Brand N.Am., 2002, sr. v.p., gen. mgr. Brand Portfolio Group N.Am., 2002—06, exec. v.p. market ops., 2006—08; group pres. No. Am. Builder group Masco Corp., Taylor, Mich., 2008—. Office: Masco Corp 21001 Van Born Rd Taylor MI 48180

YAGLE, ANDREW EMIL, engineering educator; b. Ann Arbor, Mich., Sept. 17, 1956; s. Raymond Arthur and Anne Joan Yagle. BSEE, U. Mich., 1978; PhD, MIT, 1985, MS in Engring., 1985. Exxon tchg. fellow MIT, Cambridge, Mass., 1982—85; prof. elec. engring. U. Mich., Ann Arbor, 1985—, chief program advisor elec. engring., 2001—04. Contbr. numerous tech. papers to profl. jours. Recipient Presdl. Young Investigator award, NSF, 1988—93, Young Investigator award, Office of Naval Rsch., 1990—93. Mem.: IEEE (mem.-at-large, bd. govs. Signal Processing Soc. 1998—2000). Office: U Mich 1301 Beal Ave Ann Arbor MI 48109-2122 Office Phone: 734-763-9810. Office Fax: 734-763-1503. Business E-Mail: aey@eecs.umich.edu.

YAHYAOUI, NASR E., educational association administrator; b. Oujda, Morocco, Oct. 27, 1973; s. Boujemaa Yahyaoui and Naziha Abdellaoui; m. Jewell L. Ledoux, Nov. 8, 2002; 1 child, Abdullah S. BA in English Lang. and Lit. with Linguistics, Mohamed I U., Oujda Morocco, 1997; MA in French Lang. and Lit., U. Louisville, 2006. Cert. in microsoft office 1997 IPETI - Oujda Morocco, 1999; in practical tchg. AFMIK-Oujda Morocco, 1998. Instr. IDEM, Oujda, 1998—2001; gta and ptl U. Louisville, 2003—06, vis. scholar, 2006—, bd. mem. MEIS; instr. Somali Cmty., Louisville, 2004—06; program coord. Al-Nur Islamic Ctr., Louisville, 2008—, v.p., 2008—, 2008—. Islam. Avocations: soccer, swimming, camping, computers. Office: Univ of Louisville Dept of Modern Languages Louisville KY 40292 Business E-Mail: y0nasr02@louisville.edu.

YAKU, TAKEO T., computer scientist, educator; b. Tokyo, Oct. 21, 1947; s. Masao and Teru (Nagashima) Yaku. BSc, Jiyu Gakuen Coll., Tokyo, 1970; MSc, Waseda U., Tokyo, 1972, DSc, 1977. Rschr. Rsch. Inst. Sci. and Engring. Waseda U., Japan, 1975—76; vis. lectr. Tokai U., Hiratsuka, Japan, 1975—76, asst. prof., 1976—79, assoc. prof., 1979—85, Tokyo Denki U., Hatoyama, Japan, 1985—92; prof. Nihon U., Setagaya-Tokyo, 1992—. Rsch. assoc. Inst. Sci. and Tech. Waseda U., 1975—76, vis. lectr., 1979—92, Toyo U., Kawagoe, Japan, 1991—94, Tokyo Denki U., 1992—94, assoc. prof., Japan, 1985—92, chmn. curriculum bd. Sch. Sci. and Engring., 1991—92; vis. lectr. Tsuru U., 1994—95, Hitotsubashi U., 1995—96, Nigata U., 1996, 98, Shimane U., 2002, Musashino Art U., 2006—07; vice dir. Nihon U. Inst. Info. Sci. Coll. Humanities and Scis., Setagaya-Tokyo, 1994—98, chmn. dept. applied math., 1997—98, advisor dean in student job placement, 1998—2001, vice advisor dean in rsch. activities, 2004—05, chmn. earth info. math. scis. Grad. Sch. Integrated Basic Scis., 2004—05, vice advisor dean in student job placement, 2005—, chmn. earth info. math. scis. Grad. Sch. Integrated Basic Scis., 2007—. Author: (with others) Micro Computer Handbook, 1985, (with others) Structured Editors, 1987; editorial bd. mem: Transac. Inst. Electronics, Information and Communication Engrs., 1993-98; contbr. articles to profl. jours. Mem. examination com. Nat. Pers. Authority, Japan, 1994-96; trustee Japan Assn. Devel. Info. Edn., 2005-, Japan Assn. Edn. Info. Studies, 2007-. Grantee, Sakkokai Fund, 1978—81; Travel fellow, IBM, 1978. Fellow Tokau U. Alumni Ski Alpine Club; mem. Am. Math. Soc., Assn. Computing Machinery (life), Japan Soc. Computer Assisted Instrn., Soc. Indsl. and Applied Math., Jiyu Gakuen Alumni Football Club. Buddhist. Avocations: mountain climbing, skiing, football. Home: 3-4-4-405 Yagisawa Nishi-Tokyo 202-0022 Japan Office: Nihon U 3-25-40 Sakura-Josui Setagaya Tokyo 156-8550 Japan Personal E-mail: yaku@acm.org. Business E-Mail: yaku@cs.chs.nihon-u.ac.jp.

YALAM, ARNOLD ROBERT, allergist, immunologist, consultant; b. NYC, Apr. 11, 1940; s. Herman and Sylvia (Taber) Y.; m. Carol Ann Strocker, June 16, 1964; children: John, Matthew. AB, Johns Hopkins U., 1960; MD, U. Md., Balt., 1964. Diplomate Am. Bd. Internal Medicine, Am. Bd. Allergy and Immunology. Intern Jackson Meml. Hosp., Miami, Fla., 1964-65; resident in internal medicine SUNY Downstate Med. Ctr., Bklyn., 1965-67; fellow Scripps Clinic and Rsch. Found., La Jolla, Calif., 1967-68; cons. allergist and immunologist San Diego, 1970—. Maj. US Army, 1968—70. Fellow Am. Acad. Allergy and Immunoloy; mem. Am. Soc. Addiction Medicine (cert.), San Diego Allergy Soc.

YALAMANCHI, RAMU, Internet company executive; BS in Computer Sci., U. Ill., Urbana-Champaign. Regional sales mgr. AdKnowledge; bus. devel., product mgr. eGroups; co-founder, ptnr. SponsorNet New Media, 1995; founder hi5 Networks, Inc., 2003, CEO, 2003—09, chief product officer, 2009—. Office: hi5 Networks, Inc 55 Second St, Ste 300 San Francisco CA 94105 Office Phone: 415-404-6094. Office Fax: 415-704-3482.

YALAMANCHILI, PRAVEEN RAJ, nephrologist; s. Krishna Prasad and Ranya Yalamanchili. MBBS, Osmania Med. Coll., Hyderabad, India., 1999. Diplomate Am. Bd. Internal Medicine, 2005. Contbr. to numerous presentation, to numerous rsch. papers. Personal E-mail: prawin@gmail.com.

YALDEN, MAXWELL FREEMAN, Canadian diplomat; b. Toronto, Ont., Can., Apr. 12, 1930; s. Frederick and Marie (Smith) Y.; m. Janice Shaw, Jan. 28, 1952; children: Robert, Cicely (dec.). BA, Victoria Coll., U. Toronto, 1952; MA, U. Mich., 1954, PhD, 1956; D.U. (hon.), U. Ottawa; LLD (hon.), Carleton U. With Can. Dept. External Affairs, 1956-69, asst. undersec. state, 1969-73, dep. minister communications, 1973-77, commr. ofcl. langs., 1977-84; Can. amb. to Belgium and Luxembourg, 1984-87; chief commr. Can. Human Rights Comms., Ottawa, 1987—96; mem. UN Human Rights Com., 1996—2004. Decorated companion Order of Can. Office: 201 31 Durham Pvt Ottawa ON Canada K1M 2J1

YALE, JOHN PAUL, computer systems developer; b. Uhrichsville, Ohio, Sept. 4, 1945; s. Vernon Elna and Joan (Papworth) Y.; m. Mary Anne Hinkley, Feb. 9, 1966 (dec. May 2001); children: John Vernon, Eric Kendall; m. Ann M. Willey, Oct. 2006. AAS, Orange County C.C., 1968; BS, Ohio U., 1971; MS in Engring., U. New Haven, 2006. Dir. Pub. Broadcasting, Athens, Ohio, 1969-71; freelance prodr./dir. GGT, Niantic, Conn., 1971-79; dir. media svcs. L & M Hosps., New London, Conn., 1979-96; dir. sys. devel. C&E group MPTN, Ledyard, Conn., 1996—. Mem. Internat. TV Assn., Internat. Telecomf. Assn., Assn. fo Multimedia Internat., Toastmasters Internat., Project Mgmt. Inst. Home: Westgate Farm 299 Pond Hill Rd Chatham NY 12037 Business E-Mail: john@jpyale.net.

YALE (YELEYENIDE-YALE), MELPOMENE FOTINE, researcher, anthropologist, archaeologist, art historian, conservator; b. NYC, Mar. 31, 1963; d. John P. and Serina Yale (Yeleyenide-Yale). BA in Art History, Columbia U., 1985, MA in Art History and Arch., 1998, MA in Anthropology, 2001; studied lithics and flint knapping with Prof. William Parry, CUNY Grad. Ctr., 2001; studied, Art Students League N.Y., 1987; studied fine art, Nat. Acad. Sch. Fine Arts, 1997—98; studied art history, painting, drawing, inorganic and organic chemistry, Lehman Coll., 1980—81, studied, 1987—88, studied, 1995, studied, 1996, Hunter Coll., 1983; studied with renowned iconographer Constantine Youssis, 1996—98. Sci. asst. dept. anthropology The Am. Mus. Natural History, NYC, 1987—89, collections mgmt. asst. dept. anthropology, 1989—90; fieldwork archeologist (excavations) Brit. Sch. Arch., Palaikastro, Crete, 1990, 1991; fieldwork archeologist Fordham U., Rose Hill Excavations, NY, 2000; conservator The Benaki Mus., Athens, Greece, 1991, 1992, The Monastery of St. John the Theologian, Patmos, Greece, 1992, The Hispanic Soc. Am., NYC, 1989—93, Brit. Sch. Archeol. Excavations, Palaikastro, Crete, 1990, 1991, Nat. Acad., 1997, Lilly Hollander Conservation Studio, NY, 1998—99, N.Y. Acad. Medicine, NY, 1999, Sherman Fairchild Ctr. Objects Conservation, Met. Mus. Art, NY, 2000; pvt. conservator, 1993—; rsch. asst. Ani project Columbia U.-World Monuments Found., NY, 1997; curatorial asst. Nat. Acad. N.Y., 1997; rsch. asst. to prof. emeritus Ralph Solecki and Dr. Rose Solecki Shanidar project Columbia U., 2001—03, coord. Ralph Holloway Endocast collection preservation and rsch. project, 2002—04, ind. rschr. prehistoric collection, 2003—. Designer (group fashion show) Chinese New Yr. Festival, Columbia Univ., 1984. Vol. Greek Orthodox Clergy Laity Congress, Greek Orthodox Archdiocese N.Am. and S.Am., NYC, 1984, NY Convocation for Peace in the Middle East, US Interreligious Com. for Peace in the Middle East, 1990. Recipient Cert. of merit Bd. Edn. Art Exhbn., N.Y. Daily News, Lever Ho., N.Y.C., 1981, Cert. of Achievement, N.Y. Acad. Medicine, 1999, Mcpl. hon., Moudros Lemnos Greece, 2004, Mcpl. award, 2005. Mem.: N.Y. State Archaeol. Assn., Archeol. Inst. Am., Registered Profl. Archaeologists, Am. Inst. Conservation (profl.), Am. Anthrop. Assn., The Prehistoric Soc. Achievements include research in emergence of human cognition in the Palaeolithic as indicated by stone tools and art; research on brain casting techniques; independent research towards a PhD on emergence of human cognition in Palaeolithic Period of Greece and Aegean based on Palaeontological-Palaeoanthropological data, stone tools, art, & their relation; to and their influence throughout the Palaeoanthropogeographic region of Europe and the World. Avocations: flintknapping, mosaics, painting, collecting art, and stone tools for study. Personal E-mail: mfy2@columbia.edu.

YALE (YELEYENIDE-YALE), SERINA, philanthropist, apparel designer; b. Moudros, Lemnos, Greece, Oct. 16, 1924; d. Adam and Fotika Chiros; m. John P. Yale (Yeleyenide-Yale); children: Mary Anne, Andrew Chris, Melpomene Fotine. Grad., Washington Irving HS, NYC, 1941. Draper haute couture dept. Henri Bendel, NYC, 1941—46, Bergdorf Goodman, NYC, 1946—53; asst. designer R&K Originals, NYC, 1953—56. Pres., mem. bd. dirs. Jr. Philoptochos Philanthropic Soc., Ch. of Holy Trinity, Greek Orthodox Cath. Ch. NYC, 1942—49, mem. bd., 1949—91; pres. bd. dirs. Philoptochos Philanthropic Soc., Ch. St. Spyridon, NYC, 1971—72, 1977—78; chair supervisory com. St. Michael's Home for the Aged, Yonkers, NY, 1982—84; hospitality chair 27th Greek Orthodox Clergy Laity Congress, Greek Orthodox Archdiocese N.Am. and S.Am., NYC, 1984; pres. NY Diocese Philptochos Philanthropic Soc., Greek Orthodox Archdiocese of North and South Am., NYC, 1986—88; Greek sec., mem. exec. bd. Nat. Philoptochos Philanthropic Soc., NYC, 1986—88, cardiac chmn., 1986—88; coord. benefit luncheon Greek Children's Fund, Meml. Hosp. Sloan-Kettering Cancer Ctr., NYC, 1988—90; mem. organizing com. NY Convocation for Peace in the Mid. East, US Interreligious Com. for Peace in the Mid. East, 1990, del. Ch. Women United, 1990; treas., bd. dirs. Ch. St. Spyridon, NYC, 1990—91; hon. amb. of hospitality and goodwill Greek Orthodox Archdiocese of N. and S.Am., 1933—54, Greek war relief organizer, 1941—54; hon. amb. hospitality and goodwill Consulate Gen. Greece, NYC, 1944—54; Sunday sch. tchr. Ch. of Holy Trinity, Greek Orthodox Cath. of NYC, 1938—54; asst. treas., bd. dirs. Ch. Women United, NYC, 1986—92, NGO rep. UN, 1991—92. Recipient Mcpl. honor, Moudros Lemnos Greece, 2004, Mcpl. award, 2005, Title of Archon, Order of St. Andrew of Ecumenical Patriarchate in Constantinople, 1966, Archdiocesan Medal of St. Paul, Archbishop Iakovos of N.Am. and S.Am., 1972. Home: 4555 Henry Hudson Pky New York NY 10471

YALOW, ROSALYN SUSSMAN, biophysicist; b. NYC, July 19, 1921; d. Simon and Clara (Zipper) Sussman; m. Aaron Yalow, June 6, 1943; children: Benjamin, Elanna. AB, Hunter Coll., 1941; MS, U. Ill., Urbana, 1942, PhD, 1945; DSc (hon.), U. Ill., Chgo., 1974, Phila. Coll. Pharmacy and Sci., 1976, NY Med. Coll., 1976, Med. Coll. Wis., Milw., 1977, Yeshiva U., 1977, Southampton Coll., NY, 1978, Bucknell U., 1978, Princeton U., 1978, Jersey City State Coll., 1979, Med. Coll. Pa., 1979, Manhattan Coll., 1979, U. Vt., 1980, U. Hartford, 1980, Rutgers U., 1980, Rensselaer Poly. Inst., 1980, Colgate U., 1981, U. So. Calif., 1981, Clarkson Coll., 1982, U. Miami, 1983, Washington U., St. Louis, 1983, Adelphi U., 1983, U. Alta., 1983, SUNY, 1984, Tel Aviv U., 1985, Claremont U., Calif., 1986, Mills Coll., Oakland, Calif., 1986, Cedar Crest Coll., Allentown, Pa., 1988, Drew U., Madison, NJ, 1988, Lehigh

U., 1988; LHD (hon.), Hunter Coll., 1978; DSc (hon.), San Francisco State U., 1989, Technion-Israel Inst. Tech., Haifa, 1989, Med. Coll. Ohio Toledo, 1991; LHD (hon.), Sacred Heart U., Conn., 1978, St. Michael's Coll., Winooski Park, Vt., 1979, Johns Hopkins U., 1979, Coll. St. Rose, 1988, Spertus Coll. Judaica, Chgo., 1988; DHC (hon.), U. Rosario, Argentina, 1980, U. Ghent, Belgium, 1984; D. Humanities and Letters (hon.), Columbia U., 1984; DSc (hon.), Fairleigh Dickinson U., 1992, Conn. Coll., 1992, Smith Coll., Northampton, Mass., 1994, Union Coll., Schenectady, 1994. Diplomate Am. Bd. Scis. Lectr., asst. prof. physics Hunter Coll., 1946-50; physicist, asst. chief radioisotope service VA Med. Ctr., Bronx, NY, 1950-70, chief nuclear medicine, 1970-80, acting chief radioisotope service, 1968-70, sr. med. investigator emeritus; research prof. Mt. Sinai Sch. Med., CUNY, 1968-74, Disting. Service prof., 1974-79, Solomon A. Berson Disting. prof.-at-large, 1986—; chmn. dept. clin. scis. Montefiore Med. Ctr., Bronx, 1980-85; Disting. prof.-at-large Albert Einstein Coll. Med., Yeshiva U., 1979-85, prof. emeritus, 1986. Cons. Lenox Hill Hosp., NYC, 1956—62, WHO, Bombay, 1978; sec. U.S. Nat. Com. on Med. Physics, 1963—67; mem. nat. com. Radiation Protection, subcom. 13, 1957, Pres.'s Study Group on Careers for Women, 1966—72; sr. med. investigator VA, 1972—92, sr. med. investigator emeritus, 1992—. Co-editor: Hormone and Metabolic Research, 1973—79; editl. adv. coun. Acta Diabetologica Latina, 1975—77, Ency. Universalis, 1978—, editl. bd. Mt. Sinai Jour. Medicine, 1976—79, Diabetes, 1976, Endocrinology, 1967—72, contbr. numerous articles to profl. jours. Bd. dirs. NY Diabetes Assn., 1974. Recipient VA William S. Middleton Med. Rsch. award, 1960, Eli Lilly award, Am. Diabetes Assn., 1961, Van Slyke award, NY met. sect. Am. Assn. Clin. Chemists, 1968, ACP award, 1971, Dickson prize, U. Pitts., 1971, Howard Taylor Ricketts award, U. Chgo., 1971, Gairdner Found. Internat. award, 1971, Commemorative medallion, Am. Diabetes Assn., 1972, Bernstein award, Med. Soc. State NY, 1974, Boehringer-Mannheim Corp. award, Am. Assn. Clin. Chemists, 1975, Sci. achievement award, AMA, 1975, Exceptional Svc. award, VA, 1975, A. Cressy Morrison award, NY Acad. Scis., 1975, sustaining membership award, Assn. Mil. Surgeons, 1975, Disting. Achievement award, Modern Medicine, 1976, Albert Lasker Basic Med. Rsch. award, 1976, La Madonnina Internat. prize, Milan, 1977, Golden Plate award, Am. Acad. Achievement, 1977, Nobel prize in physiology or medicine, 1977, citation of esteem, St. John's U., 1979, G. von Hevesy medal, 1978, Rosalyn S. Yalow R&D award established, Am. Diabetes Assn., 1978, Banting medal, 1978, Torch of Learning award, Am. Friends Hebrew U., 1978, Virchow Gold medal, Virchow-Pirquet Med. Soc., 1978, Gratum Genus Humanum Gold medal, World Fedn. Nuc. Medicine or Biology, 1978, Jacobi medallion, Assoc. Alumni Mt. Sinai Sch. Med., 1978, Jubilee medal, Coll. of New Rochelle, 1978, VA Exceptional Svc. award, 1978, Fed. Woman's award, 1961, Harvey lectr., 1966, Am. Gastroenterol. Assn. Meml. lectr., 1972, Joslin lectr., New Eng. Diabetes Assn., 1972, 1st Hagedorn Meml. lectr., Acta Endocrinologica Congress, 1973, Franklin I. Harris Meml. lectr., 1973, Sarasota Med. award for achievement and excellence, 1979, Gold medal, Phi Lambda Kappa, 1980, Achievement in Life award, Ency. Britannica, 1980, Theobald Smith award, 1982, Pres.'s Cabinet award, U. Detroit, 1982, John and Samuel Bard award in med. and sci., Bard Coll., 1982, Disting. Rsch. award, Dallas Assn. Retarded Citizens, 1982, Nat. medal of Sci., 1988, Abram L. Sachar Silver medallion, Brandeis U., 1989, Disting. Scientist of Yr. award, ARCS, NYC, 1989, Golden Scroll award, The Jewish Advocate, Boston, 1989, spl. award, Clin. Ligand Assay Soc., Washington, 1988, numerous others. Fellow: Clin. Soc. N.Y. Diabetes Assn., Am. Coll. Radiology (assoc. in physics), N.Y. Acad. Scis. (chmn. biophysics divsn. 1964—65); mem.: NAS, Am. Physiol. Soc., Endocrine Soc. (pres. 1978, Kocn award 1972), Soc. Nuc. Medicine, Soc. Nuc. Medicine (hon.), Am. Gastroenterol. Assn. (hon.), Am. Coll. Nuc. Physicians (hon.), Harvey soc. (hon.), Med. Assn. Argentina (hon.), Diabetes Soc. Argentina (hon.), The N.Y. Acad. Medicine (hon.), N.Y. Roentgen Soc. (hon.), Biophys. Soc., Am. Assn. Physicists in Medicine, Radiation Rsch. Soc., Am. Phys. Soc., Am. Acad. Arts and Scis., Tau Beta Pi, Sigma Delta Epsilon, Pi Mu Epsilon, Sigma Pi Sigma, Sigma Xi, Phi Beta Kappa. Office: Vet Affairs Med Ctr 130 W Kingsbridge Rd Bronx NY 10468-3904*

YAMADA, KENNETH MANAO, cell biologist; s. Paul Manao and Masaye Yamada; m. Susan Jane Sleeper, July 1, 1973. BA in Biol. Scis., Stanford U., 1966, PhD in Biol. Scis., 1971, MD, 1972. Intern Seton Med. Ctr., Daly City, Calif., 1972-73; commd. lt. USPHS, 1974, advanced through grades to capt., 1982—2003, ret., 2003; sect. chief Nat. Cancer Inst., Bethesda, Md., 1980-90; lab. chief Nat. Inst. Dental and Craniofacial Rsch., NIH, Bethesda, 1990—. Mem. Cell Biology Study sect. NIH, 1979—83; mem. external adv. com. Cancer Rsch. Ctr. Howard U., 1979—88; co-chmn. Gordon Conf. on Fibronectin, 1982; Stadtler lectr. U. Tex. Sys. Cancer Ctr. M.D. Anderson Hosp., 1988; Swerling lectr. Dana-Farber Cancer Inst. Harvard Med. Sch., 1988; Retzius lectr. Karolinska Inst., 2005; Leonardo lectr. San Raffaele Rsch. Inst., Milan. Editor: Jour. Cell Biology, 1999—; contbr. more than 350 publs. to biomed. lit. Recipient Eli Luke and Jacob David Rsch. award, 1972, Sr. Lectureship award, Am. Soc. Matrix Bio., 2004, Disting. Scientist award, AADR, 2008. Fellow: AAAS; mem.: Soc. Devel. Biology, Southeastern Cancer Rsch. Assn. (bd. dirs. 1980—83), Am. Soc. Matrix Biology (coun. 2003—), Internat. Soc. Matrix Biology (coun. 1994—2006), Am. Soc. Biochemistry and Molecular Biology, Am. Soc. Cell Biology (coun. 1992—95), Sigma Xi, Phi Beta Kappa. Office: NIDCR Nat Inst Health 30 Convent Dr Bldg 30 Rm 426 Bethesda MD 20892-4370 Office Phone: 301-496-9124. Business E-Mail: kenneth.yamada@nih.gov.

YAMADA, KOHEI, retired art educator; b. Osaka, Japan, Mar. 21, 1926; s. Tokujiro and Hisako Yamada; m. Sachiko Fujimoto, Dec. 1952; 1 child, Ruka Tamai. BA, Kyoto U., Japan, 1950; LittD, Osaka U., 1994. Tchr. Hyogo Prefectural High Sch., Ashiya, Japan, 1950-53; fellow Kyoto U., 1953-62; lectr. Naniwa Jr. Coll., 1962-64, Osaka U. Arts, 1964-71; prof. Osaka U. of Arts, 1972, dean of faculty, 1975-90, prof. grad. sch., 1993—2003, prof. emeritus, 2003—. Lectr. Doshisha U., Kyoto, 1973—96; lectr. grad. sch. Kansei Gakin U., Kobe, Japan, 1980—2003. Author: All of Dostoevsky's, 1973, The Lightning Flashes of Toledo, 1973, Science of Russian Arts, 1994, Dostoevsky and Chekhov, 1999, Meditation on the Moon, 2001, Illusion of Odalisque, 2003, Dostoevsky and Modernism, 2005, On the Surface of Black Velazquez, GOYA, Manet and Japanese Dark, 2007; editor: The Idea of Film History, 2008, The Image Movement of Dostoevsky. Councilor Soc. Ethno Arts. Mem.: Japan Art History Soc., Japan Soc. Image Arts and Scis. (v.p.), Japanese Soc. for Aesthetics. Home: Hashiridani 1-22-22 Hirakata City Japan Office: Osaka Univ of Arts Minamigawachi Kanancho-Higashiyama Osaka Japan

YAMADA, TOHRU, biologist, educator, researcher, director; b. Hadano, Kanagawa, Japan, June 30, 1975; s. Yoshio and Tamiko Yamada; m. Kaori Horiguchi, Sept. 13, 2005; 1 child, Haruki K. Bachelor's degree, Tokyo Inst. Tech., 1999, Master's degree, 2001, PhD, 2003. Post-doctoral fellow dept. microbiology/immunology U. Ill. Coll. Medicine, Chgo., 2003—, rsch. asst. prof. dept. surg. oncology, 2004—06; dir drug devel. CDG Therapeutics Inc., 2006—; cons. Reuters Insight, 2008—. Contbr. articles to profl. jours., chapters to books. First Class scholar, Japan Student Svcs. Orgn., 1999. Mem.: Am. Soc. Gene Therapy, Am. Assn. Cancer Rsch., Am. Soc. Microbiology. Office: U Ill Coll Medicine Chgo 840 South Wood St Chicago IL 60612 Personal E-mail: tohru630@gmail.com. Business E-Mail: tohru@uic.edu.

YAMAGUCH, YURIKO FUJITA, artist; b. Japan, Jan. 25, 1948; came to the U.S., 1971; d. Alexander and Michi (Hirose) Fujita; m. Hiroyuki Yamaguchi, Mar. 25, 1975; children: Seiji, Mariko. BA, U. Calif., Berkeley, 1975; MFA, U. Md., 1979. Instr. U. Md., College Park, 1988—97; adj. faculty Corcoran Sch. Art, Washington, 1988-97; asst. prof. George Washington U., 2003—. Vis. artist Md. Inst. Art, Balt., 1991, Balt., 95, Mass. Coll. Art, Boston, 1994. One-woman shows include Columbia U., NY, Howard Scott Gallery, N.Y.C., 2005, Mus. Contemporary Art, Ise, Japan, 2005, exhibited in group shows at Hirshhorn Mus., 1984, L.A. County Mus., 1987, Koplin Gallery, L.A., 1991, 1994, 1996, 1999, 2002, 2007, Gallery Emon, Japan, 1997, 2000, Numark Gallery, 1999, 2003, 2005, Adamson Gallery, 2009, exhibited in group shows at Del. Ctr. for Contemporary Arts, 2001, Suyama Space, Seattle, 2002, Mus. Modern Art, Kanagawa, Japan, 2004, Represented in permanent collections Atlanta Internat. Airport, Hirshhorn Mus., Nat. Mus. Women in Arts, Nat. Mus. Am. Art, Smith Coll. Art Mus., Corcoran Gallery of Art. Recipient award Rockfeller Found. Bellangio Ctr., 2009, Myrthine & LouisJ. Kaep Meml. Prize Nat. Acad. Museum, NY, 2008, Disting. Aluminus award U. Md., 2008, Benesse award, 2005, Joan Mitchell award, 2005, Am. Acad. Arts & Letter award, 2006; Va. Mus. Fine Arts fellow, 1988, 85, 2001; Mid-Atlantic Found. fellow, 1995; Va. Commn. Arts grantee, 1994, 2000, Salzburg Kunstlerhaus Residency grantee, 1993; Franz and Virginia Bauer grantee, 2004. Home: 1517 Snughill Ct Vienna VA 22182-1724 E-mail: yuriko414@aol.com.

YAMAGUCHI, DEAN TAKAO, medical educator, researcher; s. Jiro and Elaine Chizuru Yamaguchi; m. Susan Sueko Hondo, June 19, 1977; children: Dean Jared Norio, Tory Jordan Emi, Eden Jami Miki. MD, Tulane U., New Orleans, 1977, PhD, 1978. Diplomate Am. Bd. Internal Medicine, 1982, subspecialty nephrology Am. Bd. Internal Medicine, 1986. Intern ob-gyn Charity Hosp. La., New Orleans, 1978—79; intern internal medicine Tulane U. Affiliated Program in Internal Medicine, New Orleans, 1979, resident internal medicine, 1980—82; fellow nephrology UCLA-Wadsworth VA Med. Ctr. Program, 1982—84; assoc. investigator VA Med. Ctr. West LA, 1984—86, rsch. assoc., 1986—90, clin. investigator, 1990—95, assoc. dir. for rsch., geriat. rsch., edn., and clin. ctr., 1995—2000; assoc. chief of staff R&D VA Greater LA Healthcare Sys., 2000—. Adj. instr. anatomy Tulane U. Sch. Medicine, New Orleans, 1978—81; asst. prof. medicine in residence UCLA Sch. Medicine, 1984—91, assoc. prof. medicine in residence, 1991—2000; prof. medicine in residence David Geffen Sch. Medicine, UCLA, 2000—; sci. adv. coun. Am. Fedn. for Aging Rsch., NYC, 2005—; merit rev. bd. endocrinology B VHA, Washington, 2006—; bd. dirs. Brentwood Biomedical Rsch. Inst., LA, Sepulveda Rsch. Corp., Calif. Asst. baseball coach Taft H.S., Woodland Hills, Calif., 2003. Recipient Merck Manual award, Tulane U., 1977, Owl Club Tchg. award, 1978, 1979, Arthur Cherkin award, UCLA Multicampus Program in Geriat. and Gerontology, 2000; grantee, VHA, 1986—; fellow, Nat. Kidney Found., 1984—85, Hiroshima Internat. Coun. for Med. Care of the Radiation Exposed, HICARE, 1992. Mem.: Soc. for Exptl. Biology and Medicine, Am. Physiol. Soc., Endocrine Soc., Internat. Bone and Mineral Soc., Am. Soc. for Bone and Mineral Rsch. (Fuller-Albright Young Investigator award 1991), Internat. Soc. Nephrology, Alpha Omega Alpha, Phi Lambda Upsilon, Phi Beta Kappa. Avocation: coaching baseball and softball. Office: VA Greater Los Angeles Healthcare System 11301 Wilshire Blvd Los Angeles CA 90073 Office Fax: 310-268-4856. Business E-Mail: dean.yamaguchi@va.gov.

YAMAGUCHI, KRISTI TSUYA, ice skater; b. Hayward, Calif., July 12, 1971; d. Jim and Carole (Doi) Yamaguchi; m. Bret Hedican, July 8, 2000; children: Keara Kiyomi, Emma Yoshiko. World Junior Champion, 1988; World Skating Champion, 1991, 1992; US Skating Champion, 1992; Gold medalist, Figure Skating Albertville Olympic Games, 1992; World Profl. Figure Skating Champion, 1994; ice skater Stars On Ice tour, 1996—2002, spl. guest star, 2003—04. Founder, pres. bd. dirs. Always Dream Found., 1996—; goodwill amb. Winter Olympics, Salt Lake City, 2002. Performer: (TV series) Dancing with the Stars, 2008 (winner, becoming the first woman to win the competition since the show's premiere, 2008). Recipient Women First award, YWCA, 1993; named Skater of the Yr., 1996, Favorite Female Athlete, Nickelodeon's Kid's Choice Awards, 1996—98, Athlete of the Yr. for figure skating, US Olympic Com., 1989; named to World Figure Skating Hall of Fame, 1999, US Figure Skating Hall of Fame, 1998, US Olympic Com. Olympic Hall of Fame, 2005. Avocations: tennis, rollerblading, reading, dance. Office: Always Dream Found 1203 Preservation Park Way Ste 102 Oakland CA 94612

YAMAGUCHI, MASAYA, musician, educator; b. Japan, July 18, 1970; s. Shigenori and Mieko Yamaguchi. BA in English, Meikai U., 1994; MA in Jazz Performance, CCNY, 1999. Author: The Complete Thesaurus of Musical Scales, 1999, Symmetrical Scales for Jazz Improvisation, 2001, Pentatonicism in Jazz: Creative Aspects & Practice, 2002;: 2d edit., 2006, John Coltrane Plays Coltrane Changes, 2003, A Creative Approach to Multi-Tonic Changes: Beyond Coltrane's Harmonic Formula, 2004, Charlie Parker "Yardbird" Originals, 2005; contbr. articles to profl. jours.; author: CD Crossings, 2009. Home: 321 W 54th St Apt 305 New York NY 10019 Personal E-mail: masayayamaguchi@hotmail.com.

YAMAK, SIBEL, social sciences educator, researcher; b. Turkey; d. Tuncer and Sevgi Karakadioglu; m. Ethem Yamak; 1 child, Ali Can. BA in Mgmt. with honors, Bosphorous U., Istanbul, 1985, MA in Mgmt., 1990, PhD in Orgn. Theory, 1996. Assoc. prof. mgmt. Galatasaray U., Istanbul, Turkey, 2002—07, prof. mgmt., 2007—; assoc. editor Yönetim Arastirmalari Dergisi, 2009—. Vis. prof. Paris 1 Pantheon Sorbonne U.; vis. rschr. BETA, Strasbourg, France; presenter in field. Editl. bd. mem. Soc. & Bus. Rev., 2005—; contbr. articles to profl. jours. Recipient Literati award, Emerald Group Publishing, UK, 2007. Mem.: Strategic Mgmt. Soc., European Acad. Mgmt. (corp. governance strategic interest group vice chair 2009—), European Group Orgnl. Studies, Acad. Mgmt. (med divsn. rsch. coord.-elect 2005—06, rsch. coord. mgmt. edn. & devel. divsn. 2006—07). Avocations: painting, travel, reading, languages. Office: Galatasaray Univ Ciragan cad N36 Ortakoy Istanbul 34357 Turkey Office Fax: 90212 2582283. Personal E-mail: sibelyamak@gmail.com. Business E-Mail: syamak@gsu.edu.tr.

YAMAMOTO, ALAN H., lawyer; b. Dinuba, Calif., Oct. 13, 1945; s. Lou K. and Sadie S. Yamamoto; m. Sandra L. Johnston Socci, May 6, 1989. BS, U. Calif., Berkeley, 1967; JD, Case Western Res. U., Cleve., 1973. Bar: Ohio 1973, US Dist. Ct. (no. dist.) Ohio 1974, Washington DC 1978, Va. 1986, Ct. Appeals, (4th cir.) 1986, US Dist. Ct. (ea. dist.) Va. 1986, US Dist. Ct. DC 1999. Atty. Cleve. Legal Aid Soc., 1973—77; trial atty. U.S. Dept. Labor Solicitor's Office, Arlington, Va., 1977—86; atty. Law Offices of Alan H. Yamamoto, Alexandria, 1986—; of counsel Pearlstein & Assocs., Washington, 1986—. Pro bono atty. Animal Welfare League, Alexandria, 1995—. Dir. Roseann Finigan Meisburg Found., Alexandria, 1997—. Sgt. US Army, 1967—70. Decorated Bronze Star with Oak Leaf Cluster U.S. Army, Air medal, Viet Nam Svc. medal, Viet Nam Campaign medal. Mem.: ABA, DC Bar Assn., Nat. Assn. Criminal Def. Attorneys, Fairfax Bar Assn., Alexandria Bar Assn., Va. Bar Assn. Office: Law Offices of Alan H Yamamoto 643 S Washington St Alexandria VA 22314 Office Fax: 703-684-6643. Business E-Mail: yamamoto.law@verizon.net.

YAMAMOTO, DONALD YUKIO, United States Ambassador to Ethiopia; b. Seattle, Mar. 13, 1953; s. Hideo and Lillian Yamamoto; m. Margaret Darling, Dec. 11, 1982; 2 children. BA, Columbia Coll., 1975; East Asian cert., Columbia U., 1978; M in Internat. Affairs, Columbia U., NYC, 1978. With Fgn. Svc. US Dept. State, 1980—, staff aide to amb. Beijing, human rights officer, 1989, prin. officer Fukuoka Consulate Japan, charge d'Affaires US Embassy Asmara Eritrea, dep. dir. East African Affairs, 1998—2000, US amb. to Republic of Djibouti, 2000—03, dep. asst. sec. of state Bur. African Affairs, 2003—06, US amb. to Ethiopia Addis Ababa, 2006—. Office: DOS Amb 2030 Addis Ababa Pl Washington DC 20521-2030*

YAMAMOTO, HIRO-AKI, toxicology and pharmacology educator; b. Shimonoseki, Japan, July 9, 1947; s. Hanzo and Haruko (Watanabe) Y.; m. Kyoko Kinoshita, Sept. 24, 1976; children: Takeomi, Mika. Grad. in pharmacy, Fukuoka U., Japan, 1970; MS, Kyushu U., Fukuoka, 1972, PhD, 1975. Postgrad. researcher in pharmacology U. Calif., San Francisco, 1975-76, vis. scientist, 1979-80; vis. fellow NIH, Bethesda, Md., 1976-77; prof. Fukuyama (Japan) U., 1983-89; asst. prof. toxicology and pharmacology U. Tsukuba, Japan, 1977-83, assoc. prof., 1989—. Vis. prof. U. Mo., 1981-82. Author: Calcium and Biological Systems, 1985, Higienic Chemistry and Public Health, 1990; contbr. articles to sci. jours. Mem. Fukuyama Pollution Measures Com., 1984-89. Mem. NY Acad. Scis., Am. Soc. Pharm. and Exptl. Therapeutics, Japan Soc. Toxicology (trustee). Avocations: tennis, baseball. Home: Otto Minami 1-chome 26-1 Tsuchiura 300-0845 Japan Office: U Tsukuba Grad Sch Comprehensive Human Sci 1-1-1 Tsukuba Tsukuba 305-8575 Japan Office Phone: 81-029-853-3485. Business E-Mail: hiro_aki@jcom.home.ne.jp.

YAMAMOTO, HISASHI, chemistry professor; b. Kobe, Japan, July 16, 1943; s. Taro and Junko (Harima) Yamamoto. BS, Kyoto U., Japan, 1967; PhD, Harvard U., 1971. With Toray Industries, Inc., 1971—72; instr. Kyoto U., 1972-76, lectr., 1976-77; assoc. prof. U. Hawaii, Honolulu, 1977-80, Nagoya U., Japan, 1980-83, prof. applied chemistry, 1983—2002, councilor, 1997—99; Arthur Holly Compton disting. svc. prof. chemistry U. Chgo., 2002—. Contbr. articles to sci. jours.; mem. editl. bd.: Organic Syntheses, 1988—93, mem. adv. bd.:, 1993—, Organic Letters, 1999—, European Jour. Organic Chemistry, 1999—, Advanced Synthesis & Catalysis, 2001—, mem. editl. bd.: Synlett, 1989—, Ctrl. European Sci. Jours., 2002—, consulting editor: Tetrahedron: Asymmetry, 1990—, Tetrahedron and Tetrahedron Letters, 2003—, mem. internat. adv. bd.: Ency. Reagents for Organic Synthesis, 1992—95, Bull. Korean Chem. Soc., 1998—, mem. editl. adv. bd.: Jour. Am. Chem. Soc., 1994—99, Bull. Chem. Soc. Japan, 2005—, Trends in Organic Chemistry, 2005—. Recipient Chem. Soc. Japan Award for Young Chemist, 1977, IBM Sci. award, 1988, Houkou award, Hattori Houkou, Japan, 1991, Chunichi Culture award, Chunichi Newspaper, Japan, 1992, Prelog medal, 1993, Chem. Soc. Japan award, 1995, Toray Sci. and Tech. award, 1997, Max-Tishler prize, 1998, Le Grand Prix de la Fondation Maison de la Chimie, 2002, Nat. Prize of Purple medal, Japan, 2002, Molecular Chirality award, Molecular Chirality Rsch. Assn., 2003, Yamada prize, 2004, Humboldt Rsch. award, Alexander von Humboldt Found., Germany, 2007, Japan Acad. prize, 2007. Fellow: AAAS; mem.: Soc. Synthetic Organic Chemistry, Japan, Pharm. Soc. Japan, Royal Soc. Chemistry, Am. Chem. Soc. (2006 Tetrahedron Prize for Creativity in Organic Chemistry 2006). Office: Dept Chemistry U Chgo SCL 317 5725 S Ellis Ave Chicago IL 60637 Office Phone: 773-702-5059. Office Fax: 773-702-0805. E-mail: yamamoto@uchicago.edu.

YAMAMOTO, IRWIN TORAKI, editor, publishing executive; b. Wailuku, Maui, Hawaii, Apr. 5, 1955; s. Torao and Yukie (Urata) Yamamoto. BBA in Mktg., Chaminade U., Honolulu, 1977. Pres., editor, pub. Yamamoto Forecast, Kahului, Hawaii, 1977—. Author: Profit Making in the Stock Market, 1983; columnist: Hawaii Herald, 1978—. Named Top Market Timer, Timer Digest, Top Gold Timer, Top Bond Timer, Timer Digest Honor Roll; named to Select Info. Exch. and Rating Stock Selectors. Avocations: exercise, music, reading, philosophy. Home and Office: PO Box 573 Kahului HI 96733-7073 Office Phone: 808-877-2690.

YAMAMOTO, JANET KAZUKO, science educator; d. Shunta and Chizuko Catherine Yamamoto. BA, U. Calif., Davis, 1976; PhD, U. Tex. Med. Br., 1981. Rsch. assoc. scientist Okla. Med. Rsch. Found., Oklahoma City, 1982—83; rschr. U. Calif., Davis, 1983—85; asst. rsch. immunologist U. Calif. Sch. Vet. Medicine, 1985—91, adj. assoc. prof., 1991—93; assoc. prof. U. Fla. Coll. Vet. Medicine, Gainesville, 1993—2001, prof., 2001—. Cons. Ft. Dodge Animal Health, Iowa, 2000—. Bd. dirs. Creating Hope Internat. (Afghanistan Projects), Mich., 1996—. Recipient Pfizer Animal Health award, U. Fla., 1996; fellow, U. Tex. Med. Br., Galveston, 1979—81, U. Calif., San Diego, 1981—82. Mem.: Clin. Immunology Soc., Internat. AIDS Soc., Am. Assn. Immunologists, Phi Zeta Upsilon. Achievements include discovery of FIV (feline immunodeficiency virus) and vaccine. Avocation: music. Office: U Fla Coll Vet Medicine PO Box 110880 Gainesville FL 32611 E-mail: yamamotoj@mail.vetmed.ufl.edu.

YAMAMOTO, JOE, retired psychiatrist, educator; b. LA, Apr. 18, 1924; s. Zenzaburo and Tomie (Yamada) Y.; m. Maria Fujitomi, Sept. 5, 1947; children: Eric Robert, Andrew Jolyon. Student, Los Angeles City Coll., 1941-42, Hamline U., 1943-45; BS, U. Minn., 1946, M.B., 1948, MD, 1949. Asst. prof. dept. psychiatry, neurology, behavioral sci. U. Okla. Med. Center, 1955-58, asst. prof., 1958-60; assoc. prof. dept. psychiatry U. So. Calif. Sch. Medicine, Los Angeles, 1961-69, prof., 1969-77, co-dir. grad. edn. psychiatry, 1963-70; prof. UCLA, 1977-94, emeritus prof., 1994—; dir. Psychiat. Outpatient Clinic, Los Angeles County-U. So. Calif. Med. Center, 1958-77; dir. adult ambulatory care services UCLA Neuropsychiat. Inst., 1977-88, chief Lab. for Cross Cultural Studies; ret. Contbr. articles in field to profl. jours. Served to capt., M.C. U.S. Army, 1953-55. Fellow Am. Psychiat. Assn. (life), Pacific Rim Coll. Psychiatrists, Am. Acad. Psychoanalysis (trustee, mem. exec. com., pres. 1978-79), Am. Coll. Psychiatrists, Am. Orthopsychiat. Assn. (pres.-elect 1993-94, pres. 1994-95, past pres.), Am. Assn. for Social Psychiatry (trustee 1981-84, v.p. 1984-86); mem. So. Calif. Psychoanalytic Inst. and Soc. (pres. 1972-73), Soc. for Study of Culture and Psychiatry, Group for Advancement Psychiatry (bd. dirs. 1992-94), Kappa Phi, Alpha Omega Alpha. *Learning about the diverse peoples of America, I have been fascinated with how we can be Asian, Hispanic, Black, European, and Native American and still identify with our* *national values. We value our freedom, individual rights and our ability to be someone different but equal. In mental health also there is a need for recognition of cultural differences and the need of treatment response to the individual.*

YAMAMOTO, KAORU, emeritus psychology professor; b. Tokyo, Mar. 28, 1932; arrived in U.S., 1959; s. Saburo and Hideko (Watanabe) Y.; m. Etsuko Hamazaki, Apr. 6, 1959 (div. 1986); m. Carol-Lynne Moore, Oct. 4, 1986; children: Keita Carey Moore, Kiyomi Lynne Moore. BS in Engring., U. Tokyo, 1953; MA, U. Minn., 1960, PhD, 1962. Engr. Toppan Printing Co., Tokyo, 1953; engr., rsch. chemist Japan Oxygen Co., Tokyo, 1954-57, 58-59; asst. prof. Kent (Ohio) State U., 1962-65; from asst. to assoc. prof. U. Iowa, Iowa City, 1965-68; prof. Pa. State U., University Park, 1968-72, Ariz. State U., Tempe, 1972-87, U. Colo., Denver, 1987-99, prof. emeritus, 1999—. Vis. prof. U. Minn., Mpls., 1974, Simon Fraser U., Burnaby, B.C., Can., 1984, U.Victoria, B.C., 1985, 86, U. Wash., Seattle, 1987, Zhejiang Normal U., Jinhua, China, 1991; Fulbright lectr. U. Iceland, 1985. Author: The Child and His Image, 1972, Their World, Our World, 1993; author, editor 10 books, including Children and Stress, 2001, Too Clever for Our Own Good, 2007; co-author: Beyond Words, 1988; editor Am. Ednl. Rsch. Jour., 1972-75, Ednl. Forum, 1984-92; contbr. chpts. to books and articles to profl. jours. Recipient Disting. Tchr. award Ariz. State U., 1980; Landsdowne scholar U. Victoria, 1985, Ctr. scholar Ctr. for Rsch. on Ethics and Values Azusa Pacific U., 1998-2000. Fellow: APA; mem.: Motus Humanus. Avocations: winter sports, travel, classical music, reading. Office: 13651 W 54th Ave Arvada CO 80002

YAMAMOTO, LISA MARIA, music educator; b. Long Beach, Calif., Oct. 30, 1966; d. Peter Joseph and Edith Marie Cheoros; m. David Tohru Yamamoto, July 15, 1989; children: Sophia Marie Yumi, Andrea Katrina Megumi. MusB, Calif. State U., Dominguez Hills, 1997; MusM, Calif. State U., Fullerton, 2005. Cert. in tchg. credential music Calif. State U., 2002. Adj. faculty Irvine Valley Coll., Calif., 2007—; instr., dept. music Orange County HS Arts, Santa Ana, Calif., 2007—. Pvt. instr. Yamamoto Music Studio, Cerritos, Calif., 1994—. Mem.: Music Educators Nat. Conf. Democrat. Buddhist. Achievements include design of arts education curriculum. Avocations: exercise, art, dance, woodworking. Office: Irvine Valley Coll 5500 Irvine Ctr Dr Irvine CA 92618 Personal E-mail: dyamamama@aol.com. Business E-Mail: lyamamoto@ivc.edu.

YAMAMOTO, MASAKO, music educator, director; b. Okayama, Japan; d. Yoshio and Satoko Ogawa; m. Tadashi Yamamoto, Nov. 23, 1985; children: Ayae, Yoshie. MusB in Voice Performance, Elisabeth U. Music, Japan, 1979; MS in Music Edn., U. Ill., 1997, EdD in Music Edn., 2002. Cert. tchr. Music for Young Children, Can., Harmony Rd., Oreg., music tchr. Yamaguchi prefecture Bd. Edn., Japan. Music educator Bd. Edn., Japan, 1979—89, Melody Acad. Music, San Jose, Calif., 2003—07; Japanese lang., culture tchr. Urbana Sch. Dist., 1994—95; dir. Masako's Music Studio, Fremont, 2007—. Brass band dir. Kumage Mid. Sch., Japan, 1983—84; dance club dir. Tabuse Spl. Edn. Sch., Japan, 1980—83, rsch. dir., 1981—83. Recipient Verdell Frazier Young awards, U. Ill., 2001, 2002; Marilyn Pflederer Zimmerman Music Edn. Doctoral fellowship, 1998. Mem.: Am. Coll. of Musicians (assoc.), Kappa Delta Pi (assoc.), Pi Kappa Lambda (assoc.). Achievements include research in multicultural music education. Avocations: running, piano. Studio: 39977 Mission Blvd Fremont CA 94539 Office Phone: 510-565-6230.

YAMAMOTO, NOBUTO, immunologist, director; s. Mituji and Kiyo Yamamoto; m. Hiroko Yamaguchi, Jan. 3, 1954; children: Kureha, Nobuyuki, Shinji. MS, Kyushu U. Faculty Sci., Fukuoka City, Japan, 1953; PhD, Nagoya U. Sch. Medicine, Japan, 1958. Assoc. prof. Gifu Med. Coll., 1958—61; vis. scientist Inst. Cancer Rsch., Phila., 1959—61, Ind. U., Bloomington, 1961—62, NIH, Bethesda, Md., 1962—63; assoc. prof. microbiology Temple U. Sch. Medicine, Phila., 1963—69, prof. microbiology, 1970—80; prof. microbiology and immunology Hahnemann U. Sch. Medicine, 1980—90; rsch. prof. biochemistry Temple U. Sch. Medicine, 1990—94; chief immunotherapy, dir. Socrates Inst. Therapeutic Immunology, Phila., 1994—. Mem.: Am. Assn. Cancer Rsch. Achievements include discovery of powerful therapeutic procedures for cancer and HIV; evolutional mechanism for creation of new virus species via recombination between unrelated virus species; patents for twenty patents for immunotherapy of cancer and HIV patients and their diagnostic/prognostic procedures covering worldwide; research in mechanisms of bacterial gene expression under extreme environments such as aerobic, anaerobic and thermophilic growth temperature.

YAMANAKA, SHINYA, stem cell scientist, educator; MD, Kobe U., 1987; PhD, Osaka City U. Grad. Sch., 1993. Resident orthop. surgery Nat. Osaka Hosp., Japan, 1987—89; postdoctoral fellow Gladstone Inst. Cardiovascular Disease, San Francisco, 1993—95, staff rsch. investigator, 1995—96, L.K. Whittier Found. investigator stem cell biology, sr. investigator, 2007—; asst. prof. Osaka City U. Med. Sch., Japan, 1996—99; assoc. prof. Nara Inst. Sci. and Tech., Japan, 1999—2003, prof., 2003—05, Inst. Frontier Med. Scis., Kyoto U., Japan, 2004—; prof. anatomy U. Calif., San Francisco, 2007—. Recipient Gairdner Found. Internat. award, 2009; co-recipient Shaw prize in life sci. and medicine, 2008; named one of The 100 Most Influential People in the World, TIME mag., 2008. Office: Gladstone Inst Cardiovascular Disease 1650 Owens St San Francisco CA 94158 Office Phone: 415-734-2710. Office Fax: 415-355-0960. E-mail: syamanaka@gladstone.ucsf.edu.*

YAMANOUCHI-RYNN, MIDORI, retired social sciences educator; b. Osaka City, Japan, Jan. 8, 1928; permanent resident, 1957; d. Shin'ichi and Fumiko (Urai) Yamanouchi; m. Edward J. Rynn, Oct. 10, 1975 (dec. July 29, 1987). Diploma, Tokyo Kasai U., 1948; student, U. Tampa, 1950—51; AB, Sophia U. Internat. Divsn., 1956; MA, Mich. State U., 1958, PhD, 1972; MA in LS, U. Mich., 1959. Chief rsch. assoc. Internat. Divsn. Sophia U., Tokyo, 1952—56; libr., bibliographer Mich. State U., East Lansing, 1959—63, 1964—67; asst. dir. R&D Sperry & Hutchinson Co., NYC, 1963—64; asst. prof. sociology and anthropology Marshall U., Huntington, W.Va., 1967—70, Fisk U., Nashville, 1970—72; assoc. prof. Livingston Coll., Salisbury, NC, 1972—74; vis. prof. Frostburg State U., 1974—75; prof. U. Scranton, Pa., 1975—2006; v.p. acad. affairs Lackawanna Coll., 2006—08. Translator: Listen to the Voices from the Sea, 2000, In The Far Away Mountains and Rivers, 2005; editor: Sociol. Viewpoint, 1989—91, 2004—05; assoc. editor Comparative Civilizations Rev., 1996—2001. Trustee Lacawac Sanctuary, Lake Ariel, Pa., 1993—, Lackawanna Coll., 1995—2001, 2002—06, Tokyo Kasei U., 1997—2006; mem. pres. coun. Cedar Crest Coll., 1996—2002; mem. adv. bd. Northeastern Intermediate Unit Sch. Bd., Scranton, Pa., 1998—, Diversity Inst. Coll. Misericordia, Dallas, Pa., 1999—; bd. mem. Northeastern Pa. Philharmonic, 2006—, Everhart Mus., 2003—. Recipient Seeley Svc. medal, Lackawanna Coll., 2001, Ednl. Svc. award, Wilkes Barre Bd. Edn., Pa., 2002, UN Day Rinaldi Meml. award, UN Assn. USA NE Pa., 2007, award, Presdl. Medallion Keystone Coll., 2009; named Hon. Prof., Karaganda Econ. U., Kazakhistan, 2009. Mem.: Assn. for Gen. and Liberal Studies (mem. exec. bd. 1975—78), Internat. Orgn. for Unification of Terminological Neologisms (del. UN, non-govt. orgn. 1995—, Disting. Contbn. award 2000), Internat. Soc. for Comparative Study of Civilizations (mem. exec. bd. 1978—2005, editor newsletter 1990—93), Pa. Sociol. Soc. (editor newsletter 1986—89, pres. 1990—91). Home Phone: 570-689-4401.

YAMASHITA, KENNETH AKIRA, library administrator, librarian; b. Topaz, Utah, Sept. 11, 1945; s. Susumu and Kiyoko (Kitano) Y. BA, Rutgers U., 1967, MLS, 1972; ArtsD, Simmons Coll., 1982. Reference libr. Montclair Free Pub. Libr., NJ, 1970-73; ext. svcs. libr. Decatur (Ill.) Pub. Libr., 1973-75; asst. to commr. Chgo. Pub. Libr., 1975-78; mktg. rep. Computer Libr. Sys., Inc., Newtonville, Mass., 1978-79; asst. to dir. Mass. Bd. Libr. Commrs., Boston, 1979-81; supervising libr. Stockton (Calif.)-San Joaquin County Pub. Libr., 1982-90, libr. divsn. mgr., 1990—2007; deputy dir., 2008—09; city libr., 2009—. Guest lectr. Sch. Libr. Sci., U. Mich., Ann Arbor, 1978; bldg. program and design cons. Stockton-San Joaquin County Public Libr. Lakeland (Fla.) Pub. Libr., Calaveras County (Calif.) Pub. Libr., 1982—; advisor to prof. publs. U. Wis., Madison, Assn. Coll. and Rsch. Librs. Chgo., Calif. State Libr., Sacramento, Gale Pub., Detroit, 1989—; state, fed. grant writer Stockton-San Joaquin County Public Libr.,1990-, Calaveras County Libr., San Andreas, Calif., 1991; mem. rev. com. multi-ethnic recruitment scholarship program Calif. State Libr., 1990, 95; mem. design com. Libr. Staff Edn. Funding Program Calif. State Libr., 1998-01. Assoc. editor: (reference book) Guide to Multicultural Resources, 1995-97; contbr.: Problems in Library Management, 1981, chpts. to books, articles in profl. jours. Sec., bd. dirs. Stockton Shelter for Homeless, 1993-96; mem. diversity awareness team City of Stockton, 1994-98; mem. citizen rev. team United Way San Joaquin County, 1994, 95; participant Leadership Stockton, 1995; co-chair Joint Conf. Librs. of Color, 2000-2006, treas. Joint Conf. Libr. Color II, 2008-. Asian Studies Com. fellow Ind. U., 1967-69, Carnegie Grant fellow Ind. U., 1969-70, Montclair Free Pub. Libr. Montclair Free Pub. Libr. trustee, fellow Rutgers U., 1971, HEA Title II B fellow Simmons Coll., 1979-80. Mem. ALA (chair, adv. com. Office for Literacy Outreach Svcs. 1987-90, councilor 1995-98, 99—2006, nominating com. 1995, com. on coms. 1997-98, spectrum initiative steering com. 1997—2001, Spectrum PhD fellowship Jury, 2006-, Equality award, 2007), Asian/Pacific ALA (pres. 1996-97), Calif. Libr. Assn. (coun., assembly mem. 1987-93, pres. pub. libr. sect. 1998), Pub. Libr. Assn. (bd. dirs. & exec. com. 2000-03), Beta Phi Mu. Democrat. Avocations: films, music, reading, cooking, travel. Office: Stockton San Joaquin County Pub Libr 605 N El Dorado St Stockton CA 95202-1907 Office Phone: 209-937-8364. E-mail: ken.yamashita@ci.stockton.ca.us.

YAMAUCHI, EDWIN MASAO, history professor emeritus; b. Hilo, Hawaii, Feb. 1, 1937; s. Shokyo Yamauchi and Haruko (Owan) Yamauchi Higa; m. Kimie Honda, Aug. 31, 1962; children: Brian, Gail. Student, U. Hawaii, 1957-58; BA, Shelton Coll., 1960; MA, Brandeis U., 1962, PhD, 1964. Instr. Greek lang. Shelton Coll., Ringwood, NJ, 1960-61; grad. asst. Brandeis U., Waltham, Mass., 1962-63; asst. prof. Rutgers U., New Brunswick, NJ, 1964-69; assoc. prof. Miami U., Oxford, Ohio, 1969-73, prof. dept. history, 1973—, dir. grad. studies, 1978-82. Author: Pre-Christian Gnosticism, 1973, World of the First Christians, 1981, Foes from the North Frontier, 1982, Persia and the Bible, 1990, Africa and the Bible, 2004, others; sr. editor Christianity Today, 1992-94; editor: Africa and Africans in Antiquity, 2001 Fellow NEH, 1968, Inst. for Holy Land Studies, Jerusalem, 1968, Inst. for Advanced Christian Studies, 1974-75; grantee Am. Philos. Soc., 1970. Fellow Am. Sci. Affiliation (pres. 1983), Inst. Bibl. Rsch. (chair 1984-86, pres. 1987-89); mem. Conf. on Faith and History (pres. 1974-76), Near East Archaeol. Soc. (pres. 2007-), Archaeol. Inst. Am. (chpt. pres. 1973-74), Evang. Theol. Soc. (pres. 2005-06) Office: Miami Univ Dept History Oxford OH 45056 Home Phone: 513-523-2819. Business E-Mail: yamauce@muohio.edu.

YAMAUCHI, PAUL STEVEN, dermatologist, researcher; PhD, MD, Case We. Res. U., 1991. Med. dir. Clin. Rsch. Specialists, Santa Monica, Calif., 2000—; exec. med. dir. Dermatology Inst. & Skin Care Ctr., Santa Monica, 2004—. Med. lectr., cons. Clin. Rsch. Specialists, Santa Monica, 2000—. Contbr. articles to profl. jours. Recipient Bill Reed Award Lectureship, European Soc. Dermatol. Rsch., 1999, Everett C. Fox Residents and Fellows Award, Am. Acad. Dermatology, 1999, Ronald M. Reisner Award, UCLA Sch. of Medicine, 1998, Paul H. Curtiss, Jr. Musculoskeletal Award, Case We. Res. U., 1993. Fellow: Am. Acad. Dermatologists; mem.: Nat. Psoriasis Found. (corr.). Achievements include research in Clinical research in the development of biologic agents in the treatment of psoriasis and psoriatic arthritis. Key opinion leader in the subject of psoriatic disease; Clinical research in the development of cosmetic procedures for facial rejuvenation. Office: 2001 Santa Monica Blvd Ste 490W Los Angeles CA 90049 Office Fax: 310-829-4150. Business E-Mail: dermatology@earthlink.net.

YAMAWAKI, NOBUYUKI, engineering educator, biomedical engineer, researcher; B in Engring., Utsunomiya U., Tochigi, Japan, 1990, M in Engring., 1992; PhD in Engring., Osaka U., Toyonaka, Japan, 1995. Cert. tchg. Tochigi, Japan, 1992. Rsch. assoc. Kinki U., Kinokawa, Wakayama, Japan, 1995—2001, lectr., 2001—07, assoc. prof., 2007—. Rsch. assoc. U. Minn., Mpls., 2004—05. Author: System Signal Processing and Programming, 2003; contbr. articles to profl. jours. Mem.: IEEE, Soc. Neurosci. Achievements include research in enhanced time-trequency spatial approach for motor imagery classification. Office: Kinki Univ 930 Nishimitani Kinokawa 649-6493 Japan Office Phone: 81-736-77-3888. Business E-Mail: yamawaki@waka.kindai.ac.jp.

YAMAYEE, ZIA AHMAD, engineering educator, dean; b. Herat, Afghanistan, Feb. 2, 1948; came to U.S., 1974; s. Sayed and Merjan Ahmad. BSEE, Kabul U., Afghanistan, 1972; MSEE, Purdue U., 1976, PhD, 1978. Registered profl. engr., Calif., Wash. Mem. faculty of engring. Kabul U., 1978; engr. Systems Control, Inc., Palo Alto, Calif., 1979-81; sr. engr. Pacific N.W. Utilities, Portland, Oreg., 1981-83; assoc. prof. elec. engring. Clarkson U., Potsdam, NY, 1983-85; assoc. prof. Gonzaga U., Spokane, 1985-87, dean Sch. Engring., 1988-96; prof., chair elec. engring. dept. U. New Orleans, 1987-88. Part-time rsch. engr. La. Power and Light Co., New Orleans, 1987-88; sr. cons. Engring. and Cons. Svcs., Spokane, 1989-96. Contbr. articles, reports to profl. jours. Bd. dirs. Wash. State Math., Engring. Sci. Achievement, Seattle, 1989-96; mem. Spokane Intercollegiate Rsch. and Tech. Inst. Adv. Coun., 1990-96. NSF grantee. Mem. Am. Soc. Engring. Edn., IEEE (sr.). Office: University of Portland 5000 N Willamette Blvd Portland OR 97203-5798 Office Phone: 503-943-7314. E-mail: yamayee@up.edu.

YAMAZAKI, JUN, international organization official; b. London, 1956; BA in Internat. Rels., U. Tokyo. Various positions including counsellor in the Embassy of Japan Min. Fgn. Affairs, Japan, dir. internat. peace cooperation divsn., dep. dir. gen. global issues, internat. cooperation bur.; dep. dir. multilateral cooperation dept., adminstrn. divsn. UN, NYC, mem. adv. com. on adminstrv. and budgetary questions, 2003—07, asst. sec. gen., office of programme planning, budgets and accounts, controller, 2008—. Office: c/o UN Hdqs First Ave at 46th St New York NY 10017

YAMBRUSIC, EDWARD SLAVKO, lawyer, consultant; b. Conway, Pa., Mar. 9, 1933; s. Michael Misko and Slavica Sylvia (Yambrusic) Y.; m. Natalie Visniak, 1990. BA, Duquesne U., 1957; postgrad., Georgetown U. Law Ctr., 1959-61; JD, U. Balt., 1966; cert., The Hague Acad. Internat. Law, Netherlands, 1967-69; diploma, Ctr. Study and Rsch. Internat. Law and Internat. Rels., 1970; PhD in Pub. Internat. Law, Cath. U. Am., 1984. Bar: Md. 1969, US Ct. Customs and Patent Appeals 1972, US Supreme Ct. 1972, US. Ct Internat. Trade 1988. Copyright examiner US Copyright Office, Libr. of Congress, Washington, 1960-69; atty. adviser Office Register of Copyrights, 1969-98; pvt. practice internat. and immigration law, 1969—. Legal counsel Nat. Ethnic Studies Assembly, 1976—, Soc. Fed. Linguists, 1980; pres. AMCRO Internat. Consulting, Inc., 1995—. Author: Treat Interpretation: Theory and Reality, 1987, The Trade-Based Approaches to the Protection of Intellectual Property, 1990; contbr. articles to ofcl. newsletter Nat. Confedn. Am. Ethnic Groups, also legal jours. Pres. Nat. Confedn. Am. Ethnic Groups, Washington; nat. chmn. Croatian-Am. Bicentennial Com. nat. chmn. Nat. Pilgrimage of Croatian-Ams. to Nat. Shrine of Immaculate Conception, Washington; v.p. Croatian Acad. Am. Served to capt. US Army, 1957-59. Duquesne U. Tamburitzans scholar, 1953-57; Hague Acad. Internat. Law fellow, 1970. Mem. ABA, Md. Bar Assn., Internat. Law Assn., Internat. Fiscal Assn., Am. Soc. Internat. Law, Croatian Cath. Union Am., Croatian Frat. Union Am. Republican. Roman Catholic. Certificate issued by the Librarian of Congress in recognition of 40 years of distinguished service to the people of the United States of America, 1957-98. Home and Office: 4720 Massachusetts Ave NW Washington DC 20016-2346 Office Phone: 202-244-1626.

YAMIN, DIANNE ELIZABETH, judge; b. Danbury, Conn., June 4, 1961; d. Raymond Joseph and Linda May (Bucko) Goetz; m. Robert Joseph Yamin, Sept. 3, 1988; children: Samantha Blythe, Rebecca Anne. AB, Lehigh U., 1983; JD, Mercer U., 1986. Bar: Conn. 1986, U.S. Dist. Ct. Conn. 1989. Atty. Gerald Hecht & Assocs., Danbury, 1986-92; judge State Conn., Danbury, 1991—; ptnr. Yamin & Yamin, L.L.P., Danbury, 1992—. Chmn. ethics com. Conn. Probate Assembly, 1994—2003, 1st v.p., 2004—06, pres., 2006—08; mem. Conn. Coun. on Adoptions, 1992—. Bd. dirs. Big Bros./Big Sisters, Danbury, 1987-94, Danbury Music Ctr., 1996-2004, Hispanic Ctr. Greater Danbury, 1999-2007; bd. dirs. Conn Brass Soc., Inc., 1991—, Greater Danbury C. of C., 2003—, Christian Cmty. Outreach Ministries, Inc., 2006—; active Friends of Tarrywile Park, Inc., Danbury, 1993-99, chair task force to end homelessness, Mayor, 2005-07; pres. coun. women Lehigh U, 2000-04, Danbury Commn. Aging, 2002-08. Recipient Outstanding Young Citizen award Conn. Jaycees, 1994, pro bono award Conn. Legal Svcs., 1993; named one of 21 Young Lawyers Leading US into the 21st Century, ABA Mag., 1995, Thayer Bowman award, 2004, Red Cross Grace award, 2006. Mem. ABA, Conn. Bar Assn., Danbury Bar Assn., Greater Danbury C. of C. (bd. dirs. 2003—), Omicron Delta Kappa. Republican. Roman Catholic. Avocations: ballet, volunteerism, travel, outdoor activities. Home: 66 Barnum Rd Danbury CT 06811-2938 Office: 155 Deer Hill Ave Danbury CT 06810-7726 Office Phone: 203-744-7090. Personal E-mail: judgedianne@aol.com. Business E-Mail: lawyers@yaminlaw.com.

YAMIN, MICHAEL GEOFFREY, lawyer; b. NYC, Nov. 10, 1931; s. Michael and Ethel Yamin; m. Martina Schaap, Apr. 16, 1961; children: Michael Jeremy, Katrina. AB magna cum laude, Harvard U., 1953, LLB, 1958. Bar: NY 1959, U.S. Dist. Ct. (so. and ea. dists.) NY, U.S. Ct. Appeals (2d cir.) 1966, U.S. Supreme Ct. 1967. Assoc. Weil, Gotshal & Manges, NYC, 1958-65; sr. ptnr. Colton, Hartnick, Yamin & Sheresky, NYC, 1966-93, Kaufmann, Feiner, Yamin, Gildin & Robbins, LLP, NYC, 1993—2009, Kaufmann Gildin Robbins & Oppenheim LLP, 2009—. Trustee Gov.'s Com. Scholastic Achievement, 1976—; mem. Manhattan Cmty. Bd. 6, 1974—88, Chair Bd. 6, 1986—88, Manhattan Borough Bd., 1986—88; trustee Project Sail, Inc., 2005—. Mem.: ABA, Internat. Bar Assn., Soc. de Legis. Comparee, Internat. Law Assn., Am. Fgn. Law Assn. (Am. br.), Fed. Bar Coun., Assn. Bar City of NY, NY State Bar Assn., Harvard Alumni Assn. (bd. dirs. 1995—98, 2005—08), Harvard Club of NYC (sub-chmn. schs. and scholarships com. 1972—93, trustee Found. 1981—, bd. mgrs. 1985—88, chair ho. com. 1992—95, bd. mgrs. 1993—98, v.p. 1995—98, chair comm. com. 1997—99, chair membership svcs. com. 1999—2000, pres. Found. 1999—2006, chair cmty. svc. com. 2006—08), Harvard Faculty Club (Cambridge, Mass.). Office: Kaufmann Gildin Robbins & Oppenheim LLP 777 3rd Ave New York NY 10017-1401 Office Phone: 212-755-3100. Business E-Mail: myamin@kaufmanngildin.com.

YAMINI, DANIEL, plastic surgeon; BA in Psychology, Stanford U., 1990, BS in Biology, 1990; MD, Med. Coll. Wis., 1994. Cert. Am. Bd. Plastic Surgery, Am. Bd. Surgery, lic. Calif. Bd. Medicine. Resident, gen. surgery UCLA, 1994—2000, Harbor Gen. Hosp., Torrance, Calif., 1994—2000; resident, plastic and reconstructive surgery Providence Hosp. and Med. Ctrs. & Inst. for Craniofacial and Reconstructive Plastic Surgery, Detroit, 2000—02; fellow in advanced cosmetic surgery Dr. Richard Ellenbogen, Beverly Hills, Calif., 2002; founding ptnr., plastic surgeon Sunset Cosmetic Surgery, LA. Presenter in field; hosp. affiliations include Century City Hosp., Midway Hosp. Contbr. articles to profl. jours., chapters to books, Abstracts; featured on Dr. 90210. Recipient Soc. Academic Surgery Student Rsch. award, 1994, First prize: Resident Rsch. award, Am. Coll. Surgeons, So. Calif. Conf., 1998, Providence Hosp. Rsch. Symposium, 2002. Fellow: Am. Coll. Surgeons; mem.: AMA, Am. Soc. Plastic Surgeons, Calif. Soc. Plastic Surgeons, Calif. Med. Assn. Office: Sunset Cosmetic Surgery 9201 Sunset Blvd Ste 805 Los Angeles CA 90069 Office Phone: 310-858-9100.*

YAMPEY-JORG, GLORIA LEONOR, language educator; d. Moises Yampey and Leonor Julieta Jorg Yampey. BA, U. Houston, MA, 1985. Lectr. U. Houston, 1984—89, Rice U., Houston, 2000—02; dir. honors program Houston CC, Ctrl. Coll., 2000—07, prof. fgn. lang., 1979—, dir. guadalajara summer program, 1980—. Bd. dir. Inst. Hispanic Culture, 1994—95, pres., 1997, chair-cultural com., 2006—07, chair-scholarship com., 2006—07, treas., 2006—07; dir., sec. elect Mayor's Internat. Affairs & Devel. Coun.Americas, Houston, 2007—09; bd. mem. Colombian Ballet Folklorico, Houston, 2007—09. Mem.: TFLA, TCCTA, ACTFL, Amnesty Internat. Office: Houston CC Ctrl Coll 3517 Austin St FAC 306 Houston TX 77004 Office Fax: 713-718-6673. Business E-Mail: gloria.yampeyjorg@hccs.edu.

YAN, DONGMING, research scientist, educator; b. Xinye, Henan, China, Dec. 12, 1978; m. Qun Li. PhD, Dalian U. Tech., China, 2006. Asst. prof. Zhengzhou U., Henan, China, 2006; postdoc. fellow Mo. U. S&T, Rolla, 2007—. Contbr. scientific papers. Mem.: ASCE, Am. Concrete Inst. Office: Mo Univ S&T 500 W 16th St Rolla MO 65401 Office Phone: 573-341-6699. Business E-Mail: yando@mst.edu.

YAN, GAO, power company executive; b. Jilin, Fuyu, China, Dec. 1942; With CCP, 1965; vice gov. Jilin Province, 1988-92, gov., 1992-95; sec. CCP Com., Yunan Province, 1995-97; dir. polit. dept. Chinese People's Armed Police Force, 1997—; sec. CPC 6th Yunan Province

Com.; mem. 14th CCP Ctrl. Com., 1992-97, 15th CCP Ctrl. Com., 1997—; gen. mgr. State Elec. Power Corp., 1998—. Office: State Power Corp 137 Fuyoe St Beijing 100031 China

YAN, JIA, economics professor; b. Zhijin, Guizhou, China, July 9, 1972; s. Daqi Yan and Shanshan Wang; m. Yan Yan He, Mar. 14, 2004; children: Matthew, Nathan. PhD, U. Calif., Irvine, 2002. Asst. prof. Hong Kong Poly. U., 2004—07, Wash. State U., Pullman, 2007—. Scientist Choicestream Inc., Cambridge, Mass., 2002—04. Contbr. articles to profl. jours. Mem.: Econometric Soc. Achievements include invention of harmful algae indexing system to predict the red tides. Office: WA State Univ Hulber 101 Pullman WA 99164 Business E-Mail: jiay@wsu.edu.

YAN, JIAO, marine biologist, educator; d. Jiao and Zhang. PhD, Meml. U. Nfld., St. John's, 2004. Postdoc fellow U. Guelph, Ont., Canada, 2004—05; asst. prof. Va. Tech, Blacksburg, 2005—. Recipient Fellowship, Meml. U. Nfld., 2004, Recognition of excellence, 2001; Fellowship, Royal Bank, 2002, Grants, Social Sci. & Humanities Rsch. Coun., 2002. Mem.: Sigma Xi, Ecol. Soc. America, Am. Inst. Fisheries Rsch. Biologists, Am. Fisheries Soc. Office: Virginia Tech Univ 110 Cheatham Hall Blacksburg VA 24061 Business E-Mail: yjiao@vt.edu.

YAN, JINGYU, computer graphics designer; PhD, U. NC, Chapel Hill, 2006. Rsch. asst. UNC, 2002—06; software design engr. Microsoft Corp., Redmond, Wash., 2006—08. Achievements include research in articulated non-rigid motion recovery from single-view cameras. Office: Microsoft Corp One Microsoft Way Redmond WA 98052

YAN, MARTIN, celebrity chef; b. Guangzhou, China, 1948; m. Susan Yan; 2 children. Grad., Overseas Inst. Cookery, Hong Kong; BS Food Sci., MS Food Sci., U. Calif., Davis; PhD Culinary Arts (hon.), Johnson & Wales U.; PhD Humane Letters (hon.), Colo. Inst. Art. Product mgr. canning corp., Hong Kong, 1976; mgr, head chef Lee's Garden Restaurant, Alberta, 1977; tchr., Chinese Cooking U. Calif.; founder Yan Can Cook Inc., 1997—, Yan Can Internat. Cooking School, San Francisco. Guest chef-instr. Calif. Culinary Acad., Johnson & Wales U., Culinary Inst. Am., U. San Francisco. Host (TV series) Yan Can Cook, 1978—, Martin Yan's Chinatowns, 2002—, Martin Yan Quick & Easy, 2004—; author: Yan Can Cookbook, 1981, The Joy of Wokking, 1982, Martin Yan, the Chinese Chef, 1985, A Wok For All Seasons, 1988, Everybody's Wokking, 1991, The Well-Seasoned Wok, 1992, Simply Delicious, 1993, A Simple Guide to Chinese Ingredients, 1994, Martin Yan's Culinary Journey Through China, 1995, Martin Yan's Asia, 1997, Martin Yan's Feast, 1998, Chinese Cooking for Dummies, 2000, Martin Yan's Invitation to Chinese Cooking, 2000, Martin Yan's Asian Favorites, 2001, Martin Yan's Chinatown Cooking, 2002, Martin Yan's Quick and Easy, 2004, Martin Yan's China, 2008; guest appearances (TV series) The Today Show, A&E: Top Ten Television Chefs, Cooking Live with Sara Moulton, The Tonight Show, Good Morning America, Q&A Asia, Lo & Co., Howie Mandell Show, Donnie & Marie Show, Mornings on Two, Live with Regis and Kelly, The Dennis Miller Show, Talk Asia (CNN Asia), The Martin Short Show. Recipient Best TV Cooking Show, James Beard Found., 1994, Best TV Food Journalism award, 1996, D'Artagnan Cervena Who's Who of Food and Beverage award, 2001, Single Camera Photography award, Daytime Emmy Awards, 1998, Antonin Careme award, Chef's Assoc. of the Pacific Coast, Courvoisier Leadership award; named Culinary Diplomat, Am. Culinary Fedn. Achievements include design of cookware and kitchen tools; owner of several pan-Asian restaurants, founder and executive chef of Martin Yan's Culinary Arts Center in Shenzhen, China. Office: Yan Can Cook Inc PO Box 4755 Foster City CA 94404 Office Phone: 650-341-0701. Business E-Mail: martin@yancancook.com.

YAN, RIQIANG, science educator; b. Shanghai, May 25, 1961; m. Wanxia He; children: Linda H., Michael H. BS, Shanghai Med. U., M in Medicine, 1983; PhD, U. Ky., Lexington, 1993. Rsch. scientist Pharmacia Corp., Kalamazoo, 1997—2003; assoc. prof. Cleve. Clinic, 2003—. Recipient Spl. Recognition award, Pharmacia Corp., 1999, award, Ralph Wilson Found., 2005. Fellow: Aaron Diamond Found. Achievements include discovery of Alzheimer's ß-secretase, also called BACE1; first to clone the translation initiation factor eIF4G. Home: 3450 Courtland Rd Beachwood OH 44122 Office: Cleve Clin 9500 Euclid Ave Cleveland OH 44195 Business E-Mail: yanr@ccf.org.

YAN, WEI, research scientist; PhD, NJ Inst. Tech., Newark, 2005. Rsch. scientist McAfee, Beaverton, Oreg., 2005—07; sr. threat rschr. Trend Micro, Inc, Cupertino, Calif., 2007—. Mem.: IEEE.

YAN, WEI, science association director; s. Jiugui Yan and Yulan Wang; m. Huili Zheng, Sept. 9, 1991; children: Mark H., Ann E. PhD, U. Turku, Finland, 2000; MD, China Med. U., Shenyang, China, 1990. Instr. Baylor Coll. Medicine, Houston, 2003—04; asst. prof. U. Nev. Sch. Medicine, Reno, 2004—08. Dir. Andrology Lab, Northern Nev. Fertility Clinic, Reno, 2004—. Contbr. articles to profl. jours. Fellow, Ernst Rsch. Found., Germany, 2002—04, RO3 grant, NIH-NICHD, 2004—07, RO1 grant, 2006—, Pilot grant, Sanford Ctr. Aging, Reno, 2006—07. Mem.: Soc. Study Reprodn., Am. Soc. Andrology. Office: Univ Nev Sch Medicine 1664 N Virginia St MS352 Reno NV 89557

YAN, XIE, systems engineer; PhD, Case Western Res. U., Cleve, 2008. Hardware engr. Sony Corp., Tokyo, 2001—03. Office: Univ Utah 50S Ctrl Campus Dr Rm 3280 Salt Lake City UT 84112 Personal E-mail: sowhat7@gmail.com.

YAN, XIN, preventive medicine physician, educator; s. Dasen Yan and Qunde Li; m. Nan Yu, Mar. 8, 1980. MD, Chengdu U. Traditional Chinese Medicine, 1977; MD (hon.), Coll. Accupuncture and Herbal Medicine, Hawaii Liu Yi U., 1991. Physician Ctr. Disease Prevention and Control, Jiangyou Bur. Health, Sichuan, China, 1971—74; lectr. Mianyang Coll. Traditional Chinese Medicine, Mianyang, Sichuan, 1978—81. Chief attending physician Chongqing Inst. Traditional Chinese Medicine, 1981—; sr. rsch. fellow Qigong Rsch. Group, Tsinghua U., Beijing, 1986; mem. expert com. Coll. Advanced Study Chinese Qiqong, Beijing, 1986; adviser and hon. prof. Assn. Chinese Martial Art Qigong, Beijing U., 1986; specially invited rsch. fellow Inst., Ministry Aerospace Industry China, Shenyang, 1987; chief attending physician Chongqing Bur. Health, 1988; vis. scholar Zhongshan U., Guangzhou, Guangdong, China, 1988; academic adviser Rsch. Chinese Qigong Preserving Health, Sichuan Acad. Social Scis., Chengdu, 1988; specially invited sci. adviser Qigong Rsch. Assn., Inst. High Energy Physics, Beijing, 1988; chief sci. adviser, China Nat. Radio Qigong Sci. Rsch. Inst., Beijing, 1988, specially invited sr. adviser, Ministry Pub. Security PRC, 88; hon. dir. Rsch. Ctr. Somatic Sci., Sichuan U., Chengdu, 1988—90; sr. adviser Qigong Rsch. Group, Tsinghua U.; guest prof. China Traditional Exercise Ctr., NYC, 1990; prof. Internat. U. Qigong, Emei, Sichuan, 1993; adj. rsch. fellow Rsch. Ctr. Somatic Sci., Sichuan U.; adviser and guest prof. Nanjing U. Sci. and Tech., Nanjing, Jiangsu, China, 1994; vis. prof. Harvard U., Boston, 1997—; adj. prof. Tongji U., Shanghai, 1999—2001; hon. dean and sr. rsch. prof. New Med. Sci. Rsch. Inst., New York, NY, 2000—. Contbr. articles to profl. jours. Planner and dir. Organizing Com. Celebrating New Millennium Summit UN, NYC, 2000, 2005; qigong adviser Govt. Baoan County, Shenzhen, China, 1987; mem. standing com. Chinese Sports Qigong Rsch. Inst., Beijing, 1990; adviser Chinese Sports Svc. Team, Beijing, 1990. Named Outstanding Scientists, Internat. Biog. Ctr., 2000. Achievements include first to integrate conventional western and traditional Chinese medicine with external Qi (Chi) of traditional Chinese Qigong in medical treatment and disease prevention, as well as to deploy Qi to change the structure of the matter at various levels, including the molecular structure of proteins.

YANAGI, CARY, science educator; MS, Golden Gate U., San Francisco, 1993. Instr. computer studies Merced Coll., Calif., 1996—. Office: Merced Col 3600 M St Merced CA 95340 Business E-Mail: yanagi.c@mccd.edu.

YANAS, JOHN JOSEPH, lawyer; b. Albany, NY, July 18, 1929; m. Mary Faith Casey; children: John J., Joseph J., Kathleen Ann, Mary Patricia. Student Russell Sage Coll., 1947-50; LLB, Albany Law Sch., 1953, LLD, 1989. Bar: NY 1954, U.S. Ct. Appeals (2d cir.) 1962. Assoc. Casey, Honikel and Wisely, Albany, 1954-60; ptnr. Dugan, Casey, Burke & Lyons, Albany, 1960-69; ptnr. Casey, Yanas, Mitchell & Amerling, Albany, 1969-84, Casey, Yanas, Clyne, Mitchell & Amerling, Albany, 1984-88; ptnr. Degraff, Foy, Kunz & Devine LLP, 1989—; counsel Albany County Pub. Welfare Dist., 1959-60; mem. Albany City CSC, 1970-73, Albany County CSC, 1970-73; justice Albany City Ct., 1973-77; Trustee Home and City Savs. Bank, 1974-91, Christian Bros. Acad., Albany, 1972-2002, chair, 1992, Albany Law Sch., 1975-2001, chair, 1993. Fellow Am. Bar Found., NY Bar Found., ABA; mem. Am. Coll. Real Estate Lawyers, NY State Bar Assn. (chmn. real property law sect. 1974-75, (chmn. com. to confer with N.Y. State Realty Bd. 1975-77, chmn. com. continuing legal edn. 1977-80, treas. 1980-86, chmn. fin. com. 1987, pres.-elect 1988, pres. 1989), Albany County Bar Assn. (pres. 1978). Office: 90 State St Albany NY 12207 Home Phone: 518-438-7380; Office Phone: 518-462-5300.

YANCEY, ASA G., SR., physician, educator; b. Atlanta, Aug. 19, 1916; s. Arthur H. and Daisy L. (Sherard) Yancey; m. Carolyn E. Dunbar, Dec. 28, 1944; children: Arthur H. II, Carolyn L., Caren L., Asa Greenwood Jr. BS, Morehouse Coll., Atlanta, 1937, ScD (hon.), 1991; MD, U. Mich., 1941; ScD (hon.), Howard U., Washington, DC, 1991. Diplomate Am. Bd. Surgery. Intern City Hosp., Cleve., 1941-42; resident Freedmen's Hosp., Washington, 1942-45, U.S. Marine Hosp., Boston, 1945; instr. surgery Meharry Med. Coll., 1946-48; chief surgery VA Hosp., Tuskegee, Ala., 1948-58; chief surgery of Hughes Spalding Pavilion, 1958-72; pvt. practice specializing in surgery Atlanta, 1958-86; from asst. prof. to assoc. prof. surgery Emory U., 1958—75, prof., 1975-86, prof. emeritus, 1986—, assoc. dean Sch. Medicine, 1972-89; med. dir. Grady Meml. Hosp., Atlanta, 1972-89, trustee, 1989—93; clin. prof. surgery Morehouse Sch. Medicine, 1985—; mem. staff Hughes Spalding Hosp., St. Joseph Hosp., Emory U. Hosp., 1986—88. Contbr. articles to profl. jours. Mem. Atlanta Bd. Edn., 1967—77, Fulton-De Kalb Hosp. Authority. 1st lt. M.C. US Army, 1942. Fellow: ACS, Am. Surg. Assn.; mem.: So. Surg. Assn., Inst. Medicine of NAS, Nat. Med. Assn. (1st v.p. 1988—89, trustee 1960—66, mem. editl. bd. jour. 1964—80). Baptist. Home and Office: 2845 Engle Rd NW Atlanta GA 30318-7216 Office Phone: 404-799-5045.

YANCEY, KIM BRUCE, dermatology researcher; b. Atlanta, Nov. 25, 1952; s. Andrew Jackson and Edrie (Johnson) Yancey. BS, U. Ga., Athens, 1974; MD, Med. Coll. Ga., 1978. Diplomate Am. Bd. Dermatology. Intern dept. internal medicine Med. Coll. Ga., Augusta, 1978-79, resident dept. dermatology, 1979-81; med. staff fellow dermatology br. NIH, Bethesda, Md., 1981-84, sr. staff fellow dermatology br., 1984-85, sr. investigator dermatology br., 1993—2000; asst. prof. dept. dermatology Uniformed Svcs. U. Health Scis., Bethesda, 1985-87, assoc. prof. dept. dermatology, 1987-93, acting chmn. dept. dermatology, 1990-93; prof., chair dept. dermatology Med. Coll. Wis., Milw., 2001—. Cons. Walter Reed Army Med. Ctr., Washington, 1985—2000. Author monographs and sci. manuscripts; mem. various editl. bds.; contbr. articles to profl. jours. Grantee NIH, 1986—, NATO, 1988-93. Fellow: Am. Acad. Dermatology (editl. bd. 1986—93, 2004—); mem.: AMA, Med. Coll. Physicians (mem. exec. com. 2004—, chmn. 2004—05), Assn. Profs. Dermatology (chmn. program com. 2004), Wis. Dermatol. Assn., Dermatology Found., Am. Fedn. Med. Rsch., Soc. Investigative Dermatology (bd. dirs. 1982—84, co-chmn. ea. region 1990—92, co-chmn. program com. 2004, bd. dir. 2004—), Am. Dermatol. Assn. (Young Leadership award 1986), Am. Bd. Dermatology (v.p. 2005), Am. Soc. Clin. Investigation. Methodist. Office: Med Coll Wis Dept Dermatology 8701 Watertown Plank Rd Milwaukee WI 53226 Office Phone: 414-456-4081. Business E-Mail: kyancey@mcw.edu.

YANCEY, RICHARD CHARLES, investment banker; b. Spokane, Wash., May 28, 1926; s. George R. and M. Ruth (Yenney) Y.; m. Mary Anne Shaffer, Feb. 5, 1956; children: Leslie, Jennifer, Richard C. Jr. BA in Econs., Whitman Coll., Walla Walla, Wash., 1949; MBA with distinction, Harvard U., 1952. Assoc. Dillon, Read & Co. Inc., NYC, 1952—63; v.p. Dillon, Read & Co., Inc., NYC, 1963-75, mng. dir., 1975-89, dir., 1990; sr. adv., 1992; ret. Dillon, Read & Co., Inc., NYC, 1992. Sr. advisor Ad Media Ptnrs., Inc., NYC; chmn., dir. Czech and Slovak Am. Enterprise Fund, Massapequa, NY; past partnership bd. Whittle Comms. L.P., Knoxville, Tenn.; former bd. dirs. Prin. Funds, Des Moines. Former chmn. bd. dirs. W.M. Group of Funds, Seattle; former bd. overseers Whitman Coll.; former trustee, former pres. Plymouth Ch. of Pilgrims, Bklyn.; former trustee NY Infirmary-Beekman Downtown Hosp.; bd. dirs. Bklyn. Chamber Music Soc. With USNR, 1944—46, PTO. Recipient Pres.'s USA Freedom Corps. Call to Svc. award, USAID, 2006. Mem. N.Y. Soc. Security Analysts, Assn. Investment Mgmt. and Rsch., Harvard Club, NYC, Pilgrims of the US. Republican. Home: 42 Monroe Pl Brooklyn NY 11201-2603 Office: Ad Media Partners 3 Park Ave RM 3102 New York NY 10016-0015 Home Phone: 718-852-1729; Office Phone: 212-759-1870. Personal E-mail: rc1yancey@earthlink.net. Business E-Mail: ryancey@admediapartners.com.

YANCHICK, VICTOR A., dean, educator; b. Joliet, Ill., Dec. 3, 1940; BS in Pharmacy, U. Iowa, 1962, MS in Pharmacy, 1966; PhD in Pharmacy, Purdue U., West Lafayette, Ind., 1968. Asst. chief pharmacist Silver Cross Hosp., Joliet, Ill., 1962-64; hosp. pharmacy resident Univs. Hosp., Iowa City, 1964-66; instr. clin. pharmacy Purdue U., 1966-68; asst. prof. pharmacy U. Tex., Austin, 1968-72, assoc. prof. pharmacy, 1972-78, prof. pharmacy, 1978-84, acting asst. dean, 1971-73, asst. dean academic affairs, 1973-81, assoc. dean, 1981-84; dean U. Okla. Coll. Pharmacy, Oklahoma City, 1985-96; prof. pharmacy, dean. Va. Commonwealth U. Sch. Pharmacy, Richmond, 1996—. Cons. Tex. Nursing Home Assn., Austin, 1978—84, Baylor Coll. Medicine, Houston, 1988—90; dir. Okla. Poison Ctr., Oklahoma City, 1994—96; mem. adv. bd. Nat. Assn. Retail Druggist Edn., Nat. Assn. Chain Drug Stores. Recipient Alumni Assn. award, U. Okla., 1989, Disting. Alumnus award, Purdue U., 1995. Mem.: Am. Assn. Colleges of Pharmacy. Avocations: tennis, racquetball, gardening, antique collecting. Office: VCU Sch Pharmacy Deans Office 410 N 12th St PO Box 980581 Richmond VA 23298-0581 Office Phone: 804-828-3006. Office Fax: 804-827-0002. Business E-Mail: vyanchick@vcu.edu.*

YANCY, CLYDE WARREN, JR., cardiologist, educator; b. Baton Rouge, Jan. 2, 1958; MD, Tulane U. Sch. Medicine, 1982. Diplomate Am. Bd. Internal Medicine, Sub-specialty Cardiovascular Disease. Intern, internal medicine Parkland Meml. Hosp. and U. Tex. Southwestern Med. Ctr., Dallas, 1982—83, resident, internal medicine, 1983, dir., cardiology clinics, 1990—96; clin. rsch. assoc., dept. cardiovascular rsch. Tulane U. Sch. Medicine, New Orleans, 1985—86; staff physician, dept. internal medicine and ambulatory care New Orleans Vet. Adminstrn. Hosp., New Orleans, 1985—86; staff physician Gen. Hosp. Lakewood, Dallas, 1987—89; attending cardiologist, coronary care unit Parkland Meml. Hosp., Dallas, 1989, assoc. dir., cardiac rehabilitation program, 1990—93, cons. cardiologist, renal transplant program, 1990—92, acting med. dir., coronary care unit, 1992—93; attending cardiologist, coronary care unit Dallas Vet. Adminstrn. Hosp., Dallas, 1989; clin. cardiologist Zale-Lipshy U. Hosp., Dallas, 1989; assoc. attending staff, dept. medicine, divsn. cardiology St. Paul Med. Ctr., Dallas, 1993; fellow, cardiology U. Tex. Southwestern Med. Ctr., Dallas, 1986—89, attending cardiologist, 1989, asst. prof. medicine, divsn. cardiology, 1989—95, assoc. prof. medicine, divsn. cardiology, 1995—2004, prof. medicine, divsn. cardiology, 2004—06, Carl Westcott Disting. Chair, med. rsch., 1996, med. dir., Heart Failure/Heart Transplant Program, 1991—2006, assoc. dean, clin. affairs, 2002—06; med. dir., Baylor Heart & Vascular Inst. Baylor U. Med. Ctr., Dallas, 2006—, chief, cardiothoracic transplantation, 2006—. Rsch. asst., biomedical scis. dept. So. U., Baton Rouge, 1976; rsch. chemist Merck, Sharpe and Dohme Rsch. Lab., Rahway, NJ, 1978; camp counselor Am. Diabetes Assn., 1979; vis. tchg. staff dept., sect. medicine, cardiology St. Paul Med. Ctr., Dallas, 1989; advanced cardiac life support instr., 1990—93; cons. Ctr. for Disease Control, Vet. Affairs Med. Ctrs., NIH; mem., cardiovascular device panel Ctr. for Devices and Radiological Health; FDA; Integrity-Com. and Conf. Mgmt. Br., 2003—; mem., Nat. Immunization Program Adv. Com. Ctr. for Disease Control; FDA, 2003—05; mem., Circulatory Sys. Devices Panel of the Med. Devices Adv. Com., Dept. HHS, FDA, 2005—08; mem., physician health and recovery com. U. Tex. Southwestern Med. Ctr., Dallas, 2006; mem. scientific adv. bd. Internat. Acad. Cardiology and the World Congress, 2006—07; Newall Powell Vis. professorship Scott & White Clinic, Temple, Tex., 2004; invited lectr. in field. Contbr. chapters to books, several articles to profl. jours., web-based ednl. media, to several CD-Roms; assoc. editor Am. Jour. Cardiology, Congestive Heart Failure, mem. editl. bd., 2002—, Am. Heart Jour., Cardiology Review, Urban Cardiology, Jour. Cardiovascular Pharmacology and Therapeutics & Circulation, Progress in Transplantation, 2002—, Jour. Cardiac Failure, 2002—04, Current Heart Failure Reports, 2003—, Jour. Acute Cardiac Care, 2006—07, reviewer for major cardiovascular jours. Bd. dirs. Family Place. Named one of Top Doctors, D Mag., 1992, Top 330 Doctors in 2001, Top 381 Doctors in 2002 (Featured Top Doctor), Best Doctors, 2003—04, Top 572 Doctors of 2003 (Featured Top Doctor), Top 638 Doctors of 2004 (Featured Top Doctor), Best Doctors, 2005, Best Doctors in Am., 1998, 2000, America's Leading Physicians, Black Enterprise Mag., 2001, Tex. Super Docs, Tex. Monthly, 2004, Tex. Super Doctors 2005, America's Top Physicians, Guide to America's Top Physicians, e-book, 2006. Fellow: Internat. Soc. on Hypertension in Blacks (Outstanding Rsch. award 2001), ACP, Am. Heart Assn. (first v.p., Dallas Divsn. 1993—94, pres.-elect, Dallas Divsn 1994—95, pres., Dallas Divsn. 1995—96, first v.p., Tex. affiliate 1996—97, pres.-elect, Tex. affiliate 1997—98, pres., Tex. affiliate 1998—99, bd. dir., Tex. affiliate 2001—02, coun. clin. cardiology's heart failure and transplantation sub-com., mem. nat. bd. dirs. 2000—02, nat. spokesperson, bd. dirs. Dallas Divsn. and Tex. Affiliate, chmn., hypertension task force, Dallas Divsn., Douglas Perry Vol. Yr. award, Dallas Divsn. 1996, Walter M. Kirkendall, award for Outstanding Scientist/Educator Vol., Tex. affiliate 1996, Physician Vol. Yr., Tex. Affiliate 2001, Nat. Physician of Yr. 2003), ACS, Am. Coll. Cardiology (sec.-treas., Tex. chpt. 1993—95); mem.: Dallas County Med. Soc., Tex. Med. Assn., Tex. Translatation Soc., Tex. Acad. Physician Assts. (hon.), Am. Soc. Transplantation, Am. Diabetes Assn. (minority initiative com., bd. dirs. 1990—92), Assn. Black Cardiologists, Inc. (chmn., organ transplantation com. 2002—03, heart failure com. chair 2002—03, editl. bd. Digest of Urban Cardiology 2002—04, Daniel Savage award for Scientific Merit 2002, Cardiologists-In-Tng. Hero award 2006), Heart Failure Soc. Am. (mem. exec. com., ex-officio 2001—03), Am. Soc. Hypertension, Internat. Soc. Heart and Lung Transplantation, Alpha Omega Alpha. Office: Baylor Heart & Vascular Inst Baylor U Med Ctr 3500 Gaston Ave Ste H-030 Dallas TX 75246 Office Phone: 214-820-7357. Office Fax: 214-820-7533. Business E-Mail: clydey@baylorhealth.edu.

YANDELL, CATHY MARLEEN, language educator; b. Anadarko, Okla., Dec. 27, 1949; d. Lloyd O. and Maurine (Dunn) Y.; m. Mark S. McNeil, Sept. 7, 1974; children: Elizabeth Yandell McNeil, Laura Yandell McNeil. Student, Inst. des Professeurs de Français à l'Etranger U. Sorbonne, Paris, 1969—70; BA, U. N.Mex., 1971; MA, U. Calif., Berkeley, 1973, PhD, 1977. Tchg. asst. U. Calif., Berkeley, 1971, acting instr., 1976—77; asst. prof. Carleton Coll., Northfield, Minn., 1977—83, assoc. prof., 1983—89, prof. French, 1989—. Chair commn. on the status of women Carleton Coll., Northfield, 1983-85, ednl. policy com., 1985-86, 96-97, romance langs. and lits., 1990-94, chair faculty affairs com., 2000-02, pres. of faculty, 1991-94, Bryn-Jones disting. tchg. prof. humanities, 1996-99, mentor to jr. faculty, 1996—, W.I. and Hulda F. Daniell prof. French lit., lang. and culture, 1999—; dir. Paris French Studies Program, 1998, 2004, 08. Author: Carpe Corpus: Time and Gender in Early Modern France, 2000; co-author: Vagabondages: Initiation à la litt. d'expression française, 1996, 1996, Vieillir à la Renaissance, 2009; contbr. to Art & Argumentation: The Sixteenth Century Dialogue, 1993, French Texts/American Contexts: French Women Writers, 1994, Montaigne: A Collection of Essays, Vol. 4, Language and Meaning, 1995, Reflexivity in Women Writeres of the Ancien Régime, 1998, High Anxiety, 2002, Ronsard, figure de la variété, 2002, Lectrices d'Ancien Régime, 2003, Reflections on Teaching, 2004, Ecriture courante: Critical Perspectives on French and Francophone Women, 2005, Masculinites in Sixteenth-Century France, 2006, Paysage et nature a La Renaissance, 2007, Approaches to Teaching the Heptameron, 2007; editor: Pontus de Tyard's Solitaire Second, ou prose de la musique, 1980; contbr. articles to profl. jours. Active exec. com., then mem. Amnesty Internat., Northfield, 1980—. Grantee Faculty Devel., Carleton Coll., 1988, 1991; Regents' Travelling fellow, U. Calif. Berkeley, 1975—76, NEH Rsch. fellow, 1994—95, Mellon Faculty fellow, 2003, Roth Faculty Rsch. fellow, 2007, Mellon New Directions grantee, 2006. Mem.: MLA (del. 1989—92, chair exec. com. French 16th Century lit. 2001—05), Humanities Ctr. Carleton (dir. 2008—), Sixteenth Century Soc. (program chmn. French lit. 2007—), Phi Beta Kappa (pres. 2004—05). Democrat. Home: 514 5th St E Northfield MN 55057-2220 Office: Carleton College 1 N College St Northfield MN 55057-4044 Office Phone: 507-222-4245. Business E-Mail: cyandell@carleton.edu.

YANDERS, ARMON FREDERICK, biological sciences educator, science administrator; b. Lincoln, Nebr., Apr. 12, 1928; s. Fred W. and Beatrice (Pate) Yanders; m. Evelyn Louise Gatz, Aug. 1, 1948; children: Mark Frederick, Kent Michael. AB, Nebr. State Coll., Peru, 1948; MS, U. Nebr., 1950, PhD, 1953. Rsch. asso. Oak Ridge Nat. Lab. and Northwestern U., 1953-54; biophysicist US Naval Radiol. Def. Lab., San Francisco, 1955-58; asso. geneticist Argonne Nat. Lab., Ill., 1958-59; with dept. zoology Mich. State U., 1959-69; prof., asst. dean Mich. State U. (Coll. Natural Sci.), 1963-69; prof. biol. scis. U. Mo., Columbia, 1969—, dean Coll. Arts and Scis., 1969-82, rsch. prof., dir. Environ. Trace Substances Rsch. Ctr., 1983-93, dir. Alzheimer's Disease and Related Disorders Program, 1994—, dir. Spinal Cord Injury Rsch. Program, 2002—, rsch. prof., dir. Environ. Trace Substances Rsch. Ctr. and Sinclair Comparative Medicine Rsch. Farm, 1984-94, prof. emeritus, 1994—; dean emeritus, 2007—. Trustee Argonne Univs. Assn., 1965-77, v.p., 1969-73, pres., 1973, 76-77, chmn. bd., 1973-75; bd. dirs. Coun. Colls. Arts and Scis., 1981-82; mem. adv. com. environ. hazards VA, Washington, 1985-2002, chmn. sci. coun., 1988-2000, chmn. of com., 1990-2002. Contbr. articles to profl. jours. Trustee Peru State Coll., 1992-2001. Served from ensign to lt. USNR, 1954-58. Recipient Disting. Svc. award Peru State Coll., 1989, U. Mo., 2007. Fellow AAAS; mem. AAUP (Robert W. Martin acad. freedom award 1971), Environ. Mutagen Soc., Genetics Soc. Am., Radiation Rsch. Soc., Soc. Environ. Toxicology and Chemistry. Home: 1204 Castle Bay Pl Columbia MO 65203-6257 Office: U Mo 521 Clark Hall Columbia MO 65211-4420 Office Phone: 573-882-1640. Business E-Mail: YandersA@umsystem.edu.

YANDLE, STEPHEN THOMAS, dean; b. Oakland, Calif., Mar. 7, 1947; s. Clyde Thomas and Jane Walker (Hess) Y.; m. Martha Anne Welch, June 26, 1971. BA, U. Va., 1969, JD, 1972. Bar: Va. 1972. Asst. dir. admissions U. Va. Law Sch., Charlottesville, 1972-76; from asst. to assoc. dean Northwestern U. Sch. Law, Chgo., 1976-85; assoc. dean Yale U. Law Sch., New Haven, 1985—2002; exec. dir. Housing Authority of New Haven, 2002—04; dep. cons. on legal edn. ABA, 2004—06; v.p. global law sch. programs LexisNexis, 2007—09; assoc. dean Peking U. Sch. Transnational Law, 2009—. Bd. dirs. The Access Group, 1996-2004; lectr. in law Yale Law Sch., 2002-04; vis. scholar Am. Bar Found., 2006. Commr. New Haven Housing Authority, 1998-02; trustee Nat. Assoc. for Law Placement Found. for Rsch. and Edn., 2000-04, 07-. Capt. US Army, 1972. Mem. Law Sch. Admission Coun. (programs, edn. and prelaw com. 1978-84), Assn. Am. Law Schs. (chmn. legal edn. and admissions sect. 1979, nominations com. 1987, chmn. adminstrn. of law schs. sect. 1991), Nat. Assn. for Law Placement (pres. 1984-85, co-chmn. Joint Nat. Assn. com. on placement 1986-88), New Haven Legal Assistance Assn. (bd. dirs., treas. 1992-98). Office: Univ Town Lishui Rd Nanshan Dist Shenzhen 518055 China Home Phone: 312-587-3147; Office Phone: 886 0755 26033143. Business E-Mail: stephenyandle@szpku.edu.cn.

YANES, LICY LORENA, medical educator; d. Jose Luis Yanes and Maria Teresa Cardozo; m. Damian Gaston Romero, Jan. 3, 2005; 1 child, Patricia Maria Romero. MD, U. Nacional Asuncion, Paraguay, 1997. Postdoc. fellow U. Miss. Med. Ctr., Jackson, 2002—04, instr., 2004—07, asst. prof., 2008—. Recipient Profl. Opportunity award, Am. Physiol. Soc., 2005; fellow Postdoc. fellowship, Am. Heart Assn., 2005—07; Scientist Devel. grant, 2008—. Mem.: Am. Heart Assn. (Postdoc. fellowship 2005—07, Scientist Devel. grant 2008—), Endocrine Soc., Am. Physiol. Soc. Achievements include research in mechanisms of sex steroids-mediated hypertension. Office: Univ Miss Med Ctr 2500 North State St Physiology Jackson MS 39216 Office Fax: 1-601-984-1817. Business E-Mail: lyanes@physiology.umsmed.edu.

YANEY, GEORGE, retired history professor; b. Teaneck, NJ, Oct. 30, 1930; s. Arthur J. and Frances (Levings) Y.; m. Ann Hinrichs, June 7, 1952; children: Brian, Dale, Carolyn, Tara. B in Mgmt. Engring., Rensselaer Poly. Inst., 1952; MA in History, U. Colo., 1956; PhD, Princeton U., 1961. Instr. Coll. Wooster, Ohio, 1957-58; prof. history U. Md., College Park, 1960-92, prof. emeritus, 1992—; ret., 1992. Author: Systematization of Russian Government, 1973, Urge to Mobilize, 1982, World of the Manager, 1994. Served to capt. USMC, 1952-54. Rsch. fellow Harvard U., 1969-70, fellow Slavic Rsch. Ctr., U. Hokkaido, Japan, 1990-91; Fulbright grantee, 1975, 77, 85, Internat. Rsch. Exchanges Bd. grantee 1965, 75, 77, 85, 89. Home: 1831 Pine Mesa Grove Colorado Springs CO 80918 Personal E-mail: georgeyaney@msn.com.

YANEZ, ANTONIO, JR., lawyer; b. Newark, Dec. 30, 1970; s. Antonio and Maria P. Yanez; m. Colleen Murphy, Dec. 1, 2001; children: Daniel, Thomas. BA, Vassar Coll., Poughkeepsie, NY, 1992; JD, Bklyn. Law Sch., 1996. Bar: NY 1997, US Dist. Ct. (so. and ea. dists.), NY 1999, US Ct. Appeals (11th cir.) 2002. Assoc. Willkie Farr & Gallagher, LLP, NYC, 1996—2004, ptnr., 2005—.

YANG, ALLEN S., medical educator; married. MD, PhD, Am. Med. Assn., 1997. Asst. prof. U. Southern Calif., LA, 2004—. Office: Univ Southern Calif 1441 Eastlake Ave Los Angeles CA 90033

YANG, BENSON PIN-SHENG, neurosurgeon; b. Taipei, Taiwan, July 4, 1975; s. Tsong-Toh and Lee Ju Yang; m. Carina Wei-Yee Fung, May 25, 2001. BS, MEng, MIT, Cambridge, 1997; MD, Yale U. Sch. Medicine, New Haven, 2001. Cert. in neurol. surgery Northwestern U. Feinberg Sch. Medicine, Chgo., 2007, in complex and reconstructive spine surgery 2007. Neurosurgeon Northwestern Neurosurg. Assocs. Contbr. articles to profl. jours. Recipient Steven M. Pinsky Resident Rsch. award, Ill. Radiol. Soc., 2007, Murphy Soc. prize, Grad. Sch. Northwestern U., 2007, Mayfield Clin. Sci. award, Joint Sect. Disorders of Spine and Peripheral Nerves, 2006. Mem.: Congress Neurol. Surgeons, Am. Assn. Neurol. Surgeons, Eta Kappa Nu, Tau Beta Pi, Sigma Xi. Home: 340 E Randolph St Apt 4702 Chicago IL 60601 Office: Northwestern Neurosurg Assocs 7447 W Talcott Ave Ste 340 Chicago IL 60631 Business E-Mail: b-yang1@md.northwestern.edu.

YANG, BILL Z., economics professor; BS in Math., U. Wuhan, Hubei, People's Republic of China, 1982; MA in Economics, Queen's U., Kingston, Ont., Can., 1987; PhD in Economics (hon.), U. Iowa, Iowa City, 1993. Asst. prof. economics Flinders U. South Australia, Adelaide, 1993—96; vis. asst. prof. economics U. Iowa, 1996—97; asst. prof. economics Minot State U., ND, 1997—2000; assoc. prof. economics Ga. Southern U., Statesboro, 2000—. Contbr. articles to profl. jour. Recipient COBA award, 2003. Office: Ga Southern Univ Sch Economics Statesboro GA 30460-8152

YANG, BIN, pathologist, molecular biologist; MD, Zhengzhou U., China, 1983, MS in Cancer Biology, 1986; PhD, Case Western Res. U., Cleve, Ohio, 1996. Diplomate Pathology Bd. Cert. for Anatomic Pathology and Cytopathology 2003. Instr. Henan Med. U., Zhengzhou, China, 1986—88; postdoctoral fellow Case Western Res. U., Cleve., 1988—90; pathology resident Cleve. Clinic Found., 1996—2000, staff pathologist, 2003—; surg. pathology fellow Wash. U., St. Louis, 2000—01; cytopathology fellow Johns Hopkins U., Balt., 2001—03. Dir. cancer epigenetics core lab. Cleve. Clinic Found., 2003—. Contbr. scientific papers pub. to profl. jour. and confs. Recipient George Hoffman award, 2000, Geno Saccomanno New Frontier in Cytology award, 2002, 2007, Hans Popper Outstanding Sci. award, 2003, Johns Hopkins Pathology Young Investigator's award, 2003, Innovation award, Cleveland Clin., 2006. Mem.: Chinese Am. Pathologists Assn. (pres. 2006—08). Avocations: tennis, golf, photography, gardening.

YANG, BING-SHIANG, engineering educator; BS in Mech. Engring. with honors, Nat. Taiwan U., 1994, MS in Mech. Engring., 1996; PhD in Mech. Engring. and Biomechanics, U. Mich., 2004. Cert. nat. refrigeration and air-conditioning profl. engr., ROC, 1995. Rsch. asst. Nat. Taiwan U., Taipei, 1993—96; engr. Tenkey Refrigeration MFG. Co. Ltd., Taipei, 1994; lectr. Tjing-Ling Indsl. Rsch. Ctr., Taipei, 1995—96; tchg. asst. Nat. Taiwan U., 1998—99; rsch. asst. U. Mich., 1999—2004; rsch. assoc. Rehab. Inst. of Chgo., 2005—06; postdoctoral fellow Northwestern U., Chgo., 2005—06; asst. prof. Nat. Chiao U., 2006—; dir. Biomechanics and Med. Application Lab. Nat. Chiao Tung U., 2006—; smart gymnasium tech. organizer Integrated Smart Living Tech. Regional Ctr., 2008—. Mem. com. Internat. Conf. on Rehab. Robotics, Chgo., 2005; mem. award com. Nat. Sci. Coun., Taiwan, 2006, external grant reviewer, 07, 08, Nat. Med. Rsch. Coun., Singapore, 2007—; rsch. affiliate Brain Rsch. Ctr. Nat. Chiao Tung U., 2006—; organizer Internat. Conf. Mech. in Medicine and Biology, Singapore, 2006; spkr. in field. Contbr. articles to profl. pubs. Second lt. Armor, Army, 1996—98, Taiwan. Decorated Best Trainee award ROC Army Pre-Mil. Tng. Ctr., ranked 1st/250 second lt. ROC Army Armor Officer Tng. Ctr.; recipient Academic, Personal, Profl., and Leadership Devel. Cert., U. Mich., 2004, Sarah Baskin Rsch. Excellence award, Rehab. Inst. Chgo., 2006, Excellence Scholarship award, Nat. Chiao Tung U., 2008, NCTU Design Contest Gold & Silver medal, 2009; finalist Young Investigator award, Internat. Soc. Biomech., 2007, Clin. Biomechanics award, Internat. Soc. Biomechanics, 2009; Tchg. Fellow, U. Mich., 2004, Advanced Rehab. Rsch. Tng. Postdoctoral fellowship, US Nat. Inst. on Disability and Rehab. Rsch., 2005—06, Travel grant, Neural Control of Movement Soc. and Nat. Inst. on Disability and Rehab. Rsch., 2006, U Mich. Internat. Inst., 2002, U Mich. Rackham Grad. Sch., 2002, 2003, 2004. Mem.: Taiwanese Soc. Biomechanics (coun. mem. 2008—), Soc. for Neurosci., Soc. for Neural Control of Movement, Internat. Soc. of Biomechanics, Am. Soc. of Biomechanics, Am. Soc. for Mech. Engineers. Achievements include patents for self-guided drill jib for equal-distance holes, ROC utility model; research in simulation study of human balance control on raised rigid structures; experimental study of age and gender differences on stepping and balancing behavior on laterally-compliant raised structures; modelling of human balance control on raised structures with lateral structural compliance; sensory input-enhanced stroke rehabilitation; task-specific modulation arm/hand posture and stiffness; smart living technology, advanced vehicle technology. Avocations: martial arts (3d Dan-black belt), swimming, ping pong/table tennis, bicycling, travel. Business E-Mail: bsyang@umich.edu.

YANG, BO, electrical engineer; s. Rucai Yang and Chuanli Zhen; m. Yi He, July 27, 2006. BS in Elec. Engring., SE U., Nanjing, Jiangsu, China, 1999, MS in Elec. Engring., 2002; PhD in Elec. Engring., Ariz. State U., Tempe, 2007. Rsch. assoc. Ariz. State U., 2002—07; sr. elec. engr. LinkQuest Inc., San Diego, 2007—. Contbr. chapters to books, articles to sci. jour. Achievements include design of high-sensitivity underwater acoustic velocity profiler. Personal E-mail: byang.asu@gmail.com.

YANG, BONG-JUN, research scientist; s. Ho-Nam Yang and Myung-Ja Choi; m. Jiyoon Cecilia Jung, Sept. 5, 2004; 1 child, Dahyun Katie. PhD, Ga. Inst. Tech., Atlanta, 2004. Rsch. engr. Ga. Inst. Tech., 2005—07; sr. rsch. engr. Guided Sys. Techs., Inc, McDonough, Ga., 2007—. Contbr. articles to profl. jours. Mem.: IEEE, AIAA. Achievements include research in applying neural network based adaptive control to flexible systems. Office: Guided Sys Techs 1603 Zack Hinton Pky S Mcdonough GA 30252 Office Phone: 770-898-9100. Business E-Mail: bongjun.yang@gatech.edu, jun.yang@guidedsys.com.

YANG, BO-SUK, mechanical engineering educator; b. Kangwon, Korea, Feb. 8, 1956; s. Jae-Yong and Duk-Ryu (Cho) Y.; m. Jung-Mi Um, Apr. 26, 1980; children: Sung-Il, Sung-Wook. BS in Engring., Nat. Fisheries U. Pusan, Korea, 1978, MS in Engring., 1980; PhD in Engring., Kobe U., Japan, 1985. Teaching asst. Nat. Fisheries U. of Pusan, 1978-82, asst. prof., 1985-90, dept. chmn., 1990-92, assoc. prof., 1990-95, prof., 1995-96; prof. sch. mech. engring. Pukyong Nat. U. (formerly Nat. Fisheries U. of Pusan), Korea, 1996—, sch. head, 2001—03; dean acad. affairs Pukyong Nat. U. (formerly Nat. Fisheries U. Pusan), 2008—. Vis. prof. U. Va., Charlottesville, 1989-90; vis. scientist Kobe (Japan) U., 1990-91; cons. Korea Heavy Industries, Ltd., Changwon, 1994-98, LG Electronics Inc., Changwon, 1991-95, 2000-03, Hyundai Heavy Industries, Ltd., Ulsan, 1995-99, 2004-06, Hyosung-Ebara Co. Ltd., Changwon, 1994—, STX, Ltd., Changwon, 2002-, Daewoo Precision Ltd., 2004-06; vis. fellow QUT, Australia, 2006. Editor: Jour. Korean Soc. Lubrication Engrs., 1992-99, Jour. Korean Soc. Marine Engrs., 1991-2000, Jour. Korean Soc. Power Sys. Engring., 1999-2001; regional editor Internat. Jour. Engring. Asset Mgmt., 2008-; assoc. editor Internat. Jour. Fluid Machinery and Systems, 2008-; contbr. papers to profl. jours. Recipient Best Paper award Korean Fedn. Sci. and Tech., Socs., 1994, Outstanding Acad. Contbn. award Pukyong Nat. U., 2003. Fellow Instn. Engrs. Australia, ASME (H.H. Jeffcott award 1987), Korean Soc. Mech. Engrs. (Sci. Achievement award 2007), Japan Soc. Mech. Engrs. (Disting. Rsch. award 1988), Korean Soc. Marine Engrs. (Best Paper award 1994), Korean Soc. Noise and Vibration Engring. (editor Trans. 2003-05, Best Paper award 2002), Internat. Soc. Engring Asset Mgmt. (dir. 2005-), Presbyterian. Avocations: swimming, reading. Office: Pukyong Nat Univ San 100 Yongdang-dong Nam-gu Busan 608-739 Republic of Korea Home Phone: 82-51-629-6152; Office Phone: 82-51-629-5006. Business E-Mail: bsyang@pknu.ac.kr.

YANG, CARY, engineering educator; s. James Tao-Yao Yang and Anna Yuan-Kwan Fung; m. Marie Nakajima; children: Elaine Akiko, Jocelyn Miko. PhD, U. Pa., Phila., 1975. Prof. Santa Clara U., Calif., 1983—, chair EE, 2008—, dir. ctr. nanostructures, 2003—. Bao Yugang endowed prof. Zhejiang U., Hangzhou, China, 2008—. Fellow: IEEE (Piscataway, NJ) (pres., ieee electron devices soc. 2000—01, bd. dirs. 2002—03, Meritorious Achievement award 2004, Disting. Svc. award 2005). Office: Santa Clara Univ 500 El Camino Real Santa Clara CA 95053 Office Fax: 1-408-554-5474. Business E-Mail: cyang@scu.edu.

YANG, CHAO YUH, biochemistry professor, medical educator; b. Pingtung, Taiwan, May 8, 1939; came to U.S., 1982; s. Shang-Sheng and Kuei-Mei (Lee) Y.; m. Manlan Lou Yang; children: Tseming, Tseliang, Thomas. BS, Tamkang U., Taipei, Taiwan, 1962; MS, Georg-August U., Goettingen, Germany, 1970, PhD, 1973. Tchr. Chiatung Agr. High Sch., Pingtung, Taiwan, 1963-64; chemist Kuantu Glass Plant, Taipei, 1964-68; postdoctoral fellow dept. molecular biology Max-Planck Inst. for Exptl. Medicine, Goettingen, 1973-75, scientist dept. immunochemistry, 1975-82; asst. prof. biochemistry Baylor Coll. Medicine, Houston, 1982-89, asst. prof. dept. medicine, 1983-86, rsch. assoc. prof. dept. medicine, 1986-90, rsch. assoc. prof. dept. biochemistry, 1989-91, rsch. prof. medicine, 1990-95; rsch. prof. biochemistry, 1991-95; prof. medicine and biochemistry, 1995—2009; emeritus prof. Baylor Coll. Medicine, 2009—. Dir. peptide core Nat. Rsch. and Demonstration Ctr. in Arteriosclerosis, Baylor Coll. Medicine, 1984-96, internal adv. com., 1986-96; organizing com. 10th Internat. Conf. on Methods in Protein Structure Analysis, Snowbird, Utah, 1994; sci. com. Internat. Conf. on Methods in Protein Sequence Analysis, Berlin, 1988, Sweden, 1990; reviewer grants Biomed. Rsch. rev. Com., Nat. Inst. on Drug Abuse, NSF, Washington; lectr. in field. Reviewer papers for Jour. Chromatography, Jour. Lipid Rsch., Jour. Protein Chemistry, Molecular and Cellular Biochemistry, Biochemistry, Arteriosclerosis, Circulation; contbr. articles to profl. jours. Pres. Taiwanese Am. Citizens League of Houston, 1988-90, Taiwanese Am. Assn. Houston, 1985-86. Grantee BRSG Funds, 1982-83, NIH, 1986-96, 2001-2006, AHA, 1985-90, 97-99, Meth. Hosp. Found., 1988-91, AHA Tex., 1997-2001, ADA, 2003-06. Home: 4102 Levonshire Dr Houston TX 77025-3915 Office: Acad Bio-Med Co 1417 Kress St Houston TX 77020 Office Phone: 713-675-4040. Business E-Mail: cyang@academybiomed.com.

YANG, CHAOWEI PHIL, research scientist, educator; s. Chaoqing Yang and Mingju Tang; m. Yan Xiang, Nov. 23, 2003; 1 child, Andrew. PhD, Beijing U., 2000. Postdoc. rsch. scientist U. Calgary, Alta., Canada, 2000—01; prof. and dir. Ctr. Intelligent Spatial Computing, GMU, Fairfax, Va., 2001—. Pres. Internat. Assn. Chinese Profls. GISci., Berkeley, Calif., 2004—05. Contbr. articles to profl. jours. Mgr. profl. tng. and web com. CPGIS, Berkeley, 2003—. Recipient Unidata Equipment award, NSF, 2003; grant, Intergraph, 2002—, FGDC, 2003, 2005, NASA, 2005—. Master: AAG CISG (co-foundor 2007, vice-chair to chair 2007—, co-founder); mem.: AAAS, ACSM, ASPRS, CPGIS (pres. 2002—, bd. dirs. 2002—, com. chair 2002—, Svc. Excellence 2004). Achievements include patents pending for WebGIS performance improving techniques. Avocations: basketball, tennis, jogging, ping pong/table tennis. Office: Rm# 326A RB1 MS 6A2 George Mason Univ 4400 Univ Dr Fairfax VA 22030-4444 Office Fax: 703-993-9299. Business E-Mail: cyang3@gmu.edu.

YANG, CHARLES QI-XIANG, chemistry educator, researcher, consultant; b. Sanchang, Jiangsu, China, Jan. 30, 1944; came to U.S., 1982; s. Weizhu and Zhiyin (Zhou) Yang; 1 child, Chen. BS, Peking U., China, 1969; MS, Nanking U., China, 1981; PhD, Kans. State U., 1987. Rsch. scientist Henan Rsch. Inst. of Chemistry, Zhenzhou, Honan, China, 1975-78, 82; intern lab. scientist Perkin-Elmer Corp., Eden Prairie, Minn., 1986; asst. prof. Marshall U., Huntington, W.Va., 1987-90; assoc. prof. U. Ga., Athens, 1990-95, prof., 1995—. Cons. in field. Contbg. author: Adhesion Science, 1984, The Structures of Cellulose, 1987, Adhesives, Sealants, and Coatings for Space and Harsh Environment, 1988, Structure-Property Relations in Polymers, 1993; contbr. articles to profl. jours. Mem. Am. Chem. Soc. (treas. Cen. Ohio Valley sect. 1989, chmn.-elect Cen. Ohio Valley sect. 1990, chmn-elect N.E. Ga. sect. 1991, chmn. N.E. Ga. sect. 1992), Am. Assn. Textile Chemists and Colorists, Fiber Soc. Achievements include patents in field; development of new durable press finishing and flame retardant finishing systems. Avocations: swimming, hiking, classical music. Home: 189 Elderberry Cir Athens GA 30605-4954 Office: U Ga 305 Dawson Hall Athens GA 30602 Office Phone: 706-542-4912. Business E-Mail: cyang@uga.edu.

YANG, CHEN NING FRANKLIN, physicist, educator; b. Hofei, Anhui, Anhwei, China, Oct. 1, 1922; naturalized, 1964; s. Ke Chuan and Meng Hwa Loh Yang; m. Chih Li Tu, Aug. 26, 1950 (dec. 2003); children: Franklin, Gilbert, Eulee; m. Weng Fan Yang, 2005. BSC, Nat. SW Associated U., Kunming, China, 1942; MSc, Tsinghua U., 1944; PhD, U. Chgo., 1948; DSc (hon.), Princeton U., 1958, Bklyn. Polytechnic Inst., 1965, U. Wroclaw, Poland, 1974, Gustavus Adolphus Coll., Minn., 1975, U. Md., 1979, U. Durham, Eng., 1979, Fudan U., China, 1984, Eidg. Technische Hochschule, Switzerland, 1987, Moscow State U., 1992, Drexel U., 1995, Tsinghua U., Taiwan, 1996, Chiao Tung U., 1996, Chinese U., Hong Kong, 1997, U. Mich., 1998, SUNY, Stony Brook, 1999, Washington Coll., 1999, Baptist U., Hong Kong, 1999, Chung-Cheng U., Taiwan, 2000, U. Sci. and Tech., Hong Kong, 2002, Ecole Normale Superioeure, Paris, France, 2003. Instr. U. Chgo., 1948—49; postdoctoral position Inst. Adv. Study, Princeton, NJ, 1949—53, prof., 1955—66; position at Brookhaven Lab., 1953—54; Albert Einstein prof. physics SUNY, Stony Brook, 1966—99, prof. emeritus, 1999—; dir. Inst. Theoretical Physics, 1966—99; dir. emeritus C.N. Yang Inst. Theoretical Physics; disting. prof.-at-large Chinese U. Hong Kong, 1986—; prof. Tsinghua U., Beijing, 1998. Chmn., divsn. particles and fields Internat. Union Pure and Applied Physics, 1972—76; chmn. Fachbeirat, Max Planck Inst. Physics, 1980—83; established the found. Ctr. for Advanced Rsch., Zhongshan U., 1983, chmn.; organized a theoretical physics divsn. Nankai Inst. Math., 1986; coun. mem. Shaw Prize, mem. bd. adjudicators, 2005—; invited lectr. Contbr. articles to profl. jours.; author: Elementary Particles: a short history of some discoveries in atomic physics, 1961. Mem. governing coun. Courant Inst. Math. Sci., 1963—; mem. sci. adv. com. IBM, 1966—71; mem. High Energy Physics Adv. Panel, 1968—70; bd. trustee Rockefeller U., 1970—76, Stony Brook Found., 1981—99, Salk Inst., 1978—89, Ben Gurion U., 1981—, Brookhaven Sci. Associates, 1998—99; mem. Woods Hole Oceangraphic Institution, 1962—78; mem. coun. scholars The Libr. Congress, 1990—; bd. dir. Neuroscience Inst., 1983—88, Scientific American Inc., 1983—90. Recipient Albert Einstein Commemorative award, 1957, Rumford prize, 1980, US Nat. Medal Sci., 1986, Benjamin Franklin medal, 1993, Bower award, 1994, N. Bogoliubov prize, 1996, Lars Onsager prize, 1999, King Faisal prize, 2001; co-recipient Nobel Prize in Physics, 1957. Fellow: Am. Phys. Soc. (chmn., divsn. particles and fields 1970—71), Academia Sinica (Taiwan); mem.: AAAS (bd. dir. 1975—79), Brazilian Acad. Sciences, Asia Pacific Ctr. Theoretical Physics (pres. 1996), Assn. Asia Pacific Phys. Societies (pres. 1989—94), Nat. Assn. Chinese Americans (pres. 1977—80), Pontifical Acad. Sciences, Korean Acad. Sci. and Tech., Royal Spanish Acad. Sci., Polish Acad. Sciences, Venezuelan Acad. Sciences, Am. Philos. Soc., Russian Acad. Sciences, Royal Soc. London (fgn. mem.), NAS (chmn. panel of theoretical physics, physics survey com. 1965), Chinese Acad. Sciences. Achievements include being best known for the Yang-Mills Theory, the Yang-Baxter equation, and work with Tsung-dao Lee on parity nonconservation in weak interactions. Office: Tsinghua U Ctr for Advanced Study 1 Qinghuayuan Beijing 100084 China

YANG, CHENGHAI, agricultural engineer, researcher; b. Chengcheng, China, Sept. 25, 1962; s. Jianming Yang and Chunai Liu; m. Yueting Wang, Mar. 17, 1987; children: Ying, Michael Jiale, Melissa Mengying. BS in Agrl. Engring., NW Agrl. U., 1983, MS in Agrl. Engring., 1986; PhD in Agrl. Engring., U. Idaho, 1994. Instr. NW Agrl. U., 1986—90; vis. scholar U. Idaho, Moscow, 1990—91, grad. asst., 1991—94; rsch. scientist Tex. A&M U. Sys., Weslaco, 1995—2005; agrl. engr. USDA Agrl. Rsch. Svc., Weslaco, 2005—. Contbr. articles to profl. jours. Treas., sec. Chinese-Am. Assn. in Rio Grande Valley of Tex., Weslaco, 2000—01. Named Disting. Young Faculty Mem., NW Agrl. U., 1990. Mem.: Am. Soc. Photogrammetry and Remote Sensing (co-chair 20th biennial workshop on aerial photography, videography 2005), Assn.

Chinese Am. Agrl., Biol., and Food Engrs. (newsletter editor, at-large bd. dirs., sec., v.p., pres. 2007, Outstanding Svc. awards 2003, 2004), Am. Soc. Agrl. and Biol. Engrs. (com., sec., vice-chair, chair 1993—), Phi Kappa Phi. Achievements include research in integrating remote sensing technology for precision agriculture and mapping invasive weeds. Home: 2210 Northgate Dr Weslaco TX 78596 Office: USDA Agricultural Research Service 2413 E Hwy 83 Weslaco TX 78596 Office Fax: 956-969-4893. Business E-Mail: cyang@weslaco.ars.usda.gov.

YANG, DAN, marketing executive, researcher; married. MS, PhD, Iowa State U., Ames, 2006. Sr. market monitoring analyst Calif. Ind. Sys. Operator, Folsom, 2006—. Mem.: IEEE. Achievements include research in power and energy systems, power economics competition and market performance, numerical methods for dynamic systems; decoupled time domain simulation method, critical eigenvalue tracing; power system dynamic security analysis; simultaneous operation strategy in energy market and financial transmission right market; assessment of locational market power mitigation effect; demand response, market performance and market gaming in electricity market; a variational index to measure congestion impact on electricity market; dual step size explicit numerical integration method. Office: Calif Independent Sys Operator 151 Blue Ravine Folsom CA 95662 Office Phone: 916-608-7277. Personal E-mail: yangdan77@gmail.com.

YANG, DEBRA WONG, lawyer, former prosecutor; b. LA, 1959; 3 children. B, Pitzer Coll., 1981; JD, Boston Coll., 1985. Assoc. Haight Dickson Brown & Bonesteel, Santa Monica, Calif., 1985—87, Wildman Harrold Allen & Dixon, Chgo., 1987; law clk. to Dist. Judge Ronald Lew LA, 1988—89; atty. Greenberg Glusker, 1989; judge LA Mcpl. Ct., 1997—2000, LA Superior Ct., 2000—02; US atty. (ctrl. dist.) Calif. US Dept. Justice, LA, 2002—06; ptnr., co-chair crisis mgmt. practice group Gibson, Dunn & Crutcher LLP, LA, 2007—. Adj. prof. U. So. Calif. Law Sch. Former pres. Chinese Am. Mus., LA. Named one of 50 Most Influential Minority Lawyers in America, Nat. Law Jour., 2008. Mem.: Asian Pacific Bar Assn. (Pub. Svc. award 2003), Asian Am. Bar Assn., So. Calif. Chinese Lawyer Assn. Republican. Achievements include being the first Asian-American woman to serve as a US Attorney, 2002. Office: Gibson Dunn & Crutcher LLP 333 S Grand Ave Los Angeles CA 90071-3197 Office Phone: 213-229-7472. Office Fax: 213-229-6472. E-mail: dwongyang@gibsondunn.com.*

YANG, DI, systems administrator; PhD, Johns Hopkins U., Md., 2001. Sr. product line mgr. Avanex Corp., Fremont, Calif., 2001—. Office: Avanex Corp 40919 Encyclopedia Cir Fremont CA 94538

YANG, DUCK JOO, research scientist, educator; b. Seoul, Republic Of Korea, Mar. 20, 1947; s. Joon Hong Yang and Mee Duck Ryu; m. Esther Koo Koo, Feb. 28, 1951; children: Hehjin Michelle, Jonghwan Andrew. BA, Clark U., Worcester, Mass, 1972; Exec. MBA, Wharton Sch., U. Pa., Phila, 1982; PhD in Chemistry, UC Berkeley, Calif., 1977. Affiliated prof. Physics Dept. UT Dallas, Richardson; assoc. dean U. Tex. Dallas, Sch. Natural Scis. and Math., 2006—; rsch. prof. Dept Chemistry -AG MacDiarmid NanoTech Inst. U. Tex. Dallas, 2003—; exec. mem. Inst. Innovation & Entrepreneurship Sch. Mgmt. UT Dallas, 2006—; adj. prof. Sch. Applied Chem. Engring.-AG MacDiarmid Energy Rsch. Inst. Chonnam Nat. U., Korea, GwangJu-Si, Republic of Korea, 2006—. Exec. v.p. Samsung Advanced Inst. Tech., KiHeung-Eup, YongIn-Si, Kuynggi-Do, 2000—03, v.p. & cro, 1997—2000; dir. DuPont-Korea, Seoul, 1995—97; project mgr. DuPont Co., Wilmington, Del., 1993—95, mktg. mgr., 1992—93, rsch. chemist - rsch. assoc., 1978—91. Contbr. to numerous profl. jours. Mng. prin. Dalaware Korean Sch., Wilmington, Del., 1988—90; mem. Korean Am. Students Scholarship Fund, Richardson, 2006—08. Recipient Environ. Excellency award, DuPont Co., 1994, Sci. award, 1983. Mem.: Korean-Am. Scientists & Engrs. Assn. (chair UKC nano sci. and tech. symposium 2008), Phi Beta Cappa. Achievements include patents in field. Avocations: oil painting, hiking, golf, reading, travel. Office: The Univ of Tex at Dallas 800 W Campbell Rd BE26 Richardson TX 75080

YANG, EMELINE, lawyer; b. Oxford, Miss., Oct. 17, 1970; BA in Econs. and Managerial Studies, Rice U., Houston, 1992; JD, U. Pa. Law Sch., 1995. Bar: Tex. 1995. Assoc. Hughes & Luce, LLP, Tex., 1995—97, Winstead, Sechrest & Minick, P.C., Dallas, 1997—2002, shareholder, 2003—. Mem. Atty. Serving Cmty., Dallas; co-worker Formosan Christian Ch. Dallas, 1997—2008; bd. dir. Asian Am. Forum, Inc., Dallas, 2001—08, Women's Fin. Exch. Inc., Dallas, 2001—02. Named a Tex. Rising Star, Tex. Monthly, 2004; named one of Best Lawyers in Dallas, D Mag., 2005. Fellow: Dallas Assn. Young Lawyers Found., Dallas Bar Assn. (bd. dir. 2000), Tex. Bar Found. (life); mem.: ABA, Tex. Assn. Bank Counsel, Dallas Asian Am. Bar Assn. (pres. and bd. dir. 2000), Dallas Women Lawyers Assn. (historian 2001, bd. dir. 2001—02), Nat. Asian Pacific Am. Bar Assn. (S.W. regional gov. 2004—05). Office: Winstead PC 5400 Renaissance Tower 1201 Elm St Dallas TX 75270 Office Phone: 214-745-5687. Office Fax: 214-745-5390. E-mail: eyang@winstead.com.

YANG, GUANGRONG, physicist, researcher, educator; b. Pi County, Sichuan, China, Feb. 25, 1941; arrived in US, 1988; s. Guangyuan and Kaide (Liu) Y.; m. Shiyi Tong, Jan. 12, 1968; children: Bizhou, Tingzhou. BS, U. Sci. and Tech. China, Beijing, 1964. Rsch. assoc. prof. Inst. Semiconductors, Chinese Acad. Scis., Beijing, 1964-85; vis. prof. U. Western Ont., London, Ont., Can., 1985-88; vis. scholar, rsch. assoc. Rensselaer Poly. Inst., Troy, NY, 1988—2003; concurrent prof. Xian (China) U. Tech., 1993—. Translator, editor: VLSI Electronics, 1986. Mem. Materials Rsch. Soc. Achievements include patent for Vapor Deposition of Paryleene-F using 1, 4-bis Trifluoromethyl Benzene; increase of deposition rate of vapor deposited polymer by electric field; invention (with others) of thermoelectric semiconductor refrigerator, amorphous chalcogenide read mostly memory and dual low energy ion beam epitaxy equipment. Office: 127 Xin Wen Hua St Beijing 100031 China Personal E-mail: gryang2003@yahoo.com.

YANG, GUO-YUAN, neuroscientist; s. Zhongwei and Yuzheng Yang; m. Yuming Chen, Sept. 25; 1 child, Yibo. MD, PhD, Shanghai Med. U., 1987. Vis. rsch. investigator U. Mich. Med. Ctr. Dept. Neurosurgery, Ann Arbor, 1991—92, rsch. investigator, 1992—95, asst. rsch. scientist, 1995—2001; assoc. prof. U. Calif. Depts. Anesthesia & Neurosurgery, San Francisco, 2001—06, prof., 2006—; nuerosurgeon Shanghai Med. U. HuaShan Hosp. Dept. Neurosurgery, 1982—89. Vis. prof. Fudan U., Shanghai, 1996—, Med-X Rsch. Inst., Shanghai Jiaotong U., 2008—. Recipient 2nd Pl. award, Sci. Tech. Devel. by Dept. Health, China, 1987, award, Sturge Weber Found., 2007; grantee Mechanisms Action IL-1 Ischemic Brain, NIH NINDS, 1997, Transgenic Murine Model Brain Vascular Malformation, 2003, Integrative Study Brain Vascular Malformation, 2003, BBB Protection During Treatment Transient Ischemia, 2005. Mem.: Am. Heart Assn., Am. Stroke Assn. (faha), Soc. Neurosci. (nsf), Internat. Soc. Cerebral Blood Flow & Metabolism. Achievements include development of suture induced middle cerebral artery occlusion in mice and this focal cerebral ischemia model is widely used; research in novel adenoviral gene transfer technique, induce IL-1 receptor antagonist over expression in the ischemic brain and reduce ischemia-induced brain injury.

YANG, HENRY T.Y., academic administrator, educator; b. Chungking, China, Nov. 29, 1940; s. Chen Pei and Wei Gen Yang; m. Dilling Tsui, Sept. 2, 1966; children: Maria, Martha. BS, Nat. Taiwan U., 1962, D, 2004; MS, W.Va. U., 1965; PhD, Cornell U., 1968; D (hon.), Purdue U., 1996, Hong Kong U. Sci. and Tech., 2002, City U. Hong Kong, 2005; PhD (hon.), Chinese U. Hong Kong, 2008. Structural engr. Gilbert Assocs., Reading, Pa., 1968—69; asst. prof. Sch. Aeros. and Astronautics, Purdue U., West Lafayette, Ind., 1969, assoc. prof., 1972, prof., 1976—94, Neil A. Armstrong Disting. prof. aero. and astronautical engring., 1988—94, sch. head, 1979—84; dean engring. Purdue U., 1984—94; chancellor U. Calif., Santa Barbara, 1994—. Mem. sci. adv. bd. USAF, 1985—89, mem. sci. adv. group aero. sys. divsn., 1986—89; mem. aero. adv. com. NASA, 1985—89; mem. engring. adv. com. NSF, 1988—91; def. sci. bd. DoD (merged with Def. Mfg. Bd.), 1988—91, mem. def. mfg. bd., 1998—99; mem. mechanics bd. vis. ONR, 1990—93; mem. tech. adv. com. Pratt & Whitney, 1993—95; mem. Naval Rsch. Adv. Com., 1996—98; bd. dirs. AlliedSignal, 1996—99, Calif. Coun. Sci. and Technology, 1997—2004; rschr. in field; bd. dir. Kavli Found., 2007—. Contbr. over 170 articles in engring. to profl. jours. Bd. trustees Univs. Rsch. Assn., 2002—09; bd. dirs. Axle and Mfg., 2004—. Recipient Twelve Outstanding Tchg. awards, Purdue U., 1970—94, Outstanding Aerospace Engr. award, 1999, Hon. Disting. Tchg. award, U. Calif. Santa Barbara, 2007, Millennium Tech. prize, Selection Com. Finland, 2007—, Nat. Sci. medal, Pres.'s Com., 2009—; named Hon. alumnus, U. Calif. Santa Barbara, 2001. Fellow: AIAA, ASEE, AIAA Structures (Structural Dynamics & Materials award 2008), Am. Soc. Engring. Edn. (Centennial medal 1993, Benjamin Garver Lamme Gold medal 1998); mem.: ASME, NAE, ASCE, Academia Sinica, Tau Beta Pi. Office: U Calif Santa Barbara Chancellors Office 5221 Cheadle Hall Santa Barbara CA 93106-2030 Office Phone: 805-893-2231. Office Fax: 805-893-8717. Business E-Mail: henry.yang@chancellor.ucsb.edu.

YANG, HOICHANG, engineering educator; b. Seoul, Republic of Korea, Jan. 14, 1972; s. Young Kil Yang and Jung Sook Seo; m. Seyeon Jun; 1 child, Seon E. BA, Inha U., Incheon, Republic of Korea, 1995; MS, Pohang U. Sci. and Tech., Republic of Korea, 1997, PhD, 2002. Sr. scientist and mgr. Rensselaer Poly. Inst., Troy, 2002—; asst. prof. Inha U., 2009. Contbr. articles to profl. jours. Home: Seoknam-dong 588 Apt 104-1604 Incheon 404-220 Republic of Korea Office: Dept Advanced Fiber Engring Inha Univ Yonghyun-dong 253 Incheon 402-751 Republic of Korea Business E-Mail: hcyang@inha.ac.kr.

YANG, HUA, video coding expert; s. Zhijie Yang and Yuying Song; m. Bei Wu, Mar. 10, 2003; 1 child, Evelyn L. BSEE, Tsinghua U., Beijing, 1997, MSEE, 2000; PhD, U. Calif., Santa Barbara, 2005. Rsch. asst. dept. elec. engring. Tsinghua U., 1997—2000, rsch. asst. Multimedia Ctr., 1998—99; rsch. asst. dept. elec. and computer engring. U. Calif., Santa Barbara, 2001—05; intern IBM Rsch., Yorktown, NY, 2003; mem. tech. staff Thomson Corp. Rsch., Princeton, NJ, 2005—. Engr. Techwell Inc., China, 1997—98; reviewer IEEE Transactions on Circuit Sys. and Video Tech., Piscataway, NJ, 2005—, EURASIP Signal Processing: Image Comm., Amsterdam, 2006—06, Jour. Visual Comm. and Image Representation, Amsterdam, 2006—07, Jour. Comm. and Networks, 2007, SPIE Jour. Electronic Imaging, Bellingham, Wash., 2007. Contbr. scientific papers (Cable & Satellite Internat. Product of Yr. awards, 2008). Mem.: IEEE. Achievements include patents pending for error resilience and perceptual quality improvements of video coding, perceptual video quality measurements. Office: Thomson Corp Rsch 2 Independence Way Princeton NJ 08540 Personal E-mail: yanghua23@gmail.com. Business E-Mail: hua.yang2@thomson.net.

YANG, HYUK JUN, emergency physician; b. Pusan, Republic of Korea, Jan. 4, 1964; s. Seokchang Yang and Yangsil Lee; m. Shin Young Choi, Aug. 15, 1989; children: Yo Sup, Yo Han. MD, Kyung Hee U., Seoul, Republic Of Korea, 1988, PhD, 1998. Cert. Korea Bd. Emergency Medicine, 1997; ACLS instr. Am. Heart Assn., 2005. Med. dir. emergency med. ctr. Gachon U. Med. Sci., Incheon, Republic of Korea, 2002—, assoc. prof., 2006—. Rsch. fellow Duke U. Med. Ctr., Durham, NC, 2002—03. Translator: (medical book) Manual of Emergency Airway Management, AHA Guidelines 2000 for CPR and ECC. 1st lt. Republic Of Korea Army, 1989—92. Scholar, Duke U. Med. Ctr., 2002—03. Mem.: Incheon Med. Assn. (sci. officer 2006—). Achievements include development of certification of Korean EMS medical director program; first to endovascular cooling method for therapeutic hypothermia of cardiac arrest patient; design of mobile CPR education unit. Office: Gachon U Med Sci 1198 Kuweol-dong Incheon Namdong 405-220 Republic of Korea Home: 1109-1501 Lotte Castle Apt 23 Kuweol-dong Namdong-ku Incheon 405-220 Republic of Korea Office Fax: 82-32-460-3019. Business E-Mail: yanghj@gachon.ac.kr.

YANG, JERRY, former Internet company executive; b. Taipei, Taiwan, Nov. 6, 1968; married; 1 child. BSEE, MSEE, Stanford U., 1990, PhD studies in Elec. Engring. Co-creator Yahoo! Navigational Guide to the Internet, 1994; co-founder Yahoo!, Inc., Sunnyvale, Calif., 1995, CEO, 2007—09. Bd. dirs. Yahoo! Inc., 1995—, Cisco Systems, Inc., 2000—, Alibaba, 2005—. Co-author (with David Filo, Karen Heyman): (books) Yahoo! Unplugged: your Discovery Guide to the Web, 1995; co-author: (with David Filo, Richard Raucci, Elizabeth Crane) Yahooligans!: Way Cool Web Sites, 1996. Trustee Stanford Univ. Named one of 400 Richest Ams., Forbes mag., 2004, 2005, 2006, 50 Most Important People on the Web, PC World, 2007. Mem.: Com. 100, Phi Kappa Psi. Named company YAHOO!(acronym for Yet Another Hierarchical Officious Oracle).*

YANG, JIAN, food scientist, educator; b. Hangzhou, China, July 11, 1963; s. Huaitang Yang and Wene Tan; m. Wenping Wan; children: Leya Ruth, Enqi Joseph, Jieging Lydia. B in Food Engring. with honors, Wuxi Inst. Light Industry, China, 1985; MS in Food Sci. with honors, Wash. State U., Pullman, 1997, PhD in Food Sci. with honors, 2001. Asst. prof. Zhejiang Coll. Light Industry, Hangzhou, 1985—94, U. Guam, Mangilao, Guam, 2002—07, assoc. prof., 2007—. Rschr. Wash. State U., 1994—2001. Contbr. articles to profl. jours. Com. mem. Guam Food Safety Task Force, Mangilao, 2004—07. Mem.: Inst. Food Technologists. Office: Univ Guam Coll Natural and Applied Scis Mangilao GU 96923 Office Phone: 671-735-2027. Office Fax: 671-734-4448. Personal E-mail: jianyang94@hotmail.com. Business E-Mail: jyang@uguam.uog.edu.

YANG, JIANFEI, immunologist; PhD, Niigata U., Japan, 1997. Postdoctoral fellow Wash. U. Sch. of Medicine, St. Louis, 1997—2001; sr. scientist Boehringer Ingelheim Pharm., Inc, Ridgefield, Conn., 2001—. Mem.: Am. Assoc. Immunologists. Achievements include patents for modulating IKK alpha activity; the method to identify and analyze genes having modified expression in stimulated T cells; T cell protein and nucleotides encoding the same; compositions and methods for modulating lymphocyte activity; first to induce a interferon-gamma production in Th1 CD4+ T cells: evidence for two dictinct Pathways for promoter activation; research in IL-18-stimulated GADD45 beta required in cytokine-induced, but not TCR-induced, IFN-gamma production; unexpected characteristics of the IFN-gamma reporters in non-transformed T cells; signaling and transcription in T helper development; an essential role for endogenous interferon-gamma in the generation of protective T cells against Mycobacterium bovis BCG; the requirement of the initial production of gamma interferon in the generation of protective immunity of mice against Listeria monocytogenes; the involvement of inflammatory cytokines and nitric oxide in the expression of non-specific resistance to Listeria monocytogenes; the involvement of natural killer cells in nitric oxide production by spleen cells after stimulation with Mycobacterium bovis BCG; antigen provoking gamma interferon production in response to Mycobacterium bovis BCG; the involvement of GATA3 in Protein Kinase C theta-induced Th2 cytokine expression; the selective requirement of MAPK in cytokine-dependent, but not antigen-receptor dependent, Th1 responses; sphingosine kinase 1 a negative regulator of CD4+ T helper 1 cells; BTLA a lymphocyte inhibitory receptor with similarities to CTLA-4 and PD-1; T-bet a STAT1-induced regulator of IL-12R expression in naïve CD4+ T cells. Office: Boehringer Ingelheim Pharm 900 Rigebury Rd Ridgefield CT 06482 Office Fax: 203-837-4609. Business E-Mail: jianfei.yang@boehringer-ingelheim.com.

YANG, JIANHUA JOSHUA, materials scientist, researcher; m. Hui Wang; 1 child, Daniel. PhD, U. Wis., Madison, 2006. Mem.: IEEE, Materials Rsch. Soc., Sigma Xi. Achievements include first to realization of engineering control over the memristive devices; invention of realization of a family of memristive nanodevices with simple metal/oxide/metal structure; discovery of the interface switching mechanism of memristive nanodevices; development of created the world record of TMR ratio for the AlOx based magnetic tunnel junctions. Office: Hewlett-Packard Labs 1501 Page Mill Rd Palo Alto CA 94304 Personal E-mail: j.joushuay@gamil.com. Business E-Mail: jianhuay@hp.com.

YANG, JIDONG, transportation engineer; PhD, U. S. Fla., Tampa, 2000—04. Profl. Engr., Fla. Bd. Profl. Engrs., 2006. Sr. transp. engr. Tindale Oliver and Associates, Inc., Tampa, 2002—. Contbr. papers to profl. jours. and pubs. Bd. mem. Chinese Am. Assn. Tampa Bay, 2001—02; pres. Friendship Assn. Chinese Students & Scholars, U. S. Fla., 2001—02. Mem.: ASCE, Inst. Transp. Engrs. (assoc.). Achievements include research in deveopment of new methodologies.

YANG, JIE, electrical engineer, researcher; b. Beijing, Nov. 20, 1975; s. Shanhua Yang and Shuixian Luo; m. Yang Yanfeng, June 28, 2000; 1 child, Stephen. BS in Automotive Engring., TsingHua U., Beijing, 1998; MS in Mech. Engring., NCA&T State U., Greensboro, 2001; MS in Applied Stats., Syracuse U., NY, 2006, PhD, 2007. Rsch. & tchg. asst. NCA&T State U., 1999—2001; rsch. asst. Syracuse U., 2001—07; sr. elec. engr. Ark. Power Electronics Internat., Fayetteville, 2007—. Reviewer IEEE Trans. Antennas Program, Jour. Electromagnetic Waves and Applications. Contbr. scientific papers to profl. jours. Recipient All U. Doctoral prize, Syracuse U., 2007, Academic Excellence award, NCA&T State U., 2001. Mem.: IEEE. Achievements include development of novel chirp modulation and phase coding methods for doppler and acceleration invariant pulse compression in radar systems; research in modeling of electromagnetic system using for interpolation, extrapolation and phase reconstruction; temporal effects in bayesian networks. Avocations: travel, photograph. Office: Ark Power Electronics Internat 535 W Rsch Ctr Blvd Fayetteville AR 72701 Business E-Mail: jyang14@syr.edu.

YANG, JOSEPH, lawyer; s. Tony Tien-Sheng and Hsiu-Ying Tsai Yang; m. Roxana H. Hwu, 1999; children: Jacqueline O., Russell A. BS, Calif. Inst. Tech., 1986, MS, 1987, PhD, 1991; JD, Stanford U., 1996. Bar: U.S. Patent and Trademark Office 1996, Calif. 1996, U.S. Ct. Appeals (Fed. Cir.) 2002. Engr. TRW Corp., Redondo Beach, Calif., 1986—87; Office Naval Rsch. fellow Calif. Inst. Tech., Pasadena, Calif., 1987—91; rsch. engr. Shell Devel. Co., Houston, 1991—93; tech. advisor Weil, Gotshal & Manges LLP, Menlo Park, Calif., 1994—95; atty. McCutchen, Doyle, Brown & Enersen LLP, Palo Alto, 1995—98; counsel Skadden, Arps, Slate, Meagher & Flom LLP, Palo Alto, 1998—2005; v.p., gen. counsel Cryptography Rsch. Inc., San Francisco, 2005—; founding ptnr. PatentEsque Law Group, LLP, Menlo Park, 2005—. Adj. prof. Sch. Law U. Calif., Berkeley, 1998—99; program chair Practicing Law Inst., NY, 2002—; co-founder intellectual property transactions practice Skadden Arps LLP, Palo Alto; spkr. on intellectual property law. Editor: Advanced Licensing Agreements, 2003—, Advanced Patent Licensing, 2008—; contbr. chapters to books, articles to jours. including The Practical Lawyer, The Licensing Jour., others. Named Outstanding Student in Engring. at Caltech, Inst. for Advancement of Engring., 1986, One of World's Leading IP Strategists, Intellectual Asset Mag., 2009—; fellow, US Office Naval Rsch., 1987—91; scholar, Gen. Motors Corp., 1983—86. Mem.: Caltech Alumni Assn. (pres. San Francisco chpt., dir. 1999—2003), Assocs. Calif. Inst. Tech. (Pasadena) (ednl. patron 1999—, dir. 2008—), Licensing Execs. Soc., Am. Intellectual Property Law Assn. Office: PatentEsque Law Group LLP 2460 Sand Hill Rd Ste 101 Menlo Park CA 94025 Business E-Mail: joe@patentesque.com.

YANG, KEY PAIK, librarian, archivist; b. Naju, Cholla Namdo, Korea, Jan. 8, 1920; s. Yunmuk and Yunhui Yang; m. Hazel K. Yang; children: Won Kyung, A Kyung, Mal Kyung. Diploma, Soong Sil Acad., Pyongyang, Korea, 1939; diploma in Commerce, Nihon U., Tokyo, 1943; BA in Polit. Sci., Monmouth Coll., 1949; MA in Pub. Adminstrn., Am. U., 1958; MSLS, Cath. U. Am., 1960; Phelps, Adult Edn. Sch., Brick, 1974; PhD (hon.), Dongguk U., Seoul, Korea, 1975. With Chosen Kinyu Kumiai, Seoul, 1939, Chosen Kinsoku Butshi Eidan, Seoul, 1943—45; dir. Property Custodian Office, Seoul, 1945—46; head of sect. Pub. Works Divsn., Seoul, Kyonggi Province, 1947—48, Pub. Info., Seoul, 1948—49; head Korean sect. Libr. of Congress, Washington, 1950—94, chief, Asian divsn., 1994—95; advisor Korean Embassy Archives, Washington. Mem. panel Bd. of U.S. Civil Svc. Examiners, 1955—55; chmn. Subcom. on East Asian Librs., 1980—80. Author: Physiology of Korean Culture, Art and Civilization: Facts and Thoughts, Introduction to Koreanology, Quotations to Ponder: Medley of Quotations on Traditional Society of Korea, China and Japan, Collected Works of Key P. Yang, 6 vols., 2005, Nationhood, Culture and Koreanology: A Polemic, rev. edit., 2006, Korean Book Lexicon, Korea, Japan, China: Their Traditional Social Molds, Quotations to Ponder: An Anthology; co-author: The School of Yi Confucianism; contbr. articles to profl. jours. Recipient Meritorious award, The Libr. of Congress, 2008, Compendia Korean Records, The US Congressional Records, 1978—99, O.N. Denny China and Korea; U.S. State Dept. sr. fellow, Korea, 1965, Fulbright Lectr., Korean U., Seoul, 1983, Harvard U. grantee in Korean Ecology, 1960. Mem.: Assn. of Asian Studies. Democrat-Npl. Home: 5021 Baltan Rd Bethesda MD 20816-2401

YANG, LI, computer scientist, educator; b. Heze, Shandong, China, Sept. 20, 1966; arrived in U.S., 2000; s. Mu Yang and Yunxia Dong; m. Xiaojie Wang, Dec. 8, 1995; children: Chang, Ann, David. BS, Shandong U., 1985; M in Engring., U. Sci. and Tech. China, 1988, PhD, 1992; postgrad., Chinese Acad. Scis., Beijing, 1994. Lectr. U. Sci. and Tech. China, Hefei, 1992; vis. scientist Nat. U. Singapore, 1994—95; tech. staff Inst. High Performance Computing, Singapore, 1995—99; asst. prof. We. Mich. U., Kalamazoo, 2000—02, assoc. prof., 2002—07, prof., 2007—. Mem.: IEEE (sr.), Assn. for Computing Machinery. Office: Western Mich Univ Dept Computer Sci 1903 W Michigan Ave Kalamazoo MI 49008 Business E-Mail: li.yang@wmich.edu.

YANG, LI, electronics engineer; b. Quanzhou, China, May 7, 1980; s. Guofeng Yang and Shuhua Ni; m. Jiexin Li, Dec. 27, 2004. Attending, Ga. Inst. Tech., Atlanta, 2005—. Sr. IC designer Tex. Instruments, Dallas, 2009—; rschr. Ga. Electronic Design Ctr., Atlanta, 2005—. Reviewer Jour. Electromagnetic Waves & Applications, 2009—. Author: (book) Design and Development of RFID and RFID-Enabled Sensors on Flexible Low Cost Substrates, Modern RFID: RFID Enabled Sensors; contbr. chapters to books, to profl. publs. Recipient Poster Presentation award, ISAP, 2007, Conf. award, Asian-Pacific Microwave, 2006. Mem.: IEEE (chair, reviewer 2008—), Soc. Industry Leaders, Eta Kappa Nu. Achievements include research in high performance RFID tags and environmentally-friendly low-cost electronics design. Office: Tex Instruments 12500 TI Blvd Dallas TX 75243

YANG, LI, geography and tourism educator; d. Cunhui Yang and Fenghua Gao. BS (hon.), Yunnan U., Kunming, China, 1994, MS (hon.), 1997; PhD (hon.), U. Waterloo, Ont., Can., 2007. Lectr. Yunnan U., 1996—97, assoc. prof., 1997—2004; vis. prof. U. Man., Winnipeg, Canada, 2003, U. Waterloo, 2003—04; asst. prof. Western Mich. U., Kalamazoo, 2007—. Contbr. articles to profl. jours. Recipient Rsch. Devel. award, 2008, award, Inst. China's Rural Labor Devel., 2008. Mem.: Am. Planning Assn., Travel & Tourism Rsch. Assn., Assn. Am. Geographer. Personal E-mail: liyang0501@hotmail.com.

YANG, LI-XIA, biomedical researcher, scientist, educator; arrived in US, 1999, permanent resident, 2007; d. Chun and Guizhen Yang; m. Lizhi Gu, Aug. 4, 1986; 1 child, Chunyang Gu. MD in Medicine with honors, Jiamusi U. Sch. Medicine, China, 1982, MS in Pathophysiology, 1987; PhD in Biochemistry and Molecular Biology/Genetics, Kochi Med. Sch., Japan, 1996. Asst. prof. pathology Jiamusi U. Sch. Medicine, 1982—86, lectr. pathology, 1987—94, prin. investigator, 1987—94, assoc. prof. medicine, 1994—96; postdoc. rschr. molecular neurobiology Inst. Phys. Chem. Rsch., Nagoya, Japan, 1996—99; postdoc. rsch. fellow molecular cellular devel. neurobiology Nat. Inst. Child Health and Human Devel., NIH, Bethesda, Md., 1999—2002; intramural rsch. fellow molecular cellular pathology Molecular Imaging Lab Clin. Ctr. NIH, Bethesda, Md., 2002—03; faculty rsch. assoc. functional genomics U. Pitts., 2003—; asst. prof. Hough Ear Inst. Bapt. Med. Ctr., Oklahoma, Okla., 2006—08, rsch. scientist hearing rsch., 2006—08; prin. scientist Ctr. Innovative Rsch. Banyan Biomarkers, Inc., Alachua, Fla., 2008—. Sci. judge NIH, Bethesda, Md., 2002. Contbr. articles to profl. jours. Rsch. grant, Ministry Edn. Sci. Culture, Japan, 1990—92. Mem.: AAAS (life), Nat. Neurotrauma Soc., Assn. Rsch. Otolaryngology, Soc. Neurosci., Chinese Soc. Medicine (life). Achievements include unique discoveries of three novel Isoreceptors, GFRa-1c, GFRa-1d and GFRa-1e in human and mouse; novel gene sequences deposited to the world GenBank for public access. Avocations: music, art, swimming, dance, yoga. Mailing: 813 Turkey Creek Alachua FL 32615 Office: Ctr Innovative Rsch Banyan Biomarkers Inc 12085 Research Dr Alachua FL 32615 Office Phone: 412-913-3494. Office Fax: 386-462-0875. Business E-Mail: lxyang@pitt.edu.

YANG, MENGYAN, chemical engineer, research scientist; b. Shijiazhuang, China, Feb. 4, 1949; arrived in Eng., 1989, arrived in U.S., 1998; s. Fenglin and Wenye (Fu) Y.; m. Huiqing, Dong Yang, Jan. 6, 1976; 1 child, Guang. BS in Chemistry, Hebei Tchrs. U., China, 1982; MS in Phys. Chemistry, Taiyuan U. Tech., China, 1985; PhD in Chem. Engring., U. Bath, UK, 1993. Chartered engr. Asst. engr. Shijiezhuang Mechanic Plant, China, 1968-78; lectr. Hebei Tchrs. U., China, 1985-89; vis. rsch. fellow U. Manchester, England, 1989—90; rsch. officer U. Bath, England, 1990-93; sr. rsch. fellow, 1993—. Contbr. to Jour. Chem. Thermaldynamics, 1991, Analytica Chimica Acta, 1993, Water Research, 1997, Separation Sci. Tech., Biotech. Tech., Biosensors and Bioelectronics, 1999, J. Membraue Sci.; inventor: Physico-Chimicasinica, 1986. Mem.: Inst. Chem. Engring. Avocations: countryside walking, fishing. Office: Davisco Foods Internat 620 N Main St Le Sueur MN 56058-1401 Office Phone: 507-665-8861.

YANG, MING, engineering company executive, researcher; s. Yushu Hu and Tianling Yang; m. Jifeng Ru. BS, Peking U., Beijing, 1997; MS, Chinese Acad. Sci., Beijing, 2000; PhD, U. New Orleans, 2007. Sr. rsch. engr. Nuance Comm., Inc., Burlington, Mass., 2007—. Contbr. scientific papers, chapters to books, articles to profl. jours. Recipient Pres' Hurricane Relief Award Rsch., LSU sys., 2006; named Dean's List, Coll. Engring., U. New Orleans, 2006. Office: Nuance Comm Inc 1 Wayside Rd Burlington MA 01803

YANG, PEIDONG, material science researcher; b. Suzhou, Jiangsu, China, Aug. 22, 1971; came to US, 1993; s. Xueli and Amei Yang; m. Mei Wang, May 15, 1996. BS in Chemistry, U. Sci. and Tech. of China, Hefei, 1993; MS, Harvard U., 1995, PhD in Chemistry, 1997. Rsch. asst. U. Sci. and Tech. of China, 1989-93, Harvard U., Cambridge, Mass., 1993—99; postdoctoral fellow U. Calif., Santa Barbara, 1997—99, assoc. prof. dept. chemistry, materials sci. and engring. Berkeley, 1999—, dep. dir. Ctr. Integrated Nanomechanical Systems. Chevron Texaco chair chemistry U. Calif., Berkeley, 2003. Assoc. editor: Jour. Am. Chem. Soc. Recipient Zhongzhi Zhang prize, 1992, Presdl. prize, U. Sci. and Tech. of China, 1993, Camille and Henry Dreyfus New Faculty award, 1999, 3M Untenured Faculty award, 2000, Rsch. Innovation award, 2001, Hellman Family Faculty award, 2001, CAREER award, NSF, 2001, Young Investigator award, Alan T. Waterman award, 2007, Arnold and Mabel Beckman Young Investigator award, 2002, Camille Dreyfus Tchr.-Scholar award, 2004, Dupont Young Prof. award, 2004, Julius Springer prize for Applied Physics, 2004; named to TR100, MIT Tech. Rev., 2003; grantee Alfred P. Sloan Rsch. fellowship, 2001. Mem. Am. Chem. Soc. (chmn. nanoscience subdivision, 2003, ExxonMobil Solid State Chemistry award, 2001, Pure Chemistry award, 2005), Materials Rsch. Soc. (Outstanding Young Investigator award, 2004), Am. Phys. Soc. Achievements include invention of metal oxide nanorods and their incorporation into the high temperature superconductor, thus enhancing the critical current density. Office: Dept Chemistry U Calif Berkeley B68 Hildebrand Hall Berkeley CA 94720-1460 Office Phone: 510-643-1545. Office Fax: 510-642-7301. E-mail: p_yang@berkeley.edu.

YANG, PHILIP Q., sociologist; arrived in US, 1986, naturalized, 2005; m. Jianling Li, Dec. 20, 1984; children: Ming, William Zeus. PhB, Zhongshan U., Guangzhou, China, 1982; MA, 1988; PhD, UCLA, 1993. Asst. prof. Zhongshan U., Guangzhou, 1982—86; lectr. UCLA, 1994—95; from asst. prof. to assoc. prof. Calif. Poly. State U., San Luis Obispo, 1995—2001; from assoc. prof. to prof. Tex. Woman's U., Denton, 1999—. Author: Post-1965 Immigration to the United States: Structural Determinants, 1995, Ethnic Studies: Issues and Approaches, 2000; editor: Introduction to Ethnic Studies: A Reader, 1999; contbr. articles to profl. jours., chapters to books. Grantee, NSF, 2002—04; fellow, UN, 1986—87; Chancellor's Rsch. fellow, Tex. Woman's U., 2001—02, 2002—03. Mem.: Population Assn. Am., N.Am. Chinese Sociologists' Assn. (bd. dirs. 2001—03), Nat. Assn. for Ethnic Studies, Assn. for Asian Am. Studies (bd. dirs. 2001—03), Southwestern Social Sci. Assn., Assn. Chinese Profs. Social Scis. in the US, Am. Sociol. Assn. (Book award Internat. Migration Sect. 1998). Office: Texas Womans Univ PO Box 425887 Denton TX 76204 Office Fax: 940-898-2067. Business E-Mail: pyang@mail.twu.edu.

YANG, RALPH TZU-BOW, chemical engineer, educator; b. Chung King, China, Sept. 18, 1942; came to U.S., 1965, naturalized, 1976; s. Chen Pei and Wei (Gee) Y.; m. Frances H. Chang, Dec. 23, 1972; children: Michael, Robert. BS, Nat. Taiwan U., 1964; MS, Yale U., 1968, PhD, 1971. Rsch. assoc. Argonne (Ill.) Nat. Lab., 1972-73; scientist Aluminum Co. Am., Pitts., 1973-74; group leader Brookhaven Nat. Lab., Upton, N.Y., 1974-78; assoc. prof. chem. engring. SUNY, Buffalo, 1978-82, prof., 1982-95, chmn. chem. engring. dept., 1990-95, Praxair prof. chem. engring., chmn. dept., 1993-95; prof. chem. engring., chmn. dept. U. Mich., Ann Arbor, 1995—2000. Cons. in field. Author: Gas Separation by Adsorption Processes, 1987, Adsorbents: Fundamentals & Applications, 2003; editor Chem. Engring. Series Imperial Coll. Press, 1996—; contbr. articles to profl. jours. Rsch. grantee NSF, 1980—, Dept. Energy, 1980—, Alcoa Found., 1979-81; recipient Clarence Gerhold award for separations, 1997. Fellow AIChE (William H. Walker award for excellence in contbn. to chem. engring. lit. 1991, Inst. award for excellence in gases tech. 1996, Clarence Gerhold award separation divsn. 1997); mem. NAE, Acad. Sinica, Am. Chem. Soc. (adv. bd. Ind. Engring. Chem. Rsch. Jour. 1991-93, award in seperations sci. and tech., 2003), Am. Carbon Soc. (adv. bd. 1985—, Sigri award for overall contbn. to sci. or tech. of carbon materials 1999), Am. Soc. Engring. Edn., Internat. Adsorption Soc. (adv. bd. Jour. Adsorption 1993—, bd. dirs. 1998—, adv. bd. Adsorption Sci. and Tech. 1986—, Separation and Purification Methods 1997—, Applied Catalysis, 2000—). Achievements include patents in field. Office: U Mich Dept Chem Engring Ann Arbor MI 48109 Business E-Mail: yang@umich.edu.

YANG, ROU-LING, entomologist; d. Yu-Jen Yang and Yin-Yu Yang Lee; m. Hou-Feng Li, May 27, 2007. BSc, Nat. Taiwan U., Taipei, 1998, PhD, 2004. Postdoc. rschr. Inst. Statis. Sci., Acad. Sinica, Taipei, Taiwan, 2004—05, Dept. Entomology, Nat. Taiwan U., Taipei, 2005—07, Dept. Entomology Ft. Lauderdale Rsch. & Edn. Ctr., U. Fla., Fla., 2007—; adj. asst. prof. Dept. Sci. Edn., Taipei Mcpl. U. Edn., Taiwan, 2006—07. Contbr. articles to profl. jours. Recipient Presdl. award, Nat. Taiwan U., 1996; named Best Spkr. award, Dept. Entomology, Nat. Taiwan U., 2000; Grad. student scholarship, Ministry of Edn., Taiwan, 1998—2001, Nat. Sci. Coun., Taiwan, 2001—04, Travel grant, 2002, 2005, 2006, 2007. Mem.: Taiwan Entomol. Soc., Entomol. Soc. Am. Avocations: reading, dance, travel. Office: Dept Entomol & Nematol FLREC UF 3205 College Ave Fort Lauderdale FL 33314 Office Phone: 954-577-6326. Business E-Mail: rlyang@ufl.edu.

YANG, ROXANA HWU, lawyer, investor; d. Johnson and Grace Liaw Hwu; m. Joseph Yang; children: Jacqueline, Russell. BSEE, U. Calif., LA, 0199; JD, U. Calif., Berkeley, 1997. Bar: Calif., US Patent and Trademark Office, US Dist. Ct. (no dist.) Calif., US Ct. Appeals (fed. cir.); lic. real estate broker Calif. Atty. Pennie & Edmonds, LLP, Palo Alto, Calif., 1997—2001; prin. Law Office Roxana H. Yang, Los Altos, 2001—05; mng. ptnr. PatentEsque Law Group, LLP, 2005—. Faculty Practising Law Inst., San Francisco, 2002—. Contbr. articles to profl. jours. Ednl. patron Assocs. Calif. Inst. Tech., Pasadena, 1999—2006. Recipient Am. Jury award Torts, Pepperdine U. Sch. Law, Am. Jury award Real Property. Office: PatentEsque Law Group LLP PO Box 400 Los Altos CA 94023 Office Fax: 650-948-0833. Business E-Mail: roxana@patentesque.com.

YANG, SHANG-YOU, medical educator; m. Lei Liu, 1985. MD, Qingdao Med. Coll., Tsingdao, China, 1983; PhD, Thornhill U., London, 2001. Scholar Kansas Biosci. Authority; asst. prof. Wayne State U., Detroit, 2002—08; sr. scientist and assoc. prof. Orthop. Res. Inst., Wichita State U., U. Kans. Med. Ctr., 2008—. Grantee RO3, NIH, 2007—; Robbinson fellow, Arthritis Found., 2001—02. Mem.: Orthopaedic Rsch. Soc., Am. Coll. Rheumatology, Soc. Biomaterials. Achievements include research in novel murine models for aseptic loosening of joint arthroplasty; first to virus-mediated gene therapy for orthopaedic disorders. Office: ORI Via Christi Regional Med Ctr 929 N St francis Wichita KS 67214 Office Fax: 316-291-4998. Business E-Mail: syang-you.yang@wichita.edu.

YANG, SHING LUNG STEVEN, antenna engineer; PhD in Electronic Engring., City U., Hong Kong, 2007. Rsch. fellow U. Miss., 2007—09; antenna engr. Rsch. in Motion, 2009—. Contbr. 16 tech. jours. and 18 conf. paper. Recipient Young Scientists award, Union Radio-Scientifique Internat. Gen. Assembly, 2008, 13 awards and prizes; 14 scholarships, fellowships. Achievements include research in microstrip antennas, reconfigurable antennas and RF circuits. Office: 2550 W Golf Rd Rolling Meadows IL 60008 Business E-Mail: steven.yang@ieee.org.

YANG, SHU, materials scientist; b. China; BS in Material Sci., Fudan U., 1992; MS in Chemistry and Chem. Biology, Cornell U., 1997, PhD in Chemistry and Chem. Biology, 1999. Skirkanich asst. prof. in materials sci. and engring. U. Pa. Contbr. articles to profl. jour. Recipient ICI award in applied polymer sci., ACS, 1999, Unilever award in polymer sci. and enring., 2001; named one of Top 100 Young Innovators, MIT Tech. Review, 2004. Office: U Pa Dept Materials Sci and Engring 203 LRSM 3231 Walnut St Philadelphia PA 19104-6272

YANG, SHUJUN, electrical engineer; b. Mingshui, Heilongjiang, China, Jan. 21, 1968; s. Minghua Yang and Xiulan Tian; m. Hong Yin, Sept. 2, 2006; 1 child, Andrew. PHD, Old Dominion U., Norfolk, Va., 2006. Mfg. engr. Sanmei Electronic Corp., Fengtai, Beijing, China, 1991—92; electronic design engr. Chinese Internat. Enterprises Cooperation Corp., Haidian, Beijing, China, 1993—95; RF engr. Shireen Inc, Gaithersburg, Md., 2005—06; process devel. engr. Applied Materials, Sunnyvale, Calif., 2006—08; elec. engr. Continental AG, Huntsville, Ala., 2008—. Contbr. scientific papers. Achievements include design of an electronic circuit to transmit data through power lines; a phase-lock loop circuit to synchronize a microprocessor with a TV signal; development of a non resonant method to characterize a slow wave circuit in traveling wave tube; a switching mode power supply over ethernet; a novel etch recipe for semiconductor processing; a novel eyed monitoring method for photoresist ashing chamber; a microprocessor system to calculate electric power consumption.

YANG, SONG-YU, medical biochemist; b. Wu-Xi, Jiangsu, China, Oct. 27, 1938; came to U.S., 1981; s. Rong-Geng Zhong and Su-Fei Yang; m. Xue-Ying He, Jan. 1965; children: Ying-Zi, Yu-Xiao. MD, Peking U. Med. Ctr., China, 1960; MS, CCNY, 1982; PhD, CUNY, 1984. Instr. Peking Med. Coll., 1960—75; asst. prof. Shanghai Inst. Biochem. and Cell Biology, Chinese Acad. Sci., 1975—80; tchg. asst. CCNY, NYC, 1981—84, rsch. assoc., CUNY rsch. found., 1984—88; rsch. scientist NY State Office Mental Retardation and Devel. Disabilities, 1988—; head med. biochem. lab. Inst. Basic Rsch. in Devel. Disabilities, 1994—; prof. PhD program biology CUNY Grad. Ctr., 2007—. Contbr. chpts. to books and numerous articles to profl. jours. Investigator Am. Heart Assn., N.Y.C., 1991-94. Recipient L.J. Curtman prize CCNY, 1984, Wall Street Run Fellowship award, 1991, NIH Rsch. award, 1994, Alzheimer's Assn. Rsch. award, 1999. Mem. Am. Soc. Biochemistry and Molecular Biology. Research in fatty acid oxidation and the steroid hormone metabolism, neurological disorders; enzymes and related genes HSD17B10, HADH etc. Office: NYS Inst Basic Rsch Devel Disabilities Dept Neurochemistry 1050 Forest Hill Rd Staten Island NY 10314-6356 Personal E-mail: yang_songyu@yahoo.com.

YANG, STANLEY, computer company executive; BSEE, U. Calif., Berkeley; grad. student, U. Mass., Amherst, Santa Clara U., Calif. Various engring., bus. devel. and ops. positions Xilinx Inc., San Jose, Calif., 1992—2003; founder, pres., CEO Triscend Corp. (acquired by Xilinx Inc. in 2004), San Jose, Calif., 1997—2003; founding mem., v.p. bus. devel., CFO Sage-N Rsch., San Jose, Calif., 2003—05; CEO NeuroSky, Inc., San Jose, Calif., 2005—. Achievements include development of successful business ventures, fundraising campaigns and strategic corporate partnerships; patents for the architecture of Configurable System-on-Chip. Office: NeuroSky Inc 226 Airport Pkwy Ste 638 San Jose CA 95110 Business E-Mail: stanley@neurosky.com.

YANG, THOMAS, electrical engineer, educator; PhD, U. Ctrl. Fla., Orlando, 2004. Assoc. prof. Embry Riddle U., Daytona Beach, Fla., 2005—. Office: Elec Engr Embry-Riddle Univ 600 S Clyde Morris Blvd Daytona Beach FL 32114 Office Phone: 386-226-7098.

YANG, TINA, finance educator; d. Tingzhi Yang and Weizhi Huang. PhD, U. Ga., Athens, 2005. Vis. asst. prof. U. South Fla., Tampa, SC, 2005—06; asst. prof. Clemson U., SC, 2006—. Contbr. articles to profl. jours. Recipient Faculty Excellence award, Clemson U., 2008; Rsch. grant, Yale Sch. Mgmt. and Oxford Said Bus. Sch., 2007. Mem.: Southern Fin. Assn., Eastern Fin. Assn., Fin. Mgmt. Assn., Am. Fin. Assn. Office: Clemson Univ Sirrine Hall Clemson SC 29634

YANG, TSONG-TOH (T.T.), pharmacist, researcher; b. Taiwan, Mar. 1, 1949; s. Yen-Leng and Chhai-Shia Lin Yang; m. Lee-Ju Wu Yang, Aug. 26, 1951; children: Benson Pin-Sheng, Steven Shih-E. BS in Pharmacy, Kaohsiung Med. Coll., Taiwan, 1971; MS in Pharmacy, U. R.I., 1979; PhD in Pharm. Sci., U. So. Calif., 1984. Registered pharmacist Taiwan, 1971. Med. supply officer Chinese Army in Taiwan, 1971—73; prodn. supr. Sterling Products Internat. Inc., Taiwan, Taipei, 1973—77; tchg. asst. U. R.I., Kingston, 1977—79, U. So. Calif., LA, 1979—81, U. N.C., Chapel Hill, 1982—83; rsch. pharmacist Am. Cyanamid Co., Pearl River, NY, 1984—85; devel. fellow Schering-Plough Rsch. Inst., Kenilworth, NJ, 1985—2006; pharm. cons., 2007—. Vis. prof. Nat. Health Rsch. Inst., Taiwan, 2009—. Recipient Pres.'s award for Devel., Schering-Plough Rsch. Inst., 1994, 2002, 2005, DuPont Gold award for dry powder inhaler, 1998, Thomas Alva Edison Patent award, R&D Coun. NJ, 2005. Mem.: Am. Chinese Pharm. Assn., Controlled Release Soc., Am. Assn. for Pharm. Scientists. Achievements include patents for Preparation of powder agglomerates; inhaler for powdered medications; invention of Twisthaler dry powder inhaler-device and formulation. Home: 9 Old Farm Rd Warren NJ 07059 Personal E-mail: ttyangphd@yahoo.com.

YANG, VINCENT WEN-SHAN, gastroenterologist, educator, researcher; b. Taipei, Taiwan, Republic of China, Apr. 9, 1954; came to U.S., 1976; s. Robert H. and Julia C. Yang; m. Linda J. Chang, Aug. 5, 1978; children: Andrew, Jennie, Stephen. BSc, Nat. Taiwan U., 1976; PhD, Princeton U., 1980; MD, Rutgers U., 1984. Diplomate Am. Bd. Internal Medicine. Intern Johns Hopkins Hosp., Balt., 1984-85, resident, 1985-87, fellow, 1987-89, asst. prof., 1989-94; assoc. prof. medicine and biol. chemistry Johns Hopkins U. Sch. Medicine, 1994—. Contbr. articles to Jour. Biol. Chemistry, Procs. NAS, Genes Devel., Archives Biochem. Biophysics, Cancer Rsch., Nucleic Acids Rsch., Jour. Virology. Recipient Rsch. award NIH, 1987-90, 92—; industry scholar Am. Gastroenterol. Assn., 1989-92; grantee Alcoholic Beverage Rsch. Med. Found., 1989-91, NIH, 1992—. Mem. Alpha Omega Alpha. Achievements include research in identifying factors required for messenger RNA processing, for adipocyte differentiation, for liver gene transcription, for intestinal epithelial differentiation. Office: Johns Hopkins Sch Medicine 720 Rutland Ave Baltimore MD 21205-2109

YANG, WEIBIN, physician; MD, Zhejiang Med. U., 1988. Assoc. prof. UT Southwestern Med. Sch., Dallas; svc. chief VA North Tex. Health Care Sys., Dallas, 2004—.

YANG, WEN-CHING, chemical engineer; b. Taipei, Taiwan, Nov. 11, 1939; came to U.S., 1964; s. Ting-Lien and Ho (Lee) Y.; m. Rae Tien, Aug. 24, 1968; children: Evonne R., Peter T. BSChemE, Nat. Taiwan U., Taipei, 1962; MSChemE, U. Calif., Berkeley, 1965; PhD in Chem. Engring., Carnegie Mellon U., 1968. Sr. engr. rsch. and devel. ctr. Westinghouse Electric Co., Pitts., 1968-76, fellow engr., 1976-93, adv. engr. sci. and tech. ctr., 1993-98, Siemens Westinghouse Power Corp., Pitts., 1998—2005; sr. energy advisor Sci. Applications Internat. Corp., 2006—. Instr. U. Pitts., 1980, 83;, cons., adj. prof., 2004-; chmn. rsch. rev. panel Office Fossil Energy, Dept. Energy, Washington, 1990; hon. guest prof. Tsinghua U., Beijing, 1996—; co-chair 10th Internat. Conf. on Fluidization, Beijing, 2001; spkr. in field. Author: (with others) Encyclopedia of Fluid Mechanics, 1986, 92; editor spl. vol. Powder Tech. jour., 1987, 98; editor: Fluidization, Solids Handling, and Processing, 1999, Handbook of Fluidization and Fluid-Particle Systems, 2003; contbr. over 100 papers to sci. jours. Fellow AIChE (programming chair and sec. group 3, editor 9 symposium series vols. 1987-88, 92-93, sec. particle tech. forum 1993-95, Fluidized Processes Recognition award 1993, George Westinghouse Signature award of excellence 1995. Fluidization Lectureship award 2000); mem. Am. Chem. Soc., Chinese Am. Chem. Soc. (pres. Pitts. chpt. 1994), Orgn. Chinese Am. (pres. Pitts. chpt. 2006-). Achievements include patents in field; development of widely-used correlations and design equations in pneumatic transport and fluidization areas. Home: 3117 Treeline Dr Murrysville PA 15668-1569 Home Phone: 724-327-3011. Personal E-mail: yangwc@comcast.net.

YANG, WESLEY, lawyer; b. Canton, China, Nov. 12, 1949; came to US, 1951; s. C.K. and Louise (Chin) Y.; m. Mary Ann McDunn, May 31, 1975; children: Margaret, Thomas Michael. Student, Chinese U. Hong Kong, 1969-71; grad. chef, South China Inst. Catering, Hong Kong, 1970; BA cum laude in East Asian Hist., U. Pitts., 1972, JD, 1975. Bar:

Pa. 1975, US Tax Ct. 1984; CPA, Pa. Supervising tax specialist Coopers & Lybrand, Pitts., 1975-79; mgr. internat. taxes Dravo Corp., Pitts., 1979-84; pvt. practice atty. Pitts., 1984-88; of counsel Babst, Calland, Clements & Zomnir, Pitts., 1988; ptnr. Klett, Rooney, Lieber & Schorling, Pitts., Leech, Tishman, Fuscaldo & Lampl, LLC, Pitts, 2007—. Adj. prof. grad. prog. in taxation Robert Morris Coll., Pitts., 1982-84; asst. prof. taxation and acctg. Duquesne U. Sch. Bus. and Adminstrn., Pitts., 1984-90. Contbr. articles to profl. jours.; co-author: Representing Physicians, Estate Planning and Adminstrn. in Pa., The Tools and Techniques of Charitable Giving. Named one of Top 100 Attys., Worth mag., 2005—06. Mem. ABA, Allegheny County Bar Assn., Pa. Inst. CPA, Pitts. Tax Club. Office: Leech Tishman Fuscaldo & Lampl LLC Citizens Bank Bldg 30th Fl 525 William Penn Pl Pittsburgh PA 15219 Office Phone: 412-261-1600 ext. 269. E-mail: wyang@leechtishman.com.

YANG, YANG, statistician, medical researcher; b. China; married. PhD, Emory U., Atlanta, 2004. Rsch. assoc. Harvard U., Boston, 2004—06; scientist Fred Hutchinson Cancer Rsch. Ctr., Seattle, 2006—. Mem.: Am. Statis. Assn. Achievements include research in statistical models for the transmission and genetics of infectious diseases. Office: Fred Hutchinson Cancer Rsch Ctr 1100 Fairview Ave N PO Box 19024 Seattle WA 98109-1024 Office Fax: 206-667-4812.

YANG, YANG-MING, medical educator; d. Ming-ding Yang and Jian Song; m. C. Clifford Conaway, June 18, 1994. MD, Zhong Shan U., Med. Sch., Canton, China, 1977; PhD, NY Med. Coll., Valhalla, 1996. Rsch. scientist Am. Health Found., Valhalla, 1991—2003; rsch. asst. prof. NY Med. Coll., 2003—. Contbr. articles to profl. jours. Mem., adult fellowship Drew United Meth. Ch., Carmel, NY, 1998—. Rsch. grant, NIH, 2004. Mem.: Am. Assn. Cancer Rsch. Conservative. Avocations: gardening, swimming, travel, photography. Office: NY Med Coll 95 Grassland Reservation Valhalla NY 10595 E-mail: yang-ming_yang@nymc.edu.

YANG, YONG-EUN, professional golfer; b. Jeju-do, Republic of Korea, Jan. 15, 1972; m. Ju Pak Young, 1999; children: Hyeonwoo, Isu, Kyungmin. Profl. golfer Korean PGA Tour, Japan Golf Tour, European Tour, 2006—, PGA Tour, 2008—. Mem. Asian team Royal Trophy, 2007. Served with South Korean Army. Named Rookie of Yr., Korean PGA Tour, 1997. Achievements include winning Korean Tour event: SBS Championship, 2002; winning Japan Golf Tour events: Sun Chlorella Classic, 2004, Asahi Ryokuken Yomiuri Asolizuka, 2004, Coca-Cola Tokai Classic, 2005, Suntory Open, 2006; winning Asian Tour event: Kolon Hana Bank Korea Open, 2006; winning European Tour event: HSBC Champions, 2006; winning PGA Tour events: The Honda Classic, 2009, PGA Championship, 2009. Office: PGA Tour 100 PGA Tour Blvd Ponte Vedra Beach FL 32082*

YANG, YOUXIN, research scientist; d. Shiyan Li and Ling Yang. MD (hon.), Nanjing Rlwy. Med. Coll., China, 1986, MS (hon.), 1991; PhD (hon.), Paris U. VI, 2000. Cert. pathologist INSERM, France, 2002. Dir. Asia culture Creation Rsch. Etude Sci., Tech., Paris, 1995—2000; pres. Sci. Art Soc., Boston, 2001—. Dir. Art Exploration, Boston, 2004—. Recipient Remi (Platinum) award, WorldFest, Houston, 2004, accolade, Accolade Competition, 2005, prize for young scientist in pathology, French Assn. Pediat. Path. Rsch., 2000; named Best Dr. of Yr., Adminstrn. Medicine, Xuzhou, China, 1988. Mem.: Am. Soc. Investigative Pathology (life), Am. Assn. for Cancer Rsch. (life). Achievements include discovery of the role of tumor suppressor gene WT1 in Denys-Drash Syndrome; the role of PAX2 gene in Isolated Diffuse Mesangial Sclerosis; the role of genomic instability during cancer development; invention of combinational technique of in situ hybridization and immunohistochemistry for detecting cancer biomarker. Office: Harvard Med Sch BIDMC GI DA 601 330 Brookline Ave Boston MA 02215 Personal E-mail: yangyx@hotmail.com. Business E-Mail: yyang@bidmc.harvard.edu.

YANG, YUEKUI, atmospheric scientists; BS in Atmospheric Sci. and Engring. (hon.), U. Army, Nanjing, China, 1987, MS in Atmospheric Sci. and Engring., 1990; PhD, U. Ill. Urbana-Champaign, 2007. Rsch. scientist Aviational Meteorol. Rsch. Inst., Beijing, 1990—97; software engr. METSTAR Radar. Co., Ltd., Beijing, 1997—99; project mgr. Datatrust Info. Techs., Beijing, 1999—2001; rsch. asst. U. Ill. Urbana-Champaign, 2001—07; rsch. assoc. Goddard Earth Sci. and Tech. Ctr., Greenbelt, Md., 2007—. Contbr. scientific papers (Sci. and Tech. Advancement award, 1998). Mem.: Am. Meteorol. Soc., Am. Geophys. Union, Phi Kappa Phi. Office: NASA Goddard Space Flight Ctr Code 6132 Greenbelt MD 20771 Office Fax: 301-614-6307. Business E-Mail: yuekui.yang@nasa.gov.

YANG, YU-PING, mechanical engineer; s. Zhide Yang; m. Ying Li; 1 child, Tim. PhD, Harbin Inst. Tech., China, 1995. Prin. rsch. scientist Battelle Meml. Inst., Columbus, Ohio, 1996—2004; sr. engr. Edison Welding Inst., Columbus, 2004—. Recipient Sossenheimer award, Internat. Welding Inst., 2009. Mem.: Am. Welding Inst. Achievements include patents for weld distortion control method. Office: Edison Welding Inst 1250 Arthur E Adams Dr Columbus OH 43221 Personal E-mail: yupingyang@yahoo.com. Business E-Mail: yyang@ewi.org.

YANG, ZHANBO, mathematics professor, researcher; s. Baozhi Yang and Shuqing Li; m. Liping Peng; children: Brenda Wei, Kevin Peng. PhD, Auburn U., Auburn, Ala., 1989. Assoc. prof. Shawnee State U., Portsmouth, Ohio, 1989—97, U. Incarnate Word, San Antonio, 1997—2000; software devel. mgr. Oberthur Gaming Tech., San Antonio, 2000—05; assoc. prof. U. Incarnate Word, San Antonio, 2005—, dir., NSF funded math. scholar program, 2008—. Contbr. articles to jours. Mem.: MAA. Office: Univ Incarnate Word 4301 Broadway San Antonio TX 78259

YANKELEVITZ, DAVID F., radiologist, educator; MD, SUNY Health Sci. Ctr., Bklyn., 1981. Cert. diagnostic radiology, nuclear medicine. Intern Staten Island Hosp.; resident Long Island Coll. Hosp.; fellow Weill Cornell Med. Coll., prof. radiology & cardiothoracic surgery; attending radiologist NY-Presbyterian Hosp. Office: 520 E 70th St New York NY 10021 Office Phone: 212-746-2526. Office Fax: 212-746-2811.*

YANKEY, KOFI, economics professor; s. David Beikwaw and Margo't Yankey; m. Lydia Yankey, June 10, 2000; 1 child, Beikwaw. BA in Economics, San Diego State U., Calif., 1991, MA in Economics, 1993. Cert. in phys. edn. San Diego City Coll., Calif., 1990. Math., economics prof. Nat. U., San Diego, 1995—, Santa Monica CC, Calif., 2001—, Mt. St. Marys Coll., LA, 2003—; economics prof. El Camino Coll., Torrance, Calif., 2002—, mentor project success, 2004—07, coord., study abroad Ghana, 2006—; economics prof. Southwestern Coll., San Diego, 1998—, asst. womensvolleyball coach, 1998—2001. Eucharistic min. St. Pauls Cath. Ch., LA, 2001—05, St. Rita's Cath. Ch., San Diego, 1981—2001. Mem.: Alpha Gamma Sigma. Roman Catholic. Business E-Mail: kofiyankey1@yahoo.com.

YANKWITT, GEORGE B(RUCE), lawyer; b. Bklyn., Feb. 4, 1943; s. Irvin and Roslyn (Smith) Yankwitt; m. Adrienne G. Schwartz, Nov. 24, 1966; children: Ian, Russell, Craig. BS, Cornell U., 1964, LLB with distinction, 1967. Bar: NY 1967, US Dist. Ct. (so. and ea. dists.) NY 1968, US Tax Ct. 1982, US Ct. Appeals (2d cir.) 1968. Assoc. law clk. to judge US Ct. Appeals (2d cir.), 1967—68; assoc. Graubard, Moskovitz, McGoldrick, Dannett & Horowitz, NYC, 1968—72, Finley, Kumble, Heine, Underberg & Grutman, 1972—74, Robinson, Silverman, Pearce, Aronsohn & Berman, 1974—76, ptnr., 1976; ptnr., group co-head comml. litig. Bryan Cave LLP. Editor: Cornell Law Rev. Mem.: ABA, NY Countr Lawyers Assn., NY State Trial Lawyers Assn., NY State Bar Assn., Fed. Bar Coun., Order of Coif. Office: Bryan Cave LLP 1290 Ave of the Americas New York NY 10104 Office Phone: 212-541-2220. E-mail: gbyankwitt@bryancave.com.

YANNALFO, BRETT CONLON, bank executive; b. Lawrence, Mass., Jan. 20, 1969; MBA, So. N.H. U., Salem, NH, 1998. Treas., COO Merrimac Savs. Bank, Mass., 1999—2001; br. adminstr. Stoneham Savs. Bank, Stoneham, Mass., 2001—02; v.p. ops. The Atlas Group, LLC, Andover, Mass., 2002—. Fin. officer Norther Essex C.C., Haverhill, Mass., 2004—05. Home: 53 Lowell Street Andover MA 01810 Office: The Atlas Group LLC PO Box 819 Andover MA 01810 Office Fax: 978-824-2352. Personal E-mail: byannalfo@comcast.net. Business E-Mail: byannalfo@theatlasgroup.com.

YANNAS, IOANNIS VASSILIOS, polymer science educator; b. Athens, Apr. 14, 1935; s. Vassilios Pavlos and Thalia (Sarafoglou) Yannas; m. Stamatia Frondistou (div. Oct. 1984); children: Tania, Alexis. AB, Harvard U., 1957; SM, MIT, 1959; MS, Princeton U., 1965, PhD, 1966. Asst. prof. mech. engring. MIT, Cambridge, 1966-68, duPont asst. prof., 1968-69, assoc. prof., 1969-78, prof. polymer sci. and engring. dept. mech. engring., 1978—, prof. dept. materials sci. and engring., 1983—; prof. Harvard-MIT Div. Health Scis. and Tech., Cambridge, 1978—. Vis. prof. Royal Inst. Tech., Stockholm, 1974. Author: Tissue and Organ Regeneration in Adults, 2001; editor: Regenerative Medicine, 2 vols., 2005; mem. editl. bd. Jour. Biomed. Materials Rsch., 1986—, Jour. Materials Sci. Materials Medicine, 1990—, Tissue Engring., 1994—, Interface, 2004, Biomed. Materials (China); contbr. articles to profl. jours. Recipient Founders award, Soc. Biomaterials, 1982, Clemson award, 1992, Fred O. Conley award, Soc. Plastics Engrs., 1982, award in medicine and genetics, Sci. Digest/Cutty Sark, 1982, Doolittle award, Am. Chem. Soc., 1988; fellow, Shriners Burns Inst., Mass. Gen. Hosp., 1980—81; Pub. Health Svc. fellow, Princeton U., 1963. Fellow: Biomaterials Sci. and Engring., Am. Inst. Med. and Biol. Engrs. (founding mem.), Am. Inst. Chemists; mem.: Inst. Medicine Nat. Acad Scis. Achievements include patents in field. Office: MIT Bldg 3-332 77 Mass Ave Cambridge MA 02139-4307

YANNELLA, DONALD, literature and language professor; b. NYC, May 12, 1934; s. Donald Joseph and Johanna (Meehan) Y.; m. Kathleen Malone, May 23, 1959; children: Susan Y. Harrigan, Katherine Y. Jennings, Donald III, Christopher, Clare. BS, Fordham U., 1956, MA, 1963, PhD, 1971. Tchg. asst. dept. English Auburn U., 1956-57; prof. dept. English U. So. Miss., 1981-83, Rowan U., 1964-81, 83-91, prof. emeritus, 1991—; prof. dept. English Barat Coll., 1991-94, disting prof. Am. lit., 1995—2000. Dir. grad. studies English Rowan U., 1973-81, co-dir. Am. studies program, 1974-81; chair dept. English U. So. Miss., 1981-83; v.p. acad. affairs, dean coll. Barat Coll., 1991-94. Author: American Prose to 1820, 1979, Ralph Waldo Emerson, 1982, The Perfect Prodigy: Melville on the Birth of Malcolm, 1986, Herman Melville's Malcolm Letter: "Man's Final Lore", 1992, New Essays on Billy Budd, 2002, 2d edit., 2007; contbr. articles to profl. jours. With U.S. Army, 1957-58. Recipient Merit awards Rowan U., 1979-80, 85-86; NEH fellow, 1978-79. Mem. AAUP (chpt. pres. 1968-69, mem. cons. group Coll. and Univ. Govt. 1969, v.p. NJ State Conf. 1969-71, founding editor NJ Conf. newsletter 1969-71, nat. spl. com. non-tenured faculty 1971-72, chair 1973-79), Modern Lang. Assn. (Am. lit. sect., sec.-treas. 1982-85, exec. com. 1982-86, 88, adv. coun. 1986-88, nominating com. 1987-89, chair 1989, award 1988), Melville Soc. (program chair 1972-73, acting sec.-treas. 1973-74, acting editor 1973-74, sec.-treas. 1975-89, editor 1976-89, pres. 1990), Nat. Project Ctr. Film & Humanities (adv. com. 1974-75), Writings of Herman Melville (manuscript assoc., 1987-2001). Office Phone: 609-978-6443. Business E-Mail: yannellakd@aol.com.

YANNEY, PATRICK STEVEN, human resources specialist; b. Denver, Sept. 9, 1952; s. Merle Philip and Madeline Veronica Yanney; m. Stephanie Ann Robinson, Aug. 15, 1981; children: Mark Phillip, Luke Steven. BA, Colo. State U., 1974. Gatekeeper Glen Eyrie Conf. Ctr., 1974—76, reception ctr./bookstore mgr., 1977—78; adminstrv. asst. to dir. of adminstrv. svcs. The Navigators, 1978—79, pers. and facilities mgr., 1980—82, dir. adminstrv. svcs., 1983—91, pers. svcs. dir., 1992—2006, corp. human resources dir., 2000—. Chmn. supervisory com. Mountain Bell Credit Un ion, Colorado Springs, 1984—86; guest lectr. Webster U., Colorado Springs, 2003—04. Editor: ASTD newsletter, 1988—89; contbr. articles to profl. jours.; actor: (TV). Vol. mediator BBB, Colorado Springs, 1995—, 4th Jud. Dist. Small Claims Ct., Colorado Springs, 1997—. Named Outstanding Young Bus. and Profl. Person, Rotary Internat., 1986. Mem.: ASTD, Toastmasters (area gov. 1988—89). Avocations: Porsche racing, aviation, photography, camping, commercial acting. Office: The Navigators 3820 N 30th St Colorado Springs CO 80904 Home Phone: 719-531-0361; Office Phone: 719-594-2362. E-mail: pat.yanney@navigators.org.

YANNONE, RONALD MATTHEW, systems engineer, researcher; s. Fanny Kalamira Yannone. BSEE, Stevens Inst. Tech., 1976; MSEE, Syracuse U., 1979. Elec. engr. GE, Utica, NY, 1976—91; math tutor Asbury Pk. Mid. Sch., NJ, 1992—95, Brookdale CC, 1992—95; engring. fellow BAE Electronics, Intelligence & Support, Nashua, NH, 1996—. Editor: BAE Systems Fellows Periodical, 2004—; contbr. chapters to books, articles to profl. jours. Med. missionary Missionary, Edn. Evangelistic Tng., Huntingdon, Tenn., 1992—; math problem developer Am. Math. Competitions, Lincoln, Nebr., 1994—. Named to, Electronic Warfare Tech. Hall of Fame, 2005. Mem.: Internat. Acad. Sci., Assn. of Old Crows, Mega Soc. (editor Noesis 2004). Achievements include patents for passive 360-degree target ranging; Commander's Decision Aid (CDA) for U.S. Army ground combat vehicles; passive single-aircraft air-to-air ranging; passive missile time-to-go estimation; patents pending for aircraft and ground vehicle protection systems. Avocations: reading, puzzles, swimming, rowing, exercise. Home: 189 Ash St 2 Nashua NH 03060 Office: BAE Systems Electronics Intelligence & Support MER15-2324 Canal St Merrimack NH 03054 Office Fax: 603-885-5142. Business E-Mail: ronald.m.yannone@baesystems.com.

YANNUCCI, THOMAS DAVID, lawyer; b. Springfield, Ohio, Mar. 30, 1950; s. David Marion and Patricia (Wilson) Y.; m. Lisa Marie Copeland, June 30, 1972; children: Teresa, Andrea, Thomas D. Jr. AB summa cum laude, U. Notre Dame, 1972, JD cum laude, 1976. Bar: Ohio 1977, U.S. Ct. Appeals (D.C., 1st, 2d, 3d, 4th, 5th, 6th, 7th, 8th, 11th and 10th cirs.) 1980, U.S. Supreme Ct. 1980, D.C. 1981. Law clk. to Judge John Danaher US Ct. Appeals (DC cir.), Washington, 1976-77; trial atty. US Dept. Justice, 1977-80; ptnr. Kirkland & Ellis, 1980—, chair firm mgmt. com., 2001—. Editor-in-chief U. Notre Dame Law Rev., 1975-76. Roman Catholic. Office: Kirkland & Ellis LLP 655 15th St NW Ste 1200 Washington DC 20005-5793 Office Phone: 202-879-5000. Office Fax: 202-879-5200. Business E-Mail: tyannucci@kirkland.com, thomas.yannucci@kirkland.com.

YANNUL, EDWARD, chemical engineer, writer; s. Edward Thomas Yannul and Lucille Ann Marie Yeager; m. Roxanne Marrandino, July 15, 1994. AS in Engring., Camden County Coll., Blackwood, NJ, 1984; BSChemE, U. Pa., Phila., 1986. Process engr. Rohm and Haas Co., Bristol, Pa., 1987—94, sr. process engr., 1994—99; sr. process devel. engr. J. M. Huber Corp. Engineered Materials, Havre de Grace, Md., 1999—2003; engring. assoc. process engring. Clorox Svcs. Corp., Pleasanton, Calif., 2003—06; product engr. Rohm and Haas Co. CMPT Inc., Newark, Del., 2006—. Author: Quick Hit TRIZ Assessment: User's and Facilitator's Guide, 2005; contbr. articles to profl. jours. Recipient R&D Achievement award, Clorox Svcs. Corp., 2004, Engring. Excellence award, 2005. Mem.: NRA, AIChE, Mensa. Republican. Roman Catholic. Achievements include patents in field. Avocations: martial arts, politics, hiking, fishing, history. Home: 29 Yosemite Dr Bear DE 19701

YANO, ELIZABETH MARTIN, epidemiologist, researcher; d. William Oliver Martin and Marjorie Ann Turner; m. Grant Akira Yano, May 3, 1986; children: Michael, David, Steven. BS in Psychobiology, UCLA, 1983, MSPH in Epidemiology, 1986, PhD in Epidemiology, 1995. Rsch. analyst med. outcomes study RAND Corp., Santa Monica, Calif., 1984—86, rsch. epidemiologist, 1986—95; project mgr. dept. medicine UCLA, 1986—88, assoc. prof. health svcs. Sch. Pub. Health, 1997—; sr. assoc. Arlene Fink Assocs., Inc., Pacific Palisades, Calif., 1986—95; assoc. chief pace evaluation Sepulveda (Calif.) VA Med. Ctr., 1989—94, assoc. chief evaluation and decision support, 1994—97; rsch. health scientist VA Health Svcs. R & D Ctr. Excellence, Sepulveda, 1993—97, asst. dir., 1997—99, assoc. dir., 1999—2002, sr. social scientist, 2002—, co-dir. VA associated health postdoctoral tng. program, 2002—04, deputy dir., 2004—. Mem. sci. rev. bd. VA Greater LA Healthcare Sys., 2002—; mem. nat. ethics task force on gender disparities Dept. Vets., Washington, 2001—; presenter in field. Contbr. articles to profl. jours. Chair VA Women's Health Rsch. Agenda Conf., 2004. Recipient Achievement awards, UCLA Alumni Assn., 1980, 1981, Nat. Psychology Honors award, Psi Chi, 1982, Rsch. Career Scientist award, VA Health Svcs. Rsch. and Devel., 2007—; grantee, VA HSR&D Svc., 1997—99, 1998—2002, VHA Survey of Women Veterans Health Programs and Practices, Dept. Vets. Affairs, 2001; Regents scholar, UCLA, 1979—83, Alumni scholar, UCLA Alumni Assn., 1979—83, UCLA Coll. Honors Meeker scholar, UCLA Coll. Honors Program, 1981—82, UCLA Marhoefer Med. scholar, UCLA, 1982—83, Health Policy fellow, RAND-UCLA, Inst. Medicine, Pew Meml. Trusts, 1986—89. Office: VA Health Svcs R&D Ctr Excellence 16111 Plummer St 152 Sepulveda CA 91343 Business E-Mail: elizabeth.yano@va.gov.

YANOFF, MYRON, ophthalmologist; b. Phila., Dec. 21, 1936; s. Jacob and Lillian S. (Fishman) Yanoff; m. Karin Michelle Lindblad, Aug. 8, 1980; 1 child, Alexis A.;children from previous marriage: Steven L., David A., Joanne M. AB, U. Pa., 1957, MD, 1961. Prof. ophthalmology and pathology U. Pa. Med. Sch., Phila.; William F. Norris and George E. de Schweinitz prof. ophthalmology, chmn. dept., dir. Scheie Eye Inst., 1977-86; chmn., prof. ophthalmology Drexel U., Phila., 1988—. 1st exch. vis. prof. U. Vienna, 1992. Author: Ocular Pathology, Textbook of Ophthalmology; contbr. articles to profl. jours. Served to maj. M.C. USAR. Recipient Humboldt award, 1988. Mem.: Am. Acad. Ophthalmology (Sr. Honor award 1995), Am. Ophthalmic Soc., Verhoeff Soc. Office: 219 N Broad St Fl 3 Philadelphia PA 19107 Mailing: PO Box 0254 Gwynedd Valley PA 19437-0254 Office Phone: 215-762-3937. Business E-Mail: myanoff@drexelmed.edu, myanoffmd@aol.com.

YANOFSKY, CHARLES, retired biology professor; b. NYC, Apr. 17, 1925; s. Frank and Jennie (Kopatz) Y.; m. Carol Cohen, June 19, 1949, (dec. Dec. 1990); children: Stephen David, Robert Howard, Martin Fred; m. Edna Crawford, Jan. 4, 1992. BS, CCNY, 1948; MS, Yale U., 1950, PhD, 1951, DSc (hon.), 1981, U. Chgo., 1980. Rsch. asst. Yale U., 1951-54; asst. prof. microbiology Western Res. U. Med. Sch., 1954-57; mem. faculty Stanford U., 1958—2000, prof. biology, 1961—2000, Herzstein prof. biology, 1966—2000, prof. emeritus, 2000—; ret. Career investigator Am. Heart Assn., 1969-95. Served with AUS, 1944-46. Recipient Lederle Med. Faculty award, 1957, Eli Lilly award bacteriology, 1959, U.S. Steel Co. award molecular biology, 1964, Howard Taylor Ricketts award U. Chgo., 1966, Albert and Mary Lasker award, 1971, Townsend Harris medal Coll. City N.Y., 1973, Louisa Gross Horwitz prize in biology and biochemistry Columbia U., 1976, V.D. Mattia award Roche Inst., 1982, medal Genetics Soc. Am., 1983, Internat. award Gairdner Found., 1985, named Passano Laureate, Passano Found., 1992; recipient William C. Rose award in biochemistry and molecular biology, 1997, Abbott Lifetime Achievement award Am. Soc. Microbiology, 1998, Nat. medal of Sci., 2003. Mem. NAS (Selman A. Waksman award in microbiology 1972), Am. Acad. Arts and Scis., Genetics Soc. Am. (pres. 1969, Thomas Hunt Morgan medal 1990), Am. Soc. Biol. Chemists (pres. 1984), Royal Soc. (fgn. mem.), Japanese Biochem. Soc. (hon.) Home: 725 Mayfield Ave Stanford CA 94305-1016 Office: Stanford U Dept Of Biological Sci Stanford CA 94305

YANOTI, TIMOTHY, bank executive; B in Physics, Clarkson U., Potsdam, NY; MBA, Cornell U., Ithaca, NY. Aerospace engr.; dir. asset backed securities Greenwich Capital Markets; investment banking positions Drexel Burnham Lambert; mng. dir. GE Capital; with structured products group Nat. City Corp., Cleve., 2006, sr. mng. dir. capital markets, sr. v.p. Office: Nat City Corp Nat City Ctr 1900 E Ninth St Cleveland OH 44114-3484 Office Phone: 216-222-2000.

YANOVIAK, STEPHEN PAUL, ecologist, educator; b. Norristown, Pa., Mar. 5, 1969; s. John J. and Mary Ann Yanoviak. BS, Auburn U., Ala., 1991; MS, Purdue U., Ind., 1993; PhD, U. Okla., Norman, 1999. Postdoctoral rsch. assoc. U. Okla., Norman, 1999, Evergreen State Coll., Olympia, Wash., 1999—2001; adj. asst. prof. U. Fla. Med. Entomology Lab., Vero Beach, 2001—07; postdoctoral fellow U. Tex. Med. Br., Galveston, 2001—07; asst. prof. U. Ark., Little Rock, 2007—. Cons. BBC Nat. Hist. Unit, Panama, 2005, Wadsworth Ctr., New York, NY, 2005, Innovative Vector Control Consortium, Iquitos, Loreto, Peru, 2006, Smithsonian Instn. Monitoring and Assessing Biodiversity Program, Gamba, Gabon, 2006. Guest spkr. Multiple Sch., Norman, 1996—99, Monteverde Friends Sch., Costa Rica, 2000—01, Explorama, Colegio Roosevelt, Iquitos, Peru, 2005—06; translator US Navy Med. Mission, Iquitos, 2005. Grantee, Huron Mountain Wildlife Found., 1992—93, U. Okla. Grad. Student Senate, 1996—98, Explorers Club, 1996, Sigma Xi Sci. Rsch. Soc., 1996—97, Nat. Geog. Soc., 2006, Amazon Conservation Assn., 2006—07; fellow, Smithsonian Instn., 1996, Fulbright Found., 1998; Presdl. scholarship, Broward County, Fla., 1987, Payne Meml. scholarship, Auburn U., 1988—91, Travel grant, Marie Selby Bot. Gardens, 2000, Assn. Tropical Biology, 2001. Mem.: Internat. Canopy Network, Fla. Entomol. Soc., Assn. Tropical

Biology and Conservation, Ecol. Soc. Am., Entomol. Soc. Am., North Am. Benthological Soc., Mich. Entomol. Soc., Soc. Exptl. Biology, Beta Beta Beta, Gamma Sigma Delta, Sigma Xi, Phi Kappa Phi. Achievements include discovery of aerial gliding behavior in tropical rain forest canopy ants; research in biodiversity and ecology of tropical rain forest canopies and disease vectors. Avocations: running, travel, photography. Office: UALR Dept Biol 2801 S University Ave Little Rock AR 72204-1099 Office Fax: 501-569-3271.

YANTA, JOHN WALTER, bishop emeritus; b. Runge, Tex., Oct. 2, 1931; s. John and Mary Pollok Yanta. Ordained priest Archdiocese of San Antonio, 1956, aux. bishop, 1994—97; second asst. pastor St. Ann's Parish, San Antonio, 1956—62; pastor Sacred Heart Ch., San Antonio, 1973—81, St. James Ch., San Antonio, 1983—96; ordained bishop, 1994; bishop Diocese of Amarillo, Tex., 1997—2008, bishop emeritus, 2008—. Dir. Cath. Youth Orgn., San Antonio, 1962—63, youth dir., 1963—65; founder, exec. dir. San Antonio Neighborhood Youth Org., 1965—71; founder, pres. Polish Am. Congress Tex., 1971—73; pres. Tex. Cath. Conf. Priest Senates, 1978—82; editor Today's Cath., San Antonio, 1981—83; founder, exec. dir. Cath. TV San Antonio, 1981—83; founder Polish Am. Priests Assn., 1990; bd. dirs. Cath. Relief Svc., 2000—, Kenedy Meml. Found., St. Joseph & St. Peter Sem., Brownsville, Tex.; treas. Tex. Conf. Churches, 2003—. Roman Catholic. Office: Diocese of Amarillo PO Box 5644 Amarillo TX 79117-5644 Office Phone: 806-383-2243.

YANTZ, PATRICIA E., art educator; d. John Robert and Anne Eileen Glover; m. John Yantz, Aug. 9, 1975; children: Kathryn, Christopher, Brianne, Brendan. BS, Ladycliff Coll., Highland Falls, NY, 1973; MS in Art Edn., LI U., Greenvale, NY, 1977; MSW, SUNY, Stony Brook, 1994. Tchr. Sachem Ctrl. Sch. Dist., Holbrook, NY, 1973—. Advisor Art Honor Soc., Farmingville, NY, 2004—07. Exhibited in group shows at LI Mus., 2002, 2004—09, Neighborhood House Artists, 2006. Trustee Three Village Hist. Soc., Setauket, NY, 2005—. Mem.: Old Field Club. Roman Catholic. Avocations: tennis, painting, history, running. Office Phone: 631-716-8200. Business E-Mail: pyantz@sachem.edu.

YAO, BIN, mechanical engineering educator; b. Shaanxi, China, Dec. 23, 1968; came to U.S., 1992; s. Weikuan Yao and Qingrong Liu; m. Lan Zhong, Oct. 14, 2008. PhD, U. Calif., Berkeley, 1996. Postdoctoral rschr. mech. engring. dept. U. Calif., Berkeley, 1996; asst. prof. Sch. Mech. Engring. Purdue U., West Lafayette, Ind., 1996—2002, assoc. prof. Sch. Mech. Engring., 2002—07, prof. Sch. Mech. Engring., 2007—. Summer faculty sabbatical leave Advanced Hydraulics Group, Joliet (Ill.) plant, Caterpillar Inc., 1997. Contbr. numerous tech. articles to profl. publs. (NSF Career award 1998). Recipient O. Hugo Schuck Best Paper award Am. Automatic Control Coun., 2004; Regents fellow U. Calif., 1992. Mem.: ASME (Dynamic Systems and Control Divsn. Outstanding Young Investigator award 2007), IEEE. Avocations: sports, travel, art, music. Office: Purdue U Sch Mech Engring West Lafayette IN 47907 Office Phone: 765-494-7746. Office Fax: 765-494-0539. Business E-Mail: byao@ieee.org.

YAO, FRANCES, music educator, small business owner; arrived in U.S., 1976; d. Ted Yao and Phuong Hue Chi; children: Christopher Y. Shi, Daniel H. Shi. BA, Nat. Conservatory, Saigon, Vietnam, 1973. Cert. tchr. Suzuki and piano performance Ga., 1973. Pianist Chinese Alliance Ch., Saigon, Vietnam, 1970—75; tchr. piano Hai Quang Music Sch., Saigon, Vietnam, 1973—75, Sandy Springs Music Sch., Roswell, Ga., 1976—78, Ephrata (Pa.) Music Acad., 1975—77, Frances Yao's Piano Studio, Alpharetta, Ga., 1980—. Mem. choir, leader sect. Johns Creek Bapt. Ch., Alpharetta, Ga., 2001—. Recipient Beethoven 200-yr. Piano Competition award, German Culture Inst., 1970. Mem.: Music Tchr. Nat. Assn., North Fulton Music Tchr. Assn., N.D. Music Tchrs. Assn. (chmn. auditions 1983—, v.p. 1992), Ga. Music Educators Assn. (assoc.), Ga. Music Teachers Assn. (assoc.). Avocations: swimming, travel, music, photography, reading.

YAO, NAN, educational association administrator; s. Junen Yao and Qiulan Yan; married. PhD, Ariz. State U., Tempe, 1990. Dir. Prism Imaging & Analysis Ctr. Princeton U., NJ, 1999—. Author: (book) Handcook of Microscopy for nanotechnology, Focused Ion Beam Systems: Basics and Applications. Recipient Excellence Tchg. award, Princeton U., 2007, 2008. Office: Princeton Univ 70 Prospect Ave Princeton NJ 08544

YAO, QINGJIANG, communications educator, researcher; married. MA in Philosophy, Beijing Normal U., 1999; PhD in Mass Communication, U. SC., Columbia, 2008. Mem. editl. bd. & asst. editor-in-chief Modern Edn. Daily, Xuanwu, Beijing, 1999—2005; vis. asst. prof. Sch. Journalism & Mass Communication, U. Iowa, 2008—. Office: Sch Journalism & Mass Commnication Univ Iowa Iowa City IA 52246-2004 Business E-Mail: qingjiang-yao@uiowa.edu.

YAO, QINGPING, rheumatologist; s. Maojiu Yao and Chunu Guo; m. Sujing Wang, July 1, 1988; children: Nannan, William W. MD, Inner Mongolia Med. Coll., Huhhot, 1984; M, Inner Mongolia, Huhhot, 1988; PhD, Peking Union Med. Coll., Beijing, 1993. Cert. ABIM, 2006, in rheumatology ABIM, 2008. Physician Inner Mongolia Med. Coll. Hosp., Huhhot, Inner Mongolia, China, 1984—85, 1988—90; attending physician assoc. prof. Peking Union Med. Coll., Beijing, 1993—97; staff rheumatologist Cleve. Clin., Cleve., 2008—. Postdoc. fellowship Coll. Physicians & Surgeons, Columbia U., 1997—98; rsch. assoc. U. Pitts., 1998—2003; resident physician Capital Health Sys., Trenton, NJ, 2003—06; rheumatology fellow UCLA, 2006—08. Contbr. articles to profl. jours. Recipient Excellent Resident Physician award, Capital Health Sys., 2004—05. Mem.: ACR, AMA. Taxpayers. Avocation: swimming. Office: Cleveland Clinic 9500 Euclid Ave A50 Cleveland OH 44195 Office Fax: 216-445-7569.

YAO, WEI-DONG, medical educator, researcher; b. Hancheng, Shaanxi Province, China, June 10, 1965; permanent resident, US, 2002; s. Xurong and Fengzhen Yao; m. Hui-Hui Dai, May 1, 1992; children: Annie Ying, Eric Kaifu. PhD in Neurobiology, U. Iowa, Iowa City, 1998. Grad. rsch. asst. U. Iowa, 1992—98; rsch. assoc. Howard Hughes Med. Inst., Duke U., Durham, NC, 1999—2004; asst. prof. Harvard Med. Sch., Boston, 2004—. Med. rschr. Harvard Med. Sch., 2004—. Recipient Rsch. award, U. Iowa, 1998, Runner-up Best Poster award, Sci. Mag., 2004; grantee Young Investigator award, Nat. Alliance Rsch. Schizophrenia and Depression, 2005—07, Milton Fund, Harvard U., 2007, Rsch. grants, NIH, 2007—, 2008—. Mem.: Am. Soc. Biochemistry and Molecular Biology, Soc. Neurosci., Sigma Xi. Achievements include discovery of K channel beta subunit controls neuronal firing and activity; development of a novel bioassay system for detection of neurotransmitter release from drosophila CNS neurons; discovery of the first protein that interacts with dopamine transporter, a major target of drugs of abuse and antidepressants; a role for synaptic scaffold in drug addiction; a novel mechanism by which dopaminergic signaling is regulated; a novel multiprotein complex containing dopamine receptors, glutamate receptors and synaptic scaffolds. Home: 15 Wheelwright Dr Northborough MA 01532

YAO, XI, ceramics engineer, educator; b. Wujin, Jiangsu, China, Sept. 28, 1935; m. Liang-ying Zhang, May 9, 1959; children: Yuang-qing, Men-weng. Grad., Jiaotong U., 1957; PhD in Solid State Sci., Pa. State U., 1982. Assoc. prof. ceramics Xi'an Jiaotong U., China, 1981-84, prof., dean, 1984—; pres. Rsch. Inst. Functional Materials Tongji U. Author: Inorganic Dielectrics, 1962, An Introduction to Dielectric Theory, 1980, Dielectric Physics, 1991; patentee in field. Recipient Ross Coffin Purdy award Am. Ceramic Soc., 1985, Prominent Scientist award State Sci. and Tech. Commn., 1986. Mem.: NAE (fgn. assoc.), Asian Assn. Ferreoelectrics (chmn. 1993), Chinese Acad. Scis., Internat. Acad. Ceramics Sci. Avocation: stamp collecting/philately. Home: 1-49-103 Xian Jiaotong U Xi'an 710048 China Office: Xian Jiaotong U Xi'an 710049 China

YAO, YI, electrical engineer, researcher; d. Zhongqing Jin and Qi Yao; m. Yanzhen Li, Dec. 28, 2004. BS, Nanjing U. Aeronautics and Astronautics, Jiangsu, China, 1996, MS, 2000; PhD, U. Tenn., Knoxville, 2008. Rsch. asst. U. Tenn., 2001—08; elec. engr. Global Rsch., Gen. Electric, Niskayuna, NY, 2008—. Mem.: IEEE.

YAO, YONGXUE, immunologist; b. Hengshui, China, Oct. 23, 1971; s. Yusheng Yao and Shuhui Wang; m. Zhuo Wang, Aug. 30, 1997; 1 child, Daniel. MD, China Med. U., Shenyang, 1996; PhD, Fukui Med. U., Japan, 2003. Diplomate China Med. U., Shenyang, 1996. Resident China Med. U., Shenyang, China, 1996—97; postdoctoral fellow Ind. U. Sch. of Medicine, Indpls., 2003—05, rsch. assoc. Grantee Postdoctoral Fellowship, AHA, 2004, 2005—06; Monbosho Scholarship, Japanese Gov., 1997—2003. Communist. Achievements include research in role of interleukine-4 indendritic cell-mediated immunity. Avocations: swimming, reading. Home: 3735 Wishbone Blvd Indianapolis IN 46268 Office: Indiana Univ Sch of Medicine Wells Ctr Pediat Rsch 702 Barnhill Dr RI-2659 Indianapolis IN 46202 Business E-Mail: yonyao@iupui.edu.

YAO, YUAN, mathematician, researcher; BS in Control Engring., Harbin Inst. Tech., MS in Control Engring., 1998; MPhil in Math., City U. Hong Kong, 2002; PhD in Math., U. Calif., Berkeley, 2006. Vis. rsch. assoc. U. Calif., Berkeley, 2001—02, rschr., 2004—06; vis. scholar Toyota Technol. Inst. U. Chgo., 2004—06; postdoc. fellow Stanford U., Calif., 2006—. Author: (book) A Dynamic Theory of Learning -Online Learning and Stochastic Algorithms in Reproducing Kernel Hilbert Spaces. Mem.: Soc. Indsl. and Applied Math., Inst. Math. Stats., Am. Math. Soc. Office: Dept Math Bldg 380 Stanford Univ Stanford CA 94305-2125 Business E-Mail: yuany@stanford.edu.

YAP, ALEXANDER Y., educator, information systems, researcher, consultant; b. Cebu, Philippines, Jan. 2, 1964; m. Arsenia Q. Yap. BA in Economics, U. Philippines, Quezon City, 1984; MA in Devel. Economics, William's Coll., Mass., 1989; MBA in Internat. Mgmt. with highest distinction, U. Exeter, Eng., 1994; PhD in Mgmt. Info. Sys., Copenhagen Bus. Sch., 1999. Dep. dir. gen. Congl. Planning & Budget Office, Quezon City, 1990—92; asst. prof. Va. Commonwealth U., Richmond, 1999—2002; assoc. prof. Elon U., NC, 2002—. Lead sys. cons. Invensys Corp., Richmond, 2001—02; assoc. editor Internat. Conf. on Info. Sys., Seattle, 2003; jour. editl. rev. bd. mem. Internat. Jour. E-Svcs. and Mobile Applications, Pa., 2008—. Contbr. articles to profl. jours. Recipient Jack Larned award, William's Coll., 1989, Best Rsch. Paper award, Internat. Conf. on Info. Sys., Helsinki, Finland, 1998, Best Paper award, Copenhagen Bus. Sch., 1999. Office: Elon Univ Campus Box 2075 Elon NC 27244 Business E-Mail: ayap@elon.edu.

YAP, CLARENCE, biotechnology executive; 1 child. BS in Biomedical Engring., Northwestern U., Evanston, Ill., 2000; MD, Northwestern U. Feinberg Sch. Medicine, Chgo., 2004; MPH, Northwestern U., Chgo., 2004. Assoc. McKinsey & Co., NYC, 2004—06; assoc. dir. Biomarin Pharm., Novato, Calif., 2006—. Contbr. articles to profl. jours. Club pres. Chinatown Health Clinic, Northwestern U. Med. Sch., Chgo., 2001—02; vol. NY Cares, 2004—05. Recipient Govr. Gen.'s medal, Can., 1997, Best Published Paper award, Jour. Biomech. Engring., 2000; Summer Rsch. fellow, Sunnybrook Hosp., 1998, Inst. Med. Sci., 1999, Rsch. fellow, Alpha Omega Alpha, 2001. Mem.: APHA, AMA, Soc. Gen. Internal Medicine, Am. Coll. Preventative Medicine, Sigma Xi, Tau Beta Pi. Achievements include research in analyzing dosing errors in patients with renal insufficiency in the ambulatory care setting; effectiveness of newly developed pharmaceuticals used in corneal preservation; the prevention of mechanical stretch-induced endothelial and smooth muscle cell injury in experimental vein grafts; development of of drug candidates in multiple cardiovascular indications including hypertension, pulmonary arterial hypertension, intermittent claudication, and sickle cell disease. Avocations: travel, swimming, squash, golf. Office: BioMarin Pharm 105 Digital Dr Novato CA 94949

YAPICI, MURAT KAYA, research scientist; b. Adana, Turkey, June 25, 1982; s. Cahit Yapici and Yapici Selma. Attending in Elec. & Computer Engring., Tex. A&M U., Coll. Station, 2009. Rschr. Tex. A&M U., 2004—; intern Siemens Bldg. Techs., Zurich, Switzerland, 2004. V.p. IAESTE, Coll. Station, 2002—04. Contbr. articles to profl. jours. Mem.: IEEE, Eta Kappa Nu. Achievements include patents pending for wireless sensor system. Home: 1600 Welsh Ave Apt 362 College Station TX 77840 Personal E-mail: muratyapici@gmail.com.

YARADANAKUL, ALP, biomedical researcher; s. Mustafa and Arife Yaradanakul; m. Muberra Yaradanakul, Mar. 2, 2003; 1 child, Enes Tarik. MSc, Physics Dept., Bogazici U., Istanbul, 1996; PhD, Elec. Engring. Dept., Southern Meth. U., Dallas, 2001. Asst. lectr. Tex. A&M U., Mech. Engring. Dept., Coll. Station, Tex., 2001—03; rsch. fellow UTSW Med. Ctr. Physiology Dept., 2003—. Sci. advisor Harmony Sci. Acad., Dallas, 2006—. Rep. Raindrop Turkish Ho., Dallas, 2003—08, Inst. Interfaith Dialog, Dallas, 2005—08. Mem.: IEEE, Am. Phys. Soc., Biophysical Soc., Soc. Gen. Physiologists. Achievements include development of bolometers on kapton flexible substrate; patents pending for a smart skin: micro-machined un-cooled YBCO bolometers on flexible substrate. Office: 5323 Harry Hines Blvd Dallas TX 75390-9040

YARAGUDRI, VINOD K., neuroscientist, researcher; b. Belgaum, Karanataka, India, July 11, 1973; s. Kallappa V. and Ratna K. Yaragudri; m. Shilpa Sulebhavi, Apr. 3, 2003; 1 child, Nathan. BS, Karanatak U., Dharwad, India, 1994, MS, 1996; PhD, NIMH and Neuroscience, Bangalore, India, 2002. Rsch. scholar NIMH and Neuroscis., Banaglore, India, 1996—97, sr. rsch. scholar, 1997—2001; rsch. project mgr. Nathan S. Kline Inst. Psychiat. Rsch., Orangeburg, NY, 2002—03, asst. rsch. scientist, 2003—05, assoc. rsch. scientist, 2005—; rsch. project mgr. N.Y. State Psychiat. Inst., NYC, 2002—03, asst. rsch. scientist, 2003—05, assoc. rsch. scientist, 2005—. Contbr. articles to profl. jours. Founder Narayana Rural Devel. Soc., Mudhol, India, 2003. Recipient Academic Excellence Gold medal, Karnatak U., Dharwad, India, 1997, Burswood Rsch. Poster award, Asian Pacific Congress Clin. Biochemistry, 2004; grantee, Am. Found. Suicide Prevention, 2004—06; fellow, Lady Tata Meml. Trust, India, 1998, Indian Coun. Med. Rsch., 1999—2001, Internat. Brain Rsch. Orgn., 2001, Rsch. Found. Mental Hygeine, 2002—; scholar, Karnataka State Tchr.'s Assn., Bangalore, India, 1991, Jindal Aluminium Trust, Bangalore, India, 1994—96. Mem.: Am. Found. Suicide Prevention (hon.), Soc. Biol. Psychiatry (assoc.), Internat. Cannabinoid Rsch. Soc. (assoc.), Rsch. Soc. Alcoholism (assoc.), Schizophrenia Rsch. Forum (life), Indian Acad. Neurosci. (life), Internat. Brain Rsch. Orgn. (life). Achievements include research in the implication of the role of the brain endocannabinoid system in major depressive disorder and suicide. Home: 120 Nottingham Ct Montvale NJ 07645 Office: Nathan Kline Inst 140 Old Orangeburg Rd Orangeburg NY 10962 Office Fax: 845-398-5451. Personal E-mail: ky_vinod@yahoo.com. Business E-Mail: vyaragudri@nki.rfmh.org.

YARASANI, VENKATARAMA, chemist, researcher; b. Ponnur, Andhra Pradesh, India, June 1, 1968; s. Venkata Mohana Rao and Anjamma Yarasani; m. Padmaja Padyala, May 14, 1998; children: Snehanjali, Chitralekha. BS in Pharm. Scis., Andhra U., Visakhapatnam, India, 1990, MS in Pharmaceutics, 1993, PhD, 1998. Rsch. assoc. Dabur Rsch. Found., Ghaziabad, Uttar Pradesh, India, 1993—95; sr. group leader r&d Dr Reddy's Labs., Hyderabad, 1998—2000; rsch. scientist Kyoto Pharm. U., Kyoto, 2000—03, Murty Pharmaceuticals, Inc., Lexintgton, Ky., 2003—05; sr. rsch. scientist II Purepac/Actavis, Elizabeth, NJ, 2005—. Contbr. articles to profl. jours. Recipient Prof. V. Subba Rao Meml. Gold medal, Andhra U., 1993; fellow, U. Grants Commn., India, 1991—93, Andhra U.Coun. Sci. and Indsl. Rsch., India, 1995—98, Kyoto Pharm. U., 2000—03. Mem.: NJ Pharm. Assn. Sci. and Tech. (assoc.). Achievements include development of colon-specific drug delivery systems, oral dosage forms for macromolecular drugs and improving oral bioavailability. Avocations: travel, sports, reading. Home: 3110 Plaza Dr Woodbridge NJ 07095 Office: Actavis Elizabeth LLC 200 Elmora Ave Elizabeth NJ 07207

YARBOROUGH, CLAY, Councilman; BA in Bus. Mgmt., U. North Fla. Recruiter UPS; mem. Duval Soil & Water Conservation Bd., 2000, Greater Arlington-Beaches Citizens Planning Adv. Com., 2001; councilman, Dist. 1 Jacksonville City Coun., Fla. Mem. Sheriff's Adv. Coun., Greater Arlington Civic Coun.; chmn. Pub. Health & Safety Com.; mem. Rules Com., Fin. Com.; coun. liaison Mil. & Veterans Affairs. Mem.: Arlington Rotary Club (hon.). Republican. Office: 117 W Duval St Ste 425 Jacksonville FL 32202 Office Phone: 904-630-1386, 904-630-1389. Business E-Mail: clay@coj.net.*

YARBOROUGH, WILLIAM GLENN, JR., military officer, forester, international business executive; b. Rock Hill, SC, June 21, 1940; s. William Glenn and Bessie (Rainsford) Y.; m. Betsy Gibson, Jan. 24, 1969; children: Bill, Clinton, Frank, Elizabeth. BS, U. S.C., 1961, MBA, 1969; postgrad., Command and Gen. Staff Coll., 1970, Naval War Coll., 1979, U. Va., 1983. Commd. to U.S. Army, advanced through grades to col., 1980, co. and troop comdr., squadron staff officer Vietnam and Europe, 1961-71, strategist Washington, 1971-73; chief of assignments Office Pers. Mgmt. Mil. Pers. Ctr., Washington, 1973-76; comdr. 1st Squadron 1st Cavalry, Europe, 1976-78; chief of staff, spl. asst. to chief of staff 1st Armored Divsn., Europe, 1978; br. chief Office of Chief of Staff, Washington, 1979-80; exec. to dep. comdg. gen. Material Devel. and Readiness Command, Washington, 1980-81; mil. dep. for asst. sec. for rsch., devel. and acquisition Washington, 1981-85; dir. ops. Ford Aerospace, Washington, 1986—89; army mktg. dir. Grumman Corp., Bethpage, NY, 1990-93; pres., CEO Allied Rsch. Corp., Vienna, Va., 1993—2001; founder & prin. WGY & Assocs. Bd. dirs. Carleton Techs., Eads N.Am. Def. Co., Valentec Inc. Trustee Patton Mus.; treas. US Cavalry Assn.; bd. dirs. So Others Might Eat (Some), Easter Seals; bd. dirs. Moore Sch. Bus. U. S.C. Decorated Silver Star, Bronze Star medal with 4 oak leaf clusters and V device, Purple Heart, Legion of Merit. Mem. VFW, SAR, KC, Assn. U.S. Army (George Washington chpt., v.p. membership), Am. Legion, Armed Forces Comms. and Electronics Assn., U.S. Army Armor Assn., Nat. Def. Indsl. Assn. (bd. dirs. N.Y. chpt.), Rotary Internat., Mil. Order of the World Wars, N.G. Assn., Res. Officers Assn., Soc. of the Purple Heart, Army-Navy Club, Army Navy Country Club, Belle-Meade Country Club, Tower Club, Rotary. Republican. Roman Catholic. Home: Box 115 Thomson GA 30824-0115 Office: Box 828 Mc Lean VA 22101 Home Phone: 706-595-1935; Office Phone: 703-748-1717. Office Fax: 928-222-5742. Personal E-mail: wgyarc@aol.com.

YARBROUGH, ALLYSON DEBRA, electrical engineer; b. Peterborough, England, Feb. 14, 1958; d. Freddy Dekhoma and Rosalind Mavis Y.; m. John Russell Scarpulla, May. 8, 1990. BSEE, N.Mex. State U., 1979; MSEE, Cornell U., 1985, PhD in Elec. Engring., 1988. Rsch. asst. Nat. Atmospheric and Ionospheric Ctr., Arecibo, P.R., 1979; microwave applications engr. Hewlett-Packard Co., Santa Rosa, Calif., 1979-82; assoc. prof. Calif. State U., LA, 1988-89; tech. staff Aerospace Corp., El Segundo, Calif., 1989-93, sect. mgr., 1993-99, dept. dir., 1999—. Mem. IEEE, Microwave Theory and Techniques Soc., Alpha Kappa Alpha, Eta Kappa Nu. Democrat. Roman Catholic. Avocations: woodworking, sewing, collecting vintage radios. Home: 26821 Grays Lake Rd Palos Verdes Estates CA 90275 Home Phone: 310-594-9841; Office Phone: 310-375-9695. Personal E-mail: blue.onyx@verizon.net.

YARBROUGH, EDWARD MEACHAM, prosecutor, lawyer; b. Nashville, Dec. 17, 1943; s. Gurley McTyeire and Miriam (Mefford) Y. BA, Rhodes Coll., 1967; JD, Vanderbilt U., 1973. Bar: Tenn. 1973. Asst. dist. atty. Davidson County, Nashville, 1973-76; ptnr. Hollins, Wagster & Yarbrough, Nashville, 1976—2007; US atty. (mid. dist.) Tenn. US Dept. Justice, Nashville, 2007—. Chmn. com. Crime Commn., Nashville, 1981-82; mem. task force House Judiciary Com., Nashville, 1984; chmn. Crimestoppers Inc., Nashville, 1983-86; trustee United Way, Nashville, 1983-86, Belmont U., 1993-99, Cumberland Sci. Mus., 1996-98; bd. dirs. Big Bros. Inc., Nashville, 1983-85; mem. nat. devel. bd. Lipscomb U., 2000-03; chmn. deacons Forest Hills Bapt. Ch. Served to 1st lt. U.S. Army, 1969-71, Vietnam. Decorated Bronze Star; named Best Criminal Def. Atty., Bus. Nashville mag., 1999. Fellow Nat. Speleological Soc. (bd. dirs. 1960—); mem. ABA, Tenn. Bar Assn., Nashville Bar Assn. (pres. 1983), Tenn. Criminal Def. Lawyers, Nashville Kiwanis (pres. 1992), Am. Legion, Richland Country Club, City Club (Nashville). Baptist. Avocations: cave exploration, photography, skiing, golf. Office: US Atty's Office 110 Ninth Ave S Ste A961 Nashville TN 37203 Office Phone: 615-736-5151. Business E-Mail: ed.yarbrough@usdoj.gov.

YARBROUGH, KATHRYN DAVIS, public health nurse; b. Montrose, Colo., Aug. 31, 1947; d. L.O. and V. Jean (Dunn) Davis; m. James H. Yarbrough, Aug. 8, 1970; children: James, Jason. Diploma, Good Samaritan Hosp. Sch. Nursing, Phoenix, 1971; BSN, Kennesaw State Coll., 1996. RN, Ga.; cert. NAACOG. Supr. Cherokee County Health Dept., Canton, Ga., 1976-97. Den mother Boy Scouts Am., Canton, 1986-87; bd. dirs. Cancer soc., Canton, 1987—, Cherokee County Violence Ctr., 1990, First Steps Bd., 1993-97, Cherokee County Advocacy Ctr., 1994-97; HIV cons. ARC, Canton, 1988—, disaster vol., Cherokee County, 1993-99; co-chair Early Intervention Coun., Canton, 1991-93; mem. Leadership Cherokee, 1994, Interagy Coun., 1994; mem. Blue Ridge Jud. Cir. Domestic Violence Task Force, 1995. Mem.: ANA, Shepherd Ctr. Spinal Cord Rehab. Quad, CASA (bd. dirs. 2008), Without Reservation Luncheon Club, Ga. Nurses Assn., Svc. League Cherokee County (hon.). Methodist. Mailing: PO Box 408 Canton GA 30169 E-mail: Kyarbro216@aol.com.

YARBROUGH, MARTHA CORNELIA, music educator; b. Waycross, Ga., Feb. 8, 1940; d. Henry Elliott and Jessie (Sirmans) Y. BME, Stetson U., 1962; MME, Fla. State U., 1968, PhD, 1973. Choral dir. Ware County H.S., Waycross, 1962-64, Glynn Acad., Brunswick, Ga., 1964—70; asst. choral dir. Fla. State U., 1970-72; cons. in music Muscogee County Sch. Dist., Columbus, Ga., 1972-73; cons. in tchr. edn. Psycho-Edno. Cons., Inc., Tallahassee, 1972-73; asst. prof. music edn., dir. choruses and oratorio socs. Syracuse (NY) U., 1973-76; assoc. prof. music edn. Syracuse U., 1976-83, prof., 1983-86, acting asst. dean Coll. Visual and Performing Arts, 1980-82, acting dir. Sch. Music, 1980-82, chmn. music edn., 1982-86; prof. music La. State U., Baton Rouge, 1986—, coord. music edn., 1986—2000, Haymon prof. of music, 1995—, disting. rsch. master arts, humanities, social scis., 2004. Artist-in-residence Sch. Music U. Ala., Tuscaloosa, 1989-90, 98, 2002; chair exec. com. Music Edn. Rsch. Coun., 1992-94. Co-author: Competency-Based Music Education, 1980; mem. editl. com.: Jour. Rsch. in Music Edn., editor-in-chief:, 2000—; contbr. chapters to books, articles to profl. jours. Recipient Disting. Rsch. Master of Arts, Humanities and Social Scis. award, La. State U., 2004. Mem. Music Educators Nat. Conf. (Sr. Rschr. award 1996), La. State Music Assn., Am. Ednl. Rsch. Assn., Soc. Rsch. Music Edn. (mem. exec. com. 1988-90, program chair 1990-92, chair 1992-94), AAUP, Coll. Music Soc., Pi Kappa Lambda, Phi Beta, Kappa Delta Pi. Office: Sch Music La State U Baton Rouge LA 70803-2504 Office Phone: 225-578-2481. Business E-Mail: cyarbro@lsu.edu.

YARBROUGH, ROBERT ALLEN, literature and language professor; s. Rex Allen Yarbrough; m. Paula M. Eaton, Jan. 1, 2000. MA, U. Miss., Oxford, 1983. Instr. El Paso CC, Tex., 2000—.

YARBROUGH, TERRY PINCKNEY, physician; b. Columbia, SC, Apr. 2, 1940; s. Dabney Randolph and Frances Horton (Colcock) Y.; m. Alexandra Mayo, Aug. 28, 1965; children: Alexandra, Laurens. MD, Med. Coll. Va., 1965. Intern U. Tex. Med. Br., Galveston, 1965—66; resident in internal medicine Med. Coll. Va., Richmond, 1968—71; pvt. practice Internal Medicine of Portsmouth Ltd., 1971—. Capt. USAR, 1966-68. Named America's Top Physician. Mem. ACP, Am. Coll. of Cardiology, Coun. Clin. Cardiology, Am. Heart Assn., Med. Soc. of Va. Episcopalian. Office: Internal Medicine Portsmouth Ltd 3300 High St Portsmouth VA 23707-3321 Home Phone: 757-483-6360.

YARCHOAN, ROBERT, clinical immunologist, researcher; b. NYC, July 21, 1950; s. Zachary and Anne Mae (Veneroso) Y.; m. Giovana Tosato; children: Mark, John. BA magna cum laude, Amherst Coll., 1971; MD, U. Pa., 1975. Diplomate Am. Bd. Internal Medicine, Am. Bd. Allergy and Immunology. Resident in medicine U. Minn. Hosps., Mpls., 1975-78; clin. assoc. metabolism br. Nat. Cancer Inst., NIH, Bethesda, Md., 1978-80, investigator metabolism br., 1980-83, investigator clin. oncology program, 1983-87, sr. investigator clin. oncology program, 1988-91, chief retroviral diseases sect. medicine br., 1991-96, chief HIV and AIDS Malignancy Br., 1996—, AIDS coord., 2006—, dir. Office HIV and AIDS Malignancy, 2007—. Assoc. editor Jour. Immunology, 1985-89, AIDS Rsch. and Human Retroviruses, 1986-2004, AIDS, 1990-2000, Jour. AIDS, 2000-06, Jour. Human Virology, 2002-04, Infectious Agents and Cancer, 2006-; sect. editor Thymus, 1992-97; contbr. articles to sci. jours., chpts. to textbooks; patentee in field. Capt. USPHS, 1978—2008. Recipient Commendation medal USPHS, 1991, Asst. Sec. Health award US govt. Dept. Health & Human Svcs., 1989, Inventors award US Dept. Commerce, 1986, 87, Fed. Tech. Transfer Act award, 1999, 2000, 01, Outstanding Svc. medal USPHS, 2002, awarded NIH First World AIDS Day award, 2006, NCI HIV Aids Rsch. Excellence award, 2007. Fellow AAAS; mem. Am. Soc. Hematology, Am. Assn. Immunologists, Clin. Immunology Soc., Am. Soc. for Clin. Investigation, Phi Beta Kappa, Sigma Xi. Achievements include co-inventor of therapies for AIDS and AIDS malignancies including ddI (didanosine) and ddC (zalcitabine) for AIDS and IL-12 for Kaposi's sarcoma; co-developer of therapies for AIDS and AIDS malignancies including AZT (zidovudine) for AIDS and paclitaxel for Kaposi's sarcoma; research in interactions between viruses and the immune system, therapy of AIDS and virally induced tumors; pathogenesis of AIDS and viral-induced tumors.

YARD, MICHAEL, anatomy and physiology educator, retired military officer; BS in Biology, Chemistry, Purdue U., West Lafayette, Ind., 1985; Grad., US Army Command and Gen. Staff Coll., Ft. Leavenworth, Kans., 1992, MS in Neurobiology; PhD, Ind. U. Sch. Medicine, Indpls., 2001. Mil. officer US Army, Washington, 1976—2005, col., 1976—2005, hand-to-hand combat instr. and small arms weapons trainer, 1976—2005; autopsy supr. Ind. U. Sch. Medicine Dept. Anat. Pathology, 1978—85; dep. coroner Marion County Coroner's Office, Indpls., 1994—98; assoc. adj. prof. U. Indpls., 2002—07; lectr. biology Ind. U. Purdue U., Indpls., 2002—. Contbr. anat. edn. video series, chapters to books. Decorated Army Commendation Medal US Army, Meritorious Svc. Medal, Expert Field Med. Badge, Expert M16 Rifle Badge, Expert 9mm Pistol Badge, Army Achievement Medal, Nat. Def. Svc. Medal; recipient Hintgen Grad. Rsch. award, Ind. U. Sch. Medicine, 2002. Mem.: Am. Tae Kwon Do Inst. Black Belt Club. Achievements include research in protective effect of thyrotropin releasing hormone (TRH) against excitatory amino acid toxicity in superfused hippocampal slices, cells, and neurons. Avocations: chess, writing. Personal E-mail: michaelyard88@aol.com. Business E-Mail: myard@iupui.edu.

YARDE, RICHARD FOSTER, art educator; b. Boston, Oct. 29, 1939; s. Edgar St. Clair and Enid (Foster) Y.; m. Susan Donovan, July 8, 1967; children: Marcus, Owen. BFA in Painting cum laude, Boston U., 1962, MFA, 1964; DFA (hon., Mass. Coll. Arts, Boston, 1998. Asst. prof. art Boston U., 1965-71; assoc. prof. art Wellesley Coll., 1971-76; vis. assoc. prof. Amherst Coll., 1976-77, Mt. Holyoke Coll., 1980-81; vis. artist Mass. Coll. Art, 1977-80; prof. art U. Mass., Boston, 1981-90, Amherst, 1990—. Visual arts panelist Mass. Coun. Art and Humanities, 1976-78; bd. overseers Inst. Contemporary Art, Boston, 1991-2003; panelist Painting Mass. Cultural Coun. One-man shows include Studio Mus. in Harlem, San Diego Mus., Balt. Mus., Smith Coll. Mus. Art, Northampton, Mass., 1977, Mass. Coll. Art, 1996—99, Worcester Mus. Art, Mass., 2003, The Eric Carle Mus. Picture Book Art, Amherst, Mass., 2007, exhibited in group shows at Newport (RI) Art Mus., Nat. Acad. Design, N.Y.C. and Mass., Smithsonian Inst., Washington, 1999, New Mus. Contemporary Art, N.Y.C., 1999, Mus. Fine Arts, Boston, 1999, Master Drawings from the Smith Coll. Art Mus., Lacaixa and Madrid, 2002, DeCordova Mus., Lincoln, Mass., 2002, Inst. Contemporary Art, Boston, 2003, Heckscher Mus. Art, Huntington, NY, 2003, NAS, Washington, 2004—05, Sheldon Meml. Art Gallery U. Nebr., Lincoln, Nat. Acad. Design, 2005, Boston U. Art Gallery, 2005—06, Danforth Mus. Art, Framingham, Mass., 2005, Wadsworth Atheneum Mus. Art, Hartford, Conn., 2006 (pres. award, 2007). Recipient Alumni award for disting. contbn. to arts Boston U., 1987, Chancellor's award disting. scholarship U. Mass., Boston, 1984, Acad. award in art Am. Acad. Arts and Letters, 1995, Disting. Tchg. award U. Mass. Amherst, 1997, Works on Paper award New Eng. Found. Arts, Boston, 1998, honoree Studio Mus. in Harlem Gala, N.Y.C., 2001; Nat. Endowment Arts fellow, 1976, Samuel F. Conti faculty fellow U. Mass., 2000, When the Spirit Moves Group Exhib., Spelman Coll. Mus., 2000, Charles Wright Mus., 2000, Commonwealth Award, Artist Category, Mass. Cultural Council, 2001, William P. and Gertrude Schweitzer prize Nat. Acad. Design, N.Y., others. Mem.: NAD (academician 1994—). Office: U Mass Amherst Fine Arts Ctr Dept Art and Art History 151 Pres Dr Office1 Amherst MA 01003-4330 E-mail: rfyarde@art.u.mass.edu.

YARDIBI, TARIK, research scientist; married. BS in Electronics Engring., Hacettepe U., Turkey, 2004; MS in Elec. and Electronics Engring., Bilkent U., Turkey, 2006; PhD student in Elec. and Computer Engring., U. Fla., 2006—. Tchg. and rsch. asst. Bilkent U., Ankara, Turkey, 2004—06; rsch. asst. U. Fla., Gainesville, 2006—. Contbr. articles to profl. jours. Recipient 1st in Faculty of Engring., Hacettepe U., 2004; named UF Internat. Ctr. Cert. of Outstanding Achievement, U. Fla., 2007—08.

YARDLEY, JONATHAN, journalist; b. Pitts., Oct. 27, 1939; s. William Woolsey and Helen (Gregory) Y.; m. Rosemary Roberts, June 14, 1961 (div. 1975); children: James Barrett, William W. II.; m. Susan L. Hartt, Mar. 23, 1975 (div. 1998); m. Marie Arana, Mar. 21, 1999. AB, U. N.C., 1961; DHL (hon.), George Washington U., 1987. Writer N.Y. Times, 1961—64; editl. writer, book editor Greensboro (N.C.) Daily News, 1964—74; book editor Miami (Fla.) Herald, 1974—78, Washington Star, 1978—81; book critic Washington Post, 1981—. Author: Ring: A Biography of Ring Lardner, 1977, Our Kind of People: The Story of an American Family, 1989, Out of Step: Notes from a Purple Decade, 1991, States of Mind: A Personal Journey Through the Mid-Atlantic, 1993, Misfit: The Strange Life of Frederick Exley, 1997, Monday Morning Quarterback, 1998; editor: My Life as Author and Editor (H.L. Mencken), 1993, Selected Stories (Ring Lardner), 1997. Recipient Pulitzer prize for criticism, 1981, Disting. Alumnus award U. N.C., 1989; Nieman fellow in journalism Harvard U., 1968-69. Address: Malecon de la Reserva 801 Miaflores Lima 18 Peru Home and Office: 1500 Vermont Ave NW 1 Washington DC 20005 Office Phone: 202-544-7779. Business E-Mail: yardleyj@washpost.com.

YAREMCHUK, KATHLEEN, otolaryngologist, department chairman; d. Morris and Olga Yaremchuk; m. Glen Zatz, Sept. 23, 1978; children: Laura Zatz, Marcy Zatz, Garet Zatz. MD, U. Mich., Ann Arbor, 1978; MSA, Ctrl. Mich. U., Mt. Pleasant, 1989. Chair, otolaryngology Henry Ford Hosp., Detroit, 1984—. Office: Henry Ford Hosp 2799 W Grand Blvd Detroit MI 48202 Office Phone: 313-916-3275.

YARI, BOB, film company executive, producer; b. 1962; Diploma in Cinematography. Owner El Camino Pictures, Bull's Eye Entertainment, Syndicate Films Internat., Bob Yari Prodns., Stratus Film Co., LA. Dir., exec. prodr.: (films) Mind Games, 1989; prodr.: Perfect Fit, 1999, Where the Red Fern Grows, 2003, Employee of the Month, 2004, Agent Cody Banks 2: Destination London, 2004, House of D, 2004, A Love Song for Bobby Long, 2004, Crash, 2004 (Best First Feature, Independent Spirit award, 2006), Haven, 2004, Hostage, 2005; prodr.: (films) Find Me Guilty, 2006; prodr.: (films) Block Party, 2005, The Illusionist, 2006, First Snow, 2006, The Hoax, 2006, Resurrecting the Champ, 2007, Kickin It Old Skool, 2007; exec. prodr.: Agent Cody Banks, 2003, Devil's Pond, 2003, Sueno, 2004, In Enemy Hands, 2004, Laws of Attraction, 2004, Around the Bend, 2004, Thumbsucker, 2005, The Matador, 2005, The Chumscrubber, 2005, The LA Riot Spectacular, 2005, Prime, 2005, Sueno, 2005, Even Money, 2006; exec. prodr.: (films) The Painted Veil, 2006. Named one of 50 Most Powerful People in Hollywood, Premiere mag., 2005. Office: Stratus Film Co 10850 Wilshire Blvd 6th Fl Los Angeles CA 90024 Office Phone: 310-234-8970. Office Fax: 310-234-8975.

YARISH, CHARLES, biology professor, researcher; s. Nathan Yarish and Lillian Yarish Kutner; m. Yarish J. Michels, Aug. 14, 1971; children: Mark D., Laura Jeanne Poidomani. BS, Bklyn. Coll., 1970; MA, U. Tex., Austin, 1972; PhD, Rutgers U., New Brunswick, 1976. Tchg. asst. U. Tex., 1971—72, Rutgers U., 1973—76; asst. prof. biology U. Conn., Stamford, 1976—82, assoc. prof. biology, 1982—88, prof., 1988—, assoc. dir., 1990—94; vis. prof. marine biology U. Groningen, Netherlands, 1983—84; vis. scientist Biologische Anstalt Helogland, Hamburg, Germany, 1985—85; adj. prof. Marine Scis. Rsch. Ctr., SUNY, Stony Brook, 1990—94; guest prof. Shanghai Fisheries U., 2002—, 1st e-acad. prof., 2004. Mem. adv. bd. NRC, Halifax, Canada, 1990—95, Osborne Marine Lab., Bklyn., 1990—95; mem. model evaluation group Peconic Estuary Program, Riverhead, NY, 1996—2000; mem. grad. faculty U. Porto, Portugal, 2002—; sci. advisor Aquarium Pacific, Long Beach, Calif., 2006—. Editor: (sci. book) Economically Important Marine Plants of the Atlantic: Their Biology and Cultivation. The Connecticut Sea Grant College Program; editor: (with H. Kirkman) Seaweeds - Their Environment, Biogeography, and Ecophysiology; editor: (sci. book (German lang. edit.) Meeresbotanik: Verbreitung, Okophysiologie und Nutzung der marinen Makroalge; contbr. 75 sci. papers. Mem. adv. bd. Bridgeport's Regional Vocat. Aquaculture HS, Conn., 1993—. Recipient Marinalg award, XIVth Internat. Seaweed Symposium, Brittany, France, 1992. Mem.: EPA (co-chmn. sci. tech. adv. com. LI Sound Study 1992—), Conn. Sci.and Engring., U. Maine, Versight Com. Ctr. globalization and commerce, U. Conn., World Aquaculture Soc., NE Algal Soc., Internat. Phycol. Soc., Am. Soc. Limnology and Oceanography, Brit. Phycol. Soc., Am. Inst. Biol. Scis., Can. Aquaculture Soc., World Aquaculture Soc., Phycol. Soc. Am. (nat. lectr. 1993—95, sec. 1994—96, pres. 2001), Sigma Xi, Sci. Rsch. Soc. Avocations: scuba diving, travel, photography. Office: Univ Connecticut 1 University Pl Stamford CT 06901-2315 Office Fax: 203-251-8592. Business E-Mail: charles.yarish@uconn.edu.

YARIV, AMNON, electrical engineering educator, research scientist; b. Tel Aviv, Apr. 13, 1930; arrived in U.S., 1951, naturalized, 1964; s. Shraga and Henya (Davidson) Y.; m. Frances Pokras, Apr. 10, 1972; children: Elizabeth, Dana, Gabriela. BS, U. Calif., Berkeley, 1954, MS, 1956, PhD, 1958. Mem. tech. staff Bell Telephone Labs., 1959-63; dir. laser research Watkins-Johnson Co., 1963-64; mem. faculty Calif. Inst. Tech., 1964—, Martin Summerfield prof. applied physics, 1966—. Co-founder Xponent, Orbits Corp., Teleris Corp., Inc. Author: Quantum Electronics, 1967, 75, 85, Introduction to Optical Electronics, 1971, 77, 89, Theory and Applications of Quantum Mechanics, Propagation of Light in Crystals. With Israeli Army, 1948—50. Recipient Pender award U. Pa., Harvey prize Technion, Israel, 1992. Fellow IEEE (Quantum Electronics award 1980), Am. Optical Soc. (Ives medal 1986, Esther Beller medal 1998), Am. Acad. Arts and Scis.; mem. NAS, NAE, Am. Phys. Soc. Office: 1201 E California Blvd Pasadena CA 91125-0001 Personal E-mail: azyariv@hotmail.com. Business E-Mail: ziemer@eas.uccs.edu.

YARMUTH, JOHN ALLAN, United States Representative from Kentucky; b. Louisville, Nov. 4, 1947; s. Stanley Robert and Edna Elaine (Klein) Yarmuth; m. Catherine Elizabeth Creedon, 1981; 1 child, Stanley Aaron. BA in Am. Studies, Yale U., 1969; student, Georgetown U. Sch. Law. Stockbroker Stein Bros. & Boyce, Louisville, 1969-70; legis. asst. to Senator Marlow Cook US Senate, Washington, 1971-75; pub. Louisville Today mag., 1976-82; asst. v.p. univ. rels. U. Louisville, 1983-86; worked in pub. rels. and mktg. Caretenders Healthcorp, 1986—90; founder, exec. editor Louisville Eccentric Observer Newsweekly, 1990—2003; mem. US Congress from 3rd Ky. dist., 2007—, mem. edn. & labor com., oversight & govt. reform com. Founder, pres. Ctr. Ky. Progress. Host (radio talk shows) Yarmuth & Ziegler, WAVE 3 TV, 2003, guest appearances Hot Button, 2004—05, editor, owner (publications) Kentucky Golfer. Bd. regents No. Ky. U., Highland Heights, 1980—83, Jewish Cmty. Ctr., Planned Parenthood Louisville Forum; bd. dirs. Better Bus. Bur., Louisville, 1979—85, Louisville Sch. Art, 1980—83, Sta. WKPC-TV, Louisville, 1983—88. Recipient editorial and column writing awards, Metro Louisville Journalism; named Person of Yr., Louisville Chpt. Alzheimer's Assn., 2004; named to Atherton High Sch. Hall of Fame, 2002. Mem.: Soc. Profl. Journalists, Ky. Golf Assn., SC Melrose Club, Valhalla Golf Club. Democrat. Jewish. Avocation: golf. Office: 319 Cannon House Office Bldg Washington DC 20515 also: Romano Mazzoli Fed Bldg Ste 216 600 Martin Luther King Dr Louisville KY 40202*

YARNELL, MICHAEL ALLAN, mediator, arbitrator, law educator; b. Chgo., Sept. 10, 1944; s. Howard Winfred and Mary Elizabeth (Card) Y.; m. Karen Alice Hockenyos, June 12, 1971 (div. Mar. 1994); children: Sarah Munro, Jacob Rainey; m. Kristina Louise Renshaw, July 17, 1996. BS, Ariz. State U., 1967; JD with honors, U. Ill., 1971; MA, U. Phoenix, 2004. Bar: Ariz. 1971. Ptnr. Streich, Lang, Weeks & Cardon, Phoenix, 1971-91, also bd. dirs.; mem. Myers, Barnes & Jenkins, Phoenix, 1991; judge Maricopa County Superior Ct., Phoenix, 1991—2005, mediator, arbitrator, spl. master, 2005—; adj. prof. U. Canberra Law Sch., Australia, 2004—08; assoc. prof. law Phoenix Sch. Law, 2006—. Author: Ins and Outs of Foreclosure, 1981, 13th edit., 2007; projects editor Law Rev. U. Ill. Law Forum, 1970; contbr. articles to profl. jours. Chairperson Phoenix Children's Theatre, 1987; vol. Habitat for Humanity, Adopt-a-Home sponsor; chmn. Legal Cmty. Builds, 1999. 1st lt. US Army, 1971-72, Korea. Fellow Ariz. Bar Found.; mem. ABA, Am. Arbitration Assn. (Roster Neutrals, Comml. Panel), Maricopa Bar Assn., State Bar Ariz. (Outstanding Contbn. to Continuing Legal Edn. award 1988, Com. on Profl. Conduct award 2000), Order of Coif, Lorna Lockwood Inn of Ct. (co-pres. 2000-01), Ariz. Yacht Club (vice comdr. 2000, comdr. 2001-02, staff comdr. 2002-03), Phi Kappa Phi, Organic Supreme Ct. Com. Fed. Edn. & Training. Democrat. Avocations: computers, sailing, white-water rafting. Office: Esplanade Ctr 2415 E Camelback Rd Ste 700 Phoenix AZ 85016 Office Phone: 602-791-3364. Personal E-mail: michael@michaelyarnell.com.

YAROSLAVSKY, ANNA, biophysicist, educator; b. Saratov, Russia, Sept. 11, 1968; arrived in U.S., 1998; d. Nikita Petrovich Mityashin and Lubov Mikhailovna Mityashina; m. Ilya Vladimirovich Yaroslavsky, Oct. 23, 1987; 1 child, Anastasia Ilinichna Yaroslavksy. MS in Physics summa cum laude, Saratov State U., Russia, 1990, PhD in Physics, 1999. Engr. Russian Acad. Sci., Saratov, 1989—90, rsch. fellow, 1990—91, U. Twente, Enschede, Netherlands, 1992—98; scientist Heinrich Heine U., Dusseldorf, Germany, 1994—98; rsch. assoc. La. State U., Shreveport, La., 1998—2000; asst. physicist Wellman Ctr. Photomedicine, Boston, 2000—, instr., 2000—05; asst. prof. dept. dermatology Harvard Med. Sch., 2005—. Reviewer NIH, Bethesda, Md., 2004—, Optics Letters, Lasers in Surgery & Medicine; presenter in field. Co-author: Optics of Blood, 2002; contbr. articles to profl. jours. Fellow: Am. Soc. Lasers in Medicine and Surgery; mem.: Optical Soc. Am., Internat. Soc. Optical Engring., Animal Rescue League Boston. Avocations: music, history, art, sports. Home: 12 Farnum St North Andover MA 01845 Office: Wellman Ctr Photomedicine BHX 314B 55 Fruit St Boston MA 02114 Office Phone: 617-726-1590. Business E-Mail: yaroslav@helix.mgh.harvard.edu.

YAROWSKY, JONATHAN R., lawyer, lobbyist; b. Kansas City, Mo., May 23, 1949; AB summa cum laude, U. Mich., 1971; MS, Cornell U., 1974; JD, UCLA, 1977. Teaching instr. Cornell U., Ithaca, NY, 1972—74; summer assoc. Fed. Pub. Defender's Office, LA, 1975; assoc. Rosenfeld, Meyer & Susman, Beverly Hills, Calif., 1976, Covington & Burling LLP, 1977-82; majority counsel US House Judiciary Subcom. on Econ. and Comml. Law, Washington, 1982-90; gen. counsel US House Judiciary Com., 1991-95; spl. counsel to the Pres. The White House, 1995—98; ptnr. pub. policy practice group Patton Boggs LLP, 1998—. Mem. Nat. Commn. on Crime, 1995—; vice chair Antitrust Modernization Commn., 2004—. Chief comment editor UCLA Law Rev., 1977. Mem. Phi Beta Kappa. Office: Patton Boggs LLP 2550 M St, NW Washington DC 20037 Office Phone: 202-457-6160. Office Fax: 202-457-6315. E-mail: jyarowsky@pattonboggs.com.*

YARRINGTON, PATRICIA E., oil industry executive; b. NJ, Apr. 1956; BA in Polit. Sci., Pomona Coll., Claremont, Calif., 1977; MBA, Northwestern U. Kellogg Sch. Mgmt., Evanston, Ill. With Chevron Corp., 1980—; sr. fin. analyst Chevron USA Inc., 1984—86, mgr. investor relations, 1986; various supervisory positions Chevron Products Co., Chevron U.S.A. Prodn. Co., Chevron Rsch. and Tech. Co.; mgr. credit card enterprises Chevron Products Co., 1995—97, comptr., 1997—98; pres. Chevron Can. Ltd., Vancouver, B.C., Canada, 1998—2000; v.p. strategic planning Chevron Corp., San Ramon, Calif., 2000—01, v.p. policy, govt. & pub. affairs, 2002—, treas., 2007—08, CFO, 2009—. Bd. dirs. Chevron Phillips Chem. Co., ChevronTexaco Found.; mem. econ. adv. coun. Fed. Reserve Bank San Francisco, 2007—08, bd. dirs., 2009—. Office: Chevron Corp 6001 Bollinger Canyon Rd San Ramon CA 94583-2324 Office Phone: 925-842-1000. Office Fax: 925-842-6047.*

YARROW, PETER, folksinger; b. NYC, May 31, 1938; BA, Cornell U.; D (hon.), Nat. Lewis U., 2002, San Francisco State U., 2003. Mem. group: Peter, Paul, and Mary, 1962—, also solo performer, recording artist, Warner Bros.: albums with Peter, Paul, and Mary include: Peter, Paul, and Mary, Moving, In the Wind, In Concert, A Song Will Rise, See What Tomorrow Brings, Peter, Paul, and Mary Album, Album 1700, Late Again, Peter, Paul & Mommy, 10 Years Together: The Best Of, Reunion, Peter, Paul & Mommy, Too (Emmy nominee 1993), No Easy Walk to Freedom, Lifelines, Songs of Concience and Concern, In These Times, Carry It On; solo album: Peter, 1972, That's Enough for Me, 1973, Hard Times, 1975, Love Songs, 1975; on Broadway appearance: Peter, Paul, and Mary "From Bleecker to Broadway", 1986; TV spls. include: Reunion, Holiday Concert, Peter, Paul & Mommy, Too, Lifelines (PBS), Carry It On (PBS). Bd. dirs. Newport Folk Festival Found., Kerrville (Tex.) Folk Festival, 1971, Ctr. for Global Edn.,

Augsberg Coll.; chmn. bd. trustees Telluride Inst., 1997; founder, co-chair Oper. Respect, "Don't Laugh At Me", 1999 Recipient Emmy nominee for "Puff the Magic Dragon", 1979, Citizen Action Leadership award, Vista, 1979, Alfred Lowenstein award, 1982, Hospice Care of R.I. award, 1987, Nat. Emergency Civil Liberties Com. award, 1988, Interlochen Disting. Alumnus Arts award, 1992, Conn. Hospice award, 1993, Grammy award for prodr. Peter Paul & Mommy, Too, 1994, Kate Wolf Meml. award for the World Folk Music Assn., 1994, Tikkum Plam award, Ctrl. Synogogue, 1995, People for th Am. Way Defenders Democracy award, 1999, Ctrl. Sunagogue Shofar award, 1999, Spirit Crazy Horse award, 2000, AASC Sch. Counselor of Yr. award, 2001, Gandhi World Peace Flame, 2001,Rescuer of Humanity award, 2001, Starr Commonwealth Bd. Trustees Child Advocacy award, 2001, Good Neighbor award, 2002, N.Y. STate ASCS Educator of Yr. award, 2002, Jewish Leadership award, Panim, 2004, Wheel award Wheelock Family Theatre, 2006; Congressional hon., 1999.

YARROW, WILLIAM PAUL, literature and language professor; b. Phila., Mar. 18, 1951; s. Robert B. and Esther Yarrow; m. Leah Kalnitz Yarrow, Mar. 21, 1976; children: Benjamin, Aliza, Nathan. BA, Swarthmore Coll., Pa., 1973; MA, Northwestern U., Evanston, Ill., 1978. Cert. tchr. Ill. Online Network, 2007. Prof. English Joliet Jr. Coll., Ill., 1993—, distance edn. faculty coord., 2008—. Freelance editor Woodbine House, Washington, 1984—86. Recipient 1st prize, Acad. Am. Poets, 1971, Swarthmore Coll., 1973; Nat. fellow, Coun. Basic Edn., 1989, fellow, Nat. Endowment Humanities, 1988. Home: 6631 N Trumbull Ave Lincolnwood IL 60712 Office: Joliet Jr Coll 1215 Houbolt Ave Joliet IL 60431 Personal E-mail: bill.yarrow@gmail.com. Business E-Mail: byarrow@jjc.edu.

YARTZ, FRANK JOSEPH, retired professor, author; b. Cleve., Feb. 5, 1938; s. Frank James and Mary Josephine Yartz. PhD, St. Louis U., 1964. Prof. philosophy Loyola U., Chgo., 1965—2006, sr. prof. emeritus, 2006—. Author: (philosophy text) Ancient Greek Philosophy, Introduction to Modern Philosophy. Mem.: APA. Office: Loyola Univ Chgo 6525 N Sheridan Rd Chicago IL 60626 Business E-Mail: fyartz@luc.edu.

YARUS, MICHAEL, biologist, educator; b. Pikeville, Ky., Mar. 2, 1940; s. Bernard Alexander and Sarah Bodenger Yarus; children: Matthew DeYarus, Evan, Alyson. PhD, CalTech, Pasadena, Calif., 1965. Prof. U. Colo., Boulder, 1980—. Grantee, Astrobiology Inst., NASA. Home: 321 Carriage Hills Dr Boulder CO 80302-9476 Office: MCD Biology Univ Colo Boulder CO 80309-0347 Business E-Mail: yarus@stripe.colorado.edu.

YARWOOD, BRUCE, health science association administrator; b. Sacramento, Calif. 2 children; 2 stepchildren. Mgr. MediCal program Calif. Dept. Health; exec. v.p. Calif. Assn. Health Facilities; CEO Crestwood Hospitals, Inc.; legis. counsel Am. Health Care Assn., Washington, acting pres., CEO, 2005, pres., 2005—. Office: Am Health Care Assn 1201 L St NW Washington DC 20005-4014 Office Phone: 202-842-4444. Office Fax: 202-842-3860. E-mail: byarwood@ahca.org.

YASHON, DAVID, neurosurgeon, educator; b. Chgo., May 13, 1935; s. Samuel and Dorothy (Cutler) Y.; children: Jaclyn, Lisa, Steven. BS in Medicine, U. Ill., 1958, MD, 1960. Diplomate Am. Bd. Neurol. Surgery. Intern U. Ill., 1961, resident, 1961-64, asst. in neuroanatomy, 1960; clin. instr. neurosurgery U. Chgo., 1965-66; asst. prof. neurosurgery Case Western Res U., Cleve., 1966-69; assoc. prof. neurosurgery Ohio State U., Columbus, 1969-74, prof., 1974-89, prof. emeritus, 1989—; mem. staff St. Ann's Hosp., Children's Hosp., Grant Med. Ctr., Ohio State U. East Med. Ctr. Cons. Med. Research and Devel. Command, U.S. Army; mem. Neurology B Study Sect NIH. Author: Spinal Injury; contbr. articles to med. jours. Served as capt. U.S. Army, 1960-68. Fellow Royal Coll. Surgeons Can. (cert.), A.C.S.; mem. AMA, Am. Physiol. Soc., Congress Neurol. Surgeons, Am. Assn. Anatomists, Canadian, Ohio neurosurg. socs., Am. Assn. Neurol. Surgeons, Research Soc. Neurol. Surgeons, Acad. Medicine Columbus and Franklin County, Soc. for Neurosci., Soc. Univ. Surgeons, Am. Acad. Neurology, Assn. for Acad. Surgery, Am. Acad. Neurol. Surgery, Am. Assn. for Surgery of Trauma, Central Surg. Soc., Ohio Med. Soc., Columbus Surg. Soc., Sigma Xi, Alpha Omega Alpha. Address: 500 Columbia Pl Bexley OH 43209-1677 E-mail: dyashon@columbus.rr.com.

YASHRUTI, SALAH HADI, retired surgeon; b. Acre, Palestine, Sept. 2, 1930; arrived in U.S., 1953; s. Hadi Ibrahim and Fatima Yashruti; m. Liljana Atanas Kolarovski, Nov. 2, 1973; children: Fadi, Nenad. BA, Am. U. Beirut, 1951, MPH, 1953; MD, U. Lausanne, 1959; degree in gen. surgery, U. Wis.-Madison, 1965. Chief hematology Toledo Gen. Hosp., Ohio, 1954—64; gen. surgeon Lebanon Hosp., Beirut, 1964—66, Kitsap County Med. Ctr., Port Orchard, Wash., 1966—84; cons. Skopje Therapy Hosp., Macedonia, 1984—87; chief profl. svcs. U.S. Air Force Reserve, McChord AFB, Wash., 1988—96; ret. Lt. col. Med. USAAF, 1988—96. Recipient award for Outstanding Contbns., 446th Airlift Wing Joint ORI, Superior Performance, Sheppard Tech. Tng. Ctr., Meritorious Svc. medal, Robins AFB, 1992, Achievement medal, 1995. Fellow: Internat. Coll. Surgeons. Avocations: tennis, camping, writing, navigation, yachting, pioneering upstream danube. Home: 16505 4TH Ave S Seattle WA 98148-1420 Personal E-mail: imfadi@aol.com.

YASICK, ALISON L., science educator; b. Spangler, Pa., June 3, 1977; d. Michael E. and Carol P. Yasick. BS in Biology, Ind. U., Pa., 1999; MS, 2001. Environ. interpreter technician Pa. Dept. Conservation and Natural Resources, Butler, 1998—99, vol. Ind., 1998—2001, ednl. program developer, 1998—99; asst. in preparation Pa. herpetological atlas Ind. U., 1999—2001, advisor, 2000—01; grad. tchg. asst., biol., geol. & environ. scies. Cleve. State U., 2001—, coop. instr. aquatic ecology, 2001—07, grad. student mentor, 2002—07, invited lectr., 2003—07; adj. faculty (part-time): health careers & scis. Cuyahoga CC, Parma, Ohio, 2007—. Recipient Grad. Student Travel awards, Cleve. State U., 2005—06; Ohio Conservation Alliance Student Mini grant, Cleve. Mus. Natural History, 2003—04. Mem.: Grad. Woman Sci., N.Am. Benthological Soc., Entomol. Soc. America. Home: 215 The Mall Berea OH 44017 Office: Cleveland State Univ 2121 Euclid Ave Cleveland OH 44115 Business E-Mail: a.yasick@csuohio.edu.

YASIK, CHRISTINE MARIE, literature and language educator; b. Utica, NY; d. Charles Arthur and Joan Dinneen Kunkel; children: Lisa Marie, Jonathan Christopher. BS in Secondary Edn., Okla. State U., Stillwater, 1974; MS in Reading Specialist, Ctrl. Conn. State U., New Britain, 1980. 8th grade English tchr. Baptiste Jr. HS, Grandview, Mo., 1974—75; 9th grade English tchr. Christiana HS, Newark, Del., 1976—78; 8th grade English tchr. Westbrook Jr./Sr. HS, Conn., 1978—80; 3-8th grade English and lang. tchr. Caravel Acad., Bear, Del., 1980—86; 6th and 7th grade reading and lang. tchr. Red Clay Consolidate Schs., Wilmington, Del., 1987—98; 7th and 8th grade English tchr. Sanford Sch., Hockessin, Del., 1998—. Mem. mid. sch. admission team Sanford Sch., Hockessin, Del., 2002—, tri-chair AFG accreditation team, 2004—06; mem. mid. states accreditation team Rumson County Day, NJ, 2006, moderator, MS student coun. coach, fitness and conditioning. Mem.: Nat. Council Tchrs. English, Internat. Reading Assn., Quota Internat. Avocations: cooking, walking, reading, theater. Office: Sanford Sch 6900 Lancaster Pike Hockessin DE 19707 Office Phone: 302-239-5263 ext. 358. Business E-Mail: yasikc@sanfordschool.org.

YASNYI, ALLAN DAVID, communications company executive; b. New Orleans, June 22, 1942; s. Ben Z. and Bertha R. (Michalove) Y.; m. Susan K. Manders; children: Benjamin Charles, Evelyn Judith, Brian Mallut. BBA, Tulane U., 1964. Free-lance exec. producer, producer, writer, actor, designer TV, motion picture and theatre, 1961-73; producer, performer the Second City; dir. fin. and adminstrn. Quinn Martin Prodns., Hollywood, Calif., 1973-76, v.p. fin., 1976-77, exec. v.p. fin. & corp. planning, 1977; vice chmn., CEO QM Prodn., Beverly Hills, Calif., 1977-78, chmn. bd., CEO, 1978-80; exec. dir. Susan Manders Fine Art, 2002—; pres., CEO The Synapse Comm. Group, Inc., 1981—, ASI Entertainment, 1998-99. Mng. dir. Susan Mandears Fine Art, 2001—; exec. dir., adj. prof. U. So. Calif. Entertainment Tech. Ctr., 1994-99, exec. dir. emeritus, 1999—; participant IC IS Forum, 1990-95; exec. prodr. first live broadcast combining Intelsat, Intersputnik, The Voice of Am., and The Moscow World Radio Svc., 1990; resource guest Aspen Inst. Exec. Seminars, 1990; chmn. bd. dirs. Found. of Global Broadcasting, Washington, 1987-93; nat. adv. bd. DeSantis Ctr. Fla. Atlantic U., 1998-. Trustee Hollywood Arts Coun., 1980-83; exec. v.p., trustee Hollywood Hist. Trust, 1981-91; bd. dirs. Internat. Ctr. Intergative Studies, NYC, 1988-92; bd. dirs. Asthma and Allergy Found. Am., 1981-85. With US Army, 1964-66, Vietnam. Named to Tulane U. Hall of Fame. Mem. Acad. TV Arts and Sci., Inst. Noetic Sci., Hollywood Radio and TV Soc., Hollywood C. of C. (dir., vice chmn. 1978-93), Screen Actors Guild, Assn. Transpersonal Psychology (keynote spkr. 1988). Office: 4132 Fulton Ave Sherman Oaks CA 91423-4340 Office Phone: 818-995-0009. Personal E-mail: yasnyi@aol.com.

YASSIN, ROBERT ALAN, museum director, curator; b. Malden, Mass., May 22, 1941; s. Harold Benjamin and Florence Gertrude (Hoffman) Y.; m. Marilyn Kramer, June 9, 1963; children: Fredric Giles, Aaron David. BA, Dartmouth Coll., 1962; postgrad., Boston U., 1962—63; MA, U. Mich., 1965, postgrad., 1968—70, PhD candidate, 1970; postgrad., Yale U., 1966—68. Asst. to dir. Mus. Art U. Mich., 1965-66, asst. dir., 1970-72, assoc. dir., 1972-73, acting dir., 1973, instr. dept. history of art, 1970-73; co-dir. Joint Program in Mus. Tng., 1970-73; chief curator Indpls. Mus. Art, 1973-75, 87-89, acting dir., 1975, dir., 1975-89; exec. dir. Tucson Mus. Art, 1990—2001, Palos Verdes (Calif.) Art Ctr., 2002—. Adj. prof. Herron Sch. Art Ind. U./Purdue U., 1975-89. Contbr. to mus. publs. Rufus Choate scholar, 1962, Samuel H. Kress Found. fellow, 1968—70, Ford Found. fellow, 1966—68. Mem.: Calif. Assn. Museums, Western Mus. Assn., Nat. Trust Hist. Preservation, Coll. Art Assn. Am., Am. Assn. Museums (bd. dirs. Internat. Coun. Mus. 1986—89). Jewish. Office: Palos Verdes Art Ctr 5504 W Crestridge Rd Rancho Palos Verdes CA 90275 Home: 7321 Marina Pacifica Dr N Long Beach CA 90803-3808 Personal E-mail: rayassin@charter.net. Business E-Mail: byassin@pvartcenter.org.

YASSKY, DAVID S., City Councilman, Brooklyn, New York, lawyer; m. Diana Yassky; children: Susan, Margaret. BA, Princeton Univ.; JD, Yale Univ. Bar: NY 1992. Chief counsel House Subcommittee on Crime, Washington; prof. Bklyn Law Sch.; city councilman Dist. 11 NY City Coun., 2002—. Chmn. Small Bus. com. NY City Coun. "Top 100 New Democrats to Watch" award, Democratic Leadership Coun, 2004. Democrat. Mailing: Dist Off 114 Court St Brooklyn NY 11201 Office Phone: 718-875-5200, 212-788-7348. Office Fax: 718-643-6620. Business E-Mail: yassky@council.nyc.ny.us.*

YASTINE, BARBARA A., former diversified financial services company executive; BA in Journalism, NYU, 1981, MBA in Finance, 1987. Various communications and investor-relations positions W.R. Grace & Co.; dir. investor relations, Primerica Citigroup, 1987—91, v.p. investor relations and fin. planning & analysis, Traveler's Group, 1991, exec. v.p. fin. and insurance, CitiFinancial, chief admin. officer, global consumer group, 1998, chief auditor, CFO, global corp. and investment bank, 2000—02; CFO Credit Suisse First Boston, 2002—04. Bd. dirs. Symphony Services, Palo Alto, Calif., 2006—. Bd. dirs. Phoenix House.

YASUDA, ROBERT, painter; b. Lihue, Hawaii, Nov. 14, 1940; BFA, Pratt Inst., 1962, MFA, 1964. Prof. art Long Island U. Represented in permanent collections Bklyn. Mus., Libr. Congress, State of Hawaii Found. Arts, Hillwood Mus., Long Island U., NY Pub. Libr., one-man shows include Sculpture at the Coliseum, NY Coliseum, 1980, Albuquerque Sight-Line, Hoshour Gallery, N.Mex., 1981, Koplin Gallery, LA, 1982, 1987, Julian Pretto Gallery, NYC, 1990, Elizabeth Harris Gallery, NYC, 1993, 1996, 1998, 2002, 2004, 2006, Ledbetter Lusk Gallery, Memphis, 1997, New Arts Prog., Kutztown, Pa., 1999, David Lusk Gallery, Memphis, 2000, 2003, 2005, 2008, two-person show with Judith Murray, Galleria Miralli, Viterbo, Italy, 2005, exhibited in group shows at A More Store, Jack Tilton Gallery, NYC, 1984, The Anchorage Exhbn., Large Scale Painting Installations, Bklyn. Bridge Anchorage, NY, 1985, 8x10, Washington County Mus. Fine Arts, Hagerstown, Md., 1986, Opening exhbn., Cutler-Schreiber Gallery, NYC, 1986, Reveal, Koplin Gallery, LA, 1988, Small Scale Works, Julian Pretto Gallery, NYC, 1991, Stark Gallery, NYC, 1992, Slow Art: Painting in New York Now, P.S.1 Contemporary Art Ctr., NYC, 1992, Six Abstract Artists, Elizabeth Harris Gallery, NYC, 1993, 1995, 1998, Summer Color, 2003, After the Fall, Newhouse Ctr. Contemporary Art, Snug Harbor Cultural Ctr., NY, 1997, Monochrome/Monochrome?, Florence Lynch Gallery, NYC, 2001, Honolulu to New York, Contemporary Mus., Honolulu, 2005, Invitational Exhbn. Visual Arts, AAAL, 2008. Recipient Purchase award, AAAL, 2008; grantee J.H. Whitney Found., 1962—63; fellow NEA, 1981. Address: 429 W Broadway New York NY 10012-3766 Office: c/o David Lusk Gallery 4540 Poplar Ave Memphis TN 38117 also: c/o Elizabeth Harris Gallery 529 W 20th St New York NY 10001

YATES, ANNE BRIDGES, allergist, immunologist, educator; m. Bobby Yates. BA, U. Miss., Oxford, 1980; MD, U. Miss. Med. Sch., Jackson, 1984. Diplomate Am. Bd. Pediat., 1989, Am. Bd. Allergy and Immunology, Ill., 1991. Prof. pediat. U. Miss. Med. Ctr., Jackson, 1990—, chief divsn. allergy and immunology, 2002—. Mem. bd. dirs. Am. Lung Assn. Miss., Ridgeland, 2000—08. Grantee, U. Miss. Med. Ctr., Dept. Pediat., 2004—08; Prin. Investigation grant, Miss. State Dept. Health, 2004—09. Fellow: Am. Coll. Allergy, Asthma and Immunology, Am. Acad. Allergy, Asthma and Immunology (chair insect allergy com. 2003—04), Am. Acad. Pediat. Office: Univ Miss Med Ctr 2500 N State St Rm R-116A Jackson MS 39216

YATES, COLEEN DENISE, special education educator; b. Sacramento, Calif., Dec. 28, 1956; d. Kenneth Walter Brown and Edna Viola Pundt; children: James Jedidiah, Trista Denice, Devona Caryn. BS, Calif. State U., 1995. Substitute tchr. Roseville Union HS Dist., Roseville City Sch. Dist., Western Placer Unified Sch. Dist., Placer Union HS Dist., Eureka Union Sch. Dist., Calif., 1997; spl. edn. tchr. El Dorado HS, 1997, Chavez Elem. Sch., Davis Sr. HS, Calif., 1997—98, El Dorado HS, 1998, Mitchell Mid. Sch., Rancho Cordova, 1998—2000, Miles P. Richmond Sch., North Highlands, 2000—05, Rio Tierra Jr. HS, Sacramento, 2005—. Co-leader Girl Scouts Am., 1990—92, 1995—2000, parent vol., 1992—95; com. mem., parent vol. Boy Scouts Am., 1992—95; asst. biddy basketball coach Rocklin Parks & Recreation Dept., 1993—96; art docent vol. Rock Creek Elem. Sch., Auburn, 1990—92, Antelope Creek Elem. Sch., Rocklin, 1992—96; vol. classroom aide Rock Creek Elem. Sch., 1990—92, Antelope Creek Elem. Sch., 1992—96. Mem.: Calif. Assn. Health, Phys. Recreation, and Dance, Am. Alliance Health, Phys. Edn., Recreation and Dance, Golden Key. Home: 1531 Lathwell Way Roseville CA 95747-6285

YATES, DAVID JOHN C., chemist, researcher; b. Stoke-on-Trent, Staffordshire, Eng., Feb. 13, 1927; arrived in US, 1958; s. Eric John and Beatrice Victoria Y.; m. Natalie Chmelnitsky, June 22, 1983 BS with honors, U. Birmingham, UK, 1949; PhD, U. Cambridge, Eng., 1955, Sc.D., 1968. Rsch. physicist Kodak Labs., Wealdstone, London, 1949-50; rsch. chemist Brit. Ceramic Rsch. Assn., Stoke-on-Trent, 1950-51; rsch. assoc. dept. colloid sci. U. Cambridge, 1951-58; lectr. Sch. Mines and dept. chemistry Columbia U., NYC, 1958-60; sr. rsch. fellow Nat. Phys. Lab., Teddington, England, 1960-61; rsch. assoc. corp. labs. Exxon Rsch. and Engring., Annandale, NJ, 1961-86; rsch. prof. dept. of chem. engring. Lafayette Coll., Easton, Pa., 1986-87; rsch. prof. dept. materials sci. Rutgers U., Piscataway, NJ, 1987-88; cons. San Diego, 1988—. Contbr. over 70 articles to profl. jours., chpts. to books; 13 U.S. patents, numerous fgn. patents. Fellow Inst. of Physics (U.K.), Royal Soc. Chemistry (U.K.), N.Y. Catalysis Club (chmn. 1966-67). Clubs: N.Y. Catalysis (chmn. 1965-66). Avocations: photography, bicycling, gliding, travel, sports cars.

YATES, DONALD ALFRED, retired literature educator; b. Ayer, Mass., Apr. 11, 1930; s. Alfred Craig Yates and Bessie Mae Cambridge; m. Mary Dodd, June 24, 1951 (div. Mar. 1961); children: Brian Donald, Juliet Marie; m. Lynn P. Taylor, Mar. 31, 1962 (div. May 1975); 1 child, John Allan; m. Joanne Margaret Mueller, Mar. 21, 1977. AB in Spanish, U. Mich., 1951, MA in Spanish, 1954, PhD in Spanish, 1961. Tchg. fellow U. Mich., Ann Arbor, 1953-57; instr. Mich. State U., East Lansing, 1957-61, asst. prof. Spanish-Am. lit., 1961-64, assoc. prof., 1964-67, prof., 1967-83, prof. emeritus, 1983—. Pres. Internat. Inst. Latin-Am. Lit., Pitts., 1971-73. Author: Jorge Luis Borges: Life, Work & Criticism, 1985; editor, translator: Latin Blood: Best Crime Stories of Latin America, 1972; co-editor, translator: Labyrinths: Selected Writings of Jorge Luis Borges, 1962; co-editor: (textbook) Imaginación y Fantasía, 1960, 6th edit., 1999. With U.S. Army, 1951-53. Recipient Avery Hopwood award U. Mich., 1954; grantee NEA, 2000-01.,fellow Guggenheim, 2008-. Mem. MLA, Mystery Writers of Am., Baker St. Irregulars (The Greek Interpreter 1972). Democrat. Home: 555 Canon Park Dr Saint Helena CA 94574-9726 Home Phone: 707-963-0201. Personal E-mail: mrmelas60@comcast.net.

YATES, HARVEY E., oil industry executive, political organization administrator; Pres. Jalapeno Corp., Albuquerque; chmn. Rep. Party of N.Mex., 2009—. Spkr. in field. Republican. Office: Rep Party of NMex 5150-A San Francisco NE Albuquerque NM 87109 also: Jalapeno Corp 1429 Central Ave NW Albuquerque NM 87104 Office Phone: 505-242-2050, 505-298-3662. Office Fax: 505-292-0755.*

YATES, JACQUELYN, political science professor; BA, Chatham Coll., Pitts., 1968; PhD, U. Pitts., 1981. Instr., 1972—81; prof., 1982—2003; assoc. prof. Kent State U., Salem, Ohio, 2003—. Author: (book) The Real World of Employee Ownership. Trustee Little Beaver Creek Land Found., Lisbon, Ohio, 1999—2008. Mem.: Phi Beta Kappa. Achievements include research in employee ownership in Ohio. Office: Kent State Univ 2491 SR 45 S Salem OH 44460

YATES, JAMES ARTHUR, plastic surgeon; b. Butler, Pa., June 5, 1935; s. Adolph Walter and Laura Marie (De Foggie) Y.; m. Debra Lynne Stringer, June 19, 1983; 1 child, Jamie Dale Yates Reynolds. BA, Cornell U., 1956; MD, U. Md., 1960. Diplomate Am. Bd. Plastic Surgery, Nat. Bd. Med. Examiners, Am. Bd. Surgery; lic. physician, Pa., Ohio, R.I. Intern Cleve. Clinic Hosp., 1960—61, resident in gen. surgery, 1961—62, U. Pitts. Med. Ctr., 1963—65; resident in plastic surgery R.I. Hosp., 1966—67, chief resident, 1967—68; pvt. practice Plastic Surgery Ctr. Ltd., Camp Hill, Pa., 1968—; med. dir. Grandview Surgery Ctr., Camp Hill, Pa. Tchg. fellow gen. surgery U. Pitts. Med. Ctr., 1963-65, instr. gen. surgery, 1965-66; clin. instr. plastic surgery Milton S. Hershey (Pa.) Med. Ctr., 1968—; staff maxillofacial and plastic surgery dept. Harrisburg (Pa.) Hosp., 1968—; chief plastic and aesthetic surgery dept. Holy Spirit Hosp., Camp Hill, 1968—; staff Mechanicsburg Rehab. Hosp., Carlisle (Pa.) Hosp., Pinnacle Health Sys. Hosps.; med. dir. Grandview Surgery and Laser Ctr., Camp Hill; cons. Harrisburg State Hosp.; physician surveyor Am. Assn. Ambulatory Health Care; physician trainer plastic surgery residency program Am. Coll. Osteo. Surgery; bd. dirs., pres. Am. Assn. Accreditatiion of Ambulatory Surgery Facilities. Contbr. articles to profl. jours.; adv. bd. Town and Country Mag. Police commr. West Shore Regional Police Dept.; pres. Boro Coun. Lemoyne Boro; mem. credentialling com. Keystone Health Plan; mem. task force on ambulatory surgery Pa. Dept. Health; mem. coun. Lemoyne (Pa.) Borough Coun., pres.; credentialing officer Freedom Health Care HMO; commr. West Shore Regional Police. Fellow ACS; mem. AMA, Pa. Med. Soc., Am. Burn Assn., Am. Soc. Plastic and Reconstructive Surgeons, Am. Burn Victim Found., Am. Soc. Aesthetic Plastic Surgery, Vail Cosmetic Surgery Soc., Pa. Plastic Surgery Soc. (past pres.), Am. Soc. Automobile Medicine, Northeastern Soc. Plastic Surgeons, Royal Soc. Medicine, Lipolysis Soc. N.Am., Internat. Soc. Clin. Plastic Surgeons, South Ctrl. Pa. Regional Med. Dirs., Am. Coll. Physician Execs. Republican. Roman Catholic. Avocations: bicycling, skiing, model building, sports cars. Home: 833 Kiehl Dr Lemoyne PA 17043-1201 Office: Plastic Surgery Ctr Ltd 205 Grandview Ave Camp Hill PA 17011-1708 Home Phone: 717-761-1281; Office Phone: 717-763-7814. Personal E-mail: jay5plas@msn.com.

YATES, JANET KATHLEEN, civil engineering educator; b. Coos Bay, Oreg., Dec. 27, 1955; d. Stanley Arthur and Amelia Ann (Kiblen) Y. BSCE, U. Wash., 1978, postgrad., 1978-79; PhD in Civil Engring. in Constrn. Engring. and Mgmt., Tex. A& M U., 1986. Teaching asst. U. Wash., Seattle, 1978-79; engr. Morrison-Knudsen, Inc., Boise, Idaho, 1979-80; project controls engr. Bechtel Power Corp., San Francisco, 1980-81; facilities engr. Williams Bros. Engring. Co., Tupman, Calif., 1981-82; lectr. Indonesian Tech. Tng. Ctr., Bontang, 1983-84, Tex. A&M U., College Station, 1984-86, vis. prof., 1987; asst. prof. civil engring. Iowa State U., Ames, 1987—. Author: A Cross Cultural Evaluation, 1986. Mem. ASCE (constrn. rsch. coun.), Am. Soc. for Engring. Edn., Constrn. Industry Inst. Roman Catholic. Avocations: dog training, basketball, archery, bowling, reading. Office: ND State Univ Dept Constrn Mgmt Engring CME Bldg Rm 120G Fargo ND 58105 Business E-Mail: jk.yates@ndsu.edu.

YATES, JEROME WILLIAM, scientific administrator, researcher; b. Rockford, Ill., Nov. 9, 1936; s. Frank and Eily Yates; m. Mary Elizabeth McAuley, June 1, 1979; children: Elizabeth Ann, Sarah Eily. AB, Lawrence U., Appleton, Wis., 1961; MD, U. Ill., Chgo., 1965; MPH,

Harvard Sch. of Pub. Health, Boston, 1981. Diplomate Nat. Bd. of Med. Examiners, 1966, Am. Coll. of Med. Executives, 2002. Rsch. scientist ii Roswell Pk. Cancer Inst., Buffalo, 1970—74; prof. of medicine U. Vt., Burlington, Vt., 1974—82; assoc. dir. for centers and cmty. oncology Nat. Cancer Inst., Bethesda, Md., 1982—87; sr. v.p. for clin. affairs Roswell Pk. Cancer Inst., Buffalo, 1987—2001; nat. v.p., rsch. Am. Cancer Soc., Atlanta, 2002—. Dir. Sheehan Meml. Hosp., Buffalo, 2003—; intermittent cons. and reviewer Nat. Cancer Inst., Bethesda, NY, 1971—. Contbr. scientific papers. Cancer ctr. adv. com. NCI Designated Cancer Ctr., 1982—2006; dir. Sheehan Meml. Hosp., Buffalo, 2003—06. Sp3 AMEDS US Army, 1955—57, Landstuhl, Germany. Recipient Outstanding Leadership and Svc. award, Assn. of Am. Cancer Ctr., 2002, Award of Merit, NIH, 1983, Outstanding Work Performance award, Nat. Cancer Inst., 1983, 1984, 1985. Mem.: Assn. of Am. Cancer Inst (assoc.; pres. 1991—92). Independent. Achievements include research in leukemia treatment, standard for 30 years; initiated community clinical oncology program. Avocations: aviation, golf. Home: 240 Independence Dr Orchard Park NY 14127 Office: Am Cancer Soc 1599 Clifton Rd Atlanta GA 30333

YATES, JOHN MELVIN, United States Special Envoy for Somalia; b. Superior, Mont., Nov. 25, 1939; s. Leon Glen and Violet May (McPheeters) Y.; m. Peggy Maureen Simpson, Mar. 26, 1961 (dec. Apr. 1986); children: Catherine Diener, John Simpson, Maureen Cole, Paul Marion, Leon Gregory; m. Mary Barbara Carlin, Jan. 30, 1988. AB, Stanford U., 1961; MA, Fletcher Sch. Law and Diplomacy, 1962, MALD, 1963, PhD, 1972. Fgn. service officer US Dept. State, Washington, 1964—2002, Algiers, Algeria, 1964-66, Blantyre, Malawi, 1967-68, Bamako, Mali, 1969-71, New Delhi, 1973-75, Ankara, Turkey, 1975-77, Libreville, Gabon, 1977-80, Washington, 1971-73, 80-82, US amb. to Republic of Cape Verde, 1983-86; counselor for polit. affairs Am. Embassy, Manila, 1986-89, dep. chief of mission Lagos, Nigeria, 1989-91, Kinshasa, Zaire, 1991-93, chief of mission, 1993-95; US amb. to Republic of Benin, US Dept. State, Cotonou, 1995-98, US amb. to Republic of Cameroon and Republic Equatorial Guinea, Yaounde, 1998—2001, sr. adv., Somalia Reconciliation Talks, 2004, sr. adv., Darfur Polit. Negotiations Sudan, 2005—06, spl. envoy for Somalia, 2007—. Recipient Presdl. award for sustained superior accomplishment in conduct of fgn. policy. Mem. Am. Fgn. Service Assn. Mailing: 4534 Broad Branch Rd NW Washington DC 20008

YATES, JOHN THOMAS, JR., chemistry professor, research scientist; b. Winchester, Va., Aug. 3, 1935; s. John Thomas and Kathryn (Barnett) Y.; m. Kerin Joyce Narbut, Oct. 18, 1958; children: Geoffrey, Nathan. BS, Juniata Coll., 1956; PhD, MIT, 1960. Asst. prof. chemistry Antioch Coll., Yellow Springs, Ohio, 1960-63; NRC fellow, rsch. chemist Nat. Bur. Standards (now Nat. Inst. Standards and Tech.), Washington, 1963—65, rsch. staff, sect. chief, surface chemistry, 1965—82; R.K. Mellon prof. chemistry and physics U. Pitts., 1982—2006, founding dir., Surface Sci. Ctr., 1982—2006; prof. chem. U. Va., 2007—, Shannon fellow, 2007—. Sr. vis. scholar, U. East Anglia, 1970-71; Gwathmey vis. prof. U. Va., 2002-03 Author: Experimental Innovations in Surface Science, 1997; co-author: The Surface Scientist's Guide to Organometallic Chemistry, 1987, Molecular Physical Chemistry for Engineers, 2007; co-editor: Vibrational Spectroscopy of Molecules on Surfaces, 1987, Chemical Perspectives of Microelectronic Materials, Vol. 131; assoc. editor: Studies in Surface Science and Catalysis, 1986; series editor: Methods of Surface Characterization, 1987; bd. editors Ann. Rev. Phys. Chemistry, 1983-85, Jour. Phys. Chemistry, 1983-88, Jour. Chem. Physics, 1984-87, Jour. Catalysis, 1987-91, Chem. Revs., Langmuir, Surface Sci., Applications of Surface Sci., Accounts Chem. Rsch., Chem. Phys. letters, 1997-; assoc. editor Langmuir, 1991-98; mem. adv. bd. Chemical & Engineering News, 2001-2003; contbr. revs. and articles to profl. jours.; inventor desorption spectrometer, 1981. Sherman Fairchild Disting. scholar Calif. Inst. Tech., 1977-78; recipient Silver medal Dept. Commerce-Nat. Bur. Stds., 1973, Stratton award for Disting. Rsch., 1978, Gold medal Dept. Commerce Nat. Bur. Stds., 1981, Pres.'s Disting. Rsch. award U. Pitts., 1989, Procter & Gamble award, 1989, Alexander von Humboldt Sr. Rsch. award, 1995, 1997, Pitts.-Cleve. Catalysis Soc. award, 1998, J.W. Linnett lectr. Cambridge U., 2000, Outstanding Alumnus Juniata Coll., 2000, named Among 100 Most Highly Cited Chemists in World 1984—, G.N. Lewis lectr. U. Calif.-Berkeley, 2002; fellow Sidney Sussex Coll., 2000, Japan Soc. Promotion of Sci., 2002, Inst. Physics, 2004 Fellow Am. Phys. Soc. (bd. dirs. divsn. chem. physics 1991—, chmn. divsn. chem. physics 1989), Am. Vacuum Soc. (chmn. surface sci. divsn. 1973, 92, trustee 1975, bd. dirs. 1982-85, Medard Welch award 1994, fellow 1994); mem. NAS, Am. Chem. Soc. (chmn. divsn. colloid and surface chemistry, Langmuir lectr. 1979, Kendall award in colloid of surface chemistry 1986, E.W. Morley prize Cleve. chpt. 1990, Peter Debye lectr. Cornell U. 1993, Pitts. award 1998, Arthur W. Adamson award for Disting. Svc. in the Advancement of Surface Chemistry, 1999, Peter Debye Phys. Chemistry award, 2007), Pitts.-Cleve. Catalysis Soc. Office: Univ Va Dept Chemistry Charlottesville VA 22904-4319 Home: Po Box 124 Free Union VA 22940 Business E-Mail: johnt@virginia.edu.

YATES, LEIGHTON DELEVAN, JR., lawyer; b. Atlanta, Sept. 4, 1946; s. Leighton Delevan and Stella Louise (Hill) Y.; m. Phyllis Jeanne Hummer, Dec. 22, 1968; children: Leighton Delevan III, Lauren Jeanne. BA, Hampden-Sydney Coll., Va., 1968; JD with high honors, U. Fla., 1973. Bar: Fla. 1974, U.S. Dist. Ct. (middle dist.) Fla. 1975. Assoc. Maguire, Voorhis & Wells, P.A., Orlando, Fla., 1974-77, shareholder, 1978-98, dept. chmn., 1985-90; ptnr. Holland & Knight LLP, Orlando, Fla., 1998—, nat. practice group leader, 2005—. Bd. dirs. Hubbard Constrn. Co., Winter Park, Fla., 1985—2004, Blythe Constrn., Inc., Charlotte, NC, 1999—2004; adminstrv, dir. SunTrust Bank, Orlando, Fla., 1990—. Exec. editor U. Fla. Law Rev., 1973. Mem. Fla. Bd. Bar Examiners, 1992-97, 2002-05, vice chmn., 1995-96, chmn. 1996-97; chmn. Fla.'s Blood Ctrs., 1995—, vice chmn., 1980-95; chmn. Orlando Opera Co., 1994, pres., 1993; bd. dirs. Metro Orlando Econ. Devel. Commn., 2007-. Fellow Am. Bar Found.; mem. ABA, Fla. Bar Assn., Orange County Bar Assn., Univ. Club of Orlando, Country Club of Orlando, Order of the Coif, Omicron Delta Kappa, Phi Kappa Phi. Republican. Presbyterian. Avocations: bicycling, music, reading. Home: 3218 S Osceola Ave Orlando FL 32806-6251 Office: Holland & Knight LLP 200 S Orange Ave Ste 2600 Orlando FL 32801-3453 Office Phone: 407-425-8500. Personal E-mail: lyates@cfl.rr.com. Business E-Mail: leighton.yates@hklaw.com.

YATES, MARY CARLIN, diplomat; b. Portland, Oreg., 1946; m. John Melvin Yates, Jan. 30, 1988; stepchildren: Catherine, John, Maureen, Paul, Leon. BA in English, Oreg. State U., 1968; MA in Comparative East-West Humanities, NYU; D in English (hon.), Oreg. State U., 2007. Joined fgn. svc., 1981—85, US Embassy Seoul and Kwangio South Korea, Pub. Affairs; pub. affairs counselor Am. Embassy, Kinshasa Zaire, Republic of the Congo, 1991—95; press attaché for Amb. Pamela Harriman then sr. cultural attaché US Dept. State, Paris, 1995—99, US amb. to Burundi Bujumbura, 1999—2002, US amb. to Ghana Accra, 2002—05; polit. adv. to the comdr. US European Command (EUCOM), Stuttgart, Germany, 2005—07; Dep. to Comdr. for Civil-Military Activities US African Command (USAFRICOM), Stuttgart, Germany, 2007—. Recipient Sustained Superior Honor award, US Dept. State, Superior Honor award, Meritorious Honor award (2), Presdl. Performance award for Excellence, The White House, 2004, Lois Roth award for Excellence in Info. & Cultural Diplomacy, US Info. Agy. Office: US African Command (USAFRICOM) Kelley Barracks 70567 Stuttgart Germany

YATES, PATRICIA LAWRENCE, elementary school educator; b. Rockland, Maine, Feb. 5, 1947; d. Edward Mark and Helen Mattson Lawrence; m. George Radford Yates, Dec. 30, 1966; children: Michelle Thomas, Matthew, Amy Lally, Jeremy. BA in Edn., U. South Fla., 1969. Cert. dirs. Nat. AGHER Handbell. Kindergarten tchr. Forest Heights Sch., Lakeland, Fla., 1972—81; sub., tutor Strongsville City Sch., Ohio, 1982—85; fourth grade tchr. St. Joseph and John Sch., Strongsville, Ohio, 1985—. Sr. tchr. cons. Geographic Alliance, 1992—; mem. handbell ensemble Renaissance Ringers. Author: (CD timeline) Timeline of Northeast Ohio 1620-1861, 2003. Dir. children's bell choirs St. Joseph Ch. Mem.: Ohio AGEHR (co-chair), Am. Guild of English Handbell Ringers (handbell dir.), Nat. Coun. for Geog. Edn., Nat. Coun. Social Studies. Republican. Avocations: piano, needlecrafts, travel, handbells. Home: 17045 Shurmer Rd Strongsville OH 44136 Office Phone: 440-238-4877. Business E-Mail: pyates@ameritech.net.

YATES, RICHARD L., multi-industry company executive; BS in Acctg., Northeastern U., Boston. CPA. Ptnr. Arthur Young & Co.; treas. Paul Revere Ins. Group, 1985—95, v.p., 1985—91, contr., 1985—87, CFO, 1987—95, sr. v.p., 1991—93, exec. v.p., 1993—95; v.p., contr. Textron, Inc., Providence, 1995—2004, sr. v.p., corp. contr., 2004—. Mem. Corp. Exec. Bd. Contr.'s Leadership Roundtable. Mem.: AICPA, Mfrs. Alliance Fin. Coun. II, Fin. Execs. Inst., Mass. Soc. CPAs. Office: Texton Inc 40 Westminster St Providence RI 02903 Office Phone: 401-421-2800.

YATES, RONALD EUGENE, newspaper editor, educator, author, journalist; b. Kansas City, Mo., Feb. 19, 1941; s. Guy Raymond and Willadene (Peterson) Y.; m. Ingeborg Zoelss, May 7, 1966; children: Jennifer Christina, Nicole Brigitte. BS (Gannett Newspapers scholar 1968-69, Angelo C. Scott Meml. scholar 1969), U. Kans., 1969. Reporter Kansas City (Kans.) Star, 1968; editor Univ. Daily Kansan, 1969; reporter, asst. city editor, fgn. corr. Chgo. Tribune, Chgo. and Tokyo, 1969-76, Asia and Latin Am. corr., 1976-82, met. editor, 1983—, nat. editor, 1984—, chief Asia corr., 1985—, sr. writer, 1992—; prof., chmn. dept. journalism U. Ill., Champaign, 1997—, dean Coll. Comm., 2003—. Contbr. articles to mags. Served with U.S. Army Intelligence, 1962-66. Recipient award for excellence in staff leadership William Allen White Sch. Journalism, 1968, Edward Scott Beck award for best fgn. reporting, 1975, 87, 89, Inter-Am. Press Assn. award for reporting on Latin Am., 1979, Peter Lisagor award for bus. and fin. reporting, 1993; named Outstanding Sr. U. Kans., 1969 Mem. Fgn. Corrs. Club of Japan (v.p. 1989—), Los Angeles Press, Sigma Delta Chi. Lutheran. Home: 35989 Darcy St Murrieta CA 92562-4562 Office Phone: 217-333-2350. Business E-Mail: ryates@uiuc.edu.

YATES-WILLIAMS, LINDA SNOW, real estate broker; b. St. Louis, July 20, 1938; d. Robert Anthony Jerrue and June Alberta (Crowder) Armstrong; m. Charles Russell Snow, Nov. 26, 1958 (div. 1979); children: Cathryn Louise, Christopher Armstrong, Heather Highstone, Sean Webster; m. Alan Porter Yates, July 22, 1983 (dec.); m. John S. Williams, Mar. 10, 2006. BBA, Auburn U., 1973, MEd, 1975, EdD, 1998. Cert. profl. sec. Div. head placement div. Solutions Group, Atlanta, 1981—83; employment coord. Fulton Fed. Savs., Atlanta, 1983—84; owner, recruiter Data One, Inc., Atlanta, 1984—85; ops. mgr. Talent Tree Temporaries, Atlanta, 1985—87; legal asst., sec. Rice & Keene, Atlanta, 1987—90; legal word processing asst. Kilpatrick & Cody, Atlanta, 1990—94; pres., owner Power Comm., Cashiers, NC, 1994—98; regional coord. S.E. region, regional mktg. rep. WorldConnect Comms., Tulsa, Okla.; dir. mktg. electronic collection divsn. Am. Fin. and Credit Svcs., Inc., Greenville, SC; area v.p., loan agent Enterprise Lenders, LLC; bd. dirs., corp. sec. The Hilltop Assocs. Inc., 1992—99; real estate salesperson Apex Realty, Beaufort, SC, 2002—03; real estate sales Exit Realty Beaufort, 2003—05; broker-in-charge Exit Island Realty, Bluffton, SC, 2006—08, Exit Realty of Hilton Head, SC, 2008—. Adj. instr. DeKalb Coll., Atlanta, 1980-84, Mercer U., Atlanta, 1981-82; instr. bus. So. Union State Jr. Coll., Valley, Ala., 1974-75; radio advt. WAUD, Auburn, Ala., 1970-75, radio announcer Meet the Public; exec. legal sec. Swift, Currie, McGhee & Hiers, Atlanta, 1979-80, Samford, Torbert, Denson & Horsley, Opelika, Ala., 1969-71; dir. acad. planning, chmn. edn. divsn., mem. part-time faculty in ednl. adminstrn. CEU Grad. Coll., Nuevo Leon, Mex. Columnist Neon News Flash, 1995. V.p., bd. trustees Family Promise, Beaufort County, SC, 2008—09, EXIT Realty Beaufort. Recipient Top Sales, 2006; named Top Listing Agt., 2005, Top Prodr., 2006. Mem. Paralegal Assn. Beaufort County (charter mem., sec. 1993-94), Women Bus. Owners, Nat. Assn. Pers. Cons., Internat. Soc. Poets (Disting. mem., founding laureate mem. 2006, Internat. Poet of Merit 1996, Internat. Poetry Hall of Fame 1996), Cashiers Writers Group, 90-10 Club, Sunscribers, Phi Delta Kappa, Alpha Xi Delta. Republican. Presbyterian. Avocations: golf, writing poetry, international travel. Office: Exit Realty Hilton Head 6 Office Way Ste 930 Hilton Head Island SC 29928 Office Phone: 843-842-8880, 843-252-4948. Personal E-mail: linday1000@yahoo.com.

YATSENKO, NIKOLAI AFANASYEVICH, physics researcher, educator; b. Russia, Jan. 1, 1948; arrived in U.S., 1996; s. Afanasii and Vera (Bogacheva) Y.; m. Lyudmila Yegorovna Fedyanina, May 6, 1972; 1 child, Marina. MS in Physics, Moscow Inst. Physics & Tech., 1973, PhD in Physics and Math., 1978; DSc in Physics and Math., Russian Acad. Scis., Moscow, 1992. Rschr. Zhukovsky Mil. Air Force Acad., Moscow, 1973-75; rschr., sr. rschr. Inst. for Problems in Mechanics, Russian Acad. Scis., Moscow, 1978-95, head rschr., 1995—2006. Assoc. prof. physics Russian Inst. Textile and Light Industry, Moscow, 1980-93, full prof. physics, 1993-2000; project scientist Optical Engring., Inc., Santa Rosa, Calif., 1996-98, Macken Instruments, Inc., Santa Rosa, Calif., 1998—; referee Soviet Union State Com. for Inventions and Discoveries, Moscow, 1986-91; mem. sci. coun. Inst. for Problems in Mechanics, Moscow, 1992—; mem. spl. PhD coun. Moscow Inst. Physics and Tech., 1995—. Co-author: Thermal Plasma Diagnostics, 1994, Radio-Frequency Capacitive Discharges, 1995, Gas Lasers-Recent Developments and Future Prospects, 1996, Plasma Diagnostics, 2000; mem. editl. bd. Jour. Edn. Experiment in U., 1997—; referee Jour. Physics D: Applied Physics, 1998—, Measurement Sci. and Tech., 2000—; contbr. articles to jours. on plasma physics and gas lasers. Decorated Medal of Honor 850th Ann. Moscow, 1997; grantee Ministry of Edn., Moscow, 1992, 94, 95, 97, Internat. Sci. Found., Russia, 1993, 94, Joint Russian and Internat. Sci. Found., 1995. Fellow Internat. Biog. Assn., Am. Biog. Inst. (life), Inst. Physics (London); mem. IEEE (sr.), AAAS, Am. Phys. Soc., European Phys. Soc., Am. Vacuum Soc., Am. Assn. Physics Tchrs., Nat. Geog. Soc., Sigma Xi. Achievements include experimental discoveries relating to radio-frequency capacitive discharges at moderate pressures; invention and demonstration of a slab CO2 laser; 10 patents including laser apparatus utilizing a magnetically enhanced electrical discharge with transverse AC stabilization; Russian patent for gas-flow CO2 laser. Office: Macken Instruments Inc 3186 Coffey Ln Santa Rosa CA 95403-2555 Personal E-mail: nikolai@macken.com. Business E-Mail: nyatsenko@ieee.org.

YATSENKO, YURI PETROVICH, business professor, mathematician; b. Kiev, Ukraine, Oct. 15, 1955; arrived in US, 2000, permanent resident, 2001; s. Petr Yatsenko and Nadiya Betina; m. Natali Hritonenko; children: Oleg, Victoria, Olga. BS in Physics, Kiev State U., Ukraine, 1977, MS, 1977, PhD, 1981; DSc, Presidium Acad. Scis. USSR, 1988. Lic. prof. Edn. Ministry Ukraine, 1995. Sr. rschr., dept. head Cybernetics Inst. Ukrainian Acad. Scis., Kiev, 1983—96; prof. Kiev State U., 1991—93, Acad. Tech. & Agr., Bydgoszcz, Poland, 1993—95; sr. analyst Electric Submersible Pumps, Inc., Okla. City, Okla., 1997—99; adj. prof. U. Alta., Edmonton, Alberta, Canada, 1999—99; sr. sys. analyst Netherland, Sewell & Assoc., Inc., Dallas, 2000—01; prof. Houston Bapt. U., 2002—. Owner Cybernetics Cons. Inc., Edmonton, Alberta, Canada, 1996—2000; lectr. in field; mem. editl. bd. Internat. Jour. Applications and Applied Maths., United States, 2005—, Internat. Jour. Ecology and Devel., India, 2006—, Jour. Computational and Applied Maths., Ukraine, 2006—; assoc. editor Internat. Jour. Ecological Econs. and Stats., India, 2006—; mem. program & organizing coms. at confs. in field. Author: 6 Books; contbr. scientific papers to profl. jours. Rsch. grants, Sorros Internat. Sci. Found. & Edn. Ministry Ukraine, 1992—95, Rsch. grant, NATO, 2006—08. Russian Orthodox. Achievements include research in mathematical modeling and optimization of economic and industrial development, technological change, innovation processes, and technology replacement. Home: 15434 Tysor Park Ln Houston TX 77095 Office: Houston Bapt Univ 7502 Fondren Houston TX 77074 Office Fax: 281-649-3436. Business E-Mail: yyatsenko@hbu.edu.

YATSKIEVYCH, GEORGE ALFRED, curator, educator; b. Kassel, Hesse, Germany, June 21, 1957; s. Yaromyr and Ursula Elisabeth Yatskievych; m. Kay Hankins. BS, U. Ariz., Tucson, 1979, MS, 1982; PhD, Ind. U., Bloomington, 1990. Botanist, resource scientist Mo. Dept. Conservation, St. Louis, 1987—2005; curator Mo. Bot. Garden, St. Louis, 1987—. Rsch. assoc. prof. U. Mo., St. Louis, 2002—, grad. faculty, 2002—; rsch. assoc. Ariz. Sonora Desert Mus., Tucson, 2002—. Author: (book) Catalogue of the flora of Missouri, Steyermark's Flora of Missouri, Vol.2; contbr. articles to profl. jours. Recipient Edgar T. Wherry award, Bot. Soc. Am., 1989, Julian A. Steyermark award, Mo. Native Plant Soc., 1999; Rsch. grant, NSF, 1986, 1989, 2007. Mem.: Ariz. Nev., Ind., & Mo. Acads. Sci., Internat. Assn. Plant Taxonomy, Bot. Soc. Am., Am. Soc. Plant Taxonomists, Am. Fern Soc. (sec. 2002—), Mo. Native Plant Soc. (bd. mem. 1989—), Sigma Xi. Avocations: photography, hiking, travel, reading. Home: 11949 Claychester Dr Saint Louis MO 63131 Office: Mo Botanical Garden PO Box 299 Saint Louis MO 63166 Office Fax: 314-577-0830. E-mail: george.yatskievych@mobot.org.

YAU, EDWARD TINTAI, toxicologist, pharmacologist; b. Canton, China, Dec. 29, 1944; came to U.S., 1967; s. Wing S. and Fong K. (Wong) Y.; m. Assumpta Koo, July 3, 1979; 1 child, Jonathan C. BS in Biology, Bapt. Coll., Hong Kong, 1967; PhD in Pharmacology, U. Miss., 1974. Diplomate Am. Bd. Toxicology. Postdoctoral fellow, then asst. prof. Purdue U., West Lafayette, Ind., 1974-77; toxicology supr. Wyeth Labs., Great Valley, Pa., 1977-79; sr. toxicologist CIBA-GEIGY Corp., Summit, N.J., 1979-82, mgr., 1982-86, asst. dir., 1986-88, dir., 1988-92, exec. dir., 1993-96; exec. dir. of toxicology and pathology Novartis Pharm. U.S., 1997-98; dir. toxicology Roberts Pharm. Corp., Eatontown, N.J., 1998-99, Forest Labs., NYC, 1999-2000, Vertex Pharm. Inc., Cambridge, Mass., 2000—. Adj. prof. U. Miss., Oxford, 1989-92, 95—. Contbr. articles to sci. publs. Recipient NSF award, 1970. Mem. Am. Chem. Soc., Am. Coll. Toxicology, Soc. Toxicology, Teratology Soc., Sigma Xi. Republican. Baptist. Home: 67 Grant Ave Clifton NJ 07011-3522 Office Phone: 617-444-6706. E-mail: edward_yau@vrtx.com, yauedwardt@aol.com.

YAU, KING-WAI, neuroscientist, educator; b. Guangzhou, Guangdong Province, China, Oct. 27, 1948; came to U.S., 1968; s. Tin-Man and Wai-Hing (Chan) Y.; m. Crystal Lin, Dec. 27, 1975; children: Emily, Jason. AB, Princeton U., 1971; PhD, Harvard U., 1975. Rsch. assoc. Stanford (Calif.) U., 1976-79, Cambridge (Eng.) U., 1979-80; from asst. prof. to prof. U. Tex. Med. Br., Galveston, 1980-86; prof. neurosci. Johns Hopkins Sch. Medicine, Balt., 1986—. Investigator Howard Hughes Med. Inst., Balt., 1986—2004. Recipient Rank prize in optoelectronics, London, 1980, Rsch. Career Devel. award NIH, 1981-86, Merit award, 1992-2002, Alcon Rsch. Inst. award, 1994, 2005, Magnes prize The Hebrew U., Jerusalem, 1996, Ruth and Milton Steinbach award, 2004, Antonio Champalimaud Vision award, Portugal, 2008. Fellow Am. Acad. Arts & Scis.; mem. Soc. Neurosci., Soc. Gen. Physiologists, Assn. Rsch. Vision and Opthalmology (Friedenwald award 1993), Biophys. Soc., Physiol. Soc. (U.K.), Internat. Soc. Eye Rsch.(Balazs prize, 2006) Achievements include rsch. on mechanisms of visual and olfactory transductions. Office: Johns Hopkins U Sch Med 725 N Wolfe St Baltimore MD 21205-2105 Office Phone: 410-955-1260. Business E-Mail: Kwyau@mail.jhmi.edu.

YAU, SHING-TUNG, mathematics professor; b. Swatow, China, Apr. 4, 1949; arrived in U.S., 1969; m. Yu-Yun Kuo; children: Isaac, Michael. PhD, U. Calif., Berkeley, 1971; PhD (hon.), Chinese U. Hong Kong, 1980, Harvard U., 1987, Chao Tung U., 1997, Nat. Tsing Hua U., 2000, Macau U., 2002. Mem. Inst. Advanced Study, Princeton, NJ, 1971-72; asst. prof. math. SUNY, Stony Brook, 1972-73; prof. math. Stanford U., Ark., 1974-79; hon. prof. Chinese Acad. Scis, 1983; prof. math. Inst. Advanced Study, Princeton, 1979-84, U.Calif.-San Diego, La Jolla, 1984-87; hon. prof. Hangzhou U., 1987—, Tsinghau U., 1987—; prof. math. Harvard U., Cambridge, Mass., 1987—, William Casper Graustein Prof., 2000—; Fairchild Disting. Scholar Caltech, 1990; disting. vis. prof. SUNY, Stony Brook, 1990; hon. prof. Nankai U., 1993—; Higgins Prof., 1997—2000; hon. prof. Beijing U., 1998—, U. Sci. & Tech., China, 1999—, Zhejian U., 2002—; disting. prof.-at-large Chinese U. of Hong Kong, 2003. Vis. prof., chair math. dept. U. Tex., Austin, 1986; spl. chair Nat. Tsing Hua U., Hsinchu, Taiwan, 1991—92; Wilson T.S. Wang Disting. vis. prof. Chinese U., Hong Kong, 1991—92; adj. prof. math. Chinese U. of Hong Kong, 1994—2003, dir. Inst. Math. Scis., 1994—. Contbr. articles to profl. publs. Recipient Calif. Scientist of Yr., 1979, Sr. Scientist award, Humboldt Found. fellow, 1985, Crafoord prize, 1994, Veblen prize, 1981, Fields medal, 1982, Certy prize, 1980, Nat. Medal Sci. (USA), 1997, China International Sci. and Tech. Cooperation award, 2003; named Honorable prof., Fudan U. China, Academia Sinica China, Sci. Digest, Am. 100 brightest scientists under 40, 1984; grantee Sloan Fellow, 1975—76, Guggenheim Fellowship, 1982, MacArthur Fellow, 1985. Fellow: Russian Acad. Scis. (fgn. mem.); mem.: AAAS, Nat. Acad. Scis. (bd. mem. math. scis.), Scientific Adv. Coun., Chinese Acad. Sci. (hon. mem. academic com. 1980—, fgn. mem.), Acad. Sinica (Taiwan), Soc. Indsl. Applied Math., Am. Phys. Soc., Am. Math. Soc., Acad. Arts and Scis. Boston, N.Y. Acad. Scis. Office: Harvard U Dept Math 3d Fl Sci Ctr 1 Oxford St Cambridge MA

02138-2901 also: Inst Math Scis Chinese U Hong Kong Unit 601, 6/F Academic Bldg #1 Shatin Hong Kong Office Phone: 617-495-0836, (852)2609-8038. E-mail: yau@math.harvard.edu, yau@ims.cuhk.edu.hk.

YAUKEY, MARGARET ANN, art educator; b. Dakha, Bangladesh, Jan. 1, 1963; d. Raymond Stulting and Dolores Lilly Yaukey. BA in Philosophy, Grinnell Coll., 1984; student, U. Wash., Seattle, 1991—92; MFA, Temple U., 1996. Head jewelery designer Faces of Time, Madison, Conn., 1987—90; prof. art Appalachian State U., Boone, NC, 1996—. Exhibited artist in book, 500 Necklaces, 2005, Best of North Carolina Artists and Artisans, 2005, Best of American Jewelry Artists and Artisans, 2006, exhibitions include Funerary Urns, 2006, Ahes to Ashes, 2007. Grantee, Appalachian State U., 1997, 1999, 2004, 2007; fellow, NC Arts Coun., 2005. Mem.: Soc. North Am. Goldsmiths (life). Independent. Quaker. Achievements include development of adapting digital design and creation process for the studio jeweler. Avocation: travel. Office: Appalachian State U Dept Art Wey Hall Boone NC 28608 Home Phone: 828-773-2738; Office Phone: 828-262-2564. Office Fax: 828-262-6756. Business E-Mail: yaukeyma@appstate.edu.

YAVARKOVSKY, JEROME HAROLD, university librarian emeritus; b. NYC, May 12, 1940; B Mech. Engring., Rensselaer Poly. Inst., 1960; MS in Mgmt., MIT, 1962; M Libr. Sci., Columbia U., 1971. Lic. pub. libr. Adminstrv. specialist Bell Labs., Murray Hill, NJ, 1963-64; systems analyst J.C. Penney Co., NYC, 1965-67; tech. cons. Auerbach Assocs., NYC, 1967-68; head programming Columbia U., NYC, 1969-71, chief systems, 1971-72, asst. univ. libr., 1972-83; dean librs. Adelphi U., Garden City, NY, 1983-85; dir. NY State Libr., Albany, 1985-95; univ. libr. Boston Coll., Chestnut Hill, 1995—2008. Mem.: Media Grid (found. co-chair, libr. tech. working group 2008—).

YAVORNIK, BARBARA ANN, pre-school educator; b. Olympia, Wash., July 12, 1957; d. Eugene Earl and Betty Ann Brown; m. Edward J. Yavornik, II, Jan. 11, 1980. BA, Cen. Wash. U., Ellensburg, 1981; MEd, West Tex. A&M U., 1990. Cert. adminstrn. Dir., tchr. Fifth Ave. Pres-Sch., Ellensburg, 1981—82; tchr. Coronado Acad., Albuquerque, 1985—86, N.W. Primary, Hereford, Tex., 1987—. Presenter I-Teach K West Tex. A&M U. Sci. Conf., 2000, 01, 05; presenter HISD Sci. Inservice, 2005. Greeter coord. St. Anthony's Parish Coun., 2004—, eucharistic minister, 2004—; bd. dirs. Campfire, Hereford, 1988—90. Recipient Excel in Sci. Tchg. award, Tex. Sci. Assn., 2001, Golden Apple award, Hereford Ind. Sch. Dist., 2004; named Tchr. of Yr., N.W. Primary, 2002. Mem.: Hereford C. of C. (v.p. women's divsn. 1987—89), Delta Kappa Gamma (pres. 2002—04, v.p., Achievement award 1999—2004). Republican. Roman Catholic. Avocations: gardening, reading, collecting bears, travel. Home: 201 N Texas Ave Hereford TX 79045 Office: NW Primary Sch 400 Moreman Ave Hereford TX 79045 Office Phone: 806-363-7660. E-mail: barbarayavornik@herefordisd.net.

YAWNEY, TRENT, former professional hockey coach, retired professional hockey player; b. Hudson Bay, Sask., Can., Sept. 29, 1965; m. Charlane Yawney; children: Ashley, Conor. Defenceman Can. Nat. Team, 1985—88, Chgo. Blackhawks, 1987—91, 1997—99, Calgary Flames, 1991—96, St. Louis Blues, 1996—97; asst. coach Chgo. Blackhawks, 1999—2000, head coach, 2005—06, Norfolk Admirals, 2000—05. Mem. Team Can., Olympic Games, Calgary, 1988. Named Minor Pro Coach of Yr., The Hockey News, 2003—04.

YAZDANI, ALI, physicist, researcher; b. Tehran, Iran, Dec. 25, 1967; s. Fazollah Yazdani and Parivarh; m. Adele Goldberg, Aug. 6, 1994; 1 child, Aliza. BA in Physics, U. Calif., Berkeley, 1989; MS in Applied Physics, Stanford U., 1991, PhD in Applied Physics, 1995. Postdoc. scientist IBM Almaden Rsch. Ctr., San Jose, Calif., 1994-97; asst. prof. physics. U. (Urbana-Champaign) Ill., 1997—. Mem. Am. Phys. Soc., AAAS, Phi Beta Kappa. Achievements include rsch. in two-dimensional hyperconductors; in superconductivity and magnetism on nanometer length scale. Office: Univ Ill Dept Physics 1110 W Green St Urbana IL 61801-9013

YAZDANI, SHAHRAM, pediatrician; b. July 20, 1967; MD, Tulane U. Sch. Medicine, New Orleans, 1995. Cert. Am. Bd. Pediat., 2006. Internship in pediat. UCLA Sch. Medicine, 1995—96, residency in pediat., 1996—98, physician, 1998—, asst. prof. pediat., 1998—, asst. clin. prof. gen. pediat., 1998—. Dir. resident med. edn. UCLA Med. Sch., site dir., 3rd yr. med. sch., mem. ambulatory medicine com., 2001—; med. coord., cons. Madisons Found., 2003—. Mem.: Assn. Pediatric Program Directors. Office: UCLA Children's Health Ctr 200 UCLA Med Plz Ste 265 Los Angeles CA 90095 Office Phone: 310-825-0867. Office Fax: 310-794-5066. Business E-Mail: syazdani@mednet.ucla.edu.

YAZDI, AHMAD, computer scientist, researcher; b. Tehran, Iran, Apr. 8, 1978; s. Kazem Yazdi and Minoo Mapar. BS, Sharif U. of Tech., Tehran, 2000; MS, U. So. Calif., 2003; postgrad., U. Calif., Irvine, 2003—. Rsch. asst. U. Calif., Irvine, 2003—. Contbr. articles to profl. jours., confs. Fellow Ctr. for Pervasive Comm. and Computing, 2003—05. Mem.: IEEE, Eta Kappa Nu. Achievements include patents for a novel silicon-based differential non-uniform downsized distributed amplifier; ultra-wideband CMOS distributed mixer. Office: U Calif Irvine Dept Elec Engring and Computer Sci ET 521 Irvine CA 92697-2625 Personal E-mail: yazdi75a@yahoo.com. E-mail: yazdia@uci.edu.

YAZDI, MAHVASH, utilities executive; BS in Indsl. Mgmt., Poly. U., Pomona, Calif.; MBA, U. So. Calif., LA; grad. Mgmt. of Info. Tech. program, Harvard Bus. Sch. With IBM World Trade Corp.; v.p., chief info. officer Hughes Aircraft, 1994; with Edison Internat., Rosemead, Calif., 1997—, sr. v.p. bus. integration, chief info. officer So. Calif. Edison subs., sr. v.p. bus. integration, chief info. officer. Bd. dirs. Columbus Newport Corp.; adv. dir. Lotus Corp., IBM Corp.; mem. So. Calif. Forum of the Trusteeship of the Internat. Women's Forum, 2003. Mem. adv. bd. U. So. Calif. Marshall Sch. Bus.; bd. dirs. Claremont U. Consortium. Office: Edison Internat 2244 Walnut Grove Ave Rosemead CA 91770 Office Phone: 626-302-1212.

YAZEDJIAN, ANI, humanities educator; PhD in Human & Cmty. Devel., U. Ill., Urbana-Champaign. Asst. prof. Tex. State U., San Marcos, 2004—. Mem. San Marcos Youth Commn., 2008—. Recipient award., Fulbright-Hays Group Projects Abroad, 2005. Mem.: Soc. Rsch. Identity Formation, Soc. Rsch. Adolescence, Nat. Coun. Family Rels. (sec. & treas. ethnic minorities sect. 2008—). Office: Tex State Univ 601 Univ Dr San Marcos TX 78666

YAZIJI, HADI, lab administrator; b. Damascus, Syria, Jan. 26, 1966; married. MD, U. Damascus, 1983—89. Cert. in anatomic & clin. pathology & cytology Am. Bd. Pathology, 2000. Staff pathologist Phenopath Labs., Seattle, 1999—2004, Bapt. Hosp., Miami, Fla., 2004—06; med. dir. Vitro Molecular Lab., Miami, 2006—. Fellow: Coll. Am. Pathologists; mem.: Alpha Omega Alpha Honor Med. Soc. Office: Vitro Molecular Lab 7000 SW 62nd Ave Ste PHC Miami FL 33143

YBARRA, KIMBERLY ELIZABETH, music and elementary school educator; b. Glen Ridge, NJ, Apr. 10, 1959; d. Theodore Edward Johnson and Marian Bon Durant-Johnson; children: Samuel A., Sarah E. MusB, Calif. State U., Long Beach, 1984. Cert. music tchr., multiple subject tchr. Calif. Elem. tchr. Pacific Harbor Christian Sch., Wilmington, Calif., 1987—90, Garfield Elem. Sch., Long Beach, 1990—93; elem. tchr., music tchr. FKCP III Schs., LA, 1993—2003, choral dir., 1995—2002; elem. tchr., music tchr South Pasadena Unified Sch. Dist., Calif., 2003—, mus. theater, music dir. workshop, 2003—. Chmn. choral festival Assn. Christian Sch. Internat.; elem. choral dir. South Pasadena Unified Sch. Dist.; piano accompanist, soloist, instr. various ch. and secular orgns. Author: Little Buzzy, 1975, composer songs. Tutor Maria Regina Sch., Gardena, Calif., 2000; vocalist Summer Gospel Music Outreach, LA, 2003; adjudicator Act-So program NAACP, Inglewood, Calif., 2004—08. Recipient Excellence in Tchr. award, Pacific Harbor Christian Sch., 1990, Frederick K.S. Price III Schs., 1997, 2001, Outstanding Recognition award, South Pasadena Unified Sch. Dist., 2005. Mem.: Calif. Tchrs. Assn., Calif. Music Educators Assn., Music Educators Nat. Conf. Avocations: travel, walking, reading, psychology, photography.

YBARRA, PACO, bank executive; b. Spain; Bachelor's degree in econ., U. Valencia, Spain; MBA, IESE, Barcelona. Mgmt. assoc. Citibank, Spain, 1987, derivatives head Madrid, 1992—94, country treas. Mexico, 1995—97; regional head of sales and trading Citibank Latin America, NYC, 1997—2002; regional head of emerging markets sales and trading for Asia Pacific Citigroup, Singapore, 2002—04, global head of emerging markets sales and trading, 2004—06, global head fixed income, currencies and commodities, 2006—08, co-head global markets, 2008—. Office: Citigroup 399 Park Ave New York NY 10043*

YE, WEILAN, scientist; PhD, U. Pitts., 1995. Scientist Genentech Inc., South San Francisco, Calif., 1999—2004, sr. scientist, 2004—. Contbr. scientific papers. Guest spkr. KTSF, San Francisco, 2003. Mem.: AAAS. Achievements include discovery of important molecule that controls vascular tube formation; the mechanism that specifies the fate of dopaminergic neurons; patents for method of dopaminergic and serotonergic neuron formation from neuroprogenitor cells; 12 pending patent applications.

YE, XIAOFEI, education educator; s. Yulan Yang and Tiyu Ye; m. Qiuyu Julie Chen, 1996; 1 child, Meryl A. B in Engring., Northwestern Agrl. U., China, 1990; MS, South Dakota State U., 1998; PhD, U. Minn., 2004. Asst. prof. U. Tenn., Knoxville, 2004—. Author: (book chpt.) The Nutrition Handbook for Food Processors, Improving Thermal Processing of Foods, Thermal Technologies in Food Processing, (jour. paper) Lebensmittel-Wissenschaft und Technologie, Jour. of Food Engring. Grant, USDA, 2004. Mem.: Inst. Food Technologists, Am. Soc. Agrl. and Biol. Engrs., Alpha Epsilon (life). Office: The Univ of Tenn 2506 E J Chapman Dr Knoxville TN 37996 Business E-Mail: xye2@utk.edu.

YEA, SEHOON, consumer electronics industry executive, researcher; b. Seoul, Republic Of Korea, Sept. 10, 1970; married. PhD, Rensselaer Poly. Inst., Troy, NY, 2005. Rsch. asst. Nagoya U., Japan, 1994—95; rsch. engr. Inst. Advanced Engring., Yong-In, Kyoung-Gi Province, Republic of Korea, 1996—2001; rsch. asst. Ctr. Image Processing Rsch., Troy, 2003—05; prin. mem. tech. staff Mitsubishi Electric Rsch. Labs., Cambridge, Mass., 2006—. Mem.: IEEE, IEICE. Office: Mitsubishi Electric Rsch Labs 201 Broadway Cambridge MA 02139 Office Fax: 617-621-7550. Business E-Mail: yea@merl.com.

YEAGER, CHUCK (CHARLES ELWOOD YEAGER), retired air force officer, test pilot; b. Myra, W.Va., Feb. 13, 1923; s. Albert Hal and Susie May (Sizemore) Yeager; m. Glennis Faye Dickhouse (dec. 1990), Feb. 26, 1945; m. Victoria Scott D'Angelo, 2003 Grad., Air Command and Staff Sch., 1952, Air War Coll., 1961; DSc (hon.), W.Va. U., 1948, Marshall U., Huntington, W.Va., 1969; D in Aero. Sci., Salem Coll., W.Va., 1975. Enlisted in USAAF, 1941; advanced through grades to brig. gen. U.S. Air Force, 1969, fighter pilot, ETO, 1943-46, exptl. flight test pilot, 1945-54, various command assignments U.S., Germany, France and Spain, 1954-62; comdr., astronaut tng. Air Force Aerospace Rsch. Pilots Sch.; dir. Space Sch., Edwards AFB, 1960; comdr. 405th Fighter Wing, Seymour Johnson AFB, N.C., 1968-69; vice comdr. 17th Air Force, Ramstein Air Base, Fed. Republic Germany, 1969-71; U.S. def. rep. to Pakistan, 1971-73; spl. asst. to comdr. Air Force Inspection and Safety Ctr., Norton AFB, Calif., 1973, dir. aerospace safety, 1973-75; ret., 1975. Cons. to comdr. Test Pilot Sch., Edwards AFB, 1975—97; presdl. commn. to investigate Challenger accident, 1986; hon. chmn. Duncan Hunter Presdl. Campaign, 2006; spkr. in field. Actor: (films) Smokey and the Bandit II, 1980, The Right Stuff, 1983; (TV movies) Flying Without Fear, 1985; (TV appearances) Goodyear Television Playhouse, 1953, I Dream of Jeannie, 1964; Co-author: (with Leo Janos) Yeager: An Autobiography, 1985, (with Charles Leerhsen) Press On!, 1988, The Quest for Mach One: A First-Person Account of Breaking the Sound Barrier, 1998; featured in: Spaceflight, 1985, Looney Tunes 50th Anniversary, 1986, Realizing 'The Right Stuff,' 2003, The Real Men with 'The Right Stuff,' 2003, Pancho Barnes! A Documentary Film, 2008. Founder, chmn. Gen. Chuck Yeager Found., Calif., 2002—. Decorated DSM with oak leaf cluster, Silver Star with oak leaf cluster, Legion of Merit with oak leaf cluster, DFC with 2 oak leaf clusters, Bronze star with V device, Air medal with 10 oak leaf clusters, Air Force Commendation medal, Purple Heart; recipient Collier Trophy, 1948, Harmon Internat Trophy, 1958, Congl. medal of Honor, 1976, Presdl. medal of Freedom, 1985; first and youngest mil. pilot inducted into Nat. Aviation Hall of Fame, 1973, inducted to Aerospace Walk of Hon., 1990; promoted to rank of maj. gen. on ret. list, 2005. Achievements include flying in 64 combat missions in World War II, over 120 combat missions in Vietnam; being the first man to fly faster than the speed of sound, Oct. 14, 1947.

YEAGER, DAVID P., transportation executive; b. 1953; BA, U. Dayton, 1975; MBA, Univ. Chgo., 1987. With affiliated cos. Hub Group, Inc., 1975—, vice chmn. bd. Lombard, Ill., 1992—, CEO, 1995—. Bd. dir. SPR Inc., Thrall Car Mfg. Co. Bd. dir. Children's Memorial Hospital-Chgo., Fenwick High School; mem. adv. council Univ. Dayton. Office: Hub Group 3050 Highland Pkwy Downers Grove IL 60515

YEAGER, DEBRA LYN, science educator; b. St. Paul, Mar. 20, 1957; d. Lyle Milton and Grace Jeanette (Mitchell) Yeager, adopted d. Wilma Mitchell; life ptnr. Christopher Charles Pfannes. AS in Computer Sci., Mesa C.C., Ariz., 1982; student, Scottsdale C.C., Ariz., 1979—80. Ordained minister Order of Melchizedek, 1991. Investigator - profiler Elk River Sheriff's Dept., Minn., 1992—94; sensor sci. tchr. Open U. of Minn., Mpls., 1994—99; sensory sci. tchr. Yeager Consulting / Into the Mystic, Minnetonka, Minn., 1998—2005, Wis. Indianhead Tech. Coll., New Richmond, 2003—, West Ctrl. Cancer Symposium, Willmar, Minn., 2003, U. Alaska-Sitka, 2003—, U. Manitoba, 2004—, U. Coll. Dublin, Ireland, 2004—, Queens U.-Belfast, Ireland, 2004—; on the air talent, lectr. Kare 11 - NBC TV Mpls, 2002—03, WCCO 4 - CBS TV. Mpls., 2002, NW Mag. Cable Show, New Hope, Minn., 1996; sensory sci. specialist, prof. spirituality Park Hill, Okla., 2005—. Criminologist and profiler Crema Law Offices, Mpls., 1999—. Author: (novel) Encounters with the Sixth Dimension (Book in print), Intervention across time, Medium, Rare - the Bio of Debra Yeager, Karman from MU. Mem.: Delta Zeta (hon.). Achievements include research in metaphysical studies; development of programs of metaphysical studies. Avocations: motorcycling, designing jewelry, horse training, running, travel. Home and Office: PO Box 310 Park Hill OK 74451 Office Phone: 918-718-4077. Personal E-mail: century30@aol.com.

YEAGER, KURT ERIC, research and development company executive; b. Cleve., Sept. 11, 1939; s. Joseph Ellsworth and Karolyn Kristine (Pedersen) Y.; m. Rosalie Ann McMillan, Feb. 5, 1960; children: Geoffrey, Phillip; m. Regina Ursula Querfurt, May 12, 1970; 1 dau., Victoria. BA in Chemistry, Kenyon Coll., 1961; postgrad., Ohio State U., 1961-62; MS in Physics, U. Calif., Davis, 1964; MS Wharton Sch. Bus., U. Pa., 1995. Tchg. asst. Ohio State U., 1961-62; officer, program mgr. Air Force Tech. Applications Ctr., Alexandria, Va., 1962-68; assoc. dept. dir. Mitre Corp., McLean, Va., 1968-72; dir. energy rsch. and devel. planning EPA, Washington, 1972-74; dir. fossil power plants dept. Electric Power Rsch. Inst., Palo Alto, Calif., 1974-79, dir. coal combustion systems, 1979-83, v.p. coal combustion systems, 1983-88, v.p. generation and storage, 1988-96, pres., CEO, 1996—2004; founder, pres., CEO, Keyworks, Aptos, Calif., 2004—. Chmn. World Energy Coun. Climate Change Study,2005-07; dir. Galvin Elec. Initiative2005-; Oak Ridge fossil energy adv. bd. Nat. Acad. Engring.; mem. exec. bd. Nat. Coal Coun.; bd. dirs. nat. coalition advanced mfg. US Energy Assn.; bd. dirs. APX Corp., 2005-07; Energy Connect Corp., 2007- Contbr. articles to profl. jours; Co-author (book) Perfect Power. Pres. No. Va. Youth Football Assn., 1973-74. Capt. USAF, 1962-68, chair Watsonville Airport Adv. Council, 2008 Decorated Air Force Commendation medals (2); recipient Outstanding Svc. award EPA, 1974; named Energy Policy Leader, Sci. Am., 2003. Fellow ASME (rsch. policy bd., trustee com. econ. devel.); mem. AAAS, Am. Chem. Soc., Palo Alto C. of C. Republican. Episcopalian. Office Phone: 831-786-9832. Business E-Mail: kyeager@epri.com.

YEAGER, MARK LEONARD, lawyer; b. Chgo., Apr. 7, 1950; BA, U. Mich., 1972; JD cum laude, Northwestern U., 1975. Bar: Ill. 1975, Fla. 1985, US Supreme Ct. Ptnr. McDermott, Will & Emery LLP, Chgo., 1981—; mem. Trial Dept. McDermott, Will & Emery, Chgo. Mem. alumni adv. bd. U. Mich. Dept. Econs. Mem.: ABA. Office: McDermott Will & Emery LLP 227 W Monroe St Ste 3100 Chicago IL 60606-5096 Office Fax: 312-984-7700. E-mail: myeager@mwe.com.

YEAGER, NICHOLAS D., pediatrician, educator; b. San Antonio, Tex., Nov. 28, 1971; s. William Yeager and Darlene Hamilton; m. Nicole L. Bumpus, Aug. 5, 1995; children: Isabella, Rowan, Jack. MD, Neoucom, Rootstown, Ohio, 1996. Cert. in pediat. hematology,oncology Am. Bd. Pediat., 2004. Asst. prof. pediat. Nationwide Children's Hosp., Columbus, Ohio, 2003—08. Office: Nationwide Children's Hosp 700 Children's Dr Columbus OH 43205 Office Fax: 614-722-3699.

YEAGER, PHILLIP CHARLES, transportation company executive; b. Bellevue, Ky., Nov. 15, 1927; s. Ferd A. and Helen (Koehler) Y.; m. Joyce E. Ruebusch, June 2, 1951; children: David P., Debra A. Yeager Jensen, Mark A. BA, U. Cin., 1951. Warehouse mgr. Pure Carbonic Co., Cin., 1950-52; trace clk., rate clk., asst. office mgr. Pa. R.R., Chgo., 1952-56, salesman Kansas City, Mo., 1956-59, asst. dir. Trailvan Phila., 1959-65, div. sales mgr. Milw., 1965-68; dir. Trailvan Penn-Ctrl. R.R., NYC, 1968-71; pres. Hub City Terminals, Chgo., 1971-85; chmn. The Hub Group, Chgo., 1985—; also bd. dirs. Bd. dirs. 30 Hubcity terminals. Cpl. U.S. Army, 1946-47. Recipient Achievement award Intermodal Transp. Assn., 1991, Harry E. Salzberg medallion for outstanding achievement in transp.; named Chgo. Transp. Man of Yr., Chgo. Transp. Assn., 1990. Mem. N.Y. Traffic Club, Chgo. Traffic Club. Republican. Lutheran. Avocations: golf, biking, swimming.

YEAMANS, GEORGE THOMAS, librarian, educator; b. Nov. 7, 1929; s. James Norman and Dolphine Sophia (Manhart) Yeamans; m. Mary Ann Seng, Feb. 1, 1958; children: Debra, Susan, Julia. AB, U. Va., 1950; MLS, U. Ky., 1955; EdD, Ind. U., 1965. Asst. audio-visual dir. Ind. State U., Terre Haute, 1957—58; asst. film libr. Ball State U., Muncie, Ind., 1958—61, film libr., 1961—69, assoc. prof. libr. sci., 1969—72, prof., 1972—95, prof. emeritus, 1995—. Cons. Pendleton (Ind.) Sch. Corp., 1962, 67, Captioned Films for the Deaf Workshop, Muncie, 1963—65, Decatur (Ind.) Sch. Sys., 1978; adjudicator Ind. Media Fair, 1979—93, David Letterman Scholarship Program, 1993. Author: Projectionists' Programmed Primer, 1969, rev. edit., 1982, Mounting and Preserving Pictorial Materials, 1976, Tape Recording, 1978, Transparency Making, 1977, Photographic Principles, 1981, Computer Literacy-A Programmed Primer, 1985, Designing Dynamic Media Presentations, 1996, Robert F. Kennedy Archival Project, 1968—2004, Building Effective Creative Project Teams, 2000, Building Effective Creative Project Teams, rev. ed., 2007; songwriter: Branson Bound, 1996; contbr. articles to profl. jours. Campaign worker Wilson for Mayor, Muncie, 1979. With USMC, 1950—52. Recipient Citations of Achievement, Internat. Biog. Assn., Cambridge, Eng., 1973, Am. Biog. Assn., 1976, Mayor James P. Carey award for achievement for disting. contbns. to Ball State U. and City of Muncie, 1988; Video Info. Sys. grant, Ball State U., 1993. Mem.: ALA, NEA (del. assembly dept. audiovisual instrn. 1967), Audio-Visual Instrn. Dirs. Ind. (exec. bd. 1962—68, pres. 1966—67), Thomas Jefferson Soc. Alumni U. Va., Ind. Pub. Libr. Assn., Ind. Acad. Libr. Assn., Ind. Corp. and Network Libr. Assn., Ind. Libr. Fedn., Assn. Ednl. Comm. and Tech., Autisim Soc. Am., Assn. Ind. Media Educators (chmn. auditing com. 1979—81), Ind. Assn. Ednl. Comms. and Tech. (dist. dir. 1972—76), Am. Assn. Sch. Librs., Phi Delta Kappa. Republican. Unitarian-Universalist. Avocations: photography, stamp collecting/philately, coin collecting/numismatics, genealogy. Home: 4507 W Burton Dr Muncie IN 47304-3575

YEARGAN, MICHAEL, scenic designer; MFA, Yale U., 1973. Assoc. prof. design Yale Sch. Drama, New Haven; resident designer Yale Repertory Theatre. Scenic designer Becket, London's West End, Cyrano de Bergerac, Napoleon, Present Laughter, Stratford Festival, Can., Noises Off!, (Operas) Otello, Met. Opera, Ariadne auf Naxos, Cosi Fan Tutti, Don Giovanni, Susanna, The Great Gatsby, Norma, NYC Opera, Madama Butterfly, Tosca, La Finta, Giardiniera, Central Park, Previn's A Streetcar Named Desire, San Francisco Opera, Luisa Miller, Dead Man Walking, Simon Boccanegra, Cold Sassy Tree, Houston Grand Opera, Royal Opera House, London, Australian Opera, La Scala, Staatsoper, Vienna, The Nutcracker, San Francisco Ballet, The Rainmaker, 2006, (Off-Broadway) Dinah Was, Juvenalia, (Broadway Shows) Terrence McNally's The Ritz, Bad Habits, Hay Fever, Ah, Wilderness!, Athol Fugard's A Lesson From Aloes, The Light in the Piazza, Lincoln Ctr. Theater, 2005— (Tony Award for best scenic design of a musical,

2005, Drama Desk award outstanding set design of a musical, 2005), Awake and Sing!, 2006 (Drama Desk award outstanding set design of a play, 2006), Cymbeline, 2007, South Pacific, 2008 (Drama Desk award outstanding set design of a musical, 2008, Tony award best scenic design of a musical, 2008). Office: Yale Sch Drama PO Box 208325 New Haven CT 06520 also: Lincoln Ctr Theater 150 W 65th St New York NY 10023

YEARWOOD, DOUGLAS LYMAN, legal association administrator, researcher; b. Durham, NC, Feb. 2, 1965; s. Clarence Lyman and Deanna Rogers Yearwood; m. Natalia Voinova Yearwood, May 24, 2002; 1 child, Alexei Lyman. BS, NC Wesleyan Coll., Rocky Mt., 1987; MS, NC Ctrl. U., Durham, 1990. Bar: Internat. Assn. Law Enforcement Planners 2000; cert. pub. mgr. NC Office State Pers., 2001. Rsch. analyst US Bur. Prisons, Butner, NC, 1990—92; social rsch. assoc. NC Dept. Justice, Raleigh, 1992—94; social rsch. assoc., criminal justice planner NC Criminal Justice Analysis Ctr., Raleigh, 1994—97, rsch. dir., 1997—. Co-author: (book) Effective Program Practices for At-Risk Youth. Pres. Justice Rsch. & Stats. Assn., Washington, 2005—07. Recipient award, Omicron Delta Kappa Leadership Soc., 1986, Thrasher award, 2000, 2006, Alumnus award, 2005, Algernon Sidney Sullivan award; named Phillip Hoke award, 2001. Mem.: Am. Jail Assn., Nat. Sheriffs Assn., Am. Soc. Criminology, Alpha Phi Sigma, Phi Eta Sigma. Office: NC Criminal Justice Analysis Ctr 1201 Front St Ste 200 Raleigh NC 27609 Office Fax: 919-733-4625. Business E-Mail: dyearwood@ncgccd.org.

YEARWOOD, JOHN, manufacturing executive; BS in geology & environ. with honors, Oxford Brookes Univ., England. Mgmt. positions through pres. Dowell & pres. No. & So. Am. oilfield services Schlumberger, 1980—2006, sr. adv. to CEO, 2006—08; exec. v.p., pres. completions & production Smith Internat. Inc., Houston, 2008, pres., CEO, COO, 2009—. Bd. dir. NFR Energy, Sheridan Production Partners. Office: Smith Internat 16740 Hardy St Houston TX 77032*

YEARWOOD, TRISHA, country music singer, songwriter; b. Monticello, Ga., 1964; m. Chris Latham (div.); m. Robert Reynolds, May 21, 1994 (div.); m. Garth Brooks, Dec. 10, 2005. Degree in Music Bus., Belmont U. Intern MTM Records, demo singer, commercial jingles singer; recording artist MCA Records. Albums include Trisha Yearwood, 1991 (double platinum), Hearts in Armor, 1992 (Grammy nomination: Best Country Female Vocal, 1994 for "Walkaway Joe"), The Song Remembers When, 1993, Thinkin' About You, 1995, Everybody Knows, 1996, (songbook) A Collection of Hits, 1997, Where Your Road Leads, 1998, Real Live Woman, 2000, Inside Out, 2001, Jasper County, 2005, Live in Concert, 2007, Heaven, Heartache & the Power of Love, 2007; back-up vocalist Garth Brooks albums; opening act Garth Brooks Tour, 1991; TV appearances on TNN American Music Shop, The Tonight Show, Late Night with David Letterman, Good Morning America, A&E Live By Request, 1998 Academy Awards, 1996 Summer Olympic Closing Ceremonies. Named Best New Country Artist by Am. Music Awards, 1992, Top New Female Vocalist by Acad. Country Music, 1992, Top Female Vocalist of Yr., 1998; Top Female Vocalist of Yr., Country Mus. Assn., 1997, 98; first female in country music history to have debut single reach #1 on charts with She's in Love with the Love, 1991; recipient Grammy awards for best female country vocal, 1998, best country vocal collaboration (with Aaron Neville) 1994, (with Garth Brooks), 1998.

YEATER, KATHLEEN WECKER, musician, educator; b. York, Pa., Oct. 2, 1947; d. Philip Emanuel and Kathryn Diehl Wecker; m. Robert Alan Yeater, Mar. 20, 1982; children: Amy Tomassone, Jennifer Diehl Berman; stepchildren: Laurie Bryant, Jennifer Dorrough. BSc in Music Edn., Indiana U. of Pa., 1969. Orch. dir., string instr. Susquehannock H.S. So. York County Sch. Dist., Glen Rock, Pa., 1974—2006; ret., 2006. Violinist York Symphony Orch., 1974—, personnel coord., 2007—; violinist Salem String Quartet, York, 1983—; dir. York Jr. Symphony Orch., 1993—, condr., 1993—; guest condr. instrumental ensembles; mem. York New Salem Borough Coun., 2007; pres. elect Pa. & Del. String Tchrs. Assn. Bd. mem. York Youth Symphony, 1985—2001. Recipient Outstanding Tchr. award, South Ctrl. Pa. Joint Coun. Sch. Improvement, Shippensburg U., 1989; named Outstanding Dir. Pa., Sch. Band & Orch. Mag., 1999. Mem.: NEA, Pa. & Del. Chpt. of Am. String Tchrs. Assn. (pres. elect), Nat. Sch. Orch. Assn. (past pres. Pa. chpt. 1988—89, named Orch. Dir. of Yr. Pa. chpt. 2004, named Nat. Dir. of Yr. 1996), Am. Fedn. Musicians, Pa. Sch. Educators Assn., Am. String Tchr Assn., Music Educators Nat. Conf., Pa. Music Educators Assn. (Citation of Excellence 1986). Lutheran. Avocations: music, reading, gardening, cooking. Home: 4032 Robin Hood Dr York PA 17408 Personal E-mail: bobkathyyeater@comcast.net.

YEATES, MARIE R., lawyer; b. New Orleans, Feb. 24, 1956; BS summa cum laude, La. State U., 1977, JD, 1980. Bar: La. 1980, U.S. Ct. Appeals (5th cir.) 1981, U.S. Ct. Appeals (11th cir.) 1981, Tex. 1982, Tex. Supreme Ct. 1982, U.S. Dist. Ct. (so. dist.) Tex. 1985, U.S. Supreme Ct. 1986, U.S. Ct. Appeals (9th cir.) 1998, U.S. Dist. Ct. (no. dist.) Tex. 2001, U.S. Ct. Appeals (10th cir.) 2002, U.S. Ct. Appeals (7th cir.) 2004. Ptnr., co-head Appellate Sect. Vinson & Elkins LLP, Houston, 1990—. Office: Vinson & Elkins LLP First City Tower 1001 Fannin St, Ste 2300 Houston TX 77002 Office Phone: 713-758-4576. E-mail: myeates@velaw.com.

YEATMAN, HARRY CLAY, biologist, educator; b. Ashwood, Tenn., June 22, 1916; s. Trezevant Player and Mary (Wharton) Y.; m. Jean Hansford Anderson, Nov. 24, 1949; children— Henry Clay, Jean Hansford. AB, U. NC, Chapel Hill, 1939, MA, 1942, PhD, 1953; student, Cornell U., Ithaca, NY, summer 1937. Asst. prof. biology U. of South, Sewanee, Tenn., 1950-54, asso. prof., 1954-60, prof., 1960—, Kenan prof., 1980—, chmn. dept., 1972-76, elderhostel tchr., 1987-88. Vis. prof. marine biology Va. Inst. Marine Sci., Gloucester Point, summer 1967; cons. Smithsonian Instn., Sci. Applications, Inc., La Jolla, Calif., Ctrs. for Disease Control, Atlanta, WHO, Ecol. Analysts, Inc., Balt., Duke Power Co., Charlotte, N.C., Helminthic Disease Branch. Contbr. articles to profl. jours. Served with AUS, 1942-46. Gen. Edn. Bd. fellow, 1941-42; Brown Found. fellow, 1984, State Naturalist award Tenn. Dept. Environ. & Concervation. Fellow AAAS; mem. Soc. Systematic Biology (charter), Soc. Limnology and Oceanography (charter), Soc. Ichthyology and Herpetology, Tenn. Acad. Sci., Am. Micros. Soc., Am. Ornithologists Union, Tenn. Ornithol. Soc., Tenn. Archeol. Soc., Nat. Speleological Soc., Blue Key, Phi Beta Kappa, Sigma Xi, Omicron Delta Kappa, Sigma Nu. Republican. Episcopalian. Home: 199 Cloudcroft Pl Jumpoff Rd Sewanee TN 37375 Office: 735 University Ave Sewanee TN 37383-1000 Home Phone: 931-598-5367; Office Phone: 931-598-1000. Office Fax: 931-598-1145.

YEATMAN, HENRY CLAY, mechanical engineer; b. Sewanee, Tenn., July 13, 1957; s. Harry and Jean Yeatman; m. Paula Ann Hess, Oct. 7, 2000. BA in Math., U. South, Sewanee, Tenn., 1976—79; B of Mech. Engring., Ga. Inst. Tech., Atlanta, 1979—81. Tire devel. engr. B. F. Goodrich, Akron, Ohio, 1981—85; rsch. engr. Honda R&D Americas, Torrance, Calif., 1985—89; sr. engr. Am. Honda, Alpharetta, Ga., 1989—. Mem.: Soc. Automotive Entrs., Sports Car Club Am. Unitarian. Office: American Honda 4900 Marconi Dr Alpharetta GA 30005

YEATS, ROBERT SHEPPARD, geologist, educator; b. Miami, Fla., Mar. 30, 1931; s. Robert Sheppard and Carolyn Elizabeth (Rountree) Y.; m. Lillian Eugenia Bowie, Dec. 30, 1952 (dec. Apr. 1991); children: Robert Bowie, David Claude, Stephen Paul, Kenneth James, Sara Elizabeth; m. Angela M. Hayes, Jan. 7, 1993. BA, U. Fla., 1952; MS, U. Wash., 1956, PhD, 1958. Registered geologist, Oreg., Calif., Wash. Geologist, petroleum exploration and prodn. Shell Oil Co., Ventura and L.A., Calif., 1958-67, Shell Devel. Co., Houston, 1967; assoc. prof. geology Ohio U., Athens, 1967-70, prof., 1970-77; prof. geology Oreg. State U., Corvallis, 1977-97, prof. oceanography, 1991-97, prof. emeritus, 1997—, chmn. dept., 1977-85; geologist U.S. Geol. Survey, 1968, 69, 75, Glomar Challenger scientist, 1971, co-chief scientist, 1973-74, 78; mem. Oreg. Bd. Geologist Examiners, 1981-83; chmn. Working Group 1 Internat. Lithosphere Program, 1987-90, chmn. task force group on paleoseismology, 1990-98; chmn. subcom. on Himalayan active faults Internat. Geol. Correlation Program, Project 206, 1984-92; mem. geophysics study com. NRC, 1987-94. Rschr. on Cenozoic tectonics of So. Calif., Oreg., Wash., New Zealand and Himalaya; active faults of Calif. Transverse Ranges, deep-sea drilling in Ea. Pacific; vis. scientist New Zealand Geol. Survey, 1983-84, 99, Geol. Survey of Japan, 1992, Inst. de Phys. du Globe de Paris, 1993, So. Calif. Earthquake Ctr.; sr. cons. Earth Cons. Internat., 1997—, ptnr., 2001—. Author: The Geology of Earthquakes, 1997, Living with Earthquakes in the Pacific Northwest, 1998, 2d edit., 2004, Living with Earthquakes in California-A Survivor's Guide, 2001. Mem. Ojai (Calif.) City Planning Commn., 1961-62, Ojai City Coun., 1962-65. 1st lt. U.S. Army, 1952-54. Named Richard H. Jahns Disting. Lectr. in Engring. Geology, 1995; Ohio U. rsch. fellow, 1973-74; grantee NSF, U.S. Geol. Survey. Fellow AAAS, Geol. Soc. Am. (chmn. structural geology and tectonics divsn. 1984-85, chmn., Cordilleran sect. 1988-89, assoc. editor bull. 1987-89); mem. Am. Assn. Petroleum Geologists (Outstanding Educator award Pacific sect. 1991, Michel T. Halbouty human needs award 1998), Am. Geophys. Union, Seismol. Soc. Am., Earthquake Engring. Rsch. Inst. Home: 1654 NW Crest Pl Corvallis OR 97330-1812 Office: Oreg State U Dept Geoscis Corvallis OR 97331-5506 Office Phone: 541-737-1226.

YEATTS, FRANK RICHARD, retired physics professor; s. Frank E. and Bessie Yeatts (Stepmother); m. Loraine Gauvreau, June 18, 1960; children: Michael, Kevin. PhD in Physics, U. Ariz., Tucson, 1964. Prof. emeritus Colo. Sch. Mines, Golden, 1994. Achievements include research in solid state physics and geophysics. Avocations: mountaineering, environmental action. Office: Dept Physics Colo Sch Mines Golden CO 80401 Business E-Mail: fyeatts@mines.edu.

YEAZELL, RUTH BERNARD, English language educator; b. NYC, Apr. 4, 1947; d. Walter and Annabelle (Reich) Bernard; m. Stephen C. Yeazell, Aug. 14, 1969 (div. 1980). BA with high honors, Swarthmore Coll., 1967; MPhil, Yale U., 1970, PhD, 1971. Asst. prof. English Boston U., 1971-74, UCLA, 1975-77, assoc. prof., 1977-80, prof., 1980-91, Yale U., New Haven, 1991—, dir. grad. studies, 1993-98, 2007, Chace family prof., 1995—, chair, 2000—05. Author: Language and Knowledge in the Late Novels of Henry James, 1976, Death and Letters of Alice James, 1981, Fictions of Modesty: Women and Courtship in the English Novel, 1991, Harems of the Mind: Passages of Western Art and Literature, 2000, Art of the Everyday: Dutch Painting and the Realist Novel, 2008; assoc. editor Nineteenth-Century Fiction, 1977-80; editor: Sex, Politics and Science in the 19th Century Novel, 1986, Henry James: A Collection of Critical Essays, 1994. Dir. Lewis Walpole Libr., 1996—. Woodrow Wilson fellow, 1967-68, Guggenheim fellow, 1979-80, NEH fellow, 1988-89, Pres.'s rsch. fellow U. Calif., 1988-89, Getty scholar, 2003-04 (declined), Bellagio Ctr. Residency scholar, 2005, Walter Hines Page fellow, Nat. Humanities Ctr., 2009. Fellow: Acad. Arts and Scis; Mem. MLA (exec. coun. 1985-88), English Inst. (supervising com. 1983-86). Office: Yale U Dept English New Haven CT 06520-8302 Business E-Mail: ruth.yeazell@yale.edu.

YECKE, CHERI PIERSON, educational researcher, administrator, policymaker, writer; b. St. Paul, Feb. 5, 1955; d. Leo Sylvester and Marceline Mae (Intihar) Pierson; m. Dennis Joseph Yecke, Dec. 22, 1973; children: Anastasia, Tiffany. BA, U. Hawaii, 1975; MST, U. Wis., River Falls, 1984; PhD, U. Va., 2001. Apptd. mem. State Bd. Edn., State of Va., 1995—98, dep. sec. edn., 1998—2001, sec. edn., 2001—02; dir. tchr. quality and pub. sch. choice US Dept. Edn., 2002—03; sr. adv. to White House on USA Freedom Corps., 2003; commr. edn. State of Minn., 2003—04; disting. sr. fellow for edn. and social policy Ctr. of the Am. Experiment, 2004—05; chancellor for K-12 edn. State of Fla., Tallahassee, 2005—. Author: The War Against Excellence: The Rising Tide of Mediocrity in America's Middle Schools, 2003, Mayhem in the Middle: How Middle Schools Have Failed America and How to Make Them Work, 2005. Mem.: Am. Coun. Trustees & Alumni, Nat. Assn. Scholars. Republican. Home: 139 Belle Meade Dr Searcy AR 72143-7037 Office Phone: 850-245-0509.

YEDJOU, CLEMENT GUY, science educator, researcher; s. Christine Kouanang and Maurice Seumo; m. Laurette Thuisseu Yedjou, Jan. 14, 2004; 1 child, Malick Thounwou. PhD in Environ. Sci., Jackson State U., Miss., 2006. Cert. in Distance Learning Edn. Jackson State U., 2006. Coord. Jackson State U., 2001—, distance learning prof., 2006, rsch. asst. prof., 2006—. Rsch. mentor, advisor Jackson State U., 2004—08. Recipient Rsch. award, Ctr. U. Scholar, 2006—07. Mem.: Am. Assn. Cancer Rsch. Roman Cath. Achievements include discovery of leukemia therapy drug. Avocations: reading, travel, tennis. Office: Jackson State Univ Box 18540 Jackson MS 39217 Office Fax: 601-979-5853. Business E-Mail: clement.yedjou@jsums.edu.

YEE, ALFRED ALPHONSE, structural engineer, consultant; b. Honolulu, Aug. 5, 1925; s. Yun Sau and Kam Ngo (Lum) Y.; m. Janice Ching (div.); children: Lailan, Mark, Eric, Malcolm, Ian; m. Elizabeth Wong, June 24, 1975; children: Suling, Trevor, I'Ling. BSCE, Rose Hulman Inst. Tech., 1948, Dr. of Engring. (hon.), 1976; MEng in Structures, Yale U., 1949. Registered profl. engr., Hawaii, Calif., Guam, Tex., Minn., No. Marianas Islands. With civil engring. dept. Dept. Pub. Works, Terr. of Hawaii, Honolulu, 1949-51; structural engr. 14th Naval Dist., Pearl Harbor, Hawaii, 1951-54; pvt. practice structural engring. cons. Honolulu, 1954-55; structural engring. cons. Park & Yee Ltd., Honolulu, 1955-60; pres. Alfred A. Yee & Assocs. Inc., Honolulu, 1960-82; v.p., tech. adminstr. Alfred. A. Yee div. Leo A. Daly, Honolulu, 1982-89; pres. Applied Tech. Corp., Honolulu, 1984—. Patentee in concrete tech., land and sea structures; contbr. articles to profl. jours. Served with U.S. Army, 1946-47. Named Engr. of Yr., Hawaii Soc. Profl. Engrs., 1969, one of Men Who Made Marks in 1970, Honolulu, 1970. Mem. ASCE (hon.), NSPE, CASE, ACEC, NAE, Am. Concrete Inst. (hon.), Post-Tensioning Inst., Precast-Prestressed Concrete Inst. (PCI medal of honor award 1997), Prestressed Concrete Inst. (State of Art award 1991), Structural Engrs. Assn. Hawaii, Yale Sci. and Engring. Assn. (Martin P. Korn award 1965, Robert J. Lyman award 1984), Singapore Concrete Inst. Avocations: golf, swimming. Office: 1217 Palolo Ave Honolulu HI 96816-2525 E-mail: atc@lava.net.

YEE, CASSIAN K., oncologist, researcher; BSc in Medicine, U. Manitoba, 1986, MD, 1986. Postdoctoral fellow Ontarion Cancer Inst., 1987—89; resident Stanford U., 1989—91; oncologist U. Wash. Sch. Medicine, 1993—, assoc. prof., 2004—; oncologist, scientist Fred Hutchinson Cancer Rsch. Ctr., 1998—, assoc. mem. clin. rsch. program in immunology, 1995—98, dir. immune monitoring lab, 2003—. Contbr. several articles to peer-reviewed publ. Mem.: Soc. for Biol. Therapy, Am. Assn. Immunologist, Am. Assn. for Cancer Rsch. Address: Seattle Cancer Care Alliance 825 Eastlake Ave E PO Box 19023 Seattle WA 98109-1023 Office: Fred Hutchinson Cancer Rsch Ctr 1100 Fairview Ave N PO Box 19024 D3-100 Seattle WA 98109-1024 Office Phone: 206-667-6287. Office Fax: 206-667-7983. Business E-Mail: cyee@fhcrc.org.*

YEE, FLORENCE, library director; Mgr. Pearl City Bookmobile, Hawaii Kai Pub. Libr.; br. mgr. Kaimuki Pub. Libr.; acting dir. Hawaii State Libr., Honolulu, 2003—04, dir., 2004—, Hawaii State Libr. for Blind and Physically Handicapped, Honolulu, 2004—. Mem. Congresswoman Patsy T. Mink Commn. Mem.: Hawaii Libr. Assn. Office: Hawaii State Libr 478 S King St Honolulu HI 96813-2901 Office Phone: 808-586-3555. Office Fax: 808-733-8426.

YEE, LELAND Y., state legislator; b. China; 4 children. BA, U. Calif., Berkeley, 1970; MA, San Francisco State U., 1972; PhD in Child Psychology, U. Hawaii, 1975. Pres. Bd. Edn. City of San Francisco, 1988-96, mem. Bd. Suprs., 1996—2002; mem. Calif. State Assembly, 2002—06, speaker pro tempore, 2004—06; asst. pres. pro tempore Calif. State Senate, 2007—, mem. Dist. 8 Calif., 2007—. Pres. Nat. Asian Pacific Am. Caucus of State Legislators, 2004—. Address: San Francisco State Bldg 455 Golden Gate Ave Ste 14200 San Francisco CA 94102 Office: State Capitol Rm 4074 Sacramento CA 95814 Address: 400 S El Camino Rd Ste 630 San Mateo CA 94402 Office Phone: 916-651-4008. Business E-Mail: senator.yee@senate.ca.gov.*

YEE, SANDRA GAYLE BROWN, library director, dean; b. Benzonia, Mich., July 17, 1949; d. Al Powell and Maxine G. (Wallace) Brown; m. Johnny Yee, June 29, 1974; 1 child, Melissa Ann. BA, Western Mich. U., 1970, MLS, 1973; EdD, U. Mich., 1979. Libr., coord. libr. svcs. Muskegon CC, Mich., 1973—82; coord. access svcs. Univ. Libr. Ea. Mich. U., Ypsilanti, 1982—90, assoc. dean learning resources and tech., 1990—2001; dean univ. libr. sys. Wayne State U., Detroit, 2001—. Co-author (with M. Boone and R. Bullard): Training Student Library Assistants, 1991. Bd. trustees Online Computer Libr. Ctr., 2008—. Mem.: ALA, Mich. Libr. Assn. (treas. 1989—91, pres.-elect 1992—93, pres. 1993—95), Assn. Coll. and Rsch. Librs. (chair univ. libr. sect. 2005). Office: Wayne State U Univ Libraries Detroit MI 48202 Office Phone: 313-577-4020. Office Fax: 313-577-5525. E-mail: sandra.yee@wayne.edu.

YEE, SHIRLEY JO-ANN, history professor; b. NYC, Mar. 6, 1959; d. Audrey Joan Wong and Donald Yu Yee; life ptnr. Diane Eileen. PhD, Ohio State U., Columbus, 1987. Assoc. prof. U. Wash., Seattle, 1988—. Mem.: Orgn. of Am. Historians. Democrat. Office: Univ Wash Stevens Way Seattle WA 98195 Business E-Mail: sjyee@u.washington.edu.

YEE, SIENHO, law educator; b. Zhanjiang, Guangdong, China, July 9, 1965; BA, Brandeis U., 1989; JD, Columbia U., 1993. Bar: U.S. Ct. Appeals (3rd cir.) 1994, N.Y. 1994, U.S. Supreme Ct. 2004. Law clk. Judge Robert Cowen, US Ct. Appeals (3rd cir.), Trenton, NJ, 1993—94, Appeals Chamber, UN Internat. Criminal Tribunal for Former Yugoslavia, The Hague, Netherlands, 1995—96; counsel legal dept. Internat. Monetary Fund, Washington, 1996—97; tutor internat. law St Hugh's Coll., Oxford U., England, 1999—2000; vis. asst. prof. Northwestern U. Law Sch., Chgo., 2000; lectr. law Queen Mary, U. London, 2001; assoc. prof. law U. Colo. Law Sch., Boulder, 2001—06; prof., dir. Silk Rd. Inst. Internat. Law Xi'an Jiaotong U., China, 2006—. Assoc. Sullivan & Cromwell, NYC. Author: Towards an International Law of Coprogressiveness, 2004; editor-in-chief: Chinese Jour. Internat. Law, 2003; editor: International Law in the Post-Cold War World, 2001, International Crime and Punishment, vol. 1, 2003, International Crime and Punishment, vol. 2, 2004; contbr. articles to profl. jours. Wien Internat. scholar, Brandeis U., 1987—89, Harlan Fiske Stone scholar, Columbia Law Sch., 1990—92. Mem.: Phi Beta Kappa. Office: U Colo Law Sch 401 UCB Boulder CO 80309-0401 Office Fax: 707-788-4178; Home Fax: 707-788-4178. Personal E-mail: yee@sienhoyee.org.

YEGULALP, TUNCEL M., mining engineer, educator; b. Konya, Turkey, Nov. 5, 1937; came to U.S., 1963; s. Faik Suleyman and Selma Safiye (Karatay) Y.; m. Sevinc Guneri, July 5, 1963; children: Ali, Serdar. BS, Tech. U., Istanbul, 1961; DEngring. Sci., Columbia U., 1968. Mining engr. M.T.A., Ankara, Turkey, 1961-63, chief feasibility studies group, 1971; rsch. engr. Mobil Rsch., Paulsboro, NJ, 1967-69; chief sys. cons. Sisag Ltd., Ankara, 1971-72; asst. prof. Columbia U., NYC, 1972-75; assoc. prof. Henry Krumb Sch. Mines, 1975-85, prof., 1985—. Dir. N.Y. Mining and Mineral Resources Inst. Rsch., 1987—; elected permanent mem. U.S. del. World Mining Congress, 1993. Author articles in field. Served to 2d lt. C.E. Turkish Army, 1969-71. Internat. AEC fellow, Vienna, 1963; Krumb fellow, Columbia U., 1964, Campbell fellow, 1965. Mem. AIME, Internat. Higher Edn. Acad. Scis., Turkish Studies Assn., Inst. for Ops. Rsch. and the Mgmt. Scis., Sigma Chi. Muslim. Office: Columbia U 926B SWM MC4711 500 W 120th St New York NY 10027 Home Phone: 201-836-2099; Office Phone: 212-854-2984. Business E-Mail: yegulalp@columbia.edu.

YEH, EDWARD TU-HSING, cardiologist, educator, medical researcher; arrived in U.S., 1971; s. Jack and Pi-Lien Yeh; m. Hui-Ming Chang, Nov. 6, 1982; 1 child, Andrew Allen. MD, U. Calif., Davis, 1980. Diplomate Am. Bd. Cardiovascular Diseases. Asst. prof. Harvard Med. Sch., Boston, 1987—92; assoc. prof. U. Tex. Med. Sch., Houston, 1992—97, prof., 1997—2000; prof., chmn. cardiology MD Anderson Cancer Ctr., Houston, 2000—. Named Established Investigator, Am. Heart Assn., 1992. Mem.: Am. Heart Assn. (pres. Houston chpt. 2004—05), Assn. Am. Physicians (life). Achievements include patents in field; patents pending in field. Office: MD Anderson Cancer Ctr 1515 Holcombe 449 Houston TX 77030

YEH, GOUR-TSYH, environmental engineer, educator; m. Shu-Shen Kuo; children: Apollo Bin-Chuan, Adam Bin-Chi. BS, Nat. Taiwan U., Taipei, 1964; MS, Syracuse U., NY, 1967; PhD, Cornell U., Ithaca, NY, 1969. Cert. profl. engr., Taiwan, 1965, NY, 1973, Mass., 1974, Calif., 1976, Tenn., 1978, Pa., 1992. Rsch. assoc. Cornell U., 1969—71; vis. assoc. prof. Nat. Taiwan U., 1971; vis. rsch. scientist NASA, Houston, 1971—72; sr. engr. Ebasco, Inc., NYC, 1972—73; sr. environ. engr. Stone and Webster Engring. Co., Boston, 1973—75, sr. hydraulic engr., 1976—77; project engr. Tetra Tech., Inc., Pasadena, Calif., 1975—76; sr. rsch. staff Oak Ridge Nat. Lab., Tenn., 1977—89; prof. Pa. State U.,

Univ. Pk., 1989—2000; provost prof. U. Ctrl. Fla., Orlando, 2000—. Sr. vis. scientist Robert Kerr Environ. Lab., EPA, Ada, Okla., 1995—96; vis. fellow Pacific NW Nat. Lab., Richland, Wash., 1996; chief prof. Nat. Ctrl. U., Jhong-Li, Taiwan, 2006—, Nat. Chiao-Tung U., Hsinchu, Taiwan, 2006—07; chief engr. Provisional Nat. Ctr. Typhoon and Flood Rsch., Hsin-Chu, Taiwan, 2006—07. Contbr. articles to profl. jour. Recipient Outstanding Resarch award, Pa. State U., 2000, Disting. Rschr. award, U. Ctrl. Fla., 2005, Grad. Tchg. award, 2008. Mem.: AGU. Office: Univ Ctrl Fla 4000 Central Florida Blvd Orlando FL 32816 Office Fax: 407-823-3315. Personal E-mail: ggtyeh@gmail.com. Business E-Mail: gyeh@mail.ucf.edu.

YEH, HSU-CHONG, radiology educator; b. Taipei, Taiwan, Mar. 30, 1937; came to US, 1973; s. Ping-Hui and Ah-Chu (Chuang) Y.; m. Cha-Pying Yeh, Sept. 26, 1964; children: David, Benjamin. MD, Nat. Taiwan U., 1962. Diplomate Am. Bd. Radiology. Rotating intern U. Alberta Hosp., Edmonton, Canada, 1964—65; resident diagnostic radiology Montreal Gen. Hosp. McGill U., Canada, 1969—72, fellow diagnostic ultrasound Montreal Gen. Hosp., 1972—73; mem. active med. staff Soldier's Meml. Hosp., Campbellton, NB, Canada, 1967—69; assoc. Mt. Sinai Sch. Medicine, NYC, 1973—75, asst. prof. radiology, 1976—78, assoc. prof., 1979—86, prof., 1986—. Cons. radiology VA Hosp., Bronx, NY, 1977-87. Author: Radiology of the Adrenals, 1982; contbg. author: Progress in Liver Disease, 1979, Frontiers in Liver Disease, 1981, Ultrasound Annual, 1982, 85, Ultrasound in Urology, 1984, Ultrasonography of the Urinary Tract, 1991, Surgical Management of Urologic Disease, 1991; contbr. articles to med. jour. 2d lt. Armored Corps, Taiwan Army, 1962-63. Fellow Soc. Radiologists in Ultrasound; mem. Am. Inst. Ultrasound in Medicine (sr.), Radiol. Soc. N.Am. (sci. exhibit award 1988-2000), Computerized Radiology Soc., Am. Roentgen Ray Soc. (sci. exhibit award 1988), NY Roentgen Ray Soc. Avocations: painting, sculpting, jogging, movies. Office: Mt Sinai Med Ctr One Gustave L Levy Pl New York NY 10029-6574 Office Phone: 212-241-6302. Business E-Mail: hsu-chong.yeh@mountsinai.org.

YEH, JAMES KUEN-JANN, nutritionist; b. Kuen-Ming, Yuen Nang, China, June 27, 1942; came to U.S., 1967; s. Jin Gee-shan Yeh and Shing (Lan) Tsao; m. Jenny Ming, Feb. 1, 1969; children: Berhan S., Bervan Y. BS, Nat. Taiwan U., 1965; MS, U. Wis., 1968, PhD, 1974. Rsch. asst. U. Wis., Madison, 1969-74; rsch. assoc. Brookhaven Nat. Lab., Upton, N.Y., 1974-76; rsch. biochemist Nassau County Med. Ctr., East Meadow, N.Y., 1976-78; dir. metabolism lab. Winthrop-Univ. Hosp., Mineola, N.Y., 1978—; asst. prof. SUNY, Stony Brook, 1980-87, assoc. prof., 1988-97, prof., 1998—. Adj. prof. L.I. U., Brookville, N.Y., 1980-83; nutrition cons. Life Health Ctr., West Babylon, N.Y., 1986-88; dir. metabolism lab. Winthrop-Univ. Hosp., Mineola, 1978—. Contbr. articles to profl. jours. Grantee NIH, 1975, Retirement Rsch. Found., 1986, NASA, 1997. Fellow: Am. Coll. Nutrition; mem.: Internat. Bone Mineral Soc., Internat. Chinese Hard Tissue Soc., Am. Coll. Sports Medicine, Am. Soc. of Bone Mineral Rsch. Home: 710 First Ave New Hyde Park NY 11040 Office: Winthrop-Univ Hosp Ste 501 222 Sta Plz Mineola NY 11501-3987 E-mail: JYEH@Winthrop.org.

YEH, RAYMOND WEI-HWA, architect, educator; b. Shanghai, Feb. 25, 1942; came to U.S., 1958, naturalized, 1976; s. Herbert Hwan-Ching and Joyce Bo-Ding (Kwan) Y.; m. Hsiao-Yen Chen, Sept. 16, 1967; children— Bryant Po Yung, Clement Chung-Yung, Emily Su-Yung. BA, U. Oreg., 1965, B.Arch., 1967; M.Arch., U. Minn., 1969. Cert. Nat. Coun. Archtl. Registration Bds.; registered architect, Tex., Okla., Calif., Hawaii. Draftsman, designer various archtl. firms, 1965-68; design arch. Ellerbe Architects, St. Paul, 1968-70; v.p., dir. design Sorey, Hill, Binnicker, Oklahoma City, 1973-74; prin. arch. Raymond W.H. Yeh & Assos., Norman, Okla., 1974-80; asst. prof. to prof. U. Okla., Norman, 1970-79; head dept. architecture, prof. Calif. Poly. State U., San Luis Obispo, 1979-83; dean Coll. Architecture U. Okla., Norman, 1983-92; prin. arch. W.H. Raymond Yeh, Norman, 1983-93; dean sch. architecture U. Hawaii at Manoa, Honolulu, 1992—2007, prof., 2008—; prin. arch. Yeh Studio, 2007—. Profl. adviser Neighborhood Conservation and Devel. Center, Oklahoma City, 1977 79 Works include: St. Thomas More U. Parish and Student Center, Norman, Summit Ridge Center Retirement Community, Harrah, Okla., (recipient Nat. Design award Guild Religious Architecture 1978). Nat. Endowment for Arts fellow, 1978-79 Fellow AIA (dir., pres. Okla. chpt. 1986, design awards, nat. com. chmn. 1989); mem. Calif. Coun. Archtl. Edn. (dir., pres. 1982-83), Okla. Found. for Architecture (founding chair bd. 1989-90), Asian Soc. Okla. (award of Excellence 1992), Asia Pacific Ctr. for Arch. (founding bd. dirs. 1996). Presbyterian. Office: U Hawaii Manoa Sch Architecture Honolulu HI 96822 Business E-Mail: ray@yehstudio.com.

YEHEZKEL, SHAUL, orthodontist; m. Batel Itzhak, July 4, 1993; children: LeeEl, Sapeer, Sivan, Liad. DMD, Harvard, Boston, 1999. Pediatric dental bd. cert. Am. Bd. Pediatric Dentistry, 2008, orthodontic bd. cert. Am. Bd. Orthodontics, 2007. Mem. choc craniofacial team CHOC Hosp., Orange, Calif., 2002—; orthodontic program lectr. UCLA, 2002—. Product evaluator 3M Unitek, Monrovia, Calif., 2008—. Contbr. articles to orthodonic publ. Dental edn. tchr., Irvine, Calif., 2002. Recipient Omicron Kappa Upsilon award, Nat. Dental Honor Soc., 1999. Mem.: Am. Lingual Orthodontic Assn., Calif. Soc. Pediatric Dentistry, Am. Cleft Palate Craniofacial Assn., Pacific Coast Soc. Orthodontics, Calif. Dental Assn., Am. Assn. Orthodontits, Am. Acad. Pediatric Dentistry. Avocations: piano, guitar, bicycling, woodworking. Office: Irvine Ped Dentistry and Orthodontics 4902 Irvine Center Drive Suite 111 Irvine CA 92604

YEHIA, BALIGH R., physician; b. Aramoun, Lebanon, Dec. 19, 1981; s. Ramzi and Ekram Yehia. MD, U. Fla., Gainesville, 2009. Resident Johns Hopkins U. Sch. Medicine Dept. Medicine, Balt., 2006—; fellow U. Pa., Sch. Medicine, Phila., 2009—. Trustee MedChi, Md. State Med. Soc., Balt., 2007—09. Named to Hall of Fame, U. Fla., 2003; G.L. Schiebler Legislative fellowship, Fla. Med. Assn., 2006, Outstanding Four Yr. Scholar, U. Fla., 2003. Mem.: Am. Pub. Heath Assn., ACP (coun. mem. 2008—, Health and Pub. Policy Com. 2008—), AMA (del., house of dels. 2006—, chair, resident and fellow sect. 2008—09, resident & fellow 2009—, Resident and Fellow Leadership award 2007), Gold Humanism Honor Soc., Alpha Omega Alpha. Achievements include research in HIV health care utilization, health care policy. Personal E-mail: byehia@gmail.com.

YEHIA, SHERIF ABDEL AZIZ, civil engineer, educator; b. Cairo, July 1, 1963; s. Abdel Aziz Yehia and Ehsan Ibraham Radwan; m. Ghada Abdel Halim; children: Ayatollah Sherif, Alaa Sherif, Yousef Sherif. BSc in Civil Engring., Ain Shams U., Cairo, 1985, MS in Civil Engring., 1990; PhD in Civil Engring., U. Nebr., Lincoln, 1999. Registered profl. engr., Nebr., 1999, Mich., 2004. Asst. prof. civil engring. Western Mich. U., Kalamazoo, 2003—07, assoc. prof. civil engring., 2007—. Mem.: ASCE, Engr. Syndicate Egypt, Am. Concrete Inst. Achievements include patents in field. Avocations: tennis, travel. Office: W Mich Univ 1903 W Michigan Ave Kalamazoo MI 49008-5316 Home: PO Box 635 Portage MI 49081-0635 Office Fax: 269-276-3211. Business E-Mail: sherif.yehia@wmich.edu.

YEHUALAESHET, TESHOME E., microbiologist, educator; s. Yehualaeshet Eredie and Alyu Enate; m. Sebsibe Smret, Aug. 14, 1994. PhD, Liebig Justus U., Germany, DVM, 1995. Cert. microbiologist Germany, 1995. Asst. prof Tuskegee U., Ala., 2003—. Mem. Orhtodox Ch., Atlanta. Home: 2188 Jefferson Str Auburn AL 36830 Office: Tuskegee Univ A410 Patterson Hall Tuskegee AL 36088 Home Fax: 334-724-4110. Business E-Mail: teyehual@tuskegee.edu.

YELAMARTHI, KUMAR, engineering educator; s. Venkateswararao and Ramasundari Yelamarthi. PhD, Wright State U., Dayton, Ohio, 2008. Cert. engring. intern, Ohio, 2006. Lead grad. tchg. asst. Wright State U., Dayton, Ohio, 2002—08; asst. prof. elec. engring. Ctrl. Mich. U., Mt Pleasant, Mich., 2008—. Recipient Outstanding Tech. Dir. award, Am. Soc. Engring. Edn. North Ctrl. Sect., 2008. Mem.: Tau Beta Pi, Omicron Delta Kappa. Office: Ctrl Mich Univ Mount Pleasant MI 48859

YELENICK, MARY THERESE, lawyer; b. Denver, May 17, 1954; d. John Andrew and Maesel Joyce (Reed) Yelenick. BA magna cum laude, Colo. Coll., 1976; JD cum lau, Georgetown U., 1979. Bar: DC 1979, NY 1982, US Dist. Ct. DC 1980, US Dist. Ct. (so. and ea. dists.) NY 1982, US Ct. Appeals (DC cir.) 1981, US Ct. Appeals (5th cir.) 1995, US Ct. Appeals (4th cir.) 2006, US Supreme Ct. 1992. Law clk. to presiding justices Superior Ct., DC, 1979—81; ptnr. Chadbourne & Parke, LLP, NYC, 1981—. Contbr. articles to profl. jours. Mem.: Nat. Cath. Soc. Justice Lobby (bd. dirs. 2004—, bd. chair 2006—08), NETWORK, Phi Beta Kappa. Democrat. Roman Catholic. Home: 310 E 46th St New York NY 10017-3002 Office: Chadbourne & Parke LLP 30 Rockefeller Plz Fl 31 Ste 3550 New York NY 10112-0129

YELICH, NOLAN T., library director; b. Wis. BS, U. Wis., Oshkosh; MS, U. Wis., Madison. Dir. pub. svcs. Earl Gregg Swem Libr., Coll. William & Mary, Williamsburg, Va., 1968—73; dir. libr. svcs. Libr. Va., Richmond, 1973—94, acting state libr., 1994—95, state libr., 1994—. Recipient John Phillip Immroth Meml. award for Intellectual Freedom, ALA Intellectual Freedom Round Table, 2005. Mem.: Va. Sch. Boards Assn., Va. Libr. Assn. (past pres.), Chief Officers of State Libr. Agys. (Libr. of Congress liason 2004—06). Office: Libr of Va 800 E Broad St Richmond VA 23219 Office Phone: 804-692-3535. Office Fax: 804-692-3594. E-mail: nyelich@lva.lib.va.us.

YELIN, DAVID B., lawyer; b. Akron, Ohio, Jan. 31, 1957; BS, U. Akron, 1979; JD magna cum laude, Case Western Reserve U. Sch. Law, Cleve., 1986. CPA Ohio, 1982; bar: Ill. 1986, US Dist. Ct. (no. dist.) Ill. Ptnr. Jenner & Block, Chgo., 1986—2000, Duane Morris LLP, Chgo., 2000—. Contbr. articles to profl. jours. Bd. dirs. Respiratory Health Assn. Met. Chgo. Named an Ill. SuperLawyer, 2006; named to Ill. statewide 'Leading Lawyers' list, 2006. Mem.: ABA, Chgo. Bar Assn., Internat. Assn. Attorneys & Execs. in Corp. Real Estate. Office: Duane Morris LLP 190 S LaSalle St Ste 3700 Chicago IL 60603 Office Phone: 312-499-6778. Office Fax: 312-277-7109. Business E-Mail: DBYelin@duanemorris.com.*

YELLEN, DAVID N., dean, lawyer; b. 1957; BA, Princeton U.; JD, Cornell U. Bar: DC 1985. Law clk., fed. judge; pvt. law practice Washington; counsel to judiciary com. US House of Reps., Washington; prof. law Cornell U., NY Law Sch.; faculty mem., Max Schmertz disting. prof. law Hofstra Law Sch., Hempstead, NY, 1988—2004, dean, 2001—04; Reuschlein disting. visiting prof. Villanova U. Sch. Law, Pa., 2004—05; dean Loyola U. Sch. Law, Chgo., 2005—. Advisor on white-collar crime issues Pres. Clinton's Transition Team; lectr. in field of sentencing reform. Co-author (with T. Hutchison): Federal Sentencing and Practice, 2002; contbr. articles to profl. jours. Bd. dirs. Constl. Rights Found., Chgo. Mem.: ABA (mem. sect. on legal edn.). Office: Office of Dean U Loyola Chicago Law Sch 25 East Pearson St Chicago IL 60611*

YELLEN, JANET LOUISE, bank executive; b. Bklyn., Aug. 13, 1946; d. Julius and Anna Ruth (Blumenthal) Yellen; m. George Arthur Akerlof, July 8, 1978; 1 child, Robert Joseph. BA in Econs. summa cum laude, Brown U., Providence, 1967; PhD, Yale U., New Haven, 1971; LLD (hon.), Brown U., 1998; LHD (hon.), Bard Coll., 2000. Asst. prof. econs. Harvard U., Cambridge, Mass., 1971-76; lectr. London Sch. Econs. and Polit. Sci., Washington, 1978-80; asst. prof. econs. Sch. Bus. Adminstrn., U. Calif., Berkeley, 1980-82, assoc. prof., 1982-85, prof. Haas Sch. Bus., 1985—, Bernard T. Rocca Jr. prof. internat. bus. and trade, 1992—, Eugene E. and Catherine M. Trefethem prof. bus., 1999—; cons. div. internat. fin., Fed. Res. Sys., Washington, 1974-75, economist trade and fin. studies sect., 1977-78, mem., 1994-97; chair, Coun. Econ. Advisors Exec. Office of the Pres., Washington, 1997-99; pres., CEO Fed. Res. Bank San Francisco, 2004—. Mem. adv. panel in econs. NSF, 1977—78, 1991—92, com. visitors, econs. prog., 1996, 2004; adv. bd. Women's Econ. Round Table, 1999—, Ctr. Internat. Polit. Economy, 1999—, Jerome Levy Econs. Inst., 2002—, Calif. Assembly Select Com. on Asian Trade, 2003; bd. dirs. Economists Allied for Arms Reduction, 2002—, Delta Dental Calif., 2003—; mem. amb. adv. coun. for Marshall Scholarships, 1996—, OECD, High-Level Sustainable Devel. Group, 1999—2001, NAS Panel, Ensuring Best Presidential Sci. and Tech. Appointments, 2000; chair Pres. Interagency Com. on Women's Bus. Enterprise, 1997—99, Econ. Policy Com. Orgn. for Econ. Coop. and Devel., 1997—99; rsch. fellow MIT, Cambridge, 1974; cons. Congl. Budget Office, 1975—76, mem. panel econ. advisers, 1993—94; rsch. affiliate Yale U., 1976; fellow Yale Corp., 2000—; rsch. assoc. Nat. Bureau Econ. Rsch., 1999—; prin. investigator Russell Sage Found. Grant on Sustainable Employment, 2000; sr. adviser Macroeconomic Advisers, 2003—; mem. Brookings Panel on Econ. Activity, 1987—88, 1990—91, sr. adviser, 1989—94, adv. bd., 1999—; Yrjö Jahnsson Found. lectr. on macroecon. theory, Helsinki, 1977—78; mem. Coun. on Fgn. Rels, 1976—81. Author (with Arrow and Shavell): The Limits of the Market in Resource Allocation, 1977; assoc. editor Jour. Econ. Perspectives, 1987—91; contbr. articles to profl. jours. Recipient Maria & Sidney Rolfe award for Nat. Econ. Svc., Women's Econ. Round Table, 1997, Wilbur Lucius Cross Medal, Yale U., 1997; named one of 50 Women to Watch, Wall St. Jour., 2005; grantee NSF, 1975—77, 1990—94; fellow, 1967—71; Hon. Woodrow Wilson fellow, 1967, Guggenheim fellow, 1986—87. Fellow: Am. Acad. Arts & Scis.; mem.: Western Econ. Assn. (pres. 2003—04), Am. Econ. Assn. (adv. com. to pres. 1986—87, nominating com. 1988—90), Phi Beta Kappa. Office: Fed Res Bank San Francisco PO Box 7702 San Francisco CA 94105-7702 Office Phone: 415-974-2000.*

YELTON, DIANNE BURGESS, secondary school educator; b. Albuquerque, Nov. 23, 1954; d. Robert Allen and Elizabeth (Donnelly) B.; m. Steven John Yelton, Aug. 13, 1988. BS in Edn., Miami U., 1977, MEd, 1983; degree in Tchr. Leadership, No. Ky. U., 2003. Tchr. Defiance (Ohio) City Schs., 1977-78; jr. high devel. handicapped tchr. Princeton City Schs., Cin., 1978-79, Oak Hills Local Schs., Cin., 1979-82, tchr. primary developmentally handicapped, 1982-88; tchr. Ft. Thomas (Ky.) Ind. Schs., 1988—; English dept. chairperson, 2008—; chmn. Engish dept. Highlands Mid. Sch., 2009—. Supr. student tchrs. various sch. dists., 1980—; spkr. convs. and inservice workshops, 1979—. Recipient Outstanding Woman of No. Ky., 1998, Golden Apple Achiever award Ashland Oil, 1998, Ky. Post Golden Apple award, 1997, Tchg. Excellence award Jiffy Lube, 1997, Mem. NEA, Internat. Reading Assn., Nat. Coun. Tchrs. English, PTA, Ky. Col. (hon.). Methodist. Avocations: aerobics, spectator sports, dining out. Office: Highlands Mid Sch 2350 Memorial Pkwy Fort Thomas KY 41075-1111 Office Phone: 859-441-5222 15303. E-mail: dbyelton@yahoo.com.

YEMELYANOV, ALEXANDER M., mathematician, educator; b. Ivanovo, Russia, Jan. 31, 1953; s. Michael A. Kotik and Valentina L. Yemelyanova; m. Alla A. Zelenkevich, Nov. 12, 1961; 1 child, Alina Alexandrina. MS in Math., Moscow State U., 1975; PhD, Russian Acad. Scis., Moscow, 1980; DS, Aviation Inst., Zhukovsky, Russia, 1990. Jr., then sr. rschr. All-Union Rsch. Info. Inst., Moscow, 1975—82; dir. computer support systems divsn. Moscow Rsch. Inst. of Planning and Mgmt., 1982—89; prof. Plekhanov Russian U. Econs., Moscow, 1989—2000; adj. prof. Va. Commonwealth U., Richmond, 2000—01; prof. computer sci. Ga. Southwestern State U., Americus, 2001—. Project leader Rsch. Aviation Inst., Moscow, 1988—2000; prof. Bauman Moscow State Tech. U., 1997—99. Contbr. articles to profl. publs. Grantee, Russian State Aviation Safety Program, 1989, 1992. Mem.: Human Factors and Ergonomics Soc., Assn. Computing Machinery. Achievements include rschr. in field. Business E-Mail: ay@canes.gsw.edu.

YEMELYANOV, KONSTANTIN, research scientist, educator; MSc in Elec. Engring. (hon.), Kharkov Nat. U., Ukraine, 1996, PhD in Elec. Engring., 2000. Postdoc. rsch. fellow U. Pa., Phila., 2001—06; rsch. asst. prof. Villanova U., Pa., 2006—. Office: Villanova Univ 800 Lancaster Ave Villanova PA 19085 Business E-Mail: konstantin.yemelyanov@villanova.edu.

YEN, DAVID, information technology executive; b. Chang-hwa, Republic of China, Sept. 24, 1951; came to US, 1975. m. Grace Jen, Jan. 9, 1977; children: Irene, Christine. BSEE, Nat. Taiwan U., Taipei, 1973; MS in Elec. and Computer Engring., U. Ill., Urbana-Champaign, 1977, PhD in Elec. and Computer Engring., 1980. Sr. mem. tech. staff TRW, Inc., Sunnyvale, Calif., 1980-82; mfg. automation position IBM Rsch., San Jose, Calif., 1982-84; co-founder, dir. hardware devel. Cydrome, Inc., Milpitas, Calif., 1984—88; with Sun Microsystems, Inc., Santa Clara, Calif., 1988—, v.p., gen. mgr. enterprise systems, integrated products, enterprise server products and enterprise server engring., exec. v.p. processor and network products, exec. v.p. scalable systems, head storage group, exec. v.p. microelectronics. Mem. IEEE (sec. computer standards com. 1983-84), Eta Kappa Nu, Phi Kappa Phi. Achievements include patents in field. Office: Sun Microsystems Inc 4150 Network Cir Santa Clara CA 95054 Office Phone: 650-960-1300.

YEN, HENRY CHIN-YUAN, computer systems programmer, software engineer, consulting company executive; b. Mpls., Apr. 18, 1958; s. James and Elizabeth Y.; m. Michele Calen Yen, Oct. 8, 1988; children: Andrew, Matthew. Sr. systems programmer Grumman Data Systems Corp., Bethpage, N.Y., 1978-83; mgr. Data Ctr. On-Line Software Internat., Inc., Ft. Lee, N.J., 1983-85, lead systems programmer, 1985-88; v.p. The Galamery Co., Inc., Del., 1988—, Aegis Info. Systems, Inc, Del., 1989—. Bd. dirs. Personal Computer Systems Corp. Bd. trustees Syosset Pub. Libr., NY, 2001—05. Mem.: IEEE, Assn. Absolute Pitch/Perfect Pitch Persons (dir. 2007—), Intertel, Mensa (bd. dirs. greater N.Y. chpt. 2002—), Network and Sys. Profls. Assn., Assn. Computing Machinery. Avocations: bicycling, profl. musician. Home: PO Box 1 Hicksville NY 11802-0001 Office: Aegis Info Systems Inc PO Box 730 Hicksville NY 11802-0730 Office Phone: 516-937-3700. Business E-Mail: henry@AegisInfoSys.com.

YEN, HOPE S., journalist, lawyer; b. Austin, Tex., June 6, 1971; d. Sian L. and Beatrice H. Yen. BA with honors, U. Tex., Austin, 1993; JD, Harvard Law Sch., Cambridge, Mass., 1997. Bar: NY 1998. Atty. Chadbourne & Parke LLP, NY, 1997—99; law & bus. journalist AP, Phila., 1999—2001, bus. journalist NY, 2001—03, nat. journalist Washington, 2004—. Contbr. articles to profl. jour. Mem.: ABA, Investigative Reporters & Editors Inc., Asian Am. Journalists Assn., Tex. Execs. Alumni Assn. (life), Phi Beta Kappa Soc. Office: Associated Press 1100 13th St NW Ste 700 Washington DC 20005 Business E-Mail: hyen@ap.org.

YEN, LOUIS, research scientist; s. Wenlu Yan and Tu Zheng; m. Lily Liang Li, Sept. 16, 1981; children: Andy, David. PhD, U. Mich., Ann Arbor, 1989. Tchg. & rsch. asst. U. Mich., 1980—89, sr. rsch. assoc., 1989—98, rsch. scientist, 1998—. Vis. prof. Tianjin U. Sci. & Tech., China, 2000—, Tianjin Normal U., 2002—, Nankai U., Tianjin, 2003—. Office: Univ Mich 1015 E Huron Ann Arbor MI 48104 Office Fax: 734-763-2206. Business E-Mail: louisyen@umich.edu.

YEN, TEH FU, civil and environmental engineering educator; b. Kun-Ming, China, Jan. 9, 1927; came to U.S., 1949; s. Kwang Pu and Ren (Liu) Y.; m. Shiao-Ping Siao, May 30, 1959 BS, Cen. China U., 1947; MS, W.Va. U., 1953; PhD, Va. Poly. Inst. and State U., 1956; PhD (hon.), Pepperdine U., 1982, Internat. U. Dubna, Russia, 1996, All Russian Petroleum Exploration Inst., St. Petersburg, Russia, 1999. Sr. research chemist Good Yr. Tire & Rubber Co., Akron, 1955-59; fellow Mellon Inst., Pitts., 1959-65; sr. fellow Carnegie-Mellon U., Pitts., 1965-68; assoc. prof. Calif. State U., Los Angeles, 1968-69, U. So. Calif., 1969-80, prof. civil engring. and environ. engring., 1980—. Hon. prof. Shanghai U. Sci. and Tech., 1986, U. Petroleum, Beijing, 1987, Daqing Petroleum Inst., 1992; cons. Universal Oil Products, 1968-76, Chevron Oil Field Rsch. Co., 1968-75, Finnigan Corp., 1976-77, GE, 1977-80, United Techs., 1978-79, TRW Inc., 1982-83, Exxon, 1981-82, DuPont, 1985-88, Min. Petroleum, Beijing, 1982—, Biogas Rsch. Inst.-UN, Chengdu, 1991. Author: numerous tech. books; contbr. articles articles to profl. jours. Recipient Disting. Svc. award Tau Beta Pi, 1974, Imperial Crown Gold medal, Iran, 1976, Achievement award Chinese Engring. and Sci. Assocs. So. Calif., 1977, award Phi Kappa Phi, 1982, Outstanding Contbn. honor Pi Epsilon Tau, 1984, Svc. award Republic of Honduras, 1989, award in Petroleum Chem. Am. Chem. Soc., 1994, Kapitsa Gold medal Russian Fedn., 1995. Fellow Chem. Soc., Inst. Petroleum, Am. Inst. Chemists; mem. Am. Chem. Soc. (life; bd. dirs. 1993, councillor, founder and chmn. geochemistry divsn. 1979-81, Chinese Acad. Scis. (standing com.), Acad. Scis. Russian Fedn. (academician, fgn. mem.), Assn. Environmental Engring. and Sci. Profs. Office: U So Calif KAP 224A Viterby Sch Engring 3620 S Vermont Ave Los Angeles CA 90089-2531 Office Phone: 213-740-0586. Business E-Mail: tfyen@usc.edu.

YEN, TINGFANG, research scientist; b. Taichung, Taiwan, Oct. 19, 1976; d. Chia-Shi Yen and Chiu-Chin Yu. PhD, SUNY-Buffalo, NY, 2003—. Tchg. assit. SUNY-Buffalo, 2005—, rsch. assistance, 2006—. Field application engr. Hitachi Semiconductor, Taipei, Taiwan, 2000—01. Worship team leader Ea. Hills Wesleyan Chinese Ch., Williamsville, NY, 2006—08; treasure Taiwan Grad. Student Assn., SUNY-Buffalo, 2003—04, Tennis Club SUNY-Buffalo, 2005—06.

Achievements include research in fabricate the metal-semiconducor and metal-ultraviolet photodetectors. Office: SUNY-Buffalo 332 Bonner Hall Buffalo NY 14260 Business E-Mail: tyen2@buffalo.edu.

YEN, WEN-HSIUNG, language and music professional, educator; b. Tainan, Taiwan, June 26, 1934; came to U.S., 1969; m. Yuan-yuan Yen, Jan. 6, 1961; children: Tin-ju, Tin-jen, Tin-Tao. BA, Nat. Taiwan Normal U., 1960; MA, UCLA, 1971; PhD in Music, World U., 1988; Candidate Philosophy in Ethnomusicology, UCLA, 1995; cultural doctorate philosophy of music, The World Univ., 1988. Instr. Nat. Taichung Tchr. Coll., 1961-62; prof. Chinese Culture U., Taipei, 1964-69; lectr. West L.A. C.C., 1978-82; founder Chinese Culture Sch. L.A., 1976—. Grad. tchg. asst. U. Md., 1982-83; instr. L.A. City Coll., 1983—, Calif. State U. L.A., 1984—, Pasadena City Coll., 1989—; prof. Chinese Santa Monica (Calif.) Coll., 1986—, Calif. State U. Northridge, 1986—; founder Wen Yen Piano Studio, 1972—; founder, dir. Chinese Mus. Orch. So. Calif., 1974—; founder, pres. Chinese- Amer. Musicians Assn. of So. Calif., 1990—; co-chair Conf. Students of Chinese Lang. and Culture; Chinese lang. instrn. course designer, instr. All Seasons Children's Learning Ctr., 2001—; music dir. Soc. Confucian Studies Am., 2004—; dir. bd. Chinese Studies Ctr., Calif. State U., LA, Party Potridge Club LA, 2009-, music dir. Anniversary of Confucios Birthday, 2002-, commemorating the 2553. Musician: musical compositions include Collection of Works by Mr. Yen, 1969, (recordings) Art Songs and Chinese Folk Songs, 1982, Ode To My Home Land, 1992, Taiwanese Folk Songs Suite; musician: (Opera) Taiwanese Gezaix Suite; musician: Mother Earth-Found-Season: Spring, Summer, Autumn and Winter, 1997, Song of 911; author: Taiwan Folk Songs, 1967, vol. 2, 1969, A Collection of Wen-hsiung Yen's Songs, 1968, vol. 2, 1987, vol. 3, 2000 (award Fedn. Overseas Assns., 2000, 2002); translator: Achievement and Methodology for Comparative Musicology, 1968, Chinese Musical Culture and Folk Songs, 1989, Silk and Bamboo Expresses Emotion and Meaning, 2000, Ethnomusicology Series, 2002; composer: 100 songs and instrumental music; exhibitor traditional Chinese musical instruments and publs., Chinese Culture Ctr., 1995, 1996, Arcadia Pub. Libr., 1999; musician: East and West Music Concert, 2004, Concert for Traditional Music and New Performing Arts, 2006; organizer concerts, contbr. articles to profl. jours.; musician: (performer) Taiwanese Cultural Festival, 2008; Photographer (exhibitions) Chinese Calligraphy Painting Soc. Bd. dirs. So. Calif. Coun. Chinese Sch., 1998—; bd. dirs. Chinese Studies Ctr., Calif. State U., L.A., 1990—; conductor Chinese Music Orch. So. Calif., 1974-; prodr. Chinese Art and Culture Festival, 1990-2003; sustaining mem. Rep. Nat. Com., 2002; advisor Lu Mei Tong Xin Hui Taiwanese Am. Assn., 2003—. Recipient 30 Yrs. Outstanding Tchr. award, Overseas Chinese Affairs Commn., Taiwan, 2006, World Chinese Writer Assn., Taipei, 2008, award, Chinese Art & Literary Assn., 2009. Mem.: AARP (pub. rels. com. bd. mem. 2009, bd. dir. China Town Chpt. 2009), Northern Am. Chinese Writers Assn. So. Calif. (v.p. 2000, pres. 2008), Fedn. Overseas Chinese Assns. (bd. dirs. (hon.) 2002), So. Calif. Coun. Chinese Schs. (chmn. exec. com.), Chinese Am. PTA So. Calif. (supr. 1985—), Taiwan Benevloent Assn. Calif. (v.p. 1986, pres. 1987—89, bd. dirs.), Taiwan Benevolent Assn. Am. (bd. dirs.), Alumni Assn. Chinese Culture U. So. Calif., Soc. Asian Music (founder, pres.), Internat. Coun. Traditional Music, Coll. Music Soc., Soc. Ethnomusicology, Chinese Performing Arts Assn. of Am. (bd. dirs.), Chinese Choral Soc. So. Calif. (music dir.), Chinese-Am. Musicians Assn. So Calif. (pres.). Avocations: walking, ping pong/table tennis, tai chi chuan. Office: Chinese Culture Sch 615 Las Tunas Dr Ste B Arcadia CA 91007-8469 Office Phone: 626-447-3823. Personal E-mail: wenhyen2000@yahoo.com.

YENKO, JAYNE M., education educator; b. Yreka, Calif., Feb. 10, 1963; d. Earl I. and Sharon K. Mullin; m. Steve J. Yenko, June 22, 1996. BS in Home Econ., Clothing and Textiles, Calif. State U., Chico, 1983; MA in Tchg., U. Iowa, Iowa City, 1985. Cert. in online tchg.& learning Calif. State U., Hayward, 2002, internat. sports nutritionist 2007, internat. aerobic instr., personal trainer, consumer sci. tchr. Wyo. Registration clerk U. Iowa Hosps. and Clinics, 1983—87, unit clerk emergency room and burn units, 1989—90, sec. II dept. internal medicine, 1992—96; tchr., adminstrv. asst. U. Iowa Upward Bound, Iowa City, 1985—89; sub. tchr. six area sch. dists., Johnson County, Iowa, 1986—87; ext. home economist U. Wis., Wis. Rapids, 1987—88; unit clerk internal medicine ward Mercy Hosp., Iowa City, 1989—90; sec. II liberal arts acad. programs U. Iowa, 1990—92; adj. faculty, principles of nutrition Kaplan U., Ft. Lauderdale, Fla., 2002—; adj. faculty successful strategies Rasmussen Coll. Online, Minnetonka, 2005; adj. faculty, fashion merchandising program Westwood Coll. Online, Denver, 2005—; adj. faculty ednl. tech., reading, ednl. adminstrn. Grand Canyon U., Phoenix, 2005—. After sch. program dir. Regina Elem. Sch., Iowa City, 1988—90; tutor athletic dept. U. Iowa, 1988—91, tutor new dimensions in learning, 1988—91; owner, designer Little Sheep Sewing, Cora, Wyo., 1996—; webmaster Western Woodworking, Cora, 1996—; online tchg. asst. Calif. State U., Hayward, 2002; online tutor dept. arts and scis. Kaplan Coll., Davenport, Iowa, 2004. Donor Newborns in Need, Houston, 2005, Seedlings, Livonia, Mich., 2005; sponsor Children Internat., Little Rock, 2007. Mem.: NSTA (licentiate), ASCD (licentiate), Pa. Custom Clothiers (licentiate), Fashion Grp. Internat. (licentiate), Am. Sewing Guild (licentiate), Am. Assn. Family and Consumer Sci. (licentiate), Am. Anthrop. Assn. (licentiate), Sloan Consortium (assoc.). Democrat. Roman Catholic. Avocations: reading, piano, horseback riding, needlecrafts. Personal E-mail: online_instructor2002@yahoo.com.

YENTZER, BRAD A., medical researcher; BA in Biology, LaSalle U., Phila., 2001; MD, Jefferson Med. Coll., Phila., 2006. Rsch. fellow Wistar Inst., Phila., 2001, Med. Rsch. Inst. Chem. Def., US Army Med. Rsch. Inst. Infectious Diseases, Aberdeen, Md., 2001—02. Chief, transitional yr. residency Mercy Cath. Med. Ctr., Darby, Pa., 2006—07. Recipient 1st Position, Dermatology Nurses Assn., 2008; Clin. Rsch. grant, Am. Acne & Rosacea Soc., 2009. Mem.: AMA, Am. Acad. Dermatology, Piedmont Swing Dance Soc., Defenders Wildlife. Office: WFU Sch Medicine Dermatology Med Ctr Blvd Winston Salem NC 27101

YEO, CHARLES JOHN, surgery educator; b. East Orange, NJ, Nov. 25, 1953; s. Presley Stewart and Euphemia (Kamaras) Y.; m. Theresa Ann Pluth, May 19, 1990; children: William Stewart, Katerina Connor. AB in Biochemistry, Princeton U., 1975; MD, Johns Hopkins U., 1979. Diplomate Am. Bd. Surgery. Instr. dept. surgery Johns Hopkins U. Sch. Medicine, Balt., 1985—86, asst. prof., 1986—90, assoc. prof., 1990—96, prof., 1996—. Editor: Shackelfords Surgery of the Alimentary Tract, 2 vols., 6th edit., 2007; contbr. more than 350 articles to profl. jours. Fellow ACS; mem. Soc. Surgery Alimentary Tract, Am. Surg. Assn., Soc. Clin. Surgery, Soc. Univ. Surgeons, Halsted Soc. Office: Thomas Jefferson U 1015 Walnut St Philadelphia PA 19107 Office Fax: 215-923-6609.

YEO, KIM ENG, artist; b. Singapore, Apr. 24, 1947; arrived in US, 1978, permanent resident, 2002; d. Cheng Chye and Seok Kim (Chew) Lee; m. Bock Cheng Yeo; children: Beng Lin, Beng Jene. Student, Nanyang Acad. Fine Arts, Singapore, 1963; BSc with honors, U. Singapore, 1968. Treas., artist bd. mem. Flushing Art League, NYC, 1980-84; art instr. Poppenhusen Inst., NYC, 1984; substitute art tchr. UN Internat. Sch., NYC, 1984-85; freelance paper product designer, 1981-87; textile designer J. Brown Designs, NYC, 1987-91; tchg. artist Flushing Town Hall, NY, 1995—2002; artist-in-residence Pub. Sch. 214, 165, Francis Lewis H.S., Flushing, 1997-2001. Visual arts panelist, Flushing Coun., 1985-87, Queen's Coun., 1998-99, 2001-04; watercolor workshop demonstrator Singapore Art Mus., 2000. One person shows at Alliance Francais, 1975-77, Bhirasri Inst. Modern Art, Bangkok, Thailand, 1975-77, Flushing Coun. on Arts, 1995, 2000, Adirondack Lakes Ctr. for the Arts, NY, 2005, Synagogue For Arts Gallery, NY, 2006-08; exhibitions include Mallette Gallery, LI, NY, 1998, 99, Artfolio Gallery, Singapore, 2000, Langston Hughes Cmty. Libr. and Cultural Ctr., NY, 2004; exhibited in group shows at Womanart Gallery, NYC, 1979-80, Nat. Art League, Douglastown, NY, 1979-86, Flushing Coun. on Arts, 1984-88, 96-2008, Postcrypt Art Gallery, NYC, 1997, Singapore Watercolor Soc., 1997-99, 2001-03, Queens Coun. on Arts, NY, 2002-07; represented in corp. and pvt. collections; artist greeting cards UNICEF, 1997-98; featured on QPATV Artists Series, 1993, QPTV Queens Jour., 2000; featured in Watercolor Mag., 1997, Internat. Artist Mag., 2004. Benefit show UN Devel. Fund for Women Singapore, 1999. Mem. Flushing Art League (bd. dirs., treas. 1979-85, award 1986), Flushing Coun. on Arts, Queens Coun. on Arts. Buddhist. Avocations: gardening, bookmaking. Home: 16202 77th Ave Flushing NY 11366-1022 Business E-Mail: artist@kimengyeo.com.

YEO, PATRICIA, chef; Degree in Biochemistry, Princeton U. Line cook Miracle Grill, NYC; sous chef Mesa Grill, NYC, 1991, Bolo, NYC, 1993—95; chef China Moon; opened Hawthorne Lane, Calif.; owner, exec. chef AZ, NYC, 2000, Pazo, NYC, Sapa, NYC; exec. chef Monkey Bar, NYC. Author: Cooking from A to Z with Patricia Yeo, 2002. Office: Sapa 43 W 24th St New York NY 10010 Office Phone: 212-929-1800. Office Fax: 212-929-7070.

YEO, RON, architect; b. LA, June 17, 1933; s. Clayton Erik and Rose G. (Westman) Y.; m. Birgitta S. Bergkvist, Sept. 29, 1962; children: Erik Elov, Katarina Kristina. B.Arch., U. So. Calif., 1959. Draftsman Montierth & Strickland (Architects), Long Beach, Calif., 1958-61; designer Gosta Edberg S.A.R. Arkitekt, Stockholm, 1962; partner Strickland & Yeo, Architects, Garden Grove, Calif., 1962-63; pres. Ron Yeo, Architect, Inc., Corona del Mar, Calif., 1963—. Cons., lectr. in field. Archtl. works include Garden Grove Civic and Cmty. Ctr., 1966, Hall Sculpture Studio, 1966, Garden Grove Cultural Ctr., 1978, Gem Theater, 1979, Festival Amphitheatre, 1983, Los Coyotes Paleontol. Interpretive Ctr., 1986, Calif. State U. Fullerton Alumni House, 1997, O'Neill Regional Pk. Nature Ctr., 1998, Upper Newport Bay Interpretive Ctr., 2000, Point Vicente Interpretive Ctr., 2006, Back Bay Sci. Ctr., 2007, Stough Canyon Nature Ctr., 2000, Quon residence, 2005. Mem. Orange County Planning Commn., 1972-73, 1975-76; chmn. Housing and Community Devel. Task Force, 1978, Orange County Fire Protection Planning Task Force, City of Newport Beach City Arts Commn., 1970-72; pres. Orange County Arts Alliance, 1980-81; gen. plan advisory com. Newport Beach, 2002-06. Fellow AIA; mem. Green Bldg. Coun., Internat. Conf. Bldg. Ofcls., Nat. Assn. for Interpretation (founding), Constrn. Specification Inst. Democrat. Office: Ron Yeo FAIA Architect Inc 500 Jasmine Ave Corona Del Mar CA 92625-2308

YEO, YOON, biomedical engineer, educator; d. Wook Yeo and Seolja Park. BS, Seoul Nat. U., Republic of Korea, 1993, MS, 1995; PhD, Purdue U., West Lafayette, Ind., 2003. Registered pharmacist Ministry of Health and Social Affairs, Republic of Korea, 1993. Postdoc. assoc. MIT, Cambridge, Mass., 2004—06; asst. prof. Purdue U., 2007—. Recipient Flemming award, Purdue U., 2000. Mem.: Am. Assn. Coll. Pharmacy (Faculty award, New Investigators Program 2008), Am. Chem. Soc., Am. Assn. Pharm. Scientists (Outstanding Grad. Student Rsch. Pharm. Technologies award 2004), Controlled Release Soc., Rho Chi Pharmacy Honor Soc. Achievements include patents in field. Office: Purdue Univ 575 Stadium Mall Dr G22 West Lafayette IN 47906

YEO, YUNG KEE, physics professor; b. MoonGyeong, Gyeongbuk, Republic Of Korea, Apr. 24, 1938; s. Nam Jin Yeo and Jong Soon Eom; m. Young Ok Chang; children: Songmi Berarducci, Lami. PhD, U. Southern Calif., Los Angeles, 1972. Postdoc. rsch. assoc. U. Southern Calif., 1972, U. Oreg., Eugene, 1974—77; physicist Develco Inc., Sunnyvale, Calif., 1973—74; resident scientist Electronic Rsch. Br., Avionics Lab, Wright Patterson AFB, Ohio, 1977—78; sr. physicist Sys. Rsch. Lab., Inc., Dayton, Ohio, 1978—80; prin. investigator Universal Energy Sys., 1980—84; asst. prof. Air Force Inst. Tech., Wright Patterson AFB, Ohio, 1984—87, 1987—90, prof., 1990—. Mem.: Am. Phys. Soc. Office: Air Force Inst Tech 2950 Hobson Way Dayton OH 45433 Office Fax: 937-656-6000. Business E-Mail: yung.yeo@afit.edu.

YEOM, SEOKWON (SEKWON), engineering educator, researcher; s. Jaisun Yum; m. Shuiyan Ng, Dec. 21, 2004; children: Jinhee Katie, Jinhyun Mitchell. BS, Inha U., Incheon, Republic of Korea, 1995, Korea U., Seoul, 1997, MS, 1999; PhD, U. Conn., Storrs, 2006. Comm. sys. mgr. Korea Elec. Power Corp., Seoul, 1996—97; rsch. asst. U. Conn., 2000—06, rsch. specialist, 2006—07; asst. prof. Daegu U., Gyeongsan, Republic of Korea, 2007—. Contbr. numerous articles to profl. jours., scientific papers to profl. confs. and convs. Recipient Summer Fellowship award, U. Conn., 2003, 2006, Pre-doctoral Fellowship award, 2005, 2006, Doctoral Dissertation Fellowship award, 2005; scholar, Korea U., 1995—97, Inha U., 1990, 1993—94. Mem.: IEEE (reviewer, Jour. Display Tech.), Optical Soc. Am. (reviewer, Optics Express, Applied Optics), Internat. Soc. Optical Engring. (reviewer). Achievements include patents for method and apparatus for recognition of microorganisms using holographic microscopy. Office: Daegu Univ Info and Comm Engring 15 Jillyang Gyeongbuk Gyeongsan 712-714 Republic of Korea Home Phone: 821024123140; Office Phone: 82-53-850-6643. Business E-Mail: yeom@daegu.ac.kr.

YEOMAN, LYNN CHALMERS, medical educator; b. Evanston, Ill., May 17, 1943; m. Carol J. Yeoman; children: Caroline, Christopher, Sarah. BA, DePauw U., Greencastle, 1965; PhD, U. Ill., Urbana, 1970. Instr. Baylor Coll. Medicine, Houston, 1972-73, asst. prof., 1973-76, assoc. prof., 1976-84, prof., 1984—; assoc. dir. Bristol-Baylor Lab, Houston, 1989-90; assoc. dir. anti-cancer drug discovery and cell and molecular biology Bristol-Myers Co., Wallingford, Conn., 1989—90; dir. curriculum database program Baylor Coll. Medicine, Houston, 1995—, dir. integrated problem solving program, 1997—, exec. dir. ednl. resource ctr., 2001—, sr. dir. acad. computing, 2004—. Cons. Litton Bionetics, Ft. Detrick, Md., 1977-78, Colon Cancer Working Group, Houston, 1985-86, Oncos, Ltd., Houston, 1985-87, Bristol-Myers Co., Wallingford, Conn., 1985-89, Ubiquitex Techs. Corp., 1995-96, U. Tex. Med. Br., Galveston, 1998, ProteEx, Inc., 2001-03, Feedback Techs., Inc., 2004-; mem. com. revision U.S. Pharmacopeial Conv., 1985-90, 1995—, chmn. expert com. on biols. and biotech.: proteins and polysaccharides, 2000—, com. of experts exec. com., 2004—, chmn. content devel. task force, CATCHUM Project, Galveston, 2004-08. Editor: Methods in Cancer Research, Vols. 19 and 20, 1982; mem. editl. bd. Frontiers in Biosci., Med. Edn. Online; contbr. articles to profl. jours. V.p. Marilyn Estates Assn., Houston, 2004-05; bd. mem. Baylor Coll. Medicine Fed. Credit Union, 2007-, vice chair, Baylor Coll. Medicine Fed. Credit Union, 2008, Friends Houston Acad. Medicine-Tex. Med. Ctr. Libr. Bd., 2007-; mem. cmty. outreach adv. com., Chapelwood Found., 2009-. NCI grantee, 1987-2003. Mem. Group on Ednl. Affairs, AAMC Group on Info. Resources. Methodist. Achievements include patent for detection of antigen gp650 in sera and other specimens from cancer patients with anti-gp650 monoclonal antibody. Home: 5434 Rutherglenn Dr Houston TX 77096-4032 Office: 1 Baylor Plz Houston TX 77030-3411 Office Phone: 713-798-7336. Business E-Mail: lyeoman@bcm.edu.

YEOMANS, DONALD KEITH, astronomer; b. Rochester, NY, May 3, 1942; s. George E. and Jessie Y.; m. Laurie Robyn Ernst, June 20, 1970; children: Sarah, Keith. BA, Middlebury Coll., Vt., 1964; MS, U. Md., 1967, PhD, 1970. Supr. Computer Scis. Corp., Silver Spring, Md., 1973-76; sr. rsch. astronomer Jet Propulsion Lab., Pasadena, Calif., 1976-92, supr., 1992—. Discipline specialist Internat. Halley Watch, 1982-89; sci. investigator NASA Comet Mission, 1987-91, Near-Earth Asteroid Rendezvous Mission, 1994-2001, Multi-Comet Flyby Mission, 1997-2002, Comet Impact Mission, 1999-2006; project scientist for asteroid sample return mission, 1998—; mgr. NASA Near-Earth Object Program Office, 1998-. Author: Comet Halley: Once in a Lifetime, 1985, The Distant Planets, 1989, Comets: A Chronological History of Observation, Science, Myth, and Folklore, 1991. Recipient Space Achievement award AIAA, 1985, Exceptional Svc. medal NASA, 1986, Disting. Svc. medal, 2009, Achievement award Middlebury Coll. Alumni, 1987; named NASA/JPL Sr. Rsch. Scientist, 1993. Mem.: Am. Astron. Soc. (chair divsn. planetary scis. 1999—2000, chair hist. astronomy divsn. 2005—06). Democrat. Presbyterian. Avocations: tennis, history of astronomy. Office: Jet Propulsion Lab #301-150 4800 Oak Grove Dr Pasadena CA 91109-8001 Office Phone: 818-354-2127. Business E-Mail: donald.k.yeomans@jpl.nasa.gov.

YEOMANS, DONALD RALPH, Canadian government official, consultant; b. Toronto, Ont., Can., Mar. 25, 1925; s. Ralph and Louise (Weismiller) Y.; m. Catherine Simpson Williams, May 13, 1950; children: Patricia Ann, Nancy Louise, Jane Elizabeth. BASc, U. Toronto, 1947; LLD, Carleton U., 2008. Registered profl. engr., Ont., cert. mgmt. acct. Mem. Bur. of Govt. Orgns., Ottawa, Ont., 1962-64; dep. sec. Treasury Bd., Ottawa, 1964-69; asst. dep. minister Dept. Supply and Services, Ottawa, 1969-75; assoc. exec. dir. Anti-Inflation Bd., Ottawa, 1975-76; asst. dep. minister Dept. Nat. Health-Welfare, Ottawa, 1976-77; commr. Correctional Services of Can., Ottawa, 1977-85; chmn. Tariff Bd., 1985-89; spl. advisor Can. Jud. Centre, 1989-92; mem. bd. govs. Carleton U., 1980-93, chmn., 1989-91. Spl. advisor Royal Com. Govt. Orgns., 1961, Royal Com. Fin. Accountability, 1977; assoc. Cons. and Audit Can., 1992-97; exec. counsellor Pub. Svc. Commn., 1990-95; cons. to govt. and industry, 1990-97, bd. dirs. Corrections Corp. Can.; mem. bd. govs. Can. Comprehensive Audit Found., 1989-94; mem. ind. adv. com. Auditor Gen. Can., 1989-95; chmn. Coun. Adminstrv. Tribunals, 1986; chmn. Coun. Chairs Ont. Univs., 1991-93; mem. Expert Com. on AIDS in Prisons, 1992-94; chmn. awards com. Am. Correctional Assn., 1992-97; bd. dirs. Corrections Corp. Can., Baker Group Internat., Inc. Recipient Centennial medal Govt. Can., 1967, Jubilee medal Govt. Can., 1977, E.R. Cass award Am. Corr. Assn., 1991, Corr. Svc. of Can. Exemplary Svc. medal, 2000, Founder's award Carleton U., 2000; Australian Commonwealth fellow, 1985. Fellow: Soc. Mgmt. Accts. Can. (pres. 1977); mem.: Fed. Superannuates Nat. Assn. (pres. Ottawa br. 1998—2000, bd. dirs., nat. regional dir. 2002—), Inst. Pub. Adminstrn. Can. (pres. 1974), Assn. State Correctional Adminstrs. (pres. 1983, Spl. Founders award 2006), Ottawa Heart Inst. Alumni Assn. (v.p.), Five Lakes (pres. 1975); Canadian (Ottawa, pres. 1978), Canadian Club (Ottawa, pres. 1978), Five Lakes Club (pres. 1975). Home and Office: 205-211 Second Ave Ottawa ON Canada K1S 2H8 Home Phone: 613-232-5022.

YEOSOCK, JOHN JOHN, military officer; b. Wilkes-Barre, Pa., 1937; s. John A. and Elizabeth B. Yeosock; m. Betta Lynn; children— John John, Elizabeth John BS in Indsl. Engring., Pa. State U., 1959; MS in Ops. Rsch., U.S. Naval Postgrad. Sch., Monterey, Calif., 1969; postgrad., Nat. War Coll., 1976. Commd. officer U.S. Army, 1959, advanced through grades to lt. gen.; brigade comdr. 194th Armored Brigade, Ft Knox, Ky., 1978-80; chief of staff 1st Cavalry div. U.S. Army, Ft. Hood, Tex., 1980-81, asst. div. comdr., 1983-84; project mgr. Saudi N.G., Riyadh, Saudi Arabia, 1981-83; dep. chief of staff ops. Forces Command., Atlanta, 1984-86; comdr. 1st Cavalry Div., Ft. Hood, 1986-88; asst. dep. chief of staff for ops. The Pentagon, Washington, 1988-89; comdr. 3d Army and dep. comdg. gen. Forces Command, Ft. McPherson, Ga., 1989—&; comdr. U.S., U.K., French Army Forces, Kuwaiti Theater Ops., Desert Storm, Saudi Arabia, 1990-91; internat. cons., 1993—. Decorated D.S.M. (3), Legion of Merit (2), Bronze Star with v (2), French Legion of Honor, King Faisal award Class II, King Abdul Aziz medal Class II (Saudi Arabia), Combat Infantryman badge; recipient Nat. Vets. award, 1994, AUSA Inspiration award Atlanta, 1992; named Outstanding Engring. Alumnus, Pa. State U., 1990, Disting. Alumni, 1992, Disting. Alumnus, Valley Forge Mil. Acad., 1994; named to Pi Kappa Phi Hall of Fame. Mem. Wilkes-Barre C. of C. (hon., Achievement award 1991).

YEOSOCK, MICHAEL MICHAEL, funeral director, civil engineer; b. Wilkes-Barre, Pa., July 28, 1962; s. Michael J. and Patricia A. (Sauerwein) Y.; m. Mary Jacqueline Clemente; children: Adriana Grace, Christopher Michael. Student, Pa. State U., 1980-82; BS, W.Va. U., 1984; diploma in mortuary sci., New Eng. Inst., 1985; MS in Environ. Engring., U. New Haven, 1993. Cert. engr.-in-tng., geog. info. sys. profl.; lic. profl. engr., Pa., Conn., NY.; Diplomate Water Resources engr. Project mgr. M.J. Pasonick, Jr., Inc., Wilkes-Barre, 1986-89; asst. civil engr. in tng. City of Norwalk (Conn.) Dept. of Pub. Works, 1989—, sr. engr., 1994—; supr. Jan Fabian Funeral Chapel, Hanover, Pa., 1990-91. Bd. dirs. Norwalk (Conn.) Tree Alliance. Mem. IEEE, AIME, ASCE, AAAS, Soc. Mining Engrs., Can. Mining and Metallurgy, NY Acad. Scis., Am. Rock Mechanics Assn., Internat. Soc. Rock Mechanics, Geospatial Info. and Tech. Assn., Inst. Traffic Engrs., Internat. Mcpl. Signal Assn. Republican. Russian Orthodox. Avocations: flying, whitewater rafting. Home: 5 Country Club Dr White Plains NY 10607 Office: City of Norwalk 125 East Ave Norwalk CT 06851-5702 Home Phone: 914-345-7157; Office Phone: 203-854-7744. Personal E-mail: mmyeosock@optonline.net.

YEPES, ENRIQUE, language educator; PhD, Rutgers U., New Brunswick, NJ, 1996. Assoc. prof. Bowdoin Coll., Brunswick, Maine, 1996—. Office Fax: 207-798-7031.

YEPES-BARAYA, MARIO, educational research and evaluation consultant; b. Bogota, Colombia, Oct. 10, 1946; arrived in US, 1963; s. Mario Yepes Mantilla and Leonor Baraya; m. Jean A. Vannier, July 19, 1974; children: Julia E. Yepes, Nicholas A. Yepes. BA in Chemistry, SUNY, Buffalo, 1972, EdM in Sci. Edn., 1974, PhD in Rsch. and Evaluation in Edn., 1986. Cert. K-12 tchr. NY. Edn. rsch. and evaluation cons. World Bank, UNESCO, Colombia, Venezuela and Peru,

1979—84; asst. dir. program devel. rsch. and evaluation SUNY, Buffalo, 1984—90, asst. prof. edn. Fredonia, 1990—92; rsch. scientist Ednl. Testing Svc., Princeton, 1992—2001; dir. content devel. Harcourt Ednl. Measurement, Lawrenceville, NY, 2001—03; sr. rsch. specialist Scholastic, Inc., New York, 2005—. Contbr. articles to profl. jours. Recipient Peer Recognition award, Ednl. Testing Svc., 1997; grantee, USIA, 1998; scholar Latin Am. Scholarship Program, Harvard U., 1969—74; Latin Am. Tchg. Fellowship, Tufts U. Fletcher Sch. Law and Diplomacy, 1974—76. Mem.: Am. Edn. Rsch. Assn. Home: 17-D Carver Pl Lawrenceville NJ 08648 Office: Scholastic Inc 824 Broadway Rm 804 New York NY 10012 Personal E-mail: yepes1@gmail.com. Business E-Mail: myepes-baraya@scholastic.com.

YERDON, LAWRENCE J., museum administrator; BA in History, Eastern Nazarene Coll., 1970; MA in History, Northeastern U.; MBA, Rensselaer Polytechnic Inst. Cert. in hist. agency mgmt. Northeastern U. Pres., CEO Hancock Shaker Village, Pittsfield, Mass., 1986—2004; pres. Strawbery Banke Mus., Portsmouth, NH, 2004—. Mem.: New Eng. Mus. Assn. (bd. dirs. 1996—, pres.). Office: Strawbery Banke Mus PO Box 300 Portsmouth NH 03802 Office Phone: 603-433-1103. Office Fax: 603-433-1129. Business E-Mail: lyerdon@strawberybanke.org.

YERG, BEVERLY JOHNSON, retired physical education educator, researcher; b. Warren, Pa., Nov. 11, 1938; d. C. Walter and Emma Josephine Erickson Johnson; m. Robert Robison Yerg, June 24, 1961; 1 child, David Robert. BS, Temple U., 1960, EdM, 1973; PhD, U. Pitts., 1977. Tchr., coach Manheim Ctrl. Schs., Pa., 1961—64; tchr. Lancaster City Schs., 1960—61; substitute and homebound tchr. Warren Area Schs., 1964—73; lectr. LaRoche Coll., 1973—74; tchg. fellow U. Pitts., 1974—77; asst. prof. Fla. State U., Tallahassee, 1977—82, assoc. prof., 1982—2001, dept. head, 1982—85, dir. acad. support programs student athletes, 1986—93, chair pres.'s com. intercollegiate athletics; ret., 2001. Editl. bd., reviewer Jour. Tchg. Physical Edn., Nat. Assn. Athletic Acad. Advisors Jour., reviewer Rsch. Quar. Exercise and Sport, Merrill Pub. Co., Mosby Book Co.; contbr. chapters to books, articles to profl. jours. Bd. dirs. Neighborhood Health Clinic, Tallahassee, 1986—88; bd. mem. North Fla. Fellow Christian Athletes, 1987—90; chair Fla. Cabinet for Campus Ministry, Presbyn. Ch. USA, Fla., 1996—2008; treas., interim bd. of dirs. Presbyn. Assn. for Collegiate and Higher Edn. Ministries, 2004—06, treas., bd. dirs., 2006—09; leadership team Higher Edn. Ministries Presbyn. Ch. USA, Louisville, 2001—09; mem., pres., com. chair Presbyn. U. Ctr., 1984—2000; elder Fellowship Presbyn. Ch., 1987—90, Christ Presbyn. Ch, 1994—97; permanent jud. commn. Fla. Presbyn., Panama City, Fla., 2002—05, com. on preparation for ministry, 1991—97; bd. mem. YWCA, Warren, Pa., 1965—67. Recipient Peter W. Everett Honor award, Fla. Assn. for Health, Phys. Edn., Recreation, and Dance, 2002; named honoree, Assn. Internat. des Ecoles Supérieures d'Edn. Physique; Rsch. Consortium fellow, Am. Alliance for Health, Phys. Edn., Recreation, and Dance, 1986—. Mem.: Am. Ednl. Rsch. Assn., Fla. Assn. for Health, Phys. Edn., Recreation, and Dance, Am. Alliance for Health, Phys. Edn., Recreation, and Dance (life), Delta Psi Kappa (life; bd. dir. 1978—86, pres. 1984—86). Presbyterian. Avocations: reading, handwork, gardening, woodworking. Home: 4121 Tralee Rd Tallahassee FL 32309-2822 Personal E-mail: yerg@coe.fsu.edu.

YERGIN, DANIEL HOWARD, writer, consultant; b. LA, Feb. 6, 1947; s. Irving H. and Naomi Y.; m. Angela Stent, Aug. 10, 1975; children: Alexander George, Rebecca Isabella. BA, Yale U., Eng., 1968; MA with first class honors, Cambridge U., Eng., 1970, PhD, 1974; PhD (hon.), U. Mo., 1980, U. Houston, 1994. Contbg. editor New York mag., 1968-70; research fellow Harvard U., Cambridge, Mass., 1974-76, lectr. bus. sch., 1976-79, lectr. Kennedy Sch. Govt., 1979-83, research assoc. Cambridge, 1983-90; chmn. Cambridge Energy Research Assoc., Cambridge, 1982-98, also chmn., sec. energy task force on strategic energy R&D, 1998—. Mem. policy adv. com. Program on U.S.-Japan Rels., Harvard U.; mem. bd. energy experts Dallas Morning News; mem. internat. panel advisors Asia-Pacific Petroleum Conf.; fellow World Econ. Forum, Davos. Author: Shattered Peace: The Origins of the Cold War and the National Security State, 1977, rev. edit., 1990, The Prize: Epic Quest for Oil, Money and Power, 1991 (Pulitzer Prize for non-fiction 1992, Eccle prize 1992); co-author: Cold War, 1977, Energy Future, 1979, Global Insecurity, 1982, Future of Oil Prices: Perils of Prophecy, 1984, Russia 2010: And What It Means for the World, 1993, the Commanding Heights, 1998; contbg. editor Atlantic Monthly, 1977-83. Mem. adv. bd. Solar Energy Rsch. Inst., Golden, Colo., 1979-81; sec. Energy Adv. Bd. Fellow Univ. Consortium for World Order Studies, 1974-75, Rockefeller Found., 1975-79, German Marshall Fund, 1980-81, Harvard U., Ctr. for Bus. and Govt., 1997—; Marshall scholar Cambridge U., 1974; recipient U.S. Energy award, 1997. Mem. PEN, Coun. on Fgn. Rels. (com. on studies), Nat. Petroleum Coun., Internat. Assn. for Energy Econs., Am. Hist. Assn., Am. Polit. Assn., Royal Inst. Internat. Affairs, Assn. Marshall Scholars (bd. dirs. 1988-91), U.S. Energy Assn. (bd. dirs.), Nat. Petroleum Coun., Yale Club (N.Y.C.), Harvard Club (N.Y.C.). Office: Cambridge Energy Research Assoc 55 Cambridge Pkwy Cambridge MA 02142-1234

YERGLER, WILLARD G., orthopedist; Grad., Purdue U.; MD, Ind. U. Sch. Medicine. Resident Ind. U. Med. Ctr.; team physician & dir. sports medicine U. Notre Dame; orthopedic surgeon South Bend Orthopaedic Surgery & Sports Medicine. Fellow: Am. Acad. Orthopaedic Surgeons; mem.: Am. Orthopaedic Soc. for Sports Medicine. Office: 53880 Carmichael Dr South Bend IN 46635 Office Phone: 574-247-9441.*

YERKES, DAVID NORTON, architect; b. Cambridge, Mass., Nov. 5, 1911; s. Robert Mearns and Ada (Watterson) Y.; m. Catharine Noyes, Oct. 7, 1939 (dec. 1969); 1 dau., Catharine; m. Sarah Hitchcock Satterlee, July 9, 1972. BA, Harvard U., 1933; M.F.A., Yale U., 1935. Draftsman, designer, Chgo. and Washington, 1937-39, Deigert & Yerkes and Assos., Washington, 1945—65, David N. Yerkes & Assos., Washington, 1965—69, Yerkes, Pappas and Parker, 1980-83. Mem. panel archtl. advisers Nat. Commn. Fine Arts, 1961-63, 79-82; vice chmn. Presdl. Inaugural Parade Com., 1965 Prin. works include Voice of America Studios, Washington, 1958, Nat. Arboretum Hdqrs. Bldg. Am. Embassy, Somalia, also Madeira Sch. Auditorium, 1969; 4 stas. Washington subway sys., 1971-81, hdqrs., Nat. Trust Historic Preservation, Washington, 1977, suite, Time, Inc., Washington, 1980, also various schs., labs; paintings exhibited in New Eng. and Washington. Served to capt. AUS, 1943-45. Firm recipient numerous regional and nat. awards; recipient Kemper award AIA, 1972 Fellow AIA (bd. dirs. 1965-68, v.p. 1968-69, chmn. nat. honor awards jury 1966, chmn. Reynolds Meml. award jury 1969, pres. found. 1974-76) Home: 3050 Military Rd NW #449 Washington DC 20015 Home Phone: 202-237-2957.

YERMAN, ANNE VERONICA, interior designer; d. Joseph Anthony and Eleanor Gallagher DeLue; m. Robert Neil Yerman, May 21, 1972; children: Brant Matthew Peace, Lesley Elizabeth Hope. Cert. completion, N.Y. Sch. Interior Design, 1966. Student/staff decorator, colorist Raymond Loewy/William Snaith, Inc., NYC, 1965—69; dir. interior decoration Norwood Oliver Design Assocs., NYC, 1970—75, Barnouw Design Assocs., Katonah, NY, 1982—94; prin., owner Anne V. Yerman Interiors, Potomac, Md., 1982—. Spkr. Show House with A Conscience, Washington, 2000. Mem. various coms., fundraiser Capital Children's Mus., Washington, 1982—88; bd. mem., trustee Round House Theatre, 2003—; treas., sec. Potomac Falls Homeowners Assn. Mem.: Potomac Book Club. Democrat. Roman Catholic. Avocations: tennis, reading, theater, art. Home: 9100 Falls Rd Potomac MD 20854 Personal E-mail: avyerman@msn.com.

YERRAM, PREETHI, physician; d. Madhava Reddy and Savithri Devi Yerram; m. Poorna Rajasekhar Karuparthi, Mar. 2, 2006. BS in Medicine, NTR U., BS in Surgery, 2003; MBBS, Guntur Med. Coll., India, 2003; MS in Gerontology, U. La Verne, Calif., 2005. Lic. med. physician and surgeon temporary Mo. Bd. Registration healing arts, 2005, diplomate Am. Bd. Internal Medicine, 2008, cert. Edn. Commn. Fgn. Med. Graduates, 2004, in advanced cardiac life support Am. Heart Assn., 2007, basic life support Am. Heart Assn., 2007, lic. physician and surgeon Med. bd. Calif., 2008, registered physician Andhra Pradesh Med. Bd., 2003. Resident physician U. Mo., Columbia, 2005—08, fellow physician, 2008—. House staff Govt. Gen. Hosp., Guntur, 2002—03; primary care physician Srinivasa Multi-Specialty Hosp., Kodad, Andhra Pradesh, 2003—03; internist Inland Psychiat. & Med. Group, Corona, Calif., 2004. Contbr. scientific papers to nummerous profl. jours. Grantee Fellow travel grant, Ann. dialysis Conf., 2009; Fellow grant, 2007. Mem.: ACP, Am. Geriat. Soc., Nat. Kidney Found., Internat. Soc. Nephrology, Am. Soc. Nephrology. Office: Univ Missouri Hosp One Hospital Dr Columbia MO 65202

YERRID, C. STEVEN, lawyer; b. Charleston, W.Va., Sept. 30, 1949; s. Charles George and Audrey Faye Yerrid. BA in History and Polit. Sci., La. State U., 1971; JD, Georgetown U., 1975. Bar: Fla. 1975, Va. 1975, U.S. Supreme Ct. 1979, D.C. 1984; cert. civil trial advocate Nat. Bd. Trial Advocacy. Aide U.S. Senator Ellender, Washington, 1971-73; ptnr. Holland & Knight, Tampa, Fla., 1975-86; pres. Stagg, Hardy & Yerrid, Tampa, 1986-89, Yerrid, Knopik & Krieger PA, Tampa, 1990-2000, The Yerrid Law Firm, Tampa, 2000—. Mediator and Cir. Ct. arbitrator Fla. and Fed. Cts. Mem. ABA, Va. Bar Assn., D.C. Bar Assn., Fla. Bar Assn. (chmn. admiralty law com. 1984-85, bd. cert. com. 1988-91, vice chmn. 1990-91, chmn. 1994-95, bd. cert. civil trial lawyer), Southeastern Admiralty Law Inst., Am. Judicature Soc., ATLA (sustaining), Am. Bd. Trial Advocates (advocate), Maritime Law Assn. (proctor), Tex. Trial Lawyers Assn., Acad. Fla. Trial Lawyer (designated continuing legal edn. speaker 1982—, bd. dirs. 1989-97, 2000-01), Inner Cir. Advocates, Internat. Soc. Barristers, Am. Inns. of Ct. (supporting fellow), Cousteau Soc., Tampa Club, Univ. Club, Grand Havana Club, Old Memorial Golf Club. Democrat. Avocations: fishing, tennis, boxing. Office: The Yerrid Law Firm Bank of America Plz Ste 3910 101 E Kennedy Blvd Tampa FL 33602-5192 Office Phone: 813-222-8222. E-mail: syerrid@yerridlaw.com.

YERUSHALMI, YOSEF HAYIM, historian, educator; b. NYC, May 20, 1932; s. Leon and Eva (Kaplan) Y.; m. Ophra Pearly, Jan. 4, 1959; 1 child, Ariel. BA, Yeshiva U., 1953; M in Hebrew Lit., Jewish Theol. Sem. Am., 1957; MA, Columbia U., 1961, PhD, 1966; MA (hon.), Harvard, 1970; DHL (hon.), Jewish Theol. Sem. Am., 1987; LHD (hon.), Hebrew Union Coll., 1996; PhD (hon.), U. Haifa, 1997, Ludwig Maximilians U., Munich, 1997; DHL (hon.), Spertus Inst., 2002; PhD (hon.), Ecole Pratique des Hautes Etudes Sorbonne Paris, 2003. Instr. Jewish history Rutgers U., New Brunswick, NJ, 1963-66; asst. prof. Hebrew and Jewish History Harvard U., 1966-70, prof., 1970—80, Jacob E. Safra prof. Jewish history and Sephardic civilization, 1978-80, chmn. dept. near eastern langs. and civilizations, 1978-80, Salo Wittmayer Baron Prof. of Jewish History, Culture, Soc.; dir. Columbia U. Inst. Israel and Jewish Studies, NYC, 1980—2008, Baron prof. emeritus, 2008—. Author: From Spanish Court to Italian Ghetto: Isaac Cardoso, A Study in Seventeenth-Century Marranism and Jewish Apologetics, 1971, Haggadah and History, 1975, The Lisbon Massacre of 1506, 1976, Zakhor: Jewish History and Jewish Memory, 1982, Freud's Moses: Judaism Terminable and Interminable, 1991, A Field in Anatot: Essays on Jewish History (in German), 1993, Servants of Kings and Not Servants of Servants: Some Aspects of the Political History of the Jews (in German), 1995, Sefardica: Essays on the History of the Jews, Marranos and New Christians of Hispano-Portuguese Origin (in French), 1998; author (in Hebrew): Spinoza on the Survival of the Jews, 1983; contbr. articles to profl. publs. on Spanish and Portuguese Jewry and history of psychoanalysis; chmn. publs. com. Jewish Publ. Soc., 1972-84; pres. Leo Baeck Inst., 1986-91. Bd. dirs. Conf. Jewish Social Studies, Psycho analytic Research and Devel. Fund, Editorial Bd., History and Memory. Recipient Newman medal CUNY, 1975, Nat. Jewish Book award, 1983, 92, Ansley award Columbia U. Press, 1968, Achievement medal Nat. Found. Jewish Culture, 1995, Leopold Lucas prize U. Tübingen, Germany, 2005; Kent fellow, 1963, Nat. Found. Jewish Culture, 1964, NEH, 1976-77, Rockefeller Found., 1983-84, Guggenheim Found., 1989-90, Carl Friedrich von Siemens Stiftung fellow, 1996-97, fellow Inst. Advanced Studies Tel Aviv U., 2004. Fellow Am. Acad. Jewish Research, Am. Acad. Arts and Scis., Acad. Portuguesa da História Lisbon (hon.), Acad. Sci. Lisboa (hon.). Business E-Mail: yhy1@columbia.edu.

YESAWICH, PETER CHARLES, advertising executive; b. Ithaca, NY, Oct. 28, 1950; s. Paul Joseph Jr. and Elizabeth (Larkin) Y.; m. Paris Pyne; children: Peter Charles, Paul Christopher, Logan Baker. BS, Cornell U., 1972, MS, 1974, PhD, 1976; AMP, Yale U., 1994. Dir. rsch. Robinsons, Inc., Orlando, Fla., 1976-78, v.p., 1978-81, exec. v.p., 1981-83; pres., CEO Ypartnership, Orlando, 1983—. Vis. assoc. prof. Cornell U., Ithaca, 1977—, U. Ctrl. Fla., Orlando, 1988—; chmn. Pope Tourism Inst., Orlando, 1988-90. Co-author: Marketing, Leadership in Hospitality, 2006; contbr. articles to profl. jours. Recipient World Travel award Am. Assn. Travel Editors, 1985, Silver Medal award Am. Assn. Advt. Agys., 1992, Adrian award Hospitality Sales and Mktg. Assn. Internat., 1993; named Author of Yr. Cornell Quar., 1986. Mem. Cornell Hotel Soc., Am. Hotel & Motel Assn., Caribbean Hotel Assn., Hotel Sales Mktg. Assn., Am. Mktg. Assn. Avocations: jogging, writing. Office: Ypartnership 423 S Keller Rd # 100 Orlando FL 32810-6102 Office Phone: 407-875-1111. Business E-Mail: peter.yesawich@ypartnership.com.

YETMAN, LEITH ELEANOR, academic administrator; b. Kellits, Clarendon, Jamaica, West Indies; came to US, 1967; d. 2nd child of 12 children of Percival Augustus and Grace Elizabeth (Anderson) Y.; m. Noel W. Miller, Apr. 8, 1961 (div. 1977); children: Donovan, Jo-Ann, Kirk, Lori-Anne; adopted children: LaFara, Samantha, Brandon Ryan. Attended, Bethlehem Teachers Coll., St. Elizabeth, Jamaica, 1960; BSc, Baruch Coll., 1976; MA, Columbia U., 1979. Cert. tchr., NY; accredited Bklyn. Inst. Bus. Tech., 1998. Legal sec. various law firms, NYC, 1969-76; instr. Taylor Bus. Inst., NYC, 1977-79; founder, pres., dir. NY Inst. English and Bus. (formerly NY Inst. Bus. Tech., NYC, 1981—; founder Bklyn. Inst. Bus. Tech. (formerly Grace Inst. Bus. Tech.), 1996. Recipient award, Prime Min. Jamaica P.J. Peterson, 2003, citations Hon. Virginia Fields, Gov. NY State, Hon. George E. Pataki, City Coun. NY, 2004, letters of recognition and praise Ex-First Ladies Barbara Bush, Hillary Clinton, Ex-Pres. Bill Clinton, Senator Charles Rangel, Ex-Mayor David Dinkins, others, award Prime of Jamaica, 2003, NYC Coun. citation The Emigrant Awards Found., 2004; Leith E. Yetman Day proclaimed June 1, 1994 by Manhattan Borough Pres. Office: NY Inst English and Bus 248 W 35th St New York NY 10001 Office Phone: 212-725-9400. Personal E-mail: eleany@aol.com. Business E-Mail: nyieb02@aol.com.

YETMAN, RANDALL JOHN, plastic surgeon; b. Casper, Wyo., Nov. 1, 1948; s. Jack Eugene and Mary Yetman; m. Nancy Lynn Devins, Apr. 29, 1969; children: Koren Dodson, Jamie Finnicum. Degree, SUNY, Buffalo, 1970; MD, U. Miami, 1975. Diplomate Am. Bd. Plastic Surgery, 1984. Intern in gen. surgery Albert Einstein Sch. Medicine, 1975—79, residency in gen. surgery, 1975—79; residency in plastic surgery Cornell Sch. Medicine, NYC, 1979—81, asst. prof. surgery, 1981—83; staff surgeon Cleve. Clinic, 1983—. Residency program dir. in plastic surgery Cleve. Clinic, 1995—. Fellow: ACS; mem.: Am. Soc. Plastic Surgeons, Am. Assn. Plastic Surgeons. Republican. Roman Catholic. Avocations: golf, fly fishing. Home: 2603 Fairmount Blvd Cleveland Heights OH 44106 Office: Cleveland Clinic 9500 Euclid Ave Cleveland OH 44106 Business E-Mail: yetmanr@ccf.org.

YETTER, R. PAUL, lawyer; b. Milw., Aug. 5, 1958; s. Richard and Lobelia (Gutierrez) Y.; m. Patricia D. Yetter, May 6, 1983; children: Chris, Mark, Michael, Joseph, Thomas, Andrew, Daniel. BA in Bus., U. Tex., El Paso, 1980; JD, Columbia U., 1983. Bar: Tex. 1983, US Dist. Ct. (all dists. Tex.), US Ct. Appeals (5th cir.); bd. cert. in civil trial law and personal injury trial law Tex. Bd. Legal Specialization. Law clk. to Hon. John R. Brown US Ct. Appeals (5th cir.), Houston, 1983-84; assoc. Baker & Botts, LLP, Houston, 1984-89, ptnr., 1990-97, Yetter, Warden Coleman LLP, Houston, 1997—. Chair state judiciary rels. com. State Bar, 1995-96; mem. Funding Parity Task Force, 1995-97; mem. ex officio Jud. Selection Task Force, 1995-97; chair Alliance for Jud. Funding, Inc., 1996—; mem. ex officio contbns. com. Tex. Ctr. for the Judiciary; mem. com. on admissions, So. Dist., Tex., 2000—; mem. Tex. Jud. Found., 2008-. Contbr. articles to profl. jours. Recipient Presdl. citation State Bar Tex., 1996, Disting. alumnus U. Tex., El Paso, 2008; rsch. fellow Southwestern Legal Found.; named one of Top 10 Trial Lawyers in Am., Nat. Law Jour., 2004, Tex. Super Lawyer Bus. Litig., Tex. Monthly, 2003-08, One of Best Lawyers, H Tex. Mag., 2005-07. Fellow Tex. Bar Foun., Houston Bar Found. Office: Yetter Warden & Coleman LLP 2 Houston Ctr 909 Fannin St Ste 3600 Houston TX 77010 Office Phone: 713-632-8000. Business E-Mail: pyetter@yetterwarden.com, pyetter@ywcllp.com.

YEUN, EUNJA, nursing educator, director; b. Incheon metro-city, Republic Of Korea, Sept. 4, 1956; d. Bockman Yeun and Heewhan Kim; m. Hanbeom Lee, Oct. 20, 1985; children: Haeri Lee, Haechan Lee. BSN, Chungang U., Seoul, 1979, MSN, 1981, PhD, 1995; postgrad., Case Western Res. U., Ohio, 2004. RN Ministry Health & Welfare, 1979, cert. health educator, Ministry Edn. & Human Resource Devel., 1979; child care tchr. Ministry Gender Equality and Family, 2006. Head nurse Chungang U. Hosp., Seoul, 1982—85, don, 1986—93; vis. observer sch. nursing U. Calif., San Francisco, 1995; dean, asst. prof., dept. nursing Konkuk U., Chungju, 1996—2001, assoc. prof., dept. nursing, 2001—06; vis. prof. FPB Sch. of Nursing, Case Western Res. U., Ohio, 2003—04; prof., dept. nursing Konkuk U., Seoul, 2006—. Com. Nat. Health Pers. Licensing Exam. Bd., Seoul, 2002. Author: (books) Medical-Surgical Nursing I, II, 6th.edit., 2007, Medical-Surgical Nursing I, II.III, 2007, Adult Nursing I, II, 2nd edit., 2006, Management of Elder Care I, II, Essentials of Clinical Nursing, 2003, Emergency Nursing, 2002, Adult Nursing Practice, 2001, Adult Nursing I, II, 2002, Introduction to Nursing, 2000, Qualitative Research Terminology Dictionary, 2003, Health and Safety Control in Infancy, 2002, Gerontological Nursing, 2008, (exhibition) The experience of Middle-aged women with Sauna, 2002, A study about desiring sexual and masturbation in married women, 2002, The experience of Smoking behavior in high school girls, Effectiveness of Video-Record Method of Fundamental Nursing Skill Education, A study on the health promoting lifestyle practices of middle-aged women in Korea, 2000, How People Understand Death: A co-orientational look, 1997, A Study on the Professional Nursing Image of Nursing Unit Manager: A Q-methodological approach, 1996, Attitudes of Elderly Korean Patients Toward Death and Dying, 2005, Verification of the Profile of Mood States-Brief: Cross Cultural Analysis, 2006, Application of the Transtheoretical Model to Identify Aspects Influencing Condom Use Among Korean Coll., 2008, Cross-cultural Gelotophobia Study; contbr. numberous articles to profl. jours. Com. Policy devel. for Women, Chungju, Republic of Korea, 1997—2002; pub. health com. Pub. Health Coun., Chungju, 1998—2003; acad.advisor Aeorsinsarang, Seoul, 2004—. Rsch. grant, Konkuk U., 1996—97, 2004—05, 2008—, Study grant, Pacific Scholarship & Culture Found., 1998—99, 2001—02. Mem.: Korea Soc. Health Edn. and Promotion, Korean Soc. Sci. Study of Subjectivity, Korean Acad. of Adult Nursing Soc. (acad. com. 1998—2000, editor 2002—), Korean Acad. of Nursing Soc., Korean Nurse Assn. (academic com. edn. 1997—2000). Catholic. Achievements include development of an instrument to measure nursing professional values. Avocations: yoga, travel, mountain climbing, oil painting. Home: 787 Jayang-dong Kwangin-gu Seoul 143-882 Republic of Korea Office: Konkuk Univ Dept Nursing 322 Danwol-dong Cheongju 380-701 Republic of Korea Office Fax: 82-43-840-3929. Business E-Mail: eunice@kku.ac.kr.

YEUNG, ANN, music educator; MusD, Ind. U., Bloomington, 1998. Cert. performer and artist diploma in art Ind. U., 1993. Harp prof. U. Ill., Urbana, 1999—. Jury mem. Nippon Internat. Harp Competition, Soka, Japan, 1st Internat. Youth Talents Competition, Teignmouth, England, Internat. Harp Competition, Belgrade, Serbia. Musician: 1st Asian Harp Festival in Hong Kong, 2nd Internat. Hosp. Festival, 2008, (world premiere) Agoraphobia for flute, harp, interactive electronics and video by Stephen Andrew Taylor, Tenth World Harp Congress in Amsterdam; contbr. numerous articles to profl. jours. Named Outstanding Excellent Tchr., 1999—2008; Rsch. grant, U. Ill., 2008. Mem.: Am. Harp Soc. (dir.-at-large 2000—06, chair, harp lit. com. 2001—06, 2nd. v.p. 2004—06, mem., nominating com. 2006—, co-chair. 50th anniversary project commn. com. 2008—), World Harp Congress (rev. editor 2002—). Achievements include discovery of Chou Wen-Chung's two Chinese folk songs for solo harp arranged. Office: Univ Ill Urbana-Champaign 1114 W Nevada St Urbana IL 61801

YEUNG, RONALD WAI-CHUN, engineering educator, researcher; s. Foo and Pui Fong Yeung; m. Grace Y. Chow, Sept. 5, 1970; 1 child, Brian H. BSME, U. Calif., Berkeley, 1968, MS Naval Architecture, 1970, PhD Engring., 1973. Naval arch. Advanced Marine Tech. Divsn., Litton Ship Sys., Culver City, Calif., 1970—71; instr. U. Calif. LA ext., Long Beach Naval Shipyard, 1970—71; asst., assoc. prof. MIT, Cambridge, 1974—82; prof. hydromechanics & ocean engring. U. Calif., Berkeley, 1982—, chair dept. naval architecture & offshore engring., 1989—96, disting. prof., 1994—. Prin. R. W. Yeung - Consulting Naval Architect & Ocean Engr., Moraga, Calif., 1976—; Humboldt prof. U. Hamburg, Germany, 1988, Mercator U., Duisburg, Germany, 1998—99; vis. prof. Kyushu U. Inst. Applied Mech., Japan, 1998, Nat. Tech. U.

Norway, CESOS, Trondheim, 2007. Editor: (spl. edition on Ocean Mechanics) Jour. Engring. Math., 1999; assoc. editor: Jour. Ship Rsch., 1975—95, Jour. Computers & Fluids, 1983—, Jour. Engring. Math., 1986—, Jour. Marine Systems & Offshore Tech., 2004—, Jour. Marine Sci. & Tech., 2006—, Ocean Engring Jour., 2006—; contbr. articles to profl. jours. Recipient Univ. Gold medal, U. Calif., 1968, Disting. Scientist award, Alexander von Humboldt Found., 1988, 1998, Best Paper award, ASME, Offshore Mechanics and Arctic Engring., 1991, ASME, Offshore Mech. and Arctic Engring., 2002, Georg Weinblum lectr., Naval Studies Bd., Soc. Naval Architects and Marine Engrs. and Schiffbautechnische Gesellschaft, 2002—03, Kenneth Davidson gold medal, Soc. Naval Architects and Marine Engrs., 2004, Bill Zimmie award, U. Mich., Ann Arbor, 2006, Internat. Rschr. award, Sociedade Brasileria de Engenharia Naval, 2008; named Pi Tau Sigma Prof. of Yr., U. Calif., Berkeley, 2006; scholar Fulbright-Hayes Sr. scholar, U. Adelaide, Australian-Am. Edn. Found., 1981. Fellow: Soc. Naval Architects & Marine Engrs. (No. Calif. exec. com. and acad. liaison 1989—); mem.: Japanese Soc. Naval Architects, Am. Soc. Engring. Edn., Internat. Soc. Offshore and Polar Engrs. (chair hydrodynamics com. 2002—03), Phi Beta Kappa, Pi Tau Sigma, Tau Beta Pi. Achievements include leader in ocean engineering and marine mechanics; in particular ship, ocean, marine hydromechanics; research in free-surface computational methods, ship-to-ship interaction, channel-wall effects, surface-wave and vorticity interaction, roll-damping modeling, vortex-induced vibration, 2-layer fluid flow, hydro-elastic waves, multi-hull interference. Home: 27 Indian Wells Moraga CA 94556-1020 Office: U Calif 6135 Etcheverry Hall Berkeley CA 94720-1740 Business E-Mail: rwyeung@berkeley.edu.

YEUTTER, CLAYTON KEITH, lawyer, former United States Secretary of Agriculture; b. Eustis, Nebr., Dec. 10, 1930; s. Reinhold F. and Laura P. Y.; m. Cristena Bach; children: Victoria, Elena, Olivia. BS, Nebr. U., 1952, JD, 1963, PhD in Agrl. Econs., 1966; doctorate (hon.), Ariz. U., Clemson U., Georgetown U., Santa Clara U., Nebr. U., Nebr. Wesleyan U., U. Md., DePaul U. Bar: Nebr. 1963, D.C. 1977. Farmer, rancher, Nebr., 1957-75; mem. faculty dept. agrl. econs. U. Nebr., Lincoln, 1960-66; dir. U. Nebr. Mission in Colombia, South Am., 1968-70; exec. asst. to Gov. State of Nebr., Lincoln, 1966-68; regional dir. Com. for Reelection of Pres., 1972; adminstr. for consumer and mktg. services. USDA, Washington, 1970-71, asst. sec. for mktg. & consumer services, 1973-74, asst. sec. for internat. affairs & commodity programs, 1974-75; dep. spl. trade rep. Exec. Office of the Pres., Washington, 1975-77; sr. ptnr. Nelson, Harding, Yeutter & Leonard, Lincoln, Nebr., 1977-78; pres., CEO Chgo. Mercantile Exch., 1978-85; US Trade Rep. Exec. Office of the Pres., Washington, 1985-89; sec. USDA, Washington, 1989-91; chmn. Rep. Nat. Com., Washington, 1991-92; counsellor to the Pres. for domestic policy The White House, Washington, 1992; sr. advisor Hogan & Hartson LLP, Washington, 1993—. Bd. dirs. Neogen Corp., 2007—. Contbr. numerous articles to profl. jours. Bd. dir. Am. Comml. Lines, Burlington Capital Group, Neogen Corp., Chgo. Climate Exch., Covanta Holding Corp.; former dir. Caterpillar, Tex. Instruments, Weyerhaeuser, B.A.T. Industries, UK, Zurich Fin. Svcs., Switzerland, FMC, Con Agra Foods, Oppenheimer Funds. With USAF, 1952—57, with USAFR, 1957—87. Recipient Israel Prime Minister's medal, Master Builder of Men award FarmHouse, Leadership award Fowler-McCracken Commn., Consumers for World Trade award. Mem. Nebr. Bar Assn. Republican. Presbyterian. Avocations: skiing, water-skiing, weightlifting. Office: Neogen Corp 620 Lesher Pl Lansing MI 48912 Office Phone: 517-372-9200.*

YEW, DAVID, physician, director; b. NYC, Oct. 5, 1970; MD, SUNY, 1996—99. Cert. Am. Bd. Emergency Medicine, 2003. Emergency medicine physician St. Luke's-Roosevelt Hosp., Columbia U., NYC, 1999—2001, Kaiser Permamente, Honolulu, 2002—03, Tripler Army Med. Ctr., Honolulu, 2003—; ship dr. Norwegian Cruise Line, Honolulu, 2005—; med. dir. AirMed Hawaii, Honolulu, 2006—. Disaster medicine physician Dept. Homeland Security FEMA/DMAT, Honolulu, 2003—; mcht. mariner US Coast Guard, Honolulu, 2004—; asst. clin. prof. dept. surgery U. Hawaii Med. Sch., Honolulu, 2005—. Contbr. chapters to books. Recipient Outstanding Staff Tchr. award/Jeffrey P. Kavolius award, Tripler Army Med. Ctr., 2005. Mem.: Fed. Physicians Assn. (assoc.), Air Med. Physicians Assn. (assoc.), Mensa (life). Achievements include development of virtual simulation education. Office: AirMed Hawaii 90 Nakolo Pl Ste 203 Honolulu HI 96817 Personal E-mail: yewdave@hotmail.com. Business E-Mail: dyew@airmed.com.

YEWDELL, JONATHAN WILSON, cell biologist; b. Mt Vernon, NY, Dec. 10, 1953; s. Noel Benedict and Rosalind Henrietta (Dulberg) Y.; m. Margaret Delaney, July 22, 1982; children: Alison, William, Andrew, Alexander. AB, Princeton U., 1975; MD, PhD, U. Pa., 1981. Asst. prof. Wistar Inst., Phila., 1983-87; sr. investigator Nat. Inst. Allergy and Infectious Diseases, Bethesda, Md., 1987-93, sect. chief, 1993—. Avocations: ballroom dancing, base jumping, greco-roman wrestling. Office: NIH Bldg 4 Rm 213 Bethesda MD 20892-0001

YI, HYUNMIN, chemical engineer, educator; PhD, U. Md., Coll. Pk., 2003. Asst. rsch. scientist U. Md., 2005—06; asst. prof. Tufts U., Medford, Mass., 2006—. Contbr. articles to numerous profl. jours. Mem.: Am. Chem. Soc., Am. Inst. Chem. Engrs. Office: Tufts Univ 4 Colby St Medford MA 02155 Business E-Mail: hyunmin.yi@tufts.edu.

YI, JIANLIAN, professional basketball player; b. Shenzhen, China, Oct. 27; Student, Sports Acad. Shenzhen; grad., Guangdong U. Tech. Player Guangdong Hongyuan So. Tigers Chinese Basketball Assn., Dongguan City, Guangdong, 2002—; forward Milw. Bucks, 2007—08, NJ Nets, 2008—. Mem. Chinese Olympic Basketball Team, Athens, 2004. Achievements include being youngest player to ever play in highest league China Basketball Assn. (CBA), 2002; two-time CBA All-Star, 2004-2005. Office: NJ Nets 390 Murray Hill Pwy East Rutherford NJ 07073*

YI, JIZU, research scientist, educator; m. Lihua Chen; children: Lynn D., David C., Joycena B. PhD, Rutgers State U., NJ, 1997. Rsch. asst. prof. Mt. Sinai Sch. Medicine, NYC, 2000—; prin. scientist BD Diagnostics, Franklin Lakes, NJ, 2003—. Home: 204-12 45th Dr Bayside NY 11361 Office: BD Diagnostics 1 Becton Dr Franklin Lakes NJ 07417 Office Fax: 201-847-4851. Business E-Mail: jizu_yi@bd.com.

YI, SEUNG-HO, physicist, educator; b. Daegu, Republic Of Korea, Oct. 30, 1965; s. Jea-In Yi and So-Nan Song; m. Ji-Young Lee; children: Benjamin, Jea-Hyuk. PhD, Tex. Tech U., Lubbock, 1996. Sr. engr. Hynix Semiconductor. Co., Icheon, Kyounggi-do, Republic of Korea, 1996—2001; sr. rsch. engr. LG Semiconductor, Cheong-Ju, Chungcheongbuk-do, Republic of Korea, 1996—; rsch. fellow Seoul Nat. U., Republic of Korea, 2001—03, vis. asst. prof., 2006—07; rsch. prof. Kyung Hee U., Seoul, 2004—06, asst. prof., 2007. Tech. advisor Dong-bang Acupuncture, Inc., Sungnan, Kyounggi-do, Republic of Korea, 2006—, GS Med., Seoul, 2008—. Contbr. articles to profl. jours. Mem.: Korean Physics Soc. Achievements include development of laser guided needless injector; insertion force measurement devices for acupuncture research; patents for for semiconductor fabrication process; acupuncture and moxibustion devices; research in acupuncture and biophoton. Home: 703-101 Salgu-gol Youngtong-gu Suwon 443-736 Republic of Korea Office: KyungHee Univ 1 Hoegi-dong Dongdaemun-gu Seoul 130-701 Republic of Korea Office Fax: 82 2 963 2175; Home Fax: 82 2 963 2175. Personal E-mail: bondyi@empal.com. Business E-Mail: shyi@khu.ac.kr.

YI, TAEIL, mathematician, educator; b. Seoul, Republic of Korea, Dec. 16, 1962; s. Beomyoung and Bongwol Yi; m. Moonsil Kim, Nov. 20, 1962; children: Hanyong David, Changyong Peter. BS, Dankook U., Seoul, 1988, MS, 1990, U. Ill., 1994; MEd, U. Fla., 1997, PhD, 2000. Math. tchr. Yongmoon H.S., Seoul, South Korea, 1988—90; tchg. asst. U. Fla., Fla., 1995—2000, instr. Gainesville, 2000—01; assoc. prof. U. Tex., Brownsville, 2001—. Advisor Pi Mu Epsilon U. Tex., Brownsville, 2002—. Prodr.: (instructional video) Name That Move (Jim Harbin Award / Fla. Assn. for Media in Edn., 1995); contbr. articles to profl. jours. Condr. choir Korean Ch., Urbana/Champaign, Ill., 1993—94; chief editor Korean Bapt. Ch., Gainesville, Fla., 1996—2001, dir. gen. affair, 1997—2000; leader youth group Open Door Ch., Brownsville, Tex., 2001, sec. bd., 2002. Recipient Jim Harbin award, Fla. Assn. Media Edn., 1995, Spl. Merit award, U. Tex. Brownsville, 2006. Mem.: Scientific Rsch. Soc., Soc. Indsl. and Applied Math., Math. Assn. Am., Am. Math. Soc., Sigma Xi, Phi Kappa Phi (life), Phi Mu Epsilon. Achievements include development of an automated stereotactic radiosurgery algorithm for brain tumor treatment planning, which has been developed by a software company for broad usage. Avocations: golf, studying theology. Home: 5 Deer Haven Ct Brownsville TX 78520 Office: Univ Tex Brownsville 80 Fort Brown Brownsville TX 78520 E-mail: Taeil.Yi@utb.edu.

YI, WEI, physicist; BS, Tsinghua U., Beijing, 1996; PhD, Harvard U., Cambridge, Mass., 2005. Rsch. asst. Inst. Physics, Chinese Acad. Scis., Beijing, 1996—99; rsch. asst., sch. engring. and applied scis., Harvard U., Cambridge, 1999—2005, postdoctoral fellow Sch. Engring. and Applied Scis., 2005—. Recipient Wei Hua Sci. and Tech. award, Chinese Acad. Scis., 1999; fellow, Harvard U., 1999—2000. Mem.: Am. Phys. Soc., Materials Rsch. Soc., Sigma Xi. Achievements include development of 3-Omega method for specific heat and thermal conductivity measurements of a filament-like specimen, and measured those thermal quantities of carbon nanotube bundles with only nanogram in mass; a three-terminal ballistic carrier spectroscopy that probes bandgaps of semiconductors and band offsets at semiconductor heterojuctions; co-development of avalanche spin-valve transistor; co-development of a low cost fabrication method for integrating nanowire devices directly onto silicon; observation of coulomb blockade and fano resonance in the tunneling spectroscopy between multiwalled carbon nanotubes and normal metals; demonstrated the potential of using a dual-probe scanning tunneling microscope to study nanoscale metal-semiconductor interfaces; measured temperature dependence of thermoelectric power in multiwalled carbon nanotubes; research in measured ballistic electron emission luminescence spectroscopy of an InAs quantum dot heterostructure; co-developed integrated optics for ballistic electron emission luminescence microscopy. Office: Harvard University 9 Oxford St Cambridge MA 02138 Business E-Mail: wyi@fas.harvard.edu.

YI, ZHIXIAN, science educator; s. Limo Yi and Shuixian Chen; m. Songying Zhou. MLitt, Ctrl. S U., Hunan, 1995; MLIS, Southern Conn. State U., 2004; PhD, Tex. Woman's U., Denton, 2009. Grad. asst. Southern Conn. State U., New Haven, 2002—03; grad. tchg. asst. Tex. Woman's U., Denton, 2003—. Contbr. articles to profl. jours. Mem.: Assn. Libr. Info. Sci. Edn. (pres., SW chpt. 2009), Chinese Am. Librarians Assn. (v.p., SW chpt. 2008). Home: 326 Peach St Apt R Denton TX 76209-1944

YIELDING, K. LEMONE, physician; b. Auburn, Ala., Mar. 25, 1931; s. Riley Lafayette and Bertie (Dees) Y.; m. Lerena Wade Hauge, Dec. 8, 1973; children: K. Lemone, Michael Lafon, Teresa Louise, Riley Lafayette, Katrina Elizabeth, Elaine Louise Blodgett, Laura Carlen Blodgett. BS, Ala. Poly. Inst., 1949; MS, U. Ala., 1952, MD, 1954. Intern U. Ala. Med. Center, 1954-55; clin. assoc. Nat. Inst. Arthritis and Metabolic Diseases, NIH, 1955-57, sr. investigator, 1958-64; resident med. service USPHS Hosp., Balt., 1957-58; physician in practice of oncology and emergency medicine, 1995—. Adj. asst. prof. medicine Georgetown U. Med. Sch., 1958-64; cons. USPHS, 1964-68, 75—; prof. biochemistry, assoc. prof. medicine, chief lab. molecular biology U. Ala. Med. Ctr., Birmingham, 1964-80; prof., chmn. dept. anatomy, prof. medicine U. So. Ala. Coll. Medicine, Mobile, 1980-87; dean grad. sch. U. Tex. Med. Br., Galveston, 1987-95, dean emeritus, 1995—, v.p. for rsch., 1987-94; cons. Am. Heart Assn., Arthritis Found., NIH, NASA. Contbr. to profl. jours., books. Served with USPHS, 1955-64. Grantee USPHS, Am. Cancer Soc., Nat. Found.-March of Dimes, U.S. Army, Am. Inst. Cancer Research. Mem. Am. Soc. Biol. Chemistry, Am. Assn. Cancer Research, Am. Assn. Photobiology, Assn. Research Vision and Ophthalmology, Soc. Exptl. Biology and Medicine, Am. Soc. Pharm. and Exptl. Therapeutics, Am. Assn. Pathologists, So. Soc. Clin. Investigation, Am. Assn. Anatomy, Soc. Toxicology, Sigma Xi. Personal E-mail: lemoneyielding@hughes.net.

YIFRU, DAWIT DESALEGN, environmental scientist; PhD, U. Ga., Athens, 2006. Cert. geologist State Ga., 2008. Environ. scientist Geosyntec Cons., Kennesaw, 2006—. Contbr. articles to profl. jours. Fellow, U. Akron, 2001—02, U. Ga., 2003—06. Mem.: Nat. Groundwater Assn., Am. Geol. Soc. Home and Office: Geosyntec Cons 1255 Roberts Blvd Ste 200 Kennesaw GA 30144 Office Phone: 678-202-9500. Personal E-mail: dawitdy@yahoo.com.

YILDIRIM, HUSEYIN, engineering educator; b. Denizli, Turkey, May 10, 1972; s. Mehmet and Ayse Yildirim; m. Elif Ekebas, Aug. 5, 2000; 1 child, Artun Suayip. PhD, U. Fla., Gainesville, 2000. Cert. in engring., Bilkent U., 1993. Asst. prof. Duke U., Durham, 2000—07, assoc. prof., 2007—. Office: Duke Univ Box 90097 Durham NC 27708 Business E-Mail: yildirh@econ.duke.edu.

YILDIRIM, YILDIRAY, finance educator; PhD, Cornell U., Ithaca, 2001. Assoc. prof. fin. Syracuse U. Whitman Sch., NY, 2001—. Office: Syracuse Univ Whitman Sch Suite 500 Syracuse NY 13244 Business E-Mail: yildiray@syr.edu.

YILDIZHAN, AHMET, neurosurgeon, educator; b. Ladik-Samsun, Turkey, Feb. 24, 1956; s. Hasan and Fatma Yildizhan; m. Zeynep Sema Ugur; children: Saliha Elif, Fatma Esra, Abdullah Emir, Fatih Selim. MD, Ankara U., Turkey, 1980. Cert. Neurosurgeon Ministry of Health, 1986. Resident Faculty Medicine Erciyes U., Kayseri, Turkey, 1981—86; founder Dept. Neurosurgery SSK Hosp., Kayseri, Turkey, 1986—88; assoc. prof. Vakif Gureba Hosp., Istanbul, 1989—94; assoc. prof. Merter Vatan Hosp. and Istanbul Vatan Hosp. Universal Hosp. Group, 1994—. Adv. bd. Turkish Jour. Medicine, Ankara, 1994—2004; prin., owner Edn. and Sci. Mag., Istanbul, 1998—; vis. rschr. Harvard U., Cambridge, Mass., 1992; neurosurgeon Gulhane Mil. Med. Acad., Ankara, 1990—91; assoc. prof. Faculty Medicine Yeditepe U., Istanbul, 2003—. Author: Bel Fitigi ve Korunma Yollari, 1997, 2007, Lumbar Disc Herniation and Its Prevention (100 Recommendations for Low Back Health), 2005, 2007, Bilim Egitim ve Kultur Yazilari - Kuresel Problemler Nasil Cozulur? (Science Education and Cultural Essays - How are Global Problems Resolved?), 2007, Mutlulugun Denklemi (Equation of Happiness), 2007, Evrensel Bahceye (Didaktik Siirler) (Didactic Poems for the Universal Garden), 2007; mem. editl. bd.: Medikal Plus Mag., 2002—; contbr. 53 scientific papers in field, over 50 articles to profl. pubs. Mem. Yesilay, Istanbul, 1993; lifetime vol. mem. TEMA; supporter Neurosurgery Rsch. and Edn. Found., Provision for Clean Water in Africa, Engelliler ve Dostlari Kulubu, Campaign for Edn. of Girls in Antolia. Mem.: Turkish Neurosurgical Soc., Soc. Neuro-Oncology, Am. Assn. Neurol. Surgeons, Istanbul Chamber Medicine, Turkish Neurosurg. Soc. (Internat. Pub. award 1989, 1990, 1992), Yesilay, Nat. Geographic Soc. Muslim. Avocations: reading, writing, swimming, travel, thinking. Office Fax: 902122418121. Business E-Mail: ayildizhan@e-kolay.net.

YILMA, ALMAZ, biology professor; d. Yilma Defabachew and Feleketch Abebe; m. Mesgun Sebhatu, July 21, 1984; children: Emnet Mesgun Sebhatu, Temnete Mesgun Sebhatu. BS in Plant Sci., Addis Abada U., Ethiopia, 1978; M in Plant Pathology, Clemson U., SC, 1984. Part time biology instr. York Tech. Coll., Rock Hill, SC, 1993—; biology instr. Winthrop U., Rock Hill, 1999—. Cons. York County Mus., Rock Hill, 1989—. Contbr. scientific papers to publs. Organizer Internat. Festival, Rock Hill, 2004. Fellow, Food and Agrl. Orgn., 1982—84. Avocations: cooking, reading, travel. Office: Winthrop Univ 701 Oakland Ave Rock Hill SC 29733 Office Phone: 803-323-2111 6150. Office Fax: 803-323-3448. Business E-Mail: yilmaa@winthrop.edu.

YILMA, TILAHUN DANIEL, virologist, veterinarian, educator, researcher; b. Bulki, Gemugofa, Ethiopia, Dec. 15, 1943; parents Wolde-Ab Yilma and Getenesh Negewo. BS in Vet. Sci., U. Calif., Davis, 1968, DVM, 1970, PhD in Microbiology, 1977. Head vet. scv. Min. Agr., Harar, Ethiopia, 1970-71; lectr. UNDP/FAO of the UN Sch. for Animal Health Assts., DebreZeit, Ethiopia, 1971-72; rsch. assoc. USDA, Greenport, N.Y., 1977-79; asst. prof. vet. microbiology, pathology Wash. State U., Pullman, 1980-85, assoc. prof. vet. microbiology, pathology, 1985-86; prof. virology U. Calif., Davis, 1986—, dir. Internat. Lab. Molecular Biology for Tropical Disease Agents. Patentee in field. Recipient Ciba-Geigy prize Ciba-Geigy Ltd., 1990, Beecham award, 1988. Mem.: NAS. Office: U Calif Sch Vet Medicine 2079A Haring Hall Davis CA 95616 Business E-Mail: tdvilma@ucdavis.edu.

YILMAZKUDAY, HAKAN, assistant professor; b. Kirklareli, Turkey, Sept. 23, 1978; s. Yalcin and Yildiz Yilmazkuday; m. Demet Ulker, July 17, 2004; 1 child, Ada. BS in Economics, Istanbul Bilgi U., Turkey, 2000, London Sch. Economics, 2001; MA in Economics, Marmara U., Turkey, 2003; PhD in Economics, Vanderbilt U., Nashville, 2009, MA in Economics, 2006. Asst. prof. Temple U., 2009—. Contbr. articles to profl. jours., chapters to books. U. fellowship, Vanderbilt U., 2005. Mem.: Econometric Soc., Am. Econ. Assn. Office: Temple Univ Dept Economics Philadelphia PA 19122 Office Fax: 615-343-8495. Business E-Mail: hakan.yilmazkuday@vanderbilt.edu.

YIM, MAN BIN, neurosurgeon, educator; b. Hong Seung, Chung Nam, Republic of Korea, Feb. 29, 1948; s. Byung Soon Yim and Jeung Ok Kang; m. In Sook Kim, Dec. 4, 1974; children: Chang Ok, Chang Baek. PhD, KyungPook Nat. U., Daegu, Republic of Korea, 1988. Lic. med. practitioner Ministry Health and Welfare, Republic of Korea, 1973, cert. Korean Bd. of Neurosurgery, 1981. Instr. Keimyung U. Sch. of Medicine, Daegu, Republic of Korea, 1981—83, asst. prof., 1983—87, assoc. prof., 1988—93, head neurosurgery Dong San Med. Ctr., 1991—99, chmn. neurosurgery, 1993—99, prof. neurosurgery, 1993—; dir. brain rsch. inst. Keimyung U., 2000—05; dean Keimjung U. Sch. Medicine, 2005—. Sec. gen. 5th Japanese and Korean Friendship Conf. on Surgery for Cerebral Stroke, Cheju, Republic of Korea, 1996—99; v.p. 7th Japanese and Korean Friendship Conf. on Surgery for Cerebral Stroke, KyungJu, 2002—; sci. trustee The Korean Soc. of Cerebrovascular Surgery, Seoul, 1996—98, sec. gen., 1998—, mem. arrangement com. 6th internat. workshop, 2000, pres., 2003—04. Author: Text Book of Neurosurgery; contbr. articles to profl. jours. including Jour. Korean Neurosurg. Soc. (Best Sci. Article, Korean Soc. of Cerebrovascular Surgery, 2003, Best Sci. Article, Korean Soc. of Neurosurgery, 2003). Capt. Army, 1973—76, Republic of Korea. Recipient Encouragement award of Han-Mi Essay Lit., The Korean Doctors' Weekly, 2003; named Best Dr. in Cerebrovascular Disease, Shin Dong Ah monthly mag., 1999, Best Dr. in Cerebovascular Disease, Dong Ah Daily News, 2003. Mem.: Korean Neurosurgical Soc. (licentiate; bd. trustees 1995—99, pres. (Daegu and Kyung Pook local chapt.) 1996—97, mem. bd. exam. com. 1996—99, mem. scientific com. 2000—02, bd. trustees 2003—), Korean Med. Assn. (licentiate), World Fedn. of Neurosurgical Societies (assoc.). Avocations: tennis, essay writing. Home: 1502 202 Dong ManChon WooBang 2 Cha Ap Daegu 706-759 Republic of Korea Office: Neurosurgery Keimyung Univ 194 DongSan Dong Jung-Gu Daegu 700-712 Republic of Korea Office Fax: 82-53-250-7356. Business E-Mail: y760111@dsmc.or.kr.

YIM, MAN-SUNG, engineering educator, consultant; arrived in US, 1983, naturalized, 2004; s. Hong-Kyu Yim and Hyun-Soon Kim; m. Soyoung Chang, Mar. 18, 1988; children: Eunji Allison, Minjie. BS, Seoul Nat. U., 1981, MS, 1983; PhD, U. Cin., 1987; SM, Harvard U., Cambridge, Mass., 1991, ScD, 1994. Cert. profl. engr., Korean Profl. Engineers' Assn., 1988. Rschr. Korea Advanced Energy Rsch. Inst., Daeduk, Republic of Korea, 1981—82; sr. rschr. Korea Atomic Energy Rsch. Inst., 1987—90; instr. Seoul Nat. U., 1989; lectr. MIT, Cambridge, Mass., 1994; asst. prof. NC State U., Raleigh, 1995—2001, assoc. prof., 2001—. Cons. Electric Power Rsch. Inst., Palo Alto, Calif., 1993—2001; dir. grad. programs nuc. engring. NC State U., Raleigh, 2001—07; mem. NC Sci. Adv. Bd. Air Toxic Emissions, 2004—; external steering com. mem. on nuc. nonproliferation Idaho Nat. Lab., Idaho Falls, 2005—08. Author: A Guide to Personnel Monitoring for Radiation in the Hospital Environment, 1993; author: (with Petr Vaganov) Ecological Risk (in Russian), 1999; editl. adv. bd. mem.: Jour. Progress in Nuc. Energy, 2003—. Bd. mem. Christian Worldview Network, Buena Pk., Calif., 2003—07; elder DuRaleigh Presbyn. Ch., Raleigh, NC, 2001—; chmn. Triangle Korean Sch., Raleigh, NC, 2005—07. Named Sr. Rsch. Ethics fellow, NC State U., 2005—08; fellow, Health Physics Soc., 1992—93, Adv. Com. Nuc. Waste Nuc. Regulatory Commn., 1992—93, Sam Nunn Sch. Internat. Affairs Ga. Inst. Tech., 2003—04; scholar, Korean Sci. and Engring. Found., 1982; Fulbright scholar, Korean Am. Edn. Commn., 1983—87, Jong Ha Lee scholar, Harvard U., 1991—93, Calvin and Lucy Ellis scholar, 1993—94. Mem.: Inst. Nuc. Materials Mgmt., Health Physics Soc., Am. Nuc. Soc. (exec. com. mem. 2005—07), Korean Nuc. Soc. (life), Alpha Nu Sigma Soc. Office: NC State Univ Box 7909 2500 Stinson Dr Raleigh NC 27695 Office Phone: 919-515-1466. Office Fax: 919-515-5115. Business E-Mail: yim@ncsu.edu.

YIN, HAIZHOU, computer scientist; m. Zhou Yan. BS, Peking U., Beijing, 1996; MA, Princeton U., NJ, 1999, PhD, 2004. Rsch. scientist IBM, Hopewell Junction, NY, 2004—08, sr. scientist, 2008—. Recipient IBM Invention Achievement award, IBM Outstanding Tech. Achievement award. Mem.: IEEE. Office: IBM 2070 Rt 52 Hopewell Junction NY 12533 Office Fax: 845-892-6483. Personal E-mail: yinhaizhou@yahoo.com. Business E-Mail: yinh@us.ibm.com.

YIN, HANG, chemistry professor; b. Beijing, July 5, 1976; s. Ying Yin and Ning Bai. PhD, Yale U., New Haven, 2004. Postdoc. assoc. U. Pa. Sch. Medicine, Phila., 2004—07; asst. prof. U. Colo., Boulder, 2007—. Task force mem. Colo. Initiative in Molecular Biotech., Boulder, 2007—; mem. and preceptor U. Colo. Cancer Ctr., Aurora, 2007—, U. Colo. Hosp., Aurora, 2007—; mem. adv. bd. Cancer League Colo., Englewood, 2008—; mem. sci. adv. bd. Boulder Valley Sch. Dist., 2008—. Contbr. scientific papers. Recipient Collaborative Innovation award, Howard Hughes Med. Inst., 2008, Jr. Faculty Devel. award, U. Colo., 2008, Cutting-Edge Basic Rsch. award, Nat. Inst. Drug Abuse, 2009, Early Career award, 2009; named New Inventor Of Yr., U. Colo., 2009; Wood-Whelan fellowship, Internat. Union Biochemistry & Molecular Biology, 2007, grant, Assn. Rsch. Childhood Cancer, 2008, Kimmel scholarship, 2008. Mem.: Am. Chem. Soc., Chinese-Am. Chemistry Profs. Assn., Am. Assn. Cancer Rsch. (Gertrude Elion award 2009), Sigma Xi. Achievements include patents for CHAMP peptides that bind to membrane proteins and methods; patents pending for preparation of terephthalamide peptidomimetic compounds for therapeutic use. Office: Univ Colo 215 UCB Dept Chem & Biochem Boulder CO 80309-0215 Office Fax: 303-492-5894.

YIN, PENG, computer scientist; s. Zhenmin Yin and Fenglan Wang. BSc in Economics, Peking U., Beijing, 1998, BSc in Molecular Biology and Biochemistry, 1998; MSc in Molecular Cancer Biology, Duke U., Durham, NC, 2000, PhD in Computer Sci., 2005. Cert. in molecular cell biology Duke U., 2000. Postdoc. scholar Caltech, Pasadena, Calif., 2005—07, sr. postdoc. scholar, 2007—. Office: CA Inst Tech M/C 136-93 Moore Bldg Pasadena CA 91125 Office Fax: 626-395-8845. Business E-Mail: py@caltech.edu.

YIN, TONGMING, science educator; s. Yutang Yin; m. Shuxian Li; 1 child, Ming Hang. PhD, Nanjing Forest U., China, 1997. Lectr. Nanjing Forestry U., 1997—2000; postdoc. rschr. Swedish Agr. U. Scis., Umea, Sweden, 2000—01, Oak Ridge Nat. Lab, 2001—05, rsch. staff scientist, 2005—. Recipient Jubilee award, Internat. Sci. Fund. Sweden, 2003, Outstanding Sci. and Tech. Devel., Oak Ridge Nat. Lab, Dept. Energy, 2007. Achievements include research in sequencing the poplar genome. Office: Oak Ridge Nat Lab Bethal Valley Rd Oak Ridge TN 37831 Business E-Mail: yintm@ornl.gov.

YING, GUI-SHUANG, ophthalmologist, educator; b. YongKang, Zhejiang, China, Feb. 13, 1970; s. Longsheng Ying and Aiyue Wu; m. Qin Lin, July 28, 1998; children: Bowen, Bole. PhD, U. Pa., Phila., 2004. Biostatistician U. Pa., 2000—04, asst. prof. ophthalmology, 2004—. Recipient Rsch. award, ARVO Found., 2008. Achievements include research in worse night vision is associated with increased risk of developing late stage of age-related macular degeneration. Home: 1523 Brookhaven Rd Wynnewood PA 19096 Office Fax: 215-615-1531. Personal E-mail: gsying2002@yahoo.com. Business E-Mail: gsying@mail.med.upenn.edu.

YING, WEIHAI, biomedical researcher, educator; b. Shanghai, Aug. 18, 1963; arrived in US, 1991; s. Guoyuan Ying and Shuzhu Huang; m. Fan Wu, Feb. 14, 1991; 1 child, Ming Yin. BS, Shanghai Med. U., 1985; PhD, U. N.Mex, 1998. Postdoctoral fellow U. Calif., San Francisco, 1998—2002, asst. prof. dept. neurology, 2002—, asst. neurologist, 2002—03, asst. prof., 2003—; rsch. biologist San Francisco VA Med. Ctr., 2002—; full rsch. scientist No. Calif. Inst. Rsch. and Edn., San Francisco, 2003—. Mng. editor Frontiers in Biosci., Albertson, NY, 2005—; grant reviewer Am. Heart Assn. Nat. Ctr., Dallas, 2006—. Contbr. over 40 abstracts and 20 articles to profl. jours. and confs. Voting mem. safety subcom. VA Med. Ctr., San Francisco, 2004; mem. original com. 4th Sino-US Forum for Medicine in 21st Century, San Francisco, 2004—05. Recipient Nat. Rsch. Svc. award, NIH, 2000, Merit Rev. award, Dept. Veterans Affairs, U.S., 2004; grantee, NIH, 2005—, Am. Heart Assn. Western States Affiliate, 2003, 2005. Mem.: Am. Soc. Neuroscis., N.Y. Acad. Scis. Democrat. Achievements include research in elucidating the major mechanisms underlying the cell death induced by PARP-1-a key protein in stroke damage; discovery of NADH and NAD can be transported across the plasma membranes of astrocytes through P2X7 receptors; NAD, nobotanin B and pyruvate may be powerful drugs for treating ischemic stroke; acidosis can promote oxidative neuronal death. Avocations: music, travel, writing, sports, crabbing. Home: 3653 Lake Ontario Dr Fremont CA 94555 Office: San Francisco VA Med Ctr Dept Neurology San Francisco CA 94121 Office Fax: 415-750-2273; Home Fax: 415-750-2273. Business E-Mail: weihai.ying@ucsf.edu.

YINGLING, EDWARD L., banking association executive; b. 1949; AB, Princeton U., NJ, 1970; JD, Stanford U., Calif., 1973. Legis. asst. to Senator J. William Fulbright US Senate; chief lobbyist Am. Bankers Assn., Washington, DC, v.p., exec. v.p., 2002—05, pres., CEO, 2005—. Contbr. articles to profl. jours. Office: Am Bankers Assn 1120 Connecticut Ave NW Washington DC 20036 Office Phone: 202-663-7533. Office Fax: 202-828-4535.

YINGLING, PHYLLIS STUCKEY, writer; b. Martinsburg, W.Va., May 22, 1931; d. Carlton Bennett and Virginia DeHaven Stuckey; m. Lewis Carroll Yingling, Jr., June 26, 1954; children: Deborah Beth, Lewis Carroll III. BA in Edn., Shepherd Coll. (now Shepherd U.), Shepherdstown, W.Va., 1952; MEd in Edn. of Deaf, Western Md. Coll., Westminster, 1979. Cert. tchr. of deaf State of Md., 1979. Tchr. of the deaf and hard of hearing Prince George's County Pub. Schools, Oxen Hill, Md., 1971—73, Balt. City Pub. Schs., 1973—86, Parkville, Md., 1986—92; ret., 1992. Author: (children's book) My Best Friend, Elena Pappas, 1986, My Best Friend, Tony Santos, 1988; co-author: (children's book for dyslexic learners) Adventures of Dan and Sam, 1997, The Fantastic Fan and 7 More Fantastic Stories, 1999, Dan and Sam and the RV Trip, 2000, Dan and Sam and The Best Trip Yet; contbr. articles and stories to mags. (Best Story Award, 1984). Docent Md. Hist. Soc. Mus.; pres. Women's Internat. League for Peace and Freedom, U.S. Sect., Phila., 1999—2002; co-chair Women's Internat. League for Peace and Freedom, Catonsville, Md., 1995—99. Mem.: United Meth. Women. United Methodist. Avocations: watercolor and oil painting, travel, hiking, poetry.

YIOTIS, GAYLE, archivist, researcher, anthropologist, writer; d. Pedro and Margarette Rionda; m. Christos Fotios Yiotis; children: Fotios Christos, Peter Wesley. MA, George Washington U., Washington, 1992. Mus. specialist anthropology Smithsonian Instn., Washington, 1995—2003, archivist Nat. Mus. of Am. Indian, 2003—06. Student career alumni network Marquette U., Milw., 2000—; presenter in field. Contbr. articles to profl. jours. Mem.: Acad. Certified Archivists, Soc. of Am. Archivists. Avocations: historical research, writing, martial arts, collecting.

YIP, KWOK LEUNG, physicist, researcher; b. Canton, China, Sept. 23, 1944; came to U.S., 1968; s. Tong and Ho (Mok) Y.; m. Gee-Ying Chao, Mar. 25, 1972; children: Nora Loey, Dana Tsing. BS, Chinese U. Hong Kong, 1965; MS, Providence Coll., 1970; PhD, Lehigh U., 1973. Rsch. assoc. U. Ill., Urbana, 1973-75; sr. tech. specialist, project mgr. Xerox Corp., Webster, NY, 1975-84; sr. prin. scientist Eastman Kodak Co., Rochester, NY, 1984—2007, Carestream Health, Inc., Rochester, 2007—. Contbr. articles to profl. jours. Mem. Am. Phys. Soc., Soc. for Imaging Sci. and Tech., Internat. Soc. for Optical Engring. Achievements include patents in digital printing and medical imaging technologies. Home: 1112 Everwild Vw Webster NY 14580-8740 Office: Carestream Health Inc 1049 Ridge Rd W Rochester NY 14615 Office Phone: 585-627-8722. Business E-Mail: kwok.yip@carestreamhealth.com.

YIU, SAMUEL CHI-HUNG, ophthalmologist, researcher; s. Hung-Yu and Choi-Kam Yiu; m. Christine Yuen-Yi Yiu, July 9, 1993; children: Josiah Caleb, Kaitlyn Samantha. PhD, U. So. Calif., LA, 1988; MD, U. Alta., Edmonton, Can., 1994. Diplomate Consumer Bd. Calif., 1999. Clin. instr. U. So. Calif., Doheny Eye Inst., LA, 1999—2001, dir. ocular surface ctr., 2001—, asst. prof. ophthalmology, dir. cornea fellow, 2003—. Dir. LA Children Chorus, Pasadena, Calif., 2006. Recipient Baxter Found. Junior Faculty award; Fight Sight Postdoc. Fellowship. Fellow: Am. Acad. Ophthalmology; mem.: Tear Film and Ocular Surface Soc., Cornea Soc., Calif. Acad. Ophthalmology, Assn. Rsch. Vision and Ophthalmology. Achievements include patents pending for bioartificial lacrimal gland. Office: USC Doheny Eye Inst 1450 San Pablo St Los Angeles CA 90033 Business E-Mail: syiu@doheny.org.

YOAKAM, DWIGHT, country western musician; b. Pikeville, Ky., Oct. 23, 1956; Ph.D (hon.), Ohio Valley Coll., 2005. Musician: (albums) Guitars, Cadillacs, Etc. Etc., 1985, Hillbilly Deluxe, 1987, Buenas Noches From A Lonely Room, 1988, Just Lookin' for a Hit, 1989, If There Was a Way, 1990, This Time, 1993, Dwight Live, 1995, Gone, 1996, Under the Covers, 1997, Come on Christmas, 1997, A Long Way Home, 1998, La Croix d'Amour, 1999, dwightyoakamacoustic.net, 2000, Tomorrow's Sounds Today, 2000, South of Heaven, West of Hell, 2001, Population Me, 2003, Blame the Vain, 2005, Live from Austin, TX, 2005, Dwight Sings Buck, 2007; duet with Buck Owens Streets of Bakersfield, 1988 (No. 1 single); co-prodr. stage appearance Southern Rapture, 1993; actor (films) Red Rock West, 1992, The Little Death, 1995, Sling Blade, 1996, Painted Hero, 1997, The Newton Boys, 1998, Ozzie and Harriet: The Adventures of America's Favorite Family, 1998, The Minus Man, 1999, South of Heaven, West of Hell, 2000, Panic Room, 2002, Hollywood Homicide, 2003, 3-Way, 2004, The Three Burials of Melquiades Estrada, 2005, Wedding Crashers, 2005, Bandidas, 2006, Crank, 2006, Four Christmases, 2008, Crank: High Voltage, 2009, (TV films) Roswell, 1994, Don't Look Back, 1996, When Trumpets Fade, 1998, (TV series) Ellen, 1997. Named Top Male Vocalist by Acad. Country Music, 1986; recipient Grammy award for best country vocal performance by male for Ain't That Lonely Yet, 1993, 41st ann. Grammy award for best country collaboration with vocals for Same Old Train, 1998, also 14 nominations; Premiere Performance acting award Motion Picture Club, 1996. Office: c/o Fitzgerald Hartley 1908 Wedgewood Ave Nashville TN 37212*

YOB, CHUCK (CHARLES WALTER YOB), political organization administrator; b. Mich., Feb. 14, 1937; m. Jackalyn Joyce Krepps; 6 children. Chmn. Mich. Rep. State Convention, 1998; mem. Rep. Nat. Com., 1989, vice chmn. Midwest region, 2005; chmn. Rep. Nat. Convention Credentials Com., 1992, Senator Phil Gramm's Campaign, Mich., 1996; co-chmn. George W. Bush's Campaign, Mich., 2000, Senator John McCain's Campaign, Mich., 2008. Dir. Mich. Dept. Transp.; vice chmn. Mackinac Island State Park Comm.; dir. Fed. Home Loan Bank Bd. Republican. Office: 2143 Grosbeck Ave Hesperia MI 49421*

YOCAM, DELBERT WAYNE, retired software products company executive; b. Long Beach, Calif., Dec. 24, 1943; s. Royal Delbert and Mary Rose (Gross) Y.; m. Janet McVeigh, June 13, 1965; children— Eric Wayne, Christian Jeremy, Elizabeth Janelle. BA in Bus. Adminstrn., Calif. State U.-Fullerton, 1966; MBA, Calif. State U., Long Beach, 1971. Mktg.-supply changeover coordinator Automotive Assembly div. Ford Motor Co., Dearborn, Mich., 1966-72; prodn. control mgr. Control Data Corp., Hawthorne, Calif., 1972-74; prodn. and material control mgr. Bourns Inc., Riverside, Calif., 1974-76; corp. material mgr. Computer Automation Inc., Irvine, Calif., 1976-78; prodn. planning mgr. central staff Cannon Electric div. ITT, World hdqrs., Santa Ana, Calif., 1978-79; exec. v.p., COO Apple Computer, Inc., Cupertino, Calif., 1979-91; pres., COO, dir. Textronix Inc., Wilsonville, Oreg., 1992-95; chmn., CEO Borland Internat., Inc./Inprise Corp., Scotts Valley, Calif., 1996-2000, ret., 2000. Mem. faculty Cypress Coll., Calif., 1972-79; bd. dirs. Adobe Sys Inc., San Jose, Calif., Softricity, Inc., Boston; vice chmn. Tech. Ctr. Innovation, San Jose, Calif., 1989-90. Mem. Am. Electronics Assn. (nat. bd. dirs. 1988-89), Control Data Corp. Mgmt. Assn. (co-founder 1974), L.A. County Heart Assn. (active 1966). E-mail: yocam@aol.com.

YOCAM, ERIC WAYNE, engineer; b. Garden Grove, Calif., Aug. 23, 1966; s. Delbert Wayne and Janet Yocam; m. Siu Kuen Annie Choi, Nov. 5, 2000; children: Hailey Jasmine, Nathan Connor. BS in Computer Engring., U. Pacific, Stockton, Calif., 1990; MBA, U. San Diego, 1997; MS in Fin., Seattle U., 2002; MS in Computer Sci., Calif. State U., Chico, 2004. Cert. software devel. profl., IEEE-Computer Soc., 2002, project mgmt. profl., PMI, 2002, E-commerce cons., tech. specialist, ICECC, 2002. Mem. of tech. staff Apple Computer/Claris Corp., Santa Clara, Calif., 1991—93, Media Vision Corp., Fremont, Calif., 1993—94; tech. mgr. Ray Dream Corp., Mountain View, Calif., 1994—96, Hewlett-Packard Co., Cupertino, Calif., 1997—97; data ctr. project mgr. Intuit Corp., San Diego, 1998—99; sr. program mgr. Microsoft Corp., Redmond, Wash., 1999—. Grad. fellowship, U. San Diego, 1997. Mem.: Sigma Xi. R-Consevative. Methodist. Avocations: private pilot, scuba diving, golf, skiing, surfing. Home: 213 259th Ave NE Sammamish WA 98074 Personal E-mail: eyocam@hotmail.com.

YOCHEM, BARBARA JUNE (RUNYAN), sales executive, lecturer; b. Knox, Ind., Aug. 22, 1945; d. Harley Albert and Rosie (King) Runyan; m. Donald A. Yochem (div. 1979); 1 child, Morgan Lee; m. Don Heard, Dec. 12, 1987 (div. 1998). Grad. high school, Knox, Ind., 1963. Sales rep. Hunter Woodworks, Carson, Calif., 1979-84, sales mgr., 1984-87; sales rep. Comml. Lumber and Pallet, Industry, Calif., 1987-92; mgr. Desert Shadows Apts., Herperia, Calif., 1998—, Hesperia, Calif., 1998; real estate agt. Marina Properties, Victorville, Spring Valley Lake, 2000—01, Coldwell Banker Home Real Estate, 2001—. Owner By By Prodns., Glendora, Calif., 1976—. Author: Barbara Yochem's Inner Shooting; contbr. articles to profl. jours. Head coach NRA Jr. Olympic Shooting Camp, 1989-94. Recipient U.S. Bronze medal U.S. Olympic Com., 1976, World Bronze medal U.S. Olympic Com., 1980, Pres.'s Elite award, Coldwell Banker Internat., 2006, named Top One Percent, 2006; inductee Calif. Trapshooting Hall of Fame, 1998. Avocation: reading. Address: 9936 SVL Box Victorville CA 92395 Personal E-mail: barbarayochem@yahoo.com.

YOCK, PAUL GODO, biomedical researcher, educator; b. Mpls., Mar. 17, 1951; s. Douglas Harold and Doris Schimmel Yock; m. Cynthia Ann Yock. AB, Amherst Coll., Mass., 1973, DSc (hon.), 2007; MA in Oxon, Trinity Coll., Oxford, 1977; MD, Harvard, Boston, 1979. Asst. -assoc. prof. medicine U. Calif., San Francisco, 1986—94; weiland prof. bioengring. and medicine Stanford U., Calif., 1994—, founder, dir. program biodesign. Recipient Transcatheter Therapeutics Career Achievement award, Cardioavsc. Rsch. Found., 2007, Disting. Scientist award, Am. Coll. Cardiology, 2008. Achievements include patents for rapid exchange angioplasty system; intravascular ultrasound, mechanical transducer; doppler-guided needle, smart needle, PD access.

YOCK, ROBERT JOHN, federal judge; b. St. James, Minn., Jan. 11, 1938; s. William Julius and Erma Idella (Fritz) Y.; m. Carla Marie Moen, June 13, 1964; children: Signe Kara, Torunn Ingrid. BA, St. Olaf Coll., 1959; JD, U. Mich., 1962; postgraduate student, U. Strasbourg, France, 1961, Old Dominion Coll., 1964-65, U. Minn., 1966-67. Bar: Minn. 1962, US Supreme Ct. 1965, DC 1972. Assoc. Thomas, King, Swenson & Collatz, St. Paul, 1966-69; chief counsel Nat. Archives, Office Gen. Counsel GSA, Washington, 1969-70, exec. asst. to adminstr., 1970-72, asst. gen. counsel, 1972-77; trial judge US Ct. Claims, Washington, 1977-82; judge US Ct. Fed. Claims, Washington, 1982—98, sr. judge, 1998—. Served with JAGC USN, 1962-66. Mem. ABA, Minn., Fed., DC Bar Assns. Office: US Ct Fed Claims 717 Madison Pl NW Washington DC 20439-0002*

YOCKIM, JAMES CRAIG, foundation administrator; b. Williston, ND, Feb. 13, 1953; s. Daniel and Doris (Erickson) Y.; children: Jenna, Ericka. BSW, Pacific Luth. U., 1975; MSW, San Diego State U., 1979. Caseworker Dyslin Boys Ranch, Tacoma, 1975-77, head caseworker, program dir., 1979-80; landman Fayette Oil & Gas, Williston, 1980-82; owner Hy-Plains Energy, Williston, 1982-87; city fin. commr. City of Williston, 1984—88, 1998—2002; therapist Williston, 1983; senator N.D. State Senate, 1986-98; owner James C. Yockim Resources, Williston, 1987—. Dir. Bethel Luth. Found., 1993—; del. N.D. Dem. Conv., 1984, 86, 88, 90, 92, 94, 96, 98, 2000, 02, 04, 08; dist. chmn. Dem. Party, Williston, 1988; caucus chmn. Dem. Caucus N.D. State Senate; mem. N.D. Legis. Coun., 1997-98; coun. pres. 1st Luth. Ch. Recipient Ruth Meiers award N.D. Mental Health Assn., 1989, Legislator of Yr. award N.D. Children's Caucus, 1989; named Outstanding Young North Dakotan N.D. Jaycees, 1988. Mem. NASW. Avocation: golf. Home: 1123 2nd Ave E Williston ND 58801-4302 Office: PO Box 2344 Williston ND 58802-2344 Business E-Mail: Jamesyoc@dia.net.

YOCUM, HARRISON GERALD, horticulturist, botanist, educator, researcher; b. Bethlehemn, Pa., Apr. 2, 1923; s. Harrison and Bertha May (Meckes) Y. BS, Pa. State U., 1955; MS, Rutgers U., 1961. Horticulture instr. U. Tenn., Martin, 1957-59; biology tchr., libr. asst. high schs., El Paso, Tex., 1959-60; rsch. asst. geochronology lab. U. Ariz., Tucson, 1960-67, rsch. asst. environ. rsch. lab., 1969-76; landscaping supt. Tucson Airport Authority, 1976-82; instr. Pima C.C., Tucson, 1976—. Contbr. articles to profl. jours. Founder Tucson Bot. Gardens, 1964. Recipient 1st Unique Gardener award Gardeners Am. Mem. Am. Hort. Soc., Nat. Trust Historic Preservation, Ariz. Preservation Found., Men's Garden Club Tucson (pres. 1991), Tucson Cactus & Succulent Soc. (pres. 1991, 92), Internat. Palm Soc. (charter), El Paso Cactus and Rock Club (life), Tucson Gem and Mineral Soc. (life), Old Pueblo Lapidary Club (life), Deming Mineral Soc., Nat. Geog. Soc., Ariz.-Sonora Desert Mus., Huachuca Vigilantes, Penn State Alumni Assn. (life), Pa. Club Tucson, Nature Conservancy, N.Am. Hunting Club (life), Boyce-Thompson Arboretum, Shriners, Masons, Scottish Rite (life). Lutheran. Home: 1628 N Jefferson Ave Tucson AZ 85712-4204

YODAIKEN, RALPH E., pathologist, occupational health physician, educator; b. Johannesburg, Aug. 22, 1928; arrived in US, 1964, naturalized, 1970; m. Naomi Baumslag Yodaiken; children: Victor, Barry D., Ruth T. MD, U. Witwatersrand, Republic of South Africa, 1956; MPH, Johns Hopkins U., 1976. Diplomate Am. Bd. Pathology, Am. Bd. Forensic Medicine. Intern Coronation Hosp., Johannesburg, 1956-57; resident U. Witwatersrand Med. Ctr., 1957-58, Johannesburg Gen. Hosp., 1958; assoc. pathologist Buffalo Gen. Hosp., 1965-67; mem. staff Cin. Gen. Hosp., 1968-71; rsch. assoc. Johns Hopkins U. Sch. Hygiene and Pub. Health, Balt., 1976—; sr. staff mem. Nat. Inst. Occupational Safety and Health, Washington, 1977—, chmn. sr. adv. staff, 1983; dir. office occupational medicine Occupational Safety and Health Adminstrn., U.S. Dept. Labor, Washington, 1983-91, sr. med. advisor, 1991—98; clin. prof. preventive medicine U. Health Scis., Washington, 1983—. Lectr. U. Witwatersrand, 1958-63; asst. prof. pathology, SUNY Buffalo, 1963-67; assoc. prof. pathology U. Cin., 1968-71; prof. pathology, assoc. prof. medicine Emory U., Atlanta, 1971-75; adj. clin. prof. George Washington U., 1975—; sr. assoc. Johns Hopkins Sch. Hygiene and Pub. Health; clin. prof. preventive medicine uniformed svcs. U. Health Scis. Bd. mem. Am. Jewish Com., Bradley Blvd. Citizens Assn. With Israeli Commandos Israeli Army, 1948—50. Fellow Coll. Am. Pathologists, Am. Coll. Occupl. and Environ. Health, Am. Coll. Forensic Medicine. Democrat. Jewish. Office Phone: 301-728-4041. Personal E-mail: ryodaiken@aol.com.

YODER, EDWIN MILTON, JR., columnist, educator, editor, writer; b. Greensboro, NC, July 18, 1934; s. Edwin M. and Mytrice M. (Logue) Y.; m. Mary Jane Warwick, Nov. 1, 1958; children: Anne Daphne, Edwin Warwick. BA, U. N.C., 1956; BA, MA (Rhodes scholar), Oxford U., Eng., 1958; D.H.L. (hon.), Grinnell Coll., 1980, Elon Coll., 1986; DLitt (hon.), U. N.C., 1993, Richmond Coll., London. Editorial writer Charlotte (N.C.) News, 1958-61; editorial writer Greensboro Daily News, 1961-64, assoc. editor, 1965-75; asst. prof. history U. N.C., Greensboro, 1964-65; editorial page editor Washington Star, 1975-81; syndicated columnist Washington Post Writers Group, 1982-97; prof. journalism and humanities Washington and Lee U., 1992—2002, prof. emeritus, 2002—. Hon. fellow Jesus Coll., Oxford, Eng., 1998—. Author: Night of the Old South Ball, 1984, The Unmaking of a Whig, 1990, Joe Alsop's Cold War, 1995, The Historical Present, 1997, Telling Others What to Think: Recollections of a Pundit, 2004, Lions at Lamb House, 2007; contbr. articles to periodicals. Trustee Inst. Early Am. History and Culture, Nat. Humanities Ctr. U. NC, 1990-96. Recipient awards editorial writing N.C. Press Assn., 1958, 61, 66, Walker Stone award Scripps-Howard Found., 1978, Pulitzer prize editorial writing, 1979; Disting. Alumnus award U. N.C., Chapel Hill, 1980 Mem. Nat. Conf. Editorial Writers, Am. Soc. Newspaper Editors, Army Navy Country Club, 1925 F Street Club, Wash. Life Soc. Democrat. Episcopalian. Home: 4001 Harris Pl Alexandria VA 22304-1720 Office Phone: 703-751-9022. E-mail: yoderem@aol.com.

YODER, JOHN-DAVID SAMUEL, mechanical engineer; b. Elkhart, Ind., Apr. 27, 1969; s. John Howard and Ann Marie (Guth) Y.; m. Lynda Deanne Nyce, July 28, 1991. BSME, U. Notre Dame, 1991, MSME, 1994, PhD, 1996. Software engr. SMI, Elkhart, 1986-90; pres. Yoder Software, Inc., Elkhart, 1991—. Mem. IEEE, Sigma Xi, Tau Beta Pi. Democrat. Mem. Mennonite Ch. Avocations: sports, chess, computers, movies, motorcycling. Office: Ohio Northern Univ 525 S Main Street Ada OH 45810 Home: 335 Campus Drive Bluffton OH 45817

YODER, MICHAEL G., lawyer; b. Lynwood, Calif., Nov. 12, 1953; s. Hope G. and Vilma (Beeman) Y.; m. Susan E. Melchior, Sept. 8, 1973 (div. 1993); children: Jennifer Anne, Michael Brian, Kelly Elizabeth; m. Amy E. Bazuin, Aug. 7, 1993; children: Alyssa Michelle, Scott Charlie. BA, U. So. Calif., 1975; JD, Stanford U. Law Sch., 1978. Bar: Calif. 1978, U.S. Dist. Ct. (ctrl. dist.) Calif. 1979, U.S. Dist. Ct. (no., so. and ea. dists.) Calif. 1979, U.S. Dist. Ct. Mo. 1989, U.S. Ct. Appeals (9th cir.) 1979, U.S. Ct. Appeals (8th cir.) 1989. From assoc. to ptnr. Gibson, Dunn & Crutcher, LA, 1978-90; ptnr. Pettis, Tester, Kruse & Krinsky, Irvine, Calif., 1990-94, O'Melveny & Myers, Newport Beach, Calif., 1994—. Civil case mgmt. com. Orange County Superior Ct. Bench/Bar, Santa Ana, Calif., 1997. Bd. dirs. Constnl. Rights Found. Orange County, Newport Beach, 1983-93, pres., 1989-93; bd. dirs. YMCA Orange County, Newport Beach, 1989-90. Named one of The Nation's Top Litigators, The Nat. Law Jour., 2008. Mem. ABA (co-chair fraud subcom. 1993-96, co chair Calif. region 1996—), Assn. Bus. Trial Lawyers (ann. program co-chair 1997), Calif. Jud. Coun. Task Force on Complex Civil Litigation, Orange County Bar Assn. (chair bus. litigation sect. 1997), Robert A. Banyard Inn at Ct. Avocations: coaching youth softball, running, poetry, skiing, sailing. Office: O'Melveny & Myers 610 Newport Center Dr Ste 1700 Newport Beach CA 92660-6429 Business E-Mail: myoder@omm.com.*

YODER, PATRICIA DOHERTY, public relations executive; b. Pitts., Oct. 30, 1939; d. John Addison and Camella Grace (Conti) Doherty; children: Shari Lynn, Wendy Ann; m. James Ronald Wolfe, Oct. 30, 1999. BA, Duquesne U., 1961. Press sec. U.S. Ho. of Reps., 1965-69; dir. Office of Pub. Info., City of Ft. Wayne, 1973-76; asst. mgr. pub. and corp. comm. Mellon Bank N.A., Pitts., 1977-79; v.p. pub. affairs Am. Waterways Operators Inc., Washington, 1980-83, sr. v.p., 1983-86, exec. v.p., dir. banking, 1989-91; exec. v.p., dir. internat. banking Hill and Knowlton Inc., Pitts.; sr. v.p. corp. and pub. affairs PNC Fin. Svcs. Group, Pitts., 1987-89; v.p., corp. pub. rels. and advt. GE Capital Svcs. Corp., Stamford, Conn., 1991-95; corp. v.p. pub. affairs and comm. GTE Corp., Stamford, 1995-96; sr. v.p. corp. comm. Avis Group Holdings, Garden City, NY, 1996-99; prin. PDY Assocs., 1999—. Trustee, exec. com. Duquesne U., Shadyside Hosp., Pressley Ridge Sch., Pitts., Ellis Sch.; bd. dirs. Children's Mus., Civic Light Opera, Pitts. Ballet Theatre, Jr. League of City of N.Y. Recipient Outstanding Woman Bus. and Industry, 1988, Disting. Alumni award Duquesne U., 1996, McAnulty Svc. award, 2006. Mem. Pitts. Field Club, Duquesne Club, Indian Harbor Yacht Club, Boca Raton (Fla.) Resort and Country Club, Gardiner's Bay Country Club. Roman Catholic. Home and Office: 500 SE 5th Ave Apt 601 Boca Raton FL 33432-5510 Personal E-mail: pdyoder@mac.com.

YODER, R. PAUL, literature and language professor; b. Kinder, La., 1955; s. Richard A. and Hazel M. Yoder; m. Beth A. Miller; children: Hannah J., Laura J. BA, La. State U., Baton Rouge, 1980; MA, Ohio State U., Columbus, 1983; PhD, Duke U., Durham, NC, 1992. Assoc. prof. English U. Ark., Little Rock, 1992—. Editor: (book) Approaches to Teaching Pope's Poetry; contbr. articles to profl. jours. Recipient Tchg. Excellence award, U. Ark., 2009. Mem.: MLA, Milton Soc. Am., North Am. Soc. Study Romanticism. Jewish. Office: Univ Ark 2801 S University Little Rock AR 72204-1099 Business E-Mail: rpyoder@ualr.edu.

YODER, RONNIE A., judge; b. Knoxville, Tenn., July 10, 1937; s. Raymond Abraham and Veryl Hope (Hostetler) Y.; m. Shirley Mae Grimes, June 28, 1961; children: Susan Elizabeth Torres, Mary Amanda Anderson, Elizabeth Anne Lee, John Anthony Gerhard Yoder. BA in Polit. Sci. with honors, U. Va., 1958, JD, 1961. Bar: Va. 1961, N.Y. 1963, D.C. 1965, U.S. Dist. Ct. D.C. 1965, U.S. Dist. Ct. (so. dist.) N.Y. 1969, U.S. Ct. Claims 1964, U.S. Supreme Ct. 1968. Assoc. Mudge Rose Guthrie & Alexander, NYC and Washington, 1962-70; of counsel Zuckert Scoutt & Rasenberger, Washington, 1970-72, ptnr., 1972-75; adminstrv. law judge U.S. Dept. Labor, Washington, 1976, CAB, Washington, 1976-84, U.S. Dept. Transp., Washington, 1985-98, acting chief adminstrv. law judge, 1999-2001, chief adminstv. law judge, 2001—. Adminstrv. law judge Nat. Transp. Safety Bd., 1979-80, Maritime Adminstrn., 1983, 86-88, FDIC, 1982-83, SBA, 1983, FAA, 1985—, Fed. Hwy. Adminstrn., 1985-2000, Fed. R.R. Adminstrn., 1993-95, Rsch. and Spl. Programs Adminstrn., 1991-2005, Surface Transp. Bd., 1996-97, Fed. Motor Carrier Safety Adminstrn., 2000—, Fed. Transp. Security Adminstrn., 2002-04, Pipeline and Hazardous Materials Safety Adminstrn., 2005—; mem. Adminstrv. Conf. of U.S., 1994-95. Mem. editorial bd. U. Va. Law Rev., 1959-61; contbr. articles to profl. jours. Sec., co-counsel Capital Headstart, 1966-68; narrator Lincoln Commn., 1985, 86; founder Ronnie A. Yoder Scholarship Va. Theol. Sem., 2007; mem. permanent jud. commn. Nat. Capital Presbytery, 1985-91. Rockefeller fellow Yale Divinity Sch., 1961-62. Fellow: Fed. Bar Found., Am. Bar Found.; mem.: SAR, FBA (bd. dirs. D.C. chpt. 1999—2007, jud. divsn. leadership coun. 1999—, pres. D.C. chpt. 2003—05), ABA (nat. conf. adminstrv. law judges 1991—92, vice chmn. 1992—93, chmn.-elect 1993—94, chmn. 1994—95, jud. divsn. coun. 1994—95, vice chmn. social security com. sr. lawyers sect. 1996—2000, exec. com. nat. conf. adminstrv. law judges 1997—2001, judges adv. com. on ethics and profl. responsibility 2001—04, exec. com. nat. conf. adminstrv. law judges 2002—04, adminstrv. law sect., sec. sect. officers, chmn. task force govt. employees' participation profl. assns.), Prettyman Levanthal Am. Inn of Ct., Am. Guild Musical Artists, D.C. Bar Assn., Va. Bar Assn., Nat. Assn. Adminstrv. Law Judges (jour. bd. advisors 2004—), Fed. Adminstrv. Law Judges Conf. (exec. com. 1976—81, 1985, 1987, 1999—), Am. Judicature Soc. (nat. adv. coun. 2005—), Phi Eta Sigma, Phi Beta Kappa. Home: 1400 Summit Ave Alexandria VA 22302-2735 Office: US Dept Transp E12-320 1200 New Jersey Ave SE Washington DC 20590 Office Phone: 202-366-2137. Personal E-mail: honron@aol.com. Business E-Mail: ronnie.yoder@dot.gov.

YODER-WISE, PATRICIA SNYDER, nursing educator; d. Belford Grant and Leona Cora (Mohler) Snyder; m. Robert Thomas Wise, Feb. 17, 1973; children: Doreen Ellen Wise, Deborah Ann Wise. BSN, Ohio State U., 1963; MSN, Wayne State U., 1968; EdD, Tex. Tech. U., 1984. RN Tex., CNAA-BC. Interim assoc. dean practice program Tex. Tech. U. Health Sci. Ctr. Sch. Nursing, Lubbock, 1979—, interim dean, prof., 1991-93, dean, prof., 1993-2000; clin. prof. U. Tex. Health Sci. Ctr., San Antonio, 1993—2000; prof. Tex. Woman's U., 2004—. Mem. rev. panel Nursing Outlook, 1993—; mem. adv. com. GlaxoWellcome, 1996—2000; mem. Nat. Quality Forum Health Profls. Provide and Health Plans Panel, 2001—06. Author, editor: Leading and Managing in Nursing, 1994 (Book of Yr. award, 1996, 2003), 1998, 2002; co-author: Beyond Leading and Managing, 2006 (Book of Yr. award, 2007); peer reviewer Jour. Profl. Nursing, 1984—2003, mem. editl. bd. Jour. Continuing Edn. Nursing, 1978—; editor: Jour. Continuing Edn. Nursing, 1988—2007; editor-in-chief Jour. Continuing Edn. Nursing, 2008—. Mem. Leadership Am., 1999—2000; participant Leadership Tex.-Found. Women's Resources, 1997—98; mem. Leadership Tex., 1998—99. Recipient Women of Excellence in Medicine, YWCA, Lubbock, 1996, Woman of Excellence in Medicine, 1996, Nurse of Yr. Fellow: Acad. Nursing Edn. (treasurer 2007—), Am. Acad. Nursing (chair Inst. for Nursing Leadership 1999—2002, mem. planning com. 2004); mem.: ANCC (pres. 2005—07), ANA (del. 1995—2000, chair constituent assembly 1998—2000, sec. 2000—02, 1st v.p. 2002—05), Wise Group (pres.), Tex. Nurses Assn. (pres. 1995—99). Home: 7309 93d St Lubbock TX 79424 Office Phone: 806-559-5957, 806-790-4600. Personal E-mail: psywrn@aol.com.

YOFFIE, ERICH H., religious organization administrator; m. Amy Jacobson; 2 children. Grad., Brandeis U., Hebrew Union Coll., NYC, 1974. Ordained rabbi 74. Rabbi, Lynbrook, NJ; rabbi Durham, NC; dir. Midwest Coun. Union Am. Hebrew Congregations, NYC, 1980—92, v.p., dir. Commn. on Social Action, 1992—96, pres., 1996—; exec. dir. Assn. Reform Zionists of Am., 1983—; pres. Union Reformed Judaism. Exec. editor: Reform Judaism mag., 1992—96; contbr. articles to profl. jours. Religious leader Million Mom March, 2000; regional pres., nat. v.p. NAm. Fedn. Temple Youth; bd. dirs. many Jewish orgns. including Mazon: A Jewish Response to Hunger and the Jewish Agy. for Israel. Named one of The Top 50 Rabbis in America, Newsweek Mag., 2007; named to Top Fifty List of Leadership, Forward Annual. Office: UAHC Hdqs 633 3rd Ave New York NY 10017-6706

YOGANATHAN, AJIT PRITHIVIRAJ, biomedical engineer, educator; b. Colombo, Sri Lanka, Dec. 6, 1951; came to U.S., 1973; s. Ponniah and Mangay (Navaratnam) Y.; m. Tripti Yoganathan. BSChemE with honors, Univ. Coll., U. London, 1973; PhDChemE, Calif. Inst. Tech., 1978. Engring. asst. Shell Oil Refinery, Stanlow, Eng., 1972; tchg. asst. Calif. Inst. Tech., 1973-74, 1976, rsch. fellow, 1977-79; asst. prof. Ga. Inst. Tech., 1979-83, assoc. prof., 1983-88, chmn. bioengring. com., 1984-88, prof. chem. engring., 1988-94, dir. Bioengring. Ctr., 1989—, prof. mech. engring., 1989-94, co-dir. Emory U.-Ga. Tech. Biomed. Tech. Ctr., 1992—, Regents prof., 1994—, assoc. chair biomed. engring., 1998—; Wallace H. Coulter disting. faculty chair, 2004—. Adj. assoc. prof. U. Ala., 1985. Founding fellow Am. Inst. Med. & Biol. Engring., 1992; recipient Edwin Walker prize Brit. Inst. Mech. Engrs., 1988, Humboldt fellowship, 1985, Am. Heart Assn.-Ga. Affiliate Rsch. Investigatorship award, 1980-83, Calif. Inst. Tech. fellowship, 1973-77, Goldsmid Medal and prize Univ. Coll., 1972-73, Brit. Coun. scholarship, 1971-73, Sigma Xi Rsch. award, 1995, HR Lissner award, ASME, 1997. Mem. AIChE, ASME (Bioengring. div., H.R. Lissner award 1997), Biomed. Engring. Soc., Am. Soc. Echocardiography (dir. 1987-91). Office: Sch Biomed Engring Ga Tech/Emory Atlanta GA 30332-0535 E-mail: ajit.yoganathan@bme.gatech.edu.

YOHALEM, HARRY MORTON, lawyer; b. Phila., Jan. 21, 1943; s. Morton Eugene and Florence (Mishnun) Y.; m. Martha Caroline Remy, June 9, 1967; children: Seth, Mark. BA with honors, U. Wis., 1965; JD cum laude, Columbia U., 1969, M in Internat. Affairs, 1969. Bar: NY 1969, DC 1981, Calif. 1992, U.S. Supreme Ct. 1985. Assoc. Shearman & Sterling, NYC, 1969-71; asst. counsel to gov. State of NY, Albany, 1971-73, counsel office planning svcs., 1973-75; asst. gen. counsel FEA, Washington, 1975-77; mem. staff White House Energy Policy and Planning Office, Washington, 1977; dep. gen. counsel for legal svcs. Dept. Energy, Washington, 1978-80, dep. under sec., 1980-81; ptnr. Rogers & Wells, Washington, 1981-91; gen. counsel Calif. Inst. Tech., Pasadena, 1991—. Editor comments Columbia Jour. Transnat. Law, 1967-68, rsch. editor, 1968-69. Prin. Coun. for Excellence in Govt., Washington, 1990—; pres. Opera Bel Canto, Washington, 1984-87; mem. Lawyers Com. for Arts, Washington, 1981-88; bd. visitors dept. English U. Wis., 1999-2007. Harlan Fiske Stone scholar Columbia U., 1967, 69. Mem.: Athenaeum, Phi Kappa Phi. Home: 702 E California Blvd Pasadena CA 91106 Office: Calif Inst Tech Mail Code 108-31 1200 E California Blvd Pasadena CA 91125 Business E-Mail: harry.yohalem@caltech.edu.

YOHE, HARRY EDWARD, JR., special education educator; b. Columbia, Pa., July 20, 1950; s. Harry Edward Yohe and Doris Ruth McComsey; children: William Barris, Jordan Michele. BS in Elem. Edn., Jacksonville State U., Ala., 1977, MS in Spl. Edn., 1978, EdS in Spl. Edn., 1990. Lifetime tchg. cert. Dept. Elem. and Secondary Edn., Mo., 2007. Commd. lt. US Army, 1967, advanced through grades to command sgt. maj., ret., 1997; spl. educator Spl. Sch. Dist., Town and Country, Mo., 1999—. Decorated numerous medals US Army. Mem.: NEA, DAV (life), Coun. Exceptional Children, 173rd Airborne Brigade Soc. (life), Vietnam Vets. Am. (life), Jacksonville State U. Alumni Assn. (life), Eagle Scouts (life), Order of the Arrow (life), Sigma Nu (life). Roman Catholic. Avocations: boating, fishing, jogging, travel.

YOHE, ROBIN M., high school administration and music educator; b. Richmond, Va., June 7, 1963; d. B. Franklin and Lorena L. Moore; m. David E. Yohe; children: Buffy, Chubby, Bailey. BME, Va. Commonwealth U., Richmond, 1986; MEd, U. Va., Charlottesville, 2004—; attending, Va. Commonwealth U., 2008—. Choral dir. Manchester HS, Richmond, Va., 1986—94; choral dir., chair fine art dept. James River HS, Midlothian, Va., 1994—98, Lee-Davis HS, Mechanicsville, Va., 1998—2006; asst. prin. L. C. Bird H.S., Chesterfield, Va., 2006—. Mem.: ACDA, Music Educators Nat. Conf. Office: L C Bird HS 10301 Courthouse Rd Chesterfield VA 23832 E-mail: robin_yohe@ccpsnet.net.

YOHN, DAVID STEWART, virologist, retired science administrator; b. Shelby, Ohio, June 7, 1929; s. Joseph Van and Agnes (Tryon) Y.; m. Olivetta Kathleen McCoy, June 11, 1950; children: Linda Jean, Kathleen Ann, Joseph John, David McCoy, Kristine Renee (dec.). BS, Otterbein Coll., 1951; MS, Ohio State U., 1953, PhD, 1957; M.P.H., U. Pitts., 1960. Research fellow, scholar in microbiology Ohio State U., Columbus, 1952-56, prof. virology Coll. Veterinary Medicine, 1969-95, prof. emeritus, 1995—, dir. Comprehensive Cancer Ctr., 1973-88, dep. dir. Comprehensive Cancer Ctr., 1988-94, dir. emeritus Comprehensive Cancer Ctr., 1994—. Research assoc., asst. prof. microbiology U. Pitts., 1956-62; assoc. cancer research scientist Roswell Park Meml. Inst., Buffalo, 1962-69; mem. nat. med. and sci. adv. com. Leukemia Soc. Am., 1970-91, trustee, 1971-91; pres. Ohio Cancer Research Assocs., 1982—2008; mem. cancer research centers rev. com. Nat. Cancer Inst., 1972-77 Pres. bd. deacons North Presbyn. Ch., Williamsburg, N.Y., 1967-68. Recipient Pub. Service award Lions, 1968; named to Shelby H.S. Hall of Distinction, 2005. Mem. Am. Assn. Cancer Rsch., Am. Soc. Microbiology, Am. Assn. Immunologists, Internat. Assn. Comparative Rsch. on Leukemia and Related Diseases (sec.-gen. 1974-95), Ohio Valley-Lake Erie Assn. Cancer Ctrs. (sec. 1978-95), Sertoma (pres. 1992-93, chmn. bd. dirs. 1993-94, Dist. Sertoman of Yr. award 1987).

YOKEN, MEL B(ARTON), language educator, writer, radio personality; b. Fall River, Mass., June 25, 1939; s. Albert Benjamin and Sylvia Sarah (White) Y.; m. Cynthia Stein, June 20, 1976; children: Andrew Brett, David Ryan, Jonathan Barry. BA, U. Mass., 1960; MAT, Brown U., Providence, 1961, PhD, 1972. Instr. French U. Mass., Dartmouth, 1966-72, asst. prof., 1976-81, prof., 1981—2000, chancellor prof., 2000, Emeritus French Lang. and Lit., 2008. Dir. French summer study program French Inst., 1981-88; radio commentator, 1954-, Am. Field Svc., 1971—, pres., 1984-86, v.p., 2001—06; vis. prof. Wheaton Coll., 1987, U. of Montreal, 1981-88; translator New Bedford Superior Ct., New Bedford, Mass., 1985—, Fall River Superior Ct., Fall River, Mass., 1985—; reader, cons. AP Exams in French, 1997—2008; nominating com. Nobel Prize for lit., 1970—2009, Acad. Am. Poets, 1999—. Author: Claude Tillier, 1976, Speech is Plurality, 1978, Claude Tillier (1801-44): Fame and Fortune in His Novelistic Work, 1978, Entretiens Quebecois I, 1986, Entretiens Quebecois II, 1989, Letters of Robert Molloy, 1989, Festschrift in Honor of Stowell Goding, 1993, Entretiens Quebecois III, 1999, Breakthrough: Essays and Vignettes in Honor of John A. Rassias, 2007; contbr. articles to profl. jours. Pres. Friends of Fall River Pub. Libr., 1972-80, pres., bd. dirs., 1972-80; pres. New Bedford Pub. Libr., 1980-82; bd. dirs. Am. Field Svc., 1980—2004, pres., 1984-86, v.p., 2001-05; v.p. Friends of U. Mass. Libr., 1998—, pres., 1999—2004, v.p., 2009-; dir. Boivin Ctr., 1999—; hon. mem. adv. bd. The Irena Sendler Project. Decorated officier Ordre des Palmes académiques, Acad. Française, 2001, Order Nat. du Que., 2005; recipient Disting. Svc. award City Fall River, 1974, 80, Excellence in Tchg. French award, 1984-85, Gov.'s citation, 1986, Nat. Disting. Leadership award, 1990, Dist. Svc. award Mass. Fgn. Lang. Assn., 1992, Medaille de Vermeil du Rayonnement de la Langue Française, L'Academie Française, 1993, Outstanding Cmty. Svc. award, 1997, Disting. Alumni award, Durfee H.S., 1998, Golden Apple award Fall River Herald News, 1998; Govt. of Que. grantee, 1981-85, 87-89, Can. Embassy grantee, 1986, 87, Southeastern Mass. U. grantee, 1985, 89, 90; named Hon. Life Mem., Fall River Pub. Libr., 2003; named Mel Yoken Day in his honor by Mayor of New Bedford, 1990; named Real Hero in Edn., ARC, 2005. Mem. Acad. Am. Poets (life, hon. 2006), Pi Delta Phi (hon. charter mem. 2008), MLA (life, hon. mem. 2009), Am. Assn. Tchrs. French (life, hon. 2005), Am. Coun. Tchrs. Fgn. Langs., Middlebury Amicale (life), N.E. MLA (coord. 1987-91), New Eng. Fgn. Lang. Assn., Mass. Fgn. Lang. Assn. (bd. dirs. 1985-90, disting. svc. award 1992), NY State Assn. Fgn. Lang. Tchrs., Internat. Platform Assn., Francophone Assn. (v.p. 1990-98), Assn. Literary Scholars and Critics, PEN New England, Am. Soc. French Academic Palms, Fall River C. of C., Brown U. Alumni Assn. (rep.), Richelieu Internat., Universal Manuscript Soc. (v.p. 1993-95). Avocations: travel, languages, baseball, postcards, meteorology. Home: 261 Carroll St New Bedford MA 02740-1412 Office: U Mass Dartmouth Lang Dept Old Westport Rd North Dartmouth MA 02747-2512 Business E-Mail: myoken@umassd.edu.

YOKOSHI, YASUKO, choreographer; b. Hiroshima, Japan; arrived in US, 1981; BA, Hampshire Coll. Assoc. cur. The Kitchen, NYC, 2004—; choreographer fellow Maggie Allesee Nat. Ctr. Choreography; artist-in-residence Djerassi Art Ctr., Joyce Theater/Joyce Soho, Movement Rsch., Bklyn. Arts Exch. Author: Once in a Life Time (Ogai Mori Literary award, 1990); dir.: (documentaries) Last Sokoshi; choreographer Shuffle, 2003 (Bessie award, 2003), What We When We, 2006 (Bessie award, 2006), Reframe the Framework DDD, 2008. Fellow John Simon Guggenheim Meml. Found., 2009. Mailing: 526-528 44th St Brooklyn NY 11220 E-mail: bakayoko@earthlink.net.*

YOKOYAMA, WAYNE MAKOTO, medical educator, researcher, rheumatologist; b. Wailuku Maui, Hawaii, July 1, 1952; BA, U. Rochester, NY, 1974; MD, U. Hawaii JA Burns Sch. Medicine, Honolulu, 1978. Cert. Internal Medicine, Rheumatology. Intern, internal medicine U. Iowa Hosp., Iowa City, 1978—79, resident, internal medicine, 1979—81, fellow, clin. rheumatology, 1982, fellow, rsch. rheumatology, 1982—85; fellow, rsch. immunology Nat. Inst. Allergy and Infectious Diseases/NIH, Bethesda, Md., 1985—89; asst. prof. medicine and rheumatology U. Calif., San Francisco, 1989—92; assoc. prof. medicine and microbiology Mt. Sinai Med. Sch., NYC, 1992—95; Sam and Audrey Loew Levin chair for rsch. in arthritis Wash. U. Sch. Medicine, St. Louis, 1995—, chief, rheumatology, divsn. dept. medicine, 1995—2007, prof. medicine and pathology and immunology, dir., Ctr. for Arthritis and Related Diseases, 1996—2007, dir., med. scientist tng. program. Assoc. investigator Howard Hughes Med. Inst., 1994—95, investigator, 1997—; mem. editl. bd. Immunity, Internat. Immunology, Immunogenetics. Contbr. articles to profl. jours.; mem. adv. bd. Immunity, assoc. editor Ann. Rev. Immunol, reviewer of severel peer-reviewed jours. Recipient Novartis prize for basic immunology, 2001. Mem.: NAS, Am. Acad. Arts & Sciences, Am. Soc. Clin. Investigation, Assn. Am. Physicians, Am. Acad. Microbiology. Address: Wash U Sch Medicine Dept Medicine 10058 Clinical Sciences Research Bldg Saint Louis MO 63110 Mailing: Wash U Sch Medicine Divsn Rheumatology Campus Box 8045 666 S Euclid Ave Campus Box 8045 Saint Louis MO 63110 Office Phone: 314-362-9075. Office Fax: 314-362-9257. Business E-Mail: yokoyama@dom.wustl.edu.

YOKUBAITIS, ROGER T., lawyer; b. Wharton, Tex., Jan. 9, 1945; Student, St. Louis U.; BA, JD, U. Houston, 1969. Bar: Tex. 1969, U.S. Dist. Ct. (so., we., ea. and no. dists.) Tex., U.S. Ct. Appeals (5th, 9th, 11 cirs.), U.S. Supreme Ct. Ptnr. Carmody & Yokubaitis, L.L.P., Houston, 1995—99; prin. Roger T. Yokubaitis, P.L.L.C., Houston, 2000—. Mem. ABA, Houston Bar Assn., State Bar of Tex., Am. Bankruptcy Inst., Fed. Bar Assn., Federalist Soc. Office Phone: 713-227-9000. Business E-Mail: Yokubaitis@msn.com.

YOLDAS, BULENT ERTURK, materials scientist, educator; b. Isaparta, Turkey, Feb. 19, 1938; arrived in U.S., 1958, naturalized; s. Mustafa and Hatice Yoldas; m. Lubomyra Anne Ivanycky; children: Erol, Kim. BS in Ceramic Engring, Ohio State U., 1963, MS, 1964, PhD, 1966. Sr. engr. Owens Ill. Tech. Ctr., Toledo, 1966—74; fellow scientist Westinghouse Rsch. Ctr., Pitts., 1974—84, PPG Industries R&D Ctr., Pitts., 1984—96; adj. prof. Carnegie Mellon U., Pitts., 1996—99. Mem. editl. bd. Jour. of Sol-gel Sci. of Tech., 2000—. Contbr. articles to profl. jours. Named one of top 100 Internat. Innovators, Tech. Mag. (pemier issue), 1981. Fellow: Am. Ceramic Soc.; mem.: AAAS, Materials Rsch. Soc. Achievements include invention of a radical glass forming method, 1980; image transfer technology, 1999; research in ceramic and glass formation by chemical polymerization; optical coatings and advanced materials; 75 patents in field; development of chemical process of forming transparent microporous aluminas and other oxides known as Yoldas Process. Avocations: gardening, hiking, music, poetry. Home: 16728 Adrienne Way Ramona CA 92065 Office Phone: 760-787-1786. Personal E-mail: yoldas@cox.net.

YOLEN, JANE, writer; b. NYC, Feb. 11, 1939; d. Will Hyatt and Isabelle (Berlin) Y.; m. David Wilber Stemple, Sept. 2, 1962; children: Heidi Elisabet, Adam Douglas, Jason Frederic. BA, Smith Coll., 1960; EdM, U. Mass., 1978, LLD (hon.), 2006, Coll. Our Lady of Elms, 1980, Smith Coll., Baypath Coll., Keene State Coll. Asst. editor This Week mag., 1960; mem. staff Saturday Rev., 1960; asst. editor Gold Medal

Books, 1961, Rutledge Press, 1961—63; asst. juvenile editor A.A. Knopf, Inc., 1963—65; freelance writer, 1965—; lectr. dept. edn. Smith Coll., 1979—84; editor Jane Yolen books, imprint Harcourt Brace Jovanovich, 1988—97. Tchr. writers confs. Centrum, Cape Cod Writers Conf., Soc. Children's Book Writers, U. Mass.; mem. Mass. Coun. on Arts, 1974. Author: Pirates in Petticoats, 1963, The Witch Who Wasn't, 1964, The Emperor and the Kite, 1968, Writing Books for Children, 1973, The Girl Who Cried Flowers, 1974, The Hundredth Dove, 1978, The Dream Weaver, 1979, Commander Toad in Space, 1980, The Gift of Sarah Barker, 1981, Touch Magic, 1981, Dragon's Blood, 1982, Tales of Wonder, 1983, Heart's Blood, 1984, Cards of Grief, 1984, Dragonfield, 1985, Merlin's Booke, 1986, The Lullabye Songbook, 1986, Ring of Earth, 1986, Favorite Folktales From Around the World, 1986, Piggins, 1987, Owl Moon, 1987, Three Bears, 1987, A Sending of Dragons, 1987, The Devil's Arithmetic, 1988, Sister Light/Sister Dark, 1988, White Jenna, 1989, Dove Isabeau, 1989, Baby Bear's Bedtime Book, 1990, Tam Lin, 1990, Bird Watch, 1990, Sky Dogs, 1990, Wizard's Hall, 1991, All those Secrets of the World, 1991, Wings, 1991, Hark! A Christmas Sampler, 1991, Encounter, 1992, Briar Rose, 1992, Letting Swift River Go, 1992, What Rhymes with Moon, 1993, Welcome to the Greenhouse, 1993, Honkers, 1993, Here There Be Dragons, 1993, Grandad Bill's Song, 1994, Good Griselle, 1994, The Girl in the Golden Bower, 1994, Old Dame Counterpane, 1994, Old Macdonald's Songbook, 1994, Here There Be Unicorns, 1994, Beneath the Ghost Moon, 1994, The Wild Hunt, 1995, Ballad of the Pirate Queens, 1995, And Twelve Chinese Acrobats, 1995, Water Music, 1995, Among Angels, 1995, Here There Be Witches, 1995, O. Jerusalem, 1996, Welcome to the Sea of Sand, 1996, Passager, 1996, Hobby, 1996, Sacred Places, 1996, Here There Be Angels, 1996, Milk and Honey, 1996, Meet The Monsters, 1996, Once Upon Ice, 1997, Merlin, 1997, Child of Faerie, 1997, Twelve Impossible Things Before Breakfast, 1997, Miz Berlin Walks, 1997, Nocturne, 1997, Armageddon Summer, 1998, House/House, 1998, Prince of Egypt, 1998, Raising Yoder's Barn, 1998, The Wizard's Map, 1999, The Pictish Child, 1999, The Fairies' Ring, 1999, Moonball, 1999, Gray Heroes: Elder Tales From Around the World, 1999, How Does a Dinosaur Say Goodnight, 2000, Off We Go, 2000, Queen's Own Fool, 2000, Not One Damsel in Distress, 2000, Mirror/Mirror, 2000, Color Me a Rhyme, 2000, Welcome to the River of Grass, 2001, The Fish Prince and Other Merman Stories, 2001, Odysseus in the Serpent's Maze, 2001, Dear Mother/Dear Daughter, 2001, Hippolyta and the Curse of the Amazons, 2002, Wild Wings, 2002, Firebird, 2002, Horizons, 2002, Animal Train, 2002, Harvest Home, 2002, Girl in a Cage, 2002, Sword of the Rightful King, 2003, How Do Dinosaurs Get Well Soon, 2003, Take Joy, 2003, My Brothers' Flying Machine, 2003, Hoptoad, 2003, Mightier than the Sword, 2003, The Radiation Sonnets, 2003, The Flying Witch, 2003, Jason and the Gorgon's Blood, 2004, How Do Dinosaurs Clean their Rooms?, 2004, The Barefoot Book of Ballet Stories, 2004, Prince Across the Water, 2004, Grandma's Hurrying Child, 2005, Perfect Wizard, 2005, Pay the Piper, 2005, Apple for the Teacher, 2005, Meow, 2005, How Do Dinosaurs Eat Their Food?, 2005, Fairy Tale Feast, 2006, Troll Bridge, 2006, This Little Piggy, 2006, Dimity Duck, 2006, Baby Bear's Books, 2006, Count Me a Rhyme, 2006, Sleep Black Bear Sleep, 2007, Heros A Little Rhyme, 2007, Baby Bear's Big Dreams, 2007, How Do Dinosaurs Go to School, 2007, The Rogoes, 2007, over 200 others. Mass. del. Dem. Nat. Conv., 1972; town coord. Robert Drinan's campaign, 1970; chmn. bd. trustees Hatfield (Mass.) Libr., 1978-83. Mem. Soc. Children's Book Writers (bd. dirs. 1974—), Children's Lit. Assn. (bd. dirs. 1977-79), Sci. Fiction Writers Am. (pres. 1986-88), Mystery Writers Am., Authors Guild. Democrat. Jewish/Quaker. Home: PO Box 27 Hatfield MA 01038-0027 E-mail: janeyolen@aol.com.

YOMBA, EMMANUEL, mathematician, researcher, physicist; arrived in US, 2004; s. Louis Ngongang and Pauline Djokep; m. Hortense Mathilde Chuissi Tchapda, Dec. 16, 1995; children: Yoan Loic Mekontchou Yomba, Yvan Morel Tchapda Yomba, Wilfreid Aubin Ngongang Yomba, Grace Manuella Kenmogne Yomba. B in Physics, U. Yaounde, Cameroon, 1990, Maitrise in Mechanics, 1991, M in Mechanics, 1992; Doctorat 3 ieme Cycle in Mechanics, U. Yaounde I, Cameroon, 1998, Doctorat d'Etat in Mechanics, 2005. Asst. prof. Dept. Physics, Faculty Sci., U. Ngaoundere, Adamaoua, Cameroon, 1998—99, 2000—01, sr. asst. prof., 2001—02, 2003—04; postdoctorate fellow Inst. Nonlinear Physics, U. Saarbruecken, Germany, 1999—2000; vis. prof. Max-Planck Inst. Math., Bonn, Germany, 2002—03; vis. scholar rschr. Inst. Math. and its Applications, U. Minn., Mpls., 2004—05; vis. scholar Sch. Math., U. Minn., 2005—. Contbr. articles various scientific jours., referee for various profl. jours. Mem. Citizenship Action, Yaounde, Cameroon, 2003—07, Prepare & Enrich meeting for team couples, St. Paul, 2006—07. Mem.: Math. Assn. Am. Roman Catholic. Achievements include research in DAAD postdoctral fellowship; Max-Planck fellowship; IMA fellowship. Avocations: soccer, travel, music, movies. Office: School of Mathematics Univ of Minnesota 127 Vincent Hall Minneapolis MN 55455 Office Fax: (+1) 612 626 7370; Home Fax: (+1) 612 626 7370. Business E-Mail: eyomba@yahoo.com.

YONAS, HOWARD, neurosurgeon, neuroscientist; b. Cleve., Jan. 3, 1945; children: Michael A, Talma J, Corrine L, Windy J, Joshua H. BS in Chemistry, U. Pitts., 1966; MD, Ohio State U., 1970. Diplomate Am. Bd. Neurol. Surgery. Surg. intern Univ. Hosps. of Cleve., 1970—71, resident in neurosurgery, 1971—77; fellow in microsurgery Kantonsspital, Zurich, Switzerland, 1977—78, U. Pitts. Sch. Medicine, 1977—78, vice chmn. dept. neurol. surgery, 1998—, prof. dept. radiology, 1990—, prof. dept. neurol. surgery, 1990—, assoc. prof. dept. radiology, 1980—90, assoc. prof. dept. neurol. surgery, 1980—90; assoc. head divsn. of neurosurgery Montefiore Hosp., Pitts., 1978—80; Peter J. Jannetta prof. U. Pitts. Sch. Medicine, 1998—; co-dir. UPMC Stroke Inst., Pitts., 1996—; co-med. dir. dept. neurol. surgery UPMC Presbyn. Hosp., Pitts., 1996—, chief of cerebrovascular surgery, 1995—; co-med. dir. neurosurg. ICU, Montefiore U. Hosp., Pitts., 1995—96, chief neurosurgery, 1990—95; flight surgeon USAF, 1971—73. Ad hoc reviewer Jour. of Stroke & Cerebrovascular Disease, 1995—, Stroke, 1995—, Surg. Neurology, 1995—. Editor: Quantitative Cerebral Blood Flow Measurements; mem. editl. bd.: Jour. Neuroimaging, 2000—. Grantee, Upjohn, 1995—96, Diversified Diagnostics Products, Inc., 2000—02, Gen. Electric, 2000—02, NIH, 2001—02. Mem.: Nat. Stroke Assn., Soc. Neurol. Surgeons, Pitts. Neurosci. Soc., Am. Assn. Neurol. Surgeons, U. of Pitts. Epilepsy Ctr., Pitts. Surg. Soc., Congress of Neurol. Surgeons, Pa. Neurosurg. Soc., Pa. Med. Soc., Neurosurg. Soc. Am., Mid-Atlantic Neurosurgr. Soc., Am. Fedn. for Clin. Rsch., Allegheny County Med. Soc. Office: UPMC Presbyterian 200 Lothrop St Ste B400 Pittsburgh PA 15213-2582

YONG, RAYMOND NEN-YIU, civil engineering educator; b. Singapore, Apr. 10, 1929; naturalized, 1966; s. Ngim Djin and Lucy (Loh) Y.; m. Florence Lechensky, July 8, 1961; children: Raymond T.M., Christopher T.K. BA in Math. and Physics, Washington and Jefferson Coll., 1950; BS, MIT, 1952; MS, Purdue U., 1954; MEngring., McGill U., Montreal, Que., Can., 1958, PhD, 1960. Chartered engr., Great Britain. Mem. faculty McGill U., 1959-95, prof. civil engring., 1965-72, William Scott prof. civil engring. and applied mechanics, 1972-95; dir. Geotech Rsch. Ctr., 1973-95; assoc. mem. Ctr. for Medicine, Ethics and Law McGill U., 1991-95. Adj. prof. civil engring. U. Fla., Gainesville, 1984—; adj. rsch. prof. civil engring. Carleton U., Ottawa, 1990; disting. rsch. prof. U. Wales, Cardiff, 1995-2002, emeritus prof., sr. sci. advisor, 2002-04; sr. sci. dir. Geoenviron. Engring. Rsch. Ctr., Cardiff Sch. Engring., U. Wales, 1995, prof. emeritus, 2002—. Author: Soil Properties and Behavior, 1975 (Japanese edit. 1977), Introduction to Soil Behavior, 1966 (Japanese edit. 1974), Vehicle Traction Mechanics, 1985, Principles of Contaminant Transport in Soils, 1992 (Japanese edit. 1995), Geoenvironmental Engineering: Contaminated Soils, Pollutant Fate and Mitigation, 2001, Natural Attenuation of Contaminants in Soils, 2004, Microstructure of Smectite Clays and Engineering Performance, 2006, Geoenvironmental Sustainability, 2006. Decorated chevalier Ordre National du Que.; recipient Killam prize Can. Coun., 1985, ASTM Charles B. Dudley award, 1988, Can. Environ. Achievement award, Lifetime Achievement Environment Can., 1991. Fellow Royal Soc. Can., Engring. Inst. Can., Can. Soc. for Civil Engring.; mem. ASCE, Inst. Civil Engrs., Soc. Rheology, Clay Minerals Soc., Internat. Soc. Terrain-Vehicle Systems (pres. 1993—), Can. Geotech. Soc. (R.F. Legget award 1993). Achievements include 52 patents in field. Office Phone: 250-655-3787. Personal E-mail: r.nyong@shaw.ca.

YONKURA, RAYMOND, legislative staff member; m. Kate Yonkura. Grad., Kent State U., Ohio. Former dep. auditur City of Colombus, Ohio; chief of staff to congressman Jim Jordan US House of Reps., Washington, 2007—. Republican. Mailing: US House Reps 515 Cannon House Office Bldg Washington DC 20515 Office Phone: 202-225-2676. Office Fax: 202-225-0577. Business E-Mail: ray.yonkura@mail.house.gov.

YONTZ, KENNETH FREDRIC, medical and chemical company executive; b. Sandusky, Ohio, July 21, 1944; s. Kenneth Willard and Dorothy (Kromer) Y.; m. Jean Ann Marshall, July 21, 1962 (div. Aug. 1982); children: Terri, Christine, Michael, Jennifer; m. Karen Glojek, July 7, 1984 (wid. Dec. 1994); m. Karen Mc Diarmid, Jan. 10, 1997. BSBA, Bowling Green State U., 1971; MBA, Eastern Mich. U., 1979. Fin. planning mgr. Ford Motor Co., Rawsonville, Mich., 1970-74; fin. mgr. Chemetron Corp., Chgo., 1974-76, pres. fire systems div., 1976-80; pres. electronics div. Allen Bradley Co., Milw., 1980-83, group. pres. electronics, 1983-85, exec. v.p., 1985-86; chmn. bd. Sybron Internat., Milw., 1986—2003, Sybron Dental Specialities, Milw., 1986—2006. Chmn. Challanger Captial LLC, Dallas. Founder Karen Yontz Womens Cardiac Awareness Ctr. Mem. Muirfield Village Golf Club, Vintage Club (Indian Wells, Calif.), Tradition Golf Club (La Quinta, Calif.), Chenequa Country Club (Hartford, Wis.), Flint Hills Country Club (Wichita), Milw. Country Club, Farmington Country Club (Charlottesville, Va.). *Positive results are seldom achieved from negative thoughts.*

YOO, BYOUNGHYUN, research scientist; s. Jaesang Yoo and Soonlee Sung. BS, Yonsei U., Seoul, Republic of Korea, 1997; MS, Korea Advanced Inst. Sci. and Tech., Daejeon, 1999, PhD, 2006. Cert. info. processing engr. Human Resources Devel. Svc. Korea, 1996. Rschr. Korea Advanced Inst. Sci. and Tech., Daejeon, 1999—2006, rsch. fellow, 2006—07, Naval Postgraduate Sch., Monterey, Calif., 2007—09; rsch. scientist Mass. Inst. Tech., Cambridge, 2009—. Cons. PartDB Co. Ltd., Daejeon, 2001—07, directorship, 2002—03; presenter in field. Contbr. articles to profl. jours. Post-Doctoral fellowship, Korea Rsch. Found., 2006. Mem.: Assn. for Computing Machinery, Korea Soc. CAD/CAM Engrs., Korean Assn. Geog. Info. Studies, Korea Soc. for Simulation, Korea Info. Sci. Soc. Achievements include patents for method for generating stereographic image using z-buffer; method for making stereoscopy using selective re-rendering and extrapolation; method for bi-layered displacement mapping and protruded displacement mapping; patents pending for movable immersive virtual environment system; research in open standard-based infrastructure for visualization of geospatial information. Mailing: SMART Centre S16-05-08, 3 Science Dr 2 117543 Singapore Singapore Personal E-mail: yoo@byoo.net.

YOO, HUN-WOO, information scientist, researcher; b. Seoul, Republic of Korea, Feb. 3, 1967; s. Young-Jin Yoo and Jung-Hee Moon; m. Hye-Suk Min, Dec. 9, 2000. BSEE, Inha U., Inchon, Republic of Korea, 1992, MSEE, 1994; PhD in Indsl. Sys. and Info. Engring., Korea U., Seoul, 2001. Rsch. engr. mfg. tech. ctr. LG Electronics, Seoul, 1994—97; chief rsch. engr. Cosmo Info. and Comm., Seoul, 2000—03; adj. prof. dept. elec. engring. and computer sci. Seoil Coll., Seoul, 2002—03; rsch. prof. Ctr. Cognitive Sci., Yonsei U., Seoul, 2003—. Lectr. Korea U., Seoul, 2000—, Seoul Coll., 2001—03. Contbr. articles to profl. jours. Scholar, LG Electronics, 1990—94. Mem.: Inst. Control, Automation and Sys. Engrs. (Outstanding Paper award 2004), Korea Info. Sci. Soc. Achievements include patent for photo diode IC bonding device and method; research in content based image and video retrieval and interactive video retrieval. Avocation: church cantor. Office Phone: 82-2-2123-3984. Office Fax: 82-2-364-2440. Business E-Mail: paulyhw@yonsei.ac.kr.

YOO, JANG HEE, academic administrator, economist; b. Seoul, Rep. of Korea, Feb. 11, 1941; m. Chong-Cha Song, Apr. 22, 1967; children: Alex, Kenny. BA in Econ., Seoul Nat. U., 1963; MA in Econ., UCLA, 1967; PhD in Econ., Tex. A&M U., 1972. Asst. prof. Clark U., Worcester, Mass., 1972-76; prof. Va. Commonwealth U., Richmond, 1976-88, Seoul Nat. U., 1988-89; pres. Korea Inst. Internat. Econ. Policy, 1989-97; dean Grad. Sch. Internat. Studies, Ewha Womans U., Seoul, 1997—2004, v.p., 2004—06; prof. emeritus, 2006—; sr. rschr. Korean Econ. Rsch. Inst., 2007—. Cons. Asian Devel. Bank, Manila, 1988-89; mem. nat. Policy Rev. Com., Seoul, 1997-99; commr. Presdl. Commn. Sci. and Tech., Seoul, 1998—; mem. Eminent Persons Group Asia Pacific Econ. Cooperation, 1998—. Author: (textbook) Macroeconomic Theory, 1975; editor Jour. Econ. Devel., 1977-86. Chair foreign policy adv. coun. Korean Govt. Decorated Camelia, Korean Govt., Seoul, 1998; rsch. grantee Social Sci. Rsch. Coun., N.Y.C., 1976, NSF, 1981. Mem. Korea Internat. Econ. Assn. (pres. 2001), Korean Econ. Assn. (pres. 2003), Nat. Acad. Scis. Home: 103-1701 Samsung Raemian Apt 2-Cha Samsung 2-Dong Kangnam-Ku Seoul Republic of Korea Office: Prof Emeritus GSIS Ewha U Seodaemun-Ku 11-1 Daehyun-Dong Seoul 120-113 Republic of Korea Office Phone: (82) 3771-0070. Business E-Mail: JHY@ewha.ac.kr.

YOO, JOHN CHOON, law educator, former federal agency administrator; b. Seoul, South Korea, June 10, 1967; s. John H. and Sook (Hee) Y. BA in History, Harvard U., 1989; JD, Yale U., 1992. Bar: Pa. 1993, U.S. Dist. Ct. (9th cir.) 1997. Law clk. to Judge Laurence Silberman US Ct. Appeals (D.C. cir.), Washington, 1992-93; law clk. to Justice Clarence Thomas US Supreme Ct., Washington, 1994-95; gen. counsel US Senate Judiciary Com., Washington, 1995-96; prof. law U. Calif. Berkeley Boalt Hall Sch. Law, Berkeley, Calif., 1993-94, 96—, dir. Advanced Law Program, 2004—; dir. Internat. Legal Studies Program, Boalt Hall Sch. Law, Berkeley, Calif., 1999—2001; dep. asst. atty. gen., Office Legal Counsel US Dept. Justice, Washington, 2001—03. Visiting prof. Free U. of Amsterdam, 1998; visiting scholar Am. Enterprise Inst., 2003—; visiting prof. U. Chgo., 2003; Disting. Fulbright Chair in Law U. Trento, Italy, 2006; Fletcher Jones Disting. vis. prof. law Chapman U. Sch. Law, 2008—09. Author: The Powers of War and Peace: The Constitution and Fgn. Affairs After 9/11, 2005, War by Other Means: An Insider's Account of the War on Terror, 2006. Recipient Paul M. Bator award, Federalist Soc. for Law & Pub. Policy. Fellow: Soc. of Historians of Am. Foreign Relations, Rockefeller Found., Coun. on Fgn. Rels.; mem.: Berkeley Jour. of Internat. Law, Nat. Constitution Ctr., The Federalist Soc. Office: Boalt Hall Sch Law U Calif Berkeley 890 Simon Hall Berkeley CA 94720-0001 Office Fax: 510-642-3728. E-mail: yoo@law.berkeley.edu.*

YOO, VAK YEONG, health facility administrator; b. Seoul, Republic of Korea, June 28, 1947; d. Jang Mun Yoo and So Ran Choi. MA, Ewha Women's U., Seoul, 1974, MD, 1980. Med. diplomate internal medicine. Founder pvt. med. exam. ctr., Seoul, 1981—; dir. Yoovakyeong Internal Medicine, Seoul, 1981-92; head Med. Exam. Ctr., Seoul, 1981—; dir. Cheong-Vak P.B. Hosp., Seoul, 1992—; head Women's Health Dx & Climacteric, Seoul, 1992—. Mem. menopause and osteoporosis unit, 1992—, YVY-QOL Inst., 1997, YVY-QOL osteoporosis leader NOF-PPN, 1997; mem. sci. com. Koran Soc. Menopause, 1997-99; creator, organizer YVY-QOL support group for meno/osteoporosis Nat. Osteoporosis Found., 1997. Author: Phytoestrogens, 1995, Quality of Midbeyond Womens Life, 1996, Aging and Gender Specific Quality of Life, 1997; editor Jour. Meno/Osteoporosis, 1998—; co-editor Jour. Menopause Soc. Korea, 1999—; inventor in field. Mem. N.Am. Menopause Soc., Internat. Menopause Soc., Korean Soc. Endoscopy, Christian Med. Assn. (planning dir. 1993-96), Am. Assn. Clin. Endocrinologists, AAAS, Am. Soc. for Microbiology, Korean Soc. Endocrinology, Korean Diabetes Assn., Korean Soc. Menopause (sci. com. 1996-98, editing com. 1999—), Korean Soc. Circulation, The Endocrine Soc., NY Acad. Scis., NOF-Profl. Ptnr. Network, Am. Soc. Bone and Mineral Rsch. Avocations: travel, listening to music, opera music. Home: 138-60 Yongdu Dong Dongdaemun Ku Seoul 130-072 Republic of Korea Office: Cheongvak Antiaging Hosp 582 Shinsa Dong Kangnam Ku Seoul 135-120 Republic of Korea

YOO, YOUNG ZO, materials scientist, researcher; b. Seoul, Republic of Korea, Nov. 3, 1969; s. Jae Gun Yoo and Uk Ja Kim; m. Sun Young Yoon, Oct. 29, 2002; 1 child, Daniel. MS in Materials Sci., GwangJu Inst. Sci. and Tech., Korea, 1998; PhD in Materials Sci., Tokyo Inst. Tech., 2001. Cert. Core Radiological Tng., U.S. Dept. of Energy Office of Environment, 2005. Rschr. Korea Inst. Sci. and Tech., Seoul, 1998; spl. rschr. Nat. Inst. for Materials Sci., Tsukuba, Japan, 2001—04; rsch. assoc. Physics Dept., NIU, Dekalb, 2004—; rschr. Inst. of NanoScience, Engring. and Tech., Dekalb, 2004—. Tchg. asst. Tokyo Inst. Tech., Yokohama, Japan, 1999; advanced photon source user Argonne Nat. Lab., Argonne, Ill., 2005—. Contbr. articles to profl. jours. in field. Scholarship, Korea Govt., 1998, Rotary Found., 2002, Postdoctoral fellowships, Nat. Inst. for Materials Sci., 2003. Mem.: Materials Rsch. Soc., Am. Phys. Soc. (assoc.). Presbyterian. Achievements include patents for thin film device and its fabrication method in the United States, Japan, and Europe; research in optoelectronic and magnetic fields. Avocations: travel, golf. Home: 1305 N Annie Glidden Rd Apt 823 Dekalb IL 60115-1257 Personal E-mail: yzyoo@hotmail.com.

YOON, E. YUL, retired career officer; b. Pyungyang, Korea, Feb. 10, 1927; s. Jung Soon and Jung Duk (Lee) Y.; m. Sun Sam Lee Yoon, Nov. 29, 1931; children: Kyung Ran, Kyung Im, Kwang Ho. Grad., Mil. Acad. Seoul, 1948; BS in Politics and Fgn. Policy, Dangook U., Seoul, Korea, 1955; grad., U.S. Air U., Montgomery, Ala., 1957. Squadron comdr. The 12th Fighter SQ F-51, Korea, 1952-53; armed force attache Korean Embassy, Paris, 1959-61; wing comdr. The 1st Combat Wing, Taegu, The 10th Fighter Wing, Suwon, 1961-63; pres. Korean Air Force Coll., Seoul, 1963-64; supt. Korean Air Acad., Seoul, 1964-66; commanding gen. Combat Air Command, Korea, 1968-70; minister plenipotentiary Korean Embassy, France, Mexico, 1966-68; vice minister for def. devel. Ministry of Def., Seoul, 1970-73; pres., CEO Korea Tacoma Shipbuilding Indsl. Co., Korea, 1973-76, Buyeon Co., Ltd., Seoul, 1976-86; cons. United Tech./Martin Marieta, 1976-85. Mem. Korean Heavy Industrialization Com., Seoul, 1970-73. Decorated Eulchi and four Gold Stars, Chungmoo Meritorious Svc. medals, Korea, 1952, 53, Korean Disting. Svc. medal, 1955, U.S. Disting. Flying Cross, U.S. Air medal, Repub. of China Disting. Svc. medal. Mem. The Disting. Flying Cross Soc. (life), Ministry of Nat. Def. of Korea (rsch. assoc.). Avocations: photography, art collecting, golf. Personal E-mail: yulyoon@hotmail.com.

YOON, HANA, urologist, educator; b. Seoul, Republic Of Korea, Jan. 13, 1970; d. Young-Ja Yang. BM, Ewha Womans U., Coll. Medicine, Seoul, 1994; MD, Ewha Womans U., Seoul, 2000. Assoc. prof. Ewha Womans U., 2002—. Author: Me In the Mirror, You Think You Know Everything About Your Body, It's Our Secret. Office: Ewha Womans Univ Sch Medicine 911-1 Mokdong Seoul 158-710 Republic of Korea Office Fax: 82 2 2654 3682. Business E-Mail: wowhana@ewha.ac.kr.

YOON, HARGSOON, engineering educator; b. Cholwon, Kangwon, Republic of Korea, July 16, 1967; s. Keunhwan Yoon and Soonbok Han, Hyangsoon Moon (Stepmother); m. Youngbum Lee, Oct. 15, 1968; children: Soohyun, Byunghyun, Bohyun. BS in Physics, Yonsei U., Seoul, Republic of Korea, 1992, MS in Physics, 1994; PhD, Pa. State U., University Park, 2003. Sr. rschr. Hynix Semiconductor Inc., Ichon, Kyunggi, 1994—2005; postdoc researh assoc. Pa. State U., University Park, 2004—05; rsch. asst. prof. U. Ark., Fayetteville, 2005—, instr. elec. engring. dept., 2005—08. Referee for profl. jours. Contbr. articles to profl. jours. Mem.: IEEE, Am. Soc. for Engring. Edn. Buddhist. Achievements include patents for reactive ion etching apparatus; photo resist ashing apparatus; wafer processing method; patents pending for an assembly of a nanoporous template and a method of growing one or more vertically aligned nanowires; design and fabrication methods of dual electrode nanocavity electrochemical sensors. Avocation: soccer. Office: University of Arkansas 700 Research Center Blvd Fayetteville AR 72701 Office Fax: 479-575-2719. Business E-Mail: hyoon@uark.edu.

YOON, HOSUNG, electronics engineer; b. Busan, Republic of Korea, Sept. 8, 1975; s. Sang Weon Yun and Yeon Hee Kim; m. You-Gyoung Park, May 14, 2000; children: Seojune, Jejune. BA in Elec. Engring., Seoul Nat. U., Republic of Korea, 1998, MS in Elec. Engring. and Computer Sci., 2000, PhD in Elec. Engring. and Computer Sci., 2005. Sr. rschr. Luxpert Tech., Seoul, 2001—02; rschr. Korea Telecomm. Network Infra Lab., Daejeon, Republic of Korea, 2005—. Lectr. Myongji U., Yongin, Republic of Korea, 2001. Mem.: IEEE, Optical Soc. Korea. Roman Catholic. Achievements include development of WDM-multiplexed EPON repeator systems; gigabit-per-second WDM-PON, wavelength division multiplexing passive optical network; first to optical multilevel differential phase shift keying systems. Avocations: squash, guitar, golf. Office: KT Network Infra Lab 463-1 Jeonmin-dong Yusung-gu Daejeon 305-811 Republic of Korea

YOON, HYUNG-DOO, publisher, educator, writer; b. Kobe, Japan, Dec. 27, 1935; s. Min-Sik Yoon and Cheo-Rye Kim; m. Young-Sook Shin; children: Jae-Min Yoon, Jae-Joon Yoon, Seong-Hye Yoon. LLB,

Dongguk U., 1963; cert. mgmt. cons., Korea U. Grad. Sch. Bus., 1975; MA in Book and Magazine Publishing, Grad. Sch. Journalism, Jungang U., 1984; PhD in Pub. Sci. (hon.), Suncheon U., 2002. Reporter Shinsegye (monthly mag.), 1956, gen. editor, 1967; founder, pres. Bumwoo Publ. Co., 1966—2005, chmn., 2005—; gen. editor Dari (monthly mag.), 1970, editor, pub., 1971—72; marked literary debut by Bean and Misfortune (essay), 1972; dir. Korean Mag. Assn., 1971, 1999—2002. Mem. Korean Writer's Assn., 1974—; fin. dir. Amnesty Internat., Korean Com., 1974—80; dir. Korea Essayists Assn., 1975—87; pres. Korean Book Distribution Coun., 1982—88; exec. v.p. Korean Pub. Assn., 1984—86, 1992—94; dir. Internat. PEN, The Korean Ctr., 1989—92; pres. Korean Publ. Sci. Soc., 1989—99; vis. prof. Grad. Sch. Journalism, Jungang U., 1991—2001; founder, chief chmn. of steering com. Bumwoo Scholarship Found. for Students in Publ. Sci., 1991—; dir. Korean Inst. Bibliography, 1990—96, Korean Soc. for Journalism and Comm. Studies, 1990—94; pub. Book and Life (monthly mag.), 1992—; pres. Korean Assn. for Study of Old Books, 1996—98; v.p. Korean Alpine Fed., 1998—2002; pres. Suncheon U. Alumni Assn., 2000—03; internat. mem. Internat. PEN, 2001; established Yoon Hyung-Doo Libr., Suncheon U., 2001; hon. pres. Korean Publ. Sci. Soc., 2003; pres. Jeongdong Rotary Club, 2003; founder, dir. Bumwoo Found. for Publishing Culture, 2003-; chief dir. Korean Publishing Found., 2006-09, 09-. Author: It Will Pass from My Memory as Time Goes by, 1979; On the Wide Expanse Seashore, 1983 (Chinese translation, 1995); The Theory of Publications Distribution, 1989; The Way of Book and Mine, 1990; Book (mini book), 1993; Father's Mountain and Mother's Sea, 1995; Jambo, Jambo, Hello, 1995; As I love books, I live with them, 1997; The Truth and Falsity of Korean Publication, 2002; Love of Mountains, Books and My Country, 2003; Korean Woodblock - Printed Books of Old Books I, II, 2003, 07; An Account of a Publisher's Travels in China, 2004 (Chinese translation, 2006); An Account of a Publisher's Travels in Japan, 2005 (Japanese translation, 2006); Pieces in Past Years, 2006; The Visual History of Books (compilation), 1997; Publication as Mass Media, 1982; A Study on Books Distribution in Japan, 1983. Recipient prize, Minister of Culture and Information, 1982, Commendation, Minister of Justice, 1982, Commendation from Pres., 1988, prize, Korea Publ. Sci. Soc., 1989, Cultural prize, Seoul Metropolitan Govt., 1992, Order of Civil Merit, Seog-Ryu medal, 1995, Grand prize, Korea Publication Ethics Commission, 2000, Bo-Gwan Order of Culture Merit, 2001, Internat. Exchange prize, Chinese Editing Soc., 2002, Proud Suncheon Nat. U. Mem.'s prize, 2008, Spl. Merits award, Korea Pub. Sci. Soc., 2009. Office: Bumwoo Publ Co 525-2 Moonbal-ri Gyoha-eup Paju-si Gyeonggi 413-756 Republic of Korea Business E-Mail: bumwoosa@chol.com.

YOON, JAEWAN, civil engineering educator; b. Seoul, Korea, Dec. 15, 1961; came to the U.S., 1987; s. Heemoon Yoon and Youngja Jun; m. Sunyung H. Hong, Nov. 8, 1986; children: Soojin, Soomin. MS in Civil Engring., N.D. State U., 1990, PhD in Civil Engring., 1992. Mem. faculty dept. civil engring. N.D. State U., Fargo. Mem. ASCE, Am. Water Resources Assn., Am. Geophys. Union, Am. Soc. Photogrammery and Remote Sensing. Office: ND State U Dept Civil Engring Fargo ND 58105

YOON, JEONG WHAN, research scientist, educator; arrived in USA, 2001, permanent resident, 2004; s. Guee-Young Yoon and Bunsun Kim; m. Younhee Cheon, Feb. 5, 1995; children: Junu, Hannah. BS in Precision Mech. Engring., Han Yang U., Republic of Korea, 1991; MS in Precision Engring., Korea Advanced Inst. Sci. and Tech., Republic of Korea, 1993, PhD in Mech. Engring., 1997. Postdoctoral rschr. Alcoa Tech. Ctr., Alcoa Center, Pa., 1997—98, sr. staff scientist, 2003—08; sr. engr. LG Electronics, Seoul, 1998—2000. Lead developer MSC Software Corp., Palo Alto, Calif., 2001—03; prof. dept. mech. engring. Aveiro U., Portugal, 2003—08. Mem. editl. bd.: Internat. Jour. Plasticity; contbg. editor (spl. issue); editor, co-chair: Numerical Simulation Sheet Metal Forming Processes Conf. Proceeding, 2005; contbr. articles to profl. jours. Recipient award, Internat. Jour. Plasticity, 2008. Mem.: ASME, Sigma Xi. Roman Catholic.

YOON, KISUN, food scientist, educator; b. Seoul, Republic Of Korea, Sept. 7, 1961; d. Se Won Yoon and Ok Hae Koo; m. Choong Cheong Lee, June 28, 1987; children: Karen Hanhee Lee, Kristen Minhee Lee, Katherine Junhee Lee. PhD, U. RI, 1990. Rsch. assoc. prof. U. Md. Eastern Shore, Princess Anne, 1997—2006; prof. Kyung Hee U., Seoul, 2006—. Mem.: Internat. Assn. Food Protection. Home: 73-19 Yonhi-Dong Soedaemun-gu Seoul 120 Republic of Korea Office: Kyung Hee Univ 1 Hoegi-dong Dongdaemun-gu Seoul 130-701 Republic of Korea Office Phone: 822-961-0264. Office Fax: 822-968-0260. Business E-Mail: ksyoon@khu.ac.kr.

YOON, MYUNGKEUN, engineering educator; b. Euryung, Kyung nam, Republic Of Korea, July 7, 1968; s. JongJin Yoon and Jinsoon Hwang; m. Hyeyoung Lee, June 6, 1998; children: Andrew, Brain, Emily, Emily. PhD, Seoul Nat. U., Korea, 1997. Rsch. assoc. U. Del., Newark, 1998—2005; asst. prof. SD Sch. Mines & Tech., Rapid City, SD, 2005—. Mem.: ASME. Home: 6634 Sahalee Dr Rapid City SD 57702 Office: SD Sch Mines & Tech 501 E Saint Joseph St Rapid City SD 57701 Office Fax: 605-394-2405. Business E-Mail: myungkeun.yoon@sdsmt.edu.

YOON, SEONG-HOON, energy executive, researcher; m. Mihyun Choi, Dec. 1, 1995. PhD, Seoul Nat. U., Republic of Korea, 1998. Cert. profl. engr., Govt. of Korea, 2000. Sr. rschr. LG, Seoul, 1998—2001; sr. rsch. engr. Nalco, Naperville, Ill., 2001—07. Recipient Chairman's award, Nalco, 2007. Achievements include development of membrane flux enhancing chemical. Office: Coskata Inc 4575 Weaver Pkwy Warrenville IL 60555 Office Phone: 630-657-5800. Personal E-mail: syoon21@gmail.com.

YOON, SEONG-MIN, economics professor; b. Busan, Republic of Korea, Mar. 6, 1961; s. Jin-Heon Yoon and Jeong-Yung Jang; m. Sook-Kyung Kim, May 10, 1962; children: Ha-Jung, Jae-Hyun. BA in Econs., Korea U., Seoul, 1983, MA in Econs., 1985, PhD in Econs., 1989. Fellow Hansol Investment Adv. Co. Ltd., Seoul, 1989—91; asst. prof. dept. indsl. econs. Pukyong Nat. U., Busan, Republic of Korea, 1991—93, asst. prof. divsn. econs., 1993—97, chmn. dept. indsl. econs., 1996—98, chmn. divsn. econs., 1997—98, assoc. prof. divsn. econs., 1997—2002, prof. divsn. econs., 2002—08, vice-dean Coll. Humanities and Social Scis., chmn. divsn. econs., 2005—06; prof. dept. econs. Pusan Nat. U., 2008—. Cons. Busan Metro City, Busan, 1998—2000; scholar dept. econs. U. Colo., Denver, 1999—2000; scholar dept. fin. and bus. econs. U. Wash., Seattle, 2006—07. Author: (books) Exercises in Economics, 1990, A Comprehensive Bibliography in Economics, 1995, Economic Policy, 1996, Business Democracy and Corporate Governance, 2002, Intelligent Finance, 2004, Regional Innovation and Industrial Networks in Busan, 2004, Regional Economy in the Age of Globalization, 2008; mem. editl. bd.: Jour. Regional Social Studies, 1997—99, Jour. Humanities and Social Scis., 2005—08; contbr. articles to profl. jours. Grantee, Sunggok Rsch. and Culture Found., 1993, 2003, Korea Rsch. Found., 1994, 1995, 1997, 2001—08, Korea Acad., 1994, Busan Met. City, 1995, Pukyong Nat. U., 1995, 1998, 1999, 2001, 2004, 2007, Korean Confedn. Trade Unions, 1997, Min. Labor, Korea, 2000, 2001, KOFA, 2004, Yangsan ICD, 2004, Korean Securities Assn., 2004, 2006, LG Yonam Culture Found., 2005, Asian Inst. Regional Innovation, 2005, Korean Sci. and Engring. Found., 2006, 2007, Marine Industry and Tech. Orgn., 2007. Mem.: Rsch. Ctr. Humanities and Social Scis. (mem. exec. com. 2003—), Korea Securities Assn., Korea Small Bus. Assn., Korea Soc. and Economy Assn., Korea Money And Fin. Assn., Internat. Area Studies Assn., Korean Econ. Assn., Korean Regional Studies Assn., Korean Academic Soc. Bus., Korean Fin. Assn. Home: 113-501 Daelim ATP Jaw-Dong Haewundae-Gu Busan 612-755 Republic of Korea Office: Pusan National Univ Dept Econs Jangjeon-Dong Geumjeong-Gu Busan 609 735 Republic of Korea Office Fax: 82-51-581-3143. Personal E-mail: smyoon@pusan.ac.kr.

YOON, SO-YEON, design educator; b. Busan, Republic Of Korea, Apr. 9, 1970; d. Younghyo Yoon; m. Namjung Kim, June 25, 2005; 1 child, Alexis Dongha Kim. PhD, U. Mo., Columbia, 2004. Cert. in interior design, NCIDQ, 2006. Resident asst. prof. U. Mo., 2001—04, asst. prof., 2005—. Achievements include design of virtual reality, animation walk-through simulations. Office: Univ Mo 139 Stanley Hall Columbia MO 65211 Office Fax: 573-884-6679. Business E-Mail: yoons@missouri.edu.

YOON, WON-SUB, materials scientist; m. Kyunghee Park; children: Heesuh, Jeff. PhD, Yonsei U., Seoul, Republic of Korea, 2001. Rsch. assoc. Brookhaven Nat. Lab., Upton, NY, 2001—04, staff scientist, prin. investigator, 2004—. Judge LI Sci. and Engring. Fair, LI, 2003—. Grantee, US Dept. Energy, 2004—, 2004—, Brookhaven Nat. Lab., 2003—04, LG Chem. Co., 2006—. Mem.: Electrochem. Soc. (reviewer 2005—), Am. Chem. Soc. (reviewer 2006—), Internat. Soc. Electrochemistry (reviewer 2007—), Am. Phys. Soc. (reviewer 2006—), Materials Rsch. Soc. (life), Electrochem. Soc. (life; reviewer 2005—). Achievements include patents for cathode active material using sol-gel method, preparing method thereof and the composite cathode using the same. Office: Brookhaven Nat Lab Chemistry Dept 32 Lewis Rd Upton NY 11973 Business E-Mail: wonsuby@bnl.gov.

YOON, YEO-SUN, electronics engineer; b. Seoul, Republic of Korea, May 4, 1972; s. Seok-Kil Yoon and Young-Ock Han; m. Ji-Hyun Kim, Mar. 26, 1975; children: Catherine, Ryan. PhD, Ga. Inst. Tech., Atlanta, 2004. Postdoc. rsch. fellow Villanova U., Pa., 2007—09; sr. engr. Samsung Thales Co., Yongin, Republic of Korea, 2004—. Contbr. articles to profl. jours., chapters to books. Mem.: IEEE. Achievements include development of high-resolution imaging algorithms for through-the-wall radar.

YOPCONKA, NATALIE ANN CATHERINE, secretary officer, computer specialist, educator, entrepreneur, small business owner; b. Taylor, Pa., July 21, 1942; d. Michael Joseph and Natalie Ann Lucille (Panek) Yopconka. BS in Bus. Adminstrn., Pers. and Indsl. Rels. with high honors, U. Md., 1965; MBA in Info. Tech., George Washington U., 1976, MA in Edn. and Human Devel., Higher Edn., 1988; postgrad. in Venture Capital and Entrepreneurship, U. Md., 1990—96. Mgmt. analyst, adminstrv. trainee, computer programmer U.S. Dept. Commerce, Maritime Adminstrn., Washington, 1965-67; computer programmer, computer specialist U.S. Dept. Labor, Washington, 1967-78; instr. computer sci. Assn. for Computing Machinery, Washington, 1978; instr. computer sci. and mgmt. tech. Montgomery Coll., Takoma Park and Rockville, Md., 1979; sr. programmer analyst Dynamic Data Processing, Inc., Silver Spring, Md., 1979; instr. Nat. Bus. Sch., Inc., Alexandria, Va., 1980; cons. McLeod Corp., Washington, 1980; lectr. computer sci., coop. coord. U. Md., College Park, 1980-81; sr. adminstrv. applications analyst programmer Data Transformation Corp., Washington, 1981; sr. sys. analyst Singer Link Simulation Sys. Divsn., Silver Spring, 1981-82; accessory designer Transart Corp., 1982-83; market rschr. Washington Fin. Svc., 1982-83; lectr. computer info. and sys. sci. U. D.C., Rockville, Md., 1983; prof. computer programming and mgmt. info. sys. Benjamin Franklin U., Washington, 1983; rschr. Info. U.S.A., Potomac, Md., 1983-85; admissions rep. Brook-Wein Bus. Inst., Washington, 1985; pvt. distbr. Hyattsville, Md., 1979—86; distbr. AMWAY Corp., 1979—93. Course developer, instr. Grad. Sch. USDA, Balt., 1986-87; field interviewer Nat. Drug Abuse Bur., 1989-90; chmn. Cert. for Computing Profls. Exam. Review Course for Balt. Washington, D.C. corridor, 1994-95; agent Kivex, Inc., 1996-97, 3COM Corp., 1997-99, Information Builders, Inc., 1997-2000; bus. owner, cons., computer specialist, application developer, educator, salesperson Sys. and Edn. Enterprises, 1979—. Mem. disability com. Takoma Pk., com. energy, housing and planning, Mayor, 1980-81; mem. Vision 2030 Balt./Howard County, 2002-03; mem. Missionary Oblates of Immaculate Mary; choir Our Lady of Sorrows Cath. Ch., 1977-82, St. John the Evangelist Cath. Ch., eucharistic min. 1990-2003, 2007-08, internet com., 1996-97, lector, 2003-05, 2007—08; mem. Balt. Washington Corridor C. of C., 1996-97, citizens adv. com. to Bd. Edn. Howard County, 1991-92, computer adv. com., 1993-95; chair Leukemia Soc. Md., 1996; active Suburban Md. High Tech. Coun., 1994-95, Howard County High Tech. Coun., 1994-95; sec. officer NARFE, chpt. 1734, 2002-, T.R.I.A.D./S.A.L.T. for Howard County Police Dept., 2003-07; patron, nominator Howard County Coun. for the Arts. Recipient chmn./woman of the yr., Leukemia Soc. of Md., 1996. Mem. AARP, NAFE, IEEE (Balt. sect., earlier Washington sect., computer soc., commn. soc., tech. com. on software engring., stds. coms. and groups, software standards assn.), ASCD, ASTD, IEEE, IEEE Computer Soc. (tech. com. on software engring., software engring. stds. coms. and groups), Software Stds. Assn., Info. Sys. Audit and Control Assn., Assn. Computing Machinery (DC chpt., edn. com., instr. 1978-79, edn. com. 1980-81, profl. devel. com. 1982-83), Data Processing Mgmt. Assn. (chmn. cert. for computing profls. exam. rev. course for Balt.-Washington corridor 1994-95), Balt. Washington Info. Sys. Educators (consortium com. 1984-85, program com. for 1986 regional tng. conf. 1985-86, vendor com. 1988-89), Fed. Automatic Data Processing Users Group (com. mem. 1976-1983), Armed Forces Comm. and Electronics Assn., Balt. Coun. Fgn. Affairs, Nat. Active and Ret. Fed. Employees Assn. (sec. Howard County chpt.), Nat. Bus. Edn. Assn., U. Md. Howard County Alumni Club (scholarship com. 1989), Columbia (Md.) Assn., Phi Delta Gamma (scholarship com. 1977-78, social com. 1980-81, hospitality com. 1982-83, sec. 1989-90). Achievements include first to write software engineering standards.

YORE, JOSEPH N., communications executive; b. Emporium, Pa., Feb. 5, 1934; s. Joseph Yore and Jennie Grouanz. Cert., Hollywood Ctr. Drama Sch., Calif., 1961. Ground keeper LA County Parks and Recreation, 1960—63; rschr. Walter E. Hurst Law Firm, Hollywood, Calif., 1963—89; pres. Seven Arts Press, Hollywood, 1989—. Prodr-.(director, scriptwriter): Diary of A Hippie, 1968 (Telly bronze award, 2007). Mem. environ. rehab. adv. bd. plant 42 Air Force Base Wright Patterson, Ohio, 2000—06. Corp. USMC, 1953—56, Korea. Fellow: VFW, Am. Legion; mem.: AFTRA, Screen Actots Guild, Actor's Fund Am. (life). Avocations: painting, sculpting. Home: 38753-26th St E Palmdale CA 93550

YORIKAWA, HIROHARU, physicist, researcher; b. Hyogo, Japan, Aug. 4, 1958; s. Mineo and Yaeko (Kobayashi) Y. BS, Sci. U. Tokyo, 1983, MS, 1985, DSc, 1989. Rsch. asst. Utsunomiya (Japan) U., 1989—. Contbr. articles to Phys. Rev. B, Solid State Comms., Synthetic Metals, Appl. Phys. Lett., others. Mem. Phys. Soc. Japan. Avocation: painting. Office: Utsunomiya U Faculty of Engring 7-1-2 Youtou Utsunomiya 321-8585 Japan E-mail: yorikawa@cc.utsunomiya-u.ac.jp.

YORK, CANDACE A., marketing professional, writer; b. Lubbock, Tex., Mar. 7, 1954; d. Billy John and Francis Ann York; m. James R. Callahan, Feb. 23, 1947. BFA in Art History, U. Tex., 1976. Archival asst. S.W. collection Tex. Tech. U., Lubbock, 1976—77; claims analyst Met. Life, Austin, Tex., 1977—78; mktg. software engr., info. devel. IBM Corp., Austin, Tex., 1978—. Author: 155 Tips to Protect Your Home and Wealth From Fire, 2003, numerous poems, short stories; contbr. articles to profl. jours. Vol. Austin (Tex.) Cmty. Gardens, 2003—04, Tex. Sch. Blind, 2003. Recipient Excellence award, Soc. Tech. Comm., 1980, Honorable Mention award, Iliad Press, 2001, 1st pl. poetry in motion competition, 2001, 2nd place, Sol poet laureate competition, 2002; named Internat. Poet of Merit, Internat. Libr. Poetry, 2001. Mem.: Assn. Interactive Media, Pub. Rels. Soc. Am. (programs com. Austin chpt. 2003), Acad. Am. Poets, Internat. High IQ Soc. Avocations: poetry, photography, guitar, painting, tai chi. Home: 8210 Bent Tree Rd #213 Austin TX 78759 Personal E-mail: canyork@aol.com.

YORK, E. TRAVIS, retired academic administrator; b. Mentone, Ala., July 4, 1922; s. E.T. and Leila (Hixon) Y.; m. Vermelle Cardwell, Dec. 26, 1946; children: Lisa Carol, Travis Loften. BS, Auburn U., 1942, MS, 1946, DSc (hon.), 1982; PhD, Cornell U., 1949; postgrad., George Washington U., 1957-59; DSc (hon.), U. Fla., 1984, Ohio State U., 1996, NC State U., 2003. Rsch. fellow Cornell U., Ithaca, 1946-49; Assoc. prof. N.C. State Coll., 1949-52, prof., 1952-56, head dept. agronomy, 1953-56; Eastern dir. Am. Potash Inst., 1956-59; dir. Ala. Extension Service, Auburn U., 1959-61; adminstr. Fed. Extension Service, U.S. Dept. Agr., 1961-63; provost for agr. U. Fla., 1963-67, v.p. agrl. affairs, 1967-73, exec. v.p., interim pres., 1973-74, Disting. Svc. prof., 1988-96. Chancellor State U. System of Fla., 1975—80, chancellor emeritus, 1980—. Mem. Am. Food for Peace Coun., 1961-62, Freedom from Hunger Com., 1961-62, Pres.'s. Panel Vocat. Edn., 1961-62; chmn. coun. grad. edn. in agrl. scis. So. Regional Edn. Bd., 1964-66, mem., 1975-80, exec. com., 1978-80, mem. pres. coun., Pres.' Sci. Adv. Coun. Task Force on World Food Problems, 1966-67; senate, exec. com. Nat. Assn. State Univs. and Land Grant Colls., 1967-70; mem. Edn. Commn. of States, 1975-79, steering com., 1977-79, treas., exec. com., 1978-79; bd. dirs. Nat. 4-H Svc. Com., 1963-75, AV Med. Corp., Sante Fe, 1987-96; trustee, bd. dirs Hlth Improvement Inc mem., 1996-98, exec. com. Nat. 4-H Council, 1968-73; mem.-at-large nat. coun. Boy Scouts Am., 1962-75; dir., pres. Alpha Gamma Rho Edn. Found., 1965-72; bd. dirs. Nat. Ctr. for Voluntary Action, 1970-74; mem. Bd. for Internat. Food and Agrl. Devel., 1980-86, chmn., 1983-86; trustee Escuela Agrícola Panamericana, 1980-88, Found. for Agronomic Rsch., 1980-92; tech. adv. com., cons. Group for Internat. Agrl. Rsch., 1983-89; trustee Agronomic Sci. Found., 1989-92; chmn. bd. Internat. Fertilizer Devel. Ctr., 1999-2004. Officer AUS, 1943-45. Recipient B.B. Comer award excellence natural sci. Auburn U., 1942; disting. svc. award Fla. Vet. Med. Assn., 1966; Nat. 4-H Alumni award, 1967; George Washington honor medal award Freedoms Found., 1967; nat. ptnr. in 4-H award, 1970; disting. faculty award U. Fla., Fla. Blue Key, 1972; E.T. York, Jr. disting. svc. award U. Fla., 1973; honors medal U. Fla. Acad. Scis., 1974; E.T. York svc. award Fla. Bd. Regents, 1983, disting. svc. award Am. Farm Bur., 1991, Svc. Above Self award Rotary Internat., 1994, Medal of Honor, DAR, 1998, Lifetime Achievement award Auburn U., 2006, Lifetime Achievement award, Fla. Student Assn., 2007; named to Fla. Agrl. Hall of Fame, 1990, Ala. Agrl. Hall of Honor, 1995, Internat. Adult and Continuing Edn. Hall of Fame, 1996; designated as Great Floridian, Fla. History Mus., 1997. Fellow AAAS, Am. Soc. Agronomy, Soil Sci. Soc. Am., AM. Crop Sci. Soc.; mem. Am. Soc. Hort. Sci. (hon.), Assn. So. Agrl. Scientists (pres. 1968), Blue Key, Rotary (dist. gov. 1981-82), Sigma Xi, Phi Kappa Phi, Alpha Zeta, Gamma Sigma Delta (Internat. Disting. Svc. award 1973), Omicron Delta Kappa, Phi Delta Kappa, Epsilon Sigma Phi, Alpha Gamma Rho (named to Hall of Fame 1982). Methodist. Home: 5200 SW 25th Blvd # 4216 Gainesville FL 32608-8925 Business E-Mail: etyork@ufl.edu.

YORK, GARY ALAN, lawyer; b. Glendale, Calif., Aug. 29, 1943; m. Lois York, 1987; 1 child, Jonathan Alan. BA, Pomona Coll., 1965; LLB, Stanford U., 1968. Bar: Calif. 1969. Ptnr. Dewey Ballantine, LA, 1985-95, Buchalter, Nemer, Fields & Younger, LA, 1995-98, Le Boeuf, Lamb, Greene & MacRae, LA, 1998—2002, Baker & Hostetler, LA, 2002—07. Instr. law sch. UCLA, 1968-69. Bd. editors Stanford Law review, 1966-68. Mem. ABA (chmn. real estate fin. com., real property probate and trust sect. 1987-89, chmn. usury com. 1992-93), L.A. County Bar Assn. (chmn. real estate fin. sect. 1993-96, exec. com. 1995—), State Bar of Calif., Am. Coll. Real Estate Lawyers, Am. Coll. Mortgage Attys.

YORK, JAMES FARNSWORTH, engineering educator, retired chemical engineer; s. Randolph M. and Helen F. York; m. Evelyn Yvonne Anderson, Apr. 6, 1962; children: David Michael, Robert Alan. BS in Chem. Engring., Purdue U., 1961; MS in Chem. Engring., Ohio U., Athens, 1968. Sr. engr. Borg Warner Chems., Washington, W.Va., 1961—64, adminstrv. mgr., 1964—74, rsch. mgr. Morgantown, W.Va., 1974—87; prin. engr. Gen. Electric Plastics, Washington, 1987—99; instr. Wash. County Career Ctr., Marietta, Ohio, 1999—2008; lectr. Wash. State CC, Marietta, 2007—08. Recipient Innovative fire-retardant additive product, IR-100, 1981. Mem.: Am. Chem. Soc. Achievements include patents for US 4, 305, 866 Polyolefins Stabilized with Cyclic Diphosphites; US 4, 120, 882 Catalytically Active Composition for Electroless Plating; US 4, 665, 211 Process for Preparing bis (Dialkylphenyl) Pentaerythritol Diphosphites; US 4, 116, 926 Stabilizer for Polymers; GB 1, 526, 603 Preparation of Organic Phosphite; CAN 807, 200 Dehydrohalogenation of Halogenated Nitrile Compounds. Office: Washington State CC 710 Colegate Dr Marietta OH 45750

YORK, JAMES ORISON, retired real estate executive; b. Brush, Colo., June 27, 1927; s. M. Orison and Marie L. (Kibble) Y.; m. Janice Marie Sjoberg, Aug. 1, 1959; children: Douglas James, Robert Orison. Student, U. Calif., Berkeley, 1945—46; BA cum laude, U. Wash., 1949. Tchg. fellow U. Wash., Seattle, 1950-52; econ. rsch. analyst Larry Smith & Co. Real Estate, Seattle, 1953-60, ptrn., 1960-66, pres. San Francisco, 1966-71; pres., chief exec. officer R.H. Macy Properties, NYC, also sr. v.p. planning and devel., dir. R.H. Macy & Co., Inc., 1971-88; chmn. James York Assocs. (real estate and venture capital), 1988—2008. Dir. emeritus UBP Properties, Inc.; chmn., N.Y.C. retail div. Am. Cancer Soc. Contbg. author: Shopping Towns-USA, 1960. Trustee ICSC Ednl. and Rsch. Found. With USNR, 1945-47. Recipient Disting. Alumnus award Econs. U. Wash., 1989. Fellow Phi Beta Kappa; mem. Am. Soc. Real Estate Counselors, Urban Land Inst., Internat. Real Estate Fedn., Internat. Coun. Shopping Ctrs., Olympic Club (San Francisco); Am. Yacht Club (Rye, N.Y.), Corinthian Yacht Club (Seattle), Union League

(N.Y.C.), KM, Order St. John, Wash. Athletic Club (Seattle), Royal Victoria (B.C.) Yacht Club, Lambda Alpha. Home: 4 Riverstone Laguna Niguel CA 92677-5309 also: Sunrise Country Club 6 Malaga Dr Rancho Mirage CA 92270-3820 Personal E-mail: jysail@aol.com.

YORK, JAMES WESLEY, JR., theoretical physicist, educator; b. Raleigh, NC, July 3, 1939; s. James Wesley and Mary Smedes (Poyner) York; m. Betty Louise Mattern, Aug. 19, 1961 (div. Apr. 2002); m. Sarah Williams Walt, June 13, 2002; children: Virginia York Setzer, Guilford Mattern. BS with high honors in Physics, N.C. State U., Raleigh, 1962, PhD in Physics, 1966. Asst. prof. N.C. State U., Raleigh, 1965-68; rsch. assoc. Princeton U., 1968-69, lectr., 1969-70, asst. prof., 1970-73; assoc. prof. U. N.C., Chapel Hill, 1973-77, prof. dept. physics, 1977-89, Agnew H. Bahnson, Jr. disting. prof. physics, 1989—2001, dir. Inst. Field Physics, 1984-90; vis. asst. prof. U. Md., College Park, 1972; prof. associe U. Paris, 1976; vis. scientist ctr. astrophysics Harvard, Smithsonian, Cambridge, 1977; vis. prof. U. Tex., Austin, 1979, 87; prof. physics Cornell U., 2002—07. Spkr. Internat. Symposium on Methods of Differential Geometry in Physics and Mechanics, Warsaw, 1976; spr. in field; Alfred Schild Meml. lectr. U. Tex., 1979; del. Seventh Internat. Congress on Math. Physics, Boulder, Colo., 1983, Tex. Symposium on Relativistic Astrophysics, Jerusalem, 1984, Marcel Grossman Meeting, Rome, 1985, Jerusalem, 97, Rio de Janeiro, 2003, NATO Advanced Study Inst., Les Houches, France, 1982, Huelva, Spain, 92, Paris, 92, Banff, Canada, 92, other internat. and nat. meetings; co-organizer sci. meetings including Neutron stars and pulsars, Princeton, 1969; Spacetime dynamics Aspen Ctr. for Theoretical Physics, 1981, Classical Problems in Gravitation, 1990, Cosmic Censorship, 1992; coord. lectr. Inst. Theoretical Physics U. Calif., Santa Barbara, 2000; mem. com. of visitors physics divsn NSF, 1991; plenary lectr. Fifth Can. Conf. on Gen. Relativity and Astrophysics, Waterloo, 1993, Directions in Gen. Relativity, College Park, Md., 1993, Pacific Coast Gravity Mtg., Salt Lake City, 1996, 2d Samos meeting, Greece, 1998; plenary lectr. 50 Years of the Cauchy Problem, Cargese, Corsica, 2002; hon. physics chmn. Cornelius Lanczos Internat. Centenary, Raleigh, NC, 1993; vis. prof. dept. physics N.C. State U., 1998—99, Inter-Instl. Disting. prof. physics, 2001—02. Mem. editl. bd. Jour. Math. Physics, 1989-92; contbr. chpts. to books, articles to sci. jours. Decorated Companion of St. Patrick, 1960; Ford Found. fellow, 1962-65, NSF postdoctoral fellow, 1969-70; Battelle Found. grantee, 1967, Nat. Rsch. Com. France grantee, 1976, NSF grantee, 1974—, travel grantee, 1971, 76, 83, 84; U.S.A.-Israel Binat. Sci. Found. grantee, 1987-90, 90-93, Kenan Found. grantee, 1990, W.N. Reynolds Found. grantee, 1998; recipient Disting. Alumnus award, 1997, Marcel Grossmann prize, Rio de Janeiro, 2003; co-winner Dannie Heineman prize for math. physics Am. Phys. Soc., 2003. Fellow Am. Phys. Soc.; mem. AAAS, Internat. Soc. Gen. Relativity and Gravitation, Phi Beta Kappa, Sigma Xi, Phi Kappa Phi, Tau Beta Pi, Sigma Pi Sigma, Pi Mu Epsilon, Phi Eta Sigma. Avocations: literature, reading. E-mail: jaswyork1@mac.com.

YORK, JEROME B., investment company executive; b. Memphis, June 22, 1938; m. Eilene York; 4 children. BS, U.S. Mil. Acad., 1960; MS, MIT, 1961; MBA, U. Mich., 1966. Various engring. positions GM Corp., Pontiac, Mich., 1962-67; various managerial positions Ford Motor Co., Deerborn, Mich., 1967-70; dir. strategic planning RCA Corp., Hertz Corp. (subs.), 1970-72, v.p., 1972-75; group v.p. Baker Industries, Inc., Parsippany, NJ, 1976-78; pres. Delta Truck Body Co., Inc., Montgomeryville, Pa., 1978-79; asst. contr. Chrysler de Mex. Chrysler Corp., Highland Park, Mich., 1979-82, mng. dir. Chrysler de Mex., 1982-85, v.p., gen. mgr. Dodge divsn., 1986-90, v.p., contr., 1989-90, exec. v.p., CFO, 1990-93; sr. v.p., CFO IBM Corp., Armonk, NY, 1993—95; vice chmn. Tracinda Corp., 1995—99; chmn., pres., CEO Micro Warehouse, Inc., Norwalk, 2000—03; founder, CEO Harwinton Capital Corp., 2000—. Bd. dirs. Apple Inc. (formerly Apple Computer, Inc.), 1997—, Tyco Internat. Ltd., 2002—, Exide Technologies, 2005—, Gen. Motors Corp., 2006, Metro Goldwyn Mayer, Inc.

YORK, JERRY, men's college hockey coach; b. Watertown, Mass., July 25, 1945; m. Bobbie York; children: Laura, Brendan. BA, Boston Coll., 1967, EdM. Grad. asst. coach Boston Coll., Chestnut Hill, Mass., 1968—69, head coach, 1994—; asst. coach Clarkson U., Potsdam, NY, 1970—72, head coach, 1972—79, Bowling Green State U., Ohio, 1979—94. Recipient Spencer Penrose Trophy (Divsn. I Coach of Yr.), 1977; named Hockey East Coach of Yr., 2004, New England Coach of Yr., 2004; named to Boston Coll. Varsity Club Hall of Fame, 1982, Bowling Green State U. Athletic Hall of Fame, 2003. Achievements include being the coach of NCAA National Championship Team, Bowling Green State University, 1984, Boston College, 2001, 2008. Office: Boston Coll 140 Commonwealth Ave Chestnut Hill MA 02467

YORK, JOAN ELIZABETH SMITH, psychologist; b. Englewood, N.J., Jan. 18, 1940; s. Julius Freeman and Lottie Winfred (Mays) Smith; B.A., W.Va. State Coll., 1962; M.Ed., Trenton State Coll., 1980; postgrad. in counseling psychology Union Grad. Lic. drug and alcohol counselor. Sch. Counselor, Portsmouth (Va.) Child-Family Service, 1972-73; dir. Richmond (Va.) City Jail-Work Release Program, 1974-75; counselor Employee Adv. Service, Trenton, 1975—2002; part-time counselor Trenton State Prison Evening Sch., 1981-82; pvt. counselor Delaware Valley Psychol. Clinic, part-time 1982—; pvt. therapist Mercer Consultation Assn., 1986—; drug and alcoholism counselor, 1987—; pvt. practice 1980-. First v.p., mem. exec. bd. N.J. Task Force on Women and Alcohol. Mem. Assn. of Black Psychologists, Am. Assn. Counseling and Devel., Nat. Black Alcoholism Counselors, N.J. Alcoholism Assn. Democrat. Baptist. Home Phone: 609-396-4887; Office Phone: 609-396-4887. Personal E-mail: jesy138@comcast.net.

YORK, JOHN LYNDAL, medical educator; b. Morton, Tex., Aug. 14, 1936; s. James Lee and Jewell Fern (Braden) Y.; m. Cynthia Carolyn Giles, June 29, 1958; children: John Lee, Michelle Annette. BS in Chemistry and Math., Harding Coll., 1958; PhD in Physiol. Chemistry, Johns Hopkins U., 1962. NIH predoctoral rsch. fellow Johns Hopkins U., Balt., 1958-62, fellow dept. physiol. chemistry Sch. Medicine, 1962-64; biochemist Stanford Rsch. Inst., Menlo Park, Calif., 1964-65; asst. prof. dept. biochemistry Coll. Basic Med. Sci. U. Tenn., Memphis, 1965-68; assoc. prof. dept. biochemistry Coll. Medicine U. Ark., Little Rock, 1968-76, prof. dept. biochemistry, 1977—2002, prof. emeritus, 2002. Mem. faculty-student liason com. U. Ark., 1969-70, co-chair edn. bldg. II wet lab. design com., 1973-74, computer aided instrn. com., 1972-74, rep. to univ. senate coun., 1973-74, animal care com., 1975-76, chmn. grad. com., 1976-80, rep. to pres.'s grad. adv. coun., 1976-78, subcom. on curriculum, 1976-77, program evaluation com., 1976-78, search com. for pharmacology chmn., 1976-77, chmn. biochemistry grad. student admissions, 1975-79, med. biochemistry cirriculum com., 1975-80, 89—; grad. biochemistry com., 1981-85, coll. med. appeals bd., 1980-2002, com. on ednl. devel. Acad. Senate, 1979-80, com. on ednl. resources, 1979-80, chmn. com. on acad. affairs., 1980-81, search com. for assoc. dean grad. sch., 1982, dir. grad. program dept. biochemistry, 1983-85, dir. seminar program dept. biochemistry, 1986-95, chmn. biochemistry faculty recruitment com., 1982-86, 90-92, exec. com. dept. biochemistry, 1982—, chmn. faculty senate, 1987, handbook com., 1988-89, com. on assessment instrn., 1991-92, chair grad. assessment com. grad. sch., 2000-02; vis. prof. dept. coagulation rsch. Karolinska Inst., Stockholm, 1974-75; vis. prof. Hendrix Coll., Conway, Ark., 2006; judge biochemistry divsn. Ark. State Sci. Fair, 1985—; mem. River Mountain Park adv. com. Little Rock Parks Dept., 1991; mem. Gov's Mercury Adv. Com., 1993—. Author: The Porphyrias, 1972, (with N.S. Sloan) Review of Biochemistry, 1969, translated into German, 1972; contbr. numerous articles and abstracts to profl. and sci. jours. Grantee NIH, 1966-69, 76-78, 80-84, 89-91, 91-94, NSF, 1969-74, Swedish Med. Rsch. Coun., 1974-75, Am. Cancer Soc., 1986-88. Fellow Swedish Med. Rsch. Coun.; mem. AAAS, AAUP (Ark. conf. exec. com. 1994, co-chair Ark. Conf. com. 1995-97, chair 1998-2002), Am. Chem. Soc. (vice chmn. ctrl. Ark. sect. 1971-72, chmn. 1972-73, program chmn. 33rd Southwest regional meeting 1977, 43rd Southwest regional meeting 1987, Disting. Svc. award 1989), Soc. Biol. Chemists, Johns Hopkins Med. and Surg. Assn., Sigma Xi., Alpha Chi. Home: 42 Pine Manor Dr Little Rock AR 72207-5137

YORK, MICHAEL (MICHAEL YORK-JOHNSON), actor; b. Fulmer, Eng., Mar. 27, 1942; s. Joseph Gwynne and Florence Edith (Chown) Johnson; m. Patricia McCallum, Mar. 27, 1968. MA, Oxford U., Eng., 1964; DFA (hon.), U. SC. Profl. debut with Dundee Repertory Theatre, Scotland, 1964; mem. Nat. Theatre Co., London, 1965-66; TV film or miniseries appearances include: Much Ado About Nothing, The Forsyte Saga, Rebel in the Grave, True Patriot, Jesus of Nazareth, 1977, A Man Called Intrepid, 1979, The Phantom of the Opera, 1983, The Master of Ballantrae, 1984, Space, 1985, The Far Country, 1985, Are You My Mother, 1986, Ponce de Leon, 1987, Till We Meet Again, 1989, The Road to Avonlea, 1991, Gardens of the World, 1993; The Four Minute Mile, The Lady and the Highway Man, 1988, The Heat of the Day, 1988, The Hunt for Stolen War Treasure, 1989, The Night of the Fox, 1990, The Magic Paintbrush, 1993, David Copperfield's Christmas, 1994, Teklab, 1994, Fall From Grace, 1994, Not of This Earth, 1995, Duel of Hearts, September, 1995, A Young Connecticut Yankee in King Arthur's Court, 1995, A Knight in Camelot, (TV series) Knots Landing, 1987, SeaQuest, 1995, The Naked Truth, 1995, Babylon 5, 1995, The Ring, 1996, Un Coup De Baguette Magique, True Women, 1997, Sliders, 1997, The Magnificat, 1997, the Long way home, 1997, A Christmas Carol, 1997, The Search for Nazi Gold, 1998, The Ripper 1998, Dead Man's Gun, 1998, Perfect Little Angels, 1998, The Haunting of Hell House, 2000, The Lot, 2000, Founding Fathers, 2002, Liberty's Kids, 2002, Curb Your Enthusiasm, 2002, Founding Brothers, 2002, La Femme Musketeer, 2004, Icon, 2005, The Simpsons, 2006, Law and Order: Criminal Intent, 2006, TV "The Four Seasons", 2009; stage appearances include: Any Just Cause, 1967, Hamlet, 1970, Broadway prodns. of Outcry, 1973, Ring Round the Moon, 1975, Bent, 1980, Cyrano de Bergerac, 1981, Whisper in the Mind, 1990, The Crucible, 1991, Someone Who'll Watch Over Me, 1993, Nora, 1993, Ira Gershwin at 100, 1996, Enoch Arden, 2003, Russian David...Soviet Goliath, 2004, Peer Gynt, 2005, Shadows and Voices, 2005, Amadeus, 2006, Camelot, 2007, Strauss Meets Frankenstein 2008; appeared in motion pictures including: The Taming of the Shrew, 1966, Accident, 1966, Red and Blue, 1967, Smashing Time, 1967, Romeo and Juliet, 1967, The Strange Affair, 1967, The Guru, 1968, Alfred the Great, 1968, Justine, 1969, Something for Everyone, 1969, Zeppelin, 1970, La Poudre D'Escampette, 1971, Cabaret, 1971, England Made Me, 1971, Lost Horizon, 1972, The Three Musketeers, 1973, Murder on the Orient Express, 1974, Great Expectations, 1974, Conduct Unbecoming, 1974, The Four Musketeers, 1975, Logan's Run, 1976, Seven Nights in Japan, The Last Remake of Beau Geste, 1977, The Island of Dr. Moreau, 1977, Fedora, 1977, The Riddle of the Sands, 1978, Final Assignment, 1980, The White Lions, Success is the Best Revenge, Perfect Little Angels, 1998, Dawn, 1985, Vengeance, 1986, The Secret of the Sahara, 1987, Imbalances, 1987, Lethal Obsession, 1987, Midnight Cop, 1988, The Return of the Musketeers, 1989, The Long Shadow, 1991, Eline Vere, 1991, Wide Sargasso Sea, 1991, Rochade, 1991, Discretion Assured, Shadow of a Kiss, 1993, Gospa, 1994, Goodbye America, Austin Powers, Dark Planet, The Treat, 1997, Wrongfully Accused, 1998, One Hell of a Guy, 1998, Lovers and Liars, 1998, The Ghostly Rental, 1999, Austin Powers: The Spy Who Shagged Me, 1999, The Omega Code, 1999, Borstal Boy, 2000, Megiddo, 2001, Austin Powers in Goldmember, 2002, Moscow Heat, 2004, Testimony, 2009; radio performances The Dark Tower, 1977, (Peabody award), A Matter of Honor, 1986, Babbitt, 1987, The Crucible, 1988, Are You Now, UTZ, 1989, McTeague, 1992, Make and Break, 1993; recs. include: Mere Christianity, 1982, Anna Karenina, 1985, Don Quixote, 1986, The King Must Die, 1988, British Rock: The First Wave, UTZ, 1989, The Modigliani Scandal, 1989, The Mummy, 1989, Candide, 1989, The Vampire Lestat, 1989, The Berlin Stories, 1990, The Remains of the Day, 1990, City of Joy, 1991, Beyond Love, 1991, Memories, Dreams, Reflections, 1991, A Poet's Bible, 1992, Einstein's Dreams, 1993, Accidentally on Purpose, 1993, The English Patient, 1993, Fortune's Favorite, 1993, The Three Musketeers, 1993, Paradise Lost, 1993, The Bookof Psalms, 1994, The Book of Virtues, 1994, The MagicPaw-Paw, 1994; (recs.) The Rubaiyat of Omar Khayyam, 1995, Aesop's Fables, 1995, The Poetry of Edgar Allen Poe, 1995, The Hunting of the Snark, Caesar's Women, 1996, Treasure Island, 1996, (Grammy nomination) The Wind in the Willows, 1996, Rose, 1996, Daily Word, 1997, Les Miserables, 1998, Caesar, 1998, Brave New World, 1998, Titanic Hearings, 1998, The Fencing Master, 1999 (Audie award), Rikki Tikki Tavi, 1999, King Rat, 1999, Going Home: Jesus and Buddha, 2000, The Lion, The Witch and The Wardrobe, 2000, A Shakespearean Actor Prepares, 2002, The Theory of Everything, 2003, Creating True Peace, 2003, The Bounty, 2003, Goodbye to Berlin, 2004, The Final Solution, 2004, For the Time Being: Advent, 2005, Jane Goodall's Message of Peace, How Do I Love Thee?, 2006, Peter And The Wolf, 2007, Word of Promise, Audio Bible, 2007, Inspiration for Today, 2008; author: The Courage of Conviction, 1985, Voices of Survival, 1987; author: Accidentally on Purpose, 1992, A Shakespearean Actor Prepares, 2000, Dispatches From Armageddon, 2002, Are My Blinkers Showing?, 2005, Relording "Cry The Beloved Country", 2009. Chmn. Calif. Youth Theatre. Decorated officer Order Brit. Empire, chevalier Nat. Order Arts and Letters (France). Avocations: travel, music, art. Office: Peter Strain & Associate 5455 Wilshire Blvd # 1812 Los Angeles CA 90036 Office Phone: 323-525-3391.

YORK, MICHAEL CHAREST, librarian; b. Newton, Mass., Jan. 2, 1947; s. Richard Francis and Frances Winship (Thibaut) Y.; m. Carol Roberts, June 26, 1982; 1 child, Michael Bradley. BA, U. N.H., 1971; MS, La. State U., 1972; MBA, Plymouth State Coll., 1990. Reference libr. Ithaca (N.Y.) Coll., 1973-77; asst. dir. libr. Castleton (Vt.) State Coll., 1977-81; libr. dir. Merrimack Valley Coll., Manchester, N.H., 1981-85, U. N.H., Manchester, 1985-91, univ. libr. Durham, 1991-95; libr. dir. Colby-Sawyer Coll., New London, N.H., 1996-98; dir. The Libr. and Archives of N.H. Polit. Tradition, Concord, 1998-99; libr. N.H. State Libr., Concord, 1999—. Mem. ALA, New Eng. Libr. Assn. (pres. 1988-89), N.H. Libr. Assn. (pres. 1999—), N.H. State Libr. Adv. Coun. Avocations: sailing, skiing, woodworking, politics. Office: NH State Libr 20 Park St Concord NH 03301-6316 Office Phone: 603-271-2397. Office Fax: 603-271-2082. Business E-Mail: michael.york@dcr.nh.gov.

YORK, NEIL LONGLEY, history professor; b. San Luis Obispo, Calif., Apr. 21, 1951; s. Eric Kingsmill and Joel Barlow York; m. Carole Jean Mikita, Aug. 29, 1981; children: Jennifer Carole, Caitlin Kingsmill. BA, Brigham Young U., Provo, Utah, 1973, MA, 1975; PhD, U. Calif., Santa Barbara, 1978. Prof. history Brigham Young U., Provo, 1977—. Author: (history book) Mechanical Metamorphosis, 1985, Neither Kingdom Nor Nation, 1994, Fiction as Fact, 2001, Turning the World Upside Down, 2003, Portrait of a Patriot, 2005. Democrat-Npl. Church Of Jesus Christ Of Latter-Day Saints. Home: 2519 Cliff Swallow Dr Sandy UT 84093 Office: Brigham Young Univ Dept History Provo UT 84602 Business E-Mail: neil_york@byu.edu.

YORK, TINA, painter; b. Germany, Feb. 9, 1951; Student, Sch. Mus. Fine Arts, Boston, 1967-71; studied with, George Dergalis, Wayland, Mass., 1967-75; BA cum laude, Brandeis U., 1978; postgrad., N.Y. Med. Coll., 1980-83. Contbr. works to numerous publs., 1987-2003; columns in newspapers; one woman shows include Gallery Contemporary Art, Provincetown, Mass., 1969, Springfield (Mass.) Art Assn., 1971, Copley Soc., Boston, 1972-73, Boston U., 1974, Mendler Gallery, Rockport, Mass., 1974, Cambridge (Mass.) Art Assn., 1975, Ames Gallery, N.Y.C., 1976, Gallery Seven, Boston, 1977, Brandeis U., Waltham, Mass., 1978, Rue Oker Gallery of Art, Sturbridge, Mass., 1979, Art Collectors Gallery, N.Y.C., 1981, 153 Gallery, Inc., N.Y.C., 1982, Creative Concepts, L.A., 1984, Alpha Contemporary Exhibits, L.A., 1985, Darraby Gallery, L.A., 1986, 8th St. Gallery, L.A., 1986, Koplin Gallery, L.A., 1987, Galerie Beverly Hills, Calif., 1988, Conv. Ctr., Rome, 1988, Merck, Sharpe & Dohme, Rahway, N.J., 1988, Erlgangen Kultur Borse, Germany, 1989, Arwell Gallery, Laguna, Calif., 1989, Deutsch-Amerikanisches Inst., Regensburg, Germany, 1990, Art in Pub. Bldgs., Nuremberg, Germany, 1990, Art Expo, N.Y.C., 1990, Amerikahaus, Nuremberg, 1990, Art 5, Nuremberg, 1990, Dresdner Bank, Nuremberg, 1990, Amer. Hosp. Assn., Washington, 1990, So. Med. Assn., Nashville, 1990, 94-95, Studio Gallery, North Hollywood, Calif., 1991-92, Galerie Lehman, Germany, Galerie Sud, Studio la Citta, Italy, Studio Gallery, Calif., 1991 La Foire Internat. d'Art Contemporain, Paris, 1992, 94, Med. Heritage Gall., Waco, Tex., 1991, Herbstmesse, Frankfurt, Germany, 1992-93, Kunstforum Internat., Aachen, Germany, 1993, Kunstlerhaus, Germany, 1993, Ambiente, Frankfurt, 2003-07, ART/LA, 1993-95, Internat. Art Fair, Czechoslovakia, 2003-2007, Art Fair, Seattle, 1993-94, Art Expo, Chgo., 1993-94, Art Expo, N.Y.C., 1993-96, Chgo. Trade Show, 1993, 95, 97, Toronto Trade Show, 1993, Art Cologne, Germany, 1993-94, 96, Centre d'Art Contemporain, Switzerland, Dresdner Bank, Germany, Galerie Littmann, Switzerland, Galerie Fischer, 1994, Art Asia, Hong Kong, 1994-96, Art Expo, Calif., 1994, 96, PPFA Toronto Trade Show, 1994-95, Limited Edit. Expo, New Orleans, 1994-95, Frankfurt Book Fair, 1994, 97-98, 2000, 03, Internat. Spring Fair, Birmingham, Eng., 1994, 95, Art Miami, 1994-95, Exposition of Art, Sydney, Australia, 1993, Art Taipei, Taiwan, 1993, 94, 95, Art Santa Fe, 1993-95, NASA Ames Rsch. Ctr., Moffett Field, Calif., 1994, NASA Johnson Space Ctr., Houston, 1995, Galerie Rudelko, Germany, Scheffler Galerie, Germany, 1995, Studio Gall., Ariz., 1996, Jahns House, Germany, 1996, Internat. Contemporary Art Fair, Madrid, 1995, West Valley Mus. Art, Phoenix, 1998, Las Vegas Art Mus., 2000, Paul Joseph Galleries, Las Vegas, 2002, Rio Decor, 2003, Tina York Studio, Naples, Fla., 2003, Marco Island Art Assn., Fla. 2004, Studio Gallery, Naples, 2004, 06, Arena Arts Gallery, Naples, Fla., 2005, I.C. Fine Art 2000 Gallery, Las Vegas, 2005, Waterways Studios, Naples, 2007, Arseualt Gallery, 2007; group shows include Area Arts Gallery, Mag., Naples, Floridaand article and painting, NASA Art Programs, Washington, 2007, Mus. Fine Arts, Salt Lake City, Mus. Art, Las Vegas, Regional Mus. Art, Bautzen, Germany, 2007, Mus. Art, Downey, Calif., 2007, Carter Ctr., Atlanta, Shakespeare Theatre, NJ, 2007, Las Vegas Art Mus., Nev., 2007, Washigton, 2007; represented in permanent collections, Rio Decor, Mus. of Art, Las Vegas, Downey (Calif.) Mus. Art, Mus. Fine Arts, Salt Lake City, Mcpl. Art Mus., Osaka, Japan, Regional Mus. Art, Bautzen, Germany, Carter Ctr., Atlanta, Kennedy Space Ctr., Fla., New Zealand Space Adminstrn., Auckland, NASA, Internat. Peace Acad., NY, USIA, BBC (Brit. Broadcasting Co.), Lagan Jute, Ltd., India, NIH, Universitet Kliment Orchridski, Bulgaria, Hiatt Internat., Beverly Hills, Calif., Paris, Gallery Dmovrosek, Yugoslavia, Columbia U., Nat. Cancer Inst., Md., Kulturamt der Stadt Nurnberg, Germany, Planetary Soc., Calif., Mayo Clin., Ariz., Nat. Air and Space Mus., Washington, Nat. Air and Space Mus., South Dennis Art Gallery, Cape May Ct. Hoouse, 2009, others; represented on Artrain USA; pub. NASA/Exploration of Space, 2004; contbr. various articles and paintings in journals. First prize painting Arts Fest., Scituate, MA, 1969, Internatl. Show, Fall River, MA, 1971; third prize mixed media painting, De Cordova Mus., Lincoln, MA, 1972; second prize painting, Amer. Artists in Paris, Paris, 1975; first prize mixed media painting Inst. Contemporary Art, 1979; Gold medal painting, Spring Arts Fest., LA, 1985; first prize mixed media painting, One Fifty Three Gall., Inc., 1987. Mem.: Internat. High IQ Soc. Home: Tina York Studio 565 102nd Ave N Naples FL 34108-3210 Office Phone: 239-455-2164. Business E-Mail: tinayorkstudio@aol.com.

YORK, VERMELLE CARDWELL, retired real estate broker and developer; b. Evergreen, Ala., Jan. 30, 1925; d. Frederick Lofton and Emmie Mildred (Pitts) Cardwell; m. E. Travis York, Jr., Dec. 26, 1946; children: Lisa, Travis. BS, Auburn U., Ala., 1946. Pres. Tralisa Corp., Gainesville, Fla., 1966—87, sec., treas., 1988—94, Caret Corp., Gainesville, Fla., 1979—86, pres., 1987—2004; ret., 2004. Mem. devel. com. Harn Mus., Gainesville, 1990-96, Hospice House, Gainesville, 1992-96; co-chair March of Dimes, Gainesville, 1995, Red Ribbon Campaign, 1989, 90; bd. dirs. Keep Alachua County Beautiful, Phillips Ctr. Performing Arts U. Fla.; bd. Gainesville Cmty. Found. Recipient Pres.'s Medallion, U. Fla., 1980; named Woman of Distinction, Santa Fe C.C., Gainesville, Fla., 1988, Vam York Theatre at Gainesville Cmty. Playhouse 05 dedicated in her honor; named one of Women Who Make a Difference, Girl Scouts Am., 2005 Mem. Gainesville Builders Assn. (bd. dirs. 1997—), The Heritage Club (mem. amb. com. 1991-96), P.E.O. (pres. 1989-90), Surfside N. Club, (dir. 1988-91), Gainesville Women's Forum (membership chair 1994-96), Altrusa, Rotary, DAR, Phi Kappa Phi. Avocation: genealogy. Home: 5200 SW 25th Blvd #4216 Gainesville FL 32608-8925

YORKE, MARIANNE, lawyer, real estate executive; b. Nov. 4, 1948; d. Joseph George and Catherine Veronica (Friel) Y; m. MacLachlin, May 20, 2004. BA cum laude, West Chester U., 1971; JD cum laude, Temple U., 1980; MS in Ognl. Dynamics summa cum laude, U. Pa., 1987; M in Corp. Real Estate, Internat. Assn. Corp. Real Estate Execs., 1996. Bar: Pa. 1981, N.Y. 1992. Mgr. CIGNA Corp., Phila., 1982-85, asst. dir., 1985-90; v.p. Chase Manhattan Bank, NYC, 1990-92; real estate dir. Johnson & Johnson, 1992—. Real estate atty. Garfinkel & Volpicelli, Phila., 1980-82; prin., mng. ptnr. Yorke & Eisenman, Real Estate, Phila., 1976-89, prin., mng. ptnr. Yorke & Mac Lachlin Real Estate, Phila., 1989-02; lectr. Women in the Arts, 1982-90; guest spkr. Wharton Sch. Bus. Class of 1989, U. Pa., grad. sch. arts and sci. Class of 1988; asst. prof. bus. law Rider U. Grad Sch., 2002-03, asst. prof. real estate law and real estate transactions Rutgers U. Grad. Sch., 2003—, asst. prof. real estate negotiations Rutgers U. MBA Sch., 2005-. Contbr. articles to profl. jours. Solicitor Pa. Ballet, Phila., 1983-90, United Way, Phila.,

1983-90; mem. steering com. U. Pa., 1986-90, dir. alumni assn., 1987-90; mem. adv. com. for econ. devel. Luth. Settlement House Adv., 1986-88; mem. Ctr. Adv. Bd., 2000—; bd. dirs. Hamilton Townhouse Assn., Phila., 1988-90, chmn. ins. com., 1989-90, 718 Broadway Inc., NYC, 1990-94, Johnson Health Care Svcs. Recipient Live for Life Mgmt., Johnson Health Mgmt., 1995, Pres. Quality Process Excellence award, EthiconEndo Surgery, 2000, Process Excellence award, Ethicon, Inc., 2001. Mem. ABA (forum on constrn. 1982-90), Pa. Bar Assn. (condominium and zoning com. 1982-90), Assn. of Bar of City of NY (sects. on internat. law and real property law 1992-94), Phila. Bar Assn., Phila. Women Real Estate Atty., CORENET, Nat. Assn. Corp. Real Estate Exec. (internat. coun. 1984-, comml. coun. 1984-), Internat. Atty., Roundtable, Women's Law Caucus, Phi Alpha Delta. Independent. Roman Catholic. Home: The Admiralty 55 Ocean Ave Monmouth Beach NJ 07750-1366 Office: Johnson & Johnson W H 7G46 One Johnson & Johnson Plz New Brunswick NJ 08933-0002 Office Phone: 732-728-1277, 732-524-3881. Business E-Mail: myorke@its.jnj.com.

YORKE, THOM (THOMAS EDWARD YORKE), singer; b. Wellingborough, England, Oct. 7, 1968; children: Noah, Agnes. Student in English and Art, Exeter U., Eng. Guitarist Flickernoise; orderly; singer, guitarist Radiohead, 1992—. Singer, musician (albums with Radiohead) Pablo Honey, 1993, The Bends, 1995, Ok Computer, 1997 (Grammy award, Best Alternative Music Performance, 1998), (albums with Radiohead albums) Kid A, 2000 (Grammy award, Best Alternative Music Performance, 2001), (albums with Radiohead) Amnesiac, 2001, Hail to the Thief, 2003, In Rainbows, 2007 (Grammy award, Best Alternative Music Album, 2009), (solo albums) The Eraser, 2006. Named one of The 100 Most Influential People in the World, TIME mag., 2008. Office: Capital Records 1750 North Vine St 10th Floor Hollywood CA 90028 also: Chrysalis Music Group The Chrysalis Building Bramley Rd London W10 6SP England*

YORKE-VINEY, SALLY ANNE, elementary school educator; b. Williamsport, Pa., Dec. 8, 1953; d. H. Allen and Mary Ellen Yearick; m. Malcolm Christopher Stanley Viney, Nov. 26, 1988; 1 child, Colin Patrick Allen Viney. BS in Edn., Shippensburg U., 1975; MEd, East Stroudsburg U., 1993; PhD, Marywood U., 2007—. Tchr. elem. sch. Selinsgrove Sch. Dist., Pa., 1975—76, Shikellamy Sch. Dist., Sunbury, 1976—82; tech. editor Lambda Techs., NYC, 1983—85; singer, actress AFTRA, SAG Actor's Equity, 1978—85; profl. singer, cabaret artist various Cruise Lines, 1985—91; tchr. elem. sch. East Stroudsburg Sch. Dist., Pa., 1991—2007; elem. literacy coach East Stroudsburg Area Sch. Dist., 2007—. Adj. prof. East Stroudsburg U., 1999—2005, 2007; chair Arts in Edn. Com., 2003—06. Dir. choir Luth. Ch. of Savior, Mt. Pocono, Pa., 1989—99, St. Paul Luth. Ch., 2007—. Mem.: ASCD, Internat. Reading Assn., Phi Delta Kappa. Avocations: singing, theater. Home: HC89 Box 831 Pocono Summit PA 18346 Office Phone: 570-517-7360. Personal E-mail: malnsal@ptd.net. Business E-Mail: viney@esasd.net.

YORKEY, BRIAN, lyricist; b. Issaquah, Wash. Grad., Columbia U. Assoc. artistic dir. Village Theatre, Issaquah, Wash. Book and lyrics: Broadway plays Next to Normal, 2008 (Tony award for Best Original Score Written for the Theatre, 2009, Tony award for Best Book of a Musical, 2009), plays Funny Pages, 1993, Making Tracks, 2002, The Wedding Banquet, 2003, Play it by Heart, 2005. Mem.: Dramatists Guild America, Writers Guild America.*

YORMARK, BRETT D., professional sports team executive; b. Sept. 28, 1966; s. Arlene Sloan; m. Amy Yormark; children: Madison, Drake. Student in Mgmt., Ind. U. Thrift plan adminstr. Banker's Trust, NYC, 1988—89; account exec. NJ Nets, East Rutherford, 1989—91, v.p. corp. mktg., 1994, sr. v.p. corp. mktg., 1995—98, pres., CEO, 2005—; account exec. Sports TV Katz Comm., Chgo., 1991—92; sr. account exec. Detroit Pistons, Auburn Hills, Mich., 1992—94; mng. dir. corp. mktg. NASCAR, NYC, 1998—2000, v.p. corp. mktg., 2000—05. Bd. dirs. Assn. Volleyball Profls. Named one of 40 Under Forty, Crain's NY Bus., 2006, 40 Under 40, Sports Bus. Jour., 2006. Mem.: North Jersey Young Presidents Assn. Office: Nets Sports and Entertainment LLC 390 Murray Hill Pky East Rutherford NJ 07073 Office Phone: 201-935-8888. Office Fax: 201-935-1088.*

YORMARK, MICHAEL, professional sports team executive; m. Dana Yormark; 1 child, Sophia. Grad., Ohio U., 1989. Joined Sunrise Sports & Entertainment, 2003, now pres., COO; pres. Fla. Panthers, 2007—. Alt. gov. NHL Bd. Govs. Office: Fla Panthers One Panther Parkway Sunrise FL 33323 E-mail: yormarkm@sselive.com.

YORTSOS, YANNIS C., petroleum engineer, educator, dean; BSChemE, Nat. Tech. U., Athens, Greece, 1973; MSChemE, Calif. Inst. Tech., Pasadena, 1979; PhD in Chem. Engring., Calif. Inst. Tech., 1979. Chester F. Dolley prof. petroleum engring. Mork Family Dept. Chem. Engring. and Materials Sci. U. So. Calif., LA, 1975—, chair dept. chem. engring., 1991—97, dean engring. Viterbi Sch. Engring., 2006—. Contbr. articles to sci. jours. Office: U So Calif Viterbi Sch Engring Olin Hall Engring 200 3650 McClintock Ave Los Angeles CA 90089-1450 Office Phone: 213-740-7832. Office Fax: 213-740-8493. E-mail: yortsos@usc.edu.

YOSELOFF, JULIEN DAVID, publishing company executive; b. NYC, June 25, 1941; s. Thomas and Sara (Rothfuss) Y.; m. Darlene Starr Carbone, Aug. 6, 1967; children: Michael Ian, Anthony Alexander. BA, U. Pa., 1962; student, London Sch. Econs., 1962—63; MA, Rutgers U., 1994. With A.S. Barnes and Co., Inc., Cranbury, NJ, 1963-80; dir. Associated Univ. Presses, Inc., 1966—; pres. Rosemont Pub. and Printing Corp., 1985—. Served with AUS, 1964. Mem. Phi Beta Kappa Assocs., Phi Beta Kappa, Pi Sigma Alpha. Avocations: amateur radio, photography, bicycling. Office: 2010 Eastpark Blvd Cranbury NJ 08512-3518 Office Phone: 609-655-4770.

YOSHIDA, GLEN YOSHIO, otolaryngologist; b. Honolulu, Feb. 20, 1955; s. Charles K. and Yoshiko Yoshida; m. Nancy Marie Gustafson, Apr. 22, 1989; 1 child, Michael B. BA, Lawrence U., Appleton, Wis., 1977; MD, Uniformed Svcs. U. Health Scis., Bethesda, Md., 1982. Diplomate Am. Bd. Otolaryngology, 1987. Commd. 2d lt. US Army, 1982, advanced through grades to lt. col., 1994; intern otolaryn.-head and neck surgery Tripler Army Med. Ctr., Honolulu, 1982—83, resident otolaryn.-head and neck surgery, 1983—87; chief otolaryn.-head and neck surgery 121 Evac Hosp., Seoul, Republic of Korea, 1987—88; fellow head and neck surgery Meth. Hosp., Indpls., 1988—89; asst. chief otolaryn.-head and neck surgery Fitzsimons Army Med. Ctr., Aurora, Colo., 1989—96; mem. otolaryngology staff Altru Health Sys., Grand Forks, ND, 1996—. Mem. adv. bd. Grand Forks Pharmacy, 2000—; cons. in field; asst. clin. prof., co-program dir. otolaryngology residency U. Colo. Health Scis. Ctr., 1990—96; asst. clin. prof. Uniformed Svcs. U. Health Scis., 1995—96, U. ND Sch. Medicine, 1998—; presenter in field. Contbr. articles to med. jours. Otolaryngologist med. mission trip SW Med. Teams, Romania, 1995, Internat. Relief Teams, Honduras, 2006; med. vol. mission trip Calvary Luth. Ch., Honduras, 2004; bd. dirs. Greater Grand Forks Symphony Orch., 2001—. Decorated Army Commendation medal, Nat. Def. medal, Meritorious Svc. medal; recipient Tchr. of Yr. award, U. Colo. otolaryngology-head and neck surgery dept., 1996. Fellow: ACS, Am. Acad. Facial Plastic and Reconstructive Surgery, Am. Head and Neck Soc., Am. Acad. Otolaryngology-Head and Neck Surgery (Honor award 1998); mem.: Am. Acad. Sleep Medicine, Fighting Souix Club. Lutheran. Avocations: running, horseback riding, sled dogs, photography, golf. Office: Altru Health Sys 1000 S Columbia Rd 4D Grand Forks ND 58201

YOSHIDA, KENICHI, veterinarian, biology educator; DVM, Miyazaki U., Japan, 1995; PhD, U. Tokyo, 1999. Cert. vet. Ministry Agr., Forestry and Fisheries Japan, 1995. Fellow Japan Soc. Promotion Sci., Tokyo, 1996—2000; postdoctoral fellow Harvard Med. Sch., Boston, 1999—2001; rschr. Sankyo Corp., Tokyo, 2001—02; asst. prof. U. Tokyo, Tokyo, 2002—04; lectr. Meiji U., Kawasaki, Kanagawa, Japan, 2004—06, assoc. prof., 2007—. Cons. Sony Corp., Tokyo, 2003—04. Mng. editor (jour.) Frontiers in Biosci. Grantee, Sumitomo Found., 2004; Sci. Rsch. grantee, Ministry Edn., Culture, Sports, Sci. and Tech., 2003—, Sci. and Tech. grantee, Kao Found. Arts and Scis., 2005, Encouragement Rsch. grantee, Uehara Meml. Found., 2005, Sci. Rsch. grantee, Ministry Health, Labor and Welfare, 2005—06, Support For Pharm. Scis. fellow, Takeda Sci. Found., 2005. Mem.: Am. Soc. Biochemistry and Molecular Biology. Achievements include patents for hyperlipemia, arteriosclerosis and hyperglycemia drug screening with mouse and human angiopoietin-related protein 3 and 4. Avocations: travel, driving, reading. Office: Meiji U Sch Agr 1-1-1 Higashimita Tama-ku Kanagawa Kawasaki 214-8571 Japan Business E-Mail: yoshida@isc.meiji.ac.jp.

YOSHIMOTO, MIDORI, art educator, director; PhD, Rutgers State U. NJ, New Brunswick, 2002. Assoc. prof. NJ City U., Jersey City, 2003—, gallery dir., 2003—. Office: NJ City Univ 2039 Kennedy Blvd Jersey City NJ 07305

YOSHIMURA, KEI, oceanographer; b. Osaka, Japan, Jan. 23, 1978; s. Masakatsu and Shoko Yoshimura; m. Aki Kadosaka, Apr. 30, 2006. BSc in Engring., U. Tokyo, 2000, MSc, 2002, PhD, 2006. Tech. rsch. fellow Japan Sci. and Tech. Agy., Tokyo, 2002—04; asst. prof. Inst. Indsl. Sci., U. Tokyo, 2004—08; project scientist, Scripps instn. oceanography U. Calif. San Diego, La Jolla, 2008—. Invited rschr. Japan Agy. Marine-Earth Sci. and Tech., Yokohama, Kanagawa, 2006—. Recipient Furuichi award, Grad. Sch. Engring., U. Tokyo, 2002; Postdoc. fellowships, Japan Soc. Promotion Sci., 2006—08. Mem.: Meteorol. Soc. Japan, Japan Soc. Hydrology and Water Resources Engring., Japan Soc. Civil Engring., Am. Geophys. Union. Office: Scripps Inst Oceanography 9500 Gilman Dr 0224 La Jolla CA 92093-0224

YOSHIZUMI, DONALD TETSURO, dentist; b. Honolulu, Feb. 18, 1930; s. Richard Kiyoshi and Hatsue (Tanouye) Yoshizumi; m. Barbara Fujiko Iwashita, June 25, 1955 (dec. Feb. 1998); children: Beth Ann E., Cara Leigh S., Erin Yuri. BS, U. Hawaii, 1952; DDS, U. Mo., 1960, grad. cert. prosthodontics, 1962, MS, 1963. Clin. instr. U. Mo. Sch. Dentistry, Kansas City, 1960—63; pvt. practice Santa Clara, Calif., 1963—70, San Jose, Calif., 1970—. Contbr. articles to profl. jours. With USAF, 1952—56. Mem.: ADA, Santa Clara County Dental Soc., Calif. Dental Assn., Delta Sigma Delta, Omicron Kappa Upsilon. Home: 683 Apricot Ct Los Banos CA 93635-9691

YOSKIN, JON WILLIAM, II, insurance company executive; b. Phila., Oct. 16, 1939; s. Lewis William and Louise (Houck) Y.; m. Dorothea James, Sept. 25, 1961 (div. Mar. 1992); children: Nicholas, Dorothea, Maurice P.; m. Elizabeth Anne Groves, Sept 26, 1992. Pvt. practice, Phila., 1959-74; sr. v.p. Mid. Atlantic Gen. Investment Co., Phila., 1974-80; exec. v.p. Transatlantic Life Assurance Co., Phila., 1980-85, Meritor Life Ins. Co., Phila., 1985-88; owner, CEO Tri-Arc Fin. Svcs., Phila., 1988—; chmn., CEO Magellan Ins. Co. Ltd., Bermuda, 1996—. Bd. dirs. Concerto Soloist, Phila., 1990-92, Nat. Media Corp., 1994-98, Phila. Commn. to End. Homelessness, 1995—; mem. Spl. Olympics Adv. Com. Mem. Nat. Assn. Life Underwriters, Coun. Ins. Agts. and Brokers (bd. dirs.), Profl. Assn. Ins. Agts., Sons of Am. Revolution, Mil. Order Loyal Legion of U.S. Republican. Episcopalian. Avocation: big game hunting. Office: Tri-Arc Fin Svcs 983 Old Eagle School Rd Ste 616 Wayne PA 19087-1711 Home: 1 Brightview Ave Hobe Sound FL 33455-2123 E-mail: jyoskin@triarcfs.com.

YOST, DAN, telecommunications industry executive; BSEE, MBA, So. Meth. U., Dallas. Sr. mgmt. position NETCOM Online Comm., Metro-Cel Cellular, Inc., McCaw Cellular Comm., AT&T Wireless; pres., COO Allegiance Telecom, Inc., Dallas; exec. v.p. product & IT Qwest Comm. Internat., Inc., Denver, 2004—08, exec. v.p. for Mass Markets Orgn. (MMO), 2008—. Bd. dirs. ACE Cash Express. Office: Qwest Comm Internat Inc 1801 California St Denver CO 80202 Office Phone: 303-992-1400. Office Fax: 303-896-8515.

YOST, JAMES A., automotive parts company executive; b. 1949; BSc in Computer Sci., Johns Hopkins U., 1971; MBA in Fin., U. Chgo. Controller Autolatina; various positions Ford Europe; v.p. corp. strategy Ford Motor Co.; v.p. fin., CFO Hayes Lemmerz Internat. Inc., Northville, Mich., 2002—07, exec. v.p., CFO, 2007—08, Dana Holding Corp., Toledo, 2008—. Office: Dana Holding Corp 4500 Dorr St Toledo OH 43615

YOST, NICHOLAS CHURCHILL, lawyer; b. Washington, Aug. 15, 1938; s. Charles Woodruff and Irene Ravitch (Oldakowska) Yost; m. Sandra Moore Rennie; children: Robert, Scott, Daniel. AB in Pub. & Internat. Affairs, Princeton U., 1960; LLB, U. Calif., Berkeley, 1963. Bar: Calif., 1964, US Supreme Ct., 1972, DC, 1978. Dep. atty. gen. adminstrv. law Calif. Dept. Justice, 1965-69; counsel Calif. State Environ. Quality Study Coun., 1969-71; dep. atty. gen. in charge environ. unit Calif. Dept. Justice, 1971-77; gen. counsel Coun. Environ. Quality, Exec. Office of Pres., Washington, 1977-81; vis. scholar Environ. Law Inst., Washington, 1981-82; sr. atty. Ctr. for Law in Pub. Interest, Washington, 1982-85; ptnr. Dickstein, Shapiro & Morin, Washington, 1985-94, Sonnenschein Nath & Rosenthal, San Francisco, 1994—. US dir. Law and Adminstrn. Project under US-USSR environ. agreement, 1977—81; dir. Pres.'s Task Force on Global Resources and Environment, 1980—81; mem US Del. to UN Conf. on Environment and Devel., Rio de Janeiro, 1992; mem. & subcom. chair Calif. EPA Blue Ribbon Commn. on a Unified Environ. Statute, 1994; NEPA counsel Presidio Trust. Contbr. articles to profl. journals Capt. US Army, 1963—65. Recipient Nat. Environ. Quality Award, Natural Resources Coun. Am., 1996. Mem. ABA (chmn. standing com. on environ. law 1989-91), State Bar Calif. (chmn. com. on environ. 1975-76), DC Bar Assn. (co-chmn. environ., energy and natural resources sect. 1985-86, 88-89), Environ. Law Inst. (bd. dirs. 1986-92), UN Assn. LA (v.p. 1969-71), UN Assn. Wash. (bd. dirs. 1987-93). Office: Sonnenschein Nath & Rosenthal LLP 26th Fl 525 Market St San Francisco CA 94105 Office Phone: 415-882-2440. Office Fax: 415-882-0300. Business E-Mail: nyost@sonnenschein.com.

YOST, R. DAVID (DAVID YOST), pharmaceutical executive; b. 1947; married. BS, USAF Acad., 1969; MBA, UCLA, 1970. From v.p. to pres. Kauffman-Lattimer Co., Columbus, Ohio, 1969-74; from group v.p. to group pres. cen. region Alco Health Systems Corp., Malvern, Pa., 1989-97; pres., CEO, chmn. AmeriSource Health Corp., Malvern, Pa., 1997—2001; pres. AmerisourceBergen Corp., 2001—02, 2007—, CEO, dir., 2002—. Capt. USAF, 1969—74. Office: AmerisourceBergen Corp 1300 Morris Dr Ste 100 Wayne PA 19087-5594*

YOST, WILLIAM ALBERT, speech and hearing science professor; b. Dallas, Sept. 21, 1944; s. William Jacque and Gladys (Funk) Yost; m. Lee Prater, June 15, 1969; children: Kelley Ann, Alyson Leigh. BA, Colo. Coll., Colorado Springs, 1966, DSc (hon.), 1997; PhD, Ind. U., Bloomington, 1970. Assoc. prof. psychology U. Fla., Gainesville, 1971-77; dir. sensory physiology and perception program NSF, Washington, 1982-83; prof. psychology Loyola U., Chgo., 1979—, dir. Parmly Hearing Inst., 1977—2001, dir. interdisciplinary neurosci. minor, 1977—2001, prof. hearing scis., 1990—; chair and prof. speech and hearing sci. Ariz. State U. Prof. psychology, adj. prof. otolarynogology Loyola U., Chgo., 1990—, acting v.p. rsch., 1999—2001, assoc. v.p. rsch., dean Grad. Sch., 2001—04; individual expert bio-acoustics Am. Nat. Stds. Inst., 1983—; mem. study sect. Coun. Nat. Inst. Deafness and Other Communication Disorders, 1990—94; chair hearing bioacoustics and biomechanics com. NRC, 1992—2001, mem. bd. on behavioral cognitive and sensory scis., 1998—2004. Author: Fundamentals of Hearing, 5th edit., 2007; editor (with others) New Directions in Hearing Science, 1985, Directional Hearing, 1987, Auditory Processing of Complex Sounds, 1987, Classification of Complex Sounds, 1989, Psychoacoustics, 1993, Try Perception of Sound Sources, 2007; assoc. editor Auditory Neurosci., 1994-97; ad hoc reviewer NSF, Air Force Office Sci. Rsch., Office Naval Rsch., 1981—; contbr. chpts. to books, articles to profl. jours. Pres. Evanston Tennis Assn., Ill., 1984, 90. Grantee NSF, 1974—, NIH, 1975—, AFOSR, 1983—, ONR, 1989-90. Fellow AAAS, Am. Phys. Soc., Acoustical Soc. Am. (assoc. editor jour. 1984-91, chair tech. com. 1990-94, exec. com. 1999—, v.p. 2002-04, pres. 2004—, Silver medal 2006), Am. Speech-Lang. Hearing Assn.; mem. NAS (exec. com. on hearing bioacoustics, biomechanics 1981-87, chmn. 1993-97), Nat. Assoc. Rsch. in Otolaryngology (sec.-treas. 1984-87, pres.-elect 1987-88, pres. 1988-89), Nat. Inst. Deafness and Other Comm. Disorders (task force, rev. panel 1990-94, chmn. 1994), Am. Auditory Soc. (exec. bd. 1993-98). Office: Speech Hearing Sci PO Box 870102 Temple Scottsdale AZ 85259-0102 Office Phone: 480-965-2905. Business E-Mail: william.yost@asu.edu. *I am fortunate that I am in an occupation that is so much fun. Teaching and research are very enjoyable. Most days for me are fun.*

YOU, SUKKYUNG, research faculty; b. Seoul, Korea, May 18, 1971; d. Chanhyung Rew and Youngmin Lee. BA, Ewha Womans U., Seoul, 1995; MA, U. Calif., Santa Barbara, 2002. Contbr. articles to profl. jours. Rsch. grantee, U. Calif. Lang. Minority Rsch. Inst., 2003, Am. Ednl. Rsch. Assoc., 2007, Assoc. Institutional Rsch., 2007, Spencer Found., 2007, Nat. Inst. Health, 2009. Avocations: travel, yoga, swimming, dance, movies. Office: U Calif Santa Barbara Dept Edn Santa Barbara CA 93106 Personal E-mail: sukkyung@education.ucsb.edu.

YOU, TAEK H., biology professor, researcher; s. JiWoong You and Pil Gee Jung; m. Mi Kyong Lee, June 21, 1986; children: Elliot Y., Ashley H. PhD, Ohio State U., Columbus, 1895. Postdoc. fellow Ohio State U., Columbus, 1996—99. Sgt. US Army, 1981—83, Republic of Korea. Mem.: HPANC. Home: 809 Willowmist Ct Cary NC 27519 Office: Dept Biol Sci 205 Day Dorm Rd Cary NC 27519 Business E-Mail: you@campbell.edu.

YOU, XIAOYE, literature and language professor; b. Xinfeng, Jiangxi, China, Apr. 25, 1974; PhD, Purdue U., West Lafayette, Ind., 2005. English, Asian studies asst. prof. Pa. State U., Univ. Pk., 2005—. Mem.: Nat. Coun. Tchrs. English. Home: 445 Waupelani Dr Apt G2 State College PA 16801 Office: PA State Univ 118 Burrowes Bldg State College PA 16801 Business E-Mail: xuy10@psu.edu.

YOU, YALI, music educator; b. Xian, Shaanxi Province, China, July 31, 1962; d. Damin You and Fang Lin; m. Paul Steven Knuth, Aug. 9, 2002. D of Musical Arts, U. of Cin., Cin., Ohio, 1989—96; MusM, Northwestern U., Evanston, Ill., 1986—87; BA, Shanghai Conservatory of Music, Shanghai, China, 1980—84. Cert. cello performance Northwestern U., 1988. Prof. music Hamline U., St. Paul, 1996—; adj. prof. music Concordia U., St. Paul, 1997—2001. Hon. prof. cello Xian Conservatory Music, China, 2005; lectr. in field. Musician concert performances in various venues. Recipient Excellent Performance, 4th Chinese Nat. Chamber Music competition, 1985. Mem.: Am. Assoc. of Univ. Professors. Buddhism. Avocations: ceramics, gardening, travel. Office: Hamline Univ 1536 Hewitt Ave Saint Paul MN 55104 Business E-Mail: yyou@gw.hamline.edu.

YOU, YOUNGJAE, science educator, researcher; m. Sukyung Woo. PhD, Chungnam Natl. U., Republic of Korea, 2001. Pharmacist S. Korea, 1994. Postdoctoral rschr. SUNY at Buffalo, Buffalo, 2001—04, rsch. asst. prof., 2004—. Contbr. articles various profl. jours. Recipient Postdoctoral award, US Dept. of Def., 2004-2007; Korean Health Sci. fellowship, Korean Health Sci. Found., 1996. Mem.: Korean Pharm. Assn. (licentiate), Am. Soc. of Photobiology (assoc.), Am. Assn. of Cancer Rsch. (assoc.), Am. Chem. Soc. (assoc.). Office: 630 NSC Dept Chemistry Buffalo NY 14260 Business E-Mail: yjyou@buffalo.edu, youngjae.you@sdstate.edu.

YOUD, T. LESLIE, retired civil engineer; b. Spanish Fork, Utah, Apr. 2, 1938; s. Thomas Leslie and Mary (Evans) Y.; m. Denice Porter, June 26, 1962; children: Verlin, Lance, Melinda, Thomas, Emily. BS, Brigham Young U., 1964; PhD, Iowa State U., 1967. Rsch. civil engr. U.S. Geological Survey, Menlo Park, Calif., 1967-84; prof. Brigham Young U., Provo, Utah, 1984—2003; ret., 2004. Recipient Maeser Rsch. award Brigham Young U., 1991, Utah Engring. Educator of Yr., 1995, ASCE H. Bolton Seed medal, 2002. Mem. NAE, ASCE (hon.), Internat. Soc. for Soil Mechanics and Fnd. Engring., Earthquake Engring. Rsch. Inst.(hon.) Mem. Lds Ch. Achievements include development of techniques for mapping earthquake induced liquefaction hazard and techniques for estimating earthquake induced laterial spread displacements; inventor system for coupling accelerometers into bore hole casings. Home: 1132 E 1010 N Orem UT 84097-4306 Office: Brigham Young U Dept Civil Engring Provo UT 84602 Office Phone: 801-422-6327. E-mail: tyoud@byu.edu.

YOUENS, RACHEL P., painter; Student, Oxbow Sch. Painting, 1980; BFA, Art Inst. Chgo., 1980; MFA, Bklyn. Coll., 1993. Artist in residence Ragdale Found., Winnetka, Ill., 1989; assoc. adj. prof. art history St. Francis Coll., Bklyn., 1997—2003; adj. asst. prof. City Coll. Tech., Bklyn., 2003—06; adj. prof. Parsons Sch. Art and Design, NYC, 2002—07; adj. asst. prof. La Guardia Cmty. Coll., Queens, NY, 2007. Vis. lectr. New Sch. Social Rsch., NYC, 1997, St. Francis Coll., Bklyn., 2001, Coll. Art Assn., NYC, 2005; vis. instr. Pratt Inst., Bklyn., 2003.

One-woman shows include Verso Books, NYC, 1996, one-woman shows include with Victor Pesce Loaves and Fishes, Sideshow Gallery, Bklyn., 2006, exhibited in group shows at UNScene, ARC Gallery, Chgo., 1987, Drawings, Theater Actors Inst., NYC, 1994, Found. Faculty Exhbn., Pratt Inst., Bklyn., 2003, Zeuxis at LIU, Long Island U. Gallery, 2003, MERRY PEACE, Sideshow Gallery, Bklyn., 2003, War is Over, 2004, Ann. Benefit, Kentler Internat. Drawing Space, Bklyn., 2004, Crockery, Gallerythe.com, Bklyn., 2005, Facets, Snug Harbor Cultural Ctr., S.I., NY, 2006. Recipient Charles H. Shaw Meml. award for Painting, Bklyn. Coll., 1991, 1992; grantee Chgo. Neighborhood Coalition, 1985, Pollock-Krasner Found., 2004; fellow John Simon Guggenheim Meml. Found., 2008.*

YOUKILIS, KEVIN, professional baseball player; b. Cin., Mar. 15, 1979; Attended, U. Cin. First baseman Boston Red Sox, 2004—. Mem. US nat. team World Baseball Classic, 2009. Founder Kevin Youkilis Hits for Kids, 2007. Recipient Gold Glove award, 2007; named to Am. League All-Star Team, Maj. League Baseball, 2008, 2009. Jewish. Achievements include being a member of the World Series Champion Boston Red Sox, 2004, 2007; setting the Major League record for consecutive games without an error at first base, (238), 2006-08. Mailing: c/o Boston Red Sox Fenway Pk 4 Yawkey Way Boston MA 02215 also: Kevin Youkilis Hits for Kids PO Box 600311 Newtonville MA 02460*

YOUM, THOMAS, orthopedist, surgeon; b. New York, NY, Nov. 24, 1973; s. Kwang-Youl and Chung Ok Youm; m. Janet Kaye Han, Mar. 18, 2006. BA in History, Yale U., New Haven, 1995; MD, NYU Sch. Medicine, NYC, 1999. Clin. asst. prof. NYU Hosp. Joint Diseases, NYC, 2005—. Fellow: Alpha Omega Alpha; mem.: Am. Orthopaedic Soc. Sports Medicine, Arthroscopy Assn. N.Am., Am. Acad. Orthopaedic Surgeons. Office: Enrique Ergas & Thomas Youm MD PC 1056 Fifth Ave New York NY 10028

YOUMANS, JULIAN RAY, neurosurgeon, educator; b. Baxley, Ga., Jan. 2, 1928; s. John Edward and Jennie Lou (Milton) Y.; children—Reed Nesbit, John Edward, Julian Milton. BS, Emory U., 1949, MD, 1952; MS, U. Mich., 1955, PhD, 1957. Diplomate: Am. Bd. Neurol. Surgery. Intern U. Mich. Hosp., Ann Arbor, 1952-53, resident in neurol. surgery, 1953-55, 56-58; fellow in neurology U. London, 1955-56; asst. prof. neurosurgery U. Miss., 1959-62, assoc. prof., 1962-63, Med. U. S.C., 1963-65, prof., 1965-67, chief div. neurosurgery, 1963-67; prof. U. Calif., Davis, 1967-91; prof. emeritus, 1991—; chmn. dept. neurosurgery U. Calif., 1967-82. Cons. USAF, U.S. VA, NRC. Editor: Neurological Surgery, 1973; contbr. articles to profl. jours. No. vice chmn. Republican State Central Com. of Calif., 1979-81. Served with U.S. Navy, 1944-46. Mem. ACS (bd. govs. 1972-78), Congress of Neurol. Surgeons (exec. com. 1967-70), Am. Acad. Neurology, Am. Assn. Neurol. Surgeons, Am. Assn. Surgery of Trauma, Pan-Pacific Surg. Assn., Western Neurosurg. Soc., Neurosurg. Soc. Am., Soc. Neurol. Surgeons, Soc. Univ. Neurosurgeons, N. Pacific Soc. Neurology and Psychiatry, Royal Soc. Medicine, Am. Trauma Soc., U.S. C. of C., Bohemian Club, Rotary. Republican. Episcopalian. Office Phone: 530-756-6018. Business E-Mail: jryoumans@ucdavis.edu.

YOUN, ANTHONY SUNGJIN, plastic surgeon; b. Greenville, Mich., Oct. 31, 1972; Grad. with high honors, Kalamazoo Coll.; MD, Mich. State U., 1998. Cert. Am. Bd. Plastic Surgery, 2005. Resident gen. surgery Mich. State U., Grand Rapids, 1998—2001, resident plastic surgery, 2001—03; advanced aesthetic surgery fellowship Dr. Richard Ellenbogen, LA, 2003—04; founder, surgeon Hills Plastic Surgery and Laser Centre, Rochester Hills, Mich. Ptnr. Eye Place, Bloomfield Hills, Mich.; hosp. affiliations include William Beaumont Hosp. of Troy, Crittenton Hosp. and Unasource Surgery Ctr.; cons. plastic surgeon for US Weekly, In Touch, Life and Style, OK! Mag., Pink, Jane, Plastic Surgery Products Mag., Hour Detroit, Troy Somerset Gazette, Suburban Lifestyles, Baltimore Sun, Women's Lifestyle Mag., Plastic & Reconstructive Surgery, Aesthetic Surgery Jour., Women's Healthy Style Mag., and Metro Parent Mag., among others; spkr. in field. Authored and co-authored (numerous papers and scientific manuscripts), featured on Dr. 90210, guest appearances (radio) Motor City Midday on Live 97.1 FM, 96.3 FM WDVD, host (online blog) Celebrity Cosmetic Surgery. Named Top Doctors, Hour Detroit. Mem.: AMA, Am. Soc. Plastic Surgeons, Oakland County Med. Soc., Mich. State Med. Soc. Office: Beverly Hills Plastic Surgery Centre 1349 S Rochester Rd Ste 100B Rochester MI 48307 Office Phone: 248-650-1900. Office Fax: 248-650-1967.

YOUNATHAN, EZZAT SAAD, retired biochemistry educator; b. Deirut, Egypt, Aug. 25, 1922; came to U.S., 1950; m. Margaret Tims, Aug. 11, 1958; children: Janet Nadya, Carol Miriam. BSc in Chemistry with honors, Cairo U., 1944; MS in Chemistry, Fla. State U., 1953, PhD in Chemistry, 1955. Chemist Govt. Labs., Cairo, 1944-50; postdoctoral rsch. assoc. Coll. Medicine U. Ill., Chgo., 1955-57; asst. prof. Fla. State U., Tallahassee, 1957-59; asst. prof. Sch. Medicine U. Ark., Little Rock, 1959-63, assoc. prof., 1963-68, acting head, 1963-66; prof. biochemistry La. State U., Baton Rouge, 1968—98; ret. Vis. prof. U. Wis., Madison, 1966-67, U. Calif., Berkeley, 1978; chair rsch. grant adv. com. So. U., Baton Rouge, 1993-96. Contbg. author: (book) The Regulation of Carbohydrate Formation and Utilization in Mammals, 1981; contbr. 75 articles to profl. jours. Seagrams Internat. fellow Seagrams Co., Inc., 1950-51, Sr. Rsch. fellow NIH, 1966-67. Mem. AMA, Am. Soc. Biochemistry and Molecular Biology, Am. Chem. Soc., Soc. Exptl. Biol. Medicine. Mem. First Christian Ch. Achievements include discovery of new class of oral hypoglycemic agents; research in metabolism and chemistry of carbohydrates. Home: 1048 Castle Kirk Dr Baton Rouge LA 70808-6023 Personal E-mail: eyounathan@cox.net.

YOUNG, ALFRED BYRON, neurosurgeon; b. Nov. 6, 1939; s. Carlos Young and Margaret Louise (Rayburn) Stout; m. Judith Floy Gaines, Aug. 26, 1961; children: John Kevin, Alexander Bryce. BA, Transylvania U., 1961, D (hon.), 2006; MD, U. Ky., 1965. Diplomate Am. Bd. Neurol. Surgery (guest examiner 1980, 84, 94, 2005). Intern Vanderbilt U., Nashville, 1965-66, asst. resident in surgery, 1966-67, resident in neurosurgery, 1967-71; clin. instr. U. Ky., Lexington, Ky., 1973-74; pvt. practice Lexington, Ky., 1973-74; asst. prof. divsn. neurosurgery, dept. surgery U. Ky. Med. Ctr., Lexington, Ky., 1974—, prof., 1982—, acting chief, 1974-75, chief neurosurgery, 1977—2008; chief of staff U. Hosp., 2000—05, assoc. dean clin. affairs, 2000—05, sr. assoc. dean for clin. affairs, 2005—06, founding chair dept. neurosurgery, 2008—09. Chmn. dept. surgery U. Ky., 1986-96, chmn. operating rm. comm. 1986-96, hosp. clin. bd., 1986-96, VA dean's comm. 1986-96, press comm., 1991-96, hosp. bd. elected faculty rep., 1994-96, chmn. managed care comm., 1994-96, coun. clin. chair, 1995-96; vis. prof. U. Cin., 1981, U. Louisville, 1988, Vanderbilt U., 1988; chmn. Johnston-Wright Endowed chair, 1988-2007, chair dept. neurosurg., 2008-09; dir. Ky. Neuroscience Inst., 2004—; bd. dirs. Ky. Organ Donor Affiliates; mem. exec. com., bd. trustees Transylvania U.; presenter in field. Contbr. articles to profl. jours. Adv. bd. Ctrl. Bank & Trust; mem. liaison com. Shriner's Hosp., 1999—2005. Maj. US Army, 1971—73, Korea. Recipient Disting. Alumnus award, Transylvania U., 2001, U. Ky. Coll. of Medicine, 2001, Morrison Medallion awards, 2001; named Am. Best Doctor award, Am. Top Doctors.; named one of Am.'s Best Drs., 2005—09, Am.'s Top Drs. for Cancer, 2005, 2006—09; grantee NIH, 1987—95, 1988—99, Bowman Gray/Pfizer, 1992—96, Upjohn Pharm., 1992—94, Sterling Winthrop, 1992—95, Ciba-Geigy, 1993—97. Mem. ACS, AMA, NIH (advisory comm. 1991-95, monitoring comm. 1994—, com. mem.), Nat. Inst. Neurol. Disorders, Acad. Neurological Surgeons, Am. Surgical Assn., Soc. Neurological Surgeons, Neurosurgical Soc. Am., Am. Assn. Neurological Surgeons (bylaws comm. 1979-83, chmn. bylaws comm. 1982-83, rep. to Nat. Inst. Neurol and Comm. Disorders and Stroke 1987-89), Congress Neurological Surgeons (rep. to NIH 1987—, Mahaley Clin. Rsch. award 1998), Ky. Med. Assn., Fayette County Med. Soc., Southern Neurosurgical Soc. (pres. 1991-92, pres.-elect 1990, exec. coun. 1986-94, treas. 1986-89, chmn. fin. comm. 1986-89, long range planning comm. 1990—, chmn. long range planning comm. 1992-93, constn. and bylaws comm. 1989-90, comm. disting. practioner award, 1992—, chmn. comm. disting. practioner award, 1992-93, nominating comm. 1992—, chmn. nominating comm. 1992-93, residents award comm. 1981-82), Am. Soc. Stereotactic and Functional Neurosurgery, Ky. Neurosurgical Soc. (pres. 1990-91), Soc. Internat. Surgery, Internat. Stereotactic Radiosurgery Soc., Leksell Gamma Knife Soc., Neurotrauma Soc Achievements include patent (with others) in Multiple Function Intubation Apparatus and Method, 5,836,935 Implantable refillable controlled release device to deliver drugs directly to an internal portion of the body; research in zinc supplementation associated with improved neurologic recovery rate and visceral protein levels of patients with severe closed head-injury, nutritional and metabolic mgmt. of the head-injury patient, demographics of brain metastasis, neurosurgical diseases of aging patients, brain metastases, nutritional and metabolic variables correlate with amino acid forearm flux in patients with severe head injury, effect of lovastatin on early carotid atherosclerosis and cardiovascular events, cyclosporins- severe head injury and numerous others.

YOUNG, ALLAN PETER, physics professor; b. Lancaster, England, June 18, 1948; s. John and Eleanor Young; m. Christiane Visy, Apr. 14, 1975; children: Isabelle Anne, Alan John. MA., D.Phil., Oxford U., 1973. Lectr. math. Imperial Coll., London, 1978—84, reader math., 1984—85; prof. physics U. Calif. Santa Cruz, 1985—. Contbr. scientific papers. Recipient Outstanding Referee, Am. Phys. Soc., 2008, Outstanding faculty award, U. Calif. Santa Cruz, 2005, Excellence tchg. award, 2004, Aneesar Rahman prize, Am. Phys. Soc., 2009; co-recipient Maxwell medal and prize, Inst. physics, 1985; grants, Am. Phys. Soc., 1989. Office: Univ Calif Santa Cruz 1156 High St Santa Cruz CA 95064 Office Fax: (831_ 459-3043. Business E-Mail: peter@physics.ucsc.edu.

YOUNG, ANDRE RAMELLE See DR. DRE

YOUNG, ANDREW JACKSON, JR., consulting firm executive, former mayor, former United States Representative from Georgia; b. New Orleans, Mar. 12, 1932; s. Andrew J. and Daisy (Fuller) Y.; m. Jean Childs, June 7, 1954 (dec. 1994); children: Andrea, Lisa Dru, Paula Jean, Andrew J. III; m. Carolyn M. 1996. Student, Dillard U., 1947-48; BS, Howard U., 1951; B.D., Hartford Theol. Sem., 1955; D.D. (hon.), Wesleyan U., 1970, United Theol. Sem. Twin Cities, 1970; LL.D. (hon.), Wilberforce U., 1971, Clark Coll., 1973, Yale U., 1973, Swarthmore Coll., Atlanta U., Dartmouth U., 2005; numerous other hon. degrees. Ordained to ministry Congl. Ch., 1955; pastor Thomasville, Ga., 1955-57; assoc. dir. dept. youth work Nat. Council Chs., 1957-61; mem. staff So. Christian Leadership Conf., 1961-70, adminstr. citizen edn. program, 1961-64, exec. dir., 1964-70, exec. v.p., 1967-70; mem. US Congress from 5th Ga. Dist., 1973—77; permanent US rep. UN, NYC, 1977-79; mayor City of Atlanta, 1982—90; co-chmn. Atlanta Com. for the Olympic Games, 1996; prof. pub. affairs Ga. State U., Atlanta; founding prin., co-chmn. Goodworks Internat. LLC, 1996—. Pres. Nat. Coun. Churches, 2000—01; chmn. nat. steering com. Working Families for Wal-Mart, 2006. Author: A Way Out of No Way: The Spiritual Memoirs of Andrew Young, 1994, An Easy Burden: The Civil Rights Movement and the Transformation of America, 1996. Chmn. Atlanta Community Relations Commn., 1970-72; chmn. bd. Delta Ministry of Miss.; bd. dirs. Martin Luther King, Jr. Center for Social Change, Robert F. Kennedy Meml. Found., Field Found., So. Christian Leadership Conf. Recipient Pax-Christi award St. John's U., 1970; Springarn medal.; Presdl. Medal of Freedom, 1980, French Legion of Honor medal, 1982; co-recipient, Martin Luther King, Jr., Award for Public Svc. (Ebony mag.), 1990. Mem. Ams. Dem. Action, Alpha Phi Alpha Office: Goodworks International LLC 303 Peachtree St NE Ste 4420 Atlanta GA 30308*

YOUNG, ANTONY, marketing and communications company executive; b. New Zealand; With Saatchi & Saatchi, Aukland, New Zealand; media dir. Colenso BBDO, New Zealand, 1990—95; regional media dir. Saatchi & Saatchi Asia, Hong Kong, 1995—96; established Zenith Media ops. China; CEO ZenithOptimedia Asia, 1996-2000, 2001-2003; co-founder, CEO AdXplorer, 2000—01; CEO ZenithOptimedia UK, London, 2003—06; pres. Optimedia US, NYC, 2006—. Co-author (with Lucy Aitken): Profitable Marketing Communications: A Guide to Marketing Return on Investment, 2007. Office: Optimedia Internat 375 Hudson St 7th Fl New York NY 10014 Office Phone: 212-820-3200. Business E-Mail: antony.young@optimedia-us.com.*

YOUNG, ARTHUR PRICE, librarian, educator; b. Boston, July 29, 1940; s. Arthur Price and Marion (Freeman) Y.; m. Patricia Dorothy Foss, June 26, 1965; children: John Marshall, Christopher Price. BA, Tufts U., 1962; MA in Tchg., U. Mass., 1964; MSLS, Syracuse U., 1969; PhD, U. Ill., 1976. Head reader svcs., social sci. bibliographer SUNY-Cortland, 1969-72; rsch. assoc. U. Ill. Libr. Rsch. Ctr., Urbana, 1972-75; asst. dean pub. svcs., assoc. prof. U. Ala., Tuscaloosa, 1976-81; dean librs., prof. U. R.I., Kingston, 1981-89; dir. Thomas Cooper Libr., U. S.C., Columbia, 1989-93; sr. fellow UCLA, 1991; dean librs., mem. adj. faculty dept. history No. Ill. U., DeKalb, 1993—2006. Mem. adj. faculty Syracuse (N.Y.) U., 1970-71, Dominican U., River Forest, Ill., 1994-96; pres. Consortium R.I. Acad. and Rsch. Librs., 1983-85; mem. bd. govs. Univ. Press New England, 1987-89; mem. exec. bd. Ill. Libr. Computer Sys. Orgn., 1995-99; chair Coun. Dirs. State Univ. Librs., 1994-95, 2001—; sr. fellow UCLA, 1991; pres. Ill. Libr. Assn., 2002. Author: Books for Sammies: American Library Association and World War I, 1981, American Library History: A Bibliography of Dissertations and Theses, 1988, Higher Education in American Life, 1636-1986: A Bibliography of Dissertations and Theses, 1988, Cities and Towns in American History: A Bibliography of Doctoral Dissertations, 1989, Academic Libraries: Research Perspectives, 1990, Religion and the American Experience, 1620-1900: A Bibliography of Doctoral Dissertations, 1992, Religion and the American Experience, The Twentieth Century: A Bibliography of Doctoral Dissertations, 1994; The Next Library Leadership: Attributes of Academic and Public Library Directors, 2003; editl. bd. various jours. Chair Coun. of Dirs. Ill. State Univ. Librs., 1994-95, 2001-02. Served to capt. USAF, 1964-68. Recipient Berner Nash award U. Ill., 1976. Mem. ALA (chmn. editl. bd., chair Libr. Rsch. Seminar I, 1996), Assn. Coll. and Rsch. Librs. (publs. in librarianship 1982-88, chmn. Jesse H. Shera Endowment Fund com. 1991-94), Ill. Libr. Assn., S.C. Libr. Assn. (chmn. libr. adminstrn. sect. 1991-92), Assn. Rsch. Librs. (scholarly commn. com. 1991-93), Orgn. Am. Historians, Am. Hist. Assn., Horatio Alger Soc. (pres. 1999-2000), Caxton Club (Chgo.), Phi Kappa Phi, Beta Phi Mu, Phi Delta Kappa. Episcopalian. Home: 9 Sandy Brook Dr Durham NH 03824-3137 Office Phone: 603-868-1609. Business E-Mail: ayoung@niu.edu.

YOUNG, BARBARA, psychiatrist, educator, photographer, psychoanlyst; b. Chgo., Oct. 27, 1920; d. William Harvey and Blanche (DeBra) Y. AB, Knox Coll., 1942; MD, Johns Hopkins U., 1945; grad., Balt. Psychoanalytic Inst., 1953. Intern Univ. Hosps., Iowa City, 1945-46, asst. resident in neurology, 1946—47; asst. resident in psychiatry Phipps Clinic, Johns Hopkins U. Hosp., Balt., 1947-49; staff psychiatrist Perry Point (Md.) VA Hosp., 1949-51; practice medicine specializing in psychiatry/psychoanalysis Balt., 1951—; instr. Johns Hopkins U., 1953-69, asst. prof. psychiatry, 1969—, prof. emeritus, 1997—; freelance photographer, 1958—. Lectr. dept. psychiatry Johns Hopkins U.; lectr. Lucy Daniels Found., Carey, N.C., dept. humanities Yale U. Med. Sch., Boston Inst. for Psychotherapy, local psychiat. and social orgns. Works represented in Mus. Modern Art, N.Y.C., Balt. Mus. Art, Santa Barbara (Calif.) Mus. Art, Eastman House, Rochester, N.Y., Yale U. Gallery of Art; photographer: The Plop-A-Lop Tree, 1995, Tales of Courage: Recovering LIfe After Catastrophe, 2003; contbr. articles to profl. jours. Mem.: Am. Psychoanlytic Assn., Am. Psychiat. Assn., Balt.-Washington Ctr. for Psychoanalysis. Democrat. Address: 5307 Herring Run Dr Baltimore MD 21214-1937 Office Phone: 410-426-3583. Personal E-mail: barbarayoungmd@mac.com.

YOUNG, BARNEY THORNTON, lawyer; b. Chillicothe, Tex., Aug. 10, 1934; s. Bayne and Helen Irene (Thornton) Y.; m. Sarah Elizabeth Taylor, Aug. 31, 1957; children: Jay Thornton, Sarah Elizabeth, Serena Taylor. BA, Yale U., 1955; LLB, U. Tex., 1958. Bar: Tex. 1958. Assoc. Thompson, Knight, Wright & Simmons, Dallas, 1958-65; ptnr. Rain, Harrell, Emery, Young & Doke, Dallas, 1965-87; mem. firm Locke Purnell Rain Harrell (A Profl. Corp.), 1987-98; of counsel Locke, Lord, Bissell & Liddell LLP, 1999—. Mem. adv. coun. Dallas Cmty. Chest Trust Fund, Inc., 1964-66; bd. dirs. Mental Health Assn. Dallas County, Inc., 1969-72, Trammell Crow Family Found., 1984-87; trustee Hockaday Sch., Dallas, 1971-77, 90—, chmn., 1994-96, Dallas Zool. Soc., 1986-92, Lamplighter Sch., Dallas, 1976-99, 2006—, chmn., 1983-86, St. Mark's Sch., Dallas, 1970—, pres., 1976-78, The Found. for Callier Ctr. and Comm. Disorders, 1988-99, Friends of Ctr. for Human Nutrition, 1988-2005, Dallas Hist. Soc., 1993-2001; bd. dirs Susan G. Komen Breast Cancer Found., 2000-06, Nat. Assn. Ind. Schs., 2000-04; mem. Yale Devel. Bd., 1984-91, 98—. Fellow Tex. Bar Found., Dallas Bar Found.; mem. ABA, Tex. Bar Assn., Dallas Bar Assn., Am. Judicature Soc., Order of Coif, Phi Beta Kappa, Pi Sigma Alpha, Phi Gamma Delta, Phi Delta Phi, Dallas Country Club., Petroleum Club (Dallas), Yale Club (Dallas, N.Y.C.). Office: Locke Lord Bissell & Liddell LLP 2200 Ross Ave Ste 2200 Dallas TX 75201-6776 Office Phone: 214-740-8402. Business E-Mail: byoung3@mindspring.com.

YOUNG, BILL (CHARLES WILLIAM YOUNG), United States Representative from Florida; b. Harmarville, Pa., Dec. 16, 1930; m. Beverly Angelo; children: Robert, Patrick, Billy. Mem. Fla. State Senate, 1961—70, minority leader, 1967—70; mem. US Congress from 10th dist. Fla., 1970—, mem. appropriations com., armed svcs. com., permanent select com. intelligence, chmn. appropriations com., 1999—2005, chmn. appropriations subcom. def., 1995—98, 2007—, chmn. appropriations subcom. mil. quality of life & vets. affairs, 2007—. Nat. committeeman Fla. Young Reps., 1957—59, state chair, 1959—61; mem. Fla. Constn. Revision Commn., 1965—67, Army Caucus, Human Rights Caucus, Diabetes Caucus, Fire Svcs. Caucus, Congl. Travel & Tourism Caucus, Rep. Steering Com.; chair Congl. Social Security Caucus. Served in Army Nat. Guard, 1948—57. Named Most Valuable Senator, Capitol Press Corps, 1969. Republican. Methodist. Office: US Ho Reps 2407 Rayburn Ho Office Bldg Washington DC 20515-0910 E-mail: bill.young@mail.house.gov.*

YOUNG, BRUCE KENNETH, obstetrician, gynecologist, educator; b. NYC, Aug. 11, 1938; s. Morton David and Cecile Barbara (Lebenson) Y.; m. Phyllis Ann Lipsius, Dec. 16, 1962; children: Kathryn Rachel, Caroline Sue. AB, Princeton U., 1959; MD, NYU, 1963. Diplomate Nat. Bd. Med. Examiners, Am. Bd. Ob-gyn.; cert. spl. competence in maternal-fetal medicine Am. Bd. Ob-gyn. Intern Montefiore Hosp., Bronx, NY, 1963-64; resident ob-gyn. Bellevue Hosp. Ctr., NYC, 1964-68, NYU Hosp., 1964-68, rsch. fellow reproductive endocrinology, 1966—67; chief obstetrics Bellevue Hosp., NYC, 1970-95; dir. obstet. svcs. NYU Hosps. Network, 1995—2005. Cons. NJ Health Sys. Agy., Hoffman LaRoche Co., Kimberly Clark, Litton Ind., Revlon Corp., 1975—85; dir. maternal and fetal medicine NYU Sch. Medicine Med. Ctr., NYC, 1975—2005; prof. ob-gyn. NYU Sch. Medicine, 1980—, Silverman prof. ob-gyn., 1996—; mem. sci. adv. bd. Grain Foods Found., 2005-. Author: Miscarriage, Medicine and Miracles, 2008, The Intellectual Devotional Health, 2009;editor: Perinatal Medicine Today, 1980, Problems in Perinatal Medicine, 1986, Jour. Maternal-Fetal Neonatal Medicine, 2007-09; mem. editl. bd. Diagnostic Gynecology and Obstetrics, Jour. Perinatal Medicine, Maternal Fetal Nanotal Medicine; contbr. chpts. to books and articles to profl. jours. Bd. dirs. N.Y. State Prenatal Diagnostic Ctr., N.Y.C., 1977-87; chair health professions bd. Greater N.Y. March of Dimes, N.Y.C., 1995—2005, v.p., dir., 1995-2005. Recipient Disting. Svc. in Med. Edn. award March of Dimes, 1985, Voluntary Svc. award, 1990, Program Excellence award, 1991, Disting. Alumnus award Bellevue Obst. Gyn. Soc., 1998, Solomon A. Berson Med. Alumni Achievement award, NYU, 2005. Fellow ACOG (Outstanding Achievement award 1998), Am. Fertility Soc., Am. Gynecol. and Obstet. Soc., Am. Assn. Gynecol. Laparoscopists, Soc. Laparoendoscopic Surgeons, N.Y. Perinatal Soc. (pres. 1997-99), N.Y. Obstet. Soc. (pres. 2001-02); mem. AMA, Soc. Maternal-Fetal Medicine, NYU Sch. Medicine Alumni Assn. (pres. 1995-96, citation 1996, NYU Faculty Senator, 2008-), Mar-a-Lago Club, Princeton Club NY, Alpha Omega Alpha Med. Honor. Soc., NY Sch. Medicine. Achievements include NYU dept annual research day named after him. Office: 530 1st Ave Ste 5G New York NY 10016-6402 Office Phone: 212-263-6359. Business E-Mail: youngbo1@nyumc.org.

YOUNG, BRYANT LLEWELLYN, lawyer; b. Rockford, Ill., Mar. 9, 1948; s. Llewellyn Anker and Florence Ruth Y. AB, Cornell U., 1970; JD, Stanford U., 1974. Bar: Calif. 1974, Nev. 1975, D.C. 1979. Law clk. U.S. Dist. Ct. (no. dist.) Calif., San Francisco, 1974-75; assoc. Dinkelspiel, Pelavin, Steefel & Levitt, San Francisco, 1975-77; White House fellow, spl. asst. to sec. HUD, Washington, 1977-78, spl. asst. to sec., 1978-79; gen. mgr. to acting gen. mgr. New Cmty. Devel. Corp., 1979-80; mgmt. cons. AVCO Corp., 1980; spl. asst. to chmn. bd., CEO U.S. Synthetic Fuels Corp., Washington, 1980-81, project dir., 1981; pres. Trident Mgmt. Corp., San Francisco, 1981-87; of counsel Pelavin, Norberg, Harlick & Beck, San Francisco, 1981-82, ptnr., 1982-87; mng. ptnr. bus. sect. Carroll, Burdick & McDonough, San Francisco, 1987-90; founding ptnr. Young, Vogl & Harlick, San Francisco, 1990-93, Young, Vogl, Harlick, Wilson & Simpson, LLP, San Francisco, 1993-99; pres. Young Enterprises, Inc., 1995—2004; mgr. SRY Industries LLC,

1997—, KML Hospitality Industries LLC, 1997—, Nev. Nugget LLC, 2004—; ptnr. Young Vogl LLP, 1999—2001; prin. Law Offices of Bryant L. Young, 2002—. Dir. The Whitman Inst. Pub. affairs com. San Francisco Aid Retarded Citizens, Inc., 1977; U.S. co-chmn. New Towns Working Group, U.S.-USSR Agreement on Cooperation in Field of Housing and Other Constrn., 1979-80; treas., bd. dirs. White House Fellows Found., 1980-84; prin. Coun. Excellence in Govt., Washington, 1986-94; adv. com. Nat. Multi-Housing Coun., 1987-92; mem. Ross Sch. Found., 1994-97, sec., 1995-97; bd. dirs. Marin AIDS Project, 1996-97, sec., 1997; trustee Ross Sch., 1997-2003, pres. 2002-2003. Mem. ABA (real property, trust and probate law sects. 1975-96), White House Fellows Assn. (chmn. ann. meeting 1979, del. China 1980), Marin County Sch. Bds. Assn., Am. Field Svc. Returnees Assn., Can.-Am. C. of C. No. Calif. (v.p., bd. dirs. 1992), Chile-Calif. Found. (exec. com., bd. dirs. 1993-96). Office: 44 Montgomery St ste 3350 San Francisco CA 94104-4602 Office Phone: 415-291-1970. E-mail: bly@ebzlaw.net.

YOUNG, CARLTON JOSEPH, abdominal transplant kidney and pancreas surgeon, educator; m. Timi Young, May 2, 1992. MD, Johns Hopkins Sch. Medicine, Balt., 1987. Diplomate Am. Bd. Surgery, 1995. Assoc. prof. surgery U. Ala., Birmingham, 1997—. Bd. dir. Ctr. Urban Missions, Birmingham. Named one of Best Doctors in America, 2003—09. Office: Univ Alabama at Birmingham 701 S 19th St LHRB 719 Birmingham AL 35233 Office Phone: 205-934-1393. Office Fax: 205-975-8452.

YOUNG, CAROL ANN, elementary school educator, graphics designer, writer; d. Milton and Lucylle Young. BFA, Temple U., Phila., 1969; MS in Elem. Edn., CUNY, NYC, 2004. Common br. lic. NYC Dept. Edn., 2000, cert. pub. sch. tchr. pre-K to 6 SUNY, 2004, sch. dist. adminstr., sch. adminstr. supr. SUNY, 2007, advanced cert. in ednl. leadership CUNY, 2007. Art dir. New Breed Clothing Ltd., Bklyn., 1970—71; edn. asst. Bedford Stuyvesant Restoration Corp., Bklyn., 1972—73; tutor coord. Coll. San Mateo, Calif., 1973—74; asst. account mgr. Zebra Assocs., NYC, 1974—75; prodn. artist Grey Advt., NYC, 1976—77; mgr. White Work Cleaners, NYC, 1978—79; visual mcht. Brentano's, NYC, 1980—81; advt. mgr. Triton Press Inc., NYC, 1982—83; owner Carol Ann Young Graphic Designs, NYC, 1984—2001; tchr. Pub. Sch. 32, Bronx, NY, 2001—07; literacy coach Pub. Sch. 111, Long Island City, NY, 2007—. Drawing, painting, & photography judge NAACP, NYC Acad., Cultural, Technol., & Sci. Olympics, 1992—2008; vis. lectr. youth entrepreneurial seminars Medgar Evers Coll. CUNY, 1992—93; libr. initiative com. mem. Pub. Sch. 32, 2003—04, libr. adv. team mem., 2004—06, curriculum planning com. mem., 2006, penny harvest coach, 2006—07, cabinet mem., 2007; data com. mem Pub. Sch. 111, NY, 2008—09, instrnl. support team mem., 2008—, inquiry team mem., 2008—. Represented in permanent collections P.S. 32 Robin Hood Libr. Bd. mgrs. NYC Mission Soc., Minisink Townhouse & Camp, 1991—95; bd. overseers Brookdale Ctr. Aging, Hunter Coll., NYC, 1997—2004; steering com. mem. Mt. Sinai Hosp., NYU Med. Ctr. and Health Sys., NYC, 1998—2003; mem. United Hosp. Fund, NYC, 2005—06. Fellow: Americorp Nat. Svc., NYC Tchg. Fellows (Fellowship 2001—04); mem.: Alpha Kappa Alpha. Democrat. Baptist. Avocations: reading, classical music, jazz, walking. Home: 480 Saint Nicholas Ave 20B New York NY 10030-2709

YOUNG, CHARLES EDWARD, former academic administrator; b. San Bernardino, Calif., Dec. 30, 1931; s. Clayton Charles and Eula May (Walters) Young. AA, San Bernardino Coll., 1954; AB, U. Calif., Riverside, 1955; MA, UCLA, 1957, PhD, 1960; DHL (hon.), U. Judaism, LA, 1969; DHL (hon.), Occidental Coll., LA, 1997. Congl. fellow, Washington, 1958—59; adminstrv. analyst Office of the Pres., U. Calif., Berkeley, 1959—60; asst. prof. polit. sci. U. Calif., Davis, 1960, UCLA, 1960—66, assoc. prof., 1966—69, prof., 1969—97, asst. to chancellor, 1960—62, asst. chancellor, 1962—63, vice chancellor, adminstrn., 1963—68, chancellor, 1968—97, chancellor emeritus, 1997—; pres. U. Fla., Gainesville, 1999—2004. Bd. dirs. Intel Corp., Acad. TV Arts and Sci. Found., L.A. Met. Project; cons. Peace Corps., 1961—62, Ford Found. on Latin Am. Activities, 1964—66; bd. dirs. I-Mark Inc., AAFL Enterprises, Nicholas-Applegate Growth Equity Fund Inc., Fiberspace Inc., Student Advantage Inc., Perma-Fix Environ. Svcs. Inc., 2003—. Mem. Nat. Com. on U.S.-China Rels.; adminstrv. bd. Internat. Assn. Univs; mem. Knight Found. Commn. on Intercollegiate Athletics, Calif. Coun. on Sci. and Tech., Town Hall of Calif., Carnegie Comm. Task Force on Sci. and Tech. and the States, Pacific Coun. on Internat. Policy, NCAA Pres.'s Commn., Coun. for Govt.-Univ.-Industry Rsch. Roundtable and the Nat. Rsch. Coun. Adv. Bd.-Issues in Sci. and Tech.; chancellor's assocs. UCLA; coun. trustees L.A. Ednl. Alliance for Restructuring Now; past chair. Assn. Am. Univs., Nat. Assn. State Univs. and Land-Grant Colls.; past co-chair Calif. Campus Compact; trustee UCLA Found.; CEO Los Angeles Mus. of Contemporary Art, 2009—; bd. dirs. Found. Internat. Exchange Sci. and Cultural Info. by Telecom., L.A. Internat. Visitors Coun., Greater L.A. Energy Coalition, L.A. World Affairs Coun. With USAF, 1951—52. Recipient Inter-Am. U. Cooperaton award, Inter-Am. Orgn. Higher Edn., Neil H. Jacoby Internat. award, UCLA Student Ctr., 1987, Edward A. Dickson Alumnus of Yr. award, UCLA Alumni Assn., 1994, Disting. Svc. award, U. Calif. Riverside Alumni Assn., 1996, Treasure of L.A. award, L.A. Ctrl. City Assn., 1996, Albert Schweitzer Leadership award, Hugh O'Brien Youth Found., 1996; named Young Man of Year, Westwood Jr. C. of C., 1962; fellow, UCLA Coll. Letters and Sci., 1996. Fellow: AAAS; mem.: Nat. Collegiate Athletic Assn. Pres. Commn. Office: Perma-Fix Environmental Services Inc Ste 250 8302 Dunwoody Pl Atlanta GA 30350 Office Phone: 770-587-9898. Office Fax: 770-587-9937.*

YOUNG, SIR COLVILLE, Belizean government official; b. Nov. 20, 1932; s. Henry Oswald and Adney Wilhelmina (Waite) Y.; m. Norma Eleanor Trapp, 1956; four children. BA in English, U. London, U. West Indies, 1961; PhD in Linguistics, U. York, 1971. Prin. St. Michael's Coll., Belize, 1974-76; lectr. English and gen. studies Belize Tech. Coll., 1976-86; pres. U. Coll. Belize, 1986-90, lectr., 1990-93; gov.-gen. Belize, 1993—. Author: Creole Proverbs of Belize, 1980, rev. edit., 1988, From One Caribbean Corner, 1983, Caribbean Corner Calling, 1988, Language and Education in Belize, 1989, Pataki Full, 1990; contbr. articles to profl. jours. Knighted Queen Elizabeth II. Avocations: composing, creative writing, playing and arranging steelband music. Office: Office of Gov-Gen Belize House PO Box 174 Belmopan Belize Home: PO Box 173 Belmopan Belize Office Phone: 501-822-2521, 501-822-3081. E-mail: gougenbz@btl.net.

YOUNG, DALE LEE, banker; b. Palmyra, Nebr., Mar. 13, 1928; s. Mike P. and Grace (Clutter) Y.; m. Norma Marie Shalla, June 18, 1950; children— Shalla Ann, Phillip Mike. BBA, U. Nebr., 1950. With FirsTier Bank N.A. (formerly First Nat. Bank & Trust Co.), Lincoln, Nebr., 1950-91, cashier, 1966-91, v.p., 1966-76, exec. v.p., 1976-92; sec. ISCO, Inc., Lincoln, 1991—, also bd. dirs. Bd. dirs. Lincoln Fed. Savs. Bank; sec., bd. dirs. Leasing Corp. Treas. Lincoln City Library Found.; bd. dirs., v.p. Lincoln Symphony; bd. dirs. Lincoln Community Services, ARC, Lincoln Found.; trustee Bryan Meml. Hosp., 1976-80; mem. Lincoln City Coun., 1991-98, elected mayor, 1998. Served with AUS, 1946-48, 50-51. Mem. Nebr. Art Assn., Omaha-Lincoln Soc. Fin. Analysts, Lincoln C. of C. (pres.), Theta Xi. Clubs: Nebraska, Lincoln Country. Presbyterian. Home: 3911 Firethorn Ct Lincoln NE 68520-1466 Office: PO Box 81008 Lincoln NE 68501-1008

YOUNG, DARLENE H., information system security officer; BA in Computer Info. Sys. of Sci., U. DC, 1984. Computer specialist, office info. tech., bur. internat. info. prog. US Dept. of State. Wang Sys. adminstr. United Nations NY, 1991; tech. support US Congl. Del., Dakar, Senegal, 1998. Active mem. Washington City Ch. of Brethren. Recipient Meritorious Honor award, US Dept. of State; named to Power 150, Ebony mag., 2008. Mem.: NAACP, Am. Inst. Parliamentarians (pres. Virginia Schoulthzauer chpt.), Nat. Coun. Negro Women, Blacks in Govt. (life; nat. pres. 2005—). Office: US Dept of State 2201 C St NW Washington DC 20520 Office Phone: 202-647-4000.

YOUNG, DAVID, language educator; married. MA in Spanish, NC State U., Raleigh. Fulbright exch. tchr. Lycée Paul Vincensini, Bastia, Corsica, France, 2002—03; French and Spanish instr. FTCC, Fayetteville, NC, 1998—. Avocations: swimming, soccer.

YOUNG, DAVID, legislative staff member; b. Van Meter, Iowa; BA in English, Drake U., Des Moines, 1991. Staff Bush-Quale Re-Election Campaign, Des Moines, 1992; intern, legis asst., Senator Hank Brown US Senate, Washington, 1993—96; fundraiser for Conservative groups Washington, 1997; fin. dir., Senator Jim Bunning US Senate, 1998, legis. asst., Senator Jim Bunning, 1999—2000, legis. dir., Senator Jim Bunning, 2001—03, campaign mgr., Senator Jim Bunning, 2004, chief of staff to Senator Jim Bunning, 2005—06, chief of staff to Senator Charles Grassley, 2006—. Office: 135 Hart Senate Office Bldg Washington DC 20510-1501 Office Phone: 202-224-3744. Business E-Mail: david_young@grassley.senate.gov.*

YOUNG, DAVID, political organization administrator; m. Leigh Young; 3 children. Grad., U. NC, Chapel Hill. Banker BB&T, NC; bus. owner; mem. bd. county commrs. Buncombe County, NC, 1992—2008; chmn. NC Dem. Party, 2009—. Exec. pers. cons. with local govts. Pres. NC Assn. County Commrs., 2007—08; mem. U. NC Bd. Govs. Democrat. Office: NC Dem Party 220 Hillsborough St Raleigh NC 27603 Office Phone: 919-821-2777 ext. 106. Office Fax: 919-821-4778. Business E-Mail: dyoung@ncdemocraticparty.org.*

YOUNG, DELANO VICTOR, cell biologist, pharmaceutical scientist, biochemist, educator; b. Honolulu, Nov. 17, 1945; s. Lum Fai and Gladys Sau Pung (Wong) Y.; m. Chin-Yi Caroline Yang, Jan. 31, 1970; 1 child, Heather Tien. BS, Stanford U., 1967; PhD, Columbia U., 1973. Postdoctoral fellow Salk Inst. for Biol. Studies, San Diego, 1973-75; asst. prof. dept. chemistry Boston U., 1975-83; asst. dir. Bioassay Systems Rsch. Corp., Woburn, Mass., 1984-86; sr. scientist Damon Biotech, Inc., Needham Heights, Mass., 1986-88, dir., 1988-90; head cell biology Abbott Biotech, Inc. (formerly Damon Biotech, Inc.), Needham Heights, 1990-92; group leader tissue culture Transkaryotic Therapies, Inc., Cambridge, Mass., 1992-94; sect. head, cell culture NitroMed, Inc., Boston, 1994—2006. Cons. D. Van Nostrand Pub., Boston, 1975-83, Allyn and Bacon Pub., Boston, 1975-83; vis. scholar in biochemistry and molecular biology Harvard U., 1982-83; reviewer sci. jour. in biochemistry, 1973—; initial scientist several biotech. start-up cos., Boston area; adj. faculty mem. Mass. Bay CC, Wellesley, 2007-; part time lectr. Northeastern U., Boston, 2008-. Author: (chpt.) Inverted Microcarriers: Using Microencapsulation to Grow Anchorage-Dependent Cells, 1992, Culture of Anchorage Dependent Cells, 1999; contbr. over 30 articles to profl. jours. Eugene Higgins fellow Columbia U., 1967-68, Jane Coffin Childs fellow Salk Inst., 1973-75; GM scholar Stanford U., 1963-67. Mem. AAAS, Sigma Xi, Phi Beta Kappa, Phi Lambda Upsilon, Am. Soc. Cell Biology (emeritus mem.). Roman Catholic. Achievements include significant contributions to understanding of the nutritional requirements of cancer cells, to devel. of recombinant protein prodn. in biotechnology and cultivation of anchorage dependent cells and to nitric oxide pharmaceuticals. Home: 12 Dennis Rd Wellesley MA 02481 Home Phone: 781-235-9208. Personal E-mail: delyoung@verizon.net.

YOUNG, DELMON DAMARCUS, professional baseball player; b. Montgomery, Ala., Sept. 14, 1985; s. Larry and Bonnie Young. Outfielder Tampa Bay Devil Rays, 2006—07, Minn. Twins, 2008—. Named Minor League Player of Yr., Baseball Am., 2005, #1 Prospect, 2006. Achievements include being the second youngest player in the major leagues in 2006; 31 hits in his first 20 major league games, only six players in the last 50 years have matched or exceeded that total. Mailing: c/o Minn Twins Metrodome 34 Kirby Puckett Pl Minneapolis MN 55415

YOUNG, DONA DAVIS GAGLIANO, retired insurance company executive, lawyer; b. Bklyn., Jan. 8, 1954; BA and MA in Polit. Sci., Drew U., 1976; JD, U. Conn., 1980. Bar: Conn. 1980, U.S. Dist. Ct. Conn. 1980. Joined The Phoenix Cos., Hartford, Conn., 1980, asst. counsel, 1981—83, assoc. counsel, 1983, dir. reinsurance adminstrn., 1983—84, dir. and asst. v.p. reinsurance adminstrn., 1984—85, 2nd v.p., ins. counsel, 1985-87, v.p., asst. gen. counsel, 1987-89, sr. v.p. individual sales and mktg., gen. counsel, 1989-94, exec. v.p., gen. counsel, 1994—2000, pres., COO, 2000—02, pres., CEO, chmn., 2003—09. Bd. dirs. Sonoco Products Co., 1995—, Wachovia Corp., 2000—, Foot Locker Inc. Chair United Way Capital Area Cmty. Campaign, 2003; bd. dirs. Hartford Hosp.; bd. trustees Goodspeed Opera House Found. Inc. Recipient Leadership Award for Women in Bus., New England Coun., 1994, Antoinette Bascetta Women's Career Devel. Award, Trust House, Hartford, Conn., 2000, Outstanding Alumni Award, Drew U., 2001, Disting. Grad. Award, U. Conn. Sch. Law, 2002, Human Rels. Award, Nat. Conf. Cmty. and Justice, 2002; named Laura A. Johnson Woman of Yr., Hartford Coll. for Women, 2002. Mem. ABA, Hartford County Bar Assn., Conn. Bar Assn., N.Y. Bar Assn.*

YOUNG, DONALD ALAN, former Federal Agency Administrator; b. Oakland, Calif., Feb. 8, 1939; s. Leo Alan and Pearl Anita (Walker) Y.; children: Jennifer, Karen BA, U. Calif., Berkeley, 1960, MD, 1964. Diplomate Am. Bd. Internal Medicine. Intern, then resident in internal medicine U. Calif. Hosp., San Francisco, 1964-66; resident in internal medicine Parkland Hosp., Dallas, 1966-67; fellow chest diseases U. Calif. Hosp., San Francisco, 1967-68; mem. staff Palo Alto (Calif.) Med. Clinic, 1970-75; med. dir. Am. Lung Assn., 1975-77; scholar adminstrv. scholars program VA, Washington, 1977-80; dep. dir. policy Bur. Program Policy Health Care Financing Adminstrn., HHS, Washington, 1980—84; exec. dir. Prospective Payment Assessment Commn., Washington, 1984—97; sr. v.p. Am. Assn. Health Plans, 1997—99; COO, med. dir., pres. Health Ins. Associates Am., 1999—2003; acting asst. sec. planning and evaluation HHS, Washington, 1999—2005; chmn. Md. Health Svcs. Cost Review Commn., 2007—. Clin. instr. U. Calif. Med. Sch., San Francisco, 1968—70, Stanford U. Med. Sch., 1970—75. Bd. visitors Ind. U. Served with M.C. AUS, 1968-70. Decorated Commendation medal.; Recipient Borden award, 1964 Home: 6109 Trotter Ridge Ct Columbia MD 21044-4919

YOUNG, DONALD EDWIN, United States Representative from Alaska; b. Meridian, Calif., June 9, 1933; m. Lula Fredson (dec. Aug. 1, 2009); children: Joni, Dawn. AA, Yuba Jr. Coll., 1952; BA, Chico State Coll., Calif., 1958. Mem. Fort Yukon City Council, 1960—68, mayor, 1960—68; mem. Alaska House of Reps., 1966-70, Alaska State Senate, 1970-73, U.S. Congress from Alaska, 1973—; chmn. US House Nat. Resources Com., 1995—2001, US House Transp. & Infrastructure Com., 2001—07. Served in 41st Tank Bn. US Army, 1955—57. Republican. Episcopalian. Office: US Congress 2111 Rayburn House Office Bldg Washington DC 20515 also: Peterson Tower Bldg 510 L St Ste 580 Anchorage AK 99501 Office Phone: 202-225-5765, 907-271-5978. Office Fax: 202-225-0425, 907-271-5950.*

YOUNG, DONALD STIRLING, clinical pathology educator; b. Belfast, N. Ireland, Dec. 17, 1933; s. John Stirling and Ruth Muir (Whipple) Y.; m. Silja Meret; children: Gordon, Robert, Peter. MB, ChB, U. Aberdeen, Scotland, 1957; PhD in Chem. Pathology, U. London, 1962. Terminable lectr. materia medica U. Aberdeen, 1958-59; fellow Post-grad. Med. Sch., U. London, 1959-62, registrar, 1962-64; vis. scientist NIH, Bethesda, Md., 1965-66, chief clin. chemistry service, 1966-77; head clin. chemistry sect. Mayo Clinic, Rochester, Minn., 1977-84; prof. pathology and lab. medicine U. Pa., 1984—, vice chmn. lab. medicine dept. pathology and lab. medicine, 1994—; dir. William Pepper Lab. Hosp. of U. Pa., 1984—. Past bd. dirs. Nat. Com. Clin. Lab. Standards. Co-editor: Drug Interference and Drug Metabolism in Clinical Chemistry, 1976, Clinician and Chemist, 1979, Chemical Diagnosis of Disease, 1979, Drug Measurement and Drug Effects in Laboratory Health Science, 1980, Interpretation of Clinical Laboratory Tests, 1985, Effects of Preanalytical Variables on Clinical Laboratory Tests, 2007, Effects of Drugs on Clinical Laboratory Tests, 2000, Effects of Disease on Clinical Laboratory Tests, 2001. Recipient Dir.'s award NIH, 1977, Gerard B. Lambert award, 1974-75, MDS Health Group award Can. Soc. Clin. Chemists, 1978; Roman lectr. Australian Assn. Clin. Biochemists, 1979; Jendrassik award Hungarian Soc. Clin. Pathologists, 1985, ATB award Italian Soc. Clin. Biochemistry, 1987. Mem. Am. Assn. Clin. Chemistry (J.H. Roe award Capital sect. 1973, Bernard Gerulat award N.J. sect. 1977, Ames award 1977, Van Slyke award N.Y. met. sect. 1985, J.G. Reinhold award Phila. sect. 1993, past pres.), Internat. Fedn. Clin. Chemists (Distinguished Clin. Chemist award, 2008, past pres.), Acad. Clin. Lab. Physicians and Scientists (past exec. com.), Assn. Clin. Biochemists (Ciba-Corning lectr. 1985). Achievements include research in clinical chemistry, optimized use of the clinical laboratory. Office: Hosp U Pa 3400 Spruce St Philadelphia PA 19104-4283 Business E-Mail: donaldyo@mail.med.upenn.edu.

YOUNG, DOUGLAS PARKER, JR., social studies educator; b. Barlow, Fla. s. Douglas Parker and Joy Parrish Young. BA, U. Ga., 1984, MA, 1987, PhD in Pol. Sci., 1998. Pol. Sci. & History Prof. Gordon Coll., Ga., 1987—99, Gainesville State Coll., Ga., 1999—. Faculty advisor Politically Incorrect Club, Gainesville, 1999—, Advisor Chess Club, 2007—. Reader Rec. Blind & Dyslexic, Athens, Ga., 1995—2000. Recipient Outstanding Faculty award, GSC2004; Tchg fellow, 1996. Mem.: Sons Confederate Vets. (life), Longstreet Soc. (life), Phi Kappa Phi, Phi Beta Kappa. Avocations: reading, movies, music, hiking, travel. Office: Gainesville State Coll PO Box 1358 Gainesville GA 30503 Office Phone: 678-717-3872. Office Fax: 678-717-3937. Business E-Mail: dyoung@gsc.edu.

YOUNG, DOUGLAS REA, lawyer; b. LA, July 21, 1948; s. James Douglas and Dorothy Belle (Rea) Y.; m. Terry Forrest, Jan. 19, 1974; 1 child, Megann Forrest BA cum laude, Yale U., 1971; JD, U. Calif., Berkeley, 1976. Bar: Calif., 1976, US Dist. Ct. (no. dist.) Calif. 1976, US Ct. Appeals (6th and 9th cirs.) 1977, US Dist. Ct. (ctrl. dist.) Calif. 1979, US Dist. Ct. Hawaii, US Dist. Ct. (so. dist.) Calif., US Supreme Ct. 1982; cert. specialist in appellate law. Law clk. U.S. Dist. Ct. (no. dist.) Calif., San Francisco, 1976—77; assoc. Farella, Braun & Martel LLP, San Francisco, 1977—82, ptnr., 1983—. Spl. master US Dist. Ct. (no. dist.) Calif., 1977-78, 88, 96, 2000; mem. Criminal Justice Act Def. Panel no. dist. Calif.; mem. faculty Calif. Continuing Edn. of Bar, Berkeley, 1982—, Nat. Inst. Trial Advocacy, Berkeley, 1984—, Practicing Law Inst., 1988—; adj. prof. Hastings Coll. Advocacy, 1985—; vis. lectr. law Boalt Hall/U. Calif., Berkeley, 1986; judge pro tem San Francisco Mcpl. Ct., 1984-05, San Francisco Superior Ct., 1990—. Author: (with Purver and Davis) California Trial Handbook, ed edit., (with Hon. Richard Byrne, Purver and Davis), 3d edit., (with Purver, Davis and Kerper) The Trial Lawyers Book, (with Hon. Eugene Lynch, Taylor, Purver and Davis) California Negotiation and Settlement Handbook; contbr. articles to profl. jours Bd. dirs. Berkeley Law Found., 1977-78, chmn., 1978-79; bd. dirs. San Francisco Legal Aid Soc., pres., 1993—; bd. dirs. Pub. Interest Clearinghouse, San Francisco, chmn., 1987—, treas., 1988—; chmn. Attys. Task Force for Children, Legal Svcs. for Children, 1987—; mem. State Bar Appellate Law Adv. Commn., 1994— Recipient Appreciation award Berkeley Law Found., 1983, Criminal Justice Achievement award Criminal Trial Lawyers Assn. No. Calif., 2002; named a No. Calif. Super Lawyer San Francisco mag., 2004-05, Top Ten Super Lawyer San Francisco mag., 2005-06. Fellow ABA (Pro Bono Pub. award 1992), Am. Coll. Trial Lawyers,Internat. Acad. Trial Lawyers, Am. Acad. Appellate Lawyers; mem. San Francisco Bar Assn. (founding chmn. litig. sect. 1988-89, award of appreciation 1989, bd. dirs. 1990-91, pres. 2001), Calif. Acad. Appellate Lawyers, McFetridge Am. Inn of Ct. (master), Lawyers Club San Francisco. Democrat. Office: Farella Braun & Martel 235 Montgomery St Ste 3000 San Francisco CA 94104-2902 Office Phone: 415-954-4438. Business E-Mail: dyoung@fbm.com.

YOUNG, EARLE MICHAEL, III, history professor; b. San Rafael, Calif., June 15, 1964; s. Earle Michael Young; m. Erica W. Young. MA in History, Calif. State U., Northridge, 2003; MA in Polit. Sci., Tex. State U., San Marcos, 2008. Adj. prof. history Navarro Coll., Corsicana, Tex., 2003; adj. prof. history & govt. Austin CC, Tex., 2004—07; prof. history & govt. Trinity Valley CC, Palestine, Tex., 2008—. Mem. Tex. CC Tchrs. Ass., Austin, 2004. Home: 20946 Bayshore Dr Flint TX 75762 Personal E-mail: emyoung3@gmail.com. Business E-Mail: myoung@tvcc.edu.

YOUNG, EDWIN HAROLD, chemical and metallurgical engineering educator; b. Detroit, Nov. 4, 1918; s. William George and Alice Pearl (Hicks) Y.; m. Ida Signe Soma, June 25, 1944; children: David Harold, Barbara Ellen. BS in Chem. Engring, U. Detroit, 1942; MS in Chem. Engring, U. Mich., 1949, MS in Metall. Engring, 1952. Chem. engr. Wright Air Devel. Center, Dayton, Ohio, 1942-43; instr. U. Mich., Ann Arbor, 1946-52, asst. prof., 1952-56, assoc. prof., 1956-59, prof. chem. and metall. engring., 1959-89, prof. emeritus chem. and metall. engring., 1989—. Mem. Mich. Bd. Registration for Profl. Engrs., 1963-78, chmn., 1969-70, 72-73, 75-76; mem. Mich. Bd. Registration for Architects, 1963-78 Author: (with L.E. Brownell) Process Equipment Design, 1959; contbr. articles to profl. jours. Dist. commr. Boy Scouts Am., 1961-64; mem. Wolverine coun., 1965-68. With USNR, 1943-46, to capt. Res. ret., 1978. Fellow ASME, ASHRAE, AIChE (Donald Q Kern award 1979), Am. Inst. Chemists, Engring. Soc. Detroit; mem. Am. Chem. Soc., Am. Soc. Engring. Edn., Nat. Soc. Profl. Engrs. (pres. 1968-69, award 1977), Mich. Soc. Profl. Engrs. (pres. 1962-63, Engr. of Year award 1976), Mich. Assn. of Professions (pres. 1966, Distinguished award 1970), Nat. Council Engring. Examiners, Naval Res. Assn., Res. Officers Assn., Sigma Xi, Tau Beta Pi, Phi Kappa Phi, Phi Lambda Upsilon, Alpha Chi Sigma. Republican. Baptist. Home: 609 Dartmoor Rd Ann Arbor MI 48103-4513 Personal E-mail: ehyoung@engin.umich.edu.

YOUNG, EDWIN S. W., federal agency official; b. Honolulu, Nov. 13, 1943; s. Hoon Kwan and Clara (Lee) Y.; m. Joan Tay, May 19, 1978. BA, U. Hawaii, Honolulu, 1966; MBA, U. Utah, Salt Lake City, 1975; MS, U. So. Calif., LA, 1983. Asst. gen. mgr. Royal Men's Shops, Inc., Honolulu, 1973-75; mgmt. analyst U.S. Gen. Acctg. Office, Denver and Honolulu, 1976-83; audit mgr. USAF Audit Agy., LA, 1983-84, 87-90; fgn. svc. officer Dept. State, 1984-87; with Office of Insp. Gen., Office Policy & Program Rev., Washington, 1984-87; divsn. dir., asst. dir. Naval Audit Svc. Western Region, Vallejo, Calif., 1990—95; desk officer, planning and policy dir. Naval Audit Svc., Washington, 1995; regional inspector gen. for auditing, audit mgr. U.S. Small Bus. Adminstrn., LA, 1995-2000; dir. internal audit Calif. State U., Fullerton, 2000—01; dep. city auditor City of Palo Alto, Calif., 2001—. U.S. govt. rep. Pacific and Asian Affairs Coun., Honolulu, 1978—83; USN audit svc. rep. World Affairs Coun. No. Calif., 1990—95; exec. dir. The Asian-Am. Found. Phoenix, 1990—2006; SBA rep. World Affairs Coun. So. Calif., 1995—2000; Calif. State Fullerton rep. World Affairs Coun., 2000—01; City of Palo Alto rep. World Affairs Coun. No. Calif., 2001—06. Community coord. Kailua Neighborhood Bd., Honolulu, 1978-83; area rep. Urban Mass Transit Authority, Honolulu, 1978-83. Capt. USAF, 1966-72. Recipient Commendation awards U.S. Gen. Acctg. Office, 1980, USAF Audit Agy., 1983, 88, 90, USAF Acctg. and Fin. Ctr., 1984, U.S. Naval Audit Svc. award 1992, 94, 95, Assn. Local Auditors award/winner nat. award for best audit, 2004, 05, 06, 07. Mem. Assn. Govt. Accts., Inst. Internal Auditors, Chinese C. of C., World Affairs Coun. Roman Catholic. Avocations: photography, skiing, swimming, tennis, snorkeling. E-mail: eswyoung@aol.com.

YOUNG, ELIZABETH V., social worker; b. Ithaca, NY, Sept. 27, 1962; d. Roger G. and Emily V. Young; m. David M. Fine, Feb. 10, 2001. BA magna cum laude, Cornell U., Ithaca, 1984; PhD, U. Mich., Ann Arbor, 1989; MSW, Springfield Coll., Mass., 2008. Prof. English lit. Calif. State U., Long Beach, 1989—2006; asst. dean dept. natural resources, scis. and liberal arts Paul Smith's Coll., NY, 1999—2000; social worker Hospice Franklin County, Greenfield, Mass., 2008—. Author: (poems) Phoebe, Amaranth, Folio, Frontiers, The Formalist, Sow's Ear Poetry Review; contbr. articles to profl. jours. Bd. mem. Yellow Fox Found., Long Beach, 2003—06. Mem.: NASW. Home: 29 Amity Pl Amherst MA 01002 Office: Hospice Franklin County 329 Conway St Ste 2 Greenfield MA 01301 Office Fax: 413-774-2455. Personal E-mail: elizvyoung@hotmail.com. Business E-Mail: eyoung@hospicefc.org.

YOUNG, ERIC OTIS, soil scientist, researcher, agronomist; b. Cortland, NY, Mar. 7, 1973; s. Otis Frederick and Kathleen Lou Young; m. Barbara Catherine Storandt, June 18, 2005; 1 child, Emerson Maxwell. PhD, SUNY Coll. Environ. Sci. and Forestry, Syracuse, 2006. Cert. Am. Soc. Agronomy, 2002. Agronomist Cornell Coop. Ext., Oriskany, NY, 1999—2000; watershed resource conservationist Onondaga County Soil and Water Conservation Dist., LaFayette, NY, 2000—02; soil sci. rsch. and tchg. asst. SUNY Coll. Environ. Sci. and Forestry, 2002—06; rsch. soil scientist U. Vt., Burlington, 2006—; rsch. asst. and grad. fellow W. H. Miner Agrl. Rsch. Inst., Chazy, NY, 1996—99, rsch. agronomist. Contbr. articles to profl. jour. on environ. quality. Recipient Albert Leaf Meml. award, Faculty Forest and Natural Resources, SUNY-ESF, 2004. Mem.: Am. Soc. Agronomy, Soil and Water Conservation Soc., Am. Chem. Soc., Soil Sci. Soc. America. Avocations: skiing, hiking, gardening, cooking, guitar. Office: 1034 Miner Farm Rd Chazy NY 12921 Office Phone: 518-846-7121.

YOUNG, ESTELLE IRENE, dermatologist, educator; b. NYC, Nov. 2, 1945; d. Sidney D. and Blanche (Krosney) Young. BA magna cum laude, Mt. Holyoke Coll., 1967; MD, Downstate Med. Ctr., 1971. Intern Lenox Hill Hosp., NYC, 1971—72, resident in medicine, 1972—73; resident in dermatology Columbia Presbyn. Hosp., 1973—74, NYU Hosp., 1974—75, Boston U. Hosp., 1975—76; asst. dermatologist Harvard U. Health Svcs., Cambridge, 1975—76; assoc. staff mem. dermatology Boston U. Med. Ctr., 1975—76, 1976—77; pvt. practice medicine specializing in dermatology Petersburg, Va., 1976—97; mem. staff Poplar Springs Hosp., 1976—2002, Southside Regional Med. Ctr. (formerly Petersburg Gen. Hosp.), 1976—2002, Ctrl. State Hosp., 1984—2007. Clin. instr. dept. dermatology Med. Coll. Va., 1976-87, asst. clinic prof., 1988-94, assoc. clin. prof., 1994-2002; sec. med. staff Petersburg Gen. Hosp., 1982; dermatology cons. Cerebral Palsy Assn. N.Y. State, 1999-2005, 2007-08, Manhattan's Physician Group, 2008. Author: Visions of Mauna Kea; contbr. articles to profl. jours. Fellow: Am. Acad. Dermatology; mem.: Hawaii Dermatology Soc., Tidewater Dermatology Soc. (pres. 1982—83), Va. Dermatology Soc., Amateur Astronomers ASsn., Physicians Social Responsibility Soc., Tidewater Physicians Social Responsibility (pres. 1990), Internat. Physicians Prevention of Nuclear War, Sigma Xi. Home and Office: PO Box 20182 New York NY 10021-0063 Office Fax: 212-249-5948. Personal E-mail: eiy112@aol.com.

YOUNG, FRANK EDWARD, retired federal agency and religious organization administrator; b. Mineola, NY, Sept. 1, 1931; s. Frank E. and Erma F. Y.; m. Leanne Hutchinson, Oct. 20, 1956; children: Lorrie, Debora, Peggy, Frank, Jonathan. MD, SUNY, 1956; PhD, Case Western Res. U., 1962; DSc (hon.), Roberts Wesleyan Coll., 1983, Houghton Coll., 1984, SUNY, 1986, L.I. U., 1986, Western Bapt. Coll., 1988. Asst. prof. pathology Western Res. U., Cleve., 1962-65; assoc. mem. microbiology Scripps Clinic & Rsch. Found., LaJolla, Calif., 1965-68; assoc. prof. biology U. Calif., San Diego, 1967-70; mem. microbiology & exptl. pathology Scripps Clinic & Rsch. Found., LaJolla, Calif., 1968-70; prof. microbiology and chmn. dept., prof. pathology and radiation biology and biophysics U. Rochester, N.Y., 1970-79, dir. Med. Ctr., N.Y., 1979-81, dean Sch. Medicine and Dentistry, N.Y., 1979-84, v.p. for health affairs N.Y., 1981-84; commr. FDA, Rockville, Md., 1984-89, dep. asst. sec. for health sci. and environ., 1989-93; dir. office emergency preparedness, 1993-96; pastor adult ministries 4th Presbyn. Ch., Bethesda, Md., 1996—2002; exec. dir. Reformed Theol. Sem. Met. Washington, Bethesda, 1996-99; v.p. Reformed Theol. Sem., Bethesda, Md., 1999—2002; chmn., CEO Cosmos Alliance, 2002—08, chmn., 2009; ptnr. Essex Woodlands Health Ventures, 2006—. U.S. rep. WHO exec. bd., Geneva, 1985-88; bd. dirs. High Tech., Rochester, N.Y., 1983-84. Contbr. numerous articles on cloning, gene mapping, gene shuttle vectors, 1970-84; initiator Fed. Regulations rules to increase access to exptl. drugs to desperately ill, 1987-88. Lectr. Christian orgns., 1970—; mem. United Way, Rochester, N.Y., 1982-84, N.Y. State Statutory Adv. Com. on DNA, Albany, N.Y., 1978. Recipient sec.'s spl. citation Dept. Health and Human Svcs., 1989, Surgeon Gen.'s Exemplary Svc. medal, 1988, Disting. Svc. medal Pub. Health Svc., 1986, Edward Mott award, 1985, Surgeon Gen.'s Medallion, 1992. Mem. Inst. Medicine of NAS, AAAS, Am. Acad. Microbiology (bd. govs.). Avocations: fishing, boating. Office Phone: 301-908-3182. Personal E-mail: FrankCosmos@aol.com. Business E-Mail: fyoung@ewhv.com.

YOUNG, GAIL DIANE, secondary school educator; d. Melvin D Maze and Dorothy L (Evers) Maze; m. Kurt W. Young, Oct. 2, 1982; children: Amy, Kaylynn. BS in family and consumer sci., Miami U., 1982; MS in edn., U. of Dayton, 1999. Family and consumer sci. tchr. West Carrollton Sr. High, Ohio, 1982—. Family and consumer sci. dept. chair West Carrollton Sr. High, Ohio, 1997—; career tech. planning dist. tchr. liaison to the miami valley career tech. ctr. West Carrollton Sr. H.S., Ohio, 2002—; bldg. lead mentor - entry yr. tchg. program West Carrollton Sr. High, 2001—02; career devel. course mentor Miamisburg Sr. H.S., Ohio, 1999, Fairborn Sr. H.S., Ohio, 2000; career devel. adv. mem. Miami Valley Career Tech. Ctr., Clayton, Ohio, 2004—; owner/moderator - fcs work&family list serve The first nationwide E-mail group list for FCS teachers, 1997—. Co-founder, former v.p. Milton-Union Early Childhood Ctr., Inc. (non-profit), West Milton, Ohio, 2003; 4-h advisor Miami County 4H Program, Troy, Ohio, 2000. Recipient I Dare You award for Qualities of Leadership, William H. Danforth Found., 1978, Significant Educator award, West Carrollton Edn. Recognition Assn., 1987—, Dickinson T. Guiler award for excellence in edn., 2005. Mem.: NEA, West Carrollton Fellowship Educators, Phi Upsilon Omicron, Kappa Delta Pi. Avocations: travel, boating, gardening, painting.

YOUNG, GARY WILLIAM, minister, educator, retired military officer; b. Boscobel, Wis., Aug. 8, 1939; s. Howard Austin and Gladys Marie Young; m. Carole Jane Goldsmith-Reynolds, June 2, 1990; children: Cary J., Stacey D. Reynolds, Lisa M., Lauren R. King, Garret S. Reynolds, Lesley J. Reynolds. BS in Secondary Edn., Wis. State Coll & Inst. Tech., Platteville, 1962; BS in Bus. Adminstrn., U. Wis., Platteville, 1992, MS in Adult Edn., 1993. Lic. reverend United Fellowship of Christ Internat., 2004. English tchr. East HS, Green Bay, Wis., 1962—63; seaman apprentice, ensign, capt. USN, 1963—88; English, history tchr. Bootheville-Venice, Plaquemines Parish, 1989; adj. faculty bus., gen edn. SW Wis. Tech. Coll., Fennimore, 1990—93; CEO, chief trainer Young Sys., Boscobel, 1992—2002; mission min. United Fellowship of Christ Internat., Boscobel, 2004—. Advisor, ship rider Vietnamese Navy, Saigon, 1967; officer in charge, patrol torpedo flect divsns. 12 and 13 Cosrivron One, Coronado, Calif., 1974—75, chief staff officer, 1975—76; commdg. officer Naval and Marine Corps Res. Ctr., Des Moines, 1976—79; dir. recruiting Chief of Naval Res., New Orleans, 1979—82; chair Dept. Def. Joint Advt. Com., Washington, 1981—82; English instr. U. Wis., Platteville, 1991—92; field trainer NE Iowa CC, Calmar, 1993—97. Author, editor: training manual Total Quality Leadership, 1993. Religious, grief counseling World Christianship Ministries, Boscobel, 2004—07. Capt. USN, 1963—88. Decorated Bronze star US Pres., Staff Svc. Honor medal first class Republic of Vietnam, Meritorious Svc. medal USN, Commendation medal. Mem.: Vietnam Veterans Am. (life), Free and Accepted Masons (assoc.), 40 & 8 (assoc.), Game Wardens of Vietnam (life), VFW (life; post comdr. 2007), Am. Legion (life), Fleet Res. Assn. (life), 9th Va. Cav. Co B (sec. 1997—98), 1st Wis. Cav. Co D (sec. 1999—2001). Protestant. Avocations: golf, history. Home: 1004 Chestnut St Boscobel WI 53280

YOUNG, GENEVIEVE LEMAN, publishing executive, editor; b. Geneva, Sept. 25, 1930; came to U.S., 1945, naturalized, 1968; d. Clarence Kuangson and Juliana Helen (Yen) Y.; m. Cedric Sun, 1955 (div. 1972); m. Gordon Parks, Aug. 26, 1973 (div. 1979). BA (Wellesley Coll. scholar), Wellesley Coll., 1952. Asst. editor Harper & Row (pubs.), NYC, 1960-62, editor, 1962-64, asst. mng. editor, 1964-66, mng. editor, 1966-70; exec. editor J.B. Lippincott Co., NYC, 1970-77, v.p., 1972-77; sr. editor Little, Brown & Co., NYC, 1977-85; editor-in-chief Lit. Guild Am., NYC, 1985-88; v.p., editorial dir. Bantam Books, NYC, 1988-92. Alumna trustee Phillips Acad., Andover, Mass., 1975-78, class agt., 1979-85; mem. Wellesley Bus. Leadership Coun., 1989-98; mem. Youth Counseling League, 1986-98, pres., 1989-96, mem. com. of 100, 1991-93; mem. Literacy Ptnrs., Inc., NYC, 1992-2001, sec., 1996-2001; mem. Andover Devel. Bd., 1993-98; trustee Jewish Bd. Family and Children's Svcs., 1996-98, Meserve-Kunhardt Found., 2006—. Recipient Alumna Achievement award Wellesley Coll., 1982, Matrix award, 1988. Mem. Assn. Am. Pubs. (exec. coun. gen. pub. div. 1975-78, 85-87, freedom to read com. 1972-75), Women's Media Group (pres. 1981-82, 2d v.p. 1994-95),Independent Editors Group, Century Assn. Home: 30 Park Ave New York NY 10016-3801 Personal E-mail: panchogene@aol.com.

YOUNG, GEORGE CRESSLER, federal judge; b. Cin., Aug. 4, 1916; s. George Philip and Gladys (Cressler) Y.; m. Iris June Hart, Oct. 6, 1951; children: George Cressler, Barbara Ann. AB, U. Fla., 1938, LLB, 1940; postgrad., Harvard Law Sch., 1947. Bar: Fla. 1940. Practice in, Winter Haven, 1940-41; assoc. firm Smathers, Thompson, Maxwell & Dyer, Miami, 1947; adminstrv., legislative asst. to Senator Smathers of Fla., 1948-52; asst. U.S. atty. Jacksonville, 1952; partner firm Knight, Kincaid, Young & Harris, Jacksonville, 1953-61; U.S. dist. judge No., Middle and So. dists. Fla., 1961-73; chief judge Middle Dist., 1973-81, sr. judge, 1981—. Mem. com. on adminstrn. fed. magistrates system Jud. Conf. U.S., 1973-80 Bd. dirs. Jacksonville United Cerebral Palsy Assn., 1953-60. Served to lt. (s.g.) USNR, 1942-46. Mem. Rollins Coll. Alumni Assn. (pres. 1968-69), ABA (spl. com. for adminstrn. criminal justice), Fla. Bar Assn. (gov. 1960-61), Jacksonville Bar Assn. (past pres.), Order of Coif, Fla. Blue Key, Phi Beta Kappa, Phi Kappa Phi, Phi Delta Phi, Sigma Alpha Epsilon. Home: 2424 Shrewsbury Rd Orlando FL 32803-1334

YOUNG, GEORGE HAYWOOD, III, (WOODY YOUNG), investment banker; b. Washington, Feb. 10, 1959; s. George H. Jr. and Jeanne Marie (Collins) Y.; m. Adina Chouequet, Oct. 12, 1996; children: Nathalie Haywood, George Haywood IV. BA in Internat. Rels. with honors, Brown U., 1982; MPhil in Internat. Rels., Magdalene Coll., U. Cambridge, Eng., 1983; M in Pub. and Pvt. Mgmt., Yale U., 1987. Assoc. cons. Bain & Co., Boston, 1983-85; assoc. mergers & acquisitions dept. CS First Boston, NYC, 1987-90, v.p., 1990-91, dir., 1992-94; White House fellow, spl. asst. to dep. sec. US Dept. Treasury, Washington, 1991-92; sr. v.p. Lehman Brothers Holdings Inc., NYC, 1994-96, mng. dir., 1996—2007, head global communications group, 2000—07, chmn. sr. client coun., 2004—07, global investment banking exec. com., 2004—07, mem. firm strategy com., 2005—07; head global tech., media, & telecommunications (TMT) investment banking Merrill Lynch & Co., Inc., NYC, 2008—09, Bank of America Corp., NYC, 2009; vice chmn. head global telecomm. group Lazard Freres & Co., NYC, 2009—. Application reader White House Fellows Commn., NYC, 1993—; mem. alumni coun. exec. com. Phillips Acad., Andover, Mass., 1994—98, vis. mem. fin. and investment com. bd. trustees, 1998—2004; mem. Fin. Aid Task Force, 2008—; mem. regional selection panel White House Fellows Commn., NYC, 2002—04; vol. Ch. of the Holy Trinity, NYC, 1990—97. Mem. Coun. Fgn. Rels. (term membership selection com.), Assn. U.S. Army, Harrow Sch. Assn., Army and Navy Club, Yale Golf Club, Union Club NYC, Misquamicut Club. Roman Catholic. Office: Lazard Freres & Co LLC 30 Rockefeller Plz New York NY 10020 Office Phone: 212-632-6000.

YOUNG, HEATHER M., academic administrator, nursing educator; b. Boksburg, Republic South Africa, Aug. 20, 1960; d. Ernle W. D. and Margaret Mavis (Eddy) Y.; m. Peter Burton Quinby, Sept. 2, 1984. BS in Dietetics, U. Calif., Davis, 1981; ADN, Sacramento City Coll., 1983; BSN, So. Oreg. State Coll., 1986; M in Gerontol. Nursing, U. Wash., 1989, PhD in Nursing, 1991. RN, Oreg., Wash. With Bay Area Hosp., Coos Bay, Oreg., staff nurse ICU; nurse practitioner II Harborview Med. Ctr., Seattle; exec. dir. Ida Culver House Broadview, Seattle; rsch. asst. prof. Sch. of Nursing U. Wash., Seattle; joined Oreg. Health and Sci. U. Sch. Nursing at So. Oreg. U., Ashland, 2003, Grace Phelps disting. prof., dir. John A. Hartford Ctr. for Geriatric Nursing Excellence, dir. rural health rsch. devel.; assoc. vice chancellor nursing U. Calif., Davis, 2008—. Prin. investigator medication mgmt. in rural assisted living Nat. Inst. Nursing Rsch., 2004—06. Contbr. articles to nursing jours. Mem. Alzheimer's Disease and Related Disorders Assn., 1987. Recipient rsch. award Nta. Ctr. for Nursing Rsch., 1987-91. Fellow: Am. Acad. Nursing (co-chair Expert Panel on Aging); mem.: ANA, Western Acad. Nursing, Western Inst. Nursing Rsch., Am. Soc. on Aging, Gerontol. Soc. Am., Wash. State Nurses Assn., Sigma Theta Tau. Office: U Calif Davis Sch Nursing 4610 X St Sacramento CA 95817

YOUNG, HENRY E., tissue engineering medical educator; b. Dayton, Ohio, Dec. 5, 1951; s. Henry O. and Lucille M. Y.; m. Valerie E. Achorn, May 16, 1976; 1 child, Katherine. BS in Biology, Ohio State U., 1974; MS in Zoology, U. Ark., 1977; PhD, Tex. Tech. U., 1983. Instr.biochemistry Rush-Presbyn.-St. Luke's Med. Ctr., Chgo., 1987—88; asst. prof. anatomy Mercer U. Sch. Medicine, Macon, Ga., 1988—95, asst. prof. surgery, 1988—94, assoc. prof. anatomy, pediat., 1995—2004, prof. anatomy, pediat., 2004—. Inventor in field. Recipient Hooding award for excellence in tchg. and rsch., Mercer U. Med. Sch., 1993, 1994, Gender Equity award, Am. Med. Women's Assn., 1997, Humanism in Medicine award, Arnold P. Gold Found., 2005; NIH Postdoctoral fellow in biochemistry, Case We. Res. U., Cleve., 1983—85, postdoctoral fellow, Muscular Dystrophy Assn., 1985—87. Mem.: Am. Soc. Cell Biology, Stem Cells and Regen Medicine, Tissue Culture Soc., Am. Assn. Anatomists, Arnold P. Gold Found., Humanism Hon. Soc. Achievements include discovery of adult germ layer lineage stem cells, adult pluripotent stem cells, and adult near totipotent stem cells; invention of muscle morphogenetic protein and scar inhibitory factor. Avocation: reading. Office: Mercer U Sch Medicine 3rd Floor Medical Research Lab 1021 Georgia Ave Macon GA 31207 Office Phone: 478-301-2764. Office Fax: 478-301-5487. Personal E-mail: young.he@yahoo.com.

YOUNG, HENRY WALTHALL, JR., speech educator; b. Cleve., Oct. 13, 1959; s. Walthall Young Henry Sr. and Lucy Foy, James Foy (Stepfather). AA, Cuyahoga CC, Cleve.; BA in Communication Studies, Cleve. State U., MA in Applied Communication Theory and Methodology. Coord. prevention svcs. Covenant Adolescent Chem. Dependency Treatment Ctr., Inc., Cleve., 1989—2005; asst. prof. speech communication Cuyahoga CC, 2005—. Home: 11045 Lake Ave #14 Cleveland OH 44102 Office: Cuyahoga CC-Met 2900 Community College Ave MLA 323H Cleveland OH 44115 Office Fax: 216-987-4572. Business E-Mail: henry.young@tri-c.edu.

YOUNG, HOWARD ALAN, molecular biologist; b. Jan. 29, 1948; s. Saul B. and Yetta Young. BS, U. Mass., 1969; MS, U. Wash., 1972, PhD, 1974. Postdoctoral fellow Nat. Cancer Inst., Bethesda, 1974-76, sr. staff fellow, 1976-79; staff scientist Frederick (Md.) Cancer Rsch. Ctr., 1979-81; dir. tech. svcs. Bethesda Rsch. Labs., Gaithersburg, Md., 1981-83; cancer expert Nat. Cancer Inst., Frederick, 1983-86, staff scientist, 1986-89, head cellular & molecular immunology sect., 1989—. Dep. chief Lab. Exptl. Immunology, Cancer and Inflammation Program, Ctr. Cancer Rsch., 2006—. Mem. AAAS, Am. Soc. Microbiology, Am. Assn. Immunologists, Internat. Soc. Interferon and Cytokine Rsch., DNA Methylation Soc., Am. Soc. Biochemistry and Molecular Biology, Phi Beta Kappa. Office: NCI-Frederick Bldg 560/31-23 Frederick MD 21702 Office Phone: 301-846-5700, 301-846-5743. Business E-Mail: younghow@mail.nih.gov.

YOUNG, HOWARD THOMAS, foreign language educator; b. Cumberland, Md., Mar. 24, 1926; s. Samuel Phillip and Sarah Emmaline (Frederick) Y.; m. Carol Osborne, Oct. 5, 1949 (div. 1966); children: Laurie Margaret, Jennifer Anne; m. Edra Lee Airheart, May 23, 1981; 1 child, Timothy Howard. BS summa cum laude, Columbia U., NYC, 1950, MA, 1952, PhD, 1954. Lectr. Columbia U., NYC, 1950-54; asst. prof. Romance langs. Pomona Coll., Claremont, Calif., 1954-60, assoc. prof., 1960-66, Smith prof. Romance langs., 1966-98, prof. emeritus, 1998—. Vis. prof. Middlebury Program in Spain, Madrid, 1986-87, U. Zaragoza, 1967-68, Columbia U., summer 2000; chief reader Spanish AP Ednl. Testing Svc., Princeton, 1975-78, chmn. Spanish lang. devel. commn., 1976-79; mem. fgn. lang. adv. commn. Coll. Bd., NYC, 1980-83; mem. West Coast selection commn. Mellon Fellowships for Humanities, Princeton, 1984-86, European selection com., 1987, 90; trans. cons. Smithsonian Inst. Author: The Victorious Expression, 1964, Juan Ramón Jimènez, 1967, The Line in the Margin, 1980; editor: T.S. Eliot and Hispanic Modernity, 1995; contbr. London Times Higher Edn. Supplement; contbr. numerous articles and book revs. to profl. jours. Dir. NEH summer seminar for Sch. tchrs., 1993. Served with USNR, 1944-46, ETO. Fellow Del Amo Found., 1960-61, NEH, 1975, 89-90; Fulbright fellow; 1967-68; Rockefeller Study Ctr. scholar, 1976. Mem. MLA, Assn. Tchrs. Spanish and Portuguese, Am. Comparative Lit. Assn., Acad. Am. Poets, Assn. Lit. Scholars and Critics. Home: 447 W Redlands Ave Claremont CA 91711-1638 Office: Pomona Coll Romance Lang Dept 550 Harvard Ave Claremont CA 91711-6380 Home Phone: 909-625-2841. Business E-Mail: HTYoung@pomona.edu.

YOUNG, HUGH DAVID, physics professor, writer; b. Ames, Iowa, Nov. 3, 1930; s. Hugh Surber and Nellie Sibella (Peters) Y.; m. Alice Carroll, June 25, 1960; children: Gretchen Carroll, Rebecca Susan BS in Physics, Carnegie-Mellon U., 1952, MS in Physics, 1953, PhD in Physics, 1959, BFA in Music, 1972. From instr. to assoc. prof. physics Carnegie-Mellon U., Pitts., 1956-77, prof., 1977—; head dept. natural scis. Margaret Morrison Carnegie Coll., Carnegie-Mellon U., 1962-67, acad. coordinator, lectr. modern engring. mgrs. program, 1966-82. Vis. assoc. prof. physics U. Calif., Berkeley, 1967-68, vis. prof. physics, 1974; asst. organist St. Paul's Cathedral, Pitts., 1978-82 Author: Statistical Treatment of Experimental Data, 1962, Fundamentals of Mechanics and Heat, 2d edit., 1974, Fundamentals of Optics and Modern Physics, 2d edit., 1976; (with Sears and Zemansky) College Physics, 7th edit., 1990, University Physics, 9th edit., 1996. Bd. dirs. Renaissance and Baroque Soc., 1980-86. Recipient Ryan Tchg. award Carnegie Inst. Tech., 1965, Doherty award Carnegie Mellon U., 1997. Mem. Am. Assn. Physics Tchrs., Am. Phys. Soc., Am. Guild Organists (assoc.) Democrat. Avocations: organ, rock climbing. Home: 5746 Aylesboro Ave Pittsburgh PA 15217-1412 Office: Carnegie-Mellon Univ Dept Physics Pittsburgh PA 15213 Home Phone: 412-422-5772; Office Phone: 412-268-2759. Business E-Mail: hdy@andrew.cmu.edu.

YOUNG, JAMES EDWARD, lawyer; b. Painesville, Ohio, Apr. 20, 1946; s. James M. and Isabel P. (Rogers) Y. BBA, Ohio U., 1968; JD, Ohio State U., 1972. Bar: Ohio 1972. Law clk. to chief judge U.S. Ct. Appeals, Nashville, 1972-73; chief counsel City of Cleve., 1980-81, law dir., 1981-82; assoc. Jones, Day, Reavis & Pogue (now Jones Day), Cleve., 1973—79, ptnr., 1983—. Office: Jones Day 901 Lakeside Ave E Cleveland OH 44114-1190 Office Phone: 216-586-7259. Business E-Mail: jameseyoung@jonesday.com.

YOUNG, JAMES JULIUS, academic administrator, retired military officer; b. Ft. Ringgold, Tex., Nov. 28, 1926; s. John Cooper and Violet Thelma (Ohl) Y.; m. June Agnes Hillstead, Dec. 17, 1948; children: Robert Michael, Steven Andrew, Patrick James, Mary Frances. BS, U. Md., 1960; M.H.A., Baylor U., 1962; PhD in Hosp. and Health Adminstrn, U. Iowa, 1969. Commd. 2d lt. U.S. Army, 1947, advanced through grades to brig. gen., 1977, comdr., med. ops. officer, dir. tng. field med. units in European Command, 1949-53; comdr. Mil. Med. Leadership Sch., 1953-54; med. advisor (Nationalist Army of China), 1955-57; asst. adminstr. Fitzsimons Army Med. Center, 1957-60; med. plans and ops. officer (US Forces), Korea, 1962-63; sr. field med. instr., chief field med. service Med. Field Service Sch., 1963-66; dir. health care orgn. and mgmt. analysis Office of Surgeon Gen., 1969-71; dir. med. plans and ops. directorate Office of the Surgeon, Military Assistance Command, Vietnam, 1971-72; exec. officer, chief adminstrv. services Silas Hays Army Hosp., 1973-74; military health analyst, military health care study OMB, Exec. Office of Pres., 1974-76; dep. dir. resources mgmt. and cons. for health care adminstrn. Office of Surgeon Gen., 1976-77; chief med. svcs. corps U.S. Army, 1977-81; dir. resources mgmt. Office of Surgeon Gen., 1977-81; ret., 1981; instr. U. Iowa, 1967-69; asst. prof., preceptor Baylor U., 1973-74; vice chancellor for health affairs W.Va. Bd. Regents, Charleston, 1982-87; dean sch. of allied health scis. U. Tex. Health Sci. Ctr., San Antonio, 1987-90, interim dean Sch. Medicine, 1988-89, dean Sch. Medicine, 1989—, dean emeritus, 2000—. Cons. to Min. of Health, Republic of Vietnam, 1971-72, 1989-2000; adj. prof. Baylor U., 1977-81, George Washington U., 1975-76, W.Va. U., 1986; prof. U. Tex. health Sci. Ctr., San Antonio, 1989-2000. Contbr. articles to profl. jours. Decorated D.S.M., Legion of Merit, Meritorious Service medal, others; recipient Walter Reed medal, 1981; Army Med. Dept. medal for contbn. to health service, 1981, Order of Mil. Med. Merit, 1981, U. Tex. Health Scis. Ctr. Hon. medallion Fountains of Progress, 2000; recipient Humanism in Medicine medallion Health Care Foun. NJ, 2000. Roman Catholic. Home: 1610 Anchor Dr San Antonio TX 78213-1943 Personal E-mail: jyoung51@satx.rr.com.

YOUNG, JAMES MARION, lawyer; b. Winston-Salem, NC, Nov. 15, 1930; s. William Rector and Celia Marie (Pasley) Young; m. Barbara Marie Pultz, Feb. 2, 1957; children: Deborah Marie, Rebecca Anne, Catherine Arline, Cynthia Louise. BA, U. Va., 1953, LLB, 1957. Bar: Va. Assoc. M.S. McChung, Salem, Va., 1957—58, A. Tracy Loyd, Roanoke, Va., 1958—64, Dodson, Pence & Coulter, Roanoke, 1964—66; ptnr. Dodson Pence Vlar Young and Woodrum, Roanoke and Salem, 1966—. Pres. Roanoke County Coun. PTA, 1970; mem. exec. bd. Blue Ridge Mountains coun. Boy Scouts Am., 1960—, pres. Blue Ridge Mountains coun., 1975—77; chmn. Electoral Bd. City of Salem, 1968—83. Lt. col. (ret.) USAR. Recipient Disting. Svc. award, Salem Jaycees, 1964, Silver Beaver award, Boy Scouts Am., 1976, Champion Men's Doubles 75 & Over Clay Ct. Tennis, State of Va., 2006—08. Fellow: Va. Law Found.; mem.: ABA, Roanoke County Bar Assn. (pres. 1970), Va. Bar Assn. (life), Salem-Roanoke County C. o C. (pres. 1972), Salem Kiwanis (pres. 1981—82). Democrat. Presbyterian. Home: 412 N Shank St Salem VA 24153-2655 Office: 723 College Ave Salem VA 24153-3846

YOUNG, JAMES R., rail transportation executive; m. Shirley Young; 3 children. Grad., U. Nebr., Omaha. With Union Pacific Corp., 1978—, mgmt. fin. and ops., asst. v.p. re-engring. Union Pacific RR Co., 1994—95, v.p. re-engring. and design, 1995, v.p. customer svc. planning & quality, 1997, v.p. fin. & quality, sr. v.p., corp. treas., 1998—99, sr. v.p. fin., corp. contr., 1999, exec. v.p., CFO, 1999—2004, pres. & COO Union Pacific RR Co., 2004—05, bd. dirs., 2005—, pres., CEO, 2005—, chmn., 2007—. Bd. mem. Grupo Ferroviario Mexicano, Assn. Am. RRs. Bd. mem. Creighton U., Omaha, Joslyn Art Mus., U. Nebr. Med. Ctr. Office: Union Pacific Corp 1400 Douglas St Omaha NE 68179-1001 Office Phone: 402-544-5000.

YOUNG, JANET CHERYL, electrical engineer; b. Roanoke, Va., Oct. 3, 1960; d. Don Gordon and Barbara Hill (Mumpower) Y. BS in Physics, U. Tenn., Chattanooga, 1982; MSEE, Va. Tech. Inst., 1991. Engr. Sci. Applications Internat. Corp., Springfield, Va., 1982—91, United Telecom Coun., Washington, 1991—93, LCC, Internat., McLean, Va., 1993—2002, Sprint Nextel Corp., Reston, Va., 2002—08, Clearwire Comm., 2009—. Active Cmty. Band, Vienna, Va., 1985; vol. Shakespeare Theatre Co., 1996—97; mem. Prince William County Dem. Com., Democracy for Am., 2004—; active World Peace Mission Foundry United Meth. Ch., Washington, 1984. Mem. IEEE (mem. Electromagnetic Compatibility Soc. 1987-91, Comm. Soc. 1992—). Methodist. Avocations: gardening, travel, genealogy. Home: 4044 Chetham Way Woodbridge VA 22192 Office: 593 Herndon Pky Herndon VA 20170

YOUNG, JAY ALFRED, chemical safety and health consultant, editor, writer; b. Huntington, Ind., Sept. 8, 1920; s. Jacob Phillip and Marie (Skully) Y.; m. Anne Elizabeth Neff, June 29, 1942 (dec. June 1962); children: John, Paul, Cecelia, Michael, Joseph, Andrea, Therese, Gregory, Thomas, Lucy, Margaret, Antonia; m. Mary Ann Owens, Aug. 15, 1962; children: James, Laurence; 4 stepchildren. BS, Ind. U., Bloomington, 1939; AM, Oberlin Coll., Ohio, 1940; PhD, U. Notre Dame, South Bend, Ind., 1950. Chief chemist Asbestos Mfg. Co., Huntington, Ind., 1941-42; ordnance engr. U.S. War Dept., Washington, 1942-44; from instr. to prof. chemistry King's Coll., Wilkes-Barre, Pa., 1949-69; vis. prof. Carleton U., Ottawa, Ont., Canada, 1969-70, Fla. State U., Tallahassee, 1975-77; Hudson prof. Auburn (Ala.) U., 1970-75; mgr. tech. publs. Chem. Mfrs. Assn., Washington, 1977-80; chem. safety and health cons. Silver Spring, Md., 1980—. Pro bono cons. OSHA, EPA, Consumer Product Safety Commn., Washington, 1980—; contributor Ency. Britannica, 1974-; lectr. in field. Author: Practice in Thinking, 1958, Elements of General Chemistry, 1960, Chemical Concepts, 1963, Selected Principles of Chemistry, 1963, Arithmetic for Students of Science, 1968, Instructor's Guide for Chemistry, a Cultural Approach, 1971, Study Guide for General Chemistry, 1974, Fire!, 1977, Actions and Reactions, 1978, Chemistry, A Human Concern, 1978, Kitchen Chemistry, 1980, Electron Microscopy Safety Handbook, 1985, Introduction to Toxicology, 2004; co-author: Study Guide for Continental Classroom Chemistry, NBC/TV, vols. I and II, 1959, 60, Keys to Chemistry, 1973, Chemistry Preparation Laboratory, 1973, Keys to Oxidation-Reduction, 1974, Things that Last, 1977, Principles of Laboratory Safety (with videotape), 1980, OSHA Hazard Communication Regulations, 1984, Chemical Safety Manual for Small Businesses, 1989, 2d edit., 1992, Developing a Chemical Hygiene Plan, 1990; editor: Guidelines and Recommendations for the Preparation and Continuing Education of Secondary School Teachers of Chemistry, 1977, Improving Safety in the Chemical Laboratory: A Practical Guide, 1989, 2d edit., 1992 (also contbr.), Safety in Academic Chemistry Laboratories, Vols. 1 and 2, 7th edit., 2002, Chemical Safety for Teachers and Their Supervisors, Grades 7-12, 2001; co-editor: Heath Chemistry Laboratory Experiments, 1987, Handbook of Chemical Health and Safety, 2001 (also contbr.), Chem. Lab. Info. Profiles, 2001—; contbr. articles to profl. jours. Tech. resource person to media and expert witness regarding chem. hazards, precautions, transp. incidents involving chems.; mem. NSF Coll. Chemistry Commn., 1962-68. Lt. USNR, 1944-46. Recipient Disting. Chemistry Alumnus award U. Notre Dame, 1968, Excellence in Chemistry Tchg. award Mfg. Chemists Assn., 1970. Fellow AAAS; mem. Am. Chem. Soc. (councilor 1963-87, policy com. 1970-81, sec. divsn. chem. edn. 1969-78, chmn. divsn. chem. health and safety 1979-80, mem. chem. safety com. 1982-2003, Chem. Health and Safety award 1991, Outstanding Svc. award 2003, 2007). Roman Catholic. Avocations: wood and metalworking, gardening. Home and Office: 12916 Allerton Ln Silver Spring MD 20904-3105 Office Phone: 301-384-1768. Personal E-mail: chemsafety@verizon.net.

YOUNG, JESS RAY, retired internist; b. Fairfield, Ill., Feb. 4, 1928; s. Edgar S. and Clara B. (Musgrave) Y.; m. Gloria Wynn, July 10, 1953; children— James C., Patricia A. BS, Franciscan U., 1951; MD, St. Louis U., 1955. Intern Highland Alameda County Hosp., Oakland, Calif., 1955-56; resident in internal medicine Cleve. Clinic Hosp., 1956-59, mem. staff dept. vascular medicine, 1959-97, chmn. dept., 1976-97; ret., 1998. Co-author: Leg Ulcer, 1975, Peripheral Vascular Diseases, 1991, 1996; contbr. articles to profl. jours., chpts. to books. Served with AUS, 1946-47. Mem. AMA, Am. Heart Assn. (stroke council), Am. Coll. Cardiology, Internat. Cardiovascular Soc., ACP, Am. Fedn. Clic. Research, Ohio Soc. Internal Medicine, Soc. for Vascular Medicine, Inter-Urban Club. Methodist. Home: 1503 Burlington Rd Cleveland OH 44118-1216 Personal E-mail: jesyoung@adelphia.net.

YOUNG, JOHN DAVID, information systems analyst, consultant; b. Dallas, Sept. 15, 1975; s. John Marvin III and Donna Smith Young; m. Cerita Esther Townley, Mar. 4, 2000. BBA, Tex. A&M U., 1998. Microsoft cert. sys. engr., 1998, profl. +internet, 1998, profl., 1998; CompTIA A+ cert. svc. technician, 1998. Sys. adminstr. Tex. A&M U., College Station, 1996-98; assoc. desktop technician, Source 2000, Inc. Halliburton Co., Houston, 1999-2000, desktop analyst, 2000, tech. analyst, 2000—. Info. sys. cons., Bratton Comm., Inc., Houston, 1999—. Mem. Assn. Info. Tech. Profls., Am. Mensa, Ltd., KC Republican. Roman Catholicism. Avocation: travel. Home: 12307 Gershwin Oak St Houston TX 77089-5722

YOUNG, JOHN F., energy executive; b. 1956; m. Julie Young; children: Jack, Will. BS in Mech. Engring., US Naval Acad., Annapolis, Md., 1978. Positions including comml. sales rep., position in wholesale and retail mktg. fuel planning and procurement, head fin. and investor rels. office So. Co., 1983—2000, exec. v.p. So. Generation; sr. v.p. Sierra Pacific Resources Corp.; COO Exelon Power, 2003, pres., 2003—04, Exelon Generation, 2004—05; exec. v.p. fin. & markets Exelon Corp., 2005—08; CEO Energy Future Holdings Corp. (formerly TXU Corp.), Dallas, 2008—. Bd. dirs. Assn. Edison Illuminating Cos., Utility Bus. Edn. Coalition, Electric Power Research Inst. Engring. officer USS Ticonderoga USN. Office: Energy Future Holdings Corp Energy Plz 1601 Bryan St Dallas TX 75201-3411*

YOUNG, JOHN HARDIN, lawyer; b. Washington, Apr. 25, 1948; s. John D. and Laura Virginia (Gwathmey) Y.; m. Mary Frances (Farley) Crosby. JD, U. Va., 1973; BCL, Oxford U., Eng., 1976. Bar: Va. 1973, DC 1974, Pa. 1979, U.S. Dist. Ct. Va. 1974, U.S. Dist. Ct. DC 1974, U.S. Dist. Ct. Md. 1989, U.S. Ct. Fed. Claims 1974, U.S. Ct. Appeals (4th, 5th, Fed. and DC cirs.), Internat. Trade Ct. 1974, U.S. Supreme Ct. 1977. Ptnr., counsel Porter Wright Morris & Arthur, Washington, 1988—99; with Exec. Office of the Pres., Washington, 2000; counsel Sandler, Reiff & Young, PC, 2001—; exec. v.p. external affairs SECORIX, Inc., Washington, 2004—. Mem. adv. bd. Antitrust Bull., 1980-1994; mem. U.S. Sec. State's adv. com. Pvt. internat. Law, 1987-95; chmn. Va. Retirement Sys. Rev. Bd., 1990-94; asst. atty. gen. Commonwealth of Va., 1976-78; mem. Delmarva Interstate Compact, 2004-06; moderator Alexandria Forum, 1993-98, Fedn. Forum/TV Channel 10, 1989-91; sr. v.p., gen. counsel various tech. cos.; adj. prof. George Mason U. Sch. Law, 2003—05 Author: Young's Federal Rules of Evidence, Mastering Written Discovery; editor, contbr.: Internat. Election Principles; contbr. articles to profl. jours. Spl. counsel Dem. Nat. Com., 1998—99, chair nat. lawyers coun., 1998—2004; lead recount counsel for V.P. Gore Fla., 2000; organizer promote the vote Dem. Nat. Com., 2001—. Fellow: Am. Bar Found. (life); mem.: ABA (chmn. adminstrv. law and regulatory practice sect. 1999—2000, standing com. on continuing edn. of the bar 2002—04, standing com. on election law 2005—07, bd. govs. 2007—, fellow adminstrv. law 2001—), Am. Inns of Ct. Found (trustee 2004—07, chair rule of law conf. 2007), Temple Bar Found. (bd. dirs., founder), Comml. Bar Assn. U.K., George Mason Am. Inn of Ct. (master 1990—, pres. 2002—03, Best Spl. Projects award 2003), Am. Law Inst. (life), Cosmos Club, Phi Alpha Theta (history honors). Episcopalian. Office Phone: 202-479-1111. Office Fax: 202-479-1115. Business E-Mail: young@sandlerreiff.com.

YOUNG, JOHN JACOB, JR., former federal agency administrator; b. Moreland, Ga., May 29, 1962; s. John Jacob and Gloria Jewell (Wheelus) Young; m. Barbara Joan Schleihauf. BS in Aerospace Engring., Ga. Inst. Tech., 1985; MS in Aeronautics and Astronautics, Stanford U., 1987. Engr. in Tng., Ga. Intern US Senator Sam Nunn Intern Prog., Washington, 1984; engring. coop. Gen. Dynamics Ft. Worth Divsn., 1980-84; mem. tech. staff The BDM Corp., Huntsville, Ala., 1985-86, Rockwell Internat. Missile Systems Divsn., Duluth, Ga., 1987-88, Sandia Nat. Labs., Albuquerque, 1988-93; AIAA Congl. fellow profl. staff subcommittee on def. US Senate Appropriations Com., Washington, 1991-93, profl. staff subcommittee on def.; asst. sec. for rsch. devel. & acquisition, Dept. Navy US Dept. Def., Washington, 2001—05, dir. def. rsch. & engring., acquisition, tech. & logistics, 2005—07, acting under sec. for acquisition, tech. & logistics, 2007, under sec. for acquisition, tech. & logistics, 2007—09. Organizer, coach BDM Co-ed. Softball team, Huntsville, Ala., 1986; big brother Big Bros., Big Sisters, Huntsville, Ala., 1986; tutor El Dorado HS, Albuquerque, 1989-90. Recipient AIAA Gen. Dynamics scholarship, 1984; fellow Coll. Engring, Stanford U., 1985; named Outstanding Young Engr., AIAA Atlanta Section, 1988. Fellow AIAA; mem. Briaerean Soc., Phi Kappa Phi, Tau Beta Pi, Sigma Gamma Tau, Phi Eta Sigma. Presbyterian.*

YOUNG, JON NATHAN, archaeologist; b. Hibbing, Minn., May 30, 1938; s. Robert Nathan Young and Mary Elizabeth (Barrows) Roy; m. Karen Sue Johnson, June 5, 1961 (div. May 1980); children: Shawn Nathan, Kevin Leigh; m. Tucker Heitman, June 18, 1988 (div. Apr. 1996). BA magna cum laude, U. Ariz., 1960, PhD, 1967; MA, U. Ky., 1962. Archeologist Nat. Park Svc. Southwest Archeol. Ctr., Globe and Tucson, Ariz., 1967-75; exec., camp dir. YMCA of Metro. Tucson, 1976-77; asst. dir. Kit Carson Meml. Found., Taos, N.Mex., 1978; co-dir. Las Palomas de Taos, 1979; archeologist Nat. Forest Svc., Carson Nat. Forest, Taos, 1980-99, Taos Ski Valley, 2000—05. Exec. order cons. U.S. Sec. Interior, 1973-75. Author: The Salado Culture in Southwestern Prehistory, 1967; co-author: Excavation of Mound 7, 1981, First-Day Road Log in Tectonic Development of the Southern Sangre de Cristo Mountains, 1990, The Gila Pueblo Salado, 1997. Active YMCA White Rag Soc. Grantee NEH, 1978; Ariz. Wilson Found., NSF, Ky. Rsch. Found. fellow, 1960-62; Baird Found., Bausch and Lomb, Elks; recipient cert. merit USDA, 1987, 89. Fellow AAAS, Am. Anthrop. Assn., Explorers Club, Royal Anthrop. Inst.; mem. Am. Com. for Preservation of Archaeological Collection, Current Anthropology Ariz. Archaeol. and Hist. Soc., Ariz. Hist. Soc., Friends of Taos Pub. Libr., New Mex. Heritage Preservation Alliance, Soc. Hist. Archaeology, Soc. Am. Archaeology, Southwest Forest Svc. Amigos, Millicent Rogers Mus., Pinal County Hist. Soc. (life), Taos Archaeol. Soc., Taos County Hist. Soc. (bd. dirs.), Taos Hist. Mus., Sigma Xi, Phi Beta Kappa, Alpha Kappa Delta, Phi Kappa Phi, Delta Chi, Pershing Rifles. Home: HCR 74 Box 24826 El Prado NM 87529-9549 Home Phone: 575-776-8336.

YOUNG, JONATHAN, lawyer; BA in Govt. magna cum laude, U. Va., 1979; JD, Georgetown U., 1983. Law clk. to Hon. Caleb M. Wright US Dist. Ct. of Del.; trial atty. civil divsn. US Dept. Justice, Washington; atty. Anderson Kill & Olick PC, Shea & Gould, 1994—98; ptnr. Reed Smith LLP, NYC, 1998—, mem. exec. com. Office: Reed Smith 599 Lexington Ave 29th Fl New York NY 10022 Office Phone: 212-521-5414. Fax: 212-521-5450. Business E-Mail: jyoung@reedsmith.com.

YOUNG, JUDITH A., retired mathematics professor; d. Milton A. and Mary T. Kludt; m. Richard F. Young; children: Nathan R., Nicholas J., Timothy J. EdM, Viterbo U., La Crosse, Wis., 2003. Cert. math. tchr. State Wis., 1973. Math., sci. tchr. Sparta Jr. HS, Wis., 1974—78; math. tchr. Logan HS, La Crosse, 1981—2007; lectr. U. Wis., 2007—08. Recipient Tech. award, Tandy Corp., 1994—95, Achievement award, Am. Math. Assoc., 1999. Office Phone: 608-785-8383. Business E-Mail: young.judy@uwlax.edu.

YOUNG, JUDITH ANNE, animal conservationist; b. LA, Feb. 11, 1953; d. John Mahlstedt Young and Cynthia Sheilds Tunniciff. CEO Otter Conservation Ctr., Statesboro, Ga., 1983—. Copyright U.S. Govt., 1995. Avocations: gardening, agriculture. Office Phone: 912-839-2100. Personal E-mail: judy@g-net.net.

YOUNG, JUNE HURLEY, elementary school educator, writer; b. Cleve., Jan. 30, 1932; d. Albro C. Ching and Helen M. Walker; m. John Robert Young, Feb. 17, 1977 (dec.); children: Sean K. Hurley, Kathleen Hurley Coker. BA in Edn. cum laude, Fla. State U., 1953; Master's, U. So. Fla., 1979. Cert. tchr. Fla. Tchr. grade 5 Norwood Elem. Sch.; tchr. grades 5 and 6 Pasadena Elem. Sch., tchr. grade 1; tchr. kindergarten Romper Room TV, 1964—80, Kindergarten Corners', WEDU-TV, 1985, Baypoint Elem. Sch.; tchr. gifted and talented 16th St. Mid. Sch., 1987; realtor Frank T. Hurley Assocs., Realtor, Inc., 1950—2008. Mktg. dir., adminstrv. asst. Cohutta Lodge, Chatsorth, Ga., 2007. Author: The Don CeSar Story, 1975, 8th edit., 2007, How to Be Your Child's Best Teacher, 1980, Florida's Pinellas Peninsula, 1985, rev. edit., 1998, The Vinoy-Faded Glory Renewed, 1999, Don't Tell Me I Can't Do It, 2008; contbr. articles to newspapers. Pres. St. Petersburg Coterie, 1953—61, Pan Hellenic, St. Petersburg, 1965—67; chmn. Save the Don CeSar Hotel Com., St. Petersburg, 1971—72. Recipient Outstanding Woman Vol. award, Eckerd Drug Co., 2000; nominee Outstanding Tchr., 1957; grantee, Fla. Endowment of Arts, 1980—83. Mem.: Suntan Art Assn., Racquette Jewis Club (pres. 2009—), Camp Farthest Out (sec.-leader 1980—2006), Pass-a-Grille Woman's Club (chorus mem. 1999—2005), Phi Kappa Phi. Republican. Methodist. Avocations: watercolor painting, designing glass jewelry. Home: 342 89th Ave NE Saint Petersburg FL 33702 Home Phone: 727-577-0994; Office Phone: 706-695-9601, 727-367-1949. Personal E-mail: junecyy@aol.com.

YOUNG, LARRY ALLEN, aerospace engineer; s. Donald Lee Young and Cora Arlene Springer; m. Stephanie Ruth Martin, Apr. 18, 1984; 1 child, Courtney Shigeyo. MS in Mech. Engring., Wash. State U., Pullman, 1982. Aerospace engr. NASA, Moffett Field, Calif., 1982—. Contbr. articles to profl. sci. jours. Recipient Grover E. Bell award, Am. Helicopter Soc., 1998. Fellow: AIAA (assoc.).

YOUNG, LAURA, choreographer, educator; b. Boston, Aug. 5, 1947; d. James Vincent and Adelaide Janet Young; m. Anthony Charles Catanzaro, Sept. 26, 1970 (div. Nov. 1981); m. Christopher Edward Mehl, Aug. 23, 1987. Grad. H.S., Cohasset, Mass. Dancer Met. Opera Ballet, NYC, 1971-73, Boston Ballet Co., 1963-65, prin. dancer, 1965-71, 73-89, ballet mistress, 1989-91. Guest tchr. Dance Tchrs. Club Boston, 1978—82, Dance Masters Assn., 1979, 90, 92, 93, Walnut Hill Sch., Natick, Mass., 1984—87, Natick, 1990—91, Granite State Ballet, 1993, Portland Ballet, Maine, Nat. Dance Theatre Bermuda, 1993, Worcester Performing Arts Sch., Mass., 1994, Alwin Sch. Dance Summer Intensive, Albuquerque, 1994—95, Ashland Youth Ballet, Ky., 1995, N.E. Regional Festival, 1996, Okla. Summer Arts Inst., 2000, Pitts. Ballet Theater Summer Program, 2000; asst. dir. Boston Ballet II, 1984—86, tchr., dir., 1986—96, dir. Summer Dance Program, 1986—94; dir. DanceLab, 2001—; 1st hon. mem. Dance Masters Assn., Chpt. 5, 1992; mem. faculty Boston Conservatory, 1990—94, Boston Ballet Sch., 2004—, prin., 1993—2004. Choreographer (ballets) Occasional Waltzes, 1984, Albinoni Suite, 1986, Champ Dances, 1987, A Place of Sound and Mind, 1988, Deadlock, 1989, Rumpelstiltskin, 1989. Recipient Leadership award Greater Boston C. of C., 1987; named Disting. Bostonian Boston's 350th Jubilee Com., 1980. Mem. Am. Guild Mus. Artists, Dance Masters Am. (hon.). Office: Boston Ballet Co 19 Clarendon St Boston MA 02116-6100 Office Phone: 617-456-6250. Business E-Mail: lyoung@bostonballet.com.

YOUNG, LAURENCE RETMAN, biomedical engineer, educator; b. NYC, Dec. 19, 1935; s. Benjamin and Bess (Retman) Y.; m. Joan Marie Fisher, June 12, 1960; children: Eliot Fisher, Leslie Ann, Robert Retman. AB, Amherst Coll., 1957; SB, MIT, 1957, SM, 1959, ScD, 1962; Certificat de License (French Govt. fellow), Faculty of Sci. U. of Paris, France, 1958. Registered profl. engr., Mass. Engr. Sperry Gyroscope Co., Great Neck, NY, 1957; engr. NASA Instrumentation Lab., MIT, 1958-60, asst. prof. aero. and astronautics, 1962-67, assoc. prof., 1967-70, prof., 1970—, payload specialist spacelab life sci., 1991-93; Apollo Program prof., chair in astronautics MIT, Cambridge, 1995—; prof. Baylor Coll. Medicine, Houston, 1996—2003; prof. of health sci. and tech. Harvard MIT, 2003—. Dir. Nat. Space Biomed. Rsch. Inst., 1997-01; summer lectr. U. Ala., Huntsville, 1966-68; lectr. Med. Sch. Harvard U., 1970-78; mem. tng. com. biomed. engring. NIH, 1971-73; mem. com. space medicine and biology Space Sci. Bd., NAS, 1974-77, chmn. vestibular panel summer study of life scis. in space, 1977; mem. com. engring. and clin. care NAE, 1970; mem. Air Force Sci. Adv. Bd., 1979-85; mem. Air Force Studies Bd., NRC, 1982, Aeros. and Space Engrs. Bd., 1982-87; mem. NRC Com. on Space Sta., 1987, 1991—, Com. on Human Exploration Space, 1990, Com. on Human Factors,

1990—; CHABA coun. NASA Task Force on Sci. Uses of Space Sta., 1982-85; vis. prof. Swiss Fed. Inst. Tech., Zurich, 1972-73, Conservatoire Nationale des Arts and Metiers, Paris, 1972-73, Stanford U., 1987-88; vis. scientist Kantonsspital Zurich, 1972-73; prin. investigator vestibular expts. on Spacelabs— 1, SLS-1, 2 and D-1, 1977—; cons. Applied Sci. Lab., NASA, Gulf & Western, Link div. Singer Co., Boeing, Lockheed, others; payload specialist Space Shuttle STS-58 (Spacelab SLS-2), NASA Johnson Space Ctr., 1992—; vis. prof. Coll. de France, Paris, 2003. Contbg. author: chpt. on vestibular system Medical Physiology, 1974, Handbook of Physiology, 1983, Encyclopedia of Neuroscience, 1987; editorial bd. chpt. on vestibular system Internat. Jour. Man-Machine Studies, 1966-75, Neurosci., 1976-92; contbr. numerous articles to profl. jours. Recipient Pub. Svc. Group Achievement award NASA, 1984, Exceptional Civilian Svc. award USAR, 1985, Koetser Found. prize, 1998. Fellow IEEE (Franklin V. Taylor award 1963, First Ann. Space Life Sci. lectr. 1990), AIAA (Dryden lectr. 1981), Aerospace Medical Assn. (Jeffries Medical Rsch. award 1992), Aerospace Human Factor Assn. (Paul Hensen award 1995), Am. Inst. Med. and Biol. Engring., US Ski Assn. (award of merit 1976), Explorers Club; mem. NAE, Inst. Medicine, Am. Physiol. Soc. (1st lectr. in aerospace life scis. 1990), Biomed. Engring. Soc. (founding/charter mem., dir. 1972-75, pres. 1979-80, Alza lectr. 1984), Aerospace Med. Assn., ASTM (com. on snow skiing 1975—, chmn. 1988-93), Internat. Soc. Skiing Safety (bd. dirs. 1977-85), Internat. Fedn. Automatic Control (tech. com. biomed. engring. 1975-85), AIAA (working group for simulator facilities 1976-80), Nat. Acad. Engrs., Inst. Medicine, Internat. Acad. Astronautics (corr.), Aerospace Medicine and Medicine Extreme Environments (standing com., nominated 2007), TU Delft (promotor, doctorate supr., 2007), Barany Soc., Cosmos Club, Tau Beta Pi. Achievements include research in instrumentation and basic and applied research in field of vestibular function; psychophysical work on semicircular canal and otolith function led to models which are applied to flight simulator motion control and are being extended to include visually-induced motion effects; ski injurys. Home: 217 Thorndike St Apt 108 Cambridge MA 02141-1504 Office: MIT Man-Vehicle Lab Rm 37-219 Cambridge MA 02139 Business E-Mail: lry@mit.edu.

YOUNG, LORETTA ANN, auditor; b. Reading, Pa., Dec. 2, 1962; d. Milton and Delois Jean (Ridley) Y. BS, Towson U., Md., 1985. CPA, cert. fin. svcs. auditor, internal auditor. Auditor Irving Burton Assocs., Inc., Washington, 1984-88; tax technician Gen. Bus. Svcs., Germantown, Md., 1989; auditor Montgomery County Govt., Rockville, Md., 1989-90; dir. membership devel. Nat. Forum for Black Pub. Adminstrs., Washington, 1990-91; sr. acct.-analyst Cox & Assocs. CPAs, P.C., Hyattsville, Md., 1992; mgr. ops. LKA Computer Cons., Inc., Hyattsville, 1992-94; supervisory auditor Office Specialists, Inc., Washington, 1994-97; sr. auditor Amtrak, Washington, 1997-2000; sr. mgr. Deloitte & Touche, 2000—05, Unisys, 2005—. Mem. AICPA, Inst. Internal Auditors, Md. Assn. CPAs., Assn. Govt. Accts. Home: PO Box 479 Germantown MD 20875-0479 Office: 11720 Plz Am Dr Reston VA 20190 Personal E-mail: lyoungcpa@aol.com. Business E-Mail: Loretta.Young@unisys.com.

YOUNG, LUCIA PATAT, psychotherapist; b. Charleston, SC, Aug. 19, 1947; d. Leon Philip and Amelia (Wallace) P.; m. David Michael Young, Sept. 2, 1972; children: David Michael II, Allison Amelia. BS, U. S.C., 1969; MEd, EdS, U. Fla., 1991, PhD, 1996. Lic. mental health counselor Nat. Bd. Cert. Counselors. Mental health assoc. Med. U. SC, Charleston, 1969; exec. sec. Mass. Gen. Hosp., Boston, 1969-73, sr. biol. and biochem. technician dept. neurology, summer 1974; adminstrv. asst. Harvard U., Cambridge, Mass., 1973-74; tchr. biology, anatomy and physiology Brimmer & May Sch., Chestnut Hill, Mass., 1974-76; mng. editl. asst. Molecular and Cellular Biochemistry, Gainesville, Fla., 1982-86; adminstrv. asst. U. Fla. Found., Gainesville, Fla., 1986-89; addictions counselor Bridge House Residential Ctr., Gainesville, 1990-91; family therapy internship; sch. guidance counselor Trenton Middle and HS, Fla., 1991-92; mental health counselor, children's outpatient dept. Mental Health Svcs., Gainesville, 1992-93; children's bereavement counselor, family counselor Hospice of N. Ctrl. Fla., Gainesville, 1993-96; pvt. practice Gainesville, 1996—2000, Gloucester, Mass., 2000—01, Ellsworth, Maine, 2001—; trauma therapist Arbour Trauma Counseling Ctr., Allston, Mass., 2000—01. Mem. AAAS, Am. Assn. Marriage and Family Therapy, Internat. Assn. Eating Disorders Profls., Nat. Bd. Cert. Counselors, Eye Movement Desensitization and Reprocessing, Internat. Assn., Kappa Delta Pi, Chi Sigma Iota. Office: 114 State St Ellsworth ME 04605 Home: Po Box 408 Sullivan ME 04664-0408 Office Phone: 207-667-4334. Personal E-mail: luciayoungly@yahoo.com.

YOUNG, LUCY CLEAVER, retired physician; b. Aug. 8, 1943; d. Oliver B. and Ada (Smith) Cleaver; m. Lynn H. Young, Feb. 4, 1968 (div. 1977); m. Lynn H. Young, Apr. 2, 1986; 1 child, Clinton Oliver. BS in Chemistry, Wheaton Coll., Ill., 1965; MD, Ohio State U., 1969. Diplomate Am. Bd. Family Practice, Bd. Ins. Medicine. Rotating intern Riverside Meth. Hosp., Columbus, Ohio, 1969—70; resident Trumbull Meml. Hosp., Warren, Ohio, 1970—71; practice medicine specializing in family practice West Chicago, Ill., 1971—73, Paw Paw and Mendota, Ill., 1973—78; co-founder, med. dir. Wholistic Health Ctr. of Mendota, 1976—78; asst. med. dir. Gt. Lakes head office Met. Life Ins. Co., Aurora, Ill., 1979—80; med. dir. Commonwealth Life Ins. Co., Louisville, 1980—85; locum tenens family practice Kron Med. Corp. of Chapel Hill, NC, 1986—89; physician Red Bird Mission & Med. Ctr., Beverly, Ky., 1989—90; family practice floater Ochsner Clinic satellites, New Orleans, 1990—2006; ret. Assoc. prof. U. Ill. Abraham Lincoln Sch. Medicine, 1976-79; faculty monitor MacNeal Meml. Hosp. Family Practice Ctr. (Ill.), 1979-80; faculty preceptor U. Louisville Family Practice Dept., 1981-85; clin. faculty preceptor La. State U. Sch. Medicine, 1992-2006; mem. staffs Ctrl. DuPage Hosp., Winfield, Ill., 1971-73, Mendota Cmty. Hosp., 1973-80, Ochsner Found. Hosp., New Orleans, 1991-2006; musician La. Via de Cristo, 2003-05. Vol. Red Bird Med. Ctr., 1985—2006; part-time worship coord. Hosanna Luth. Ch., Mandeville, La., 1996-97; musician, lay preacher, nursing home visitor, 1990—2006; musician, lay preacher St. Mathew, Lake Luth. Ch., Beaton, Ky., 2006-. Fellow Am. Acad. Family Practice; mem. Christian Med. and Dental Assns. (del. to Ho. 1995-2000). Lutheran. Home: PO Box 187 239 Jetty Dr #6-27 Grand Rivers KY 42045-0187

YOUNG, LYNDA JEANNE, dental educator, director; d. Roy Clarence and Jeanne Elizabeth Enroth; m. Ronald Joseph Young, Mar. 15, 2008; children: Karna Lynn, Eric Peter. BS, U. Minn., Mpls., 1974, MA, 1980, candidate, 2008. Dir., continuing dental edn. U. Minn., 1984—, assoc. prof., dental sch., 1984—. Cons., nat. com. continuing edn. ADA, Chgo., 1980—83; pres. Minn. Dental Hygienists Assn., St. Paul, 1982—83; mem. Minn. Bd. Dentistry, St. Paul, 1985—92, officer, 1985—92; mem., com. nat. bds. Am. Dental Hygienists Assn., Chgo., 1993—98; pres. Assn. Continuing Dental Edn., Chapel Hill, NC, 2006—07. Contbr. articles to profl. jours. Office: Univ Minn Dental Sch 6-406 Moos Tower Minneapolis MN 55455

YOUNG, MARGARET LABASH, librarian, information consultant, editor; b. Bridgeport, Conn., Aug. 17, 1926; d. George and Mary (Feltovic) Labash; m. Harold Chester Young, June 7, 1958 (div. July 1991); children: Jeffery Avery, Amy Margaret. BA, Cornell U., 1948; AMLS, U. Mich., 1959. Mktg. grader Harvard Bus. Sch., Boston, 1949-52; ops. rsch. sales asst. Arthur D. Little, Inc., Boston, 1953-57; reference libr. U. Mich., Dearborn, 1959-62; editor Gale Rsch., Detroit, 1964-74, Mpls., 1977-88; libr. Salzburg (Austria) Seminar, 1981-83; editor, info. cons. self employed, Hopkins, Minn., 1989—. Tax libr. cons. KPMG Peat Marwick, LLP, Mpls., 1991—; indexer Small Bus. Innovation Rsch., Minn. Project Innovation, Mpls., 1990-97. Co-editor: Directory of Special Libraries and Information Centers, edits. 3-6, 1974-81, Life Sciences Organizations and Agencies Directory, 1988; editor: Scientific and Technical Organizations and Agencies Directory, 1985, 2d edit., 1987. Host family Am. Field Svcs., 1979-80, 80-81; mem. steering com. Twin Cities Internat. Citizens Award, 1996-99. Mem. Spl. Librs. Assn. (internat. rels. chair Minn. chpt. 1994—2003, Quality in Action award, Minn. Chpt. Spl. Librs. Assn., 2003, Fannie Simon award Pub. divsn. 1989), Am. Soc. Indexers, Beta Phi Mu. Democrat. Episcopalian. Avocations: travel, gardening, classical music, dance, aerobics. Home: 313 Farmdale Rd W Hopkins MN 55343-7111 Home Phone: 952-933-5062.

YOUNG, MARK PHILIP, allergist; b. NYC, May 30, 1954; MD, U. Ctrl. Del Caribe, 1982. Cert. Am. Bd. Allergy/Immunology. Resident pediat. Miami Children's Hosp., 1983—86, former assoc. dir. Department of Allergy/Immunology; fellowship allergy and immunology Emory U., Atlanta, 1986—87, Georgetown U., 1987—88; pvt. practice Asthma & Allergy Assocs. of Fla., PA, Miami. Fellow: Am. Coll. Allergy, Asthma and Immunology; mem.: Fla. Allergy Asthma and Immunology Soc. Office: Asthma & Allergy Assocs of Fla, PA 7800 SW 87th Ave, Ste C-340 Miami FL 33173 Office Phone: 305-595-0109. Office Fax: 305-595-7092.

YOUNG, MARK R., lawyer, hospitality company executive; With Sullivan & Worcester, Wilmer, Cutler, Pickering, Hale, and Dorr, Staples Inc; assoc. gen. counsel CMGI Inc., Waltham, Mass., 2000—01; asst. v.p., assoc. gen. counsel Reit Mgmt. and Rsch., 2001—06, v.p. leasing, assoc. gen. counsel, 2006; exec. v.p., gen. counsel TravelCenters of Am., 2007—. Office: TravelCenters of Am 24601 Center Ridge Rd Ste 200 Westlake OH 44145-5639

YOUNG, MARK VERNON, sports association executive, lawyer; b. Ridley Park, Pa., 1958; m. Regi Young; children: Jack, Mark. BBA, U. Fla., 1979; JD, U. Fla. Levin Coll. Law, 1982. Atty. Smith Hulsey and Busey; sr. atty. The Charter Co.; exec. v.p., gen. counsel Assn. Tennis Professionals (ATP), Ponte Vedra Beach, Fla., 1990—, CEO ATP Americas, 2006—. Bd. mem. First Serve. Office: ATP World Tour 201 ATP Tour Blvd Ponte Vedra Beach FL 32082 Office Phone: 904-285-8000. Office Fax: 904-285-5966.*

YOUNG, MARYANN, humanities educator; d. William Gordon and Masako Burnside; m. Marcus Aaron Young, Aug. 7, 2004; 1 child, Rai Yun-Taek. MA in Humanities, U. Tex.-Dallas, Richardson. Lectr. arts, lang., and lit. Eastfield Coll., Mesquite, Tex., 2006—, co-chair Asian-Am., mid. eastern-Am. studies; sr. lectr. in arts & humanities U. Tex.-Dallas, 2008—. Mem.: Soc. Ethnomusicology, Japan-Am. Soc. DFW, Assn. Asian Studies. Business E-Mail: maryann@utdallas.edu.

YOUNG, MERWIN CRAWFORD, political science professor; b. Phila., Nov. 7, 1931; s. Ralph Aubrey and Louise (Merwin) Y.; m. Rebecca Conrad, Aug. 17, 1957; children: Eva Colcord, Louise Conrad, Estelle Merwin, Emily Harriet. BA, U. Mich., 1953; postgrad., Inst. Hist. Rsch. U. London, 1955-56, Inst d'Etudes Politiques, U. Paris, 1956-57; PhD, Harvard U., 1964; DSc (hon.), Fla. Internat. U., 1998. Asst. prof. polit. sci. U. Wis., Madison, 1963-66, assoc. prof., 1966-69, prof., 1969—2001, emeritus, 2001—, Rupert Emerson prof., 1983; H. Edwin Young prof., 1994; chmn. African Studies Program U. Wis., Madison, 1964-68, chmn. dept. polit. sci., 1969-72, 84-87, assoc. dean Grad. Sch., 1968-71, acting dean Coll. Letters and Sci., 1992-93. Vis. prof. Makerere U. Coll., Kampala, Uganda, 1965-66; dean Faculty of Social Sci. Nat. U., Lubumbashi, Zaire, 1973-75; Fulbright prof. U. Dakar, Senegal, 1987-88. Author: Politics in the Congo, 1965, The Politics of Cultural Pluralism, 1976 (Herskovits prize 1977, Ralph Bunche prize 1979), Ideology and Development in Africa, 1982, The African Colonial State in Comparative Perspective, 1994 (Gregory Luebbert prize 1995); co-author: Cooperatives and Development, 1981, The Rise and Decline of the Zairian State, 1985; editor: The Rising Tide of Cultural Pluralism: The Nation-State at Bay?, 1993, Ethnic Diversity and Public Policy, 1998, The Accommodation of Cultural Diversity, 1999; co-editor: Dilemmas of Democracy in Nigeria, 1995, Beyond State Crisis? Postcolonial Africa and Post-Soviet Eurasia in Comparative Perspective, 2002. Served to 1st lt. U.S. Army, 1953-55. Fellow Woodrow Wilson Internat. Ctr. for Scholars, 1983—84; Social Sci. Rsch. fellow, 1967—68, Ford Faculty fellow, 1972—73, Guggenheim Found. fellow, 1977—78, vis. fellow, Inst. for Advanced Study, Princeton, 1980—81. Mem. AAAS, Am. Acad. Arts and Scis., Am. Polit. Sci. Assn., African Studies Assn. (pres. 1982-83, Disting. Africanist award 1991), Coun. Fgn. Rels. Home: 639 Crandall St Madison WI 53711-1836 Office: U Wis Dept Polit Sci North Hall 1050 Bascom Mall Madison WI 53706-1389 Business E-Mail: young@polisci.wisc.edu.

YOUNG, MICHAEL BRIAN, professional baseball player; b. Covina, Calif., Oct. 19, 1976; s. Fred and Anna Young; m. Cristina Barbosa, Nov. 25, 2000. Student, U. Calif., Santa Barbara. Shortstop Tex. Rangers, 2000—. Mem. US Team World Baseball Classic, 2006. Recipient Harold McKinney Good Guy award, 2003, Gold Glove award, 2008; named All-Star Game MVP, 2006; named to Am. League All-Star Team, Maj. League Baseball, 2004—07, 2009. Achievements include leading the American League in: batting average (.331), hits (221), 2005. Avocations: golf, billiards. Office: c/o Texas Rangers 1000 Ballpark Way Arlington TX 76011*

YOUNG, MICHAEL CHUNG-EN, allergist, immunologist, pediatrician; b. Chgo., July 10, 1953; s. Koon C. and Siu Fun (Hui) Y.; m. Karen Lee Young, Apr. 7, 1979; 1 child, Liane. AB cum laude, Harvard Coll., 1975; MD, Yale U., 1979. Diplomate Am. Bd. Allergy and Immunology, Am. Bd. Pediatrics, Nat. Bd. Med. Examiners. Resident pediat. Children's Hosp., Boston, 1979—82, fellow in allergy and immunology, 1982—84, asst. in medicine (immunology), attending physician, 1984—; clin. instr. pediat. Harvard Med. Sch., Boston, 1985—2001, asst. clin. prof. pediat., 2002—. Mem. active staff South Shore Hosp., South Weymouth, Mass., 1985—. Author: Peanut Allergy Answer Book, 2001, 2d edit., 2006; contbr. articles to profl. jours. Recipient Nat. Rsch. Svc. award, NIH, 1982—84, Mariel C. Furlong award for Making a Difference, Food Allergy & Anaphylaxis Network, 2005; named physician honoree, Asthma and Allergy Found. Am., 2001; named to Guide to Top Doctors, Ctr. for the Study of Svcs. Fellow Am. Coll. Allergy and Immunology (Parke Davis Allergy Fellows award 1983), Am. Acad. Allergy and Immunology, Am. Coll. Chest Physicians, Am. Acad. Pediatrics; mem. New Eng. Soc. Allergy, Mass. Allergy Soc. (pres. 1992-94), Mass. Med. Soc. Office: South Shore Allergy & Asthma Specialists 851 Main St South Weymouth MA 02190-1612

YOUNG, MICHAEL KENT, academic administrator, law educator; b. Sacramento, Nov. 4, 1949; s. Vance Lynn and Ethelyn M. (Sowards) Young; m. Suzan Kay Stewart, June 1, 1972; children: Stewart, Kathryn, Andrew. BA summa cum laude, Brigham Young U., Provo, Utah, 1973; JD magna cum laude, Harvard U., Cambridge, Mass., 1976. Bar: Calif. 1976, NY 1985. Law clk. to Justice Benjamin Kaplan, Supreme Jud. Ct. Mass., Boston, 1976—77; law clk. to Justice William H. Rehnquist U.S. Supreme Ct., Washington, 1977—78; assoc. prof., prof., Fuyo prof. Japanese law Columbia U., NYC, 1978—98, dir. Program Internat. Human Rights and Religious Liberties, 1995—98; dir. Ctr. Japanese Legal Studies and Ctr. for Korean Legal Studies, NYC, 1985—98; dean, Lobingier prof. comparative law and jurisprudence George Washington U. Sch. of Law, Washington, 1998—2004; dep. legal advisor U.S. Dept. State, Washington, 1989—91, dep. under sec. for econ. affairs, 1991—93, amb. for trade and environ. affairs, 1992—93; pres. and prof. law U. Utah, Salt Lake City, 2004—. Mem. US Commn. on Internat. Religious Freedom, 1998—2005, chair, 2001—02, 2002—03, vice chair, 2002—03; vis. scholar law faculty U. Tokyo, 1978—80, 1983; vis. prof. Waseda U., 1989; chmn. bd. advisors Japan Soc., 1996—98; counsel select subcom. on arms transfers to Bosnia US Ho. of Reps., 1996; mem. steering com. Law Profs. for Dole, 1996; mem. com. on internat. jud. rels. US Jud. Conf., 1999—2005; mem. Brown v. Bd. Edn. 50th Anniversary Commemoration Com.; chair NAFTA labor agreement adv. com. Dept. of Labor; mem. trade and environ. policy adv. com. US Trade Rep. Office, 2003—. Author: Fundamentals of U.S. Trade Law, 2001, Japanese Law in Context, 2001, International Environmental Law: Cases, Materials and Problems, 2007. Bd. visitors USAF Acad., 2000—02; bd. govs. East West Ctr.; bd. dirs. Salt Lake C. of C., Envision Utah, Alliance for Unity, Herbert I. and Elsa B. Michael Found., The Craig H. Neilsen Found., Magnet Bank, tanner lectrs. human Vvlues. Recipient Disting. Contbns. to Human Rights award, Ctr. for Internat. Religious Freedom, Brigham Young U., 2005, Excellence in Edn. award, Utah Hispanic C. of C., Excellence in Ethics award, Utah Valley State U., 2005, Internat. Humanitarian award, Pub. Affairs Office, LDS Ch., 2006, Disting. Svc. award, J. Reuben Clark Soc., 2006, The Helping Hand award, Utah Youth Village, 2006, award of Merit and Knighthood Order St. Michael of the Wing, 2007, US Chaina Collaboration Leadership award, Chines Assn. Sci. Tech., 2008, Disting. Svc. award, Brigham Young U., 2008; named Communicator of Yr., Publs. Soc. Am. and Internat. Assn. Bus. Communicators, Internat. Leader of Yr., World Trade Assn., 2008; POSCO Rsch. Inst. fellow, 1995—98, Japan Found. fellow, 1979—80, Fulbright fellow, 1983—84. Fellow: Am. Bar Found.; mem.: SkyWest Inc. (bd. dirs. 2009—), Coun. Fgn. Rels. Mem. Lds Ch. Avocations: skiing, scuba diving, photography. Home: 1480 Military Way Salt Lake City UT 84103 Office: U Utah 201 S President's Cir Rm 203 Salt Lake City UT 84112 Office Phone: 801-581-5701. Business E-Mail: president@utah.edu.

YOUNG, MICHAEL WARREN, geneticist, educator; b. Miami, Fla., Mar. 28, 1949; s. Lloyd George and Mildred (Tillery) Y.; m. Laurel Ann Eckhardt, Dec. 27, 1978; children: Natalie, Arissa. BA, U. Tex., 1971, PhD, 1975. NIH postdoctoral fellow Stanford (Calif.) U. Med. Sch., 1975-77; asst. prof. genetics Rockefeller U., NYC, 1976—83, assoc. prof., 1984—88, prof., 1988—, Richard and Jeanne Fisher prof., 2004—. Investigator Howard Hughes Med. Inst., N.Y.C., 1987-96; adv. panel on genetic biology NSF, Washington, 1983-87; spl. advisor Am. Cancer Soc., N.Y.C., 1985—; spl. reviewer genetics study sect. NIH, Bethesda, Md., 1990—, cell biology study sect., 1993-97; head Rockefeller unit NSF Sci. and Tech. Ctr. Biol. Timing, 1991-2001; dir. Levy/White Ctr. Mind, Brain and Behavioral Studies Rockefeller U., N.Y.C., 2000-2002, v.p. academic affairs, 2004-. Contbr. articles to profl. jours. Meyer Found. fellow, N.Y.C., 1978-83. Fellow N.Y. Soc. Fellows, Am. Acad. Microbiology; mem. AAAS, Genetics Soc. Am., Am. Soc. Microbiologists, N.Y. Acad. Scis., Harvey Soc., Nat. Acad. Sci., Am. Chem. Soc., Gruber Found.(Neuroscis. prize, 2009) Achievements include research on transposable DNA elements, molecular genetics of nerve and muscle development, biological clocks, molecular control of circadian rhythms. Home: 51 Greenwoods Rd Old Tappan NJ 07675-7018 Office: The Rockefeller Univ 1230 York Ave New York NY 10021-6399

YOUNG, MILES, advertising executive; Degree in Hist., Oxford U., Eng. Various advt. positions Lintas, Allen Brady & Marsh; joined Ogilvy & Mather WPP Grp. PLC, 1983, advt. bd. mem. London, 1986—88, dir. client svcs., 1988—90, mng. dir. Ogilvy & Mather Direct London, 1990, regional dir. Ogilvy & Mather Direct Europe, 1990—95, chmn. Ogilvy & Mather Asia/Pacific Hong Kong, 1995—2008, CEO Ogilvy & Mather Worldwide NYC, 2009—. Bd. dirs., exec. com. Ogilvy & Mather Worldwide, 1995—; vis. prof. Xiamen U., China; co-founder Ogilvy-Tsinghua Prog. Pub. Branding, Tsinghua U., Beijing. Mem. adv. bd. Tsinghua U. Sch. Journalism. Office: Worldwide Plz 309 W 49th St New York NY 10019 Office Phone: 852 2568 1177. Office Fax: 212-237-4000.*

YOUNG, NANCY, lawyer; b. Washington, Dec. 3, 1954; d. John Young and Byounghye Chang; m. Paul Brendan Ford, Jr., May 28, 1983; children: Paul Brendan III, Ian A., Hunter Chang Young, Jade Augustine Young. BA, Yale U., 1975, MA, 1976; JD, Columbia U., 1979. Bar: N.Y. 1981. Assoc. Simpson Thacher & Bartlett, NYC, 1979-82, Richards O'Neil & Allegaert, NYC, 1982-86; ptnr., chair internat. practice group Richards & O'Neil, NYC, 1986-2001; of counsel Bingham McCutchen LLP, NYC, 2001—. Lectr. Am. corp. and securities law Tokyo U. Faculty of Law, 1992. Author: Basic Business Japanese, 1998; contbr. articles to legal publs. Mem. Tribar Legal Opinion Com., 2001—. Named Internat. Woman of Yr., 1992-93. Mem. ABA (co-chmn. conf. minority ptnrs in corp. majority law firms 1992, mem. Triba legal opinion com. 2001-), Assn. Bar of City of N.Y., Coun. on Fgn. Rels., Fgn. Policy Assn. (bd. govs. 1995-2001), Yale U. Alumni Assn. (bd. govs. 1989-92), Columbia U. Law Sch. Assn. (bd. dirs. 1991-92), Columbia U. Alumni Assn. (bd. dirs. 1991-92), Yale Club N.Y. (bd. dirs. 1996-98), Asia Soc. Office: Bingham McCutchen LLP 399 Park Avenue New York NY 10022

YOUNG, NERISSA ANN, journalist; b. Bluefield, W.Va., June 3, 1965; d. James Weldon and Norene Amie (Wallace) Y. BS in edn., Concord Coll., 1987; MA in journalism, Marshall Univ., 1993. Radio personality WMTD Radio, Hinton, W.Va., 1986-88, 89-90; tchr. Monroe County Schs., Union, W.Va., 1988-89, 90-91; journalist The Register-Herald/Beckley Newspapers, W.Va., 1993—2002; employee Okla. State U. Sch. Journalism & Broadcasting, 2002—03, Dept. Mass Comm., Shepherd U., 2004—07, Marshall U. W-Page Pitts. Sch. Journalism & Mass Comm., 2007—. Contbr. articles to profl. jours. Pianist, choir mem., drama dir. Fairview Bapt. Ch., Forest Hill, W.Va., 1982—; camp counselor Summers County 4-H Camp, Hinton, 1985-89, 94-95. Recipient 1st place for crime/ct. coverage W.Va. Press Assn., 1996. Mem. Soc. Profl. Journalists (nat. ethics com. 1995-). Baptist. Avocations: walking, reading, piano, guitar.

YOUNG, PATRICIA JANEAN, speech pathology/audiology services professional; b. San Diego, Nov. 30, 1953; d. Bernarr E. and Janean Romig Young. AA, Palomar C.C., San Marcos, Calif., 1974; BA, Calif. State U., Chico, 1976; MA, Calif. State U., Long Beach, 1981. Cert. clin. competence Am. Speech-Lang.-Hearing Assn., lic. speech pathologist Calif., cert. tchr. Calif. Mgmt. trainee Robinson's Dept. Store, LA, 1976—78; speech and hearing screening coord. Riverview Hearing, Speech, Lang. Ctrs., Long Beach, 1978—81, speech pathologist, 1981—84, Lake Elsinore Unified Sch. Dist., Calif., 1998—; speech pathologist, dir. Speech Pathology Svcs., Carlsbad and Temecula, Calif., 1984—. Prodr. TV shows on comm. disorders Long Beach Cable TV, 1983; coord. pub. svc. announcement and interviewee for Disabilities Awareness Week ABC TV, San Diego, 1986, San Diego, 88. Game inventor: Match This!, 1995; author: (children's book) Bird Boy, 2006; contbr. poetry to lit. publs.;, author. Named to Outstanding Young Women Am. Mem.: Calif. Speech-Lang-Hearing Assn. (region rep., Outstanding Achievement award 1987), Am. Speech-Lang-Hearing Assn., Zeta Tau Alpha. Avocations: writing, theater, decorating. Home: 31935 Calle Espinoza Temecula CA 92592 Office: Lake Elsinore Unified Sch Dist 545 Chaney St Lake Elsinore CA 92530 Home Phone: 951-303-9422; Office Phone: 951-253-7000. Personal E-mail: pjyoung2000@aol.com.

YOUNG, PATRICK, editor, writer; b. Ladysmith, Wis., Oct. 19, 1937; s. Rodney and Janice (Wolf) Y.; m. Leah Ruth Figelman, Oct. 8, 1966; 1 child, Justine Young Gottshall. BA, U. Colo., 1960. Reporter UPI, Washington, 1961-62; journalist USN, 1963-64; staff writer Nat. Observer, Silver Spring, Md., 1965-77; free-lance writer Laurel, Md., 1977-79; mem. sr. staff Pres.'s Commn. on the Accident at Three Mile Island, Washington, 1979; chief sci. and med. writer Newhouse News Svc., Washington, 1980-88; editor Sci. News, Washington, 1988-95; ind. writer, editor, cons., 1995—. Sci. writer in residence U. Wis., 1986. Author: Asthma and Allergies, 1980, Drugs and Pregnancy, 1987, Schizophrenia, 1988; co-author: Keeping Young Athletes Healthy, 1991. With USN, 1963-64. Recipient Howard W. Blakeslee award Am. Heart Assn., 1971, Sci. Writing award in physics and astronomy Am. Inst. Physics, 1974, James T. Grady award Am. Chem. Soc., 1977. Mem. Nat. Assn. Sci. Writers, Nat. Press Club, Am. Assn. Adv. Sci. Home Phone: 301-498-4251; Office Phone: 301-498-4251. Business E-Mail: young@nasw.org.

YOUNG, PAUL ANDREW, anatomist; b. St. Louis, Oct. 3, 1926; s. Nicholas A. and Olive A. (Langford) Y.; m. Catherine Ann Hofmeister, May 14, 1949; children— Paul, Robert, David, Ann, Carol, Richard, James, Steven, Kevin, Michael. BS, St. Louis U., 1947, MS, 1953; PhD, U. Buffalo, 1957. Asst. in anatomy U. Buffalo, 1953, instr. anatomy, 1957; asst. prof. anatomy St. Louis U., 1957, assoc. prof., 1966, prof., 1972—, chmn. dept., 1973—2004, prof. anatomy in surgery, 2004, prof. and chair emeritus, dept. anatomy and neurobiology, 2006. Author: (with B.D. Bhagat and D.E. Biggerstaff) Fundamentals of Visceral Innervation, 1977, (with P.H. Young) Basic Clinical Neuroanatomy, 1996, (with P.H.Young and D.L.Tolbert) Basic Clinical Neuroscience, 2007, also computer assisted neurological anatomy tutorials; contbr. articles to profl. publs. Recipient Preclinical Golden Apple Tchg. award, St. Louis U. Sch. Medicine, 1974, 2000, Outstanding Preclinical, 1981, 1985, 1986, 1991, 1992, tchg. award, St. Louis Acad. Sci., 1993, Emerson Excellence for St. Louis U. faculty, 2001, Acad. Sci. Outstanding Sr. Louis Scientist award, 2008. Mem. Am. Assn. Anatomists, Am. Assn. Clin. Anatomists, Soc. Neurosci., Sigma Xi, Alpha Omega Alpha. Office: St Louis Univ Ctr for Anatomical Science and Education 1402 S Grand Blvd Saint Louis MO 63104-1004 Home Phone: 636-225-1437; Office Phone: 314-977-8025. Personal E-mail: pay1957@gmail.com. Business E-Mail: youngpa@slu.edu.

YOUNG, PETER ROBERT, library director; b. Washington, Aug. 13, 1944; s. Ju Chin and Jane Kathrine (Lybrand) Young; m. Mary Sue Townsend, Mar. 25, 1978; children: Kathryn, Timothy;children from previous marriage: Robert, Jonathan. AB in Philos., Coll. Wooster, Ohio, 1966; MSLS, Columbia U., NYC, 1968. Adminstrv. libr. Am. U. Libr., Washington, 1968; head cataloger, reference libr. Franklin & Marshall Coll. Libr., Lancaster, Pa., 1971-74; asst. libr. pub. svcs. Rice U. Librs., Houston, 1974-76; sales support libr. CL Systems Inc., Newtonville, Mass., 1976-78, libr. systems analyst, 1978-80; asst. dir. Grand Rapids Pub. Libr., Mich., 1978; customer svcs. officer Cataloging Distbn. Svc. Libr. Congress, Washington, 1980-84, asst. chief Marc editl. divsn., 1984-85, chief copyright cataloging divsn., 1985-88; dir. acad. info. svcs. The Faxon Co., Westwood, Mass., 1988-89, dir. Faxon Inst. Advanced Studies Scholarly & Sci. Comm., 1989-90; exec. dir. US Nat. Commn. Librs. & Info. Sci., Washington, 1990-97; chief cataloguing distbn. svc. Libr. Congress, 1997—2001, acting chief Asian div., 2001—02, chief Asian divsn., 2008—; dir. Nat. Agrl. Libr., Beltsville, Md., 2002—. Implementation task force libr. data Nat. Ctr. Edn. Stats. US Office Edn., 1988, coun. edn. stats. Office Edn. Rsch. & Improvement, 90; co-chair libr. stats. standard revision com. Nat. Standards Info. Office, 1989—93; adv. bd. Highsmith Press, 1991—99; exec. bd. Fed. Libr. & Info. Ctr. Com., 1993—96. Mem. editl. bd. Serials Review; contbr. articles to profl. jours. Mem. stats. task force US Nat. Commn. Librs. & Info. Sci., 1988—89. Served with US Army, 1968—70, Vietnam. Decorated Bronze Star (3) US Army. Mem.: ALA (pub. librs. policy com., rsch./stats. com.), Chinese Am. Libr. Assn. (chair pub. rels. com. 1987—88, pres. 1989—90). Office: Nat Agrl Library Abraham Lincoln Bldg 10301 Baltimore Ave Beltsville MD 20705-2351*

YOUNG, PHYLLIS CASSELMAN, music educator; b. Milan, Kans., Oct. 20, 1925; d. Phillip James and Velma (Stewart) Casselman; m. James M. Young, July 14, 1945 (dec. Sept. 1991). MusB with high honors, U. Tex., 1949, MusM, 1950. Tchr. string instruments Kansas City (Kans.) Pub. Schs., 1951-52; prof. cello and string pedagogy U. Tex., Austin, 1953—; dir. U. Tex. String Project, Austin, 1958-93; Parker C. Fielder Regents prof. music U. Tex., Austin, 1991—. Presenter numerous workshops and master classes, 1976—. Author: Playing the String Game, 1978, The String Play, 1986; also articles. Mem. Am. String Tchrs. Assn. (state pres. 1972-74, nat. pres. 1978-80, Nat. citation 1974, 82, Disting. Svc. award 1984, Paul Rolland Lifetime Achievement award 2002), European String Tchrs. Assn. (hon. mem. Brit. br.), Music Educators Nat. Conf., Suzuki Assn. Ams., Tex. Music Educators Assn. Home: 7304 W Rim Dr Austin TX 78731-2043 Office: Sch Music Univ Tex Austin TX 78712 Home Phone: 512-345-1498. Business E-Mail: phyllis@mail.utexas.edu.

YOUNG, RAY G., automotive executive; B in Bus. Adminstrn., U. Western Ontario, 1984; M Bus. Adminstrn., U. Chgo., 1986. Joined GM Can., 1986, dir. capital markets and fgn. exchange, 1988—93; regional treas. GM Europe, Brussels, 1993—96; v.p. fin. CAMI Automotive, 1996—2001; v.p., CFO GM N. Am., Detroit, 2001—04; pres., mng. dir. GM do Brasil, 2004—07; group v.p. fin. GM Corp., Detroit, 2007—08, exec. v.p., CFO, 2008—. Office: GM Corp 300 Renaissance Ctr Detroit MI 48265-3000*

YOUNG, RAYMOND HENRY, lawyer; b. Boston, Sept. 28, 1927; s. Raymond H. and Clara Elms (Oakman) Y.; m. Louisa Breda, Sept. 1, 1951; children: Christopher, Pamela, Amy. AB, Yale U., 1947, LLB, 1950. Bar: Mass. 1951. Assoc. Warner, Stackpole, Stetson & Bradlee, Boston, 1950-52; pvt. practice Boston, 1952-64; ptnr. Young & Bayle, Boston, 1964—. Mem. ABA (past sec. sect. real property, probate and trust law, mem. commn. legal problems of the elderly), Am. Coll. Trust and Estate Counsel (mem. joint editorial bd. for trust and estate acts, 1988-2007, emeritus 2007-), Am. Law Inst. (advisor for restatement property 3d donative transfers, cons. restatement trusts 3d), Nat. Commn. on Nat. Probate Ct. Standards, Internat. Acad. Trust and Estate Law (past pres.), Mass. Bar Assn., Boston Bar Assn. (past pres.), Boston Estate Planning Coun. (past pres., Estate Planner of Yr. award 1991), Boston Probate and Estate Planning Forum. Home: 122 Garfield St Watertown MA 02472-4916

YOUNG, RICHARD WILLIAM, chemicals executive; b. Ridgewood, NY, Oct. 17, 1926; s. Charles Michael and Louise Margaret (Baust) Y.; m. Sheila deLisser, Sept. 11, 1949; children: Christine, Noreen, Brian, Eileen. AB, Dartmouth Coll., 1946, A.M., 1947; PhD, Columbia U., 1950; DSc (hon.), Regis Coll., 2002. Sr. rsch. chemist Chemotherapy div. Am. Cyanamid Co., Conn., 1950-56, group leader pesticide chems. Agrl. div. Conn., 1956-58, dir. chem. Agrl. div. Conn., 1958-60, dir. chem. rsch. cen. rsch. div. Conn., 1960-62; asst. dir. rsch. Polaroid Corp., Cambridge, Mass., 1962-69, v.p., 1963-69, sr. v.p. rsch. and devel., 1969-72, sr. v.p., pres. Internat. div., 1972-80, exec. v.p., dir. worldwide mktg., 1980-82; pres. Houghton Mifflin Co., Boston, 1982-85; chmn., CEO Mentor O & O, Inc., Norwell, Mass., 1985-92. Bd. dirs. Bay State Milling Corp., Quincy, Mass., Instron Corp., Canton, Mass., Oceantrawl Inc., Seattle, Mentor Corp., Santa Barbara, Calif. Patentee in field. Chmn. bd. trustees Regis Coll., Weston, Mass.; trustee Mass. Eye and Ear Infirmary, Boston, 1963-90, Trinitas Found., Quincy; mem. corp. Northeastern U., Boston, 1960-92; bd. dirs. Martin Meml. Hosp. Found., 2002—. Mem. Am. Chem. Soc. Office: Trinitas Found 100 Congress St Quincy MA 02169-0906 Home: 865 Central Ave Apt N-508 Needham MA 02492-1393 Office Phone: 617-328-4400 ext. 273. Personal E-mail: rwy1926@aol.com.

YOUNG, ROBERT BOND, lawyer; b. Phila., May 18, 1943; s. Robert A. and Anna Battelle (Bond) Y.; m. Karen Alexander, June 17, 1966; children: Jeffrey A., Randall C. BA, Denison U., 1965; JD, Ohio State U., 1969. Bar: Ohio 1969, U.S. Dist. Ct. (so. dist.) Ohio 1970, Del. 1975, U.S. Dist. Ct. Del. 1976, U.S. Supreme Ct. 1978, U.S. Ct. Appeals (3d cir.) 1986. Assoc. Young & Alexander, Dayton, Ohio, 1969-72, ptnr., 1973-75; pvt. practice Dover, Del., 1975-84, 1992—; sr. ptnr. Young & Sherlock, Dover, 1985-92. Adj. prof. bus. law Del. Community Coll., Dover, 1975-79; adj. prof. ins. law Wesley Coll., Dover, 1993—; pres. Overseas Fiber Export Corp., Dover, 1978—. Author: (light verse/text book) Grappling With Grammar, 1976, (musical comedies) To The Revolution, 1976, MacBeth: A Family Musical, 1977, O, 1978, Swarthmore Fight Song, 1989, Calibants Rage. Mgr. Dover Little League, 1978-87, Sr. League All-Star mgr., 1984, 86, bd. dirs. 1982, 84; bd. dirs. Del. Soc. Prevention Cruelty to Animals, 1980. Mem. ABA, Am. Bd. Trial Lawyers (Del. chpt. pres. elect 1991-93, pres. 1993-95), Def. Rsch. Inst., Del. State Bar Assn. (pres. 2004), Assn. Def. Trial Advocates, Terry Carey Am. Inn of Ct. (master 1991—, counselor 1994-95). Avocations: youth sports, creative writing.

YOUNG, ROBERT CRAIG, banker; b. NYC, Mar. 15, 1960; s. Robert J. and Gloria L. (Sandhop) Y.; m. Anke Ott, Dec. 2, 2000. BS cum laude, NYU, 1982, MBA, 1985. Asst. v.p. Chem. Bank, NYC, 1982-86; project mgr. GE Credit Corp., Stamford, Conn., 1986-87; dir. Merrill Lynch & Co., NYC, 1987-94; sr. v.p. Greenwich (Conn.) Capital Markets, Inc., 1994-97; mng. dir. Nomura Securities, NYC, 1997-2001, Macquarie, NYC, 2001—. Home: 98 Revere Rd Manhasset NY 11030-2733 Office: Macquarie 125 West 55th St 16th Fl New York NY 10019 Office Phone: 212-231-1707. E-mail: rcyoung@optonline.net.

YOUNG, ROBERT P., JR., state supreme court justice; B cum laude, Harvard U., 1974, JD, 1977. Atty. Dickinson, Wright, Moon, Van Dusen & Freeman, 1977-1992; v.p., corp. sec., gen. counsel AAA Mich., 1992; judge Mich. Ct. Appeals 1st Dist., 1995—98; justice Mich. Supreme Ct., 1999—. Mem. Mich. Civil Svc. Commn.; bd. trustees Cen. Mich. U. Mem.: ABA, Mich. State Bar Assn., Mich. Supreme Ct. Historical Soc. Office: Mich Supreme Ct PO Box 30052 Lansing MI 48909-7552*

YOUNG, RONALD FARIS, commodities trader; b. Schenectady, Dec. 17, 1939; s. James Vernon and Dorothy (Girod) Y.; m. Anne Randolph Kendig, Feb. 23, 1963; children: Margaret Randolph Reynolds, Anne Corbin Gray. BA, U. Va., 1962; MBA, Harvard U., 1966. Grain trader Continental Grain Co., 1966-70; pres. Conti-Commodities, Chgo., 1970; v.p. commodity sales DuPont, Glore Forgan, Chgo., 1971-72; self-employed commodity trader Chgo. Bd. Trade, 1972-78; ind. trader Va. Trading Co., 1978-90, pres., 1978-84, dep. chmn., 1984-89; pres. Randolph Ptnrs., Ltd., 1983-91. Chmn. bd. Chgo. Bd. Trade, 1978, dir., 1975—77, 1980, 2003. Bd. dirs. Princeton Fund, 1981-82, Lake Forest Hosp., 1981-84, Lake Forest Country Day Sch., 1981-86. Served with USMCR, 1959-65. Mem. Racquet Club (bd. dirs. 1989-97), Onwentsia Club (Lake Forest, Ill., bd. dirs. 1981-90, pres. 1991-93), Everglades Club (Palm Beach, Fla.), Bath and Tennis Club of Palm Beach (bd. dirs. 2007—). Republican. Episcopalian.

YOUNG, RONALD FREDERICK, neurosurgeon; b. Buffalo, Jan. 4, 1939; s. Frederick Earl and Ruth Henrietta (Cowan) Y.; m. Sheila Marie Young, June 23, 1962 (div. 1990); children: Scott Ronald, Anne Louise, Karen Lynn. BA, SUNY, Buffalo, 1961; MD, 1965. Diplomate Am. Bd. Neurol. Surgery. Intern U. Minn Hosp., Mpls., 1965-66; resident in neurosurgery VA Hosp., Longbeach, Calif., 1966-67, SUNY, Syracuse, 1969-73, asst. prof. neurosurgery, 1973-77; assoc. prof. UCLA, 1977-85; prof. neurosurgery U. Calif., Irvine, 1986-93; chief of neurosurgery U. Calif. Med. Ctr., Irvine, 1986-93; clin. prof. U. Calif., Irvine, 1993—98; dir. N.W. Gamma Knife Ctr. and N.W. Neurosci. Inst. Northwest Hosp., Seattle, 1993—; med. dir. Los Robles Hosp. Neuroscience Inst. GAMMA Knite Ctr., Thousand Oaks, Calif., 2006—, Rotating Gamma Inst., Anaheim, Calif., 2008—, Providence St. Joseph's Med. Ctr., Burbank, Calif., 2009—. Elizabeth Crosby Meml. lectr. U. Mich., Ann Arbor, 1990; mem. med. staff Northwest Hosp, Seattle, Los Robles Hosp., Thousand Oaks, Calif., Providence St. Joseph's Med. Ctr., Burbank, Calif. Author: Spinal Cord Injury, 1981; contbr. articles to profl. jours. Capt. USAF M.C., 1967-69. Recipient Kongress medal German Neurosurg. Soc., 1982. Fellow ACS; mem. Western Neurosurg. Soc. (v.p. 1990-91, pres. 1993-94), Am. Acad. Pain Medicine (sec. 1991-93), Am. Assn. Neurol. Surg., Congress Neurol. Surgery, Soc. Neurol. Surgeons, Internat. Leksell Gamma Knife Soc. (chmn. 1995). Avocations: travel, photography, french lessons, horseback riding. Office: Neuroscience Inst Med GRP 637 S Lucas Ave Ste 501 Los Angeles CA 90017 Office Phone: 213-977-4195, 818-783-4949. Personal E-mail: rfy127@hotmail.com.

YOUNG, RUSSELL DAWSON, physicist, consultant; b. Huntington, NY, Aug. 17, 1923; s. C. Halsey and Edna (Dawson) Young; m. Carol Vaughn Jones, Aug. 14, 1954; children: Bessmarie, Gale, Janet, Shari. BS in Physics, Rensselaer Poly. Inst., Troy, NY, 1953; PhD in Physics, Pa. State U., 1959. Rsch. assoc. Pa. State U., State College, 1959-61; project leader Nat. Bur. Stds., Gaithersburg, Md., 1961-73, chief optics and micrometrology, 1973-78, chief mech. processing div., 1975-80, ind. sys. div. chief, 1980-81, chief mech. prodn. div., 1980-81; pres. R.D. Young Cons., Pasadena, Md., 1981—. Contbr. articles to profl. jours.; inventor in field of instrumentation. 1st lt. Signal Corps, U.S. Army, 1943-46. Recipient Edward V. Condon award Dept. Commerce, 1974, Silver medal 1979, Gaede-Langmuir award 1994, Presdl. citation 1986, Washington Acad. Scis. award 1988. Fellow Internat. Inst. Prodn. Engring. Rsch., Nat. Inst. Standards and Tech. Avocation: boating. Home: 10586 Edwardian Ln New Market MD 21774-3219 Personal E-mail: cryoung2@aol.com.

YOUNG, RUTH BROOKS, retired elementary school educator; b. Balt., Aug. 30, 1933; d. Benjamin Franklin and Ora Estelle Brooks; m. David Donald Young Sr., 1952 (dec.); children: David Donald Jr. (dec.), Gerard Brooks Sr., Mark Douglas (dec.), Elizabeth Allyson Mack. BS, Coppin State Tchrs. Coll., 1958; MS, Morgan State Coll., 1975. Cert. tchr., Md. Tchr. Balt. City Pub. Schs., 1958-98, supervising tchr., 1968-72, sch. test coord., 1990-96; ret., 1998. Mem. Phi Delta Kappa. Democrat. Lutheran.

YOUNG, SHAWN, education educator; m. Kimberly Young, July 10, 1999; children: Sydney children: Macyn. BS in Elem. Edn., SE Mo. State U., Cape Girardeau; MS in Ednl. Adminstrn., SW Bapt. U., Bolivar, Mo., degree. Tchr. Fox C-6 Sch. Dist., Arnold, Mo., 1997—2007; assoc. prof. Mineral Area Coll., Park Hills, Mo., 2007—. Mem.: Mo. Assn. Colls. Tchr. Edn., Mo. State Tchrs. Assn. (acad. advisor). Home and Office: Mineral Area Coll 5270 Flat River Rd Park Hills MO 63601

YOUNG, SHELDON MIKE, lawyer, author; b. Cleve., Aug. 27, 1926; s. Jack and Ray Y.; m. Margery Ann Polster, Dec. 25, 1948 (div. 1988); children: Jeffrey, Martin, Janet; m. Bette Abel Roth, Nov. 11, 1988. BA, Ohio State U., 1948, JD, 1951; LLM, Case Western Res. U., 1962. Bar: Ohio 1951, U.S. Dist. Ct. (no. dist.) Ohio. Gen. counsel Eugene M. Klein & Assoc., Actuaries, Cleve., 1952-72; assoc. Shapiro, Persky & Marken, Cleve., 1972-74; counsel pension tech. svcs. dept. CNA Ins., Chgo., 1974-76; ptnr. Weiss & Young, Cleve., 1976; of counsel Arter & Hadden, Cleve., 1977-85, Squire, Sanders & Dempsey, Cleve., 1985-87; pvt. practice Columbus, 1987-91; of counsel Schwartz, Kelm, Warren & Rubenstein, Columbus, 1991—93, Walter & Haverfield, Columbus, 1993—. Instr. Case Western Res. U. Law Sch., 1962-82, 85, U. Akron Law Sch., 1984, 88. Author: Pension and Profit Sharing Plans, 7 vols., 1977-93, (novel) Toledoth-City of Generations, 2003, rev., 2006; freelance writer for newspapers and mags.; contbr. articles to pension jours. Served with USN, WWII. Recipient award Nathan Burkan Meml. Copyright Competition, 1951. Fellow Am. Coll. Employee Benefits Counsel (charter); mem. ABA, Cleve. Bar Assn., Masons. Jewish. Home and Office: Walter & Haverfield 4776 Smoketalk Ln Westerville OH 43081-7838 Home Phone: 614-890-3018; Office Phone: 614-898-1096. Office Fax: 614-898-7190. Personal E-mail: yomike@earthlink.net.

YOUNG, SHERILYN BURNETT, lawyer; b. Providence, Nov. 7, 1953; d. Archie C. III and Hope Burnett; m. Gary Richard Young, Oct. 9, 1977; 3 children. BA, Cornell U., Ithaca, NY, 1975; JD, Franklin Pierce Law Ctr., 1982. Bar: N.H. 1982, U.S. Dist. Ct. N.H. 1982, U.S. Tax Ct. 1983. Assoc. Orr & Reno, P.A., Concord, N.H., 1982-87; founder Rath, Young and Pignatelli, P.C., Concord, 1987—96. Trustee U. Sys. N.H., Concord Hosp., 1991-98; bd. dirs. N.H. Hist. Soc., Franklin Pierce Law Ctr.; legis. counsel to Gov. Gregg, Concord, 1989-90; mem. adv. coun. to ins. commr., 1989-93; spkr. in field. Legal counsel Rudman for U.S. Senate campaign, Concord, 1984-93; bd. dirs. Concord chpt. ARC, 1988-91; mem. N.H. adv. bd. New Eng. Legal Found., 1991-97; pres. Concord Hosp. Assn., 1991-97, bd. dirs. Mem. ABA, NH Bar Assn., New Eng. Coun., Concord C. of C. (bd. dirs. 1988-91), NH Bus. and Industry Assn. (bd. dirs. 2004-), Cornell Club NH. Republican. Avocations: skiing, tennis. Office Phone: 603-226-2600.

YOUNG, STEPHEN BERNARD, urogynecologist, surgeon; b. Bklyn., Apr. 21, 1943; s. Alice Dora (Klein) and Louis Wolf Young; m. Martha Anne Abeles, June 25, 1995; children: Sarah Chi, Ezekiel Elye, Ray Malka. BA, Columbia U., NYC, 1964; MD, George Washington U., 1968. Diplomate Nat. Bd. Med. Examiners, Am. Bd. Ob/Gyn. Fellow vaginal surgery Women and Infants Hosp., Brown U., Providence, 1986—89; prof., ob-gyn., chief urogynecology and reconstructive pelvic surgery U. Mass. Med. Sch., Worcester, 1990—. Tchr. in field, Guatemala, 1994, Beijing, 2005, Beijing, 07, Chennai, India, 06, Chennai, 07. Contbr. articles to profl. jours., chapters to books. Recipient Women and Infants Excellence in Tchg. award, 1984, Clin. Tchg. award, U. Mass., 1994, Faculty Tchg. award, 1996, 2005, Golden Apple Med. Student Tchg. award, 2005—07, Nat. Faculty award, ACOG-CREOG, 2008. Mem.: ACOG, Soc. Gynecologic Surgeons (pres. 2007—), Am. Urogynecologic Soc. (pres. 2004—05, chair sci. program com. 2004, Prize Paper award 2000). Avocations: music, meditation. Office: Univ Mass 119 Belmont St Worcester MA 01605

YOUNG, SUSAN JEAN, music specialist; b. Chgo., Nov. 9, 1940; d. Walter Lawrence and Grace Helen (Blue) Pennie; m. Peter R. Young Jr., June 23, 1962; children: Laura Jane, Beth Ann. B.Mus.Ed (scholar), Northwestern U., 1962; M.Mus.ED (grad.scholar), Am. Conservatory of Music, Chgo., 1974; cert. advanced study in edn. adminstrn., Nat.-Louis U., 1995. Music specialist Skokie (Ill.) Sch. Dist., 1962-63, Northbrook (Ill.) Sch. Dist. # 28, 1974—2003. Lectr. music edn. North Park Coll., 1995-96, Northwestern U., 1997—; pvt. piano tchr., 1963-74; pres. Stevenson High Choral Guild, 1979-81; music dir., choir dir. Wheeling Cmty. Ch., 1981-93; choir dir. Ivanhoe United Ch. of Christ, 1995-96, Cmty. Protestant Ch. Mundelein, Ill., 2004-06; dir. Y'all Come Choir, 1991—; music dir. Northbrook Children's Theatre, 1981-88, Glenview Cmty. Theatre, Northbrook Cmty. Theatre; founder, dir. Y'All Come Choir, Northbrook, Ill., 1989-2009; choir master Evanston Symphony Orch. Festival, 2005-; adj. prof. conducting CCPA Roosevelt U., 2008. Mem. ASCD, Music Educators Nat. Conf., Ill. Music Educators Assn. (chmn. Jr. High Choral Fest 1987-90, Mary E. Hoffman award 2003), Nat. Registered Music Educator, Am. Choral Dirs. Assn., Delta Kappa Gamma (pres. Beta Tau chpt. 1992-96, Ill. State music chmn. 1995-99, 2009-, internat. music rep. 2002-2004), Mu Phi Epsilon Home: 3161 N Southern Hills Dr Wadsworth IL 60083-9289 Personal E-mail: choirmusicsue@yahoo.com. Business E-Mail: susan-young@northwestern.edu.

YOUNG, TERESA GAIL HILGER, retired adult education educator; b. Modesto, Calif., Mar. 4, 1948; d. Richard George and Jessie Dennie (Dennis) Long; m. Charles Ray Young, June 22, 1974; 1 child, Gregory Paul. BS in Edn., Abilene Christian U., Tex., 1970; MEd in Curriculum, Tarleton State U., Stephenville, Tex., 1976; postgrad., Tex. Tech U.,

1990-92. Cert. supr., mid-mgmt., supt., Tex. Tchr. sci. Tex. Youth Coun., Gatesville, 1970-73, Gatesville Ind. Sch. Dist., 1973-81; coord. Edn. and Tng. Ctr., Cen. Tex. Coll., Gatesville, 1983; tchr. Tex. Dept. of Criminal Justice-ID, 1984—2002; ret., 2003. Conf. presenter. Trustee Jonesboro (Tex.) Ind. Sch. Dist., 1988-96. Teacher of the Year for Region II of Tex. Dept. of Criminal Justice, 1997-98. Mem. Am. Fedn. Tchrs., Assn. Tex. Profl. Educators. E-mail: tyoung@htcomp.net.

YOUNG, TERRI L., ophthalmologist; b. Sacramento, 1959; AB in BioChemistry and Sociology, Bowdoin Coll., Brunswick, Maine, 1981; MD in Medicine, Harvard U., 1986. Postdoctoral in pediat. Children's Hosp. Boston, 1986—87; resident in ophthalmology U. Ill., Chgo., 1987—90; clin. instr. ophthalmology U. Ill. Sch. Medicine, Chgo., 1989—90; extern in strabismus and adult motility disorders U. Iowa, 1991; fellow in pediatric ophthalmology, strabismus and adult motility disorders U. Pa. and Children's Hosp. Phila., 1990—92; clin. instr. opthalmology U. Pa., 1990—92; instr. neurobiology and ophthalmology Harvard Med. Sch., 1992—94; asst. prof. ophthalmology U. Minn., 1994—2000, asst. prof. pediat., 1998—2000, assoc. prof. pediat., 2000; dir.Ophthalmic Genetics Rsch. Ctr., Children's Hosp. Phila., 2000—; assoc. prof. ophthalmology and pediat. U. Pa., 2001—. Recipient Surdna Undergrad. Rsch. fellowship, Bowdoin Coll., 1980—81, Stanley J. Sarnoff Soc. Cardiovascular Rsch. award and fellowship, Harvard Med. Sch., 1983—84, Commonwealth Fund Rsch. fellowship, 1985, George and Mary Knox Harvaard Med. Grad. award, 1984, Grad. Kaiser Merit award, Nat. Med. Fellowship, 1986, Keeshin Prize Rsch. award, Inst. Medicine Chgo., 1990, Honor award, Am. Acad. Ophthalmology, 1998, Robert Wood Johnson Faculty Devel. award, 1992—97, Honor award, Am. Acad. Ophthalmology, 1998, Am. Assn. Pediatric Ophthalmology and Strabismus, 2002; selected as part of, NIH's "Changing the Face of Medicine" exhbn., 2003. Fellow: Am. Ophthalmol. Soc. Office: Duke U Eye Ctr Box 3082 2351 Erwin Rd Durham NC 27705 Office Phone: 919-684-0584. Business E-Mail: terri.young@duke.edu.

YOUNG, TODD DEAN, legislative staff member; BA in Polit. Sci., Am. U., Wash., 1995, MA in Polit. Sci., 1996. Comm. dir. for Rep. Doc Hastings US House of Reps., Washington, 2001—03, legis. dir., 2003—05, chief of staff, 2005—, Rep. staff dir. Subcom. on Rules and the Orgn. of House. Office: Office of Congressman Doc Hastings 1203 Longworth House Office Bldg Washington DC 20515*

YOUNG, TONY, councilman; b. Madrid; s. James and Jeanne Young; m. Jacqueline Young. Grad. in Socio-econs., Howard U.; attended, U. San Diego. Intern Congressman Jim Bates; legis. aide to San Diego County Supr. Leon Williams; chief of staff to City Councilman Charles L. Lewis III; councilman, Dist. 4 San Diego City Coun., 2005—, co-chmn. City-County Reinvestment Task Force, vice chair Com. Pub. Safety and Neighborhood Svcs., chmn. Com. on Budget and Fin. Tchr. O'Farrell Middle Sch., San Diego, Muirlands Middle Sch., San Diego. Democrat. Office: 202 C St MS 10A San Diego CA 92101 also: 415 Euclid Ave San Diego CA 92102 Office Phone: 619-236-6644. Office Fax: 619-236-7273. E-mail: anthonyyoung@sandiego.gov.*

YOUNG, VERNON LEROY, plastic surgeon, researcher; b. Oneida, Ky., Oct. 14, 1945; s. Roy Young and Susie Lou; m. Jill Marie Meyer, Mar. 12, 1988; children: Ann Elizabeth, Hunter, Chase, Hampton. BA, U. Ky., Lexington, 1966, MD, 1970. Cert. Am. Bd. Plastic Surgery, 1981. Intern Univ. Ky. Med. Ctr., Lexington, 1970—71, resident in surgery, 1973—77; resident in plastic surgery Barnes Hosp. Washington Univ., St. Louis, 1977—79; William G. Hamm prof. plastic surgery Washington Univ., St. Louis, 1979—2002; pres. Body Aesthetic Plastic Surgery, St. Louis, 2002—. Cons. Cook Biotech, Indpls., 2000—06, Ethicon, NJ, 2003—06; mem. adv. bd. Renovo, Manchester, England, 2006, Aovtech, Sydney, 2006; examiner Am. Bd. Plastic Surgery. Editor (assoc.): Aesthetic Surgery Jour., 2005. Capt. US Army, 1971—73. Mem.: Am. Assn. Plastic Surgery, Am. Soc. for Aesthetic Surgery, Am. Soc. Plastic Surgeons. Episcopalian. Avocation: gardening. Home: 18229 Melrose Rd Wildwood MO 63069 Office: Body Aesthetic Plastic Surgery 969 Mason Rd Saint Louis MO 63141 Office Phone: 314-628-8200. Office Fax: 314-628-9504. Business E-Mail: vlyoungmd@bodyaesthetic.com.

YOUNG, VINCE PAUL, JR., professional football player; b. Houston, June 18, 1983; Student, U. Tex., 2002—06. Quarterback Tenn. Titans, Nashville, 2006—. Recipient Davey O'Brien Nat. Quarterback award, 2005, Manning award, 2005; named Rose Bowl MVP, 2005, 2006, ESPY award, Best Male Coll. Athlete, 2006, NFL Offensive Rookie of Yr., AP, 2006; named to Am. Football Conf. Pro Bowl Team, NFL, 2006. Achievements include being the only player in NCAA Division I history to pass for 2,500 yards and rush for 1,000 yards in the same season, 2005; being a member of the NCAA Division I Bowl Championship Series winning University of Texas Longhorns, 2006. Office: Tenn Titans One Titans Way Nashville TN 37213*

YOUNG, WANDA, marketing executive; Prodn. artist Kirkpatrick Williams Assocs., Little Rock, 1994—98; account exec. Stone & Ward, Little Rock, 1998—2000, account mgr., 2000; interactive mktg. dir. Alltel Wireless, Little Rock, 2005—08, sr. dir. digital mktg. Wal-Mart Stores, Inc., Bentonville, Ark., 2008—. Named a Woman to Watch, Advt. Age, 2009. Office: Walmart Stores Inc 702 SW 8th St Bentonville AR 72716*

YOUNG, WILLIAM H., labor union administrator; b. 1947; m. Debbie Young; 4 children. Mem., Ctrl. Calif. Coast Br. 52 Nat. Assn. Letter Carriers, San Luis Obispo, 1965, pres., Ctrl. Calif. Coast Br. 52, 1971—78, regional adminstrv. asst., 1978—86, nat. bus. agent San Francisco region, 1986—90, asst. sec.-treas. Washington, 1990—94, dir. city devel., v.p., 1994—98, exec. v.p., 1998—2002, nat. pres., 2002—09. Officer Calif. State Assn., 1972—; v.p. Am. Fedn. Labor, Con. Indsl. Orgn. (AFL-CIO). Nat. v.p. Muscular Dystrophy Assn. (MDA); mem. adv. bd. Walter P. Reuther Libr. Labor and Urban Affairs, Wayne State U., Detroit. Served with US Army. Office: Nat Assn Letter Carriers 100 Ind Ave NW Washington DC 20001-2144 Office Phone: 202-393-4695.

YOUNG, WILLIAM WEBB, military officer, aire warfare specialist, poet; b. St. Louis, Aug. 4, 1967; s. Raymond Andrew and Betty Rosella (Myers) Young; children: Jamie Elizabeth, Christen Lee, Sara Rayan. Commd. ensign USN, 1987; Persian Gulf War/Cold War vet.; owner Young Studies Ran Cha Rainc Resorts, Doniphan, Md. Svc. officer Three Rivers Serenity Group, Poplar Bluff, Mo., 1989—2002, dist. 8 spl. needs com. chmn., 2001—; plane capt. Master At Arms NAval Air Engring., Lakehurst, NJ; Petty officer asst. batch safety PO Navy Lakehurst Ceremonial HonorGuard Unit, Petty officer in charge, rifle team leader. Author numerous poems. Local stream team coord. Mo. Dept. Conservation, Butler County, Mo., 1997—, frontiers program leader, 1998—; water quality monitoring vol. Mo. Dept. Natural Resources, Butler County, Mo., 1999—2002. Patrol squadron Navy Unit Commendation Combat, comdr. Catholic War Vets. MBR MOdern Day Vets. Decorated Battle "E" Award Persian Excursion US Navy, Order of the Spanish Main, Joint Meritorious Unit award, Nat. Def. medal PGWAG Panama Ops. Just Cause, Overseas Deployment Ribbon, Good Conduct medal, Kuwait Liberation medal, Saudi Arabia Liberation Medal, Disting. Expert Pistol medal, Expert Rifle medal, Meritorious Unit Commendation for Bravery and Heroism, Russian Cold War Star, Navy Achievement medal, Silver Life Saving medal, Coldwar Victory medal; recipient Iliad Lit. award, Internat. Poet of Merit, 1996, Editors Choice award, 1996, Americanism award, Grande Voiture of NJ Navy, 1990, Loyalty Day award, VFW, 1990, Ops. Desert Shield Mobilization award. Fellow: K.C. Knights Colombus (1st degree crusader, Altar Server award 1981); mem.: US Grant Museum Am. Words (dir.), Internat. Soc. Poets, Disabled Am. Vets. (life Golden Anchor award 1988), Amherst Soc., Iraqi Desert Yacht Club, Gulf of Oman Yacht Club, Gulf of Sidra Yacht Club, Persian Gulf Yacht Club, Persian Gulf Health Club (life; adminstr.), Am. Legion (honor guard). Roman Catholic. Avocation: art. Home: 201 W Lexington Ave Poplar Bluff MO 63901

YOUNG, YIH-JIN, sociologist, educator; b. Hsinchu County, Taiwan, Dec. 10, 1964; s. Chen-Yu Yang and Yuan Chiu; m. Chien-Hui Weng, Jan. 13, 1997; children: Melody W., Allen W., Austin W., Addison W. PhD, U. Wash., Seattle, 1997. Prof. Nassau CC, Garden City, NY, 1999—; adj. prof. Suffolk County CC, Selden, NY, 2005—. V.p. Taiwanese Am. Assn. LI, Centereach, 2006, pres., 07, advisor, 2008—; coord. Overseas Compatriots Affairs Promotion Com., Taipei, Taiwan, 2007—. Co-author (with William Feigelman): (book) Hands on Sociology. Bd. mem. Suffolk County Asian Am. Adv. Bd., Haupaggue, NY, 2005—09. Mem.: Eastern Sociol. Assn. Achievements include research in ICPSR winner of instructional innovation in the social sciences. Office: Nassau CC 1 Education Dr Garden City NY 11530 Business E-Mail: youngy@ncc.edu.

YOUNG, YIN LU, engineering educator; PhD, U. Tex., Austin, 2002. Asst. prof. Princeton U., NJ, 2002—; assoc. prof. U. Mich., 2009—. Recipient ONR YIP award, Office Naval Rsch., 2005—08. Achievements include research in Smart Energy Systems, Fuel-Efficient Propulsors And Turbines, Marine & Coastal Structures. Office: Univ Mich Dept Naval Architecture & Marine Engring Ann Arbor MI 48109 Office Fax: 609-258-1563. Business E-Mail: ylyoung@umich.edu.

YOUNG-CAMPBELL, LAURA L., speech pathology/audiology services professional; m. Donald Campbell; 1 child. BE in Comm. Disorders & Spl. Edn., Gonzaga U., Spokane, Wash., 1979—83; MS in Speech & Hearing Scis., U. Ariz., Tucson, 1990—93. Cert. spl. svcs. in speech pathology Alaska Dept. Edn., 1983, cert. of clin. competence in speech pathology Am. Speech-Hearing Assn., 1994, advanced cert. speech pathology Alaska Dept. Edn., 2002. Speech-lang. pathologist Matanuska-Susitna Borough Sch. Dist., Palmer, Alaska, 1983—. Mem. editl. bd. Perpspectives on Sch. Based Issues, Am. Speech-Hearing Assn., Md. Del., amb. to China People to People Internat., 2006—; vol. Alaska Health Fair, 1998—; healthy hearing vol. Spl. Olympics, Alaska, 2001—. Fellow: Am. Speech-Hearing Assn. (licentiate; legislative councilor 2005—09, award for continuing edn. 1994—2009); mem.: Mat-Su Speech-Hearing Assn., Mat-Su Alaska Edn. Assn. (life; del. assembly 1999—), Alaska Speech Hearing Assn. (exec. bd. 1995—, Friend of Assn. award 2004). Avocations: travel, gardening, reading, movies. Office: Matanuska-Susitna Borough Schs 501 N Gulkana St Palmer AK 99645

YOUNGDAHL, JAY THOMAS, lawyer; b. St. Louis, May 29, 1952; s. James Edward and Patricia Ruth (Lucy) Y.; m. Mary Ellen Vogler, Dec. 12, 1981; children: Benjamin Douglass, Colleen Alexandra. BS, U. Houston, 1978; JD, U. Tex., 1980; MA, St. John's Coll., 2004; MDiv, Harvard U., 2007. Bar: Ark. 1981, Tex., 1992, D.C. 1993, U.S. Dist. Ct. (ea. and we. dists.) Ark. 1981, U.S. Ct. Appeals (8th, 10th and 11th cirs.) 1981, U.S. Claims Ct. 1992, U.S. Tax Ct. 1981, Tex. 1994. Mng. ptnr. Youngdahl Law Firms, 1981—. Gen. counsel East Bay Pub., L.P.; adj. instr. Webster Coll., Little Rock, 1983-95; adj. prof. U. Ark., Little Rock Sch. of Law, 1988-90; mem. Ark. Employment Security Div. Adv. Coun., Little Rock, 1980-97, Gov.'s Workers Compensation Study Com., Little Rock, 1985-86. With U.S. Army, 1972-74. Mem. ABA, Ark. Bar Assn. (chmn. labor law sect. 1983-84), ATLA, Ark. Trial Lawyers Assn., AFL-CIO Lawyers Coordinating Com. (adv. bd.), Acad. Rail Labor Attys., Tex. Trial Lawyers Assn., State Bar Tex. (Pro Bono Coll. 1996). Avocations: triathlons, art, culinary arts. Office: Youngdahl Law Firm 12621 Featherwood Ste Houston TX 77034 Office Phone: 281-996-0750. Business E-Mail: jyoungdahl@youngdahl.com.

YOUNGER, JENNIFER A., university librarian; BA in history, U. Wis.-Madison, MLA, PhD in info. studies. Various positions in libr. sys. U. Wis.-Madison, 1977—91; asst. dir. tech. svc. Ohio State U. libr., 1991—97; Edward H. Arnold dir. univ. libraries U. Notre Dame, 1997—. Editor: (jour.) Library Resources & Technical Services. Mem.: ALA, Assn. Libr. Collections & Tech. Svc. (pres. 1993—94), Beta Phi Mu. Office: Univ Notre Dame 221 Hesburgh Library Notre Dame IN 46556 Office Phone: 574-631-7790. Office Fax: 574-631-6772. E-mail: Jennifer.A.Younger@nd.edu.

YOUNGER, JUDITH TESS, law educator; b. NYC, Dec. 20, 1933; d. Sidney and Kate (Greenbaum) Weintraub; m. Irving Younger, Jan. 21, 1955; children: Rebecca, Abigail M. BS, Cornell U., 1954; JD, NYU, 1958; LLD (hon.), Hofstra U., 1974. Bar: N.Y. 1958, U.S. Supreme Ct 1962, D.C. 1983, Minn. 1985. Law clk. to judge U.S. Dist. Ct., 1958-60; assoc. firm Chadbourne, Parke, Whiteside & Wolff, NYC, 1960-62; mem. firm Younger and Younger, and (successors), 1962-67; adj. asst. prof. NYU Sch. Law, 1967-69; asst. atty. gen. State of N.Y., 1969-70; assoc. prof. Hofstra U. Sch. Law, 1970-72, prof., assoc. dean, 1972-74; dean, prof. Syracuse Coll. Law, 1974-75; dep. dean, prof. law Cornell Law Sch., 1975-78, prof. law, 1975-85; vis. prof. U. Minn. Law Sch., Mpls., 1984-85, prof., 1985-91, Joseph E. Wargo Anoka County Bar Assn. prof. family law, 1991—. Of counsel Popham, Haik, Schnobrich & Kaufman, Ltd., Mpls., 1989-95; cons. NOW, 1972-74, Suffolk County for Revision of Its Real Property Tax Act, 1972-73; mem. N.Y. Gov.'s Panel To Screen Candidates of Ct. of Claims Judges, 1973-74; mem. Minn. Lawyers' Profl. Responsibility Bd., 1991-93. Contbr. articles to profl. jours. Trustee Cornell U., 1973-78. Mem.: AAUP (v.p. Cornell U. chpt. 1978—79), ABA (council legal edn. 1975—79), Minn. Bar Assn., Assn. of Bar of City of N.Y., Am. Law Inst. (adv. restatement property 1982—84). Home: 3520 W Calhoun Pkwy Minneapolis MN 55416-4657 Office: U Minn Law Sch Minneapolis MN 55455 Home Phone: 612-925-5894; Office Phone: 612-625-5844. Business E-Mail: young001@umn.edu.

YOUNGJOHNS, ROBERT H., computer software company executive; married. MA in Physics and Philosophy with honors, Oriel Coll., Oxford Univ. Various engring. and mgmt. roles IBM, 1980—95; v.p. Sun Microsystems, England, 1995—98; v.p. sales & mktg. Sun Microsystems Europe Middle East and Africa, 1998—2002; exec. v.p. global sales ops. Sun Microsystems, 2002—04, exec. v.p. strategic devel. and Sun financing Santa Clara, Calif., 2004—05; pres., CEO Callidus Software Inc., 2005—07; corp. v.p., pres. North America sales & mktg. Microsoft Corp., Redmond, Wash., 2007—. Bd. dir. Callidus Software Inc., 2005—. Office: Microsoft Corp 1 Microsoft Way Redmond WA 98052-6399*

YOUNGMAN, LOLA JEANNE, music educator; b. Royal Oak, Mich., Mar. 18, 1951; d. Robert Edward Grant and Elaine Margaret Eddy; m. David Frederick Youngman, June 22, 2002; m. Richard Vincent Lewis, Apr. 9, 1977 (div. Sept. 30, 2001); children: Adam Ryan Lewis, Jessica Marie Lewis. BS in Edn., Ctrl. Mich. U., Mt. Pleasant, 1973; student, Wayne State U., Detroit, 1975—76. Cert. tchr. Yamaha Music Sch., Atlanta & L.A., lic. Real Estate NC, 1987, cert. tchr. K-8 Mich., 1973, tchr. K-9 music Mich., 1973. Elem. vocal music tchr. Lamphere Sch. Dist., Madison Heights, Mich., 1974—78; dir., tchr. Yamaha Music Sch., Raleigh, NC, 1985—95; pvt. piano tchr. Raleigh, 1985—97; real estate agent Doreen Silber & Co., Raleigh, 1987; elem. vocal music tchr. Wake County Schs., Raleigh, 1997—. Musician (pianist); singer: Dave Youngman Band, 2002—, (CD) This Can't Be Love, 2004—. Contbr. donations to United Way, Good Will, Breast Cancer Rsch., Democratic Party, Habitat for Humanity, Sierra Club, Cystic Fibrosis Found., vol.; pres., v.p., chmn. Women's Club, 1983—95. Nominee Tchr. of Yr., Wake County Schs. Mem.: NEA, NC Assn. Educators, Boulder Creek Neighborhood Assn. (pres. 1988, v.p.). Avocations: tennis, singing. Home: 4908 Boulder Creek Ln Raleigh NC 27613

YOUNGMAN, OWEN RALPH, newspaper executive, educator; b. Chgo., Apr. 24, 1953; s. Ralph Elmer and Charlotte Earldine (Ottoson) Y.; m. Linda Ann Erlandson, Aug. 24, 1975. DSc, LHD, North Park U., 2005. Sportswriter Ashtabula (Ohio) Star-Beacon, 1969-71; office clk. Chgo. Tribune, 1971-73, transcriber, 1973-75, copy editor, slotman, 1976-79, copy chief, news editor, 1979-83, dep. sports editor, 1984-86, assoc. met. editor, 1986-88, assoc. features editor, 1988-90, dep. fin. editor, 1990-91, assoc. mng. editor, 1991-93, features editor, 1993-95, mng. editor, features, 1995, dir. interactive media, 1996-99, dir. planning and devel., 1999, v.p. devel., 2000—06, sr. v.p. strategy and devel., 2007—08; Knight prof. digital media strategy Medill Sch. Journalism, Northeastern U., 2009—. Bd. dirs. Swedish Covenant Hosp., Legacy, Inc. Web site, Solti Found. USA; nat. exec. bd. Evang. Covenant Ch.; bd. trustees North Pk. U. Named to Ashtabula HS Alumni Hall of Fame, Ohio, 2005. Mem. Newspaper Assn. Am. New Media Fedn., Am. Soc. Newspaper Editors, Presidents Club North Park U., Arts Club Chgo. Avocation: vocal and instrumental music. Home: 40 Kenmore Ave Deerfield IL 60015-4750 Office: Northwestern Univ 1870 Campus Dr Evanston IL 60208-2170 Home Phone: 847-940-1191; Office Phone: 874-467-6759. Business E-Mail: o-youngman@northeastern.edu.

YOUNG-POHLMAN, COLETTE LISA, music educator; b. Honolulu, July 20, 1952; d. Richard Ah On and Winifred Oi Chin Chang Young; m. Kurt I. Pohlman, Oct. 5, 1985; 1 child, Vinson Sterling Pohlman. EdB, U. Hawaii-Manoa, Honolulu, 1974, postgrad., 1975. Part-time tchr. dept. edn. Kalani High, Honolulu, 1978—79; chpt. 1 reading tchr. McKinley High, Honolulu, 1979—80, basic skills tchr., 1980—81; part-time tchg. asst. pvt. preschs., Honolulu, 1981—82; part-time tchr. dept. edn., chpt. 1 reading Ala Wai Elem. and Palolo Elem., 1982—83; classroom tchr. Heeia Elem., Kaneohe, Hawaii, 1990; part-time tchr. dept. edn. Wailupe Valley Elem., Honolulu, 1990—91; instrnl. resource augmentation tchr. Maemae Elem., Honolulu, 1991—92; project tchr. Title I reading Washington Intermediate, Honolulu, 1992—94; instrnl. resource augmentation tchr. Accelerated Gifted & Talented Performing Arts, Kailua, Hawaii, 1994—97; classroom tchr. Mokapu Elem., Kailua, 1997—2002, instrnl. resource augmentation music tchr., 2002—07, Ann. Winter Concert and Talent Showcase, 2002—07; music specialist Aiea Elem., 2007—, jr. alii allstars, 2008. Dir., choreographer, scripting/editing of musical play productions in elem. settings Windward Dist., Kalaheo Complex. Dir.(choreographer, writer): (multicultural musical plays) Little Firefly, the Rough-face Girl, Double Happiness, Souled Out; composer: There's Something About a Pet, 1998 (2d Pl. award, 1998); composer: (choreographer) (new sch. song dance) Enchantment of Mokapu, 2000, Reading Rap, 2003, (music video) Enchantment of Mokapu, 2006, (plays) Petite Rouge, 2006—07 (Hawaii Student Digital Showcase grant award, 2007); prodr. (dir.): (weekly TV program Olelo Cablevision) Na Keiki Hauoli o Mokapu, The Happy Children of Mokapu, 2007—. Mem., tchr. Boy Scouts Am. Troop 113, 1999—. Mem.: Hawaii State Tchrs. Assn., Hawaii Music Educators Assn., Hawaii Orff Schulwerk Assn. (bd. dirs. 2005—), Am. Orff Schulwerk Assn., Music Educators Nat. Conf., Nat. Educators Assn. Avocations: composing songs, poetry, singing, keyboard, storytelling. Home: 45-427 Loli'i St Kaneohe HI 96744-5911 Office Phone: 808-483-7200 ext. 246. Business E-Mail: colette-youngpohlman@notes.k12.hi.us.

YOUNGQUIST, ARVID TADAO, legislation advocate, public servant; b. Tokyo, Aug. 7, 1948; s. Setsuko Kobayashi and Albin Harold Youngquist, Mary Elizabeth Oya; m. Gloria Sotto Youngquist, Aug. 22, 1946; foster children: Marry, Oye. BA, U. Tex., 1974. Founder, spokesman The Mestizo Assn., Honolulu, 1982—; office asst. III Dept. Transp., Honolulu, 1998—. Interpretor Asia U., Musashino, Japan, 1958—59; fixed sta. tech. contr. Signal Corps, US Army, Asmara, Ethiopia, 1970—71; shipping clk. Hawaiian Papayas, Honolulu, 1974; security guard Freeman Guards, Honolulu, 1974; reserve technician 100th Bn, 442d Inf., USAR, Honolulu, 1974—82; sqt test stds. officer DPT, USASCH, Ft. Shafter, Honolulu, 1981—82; adminstrv. technician 411th Engr Bn (Cbt) (Hvy) USAR, Honolulu, 1982—86; ratings clk. Sec. of State, Austin, Tex., 1986—92; data entry clk. APHIS, USDA, Austin, Tex., 1992—96; interpretor Wasedu U., Tokyo, Hosei U., Tokyo, Musa shino Women's U. Editor Kalihi-Palama neighborhood bd. news. Mem. Oahu Metro. Planning Orgn., 2007—08; mem. steering com. Faith Action Cmty. Equity, 2008; mem. Com. Common Cause Hawai, 1978; male rep. State Ctrl. Com. Womans Caucus Hawii Dem. Party; convenor Sub-Sandwich Group, 2009—; senate candidate Dem. & Green Party, Honolulu, 1998, 2002; state ctrl. committeeman Hawaii Democratic Party, 2008—; mem. steering com. Single Mem. Dists. for Austin, Tex., 1990—92; bd. mem. Hawaii Friends and Family of Schizophrenics, Honolulu, 1984; pers. com. and bd. dir. Austin/Travis County MH/MR Ctr., Tex., 1990; dir. Save Austins Neighborhood & Environment, Austin, Tex., 1992—96; bd. dirs. Hawaii Coalition Against Legalized Gambling, Honolulu, 1999—2000; bd. dirs., sec. United Self Help, Inc., Honolulu, 2001—03; mem. adv. coun. Kalihi-Palama Mental Health Com. Ctr., Honolulu, 1981—81; mem. West Honolulu Sub-Area Health Planning Coun., Honolulu, 1981—82; state legislative com. AARP, Honolulu, 1998—99; steward and agy. coun. sec., del. to gen. assembly HGEA, AFSCME Local 152, AFL-CIO State of HI Local 152, Honolulu, 1999—. With US Army, 1969—71, sgt. 1st class USAR, 1974—87. Recipient Certificates of Appreciation, Vols. in Corrections, Hawaii, 1978, Gov. George Ariyoshi, 1982, Appreciation Plaquee, Austin/Travis County MH/MR Ctr., 1990, Health and Safety Employee of Yr. award, APHIS, USDA, 1995. Mem.: ADA, Progressive Dem. Hawai, Liliha Neighbourhood Bd. (additional sec. & legis. chair). Democrat. Roman Catholic. Avocations: films, reading, writing. Personal E-mail: thirr33@gmail.com.

YOUNGQUIST, WALTER LEWELLYN, geologist, consultant; b. Mpls., May 5, 1921; s. Walter Raymond and Selma Regina (Knock) Y.; m. Elizabeth Salome Pearson, Dec. 11, 1943; children: John, Karen, Louise, Robert. BA, Gustavus Adolphus Coll., St. Peter, Minn., 1942; MSc, U. Iowa, 1943, PhD, 1948. Registered profl. geologist, Oreg. Jr. geologist U.S. Geol. Survey, 1943-44; rsch. assoc. U. Iowa, Iowa City, 1945-48; asst. prof. geology U. Idaho, Moscow, 1948-51; sr. geologist Internat. Petroleum Co., Talara, Peru, 1951-54; prof. geology U. Kans., Lawrence, 1954-57, U. Oreg., Eugene, 1957-66; cons. geologist Minerals dept. Exxon Corp., Houston, 1968-73; geothermal cons. Eugene Water & Electric Bd., 1973-92; ind. cons. Eugene, 1992—. Author: Investing in Natural Resources, 1980, Mineral Resources and the Destinies of Nations, 1990, GeoDestinies, 1997; co-author: Ordovician Cephalopod Fauna of Baffin Island, 1954. Ensign, USNR, 1944-45. Recipient Lowden Prize in Geology, U. Iowa, 1943, Journalist award, Am. Assn. Petroleum Geology, 2000, Disting. Alumni award Gustavus Adolphus Coll., 2002. Fellow AAAS, Geol. Soc. Am.; mem. Am. Assn. Petroleum Geologists, Internat. Assn. Math. Geology, Soc. Exploration Geophysicists, Geothermal Resources Coun., N.W. Energy Assn., N.Y. Acad. Scis., Sigma Xi. Lutheran. Avocations: fly-tying, photography, fishing. Office: PO Box 5501 Eugene OR 97405-0501 Personal E-mail: wyoungst@mindspring.com.

YOUNGREN, DELVANA HOPE, secondary school educator; b. LA, Apr. 13, 1941; d. Herman Melvin and Betty Floy (England) Ferguson; m. Allan Morse Youngren, June 17, 1961; children: Erik Allan, Deanna Marie. BA, Calif. State Coll., Long Beach, 1963; MA, Calif. State Coll., 1968. Cert. secondary tchr., Calif. Tchr. Long Beach (Calif.) Unified Sch. Dist., 1963-70, Faith Christian Acad., Pasadena, Tex., 1975-80, Cherry Valley (Calif.) Brethren Christian Sch., 1980-86, Arrowhead Christian Acad., Redlands, Calif., 1984—87, New Life Christian Acad., San Bernardino, Calif., 1987-90, Mt. View Jr. H.S., Beaumont, Calif., 1990—2002, Mt. View Mid. Sch., Beaumont, 2002—. Chmn. GATE, Gifted and Talented, Calif.; educator Drug, Alcohol & Tobacco Edn.; tech. computer tchr. On-Line Learning, Novanet. Head computer dept. San Gorgonio Pass Geneal. Soc., Banning, Calif., 1992-95; mem. Yucaipa Geneal. Soc., 1992-95. Mem. NEA, Calif. Tchrs. Assn., Beaumont Tchrs. Assn., Calif. Inland Area Math. Project, Soroptomists (Beaumont chpt.). Republican. Avocations: sports, cats. Home: 10640 Jonathan Ave Cherry Valley CA 92223-4974 Office: Beaumont United Sch Dist PO Box 187 Beaumont CA 92223-0187 Office Phone: 951-845-1627.

YOUNGS, DIANE CAMPFIELD, learning disabilities specialist, educator; b. Margaretville, NY, Feb. 16, 1954; d. Richard Maxwell and Charlotte June (Rickard) Campfield; m. William H. Youngs, June 30, 1984. BS in Edn., SUNY, Geneseo, 1976, MS in Edn., 1977. Professionally recognized spl. educator. Tchr. educable mentally retarded Tompkins-Seneca-Tioga Bd. Coop. Ednl. Svcs., Ithaca, NY, 1978-80; tchr. learning disabled Joint Svc. for Spl. Edn., Mishawaka, Ind., 1980-97; assoc. faculty Ind. U.-South Bend Grad. Sch. Edn., 1996-98. Vis. lectr. dept. edn. Ind. U., South Bend, 1998-2002, lectr., 2002—; mem. Task Force for Reorgn. Spl. Edn., Mishawaka, 1990-91; coord. Tiny Talkers Summer Speech/Lang. Camp, 1994—. Recipient Tchg. award, Ind. U. Trustees, 2005, 2006, 2009. Mem. AAUP, Learning Disabilities Assn., Coun. for Learning Disabilities, Ind. Prof. Reading, Internat. Reading Assn., Nat. Coun. Tchrs. English, Kappa Delta Pi. E-mail: dyoungs@iusb.edu.

YOUNGS, MICHAEL THERON, JR., non-commissioned officer; b. Binghamton, NY, Nov. 30, 1973; s. Michael Theron Youngs, Sr. and Diane Marie Sykes; m. Marianne Jeanette Viren, Apr. 17, 1992; children: Mychelle Leigh, Lauren Nicole, Michael Theron III. Student, Ctrl. Tex. Coll., 2003. Enlisted US Army, 1992, advanced through grades to sgt. first class, 2003, gens. enlisted aide Ft. Drum, NY, 1997—98, 2001—03, asst. dining facility mgr. Ft. Drum, NY, 2003—05. Task force mayor U.S. Army, Iraq, 2004—05. Fellow: 1000 Islands 700 Club. Avocations: bowling, softball, golf. Office: E Company 210th BSB Bldg 10182 4th Armored Divsn Fort Drum NY 13602 Home: 208 High St Theresa NY 13691-2102 Business E-Mail: michael.youngs@us.army.mil.

YOUNG-WILSON, BRENDA L., special education educator; b. Balt., July 5, 1953; d. David and Wilma Young; m. Antonio Wilson, Apr. 8, 1979; children: Barry Wilson, Arnita Wilson. MA, Coppin State U., Balt. Spl. edn. tchr. Benjamin Franklin Mid., Balt., 1971—79, Bklyn. Pk. Mid. Sch., 1990—. Home: 5600 Gibbons Ave Baltimore MD 21225 Office: Brooklyn Park Middle Sch 200 Hammonds Ln Brooklyn MD 21225 Personal E-mail: mswilson705@aol.com. Business E-Mail: blwilson1@aacps.org.

YOUNGWOOD, ALFRED DONALD, lawyer; b. NYC, Apr. 27, 1938; s. Milton and Lillian (Ginsburg) Y.; m. Judith Goldfarb, June 24, 1963 (dec. March 9, 2008); children: Jonathan David, Stephen Michael. BA magna cum laude, Yale U., 1959; LLB magna cum laude, Harvard U., 1962. Bar: NY 1962, DC 1970, US Tax Ct. 1964, US Ct. Appeals (2d cir.) 1969. Law clk. to judge US Dist. Ct. NY, 1962-63; assoc. Paul, Weiss, Rifkind, Wharton & Garrison LLP, NYC, 1964-70, ptnr., 1970—2008, chair, 1999—2008, of counsel, 2009—. Pres. Ctrl. Synagogue, NYC, 2003—06, trustee; bd. dirs. Legal Aid Soc., NYC, dir., 2005—08. Fulbright scholar, London, 1963-64. Fellow Am. Coll. Tax Counsel; mem. ABA, NY State Bar Assn. (chmn. tax sect. 1978-79, exec. com. 1971—, ho. of dels. 1979-80), Assn. of Bar of City of NY, Coun. on Fgn. Rels. Home: 1125 Park Ave New York NY 10128-1243 Office: Paul Weiss Rifkind Wharton & Garrison LLP 1285 Avenue Of The Americas New York NY 10019-6064 Home Phone: 212-860-8848. Business E-Mail: ayoungwood@paulweiss.com.

YOUNIS, OSSAMA, research scientist; s. Mohamed Fadlia and Afkar Ibrahim; m. Mona Badawy, July 10, 2000; children: Seif, Salma, Marwan. PhD, Purdue U., West Lafayette, Ind., 2005. Asst. rsch. scientist U. Ariz., Tucson, 2005—07; sr. rsch. scientist Telcordia Technologies, Inc., Piscataway, NJ, 2007—. Contbr. scientific papers to profl. jours. Mem.: IEEE, ACM. Office: Telcordia Tech Inc One Telcordia Dr Piscataway NJ 08854 Office Fax: 732-336-7013. Personal E-mail: ossyounis@gmail.com.

YOUNISS, JAMES, psychology professor; b. Green Bay, Wis., Dec. 20, 1936; s. Thomas and Jean Youniss; m. Dorothy Watterson, June 13, 1959; children: Carrie Maslen, Andrew, Emily Hussey; 1 child, Jessica. BA, Marquette U., Milw., 1959; MA, Hollins Coll., Roanoke, Va., 1960; PhD, Cath. U. Am., Washington, DC, 1962. Dir. life cycle inst. Cath. U. Am., 1988—99, James R. & Wylma R. Curtin prof. psychology, 2000—. Contbr. more than 180 articles to profl. jours.;, editor 10 profl. books. Bd. mem. Youth Svc. Am., Washington, 2002. Recipient Provost award, lifetime tchg. and rsch. Fellow: APA. Office: Cath Univ Am Washington DC 20064

YOUNKER, KATHLEEN TEUBER, pianist, music educator; b. St. Cloud, Minn., Jan. 22, 1947; d. Hans Richard and Philomena (Hortsch) T.; m. Daniel William Younker, July 19, 1968; children: Laura, Jonathan. BA in History and Philosophy, St. Cloud State U., 1968; ARCT in Piano Performance, Royal Conservatory Toronto, Ont., Can., 1983; BA in Music, Bishop's U., Lennoxville, Que., Can., 1984; pvt. piano student, Rose Goldblatt, Montreal, 1985-95; MA in Spl. Studies, St. Cloud State U., 2002; BA in German, St. Cloud State U., Minn., 2009. Self-employed piano tchr., Lennoxville, 1978—97, St. Cloud, 1997—; sch. music tchr. Eastern Twps. Regional Sch. Bd., Lennoxville, 1982-86; ch. organist Peace United Ch. of Christ, St. Cloud, 1998-99; accompanist Sauk Rapids (Minn.) Rice HS, 1999—2000. Mem Music Tchrs. Nat Assn., Nat. Guild Piano Tchrs., Can. Fedn. Music Tcrs. Assns. (com. mem., ex officio nat. conv. 1997), Minn. Music Tchrs. Assn. (com. mem. state conv. 1999-01, com. mem. piano exam devel. com. 2002—), Eastern Twps. Music Tchrs. Assn. (pres. 1989-91), Que. Music Tchrs. Assn. (pres. provincial coun. 1993-97), Nat. Fedn. Music Club. Avocations: home restoration, pets, reading, gardening, cooking, entertaining.

YOUNKIN, GEORGE WORTHINGTON, retired electrical engineer; b. NYC, Nov. 6, 1923; s. George Younkin and Marion Truex; m. Nancy Louise Greenwald, June 25, 1950; children: Janine Susan children: Gregory Wane. BSEE, Mich. State Un., E. Lansing, 1950; MSEE, U. Wis., Madison, 1957. Registered profl. Engr., Wis., Tex. Tech sgt.(wwii), 2nd lt. Army Signal Corps, Pacific and Atomic tests, 1941—52; control engr. Westinghoue, Buffalo, 1950—55; sr. rsch. engr. Giddings and Lewis Machine Tool Co., Fond du Lac, Wis., 1955—93; profl. engr. Bullseye Rsch., Inc., Fond du Lac, 1993—. Contbr. to numerous profl. jours. Men's club YMCA, Fond du Lac, 1955—70; hosp. vol. St. Agnus Hosp., Fond du Lac, 1993—2009. Fellow: IEEE (soc. pres. 1974); mem.: ASME, NSPE. Independent. Presbyterian. Achievements include patents for 13, 101, 436 First Commercial Numerical Control. Avocations: photography, travel. Home Phone: 920-921-2371; Office Phone: 920-929-6544. Personal E-mail: gwyounkin@charter.net. Business E-Mail: george@bullseyenet.com.

YOUNOSZAI, ADEL K., pediatrician, director; BS in Liberal Arts, U. Iowa, 1989, MD, 1994. Pediat. intern & resident Columbus Children's Hosp. Tng. Program, Ohio, 1994—97; pediat. cardiology fellow U. Calif., San Francisco, 1997—2000. Dir. cardiac & fetal imaging, pediat. cardiology Children's Hosp., Denver, 2006—. Recipient Best Doctor award, 2006—06. Fellow: Am. Acad. Pediat., Am. Coll. Cadiology; mem.: Am. Heart Assn., Soc. Pediat. Echocardiography, Am. Soc. Echocardiography (pediat. echo bowl co-champion 2005—06). Office: Children's Hosp 13123 E 16th Ave B100 Aurora CO 80045

YOUNOSZAI, BARBARA B., literature and language professor, researcher; b. Oakland, Calif., Nov. 30, 1932; d. William Gordon Beckwith and Birdie Perrone; m. Rafi Younoszai, Jan. 4, 1964; children: Adam Sean, Barak Gordon. PhD, U. Minn., Mpls., 1971. Chair, modern langs. Hamline U., St. Paul, 1978—88, prof., 1965—. Translator: (book of plays) Three Plays by Isaac Chocron, 1995, (plays) Seven Plays by Argentine Playwright Susana Torres Molina, 2006; contbr. articles, chapters to books. Scholar Fulbright, 1964; US NDEA grants, 1962—64, Danforth grant, 1967. Home: 1574 Glenhill Rd Arden Hills MN 55112 Office: Hamline Univ Snelling & Hewitt Saint Paul MN 55104 Office Fax: 651-523-3170; Home Fax: 651-523-3170. Business E-Mail: byounoszai@gw.hamline.edu.

YOUNT, KATHRYN MARY, science educator; d. William Jay and Mary Rooney Yount; m. Robert William Dodson, June 19, 2004; children: Harper Leigh Dodson, Brenne Elizabeth Dodson. PhD, Johns Hopkins U., Balt., 1999. Assoc. prof. Emory U., Atlanta, 2000—; scientist WHO, Geneva, 1999—2000. Cons. Am. U., Beirut, 2002. Contbr. to numerous profl. jours. (Nobuo Maeda Internat. Rsch. award, Gerontology Sect., APHA, 2004), chapters to books. Recipient Rsch. award, Dept of Sociology, Emory U.;, 1987—2008, award, French Honor Soc., 1987—91; Rsch. grants, NSF, 2000—08, NIH, 2000—08, tchg. fellowship, Fulbright found., 1991—92. Mem.: Phi Eta Sigma, Phi Beta Kappa, Am. Sociol. Assn. (invited paper presenter 2000—08), Population Assn. America (discussant 2007—08, sci. session organizer 2007—08). Office: Emory Univ 1518 Clifton Rd NE Atlanta GA 30322

YOUNT-BAXLEY, KATHLEEN ANN, psychologist; d. Loren C. Nichols and Ann W. Rumsey; m. Edward A. Baxley, Oct. 20, 1979; children: Chaney M. Mobley, Coriann C. Morales. MA in Sch. Psychology, U. Colo. Denver Ctr., 1995. Cert. in profl. spl. svc. State of Colo. Dept. Edn., 1996. Sch. psychologist Ctrl. Elem., Commerce City, Colo., 2000—02, Legacy HS, Broomfield, Colo., 2002—. Vocat. rehab. counselor Jefferson County Cmty. Ctr., Littleton, Colo., 1984—94. Counselor Christian Ch. Broomfield, 2008—. Home: 1075 W 4th Ave Broomfield CO 80020

YOUNTS, SHANE-ANN, speech educator; d. James Ogden and Ethel Shane Younts. BFA, South Meth. U., Dallas, 1969. Voice & speech tchr. NYU Grad. Tisch Sch. Arts, 1990—, head voice & speech, 2005—, Pvt. Studio Shakespeare Lab., NYC, 1983—, Pub. Theatre's Shakespeare Lab., NYC, 1999, Guthrie Experience, Mpls., 2000, Sedona Shakespeare Inst., Ariz., 2003. Vocal/dialect cons. various field. Co-author (with Louis Scheeder): (book) All the Words on Stage, A Complete Pronunciation Dictionary for the Plays of William Shakespeare, 2002. Faculty Devel. grant, Tisch Sch. Arts, NYU, 2005, 2009. Office: Grad Acting NYU 721 Broadway New York NY 10003 Home Phone: 212-877-2567. Business E-Mail: say1@nyu.edu.

YOURZAK, ROBERT JOSEPH, management consultant, educator, engineer; b. Mpls., Aug. 27, 1947; s. Ruth Phyllis Sorenson. BCE, U. Minn., 1969; MSCE, U. Wash., 1971, MBA, 1975. Registered profl. engr., Wash., Minn. Surveyor N.C. Hoium & Assocs., Mpls., 1965-68, Lot Surveys Co., Mpls., 1968-69; site layout engr. Sheehy Constrn. Co., St. Paul, 1968; structural engring. aide Dunham Assocs., Mpls., 1969; aircraft and aerospace structural engr., program rep. Boeing Co., Seattle, 1969-75; engr., estimator Howard S. Wright Constrn. Co., Seattle, 1976-77; dir. project devel. and adminstrn. DeLeuw Cather & Co., Seattle, 1977-78; sr. mgmt. cons. Alexander Grant & Co., Mpls., 1978-79; mgr. project sys. dept., project mgr. Henningson, Durham & Richardson, Mpls., 1979-80; dir. project mgmt., regional offices Ellerbe Assocs., Inc., Mpls., 1980-81; pres. Robert Yourzak & Assocs., Inc., Mpls., 1982—. Lectr. engring. mgmt. U. Wash., 1977-78; lectr., adj. asst. prof. dept. civil and mineral engring. and mech./indsl. engring. Ctr. for Devel. of Tech. Leadership, Inst. Tech.; mem. strategic mgmt. and orgn. dept., mgmt. scis. dept. Sch. Mgmt., U. Minn., 1979-90, 96—; bd. adv. inst. tech., 1989-93; founding mem., membership com., mem. U. of Minn. com. Minn. High Tech. Coun., 1983-95; instr. principles mgmt. dept. bus. and pub. policy Concordia U., 1997, instr. constrn. mgmt., constrn. estimating and scheduling, bldg. orgn. and tech., project mgmt. and planning skills, project mgmt. software, supervision and applied leadership, and supervisory techniques for bus. Inver Hills C.C., 1998—; instr. introduction to engring. and design, statics, mechanics of materials, ops. mgmt. North Hennepin C.C., 2002—; adj. instr. ops. mgmt. Hamline U., St. Paul, 2001; spkr. in field. Author: Project Management and Motivating and Managing the Project Team, 1984, (with others) Field Guide to Project Management, 1998, 2004 (sec. edition). Chmn. regional art group experience Seattle Art Mus., 1975-78; mem. Pacific N.W. Arts Coun., 1977-78, ex-officio adviser Mus. Week, 1976; bd. dirs. Friends of the Rep. Seattle Repertory Theatre, 1973-77; mem. Symphonics Seattle Symphony Orch., 1975-78. Named Outstanding Young Man of Am., U.S. Jaycees, 1978; scholar Boeing Co., 1967-68, Sheehy Constrn. Co., summer 1967. Fellow ASCE (chmn. continuing edn. subcom. Seattle chpt. 1976-79, chmn. program com. 1978, mem. transp. and urban planning tech. group 1978, Edmund Friedman Young Engr. award 1979, chmn. continuing edn. subcom. 1979-80, chmn. energy com. Minn. chpt. 1980-81, bd. dirs. 1981-89, sec. 1981-83, v.p. profl. svcs. 1983-84, v.p. info. svcs. 1984-85, pres. 1986-87, past pres. 1987-89, spkr.), PMI Project Mgmt. Inst. (cert. project mgmt. prof., spkr., founding pres. 1985, chmn., adv. com. 1987-89, bd. dirs. 1984-86, program com. chmn. and organizing com. mem. Minn. chpt. 1984, spkr., project mgr. internat. mktg. program 1985-86, chmn. internat. mktg. standing com. 1986, long range and strategic planning com. 1988-93, chmn. 1992, v.p. pub. rels. 1987-88, ex-officio dir. 1989, 92, internat. pres. 1990, chmn. bd. 1991, ex-officio chmn. 1992, internat. bd. dirs., chmn. nominating com. 1992, PMI fellow 1995, chmn. exec. dir. selection com. 1996-97, Robert J. Yourzak Scholarship Award established Minn. chpt. 1998—), Inst. Indsl. Engrs. (pres. Twin Cities chpt. 1985-86, chmn. program com. 1983-84, bd. dirs. 1985-88, awards com., chmn. 1984-89, fellow 1999, spkr.); mem. ASTD (So. Minn. chpt.), Am. Cons. Engrs. Coun. (peer reviewer 1986-89), Am. Arbitration Assn. (mem. Mpls. panel of constrn. arbitrators), Minn. Surveyors and Engrs. Soc., Cons. Engrs. Coun. Minn. (chmn. pub. rels. com. 1983-85, vice chmn. 1988, chmn. 1989, program com. chmn. Midwest engrs. conf. and exposition 1985-90, spkr., Honor award 1992), Inst. Mgmt. Cons. (cert. mgmt. cons.), Mpls. Soc. Fine Arts, Internat. Facility Mgmt. Assn., Am. Soc. Engring. Edn., Rainer Club (co-chmn. Oktoberfest), Sierra club, Chowder Soc., Mountaineers, North Star Ski Touring, Chi Epsilon (life). Office: 7320 Gallagher Dr Ste 325 Minneapolis MN 55435-4510

YOUSEF, FATHI SALAAMA, communications educator, management consultant; b. Cairo, Jan. 2, 1934; arrived in U.S., 1968, naturalized, 1973; s. Salaama and Rose (Tadros) Yousef; m. Marjan Lowies El-Faizy, June 24, 1994. BA, Ain Shams U., Cairo, 1955; MA, U. Minn., 1970, PhD, 1972. Svc. ctr. supt. Shell Oil Co., Cairo, 1955-61; indsl., mgmt. tng. instr. ARAMCO, Dhahran, Saudi Arabia, 1961-68; tchg. assoc. U. Minn., Mpls., 1968-72; comm. studies prof. emeritus Calif. State U., Long Beach, 1972—. With orgn. and indsl. engring. dept. ARAMCO, 1978—80. Co-author: An Introduction to Intercultural Communication, 1975, 1985; contbr. Grantee, NSF, 1981, 1982, 1983. Mem.: Assn. Egyptian Am. Scholars. Democrat. Office: Calif State U Dept Comm Studies Long Beach CA 90840 Business E-Mail: fyousef@csulb.edu.

YOUSEF, MAHMOUD, mathematics professor, computer scientist, educator; s. Abdullah and Haniefa (Abu Mukh) Yousef; m. Gamileh Abu Mukh, June 29, 1993; children: Ahmed, Abdala, Janna, Mohammed. BS, Yarmouk U., Irbid, Jordan, 1986; MA, Kent State U., Ohio, 1992; MS, PhD, La. Tech U., Ruston, 2001. Tchr. Ministry of Edn., Tulkarem, Jordan, 1986—88; grad. asst. Kent State U., Kent, Ohio, 1989—92, adj. faculty, 1992—94, 1996—97; instr. United Arab Emirates U., Al-Ain, 1994—96; grad. asst. La. Tech U., Ruston, 1997—2000; vis. prof. Grambling State U., La., 2000—01; asst. prof. U. Ctrl. Mo., Warrensburg, 2001—05, assoc. prof., 2005—. Adj. prof. Kent State U., 1988—89. Contbr. articles to profl. jours. Panel judge Assn. for Computing Machinery, 2004. Named Tchr. of Distinction, United Arab Emirates U., 1994—96; grantee, U. Ctrl. Mo., 2001—07, Ednl. Advancement Found., 2004. Mem.: Math. Assn. Am., Consortium for Computing Sciences in Colls. (steering com. 2003—07), Phi Kappa Phi. Avocations: reading, soccer, travel. Office: Univ Ctrl Mo Dept Math & Computer Sci Warrensburg MO 64093 Office Fax: 660-543-8013. Business E-Mail: yousef@ucmo.edu.

YOUSEFI'ZADEH, HOMAYOUN, science educator; BS, Shariff U. Tech., 1989; MS, Tehran Polytechnic Inst., Iran, 1993; degree in Elec. Engring., U. So. Calif., 1995, PhD, 1997. Grad. rsch. asst. Info. Scis. Inst., Marina Del Rey, 1994—95; tech. cons. NEC Elec., San Jose, 1995; sr. engr., mgr. Procom Tech., Irvine, 1995—2001; founder, chief tech. officer TierFleet, Irvine, 2001—02; asst. adj. prof. U. Calif., Irvine, Calif., 2002—; scientist Boeing Co., Anaheim, Calif., 2004—. Contbr. chapters to books, articles to profl. jours. Mem.: IEEE (sr.; mem. editl. bd., mem. tech. program coms.), Storage Networking Industry Assn. (chmn. sys. mgmt. working group), Am. Soc. Engring. Edn., Am. Mgmt. Assn. Achievements include patents in field. Office: Dept of EECS UC Irvine 444B Engineering Tower UCI Irvine CA 92697 Personal E-mail: hyousefi@yahoo.com. E-mail: hyousefi@uci.edu.

YOUSSEF, CAROLYN MAGDY, finance educator; BA, Am. U. Cairo, 1998, MBA, 2000; PhD, U. Nebr., Lincoln, 2004. Author: (book) Psychological Capital: Developing the Human Competitive Edge; contbr. chapters to books, articles to profl. jours. Achievements include research in positive organizational behavior. Office: Bellevue Univ 1000 Galvin Rd S Bellevue NE 68005 Business E-Mail: carolyn.youssef@bellevue.edu.

YOUST, DAVID BENNETT, career development educator; b. May 14, 1938; s. Howard Page and Agnes (Bennett) Y.; m. Faye Phillips; children: Stacy Sillen, Shawna Sannier, Liesl Berger, Genny Rankin, Elizabeth Curley. BS, SUNY-Albany, 1959; MS, Syracuse U., NY, 1961; PhD, Mich. State U., 1969. Cert. career counselor Nat. Bd. Counselor Cert. Tchr. sci. North Syracuse schs., 1959-61; adminstr. student pers. Mich. State U., 1961-63; counselor, prin., program dir. Rochester (N.Y.) schs., 1963-70; sr. rsch. technologist Eastman Kodak Co., Rochester, 1970-72; asst. dean Nat. Tech. Inst. for the Deaf, Rochester Inst. Tech., 1972-74; mem. faculty Empire State Coll., SUNY, Rochester, 1974-78; exec. dir. Career Devel. Coun., Corning, N.Y., 1978-84; mgr. engring. tng. Corning Inc., N.Y., 1984-90; ptnr. Phillips Tng. Sys., Inc., 1989—. Former adj. faculty Corning C.C., Elmira Coll., C.W. Post Coll.; mediator cmty. dispute resolution, former bd. dirs. Cmty. Dispute Resolution Ctr., Ithaca, NY; instr. MSF motorcycle safety; EEO mediator U.S. Postal Svc. Author guide, articles in field; former mem. editl. bd. Career Devel. Quar. Former bd. dirs. 171 Cedar Arts Ctr. Mem. ACA, Nat. Career Devel. Assn. (Merit award 1970, 84), Am. Ednl. Rsch. Assn., Assn. Measurement and Evaluation in Guidance. E-mail: dyoust@gmail.com.

YOUSUFF, AJMAL, engineering educator; PhD, Purdue U., West Lafayette, Ind., 1983. Asst. prof. Dept. Mech. Engring. and Mechanics, Drexel U., Phila., 1983—88, assoc. prof., 1988—. Recipient Teetor award, Soc. Automotive Engrs. Mem.: IEEE, AIAA. Office: Drexel Univ 32 Chestnut St Philadelphia PA 19104

YOVANOF, SILVANA, physician; b. Lubojno, Macedonia, Jan. 14, 1956; came to U.S., 1961; d. Peter and Nuna Yovanof. BS in Biology and Psychology, Loyola U., Chgo., 1978; MS, U. Ill., 1982; MD, Am. U. Caribbean, Montserrat, 1985. Diplomate Am. Bd. Internal Medicine. Intern Deaconess Hosp., St. Louis, 1986-87; resident in internal medicine St. Joseph Mercy Hosp., Pontiac, Mich., 1987-89, chief resident in medicine, 1989-90; fellow U. Ill. Med. Ctr., Chgo., 1990-92; chmn. dept.

medicine Monongahela Valley Hosp., 2002—08. Mem. adv. panel Internal Medicine for the Specialist, 1988—; affiliated with hosps. Jefferson Hosp., Pitts., 1991, MonValley Hosp., Monongahela, Pa., 1993, Mercy Hosp., Pitts., 1995. Contbr. articles to profl. jours. including Neurosci. Letters. Mem.: ACP, Am. Assn. Clin. Endocrinologists, Allegheny County Med. Soc. (med. legal com. 1996—), Pa. State Med. Soc., Am. Diabetes Assn. Office: Med and Endocrinology Assoc 420 W Main St Monongahela PA 15063-2552 Home Phone: 412-881-3237; Office Phone: 724-258-8680. E-mail: syovanof@comcast.net.

YOVANOVICH, ROBYN DOBSON, theater educator, department chairman; d. Robert Vernon and Gwendolyn Armstrong Dobson; m. Donald Yovanovich, Nov. 10, 1990; 1 child, Anna Clancey. BA, Cath. U. Am., Washington, DC, 1971—75. Editor Middleburg Life, Middleburg, Va., 1989—91; fine arts dept. chmn. Foxcroft Sch., Middleburg, 1997—. Chmn. of volunteers Va. Gold Cup/Internat. Gold Cup, The Plains, 1989—2006. Editor: (book) Middleburg and Nearby; contbr. color commentator; actor: (TV commercials) Soft and Dri/ Mountain Dew, (musical revue- ford's theatre) Uncle Funky's Mistletoe Revue; (Broadway plays, and Off Broadway), 1977—80. Com. mem. Am. Cancer Soc. Charity Polo Classic, The Plains, 1996, Range Rover Internat. Polo Classic, The Plains, 2002; bd. mem. The Middleburg Players, 1998—2002. Grantee Kenan Grant for Profl. Devel., Foxcroft Sch., 2006. Republican. Episcopalian. Avocation: interior design. Home: PO Box 1877 Middleburg VA 20118 Office: Foxcroft Sch PO Box 5555 Middleburg VA 20118 Personal E-mail: dony13@aol.com. Business E-Mail: ryovanovich@foxcroft.org.

YOVANOVITCH, MARIE L., United States Ambassador to Armenia; BA, Princeton U., 1980; Attended, Pushkin Inst., 1980; MS, Nat. War Coll., 2001. Joined Fgn. Svc. US Dept. State, 1986—; dep. dir. Russian desk US Embassy, Moscow, 1998—2000, dep. chief of mission Kiev, Ukraine, 2001—04; sr. adv. to under sec. for polit. affairs US Dept. State, Washington, 2004—05, US amb. to Kyrgyz Republic Bishkek, 2005—08, US amb. to Armenia Yerevan, 2008—. Office: US Embassy 7020 Yerevan Pl Washington DC 20521*

YOVICH, DANIEL JOHN, chemist, educator; b. Chgo., Mar. 5, 1930; s. Milan D. and Sophie (Dorociak) Y.; m. Anita Barbara Moreland, Feb. 7, 1959; children: Daniel, Amy, David, Julie Ann. Ph.B., DePaul U., 1952; MA, Governors State U., 1975, MS, 1976. Cert. reality therapist, profl. mgr. Formulator Nat. Lead Co., 1950-52, 56-59; researcher Montgomery Ward, Chgo., 1959-62; tech. dir. Riley Bros., Inc., Burlington, Iowa, 1962-66, Mortell Co., Kankakee, Ill., 1966-70; exec. dir. Dan Yovich Assos., 1970-79; asst. prof. Purdue U., Hammond, Ind., 1979-84, assoc. prof., 1984-90, prof., 1990-2000, prof. emeritus, 2000—. Instr. Army Security Agy. Sch., 1954—56, Napoleon Hill Acad., 1965—66; cons. Learning House, 1964—; assoc. Hill, Zediker & Assocs. Psychologists, Kankakee, 1975—79; mem. adv. bd. Nat. Congress Inventor Orgns., 1984; vis. prof. Grand Valley State U., 2000—, Northwood U., 2001—; creator games Math Svey Break Hex & Octcon Step. Author: Applied Creativity; prdr., moderator: (program) Careers Unlimited, Sta. WCIU-TV, Chgo., 1967; contbr. articles to profl. jours.; patentee game Krypto, coating Sanitane. Mem. cmty. adv. coun. Governors State U., 1978; mem. Hammond (Ind.) Hist. Soc. Served to 1st lt. AUS, 1952-56. Recipient Outstanding Citizen Award News Pub. Co. Am., 1971, Outstanding Tchr. award Purdue U., 1980, 82, 83, Faculty Service award Nat. U. Continuing Edn. Assn., 1984, Disting. Service award Purdue U.-Calumet Alumni Assn., 1988, Arthur Young award Venture Mag., 1988, Entrepreneurial Edn. award Inc. Mag., 1990, Indiana Spirit of Innovation award, 1996. Mem. World Future Soc., Am. Soc. Profl. Supervision (exec. sec. 1986), Inventors and Entrepreneurs Soc. Am. (founder, exec. dir. 1984, prodr. Salute Vet. Recognition Programs 1999—), Global Intuition Network, Internat. Creativity Network, Infantry Officer Cand. Sch. Alumni Assn. (life), Napoleon Hill Found., Inst. Reality Therapy, Inst. Contemporary Living, Soc. Am. Inventors (life), Am. Legion, Vets. of the Battle of the Bulge (historian). Home: 3527 Whispering Brook Dr SE Kentwood MI 49508-3733 Personal E-mail: danyovich@sbcglobal.net.

YOVITS, MARSHALL CLINTON, information scientist, educator, dean; b. Bklyn., May 16, 1923; s. Louis Frederick and Rebecca (Gerber) Y.; m. Anita S. Friedman, Aug. 2, 1952; children: Bruce J., Mara F., Steven. BS, Union Coll., Schenectady, 1944, MS, 1948, Yale U., 1949, PhD, 1951. Sr. physicist Johns Hopkins U., 1951—56; physicist electronics br. Office Naval Rsch., Washington, 1956, head info. sys. br., 1956—62; dir. Naval Analysis Group, 1962—66; prof., chmn. dept. computer and info. sci. Ohio State U., 1966—78, prof., 1978—79; prof. computer and info. sci. Sch. of Sci., Ind. U., Purdue U., Indpls., 1980—, dean, 1980—88; prof. emeritus Ind. U., Purdue U., Indpls., 1993—. Gen. chmn. Computer Sci. Conf. NSF, 1973. Editor: (with Scott Cameron) Self-Organizing Systems, Proc. Interdisciplinary Conf., 1960, Large-Capacity Memory Techniques for Computing Systems, 1961 (with George T. Jacobi, Gordon D. Goldstein) Self-Organizing Systems, 1962, (with D.M. Gilford, R.H. Wilcox, E. Staveley, H.D. Lerner) Research Program Effectiveness, 1966, Advances in Computers, Vol. 11, 1971; editor: series Advances in Computers, Vols. 13-40; contbr. rsch. articles to profl. jours. Recipient Superior Civilian Svc. award, U.S. Navy, 1964, Outstanding Performance award, 1961; fellow AEC fellow, 1950—51, Indpls. Ctr. Advanced Rsch., 1988—89. Fellow AAAS (chmn. coun. sect. T 1985-88, chmn. 1996-98), IEEE (computer soc. chmn. awards com. 1989, bd. govs. 1988-89, computer pioneer award 1990), Assn. for Computing Machinery (coun., gen. chmn. computer sci. conf. 1982), EDUCOM (nominating com.), Sigma Xi. Home: 9016 Dewberry Ct Indianapolis IN 46260-1527 Office Phone: 317-274-9737. E-mail: myovits@iupui.edu.

YOW, DEBORAH A., athletic director; b. Gibsonville, NC, 1949; m. William W. Bowden. Grad. in English, Elon Coll., 1974; M in Counseling, Liberty U.; PhD, Baptist Christian U., 1993. Basketball coach U. Ky., 1976—80, Oral Roberts, 1980—83, U. Fla., 1983—85, asst. dir. Gator boosters, 1985—87; assoc. athletic dir. U. NC, Greensboro, 1987—90; dir. athletics St. Louis U., 1990—94, U. Md., College Pk., 1994—. Contbr. articles to profl. jours. Recipient Carl Maddox Sport Mgmt. award, US Sports Acad.; named one of 20 Most Influential People in Intercollegiate Athletics, 10 Most Powerful People in Coll. Sports, 2007; named to Md. Women's Hall of Fame, 2003, NC Sports Hall of Fame, 2006. Mem.: Nat. Assn. Collegiate Dirs. of Athletics (pres. 2001). Achievements include being the only Division I coach to take three previously unranked teams to the Top 20. Office: U Md Dept Intercollegiate Athletics Terrapin Trail College Park MD 20742 Office Phone: 301-314-7075.

YOW, VALERIE RALEIGH, historian, writer, counselor; d. Fletcher Raleigh Yow and Mae Moore Wyatt; m. Richard Quinney, June 14, 1958 (div. 1989); children: Laura Ellen Quinney, Anne Holloway Quinney. AB, U. NC, Greensboro, 1956; PhD in History, U. Wis., Madison, 1967; postgrad., Harvard U., Cambridge, Mass., 1980—81; MA in Counseling Psychology, Boston Coll., 1983. Nat. cert. psychologist N.Am. Masters Psychology, 1994. Faculty Bklyn Coll., 1966—70; instr. history dept. U. RI, Kingston, 1974—80; asst. prof. Northern Ill. U., DeKalb, 1984—91; psychol. counselor Counseling Couples and Individuals, Chapel Hill, NC, 1994—. Author: (plays) In the Service of Others (1st pl. Gt. Chgo. Playwrights Expn., 1987), Past Tense/Present Tense, Betty Smith Meets Carl Jung: Some Memories, Dreams, Reflections, (books) Bernice Kelly Harris: A Good Life Was Writing, 1999, Recording Oral History: A Guide for the Humanities and Social Sciences, 2005, Betty Smith: Life of the Author of A Tree Grows in Brooklyn, 2008; book rev. editor: Oral History Rev., 1999—2007; contbr. articles to profl. jours. Mem. Eno River Assn., Durham, NC, 1995, Tikkun, the Rsch. Triangle, 2002—, Women in Three Arts, 2004—. Recipient Harvey Kantor award in Recognition of Outstanding Achievement in Oral History, New Eng. Oral History Assn., 2005, Outstanding Acad. Texts, ALA's Choice for book Rec. Oral History, 2007. Mem.: C.G. Jung Soc. Rsch. Triangle (bd. dirs. 2002—04), Orgn. Am. Historians, Oral History Assn. (mem. governing coun. 2006—), Chapel Hill Preservation Soc., Alliance the Mentally Ill. Democrat. Unitarian. Avocations: art, painting, dance. Home and Office: 12 Davie Cir Chapel Hill NC 27514

YOZWIAK, BERNARD JAMES, retired mathematics educator, academic administrator; b. Youngstown, Ohio, July 5, 1919; s. Walter J. and Anna (Baluch) Y.; m. Helen A. Mika, Aug. 28, 1943; children— Ruth (Mrs. Charles W. Lewis), John B., Mark S., Bernard P. AB, Marietta Coll., Ohio, 1940; MS, U. Pitts., 1951, PhD, 1961; LLD, Youngstown State U., Ohio, 1992. Office clk. Youngstown Sheet & Tube Co., 1940—41, 1944—45; instr. math. and sci., prin. Fowler Twp. H.S., Ohio, 1941—42, 1945—47; prof. math., chmn. math. dept. Youngstown State U., 1947—, dean Coll. Arts and Scis., 1971—92; ret., 1992. Recipient Watson Distinguished Prof. award, 1961; NSF sci. faculty fellow, 1958-60 Mem. AAUP, Math. Assn. Am. (chmn. Ohio sect. 1970-71), Sigma Xi. Home: 2080 S Schenley Ave Youngstown OH 44511-1271

YRIGOYEN, CHARLES, JR., retired church denomination executive; b. Phila., Dec. 9, 1937; s. Charles and Erma Mae (Suters) Y.; m. Jeanette Alice Brittingham, Dec. 13, 1958; children: Debra Jean, Charles III. BS in Econs., U. Pa., 1959; BD, Lancaster Theol. Sem., Pa., 1962; ThM, Ea. Bapt. Theol. Sem., Phila., 1964; PhD, Temple U., 1973; DD (hon.), Albright Coll., 1987. Ordained to ministry United Meth. Ch., 1960. Pastor various chs. Meth. Ch., Pa., 1958-66, campus min. Phila., 1966-68; chaplain, prof. religion Albright Coll., Reading, Pa., 1968-82; gen. sec. Gen. Com. on Archives and History, United Meth. Ch., Madison, NJ, 1982—2005; dir. United Methodist Studies Evangelical Theol. Sem., 2006—08, Lancaster Theol. Sem., 2007—. Vis. scholar Union Theol. Sem., N.Y.C., 1980, adj. prof., 1982-93, 2000-02; adj. prof. ch. history Drew U., Madison, 1982-2005; adj. prof. Moravian Theol. Sem., Bethlehem, Pa., 1994-02; exec. com. World Meth. Coun., 1986-2006; bd. dir. Wesley Works Editl. Project, 1982-2006; adj. prof. Luth. Theol. Sem., Phila., 1999. Author: Acts for Our Time, 1987, John Wesley: Holiness of Heart and Life, 1996, Belief Matters: United Methodism's Doctrinal Standards, 2001; editor: Reformed and Catholic, 1978, Catholic and Reformed, 1979, Historical Dictionary of Methodism, 1996, 2d edit., 2005, The Global Impact of the Wesleyan Traditions and Their Related Movements, 2002, Praising The God of Grace: The Theology of Charles Westey's Hymns, 2005; United Methodism at Forty: Looking Back, Looking Forward, 2008; editor Methodist History Jour., 1982-2006. Mem. alumni coun., sec. Lancaster Theol. Sem., 2002—08. Masland fellow Union Theol. Sem., 1975, 80; disting. svc. award, United Methodist Ch., 2005. Mem. World Meth. Hist. Soc. (gen. sec. 1987-2006), Wesley Hist. Soc., Wesleyan Theol. Soc., Charles Wesley Soc., Oxford Inst. Meth. Theol. Studies, Mercersburg Soc. (bd. dirs.), United Meth. Hist. Soc. (treas.) Republican. Methodist. Avocation: model railroads. Home: I 106 950 Willow Valley Lakes Dr Willow Street PA 17584-9663 Business E-Mail: cyrigoyen@lancasterseminary.edu. E-mail: jyrigoyen@cs.com.

YSASI-DIAZ, GLORIA, wholesale distribution executive; BS in Chem. Engring., Univ. Rochester; MBA, Coll. William & Mary. Ops. positions GE Co., 1978—84; ops. positions to sr. v.p., process mgmt. R.R. Donnelley, Chgo., 1984—2004; v.p. logistics mgmt., US branch-based bus. WW Grainger Co., Chgo., 2004—. Named one of 50 Most Important Hispanics in Tech., Bus., Hispanic Engineer and Info. Tech. mag., 2005—09. Office: 100 Grainger Pkwy Lake Forest IL 60045-5201 Office Phone: 847-535-1000. Office Fax: 847-535-0878.

YSIKES, JUANITA LOU, art educator; b. Belen, N.Mex., Dec. 22, 1951; d. Melvin Vernette and Doris Marie (McArthur) Lovelady; m. James Carroll Fulcher, May 30, 1970 (div. Aug. 1988); children: Lee Collins Fulcher, Amy Laura Fulcher; m. Robert Harry Sikes, Dec. 26, 1990. BS in Edn., Ea. N.Mex. U., 1983. Cert. tchr., N.Mex. Bookkeeper J & L Auto Salvage, Socorro, N.Mex., 1970-72, Navajo Mobil, Truth or Consequences, N.Mex., 1972-75; subs. tchr. Portales (N.Mex.) Schs., 1977-78, art aide, 1988-91; tchr., aide spl. edn. Ft. Summer (N.Mex.) High Sch., 1978-83, tchr. spl. edn., 1983-86; tutor ESL and GED Ea. N.Mex. U. Clovis Campus, Ft. Summer, 1986-87; fashion illustrator Slyduds Clothing, Roswell and Ft. Summer, N.Mex., 1987-88; instr. drawing Ea. N.Mex. U., Portales, 1989-90; tchr. art Portales Jr. High Sch., 1991—. Supt. art dept. DeBaca County Fair Bd., Ft. Summer, 1979-87; advisor Portales Elem. Spl. Art Program, Portales, 1989-91; coord. Portales Jr. High Spl. Art Program, Portales, 1991-2001; sponsor art club Portales HS, 2001—; judge arts and crafts dept. Roosevelt County Fair, Portales, 1992. Exhibited in group shows Crafter's Crossing Gallery, Ft. Worth, numerous art fairs. Vol. Sierra County Rescue Squad, Truth or Consequences, 1973-75, Mayors Christmas Tree, Portales, 1989-90; coord., 1991—. Recipient Outstanding Citizenship award Sierra County Rescue Squad, 1974, 75; named Artist of Month Ft. Sumner Pub. Libr., 1987. Mem. NEA (pres. local chpt. 1992—), Nat. Art Edn. Assn., Gamma Zeta (pres. Beta Sigma Phi chpt. 1984-88). Democrat. Mem. Ch. of Christ. Avocations: painting, sewing, bowling, archery. Home: 2108 W Beech St Portales NM 88130-9303 Office: Portales Jr High Sch 300 E 5th St Portales NM 88130-6082

YSLAS, STEPHEN DANIEL, lawyer; b. Los Angeles, Mar. 28, 1947; m. Alice Troy. BA, UCLA, 1969, JD, 1972. Bar: Calif. 1973. Atty. NLRB, LA, 1972-73, Atlantic Richfield, LA, 1973-75; asst. gen. counsel Northrop Corp., LA, 1975, chief counsel aircraft and electronics businesses; corp. v.p., sec., deputy general counsel Northrop Grumman Corp., 2006—08, corp. v.p., gen. counsel, 2009—. Commr., City of L.A. Police Dept., 1980-90; bd. dirs. Youth Opportunities Found., L.A., Constl. Rights Found., Police Meml. Found. Mem. ABA, Mexican Am.-Bar Assn. (Benito Juarez award for community service), Calif. Bar Assn. Office: Northrop Grumman 1840 Century Park E Los Angeles CA 90067-2199*

YSSEL, NINA, special education educator; b. Bethal, South Africa, Oct. 31, 1950; d. Jan Adriaan and Anna Venter; children: Nicola Johnson, Renate Myler. PhD, Southern Ill. U., Carbondale, 1992. Tchr. High Schs., Johannesburg, 1972—86, Alexandria Mid. Sch., 1992—95; assoc. prof. Ball State U., Muncie, Ind., 1995—. Mem.: Coun. Exceptional Children. Presbyterian. Avocations: travel, reading, gardening. Home: 1001 N Greenbriar Rd Muncie IN 47304 Office: Ball State Univ University Ave Muncie IN 47306 Home Phone: 765-286-0223; Office Phone: 765-285-5703. Office Fax: 765-285-4280. Business E-Mail: nyssel@bsu.edu.

YSURSA, BEN T., Secretary of State, Idaho; b. Boise, Idaho, June 10, 1949; m. Penny Ysursa; children: Shawn Del, Matthew, Andrew. BA, Gonzaga U., 1971; JD, St. Louis U. Law Sch., 1974. Bar: Idaho 1974. Dep. sec. state State of Idaho, Boise, 1974—76, chief dep., 1976—2002, sec. state, 2002—. Mem. Basque Ctr., St. John's Parish; pres. Adh County Lincoln Day, 1990. Recipient Boyd Martin award, Assn. Idaho Cities, Outstanding Adminstr., Idaho Rep. Party, 1992. Mem.: Reagan-Bush Idaho Com. (treas. 1984), NHSS (secs. state 2003), Idaho State Bar Assn. Republican. Roman Catholic. Office: Office Sec State Rm 203 700 W Jefferson Boise ID 83720-0080 Office Phone: 208-334-2300. Office Fax: 208-334-2282. E-mail: bysursa@idsos.state.id.us.

YTTERBERG, MICHAEL ROGER, architect, educator; b. San Antonio, Tex., Nov. 9, 1953; s. Roger Byron and Gretchen Ann Ytterberg; m. Karen S. Harrison, Nov. 21, 1982 (div. May 15, 2004); children: Gabriel, Arden, Eliel; life ptnr. Janet L. Kroll; 1 child, Lucy Kroll. BA, Rice U., Houston, 1975, MArch, 1980; cert. in expressive movement in theater and arch., Ecole Jacques Lecoq, Paris, 1976; PhD in History and Theory of Architecture, U. Pa., Phila., 2005. Cert. Nat. Coun. oArchtl. Registration Boards, 2006, registered arch., Pa., 1992, Nev., 2007, Md., 2007, NJ, 2007. Assoc. CRSS, Houston, 1979—85; project arch. Mitchell Giurgola Archs., Phila., 1987—89; assoc. Kling Stubbins, Phila., 1989—92; pvt. practice M. Ytterberg Archs., Phila., 1993; sr. designer Parsky Assoc., Phila., 1994—97; design prin. BLT Archs., Phila., 1997—. Vis. lectr. SUNY, Buffalo, 1986; adj. assoc. prof. dept. architecture Drexel U., Phila., 1987—; guest lectr. Wharton Sch., U. Penn., Phila., 2004—. High rise residential condominium, Symphony House, Phila., casino resort, Echelon, Las Vegas. Grantee, Insitute Internat. Edn., Rome, 1985—86. Mem.: AIA, Congress New Urbanism, Soc. Archtl. Historians, Urban Land Inst. Office Fax: 215-563-3036. Business E-Mail: mry@blta.com.

YU, AITING TOBEY, engineering executive; b. Chekiang, China, Jan. 6, 1921; came to U.S., 1945, naturalized, 1955; s. H.K. and A. (Chow) Y.; m. Natalie Kwok, Nov. 10, 1951; children: Pamela, Leonard T. BS, Nat. Cen. U., Chungking, China, 1943; SM, MIT, 1946; PhD, Lehigh U., 1949; MBA, Columbia U., 1972. Registered profl. engr., Fla. Asst. prof. engring. NYU, 1949-51; design engr. Hewitt-Robins Inc., 1951-54, chief design engr., 1955-58, engring. mgr., 1958-59, dir. systems engring. Totowa, N.J., 1967-68, v.p. ops., 1968-71; tech. dir. West S.Am. Overseas Corp., NYC, 1959-67; prin. A.T. Yu Cons. Engrs., 1971-72; co-founder, chmn. Orba Corp., Mountain Lakes, N.J., 1972—, now chmn. emeritus. Contbr. articles to profl. jours; patentee in field. Recipient nat. outstanding engring. achievement awards by ASCE, NSPE, AIME, ASME; inducted into Nat. Mining Hall of Fame, 1998. Mem. NAE, AIME (chmn. minerals processing div., SME pres. 1986), NSPE, Nat. Acad. Engring., Sigma Xi. Home: 4303A Hana Hwy Haiku HI 96708-5303 Office: Orba Corp 1250 W Sam Houston Pkwy S Houston TX 77042-1916

YU, ANDREW, minister; b. Fu-Yang, Chekian, China, Feb. 28, 1927; came to the U.S., 1972; s. Kung-Chu Yu and Mei-Chen Liu; m. Julie Yu, July 13, 1957; children: Peter, Ruth. BTh, Taiwan Bapt. Theol. Sem., Taipei, 1957; postgrad., Tanghai U., Taichung, Taiwan, 1965; MA in Ministry Studies, Moody Bible Inst., 1991; postgrad., Bibl. Archaeology Soc., 1993, Fuller Theol. Sem., 1996, Fuqua Internat. Sch. Christian Comm., 1998. Cert. pastoral counseling. Jour. clk. Bankers Trust Co., NYC, 1972-80; pastoral coounselor Am. Assn. Christian Counseling, Forest, Va., 1991—; minister Manhattan Chinese Bapt. Ch., NYC, 1980—, sr. pastor, 1986—. Author: Rekinling the Fires of Revial, 1993, A Master Piece of Spirituality, 1995, The Poem of Draw Wings, 2001, A Song of Harmonies, 2008; editor Chinese Christian Workers, 1999—; editor: Chinese Newsletter, NY, 1999-2002. Mem. Bapt. World Alliance 100th Anniversary Congress, Bermingham, England, 2005. Recipient Lifetime Royal Patronage status Kevin, Prince Regent Prinecpality of Hutt River Province, Australia, 1994, Cert. of Appreciation, Ronald Reagan Presdl. Found., 2003. Mem.: Poetry Soc. Am. Avocations: reading, writing, music, travel, collecting. Home: Apt 20E 675 Water St New York NY 10002 Office: Manhattan Chinese Bapt Ch 236 W 72nd St New York NY 10023 Office Phone: 212-496-1486. Personal E-mail: andreweyu@gmail.com, andrewyu236@hotmail.com.

YU, ANTHONY C., religion and literature educator; b. Hong Kong, Oct. 6, 1938; came to U.S., 1956, naturalized, 1976; s. P.C. and Norma (Au) Y.; m. Priscilla Tang, Sept. 18, 1963; 1 son, Christopher Dietrich. BA, Houghton Coll., 1960; STB, Fuller Theol. Sem., 1963; PhD, U. Chgo., 1969, DLitt, 1996; DLitt (hon.), 2006. Instr. U. Ill., Chgo., 1967-68; asst. prof. U. Chgo., 1968-74, assoc. prof., 1974-78, prof., 1978—2005, prof. emeritus, 2005—. Assoc. vis. prof. Ind. U., Bloomington, 1975; Whitney J. Oates short-term vis. fellow Princeton U., 1986; disting. vis. prof. Faculty of Arts, U. Alta., Can., 1992; mem. joint com. on study Chinese civilization Am. Coun. Learned Socs., 1980-86, bd. dirs., 1986-94; regional chmn. Mellon Fellowship in Humanities, 1982-92; bd. dirs. Ill. Humanities Coun., 1995-97; vis. prof. dept. religion Chinese U. Hong Kong, 1997; mem. com. social thought U. Chgo., 2004—, Siu Lien Ling Wong vis. fellow, Chinese U. Hong Kong, 2006 Asst. editor Jour. Asian Studies, 1975-78; co-editor Jour. Religion, 1980—; author, editor: Parnassus Revisited, 1973; editor, translator: The Journey to the West, 4 vols., 1977-83, Essays on The Journey to the West and Other Studies (in Chinese), 1989, The Monkey and the Monk, An Abridgment of the Journey to the West, 2006; co-editor (with Mary Gerhart) Morphologies of Faith: Essays on Religion and Culture in Honor of Nathan A. Scott, Jr., 1990, Rereading the Stone: Desire and the Making of Fiction in Dream of the Red Chamber, 1997, State and Religion in China: Historical and Textual Perspectives, 2005, Dream of the Red Chamber, Journey to the West, and Other Studies, Chinese edit., 2006; author: Comparative Journeys: Essays on Literature and Religion East and West, 2008. Recipient Gordon J. Laing prize, 1983, Norman Maclean Faculty award, 2009; Danforth fellow, 1960-67; Guggenheim fellow, 1976-77; NEH translation grantee, 1977-82; Am. Coun. Learned Socs. sr. fellow, 1986-87, Mellon Emeriti fellow, 2006—; Masterworks Study grant NEH Seminar for Pub. Sch. Tchrs., 1992; elected academician Academia Sinica, 1998; Phi Beta Kappa vis. scholar 2001-02. Fellow Am. Acad. Arts and Scis.; mem. MLA (exec. coun. 1998—2001), Assn. for Asian Studies, Am. Acad. Religion (bd. dirs. 1995-97), Am. Comparative Lit. Assn., Milton Soc. Am., Arts Club. Home: 950 N Clark St Unit G Chicago IL 60610-8702 Office: U Chicago 1025 E 58th St Chicago IL 60637-1509 Office Phone: 773-702-8245. Business E-Mail: acyu@mid.uchicago.edu.

YU, BENITA KA PO, lawyer; b. Hong Kong; d. Yu Sai Hung and Yu Shirley; m. E. Kwok; 2 children: V. Kwok, A. Kwok BA, U. Oxford, 1986, MA, 1991; law soc. finals 1st class, 1987. Solicitor: Supreme Ct., England, 1989, Wales, 1989, High Ct. Hong Kong Spl. Adminstv. Region, 1994. Articled clk. Norton Rose, London, 1987—89; asst.

solicitor Norton Rode, London, 1989-93, Slaughter and May, Hong Kong, 1994-96, ptnr., 1996—. Contbg. author: Asia Finance Manual, 2d edit., 1998, Practitioner's Guide to the Listing Rules, 2005; contbr. articles to profl. jours. and mags. Recipient Book prize St. Hugh's Coll., Oxford U., 1984; scholar Hong Kong Govt., 1976-81, Ho Leung Ho Lee, 1983. Mem.: Hong Kong Fedn. Women Lawyers (mem. coun., mem. takeovers panel, takeovers appeal com.), Hong Kong Golf Assn., The Oxford and Cambridge Soc. Hong Kong, Law Soc. Hong Kong, Law Soc. England, Diocesan Old Girls' Assn. (co-chmn. legal sub-com., mem. careers and scholarships). Avocations: piano, singing, jazz, classical music. Office: Slaughter and May 47th Flr Jardine Ho Ctr One Connaught Pl Hong Kong China Office Phone: 852 2901 7207. E-mail: benita.yu@slaughterandmay.com.

YU, BIN, statistician, educator; BS in Math, Peking U., 1984; MA in Stats., U. Calif. Berkeley, 1987, PhD of Stats., 1990. Asst. prof. U. Wis. Madison, 1990—92; asst. prof., assoc. prof. U. Calif. Berkeley, 1993—2000, prof., 2001—. Postdoctoral fellow MSRI, Berkeley, 1991; vis. asst. prof. Yale U., New Haven, 1993; mem. tech. staff Bell Labs. Lucent, Murray Hill, NJ, 1997—2000. Guest editor spl. issue Statistica Sinica, 2001, IEEE Signal Processing; contbr. articles to profl. jours. Grantee, Army Rsch. Office, 1991, 1994, 1998, 2001, 2004, 2005, NSF, 1994, 1998, 2001, 2004, 2006; Guggenheim fellow, 2006. Fellow: AAAS, IEEE, Am. Stats. Assn., Inst. Math. Stats. Achievements include patents for lossless coding and data network tomography. Avocations: reading, walking, swimming, movies. Office: Univ Calif Berkeley 367 Evans Hall #3860 Berkeley CA 94720

YU, BOAS J., nursing educator; BA, Rutgers U., Nj, 1990; BSN, Fairleigh Dickinson U., Nj, 1992; MSN, TCNJ, Nj, 1996; EdD, Columbia U., Ny, 2002; Degree, UMASS, Boston, 2008. Clinical Nurse Specialist, ANCC, 1996. Asst. prof. St. Joseph's Coll., Brooklyn, NY, 2002—. Grants, St. Joseph's Coll., 2004. Mem.: Kappa Delta Pi, Sigma Theta Tau.

YU, CHACK YUNG, pediatrics educator, molecular biologist; b. Guangdong, People Republic of China, Dec. 24, 1957; s. Hung Ho and Shui-Wo (Kwok) Y.; m. Lai-Chu, Apr. 23, 1987; children: Gayang Heidi, Gakit Richard. BS, Chinese U. Hong Kong, 1981, MPhil, 1983; DPhil, Oxford U., England, 1988. Asst. prof. Ohio State U., Columbus, 1990-96, assoc. prof., 1996—. Contbr. articles to profl. jours. Grantee NIH, Bethesda, Md., 1994—, March of Dimes, 1992-94; postdoctoral fellow Med. Rsch. Coun. Lab. Molecular Biology, Cambridge, England, 1987-90. Mem. AAAS, Am. Assn. Immunologists, Am. Soc. Human Genetics, Am. Soc. Microbiology, Am. Soc. Biochemistry and Molecular Biology, Soc. for Pediat. Rsch. Office: Children's Rsch Inst 700 Childrens Dr Columbus OH 43205-2664 E-mail: cyu@chi.osu.edu.

YU, CHIEN-NING, engineer, consultant; MSME, MIT, Cambridge, 1996, PhD in Mech. Engring., 1999. Rsch. asst. MIT, 1995—99; consulting engr. Asea Brown Boveri, Santa Clara, Calif., 1999—. Achievements include design of and implementation of market applications for many electricity markets including Texas ERCOT, Ontario Canada IESO, Western Australia IMO, South Korea KPX, East China ECG and Philippine WESM.

YU, CLEMENT TAK, educator, researcher, consultant; b. Hong Kong, Aug. 31, 1948; came to U.S., 1967; s. Ching Hang and Chen-Chun (Sheit) Y.; m. Teresa Yuen-Ling Chan, May 31, 1975; children: Victor Kar-Yun, Christine Mei-Yun. BSc, Columbia U., 1970; PhD, Cornell U., 1973. Asst. prof. U. Alberta, Edmunton, Can., 1973-77, assoc. prof., 1977-78, U. Ill., Chgo., 1978-84, prof., 1984—. Cons. System Devel. Corp., MCC, Shell Oil, Amoco Oil, Argonne Nat. Lab., Trilogy, Info. Arts., Fla. Internat. U. Contbr. more than 200 article to profl. confs. and jours. Mem. IEEE (assoc. editor 1994-98), Assn. for Computing Machinery (spl. interest group on info. retrieval, chmn. 1985-87, chmn. conf. 2006), Distributed and Parallel Databases (mem. editl. bd. 1992—). Office: U Ill Dept Computer Sci Chicago IL 60607-7053 Office Phone: 312-996-2318. Business E-Mail: yu@cs.uic.edu.

YU, GANG, medical educator, researcher; PhD, U. Calgary, Alberta, Canada, 1996. Postdoc. fellow U. Toronto, Ontario, Canada, 1996—2000, rsch. assoc., 2000—01; asst. prof. neurosci. UT Southwestern Med. Ctr., Dallas, 2001—08, assoc. prof. neurosci., 2008—. Contbr. articles to profl. sci. jours. Recipient Meml. Frist Rsch. award, U. Toronto, 1998, Alzheimer's Disease Rsch. award, UT Southwestern Med. Ctr., 2003, Ruth Salta Jr. Investigator Achievement award, Am. Health Assistance Found., 2005; Helen B. Hunter fellowship, U. Toronto, 1997—2000, New investigator grant, Alzheimer's Assn., 2003—05, AFAR Rsch. grant, Am. Fedn. Aging Rsch., 2003—05, AHAF grant, Am. Health Assistance Found., 2003—05, grant, NIH, 2003—, Rsch. grant, Welch Found., 2003—, grant, Ruth K. Broad Rsch. Found., 2006—08. Mem.: Soc. Neurosci. Office: UT Southwestern Med Ctr 6000 Harry Hines Blvd Dallas TX 75390

YU, GANG, science educator; s. Honhcheng Yu and Manling Qu; m. Xiaoyan Lin; 1 child, Yanlin. PhD, U. Wis.-Milw., 2002. Rsch. assoc. U. Wis.-Milw., 2002—03, Northeastern U., Boston, 2004—05; assoc. prof. Harbin Inst. Tech. Shezhen Grad. Sch., Guangdong, China, 2005—. Office: HIT Shezhen Graduate Sch Xili Shezhen University Town HIT Campus Shenzhen Guangdong 518055 China Office Fax: 86-755-26033774. Personal E-mail: joseph.yugang@gmail.com.

YU, HAIPING, research scientist; arrived in US, 1998, naturalized, 2006; s. Shunqing Yu and Changzhu Liu. B, Hangzhou U., China, 1981; M, East China Normal U., Shanghai, 1984; PHD, Fundan U., Shanghai, 1988. Cert. profl. mgmt. Am. Mgmt. Assn. Internat., 2000. Postdoctoral rschr. Stockholm U., Stockholm, 1988—90; rsch. assoc. Imperial Coll., London, 1990—98; staff rschr. Reveo Inc., NY, 1998—2001; lead engr. Semrock Inc., NY, 2001; mng. dir. Kent Optronics, Inc., Hopewell Junction, NY, 2002—. Contbr. articles to profl. jours. Achievements include 1 patent and 5 patents pending in field. Office: Kent Optronics Inc 40 Corporate Park Dr Hopewell Junction NY 12533 Business E-Mail: haipingyu@kentoptronics.com.

YU, HANNAH, medical researcher; PhD, U. Del., Newark, 1998. Sr. rsch. scientist Eli Lilly and Co., Indpls., 2004—08, prin. rsch. scientist, 2008—.

YU, JEN, medical educator; b. Taipei, Taiwan, Jan. 23, 1943; came to U.S., 1969; s. Chin Chuan and Shiu Lan (Lin) Y.; m. Janet Chen, June 16, 1973; children: Benjamin, Christopher. MD, Nat. Taiwan U., 1968; PhD in Physiology, U. Pa., 1972. Diplomate Am. Bd. Phys. Medicine and Rehab. Intern Phila. Gen. Hosp., 1972-73; resident in phys. medicine and rehab. Hosps. of U. Pa., 1973-75; asst. prof. dept. phys. medicine and rehab. U. Pa. Sch. Medicine, Phila., 1975-76, U. Tex. Health Sci. Ctr., San Antonio, 1976-79, assoc. prof., 1979-81; prof. dept. phys. medicine and rehab. U. Calif. Irvine Coll. Medicine, 1981-82, prof., chmn. dept. phys. medicine and rehab., 1982—. Contbr. articles to profl. jours. Mem. Am. Acad. Phys. Medicine and Rehab., Am. Congress Rehab. Medicine, Assn. Acad. Physiatrists, Am. Assn. Anatomists, Soc. for Neurosci. Office: U Calif Irvine Med Ctr Dept Phys Medicine & Rehab 101 The City Dr Orange CA 92868-3201 Home Phone: 949-856-3264; Office Phone: 714-456-6504. Business E-Mail: jyu@uci.edu.

YU, JIE, computer scientist; PhD, U. Tex., San Antonio, 2007. Rsch. fellow U. Ill., Urbana-Champain, 2007; rsch. scientist Eastman Kodak Co., NY, 2007—. Recipient Student Paper Contest Winner award, IEEE Internat. Conf. Acoustics, Speech and Signal Processing, 2006, Best Poster Paper award, ACM Internat. Conf. Image and Video Retrieval, 2008; UTSA fellowship, U. Tex., 2001—07, UIUC Rsch. fellowship, U. Ill., 2007. Mem.: Sci. Rsch. Soc., Sigma Xi.

YU, JIE, researcher; s. Zonglai Yu and Wenxia Yang; m. Yanling Wu; 1 child, Jennifer. PhD, U. Tex., Austin, 2007. Rsch. engr. Shell Global Solutions, Houston, 2007—. Contbr. articles to profl. jours. Mem.: IEEE, AIChE, Sigma Xi.

YU, JOHN JUNYAO, mechanical engineer, researcher; PhD in Mech. Engring., U. Alta., Can., 1997. Lic. Alta., 1999. Faculty mem. Shanghai Jiao Tong U., Shanghai, 1985—92; rsch. assoc. U. Alta., Edmonton, Canada, 1997—98; rsch. engr. Bently Rotor Dynamics Rsch. Corp., Minden, Nev., 1998—99, sr. rsch. engr., 1999—2000, rsch. scientist, 2000—02; sr. engr. GE Energy-Bently Nev., Minden, Nev., 2002—. Contbr. more than 50 scientific papers to profl. pubs. (IGTI 2001 John P. Davis Award, 2003). PhD dissertation fellow, U. Alta., 1996-1997. Mem.: ASME (rotordynamics session chair ASME/IGTI Turbo Expo 2003, 2004), IGTI Dynamics and Structure Com. Achievements include development of rolling element bearing defect detection methodology; gas bearing design code; discovery of dry-whip generated spontenuously. Home: 1839 Bougainvillea Dr Minden NV 89423 Office: GE Energy-Bently Nevada 1631 Bently Pkwy S Minden NV 89423 Office Phone: 775-215-1225. Business E-Mail: john.yu@ge.com.

YU, JOHN SUN, neurosurgeon, immunologist; b. Seoul, Republic of Korea, Sept. 11, 1963; s. Victor Seung Jae Yu, Grace Eun Duk Yu; m. Helena Yoon; children: Jeffrey, Lauren. BA, BS, Stanford U., 1985; MD, Harvard U., 1990, MS in Genetics, 1990. Diplomate Am. Bd. Neurol. Surgery. Resident in neurosurgery Mass. Gen. Hosp., Boston, 1997; neurosurgeon Cedars-Sinai Med. Ctr., LA, 1997—, co-dir. Comprehensive Brain Tumor Program, 1997—; med. dir. Gamma Knife, 2006—; chmn., chief sci. officer Immunocellular Therapeutics Ltd., Woodland Hills, Calif., 2006—; dir. surg. neuro-oncology Cedars-Sinai Med. Ctr., LA, 2007—. Editor: Current Stem Cell Rsch. and Therapy; contbr. articles to Lancet, Cancer Rsch., Human Gene Therapy, others.; patent for differentiation of whole bone marrow cells into neural progenitor cells, 2001. Recipient Acad. award, Am. Acad. Neurol. Surgery, 1998, Betty Lea Stone award, Am. Cancer Soc., 1986, Preuss Resident Rsch. award, AANS and CNS, 1995, Mahaley Clin. Rsch. award, 2005; grantee, NIH, 2001—. Mem.: Am Assn. Neurol. Surgeons (tumor sect.). Office: Cedars-Sinai Neurosurg Inst 8631 W Third St Ste 800E Los Angeles CA Office Phone: 310-423-7900, 310-423-7000. Business E-Mail: yuj@cshs.org.

YU, JURONG, chemist; b. Suzhou, Jiangsu, China, Aug. 15, 1963; arrived in U.S., 1990; s. Jingrong and Zhenzhu Yu; m. Huilei Shi, Aug. 14, 1986; children: Christina H., Timmy C. BSc, Xuzhou Normal U., China, 1984; PhD, Shanghai Inst. Materia Medica, Chinese Acad. Scis., 1988. Rsch. asst. prof. Shanghai Inst. Materia Medica, Chinese Acad. Scis., 1988—90; postdoctoral rsch. fellow U. Tex. Southwestern Med. Ctr., Dallas, 1990—96; sr. rsch. investigator Bristol-Myers Squibb Co., New Brunswick, NJ, 1997—. Contbr. articles to profl. jours. Recipient Presdl. Young Investigator award, Chinese Acad. Scis., 1989, Excellent Grad. Student award, Shanghai Inst. Materia Medica, Chinese Acad. Scis., 1988, Triumph award, Devel. Operating Com. Bristol-Myers Squibb Co., 2003. Mem.: Am. Chem. Soc. Achievements include patents for pharmaceutical development; research in total synthesis of complex antifungal agent FR-900848; invention of intramolecular mitsunobu displacement with carbon nucleophiles: preparation of a-Nitrocyclopropanes; synthesis of Alkyl Nitronates via Mitsunobu Condensation; stereospecific Dehydrative Alkylation of Bis-Sulfones: Synthesis of a Lessor Tea Tortrix Pheromone; Total Synthesis of Polycyclopropyl Antibiotic FR-900848; Synthesis of Camptothecin Using Nitrone Cycloaddition to Construct the CDE Ring Moiety; One-pot Synthesis of Cyclic Enecarbamates from Lactam Carbamates. Home: 15 Scenic Dr Dayton NJ 08810 Office: Nanjing Pharmatechs Nanjing 210047 China Home Phone: 732-438-0678. Office Fax: 8625 58393229; Home Fax: 732-438-0678. Personal E-mail: jurongyu@yahoo.com.

YU, KELLY JEN-YI, epidemiologist; b. Taipei, Taiwan, Jan. 27, 1976; d. Hoping and Meichu Yu; m. Li Si, Aug. 8, 2008. BS, U. Md., Coll. Pk., 1997; MPH, Yale U., New Haven, 2000; PhD, Johns Hopkins Bloomberg Sch. Pub. Health, Balt., 2008. Rschr. NIH-NCI-DBS-LMP, Bethesda, Md., 1993—97; rsch. assoc. Inst. Genomic Inst., Rockville, Md., 1997—98; study mgr. Rsch. Triangle Inst., Rockville, 2000—01; epidemiologist NIH-NIMH-MAP-SDGE, Bethesda, 2001—03; postdoc. fellow NIH-NCI-DCEG-IIB, Rockville, 2008—. Achievements include research in prevention, screening and etiology of virally related cancers. Office Fax: 301-402-0817. Business E-Mail: yuke@mail.nih.gov.

YU, LONG-XI, agriculturist, researcher; m. Xin Shen; 1 child, Jing. PhD, Orleans, France, 1988. Rsch. fellow U. Bristol, England, 1989—91; sr. scientist Nova Flora, INC., Phila., 1998—2000; project mgr. Cornell U., Ithaca, NY, 2009—. Mem.: Am. Soc. Plant Biologists. Achievements include research in plant molecular biology. Home: 408 Richard PL Ithaca NY 14850 Office: Cornell Univ Tower Rd Ithaca NY 14853

YU, MAY HUANG, librarian, educator; b. Chengdu, Sichuan, China, June 24; came to the U.S., 1989; s. Dazhou Huang and Jiangzhen Yu; m. Lixin Yu; 1 child, Michael. Student, Beijing U., 1988; LLB, State Normal U. Sichuan, Chengdu, 1982; MLS, SUNY, Albany, 1996. Cert. pub. libr., N.Y. Tchr. Fuxing HS, Qingcheng, Sichuan, China, 1975-78; asst. prof. State Normal U. Sichuan, Chengdu, Sichuan, 1982-89; docs. libr., instr. head docs. dept. Alcorn State U., Miss., 1996—97; web developer, metadata libr. Fla. State U., Tallahassee, 1998—2000; media libr., instr., head Instrnl. Media Ctr., Alcorn State U., Lorman, Miss., 2000—05, asst. prof., media libr., head, 2005—. Spl. corr. Jour. Ethics, Chengdu, 1985-89; gen. sec. Sichuan State Ethics Assn., Chengdu, 1985-89. Editor: The Dictionary of Ethics, 1987. Named Outstanding Rschr., Assn. Philosophy and Social Scis. Sichuan State, 1987. Mem. ALA, Miss. Libr. Assn., Internat. Fedn. Libr. Assn. & Instns. (standing com. mem. 2009-). Avocations: ping pong/table tennis, movies, travel. Office: JD Boyd Libr 1000 ASU Dr Alcorn State MS 39096-7510

YU, MING, engineering educator, researcher; s. Chongguang Yu and Zhongying Su; m. Tian Xing, Aug. 28, 1992; children: Ellen Tian, Karen Tian, Tim Tian. BEE, Hubei Inst. Auto Tech., 1984; MEE, Huazhong U. Sci. and Tech., 1987; D of Engring., Tsinghua U., China, 1994; PhD, Rutgers U., New Brunswick, NJ, 2002. Sr. tech. staff mem. AT&T Labs, Middletown, NJ, 1997—2000; asst. prof. SUNY, Binghamton, NY, 2003—06, Fla. State U., Tallahassee, 2006—. Sr. software engr. Jedai Broadband Networks, Red Bank, 2000; sys. engr. AT&T Labs, Middletown, 2002—03. Contbr. articles to profl. jours. Fin. chair IEEE Iwat, NYC, 2005—; cyber trust panelist NSF, Washington, 2004—05, it rsch. panelist, 2004; tech. program com. IEEE Wireless Comm. and Network Conf., Piscataway, NJ, 2005—, Internat. Workshop on Antennas Tech., 2005, Internat. Conf. Networking Sensing and Control, 2005, Internat. Conf. Circuits and Systems, 2003, Systems Man and Cybernetics Sys. Assurance, 2005; reviewer IEEE Trans on Comm., Antennas and Propagations, Piscataway, 2005—; guest editor Int. J. of Wireless and Mobile Computing, Piscataway, 2003—. Recipient Third Millenium medal, IEEE, 2000. Mem.: IEEE (sr. regional 1 award 2006). Achievements include development of novel routing protocols and traffic models. Office: Fla State U Dept ECE 2525 Pottsdamer St Tallahassee FL 32310 Office Fax: 850-410-6479. Personal E-mail: mingyu@ieee.org. Business E-Mail: mingyu@eng.fsu.edu.

YU, PAULINE RUTH, former dean, educational association administrator; b. Rochester, NY, Mar. 5, 1949; d. Paul N. and Irene (Tang) Y.; m. Theodore D. Huters, Aug. 23, 1975 (div. Feb. 2000); children: Emily Elizabeth, Matthew Charles, Alexander David. BA in History and Lit. magna cum laude, Harvard U., 1971; MA in Comparative Lit., Stanford U., 1973, PhD in Comparative Lit., 1976. Asst. prof., then assoc. prof. U. Minn., Mpls., 1976-85; assoc. prof., then prof. Columbia U., NYC, 1985-89; prof., founding chair dept. East Asian langs. and lit. U. Calif., Irvine, 1989-94; dean humanities UCLA, 1994—2003, prof. East Asian langs. and culture, 1994—2003; pres. Am. Coun. Learned Socs., NYC, 2003—. Author: The Poetry of Wang Wei, 1980, The Reading of Imagery in the Chinese Poetic Tradition, 1987; editor and contbg. author: Voices of the Song Lyric in China, 1994, Culture and State in Chinese History: Conventions, Accommodations, and Critiques, 1997, Ways with Words: Writing about Reading Texts from Early China, 2000; editor, contbr.: The Longman Anthology of World Literature; mem. editl. bd. Tang Studies, Chinese Lit., Comparative Lit. Studies, 1993—; mem. Scholars' Coun., Libr. of Congress, 2006—. Mem. nat. adv. bd. Woodrow Wilson Found., 2004—07; mem. internat. adv. bd. Asia Rsch. Inst., Nat. U. Singapore, 2002—06; mem. western ctr. exec. coun. Am. Acad. Arts and Scis., 2000—03; bd. dirs. Am. Coun. Learned Socs., 1998—; trustee Nat. Humanities Ctr., 2000—, Asian Cultural Coun., 2006—, mem. exec. com., 2006—; bd. dirs. The Teagle Found., 2003—, mem. exec. com., 2005—; mem. adv. coun. dept. East Asian studies Princeton U., 2003—; bd. overseers Harvard U., 2003—09, mem. exec. com., 2006—09; mem. adv. bd. Coun. for Internat. Exch. of Scholars, 2001—05. Guggenheim fellow, 1983-84, ACLS fellow, 1983-84; recipient Profl. Achievement award U. Calif. at Irvine Alumni Assn., 1993. Fellow Am. Acad. Arts and Scis., Am. Philos. Soc.; mem. MLA, Assn. Asian Studies (mem. China and Inner Asia coun. 1982-85), Am. Comparative Lit. Assn., Am. Oriental Soc., Phi Beta Kappa Soc. (senator 1997—, exec. com. 2001—). Office: Am Coun Learned Societies 633 Third Ave New York NY 10017-6795 Home Phone: 212-260-3375; Office Phone: 212-697-1505 x 121. E-mail: paulineyu@acls.org.

YU, PEIRONG, plastic surgeon, educator; s. Fengsheng Sun and Acai Yu; m. Yanli Tan; children: Ronald, Violet. MD, Suzhou Med. Coll., Jiangsu, 1984; MS, Peking Union Med. Coll., Beijing, 1987. Diplomate Am. Bd. Plastic Surgery, Inc., Pa., 2002. Rsch. assoc. RI Hosp., Brown U. Sch. Medicine, Providence, 1991—95; rsch. scientist Dept. Plastic Surgery, Med. Coll. Wis., Milw., 1998—99; asst. prof. Brown U. Sch. Medicine, 1994—95, The U. Tex. M.D. Anderson Cancer Ctr., 2001—05, assoc. prof., 2005—, Dept. Plastic Surgery, Baylor Coll. Medicine, Houston, 2006—. Contbr. articles to profl. jour. (Brit. Jour. Plastic Surgery prize, 2004). Decorated Godina Traveling Fellow award; recipient Best Fellow Emergency Medicine Rsch. award, Med. Coll. Wis, 1999. Office: UT MD Anderson Cancer Ctr 1515 Holcombe Blvd Unit 443 Houston TX 77030 Office Fax: 713-794-5492.

YU, PETER LEGASPI, rehabilitation physician; b. Jan. 31, 1957; BS, U. Santo Tomas, Manila, 1975, MD, 1979. Diplomate Am. Bd. Ind. Med. Examiners, U.S. Ednl. Coun. Fgn. Med. Grads., 1980, U.S. Fed. Lic. Examination, 1982, Philippine Med. Bd. Examination, 1980. Intern Vets. Meml. Med. Ctr., Quezon City, The Philippines, 1979-80; resident in gen. surgery St. Clare's Hosp., NYC, 1982-84; resident in phys. medicine U. Ala., Birmingham, 1984—87; pvt. practice South Bend, Ind., 1988—; lect., spasticity mgmt. closed head injury patient Ind. Head Injury Assn., 2000; with physiatric mgmt. arthritic pain Arthritis Found. Greater Chgo., 2004. Attending physiatrist Meth. Hosp., Gary, Ind., 1989—, Merrillville, 1989—, Porter Meml. Hosp., Ind., 1994-2000, Meml. Hosp., South Bend, 1988—, Lakeland Med. Ctr., Niles, 1995-2002, St. Anthony Med. Ctr., Crown Point, Ind., 1992—, St. Mary's Med. Ctr., Hobart, Ind., 1994—, St. Catherines Hosp., East Chgo., Ind., 1994—; rehab. dir. Healthwin Hosp., South Bend, 1999-2002, Cardinal Nursing and Rehab. Ctr., South Bend, 1999-2001, Silverbrook Manor, Niles, Mich., 1997-2001, Ironwood Health and Rehab. Ctr., 2004-08; rehab. dir. Hamilton Cmtys., New Carlisle, Ind., 2006-; rehab. med. cons. Fountainview Nursing Home, Mishawaka, Ind., 2008-; co-chair med. mission to virac, Catanduanes Philippines Ind. Med. Assn, 2008-; lect., rehab. topics U. Ala., Northern Ind. Hosps., 1984-2008. Contbg. editor: US Thomasian Mag., 2006—. Vol., chmn. Philippine Centennial Celebration for South Bend, Ind., 1998, Philippine Centennial Celebration SW Mich.; lector St. Pius X Cath. Ch., Granger, Ind., 2006—. Recipient Cmty. Svc. award, St. Joseph Chapin Street Clinic, South Bend, 1989, Filipino-Am. Assn., South Bend, 1994—95, Provincial Bd. Resolution, Aklan Province Med. Mission, 2007, Twenty Outstanding Filipinos Abroad award, Filipino Image Mag., 2008; named Asian Leader in Ind., Asian Access Mag., 2007, Physician of Yr., Ind. Philippine Med. Assn., 2008; named to Youngest Grad., U. Santo Tomas, Faculty Medicine & Surgery, 1979, Top Physiatrists, Nation Based on Press Gainey Orgn. Patient Satisfaction Survey, 2003. Mem. AMA, No. Ind. Rehab. Med. (pres.), Philippine Am. Physiatry Assn., (pres. 1999-2001), Asian Am. Med. Soc. (bd. dirs. 1999-02, 2006—), Am. Acad. Phys. Medicine and Rehab., Am. Congress Rehab. Medicine, Am. Acad. Electrodiagnostic Medicine, Am. Acad. Exec. Physicians, Ind. State Med. Assn., Ind. Soc. Phys. Medicine and Rehab., Ind. Philippine Med. Assn. (pres. 2007-2008, chmn. med. and surg. mission to Aklan Province, Philippines 2007), St. Joseph County Med. Soc., U. Santo Tomas Med. Alumni Assn. Am. (with chronic pain mgmt 2008, auditor 2006-2008, bd. dirs. 2008-, sec. 2009-), U. Santo Tomas Medicine Class 1979 (sec. USA chpt. 2003—, editor-in-chief newsletter). Address: 8127 Merrillville Rd Merrillville IN 46410-6158 Office Phone: 219-736-1266. Personal E-mail: nirm-mvl@sbcglobal.net.

YU, QINGJUAN, astrophysicist, educator; b. Mudanjiang, Heilongjiang, China, 1975; m. Youjun Lu, 1998. PhD, Princeton U., NJ, 2002. Postdoc. fellow CITA, U. Toronto, Ont., Canada, 2002—03; rsch. assoc. U. Calif., Santa Cruz, 2006—08; prof. Kavli Inst. Astronomy & Astrophysics, Peking U., Beijing, 2008—. Recipient award, Consortium Math. & Its Applications, 1996; Hubble fellowship, Space Telescope Sci. Inst., NASA, 2003—06. Office: Kavli Inst Astronomy & Astrophysics Peking Univ Yi He Yuan Lu 5 Hai Dian Qu Beijing 100871 China

YU, ROBERT KUAN-JEN, biochemistry professor; b. Chungking, China, Jan. 27, 1938; came to U.S., 1962; m. Helen Chow, July 1, 1972; children: David S., Jennifer S. BS, Tunghai U., Taiwan, 1960; PhD, U. Ill., 1967; Med.ScD. (hon.), Tokyo, 1980; MA (hon.), Yale U., 1985. Rsch. assoc., instr. Albert Einstein Coll. Medicine, Bronx, 1967-72; asst. prof. Yale U., New Haven, 1973-75, assoc. prof., 1975-82, prof., 1983-88; prof. biochemistry, chmn. dept. Med. Coll. Va. Va. Commonwealth U., Richmond, 1988-2000; dir. Inst. Mol. Med. Genetics Med. Coll. Ga, Augusta, 2000—09, prof., 2009—; dir. inst. neurosci. Med. Coll. Ga., Augusta, 2005—09. Mem. study sect. NIH, Washington, 1980-84, 96—; mem. Bd. Lab. Svcs., Va., 1994-98, Acadmician, Acad. Sinica ROC, 2004-, Ga. Comm. saving and Cure, 2007-, Editor: Gangioside Structure Function and Biomedical Potential, 1984, New Trends in Ganglioside Research, 1988; contbr. over 500 articles to profl. publs. Josiah Macy scholar, 1979; grantee NIH, 1975—, 84-91; recipient Va. Outstanding Scientist of Yr. award, 1995, Alexander von Humboldt award, 1990, GRA Eminent scholar, 2000, Dist. Alumnus award Tunghai U., 2003, Achievement award Chinese Assn. Engrs. and Scientists So. Calif., 2004, Outstanding Faculty award Sch. Medicine, Med. Coll. Ga., 2006, 2009. Mem. AAAS, Am. Soc. Cell Biology, Am. Soc. Neurochemistry (mem. coun. 1983-86, 91-95, pres. 2001-03), Internat. Soc. Neurochemistry, Soc. Neurosci., Am. Soc. Biochemistry and Molecular Biology, Am. Chem. Soc., N.Y. Acad. Sci., Soc. Glybiol, Am. Soc. Cell Biol. Business E-Mail: ryu@mcg.edu.

YU, SIMON SHYI-JIAN, entomologist, educator; b. Ilan, Taiwan, Republic of China, Sept. 11, 1935; arrived in Can. 1963, U.S. in 1968; s. Son-Wei and Ah-So (Liao) Yu; m. Rachel R.C. Yeh, Setp. 16, 1967; children: Robert Yu, Edmund Yu. BS, Nat. Taiwan U., 1959; MS, McGill U., Montreal, Can., 1965, PhD, 1968; postdoctoral, Cornell U. and Oreg. State U., 1968-74. Rsch. entomologist Taiwan Sugar Co., Kuohsiung, Taiwan, 1961-62; rsch. asst. McGill U., Montreal, 1963-68; postdoctoral fellow Cornell U., Ithaca, N.Y., 1968-69; rsch. assoc. Oreg. State U., Corvallis, 1969-74, asst. prof., 1974-79; asst. prof. U. Fla., Gainesville, 1980-82, assoc. prof., 1982-86, prof., 1986—2006, prof. emeritus, 2006—. Contbr. articles to profl. jours., chapters to books; author: (text book) The Toxicology and Biochemistry of Insecticides, 2008. 2nd lt. Chinese infantry, 1959-61. Rsch. grantee NIH, 1979, USDA, 1980, 82, 85, 90, 91, EPA, 1981, 2005, NSF, 1988, 90. Mem. Entomol. Soc. Am., AAAS, Am. Chem. Soc., The Soc. Sigma Xi, Fla. Entomol. Soc. Avocations: classical music, fishing, bicycling. Office: U Fla Dept Entomology And NE Gainesville FL 32611 Home: 5205 NW 43rd Rd Gainesville FL 32606-4323 Office Phone: 352-392-1901. Business E-Mail: yusj@ufl.edu.

YU, TING, research scientist; b. Nan Chang, Jiang Xi, China, Feb. 23, 1979; s. Ming Yu and Jinrong Zhou. PhD, Northwestern U., Evanston,Ill., 2006. Intern rschr. NEC Labs Am., Cupertino, Calif., 2004, Microsoft Rsch., Redmond, Wash., 2005; rsch. scientist Gen. Electric Global Rsch., Niskayuna, NY, 2006—. Contbr. scientific papers to profl. jours. Walter P. Murphy fellowship, Northwestern U., 2002, IEEE Student Travel grants, IEEE Computer Sci. Soc., 2003, 2004. Mem.: IEEE. Home: 15B3 Sheridan Village Schenectady NY 12308 Office: Gen Electric Global Rsch One Rsch Circle KW-C211A Schenectady NY 12309 Office Fax: 518-387-6981. Personal E-mail: benny.tingyu@gmail.com. Business E-Mail: yut@research.ge.com.

YU, WEI, economist, researcher; s. Guoxing Yu and Lixin Zhu; m. Li Fan, Aug. 9, 1952; 1 child, Yifan F. BSEE, East China U., Shanghai, 1982; MA in Econs., Clemson U., SC, 1988, PhD in Applied Econs., 1992. Instr. dept. econs. Clemson U., 1988—92, asst. prof. dept. applied econs., 1992—94; postdoctoral fellow Nat. Inst. Aging Boston U., 1994—96; rsch. asst. prof. Boston U. Sch. Medicine, 1996—2000; health economist dept. vet. affairs Health Econs. Resource Ctr., Menlo Park, Calif., 2000—; fellow Ctr. for Health Policy, Stanford U., Calif., 2000—. Dir. expert com. for the expt. of cmty. based healthcare sys. Ministry of Health China, Beijing, 1996—2000; chair fin. com. Chinese Economist Soc., Ann Arbor, Mich., 1998—2005, dir. bd. Gregory Chow Fund, 2002—05; lectr. UN Devel. Programme, NYC, 1994; mem. sci. rev. and evaluation bd. dept. vet. affairs Health Svcs. R & D, Washington, 2001—05, mem. adv. com. for evaluating cmty.-based outpatient clinics in the vets. health sys. dept. vet. affairs, 2002—05; assoc. dir. China-U.S. postdoctoral tng. program Ctrs. for Health Policy and for Primary Care and Outcomes Rsch., Stanford U., 2003—; mem. of steering com. Ctr. for Patient Healthcare Behavior, VA Tenn. Valley Health Care Sys., Nashville, 2003—; mem. adv. com. dept. vet. affairs Info. Resource Ctr., Hines, Ill., 2003—, mem. Medicare data rev. bd. dept. vet. affairs, 2004—; mem. data safety and monitoring bd. for a clin. trial Vets. Health Adminstrn. Coop. Study Program, Perry Point, NJ, 2004—; mem. steering com. Ctr. of Patient Healthcare Behavior. Author: more than 50 articles on health care, public financing, and econs. in peer-reviewed jours., books, and confs. Recipient Internat. Study award, China Ministry of Edn., 1986—88; fellow, Nat. Inst. on Aging, 1994—96. Mem.: Internat. Health Econs. Assn. Home: 1443 Rockledge Ln Apt 5 Walnut Creek CA 94595-2422 Office Fax: 650-617-2639. Business E-Mail: wyu2@stanford.edu.

YU, WEIDER D., engineering educator; children: Peggy, Rebecca, Herbert, Stephanie. MS, SUNY, Albany, 1977; PhD, Northwestern U., Evanston, Ill., 1983. Cert. in info. security engring. Carnegie-Mellon U., Pa. Mem. tech. staff AT&T Bell Labs., Naperville, Ill., 1983—90, disting. mem. tech. staff, 1990—2002; adj. asst. prof. EECS Dept., U. Ill., Chgo., adj. assoc. prof.; pres. Mobillion Wireless Mobile Tech. Consulting, San Jose, Calif.; prof. computer & software engring. San Jose State U., Calif., 2009—. Pres. & prin. Chinese Lang. Jr. Schs. Assn. Mid-America, Chgo., 1990—95; pres. & dir. Chinese Am. Academic & PA Mid-America, Chgo., 1997—98; pres. Naperville Chinese Lang. Sch., Ill.; bd. dir. Monte-Jade Sci. & Tech. Assn. Mid-America, Chgo.; computer rsch. lab. coord. Northwestern U., Evanston, Ill.; symposium chair IEEE Internat. Communication Conf., Helsinki, 2001; region coord. Asian-Pacific Ubiquitous Healthcare Tech. Rsch. Ctr., San Jose, 2009—; sr. cons. CITS Group Inc., San Jose, Calif., 2009—. Contbr. scientific papers (AT&T Bell Labs. Disting. Mem. Tech. Staff award, 1990, AT&T Tech. Jour. award, 1990, AT&T Switching Sys. Employee Excellence award, 1992, AT&T Network Sys. Quality Excellence award, 1994, Bell Labs Tech. Jour. award, 1998, Outstanding Asian Am. award, 2000, Best Paper award, 2006). Local sr. HS mentor AT & T, Naperville, 1995—2001; cmty. worker AT & T, Lucent Techs., Naperville, 1983—2001. Recipient Profl. Devel. award, Computer Engring. Dept., San Jose State U., 2004, 2006; Rsch. grant, Calif. State U., 2003, Applied Mobile Tech. Solutions grant, Hewlet Packard Corp., 2003, 2004, Calif. Edn. grant, INTEL Corp., 2005, Faculty Devel. grant, Coll. Engring., San Jose State U., 2007, grant, NSF, 2008. Mem.: IEEE (communication soc., Chgo. chpt. chair 1993—2001, Chpt. of Yr. award 1995). Achievements include research in RFID technology based wireless mobile multimedia system in healthcare, language for authorization rule specification in software security; first to introduce algorithmic approach to authorization rules conflict resolution in software security. Avocations: basketball, volleyball, bowling, travel, fishing. Office: San Jose State Univ 1 Washington Sq San Jose CA 95192-0180 Office Phone: 408-924-7365. Office Fax: 408-924-4153. Business E-Mail: weider.yu@sjsu.edu.

YU, XUNQI, software engineer; b. Fengxin, Jiangxi, China, Nov. 13, 1978; s. Moda Yu and Xuemei Wu; m. Zhang Liyun, Dec. 26, 2006. MS, Huazhong U. Sci. Tech., Wuhan, Hubei, China, 2002; PhD, U. Miami, Fla., 2007. Engr. Microsoft Corp., Redmond, Wash., 2007—. Contbr. scientific papers (Most prestigious jour. networking rsch., 2008, Most prestigious internat. jour. Info. Theory rsch., 2008, Famous internat. Conf. computer networking Conf., 2005). Mem.: IEEE, Sigma Xi. Achievements include Participattion of the R & D of Windows 7.

YU, YING, librarian, educator; d. Ming Yu and Zhongyao Pei; m. Zhiqun Deng, May 11, 2000; children: Grace Deng, Lily Deng. BA in English Summa Cum Laude, Shaanxi Normal U., 1996; MS, U. Ill., Urbana-Champaign, 2002. Asst. libr. Calif. State U., Bakersfield, 2002—03; asst. prof. Columbia Basin Coll., Pasco, Wash., 2004—. Recipient Exceptional Faculty award, Columbia Basin Coll., 2008. Mem.: ALA, Beta Phi Mu.

YU, YUAN HSIANG, chemist, electronics engineer, educator; b. Yilan County, Taiwan, June 15, 1967; s. Pen Miao Yu and Yu Tzu Chang; m. Ai Yu Huang, Mar. 25, 1998; children: Shu Ching, Neng Jui. BS, Fu Jen Cath. U., Taipei, 1990; PhD, Nat. Taiwan U., Taipei, 1995. Ensign military svc. for Republic of China, Taiwan; dep. mgr. TECO Info. Sys. Co., Ltd., Taoyuan County, Taiwan, 1997—2001; rschr., asst. prof. dept. chemistry ctr. nanotechnology Chung-Yuan Christian U., Taoyuan County, 2001—02; mgr. TECO Nanotech Co., Ltd., Taoyuan County, 2002—03; asst. prof. dept. electronic and electro-optical engring. Lan Yang Inst. Tech., Yilan County, Taiwan, 2003—. Cons. in field. Contbr. articles to profl. jours. Second lt. Taiwanese Marine Corps., 1995—97. Decorated Excellent Officer Compulsory Mil. Svc. Republic of China Navy, Taiwan; recipient Creating award, Nat. Sci. Coun., Taiwan, 1990. Mem.: Carbon Nano Capsule Rsch. Alliance (hon.). Avocations: reading, travel, swimming. Office: Lan Yang Inst Tech No 79 Fusing Rd Toucheng Township Yilan County 261 Taiwan Personal E-mail: yoku0705@ms43.hinet.net. Business E-Mail: yuyh@mail.fit.edu.tw.

YUAN, JIAHUI, electronics engineer, researcher; married. BS in Engring., Tsinghua U., Beijing, 2005; PhD student, Ga. Inst. Tech., Atlanta. Intern IBM Microelectronics, East Fishkill, NY; grad. rsch. asst. Ga. Inst. Tech., 2005—. Mem.: IEEE. Achievements include research in discoveries on semiconductor devices. Office: Ga Inst Tech 85 5th ST NW TSRB 5th Fl Atlanta GA Business E-Mail: jhyuan@ece.gatech.edu.

YUAN, JIAN-MIN, epidemiologist; MD, Shanghai Med. U., 1983, MPH; PhD in epidemiology, U. Southern Calif., 1996. Rsch. fellow Shanghai Cancer Inst., 1986—88, asst. prof. epidemiology, 1989—92; rsch. asst. U. Southern Calif. Sch. Medicine, LA, 1992—96, rsch. assoc., 1996—99, asst. prof. preventive medicine, 1999—2005; assoc. prof. epidemiology and cmty. health U. Minn./Masonic Cancer Ctr., Mpls., 2005—, rschr. prevention and etiology, 2005—. Recipient Nat. Sci. and Tech. Achievement award, China, 1995. Office: U Minn Masonic Cancer Ctr Mayo Mail Code 806 420 Delaware St SE Minneapolis MN 55455 Office Phone: 612-625-8056. E-mail: jyuan@umn.edu.*

YUAN, JUNSONG, research scientist; s. Jiuti Yuan and Jinyun Xiong; m. Jingjing Meng. BE (hon.), Huazhong U. Sci. and Tech., Wuhan, China, 2002; ME, Nat. U. Singapore, 2005; PhD student, Northwestern U., Evanston, Ill. Rsch. scholar Inst. Infocomm Rsch., Singapore, 2003—04; rsch. asst. Northwestern U., 2005—; rsch. intern Kodak Rsch. Labs., Rochester, NY, 2007—07, Motorola Multimedia Labs., Schaumburg, Ill., 2007, Microsoft Rsch., Redmond, Wash., 2008. Reveiwer EURASIP Jour. Applied Signal Processing, 2007, SPIE Jour. Electronic Imaging, Elsevier Info. Sci., 2008, IEEE Transaction Pattern Analysis & Machine Intelligence, IEEE Transaction Circuits & Sys. Video Tech.; editl. bd. Internat. Jour. Data Mining, Modelling and Mgmt., 2008—. Contbr. scientific papers (Student Travel grant, 2007, 2008). Recipient Outstanding Student award, Ministry of Edn. Chaina, 2001; Huchu Nan fellowships, Ministry Edn., China, 2001. Mem.: Assn. Computing Machinary, IEEE (reviewer). Business E-Mail: j-yuan@u.northwestern.edu.

YUAN, JUNYING, medical educator, researcher; b. Shanghai; BS, Fudan U., Shanghai, 1982; PhD in Neuroscience, Harvard U., 1989. Postdoctoral trainee in devel. biology MIT, 1989—90; instr. medicine Harvard U., 1990—91, asst. prof. medicine and program in neuroscience, 1992—96, asst. prof. cell biology and program in neuroscience, 1996—2000, prof., 2000—; asst. geneticist Cardiovasc. Rsch. Ctr. Mass. Gen. Hosp., 1990—96. Mem. editl. bd.: Current Biology, 1996, ad hoc reviewer: NIH Human Embryology and Devel. 2 Study Sect., 1995, regular reviewer:, 1996—; patentee in field, —; contbr. articles to profl. jours.; presenter in field, —. Recipient Wilson S. Stone Meml. award, MD Anderson Cancer Ctr. U. Tex., 1994, Established Investigator award, Am. Heart Assn., 1996—, Dir.'s Pioneer Award, NIH, 2005; fellow Ryan, Harvard Med. Sch., 1985—89. Fellow: Am. Acad. Arts & Scis. Office: Harvard Med Sch Dept Cell Biology 240 Longwood Ave Boston MA 02115-5701 Office Phone: 617-432-4170. Office Fax: 617-432-4177. E-mail: jyuan@hms.harvard.edu.

YUAN, LIJUAN, engineering educator; m. Lijuaj Yuan. PhD, Ohio State U., 2000. Rsch. scientist Ohio State U., Wooster, Va., 2002—07; asst. prof. Va. Poly. Inst. & State U., Blacksburg, 2007—. Rsch. grant R21, NCCAN, NIH, 2005. Mem.: ASV. Office: Viginia Tech 1981 Kraft Dr ILSB CRC Blacksburg VA 24061-0913 Business E-Mail: lyuan@vt.edu.

YUAN, LONGPING, agronomist; b. Jiangxi, China, 1930; Grad., Southwest Agriculture Inst., 1953. Rsch. prof. Hunan Acad. Agrl. Scis., 1971; tech. advisor Internat. Rice Inst., 1980—81; academician Chinese Acad. Engring., 1995—; dir. gen. China Hybrid Rice Rsch. and Devel. Ctr., Hunan. Internat. chief cons. UN Food and Agriculture Orgn., 1991—. Recipient Sci. award, UNESCO, 1987, China State Preeminent Sci. and Tech. award, 2001, Ramon Magasaysay award, 2001, Medal Honor, United Nat. FAO, Wolf prize in agr., Wolf Found., Israel, 2004, World Food Prize, World Food Found., USA, 2004. Mem.: NAS. Achievements include development of indica hybrid rice in 1973; first scientist to successfully alter the self-pollinating characteristic of rice, which lead to large-scale farming of hybrid rice; known as "Father of Hybrid Rice". Office: Chinese Acad Engring 3 Fuxing Rd Beijing 100038 China E-mail: lpyuan@public.cs.hn.cn.

YUAN, ROBIN TSU-WANG, plastic surgeon; b. Boston, July 2, 1954; s. Robert Hsun-Piao and Grace I. (Chen) Y. AB, Harvard U., 1974, MD, 1978. Diplomate Am. Bd. Plastic Surgery. Resident in gen. surgery UCLA Med. Ctr., 1978-80, Cedars-Sinai Med. Ctr., LA, 1980-81, 83-84; resident in plastic surgery U. Miami (Fla.)-Jackson Meml. Hosp., 1985-87; pvt. practice LA, 1987—. Clin. instr. divsn. plastic surgery UCLA, 1987-98, asst. clin. prof., 1998—; vice-chief divsn. plastic surgery Cedars-Sinai Med. Ctr., LA, 1991—; pres., CEO, founder Family of Independent Reconstructive Surgery Teams, 1990—, pres. Millard Soc., 2003, Ethics Com., Calif. Soc. Plastic Surgeons, 2002-, plastic surgeon ABC's Extreme Makeover, 2004 Author: Cheer Up...You're Only Half Dead!, Reflections at Mid-Life, 1996; contbr. numerous articles to med. jours. Named LA's Super Dr., 2007—; named one of Am.'s Top Drs., Med. Castle Connolly Pub., 2006. Mem. Am. Soc. Plastic and Reconstructive Surgery, Am. Cleft Palate Assn., Calif. Med. Assn. (del.), LA County Med. Assn. (bd. govs. dist. 1), Phi Lambda (co-mgr. 1991—). Avocations: tennis, skiing, golf, creative writing, violin. Office: 462 N Linden Dr Ste 236 Beverly Hills CA 90212 Office Phone: 310-385-8425. Personal E-mail: robinpbhps@aol.com.

YUAN, XIAOHUI, engineering educator; PhD, Tulane U., New Orleans, 2004. Postdoc. fellow NIH, Bethesda, Md., 2004—06; asst. prof., dept. computer sci. & eng. U. North Tex., Denton, 2006—. Recipient Ralph E. Powe Jr. Faculty Enhancement award, Oak Ridge Associated U., 2008; Jr. Faculty Summer Rsch. fellowship, U. North Tex., 2007, 2008. Mem.: IEEE. Office: Dept CSE Univ North Texas PO Box 311366 Denton TX 76203-1366 Office Fax: 940-565-2799. Business E-Mail: xyuan@cse.unt.edu.

YUAN, ZENG-GUANG, mechanical engineer, researcher; s. Shu-Chi Yuan and Chui-Fan Wei; m. Gui-Fang Zhang; children: Sarah Qing, James Jie. BS, Qinghua U., 1963, MS, 1966, U. Calif., 1988, PhD, 1990. Registered profl. engr., Calif., 1993. Sr. reservoir engr. Offshore Oil Exploration China., Shanghai, 1978—86; sr. rsch. engr. Dept. Mech. Engring. U. Calif., Berkeley, Calif., 1994—; staff scientist Nat. Ctr. for Microgravity Rsch. NASA Glenn, Cleve., 1998—. Cons. Calif. EPA, Berkeley, Calif., 1993—94; advanced math. instr. Shanghai Tele-U., Shanghai, 1983—86; cons. Ministry of Geology China, Beijing, 1984—86. Co-author: Thermal properties and temperature-related behavior of rock/fluid systems; contbr. articles to profl. jours. Recipient China Nat. Sci. Tech. award, Sci. and Tech. Commn. China, 1982, Silver Snoopy award, NASA, 2004; fellow Jane Lewis fellowship, U. Calif., Berkeley, 1986—88. Mem.: AIAA, ASME, Combustion Inst., Soc.Petroleum Engrs. Achievements include discovery of new phenomenon of electric effects on flames.

YUAN, ZHEN, biomedical researcher; b. Zibo City, Shandong, China, Dec. 16, 1972; s. Anzhe Yuan; 1 child, Anzhe; m. Guifen Yin. PhD, U. Sci. & Tech., Hefei, China, 2002. Engineering, U. Sci. and Tech., China, 2002. Rsch. asst. dept. modern mechanics U. Sci. and Tech., Hefei, 1996—2002; postdoctoral rsch. fellow Inst. High Performance Computing, Nat. U. Singapore, Singapore City, 2002—04; postdoctoral rsch. assoc. physics dept. Clemson Univ., 2004—05; postdoctoral rsch. scientist biomedical engring. dept. U. Fla., Gainesville, 2005—07, rsch. asst. prof. biomed. engring. dept., 2007—. Fellow, Nat. U. Singapore, 2003; scholar Lixue Pandeng, Chiense Acad. Scis., 2002. Mem.: BMES, SPIE, OSA. Achievements include research in biomedical imaging of cancer-related diseases; invention of finite-elment-based photoacoustic imaging; electric-sensitive BIOMEMS; first to hydrogel biomaterials development. Office: U Fla Biomed Engring Dept 130 BME Bldg PO Box 116131 Gainesville FL 32611 Home: 1324 NW 16th Ave Apt 36 Gainesville FL 32605-4051 Office Phone: 352-392-5532. Office Fax: 352-392-9791. Business E-Mail: yzhen@bme.ufl.edu.

YUAN GEE, KA CHUEN CAROL, school librarian; b. Beijing, Nov. 2, 1940; d. Kejian Yuan and Shutkin Pan; m. Stephen C. Gee, Dec. 29, 1962; children: Jonathan Gee, Justin W.L. Gee. BA, NY U., 1966; MLS, Columbia U., NY, 1968; MS in Edn., CUNY, 1990. Cert. libr. NY State, 1970. Asst. chief libr. Equitable Life Assurance Soc., NYC, 1980—86; head, tech. svcs. Leonard Life Libr., Bronx, NY, 1986—, Lehman Coll. CUNY, 1986—. Sr. cataloger NY Pub. Libr., 1968—80. Bd. mem. Chinese Am. Librs. Assn., NYC, chpt. pres. Recipient Rsch. award, Profl. Staff Congress, CUNY, 2002, 2008. Office: Leonard Lief Libr 250 Bedford Pk Blvd Bronx NY 10468

YUDKOWSKY, RACHEL, medical educator; b. NY, 1955; m. Moshe Yudkowsky; children: Eliezer, Channah. MD, Northwestern U., Evanston, Ill., 1979. Cert. psychiatry Am. Bd. Psychiatry and Neurology. Faculty dept. psychiatry Evanston Northwestern Healthcare, Ill., 1985—99; asst. prof. dept. med. edn. U. Ill. Coll. Medicine, Chgo., 1999—. Clerkship dir., residency program dir. and dir. edn., dept. psychiatry Evanston Northwestern Healthcare, Chgo., 1990; dir. clin. performance ctr. U. Ill. Coll. Medicine, 2001—. Office: U Ill Chgo Coll Medicine Dept Med Edn MC 591 808 S Wood St Chicago IL 60612 Business E-Mail: rachely@uic.edu.

YUDOF, MARK GEORGE, academic administrator, law educator; b. Phila., Oct. 30, 1944; s. Jack and Eleanor (Parris) Y.; m. Judith Lynn Gomel, July 11, 1965; children: Seth Adam, Samara Lisa. BA cum laude, U. Pa., 1965, LLB cum laude, 1968. Bar: Pa. 1970, U.S. Supreme Ct. 1974, U.S. Dist. Ct. (we. dist.) Tex. 1975, U.S. Ct. Appeals (5th cir.) 1976, Tex. 1980. Law clk. to judge US Ct. Appeals (5th cir.), 1968-69; assoc. gen. counsel to ABA study FTC, 1969; rsch. assoc. Harvard Ctr. Law and Edn., 1969-70, sr. staff atty., 1970-71; lectr. Harvard Grad. Sch. Edn., 1970-71; asst. prof. law U. Tex., Austin, 1971-74, prof., 1974—97, 2002—, assoc. dean, 1979-84, James A. Elkins Cent. chair in law, 1983-97, dean, 1984-94, exec. v.p., provost, 1994-97, John Jeffers rsch. chair in law, 1991-94; pres. U. Minn., 1997—2002, pres. emeritus, 2002—; chancellor U. Tex. Sys., 2002—08, Jamail regents chair higher edn. leadership, 2002—08, Wright chair fed. courts, 2002—08; pres. U. Calif. Sys., 2008—. Of counsel Pennzoil vs. Texaco, 1987. Author: When Government Speaks, 1983 (Scribes Book award 1983, cert. merit ABA 1983), (with others) Educational Policy and the Law, 1992, (with others) Gender Justice, 1986. Mem. Tex. Gov.'s Task Force on Sch. Fin., 1989-90, Tex. Gov.'s Select Com. on Edn., 1988; bd. dirs. Freedom to Read Found., 1989-91; mem. Austin Cable Commn., 1981-84, chmn., 1982; mem. nat. panel on sch. desegregation rsch. Ford Found., 1977-80; mem. state exec. com. Univ. Interscholastic League, 1983-86; bd. dirs. Jewish Children's Regional Svc., 1980-86; mem. Gov.'s Select Task Force on Pub. Edn., 1995; mem. Telecomms. Infrastructure Fund Bd., State of Tex., 1995-97; adv. bd. Nat. Inst. for Literacy, 2002-06, Pres. Coun. on Svc. and Civic Participation, 2006—; chmn. Coun. Pub. Univ. Pres. and Chancellors, 2006—. Recipient Tchg. Excellence award, 1975, Most Meritorious Book award Scribes, 1983, Humanitarian award Austin region NCCJ, 1988, Antidefamation League Jurisprudence award, 1991, James Wilson award, U. Pa. Law Sch., 2004; hon. fellow Queen Mary and Westfield Coll., U. London. Fellow: Am. Acad. Arts & Sci., Am. Bar Found., Tex. Bar Found.; mem.: Edn. Testing Svc. (mem. bd. dirs. 2000—02), Am. Coun. Edn. (mem. com. on leadership and instl. effectiveness 2000), Assn. Am. Law Schs. (chmn. law and edn. sect. 1983—84, exec. com. 1988—90), Tex. Bar Found., Am. Law Inst. Avocation: collecting antique maps. Office: Office of Pres U Calif 1111 Franklin St, 12th Fl Oakland CA 94607 Office Phone: 510-987-9220. E-mail: president@ucop.edu.

YUE, AGNES KAU-WAH, otolaryngologist; b. Shanghai, Peoples Republic China, Dec. 1, 1947; arrived in US, 1967; d. Chen Kia and Nee Yuan; m. Gerald Kumata, Sept. 25, 1982; children: Julie, Allison, Benjamin. BA, Wellesley Coll., 1970; MD, Med. Coll. Pa., 1974; postgrad., Yale U., 1974-78. Intern Yale-New Haven Hosp., 1974-75, resident, 1975-78; fellow U. Tex. M.D. Anderson Cancer Ctr., Houston, 1978-79; asst. prof. U. Wash., Seattle, 1979-82; physician Pacific Med. Ctr., Seattle, 1979-90; pvt. practice Seattle, 1991—. Fellow Am. Acad. Otolaryngology; mem. Northwest Acad. Otolaryngology. Avocations: sailing, opera, cooking. Office: 1801 NW Market St Ste 410 Seattle WA 98107-3909 Office Phone: 206-782-1090.

YUE, ALFRED SHUI-CHOH, metallurgical engineer, consultant; b. China, Nov. 12, 1920; s. Choy Noon-woo and Sze Man-hun (Tom) Yue; m. Virginia Chin-wen Tang, May 21, 1944; children: Mary, Raymond Yuan, John, Ling Tsao, David, Nancy Chang. BS, Chao-tung U., 1942; MS, Ill. Inst. Tech., 1950; PhD, Purdue U., 1956. Assoc. engr. Taiwan Aluminum Co., 1942-47; instr. Purdue U., 1952-56; research engr. Dow Chem. Co., Midland, Mich., 1956-62; sr. mem. Lockheed, Palo Alto Rsch. Lab., 1962-69; from prof. engring. and applied sci. to cons. UCLA, LA, 1969—. Hon. prof. Xian Jiao-tong U., China, 1980. Sec.-gen. Chinese Culture Assn. U.S., 1967; bd. dirs. Chinese scholar to U.S. Fellow: AIAA (assoc.); mem.: AIME, Materials Rsch. Soc., Am. Soc. Metals, Sigma Xi, Phi Tau Phi (pres. 1978—82), Tau Beta Pia, Sigma Pi Sigma.

YUECHIMING, ROGER YUE YUEN SHING, mathematics professor; b. Mauritius, Feb. 25, 1937; s. James and Marie Yuechiming; m. Renée Bethery, Nov. 9, 1963; children: Françoise, Marianne, Isabelle. BSc with 1st class honours, U. Manchester, Eng., 1964, PhD, 1967. Asst. U. Strasbourg, France, 1967-69; lectr. math. U. Paris VII, 1970—. Participant math. confs. and seminars in numerous countries; referee various math. jours. Contbr. over 100 articles to profl. jours. Mem. French Math. Soc., Am. Math. Soc., London Math. Soc., Belgian Math. Soc., Japan Math. Soc. Achievements include introduction of concept of p-injective modules and the more generalized notion of YJ-injectivity, new approaches in ring and module theory leading to a better understanding of von Neumann regular rings, V-rings, self-injective rings and generalizations. Home: 38 rue du Surmelin 75020 Paris France Office: U Paris VII Unité Mixte de Rsch 9994 CNRS 2 Pl Jussieu 75251 Paris France

YUEN, PO KI, engineering company executive; PhD, U. Pa., Phila. Rsch. mgr. - bioengring Corning Inc., NY, 2000—. Office: Corning Inc Sullivan Pk SP-FR-01 Corning NY 14831

YUEN, RICHARD JOSEPH, university dean; b. San Francisco, Mar. 1, 1956; s. Joseph Edward Yuen and Nancy Jair Louie; children: Tania, Lia. BA in Sociology/BA in Asian Am. Studies, U. Calif., Berkeley, 1978; MSW in Social Work Edn., San Francisco State U., 1983. Rare book handler John Howell Books, San Francisco, 1973-82; acad. counselor City Coll. of San Francisco, 1986-89; asst. dean of students Stanford (Calif.) U., 1989—, jud. officer, 1994—. Founding mem. Nat. Coalition for Redress and Reparations, San Francisco, 1980; del. San Francisco Shanghai Sister City, SF Taipei Sister City, SF Oska & SF Ho Chi Minh Sister City. Recipient Dir.'s award Black Cmty. Svcs. Ctr., Stanford, 1992, Dedicated Svc. award Stanford U. Nikkei; Children, Youth and Family fellow Frederick Burke Found., San Francisco; named one of 500 most influential Asian Ams., Ave. Mag., 1996—. Mem. Assn. Student Conduct Adminstrs., Nat. Assn. Student Pers. Adminstrs., Kappa Delta Phi (Outstanding Svc. award). Democrat. Avocations: photography, bicycling. Office: Stanford University 459 Lagunita Dr Ste 9 Stanford CA 94305-3010 Business E-Mail: rickyuen@stanford.edu.

YUHARA, MAKOTO, mechanical engineer; b. Tokai-mura, Ibaraki, Japan, July 3, 1980; s. Hideo and Sachiko Yuhara. B in Engring., U. Tsukuba, Japan, 2003, M in Engring., 2005. EIT Instn. Profl. Engrs., Japan, 2005. Engr. Ebara Corp., Fujisawa, Kanagawa, Japan, 2005—08; project engr. Ebara Internat. Corp., Sparks, Nev., 2008—. Scholar, Yoshida Scholarship Found., 2003—05. Mem.: Instn. Profl. Engrs., Turbomachinery Soc. Japan. Avocations: running, baseball. Office: Ebara Internat Corp 350 Salomon Cir Sparks NV 89434 Business E-Mail: yuhara.makoto@ebara.com.

YUI, LISA, music educator; b. Tokyo, July 8, 1975; BM, Juilliard Sch., NYC, 1998; MM, Manhattan Sch. Music, NYC, 2000, DMA, 2005. Adj. faculty Marymount Manhattan Coll., NYC, 2000—05; faculty Juilliard Sch., 2003—, Manhattan Sch. Music, 2004—. Grant, Can. Coun. Arts, 1996—97. Business E-Mail: lyui@msmnyc.edu.

YUILL, THOMAS MACKAY, academic administrator, microbiology educator; b. Berkeley, Calif., June 14, 1937; s. Joseph Stuart and Louise (Dunlop) Y.; m. Ann Warnes, Aug. 24, 1960; children: Eileen, Gwen. BS, Utah State U., 1959; MS, U. Wis., 1962, PhD, 1964. Lab. officer Walter Reed Army Inst. Rsch., Washington, 1964-66; med. biologist SEATO Med. Rsch. Lab., Bangkok, 1966-68; asst. prof. U. Wis., Madison, 1968-72, assoc. prof., 1972-76, prof., 1976—2003, dept. chmn., 1979-82, assoc. dean, 1982-93, dir. Gaylord Nelson Inst. Environ. Studies, 1993—2003, emeritus prof. and dir., 2003—. Cons. NIH, Bethesda, 1976-86, CDC, 2005-; chmn. Viral Diseases Panel, U.S.-Japan Biomed. Scis. Program, 1979-86, Am. Com. Arbovirology, 1982—; bd. dirs. Cen. Tropical Agrl. Res. Teaching, Turrialba, Costa Rica, 1988-96. Contbr. chpts. to books, articles to profl. jours. Served to capt. U.S. Army, 1964-66. Recipient grants state and fed. govts., 1968—. Mem. Orgn. Tropical Studies (pres. 1979-85), Wildlife Disease Assn. (treas. 19880-85, pres. 1985-87, editl. bd. 1989-2003), Am. Soc. Tropical Medicine and Hygiene (editl. bd. 1984-96), Nat. Assn. State Univ. Land Grant Colls., EPA Task Force (co-chair 1994-2002), Sigma Xi. Avocations: flying, cross country skiing, music. Office Phone: 801-491-3226. Business E-Mail: tmyuill@wisc.edu.

YULE, JOE See ROONEY, MICKEY

YULISH, CHARLES BARRY, retired energy and environmental consultant, public relations executive; b. Cleve., Oct. 14, 1936; s. Isadore and M. Yulish; m. Barbara Pearlman, Aug. 22, 1973 (div. 1995); 1 child, Alexi Jules-Nicholas; m. Cynthia Brown Fleek, Oct. 28, 1995. AA in Govt., U. Fla., 1957; BS in Polit. Sci., Kent State U., 1959; MPA, Maxwell Sch., Syracuse U., 1963; postgrad., NYU, 1961-63, New Sch. Social Rsch., 1963-64. Spl. projects officer U.S. AEC, Washington and NYC, 1961-63; pub. affairs mgr. Atomic Indsl. Forum, NYC, 1963-66; pres., chief exec. officer Charles Yulish Assocs. Inc., NYC, 1966—84; exec. v.p. Wesley, Brown & Bartle Inc., NYC, 1984—88; vice chmn., ptnr. Holt, Ross & Yulish, Edison, NJ, 1988-92; exec. v.p., mng. dir. E. Bruce Harrison Co., Washington, 1993-95; v.p. corp. comm. USEC Inc., Bethesda, Md., 1995—2005; ret., 2005. Writer, dir. (film) Energy: We Have the Choices, 1978 (Golden Eagle award); editor: Hard vs. Soft Energy Paths, 1980; author over 60 articles on classical music, It's On The Record Interviews & Notes On Classical Composers, 2009. Founder, bd. dirs. Serge Koussevitsky Archives Soc., N.Y.C., 1977; bd. dirs. Imperial Russia Hist. Soc., 1986, U.K. and U.S. Friends of Benjamin Franklin. Maxwell fellow Syracuse U., 1960. Home: 1438 Q St NW Washington DC 20009-3808

YULMETYEV, RENAT MUZIPOVICH, physicist, educator; b. Kazan, Tatarstan, USSR, Dec. 14, 1940; s. Muzip Garipovich and Zainab Khairullovna (Davletshina) Yulmetyev; m. Dinara Gabidullovna Bulgakova, Oct. 30, 1965; 1 child, Timur. MS, Kazan State U., 1962, PhD, 1967; D in Physics, Ukranian Inst. Physics, Kyiv, 1981. Theoretical physicist. Sr. lectr. Kazan State Pedagog. Inst., 1965-70; assoc. prof. Kazan State Pedagog. U., 1970-83, prof., 1983—, dean phys.-math. faculty, 1971-72, 78-86, mem. faculty, 1978—, head chair theoretical physics, physicist, 1984, prof., 1993—, leading scientific collabarator, dept. physics, 1994—. Sr. sci. collaborator, chief sci. group Kazan State U., 1993—; Soros prof. Kazan Pedagogical U., 1994—. Author: An Introduction to Statistical Physics of Liquids, 1972, Microscopic Dynamics of Liquids, 2006; contbr. articles to internat. profl. jours. Recipient Honored Scientist, Russian Fedn., 2000; named, Tatarstan Republic, 1990, Hon. Man of Higher Prof. Edn., Russian Fedn., 2001—; grantee, Internat. Soros Sci. Edn. Programme Fund, 1994—2001, Russian Fund Fundamental Rsch., 1994—96, 2002—, Russian Humanitarian Sci. Found., 1997—2005, DAAD, 1999—2000, NOIKR Found. Tatarstan Republic, 2000—, Ministry Higher Edn. and Sci., 2005; Competitive Ctr. Fundamental Rsch. grantee, St. Petersburg U., 1992—98. Mem.: NY Acad. Scis., Acad. Nature Russian Fedn. (academician). Avocations: painting, classical music, travel, literature. Office: Tatar State U of Pedagogical and Humanities Sci Tatarstan St 2 420021 Kazan Russia

YUN, EDWARD JOON, lawyer; b. Seoul, Republic of Korea, Apr. 2, 1969; s. Alex Yun and Lily Yun. BA, U. Calif., Berkeley, 1992; JD, N.Y. Law Sch., 1995. Bar: NY 1996, NJ 2006, US Dist. Ct (so. and ea. dists.) NY 1997. Assoc. Martin, Clearwater & Bell, NYC, 1995—97, Dembin & Assocs. PC, NYC, 1997—2002, Hoffman Einiger & Polland, PLLC, NYC, 2002—06, Wolf Block LLP, Roseland, NJ, 2006—09, Brach Eichler LLC, Roseland, NJ, 2009—. Contbr. articles to profl. jours. Office: Brach Eichler LLC 101 Eisenhower Pky Roseland NJ 07068 Office Phone: 973-364-5229. Office Fax: 973-618-5589. Business E-Mail: eyun@bracheichler.com.

YUN, HYUN JUNG, political science professor; PhD, U. Fla., Gainesville, 2007. Rschr. & office mgr. U. Fla., 2005—07. Office: Tex State Univ 266 Evans Liberal Arts Bldg 601 University Dr San Marcos TX 78666 Office Fax: 512-245-7815. Business E-Mail: hy12@txstate.edu.

YUN, JAESEOK, research scientist; s. Gilwoong Yun and Heesook Kim; m. Sunju Park, Aug. 20, 2006. PhD in Mechatronics, Gwangju Inst. Sci. and Tech., Gwangju, Republic of Korea, 2006. Rsch. scientist Coll. Computing, Ga. Tech, Atlanta, 2006—. Contbr. articles to profl. jours. Achievements include research in development of user identification system using human's gait pattern; analysis of inertial power harvester performance using acceleration dataset captured in normal daily life. Office: Coll Computing Georgia Tech 85 5th St NW Atlanta GA 30308 Business E-Mail: jaeseok.yun@gmail.com.

YUN, JAMES KYOON, electrical engineer; b. Andong, South Korea, Oct. 26, 1965; came to U.S., 1973; s. Joh Kyong and Karen Suk (Kim) Y. BSEE, U. Ill., 1987, MSEE, 1989. System engr. GE Co., Syracuse, NY, 1989-91, software engr., 1991-93, Martin Marietta Corp., Syracuse, 1993-95; sr. mem. engring. staff Lockheed Martin Corp., Moorestown, NJ, 1995—. Cons. Silver Knight Co., Liverpool, N.Y., 1994—. Inventor seal indicator. Mem. IEEE, Assn. for Computing Machinery, Tau Beta Pi, Eta Kappa Nu.

YUN, SOO IN, physics professor, researcher, academic administrator; b. Kyungjoo, Korea, Nov. 6, 1937; s. Jang Suk and Kae Won (Son) Y.; m. Hyun Young Huh, June 30, 1968; children: Zee Sun, Hee Sun, Dong Joo. BS, Pusan Nat. U., Republic of, 1960, MS, 1962, Carnegie-Mellon U., 1970; PhD, Okla. State U., 1972. From lectr. to assoc. prof. dept. physics Pusan Nat. U., 1966-79, prof., 1979-95, 1999—2003, prof. emeritus, 2003—, chmn. dept. physics, 1977—81, prof. dept. physics, 1979-95, dean acad. affairs, 1987-89, pres., 1995-99. Vis. asst. prof. Okla. State U., Stillwater, 1973, vis. scientist, 1976; vis. sch. U. Ala., 2001. Chmn. Hyowon Academic & Cultural Found., Busan, 2003—; trustee Kyung Ahm Edn. & Cultural Found., 2008—. Hon. fellow U. Wis., 1985-86, Cultural award Nulwon Found., Pusan, 1992, Rsch. award Pusan Nat. U., 1976, Blue Stripes Order of Svc. merit, Korea, 2003. Fellow Korean Phys. Soc. (v.p. 1993, Rsch. award 1982, Physics Edn. award 2006); mem. Am. Phys. Soc., Hyowon Found. (pres. 2003—), Fedn. Busan Sci. and Tech. (advisor 2004—). Office: Pusan Nat Univ Dept of Physics Busan 609 735 Republic of Korea Home: 208-903 Hyundai Apt Hwamyeong-dong Busan 616-795 Republic of Korea Business E-Mail: yunsi@pusan.ac.kr.

YUN, YEOHEUNG, research scientist; b. Iksan, Chonbuk, Republic of Korea, Apr. 12, 1975; s. Chilsuk Yun and Insun Kwon. MS, Chonbuk Nat. U., 2001; PhD, U. Cin., 2006. Postdoc. fellow U. Cin., rschr., 2003—, rsch. assoc., 2008—. Contbr. articles to sci. jours. (Best Paper award, KSPE). Grant, NIOSH, 2006, GEAE, 2007, Oak Ridge Nat. Lab. Achievements include invention of hybrid nanotube actuator; first to longest carbon nanotube array in the world; invention of a device to support directional neurite growth. Avocation: swimming. Office: Univ Cin 598 Rhodes Hall Cincinnati OH 45221-0072 Business E-Mail: yunyg@email.uc.edu.

YUNDT, BETTY BRANDENBURG, elementary school educator; b. Corydon, Ind., Sept. 23, 1957; d. Melvin Marion and Lena Beatrice (Blake) Brandenburg; m. Randall Gene Yundt, Apr. 2, 1978; 1 child, Cameron Blake. BS, Ind. U. SE, New Albany, 1981, MS with highest distinction, 1989. Cert. elem. tchr. Rank I, Ind., Ky; lic. prin. Ind. Western U. Tchr. pre-kindergarten Keneseth Israel Sch., Louisville, 1981—82; tchr. Dept. Def. Dependent Sch., Goppingen, Germany, 1983—86; curriculum coord. Iroquois and West End Child Devel. Ctr., Louisville; elem. tchr. Ft. Knox (Ky.) Sch. Dist., 1986—87; curriculum facilitator Walker Intermediate Sch., 1987—. KERA Fellows II cohort. Recipient Campbellsville Coll. Excellence in Edn. award, 2003, 2009, Elem. award, Middle Sch., 2009; named Tchr. of Yr., Ft. Knox, Ky., 2003; named to, USA Today All Star Tchr. Team, 2003. Mem. NEA, ASCD, Internat. Reading Assn., Ind. Coun. Tchrs. Math., Louisville Assn. for Children Under Six, Kappa Delta Pi, Phi Lambda Theta, Alpha Chi. Home: 40 Springdale Rd Guston KY 40142-7151 Office Phone: 502-624-7835. Personal E-mail: teechyundt@bbtel.com. Business E-Mail: betty.yundt@am.dodea.edu.

YUNEN, JOSE R., surgical intensivist, director, epidemiologist; b. Santo Domingo, Dominican Republic, Aug. 12, 1972; s. Antonia M. Gonzalez. BS, Boston Coll., 1994; MS, Georgetown U., Washington, 1996; MD, Ctrl. Del Caribe, Bayamon, Puerto Rico, 1999. Diplomate Am. Bd. Internal Medicine, NYC, 2002, Am. Bd. Infectious Diseases, 2006. Med. dir., cardio-thoracic ICU Montefiore Med. Ctr., Bronx, NY, 2005—; dir. infectious diseases dept., med.-surg. ICU CEDIMAT, Santo Domingo, Dominican Republic, 2008—. Contbr. scientific papers. Fellow: Am. Coll. Chest Physicians. Achievements include research in substituting the stethoscope for hand carried ultrasound as an extension for physical examination. Office: Montefiore Med Ctr 111 E 210th St Gold Zone Bronx NY 10467 Business E-Mail: jyunen@gmail.com.

YUNIS, AMIRA, real estate company officer; b. Richfield, Minn., 1971; 1 child. Exec. v.p. & prin. Nat. Retail group Newmark Knight Frank Retail, NYC, 2000—. Named one of 40 Under 40, Crain's NY Bus., 2007. Mem.: Comml. Industrial Brokerage Soc., Internat. Coun. Shopping Ctrs., Real Estate Bd. NY (Retail Deal of Yr. award 2006). Office: Newmark Knight Frank Retail 110 E 42nd St New York NY 10017 Office Phone: 212-372-2397. E-mail: AYunis@newmarkkf.com.

YURCHEKFRODL, PATRICIA, librarian; d. Frank and Helen Yurchek; m. Kevin Michael Frodl, Jan. 4, 1992; children: Eric, Alec. MLS, Kent State U., Ohio, 1979. Libr. Youngstown Pub. Libr., Ohio, 1986—. Office: Canfield Libr 43 W Main St Canfield OH 44406

YURECHKO, JOHN JOSEPH, federal agency administrator, director; b. Hazleton, Pa., Apr. 12, 1948; s. Andrew Joseph and Helen Theresa Yurechko; m. Jane Teresa Haltmaier, Sept. 25, 1982; children: Christine, Alice, Janie. BA in History, Wesleyan U., Middletown, Conn., 1970; MA, U. Calif., Berkeley, 1973, PhD in History, 1980. Intelligence analyst Def. Intelligence Agy. (DIA), Washington, 1981—88, senior analyst, command, control, comm. program mgr., 1988—94, spl. planning office chief, 1994—96, info. warfare office chief, 1996—98, def. intelligence sr. level officer (DISL), def. intelligence officer (DIO), 1998—2004; nat. counterintelligence officer for sci. and tech, dir. strategy and policy Nat. Counterintelligence Exec. (NCIX), Washington, 2004; dir. analysis and collection, sr. exec. svc. NCIX, 2005; dep. nat. intelligence officer for warning, 2007. Adj. prof. nat. security studies program Georgetown U., Washington, 1986—92; prof. Inst. World Politics, 2007. Author, editor: poetry jour. Gallery Works, 1972—80; contbr. articles to jours. and books in field. Recipient Nat. Intelligence Achievement award, Dir. Central Intelligence, Washington, 1992. Avocations: poetry, martial arts, swimming, weightlifting.

YURIKO, (YURIKO KIKUCHI), dancer, choreographer; b. San Jose, Calif., 1920; m. Charles Kikuchi, 1946. Student, UCLA, Martha Graham Sch.; Doctor Honoris Causa (hon.), La Fedn. Francaise De Danse, 1987; Doctorate (hon.), Boston Conservatory, 2006. Mem. Martha Graham Dance Co., 1944-67; dance tchr. NYC, 1945—; dir., founder Yuriko Dance Co., 1960—78; assoc. artistic dir. Martha Graham Dance Co., 1991—. Artistic dir. dance company Time and Talents Club, Bombay, 1974; organizer Modern Dance Sch., Ctr. Internat. de la Danse, Paris, 1975; resident guest tchr., modern dance cons. Ballet Nacional de Cuba, 1976; ind. modern dance choreographer Warsaw Weiklki Classic Ballet Co., 1977, 78, Australian Dance Theater's Concert at Adelaide Festival of the Arts, 1978; guest tchr., choreographer Akar Modern Dance Co., Switzerland, 1981; guest tchr. Nat. U. Costa Rica, Nat. Ballet of Mexico, Martha Graham Sch. Contemporary Dance; guest artist and tchr. various cities including London, Paris, Mexico City, Zurich, Tokyo and Cologne, Germany; founder & dir., The Arigato Project; founder Martha Graham Ensemble, 1983. Dancer premiere prodns. Appalachian Spring, Cave of the Heart, Dark Meadow, Embattled Garden, Clytemnestra; appeared on Broadway as Eliza in The King and I, 1951; performed feature role The Small House of Uncle Thomas, Sandhog, Flower Drug Song; dir., re-staged Broadway prodn. of The King and I with Yul Bryner, 1977, London prodn., 1979, dir. Toyko prodn., 1978; dir. Madame Butterfly. Recipient Bessie award NY Dance and Performance, 1991; Tribute NY/Japan Soc., 2004; Honor Saeko Ichinohe Dance Co., 2005; grantee NY State Arts Coun., Nat. Endowment for the Arts; Guggenheim fellow for choreography, 1968; commissioned to choreograph and perform Judith Symphony.

YURIST, SVETLAN JOSEPH, mechanical engineer; b. Kharkov, USSR, Nov. 20, 1931; came to U.S., 1979, naturalized, 1985; s. Joseph A. and Rosalia S. (Zoilman) Y.; m. Imma Lea Erlikh, Oct. 11, 1960; 1 child, Eugene. MSME with honors, Poly. Inst. Odessa, USSR, 1954. Engr., designer Welding Equipment Plant, Novaya Utka, USSR, 1954-56; sr. tech. engr. Heavy Duty Automotive Crane Plant, Odessa, USSR, 1956-60, asst. chief metallugist, 1971-78; supr. rsch. lab. Inst. Spl. Methods in Foundry Industry, Odessa, 1960-66, project engr. sci. rsch., 1966-70; engr. designer Teledyne Cast Product, Pomona, Calif., 1979-81; sr. mech. engr. Walt Elliot Disney Enterprises, Glendale, Calif., 1981-83; foundry liaison engr. Pacific Pumps divsn. Dresser Industries, Inc., Huntington Park, Calif., 1984-86; casting engr. Superior Industries Internat., Inc., Van Nuys, Calif., 1986-89; mech. engr. TAMCO Steel, Rancho Cucamonga, Calif., 1989-96. Contbr. articles to profl. jours. Recipient award for design of automatic lines for casting electric motor parts USSR Ministry Machine Bldg. and Handtools Mfr., 1966, for equipment for permanent mold casting All Union Exhbn. of Nat. Econ. Achievements, 1966-70. Achievements include patents for permanent mold casting. Home: 1718 Downs St Oceanside CA 92054-6191 Personal E-mail: siyurist@netzero.com.

YURK, TODD MICHAEL, retired health products executive; b. Sheboygan, Wis., Feb. 21, 1956; s. Harold Robert and Barbara Ann Jurk; 1 child, Natasha Mary Michaela. BS, U. Wis., Madison, 1990. Registered med. supplier Health Care Fin. Adminstrn., 1999, initial med. device distributor FDA, 1992. Grant reviewer Health Resources Svc. Adminstrn., Washington, 2006—. Petty officier 3d class USN, 1984—88. Mem.: Am. Acad. Med. Adminstrs., Am. Coll. Med. Practice Execs., Mensa. Home: 540 Petra Ln Sheboygan WI 53081

YURKO, RICHARD JOHN, lawyer; b. Ottawa, Ont., Can., Oct. 30, 1953; came to U.S., 1960; s. Michael and Catherine (Ewanishan) Y.; m. Robert F. Leary, Nov. 27, 2004; children: Nathan, Daniel. AB summa cum laude, Dartmouth Coll., 1975; JD cum laude, Harvard U., 1979. Bar: Mass. 1979, U.S. Dist. Ct. Mass. 1980, U.S. Ct. Appeals (1st cir.) 1980. Law clk. to Judge James L. King, U.S. Dist. Ct. for So. Dist. Fla., Miami, 1979-80; assoc. Bingham, Dana & Gould, Boston, 1980-85, Widett, Slater & Goldman, P.C., Boston, 1985-87, shareholder, 1987-92, chmn. litigation dept., 1989-91, hiring ptnr., 1992; shareholder Hutchins, Wheeler & Dittmar, Boston, 1992-94, chmn. litigation dept., 1992-94; shareholder Yurko & Perry, P.C., Boston, 1995—; shareholder, pres. Yurko, Salvesen & Remz, P.C. Teaches legal resch. & writing at Boston U. Sch. of Law. Contbr. articles to legal jours. Mem. ABA, Mass. Bar Assn., Boston Bar Assn. (former chmn. antitrust com., ad hoc com. on creation of bus. ct. 1999-2000), Phi Beta Kappa, Frank J. Murray Inn of Ct. (former pres.), Boston Bar Assns. (head mentoring com. 1998-2004). Editor Harvard Civil Rights - Civil Liberties Law Review. Office: Yurko Salvesen & Remz PC 1 Wash Mall 11th Fl Boston MA 02108-2603 Home: 62 Commonwealth Ave Boston MA 02116 Office Fax: 617-723-6905. Business E-Mail: rjy@bizlit.com.

YURT, ROGER WILLIAM, surgeon, educator; b. Louisville, June 8, 1945; s. Albert William and Mary Louise (McGrath) Yurt; m. Joan A. Terry, Sept. 3, 1971; children: Jennifer, Daniel, Gregory. BS in Biology, Loyola U., New Orleans, 1967; Md, U. Miami Sch. Medicine, 1972. Diplomate Am. Bd. Surgery, Nat. Bd. Med. Examiners. Intern surgery Parkland Meml. Hosp.-Southwestern Med. Sch., U. Tex., Dallas, 1972-73, resident surgery, 1973-74; postdoc. fellow Robert B. Brigham Hosp.-Harvard Med. Sch., Boston, 1974—77; resident, chief resident NY Presbyn. Hosp.-Weill Cornell Med. Ctr., NYC, 1977-79, acting dir. Burn Ctr., dir. rsch., 1982-83, vice chmn. dept. surgery, 1987—, acting chmn., 1991-93, dir. Trauma Ctr., 1992-99, attending surgeon, chief burn surgery, 1995—, dir. William Randolph Hearst Burn Ctr.; prof. surgery Weill Cornell Med. Coll., 1982—95, Johnson & Johnson disting. prof. surgery, 1995—. Clin. asst. prof. surgery Uniformed Svcs. U. Health Sci., Bethesda, Md., 1980—82, U. Tex. Health Sci. Ctr., San Antonio, 1981—82; chmn. burn com. Regional Emergency Med. Svcs., NY, 1982—84, mem. trauma ctr. adv. com., 1984—89, chmn., 1995—98, chmn. burn ctr. adv. com., 1996—2000. Editor: Infections in Surgery, 1981—88; contbr. articles to profl. jours., chapters to books. Maj. US Army, 1979—82. Recipient Hewitt award, Royal Soc. Medicine, 2003, Meritorious Humanitarian Recognition award, Am. Skin Assn., 2003, Physician of Yr. award, NY Presbyn. Hosp., 2006; named one of Best Doctors in America, Castle Connelly Med. Ltd., 1998—, NY's Super-Doctors, 2008; named to NY Mag.'s 'Best Doctors' issue, 1998—; grantee United Health Found., 1968—69, USPHS, 1973—75, NIH, 1984—87. Mem.: ACS (gov. 1990—96), Internat. Surg. Soc., Assn. Acad. Surgery, Am. Surg. Assn., Soc. Univ. Surgeons, Am. Surg. Infection Soc. (sec. 1987—90, pres. 1991—92, charter mem., chmn. membership com.), Am. Burn Assn. (v.p. bd. trustees 2004—06), Am. Assn. Med. Colleges (del. coun. academic societies 1985—87), Am. Assn. Surgery of Trauma, Omicron Delta Kappa, Alpha Omega Alpha. Roman Catholic. Office: NY Presbyn Cornell Med Ctr 250E 70th St L7 New York NY 10021-4885 Office Phone: 212-746-5410. Office Fax: 212-746-8991.

YUSPA, STUART HOWARD, oncologist, researcher; b. Balt., July 19, 1941; BS, Johns Hopkins U., 1962; MD, U. Md., 1966. Diplomate Am. Bd. Internal Medicine. Intern Hosp. of U. Pa., Phila., 1966-67, resident in internal medicine, 1970-72; rsch. assoc. Ctr. Cancer Rsch., Nat. Cancer Inst., NIH, Bethesda, Md., 1967-70, sr. investigator, 1972—, chief Lab. Cellular Carcinogenesis and Tumor Promotion, 1981—, chief Lab. Cancer Biology and Genetics, head In Vitro Pathogenesis Sect. Assoc. editor Cancer Rsch., 1983—96; editor-in-chief Molecular Carcinogenesis, 1987—92. Recipient Lila Gruber Cancer Rsch. Award, Am. Acad. Dermatology, 1989, DSM, USPHS. Fellow AAAS; mem Am. Assn. Cancer Rsch. (G.H.A. Clowes Meml. Award 1993), Am. Soc. Cell Biology, Soc. Investigative Dermatology, USPHS Commd. Officers Assn. Achievements include research in determining mechanisms whereby chemicals initiate or promote malignant transformation of epithelial cells. Office: Lab Cellular Carcinogenesis and Tumor Promotion Ctr Cancer Rsch Bldg 37 Rm 4068A1 37 Convent Dr Bethesda MD 20892 Office Phone: 301-496-2162. Office Fax: 301-496-8709. E-mail: sy12j@nih.gov.*

YUSPEH, ALAN RALPH, lawyer, health company executive; b. New Orleans, June 13, 1949; s. Michel and Rose Fay (Rabenovitz) Y.; m. Janet Horn, June 8, 1975. BA, Yale U., 1971; MBA, Harvard U., 1973; JD, Georgetown U., 1978. Bar: DC 1978. Mgmt. cons. McKinsey & Co., Washington, 1973-74; adminstrv. asst., legis. asst. Office of U.S. Senator J. Bennett Johnston, Washington, 1974-78; atty. Shaw, Pittman, Potts & Trowbridge, Washington, 1978-79, Ginsburg, Feldman, Weil and Bress, Washington, 1979-82; gen. counsel Com. on Armed Svcs.-U.S. Senate, Washington, 1982-85; ptnr. Preston, Thorgrimson, Ellis & Holman, Washington, 1985-88, Miller & Chevalier, Washington, 1988-91, Howrey & Simon, Washington, 1991-97; sr. v.p. ethics, compliance and corp. responsibility HCA, Nashville, 1997—2007, sr. v.p. and chief ethics and compliance officer, 2007—. Coord. Def. Industry Initiative on Bus., Ethics and Conduct, 1987-97; pres. Health Care Compliance Assn., 2002. Editor Law and Policy in Internat. Bus. Jour., 1978-79, Nat. Contract Mgmt. Jour., 1988-92; assoc. editor Pub. Contract Law Jour., 1987-91. Chmn. bd. ethics, City of Balt., 1988-96, planning commn., 1996-97; chmn. bd. dirs. Tenn. Repertory Theater, 2002-05; bd. dirs. Balt. Housing Authority, 1996-97, Ethics Officer Assn., 2001-04, YMCA Mid. Tenn. Camp, 2002-, Tenn. Performing Arts Ctr., 2003-, Nashville Pub. Libr. Found., 2005-. 1st lt. USAR, 1971-77. Office: HCA One Park Plaza Nashville TN 37203 Home: 126 Third Ave N Franklin TN 37064 Office Phone: 615-344-1005. Business E-Mail: alan.yuspeh@hcahealthcare.com.

YUSSOUFF, MOHAMMED, retired physicist, educator; b. Cuttack, India, Aug. 14, 1942; arrived in U.S., 1991; s. Haji and Nurunnisa Fakhruddin; m. Farhana Begum, Apr. 6, 1969; children: Ashraf, Zeenat, Mustafa. MSc, Delhi U., 1963; PhD, Indian Inst. Tech., Kanpur, 1967. Prof. physics Indian Inst. Tech., Kanpur, 1967-90; vis. prof. physics Mich. State U., East Lansing, 1991—; ret., 1999. Guest scientist Ford Rsch., Dearborn, Mich., 1991-97, GM Tech. Ctr., Warren, Mich., 1997-98, Delphi Tech. Ctr., Warren, 1999—; vis. scientist U. Köln, Germany, 1972-74, U. Western Ont., London, Can., 1990-91; Humboldt scientist Atomic Energy Agy, Jülich, Germany, 1979-81; vis. prof. U. Konstanz, Germany, 1986-89; mem. com. physics examination Pub. Svc. Commn., Delhi, India, 1976-86, rsch. grants Univ. Grants Commn., Delhi, 1985-90; dir. Internat. Sch. on Band Structure, Indian Inst. Tech., 1986; creator Slow Pace program for tchg. sci. and engring. to deficient students with poor econ. or sch. backgrounds. Editor: Electronic Band Structure and Its Applications, 1987, The Physics of Materials, 1987. Mem.: Am. Phys. Soc., Internat. Ctr. Theoretical Physics (assoc.). Muslim. Achievements include patents for monitoring the catalytic converters in cars; theory of disordered systems, chanelling, clusters, electronic structure, ionic conductors, exhaust gas sensors, superconductors, zeolites; fundamental rate constants of catalytic reactions and foundations of quantum theory; research in kinetic model of catalysis; theory of freezing. Home: 5920 Crystal Lake Dr Romulus MI 48174 E-mail: yussouf2@hotmail.com.

YUST, DAVID E., artist, educator; b. Wichita, Kans., Apr. 3, 1939; s. Earl and Truly Yust; m. Joan G. Dalby, Mar. 13, 1966; children: Erin L., Joel C. BFA, U. Kans., Lawrence, 1963; MFA, U. Oreg., Eugene, 1969. Prof. Colo. State U., Ft. Collins, 1965—. One-man shows include Denver Art Mus., 1976, Wichita Art Mus., Kans., 1979, Wichita Ctr. for the Arts, 1998, Rourke Art Mus., Moorehead, Minn., 2003, Ft. Collins Mus. Contemporary Art, Colo., 2003, Plus Gallery, Denver, 2006, Arvada Ctr., Arvada, 2008, Art in Embassies Program, US Dept. State, Zagreb, Croatia, 2003—06, Manama, Bahrain, 2008—, Colorado Abstract, Ctr. Visual Art, Denver, 2009. Bd. dirs. Denver Art Mus., 1998—, D.A.M. Contemporaries, 1998—. Recipient Afkey award, Alliance for Contemporary Art, Colo., 2000, John Stern Disting. Prof. award, Colo. State U., 2004; named Art Educator of Yr., Colo. Art Edn. Assn., 2003, Nat. Art Edn. Assn., Pacific Region, 2004. Office: Colo State U Fort Collins CO 80523 Home Phone: 970-484-0675; Office Phone: 970-491-6774, 970-491-5478. Business E-Mail: davyust@lamar.colostate.edu.

YUTAKA, NIBU, medical educator; m. Anna Di Gregorio; 1 child, Marianna Cettina Nibu. PhD, U. Tsukuba, Ibaraki, Japan, 1995. Rsch. assoc. U. Tsukuba, 1995—97; postdoc. fellow U. Calif., Berkeley, 1997—2002; asst. prof. Weill Med. Coll. Cornell U., NYC, 2002—. Office: Weill Med Coll Cornell Univ 1300 York Ave Box 60 A308 New York NY 10065 Office Fax: 212-746-8175. Business E-Mail: yun2001@med.cornell.edu.

YZAGUIRRE, RAUL HUMBERTO, civil rights leader; b. San Juan, Tex., July 22, 1939; s. Ruben Antonio and Eva Linda (Morin) Y.; m. Audrey H. Bristow, Jan. 2, 1965; children: Regina Dolores, Raul Humberto, Elisa Almalinda, Roberto Hayse, Rebecca Morin, Benjamin Ruben. Student, U. Md., 1963-64; BS, George Washington U., 1968. Registered med. technologist. Student and community activist, 1963-65; active War on Poverty, 1969-74; founder, exec. dir. Interstate Research Assocs (Hispanic cons. firm), Washington, 1969-73; v.p. Center for Community Change, Washington, 1974; community organizer in S.Tex., 1974; pres. Nat. Council of La Raza, Washington, 1974—2004; presdl. prof. practice, exec. dir. Ctr. Community Devel. and Civil Rights Ariz. State U., 2005—. Lectr. Harvard U., U. Notre Dame, U. Tex., others.; commr. U.S. Nat. Commn. for UNESCO, 1983—; chmn. Associated SW Investors, 1976—; bd. dirs. Si TV, 2008- Co-chmn. Nat. Urban Coalition, 1975-83; co-chmn. Working Com. on Concerns of Hispanics and Blacks, 1979—, sec. ind. sector, 1983-84; sec., chmn. Forum of Nat. Hispanic Orgns., 1976-79; chmn. adv. com. I.N.S.; former trustee Common Cause; co-founder, chmn. Nat. Neighborhood Coalition, 1977—; immediate past chair Ind. Sector; bd. dirs. Enterprise Found., Nat. Dem. Insts. Served with USAF, 1959-62. Recipient Rockefeller Public Service award, 1979, Common Cause Pub. Service award, 1986, Order of the Aztec Eagle, Govt. Mexico, 1993, Sargent Shriver award for Equal Justice: For Distinguished Achievement in Building Collaborations to Overcome Poverty, Shriver Ctr., 2006, Smithsonian Latino Ctr. Legacy award, 2007; fellow Inst. Politics John F. Kennedy Sch. Govt. Mem. Am. GI Forum, Hispanic Assn. Corp. Responsibility (co-founder, chmn. bd. dirs.). Democrat. Roman Catholic. Office: ASU Ctr Community Development Civil Rights 411 N Central Ave Ste 650 Phoenix AZ 85001 *The civil rights struggle of the 80's will be the transformation of America to a truly pluralistic society where cultural differences will not only be tolerated, but indeed valued.*

YZERMAN, STEVE (STEPHEN GREGORY YZERMAN), professional sports team executive, retired professional hockey player; b. Cranbrook, BC, Can., May 9, 1965; m. Lisa Brennan; children: Isabella Katherine, Maria Charlotte, Sophia Rose. Center Detroit Red Wings, 1983—2006, captain, 1986—2006, v.p., 2006—; gen. mgr. Team Can., IIHF World Championship, Moscow, 2007. Mem. Team Can., Olympic Games, Nagano, Japan, 1998, Salt Lake City, 2002; exec. dir. Team Can., 2010 Olympic Games, 2008—. Recipient Lester B. Pearson award, 1989, Conn Smythe Trophy, 1998, Frank J. Selke Trophy, 2000, Bill Masterton Trophy, 2003, Lester Patrick Award, 2006; named NHL Rookie of Yr., Sporting News, 1984; named to All-Rookie Team, NHL, 1984, First All-Star Team, 2000, NHL All-Star Game, 1984, 1988—93, 1997, 1999, 2000. Achievements include being the youngest person ever to play in the NHL All-Star game, 1984; being a member of Stanley Cup Champion Detroit Red Wings, 1997, 1998, 2002; being a member of gold medal Canadian Hockey team, Salt Lake City Olympic Games, 2002; being the longest serving captain in NHL history; having his number, 19, retired by Detroit Red Wings, 2007; being inducted into the Canadian Sports Hall of Fame, 2008. Office: Detroit Red Wings Joe Louis Arena 600 Civic Center Dr Detroit MI 48226-4419

ZABALAWI, SALAHEDDIN AIMAN, electrical engineer; b. Damascus, Syria, Sept. 17, 1983; s. Aiman Salaheddin Zabalawi and Sausan Rateb Mosely. BS in Elec. Engr., Am..U. Sharjah, United Arab Emirates, 2006; MS in Elec. Engr., U. Wis., Milw., 2008. Field engr. SAWARY Energy, Jeddah, Saudi Arabia, 2006—07. Contbr. articles to profl. sci. jours., scientific papers. Mem.: IEEE. Avocations: computers, travel.

ZABANAL, EDUARDO OLEGARIO, lawyer; b. Legazpi City, Albay, The Philippines, Aug. 8, 1952; came to U.S., 1986; s. Jose Agas and Maria Soledad (Olegario) Z.; m. Leorosie Rebodos Nabor, June 18, 1983; children: Shalimar Rosary, Angelica Almira, Regina Tatiana, Lorelei Blossom, Eduardo Olegario, Jr. BA, Aquinas U., The Philippines, 1972; BL, U. The Philippines, 1978. Bar: Hawaii 1990, The Philippines 1979, U.S. Dist. Ct. Hawaii 1990, U.S. Ct. Appeals (9th cir.) 2002. Assoc. Pacis & Reyes, Manila, 1979-86; pvt. practice Honolulu, 1990—. Contbr. articles to profl. jours. Bd. dirs. Kahaluu Neighborhood Bd., Honolulu, 1991-93; active Filipino Coalition for Solidarity, Honolulu, 1991—. Recipient recognition among Disting. Filipinos in Oahu, FIL-AM Courier, 1995, Outstanding Vol. award HSBA, 2003. Mem. ABA, ATLA, Hawaii State Bar Assn., Am. Civil Immigration Lawyers Assn., Hawaii Filipino Lawyers Assn., Integrated Bar The Philippines, Philippine Bar Assn., Filipino C. of C. Hawaii. Roman Catholic. Avocations: jogging, travel, reading. Home: 91-1146 Lanakoi St Kapolei HI 96707-2907 Personal E-mail: e.zabanal@worldnet.att.net.

ZABAR, ELI, food products executive; b. NYC, Jan. 7, 1943; s. Louis and Lillian Zabar; m. Ali Zabar (div.); m. Devon S. Fredericks, June 21, 1990. Grad., Columbia U., NYC, 1967. Owner E.A.T., NYC, 1973—, E.A.T. Boutique, 1977—85, E.A.T. Gifts, 1985, Eli's Bread, 1985—, Eli's Restaurant, 1987—, Eli's Vinegar Factory, 1993—, Eli's Manhattan, 1998—, Eli's The Restaurant, 1999—, Taste Restaurant and Wine Bar, W.I.N.E. Office: Elis Manhattan 1411 Third Ave New York NY 10028*

ZABECKI, DAVID TADEUSZ, engineer, educator, military historian, military officer; b. Springfield, Mass., Aug. 8, 1947; s. Julian Tadeusz and Virginia Charlotte (Luthgren) Z.; m. Marlies Schweigler, 1991; children: Konrad Josef, Jonathan Tadeusz. BA, Xavier U., 1972, MA, 1973; MS, Fla. Inst. Tech., 1976; PhD in Engring., Calif. Coast U., 1987; diploma, U.S. Army War Coll., 1995; PhD in Mil. Sci., Royal Mil. Coll. Sci., 2004; grad. exec. program Russian and Am. gen. officers, Harvard U., 2002. Patrolman Xavier U. Campus Police, Cin., 1972—74; quality assurance specialist Rock Island Arsenal, Ill., 1974—77; quality engr. Deere & Co., Moline, Ill., 1977—84, Zweibruecken, Germany, 1985—93; adj. instr. Fla. Inst. Tech., Fla., 1977—79; adj. lectr. European program City Colls. Chgo., 1986—89; asst. prof. Am. Mil. U., 1993—2003; dep. chief of staff for ops. 7th Army Res. Command, Schwetzingen, Germany, 1997—98, chief of staff, 1998—2000; dep. chief USAR, Washington, 2000—02; comdg. gen. 7th Army Res. Command, Schwetzingen, Germany, 2002—03; dep. chief of staff for mobilization and res. affairs US Army Europe, 2003—07; sr. security advisor US Coord. and Monitoring Mission (Roadmap to Peace in the Mid. East), 2003; hon. sr. rsch. fellow U. Birmingham, 2009—. Comdr. Task Force Normandy-60, U.S. Army Europe, 2004; exec. dir. Europe, Dept. Def. World War II 60th Anniversary Observance Com., 2004—05; comdg. gdn. US So. Europe Task Force Rear Airborne, 2005-06; sr. historian, Weider History Group, 2008-; lectr. in field, hon. sr. rsch. fellow, U. Birmingham, 2009-. Author: Karl Doenitz: A Defense, 1972, Field Artillery in the 1980's, 1983, Steel Wind: Colonel Georg Bruchmueller and The Birth of Modern Artillery, 1994, The German 1918 Offensives: A Case Study in the Operational Level of War, 2006; editor in chief: WWII in Europe: An Ency., 1998, translator, editor: On the German Art of War: Truppenfuhrung, 2001, contbg. editor: Mil. History mag., 1987—99, World War II mag., 1987—99; editor: Vietnam mag., 2000—08, Vietnam: A Reader, 2002; author and editor Chief of Staff: The Principal Staff Officers Behind History's Great Commanders, 2008; series editor: The Art of War, 2000—03, book reviewer: Mil. Rev., Jour. of Royal Arty., —; developer contbn. margin differential concept of quality cost analysis, —. Served to maj. gen. US Army, 1966—69, 1996—97, 2002—06 USAR, 1969—2007. Decorated DSM, Combat Infantryman's Badge, Bronze Star, Army Commendation medal, Meritorious Svc. medal with 5 oak leaf clusters, Legion of Merit with 2 oak leaf clusters, Def. Superior Svc. medal, US Army Gen. Staff Identification badge, German Army Proficiency badge in gold; Knight Comdr. Order St. John Jerusalem, Knight Sovereign Mil. Order Temple Jerusalem, Knight Comdr. Order of St. Michael of the Wing (Portugal), Gen. John J. Pershing award U.S. Army Command and Staff Coll., 1988, George Washington Honor medal Freedoms Found., 1988, Wm. Hornaday Dist. Svc. in Conservation award, 1963, Knowlton award Mil. Intelligence Corps Assn. Fellow: Ermine Soc.; mem.: DAV, Sons of Union Vets. Civil War, Polish Inst. Arts and Scis. in Am., Assn. US Army, NY Acad. Scis., Royal Arty. Assn., Co. Mil. Historians, German Philatelic Socs., Res. Officers Assn., Ancient Order of St. Barbara, US Field Arty. Assn., Am. Soc. Quality Control (cert. quality engr., cert. reliability engr.), Soc. 173d Airborne Brigade (hon.), VFW, Nat. Eagle Scouts Assn., Army and Navy Club Washington, Nat. Sojourners, York Rite, Scottish Rite, Masons, Alpha Sigma Nu. Address: Guenterstal Strasse 86 79100 Freiberg Germany Home Phone: 49-761-75782; Office Phone: 49-761-3848281. Personal E-mail: david.zabecki@gmx.de.

ZABEL, MATTHEW L., legislative staff member; b. SD, Apr. 15, 1968; BS magna cum laude, U. SD, 1990; MS with distinction, U. Bristol, England, 1992; JD cum laude, Northwestern U., 1996. Bar: SD 1996. Legis. asst. Senator Larry Pressler, 1990—91; fed. jud. law clk., 1996—97; trial atty. US Dept. Justice, 1997—2002, dep. assoc. atty. gen., chief of staff to the assoc. atty. gen., 2003—05; chief of staff Senator John Thune, 2005—. Editor in chief Northwestern U. Law Rev.; mem. US trial team Waco/Branch Davidian civil litigation and trial. Mem.: Phi Beta Kappa. Lutheran. Office: Office of Senator John Thune 493 SROB Washington DC 20510-4105 Office Phone: 202-224-2321. E-mail: matthew_zabel@thune.senate.gov.*

ZABEL, WILLIAM DAVID, lawyer; b. Omaha, Dec. 14, 1936; s. Louis J. and Anne I. Z.; m. Deborah M. Miller, Oct. 31, 1979; children by previous marriage: Richard, David. AB summa cum laude, Princeton U., 1958; LLB cum laude, Harvard U., 1961. Bar: N.Y. 1961, U.S. Supreme Ct. 1966, Fla. 1975. Ptnr. Schulte Roth & Zabel, NYC, 1969—. Lectr. Cornell Law Sch., So. Fed. Tax Inst., U. Miami Inst. Estate Planning, Great Plains Tax Inst., Assn. of Bar of City of N.Y., Practising Law Inst., profl. orgns.; N.Y. State adv. com. U.S. Civil Rights Commn., 1969-73; vol. civil rights litigator Lawyers Constl. Def. Com., Miss., summer 1965; bd. dirs. Del. Mgmt. Holdings Inc.; chmn., Human Rights First, 2000- Author: Estate Planning for the Large Estate, 1976, Domicile, Wills and Tax Problems of Migrating Clients Transplanted to Florida, 1976, Income, Estate and Gift Tax Consequences of Marital Settlements, 1979, Estate Planning for Interests in a Closely Held Business, 1981, Use of Trusts in Connection with Marital Dissolutions, 1983, Thy Will Be Done?, 1991, The Rich Die Richer -- and You Can Too, 1995; Am. editor: The Lawyer, Eng., 1963-66; mem. editl. adv. bd. Trusts and Estates Mag.; contbr. articles to profl. jours. Pres. Merlin Found.; mem. Lymphoma Found., Soros Founds. (Newly Ind. States and the Baltic Republics, Hungary, Romania, Bulgaria and Ctrl. European U.), Open Soc. Fund, Inc., Human Rights Watch/Helsinki, Doctors of World, Winston Found. World Peace, Ottinger Found., David H. Cogan Found., The Picower Med. Rsch. Inst., Lawson Valentine Found., Am. Friends of the Israel Mus., Am. Com. for Weizmann Inst. Sci.; legal counsel Internat. Confedn. Art Dealers; bd. dirs. Tauber Inst., Sakharov Archives, Brandeis U., Population Action Internat., 1996-2004, Lincoln Ctr. Theater, 1996-, Acad. Am. Poets, 1977-; trustee The New Sch. for Social Rsch., 1994—; adv. bd. Project on Death in Am.; chmn. Princeton U. Planned Giving Com., 1991—. Recipient Disting. Cmty. Svc. award Brandeis U., 1986, U.S. Masters Squash Team Bronze medal 14th Maccabiah Games, 1993, Disting. Svc award, New Sch. U., Extraordinary Leader award, Lawyers Com. for Human Rights, 2003, Lifetime Achievement award, The Am. Lawyer mag., 2006; fellow Brandeis U., 1987—. Fellow Am. Coll. Trust and Estate Coun., Internat. Acad. Estate and Trust Law, N.Y. Bar Found., Am. Bar Found.; mem. ABA, Am. Law Inst., N.Y. State Bar Assn., Assn. of Bar of City of N.Y. (internat. human rights com.), Human Rights First (formerly Lawyers Com. for Human Rights) (bd. dirs., chmn., 2005), Vol. Lawyers for Arts (bd. dirs.), Estate Planning Coun. N.Y.C. (bd. dirs. 1975-79), Fla. Bar Assn., Harmonie Club (pres. 1989-91), Phi Beta Kappa. Office: Schulte Roth & Zabel 919 Third Ave New York NY 10022-4774 also: Phillips Point W Tower 10th Fl 777 S Flagler Dr West Palm Beach FL 33401-6161 Office Phone: 212-758-2351. Office Fax: 212-592-5955. Business E-Mail: william.zabel@srz.com.

ZABETAKIS, PAUL MICHAEL, nephrologist, educator; b. Washington, Pa., July 30, 1947; s. Michael G. and Rebecca A. (Banakas) Z.; m. Martha Robinson, Oct. 3, 1970; 1 child, Amy Shannon. BA, Washington & Jefferson Coll., 1969; mD, U. Tenn., 1972. Diplomate Am. Bd. Internal Medicine, Am. Bd. Nephrology. Intern in medicine U. Pitts., 1972-73, resident in medicine, 1973-75; fellow in nephrology Yale U., New Haven, 1975-77; asst. chief nephrology-hypertension Lenox Hill Hosp., NYC, 1977-82, assoc. chief nephrology-hypertension, 1978-99, dir. home peritoneal dialysis, 1985-99; asst. prof. clin. medicine NY Med. Coll., Valhalla, 1980-88, assoc. prof. clin. medicine, 1988-92; clin. asst. prof. medicine Cornell U., NYC, 1992-93; clin. assoc. prof. medicine NYU, 1993-99; exec. v.p., COO Everest Healthcare Svc., Oak Park, Ill., 1999-2001; CEO Extracorporeal Alliance Fresenius Med. Care, N.Am., 2001—06; pres. Renal Rsch. Inst., 2006—. Mem. editl. bd. Clinical Nephrology, 1979—, Clinical and Experimental Dialysis and Apheresis, 1983-86, Geriatric Nephrology and Urology, 1995—, Advances in Renal Replacement Therapy, 1999—; nephrology cons. Nicholas Inst. Sports Medicine and Athletic Trauma Lenox Hill Hosp., N.Y.C., 1978-99, rsch. physician, 1982-99; mem. hypertension svc. adv. com. ARC, N.Y.C., 1981-99; mem. exec. com. End Stage Renal Disease Network N.Y. Inc., 1986-99, treas., 1992-93, chmn. long-range planning com., 1994; bd. dirs. Physician Hosp. Orgn. Lenox Hill Hosp., chmn. bd. dirs., 1996-99, v.p. med. bd., 1997-99; vice-chmn. quality improvement, med. dir. Everest Healthcare Svcs., Chgo., 1996-99. Contbr. numerous chpts. to books; patentee in field; lectr. in field; contbr. articles to profl. jours. Fellow ACP, Am. Coll. Preventive Medicine, Am. Coll. Sports Medicine; mem. N.Y. County Med. Soc., Med. Soc. of State of N.Y., Am. Heart Assn., Westchester Heart Assn., N.Y. Soc. Nephrology, Am. Soc. Nephrology, Internat. Soc. Nephrology, N.Y. Acad. Scis., N.Y. State Fedn. Profl. Health Educators, Am. Fedn. Clin. Sch., Internat. Soc. Peritoneal Dialysis, Am. Soc. Artificial Internal Organs (program com. 1995-99), Soc. Critical Care Medicine, Am. Coll. Nutrition, Internat.

Soc. for Renal Nutrition and Metabolism, Internat. Soc. Geriatric Nephrology and Urology (founding mem., sec-treas. 1994-99). Avocation: sailboat racing. Office Phone: 708-498-9114. Business E-Mail: paul.zabetakis@fmc-na.com.

ZABINSKI, RICHARD A., pharmacist; b. Hibbing, Minn., Mar. 8, 1965; s. Claude A. and Celine A. Zabinski; m. Corinne S. Schroeder; children: Nathaniel R., Jack S. PharmD, U. Minn., Mpls., 1990. Registered pharmacist Minn., 1988. Mgr., med. mktg. Bayer, West Haven, Conn., 1992—96; dir., applied therapeutics Searle Pharms., Skokie, Ill., 1996—2000; dir., bus. devel. Ingenix, Eden Prairie, Minn., 2002—04; sr. dir. and team leader, clinrx solutions United Health Care, Edina, Minn., 2004—06; v.p., pharm. solutions OptumHealth, United-Health Group Co., Golden Valley, Minn., 2006—. Chairperson, program planning & devel. com. Acad. Managed Care Pharmacy, Alexandria, Va., 2002—03, pres., acad. managed care pharmacy, 2007—08, bd. chmn., 2008—; bd. dirs. AMCP, Alexandria, Va., 2005—07; v.p., bd. trustees Found. Managed Care Pharmacy, Alexandria, 2008—. Asst. scout master Boy Scouts America, Bloomington, Minn., 2008—09; del. Rep. Party - Dist. 41B, Bloomington, 2006—09. Fellowship, Am. Soc. Health Sys. Pharmacists, 1991—92. Mem.: Minn. Pharmacists Assn., Acad. Managed Care Pharmacy (pres. 2007—08), Kappa Psi. Conservative. Roman Catholic. Avocation: bicycling. Home: 7710 Bush Lake Dr Bloomington MN 55438 Office: OptumHealth 6300 Olson Meml Hwy Golden Valley MN 55427-4946 Personal E-mail: rick@pharmacystrategies.com. Business E-Mail: richard.zabinski@optumhealth.com.

ZABLE, JACK LOUIS, mechanical engineer, educator; b. Bklyn., Feb. 24, 1942; s. Phillip David and Gertrude Zable; m. Barbara Zable; children: Brian, Ilyse, Robert. BSME, CCNY, 1963; MSME, Purdue U., 1965, PhD, 1969. Sr. tech. staff IBM, Endicott, NY and Boulder, Colo., 1964—97; prof. attendant, dept. mech. engring. U. Colo., Boulder, 1997—. Dir. Industry/Univ. Coop. Projects Ctr. U. Colo., Boulder, 1999—; mem. IBM Acad. Tech., Armonk, NY, 1990—97. Contbr. chapters to books, articles to profl. jours. Pres. Temple Concord, Binghamton, NY, 1982—84; bd. mem. Jewish Fedn., Binghamton, NY, 1984—88. Fellow: ASME; mem.: Sigma Xi, Pi Tau Sigma. Republican. Jewish. Achievements include patents in field of printer technologies. Avocations: hiking, reading, golf, bridge. Home: 6798 Snead Ct Niwot CO 80503 Office: U Colo ME Dept Campus Box 427 Boulder CO 80309 E-mail: zable@spot.colorado.edu.

ZABOLOTSKAYA, EVGENIYA ANDREEVNA, physicist; b. Moscow, Nov. 26, 1935; d. Andrei and Evdokiya (Bobrovskaya) Z.; m. Genadii Mil'shin, Sept. 1960 (div. June 1962); m. Yurii Il'inskii, Dec. 14,1963; children: Ekaterina Il'inskii, Kceniya Il'inskii. Student, Moscow State U., 1955-61, postgrad., 1963-66, PhD, 1968; D. in Phys. and Math. Scis., USSR Acad. Scis., Moscow, 1985. Cert. phys. diploma. Milling-machine operator Moscow Brake Plant, 1954-55; engr. All-Union Elec. & Mech. Inst., Moscow, 1961-63; jr. researcher Acoustical Inst., Moscow, 1966-70; sr. researcher Moscow Electronic Design Inst., 1970-73; jr. researcher Moscow State U., 1973-82, USSR Acad. Scis. Gen. Physics Inst., Moscow, 1982-86, leading researcher, 1986—. Sec. doctor degree com. USSR Acad. Scis. Physics Inst. Author: (with N.S. Bakhvalov, Ya. M. Zileikin) Nonlinear Theory of Sound Beams, 1982, English edit., 1987; contbr. over 50 articles to phys. jours. Recipient USSR State prize, 1985. Fellow Acoustical Soc. Am.

ZACCARIA, MARK STUART, marketing professional; b. Boston, Jan. 27, 1949; s. Leo V. and Charlotte (Cross) Z.; m. Ruth Ann Carter, Apr. 5, 1975; children: Adam Jay, Katharine Ann, April Elizabeth. BA, Colby Coll., 1970. Flight instr. USAF/Air Tng. Command, 1970-75; gen. mgr. Marlyn Engring. Corp., Boston, 1975-83; mktg. mgr., mgr. direct mktg., product mgr. Dennison Mfg. Co., Framingham, Mass., 1983—2007; cons. in bus. to bus. mktg. Rustin Mktg. Services, LLC, North Kingstown, RI, 2008—. Del. Auto ID Mfg. Inc., Pitts. Contbr. articles to profl. jours. Mem. North Kingstown Zoning Bd. Review, 1999—2004; mem., past chair North Kingstown Rep. Town Com., 2003—05, campaign mgr., local & state elections, 2000, 2002, 2004, 2006; mem. North Kingstown Town Coun., 2004—06, 2004. Capt. USAF, 1970—75. Republican. Methodist. Avocations: bicycling, alpine skiing, raquetball, cabinet making, parenting. Office: Rustin Mktg Services LLC 35 Congdon Hill Rd Saunderstown RI 02874 Office Phone: 401-268-3080.

ZACEK, JOSEPH FREDERICK, historian, educator; b. Stickney, Ill., Dec. 18, 1930; s. Joseph and Emilie (Dvorak) Z.; m. Judith Ellen Cohen (div. 1975); 1 child, Natalie Ann; m. Jane Perlberg Shapiro; stepchildren: Leslie Helen, Peter Carl. BA summa cum laude, U. Ill., Champaign-Urbana, 1952, MA in History, 1953, PhD in History, 1962; cert., Columbia U. Inst. on East Cen. Europe, 1962. Asst. prof. history Occidental Coll., LA, 1962-65; asst. prof., dir. Russian & East European Programs UCLA, 1965-68; assoc. prof. SUNY at Albany, 1968-71, dir. Russian and East European Programs, 1968-77, 91-92, prof., 1971—2001, chair dept. history, 1974-77, prof. emeritus, 2001—. Selection com. for East Europe Internat. Rsch. and Exch. Bd., Princeton, NJ, 1978-81; nat. bd. cons. NEH, Washington, 1975—; vis. scholar IREX Comenius U., Bratislava, and Charles U., Prague, Czechoslovakia, 1973, Columbia U., 1977-78, U. Ill, Champaign-Urbana, 1987. Author: Palacky: The Historian as Scholar and Nationalist, 1970; editor, co-author: Frantisek Palacky, 1798-1876: A Centennial Appreciation, 1981, The Enlightenment and the National Revivals in Eastern Europe, 1983, The Intimate Palacky, 1984; also numerous periodical articles and chpts. in multi-authored books. With M.I., U.S. Army, 1954-57. Fgn. Area Tng. fellow Ford Found., Columbia U., 1960-62, Sr. Humanities fellow Rockefeller Found., 1977-78, fellow Russian Rsch. Ctr. Harvard U., 1986-91; Rsch. grantee Am. Coun. Learned Soc./Soc. Sci. Rsch. Coun., 1965, Am. Philos. Soc., 1968; recipient Comenius medal Govt. of Czech and Slovak Fed. Republic, 1992, Medal of Comenius Pedagogical Inst. in Prague, 1992, Josef Hlávka medal of Czechoslovak Acad. of Scis. in Prague, 1992, others. Mem. Am. Hist. Assn., Am. Assn. for Advancement Slavic Studies, Western Slavic Conf., Czechoslovak Studies Assn., Slovak Studies Assn., Consortium on Revolutionary Europe, Assn. for Study of Ethnicity and Nationalism, Phi Beta Kappa. Avocations: travel, gardening, music. Home: 22 Sandhurst Dr Slingerlands NY 12159-9418 Office Phone: 518-482-7478.

ZACHARELLA, ALEXANDRA, music educator, director; b. Livingston, NJ, July 5, 1976; d. Carl Arthur and Nellie Zacharella. MusB, U. Hartford, West Hartford, Conn., 1999; MusM, U. Mich., Ann Arbor, 2001; PhD in Musical Arts, U. Southern Calif., LA, 2007. Trombone instr. Interlochen Ctr. Arts Summer Camp, Mich., 2001—04; dir. bands Lanse Creuse Mid. Sch. Ctrl., Harrison Township, Mich., 2001—04; festival wind ensemble trombone coach Idyllwild Music Festival, Calif., 2005—; asst. prof. law brass U. Ark., Ft. Smith, 2007—, dir. athletic band, 2007—. Recipient Order of Arete, U. Southern Calif., 2007, Robert Marsteller Meml. Endowed Music award, 2007. Mem.: Ark. Bandmaster's Assn., Internat. Trombone Assn., Coll. Music Soc., Pi Kappa Lambda, Kappa Kappa Psi, Alpha Chi Nat. Honor Soc. Home: 109 N 3rd St Apt 318 Fort Smith AR 72901 Office: Univ Ark Ft Smith 5210 Grand Ave Fort Smith AR 72903 Personal E-mail: az1776@aol.com. Business E-Mail: azachare@uafortsmith.edu.

ZACHARIAS, DAVID ALAN, biotechnologist, educator; b. Indianapolis, 1966; BS, Andrews U., MS, 1991; PhD, Mayo Grad. Sch., Rochester, Minn., 1996. Sr. scientist Merck Rsch. Labs, 2001—03; asst. prof. U. Fla., St Augustine, 2003—. Advisor Sid Martin Biotech Incubator U. Fla., Gainesville, 2004—07; advisor and bd. mem. Calif., 2003 Vala Bioscis., La Jolla, Calif. Contbr. scientific papers to jours. Grant, NIH, ACS. Achievements include numerous patents. Office: Univ Fla-The Whitney Lab 9505 Ocean Shore Blvd Saint Augustine FL 32080

ZACHARIAS, NIKOLAOS MARIOS, obstetrician, gynecologist, perinatologist; b. Athens, Greece; s. Marios Nikolaos and Constantoula Marios Zacharias; m. Ioanna Dimitrios Athanassaki, May 12, 2000. MD, Nat. and Kapodistrian U., Athens, 1995. Cert. in ob-gyn. Gen. practitioner Greek Nat. Health Svc., Vassiliki, Greece, 1996-97; gen. surgery intern Laikon Gen. Hosp., Athens, 1997-98; chief resident in ob-gyn. Baylor Coll. Medicine, Houston, 1998—2002; fellow in maternal-fetal medicine U. Tex. Med. Br., Galveston, 2002—05; asst. prof. ob-gyn Baylor Coll. Medicine, Houston, 2005—; program dir. dist. prenatal ultrasound maternal fetal medicine Harris County Hosp., Houston, 2005—. Undergrad. Ann. scholar Found. State Scholarships, 1990-94; Papadakis grantee Nat. and Kapodistrian U. Athens, 1990-95, Kontoleon grantee, 1998-2002, Acad. fellow U. Tex. Med. Br., 2002-. Fellow ACOG; mem. AMA, Athens Med. Assn., Gen. Med. Coun., Tex. Med. Assn., Soc. for Maternal-Fetal Medicine. Avocations: swimming, basketball, travel. Home: 125 White Dr Bellaire TX 77401 Office: Baylor Coll Medicine 1709 Dryden Ste 1100 Houston TX 77030-2400 Office Phone: 713-873-3436, 713-870-6884. Business E-Mail: nmz@bcm.edu, nikolaos_zacharias@hchd.tmc.edu.

ZACHAROULIS, DIMITRIS, surgeon, researcher; b. Larisa, Greece, Nov. 8, 1967; s. Christos Zacharoulis and Anastasia Tsita. Grad. Diploma (hon.), 5th Gen. Lyceum, Greece, 1985; PhD, U. Athens, 2000. Cert. Ptychion Iatrikes Aristotelian U. Thessaloniki, Greece, 1991, Gen. Surgery Boards Com., 2000. Rsch. fellow U. Athens, 1991—92; surgery intern Greek Army, Alexandroupolis, Greece, 1992—93; gen. practitioner Greek Ministry of Health, Larisa, Greece, 1993—94; rsch. fellow Harvard Med., Boston, 1994—95; resident gen. surgery SUNY, Syracuse, 1995—2000; clin. fellow, registrar, cons. of hpb surgery Hammersmith Hosp., London, 2000—03; sr. lectr. U. of Thessaly, Larisa, Greece, 2003—06. Mem. Med. Assn. of LARISA, Larisa, Greece, 2005—06, Greek Med. Assn., 2005—06. Mil. dr. US Army, 1992—93, Greece. Achievements include research in Investigation of New Technology in Liver Surgery.The use of Radiofrequency Energy in bloodless resection of solid organs and endoscopy. Home: Kalliarhou Larissa 41221 Greece Office: Univ of Thessaly Univ Hosp Larissa 41222 Greece Office Fax: +1030-2410-670-100; Home Fax: +1030-2410-670-100. Personal E-mail: zachadim@yahoo.com.

ZACHARY, LOUIS GEORGE, chemical company consultant; b. Aug. 14, 1927; s. George E. and Angelike (Hantsis) Zacharakis; m. Lillie Vletas, Apr. 20, 1955; children: Leslie A., Louis George. Prodn. supr. Dewey & Almy Co., Acton, Mass., 1951-52; salesman chem. divsn. Union Camp Corp., Wayne, NJ, 1952-59, sales mgr. chem. divsn., 1959-62, gen. mgr. chem. ops., 1962-66, gen. mgr. chem. divsn., 1970-78, v.p., 1974-78, Drake Mgmt. Co., NYC, 1966-70; sr. v.p. GAF Corp., NYC, 1978-82, mem. office of chmn., 1981-82; cons., 1983-84; chmn., CEO Universal Die Casting, Inc., Saline, Mich., 1984—90; acting pres. chem. divsn. Church & Dwight Inc., 1990—91; v.p. Nat. Exec. Svc. Corp., NYC, 1993—96. Vis. com. chem. engring. dept. Johns Hopkins U., Balt., 1981-83. Co-editor: Tall Oil and Its Uses, 1965. With USN, 1945—46. Mem. Chem. Mfrs. Assn. (dir. 1979-83), Synthetic Organic Chem. Mfrs. Assn., Soc. Chem. Industry, Harvard Club NJ (exec. com., trustee 2000—). Home: 227 Oak Ridge Ave Summit NJ 07901-3258 Personal E-mail: louiszachary@aol.com.

ZACHERT, MARTHA JANE, retired librarian; b. York, Pa., Feb. 7, 1920; d. Paul Rodes and Elizabeth Agnes (Lau) Koontz; m. Edward G. Zachert, Aug. 25, 1946; 1 child, Lillian Elizabeth. AB, Lebanon Valley Coll., 1941; MLS, Emory U., 1953; DLS, Columbia U., 1968. Asst. Enoch Pratt Free Library, Balt., 1941-46; head librarian Wood Research Inst., Atlanta, 1947; sch. librarian DeKalb (Ga.) County Schs., 1950-52; head librarian, prof. history of pharmacy So. Coll. Pharmacy, Mercer U., Atlanta, 1952-63; instr. Ga. State Coll., 1962-63, Emory U., summers 1955-59, 1956-57, 59-60; mem. faculty Library Sch., Fla. State U., 1963-78, prof., 1973-78, Coll. Librarianship U. S.C., Columbia, 1973-74, 78-84. Vis. fellow Brit. Library, 1980; cons. So. Regional Med. Library, Emory U., 1976-77, Nat. Library Medicine, 1977, others. Author: Fine Printing in Georgia, 1950s-1990, 1994; assoc. editor Jour. Libr. History, 1966-71, 73-76; mng. editor, 1971-73; cons. editor Jour. Libr. Adminstrn., 1979-86; contbr. numerous articles to profl. jours. Fellow Med. Libr. Assn. (named among 100 Most Notables 1998); mem. ALA, Spl. Librs. Assn. (past pres. Fla. chpt., spl. citation 1977, Hall of Fame 1985), Am. Printing History Assn., Beta Phi Mu (pres. 1974-75). Home and Office: 4436 Meandering Way #108AG Tallahassee FL 32308-8705 Home Phone: 850-385-2850.

ZACHERT, VIRGINIA, retired psychologist; b. Jacksonville, Ala., Mar. 1, 1920; d. R.E. and Cora H. (Massee) Z. Student, Norman Jr. Coll., 1937; AB, Ga. State Woman's Coll., 1940; MA, Emory U., 1947; PhD, Purdue U., 1949. Diplomate Am. Bd. Profl. Psychologists. Statistician Davison-Paxon Co., Atlanta, 1941-44; research psychologist Mil. Contracts, Auburn Research Found., Ala. Poly. Inst.; indsl. and research psychologist Sturm & O'Brien (cons. engrs.), 1958-59; research project dir. Western Design, Biloxi, Miss., 1960-61; self-employed cons. psychologist Norman Park, Ga., 1961-71, Good Hope, Ga., 1971-99; ret. Rsch. assoc. med. edn. Med. Coll. Ga., Augusta, 1963-65, assoc. prof., 1965-70, rsch. prof., 1970-84, rsch. prof. emeritus, 1984—, chief learning materials divsn., 1973-84, faculty senate, 1976-84, acad. coun., 1976-82, pres. acad. coun., 1983, sec., 1978; mem. Ga. Bd. Examiners Psychologists, 1974-79, v.p., 1977, pres. 1978; adv. bd. Comdr. Gen. ATC USAF, 1967-70; cons. Ga. Silver Haired Legislature, 1980-86, senator, 1987-93, pres. protem, 1987-88, pres., 1989-93, rep., spkr. protem, 1993-96, spkr., 1997-98, Nat. Silver-Haired Congress rep., 1995—, spkr. 1997-99; govs. appointee White House Conf. on Aging, 1971, 96, Ga. Coun. on Aging, 1988-96; U.S. Senate mem. Fed. Coun. on the Aging, 1990-93; senator appointee White House Conf. on Aging, 1995; Ga. Health Decision's appointee to Ga. Coalition for Health, 1996-98. Author: (with P.L. Wilds) Essentials of Gynecology-Oncology, 1967, Applications of Gynecology-Oncology, 1967. Del. White House Conf. on Aging, 1981, 95. Served as aerologist USN, 1944-46; aviation psychologist, Lackland Air Force, San Antonio, USAF, 1949-55. Recipient Jane Kennedy Excellence Aging award, 1999. Fellow AAAS, Am. Psychol. Assn.; mem. AAUP (chpt. pres. 1977-80), Sigma Xi. (chpt. pres. 1980-81) Baptist. Home: 4275 Owens Rd # 403 Evans GA 30809 *It's really quite simple-I find, if I wish to be understood or heard, that simplicity is necessary but not ever easy. Simplicity is basic, essential and always the major factor in my search for truth.*

ZACHMAN, RANDALL CARRINGTON, theology studies educator; b. Perrysburg, Ohio, Sept. 25, 1953; s. John Wesley and Anne Morley Zachman; m. Carolyne Mary Call, May 15, 2002; 1 child, John Alex. PhD, U. Chgo. Div. Sch., Ill., 1990. Asst. prof. reformation history Colgate Rochester, Bexley, Crozer Div. Sch., NY, 1987—90; prof. reformation studies U. Notre Dame, Ind., 1991—; fellow, theolog Henry Luce III Found., 2003—04. Episcopalian. Office: Univ Notre Dame 130 Malloy Hall Notre Dame IN 46556 Office Fax: 574-631-4291. Business E-Mail: rzachman@nd.edu.

ZACHMANN, WILLIAM FRANCIS, computer and communications industry market research company executive; b. Cleve., Oct. 19, 1942; s. Kurt Wilhelm and Jean (O'Konski) Z.; m. Elizabeth Ann Loftus, June 7, 1980. BA, Harvard U., 1966. Programmer, analyst Cambridge (Mass.) Computer Assocs., 1967-69; sys. rsch. officer 1st Nat. Bank, Boston, 1969-74; dir. rsch. Forum Corp., Boston, 1974-75; coord. personnel adminstrn. Harvard U., Cambridge, 1976-77; mgr. tech. support Call-Data Sys., Boston, 1977-79; v.p. tech. assessment Internat. Data Corp., Framingham, Mass., 1979-83, v.p. corp. rsch., 1983-87, sr. v.p., 1987-88; pres. Canopus Rsch., Duxbury, Mass., 1988—, editor, pub. Canopus report, 1992—, host Canopus rsch. forum, 1992-99; v.p. Meta Group, Stamford, Conn., 2000—02; chmn., CEO Canopus Rsch. Inc., Duxbury, 2002—; pres., CEO Agylity, 2004—. Mem. Harvard (Boston), Harvard Faculty (Cambridge), Compuserve. Author: Keys to Application Development Productivity, 1981; contbg. editor Computer Industry Report, 1982-88, Communications and Distributed Resources Report, 1983-87, PC World mag., 1987-88; columnist On Communications mag., 1984-86, Software News mag., 1984-86, Computerworld mag., 1986-88, Infoworld mag., 1987-88, Micromarketworld mag., 1985-87, PC Mag., 1988-92, PC Week mag., 1988-92, MacUser mag., 1988-89, Windows World, 1992-95, Ad Week's Marketing Computers, 1993-95, Computing Pro, 1996-99, CIO mag., 1999-2002, Redmond Developer News, 2006-09; columnist, sr. contbg. editor OS/2 Professional, 1992-94, Real Estate Jour., 2004-08, Duxbury Clipper, 2004-06. Mem. City Mgrs. Adv. Com. on Cable TV, Cambridge, 1979-93; mem. Duxbury Econ. Devel. Com., 1992-95, 2004-07; mem. Planning Bd., Duxbury, 1995-2001, vice chmn., 1996-2000. Home: 160 Standish St Duxbury MA 02332-5065 Office: Canopus Rsch Inc PO Box 2805 Duxbury MA 02331-2805 Office Phone: 781-934-9800. Business E-Mail: wfz@canopusresearch.com.

ZACK, ARNOLD MARSHALL, lawyer, mediator, arbitrator, judge; b. Lynn, Mass., Oct. 7, 1931; s. Samuel George and Bess Ethel (Freedman) Z.; m. Norma Eta Wilner, Aug. 10, 1969; children: Jonathan Samuel, Rachel Ann. AB, Tufts Coll., 1953; LLB, Yale U., 1956; MPA, Harvard U., 1961. Asst. to Saul Wallen (arbitrator), 1956-63; cons. govt. South Africa UN Mission to Congo, 1960; cons. U.S. Peace Corps, 1961-63, Labor Dept., 1962-79, Pres.'s Study Commn. on Nat. Service Corps, 1962-63, U.S. AID, 1963—, Friedrich Ebert Stiftung, 1963-64, Nat. Center for Dispute Settlement, 1968-76; v.p. adminstrn. tribunal Asian Development Bank, 2004—. Cons. IMF, 2000—02, Govt. Italy, 2002—, Internat. Labor Orgn., 1961—; chmn. steering com. Permanent Ct. Arbitration, 2002—; vis. Fulbright lectr. Haile Selassie U., Addis Ababa, Ethiopia, 1963—64; referee Nat. R.R. Adjustment Bd., 1964—; mem. faculty Labor and Worklife Program Harvard Law Sch., 1985—; full time mediator/arbitrator, Boston, 1968—; bd. dirs. Ctr. for Socio-Legal Studies faculty of law U. Natal, South Africa, 1986—92; mem. Fgn. Svc. Labor Rels. Bd., 1982—84, Presdl. Emergency Bds. 221 and 222; chair Presdl. Emergency Bd. 232, 234; chmn. Essential Industries Dispute Settlement Bd. Bermuda, 1993—2000; chair Essential Svcs. Dispute Settlement Bd. Bermuda, 1996—2000; vis. lectr. Yale Law Sch., 1995—96; permanent arbitrator Am. Airlines & APA, IRS & NTEU, Commonwealth Mass., Overseas Fedn. Tchrs., Def. Dept. Author: Labor Training in Developing Countries, 1964, Ethiopia's High Level Manpower-Analysis and Projections, 1964, Handbook on Grievance Arbitration in the Public Sector, 1974, Handbook on Fact Finding and Arbitration in the Public Sector, 1974, Grievance Arbitration, A Practical Guide, 1977; (with R. Bloch) Arbitration of Discipline and Discharge Cases, 1979, (with R. Bloch) The Agreement in Negotiation and Arbitration, 1983, 2d edition, 1995, Arbitration in Practice, 1984, Mediation in the Public Sector, 1985, Grievance Arbitration: Cases on the Merits in Discipline Discharge and Contract Interpretation, 1989, Handbook on Grievance Arbitration: Issues on Procedure and Ethics, 1992, (with J. Dunlop) Mediation and Arbitration of Employment Disputes, 1997, Arbitration Discipline and Discharge Cases, 2000, Arnold Zack: From A To Z, 2007; contbr. articles to profl. jours. Bd. visitors Harvard U. Recipient Whitney North Seymour medal for oustanding contbn. to arbitration, 1980, Cushing Gavin award, 1986, Mildred Spaulding award, 1987, Disting. Svc. award for arbitration of labor-mgmt. disputes, 1989, Pioneer award Assn. Conflict Resolution, 2003, Willoughby Abner award, Assn. for Conflict Resolution, 2004; Wertheim fellow Harvard U., 1996-97, Inaugural LERA fellowship, 2008. Fellow: African Studies Assn.; mem.: ABA (mem. coun. labor and employment law sect. 2000—06), Coll. Labor and Employment Lawyers, Internat. Soc. for Labor Law and Social Security (bd. dirs.), Indsl. Rels. Rsch. Assn. (bd. dirs.), Am. Arbitration Assn. (dir. Labor-Mgmt. Inst. 1966—68), Nat. Acad. Arbitrators (treas. 1972—75, bd. govs. 1977—79, v.p. 1980—82, pres. Rsch. and Edn. Found. 1989—91, pres. 1994—95), Yale Law Sch. Assn., Yale Club (N.Y.C.), Harvard Club ((Boston)). Address: 170 W Canton St Boston MA 02118-1216 Home Phone: 617-262-0478.

ZACK, DANIEL GERARD, library consultant; b. Waukegan, Ill., Oct. 1, 1943; s. Raymond Gerard and Rosanna Marie (Atkinson) Z.; m. Mary Frances Anthony, Aug. 25, 1966; children: Jennifer Lee, Rebecca Jane. BA in Psychology, Western Ill. U., 1967; MS in Libr. Sci., U. Ill., 1975. Editor IBM Corp., Rochester, Minn., 1968-70, Memorex Corp., Mpls., 1970-74; rsch. assoc. Libr. Rsch. Ctr. U. Ill., Urbana, 1974-75; asst. dir. Portage County Pub. Libr., Stevens Point, Wis., 1976-78; dir. Burlington Pub. Libr., Iowa, 1978-87, Gail Borden Pub. Libr., Elgin, Ill., 1987—2004, Beloit Pub. Libr., Wis., 2007—; with Libr. Cons. Svcs., 2004—. Trustee Batavia Pub. Libr., Ill., 1997-2003; founder Friends of Ill. Libr., 1990, bd. dirs. 1990-97. Mem. ALA, ACLU, Ill. Libr. Assn. (mgr. pub. libr. forum 1991-92, 2002-03, exec. bd. dirs. 1992-95, pub. policy com. 1995-98), Pub. Libr. Assn. (intellectual freedom com. 1993-96), Kiwanis.

ZACK, STEPHEN NEAL, lawyer; b. Detroit, Dec. 2, 1947; s. Benn Zack and Anita (Rabinovich) Petluck; children: Jason, Tracey. BA, U. Fla., 1969, JD, 1971. Bar: Fla. 1972, NY 1982, DC 1986, US Dist. Ct. (no. and so. dists.) Fla. 1986, U.S. Ct. Appeals (5th and 11th cirs.)1986. Sr. ptnr. Floyd, Pearson, Richman, Greer, Weil, Zack & Brumbaugh P.A., Miami, Fla., 1972-91, Zack, Hanzman & Ponce P.A., Miami, 1991—95, Zack Kosnitzky P.A., 1995—2002, Boies, Schiller & Flexner LLP, Miami, 2002—. Legis. aide to Congressman Claude Pepper, 1971-72; chmn. environ. rev. bd. City of Miami, 1978-79, Fla. law ctr. coun. U. Fla., 1982; mem. Speakers Adv. Com. on Future, Jud. Nomination Commn. for 11th Cir.; spl. counsel to Gov. Bob Graham, 1986; bd. dirs. Jewish Family Services, 1984-; chmn. State Fla. Ethics Comm.; former pres. Nat. Conf. Bar Presidents. Named to Hall of Fame, U. Fla. Mem. ABA (life fellow, chmn. House Del. 2004—2006, mem. bd. govs., pres.-elect 2009-), ALTA, Fla. Bar Assn. (pres. young lawyers sect. 1975-76, bd. govs. 1977-88, chmn. internat. law sect. 1981-82, pres. 1989-90), Acad. Fla. Trial Lawyers (bd. dirs. 1982-86), Dade County Bar Assn. (bd. dirs. & pres. young lawyers sect. 1975-76), Cuban-Am. Lawyers Assn., Federacion Interamericana de Abogados, Blue Key (pres. Fla. chpt.), Omicron Delta Kappa. Office: Boies Schiller & Flexner LLP Bank of Amer Tower 100 SE 2nd St Ste 2800 Miami FL 33131-2115 Office Phone: 305-539-8400. E-mail: szack@bsfllp.com.*

ZACKS, SHELEMYAHU, mathematical sciences educator; b. Tel Aviv, Oct. 15, 1932; came to U.S., 1965; s. Yechezkiel and Devora (Kolomoitzev) Z.; m. Hanna Bilik; children: Yuval Joseph, David Noam. BA, Hebrew U., Jerusalem, Israel, 1956; MSc, Technion Israel Inst. Tech., Haifa, 1960; PhD, Columbia U., 1962; PhD (hon.), U. Haifa, 2005. Prof. stats. Kans. State U., Manhattan, 1965-68; prof. math-stats. U N. Mex., Albuquerque, 1968-70; prof. math.-stats. Cse Western Reserve U., Cleve., 1970-79; prof. stats. Va. Polytech. U., Blacksburg, 1979-80; prof. math. scis. SUNY, Binghamton, 1980—. Chmn. dept. math. scis., SUNY, Binghamton, 1980-83, dir. Ctr. Stats. Quality Control and Design, SUNY, Binghamton, 1983— Author: (books) The Theory of Statistical Inference, 1971, Parametric Statistical Inference: Basic Theory and Modern Approaches, 1981, Inroduction to Reliability Analysis: Probability Models and Statistical Methods, 1992, Prediction Theory for Finite Populations, 1992, Stochastic Visibility in Random Fields, 1994, Modern Industrial Statistics: Design and Control of Quality and Reliability, 1998; Stage Wise Adaptive Designs, 2009; contbr. over 170 articles and papers to profl. jours.; assoc. editor Jour. Am. Stats. Assn., 1971-72, 86-89, Annals of Math. Stats., 1972-74, Comm. in Stats, 1973-89, Naval Rsch. Logist. Qtrlyl, 1977-87, Sequential Analysis, 1986—; joint chief editor Jour. Stats., Planning and Inference, 1981-83, coordinating editor, 1983-91, adv. editor, 1991-98, exec. editor, 1998-2000. Grantee: NSF, Washington, 1966-70, Office Naval Rsch., Washington, 1970-82, Army Rsch. Office, Durham, N.C., 1982-90. Fellow AAAS, Am. Stats. Assn., Inst. Math. Stats.; mem. Internat. Stats. Assn. Avocation: viola player Binghamton Comty. Orch. Office: SUNY Binghamton Dept Math Scis Binghamton NY 13902-6000 Office Phone: 607-777-6035. Business E-Mail: shelly@math.binghamton.edu.

ZACUR, RICHARD AARON, lawyer; b. Miami, Fla., Nov. 19, 1949; s. Howard Aaron and Helen (Pezzuti) Z. BA, Fla. State U., 1971; JD, Stetson Coll. of Law, St. Petersburg, Fla., 1974. Bars: Fla. 1974, U.S. Dist. Ct. (mid. dist.) Fla. 1974, U.S. Ct. Appeals (5th cir.) 1974, U.S. Supreme Ct. 1977, D.C. 1982. Ptnr. Zacur & Graham, P.A., St. Petersburg, 1974—. Mem. Fla. Lawyer's Action Group, St. Petersburg, 1978. Named one of Outstanding Young Men of Am., U.S. Jaycees, 1977. Mem. ABA, ATLA, Am. Judicature Soc., Acad. Fla. Trial Lawyers, Pinellas County Trial Lawyers Assn., Fla. Bar Assn. (grievance com., vice chmn. 1997, chmn. 1997-98), Canakaris Family Law Inns of Ct., Lawyer's Title Guaranty Fund, Gold Key Soc., Omicron Delta Kappa. Presbyterian. Avocations: alpine skiing, golf. Office: Zacur Graham & Costis PA 5200 Central Ave Saint Petersburg FL 33707-1834

ZADEH, JAVAD HAMADANI, mathematics professor; b. Kerman, Iran, Oct. 2, 1940; arrived in U.S., 1964; s. Bagher Hamadani Zadeh and Fatemeh Asadi; children: Neda, Mina. BA, The Am. U. Beirut, Lebanon, 1963; MS, Purdue U., West Lafayette, Ind., 1966; PhD, MPhil, Columbia U., NYC, 1976. Cert. tchr. Ga. Profl. Standards Commn., 1988. Instr. math. Shiraz U., Iran, 1963—64, Ctr. Coll. Ky., Danville, Ky., 1966—67, Bowling Green State U., Ohio, 1969—70; from instr. to asst. prof. Sharif U. Tech., Tehran, Iran, 1970—82, chmn. dept. math. and computer sci., 1979—81, assoc. prof., 1982—86; vis. prof. math. U. Ga., Athens, 1986—87; tchr. math. Ga. Pub. Schs., Alamo, 1990—92; asst. prof. math. Mid. Ga. Coll., Cochran, Ga., 1992—93; assoc. prof. Brewton-Parker Coll., Mt. Vernon, Ga., 1993—97, prof., 1997—2006; asst. prof. math. Dalton State Coll., Ga., 2006—. Postdoctoral rsch. fellow dept. math. U. Calif., 1976—77. Author: Shenidi Che-Gaft, 1970, 2d edit., 2000; editor: Bull. Iranian Math. Soc., 1979—81; contbr. articles to profl. jours. Home: 8740 Roswell Rd 9D Atlanta GA 30350 Office Phone: 706-272-2580.

ZADEH, MANSOUR T., food products executive; Sr. info. tech. leader PepsiCo; head info. tech. Miller Brewing Co.; chief tech. officer Kraft Foods; chief info. officer Smithfield Foods, Inc., Va., 2002—. Named one of 25 Most Influential Consumer Goods Execs. That Make a Difference, Consumer Goods Tech. mag., 2004. Office: Smithfield Foods Inc 200 Commerce St Smithfield VA 23430 Office Phone: 757-365-3000.

ZADROZNY, WLODEK W., computer scientist; m. Elizabeth L. Belling, Jan. 3, 2002; children: Sophie L. Simon, Andrew Belling, Mateusz. MSc, Warsaw U., 1976; PhD, Polish Acad. Scis., Warsaw, 1980. Rschr. IBM T.J.Watson Rsch. Ctr., Hawthorne, NY, 1985—. Haskell B. Curry fellowship, Pa. State U., 1979, fellowship, Alexander von Humboldt Found., 1982—83. Mem.: IEEE, ACM, AAAI. Achievements include first to spoken natural dialog systems for commercial applications. Office: IBM TJWatson Rsch Ctr 19 Skyline Dr Hawthorne NY 10532 Office Phone: 914-784-7901.

ZAETS, SERGEY, medical researcher, consultant, director; b. Kiev, Ukraine, Oct. 31, 1956; s. Boris Shaferman and Tatiana Zaets; m. Tamara Berezina; 1 child, Nadejda. MD, Moscow Med. Stomatological Inst., Russia, 1979; DMS, PHD, Bakoulev Ctr. Cardiovasc. Surgery, Moscow. Rsch. assoc., clin. rsch. coord. UMDNJ - NJ. Med. Sch., Newark, 2000—08; sr. staff scientist Novo Nordisk US, North Brunswick, NJ, 2005—08; prin. scientist Bakoulev Ctr. Cardiovasc. Surgery, Moscow, 1981—; cons. Mt. Sinai Sch. Medicine, NYC, 2008—09; assoc. dir. Nova Nordisk Inc., Princeton, NJ, 2009—. Mem.: European Assn. Cardiovasc. Surgery, Soc. Thoracic Surgeons, Shock Soc., Am. Heart Assn., Russian Assn. Cardiovasc. Surgeons. Achievements include patents for biological prosthesis of the pulmonary tunk. Personal E-mail: zaets001@yahoo.com.

ZAFFIRO, JAMES J., political science professor; b. Milw., June 23, 1955; m. Louise Zaffiro; 1 child, Tonia. PhD, U. Wis., Madison, 1983. Prof. polit. sci. Ctrl. Coll., Pella, Iowa, 1983—. Fulbright fellowship, US Fulbright, 1985. Office: Ctrl Coll 812 University Pella IA 50219 Business E-Mail: zaffiroj@central.edu.

ZAGANO, PHYLLIS, religious studies educator; BA in English, Marymount Coll., Tarrytown, NY, 1969; MS in Pub. Rels., Boston U., 1970; MA in English, L.I.U., 1972; PhD in English, SUNY, Stony Brook, 1979; MA in Theology, St. John's U., Jamaica, NY, 1990. Program officer Nat. Humanities Ctr., NYC, 1979—80; asst. prof. comms. Fordham U., Bronx, NY, 1980—84; rschr. Archdiocese of NY, 1984—86; ind. rschr. NYC, 1986—88; assoc. prof. Boston U., 1988—98, adj. assoc. prof. theology, 1988—98, dir. inst. for democratic comm., 1988—98; sr. rsch. assoc. in residence, spl. assoc. prof. religion Hofstra U., Hempstead, NY, 2002—04; weekly columnist Religion News Svc. Vis. Aquinas chair St. Thomas Aquinas Coll., 2005; vis. assoc. prof. Cath. studies Yale Div. Sch., 2005; adj. prof. religion Hofstra U., Hempstead, NY, 2005—; fulbright fellow U. Comerick Spring, 2009. Author: Religion and Public Affairs, 1987, Social Impact of the Mass Media, 1991, Woman to Woman, 1993, On Prayer, 1994, Ita Ford: Missionary Martyr, 1996, Twentieth Century Apostles, 1999, Things New and Old, 1999, Holy Saturday: An Argument for the Restoration of the Formale Diaconate in the Catholic Church, 2000 (Book award Catholic Press Assn. 2001, Coll. Theology Soc. 2002), Dorothy Day: In My Own Words, 2003, Called to Serve: A Spirituality for Deacons, 2004, The Dominican Tradition, 2006, Acerca de la Oracion: Una Carta a Mi Amijado (Book award Cath. Press Assn. 2003); monthly radio host Boston U. World of Ideas, 1992-97; series editor Spirituality in History, 2006-. Lector, lay min. Ch. St. Vincent Ferrer, NYC, 1980—92, Our Lady of the Miraculous Medal Ch., 1996—, Newman Ctr., Boston U., 1992—96. Comdr. USNR, 1976—2007. Faculty Rsch. grantee Fordham U., 1983, Rsch. grantee Nat. Inst. Peace, 1989, Rsch. grantee Wabash Ctr., 2003; Coolidge fellow Episcopal Divinity Sch., 1987; recipient citation for heroism Nassau County (N.Y.) Fire Commn., 1995; Fulbright fellowship, Republic of Ireland, 2009. Mem. Am. Acad. Religion (co-chair Roman Cath. Studies, 1991-2001), Am. Cath. Philos. Assn., Coll. Theology Soc., Cath. Theol. Soc. Am., Naval Res. Assn., Soc. for Study of Christian Spirituality. Roman Catholic. Office: 115 Hofstra Univ Hempstead NY 11549 Office Phone: 516-463-6023, 516-463-5008. Business E-Mail: phyllis.zagano@hofstra.edu.

ZAGAR, ROBERT JOHN, psychologist, researcher; b. Great Lakes, Ill., Nov. 26, 1948; s. Anthony John and Helen Gertrude (Kurzynowski) Z.; m. Agata. MS in Psychology, Ill. Inst. Tech., Chgo., 1975; PhD in Psychology, Northwestern U., 1981; MPH in Pub. Health, U. Ill. Med. Ctr., Chgo., 1982; postgrad., DePaul U., 1982-83, Barry U., 1984-85. Clin. psychologist, Ill.; sch. psychologist, Ill. Sch. psychologist Chgo. Pub. Schs., 1991-93; asst. prof. Nat. Louis U., Evanston, Ill., 1991-93; psychologist Juvenile Divsn. Cir. Ct., Chgo., 1985-91; economist Ill. Dept. Labor, 1986-87; pvt. practice Chgo., 1992—. Cons. psychologist But. Disability Determination, Chgo., 1992—, Dept. Children and Family Svcs., 1992—, Juvenile Divsn. Cir. Ct., 1992—; asst. prof. Ill. Sch. Profl. Psychology, 1989—2006, Argosy U., 1992—2006; sch. psychologist Aurora Pub. Schs., Ill., 1989—91; asst. prof. Forest Sch. Profl. Psychology, Wheeling, 1988—89; sch. psychology Chgo. Pub. Schs., 1999—, Woodstock, 2000—01; invited spkr. Nat. Summit Youth Violence, U.S. Dept. Dept. Corrections, others; asst prof. Lewis U., 1998—, Chgo. Sch. Profl. Psychology, 2007—. Contbr. articles to profl. jours. in field of neuropsychol. tests, forensic exams. and aggress. Mem. APA, APHA, Am. Psychol. Soc., Fla. Psychol. Assn., Ill. Psychol. Assn., Nat. Assn. Sch. Psychologists, Ill. Sch. Psychology Assn., Delays Task Forceone Youth Violence. Roman Catholic. Achievements include development of the first cradle to jail actuarial empirical and objective measures of dangerousness. Office: 233 E Erie St Ste 610 Chicago IL 60611 Office Phone: 312-266-3411. Personal E-mail: drzagar@hotmail.com, drzagar@msn.com.

ZAGAT, NINA, publishing executive; b. 1942; m. Tim Zagat, 1965; children: Ted, John. AB, Vassar Coll., 1963; LLB, Yale Law Sch., 1966; attended, Le Cordon Bleu Ecole de Cuisine. Atty. Sherman and Sterling, NYC, 1966—90; co-founder, co-pub. Zagat Survey. LLC, NYC, 1979—. Served on White House Conf. on Travel and Tourism; established lecture series Culinary Inst. Am., 2001; bd. overseer Hospitality Industry Hall of Honor. Biographies have been featured on CBS, A&E and History Channel; Zagat content is available: in print guides and through ZAGAT.com, ZAGAT TO GO for smart phones, and the ZAGAT.mobi mobile website. Named (with Tim Zagat) Entrepreneurs of Yr., Ernst & Young, 2000, Entrepreneur of Yr., Harvard Bus. Sch., 2000; named one of Top Tech 100, featuring NYC most influential people in technology, Crain's, 2001, Leading Women Entrepreneurs of the World, Star Group, 2001, The 100 Most Influential Women in NYC Bus., Crain's NY Bus., 2007; named to (with Tim Zagat) James Beard Who's Who in Food & Beverage, 1994, (with Tim Zagat) NYU Entrepreneurship Hall of Fame, 2001, (with Tim Zagat) Hospitality Industry Hall of Honor, 2003. Fellow: Culinary Inst. America. Office: Zagat Survey LLC 4 Columbus Circle New York NY 10019*

ZAGAT, TIM, publishing executive; b. NYC, May 13, 1940; m. Nina Zagat, 1965; children: Ted, John. BA, Harvard U., 1961; LLB, Yale U., 1966. Assoc. Hughes, Hubbard & Reed; ptnr. Pomerantz, Levy, Haudek & Block, 1976—82; chief litigation counsel Gulf & Western Industries Inc., 1980—87; co-founder, co-chair, CEO Zagat Survey, LLC, NYC, 1979—. Served on White House Conf. on Travel and Tourism; bd. overseer Hospitality Industry Hall of Honor. Biographies have been featured on CBS, A&E and History Channel; Zagat content is available: in print guides and through ZAGAT.com, ZAGAT TO GO for smart phones, and the ZAGAT.mobi mobile website. Bd. mem. World Travel & Tourism Coun., Bus. for Diplomatic Action, Partnership for NYC; bd. mem., v.p. Careers through Culinary Arts Program; chmn. NYC & Co., 1999—2002, mem. exec. com. Recipient l'Ordre de Merite, French Govt.; named (with Nina Zagat) Entrepreneurs of Yr., Ernst & Young, 2000; named to (with Nina Zagat) James Beard Who's Who in Food & Beverage, 1994, (with Nina Zagat) NYU Entrepreneurship Hall of Fame, 2001, (with Nina Zagat) Hospitality Industry Hall of Honor, 2003. Fellow: Culinary Inst. America. Office: Zagat Survey LLC 4 Columbus Circle New York NY 10019*

ZAGEL, JAMES BLOCK, federal judge; b. Chgo., Mar. 4, 1941; s. Samuel and Ethel (Samuels) Z.; m. Margaret Maxwell, May 27, 1979. BA, U. Chgo., 1962, MA in Philosophy, 1962; JD, Harvard U., 1965. Bar: Ill. 1965, US Dist. Ct. (no. dist.) Ill. 1965, US Supreme Ct. 1970, US Ct. Appeals (7th cir.) 1972. Asst. state atty. Cook County, 1965—69; asst. atty. gen. criminal justice divsn. State of Ill., Springfield, 1970-77; chief prosecuting atty. Ill. Jud. Inquiry Bd., Springfield, 1973-75; exec. dir. Ill. Law Enforcement Commn., Springfield, 1977-79; dir. Ill. Dept. Revenue, Springfield, 1979-80, Ill. Dept. State Police, Springfield, 1980-87; judge US Dist. Ct. (no. dist.) Ill., Chgo., 1987—, Fgn. Intelligence Surveillance Ct. (FISC), 2008—. Co-author: Criminal Law and Its Administration, 1989, Cases and Comments on Criminal Procedure, 1992, Author's Money to Burn, 2002. Named Outstanding Young Citizen, Chgo. Jaycees, 1977; recipient Disting. Svc. Merit award Assn. Commerce and Industry, 1983. Mem. Chgo. Bar Assn., Jud. Conf. of US (codes of conduct com. 1987-92). Office: US Dist Ct 219 S Dearborn St Ste 2588 Chicago IL 60604-1801*

ZAGEL, MARGARET MAXWELL, lawyer; b. Centralia, Ill., Jan. 17, 1949; d. Francis Edgar and Joan (Beckmeyer) Maxwell; m. James Block Zagel, May 27, 1979. BA, Tulane U., 1970; JD, U. Ill., 1973. Bar: Ill. 1973, U.S. Ct. Appeals (7th cir.), U.S. Supreme Ct. Atty. Ill. Appellate Defender's Office, Chgo., 1973-75, law clk. to Hon. Seymour Simon, 1975-76; assoc., then ptnr. Schuyler Roche & Zwirner, Chgo., 1976-84; gen. counsel Grant Thornton LLP, Chgo., 1984-98, mng. prin. risk, regulatory & legal affairs, gen counsel, 2003; v.p., gen. counsel Tellabs, Inc., Lisle, Ill., 1998—99; sr. v.p., chief legal and admin. officer Organic, Inc., San Francisco, 1999—2001; spec. coun. litigation transactions Arthur Andersen LLP, 2002; practice lead, corp. governance, risk and crisis mgmt., co-gen. coun. Altheimer & Gray, 2002—03. Mem. planning com. Securities Inst. Northwestern U., Chgo., 1993-2000, mem. corp. counsel planning com., 1994-2000; mem. civil justice reform adv. com. U.S. Cir. Ct. (no. dist.) Ill., Chgo., 1994-95; mem. Ill. Commn. Regulatory Issues, mem. ACCA 1986, Nat. Assoc. Corp. Dir., 2002-2004, Economic Club Chgo. 2003-, Women Corp. Dirs. 2003-; mem. vis. com. Coll. Law U. Ill., 1997-2001.; bd. dirs. Atrion Corp. 2002-2003. Bd. trustees Court Theatre. Mem.: Econ. Club Chgo. Office: Grant Thornton LLP 175 W Jackson 20th Fl Chicago IL 60604

ZAGER, STEVEN MARK, lawyer; b. Memphis, Nov. 16, 1958; s. Jack and Sylvia (Bloomfield) Z.; m. Debra D'Angelo; children: Samantha, Amanda, Kathryn, Jackson. BA, Vanderbilt U., 1979, JD, 1983. Bar: Tex. 1984, U.S. Dist. Ct. (all dists.) Tex. 1984, U.S. Dist. Ct. Ariz. 1992, U.S. Dist. Ct. (D.C.) 1998, U.S. Ct. Appeals (5th, 6th, and 11th cirs.) 1983, U.S. Ct. Appeals (D.C. cir.) 1991, U.S. Ct. Appeals (Fed. cir.) 1997, U.S. Supreme Ct. 1991. Assoc. Fulbright & Jaworski, Houston, 1983-86, Weil, Gotshal & Manges, Houston, 1986-90, ptnr., 1990-98, head Houston office litigation sect., 1994-96; mng. ptnr. Tex. offices Brobeck, Phleger & Harrison, Austin, 1999—2001, firm ops. com., 1999—2003, head nat. litigation group, 2001—03; ptnr. Akin, Gump, Strauss, Hauer & Feld, LLP, Houston, 2003—, head intellectual property practice, 2007—, mem. mgmt. com., 2009—. Adj. prof. U. Houston Sch. Law, 1990—95; nat. adv. bd. NALP, 1996—99. Contbr. articles to Tex. Bar Jour., Texas Lawyer, Houston Lawyer. Bd. dirs., exec. com. Alley Theatre, Houston, 1988-96, Tex. Accts. and Lawyers for the Arts, Houston, 1984-88; adv. bd. Montgomery Bell Acad., 1996-2004, chmn., 2004-; bd. dirs. Vol. Legal Svcs. Ctrl. Tex., 2000-01 (bd. trustees 2004-), TV Sta. KLRU, 2001-03, M.D. Anderson Cancer Ctr., 2005-, Houston Arboreum, 2005-07, bd. Vanderbilt Law Sch., 2007-. Recipient Frank J. Scurlock award, State Bar Tex., 1991, Outstanding Pro Bono Svc., Professionalism award, Tex. Ctr. for Legal Ethics, 2002; named Outstanding Young Man in Am., U.S. Jaycees, 1983, Best Civil Def. Trial Lawyer in Tex., Tex. Lawyer, 2003; named one of 45 Best Lawyers Under 45 in Am., Tex. Super Lawyers, Tex. Monthly Mag., 2003—, The Nation's Top Litigators, The Nat. Law Jour., 2007, Top 10 Trial Lawyers in Country, 2008, Best Lawyers in America, 2008—, Chambers, 2008—, 2008—. Mem. ABA (litigation sect.), State Bar Tex. (dir. 1997-98, Frank J. Scurlock award 1991), Houston Bar Assn. (sec. 1996-97, v.p. 1997-98, bd. dirs. 1993-96, 2004-06, chair law and arts com. 1994, chair adminstrn. of justice com. 1995, rodeo com. 1997, chair law and media com. 2004, chair cmty. svc. task force 2004, Outstanding Young Lawyer in Houston 1991, Pres.'s award 1996-98), Houston Vol. Lawyers Program (bd. dirs. 1997-98, chair 1998), Travis County Bar Assn. (bd. dirs. 2001-03, chair bench bar program 2000, chair, 2003, jud. affairs com. 1999-2000), Fed. Bar Assn., Am. bd. Trial Advocates. Office: Gump Strauss Hauer & Feld 1 Bryant Pk New York NY 10036 Office Phone: 212-872-1037. Business E-Mail: szager@akingump.com.

ZAGHLOUL, ABDEL RAHMAN M., electrical engineering educator, consultant, entrepreneur; s. M.A. and Z.A. (Hebesha) Z.; m. Mervat A. El-Shazly, July 26, 1973; children: Waleed, Yasser. BSEE, Cairo U., 1971, MSEE, 1974; PhD, U. Nebr., 1975; Higher Diploma in Ednl. Tech., U. Abertay Dundee, Scotland, 1982. Chartered engr., U.K., European engr. Rsch. coord. U. Nebr., Lincoln, 1975-76; asst. prof. Cairo U., 1977-82, assoc. prof., 1982-88, prof. elec. engring., 1988—96; dir. curriculum devel. and rsch. Telecom Coll., Jeddah, Saudi Arabia, 1990-92; cons. Saudi Telecom, Riyadh, Saudi Arabia, 1992-93. Vis. assoc. prof. Coll. Edn., Makkah, Saudi Arabia, 1982—85; lead curriculum developer elec. engring. dept. Coll. Engring., October Univ. (formerly Higher Inst. for Engring.), 1995; adj. prof. mgmt. info. sys. Doane Coll., Lincoln, Nebr., 1997—98; adj. prof. math. Nebr. Wesleyan U., 1998—99; adj. prof. elec. engring. U. Nebr., Lincoln, 1998—2000; co-founder, v.p. ITR Techs., Inc., Lincoln, Nebr., 1998—; vis. prof. elec. engring. N.Mex. Tech., Socorro, 2000—01; prof. elec. and computer engring. & optics & photonics Ga. Inst. Tech., 2001—07, dir., founder Ellipsometry Rsch. Applications Labs. and Artificial Cognitive Sys. Lab., 2001—; cons. in field; tchr. US Army Sch. Information Tech., Ft. Gordon, Ga. Contbr. articles to profl. jours. Ellipsometry Project grantee U.S. NSF, 1978, recipient other grants. Fellow Inst. Elec. Engrs. (U.K.), Salzburg Seminar in Am. Studies; mem. IEEE (sr.), Internat. Soc. Optical Engring., Optical Soc. Am., Engring. Coun. (UK) Achievements include patents in field. Avocations: music, poetry, reading, fencing, travel. Home: 8344 Rockledge Rd Apt 725 Lincoln NE 68506-7365 Office Phone: 402-617-9525. Personal E-mail: arzaghloul@ieee.org.

ZAGHLOUL, NORANN AMIR, geneticist, research scientist; b. Kitchener-Waterloo, Ontario, Canada, Jan. 20, 1978; d. Amir Ibrahim and Mona Elwakked Zaghloul; m. Mohamed Tamer Abdelrahman Refaei, Jan. 2, 2003. BA, Johns Hopkins U., Balt.; MS, PhD, George Wash. U., DC. Grad. tchg. asst. George Wash. U., 2000—03, rsch. asst., 2000—06; postdoctoral fellow Johns Hopkins U., 2006—. Fellow Presdl. Merit Fellowship, George Wash. U., 2003. Mem.: Egyptian Am. Cultural Assn. (v.p. 2000), Soc. Devel. Biology. Achievements include research in genetic control of retinal development. Home: 6261 Clearwood Rd Bethesda MD 20817-5634

ZAGHLOUL, YASSER A., research and development company executive; b. Cairo, July 17, 1981; BEE, U. Nebr., Lincoln, 2001, MEE, 2004; PhD in Elec. & Computer Engring., Ga. Inst. Tech., Atlanta, 2009. V.p. R & D ITR Technologies, Lincoln, Nebr., 2004—. Recipient award, US Pres., 1998; numerous awards, U. Nebr., 1998—2001. Mem.: IEEE, Internat. Soc. Optical Engring., Golden Key Soc. Achievements include invention of first true digital optical processor and devices; development of first complete set of polarization optical logic gates; patents pending for optical logic devices having polarization-based logic level and all optical polarization switch and logic devices utilizing thin-film coatings transmission-polarization-devices, complete system identification of film-substrate systems, closed-form formula to calculate the substrate optical constant; research in optical computing polarization and ellipsometry, inverse electro-cardiography. Home: 747 Ralph McGill Bvld #1569 Atlanta GA 30312 Office Phone: 402-617-0400. Business E-Mail: yaz@ieee.org.

ZAGON, IAN STUART, neuroscience and anatomy educator, researcher, inventor; s. Benjamin and Beatrice (Shaffer) Z.; m. Eileen Kostel, Nov. 26, 1964. BS, U. Wis., 1965; MS, U. Ill., Urbana, 1969; PhD, U. Colo., Denver, 1972. Asst. prof. biol. structure U. Miami, Fla., 1972-74; asst. prof. anatomy Pa. State U., Hershey, 1974-78, prof. genetics, 1975—, assoc. prof. anatomy, 1978-85, prof., 1985-91, prof. cell and molecular biology and neurosci., 1984—, prof. neurosci. and anatomy, 1991—2003, prof. neural and behavioral scis., 2003—, disting. educator, 2002—, disting. univ. prof., 2005—, program dir. on edn. in human structure, 2005—. Cons. Nat. Inst. on Drug Abuse, Rockville, Md., 1980—; cons., reviewer NIH, Bethesda, Md., 1984—; grant reviewer Am. Heart Assn. of Pa., 1985—, mem. rsch. com., 1988—, bd. dirs., 1992-97, v.p., 1993-96; founder ZoeGenics LLC. Author: Maternal Substance Abuse and the Developing Nervous System, 1992, Receptors in the Developing Nervous System, 1993; mem. editl. bd. Brain Rsch. Bull., 1980—, sect. editor for cellular and molecular neurobiology, 1994—; mem. editl. bd. Physiology and Behavior, 1987-97, Pharmacology, Biochemistry and Behavior, 1989—, Internat. Jour. Oncology,

1998—, Advances in Neuroimmunology, 1990, Internat. Jour. Devel. Neurosci., 1987-89, Brain Rsch., 1992-, Devel. Brain Rsch., 1992-2006, Cancer Therapy, 2003—, Exptl. Biology and Medicine, 2006—, assoc. editor Anatomy & Pathology, 2009-; contbr. numerous articles to med. and profl. jours.; patentee on growth factors, receptors, devel., cancer, wound healing. Recipient Entrepreneurial Achievement award, Kutztown U., The John Marshall Soc., Franklin and Marshall Coll.; grantee NIH, Am. Cancer Soc., Nat. Inst. Drug Abuse, Philip Morris, Nat. Multiple Sclerosis Soc. Mem.: Am. Assn. Cancer Rsch., Am. Diabetes Assn., Assn. for Rsch. in Vision and Ophthalmology, Soc. for Neurosci., Am. Soc. Cell Biology. Achievements include discovery of low-dose naltrexone, topical naltrexone, and opioid growth factor therapies, non-erythroid spectrin, CCK-C receptor, and opioid growth factor receptor gene. Office: Pa State U Coll Medicine PO Box 850 H109 500 University Dr Hershey PA 17033-0850 Business E-Mail: isz1@psu.edu.

ZAGOREVSKI, DMITRI, academic administrator; b. Moscow; PhD in Chemistry, USSR Acad. Scis., Moscow. Mass spectrometrist U. Mo., Columbia, 1997—2001; proteomics core dir. Rensselaer Poly. Inst., Troy, NY, 2001—. Author: (novel) Organic And Organometallic Molecules; contbr. articles to profl. sci. jours. Office: Rensselaer Poly Inst 110 8th St Troy NY 12180

ZAGORIA, SAM D(AVID), reporter, educator, federal agency administrator; b. Somerville, NJ, Apr. 9, 1919; s. Nathan and Rebecca (Shapiro) Z.; m. Sylvia Bomse, Dec. 21, 1941; children: Paul, Marjorie Zagoria Isacks, Ronald. BL in Journalism, Rutgers U., 1941. With New Brunswick (N.J.) Daily Home News, 1940-41, N.J. Def. Coun., Trenton, 1941-42, Fed. Office Govt. Reports, Newark, 1942; reporter Washington Post, 1946-55; adminstrv. asst. to Senator Clifford P. Case, Washington, 1955-65; pres. Washington Newspaper Guild, 1953; mem. NLRB, Washington, 1965-69; dir. Labor-Mgmt. Rels. Svc. U.S. Conf. of Mayors, Washington, 1970-78; mem. U.S. Consumer Product Safety Commn., 1978-84; ombudsman Washington Post, 1984-86; arbitrator, 1986—. Fulbright lectr., Copenhagen, 1987; vis. prof. Fla. Atlantic U., Boca Raton, 1988—91; adj. prof. Wake Forest U., Winston-Salem, NC, 1993—2001. Author: Public Workers, Public Unions, 1972, The Ombudsman: How Good Governments Handle Citizens' Grievances, 1988. Campaign mgr. reelection Senator Case, 1960; campaign mgr. race for gov., former Sec. of Labor James P. Mitchell, 1961. With USAAF, 1942-45. Nieman fellow Harvard U., 1954. Mem. Common Cause, Nat. Consumers League, Rutgers U. Alumni Assn. Jewish. also: 2864 Wynfield Crossing Ln Winston Salem NC 27103-6597 Address: 3101 S Ocean Blvd 622 Boca Raton FL 33487 Office Phone: 561-274-6376.

ZAGORIN, JANET SUSAN, legal firm administrator, marketing professional; b. Lakewood, NJ; d. Irving C. and Dorothy (Tarshish) Zagorin. BA, Douglass Coll., 1975; MLS, Rutgers U., 1977. Asst. law libr. N.J. Atty. Gen., Trenton, 1977-78; head of reference sect. Cardozo U. Law Sch., NYC, 1978-79; law and legis. svcs. libr. FTC, Washington, 1979-81; dir. of reference Paul Weiss Rifkind, NYC, 1981-82; libr., profl. devel. dir. Baker & McKenzie, NYC, 1982-96; dir. practice devel. and info. svcs. Stroock & Stroock & Lavan LLP, NYC, 1996-98; dir. practice devel. Cadwalader, Wickersham & Taft, NYC, 1998-99, Gibson, Dunn & Crutcher, NYC, 1999—2001; dir. mktg. Sidley Austin Brown & Wood, NYC, 2001—04; dir. practice devel. Sidley Austin LLP, NYC, 2004—. Bd. dirs. N.Y. Cares, 1998—, audit com., 2007—. Mem.: ABA (vice chmn. standing com. Law Libr. Congress 1995—96, chmn. 1996—2001, law 2000 steering com. Libr. Congress), Am. Assn. Law Librs. (chair fgn. comparative internat. law com. 1990—91, vice chair pvt. law librs. 1990—91, chair com. on recruitment 1991, chair 1991—), Fin. Women's Assn. (bd. dirs. 1993—95, 1999—2000), Hadassah. Office: Sidley Austin LLP 787 Seventh Ave New York NY 10019-6018 Office Phone: 212-839-8797. Business E-Mail: jzagorin@sidley.com.

ZAHEER, ASGAR, medical educator; married. Asst. prof. U. Iowa, Iowa City, 1979—; health sci. specialist Va. Med. Ctr., Iowa City, 1988—. Office: Va Med Ctr & Univ Iowa 200 Hawkins Dr Iowa City IA 52242 Business E-Mail: asgar-zaheer@uiowa.edu.

ZAHKA, KENNETH GEORGE, pediatrician, cardiologist, educator; b. 1950; BA summa cum laude, Boston U., 1971; MD, Johns Hopkins U., 1975. Cert. Am. Bd. Pediat., 1980, Pediat. Cardiology, 1981. Intern pediat. Johns Hopkins Hosp., Balt., 1975—76, resident pediat., 1976—78, clin. fellow pediat. cardiology, 1978—81, dir. Pediat. Heart Station, 1983—90; asst. prof. pediat. Johns Hopkins U. Sch. Medicine, 1981—88, assoc. prof., 1988—90; dir. Divsn. Pediat. Cardiology Rainbow Babies and Children's Hosp., 1990—2004, vice chair subspecialty practices, vice chair clin. affairs, 1997—; dir. pediat. cardiology Case Western Reserve Sch. Medicine, 1990—2004, prof. pediat., 2004—. Assoc. staff MetroHealth Med. Ctr., 1991—97; cons. Lakewood Hosp., 1991—98; physician Dept. Pediat. Cons. Staff Mt. Sinai Med. Ctr., 1994—97; cons. staff St. Elizabeth Health Ctr., 1997—, Tod Children's Hosp., 1997—, S.W. Gen. Health Ctr., 1997—, Bedford Med. Ctr., 1997—; spkr. in field. Contbr. articles to med. jours. Recipient Presdl. Recognition Award, Republic of Armenia, 1994, Friend of Armenians Award, Diocese of Am. Ch. of Am., 1997. Fellow: Am. Coll. Cardiology (Hoechst Marion Roussel Ohio Chap. award 1997), Am. Acad. Pediat.; mem.: Am. Soc. Echocardiography, Am. Heart Assn., Southeastern Pediat. Cardiology Soc. Office: Rainbow Babies and Children's Hosp 11100 Euclid Ave Cleveland OH 44106 Office Phone: 216-844-3278. Office Fax: 216-844-5478. E-mail: kgz@po.cwru.edu.

ZAHL, PAUL FRANCIS MATTHEW, retired dean; b. NYC, May 24, 1951; m. Mary McLean Cappleman, Dec. 29, 1973; children: John Arthur, David William Franklin, Simeon McLean. Student, U. N.C., 1968-70; AB magna cum laude, Harvard Coll., 1972; MPhil in Theology, U. Nottingham, Eng., 1975; diploma in pastoral studies, St. John's Theol. Coll., Nottingham, 1975; ThD, Eberhard-Karls-Univ., Tübingen, Germany, 1994. Ordained min. Protestant Episcopal Ch., 1976. Deacon in tng. Good Shepherd Episcopal Ch., Silver Spring, Md., 1975-76; curate Grace Ch., NYC, 1976-82; rector St. Mary's Ch., Scarborough, N.Y., 1982-88, St. James' Ch., Charleston, S.C., 1988-92; fellow Episcopal Ch. Found., 1993-95; dean Cathedral Ch. of the Advent, Birmingham, Ala., 1995—2004, Trinity Episcopal Sch. for Ministry, Pitts., 2004—07; rector All Saints Church, Chevy Chase, Md., 2007—09; retired. Tchr. Gen. Theol. Sem., N.Y.C., 1979-82, The King's Coll., Briarcliff Manor, N.Y., 1985-88, Coll. Charleston, S.C., 1990-92, U. Tübingen, Germany, 1992-93; vis. scholar Wycliffe Hall, Oxford, Eng., 1994-95. Author: Who Will Deliver Us?, 1983, Die Rechtfertigungslehre Ernst Kasemanns, 1996, Protestant Face of Anglicanism, 1998; co-author: The Collects of Thomas Cranmer, 1999; columnist The Anglican Digest, 1986—; contbr. articles to profl. jours. Mem. Phi Beta Kappa. Episcopalian. Office: All Saints Church 3 Chevy Chase Circle Chevy Chase MD 20815*

ZAHL, PERCY, physicist, researcher; PhD, Inst. Festkörperphysik, U. Hannover, Germany, 2001. Postdoc. Colo. Sch. Mines, Golden, 2001—03, IBM, Zurich Rsch. Lab., Rüschlikon, Switzerland, 2003—05; rsch. assoc. Brookhaven Nat. Lab., Upton, NY, 2005—. Gxsm project adminstr. SourceForge.net, 2000—. Mem.: SBRA, Bike Club Webmaster. Achievements include patents for defining a pattern on a substrate.

ZAHLER, ADAM TROY, stage director, theatre professor; b. Houston, Nov. 30, 1955; s. Burton Ross and Suzanne Troy Zahler, Michal Frank Zahler (Stepmother); m. Amy Bernstein, July 30, 1988; children: Michal Celia, Naomi Esther. BA (magna cum laude), U. Vt., 1977; MFA, U. Va., 1996. Founding artistic dir. Second Stage, Burlington, Vt., 1978—81; assoc. dir. Vt. Repertory Theatre, Winooski, Vt., 1987—88; founding artistic dir. The Open Stage, Burlington, Vt., 1988—93; producing assoc. New Repertory Theatre, Newton Highlands, Mass., 1997—2004. V.p. Burlington (Vt.) Arts Round Table, 1991—92, pres., 1992—93; adj. prof. U. Mass., Lowell, 2000—06; chair Theatre Arts Mktg. Alliance, Boston, 2003; asst. prof. theatre Worchester State Coll., 2006—. Dir.: (plays) Wit (IRNE Award Best Acting, 2002), Rose (IRNE Award Best Solo Performance, 2001), Stonewall Jackson's House (Elliot Norton award for Best Prodn. Small Theatre, 2001, Elliot Norton award for Best Actress Small Theatre, 2001), To Bed With Betsy, Permanent Collection, 2005 (Elliot Norton Outstanding Dir. Small Theatre award, 2005), (hot play) The Patriot Act, Hot Play, Edinburgh Fringe Festival, 2008. Mem.: Stage Source: Kennedy Ctr. Am. Coll. Theatre Festival Region One Directing Com., Stage Dirs. and Choreographers. Avocations: gourmet cooking, birdwatching, vegetable gardening. Office Phone: 508-740-7783. Personal E-mail: adamzahler@rcn.com.

ZAHLER, CLARA TATAR, music educator; b. Cremona, Lombardia, Italy, Jan. 9, 1951; d. Pietro and Santina Arigoni Tatar; m. Noel B. Zahler; children: Mathieu Pierce, Metisse Pietra. BA, CUNY Queens Coll., NY, 1974; MA, Conn. Coll., New London, 2000. Cert. in pub. sch. music tchg. NYC, 1974, NJ, 1975, Conn., 1990. Gen. music tchr. New Haven Pub. Schs., 1994—96; string tchr., elem. and mid. sch. Norwich Pub. Schs., Conn., 1996—2000; dir. string program Griswold Pub. Schs., Conn., 2000—03; prof. music edn. U. Minn.-Twin Cities, Mpls., 2004—07; assoc. tchg. prof. music Carnegie Mellon U., Pitts., 2007—. Violinist Maggio Musicale Fiorentino, Firenze, Tuscany, Italy, 1976—77, Am. Symphony Orch., NYC, 1978—93, NY Pops Orch., NYC, 1980—, Martha Graham Dance Co., NYC, 1982—87. Mem.: ASTA. Office: Carnegie Mellon Univ 5000 Forbes Ave Pittsburgh PA 15213 Business E-Mail: czahler@andrew.cmu.edu.

ZAHN, CARL FREDERICK, museum program director, photographer, graphics designer; b. Louisville, Mar. 9, 1928; s. Fred Joseph and Myrtle (Fulks) Z.; m. Betty Jane Woodrow, Nov. 18, 1950 (div. July 1977); children: Lisa, Karen, Richard; m. Felicitas Magdalena Fuhlrott, July 30, 1979 (dec. Mar. 1999). BA, Harvard Coll., 1948. Asst. in conservation Fogg Art Mus., Cambridge, Mass., 1949-50; with art dept. Benton & Bowles Inc., NYC, 1950-51; design asst. Inst. Contemporary Art, Boston, 1951-56; dir. publs. Mus. Fine Arts, Boston, 1956—; also dir. exhbns., 1995-96; ret., 1997; co-founder Mus. Pub. Ptnrs., 2000. Exhibitions include: Addison Gallery Am. Art, Andover, Mass., 1959, Am. Inst. Graphic Arts, N.Y.C., 1960—, Rose Art Mus. Brandeis U., Waltham, Mass., 1969; author: Introduction to Hermann Zapf and His Design Philosophy, 1987, Books and Such Designed by Carl Zahn at the Museum of Fine Arts, Boston, 1956-97, 1997; co-author Weston's Westons: Portraits and Nudes, 1989; co-editor: Eye of the Beholder: Masterpieces from the Isabella Stewart Gardner Museum, 2003. Mem. Soc. Printers, Bund Deutscher Buchkünstler, East Chop Tennis Club (bd. dirs. 1970-72), Longwood Cricket Club. also: 1808 Par Pl Sarasota FL 34240-9689 E-mail: czbird@comcast.net.

ZAHN, CINDY MAE, dental educator; m. Dieter Zahn, 1987; children: Nicole, Matthew. BS in Dental Hygiene, Old Dominion U., Norfolk, Va., 1983; MS in Health Planning, U. Cin., 1986. Dental hygienist Paul Will, Snyder, NY, 1987—91; prof. dental hygiene Erie CC, Williamsville, NY, 1991—. Mem.: Am. Dental Hygiene Assn. Office: Erie CC 6205 Main St Williamsville NY 14221

ZAHN, DONALD JACK, lawyer; b. Oct. 24, 1941; s. Jerome and Clara (Zinsher) Z.; m. Laurie R. Hyman, Aug. 19, 1966; children: Lawrence, Melissa. AB, NYU, 1963; LLB, Union U., 1966; LLM in Taxation, NYU, 1967. Bar: N.Y. 1966, U.S. Dist. Ct. (no. dist.) N.Y. 1966, U.S. Tax Ct. 1969, U.S. Ct. Appeals (2d cir. 1970), Tex. 1972, U.S. Ct. Appeals (5th and 11th cirs.). Assoc. Bond, Schoeneck and King, Syracuse, NY, 1967-71; ptnr. Haynes and Boone, Dallas, 1971-82, Akin, Gump, Strauss, Hauer & Feld, Dallas, 1982-92; assoc. prof. internat. taxation, fed. income taxation, entities taxation, business associations Tex. Wesleyan Sch. Law, Ft. Worth, 1992-99. Vis. prof. fed. income taxation Baylor U. Sch. Law, 1995, prof. fed. income taxation and bus. orgns. II, 2000; grad. taxation program U. San Diego Sch. Law, 1996—98, fed. income taxation, corp. taxation, current income tax problems, tax ethics; adj. prof. Sch. Law So. Meth U., Dallas, 1972—87, 1990—91. Trustee, sec. mem. exec. and fin. com., nominating com. Greenhill Sch., Addison, Tex., 1980-90; trustee, chmn. budget com., mem. fin. com. Jewish Fedn. Greater Dallas, 1978-89; trustee, chmn. Found. Jewish Fedn., Dallas, 1980-89; trustee, v.p., pres. Dallas chpt. Am. Jewish Com., 1980-92; mem. Tex. World Trade Coun., 1986-87, Dallas Mayor's Internat. Com. Mem. State Bar Tex. (sec. 1982-83, chmn. tax sect. 1984-85, newsletter taxation sect. editor 1980-81), Internat. Bar Assn., Internat. Comte (N.Tex. commn.), Ctr. for Am. and Internat. Law (adv. bd., treas. Internat. and Comparative Law Ctr., lectr. Acad. in Internat. Law), N.Y. State Bar Assn. Address: 11218 Hillcrest Rd Dallas TX 75230-3501 Office Phone: 214-769-9712. Office Fax: 214-739-4533. E-mail: donzahn@flash.net.

ZAHN, PAULA, newscaster; b. Omaha, Feb. 24, 1956; m. Richard Cohen, 1987 (separated 2007); children: Haley Brynne, Jared Brandon, Austin Bryce. BA in journalism, Stephens Coll., Columbia, Mo., 1978. With Sta. WFAA-TV, Dallas, 1978, Sta. KFMB-TV, San Diego, 1979—81, Sta. KPRC-TV, Houston, 1981—83, Sta. WHDH-TV, Boston, 1983—85; anchor, reporter Sta. KCBS-TV, LA, 1985—87; anchor The Health Show ABC News, NYC, 1987—88, co-anchor World News This Morning, 1988—90; co-anchor CBS This Morning CBS News, NYC, 1990—96, anchor CBS Evening News Sat. edit., 1996—99; anchor The Fox Report with Paula Zahn Fox News Network, NYC, 1999, anchor The Edge with Paula Zahn, 1999—2001; co-anchor American Morning CNN, 2001—03, co-anchor People in the News, 2002—07, anchor Paula Zahn Now, 2003—07. Primetime co-host Olympic Winter Games, Albertville, France, 1992; co-anchor Olympic Winter Games, Lillehammer, Norway, 94. Musician (Cellist): Carnegie Hall Debut, 1992. Recipient Broadcasting Award, Nat. Commn. Working Women, 1982, Spirit Achievement Award, Albert Einstein Coll. Medicine, 1993, Cancer Awareness Award, Congl. Families Action for Cancer Awareness, 1994, Emmy award for outstanding coverage of a continuing news story, 1994, Spirit of Life Award, City of Hope Cancer Ctr., 2003; named Newscaster of Yr., Am. Women in Radio and TV, 1983.

ZAHN, STEVE, actor; b. Marshall, Minn., Nov. 13, 1967; m. Robyn Peterman, July 16, 1994; children: Henry James, Audrey. PhD in Fine Arts (hon.), Norther Ky. U., 2007. Co-founder Malaparte theater co. Actor: (TV films) First Love, Fatal Love, 1991, Subway Stories: Tales from the Underground, 1997, Speak, 2004; (films) Rain Without Thunder, 1992, Reality Bites, 1994, Crimson Tide, 1995, Race the Sun, 1996, SubUrbia, 1996, The Object of My Affection, 1998, Out of Sight, 1998, Safe Men, 1998, You've Got Mail, 1998, Happy, Texas, 1999 (Spl. Jury prize, Sundance Film Festival, 1999, Ind. Spirit award for Best Supporting Male, 2000), Forces of Nature, 1999, Freak Talks About Sex, 1999, (voice) Stuart Little, 1999, Hamlet, 2000, Chain of Fools, 2000, Saving Silverman, 2001, (voice) Dr. Dolittle 2, 2001, Joy Ride, 2001, Chelsea Walls, 2001, Riding in Cars with Boys, 2001, (voice) Stuart Little 2, 2002, National Security, 2003, Daddy Day Care, 2003, Shattered Glass, 2003, Employee of the Month, 2004, Sahara, 2005, Bandidas, 2006, Rescue Dawn, 2006, Sunshine Cleaning, 2008, Strange Wilderness, 2008; actor, actor: (films) The Great Buck Howard, 2008, Management, 2008, A Perfect Getaway, 2009; (TV series) Picture Window, 1994, Liberty! The American Revolution, 1997; (TV miniseries) From the Earth to the Moon, 1998, Comanche Moon, 2008. Avocations: fly fishing, guitar. Office: Endeavor Agy 9601 Wilshire Blvd 3rd fl Beverly Hills CA 90212*

ZAHND, RICHARD H., sports association executive, lawyer; b. NYC, July 22, 1946; s. Hugo and Rose (Genovese) Z.; m. Phyllis Beth Workman, Aug. 13, 1978; children: Andrew Richard, Melissa Dawn. AB, NYU, 1968, JD, 1971. Bar: N.Y. 1972. Assoc. Paul, Weiss, Rifkind, Wharton & Garrison, NYC, 1971-74; staff atty. Madison Square Garden Corp., NYC, 1974-75; v.p. legal affairs Madison Square Garden Center, Inc., NYC, 1975-79; v.p., gen. counsel Madison Square Garden Corp., NYC, 1979-86; v.p. N.Y. Knickerbockers Basketball Club, NYC, 1979-86, N.Y. Rangers Hockey Club, NYC, 1979-86; ptnr. Morrison & Foerster, NYC, 1986-91; exec. v.p., gen. counsel NHL Enterprises, L.P., NYC, 1992—. Served to capt. U.S. Army, 1972. John Norton Pomeroy scholar NYU Law Sch., 1969; Mortimer Bishop scholar NYU Law Sch., 1969; Judge Jacob Markowitz scholar NYU Law Sch., 1970; recipient Am. Jurisprudence prize NYU Law Sch., 1969 Episcopalian. Office: NHL Enterprises LP 1185 Ave of the Americas New York NY 10036 Office Phone: 212-789-2023. Business E-Mail: rzahnd@nhl.com.

ZAHNER KRAEFT, DOROTHY SIMKIN, retired elementary school educator, school librarian; arrived in US, 1931; d. Robert Louis and Margaret Isadore (Timberlake) Simkin; m. Henry Zahner (div.); children: Mary De Avilan, Robert Louis; m. Norman John Kraeft, May 28, 2005 (div. Jan. 2007). BA in Sociology, Whittier Coll.; MLS, U. So. Calif., LA, 1952. Cert. tchr. Calif., Ariz. Tchr. LA and Pasadena Sch., Calif., 1969-93; dir., owner Betty Ingram Sch., North Hollywood, Calif., 1976-79; dir. Foothill Nursery Sch., La Crescenta, Calif., 1970s; tchr. L.A. Unified Sch. Dist., 1980s; guest tchr. Washington Unified Sch. Dist., Phoenix, 1994-97; ret., 2002. Guest tchr. Osborn Sch. Dist., 1998-2000, Madison Sch. Dist., Phoenix, 1999-2001. Author: poems pub. in U.S., Europe and China. Bd. dirs. Ariz. Tenants Assn., Phoenix, 1994, 95; vol. Am. Friends Svc. Com., Phila., Calif., 1985, Common Cause, LA, 1990, Internat. Rescue Com.; domestic violence vol., Phoenix, 1999-2000; vol. Dem. candidates, LA, Phoenix and Tucson; poll marshall Election Bd., Phoenix. Recipient cert. appreciation, Project Hope, 2005. Mem.: Southwestern Authors, Soc. Southwestern Authors, Ariz. State Poetry Soc. (pres. 2002—03, chmn. 2004), Alameda Writers Group, Phoenix Poetry Soc. (pres. 1998, anthology editl. co. 2001, featured Tucson reader 2007, com. mem., featured reader 2005, Poet of Yr. 2000, poetry awards 1995, 2000), Am. Assn. Ret. Persons, Phoenix Writers Club (sec. 1998). Democrat. Avocations: theater, films, music, swimming, reading.

ZAHORIK, PAVEL, psychology professor; b. Milw., June 13, 1969; s. John and Lois Zahorik; m. Kari Davis, Oct. 23, 1993; children: Andrei, Dara. BS, U. Wis., Madison, 1991, PhD, 1998. Asst. scientist U. Wis., 2001—03; assoc. prof. U. Louisville, 2009—. Cons. Rockwell Sci., Thousand Oaks, Calif., 2000—01. Contbr. articles to profl. jours. Grant, NIH-NEI, 1999—2001, NIH-NIDCD, 2002—06, 2007—. Mem.: Assn. Rsch. Otolaryngology, Audio Engring. Soc., Acoustical Soc. Am. Office: Univ Louisville Dept Psychol & Brain Sci Louisville KY 40292 Office Fax: 502-852-8904. Business E-Mail: pavel.zahorik@louisville.edu.

ZAHRALDDIN-ARAVENA, RAFAEL XAVIER, law educator; b. Bogota, May 6, 1967; s. Ramez Moayad and Mercedes Ana (Aravena-Echaurren) Z. BS in Architecture, U. Va., 1989; JD, Widener U., 1993; LLM, Georgetown U., 1995. Bar: Pa. 1994, Delaware, Calif., US Ct. of Appeals (3rd cir.), US Dist. Ct. (Delaware dist.). Teaching asst. U. Va., 1988-89, Widener U., 1992; asst. prof. Chapman U. Sch. Law, Orange, Calif., 1995—98, assoc. prof., 1998—2000; law clk. Hon. Samuel L. Bufford (US Bankruptcy Ct. Ctrl. Dist.), Calif., 1999—2000; assoc. Morris James Hitchens & Williams LLP, Wilmington, Del. US sec. of state adv. group pvt. internat. law transnational insolvency com. Contbg. editor: L.Am. Telecom Report, Washington, 1994-95; contbr. articles to profl. jours. Benefit vice chmn. I Have a Dream Found., Washington, 1995. Mem. ABA, ASIL, IABA, Capital Club (membership com. 1994-95), Belmont Shore Rugby Football Club (bd. dirs.), Mem. ABA Business Law Sect. and Sect. Internat. Law and Practice, Vice Chair Inter-Am. Law Com. Sect. Internat. Law and Practice, American Bankruptcy Inst., Delaware Bankruptcy Inns of Ct. sr. writing fellow Georgetown U. Wash. 1994-95, Articles editor Del. Jour. Corp. Law, 1992-93. Office: Elliott Greenleaf 1105 Market St Suite 1700 Wilmington DE 19801 Office Phone: 302-888-6947. Office Fax: 302-571-1750. Business E-Mail: rzahraldd in@morrisjames.com.

ZAHRAN, MOHSEN MOHARRAM, architect, educator; b. Cairo, Aug. 8, 1938; s. Moharram M. and Dawlat (Sadek) Z.; m. Gayle McConaghy; children: Mona, Tamer. BArch, Ein Shams U., Cairo, 1959; MArch, MIT, Cambridge, 1962; MFA in Architecture, Princeton U., 1963, PhD in Environ. Planning, 1965. Prof. emeritus arch. and urban planning faculty engring. U. Alexandria, Egypt, 1965—; chmn. Alexandria Comprehensive Plan 2005/2017/2050 Alexandria Planning Commn., 1983—; chmn. Gov. of Alexandria's Consultative Com. for Planning, 1986—97; exec. dir. Gen. Orgn. of Alexandria Libr., 1988—2001; project mgr. Bibliotheca Alexandrina, 1995—2001; head dept. architecture U. Alexandria, 1994—97. Pub. & academic lectr., Egypt & Overseas, 1971-2009, Inst. NYC, Columbia U., NYC, MIT, Cambridge, AUB, BAV, Berirut, London U., Kuwait U., Oman U., Ministry of Housing; mem. faculty promotion com., nationally, 1977-2009; mem. sci. com. Arab Cities Orgn. and Mediterrean Cities Orgn.; adviser to the Gov. of Alexandria, 1986-2005; prin. adv. Bibliotheca Alexandria, 2001-02; cons. and expert in the field; jury mem. and chmn. nat. and internat. competitions. Author: College Housing: An Arena of Involvement and Conflict, 1972, Challenges of the Urban Environment, 1973, Philosophy of Design, 1977, Validity and Illusions in Architecture, 1980, The New Bibliotheca Alexandrina Reflections on A Journey of Achievements, 2007; designed and built several housing projects, medical centers, government complexes, banks, museums and residential buildings in Egypt, Middle East, Africa and the US; contbr. more than 110 sci. papers to numerous profl. jours. Chmn. Housing and

Planning Com., Alexandria City Coun., 1989-94, Nat. Dem. Party, 1995—; dep. chmn. jury internat. competition Bibliotheca Alexandria, 1989—98; cons. and expert UNESCO, WHO, ECWA, ESCWA, UNEP, UNDP, UNCHS, UNCHBP, Arab cities org., medcities medurbs, etc. Recipient Egyptian Arab Republic's medal of distinction of first order, 1959, Honor Shield, U. Alexandria, 1986; fellow Salzburg (Austria) Seminar, 1981, Award chevalier Legion d'Honour (France), Alexandria Univ. Merit award, 1997; winner prizes of several archtl. competitions; nominated Nat. Merit & Distinction award, Alexandria U., 2009. Fellow Lebanese Pub. Health Assn.; mem. AIA, Egyptian Soc. Archs., Egyptian Engrng. Syndicate, Alexandria Yacht Club (mem. bd. 1984-89), Sporting Club Alexandria, West Alexandria Rotary (past pres. 1994). Home: 23 Roushdy St Apt 3 Roushdy Alexandria 21529 Egypt Office: 15 Farid Bek St Roushdy Alexandria Egypt Office Phone: 03/4211848. Personal E-mail: mohsen_zahran@hotmail.com, mohsenzahran@yahoo.com. E-mail: zahran@mohsenzahran.com.

ZAHROWSKI, JAMES J., orthodontist; m. Sally H. Zahrowski, June 30, 1979; children: Kelly L., Mark T. BS, U. Calif., Riverside, 1974; PharmD, USC Sch. Pharmacy, LA, 1979; Dr. in Dental Medicine, U. Oreg., Portland, 1985; MS, UCLA, 1989. Diplomate Am. Bd. Orthodontics, 2006; cert. in orthodontic specialty UCLA, 1987. Orthodontic clin. instr. UCLA, 1992—98; pvt. practice Tustin, Calif., 1988—. Contbr. articles to profl. jours. Mem.: ADA, Pacific Coast Soc. Orthodontists, Edward H. Angle Orthodontic Soc., Orange County Dental Soc., Calif. Dental Soc., Am. Assn. Orthodontists. Office: James J Zahrowski DMD MS INC 13372 Newport Ave E Tustin CA 92780

ZAI, ADRIAN, medical researcher, director; s. David and Judy Zai; m. Margaret Liu; 1 child, Amelia. BA, Boston U., 1992; MD, PhD, Boston U. Sch. Medicine, 2001; MPH, Harvard Sch. Pub. Health, Boston, 2007. Med. informatics fellow Mass. Gen. Hosp., Boston, 2004—07, clin. dir. population informatics, 2007—; internal medicine resident Metrohealth Med. Ctr., Cleve. Mem.: Am. Med. Informatics Assn. Office: Mass Gen Hosp 50 Staniford St Ste 750 Boston MA 02114 Business E-Mail: azai@partners.org.

ZAID, SHAKIR TOR ISHAQ, not-for-profit developer, minister; b. Oakland, Calif., June 6, 1961; s. James Arthur and Mable Wheatley Hooker; m. Nette Pierce, Feb. 14, 1960; children: Amir Sharif, Shimar Anton, Shominic Antone, Shiceau Le', Myia Mae, Aliyah, Mario Lamar Mc Clellon. ThM, DD, Sacramento Sch. Theology, Calif., 1999. Founder, CEO, pastor Rapture Internat. Ministries, Oakland, Calif., 2000—; mentor, cons., motivational spkr. Chosen Out of Love, San Leandro, Calif., 2004, CEO, 2005; case worker San Francisco Sheriff Dept. Recipient Man the Yr. award. Mem.: Gt. Lives of 21st Century (mentor, motivational spkr., lectr.). Personal E-mail: drshakirzaid@minister.com, drshakirzaid@gmail.com. E-mail: pastorsz@minister.com.

ZAIDAT, OSAMA O., neurologist; b. Zarqa, Jordan, Sept. 3, 1969; s. Othman M. and Anneh H. Z.; m. Sabreen O. Owais, Mar. 19, 1998; 1 child, Bashar O.O. MBBS, MD, Jordan U., 1993. Diplomate Am. Bd. Neurology. Intern in internal medicine and emergency rotation U. Hosp., Amman, Jordan, 1993-94; resident in internal medicine Seton Hall U., St. Joseph Hosps., 1994-95; resident in neurology Case Western Reserve U., U. Hosps. of Cleve., 1995-98; fellow in cerebrovascular disease and neurocritical care Case Western Reserve U., 1998-99, Case Western Reserve U., U. Hosps. of Cleve., 1999—. Vis. fellow neurocritical care Cleve. Clinic Found., 1997, Johns Hopkins U., 1998. Author: (with others) Geriatric Neurosurgery, Muscles Diseases, Neuromuscular Disorders in Clinical Practice; jour. reviewer Neurology, Jou. Neurology Neurosurgery and Psychiatry; contbr. articles to profl. jours.; presenter in field. Mem. Am. Heart Assn., Am. Stroke Assn. Mem. AMA, ACP, Am. Acad. Neurology, Jordanian Med. Assn. Avocations: sports, reading, movies, travel. Office: CWRU U Hosp of Cleve Dept Neurology Hanna House 11100 Euclid Ave Fl 5 Cleveland OH 44106-1736 Fax: 216-844-5066. E-mail: ozaidat@hotmail.com.

ZAIDI, EMILY LOUISE, retired elementary school educator; b. Hoquiam, Wash., Apr. 20, 1924; d. Burdick Newton and Emily Caroline (Williams) Johnston; m. M. Baqar Abbas Zaidi, June 12, 1949 (dec. Dec. 1983). BA in Edn. and Social Studies, Ea. Wash. U., 1948; MEd, U. Wash., 1964, EdD, 1974. Tchr. 4th grade Hoquiam Schs., 1948—49; tchr. grades 5-6 Lake Washington Sch. Dist., Kirkland, Wash., 1949—51; tchr. grades 2-3 Port Angeles Schs., Wash., 1951—54; tchr. grade 2 Seattle Schs., 1954—55; tchr., reading specialist Northshore Sch. Dist., Bothell, Wash., 1955—69, Sacramento City Schs., 1969—87; ret., 1987. Mem. Calif. State Instrnl. Materials Panel, Sacramento, 1975. Mem. Sacramento Opera Assn., 1986—, Sacramento Ballet Assn., 1987—2000. Fulbright Commn. Exch. Tchr., 1961—62. Democrat. Avocations: writing, children's literature, reading, travel. Home: 4230 N River Way Sacramento CA 95864-6055 Personal E-mail: e.zaidi@sbcglobal.net.

ZAIDI, MOHAMMAD A., metal products executive; Grad. in Metall. Engring., Indian Inst. Tech., Kanpur, India, 1975; M in Materials Tech., Imperial Coll., London, 1977, PhD in Mech. Metallurgy, 1980. Sr. engr. Alcoa, Inc., Alcoa Center, Pa., 1985, mgr. tech. devel. and transfer for aluminum-intensive vehicle, 1991—92, with Automotive GmbH plant Soest, Germany, 1992—95, dir. product strategy, 1995—97, v.p. tech. devel. Automotive bus., 1997—98, dir. tech. worldwide automotive and extrusions Alcoa Center, 1998—2001, pres. Alcoa Automotive Fabrication and Assembly bus., COO Automotive Castings bus., 2001—03, v.p., chief tech. officer, 2003—06, exec. v.p. market strategy, tech. and quality, 2006—. Contbr. articles to sci. jours. Office: Alcoa Inc Alcoa Tech Ctr 100 Technical Dr New Kensington PA 15069

ZAIDI, MONE, endocrinologist, educator; b. Lucknow, India, Apr. 30, 1960; came to U.S., 1994; s. Sibte Hasan and Qamar Ara (Shahanshah Husain) Z.; m. Meenakshi Arora, May 28, 1984; children: Neeha, Samir. MB, BChir, U. Lucknow, 1983; PhD, U. London, 1987, MD, 1991. Resident intern, then house officer in medicine King George's Med. Coll., Lucknow, 1983-84; Tata meml. rsch. scholar endocrine unit Royal Postgrad. Med. Sch., Hammersmith Hosp., U. London, 1984-86; registrar chem. pathology Hammersmith Hosp., 1987; lectr., sr. registrar endocrine unit Royal Postgrad. Med. Sch., U. London, 1987-89; sr. registrar chem. pathology St. George's Hosp., London, 1990; sr. lectr., cons. divsns. biochem. medicine and biochemistry St. George's Hosp. Med. Sch., U. London, 1990-95; rechr. Physiol. Lab., U. Cambridge, Eng., 1991—; staff physician Geriat. Rsch. Edn. and Clin. Ctr., VA Med. Ctr., Little Rock, 1995—; mem. Ark. Cancer Rsch. Ctr., U. Ark. for Med. Scis., 1995—, Ctr. for Osteoporosis and Metabolic Bone Disease, 1995—; prof. medicine divsn. endocrinology and metabolism Coll. Medicine, U. Ark., Little Rock, 1995—; staff. physician Univ. Hosp., Little Rock, 1995—. Mem. acad. bd., mem. electron microscope users subcom. St. George's Hosp. Med. Sch., 1990-95, tutor biochemistry of cells, 1990-93, dir. structure and function of blood course, 1990-94; cons. NPS Pharms., Salt Lake City, 1991-93, Cortex Internat., London, 1993-95; adj. prof. divsn. basic scis. NYU, 1990-95; lectr. advanced endrocrinology for clinicians U. London, 1987, 89, PhD supr., 1990-94, lectr., co-organizer MS in Clin. Biochemistry and postgrad. diploma in clin. pathology courses, 1987-89, MB, BChir examiner, mem. collegiate com. of examiners, 1991-95, mem. bd. studies in pathology U. London, 1989-95, mem. panel for cons. appointment coms., 1992-95; dir. endocrinology fellowship program Coll. Medicine U. Ark., 1995, examiner objective structured clin. exam. U. Ark. Med. Scis., 1995—; Foster Club guest spkr. Physiol. Lab., U. Cambridge, 1990, 92; keynote spkr. Dutch Bone and Mineral Soc., Leiden, 1993, Internat. Bone Cell Biology Meeting, Fuji, Japan, 1994, Australian-New Zealand Bone and Mineral Soc., 1996; plenary spkr. Hellenic Bone Metabolism Soc., Athens, Greece, 1994; mem. program organizing subcom. 11th Internat. Congress on Calcium Regulating Hormones, Melbourne, Australia, 1995; ad hoc reviewer orgns. including North Cancer Rsch. Campaign, Eng., Action Rsch., Eng., Rsch. into Aging, Eng., Wellcome Trust, Eng., New Zealand Rsch. Coun., Arthritis and Rheumatism Coun., Eng., Med. Rsch. Coun., Eng., many profl. jours.; lectr., spkr. numerous profl. confs. and symposia, 1987—. Co-author: Therapy of Osteoporosis, 1995; contbr. over 200 articles and abstracts to profl. publs.; co-patentee method for prevention of bone resorption. Recipient Vivian Jacob Meml. Gold medal La Martiniere Coll., Lucknow, 1973, Overseas Rsch. Scholars award Com. of Vice Chancellors and Prins. of Univs. of U.K., 1984, Lady Tata Meml. Internat. Rsch. Fellowship award, London, 1985, Nuffield Found. award for sci. lectures, London, 1988, Royal Soc. travel award, 1991; rsch. grantee Hammersmith Spl. Health Authority, 1987-88, 88-89, Sandoz Found. for Gerontol. Rsch., Basel, Switzerland, 1990-92, 93-95, Nuffield Found., 1987-88, Leverhulme Trust, 1989-91, Med. Rsch. Coun., Eng., 1988-89, 90-91, Arthritis and Rheumatism Coun., Eng., 1988-91, 92-95. Fellow ACP, Inst. Biologists Gt. Britain, Royal Coll. Physicians Ireland (advisor for membership exam. 1993); mem. Am. Soc. for Bone and Mineral Rsch., Soc. Gen. Physiologists, Physiol. Soc. (Eng.), Royal Coll. Pathologists (London), Brit. Soc. for Cell Biology, Biochem. Soc. (Eng.), Brit. Endocrine Soc., Inst. Biologists (Eng., chartered), N.Y. Acad. Scis., Inst. Advanced Motorists. Avocation: driving. Office: Mt Sinai Sch of Medicine One Gustave L Levy Pl New York NY 10029

ZAILLIAN, STEVEN, screenwriter, director; b. Fresno, Calif., Jan. 30, 1953; BA, San Francisco State U., 1975. Scripts include: The Falcon and the Snowman, 1985, Awakenings, 1990 (Acad. award nominee for best adapted screenplay, 1990), Jack the Bear, 1993, Schindler's List, 1993 (Acad. award best adapted screenplay 1993), Mission: Impossible, 1996, Hannibal, 2001, The Interpreter, 2005; co-writer (with Donald Stewart and John Milius) Clear and Present Danger, 1994; scriptwriter, dir.: Searching for Bobby Fisher, 1993, A Civil Action, 1998; co-writer: Gangs of New York (nominee Acad. Award Best Original Screenplay, 2002), American Gangster, 2007; scriptwriter, dir., exec. prodr.: A Civil Action, 1998; scriptwriter, dir., prodr.: All the King's Men, 2006

ZAIMAN, JOEL HIRSH, rabbi; b. Chgo., Mar. 10, 1938; s. Solomon and Ruth (Levy) Z.; m. Ann Shanok, July 1, 1959; children: Elana Beth, Sarina, Ari Lev. BS, DePaul U., 1957; Master of Hebrew Letters, Jewish Theol. Sem., NYC, 1962. Assoc. rabbi Temple Emanu-El, Providence, 1962-73, sr. rabbi, 1973-80, Chizuk Amuno Congregation, Balt., Md., 1980—. Pres. Balt. Bd. Rabbis, 1985-87; 1st v.p. Synagogue Coun. Am., 1988, pres., 1989-91. Contbr. articles to profl. jours. Chmn. edn. com. Kreiger Schecter Day Sch., Balt., 1983; bd. dirs. Balt. Bd. Jewish Edn., Md. Commn. on Hereditary and Congenital Disorders, Assoc. Jewish Charities and Welfare Fund, Levindale Hebrew Geriat. Ctr. and Hosp., Balt., 1984—, long range planning com.; v.p. Balt. Jewish Coun., 1992-94, pres., 1994-96; chancellors rabbinic cabinet Jewish Theol. Sem.; bd. dirs., patient care adv. com. Sinai Hosp., 1991; bd. dirs., chmn. program com. Inst. Christian and Jewish Studies; adv. coun. Md. Health Care Decisions Act, 1994—. Fellow Pearlstone Inst. Jewish Living (program planning com.); mem. Rabbinical Assembly (exec. council, long range planning com.), United Synagogue Commn. Jewish Edn. (chmn.), Md. Jewish Hist. Soc. (bd. dirs.), Associated Jewish Fedn. Balt. (bd. dirs. 1991—). Jewish. Home: 1 Talton Ct Baltimore MD 21208-3109 Office: Chizuk Amuno Congregation 8100 Stevenson Rd Baltimore MD 21208-1899 E-mail: jhzaiman@chizukamuno.org.

ZAIMAN, K(OICHI) ROBERT, dentist; b. Cin., Oct. 19, 1944; s. Noboru Gary and Toshiko (Matsuyama) Zaiman; m. Kimberly Ann Sass, Nov. 6, 1976; children: Kara Jean, Matthew Robert. Student, Creighton U., Omaha, 1962-64, DDS, 1968. Asst. prof. Creighton U. Sch. Dentistry, Omaha, 1971-73, assoc. prof., 1973-75; pvt. practice dentistry Omaha, 1971—. Dir. Chicano and Native-Am. Free Clinic Creighton U., Omaha, 1970—75. Mem. bd. elders King of Kings Luth. Ch., 1990—95, deacon, 1995—; past v.p., bd. dirs. Japanese-Am. Citizens League, Omaha, 1977—86. Fellow: Am. Coll. Dentistry, Internat. Coll. Dentistry, Acad. Gen. Dentistry (nat. del. 1971—76, pres. 1976—77), Acad. Continuing Edn., Pierre Fauchard Internat. Hon. Acad.; mem.: ADA, King of Kings Luth. Ch. (past elder, past bd. elders), Omaha Dental Study Club (pres. 1999—2001), Nebr. Dental Assn. (del. 1971—94, 1996—), Omaha Dist. Dental Soc. (bd. dirs. 1968, treas. 1980—85, peer rev. 1996—), Delta Sigma Delta (pres. 1973—74). Office: 10841 Q St Ste 109 Omaha NE 68137-3741 Office Phone: 402-339-4999.

ZAINAL-ABIDIN, SITI-ZALEHA, computer scientist, educator; d. Zainal-Abidin Ulop and Zainab Atin; m. M-Zailani Johari, Oct. 29, 1992; children: Hazirah M-Zailani, Hazmi-Afandi M-Zailani, Haidah-Dayini M-Zailani. BSc in Computer Sci., Mich. State U., East Lansing, 1985; MSc in Computer Sci., Western Ill. U., Macomb, 1987; PhD in Computer Sci., U. Wales, Swansea, 2007. Assoc. prof. U. Tech. MARA, Shah Alam, Malaysia, 1988—. Part-time cons. Mozani Group Holding, Shah Alam, 1996—2001; cons. Ctr. Media and Info. Warfare Studies U. Tech. MARA, 2007—. Author: Asas Sistem Pengendalian, 2002; contbr. articles to profl. jours. Voluntary officer Kuala Lumpur Commonwealth Games, Malaysia, 1998—98. Scholar, Malaysian Govt., 1981—87, Univ. Tech. MARA, 2002—06. Mem.: Pi Mu Epsilon, Upsilon Pi Epsilon. Avocation: travel. Office: Univ Tech MARA Selangor Shah Alam 40450 Malaysia Personal E-mail: szalehaza@yahoo.co.uk. Business E-Mail: zaleha@tmsk.uitm.edu.my.

ZAISER, KENT AMES, lawyer; b. St. Petersburg, Fla., June 10, 1945; s. Robert Alan and Marion (Brown) Z. AB, Duke U., 1967; postgrad., U. Calif., Berkeley, 1971; JD, U. Fla., 1972. Bar: Fla. 1973, U.S. Dist. Ct. (no. dist.) Fla. 1974, U.S. Supreme Ct. 1978, U.S. Dist. Ct. (so. dist.) Fla. 1980, U.S. Dist. Ct. (mid. dist.) Fla. 1981, U.S. Ct. Appeals (11th cir.) 1981. Rsch. aide Fla. Supreme Ct., Tallahassee, 1973-75, adminstrv. asst. to chief justice, 1975-76; asst. gen. counsel Fla. Dept. Natural Resources, Tallahassee, 1976-80; asst. atty. gen. Fla. Dept. Legal Affairs, Tallahassee, 1980-85; dep. gen. counsel S.W. Fla. Water Mgmt. Dist., Brooksville, 1985-89, gen. counsel, 1989-92; ptnr. Foley and Lardner, Tallahassee, 1992-93; prin. Kent A. Zaiser, P.A., Tallahassee, 1994—. Cons. Fla. State Cts. Adminstr., Tallahassee, 1975; mem. Fla. New Motor Vehicle Arbitration Bd., 1998-99. Contbg. author: Environmental Regulation and Litigation in Florida, 1980-84. Campaign chmn. Vince Fechtel for State Rep. of Fla., Leesburg, 1972. Mem. Jefferson County Bar Assn., Govs. Club. Democrat. Episcopalian. Home: 3286 Longleaf Rd Tallahassee FL 32310-6406 Office: PO Box 6045 Tallahassee FL 32314-6045 Home Phone: 850-576-2464; Office Phone: 850-576-7600.

ZAITZ, CYNTHIA LOUISE, creativity, music, theatre and dance educator; BA in Drama, U. Calif., Irvine, 1992; MA in Consciousness Studies, John F. Kennedy U., San Francisco, 1999; PhD in Comparative Studies: Fine and Performing Arts, Fla. Atlantic U., Boca Raton, 2009. Cert. profl. educator Fla. Dept. Edn., 2006. Performer St. Francis Hotel, San Francisco, 1996; music tchr. Aventura City Excellence Schs., Fla., 2003—05, Palm Beach Day Acad., Fla., 2005—07; grad. asst., instr. Fla. Atlantic U., 2007—, v.p. composer's forum, 2008—09. Original music composer and choreographer (modern dance performance) Of Moon and Madness, 2008; Played the King of he Zzorgs in Captain Crash vs the Zzorg Women in 1981in LA; original music composer and choreographer (modern dance performance) Six Butts on a Two Butt Bench: a tongue in cheek look at the overpopulation problem, for 10 actors and 70 dancers, FAU, 2009; painting, Alcheme 1 vol. 10. Office: Fla Atlantic Univ 777 Glades Rd Boca Raton FL 33431 Business E-Mail: czaitz@fau.edu.

ZAITZEFF, ROGER MICHAEL, lawyer; b. Detroit, June 25, 1940; s. Peter and Mary (Fedchenia) Z.; children: Zachary, Natasha, Zoe, Peter. BA with high honors and high distinction, U. Mich., 1962; MA with distinction, U. Calif., Berkeley, 1963, JD, 1969. Bar: NY 1970, US Dist. Ct. (so. dist.) NY 1975, US Ct. Appeals (2d cir.) 1975, DC 1985. Assoc. Seward & Kissel, NYC, 1969-77, ptnr., 1977-94, Latham & Wakins, NYC, 1994-2000, LeBoeuf Lamb Greene & MacRae, NYC, 2000—02, Swidler Berlin LLP, NYC, 2002—05, Sheppard Mullin Richter & Hampton LLP, NYC, 2005—. Contbr. articles to profl. jours. Mem. Tribar Opinion Com., 1990-93. Heller grantee U. Mich., 1962; recipient William Jennings Bryan Prize. Fellow: Am. Bar Found. (life); mem.: Phi Beta Kappa Assocs. Office: Sheppard Mullin Richter & Hampton LLP 30 Rockefeller Plz 24th Fl New York NY 10112 Office Phone: 212-332-3837.

ZAJAC, JOHN, semiconductor equipment company executive; b. NYC, July 21, 1946; s. John Andrew and Catherine (Canepa) Z.; m. Vera Barbagallo, Jan. 13, 1973; children: Jennifer, Michelle. AAS, NYU, 1966; BEE, U. Ky., Lawrence, 1968. Project engr. B.C.D. Computing, NYC, 1968-70; v.p. Beacon Systems, Commack, N.Y., 1970-73, E.T. Systems, Santa Clara, Calif., 1973-77; v.p. research and devel. Eaton Corp., Sunnyvale, Calif., 1977-81; pres. Semitech/Gen. Signal, Los Gatos, Calif., 1981-83; mgr. advanced product div. Tegal/Motorola Inc., Novato, Calif., 1983-86; v.p. research and devel. U.S. Alcohol Inc., San Jose, Calif., 1986—2002; staff scientist Mattson Tech., Fremont, Calif., 1994—2002; dir. R&D Silicon Etch Tech., 2003—04; v.p. R&D Zajac Optimum Output Motors, Inc., San Jose, 2004—. Author: The Delicate Balance, 1988, A Thief's Way to Heaven, 1999, Pyramids, Prophecy and 666, 2000; guest TV and radio. Achievements include patents in field.

ZAJAC, MATTHEW A., chemist; b. Buffalo, Nov. 15, 1976; m. Holly Cromwell Bentz, May 26, 2001. PhD, U. Mich., Ann Arbor, 2003. ACS postdoc. fellow Harvard U., Cambridge, Mass., 2003—05; prin. chemist Glaxo Smith Kline, King of Prussia, Pa., 2005—. Office: Glaxo Smith Kline 709 Swedeland Rd King Of Prussia PA 19406-0939

ZAK, ROBERT JOSEPH, lawyer; b. Steubenville, Ohio, July 29, 1946; s. Joseph and Pearl (Munyas) Zak; m. Kristy Hubbard Winkler, Sept. 13, 1980; children: Elizabeth Adele, Robert Joseph Jr, Barbara Ann. BS, W.Va. U., 1968, JD, 1975. Bar: WVa 1975, US Dist Ct (so dist) WVa 1975, US Dist Ct (no dist) WVa 1989, US Ct Appeals (4th cir) 1990. Staff atty. Pub. Svc. Commn. of W.Va., Charleston, 1975-76; assoc. Preiser & Wilson L.C., Charleston, 1976-81, ptnr., 1981-85; sr. ptnr. Zak & Assocs., Charleston, 1985—. Hearing examiner W.Va. Bd. Regents, Charleston, 1987—90; spl. asst. atty. gen. State of W.Va., 1987—90; mem. Workers Compensation Appeals Bd., 1991—97, 2001—04. Chmn. West Va. Support Enforcement Commn., 2003—. With US Army, 1969—71, Vietnam. Fellow: Am Acad Matrimonial Lawyers; mem.: Order Barristers. Republican. Presbyterian. Office: Zak & Assocs 607 Ohio Ave Charleston WV 25302-2228 Office Phone: 304-345-0745. E-mail: zakslaw@hotmail.com.

ZAKAHI, WALTER R., dean, communications educator; s. Raymond J. and Nylda Lelia Zakahi; m. Catharine Foster, Aug. 13, 1983; children: Philip Javier, Nathaniel Foster. PhD, Bowling Green State U., Ohio, 1982. Dept. head N.Mex State U., Las Cruces, 1998—2006, assoc. dean, 2006—. Contbr. articles to profl. jours. Fellowship, Am. Coun. Edn., 2008—. Roman Catholic. Avocations: golf, reading. Office: N Mex State Univ Coll Arts and Scis MSC 3335 Las Cruces NM 88003

ZAKANITCH, ROBERT RAHWAY, artist; b. Elizabeth, NJ; s. Andrew and Mary Z. Student, Newark Sch. Fine and Indsl. Art, NJ, 1954-57. Vis. artist, lectr. Sch. Art Inst. Chgo., 1976, U. Calif., San Diego, 1974; lectr. in field. One-man shows include Henri Gallery, Alexandria, Va., 1965, Reese Palley Gallery, NYC, 1970—71, Cunningham Ward, 1973—74, Holly Solomon Gallery, 1977, exhibited in group shows at Franklin Gallery, Cornell U., 1978, Va. Mus. Fine Arts, 1979, Palais des Beaux-Arts, Brussels, 1979, Inst. Contemporary Art, U. Pa., 1979, New Mus., NY, 1979, Galerie Daniel Templon, Paris, 1980, Nat. Gallery Art, Washington, 1980, Indpls. Mus. Art, 1980, San Francisco Art Inst., 1980, Whitney Mus. Am. Art, NYC, 1981, Jacksonville Art Mus., 1981, Galeria Civica, Italy, 1982, Mus. Fine Arts, Boston, 1982, Fay Gold Gallery, Atlanta, 1982, High Mus. Art, 1983, Meml. Art Gallery, Rochester, NY, 1983, Kunstmuseum, Luzern, 1983, Robert Miller Gallery, 1978—79, 1981, 1984—85, 1988, Galerie Liatowitsch, Basel, Switzerland, 1978, Galerie Rudolf Zwirner, Cologne, Germany, 1979, Daniel Templon Gallery, NYC, 1980, Bruno Bischofberger Gallery, Zurich, 1980, James Mayor Gallery, London, 1981, Marcus Gallery, 1984, Inst. Contemporary Art, Phila., 1981, Akira Ikeda Gallery, Nagoya, Japan, 1981, Daniel Templon Gallery, Paris, 1982, 1987, 1991, McIntosh-Drysdale Gallery, Washington, 1983, Harcus Gallery, Boston, 1984, 1987, 1989, Delahunty Gallery, Dallas, 1984, Helander/Rubinstein Gallery, Palm Beach, Fla., 1985, 1989, Asher Faure Gallery, LA, 1985, Yares Gallery, Scottsdale, Ariz., 1987, Sidney Janis Gallery, NYC, 1990, Jason McCoy Gallery, 1994—95, Guild Hall, East Hampton, NY, 1995, Hirschl & Adler, NYC, 1995, Patricia Faure Gallery, LA, 1997, Santa Monica, Calif., 2003, Locks Gallery, Phila., 1997, 1999, Patricia Faure Gallery, LA, 2003, Spike Gallery, NYC, 2003, 2005, 2006, Locks Gallery, Verkstatte, NY, 2007. With U.S. Army, 1958-60. John Simon Guggenheim fellow, 1995. Studio: 119 N 11th St Brooklyn NY 11211-1163 Office Phone: 718-486-7735. Personal E-mail: robertraw@earthlink.net. E-mail: robert@zakanitch.com.

ZAKARIA, ASMA, neurologist; MD, Aga Khan U., Karachi, 2001. Diplomate neurology Am. Bd. Psychiatry and Neurology, 2008. Neurology resident Baylor Coll. Medicine, Houston, 2003—07; neurointensive care fellow Cleve. Clinic Found., 2007—09. Mem.: Neurocritical Care Soc., Soc. Critical Care Medicine, Am. Acad. Neurology. Islam. Home: 30 Severance Cir Apt 702 Cleveland Heights OH 44118

ZAKARIA, FAREED RAFIQ, editor, journalist; b. Mumbai, Jan. 20, 1964; s. Rafiq Ahmed and Fatma Rafiq Zakaria; m. Paula Henley Throckmorton, Apr. 5, 1997; children: Omar, Lila, Sofia. BA, Yale U.,

1986; PhD in Polit. Sci., Harvard U., 1993. Reporter, rschr. The New Republic, Washington, 1987; exec. coord. changing security environ. project Olin Inst., Harvard U., Cambridge, Mass., 1991-92; mng. editor Fgn. Affairs, NYC, 1993—2000; editor Newsweek Internat., 2000—. News analyst This Week with George Stephanopoulos, 2002—07; host Foreign Exchange with Fareed Zakaria, PBS, 2005—07; host Fareed Zakaria GPS CNN, 2008—. Author: The American Encounter: The United States and the Making of the Modern World Essays from 75 Years of Foreign Affairs, 1997, From Wealth to Power, 1998, The Future of Freedom: Illiberal Democracy at Home and Abroad, 2003, The Post-American World, 2008; co-editor (with James F. Hoge): The American Encounter: The United States and the Making of the Modern World: Essays from 75 Years of Foreign Affairs, 1997. Recipient Overseas Press Club award, 1998; named one of the 21 Most Important People of the 21st Century, Esquire mag.; MacArthur fellow, 1989—91, John M. Olin fellow, 1991—92. Mem.: Coun. Fgn. Rels. (bd. dirs.), Century Assn. Office: Newsweek International 251 W 57th St New York NY 10019-1894*

ZAKHEIM, DOV SOLOMON, economist, former federal agency administrator; b. Bklyn., Dec. 18, 1948; s. Zvi Hirsh and Bella (Rabinowitz) Zakheim; m. Barbara Jane Portnoi, Aug. 20, 1972 (div. 1990); children: Keith Samuel, Roger Israel, Scott Elisha; m. Deborah Bing Lowy, May 26, 1991. Student, London Sch. Econs., 1968—69; BA summa cum laude, Columbia U., N.Y.C., 1970; DPhil, Oxford U., Eng., 1974. Rsch. fellow St. Antony's Coll. Oxford U., 1974; asst. to mng. dir. U.K. br. Internat. Credit Bank Geneva, 1974-75; assoc. analyst Nat. Security and Internat. Affairs Congl. Budget Office, Washington, 1975-78, prin. analyst, 1978-81; spl. asst. to asst. sec. for internat. security policy US Dept. Def., Washington, 1981-82, spl. asst. to under sec., 1982-83, asst. under sec. for policy & resources), 1983-85, dep. under sec. for planning & resources, 1985-87; exec. v.p. Sys. Planning Corp., Arlington, Va., 1987-90, corp. v.p., 1990-2001; CEO SPC Int Inc, 1998—2001; under-sec. (comptr.) & CFO US Dept. Def., Washington, 2001—04; v.p. Booz Allen Hamilton, McLean, Va., 2004—. Cons. to sec. def. and undersec. def., 1987—2000, 2004—; adj. prof. Nat. Def. U., 1992, Columbia U., 1995—96, Yeshiva U., 1995—96; adj prof., presdl. fellow Trinity Coll., Conn., 1998; guest lectr. War Coll. Author: (book) Flight of the Lavi; contbr. articles to profl jours. Mem US Comn Preservation Am's Heritage Abroad, 1991—95; mem. bd. visitors Dept. Def. Overseas Regulatory Ctrs., 1998—2001; mem. Dept. Def. Bus. Bd., 2004—, Chief Naval Ops. Exec. Panel, 2004—; mem Secy Def Task Force Def Reform; mem bd deps Brit Jews, 1971—72; mem Chief Rabbi's Chaplaincy Bd, England, 1971—72, Commn. Wartime Contracting Iraq & Afghanisthan, 2008—; bd dirs Friends of Jewish Chapel, US Naval Acad, 1997—. Fellow, NSF, 1970—73, Kellet, Columbia Col, 1974. Mem.: Comn. Wartime Contracting, Royal Inst Int Affairs (UK), Int Inst Strategic Studies, Coun Foreign Relations, Cosmos Club, United Oxford and Cambridge Univ Club, Columbia Club, Phi Beta Kappa. Home: 817 Lamberton Dr Silver Spring MD 20902-3038 Office: Booz Allen Hamilton 8283 Greensboro Dr Mc Lean VA 22102 Office Phone: 703-902-7000. Business E-Mail: zakheim_dov@bah.com.

ZAKI, KAMAL EL-DIN MAHMOUD, veterinarian, educator; b. Atbara, Sudan, Oct. 3, 1927; arrived in Egypt, 1933; s. Mahmoud Zaki Ahmed and Monira Yousef Ibrahim; m. Hayat Abdel Hadi, May 8, 1952; children: Hani, Mahmoud, Hanaa, Maha. BVSc, Cairo U., Giza, 1950; Dr Med Vet, Vet. H.S., Hanover, Germany, 1959. Demonstrator ob/gyb. Faculty Vet. Medicine Cairo U., Giza, 1955-60, lectr., 1960-67, asst. prof., 1967-72, prof., 1972-78, vice dean, 1978, dean, 1978-82, head surgery & obstet. dept., 1986-88, prof. emeritus, 1988—, v.p. Khartoum, Sudan, 1982-86. Univ. advisor Cairo U., 1974-78; cons. Ministry Local Adminstrn., Cairo, 1959-66. Editor Vet. Medicine Jour., 1978-82. V.p. Egyptian Vet. Medicine Syndicate, 1978-82, Egyptian Vet. Medicine Assn., 1979-81. Recipient First Grade Sci. & Arts award Pres. Republic Egypt, 1983. Mem. Staf Mems. Club. Avocations: sports, camping, travel. Home: Galal El Dessouky St 3 Pyramids Giza 12111 Egypt Office: Cairo U Faculty Vet Medicine Giza 12211 Egypt Home Phone: 0020235685174; Office Phone: 002025720399. Personal E-mail: hanikamalhighcare-egypt@hotmail.com.

ZAKIAN, VIRGINIA ARAXIE, molecular biology professor; d. Aram and Charlotte Zakian; m. Robert N. Sandberg, 1973; children: Megan Sandberg-Zakian, Eric Sandberg-Zakian. BA, Cornell U., NY, 1970; PhD, Yale U., New Haven, 1975. Faculty Fred Hutchinson Cancer Rsch. Ctr., Seattle, 1979—95, asst. mem., 1979—83, assoc. mem., 1984—87, mem., 1987—95; prof., molecular biology Princeton U., NJ, 1995—, Harry Weiss prof., life scis., 1995—. Mem., nominating com. Genetics Soc. Am., 1983; co organizer Seattle Area Yeast Meetings, 1985—87; mem. Nat. Yeast Com., 1985—89; fellow Am. Acad., 1992—, Am. Acad. Microbiology, 1993—; cons. Geron Corp., 1993—97; mem., raymond w. sarber award selection com. Am. Soc. Microbiology, 1996—99; mem., resource bur. Women Cell Biology, Am. Soc. Cell Biology, 1997—; mem., bd. dirs. Genetics Soc. Am., 1997—99; mem., subcom., divsn. gen. & dev. bio Nat. Adv. Gen. Med. Scis. Coun., 1998; co-chair yeast sub group NIH Workshop Non-mammalian model organisms, 1999; mem., eli lilly & co. rsch. award selection com. Am. Soc. Microbiology, 2000—03; mem., awards com. Am. Soc. Cell Biology, 2001; chair, faculty task force Princeton U., 2001—03; mem., NIH, panel sci. boundaries, 2001; mem. Pres. Coun. Cornell Women, 2001—, Molecular Biology Study Group, Keystone Meetings, 2002—03; external reviewer, molecular cell & devel. biology dept. U. Colo., 2003; mem., target opportunity search com. Princeton U., 2003—09; rep., gender equity analysis Nine U., Princeton U., 2003—04; mem. Nat. Adv. Gen. Med. Scis. Coun., 2004—09; mem., electorate nominating com. AAAS Sect. Biol. Scis., 2004—07; mem., adv. panel, women sci. & engring. NY Acads. Scis., 2004; mem. Molecular Biology Study Group for Keystone Symposia, 2005—06; co-chair, minority opportunities rsch. programs NIH, 2005—06; sec. AAAS Sect. G, Biol. Scis., 2005; founding bd. mem. Rosalind Franklin Soc., 2007—; mem., adv. panel women sci. & engring.; co-chairperson Gordon Conf., Plasmid & Chromosome Dynamics, 1995—97; mem., program com. for 1986, 1987, and 1989 Yeast Genetics and Molecular Biology Meeting; mem. Am. Women in Sci.; mem., program com. Am. Soc. Cell Biology, 1980, 1981—83, mem., edn. com., 1986—89, mem., program com., 1995, coun. mem., 2009—; coun. standing com., tng. & faculty devel. NAGMS, Bethesda, 2007—; co-organizer AACR Telomerase & Cancer Meeting, 2007—, CSH Telomere Meetings, 2009—; mem. Faculty 1000 Biology, 2009—. Recipient Travel award, Ministry of Edn., Japan, 1993, Sr. Woman award, Am. Soc. Cell Biology, 1995, Disting. Lecture Series, NIEHS, 1997, June Wood Lecture, Ind. U., 1997, Blaffer Seminar, U. Tex. M.D. Anderson Cancer Ctr., 1997, Disting. Lecture award, Winship Cancer Ctr., Emory U., 1999, Lawrence Berkeley Nat. Lab., Life Scis. Divsn., 2003, Wall of Fame, Upper Darby Sr. HS, Pa., 2006; fellowship, NSF, 1970—73, Postdoc. fellowship, NIH, 1975—78, grant, 1979—, 1990—, 1993—95, Merit award, 1999—2009, grant, Am. Cancer Soc., Geron Corp., 1994—96. Mem.: Pres. Coun. Cornell Women, Cornell U., Rosalind Franklin Soc., Genetics Soc. Am., Assn. Women Sci., Am. Soc. Microbiology, Am. Soc. Cell Biology, Am. Acad. Advancement Sci. Liberal. Office: Princeton Univ Dept Molecular Bio Washington Rd LTL Princeton NJ 08544-1014

ZAKIM, DAVID, biochemist; b. Paterson, NJ, July 10, 1935; s. Sam and Ruth (Sorokin) Zakim; m. Nancy Jane Levine, June 12, 1957 (div. 1976); children: Michael, Eric, Thomas; m. Dagmar Aurelia Stanke, July 30, 1978; children: Tamara, Robert. AB in Chemistry, Cornell U., 1956; MD summa cum laude, SUNY, Bklyn., 1961. Diplomate Am Bd Internal Med. Intern N.Y. Hosp., NYC, 1961-62, asst. resident, 1962-63, fellow, 1963-65; asst. prof. to prof. medicine and pharmacology U. Calif., San Francisco, 1966-83; Vincent Astor Disting. prof. medicine Cornell U. Med. Coll., NYC, 1983-2000; prof. biochemistry Cornell U. Grad. Sch. Med. Sci., NYC, 1983-2000, prof. emeritus, 2000—; chief scientist, chmn. Zmedix Corp., San Francisco, 2000—08; dir. Inst. Digital Medicine Found., Stuttgart, Germany, 2008—. Editor: Hepatology: A Textbook of Liver Disease, 1982, 4th edit., 2002, Disorders of Acid Secretion, 1991, (series) Current Topics in Gastroenterology, 1985, Gastroenterology Medicine Today, 1992—95; contbr. articles to profl. jours. Capt US Army, 1965—68. Named Distinguished Alumnus, SUNY-Brooklyn, 1986. Mem.: Am. Soc. Clin. Investigation, Am. Soc. Biol. Chemists, Am. Assn. Physicians. Office: Inst Digital Medicine Found Stuttgart Germany Office Phone: 415-462-1759, 415-244-7672. Personal E-mail: dzakim@pacbell.net, david@zmedix.net. Business E-Mail: davidzakim@idm-foundation.org.

ZAKIN, JACQUES LOUIS, chemical engineering educator; b. NYC, Jan. 28, 1927; s. Mordecai and Ada Davies (Fishbein) Z.; m. Laura Pienkny, June 11, 1950; children: Richard Joseph, David Fredric, Barbara Ellen, Emily Anne, Susan Beth. BChemE, Cornell U., 1949; MChemE, Columbia U., 1950; DEng. Sci., NYU, 1959. Chem. engr. Flintkote Research Labs., Whippany, NJ, 1950-51; research technologist, research dept. Socony-Mobil, Bklyn., 1951-53, sr. research technologist, 1953-56, supervising technologist, 1959-62; assoc. prof. chem. engring. U. Mo., Rolla, 1962-65, prof., 1965-77, dir. minority engring. program, 1974-77, dir. women in engring. program, 1975-77; chmn. dept. chem. engring. Ohio State U., Columbus, 1977-94, Helen C. Kurtz prof. chem. engring., 1994-2000, Helen C. Kurtz prof. emeritus, 2000—. Chmn. sci. manpower and resources com. Coun. Chem. Rsch., 1984-86, governing bd., 1986-89; exec. com., 1988-89; adv. bd. State of Ohio Alternative Fuels, 1992-93; vis. prof. Technion, 1968-69, 94-95, Hebrew U., 1987; disting. vis. prof. Mex. Acad. Scis. and Mex.-USA Found. for Scis., 1999. Co-editor: Proc. Turbulence Symposium, 1969, 71, 73, 75, 77, 79, 81, 83; contbr. articles to profl. jours Bd. dirs. Rolla Cmty. Concert Assn., 1966-77, 2d v.p., 1975-77; bd. dirs. Ozark Mental Health Assn., 1976-77; trustee Ohio State Hillel Found., 1981-84, treas., 1984-89, pres., 1989-92; trustee Congregation Beth Tikvah, 1983; bd. trustees Columbus Jewish Fedn., 1989-92; co-chmn. Academics and Scientists for Soviet Refuseniks. With USNR, 1945-46. Recipient Outstanding Rsch. award U. Mo., 1970, U. Mo. Rolla Acad. Chem. Engrs., 2007, Josef Hlavka Meml. medal Czechoslovakian Acad. Sci., 1992, Clara M. and Peter L. Scott Faculty award, 1996, Rsch. award Japanese Govt., 2001; named Outstanding Educator of Yr., Ohio Soc. Profl. Engrs., 1994, Tech. Person of Yr., Columbus Tech. Coun., 1987; Am. Chem. Soc. Petroleum Rsch. Fund Internat. fellow, 1968-69, Socony-Mobil Employee Incentive fellow NYU, 1956-59, Sr. Fulbright Rsch. fellow Technion, 1994-95. Fellow Am. Inst. Chem. Engrs.; mem. Am. Chem. Soc., Soc. of Rheology, Am. Soc. Engring. Edn., Sigma Xi, Phi Lambda Upsilon, Phi Eta Sigma, Alpha Chi Sigma, Tau Beta Pi, Phi Kappa Phi. Jewish. Achievements include patents in field. Office: Ohio State U 140 W 19th Ave Columbus OH 43210-1110

ZALAVRAS, CHARALAMPOS, orthopedic surgeon; arrived in U.S., 2000; s. Georgios Zalavras and Maria Zalavra. Attended, Aristoteleion U. Med. Sch., Greece, 1991; PhD, U. Ioannina, Greece, 2000. Cert. orthop. surgeon Ministry of Health, Greece, European Union, physician's cert. of registration Med. Bd. Calif. Resident dept. orthop. surgery U. Ioannina, Ioannina, Greece, 1996—2000; from clin. rsch. fellow to assoc. prof. Dept. Orthop. Surgery U. So. Calif., LA, 2000—06, assoc. prof. Dept. Orthop. Surgery, 2006—. Recipient Best Scientific Work award, Balkan Congress Orthops., 1997, Best Resident, Fellow Paper award, Arthroscopy Assn. No. Am., 2002, Marshall Urist Young Investigator award, Assn. Bone and Joint Surgeons, 2003. Mem.: ACS, Musculoskeletal Infection Soc. N.Am. (v.p., Scholar award 2009), Hellenic Soc. for Reconstructive Microsurgery, Hellenic Soc. for Surgery of Hand, Hellenic Assn. Orthop. Surgery and Traumatology, European Soc. Sports Traumatology, Knee Surgery and Arthroscopy, Western Orthop. Assn. Office Fax: 323-226-4051. Business E-Mail: zalavras@usc.edu.

ZALAZNICK, LAUREN JANE, broadcast executive; b. Jan. 18, 1963; m. Phelim Dolan; 3 children. BA, Brown U., Providence, 1984. With MTV Networks, USA Cable; sr. v.p. original programming & devel. VH1; exec. v.p. network enterprises NBC Universal TV Networks, pres. Bravo Media, 2004—08, pres. Oxygen Media, 2007—08, pres. Women & Lifestyle Entertainment Networks, 2008—. Head green coun. NBC Universal TV Networks, 2008; bd. dirs. Peacock Equity, 2009—. Named a Maverick, Details mag., 2007, Woman to Watch, Advt. Age, 2008; named one of The 100 Most Powerful Women in Entertainment, Hollywood Reporter, 2006, 2007, 12 to Watch, TVWeek, 2008, The World's Most Influential People, TIME mag., 2009. Democrat. Jewish. Office: NBC Universal TV Group 30 Rockefeller Plz New York NY 10112 Office Phone: 212-664-4444. Office Fax: 212-664-3720.*

ZALD, DAVID H., cognitive neuroscientist; b. Nashville, Apr. 10, 1966; s. Mayer Nathan and Joan Khalila (Kadri) Z.; m. Mary Beth Early, Sept. 5, 1993; 1 child, Khalila Marie Early. BA, U. Mich., 1989; PhD in clin. psychology, U. Minn., 1997. Psychiatric interviewer, dept. family studies U. Minn., Mpls., 1991—94, tchg. asst., 1992—93, instr. psychology, 1994—96, 1999; intern in clin. neuropsychology Ann Arbor VA Med. Ctr./U. Mich. Hosp., 1995—96; rsch. fellow in neuroimaging U. Minn./Minn. VA Med. Ctr., Mpls., 1997—2000; asst. prof. psychology Vanderbilt U., Nashville, 2000—07, assoc. prof. psychology, 2007—, dir. undergraduate studies. Contbr. articles to profl. jours.; co-editor: The Orbitofrontal Cortex, 2006. Recipient Young Investigator award Am. Neuropsychiat. Assn., 1997, Nat. Rsch. Svc. award NIMH, 1997. Mem. APA, Assn. Chemoreceptor Sci. Avocation: music. Achievements include first neuroimaging studies of human amygdala activation during olfactory and gustatory stimulation; recognized expert on functions of human orbitofrontal cortex. Office: Vanderbilt U 301 David K Wilson Hall 2201 West End Ave Nashville TN 37240 also: Zald Lab 219 Wilson Hall 111 21st Ave S Nashville TN 37203 Office Phone: 615-343-6076, 615-322-2874, 614-343-1446. Office Fax: 615-343-8449. E-mail: david.zald@vanderbilt.edu.*

ZALDARRIAGA, MATIAS, cosmologist, physics professor; b. Buenos Aires, 1971; Degree in Phys. Sci., U. Buenos Aires, 1994; PhD., MIT, 1998. Keck vis. prof. Inst. Adv. Study, Princeton, NJ, 2001—02; asst. prof. NYU, 2001—02; assoc. prof. Dept. Physics, Harvard U., 2003, prof.; assoc. prof. Dept. Astronomy, Harvard U., 2003, prof. Contbr. scientific papers to sci. journals. Packard Fellow, David and Lucile Packard Found., 2001, MacArthur Fellow, John D. and Catherine T. MacArthur Found, 2006. Achievements include design of CMBFAST computer software tool for astronomy research. Office: Harvard-Smithsonian Center for Astrophysics 60 Garden St MS 51 Cambridge MA 02138 Office Phone: 617-384-9665. Office Fax: 617-495-7093.

ZALENSKI, AMY RALYNN, athletic trainer, small business owner; b. Wheeling, W.Va., May 29, 1978; d. Donald and Phyllis Marie Zalenski. BS in Edn., Ohio State U., Columbus, 2000; MA in Adult Edn., Muskingum Coll., Ohio, 2008. Cert. athletic trainer Nat. Athletic Trainers Assn., Tex., 2004; asst. athletic trainer Muskinguin Coll, New Concord, Ohio, 2008. Claims examiner Compensation Consultants, Inc., Dublin, Ohio, 2002—04; cert. athletic trainer Southeastern Ohio Regional Med. Ctr., Cambridge, 2004—; cert. athletic trainer and instr. Belmont Tech. Coll., St. Clairsville, 2005—. Ind. cons. Mary Kay Cosmetics, Wheeling, W.Va., 2003—; grad. asst. athletic trainer Muskingum Coll., 2007—08. Mem.: Nat. Strength & Conditiong Assn., Ohio Athletic Trainers Assn., Nat. Athletic Trainers Assn., Ohio Occupl. Therapy, Phys. Therapy and Athletic Trainers Bd. (licentiate). Roman Catholic. Avocations: travel, crafts, music. Home: 3118 Eoff St Wheeling WV 26003-4116 Office: SEa Ohio Regional Med Ctr 10095 Brick Church Rd Cambridge OH 43725 Personal E-mail: wrightbuckeyes@yahoo.com, oneohiostatefun@yahoo.com.

ZALENSKY, ANDREI O., biology professor, researcher; b. St. Petersburg, Russia, Sept. 14, 1945; s. Oleg V. Zalensky and Valentina M. Sveshnikova; m. Irina Zalenskaya; children: Anna Zalenskaya, Andrei Vinogradov. Cert. in biology Inst. Cytology, Russ Acad Sci, 1991. Assoc. prof. Ea. Va. Med. Sch., Norfolk, 2003—. Contbr. to numerous sci. publ. Grant, NIH, 1998—2008, USDA, 1998—2008. Home: 2941 Heutte Dr Norfolk VA 23518 Office: The Jones Inst for Reproductive Med 601 Colley Ave Norfolk VA 23507 Business E-Mail: zalensao@evms.edu.

ZALES, MARY CLARE, library director; Adminstr. state aid to pub. librs. Pa. Dept. Edn., Harrisburg, exec. asst. to dep. sec. librs., dep. sec. for librs. & commr. librs., 2004—. Mem.: Chief Officers of State Libr. Agencies. Office: Office of Commonwealth Librs 333 Market St Harrisburg PA 17126-1745 Office Phone: 717-787-2646. Office Fax: 717-772-3265. E-mail: mzales@state.pa.us.

ZALESKI, JAN FRANCISZEK, biochemist; b. Bytom, Poland, Feb. 3, 1949; came to U.S., 1979; s. Stanislaw and Maria (Fliska) Z.; m. Margaret M. Toczkowska, Dec. 28, 1971; children: Marta, Monika. MS in Biochemistry, U. Warsaw, Poland, 1971, PhD in Biochemistry, 1978. Rsch. assoc., asst. prof., assoc. prof. U. Warsaw Inst. Biochemistry, 1971-82; vis. scientist Roswell Park Meml. Inst., Buffalo, 1979-82; assoc. scientist Okla. Med. Rsch. Found., Oklahoma City, 1982-85; rsch. assoc. U. Pa. Med. Sch., Phila., 1985-88; vis. scientist Great Lakes Lab., Buffalo, 1988; rsch. assoc. prof. Rutgers U. Sch. Pharmacy, New Brunswick, NJ, 1989-97. Cons. J.A. Haley Vets. Hosp., Tampa, 1985, Great Lakes Lab., Buffalo, 1988, Wyeth-Ayerst Rsch., Princeton, 1994. Contbr. articles to profl. jours., chpts. to books. Mem. Am. Soc. Biochemistry and Molecular Biology. Avocations: antique and modern prints collecting, interior decorating, gardening, photography, basketball. Personal E-mail: jmzaleski@comcast.net.

ZALESKI-VEGAZO, ILENE, librarian; b. Worcester, Mass., Sept. 26, 1946; d. John Dominic and Emily Viola (Jarvais) Z. BS in Zoology cum laude, U. Mass., 1968; MLS, U. R.I., 1973. Biology tchr. Northampton (Mass.) Sch. for Girls, 1968-69; asst. circulation libr. U. R.I. Libr., Kingston, 1972-73, audiovisual cataloger computerized cataloging libr., 1973-75; asst. editor Deep Sea Rsch/Oceanographic Abstracts and Bibliography, Woods Hole, Mass., 1977; scientific book reviewer Small Press Rev., Vt., 1977-78; assoc. editor Oceanographic Lit. Rev., Woods Hole, 1978-83; cons. editor RP Record in Natural Resources and Environ. Mgmt., Woods Hole, 1983-84; sr. editor Woods Hole Data Base, 1983-84; asst. to dir. North Miami Pub. Libr., 1984—2002, dir., 2002—06. YMCA fitness instr., 2007-, Silver Sneakers instr., 2007-, ofcl. del. Gov.'s Conf. on Librs. and Info. Svcs., 1990; judge Benjamin Franklin Awards Competition, 1996-. Named Vol. of Yr. Learn to Read Vols. of Miami, 1989; Ilene Zaleski Day named in City of North Miami, 1991, 94, 2006; recipient Key to City of North Miami, 2006. Mem. ALA, Fla. Pub. Libr. Assn. (dir.-at large 1994—, sec. 1993, Libr. Employee of Yr. 1989-90), North Miami Woman's Club (pres. 1993-95, v.p. 1991-93, treas. 1989-91), Fla. Libr. Assn. (chair awards com. 2005-06), Dade County LIbr. Assn. (scholarship chair 2004-05), Assn. Fla. Laubach Orgns. (pres. 1990-91), Train Collectors Assn., Womans Club Deland (corr. sec. 2009-). Avocations: reading, bicycling, aerobics, travel, toy trains. Home Phone: 386-740-1293. Personal E-mail: izbabycar@aol.com.

ZALEWA, DONALD ANDREW, management consultant, educator; b. Chgo., May 30, 1950; s. Chester and Cecilia Geraldine (Stec) Z.; m. Judith Ellen Rossom, Sept. 14, 1986; children: Ryan, Austin. AA, Coll. of DuPage, Glen Ellen, Ill., 1970; BA, North Cen. Coll., Naperville, Ill., 1978; MBA, Keller Grad. Sch. Mgmt., Chgo., 1985. Pers. asst. Spraying Systems Co., Wheaton, Ill., 1978-79, pers. coord., 1979—86, adminstr. human resources, 1986—87; v.p. human resources Spraco, Nasuha, NH, 1987—88; v.p. adminstrn. Lechler, Inc., St. Charles, Ill., 1988—91; mng. dir. Austin Ryan Assocs. Mgmt. Cons. Svcs., Geneva, 1991—; mgr. human resources Apollo Colors Inc., Northbrook, Ill., 1989—90. Advisor bus. adv. coun. Delnore Hosp., 1987-91; mem. faculty Keller Grad. Sch. Mgmt., 1988-94, sr. faculty, 1994—; sr. cons. People Soft Inc., Westchester, Ill., 1997-2001; cons. in field., 1987-88. Mem. bus. adv. coun. Elgin Community Coll. Mem. Am. Mgmt. Assn., County Bus. Edn. (adv. com. 1995-1996), Carol Stream Personnel Assn. (v.p. 1979-80). Avocation: golf.

ZALEWSKI, MICHAEL R., alderman; b. Chgo. m. Millie Zalewski; children: Michael, Melinda. Ward supt. City of Chgo., 1984, divsn. supt., 1984—90, asst. commr., Bur. Sanitation, 1990—93, dep. commr., Bur. Sanitation, 1993—95; alderman, 23d ward Chgo. City Coun., 1995—. Chmn. Patriots Day Parade, Chgo., Pumpkin Day Parade, Chgo., Ward 23 Recycling Program. Recipient Vito Marzullo award, Richard Daley award; named Nat. Dem. Ethnic Am. Man of Yr., 1991. Mem.: Am. Pub. Works Assn., Midway Kiwanis. Democrat. Roman Catholic. Office: 6247 S Archer Ave Chicago IL 60638 also: City Hall 121 N La Salle St Rm 203 Office 6 Chicago IL 60602 Office Phone: 773-582-4444, 312-744-6828. Business E-Mail: mzalewski@cityofchicago.org.*

ZALEZNIK, ABRAHAM, psychoanalyst, management specialist, educator; b. Phila., Jan. 30, 1924; s. Isadore and Anna (Appelbaum) Z.; m. Elizabeth Ann Aron, June 24, 1945; children: Dori Faith, Ira Harry. AB in Econs., Alma Coll., 1945, DLitt (hon.), 1992; MBA, Harvard U., 1947, DCS, 1951; grad., Boston Psychoanalytic Soc. and Inst., 1965; D (hon.), U. Montreal, 1999; prof. (hon.), Haute Etude Commercial, France, 2001. Research asst. Harvard U. Grad. Sch. Bus. Adminstrn., 1947-48, instr., 1948-51, asst. prof., 1951-56, assoc. prof., 1956-61, prof., 1961—, Cahners-Rabb prof. social psychology of mgmt., 1967-83, Konosuke Matsushita prof. leadership, 1983-90, Konosuke Matsushita prof. leadership emeritus, 1990—; research fellow Boston

Psychoanalytic Soc. and Inst., 1965-68, mem. faculty, 1972—; pvt. practice psychoanalysis Boston, 1968—. Cons. in field. Author: Human Dilemmas of Leadership, 1966, (with Manfred F.R. Kets de Vries) Power and the Corporate Mind, 1975, The Managerial Mystique, 1989, An Executive Guide to Motivating People, 1990, Learning Leadership, 1992; contbr. articles to profl. jours. Bd. overseers Beth Israel Hosp., Boston, 1968—. With USN, 1942-46. Mem. Boston Psychoanalytic Soc., Am. Psychoanalytic Assn. (cert.), Am. Sociol. Assn., Tavern Club (Boston), Belmont Country Club (Mass.). Home: 170 N Ocean Blvd Palm Beach FL 33480-3946 Office: Harvard University Business School Boston MA 02163 Home Phone: 561-832-5270; Office Phone: 617-495-6285. E-mail: azaleznik@hbs.edu.

ZALK, DAVID MARK, industrial hygienist, EHS manager occupational health researcher; b. Boston, Sept. 21, 1964; s. Bertram Marcus and Sophia Abrams Zalk; m. Janice Kirsh; children: Joshua Aaron, Jacob Benjamin, Jesse Hirsh. BA in Environ. Studies, U. Calif., Santa Barbara, 1987, BA in Chemistry, 1987; MPH in Indsl. Hygiene, U. Calif., Berkeley, 1994; PhD student, Delft U. Tech., Netherlands, 2006—. Cert. indsl. hygienist Am. Bd. of Indsl. Hygiene. Br. mgr. P.W. Stephens Environ., Health & Safety, Santa Clara, Calif., 1988—90; indsl. hygienist U. Calif., Lawrence Livermore Nat. Lab., 1993—. Co-chair, task force 10 preventive techs. Collaborating Centres on Occupl. Health WHO, Geneva, 2001—06, expert indsl. hygiene, 2005—; US rep. Internat. Control Banding Working Group, 2002—; co-chair US Nat. Control Banding Workshop, Washington, 2003—04, 2004—05, 2d Internat. Control Banding Workshop, Cin., 2003—04; chair 3d Internat. Control Banding Workshop, Johannesburg, 2004—05, 4th Internat. Control Banding Workshop, Seoul, Republic of Korea, 2007—08, 5th Internat. Control Banding Workshop, Cape Town, South Africa, 2008—09; v.p. Found. for Occupl. Health and Safety, Cin., 2006—. Co-author: Control Banding; A Literature Review and Critical Analysis, Guidance for Conduction Control Banding Analyses; dir.: (tng. video) The Adventures of Ergoman; contbr. articles to profl. jours. Classroom vol. Schallenberger Elem., San Jose, Calif., 2000—05. Recipient award of distinction, U. Calif. Santa Barbara, 1987, John J. Bloomfield award, Am. Conf. Govtl. Indsl. Hygienists, 1996, award of excellence, Nat. Nuc. Security Adminstrn., 2003; named Jeff Lee lectr., Found. for Occupl. Health and Safety, 2003; U.C. Berkeley scholar, Pub. Health Alumni, 1993. Mem.: Internat. Occupl. Hygiene Assn. (bd. dirs. 1999—2005, pres. 2002—03, envoy 2005—), Internat. Ergonomics Assn. (corr.; Internat. Occupl. Hygiene Assn. liaison 2001—05), Am. Indsl. Hygiene Assn. (assoc.; internat. affairs com. liaison 1999—2005), Am. Conf. Govtl. Indsl. Hygienists (assoc.; task force chair 1996—97, chair internat. com. 1998—2006, mem. internat. com. 2006—), Brit. Occupl. Hygiene Assn. (assoc.), Internat. Congress Occupl. Health (assoc.; Internat. Occupl. Hygiene Assn. liason 2002—05). Jewish. Achievements include research in nanomaterial sciences, metals analysis and detection methods relating to explosive events; patents for ergonomic material-handling device; patents pending for particle glue, airborne small-particle binder and reaerosolization inhibitor; creator and expert of post-detonation sciences. Avocation: soccer. Office: Lawrence Livermore Nat Lab 7000 East Ave L 871 Livermore CA 94550 Business E-Mail: zalk1@llnl.gov.

ZALK, ROBERT H., retired lawyer; b. Albert Lea, Minn., Dec. 1, 1944; s. Donald B. and Juliette J. (Erickson) Z.; m. Ann Lee Anderson, June 21, 1969; children: Amy, Jenna. BA, Carleton Coll., 1966; JD, U. Minn., 1969. Bar: Minn. 1969, U.S. Dist. Ct. Minn. 1969. Assoc. Popham, Haik, Schnobrich, Kaufman & Doty, Mpls., 1969-72; atty. No. States Power Co., Mpls., 1972-73, Wright, West & Diessner, Mpls., 1973-84, Fredrikson & Byron P.A., Mpls., 1984-94, Zalk & Assocs., Mpls., 1994-95; ptnr. Zalk & Eayrs, Mpls., 1995-98, Zalk & Wood, Mpls., 1999, Zalk & Bryant, Mpls., 2000—06, ret., 2006. Fellow Am. Acad. Matrimonial Lawyers (bd. govs. 2004-06, pres. Minn. chpt. 2000-01), Minn. Bar Assn. (co-chmn. maintenance guideline com. 1991-94), Hennepin County Bar Assn. (co-chmn. family law sect. 1990-91). Personal E-mail: rzalk@comcast.net.

ZALL, PAUL MAXWELL, language educator, consultant; m. Elisabeth Weisz, June 21, 1948; children: Jonathan, Barnaby, Andrew. BA, Swarthmore Coll., 1948; AM, Harvard U., 1950, PhD, 1951. Teaching fellow Harvard U., 1950-51; instr. Cornell U., 1951-55, U. Oreg., 1955-56; research editor Boeing Co., 1956-57; asst. prof. Calif. State Coll., Los Angeles, 1957-61, asso. prof., 1961-64, prof. English, 1964-86; research scholar, cons. to library docents Huntington Library, San Marino, Calif., 1986-96; acting chmn. dept. Calif. State Coll., 1969-71. Cons. in report writing, proposal preparation and brochures to industry and govt. agys., 1957-99. Author: Elements of Technical Report Writing, 1962, Hundred Merry Tales, 1963, Nest of Ninnies, 1970, Weakly Blast, 1960-85, Literary Criticism of William Wordsworth, 1966, (with John Durham) Plain Style, 1967, Simple Cobler of Aggawam in America, 1969; (with J.R. Trevor) Proverb to Poem, 1970, Selected Satires of Peter Pindar, 1971, Comical Spirit of Seventy Six, 1976, (with Leonard Franco) Practical Writing, 1978, Ben Franklin Laughing, 1980; (with J.A.L. Lemay) Autobiography of Benjamin Franklin, 1981; Norton Critical Edition of Franklin's Autobiography, 1986, Abe Lincoln Laughing, 1983, 95; (with E. Birdsall) Descriptive Sketches, 1984, Mark Twain Laughing, 1985, Being Here, 1987, George Washington Laughing, 1989, Franklin's Autobiography: Model Life, 1989, Founding Mothers, 1991, Becoming American, 1993, 98, Lincoln's Legacy, 1994, Wit and Wisdom of the Founding Fathers, 1996, Blue and Gray Laughing, 1996, Lincoln on Lincoln, 1999, 2003, Dolley Madison, 2001, Franklin on Franklin, 2001, Jefferson on Jefferson, 2002, Washington on Washington, 2003, Adams on Adams, 2004, Benjamin Franklin's Humor, 2005, Lincoln's Legacy of Laughter, 2007. Pres. Friends of South Pasadena Library, 1967-70. Served with USAAF, 1942-45, ETO. Recipient Outstanding Prof. award, 1965; grantee, John Carter Brown Libr., Huntington Libr., 1993; fellow, Am. Philos. Soc., 1964, 1966, Huntington Libr., 1993. Home: 2040 Amherst Dr South Pasadena CA 91030-3906 Office: Huntington Libr San Marino CA 91108 Fax: 626-449-5720. E-mail: pzall9@hotmail.com.

ZALL, ROBERT ROUBEN, food scientist, educator; b. Lowell, Mass., Dec. 6, 1925; s. Samuel and Sarah (Cohen) Z.; m. Mollie Leah Wiseblood, June 8, 1949; children— Linda Zall Sheffield, Judy Zall Kusek, Jonathan J. BS, U. Mass., 1949, MS, 1950; PhD, Cornell U., 1968. Gen. mgr. Grandview Dairies, Bklyn. and Arkport, N.Y., 1950-66; dairy industry cons. Ithaca, N.Y., 1966-68; dir. research prodn. Crowley Foods Co., Binghamton, N.Y., 1968-71; prof. food sci. Cornell U., 1971-92; prof. emeritus, 1992—. Past trustee Milk Industry Pension and Welfare Fund; dairy industry cons., project dir. EPA-Industry demonstration whey processing plant. Author: (with Bela G. Liptak) Environmental Engineers Handbook, 1972, Managing Food Industry Waste: Common Sense Methods for Food Processors, 2004; co-contbr. to Food Processing Waste Management, 1979, Food Processing, 15 vols., 1979, Dairy Microbiology, 1981, rev. edit., 1990; contbr. numerous articles to profl. jours., popular mags.; patentee automatic cleaning apparatus, stabilization of milk and improved cheese yield, Rennin-like enzymes from clams, a process for preserving fish and microbial production of acetaldeyde. Served with AUS, 1944-46. Recipient Cert. Appreciation EPA, 1975, 79; Howard B. Marlott award N.Y. State Milk and Food Sanitarians Mem. Internat. Assn. Milk, Food and Environ. Sanitarians, Internat. Dairy Fedn., Inst. Food Technologists, Am. Soc. Agrl. Engrs., Masons, Phi Kappa Phi. Office: Cornell U Dept Food Sci Stocking Hall Ithaca NY 14853-7201 *Most people I know, never made a success of themselves by just working forty hours a week. It takes hard work, the love of a good wife, and the willingness to accept challenges.*

ZALLEN, HAROLD, academic administrator, chemist; b. Boston, Apr. 7, 1926; s. Joseph and Lillian L. (Stahl) Z.; m. Eugenia Malone, Aug. 23, 1959. BS in Pharmacy, Northeastern U., Boston, 1951; EdM in Sci. and Math., Boston U., 1954; MS in Organic Synthetic Medicinal Chemistry and Biochemistry, Purdue U., West Lafayette, Ind., 1959; PhD in Analytical Medicinal Chemistry and Nucleonics, Purdue U., 1960. Registered pharmacist, Mass., Ind. With USAAF, 1943-46, combat flier, sgt. 487th bomb group H, 839th bomb squadron; commd. 1st lt. U.S. Army, 1955, advanced through grades to col., 1986; ret.; mgr. Shoppers World Pharmacy, Inc., Framingham, Mass., 1951-53; asst. prof. phys. sci. Portia Law Sch. Calvin Coolidge Coll., Boston, 1952-54; tchr. physics and chemistry Natick (Mass.) High Sch., 1955-56; asst. prof. microbiology Lowell Gen. Hosp. Sch. Nursing, Mass., 1955-56; grad. instr., asst. radiol. control officer Purdue U., West Lafayette, Ind., 1957-58; assoc. prof. chemistry Coll. Pharmacy Mercer U., Atlanta, 1960-61; assoc. prof. to prof., head dept. radiol. scis., dir. Office Radiol. Safety Auburn U., Ala., 1961-66; specialist phys. sci. rsch. div. higher edn. rsch. Bur. Rsch., U.S. Office Edn., 1966-67, head curriculum higher edn. rsch., 1967; head instructional sci. equipment program, assoc. program dir., then dir. spl. projects program NSF, Washington, 1967-72; asst. dean, dir. rsch. and grad. studies Okla. State U., Stillwater, 1972-73, prof. chemistry, 1972-73, rsch. prof. biochemistry and molecular biology, 1973-75; assoc. v.p. for adminstrn. and fin., CEO Health Scis. Ctr. Campus U. Okla., Oklahoma City and Tulsa, 1973-75, assoc. v.p. for systems planning, procedure devel. and spl. projects, cen. adminstrn. Norman, 1975—; exec. v.p. Acad. World Inc., 1975—; pres., CEO Malone, Zallen & Assocs. div. AcaWorld Corp., Greenville, NC; v.p., dir. nuclear divsn. Vachon, Nix & Assocs., Atlanta; pres., CEO Computer Profls. Inc., Computer Distbrs. Corp., Malone Group Internat., Columbus, Ga.; sci. advisor Litton Corp./Army Rsch. Inst., 1991, Omega Tng. Group Inc./GIAT Industries, France, 1992—, Wetzel Internat., Inc., 1994—; chmn. bd. dirs. Cons. Unltd., Columbus, Ga.; rsch. dir., joint project Malone Group Internat. and Auburn U. Analytical chemist Communicable Diseases Ctr. USPHS, Atlanta, 1962; spl. lectr. NSF Radiobiology Inst., Tuskegee U., 1963-64, head instrnl. sci. equipment program, assoc. program dir., dir. spl. projects program, 1967-72; pres. Pres.'s Sci. and Technol. Adv. Commn., Washington; v.p. Okla. Coll. Osteo. Medicine and Surgery, Tulsa; Gov. NC primary alt. to So. States Energy Bd., 1984-90, exec. com. bd., 1986; bd. vis. Tex. Christian U., Ft. Worth, 1973-76, bd. visitors, Dartmouth Coll., 1973-74; leadership coun. Coll. Sci. and Math. Auburn U., 2003—; cons. in field; rsch. dir., joint project Auburn U. COB Aviation Mgmt.-CLA STET Audiology Divsn-COSAM Math. & Stats.-Auburn-Opelika Robert G. Pitts Airport & Malone Group Internat., Head Tilt Variations Vestibular Function Measured By Flight Simulation. Editor, pub. Jour. Internat 6800 Computer Ctr.; contbr. articles to profl. jours. Hon. chmn. bus. adv. coun., Ala., 2003; rep. candidate NC Gen. Assembly, 1986; mem. nat. rep. congl. com. Recipient Mayoralty cert. of merit and Key to City, City of New Orleans, 1973, Most Outstanding Alumni award Northeastern U., 1996, Comdg. Gen. award U.S. Army Inf. Ctr., 1998; GE sci. fellow Union U., Schenectady, NY, 1955, fellow Purdue Rsch. Found., 1958, Elks Cancer Soc., 1959, Am. Cancer Soc., 1960; named Disting. Vis. Rsch. Prof., Dept. Aerospace Engrng., 2009. Mem. Am. Chem. Soc. (bd. dirs., chmn. Auburn sect. 1966), Am. Soc. Engring. Edn. (long range planning com.), Nat. Coun. Univ. Adminstrs., Soc. Rsch. Adminstrs. (pres. So. sect. from 1974, chmn. publs. com.), Health Physics Soc., Greenville (NC) Area C. of C. (chmn. rsch.), Columbus Club, Rotary (chmn. bull. com. Auburn 1963, bd. dirs. Auburn 1964, bd. dirs. Stillwater 1972-73, Greenville 1981-86, charter pres. Greenville, N.C. Morning Club 1986, 91, 94, Paul Harris fellow, (4) R.I. Svc. Above Self award 1986), Masons (32 degree), Shriners, Sigma Xi, Phi Lambda Upsilon, Rho Chi, Phi Delta Kappa, Delta Sigma Theta, Beta Phi (past nat. sec.) Baptist. Office: Malone Group International PO Box 3682 Auburn AL 36831-3682 Office Phone: 334-887-2085. Personal E-mail: zallen1780@hotmail.com.

ZALLER, JOHN RAYMOND, political science professor; BA in History, U. Calif., San Diego, 1971; MA in Polit. Sci., U. Calif., Berkeley, 1976, PhD in Polit. Sci., 1984. Reporter Orange Coast Daily Pilot, 1972—74; asst. prof., dept. politics Princeton U., NJ, 1984—86; prof., dept. polit. sci. UCLA, 1986—. Author: The American Ethos: Public Attitudes Toward Capitalism and Democracy, 1984, The Nature and Origins of Mass Opinion, 1992 (APSA award, 1994, Warren Miller prize, 2000, Doris Graber prize, 2001, Book prize, Am. Assn. Pub. Opinion Rsch., 2002); co-author (with M. Cohen, D. Karol, H. Noel): The Party Decides: Presidential Nominations Before and After Reform, 2008; mem. editl. bd.: Pub. Opinion Quar., Polit. Behavior, Jour. Politics, Am. Polit. Sci. Rev., assoc. editor:, 2007—; contbr. articles to profl. jours., chapters to books. Grantee, NSF, 1992—95, Social Sci. Rsch. Coun.; Regents fellow, U. Calif. Berkeley, 1982—83, Guggenheim fellow, 1992—93, fellow, Ctr. Advanced Study in the Behavioral Sciences, 1993—94. Fellow: Am. Acad. Arts and Scis. Office: UCLA Dept Polit Sci 4289 Bunche Hall Box 951472 Los Angeles CA 90095-1472 Office Phone: 310-825-7527. Office Fax: 310-825-0778. Business E-Mail: zaller@ucla.edu.*

ZALOSH, ROBERT GEOFFREY, engineering educator; b. NYC, Oct. 10, 1944; s. Ralph and Rena (Romoff) Z.; m. Gloria Anne Katz, Dec. 25, 1965; children: Michael, Matthew. BE, The Cooper Union, NYC, 1965; MS, U. Rochester, 1966; PhD, Northeastern U., Boston, 1970. Sr. rsch. scientist Mt. Auburn Rsch. Assocs., Cambridge, Mass., 1970-75; mgr., exlosion rsch. sect., mgr. applied rsch. dept. Mut. Rsch. Corp., Norwood, Mass., 1975-90; prof. fire protection engrng. Worcester (Mass.) Polytechnic Inst., 1990—. Cons. various orgsn., 1990—; mem. hydrogen tech. adv. panel Dept. of Energy, Washington, 1992-99; fire safety coun. Underwriters Labs., Northbrook, Ill., 1998—. Mem. NFPA (mem. explosion protection com. 1980—), Soc. of Fire Protection Engrng., Am. Soc. Mech. Engrs., Am. Inst. Chem. Engrs., Internat. Assn. Fire Safety Sci. Home: 20 Rockland St Wellesley MA 02481-4902 Office: Worcester Polytechnic Inst 100 Institute Rd Worcester MA 01609-2247

ZALTA, EDWARD, otolaryngologist, physician; b. Houston, Mar. 2, 1930; s. Nouri Louis and Marie Zahde (Lizmi) Zalta; m. Carolyn Mary Gordon, Oct. 8, 1971; 1 child, Ryan David;children from previous marriage: Nouri Allan, Lori Ann, Barry Thomas, Marci Louise. BS, Tulane U., 1952, MD, 1956. Diplomate Am. Bd. Quality Assurance and Utilization Rev. Physicians. Intern Brooke Army Hosp., San Antonio, 1956—57; resident otolaryngology U.S. Army Hosp., Ft. Campbell, Ky., 1957—60; practice medicine specializing in otolaryngology Glendora, West Covina and San Dimas, Calif., 1960—82. ENT cons. City of Hope Med. Ctr., 1961—76; mem. staff Foothill Presbyn.; past pres. L.A. Found. Cmty. Svc., L.A. Poison Info. Ctr., So. Calif. Physicians Coun., Inc.; founder, chmn. bd. dirs., CEO Health Solutions Internat.; founder, chmn. bd. dirs. CAPP CARE, Inc.; founder Inter-Hosp. Coun. Continuing Med. Edn.; trustee U.S. Pharmacopeial Conv., Inc.; mem. adv. bd. Global Health Sys., Inc. Author (with others): Medicine and Your Money; mem. editl. staff Jour. Assn. Managed Healthcare Orgns., Managed Care Interface, Mng. Employee Health Benefits, mem. editl. adv. bd. Inside Medicaid Managed Care, Disease Mgmt. News, Managed Care Outlook; contbr. articles to profl. jours. Pres. bd. govs. Glendora Unified Sch. Dist., 1965—71; mem. Calif. Cancer Adv. Coun., 1967—71, Commn. Californias, Los Angeles County Commn. Economy and Efficiency. Served to capt. Med. Corps US Army, 1957—60. Recipient award of Merit, Order St. Lazarus, 1981. Mem.: AMA, Los Angeles County Med. Assn., Am. Coll. Med. Quality, Am. Assn. Preferred Provider Orgns., Am. Coun. Otolaryngology, Am. Acad. Otolaryngology, Calif. Med. Assn., Pacific Golf Club (San Juan Capistrano), Glendora Country Club, Ctr. Club (Costa Mesa, Calif.), Sea Bluff Beach and Racquet Club, Centurion Club, Phi Delta Epsilon, Kappa Nu. Republican. Jewish. Home: 3 Morning Dove Laguna Niguel CA 92677 Office: Ste 1123 27136 B Paseo Espada San Juan Capistrano CA 92675 Office Phone: 949-292-1951. Personal E-mail: edzata@cox.net.

ZALUPS, RUDOLFS KARLIS, medical educator, director; b. Markdale, Ont., Can., Nov. 17, 1953; s. Rudolfs Zalups and Valerija Munds. PhD, U. Western Ont., London, 1981. Postdoc. rsch. fellow Yale U. Sch. Medicine, New Haven, Mayo Clinic, Rochester, Minn., 1982; instr. U. Rochester Sch. Medicine, NY, 1984—85; asst. prof. Mercer U. Sch. Medicine, Macon, Ga., 1988—90, assoc. prof., 1990—92, prof., 1993—, assoc. dir., rsch., 2008—. Editor: (book) Methods in Renal Toxicology, Molecular Biology and Toxicology of Metals, Cellular and Molecular Biology of Metals. Recipient C.P. LeBlond Rsch. Presentation award, Can. Assn. Anatomist, 1982, Rsch. award, Mercer U., 1996; Rsch. fellowship, U. Rochester Sch. Medicine, 1984—85. Mem.: Am. Soc. Pharmacology and Exptl. Therapeutics, Soc. Toxicology, Am. Physiol. Soc. Achievements include discovery of membrane transport proteins in cellular uptake of mercury and cadmium; reduced kidney mass on susceptibility of remaining functional renal tissue; genetic mouse-model of glomerulosclerosis and reduced renal mass. Avocation: fishing. Office: Mercer Univ Sch Medicine 1550 College St Macon GA 31207 Business E-Mail: zalups_rk@mercer.edu.

ZALUTSKY, MORTON HERMAN, lawyer; b. Schenectady, Mar. 8, 1935; s. Albert and Gertrude (Daffner) Z.; m. Audrey Englebardt, June 16, 1957; children: Jane, Diane, Samuel BA, Yale U., 1957; JD, U. Chgo., 1960. Bar: Oreg. 1961. Law clk. to presiding judge Oreg. Supreme Ct., 1960-61; assoc. Hart, Davidson, Veazie & Hanlon, 1961-63, Veatch & Lovett, 1963-64, Morrison, Bailey, Dunn, Cohen & Miller, 1964-69; prin. Morton H. Zalutsky, P.C., 1970-76; ptnr. Dahl, Zalutsky, Nichols & Hinson, 1977-79, Zalutsky & Klarquist, P.C., Portland, Oreg., 1980-85, Zalutsky, Klarquist & Johnson, Inc., Portland, 1985-94; Zalutsky & Klarquist, P.C., Portland, 1994—. Instr. Portland State U., 1961-64, Northwestern Sch. of Law, 1969-70; assoc. prof. U. Miami Law Sch.; lectr. Practising Law Inst., 1971—, Oreg. State Bar Continuing Legal Edn. Program, 1970, Am. Law Inst.-ABA Continuing Legal Edn. Program, 1973—, 34th, 37th NYU ann. insts. fed. taxation, So. Fed. Tax Inst., U. Miami Inst. Estate Planning, Southwestern Legal Found., Internat. Foun. Employee Benefit Plans, others; dir. A-E-F-C Pension Plan, 1994-99, chmn., 1989-99. Author: (with others) The Professional Corporation in Oregon, 1970, 82; contbg. author: The Dentist and the Law, 3d edit.; editor-in-chief: Matthew Bender's Federal Tax Service, 1987-90; contbr. articles to profl. jours. Mem. vis. com. U. Chgo. Law Sch., 1986-88. Mem. ABA (vice chair profl. svcs. 1987-89, mem. coun. tax sect. 1985-87, spl. coord. 1980-85), Am. Law Inst., Am. Bar Retirement Assn. (trustee, bd. dirs., vice chair 1990-91, chair 1991-92), Am. Coll. Employee Benefits Coun. (charter mem.), Am. Coll. Tax Coun. (charter mem.), Multnomah County Bar Assn., Am. Tax Lawyers (charter mem.), Oreg. Estate Planning Coun. Jewish. Home: 3118 SW Fairmount Blvd Portland OR 97201-1466 Office: 215 SW Washington St Fl 3 Portland OR 97204-2636 Office Phone: 503-248-0300. E-mail: mort@erisalaw.com.

ZAMAN, KAHKASHAN T., psychologist; d. Manzer M. and Nayara P. Sulaiman; m. Syd K. Zaman, Sept. 11, 1985; children: Asif S., Meher N. MA in Clin. Psychology, Aligarh Muslim U., India, 1985; MA in Sch. Psychology, City Coll., Convent Ave., 1991, MS in Edn., 1991. Psychologist ll Bernard Fienson Devel. Ctr., NYC, 1990—91; sch. psychologist Dept. Edn., NYC, 1991—. Home: 16 Crescent Rd Great Neck NY 11021 Office: Dept Edn 985 Rockway Ave Great Neck NY 11021 Business E-Mail: kzaman@schools.nyc.gov.

ZAMAN, MUSHARRAF, civil engineering educator; b. Rajshahi, Bangladesh, Mar. 8, 1952; came to U.S., 1979; s. Md. Gias Uddin and Jahanara Begum; m. Afroza Khanam, Aug. 7, 1981; children: Jessica, Ashiq. MSCE, Carleton U., Can., 1979; PhDCE, U. Ariz., Tucson, 1982. Registered profl. engr., Okla. Lectr. civil engrng. U. Engring. and Tech., Dhaka, Bangladesh, 1975-76; rsch. assoc. Asian Inst. Tech., Bangkok, 1976-77; grad. tchg. asst. Carleton U., Ottawa, Can., 1977-79; rsch. asst. Va. Tech., Blacksburg, 1979-81; rsch. assoc. U. Ariz., Tucson, 1981-82; asst. prof. U. Okla., Norman, 1982-88, assoc. prof., 1988-93, prof., 1993—, David Ross Boyd prof., Aaron Alexander prof., 2003—, assoc. dean for rsch. Coll. Engrng., 2005—. Faculty advisor Bangladesh Student Assn., U. Okla., Norman, 1983—, Muslim Student Assn., 1990—; summer faculty fellow Argonne (Ill.) Nat. Lab., 1986; v.p. geotech. Consortium Internat., Oklahoma City, 1992-94; co-organizer U.S.-Can. Geomechanics Workshop, 1992. Co-editor Internat. Jour. Geomechanics; assoc. editor Jour. Petroleum Sci. and Engring.; contbr. articles to European Jour. Mechanics, Computer Methods in Applied Mechanics and Engring., Internat. Jour. Numerical Analytical Met. Geomech., Internat. Jour. Petroleum Sci. and Engring., Applied Math. Modelling, ASME Jour. Applied Mechanics, ASME Jour. Energy Resources Tech., Jour. Geotech. Engring. divsn. ASCE, Jour. Engring. Mechanics divsn. ASCE, Jour. Transp. Engring. divsn. ASCE, Arabian Jour. Sci. and Engring., Transp. Rsch. Record, Internat. Jour. Geomechanics, pavement Engring. Jour. Recipient David Ross Boyd Professorship, 2003—. Mem. ASCE (mem. deep found. com. 1987-96), Internat. Assn. Computer Methods and Advances in Geomechanics (co-chmn. internat. conf. 1992-94, co-editor newsletter 1989—, mem. internat. adv. com. 11th conf., bd. dirs. 2003—), Am. Rock Mechanics Assn. (founding mem.). Home: 3213 Riverwalk Dr Norman OK 73072 Office: U Okla 202 W Boyd St Rm 334 Norman OK 73019-1027 Office Phone: 405-325-2626.

ZAMARIN, RONALD GEORGE, lawyer; b. NYC, May 2, 1946; s. Leonard Leon and Laura Aileen (Gargus) Z.; m. Kathleen Veronica Durkin, July 20, 1968; children: Ryan, Chad, Jennifer. BA, UCLA, 1969, JD, 1972. Bar: Ill. 1972, U.S. Ct. Appeals (7th cir.) 1972, Fed. Trial Bar. Assoc. Isham, Lincoln & Beale, Chgo., 1972-79, ptnr., 1980-88; pvt. practice Des Plaines, Ill., 1988—2003, Palatine, Ill., 2003—. Coop. atty. ACLU, Chgo., 1982—; litigating mem. Lawyers Com. for Civil Rights under Law, Chgo., 1974-78. Co-author: Media Law Handbook, 1982. Trustee, treas. Palatine Pub. Libr. Dist. (Ill.), 1980-89; co-chair Citizens Com. for the Palatine Libr., 1990-95,

Citizens Com. for the Palatine Park Dist., 1994—; co-founder Palatine Pub. Libr. Found.; mem. Palatine Adv. Bd., 1978-79; mem. bd. commrs. Palatine Boys' Baseball, 1983-98, sec., 1986-98. Mem.: ABA (forum on comm. law), First Amendment Lawyers Assn. Office: Suite 700 800 E Northwest Hwy Palatine IL 60074 Home: 486 Banyan Tree Ln Buffalo Grove IL 60089 Office Phone: 847-705-3895. Personal E-mail: rgzlaw@comcast.net.

ZAMBELLI, ANGELO, lawyer; b. Milan, Oct. 27, 1962; s. Alessandro Cristoforo and Gabriella (Gramiccia) Z. JD magna cum laude, U. Milan, 1987. Bar: Milan 1992, Supreme Ct. 2004. Assoc. Toffoletto & Assocs., Milan, 1989—94, ptnr., 1995—98, Croze, Radice & Zambelli Studio Legale, 1998—99, Carnelutti Law Firm, Milan, 2000—03, McDermott WIll & Emery/Carnelotti Law Firm, 2003—05; mng. ptnr. LabLaw Studio Legale Failla Rotondi & Zambelli, 2005—08; ptnr. Dewey & LeBoeuf, 2009—. Asst. prof. U. MIlan, 1987—; freelance prof. U. Castellanza, 1995-97, apptd. cons. labor min. Romania EEC. Author: La Disciplina del Licenziamenti, 3d edit., 1995, Dieci Temi di Diritto Del Lavoro, 1996, Guida Pratica Diritto Sindacale, 3d edit., 2007, Guida Pratica Licenziamenti e Sanzioni Disciplinari, 2d edit., 2006, Codice Del Processo Del Lavoro, 1st edit., 2008; contbr. articles to profl. jours. Lt. Italian mil., 1987-88. Mem. Am. C. of C. Avocations: skiing, sailing, books, motor biking, golf. Office: Dewey and LeBoeuf Via F Ili Gabba 4 20121 Milan Italy Office Phone: 39 02 30 30 93 90. Business E-Mail: azambelli@dl.com.

ZAMBIE, ALLAN JOHN, retired lawyer; b. Cleve., June 9, 1935; s. Anton J. and Martha (Adamski) Z.; m. Nancy Hall, Sept. 22, 1973. Student, Ohio U., 1953-54; BA, Denison U., 1957; LL.B., Western Res. U. (now Case Western Res. U.), 1960. Bar: Ohio 1960. Asso. firm Hribar and Conway, Euclid, Ohio, 1961-63; staff atty. The Higbee Co., Cleve., 1963-67, asst. sec., 1967-69, sec., 1969-74, v.p.-sec., 1974-88, gen. counsel, 1978-88; v.p., sec., gen. counsel The Lamson & Sessions Co., Cleve., 1989-94; of counsel Conway, Marken, Wyner, Kurant & Kern Co., LPA, Cleve., 1994—95; v.p.-sec. John P. Murphy Found., Cleve., 2000, exec. v.p., 2008, sr. advisor, sec., 2008—09. V.p. sec. Kulas Found., 2001—06, v.p., sec., treas. Kulas Found., 2006-08. Trustee Cleve. Music Sch. Settlement, pres. bd. trustees, 1980—82, treas., 1996—2001; trustee N.E. Ohio affiliate Am. Heart Assn., 1989—96. With US Army, 1960—61. Mem.: Am. Soc. Corporate Secs. (nat. v.p. 1977), Cleve. Bar Assn., Ohio Bar Assn. Home: 25243 Bryden Rd Beachwood OH 44122

ZAMBONINI, RON (RENATO ZAMBONINI), information technology executive; B, Univ. Ottawa. With Comtech Group Internat., Warrington Inc.; gen. mgr. Applied Devel. Corp.; v.p. R & D Cullinet Software Inc., Cognos Inc., 1989—90, sr. v.p. R & D, 1990—93, COO, 1993—95, pres., 1993—2002, CEO, 1995—2004, chmn., 2004—. Bd. dir. CA Inc., Reynolds & Reynolds. Mailing: Cognos Inc PO Box 9707 Sta T Ottawa ON K1G 4K9 Canada

ZAMBRANO, CARLOS ALBERTO, professional baseball player; b. Puerto Cabello, Venezuela, June 1, 1981; m. Ismary Zambrano; 2 children. Pitcher Chgo. Cubs, 2001—. Mem. Venezuelan nat. team World Baseball Classic, 2009. Recipient Silver Slugger award, 2006, 2008; named to Nat. League All-Star Team, 2004, 2006, 2008. Achievements include leading the National League in: wins (16), 2006; pitching a 10 strikeout no-hitter against the Houston Astros, September 14, 2008. Mailing: c/o Chgo Cubs Wrigley Field 1060 W Addison Chicago IL 60613-4397*

ZAMBRANO, LORENZO H., manufacturing executive; b. Monterrey, Mex., Mar. 27, 1944; BS in Mech. Engring., Tecnológico Monterrey, 1966; MBA, Stanford U., 1968. With CEMEX, 1968—85, CEO, 1985—, chmn. bd. dirs., 1995—. Chmn. bd. Monterrey Tech., 1997—; bd. dirs. Alfa, Femsa, Televisa, Grupo Fin. Banamex, Vitro, IBM; internat. adv. bd. Allianz Cos., Citigroup. Bd. dirs., mem. adv. coun. Contemporary Art Mus. Monterrey (MARCO). Recipient Ernest C. Arbuckle award managerial excellence Stanford Grad. Bus. Sch. Alumni Assn., 1998, Woodrow Wilson award corp. citizenship, 2005, Gold medal disting. svc. The Ams. Soc., 2005. Address: Av Ricardo Margain Zozaya 325 Col Valle del Campestre 66265 San Pedro Garza Garcia Mexico

ZAMBRI, CARLA NICOLE, psychologist; d. Rose A. Bove; m. John Anthony Zambri, July 1, 2006; 1 child, Mia Nicole. BA, Ithaca Coll., 1996; MA, Iona Coll., New Rochelle, 2001. Cert. mental health counselor NY, 2005. Sch. psychologist Clarkstown Ctrl. Sch. Dist., New City, NY, 2002—. Recipient SEPTA award, Spl. Ed. PTA, 2007. Home: 40 Vt Ave Congers NY 10920 Office: Clarkstown Ctrl Sch Dist 62 Old Middletown Rd New City NY 10956 Personal E-mail: cnbove@aol.com. Business E-Mail: czambri@ccsd.edu.

ZAMBRI, MELISSA MARIE, lawyer, educator; b. Albany, NY, Dec. 16, 1971; d. Zachary Edward and Donna Marie Zambri; life ptnr. Gina Marie Moran; children: Anthony, Sofia. BS in Fin., Siena Coll., 1994; MBA in Health Sys., Union Coll., 1998; JD, Albany Law Sch., 1998. Bar: NY 1999, US Dist. Ct. (no. dist.) NY 1999. Atty. Sherrin & Glasel, LLP, Albany, 1998—99, Hiscock & Barclay, LLP, Albany, 1999—. Adj. prof. mgmt. Grad. Coll. Union U., 2005—; lectr. in field. Contbg. editor Health Care Law Guide, 2003—; exec. editor: Albany Law Jour. Sci. Tech., 1997—98. Mentor grad. program Union Coll., 2000—05; vol. coach Miss Shen Softball, Clifton Park, NY, 1990—2001. Recipient Student Achievement award, The Wall St. Jour., 1994; Merit scholar, Albany Law Sch., 1994—97, Union Coll., 1995—96. Mem.: ABA, NY State Bar Assn., Am. Health Lawyers Assn. Office: Hiscock & Barclay LLP 50 Beaver St Albany NY 12207 Office Fax: 518-434-2621. Business E-Mail: mzambri@hblaw.com.

ZAMECNIK, PAUL CHARLES, oncologist, medical researcher; b. Cleve., Nov. 22, 1912; married; 3 children. AB, Dartmouth Coll., 1933; MD, Harvard U., 1936; DSc (hon.), U. Utrecht, 1966, Columbia U., 1971, Harvard U., 1982, Roger Williams Coll., 1983, Dartmouth Coll., 1988, U. Mass., 1994. Resident Huntington Meml. Hosp. Harvard U., Boston, 1936—37; intern U. Hosps., Cleve., 1938—39; Moseley traveling fellow Carlsberg Labs. Harvard U., Copenhagen, 1939—40; Finney-Howell fellow Rockefeller Inst., 1941—42; instr., assoc. prof. medicine Harvard U., 1942—56, Collis P. Huntington prof. oncologic medicine, 1956—79; dir. J.C. Warren Labs., 1956—79; chmn. exec. com. Dept. Medicine Harvard U., 1956—61; emeritus prof. oncological medicine Sch. Medicine, 1979—; prin. sci. Worcester Found. Experimental Biology, 1979—97; physician Mass. Gen. Hosp., 1956—79, hon. physician, 1979—, sr. scientist, 1998—. Vis. fellow dept. chemistry Calif. Tech. U., 1952; vis. Commonwealth scholar in chemistry U. Cambridge, 1962. Recipient Warren Triennial prize, Mass. Gen. Hosp., 1946, 1950, 1999, James Ewing award, 1962, Borden award, 1965, Am. Cancer Soc. Nat. award, 1968, Passano award, 1970, Nat. medal of sci., NSF, 1991, Hudson Hoagland award, 1992, City of Medicine award, Durham, N.C., 1995, Enterprize 2000 award, City of Worcester, Mass., 1996, Lasker-Koshland Spl. Achievement award in Med. Sci., Lasker Found., 1996, Lifetime Achievement award, Inst. Human Virology, 2004, Gene Expression Systems Conf., 2009. Mem.: NAS, Nat. Acad. Medicine, Am. Philosophy Soc., Am. Soc. Biol. Chemists (Merck award 1997), Mass. Med. Soc. (Ann. Orator 1998), Nat. Acad. Scis., Assn. Am. Physicians, Am. Assn. Cancer Rsch. (pres. 1964—65), Am. Soc. Biol. Chemists, Am. Acad. Arts and Scis., Interurban Club. Office: Mass Gen Hosp Charlestown 149 13th St Rm 1494005 Charlestown MA 02129-2020 Office Fax: 671-724-9627.

ZAMFIR, NICOLAE VICTOR, physicist, researcher; b. Brasov, Romania, Mar. 24, 1952; arrived in U.S., 1992; s. Nicolae Zamfir, Livia Zamfir; m. Ecaterina Edita Petre; children: Radu Bogdan, Ioana Livia. Masters Degree (magna cum laude), U. Bucharest, Romania, 1976; PhD, Ctrl. Inst. Physics, Bucharest, Romania, 1984. Physicist Inst. Physics and Nuc. Engring., Magurele, Bucharest, Romania, 1978—84, sr. rschr. Bucharest, 1984—; physicist Brookhaven Nat. Lab., Upton, NY, 1994—97; sr. rsch. scientist Yale U., New Haven, 1997—2004; dir. Nat. Inst. Physics and Nuc. Engring., Bucharest, 2004—; plenipotentiary rep. Romania Joint Inst. Nuc. Rsch., Dubna. Cons. Clark U., Worcester, Mass., 1992—2003; mem. adv. com. 10 Internat. Confs. Contbr. over 200 articles to profl. jours.;, co-editor 7 internat. conf. proceedings. Recipient Hurmuzescu award in physics, Romanian Acad., 1984. Mem.: AAAS, Romanian Acad., European Phys. Soc., Am. Phys. Soc. Achievements include research in evolution of nuclear collectivity, phase/shape transition and phase co-existence in nuclei, octupole collectivity in nuclear structure. Office: Nat Inst Physics and Nuc Engring PO Box MG6 Bucharest Romania Business E-Mail: zamfir@tandem.nipne.ro.

ZAMKA, GEORGE D., astronaut; b. Jersey City, June 29, 1962; s. Conrad P. and Sofia Zamka; m. Elisa P. Walker; 2 children. BS in Math., U.S. Naval Acad., 1984; MS in Engring. Mgmt., Fla. Inst. Tech., 1997. Commd. 2d lt. USMC, 1984, advanced through grades to lt. col.; with Navy Attack Squadron, Marine All Weather Attacki Squadron, VMA, El Toro, Calif.; squadron weapons and tactics instr.; with Marine All Weather Fighter Attack Squadron VMFA, El Toro; forward air contr. 1st Bn., 5th Marines, Camp Pendleton, Calif.; with 31st Marine Expeditionary Unit, USS Belleau Wood, Western Pacific; test pilot/project officer Naval Strike Aircraft Test Squadron; aircraft maintenance officer VMFA, 1998; astronaut (pilot) NASA, Houston, 1998—, various duties with Astronaut Office. Pilot STS-120 Discovery Mission to Internat. Space Station, 2007. Decorated 6 Navy Strike Air medals, Navy Commendation medal with Combat V. Mem.: Soc. Exptl. Test Pilots, Marine Corps Assn., U.S. Naval Acad. Alumni Assn. Achievements include logged over 3,000 flight hours in over 30 different aircraft. Avocations: weightlifting, running, bicycling, scuba diving, boating. Office: Astronaut Office /CB NASA Johnson Space Ctr Houston TX 77058

ZAMMIT, JOSEPH PAUL, lawyer; b. NYC, May 19, 1948; s. John and Farla (Rudolph) Z.; m. Dorothy Therese O'Neill, June 6, 1970; children: Michael, Paul, Brian. AB magna cum laude, Fordham U., 1968; JD cum laude, Harvard U., 1971; LLM, NYU, 1974. Bar: N.Y. 1972, U.S. Dist. Ct. (so. and ea. dists.) N.Y. 1973, U.S. Dist. Ct. (no. dist.) Ala. 1989, U.S. Dist. Ct. (we. dist.) N.Y., 1991, U.S. Dist. Ct. (no. dist.) N.Y. 1983, US Dist. Ct. Colo., 2007, U.S. Ct. Appeals (2d cir.) 1973, U.S. Ct. Appeals (11th cir.) 1987, U.S. Ct. Appeals (fed. cir.) 1995, U.S. Supreme Ct. 1978. Assoc. Reavis & McGrath, NYC, 1971-74; asst. prof. law St. John's U., Jamaica, NY, 1974-76, assoc. prof., 1976-78; assoc. Reavis & McGrath, NYC, 1978-79, ptnr., 1979-88, Fulbright & Jaworski L.L.P. (formerly Fulbright Jaworski & Reavis McGrath), NYC, 1989—. Adj. assoc. prof. St. John's U., Jamaica, 1979-83, adj. prof., 1984—; mem. panel comml. arbitrators tech. panel Am. Arbitration Assn., N.Y.C., 1977—. Bd. editors E-commerce Law and Strategy, 1987—; contbr. articles to profl. jours. Mem.: ABA, Computer Law Assn., Assn. Bar City of N.Y. (chmn. comml. liability subcom. 1981—87, chmn. com. on computer law 1995—98, fed. cts. com. 1998—2001, info. tech. law com. 2002—06, internat. comml. disputes com. 2007—), N.Y. State Bar Assn., Phi Beta Kappa. Office: Fulbright & Jaworski LLP 666 5th Ave Fl 31 New York NY 10103-0001 Office Phone: 212-318-3000. Personal E-mail: jzammit@fulbright.com.

ZAMORA, ANTONIO, music director, educator; b. Corpus Christi, Tex., June 8, 1969; s. Dionicio Leonirez and Trinidad Zamora. Choir dir. Immaculate Conception, Gregory, Tex., 1990—93; music dir. Holy Family Ch., Corpus Christi, Tex., 1990—93, Our Lady of Guadalupe, Corpus Christi, 1990—94; choir dir. Our Lady of Prepetual Help, Corpus Christi, 1991—93; youth choir dir. Sacred Heart Ch., Odom, Tex., 1993—94; music tchr. St. Patrick Sch., Corpus Christi, 1993—; music dir. St. Paul Cath. Ch., Corpus Christi, 1995—96; youth choir dir. Our Lady of Guadalupe, Edroy, Tex., 1993—94; youth music dir. Most Precious Blood Ch., Corpus Christi, 1996—2000; activity dir. Wooldridge Pl. Nursing Ctr., Corpus Christi, 1998—2002; music dir. St. Andrew By The Sea, Corpus Christi, 2002—07; music tchr. Ctrl. Cath., Corpus Christi, 2005—. Liturgy dir. Holy Family Ch., Corpus Christi, Tex., 2005—. Musician, writer: musicals Life of Jesus Through the Eyes of Many, Our Lady of Guadalupe, A Christmas Story. Pres. Coastal Bend Activities Directors Assn., Corpus Christi, 1998—2000. Democrat. Roman Catholic. Avocations: music, singing, dance, musical instruments. Home: 2817 Sarita Corpus Christi TX 78405 Office: St Patrick Sch 3340 S Alameda Corpus Christi TX 78411 Personal E-mail: alzag18@yahoo.com.

ZAMORA, BOBBIE JEAN, literature and language professor; b. Lexington, Ky., Jan. 19, 1949; d. Bobbie L. Turner and Jean Purcell Reed; m. Oscar Zamora, Jan. 2, 1971. BA, U. Tex. at Austin, 1970; MS, Corpus Christi State U., Tex., 1978; PhD, U. Pitts., 1992. Sixth grade tchr. St. Theresa's Elem. Sch., Corpus Christi, 1974—76; English tchr. St. Joseph's Jr. HS, Corpus Christi, 1976—78, St. Louis HS, Lake Charles, 1978—86; tchg. fellow U. Pitts., 1987—90; English prof. Cleve. CC, Shelby, 1995—. Cert. therapeutic riding instr. Cleve. County Hearts & Hooves, Shelby, pres. therapeutic riding program, 2004—06; humanities tchr. Gov.'s Program Gifted Children, Lake Charles, La., 1979—83. Recipient Excellent Tchg. award, Cleve. CC, 1997. Mem.: TYCA-SE, NC Coll. English Instructors (pres. 2005—07), NCTE. Liberal. Buddhist. Avocation: travel. Office: Cleveland CC 137 S Post Rd Shelby NC 28152 Business E-Mail: zamora@clevelandcommunitycollege.edu.

ZAMORE, MICHAEL SETH, legislative staff member; s. Joseph and Frances Zamore; m. Abigail Smith, Aug. 1998. BA magna cum laude, Brown U., Providence, 1993; JD, Harvard U. Law Sch., 1999. Policy advisor, Rep. Patrick Kennedy US House of Reps., Washington, 2000—07; policy dir. Dem. Senatorial Campaign Com., Washington, 2007—08; chief of staff to Senator Jeff Merkley US Senate, Washington, 2008—. Mem.: Phi Beta Kappa. Democrat. Office: SDB-40B Dirksen Senate Bldg Washington DC 20510 Office Phone: 202-224-3753. Business E-Mail: michael_zamore@merkley.senate.gov.*

ZAMPINI, CARMEN C., library director; b. Painesville, Ohio, Jan. 11, 1947; d. Michael Peter Zampini and Anne S. nee Sabadosh; children: Micheleanne Celigoj, F. Andrew Celigoj. BA, Lake Erie Coll., Painesville, Ohio, 1969; MLS, Kent State U., Ohio, 1971. Libr. Cleve. Mus. Art, 1971—73; part-time instr., libr. sci. Kent State U., 1972, 1990; dir. Kent Free Libr., 1973—; part-time instr. U. Akron, Ohio, 1980—95. Pres. Lake Erie Coll. Nat. Alumnae Assn., Painesville, 1979—85; sec. Pinto Horse Assn. America, Ft. Worth, 1991—2003. Recipient Diane Vescelius award, Ohio Libr. Assn., 1978. Mem.: ALA (libr. adminstrn., mgmt. com. mem. 1986—90), Ohio Libr. Coun. (chair 1986—88), Pub. Libr. Assn., Beta Phi Mu (pres. 1978—79). Office: Kent Free Libr 312 W Main St Kent OH 44240 Business E-Mail: carmen.zampini@kentfreelibrary.org.

ZAMUDIO, CELIA ISABEL, language educator; b. Mexico City, Nov. 19, 1948; d. Jose Zamudio and Hermelinda Velasco; life ptnr. Edgar Miranda, Dec. 11, 1971; children: Edgar Miranda, Ronnie Miranda. BA in Spanish Lang. and Culture, Calif. State U. Northridge, 1996; MA in Spanish Lang., Calif. State U., Northridge, 2005. Cert. in Christian edn. Assn. Christina Schs. Internat., 1998; academia comercial justo sierra Mexico City, 1966. Dept. mgr. Banco Comercio, Mexico City, 1969—72, LA Unified Sch. Dist., Reseda, Calif., 1985—97; assoc. arts LA Mission Coll., Sylmar, Calif., 1989—92; Spanish lang. instr. Alemany HS, Miission Hills, Calif., 1997—98, Frederick K. C. Price Schs., LA, 1998—2002, Antilope Valley Coll., Lancaster, Calif., 2005—, Pierce Coll., Woodland Hills, Calif., 2007—. Sponsor Al-Anon, Granada Hills, Calif., 1997—2008. Mem.: Nat. Cath. Ednl. Assn., LA Cath. Alumni Club. Roman Catholic. Avocations: travel, walking, yoga. Office: Antilope Valley Coll 3041 W Ave K Lancaster CA 93536-5426

ZAMYATIN, ALEXANDER, medical researcher; s. Andrey and Ludmila Zamyatin; m. Olga Zamyatin, July 8, 2000; 1 child, Ivan. PhD, U. Ctrl. Fla., Orlando, 2003. Rsch. project mgr. Toshiba Med. Rsch. Inst., Vernon Hills, Ill., 2003—. Contbr. scientific papers. Recipient Outstanding Paper award, MSMW Conf., 1998. Mem.: IEEE, SIAM, SPIE. Achievements include patents in field. Office: Toshiba Med Rsch Inst 706 N Deerpath Dr Vernon Hills IL 60061

ZANARDELLI, JOHN JOSEPH, healthcare organization executive; b. Monongahela, Pa., July 27, 1950; s. John and Linda (Lazzari) Z.; m. Suzanne King, Jan. 29, 1972; children: Brandon John, Stephen William, Robyn Lynn. Student, Davis & Elkins Coll., 1968; AA, C.C. Allegheny Cty, Pitts., 1970; AS in Acctg., C.C. Allegheny Cty., Pitts., 1991; BS in Edn., California State Coll. Pa., 1972; MPH, U. Pitts., 1979, cert. acct., 1994; cert. non-profit mgmt., Harvard U., 1998; cert. gen. mgmt., Carnegie Mellon U., 1999. Cert. in evaluation pub. health promotion and health edn. programs U. Pitts., 2008. Rsch. asst. grad. sch. pub. health U. Pitts., 1973-78; adminstrv. resident Ctrl. Med. Ctr. and Hosp., Pitts., 1978-79; vice-chmn., sec., dir. Allegheny Mountain Health Enterprises, Inc., Oil City, Pa., 1985-88; exec. v.p. Oil City Area Health Ctr., Inc., 1979-88; exec. v.p., COO Grane Healthcare, Inc., Pitts., 1988-90; adminstr., COO Southwood Psychiat. Hosp., Inc., Pitts., 1990-91; exec. dir. Allegheny divsn. Presbyn. Sr.Care, Pitts., 1991-92; pres. United Meth. Svcs. for Aging, 1993—, CEO, 1993. Preceptor, mentor health adminstrn. program U. Pitts. Grad. Sch. Pub. Health, 1980—2006, vis. faculty, 1997—98; adj. asst. prof. health svcs. adminstrn. Grad. Sch. Pub. Health, 1998—2001, adj. assoc. prof. health policy and mgmt., 2001—05, adj. assoc. prof. behavioral and cmty. health scis., 2005—; pres. HCCP, Inc., Pitts., 1983—; bd. dirs. Faith-Based Network, Inc., 1998—2008; co-chair pub. rels. and mktg. com. Davis and Elkins Coll., 2000—02; co-chair exec.-in-residence com. U. Pitts. Grad. Sch. Pub. Health, 2001—02, exec. in residence, health adminstrn. program, 2001—03, fellow evaluation sci., dept. behavioral and cmty. health scis., 2004—08; preceptor, Initiative on Social Enterprise, Harvard Bus. Sch., 2001—; mem. planning com. and faculty longterm care program U. Pitts. Inst. Aging, 2002—05, 2007—08; mem. evidence based mgmt. collaborative Acad. Mgmt. and Carnegie Mellon U., 2007—. Fellow: Am. Coll. Healthcare Execs.; mem.: Delta Omega (Omicron chpt., pres. 2000—01). Home: 2997 Greenwald Rd Bethel Park PA 15102-1615 Office: Asbury Heights 700 Bower Hill Rd Pittsburgh PA 15243-2040 Office Phone: 412-571-5134. Business E-Mail: johnzan@alumni.pitt.edu, jzanardelli@asburyheights.org.

ZAND, DALE EZRA, business management educator; b. NYC, July 22, 1926; m. Charlotte Edith Rosenfeld, Oct. 16, 1949; children: Fern, Mark, Karen, Jonathan, Matthew. BEE, Cooper Union, 1945; MBA, NYU, 1949, PhD, 1954. Asst. to v.p. Spectator Bags, 1947-49; v.p. Glo-Cold Co., 1949-50; mem. faculty Stern Sch. Bus., NYU, NYC, 1950—, prof. mgmt., 1963—, chmn. dept., 1968—, sr. faculty fellow, 1999—. Cons. to industry, 1951—; bd. dirs. Newfield Exploration Co., Inst. Applied Behavioral Sci. Author: Information, Organization, and Power, 1981, The Leadership Triad, 1997, also articles. Served with USNR, 1945. Ford Found. fellow, 1959-60 Mem. Am. Psychol. Soc., Inst. Mgmt. Sci., Acad. Mgmt., Internat. Assn. Applied Social Scientists. Office: NYU Stern 40 W 4th St KMC890 New York NY 10012-0157

ZANDER, EDWARD J., retired communications executive; b. Bklyn., Jan. 12, 1947; m. Mona Zander; 2 children. BSEE, Rensselaer Poly. Inst., 1968; MBA, Boston U., 1975. Formerly with Apollo Computer, Data Gen., Raytheon; with Sun Microsystems Inc., Palo Alto, Calif., 1987—2002, COO, 1998—2002, pres., COO, 1999—2002; mng. dir. Silver Lake Ptnrs., 2002—03; CEO Motorola Inc., Schaumburg, Ill., 2004—08, chmn., 2004—08. Bd. dirs. Documentum, Inc., Portal Software, Inc., Rhythms Netconnections, inc., Seagate Tech., Time Warner Inc., 2007—, NetSuite Inc. Mem. sci. adv. bd. Rensselaer Poly. Inst., Troy, NY, presdl. advisor; mem. dean's adv. bd., sch. of mgmt. Boston U.; bd. dirs. Jason Found. for Edn.; mem. Economics Club Chgo., Exec. Club Chgo.; mem. civic com. Comml. Club Chgo. Named one of 50 Who Matter Now, CNNMoney.com Bus. 2.0, 2006. Mailing: NetSuite Inc Bd Directors 2955 Campus Dr San Mateo CA 94403-2511*

ZANDI, MARK M., economist, financial consultant; b. 1959; married; 3 children. BS in Economics, U. Pa. Wharton Sch. Bus., 1981; PhD in Economics, U. Pa., 2006. Co-founder, chief economist Moody's Economy.com (subs. Moody's Corp.), West Chester, Pa., 1990—. Author: (books) Financial Shock, 2008. Democrat. Office: Moodys Economy com 121 N Walnut St Ste 500 West Chester PA 19380 Office Fax: 610-235-5299, 610-235-5302. Business E-Mail: hzandi@economy.com.*

ZANDI, PETER P., medical educator; b. Wilmington, Del., Nov. 5, 1966; s. Iraj Zandi and Annette Grantham; m. Megan C. Fox; children: Maxwell J., Grace A. BA, U. Pa., Phila., 1988; MPH, Johns Hopkins U., Balt., 1997, PhD, 2001. Asst. prof. Johns Hopkins U., Balt., 2001—07, assoc. prof., 2007—. Contbr. articles to profl. jours. Recipient Harold and Sylvia Halpert award, Dept. Mental Health, Johns Hopkins U. Bloomberg Sch. Pub. Health, 1999, Morton Kramer award, 2000; Pre-Doctoral fellowship, NIMH, 1998—2001. Mem.: Internat. Soc. Vascular Behavioral and Cognitive Disorders, Am. Psychopathological Assn., Am. Soc. Human Genetics, Internat. Soc. Psychiat. Genetics, Delta Omega Soc. (Alpha chpt.). Office: Johns Hopkins Univ 624 N Broadway Baltimore MD 21205 Office Fax: 410-955-9088. Business E-Mail: pzandi@jhsph.edu.

ZANDMAN, FELIX, electronics executive; b. Grodno, Poland, 1928; MS, U. Nancy, France, 1953; PhD, U. Paris The Sorbonne; doctorate (hon.), Univ. Beer Sheva, Israel Inst. Tech. (Technion). With French Nat. Ctr. Sci. Rsch., Paris, 1950-53; with engring. and consulting SNECMA, 1953-57; dir. basic rsch. Tatnall Measuring Systems Co., Phoenixville, Pa., 1957-62; founder, dir., chmn. bd. Vishay Intertechnology, Malvern, Pa., 1962—, pres., 1962—98, CEO, 1962—2004, chief tech. officer, 2004—. Author: Never the Last Journey, 3 textbooks in electronics; contbr. articles to profl. jours. Recipient Medal of Honor, Electronic Industries Alliance, 2001. Achievements include 39 patents in electronics. Office: Vishay Intertechnology 63 Lincoln Hwy Malvern PA 19355

ZANDSTRA, GRETA MARIE, theater educator, actor; b. East Chgo., Ind., Oct. 31, 1976; d. Nicholas Paul and Ruth Ann Zandstra; m. Charles Anthony Pofahl, June 30, 1983. BA, St. Mary's Coll., Notre Dame, Ind., 1999; MA, U. Nebr., Omaha, 2001. Dir. summer edn. Nebr. Shakespeare Festival, Omaha, 2001—02; dir. satellite edn. Madison Family Theatre, Wis., 2003—04; actor-educator Children's Theatre Charlotte, NC, 2003—; theatre prof. Ctrl. Piedmont CC, Charlotte, 2007—; artistic assoc. Charlotte Shakespeare Festival, 2007—; theatre educator Davidson Cmty. Players, NC, 2008—. Actor: (children's theatre) Tarradiddle Players. Recipient Part Time Prof. award, 2008; named one of Best Comedy Actress, Creative Loafing Charlotte, 2004. Personal E-mail: greta.zandstra@cpcc.edu.

ZANE, PHILLIP CRAIG, lawyer; b. NYC, Sept. 25, 1961; s. Martin I.L. and Rosalind Carol (Siegler) Z.; m. Denise Janine Wydra; 1 child, Christopher Abelard. BA, Pomona Coll., 1983; postgrad., U. Mich., 1985-88; JD cum laude, NYU, 1991. Bar: Ill. 1991, D.C. 1996, U.S. Dist. Ct. (no. dist.) Ill. 1991, U.S. Ct. Appeals (7th cir.) 1994, U.S. Ct. Appeals (8th cir.) 1993, U.S. Ct. Appeals (9th cir.) 1996, U.S. Fed. Cir. Ct. 1994, U.S. Dist. Ct. D.C. 2000, U.S. Supreme Ct. 2004. Assoc. Mayer, Brown & Platt, Chgo., 1991-93; judicial law clerk to Hon. Morris S. Arnold 8th Cir. Ct. Appeals, Little Rock, 1993-94; assoc. Mayer, Brown & Platt, Chgo., 1994-95, Morgan, Lewis & Bockius, Washington, 1996-2000, of counsel, 2000—04; solo practice, 2004—05; of counsel Baker, Donelson, Bearman, Caldwell & Berkowitz, PC, 2005—. Staff editor NYU Rev. of Law and Social Change, 1989-90, critical legal studies editor, 1990-91; editor Sherman Act Almanac, 1998; contbr. articles to profl. jours. Sec. gen. coun. Arthur F. Burns Fellowship Program, Inc., 1998—. Fellow Thomas J. Watson Found., 1983-84; fgn. lang. area studies fellow U. Mich., Ann Arbor, 1986, 87-88. Mem. ABA (vice chair Sherman Act sect. one com. 1999-2001), Ill. State Bar Assn. (spl. com. on Law Day in Moscow and Kiev 1992). Democrat. Avocation: legal history. Office: Baker Donelson Bearman Caldwell & Berkowitz PC 555 11th St NW Fl 6 Washington DC 20004-1314 Office Phone: 202-508-3490. E-mail: pzane@bakerdonelson.com.

ZANG, KATHLEEN ANN, pre-school educator; b. Aug. 24, 1958; Bachelor, Ohio State U., Columbus, 1980. Author: (games) Healthy Habits, 2005 (Dr. Toy award, 2005, One of 100 Best Toys, 2005, One of 10 Best Active Toys, 2005), That's Just Rude, The Birthday Walk. Recipient Learning Mag. Tchrs' Choice award, 2008, Tchrs' Choice award, Learning Magazines, 2008. Mem.: Assn. Childhood Edn. Internat.

ZANJACOMO, PAULO REGIS, engineering executive; s. Expedicto and Alzira Zanjacomo; m. Hilda Hortensia Valero Tonone, Mar. 27, 1999. BSc in Computer Scis., U. Sao Paulo, 1990, MSc in Applied Math., 1992; PhD in Indsl. Engring., Ga. Inst. Tech., 1998. Asst. prof. U. Sao Paulo, 1992—94; sr. engr. for rsch. and product design Energy Imperium, Atlanta, 1999—99; dir. rsch. and design Altra Energy Technologies, Houston, 1999—2000; chief tech. officer Delfin Energy, Atlanta, 2000—04, Stats. and Research Autom. Trading Desk Charleston, SC, 2002—. Contbr. articles to profl. jours. Mem.: INFORMS.

ZANK, VIRGINIA, retired literature and language professor, educational consultant; b. Plainview, Ark., Apr. 29, 1942; d. Hayes Dale and Imogene Bridges; m. Martin J. Kugel (dec.); children: Cynthia Gail Kugel, Melissa Gene Kugel-Couch; m. Dale M. Zank, Nov. 25, 1995. BS in Secondary Edn., John Brown U., 1963; MA in English, Ctrl. Mo. State U., 1978. Lifetime cert. tchr. English Mo. Tchr. Higbee (Mo.) H.S., 1963—64; tchr. English Hallsville (Mo.) H.S., 1964—67, Marshall (Mo.) H.S., 1967—93; assoc. prof. English Mo. Valley Coll., Marshall, 1993—2009. Recipient Gov.'s award for tchg. excellence, State of Mo., 1996; named Disting. Educator, Optimist Club, Marshall, 1997. Mem.: Mo. State Tchrs. Assn., Nat. Coun. Tchrs. English, Mo. Assn. Tchrs. English (pres.). Home: 628 Stoney Kirk Cir Branson West MO 65737 Business E-Mail: zankv@moval.edu.

ZANNA, MARTIN THOMAS, physician; b. Mpls., Apr. 2, 1947; s. Peter J. and Mary L. (Peck) Z. AB, Harvard U., 1969, MPH, 1976; MD, U. Minn., 1973. Diplomate Am. Bd. Preventive Medicine. Resident in pub. health N.J. State Dept. Health, 1974-77, acting dir. chronic disease svcs., 1976-79, dir. chronic disease svcs., 1979-81; med. adminstr. Fla. Dept. Health and Rehab. Svcs., Tallahassee, 1981-82; med. cons. N.J. Medicaid, Trenton, 1982—, chief med. cons., 1990-96; med. cons. N.J. State Dept. Health and Sr. Svcs., 1996—. Mem. Fla. Cancer Coun., 1981-82, Fla. Bd. Med. Examiners, 1982, N.J. Hypertension Study Group, 1977-81; chmn. grad. med. edn. com. N.J. State Dept. Health & Sr. Svcs., 1993—; diabetes adv. coun. exec. com. N.J. Dept. Health, 2001—. Contbr. articles to profl. jours. Participant Fla. Gov.'s Mission to Haiti, 1982; mem. divsn. profl. edn. Am. Cancer Soc., 1976-81. Fellow Am. Coll. Preventive Medicine; mem. APHA, Harvard Club (Boston), Harvard Faculty Club (Cambridge). Home: 104 Olympic Ct Apt 2 Princeton NJ 08540 Office: NJ State Dept Health & Sr Svcs PO Box 807 Trenton NJ 08625-0722

ZANNIERI, NINA, museum director; b. Summit, NJ, Feb. 1, 1955; d. Angelo Joseph and Louise Mary (Brumm) Z.; m. Douglas M. Vogel, Oct. 29, 1994. BA, Boston Coll., 1977; postgrad., Coll. of William & Mary, 1977-78; MA, Brown U., 1980. Curatorial asst. R.I. Hist. Soc., Providence, 1980-81, asst. curator, 1981-83, curator, 1983-86; dir. Paul Revere Meml. Assn., Boston, 1986—. Gen. editor: (exhbn. catalog) Paul Revere: The Man Behind the Myth, 1988; collaborator: A Most Magnificent Mansion; project dir.: (exhbn. catalog) Let Virtue Be A Guide To Thee, 1983 Mem. Am. Assn. Mus.'s (bd. dirs. 1999-02, vice-chair 2002-03), New Eng. Mus. Assn. (pres. 1998-02), Am. Assn. State and Local History (gov. coun. 2004-), Phi Beta Kappa. Office: Paul Revere Meml Assn The Paul Revere House 19 North Sq Boston MA 02113-2405

ZANNINO, RICHARD F., private equity firm executive, former publishing executive; b. Oct. 26, 1958; m. Anna Zannino; 4 children. BS in Fin. & Economics, Bentley Coll., 1980; MBA, Pace U., 1984. With Continental Group, Inc., Stamford, Conn.; various fin. positions Emery Worldwide, 1984—86, Peter Kiewit Sons, Inc., 1986—91, JWP, 1992; v.p., CFO Saks Fifth Ave., 1993—98; CFO Gen. Signal Corp., 1998; various sr. level positions including exec. v.p. Liz Claiborne, Inc., 1998—2001; CFO Dow Jones & Co., NYC, 2001—02, exec. v.p., COO, 2002—06, CEO, 2006—07; mng. dir., co-head consumer, media & retail practice CCMP Capital Advisors LLC, NYC, 2009—. Bd. dirs. IAC/InterActiveCorp, 2009—. Vice chmn. Advt. Edn. Found.; mem. dean's adv. coun. coll. commerce and fin. Villanova U.; mem. Columbia Bus. Sch. Media Forum; trustee Pace U., 2009—. Office: CCMP Capital Advisors LLC 16th Fl 245 Park Ave New York NY 10167-2403 Office Phone: 212-600-9600. Office Fax: 212-599-3481.*

ZANTA, CAROLYN A., biology professor; PhD, Purdue U. Biotech. edn. outreach program dir. U. Ill., Champaign, 1999—2006; asst. prof. Clarkson U., Potsdam, NY, 2007—. Office: Clarkson Univ Box 5805 Potsdam NY 13699-5805

ZANUSSI, KRZYSZTOF, film director, producer, scriptwriter; b. June 17, 1939; s. Jerzy and Jadwiga A. Student, Warsaw and Cracow U., Lodz Higher Film Sch. Dir. short feature films including Death of a Provincial, 1967, Structure of Crystals, 1972, Family Life, 1972, Illumination, 1972, The Catamount Killing, 1973, Womens Decision, 1974 (OCIC prize West Berlin), Camouflage, 1977 (Spl. prize Teheran, Grand prize Polish Film Festival), Spiral, 1978 (Cannes award, OCIC prize), Wege in der Nacht, 1979, Constant Factor, 1980 (Best Dir. award Cannes), Contract, 1980 (Distbn. prize Venice), From a Far Country; Imperative, 1984 (award W.Ger., France), Year of the Quiet Sun, 1984 (Golden Lion Venice Film Fest.), The Power of Evil, 1985 (OCIC prize Montreal), Wherever You Are, 1988, The Inventory, 1989 (Oekumenical prize Moscow, Grand prize Strausbourg), Life For Life, 1990, The Silent Touch, 1992 (Best Actor prize Tokyo), On Full Gallop, 1995 (Spl. Jury prize Tokyo), Our God's Brother, 1997, Life as Fatal, Sexually Transmitted Disease, 2000 (Grand prize Moscow), Suplement, 2002 (Fipresci prize, Moscow), Persona Non Grata, 2005 (Spl. Jury prize Edyma), The Black Son, 2007; (TV films) Face to Face, 1967, Mountains at Dusk, 1970, Role, 1971, Behind the Wall, 1971 (Grand prize San Remo 1972), Nachtdienst, 1975, Anatomiestunde, 1975, Haus der Frauen, 1978, Versuchung, 1981, Unaproachable, Blaubart, 1984 (Grand prize Venezia TV), Long Conversation With a Bird, 1990, Portrait of Russia of B. Yeltzin, 1991, Sounds and Images, 1991, Weekend Stories, 1996-97; author: Nowele Filmowe, 1976, Scenariusze Filmowe, 1, 2, 3, 4, Sei Film, 1979, Rigorista, 1982, Pora Umierac, 1997, Opowiesci Weekendowe, 1998, Miedzy Jarmarkiem A Salonem, 1999, In Full Gallop, 2002, Bigos in Europe, 2003, Klezmer in Germany, 2007, other scripts. Mem.: Polish Film Assn. (vice-chmn. 1971—81). Office: Tor-Film Prodn Co Pulaska 61 00-173 Warsaw Poland Address: 8 rue Richepense 75001 Paris France Home Phone: +48228392556; Office Phone: +48228455303. E-mail: tor@tor.com.pl.

ZAPATA, ANGEL, pastor; b. Mayaguez, PR, Mar. 23, 1950; s. Jorge Zapata and Isabel Velez; m. Rosita Zapata, Aug. 16, 2003; children: Angel, Michael, CeLina, Angie, Sarah, Arianna, Natalie Roman, Shaila Salliant. BA in Sociology, magna cum laude, Mercy Coll., 1984; MSW magna cum laude, Yeshiva U., NY, 1995. Chaplain United Chaplains, NY State, 2006, Ordained Pastor NY State, 2006; LCSW NY, 1995; cert. social studies and history tchr. NY State Higher Edn., 1989. Cons. Fed. Govt., 1970—2000. Sgt. US Army, 1968—71, Vietnam, Japan, Europe. Decorated Combat Inf. Badge US Army, Purple Heart, Bronze Star, Vietnamese Cross of Gallantry. Mem.: Phi Gamma Mu. Home: Radio City Sta PO Box 241 New York NY 10101-0241

ZAPF, HERMANN, book and type designer; b. Nuremberg, Germany, Nov. 8, 1918; s. Hermann and Magdalene (Schlamp) Zapf; m. Gudrun von Hesse, Aug. 18, 1951; 1 child, Christian Ludwig. D in Fine Arts (hon.), U. Ill., 2003. Freelance designer, 1938—; type dir. D. Stempel AG, type foundry, Frankfurt, Fed. Republic of Germany, 1947-56; design cons. Mergenthaler Linotype Co. (NYC and Frankfurt), 1957-74; cons. Hallmark Internat., Kansas City, Mo., 1966-73; v.p. Design Processing Internat. Inc., NYC, 1977—87; prof. typographic computer programs Rochester (N.Y.) Inst. Tech., 1977-87; chmn. Zapf, Burns & Co., NYC, 1987-91. Instr. lettering Werkkunstschule, Offenbach, Fed. Republic Germany., 1948-50; prof. graphic design Carnegie Inst. Tech., 1960; instr. typography Technische Hochschule, Darmstadt, Fed. Republic Germany, 1972-81. Author: William Morris, 1948, Pen and Graver, 1952, Manuale Typographicum, 1954, 1968, About Alphabets, 1960, 1970, Typographic Variations, 1964, Orbis Typographicus, 1980, Hora fugit/Carpe diem, 1984, Hermann Zapf and His Design Philosophy, 1987, ABC-XYZapf, 1989, Poetry Through Typography, 1993, August Rosenberger, 1996, (film) The Art of Hermann Zapf, German version Die Welt der Buchstaben von Hermann Zapf, (CD-ROM) The World of Alphabets, 2001, Alphabet Stories: A Chronicle of Technical Developments, 2007; designer types Palatino, Melior, Optima, ITC Zapf Chancery, ITC Zapf Internat., Digiset Marconi, Digiset Edison, Digiset Aurelia, Pan-Nigerian, Sequoyah, URW-Roman and San Serif, Renaissance Roman, Linotype, Zapfino Extra, Optima nova, ITC Dingbats, Zapf Essentials, Palatino Sans, Palatino Arabic. Hon. pres. Edward Johnston Found., Ditchling, England. Recipient Silver medal, Brussels, 1962, 1st prize typography, Biennale Brno, Czechoslovakia, 1966, Gold medal, Type Dirs. Club, N.Y., Frederic W. Goudy award, Inst. Tech. Rochester, 1969, Silver medal, Internat. Book Exhbn., Leipzig, 1971, Gold medal, 1989, Johannes Gutenberg prize, Mainz, Fed. German Republic, 1974, Gold medal, Museo Bodoniano, Parma, Italy, 1975, J.H. Merck award, Darmstadt, 1978, Robert Hunter Middleton award, Chgo., 1987, Euro Design award, Oostende, 1994, Wadim Lazursky award, Acad. of Graphic Arts, Moscow, 1996, SOTA Typography award, Chgo., 2003, Goethe medal, State Hesse, Germany, 2007; named hon. citizen, State of Tex., 1970, hon. Royal Designer for Industry, London, 1985. Mem.: Internat. Gutenberg Gesellschaft, Bund Deutscher Grafik Designer, Alliance Graphique Internat., Am. Math. Soc., Royal Soc. Arts, Dante e.V. (German TEX Group) (hon.), Soc. Scribes N.Y. (hon.), Brno Biennale Assn. (hon.), Goudy Internat. Ctr. (hon.), Alcuin Soc. Can. (hon.), Typographers Internat. Assn. (hon.), Chgo. Calligraphy Collective (hon.), Eesti Kalligraafide Koondis (hon.; Tallinn, Estonia), Wynkyn de Worde Soc. (hon.), Soc. Calligraphy (hon.), Grafiska Inst. (hon.), Bund Deutscher Buchkünstler (hon.), Soc. Graphic Designers Can. (hon.), Soc. Printers (hon.), Soc. Typographic Arts (hon.), Soc. Typographique de France (hon.), Assocs. of Stanford Univ. Librs., Art Dirs. Club Kansas City (hon.), Alpha Beta Club (hon.; Hong Kong), Friends of Calligraphy (hon.), Double Crown Club (hon.), Type Dirs. Club N.Y.C. (hon.), Soc. Scribes and Illuminators (hon.), Typophiles (hon.), Letter Exch. (hon.), Washington Calligrapher's Guild (hon.), Monterey Calligrapher's Guild (hon.), Caxton Club (hon.), Gamma Epsilon Tau (hon.).

ZAPFFE, NINA BYROM, retired elementary school educator; b. Independence, Mo., Aug. 17, 1925; d. Richmond Douglas and Nina Belle (Howell) Byrom; m. Robert Glenn Fessler, June 25, 1946 (dec. June 1947); 1 child, Robert Glenn Fessler Zapffe; m. Fred Zapffe, July 1, 1952 (dec. Dec. 1999); children: Paul Douglas (dec. Nov. 2008), Carl Raymond. BA, So. Meth. U., Dallas, 1946. Fin. sec. Tyler St. Meth. Ch., Dallas, 1948-49; tchr. Dallas Ind. Sch. Dist., 1949-52, Norman (Okla.) Pub. Schs., 1966-74; chief reader for GED Writing Skills Test Part II GED Testing Svc., Am. Coun. on Edn., Washington, 1990—98; ret., 1998. Adv. com. Acad. Resource Ctr. Moore-Norman Tech. Ctr., 1988-2004. Adv. bd. Norman Salvation Army, 1978-90, chmn., 1986; organizer, historian Norman Salvation Army Womens Aux., 1983-2000, pres., 1985; organizer, past pres. Norman Literacy Coun., 1976—; organizing com., past pres. Norman Interfaith Coun., 1974-93; organizing com., past treas. Friends of the Norman Libr., 1979—; mem. McFarlin Meml. United Meth. Ch., historian 2-in-1 Sunday Sch. class, 1990-2002, lay leader, 1980-81, adminstrv. bd., 2001-2004; pres. Two-in-One Class, 2007. Recipient medal of appreciation, SAR, 2002; named Woman of Yr., Norman Bus. and Profl. Women, 1999; named to Literacy Hall of Fame, Pioneer Libr. Sys., Norman, 1995. Mem. DAR (regent Black Beaver chpt. 1998-2000, state literacy chmn. 2000-02, chpt. sec. 2003-08), Nat. Soc. Daus. 1812 (pres. 1889er chpt. 1991-93, state treas. 1996-2000, chpt. sec. 2002-08, chpt. treas. 2008-), Old Regime Study Club (pres. 1998-99), Coterie Club (pres. 1996, 2002, 2008), Delta Delta Delta Alumnae. Independent. Avocation: genealogy. Home: 2717 Walnut Rd Norman OK 73072-6940

ZAPHIRIOU, GEORGE ARISTOTLE, lawyer, educator; b. July 10, 1919; came to U.S., 1973, naturalized, 1977; s. Aristotle George and Callie Constantine (Economou) Z.; m. Peaches J. Griffin, June 1, 1973; children: Ari, Marie. JD, U. Athens, 1940; LLM, U. London, 1950. Bar: Supreme Ct. Greece 1946, Eng. 1956, Ill. 1975, Va. 1983. Gen. counsel Counties Ship Mgmt. and R & K Ltd., London, 1951-61; practicing barrister, lectr. City of London Poly., 1961-73; vis. prof. Ill. Inst. Tech.-Chgo. Kent Coll. Law, 1973—75; pvt. practice Northbrook, Ill., 1975—78; prof. law George Mason U. Sch. Law, 1978-94, prof. law emeritus, adj. prof., 1994—. Prof. internat. transactions George Mason U. Internat. Inst., 1992-94; mem. Odin, Feldman & Pittelman P.C., Fairfax, Va., 1994-96; mem. study group on internat. elec. commerce conv. and other pvt. internat. law convs. U.S. Dept. of State. Author: Transfer of Chattels in Private International Law, 1956, U.S. edit., 1981, European Business Law, 1970; co-author: Declining Jurisdiction in Private International Law, 1995; joint editor: Jour. Bus. Law, London, 1962-73; bd. dirs. and bd. editors Am. Jour. Comp. Law of Am. Soc. Comparative Law, 1980-94; contbr. articles to profl. jours. Mem.: ABA, Am. Arbitration Assn. (commL. panel arbitrators 1983—2008), George Mason Am. Inn of Ct. (founder, master, emeritus), Ill. Bar Assn. Home: 400 Green Pasture Dr Rockville MD 20852-4233 Business E-Mail: gzaphiri@gmu.edu.

ZAPP, KENNETH MICHAEL, engineering educator, department chairman; b. NYC, Oct. 10, 1944; s. Frederick Michael and Jane Zapp; m. Cindy Murphy Kelley, June 9, 2000; 1 child, Tara Paleczny Zapp. BA, Rice U., Houston, Tex., 1966; MBA, U. Houston, Tex., 1968; MA, Case Western Res. U., Cleve., 1973. Data processing mgr. B & B Engring. & Supply Co., Houston, 1968—69; instr. U. Houston, 1969—70; vis. prof. Cleve. State U., 1972—73, adj. prof., 1972—73; assoc. prof. William James coll. Grand Valley State U., Allendale, Mich., 1973—84, assoc. prof., 1973—84; prof. and dept. chair Met. State U., Mpls., 1984—. Hon. coun. Republic of Slovenia, Minn., 1999—2005. Contbr. articles to profl. jours. Devel. com. Minn. Sr. Fedn., St. Paul, 2008—; bd. chair Bosnian Women's Network, Mpls., 2000—06; fin. com. chair Affinity Plus Credit Union, St. Paul, 1990—93. With USN, 1962—68, Houston. Home: 3531 Hennepin Ave 1 Minneapolis MN 55408 Office: Met State Univ 1501 Hennepin Ave Minneapolis MN 55403 Office Fax: 612-659-7268. Business E-Mail: kenneth.zapp@metrostate.edu.

ZAPPE, JOHN PAUL, city editor, newspaper executive, educator; b. NYC, July 30, 1952; s. John Paul and Carolyn (Pikor) Z. BA, Marist Coll., 1978; JD, Syracuse U., NY, 1978. Reporter Poughkeepsie Jour., 1973-75, Nev. State Jour., Reno, 1979-80; prin. Am. Media Bold, Oakland, Calif., 1981-83; reporter Press-Telegram, Long Beach, Calif., 1983-88, city editor, 1988-97, webmaster PT Connect, 1995-97, mgr. new media, 1997-98; dir. new media Riverside (Calif.) Press-Enterprise, 1998-2000; v.p. new media L.A. Newspaper Group, Woodland Hills, Calif., 2000—03; prin. Zappe Media Svcs., 2003—; dir. bus. devel. Classified Intelligence, sr. analyst. Tchr. Syracuse U., 1976-78, Calif. State U., 1985-87, U. So. Calif., 2003—04; prin. Am. Media Bold, 1981-83. Chmn. Local 69 Newspaper Guild, Long Beach, 1984-87. Mem. NAA New Media Fedn., Belgian Tervuren Club of Southern Calif. (pres.), Sierra Club (mem. exec. com. Long Beach group, LA chpt.), S. Coast Agility Team (pres. & dir.) Office Phone: 562-252-0686. Business E-Mail: zappemedia@gmail.com.

ZAR, DAVID M., research associate, consultant; b. De Kalb, Ill., July 16, 1969; s. Jerrold H and Carol B Zar; m. Rene N Roth; children: Sarah E, Hannah K, Ian M. BSCS, Wash. U., St. Louis, 1992, BSEE, MSEE, Wash. U., St. Louis, 1993. Rsch. assoc. Wash. U., St. Louis, 1993—; sr. engr. Blendics LLC, St. Louis, 2007—08. Owner Z&R Techs. LLC, St. Louis, 2003—. Bd. mem. St. Louis Wind Symphony, 2004—08. Achievements include patents for design of instantaneously restartable clocks and their use. Office: Wash Univ St Louis 1 Brookings Dr Box 1024 Saint Louis MO 63130

ZARA, CLAUDIO, finance educator, management consultant; b. Milan, Oct. 26, 1965; s. Manlio Zara and Marisa Angela Sturme; m. Miriam Santoro, Aug. 1, 2002; 1 child, Vittorio Francesco. Degree in Bus. Adminstrn. Acctg. and Control, Bocconi U., Milan, 1989. Cert. internat. tchrs. program London Bus. Sch., 1996. Dir. asst. Canon S.p.A., Milan, 1990—92; sr. rschr. SDA Bocconi Sch. Mgmt., Milan, 1993—96, prof., 1997—2003, full prof., 2004—. Vis. fellow Warwick Bus. Sch., U. Warwick, Coventry, Midlands, England, 1994; cons. Credito Emiliano S.p.A., Reggio Emilia, Italy, 2000—; mem. investment com. Credem Venture Capital Fund, 2006—. Editor: Brand Valuation: The Brand Contribution to the Company Value, 1997, Banks and Corporate Financial Advisoring, 2001, Brand Valuation in Internet Retail Banking, 2003, Trends on Company Financing: How Bank Firm Relationships are Changing, 2003, Valuation for Investment Decision, 2005, Weather Derivatives in Wine Industry, 2008; columnist: newspaper articles La Repubblica - Affari e Finanza; contbr. articles to profl. jours. Adv. bd. Regione Lombardia, Milan, 2001—02. Named Best Exec. Tchr., SDA Bocconi Sch. Mgmt., 2005; grantee, Ministry Internat. Trade and Industry, Japan, 1995; fellow European Mobility Program, European Union, 1993—94. Avocations: running, wine tasting, mountain climbing, classis cars. Office: Bocconi U via Röentgen 1 20136 Milan Italy Office Fax: +390258365920. Personal E-mail: studio.czara@tiscali.it. Business E-Mail: claudio.zara@unibocconi.it.

ZARAMA, LUIS RAFAEL, bishop; b. Pasto, Colombia, Nov. 28, 1958; arrived in USA, 1991, naturalized, 2000; Licentiate in philos. & theol., Pasto Sem., Universidad Mariana, Colombia, 1982—87; licentiate in canon law, Universidad Javeriana, Bogota, Colombia, 1987—91. Ordained priest Archdiocese of Atlanta, 1993; parochial vicar Sacred Heart parish, Atlanta, 1993—96; adminstr. St. Helena mission, Clayton, Ga., 1996—2006; pastor St. Mark parish, Clarkesville, Ga., 1996—2006; vicar gen. Archdiocese of Atlanta, 2006—; appointed bishop, 2009; aux. bishop Archdiocese of Atlanta, 2009—. Advocate, Ct. Appeals Ecclesiastical Province Atlanta, 1993—97, Defender of the Bond, Ct. Appeals, 1997—; asst. dir. vocations Archdiocese of Atlanta,

2000—. Roman Catholic. Office: Archdiocese of Atlanta Catholic Ctr 680 W Peachtree St NW Atlanta GA 30308-1984 Office Phone: 404-888-7805. Office Fax: 404-888-7230.*

ZARATE, JUAN CARLOS, former federal official; b. Santa Ana, Calif., 1971; AB magna cum laude, Harvard U., 1993, JD cum laude, 1997. Bar: 1997. Law clerk US Dist. Ct. (So. dist.) Calif.; atty. appellate sect. criminal divsn. US Dept. Justice, Washington, prosecutor terrorism and violent crime sect.; asst. sec. treas. counter-terrorist financing US Dept. Treasury, Washington, 2004—05; dep. asst. to Pres. The White House, Washington, 2005—09; dep. nat. security adv. for combating terrorism NSC, Washington, 2005—09; sr. ad. transnational threats project Ctr. for Strategic & Internat. Studies (CSIS), Washington, 2009—. Head Fin. Crimes Enforcement Network (FinCEN), Office Fgn. Assets Control (OFAC), Tri-Border conf., Brazil, U.S. delegation to UAE; head treas. delegation G-8 Counter-Terrorism conf., Florence, Italy; policy advisor criminal investigation divsn. IRS; policy advisor Fin. Action Task Force (FATF). Author: Forging Democracy: A Comparative Study of the Effects of U.S. Foreign Policy on Central American Democratization, 1994; contbr. articles to profl. jours. Rotary internat. fellow, U. Salamanca, Spain. Mem.: Calif. Bar Assn. Office: Center for Strategic & International Studies (CSIS) 1800 K St NW Washington DC 20006*

ZARB, FRANK GUSTAVE, private equity firm executive; b. NYC, Feb. 17, 1935; s. Gustave and Rosemary (Antinoro) Z.; m. Patricia Koster, Mar. 31, 1957; children: Krista Anne, Frank, Jr. BBA, Hofstra U., 1957, MBA, 1962, L.H.D., 1975. Trainee Cities Service Oil Co., NYC, 1957-62; gen. partner Goodbody & Co., NYC, 1962-69; exec. v.p. CBWL-Hayden Stone, Inc. (investment banking), NYC, 1969-71; asst. sec. US Dept. Labor, Washington, 1971-72; exec. v.p. Hayden Stone, Inc., NYC, 1972-73; assoc. dir., Office Mgmt. & Budget Exec. Office of the Pres., Washington, 1973-74; asst. to Pres. for energy affairs The White House, Washington, 1974-77; adminstr. Fed. Energy Adminstrn., Washington, 1974-77; adv. U.S. Congress, Washington, 1977-78; gen. ptnr. Lazard Freres & Co., NYC, 1977-88; chmn., pres., CEO Smith, Barney, Harris, Upham & Co., Inc., NYC, 1988-93; vice chmn., group chief exec. The Travelers Inc., NYC, 1993-94; chmn., pres., CEO, Alexander & Alexander Svcs. Inc., NYC, 1994-97; pres. Nat. Assn. Securities Dealers, 1997-98, chmn., CEO, 1997—2000, Nasdaq Stock Market, Inc, 1997—2001; chmn. Frank Zarb Associates; sr. adv., mng. dir. Hellman & Friedman LLC, San Francisco, 2002—; interim chmn. Am. Internat. Group (AIG), NYC, 2005—06; non-exec. chmn. Promontory Financial Group, LLC. Bd. dirs. CS First Boston, Inc., Coun. on Fgn. Rels., FPL Group, Inc., 2002-, Kraft Foods Inc., 2007-; chmn. L.I. Power Authority, 1996-97; bd. dirs., mem. exec. com. Am. Internat. Group (AIG), 2001-; co-chair, Promontory Fin. Group, 2006- Author: The Stockmarket Handbook, 1969, Handbook of Financial Markets, The Municipal Bond Handbook Mem. bd. trustees Gerald R. Ford Found.; mem. and former chmn. bd. trustees Hofstra U, bd. dirs. Lower Manhattan Develop. Corp. Recipient Disting. Scholar award Hofstra U., 1974; bus. sch. named in his honor Hofstra U. Mem. Coun. Fgn. Rels. Office: Hellman & Friedman LLC 390 Park Ave 21st Fl New York NY 10022*

ZARE, RICHARD NEIL, chemistry professor; b. Cleve., Nov. 19, 1939; s. Milton and Dorothy (Amdur) Zare; m. Susan Leigh (Shively), Apr. 20, 1963; children: Bethany Jean, Bonnie Sue, Rachel Amdur. BA, Harvard U., 1961, PhD, 1964; post grad., U. Calif., Berkeley, 1961—63; DS (hon.), U. Ariz., 1990, Northwestern U., 1993, ETH, Zürich, 1993, Columbia U., 2000, State U. West Ga., 2001; DP (hon.), Uppsala U., Sweden, 2000; PhD (hon.), U. York, 2001, Hunan U., 2002, U. Paul Sabatier, 2003; PhD, Chamber Inst. Tech., 2007. Postdoctoral fellow Harvard U., 1964; rsch. assoc. Joint Inst. for Lab. Astrophysics, 1964—65; asst. prof., chemistry MIT, 1965—66; asst. prof., dept. physics and astrophysics U. Colo., 1966—68, assoc. prof. physics, astrophysics, chemistry, 1968—69; prof. chemistry Columbia U., 1969—77, Higgins prof. natural sci., 1975—77; prof. Stanford U., 1977—, Shell, disting. prof. chemistry, 1980—85, Marguerite Blake Wilbur prof., natural sci., 1987—, prof., physics, 1992—, Howard Hughes Med. Inst. prof., 2006—. Cons. Aeronomy Lab, NOAA, 1966—77; radio standards physics divsn. Nat. Bur. Std., 1968—77, Lawrence Livermore Lab., U. Calif., 1974—, SRI, Internat., 1974—, Los Alamos Sci. Lab., U. Calif., 1975—; fellow adj. Joint Inst. Lab. Astrophysics, U. Colo.; sci. adv. com. IBM, 1977—92; chmn. commn. on phys., scis., and math applications Nat. Rsch. Coun., 1992—95; chmn. bd. dir. Ann. Rev., Inc., 1995—. Contbr. articles to profl. jour.; editor: Chem. Physics Letters, 1982—85. Recipient Fresenius award, Phi Lambda Upsilon, 1974, Michael Polanyi medal, 1979, Nat. Medal Sci., 1983, Spectroscopy Soc. Pitts. award, 1983, Michelson-Morley award, Case Inst. Tech., Case Western Res. U., 1986, ISCO award for significant contbn. to instrumentation for biochemical separations, 1990, Bing Fellowship Tchg. award, 1996, Eastern Analytical Symposium award, 1997, Exceptional Sci. Achievement award, NASA, 1997, Space award Aviation Week and Space Tech., 1997, Disting. Svc. award, Nat. Sci. Bd., 1998, Centennial medal, Harvard U., Welch award, 1999, Wolf prize in chemistry, Wolf Found., Israel, 2005, Chandler medal, Columbia U., 2005, Pupin medal, 2005, Oesper award, U. Cin., 2006, H. Juliam award, NASA Rsch. Ctr., 2007, F.A. Cotton medal, ACS Tex. A&M Sec., 2009; named Calif. Scientist of Yr., 1997; fellow Alfred P. Sloan fellow, 1967—69, Non-resident fellow, Joint Inst. for Lab. Astrophysics, 1970—, Christensen fellow, St. Catherine's Coll. Oxford U., 1982, Stanford U., 1984—86. Fellow: AAAS, Inst. of Physics, Royal Soc. Chemistry (hon. Faraday medal 2001), Calif. Acad. Sci. (hon.); mem.: NAS (coun. mem., Chem. Sci. award 1991), Indian Acad. Scis., Chem. Rsch. Soc. India, European Acad. Scis., Chinese Acad. Scis. (fgn.), Swedish Royal Acad. Engring. Scis. (fgn.), Royal Soc. London (fgn.), World Jewish Acad. Scis. (hon.), Chem. Soc. London, Am. Philos. Soc., Am. Chem. Soc. (Harrison Howe award 1985, Remsen award 1985, Kirkwood award 1986, Willard Gibbs medal 1990, Peter Debye award in phys. chemistry 1991, Linus Pauling medal 1993, Dannie-Heineman prize 1993, Harvey prize 1993, Analytical Chemistry Divsn. award in chem. instrumentation 1995, Analytical Chemistry award 1998, G.M. Kosalapoff award 1998, E. Bright Wilson award in spectroscopy 1999, Nobel Laureate Signature award 2000, Charles Lathrop Parsons award 2001, Madison Marshall award 2001, James Flack Norris award for outstanding achievement in the tchg. of chemistry 2004, Nichols medal NY sect. 2004, George C. Pimentel award 2008), Am. Phys. Soc. (Earle K. Plyler prize 1981, Irving Langmuir Prize 1985, Arthur L. Schawlow prize in laser sci. 2000), Am. Acad. Arts and Scis., Phi Beta Delta. Achievements include research in laser chemistry and chem. physics. Office: Stanford U Dept Chemistry Stanford CA 94305-5080 Office Phone: 650-723-3062. Business E-Mail: rnz@stanford.edu.

ZARELLA, PETER T., state supreme court justice; b. Boston; BS, Northeastern U., 1972; JD, Suffolk U., 1975. Bar: Mass. 1975, Conn. 1977, U.S. Dist. Ct. Mass. 1976, U.S. Dist. Ct. Conn. 1977, U.S. Supreme Ct. 1985, U.S. Ct. Appeals (2nd cir.) 1985, U.S. Dist. Ct., So. Dist. N.Y. 1990. Pvt. practice, 1977—96; ptnr. Brown, Paindiris & Zarella, Hartford, Conn., 1978—96; judge Superior Ct., 1996—99, Appellate Ct., 1999—2001; assoc. justice Conn. Supreme Ct., 2001—. Chmn. Criminal Justice Commn., 2001—; chmn. rules com. Superior Ct., 2001—. Mem.Ethics Commn., Town of West Hartford, Conn., 1992—95, mem. Charter Revision Commn., 1995—96. Mem.: Conn. Bar Assn. (mem. exec. com. coml. law and bankruptcy sect. 1985—90, mem. banking law com. 1990—94). Office: Conn Supreme Ct 231 Capitol Ave Hartford CT 06106*

ZAREM, HARVEY ALAN, plastic surgeon; b. Savannah, Ga., Feb. 13, 1932; s. Harry A. and Rose (Gold) Z.; m. Beth McCanghey, July 11, 1981; children: Harold, Allison, Melissa, Kathryn, Michael, Robert. BA, Yale U., 1953; MD, Columbia U. Coll. Physicians and Surgeons, 1957. Diplomate Am. Bd. Surgery, Am. Bd. Plastic Surgery; lic. physician, Md., Ill., Calif. Intern, surgery Johns Hopkins Hosp., Balt., 1957-58, resident, plastic surgery, 1964-66; rsch. fellow Peter Bent Brigham Hosp., Boston, 1958-59, asst. resident, surgery, 1959-61; resident, surgery then chief resident Boston City Hosp., 1961-63; postdoctoral fellow NYU, NYC, 1963-64; from asst. prof. to assoc. prof. surgery U. Chgo., 1966-73; head, sect. plastic surgery U. Chgo. Hosp. and Clinics; prof. surgery U. Calif., LA, 1973-87, prof. emeritus, 1987—, chief, divsn. plastic and reconstructive surgery, 1973—87; mem. med. staff Pacific Surgicenter, Santa Monica, Calif., 1987—. Physician Sepulveda (Calif.) VA Hosp., 1974—; mem. med. staff St. Johns Hosp., Santa Monica, Calif., 1987—, Santa Monica Hosp., 1988—; vis. prof. So. Ill. U., 1983, Lackaland AFB, 1986, Creighton U., 1987, Comesa, Milan, 1989, Baylor Coll. Medicine, 1990; Kazanjian vis. prof. Mass. Gen. Hosp., 1986, 88; cons. and presenter in field; cons. plastic surgery, Wadsworth VA Hosp., LA; surgeon, Extreme Makeover, ABC TV, 2003-. Contbr. numerous articles to profl. jours. Grantee NIH, 1964-75, NIH, 1967-72, Sheldon and Carol Appel Family Found., 1982—, Chantal Pharms., 1983-84, Mentor Corp./Heyer-Schulte Products, 1985—, Michael Jackson Burn Found., 1986-87. Fellow ACS; mem. AMA, Am. Soc. Plastic Reconstructive Sugeons, Inc., Am. Burn Assn., Am. Cleft Palat Assn., Am. Assn. Plastic Surgeons (trustee 1987, 1989), Am. Soc. Aesthetic Plastic Surgery, Inc., Am. Assn. Hand Surgery, Am. Assn. Surgery of Trauma, Calif. Med. Asssn., Calif. Soc. Plastic Surgeons, New Eng. Soc. Plastic Surgeons (hon.), L.A. County Med. Assn., Johns Hopkins Med. and Surg. Soc., Plastic Surgery Rsch. Coun., Soc. Head and Neck Surgeons (sr.), Soc. U. Surgeons, Lipoplasty Soc. N.Am., Bay Surgical Soc., N.W. Soc. Plastic Surgeons (hon.), Calif. Plastic Surgeon Assn. (pres.), Calif. Yacht Club, Beverly Hills Country Club, (bd. dirs.). Office: Pacific Surgicenter 1301 20th St Ste 350 Santa Monica CA 90404-2082 Home Phone: 310-474-3904; Office Phone: 310-315-0222, 310-586-0700. Business E-Mail: hzarem@ucla.edu, drzarem@drzarem.com.

ZAREMBKA, PAUL, economics professor; b. St. Louis, Apr. 17, 1942; BS, Purdue U., 1964; MS, PhD, U. Wis., 1967. Asst. prof. U. Calif., Berkeley, 1967-72; vis. prof. Heidelberg U., Germany, 1970-71, Goettingen U., Germany, 1972; assoc. prof. SUNY, Buffalo, 1973-76, prof., 1976—, dir. grad. studies dept. econs., 1995—99. Sr. rsch. officer Internat. Labor Office, Geneva, 1974-77; rschr. Louis Pasteur U., Strasbourg, France, 1978-79; Fulbright-Hayes lectr. Coun. Internat. Exch. of Scholars, Poznan, Poland, 1979. Author: Toward a Theory of Economic Development, 1972; editor: Frontiers in Econometrics, 1974, The Hidden History of 9-11, 2008; gen.editor: Research in Political Economy, 1977—, Transitions in Latin America and in Poland and in Syria, 2007, Why Capitalism Survives Cries: The Shock Absorbers, 2009; co-editor: Essays in Modern Capital Theory, 1976; contbr. articles to profl. publs. Active Buffalo Ctr. chpt. exec. bd. United Univ. Professions, 1981—, pres., 1991-95, grievance officer acad., 1995-97, 2007—; active AFL-CIO Buffalo Labor Coun., 1982-83, 96-97, Commn. on Quality Edn. in Buffalo for the 1990s, 1990-91; mem. subcom. on capital appropriations City of Buffalo, 1990-2000, citizens adv. com., 1997-2000; bd. dirs. United Parents, 1991-94; chair Labor Party, Buffalo, 1996. NSF grantee, 1969-72. Office: SUNY Dept Econs 415 Fronczak Hall Buffalo NY 14260-1520 Office Phone: 716-645-2121 ext. 438. Business E-Mail: zarembka@buffalo.edu.

ZARET, BARRY LEWIS, cardiologist, medical educator; b. NYC, Oct. 3, 1940; s. Irving Z. and Beatrice (Fader) Zaret; m. Myrna Zimmerman, June 23, 1963; children: Adam L., Elliot C., Owen M. BS, Queens Coll., Flushing, NY, 1962; MD, NYU, 1966; MA, Yale U., New Haven, Conn., 1982. Diplomate Am. Bd. Internal Medicine. Intern Bellevue Hosp., NYC, 1966-67, resident, 1967-79; rsch. fellow John Hopkins U., Balt., 1969-71; asst. prof. medicine Yale U., New Haven, 1973-76, assoc. prof. medicine and diagnostic radiology, 1976, chief sect. cardiology, 1978—2004, assoc. prof. medicine and diagnostic radiology, 1980-82, prof. medicine and diagnostic radiology, 1982-84, Robert W. Berliner prof. medicine, 1984—, assoc. chair clin. affairs dept. internal medicine, 1994—2004; mem. staff Yale-New Haven Med. Ctr.; med. dir. Yale-New Haven Med. Hosp. Heart Ctr., 1999—2004. Mem. cardiovasc. subsplty. bd. Am Bd. Internal Medicine, 2002—. Mem. editl. bd. Am. Jour. Cardiology, 1977—, Jour. Am. Coll. Cardiology, 1986-91, 92-97, Jour. Cardiac Imaging, 1986—, Circulation, 1993; assoc. editor: Yearbook of Nuc. Medicine, 1980-95; editor-in-chief Jour. Nuc. Cardiology, 1993-2004; contbr. articles to profl. jours. Recipient Casimir Funk award Soc. Mil. Surgeons, 1973; recipient Herrman Blumgart Pioneer award New Eng. chpt. Soc. Nuc. Medicine, 1978, Solomon Berson Alumni Achievement award in clin. sci. NYU Sch. Medicine, 1998, Ellis Island medal Honor, 2004, Disting. Svc. award Am. Soc. Nuc. Cardiology, 2006. Fellow Am. Coll. Cardiology, Coun. Clin. Cardiology, Am. Heart Assn., Coun. Circulation, Am. Heart Assn., Am. Physiology Soc.; mem. Am. Soc. Clin. Investigation, Am. Fedn. Clin. Rsch., Assn. Am. Physicians, Soc. Nuc. Medicine, Am. Soc. Nuc. Cardiology (Disting. Svc. award 2006), Assn. Univ. Cardiologists, Assn. Profs. Cardiology (pres. 1992), Phi Beta Kappa, Alpha Omega Alpha, Interurban Clin. Club. Jewish. Home: 15 Cassway Rd Woodbridge CT 06525-1214 Office: 333 Cedar St # 3 New Haven CT 06520-8017 Office Phone: 203-785-4127. Business E-Mail: barry.zaret@yale.edu.

ZARETSKAYA, ELENA, social sciences educator, dean; b. Moscow, Apr. 14, 1952; d. Naum Borokchovich Zlotnic and Maya Petrovna Senkyevich; m. Anatoly Dmitrievich Chashchinskiy; children: Olga Alexandrovna, Dmitri Alexandrovich Zaretskiy. MS, Moscow State U., 1973; PhD, St. Petersburg State U., Russia, 1981; D, Moscow State U., Russia, 1999; academician (hon.), Acad. of Informatization, Moscow, Russia, 1993. Rschr. All-Union Inst. Sci. Tech. Info., Moscow, 1973—89; vice dir. Ind. Inst. Russian Enterpreneurship, Moscow, 1990—96; dean dept. social scis. and humanities Acad. Nat. Economy under Govt. Russian Fedn., Moscow, 1997—. Mem. Moscow bd. Russian Union Scientists, 1995—; fellow prof. Internat. Program Mgmt., 1996; mem. program com. Internat. Conf. Dialog, Moscow, 2001—. Author: Rethorics. Theory and Practice of Speech Communication, Business Communication (Silver Br., 2004), Speech Logic for Managers, Typology of Verbal Formation, Speech Logic. Hon. fellow consul Planet of Humans, Moscow, 2006, Russian Cultural Ctr. France, Paris, 2005. Recipient Honor of Russia, Govt. Russian Fedn., 1997, Medal 850-Yr. Moscow, 1996. Fellow: Internat. Advt. Assn.; mem.: Amnesty Internat. Russian Orthodox. Avocation: travel. Home: Sadovaya-Kudrinskaya 23-17a Moscow 123001 Russia Office: Acad Nat Economy Pr Vernadskogo 82 117571 Moscow Russia Office Phone: (007) 90 37495621. Office Fax: (007) 495 4343531.

ZARGES, THOMAS H., engineering executive; Degree in Engring., Va. Mil. Inst. V.p. bus. devel. United Engrs. & Constructors, 1990; pres., CEO power and indsl./mfg. divsns. Washington Group, 1991; sr. exec. v.p. ops. Washington Group Internat., Boise, Idaho, 2002—. Office: Washington Group Internat PO Box 73 Boise ID 83729

ZARGHAMI, CYMA, broadcast executive; b. Iran, 1962; d. Gorham and Catherine; m. George Obergfoll, 1994; children: Liam, Ethan. BA, U. of Vt., Burlington, 2000. Scheduling clerk, scheduling exec., programming exec. Nickelodeon, 1985—96, exec. v.p., gen. mgr., 1996—2004, pres., 2004—. Directs co. initiatives Big Help and Kids Pick the Pres. Campaign; launched Nick Jr., SNICK, Nicktoons. Named one of The 100 Most Powerful Women in Entertainment, Hollywood Reporter, 2006, 2007. Office: Nickelodeon 1515 Broadway New York NY 10036

ZARINS, BERTRAM, orthopedic surgeon; b. Latvia, June 22, 1942; came to U.S., 1946, naturalized, 1956; s. Richard Arthur and Maria (Rozenbergs) Z. AB in Chemistry, Lafayette Coll., 1963; MD, SUNY, Syracuse, 1967. Diplomate Am. Bd. Orthop. Surgery. Clin. instr. orthop. surgery Harvard Med. Sch., Boston, 1976—, asst. clin. prof., 1982—, assoc. clin. prof., 1996—, Harvard Thorndike prof. orthopaedic surgery, 2007—; orthop. surgeon Mass. Gen. Hosp., Boston, 1982-95, chief sports medicine svc., 1982—; team physician Boston Bruins Hockey Team, 1976—. Chmn. edn. com. Sports Medicine Coun., U.S. Olympic Com., 1980-92; team physician New England Patriots football team, 1982—; head physician USA Olympic teams XIV Winter Olympic Games, Sarajevo, Yugoslavia, 1984; cons. editor for sports medicine Jour. of Bone and Joint Surgery, 1999—. Contbr. articles to profl. jours. Team physician N.E. Revolution profl. soccer team, 1996—. Lt. comdr. M.C., USNR, 1973-75. Fellow ACS, Am. Acad. Orthop. Surgeons (chmn. com. on sports medicine 1993-97), Am. Coll. Sports Medicine; mem. AMA, Internat. Arthroscopy Assn. (bd. dirs. 1991-95), Arthroscopy Assn. N.Am., N.Am. Trauma Assn. (pres. 1977), Internat. Soc. of Arthroscopy, Knee Surgery and Orthopaedic Sports Medicine, Am. Shoulder and Elbow Surgeons, Herodicus Soc., Brookline (Mass.) Country Club, Somerset Club. Office Phone: 617-726-3421. Business E-Mail: bzarins@partners.org.

ZARINS, CHRISTOPHER KRISTAPS, surgeon, educator; b. Tukums, Latvia, Dec. 2, 1943; came to U.S., 1946; s. Richard A. and Maria (Rozenbergs) Z.; m. Zinta Zarins, July 8, 1967; children: Daina, Sascha, Karina. BA, Lehigh U., 1964; MD, Johns Hopkins U., 1968. Surgery residency U. Mich., Ann Arbor, 1968-74; asst. prof. surgery U. Chgo., 1976-79, assoc. prof. surgery, 1979-82, prof. surgery, 1983-93, chief of vascular surgery, 1978-93; prof. surgery Stanford (Calif.) U., 1993—, chmn. divsn. vascular surgery, 1993—2005, acting chmn. dept. of surgery, 1995-97. Author: Essays In Surgery, 1986, Atlas of Vascular Surgery, 1988; editor Jour. of Surg. Rsch., 1982-95; contbr. articles to profl. jours. Pres. Latvian Med. Found., Boston, 1991. Lt. comdr. USN, 1974-76. Grantee NIH, NSF. Mem. Am. Surg. Soc., Soc. for Clin. Surgery, Soc. for Vascular Surgery (pres. 1998-99), Internat. Soc. for Cardiovascular Surgery, Soc. of Univ. Surgeons, Latvian Nat. Acad. of Scis., Latvian Vascular Surg. Soc. (pres. 1989), Soc. for Vascular Surgery (pres. 1998-99). Avocations: triathlons, skiing. Office: Stanford U Med Ctr Divsn Vascular Surgery 300 Pasteur Dr # H3642 Stanford CA 94304-2203 Office Phone: 650-725-7830.

ZARISH, JANET ANN, art educator, director, actress; b. Chgo., Apr. 21, 1954; d. Joseph Frederick and Jane Avis Zarish; m. Mark Blum, May 29, 2005. BFA, Julliard Sch., NYC, 1976. Pvt. practice, 1992—; acting, scene study NYU, 1991, Ensemble Studio Theatre Summer Workshops, NY, 1994—96, Pearl Theatre Intern Program, NY, 1996, Actors Ctr., 1997—2005, Manhattan Sch. Music, 2000, NY Shakespeare Festival, Shakespeare Lab., 1997—; assoc. art prof., dir. NYU Tish Grad. Acting Program, 1996—. Conservatory adv. bd. Ensemble Studio Theater, NYC, 2008; pub. spkr. in fields, 2003—; pvt. practise UCLA, 1978. Actor: (films) Danny, 1997, Without A Trace, 1983, Mystic Pizza, 1988, Malcolm X, 1992, Square Root of Three, 1994, Object of My Affection, 1998, The Zoo, 1999, The Next Big Thing, 2001, Season of Youth, 2005, Life in Flight, 2006, Brooklyn to Manhattan, 2007; (TV series) Law & Order, 1996—2005, Good Night, 2006, The Fall of Troy, 2008, One Life to Live, 2008; (plays) Hamlet - The National Shakespeare Theatre, 2007; dir.: Hamlet, 2001, Romeo & Juliet, 2002, Picnic, 2007; actor: (Broadway plays) Miss Julie, 1981, Other People's Money, 1989—90, The Square, 2001, Romola and Nijinsky, 2003, Our Time Is Up, 2008; dir.: Piscary, 2008. Panel com. mem. Fulbright Scholarship Program, NYC, 2008—. Mem.: Actors Equity, Am. Fedn. TV and Radio Artist, Screen Actor Guild, Ensemble Studio Theater, Roosevelt Island Residents Assoc. (elect. bd. mem. 2008—), NYU Green Sustainability Com. Office: NYU Tish Grad Acting Program 721 Broadway 5th Fl New York NY 10003

ZARKIN, HERBERT J., wholesale distribution executive; b. 1938; m. Susan Zarkin; children: Amy, Ann. Attended, U. Pa. Exec. v.p. Zayre Corp., Framingham, Mass.; pres. Zayre Corp., HomeClub subs., Framingham, Mass., 1986-88; chmn. Zayre Corp., Zayre Stores div., Framingham, Mass., 1988; pres., CEO Waban Inc, Natick, 1988-95, chmn. bd., 1997-98; chmn. HomeBase, Irvine, Calif., 1999—2001, BJ's Wholesale Club, Inc., Natick, Mass., 1997—2006, chmn., interim CEO, 2006—07, chmn., CEO, 2007—09, chmn., 2009—. Bd. dirs. BJ's Wholesale Club, Inc., 1996—. Office: BJs Wholesale Club Inc 1 Mercer Rd Natick MA 01760-2400*

ZARNIKOW, ERIC R., federal agency administrator; B, Iowa State U., 1981; MBA, Drake U., Des Moines. V.p., treas. Gaylord Container Corp.; sr. v.p., chief officer, treas. The ServiceMaster Co., Downers Grove, Ill., 1999; assoc. adminstr. office capital access US Small Bus. Adminstrn., 2007—. Ind. bd. mem., chmn. audit com. Caraustar Industries, 2005—09. Mem.: Interstitial Cystitis Assn. (bd. mem., mem. exec. com.). Office: US Small Bus Adminstrn 409 3rd St SW Washington DC 20416*

ZARNOCH, ROBERT ANTHONY, judge, lawyer, educator; b. Balt., Sept. 19, 1945; s. Theodore Anthony and Dora Helen (Stemplezski) Z.; m. Jeanne Marie Borgerding, Feb. 7, 1970; children: Robert E., Elizabeth A. BA in English, Loyola Coll., 1967; MA in Journalism, Am. U., 1969; JD, Georgetown U., 1974. Bar: Md. 1974, D.C. 1975, U.S. Dist. Ct. Md. 1976, U.S. Ct. Appeals (4th cir.) 1977, U.S. Supreme Ct. 1978. Pub. info. officer IRS, DC, 1968-74; law clk. Md. Ct. Appeals, Annapolis, Md., 1974-75; asst. atty. gen. Md. Atty. Gen., Balt., 1975-79, chief legis. Annapolis, 1979—2008; assoc. judge Ct. Spl. Appeals, Annapolis, 2008—; instr. U. Md. Sch. Law, Balt., 1985-88, 95, U. Balt. Sch. Law, 1991—, Univ. Coll., College Park, 1995, Towson U., Md., 1996—2002. Lectr. Md. Judicial Inst., Annapolis, 1985, 92, 96, 98, 2002, 05, 08, 09, Md. Inst. Continuing Profl. Edn. of Lawyers, Balt.,

1983, 93, 2000, 03, 05, 08, 09; mem. standing com. rules of practice and procedure US Ct. Appeals Md., 1993—2008; mem. 4th Cir. Jud. Conf.; speaker in field. Mem. editl. bd. Daily Record, 1996-2006; contbr. articles to profl. jours. Vice-chmn. Gov.'s Commn. to Revise Adminstrv. Procedure Act, Balt., Annapolis, 1991, chmn. Task Force to Study Dual Office Holding, 1995; mem. Code Revision Com., 2008-, Code Revision Article Com., Annapolis, 1990-94, 1999-2001, 08-, Gov.'s Task Force Adminstrv. Hearing Officers, 1988, Gov.'s Jr. Cabinet, Annapolis, 1987-90, Gov.'s Task Force County-Mcpl. Relationships, 1982-83. Recipient Leadership in Law award, Daily Record, 2005. Mem. Md. State Bar Assn. (adminstrv. law sect. 1986-2006, litigation sect. 1989—), D.C. Bar Assn., Soc. Profl. Journalists, Rule Day Law Club, Lawyers' Roundtable, Kappa Tau Alpha. Democrat. Roman Catholic. Avocations: writing, reading, movies. Home: 2829 Dana Ct Ellicott City MD 21042-2561 Office: Assoc Judge Ct Spl Appeals 361 Rowe Blvd Annapolis MD 21401 Office Phone: 410-260-3701. Business E-Mail: robert.zarnoch@mdcourts.gov.

ZARO, BRAD A., research and development company executive, biologist; b. San Jose, Calif., Dec. 4, 1949; s. Raymond J. and Irene R. Z.; children: Amy C., Kristen E. BA in Zoology, San Jose State U., 1974, MA in Biology, 1981. Chemist, Dept. Drug Metabolism Syntex Rsch., Inc., Palo Alto, Calif., 1976-78, chemist II, Dept. Drug Metabolism, 1978-81, chemist III, Dept. Drug Metabolism, 1981-84, clin. rsch. assoc. I, Inst. of Clin. Medicine, 1984-85, clin. rsch. assoc. II, Inst. of Clin. Medicine, 1985-87, sen. clin. rsch. assoc., Inst. of Clin. Medicine, 1985-87; sen. clin. rsch. assoc. Triton Biosciences, Inc., Alameda, Calif., 1988, mgr. clin. trials, 1988; pres., CEO Clinimetrics Rsch. Assoc., Inc., San Jose, 1988—. Contbr. articles to scholarly jours. Mem. AAAS, Am. Coll. Clin. Pharmacology, Am. Soc. Pharmacognosy, Assn. Clin. Rsch. Profls., Drug Info. Assn. Democrat. Roman Catholic. Avocations: scuba diving, skiing, flying. Home: 5681 Morningside Dr San Jose CA 95138-2229

ZARR, MELVYN, lawyer, educator; b. Worcester, Mass., Aug. 29, 1936; m. Gail Sclar, Aug. 29, 1971. AB, Clark U., 1958; LL.B., Harvard U., 1963. Bar: Mass. bar 1964, Maine bar 1973. Staff atty. NAACP Legal Def. & Edn. Fund, Inc., NYC, 1963-69; co-dir. Mass. Law Reform Inst., Boston, 1970-73; prof. law U. Maine, 1973—; U.S. magistrate, Portland, Maine, 1977-82. Mem.: Am. Law Inst. Home: 19 Mckinley Rd Falmouth ME 04105-1913 Office: U Maine Sch Law 246 Deering Ave Portland ME 04102-2837 Office Phone: 207-780-4359. Business E-Mail: mzarr@usm.maine.edu.

ZARRA, ERNEST JOSEPH, III, secondary school educator, researcher; b. Montclair, NJ, Dec. 14, 1955; s. Ernest Joseph Jr. and Faith Zarra; m. Susan Sembrat, May 29, 1976; children: Elya Joelle, Jonathan Joseph. BA, Northeastern Bible Coll., 1978; MA, Simon Greenleaf U., 1981; MABS, Grace Grad. Sch., Long Beach, Calif., 1986; MEd, Calif. State U., Bakersfield, 1988; PhD, U. So. Calif., 1999. Cert. tchr., N.J., Calif. Pvt. sch. tchr., 1978-89; pastor Millington Bapt. Ch., Basking Ridge, NJ, 1994-95; tchr., GATE coord. Fruitvale Sch. Dist. Pub. Sch., Bakersfield, Calif., 1989-94, 95-00; tchr. govt. and econs. Centennial H.S., Bakersfield, Calif., 2000—, girls varsity soccer coach, 2000—. Adj. faculty Calif. State U., Bakersfield, 1998—, Pt. Loma Nazarene U.; lectr. U. Pa., Bakersfield Coll., Fresno Pacific U., U. San Diego, others; presenter in field. Author: It Should Never Happen Here, 1997; contbr. articles to profl. jours. Youth coach Am. Youth Soccer Orgn., Kern County, Calif., 1993—; youth and adults tchr. Laurelglen Bible Ch., Bakersfield, 1984—; presenter to law enforcement officers Kern County Sheriffs Dept., 1988. Named All-Am. Soccer Player Nat. Christian Coll. Athletic Assn., 1978, All-State. All Dist., All Conf.; drafted Dallas Tornado (NASL), 1978. Mem. ASCD, Am. Edni. Rsch. Assn., Evang. Theol. Soc., Link Inst., Kappa Delta Pi (Character Edn. Partnership). Republican. Mennonite Brethren. Avocations: athletics, writing, travel, ministry, debate. Home: 400 Sinaloa Ave Bakersfield CA 93312-9334

ZARRELLA, RONALD L., retired pharmaceutical executive; b. Waterbury, CT, 1949; BSEE, Worcester Poly. Inst., Worcester, Mass., 1971; student, NYU Grad. Sch. Bus., NYC. With Bristol Myers Co., Esmark Corp.; exec. Bausch & Lomb Inc., 1985—94; v.p., No. Am. Vehicle Sales GM Co., 1994—98, exec. v.p. GM N. Am., 1998—2001; chmn., CEO Bausch & Lomb Inc., Rochester, NY, 2001—08, chmn. emeritus, 2008—. Bd. dir. Avaya, Inc., FIRST (For Inspiration and Recognition of Science and Technology), Univ. Rochester Med. Ctr., NY. Mem.: Rochester Inst. Tech., Comm. for Econ. Devel., Nat. Italian Found. Office: c/o Bausch & Lomb Inc One Bausch & Lomb Place Rochester NY 14604*

ZARRES, SHARON L., marriage and family therapist, health facility administrator; b. Altadena, Calif., June 11, 1947; d. Verne Ivan and Ruth Elizabeth Hatfield; m. Michael Paul Zarres, 1977; adopted children: Rebecca, Philip, Victor, Amber, James, MacKenzie. BA, Azusa Pacific U., 2000, MA in Clin. Psychology, 2002, MA in Marriage and Family Therapy, 2003. Ordained to ministry Western Evang. Orgn. Dir. Jack & Jill Pre-Sch./Grade Sch., La Puente, Calif.; office mgr. World Vision Internat., Monrovia, Calif., 1985—95; owner, mgr. Zarres Family Day Care, Covina, Calif., 1995—2005; adminstr., marriage and family therapist Father's Heart Ranch, Desert Hot Springs, Calif., 2003—. Mem. integration com. Azusa (Calif.) Pacific U., 2000—, tchg. and rsch. asst., 2001—02. Foster parent Koinonia Foster Homes, San Bernardino, Calif.; v.p., founder Lighthouse Prayer, Covina. Avocations: reading, travel, movies. Home and Office: 71-175 Aurora Rd Desert Hot Springs CA 92241

ZARRIN-KHAMEH, NEDA, pathologist; arrived in US, 1999, permanent resident, 2004; d. Hassan Zarrin-Khameh and Amirzadeh Amir-Ghazanfari; m. Hamed Jafar-Nejad, Aug. 18, 1994; 1 child, Neema Jafar-Nejad. MD, Tehran U. Med. Scis., 1994; MPH, U. Tex. Sch. Pub. Health, Houston, 2002. Lic. Tex. Med. Examiner, 2007. Internship Tehran U. Tchg. Hosps., 1992—94; supr. physician, blood donation sect. Iranian Blood Transfusion Services, Tehran, 1994—96; gen. practitioner, emergency dept. Shahriar Gen. Hosp., Tehran, 1994—97; gen. practitioner Ghadir Khom Clinic, Tehran, 1996—99; rsch. asst. Nat. Rsch. Ctr. Genetic Engring. & Biotech., Tehran, 1998—99; v.p. knowledge devel. Intelligent Diagnostics Inc., Houston, 2000—01; pathology resident Baylor Coll. Medicine, Houston, 2005—07, cytopathology fellow, 2007—; surg. pathology fellow Meth. Hosp., Houston, 2008—; asst. prof. Baylor Coll. Medicine; with Ben Tanb Gen. Hosp., Houston; asst. prof. Baylor Coll. Medicine, ben Tanb Gen. Hosp. Recipient Resident Good Citizen award, Baylor Coll. Medicine, 2007. Mem.: AMA, US and Can. Acad. Pathology, Tex. Med. Assn., Harris County Med. Soc., Tex. Soc. Pathologists. Achievements include patents for automated medical decision making utilization; research in the association of heat shock protein 70 gene polymorphism with risk of coronary heart disease and stroke; molecular studies in a sample of Iranian phenylketonuria patients; several case reports. Avocations: basketball, cooking, gardening. Office: Baylor Coll Med Dept Pathology One Baylor Plz Houston TX 77030

ZARRO, JANICE ANNE, lawyer; b. Newark, June 30, 1947; BA, Rutgers U., 1969; JD, IIT-Chgo.-Kent Coll. Law, 1973. Bar: Pa. 1974. Counsel jud. com. U.S. Ho. Reps., Washington, 1973-77; profl. staff mem. counsel labor and human resources com. U.S. Senate, Washington, 1977-80; dir. Avon Products, Inc., NYC, 1980-81, Washington, 1982-86, v.p., 1986-90; pres. The Novus Group, Inc., 1990-92; dir. fed. affairs Mallinckrodt Med., 1992—, v.p., 1993-94; v.p. govt. affairs Worldwide Mallinckrodt Inc., 1994-2000; exec. dir. Women's Resource Ctr. Sarasota County, 2003—. Gen. counsel Nat. Italian-Am. Found., 1989-96, chair bd. trustees, 1996-99; mem. Bus. Govt. Rels. Coun., Washington, 1987—; past chair Women's Fgn. Policy Group. Past chmn. Nat. Capital chpt. Multiple Sclerosis Soc. Recipient Leadership Recognition award Nat. Women's Econ. Alliance, 1984. Office Phone: 341-366-1700. Business E-Mail: jzarro@thewomensresourcecenter.org.

ZARTMAN, CHARLEEN THERESE, physical education educator; d. Leonard and Mary Boehnert; m. Patrick Zartman, July 31, 1976; children: Teri, Chrissie. BS, UCLA, 1973. Registered yoga tchr. Yoga Alliance, 2007. Prof. El Camino Coll., Torrance, Calif., 1976—. Author: (books) Youth Volleyball. Named Volleyball Coach of Yr., 1983, 1985. Mem.: CAHPERD (Southern Sect. Health Educator of Yr. award). Avocation: volleyball. Office: El Camino Coll 16007 Crenshaw Blvd Torrance CA 90506-0001 Business E-Mail: czartman@elcamino.edu.

ZARTMAN, DAVID LESTER, retired zoology educator, researcher; b. Albuquerque, July 6, 1940; s. Lester Grant and Mary Elizabeth (Kitchel) Z.; m. Micheal Aline Plemmons, July 6, 1963; children: Kami Renee, Dalan Lee. BS cum laude in Dairy Husbandry, N.Mex. State U., 1962; MS in Genetics, Ohio State U., 1966, PhD in Genetics, 1968. Cert. dairy cattle specialist, Am. Registry Profl. Animal Scientists. Jr. ptnr. Marlea Guernsey Farm, Albuquerque, 1962-64; grad. rsch. assoc. Ohio State U., Columbus, 1964-68; asst. prof. dairy sci. N.Mex. State U., Las Cruces, 1968-71, assoc. prof., 1971-79, prof., 1979-84, Ohio State U., Columbus, 1984—2006, emeritus prof., 2006—. Chmn. dept. Ohio State U., Columbus, 1984-99; pres. Mary K. Zartman, Inc., Albuquerque, 1976-84; cons. Bio-Med. Electronics, Inc., San Diego, 1984-89, Zartemp, Inc., Northbrook, Ill., 1990, Recom Applied Solutions, 1993-2000, Am. Registry of Profl. Animal Scientists, 1996—, Midwest Univs. Consortium for Internat. Assistance, 2004. Contbr. articles to profl. jours.; patentee in field. Recipient State Regional Outstanding Young Farmer award Jaycees, 1963, Disting. Rsch. award N.Mex. State U. Coll. Agr. and Home Econs., 1983, Outstanding Svc. award Ohio Poultry Assn., 1999, Grazier of Yr. award Gt. Lakes Internat. Grazing Conf., 2001, hon. state degree Ohio FFA, 2000, The Jack Tucker Disting. Svc. award Ohio Forage and Grassland Coun., 2004; course acclaimed by Humane Soc. of U.S.; named one of Top 100 Agr. Alumni, N.Mex. State U. Centennial, 1987; spl. postdoctoral fellow NIH, New Zealand, 1973; Fulbright-Hayes lectr., Malaysia, 1976. Fellow AAAS; mem. Am. Dairy Sci. Assn., Am. Soc. Animal Sci., Dairy Shrine Club, Ohio Farm Bur., Sigma Xi, Gamma Sigma Delta, Alpha Gamma Rho (1st Outstanding Alumnus N.Mex. chpt. 1985), Alpha Zeta, Phi Kappa Phi. Home: 7671 Deer Creek Dr Worthington OH 43085-1551 Office: Ohio State U 2027 Coffey Rd Columbus OH 43210-1043 Home Phone: 614-431-3479; Office Phone: 614-292-1387. Business E-Mail: zartman.3@osu.edu.

ZARUTSKIE, JENNIFER ANNE, lawyer; b. Ashland, Pa., Jan. 30, 1974; d. Frank and Joan Ellen Zarutskie. AB in Chemistry magna cum laude, Bryn Mawr Coll., Pa., 1996; PhD in Biol. Chemistry, MIT, Cambridge, Mass., 2001; JD cum laude, Boston U., 2004. Bar: U.S. Patent and Trademark Office 2001, Mass. 2004. Patent agt. Foley Hoag LLP, Boston, 2001—04, atty., 2005—, Goodwin Procter LLP, 2004—05. Coach Ctr. for Women in Enterprise. Contbr. articles to profl. jours. Pro bono atty. Econ. Justice Project, Bus. Law Clinic, Lawyer's Clearinghouse on Affordable Housing and Homelessness. Fellow Merck/MIT Collaboration Grad. fellow, 1998—2000; scholar Paul J. Liacos scholar, 2003, G. Joseph Tauro scholar, 2002, Keystone Symposium scholar, 2000. Mem.: Am. Chem. Soc., Boston Bar Assn., Boston Patent Law Assn., Am. Intellectual Property Law Assn., Women Entrepreneurs in Sci. and Tech., Licensing Execs. Soc. Office: Foley Hoag LLP 155 Seaport Blvd Boston MA 02210

ZARWYN, BERTHOLD, physicist, consultant; b. Vienna, Aug. 22, 1921; came to US, 1949, naturalized, 1955; s. Joseph and Bronislawa Regina (Unger) Zarwyn. ME, Gliwice, Poland, 1946; ScD, UN Univ., Munich, 1947; PhD, NYU, 1954; ScD in Engring., Columbia U., NYC, 1963. Project engr. Curtiss-Wright Corp., Woodridge, NJ, 1951-55; staff scientist AMF Corp., NYC, 1955-57; chief scientist Link Aviation Co., Binghamton, NY, 1957-58; head rsch. staff Am. Bosch-Arma Corp., Garden City, NY, 1958-63; corp. cons. Cutler-Hammer Corp., Deer Park, NY, 1963-65; chief engr. Bell Aerosystems Corp., Niagara Falls, NY, 1965-66; sr. cons. Mitre Corp., Bedford, Mass., 1966-68; spl. asst. to commdg. gen., acting chief engr. Hdqs. US Army Materiel Command, Arlington, Va., 1968-71; chief phys. scis. br. US Army Devel. and Readiness Command, Alexandria, Va., 1971-75; phys. scientist US Army Harry Diamond Labs., Washington, 1975-78; chief sys. analysis br. US Army Elec. Rsch. and Devel. Command, Adelphi, Md., 1978-79, chief tech. divsn., 1979-81, asst. tech. dir., 1981-85; spl. asst. to dep. chief of staff for tech. & program mgmt. US Army Lab. Command, Adelphi, Md., 1985-87; pres. Pan-Tech. Corp., Delray Beach, Fla., 1987—. Adj. faculty, lectr., cons. in field; dir. Film Microelectronics Co. Inc., Burlington, Mass., 1965-67. Mem. editl. bd. Bavarian Soc. Engrs., 1947-49, transl. panel Russian Jour. Applied Math. and Mechanics with Pergamon Inst., 1956-57; inventor nuc. gyroscope, microwave holography, other items. Mem. IEEE, Am. Phys. Soc., NY Acad. Scis., Sigma Xi. Home and Office: Pan-Tech Corp 7589 Mansfield Hollow Rd Delray Beach FL 33446-3314 Office Phone: 561-637-9387. Personal E-mail: zarwyn22@comcast.net.

ZARYCHTA, WILLIAM ALEX, aviation medical officer, physician assistant; BS in Health, West Chester U., 1996; AAS in Nursing, Gloucester County Coll., 1999; BS in Physician Asst. Studies, Hahnemann U., 2001; M in Physician Asst. Studies, U. Nebr., 2002; MPH, U. Minn., 2009. Cert. physician asst. Nat. Commn. Certification Physician Assts., paramedic Nat. Registry Emergency Med. Technicians, lic. physician asst.; RN, Pa. Paramedic Mercy Health Sys., Darby, Pa., 1993—99, emergency RN, 1999—2000; emergency medicine physician asst. Brandywine Emergency Physician Assocs., Coatesville, Pa., 2001—06; mil. medicine physician asst. US Army, Afghanistan, 2004—05; med. officer dept. homeland security USPHS, DC, 2006—08; med. officer US Coast Guard, 2008—. Clin. instr. Arcadia U., Glenside, Pa., 2001—06, Drexel U., Phila., 2001—06, clin. asst. prof., 2006—. Contbr. articles to profl. jours. Med. screening Spl. Olympics, Phila., 2000, Mid-Atlantic Boating Assn., Ocean City, Md., 2001. With US Army, 1990—2006, with USPHS, 2006—08, with USCG, 2008—. Decorated Bronze Star medal, 3 Army Commendation medals, 3 Army Achievement medals, Humanitarian Svc. medal, Mil. Outstanding Vol. Svc. medal, Global War on Terrorism Expeditionary and Svc. medals, Combat Action ribbon, Combat Med. badge, Flight Surgeon badge US Army, Excellence in Competition Pistol badge, Physician Asst. badge USCG, State of NJ Disting. Svc. medal; recipient Presdl. Academic Fitness award; named Fed. Svc. Physician Asst. of Year, Assn. Mil. Surgeons US. Fellow: Pub. Health Svc. Acad. Physician Assts. (bd. dirs.), Soc. Emergency Medicine Physician Assts., Am. Acad. Physician Assts.; mem.: Commissioned Officer Assn., Assn. Mil. Surgeons US (life), EMT Hist. Soc. (disting.), Am. Coll. Clinicians (charter), Phi Theta Kappa. Office: USCG HQ HSC k 2100 Second St SW Washington DC 20593-0001

ZASADA, MARY EILEEN, nursing administrator; b. Waterbury, Conn., July 23, 1957; d. Walter Francis and Elizabeth Ann (Doyle) Lewis; m. Peter Pilkington Zasada, Sept. 8, 1984; children: Kathleen, Andrew. Diploma in nursing, St. Vincent's Med. Ctr., 1978; BS in Mgmt., Tiekyo Post U., 1983; MSN, Sacred Heart U., 1997. RN, Conn. Staff New Britian (Conn.) Gen. Hosp., 1978-79, St. Mary's Hosp., Waterbury, Conn., 1980-84, nurse analyst, 1984-98, project leader clin. applications, 1998—. Bd. dirs. Conn. Healthcare Informatics Network. Mem. Rotary Internat. (bd. dirs. 1990-98, Paul Harris fellow), Girls Inc. of Waterbury (bd. dirs. 1996-2001), Sigma Theta Tau (Mu Delta chpt.). Home: 122 Terrell Farm Rd Bethlehem CT 06751-1408 Office: St Marys Hosp 56 Franklin St Waterbury CT 06706-1238

ZASLAV, DAVID M., broadcast executive; b. Brooklyn, NY, Jan. 15, 1960; m. Pam Zaslav, 1987; 3 children. Student, Cornell U., 1978—79; BS, SUNY, Binghamton, 1981; JD cum laude, Boston U., 1985. Corp. entertainment atty. LeBouef, Lamb, Leiby & MacRae; gen. counsel, NBC Cable NBC, 1988, v.p. bus. affairs CNBC, 1990, v.p. bus. devel., 1992, sr. v.p. affiliate mktg. & sales, 1993, exec. v.p. bus. devel. and affiliate sales mktg. NBC Cable Networks, 1995, pres. NBC Cable Distribution, 1996, pres. NBC Universal Cable, 1999—2006, pres. Domestic TV and New Media Distribution, 2006; pres., CEO Discovery Comm. Inc., 2007—. Bd. dirs. A&E Network, Nat. Geographic TV, TiVo, 2000—, Nat. Cable Ctr., Cable in the Classroom, NYC Ctr. Communications; adj. prof. Fordham U. Mem.: Nat. Assn. TV Program Execs. (bd. mem.), Nat. Cable & Telecommunications Assn. (bd. mem.). Office: Discovery Comm 1 Discovery Pl Silver Spring MD 20910*

ZASLAVSKY, LEONID, research scientist; b. Russia; PhD in Computational Modeling and Numerical Analysis, Russian Acad. Scis., Moscow, 1993. Postdoc. fellow Weizman Inst. Sci., Israel, 1993, Courant Inst. Math. Scis., NYU, 1996, Howard Hughes Med. Inst., 1996; scientist Nat. Ctr. Biotech. Info., NIH, Bethesda, Md., 2004—. Mem.: Assn. Computer Machinery, Am. Com. Weizmann Inst. Sci. (mem. bd. scientists, Wash. regional sect.). Achievements include development of NCBI influenza virus resource.

ZASLAW, NEAL, musicologist; b. NYC, June 28, 1939; s. Alexander and Bertha Lampert Zaslaw; m. Ellen Faust, June 10, 1962; children: Sarah, Diana. BA, Harvard U., Cambridge, Mass., 1961; MS, Juilliard Sch., NY, 1963; MA, Columbia U., NY, 1965, PhD, 1970. Herbert Gussman prof. music Cornell U., Ithaca, NY, 1970—. Musicological advisor Lincoln Ctr., NYC, 1988—92; instr. Juilliard Grad. Sch., NYC, 1988—92; musicological supr. Decca Records Ltd., London, 1978—82; instr. City Coll., CUNY, NYC; musical adv. St. Paul Chamber Orch., 2003—06. Author: Mozart's Symphonies: Context, Performance Practice, Reception, 1989, The Classical Era from the 1740s to the End of the 18th Century, 1989, The Compleat Mozart, 1990, W.A. Mozart: Portfolio of a Genius, 1991, Mozart's Piano Concertos: Text, Context, Interpretation, 1996, The Birth of the Orchestra: History of an Institution 1650-1815, 2004; editor-in-chief: Current Musicology, 1967—70; contbr. articles to profl. jours. Book review editor Music Libr. Assn. Notes, 1970—75. Recipient Österreichische Ehrenkreuz für Wissenschaft und Kunst award, Austrian Ministry Culture, 1991; fellow, Am. Coun. Learned Soc., 1983—84; Dissertation Yr. fellow, Martha Baird Rockefeller Fund for Music, 1968—69, Sr. fellow, NEH, 1976—77. Fellow: Am. Acad. Arts & Sci.; mem.: Soc. France Musicology, der Musikforschung, Royal Musical Assn., Am. Musicol. Soc. (v.p. 1992—94). Office: Cornell Univ Lincoln Hall Ithaca NY 14853-4101 Office Phone: 607-255-4279. Business E-Mail: naz2@cornell.edu.

ZASLOW, ERIC GALLANT, mathematics professor; b. NYC, June 19, 1968; s. Stephen Zaslow and Fran Walker; m. Lizzie Burslem; children: Henry Dimond, Molly Pearl. AB, Dartmouth Coll., Hanover, NH, 1989; AM, Dartmouth Coll., 1989; PhD, Harvard U., Cambridge, Mass., 1995. Prof., math. Northwestern U., Evanston, Ill., 1998—. Author: (book) Ultimate Techniques and Tactics. Achievements include research in field mirror symmetry, mathematical physics. Office: Northwestern Univ 2033 Sheridan Rd Evanston IL 60208

ZASLOW, JEFFREY LLOYD, journalist, columnist; b. Phila., Oct. 6, 1958; s. Harry and Naomi (Weintraub) Zaslow; m. Sherry Lynn Margolis, July 4, 1987; children: Jordan Danielle, Alexandra Nicole, Eden Gabrielle. BA with honors, Carnegie Mellon U., Pitts., 1980. Reporter/columnist Orlando Sentinel, Fla., 1980-83; staff writer Wall St. Jour., 1983-87, columnist, 2001—, Chgo. Sun Times, 1987—2001, USA Weekend mag., 1994—2002. Author: The Girls from Ames, 2009 (Publishers Weekly bestseller); co-author (with Randy Pausch): The Last Lecture, 2008 (#1 Publishers Weekly bestseller, #1 NY Times bestseller); TV appearances include The Tonight Show, Larry King Live, 60 Minutes, The Today Show, Good Morning America, The Oprah Winfrey Show. Recipient Will Rogers Humanitarian award, Nat. Soc. Newspaper Columnists, 2000, Nat. Soc. Newspaper Columnists award for best gen. interest column, 2003, 2005, Disting. Column Writing award, NY Newspaper Pub. Assn., 2008. Jewish. Achievements include using his column to run programs that benefited 47,000 disadvantaged Chicago children; hosting an annual singles party for charity, Zazz Bash, drawing 7,000 readers a year resulting in 78 marriages. Office: Wall St Jour Hdqs 200 Liberty St New York NY 10281 Business E-Mail: jeff.zaslow@wsj.com.*

ZATLIN, PHYLLIS, language educator, translator; b. Green Bay, Wis., Dec. 31, 1938; d. Frank L. and Ellen Mary (Butler) Z.; m. George Boring Kelly, Aug. 20, 1962; children: William, Lee. BA, Rollins Coll., 1960; postgrad., U. Grenoble, France, 1960-61; MA, U. Fla., 1962, PhD, 1965. Cert. Spanish to English translator Am. Translators Assn. Instr. Rutgers U., New Brunswick, N.J., 1963-66, asst. prof., 1966-71, assoc. prof., 1971-79, assoc. dean, 1974-80, prof. Spanish, 1979—2008, prof. emeritus, 2008—, chair dept. Spanish, grad. dir., 1980-87. Mem. discipline adv. com. Coun. Internat. Exch. Scholars', 1990—93; spkr. in field. Author: Elena Quiroga, 1977, Victor Ruiz Iriarte, 1980, Jaime Salom, 1982, Cross Cultural-Approaches to Theatre: The Spanish-French Connection, 1994, The Novels and Plays of Eduardo Manet: An Adventure in Multiculturalism, 2000, Theatrical Translation and Film Adaptation A Practitioner's View, 2005, Piecing Together the Butler Puzzle, 2008; editor (Francisco Ayala): El Rapto, 1971; co-author: Lengua y Lectura: Un Repaso y Una Continuación, 1970; editor (Victor Ruiz Iriarte): El Landó de Seis Caballos, 1979; editor: (Jaime Salom) La Piel del Limón, 1980; editor: (Antonio Gala) Noviembre y un Poco de Yerba. Petra Regalada, 1981; editor: (Francisco Nieva) Combate de Opalos y Tasia. Sombra y Quimera de Larra. La Magosta, 1990, El teatro alternativo español, 2001; co-editor: The Contemporary Spanish Theater. A Collection of Critical Essays, 1988, Homenaje (A Tribute to Martha T. Halsey), 1995, Entre Actos: Diálogos sobre teatro español, 1999, Un escenario propio (A Stage of Their Own), 1998, History and Myth of the Mad Queen: Modern Representations of Juana de Castile, 2008; co-guest editor jour. Art Teatral. Cuadernos de Minipiezas Illustradas, 1996; translator: play edits.: (J.L. Alonso de Santos) Going Down to Marrakesh, 1992, Hostages in the Barrio, 1997; translator: (Paloma Pedrero) Parting Gestures (The Color of August, A Night Divided, The Voucher, With Tonight in the Subway), 1999, Ana 3/11, 2007; translator: (Jaime Salom) A Bonfire at Dawn, 1992, 2006; translator: The Other William, 2004; translator: (Jean Bouchaud) Is That How It Was?, 2007; translator: (Francisco Nieva) Red Riding Hood, Part II, 2006; translator: (Jean-Paul Daumas) The Elephant Graveyard, 1994; translator: (Eduardo Manet) Lady Strass, 1992, 1997; translator: (Itziar Pascual) Gone Astray, 2006; translator: also performances; assoc. editor Estreno, 1992—2001; editor: Estreno Plays, 1998—2005; mem. editl. bd. Western European Stages, España Contemporánea, others, adv. bd. mem. Acotociones. State pres. Women's Equity Action League, N.J., 1971-72, nat. bd. dirs., Washington, 1973, 76-77. Fellow Fulbright Found., 1960-61, Woodrow Wilson Found., 1961-62; recipient Disting. Alumna award Rollins Coll., 1985, Profl. award Fgn. Lang. Educators of N.J., 1989, Outstanding Alumna award Romance Langs., U. Fla., 2003, Hon. Order Ky. Cols., 2008. Mem. AAUP (mem. nat. coun. 1987-90), MLA (mem. commn. on status of women 1978-81), Dramatists Guild, Soc. Gen. de Autores y Editores (Profl. award 1997), Southeast Jacksonport Neighborhood Assn.(bd. mem. 2009-). Democrat. Avocations: biking, jogging, travel. Home: 5 Timber Rd East Brunswick NJ 08816-2941 also: 6138 Lake Shore Rd Sturgeon Bay WI 54235 Business E-Mail: zatlin@rci.rutgers.edu.

ZATSIORSKY, VLADIMIR MOISEEVICH (MICHAILOVICH), biomechanics educator, researcher; b. Leningrad, Russia, Dec. 26, 1932; came to U.S., 1990; s. Moisey T. and Berta L. (Bardenstein) Z.; m. Rita Y. Zatsiorsky, Oct. 27, 1960; children: Betty V. Ulitsky, Michael V. PhD, Lesgaft Inst. Phys. Culture, Leningrad, 1961; DSc, Ctrl. Inst. Phys. Culture, Moscow, 1969; D honoris causa, Acad. Phys. Culture, Wroclaw, Poland, 1999, Russian State U. Phys. Culture, 2003. Asst. prof. Lvov Inst. Phys. Culture, Ukraine, 1954—57; asst. prof., assoc. prof., prof. Ctrl. Inst. Phys. Culture, Moscow, 1959—90; vis. prof. UCLA, 1990, U. Calgary, Canada, 1991; prof. kinesiology Pa. State U., University Park, 1991—2003. Med. commn. Internat. Olympic Com., 1982—. Author (15 books including): Science and Practice of Strength Training, 1995—2006, Kinematics of Human Motion, 1998, Kinetics of Human Motion, 2002; editor: Biomechanics in Sport, 2000, Classics in Movement Science, 2001 (all books published in English, Russian, German, Italian, Spanish, Portuguese, Chinese, Japanese, Polish, Romanian, Czech, Serbo-Croatian & Bulgarian); contbr. more than 400 rsch. papers. Recipient J. Dyson award Internat. Soc. of Sport Biomechanics, 1992, Jim Hay award Am. Soc. Biomechanics, 2008. Fellow: Am. Acad. Kinesiology; mem.: Internat. Soc. Sport Kinetics (hon.). Avocations: reading, music.

ZAUBLER, THOMAS SCOT, psychiatrist, educator; b. NY, June 13, 1963; s. Leland and Lynn Zaubler; m. Katharine L. Sonnenberg, Sept. 11, 1993; children: William Sonnenberg, Elizabeth Dale Sonnenberg. BA, Columbia U., 1986; MD, Albert Einstein Coll. of Medicine, 1991; MPH, U. Wash., 1997. Diplomate Nat. Bd. Med. Examiners, 1992, lic. gen. psychiatry Am. Bd. Psychiatry and Neurology, 1997, cert. subspecialty in psychosomatic medicine Am. Bd. Psychiatry and Neurology, 2005. Resident gen. psychiatry Cornell Med. Ctr. N.Y. Hosp., 1991—95; fellow psychosomatic medicine U. Wash., Seattle, 1995—97; dir. residency tng., asst. prof. Dept. Psychiatry Med. Ctr. Georgetown U., Washington, 1997—2000; chmn. Dept. Psychiatry Morristown (N.J.) Meml. Hosp., 2000—, med. dir. Dept. Psychiatry, 2000—; clin. assoc. prof. Dept. Psychiatry U. of Medicine and Dentistry N.J. Med. Sch., Newark, 2002—. Contbr. chapters to books, articles to profl. jours. Recipient Tchr. of the Yr. award, Dept. Psychiatry, U. of Medicine and Dentistry, N.J. Med. Sch., 2002; named Top Psychiatrist, Consumers' Checkbook, Guide to Top Doctors, 2002—09; grantee, NIH, 1995—97. Fellow: Am. Psychiat. Assn. (life); mem.: Am. Coll. Physician Execs., Am. Coll. Psychiatry, Acad. Psychosomatic Medicine. Office: Morristown Meml Hosp 100 Madison Ave Morristown NJ 07962 Office Fax: 973-290-7166. Business E-Mail: thomas.zaubler@atlantichealth.org.

ZAUCHA, JEROME J., lawyer; b. Uniontown, Pa., 1952; AB summa cum laude, U. Notre Dame, 1974; JD, Yale U., 1977. Bar: Pa. 1977, DC 1978. Ptnr., Internat. Trade practice Venable LLP, Washington; ptnr. Kirkpatrick & Lockhart Preston Gates Ellis LLP, Washington, 2007—. Mem.: Phi Beta Kappa. Office: Kirkpatrick & Lockhart Preston Gates Ellis LLP 1601 K St NW Washington DC 20006 E-mail: jerome.kaucha@klgates.com.

ZAUDER, GAIL S., investment banker; b. 1957; AB cum laude, Smith Coll.; MBA, Yale U. With Lehman Brothers Kuhn Loeb; joined Credit Suisse First Boston, NYC, 1985, mng. dir., head, Mergers & Acquisitions, Retail and Apparel Investment Banking Group, 1992—98, mng. dir., worldwide head, Luxury Goods Investment Banking Group, 1998—2001; founder, mng. dir. Elixir Advisors, NYC, 2002—. Bd. dir. GAR Found. Named a Top Dealmaker, Dealmaker mag., 2006.

ZAUDERER, MARK CARL, lawyer; b. Jan. 26, 1946; BA, Union Coll., 1967; JD, NYU, 1971. Bar: N.Y. 1972, US Dist. Ct. (So. & Ea. dist. NY) 1974, US Ct. Appeals (2d, 5th, Fed. cir.), US Supreme Ct. 1993. Law clk. U.S. Dist. Ct., Newark, 1971—72; founding ptnr. Solomon Zauderer Ellenhorn Frischer & Sharp, NYC, 1981—2003; ptnr., litigation practice DLA Piper Rudnick Gray Cary, NYC, 2003—05; ptnr. Flemming Zulack Williamson Zauderer LLP, NYC, 2005—. Faculty chmn. Practicing Law Inst. Program., Litigating Comml. Cases up to Trial, N.Y.C. and San Francisco, 1986, faculty mem. Deposition Skills Tng. Program, N.Y., 1986, 88-90; adv. com. on civil practice to Chief Adminstrn. Judge N.Y. State Ctrs., 1992—; trustee bd. advisors Union Coll., 1993—; chief Judge's Task Force on Comml. Cts., 1995—; chmn. Chief Judge's Commn. on Jury, 2003—. Author, moderator practising law inst. satellite TV program Deposition Strategy and Tactics, 1989; contbr. articles to profl. jours. Life fellow N.Y. Bar Found.; mem. ABA, N.Y. State Bar Assn. (exec. com. 1991—, chmn. exec. com. 1996-97, comml. and fed. litigation sect., chmn. complex civil litigation com.), Assn. of Bar of City of N.Y. (chmn. com. complex civil litigation, comml. and fed. litigation sect., mem. exec. com. 1991—, chair 1996-97), Fed. Bar Coun. (trustee 1998-2004, treas. 1998—, pres.-elect 2004-2006, pres. 2006—). Office: Flemming Zulack Williamson Zauderer LLP One Liberty Plz 35th Fl New York NY 10006-1404 Office Phone: 212-412-9562. Office Fax: 212-964-9200. Business E-Mail: mzauderer@fzwz.com.

ZAUN, ANNE MARIE, lawyer; b. NYC, Aug. 1, 1949; d. George F. and Clara J. (Varriale) Z.; m. Stephen A. Lokos, Oct. 17, 1987; children: Debra M., Anthony G. BS, Fordham U., 1970; JD cum laude, Seton Hall U., 1979. Assoc. mgr. Prudential Property and Casualty Ins. Co., Woodbridge, N.J., 1972-76; dep. atty. gen. State of N.J., Trenton, 1980-84; staff atty. Knapp & Blejwas, Edison, N.J., 1984-87; dir. legal writing program Law Sch. Seton Hall. U., Newark, 1987-89; prin. Anne M. Zaun, East Brunswick, N.J., 1989—. Adj. prof. paralegal program Middlesex County Coll., 1992—2002. Mem. N.J. Bar Assn. (elder law sect.), Middlesex County Bar Assn. (elder law sect.). Democrat. Avocations: reading, music, tennis, swimming. Office: G 12A Brier Hill Ct East Brunswick NJ 08816-3000 Office Phone: 732-613-3900. Personal E-mail: amzesq@earthlink.net.

ZAVADA, BARBARA JOHANNA, artist, educator; b. Jena, Thueringia, Germany, June 20, 1938; arrived in U.S., 1953; d. Paul Egon Weber and Johanna-Helene Kuehlich; m. Gerhard Manfred Grote (div.); 1 child, Erika Barbara Grote. Studied with Karl Bobeck, Berlin, 1962; AA in Fine Art Print Making, Rochester Inst. Tech., NY, 1966; postgrad., Art Students League, NYC, 1970—71. Cert. Traphagen Sch. Fashions, NYC, 1960. Painter, 1960—; fashion designer H & U Schmidt, Berlin, 1961—62, Dave Goldberg, NYC, 1967—71; graphic designer Zavada Assocs., Stamford, Conn., 1974—90. Lectr. in field. One-woman shows include Mus. Art, Sci. and Industry, Bridgeport, Conn., 1974, Bruce Mus., Conn., 1976, Conn. Women's Bank, 1985, Stamford Landmark Tower Rotunda, Conn., 1985, So. Conn. State U., 1990, John Wesley Powell Meml. Mus., Page, Ariz., 1996, Edge of Cedars Mus., Blanding, Utah, 1996, 1999, Western Colo. Arts Ctr., Grand Junction, 1998, Zavada Fine Art Studio-Gallery Arroyo, Seco, N.Mex., 1998—2005, Iron Mission State Pk., Utah, 2000, Beaver St. Gallery, Flagstaff, Ariz., 2005, Represented in permanent collections Concordia Hist. Soc., St. Louis, pmwgallery.com, artprice.com, Saint-Romain-au-Mont-d'Or, France. Search and rescue pilot CAP, Rochester, NY, 1964—68, SI, NY, 1969—70; v.p. German Lang. Sch., Westport, Conn., 1981—83; graphics, scholarship fund Greenwich Acad., 1985—90. Recipient 1st prize, NYC Fashion Competition, 1960, Faber Birren Color award, Stamford, 1981. Mem.: CAP, Toastmasters Internat., Nat. Mus. Women In Arts, Nat. Women's History Mus. Avocations: travel, winemaking, hiking, golf. Home: HC 64 Box 3001 Castle Valley UT 84532-9614 Office Phone: 435-259-7574. Personal E-mail: bjzavada@yahoo.com. Business E-Mail: bjhazavada@aol.com.

ZAVADA, JEFFREY J., retail executive; BS in Polit. Sci., U. Wis., 1994, BS in Bus. Mgmt. Worked in sales PacifiCare Health Sys. LLC, 1992—2000; nat. v.p., sales ppoNEXT, 2000—03; nat. v.p., key accts. UnitedHealthcare Group Inc., 2003—08; v.p., chief sales officer Walgreen Co., 2008—. Office: Walgreen Co 200 Wilmot Rd Deerfield IL 60015 Office Phone: 847-914-2500. Office Fax: 847-914-2804.

ZAVALA, ALBERT, research psychologist; b. Chgo., Mar. 10, 1930; s. Edward and Maria Soledad (Herrejon) Z.; married; children: Camille, Sally, Elena, Jenifer, Alexis. BA, Willamette U., 1959; MA, Mich. State U., 1961; PhD, Kans. State U., 1966. Prof., head life scis. Carlspan, Buffalo, 1967-73; prof. SUNY, Buffalo, 1968-78; exec. dir. Corp. IV, Cheektowaga, N.Y., 1973-77; dir. projects Inpsych, Cupertino, Calif., 1978-80; sr. rsch. psychologist SRI Internat., Menlo Park, Calif., 1980-85; sr. staff engr. Lockheed Missiles and Space Co., Sunnyvale, Calif., 1985-94; sr. engr. Nova Mgmt. Monterey, Calif., 1994-97; bid mgr. Siemens Info. and Network Comm., Inc., Santa Clara, Calif., 1997-2000; sr. staff engr. Hernandez Engring., Inc., Santa Clara, Calif., 2000—. Author: (with J.J. Paley) Personal Appearance Identification, 1972; contbr. numerous articles to profl. jours. Mem. Erie County (N.Y.) Sheriff's Sci. staff, 1972-78. With U.S. Army, 1955-57. Dunlap fellow, 1964, fellow Greater Kans. City Mental Health Found., 1962-63. Mem. APA, Human Factors Soc., Sigma Xi, Psi Chi, Phi Kappa Phi.

ZAVALA, GABINO, bishop; b. Tijuana, Mexico, Sept. 7, 1951; BA, St. John's Sem., Camarillo, Calif.; MA, St. John's Sem.; grad., Cath. U. Am. Ordained priest Archdiocese of LA, 1977, assoc. pastor, assoc. dir. marriage tribunal, aux. bishop San Gabriel Pastoral Region, 1994—; ordained bishop, 1994; prof. canon law, rector St. John's Sem., Camarillo, Calif. Mem. adv. bd. detention ministry Archdiocese of LA. Bd. dirs. Inst. Liturgia Hispana, A Place Called Home, House of Ruth, Don Bosco Tech. HS; pres. nat. coun. Pax Christi USA. Mem.: US Conf. Cath. Bishops. Roman Catholic. Address: San Gabriel Pastoral Region 16009 Cypress Ave Irwindale CA 91706-2122

ZAVALA, PEDRO JOSE, pharmacy educator; BS in Chemistry and Biology, Seton Hall U., South Orange, NJ, 1977; MSP, U. Fla., Gainesville, 1981, PhD in Phys. Chemistry, 1988. Asst. prof. Nova Southeastern U. Coll. Pharmacy, Ft. Lauderdale, Fla., 2002—07, U. Okla. Coll. Pharmacy, Okla. City, 2007—. Dir. Environ. Fate & Risk, Inc., Denver, 1995—98. Pres.'s Faculty Rsch. & Devel. grant, Nova Southeastern U., 2003—04. Mem.: Am. Assn. Colls. Pharmacy, Am. Assn. Pharm. Scientists. Personal E-mail: zzflorida@yahoo.com.

ZAVALA-ALARCON, EDGARDO DONATO, medical association administrator, director; b. Mex. City, Mex., Dec. 19, 1951; s. Edgardo Zavala and Mireya Alarcon; m. Alicia Cristina Villalon, Dec. 10, 1976; children: Ariadna Zavala, Andres Zavala, Edgardo Zavala. BS in Chemistry & Biology, Centro U. Mex., Méx. City, 1971; MD, U. Nat. Autónoma Méx., Méx. City, 1978. Chief, cardiology Maricopa Med. Ctr., Phoenix, 1998—2007; med. dir. Ciao Bella Med. Spa & Vein Clinic, Chandler, Ariz., 2007—; fellow Millenium Cosmetic and Laser Inst, 2007. Chief, cardiology Phoenix Meml. Hosp., 2004—07. Contbr. articles to profl. jours. Recipient Best resident award, Nat. Inst. Cardiology Mex. City, 1983. Fellow: SCAI, Am. Coll. Cardiology; mem.: Am. Soc. Liposuction Surgery, Am. Acad. Cosmetic Surgery. Home: 2723 W Carla Vista Dr Chandler AZ 85224 Office: Ciao Bella Med Spa & Vein Clinic 2310 W Ray Rd Chandler AZ 85224 Office Fax: 480-686-8425. Personal E-mail: ezamd@hotmail.com.

ZAVALIN, ANDREY I., optics scientist, educator; BS, MS, Moscow Engring. Physics Inst., Russia, 1982, PhD, 1990. Sr. rsch. assoc. Russian Acad. Scis., Moscow, 1989—99; rsch. prof. NASA Ctr. Photonic Materials and Devices, Nashville, 1999—2003, Vanderbilt U., Nashville, 2003—. Adj. prof. Conservative Optical Logic Devices Program Fisk U., Nashville, 2004—. Mem.: Soc. Sci. Exploration, Optical Soc. Am., Am. Phys. Soc. Achievements include research in multipolar electromagnetic and acoustic waves; development of effect of a self-assembly in one-beam optical trap; optical logic devices; ionoluminescence in nano-particles. Home: 104 Glenway Ct Nashville TN 37221-3021 Office: Vanderbilt University VU Sta B 351807 2301 Vanderbilt Pl Nashville TN 37235-1807 Office Fax: 615-329-8634. E-mail: andrey.zavalin@vanderbilt.edu.

ZAVATTIERI, PABLO DANIEL, research scientist, educator; b. Buenos Aires, June 26, 1970; PhD, Sch. Eronautics and Astronautics, Purdue U., West Lafayette, Ind., 2000. Vis. scholar Sch. Aeronautics and Astronautics, Purdue U., 1996, rsch. asst., 1996—2000; vis. prof. aero. engring. U. Nat. La Plata, Buenos Aires, 2001—02; sr. rschr. Gen. Motors R & D Ctr., Warren, Mich., 2001—08, staff rschr., 2008—. Mem.: ASME. Achievements include patents for active material actuated headrest assemblies; patents pending in fields. Office: Gen Motors Rsch and Devel 30500 Mound Rd Warren MI 48090-9055

ZAVODNEY, LAWRENCE DENNIS, mechanical engineer, educator; b. Akron, Ohio, June 24, 1951; s. Larry and Charlotte Ann Zavodney; m. Deborah Jo Sinea; children: Sara Karimeh Campbell, Kristin Joy McLaughlin, Daniel Lawrence, Anna Kathryn, Julie Ann, Jonathan David, Joseph Alan. BS in Mech. Engring., U. Akron, 1974, MS, 1977; PhD, Va. Poly. Inst. & State U., Blacksburg, 1988. Cert. Ohio State Bd. Registration Profl. Engrs. & Surveyor, 1996. Mech. engr., coop. Goodyear Tire & Rubber Co., Akron, 1972—73; grad. rsch. asst., dept. mech. engr. U. Akron, 1974—77; civil engr. USAF, Youngstown, Ohio, 1976; sr. engr. Babcock & Wilcox Rsch. & Devel. Div., Alliance, Ohio, 1977—79; instr. Dept. Engring. Sci. & Mechanics, Blacksburg, Ohio, 1979—80, rsch. assoc., 1982—87, grad. rsch. asst., 1982—87, instr., 1982—87; lectr. Yarmouk U., Irbid, Jordan, 1980—82; asst. prof. Ohio State U., Columbus, 1988—92; assoc. prof., chmn. Cedarville U., Ohio, 1992—98, chmn., 1998—2006, prof., chmn., 1998—2006, prof. mech. engring., 2006—. Cons. various, 1975—. Contbr. scientific papers. Internat. humanitarian ELWA, Monrovia, Liberia, 2006—08. Recipient Outstanding Sr. award, Akron U. Dept. Mech. Engring., 1974, Best Paper award, Am. Soc. Engring. Educators, NCS, 2008; named to Alumni Hall of Fame, Revere Sr. HS, 2002. Mem.: ASME (chair, dept. head 1999—2006), Tau Beta Pi, Am. Soc. Mech. Engring. Edn., Soc. Automotive Engrs. Avocations: scuba diving, photography, flying. Home: 168 Creamer Dr Cedarville OH 45314 Office: Cedarville Univ 251 N Main St Cedarville OH 45314 Office Fax: 937-766-7689. Personal E-mail: lzavodney@woh.rr.com. Business E-Mail: zavodney@cedarville.edu.

ZAVORTINK, THOMAS JAMES, retired biology professor; b. Ravenna, Ohio, May 27, 1939; children: David Martin, Matthew Brian. PhD, U. Calif., LA, 1967. Rsch. zoologist U. Calif., LA, 1968—74; prof. U. San Francisco, 1975—2001. Office: Entomology Univ Calif 1 Shields Ave Davis CA 95616 Office Fax: 530-752-9464. Business E-Mail: tjzavortink@ucdavis.edu.

ZAVRAS, EUGENIA T., parasitologist, educator; b. Greece; married. BA summa cum laude, U. Bridgeport, Conn., MS; PhD, U. Mass., Amherst, 1982. Adj. instr. U. Bridgeport, 1986—92; adj. asst. prof. Sacred Heart U., Fairfield, 1987—92; instr. & asst. prof. Fairfield U., Conn., 1991—. Vol. Pub. Schs., Stamford, Conn., 1988—; mem. Ladies Philanthropic Group, Stamford. Recipient Stauber award, NJ. Soc. Parasitology, 1975. Mem.: AAAS, New Eng. Assn. Parasitologists (treas. 2001—), Am. Soc. Parasitologists, Am. Microscopical Soc., Alpha Sigma Lambda, Sigma Xi. Office: Fairfield Univ 1073 N Benson Rd Fairfield CT 06824 Business E-Mail: ezavras@mail.fairfield.edu, ezavras@fairfield.edu.

ZAVYALOV, VLADIMIR V, physicist, educator; b. Petropavlovsk, Kamchtskii region, Russia, Sept. 13, 1948; s. Viktor Alekseevich Zavyalov and Ninel Vasilevna Zavyalova; m. Lyubov V Karpikova, Apr. 16, 1972; 1 child, Jane V Owens. PhD, Ural State U., Ekaterinburg, Russia, 1972. Sr. scientist Ural State U., 1995; rsch. assoc. U. Utah, Salt Lake City, 1997—2000; adj. assoc. prof. Utah State U., Logan, 1996—; sr. scientist Space Dynamics Lab., North Logan, 2002—. Recipient Jack W. Keufel award, U. Utah, 1999, award, Space Dynamic Lab, USU, 2007. Mem.: APS.

ZAWACKI, BRUCE EDWIN, surgeon, educator, ethicist; b. Northampton, Mass., Dec. 6, 1935; BS, Coll. of Holy Cross, 1957; MD, Harvard U., 1961; MA, U. So. Calif., 1986. Diplomate Am. Bd. Surgery. Intern in surgery Mass. Gen. Hosp., 1961—62, resident in surgery, 1962—65; vis. scholar in trauma surgery Birmingham Accident Hosp., Birmingham, England, 1966; resident in surgery Mass. Gen. Hosp., 1967; gen. surgeon So. Calif. Permanente Med. Group, Panorama City, 1969-71; dir. burn ctr. L.A. County and U. So. Calif. Med. Ctr., LA, 1971-98; assoc. prof. surgery U. So. Calif. Sch. Medicine, LA, 1975-98, assoc. prof. emeritus, 1998—; assoc. prof. religion U. So. Calif. Sch. Religion, LA, 1992-98; assoc. for edn. Pacific Ctr. for Health Policy and Ethics, 1997—; adj. assoc. prof. religion U. So. Calif., 2001—02. Contbr. articles to profl. jours. Served to maj. U.S. Army, 1967-68. Mem. Am. Burn Assn. (2d v.p., bd. trustees 1992-93; Harvey Stuart Allen Disting. Svc. award 1996), Am. Soc. Bioethics and Humanities, L.A. Surg. Soc., Internat. Soc. for Burn Injuries. Achievements include first to describe the natural history of reversible burn injury, the independence of burn hypermetabolism from evaporative water loss and an autonomous role for burn patients without precedent for survival.

ZAWADZKI, ROBERT J., ophthalmologist, educator; s. Andrzej Zawadzki and Teresa Zawadzka; m. Sylwia A. Orzechowska, Aug. 10, 2002; 1 child, Helena M. Zawadzka. PhD, Tech. U. Vienna, 2003. Asst. rsch. prof. U. Calif. Davis Eye Ctr., Sacramento, 2006—. Mem.: OSA, SPIE, ARVO.

ZAWADZKI-JANUSZ, STACY LYNN, performing arts director, owner, educator; b. Buffalo, June 13, 1974; d. Michael Thomas and Diane Theresa Zawadzki; m. Robert Paul Janusz, Aug. 13. BA magna cum laude, U. Buffalo, NYC, 1996, MA and Humanities magna cum laude, 2004. CPR, ARC; cert. tchr. N.Y. Substitute tchr. P.S. 139 Elem. Sch., 1999—2000; dance tchr. I.S. 232 Winthrop Intermediate Sch., 2000—00; choreographer, workshop tchr. West Seneca East H.S., NY, 2002—, Cheektowaga Ctrl. H.S., NY, 2002; tchr. art Arts in Edn., West Seneca, NY, 2002—; choreographer Irish Classical Theatre, Buffalo, 2005—; prof. mus. theatre and dance Niagara U., Niagara Falls, NY, 2005—; co-founder, artistic dir., choreographer Youth for Truth Performing Arts Co., Inc., 2005—. Mem. Buffalo Contemporary Dance Co., Marie-Christine Giordano Dance Co., Alpha Omega Dance Co., New Dance Collective Dance Co., Zodiaque Dance Co.; dir. and founder ECNAD Dance Co.; dance educator, choreographer St. Margaret's Cath. Sch., 2007—; owner, dir. Stacy Zawadzki's Performing Arts Ctr., 2007—; adjudicator dance competitions throughout US and Can.; artistic dir., co-founder, choreographer Youth for Truth Performing Arts Co.; summer dance educator U. Buffalo; fitness assessor, instr. BWI Health & Promotion, 2007—; fitness instr. Pulse Health & Fitness Gym, Praxair, 2008—. Choreographer Music is Art Festival and Elmwood Art Festival, Zodiaque Dance Co., Am. Coll. Dance Festival, Grease, various musicals including Gypsy, Once on This Island, Pippin, Singin' the the Rain, High Society, 42nd Street, Guys and Dolls, Hello Dolly, My Fair Lady, West Side Story, Oklahoma, Damn Yankees, Bye Bye Birdie, Anything Goes, Jesus Christ Superstar and Grease; choreographer A Man of No Importance, — (Artie award, 2006), Sound of Music, —, Godspell, —; choreographer MTC Prodns., Lancaster Opera House, NYC, 2003—, choreographer (performance) Disney Magic Music Days, 2009, dancer performer NYC, Can., Conn., Mex., Brit. Virgin Islands, featured soloist U. Games and World Vet. Games, Comml. Spot TCT and WGRZ TV. Recipient Choreography award, NY State TANYS Theatre Assn., numerous choreography competitions awards. Office Phone: 716-822-0771. Personal E-mail: dancestace@roadrunner.com.

ZAWICKI, JOSEPH LEO, science educator; b. Batavia, NY, Sept. 24, 1958; s. Leo Stanley Zawicki, Rita Zawicki; m. Ann Marie Hartley, July 27, 1984; children: Richard John, Erin Kathleen, Lee Joseph, Sean Michael. BA, Canisius Coll., 1980; MSEd, U. Rochester, 1989; PhD in Sci. Edn., SUNY, Buffalo, 2002. Cert. tchr. certificate N.Y. Lab technologist Strong Meml. Hosp., Rochester, NY, 1984—89; tchr., dept. chair Elba Ctrl. Sch., Elba, NY, 1989—2002; assoc. prof. Buffalo State

Coll., Buffalo, 2002—. Lectr. Buffalo State Coll., NY, 2001—02, U. Buffalo, 2002; item writer, cons. N.Y. State Edn. Dept., Albany, 1995—; physics mentor N.Y. State Mentor Network, Oneonta, 1996—; bd. dirs. N.Y. Sci. Edn. Leadership Assn. Developer Optic Bench Sci., 2001. Bd. dirs. Cornell Coop. Ext., Batavia, 1996—98; dir. religious edn. Our Lady of Fatima, Elba, 1999—. Recipient St. Joseph the Worker award, Diocese of Buffalo, 2001; grantee Environ. Empowerment, N.Y. State, 1998. Mem.: Nat. Assn. Rsch. in Sci. Tchg., N.Y. State Edn. Leadership Assn., Sci. Tchrs. Assn. N.Y., Am. Assn. Physics Tchrs., Am. Chem. Soc. Avocations: youth programs, reading. Home: PO Box 172 7 S Main St Elba NY 14058-0172 Office: Buffalo State Coll Sci 130 Dept Earth Scis and Sci Edn 1300 Elmwood Ave Buffalo NY 14222 Office Phone: 716-878-3800. Business E-Mail: zawickjl@buffalostate.edu.

ZAWISTOWSKI, STEPHEN LOUIS, psychologist, educator; b. Lackawanna, NY, July 28, 1955; s. Louis Henry and Alice Theresa (Bartus) Z.; m. Jane Elaine Clark, May 26, 1979; 1 child, Matthew. BA, Canisius Coll., 1977; AM, U. Ill., 1979, PhD, 1983. Cert. tech. animal rescue specialist, Am. Humane Assn./Rescue 3. Vis. asst. prof. Ind. U., Bloomington, 1983-84, postdoctoral fellow, 1984-85; asst. prof. St. John's U., NYC, 1985-88; exec. v.p. ASPCA, NYC, 1988—. Adj. prof. U. Ill. Vet. Coll., 2004; nat. rsch. coun. panel for rev. of the nat. zoo Nat. Rsch. Coun., 2003—04. Author: Animal Shelter Medicine for Veterinarians and Staff, 2004, Companion Animals in Soc., 2008; co-author: Animal Rights Handbook, 1990, Heritage of Care, 2008; editor Animal Behavior Cons. Newsletter, 2001; co-editor: For Kids Who Love Animals, 1991; contbg. editor Animal Watch Mag., 1990-2004; co-exec. prodr. (film) Question of Respect, 1990 (Silver Apple award 1990); writer, host ASPCA pet check segments, PBS; mem. bd. editors Psychologists for the Ethical Treatment of Animals, 1988-95; founding co-editor Jour. Applied Animal Welfare Sci.; contbg. editor, sci. advisor Animaland Mag., 1998-2000; script cons. Animal Rescue Kid, 1997; contbr. articles to profl. jours. Scoutmaster Boy Scouts Am., SI, 1988-98; asst. coach SI Youth Soccer, 1986-95; bd. dirs. Nat. Coun. on Pet Population Study and Policy, v.p., 1995-96, 99-2000, pres., 1996-97, advisor, 2004—; mem. steering com. NY State Watchable Wildlife Program; mem. Nat. Humane Dog Tng. Task Force; bd. dirs. United for Wildlife, 1999-2001, Harmony Inst. Cmty. Adv. Bd.; mem. sci. adv. com. Humane Farm Animal Care, 2003-08; bd. dirs., vice chair Alliance for the Contraception of Cats and Dogs, 2005, chmn. 2006-09. Recipient Stan Lesny scholarship Kosciuszki Found., 1977, U. Ill. Grad. fellowship, 1977, Postdoctoral fellowship NSF, 1984, Patrick Daley award for contbns. to edn. St. John's U.; named Psychologist of Yr., Psychologists for Ethical Treatment of Animals, 1989. Mem. World Soc. for Protection of Animals (sci. adv. panel 2003—), Animal Behavior Soc. (cert. applied animal behaviorist, chmn. Issues in Applied Animal Behavior Com. 2007-, chmn. bd. profl. cert. 1998-2007, devel. com. 1995-98, animal welfare com. 1989-95), Order of Arrow (mem. exec. bd. 1996-98), Sigma Xi. Achievements include research in genetics and animal learning, animal behavior and welfare. Office: ASPCA 520 8th Ave 7th Fl New York NY 10018 Office Phone: 212-876-7700 ext. 4401. Business E-Mail: stevez@aspca.org.

ZAWODNIOK, MACIEJ JAN, engineering educator; married. MS in Computer Sci., Politechnika Slaska w Gliwicach, Poland, 1999; PhD in Computer Engring., U. Miss., Rolla, Mo., 2006. Postdoc. fellow, ECE dept. U. Miss., 2006—08; asst. prof., ECE dept., Mo. S&T, Rolla, 2008—. Site coord. NSF I/UCRC Intelligent Maintenance Sys., Rolla, 2006—08, asst. dir., 2008—. Contbr. articles to profl. sci. jours. Mem.: IEEE. Office: Miss Univ S&T 133 Emerson Hall Rolla MO 65409 Office Fax: 573-341-4532. Business E-Mail: mjzx9c@mst.edu.

ZAWOROTKO, MICHAEL JOHN, chemistry professor; b. Tredegar, Gwent, Wales, Aug. 14, 1956; s. Iwan and Gwyneth Zaworotko; m. Griselda Enriquez, July 28, 2008; children: Rebecca Elizabeth, Holly Charlotte, Samuel Craig. BSc, Imperial Coll., London, 1977; PhD, U. Ala., Tuscaloosa, 1982. Prof. St. Mary's U., Halifax, NS, Canada, 1985—98; prof. and dean U. Winnipeg, Man., Canada, 1998—99; prof. U. South Fla., Tampa, 1999—. Contbr. articles over 260 publs. Achievements include patents for air and water stable ionic liquids; patents pending for novel crystal forms of pharmaceutical ingredients. Office: Univ South Fla CHE205 4202 E Fowler Ave Tampa FL 33620 Office Fax: 813-974-3203. Business E-Mail: xtal@usf.edu.

ZAX, LEONARD A., lawyer; b. Paterson, NJ, July 16, 1950; s. Harry and Shirley Jeanne (Hollander) Z.; m. Helen Kemp, May 25, 1980; children: David Hollander, Laura Alexandra. BA, U. Chgo., 1971; M of City Planning, Harvard U., 1975, JD, 1975. Bar: N.J. 1978, D.C. 1978. Spl. asst. to gen. counsel HUD, 1975-76, spl. asst. to sec., 1976-77; lectr., mem. faculty Harvard U., Cambridge, Mass., 1977-78; assoc. Fried, Frank, Harris, Shriver & Kampelman, Washington, 1977-82, ptnr., 1982-95, Latham & Watkins, Washington, 1995—, also chmn. real estate group. Co-chmn. Mayor's Downtown Housing Commn., Washington, 1986-89, D.C. Enterprise Zones Study Commn., 1986-89; D.C. Downtown Interactive Retail Task Force, 1996-98; co-chmn. Washington adv. com. Asian Real Estate Assn., Washington, 1991-92. Contbg. author: N.Y. Times, Nat. Law Jour., L.A. Times, Harvard Law Bull., Real Estate Fin. Jour., Urban Land, Washington Business Jour., Washington Post; editor: Real Estate and the RTC: A Guide to Asset Purchases and Contracting, Urban Land Inst., 1990. Trustee Nat. Bldg. Mus., D.C. Preservation League, 1988-95; mem. Fannie Mae Nat. Adv. Coun., 1994-95; mem. vis. com. Harvard Design Sch., 2000-06. Mem. ABA (chmn. com. on housing and urban devel. law 1986-89, steering com. representation of the Homeless Project 1988-91, governing bd. forum com. affordable housing and community devel. 1991-94), Cosmos Club, Urban Land Inst. (chmn. comml. & retail devel. coun. 1998-2002). Home: 4511 28th St NW Washington DC 20008-1035 Office: Latham Watkins LLP 555 11thSt NW Ste 1000 Washington DC 20004-1304

ZAX, MELVIN, psychologist, educator; b. Cambridge, Mass., Apr. 14, 1928; s. Joseph and Sadie (Kirshner) Z.; m. Ruth Leah Vogel, Apr. 23, 1977; children: Jeffrey S., David B., Jonathan B. AB, Boston U., 1951, A.M., 1952; PhD, U. Tenn., 1955. Clin. psychologist U. Tenn., Knoxville, 1955-56; staff psychologist St. Elizabeths Hosp., Washington, 1956-57; asst. prof. psychology U. Rochester, NY, 1957-62, assoc. prof. psychology NY, 1962-67, prof. NY, 1967-93, prof. emeritus NY, 1993—; pvt. practice, 1973—. Chmn. exptl. and spl. tng. rev. com. NIMH, 1970-71. Author: (with G. Stricker) Patterns of Psychopathology, 1963, (with E.L. Cowen) Abnormal Psychology: Changing Conceptions, 1972, (with G.A. Specter) An Introduction to Community Psychology, 1974, (with M. Nichols) Catharsis in Psychotherapy, 1977; editor: (with Stricker) The Study of Abnormal Behavior: Selected Readings, 1964, (with Cowen and E.A. Gardner) Emergent Approaches to Mental Health Problems, 1967, (with D. Dorr and J. Bonner) The Psychology of Discipline, 1983; adv. editor Jour. Cons. and Clin. Psychology, 1965-81; contbr. articles to profl. jours. Served with AUS, 1946-47. NIMH spl. research fellow Psykologisk Inst., Copenhagen, 1966-67 Fellow Am. Psychol. Assn.; mem. Eastern Psychol. Assn., AAUP, Phi Beta Kappa, Sigma Xi, Phi Kappa Phi. Home: 27 Sky Ridge Dr Rochester NY 14625-2167 Office Phone: 585-385-6370.

ZAYAC, LINDA MARY, sociologist, educator; d. Ernest F. and Barbara T. Dauplaise; m. Paul Edward Zayac, Nov. 3, 1976; children: Nicholas Alexander, Alexander Joseph. BA in Sociology and Psychology, Am. Internat. Coll., Springfield, Mass., 1972, MA in Edn., 1973. Instr. of social studies Southwick H.S., Mass., 1975—79; project dir. visual edn. lab. Southwick Pub. H.S., 1978—85; co-owner sr. cons. and svcs. Pvt. Geriatric Care Mgmt. Firm, West Springfield, Mass., 1999—2002; instr. sociology Westfield State Coll., Westfield, 1994—, dir., ctr. instrnl. tech., 2003—09. Mem. Town Meeting, West Springfield, 1983—2002; traffic safety com. chair Town of West Springfield, 1989—2002; chair Master Plan Commn., 1994—2002; mem. Planning Bd., 1983—2002, Traffic Adv. Commn., 1989—2002, Pioneer Valley Planning Commn. Joint Study Com., West Springfield, 1990—2002, Holyyoke, Mass., 1990—2002; chair Corridor Bus. Assn., Riverdale, Mass., 1993—2002; mem. Pioneer Valley Planning Commn. Study Group, 1989—2002, Mass. Sr. Action Coun., 1995—2002, Dem. Town Com., 1983—2002; lacrosse dir. Youth League, 1992—98; pres. Lacrosse Booster Club, 1998—2002; it steering com. Westfield State Coll., 2003—. Mem.: Mass. Coun. Aging Affairs, Nat. Assn. Profl. Geriatric Care Mgrs., Children Aging Parents, Native Am. Inst., Mass. Women in Pub. Higher Edn., Mass. Coll. Online (liason 2003—06), Mass. Teachers Assn., NERCOMP (assoc.). Home: 79 Highmeadow Dr West Springfield MA 01089 Office: Westfield State Coll 577 Western Ave Westfield MA 01086 Office Phone: 413-572-8142. Office Fax: 413-572-8048. Business E-Mail: lzayac@wsc.ma.edu.

ZAYAS, JOSEPH M., physics professor; b. Havana, Cuba, Jan. 10, 1946; s. Jose M. and Manin Zayas; m. Susan L. Wood, July 31, 1982; 1 child, Joseph Michael. PhD, Adelphi U., Garden City, NY, 1976. Asst. prof. physics Manhattan Coll., NYC, 1976—77; prof. physics Pensacola Jr. Coll., Fla., 1977—. Named Acad. of Tchg. Excellence, Pensacola Jr. Coll., 1991, Faculty Advisor of Yr., Fla. Engring. Soc., 2003. Mem.: Sigma Pi Sigma, Sigma Xi, Am. Assn. Physics Tchrs. Conservative. Roman Catholic. Home: 5985 Keystone Rd Pensacola FL 32504 Office: Pensacola Jr Coll 1000 College Blvd Pensacola FL 32504 Personal E-mail: jzayas@cox.net. Business E-Mail: jzayas@pjc.edu.

ZAYDON, THOMAS JOHN, JR., plastic surgeon; b. Phila., Apr. 3, 1952; s. Thomas J. and Helen (Joseph) Z. BS, Fla. State U., 1974; MD with spl. honors, Hahnemann Med. U., 1978. Cert. Am. Bd. Plastic Surgery, 1982; diplomate Am. Bd. Surgery, 1991. Intern in gen. surgery Eastern Va. Med. Sch., Norfolk, 1978—79, resident in gen. surgery, 1979—80; jr. resident in gen. surgery Monmouth Med. Ctr., Long Beach, NJ, 1980-81, sr. resident in gen. surgery, 1981-82; resident in plastic surgery La. State U., New Orleans, 1982-83, chief resident in plastic surgery, 1983-84, clin. instr.; pvt. practice surgery Cosmetic Surgery Inst., Miami, 1984—; assoc. chief plastic surgery Miami Heart Inst., Fla., 1984—85; assoc. chief, plastic surgery Mercy Hosp., 2004—05, chief, plastic surgery, 2007—08; pvt. practice. Vol. clin. instr. plastic surgery U. Miami, Fla. 1986—. Author articles and book chpts. in field. Fellow ACS; mem. Dade County Med. Assn., John Rives Surg. Soc., Aesculapian Soc. Miami, Fla. Med. Assn., Fla. Soc. Plastic and Reconstructive Surgeons, Fla. Soc. Plastic Surgeons, Greater Miami Soc. Plastic Surgeons, Am. Soc. Plastic Surgeons, Am. Soc. Aesthetic Plastic Surgery, Southeastern Soc. Plastic Surgeons. Office: Cosmetic Surgery Inst Miami Mercy Hosp Profl Bldg 3661 S Miami Ave Ste 509 Miami FL 33133-4206 also: Dadeland Med Ctr 7400 N Kendall Dr Ste 502 Miami FL 33156 Office Phone: 305-856-3030. E-mail: tzaydon@pol.net.

ZAYEK, FRANCIS MANSOUR, archbishop, bishop emeritus; b. Manzanillo, Cuba, Oct. 18, 1920; s. Mansour and Mary (Coury) Zayek. Attended, St. Joseph's Cath. U., Beirut, 1938; DD, PhD, U. Propagation of Faith, 1947; DCL, Pontifical Lateran Univ., 1951. Ordained priest Maronite rite, 1946; rector Maronite Cathedral of Holy Family, Cairo, 1951—56; Oriental sec. to Vatican Apostolic Internunciature; mem. Archdiocesan Tribunal, 1951—56; promoter of justice Sacred Roman Rota, 1956—58; prof. Oriental canon law Internat. Coll. St. Anselm, Rome, 1958—60, Pontifical Lateran Univ., Rome, 1960—61; ordained bishop, 1962; aux. bishop Sao Sebastiano do Rio de Janeiro, Brazil, 1962—66; presided over First Ann. Maronite Conv., Washington, 1964; bishop, exarch Maronite Apostolic Exarchate in the U.S., Detroit, 1966—71; bishop Eparchy of St. Maron of Bklyn., 1971—82; archbishop, bishop Eparchy of St. Maron in Bklyn., 1982—96, archbishop emeritus, 1996—. Decorated knight comdr. Equestrian Order of Holy Sepulchre of Jerusalem; recipient medal of merit, Govt. of Republic Italy, 1966. Roman Catholic.

ZAYFERT, CLAUDIA, psychologist, educator; PhD, W.Va. U., Morgantown, 1993. Assoc. prof. Dartmouth Med. Sch., Lebanon, NH, 1993—. Author: (book) Cognitive Behavioral Therapy for PTSD: A Case Formulation Approach. Office: Dartmouth Med Sch Lebanon NH 03756

ZAYHOWSKI, JOHN J., electrical engineer, researcher; b. Troy, NY, 1958; s. John J. and Carole E. J. Zayhowski; m. Lien N. Zayhowski, 1982; children: Justine A., Kimberly M. BS, MS, MIT, Cambridge, Mass., 1982, PhD, 1986. Engr. Tex. Instruments, Dallas, 1979-82; mem. tech. staff Lincoln Lab. MIT, Lexington, Mass., 1986—2000, sr. staff Lincoln Lab., 2000—. Chmn. Advanced Concepts Com., Lincoln Lab., 1998-99; vis. prof. Tufts U., Medford, Mass., 1997; chmn. various meetings in field; cons. in field. Author: (chpt.) Handbook of Photonics, 1997, 2d edit., 2007, Encyclopedia of Applied Physics, 1994, LIA Handbook of Laser Materials Processing, 2001, The Optics Encyclopedia, Basic Foundations and Practical Applications, 2003, Encyclopedia of Physics, 3d edit., 2005, Solid-State Lasers and Applications, 2007; topical editor Optics Letters, 2005—; contbr. over 70 articles to profl. jours. Pres. Sherwood Forest Homeowners Assn., 1997-98. Recipient fellowship Hertz Found., 1981, scholarship Edith Craig Reynolds, 1977, 1998 R&D 100 award R&D Magazine, commendation for Excellence in Tech. Communications Laser Focus World, 1996, 99, Appreciation cert. NBC, 2004, Team award MIT, 2002, 03, Tech. Excellence award, MIT, 2005. Fellow Optical Soc. America; mem. Sigma Xi, Tau Beta Pi, Eta Kappa Nu. Achievements include development of microchip laser technology resulting in four start-up companies; 16 patents in field. Office: MIT Lincoln Lab L-224 244 Wood St Lexington MA 02420-9108

ZAZUETA, DOLORES MANRIQUE, language educator; b. Nogales, Sonora, Mex., Oct. 11, 1935; arrived in US, 1986; d. Duarte Erneotina; children: Clarisa, Marco Ontonio, Amalilia, Imelda. M in Bilingual Edn., U. Ariz., Tuscon, 1995, M in Lit., 2002. Cert. tchr. Gomez Palacio Sch., bilingual tchr. U. Ariz. Spanish tchr. 6th Grade Edn. Dept., Hermosillo, 1980—85, Prima Coll., Tuscon, 2002—; tchr., elem. sch. Hollonger Sch., Tuscon, 1994—97. Spanish tutor Prima CC, Tuscon, 1987—90. Tchr. & mentor NAMISA, 2006—08. Democrat. Roman Catholic. Avocations: reading, travel, cooking.

ZAZZALI, JAMES R., lawyer, retired state supreme court chief justice; b. Newark, June 17, 1937; s. Andrew F. Zazzali; m. Eileen Fitzsimmons; children: Mara, James Jr., Robert, Courtney, Kevin. BA, Georgetown U., 1958, JD, 1962. Bar: NJ, NY, DC. Law clk. to Hon. Lawrence A. Whipple US Dist. Ct. NJ, 1964—65; asst. prosecutor Essex County Prosecutor's Office, NJ, 1965—68, trial prosecutor NJ, 1965—66, chief appellate sect. NJ, 1967—68; ptnr. Zazzali, Zazzali, Fagella, & Nowak, Newark; gen. counsel NJ Sports and Exposition Authority, 1973—81; atty. gen. State of NJ, Trenton, 1981—82; assoc. justice NJ Supreme Ct., Trenton, 2000—06, chief justice, 2006—07; of counsel Gibbons P.C., Newark, 2007—, Zazzali, Fagella, Nowak, Kleinbaum & Friedman, Newark, 2007—. Adj. prof. Seton Hall Law Sch., 1984—2000; commr. NJ State Commn. of Investigation, 1984—94, chmn., 1989—93, Cong. Superfund Study Group, 1981—82; mem., vice-chair Disciplinary Rev Bd., 1984—2000; chmn. Jud. Labor Rels. Task Force, 1985—88, Com. on Minority Participation in the Courts, 1985—92; mem. Adv. Com. on Jud. Conduct, 1999—2000. Recipient John Carroll award, Georgetown U., 1984, Dean Paul award, Georgetown U. Law Ctr., 2000. Democrat. Office: Gibbons PC One Gateway Ctr Newark NJ 07102 E-mail: JZazzali@gibbonslaw.com.

ZBAR, LLOYD IRWIN STANLEY, otolaryngologist, educator; b. Jersey City, June 2, 1939; m. Margo Wally, Mar. 25, 1965; children: Ross I.S., Brett I.W. MD, Queen's U., Kingston, Ont., Can., 1964. Cert. otolaryngologist. Intern Beth Israel/Harvard, Boston, 1964; resident surgery French Hosp., NYC, 1965—66; resident otolaryngology Bellevue Hosp. Ctr.-NYU, NYC, 1966—69, fellow otolaryngology, 1969—70; chmn. med. edn. com. Mountainside Hosp., Montclair, NJ, 1979—89, dir. otolaryngology, 1990—97, 1999—2009. Sec. med. bd. Mountainside Hosp., Glen Ridge, N.J., 1986-90, clin. assoc. prof. otolaryngology NYU Sch. Medicine Contbr. rev. to New Eng. Jour. Medicine, 1988 Mem. exec. bd. Boy Scouts Am., Essex County, N.J., 1984-95; pres. Mountainside Physicians Scholarship Loan Fund, 1972-85 With USAF. Named a Top Dr. NY Metro Area, 1998—2009. Fellow ACS, Am. Acad. Otolaryngology-Head and Neck Surgery, Royal Soc. Medicine Office: 200 Highland Ave Glen Ridge NJ 07028-1528 Office Phone: 973-744-2424. Office Fax: 973-743-3111. Personal E-mail: liszmd@yahoo.com.

ZBIB, HUSSEIN MUSTAPHA, engineering educator; s. Mustapha Mohammed and Sahjouna Youssef Zbib; m. Marcia Ann Rowe. BS, Mich. Technol. U., Houghton, 1981, MS, 1983, PhD, 1987. Prof. Wash. State U., Pullman, 1988—; dir. Wash. State U., Sch. Mech. and Materials Engring., 2003—. Editor: (jounral) Engineeirng Materials and Technology. Recipient Computational Mechanics Achievement award, Japanese Soc. of Mech. Engineers, 2003. Fellow: Am. Socity of Mech. Engineers; mem.: Lebanese Acad. of Sci. (treasures 2007). Achievements include research in Over 200 Publications In Materials Science And Engineeirng Mechanics. Office: Washington State Univ School of Mechanical & Materials Engg Pullman WA 99164-2920

ZBOCK, JASON PAUL, mathematics professor; b. Buffalo, Feb. 28, 1976; s. John Patrick and Marie Eleanor Zbock; m. Laurie Ann Bono, Dec. 20, 2003; 1 child, Ayden Ronald. MS in Math. Edn., U. Buffalo, 1999. Asst. prof. math., mem. academic cmty. Morrisville State Coll., NY, 2000—. Mem.: NY State Math. Assn. Two-Yr. Colls. Independent. Home and Office: Morrisville State Coll Route 20 Morrisville NY 13408 Business E-Mail: zbockjp@morrisville.edu.

ZBORAY, RONALD JOHN, history educator; b. Bridgeport, Conn., June 23, 1953; s. Julius Anthony and Margaret Magdalen (Misko) Z.; m. Mary Elizabeth Saracino, Dec. 4, 1984. BA in History summa cum laude, U. Bridgeport, 1975; AM in Am. Civilization, NYU, 1977, PhD, 1984. Microfilm editor Goldman Papers U. Calif., Berkeley, 1984-89; asst. prof. History U. Tex., Arlington, 1989-92, Ga. State U., Atlanta, 1992-96. Hon. vis. scholar Radcliffe Coll., 1998. Author: A Fictive People, 1993; co-author: A Handbook for the Study of Book History in the United States, 2000; contbr. articles to profl. jours. Am. Antiquarian Soc./NEH fellow, 1992, Schlesinger Libr. grantee, 1993, Benjamin F. Stevens fellow Mass. Hist. Soc., 1994, NEH fellow for Univ. Tchrs., 1998. Mem. Orgn. of Am. Historians, Am. Studies Assn., Am. Culture Assn., Am. Hist. Assn., Am. Antiquarian Soc. Office: Dept History Ga State U PO Box 4117 Atlanta GA 30302-4117

ZDERIC, STEPHEN ANTHONY, urologist, surgeon; b. Detroit, July 2, 1956; s. John Anthony and Marie Alice Zderic; m. Kathleen (Kate) Marie Cronan, Dec. 6, 1953; children: Olivia Cronan, Colin Cronan, Natalie Sang Me. BS Chemistry and BioChemistry, U. Calif. Riverside, 1979; MD, UCLA, 1983. Cert. Urologist Am. Bd. of Urology, 1993. Asst. prof. surgery in urology Sch. Medicine U. Pa., Phila., 1991—99; attending surgeon Children's Hosp. Phila., 1991—; assoc. prof. surgery in urology Sch. Medicine Sch. Medicine U. Pa., 1999—2006, prof. surgery in urology, 2006—. Editor: (sci. mongraph) Muscle Matrix and Bladder Function, Pediatric Gender Assignment A Critical Reappraisal, (book) Pediatric Urology for the Primary Care Provider; cons. reviewer Jour. Urology, Brit. Jour. Urology; contbr. articles to profl. jours. Grantee, NIH, 1993—98, 1994—95, 2003—05, 1998—; Rsch. Grant, Am. Found. Urologic Disease, 1989—90. Avocations: tennis, skiing, swimming. Office: Children's Hosp Philadelphia 34th & Civic Center Blvd Philadelphia PA 19104 Office Fax: 215-590-3985. Personal E-mail: zderic@email.chop.edu.

ZEAKES, BEVERLY JEAN, physical education educator, department chairman; BS, Kans. State U., Manhattan, 1970; MS, Radford U., Va., 1985; EdD, Va. Poly. and State U., Blacksburg, 1998. Tchr. Radford U., Va., chair dept. exercise sport and health edn. Wellness cons. Volvo, Dublin, 2006. V.p. health divsn. Va. Assn. for Health, Phys. Edn., Recreation and Dance, 1997—2004. Named Coll./Univ. Health Educator of Yr., Va. Assn. for Health, Phys. Edn., Recreation and Dance, 2005. Mem.: Phi Delta Kappa (treas. Radford br. 2000—09), Phi Kappa Phi. Office: Radford Univ Box 6957 Radford VA 24142

ZEAKES, SAMUEL JOHN, biology professor; MS, Kans. State U., Manhattan, 1969, PhD, 1972. Prof., chairman dept. biology Marymount Coll., Salina, Kans., 1972—84, dir. program nuc. medicine tech., 1976—84; prof. dept. biology Radford U., Va., 1984—, chairman, faculty appeals com., 1999—2004, dir., program clin. lab. sci., 2002—08. Recipient Excellence Tchg. award, Marymount Coll. Alpha Chi, 1980—81, Radford U. Found., 1989. Mem.: Human Anatomy & Physiology Soc. (America). Home: 901 Pendleton St Radford VA 24141 Office: Radford Univ Dept Biology P O Box 6931 Radford VA 24142

ZEALEY, SHARON JANINE, lawyer; b. St. Paul, Aug. 30, 1959; d. Marion Edward and Freddie Zealey. BS, Xavier U. of La., 1981; JD, U. Cin., 1984. Bar: Ohio 1984; U.S. Dist. Ct. (so. dist.) Ohio 1985; U.S. Ct. Appeals (6th cir.) 1990; U.S. Supreme Ct. 1990. Law clk. US Atty. S. Dist. Ohio, Cin., 1982; trust adminstr. US Bank (formerly First Nat. Bank), Cin., 1984-86; atty. UAW Legal Svcs., Cin., 1986-88; assoc. Manley, Burke, Lipton & Fischer, Cin., 1988-91; mng. atty. and dep. atty. gen. Ohio Atty. Gen. Office, Cin., 1991-95; asst. US atty. criminal div. for So. Dist. Ohio US Attys. Office, Cin., 1995-97; United States atty. So. Dist. Ohio, Cin., 1997—2001; ptnr. Blank Rome LLP, 2001—06; sr. litig. counsel Coca-Cola Co., Atlanta, 2006—. Adj. instr.

support Nat. Assn. Emergency Med. Technicians, 2007, in pediat. advanced life support Am. Heart Assn., 2007, in advanced cardiac life support Am. Heart Assn., 2007; lic. comml. pilot FAA, 1996. Aviation faculty U. ND, 2002—. Rschr. Ctrs. Excellence Gen. Aviation Rsch., Atlantic City, 2003—. Vol. firefighter Manvel Fire & Rescue, ND, 2003—. Recipient Master Flight Instr. award, Nat. Assn. Flight Instructors, 2000. Evangelical. Achievements include research in alternate forms of runway lighting not dependent on grid electricity; LED lighting for use on active civilian runways. Business E-Mail: zeidlik@aero.und.edu.

ZEIDMAN, FRED S., civic leader, corporate financial executive; b. July 11, 1946; m. Kay Zeidman; 4 children. BSBA, Washington U., 1968; MBA, NYU, 1970. Former pres. Enterprise Capital Corp.; former CEO, pres. InterSystems Inc.; bd. dirs. Seitel Inc., 1997, former chmn., 2002; former mng. partner WoodRock & Co., Houston; sr. dir. governmental affairs Greenberg Traurig LLP, Washington, 2004—. Bd. dirs. Prosperity Bank, Houston, Turnaround Partners, Inc. Chmn. US Holocaust Meml. Coun., Washington, 2002—. Mem.: Bd. of Regents, Tex So. U. (vice chmn.), Anti Defamation League (chmn.), Am Isreal Public Affairs Com. (exec. com.), Jewish Inst. Nat. Sec. Affairs (vp, dir.), Isreal Bonds. Republican. Office: Greenberg Traurig LLP 2101 L St NWSuite 1000 Washington DC 20037

ZEIDMAN, PHILIP FISHER, lawyer; b. Birmingham, Ala., May 2, 1934; s. Eugene Morris and Ida (Fisher) Z.; m. Nancy Levy, Aug. 19, 1956; children: Elizabeth Miriam, John Fisher (dec.), Jennifer Zeidman Bloch. BA cum laude, Yale U., 1955; LLB, Harvard U., 1958; postgrad., Grad. Sch. Bus. Adminstrn., 1957-58. Bar: Ala. 1958, Fla. 1960, U.S. Supreme Ct. 1961, D.C. 1968, N.Y. 1981. Trial atty. FTC, 1960-61; staff asst. White House Com. Small Bus., 1961-63; spl. asst. to adminstr. SBA, 1961-63, asst. gen. counsel, 1963-65, gen. counsel, 1965-68; spl. asst. to Vice Pres. of U.S., 1968; govt. rels. mgr. Nat. Alliance Businessmen, 1968; founding prin. Brownstein & Zeidman P.C., Washington, 1968-96; sr. ptnr. Rudnick, Wolfe, Epstien & Zeidman, Washington, 1996-99; ptnr. Piper Marbury Rudnick & Wolfe, Washington, 1999—2004; ptnr., Franchise & Distribution practice group DLA Piper, Washington, 2005—. Chmn. grants and benefits com. Adminstrv. Conf. U.S., 1968; chmn. food industry adv. com. Dept. Energy, 1979-81; chmn. distbn. and food merchandising subcom. Alliance to Save Energy, 1978; mem. Pres.'s Commn. on Exec. Exch., 1978-81; gen. counsel Internat. Franchise Assn.; spl. counsel Japanese Franchise Assn.; advisor to govts. and internat. orgns.; founder EastEuropeLaw, Ltd., Budapest, Hungary. Editor, author: Survey of Laws and Regulations Affecting International Franchising, 1982, 2nd edit., 1990, 3rd edit., 2004, Regulation of Buying and Selling a Franchise, 1983, Legal Aspects of Selling and Buying, 1983, 2nd edit., 1991, 3rd edit., 2004; cons. editor Global Franchising Alert; assoc. editor Jour. of International Franchising Law and Distribution; contbg. editor Legal Times of Washington, 1978-85; mem. adv. bd. Antitrust and Trade Regulation Report for Bur. Nat. Affairs, 1978-85. Mem. young leadership coun. Dem. Nat. Com.; exec. dir. Dem. platform com., 1972; adviser Nat. Presdl. Campaign of Jimmy Carter, 1976; mem. pres.'s adv. com. John F. Kennedy Ctr. for Performing Arts, 1981; mem. adv. bd. Yale U. Sch. Mgmt.; trustee Yale-China Assn., 1983-89; dir. & gen. coun. com. Appleseed Found. 1994—; mem. adv. bd. DeWitt Wallace Ctr. for Comm., Terry Sanford Inst. Pub. Policy, Duke U., 1994-98; With USAF, 1958-60. Recipient Younger Fed. Lawyer award Fed. Bar Assn., 1965; Jonathan Davenport Oratorical award, 1954; William Houston McKim award, 1955 Mem. ABA (chmn. com. on franchising 1977-81), D.C. Bar Assn., Ala. Bar Assn., Fla. Bar Assn., Fed. Bar Assn., Bar Assn. D.C., Internat. Bar Assn. (hon., life; mem. council, 2007-, chmn. internat. franchising com. 1986-90, mem. coun. sect. bus. law 1996—2000), Am. Intellectual Property Law Assn. (chmn. franchising com. 1987-90), Assn. Yale U. Alumni (class rep.), Internat. Bar Assn. Found. (pres. 2000-09). Office: DLA Piper 500 8th St Washington DC 20004 Office Phone: 202-799-4272, 703-773-4013. Office Fax: 202-799-5272. Business E-Mail: philip.zeidman@dlapiper.com.

ZEIGER, LAWRENCE HARVEY See KING, LARRY

ZEIGLER, ANN DEPENDER, lawyer; b. Spokane, June 7, 1947; d. F. Norman and Dorothy dePender; m. Paul Stewart Zeigler, June 20, 1970; 1 child, Kate Elizabeth. BA magna cum laude, Ft. Wright Coll. Holy Names, 1969; MFA in Creative Writing, U. Mont., Missoula, 1975; JD, U. Houston, 1984. Bar: Tex. 1984. Course adminstr. legal comm. U. Houston, 1982—84; exec. editor Houston Jours. Internat. Law, 1983—84; assoc. Dula, Shields & Egbert, 1984—87; ind. project atty., 1987; assoc. Dow, Cogburn & Friedman, 1987—90; assoc. bankruptcy sect., chpt. 7 trustee rep. Hughes, Watters & Askanase, Houston, 1990—2008; of counsel Nelson S Ebaugh PC, 2009—. Spkr. in field. Co-editor: Insurance Guide-Arts Nonprofits, 1993, Basic Issues in Estate Planning-Representing the Artist, 1994, Leading the Arts Nonprofit: Duties of Officers and Directors, 1999; mem. editl. bd. Houston Lawyer, 1999— (award Best Series of Articles for 2-part series on bankruptcy amendments); guest editor spl. hist. issue: Houston Lawyer, 2000, 2001, guest editor 40th ann. issue:, 2003, assoc. editor: Keeping Up With/Legal Trends, 2002—05, 2007—08; contbr. articles to profl. jours.; editor in chief Houston Lawyer, 2009—, articles editor, 2008—09. Mem.: ABA, Can. Bar Assn., Houston Bar Assn. (chair law and arts com. 1996—97, co-chair ann. fiction contest), State Bar Tex. (bankruptcy sect.), Phi Alpha Delta. Democrat. Home: 4038 Cheena Dr Houston TX 77025-4702 Home Phone: 713-661-9204; Office Phone: 713-752-0700. Business E-Mail: azeigler@ebaughlaw.com.

ZEILBERGER, DORON, mathematics professor, researcher; b. Haifa, Israel, July 2, 1950; s. Yehuda Heinz and Ruth (Alexander) Z.; m. Jane Deborah LeGrange, June 3, 1979; children: Celia, Tamar, Hadas. BS with first class hons., U. London, 1972; PhD, Weizmann Inst., Rehovot, Israel, 1976. Mem. Inst. for Advanced Study, Princeton, NJ, 1977-78, 93; vis. asst. prof. Ga. Inst. Tech., Atlanta, 1978-79; lectr. U. Ill., Urbana, 1979-80; sr. scientist Weizmann Inst., Rehovot, Israel, 1980-82; lectr. U. Pa., Phila., 1982-83; assoc. prof. Drexel U., Phila., 1983-88, prof., 1988-90, Temple U., Phila., 1990-99, Laura H. Carnell prof., 1999-2001; bd. govs. prof. Rutgers U., New Brunswick, NJ, 2001—. Mem. editl. bd. Elec. Jour. of Combinations, others, editor-in-chief Advances in Applied Math.; contbr. numerous articles to profl. jours. Mem. Am. Math. Soc. (Leroy P. Steele prize 1998), Math. Assn. Am. (Lester R. Ford award 1990), Inst. for Combinatorics and Its Applications (Euler medal, 2004). Business E-Mail: zeilberg@math.rutgers.edu.

ZEILIG, NANCY MEEKS, writer, editor; b. Nashville, Apr. 28, 1943; d. Edward Harvey and Nancy Evelyn (Self) Meeks; m. Lanny Kenneth Fielder, Aug. 20, 1964 (div. Dec. 1970); m. Charles Elliot Zeilig, Jan. 6, 1974 (div. Dec. 1989); 1 child, Sasha Rebecca; m. Kenn Lively, Apr. 22, 2006. BA, Birmingham-So. Coll., 1964; postgrad., Vanderbilt U., 1971-73. Editorial asst. Reuben H. Donnelley, NYC, 1969-70; asst. editor Vanderbilt U., Nashville, 1970-74; editor U. Minn., St. Paul, 1975; asst. editor McGraw-Hill Inc., Mpls., 1975-76; mng. editor Denver mag., 1976-80; editor Jour. Am. Water Works Assn., Denver, 1981—99; owner Nancy Zeilig Writing & Editing, Denver, 2000—. Editor, co-pub.: WomanSource, 1982, rev. edit., 1984; contbr. articles to trade and consumer mags. Co-chair arts adv. com. Denver Sch. Arts, 1994-96. Avocations: travel, reading, cooking. Office Phone: 303-758-7750. E-mail: nzeilig@earthlink.net.

ZEILINGER, ELNA RAE, elementary school and gifted and talented educator; b. Tempe, Ariz., Mar. 24, 1937; d. Clayborn Eddie and Ruby Elna (Laird) Simpson; m. Philip Thomas Zeilinger, June 13, 1970; children: Shari, Chris. BA in Edn., Ariz. State U., 1958, MA in Edn., 1966, EdS, 1980. Bookkeeper First Nat. Bank of Tempe, 1955-56; with registrar's office Ariz. State U., 1956-58; piano tchr., recreation dir. City of Tempe; tchr. Thew Sch., Tempe, 1958-61; elem. tchr. Mitchell Sch., Tempe, 1962-74, intern prin., 1976, personnel intern, 1977; specialist gifted edn. Tempe Elem. Schs., Tempe, 1977-86; elem. tchr. Holdeman Sch., Tempe, 1986-89; tchr. grades 1-12 and adult reading, lang. arts, English Zeilinger Tutoring Svc., 1991—. Grad. asst. ednl. adminstrn., Iota Workshop coordinator Ariz. State U., 1978; presenter Ariz. Gifted Conf., 1978-81; condr. survey of gifted programs, 1980; reporter pub. rels. Tempe Sch. Dist., 1978-80, Access com. for gifted programs, 1981-83. Author: Leadership Role of the Principal in Gifted Programs: A Handbook, 1980; Classified Personnel Handbook, 1977, also reports, monographs and paintings. Active Tempe Hist. Assn., liaison, 1975, Tempe Art League; freedom train com. Ariz. Bicentennial Commn., 1975-76; bd. dirs. Maple Property Owners Assn., 1994-2002; storyteller Tempe Hist. Mus., 1997—; dir. pagentry Daus. of the Nile, 2002-03. Named Outstanding Leader in Elem. and Secondary Schs., 1976' Ariz. Cattle Growers scholar, 1954-55; Elks scholar, 1954-55; recipient Judges award Tempe Art League, 1970, Best of Show, Scottsdale Art League, 1976. Mem.: Daus. of the Nile (dir. pageantry 2002—03), Tempe Women's Club. Independent. Congregationalist.

ZEILSTRA-RYALLS, JILL HELEN, biology professor; d. Milton Roger and Mary Mabel Ryalls; m. Anne Zeilstra, June 6, 1976; children: Ian Abel Zeilstra, Benjamin Gabriel Zeilstra. PhD, Purdue U., West Lafayette, Ind., 1990. Asst. prof. Oakland U., Rochester, Mich., 1997—2003, assoc. prof., 2003—07; prof. Bowling Green State U., Ohio, 2007—. Editl. bd. mem. Applied & Environ. Microbiology, Washington, 2009—. Grantee RUI, NSF, 1998—2002, 2003—06; Rsch. grant, Mich. Life Scis. Corridor Fund., 2001—04. Mem.: Am. Soc. Biochemistry & Molecular Biology, Am. Soc. Microbiology, Gamma Sigma Delta. Office: Bowling Green State Univ 442C Life Scis Bldg Bowling Green OH 43403

ZEISEL, STEVEN H., nutritionist, scientist, educator; b. NYC, July 16, 1950; BS in Life Sci., MIT, 1971; MD, Harvard Med. Sch., 1975; PhD in Nutrition, MIT, 1980. Asst. in medicine Children's Hosp., Boston, 1980-81; asst. prof. pathology and pediatrics Boston U. Sch. Medicine, 1982—90, assoc. prof., 1987-90, prof., 1990; prof. dept. pediatrics U. N.C., Chapel Hill, 1990—, prof. dept. nutrition, 1990—, chair dept. nutrition, 1990—2005; chair med. edn. com. Am. Soc. Clin. Nutrition, 1995—97. Chair joint membership com. AIN/ASCN, 1992-94; chmn. adv. bd. Gen. Clin. Rsch. Ctr., U. N.C., 1990-2000; mem. Inst. of Medicine panel on folate and B Vitamins, 1997-99; mem. sci. adv. bd. Monsanto Corp., 1998-2000; mem. sci. coun. Dannon Inst.; bd. dirs. Interactive Info; dir. U. NC Clin. Nutrition Rsch. Unit. Editor-in-chief Jour. Nutritional Biochemistry. Mem. Internat. Soc. for Rsch. on Human Milk and Lactation, Am. Soc. Nutritional Scis., Am. Soc. Clin. Nutrition (councilor 1991-94, chmn. residency edn. and subspecialty tng. com. 1995—), Am. Soc. Parenteral and Enteral Nutrition, Am. Coll. Nutrition, Am. Pub. Health Assn., Soc. Pediatric Rsch. Achievements include development of hippocampus is influenced by the availability of choline because of changes in mitosis and apoptosis in neuronal cells. Office: UNC Dept Nutrition #7461 Sch Pub Health/Sch Medicine 2115A Michael Hooker Rsch Ctr Chapel Hill NC 27599-7461 Office Phone: 919-843-4731. Office Fax: 919-843-8555. E-mail: steven_zeisel@unc.edu.

ZEITELS, STEVEN MARC, surgeon, educator; b. NYC, Nov. 7, 1957; m. Maria Nuria Hananias, June 27, 2003. BA, Boston U., Boston, 1978, MD, 1982, degree Otolaryngology, Tufts U.; degree Head & Neck Surg. Oncology, Boston U., Boston, 1988. Dir. voice ctr. Mass. Gen. Hosp., Boston, 2004—; Eugene B. Casey prof. laryngeal surgery Harvard Med. Sch., Boston, 2005—. Consulting laryngologist Berklee Coll. Music, Boston, 1991—, Boston U., Boston, 1994—, New Eng. Conservatory, Boston, 1994—, The Juilliard Sch., NYC, 2006—; pres. Am. Broncho-Esophagological Assn., 2004—05; guest lectr. in field. Author: Adduction Arytenopexy: A New Procedure for Paralytic Dysphonia (Am. Laryngol. Assn. Casselberry award, 1998), (surgical textbook) Atlas of Phonomicrosurgery; contbr. documentary. Cons. Inst. Laryngology and Voice Restoration, Boston, 2003. Recipient Disting. Alumnus award, Boston U., Henry J. Rubin Meml. Lectureship, Cedars-Sinai Med. Ctr., LA, 2002, Disting. Svc. Award, Am. Acad. of Otolaryngology - Head and Neck Surgery, 2004, Disting. Alumnus award, Boston U. Sch. Medicine, 2007, Tchg. Svc. award, Am. Acad. Otolaryngology Head and Neck Surgery, 1995; named Ann. Arnold Grossman Lectr. in Laryngology, Montreal Gen. Hosp., 1996, Lewis H. Wright Meml. Disting. Lectr., Am. Soc. Anesthesiology, 1998, Sylvan Stool History Medicine Lectr., U. Pitts., 2000, Ann. George Barber Lectr., U. of Ala., 2003, Lawrence Boies Lectr., U. Minn., 2003, Chevalier Jackson Lectr., Am. Broncho-Esophagological Assn., 2006. Fellow: ACS, Am. Bd. Otolaryngology. Achievements include patents for the Universal Modular Laryngoscope/Glottiscope System; the Adjustable Supraglottiscope; universal modular glottiscope system having intra-wall channels for vocal fold microsurgery or orotracheal intubation; invention of Subepithelial Vocal-Fold Infusion Needle; Microlaryngeal Suspension Gallows. Office: Mass Gen Hosp Voice Cent One Bowdoin Square 11th Fl Boston MA 02114 Office Phone: 617-726-0218. Office Fax: 617-726-0222.

ZEITLIN, EUGENIA PAWLIK, librarian, educator, writer; b. NYC, Jan. 29; d. Charles and Pauline (Klimowski) Pawlik; m. Herbert Zakary Zeitlin, July 3, 1949; children: Mark Clyde, Joyce Therese Zeitlin Harris, Ann Victoria, Clare Katherine. BA in English, Bklyn. Coll., 1945; MA in English, NYU, NYC, 1951; MALS, Rosary Coll., 1968. Teaching credential N.Y., Ariz., Calif., Ill. English tchr., Sea Cliff, L.I., NY, 1945—47; English, math. tchr. Merrick (N.Y.) Sch. Dist., 1948—49; English tchr. Wilson Sch. Dist., Phoenix, 1949—50; counselor West Phoenix (Ariz.) High Sch., 1953—56; asst. prof. English Wright Coll., Chgo., 1965—66; asst. prof. English, asst. to v.p. curriculum and instrn. Oakton C.C., Des Plaines, Ill., 1970—76; libr. Pasadena City Coll., LA, 1979—84, L.A. Pub. Libr., 1984—2004; ret., 2004. Contbr. articles to profl. jours. Named Northridge City Employee of Yr., 1986. Mem. AAUW (br. pres. Lancaster, Calif. 1959-60), Thoreau Soc. (life), Beta Phi Mu. Avocations: writing and editing, book collecting. Home: 20124 Phaeton Dr Woodland Hills CA 91364-5633

ZEITLIN, HERBERT ZAKARY, college administrator, educational consultant, writer; b. NYC, Jan. 14; s. Leonard and Martha Josephine (Soff) Zeitlin; m. Eugenia F. Pawlik, July 3, 1949; children: Mark Clyde, Joyce Therese Zeitlin Harris, Ann Victoria, Clare Katherine. BS, NYU, 1947, MA, 1949; EdD, Stanford U., 1956. Tchr. Mepham HS, Bellmore, NY, 1946—47, Nassau County Vocat. Edn. Extension Bd., Mineola, NY; electronics instr., adj. faculty Mephan CC; tchr., counselor, dir. testing Phoenix Union HS and Coll. Dist.; dean eve. coll., prin. high sch. Antelope Valley Union HS and Coll. Dist., Lancaster, Calif.; dean instrn. Southwestern Coll., Chula Vista, Calif.; pres., supt., cons. Triton Coll., River Grove, Ill., 1964—79; dean, pres. West LA Coll., 1976-80; pres. Trident Cons., LA, mgmt. cons., 1976—; adj. faculty Ariz. State U., Flagstaff, No. Ill. U., DeKalb, U. Calif., Santa Barbara. Author: Turbulent Birth of Triton College, 2001, Corruption: How to Fight It and Win, 2004, What Makes A Teacher Great?, 2007; editor: in field. Pres. Antelope Valley Breeze & Sage, Bon Vivant Homeowners Assn.; mayor Upper Woodland Hills, Calif. With USAAF, 1942—46. Recipient Spl. commendation, Chgo. Tribune, Richard Ogilvie, former Gov. Ill., Spl. Achievement award for visionary accomplishment, Ill. Sch. Adminstrs. Assn.; named Adminstr. of the Yr., Triton Coll. Faculty Assn., 1974, Most Influential Educator in Ill., Chgo. Sun Times. Mem.: Ariz. State Vocat. Assn. (pres.), Ariz. Vocat. Guidance Assn. (pres.), Maywood Ill. Rotary (pres.), Antelope Valley Rotary (pres.). Mailing: Trident Cons PO Box 571412 Tarzana CA 91357 Home: 20124 Phacton Dr Woodland Hills CA 91364 Home Phone: 818-884-7819. Personal E-mail: herbertzzeitlin@aol.com. *I always felt that being the president of an organization, having held many presidencies in my lifetime, was like being the quarterback on the football team. You had a choice of running with the ball and taking some bruises or passing it to someone who should score. I was lucky most of the time in selecting some very fine receivers.*

ZEITLIN, LAURIE, printing company and information technology executive; BA in Econs., Duke U., 1984; MBA in Fin., U. Pa., 1989. Rsch. asst. Touche Ross & Co., 1985—87; sr. mng. consulting Deloitte & Touche LLP, 1989—95; dir. info. tech., sr. mgr. application devel., v.p. info. tech. Home Depot, Inc., Atlanta, 1995—2003; sr. v.p., chief info. officer Kinko's Inc., Dallas, 2003—. Named one of Premier 100 IT Leaders, Computerworld, 2006. Office: Kinkos 13155 Noel Rd Ste 1600 Dallas TX 75240 Office Phone: 214-550-7020. E-mail: laurie.zeitlin@fedexkinkos.com.

ZEITLIN, MAURICE, sociology educator; b. Detroit, Feb. 24, 1935; s. Albert J. and Rose (Goldberg) Zeitlin; m. Marilyn Geller, Mar. 1, 1959; children: Michelle, Carla, Erica. BA cum laude, Wayne State U., 1957; MA, U. Calif., Berkeley, 1960, PhD, 1964. Instr. anthropology and sociology Princeton (N.J.) U., 1961-64; rsch. assoc. Ctr. Internat. Studies, 1962-64; from asst. prof. to assoc. prof. sociology U. Wis., Madison, 1964—70, prof., 1970-77; dir. Ctr. Social Orgn., 1974-76; disting. prof. sociology UCLA, 1977—, rsch. assoc. Inst. Inds. Rels. Vis. prof. polit. sci. and sociology Hebrew U., Jerusalem, 1971—72; vis. disting. prof. sociology Tel Aviv U., 1996—97. Author (with R. Scheer): Cuba: An American Tragedy, 1963, 1964, Revolutionary Politics and the Cuban Working Class, 1967, 1970, The Civil Wars in Chile, 1984; author: (with R. E. Ratcliff) Landlords and Capitalists, 1988, The Large Corporation and Contemporary Classes, 1989; author: (with J. Stepan-Norris) Talking Union, 1996, Left Out: Reds and America's Industrial Unions, 2003; Latin Am. editor: Ramparts mag., 1967—73, editor-in-chief: Political Power and Social Theory, 1980—90; mem. editl. adv. bd. Progressive mag., 1985—96; editor (with J. Petras): Latin America: Reform or Revolution?, 1968, American Society, Inc., 1970, 1977, Father Camilo Torres: Revolutionary Writings, 1972, Classes, Class Conflict, and the State, 1980, How Mighty a Force?, 1983, Insurgent Workers: The Origins of Industrial Unionism, 1987. Chmn. Madison Citizens for a Vote on Vietnam, 1967—68, Am. Com. for Chile, 1973—75; mem. exec. bd. U.S. Com. Justice to Latin Am. Polit. Prisoners, 1977—84; mem. exec. com. Calif. Campaign for Econ. Democracy, 1983—86. Recipient Project Censored award, Top Censored Story, 1981; co-recipient Inaugural Disting. Publ. award in Labor Studies, Soc. for Study Social Problems, 1996; named to Ten Best Censored Stories list, 1978; Ford Found. fellow, 1965—67, 1970—71, Guggenheim fellow, 1981—82, NSF grantee, 1981, 1982, 1998. Mem.: Internat. Sociol. Assn. (mem. editl. bd. 1977—81), Am. Sociol. Assn. (mem. governing coun. 1977—80, co-recipient Disting. Contbn. Scholarship award in Polit. Sociology 1992, 1996, 2002, The 2004 Max Weber award for an Outstanding Book Published Over the Past Three Years in Orgns., Occupations and Work). Democrat. Jewish. Office: UCLA Dept Sociology 264 Haines Hall Los Angeles CA 90095-1551 Office Phone: 310-825-3968. Business E-Mail: zeitlin@soc.ucla.edu. *Personal philosophy: "If I am not for myself who will be? And when I am for myself, what am I?" Hillel, the Elder.*

ZEITZ, JOSHUA, history professor, writer; b. Trenton, NJ; BA, Swarthmore Coll., Pa.; PhD in Am. History, Brown U., Providence. Tchr. jr. high and HS students at a summer academic enrichment program, Md.; with non-profit urban redevel. corp., New Brunswick, NJ; lectr. in Am. history Rutgers U., NJ, Harvard U., Cambridge, Mass., Cambridge U., England. Author: Flapper: A Madcap Story of Sex, Style, Celebrity and the Women Who Made America Modern, 2006, White Ethnic New York: Jews, Catholics, and the Shaping of Postwar Politics, 2007; contbr. articles to profl. jours., newspapers and mags. Democrat. Mailing: PO Box 560 Bordentown NJ 08505 Office Phone: 609-888-1925.

ZEKMAN, TERRI MARGARET, graphic designer; b. Chgo., Sept. 13, 1950; d. Theodore Nathan and Lois (Bernstein) Z.; m. Alan Daniels, Apr. 12, 1980; children: Jesse Logan, Dakota Caitlin. BFA, Washington U., St. Louis, 1971; postgrad, Art Inst. Chgo., 1974-75. Graphic designer (on retainer) greeting cards and related products Recycled Paper Products Co., Chgo., 1970—, Jillson Roberts, Inc., Calif.; apprenticed graphic designer Helmuth, Obata & Kassabaum, St. Louis, 1970-71; graphic designer Container Corp., Chgo., 1971; graphic designer, art dir., photographer Cuerden Advt. Design, Denver, 1971-74; art dir. D'Arcy, McManus & Masius Advt., Chgo., 1975-76; freelance graphic designer Chgo., 1976-77; art dir. Garfield Linn Advt., Chgo., 1977-78; graphic designer Keiser Design Group, Van Noy & Co., Los Angeles, 1978-79; owner and operator graphic design studio Los Angeles, 1979—. Art and photography tchr. Ctr. for Early Edn., L.A., 1996—, Buckley Sch., Sherman Oaks, 1996—; 3d grade tchr. asst., 1999—. Recipient cert. of merit St. Louis Outdoor Poster Contest, 1970, Denver Art Dirs. Club, 1973 Personal E-mail: redzek50@aol.com.

ZELAC, RONALD EDWARD, physicist; b. Chgo., Jan. 22, 1941; BS in Engring. Physics summa cum laude, U. Ill., 1962, MS in Physics, 1964; MS in Environ. Health, U. Mich., 1965; PhD in Environ. Engring., U. Fla., 1970. Diplomate Am. Bd. Health Physics, Am. Bd. Medical Physics. Chief health physicist IIT Rsch. Inst., Chgo., 1965-68; radiation physicist Mercy Medical Ctr., Chgo., 1967-68; asst., assoc. prof. Temple U., Phila., 1970-92, radiation safety officer, 1970-91; adj. assoc. prof. U. Pa., Phila., 1980-86; assoc. vice provost Temple U., Phila., 1987-91; sr. physicist and exec. mgr. tech. Landauer Inc., Glenwood, Ill., 1991-97. Adj. prof. Northwestern U., Evanston, Ill., 1991-97, Temple U., 1992—, Purdue U., 1998—; health physicist, tech. asst., sr. asst. to chmn., sr. health physicist, US NRC, Rockville, Md., 1998—; cons. Wyeth-Ayerst Rsch., Radnor, Pa., Princeton, NJ, 1971-94, Presby. U. Pa. Med. Ctr., Phila., 1974-86, Mobil Rsch. Devel. Corp., Paulsboro, Princeton, 1977-95, Rhone-Poulenc Rorer Cen. Rsch., Ft. Washington, Collegeville, Pa.,

Coll. Law U. Cin., 1997—; mem. U.S. Atty. Gen.'s Adv. Com., 1999—2001, chair civil rights subcom., 2001; mem. merit selection com. Sixth Cir. Ct. of Appeals Bankruptcy Ct., 1992—96, 2003. Mem. commn. Cin. Cmty. Action Now, 2001—; commr. Tall Stacks Commn., City of Cin., 1990—94, Mayor's Commn. on Children, City of Cin., 1992—94; mem. equal employment adv. rev. panel City of Cin., 1989—91; trustee, bd. visitors U. Cin. Coll. Law, 1992—2006; trustee Legal Aid Soc. Cin., 1987—92; bd. dirs. Freestore Foodbank, 2003—, Playhouse in the Park, 2002—06, Nat. Inst. for Law and Equity, 2002—; co-chair Greater Cin. Minority Counsel Program, 2005—06; mem. exec. bd. Cin. Youth Collaborative, 2005—06. Recipient Disting. Alumni award, Friends of Women's Studies, U. Cin., 2001, Theodore M. Berry award for outstanding achievement in politics and in svc. to cmty., Cin. chpt. NACCP, 1998, Nicholas Longworth III Alumni Achievement award for disting. pub. svc., U. Cin. Coll. Law, 1997; named Career Woman of Achievement, Cin. YWCA, 1988; named one of Top Ten Women Attys., Women's Bus. Cin., 2005; named to Super Lawyers, Ohio, 2006. Mem. Black Lawyers Assn. of Cin. (pres. 1989-91, round table 1988-), Legal Aid Soc. (sec. 1991-92), ABA, Fed. Bar Assn., Ohio Bar Assn., Nat. Bar Assn. (bd. govs. 1988-1990, Mem. of Yr. region VI 1990), Cin. Bar Assn. (trustee 1989-94), Cin. CAN Commn. Democrat. Episcopalian. Office: Coca-Cola Co One Coca-Cola Plz NAT 2062 PO Box 1734 Atlanta GA 30301 Office Phone: 404-676-2121. Business E-Mail: zealey@blankRome.com.

ZEBALLOS, ABEL, theater educator, make-up artist, consultant; b. Oruro, Bolivia, Oct. 17, 1948; s. Abel and Blanca S. Zeballos; life ptnr. Delmer Don Kennedy, July 6, 1977 (dec. Aug. 16, 2008). MA, Calif. State U., Fullerton, 1976. Makeup dir. Knott's Berry Farm, Buena Pk., Calif., 1975—93; makeup and hair designer South Coast Repertory Theatre, Costa Mesa, Calif., 1978—87; part time instr. theatrical design Calif. State U., LA, 1982—89, prof. theatre Fullerton, 1984—; part time instr. theatre UCLA, Westwood, 1987—87; costume designer Alternative Repertory Theatre, Santa Ana, Calif., 1987—95. Lectr. Nat. U. Mex., 1998—98. Makeup, Basic Theatrical Makeup. Recipient Outstanding Faculty Recognition award, Calif. State U. Fullerton, 1995—97. Mem.: Calif. faculty Assn. Democrat. Roman Catholic. Avocations: travel, reading. Office: Calif State Univ Fullerton 800 N State Coll Blvd Fullerton CA 92834-6850 E-mail: azeballos@fullerton.edu.

ZEBROSKI, EDWIN LEOPOLD, risk management consultant; b. Chgo., Apr. 1, 1921; s. Peter Paul and Sophie (Rydz) Z.; m. Gisela Karin Rudolph, Sept. 6, 1969; children: Lars, Zoe, Susan, Peggy. BS, U. Chgo., 1941; PhD, U. Calif., Berkeley, 1947. Registered prof. engr., Calif. Project engr. Gen. Electric Co., Schenectady, N.Y., 1947-53, mgr. devel. engring. San Jose, Calif., 1958-73; mgr. engring. SRI Internat., Menlo Park, Calif., 1954-58, dir. systems and materials dept., 1974-79; dir. nuclear safety analysis ctr. EPRI, Palo Alto, Calif., 1979-81; v.p. engring. INPO, Atlanta, 1981-83; chief nuclear scientist EPRI, 1982—88; dir. risk mgmt. svcs. APTECH Engring. Svcs., Sunnyvale, Calif., 1988-97; safety and risk mgmt. advisor Oak Ridge Nat. Lab., 1997—2000, DOE-Sandia Nat. Lab., 2000—04. Vis. prof. Purdue U., Lafayette, Ind., 1977-78; cons. OTA, Washington, 1980, 82-83, Dept. Energy, Washington, 1985-90, panels Nat. Rsch. Coun., 1990—, Electricite de France, 1986-87, Dept. Interior, Washington, 1987-89, EPRI, Palo Alto, 1988-98, Acad. Sci., USSR, 1987, Karlsruhe Lab., Germany, 1988; mem. commn. engring. edn. NRC, Washington, 1970-73; mem. NAS-NRC Panel on Decision-Making in Govt. Agy., 1997-98; mem. NAS-NRC Panel on High Level Waste R&D, 2001; mem. NAE Panel on Countering Terrorism, 2002—03. Contbr. chpts. to books, numerous articles to profl. jours.; patentee in field. Pres. bd. dirs. Unitarian Ch., Palo Alto, 2005—06; bd. dirs. Stevenson House, Palo Alto, 2003—07. Recipient Charles A. Coffin award Gen. Electric Co., Schenectady, 1954, Edward Teller award, 2002. Fellow AAAS, Am. Nuclear Soc. (bd. exec. com. 1969-71), Am. Inst. Chemists; mem. NAE (chmn. energy com. 1984-86, chmn. mem. com. 1986-87, policy com. 1995-96), Am. Phys. Soc., Soc. for Risk Analysis. Avocations: safety and risk management, public sector decision processes, music, writing. Business E-Mail: edzeb1@comcast.net.

ZECHER, LINDA, computer software company executive; m. Richard Zecher; 3 children. BS, Ohio State U., Columbus. Mgmt. positions Tex. Instruments, Bank of America; v.p. sales and mktg. PeopleSoft; sr. v.p. Oracle; CEO Evolve Corp.; joined Microsoft Corp., Redmond, Wash., 2003, v.p. US pub. sector, v.p. pub. sector Americas, corp. v.p. worldwide pub. sector, 2009—. Bd. mem. Emily Couric Leadership Forum, Intelligence Nat. Security Assn., Va. Piedmont Tech. Coun., Ohio State U. digital Union Adv. Com., US Dept. State Bd. Overseas Schools. Office: Microsoft Corp One Microsoft Way Redmond WA 98052-6399*

ZECHMAN, EDWIN KERPER, JR., medical facility administrator; b. Harrisburg, Pa., Jan. 22, 1948; BS, MEd, Shippensburg State Coll., Pa.; MS in Health Adminstrn., Ohio State U., 1974. Asst. adminstr. Children's Hosp. Med. Ctr., Akron, Ohio, 1974-78, assoc. adminstr., 1978-80; exec. dir. Children's Hosp., New Orleans, 1980-81, Children's Hosp. Ala., Birmingham, 1981-85; pres., CEO Children's Hosp. Pitts., 1985-94, Children's Nat. Med. Ctr., Washington, 1994—, also CEO Children's Rsch. Inst. Chmn. Nat. Assn. Children's Hoss. & Related Instns.; bd. dirs. DC Hosp. Assn. Fellow: Am. Coll. Healthcare Execs., Am. Hosp. Assn.; mem.: AMA. Office: Children's Nat Med Ctr 111 Michigan Ave NW Washington DC 20010-2916*

ZECK, VAN, federal agency administrator; b. Morgantown, W.Va., 1948; BS, W.Va. U., 1970. With US Dept. Treasury, 1971—, various positions in data processing, marketable securities ops., adminstrn., with bur. internal audit staff; asst. commr. financing Bur. Pub. Debt, US Dept. Treasury, 1982—87, dep. commr., 1987—98, commr., 1998—. Office: US Dept Treasury Bur Pub Debt PO Box 7015 Parkersburg WV 26106*

ZECKHAUSER, RICHARD JAY, economist, educator; b. Phila., Nov. 1, 1940; s. Julius Nathaniel and Estelle (Borgenicht) Zeckhauser; m. Nancy Mackell Hoover, Sept. 9, 1967; children: Bryn Gordon, Benjamin Rennell. AB, Harvard U., 1962, PhD, 1969. Jr. fellow Soc. Fellows Harvard U., Cambridge, Mass., 1965-68, mem. faculty, 1968—, prof. polit. econ. Kennedy Sch., 1972—, Frank P. Ramsey prof. polit. economy. Founder, bd. dirs. Niederhoffer, Cross & Zeckhauser, 1968—84; sr. advisor, prin. Equity Resource Investments, 2005—; bus. adv. bd. Tengion, Inc., 2006—. Co-author: A Primer for Policy Analysis, 1978, Demographic Dimensions of the New Republic, 1982, The Early Admissions Game: Joining the Elite, 2003; editor or co-editor: Benefit-Cost and Policy Analysis, 1974, What Role for Government, 1983, Principals and Agents: The Structure of Business, 1985, American Society: Public and Private Responsibilities, 1986, Privatization and State-Owned Enterprises: Lessons from the United States, Great Britain, and Canada, 1989, Strategy and Choice, 1991, Wise Choices: Games, Decisions, and Negotiations, 1996, Targeting in Social Programs: Avoiding Bad Bets, Removing Bad Apples, 2006; editor or co-editor The Patron's Payoff: Conspicuous Commissions in Italian Renaissance Art, 2008; contbr. 248 articles to profl. jours., chapters to books; rsch. fin., coll. admissions, climate change and healthcare. Bd. dirs. Commonwealth Sch. Recipient 2d pl., US Mixed-Teams Championship, 2003, 3d pl., US Open Pairs Championship, 2004, 1st Pl., US Mixed Pairs, 2007; named winner, numerous regional and nat. contract bridge competitions; finalist, World Paris Championship, 1998. Fellow: AAAS, Inst. Medicine/NAS, Assn. Pub. Policy and Mgmt., Econometric Soc. Office: Harvard U John F Kennedy Sch Govt 79 JFK St Cambridge MA 02138-5801 Business E-Mail: richard_zeckhauser@harvard.edu.

ZEDILLO PONCE DE LEÓN, ERNESTO, economics professor, former president of Mexico; b. Mexico City, Apr. 27, 1951; s. Rodolfo Zedillo Castillo and Martha Alicia Ponce de Leon; m. Nilda Patricia Velasco Nuñez; children: Ernesto, Emiliano, Carlos, Nild Patricia, Rodrigo. Student, Instituto Politécnico Nacional, Bradford U., U. Colo.; MA, Yale U., 1977, PhD, 1981, LLD (hon.), 2001. With Partido Revolucionario Institucional, 1971—, Instituto de Estudios Políticos, Económicos y Sociales; econ. rschr. Dirección Gen. de Programación Económica y Social; lectr. Colegio de Mex., 1978-80; dep. mgr. finance and econ. rsch., advisor to bd. dirs. Banco de Mex.; dep. sec. for planning and budget Govt. Mex., Mexico City, 1985-88, sec. for planning and budget, 1988-92, sec. public edn., 1992-93; campaign mgr. presdl. nominee Luis Donald Colosio Partido Revolucionario Institucional, 1993-94; pres. Govt. Mex., Mexico City, 1994—2000; chair, high level panel financing for devel. UN; prof. internat. economics & politics Yale U., New Haven, 2002—, dir. Yale Ctr. Study of Globalization, 2002—; co-chmn. Internat. Task Force on Global Public Goods, UN Commn. on Private Sector and Devel.; chair Global Devel. Network. Mem. Trilateral Commn.; mem. internat. adv. bd. Coun. Fgn. Rels.; bd. dirs. Inst. Internat. Economics, Union Pacific Corp., 2001—06, Electronic Data Systems Corp., 2007—, Alcoa Inc., The Proctor & Gamble Co., Peter G. Peterson Inst. Internat Economics, Internat. Crisis Group; disting. vis. fellow Centre for Global Governance London Sch. Economics & Politc. Sci., 2001; disting. lectr. U. Miami, 2001; Colins Family disting. fellow John F. Kennedy Sch. Govt., Harvard U., 2002. Recipient Wilbur Cross Medal, Yale U., 2001, Franklin D. Roosevelt Freedom from Fear award, Gold Insigne, Coun. Americas, Tribuna Americana award, Casa de America, Madrid, Berkeley medal, U. Calif. Office: Yale U Ctr Study of Globalization PO Box 208360 New Haven CT 06520

ZEDROSSER, JOSEPH JOHN, lawyer; b. Milw., Jan. 24, 1938; s. Joseph and Rose (Zollner) Z.; m. Antonina Krass, Sept. 6, 1997. AB, Marquette U., 1959; LLB, Harvard U., 1963. Bar: N.Y. 1964, U.S. Dist. Ct. (so. dist.) N.Y. 1966, U.S. Dist. Ct. (ea. dist.) N.Y. 1971, U.S. Ct. Appeals (2d cir.) 1971, U.S. Ct. Appeals (D.C. Cir.) 1975, U.S. Supreme Ct. 1975. Assoc. William G. Mulligan, NYC, 1964-67, Christy, Bauman, Frey and Christy and successors, NYC, 1967-71; dir. cmty. devel. unit Bedford-Stuyvesant Cmty. Legal Svcs. Corp., NYC, 1971-73; assoc. atty. fed. defender svcs. unit Legal Aid Soc., NYC, 1973-74; asst. atty. gen. Environ. Protection Bur., N.Y. State Dept. Law, NYC, 1974-80; regional counsel EPA, NYC, 1980-82; assoc. prof. St. John's U. Sch. Law, NYC, 1982-86; ptnr. Rivkin, Radler, Dunne & Bayh, Uniondale, N.Y., 1986-89, Breed, Abbott & Morgan, NYC, 1989-93, Whitman Breed Abbott & Morgan, NYC, 1993-95; v.p. CPR Inst. for Dispute Resolution, NYC, 1996; sr. investigative counsel com. on investigations, taxation, and gov. ops. N.Y. State Senate, 1998-99; asst. atty. gen. Environ. Protection Bur. N.Y. State Office Atty. Gen., NYC, 1999—. Lectr., contbr. to course handbooks for courses sponsored by Practicing Law Inst. and other assns. Lt. USNR, 1965-74, USAR, 1963-65. Mem. ABA, Assn. Bar City N.Y., N.Y. State Bar Assn., Alpha Sigma Nu. Roman Catholic. Home: 1520 York Ave Apt 15B New York NY 10028-7982

ZEEVI, ADRIANA, microbiologist, immunologist; BA in Microbiology, MA in Microbiology, Ilan Univ., Ramat-Gan, Israel, PhD in Immunology; postdoctoral study, Blood Ctr., Southeastern Wis. Rsch. investigator Blood Ctr., Southeastern Wis.; prof., pathology, surgery Univ. Pitts. Med. Ctr. Bd. dir. United Network for Organ Sharing (UNOS). Sect. editor Clin. Immunology. Recipient New Investigator award, NIH, 1994, Astellas Clin. Sci. Established Investigator award (Prof. Level), Am. Soc. Transplantation, 2007. Mem.: Am. Soc.Histocompatibility & Immunogenetics (pres.-elect, chair, sci. affairs). Office: McGowan Inst Regenerative Medicine Univ Pitts--Ste 200 100 Technology Dr Pittsburgh PA 15219-3110 Office Phone: 412-235-5100, 412-624-1073. Office Fax: 412-235-5110. Business E-Mail: zeevia@upmc.edu.

ZEFFIRELLI, FRANCO, theater and film director; b. Florence, Italy, Feb. 12, 1923; s. Ottorino Corsi and Alaide Cipriani. Student, U. Architecture, Florence; DHL, U. San Diego, 1980; PhD, U. Tel Aviv, 1993. Actor in Crime and Punishment, 1946, Euridyce, 1947; appeared in film Onorevole Angelina, 1948; set designer for various prodns. of Luchino Visconti, 1949-52, A Streetcar Named Desire, The Three Sisters; dir. (films) The Taming of the Shrew, 1966, Romeo and Juliet, 1967, Brother Sun, Sister Moon, 1971, The Champ, 1979, Endless Love, 1981, I Pagliacci, 1981, La Traviata, 1982, Cavalleria Rusticana, 1986, Otello, 1986, The Young Toscanini, 1988, Hamlet, 1990, Sparrow, 1993, Jane Eyre, 1996, Tea with Mussolini, 1998, Callas Forever, 2002; (ballet) Swan Lake, 1985; co-screenwriter, dir.(film) Hamlet, 1990; TV dir. Giorni Di Distruzione, 1966, Fidelio conducted by Leonard Bernstein, 1970, Missa Solemnis of Beethoven conducted by Wolfgang Sawallisch in Basilica of St. Peter in presence of Pope Paul VI, 1970, Jesus of Nazareth (epic film), 1976; numerous operas including Cenerentola, La Scala, 1953, I Pagliacci, 1959, Cavalleria Rusticana, 1959, Lucia Di Lammermoor, Covent Garden, 1959, La Bohème, La Scala, 1963, Falstaff, Met. Opera, 1964, Tosca, Covent Garden, 1965, Norma, Paris Opera, 1965, Anthony and Cleopatra, Met. Opera, 1966, Otello, Met. Opera, 1972, Don Giovanni, Staatsoper, Vienna, 1972, Un Ballo in Maschera, La Scala, 1972, Otello, La Scala, 1976, Carmen, Staatsoper, Vienna, 1978, La Traviata, 1979, 83, Tosca, Met. Opera, 1985, Turandot, 1987, Don Giovanni, 1990, Don Carlo, La Scala, 1992, Aida, Rome Opera, 1993, Carmen, Arena Di Verona, 1995, Carmen, Met, 1996, Aida, New Nat. Theatre, Tokyo, 1997, La Traviata, Met, 1998, Tosca, Rome Opera, 2000, Don Giovanni, Met, 2000, Aida, Busseto Theatre, 2001, Trovatore, Verona Arena, 2001, 2002, 2003, Pagliacci Convent Garden, 2003, La Traviata-Busseto, 2002, Carmen Arena Di Verona, 2003, La Bohème, La Scala and Rome Opera, 2003, Aida, Teatro Argentina, Rome, 2003, Madame Butterfly Arena di Verona, 2004, Busseto Traviata Taken to Moscow, 2004, Busseto Traviata Taken to Tel Aviv, 2005, Pagliacci, Tel Aviv, 2005, Aida, Moscow, 2005, Don Giovanni, Rome, 2005, Aida, La Scala, 2006, La Traviata, Rome, 2007, Tosca, Rome, 2008, others; theater dir. Romeo and Juliet, Old Vic Co., London, 1960, Othello, Stratford-on-Avon, Eng., 1961, Camille, Winter Garden Theatre, N.Y.C., 1962, Who's Afraid of Virginia Woolf?, Festival del Teatro, Venice, and Paris, 1963, Romeo and Juliet, Verona, Italy, Paris, Vienna, Austria, Rome and Milan, Italy, Moscow and Leningrad, 1964, Hamlet, 1964, After The Fall, 1965, Much Ado About Nothing, Old Vic Theatre, 1965, La Lupa, Florence, Rome, Vienna, Zurich, Switzerland, Paris, London and Moscow, 1965, A Delicate Balance, 1966, Black Comedy, 1967, Venti Zecchini D'Oro, 1968, Due Piu Due Non Fanno Quattro, 1969, Sabato, Doemnica, Lunedi, Nat. Theatre, London, 1973, The Dead City, Italy, 1975, Lorenzaccio, Comedie Française, Paris, 1976, Filumena Marturano, Lyric Theatre, London, 1977, Absolutely, Perhaps!, Wyndham Theatre, London, 2003; author: Zeffirelli by Zeffirelli, 1986, Zeffirelli, Autobiografia, 2006. Recipient Liberty award, 1986. Mem. Dirs. Guild Am. Roman Catholic. Address: Via Lucio Volumnio 45 00178 Rome Italy

ZEFFREN, EUGENE, cosmetics executive; b. St. Louis, Nov. 21, 1941; s. Harry Morris and Bess (Dennis) Z.; m. Steccia Leigh Stern, Feb. 2, 1964; children: Maryl Renee, Bradley Cruvant. AB, Washington U., 1963; MS, U. Chgo., 1965, PhD, 1967. Research chemist Procter & Gamble Co., Cin., 1967-75, sect. head, 1975-77, assoc. dir., 1977-79; v.p. R & D, Helene Curtis, Inc., Chgo., 1979-95; pres. Helene Curtis USA, Chgo., 1995-96; sr. v.p. Helene Curtis bus. unit Unilever Home and Personal Care USA, Chgo., 1996-98, exec. v.p., COO hair and deodorant bus. unit, 1998-2000; sr. v.p. brand devel. Unilever Home and Personal Care N.Am., 2000—02; chmn. NFG Stuff, LLC, 2002—07; CEO AG Brands, LLC, 2005—08. Mem. vis. com. for phys. scis. U. Chgo., 1997-06; active Wash. U. Nat. Coun. for Arts and Scis., 1997—; pres. bd. dirs. River North Dance Co., 1998-2000, chmn. 2000-04. Co-author: The Study of Enzyme Mechanisms, 1973; contbr. articles to profl. jours. Bd. dirs. Goodman Theatre, 1999—, Children's Meml. Rsch. Ctr., 2002—05; trustee Spertus Inst. Jewish Studies, 2002—08. Recipient award, Cosmetic Ingredient Buyers and Suppliers, 1990. Mem. AAAS, Am. Chem. Soc., Soc. Cosmetic Chemists, Cosmetic Toiletry and Fragrance Assn. (sci. adv. com. 1979-95, vice chmn. 1984-88, chmn. 1988-90, bd. dirs. 1996-02), Soap and Detergent Assn. (bd. dirs., exec. com. bd. 2000-02), Indsl. Rsch. Inst., Omicron Delta Kappa. Democrat. Jewish. Achievements include patents in field of enzymes and hair care. Avocations: tennis, skiing, reading adventure and espionage novels.

ZEGAS, ALAN LEE, lawyer; b. Newark, Oct. 28, 1952; s. Norman and Harriet (Lava) Z. BS, U. Pa., 1974; MBA, Harvard U., 1978; JD, Rutgers U., 1981. Bar: N.J. 1981, U.S. Dist. Ct. N.J. 1981, N.Y. 1982, U.S. Ct. Appeals (3d cir.) 1982. Law clk. to Hon. H. Lee Sarokin U.S. Dist. Ct. N.J., Newark, 1981-83; assoc. Robinson, Wayne, Levin, Riccio & La Sala, Newark, 1983-84; pvt. practice Chatham, NJ, 1984—. Editor-in-chief Rutgers U. Law Rev., 1980-81; adj. prof. law Rutgers U., Newark, 1983-88; reader N.J. Bd. Bar Examiners, Trenton, 1985; pres. Assn. Criminal Def. Lawyers N.J., 1998-99. Editor (pamphlet) Law Tips for the Elderly, 1983; contbr. of articles to profl. jours. Mem. N.J. Bar Assn. (dist. rep. young lawyers div. 1983-85, vice chmn. 1985-86, trustee 1986-88, chmn. criminal law sect. 1996-97), Essex County Bar Assn. (chmn. lawyers referral service 1986—), Rutgers U. Law Sch. Alumni Assn. (rep. 1983—), U. Pa. Alumni Assn. (sec. 1986-87), Harvard U. Bus. Sch. Alumni Assn., Assn. Criminal Def. Lawyers of N.J. (pres. 1998-99), Morris County Bar Assn. (chmn. criminal law sec.). Achievements include serving on state atty. gen.'s comm. overseeing implementation of Meghan's Law; listing among pre-eminent attys. by Martindale-Hubbell and Best Lawyers in Am. Home: 476 South St New Providence NJ 07974-2132 Office: 552 Main St Chatham NJ 07928-2120

ZEHNER, LEE RANDALL, entrepreneur, chemist; b. Darby, Pa., Mar. 15, 1947; s. Warren L. and Alycia G. (Van Riper) Z.; m. Susan D. Hovland, June 23, 1973; children: Adam, Erica. BS in Chemistry, U. Pa., Phila., 1968; PhD in Organic Chemistry, U. Minn., Mpls., 1973. Sr. rsch. chemist ARCO Chem. Co., Glenolden, Pa., 1973—78; rsch. group leader Ashland Chem. Co., Dublin, Ohio, 1978-82; mgr. organic rsch. W.R. Grace & Co., Clarksville, Md., 1982-85; dir. biotech. divsn. Biospherics Inc., Beltsville, Md., 1985—91, v.p. sci. svcs., 1991—98; founder, pres. VivaLac Inc., Ashton, Md., 1998—. Contbr. scientific papers to profl. jours. Mem.: Am. Diabetes Assn., Inst. Food Technologists, Am. Chem. Soc. Achievements include patents in field; research in food ingredients and chemical processing; invention of Whey Low natural sweetener; D-tagatose as low-calorie sweetener; D-tagatose as anti-hyperglycemic drug; development of chemical processes for manufacture of ethylene glycol from coal, methacrylate intermediate, adipic acid from coal and butadiene. Avocations: swimming, opera, chess. Office: VivaLac Inc PO Box 272 Brookeville MD 20833 Office Phone: 301-774-2433. Personal E-mail: lzehner@wheylow.com.

ZEHRING, KAREN, information executive; b. Washington, Dec. 5, 1945; d. Robert William Zehring and Gretchen (Lorenz) Proos; m. George Lang, 1970 (div. 1979); m. Peter Frank Davis, 1979 (div. 1995). BA, U. Denver, 1967; grad., Yale U., 1967-68. Assoc. pub. mktg. and sales Instl. Investor mag., NYC, 1968-74; co-owner, co-creator Cafe des Artistes Restaurant, NYC, 1975-79; owner, pub. The Corp. Fin. Letter, NYC, 1976-78; group dir. planning and devel. Bus. Week mag., NYC, 1977-78; owner, pub., exec. editor Corp. Fin. Sourcebook The Corp. Fin. Bluebook, NYC, 1979-84; chmn., pres., pub., editor-in-chief Corp. Fin. mag., NYC, 1986-90; cons. Karen Zehring & Assocs., Castine, Maine, 1990-94; CEO SourceCapital InterNetwork, NYC, 1998—2001; mng. ptnr. Creative Devel. Ptnrs., NYC, 1995-98, 2001—. Mem.: The Internat. Women's Forum. Unitarian Universalist.

ZEICHNER, JOSHUA A., dermatologist; BA, U. Pa., 1999; MD, Johns Hopkins Sch. Medicine, Balt., 2003. Dermatopharmacology fellow Mt. Sinai Med. Ctr., Dept. Dermatology, NYC, 2004—06, chief resident, 2006—. Office: Mt Sinai Hosp 5 E 98th St 5th Fl New York NY 10029

ZEIDENWEBER, CARLO M., cardiologist; b. Mexico City, Dec. 22, 1973; s. Pepe Zeidenweber and Matilde Fainstein. MD, U. Anahuac, Mexico City, 1998. Pediatrician Miami Children's Hosp, Fla., 2001—04; pediat. cardiologist Emory U., Atlanta, 2004—07, Children's Heart Ctr. Nev., Las Vegas, 2007—. Contbr. articles to profl. jours. (3rd Pl. in Ann. Rsch. Competition). Fellow: Fellowship Soc. Emory U. (founding mem.).

ZEIDLER, JAMES ROBERT, electrical engineer, researcher; b. Carlinville, Ill., Dec. 1, 1944; s. John Carroll and Jacqueline Zeidler; m. Wanda Jean Butler, June 9, 1968; children: Brandon James, Kevin Andrew. BA, MacMurray Coll., 1966; MS, Mich. State U., 1968; PhD, U. Nebr., 1972. Scientist Spawarsyscen, San Diego, 1974—2003; rsch. scientist U. Calif., San Diego, 2003—. Adj. prof. Dept. Elec. & Computer Engring., U. Calif. San Diego, La Jolla, 1989-2003; vis. prof. Ireste, U. Nantes, France, 1996. Recipient Navy Meritorious Civilian Svc. award U.S. Dept. Navy, 1991. Fellow IEEE (assoc. editor Transactions on Signal Processing 1991-94, underwater acoustics signal processing com. 1991-94, Best Paper award Mil. Comms. Conf. 1995). Achievements include patents and publications in field. Office: Univ Calif Dept Elec Engring 9500 Gilman Dr La Jolla CA 92093-0407 Office Phone: 858-534-5369. Business E-Mail: zeidler@ece.ucsd.edu.

ZEIDLIK, THOMAS RICHARD, pilot, educator; m. Raquel Zeidlik, 1990. BS in Aero. Studies & Aviation, U. ND, Grand Forks, 1997; MS in Space Studies & Physics, U. ND, 2002; AAS in Paramedicine, Northland Coll., E. Grand Forks, 2007. Cert. in pre-hosp. trauma life

1986-93, Smith, Kline and French Labs., Phila., 1979-86. Editor: A Guide to Personnel Monitoring, 1993; contbr. articles to profl. jours. Fellow Phi Kappa Phi, 1962-63, U.S. AEC, 1964-65, USPHS, 1968-70. Mem. Health Physics Soc. (com. mem. 1978-79), Campus Safety Assn., Am. Assn. Physicists in Medicine (com. mem. 1995—), Am. Coll. Medical Physics, Sigma Xi (v.p., pres. 1984-88). Home and Office: PO Box 26786 Elkins Park PA 19027-5773 Business E-Mail: ronald.zelac@nrc.gov.

ZELANTE, THOMAS ANDREW, lawyer; b. NYC, Nov. 30, 1954; s. Sabino and Rae Zelante; m. Maureen Connors; children: Thomas Andrew Jr., Christopher William. BA, LaSalle Coll., 1976; JD, Seton Hall U., 1979. Bar: NJ 1980. Assoc. atty. Ribis, McCluskey, Short Hills, NJ, 1982—83, Bowkley & Zelante, Randolph, NJ, 1986—. Mem. ethics com. Morris and Sussex counties Supreme Ct. of NJ Dist. X, 1996—2000; town atty. Borough of Victory Gardens, NJ, 2005—; atty. Morristown Zoning Bd. Adjustment, 2006—. Mem. govtl. affairs com. Morris County C. of C., Morristown, mem. infrastructure adv. group, 2004—06; mem. NJ Health Care Facilities Financing Authority, 2002—04; chmn. Morris County Dem. Com., Morristown, 2002—04; mem. Head Start of Morris County, 1998—2003, pres., 2003—04; trustee Ramapo Coll., Mahwah, NJ, 2004—, chmn. bd. trustees, 2005—; commr. Morris County Bd. Taxation, Morristown, 2005—. Mem.: Morris County Bar Assn. (trustee, Cmty. Svc./Pro Bono award (lifetime achievement) 2004). Avocations: golf, travel, ice hockey. Home: 7 Stoneybrook Way Morristown NJ 07960 Office: Bowkley & Zelante 390 Rte 10 West Randolph NJ 07869 Office Fax: 973-366-0191.

ZELAZNY, CATHERINE, retired elementary school educator; d. Edward and Irene R. Zelazny. BS in Edn., Edinboro U., 1971, postgrad. in Sch. Adminstrn., 1987; MEd in Guidance and Counseling, Gannon U., 1974, postgrad. small bus., 2005; postgrad. pre-law, Pa. State U., 1985. Counselor, math. tchr. Gannondale Home for Girls, Erie, Pa., 1972; tchr. Ft. LeBoeuf Sch. Dist., Waterford, Pa., 1972—77, 1979—86, 1987—2006, counselor, 1977—78; spl. edn. coord. Edinboro Intermediate Unit # 5, 1978—79; ret., 2006. Pvt. practice counselor, Erie, Pa.; mentor to educators, probationary boys, Erie. Author: Teacher Handbook and Parent Handbook, 1987. Logistics/project mgr., coord. Summer Arts Festival, Erie, 1980—85; mem. County Com. for Abuse Prevention, Erie; vice chmn. Erie County Dem. Party, Erie, 2002—06, chmn., 2006—. Recipient Project GIVE award, Pa. Dept. Edn., 1972. Mem.: NEA, Pa. Edn. Assn., Ft. LeBoeuf Edn. Assn. (treas., v.p., pres., mem. grievance com., membership com.), Erie County Hist. Soc., Phi Delta Kappa (v.p.). Avocations: antiques, piano, jewelry collecting, exercise. Home: 903 W Grandview Blvd Erie PA 16509 Personal E-mail: cazny@verizon.net.

ZELAZO, PHILIP DAVID, science educator; b. Kitchener, Ont., Can., Oct. 21, 1966; s. Philip Roman and Nancy Burl Zelazo; 1 child, Samuel Bidwell. BA with honors, McGill U., Montreal, Quebec, Can., 1988; diploma, Milton Acad., Mass., 1984; PhD, Yale U., New Haven, 1993. Lectr. U. Toronto, Ont., Canada, 1992—93, prof., 1993—2007, can. rsch. chair devel. neurosci., 2001—07; prof., inst. child devel. U. Minn., Mpls., 2007—. Co dir. Sino Canadian Ctr. Rsch. Child Devel., Chongqing, Sichuan, China, 2004—. Editor: (book) The Cambridge Handbook of Consciousness. Recipient Premier's Rsch. Excellence award, Govt. Ont., Can., 1999, Can.'s Top 40 Under 40 award, Caldwell Ptnrs., 2006. Fellow: Can. Inst. Advanced Rsch., Am. Psychol. Soc., APA Divsn. 7 (Boyd McCandless Young Scientist award 1997). Achievements include research in development and neural bases of human consciousness and the cognitive control of behavior executive function. Office: Univ Minn 51 East River Pky Minneapolis MN 55455

ZELBY, LEON WOLF, electrical engineer, educator, consultant; b. Sosnowiec, Poland, Mar. 26, 1925; came to U.S., 1946, naturalized, 1951; s. Herszel and Helen (Wajnryb) Zylberberg; m. Rachel Kupfermintz, Dec. 28, 1954; children: Laurie Susan, Andrew Stephen. BSEE, Moore Sch. Elec. Engring., 1956; MS, Calif. Inst. Tech., 1957; PhD, U. Pa., 1961. Registered profl. engr., Pa., Okla. Mem. staff RCA, Hughes R & D Labs., Lincoln Lab., MIT, Sandia Corp., Argonne (Ill.) Nat. Labs., Inst. for Energy Analysis; mem. faculty U. Pa., 1959-67, assoc. prof., 1964-67; assoc. dir. plasma engring. Inst. Direct Energy Conversion, 1962-67; prof. U. Okla., Norman, 1967-95, dir. Sch. Elec. Engring., 1967-71; ret., 1995. Cons. RCA, 1961-67, Moore Sch. Elec. Engring., 1967-68, also pvt. firms. Editor Tech. and Soc. mag., 1990-93; contbr. articles on energy-associated problems and issues to profl. jours. With AUS, 1946-47. Cons. Electrodynamic Corp. fellow Calif. Inst. Tech., 1957, Mpls.-Honeywell fellow U. Pa., 1957-58, Harrison fellow, 1958. Mem. IEEE, Franklin Inst., Sigma Xi, Tau Beta Pi, Eta Kappa Nu, Pi Mu Epsilon, Sigma Tau, Phi Kappa Phi. Business E-Mail: zelby@ou.edu. *To learn as much, and to experience as much as possible, without harm to others; read, study, vary professional and recreational activities within constraints of the system.*

ZELDIN, LEE M., lawyer; b. East Meadow, NY, Jan. 30, 1980; m. Diana Zeldin; children: Mikayla, Arianna. B in Polit. Sci., cum laude, SUNY, Albany; JD, Albany Law Sch., 2003. Bar: NY 2004. 2nd lt., mil. intelligence corps US Army, Ft. Huachuca, Ariz., 2003—04; assigned Judge Advocate General's Corps, 2004, 82nd Airborne Divsn., Ft. Bragg, NC; mil. magistrate 18th Airborne Corps, Ft. Bragg; capt. US Army Res., Iraq, 2006—07; counsel Port Authority of NY and NJ, 2007; atty. Raiser and Kenniff, PC, 2007—. Mem.: Am. Legion, VFW. Republican. Jewish. Avocations: piano, Tae Kwon Do, boating. Office: Raiser & Kenniff PC 1517 Franklin Ave Ste 300 Mineola NY 11501-4804 Office Phone: 516-742-7600.

ZELEK, CHARLES ANDREW, economist; b. Louisville, Ky., Nov. 19, 1970; s. Walter Andrew and Charlotte Anne Zelek. BA in Econs., OH U., 1993; MS in Resource Econs., U. Alaska, Fairbanks, 1997; PhD in Agrl. Econs., Purdue U., West Lafayette, 2002. Rsch. asst. Purdue U., 1998—2002; state economist USDA/Nat. Resources Conservation Svc., Indpls., 2002—05, program specialist, exec. Washington, 2005—07, sr. economist, 2007—. Sub.-com. chmn. Pres.' Biomass Initiative, Washington, 2003; pres. State Office Employees Assn., Indpls., 2004; co-pres. USDA-Economist Group, Washington, 2006; mem. USDA Biobased-Bionic Coord. Coun., USDA Global Climate Change Task Force. Contbr. articles to profl. jours. With US Army, 1993—98. Decorated Army Commendation medal. Mem.: USDA (mem. biobased bioenergy coordination coun., mem. global climate change task force), Am. Agrl. Econs. Assn. Avocations: running, reading, martial arts, computers.

ZELEN, MARVIN, statistics educator; b. NYC, June 21, 1927; m. Thelma Geier, Sept. 10, 1950; children: Deborah, Sandra. BS, CCNY, 1949; MS, U. N.C., 1951; PhD, Am. U., 1957; MA (hon.), Harvard U., 1977; Docteur Honoris Causa, U. Victor Segalen, 2003. Stat. eng. lab. Nat. Bureau of Standards, 1952-61; assoc. prof. Univ. Md., 1960-61; head, stat. and applied Math. section Nat. Cancer Inst., 1963—67; leading prof. State U., Buffalo, 1967-77; pres. Frontier Sci. and Tech. Rsch. Found., Boston, 1975—; chmn. dept. biostats. Dana Farber Cancer Inst., Boston, 1977-98; prof. Harvard U. Sch. Pub. Health, Boston, 1977—; chmn. dept. biostat. Harvard U., 1980-90. Vis. prof. Univ. Wis., 1961-63, vis. assoc. prof. Univ. Calif., 1958. Sgt. U.S. Army, 1945-46. Fulbright scholar, 1965-66. Fellow Am. Acad. Arts and Sci., AAAS, Inst. Math. Stats., Am. Statis. Assn.; mem. Internat. Stats. Inst. Home: 230 Eliot St Chestnut Hill MA 02467-1447 Office: Harvard Sch Pub Health 677 Huntington Ave Boston MA 02115-6096 Business E-Mail: zelen@hsph.harvard.edu.

ZELENKA, H. DAYLE KENDALL, librarian; b. St. Paul, May 1, 1967; s. Henry Baltzer and Sandra Jean Zelenka; m. Gena Karen Martinez, June 6, 1998. BA, Grinnell Coll., Iowa, 1989; MLS, Ind. U., Bloomington, 1993; MBA, North Pk. U., Chgo., 2000, MS in Mgmt., 2001. Mgr. academic tech. svcs. U. Dubuque, Iowa, 1994—96; sys. libr. North Pk. U., 1996—2003, serials and sys. libr., 2003—05, dir. tech. svcs. & sys., 2005—, practitioner faculty Sch. Bus. and Nonprofit Mgmt., 2006—. Trustee, bd. sec. Skokie Pub. Libr., Ill., 2005—; dir. North Suburban Libr. Sys., Wheeling, Ill., 2006—. Mem.: ALA, Assn. Coll. and Rsch. Librs., Libr. Adminstrn. and Mgmt. Assn., Ill. Libr. Assn. (dir.-at-large 2007—). Office: North Pk Univ Box 38 3225 W Foster Ave Chicago IL 60625 Office Fax: 773-634-6040. Business E-Mail: hzelenka@northpark.edu.

ZELENY, ANN DOUGLAS, sculptor; b. Tucson, Dec. 7, 1955; d. Charles Ellingson and Marjorie Ann (Pfeiffer) Zeleny; m. Arthur Jeffrey Munson, Dec. 22, 1974 (div. 1985); 1 child, Frederick Michael Munson Zeleny; m. Carl Douglas Anderson, Nov. 3, 1985; 1 child, Gwyneth Violet Zeleny Anderson. BFA, Va. Commonwealth U., 1977. Songwriter/vocalist Seventh Dawn, Richmond, Washington, 1973-80; archtl. sculptor Monumental Constrn. and Moulding Co., Washington, 1981—86; freelance sculptor, graphic designer & photographer, 1986—. Co-creator, set designer, propmaster, puppeteer The Mondo Breakfast Show, Arlington, 1984-86; graphics cons. Gfx, Washington, 1991-95; modelmaker, archtl. ornament cons. (trompe l'oeil murals) Community Bridge, Frederick, Md., 1993-95; photographer, graphic designer, sculptor ADZarts.com, 2006— Sr. sculptor, sites of installation include: The Nat. Theatre, The Washington Times Bldg., The Hay-Adams Hotel, Phoenix Park Hotel, Phillips Collection Gallery, Casa Casuarina, Miami Beach; creator bust of Margaret Mantz Hauer for Faces of Frederick invitational exhibit, presented by Delaplaine Visual Arts Edn. Ctr. and Hist. Soc. Frederick County; songwriter, performer (albums) Sunrise, 1976, Dreams, 1978; creator ceramic or cold cast sculptures including Presence, Purr, Daphne, featured by Design Toscano Galleries; Reflection, Gaia, Green Man Medallion, The Five Elements & Venus featured by Sacredsource.com, Sylph, Consort, Romeo & Juliet, Leap Dog Poser & Major Wigeon; cameraperson Arlington Weekly News, 1980-85. Vol. graphics The Greens, 1989-92, The Common Market Food Coop., Frederick, Md., 1990-93; vol. set fabrication Beaux Artes Ball, Frederick, 1993; vol. designer, fabricator Delaplaine Visual Arts Ctr., Frederick, Md., 1995. Recipient "Ammy" Craft Award for set design Arlington Community TV, 1985, Ammy for best variety program, 1985, Ammy for humor, 1986. Achievements include invention of short tail needle. Avocations: metaphysics, fibre arts. E-mail: studio@adzarts.com.

ZELENY, DENNIS, oil industry executive, human resources specialist; b. Bklyn., Dec. 9, 1955; s. Stanly and Olga (Freida) Z. BS, Cornell U., 1977; MBS, Columbia U., 1985. With labor rels. adminstrn. Parker Pen Co., Janesville, Wis., 1977-78; rep. employee rels. Pepsi-Cola Co., NYC, 1978-79, mgr. area employee rels. Detroit, 1979-81, mgr. div. employee rels., 1981-83, NJ, 1983-85, dir. personnel Purchase, NY, 1985-88; v.p. human resources Pepsi-Cola West, Taco Bell, Frito Lay, 1988—95, Allied Signal, 1995—2000, Honeywell Internat., 2000—01; sr. v.p. human resources E.I. Du Pont de Nemours, 2001—05; exec. v.p. adminstrn. & services Caremark Rx, 2005—07; sr. v.p., chief human resources officer Sunoco Inc., Phila., 2009—. Mem. Am. Mktg. Assn., Am. Soc. Personnel Adminstrs. Avocations: running, piano, reading, sports. Office: Sunoco Inc 1735 Market St Philadelphia PA 19103-7583*

ZELENY, MILAN, management systems scientist, economist; b. Prague, Czechoslovakia, Jan. 22, 1942; came to U.S., 1967; s. Josef and Marie (Barvinkova) Z.; 1 child, Maximilian. Ing., Prague Sch. of Econs., 1964; MS, U. Rochester, 1970, PhD, 1972. Researcher Czechoslovak Acad. Scis., Prague, 1964—67; asst. prof. U. S.C., Columbia, 1971-72; assoc. prof. Columbia U., NYC, 1972-80; prof. Copenhagen (Denmark) Sch. Econs., 1980-82, Fordham U., NYC, 1982—. Von Humboldt prof. U. Bonn, Fed. Republic of Germany, 1979; Rockefeller scientist-in-residence, Bellagio, 1980; Fulbright prof. USIA, Prague, 1990; prof. T. Bata U., Zlin, Czech Republic, 1998—, Xidian U., Xi'an, China; bus. cons. Author: Linear Multiobjective Programming, 1975, Multiple Criteria Decision Making, 1982, Human Systems Management, 2005, (2nd print 2008) Portfolio Selection, 1979; editor: Autopoiesis, 1982, MCDM: The Next Decade, 1982, Handbook of Information Technology in Business, 1999; contbr. more than 400 articles to profl. jours. Recipient Norbert Wiener award Kybernetes, U.K., 1980. Mem. AAAS, Ops. Rsch. Soc. Am., Human Sys. Mgmt., Inst. Mgmt. Sci., Soc. Am. for Social Econs., Multiple Criteria Decision Making Soc. (Georg Cantor award 1992), Beta Gamma Sigma, Omega Rho. Office: Fordham U GBA 626E New York NY 10023 Office Phone: 212-636-6150. Office Fax: 212-765-5573. Business E-Mail: mzeleny@fordham.edu.

ZELEVANSKY, LYNN, museum director; 2 children. Attended, Carnegie Mellon U., Pitts.; BFA, Pratt Inst.; MA in photography, NYU. Curator Mus. Modern Art, NYC, 1987—95; named assoc. curator dept. 20th century painting LA County Mus. Art, 1995, assoc. curator modern and contemporary art, Terri and Michael Smooke curator, dept. head modern and contemporary art; Henry J. Heintz dir. Carnegie Mus. Art, Pitts., 2009—. Curator (exhibitions) Sense and Sensibility: Women Artists and Minimalism in the '90s, 1994, Love Forever: Yayoi Kusama 1958-68, 1998—99, Robert Therrian retrospective, 2000, Jasper Johns to Jeff Koons: Four Decades of Art from the Broad Collections, 2001, Keith Edmier and Farah Fawcett, 2002, Beyond Geometry: Experiments in Form, 1940s-70s, 2004 (Award for Best Thematic Mus. Show Nationally, Internat. Assn. Art Critics/USA, 2005), many others. Office: Carnegie Mus Art 4400 Forbes Ave Pittsburgh PA 15213-4080*

ZELIKOFF, JUDITH TERRY, medical educator, consultant; b. Paterson, Nj, Sept. 15, 1952; d. Harry Gary Zelikoff and Shirley Clare; m. Jack Steven Jacobsen, Oct. 2, 1982. PhD, U. Medicine and Dentistry Nj., Newark, 1982. Prof. Ny U. Sch. Medicine, Tuxedo, 1982—. Cons. UN Environ. Program, Bangkok, 2007—. Grant, Inst. for Sci. and Health, 2005—. Mem.: Soc. Toxicology, nominating com. Avocations: horseback riding, reading, travel. Office: NY Univ Sch of Medicine 57 Old Forge Rd Tuxedo Park NY 10987 Office Fax: 845-351-5472. Personal E-mail: zelikoff33@gmail.com. Business E-Mail: judith.zelikoff@nyumc.org.

ZELIN, JEROME, retired retail executive; b. Bklyn., Dec. 24, 1930; s. Isidore and Ida (Roffman) Z.; m. Muriel Altsher, Dec. 18, 1955; children— Dorothy, Michael, Steven. BS magna cum laude, N.Y.U., 1952. Acct. Seymour Schwartz CPA, 1954-57; partner firm Schwartz, Zelin & Weiss CPAs, NYC, 1958-61; vice chmn., pres., exec. v.p., treas., financial v.p., dir. Unishops, Inc. (retail co.), Jersey City, 1961-74; exec. v.p. Masters, Inc., Westbury, NY, 1974-97; cons. Master's, Inc., Westbury, NY, 1997-2000; ret. Served with AUS, 1952-54. Mem. N.Y. Soc. CPAs, Am. Inst. CPAs, Beta Gamma Sigma, Tau Alpha Omega. Jewish. Home: 6 Maiden Stone Lane Monroe Township NJ 08831 Home Phone: 732-656-9577. Personal E-mail: jzelin1000@aol.com.

ZELINSKI, JOSEPH JOHN, engineering educator, consultant; b. Glen Lyon, Pa., Dec. 30, 1922; s. John Joseph and Lottie Mary (Oshinski) Z.; m. Mildred G. Sirois, July 22, 1946; children: Douglas John, Peter David. BS, Pa. State U., University Park, 1944; PhD, Pa. State U., 1950. Grad. fellow Pa. State U., University Park, 1946—50; project supr. applied physics lab. Johns Hopkins U., Silver Spring, Md., 1950—58; staff scientist Space Tech. Labs. (now TRW, Inc.), Redondo Beach, Calif., 1958—60; head chem. tech. divsn. Ops. Evaluation Group MIT, Cambridge, 1960—62; prin. rsch. scientist Avco Everett Rsch. Lab., Mass., 1962—64; prof. mech. engring. Northeastern U., Boston, 1964—85, prof. emeritus, 1985—; pres. World Edn. Resources, Ltd., Tampa, Fla., 1984—. Cons. Avco Everett Rsch. Lab., 1964-71, Pratt & Whitney Aircraft, East Hartford, Conn., 1966-70, Modern Electric Products and Phys. Scis. Co., Inc., Boston, 1980-82, Morrison, Mahoney and Miller, Boston, 1984; vice-chmn., chmn. exec. com. Univ. Grad. Coun., Northeastern U., Boston, 1980-84, dir. mech. engring. grad. program, 1982-85; del. 4th World Conf. Continuing Engring. Edn., Beijing China People to People, Spokane, Wash., 1989. Contbr. articles to profl. jours. Prin. Confraternity Christian Doctrine, Andover, Mass., 1961-64; pres. Andover Edn. Coun., 1962-64; vice chmn. Dem. Town Com., Boxford, Mass., 1980-84. Lt. (j.g.) USNR, 1943-46, PTO. Mem. AAAS, ASME, Am. Chem. Soc. Democrat. Roman Catholic. Achievements include foreign and domestic patents for coal combustion system for magnetohydrodynamic power generation, for fuel-cooled combustion systems for jet engines flying at high Mach numbers; prediction of optical observables of re-entry vehicles from analysis of decomposition mechanisms of heat-shield materials; invention of high-temperature furnace for production of crystalline graphite; development of a design method for ramjet combustors, liquid fuel-oxygen combustion system for Avco Mark 5 MHD power generator, carbon-air combustion system for lasers. Personal E-mail: jjzelin@yahoo.com.

ZELINSKY, DANIEL, mathematics professor; b. Chgo., Nov. 22, 1922; s. Isaac and Ann (Ruttenberg) Z.; m. Zelda Oser, Sept. 23, 1945; children: Mara Sachs, Paul O., David. BS, U. Chgo., 1941, MS, 1943, PhD, 1946. Rsch. mathematician applied math group Columbia U., NYC, 1944-45; instr. U. Chgo., 1943-44, 46-47; Nat. Rsch. Coun. fellow Inst. Advanced Study, Princeton, NJ, 1947-49; from asst. to assoc. prof. dept. math. Northwestern U., Evanston, Ill., 1949-60, prof., 1960-93, prof. emeritus, 1993—, acting chmn. math. dept., 1959-60, chmn., 1975-78. Vis. prof. U. Calif. Berkeley, 1960, Fla. State U., Tallahassee, 1963, Hebrew U., Jerusalem, 1970-71, 85, others; vis. scholar Tata Inst., 1979; mem. various coms. Northwestern U.; lectr. in field. Author: A First Course in Linear Algebra, 1968, rev. edit., 1973; contbr. articles to profl. jours. Fulbright grantee Kyoto U., 1955-56, grantee NSF, 1958-80; Guggenheim fellow Inst. Advanced Study, 1956-57, Indo-Am. fellow, 1978-79. Fellow AAAS (mem. nominating com. sect. A 1977-80, chmn. elect sect. A 1984-85, chmn. 1985-86, retiring chmn. 1986-87), Am. Math. Soc. (mem. coun. 1961-67, editor Transactions of A.M.S. 1961-67, mem. various coms., mem. editorial bd. Notices of A.M.S. 1983-86, chmn. editorial bds. com. 1989, chmn. ad hoc com. 1991-92). Jewish. Home: 613 Hunter Rd Wilmette IL 60091-2213 Office: Northwestern U Dept Math Evanston IL 60208-0001 Business E-Mail: dz@northwestern.edu.

ZELINSKY, PAUL O., illustrator, artist, writer; b. Evanston, Ill., Feb. 14, 1953; s. Daniel and Zelda B. (Oser) Z.; m. Deborah M. Hallen, Dec. 31, 1981; children: Anna H., Rachel L. BA summa cum laude, Yale U., 1974; MFA in Painting, Tyler Sch. Art, 1976. Art instr. San Diego State U., 1976; freelance illustrator/author, 1977—. Illustrator: Emily Upham's Revenge, 1978, How I Hunted the Little Fellows, 1979, The History of Helpless Harry, 1980, What Amanda Saw, 1981, Ralph S. Mouse, 1982, The Song in the Walnut Grove, 1982, The Sun's Asleep Behind the Hill, 1982, Zoo Doings, 1983, Hansel and Gretel, 1984 (Caldecott Honor 1985), The Story of Mrs. Lovewright and Purrless her Cat, 1985, The Random House Book of Humor for Children, 1988, Strider, 1991, The Enchanted Castle, 1992, Dear Mr. Henshaw, 1993, More Rootabagas, 1993, Swamp Angel, 1994 (Caldecott honor 1995), Five Children and It, 1999, Awful Ogre's Awful Day, 2001, Doodler Doodling, 2004, Toys Got Out, 2006, The Shivers in the Fridge, 2006, Awful Ogre Running Wild, 2008; Toy Dance Party, 2008, illustrator, adapter: The Maid and the Mouse and the Odd-shaped House, 1981, Rumpelstiltskin 1986 (Caldecott medal 1987), Rapunzel, 1997 (Caldecott medal 1998); illustrator, author: The Lion and the Stoat, 1984; illustrator, adapter, designer: The Wheels on the Bus, 1990, Knick-Knack Paddywhack!, 2002. Recipient Boston Globe/Horn Book Honor, 1994, Best Illustrated Book N.Y. Times Book Rev., 1981, 85, 94, 2001, 02, Reading Magic award Parenting Mag., 1990, 94, 2002; runner-up Bologna Ragazzi award 2005, Mazza medallion, 2006. Mem. PEN, Graphic Artists Guild, Author's Guild, Soc. Children's Book Writers and Illustrators, Phi Beta Kappa.

ZELIS, ROBERT FELIX, cardiologist, educator; b. Perth Amboy, NJ, Aug. 5, 1939; s. Felix Andrew and Rita Marie (Jurasz) Z.; m. Gail Ann Heelon, Sept. 10, 1960; children: Robert Felix, Kathleen, Karen, David. BS cum laude, U. Mass., 1960; MD with honors, U. Chgo., 1964. Diplomate: Am. Bd. Internal Medicine (cardiovascular disease). Intern, then asst. resident in medicine Beth Israel Hosp., Harvard U. Med. Sch., 1964-66; clin. assoc. (lt. comdr. USPHS) cardiology br. Nat. Heart Inst., NIH, Bethesda, Md., 1966-68; mem. faculty U. Calif. Med. Sch., Davis, 1968-74, asst. assoc. prof. medicine, 1972-74, chief lab. clin. physiology, 1968-74, asst. chief sect. cardiovasc. medicine, 1970-74; prof. medicine and cellular/molecular physiology Milton S. Hershey (Pa.) Med. Ctr., Pa. State U. Coll. Medicine, 1974—, chief divsn. cardiology, 1974-84, dir. cardiology rsch., 1984—2002. Editor: The Peripheral Circulations, 1975; co-editor: Calcium Blockers, 1982; mem. editorial bd. Annals Internal Medicine, 1976-79, Am. Jour. Physiology, 1976-79, Circulation, 1979-82, Am. Heart Jour., 1980-90, Am. Jour. Cardiology, 1983-86, Jour. Cardiovasc. Pharmacology, 1991-2001, Jour. Am. Coll. Cardiology, 1994-99; contbr. articles to profl. jours. Walter S. Barr fellow, 1960-64; recipient Borden Rsch. award, 1964, Palmer award for Faculty Mentoring Pa. State U., 1997, Disting. Educator award Pa. State U. Coll. Medicine, 2003, Disting. Svc. award U. Chgo. Med. and Biol. Scis. Alumni Assn., 2004. Fellow A.C.P., Am. Coll. Chest Physicians, Am. Coll. Cardiology (gov. Eastern Pa. 1977-80); mem. Am. Fedn. Clin. Research (pres. 1977-78), Am. Soc. Clin. Investigation (nat. council 1981-85, v.p. 1984-85), Am. Physiol. Soc., Assn. Am. Physicians, Assn. Univ. Cardiologists, Am. Soc. Pharmacology and Exptl. Therapeutics, Am. Heart Assn. (nat. fellow councils circulation, arteriosclerosis, clin. cardiology and epidemiology, v.p. for community programs 1979-81, award of merit 1983 v.p., exec. com. Pa. 1976-79, pres. Pa. affiliate 1979-80, Charles T. Mears Humanitarian award 1984), Western Soc. Clin. Research, Sigma Xi, Alpha Omega Alpha, Phi Eta Sigma. Roman Catholic. Home: 815 Verden Dr Hummelstown PA 17036-9700 Office: MS Hershey Med Ctr Cardiology Divsn HO-47 PO Box 850 Hershey PA 17033-0850 Home Phone: 717-533-7512.

ZELITCH, ISRAEL, retired scientist; b. Phila., June 18, 1924; s. Judah and Helen (Sherman) Z.; m. Ruth Helen Goldman, June 30, 1945; children: Helen, Bernard, Deborah. BS, Pa. State U., 1947; PhD, U. Wis., 1951. Nat. research coun. postdoctoral fellow NYU Coll. Medicine, NYC, 1951-52; asst. biochemist Conn. Agrl. Experiment Sta., New Haven, 1952-54, assoc. biochemist, 1954-60, biochemist, 1960-63, head dept biochemistry, 1963-79, Samuel W. Johnson Disting. scientist, 1974—, head dept. biochemistry and genetics, 1980—94, now disting. scientist emeritus. Adj. prof. Dept. molecular biophysics and biochemistry Yale U., New Haven, 1958—, dept. biology, 1979—; chmn. Gordon Research Conf., 1979. Editorial bd. Plant Physiology, 1964-78, Archives of Biochemistry and Biophysics, 1969-77; editorial com. Annual Rev. of Plant Physiology, 1969-74; bd. editors Am. Scientist, 1984-90; author: Photosynthesis, Photorespiration, and Plant Productivity, 1971; contbr. articles to profl. jours. 1st lt. U.S. Army, 1944-46. Guggenheim fellow Guggenheim Found., U. Oxford, 1960, Am. Acad. Arts and Scis., 1980; recipient Fulbright Disting. Prof. award, Yugoslavia, 1981. Fellow AAAS; mem. Am. Soc. Plant Physiologists (exec. com. 1973-76, pres. 1977-78), Am. Soc. for Biochemistry and Molecular Biology, Am. Chem. Soc., Phi Beta Kappa. Jewish. Home: 70 Hall St Hamden CT 06517-3419 Office: Conn Agrl Experiment Sta 123 Huntington St PO Box 1106 New Haven CT 06504-1106

ZELIZER, VIVIANA, sociologist, educator; BA, Rutgers Univ., 1971; MA in Sociology, Columbia Univ., 1974, MPhil, 1974, PhD, 1977. Vis. instr. Columbia Univ., 1976; asst. prof. sociology Rutgers Univ., 1976—78, Barnard Coll., 1978—82, acting chair, dept. sociology, 1978—80, assoc. prof., 1982—85, prof., 1985—88; grad. faculty Columbia Univ., 1978—82; prof. Princeton Univ., 1988—2002, Lloyd Cotsen '50 prof. sociology, 2002—. Recipient Elizur Wright award, Am. Risk and Ins. Assn., 1985, C.W. Mills award, Soc. Study of Social Problems, 1985; grantee John Simon Guggenheim Mem. Found. Fellowship, 1996—97. Fellow: Am. Acad. Arts & Scis.; mem.: Sociol. Rsch. Assn., Phi Beta Kappa. Reads, speaks, writes English, Spanish, French, Italian. Office: Dept Sociology 120 Wallace Hall Princeton Univ Princeton NJ 08544 Office Phone: 609-258-4557. Business E-Mail: vzelizer@princeton.edu.

ZELL, JOSEPHINE MAY, retired language educator; b. Harwood, Lancashire, England, Apr. 26, 1934; d. Joseph Henry Howe and Emily Emma Herod; m. Robert Zell, Apr. 17, 1968 (div. Oct. 2002); children: Rosemary, Philip. BA Honors English Lang. and Lit., U. Manchester, Eng., 1955; MA in Latin, U. Wis., 1989. Chair dept. English, Milham Ford Sch., Oxford, England, 1964—68; lectr. English, U. Wis., Milw., 1968—71; tchr. English, Madison (Wis) Met. Sch. Dist., 1977—97; tchr. Latin, West H.S., Madison Sch. Dist., 1992—97. Author: (poetry) The Curtain Rises, 1993. Mem.: AAUW. Methodist. Home: 7001 Havenswood Dr Madison WI 53718

ZELL, SAMUEL, real estate company executive, publishing executive; b. Chgo., Sept. 28, 1941; s. Bernard Zell; m. Helen Zell; 3 children. BA, U. Mich., 1963, JD, 1966, LLD (hon.), 2005. With Yates Holleb and Michelson, 1966-68; co-founder, pres. Equity Fin. & Mgmt. Co., Chgo., 1968—76; chmn., pres. Equity Group Investments, LLC (formerly Equity Fin. & Mgmt. Co.), Chgo., 1976—; chmn. Great Am. Mgmt. and Investment Inc., 1981—; co-chmn. Revco D.S.; owner Chgo. Cubs, 2007—; chmn., CEO Tribune Co., 2007—. Chmn. Anixter Internat. 1985-, Delta Queen Steamboat Co., New Orleans, 1984—, Eagle Industries Inc., Itel Corp., 1985—, Nat. Assn. Real Estate Investment Trusts, 1998-2000; bd. dirs. The Tribune Co., 2007- Named one of Forbes' Richest Americans, 2006, World's Richest People, Forbes Mag., 2005—, 50 Who Matter Now, Business 2.0, 2007. Republican. Avocations: racquetball, skiing. Office: Equity International Two N Riverside Plz Ste 700 Chicago IL 60606 also: Tribune Co 435 N Mich Ave Chicago IL 60611

ZELL, VALERIE, art historian, educator; d. Berna Dene Winfrey; m. John Zell, July 1, 1995; children: Stephanie, Anna. MA, U. Mo., Kansas City, 1992. Asst. curator Nelson-Atkins Mus. Art, Kansas City, Mo., 1999—2001; adj. instructor art history Johnson County CC, Overland Park, Kans., 2008—. Art reviewer Kans. City Star, Mo., 2003—05. Home: 3308 W 132nd St Leawood KS 66209 Business E-Mail: vzell@jccc.edu.

ZELLE, BORIS ALEXANDER, orthopedist, researcher; arrived in US, 2005, permanent resident, 2005; s. Eberhard Zelle and Ursula Harlacher; m. Ana Luiza Allegretti, Mar. 27, 1975; 1 child, Julia Allegretti. BS in Med. Edn., George-August U. Gottingen, Germany, 1996, MD, 2000. Cert. Ednl. Commn. for Fgn. Med. Grads., 2001. Resident in orthop. Hannover Med. Sch., Germany, 2000—02; rsch. assoc. orthop. U. Pitts., 2002—05, resident in orthop., 2005—. Mem. evidence-based medicine working group Orthop. Trauma Assn., Rosemont, Ill., 2005—; presenter in field. Guest editor, peer reviewer: Clin, Orthop. and Related Rsch., 2007—, peer reviewer: Jour. Trauma, 2004—, Med. Sci. Monitor; contbr. over 60 articles to profl. jours., 8 chpts. to books, over 36 presentations at sci. meetings. Civil svc. U. Hosp., Hannover Med. Sch., 1992—94. Recipient Resident/Fellow Essay award, Arthroscopy Assn. N.Am., 2006; grantee, Pitts. Found., 2004, 2005. Mem.: Pa. Orthop. Soc. (licentiate), Am. Acad. Orthop. Surgeons (licentiate), Orthop. Trauma Assn. (assoc. grantee 2003). Avocations: foreign languages, soccer, running. Home: 1421 Macon Ave Pittsburgh PA 15218 Office: U Pitts Kaufmann Bldg Ste 1011 Pittsburgh PA 15213 Office Fax: 412-687-0802. Business E-Mail: zelleba@upmc.edu.

ZELLER, CHRISTOPHER LEE, preservation archaeologist; b. Northampton, Pa., Nov. 25, 1956; s. Karl Fredrich and Joan Veron (Hagenbuch) Zeller; m. Christi Joanne Wiggins, Apr. 24, 1982 (div. Mar. 11, 2004); 1 child, Kaeti Grace. BA in Anthropology, Ft. Lewis Coll., 1980. Fireline archaeologist/medic US Forest Svc. Bur. Land Mgmt., cert. ski patroller Nat. Ski Patrol and Assn. Profl. Patrollers, EMT Colo. Preservation tech., foreman San Juan Stabilization, Mancos, Colo., 1977—81; archaeologist Bur. Land Mgmt., Durango, Colo., 1982; preservation specialist Paul Nickens and Assocs., Montrose, Colo., 1983; ind. contractor, preservation specialist Woods Canyon Archaeol. Cons., Yellow Jacket, Colo., 1985—87; ind. contractor, project dir. Four Corners Rsch. Inst., Durango, 1986—87; owner, operator Petro Graphics, Durango, 1987—. Ski patroller Durango Mountain Resort, 1974—83, patrol foreman, 1984—2002, asst. patrol dir., 2003—. Achievements include invention of toboggan platform; conducted over 80 major preservation projects involving over 70 archaeological and historic sites in American Southwest. Avocations: fine art, trout fishing, motorcycle touring. Office: Petro Graphics Po Box 745 Durango CO 81302 Office Phone: 970-799-5146.

ZELLER, JOSEPH PAUL, advertising executive; b. Crestline, Ohio, Mar. 19, 1940; s. Paul Edward and Grace Beatrice (Kinstle) Z.; m. Nancy Jane Schmidt, June 17, 1961; children: Laurie, Joe. BA, U. Notre Dame, 1962; MFA, Ohio U., 1963. Mgr.radio/television Drewrys Ltd. USA, Inc., South Bend, Ind., 1963-64; media supr. Tatham-Laird & Kudner, Chgo., 1964-67; v.p. assoc. media dir. J. Walter Thompson Co., Chgo., 1967-77; v.p. media dir, v.p. Campbell-Mithun, Chgo., 1977-80; sr. v.p., dir. media, fin., chmn. media coun. D'Arcy Masius Benton & Bowles, Chgo., 1980-96, sr. v.p., 1996-2000; pres. Fox River Trading Co., East Dundee, Ill., 2000—. Chmn. Z Prop, 1986—; dir. circle Desert Caballeros Mus., 1994-96; founder Native Am. Images web mag., 1999. Pres. Amateur Hockey Assn. Ill., 1985. Named to Ill. Hockey Hall of Fame, 2005. Mem. Broadcast Pioneers, Chgo. Advt. Club, Moose. Roman Catholic. Avocations: hockey, photography, music. Business E-Mail: trader@rivertradingpost.com.

ZELLER, MARILYNN KAY, retired librarian; b. Scottsbluff, Nebr., Mar. 1, 1940; d. William Harold and Dorothy Elizabeth (Wilkins) Richards; m. Robert Jerome Zeller, May 21, 1966; children: Kevin Jerome and Renae Kay. BS, Calvary Bible Coll., 1985; MLS, U. Mo., Columbia, 1989. Cert. libr. File clk. Waddell & Reed, Kansas City, Mo., 1962-65; payroll clk. Century Fin. Co., Kansas City, Mo., 1965-67, Percy Kent Bag Co., Independence, Mo., 1968-70; accounts receivable Swansons on the Plaza, Kansas City, 1971-73; clk. casualty ins. Mill Mutuals, Kansas City, 1977-80; registrar's asst. Calvary Bible Coll., Kansas City, 1980-85, libr. asst., 1985-88, asst. libr., 1988-89, head libr., 1990—96. Chairperson libr. com. Calvary Bible Coll., Kansas City, 1990-96; libr. rep. Friends of the Hilda Kroeker Libr., Kansas City, 1990-96. Author: History of the Christian Librarian's Association, 1989. Mem. Christian Librs. Assn. Avocations: walking, reading, crocheting, sewing, swimming. Home: 401 13th Ave N Greenwood MO 64034-9750

ZELLER, MICHAEL EDWARD, physicist, researcher; b. San Francisco, Oct. 8, 1939; s. Edward Michael and Marie (Eschen) Z.; m. Linda Marie Smith, June 12, 1960; children: Jeffrey, Daniel. BS, Stanford U., 1961; MS, UCLA, 1964, PhD, 1968. Rsch. assoc. UCLA, 1968-69; instr. physics Yale U., New Haven, 1969-70, asst. prof., 1970-76, assoc. prof., 1976-82, prof., 1982—, chmn., 1989-95, Henry Ford II prof., 1996—. Recipient DeVane medal Phi Beta Kappa, 1980. Fellow Am. Phys. Soc.; mem. N.Y. Acad. Sci., Sigma Xi, Sigma Pi Sigma. Democrat. Jewish. Home: 135 Newton Rd Woodbridge CT 06525-1534 Office Phone: 203-432-3372. Business E-Mail: michael.zeller@yale.edu.

ZELLER, MICHAEL JAMES, psychologist, educator; b. Des Moines, Dec. 3, 1939; s. George and Lila (Fitch) Zeller. BS, Iowa State U., 1962, MS, 1967. Instr. psychology Minn. State U., Mankato, 1967—73, asst. prof., 1974—89, assoc. prof., 1990—2001, prof. emeritus, 2001—. Mem. social sci. edn. Mankato State U., 1976—; ednl. cons. Random Ho., Scott Foresman, West Pub. Co-author: (book) Unit Mastery Workbook, 1974, Test Item File to Accompany Psychology, 1974, 2d edit., 1976, Unit Mastery Workbook, 2d edit., 1976, Psychology: A Personal Approach, 1982, 2d edit., 1984, Test File for Psychology, 3d edit., 1988, Test Item File to Accompany Introduction to Psychology, 5th edit., 1989; editor: Test Item File to Accompany Introduction to Psychology, 6th edit., 1992; contbr. chapters to books. With USAR, 1964—70. Mem.: APA (life), Assn. for Psychol. Sci. (u. tchr.), Psi Chi (award 1988). Achievements include development of and research on educational materials; methods of instruction and career opportunities for psychology majors. Home and Office: 209 Deveraux Pt Mc Cormick SC 29835 Personal E-mail: mzeller39@yahoo.com.

ZELLER, RONALD JOHN, lawyer; b. Phila., Jan. 28, 1940; m. Lucille Bell; children: John, Kevin, Suzanne. BSBA, LaSalle Univ., 1964; JD, Ohio State U., 1967. Bar: Mich. 1968, Fla. 1971. Ptnr. Patton & Kanner, Miami, Fla., 1973-80, of counsel, 1980-89; dir., pres., CEO Norwegian Cruise Lines, 1980-86; pres. Twenty First Century Mgmt. Group, Inc., Coconut Grove, Fla., 1986-90, Miami Voice Corp., 1990-92; gen. counsel Splty. Mgmt. Co., Delray Beach, Fla., 1992-93, pres., 1994-96; ptnr. Zeller & Assocs., LLC, Palm Beach, Fla., 1996—; of counsel Koeppel Gottleib Mesches, 2000—06, Gottleib Mesches, L.P., 2007—08. Dep. chmn. Cruise Lines Internat. Assoc., NYC, 1981-85, chmn., 1986. Trustee United Way Dade County, 1981-86; pres. Cath. Charities, Archdiocese of Miami 1976-78, Broward County, 1975-76, Excalibur Devel. Ctrs., Inc., 1973-75; mem. citizens bd. U. Miami, 1980-92; mem. exec. bd. New World Sch. Arts, 1986-87; mem. centennial campaign com. Ohio State U. Coll. Law, 1982-92; mem. nat. coun. Moritz Coll. Law; mem. coun. Pres.'s Assocs., LaSalle U., 1982-87; mem. Fla. Postsecondary Edn. Planning Commn., 1986-87; mem. Cmty. Assns. Inst., 1995-2000; chmn. exec. com. Maritime Inst., 1997-99; mem. utility rev. bd. Village of Wellington, 1997-98; mem. gen. counsel Palm Beach Maritime Mus., 1997-2005; mem. Fla. com. Affirm Thy Friendship Campaign, Ohio State U., 1997-2000; mem. cruise line incentive com. Port of Palm Beach, 1997-2000; mem. ecumenical rev. bd. Diocese Palm Beach, 2002—03, mem. comm. adv. bd., 2002—. Mem. ABA (sect. taxation, closely held businesses. com.), Fla. Bar Assn. (lawyers and CPA's com. 2003-04, long range planning com. 2001-04), Maritime Law Assn. (proctor in admiralty), Pres.' Club Ohio State U. Office: Zeller & Assocs LLC Trump Plz Office Ctr 525 S Flagler Dr Ste 200 West Palm Beach FL 33401 Home Phone: 561-792-1272; Office Phone: 561-802-4480. Office Fax: 561-802-4387. Business E-Mail: zellerlawfirn@att.net.

ZELLER, SCOTT L., psychiatrist; b. Macomb, Ill., Dec. 4, 1960; s. Gerald L. and Marilyn Zeller; m. Susan Brydges Winchester, Jan. 19, 1996; 1 child, Douglas Winchester. BA, Ill. Wesleyan U., Bloomington, 1982; MD, Northwestern U., Chgo., 1986. Diplomate Nat. Bd. Med. Examiners, 1987. Resident U. Calif., San Francisco, 1986—89; attending physician psychiat. emergency svcs. Alameda County Med. Ctr., San Leandro, Calif., 1988—97; chief psychiat. emergency svcs. Alamda County Med. Ctr., 1997—; ptnr. JSA Health Mgmt., Houston, 2006—; dir. psychiatry St. Rose Hosp., Hayward, Calif., 2008—. Bd. dirs. Psychiat. Emergency Solutions, Inc, Houston; chmn. We. Emergency Psychiatry Conf., Oakland, Calif., 2001—. Editor: Emergency Psychiatry: Principles and Practice; editor: (pub.) Harpoon Mag., 1989—93; contbr. chapters to books, columns in newspapers, articles to profl. jours. Physician, asst. clinic dir. Katrina relief efforts Astrodome, Houston, 2005; spkr., writer and planner Ctrl. Fwy., San Francisco, 1996—99; bd. dirs. San Francisco Symphony Symphonix, 1991—95, San Francisco Press Club, 1992—94. Named Physician of Yr., Alameda County Med. Ctr., 2009. Mem.: Am. Assn. Emergency Psychiatry (v.p. 1999—2008, pres. -elect 2008—), Sigma Pi (life). Avocations: hiking, travel. Office: Alameda County Med Ctr 2060 Fairmont Dr San Leandro CA 94578 Business E-Mail: szeller@acmedctr.org.

ZELLERBACH, WILLIAM JOSEPH, retired paper company executive; b. San Francisco, Sept. 15, 1920; s. Harold Lionel and Doris (Joseph) Z.; m. Margery Haber, Feb. 25, 1946; children: John William, Thomas Harold, Charles Ralph, Nancy. BS, Wharton Sch., U. Pa., 1942; grad., Advanced Mgmt. Program, Harvard U., 1958. With Crown Zellerbach Corp. and subs., 1946-85; officer, dir. Crown Zellerbach Corp., 1960-85. Mem gen. adv. com. fgn. assistance programs AID, 1965-68; chmn. bd. Zellerbach Family Found. Served as lt. USNR, 1942-46. Mem. Nat. Paper trade Assn. (pres. 1970) Clubs: Villa Taverna (San Francisco), Presidio Golf (San Francisco), Pacific Union (San Francisco), Commonwealth (San Francisco); Peninsula Country (San Mateo, Calif.). Office: 575 Market St Ste 2950 San Francisco CA 94105

ZELLNER, ARNOLD, economics, econometrics and statistics professor; b. Bklyn., Jan. 2, 1927; s. Israel and Doris (Kleiman) Z.; m. Agnes Marie Sumares, June 20, 1953; children— David S., Philip A., Samuel N., Daniel A., Michael A. AB in Physics, Harvard U., Cambridge, Mass., 1949; PhD in Econs., U. Calif., Berkeley, 1957; D (hon.), U. Autonoma de Madrid, 1986, Tecnia de Lisboa, Portugal, 1991, U. Kiel, Germany, 1998, Erasmus U., Rotterdam, Netherlands, 2006. Asst., then assoc. prof. econs. U. Wash., 1955-60; Fulbright vis. prof. Netherlands Sch. Econs., Rotterdam, 1960-61; assoc. prof., then prof. econs. U. Wis., 1961-66; H.G.B. Alexander disting. service prof. econs. and statistics U. Chgo., 1966-96, prof. emeritus, 1996—; dir. H.G.B. Alexander Rsch. Found., 1973—. Cons. Battelle Meml. Inst., 1964—71; vis. rsch. prof. U. Calif., Berkeley, 1971, vis. prof., 1997—2007, Am. U., Cairo, 1997, Hebrew U., 1997; trustee Nat. Opinion Rsch. Corp., 1973—80; bd. dirs. Nat. Bur. Econ. Rsch., 1980—; seminar leader NSF-NBER Seminar on Bayesian Inference in Econometrics and Stats., 1970—95. Co-author: Systems Simulation for Regional Analysis, 1969, Estimating the Parameters of the Markov Probability Model, 1970; author: Bayesian Inference in Econometrics, 1971, Basic Issues in Econometrics, 1984, Bayesian Analysis in Econometrics and Statistics: The Zellner View and Papers, 1997, Statistics, Econometrics and Forecasting, 2004; editor: Economic Statistics and Econometrics, 1968, Seasonal Analysis of Economic Time Series, 1978, Simplicity, Inference and Modelling, 2001; assoc. editor: Econometrica, 1962-68; founding co-editor: Jour. Econometrics, 1972—; co-editor Studies in Bayesian Econometrics and Statistics, 1975, The Economics of Marine Resources, 2001, The Structural Econometrics, Time Series Analysis Approach, 2004; founding editor ASA Jour. Bus. and Econ. Stats., 1983; contbr. articles to profl. jours. Pres. Leonard J. Savage Meml. Trust Fund, Chgo., 1977-2000. Fellow AAAS, Am. Acad. Arts and Scis., Am. Econ. Assn., Internat. Inst. Forecasters, Econometric Soc., Am. Statis. Assn. (pres. elect 1990—, pres. 1991—, chmn. bus. and econs. sect. 1980, chmn. Bayesian statis. sci. sect. 1993); mem. Internat. Statis. Inst., Internat. Soc. Bayesian Analysis (co-pres. 1993, pres. 1994-96, Founders award 1998), Soc. Actuaries (trustee, rsch. found., 1994-98). Avocations: golf, tennis, travel, theater, music. Home: 5628 S Dorchester Ave Chicago IL 60637-1722 Office: U Chgo Grad Sch Bus 5807 S Woodlawn Ave Chicago IL 60637-1511 Office Phone: 773-702-7145. Business E-Mail: arnold.zellner@chicagogsb.edu, arnold.zellner@chicagobooth.edu.

ZELLWEGER, RENÉE, actress; b. Katy, Tex., Apr. 25, 1969; d. Emil Erich Zellweger and Kjellfrid Irene Andreassen; m. Kenny Chesney, May 9, 2005 (annulled Dec. 20, 2005). BA in English, U. Tex., Austin, 1991. Actress (films) Reality Bites, 1994, 8 Seconds, 1994, Love and a .45, 1994, Texas Chainsaw Massacre: The Next Generation, 1994, Empire Records, 1995, The Low Life, 1995, The Whole Wide World, 1996, Jerry Maguire, 1996 (Broadcast Film Critics Assn. award for Breakthrough Artist, Nat. Bd. Rev. award for Breakthrough Performance), Deceiver, 1997, A Price Above Rubies, 1998, One True Thing, 1998, The Bachelor, 1999, Nurse Betty, 2000 (Golden Globe award for Best Actress), Me, Myself & Irene, 2000, Bridget Jones's Diary, 2001 (Acad. award nominee, Golden Globe award nominee), White Oleander, 2002, Chicago, 2002 (Golden Globe award for Best Actress, SAG award for outstanding performance by a female actor in a leading role, Acad. award nominee), Down with Love, 2003, Cold Mountain, 2003 (Acad. award for Best Supporting Actress, Golden Globe award for Best Supporting Actress, SAG award for outstanding performance by a female actor in a supporting role, BAFTA award for Best Actress in a Supporting Role), Shark Tale (voice only), 2004, Bridget Jones: The Edge of Reason, 2004 (Golden Globe award nominee), Cinderella Man, 2005, Miss Potter, 2006 (Golden Globe award nominee), Bee Movie (voice only), 2007, Leatherheads, 2008, Appaloosa, 2008, New in Town, 2009, Monsters vs. Aliens (voice only), 2009, My One and Only, 2009, (TV films) A Taste for Killing, 1992, Murder in the Heartland, 1993, Shake, Rattle and Rock!, 1994. Recipient Crystal award, Women in Film Crystal + Lucy awards, 2007; named Woman of Yr., Hasty Pudding Theatrical Soc., 2009, Best Supporting Actress (for Cold Mountain), Broadcast Film Critics Assn., Chgo. Film Critics Assn., Dallas-Fort Worth Film Critics Assn., San Diego Film Critics Soc., Southeastern Film Critics Assn. Office: c/o John Carrabino Mgmt 5900 Wilshire Blvd Los Angeles CA 90036*

ZELMAN, SUSAN TAVE, broadcast executive, former state official, school system administrator; m. Allan Zelman; 3 children. BA in Arts, History and Polit. Sci., Hunter Coll.; MEd, EdD, U. Mich.; D in Pub. Edn. (hon.), U. Rio Grande, Ohio; D in Humanities (hon.), Youngstown U. Assoc. prof. edn. Emmanuel Coll., Boston, chair dept. edn.; assoc commr. ednl. dept. personnel Mass. Dept. Edn., 1988—94; dep. commr. Mo. Dept. Elem. and Secondary Edn., Jefferson City, 1994—99; supt. pub. instrn. Ohio Dept Edn., Columbus, 1999—2008; sr. v.p. edn. and children's content Corp. for Pub. Broadcasting (CPB), Washington, 2008—. Rschr. Edn. Tech. Ctr. Harvard Grad. Sch. Edn. Recipient Nat, Sci. Rsch. Opportunity award, Columbus Tchrs. Coll. Office: Corp for Pub Broadcasting 401 Ninth St, NW Washington DC 20004-2129*

ZELMANOWITZ, JULIUS MARTIN, mathematics professor, academic administrator; b. NYC, Feb. 20, 1941; s. Morris and Tillie (Holtz) Z.; m. Joan R. Traubel, June 24, 1962; 1 child, Dawn Michèle. AB, Harvard U., 1962; MS, U. Wis., 1963, PhD, 1966. From asst. prof. to assoc. prof. U. Calif., Santa Barbara, 1966—77, prof. math., 1977—2006, assoc. vice chancellor acad. affairs, 1985-87, assoc. vice chancellor acad. personnel, 1988-98; assoc. prof. Carnegie-Mellon U., Pitts., 1970-71; interim vice provost acad. initiatives U. Calif., 1999-2000, v.p. acad. initiatives, 2000—06, sr. vice provost acad. programs, 2005; dep. dir. Math. Sci. Rsch. Inst., Berkeley, Calif., 2006—08. Vis. asst. prof. UCLA, 1969—70, vis. assoc. prof., 1973—74; vis. prof. U. Rome, 1977, McGill U., Montreal, Que., Canada, 1982—83, 1987—88, U. Munich, 1983, 88, U. Calif., Berkeley, 2006—. Contbr. articles to profl. jours. Sr. rsch. grantee Italian Nat. Rsch. Coun., Rome, 1977, Palermo, 1988; named Milw. Prof. of Maths. The Technion, Haifa, Israel, 1979; Fulbright sr. fellow, Munich, 1983. Mem. Am. Math. Soc., Math. Assn. Am. Home: 2369 Century Hl Los Angeles CA 90067-3527 Office Phone: 510-643-6040. Business E-Mail: julius@math.ucsb.edu, jz@msri.org.

ZELNAK, STEPHEN P., JR., construction materials company executive; BS, Ga. Inst. Tech.; M Adminstrv. Sci. and Bus. Adminstrn., U. Ala. With Martin Marietta Corp., Raleigh, NC, 1981—, head aggregates ops., 1982-92, pres. materials group, 1992-93; pres. Martin Marietta Materials, Raleigh, NC, 1993, CEO, 1993—, chmn. bd. dirs., 1997—. Bd. dir. Beazer Homes USA Inc. Former chmn. NC Citizens for Bus. and Industry. Office: Martin Marietta Materials Inc 2710 Wycliff Rd Raleigh NC 27607

ZELNICK, RONALD STUART, surgeon; b. NYC, Dec. 6, 1958; BS, George Washington U., 1980; MD, Albany Med. Coll., 1984. Diplomate Am. Bd. Surgery, Am. Bd. Colon Rectal Surgery. Resident gen. surgery L.I. Jewish Hosp., New Hyde Park, N.Y., 1984-89; fellowship colon and rectal surgery Henry Ford Hosp., Detroit, 1989-90; pvt. practice Jupiter,

Fla., 1991—. Fellow ACS, Am. Soc. Colon Rectal Surgeons; mem. Fla. Surg. Soc., Fla. Colon Rectal Surgery Soc. Office: Ste 105 210 Jupiter Lakes Blvd #3105 Jupiter FL 33458 Office Phone: 561-575-7875.

ZELNICK, STRAUSS, entertainment company executive; b. Boston, June 26, 1957; s. Allan Zelnick and Elsa Lee Strauss; m. Wendy Belzberg, 1990; children: Cooper, Lucas, Leigh. BA summa cum laude, Wesleyan U., Middletown, Ct., 1979; MBA, Harvard U., 1983, JD cum laude, 1983. Bar: N.Y. 1984. Dir. internat. TV Columbia Pictures Internat. Corp., NYC, 1983-85, v.p. internat. TV, 1985-86; sr. v.p. corp. devel. Vestron Inc., Stamford, Conn., 1986-87, exec. v.p., 1987, pres., chief oper. officer, 1988-89, Twentieth Century Fox, LA, 1989-93; pres., CEO Crystal Dynamics, Palo Alto, Calif., 1993-95, BMG Entertainment N.Am., NYC, 1994—98, BMG Entertainment, NYC, 1998—2001; founder, ptnr. ZelnickMedia, 2001—. Non-exec. dir. Reed Elsevier PLC, 2005—, Reed Elsevier NV, 2005—, Reed Elsevier Group PLC, 2005—; chmn. Columbia Music Entertainment of Japan, OTX and ITN Networks, Take-Two Interactive Software, 2007—; bd. dir. Carver Bancorp, Inc., Blockbuster Inc., UGO Networks, Naylor Inc.; former exec. chmn. Direct Holdings (sold to Reader's Digest in 2007). Trustee Wesleyan U., 1992—; mem. contemporary arts coun. Mus. Modern Art, 1989, Young Pres. Orgn.; chmn. Covenant House Calif., 1992-95; bd. dirs. Covenant House, N.Y.C., 1995-2000. Mem. N.Y. State Bar Assn., Nat. Acad. Recording Arts and Sciences (assoc. mem.), Harvard Club, Recording Industry Assn. Am. (bd. dir.), Motion Picture Assn. Am. (bd. dir.), Phi Beta Kappa. Avocations: squash, sailing, skiing. Office: Zelnickmedia Corporation 19 W 44th St Fl 18 New York NY 10036-6101 Office Phone: 212-223-1383. Office Fax: 212-223-1384.

ZELON, LAURIE DEE, judge; b. Durham, NC, Nov. 15, 1952; d. Irving and Doris Miriam (Baker) Z.; m. David L. George, Dec. 30, 1979; children: Jeremy, Daniel. BA in English with distinction, Cornell U., 1974; JD, Harvard U., 1977. Bar: Calif. 1977, US Ct. Appeals (9th cir.) 1978, US Supreme Ct. 1989. Assoc. Beardsley, Hufstedler & Kemble, LA, 1977-81, Hufstedler, Miller, Carlson & Beardsley, LA, 1981-82, ptnr., 1983-88, Hufstedler, Miller, Kaus & Beardsley, LA, 1988-90, Hufstedler, Kaus & Ettinger, LA, 1990-91, Morrison & Foerster, LA, 1991-2000; judge LA Superior Ct., 2000—03; assoc. justice Calif. Ct. Appeal, LA, 2003—. Contbg. author: West's California Litigation Forms: Civil Procedure Before Trial, 1996; editor-in-chief Harvard Civil Rights and Civil Liberties Law Rev., 1976-77 Bd. dirs. NY Civil Liberties Union, 1973-74. Mem. ABA (chmn. young lawyers divsn. pro bono project 1981-83, delivery and pro bono projects com. 1983-85, subgrant competition-subgrant monitoring project 1985-86, chair standing com. on lawyers pub. svc. responsibility 1987-90, chair law firm pro bono project 1989-91, standing com. legal aid and indigent defendants 1991-97, chmn. 1993-97, mem. house dels. 1993—, state del. 1998-2006, commn. on ethics 2000 1997-2002, bd. govs. 2006—2009), Calif. Bar Assn. (bd. dirs. appellate project 1995-2000, chair commn. on access to justice 1997-99), LA County Bar Assn. (trustee 1989-91, v.p. 1992-93, sr. v.p. 1993-94, pres.-elect 1994-95, pres. 1995-96, fed. cts. and practices com. 1984-93, vice chmn. 1987-88, chmn. 1988-89, chmn. judiciary com. 1991-92, chmn. real estate litigation subsect. 1991-92), Women Lawyers Assn. LA, Calif. Women Lawyers Assn. Democrat. Office: Calif Ct of Appeal 2d Appellate Dist 300 S Spring St Los Angeles CA 90013 Business E-Mail: laurie.zelon@jud.ca.gov.

ZELTZER, LONNIE K., pediatrician, educator; b. Passaic, NJ, Oct. 4, 1944; m. Paul Zeltzer; 3 children. BA, Rutgers U., 1966; MD, U. Cin., 1970. Bd. cert. Am. Bd. Pediats., Nat. Bd. Med. Examiners; lic. physician, Tex., Calif. Intern pediat. UCLA, 1970—71; resident pediat. U. Ariz., 1971—72, chief resident, 1972—73; adolescent medicine fellow Children's Hosp. of LA, 1975—76; asst. prof. dept. pediat. U. So. Calif. Sch. Medicine, 1976—78; from asst. prof. to assoc. prof. dept. pediat. U. Tex. Health Sci. Ctr., San Antonio, 1978—86; assoc. prof. dept. pediat. U. So. Calif. Sch. Medicine, 1986—88; prof. pediat. Dept. Pediat. UCLA Sch. Medicine, 1988—. Med. dir. LA Job Corps, 1975-78; head divsn. adolescent medicine dept. pediats. U. Tex. Health Sci. Ctr., San Antonio, 1978-86; dir. behavioral sci. sect. divsn. hematology-oncology Children's Hosp. of L.A., 1986-88, dir. psychology fellowship and internship program; head divsn. child devel. and biobehavioral pediats. UCLA Sch. Medicine, 1988-81, dir. pediat. pain program dept. pediats., 1989—; assoc. dir. patients and survivors divsn. prevention and control rsch. br. UCLA Jonsson Comprehensive Cancer Ctr., 1996; Jour. of Pediats. vis. prof. dept. pediats. U. Iowa, 1982; con. in field. Mem. editl. bd.: Clin. Pediats., 1982-90, Pediats. Update, 1985-88, Jour. Pediat. Psychology, Topics in Pain Mgmt., 1990-96, others; outside reviewer: Jour. Adolescent Health Care, 1980-82, Health Psychology, 1985—, Pain, 1992—, Jour. Adolescent Health, 1992—, others; contbr. numerous articles to profl. jours. Mem. adv. bd. Comty. Guidance Ctr., San Antonio, 1980-82; mem. med. adv. bd. Vital Options, L.A., 1987-91; camp physician Ronald McDonald Camp Goodtimes, 1988; mem. med. adv. bd. Starbright Pediat. Network, 1993-96; med. advisor Cancervive, 1995-96 Recipient W.T. Grant Found. Faculty Scholars award, 1985-91, Rsch. Career Devel. award Nat. Cancer Inst., 1985-90; Health Professions scholar USPHS, 1966-70; also numerous rsch. grants. Fellow Am. Acad. Pediats., Soc. Clin. and Exptl. Hypnosis, Soc. for Clin. and Exptl. Hypnosis; mem. APA (sect. on clin. child psychology, sect. on pediat. psychology), Internat. Assn. for Study of Pain, Internat. Soc. Pediat. Oncology, Am. Pain Soc., Am. Pediat. Soc., Am. Soc. Clin. Hypnosis, Am. Soc. Clin. Oncology, Western Soc. for Pediat. Rsch., So. Soc. for Pediat. Rsch., Soc. for Adolescent Medicine, L.A. Pediat. Soc., Soc. for Rsch. in Adolescence, Soc. for Behavioral Medicine, Soc. for Pediat. Rsch., Soc. for Devel. and Behavioral Pediats., Ambulatory Pediat. Assn., San Antonio Pediat. Soc. Office: Mattel Children's Hosp at UCLA Pediat Pain Program 22-464 MDCC, 10833 Le Conte Ave Los Angeles CA 90095-1752 Office Phone: 310-825-0731. Office Fax: 310-794-2104. E-mail: lzeltzer@pediatrics.medsch.ucla.edu.

ZEMAN, HERBERT DAVID, biomedical engineer; b. NYC, Mar. 17, 1944; s. Mark Waldo and Adele (Cohen) Zemansky. AB magna cum laude, Oberlin Coll., 1965; MS, Stanford U., 1966, PhD, 1972. Fellow U. Muenster, Fed. Republic Germany, 1972-74; physicist SRI Internat., Menlo Park, Calif., 1974-76; rsch. assoc. Stanford U., Calif., 1976-78, sr. rsch. assoc. Calif., 1980-87; staff scientist Xerox Med. Systems, Palo Alto, Calif., 1978-80; med. physicist Nat. Synchrotron Light Source Brookhaven Nat. Labs., Upton, NY, 1987-90; assoc. prof. biomed. engring. and radiology U. Tenn., Memphis, 1990—2005; founder Luminetx Corp., Memphis, 2001, chief scientist, 2005—08. Contbr. articles to profl. jours. Chmn. Charleston Meadows Neighborhood Orgn., Palo Alto, 1977-84; founder Palo Alto Coalition for Equal Rights, 1981; steering com. mem. Palo Alto Civic League, 1983-84, Oberlin Lamda Alumni, 2007—; sec. AIDS/KS Found., Santa Clara County, 1983-84; bd. dirs. Nat. Stonewall Democrats, 2007—09; second tenor Memphis Symphony Chorus, 1994-2004, Memphis Vocal Arts Ensemble, 2006—08, Memphis Men's Chorale, 2006—, Rhodes MasterSingers, 2007—. Fellow NSF, Woodrow Wilson Found., Alexander von Humboldt Found. Mem. IEEE, Soc. Photo-Optical Instrument Engring., Am. Phys. Soc., Am. Assn. Physicists in Medicine, Optical Soc. Am.PFP Investment Club (sec. 1983-87), Phi Beta Kappa, Sigma Xi. Democrat. Jewish. Achievements include invention of the VeinViewer, 1995. Home and Office: 435 S Front St #401 Memphis TN 38103 Office Phone: 901-229-0508. Personal E-mail: herbzeman@gmail.com.

ZEMANIAN, ARMEN HUMPARTSOUM, electrical engineer, mathematician; b. Bridgewater, Mass., Apr. 16, 1925; s. Parsegh and Filor (Paparian) Z.; m. Edna Odell Williamson Zemanian, July 12, 1958; children: Peter, Thomas, Lewis, Susan. BEE, CCNY, 1947; ScD in Engring., NYU, 1953; prof. (hon.), Dubna U., Russia, 1996. Registered profl. engr., N.Y. Tutor CCNY, 1947-48; engr. The Maintenance Co., NYC, 1948-52; from asst. to assoc. prof. NYU, 1952-62; prof. SUNY, Stony Brook, 1962-83, leading prof., 1983-98, distinguished prof., 1998—. Author: Distribution Theory and Transform Analysis, 1965, Generalized Integral Transformations, 1968, Realizability Theory for Continuous Linear Systems, 1972, Infinite Electrical Networks, 1991, Transfiniteness for Graphs, Electrical Networks and Random Walks, 1996; Pristine Transfinite Graphs and Permissive Electrical Networks, 2001, Graphs and Networks: Transfinite and NonStandard, 2004; co-author: Electronics, 1961; co-founder, editor-in-chief emeritus Circuits, Systems and Signal Processing, 1982—. Sr. Faculty fellow NSF, 1975-76; recipient Sci. award Armenian Students Assns. Am., 1982. Fellow IEEE, IEEE Circuits and Systems Soc. (Golden Jubilee medal 2000), Am. Math. Soc., Russian Acad. Natural Scis. (fgn.; Kapitsa Gold medal 1996), Armenian Acad. Scis. (fgn.), Armenian Acad. Engrs. (fgn.), Sigma Xi, Tau Beta Pi, Eta Kappa Nu. Democrat. Presbyterian. Office: SUNY Electrical Engring Dept Stony Brook NY 11794-0001 Personal E-mail: aezem@optonline.net. Business E-Mail: zeman@ee.sunysb.edu.

ZEMECKIS, ROBERT L., film director; b. Chgo., May 14, 1952; m. Mary Ellen Trainor July 26, 1980 (div. 2000), 1 child, Alexander; m. Leslie Harter, Dec. 4, 2001. Student, U. So. Calif. Cinema Sch. Co-owner ImageMovers prodn. co., DarkCastle Entertainment. Dir. (films) I Wanna Hold Your Hand (also writer), 1978, Used Cars, 1980, Romancing the Stone, 1984, Back to the Future (also writer), 1985, Who Framed Roger Rabbit?, 1988, Back to the Future Part II (also writer), 1989, Back to the Future Part III (also writer), 1990, Death Becomes Her (also prodr.), 1992, Forrest Gump, 1994 (Best Dir. Acad. award), Contact, 1996 (TV series episode) Amazing Stories; co-screenwriter 1941, 1979, Trespass (also exec. prodr.), 1992; prodr. (films) Contact, 1997, (TV series) Johnny Bago, 1993, The House on Haunted Hill, 1999, Thirteen Ghosts, 2001, Ritual, 2001, Ghost Ship, 2002, Gothika, 2003, House of Wax, 2005, The Prize Winner of Defiance, Ohio, 2005, The Reaping, 2007, Beowulf, 2007; exec. prodr. (films) The Public Eye, 1992, Tales from the Crypt Presents: Demon Knight, 1995, The Frighteners, 1996, Tales from the Crypt Presents: Bordello of Blood, 1996 (also writer), The 20th Century: The Pursuit of Happiness, 1999 (TV), Matchstick Men, 2003, Last Holiday, 2006, Monster House, 2006, (TV series) Tales from the Crypt, 1989, W.E.I.R.D. World, 1995, Perversions of Science, 1997; writer (films) 1941, 1979, Used Cars, 1980; TV guest appearances include Parker Lewis Can't Lose, 1990; prodr., dir. What Lies Beneath, 2000, Cast Away, 2000, The Polar Express, 2004. Mem. bd. councilors U. So. Calif. Sch. Cinema-TV. Named one of 50 Smartest People in Hollywood, Entertainment Weekly, 2007. Mem. Dirs. Guild Am. Office: care Gelfand Rennert & Feldman 1880 Century Park E Ste 900 Los Angeles CA 90067-1609 also: South Side Amusement Bugalow 127 100 Universal City Plz Universal City CA 91608-1002

ZEMLICKA, JIRI, medical educator, researcher; b. Prague, Czech Republic, July 31, 1933; arrived in U.S., 1968; s. Vojtech Zemlicka and Otilie Zemlickova; m. Helena Zvarova, Mar. 30, 1961; children: Helena, George. MS, Charles U., Prague, 1956, Rerum Naturarum Dr., 1966; PhD, Czech Acad. Scis., Prague, 1959. Rsch. scientist Czech Acad. Scis., Prague, 1959—69; vis. scientist Mich. Cancer Found., Detroit, 1968—69, rsch. scientist, 1969—83, mem., 1983—94, Karmanos Cancer Inst., Detroit, 1994—. Assoc. prof. Wayne State U., Detroit, 1971—85, prof., 1985—; cons. Microbiotix, Inc., Worcester, Mass., 2002, Therapeutic Sys. Rsch. Lab., Inc., Ann Arbor, Mich., 2005—. Mem. editl. bd.: Nucleosides, Nucleotides & Nucleic Acids, 1982—, Antiviral Chemistry and Chemotherapy, 2000—; contbr. chapters to books, articles to profl. jours. Grantee, NIH, 1972—81, 1984—. Mem.: Internat. Soc. for Antiviral Rsch., Internat. Soc. for Nucleosides, Nucleotides and Nucleic Acids, Am. Chem. Soc. Achievements include patents in field. Home: 2025 Common Warren MI 48092 Office: Karmanos Cancer Inst 110 E Warren Ave Detroit MI 48201-1379

ZEMPLENI, JANOS, nutritionist, educator; m. Sabine B. Zempleni; children: Flora J., Anika M. PhD, U. Giessen, Germany. Postdoc. fellow U. Innsbruck, Austria, 1993—94, Emory U., Atlanta, 1994—95, Ark. Children's Hosp. Rsch. Inst., Little Rock, 1995—98, instr., 1998—99, asst. rsch. prof., 1999—2000; rsch. asst. prof. U. Ark. Med. Scis., 2000—01; asst. prof. U. Nebr., Lincoln, 2001—06, assoc. prof., 2006—. Contbr. scientific papers to peer reviewed publ. Mem.: Soc. Exptl. Biology & Medicine, Am. Physiol. Soc., Am. Soc. Advancement Scis., Am. Soc. Nutrition (Mead Johnson Award 2006), Gamma Sigma Delta. Home: 2841 Sissel Rd Lincoln NE 68516 Office: Univ NE Lincoln 316 Ruth Leverton Hall Lincoln NE 68583-0806 Office Fax: 402-472-1587. Business E-Mail: jzempleni2@unl.edu.

ZEMPSKY, WILLIAM TODD, physician; married. MD, Johns Hopkins U., Balt., 1988. Cert. physician Conn. Assoc. dir. Pain Relief Program, CCMC, Hartford, Conn., 2001—, med. dir. Contbr. articles to med. jours., chapters to books. Office: Conn Childrens's Med Ctr 282 Washington St Hartford CT 06117 Office Fax: 860-545-9969. Business E-Mail: wzempsk@ccmckids.org.

ZEN, E-AN, research geologist, educator; b. Peking, China, May 31, 1928; came to U.S., 1946, naturalized, 1963; s. Hung-chun and Heng-chi'h (Chen) Z. AB, Cornell U., 1951; MA, Harvard U., 1952, PhD, 1955. Rsch. fellow Woods Hole Oceanographic Inst., 1955-56, rsch. assoc., 1956-58; asst. prof. U. N.C., 1958-59; geologist U.S. Geol. Survey, 1959-80, rsch. geologist, 1981-89, scientist emeritus, 1990—; sr. scientist Va. Mus. Natural History. Adj. prof. geology U. Md., 1990—; vis. assoc. prof. Calif. Inst. Tech., 1962; Crosby vis. prof. MIT, 1973; Harry H. Hess sr. vis. fellow Princeton U., 1981; counselor 28th Internat. Geol. Congress. 1986-89. Contbr. articles to profl. jours. Recipient Maj. John Coke medal Geol. Soc. London, 1992, Outstanding Contbn. to Pub. Understanding of Geology award Am. Geol. Inst., 1994, Thomas Jefferson medal Va. Mus. Natural History Found., 1996. Fellow: AAAS, Mineral Soc. Am. (coun. 1975—77, pres. 1975—76, Roebling medal 1991), Geol. Soc. Am. (councillor 1985—88, v.p. 1991, ores. 1992, Day medal 1986), Am. Acad. Arts and Scis.; mem.: NAS, Geol. Soc. Washington (pres. 1973), Va. Mus. Natural History (sr. scientist). Office: U Md Dept Geology College Park MD 20742-0001

ZENACK, LES, mathematics professor; s. Sol and Ruth Zenack; m. Daron Krohn; children: Scott, Alissa, Tara. BS with honors, Stevens Inst. Tech., Hoboken, NJ; MS, NJ. Inst. Technolgy, Newark. Lic. in secondary math. MA Dept. Edn. Environ. engring. Numerous instns., Boston, 1990—2000; math. tchr. pub. sch., Mass.; prof. math. MassBay Coll., Mass., Dean Coll. Self employeed LINK Home Tutoring, Mass., 2004—. Home: 44 Condor Rd Sharon MA 02067-2949 Business E-Mail: thelinktutors@teacher.com.

ZENDLE, HOWARD MARK, systems engineer; b. Binghamton, NY, June 8, 1949; s. Abraham and Evelyn (Hershowitz) Z. BA in Physics summa cum laude, SUNY, Binghamton, 1972, MA in Physics, 1976; MSEE, Syracuse U., 1987. With IBM, Owego, NY, 1974—94, staff programmer, 1978-83, mgr. microprocessor application software, 1979-81, mgr. tactical avionics software, 1981-82, adv. programmer, 1983-86, sr. programmer, 1986-94, Loral, Owego, NY, 1994-96, Lockheed Martin, Owego, NY, 1996—2005, sys. engr. sr. staff, 2005—. Sec. Men's Club Beth David Synagogue, Binghamton, 1984-85, v.p., 1986-88; bd. dirs. Jewish Cmty. Ctr., Binghamton, 1983-86. Recipient SPOT award, Lockheed Martin, 2006, 2007. Mem. IEEE, AIAA, Ctrl. Electric Railfan's Assn., Masons, Phi Beta Kappa, Sigma Pi Sigma. Republican. Avocations: railfanning, history. Home: 5 Leigh St Johnson City NY 13790-1608 Office: Lockheed Martin 1801 State Route 17C Owego NY 13827-3998 Office Phone: 607-751-2625. Personal E-mail: hzendle@stny.rr.com.

ZENG, FAN-GANG, neuroscientist; b. Jiujiang, China, Feb. 20, 1964; s. Qin-Biao and Mei-Li Zeng; m. Ruby Xiong, Aug. 18, 1987. BS, U. Sci. and Tech., Hefei, 1982; MS, Academia Sinica, Shanghai, 1985; PhD, Syracuse U., NY, 1990. Rsch. assoc. House Ear Inst., LA, 1990-92, asst. scientist, 1992-94, dir. auditory perception lab., 1994—. Ad hoc mem. NIH Study Sect., Md., 1995-96; mem. Psychol. and Physiol. Acoustics Tech. Coun., 1996—; adj. prof. Henan Med. U., 1994—. Editl. cons. Jour. Speech and Hearing Rsch., 1993—. Recipient NIH first award, Md., 1994—, doctoral award Syracuse U., 1991. Mem. AAAS, IEEE, Assn. Otolaryngology, Acoustical Soc. Am. Avocations: basketball, volleyball, skiing. Office: House Ear Inst 2100 W 3rd St Los Angeles CA 90057-1922

ZENG, KAI, biomedical engineer; BS, Tsinghua U., Beijing, 2002; MA, Tsinghua U., 2004; PhD, U. IOWA, 2007. Rsch. asst. CT-Micro-CT lab, U. IOWA, 2004—07; grad. intern GE Global Rsch. Ctr., Niskayuna, NY, 2006—06, biomedical engr., 2008—. Contbr. to numerous profl. jours. Achievements include research in medical image reconstruction fields; patents pending in field. Office: GE Global Rsch Ctr One Rsch Circle Schenectady NY 12309

ZENG, SHENG, research and development company executive; s. Xiankui Zeng and Qingke Liu; m. Lizhi Yang, Oct. 2, 1999; children: Jason Zicheng, Henry Ziheng. BS, Shandong U., Jinan, 1994; MS, Tianjin U., China, 1997; PhD, U. Cin., 2006. R & D engr. Hewlett-Packard, Vancouver, Wash., 2006—. Contbr. articles to profl. jours. (Hewlett-Packard awards, 2008). Recipient Excellent Student award, Tianjin U., 1996. Mem.: IEEE, Am. Math. Soc.

ZENG, XIANMIN, science educator; b. Fujian, China, Oct. 31, 1967; d. Dryi Zeng and Yuying Yang; m. Michael Pedersen; children: Oliver Pedersen, Ophelia Pedersen, Andrea. PhD, Tech. U. Denmark, 2000; PostDoc., Nat. Inst. Aging, Balt., 2005. Assoc. prof. & dir. north bay cirm shared lab Inst., Novato, Calif., 2005—.

ZENGER, JOHN HANCOCK, training company executive; b. Salt Lake City, Nov. 13, 1931; s. John H. and L. (Hancock) Z.; m. Dixie Robison, June 1, 1955 (div. 1978); children: Mark R., Robin, Todd R., Blake R., Mitchell R., Drew R.; m. Holly Olsen, June 29, 1979; stepchildren: Roger, Kirk, Lori, Michael. BS, Brigham Young U., 1955; MBA, UCLA, 1957; DBA, U. So. Calif., 1963; Doctorate (hon.), Utah Valley State Coll., 2006. Asst. prof. Grad Sch. Bus. U. So. Calif., LA, 1966—67; exec. v.p. Blanfield-Smith and Co., Pasadena, Calif., 1965—67; v.p. human resources Syntex Corp., Palo Alto, Calif., 1967—77; pres. Zenger-Miller Inc., Cupertino, Calif., 1977—92; group v.p. Times Mirror Co., San Jose, 1992—97; pres., CEO Provant, Inc.; CEO Zenger Folkman Corp., 2003—. Chmn. Palo Alto Human Rels. Coun., 1961-66; trustee Utah Valley State Coll., chmn., 2003-04; pres. Midway Boosters, Inc. Ford Found. fellow, 1962-63; recipient Disting. Svc. award Brigham Young U., 1983; named to Human Resources Devel. Hall of Fame, 1994, Bd. Regions award, State Utah. Mem. Brigham Young U. Alumni Assn. (pres. 1981). Independent. Mem. Lds Ch. Avocation: magic. Home: 275 Luzern Rd Midway UT 84049-1268 Office Phone: 801-705-9494. E-mail: jzenger@zfco.com.

ZENKOVSKY, BETTY JEAN, modern languages educator; b. Mankato, Minn., Mar. 6, 1927; d. William and Sarah (Cloyd) Bubbers; m. Serge A. Zenkovsky, May 10, 1952. AB in Russian, U. Mich., Ann Arbor, 1950; AM in Slavic Studies, Ind. U., Bloomington, 1954; postgrad., Radcliffe U., Cambridge, Mass., 1956—58. Instr. modern langs. Stetson U., DeLand, Fla., 1958—60, asst. prof., 1962—65; instr. fgn. langs. U. Colo., Boulder, 1960—62; vis. lectr. Russian, Vanderbilt U., Nashville, 1967—68; rsch. assoc., translator NEH, DeLand, 1978—82. Co-translator: The Nikonian Chronicle, (5 vols.), 1984, 86, 88, 89. Grace Hill fellow, Radcliffe Grad. Sch., Cambridge, Mass., 1957—58. Mem. AAUW (pres. DeLand chpt. 1982-84, sec. Daytona Beach chpt. 1984-86), DAR (chpt. James Ormond br., vice regent, 1988-89), Am. Assn. Advancement Slavic Studies, Am. Assn. Tchrs. Slavic and Ea. European Langs., UN Assn., So. Conf. Slavic Studies, St. Barbara's Philoptochos. Democrat. Greek Orthodox. Home: 1224 S Peninsula Dr Apt 507 Daytona Beach FL 32118-4861 Home Fax: 386-253-3540. Personal E-mail: bjzenk@aol.com.

ZENN, MICHAEL ROBERT, plastic and reconstructive surgeon; b. NYC, Feb. 28, 1962; s. Renee Schwam; m. Susan Speer; children: Andrew, Erica. BA summa cum laude, U. Pa., 1984; MD, Cornell U., 1988. Diplomate Am. Bd. Gen. Surgery, 1994, Am. Bd. Plastic Surgery, 1998. Resident in gen. surgery NY Hosp. Cornell Med. Ctr., NYC, 1988—92, chief surgical resident, 1992—93; resident in plastic surgery Mass. Gen. Hosp., Boston, 1993-95; fellow in microsurgery Meml. Sloan-Kettering Cancer Ctr., NYC, 1995; asst. prof. plastic surgery U. N.C., Chapel Hill, 1996-2000, Duke Univ. Med. Ctr., Durham, NC, 2000—05, assoc. prof. plastic surgery, program dir. plastic surgery residency, 2005—. Contbr. articles to profl. jours. Named a Best Doctor for Women-Southeast Region, Ladies Home Jour., 2002, Best Doctor, Redbook mag., 2001; recipient NC Med. Soc. Tobacco Control award, 1999; named Best Cosmetic Surgeon in the Triangle, News and Observer, 1997. Fellow ACS (assoc.); mem. AMA, Am. Soc. Plastic Surgeons, Am. Soc. Reconstructive Microsurgery, World Soc. Reconstrictive Microsurgery, Plastic Surgery Rsch. Coun., NC Med. Soc., NC Soc. Plastic and Reconstructive Surgeons (v.p., 2001-02, pres., 2002-03), Nathan A. Womack Surg. Soc., Alpha Omega Alpha Avocations: painting, golf. Office: Plastic Surgery 3358 Duke Univ Med Ctr Durham NC 27710 Office Fax: 919-684-4954. Business E-Mail: michael.zenn@duke.edu.

ZENNSTRÖM, NIKLAS, Internet company executive, entrepreneur; b. 1966; married. Degree in Bus. Adminstrn., Uppsala U., Sweden, MSc in Engring. Physics and Computer Sci.; attended, U. Mich., Ann Arbor. With Tele2, ATT-Unisource; various bus. develop. roles get2net; various bus. develop. roles, CEO everyday.com; co-founder, CEO KaZaA, 2002—; founder, CEO Joltid, 2002—; co-founder Altnet, 2003—; co-founder, CEO Skype Technologies S.A., 2003—07; co-founder, co-chmn. Joost, 2006—; co-founder, ptnr. Atomico Investment Holdings Ltd. Mem. exec. com. eBay; bd. mem. FON; non-exec. chmn. Skype Technologies S.A., 2007—; spkr. in field. Recipient Innovation in Computing and Comm. award, Economist Innovation Awards, 2006; named Bus. Leader of Yr., European Voice, 2006, Tech. Change Agent of Yr., Wharton Infosys Bus. Transformation Awards, 2006, Entrepreneur of Yr., European Bus. Leaders Awards, 2006; named a Maverick, Details mag., 2007; named one of The World's Most Influential People, TIME mag., 2006, 50 Who Matter Now, CNNMoney.com Bus. 2.0, 2006, 2007, 50 Most Important People on the Web, PC World, 2007. Avocations: sailing, skiing, outdoor activities and travelling. Office: Skype Technologies 2 Stephen St London W1T 1AN England

ZENÓN, MIGUEL, musician; b. San Juan; Studied saxophone, Escuela Libre de Musica, PR; BA, Berklee Sch. Music, Boston, 1998; MA in saxophone performance, Manhattan Sch. Music, 2001. Drummer Bob Moses' Mozamba, Boston, Either/Orchestra, Boston; founding mem. SF Jazz Collective, 2004—; leader Miguel Zenón Quartet. Pvt. saxophone instr. New Sch. Jazz and Contemporary Music, NYC. Musician: (albums) Looking Forward, 2002 (named independent jazz record of 2002, NY Times), Ceremmonial, 2004, Jibaro, 2005, Awake, 2008; sideman: numerous albums, 1998—. Named Best New Artist of Yr., Jazz Times mag., 2006; named a Rising Star - Alto Sax, Downbeat Critic's Poll, 2004—07, 2008, MacArthur Fellow, The John D. and Catherine T. MacArthur Found., 2008; named one of 30 Under 30: Top Young Acts and Executives, Billboard mag., 2005; fellow John Simon Guggenheim Meml. Found., 2008. Office: c/o Mariah Wilkins Artist Mgmt LLC 305 E 86th St New York NY 10028 also: c/o Myles Weinstein Unlimited Myles Inc 81 Deerfield Ln Matawan NJ 07747 Office Phone: 212-426-3282, 732-566-2881. Office Fax: 732-566-8157. E-mail: mariahwilkins@earthlink.net, myles@unlimitedmyles.com, miguelmusic@miguelzenon.com.*

ZENTAY, JOHN H., lawyer; AB cum laude, Harvard U., 1953, LLB, 1958. Bar: Mo. 1958, DC 1966, US Supreme Ct. 1962. Legis. asst. to U.S. Senator Stuart Symington, Mo., 1958—62; mem. legis. staff AID, U.S. Dept. of State, 1963—66; cons. Bureau of the Budget, Washington, 1967—68; ptnr. Verner Liipfert Bernhard McPherson & Hand, Washington; ptnr., chmn. Fed. Affairs & Legis. practice group DLA Piper US LLP, Washington, 2002—. Mem. adv. com. on revision of rules of practice & procedure FERC, Washington, 1979—81. Bd. dir. Found. for Nat. Archives; trustee George C. Marshall Found.; chmn. fin. com. Nat. Protestant Episcopal Cathedral; bd. mem. Beauvoir Sch.; mem. long range planning com. St. Albans Sch.; mem. bd. mgr. Historical Soc. of Washington; bd. mem. Children's Hosp. Nat. Med. Ctr. Served US Army, 1953—55. Office: DLA Piper US LLP 1200 19th St NW Washington DC 20036-2412 Office Phone: 202-861-6449. Office Fax: 202-689-8563. Business E-Mail: john.zentay@dlapiper.com.

ZENTELLA, ANA CELIA, retired language educator; d. Ahmed and Monica Zentella; m. Robert Cabot, June 26, 1993. BA, Hunter Coll., Bronx, NY, 1960; MA, Pa. State U., State Coll, 1962; PhD, U. Pa., Phila., 1981. Prof. Hunter Coll., 1970—2001, U. Calif., La Jolla, 2001—08. Editl. bd. mem. Centro Jour., Ctr. Puerto Rican Studies, NYC, 2003—; mem. Conf. Coll. Comm. and Composition Lang. Policy Task Force, 1999—, Linguistic Soc. Am. Com. Ethnic Diversity in Linguistics, 2003—06, Am. Anthro Assn. Lang. and Social Justice Task Force, 2005—. Author: (book) Growing up Bilingual: Puerto Rican Children in New York (Brit. Assn. Applied Linguists Book award, 1998, Assoc. Latina & Latino Anthropologists Book award); editor: Building on Strength: Language and Literacy in Latino Families and Communities, Multilingual San Diego: Portraits of Language Loss and Revitalization. Mem. Nat. Congress Puerto Rican Rights, St. James Mission Cir., Solana Beach, Calif., Preuss Sch., La Jolla, Calif., 2004—08. Recipient Ana Celia Zentella DAY, Manhattan Borough President's Office, 1996; named to Hunter Coll. Hall of Fame, Hunter Coll., 1998; grant, UCSD Ctr. Study Race and Ethnicity, 2006, rsch. grant, UC Linguistic Minorities Rsch. Inst., 2008—. Mem.: Soc. Linguistic Anthropology, House PR, San Diego, Phi Beta Kappa. Roman Catholic. Achievements include research in anthro-political linguistics, NYC Spanish dialects, language socialization, Spanglish. Avocations: swimming, travel. Office: UCSD Ethnic Studies 9500 Gilman Dr 0522 La Jolla CA 92093-0522 Business E-Mail: azentella@ucsd.edu.

ZENTMYER, HUGH J., engineering executive; BS, U. Cin.; MBA, Xavier U., Cin. Various acctg. positions including v.p. fin. Strapping Divsn. Signode Corp. (acquired by Ill. Tool Works), 1968—86; ops. mgmt. position Ill. Tool Works (ITW), Glenview, 1986, exec. v.p. Bd. dirs. Marmon Group. Bd. mem. St. Patrick's HS. Office: Ill Tool Works 3600 W Lake Ave Glenview IL 60026-1215 Office Phone: 847-724-7500. Office Fax: 847-657-4572.

ZENTZ, LAURIE FUNDERBURK, music educator; d. Charles Edward and Jean Sanders Funderburk; m. Donald Mark Zentz, June 29, 1985; children: Danielle Marie, Andrea Rose. MusB, Valdosta State Coll., Ga., 1984; MA, Jacksonville U., Fla., 1994. Cert. Orff Schulwerk Level III Am. Orff-Schulwerk Assn., 1993, Tchr. Fla., 1987, Nat. Bd. Cert. Tchr. Nat. Bd. for Profl. Tchg. Stds., 2005. Music specialist Cunningham Creek Elem. Sch., Jacksonville, 2000—. Music edn. cons., author Z&Z Publications, Jacksonville, 1990—. Author: (music edn. materials) Junior Jam Session, 1993, The Heart Chart, 1995, Note Name Nonsense, 2000, Percussion Playalongs, 2000. Children's music ministry Mandarin Presbyn. Ch., Jacksonville, 2001—. Fellow Tchg. Fellowship, Nat. Endowment for the Arts, 1993. Mem.: North Fla. (pres. Orff chpt. 1994—98, pres., v.p. 1994—2006, v.p. 2004—06, pres. Orff chpt. 2007—), Fla. Music Educators Assn. (dist. chmn. 1993—95). Avocations: running, music.

ZEN ZE-KIUN, JOSEPH CARDINAL, cardinal, bishop; b. Shanghai, Jan. 13, 1932; Attended, Salesian Novitiate, Hong Kong, Salesian Sch., Turin, Italy; lic. in Theology, Pontifical Salesian U., Rome, D in Philosophy. Ordained priest Salesians of St. John Bosco, 1961; pastoral assignments Diocese of Hong Kong, coadjutor bishop, 1996—2002, bishop, 2002—09, bishop emeritus, 2009—; pres. Assn. Superiors Major; elevated to cardinal, 2006; cardinal-priest S. Maria Madre del Redentore a Tor Bella Monaca, 2006—. Mem. Congregations for Evangelization of peoples, for Divine Worship & Discipline of the Sacraments, Spl. Council for Asia, Secretariat Gen. of Synod of Bishops. Roman Catholic. Office: Diocese of Hong Kong Catholic Diocese Ctr 12 F 16 Caine Rd Hong Kong Island Hong Kong*

ZEPF, THOMAS HERMAN, retired physics professor; b. Cin., Feb. 13, 1935; s. Paul A. and Agnes J. (Schulz) Z. BS summa cum laude, Xavier U., 1957; MS, St. Louis U., 1960, PhD, 1963. Asst. prof. physics Creighton U., Omaha, 1962-67, assoc. prof., 1967-75, prof., 1975—2002, prof. emeritus, 2002—, acting chmn. dept. physics, 1963-66, chmn., 1966-73, 81-93, coord. allied health programs, 1975-76, coord. pre-health scis. advising, 1976-81. Cons. physicist VA Hosp., Omaha, 1966-71; vis. prof. physics St. Louis U., 1973-74; program evaluator Am. Coun. on Edn., 1988-2002. Contbr. articles and abstracts to Surface Sci., Bull. Am. Phys. Soc., Proceedings Nebr. Acad. Sci., The Physics Tchr. Jour., others. Recipient Cert. Recognition award, Phi Beta Kappa U. Cin. chpt., 1953. Mem. Am. Phys. Soc., Am. Assn. Physics Tchrs. (pres. Nebr. sect. 1978), Nebr. Acad. Sci. (life, chmn. physics sect. 1985-05), Internat. Brotherhood Magicians, Soc. Am. Magicians (pres. assembly #7, 1964-65), KC, Creighton Univ. Retirees Assn. (pres. 2007-), Sigma Xi (Achievement award for rsch. St. Louis chpt. 1963, pres. Omaha chpt. 1993-94), Sigma Pi Sigma. Roman Catholic. Office: Creighton U Dept Physics Omaha NE 68178-0001 Business E-Mail: thzepf@creighton.edu. *The real magic we all have at our disposal is the ability to comprehend our world, to understand how things behave. This understanding, which we gain through science, enables us to predict outcomes and exert a measure of control over nature. It's a sacred trust. It makes the scientist a kind of modern day magician.*

ZEPPOS, NICHOLAS S., academic administrator; BA, U. Wis., 1976, JD, 1979. Atty., Washington; joined faculty Vanderbilt U., Nashville, 1987, assoc. dean rsch. Law Sch., assoc. provost, 1999, vice chancellor for instnl. planning and advancement, 2000, provost, vice chancellor for acad. affairs, prof. law, 2001—, interim chancellor, 2007—08, chancellor, 2008—. Contbr. articles to publs. Office: Vanderbilt U Chancellor's Office 211 Kirkland Hall Nashville TN 37240 Office Phone: 615-322-1813. Office Fax: 615-322-6060. E-mail: nick.zeppos@vanderbilt.edu, chancellor@vanderbilt.edu.

ZERBE, KATHRYN JANE, psychiatrist; b. Harrisburg, Pa., Oct. 17, 1951; d. Grover Franklin and Ethel (Schreckengaust) Z. BS with BA equivalent cum laude, Duke U., Durham, NC, 1973; MD, Temple U., Phila., 1978. Diplomate Am. Bd. Psychiatry. Resident Karl Menninger Sch. Psychiatry, Topeka, 1982, dean, dir. edn. and rsch., 1992-97; staff psychiatrist Menninger Found., Topeka, 1982-2001; v.p. edn. and rsch. The Menninger Clinic, Topeka, 1993-97, prof., 1997-2001, Jack Aron chair in psychiat. edn., 1997-2001, apptd. tng. and supr. analyst, 1995—; prof. psychiatry, prof. ob-gyn. Oreg. Health Scis. Univ., Portland, 2001—; dir. behavioral medicine dept. Oreg. Health Scis. U., Portland, 2001—06; dir. outpatient clinic Oreg. Health Scis. Univ., Portland, 2003—, vice chair for psychotherapy, 2003—; tng. and supr. analyst Oreg. Psychoanalytic Inst., 2002—. Instr. numerous seminars and courses. Author: The Body Betrayed: Women, Eating Disorders and Treatment, 1993, Women's Mental Health in Primary Care, 1999, Eating Disorders for Ob-Gyns, 2007, (book) Integrated Tretment of Eating Disorder, 2008, numerous articles profl. rsch. papers; editor: Womens Mental Health: Primary Care Clinics, 2001; assoc. editor:, 1996—98; editor: Bull. of Menninger Clinic, 1998; mem. editl. bd.: Eating Disorders Rev., Eating Disorders: The Jour. of Treatment and Prevention Postgrad. Medicine; editor (sect.): Current Women's Health; contbr. book revs. and articles to profl. jours. Probation officer Juvenile divsn. Dauphin County, Pa., 1973. Recipient Ann. Laughlin Merit award The Nat. Psychiat. Endowment Fund, 1982, Outstanding Paper of Profl. Programs award The Menninger Found. Alumni Assn., 1982, Writing award Topeka Inst. for Psychoanalysis, 1985, 90, Mentorship award, 1997, Women Helping Women award, 1995, Tchr. of Yr. award Psychiatry Residents, 1988, 96, 99, 03, 05, 06; named one of Outstanding Young Women in Am., 1986, 88, Portland's Top Drs., 2007; Seeley fellow, 1979-82; Hilde Bruch lectureship, 1996. Fellow Am. Psychiat. Assn. (Alexandra Symonds award 2005, Edith Sabshin award 2007); mem. AMA, Am. Coll. Psychiatrists, Am. Med. Women's Assn., Oreg. Med. Assn., Oreg. Psychiat. Assn., Sigma Xi, Alpha Omega Alpha. Avocations: writing, reading, art history, travel. Office: Oreg Health and Scis U Adult Psychiatry 3181 SW Sam Jackson Park Rd Portland OR 97239-3098 Home Phone: 503-296-6164; Office Phone: 503-295-9909. Personal E-mail: kzbone@comcast.net. Business E-Mail: zerbek@ohsu.edu.

ZERELLA, JOSEPH A., endodontist; b. Bridgeport, Conn., Dec. 16, 1973; s. Zerella. DMD, U. Conn. Sch. Dental Medicine, Farmington, 2003. Cert. endodontist Conn., 2003. Endodontist Fairfield Endodontic Specialists, Conn., 2003—. Mem.: Am. Assn. Endodontists. Office: Fairfield Endodontic Specialists 1275 Post Rd Fairfield CT 06824 Home Fax: 203-254-7998. Personal E-mail: josephzerella@yahoo.com. Business E-Mail: fairfieldendo1@yahoo.com.

ZERELLA, JOSEPH T., retired pediatric surgeon; b. Youngstown, Ohio, Mar. 7, 1941; s. Atilio and Ann (Capuzello) Z.; m. Diana Isabelle Talbot, Aug. 5, 1967; children: Ann, Michael, Mark. BS, Northwestern U., 1962, MD, 1966. Diplomate Am. Bd. Surgery, Am. Bd. Pediatric Surgery. Intern Med. Coll. Wis., Milw., 1966-67, resident in surgery, 1967-68, 70-73; tng. fellow in pediatric surgery Children's Hosp. Med. Ctr., Cin., 1973-75; staff pediatric surgeon Phoenix Children's Hosp., 1975—; pvt. practice medicine, specializing in pediatric surgery Phoenix, 1975—. Mem. staff Good Samaritan Hosp., Phoenix, 1975—, sect. chief pediatric surgery, 1979—; mem. staff St. Joseph's Hosp., Phoenix, 1975—, sect. chief pediatric surgery, 1980—. Contbr. articles to profl. jours. Capt. USAR, 1968—70. Fellow ACS, Am. Acad. Pediatrics, Am. Pediatric Surg. Assn., Pacific Assn. Pediatric Surgeons. Roman Catholic. Mailing: 8426 N 15th Dr Phoenix AZ 85021 E-mail: dzerella@aol.com.

ZEREN, KARL JOSEPH, dentist, educator; children: Sarah, Lindsey, Kurt. BS in Psychology, U. Md., College Park, 1969; DDS, U. Md., Balt., 1975. Diplomate Am. Bd. Periodontology, 1986. Attending in periodontics Johns Hopkins Med. Instn., Balt., 1980—2008. Asst. clin. prof. U. Md., Sch. Dentistry, Balt., 1987—. Contbr. scientific papers. Lay chaliscist Trinity Episcopal Ch., Towson, Md., 2005—07. Lt. U.S. Navy, 1976—77. Named one of, Top Dentists in the Am., 2005. Mem.: Am. Coll. Dentists, Internat. Coll. Dentists, Md. Soc. Periodontists (pres. 1988—90), Am. Acad. Periodontology. Independent-Republican. Episcopalian. Achievements include research in human allograft block gtafting in dento-alveolar ridge augmentation. Avocations: golf, skiing, travel. Office: Karl J Zeren DDS LLC 9515 Deereco Rd Ste 308 Timonium MD 21093 E-mail: kjzeren@verizon.net.

ZERHOUNI, ELIAS ADAM, former federal agency administrator, radiologist; b. Nedroma, Algeria, Apr. 12, 1951; s. Mohamed and Yamna (Raahmouni) Zerhouni; m. Nadia Azza, Oct. 25, 1975; children: Djillali, Yasmin, Adam. MD, U. Algiers, 1975. Diplomate Am. Bd. Radiology. Resident diagnostic radiology John Hopkins U. Sch. Medicine, Balt., 1974—75, chief resident diagnostic radiology, 1975—78, instr., 1978—79, asst. prof. radiology, 1979—81, assoc. prof. radiology, 1985—92, Martin Donner prof. radiology, 1992, prof. biomedical engring., 1995, chmn. Russell H. Morgan dept. radiology & radiol. sci., 1996, exec. vice dean, vice dean clin. affairs, 1996—99, vice dean rsch., 1999—2000, exec. vice dean, 2000—02, sr. adv., 2009—; asst. dir. body CT Johns Hopkins Hosp., Balt., 1978—81, radiologist-in-chief, 1996—2002; asst. prof. radiology Ea. Va. Med. Sch., Norfolk, Va., 1981—83, assoc. prof. radiology, 1983—85; vice chmn., dir. body imaging De Paul Hosp., Norfolk, Va., 1982—85; dir. Advanced Med. Imaging Inst., Norfolk, Va., 1991—92, NIH, Bethesda, Md., 2002—08. Cons. White House, 1985, WHO, 1988; centennial lectr. Swedish Royal Acad. Radiology, Stockholm, 1994; mem. bd. sci. advisors Nat. Cancer Inst., 1998—2002. Assoc. editor Jour. Surg. & Radiol. Anatomy, 1980—86, Radiology, 1983—90, Jour. Thoracic Imaging, 1990—97; contbr. articles to profl. jours. Decorated Knight, Nat. Order Legion of Honor France, 2008; recipient Lauterbur award for MRI rsch., 1989, 1993, Hounsfield award for CT imaging, 1991; named Hon. Dr. Emeritus, U. Algiers, 2005. Mem.: AAAS, Inst. Medicine, Soc. Cardiovasc. Magnetic Resonance, N.Am. Soc. Cardiac Imaging, Balt. City Med. Soc., Am. Coll. Radiology, Am. Heart Assn., Internat. Soc. Magnetic Resonance in Medicine (bd. trustees 1995—98), Assn. Univ. Radiologists, Soc. Computed Body Tomography, Soc. Thoracic Radiology (founding mem.), Radiol. Soc. of N.Am., Am. Roentgen Ray Soc. Achievements include research in magnetic resonance imaging (MRI); development of imaging methods used for diagnosing cancer and cardiovascular disease; discovery of magnetic tagging, a non-invasive method of using MRI to track the motions of a heart in three dimensions; design of an imaging technique called computed tomographic (CT) densitometry that helps discriminate between non-cancerous and cancerous nodules in the lung; patents in field. Avocations: swimming, windsurfing, music. Office: Johns Hopkins U 601 N Caroline St Baltimore MD 21287-0006*

ZERHUSEN, JAMES A., prosecutor; BA, U. Dayton, 1971; JD, U. Ky., 1975. Asst. atty. gen. Office of Atty. Gen., Ky., 1978—80; asst. US atty. (ea. dist.) Ky. US Dept. Justice, 1980—2008, gen. crimes chief, 1990—92, chief criminal divsn., 1993—2008, acting US atty. (ea. dist.) Ky., 2008—. Mem. JAG, 1975—78. Office: US Attys Office 260 W Vine St Ste 300 Lexington KY 40507-1671 Office Phone: 859-233-2661. Office Fax: 859-233-2666.*

ZERMAN, MELVYN BERNARD, retired publishing executive, writer; b. NYC, July 10, 1930; s. Abraham and Ida (Belsky) Zirman; m. Miriam Baron, Jan. 2, 1985 (dec.); children: Andrew, Jared, Lenore. BA, U. Mich., 1952; MA, Columbia U., 1953. With Oxford Book Co., NYC, 1953-55; asst. editor Abelard-Schuman, Pubs., NYC, 1955-57; office mgr., salesman Harper & Row, NYC, 1957-61, sales rep., 1961-69, sales mgr., 1969-79, Random House, Inc., NYC, 1979-83, sales cons., 1983-87; pres., pub. Limelight Edits., NYC, 1983—2004. Mem. exec. com. N.Y. Is Book Country, N.Y.C., 1985-2004. Author: Call the Final Witness, 1977, Beyond a Reasonable Doubt, 1981 (Freedoms Found. medal 1981), Taking on the Press, 1986. Mem.: Phi Beta Kappa. Democrat. Avocations: book collecting, travel.

ZEROM, DAWIT, finance educator; PhD, U. Amsterdam, 2002. Asst. prof. U. Alta., Edmonton, Alberta, Canada, 2003—07; assoc. prof. Calif. State U. Fullerton, 2007—. Mem.: INFORMS, Internat. Inst. Forecasters, Econometric Soc., Am. Statis. Assn. Business E-Mail: dzerom@fullerton.edu.

ZERVANOS, STAMATIS MICHAEL (STAM ZERVANOS), biology professor; s. Michael S. and Vasiliki Zervanos; m. Joyce Zervanos; children: Mary Dialectos, Michael. BS, Albright Coll., Reading, Pa., 1965; MS, Pa. State U., State Coll., 1969; PhD, Ariz. State U., Tempe, 1972. Prof. biology Pa. State U., Reading, 1972—2006, emeritus prof. biology, 2006—. Contbr. scientific papers. Pres., parish coun. Sts. Constantine & Helen Greek Orthodox Ch., Reading, 1995—2002; pres., bd. chair Berks County Conservancy, Reading, 1997—98. Mem.: Pa. Acadamy Sci., Am. Soc. Mammalogist, Torch Club Reading (pres. 1993—94). Greek Orthodox. Avocations: travel, fishing. Home: 1506 Dauphin Ave Reading PA 19610

ZESCH, HAL, energy executive; BBA in Acctg., U. Tex., Austin. CPA. Audit and consulting mgr. Deloitte & Touche; various positions including v.p. best bus. practices, asst. corp. contr., contr. natural gas ops., and dir. corp. acctg. Valero Energy Corp., San Antonio, v.p. SAP systems integration, v.p., chief info. officer, 2003. Office: Valero Energy Corpn PO Box 696000 San Antonio TX 78269-6000*

ZETA-JONES, CATHERINE, actress; b. Swansea, Wales, Sept. 25, 1969; d. David and Patricia (Fair) Jones; m. Michael Douglas, Nov. 18, 2000; children: Dylan Michael, Carys Zeta. Actress (films) Les 1001 nuits (Italy), 1990, Christopher Columbus: The Discovery, 1992, Splitting Heirs, 1993, Blue Juice, 1995, The Phantom, 1996, The Mask of Zorro, 1998 (Blockbuster Entertainment award for favorite female newcomer), Entrapment, 1999 (European Film award/Jameson People's Choice award for Best European Actress), The Haunting, 1999, High Fidelity, 2000, Traffic, 2000 (Golden Globe award nominee), America's Sweethearts, 2001, Chicago, 2002 (Acad. award for Best Supporting Actress, BAFTA award for Best Actress in a Supporting Role, SAG award for outstanding performance by a female actor in a supporting role, Broadcast Film Critics Assn. award for Best Supporting Actress, Phoenix Film Critics Soc. award for Best Supporting Actress, Golden Globe award nominee), Sinbad: Legend of the Seven Seas (voice only), 2003, Intolerable Cruelty, 2003, The Terminal, 2004, Ocean's Twelve, 2004, The Legend of Zorro, 2005, No Reservations, 2007, Death Defying Acts, 2008, (TV films) Out of the Blue, 1991, The Cinder Path, 1994, The Return of the Native, 1994, Catherine the Great, 1995, (TV series) The Darling Buds of May, 1991—93, The Young Indiana Jones Chronicles, 1992—93, (TV miniseries) Titanic, 1996.*

ZETCHER, ARNOLD B., apparel executive; b. 1940; m. Ellen Zetcher. BA, Washington U., 1962. With Federated Dept. Stores, NYC, 1962-76; chmn. bd., CEO Bonwit Teller, NYC, 1976-80; with Kohl's Corp., NYC, 1980-83; chmn., CEO Kohl's Food Stores, NYC, John Breuner Co., San Ramon, Calif., 1983-86; pres. The Talbots, Inc., Hingham, Mass., 1987—2007, CEO, 1988—2007, chmn., 2000—. Trustee Wash. U.; bd. mem. Celebrity Series of Boston. Named CEO of Year for Retail, Apparel and Accessories, Financial World mag., 1995; named one of Top 25 Managers, BusinessWeek, 2000. Mem.: Nat. Retail Fedn. (exec. com., chmn. 2004—05). Office: The Talbots Inc 1 Talbots Dr Hingham MA 02043-1501

ZETIN, MARK I., psychiatrist; b. Seattle, June 19, 1948; m. Lynda Bjornson PhD, Pomona Coll., 1970; MS, Stanford U., 1971; MD, U. Calif., Irvine, 1975. Diplomate Am. Bd. Psychiatry & Neurology. Clin. prof. psychiatry U. Calif., Irvine, 1979-94; pvt. practive psychiatry Garden Grove, Calif., 1994—. Author: (book) Challenging Depression, Norton, 2009. Fellow: APA (disting.), Office: PO Box 879 Orange CA 92856-6879 Office Phone: 714-971-8103. Personal E-mail: mzetinmd@pacbell.net.

ZETSCHE, DIETER, automotive executive; b. Istanbul, Turkey, May 5, 1953; m. Gisela Zetsche. Grad., U. Karlsuhe, 1971—76; DEng, Tech. U. Paderborn, 1982. Joined rsch. dept. Daimier-Benz AG, 1976—81, asst. to chief engr. comml. vehicle divsn., 1981—84, coord. comml. vehicle devel. activities, 1984—86, sr. mgr., chief engr. cross-country vehicle unit, 1986—87; head devel. dept., chief engr. Mercedes-Benz do

Brazil, 1987—88, mem. mgmt., 1988—89; pres. Mercedes-Benz, Argentina, 1989—1991, Freightliner Corp., Portland, Oreg., 1991—92; dep. mem. bd. mgmt. Mercedes-Benz AG, 1992, chief engr. devel. divsn. passenger cars bus. unit, 1992, mem. bd. mgmt. sales divsn., 1995, Daimier-Benz AG, 1997—98, DaimlerChrysler AG, 1998—99, mem. bd. mgmt. comml. vehicle divsn., 1999—2000, chmn. bd. mgmt., 2006—, mem. bd. mgmt., Mercedes Car Group, 2005—07; mem. bd. mgmt., CEO Chrysler Group Divsn., 2000—05; chmn. mgmt. bd. Daimler AG, 2007—. Spokesperson for TV commercials Daimler-Chrysler, 2006. Named one of 100 Most Influential People, Time Mag., 2006. Office: Daimler AG Epplestrasse 225 D-70546 Stuttgart Germany Office Phone: +49-711-17-0. Office Fax: +49-711-17-94022.

ZETTERBERG, HENRIK, professional hockey player; b. Njurunda, Sweden, Oct. 9, 1980; Left wing Timra IK, Swedish Elite League, 2000—02, 2004—05, Detroit Red Wings, 2002—. Mem. Swedish Olympic Hockey Team, Salt Lake City, 2002, Torino, Italy, 06. Recipient Conn Smythe Trophy, 2008, NHL Rookie of Yr., Sporting News, 2003; named TSN NHL Player of Yr., 2008; named to All-Rookie Team, NHL, 2003, NHL All-Star Game, 2007, 2008, Second All-Star Team, NHL, 2008. Achievements include being a member of gold medal winning Swedish Hockey Team, Torino Olympics, Italy, 2006; being a member of Stanley Cup Champion Detroit Red Wings, 2008. Office: Detroit Red Wings Joe Louis Arena 600 Civic Ctr Detroit MI 48226

ZETTERMAN, ROWEN KENT, gastroenterologist, hepatologist, dean; b. York, Nebr., July 30, 1944; s. Verlie L. and Maurine E. (Venell) Z.; m. Emily Joan Clark, June 4, 1966; children: David, Justin, Corey. BA, Nebr. Wesleyan U., 1966; MD, U. Nebr., 1969. Diplomate Am. Bd. Internal Medicine, Am. Bd. Gastroenterology. Intern U. Nebr. Med. Ctr., Omaha, 1969-70, resident, 1970-71, resident gastroenterology, 1971-72, gastroenterologist, 1976—, sect. chief digestive diseases, 1984-91, vice chair internal medicine, 1996; hepatology fellow NJ Med. Sch., Newark, 1972-74; gastroenterologist Walter Reed Army Med. Ctr., Washington, 1974-76; chief medicine dept. Omaha VA Med. Ctr., 1998—2002; chief of staff for vet. affairs Nebr.-Western Iowa Health Care Sys., 2002—09; dean Creighton U. Sch. Medicine, 2009—. Faculty mem. Dept. Internal Medicine Creighton U., 1977, clin. prof. internal medicine. Editor Digestive Diseases, 1981-92, Am. Jour. Gastroenterology, 1991-97; contbr. 110 articles to med. jours. Troop chmn. Boy Scouts Am., 1980-90; active 1st United Meth. Ch., Omaha, 1976—. Fellow ACP (bd. govs. 1992-96, 96-97, chair-elect bd. govs. 1995-96, regent 1997—), Am. Coll. Gastroenterology (gov. 1990-92, v.p. 1998-99, Berk/Fise Clinical Achievement Award, 2008). Office: Creighton U Sch Medicine 2500 California Plaza Omaha NE 68178 Office Fax: 402-280-2600. E-mail: rze63323@creighton.edu.*

ZETTL, GARY T., engineering educator; b. Chgo., Nov. 1, 1951; s. Marian E. Zettl; m. Teresa M. Traas, July 27, 1985; children: Kathryn E., Tyler N. Tchr. Kettle Moraine Mid. Sch., Dousman, Wis., 1974—. Home: S33 W35551 Meadow Trail Dousman WI 53118 Office: Ketle Moraine Mid Sch 301 E Ottawa Ave Dousman WI 53118 Business E-Mail: zettlg@kmsd.edu.

ZEUGNER, JOHN FINN, historian, educator, writer; b. NYC, Oct. 7, 1938; s. Orland Kump and Ethel (Finn) Z.; m. Alice Chatfield Valentine, Sept. 7, 1968; children: Emily Valentine, Maxwell Finn, Laura Ruth. AB, Harvard U., 1959; MA, Fla. State U., 1968, PhD, 1971. Night mgr. Beach Cart, Sarasota, Fla., 1960-67; asst. prof. history Worcester Poly. Inst., Mass., 1971-74, assoc. prof., 1974-82, prof., 1982—; Fulbright lectr. Osaka U., Kobe U., Japan, 1976-78. Vis. prof. Keio U., Tokyo, 1981-83; Bryant Drake guest prof. Kobe Coll., Japan, 1994-95. Contbr. articles to profl. jours. With USCG, 1961—62. Named Paris Fletcher Disting. Prof. Humanities, Worcester Poly. Inst., 1985; grantee NEA, 1970 Mem.: Soc. Historians Am. Fgn. Rels., Orgn. Am. Historians. Avocations: tennis, chess. Home: 31 William St Worcester MA 01609-2313 Office: Worcester Poly Inst Humanities & Arts Dept Worcester MA 01609 Office Phone: 508-831-5246. Business E-Mail: jzeugner@wpi.edu.

ZEUSCHNER, ERWIN ARNOLD, brokerage house executive; b. Freiburg, Germany, Nov. 17, 1935; came to U.S., 1936; s. Reinhold Hermann and Helene Barbara (Maas) Z.; m. Christa Elfreide Ellmers, June 20, 1959 (dec. Aug., 1971); children— Peter Erwin, Suzanne Christina, Andrea Ellmers; m. Margaret Anne Finn, Mar. 25, 1972; 1 dau., Elizabeth Nora. BA in Econs., Queens Coll., 1957; MBA in Fin, NYU, 1964. Sr. v.p. Chase Manhattan Bank, NYC, 1970-72; sr. v.p., dir. Chase Investors Mgmt. Corp., 1972-80; sr. v.p. Chase Manhattan Corp., 1970-80; ptnr. David J. Greene & Co. (investment advs.), NYC, 1980—. Trustee Marymount Manhattan Coll., 1997. Served to capt. USAF, 1958-60. Mem. N.Y. Soc. Security Analysts (dir.) Home: 1 Middle Dr Manhasset NY 11030-1414 Office: Nevberler Berman 605 Third Ave 35th Fl New York NY 10158

ZEVGOLIS, IOANNIS, geotechnical engineer, researcher; b. Athens, Greece, May 6, 1977; s. Emmanouil Zevgolis and Aikaterini Zevgolis - Protonotarios. Diploma in Mining and Metall. Engring., Nat. Tech. U. Athens, Greece, 2002; MS in Engring., Sch. Civil Engring. Purdue U., West Lafayette, Ind., 2003, PhD, 2007. Lic. profl. engr., Tech. Chamber Greece, EU, 2002. Rsch. and tchg. asst. Purdue U., West Lafayette, Ind., 2002—07. Recipient Thomaidio award, Nat. Tech. U. Athens, 2002, Best Diploma Thesis, Tech. Chamber Greece, 2002, Nellie Munson Tchg. Asst. award in civil engring., Purdue U., 2007, Outstanding Civil Engring. Grad. Student award, 2007; scholar, Gerondelis Found., 2004, Empeirikion Found., 2004—06. Mem.: ASCE, Geo-Inst. of ASCE, Tech. Chamber of Greece, Bd. European Students Tech. (v.p. pub. rels. and mktg. 1998—2001), Internat. Geosynthetics Soc., Internat. Soc. Soil Mechanics and Geotechnical Engring. Achievements include research in soil reinforcement methods; reliability and risk analysis in geotechnical engineering; underground space development. Home: 7-9 Gavriilidou St 11141 Athens Greece E-mail: i.zevgolis@alumni.purdue.edu.

ZEVIAR-GEESE, GABRIOLE, stock market investor, lawyer; b. LA, Apr. 10, 1948; d. Harry Lindstedt and Josephine Blom; m. Stephan Otto Geese, Nov. 22, 1992. Diploma in Computer Programming and Analysis, Seneca Coll. Applied Arts and Tech., 1981; BA, York U., 1991; JD, Calif. Pacific Sch. Law, 1999. Data base cons., edn. specialist Bull Internat., Toronto, Canada, 1982—91; programmer Sparta, Laguna, Niguel, Calif., 1992; stock market investor, 1994—; pvt. practice Bakersfield, Calif., 2001—. Tech. educator, course developer, text book writer, data base adminstr. U.S. and Can. Contbr. articles to profl. jours. Mem.: ABA, Kern County Bar Assn., Calif. Bar Assn. Avocations: piano, painting. Office Phone: 661-859-1031. E-mail: geeselawoffice@aol.com.

ZEWAIL, AHMED HASSAN, chemistry and physics educator, consultant, editor; b. Damanhour, Egypt, Feb. 26, 1946; arrived in U.S., 1969, naturalized, 1982; s. Hassan A. Zewail and Rawhia Dar; m. Dema Zewail; children: Maha, Amani, Nabeel, Hani. BS, Alexandria U., Egypt, 1967, MS, 1969; PhD, U. Pa., 1974; MA (hon.), Oxford U., 1991; DSc (hon.), Am. U., Cairo, 1993, Katholieke U., Leuven, Belgium, U. Pa., U. Lausanne, Switzerland, 1997; DU (hon.), Swinburne U., Australia, 1999; HDA Sc (hon.), Arab Acad. for Sci. and Tech., Egypt, 1999, Alexandria U., 1999; DSc (hon.), U. New Brunswick, Canada, 2000; DHC (hon.), U. Rome, Italy, 2000, U. de Liège, Belgium, 2000. Teaching asst. U. Pa., Phila., 1969—70; IBM fellow U. Calif., Berkeley, 1974—76; asst. prof. chem. physics Calif. Inst. Tech., Pasadena, 1976—78, assoc. prof., 1978—82, prof., 1982—89, Linus Pauling prof. chem. physics, 1990—94, Linus Pauling prof. chemistry and prof. physics, 1995—, dir. NSF Lab. for Molecular Scis., 1996—. Cons. Xerox Corp., Webster, NY, 1977—80, ARCO Solar, Inc., Calif., 1978—81. Editor Laser Chemistry, 1980—85, Jour. Phys. Chemistry, 1985—90, Chem. Physics Letters, 1991—; editor: International Series Monographs on Chemistry, 1992—, Advances in Laser Spectroscopy, 1977—, 1978—, Photochemistry and Photobiology, 1983—, Ultrafast Phenomena, 1990—, 1993—, 1994—, The Chemical Bond: Structure and Dynamics, 1992, Femtochemistry-Ultrafst Dynamics of the Chemical Bond, 1994; contbr. numerous articles to sci. jours., patentee in solar energy field. Recipient Tchr.-Scholar award, Dreyfus Found., 1979—85, Alexander von Humboldt Sr. U.S. Scientist award, 1983, John Simon Guggenheim Meml. Found. award, 1987, King Faisal Internat. prize in sci., 1989, NASA award, 1991, 1st AMM Achievement award, 1991, Nobel Laureate Signature award, 1992, Carl Zeiss award, Cairo U. Medal and Shield of Honor, 1992, U. Qatar medal, 1993, Wolf prize in chemistry, Wolf Found., Israel, 1993, Niles award of honor Bonner Chemiepreis, Germany, 1994, Order of Merit first class, Egypt, 1995, Coll. de France medal Leonardo Da Vinci award of excellence, France, 1995, J.G. Kirwood medal, Yale U., 1996, Beijing U. medal, 1996, Robert A. Welch award in chemistry, 1997, Pitts. Spectroscopy award, 1997, Benjamin Franklin medal, 1999, Paul Karrer Gold medal, Zurich, 1999, Roentgen prize, Germany, 1999, E.O. Lawrence award, U.S. Govt., 1999, Merski award, U. Nebr., 1999, Nobel prize in Chemistry, 1999, Egypt Postage Stamp with portrait issued, 1999, Grand Collar of the Nile, Highest Award, 2000, Order of Zayed, United Arab Emirates, 2000, Ahmed Zewail fellow established, U. Pa., 2000, Order of Cedar, Lebanon, 2000, Order of ISESCO 1st class, Saudi Arabia, 2000, Order of merit, Tunisia, 2000, Insignia Pontifical Acad., Vatican, 2000, Albert Einstein World Award of Sci., 2006. Mem.: NAS (Chem. Scis. award 1996), AAAS, Third World Acad. Scis., European Acad. Arts, Scis. and Humanities, Royal Danish Acad. Scis. and Letters, Pontifical Acad. Sci., Am. Phys. Soc. (Herbert P. Broida prize 1995), Am. Philos. Soc., Am. Chem. Soc. (Buck-Whitney medal 1985, Harrison-Howe award 1989, Hoechst prize 1990, Peter Debye award 1997, Linus Pauling medal 1997, 1st E.B. Wilson award 1997, William H. Nichols award 1998, Richard C. Tolman medal 1998), Am. Acad. Arts and Scis. (Royal Netherlands Acad. Arts and Scis. medal 1993), Sigma Xi (Earle K. Plyler prize 1993, Wolf prize 1993). Office: Arthur Amos Noyes Lab of Chem Physics Calif Inst Tech MC 127-72 1200 E California Blvd Pasadena CA 91125 Business E-Mail: zewail@caltech.edu.*

ZEYDEL, DIANA S. C., lawyer, former professional ballet dancer; Grad., Joffrey Ballet Sch., NY; BA summa cum laude, Yale U., 1982; JD, Yale Law Sch., 1986; LLM, NYU Sch. Law, 1993. Bar: NY 1987, Fla. 1995. Profl. ballet dancer Chgo. Ballet; shareholder Greenberg Traurig, LLP. Spkr. in field. Contbr. articles to profl. jours. Mem. cmty. devel. bd. Miami City Ballet, chair planned giving com. Named to, Super Lawyers Mag., 2006, 2007. Fellow: Am. Coll. Trust and Estate Counsel (mem. nominating com. 2001—02, mem. internat. planning com. 2001—, mem. program com. 2002—04, mem. estate and gift tax com. 2005—); mem.: ABA (co-chair generation-skipping tax com. 2001—), Fla. Bar (mem. exec. counsel, circuit rep.). Office: Greenberg Traurig LLP 1221 Brickell Ave Miami FL 33131 Office Phone: 305-579-0500. Office Fax: 305-579-0717. Business E-Mail: zeydel@gtlaw.com.

ZGARRICK, DAVID PAUL, pharmaceutical executive; b. Marshfield, Wis., Nov. 13, 1964; m. Michelle Witham. BS in Pharmacy, U. Wis. Madison, 1988; PhD, Ohio State U., Columbus, 1993. Cert. Wis. Bd. Pharmacy, 1988. Prof. Midwestern U., Downers Grove, Ill., 1993—2007, vice chair, 1993—2007; John R. Ellis disting. chair pharmacy practice, Coll. Pharmacy and Health Scis. Drake U., Des Moines, 2007—. Bd. dirs. Am. Assn. Colls. Pharmacy, Alexandria, Va., 2007—08. Contbr. articles to profl. jours. Avocations: cooking, skiing, travel. Office: Drake Univ 2507 University Ave Des Moines IA 50323 Business E-Mail: david.zgarrick@drake.edu.

ZHA, JIPING, pathologist; b. China; MD, Shanghai Med. U., 1987; PhD, U. Tenn., Memphis, 1993. Diplomate Am. Bd. Pathology, 1999. Postdoc. fellow Howard Hughes Med. Inst., St. Louis, 1993—96; resident anatomic pathology Wash. U. Sch. Medicine, St. Louis, 1996—98, Brigham & Women's Hosp., Boston, 1998—99; instr. Harvard Med. Sch., Boston, 1999—2000; asst. prof. U. Tex. Southwestern Med. Ctr., Dallas, 2000—03; pathologist Genentech Inc., San Francisco, 2003—. Contbr. articles to sci. jours. Recipient Howard Temin award, Nat. Cancer Inst., 1999. Mem.: Am. Assn. Cancer Rsch. Achievements include patents pending for antibodies to insulin-like growth factor-I receptor.

ZHA, SHITONG, research scientist; b. Xinxiang, Henan, China, Sept. 24, 1970; d. Baotian Zha and Guizhen Ma; m. Xi Sun; 1 child, Xinyi Sun. PhD, Tianjin U., China, 2003. Postdoc. rschr. Norwegian Sci. and Tech. U., Trondheim, 2004—06; rsch. engr. R&D, Hill Phoenix, Covington, Ga., 2006—. Assoc. prof. Tianjin U. Commerce, 2002—03. Contbr. articles to profl. jour. Mem.: ASHRAE. Achievements include patents for carbon dioxide transcrisis refrigeration circulation rolling rotor energy recovery device. Home: 2434 Keswick Village Conyers HI 30013 Georgia Office: Hill Phoenix 8166 Industrial Blvd Covington GA 30014 Georgia Personal E-mail: zhast@hotmail.com. Business E-Mail: shitong.zha@hillphoenix.com.

ZHAI, YAN, education educator, researcher; s. Zhai and Song. MS, Okla. State U., Stillwater, 2002; postgrad., U. Okla., Norman, 2003—. Design engring. Beijing Constrn. Corp., 1998—2000; rsch. asst. Okla. State U., Stillwater, 2000—02, U. Okla., Norman, 2003—. Contbr. articles to profl. jours. Mem.: IEEE (signal processing), Phi Kappa Phi, Tau Beta Pi. Achievements include development of novel signal processing algorithms. Office: Univ Okla 202 W Body St Norman OK 73071

ZHAN, XIANQUAN, medical educator; s. Daoshun Zhan and Shougui Xiang; m. Ying Tang; children: Xiaohan, Amira. MD, West China U. Med. Scis., Chengdu, 1994, PhD, 1999. Rsch. asst. prof. Xiangya Med. Sch., Ctrl. South U., Changsha, Hunan, China, 1999—2001, postdoc. rsch. fellow, 1999—2001, U. Tenn. Health Sci. Ctr., Memphis, 2001—05, asst. prof., 2005—06, 2008—; project scientist, project staff Cleve. Clinic Found., 2006—07. Contbr. scientific papers to profl. jours., chapters to books. Recipient Excellent Grad. Student Cadre Recognition medal, West China U. Med. Scis., 1997, First Hongkong Union Medicine Edn. medal, 1998, Chinese Postdoc. Sci. Rsch. Fund award, Ministry Human Resources, 2000, Sichuan U. Outstanding Doctoral Thesis Recognition medal, Sichuan U., 2003, Province Sci. Technol. Progress award, Hunan, 2005; Travel grant, Nat. Eye Inst., 2007. Mem.: Am. Soc. Mass Spectrometry, Soc. Neurosci., Human Proteome Orgn., Assn. Rsch. Vision and Ophthalmology, Am. Assn. Cancer Rsch. Achievements include research in cancer proteomics, biomarkers and protein post-translational modification.

ZHANG, AMY YANYUN, cancer and health services researcher; arrived in U.S., 1989; d. Xiangnan Zhang and Yusheng Chen. BA, Peking U., Beijing, 1982; MS, Pa. State U., 1992, PhD, 1995. Agy. for Health Care Policy Rsch. NIMH postdoctoral fellow Sch. Pub. Health, U. Calif., Berkeley, 1996—98; sr. rsch. assoc. Case Western Res. U. Med. Sch., Cleve., 1999—2000, asst. prof. medicine, 2001—03, asst. prof. nursing, 2004—09, assoc. prof. nursing, 2009—. Translator: The Psychology of Emotion, 1986, The Interpretation of Dreams, 1987; contbr. articles to profl. jours. Grantee, Am. Cancer Soc., 2000, 2003, NIH, Nat. Cancer Inst., 2006, 2008. Office: Case Western Res Univ Sch Nursing 10900 Euclid Ave Cleveland OH 44106-4904 Business E-Mail: amy.zhang@case.edu.

ZHANG, BIN, research scientist; m. Sunny W. Sun; 1 child, Leo S. Sun. BS, Nanjing U. Sci. and Tech., 1993, MS, 1999; PhD, Nanyang Technol. U., Singapore, 2005. Rsch. assoc. Shanghai Jiaotong U., 1999—2001; tech. mgr. Huiming Automation Info. Tech. Co. Ltd, Shanghai, 2001—02; rsch. engr. Ga. Inst. Tech., Atlanta, 2005—. Vis. scholar Nanyang Technol. U., Singapore, 2007; assoc. edit. Internat. Jour. Fuzzy Logic and Intelligent Sys. Contbr. articles to profl. jour. Mem.: ASME, IEEE, Sigma Xi. Achievements include development of signal enhanced algorithms; iterative learning controls in time-frequency and multirate processing domains; physics-based and data-driven models advanced controls. Personal E-mail: ben.binzhang@gmail.com.

ZHANG, CHARLES C., financial planner; MA in Econs., Western Mich. U., 1991; MBA, Northwestern U., 2004. ChFC; CFP; CLU; chartered mutual fund counselor; cert. fund specialist. Sr. fin. advisor Am. Express Fin. Advisors, Inc., Kalamazoo, 1991—2007; sr. ptnr. Zhang Financial, 2008. Adj. prof. finance Western Mich. U. Mem. Am. Soc. CLU and ChFC, Inst. cert. Fin. Planners, Internat. Assn. Fin. Planning. Office: Zhang Financial 1302 W Milham Portage MI 49024 Personal E-mail: czhangcfp@yahoo.com.

ZHANG, CHI, engineer; s. Youkun Zhang and Jialing Zhao; m. Yujuan Zhang, June 9, 2004; 1 child, Isaac. PhD, Northeastern U., Boston, 2003. Asst. prof. Fla. Internat. U., Miami, 2003—06; staff engr. Juniper Networks, Sunnyvale, Calif., 2006—. Editl. bd. mem. Jour. Internet Engring., Greece, 2006—. Contbr. scientific papers to numerous profl. jours. Grant, Cisco Sys. Inc., 2004—06, NSF, 2005—06. Mem.: IEEE (session organizer & chair conf. networking, sensing and control 2006, session chair conf. internet monitoring and protection 2008), Phi Kappa Phi. Office: Juniper Networks 1194 N Mathilda Ave Sunnyvale CA 94089

ZHANG, CHUHAN, civil engineer, educator; b. Meizhou, Guangdong, China, Oct. 11, 1933; s. Zhuohu Zhang and Qingrong Yu; m. Guiqin Wang, Apr. 30, 1962; children: Qing, Jin. B in Hydraulic Structures, Tsinghua U., Beijing, 1957; grad., Tsinghua U., 1965. Instr., lectr. Tsinghua U., 1957-65, assoc. prof., divsn. chair, 1983-88, prof., divsn. chair dept. hydraulic engring., 1988-94, prof. engring., 1994, prof. water resources and hydropower engring. dept.; chief engr. Miyun Hydro Project, Beijing, 1976-78. Vis. scientist U. Calif., Berkeley, 1978—81; adj. prof. Concordia U., Montreal, Canada, 1988—; v.p. univ. grad. sch. com. Tsinghua U., 1993—97; mem. state com. South-North Trans-Basin Water Transfer; mem. adv. com. Nat. Sci. Found. China; mem. sci. and tech. com. Ministry of Water Conservancy China; academician Chinese Acad. Scis., 2001. Prin. investigator Seismic Analysis for High Dams, 1981; sec.-gen. (China US workshop) Earthquake Behavior for Arch Dams, 1986; editor, chair (Chinese Swiss workshop proceedings book) Soil-Structure Interaction, 1997; contbr. articles to profl. jours. Recipient China State Natural Sci. prize, 1999, State Outstanding Ednl. prize, State Sci. and Tech. Congress prize, Sci. and Tech. Advancement prize, State Edn. Commn., State Power Ministry. Mem. ASCE, Chinese Soc. Mechanics (hon.), Chinese Soc. Hydraulic Engring. Avocations: photography, travel. Office: Dept Hydraulic Engring Tsinghua U Beijing 100084 China Business E-Mail: zch-dhh@tsinghua.edu.cn.

ZHANG, DAN, engineering educator, researcher; arrived in Can., 1997, naturalized, 2001; s. Hongtao Zhang and Yu Li; m. Junmei Guo, Aug. 8, 1990; children: Mengjia, James William. BS in Mech. Engring., Dong Hua U., Shanghai, 1986, MS in Mech. Engring., 1994; PhD, Laval U., Quebec City, Can., 2000. Rsch. scientist NRC Can., London, Ontario, 2000—04; asst. prof. U. Ont. Inst. Tech., Oshawa, 2004—, assoc. prof., 2006—07, assoc. prof., programs dir., 2007—. Chair robotics & automation, Canada, 2009. Dir. Durham Region Mfrs. Assn., Oshawa, 2004; bd. dirs. Lake Ontario chpt. Profl. Engrs. Ontario, 2007—. Recipient Tchg. Excellence award, Faculty Engring. and Applied Sci., U. Ont. Inst. Tech., 2006, Rsch. Excellence award, 2008; grantee, Can. Rsch. Chair program, 2009—; Discovery grantee, Natural Scis. and Engring. Rsch. Coun. Can., 2006—. Mem.: ASME (Cert. Appreciation, Computers and Info. in Engring. Conf. 2004, 2006), IEEE (sr.), Soc. Mfg. Engrs., Can. Soc. for Mech. Engring., Materials and Mfg. Ont. (Indsl. fellow 2001—03). Achievements include patents pending for high accuracy parallel kinematic machine. Office: Univ Ontario Inst Tech 2000 Simcoe St North Oshawa ON Canada L1H 7K4 Office Fax: 9057213370. Personal E-mail: dan_zhang99@hotmail.com. Business E-Mail: dan.zhang@uoit.ca.

ZHANG, DONG-ER, medical educator; married. PhD, U. Houston, 1987. Asst. prof. Harvard Med. Sch., Boston, 1995—99; prof. Scripps Rsch. Inst., La Jolla, 1999—2007, U. Calif., La Jolla, 2007—. Achievements include research in blood cell differentiation and leukemia development. Office: Univ Calif San Diego 3855 Health Scis Dr Mail Stop 815 La Jolla CA 92093 Office Fax: 858-822-5433. Business E-Mail: d7zhang@ucsd.edu.

ZHANG, DU, engineering educator; b. Nanjing, Jiangsu, China; arrived in U.S., 1984; s. Wen-Tang Zhang and Xue-Wen Yu; m. Meiliu Lu; 1 child, Bryan. BS, Nanjing U., 1977, MS, 1982; PhD, U. of Ill., 1987. Lectr. Nanjing U., 1977—80, 1982—84; rschr. U. of Ill., Chgo., 1984—87; asst. prof. Calif. State U., Sacramento, 1987—89, assoc. prof., 1989—93, prof., 1993—, dept. assoc. chair, 1996—97, dept. grad. coord., 1997—98, dept. chair, 2004—. Mem. program com. various internat. confs., 1991—2006. Editor: (book) Machine Learning Applications in Software Engineering, Advances in Machine Learning Applications in Software Engineering; assoc. editor: Internat. Jour. Artificial Intelligence Tools, 2003—, guest editor: Internat. Jour. Software Engring. and Knowledge Engring., 2004, Software Quality Jour., 2005, Internat. Jour. Cognitive Informatics and Natural Intelligence, 2007, mem. editl. bd.:, 2005—; contbr. articles to prof. jours. and tech. reports in field, chapters to books. Recipient Chancellor's Student Svc. award, U. of Ill., 1986, Student Leadership Recognition award, U. of Ill. Alumni Assn., 1987, Nat. award, U.S. Achievement Acad., 1987, Outstanding Scholar award, Coll. of Engring., Calif. State U., Sacramento, 1998,

2004, Meritorious Performance award, Calif. State U., Sacramento, 1989, 1996. Mem.: ACM, IEEE (sr.; program chair 15th internat. conf. tools with artificial intelligence 2003, vice-program chair internat. conf. tools artificial intelligence 2003, gen. chair 16th internat. conf. tools with artificial intelligence 2004, internat. symposium on bioinformatics and bioengring. 2004, program co-chair internat. conf. info. reuse and integration 2004—06, 4th internat. conf. cognitive informatics 2005, program co-chair internat. conf. cognitive informatics 2005, 2007—08, SMC tech. com. on knowledge acquisition in intelligent sys., program co-chair internat. conf. software and knowledge engring. 2007—08), IEEE Computer Soc. (tech. coun. on software engring., multimedia computing com.), Upsilon Pi Epsilon, Phi Beta Delta. Achievements include research in A high-level Petri net model for definite clause logic programs; ZCZOS, a distributed operating system; Pr/T net model for planning; Pr/T net model for parallel query processing in deductive databases; Theory And Verification Methods For Knowledge Bases; Machine Learning Applications In Software Engineering. Avocations: travel, sports. Office: Calif State U 6000 J St Sacramento CA 95819-6021

ZHANG, GUOHAO (GARY), electronics engineer; s. Zhilin Zhang and Ailu Wang; m. Qun Zou; children: Johnny, Kenneth. PhD, Leeds U., 1996. Engr. Nanjing Electronic Device Rsch. Inst., Jiangsu, China, 1988—93; sr. engr. Epsilon Lambda Electronics Corp., Geneva, Ill., 1996—98; sr. prin. engr. Skyworks Inc., Irvine, Calif. Sr. engr. Calif. Amplifier Inc, Oxnard, Calif., 1998—2004. Contbr. scientific papers. Mem.: IEEE. Achievements include patents for multi-mode high efficiency linear power amplifier. Home: 4 Carlton Irvine CA Office: Skyworks Inc 5221 California Ave Irvine CA 92617 Personal E-mail: guohaoz@yahoo.com. Business E-Mail: gary.zhang@skyworksinc.com.

ZHANG, GUOQING, engineering educator; PhD, City U. Hong Kong, 2000. Cert. Engr., PEO, 2007. Assoc. prof. U. Windsor, Canada, 2005—. Office: Univ Windsor 401 sunset ave IMSE dept Windsor ON Canada N9B 3P4

ZHANG, HARRY X., environmental engineer; PhD, U. Va., Charlottesville. Cert. profl. engr., Va. State Bd., 2005. Prin. engr. and project mgr. Parsons Corp., Fairfax, Va., 2000—07; prin. engr. and indsl. water resources lead CH2M HILL Inc., Chantilly, Va., 2007—. Mem.: Am. Water Resources Assn. (chair, hydrology & watershed mgmt. techinal com. mem. 2002—).

ZHANG, HENG, research scientist, educator; s. Qixiu Zhang and Quanlu He; m. Ying Huang; 1 child, Jiyu. B in Engring., Ctrl. South U., 1982, M in Engring., 1986; PhD, U. NSW, 1999. Asst. to assoc. prof. Hunan U., Changsha, China, 1986—93, prof., 1999—; rschr. U. Newcastle, Australia, 1993—95; rsch. scholar U. NSW, Australia, 1995—99; postdoctoral rsch. fellow U. Conn., 1999—2001; sr. scientist NanoGroup Inc., Willington, Conn., 2001—. Contbr. over 100 sci. publs. in field. Recipient Second prize, Nat. Edn. Bd. of People's Republic of China, 1988, Third prize, Ministry of Mech. and Electronic Industry of People's Republic of China, 1992, Disting. Young Scientist, Ministry of Mech. Industry of People's Republic of China, 1992, Second prize for Sci. and Tech., 1996, 1998, Third prize for Sci. and Tech., 1996, Second prize, Bur. of Mech. Industry of People's Republic of China., 1999; Overseas Postgraduate Rsch. Scholarship, Dept. Edn. of Australia, 1993, scholarship, Australian Rsch. Coun., 1995, Postdoctoral fellowship, Australian Nat. U., 1999, Oversea Scholar fellowship, Ministry of Edn. of People's Republic of China, 2001. Mem.: Materials Rsch. Soc. (assoc.). Achievements include discovery of a large group (about 78) of novel rare-earth compounds R3T29M4B10, a few hundred of pseudocompounds, determination of the crystalline structure and magnetic structure of R3T29M4B10; invention of nanostructured magnetic ceramic and soft magnet composites with ultrafine components and high performance; design and development of exchange-spring coupled nanostructured hard and soft magnetic composite with high energy density at ambient and elevated temperatures; design and development of nanostructured ceramic coating technique for orthopedic and dental implants with various complicated surface profiles and geometries with high bioactivity; strong bonding and fast healing after implantation, innovation of doped nanocrystal hydroxypatite coating for orthopedic and dental implants with antibacterial function; which can significantly reduce the infection caused by implantation surgery; patents pending for plasma thermal spray making integrated oxide fuel cell and electrodes; innovation of nanostructured Sr1-1.5xYxTiO3 anode material for solid oxide fuel cell using a wet chemical method; invention of a novel nanostructured Pd-TM oxide ceramic catalyst system with higher stability for low-temperature methane combustion; achieving hydrogenization for titanium at low temperature; creation of mullite-insulating coating on the surface of silicon carbide whiskers with exceptional electrical insulating feature and mechanical property; discovery of ternary Cu-Ti-Zr and binary Zn-M (M = Nb, V, Ti, Zr) amorphous solids; development of innovation of novel Cu-Ni-Sn-P-Ce series glass films with super mechanical property; establishment of a modeling system to describe the formation and stability of Cu-P based glasses; and predict the amorphization by solid-state phase transition. Office: NanoGroup 156 J River Rd Willington CT 06279 Personal E-mail: hgzh@yahoo.com.

ZHANG, HONG (RICK), design engineer, researcher; b. Hancheng, Shaanxi, China, May 28, 1960; s. Runmin Zhang and Mingzhu Ma; m. Li Qu, Apr. 1, 1995; 1 child, Chi (Jim). PhD, Beijing U. Aero & Astro, 1992. Assoc. prof. Beijing Inst. Machinery Industry, 1992—95; post doctoral rschr. U. Minn., Mpls., 1998—2001; design engr. ADC Telecomm., Inc., 2001—02; sr. design engr. Princetel, Inc., Lawrenceville, NJ, 2002—. Presenter in field. Contbr. articles to profl. jours. Fellow, Nanyang Technol. U., Singapore, 1995—97. Achievements include patents for MEMS optical switch on a single chip and method; latching apparatus for a MEMS optical switch; apparatus and method for sensing switching positions of a MEMS optical switch; scanning apparatus; a new type of load balancing mechanisms for planetary gearing; off-axis fiber optic slip ring; anti-backlash planetary gearing for optic rotary joint; fiber optic polisher; two-channel, dual-mode fiber optic rotary joint; optic rotary joint using rotatable fiber. Avocation: ping pong/table tennis. Home: 5 Wayne Ct Plainsboro NJ 08536 Office: 1595 Reed Rd Pennington NJ 08534 Office Fax: 609-895-9552. Personal E-mail: mr_hongzhang@yahoo.com.

ZHANG, HONGTAO, research scientist, engineer; b. Yuzhou, Henan Province, China, Jan. 12, 1966; s. Songpeng Zhang and Zhuanying Liu; m. Huimin Li, Sept. 17, 1966; children: Zhiqi, Jenny, Michael, David. BS, Zhejiang U., Hangzhou, China, 1988, MS, 1990; PhD, U. Nebr., 2000. Rsch. asst. Zhejiang U., Hangzhou, China, 1988—91; editor China Electric Press, Beijing, 1991—94; vis. rsch. scholar Western Ky. U., Bowling Green, 1994—95; rsch. asst. U. Nebr., Lincoln, 1995—2000, postdoctoral rsch. assoc., 2000, rsch. asst. prof., 2000—03; lead engr. GEAE, 2003—. Editor: A Chinese-English-Russian Dictionary of Fossil-Fired Power Plant Terms, 1994; contbr. more than 30 papers to profl. publs. Recipient Outstanding Scholar award, NASA Nebr. Space Grant Program, 1998—2003; Milton E. Mohr rsch. fellow, U. Nebr., Lincoln, 1997—99, Martin C. Hemsworth fellow, 1999, Brooks rsch. fellow, 2000, Kwang-hua scholar, 1990, Zhu Kezheng fellow, 1991. Mem.: AIAA, ASME, Combustion Inst. Personal E-mail: zhanght101@yahoo.com.

ZHANG, HUI, researcher; b. Changchun, Jilin Province, China, Jan. 30, 1959; d. Zhongyao Zhang and Yaqing Gao; m. Xiaoping Zhu; children: Kateri Yanshan Zhu, Megan May Zhu. PhD, U. of Calif., Berkeley, 2003. Rsch. scholar U. of Calif., 1989—93, rsch. specialist, 1993—. Asst. prof. Tsinghua U., Beijing, 1986—89. Contbr. articles to profl. jours. Mem.: ASHRAE (Nevins Physiology & Human Environment award 2003—08). Home: 887 Camino Ricardo Moraga CA 94556 Office: UnivCalif 390 Wurster Hall UC Berkeley Berkeley CA 94720 Office Fax: 510-643-5571. Business E-Mail: zhanghui@berkeley.edu.

ZHANG, HUI, aerospace scientist; PhD, Boston U., 2008. Postodoc. fellow NASA Goddard Space Flight Ctr., Greebelt, Md., 2007—. Contbr. scientific papers. Mem.: AGU. Personal E-mail: zh7926@gmail.com.

ZHANG, JAMES XUEJIE, healthcare educator; s. Wudong Zhang and Xinde Huang; m. Cindy Zhang. BA, Fudan U., Shanghai, 1988; PhD, Northern Ill. U., DeKalb, 1999. Assoc. prof. Chinese U. of Hong Kong, 2001—03; dir. health econometrics U. Chgo., 2003—06, rsch. assoc., asst. prof., 2006—. Contbr. articles to profl. jours. Grantee, NIH, 1998—99, 2000—03, 2001—05. Mem.: Internat. Health Econs. Assn. (sci. com. 2006—), Acad. Health (Paper of Yr. Award com. 2007—, interest group adv. bd. 2006—). Office: U Chgo 5841 S Maryland Ave MC 2007 Chicago IL 60521 Office Fax: 773-834-2238. Personal E-mail: ktmg_chicago@yahoo.com.

ZHANG, JIAN, physics professor, researcher; PhD, U. NC, Chapel Hill, 2005. Cert. CyberKnife physicist Accuray, Calif., 2007. Postdoc. rsch. assoc. Dept. Radiation Oncology, U. NC, 2005—07, asst. prof., 2007—, adj. asst. prof., 2008—. Co-dir. U. NC CyberKnife Ctr., 2007—. Contbr. articles to profl. jours. Pres. Friendship Assn. Chinese Students and Scholars, U. NC, 2002—03. Recipient Grad. Student award, Material Rsch. Soc., 2004. Mem.: CyberKnife Soc. (CKS), Soc. Photo-optical Instrumentation Engrs., Am. Assn. Physicists in Medicine. Achievements include 5 patents and 1 pending patent application; development of nanotechnology based field emission x-ray technology. Office: UNC Chapel Hill Dept Radiation Oncology CB7512 101 Manning Dr Chapel Hill NC 27599-7512 Business E-Mail: jzh@physics.unc.edu.

ZHANG, JIANLONG, engineer; m. Yanyan Zheng. BS, U. Sci. and Tech. China, Hefei, Anhui, 1999; MS, Vanderbilt U., Nashville, 2001; PhD, U. Southern Calif., LA, 2006. Control engr. Advt. Com., Mountain View, Calif., 2006—. Pres. fellowship, U. Sci. and Tech. China, 1998. Mem.: IEEE. Achievements include patents pending for on-line advertising.

ZHANG, JIE, engineering educator; married. PhD, Purdue U., West Lafayette, Ind., 2004. Cert. profl. engr., Ohio, 2002. Lectr. Shanghai Jiao Tong U., 1995—97; asst. prof. N.Mex State U., Las Cruces, 2005—. Mem.: ASCE. Office: N Mex State Univ 3035 Espina St Hernandez Hall Rm 202 Las Cruces NM 88003-8001 Office Fax: 575-646-6049.

ZHANG, JIN, information educator; b. Zheng Zhou, Henan, China, Dec. 3, 1959; arrived in U.S., 1994; s. Shi Zhang and Lily Yang; m. Yi Hong, Aug. 26, 1987; 1 child, Tian Run. BS, Wuhan U., China, 1983, MS, 1986; PhD, U. Pitts., 1999. Prof. Wuhan U., 1986-95; asst. prof. U. Wis., Milw., 1999—2004, assoc. prof., 2004—. Author: Principle of Computerized Information Retrieval System Design, 1994; contbr. articles to profl. jours. Fulbright scholar U.S. Govt., 1994. Mem. Am. Soc. for Info. Sci. (Pratt-Severn Best Student Rsch. Paper award 1994). Avocations: music, reading. Office: U Wis Milw Bolton Hall 532 PO Box 413 Milwaukee WI 53201-0413 Office Phone: 414-229-2712. Office Fax: 414-229-6699. Business E-Mail: zhang@sois.uwm.edu.

ZHANG, JINFA, geneticist, educator; s. K. S. Zhang and K. B. Xiao; m. Xiaoping Jin; 1 child, Xin. Doctorate in Agronomy, Ctrl. China Agrl. U., Wuhan, 1993; PhD, U. Ark., Fayetteville, 1999. Instr. Ctrl. China Agrl. U., Wuhan, China, 1985—87, asst. prof., 1987—92, assoc. prof., 1992—98; vis. scholar U. Ark., Fayetteville, 1995—96, sr. rsch. asst., 1996—99, postdoc. rsch. assoc., 1999—2000, McGill U., Montreal, Quebec, Canada, 2000—01; molecular cotton breeder Monsanto Co., Leland, Miss., 2001—02; asst. prof. N.Mex State U., Las Cruces, 2002—07, assoc. prof., 2007—. Dir. cotton breeding and genetics lab, Ctrl. China Agrl. U., Wuhan, 1992—98. Editor cotton sci.; contbr. articles to profl. jours. Recipient First Pl. award, 2nd Nat. Young Scienstist Symposium, China Cotton Soc., 1993, Nat. Agrl. Sci. and Tech. Achievement award, Ministry Agr., China, 1994, Nat. sci. & Tech. Achievement award, Mininstry Sci. and Tech., 1995, Outstanding Grad., Cotton Inc. and Ark. State Support Com., 1999. Mem.: AAAS, Agronomy Soc. Am., Crop Sci. Soc. Am., Sigma Xi. Office: New Mexico State Univ Dept Plant and Environ Sci Las Cruces NM 88003 Office Fax: 575-646-6041. Business E-Mail: jinzhang@nmsu.edu.

ZHANG, JING, science educator; BS with honors, U. Sci. and Tech. Beijing, 1996; MS with honors, Beijing U. Aeronautics and Astronautics, 1999; PhD, Drexel U., Phila., 2004. Asst. prof. U. Alaska, Fairbanks, 2005—; USAF summer faculty NSF/EPCOR Career Assn., Alaska, 2008. Hon. faculty dept. athletics U. Alaska, Fairbanks, 2007. Office: U Alaska Dept Mech Engring Fairbanks AK 99775 Office Fax: 907-474-6141. Business E-Mail: jzhangg@alaska.edu.

ZHANG, JUN, research scientist, educator; s. Huanxin Zhang and Yingzhi Liang; m. Yansheng Wei, Aug. 19, 1989; 1 child, Muyuan. PhD, U. N.Mex, Albuquerque, 2000. Lectr. Taiyuan U. Tech., Shanxi, China, 1998—; rsch. investigator Abbott Labs., Abbott Pk., Ill., 2002—; CTO Shanxi Hightech Inst., Taiyuan, 2004—06. Contbr. scientific papers to rsch. publs. (Abbott Pres. Award, 2008). Recipient Pres. award, Abbott Labs., 2008, Outstanding award, 2008. Mem.: Am. Soc. Mass Spectrometry. Achievements include patents for ion mirror; research in salting-out assisted liquid, liquid extraction of drugs as a generic, rapid, environment-friendly way to prepare biological samples in the exposure evaluation; development of thorough strategy for accurately evaluating drug exposure in tissue.

ZHANG, LEI, physics professor; b. Shanghai, June 11, 1966; s. Guo Rui Zhang and Gua Zhen Dong; m. Qiuhong Zhao. MS, Fla. Internat. U., Miami, 1995, La. Tech U., Ruston, 1995; PhD, U. Tex., Arlington, 2000. Vis. asst. prof. physics Elizabeth City State U., NC, 2002—05; asst. prof. physics Winston-Salem State U., NC, 2005—. Mem. U. Tex. Sys. Student Adv. Coun., 1999—2000; pres. Grad. Student Coun. U. Tex., Arlington, 1999—2000. Mem.: Am. Phys. Soc. Achievements include development of novel nuclear methods to detect and analyze the change of electric density in polymer-dispersed liquid crystal (PDLC) materials. Home: 2112 Fiddlers Ct # G Winston Salem NC 27107 Personal E-mail: zhanglei90@hotmail.com. E-mail: zhangl@wssu.edu.

ZHANG, LI, medical researcher; d. Hongtu Zhang and Peixian Wang; m. Xi Feng, June 1, 1984; 1 child, Kevin Kun Feng. MD, Xi'an Med. Coll., 1982. Cert. dr. Medicine Xi'an Med. Coll., 1982, investigator in human subject rsch Nat. Inst. Health, 2007, ACLS provider Am. Heart Assn., 2007. Med. intern 2nd Affiliated Hosp. Xi'an Med. U., 1983—85, med. resident cardiology, 1985—87, chief med. resident, 1987—88, physician in charge cardiology, 1988—89; rsch. asst. LDS Hosp., Salt Lake City, 1992—96, rsch. assoc., 1996—2004, dir., multinational, multicenter studies sudden cardiac death diseases, 2004—08; assoc. prof. Lankenau Inst. Med. Rsch.; dir. cardiovasc. outcomes rsch. Main Line Health Heart Ctr., Wynnewood, Pa., 2008—. Mem. Am. Heart Assn., Dallas, 2004—; chair, electrophysiology Chinese Am. Heart Assn., Huston, Tex., 2009. Recipient Heart award, Gt. Wall Cardiology Congress, 2006; Scientist Devel. grant, Am. Heart Assn., 2007—. Mem.: Internat. Soc. Holter and Elecrocardiology(Rochester, NY), Chinese Am. Heart Assn., Heart Rhythm Soc., Cardiac Electrophysiology Soc.(Utica, NY), Am. Heart Assn. Democrat. Avocations: painting, dance, travel. Office: Main Line Health Heart Ctr 100 Lancaster Ave Wynnewood PA 19096

ZHANG, LI LARRY, engineer, researcher, educator; b. Beijing, Nov. 8, 1969; s. Qicheng Zhang and Liuying. MS in Nuclear Engring., MIT, 1996, MS in Elec. Engring and Computer Sci., 1996, PhD in Radiol. Scis., 1998. Tchg. asst. MIT, Cambridge, 1993-94, rsch. asst., 1994-98; sys. engr. Robotic Vision Sys., Inc., Hauppauge, NY, 1998; tech. mgr. Youngtech Inc., Edison, NJ, 1998—2001; project leader ADP Inc., Parsippany, NJ, 2001—03; pres. Internat. Innovative Imaging Sys., LLC, Piscataway, NJ, 2003—; prof. DeVry U., Westminster, Colo., 2005—; pres. NeoTech. LLC, Denver, 2008—. Dir. electronics Beijing Perfect Electronics Engring. Corp., Beijing, 1992-93; project mgr. AT&T, Bedminster, N.J., 1998-99. Mem. AAAS, IEEE, SPIE, Assn. for Computing Machinery, Health Physics Soc., Am. Nuclear Soc., N.Y. Acad. Scis., Sigma Xi. Achievements include creation and research for explosive detection and nuclear medicine imaging. Avocations: hiking, travel, movies, Broadway shows, computer/internet surfing. Office: 1870 W 122nd Ave Westminster CO 80234 Office Phone: 732-801-4508. E-mail: lizhang@alum.mit.edu.

ZHANG, LIANFENG, chemical engineer; s. Fengrui Zhang and Shuting Liu; m. Lan Wang; 1 child, Mia. PhD, Himeji Inst. Tech., Japan, 2001. Engr. Shaanxi Inst. Environ. Rsch. and Monitoring Def. Sci. & Tech. Industry, Xi'an, China, 1988—93, Japan ALi Ltd. Co., Nagoya, Japan, 1993—96, Advanced UV inc., Cerritos, Calif., 2008—; postdoc. fellow U. Waterloo, Canada, 2001—07. Contbr. to profl. jours. (Kansai Chmn. award, 2000). Scholarship, Ministry of Edn., Culture, Sports, Sci. & Tech., Japan. Fellow: Profl. Engr. Ont., Can.; mem.: Assn. Chem. Profl. Ont., Can. Achievements include development of a new method to immobilize photocatalyst. Home: 9090 Moody st Cypress CA 90630 Office: Advanced UV inc 16350 Manning Way Cerritos CA 90703 Office Fax: 562-407-0399. Personal E-mail: tyou6@hotmail.com. Business E-Mail: lzhang@advanceduv.com.

ZHANG, LIN, research scientist; b. Anshan, China, Oct. 1, 1978; s. Yuantai Zhang and Xiugui Lin. BS, Tsinghua U., Beijing, China, 1997—2001, MS, 2001—04; PhD, U. So. Calif., LA, 2004—. Rsch. asst. Tsinghua U., 2001—04, U. So. Calif., 2004—. Contbr. papers to profl. jours. and pubs. Recipient Excellent Grad., Tsinghua U., 2001, Top-Ten Outstanding Grad. Students, 2003; scholar First Prize scholarship, Tsinghua U. & Chinese Acad. Scis., 2002, Tsinghua U., 2003, Asst. scholarship, U. So. Calif., 2004—. Mem.: IEEE, Optical Soc. Am. Achievements include research in polarization dependent coupling in photonic crystal fiber and slow light based optical buffers; reduction of pattern dependent signal distortion in slow light by detuning data channel; polarization splitting in photonic crystal fibers; pattern dependence of data distortion in slow light based optical buffers; modulation and demodulation of phase shift keying signals in micro- and nanophotorics and enabaled optical resonators; nonreciprocal coupling in asymmetric photonic crystal fibers; photonic crystal fibers with squeezed hexagonal lattice; patents for fiber gratings with sinusoidal chirps; dual-core photonic crystal fibers; invention of sinusoidally chirped fiber grating. Avocations: swimming, tennis. Office: Univ So Calif 3740 McClintock EEB 500 Los Angeles CA 90089 Office Fax: 213-740-8729. Business E-Mail: linzhang@usc.edu.

ZHANG, LIXIN, computer scientist, researcher; s. Qikui Zhang and Minyu Xu; m. Haiying Wang; children: Alena, Bailey. PhD, U. Utah, Salt Lake City, 2001. Rsch. staff U. Utah, Salt Lake City, 1999—2001, postdoc. rsch. assoc., 2001—03; rsch. staff mem. IBM Austin Rsch. Lab., Tex., 2003—, lead rsch. advisor, 2004—06. Program com. mem. Various Confs., 2002—08. Contbr. scientific papers. Recipient Invention Achievement award, IBM, 2005, Tech. Group award, 2005, Bravo award, 2006—08, Outstanding tech. achievement award, 2007—08. Mem.: IEEE (sr.).

ZHANG, LIXUAN, education educator; PhD, U. of North Tex., Denton, 2001—06. Asst. prof. Augusta State U., Augusta, Ga., 2008—09, Coll. of Charleston, Charleston, SC, 2006—08.

ZHANG, LUWEN, virologist; s. Runxiang and Peizhi Zhang; m. Jie Li; 1 child, Leon Li. PhD, U. Kans. Med. Ctr., 1993. Prof. U. Nebr., Lincoln, 2001—. Achievements include discovery of important cellluar gene, IRF-7. Home: 7031 South 30th Pl Lincoln NE 68516

ZHANG, MEI, pharmaceutical executive, researcher; b. Changshou, Chongqing, China, June 14, 1965; s. Lieming Zhang and Jiping Zou; m. Mei Sun, Feb. 16, 1965; 1 child, Cindy Peiwen. MD, West China Coll. Medicine, Sichuan U., Chengdu, China, 1988, PhD, 1993. Assoc. rsch. prof. Shanghai Inst. Pediat. Shanghai Jiao Tong U., 1993—97; rsch. fellow NIH, Bethesda, Md., 1997—2003; instr. Mass. Gen. Hosp. Harvard Med. Sch., Charleston, 2003—04; sr. scientist Synta Pharmaceuticals, Lexington, Mass., 2004—. Avocations: art, writing, photography, calligraphy, poetry. Office: Synta Pharmaceuticals 125 Hartwell Ave Lexington MA 02421 Personal E-mail: mei.zhang.m@gmail.com. Business E-Mail: mzhang@syntapharma.com.

ZHANG, MING, business and management consultant; b. Jiangsu, China, 1962; arrived in U.S., 1988; m. Jiping Wu, 1993; children: Oak, Sky. BA, Nanjing U., China, 1983, MA, 1986; cert., Johns Hopkins U.-Nanjing U., 1987; PhD, Purdue U., West Lafayette, Ind., 1994. Rsch. fellow Nat. Def. U., Washington, 1994—97; rsch. analyst Libr. Congress, Washington, 1995—97; cons. Carnegie Endowment, Washington, 1998—99; non-resident sr fellow Atlantic Coun. US, Washington, 2000—; dir. rsch. IHS Internat., Arlington, Va., 1998—2004; owner, pres. Crossroads Initiative LLC, Va., 2002—. Spkr. in field. Author: Major Powers at a Crossroads, 1995, China's Changing Nuclear Posture, 1999, A Triad of Another Kind, 1999. Grantee Tchg. grant, Rockefeller

Bros. Fund, 1991, Travel grant, Am. Polit. Sci. Assn., 1993, Rsch. grant, NDU Found., 1994—97. Avocations: basketball, travel. Office Phone: 703-264-9080. Personal E-mail: mingzhang28@aol.com.

ZHANG, MING, medical educator; MD, PhD, U. Iowa. Faculty, comm. disorders and otolaryngology Tex. Tech. U. HSC, dir. Ctr. Functional Brain Mapping and Cortical Studies. Contbr. scientific papers. Named Tchr. of Yr., U. Student Senate, 2002—03, Outstanding Faculty, 2004—05. Achievements include developing an approach using sound to modify tinnitus-related cortical areas in the brain and to objectively assess the areas; developing cell lines that can generate stereocilia. Business E-Mail: ming.zhang@ttuhsc.edu.

ZHANG, NENGLI, research scientist; b. Sichuan, China, Jan. 8, 1940; arrived in US, 1989; s. Sunxian Zhang and Huirong Xiong; m. Xiaohui Sun, Jan. 29, 1968; 1 child, Chi. BS equivalent in thermophysics, Tsinghua U., Beijing, 1962; PhD equivalent in thermophysics, Tsinghua U., 1984. Rsch. asst. Tsinghua U., Beijing, 1962—78, asst. prof., 1978—80; vis. scholar U. Mich., Ann Arbor, 1981—83; assoc. prof. Tsinghua U., 1984—89; rsch. assoc. U. Mich., 1989—93; sr. rsch. assoc. NRC at NASA Lewis Rsch. Ctr., Cleve., 1994—98; sr. scientist Ohio Aerospace Inst. at NASA Glenn Rsch. Ctr., Cleve., 1998—. Concurrent deputy chief engr. Hai Hua New Tech. Devel. Ctr., Beijing, 1984—88; cons. Beijing Inst. of Rubber Industry, 1984—86, Da peng Sci.-Tech. Industry Ltd., Co., 1987—89. Author: Process System Engineering (in Chinese), 1982; contbr. articles various profl. jours. Recipient Achievements in Sci. award, Beijing Sci.-Tech. Com., 1983, Nat. Sci.-Tech. Progress award, Nat. Sci.-Tech. Com., 1985, Achievement in Sci. award, China State Edn. Com., 1988, Achievement in Natural Sci. award, Nat. Sci-Tech. Com., 1989, 3 NASA Tech Innovations awards, NASA, 1998. Mem.: Am. Assn. for Advancement of Sci., Am. Soc. of Mech. Engrs. Achievements include patents for innovative heat pipe systems using new working fluids; shadowgraphic method to measure contact angles with flow visualization in a sessile drop; research in thermal instability in evaporating sessile drops; identifying the profiles near three-phase contact line through caustic-diffraction of wave; convective instability in transient evaporating thin liquid layer; catastrophe optics applying to study of spreading of liquid drops. Avocations: music, gardening, sports. Home: 34671 Plantation Pl North Ridgeville OH 44039 Office: Ohio Aerospace Inst NASA Glenn Rsch Ctr 21000 Brookpark Rd Cleveland OH 44135 Office Phone: 216-433-8750. Business E-Mail: nzhang@grc.nasa.gov.

ZHANG, NING JACKIE, lab administrator, consultant; MD, PhD, MPH, Va. Commonwealth U., Richmond. Dir. informatics lab. U. Ctrl. Fla., Orlando, 2004—, grad. coord., 2005—. Cons. MD Anderson Cancer Ctr., Orlando, 2009—. Grantee, NIH, 2003—09. Fellow: Grantmaker Aging. Achievements include research in nurse staffing & quality of care in nursing homes. Office: Univ Ctrl Fla 3280 Progress Dr Orlando FL 32826 Business E-Mail: nizhang@mail.ucf.edu.

ZHANG, QING, language educator; married. PhD, Ball State U., Muncie, Ind., 1997. Asst. prof. Chinese Ball State U., 2001—. Faculty advisor China Club. Mem.: CLTA. Achievements include research in in comparative linguistics.

ZHANG, QINGCHUN, research scientist; b. Pizhou, Jiangsu, China; married. PhD, U. SC., Columbia, 2001. Cert. in elec. engring., SC, 2001. Rsch. scientist CREE, Inc., Durham, NC, 2005—. Achievements include patents in field. Home: 108 Hickorywood Blvd Cary NC 27519 Office: CREE Inc 4600 Silicon Dr Durham NC 27703 Business E-Mail: jon_zhang@cree.com.

ZHANG, SHENG, computer scientist, researcher; married. PhD, Nat. U. Singapore, 2006. Rschr. UCSB, Santa Barbara, Calif., 2006—. Mem.: IEEE. Achievements include patents for combining image rendering and machine learning to improve the robustness of face recognition. Business E-Mail: zhangs@ece.ucsb.edu.

ZHANG, SHENGLIANG, materials scientist; b. Zhangjiagang, Jiangsu Province, China, May 21, 1964; s. Xiangxing Zhang and Yongdi Wang; m. Qian Zhou, Mar. 20, 1993; 1 child, Gloria. BS, Nanjing U., 1984, MS, 1987; PhD, U. Rochester, 2001. Vis. rschr. Kyoto U., 1986—88; lectr. Nanjing U., 1988—93; sr. project engr. Xerox Corp., Webster, NY, 1999—2001, tech. specialist, 2001—. Contbr. articles to profl. jours.; patents in field (Xerox Inventor's awards, 2003). Japanese Govt. Monbusho scholar, 1988. Mem.: AIChe, ASM Internat., Materials Rsch. Soc. Avocations: fishing, hiking. Office: Xerox Corp 800 Phillips Rd Bldg 111-30N Webster NY 14580 Home: 15 Barclay Square Dr Rochester NY 14618-3100 Personal E-mail: johnslz@yahoo.com. E-mail: john.s.zhang@xerox.com.

ZHANG, SHENGZHI, research scientist; PhD, Pa. State U., Univ. Pk., PA, 2007. Cert. computer network profl. China, 2005. Rsch. asst. Inha U., Inchon, Republic of Korea, 2006—07. Contbr. articles to profl. jours. IT Fellowships, Korea Govt., 2006—07, grant Rsch. Asst., School IST, 2007—. Office Phone: 814-441-1870. Business E-Mail: suz116@ist.psu.edu.

ZHANG, SHIBAO, electrical engineer; BS, Tsinghua U., Beijing, 1994, MS, 1997; PhD, Kans. State U., Manhattan, 2001. Sr. engr. PCORE Electric Co., Inc., LeRoy, NY, 2002—. High-voltage bushing expert. Contbr. scientific papers to profl. jours. Mem.: IEEE (sr.). E-mail: shibao.zhang@ieee.org.

ZHANG, SHISHAN, researcher; BS, Tsinghua U., Beijing, 1998; MS, Nat. U. Singapore, 2001; PhD, U. Houston, Tex., 2007. EIT Tex. Bd. Profl. Engrs., 2008. Rsch. asst. U. Houston, 2002—07; engr. Formosa Plastics USA, Point Comfort, Tex., 2007—. Contbr. articles to profl. jours. Mem.: AIChE, Materials Rsch. Soc., Am. Chem. Soc., Sigma Xi. Achievements include research in areas span molecular monolayers, polymer nanocomposites, nanoparticles and fabrication of nanoarrays, magnetic multilayers.

ZHANG, SHIWEI, physics professor, researcher; PhD, Cornell U., Ithaca, NY, 1993. Postdoc. rsch. assoc. Los Alamos Nat. Lab, N.Mex., 1994—95; u. postdoc. fellow and nsf cise postdoc. fellow Ohio State U., Columbus, 1996; prof. physics Coll. William and Mary, Williamsburg, Va., 1996—. Recipient Alumni award, Coll. William and Mary, 2001, Plumeri award, 2008; fellowship, NSF, 1995, Cotrell scholar, Rsch. Corp., 2000. Mem.: Am. Phys. Soc. Achievements include research in computational materials physics, monte carlo algorithms, parallel computations, development of novel methods to simulate quantum many-body systems. Business E-Mail: shiwei@physics.wm.edu.

ZHANG, SHU-XIN, neuroscientist; s. Chun Gan; m. Fengfa Huang, Feb. 25, 1977; children: Wei, Si. MD, Nanfang Med. U., Guangzhou, China, 1974, MS in Histology, 1983; PhD in Anatomy, Kochi Med. Sch., Japan, 1992. Tchg. asst. Nanfang Med. U., Guangzhou, Guangdong, 1974—85, lectr., 1985—87; asst. prof. Kochi Med. Sch., 1992—94; vis. scholar Ohio State U., Columbus, 1994—95; postdoc. rschr. St. Louis U., 1995—97; postdoc. fellow, rsch. assoc. U. Ky., Lexington, 1997—2002; rsch. scientist Spinal Cord Soc. Rsch. Ctr., Ft. Collins, Colo., 2002—. Author: (book) An Atlas of Histology. Scholarship, Japanese Govt., 1987—92, grant, Paralysis Project America, 2001—02. Mem.: Nat. Neurotrauma Soc. Achievements include research in scar ablation, tissue repair, axonal regeneration and functional recovery in chronically injured spinal cord of rat. Avocations: violin, calligraphy, drawing. Home: 6950 Barbuda Dr Fort Collins CO 80525 Office: Spinal Cord Soc Rsch Ctr 2401 Research Blvd Ste #206 Fort Collins CO 80526-1826 Office Fax: 970-484-3262. Personal E-mail: sxzhangp@hotmail.com. Business E-Mail: szhang@scs.cbeyond.com.

ZHANG, SONG, computer science educator; s. Zongdi Zhang and Jingzhen Wu; m. Jing Xu, June 1, 2007. PhD, Brown U., Providence, 2006. Asst. prof. Miss. State U., Starkville, 2006—. Contbr. articles to jours. publs. Recipient Best Poster award, Siggraph, 2006—; fellowship, Burroughs Welcome Fund, 2004—05, grant, NOAA, 2006—, Miss. State U., 2006, MAFES, 2007—08. Mem.: IEEE (Best Poster award 2008), Upsilion Pi Epsilion.

ZHANG, (MIKE) TAO, electrical engineer, researcher; arrived in U.S., 1997; s. Shaojun Zhang and Huaying Sun. MS in Mech. and Aerospace Engring., N.C. State U., Raleigh, NC, 1998; MS in Indsl. Engring. and Ops. Rsch., U. Calif., Berkeley, Calif., 2000, PhD in Indsl. Engring. and Ops. Rsch., 2001. Cert. in mgmt. of tech. Haas Sch. Bus. and Coll. Engring. U. Calif., Berkeley, 2000. Postdoctoral rsch. fellow U. Calif., Berkeley, 2001—02; sr. engr. Intel Corp., Portland, Oreg., 2002—03, group leader Shanghai, 2003—05, dept. mgr., 2005, staff engr. Phoenix, 2005—. Vis. assoc. prof. Tsinghua U., Beijing, 2003—04. Author: Modern Supply Chain Management, 2003; contbr. 3 chapters to books, over 50 articles to profl. pubs. Recipient Outstanding Achievement award, Flash Product Steering Com. Intel Corp., 2004, Assembly and Test Mfg. Achievement award, Intel Corp., 2004. Mem.: IEEE (co-chmn. tech. com. on semiconductor factory automation 2006—, assoc. editor, guest editor Trans.), Inst. Indsl. Engrs. (Outstanding Young Indsl. Engr. award), Berkeley Chinese Alumni Internat. Assn. (officer internat. com. 2003), Phi Kappa Phi. Office: Intel Corp 4500 S Dobson Rd Mail Stop: OC2-254 Chandler AZ 85248 Business E-Mail: mike.zhang@intel.com.

ZHANG, WEIMING, engineer; b. Chengdu, Sichuan, China, June 15, 1962; m. Dan Dan Wu. PhD, Kyoto U., Japan, 1991. Sr. engr. Murata Machinery Ltd, Kyoto, 1991—94; asst. prof. Osaka Inst. Tech., Japan, 1994—2006. Tech. specialist TRW Automotive, Livonia, Mich., 2006—08; engring. mgr. Robert Bosch LLC, Farmington Hills, Mich., 2008—09. Author: (book) Practical Design of Belt Transmission and Precision Conveying; contbr. scientific papers. Recipient Takagi award, Japan Soc. Precision Engring., 2003. Mem.: ASME, JSPE, JSAW, JSME, SAE. Achievements include patents for yarn take-up machine. Home: 17151 Black Pine Dr Northville MI 48168 Office: MKP Structural Design Assoc Inc 6869 Marshall Rd Dexter MI 48130 Personal E-mail: chiyo62@comcast.net. Business E-Mail: david.chiyo@mkpsd.com.

ZHANG, XIAODONG, oceanographer, educator; s. Huanxin Zhang and Weihua Chen; m. Hong Xu; 1 child, Ella Jiayi. BS, Nanjing U., 1989; PhD, Dalhousie U., Halifax, Nova Scotia, Can., 2002. Assoc. prof. U. ND, Grand Forks, 2007—, asst. prof., 2003—07; rschr. Ocean U., Qingdao, Shandong, China, 1989—96; vis. scientist Tokai U., Shimizu, Shizuoka, Japan, 1994. Rsch. grants, NASA, 2003—08, USDA, 2008. Mem.: AAAS, IEEE, Am. Geophys. Union, Optical Soc. Am., Sigma Xi. Achievements include development of web-based remote sensing database. Office: Univ ND 4149 Univ Ave Stop 9011 Grand Forks ND 58202-9011 Office Fax: 701-777-2940. Business E-Mail: zhang@aero.und.edu.

ZHANG, XIAOYU, science educator; b. Nanxi, Sichuan, China, Feb. 27, 1973; s. Chi Zhang and Caijun Nie; m. Jia Le; 1 child, Rudy. PhD, U. Tex., Austin, 2001. Asst. prof. Calif. State U., San Marcos, 2002—08, assoc. prof., 2008—. Mem.: Sigma Xi. Office: Calif State Univ San Marcos 333 Twin Oaks Valley Rd San Marcos CA 92096

ZHANG, YADONG, medical researcher; b. Wuxue, Hubei, China, June 8, 1965; s. Xuefu Zhang and Xiurong Zheng; m. Meiqiao Lu, Aug. 15, 2001; 1 child, Huanran. BS in Medicine, 3rd Mil. Med. U., Chongqing, China, 1987, MS in Immunology, 1993; PhD in Immunology, Peking U., Beijing, 1996. Postdoc. fellow Acad. Mil. Med. Scis., Beijing, 1996—98, asst. prof., assoc. prof., 1998—2003; assoc. prof. Chinese Acad. Scis., Shanghai, 2003—05; rsch. fellow Harvard Med. Sch., Boston, 2006—07; regular fellow Ctrs. Disease Control, Nat. Inst. Occupl. Safety and Health, Morgantown, W.Va., 2007—. Nominee Charles C. Shepard Sci. award, Ctrs. Disease Control, Nat. Inst. Occupl. Safety and Health, 2006. Mem.: Chinese Soc. Immunology. Home: 1500 Charles St Apt 5 Morgantown WV 26505 Office: Ctrs Disease Control Nat Inst Occupl Safety and Health 1095 Willowdale Rd Morgantown WV 26505 Personal E-mail: yadong-zhang@hotmail.com. Business E-Mail: fha3@cdc.gov.

ZHANG, YAN ANTHEA, finance educator; b. China, 1971; PhD, U. Southern Calif., LA, 2001. Prof. Rice U., Houston, Tex., 2001—. Business E-Mail: yanzh@rice.edu.

ZHANG, YANLI, management consultant, educator; BA, Beijing U., China, 1996; MBA, Rutgers U., Newark, 2004, PhD, 2007. Cert. SAP, 1999. Econ. policy analyst Ministry Fgn. Affairs, China, Beijing, 1996—97; strategy analyst Lenovo Group, Beijing, 1997—98; mgmt. cons. Accenture Beijing Office, 1998—2001; asst. prof. Montclair State U., NJ, 2007—. Instr. Rutgers U., Newark, 2005—06. Contbr. articles to academic profl. jours., chapters to books (Doug Nigh award, 2007). Recipient Best Paper award, Acad. Mgmt., 2007, Dissertation Rsch. award, Rutgers Tech. Mgmt. Rsch. Ctr., 2006; Travel grant, Strategic Mgmt. Soc., 2005. Mem.: Assn. Japanese Bus. Studies, Acad. Internat. Bus., Acad. Mgmt., Mensa, Beta Gamma Sigma. Avocations: travel, reading, music. Office: Montclair State Univ 1 Normal Ave Montclair NJ 07043

ZHANG, YANPENG, physics professor; m. Chenli Gan; 1 child, Yuanfei. PhD, Xi'an Jiaotong U., 1995. Postdoc. fellow Xi'an Inst. Optics and Precision Mechanics, Chinese Acad. Sci., 2000—01; special-term prof. Xi'an Jiaotong U., 2001—; postdoc. fellow Physics Dept., U. Conn., Storrs, 2001—04; PhD student advisor Xi'an, 2005—; rsch. assoc., dept. physics U. Ark., Fayetteville, 2005—08. Contbr. scientific papers (Numerous awards). Communist. Office Fax: 029-82668643ext.2731. Business E-Mail: ypzhang@mail.xjtu.edu.cn.

ZHANG, YANWEN, physicist; PhD in Sci., Beijing Normal U., 1999; PhD in Engring. Physics, Lund U., Sweden, 1998. Asst. prof., divsn. ion physics Uppsala U., Sweden, 2000—02; staff scientist Pacific NW Nat. Lab., Richland, Wash., 2003—; guest prof. Peking U., 2006—. Recipient Outstanding Young Alumnae award, Beijing Normal U., 1990, Hon. Docent award, Lund U., Sweden, 2004, Presdl. Early Career award for scientists & engrs., US Govt., 2005, Early Career Scientist and Engr. award, Office Sci., Dept. Edn., 2005, EMSL Dir. award, Pacific NW Nat. Lab., 2006. Mem.: AAAS, Materials Rsch. Soc. Achievements include attend the German American Frontiers of Engineering Symposium hosted by National Academy of Engineering and Alexander von Humbolt, 2008, German American Frontiers of science symposium; hosted by the US national academy of science and the Alexander Von Humboldt foundation, 2008; named to the advisory editorial board of nuclear instruments & methods in physics research, section B. Avocations: skiing, camping, hiking, hunting. Business E-Mail: yanwen.zhang@pnl.gov.

ZHANG, YAOXIN, engineer, researcher; b. Huangshi, Hubei, China, Jan. 27, 1975; s. Weiyang Zhang and Taichu Zhou; m. Hui Xiong, May 9, 1999; 1 child, Luke Xi. PhD in Engring., U. Miss., 2004. Rsch. scientist U. Miss., University, 2004—08. Mem.: ASCE. Office: Univ Miss 102 Carrier Hall University MS 38677 Business E-Mail: yzhang@ncche.olemiss.edu.

ZHANG, YA-QIN, computer software company executive; b. Taiyuan, China, Jan. 7, 1966; came to U.S., 1986; s. Jung-Fang Bi; m. Jenny Jian Wang, Apr. 28, 1989; 1 child, Sophie W. Zhang. BS, U. Sci. and Tech. China, Hefei, 1983, MS, 1985; PhD in elec. engring., George Washington U., 1989. Mem. tech. staff Contel Corp., Chantilly, Va., 1990-91; sr. mem. tech. staff GTE Corp., Waltham, Mass., 1990-95; dir. multimedia tech. of lab. Sarnoff Corp., Princeton, NJ, 1995—99; asst. mng. dir., mng. dir. Microsoft Rsch. Asia, 1999—2004; corp. v.p. mobile & embedded devices Microsoft Corp., Redmond, Wash., 2004—07, corp. v.p., rsch. & develop. in China, 2007—. Guest editor SPIE, 1996. Editor 8 books, 1995—; contbr. over 150 articles to profl. jours. and internat. confs. Coun. chair Ind. Fedn. Chinese Students and Scholars, 1989. Fellow IEEE (sr.; Indsl. Pioneer award; guest editor tech. jour. 1995, mem. editorial bd. Computer Press 1997, editor-in-chief Circuits & Systems for Video Technology 1997); mem. ISD, ITU, Eta Kappa Nu (Outstanding Young Elec. Engr. award 1997, Engr. of Yr. 1997). Achievements include the building of several products in videophone, digital TV and satellite communications; patentee in field. Office: Microsoft Corp 1 Microsoft Way Redmond WA 98052-6399

ZHANG, YEJIA (ZHANG YEJIA), physiatrist; MD, Second Mil. Med. Univ., Shanghai, P.R. China, 1989; PhD, Univ. Penn., Phila, Pa., 1997. Rsch. asst., dept. parasitology Second Mil. Med. Univ., Shanghai, P.R. China, 1989—91, Univ. Penn., 1991—93, rsch. asst., grad. group cell and devel. bio., 1993—97; intern, transitional residency St. Francis Hosp., Evanston, Ill., 1997—98; post-doctoral fell., dept. pathology, dept. dermatology Northwestern Univ., 1998—99; resident, dept. phys. medicine, rehab. Univ. Rochester, 2000—02, chief resident, 2001; resident, dept. phys. medicine, rehab. Rush Univ., 1999—2000, instr., dept. phys. medicine, rehab., 2002—. Tchg. asst. Second Mil. Med. Univ., Shanghai, P.R. China, 1989—91; rschr. Thomas Jefferson Univ., Phila., 2006—08. Contbr. articles to numerous profl. jours. Named to Top Doctor's, Chgo. Mag., 2009; Rsch. fellow, NIH, 1998—99, 2002—05. Mem.: Am. Acad. Phys. Medicine and Rehab., Am. Acad. Academic Psychiatrists. Office: Midwest Orthopaedics at Rush 1 Westbrook Corp Ctr Ste 240 Westchester IL 60154 Business E-Mail: yejia_zhang@rush.edu.*

ZHANG, YIMIN, researcher; b. Shengzhou, China, Dec. 27, 1964; married. PhD, U. Tsukuba, Japan, 1988. Asst. prof. Southeast U., Nanjing, China, 1988-89; sr. mgr. Oriental Sci. Lab., Yokohama, Japan, 1989-95, Comm. Lab., Kawasaki, Japan, 1995-97; rschr. Adaptive Comm. Rsch. Labs., Kyoto, 1997—98; rsch. assoc. Villanova (Pa.) U., 1998—2003, rsch. assoc. prof., 2003—. Contbr. articles to profl. jours.; patentee in field. Mem. IEEE (sr., assoc. editor jour. Franklin Inst.). Office: Villanova U Dept Elec & Computer Engr Villanova PA 19085

ZHANG, YING, science educator; s. Shuwen Zhang and Shulian Deng; m. Fei Wang. BS, MS, U. Tex., Arlington, PhD, 2008. Tchg. and rsch. asst. U. Tex., 2004—08; asst. prof. Monmouth U., West Long Branch, NJ, 2008—. Hermann's scholarship, U. Tex., 2008. Office: Monmouth Univ 400 Ceder Ave West Long Branch NJ 07764 Business E-Mail: yzhang@monmouth.edu.

ZHANG, YONG, physicist, researcher; s. Wen Zhang and Wen-Zhen Chen; m. Yuan Zhang; children: Sunny Yao, Lisa Peng. BS, 1982; MS, Xiamen U., Fujian, 1985; PhD, Dartmouth Coll., Hanover, NH, 1994. Sr. scientist Nat. Renewable Energy Lab., Golden, Colo., 1997—. Mem.: MRS, APS. Achievements include discovery of total & negative refraction in real crystals for ballistic electrons & light; first to observe exciton polariton emission in fully ordered inorganic-organic hybrid crystals; discovery of zero-thermal expansion in inorganic-organic hybrid crystals; design of quantum coaxial cables for solar energy applications. Office: Nat Renewable Energy Lab 1617 Cole Blvd Golden CO 80401 Office Phone: 303-384-6617. Business E-Mail: yong_zhang@nrel.gov.

ZHANG, YOUXUE, geology educator; b. Huarong County, Hunan, China, Sept. 17, 1957; came to U.S., 1983; s. Zaiyi Zhang and Dezhen Wu; m. Zhengjiu Xu; children: Dan, Ray. BS in Geol. Scis., Peking U., Beijing, 1982; MA in Geol. Scis., Columbia U., 1985, MPhil, 1987, PhD in Geol. Scis., 1989. Grad. rsch. asst. Columbia U., NYC, 1983-88; postdoctoral fellow Calif. Inst. Tech., 1988-91; asst. prof. geology U. Mich., Ann Arbor, 1991-97, assoc. prof., 1997—2004, prof., 2004—. Contbr. articles to profl. jours. Named Young Investigator, NSF, 1994. Fellow: AAAS, Geol. Soc. Am.; mem.: Am. Geophys. Union, Geochem. Soc. (F.W. Clarke medal 1993), Mineral. Soc. Am., Sigma Xi. Office: Dept Geol Sci U Mich Ann Arbor MI 48109-1005 E-mail: youxue@umich.edu.

ZHANG, YU, medical researcher; m. Jin Yi. MD, Nagoya U. Sch. Medicine, Japan; PhD, Nagoya U. Sch. Medicine, 2003. Rsch. assoc. Nagoya U. Sch. Medicine, 1999—2004; asst. specialist iii CIND, VAMC and UC, San Francisco, 2004—. Office: CIND VAMC and UC San Francisco Mail Stop 114M 4150 Clement St San Francisco CA 94121

ZHANG, YUHONG, mechanical engineer, researcher; PhD, U. Del., Newark, 2004. Rsch. asst. U. Del., Newark, 2000—04, rsch. assoc., 2004—; control systems engr. John Deere. Mem.: IEEE, ASME (program chair Del. sect. 2005—, chair 2006—), Sigma Xi. Office: Univ Del Rm 218 101 Acad St Newark DE 19716 Home Fax: 302-831-8525. E-mail: yhzhang@udel.edu.

ZHANG, ZHONGQI, chemist; arrived in U.S., 1989, naturalized, 2003; m. Rong Wang, Dec. 25, 1990; children: Justin R., Wesley S. PhD, Purdue U., 1990—95. Postdoctoral rsch. assoc. Nat. High Magnetic Field Lab., Tallahassee, 1995—97; scientist Amgen, Thousand Oaks, Calif., 1997—. Mem.: Am. Chem. Soc., Am. Soc. for Mass Spectrometry. Achievements include invention of techniques in mass spectrometry based peptide sequencing; research in quantitative prediction of peptide tandem mass spectrum; invention of method for gradient elution in micro-flow liquid chromatography; first to new technique for studying protein structure using hydrogen exchange and mass spectrometry; invention of new method for charge state deconvolution in electrospray mass spectrometry; development of software for automated mining of mass spectrometric data; research in peptide conformation by collision-induced dissociation. Office: Amgen One Amgen Ctr Dr Thousand Oaks CA 91320 Personal E-mail: zzhang@amgen.com.

ZHANG, ZHU-MING, medical educator; d. Yun Zhang and Min Zhou; m. Xiao-yuan Wang, 1978; 1 child, Wei Wang. MD, Jinan Med. Sch., Shandong, China, 1974; MPH, Capital Med. U., Beijing, 1986. Physician Shandong Hosp., Jinan, Shandong, China, 1974—79; physician and med. ofcl. Haidian Hosp. and Bur. Health, Beijing, 1980—83; grad. student Capital Med. U., Beijing Inst. Heart Lung and Blood Vessel Diseases, 1983—86; attending physician Beijing Inst. Heart, Lung and Blood Vessel Diseases and An-Zhen Hosp., Beijing, 1986—88; instr., divsn. hypertension and endocrinology, dept. medicine U. Miss. Med. Ctr., Jackson, 1988—89; sr. rsch. assoc., assoc. dir., electrocardiogram reading ctr., dept. epidemiology and pub. health U. Miami Sch. Medicine, Fla., 1989—97; rsch. assoc., asst. dir., epidemiol. cardiology rsch. ctr., divsn. pub. health scis. Wake Forest U. Sch. Medicine, Winston-Salem, NC, 1997—2007; asst. prof., assoc. dir. epicare epidemiology cardiology rsch. ctr., divsn. pub. health scis., Wake Forest U. Sch. Medicine, 2008—. Contbr. articles to profl. jours. Mem.: Chinese Medicine Assn., Am. Heart Assn., Phi Beta Delta. Home: 5185 Laurel View Dr Winston Salem NC 27104 Office: Wake Forest Univ Sch Medicine 2000 W First St Ste 505 Winston Salem NC 27104 Office Fax: 336-716-0834; Home Fax: 336-794-1385. Personal E-mail: zzhang5185@yahoo.com. Business E-Mail: zmzhang@wfubmc.edu.

ZHAO, BINSHENG, physicist; b. Harbin, China, Apr. 10, 1963; arrived in U.S., 1994; d. Zhicheng Zhao and Wenxi Xue; m. Xiao Wang, June 6, 1987; 1 child, Lucy Wang. BEE, Nat. Inst. Tech., Changsha, China, 1984, MEE, 1987; DSc, Univ. Heidelberg, Germany, 1994. Lic. med. physicist in diagnostic radiological. Asst. rsch. engr. Chinese Acad. of Space Tech., Beijing, 1987—89; rsch. asst. German Cancer Rsch. Ctr., Heidelberg, Germany, 1991—94; instr. Cornell Med. Sch., NYC, 1997—2000, asst. prof., 2000—; asst. attending physicist Meml. Sloan Kettering Cancer Ctr., NYC, 2002—07, assoc. attending physicist, 2007—. Contbr. articles pub. to profl. jour. Recipient Women award, Pres.'s Coun. Cornell, 1997; grantee Whitaker Biomedical Engring. Rsch Grant, Whitaker Found., 1998—2001; Gottlieb Daimler-Karl Benz Fellowship, Gottlieb Daimler-Karl Benz Fellowship Found, Germany, 1991. Mem.: Chinese Assn. for Sci. and Tech. (bd. dirs.), Am. Assn. Physicists in Medicine. Achievements include development of computer image processing methods for automatic detection and diagnosis of lung cancer on computed tomography images; computerized assessment of response to therapies for lung, liver, and lymph node metasteses. Avocations: travel, tennis, stamp collecting/philately, reading. Office Phone: 212-639-8759.

ZHAO, CHONGHAO, neurologist, educator; MD, Guangzhou Med. Coll., China, 1986; PhD, Med. Coll. Va., 1994. Diplomate Am. Bd. Neurology, Ill., 2004, Am. Bd. Med. Acupuncture, Calif., 2002. Sr. lectr. UCLA, LA, 2001—; pres. Calif. Headache and Pain Ctr., Burbank; staff physician Providence St. Joseph Med. Ctr. Contbr. articles to profl. jours. Hon. chmn. physicians' adv. bd. Nat. Rep. Congl. Com., Washington, 2005—05; pres. So-Sue-Fang Ednl. Found., Guangzhou, China, 2003—05. Recipient Ronald Reagan Rep. Gold medal, Nat. Rep. Congl. Com., 2005; fellow, Cleve. Clinic Found., 2003. Mem.: Am. Acad. Pain Medicine, Am. Pain Soc., Am. Acad. Neurology, Am. Headache Soc. Achievements include research in Superficial cervical plexus block as an acute abortive therapy for intractable headache. Office: Calif Headache and Pain Ctr 201 S Buena Vista St Ste 238 Burbank CA 91505 Office Fax: 818-842-1638. E-mail: drzhao@chpci.com.

ZHAO, HONGBIN, artist; b. Shanghai, Aug. 15, 1952; arrived in Australia, 1988; s. Chi-Zhen Zhao and Xue-Min Chen; m. Mei-Jun Gu; 1 child, Hui-Jie. Student in Fine Arts Rsch., Shanghi Jiao Tong U., China, 1984-85; ArtsD (hon.), Yorker Internat. U., 2006. Art editor, designer Science Life Mag., Mcpl. Sci. and Tech. Assn., Shanghi, China, 1979-85; chief editor Modern New Products Pictorial, Shanghi U. Tech., China, 1985-88; freelance artist Warrandyte South, Australia, 1988—. Art works pub. in nat. and internat. newspapers, mags. and books including Portraits of Australia, 1992, 50 Australian Artists, 1994, Dictionary of the Achievements of World Chinese Artists, 1994, The Paintings of Zhao Hongbin, 1997, Zhao Hongbin, Monet of the Orient, 1999, The Overseas Oil Painter of China-Zhao Hangbin, 2008; art calendars include Emotion of the Native Land, Blossom, 1984, The Sun, 2004; limited edition art prints: Spring, The Beach, 2005; one man shows include 48 in Australia, Japan, China, Singapore, Indonesia, Taiwan; group shows include China Nat. Art Gallery, Shanghai Nat. Art Gallery of Art, 1977-85, Victoria Art Ctr., 1991, Sydney Opera House (Doug Moran Nat. Portrait Prize top four finalists), 1992, Australian Nat. Maritime Mus., 1993, Chinese War Meml. Mus., 1993, Internat. Exhbn., London (award winning), 1993, Nat. Gallery Victoria, Australia, 1992, 94, Art Gallery of New South Wales (Archibald prize finalist), 1994, Art Gallery of South Australia, 1995, New Parliament House, Canberra, 1995, Shanghai World Trade Ctr., 1997-99, Dr. Sun Yet-Sen Meml. Hall, Taipei, 1997. Recipient cert. of Hon. Shanghai Mcpl. Gov., 1986, Macquarie award 2000, 1994, Ernest Henry Meml. Art Show 1st prize, 1992-94, Dick Ovenden Meml. Art show first prize, 1991, Victor Harbor Art Exhbn. first prize, 1991, Mulcahy Mazda award, 1991, Omega Contemporary Art award Royal Overseas League, 1992, Bronze medal China Famous Figures Works Exbhn. of Arts Circles, 1994. Fellow Internat. Biog. Assn. U.K. (life); mem. Chinese Celebrity's Assn. Avocations: dance, poetry, chinese calligraphy. Office Phone: 61-2-411613886. Personal E-mail: benzhao888@hotmail.com.

ZHAO, JIANLIANG LEON, computer scientist, educator, computer scientist, researcher; b. Xinji, Hebei, China, Nov. 24, 1953; married. PhD, Haas Sch. Bus., Berkeley, Calif., 1992. Asst. prof. Coll. William and Mary, Williamsburg, Va., 1992—95; computer scientist Lawrence Berkeley Nat. Lab., Berkeley, 1995—96; asst. prof. Hong Kong U. Sci. and Techn., Hong Kong, China, 1996—99; assoc. prof. U. Ariz., Tucson, 1999—. Mem.: Assn. Info. Sys. Achievements include patents for cool storage supervisory controller.

ZHAO, LAN, mathematics professor; b. Jiang Jing, Sichuan, China, Oct. 10, 1956; d. Weimin Z.; m. Ping Ji; 1 child, Angela A. BS, Chongging U., 1982; MS, Brown U., 1985, PhD, 1989. Faculty mem. Dept. of Applied Math. Chongging (China) U., 1982-83; asst. prof. Sch. Mgmt. U. Mass., Amherst, Mass., 1988-89. Mem. The Math. Assn. Am. Home: PO Box 191 Providence RI 02901-0191

ZHAO, LIN, engineering educator; d. Shuzhen and Yonglian Zhao; m. Rencheng Cui; children: Eric Cui, Eileen Cui. BEE, Shandong U., Jinan, China, 1993, MEE, 1996; PhD in Elec. Engring., U. Western Ont., London, Can., 2006. Asst. prof. lectr. Shandong U., 1996—2001; rsch. and tchg. asst. U. Western Ont., London, 2002—06, postdoc. fellow, 2006—07; asst. prof. Gannon U., Erie, Pa., 2007—. Contbr. scientific papers (First Pl. award of Student Paper Competition, 2005, 2006), chapters to books. Recipient Outstanding Student award, Shandong U., China, 1993, award, Chinese Govt., 2004, Faculty Devel. award, Gannon U., 2007—08; Grad. Travel grant, U. Western Ont., 2005—06, Faculty Devel. grant, Gannon U., 2007. Mem.: IEEE, Electrostatic Soc. America. Achievements include development of prototype of the EHD gas pump sampling system on Mars; a sophisticated numerical model of the electrical corona discharge and the electrohydrodynamic (EHD) flow generated by the discharge; an EHD flow regime map; research in designed a mini-EHD thruster and successfully carried out the levitation experiment and the numerical simulation. Office: Gannon Univ 109 University Sq Erie PA 16541 Business E-Mail: zhao001@gannon.edu.

ZHAO, LI-RU, neuroscientist, educator; d. Jitian Zhao; m. Wei-Ming Duan; 1 child, Yi-Fei Duan. MD, Hebei Med. Sch., Shijiazhuang, Hebei, China, 1982; PhD in Neurosci., Lund U., Sweden, 2004. Cert. in medicine Chinese Academic Chinese Medicine, 1986. Tchr. asst. Hebei Med. Coll., 1983—84; instr. Beijing Coll. Acupuncture, Moxibustion and Orthop., Beijing, 1987—91; rsch. assoc. U. Minn. Med. Sch., Mpls., 2000—02; rsch. asst. prof. Northwestern U., Feinberg Sch. Medicine, Chgo., 2002—04; asst. prof. La. State U. Health Scis. Ctr., Shreveport, La., 2005—. Contbr. articles to profl. jour. Named Disting. Physician, Mex. Soc. Natural Medicine, 1991; numerous grants. Mem.: Internat. Soc. Cerebral Blood Flow and Metabolism, Am. Heart Assn., Soc. Neurosci., Am. Soc. Neural Transplantation (Therapy) and Repair (Travel awards 2000—01).

ZHAO, SHENGJIE, electrical engineer, computer engineer; BS in Signal Processing and Transmissions, U. Sci. and Tech. of China, Anhui, 1988; MS in Signal Processing and Digital Comms., China Aerospace Inst., Beijing, 1988; PhD in Elec. Engring., Tex. A&M U., 2004. Engr. China Aerospace Inst., 1991—96, sr. engr., 1997—99; mem. R&D staff Motorola-NCIC Joint R&D Lab. for Advanced Computer and Comms., Beijing, 1996—97. Presenter in field. Contbr. articles to profl. jours. Mem.: IEEE, IEEE Computer Soc., IEEE Comms. Soc., IEEE Signal Processing Soc. (reviewer). Office: Tex A&M U Dept Elec Engring # 384 College Station TX 77843-3128

ZHAO, TONG, management consultant; PhD, U. Md., Coll. Pk., 2003. Faculty rsch. asst., assoc. U. Md., Coll. Pk., 2003—05; sr. cons. Delta Consulting Group, Inc., Woodbridge, Va., 2005—. Mem.: ASCE, Sigma Xi. Office: Delta Consulting Group Inc 4330 Prince William Pky Ste 301 Woodbridge VA 22192

ZHAO, WAYNE (WEI), materials scientist, researcher, transmission electron microscopist; s. Zuyao Zhao and Dingru Liu; m. Yi (Merry) Sun, Jan. 28, 1992; children: Allen Aquila, Andrew Brenton. B in Engring., Harbin Inst. Tech., 1987; M in Engring., NE Forestry U., 1989; PhD, U. Tenn., 1999. Asst. prof. Tianjin U., China, 1989—91, lectr., prin. investigator, 1992—95; postdoc. rsch. faculty U. Pa., Phila., 1999—2001; sr. TEM engr. Infineon Tech. Richmond, Sandston, Va., 2001—03; TEM analyst Internat. Sematech, Austin, Tex., 2003—04; staff scientist, supr. electron microscopy and particle physics group, project mgr. particle physics Kerr McGee Chem., LLC, Oklahoma City, 2004—. Grad. tchg. and rsch. asst. NE Forestry U., Harbin, 1987—89; grad. rsch. asst. U. Tenn., Knoxville, Tenn., 1996—99. Contbr. articles to profl. jours. Mem.: Microscopy Soc. Am., Materials Rsch. Soc. Achievements include discovery of stacking sequence effects on mechanical performance for a plain-weave Nicalon fiber-fabric reinforced SiC ceramic-matrix composite; first to computer-aided modeling on effects of lamina stacking sequence and laminate layup for plain-weave Nicalon/SiC ceramic-matrix composite; introduce SEM/XEDS linescan technique to semi-quantify fiber/matrix interfacial oxidation behavior for a Nicalon/SiC ceramic-matrix composite; discovery of fiber orientation effects on mechanical properties for a crow-foot woven Nextel fiber-fabric reinforced Blackglas low-cost ceramic-matrix composite; first to initiate combined SEM/XEDS elemental mapping, ultrasonic, and x-ray computed tomography characterization on fiber and void distributions in a crow-foot woven Nextel/Blackglas ceramic-matrix composite; research in atomic-scale high-resolution transmission electron microscopy in nanometer semiconductor wafer process development; analytical transmission electron microscopy in physical failure analysis for nanometer semiconductor wafer and device process integration; materials science issues in advanced metallization for nanometer semiconductor wafer integration; development of advanced surface coatings to nanometer titanium dioxide pigment and particle physics; first to introduce polycrystallined diamond compact and tungsten carbide composite blank onto woodworking tools in China; research in synthesis of diamond thin film by combustion flames techniques. Personal E-mail: wayne_zhaowei@yahoo.com.

ZHAO, WEI, medical researcher; s. Zhao and Fu. PhD, U. Fla., Gainesville, 2005. Asst. mem. St Jude Children's Rsch. Hosp., Memphis, 2007—. Office: St Jude Children's Rsch Hosp 262 Danny Thomas Pl Memphis TN 38105 Business E-Mail: wei.zhao@stjude.org.

ZHAO, WENMING, retired biochemistry and molecular biology educator; b. Xi-Xiang County, Shaanxi province, China, Jan. 24, 1938; s. Fa-Ke Zhao and Yuan-Hui Yu; m. Zhi-Hui Hu, Jan. 19, 1963; 2 children: Meng, Yuan. BS, Northwestern Coll. Agrl., 1960, MSc, 1964. Asst. Northwestern Coll. Agrl., Yang-Ling, China, 1960-61, tchr., 1974-93, Shanxi Labour U., Dai-Yuan, China, 1965-70, Zhou-Zhi Middle Sch., China, 1971-73, Xi'an Jiaotong U., China, 1994—; ret. Vice dean of studies Shanxi Labour U., 1965-66; dir. tchg. Northwestern Agrl. U., 1990-93; dir. inst. Xi'an Jiaotong U., 1994-98; vice-dir. Shaanxi Biochem. Soc., 1995-2005; vis. scholar dept. botany U. Durham, Eng., 1981-83; vis. prof. dept. biol. sci. U. Calgary, Can., 1991. Author: Gene Engineering of Seed Proteins, 1995; editor: Teaching Material of Biochemistry, 1979, Teaching Material for Plant Molecular Biology, 1986; translator Introduction of Plant Biochemistry, 1988; contbr. over 200 articles to profl. jours. Mem. alliance Shaanxi Province, 1985. Recipient Prize State Coun. of China, 1992. Fellow Chinese Soc. of Biochemistry and Molecular Biology (dir. agrl. com. 1993-2009), Chinese Soc. of Cell Biology. Achievements include research in gene engineering of seed proteins and plant molecular biology. Avocation: reading. Office: Dept Biosci & Engring Sch Life Scis & Tech Xi'an Jiaotong U Xi'an 710049 China Home: 144 Sunrise Pl Vestal NY 13850 also: Xi'an Jiaotong U 151 Hao 1 Cun 34 Bldg Xi'an 710049 China Business E-Mail: wmzhao@mail.xjtu.edu.cn.

ZHAO, YONG, application developer, researcher; s. Xinghua Zhao and Wanling Long; m. Kun Jiao, Aug. 18, 1999; 1 child, Sophie. PhD, U. Chgo., 2000—07. Mgr. Beijing Telecom, 1997—2000; rsch. intern IBM T. J. Watson Rsch. Ctr., NYC, 2005; software devel. engr. Microsoft Corp., Redmond, Wash., 2007—. Contbr. chapters to books. Mem.: IEEE, Open Grid Forum, Assn. Computing Machinery. Achievements include patents pending for personal ads service system that allows users to take initiatives in deciding what ads they want to receive; development of a brand new workflow language, called virtual data language, to specify and execution millions of jobs on thousands of distributed computers; three open source grid systems, a swiftscript to specify and execute millions of jobs or thousands of distributed computers.

ZHAO, YONGLI, engineering educator; PhD, U. Iowa, Iowa City, 2006. Postdoc. rschr. U. Iowa; asst. prof. SCSU, St. Cloud, Minn., 2006—. Rsch. grant, SCSU, 2007. Mem.: APS.

ZHAO, YUSHENG, physicist; b. Kunming, Yunnan, China, Jan. 15, 1956; arrived in US, 1985; s. Liu-Quan Zhao and Ru-Xian Chen; m. Hong-Hong Zhu, Sept. 23, 1983; children: Holly Hao, Andrew Zigang. BS, Peking U., Beijing, 1982, MS, 1985; PhD, SUNY, 1992. Postdoctoral assoc. Calif. Inst. Tech., Pasadena, 1992—94; staff scientist Los Alamos (N.Mex) Nat. Lab., 1994—. Grantee, Los Alamos Nat. Lab. Directed R & D, 1999—2001, 2003—, Dept. of Energy, 2001—, Dept. of Def., Dept. of Energy, 2003, 2004; Exch. scholar, U. Calif., 1985—86. Mem.: Am. Geophysical Union (assoc.). Achievements include development of high pressure/temperature neutron diffraction; research in mineralogical modeling of Earth mantle; equations of state on minerals, metals, and ceramics; novel superhard materials of BC2N and its property characterization; hydrogen clathrate for Hydrogen storage; design of TAP-98, TAPLUS-2000, and ZAP pressure cells for integrated neutron/X-ray diffraction, laser spectroscopy, ultrasonic interferometry experiments; large-volume press for high P-T synthesis and diffraction; neutron diffractometer for high pressure research; discovery of pressure forming of Zirconium metallic glass; direct orthorhomic-to-cubic phase transition in NaMgF3 Perovskite; new quenchable superhar carbon form from high pressure carbon nanotube sample at 70 GPs; invention of high P-T synthesis of nanostructured superhard materials; patents for bulk superhard B-C-N nanocomposite compact; patents pending for superhard diamond / silicon-carbide nano-composite and for rapid formation of hydrogen clathrate hydrates. Office: Los Alamos Nat Lab Lansce-12 Ms-H805 Los Alamos NM 87545 Business E-Mail: yzhao@lanl.gov.

ZHAO, ZHEN, music educator; b. Tian Jin, China, Aug. 27, 1947; arrived in U.S., 1985; d. Tian Qi Zhao and Pei Ying Gong; m. Yang Zhong Zhang, Apr. 29, 1976; 1 child, William Wen Wei Zhang. MusB, U. Tex., 1991, MusM, 1994. Pvt. piano tchr., Austin, Tex., 1995—. Contbr. articles to profl. jours. Mem.: Nat. Guild Piano Tchrs., Music Tchrs. Nat. Assn., Tex. Music Tchrs. Assn., Austin Dist. Music Tchrs. Assn. Achievements include established the Zhen Zhao piano studio; her students have won numerous piano competitions. Avocations: ping pong/table tennis, tai chi, travel, photography. Personal E-mail: zhaozhen@austin.rr.com.

ZHAO, ZHONGKUI, researcher; b. Xinxiang, China, Oct. 20, 1977; s. Henyi Zhao and Fenglan Xu; m. Anji Lin. B, Dalian U. of Tech., 2000—00, M, 2002, PhD, 2005. Postdoctoral rsch. assoc. Ohio State U., Columbus, 2005—; assoc. prof. Dalian U. Tech. Contbr. articles to profl.jours., chapters to books. Recipient Outstanding Grad., Ednl. Office of Liaoning Province, 2005, Outstanding Grad. of Dalian City, China, Dalian Ednl. Office, 2005, Scholarship for Outstanding Grad., Dalian U. of Tech., 2005, Chinese Acad. of Sciences, 2004, Outstanding Grad. of Dalian City, Ednl. Office of Dalian City, 2004, Scholarship for Outstanding Grad., Dalian U. of Tech., 2003; Scholarship for Outstanding Undergraduate, 1998, 1997, 1999. Achievements include research in heterogeneous catalysis on Hydrogen production, catalytic synthesis of fine chemicals, environmental catalysis, Green Chemistry, Ionic Liquids, Biomass Transformation etc. Avocations: sports, reading. Office: Dalian Univ Tech State Key Lab Fine Chm 158 Zhongshan Rd, PO Box 40 Dalian 116012 China Personal E-mail: zzkdlut@yahoo.com.

ZHARIKOV, ALEXANDER NIKOLAEVICH, trade union federation executive; b. Michailov, Rjazan, Russia, Jan. 2, 1945; s. Nikolaj Philippovich and Claudia Egorovna (Gorodnicheva) Z.; m. Eva Svachova; children: Michail, Anette, Lucia. Student, Shipbldg. Inst., Leningrad, Russia, 1969. Sec. Student Orgn. Shipbldg. Inst., Leningrad, 1967-70; dir. student dept. Leningrad City Youth Orgn., Leningrad, 1970-71, sec., 1971-74; vice chmn. Com. Youth Orgns. USSR, Moscow, 1974-76; chmn. Student Coun. USSR, Moscow, 1976-78; v.p. Internat. Union Students, Prague, Czechoslovakia, 1978-84; officer Internat. Dept. Ctrl. Com. CPSU, Moscow, 1984-88; dir. internat. dept. All Union Ctrl. Coun. Trade Unions, Moscow, 1988-90; gen. sec. World Fedn. Trade Unions, Prague, 1990—2006. Co-author: International Union of Students, 1978. Mem. City Com. Leningrad Youth Orgn., 1970-71, sec., 1971-74; mem. Ctrl. Com. Youth Orgn. USSR, Moscow, 1978-84. Capt. Russian mil., 1962-66. Personal E-mail: evaaneta@seznam.cz.

ZHARIKOV, SERGEY IVAN, biologist, researcher; b. Moscow, Nov. 3, 1947; m. Alevtina D. Gurianov, July 26, 1974; 1 child, Sergey S. PhD, Inst. Biol. Physics USSR Acad. Scis., Moscow, 1977. Asst. prof. U. Fla., Gainesville, 1998—2005, assoc. prof., 2005—. Grant, Am. Heart Assn., 2002—05, Am. Lung Assn., 2002—07, Nat. Inst. Health, 2003—08, Fla. Dept. Health, 2004—07. Mem.: Soc. Free Radical Biology and Medicine, Am. Physiol. Soc., Am. Thoracic Soc. Avocations: travel, running.

ZHDANOV, BORIS, research scientist; MSc in Physics, Moscow State U., 1970, PhD, 1975. Assoc. prof. Moscow State U., 1988—99; vis. prof. USAF Acad., Colo., 1998—2000, sr. scientist, 2004—; prin. scientist Directed Energy Solutions, Inc., Colorado Springs, 2000—04. Business E-Mail: boris.zhdanov@usafa.edu.

ZHELEVA, TSVETANKA SPASSOVA, scientist; b. Sofia, Bulgaria, May 30, 1956; came to U.S., 1991; d. Spass Asenov and Violeta Georgieva Maximova; m. Dontcho Videv Zhelev, Aug. 14, 1978; children: Maria Dontcheva, Svilen Dontchev. BS in Physics, Sofia U., 1980, MS in Optics and Spectroscopy, 1981; PhD in Materials Sci. and Engring., N.C. State U., 1995. Jr. scientist Cen. Lab. Photo Processes Bulgarian Acad. Scis., Sofia, 1981-86, scientist Applied Mineralogy Inst., 1986-91; rsch. assoc. N.C. State U., Raleigh, 1991-95, postdoctoral rsch. assoc., 1995-98; NAS rsch. assoc. Army Rsch. Lab., Adelphi, Md., 1998—. Adj. asst. prof. N.C. State U., Raleigh, 1998—. Contbr. articles and papers to profl. jours. and conf. procs.; patentee in field. Recipient Best Paper award Electron Microscopy Soc., 1994, Materials Rsch. Soc., 1998, 99, BF Goodrich award, 1999. Mem. Internat. Folk Dance Club. Office: US Army Rsch Lab 2800 Powder Mill Rd Adelphi MD 20783-1138 E-mail: tsvetanka_zheleva@ncsu.edu.

ZHENG, GUOQIANG, history professor; PhD in History, U. Toledo, Ohio. Assoc. prof. Angelo State U., Tex., 1999—. Office: Angelo State Univ ASU Sta #10897 San Angelo TX 76909

ZHENG, LINGYI ALBERT, materials scientist, researcher, materials engineer, consultant; s. Cheng and Yuhe Zheng; m. Zhenwan Jennifer Xu; 1 child, Albert D. BA in Materials Engring., Shanghai Jiaotong U., 1991; PhD in Material Sci., Rice U., Houston, 1999; MBA in Mgmt., Bus., Boise State U., Idaho, 2003. Sr. engr. Micron Tech., Boise, Idaho,

1999—2004, Micron Tech. Inc, Manassas, Va., 2004—. Contbr. articles to profl. jours. Scholar, Rice U., 1995. Achievements include patents in field. Avocation: golf. Personal E-mail: albertzheng@yahoo.com.

ZHENG, MIN, engineer; d. ZiYing Zhao and Shuzhong Zheng; m. Xiangdong Bi, Apr. 19, 1995. PhD, Inst. Physics, Chinese Acad. Scis., 1997. Postdoc. rsch. assoc. Ctr. Materials Rsch. and Analysis, Dept. Physics, U. Nebr., Lincoln, 1998—2000; staff R&D engr. Maxtor Corp./MMC Tech., San Jose, Calif., 2000—. Postdoc. fellow Max-Planck-Instt. Mikrostruktur, Halle/Saale, Germany, 1997—98. Contbr. articles to profl. jours., The Royal Fellowship fellow, 1997. Mem.: Sigma Xi. Achievements include patents pending for. Office: Mmc Technology 311 Turquoise St Milpitas CA 95035-5432 Home: 1641 Butano Dr Milpitas CA 95035-7004 E-mail: zhengmin70@hotmail.com.

ZHENG, NAIQUAN NIGEL, mechanical engineer, educator; m. Li Tao Tao; children: Michelle, Adam. PhD, U. Sask., Can., 1995. Rsch. coord. Am. Sports Medicine Inst., Birmingham, Ala., 1995—2004; asst. prof. Shanghai Second Med. U., 1985—89, U. Fla., Gainesville, 2004—07, U. NC, Charlotte, 2008—. Mem.: Am. Soc. Biomechanics. Office: Univ NC Charlott 9201 University City Blvd Charlotte NC 28223 Business E-Mail: nzheng@uncc.edu.

ZHENG, QI, statistician, biomathematician; b. Lanxi, Zhejiang, China, July 8, 1958; arrived in U.S., 1988; s. Huanming Zheng and Sulan Zhuge; m. Huiping Hu, May 12, 1987; children: Yan, Eric Hugh. BS in math., Zhejiang U., 1978—82; PhD in stats., Tex. A&M U., 1988—93, postgrad., 1993. Cert. independent Mathematica trainer. Post-doc Nat. Ctr. Toxicological Rsch., Jefferson, Ark., 1994—96, staff fellow, 1996—2002; rsch. scientist Tex. A&M U., College Station, 2002—03, assoc. prof. dept. epidemiology and biostats. Sch. Rural Pub. Health, 2003—. Contbr. articles to jour. (Commendable Svc. award, FDA, 1997). Recipient Achievement award, Nat. Ctr. Toxicological Rsch., 1995; grantee Mathematica Vis. Scholar Grant, Wolfram Rsch. Inc., 1995, 1997. Mem.: Am. Statis. Assn., Phi Kappa Phi. Achievements include research in directed mutation hypothesis; stochastic modeling of carcinogenesis; development of algorithms and first comprehensive computer software SALVADOR for estimating mutation rates using data from fluctuation experiments. Avocations: reading, mountain hiking, music. Office: Tex A&M U Health Sci Ctr Sch Rural Pub Health Dept Epidemiology and Biostats College Station TX 77843 E-mail: qzheng@srph.tamhsc.edu.

ZHENG, SHUANG-CAI, physics educator, researcher; b. Shen-Ze County, He-Bei, China, Nov. 7, 1940; s. Quan-De Zheng and Jun-Mei Cao; m. Wen-Li Hu, May 1, 1969; children: Yue, Hui. BS, Nan-Kai U., Tian-Jin, China, 1966. Asst. Beijing Inst. Tech., 1966-80, lectr., 1980-94, prof., 1994—. Contbr. articles to profl. jours. Mem. AAAS. Home and Office: 12701 Little Dipper Path Austin TX 78732 Office Phone: 86 10 68468874. Personal E-mail: sc_zheng@hotmail.com.

ZHENG, WEI, science educator; s. Yongnian Zheng and Jin Xu; m. Wendy Jiang; children: Danielle N., Andrew J. Zeng. BS, Zhejiang U., Hangzhou, 1981; MS, 1984; PhD, U. Ariz., Tucson, 1991. Asst. prof. Columbia U., New York, 1993—99, assoc. prof., 2000—03, Purdue U., West Lafayette, Ind., 2003—06, prof., 2006—, head & assoc. dean, 2008—. Chmn. Life Plus LLC, West Lafayette, 2004—. Recipient Johnson & Johnson Focused Giving award, Seeds Success award; grantee Best paper award, Soc. Exptl. Biology & Medicine, 2006; grant, Eli Lily, 2004, grants, NIH-NIEHS, 1994—2008. Mem.: Soc. Neuroscience, Soc. Toxicology (v.p. 2007—). Office: Purdue Univ 550 Stadium Mall Drive West Lafayette IN 47907 Office Fax: 765-496-1377. Business E-Mail: wzheng@purdue.edu.

ZHENG, WEIAN, mathematics professor; b. Shanghai, May 13, 1952; s. Huicheng Zheng and Baozhang Song. DSc, U. Strasbourg, France, 1984. Prof. East China Normal U., Shanghai, 1986—90, Dept. Math., U. Calif., 2009—. Office: Dept Math Univ Calif Irvine CA 92697 Personal E-mail: financialmaths@gmail.com.

ZHENG, WENXIN, gynecologist, pathologist; MD, Shanghai Med. U., China, 1983. Diplomate Am. Bd. Pathology, 1996. Asst. prof. pathology and gynecology U. So. Calif., LA, 1996—2000; assoc. prof. pathology and gynecology Yale U., New Haven, 2000—05; tenured prof. pathology and gynecology U. Ariz., Tucson, 2005—. Funding pres. Assn. Chinese Physicians - Calif., LA, 1997—2001. Achievements include research in precursor lesions of gynecologic cancers. Office: Univ Ariz 1501 N Campbell Ave Tucson AZ 85718

ZHENG, YIN PING, performing arts educator; b. China, Jan. 1964; s. Zu De Zheng and Lin Rui Ru. BFA, High Level Night Coll., Fuzhou, Fujian, China, 1987; Apprenticship - Traditional Chinese Painting, Master Traditional Chinese Painter - Wang Yao Ting, Fujian, Fuzhou, China, 1982—2002. Performer instr. Fujian Acrobatic Troupe China, Fuzhou, China, 1976—, mem. FATC, 1980; instr. Antelope Valley Coll., Lancaster, Calif., 2006—. Donator LA County Commn. Women, 2008, Antelope Valley Coll. Found., Lancaster. Recipient winner, 2nd Regional Acrobatic Competition, Eastern Region, China, 1986—87, 4th Nat. Acrobatic Competition, Eastern Region, China, 1995, 14th Festival Internat. Du Cirque De Massy, Massi, France, 2006, Bronze Lion award, 2nd China WuQiao Internat. Circus Festival, Hebei, 1989. Mem.: Nat. Chinese Calligraphy Assn., Artist Employment Assn., Rong Cheng Painting Art Com. Gallery Mem., Yi Xian Art Gallery (Fujian), Antelope Valley Chinese Assn. (hon.; contbr. donation traditional Chinese painting auction 2007). Personal E-mail: yinpingzheng@yahoo.com.

ZHIGLO, ANDREY, research scientist; b. Kharkov, Ukraine, May 10, 1979; s. Valentin Fedorovich and Galina Aleksandrovna Zhiglo. Degree, Kharkov Nat. U., Ukraine, 2002; MS, attending, U. Chgo., 2009. Technician Kharkov Inst. Physics & Tech., 1999—2002, sci. collaborator, 2002; grad. student U. Chgo., 2002—09; rsch. assoc. Fla. State U., Tallahassee, 2009—. Tchr., trainer Physics & Math Liceum 27, Kharkov, 1996—97; lectr. Physics & Math Summer Sch., Sudak, Ukraine, 1999; organizer, com. mem. Regional-Nat. Olympiads Tournaments young physicists, Kharkov, Berminvody, Odessa, Ukraine, 1996—2001. Recipient Award, Fund. Support Gifted Youth, Kharkov, 1995—96, 1998, 2001; grantee, Internat. Soros Sci. Edn. Program, 1996—99, Dept. Edn., Kharkov Region Adminstrn., 1999—2002. Achievements include research in problems of atomic science & technology. Home: 6107 S Kimbark Ave Apt 2W Chicago IL 60637

ZHILINA, IRINA, language educator; b. Vladimir, Russia, Apr. 23, 1952; arrived in US, 1998, permanent resident, 2008; d. Cyril and Olga Arkhangelsky; 1 child, Dmitry Zhilin. MEd in English Lang., State Linguistic U., Minsk, Belarus, 1974; PhD in Pegagogy and Psychology Tchg., High Attestation Commn., Moscow, 1988. Assoc. prof. Scorina State U., Gomel, Belarus, 1974—2003; adj. lecr. Rutgers U., NJ, 2004—; adj. lctr. Pace U., NYC, 2007—; adj. instr. Union County Coll., Elizabeth, NJ, 2004—. Contbr. articles to profl. jours. Vol. Chernobyl Children-UK, 1999—2003; vol. Internat. Students Ctr. Princeton U., 2003—; trustee Twin Cities Aberdeen-Gomel, 1991—2003. Regional Scholars Exch. Program fellow, 1998—99, 2003. Mem.: TESOL. Avocations: reading, travel, music, theater. Home: 169 Linda Ln Edison NJ 08820-4505 Office: Rutgers U ESL Grad Office 53 Ave E Tillett Hall Piscataway NJ 08854-8040 Office Phone: 908-420-7126. Personal E-mail: zhylinirene@yahoo.com.

ZHILINA, LUDMILA, research scientist; b. Archangelsk, Russia, Jan. 27, 1946; Grad., Permsky State Med. Inst., 1971; Dr. in Ecol. and Physiol. Characteristics of Immune Status and Health, Arkhangelsk Oblast, 2007. With Govt. Archangelsk Region, Russia, 1987—96, Inst. Environ. Physiology, Archangelsk, 1996—. Author: (monography) Immunological Reactivity & Health in Archangelsk Region, 2004; contbr. articles to profl. jours. Mem.: Russian Soc. Physyologists (assoc.), Russian Soc. Allergologists & Immunologists (assoc.). Office: Inst Environ Physiology Lomonosov av 249 Archangelsk 163061 Russia Office Fax: 78182652992. Personal E-mail: ifpa@atnet.ru.

ZHIRNOV, VICTOR, physicist, researcher; b. Pervouralsk, Russia, Jan. 29, 1966; s. Vladimir Zhirnov and Valentina Zhirnova; m. Oksana Balnova, Aug. 21, 1993; 1 child, Eugenea. MS summa cum laude, Ural Poly. Inst., Ekaterinburg, Russia, 1989; PhD, Physics and Tech. Inst., Russian Acad. Scis., Moscow, 1992. Rsch. scientist Ctrl. Inst. Tech., Moscow, 1989—92; sr. rschr. Inst. Crystallography, Moscow, 1992—98, Semiconductor Rsch. Corp., Durham, NC, 1998—; rsch. prof. N.C. State U., Raleigh. Recipient Outstanding Young Scientist award, Russian Acad. Scis., 1997, Inventor Recognition award, Semiconductor Rsch. Corp., 2000. Achievements include patents for Field Emission Cathode and a Device based thereon; patents pending for Supermolecular Structures and Devices Made from Same. Home: 104 Westwind Ct Cary NC 27511 Office: Semiconductor Rsch Corp 1101 Slater Rd Durham NC 27703 E-mail: zhirnov@src.org.

ZHITNIK, ALEXEI, professional hockey player; b. Kiev, Russia, Oct. 10, 1972; m. Luda Zhitnik. Defenseman La Kings, 1992—95, Buffalo Sabres, 1995—2005, NY Islanders, 2005—06, Phila. Flyers, 2006—07, Atlanta Thrashers, 2007—. Mem. def. team Russia World Championships, Austria, 1996, World Cup Tournament, 1996, World Championships, Italy, 1993—94; rep. Gold medal unified team Albertville Winter Olympics, France, 1992. Office: Atlanta Thrashers Centennial Tower, Ste 1900 101 Marietta Street NW Atlanta GA 30303 Office Phone: 516-501-6700. Office Fax: 516-501-6762.

ZHONG, JUN, medical educator; b. China; PhD, U. Wash., Seattle, 1999. Postdoc. Columbia U., NYC, 2000—03; rsch. asst. prof. SUNY, Bklyn., 2003—. Office: SUNY Downstate 450 Clarkson Ave Box 29 Brooklyn NY 11203

ZHONG, WEIHONG (KATIE ZHONG), engineering educator; b. He Gang, Hei-Long-Jiang, China, Feb. 15, 1966; PhD, Bejing U. Aeronautics and Astronautics, 1994. Prof. Beijing U. Aeronautics and Astrautics, 1999—2003; assoc. prof. ND State U., Fargo, 2003—07, Wash. State U., Pullman, 2007—. Achievements include research in polymers and nanocomposites. Office: Wash State Univ Sch Mech and Materials Engring Pullman WA 99164 Office Fax: 509-335-4662. Business E-Mail: katie_zhong@wsu.edu.

ZHOU, BANG RONG, physicist, researcher; b. Chengdu, Sichuan, China, Apr. 18, 1941; s. Fu Cheng and Ying Juan (Wang) Z.; m. Yong Pu Kang, Feb. 2, 1981; 1 child, Xiao Zhi. Grad., U. Sci. and Tech. China, Beijing, 1963, degree, 1966. Tchg. asst. U. Sci. and Tech. of China, Hefei, 1973-78, lectr., 1979-85, assoc. prof. Grad. Sch., Chinese Acad. Scis. Beijing, 1985-87, 87-90, prof., 1990—. Vis. scholar Fermi Nat. Accelerator Lab., Batavia, 1981-83, Stanford Linear Accelerator Ctr., Calif., 1983; assoc. vis. prof. Internat. Centre for Theoretical Physics, Trieste, Italy, 1992, 94, 98; judging specialist Nat. Natural Sci. award of China in Physics and Astronomy, 2002-. Author: Quamtum Field Theory; contbr. articles to profl. jours. including Atomic Energy, Nuclear Physics B, Physics Letters B, Phys. Rev. D, others. Recipient award Chinese Nat. Sci. Conf., 1978, Sci. Achievements award Chinese Acad. Scis., 1981, award Nat. Natural Sci. of China, 1982, Spl. Allowance Upon Contbn. to Chinese Advanced Edn. award The State Coun. of China, 1992. Mem. Chinese Soc. High Energy Physics, Chinese Phys. Soc., Western Returned Scholars' Assn. Achievements include participating in work on straton (quark) model of hadrons; creative research on asymptotic freedom in heavy quark potential, dynamical chiral and electroweak symmetry breaking, finite temperature field theory and phase transitions. Avocations: collecting stamps and coins, swimming, ping-pong, classical music, athletic competition, detective films on television. Office: Chinese Acad Scis Grad Sch Beijing 100049 China Home Phone: 0086-010-62620024. E-mail: zhoubr@163bj.com, zhoubr@gucas.ac.cn.

ZHOU, BIAO, computer scientist; s. Zaojin Zhou and Enrong Cai; m. Liyan Yuan. PhD, UCLA, 2008. Rsch. assoc. Tsinghua U., Beijing, 1995—99; rsch. assoc. mech. engring. dept. UCLA, 1999—2004, rsch. assoc. computer sci. dept., 2004—. Intern Scalable Network Inc., LA, 2004—05. Contbr. chapters to books, articles to profl. jour. Mem.: IEEE. Business E-Mail: zhb@cs.ucla.edu.

ZHOU, BING-NAN, chemistry professor; b. Shanghai, Jan. 31, 1934; came to U.S., 1993; m. Xiu-Ying Chen, Feb. 11, 1958; children: Cindy Qin & Hong. MD, Shanghai Med. U., 1954, MS; PhD, Shanghai Inst. Materia Medica, 1964. Vis. scientist Czechoslovak Acad. Scis., Prague, 1962-64; postdoctoral fellow U. Wis., Madison, 1981-83; prof. Shanghai Inst. Materia Medica, Academia Sinica, 1988—99; sr. rsch. scientist dept. chemistry Va. Tech., 1994—2002; sr. rsch. scientist & sr. mgr. R&D Tahitian Noni Internat., Inc., Provo, Utah, 2002—. Reviewer The Sci. Found. for New Drug Rsch. in China, Beijing, 1987-92, NSF of China, Beijing, 1988-94; vis. prof. chemistry U. B.C., Vancouver, Can., 1986, U. Ill., Chgo., 1987-94; dir. dept. phytochemistry Nat. Lab. Drug Rsch., Shanghai, 1989-94. Author: Extraction and Separation of Active Compounds from Chinese Herbs, 2d edit., 1981, Bioactive Natural Products, 1981, The Chemistry of Natural Products, 1993, The Strategies for Development of Natural Organic Chemistry in China, 1995; contbr. over 150 articles to profl. internat. peer jours. Home: 138 W Thorneberry Way Pleasant Grove UT 84062 Office: Tahitian Noni Internat (Marinda Inc) R&D 737 East 1180 South American Fork UT 84003 Business E-Mail: bingnan_zhou@tni.com.

ZHOU, BO, systems engineer; b. Shanghai, Dec. 28, 1978; s. Shirong Zhou and Liang Weng; m. Zhaoqiong Dong. BS in Engring., Shanghai Jiao Tong U., 2001, MS in Engring., 2004; PhD, U. Calif., Davis, 2008. Software engr. Nat. Instruments, Shanghai, 2004; grad. student rschr. Coding Theory Group, Dept. ECE, UC Davis, 2004—08; assoc. software engr. Marvell Semiconductor, Inc., Marlborough, Mass., 2007; sr. sys. engr. Qualcomm Inc., San Diego, 2008—. Rschr. Shanghai IS'vision Technologies Co., Ltd., 2003. Contbr. articles to profl. jours. Recipient QUALSTAR Diamond award, Qualcomm Inc., 2008, Outstanding Student, Shanghai Jiao Tong U., 2000; Grad. Student fellowship, Dept. Elec. & Computer Engring., UC Davis, 2005—06. Mem.: IEEE, Soc. Photographic Instrumentation Engrs., Sigma Xi, Phi Kappa Phi (life). Achievements include research in algebraic constructions of high performance and efficiently encodable non-binary quasi-cyclic LDPC codes; first to geometric distortion resilient image watermarking algorithm based on SVD; research in digital watermarking algorithm for binary image. Office: Qualcomm Inc 5775 Morehouse Dr San Diego CA 92121 E-mail: bzhou@qualcomm.com.

ZHOU, CHENMING, research scientist; married. PhD, Tenn. Technol. U., Cookeville, 2008. Rsch. asst. Tenn. Technol. U., 2004—08; rsch. scientist Carnegie Mellon U., Pitts., 2008—. Mem.: IEEE, Phi Kappa Phi. Achievements include cutting edge research in applying time reversal technique to UWB field. Office: Carnegie Mellon Univ ECE Dept 5000 Forbes Ave Pittsburgh PA 15213 Business E-Mail: czhou@cmu.edu.

ZHOU, DIAN, engineering educator; s. Guangfu Zhou and Xingming Liu. BS in Physics, Fudan U., Shanghai, 1982, MSEE, 1985; PhD in Electric Engring., U. Ill., Urbana-Champaign, 1990. Asst. prof. U. NC, Charlotte, 1990—94, assoc. prof., 1994—99; assoc. editor IEEE Transactions CAS, 1996—98, Sci. China, Beijing, 2008—; prof. U. Tex. Dallas, Richardson, 1999—; Changjiang honor prof. Fudan U., 2003—06, dean, sch. microelectronics, 2003—06, dir., state key lab. asics and sys., 2004—07, dir., nano micro-electronics sci. and tech. innovation platform, 2004—06; bd. mem. Shanghai Semiconductor and IC Soc., 2005—07. Recipient Young Investigator award, NSF, 1994, Outstanding Overseas Young Investigator award, NSFC, China, 2000; Changjiang Honor Scholar, Ministry Edn., China, 2002. Mem.: IEEE (Circuits and Sys. Darlington award 1992).

ZHOU, DING-WEI, mechanical engineer, researcher; b. Xiangtan, Hunan, China, Mar. 1, 1971; s. Kunyan Zhou and Lijun Wang; 1 child, Renruisheng. BS in Metallurgy Engring., U. Arch. Tech., China, 1994, MS in Metallurgy Engring., 1997; PhD in Energy and Power Engirng., Xi'an Jiaotong U., China, 2000. Grad. rsch. asst. Beijing Polytechnic U., Coll., Environ. And Energy Engring., China, 1997; grad. tchg. asst. Xi'an U. Arch. Tech., Coll. Metallurgy Engring., China, 1997; rsch. asst. prof. Chinese Acad. Scis., Inst. Engring. Thermophysics, China, 2000—02; postdoctoral rsch. assoc. Pohang U. Sci. Tech., Dept. Mechanical Engring., Republic of Korea, 2002—03; vis. scholar, Inst. Tech. Thermodynamics, Dept. Mechanical Engring. Darmstadt U. Tech., Germany, 2003—04, sr. rschr., 2003—04; rsch. scientist, Dept. Mechanical and Aerospace Engring Ariz. State U., Tempe, 2005—; sr. mech. engr. ESG Engring., 2007—. Recipient Best Lecture award, Inst. Engring. Thermophysics, Chinese Acad. Sci., 2001; scholar, Xi'an Jiaotong U., 1998. Fellow: ASME (corr.), Chinese Soc. Engring. Thermophysics; mem.: ACE, European Multiphase Systems Inst. Home: 1050 S Stanley Pl P242 Tempe AZ 85281 Office: Arizona State U Dept Mech and Aerospace Eng Tempe AZ 85287-6106 Office Phone: 480-208-8958. Personal E-mail: drdwzhou@hotmail.com.

ZHOU, HUAN-XIANG, biophysicist, scientist; b. Tianmen, Hubei, People's Republic of China, Jan. 3, 1965; s. Yuanmi and Nianbao (Qi) Z.; m. Ke Xu, May 14, 1993; 1 child, Kenneth Hui. BS, Wuhan U., 1984; MS, Drexel U., 1986, PhD, 1988. Asst. prof. Hong Kong U. of Sci. and Tech., 1995—. Vis. fellow NIH, Bethesda, Md., 1988-90, vis. assoc., 1990-95. Contbr. more than 30 articles to profl. jours. including Sci., Proceedings of the Nat. Acad. of Scis. Mem. AAAS, Am. Biophys. Soc., Am. Chem. Soc.

ZHOU, JI-XUN, ocean acoustics physicist, acoustician; b. Rugao, Jiangsu, China, Oct. 16, 1938; s. Chun Zhou and Ruxin Li; m. Xue-Zhen Zhang, Oct. 1, 1967; children: Wen-Xu, Fang-Xiao. Degree in Physics, Nanjing U., China, 1963; degree in Ocean Acoustics, Grad. Sch. Chinese Acad. Scis., Beijing, 1967. Prof. Inst. Acoustics, Chinese Acad. Scis., 1967—89; vis. prof. Ga. Inst. Tech., Atlanta, 1989—92, prin. rsch. scientist, 1992—. Chmn. sci. com. 1st Internat. Conf. Shallow-Water Acoustics, Beijing, 1997; hon. co-chair Internat. Conf. Shallow-Water Acoustics, Shanghai, 2009. Contbr. scientific papers to profl. jours. Recipient Nat. Nature Sci. award, China, 1982, 1989. Fellow: Acoustical Soc. America. Business E-Mail: jixun.zhou@me.gatech.edu.

ZHOU, KECHENG, mathematics professor; MSc, Nanjing U., China, 1980; PhD, U. Ill., Chgo., 1990. Asst. prof. Nanjing Inst. Tech., China, 1980—84; prof. Calif. State U., Sacramento, 1990—. Office: Calif State U Dept Math 6000 J St Sacramento CA 95819-2605 Home Phone: 916-974-0178. E-mail: zhouk@csus.edu.

ZHOU, LI, medical researcher; b. ZouCheng, ShanDong, China, 1973; m. Xiaoguang Zhen; children: Ellen Zhen, Ethan Zhen. MB, Shanghai Med. U., 1996; MS, Baruch Coll., CUNY, NYC, 2002; PhD, Columbia U., NYC, 2007. Lectr. Shanghai Med. U., 1996—2000; rsch. assoc. Columbia U., 2000—02; informatician Ptnrs. HealthCare Inc., Boston, 2007—; rsch. assoc. Harvard Med. Sch., Boston, 2007—. Contbr. articles to profl. jour. Mem.: AAAS, Am. Med. Informatics Assn. Achievements include development of TimeText system. Office: Partners HealthCare Inc 93 Worcester St Wellesley MA 02481 Business E-Mail: lzhou2@partners.org.

ZHOU, LINDA HUA, dermatologist, educator; d. Zhenbang Zhou and Jinxiang Hu; m. Chunsong Luo, May 8, 1984; 1 child, Su Luo. MD, Hubei Coll. Traditional Chinese Medicine, Wuhan, Hubei, 1983. Diplomate dermatologist Am. Bd. Dermatology, 2005. Dermatology attending Roger Williams Med. Ctr., Providence, 2005—; asst. prof. Boston U. Sch. Medicine, Providence, 2008—. Office: Roger Williams Med Ctr 50 Maude St Providence RI 02908 Office Fax: 401-456-6824.

ZHOU, LING-YI, psychology professor; MEd in Tchr. Edn., Miami U., Oxford, Ohio, 1995, PhD in Psychology, 1995. Prof. U. St. Francis, Joliet, Ill., 1995—. Contbr. articles to profl. psychol. jours. Mem.: APS, Phi Kappa Phi. Office: Univ St Francis Psychology Dept 500 Wilcox St Joliet IL 60435 Office Phone: 815-740-3594.

ZHOU, MENGCHU, engineering educator; b. Dongyang, China, Oct. 31, 1963; s. Shenglong and Wenguang Zhou; m. Fang Chen, 1965; children: Albert Huiheng, Benjamin Xinheng. BS in Control Engring., Nanjing U. of Sci. and Tech., China, 1983; MS in Automatic Control, Beijing Inst. Tech., 1986; PhD in Computer and Sys. Engring., Rensselaer Poly. Inst., 1990. Assoc. prof. N.J. Inst. Tech., Newark, 1995-2000, prof., 2000—. Presenter in field. Author: Petri Net Synthesis for Discrete Event Control of Manufacturing Systems, 1993, Modeling, Simulation and Control of Flexible Manufacturing Systems, 1998; editor: Petri Nets in Flexible and Agile Automation, 1995, Deadlock Resolution in Computer Integrated Systems, 2005, Object-Oriented Programming in C++: A Project Based Approach, 2005, Modeling and Control of Discrete Event Dynamic Systems, 2007; editor: Internat. Jour. of Intelligent Control and Systems; contbr. articles to profl. jours. Recipient Lead award Soc. Mfg. Engrs., 1994, Harlem J. Perlis Rsch. award N.J. Inst. Inst. Tech., 1996, Humboldt Rsch. award Alexander von Humboldt

Found., 2000. Fellow IEEE (assoc. editor Trans. on Robotics and Automation 1997-2000, Trans. Automation Sci. and Engring. 2004—, Trans. Indsl. Informatics 2007—), IEEE Sys. Man and Cybernetics Soc. (assoc. editor 1999-2005, mng. editor 2005—, Outstanding Contbn. award 2003, Disting. Lectr. 2005); mem. Chinese Assn. for Sci. and Tech. U.S. (life, v.p. 1996-97, pres.-elect 1998, pres. 1999, Outstanding Svc. award, Leadership award). Avocations: tennis, bridge, skiing. Office: NJ Inst Tech 323 MLK Blvd Newark NJ 07102-1824 Office Phone: 973-596-6282. Personal E-mail: zhoumc@yahoo.com.

ZHOU, PENGBO, medical educator; b. Beijing; PhD, U. Mich. Med. Sch., Ann Arbor, 1993. Instr. Harvard Med. Sch., Boston, 1999—99, postdoctoral fellow, 1996—99, U. Chgo., Chgo., 1994—96; asst. prof. Cornell U. Weill Med. Coll., NYC, 1999—2005, assoc. prof., 2006—. Cons. Rigel Pharm., South San Francisco, 2001—02. Contbr. articles to profl. jours. Recipient Rsch. award, Dorothy Rodbell Cohen Found., 2000—01, 2003—04, award, Mary Kay Ash Charitable Found., 2000—02, Acad. award, Beijing U., 1986—87, Irmat Hirschl Career Scientist award, 2007—, Young Investigator award, AMDeC Found., 2000—03, Lee Murphy Meml. award, U. Mich. Dept. Biology, 1992; grantee Travel grant, Am. Assn. Cancer Rsch., 1994, various grants, NIH; fellow, Horace H. Rackham Sch. Grad. Studies, U. Mich., 1991—92; scholar, Leukemia and Lymphoma Soc., 2000—01, Sidney Kimmel Found. Cancer Rsch., 2000—02. Mem.: Am. Soc. Hematology. Achievements include patents for developed the protein knockout technology.

ZHOU, PING, physical engineer; b. Beijing; arrived in US, 1985; 1 child, Jie Yang. BA, Beijing U. Chem. Tech.; postgrad., U. Sci. & Tech. China, Beijing U. Asst. prof. SUNY, Albany, 1985—87; engr. Chinese Acad. Scis., Beijing, 1970—90; rsch. engr. Stanford U., Calif., 1990—. Vis. porf. Stanford U., 1987-88. Mem. Am. Soc. Materials Internat., Materials Rsch. Soc., Am. Vacuum Soc., Am. Phys. Soc. Achievements include development of multilayer Ti-Cu thin films for gravity probe-B gyroscope housings, BSCCO thin films with Tc above 100K; development, manufacturing, and testing of the thin film coatings and the superconducting bearings for the accelerometer for the Satellite Test of Equivalence Principle (STEP) Project. Office: Stanford Univ Hansen Lab Stanford CA 94305 Office Phone: 650-725-5995. Business E-Mail: ping@relgyro.stanford.edu.

ZHOU, PING, research scientist; PhD, Northwestern U., Evanston, 2004. Rsch. assoc Rehab. Inst. Chgo., 2004—06, rsch. scientist, 2006—; adj. asst. prof. Northwestern U., Chgo., 2006—. Office: Rehab Inst Chgo 345 E Superior St Ste 1406 Chicago IL 60611 Business E-Mail: p-zhou@northwestern.edu.

ZHOU, QUANSHENG, medical researcher; married. PhD, Suzhou Med. Coll., Soochow U., China, 1991. Postdoc. fellow Blood Rsch. Inst., Milwauke, Wis., 1994—97; staff scientist Scripps Rsch. Inst., La Jolla, Calif., 1998—2005, sr. staff scientist, 2006—. Contbr. scientific papers to profl. jours. Office: Scripps Rsch Inst 10550 N Torrey Pines Rd La Jolla CA 92037

ZHOU, SHENGDE, science educator, researcher; PhD, Auburn U., 1997. Scientist U. Fl., 2001—05; asst. prof. Northern Ill. U., Dekalb, 2005—. Mem.: Soc. Indsl. Microbology, Am. Soc. Microbiology, Sigma Xi. Achievements include patents in field. Office: Northern Ill Univ Castle Dr 155 Dekalb IL 60115

ZHOU, XIAOFENG, biomedical researcher, medical geneticist; b. China; PhD, Boston U., 2000; MS, Brandeis U., Waltham, Mass., 2002; BS, Hangzhou U., China, 1992. Rsch. asst. Boston Biomedical Rsch. Inst., 1992—95; postdoc. fellow genetics Ctr. Human Genetics, Boston Med. Ctr., 2000—02; lectr. UCLA, 2002—04, asst. prof., 2005—06, U. Ill., Chgo, 2006—. Mem. UCLA Jonsson Comprehensive Cancer Ctr., 2005—06, UIC Cancer Ctr., U. Ill., 2006—, Grad. Coll., U. Ill., 2007—; vis. prof. Sun Yat-sen U., Guangzhou, China, 2007—. Contbr. articles to profl. jours. Fellowship, Cancer Rsch. and Prevention Found. Am., 2002—04, grant, Tobacco Related Disease Rsch. Program, 2004—06, Nat. Inst. Dental and Craniofacial Rsch., 2004—, 2005—, Nat. Cancer Inst., 2005—, 2008—, Prevent Cancer Found., 2008—. Mem.: Assn. Chinese Geneticists America., Am. Dental Edn. Assn., Am. Assn. Dental Rsch., Am. Soc. Human Genetics, Am. Assn. Cancer Rsch. Achievements include patents for biomarkers for oral tongue cancer metastasis and extracapsular spread. Office: Univ Illinois Chgo 801 S Paulina St Chicago IL 60612

ZHOU, YILI, physician; married. MD, Wenzhou Med. Coll., China, 1982. Diplomate Am. Bd. Pain Medicine, 2004. Fellow pain mgmt. Harvard Med. Sch., Boston, 2000—01; dir. Jackson Meml. Hosp. Pain Clinic, Miami, Fla., 2002—04; med. dir. Comprehensive Pain Mgmt. NF, Gainesville, Fla., 2005—. Mem.: Am. Pain Soc. Office: Comprehensive Pain Mgmt NF 6830 NW 11th Pl Gainesville FL 32605 Office Fax: 352-331-0970. Personal E-mail: yilizhoumd@yahoo.com.

ZHOU, YONG, engineering educator; b. Hubei, China; PhD, U. Tex. Austin, 2005. Asst. prof. U. Tex. Brownsville, 2005—. Olegario Vazquez Rana Faculty fellowship, 2008. Mem.: IEEE AP Soc., Sigma Xi. Office: Univ Tex Brownsville 80 Ft Brown Brownsville TX 78526

ZHOU, YUYU, environmental scientist, researcher; m. Huixia Zhao, Mar. 26, 2004. PhD, U. RI, 2008. Rsch. asst. Beijing Normal U., 2001—04, grad. rschr., 2002—03; vis. scholar U. Toronto, Canada, 2003—04; rsch. asst. U. RI, 2004—07, tchg. asst., 2007—08, lab. mgr., 2007—08; postdoc. rsch. assoc. Purdue U., West Lafayette, Ind., 2008—. Contbr. articles to profl. jours. Recipient Geo Eye award, Am. Soc. Photogrammetry and Remote Sensing, 2006, BAE Sys. award, 2007, Sigma Xi Dissertation award, Chpt. U. RI, 2008, IGIF Student Travel award, Assn. Am. Geographers, 2008, Rsch. Paper Competition Winner, 2008; Rsch. grant, RI Sea Grant Honors Program Office Provost, 2007. Mem.: IEEE, ASPRS, AAG, Soc. Sigma Xi, Phi Kappa Phi. Personal E-mail: zhouyuyu@gmail.com.

ZHOU, ZHE, research scientist; Rsch. specialist Dow Chem. Co., Freeport, Tex., 2002—; NMR lab mgr. La. State U., Baton Rouge, 1999—2002. Mem.: ACS. Office: Dow Chem Co B-1219 Freeport TX 77541

ZHOU, ZUHAN, literature educator; arrived in US, 1989; BA, Fudan U., Shanghai, 1982, MA, 1984; PhD, Washington U., St. Louis, 1996. Lectr. U. Fla., Gamsville, Fla., 1995—2001; asst. prof. Hofstra U., Hampstead, NY, 2001—05, assoc. prof., 2006—. Author: (book) Andrography in Lote Ming Early Qing Literature, 2003; contbr. articles to profl. jours. Avocation: ping pong/table tennis. Office: Hofstra Univ 311 Calkins Hall 107 Mail Box 1000 Hampstead Tmp Hempstead NY 11549

ZHU, ALF (AIWU ZHU), research scientist, educator; Sr. scientist U. Va., Charlottesville, 2002—; instr. SVGS, Fisherville, Va., 2008—. Rsch. cons., Dayton, Ohio. Author (investigator): (applied sci. and engring.) Materials Physics, Chemistry, Computation.

ZHU, BAO TING, pharmacologist, toxicologist, researcher; b. Shanghai, Jan. 20, 1962; came to U.S. 1989; s. Young-Shen Zhu and Fu-Di Qiu; m. Xiaomeng Xu, Aug. 30, 1989. MB/MD, Shanghai Med. U., 1985, MS, 1988; PhD, U. Tex. Med. Br., 1992. Lectr. Shanghai Med. U., 1988-89; grad. asst. U. Tex. Med. Br., Galveston, 1989-92, postdoctoral researcher, 1992-94. Contbr. articles to profl. jours. Mem. Am. Assn. Cancer Rsch. (assoc.). Baptist. Avocations: tennis, ping-pong, soccer. Office: U Tex Med Br 301 University Blvd Galveston TX 77555-5302

ZHU, CAROLYN WEI, healthcare educator; d. Yu Zhu and Alice Jiang; 1 child, Andrew K. Shen. PhD, Duke U., 1999. Health economist, 2004—. Contbr. chapters to books, articles to profl. jours. Mem.: Phi Beta Kappa.

ZHU, DONGHUI, research scientist; s. Zuxian Zhu and Youlan Gu; m. Lu Gao, July 24, 2000; 1 child, Julia Gao. BS with honors, East China U. Sci. Tech., Shanghai, 1996; MS, Fla. State U., Tallahassee, 2001, Wash. U., St. Louis, 2003; PhD, U. Mo.-Columbia, 2006. Cert. preparing future faculty 2006. Rsch. scientist Columbia U., NYC, 2006—07, U. Rochester, NY, 2007—. Editl. reviewer: Jour. Cellular and Molecular Medicine, Jour. Neurogenetics, So. Med. Jour., Chinese Jour. Cancer, Neurol. Rsch., sr. editor: Medjaden Biomed. Services; contbr. articles to profl. jours. Recipient Coll. Outstanding Grad. Student award, U. Mo., 2006, Superior Grad. Achievement award, 2006; fellow, East China U. of Sci. and Tech., 1992—96, Fla. State U., 2000—02, Wash. U., 2002—03; Profl. Presentation Travel fellowship, U. Mo., 2006. Mem.: Biophysical Soc., Soc. Neurosci., Biomedical Engring. Soc. (Grad. Student Travel award 2005), Am. Soc. Neurochemistry, Sigma Xi. Achievements include discovery of key enzyme in Alzheimer's disease; research in mathematical modeling of blood coagulation cascade; application of molecular rotors to the determination of the molecular weight-dependence of viscosity in polymer melts; hydrogen peroxide altering membrane and cytoskeleton properties and enhanced intercellular connections in astrocytes; Brownian diffusion and surface kinetics of liposome and viral particle uptake by human lung cancer cells in-vitro; phospholipases A2 mediate Alzheimer's Abeta-induced mitochondrial dysfunction. Avocations: sports, music, travel, gourmet cooking. Office: Univ Rochester 601 Elmwood Ave Box 670 Rochester NY 14642 Office Fax: 585-273-5662. Business E-Mail: donghui_zhu@urmc.rochester.edu.

ZHU, DONGXIAO, science educator; b. Jinan, Shandong, China, Jan. 18, 1974; s. Changyong Zhu and Binglin Nie; m. Zhou Jun. MA, Eastern Mich. U., Ypsilanti, 2002, U. Mich., Ann Arbor, 2005, PhD, 2006. Biostatistician Stower Inst. Med. Rsch., Kans. City, Mo., 2006—08; asst. prof. computer sci. U. New Orleans, 2008—. Bioinformatics fellowship, U. Michigan, 2003. Mem.: Sigma XI. Office: Univ New Orleans Computer Sci 2000 Lakeshore Dr Math 311 New Orleans LA 70148 Office Phone: 304-280-2406. Personal E-mail: dongxiaozhu@yahoo.com.

ZHU, GUANGYU, computer scientist, researcher; arrived in US, 2008, permanent resident; s. Jiwen Zhu and Ping Sun; m. Yuan Yuan, Dec. 18, 2006. BS in Engring. with first class honors, Nanyang Technol. U., Singapore, 2001; MSc in Engring., U. Md., Coll. Pk., 2008; attending in Engring., U. Md. Cert. lotus specialist IBM, 2002, sys. expert on webSphere application server IBM, 2003, e-bus. solution technologist IBM, 2003, info. sys. security profl. Internat. Info. Sys. Security Cert. Consortium, 2003. Software engr. internship software group, Motorola Singapore Design Ctr., Singapore, 2000; tech. solution arch. IBM Global Svcs., IBM Singapore, 2001—03; instr. U. Md., 2004—05, rschr., 2004—; rsch. intern IBM Almaden Rsch. Ctr., San Jose, Calif., 2006, Search and Advertising Scis. Group, Yahoo! Applied Rsch., Santa Clara, Calif., 2008; software engring. intern Yahoo! Search Group, 2008. Internet technology security cons. IBM Global Svcs., IBM Singapore, 2002—03. Contbr. articles to profl. jours. Recipient Jacob K. Goldhaber Travel award, U. Md., 2007, Student Travel award, ACM Spl. Interest Group Knowledge Discovery Data and Data Mining, 2007; Edn. scholarship, Ministry Edn., 1997—2001, Rsch. scholarship, Inst. Advanced Computer Studies, 2004—. Mem.: Soc. for Indsl. and Applied Math., IEEE, Internat. Assn. Pattern Recognition. Achievements include research in content recognition for heterogeneous image collections; computational framework for unconstrained language identification on document images; signature detection and segmentation from document images; invention of extraction of relevant named entities from unstructured document image sources; design of DOCLIB software library for complex document image processing. Office: Univ Md 3348 AV Williams Bldg College Park MD 20742 Business E-Mail: zhugy@umiacs.umd.edu.

ZHU, HONGTU, science educator; married. PhD, Chinese U. Hong Kong, 1999. Asst. prof. Columbia U., NYC; assoc. prof. UNC-CH, 2006—. Office: UNC-CH McGavran Greenberg Hall Chapel Hill NC 27599

ZHU, JI, science educator; b. Beijing; PhD, Stanford U., Calif., 2003. Asst. prof. U. Mich., Ann Arbor, 2003—08, assoc. prof., 2008—. Office: Univ Mich 439 W Hall 1085 S Univ Ave Ann Arbor MI 48109

ZHU, KEHE, mathematician; b. Miluo, Hunan, People's Republic of China, July 8, 1961; arrived in US, 1983; s. Guiqing and Mowen (Feng) Z.; m. Peijia Tan, Aug. 2, 1985; children, Peter F., Michael Y. BS, Nat. U. Def. Tech., Changsha, People's Republic of China, 1981; PhD, SUNY, Buffalo, 1986. Asst. prof. math. U. Wash., Seattle, 1986-88, U. Waterloo, Can., 1988, SUNY, Albany, 1989-92, assoc. prof. math., 1992-95, prof. math., 1995—. Author: Operator Theory in Function Spaces, 1990, An Introduction to Operator Algebras, 1993, Theory of Bergman Spaces, 2000, Spaces of Holomorphic Functions in the Unit Ball, 2005; contbr. articles to publs. NSF grantee, 1987—. Mem. Am. Math. Soc. Home: 616 Stream Ln Slingerlands NY 12159-3008 Office Phone: 518-442-4618. Business E-Mail: kzhu@math.albany.edu.

ZHU, LIE, physics professor; BS in Space Physics, U. Sci. and Tech. of China, Hefei, 1982, MS in Space Sci., 1985; PhD in Space Physics, U. Alaska, Fairbanks, 1990. Contbr. articles to profl. jours., chapters to books. Mem.: Am. Geophys. Union (guest editor Radio Sci. 1994—98), Com. on Space Rsch. (assoc.). Office: Utah State U Old Main Hill Logan UT 84322-4405 Business E-Mail: zhu@cc.usu.edu.

ZHU, LIN, engineer; b. Beijing, Oct. 29, 1975; s. Qiming Zhu and Jiaxiang Zhan; m. Qiong Luo, May 2, 2008. BE, Tsinghua U., Beijing, 1999; PhD, Rensselaer Poly. Inst., Troy, NY, 2006. Engr. Power Integrations, San Jose, Calif., 2005—08. Office: Power Integrations 5245 Hellyer Ave San Jose CA 95138 Office Fax: 408-414-9651. Business E-Mail: lin.zhu@powerint.com.

ZHU, QIANG, education educator; s. Tingyi Zhu and Jingqin Xu; m. Yanping Zhang; children: Han, Kayla Jie. BSc, S.E. U., China, 1978—82, MEng, 1982—84; MSc, McMaster U., Can., 1988—90; PhD, U. Waterloo, Can., 1990—95. Lectr. SE U., 1984—88; vis. scientist IBM Centre for Advanced Studies, Toronto, Canada, 1998—2005, faculty fellow, 2003—; asst. prof. U. Mich., Dearborn, 1995—2001, assoc. prof., 2001—07, prof., 2007—. Assoc. editor Internat. Jour. Computers and Their Applications, 2005—; program com. mem., numerous internat. confs., 1998—2003; workshop/track/session/publicity chair, numerous internat. confs., 1985—2007. Contbr. articles to profl. jours. and pubs. Recipient Partnership Rsch. award, IBM U. Rels., 1999, Faculty award, 2003, 2004; Rsch. grant, NSF, 1998, 1999, IBM Toronto Lab., 1998, 2002, 2007, NSF, 2005, Ford, 2008. Mem.: IEEE, Assn. Computing Machinery. Achievements include research in techniques for multi-database cost modeling, multidimensional non-ordered discrete data space indexing, etc. Office: Univ Mich 4901 Evergreen Rd Dearborn MI 48128-1491

ZHU, SHA, materials engineer; d. Yanwen Zhang; m. Daming Wang, Mar. 25, 2002; children: Sophia Xueqi Wang, Gracie Jiaqi Wang. PhD, U. Mich., Ann Arbor, 2003. Postdoc. rschr. U. Mich., 2004—06, U. Calif., Davis, 2006—07; sr. material sci. engr. Seagate Tech. Inc, Fremont, Calif., 2008—. Recipient Disting. award, Microanalysis Soc. Am., 2001. Mem.: Sigma XI. Achievements include research in synthesizing nano-particles in various substrates. Home: 47083 Benns Ter Fremont CA 94539 Office: Seagate Tech 47010 kato St Fremont CA 94538

ZHU, SHANKUAN, epidemiologist, educator; s. Lianghao Zhu and Hanzhu Zhen; m. Xiaoou Huang, Aug. 28, 1991; 1 child, Xueyi Zoey. MD, Zhejiang U. Sch. Medicine, Hangzhou, China, 1988; PhD, Nagoya U., Japan, 1997. Asst., sch. medicine Zhejiang U., 1988—92, cons. Emergency and Acute Care Medicine Ctr., 2nd Affiliated Hosp., 2005—, chair prof., 2007—, dir., Obesity and Body Composition Rsch. Ctr., sch. medicine, 2007—, dir., Injury Prevention and Control Rsch. Ctr., 2007—; tchg. asst. Nagoya U. Sch. Medicine, 1993—97, asst. prof., 1997—2000; postdoc. rsch. fellow Obesity Rsch. Ctr., Columbia U. Coll. Physician and Surgeons, NYC, 2000—03, rsch. assoc., 2003; sr. epidemiologist Med. Coll. Wis., Milw., 2003—08, asst. prof., 2003—07, assoc. adj. prof., 2008—. Contbr. numerous sci. articles to profl. jours. Dir. N.Am. Zhejiang U. Alumni Assn., 2005, N.Am. Zhukezhen Edn. Found., 2007, Wis. Crash Outcome Data Evaluation Sys. Com., Milw., 2003. Grantee, Ministry of Edn., Sci., Sports and Culture japan, 1998, Tanita Corp., 2002, Weight Watchers Internat., Inc., 2002, Pfizer Pharm. Inc., 2003, Nat. Inst. Health, 2007; Postdoc. fellowship, Mead-Johnson and Merck Pharmas., 2000. Mem.: APHA, Chinese Jour. Emergency Medicine (editl. bd. mem.), Soc. Advancement Violence and Injury Rsch., Am. Coll. Epidemiology, Assn. Advancement Automotive Medicine, N.Am. Assn. Study Obesity, Internat. Epidemiology Soc. Office: Med Coll Wis 8701 Watertown Plank Rd Milwaukee WI 53226 Business E-Mail: szhu@mcw.edu.

ZHU, TINGJU, environmental scientist; PhD, U. Calif., Davis, 2004. Sr. scientist Internat. Food Policy Rsch. Inst., Washington, 2005—. Mem.: ASCE, Internat. Water Resources Assn., Internat. Assn. Hydrological Scis., Am. Geophys. Union, Sigma Xi. Office: Internat Food Policy Rsch Inst 2033 K St Washington DC 20006 Business E-Mail: t.zhu@cgiar.org.

ZHU, WEIDONG, engineering educator; s. Chao Zhu and Xiuju Wang; m. Yue D. Dai; 1 child, Angela. PhD in Mech. Engring., U. Calf., Berkeley, 1994. Asst. prof. mech. engring. Chinese U. Hong Kong, Shatin, China, 1994—97, U. ND, Grand Forks, 1997—99; prof. mech. engring. U. Md., Balt. County, 1999—. Recipient aaward, NSF, 2004. Mem.: ASME, Am. Soc. Engring. Edn., Soc. Exptl. Mechanics. Office: Univ Md Balt County 1000 Hilltop Cir Baltimore MD 21050 Office Fax: 410-455-1052. Business E-Mail: wzhu@umbc.edu.

ZHU, XIANGDONG, physics professor; b. Beijing; married. PhD, U. Calif., Berkeley, 1989. Asst. prof. physics U. Calif., Davis, 1989—93, assoc. prof. physics, 1993—98, prof. physics, 1998—. Mem.: Am. Vacuum Soc., Am. Chem. Soc., Optical Soc. America, Am. Phys. Soc. Office: Univ Calif One Shields Ave Davis CA 95616

ZHU, XIANJIN, application developer; PhD, SUNY, Stony Brook, 2008. Software devel. engr. Microsoft Corp., Redmond, Wash., 2008—. Achievements include research in collaborative information processing and query evaluation in wireless sensor networks.

ZHU, XINYUAN, chemistry professor; married. PhD, Shanghai Jiao Tong U. Prof. Shanghai Jiao Tong U., 2005—. Office: Shanghai Jiao Tong Univ 800 Dongchuan Rd Shanghai 200240 China Office Fax: 0086-21-34205722. Business E-Mail: xyzhu@sjtu.edu.cn.

ZHU, YIFU, physics professor; married. PhD, U. Va., charlotteville, 1987. Rsch. scientist Schlumberger-doll Rsch., Ridgefield, Conn., 1990—93; prof. Fla. Internat. U., Miami, 1994—. Contbr. articles to profl jours. Office: Florida Internat Univ University Pk Miami FL 33199

ZHU, YILIANG, research scientist, educator; BSc, Shanghai U., 1982; MSc, Queen's U. Kingston, Ont., Can., 1987; PhD, U. Toronto, 1991. Rsch. scientist Environ. Health Ctr. Health Can., Ottawa, Ont., 1991—93; from assoc. prof. to prof. U. South Fla., Tampa, 1993—. Principle biostatistician Shriner's Hosps. for Children, Tampa, 1997—2000; CEO Scinfo Assocs., Tampa, 2000—; vis. scientist Nat. Ctr. for Environ. Assessment, U.S. EPA, Research Triangle Park, NC, 2000—01; mem. organ transplant adv. com. Dept. HHS, 2005—; mem. biology sys. modelling sect. NIH, 2006; mem. dioxin risk rev. com. NAS, 2005—06, mem. tetrachloroethylene risk review com., 2008—09. Exec. com. mem. Asian Am. Coalition Fla., Tampa, 2001—02; founding pres. Chinese Am. Assn. Tampa Bay, 2001—02; pres. USF Asian Faculty and Staff Alliance, Tampa, 1997—98. Grantee, NSF, 1999—2002. Mem.: Am. Statis. Assn. Office: Coll Pub Health Univ S Fla 13201 Bruce B Downs Blvd Tampa FL 33612 Business E-Mail: yzhu@health.usf.edu.

ZHU, YINGXUAN, engineering educator; d. Shenquan Zhu and Youhua Wang. MS, Syracuse U., NY, 2007. Tchg. asst. Syracuse U., 2005—. Mem.: IEEE.

ZHU, YONGJIE, engineer; d. Zhengzhu Zhu and Jianlan Sun. PhD, Ohio State U., Columbus, 2008. Rsch. asst. Harbin Inst. Tech., Heilongjiang, China, 1999—2002, Ohio State U., 2003—08, tchg. asst., 2004—07; sr. engr. Cummins Inc., Columbus, Ind., 2008—. Contbr. to profl. jours. Mem.: Soc. Automobile Engrs. Business E-Mail: zhu.120@osu.edu.

ZHU, YUN, engineer, researcher; d. Shunyu Zhu and Zhiying Liang; m. Jiwei Chen, June 29, 2000. PhD, U. Calif., Irvine, 2007. Intelligent network engr. China Telecom., Nanjing, 1998—2001; grad. student rschr. U. Calif., Irvine, 2002—07. Contbr. articles to profl. jours. Recipient IEEE Marconi Best Paper award, IEEE Comm. Soc., 2006, Best Student Paper award, U. Calif., 2005. Achievements include research in design, analyze, implement, test efficient space-time codes in MIMO systems. E-mail: yzhu1@uci.edu.

ZHU, ZHENYU, systems engineer; b. Suzhou, Jiangsu, China, Feb. 27, 1972; s. Yubin Liu and Jianlan Ni; m. Yi Wang; 1 child, Vivian. PhD, Lehigh U., Bethlehem, Pa., 2000. Cert. microsoft sys. engr. Wa., 1997. Mem. tech. staff Bell Labrs., Allentown, Pa., 1999—2002; IC arch. Intel Corp., Folsom, Calif., 2005—. Contbr. articles to profl. jours. (Pres. award, Chinese Acad. Sci., 1996). Recipient Divsn. Recognition award, Intel Corp., 2008. Mem.: IEEE. Achievements include invention of SIMO based optical PMD precoder. Personal E-mail: zhenyu.k.zhu@gmail.com.

ZHUANG, HONG, food scientist; s. Jiwen Zhuang and Qingling Chen; m. Yuan Sun, Jan. 31, 1983; children: Lefan, Louise Leyi. PhD, U. Ky., Lexington, 1996. Sr. rsch. scientist Fresh Express Inc., Franklin Pk., Ill., 1998—2003, Chiquita Brands Internat. Inc., Cin., 2003—06; rsch. food technologist ARS-USDA, Athens, Ga., 2006—. Contbr. articles to profl. jours. Mem.: Chinese Am. Food Soc. (pres. 2000—), Inst. Food Technologists (chair fruit and vegetable product divsn. 1993—). Personal E-mail: hongzhuang08@gmail.com. Business E-Mail: hong.zhuang@ars.usda.gov.

ZHUANG, JUN, engineering educator, researcher; b. Nanjing, Jiangsu, China, May 20, 1980; m. Jie Zhao; 1 child, Emily T. BA in Indsl. Engring., Southeast U., Nanjing, China, 2002; MS in Agrl. Econs., U. Ky., Lexington, 2004; PhD in Indsl. Engring., U. Wis., Madison, 2008. Rsch. asst. U. Ky., Lexington, 2002—04; instr., tchg./rsch. asst., grader U. Wis.-Madison, 2004—08; ops. rschr. Dow Chem. Co., Freeport, Tex., 2007. Contbr. scientific papers to profl. jours. Recipient 2d Place award, Internat. Process Design Contest, Intelligen Inc., 2006. Mem.: IEEE, Soc. of Risk Analysis, Inst. Indsl. Engrs., Soc. for Judgment and Decision Making, Inst. Ops. Rsch. and the Mgmt. Scis. (see the award session). Baptist. Home: 1525 Amherst Manor Dr Apt 403 Buffalo NY 14221-2018 Office: U Buffalo SUNY 403 Bell Hall Buffalo NY 14260

ZHUGE, JIAN, medical educator, researcher; married. MS, Tongji Med. U., Wuhan, 1994; PhD, Zhejiang U., China, 2003. Assoc. prof. Zhejiang U., Hangzhou, 2000—04; postdoc. fellow Mt. Sinai Sch. Medicine, NYC, 2004—08, instr., 2008—. Contbr. scientific papers. Achievements include research in cytochrome P450 2E1 and oxidative stress. Office: Mount Sinai Sch Medicine One Gustave L Levy Pl Box 1194 New York NY 10029 Personal E-mail: zhugejian@yahoo.com. Business E-Mail: jian.zhuge@mssm.edu.

ZHUKOVSKY, MIKHAIL ANDREYEVICH, biophysicist; b. Leningrad, Russia, Jan. 12, 1970; s. Andrey Pavlovich Zhukovsky and Valeria Grigoryevna Zhukovskaya. MSc, St. Petersburg State U., Russia, 1993, PhD, 1997. Rschr. St. Petersburg State U., 1997—98; post-doctoral fellow NIH, Bethesda, Md., 1998—2002, Dana-Farber Cancer Inst., Boston, 2002—07, Max Planck Inst. Biophys. Chemistry, Goettingen, Germany, 2007—08; rschr. Saarland U., Saarbruecken, Germany, 2008—. Scholar, Swedish Inst., Stockholm, 1995. Mem.: AAAS, Biophys. Soc. Avocations: chess, travel. Office: Dept Biol Experimental Physics Saarland Univ Saarbruecken D-66123 Germany Home Phone: 49-681-925-6432; Office Phone: 49 681-302-68540. Business E-Mail: mikhail.zhukovsky@physik.uni-saarland.de.

ZHUO, JIA LONG, physiologist; b. Nanning, China, Oct. 25, 1956; arrived in Australia, 1984, naturalized, 1994; s. Ju Tang and Feng Zhao (Luo) Z.; m. Xiao Chun Li; children: David, Freda. MD, Guangxi Medical Univ., Nanning, 1983; MSc, Univ. Melbourne, Melbourne, Australia, 1985; PhD, Univ. Melbourne, 1990. Medical officer Guangxi Medical Univ., Nanning, 1982-83, assoc. lectr., 1983-84; rsch. officer Nat. Health and Med. Rsch. Coun. Univ. Melbourne, 1991-92, postdoc. fellow Nat. Health and Med. Rsch. Coun., Austin and Repatriation Med. Ctr., 1993-96, sr. rsch. officer Howard Florey Inst. Exptl. Physiology and Medicine, 1997-99; vis. asst. prof. physiology Tulane U. Sch. Medicine, New Orleans, 1999—. Contbr. numerous articles to profl. jour., chpts. to books. Recipient Overseas Rsch. fellowship Guangxi Gov., 1984, Australian Postdoc. fellowship Nat. Health and Med. Rsch. Coun., Australia, 1993-96, Young Australian Investigators award Internat. Hypertension Soc., 1994; named hon. prof. physiology Guangxi Med. U., 1995. Fellow Australian High Blood Pressure Rsch. Coun.; mem. N.Y. Acad. Scis., Australian Pharmacology Physiology Soc., Australian New Zealand Soc. Nephrology. Avocations: movies, novel reading, gardening, australian football. Office: Henry Ford Hosp 2799 W Grand Blvd Detroit MI 48202 Office Fax: 313-916-1479. Business E-Mail: jzhuo1@hfhs.org.

ZHURAVENKO, IGOR N., health services administrator, physician; b. Lvov, Ukraine, Mar. 6, 1959; came to U.S., 1992; s. Naum and Raisa Zhuravenko; m. Svetlana Zhuravenko, Dec. 1, 1990; children: Dimitri, Gary, Richard, Gabrielle. MD, Lvov Med. Sch., 1983. Diplomate Am. Bd. Internal Medicine. Physician Gen. Hosp., Rovno, Ukraine, 1984-88, Diagnostic Ctr., Lvov, 1989-92; clin. instr. ultrasound Med. Sch., Lvov, 1990-92; resident in internal medicine SUNY, Buffalo, 1995-98, clin. asst. instr. medicine, 1995-98; physician Ocean Med. Plz., 2003—07; pres. IZNY Med. PC, 2007—. Physician MEDEX, Forest Hills, NY, 1998—99; med. dir. Adult Home Sites/CHS, NYC, 1999—; mem. sci. adv. bd. Nutrition Superstores, Inc., West Palm Beach, Fla., 1999—; pres. Z Best Med. Care, P.C., 1999—2003; med. dir. Privilege Care a Diagnostic and Treatment Ctr., 1999—2001. Contbr. articles to profl. jours. Named one of America's Top Physicians, 2003—08. Mem. ACP, AMA (Physician's Recognition award 1998, 2002, 03, 04, 05, 06, 07, 08, 08, 09), Am. Thyroid Assn. Avocations: chess, reading, computer, internet. Office Phone: 718-375-1777. E-mail: IZBEST@aol.com.

ZIAMANDANIS, CLAIRE M., language educator; b. Syracuse, NY, Mar. 27; m. Stephen J. Ziamandanis; children: Grace, Dennis. PhD, U. Albany, NY, 1995. Assoc. prof. Spanish Coll. St. Rose, Albany, 1995—, faculty advisor, study abroad, 2001—, chair, fgn. lang. dept., 2004—. Office: Coll Saint Rose 432 Western Ave Albany NY 12203 Business E-Mail: ziamandc@strose.edu.

ZIAVRAS, SOTIRIOS GEORGE, computer and electrical engineer, educator; came to the U.S., 1984; s. George Spyros and Sofia George Z. Diploma in elec. engring., Nat. Tech. U., Athens, 1984; MS, Ohio U., 1985; DSc, George Washington U., 1990. Rschr. Riso Nat. Lab., Denmark, 1983; tchg. and rsch. asst. Ohio U., Athens, 1984—85; disting. grad. tchg. asst. George Washington U., Washington, 1985—89, rsch. asst., 1986; from asst. prof. to assoc. prof. N.J. Inst. Tech., Newark, 1990—2001, prof., 2001—, assoc. chmn. grad. studies, 2001—04, 2007—08. Rschr. Walter Reed Army Inst. Rsch., Silver Spring, Md., 1987-88; rsch. asst. U. Md., College Park, 1988-89; vis. prof. George Mason U., Fairfax, Va., 1990; dir. internet engring. program N.J. Inst. Tech., 2000-01; vice chmn. faculty coun., N.J. Inst. Tech., 2000-01, chmn., 2001-02, coord. ECE Grad. Focus Area in Computer Architecture and Sys., 2008-; assoc. chmn. grad. studies, 2007-; disting. vis. prof. Chung-Ang U., Seoul, Republic of Korea, 2005. Editor Trends in Applied Scis. Rsch.; assoc. editor: Pattern Recognition Jour., 1994-2006; contbr. articles to profl. jours. Recipient Rsch. Initiation award NSF, 1991, New Millenium Computing Point Design award NSF/DARPA, 1996; grantee Dept. Energy, 2002-06. Mem. IEEE (sr.), Assn. for Computing Machinery, N.Y. Acad. Scis. (adv. bd. CIS sect. 1994-97), Eta Kappa Nu. Achievements include development of class of high-performance, low-cost interconnection networks for massively parallel computers called reduced hypercubes; reconfigurable chip multiprocessors; introduction of class of multilevel architectures for high-performance multiresolution image analysis, reconfigurable computing project for the Power Grid to investigate parallel processing with FPGAS. Office: NJ Inst Tech Elec Computer Engring Dept Newark NJ 07102 Home Phone: 201-592-0156; Office Phone: 973-596-5651. Business E-Mail: ziavras@njit.edu.

ZIBART, MICHAEL ALAN, wholesale book company executive; b. Nashville, Mar. 12, 1947; s. Alan Walter and Joy (Hughes) Z.; m. Margaret Anne Boyd, Dec. 27, 1976; children: Emily Joy, Mary Claire. BA, Vanderbilt U., 1969. Mgmt. trainee Zibart Bros. Books, Nashville, 1961-69; property mgr. Pollack Co., Nashville, 1966-69; buyer Ingram Book Co., Nashville, 1970-75, mgr. trade dept., 1976, v.p., 1976-85, exec. v.p., 1985-88; founder, pres. ProMotion, Inc., Nashville, 1988—. Author: Almanac on Bookselling, 3d edit., 1980; pub. (monthly book review) BookPage, 1988—. Office: ProMotion Inc 2143 Belcourt Ave Nashville TN 37212-3503 Office Phone: 615-292-8926. Business E-Mail: michael@bookpage.com.

ZIBELL, DONALD FREDRICK, lawyer; b. St. Paul, Feb. 13, 1937; s. Otto Ernst and Anna Emma Zibell; m. Luella Louise Lepisto, Oct. 14, 1967; 1 child, Deanne. BA, U. Minn., 1959; JD, William Mitchell Coll. Law, 1962. Bar: Minn.; cert. public acct. Minn. Mng. tax ptnr. Boulay, Heutmaker, Zibell and Co., PLLP, Mpls., 1959—90; real estate devel., 1965—; pvt. practice Roseville, Minn., 1990—. Dir. Cmty. Resource Bank, Northfield, Minn., 1999—; dir., treas. Poly-Cam, Inc., Anoka, Minn., 1992—; dir. Roseville (Minn.) Cmty. Bank, 1983—91. Trustee, treas. North Suburban Cmty. Found., Roseville, 1982—; dir., asst. treas. Donald and Luella Zibell Family Found., Shoreview, Minn., 1999—; trustee, exec. com. William Mitchell Coll. Law, St. Paul, 2002—; mem. various other charitable bds. and adv. coms. Named one of Ten Outstanding Young Men of Minn., Minn. Jaycees, 1971, 100 Who Made a Difference, William Mitchell Coll. Law, 2001. Mem.: ABA, Roseville Rotary Club (former pres. 1970—, Paul Harris fellow 1980), Minn. Soc. CPAs and AICPA (life; former com. chair 1964—). Republican. Luth. Avocations: gardening, reading, boating, golf, spectator sports. Home: 3422 Chandler Rd Saint Paul MN 55126-3914 Office: 2233 N Hamline Ave 511 Saint Paul MN 55113 Office Phone: 651-633-3623. Personal E-mail: zibellshor@aol.com.

ZIDICH, JOHN M., publishing executive; b. San Francisco, 1954; m. Pam Zidich; children: Katie, Ali. Attended, Santa Clara U. Circulation dist. mgr. to advt. and sales mgmt. positions The Record (Gannett Newspapers), Stockton, Calif., 1977—90; retail advt. mgr. Reno Gazette-Jour., Nev., 1990—2000, pres., pub., 2000—01; exec. v.p. Ariz. Republic, Phoenix, 2001—04, pres., COO, 2004—05, CEO, pub., 2005—. Bd. dir. Banner Health Found., Greater Phoenix C. of C., Phoenix Suns Charities. Mem.: Ariz. Sports Found. Avocations: cooking, golf, entertaining. Office: Arizona Republic 200 E Van Buren St PO Box 1950 Phoenix AZ 85001 Office Phone: 602-444-8000.*

ZIEBARTH, ROBERT CHARLES, management consultant; b. Evanston, Ill., Sept. 12, 1936; s. Charles A. and Marian (Miller) Z.; m. Patience Arnold Kirkpatrick, Aug. 28, 1971; children— Dana Kirkpatrick, Scott Kirkpatrick, Christopher, Nicholas. AB, Princeton, 1958; MBA, Harvard, 1964. With Bell & Howell Co., Chgo., 1964-73, treas., chief fin. officer, 1969-73; mgmt. cons. Ziebarth Co., 1973—. Mem. dirs. adv. bd. Arkwright Boston Ins. Co., devel. com. Nat. Assn. Ind. Schs.; bd. dirs. M.B.A. Resources, Inc., Telemedia, Inc., Corp. Resources, Inc., Nordemann Grimm Inc. Assoc. Community Renewal Soc., Citizens Coun. Gateway House; mem. Ill. Bd. Higher Edn., Ill. Joint Edn. Commn.; trustee Choate Sch.; trustee, pres. Latin Sch.Chgo., Chgo. Maternity Ctr.; bd. dirs. Harvard Bus. Sch. Fund, U.S.O., Inc., Prentice Women's Hosp., Northwestern Meml. Corp., Found. for Reproductive Rsch. and Edn., Endowments Inc., Bond Portfolio Endowments Inc. Served to lt. USNR, 1958-62. Mem. Naval Hist. Found., Art Inst. Chgo., Chgo. Hist. Soc., Mus. Modern Art. Clubs: Mid-Am. (Chgo.), Racquet (Chgo.), Saddle and Cycle (Chgo.), Economic (Chgo.), Executives (Chgo.). Presbyterian. Office: PO Box 4569 Ketchum ID 83340-4569

ZIEBARTH-BOVILL, JANE K., social sciences educator; d. Wayne W. and Renee Ziebarth; m. Ron Bovill, Mar. 4, 2000. PhD, U. Nebr., Lincoln, 1996. Cert. in adminstrn., curriculum & instrn. U. Nebr., 1996. Assoc. prof. U. Nebr., Kearney, 1996—. Emerging leaders acad. NEA, Washington, 2008—. Mem.: Kappa Delta Pi (assoc. advisor 2008—). Democrat. Lutheran. Avocations: reading, walking, gardening, travel. Office: Univ Nebr Kearney 1615 W 24th St Kearney NE 68849 Office Phone: 308-865-8815. Business E-Mail: ziebarthj@unk.edu.

ZIEBOLD, BARBARA M., music educator; d. Joseph F. and Martha M. Ziebold. MusM, Bowling Green State U., Ohio., 1975. String instr. Fremont City Schs., String Dept. Head, Ohio, 1979—2006, Terra CC, 2007—. Contest adjudicator Ohio Music Edn. Assn., 1998—. Mem.: Terra Baroque Orch., Terra Chamber Arts Orch., Terra Chamber String Ensemble, Heidelberg Coll.-Cmty. Orch., Perrysburg Symphony Orch., Ohio String Tchrs. Assn., Am. String Tchrs. Assn., Music Educators Nat. Conf., Ohio Music Edn. Assn. Avocations: camping, knitting. Office: Terra Cmty Coll 2830 Napoleon Rd Fremont OH 43420 Business E-Mail: bziebold@terra.edu.

ZIEGLER, ANNETTE KINGSLAND, state supreme court justice; b. Grand Rapids, Mich., Mar. 6, 1964; d. Rex Raymond and Joyce Wanda (Wirth) Kingsland; m. Jeffrey John Ziegler, July 1, 1994; 3 children. B in Psychology and Bus. Adminstrn., Hope Coll., Holland, Mich., 1986; JD, Marquette U., Milw., 1989. Bar: Wis. 1989. Assoc. O'Neil, Cannon & Hollman S.C., Milw., 1989-95; pro bono spl. asst. dist. atty. Milw. County, 1992, 1996; asst. US atty. Ea. Dist. Wis., Milw., 1995—97; judge Washington County Cir. Ct., 1997—2007; Ct. Appeals Judge Dist. II Ct. Appeals Jud. Exch. Program, 1999; assoc. justice Wis. Supreme Ct., 2007—. Faculty mem. Wis. Jud. Coll. Staff editor jour. Marquette U. Law Sch., 1987-89; contbr. articles to profl. jours. Mem. ABA, ATLA, Wis. State Bar, Wis. Acad. Trial Lawyers, Washington County Bar Assn., Milw. Bar Assn., Assn. Women Lawyers. Office: Wis Supreme Ct 16 E State Capitol PO Box 1688 Madison WI 53701-1688*

ZIEGLER, DONALD EMIL, retired federal judge; b. Pitts., Oct. 1, 1936; s. Emil Nicholas and Elizabeth Ziegler; m. Claudia J. Chermak, May 1, 1965; 1 son, Scott Emil. BA, Duquesne U., 1958; LL.B., Georgetown U., 1961. Bar: Pa. 1962, U.S. Supreme Ct. 1967. Practice law, Pitts., 1962-74; judge Ct. of Common Pleas of Allegheny County, Pa., 1974-78, U.S. Dist. Ct. (we. dist.) Pa., Pitts., 1978—2003, chief judge, 1994-2001. Mem. Jud. Conf. U.S., 1997-2000. Treas. Big Bros. of Allegheny County, 1969-74. Mem. ABA, Pa. Bar Assn., Allegheny County Bar Assn., Am. Judicature Soc., St. Thomas More Soc. Clubs: Oakmont Country. Democrat. Roman Catholic. Office: 100 Ross St Ste 105 Pittsburgh PA 15219-2013 Office Phone: 412-281-6770. E-mail: coopzieg@aol.com.

ZIEGLER, DONALD ROBERT, cpa; b. Lancaster, Pa., Nov. 15, 1932; s. John Jacob and Esther Mae (McKelly) Z.; m. Suzanne Foster; children: D. Rand, Scott F., Kurt J. BS in Econ. Acctg., Franklin and Marshall Coll., 1954. CPA, Pa. Mgr., sr. staff mem. Price Waterhouse, Phila., 1954-67, ptnr., 1967-92, sr. practice ptnr., 1978-92, mng. ptnr. Mid-Atlantic area, 1985-88, vice chmn. S.E. region, 1988-92, mem. policy bd. NYC, 1980-88, mem. mgmt. com., 1986-92. Author: (with others) Managing and Accounting for Inventories, 1980; contbg. author various books in field. Trustee Franklin and Marshall Coll., 1983—, mem. alumni exec. coun., 1979—83, mem. exec. com., 1995—, chmn. audit com., 1989—2003, vice-chmn. bd. trustees, 2002—, mem. Phila. alumni coun.; trustee Pa. Ballet, 1988—92, 1994—95, mem. devel. and fin. coms., vice chmn. bd. trustees, 1989—92, chmn. exec. com., 1989—91; chmn. audit com., budget and fin. com., ethics com., bd. of adjustment Town of Dewey Beach; bd. dirs. Beebe Med. Ctr., 2000—06, Beebe Med. Found., 2001—06, So. Del. Surgery Ctr., 2003—06. With US Army, 1955—57. Recipient Outstanding Soldier award U.S. Army, 1955, Disting. Svc. Alumni medal Franklin and Marshall Coll., 1991. Mem. AICPA (auditing stds. com. 1973-76, chmn. subcom. fraud 1976-80), Pa. Inst. CPAs (Phila. chpt. exec. coun.), Rehoboth Beach Country Club (bd. govs. 2000-08, treas. 2003-08), Phila. Aviation Club (bd. govs. and treas. 1969-90), Franklin and Marshall Soc. Disting. Alumni. Home: One West St Dewey Beach DE 19971 Office: PricewaterhouseCoopers LLP Two Commerce Sq 2001 Market St Ste 1700 Philadelphia PA 19103-7042 Personal E-mail: drsfzig@comcast.net.

ZIEGLER, EKHARD ERICH, pediatrics educator; b. Saalfelden, Austria, Apr. 12, 1940; children: Stefan, Gabriele, Lena. MD, U. Innsbruck, Austria, 1964. Diplomate: Am. Bd. Pediatrics. Intern U. Innsbruck, 1966-67, resident in pediatrics, 1967-68 70-71, resident in pharmacology, 1964-66, asst. dept. pediatrics, 1970-73; vis. instr. pediatrics U. Iowa, Iowa City, 1968-70, asst. prof. pediatrics, 1973-76, assoc. prof., 1976-81, prof., 1981—. Mem. nutrition study sect. NIH, 1988-92. Recipient Nutrition award Am. Acad. Pediactrics, 1988. Mem. Am. Soc. Clin. Nutrition, Soc. Pediatric Research, Soc. Exptl. Biology and Medicine, N.Am. Soc. Pediatric Gastroenterology, Midwest Soc. Pediatric Research, Am. Pediatric Soc., The Nutrition Soc., N.Y. Acad. Scis., Am. Acad. Pediatrics., Am. Dietetic Assn. (hon.). Clubs: Univ. Athletic (Iowa City). Office: U Iowa Dept Pediatrics Iowa City IA 52242 Office Phone: 319-335-4570. Business E-Mail: ekhard-ziegler@uiowa.edu.

ZIEGLER, JAMES F., science educator; s. Francis Marion and Malinda Lorie Ziegler; m. Ann T. Ziegler, Aug. 23, 1969; children: Samuel B., Matthias D. BS, Yale U., New Haven, 1957, MS, 1967, PhD. Rsch. scientist Internation Bus. Machines, Inc., Yorktown, NY, 1967—2000; prof. US Naval Acad., Annapolis, Md., 2000—. Contbr. articles to profl. jours. Lt USN, 1957—60. Recipient Sci. Achievement award, Internation Conf. Ion Beam Analysis, 1992, Internat. Ion Implantation Tech., 1996, Humboldt Soc., Germany, 1994; fellow, Am. Phys. Soc., 1987, IEEE, 1996. Achievements include discovery of effect of cosmic rays on terrestrial electronics and computers. Office: US Naval Acad Chauvenet Hall Annapolis MD 21402

ZIEGLER, JENNIFER ANNE, management consultant, educator; d. Michael J. and Joan M. Thackaberry. PhD, U. Colo., Boulder, 2000. CPA DC, 1990. Asst. prof. Purdue U., West Lafayette, Ind., 2002—07, Valparaiso U., Ind., 2007—. Pres., CEO Safety Culture Consulting LLC, Plymouth, Ind., 2006—. Office: Valparaiso Univ 1809 Chapel Dr Schnabel 6 Valparaiso IN 46383

ZIEGLER, JOHN ALAN, historian, political scientist, educator; b. Belleville, Ill., Jan. 28, 1933; s. John Wendell and Georgia Elizabeth (Reppel) Z.; m. Carol Ruth Alcorn, June 15, 1963; children: Mimi, Robin. BS, So. Ill. U., 1955, MS, 1956; Rotary Found. fellow, St. Andrews U., Scotland, 1956-57; PhD, Syracuse U., 1970. Asst. prof. polit. sci. and social sci. Calif. State U., Hayward, 1966-72; lectr. Am. civilization Calif. State Poly. U., Pomona, 1972-74; assoc. prof. polit. sci. Hendrix Coll., Conway, Ark., 1974-84, prof., 1984-91, Harold and Lucy Cabe Disting. prof. history and politics, 1991-98, emeritus prof., 1998—, legendary lectr., 1998. Coord. and founder Hendrix-Oxford program, 1979-98, head social sci. area, 1978-82, chmn. dept. polit. sci. and history, 1974-83; guest lectr. St. Peter's Coll., Oxford U., 1983, 90, 94, Clare Coll., Cambridge U., 1988, 89, Dundee U., 1994; Churchill life fellow Westminster Coll., Fulton, Mo.; participant Wilton Pk. Confs., Wiston House Internat. Conf. Ctr., Sussex, England, 1979—. Author: Experimentalism and Institutional Change, 1994, In Search of the Special Relationship with Britain, 2000. With AUS, 1957-60. Mem. AAUP, Friends Churchill Meml. (life), Am. Friends Wilton Park, ACLU, Royal Oak Found., South Downs Soc. (life), Dundee (Scotland) Curling Club. Mem. United Ch. of Christ. Home: PO Box 1045 Conway AR 72033-1045 Office: Hendrix Coll Conway AR 72032 E-mail: johnziegler@webtv.net.

ZIEGLER, MELANIE MCCLURE, social sciences educator; d. Don Miller and Ruth Crockett McClure; m. Richard Alan Ziegler, July 6, 1974; children: Erich Alan, Heidi Elaine. PhD, Miami U., Oxford, OH, 2004. Faculty internat. studies program Miami U., 2005—. Author: (book) US-Cuban Cooperation Past, Present, and Future. Home: 162 Ryan Dr Oxford OH 45056 Office: 122 MacMillan Hall Miami Univ Oxford OH 45056 Office Phone: 513-529-9305. Home Fax: 513-529-1890. Personal E-mail: zieglemm@muohio.edu.

ZIEGLER, R. W., JR., lawyer, consultant; b. Pitts. children: Caroline, Gretchen, Jeremy, Benjamin, Phoebe, Polly. Student, Carnegie Mellon, U. Pitts.; JD, Duquesne U., 1972. Bar: Pa. 1972, Calif. 1981, U.S. Ct. Appeals (3d cir.) 1977, U.S. Dist. Ct. (we. dist.) Pa. 1972, U.S. Supreme Ct. 1977, U.S. Tax Ct. 1978, Calif. 1982, U.S. Dist. Ct. (no. dist.) Calif. 1982, U.S. Ct. Appeals (9th cir.) 1982. Ptnr. Ziegler & Ombres, Pitts., 1973-79; pres. Ziegler Ross Inc., San Francisco, 1979—2007, Ziegler Consultants, 2007—, Mesa Consulting LLC, 2009—. Lectr. for Bar Assns. Author: Law Practice Management; editor: Law Office Guide in Computing. Mem. ABA, Am. Mgmt. Assn., Pa. State Bar Assn., Calif. State Bar Assn., Assn. of Legal Admin., Young Presidents' Org., Am. Assn. of Law Librarians., San Francisco Bar Assn. Office: 315A Meigs Rd Ste 355 Santa Barbara CA 93109 Office Phone: 415-682-4944.

ZIEGLER, RICHARD FERDINAND, lawyer; b. Elizabeth, NJ, Aug. 1, 1949; m. Carolyn Lewis; children: Anna B., David A., Andrew P. D-J. BA summa cum laude in Hist., Yale U., 1971; JD magna cum laude, Harvard U., 1975. Bar: NY 1976, US Dist. Ct. (so. and ea. dists. NY)

1976, US Dist. Ct. (ea. dist. Mich.) 1982, US Supreme Ct. 1984, US Dist. Ct. (no. dist. NY) 1987. Law clk. to judge US Dist. Ct. (so. dist.) NY, NYC, 1975-76; assoc. Paul, Weiss, Rifkind, Wharton & Garrison, NYC, 1976-77; asst. US atty. (so. dist.) NY US Dept. Justice, NYC, 1977-80; assoc. Cleary, Gottlieb, Steen & Hamilton, NYC, 1980-83, ptnr., 1983—2002; sr. v.p. legal affairs, gen. counsel 3M Co., St. Paul, 2003—07; ptnr. Jenner & Block LLP, NYC, 2007—; mng. ptnr. NY Office. Lectr. Columbia Law Sch., NYC, 1997—2000. Contbr. articles to profl. jours.; author: New Obstucles in Setting Tone at The Top. Bd. dirs. Legal Aide Soc. NY, 1993-95; bd. trustee William Mitchell Coll. Law, chmn., Audit & Fin. Com., 2006-07. Mem. ABA, Assn. Bar City of NY, Fed. Bar Coun., NY State Bar Assn. (chmn. com. on profl. ethics, 1995-98), Assn. Gen. Coun. (mem. exec. com. 2006-07) Office: Jenner & Block LLP 919 Third Ave 37th Fl New York NY 10022 Office Phone: 212-891-1600, 212-891-1680. Business E-Mail: rfziegler@jenner.com.

ZIEGLER, ROBERT GEORGE, psychiatrist, family therapist; b. NYC, Nov. 10, 1941; s. John and Barbara Edna (Seeler) Z.; m. Patricia Curnen; children: Lisa, Jeffrey Peter. BA in English, Hofstra U., 1963, MA in English, 1964; MD, Columbia U., 1968. Diplomate Am. Bd. Psychiatry and Neurology, Am. Bd. Child Psychiatry. Child psychiatrist Boston U., 1974-75, South Shore Mental Health Ctr.-Tufts U., Quincy, Mass., 1974-79; dir. Boundaries Therapy Ctr., Acton, Mass., 1975—. Dir. family svc. team seizure unit Children's Hosp.-Harvard U. Med. Sch., 1978-89; cons. Therapeutic Presch., Concord, Mass., 1978—87, Somerville (Mass.) Mental Health Ctr., 1987—92, assoc. prof., sr. clinician CHA Harvard Med. Sch. Author: Does Your Child Have Epilepsy?, Homemade Books to Help Kids Hope, 1984, Sharing Care: The Integration of Daily Approaches with Childs Treatment, 1999; contbr. articles to med. jours. Mem. profl. adv. bd. Epilepsy Soc., Boston, 1987—. Mem. Am. Psychiat. Assn., Am. Acad. Child Psychiatry. Avocations: windsailing, biking. Office: Boundaries Therapy Ctr 518 Great Rd Acton MA 01720-5670

ZIEGLER, ROCHELLE ELIZABETH, special education educator; b. Virginia Beach, Va., Dec. 21, 1974; d. Robert Herman and Elizabeth Ethiel Ziegler. BS in Interdisciplinary Studies /Mental Retardation, Norfolk State U., Norfolk, Va., 2003; M in Severe Disabilities, Norfolk State U., 2005. Tchr. asst. Southeastern Coop. Ednl. Programs, Norfolk, Va., 1995—2004; tchr. spl. edn. Portsmouth Pub. Schs., 2005—. Mentor Young Sister's In Christ, Virginia Beach, Va., 1996. Recipient Nat. Collegiate Edn. Awards, US Achievement Acad., 2000; scholar All-Am. Scholar at Large Divsn., 2000. Mem.: Coun. of Exceptional Children (assoc.). Democrat-Npl. Bapt. Avocations: reading, helping in the community/church, exercise. Home: 834 Tuition Dr Virginia Beach VA 23462 Personal E-mail: rez1221@msn.com.

ZIEGLER, WILLIAM ALEXANDER, lawyer; b. NYC, July 15, 1924; s. William Alexander and Sally (Cootes) Z.; m. Glenn Crawley, Feb. 10, 1950; children: Richard S., Daryl A. Henning, Susan G. Barrows, W. Thomas. AB, Harvard U., 1944, JD, 1949. Bar: NY 1949, US Tax Ct. 1950, US Dist. Ct. (so. dist.) NY 1949, US Dist. Ct. (ea. dist.) NY 1957, US Dist. Ct. (no. dist.) Ohio 1973, US Dist. Ct. (ea. dist.) Mich. 1983, US Ct. Apppeals (1st cir.) 1963, US Ct. Appeals (2d cir.) 1957, US Ct. Appeals (3d cir.) 1986, US Ct. Appeals (4th cir.) 1979, US Ct. Appeals (5th cir.) 1987, US Ct. Appeals (6th cir.) 1984, US Ct. Appeals (7th cir.) 1992, US Ct. Appeals (8th cir.) 1981, US Ct. Appeals (9th cir.) 1973, US Ct. Appeals (10th and 11th cirs.) 1983, US Ct. Appeals (DC cir.) 1972, US Supreme Ct. 1972. Assoc. Sullivan & Cromwell, NYC, 1949-56, ptnr., 1957-89. Cons. in field, 1989—. Bd. dir. Friends of Canterbury Cathedral in US; former bd. drs. Harvard Law Sch. Assn. NYC, St. Mark's Sch., Salisbury Sch., Am. Dressage Inst., St. Paul's Ch. (Norwalk, Conn.), Std. Comml. Corp., Wietna(Conn.) & Land Conservation Trust; chair exec. com. Engring. Info., Inc., The H.W. Wilson Co.; sec. The H. W. Wilson Found., Big Brothers of NYC, Fgn. Policy Assn.; v.p. Manhattan Coun. Boy Scouts of Am., Ox Ridge Hunt Club; pres. Land Trust of Darien, Conn. Served with USN, 1943—46. Mem. Assn. Bar City NY, Riverside Country Club (Mont.), Harvard Club of Fairfield Country, Harvard Club Mont. Episcopalian. Avocations: music, golf, literature. Home and Office: 168 Cannon Rd Wilton CT 06897-2639 Office Phone: 203-761-9102.

ZIELINA, MARIA C., literature and language professor; d. Eva Rodriguez; m. Zbigniew Zielina; children: Marek, Aymara. BA, Calif. Luth. U., Thousand Oaks, 1985; MA, U. Calif., Santa Barbara, 1987, PhD, 1991. Cert. CC Credential, Calif., 1987. Prof. Calif. State U. Monterey Bay, Seaside, 1995—. Author: (book) La Africania en el Cuento Cubano y Puertorriqueno. Grants, Gettysburg Coll., 1994, Rsch. grant, U. Am., 1999, Fulbright scholarship, US Dept. State, 2004. Mem.: Fulbright Assn. Office: Calif State Univ Monterey Bay 100 Campus Ctr Seaside CA 93955

ZIELINSKI, THOMAS C., lawyer, insurance company executive; Various positions Cozen & O'Connor, P.C., 1982—2001; sr. v.p., gen. counsel Coventry Health Care Inc., Bethesda, Md., 2001—. Office: Coventry Health Care Inc 6705 Rockledge Dr Ste 900 Bethesda MD 20817 Office Phone: 301-581-0600. Office Fax: 301-493-0731. Business E-Mail: tielinski@cvty.com.

ZIELKE, JULIE FAYE, psychologist; d. Harry Dean and Evelyn Elaine Schmidt; m. Lyndon Jon Zielke, Nov. 23, 1985; children: Logan Scott, Luke Aaron. AA in Liberal Arts, Hesston Coll., Kans., 1981; BA in Psychology, Ea. Mennonite U., Harrisonburg, VA, 1983; Specialist in Ednl. Psychology, Wichita State Universtiy, Kans., 1989; MEd in Counseling and Sch. Psychology, Wichita State U., Kans., 1989. Sch. psychologist Wichita Pub. Schs. USD 259, 1989—92, 1997—.

ZIEMAN, MARK, editor, publishing executive; b. El Dorado, Kan., Jan. 17, 1945; m. Kristi Zieman (div.); m. Rhonda Chriss Lokeman; 4 children. Degree in Journalism, U. Kans., 1983; Exec. MBA, Rockhurst U. Mem. staff Houston bur. The Wall St. Jour., 1984—86; columnist Kans. City Star, 1986—89, editor projects desk, 1989—92, mng. editor, 1992—97, v.p., editor, 1997—2008, pres., pub., 2008—. Trustee William White Found. U. Kans.; mem. adv. bd. Rockhurst U. Recipient Pulitzer prize, 1992. Mem.: Investigative Reporters and Editors, Am. Soc. Newspaper Editors. Office: The Kansas City Star 1729 Grand Blvd Kansas City MO 64108-1458 Office Phone: 816-234-4878. E-mail: zieman@kcstar.com.*

ZIEMANN, GEORGE PATRICK, bishop emeritus; b. Pasadena, Calif., Sept. 13, 1941; Attended, Our Lady of the Angels Sem., San Fernando, Calif., 1959—61; BA, MA, St. John's Sem., Camarillo, Calif.; MS in Edn., Mt. St. Mary's Coll., LA. Ordained priest Archdiocese of LA, 1967; assoc. pastor St. Matthias Parish, Huntington Park, Calif., 1967—71; tchr. of religion Mater Dei HS, Santa Ana, Calif., 1971—74; vice rector, dean of studies Our Lady Queen of Angels Sem., Mission Hills, Calif., 1974—87; aux. bishop Archdiocese of LA, 1986—92; ordained bishop, 1987; bishop Diocese of Santa Rosa, Calif., 1992—99, bishop emeritus, 1999—. Episcopal advisor Nat. Assn. Cath. Chaplains, Region XI, Nat. Assn. Diocesan Dirs. of Campus Ministry, Nat. Cath. Cemetery Conf., Nat. Conf. Catechetical Leadership. Roman Catholic. Office: Diocese Of Santa Rosa Roman Catholic 329 10th St PO Box 1297 Santa Rosa CA 95402-1297

ZIEMBA, KAREN, actress; Appeared in Broadway plays A Chorus Line, Teddy & Alice, 42nd Street, Crazy for You, Chicago, Contact (Drama Desk award, Outer Critics Cir. award, Tony award, 2000), Never Gonna Dance (Tony nom. best featured actress in a play, 2004); (off-Broadway) And the World Goes 'Round (Drama Desk award) I Do! I Do!; (musical) Steel Pier (Tony award nominee), The Pajama Game, Allegro, Leading Ladies, 2005; (tour) Crazy for You (Joseph Jefferson award), Chicago (1998-99); (regional plays) Much Ado About Nothing, House and Garden, The Foreigner, Fifth of July, Curtains, 2006 (Outer Critics Cir. award outstanding featured actress in a musical, 2007); (opera) The Most Happy Fella, 110 in the Shade; singer Allegro, Grand Night for Singing; (TV show) Sondheim: A Celebration at Carnegie Hall, Evening at Pops, My Favorite Broadway: The Leading Ladies, Law and Order; (film) The Devil and Daniel Webster; (albums) And the World Goes 'Round, Fifty Million Frenchmen, Lost in Boston II, Shakespeare on Broadway, 110 In The Shade, The Most Happy Fella, Ziegfeld Follies of 1936.

ZIEMBA, LAWRENCE M., oil industry executive; Plant mgr. Avon refinery Tosco Corp., Calif.; gen. mgr. US refinery svcs. ConocoPhillips Co., pres. ctrl/West coast refining, 2003, now pres. US refining Houston, also v.p. WRB Refining, LLC Ill. Mem.: Nat. Petrochemical & Refiners Assn. Office: ConocoPhillips Co 600 N Dairy Ashford Houston TX 77079 Business E-Mail: larry.ziemba@conocophillips.com.*

ZIEMBA, MARY ROSE, biology professor; b. Endwell, NY, Nov. 30, 1958; children: R. Freitas Shawn, A. Freitas Emily, L. Freitas Daniel. BA in Natural Sci. with honors, U. Hawaii, 1995; MPS in Environ. & Forest Biology with honors., SUNY Coll. Environ Sci. & Forestry, Syracuse, NY, 2004. Cert. emergency med. technician 2007. Sci. educator Anchorage Sch., 2005—; adj. prof. dept. biology U. Alaska Anchorage, 2006—. Recipient Spirit Youth award, Anchorage Sch., 2007. Mem.: Nat. Merit Educators Assn. Home: PO Box 190488 Anchorage AK 99519

ZIEMBA, MICHAEL ROBERT, engineering educator; b. Owego, NY, June 11, 1966; s. Robert W. and Carol D. Ziemba; m. Ann M. Schwenz, Sept. 17, 1994. BS in Computer Sci., SUNY Empire State Coll., 2000. Test devel. engr. Lockheed Martin, Johnson City, NY, 1986—2000; product integrity engr. BAE Sys. Controls, Johnson City, 2000—04; adj. prof. Broome CC, Binghamton, NY, 2008—. Cons. Four County Libr. Sys., Binghamton, 2006—08. Actor(actor, singer): (plays); prodr.: A Christmas Story. Numerous vol. Muscular Dystrophy Assn., Binghamton, NY, 1990—2008. Recipient Lifetime Achievement award, Muscular Dystrophy Assn., 2004; named Vol. of Yr., 1998. Achievements include development of F18 E/F super hornet flight control system and BSY-2 control system for Seawolf submarine. Business E-Mail: ziemba_m@sunybroome.edu.

ZIEN, CHIP, actor; b. Milwaukee, Wis., Mar. 20, 1947; BA, U. Pa. Actor: (Broadway plays) Ride the Winds, 1974, The Suicide, 1980, Into the Woods, 1987, Grand Hotel, 1989, Falsettos, 1992, The Boys from Syracuse, 2002, Chitty Chitty Bang Bang, 2005, Les Miserables, 2007, The Country Girl, 2008, (Off-Broadway) How to Succeed in Business Without Really Trying, 1972, Smile, Smile, Smile, 1973, Tuscaloosa's Calling Me... But I'm Not Going, 1975, Dear Mr. G, 1975, In Trousers, 1979, Split, 1980, March of the Falsettos, 1981, Isn't It Romantic, 1983, Hot L Baltimore, 1984, Diamonds, 1984, An Imaginary Life, 1993, A New Brain, 1998, They're Playing Our Song, 2004; (films) Mrs. Parker and the Vicious Circle, 1994, Die Schelme von Schelm, 1995, Snake Eyes, 1998, The Siege, 1998, Brooklyn Thrill Killers, 1999, Breakfast of Champions, 1999, United 93, 2006; (TV films) Quiet Killer, 1994, Cagney & Lacey: The View Through the Glass Ceiling, 1995, Cagney & Lacey: True Convictions, 1996, Inseparable, 2006.

ZIENIEWICZ, STEPHEN, hospital administrator; BS in Biology, St. John's U.; MPH, Columbia U. Staff role to mgmt. then sr. mgmt. positions North Shore U. Hosp., Manhasset, NY; adminstr. Winthrop-University Hosp.; asst. v.p. Long Island Health Network; v.p. NY Methodist Hosp., Bklyn.; v.p. support and ancillary services, South Nassau Hosp. Winthrop South Nassau U. Health System, 1999—2004; COO Saint Louis U. Hosp., 2004—07, Tenet Healthcare Corp., 2004—07; exec. dir. U. Wash. Medical Ctr., 2007—. Former adj. prof. health mgmt. and policy Saint Louis U. Sch. Public Health; former chmn. Statewide Disaster Preparedness Com. Mo. Dept. Health, Division of Health and Sr. Services. Fellow: American Coll. Healthcare Executives. Office: UW Medical Ctr 1959 NE Pacific Seattle WA 98195*

ZIENOWICZ, RICHARD JOSEPH, plastic surgeon; b. Providence; s. Edwin Paul and Phyllis Teresa (Janasiewicz) Z.; m. Frances Cecelia Regas. BS, Concordia U., Montreal, Quebec, 1976; MD, Brown U., 1983. Diplomate Am. Bd. Surgery, Am. Bd. Plastic Surgery; cert. Added Qualifications in Hand Surgery. Instr. surgery Harvard U., Boston, 1990-91; asst. prof. Brown U., Providence, 1991—; chief plastic surgery VA Med. Ctr., Providence, 1992. Contbr. chpts. to books. Recipient W.H.J. Chang award U. Mass., 1988. Fellow ACS; mem. AMA, Am. Soc. Plastic and Reconstructive Surgery, Am. Burn Assn., Am. Soc. Reconstructive Microsurgery, N.E. Hand Soc., New Eng. Soc. Plastic and Reconstructive Surgery, R.I. Soc. Plastic Surgeons, R.I. Med. Soc. Office: 10 Elmgrove Ave Providence RI 02906-4102

ZIENTS, JEFFREY D., federal official; b. 1968; m. Mary Menell Zients; 4 children. BS in Polit. Sci. summa cum laude, Duke U., Durham, NC, 1988. With Bain & Co., Boston, Mercer Mgmt. Consulting; COO DGB Enterprises Inc., 1997; various positions The Adv. Bd. Co., Washington, 1992—96, COO, 1996—98, CEO, 1998—2001, chmn. bd., 2001—04; various positions Corp. Exec. Bd. Co., Arlington, Va., 1992—2000, chmn. bd., 2000—01; founder, mng. ptnr. Portfolio Logic, Washington, 2004—09; chief performance officer, dep. dir. for mgmt. Office Mgmt. & Budget (OMB), Exec. Office of the Pres., Washington, 2009—. Mem. bd. dirs. Best Practices, PSA Healthcare, Revolution Health, XM Satellite Radio Inc., 2006—08, Sirius XM Radio, 2008—09, Timbuk2 Designs. Pres., chief exec. Washington Baseball Club, 2004—06; co-founder, treas. Urban Alliance Found.; chmn. fin. and investment com. Children's Nat. Med. Ctr., Washington. Named one of America's 40 Richest Under 40, Fortune mag., 2002. Office: Office of Mgmt and Budget 725 17th St NW Washington DC 20503*

ZIERDEN, DON, professional basketball coach; m. Anne Zierden; children: Isaiah, Rachel. Student, Mt. Senario Coll. Coach De La Salle HS, U. Tulsa, 1986—88, La Crosse Catbirds, Continental Basketball Assn., 1990—94; head coach Pitts. Piranhas, Continental Basketball Assn., 1995, La Crosse Bobcats, Continental Basketball Assn., 1996; video coord. Minn. Timberwolves, 1999—2000, asst. coach, dir. player devel., 2000—05; asst. coach Detroit Pistons, 2005—07; head coach Minn. Lynx, 2007—09; asst. coach Washington Wizards, 2009—. Office: Washington Wizards 601 First St NW Washington DC 20004-1605*

ZIERDT, CHARLES HENRY, retired microbiologist; b. Pitts., Apr. 24, 1922; s. Conrad Henry and Nancy Leora (Harshberger) Zierdt; m. Margaret May Wise, June 1, 1942 (div. 1962); children: Charles Henry Jr., Carolyn, Douglas, Richard; m. Willadene Smith, Sept. 30, 1967. BS, Pa. State U., 1943; MS, U. Mich., 1945; PhD, George Washington U., 1967. Rsch. assoc. Parke-Davis & Co., Detroit, 1945—48; microbiologist Henry Ford Hosp., Detroit, 1948—53, USPHS, Detroit, 1953—56; rsch. microbiologist NIH, Bethesda, Md., 1956—93, ret., 1993. Scientist sponsor U. Md., 1975—; instr. Found. Advanced Edn. Scis., Bethesda, Md., 1978—. Author: Glucose Nonfermenting Gram Negative Bacteria in Clinical Microbiology, 1978, Non-fermentative Gram Negative Rods: Laboratory Identification and Clinical Aspects, 1985, McGraw-Hill Yearbook of Science and Technology, 1986, Diagnostic Procedures for Bacterial Infections, 1987; contbr. articles to profl. jours. Fellow: Am. Acad. Microbiology; mem.: Mensa, Avanti Owners Assn. Internat., U.S. Fedn. Culture Collections (membership chmn. 1985), Am. Soc. Microbiology (chpt. pres. 1976), Antique Auto Club Am. (pres. Sugar Loaf Mountain region 1997), Model T Ford Club Internat., Model A Ford Club Am. (Fairfax, Va. chpt. pres. 1985), Sigma Xi. Achievements include the classification and pathogenesis of Blastocystis Hominis, an intestinal protozoan parasite of man; description of non-oxidative (anaerobic) mitochondria. Avocations: gardening, antique car restoration, church historian. Office: NIH Bethesda MD 20816 Home: 4707 Coachway Dr Rockville MD 20852-2339

ZIERLER, NEAL, retired mathematician; b. Balt., Sept. 17, 1926; children: Robert Eugene, Joan Mariye, Ann Michie. AB, Johns Hopkins U., 1945; AM, Harvard U., 1949, PhD, 1959. Mathematician, physicist Ballistic Rsch. Labs., Aberdeen, Md., 1951; mem. tech. staff instrumentation lab. MIT, Cambridge, Mass., 1952-54, mem. tech. staff Lincoln Lab. Lexington, Mass., 1954-60; supr. info. processing group of jet propulsion lab. Calif. Inst. Tech., Pasadena, 1960-61; sr. scientist ARCON Corp., Lexington, 1961-62; head sub-dept. process analysis MITRE Corp., Bedford, Mass., 1962-65; tech. staff Ctr. for Comm. Rsch. Inst. Def. Analysis, Princeton, N.J., 1965-96. Patentee error-detecting and -correcting devices; contbr. articles to profl. jours. Lt. USN, 1944-46. Fellow IEEE; mem. Am. Math. Soc., Math. Assn. Am., Am. Physics Soc. Avocations: tennis, skiing, photography. Business E-Mail: nzierler@ieee.org.

ZIESSMAN, HARVEY A., nuclear medicine physician, medical association administrator; BS, Indiana U., MD, 1969; MBA, Georgetown U. Joined faculty Georgetown U., 1984, dir. nuclear medicine, 1991—2003; prof. radiology, divsn. nuclear medicine Johns Hopkins U., 2003—. Author: Nuclear Medicine, The Requisites. Mem.: American Bd. Nuclear Medicine (chair 2009). Office: Johns Hopkins Nuclear Medicine Ste 3223 600 N Caroline St Baltimore MD 21287*

ZIEZIULA, CHARMAYNE C., education educator; b. NY; d. George and Carol Feltz; m. David J. Zieziula; children: Noel Anderson, Nathan, Naomi, Nicholas. BS, MSEd., Buffalo State Coll., NY. Cert. in special edn., in music. Faculty Buffalo State Coll., 1998—. Office: Buffalo State Coll Kh 102 1300 Elmwood Ave Buffalo NY 14222 Business E-Mail: zieziucc@buffalostate.edu.

ZIFCHAK, WILLIAM C., lawyer; b. 1948; BA, Harvard U., 1970; JD, Columbia U., 1973. Bar: N.Y. 1974, U.S. Ct. Appeals (2d cir.) 1975, U.S. Ct. Appeals (3d cir., D.C. cir.) 1983, U.S. Dist. Ct. (so. dist.) N.Y. 1984. Ptnr., co-chair labor and employment law dept. Kaye, Scholer, Fierman, Hays & Handler, NYC. Planning com. NYU Ann. Nat. Conf. Labor, 1991-97. Contbr. articles to profl. jours. Named a Super Lawyer, NY, 2006—09. Mem. ABA (sect. labor and employment law 1975—, subcom. antitrust, RICO and labor rels. law), Assn. Bar City of N.Y. (sec. com. labor and employment law 1984-87), N.Y. State Bar (comml.-fed. litig. sect. co-chair labor and employment law com. 1995-97). Office: Kaye Scholer LLP 425 Park Ave New York NY 10022-3506 Business E-Mail: wzifchak@kayescholer.com.

ZIFF, EDWARD BENJAMIN, biochemist, educator; s. Morris Ziff and Ruth Alice Rawson; m. Susan Sarah Taylorson, June 18, 1974; children: Sara Tamsin, Benjamin Simon. BA, Columbia Coll., NYC, 1963; PhD, Princeton U., Nj., 1969. Postdoc. fellow MRC Lab. Molecular Biology, Cambridge, England, 1970—73; staff scientist Imperial Cancer Rsch. Fund Lab., London, 1973—74; asst. and assoc. prof. Rockefeller U., NYC, 1974—81; prof. biochemistry NY U. Sch. Medicine, 1981—. Bd. dir. Biotechnology Investments Ltd, London; coun. Am. Cancer Soc., Atlanta; vis. prof. Coll. de France, Paris, Tulane U. Med. Sch., New Orleans; investigator Howard Hughes Med. Inst., NYC, 1990—2003; chair external sci. adv. com. Wistar Inst., Phila., 2007—. Author: (book) DNA for Beginners. Mem. Trevor Day Sch., NYC. Mem.: Soc. Neurosci. Achievements include research in gene regulation by growth factors and of mechanisms of synaptic plasticity. Business E-Mail: edward.ziff@nyumc.org.

ZIFF, LARZER, literature and language professor; b. Holyoke, Mass., Oct. 2, 1927; s. Isadore Menden and Sara (Rosenbloom) Z.; m. Ruth Rosalind Geisenberger; children— Joshua, Oliver, Joel, Abigail. Student, Middlebury Coll., 1945-47; MA, U. Chgo., 1951, PhD, 1955; MA (hon.), U. Oxford, Eng., U. Pa. Prof. English U. Calif., Berkeley, 1956-73; univ. lectr. Oxford U., Eng., 1973-78; prof. English U. Pa., 1978-81; Caroline Donovan prof. English Johns Hopkins U., Balt., 1981—, chair dept., 1991-95. Dir. U. Calif. Edn. Abroad Program, U.K., Ireland, 1969-71; cons. and lectr. in field. Author: The Career of John Cotton, 1962; The American 1890's, 1968; Puritanism in America, 1973; Literary Democracy, 1981; Writing in the New Nation, 1991, Return Passages, 2000, Mark Twain: Life and Legacy, 2004; also articles, essays in profl. jours.; mem. editl. bds. including ELH, 1981—94. Recipient numerous awards for excellence in English including Christian Gauss award, the American 1890's, 1967; Fulbright fellow, 1959-60, fellow Am. Coun. Learned Socs., 1963-64, Newberry Libr., 1964, NEH, 1967-68, Guggenheim fellow, 1977-78, Woodrow Wilson Internat. Ctr. for Scholars, 1986-87; Fulbright Disting. Sr. Lectr., 1993. Fellow Am. Acad. Arts and Scis., Am. Philos. Soc., Am. Antiquarian Soc., Soc. Am. Historians. Office: Johns Hopkins U Dept English Baltimore MD 21218 Office Phone: 410-516-4172. Personal E-mail: nchester@netzero.com.

ZIFF, ROBERT MICHAEL, engineering educator; b. Burbank, Calif., Jan. 28, 1951; s. Barrymore and Evelyn Loretta Ziff. PhD, Rockefeller U., NYC, 1976. Postdoc. fellow Los Alamos Nat. Lab., N.Mex., 1976—78, SUNY, Stonybrook, 1978—82; prof. U. Mich., Ann Arbor, 1982—. Contbr. scientific papers to profl. jours. Bd. dirs. Phoenix Ensemble Music Edn., Ann Arbor, 2003—08. Fellow: Am. Phys. Soc.;

mem.: AIChE. Liberal. Jewish. Avocation: bicycling. Home: 2540 Newport Rd Ann Arbor MI 48103 Office: Univ Mich Dept Chem Engring Ann Arbor MI 48109-2136 Office Fax: 734-763-0459. Business E-Mail: rziff@umich.edu.

ZIFFREN, KENNETH, lawyer; b. Chgo., June 24, 1940; BA, Northwestern U., 1962; JD, UCLA, 1965. Bar: Calif. 1967. Law clerk to Chief Justice Warren, 1965—66; ptnr. Ziffren Brittenham LLP, LA. Mem.: ABA, L.A. Copyright Soc., Beverly Hills Bar Assn., L.A. County Bar Assn. (pres. 1977—78), State Bar Calif. Office: Ziffren Brittenham LLP 1801 Century Park W Los Angeles CA 90067-6406

ZIGLAR, JAMES W., govt. official, investment banker, corporate, lawyer, educator; b. Pascagoula, Miss., Dec. 8, 1945; married; 3 children. BA, George Washington U., 1968, JD, 1972. Bar: Va. 1972, D.C. 1973, N.Y. 1975, Ariz. 1977. Staff asst. Senator James Eastland, Washington, 1964-71; spl. asst. Dept. of Justice, Washington, 1971-72; law clk. to assoc. justice Harry Blackmun U.S. Supreme Ct., Washington, 1972-73; assoc. Mudge, Rose, Guthrie et al, NYC, 1973-77; ptnr. O'Connor, Cavanagh, Anderson et al, Phoenix, 1977-80; sr. v.p. Dillon, Read & Co., NYC, 1980-84; mng. dir. UBS Fin. Svcs., NYC, 1984—87, 1990—98, 2004—05; asst. sec. Dept. of Interior, Washington, 1987-88; mng. dir. Drexel Burnham Lambert Inc., NYC, 1989-90; sgt. at arms U.S. Senate, Washington, 1998—2001; comnr. immigration and naturalization serv. U.S. Dept. Justice, Washington, 2001—02; resident fellow Inst. of Politics Harvard U., Cambridge, Mass., 2003; pres. and CEO Cross Match Tech., Inc., Palm Beach Gardens, Fla., 2005—08; sr. fellow Migration Policy Inst., Washington, 2008—; sr. counse Van Ness Feldman, Washington, 2009—. Disting. vis. prof. Law Sch. George Washington U., 2003—04. Office: 1050 Thomas Jefferson St 5th Fl Washington DC 20007 Office Phone: 202-298-1802. Business E-Mail: jwz@vnf.com.

ZIGLAR, WILLIAM LARRY, academic administrator, historian, religious studies educator; b. Yazoo City, Miss., Aug. 25, 1938; s. W. Hubert and Freida Belle (Waaser) Z.; m. Brenda Joy Helms, June 25, 1960; children: Scott Lawrence, Heidi Lynn. BA, Miss. Coll., 1960, MA, 1961; PhD, U. Maine, 1972. Dir. music and youth Midway Bapt. Ch., Jackson, Miss., 1957-59; mem. faculty Ea. Coll., St. David's, Pa., 1964-89, prof., Kea chair Am. history, dean spl. programs, 1979-89, dean acad. affairs, 1986-89, v.p. for acad. affaris, dean of coll., 1989; provost, v.p. acad. affairs Wingate Coll., NC, 1990—94, interim pres. NC, 1991—92; scholar, tchr. Penncrest HS, Media, Pa., 1994—2005. Disting. Christian scholar/lectr. Staley Found., 1983—; scholar-in-residence Radnor Pub. Libr./NEH, Wayne, 1980-81, Wayne Presbyn. Ch., Pa., 1981; ch. sch. tchr. Ch. of the Good Samaritan, Paoli, Pa., 1984-89. Author: Theodore Roosevelt and Black Americans, 1972, Roots of American Diversity, 1991, They Hate the Smell of Smoke: History of Radnor Fire Co., 2007; contbr. articles to profl. jours. V.p. Wayne PTA, 1979-80; bd. dirs. Presbyn. Hist. Commn., Phila., 1981-84; historian North Wayne Protective Assn., 1984-85; founder Phi Alpha Epsilon, Nat. HS Social Studies Honorary. Recipient Goddard medal Nat. Space Assn., 1979, Lindback Disting. Coll. Tchr. award, 1979, Legion of Honor Chapel of 4 Chaplains, 1983; grantee Shell Found., 1970, NEH, 1979-80; McLemore lectr., 1985, Fulbright scholar, 1989-90. Mem. Am. Studies Assn., Am. Hist. Assn., Am. Assn. for State and Local History, Hist. Soc. Pa., Soc. History of Tech., Am. Soc. Ch. History, Nat. Coun. Social Studies (Christa Mc Auliffe award 1998), Phi Alpha Theta, Pi Kappa Delta, Pi Gamma Mu, Kappa Delta Pi, Omicron Delta Kappa, Delta Mu Delta, Sigma Zeta, Alpha Chi. Home: 408 Oak Ln Wayne PA 19087-3417 Personal E-mail: happytrailslbz@msn.com.

ZIGLER, VIVI, broadcast executive, marketing professional; b. Inglewood, Calif., July 19, 1958; d. R. Paul and Lexie St. Amand; m. Kenneth F. Zigler; 1 child, Nick. BS in Journalism, Calif. Polytechnic State U., San Luis Obispo. Station mgr. KSBY-TV, San Luis Obispo; dir. mktg. & advt. KING 5 TV, Seattle; v.p. advt. affiliate & promotional NBC Entertainment, Burbank, Calif., 1996—99, exec. v.p. current programs, 2005—06, exec. v.p. digital entertainment & new media, 2006—08; sr. v.p. advt. services The NBC Agy., 1999—2003, sr. v.p. mktg & advt. services, 2003—05; pres. NBC Universal Digital Entertainment, 2008—. Named a Woman to Watch, Advt. Age, 2008, Maverick, Details mag., 2008. Office: NBC Universal 100 Universal City Plaza Universal City CA 91608 Office Phone: 818-404-7327.*

ZIGMOND, RICHARD ERIC, neuroscientist, researcher; b. Willimantic, Conn., May 9, 1944; m. Mary Patricia Carson, Jan. 13, 1990. PhD, Rockefeller U., 1971. Prof. Case Western Res. U., Cleve., 1989—; asst. and assoc. prof. Harvard Med. Sch., Boston, 1975—89. Grantee rsch. grants, NIH, 1976—. Mem.: Soc. for Neurosci. Office: Case Western Reserve Univ 10900 Euclid Ave Cleveland OH 44106-4975

ZIGO, PAUL EDWARD, historian, educator; b. Newark, July 14, 1942; s. Edward and Jeannette Zigo; m. Kim Irene Schmerler; children: Paul Jr., Drew, Travis, Marc, Kristen. BA in History, Rutgers U., New Brunswick, NJ, 1964; M in Pers. and Guidance, Rider U., Lawrenceville, NJ, 1973; diploma, US Army War Coll., Carlisle Barracks, Pa., 1989; M in Recent Am. Diplomatic and Mil. History, Temple U., Phila., 2000. Lic. radio broadcaster FCC, cert. Nat. Security Mgmt., Nat. Def. U., Wash., DC, 1982. Asst. dir. cmty. rels. Monmouth U., West Long Branch, NJ, 1966—75, dir. cmty. rels., 1975—77; dir., off-campus svcs. Brookdale CC, Lincroft, NJ, 1977—2003, tenured asst. prof. history, 2003—, dir. Ctr. World War II Studies and Conflict Resolution, 2003—. Exec. prodr. cable series Triumphant Spirit: America's World War II Generation Speaks, 2002—; dir. Narozanick World War II, Resource Ctr., 2007—; dir., curator Al Meserlin World War II Photo Gallery, 2009—; bd. mem. Eastern CC Social Sci. Assn., Arlington, Va.; adv. coun. Brookdale CC Internat. Ctr. Editor: Witnessing History, The Eisenhower Photos, 2009. Adv. bd. mem. NJ Profl. Devel. Ctr. Early Childhood Edn., Union, 2001—03; mem., exec. com. Monmouth Jr. Sci. Symposium, Monmouth U., West Long Branch, NJ, 1979—2005; bd. dirs. Western Monmouth C. of C., Freehold, NJ, 1999—2005; mem. edn. adv. coun. Battleship NJ (BB 62) History Mus., Camden; mem. allocations com. Monmouth County United Way, Farmingdale; founder ann. study abroad program Brookdale CC, 2000, chair adv. coun. Ctr. for WWII Studies and Conflict Resolution; mem. Ft. Monmouth Retiree Coun., Eatontown, NJ; founder Ctr. for WWII Studies and Conflict Resolution, Brookdale CC, 2000. Col. USAR, 1964—94. Decorated Def. Meritorious Svc. medal US Dept. of Def., Legion of Merit medal US Army; recipient Cert. of Recognition for Svc. to Monmouth County, Monmouth County Bd. of Chosen Freeholders, 1994, Excellence award for Outstanding Contbns. to Tchg., Leadership and Learning, Nat. Inst. for Staff and Orgnl. Devel., 2005, George Washington Honor medal, Freedoms Found. at Valley Forge, 2006, Excellence Edn. Barringer award, Brookdale Cmty. Coll. Alumni Assn., 2008; named to Point Pleasant Beach HS Hall of Fame, Point Pleasant Beach Pub. Edn. Found., 2002. Mem.: Eastern Cmty. Colls. Social Sci. Assn. (assoc.), Brookdale CC Faculty Assn. (assoc.), Mil. History Soc. (assoc.), Assn. of US Army (assoc.), Monmouth cpt. Vets. Battle of Bulge (assoc.). Roman Catholic. Avocations: military history, overseas and national travel, photography. Home: 15 Beach Rd Neptune NJ 07753 Office: Brookdale CC 765 Newman Springs Rd Lincroft NJ 07738 Office Fax: 732-224-2444. Personal E-mail: pzigo@optonline.net. Business E-Mail: pzigo@brookdalecc.edu.

ZIKMUND, BARBARA BROWN, minister, religious organization administrator, educator; b. Ann Arbor, Mich., Oct. 16, 1939; d. Henry Daniels and Helen Langworthy Brown; m. Joseph Zikmund II, Aug. 26, 1961; 1 child, Brian Joseph. BA, Beloit Coll., 1961; BDiv, Duke U., 1964, PhD, 1969; D in Div (hon.), Doane Coll., 1984, Chgo. Theol. Sem., 1985, Ursinus Coll., 1989; LHD, U. Hartford, 1998. Ordained to ministry United Ch. of Christ, 1964. Instr. Albright Coll., Reading, Pa., 1966-67, Temple U., Phila., 1967-68, Ursinus Coll., Collegeville, Pa., 1968-69; asst. prof. religious studies Albion Coll., Mich., 1970-75; asst. prof. ch. history, dir. studies Chgo. Theol. Sem., 1975-80; dean and assoc. prof. ch. history Pacific Sch. Religion, Berkeley, Calif., 1981-85, dean and prof. ch. history, 1985-90; pres. Hartford (Conn.) Sem., 1990-2000; fellow Life Cycle Inst. Cath. U. America, 2005—. Prof. grad. sch. am. studies Doshisha U., Kyoto, Japan, 2000-05; vis. scholar Wesley Theol. Sem. Washington, 2007-; chmn. United Ch. of Christ Hist. Coun., 1983-85, mem. coun. for ecumenism, 1983-89; mem. Nat. Coun. Chs. Commn. on Faith and Order, 1979-87, World Coun. of Chs. Programme Theol. Edn., 1984-91, Nat. Coun. Chs. Working Group on Inter-Faith Rels., 1992-96, Nat. Coun. Chs. Commn. on Inter-faith Rels., 1996-2007, chair Commn. on Inter-faith Rels., 2000-07, World Conf. Assns. for Theol. Instns., sec. treas., 1992-96, pres., 1996-2000. Author: Discovering the Church, 1983, Clergy Women: An Uphill Calling, 1998; editor: Hidden Histories in the UCC, 1984, vol. 2, 1987; (with Manschreck) American Religous Experiment, 1976; mem. editl. bd. Jour. Ecumenical Studies, 1987—, Mid-Stream, 1991—; series editor: Living Theological Heritage of the United Church of Christ, co-editor Vol. 7 United and Uniting, 2005; contbr. articles to profl. jours. Mem. City Coun., Albion, Mich., 1972-75; elector Wadsworth Atheneum, 1994-2000; corporator St. Francis Hosp., 1994-2000, Hartford Hosp., 1996-2000; pres. Greater Hartford Consortium for Higher Edn., 1994-96, bd. dir. elect. Humanities Edn. Rsch. Assn. 2008. NEH grantee, 1974-75; Woodrow Wilson fellow, 1964-66; vis. scholar Schlesinger Libr. Women's History, Radcliffe Coll., 1988-89, Disting. Alumna, Duke Divinity Sch., 1994; recipient Disting. Svc. Citation Beloit Coll., 1986; Antoinette Brown award, United Ch. of Christ, 2005. Mem. Assn. Theol. Schs. (v.p. 1984-86, pres. 1986-88, issues implementation grantee 1983-84, Disting. Svc. award 2004), Am. Soc. Ch. History (coun. 1983-85, pres. elect 1996-97, pres. 1997-98), Internat. Assn. Women Ministers (v.p. 1977-79), AAUW (v.p. 1973-75), Greater Hartford C. of C. (bd. dirs. 1992-95). Democrat. Home: 4545 Connecticut Ave NW Apt 510 Washington DC 20008-6018 Office: Wesley Theol Sem 4500 Massachusetts Ave Washington DC 20016 Business E-Mail: beebeezee@verizon.net.

ZILBERBERG, JULIE MARLENE, social studies educator; d. Charles and Barbara Zilberberg; m. John Lawrence Nathenson, Jan. 10, 1993; children: Alexander Silver Michael, Michael Silverg Nathenson, Alexander Ray Nathenson, Michael Silver Nathenson, Alexander Ray Nathenson. BA, Muhlenberg Coll., Allentown, Pa., 1990; MA, CUNY, 1997, PhD, 2006. Cert. women's studies Grad. Ctr. of CUNY, 2006. Ethics fellow Mt. Sinai Sch. of Medicine, NYC, 1997—2004; vis. scholar Hastings Ctr., Garrison, NY, 1988—98; grad. tchg. fellow York Coll. of CUNY, Jamaica, 1994—2000; adj. asst. prof. Coll. New Rochelle, NY, 2000. Bioethics cons. Mt. Sinai Sch. Medicine, NYC, 1997—2004. Contbr. articles to profl. jours. Vol. NY Soc. Women in Philosophy, NYC, 1994—2006; steering com. Larchmont Temple Nursery Sch., NY, 2004—08; com. chair PTA Chatsworth Ave. Sch., Larchmont, 2007—09. Recipient Helena Rubinstein Found. award, Helena Rubinstein Found. & Grad. Ctr. of CUNY, 1998—99; fellow Ethics fellowship, Mt. Sinai Sch. Medicine, 1997—2004, Grad. Tchg. fellowship, Grad. Ctr. & York Coll. of CUNY, 1994—97, Fellowships, Grad. Ctr. of CUNY, 1993. Mem.: Internat. Network Feminist Approaches Bioethics, Soc. Women Philosophy (sec. 1996—98), Assn. Bioethics & Humanities, Am. Philos. Assn., Mensa. Avocations: yoga, travel. Home: 22 Concord Ave Larchmont NY 10538 Personal E-mail: juliemz@optonline.net.

ZILBERBERG, MARYA, epidemiologist, researcher; MD, Boston U. Sch. Medicine, 1992; MPH in Epidemiology, U. Mass., Amherst, 2008. Resident & fellow Tufts U. Sch. Medicine, 1992—98; intensivist Winchester Hosp., 1996—98; outcomes rsch. Johnson & Johnson, 2001—07; founder & pres. EviMed Research Group LLC, 2007; physician & researcher U. Mass. Office: University of Massachusetts School of Public Health 715 N Pleasant St Amherst MA 01003-9304 also: 421 N Main St Leeds MA 01053 Office Phone: 413-268-3414. E-mail: MZilberb@schoolph.umass.edu, Marya@EviMedGroup.org.*

ZILIAK, JAMES PATRICK, economics educator; b. Quincy, Ill., July 12, 1965; s. Lawrence Oliver and Barbara Z.; m. Gena Marie Mark, Aug. 12, 1989; 1 child, Aidan. PhD, Ind. U., Bloomington, 1993. Asst. prof. U. Oreg., Eugene, 1993-99; vis. asst. prof. U. Mich., Ann Arbor, 1997-98; assoc. prof. U. Oreg., Eugene, 1999—; rsch. affiliate Inst. for Rsch. on Poverty, Madison, Wis., 2000—, Joint Ctr. for Poverty Rsch., Chgo., 1999—. Author: Research on Tax Reform, Journal on Political Economy, 1999, Research on Welfare Reform, Journal of Human Resources, 2000 Research on Business Cycles, Review of Economics and Statistics, 1999, Research on gender Discrimination, Industrial and labor Relations Review, 2001. Grantee: Economic Rsch. Svc., U.S. Dept. Agr., 1997-01, Office of Asst. Sec. for Planning and Evaluation, U.S. Dept. Health and Human Svcs., 2000-01; recipient Hon. Mention Outstanding Dissertation Prize, Nat. Tax Assn. Am., 1993. Mem. Am. Econ. Assn., Econometric Soc., Nat. Tax Assn., Soc. Labor Economists. Avocations: running, hiking, skiing. Office: Dept Econ Univ Oregon Eugene OR 97403-1285 Fax: 541-346-1243. E-mail: jziliak@oregon.uoregon.edu.

ZILKHA, EZRA KHEDOURI, banker; b. Baghdad, Iraq, July 31, 1925; arrived in U.S., 1941, naturalized, 1950; s. Khedouri A. and Louise (Bashi) Z.; m. Cecile Iny, Feb. 6, 1950; children: Elias Donald, Donna, Bettina Louise. Grad., Hill Sch., Pottstown, Pa., 1943; AB, Wesleyan U., Middletown, Conn., 1947, LLD (hon.), 1987. Dir. Zilkha & Sons, Inc., NYC, 1946—, chmn., pres., 1956—. Dir. Cigna Corp., Phila., 1968—96, former chmn. investment com.; dir. Mothercare, Ltd., England, 1970—82, INA Life Ins. Co. of NY, 1973—87, Blyth Eastman Dillon & Co., 1976—79, Newhall Land & Farming Co., Calif., 1977—2004, Revlon, Inc., 1981—95, Chgo. Milw. Corp., 1981—96, Cambridge Assocs., Boston, 1988—2000; vice chmn. bd. Fortune Bancorp, 1990—94, Handy & Harman, 1969—88; chmn. bd. Fidelity Internat. Bank., 1968—79; chmn. Union Holdings, 1984—90. Trustee emeritus, former chmn. investment com. Wesleyan U.; hon. trustee, former chmn. investment com. Brookings Inst., Washington; former trustee Spence Sch., NYC, French Inst., NYC, Lycee Francais de NY; trustee Am. Soc. French Legion of Honor; former mem. exec. com., former chmn. bd. Internat. Ctr. for Disabled, NYC. Decorated comdr. Legion d'Honneur, officer Ordre Nat. du Merite (France); recipient Freedom of Human Spirit award Internat. Ctr. for Disabled, 1989, Pilier d'Or award French Inst./Alliance Francaise, 1995, Charles de Ferry de Fontnouvelle award Lycee Francais de N.Y., 2003. Mem.: Coun. Fgn. Rels., The Brook Club, Travellers Club, Meadow Club, Knickerbocker Club, Racquet & Tennis Club. Office Phone: 212-758-7750.

ZILLMER, JOHN J., waste management administrator; MBA, Kellogg Graduate School Northwestern Univ. Mgmt. Aramark Corp., pres. food and support services group, exec. vice-pres.; chmn. bd. and CEO Allied Waste Industries, 2005—. Mem. bd. dir. United Stations Directors, Inc. Office: Allied Waste Industries 18500 N Allied Way Phoenix AZ 85054 Office Phone: 480-627-2700.

ZILLY, THOMAS SAMUEL, federal judge; b. Detroit, Jan. 1, 1935; s. George Samuel and Bernice M. (McWhinney) Z.; divorced; children: John, Peter, Paul, Luke; m. Jane Greller Noland, Oct. 8, 1988; stepchildren: Allison Noland, Jennifer Noland. BA, U. Mich., 1956; LLD, Cornell U., 1962. Bar: Wash. 1962, U.S. Ct. Appeals (9th cir.) 1962, U.S. Supreme Ct. 1976. Ptnr. Lane, Powell, Moss & Miller, Seattle, 1962-88; dist. judge U.S. Dist. Ct. (we. dist.) Wash., Seattle, 1988—. Judge pro tem Seattle Mcpl. Ct., 1972-80; mem. adv. com. bankruptcy rules U.S. Judicial Conf., 1998—; chair adv. com. U.S. Jud. Conf., 2004-2007. Contbr. articles to profl. jours. Mem. Cen. Area Sch. Council, Seattle, 1969-70; scoutmaster Thunderbird Dist. council Boy Scouts Am. Seattle, 1976-84; bd. dirs. East Madison YMCA. Served to lt. (j.g.) USN, 1956-59. Recipient Tuahku Dist. Service to Youth award Boy Scouts Am., 1983. Mem. ABA, Wash. State Bar Assn., Seattle-King County Bar Assn. (treas. 1979-80, trustee 1980-83, sec. 1983-84, 2d v.p. 1984-85, 1st v.p. 1985-86, pres. 1986-87). Office: US Dist Ct 700 Stewart St Ste 15229 Seattle WA 98101

ZILVETI, CARLOS BENJAMIN, preventive medicine physician, pediatrician; b. Sucre, Bolivia, June 14, 1928; arrived in USA, 1956; s. Carlos and Marina (De La Reza) Z.; m. Halina J. Daszewski, Sept. 8, 1957 (div. Sept. 1976); 1 child: Carlos Joseph III; m. Vita Palazzolo, Sept. 5, 1987. BS, Sacred Heart Coll., Sucre, Bolivia, 1946; MD, U. San Francisco Xavier, Sucre, Bolivia, 1954; MPH, Yale U., New Haven, Conn., 1966. Physician in rural medicine Bolivian Power Co., La Paz, 1955; intern Hosp. Obrero Victor Paz Estenssoro, La Paz, 1956; asst. resident in pediats. St. Luke's Hosp., Meml. Cancer Ctr., Woman's Hosp., NYC, 1957-58; resident and chief resident in pediats. Hosp. of St. Raphael, New Haven, 1958-59; pvt. practice New Haven and Branford, Conn., 1960-63; dir. maternal-child health New Haven Dept. Health, 1964-74; regional med. officer South and Ctrl. Am. Peace Corps, Bogota, Colombia, 1975-76; regional med. officer, sci. attache in West Africa U.S. Dept. of State, Liberia, Ghana, Togo, Sierra Leone, 1976-79; reserve appt. of maj., advanced to col. USAF, San Antonio, 1979-91, chief environ. medicine Wilford Hall Med. Ctr., 1979-83, cons. preventive and occupl. medicine, 1983-91, cons. aerospace-preventive medicine Wilford Hall Med. Ctr. Lackland AFB, Tex., 1984-91, ret. col., 1991. Cons. FDA, HEW, Washington, 1966-75; cons. to Headstart Am. Acad. Pediats., Stanford-Norwalk, Conn., 1968-75; regional med. officer, sci. attache West Africa U.S. Dept. State. Contbr. articles to profl. jours. Chmn. gov.'s task force Conn. State Dept. Health, Hartford, 1969-75. Fellow Am. Acad. Pediats. (emeritus), Am. Coll. Preventive Medicine (emeritus); mem. APHA, AMA, New Eng. Pub. Health Assn., Conn. Acad. Preventive Medicine, Am. Occupl. Med. Assn. Avocations: swimming, tennis, golf, travel, classical music. Home: 9222 Dover Rdg San Antonio TX 78250-3557 Home Phone: 210-681-6464.

ZIMA, HANS PETER, science educator; b. Vienna, May 12, 1941; m. Eva Ilona Schilk. PhD, U. Vienna, 1964. Prof. Bonn U., Germany, 1975—89, U. Vienna, 1989—2007; prin. scientist Jet Propulsion Lab., CalTech, Pasadena, Calif., 2001—. Contbr. scientific papers. Business E-Mail: zima@jpl.nasa.gov.

ZIMAND, HARVEY FOLKS, lawyer; b. NYC, Aug. 28, 1928; s. Savel and Gertrude (Folks) Z.; m. Ingeborg Rockosch, 1963 (div. 1980); children: Patricia Folks Carpenter, Stephanie Folks Plexico; m. Noel French, Apr. 30, 1983 (dec. 2006). BA, Colgate U., 1950; postgrad., Oxford U., Eng., 1950; MA, U. Chgo., 1951; postgrad., Columbia U., 1952-53; LL.B., Yale U., 1957. Bar: N.Y. 1957. Rapporteur Council for Fgn. Relations, NYC, 1952-53; atty. Dept. Navy, Washington, 1956-70; ptnr. Kelley Drye & Warren, NYC, 1970—. Dir. Toronto-Dominion Trust Co., N.Y.C., 1975-83. Bd. editors The Chase Jour. Bd. dirs. Virginia Day Nursery, N.Y.C., 1980-84. Served to cpl. U.S. Army, 1951-53 Named to The Best Lawyers in Am., 1996—, Best Lawyers in NY, 1996—. Fellow NY Bar Found., Am. Coll. Trust and Estate Counsel; mem. ABA, NY State Bar Assn., Assn. Bar City of NY, Estate Planning Coun., Univ. Club, Yale Club (NYC), Randolph Mountain Club (NH). Republican. Episcopalian. Home: 120 E 81st St New York NY 10028-1428 Office: Kelley Drye & Warren LLP 101 Park Ave New York NY 10178-0002 Business E-Mail: hzimand@kelleydrye.com.

ZIMBALIST, MICHAEL, publishing executive; m. Melissa Zimbalist; children: Lila, Peri, Quentin. BA in Chemistry and Philosophy, Brown U., 1979. Mgmt. positions AT&T Downtown Digital; dir. production Capital Cities/ABC, 1995—97; gen. mgr., online svcs. United Media, Divsn. E.W. Scripps Co., 1997—99; exec. v.p., mktg. and bus. develop. ePod Corp. (sold to Star Media Network), 1999—2001; exec. dir. Online Publishers Assn., 2001—04, pres., 2004—06; v.p., R&D ops. NY Times Co., 2006—. Disney imagineer, wrote and produced a number of interactive exhibits; frequent commentator on issues affecting the online media and advertising bus.; regular spkr. at industry conf. and events. Imagineer, writer, prodr.: numerous interactive exhibits; contbr. numerous TV shows for Hanna Barbara and interactive games for MCA/Universal Studios; guest appearances NBC News, CNN, BBC; contbr. articles to numerous newspapers. Office: 620 Eight Ave New York NY 10018

ZIMBARDO, PHILIP GEORGE, psychologist, educator, writer; b. NYC, Mar. 23, 1933; s. George and Margaret (Bisicchia) Z.; m. Christina Maslach, Aug. 10, 1972; children: Zara, Tanya; 1 son by previous marriage, Adam. AB, Bklyn. Coll., 1954; MS, Yale U., 1955, PhD, 1959; D (hon.), U. Peru, 1996; LHD in Clin. Psychology, Pacific Grad. Sch. Psychology, 1996, D (hon.), 1997, Nat. U. of San Martin, 1996, Nat. U. Peru, Thessalonoki, Greece, 1997, Aristotle U., 1998. Asst. prof. psychology Yale U., New Haven, 1959-61, NYU, NYC, 1961-67; vis. assoc. prof. psychology Columbia U., NYC, 1967-68; prof. psychology Stanford (Calif.) U., 1968—; prof. Naval Post Grad. Sch., Monterey, 2002—, Pacific Grad. Sch. Psychology, 2006—; dir. Ctr. Interdisciplinary Policy, Edn., Rsch. in Terrorism, 2006—. Pres. P.G. Zimbardo, Inc., San Francisco; sr. project advisor Exploratorium, 1993; host, writer, gen. acad. advisor PBS-TV series Discovering Psychology, 1987, 2001; cons. NBC. Author: Cognitive Control of Motivation, 1969, Canvassing for Peace, 1970, Psychology and Life, 18th edit., 2007, Shyness, What It Is, What To Do About It, 1977, Influencing Attitudes and Changing Behavior, rev. edit., 1977, The Shyness Workbook, 1979, A Parent's Guide to the Shy Child, 1981, reprinted, 1999, The Psychology of Attitude Change and Social Influence, 1991, Core Concepts in Psychology, 6th edit., 2008, The Lucifer Effect, 2007, The Time Paradox, 2008. Ctr. for Advanced Study of Behavioral Scis. fellow, 1971; recipient Peace medal Tokyo Police Dept., 1972, City Medal of

Honor, Salamanca, Spain, Disting. Tchr. award Am. Psychol. Found., 1975, award Havel Found., 2005. Fellow APA (pres. 2002, Presdl. citation Discovery Psychology series 1994, Tchg. award 1999); mem. Am. Psychol. Soc., AAUP, Internat. Congress Psychology, Western Psychol. Assn. (pres. 1985, 2001), Ea. Psychol. Assn., Calif. Psychol. Assn. (Disting. Contbn. to Rsch. award 1978), Soc. for Psychol. Study of Social Issues, Coun. Sci. Soc. Pres. (chair 2005), Sigma Xi, Phi Beta Kappa, Psi Chi. Roman Catholic. Office: Stanford U Psychology Dept Stanford CA 94305 Home Phone: 415-776-4748. Office Fax: 415-673-2294. Business E-Mail: zim@stanford.edu. *One of the few virtues of growing up in a poor urban ghetto is the realization that people are the most important resource we have— to be used wisely, well and as often as possible. The second is the tempering of book learning by street wits. The third is to value a career that allows me to contribute to improving the quality of our lives through research and teaching.*

ZIMBLER, MARC S., plastic surgeon, director; b. NYC, Oct. 4, 1966; m. Deborah Rachel Stern; 1 child, Gabriel. MD, Mt. Sinai U., NY, 1993. Cert. Am. Bd. Facial Plastic Surgery, Wash., 2001. Dir. facial plastic & reconstructive surgery Beth Israel Med. Ctr., NYC, 2000—, site dir. residency edn., dept. head & neck surgery, 2003—. Office: Beth Israel Med Ctr 990 Fifth Ave New York NY 10075

ZIMET, CARL NORMAN, psychologist, educator; b. Vienna, June 3, 1925; came to U.S., 1943, naturalized, 1945; s. Leon and Gisela (Kosser) Z.; m. Sara F. Goodman, June 4, 1950; children: Andrew, Gregory. BA, Cornell U., 1949; PhD, Syracuse U., 1953; postdoctoral fellow, Stanford U., 1953-55. Diplomate in clin. psychology Am. Bd. Profl. Psychology (trustee 1966-74). Instr., then asst. prof. psychology and psychiatry Yale U., 1955-63; mem. faculty U. Colo. Med. Center, 1963—, prof. clin. psychology, 1965—2007, head div., 1963—2006, prof. emeritus, 2007—. Mem. Colo. Bd. Psychol. Examiners, 1966-72, Colo. Mental Health Planning Commn., 1964-66; mem. acad. adv. com. John F. Kennedy Child Devel. Center, U. Colo., 1966-68; chmn. Council for Nat. Register of Health Service Providers in Psychology, 1975-85, pres., mem. exec. bd. div. psychotherapy, 1970-89; chair exec. com. Assn. Psychol. Internship Ctrs., 1988-91. Bd. editors: Jour. Clin. Psychology, 1962-91, Jour. Clin. and Cons. Psychology, 1964-73, Psychotherapy, 1967—, Profl. Psychology, 1969-75. With USNR, 1943-46. Recipient Disting. Service award Colo. Psychol. Assn., 1976 Fellow: APA (coun. reps. 1969—72, 1973—76, bd. dirs. 1985—88, Disting. award for profl. contbn., div. psychotherapy and div. clin. psychology 1987), Soc. Personality Assessment (pres. 1975—76, 1975—76, chair gen. psychol. svcs. 1987—97, bd. dirs.); mem.: Med. Sch. Profs. Psychology (pres. 1992—94, bd. dirs. 2004—06), Denver Psychoanalytic (trustee 1968—71), Am. Acad. Clin. Psychology (pres. 1993—2001). Home: 400 E 3rd Ave # 901 Denver CO 80203 Office Phone: 303-315-8611, 303-315-9128. Business E-Mail: carl.zimet@uchsc.edu, carl.zimet@ucdenver.edu.

ZIMET, LLOYD, sport psychologist, health educator, program planner and administrator; b. Bklyn., 1951; s. Victor R. and Marcia Z. BA, Whittier Coll., Calif., 1973; MA, U. Md., 1983, PhD, 1984; MPH, NYU, 1989; DD. Diplomate Coll. Health Behavior & Coll. Advocacy Edn., AAIM, bd. cert. health behavior Am. Assn. Integrative Medicine; ordained min. Universal Life Ch., 2007; cert. in sport psychology Nat. Inst. Sport Profl., 2008. Head basketball coach Aarhus U., Denmark, 1973—78, 1980—82, 1985—86; resident dir. U. Md., College Park, 1978—80; sports supr. Montgomery County Dept. Recreation, Md., 1978, 1982—84; dir. health promotion Optimal Fitness Inc., NYC, 1986—91; internat. cons. cmty. and occupational health, 1984—; dir. World of Discovery Day Camp, Bklyn., 1997—2000. Dir. edn. AIDS Ctr. of Queens County, NY, 1989-90; bd. dirs. Patricia Manning Meml. Fund childhood cancer Am. Cancer Soc., Queens, 1988-95; mem. AIDS med. adv. com. NYC Bd. Edn., 1989-90; mem. adv. bd. Adolescent Health Network, Queens, 1989-90; keynote speaker NYU Health Edn. Alumni, 1990, USPHS Region II Conf., 1991; prevention specialist Hillsborough County Sch. Dist., Fla., 2004-08, mem. sch. health adv. com., 2004, staff & program developer, 2005; program dir. HIV/STD/Pregnancy Prevention Program, Youth Risk Behavior Survery, Fla. Youth Surveys, 2005-08; mem. AIDS adv. com. Dept. Edn., State of Fla., 2004-08, Dist. Wellness Task Force, 2005-08. Bd. govs. US Amateur Boxing Fedn., Colorado Springs, Colo., 1988-91; bd. dirs. Met. Amateur Boxing Fedn., NYC, 1988-91; mem. USA Boxing Nat. Scholarship com., 1984-88. Fellow: Am. Assn. Intergrative Medicine, Soc. Pub. Health Educators; mem.: AAHPERD, APA, APHA, Am. Inst. Stress.

ZIMMAN STETSON, NANCY See STUART, NANCY

ZIMMER, ANNA HELD, retired social worker; b. Revere, Mass., Jan. 1, 1922; d. Morris and Sarah (Javits) Held; m. Fred Zimmer, Apr. 4, 1948; children: Harold, Sarah, Bonnie. BA, Bklyn. Coll., 1943; MSW, Smith Coll., 1944. Cert. social worker, N.Y. Caseworker New Haven Family Svc., 1944-46, Phila. Family Svc., 1946-48, United Svc. for New Ams., NYC, 1948-49, Coun. Ctr. Sr. Citizens, Bklyn., 1957-69; caseworker, student supr. Community Svc. Soc. N.Y., NYC, 1967-82; co-dir. Network Assocs., 1982-87; dir. media assistance to caregivers Brookdale Ctr. Aging/Hunter Coll., NYC, 1985-87; dir. Inst. on Mut. Aid, Self Help in Field of Aging Brookdale Ctr. Aging Hunter Coll., NYC, 1986—2003. Mem. long term home health care com. Jewish Home and Hosp. for Aged; regional rep. Nat. Inst. on Community-Based Long-Term Care, Nat. Coun. on Aging, mem. adv. com. caregivers project, 1986; mem. adv. com. Ret. Sr. Vol. Program, NYC; co-chair Hunter Coll., Sch. Social Work, 2003. Editorial Bd. Jour. Gerontol. Social Work; dir. documentary video, In Case of: Families & Their Aged. Recipient Outstanding Svc. award, Hunter Coll., Sch. Social Work, 2003; named Outstanding Field Educator, 2000. Mem. NASW (Social Worker in Aging award N.Y.C. chpt. 1987, Walter Beattie award 1998), Aca.d Cert. Social Workers, Gerontol. Soc. Am., Am. Soc. Aging, N.Y. Soc. Aging. Home: 975 Massachusetts Ave Apt 305 Arlington MA 02476-4545

ZIMMER, DONALD WILLIAM, former professional baseball coach, professional baseball manager, retired professional baseball player; b. Cin., Jan. 17, 1931; s. Harold Lesley and Lorraine Bertha (Ernst) Z.; m. Jean Carol Bauerle, Aug. 16, 1951; children: Thomas Jeffrey, Donna Jean. Student Pub. Schs., Cin. Baseball player Dodger Farm Clubs, 1949-54, Bklyn. Dodgers, 1954-57, L.A. Dodgers, 1958-59, 1963, Chgo. Cubs, 1960-61, N.Y. Mets, 1962, Cin. Reds, 1962, Washington Senators, 1963-65, Toei Flyers, Tokyo, 1966; mgr. Cin. Reds Farm Clubs, Knoxville and Buffalo, 1967, Indpls., 1968, San Diego Padre Farm Clubs, Key West, Fla., 1969, Padre Farm Club, Salt Lake City, 1970; coach Montreal Expos, Que., Canada, 1971; mgr. San Diego Padres, 1972-73; coach Boston Red Sox, 1974-76, 1992, mgr., 1976-80, Tex. Rangers, 1981-82; coach Chgo. Cubs, 1984, 85, 86, mgr., 1988-91; coach San Francisco Giants, 1987, Colo. Rockies, Denver, 1993-95, N.Y. Yankees, 1983, 1986, 1996—2003; sr. baseball advisor Tampa Bay Rays, 2004—09. Mem. minor league All-Star Teams, Hornell, N.Y., 1950, Elmira, N.Y., 1951, Mobile, Ala., 1952, St. Paul, 1953; player World Series teams 1955, 56, 59; coach World Series teams 1975, 96, 98, 99, 2000, 01, 03; mem. adv. bd. Baseball Assistance Team. Recipient Bill Stern award NBC, 1949; named St. Paul Rookie of Yr., 1953, All Star Team Player, 1961, All Star Coach, 1978, 81, 90, 97, 99, 2000, 01, 02, 03; named Nat. League Mgr. of Yr. 1989. Mem. Profl. Baseball Players Assn. (life), Maj. League Baseball Players Alumni Assn., Old Time Ball Players Wis. Office: c/o Tampa Bay Rays 1 Tropicana Drive Saint Petersburg FL 33705 Office Phone: 727-825-3137.

ZIMMER, GEORGE A., men's apparel executive; b. NYC, Nov. 21, 1948; s. Robert Zimmer; m. Lorri Zimmer; 4 children. BA in Econ., Washington U., St. Louis, 1970. Founder The Men's Wearhouse Inc., Houston, 1973, chmn., pres., 1974—91, chmn., pres., CEO, 1991—97, chmn., CEO, 1997—. Bd. dir. Apollo Group Inc., 2006—. Bd. dirs. Inst. Noetic Sciences. Office: The Mens Wearhouse 40650 Encyclopedia Cir Fremont CA 94538-2453 also: 5803 Glenmont Dr Houston TX 77081

ZIMMER, HANS FLORIAN, composer; b. Frankfurt, Germany, Sept. 12, 1957; m. Suzanne Zimmer; 4 children. Former mem. The Buggles; co-founder Media Ventures LLC. Composer: (films) (with Stanley Myers) Moonlighting, 1982, Success is the Best Revenge, 1984, The Wind, 1987, The Zero Boys, 1987, Taffin, 1988, Terminal Exposure, 1987, Wonderland, 1988, (with Myers) The Nature of the Beast, 1988, (with Luis Bonfa) Prisoner of Rio, 1988, Burning Secret, 1988, (with Myers) Paperhouse, 1988, Rain Man, 1988 (Acad. award nominee best original score, 1988), A World Apart, 1988, Arcadia, 1988, Black Rain, 1989, Diamond Skulls, 1989, Driving Miss Daisy, 1989, Twister, 1989, Bird on a Wire, 1990, (with Shirley Walker) Chicago Joe and the Showgirl, 1990, Days of Thunder, 1990, Fools of Fortune, 1990, Green Card, 1990, The Neverending Story II: The Next Chapter, 1990, Pacific Heights, 1990, Backdraft, 1991, Regarding Henry, 1991, Thelma and Louise, 1991, Radio Flyer, 1991, The Power of One, 1992, A League of Their Own, 1992, (with Mark Mancina) Where Sleeping Dogs Lie, 1992, Sniper, 1993, (with Bob Telson) Younger and Younger, 1993, Point of No Return, 1993, True Romance, 1993, Calendar Girl, 1993, Cool Runnings, 1993, The House of the Spirits, 1993, I'll Do Anything, 1994, Renaissance Man, 1994, The Lion King, 1994 (Acad. award best original score, 1994, Golden Globe award, 1995), Crimson Tide, 1995 (Grammy award, 1996), Nine Months, 1995, Broken Arrow, 1996, Muppet Treasure Island, 1996, The Preacher's Wife, 1996, The Peacemaker, 1997, As Good As It Gets, 1997, The Prince of Egypt, 1998, The Thin Red Line, 1998, Chill Factor, 1999, The Road to El Dorado, 2000, Gladiator, 2000 (ASCAP award, 2001, Golden Globe award, 2001), Mission: Impossible II, 2000 (ASCAP award, 2001), An Everlasting Piece, 2000, Hannibal, 2001 (ASCAP award, 2002), Pearl Harbor, 2001 (ASCAP award, 2002), Invincible, 2001, Riding in Cars with Boys, 2001, Black Hawk Down, 2001, Spirit: Stallion of the Cimarron, 2002 (ASCAP award, 2003), The Ring, 2002 (ASCAP award, 2003), Tears of the Sun, 2003, Matchstick Men, 2003, The Last Samurai, 2003 (ASCAP award, 2004), Something's Gotta Give, 2003, King Arthur, 2004, Thunderbirds, 2004, Shark Tale, 2004 (ASCAP award, 2005), Lauras Stern, 2004, Spanglish, 2004, Madagascar, 2005 (ASCAP award, 2006), Batman Begins, 2005 (ASCAP award, 2006), The Little Polar Bear 2, 2005, The Weather Man, 2005, The Da Vinci Code, 2006 (ASCAP award, 2007), Pirates of the Caribbean: Dead Man's Chest, 2006 (ASCAP award, 2007), The Holiday, 2006, Pirates of the Caribbean: At World's End, 2007, The Simpsons Movie, 2007, Kung Fu Panda, 2008 (Annie award for Best Music in an Animated Feature Prodn., 2009), The Dark Knight, 2008 (Grammy award for Best Score Soundtrack Album, 2009), Frost/Nixon, 2008, Madagascar: Escape 2 Africa, 2008, Angels & Demons, 2009, (TV films) Wild Horses, 1985, Millennium: Tribal Wisdom and the Modern World, 1992, The 3rd Reich, in Color, 1998, (TV miniseries) First Born, 1989, (TV series) El Candidato, 1999; music prodr. (films) The Last Emperor, 1987. Recipient Joseph Plateau award of Honor, 2000, Hollywood Film award for Outstanding Achievement in Music in Film, Hollywood Film Festival, 2001, Harry Mancini award, ASCAP, 2003, Career Achievement award, US Nat. Bd. of Rev., 2003. Office: Gorfaine Schwartz Agency 4111 W Alameda Ave Ste 509 Burbank CA 91505-4171*

ZIMMER, JOHN HERMAN, lawyer; b. Sioux Falls, SD, Dec. 30, 1922; s. John Francis and Veronica (Berke) Zimmer; m. Deanna Langner, 1976; children from previous marriage: Mary Zimmer Quinin, Robert Joseph, Judith Maureen Zimmer Rose. Student, Augustana Coll., Sioux Falls, 1941—42, Mont. State Coll., 1943; LLB, U. S.D., 1948. Bar: S.D. 1948. Pvt. practice, Turner County, SD, 1948—; of counsel Zimmer, Duncan & Cole, Parker, SD, 1992—. States atty., Turner County, 1955—58, Turner County, 1962—64; asst. prof. med. jurisprudence U. S.D.; minority counsel U.S. Senate Armed Svcs. Com. on Strategic and Clin. Materials Investigation, 1962—63; chmn. Southeastern Coun. Govts., 1973—75; mem. adv. coun. U. S.D. Law Sch., 1973—74. Pres. S.D. Easter Seal Soc., 1986—87; Chmn. Turner County Rep. Com., 1955—56; mem. adv. com. S.D. Rep., 1959—60; alt. del. Rep. Nat. Conv., 1958. With AUS, 1943—46, PTO. Decorated Bronze Star, Philippine Liberation Ribbon with 2 Bronz Stars, Asian Pacific medal with 3 Battle Stars. Mem.: ATLA, ABA, VFW, S.D. Bar Assn., Fed. Bar Assn., Am. Legion, Shriners, Elks, Phi Delta Phi. Home: PO Box 640 Parker SD 57053-0640 Office: Zimmer Duncan & Cole LLP Law Bldg PO Box 550 Parker SD 57053-0550 Home Phone: 605-297-3265; Office Phone: 605-297-4446. Personal E-mail: jhzim@hotmail.com.

ZIMMER, LARRY WILLIAM, JR., sports announcer; b. New Orleans, Nov. 13, 1935; s. Lawrence W. Sr. and Theodora (Ahrens) Z.; m. Dawn M. Caillouet, June 4, 1955 (div. June 1972); children: Larry III, Tracey; m. Brigitte Bastian, Nov. 17, 1972. Student, La. State U., 1953-55; BJ, U. Mo., 1957. Sports dir. KFRU Radio, Columbia, Mo., 1960-66; asst. mgr. programming WAAM Radio, Ann Arbor, Mich., 1966-71; broadcaster football, basketball Mich., 1966-70; sportscaster, sports dir. KOA Radio, Denver, 1971—; broadcaster Denver Broncos Football, 1971-96; broadcaster football, basketball U. Colo. Buffaloes, 1971—; broadcaster Denver Rockets, 1972-74. Adj. prof. journalism U. Colo., 2001—. Author: Stadium Stories--The Denver Broncoes, 2004. Bd. mem. Colo. Ski Mus. and Hall of Fame, Vail, 1981-2000, Opera Colo., Denver, 1985—, Colo. chap. Nat. Football Found; former mem. adv. bd. Jefferson Co. Youth Advocacy Ctr. 1st lt. US Army, 1958-60. Named Colo. Sportscaster of the Yr., Nat. Sportscasters and Sportswriters Assn., Salisbury, NC, 1988, 90, 91, 2001, 02, Broadcaster of the Yr., Colo. Broadcaster's Assn., Denver, 1995, Broadcast Profls. Colo. Hall of Fame, 2009, Coll. Football Hall of Fame, 2009; recipient Powerade award for best radio/TV sports story of yr. Nat. Sportscasters and Sportswriters Assn., 2000, Chris Schenkel award Nat. Football Found., 2009. Avocations: skiing, walking, opera. Office: KOA Radio 72 Paradise Rd Golden CO 80401 Business E-Mail: larryzimmer@clearchannel.com.

ZIMMER, MARKUS BERNHARD, legal association administrator; b. Basel, Switzerland, Oct. 10, 1946; came to U.S., 1948; s. Max Bernhard and Elisabeth (Sulzmann) Z.; m. Shelley Elaine Melcomian, Jan. 5, 1976; children: Jessica, Christopher. BA in Philosophy, U. Utah, 1971, MA in Philosophy, 1975; MEd, Harvard U., 1977; EdD in Philosophy of Edn., 1980. Rsch. asst. Harvard Law Sch., Cambridge, Mass., 1977-78; teaching fellow law and ethics Harvard U., Cambridge, Mass.; asst. divsn. dir. Div. Continuing Edn. and Tng., Fed. Jud. Ctr., Washington, 1981—83, chief legal svcs. tng. br., 1983—84, chief mgmt. tng. br., 1984-87; adj. assoc. prof. mgmt. U. Md., College Park, 1985-87; clk. of ct., dist. ct. adminstr. US Dist. Ct. Utah, Salt Lake City, 1987—2006; chief ct. mgmt. Internat. Criminal Tribunal, The Hague, Netherlands, 2006—07; deputy chief party Ukrainian Rule of Law Project, Kiev, 2007—08; project mgr. Comml. Ct. Modernizatlon, Abu Duabi Govt. Restructing Com., Abu Dabi, United Arab Emirates, 2008—09; sr. advisor & mem., adv. group Saudi Arabia Jud. Sys. Modernization Project, 2009—; jud. independence advisor Global Justice Project, Iraq, 2009—. Fed. dist. ct. clks. adv. com. Adminstrv. Office US Cts., 1990-96, fed. dist. ct. case mgmt. and stats. umbrella group, 1992-98, dist. ct. efficiencies task force, 1992-93, ct. adminstrn. adv. com., 1995-96, chmn. tech. panel on automation, 1999-2002; interagy. adv. group on tng. and devel. Office of Pers. Mgmt., Washington, 1984-87; ABA CEELI ct. adminstrn. cons. Bulgarian Ministry Justice, Sofia, 1992, legal specialist, Skopje, Macedonia, 1997, faculty, Jud. Tng. Inst., Prague, Czech Republic, 2000-01, jud. edn. assessment Supreme Ct. Rwanda, 2003; chief arch. jud. reform strategy, Serbia, 2005; leader World Bank Regional Justice Sector Capacity Bldg. Program, Prague, Czech Republic, 2003-05; mem. faculty ABA Prague Inst. Iraqi Judges, 2004; faculty Internat. Seminar on Jud. Transparency, Chengdu, China, 2005, Justice Sys. Assessment, Monrovia, liberia, 2006; founding ptnr. and pres. Internat. Assn. Ct. Admin., 2004—; chair US Dist. Cts. Civil/Criminal User Group, 1995-98; ad hoc task force on budget allotment simplification US Cts., 1996-98; dist. clk. liaison US Jud. Conf. IT Com., 1999-2001, internat. jud. rels. com., 2002-04; adv. roundtable on law on cts. Coun. Europe, Rep. of Montenegro, 2001; others in field; spkr. in field. Exec. editor Internat. Jour. Court Adminstrn., 2007—; contbr. articles to profl. jours. Exec. bd. Utah Combined Fed. Campaign, 1989-2006, bd. chmn. and statewide campaign dir., 1992, 2002. Fulbright fellow, 1972-73; recipient U.S. Cts. Dir.'s award for outstanding leadership, 1994, Roy B. Gibson Freedom of Info. Act award Utah chpt. Soc. Profl. Journalists, 2000. Mem. ABA (CEELI ct. adminstrn. working group 1991-94, Russian jury trial working group 1993-94, African human rights subcom., 2004-2007, ABA Internat. Human Rights Steering Com., 2007-), ASTD (dir. justice sys. trainers 1984-86), Fed. Ct. Clks. Assn. (exec. bd. 1991-92). Office Phone: 801-733-6282. Business E-Mail: zimmermb@gmail.com.

ZIMMER, RICHARD, anthropologist, educator; s. Emanuel and Tessie Zimmer; m. Ann Zimmer; children: Jessica, Daniel. PhD, UCLA, 1976, Ctr. Psychol. Studies, Berkeley, Calif., 1989. Cert. psychologist C Bd. Psychology, Calif., 1994. Instr. LA Valley Coll., Van Nuys, Calif., 1965—71; prof. Sonoma State U., Rohnert Pk., Calif., 1971—. Self-employed psychologist, Santa Rosa, Calif., 1995—. Bd. mem. DS/LC, Santa Rosa, 2004—. Mem.: Am. Anthrop. Assn. Office: 1144 Sonoma Ave St 117 Santa Rosa CA 95405 Office Fax: 707-526-1913.

ZIMMER, ROBERT JEFFREY, academic administrator, mathematician, educator; b. NYC, Nov. 5, 1947; s. Max S. and Harriet (Brokaw) Z.; m. Terese Schwartzman, Oct. 27, 1974; children— David, Benjamin, Alexander. AB summa cum laude, Brandeis U., 1968; PhD, Harvard U., 1975. Asst. prof. US Naval Acad., Annapolis, Md., 1975-77; instr. U. Chgo., 1977-79, assoc. prof., 1979-80, prof. math, 1980—, chmn. math dept., 1991-95, assoc. provost for rsch. & edn., 1995—98, dep. provost for rsch., 1998—2000, dep. provost, 2000—01; pres. U. Chgo, 2006—; prof. math. U. Calif.-Berkeley, 1981-83; provost, Ford Found. prof. math. Brown U., Providence, 2002—06. V.p. rsch. Argonne Nat. Lab., 2000—02. Author: Ergodic Theory and Semisimple Groups, 1984, Essential Results of Functional Analysis; contbr. articles to profl. jours. Sloan Found. fellow, 1979-83 Fellow AAAS, Am. Acad. Arts & Scis. Office: U Chgo Office of Pres 5801 S Ellis Ave Chicago IL 60637

ZIMMERER, KATHY LOUISE, museum director; b. Whittier, Calif., Dec. 9, 1951; BA cum laude, U. Calif., Berkeley, 1974; MA, Williams Coll., 1976. From tour guide to curatorial asst. Sterling and Francine Clark Inst., Williamstown, Mass., 1975-76; spl. asst. dept. modern art L.A. County Mus. Art, 1976-77; mus. edn. fellow Fine Arts Mus. San Francisco, 1977-78; dir. coll. art gallery SUNY, New Paltz, 1978-80; cons. in field, 1980-81; dir. univ. art gallery Calif. State U., Dominguez Hills, 1982—. Project dir. Painted Light: California Impressionist Paintings from the Gardena H.S./L.A. Unified Sch. Dist., 1996—. Mem. Internat. Assn. Art Critics, Art Table. Office: Univ Art Gallery Calif State U 1000 E Victoria St Carson CA 90747-0001 Home Phone: 562-421-1743; Office Phone: 310-243-3334. E-mail: kzimmerer@csudh.edu.

ZIMMER-GALLER, INGRID E., ophthalmologist, educator; d. Martin Zimmer and Roswitha Zimmer-Galler; m. Isaac Yoon, May 6, 1989. BS, Johns Hopkins U., Balt., 1985; MD, Tulane U., New Orleans, La., 1989. Diplomate Am. Bd. Ophthalmology, 1994. Assoc. prof. Johns Hopkins U., 2007—. Prin. Investigator grant, NIH, 2005, Nat. Inst. Health grant. Fellow: Am. Acad. Ophthalmology (Achievement award 2008); mem.: Am. Soc. Retina Specialists (Achievement award 2006). Office: Johns Hopkins Wilmer Eye Ins 87 Thomas Johnson Dr #102 Frederick MD 21702

ZIMMERMAN, ANDREW, pediatrician, neurologist; AB, Princeton U.; MD, Columbia U., 1970. Diplomate Am. Bd. Pediatrics, Am. Bd. Psychiatry & Neurology. Clinical assoc. Devel. & Metabolic Neurology Branch NIH; fellow Johns Hopkins U. Sch. Medicine, 1974, assoc. prof. neurology & psychiatry; faculty U. Conn. Sch. Medicine, 1977—83; pvt. practice Knoxville Neurology Clinic; pediatric neurologist Kennedy Krieger Inst. Ctr. for Autism & Related Disorders, dir. med. rsch. Recipient Disting. Svc. award, Autism Soc. America East Tenn. Chpt. Mem.: AMA, Soc. for Neuroscience, Child Neurology Soc., Am. Acad. Neurology, Am. Acad. Pediatrics. Office: Kennedy Krieger Institute 707 N Broadway Baltimore MD 21205 Office Phone: 443-923-9150. Office Fax: 443-923-9160.

ZIMMERMAN, BERNARD, investment banker; b. Bklyn., Dec. 7, 1932; s. Jacob and Pearl (Schechner) Z.; m. Joyce M. Singer, Dec. 24, 1960; children: Wayne Jay, Ellen Holly. BBA, CCNY, 1954; MBA, NYU, 1957. CPA NY. Fin. exec. consumer products Spartans Industries, Inc., NYC, 1961-65; sr. v.p. Scheinman, Hochstin, and Trotta, Inc., NYC, 1965-72; pres. Bernard Zimmerman and Co., Inc., Weston, Conn., 1972—; pres., CEO FCCC, Inc. (formerly First Conn. Capital Corp.), Norwalk, Conn., 2003—. Pres. Beacon Hill Mgmt., Inc., Boston, 1994-97; sr. v.p. corp. fin. Gruntal & Co., Inc., N.Y.C., 1983-84; pres., chmn. bd., pres. St. Lawrence Seaway Corp., Indpls., 1985-93, fin. cons.; sr. v.p. The Zimmerman Group, Inc., 1991-96; chmn. bd. dirs., pres. Beacon Hill Mut. Fund, Inc., Boston, 1994-97; Liquidating trustee Unity Buying Svc. Co. Liquidating Trust, Hicksville, NY; bd. dirs. Sbarro, Inc., Melville, NY; fin. cons. Beautiful Visions-U.S.A., Ltd., Bethpage, NY, Task Mgmt. Co., Ridgefield, Conn., 1998-99; pres. and CEO FCCC, Inc., Norwalk, Conn., 2003—; chmn. bd., pres. GVC Venture Corp., NYC, 2004—, pres., St. Lawrence Seaway Corp., chmn. bd., CEO, Norwalk Conn., 2007—. Bd. dirs. Inst. Cancer Rsch. and Molecular Medicine, Temple U., Phila., 1995-2007; trustee Sharro Family Found., Melville, 1993-2007; mem. Nat. Assn. Corp. Dir. Blue Ribbon Commn.

on Corp. Governance-Best Practice Coun., 1997. With AUS, 1955-57. Mem.: NY State Soc. CPAs. Home and Office: 18 High Meadow Rd Weston CT 06883-2946 Office Phone: 203-226-5165.

ZIMMERMAN, CHRIS, professional sports team executive; BA in Econs. and Mass Comm., U. Vermont; MBA, Babson Coll. Sr. v.p. Saatchi and Saatchi Advertising, NYC; USA advertising dir. Nike Brand; joined Nike Golf USA, 1998, gen. mgr.; pres., CEO Nike Bauer Hockey Inc., 2003—06, Canucks Sports & Entertainment; pres., CEO, alt. gov. Vancouver Canucks, 2006—. Former asst. hockey coach Babson College. Bd. mem. Canucks for Kids Fund, Special Olympics BC. Office: Vancouver Canucks 800 Griffiths Way Vancouver BC V6B 6G1 Canada

ZIMMERMAN, CONNIE ANN, public administrator; AA, Harrisburg Area CC, 1978; BS in Pub. Policy, Pa. State U., 2002. Exec. sec. DER, 1993—95, adminstrv. asst., 1995—99; adminstrv. mgr. PennDOT Bureau of Design, Harrisburg, 1999—2008, Bur. Infrast Ops., 2008—. V.p. Women's Legis. Exchange, 2001—09; chair legis. com. Ctrl. Pa. Female Execs., 2005—07; bd. dirs. Ctrl. Pa. Women Execs., Harrisburg, Pa., 1997—2002, YWCA of Greater Harrisburg, 2002—08, Program Female Offenders, 2008—. Recipient Sarah Wright award, YWCA, 2006, 2007. Mem.: Am. Soc. Pub. Adminstrn., Nat. Women's History Mus. and Nat. Constl. Ctr. (charter), Harrisburg Mannechor, Mitgleider Deutscher Verein, Pi Gamma Mu. Roman Catholic. Avocations: dance, music, gardening. Home: 933 Highland St Steelton PA 17113-1537 Personal E-mail: caz125@psualum.com.

ZIMMERMAN, D. PATRICK, psychotherapist, health facility administrator; b. Chgo., Jan. 7, 1942; s. Delores Morley Zimmerman and Steven Joseph Patrick Maloney. BA, Wofford Coll., Spartanburg, SC, 1963; MA, Antioch Coll., Yellow Springs, Ohio, 1976; PhD, Ill. Sch. Profl. Psychology, Chgo., 1986. Cert. Clin. Psychologist Ill. Dept. Profl. Regulation, 1988, Psychoanalyst Chgo. Ctr. Psychoanalysis, 1998. Tchr. Chgo. Pub. Schs., 1967—69; founder, dir. The So. Sch. (Therapeutic Day Sch.), Chgo., 1969—94; post-doctoral fellow Sonia Shankman Orthogenic Sch., U. Chgo., Chgo., 1985—86, coord. rsch., 1987—2002, asst. dir., admissions and psychotherapy svcs., 2002—. Lectr. Com. on Human Devel. U. Chgo., 1998—2004, lectr. Dept. Psychiatry, 1998—. Editor: (jour.) Residential Treatment for Children and Youth; author: (books) The Forsaken Child: Essays on Group Care and Individual Therapy; co-editor: On Transitions from Group Care: Homeward Bound, Psychotherapy in Group Care, Residential Treatment. Mem., sec. Chgo. Ctr. for Psychoanalysis, 2001—04, bd. dirs., 2002—05. Grantee, Found. for Emotionally Disturbed Children, 1998. Fellow: Am. Assn. Children's Residential Centers; mem.: APA, Quadrangle Club, U. Chgo. Office Fax: 773-702-1304. E-mail: pzimmerm@midway.uchicago.edu.

ZIMMERMAN, DEBBIE, communications educator; b. Winchester, Tenn., June 23, 1953; m. Robert E. Zimmerman; 1 child, Julie Beth Salter. AA, Motlow State CC, Tullahoma, Tenn., 1973; BS, MEd, Mid. Tenn. U., Murfreesboro, 1980. Assoc. prof. communication Motlow State CC, 1981—. Dir.: (25 childrens' plays). Sunday sch. tchr., vocalist, drama coord. Cumberland Presbyn. Ch., Winchester, 1992—2008. Mem.: AAUP, Delta Kappa Gamma (pres. to v.p. 1998—2002). Presbyterian. Avocations: singing, theater. Business E-Mail: dzimmerman@mscc.edu.

ZIMMERMAN, DENNIS NEAL, psychologist; b. Martindale, Pa., June 8, 1947; s. Ivan Z. and Pearl Lydian Zimmerman; m. Kathy Kay McKinney, Aug. 26, 1967; children: Shawn Patrick, Kristen Nicole Eshleman. EdD in Sch. Psychology, Ind. U. Pa., 2007. Cert. sch. psychologist Pa. Dept. Edn., 2001. Spl. edn. tchr. Oxford Area Sch. Dist., Pa., 1999—2001; sch. psychologist Eastern Lebanon County Sch. Dist., Myerstown, Pa., 2001—. Radioman 3rd class USN, 1965—68, Groton, Conn. Mem.: Assn. Sch. Psychologists Pa., Psi Chi (life). Home: 352 Coventry Ln Lititz PA 17543 Office: Eastern Lebanon County Sch Dist 558 W Main Ave Myerstown PA 17067

ZIMMERMAN, DIANE LEENHEER, law educator; b. Newton, N.J., Apr. 16, 1941; d. Adrian and Mildred Eleanor (Booth) Leenheer; m. Earl A. Zimmerman, Sept. 24, 1960 (div. Aug. 1982); m. Cavin P. Leeman, Feb. 18, 1984. BA, Beaver Coll., Glenside, Pa., 1963; JD, Columbia U., 1976. Bar: N.Y. 1977, US Supreme Ct. 1983. Reporter, Newsweek mag., N.Y.C., 1963-71; spl. features writer N.Y. Daily News, NYC, 1971-73; law clk. to Hon. Jack B. Weinstein US Dist. Ct. Ea. Dist. N.Y., 1976-77; asst. prof. law N.Y.U. Sch. Law, 1977-80, assoc. prof., 1980-82, prof., 1982-2008, Samuel Tilden prof. law emerita, 2009; mem. faculty Practicing Law Inst., N.Y.C., 1979, 84, 90, 92, 94, 96-02; Disting. Lee Vis. Prof. Constl. Law Coll. William and Mary, 1994; moderator justice and soc. program Aspen Inst., 1992, 99; Disting. Vis. Hosier Chair Intellectual Property, DePaul Coll. Law, Chgo., 2001; lectr. 17th Ann. Manges Lectr. Intellectual Property, 2004. Recipient citation of merit Columbia U. Sch. Journalism, 1972; Kent scholar and Stone scholar, 1973-76; Mem. ABA (vice chmn. tort liability study com. tort and ins. sect. 1986-87, chair 1st amendment rights com. 1989-94), Am. Law Inst., Assn. of Bar City of N.Y. (chairperson com. civil rights 1981-83), Copyright Soc. USA (trustee 1988-91, 2004-07). Office: NYU Sch Law Vanderbilt Hall Rm 332 40 Washington Sq S New York NY 10012-1099 Office Phone: 212-998-6250. Business E-Mail: zimmermd@exchange.law.nyu.edu.

ZIMMERMAN, DONALD PATRICK, lawyer; b. Albany, NY, Mar. 20, 1942; s. Bernard M. and Helen M. (Eshelman) Z. Student, McDonogh Sch., 1953—57, Lawrenceville Sch., 1960; BA, Rollins Coll., 1964; JD, Dickinson Sch. Law, 1967. Bar: Pa. 1968, US Dist. Ct. (ea. dist.) Pa., US Ct. Appeals (3rd cir.), US Supreme Ct. 1971. Atty. Legal Aid, 1968-69; pub. defender Lancaster County, Pa., 1969-72; pvt. practice Lancaster, 1974—. Instr. Ct. Common Pleas for Constables, 1976-; solicitor Lancaster County Dep. Sheriff Assn., 1977-, Lancaster County Constable Assn., 1975-; sheriff solicitor Lancaster County Sheriff Office 2004-; instr. sheriff's dept. Lancaster County for Dep. Sheriffs, 1978-85; of counsel to Dep. Sheriff Assn. Pa., 1979-81; spl. counsel Pa. State Constables Assn., 1981; chmn. Bd. Arbitrators Lancaster County, 1975-81; spl. counsel Legislative Com. to Constable Assn. Pa., 1982; pres. Pa. Coun. Sheriff's Solicitors, 2007-08; legal instr. NRA. Author: The Pennsylvania Landlord and Tenant Handbook, 1982, revised edit., 1993; editor (with J. Hatfield and A. Taylor) Pennsylvania Constable Handbook, 1998, Landlord Training Program, Nat. Program Manual; contbr. articles to profl. jours. Legal instr. NRA, 2007; mem. pastoral coun. St. Anthony's Cath. Ch., 1995-98, mandated extraordinary min. of Communion, 2002. Recipient Ofcl. Commendation of Merit, Lancaster County Sheriff's Dept., 1979, Ofcl. Commendation of Merit, F.O.P. State Police Lodge 66, 1985, Disting. Svc. award, 1987, Cert. of Appreciation, Lancaster Crime Commn., 2003, Recognition award City of Lancaster, 2004, Recognition award Borough of Manheim, 2006. Mem. ABA, ATLA, Pa. Bar Assn., Acad. Family Mediators, Lancaster County Bar Assn., W. Hensel Brown Inn of Ct., Lancaster County Constables Assn. (Outstanding Leadership award 1988, Disting. Svc. award as solicitor 1998, 25 Yrs. Dedicated Svc. award 2000, Dedicated Svc. award 2004, 30 Yr. Dedicated Svc. award 2005). Avocation: fencing. Office: 214 E King St Lancaster PA 17602-2977 Office Phone: 717-394-6859. Personal E-mail: patrickzimm@comcast.net.

ZIMMERMAN, EARL ABRAM, neurologist, educator; b. Harrisburg, Pa., May 5, 1937; s. Earl Beckley and Hazel Marie (Myers) Z. BS in Chemistry, Franklin and Marshall Coll., 1959; MD, U. Pa., 1963. Diplomate Am. Bd. Psychiatry and Neurology, Am. Bd. Internal Medicine. Intern Presbyn. Hosp., NYC, 1963-64, resident, 1964-65, Neurol. Inst. CPMC, NYC, 1965-68, research fellow endocrinology, 1970-72; asst. prof. to prof. neurology Columbia U., NYC, 1972-85; prof., chmn. dept. neurology Oreg. Health Sci. U., Portland, 1985-2000; chmn. dept. neurology Albany (N.Y.) Med. Coll., 2000—04; clin. dir. neuroscis. Advanced Imaging Rsch. Ctr., dir. Alzheimer's Ctr., Albany Med. Ctr./GE Global Rsch., 2002—. Dir. neurology Helen Hayes Hosp., Haverstraw, N.Y., 1982-83 Mem. editl. bd. Jour. Histochem. Cytochemistry, 1980-85, 87, Neuroendocrinology, 1985-88, Annals of Neurology, 1985-91, Western Jour. Medicine, 1993-98, Jour. Clin. Endocrinal Metabolism, 1995-99; contbr. numerous articles to profl. jours. Maj. USAF, 1968-70 Rsch. grantee NIH, 1977—. Mem. Am. Neurol. Assn. (program chmn. 1980-82), Am. Acad. Neurology (Wartenber lectr. 1985), Endocrine Soc. Democrat. Mem. United Ch. of Christ Avocations: woodworking, gardening, theater, music, art, skiing, tennis. Office: Albany Med Coll Dept Neurology 47 New Scotland Ave MC-65 Albany NY 12208 Home Phone: 518-785-3638; Office Phone: 518-262-0801. Business E-Mail: zimmere@mail.amc.edu.

ZIMMERMAN, EDWIN MORTON, lawyer; b. NYC, June 11, 1924; s. Benjamin and Tobie (Fuchs) Z.; m. Caroline Abbot, July 3, 1956; children: Sarah Abbot, Lyle Benjamin, Miriam Appleton. AB, Columbia U., 1944, LLB, 1949. Bar: NY 1949, DC 1969, US Supreme Ct 1969. With Hoover Commn. Reorgn. Exec. Br., 1948; law clk. to Hon. Stanley F. Reed U.S. Supreme Ct., 1950-51; law clk. to Judge Simon H. Rifkind U.S. Dist. Ct., 1949-50; pvt. practice law NYC, 1951-59; prof. law Stanford U., 1959-69; with Justice Dept., 1965-69, asst. atty. gen. charge antitrust div., 1968-69; mem. Covington & Burling, Washington, 1969-94, sr. counsel, 1994—. Mem. coun. Adminstrv. Conf. U.S., 1975—78; mem. mfg. studies bd. Nat. Acad. Sci., 1983—87; adj. prof. George Washington Sch. Law, 1996—2001. Trustee Textile Mus., 1983-2007, pres. bd. trustees, 1987-96; mem. Folger Poetry Bd., 1990—; mem. adv. bd. Partisan Rev., 1996-2003. 1st lt. signal corps US Army, 1944—46. Mem. ABA, Assn. of Bar of City of NY, Am. Law Inst., Coun. Fgn. Rels., Phi Beta Kappa. Home: 1820 Kalorama Sq NW Washington DC 20008-4022 Office: Covington & Burling PO Box 7566 1201 Pennsylvania Ave NW Washington DC 20004-2401 Office Phone: 202-662-5190. Business E-Mail: ezimmerman@cov.com.

ZIMMERMAN, ELYN, artist; b. Phila., Dec. 16, 1945; d. Louis B. and Sylvia (Snyder) Z.; m. Kirk Varnedoe, Oct. 8, 1983. BA in Psychology, UCLA, 1968, MFA in Painting, 1972. Apptd. mem. Commn. Fine Arts, 2003. One-man shows include Univ. Art Mus., Berkeley, Calif., 1974, P.S. 1, Long Island City, N.Y., 1977, Mus. Contemporary Art, Chgo., 1979, Hudson River Mus., Yonkers, N.Y., 1982, Joslyn Art Mus., Omaha, 1984, Wave Hill, Riverside, N.Y., Contemporary Art Mus. U. South Fla., Tampa, 1991, Gagosian Gallery, N.Y.C., 1993, 96, 98, 2001, 03, 04; exhibited in group shows at Whitney Mus. Am. Art, N.Y.C., 1975, Biennale of Sydney, Australia, 1976, Walker Art Ctr., Mpls., 1979, San Diego Mus. Art, 1980, Venice Biennale, USA Pavillion, Italy, 1980, Mus. Contemporary Art, Chgo., 1981, Newport Harbor Art Mus., Calif., 1982, Hirshhorn Mus., Washington, 1983, San Francisco Mus. Modern Art, 1984, Socrates Sculpture Park, N.Y.C., 1996, L.A. County Mus. Art, 1996, Addison Gallery, Andover, Mass., 1998, Marlborough Gallery, N.Y.C., 1998, Chesterwood, Stockbridge, Mass., Montclair Mus., N.J., 1999, Ctr. for Photography, Woodstock, N.Y., Witherspoon Gallery Durham, N.C., 2002; pub. sculpture commns. include Nat. Geographic Soc., Washington, O'Hare Internat. Ctr., Rosemont, Ill., Dade County Justice Ctr., Miami, Fla., Moffit Rsch. Ctr./U. South Fla., Tampa, Market Plz., San Francisco, Birmingham Mus. Art, Ala., AT&T Hdqrs., N.J., World Trade Ctr. Meml., N.Y.C., Olympic Park, Beijing, Cavala Park, NYC. Nat. Endowment for Arts grantee, 1976, 80, 83, Creative Artist Pub. Svc. grantee, 1980; NEA and Japan-U.S. Friendship Commn. fellow, 1982. Mem. Creative Time, Inc. (bd. dirs. 1984-90). Home: 140 Greene St New York NY 10012-3241 Office Phone: 212-219-3224. Business E-Mail: zimmermanstudio@nyc.rr.com.

ZIMMERMAN, EVE KATHLEEN, literature and language professor; d. Franklin B. Zimmerman and Rachel Phillips Belash; m. Seth Lloyd, May 31, 1994; children: Emma Rachel Lloyd, Zoe Susan Lloyd. PhD, Columbia U., NYC. Asst. prof. Boston U., 1995—2000; assoc. prof. Wellesley Coll., Mass., 2000—. Translator: (fiction) The Cape and Other Stories from the Japanese Ghetto, (autobiography) Strawberry Road (US Japan Friendship Commn. award, 1992); author: (book) Out of the Alleyway: Nakagami Kenji and the Poetics of Outcaste Fiction, 2007; contbr. articles. Bd. mem. Assn. Tchrs. Japanese, Boulder, Colo., 2005—08. Recipient award, Fulbright Assn., 2003—04. Home: 18 Weston Rd Wellesley MA 02481 Office: Wellesley Coll 106 Ctrl St Wellesley MA 02481 Business E-Mail: ezimmerm@wellesley.edu.

ZIMMERMAN, GARY A(LAN), chemistry educator, academic administrator, profl. genealogists; b. Seattle, Oct. 19, 1938; s. Philo Ralph and Nellie Evelyn (Heritage) Z.; m. Leslie Anne Ryder, June 25, 1960 (div. Mar. 1987); children: Teresa Jean, Thomas Edward; m. Marie Claire Markham Hudgins, Feb. 20, 1988 (div. Jan 1994) m. Michele Genthon, May 20, 1995 BS with honors, Calif. Inst. Tech., 1960; PhD, U. Wis., 1964. Faculty Seattle U., 1964-88, prof., 1976-88, dean sci. and engring., 1973-79, acad. v.p., 1980-81, exec. v.p., 1981-87; provost, chief oper. officer Antioch U. Seattle, Seattle, 1988—99; pres. Fiske Genealogy Libr., 1998—. Bd. dirs. Pacific Sci. Ctr. Found., 1985-91. Mem. Bellevue (Wash.) City Council, 1974-80, mayor, 1978-80; chmn. coun. Municipality Met. Seattle, 1980-90; chmn. King County Solid Waste Mgmt. Bd., 1978-80; bd. dirs. Chief Seattle coun. Boy Scouts Am., 1979—; governing coun. Pacific Hosp. Preservation Devel. Authority, 1997-, chair 2006-. Recipient Pres.'s award Nat. Def. Transp. Assn., 1981; NIH fellow, 1961-64; Woodrow Wilson fellow, 1960-61 Fellow AAAS; mem. AAUP, Am. Assn. Clin. Chemistry (bd. dirs. 1977-84, pres.-elect 1982, pres. 1983), Am. Chem. Soc., Pioneer Assn. Wash. (historian 1987-89, 2003-, pres. 1989-90, past pres. 1990-92, treas. 1992-2009), Bellevue C. of C. (bd. dirs. 1978-88), Bellevue Rotary Club (pres. 2007-2008). Home: 3900 112th Ave NE Bellevue WA 98004-7772 Office: Fiske Genealogy Libr 1644 43rd Ave E Seattle WA 98112-3222 Office Phone: 206-328-2716. Business E-Mail: gzim@fiskelibrary.org.

ZIMMERMAN, GARY J., retired utilities association executive; b. Chgo., 1960; B, U. Colo., Boulder, 1982; MBA, U. Denver, 1984. Intern Office of Senator William L. Armstrong US Senate; with Unisource Worldwide; group v.p. south ctrl. US xpedx; COO WebTransport, 2000; v.p. bus. ops. Denver Ops. Ctr. 180 Connect, Inc.; exec. v.p. Arabian Horse Assn., 2006—08; exec. dir. Am. Water Works Assn., 2008—09. Office Phone: 303-794-7711. Office Fax: 303-347-0804.

ZIMMERMAN, GARY WAYNE, professional football player; b. Fullerton, Calif., Dec. 13, 1961; m. Lisa Zimmerman; children: Lindsay, Rue. Student, U. Oreg. Offensive tackle LA Express (US Football League), 1984-85, Minn. Vikings, 1986—92, Denver Broncos, 1993—97. Named to NFL 1980's All-Decade Team, NFL 1990's All-Decade Team, NFL Pro Bowl, 1987—89, 1992, 1994—96, NFL All-Pro Team, 1986—89, 1992—96, Oreg. Sports Hall of Fame, 2002, Pro Football Hall of Fame, 2008. Address: Pro Footbal Hall of Fame 2121 George Halas Dr NW Canton OH 44708-2699

ZIMMERMAN, GIDEON K., retired minister; b. Lehr, ND, Aug. 18, 1920; m. Eleanor Pekrul,(dec. Nov 10, 2007); children: Paul, Mark (dec.), Thomas. Diploma, N.Am. Baptist Sem., Rochester, NY, 1943; BA, U. ND, 1951; postgrad., Bethany Bibl. Sem., 1958—59, Chgo. Lutheran Sem., 1959—61; BD, N.Am. Bapt. Sem., Sioux Falls, SD, 1960, DD, 1971. Pastor First Bapt. Ch., Auburn, Mich., 1943-47, Grace Bapt. Ch., Grand Forks, N.D., 1947-51, Temple Bapt. Ch., Milw., 1951-55; gen. sec. dept. Christian edn. N. Am. Bapt. Conf., 1955-68, exec. sec., 1968-79, estate planning counselor, 1979-85; ret. Home: 2116 Buechel Bank Rd Apt 205 Louisville KY 40218-3577

ZIMMERMAN, HELENE LORETTA, retired business educator; b. Rochester, NY, Feb. 26, 1933; d. Henry Charles and Loretta Catherine (Hobert) Z. BS, SUNY, Albany, 1953, MS, 1959; PhD, U. N.D., 1969. Cert. records mgr., 1977-. Bus. tchr., chmn. bus. dept. Williamson (N.Y.) Cen. Sch., 1953-69; asst. prof. U. Ky., Lexington, 1969-70; assoc. prof. bus. Cen. Mich. U., Mt. Pleasant, 1970-74, prof., 1974-98. Author General Business, 1977; contbg. author to records mgmt. text book, 1987. Sec. Isabella County Christmas Outreach, Mt. Pleasant, 1983-2004, mem. steering com., 1983—; mem. Internat. Rels. Coun., Mt. Pleasant, 2003—; active Goodrow Fund, 2006—. Mem.: AAUW (pres. 1984—86), Mich. Bus. Edn. Assn. (bd. dirs. 1985—90, pres. 1988—89, bd. dirs. 1995—97), Nat. Bus. Edn. Assn., Internat. Soc. Bus. Edn. (internat. v.p. English speaking nations 1986—88, editor Internat. Rev. 1997—2006), Inst. Cert. Records Mgrs. (sec. 1985—89, exam. devel. com. 1993—2002), Assn. Records Mgmt. and Adminstrn., Gen. Fedn. Women's Clubs (pres. Mt. Pleasant chpt. 2004—05), Delta Kappa Gamma (state pres. 1987—89, internat. fin. com. 1990—94, internat. ad hoc com. on tech. 1996—2000). Avocations: travel, crafts.

ZIMMERMAN, HOWARD ELLIOT, chemist, educator; b. NYC, July 5, 1926; s. Charles and May (Cohen) Zimmerman; m. Jane Kirschenheiter, June 3, 1950 (dec. Jan. 1975); children: Robert, Steven, James; m. Martha L. Bailey Kaufman, Nov. 7, 1975 (div. Oct. 1990); stepchildren: Peter B. Kaufman, Tanya Kaufman; m. Peggy J. Vick, Oct. 1991. BS, Yale U., 1950, PhD, 1953. NRC fellow Harvard U., 1953-54; faculty Northwestern U., 1954-60, asst. prof., 1955-60; assoc. prof. U. Wis., Madison, 1960-61, prof. chemistry, 1961—, Arthur C. Cope and Hilldale prof. chemistry, 1975—. Chmn. 4th Internat. Union Pure and Applied Chemistry Symposium on Photochemistry, 1972; organizer, chmn. Organic Photochemistry Symposium at Pacifchem, Honolulu, 1972, Honolulu, 95, Honolulu, 2000, Honolulu, 05. Author: (book) Quantum Mechanics for Organic Chemists, 1975; mem. editl. bd.: Jour. Organic Chemistry, 1967—71, Molecular Photochemistry, 1969—75, Jour. Am. Chem. Soc., 1982—85, Revs. Reactive Intermediates, 1984—89; contbr. articles to profl. jours. and chpts. to profl. texts. Recipient Halpern award for photochemistry, N.Y. Acad. Scis., 1979, Chem. Pioneer award, Am. Inst. Chemists, 1986, Sr. Alexander von-Humboldt award, 1988, Hilldale award, U. Wis., 1988—89, 1990, Porter medal, IUPAC, 2006. Mem.: NAS, Inter-Am. Photochemistry Assn. (co-chmn. orgnic divsn. 1977—79, exec. com. 1979—86), German Chem. Soc., Chem. Soc. London, Am. Chem. Soc. (James Flack Norris award 1976, Arthur C. Cope Scholar award 1991, XXI IUPAC Porter medal 2006), Phi Beta Kappa, Sigma Xi. Home: 7813 Westchester Dr Middleton WI 53562-3671 Office: U Wis Chemistry Dept 1101 University Ave Madison WI 53706-1322 Business E-Mail: Zimmerman@chem.wisc.edu.

ZIMMERMAN, J. JEFFREY, lawyer, automotive executive; b. Akron, Ohio, Mar. 22, 1959; BA summa cum laude, Denison U., Granville, Ohio, 1981; JD, Northwestern U. Sch. Law, Evanston, Ill., 1984. Bar: Ohio 1984, Ill. 1990. Equity ptnr. Jenner & Block, LLP, Chgo., 1993—2000; v.p. law Tenneco Automotive, Inc., 2000—07; sr. v.p., gen. counsel, sec. Hertz Global Holdings, Inc., 2007—. Office: Hertz Global Holdings Inc 225 Brae Blvd Park Ridge NJ 07656 Office Phone: 201-307-2000. Office Fax: 201-307-2876.*

ZIMMERMAN, JAMES M., lawyer; b. Cin., Apr. 7, 1974; BA, Vanderbilt U., 1996, JD, 1999. Bar: Ohio 1999. Ptnr. Taft, Stettinius & Hollister LLP, Cin., 1999—. Mem., Bd. of Trustee Cin. County Day Sch. Named one of Ohio's Rising Stars, Super Lawyers, 2005, 2006, 2007. Mem.: Ohio State Bar Assn., Cin. Bar Assn., Order of Coif. Office: Taft Stettinius & Hollister LLP 425 Walnut St Ste 1800 Cincinnati OH 45202-3957 Office Phone: 513-381-2838. Office Fax: 513-381-0205. E-mail: zimmerman@taftlaw.com.

ZIMMERMAN, JEAN, lawyer; b. Berkeley, Calif., Dec. 3, 1947; d. Donald Scheel Zimmerman and Phebe Jean (Reed) Doan; m. Gilson Berryman Gray III, Nov. 25, 1982; children: Charles Donald Buffum and Catherine Elisabeth Phebe (twins); stepchildren: Alison Travis, Laura Rebecca, Gilson Berryman. BSBA, U. Md., College Park, 1970; JD, Emory U., Atlanta, Ga., 1975. Bar: Ga. 1975, D.C. 1976, N.Y. 1980. Asst. mgr. investments FNMA, Washington, 1970-73; assoc. counsel Fuqua Industries Inc., Atlanta, 1976-79; assoc. Sage Gray Todd & Sims, NYC, 1979-84; from assoc. counsel to sr. v.p., gen. counsel, sec. IBJ Whitehall Bank & Trust Co., NYC, 1984—99; sr. v.p., gen. counsel, sec., bd. dirs. IBJ Schroder Bus. Credit Corp., NYC, 1996-98, Innovest Capital Mgmt., Inc., NYC, 1997-99; sr. v.p., gen. counsel, sec. Innovest Corp., NYC, 1997-99; from gen. counsel, sec. to exec. v.p. ops. and legal ArrowSight, Inc. (formerly ParentWatch.com), Mt. Kisco, NY, 2001—. From asst. sec. to sr. v.p., gen. counsel, sec., bd. dirs. IBJ Whitehall Bus. Credit Corp., IBJ Whitehall Capital Corp., IBJ Whitehall Securities, Inc., Delphi Asset Mgmt., Inc., Innovest Asset Mgmt., Inc., N.Y.C., 1997-99; from asst. sec. to v.p., gen. counsel, sec. IBJ Schroder Internat. Bank, Miami, Fla., 1989-98; sr. v.p., gen. counsel, sec. Execution Svcs., N.Y.C., 1991-93. Founder, officer ERA Ga., Atlanta, 1977-79; bd. dirs. Ct. Apptd. Spl. Advs., 1988-94. Named one of Outstanding Atlantans, 1978-79; recipient Disting. Alumni award Emory U. Sch. Law, 1999. Mem.: ABA, Emory U. Sch. Law (adv. bd. 1999—2009), LWV, Am. Soc. Corp. Secs., Inc., Ga. Assn. Women Lawyers (bd. dirs. 1977—79), Assn. Bar City N.Y., Assn. Emory Alumni (N.Y. pres. 1999—2003, bd. govs. 2001—05), DAR. Office: Arrowsight Inc 45 Kensico Dr 2nd Fl Mount Kisco NY 10549 Personal E-mail: jzimmer642@aol.com. Business E-Mail: jean.zimmerman@arrowsight.com.

ZIMMERMAN, JO ANN, retired health science association administrator, educator, retired lieutenant governor; b. Van Buren County, Iowa, Dec. 24, 1936; d. Russell and Hazel (Ward) McIntosh; m. A. Tom Zimmerman, Aug. 26, 1956; children: Andrew, Lisa, Don and Ron (twins), Beth. Diploma, Broadlawns Sch. of Nursing, Des Moines, 1958; BA with honors, Drake U., 1973; postgrad., Iowa State U., 1973—75.

RN, Iowa. Asst. head nurse maternity dept. Broadlawns Med. Ctr., Des Moines, 1958—59, weekend supr. nursing svcs., 1960—61, supr. maternity dept., 1966—68; instr. maternity nursing Broadlawns Sch. Nursing, 1968—71; health planner, community rels. assoc. Iowa Health Systems Agy., Des Moines, 1978—82; mem. Iowa Ho. Reps., 1982—86; lt. gov., pres. of Senate, State of Iowa, 1987—91; cons. health svcs., grant writing and continuing edn. Zimmerman & Assocs., Des Moines, 1991—2000; dir. patient care svcs. Nursing Svcs. Iowa, 1996—98; nurse case mgr. Olsten Health Svcs. (now Gentiva Health Svcs.), 1998—2004; founder JAZ Tours, 2002—04, ret., 2004, 2004. Ops. dir. Medlink Svcs., Inc., Des Moines, 1992-96. Contbr. articles to profl. jours. Mem. advanced registered nurse practioner task force on cert. nurse mid-wives Iowa Bd. Nursing, 1980-81, Waukee, Polk County, Iowa Health Edn. Coord. Coun., Iowa Women's Polit. Caucus, Dallas County Women's Polit. Caucus; chmn. Des Moines Area Maternity Nursing Conf. Group. 1969-70, task force on sch. health svcs. Iowa Dept. Health, 1982, task force health edn. Iowa Dept. Pub. Instruction, 1979, adv. com. health edn. assessment tool, 1980-81, Nat. Lt. Govs., chair com. on Agrl. and Rural Devel., 1989; Dallas County Dem. Ctrl. Com., 1972-84, 98—; bd. dirs. Waukee Cmty. Sch. Bd., 1976-79, pres. 1978-79; bd. dirs. Iowa PTA, 1979-83, chair Health Com., 1980-84; mem. steering com. ERA, Iowa, 1991-92; founder Dem. Activist Women's Network (DAWN), 1992; mem. Disciples of Christ Mission Group to El Salvadore, 2003, 04; founder health ministry First Christian Ch., Des Moines, Iowa, 2004. Recipient Woman Achievement award, YWCA Greater Des Moines, 2005, Search Your Heart award, Am. Heart Assn., 2007; named to Iowa Women's Hall of Fame, 2005. Mem. ANA, LWV (health chmn. met. Des Moines chpt.), Iowa Nurses Assn., Iowa League for Nursing (bd. dirs. 1979-83), Family Centered Childbirth Edn. Assn. (childbirth instr., advisor), Iowa Cattleman's Assn., Am. Lung Assn. (bd. dirs. Iowa 1988-92), Dem. Activist Women's Network (founder 1992), State Hist. Soc. Iowa (bd. mem. 2007-), First Christian Ch. Des Moines (pres. elect 2008, pres. 2009), Dallas County Master Gardeners (pres. 2008-09). Mem. Christian Ch. Avocations: gardening, sewing, reading, bridge.

ZIMMERMAN, JOSEPH FRANCIS, political scientist, educator; b. Keene, NH, June 29, 1928; s. John Joseph and May Veronica (Gallagher) Z.; m. Margaret Bernardette Brennan, Aug. 2, 1958; 1 child, Deirdre Ann. BA, U. N.H., 1950; MA, Syracuse U., 1951, PhD, 1954. Instr. govt. Worcester Poly. Inst., 1954—55, asst. prof., 1955-57, assoc. prof., 1957-62, prof., 1962-65; lectr. Clark U., Worcester, Mass., 1957-65; prof. polit. sci. SUNY, Albany, 1965—. Staff dir. N.Y. State Joint Legis. Com. Transp., 1967-68, rsch. dir., 1968-73; rsch. dir. N.Y. State Select Legis. Com. Transp., 1977-82, Legis. Commn. on Critical Transp. Problems, 1982-95. Author: State and Local Government, 1962, The Massachusetts Town Meeting: A Tenacious Institution, 1967, The Federated City: Community Control in Large Cities, 1972, Pragmatic Federalism, The Reassingment of Functional Responsibility, 1976, (with Frank W. Prescott) The Politics of the Veto of Legislation in New York, 1980, The Government and Politics of the Empire State, 1981, Local Discretionary Authority, 1981, (with Deirdre A. Zimmerman) The Politics of Subnational Governance, 1983, State-Local Relations: A Partnership Approach, 1983, 2d edit., 1995 (CHOICE award as outstandin acad. book, 1984), Participatory Democracy: Populism Revived, 1986, Federal Preemption: The Silent Revolution, 1990, Contemporary American Federalism, 1992; (with Wilma Rule) United States Electoral System: Their Impact Upon Women and Minorities, 1992, Electoral Systems in Comparative Perspective: Their Impact on Women Minorities, 1994, Curbing Unethical Behavior of Government, 1994, Interstate Relations: The Neglected Dimension of Federalism, 1996, The Recall: Tribunal of the People, 1997, The New England Town Meeting: Democracy in Action, 1999; The Initiative: Citizen Law-Making, 1999, (with Wilma Rule) The U.S. House of Representatives: Reform or Rebuild?, 2000, The Referendum: The People Decide Public Policy, 2001 Interstate Cooperation: Compacts and Administrative Agreements, 2002, Interstate Economic Relations, 2004, Congressional Preemption: Regulatory Federalism, 2005, Interstate Disputes: The U.S. Supreme Court's Original Jurisdiction, 2006, The Silence of Congress: State Taxation of Interstate Commerce, 2007, Government and Politics of New York State, 2008, Contemporary Am. Federalism, 2008; contbr. articles to profl. jours. Pres. Citizens' Plan E Assn., Worcester, 1960-62, Citizens for Neighborhood Improvement Worcester, 1957-59. Served to capt. USAF, 1951—53. Named 1 of 3 Outstanding Young Men Worcester Jr. C. of C., 1959, 61, 1 of 3 Outstanding Young Men Mass, Jr. C. of C., 1961, disting. citizen award Nat. Conf. on Govt., 1986. Mem. Am. Polit. Sci. Assn. (Outstanding Academician sect. intergovtl. adminstrn. 1997), Am. Soc. Pub. Adminstrn. (Outstanding Federalism Academician 1997), Nat. Mcpl. League. Clubs: German-Am. Social. Roman Catholic. Home: 82 Greenock Rd Delmar NY 12054-4414 Office: SUNY Rockefeller College 135 Western Ave Albany NY 12222 Office Phone: 518-439-9440, 518-442-5378. E-mail: zimmer@albany.edu.

ZIMMERMAN, KATHLEEN MARIE, artist; b. Floral Park, NY, Apr. 24, 1923; d. Harold G. and Evelyn M. (Andrade) Z.; m. Ralph S. Iwamoto, Nov. 23, 1963. Student, Art Students League, NYC, 1942—44, Nat. Acad. Sch. Fine Arts, 1944—47, Nat. Acad. Sch. Fine Arts, 1950—54. Tchr. drawing and painting Midtown Sch. Art, N.Y.C., 1947-52. Illustrator (with Ralph S. Iwamoto) Diet for a Small Planet, 1971; one-woman shows include Westbeth Gallery, N.Y.C., 1973, 1974, St. Mary's Coll., St. Mary's City, Md., 1990, Broome St. Gallery, N.Y.C., 2002, Lecei Gallery, Concord, Mass., 2005, exhibited in group shows at Woodstock Art Gallery, N.Y., 1945, Nat. Arts Club, N.Y.C., 1948—56, 1984, Emily Lowe Award Show, 1951, Contemporary Arts Gallery, N.Y.C., 1952, 1960, Village Art Ctr., 1956—61, Allied Artists Ann., N.Y.C., 1956, 1978, 1980—91, 1993—2005, 2006—07, Studio Gallery, 1957—60, Nat. Assn. Women Artists, N.Y.C., 1957—85, 1987—98, 2000, 2003, Art USA, 1958, ACA Gallery, 1958—59, City Ctr. Gallery, 1960, Janet Nessler Gallery, N.Y.C., 1961, Silvermine Guild, Conn., 1962, Pioneer Gallery, Cooperstown, N.Y., 1962—63, Audubon Artists, N.Y.C., 1963—2005, 2007, NAD, 1969—2001, 2003, 2004, 2005, 2007, Women Artists Award Winners, N.Y.C., 1974, Am. Watercolor Soc., 1975—78, 1980, Cheyenne (Wyo.) Western Galleries, 1975—77, Edward-Dean Mus., Cherry Valley, Calif., 1975—77, Frye Mus., Seattle, 1975—76, 1997, Boise Gallery Art, 1975, Central Wyo. Mus. Art, 1975—76, Willamette U., 1975, Yellowstone Art Ctr., Billings, Mont., 1975, Utah State U., 1975, Applewood Art Gallery, Colo., 1976, Charleston Art Gallery, W.Va., 1976, Kent State U., 1976, Cin. Art Club, 1976, Martello Mus., Key West, Fla., 1976, Buecker Gallery, N.Y.C., 1976, Anchorage Fine Arts Mus., 1976, Davis and Long Gallery, N.Y.C., 1977, Butler Inst. Am. Art, 1978, 2000, Washington Square East Gallery, NYU, 1979, Internat. Festival Women Artists, Copenhagen, 1980, Westbeth Gallery, N.Y.C., 1980, 1983, 1999—2007, 2008, City Gallery, 1981, Bergen Cmty. Mus., Paramus, N.J., 1983, Kenkeleba Gallery, N.Y.C., 1985, Adelphi U., Garden City, N.Y., 1987, Lotos Club, N.Y.C., 1987, Temperance Hall Gallery, Bellport, N.Y., 1987, Monmouth Mus., Lincroft, N.J., 1987, Marbella Gallery, N.Y.C., 1989, Knickerbocker Artists, 1990, Brownstone Gallery, N.Y.C., 1993, Viridian Gallery, 1995, Sundance Gallery, Bridgehampton, N.Y., 1996, Mcpl. Art Ctr., Athens, Greece, 1996, ISE Art Found., N.Y.C., 1996, Nat. Soc. Painters in Casein & Acrylic, 1997-2001, 2004, Zimmerli Mus., Rutgers U., New Brunswick, N.J., 1998, Gallery OneTwentyEight, N.Y.C., 2001—03, Broome St. Gallery, 2002—03, Nat. Acad. Mus., 2003, Lecei Gallery, West Concord, Mass., 2003, 2004, 2005, Represented in permanent collections Butler Inst. Am. Art, Youngstown, Ohio, Sheldon Swope Art Gallery, Terre Haute, Ind., Lauren Rogers Mus. Art, Laurel, Miss., U. Wyo. Art Mus., Laramie, U. Miami Lowe Art Mus., Coral Gables, Fla., N.C. Mus. Art, Raleigh, Swarthmore Coll., Pa., Erie Art Mus., Nat. Acad. Design, N.Y.C., Zimmerli Mus., Rutgers U., New Brunswick, Nat. Mus. Women in the Arts, Washington; bibliography James Mellow, N.Y. Times Art Rev., 1973, Hilton Kramer, N.Y. Times Rev., 1977, Helen A. Harrison, N.Y. Times Rev., 1987, William Zimmer, N.Y. Times Rev., 1999, Terry Teachout, Washington Post Review, 2003, Ken Johnson, N.Y. Times Rev., 2003, contbr. (bibliography) The Art of Collage, 1978, Mastering Color & Design in Watercolor, 1981, The Collage Handbook, 1985, Painting Without a Brush, 1992, Collage Techniques, 1994. John F. and Anna Lee Stacey scholar, 1954; recipient Nat. Soc. Painters in Casein and Acrylic award 1997, Liquitex Art award, 1999, Winsor & Newton award 2001, Howard Mandel Meml. award, 2004. Mem.: NAD (Henry Ward Ranger Fund purchase prize 1976, cert. of merit 1980, Henry Ward Ranger Fund purchase prize 1982, L.G. Sawyer prize 1988, Ogden Pleissner Meml. award 1991, William A. Paton prize 1993, 1997, Zellah W. Pike prize 2001), Nat. Acad. Design, N.Y. Artists Equity Assn. (Dr. Maury Leibovitz award 1985), Allied Artists Am. (Silver medal 1981, Jane Peterson award 1985, Creative Watercolor prize 1989, Silver medal 1991, Creative Watercolor prize 1997, Mary Lou Fitzgerald Meml. award 1998, John Young-Hunter Meml. award 2002, Pauline Law Meml. award 2003, Dale Meyers Cooper award 2007), Nat. Assn. Women Artists (14 prizes 1957—2003), Am. Watercolor Soc. (Barse Miller Meml. award 1976), Audubon Artists (John Wenger Meml. award 1978, Ralph Fabri medal 1981, J&E Liskin Meml. award 1987, Dick Blick award 1994, Gold Medal of Honor 2001, Art Students League award 2002, Giulia Palermo award 2005). Home: 463 West St Apt 1110A New York NY 10014-2040

ZIMMERMAN, KENNETH JAY, humanities educator; b. NYC, Oct. 1, 1943; s. Alex and Lillian Zimmerman; m. Janice Mendelson, Mar. 15, 1977. MA, U. Wis., Madison, 1970. Prof. humanities and film studies Tallahassee CC, 1990—. Contbr. scientific papers. Recipient Sarah Herndon Tchg. award, Fla. State U., 1986. Office: Tallahassee CC 444 Appleyard Dr Tallahassee FL 32304 Office Fax: 850-201-8044. Business E-Mail: zimmermk@tcc.fl.edu.

ZIMMERMAN, LAWRENCE A., printing company executive; b. NY, Dec. 2, 1942; BS in Fin., NYU, 1965; MBA, Adelphi U., Garden City, NY, 1967. Dir. budgets to corp. contr. IBM Corp., 1988—94, v.p. fin. Europe, Mid. East and Africa ops. Paris, 1994—96, v.p. fin. and planning server and tech. divsn., 1996—98; exec. v.p., CFO Sys. Software Assoc., Inc., Chgo., 1999; corp. sr. v.p., CFO Xerox Corp., Norwalk, Conn., 2002—07, exec. v.p., CFO, 2007—09, vice chmn., CFO, 2009—. Bd. dirs. Brunswick Corp., 2005—, The Stanley Works, 2005—. Mailing: Xerox Corp PO Box 4505 Norwalk CT 06856-4505 Office: Xerox Corp 45 Glover Ave Norwalk CT 06856 Office Phone: 203-968-3000.*

ZIMMERMAN, LYNDA DIANE, music educator; b. Eau Claire, Wis, Oct. 6, 1948; d. William Roy and Elda Amelia Goodwin; m. David Lloyd Zimmerman, June 13, 1981. BME, U. Wis., Eau Claire, 1971; MusM, East Tex. State U., Commerce, 1973. Grad. asst. prof. East Tex. State U., 1971—73; music prof. U. Wis., 1973—74, Rice Lake, 1974—82, Menasha, 1982—, accompanist choirs, recitals, musicals, 1982—, music dir., 2008. Pianist Nursing Homes, Appleton, Wis., 1982—; subs. organist Luth. Ch., Menesha Attic, 1998—; accompanist Ch. Retreats, Appleton, 2005—; music dir. Atlic Children's Theatre, Appleton, 2007—08. Composer song, (plays) The Laramie Project, 2003. Composer U. Wis., Fox Valley Sch. Song, 2002. Named one of Outstanding Young Women America, Bd. Advisors, 1978. Mem.: SAI Music Alumni Sorority. Office: Univ Wis Fox Valley 1478 Midway Rd Menasha WI 54952

ZIMMERMAN, MARLIN U., JR., chemical engineer; b. Akron, Ohio, Aug. 2, 1923; s. Marlin Ulrich and Helen (Nelson) Z. BChemE, Johns Hopkins U., 1944; MBA, Harvard U., 1966. Registered profl. engr., Ohio. Jr. engr. Standard Oil Co. (Ohio), Cleve., 1944-46, engr., 1946-48, sr. engr., 1948-49, process engr. Lima (Ohio) refinery, 1949-50, group engr. Cleve., 1951-55, group supr., 1956-60, supr. process sys. sect., 1961-63, head acrylonitrile task force, 1961, tech. specialist, 1964-66; mgr. long term planning Norton Co., Worcester, Mass., 1966-69; cons. John Van Der Valk & Assocs., NYC, 1970-73; pvt. practice cons. chem. engr. ammonia-urea Hackensack, NJ, 1974—. Head task force to help commercialize Sohio acrylonitrile process. Contbr. articles to profl. jours. Baker scholar, 1966. Mem. AIChE, Johns Hopkins Club, Tudor and Stuart Club, Tau Beta Pi, Omicron Delta Kappa, Beta Theta Pi. Methodist. Achievements include patent for process improvement of Tosco shale process for oil recovery; patent for pig handling for gasoline blender meter testing loop, others. Avocations: travel, photography, reading, investing, computer programming.

ZIMMERMAN, MARY ALICE, performing arts educator, director, playwright; BA, MA, PhD, Northwestern U. Asst. prof. performance studies Northwestern U., Evanston, Ill.; artistic assoc. Goodman and Seattle Repertory Theater; mem. Lookingglass Theater Company, Chicago. Writer, dir. (plays) The Notebooks of Leonardo da Vinci, Secret in the Wings, 1991, Arabian Nights, 1992, Journey to the West, 1995, Mirror of the Invisible World, 1997, Eleven Rooms of Proust, 1998, The Odyssey, 1999, Metamorphoses, 2001 (Best Dir., Tony Awards, 2002, Best Dir., Best New Play, Drama Desk Awards, 2002), Silk, 2005, Argonautika, 2006; dir.: (plays) All's Well That Ends Well, 1995, Henry VIII, 1997, A Midsummer Night's Dream, 2000, Measure for Measure, 2001, Trojan Women, 2003, Pericles, 2004; dir., co-librettist (Operas) Galileo Galilei, 2002. Active Lookingglass Theatre Co. Recipient MacArthur Fellowship, 1998, 20 Joseph Jefferson Awards for best direction. Fellow: Am. Acad. Arts & Sci. Office: Northwestern U Sch Communication 1800 Sherman Ave Rm 401 Evanston IL 60201 Office Phone: 847-491-3623.

ZIMMERMAN, MICHAEL DAVID, lawyer; b. Chgo., Oct. 21, 1943; s. Elizabeth Porter; m. Lynne Mariani (dec. 1994); children: Evangeline Albright, Alessandra Mariani, Morgan Elisabeth; m. Diane Hamilton, 1998. BS, U. Utah, 1966, JD, 1969, LLD (hon.), 2001. Bar: Calif. 1971, Utah 1978. Law clk. to Chief Justice Warren Earl Burger U.S. Supreme Ct., Washington, 1969-70; assoc. O'Melveny & Myers, LA, 1970-76; assoc. prof. law U. Utah, 1976-78, adj. prof. law, 1978-84, 89-93; of counsel Kruse, Landa, Zimmerman & Maycock, Salt Lake City, 1978-80; spl. counsel Gov. of Utah, Salt Lake City, 1978-80; ptnr. Watkiss & Campbell, Salt Lake City, 1980-84; assoc. justice Supreme Ct. Utah, Salt Lake City, 1984-93, 98-00, chief justice, 1994-98; atty., mediator, arbitrator, ptnr. Snell & Wilmer, Salt Lake City, 2000—. Co-moderator Justice Soc. Program of Snowbird Inst. for Arts and Humanities, 1991, 92, 93, 94, 95, 97, 98; moderator, Tanner lecture panel dept. philosophy U. Utah, 1994; faculty Judging Sci. Program Duke U., 1992, 93; bd. dirs. Conf. of Chief Justices, 1995-98. Note editor: Utah Law Rev., 1968-69; contbr. numerous articles to legal pubs. Mem. Project 2000, Coalition for Utah's Future, 1985—96; trustee Hubert and Eliza B. Michael Found., 1994—98; bd. dirs. Rowland-Hall St. Mark's Sch., 1995—2002; bd. assoc. Utah Mus. Natural History Found., 1997—; bd. dirs. Summit Inst. for Arts and Humanities, 1989—2002, chair, 2002—; bd. dirs. Hansen Planetarium, 1997—2001, Snowbird Inst. for Arts and Humanities, 1989—98, Deer Valley Inst. for Arts and Humanities, 1996—98, Kanzeon Zen Ctr., 1999—, chair, 2000—; bd. dirs. Utah Coun. on Conflict Resolution, 1999—2005, chair, 1999—2005; bd. dirs. Pvt. Adjudication Ctr.; mem. Duke U., 2000—02; co-dir. Registry of Ind. Sci. and Tech. Advisors, Duke U., 2000—02; chair Utah Jud. Coun. Task Force on Racial and Ethnic Fairness in the Jud. Sys., 1996—2000. Recipient Excellence in Ethics Award, Ctr. for Study of Ethics, 1994, Disting. Svc. Award Utah State Bar, 1998, Individual Achievement Award Downtown Alliance, 1997, The Peter W. Billings, Sr. American Arbitration Assoc. Outstanding Dispute Resolution Svc. Award, 1997, Humanitarian award, Nat. Conf. for Cmty. and Justice, 2005; named Utah State Bar Appellate Ct. Judge of Yr., 1998. Fellow: Am. Bar Found.; mem.: Am. Acad. Appellate Lawyers, Gov. Radiation Exposure Study Mgmt. Com., Ririe-Woodbury Dance Co. (exec. bd. 1982—84), U.S. Dept. of Energy Dose Assessment Adv. Group of the Off-Site Radiation Exposure Reconstruction Project (Utah citizen rep. 1980—84), Utah Legal Svc. Corp. (Bd. of Trustees 1985—87, 2002—), U. Utah Master of Pub. Adminstrn. Program Practitioners' Adv. Com. (mem 1985—89), U.S. Vet. Adminstrn. Adv. Com. on Environ. Hazards (e.g., agent orange, nuclear radiation 1985—89), Nat. Endowment for the Humanities Scholar in Residence at Utah Valley Cmty. Coll. (Orem, Utah 1990), Order of Coif, Am. Judicature Soc. (bd. dirs. 1995—2001), Am. Inns of Ct. VII, Utah Jud. Coun. (supreme ct. rep. 1986—91, chair 1994—98), Jud. Conf. U.S. (adv. com. civil rules 1985—91), Salt Lake County Bar Assn., Utah Bar Assn., Am. Law Inst., ABA (faculty mem. appellate judges' seminar 1993), Phi Kappa Phi. Office: Snell & Wilmer 15 West South Temple Ste 1200 Salt Lake City UT 84101 Office Phone: 801-257-1964. E-mail: mzimmerman@swlaw.com.

ZIMMERMAN, PAUL ALBERT, retired academic administrator, minister; b. Danville, Ill., June 25, 1918; s. Albert Carl and Hanna Marie (Haffner) Z.; m. Genevieve Emmaline Bahls, June 11, 1944; children—Karmin (Mrs. Raymond Philp), Thomas. Student, Concordia Coll., Ft. Wayne, Ind., 1936-39; BA, Concordia Sem., St. Louis, 1941, M.Div., 1944; MA, U. Ill., 1947, PhD, 1951; D.D., Concordia Sem., Springfield, Ill., 1975; LLD (hon.), Concordia Coll., Ann Arbor, Mich., 1994. Prof. theology and sci. Bethany Coll., Mankato, Minn., 1944-53; prof. Concordia Tchrs. Coll., Seward, Nebr., 1953-54, pres., 1954-61, Concordia Luth. Jr. Coll., Ann Arbor, Mich., 1961-73, Concordia Coll., River Forest, Ill., 1973-83, ret., 1983; pastor St. Luke's Luth. Ch., Harrison, Mich., 1983-88. Author and editor: Darwin, Evolution and Creation, 1959, Rock Strata and the Bible Record, 1971, Creation, Evolution and God's Word, 1972; author A Seminary in Crisis: The Inside Story of the Preus Fact Finding Committee, 2007. Chmn. Washtenaw County Red Cross, 1968-70; pres. Ann Arbor Found., 1970-71; mem. Citizens Com. Study Taxation, Ann Arbor, 1972; mem. adv. bd. St. Joseph Mercy Community, 1969-72; chmn. Luth. Ch. Mo. Synod's Bd. for Mission Services, 1982-92, Mission Task Force, 1990-91, adminstrv. asst. pres. Mo. Synod, 1972-73, 93-94, mem. curriculum commn. bd. higher edn., 1963-73, mem. task force constl. revision Mo. Synod, chmn. com. adjudication procedures Mo. Synod, Mo. Synod com. on structure, 1995-98. Fellow Creation Rsch. Assn. Lutheran. Home: 2798 Princeton Dr Traverse City MI 49684-9131

ZIMMERMAN, PHYLLIS ELAINE, music educator, composer, director; b. Pitts., Feb. 22, 1934; d. William H. and Isabelle Anderson Zimmerman. BA in Sociology, Thiel Coll., 1956; BA in Vocal Performance, Concordia Coll., 1959; student in Voice, U. Colo., 1966; student in Choral Techniques and Voice, Meadowbrook Sch. Music, 1967; student in Music, Choral Conducting, Choral Technique & Voice, Occidental Coll., 1968—69. Dir. choral Wellsville (Ohio) H.S., 1959—63, Churchill Area H.S., Pitts., 1963—68; thr. music, dir. choral Santa Barbara (Calif.) H.S., 1969—95; founder, artistic dir. Canticle A Cappella Choir, Santa Barbara, 1995—. Dir. madrigal singers Santa Barbara H.S. Choir, 1969—95, dir. concert tours, 1972—92. Dir.(prodr.): (compact disc) Earth Chants, 1994, Canticle, 1996, My Song in the Night, 2000, O Wondrous Mystery, 2003, Phoenix (27 original compostions and arrangements), 2004, Every Time I Feel the Spirit, 2006; composer: (songs) Seasons of his Mercies, 2003, Four Songs of Concord, 2005, Four Lyrics of Sara Teasdale, 2006, The Gift of God's Grace, 2006. Recipient Outstanding Contbn. to Cmty. award, Santa Barbara (Calif.) City Coun., 2004, Disting. Alumni award, Concordia Coll., 2006; named Local Hero, Santa Barbara (Calif.) Ind., 1995. Mem.: Am. Choral Dirs. Assn. (performer).

ZIMMERMAN, ROBERT ALLEN See DYLAN, BOB

ZIMMERMAN, ROBERT S., internist, endocrinologist; b. Chgo., Sept. 13, 1956; s. Nathan and Minette (Kositchek) Z.; m. Teresa Nelson, Aug. 9, 1986; children: Sean David, Rachel Dawn. BS in Zoology with honors, U. Mich., 1977; MD, Johns Hopkins U., 1981. Diplomate Nat. Bd. Med. Examiners, Am. Bd. Internal Medicine, Am. Bd. Endocrinology. Intern Duke U. Hosp., Durham, N.C., 1981-82, resident, 1982-84; fellow in endocrinology and metabolism Mayo Clinic, Rochester, Minn., 1984-87; staff physician Ochsner Clinic, New Orleans, 1987-96, dir. Diabetes Inst., 1996—. Mem. kidney pancreas transplant com. Ochsner Clinic, New Orleans, 1995—; course dir. Ann. Endocrinology Update, ACP, 1995, 96; rschr. in field. Contbr. articles to profl. jours., chpts. to books. Ill. State scholar, 1974; James B. Angell scholar U. Mich., 1976; Gelston fellow U. Mich., 1976; recipient Travel award Am. Thyroid Assn., 1986, 87; grantee Nat. Kidney Found., 1987. Fellow Am. Heart Assn. (coun. high blood rsch., grantee 1989, 91, 94); mem. AMA, Am. Diabetes Assn. (camp physician Leesville, La. 1987-90), Am. Soc. Hypertension, Am. Fedn. Clin. Rsch., So. Med. Assn., Endocrine Soc. (clin. affairs com. 1996—), Orleans Parish Med. Soc., Phi Beta Kappa. Avocations: bassoon, piano. Office: Ochsner Diabetes Inst Ochsner Clinic 1514 Jefferson Hwy New Orleans LA 70121-2429 Home: 26400 Hendon Rd Beachwood OH 44122-2428

ZIMMERMAN, RYAN WALLACE, professional baseball player; b. Washington, NC, Sept. 28, 1984; s. Keith and Cheryl Zimmerman. Attended, U. Va. Third baseman Washington Nationals, 2005—. Active Nat. Multiple Sclerosis Soc.; founder ziMS Found. Named an All-Am., Baseball Am., 2005, Nat. Collegiate Baseball Writer's Assn., 2005; named to Nat. League All-Star Team, Maj. League Baseball, 2009. Office: Washington Nationals Nationals Pk 1500 S Capitol St Washington DC 20003 Office Phone: 202-349-0400.*

ZIMMERMAN, STEVEN CHARLES, chemistry professor; b. Chgo., Oct. 8, 1957; s. Howard Elliot and Jane (Kirschenheiter) Z.; m. Sharon Shavitt, Aug. 5, 1990; 2 children, Arielle Reneé, Elena Michelle. BS, U. Wis., 1979; MA, MPhil, Columbia U., PhD, 1983. Asst. prof. chemistry U. Ill., Urbana, 1985-91, assoc. prof. chemistry, 1991-94, prof. chemistry, 1994—, Roger Adams prof. chem., interim chem. dept. head; affiliate faculty mem. Beckman Inst. Mem. bioorganic natural products study sect. NIH, 1994—98. Contbr. articles to profl. publs. Recipient Presdl. Young Investigator award NSF, 1988-93, Buck-Whitney award

Am. Chem. Soc., 1995, Arthur C. Cope Scholar award, 1997; Alfred P. Sloan fellow, 1992-93. Fellow: AAAS. Home: 55 Chestnut Ct Champaign IL 61822-7121 Office: U Ill 345B Roger Adams Lab 600 S Mathews Ave Urbana IL 61801 Office Phone: 217-333-6655. Office Fax: 217-244-9919. Business E-Mail: sczimmer@uiuc.edu.

ZIMMERMAN, THOMAS GLENN, physician, educator; BS, Cornell U., Ithaca, NY, 1995; D in Osteo. Medicine, NY Coll. Osteo. Medicine, Old Westbury, NY, 2000. Diplomate Am. Osteo. Bd. Family Physicians, 2003. Asst. prof. NY Coll. Osteo. Medicine, 2005—07, clin. asst. prof. family medicine, 2007—, med. dir., academic health ctr., 2005—07; clin. preceptor South Nassau Cmty. Hosp., Oceanside, NY, 2007—, osteo. med. edn. program dir., 2007—; with tech. adv. bur. Am. Osteo. Assn., Chgo., 2008—. Recipient Std. Excellence award, NY Coll. Osteo. Medicine, 2006, Eagle Scout, Boy Scouts America, 1989, Bronze Palm, 1989. Mem.: Am. Osteo. Assn. Med. Informatics, NY Osteo. Med. Soc., Am. Coll. Osteo. Family Physicians, Am. Osteo. Assn., Acacia Frat. (sr. steward 1994—95). Office: S Nassau Cmty Hosp One Healthy Way Oceanside NY 11572 Office Phone: 516-255-8415. Office Fax: 516-255-8453. Business E-Mail: tzimmerman@snch.org.

ZIMMERMAN, WILLIAM EDWIN, editor, writer; b. Bklyn., Feb. 2, 1941; s. George and Ruth (Edelbaum) Z.; m. Teodorina Bello, Dec. 13, 1969; 1 child, Carlota Pastora. BA, Queens Coll., Flushing, 1962. Pres. Guarionex Press, Ltd., NYC, 1979—; with Am. Banker, NYC, 1962-82, editor, sr. v.p., 1982-89; editor in chief Banking Week, 1986-89; dep. editor Sunday Bus. sect. The NY Times, 1989; spl. projects editor, editor Student Briefing Page Newsday, LI, NY, 1989—2004. Author: How to Tape Instant Oral Biographies, 1979, A Book of Questions to Keep Thoughts and Feelings, 1984, Make Beliefs, 1987, Life Lines: A Book of Hope, 1990, The Little Book of Joy, 1995, Dogmas: Simple Truths from a Wise Pet, 1995, Make Beliefs for Kids of All Ages, 1996, A Book of Sunshine, 1997, Cat-e-chisms: Feline Answers to Life's Big Questions, 1997, My Life: An Open Book, 2000, Lunch Box Letters, 2000, Idea Catcher for Kids, 2000, Butterfly Wishes, 2002, My Paper Memory Quilt, 2004, 100 Things Guys Need to Know, 2005, Doodles & Daydreams: Your Passport for Becoming An Escape Artist, 2007, Pocket Doodles for Kids, 2009. Mem. Am. Oral History Assn., Am. Soc. Bus. Writers, Am. Soc. Bus. Press Editors, NY Fin. Writers Assn., Overseas Press Club, Deadline Club, Dowtown Athletic Club, NY Athletic Club, Sigma Delta Chi. Democrat. Jewish. Personal E-mail: wmz@aol.com.

ZIMMERMANN, FRANK MARTIN, physicist, educator, research scientist; b. Karlsruhe, Germany, May 6, 1964; arrived in US, 1987, naturalized, 2004; s. Manfred Eugen and Herta Zimmermann; m. Yeong-Ah Soh, Oct. 29, 1995 (div. Sept. 2, 2003); 1 child, Ingrid Hana; m. Sophia Tsai, July 2, 2006. MS in Physics, Cornell U., 1993, PhD in Physics, 1995. Rsch. asst. solid state physics Ariz. State U., 1988-89; rsch. asst. surface sci. Cornell U., 1990-95; asst. prof. physics dept. physics and astronomy and lab. surface modification Rutgers U., Piscataway, NJ, 1995-2001, assoc. prof., 2001—. Lectr., presenter in field. Contbr. numerous articles to profl. jours. including Surface Sci. Reports and Phys. Rev. Lett. Fulbright fellow, 1987-88, Internat. Rsch. fellow Sci. and Tech. Agy., Japan, 1996, 98; Rutgers bd. trustees rsch. fellow for scholarly excellence, 2001. Mem. Am. Phys. Soc., Am. Vacuum Soc. (Grad. Rsch. award 1994, Morton M. Traum award 1995), Am. Chem. Soc. (Victor K. LaMer award 1996), Phi Kappa Phi. Achievements include elucidation of mechanisms and dynamics of thermal and photochemical desorption and adsorption using laser spectroscopy. Avocations: whitewater kayaking, downhill skiing, bicycling. Office: Rutgers U Dept Physics 136 Frelinghuysen Rd Piscataway NJ 08854-8019

ZIMMERMANN, JOHN PAUL, plastic surgeon; b. Milw., Mar. 9, 1945; s. Paul August and Edith Josephine (Tutsch) Z.; m. Bianca Maria Schaldach, June 13, 1970; children: Veronica, Jean-Paul. BS in Biology, Chemistry, Marquette U., 1966; MD, Med. Coll. Wis., 1970. Diplomate Am Bd. Plastic Surgery. Internship surgery Stanford U. Sch. of Medicine, Calif., 1970-71, residency in gen. surgery, plastic & reconstructive surgery Calif., 1974-79; flight surgeon USAF, 1971-73; fellowship head & neck surgery Roswell Park Meml. Cancer Inst., Buffalo, N.Y., 1977; pvt. practice Napa, Calif., 1979—. Dir. Aesthetic Surgery Ctr. of Napa Valley, Calif., 1993—; clinical asst. prof. of plastic surgery Stanford U. Sch. of Medicine, Calif., 1993—; bd. dirs. Interplast, Palo Alto, Calif. (pres., bd. dirs. 1991-94, chmn. bd. dirs. 1994-95). Mem. Am. Soc. Plastic Surgeons, Am. Soc. Aesthetic Plastic Surgeons, Lipoplasty Soc., Calif. Soc. Plastic Surgeons (bd. dirs.), Calif. Med. Assn., Napa County Med. Assn. Republican. Roman Catholic. Avocations: sailing, golf. Office: Plastic Reconstructive Surgery Ctr 3443 Villa Ln Ste 10 Napa CA 94558-6417

ZIMMERMANN, MURIEL MADELINE, retired biology professor; b. Sacramento, Calif., Aug. 16, 1942; d. Max Hubertus and Emily Matilda Zimmermann; m. Vernon Richard Wheeler, June 10, 1978; children: Mark Dean Williams, Bret Albert Williams, Christopher William Wheeler. MS, Calif. State Poly. U., Pomona, 1977. Cert. in hazardous materials mgmt. U. Calif., Davis, 1993. Divsn. chmn. phys. edn. Chaffey Coll., Rancho Cucamonga, faculty, 1974—96, faculty senate chmn., 1980—81, divsn. chmn. life sci., 1981—90; faculty lectr., 1992—93; coord., environ. hazardous materials tech. program Chaffey Coll., 1993—96, dean, phys., life, health scis., 1996—2004, emeritus prof., 2004—. Recipient, Chaffey Coll. Presdl., 1991—93, Acad. Excellence, Chaffey Coll. Student Govt., 1992—95, Faculty Spkr. of Yr., Chaffey Coll., 1993, Meritorius Svc. award, 2005—06; named to Hall of Fame, Bldg. Dedication Muriel M. Zimmermann, 2007. Mem.: AAAS, Am. Soc. Microbiology, Alpha Gamma Sigma. Democrat. Avocations: singing, swimming. Office: Chaffey Coll POBox 672 Calimesa CA 92320-0672 Business E-Mail: mmzimm@yahoo.com.

ZIMMERMANN, THOMAS CALLANDER PRICE, retired historian, educator; b. Bryn Mawr, Pa., Aug. 22, 1934; s. R.Z. and Susan (Goodman) Z.; m. Margaret Upham Ferris. BA, Williams Coll., 1956, Oxford U., 1958, MA, 1964; AM, Harvard U., 1960, PhD, 1964. Asst. prof. Reed Coll., Portland, Oreg., 1964-67, assoc. prof., 1967-73, prof. history, 1973-77, chmn. dept. history, 1973-75; v.p. acad. affairs Davidson (N.C.) Coll., 1977-86, Charles A. Dana prof. History, 1986-99, Charles A. Dana prof. history emeritus, 1999-2000, ret., 2000. Mem. Oreg. Com. for Humanities NEH, 1971—77; mem. Region 14 selection com. Woodrow Wilson Nat. Fellowship Found., Princeton, NJ, 1967—70. Author: Paolo Giovio: The Historian and the Crisis of Sixteenth-Century Italy, 1995 (Helen and Howard R. Marraro Book prize Am. Hist. Assn. 1996, Presdl. Book award Am. Assn. for Italian Studies 1997); co-editor of collected works of Paolo Giovio, 1985; contbr. articles to profl. jours. Pres. Am. Alpine Club, NYC, 1979-82, bd. dirs., 1975-83; bd. dirs. Charlotte Opera Assn., NC, 1980-82, NC Outward Bound Sch., Morgantown, 1978-81; bd. advisors Lowell Obs., 1988-93; mem. Rome Prize Jury (Post-Classical Humanistic Studies) Am. Acad. in Rome, 1993; adv. coun. bot. gardens U. NC, Charlotte, 2007-08. Danforth fellow, 1956-62, Fulbright fellow, Italy, 1962-64, Villa "I Tatti" fellow Harvard U. Ctr., 1970-71; Am. Council of Learned Socs. fellow, N.Y.C., 1975-76. Mem. Renaissance Soc. Am., Soc. Italian Hist. Studies, Am. Assn. Italian Studies, Phi Beta Kappa, Opera Carolina Endowment (bd. advisors, 2008-).

ZIMMERN, ANDREW, chef, television personality; Meal adventure guide SuperTarget; internat. spokesperson Procter & Gamble's Pepto-Bismol brand, Travel Leaders, Elite Destination Homes. Co-creator, host, contbg. prodr. (TV series) Bizarre Foods with Andrew Zimmern, host Bizarre Worlds with Andrew Zimmern, 2009—, dining columnist Mpls.-St. Paul Mag.*

ZIMMERN, EMILY FAIRCHILD, museum director; b. La. m. Sam Zimmern; children: Bill, Amelia. BA in History, Vanderbilt U., MA in Am. Diplomatic History Studies; MBA, Queens U. Cert. in strategic perspectives in non-profit mgmt. Harvard Bus. Sch. Exec. dir., pres., CEO Levine Mus. of the New South, 1995—. Affiliate orgns. rep., cultural facilities planning task force Arts & Sci. Coun. Founding mem. Cmty. Building Initiative; mem. leadership team Leadership Develop. Initiative; mem., Am. Leadership Forum Lee Inst. Named Charlotte Woman of Yr., 2002. Office: Levine Mus of the New South 200 E Seventh St Charlotte NC 28202 Office Phone: 704-333-1887. Office Fax: 704-333-1896.

ZIMMETT, MARK PAUL, lawyer, educator; b. Waukegan, Ill., July 4, 1950; s. Nelson H. Zimmett and Roslyn (Yastrow) Zimmett Grodzin; m. Joan Robin Urken, June 11, 1972; children: Nora Helene, Lili Eleanor. BA, Johns Hopkins U., 1972; JD, NYU, 1975. Bar: N.Y. 1976, U.S. Dist. Ct. (so. and ea. dists.) N.Y. 1976, U.S. Dist. Ct. (no. dist.) Calif. 1980, U.S. Ct. Appeals (2d cir.) 1980, U.S. Supreme Ct. 1981, U.S. Ct. Appeals (5th cir.) 1986, U.S. Ct. Appeals (9th cir.) 1988. Assoc. Shearman & Sterling, NYC, 1975-83, ptnr., 1984-90; adj. assoc. prof. internat. law NYU, 1986-88; lectr. internat. comml. litig. and arbitration Practicing Law Inst., 2000—02. Author: Letters of Credit, New York Practice Guide Business and Commerical Law, 1990; contbr. articles to profl. jours. Mem. ABA (subcom. on letters of credit, com. on uniform comml. code sect. bus. law), NY State Bar Assn., Assn. of the Bar of the City of NY (task force on corp. governance, com. on fed. cts., coun. on profl. and jud. ethics), NY County Lawyers Assn. (com. on bus. bankruptcy law, task force corp. governance, com. fed. cts., com. profl. and jud. ethics), Citizens Union. Democrat. Jewish. Office: 126 E 56th St New York NY 10022-3613 Office Phone: 212-755-0808.

ZIMMIE, THOMAS FRANK, civil engineer, educator; b. Scranton, Pa., Jan. 24, 1939; s. Thomas and Stella Josephine (Price) Z.; m. Patricia Joyce Kelly, June 8, 1962 (div. 1979); 1 child, David Thomas; m. Judith Anne Braden, July 13, 1989. BSCE, Worcester Poly. Inst., 1960; MSCE, U. Conn., 1962, PhD in Geotech. Engring., 1972. Registered profl. engr., N.Y., Conn. Staff engr. Union Carbide Corp. (Linde div.), Buffalo, 1964-68; profl. engr. Town of Mansfield, Conn., 1968-72; ptnr. Wang and Zimmie Cons., Troy, NY, 1973-80; v.p. Arch Engring. Cons., Troy, 1984-88; program dir. NSF, Washington, 1988-90; pres., CEO Civrotech Engrs., Inc., Troy, 1993—; prof., chair dept. civil engring Rensselaer Poly. Inst., Troy, 1973—, acting chair dept. civil and environ. engring., 2005—08. Geotech. engr. N.Y. Dept. Environ. Conservation, Albany, 1983-85; town engr. Town of North Greenbush, N.Y., 1985-88. Editor: Permeability and Groundwater Contamination, 1981, Environmental Geotechnology, 2000; contbr. articles to profl. jours. 1st lt. US Army, 1962—64. Recipient Civilian Patriotic Svc award, US Army Corps. Engrs., 2007, award, US Senate Hurricane Katrina, 2007; NSF fellow, Norwegian Geotech. Inst., 1972—73. Fellow Am. Coll. of Forensic Examiner, fellow ASCE (cert., Outstanding Svc. award 1986, 87); mem. ASTM (Spl. Svc. award 1980, Charles Dudley award 1984), Transp. Rsch. Bd., Am. Rd. and Transp. Builders Assn. Avocation: flying. Home: 39 Zelenke Dr Wynantskill NY 12198-8627 Office: Rensselaer Poly Inst Civil & Environ Engring Dept Soil Mechanics Lab Troy NY 12180 Home Phone: 518-283-6208; Office Phone: 518-276-6939. Business E-Mail: zimmit@rpi.edu.

ZIMNY, MAX, labor union administrator, lawyer, arbitrator; b. Bklyn., Mar. 9, 1925; s. Joseph and Rebecca (Nadelman) Z.; m. Bernice Nelson, June 26, 1948; children: Stuart, Andrew. Student, Bklyn. Coll., 1942—47, LLB cum laude, 1950; postgrad., NYU Grad. Sch. Labor Law, 1950—52. Bar: N.Y. 1950, U.S. Dist. Ct. (so. and ea. dists.) N.Y. 1951, U.S. Ct. Appeals (2nd cir.) 1955, U.S. Supreme Ct. 1962, U.S. Ct. Appeals (D.C. cir.) 1968, U.S. Ct. Appeals (4th cir.) 1969, U.S. Ct. Appeals (9th cir.) 1975, U.S. Ct. Appeals (8th cir.) 1980, U.S. Dist. Ct. (no. dist.) N.Y. 1983, U.S. Ct. Appeals (6th cir.) 1987, U.S. Ct. Appeals (7th cir.) 1988, U.S. Ct. Appeals (3rd and 5th cirs.) 1991. Mem. Zimny & Goldberg, NYC, 1950—52; asst. gen. counsel Textiles Workers Union Am., NYC, 1952—58, Internat. Ladies' Garment Workers' Union, NYC, 1958—63, assoc. gen. counsel, 1963—72, gen. counsel, 1972—95, Union of Needletrades, Indsl. and Textile Employees Unite, 1995—2001. Mem. Vladeck, Elias, Vladeck, Zimny and Englehard, N.Y.C., 1976-78; lectr. NYU Sch. Law, Stetson U. Sch. Law, Indsl. Rels. Rsch. Inst., Nat. Acad. Arbitrators. Editor: Labor Arbitrator Development, 1983, Arbitration: A Guide for Advocates, 1990, Arbitration Casebook, 1997. Mediator, fact finder N.Y. Pub. Employment Rels. Bd., 1968—; chmn. Consumer Adv. Coun. City of N.Y.; mem. Levittown (N.Y.) Bd. Edn.; chmn. Profls. for Histadrut, NYC; arbitrator NYS disciplinary panel; Bd. dirs. Nat. Resources Ctr. for Consumers Legal Svcs., Lawyers Coord. Com. AFL-CIO; bd. dirs. Corsi Labor Mgmt. Inst.; mediator, arbitrator Am. Arbitration Assn.; labor, employment and comml. panels, arbitrator labor and mgmt. panel Fed. Mediation and Conciliation Svc.; arbitrator N.Y.C. Office of Collective Bargaining, Electric Boat, Groton, Conn.; mem. nat. adv. coun., chair com. on rules and procedures, chair nat. task force on ADR in employment and due process protocol; mem. steering com. ctr. for Law and Econ. Policy Columbia U. Sch. Law; adv. com. NYU and Fordham Conf. on Labor, 1985—. With US Army, 1943—46. Fellow: Coll. Labor and Employment Lawyers (chair, com. on ethics and civility); mem.: ABA (chmn. com. on arbitration 1977—81, coun. labor sect. 1989—, chair labor and employment sect., pub. rels. com.), Nassau Bar Assn., Commn. Healthcare Dispute Resolution, Labor Employee Rels. Assn., Bar Assn. City of N.Y. (labor com.), B'nai B'rith Club (pres. lodge), Order of Coif. Home Phone: 516-731-4358; Office Phone: 516-731-4358. E-mail: maxzimny@optonline.net.

ZIMPHER, NANCY LUSK, academic administrator; b. Gallipolis, Ohio, Oct. 29, 1946; d. Aven Denzle and Elsie Gordon (Hammond) L.; 1 child from a previous marriage, William Fletcher Zimpher; m. Kenneth R. Howey, May 8, 1987. BS, Ohio State U., 1968, MA, 1971, PhD, 1976. Cert. K-12 Tchr., Ohio. English tchr. Montgomery County Schs., Md., 1968, Reynoldsburg Schs., Ohio, 1970; substitute tchr. Rolla City Schs., Mo., 1970-71; tchr. Phelps County Schs., Mo., 1971-72; grad. teaching assoc. Coll. Edn. Ohio State U., Columbus, 1972-73; dir. Coll. of Edn. Ohio State U., Columbus, 1973-74, grad. adminstrn. asst. to dean, 1974-76, dir. field experiences alumni rels., 1976-80, coord. undergraduate programs, 1980-84; asst. prof. Ednl. Policy and Leadership Ohio State U., 1984-86, assoc. prof., 1986-91, full prof., 1991-98, assoc. dean, 1992, dean, 1993, exec. dean, 1994; chancellor, prof. curriculum and instrn. U. Wis., Milw., 1998—2003; pres. U. Cin., 2003—09; chancellor SUNY Sys., Albany, 2009—. Prin. investigator U.S. Office Edn. Field Devel. Grant, 1981-83, 85-88; co-principal investigator Metro. Life Found. Grant. 1989—, 1992—; cons. The Holmes Group, Lansing, Mich., 1991—. Book rev., editor: Journal of Teacher Education, 1986-89; co-author: Book Profiles of Preservice Teacher Education, 1989, RATE Profiles, 1987-92, A Time for Boldness: A Case Story of Institutional Change, 2002; co-editor: University Leadership in Urban School Renewal: The President's Role, 2004, Boundary Spanners: A Key to Success in Urban Partnerships, 2006, Recruiting, Preparing and Retaining Teachers for Urban Schools, 2006, Creating a New Kind of University, 2006. Chair Faculty Compensation and Benefits Commn., 1989-90, Fiscal Com., 1991-92, Spousal Equivalency Com., 1990-91, Search Com., v.p. for Fin., 1992, Ohio State U; pres., chair bd. dirs. Holmes Partnership, 1997; chair edn. vision coun. United Way Franklin County, 1997; chair bd. dirs. United Way Franklin County, 1998; chair bd. dirs. Nat. Assn. State Univs. and Land-Grant Colls., 2007; chair Urban Serving Univs., 2005—. Fellow Com. for Instnl. Coop., Acad. Leadership Program. 1989-90; recipient Disting. Rsch. award, Disting. Teacher Educator award Assn. Tchr. Educators, 1990, Adams Professorshi Coll. Edn. Ind. State U., 1990—, Alumni Disting. Tchg. award, The Ohio State U., 1992, Chief Exec. Leadership award Coun. for the Advancement and Support Edn., 2003, Career Woman of Achievement award YWCA, 2004, Profl. Achievement award Ohio State U., 2004; named YWCA Woman of Achievement, 1997. Mem. Am. Edn. Rsch. Assn., Am. Assn. Coll. Teacher Edn. Rsch. Comm., Assn. Tchr. Educators, ASCD, Phi Delta Kappa. Episcopalian. Avocations: watercolorist, golf, sewing. Office: SUNY Office of Chancellor State University Plaza 353 Broadway Albany NY 12246 Office Phone: 518-443-5355.*

ZIMPLEMAN, LARRY DONALD, insurance company executive; b. Williamsburg, Iowa, Sept. 7, 1951; s. J. Henry and Clara (Hansemann) Z.; m. Kathleen Margaret Berry, Dec. 29, 1973; children: Jeffrey, Christopher, Thomas. BSBA, Drake U., 1973, MBA, 1979. Enrolled actuary. Actuary student Principal Fin. Group, Des Moines, 1973-77, asst. actuary, 1977-82, dir., 1982-88, 2d v.p., 1989—97, v.p., 1997—99, sr. v.p., 1999—2001, exec. v.p., 2001—03, pres. retirement & investor services, 2003—06, pres., COO, 2006—08, pres., CEO, 2008—09, chmn., pres., CEO, 2009—. Chmn. Princor Fin. Services Corp.; past chmn. Employee Benefit Rsch. Inst.; trustee Actuarial Found.; chmn. Harris Trust com. Am. Council Life Insurers; delegate Nat. Summit on Retirement Savings, 2002—06. Contbr. articles to Drake Law Rev., 1984, Matthew Bender Rev., 1984, Taxes, 1987, Pension Section Newsletter, 1990. Bd. dirs. Prin. Fed. Polit. Action Com. Fellow Soc. of Actuaries; mem. Am. Acad of Actuaries (bd. dirs. Washington 1989—), Des Moines Actuaries Club (pres. 1989-90), Greater Des Moines C. of C. (bd. drs., bus. econ. devel. com. 1990). Avocations: sports, running. Office: Principal Fin Group 711 High St Des Moines IA 50392*

ZIMRING, FRANKLIN E., lawyer, educator; b. 1942; BA, Wayne State U., 1963; JD, U. Chgo., 1967. Bar: Calif. 1968. Asst. prof. U. Chgo., 1967-69, assoc. prof., 1969-72, prof., 1972-85; co-dir. Ctr. for Studies in Criminal Justice, 1973-75, dir., 1975-86; prof. law dir. Earl Warren Legal Inst., U. Calif., Berkeley, 1985—2002. Author: (with Newton) Firearms and Violence in American Life, 1969; The Changing Legal World of Adolescence, 1982; (with Hawkins): Deterrence, 1973, Capital Punishment and the American Agenda, 1986, The Scale of Imprisonment, 1991, The Search for Rational Drug Control, 1992, Crime is Not the Problem, 1997, American Youth Violence, 1998, Punishment and Democracy, 2001, The Contradictions of American Capital Punishment, 2003, An American Travesty, 2004, American Juvenile Justice, 2005, The Great American Crime Decline, 2007, The Next Frontier, 2009. Mem. Am. Acad. Arts and Scis. Office: U Calif Earl Warren Legal Inst Boalt Hall Berkeley CA 94720 Business E-Mail: zimring@law.berkeley.edu.

ZINBERG, CECILE, retired history professor; PhD, U. Chgo., 1968. Prof. emeritus, history Calif. State U., Fullerton, 1969—; vis. scholar, history U. Va., Charlottesville, 2007—. Mem.: Am. Hist. Assn. Home: 612 Rainier Rd Charlottesville VA 22903 Business E-Mail: czinberg@fullerton.edu.

ZINBERG, DAVID J., lawyer; b. NYC, Apr. 12, 1954; ScB magna cum laude, Brown U., 1974; JD, Harvard U., 1978. Bar: N.Y. 1979, U.S. Dist. Ct. (so. and ea. dists.) N.Y. 1981. Assoc. DeForest & Duer, 1978—81, Rosenman & Colin LLP, NYC, 1981—87, ptnr., 1987—97; v.p. Morgan Guaranty Trust Co., 1997—2000; ptnr. Ingram Yuzek Gainen Carroll & Bertolotti, LLP, NYC, 2000—. Mem.: Assn. Bar City NY (real property sect.), NY State Bar Assn. (real property sect., exec. com. 1999—). Office: Ingram Yuzek Gainen Carroll & Bertolotti LLP 250 Park Ave New York NY 10177 Office Phone: 212-907-9600. Office Fax: 212-907-9681. E-mail: dzinberg@ingramllp.com.

ZINBERG, DOROTHY SHORE, sociologist, educator; b. Boston; m. Norman E Zinberg (dec.); children: Sarah Zinberg Mandel, Anne Budd. BA, MA, Boston U.; PhD, Harvard U., 1966. Research chemist Lever Bros., Cambridge; sr. research assoc. Daniel Yankelovich, Inc., NYC, and; Cambridge Center for Research in Behavioral Scis., 1966-68; NSF research sociologist dept. chemistry U. Coll. London, 1968-69; lectr. Harvard U., 1960—. Mem. adv. com. Office Sci. Pers. NRC, Washington, 1971—74, bd. on engring. edn., 1991; spl. adviser Aspen Inst.; cons. MacArthur Found., 1989—93; vis. scholar NAS, China, 1987, Nat. Inst. Sci. and Tech., Tokyo, 1991; vis. lectr. Inst. for Human Scis., Vienna, 1995; mem. coun. scholar Erik Erikson Inst. for Edn. and Rsch., 1996—; vis. prof. Imperial Coll., London, 2001—04; assoc. Whitehead Inst. Biomed. Rsch., MIT, 2004—; vis. sr. fellow U. Coll. London, 2006—. Columnist: London Times Higher Educ Supplement, 1993—2001, NY Times Syndication, 1994—96. Mem. internat. sci. exchs. NAS, 1994—96, mem comt int relations, 1977—80, mem comt int human resources; chmn adv coun int div NSF, 1978—81; mem coun Int Exchange Scholars, 1978—81; mem comt int exchange engrs NAE, 1987—88; mem adv panel Office Technology Assessment Educ and Employment Scientists and Engrs, 1986—88; trustee Simon's Rock Col, 1971—75; mem panel sci and tech policy NATO, 1995—99; bd. dirs. Fine Arts Workshop, Provincetown, Mass., 1970—86, Bill T. Jones Found for Dance Promotion, 1997—99; bd dirs Gen Scanning, Inc, 1998—99; bd dirs eng educ NRC, 1990—95. Fellow: AAAS (mem comt sci freedom and responsibility 1972—74, comt opportunities in sci 1973—76, comt sci, eng, and pub policy 1982—88, com. exch. scientists with Fed. Republic Germany 1987—91, 1991); mem.: NAS (com. to evaluate Internat. Sci. and Tech. Ctr. Moscow 1995—97), Int Sci Policy Found (adv. bd. 1988—2004), Coun Foreign Relations, Fedn. Am. Scientists (mem. coun. 1980—85, bd. talking sci.). Home: 3 Acacia St Cambridge MA 02138-4818 Office: Harvard U 79 JF Kennedy St Cambridge MA 02138 Office Phone: 617-495-1406.

ZINCZENKO, DAVID, editor-in-chief; b. Dec. 13, 1969; s. Bohdan Zinczenko and Janice Sobieski. B, Moravian Coll., Bethlehem, Pa. Assoc. editor Men's Journ., 1991—93; editl. dir. Men's Health Internat.; editor-in-chief Men's Health mag. Rodale Inc., 2000—, editl. dir. Best

Life mag., 2004—, editl. dir. Women's Health mag., 2008—. Chmn. Am. Mag. Conf., 2007. Author: (books) The Abs Diet series, 2004—06 (NY Times Bestsellers), Men, Love & Sex: The Complete User's Guide for Women, 2006, Eat This, Not That!, 2007 (Publishers Weekly bestseller), Eat This, Not That! For Kids, 2008, Eat This, Not That! Supermarket Survival Guide, 2008 (Publishers Weekly bestseller), (web logs) Eat This, Not That!, Mysteries of the Sexes Explained; regular contbr. Today Show, NY Times, LA Times, USA Today, TV appearances include Ellen, 20/20, Biggest Loser, Oprah, Rachael Ray, Good Morning America. Recipient Nat. Mag. award, Am. Soc. Mag. Editors, 2000; named Editor of Yr., Ad Week, 2008; named one of Thirty Under 30, Folio mag., 1999, 21 Most Intriguing People, MIN mag., 2003, Ten Best-Dressed in Media, Ad Age, 2005, 40 Under 40, Crain's NY Bus., 2005, 50 Most Eligible Bachelors, People mag., 2002, 2007. Office: Men's Health 733 Third Ave New York NY 10017 also: Men's Health Rodale 33 E Minor St Emmaus PA 18098 Office Phone: 212-697-2040, 610-967-5171. Office Fax: 610-967-8963.*

ZINDER, NEWTON DONALD, investment advisor, consultant; b. NYC, Aug. 12, 1927; s. Paul and Jennie (Feld) Z.; m. Clarice Katz, Dec. 26, 1954; children— Marla, Andrea, Pamela. BA, NYU, 1948, MBA, 1957; MA, Columbia U., 1949. Securities analyst Ira Haupt & Co., NYC, 1953-60; securities analyst E.F. Hutton & Co., NYC, 1960-63, stock market analyst, 1963-88, Shearson Lehman Bros., NYC, 1988-92; investment cons., 1993—. Served with USN, 1945-46 Mem. Market Technicians Assn. Home: 66 Oak Creek Trail Madison WI 53717-1510 Personal E-mail: nzinder@gmail.com.

ZINDRICK, MICHAEL R., orthopedist; MD, Loyola Univ. Stritch Sch. Med. Cert. Am. Bd. Orthopaedic Examiners, Am. Bd. Spinal Surgery Examiners. Internship & residency Loyola Univ. Med. Ctr., Maywood, Ill.; fellowship in spine surgery Long Beach Meml. Hosp., Calif.; ptnr. Hinsdale Orthopaedic Assoc., S.C., 1985—; staff physician Hinsdale Hosp. and Good Samaritan Hosp.; clin. assoc. prof., dept. orthopaedic surgery Loyola Univ. Clin. dir. Rsch. and Spinal Surgery Fellowship Program; examiner Am. Bd. Orthopaedic Surgery; v.p. Am. Bd. Spinal Surgery, 2005—08. Contbr. articles to profl. jours. Mem.: Am. Acad. Orthopaedic Surgeons, Am. Orthopaedic Assn., Assn. Bone and Joint Surgeons, North Am. Spine Soc., Internat. Soc. the Study of the Lumbar Spine, Ill. State Med. Soc. Office: Hinsdale Orthopaedics 550 W Ogden Ave Hinsdale IL 60521*

ZINE, DENNIS P., councilman; b. LA; children: Chris, Eric. Mem. LA Police Dept., sgt., reserve officer, 2001—; councilman, Dist. 3 LA City Coun., 1997—, chmn. personnel com., vice chmn. info tech. and gen. svc. com., mem. public safety & transp. com., vice chair audits and govtl. efficiency com., mem. rules and govt. com., mem. edn. and neighborhoods com., mem. exec. employee rels. com. Bd. dir. LA Police Protective League; LA representative on public safety & crime prevention steering com. Nat. League of Cities; vice chmn. Charter Reform Commn., 1997; dir. Ind. Cities Assn.; bd. dir. League of Calif. Cities; chair Nat. Immigration Task Force; commr. LA County Jud. Procedures Commn.; pres. Executives of the LA Jewish Home for the Aging, 2006. Founder People Organizing a Safe, Secure Environment; bd. dir. West Valley YMCA. Office: City Hall 200 N Spring St Rm 450 Los Angeles CA 90012 also: Dist Office 19040 Vanowen St Reseda CA 91335 Office Phone: 213-473-7003, 818-756-8848. Office Fax: 213-485-8988, 818-756-9179. E-mail: councilmember.zine@lacity.org.*

ZINGALE, DONALD PAUL, academic administrator, educator; b. Bklyn., Aug. 3, 1946; s. Charles and Helen (Puglisi) Z. BS in Health, Phys. Edn., Bklyn. Coll., 1967; MS in Phys. Edn., U. Mass., 1969; PhD in Phys. Edn., Ohio State U., 1973; MSW, Calif. State U., Sacramento, 1984. Lic. clin. social worker, Calif.; lic. marriage and family counselor, Calif.; cert. health and phys. edn. instr. secondary schs., N.Y.C., N.Y.; cert. Alpine ski instr. Prof., assoc. dean health, human svcs. Calif. State U., Sacramento, 1973-93, assoc. v.p. rsch. and grad. studies, 1993-95, dean LA, 1995—96; dean Coll. Health and Human Svcs. San Francisco State U., 1996—2004; v.p. acad. affairs Calif. Maritime Acad., 2004—08; pres. SUNY Cobleskill, 2008—. Contbr. articles to profl. jours. and publs. Mem.: APHA, ACE, AASCU, Nat. Coun. U. Rsch. Adminstrs., Am. Assn. Higher Edn., Am. Assn. Health Phys. Edn., Recreation and Dance, Profl. Ski Instrs. Am. Roman Catholic. Avocations: alpine skiing, sailing, travel, cooking, home renovation. Office: SUNY Cobleskill 106 Suffolk Cir Knapp Hall Cobleskill NY 12043

ZINGG, PAUL JOSEPH, academic administrator; b. Newark, July 22, 1947; s. Carl William Zingg and Dolores Lucking Dulebohn. BA in History, Belmont Abbey Coll., Belmont, NC, 1968; MA in History, U. Richmond, Va., 1969; PhD in History, U. Ga., 1974. Chair and asst. prof., dept. of history and polit. sci. St. Bernard's Coll., Cullman, Ala., 1975-77; dean, academic affairs Daniel Hale Williams U., Chgo., 1977-78; adj asst./assoc. prof., dept. of Am. civilization U. Pa., Phila., 1978—86, asst. dean, academic affairs, Coll. of Arts and Sciences, 1978—79, vice dean, undergraduate studies and admissions, Coll. of Arts and Sciences, 1979—83, Am. Coun. on Edn. Fellow in Academic Adminstrn. and spl. asst. to the pres., 1983—84, exec. asst. to pres., 1984—86; cons. U. Calif., Berkeley, 1986; dean liberal arts and prof., dept. of history St. Mary's Coll., Moraga, Calif., 1986-93; prof., dept. of history Calif. Poly. State U., San Luis Obispo, Calif., 1993—2003, dean liberal arts, 1993-95, provost and acad. v.p., 1995—2003; pres. Calif. State U., Chico, 2004—. Vis. instr. history Ga. Coll., Milledgeville, 1971; cons., contbr. on exhibits Oakland Mus., 1992-94, Calif. Hist. Soc., 2004, PBS-TV documentary film Baseball, 1991-93; editorial cons. U. Nebr. Press, 1994—, U. Ill. Press, 1995-, others. Author: Pride of the Palestra, 1987, Harry Hooper, 1887-1974: An American Baseball Life, 1993, Runs, Hits and an Era: The Pacific Coast League, 1903-1958, 1994, 2nd edit., 1996, A Good Round: A Journey Through the Landscapes and Memory of Golf, 1999, The Moraine Country Club 1930-2005, An Enersid Odyssey: In Search of the Gods of Golf and Ireland, 2008; co-author: Through Foreign Eyes, 1982; editor, co-author: The Academic Penn, 1986; editor, contbr.: The Sporting Image: Readings in American Sport History; editor: In Search of the American National Character, 1984; contbr. numerous articles to profl. jours. Mem. Calif. Hist. Soc., 2000—; charter mem., Calif. Coun., Oakland Mus., 1995—. NEH summer fellow, 1975, summer rsch. grant, 1989, Ctr. for Internat. Study and Rsch. fellow, 1980-82, Am. Coun. on Edn. fellow, 1983-84; U. Pa. Rsch. Found. awards, 1983-85, faculty mem. of the yr., 1984, grantee St. Mary's Coll., 1987, 90, 91, 93, alumni faculty scholarship award, 1992. Mem. Orgn. Am. Historians, Soc. for History Edn., N.Am. Soc. for Study of Sport, Am. Studies Assn., Soc. for Am. Baseball Rsch., Am. Coun. on Edn., Assn. Am. Colls. and Univs., Am. Assn. Higher Edn., Nat. Assn. State Univs. and Land-Grant Colls., Rotary Club, Merion Golf Club, Butte Creek Country Club, Canyon Oaks Country Club, Phi Alpha Theta, Phi Beta Delta. Avocations: golf, labrador retrievers, baseball. Office: Calif State U 400 W First St Chico CA 95928-0155 Office Phone: 530-898-5201. E-mail: pzingg@csuchico.edu.

ZINK, HARRY A., ophthalmologist; MD, Univ. Pa., 1971. Resident, rsch. fellow, glaucoma Barnes Hosp.-Washington Univ. Sch. Med., St. Louis, 1976; asst. clin. prof. Case Western Res. Univ.; pvt. practice Wooster, Ohio. Mem.: Ohio Ophthalmological Soc., Am. Acad. Ophthalmology (mem. coun. from Ohio Ophthalmological Soc. 1993—95, trustee-at-large 1995—97, sec. mem. svcs. 1998—2004, pres. 2005—06, chmn. membership adv. com., ad hoc com. on primary eye care). Office: Wooster Eye Ctr 3519 Friendsville Rd Wooster OH 44691 Office Phone: 330-345-7200.

ZINKAN, JEFFREY PATRICK, real estate analyst; b. Washington, Ind., Aug. 19, 1950; m. Mary Susan Gates, Nov. 29, 1969; children: Kelley Nichol Puthoff (Zinkan), Geoffrey Gates. BS, Ind. State U., Terre Haute, 1972; MA, Northeastern Ill. U., Chgo., 1980. Project mgr. George Wash. U., 1999, real estate lic. State Ill., 1979, State Ohio, 1995, State Fla., 2008, real property adminstr. Bldg. Owners & Mgrs Assn., 1991, secondary edn tchg. lic. State Ohio, 1999. Realty specialist Veterans Adminstrn., Chgo., 1975—85, IRS, Washington, 2001—05; contracting officer GSA, Chgo., 1985—88; mgmt. analyst IRS, Cin., 1988—2001; adj. faculty Joliet Jr. Coll., 1987—88, Hillsborough C.C., Tampa, 2008; adj. instr. U. Coll.-U. Cin., 1998—2001. 1st. lt. USAR, 1973—75, Ft. Eustis, VA. Mem.: Ind. Hist. Soc., KC. Liberal. Roman Catholic. Avocations: golf, reading. Home: Apt # 6208 2717 Seville Blvd Clearwater FL 33764-1168 Personal E-mail: jeffreyzinkan@gmail.com.

ZINKLE, STEVEN JOHN, engineer, researcher; b. Prairie du Chien, Wis., Nov. 5, 1958; s. Aloysius Peter and Katherine Edith (Brownlee) Z.; m. Teresa Allen Medford, May 26, 1990; children: Austin Chase, Allen Peter. BS, U. Wis., 1980, PhD, 1985. Wigner fellow, 1985—87; rsch. staff Oak Ridge Nat. Lab., Tenn., 1985—2006, corp. fellow, 2004—, dir. materials sci. and tech. divsn., 2006—. Vis. scientist Forschungszentrum Jülich, Germany, 1991-92, Risø Nat. Lab., Roskilde, 1991-92. Assoc. editor: Jour. ASTM Internat., 2003—06. Recipient Rsch. Publ. award Martin Marietta Energy Systems, Oak Ridge, 1991, David Rose Excellence in Fusion Engrng. award Fusion Power Assocs., Gaithersburg, Md., 1992, Oak Ridge Nat. Lab. Tech. Achievement award, 1997, 99, 2002, Ernest Orlando Lawrence award in Nuc. Tech. Dept. Energy, 2006. Fellow Am. Ceramic Soc. (Nuc. and Environ. Techs. Best Paper award 1994-95), Am. Soc. Metals Internat. (chair nuc. material com. 2003-05), Am. Nuc. Soc. (materials sci. and tech. exec. com. 2003—, Mishima award 2007); mem. IEEE (Fusion Technol. award Nuc. & Plasma Sci. Soc. 2006), Materials Rsch. Soc., The Minerals, Metals and Materials Soc., Am. Phys. Soc., Sigma Xi, Phi Kappa Phi. Office: Oak Ridge Nat Lab PO Box 2008 Oak Ridge TN 37831-6132 Home Phone: 865-966-1239; Office Phone: 865-574-4065. E-mail: zinklesj@ornl.gov.

ZINN, DONALD EDWARD, biologist, researcher; s. Donald Edward and Robbie Janet Zinn; m. Michele R. Gillette. BS in Biology, UMBC, Balti., 1990. CEO AzoRx, Inc., Kalamazoo, 2005—08; pres. & CEO Aursos, Inc., Kalamazoo, 2008—. Adj. prof. biology Grand Valley State U., Grand Rapids, Mich., 2005—. Contbr. articles to profl. sci. jours. With US Army, 1983—85, Schweinfurt & Garmisch, Germany. Achievements include patents for dry process microarray. Office: Aursos Inc 350 E Michigan Ave Kalamazoo MI 49007 Business E-Mail: don@aursos.com.

ZINN, GEORGE, computer software company executive; b. Detroit, Mich. AB, Bowdoin Coll.; MBA, Univ. Wash. Fin. analysis & mgmt. positions Microsoft Corp., Redmond, Wash., 1996—2004, asst. treas., CFO intellectual property & licensing divsn., corp. v.p., treas., 2004—. Named one of Top 40 Fin. Profl. Under 40, Treasury & Risk Mgmt. Mag. Office: Microsoft Corp 1 Microsoft Way Redmond WA 98052-6399

ZINN, GROVER ALFONSO, JR., retired religion educator; b. El Dorado, Ark., June 18, 1937; s. Grover Alfonso and Cora Edith (Saucke) Z.; m. Mary Farris, July 28, 1962; children: Jennifer Anne, Grover Andrew. BA, Rice U., 1959; BD, Duke U., 1962, PhD, 1969; spl. student, U. Glasgow, Scotland, 1962-63. Asst. minister The Barony Ch., Glasgow, 1962-63; instr. in religion Oberlin Coll., Ohio, 1966-68, asst. prof., 1968-74, assoc. prof., 1974-79, prof., 1979—2006, Danforth prof. religion, 1986—2006, Danforth prof. religion emeritus, 2006—, chmn. dept. religion, 1980-84, 85-86, 1993-94, 98-00, assoc. dean coll. arts and scis., 2001—05. Translator: Richard of St. Victor: The Twelve Patriarchs, The Mystical Ark, and Book Three of the Trinity, 1979; co-editor: Medieval France: An Encyclopedia, 1995; mem. editl. bd. Commentatio: Sacred Texts And Their Interpretation In Medieval, Jewish, Christian And Islamic Traditions; contbr. articles to profl. jours. H.H. Powers Travel grantee Oberlin Coll., 1969, 85; Dempster fellow United Meth. Ch., 1965-66, NEH Younger Humanist fellow, 1972-73, Research Status fellow Oberlin Coll., 1972-73, 97-98, Faculty Devel. fellow Oberlin Coll. 1985, Lilly Endowment fellow U. Pa., 1981-82; recipient ACLS Travel award, 1982. Mem.: Ecclesiastical History Soc., Am. Soc. Ch. History (coun. mem. 1989—92, 1995—98), Medieval Acad. Am. (councillor 1983—86, 2003—06). Democrat. Methodist. Achievements include research in medieval Christian mysticism, theology, and iconography. Avocations: photography, electronics. Home: 61 Glenhurst Dr Oberlin OH 44074-1423 Office: Oberlin Coll Dept Religion Rice Hall Oberlin OH 44074 Office Phone: 440-775-5027, 440-775-8866. Business E-Mail: grover.zinn@oberlin.edu.

ZINN, KEITH MARSHALL, ophthalmologist, educator; b. Bklyn., Oct. 15, 1940; s. Victor Zinn and Eve (Lane) Z.; m. Elaine H. Kirban, Apr. 8, 1979. Student, NYU, Bronx, 1961; MD, SUNY, Bklyn., 1965. Diplomate Am. Bd. Ophthalmology; lic. physician, NY, Calif. Intern St. Lukes Hosp., NYC, 1965-66; research assoc. NIH, Bethesda, Md., 1966-68; post-doctoral fellow Retina Found., Boston, 1968-69; post-doctoral fellow dept. ophthalmology Harvard U. Med. Sch., Boston, 1968; asst. resident chief resident dept. ophthalmology Mount Sinai Hosp., NYC, 1969-71, ednl. fellow dept. ophthalmology, 1971-72; chief clin. fellow retina service Mass. Eye & Ear Infirmary, Harvard U. Med. Sch., Boston, 1972-73, Heed fellow dept. ophthalmology, 1972-73; research assoc. dept. retina research Retina Found., Boston, 1972-73; mem. faculty Lancaster Post-Grad. Course Ophthalmology, Harvard U. Med. Sch., Boston, 1970-90; consulting mng. dir. HT Capital Advisors, LLC, 2000—. Guest faculty dept. ophthalmology Harvard U. Med. Sch., Boston, 1969-84; asst. prof. dept. ophthalmology Mt. Sinai Sch. medicine, NYC, assoc. clin. prof., 1976-80, clin. prof., 1980—; attending ophthalmic surgeon NYC, 1980—; attending ophthalmic surgeon Manhattan Eye Ear & Throat Hosp., NYC, 1981—; surgeon cons. Hosp. Joint Diseases, NYC, 1975-83, Patrolmen's Benevolent Assn., NYC, 1977—; lectr. field. Author: The Pupil, 1972, Ocular Fine Structure for the Clinician, 1973, The Developing Visual System, 1975, The Retinal Pigment Epithelium, 1975; author-editor: The Retinal Epithelium, 1979, Clinical Atlas of Peripheral Retinal Disorders, 1988; numerous audio-visual teaching progs. in ophthalmology; contbg. editor Mt. Sinai Jour. Medicine, 1975—; assoc. mem. editorial bd. Ophthalmic Surgery, 1980-89; mem. faculty editorial bd. Clin. Opthalmology Update, 1982—; inventor field. Served lt. comdr. USPHS, 1966-68. Recipient numerous awards excellence medicine, including: Joseph Globus award Mount Sinai Jour. Medicine, 1979, Abraham Kornzweig Teaching award Mount Sinai Sch. Medicine, 1982. Fellow Am. Acad. Ophthalmology, Otolaryngology, ACS, Internat. Coll. Surgeons, Internat. Eye Found., Soc. Eye Surgeons, NY Acad. Medicine, NY Diabetes Assn., NY Heart Assn., NY Soc. Clin. Ophthalmology, Soc. Heed Fellows, Retina Soc., Ophthalmic Soc. UK, Oxford Ophthal. Congress, Brit. Am. Retinal Group; mem. AMA (Physicians Recognition award 1971, 76, 81, 82, 85), Ophthalmic Laser Surg. Soc. (v.p. 1986-88, pres. 1988-90), Am. Intraocular Lens Implant Soc., NY Acad. Medicine (trustee 1989-90, sec. 1985-86, chmn. ophthalmology sect. 1987-88, David Warfield fellowship com. 1990-92), Am. Bd. Laser Surgery (bd. dir. 1987—). Home: 125 E 87th St Apt 14C New York NY 10128 Office Phone: 212-535-5030.

ZINN, MICHAEL WALLACE, aerospace engineer; b. Washington, Dec. 30, 1962; s. Wallace Bernard and Frances E. AA, Charles County C.C., La Plata, Md., 1983; BS, Tri-State U., Angola, Ind., 1986. Coop student Naval Ordnance Sta., Indian Head, Md., 1980-86, mine decoy engr., 1986-87, airbreathing propulsion engr., 1987-92; airbreathing propulsion engr. Air/Cruise Missile Br. Naval Surface Warfare Ctr., Indian Head, 1992—2005, quality evaluation engr., 2005—. Mem. Joint Army-Navy-NASA-Air Force (JANNAF) airbreathing com., expendable engine subcom., Laurel, Md., 1987—; mem. Internat. Tech. Coop. Program involved in pyrotechnic aging and degradation Key Tech. Area 421, 1994-98. Author several tech. papers for AIAA and JANNAF. Pres. Port Tobacco Players, Inc., La Plata, Md., 1992-93; bd. dirs. Charles County Fair, Inc. Mem. AIAA (life, sr.), Am. Def. Preparedness Assn. (life), Cruise Missile Assn., Internat. Pyrotechnics Soc., Charles County Darts Assn. (webmaster) Achievements include work on aging surveillance programs for expendable gas turbine engines, on aging properties of expendable engines and solid propellant gas generators; assisted in new predictive techniques for ordnance surveillance; assisted in design of mine clearing line charge solid propellant rocket motor. Home: 11922 Charles St La Plata MD 20646-6414 Home Phone: 301-934-6961; Office Phone: 301-744-1434. Business E-Mail: michael.zinn@navy.mil.

ZINN, WILLIAM, musician, composer; b. NYC, Nov. 19, 1924; s. Philip and Anna (Miller) Zinn; m. Sophia Kalish, July 11, 1948; children: Karen Louise Heau, David Benjamin. Student, SUNY, 1952-54. Violinist Balt. Symphony, 1944-45, Indpls. Symphony, 1945-46, Ft. Wayne Philharm., 1946-47, Pitts. Symphony, 1947-49, Mpls. Symphony, 1950-51; concertmaster New Britain Symphony, Conn., 1968-90, Queens Symphony, 1969-71, Ridgefield Symphony, Conn., 1973-76, Chappaqua Symphony, NY, 1976, Yonkers Philharm., 1993—. Tchr. mech. drafting Mondell Inst., 1956; soloist with orchs. on records, radio, TV and recitals, 1993—2003; founder Masterwork Piano Trio, Masterwork Piano Quartet, Classical String Quartet, Zinn's Ragtime String Quartet, Excelsior String Quartet, Queens Festival Orch., Bayside, NY, 1965, Assn. Musical William Zinn, Caracas, Venezuela, 1968, Vitametrics Am., 1976, Internat. Symphony World Peace, 1978, Big Apple chamber Pops, 1983, Excelsior Composer's Festival Competition, 1984; coach ensembles Chamber Music Assocs., 1973—78; engr. NYC Bd. Edn., 1951—57, Bodin-Zinn Corp., 1957—58, Chem. Constrn. Corp., 1958—59; pres. Zinn Originals, Inc., 1959—68, Sparx, Inc., Trademark Hall of Fame, Inc., Nice Realty Corp., MFW Restaurant Corp., Caramoor Press Internat. Corp., 1996, Dunhill Pub. Co., 1996, ZinnPrint Internat., Inc., 1996, Barclay Holdings Group, Inc., 1998; co-founder Excelsior Music Pub. Co., Visionary Music Pub. Co., Nat. Music Promotion Agy., Telecom. Svcs., 1982, Assoc. Sci. Publs., 1985, Barclay House Pubs., 1985, Excelsior Typographers and Engravers Unltd., 1985, Empco Recs. Internat., 1985, Imperial Editions, 1986, Missing Link Publs., 1986, Krazy Klassics Kompany, 1986, New Age Publs., 1987, Krazy Klassics Komix, 1988, Zinn Pub. Group, 1989, Zinn Comm., 1989, Decca Books, 1993, Arlington House, 1993, Zinn Labs., Inc.; sec. treas. Spark Industries, Inc., Music Clearing House, 1989, Innovation Records, 1991, Krazy Klassics Records, 1991, Hanover House, 1991; adj. prof. NYU, 1987—; cons. Worldwide Leisure Corp., 1997. Author (with Edward Gordon): Thermography, 1947; author: (with George S. Grosser) Vitametrics I, The Human Formula for Self-Evaluation, 1976, Vitametrics II, The Human Formula for Self-Improvement, 1978; author: The Lost Chord, 1981, To Whom It May Concern, 1995, 1,001 Original Wise Sayings of William Zinn, 1996, 2,600 Wise Sayings, 1997, 3,500 Wise Sayings, 1998, 4,100 Wise Sayings, 1999, 6,000 Wise Sayings, 2000, 6,700 Wise Sayings, 2001, 10,000 Wise Sayings, 2002, 11,000 Wise Sayings, 2003, 12,500 Wise Sayings, 2004, 13,500 Wise Sayings, 2005, 15,000 Wise Sayings, 2006, 16000 Wise Sayings, 2008, 15,650 Wise Sayings, 2009; composer: Chromatique, 1946, Piccolo Concerto, 1948, Violin Concerto, 1950, String Quartet, 1963, Chopinesque, 1965, (ballets) Night Creatures, Andante for Strings, 1967, Concerto for Octahorn, 1976, The International Anthem for World Peace, 1977, String Symphony, 1977, Romance for French Horn or Viola and Piano, 1981, Concerto for Violin/Viola/Cello/Double Bass and Orchestra, 1985, Kol Nidrei Memorial for String Quartet or String Orchestra, 1985, six concert duos for violin and viola, 1988, 15 Leroy Anderson favorites for string quartet or string orch., 1988, Mia, 1989, Aloha Hawaii, 1989, The Willows, 1990, Our Song of Love, 1990, Symphony in Ragtime, 1990, In Old Hawaii, 1991, Christmas in Hawaii, 1991, A Tribute to the Masters for String Quartet or String Orchestra, 1991, A Stroll in a Japanese Garden for Violin, Cello, Harp trio in 24 movements, 1996; arranger: numerous operatic arias for string quartet or string orch., originator: Musiphonics, 1981, 24 Paganini Caprices for String Quartet, 1992, 10 Sousa marches for string quartet, 1992, The Merry Widow Waltz for string quartet or string orch., 1992, Mozart Symphony # 40, 1992, arranger: 21 Henry Mancini songs for string quartet/string orch., 1992, 16 Duke Ellington songs for string quartet/string orch., 1993, Gold and Silver Waltz, Skater's Waltz for string quartet and string orch., 8 arias from Porgy & Bess for string quartet/string orch., 1992, A Tribute to Fritz Kreisler for violin and piano, 1994, 16 arrangements of Fritz Kreisler works for string quartet/string orch., 1994, 24 Jewish Dances and Songs for String Quartet/String Orch., 1995, 6 duets for violin and viola, vol. II, 1996, An Elegy for Mother Teresa, 1997, concerto Hebraic for piano and string orch., Let Freedom Ring, A Tribute to Martin Luther King, Jr. for orch., chorus and narrator, 24 Etudes for solo cello, 1998, Hebraic Lament of Atonement for solo cello and string quartet or string orch., 1999, A Symphonic Portrait of Yonkers, 1999, The Seven Seasons for Orchestera: seven symphonic works commemorating the Jewish holidays of Rosh Hashanah, Yom Kippur, Sukkot, Hanukkah, Purim, Passover, Shavuot, 2000, Siegfried Idyll Rhapsody solo violin and orch., 2001, A Requiem for Jerome G. Sala for soloists, chorus and orch., 2001, 6 Bach solo cello suites converted to duets with original violin part added, 2002, Dance of the Hours Fantasy for solo violin and orch. or piano, 2002, Meditation for solo violin or flute, harp and string orch., 2002, 28 Beethoven Bagatelles arranged for string quartet or string orch., 2002, Beethoven: Pathetique Sonata, slow movement arranged for string quartet or string orch., 2002, violin and piano The Carnival of the Animals, Nutcracker Suite, 2003, In Hallowed Ground, 9/11/2001 for solo voice, chorus, string orch., bass clarinet, 2003, Peter & The Wolf for violin and piano, 2004, String Trio, 2004, A Klezmer Symphony, 2004, 6 Dvorak waltzes for quartet or string orch., 2004, String Quartet No. 2, 4 Clarinet Quartet, 2004, concertino for 2 violins and strings, 2004, Elegy for solo trumpet and strings, 2005, concertino for 2 French horns and strings, 2005, Octet Netherworld for low brass and woodwinds,

2005, solo for flute and strings, 2005, solo for clarinet and strings, 2005, solo for trombone and strings, 2005, Mourning, solo for E. Horn and Strings, solo for bassoon and strings, 2006, America for viola and piano, 2007, Solo for Euphonium and String Orch., 2007, Tuba on a Holiday - Tuba and Strings, 2007, A Joyful Sonata for Violin and Piano, 2007, 14 Kreutzer Etudes for String Quartet, 2008, Concertante forString Trio & String Orch., 2009, Blue Eyed Susan, Harmonica & String Orch., 2009, Duet for Oboe & E. Horn, 2009, Hebraic Fantasy for String Quartet, Six Original Bagatellas for String Quartet, 2009. Chmn., bd. dirs. Let Us Remember to Remember, 1984. Recipient 41st Hawaiian Nat. Song Contest award, 1990, Mayor and City Coun. citations for Yonkers, 2000, Symphonic Portrait. Mem.: ASCAP, Am. Fedn. Musicians, NY Humanist Assn., Nat. Coun. Women US, Internat. Platform Assn. Home: 35-19 215th Pl Bayside NY 11361-1725

ZINNES, ALICE FICH, artist, educator; b. Norman, Okla., June 24, 1956; d. Irving I. and Harriet F. (Fich) Z BA Art History, Swarthmore Coll., 1977; cert. merit in painting, N.Y. Studio Sch., NYC, 1977—80; postgrad., Skowhegan Sch. Art, Maine, 1980; MFA Painting, Queens Coll., CUNY, 1982. Tchr. Pratt Inst., Bklyn., 1999—. Tchr. N.Y.C. Tech. Coll., CUNY, Bklyn., 1983—88, Bklyn., 1997—, Baruch Coll., CUNY, NYC, 1986, NYC, 1988—97, Coll. S.I., CUNY, 1987—2001, Bklyn. Coll., 1998; guest lectr., vis. critic Millersville U., Pa., 1992, 93, 97, Dartmouth Coll., Hanover, NH, 1997, Swarthmore Coll., Pa., 2008; curator Frankel Pariser & Rudder, NYC, 1994—97; vis. critic N.Y. Studio Sch., NYC, 1997. One-woman shows include Queens Coll. Gallery, 1982, 2002, Swarthmore Coll., 1987, Frankel Pariser & Rudder, 1993, Dartmouth Coll., 1997, Tribes Gallery, N.Y.C., 1998, 2002, Hopper House, Nyack, N.Y., 2002, Delaware Arts Ctr., Narrowsburg, NY, 2006, Galleria Janet Kurnatowski, Bklyn., 2007, Chi Contemporary Art, 2009, Chi Contemporary Fine Art, 2009, exhibited in group shows at Millersville U., 1992, Greenwich House, N.Y.C., 1992, Nat. Acad. Design, 1992, 1994, 1996, Tribeca 148 Gallery, 1992, 1996, 2000, N.Y. Studio Sch., 1993, 1995—2001, Bowery Gallery, N.Y.C., 1993, 1995, Salena Gallery-L.I. U., Bklyn., 1994, 1997, Art Showcase, The Bond Market, N.Y.C., 1998, Elsa Mott Ives Gallery, 1997, 1999, 2001, Grace Gallery, N.Y.C. Tech. Coll., Bklyn., 1999, Artist Space, N.Y.C., 1999, Simon Gallery, Morristown, N.J., 2000, 55 Mercer Gallery, N.Y.C., 2000, William Paterson U., N.J., 2000, Contemporary Mus., Balt., 2000, Key Span Corp. Galleries, Bklyn., 2000, Piergo, 2000—, Seton Hall U., Newark, 2000, NYU, 2000, Drawing Ctr. Registry, N.Y.C., 2001—, John Elder Gallery, 2001, Chelsea Pier 60, 2001, Exit Art, 2002, Sperone Westwater Gallery, 2002, Ayce de Roulet Williamson Gallery, Pasadena, Calif., 2002, Artisi Space, N.Y.C., 2004, Brent Sikkeme Gallery, 2004, Del. Arts Coun., Narrowsburg, N.Y., 2005, Times Square Lobby Gallery, N.Y.C., 2005, Pratt Inst., 2005, Painting Ctr., 2005, Lori Bookstein Fine Art, 2005, Chh'i Contemporary Fine Art, Bklyn., 2006, Gallery 64, 2006, Michael Ingbar GAllery, NYC, 2007, Windham Fine Art, NY, 2007, Chgo. Bridge Art Fair, Chi Contemporary Fine Art Booth, Chgo., 2007, Swarthmore Coll. List Gallery, 2007, Sideshow Gallery, Williamsburg, Bklyn., 2008, 2009. Recipient Julius Hallgarten prize, Nat. Acad. Design, N.Y.C., 1988, 1990; named Barklie McKee Henry Meml. scholar, Skowhegan Sch. Art, 1980, Residency fellow, Va. Ctr. for the Creative Arts, Sweet Briar, 1992, 1997, 1999, 2001, Cummington (Mass.) Cmty. Arts, 1993. Avocations: swimming, hiking, reading. Home: 457 15th St Apt 5D Brooklyn NY 11215-5734 Office: NYC Tech Coll 300 Jay St Brooklyn NY 11201-1909 Home (Summer): 1253 Milanville Rd Milanville PA 18443 Office Phone: 718-768-3655. Personal E-mail: azinnes@mindspring.com.

ZINNES, HARRIET FICH, poet, fiction writer, retired English educator, literary and art critic; b. Boston; d. Assir and Sarah (Goldberg) Fich; m. Irving I. Zinnes, Sept. 24, 1943 (dec. 1979); children: Clifford, Alice. BA cum laude, CUNY, 1939, MA, 1944; PhD, NYU, 1953. Editor publs. divsn. Raritan (N.J.) Arsenal, 1942-43; assoc. editor Harper's Bazaar, NYC, 1944-46; tutor Hunter Coll. CUNY, NYC, 1946-49; asst. prof. Queens Coll. CUNY, Flushing, 1949-53, assoc. prof., 1962-78, full prof., 1978-89, prof. emerita, 1989—; lectr. in English Rutgers U., New Brunswick, N.J., 1961-62. Vis. prof. Am. lit. U. Geneva, 1968. Author: Waiting and Other Poems, 1964, An Eye for an I, 1966, I Wanted to See Something Flying, 1976, Entropisms, 1978, Book of Ten, 1981, Lover: Short Stories, 1988, Book of Twenty, 1992, My, Haven't the Flowers Been?, 1995, The Radiant Absurdity of Desire, 1998, Plunge, 2001, Drawing on the Wall: Poems, 2002 (named Notable Book of Yr.), Whither Nonstopping, 2005, Light Light or The Curvature of Earth, 2009; editor: Ezra Pound and the Visual Arts, 1980; translator Blood and Feathers: Selected Poems of Jacques Prevert, 1988, rev. edit., 1993, 2008; contr. editor, Hollin's Critic, Denver Quarterly, Colo., Nev.,; contr. writer, N.Y. Arts Mag.; author numerous poems; contbr. articles to popular mags. MacDowell Art Colony fellow, 1972-74, 77, 2004, Yaddo fellow, 1978, 81, Va. Ctr. for Creative Arts fellow, 1975-76, 81-82, 84, 86, 88-93, resident fellow, Djerassi Found., 1990, La Napoul, 2002; Am. Coun. Learned Socs. grantee, 1978, CUNY summer grantee, 1979, 81, 86. Fellow Poets Editors & Novelists, Nat. Book Critics Circle, Acad. Am. Poets, Internat. Assn. Art Critics, Poetry Soc. Am.; mem. Phi Beta Kappa. Home: 25 W 54th St New York NY 10019-5404 Office: Dept English Queens Coll Flushing NY 11367 Office Phone: 212-582-8315. Personal E-mail: hzinnes@rcn.com.

ZINNI, ANTHONY CHARLES, global defense company executive, retired military officer; b. Conshohocken, Pa., Sept. 17, 1943; s. Antonio and Lilla (Disabatino) Z.; m. Dale Elaine Bathke, Nov. 19, 1966; children: Lisa, Maria, Anthony. BS in Econs., Villanova U., 1965; MA in Bus., Cen. Mich. U., 1984; MA in Internat. Rels., Salve Regina Coll., Newport, RI, 1986; postgrad., Nat. War Coll., Washington, 1983-84. Commd. 2d lt. USMC, 1965, advanced through grades to gen., 1997, ret., 2000; comdg. officer 2d bn. 8th Marines, Camp Lejeune, N.C., 1980-81, 9th Marines, Okinawa, Japan, 1987-89; instr. Comdt. Staff Coll., Quantico, Va., 1981-83; staff ops. officer Hdqrs. USMC, Washington, 1984-86; chief naval ops. fellow Strategic Studies Group, Newport, 1986-87; chief staff Tng. and Edn. Ctr., Combat Devel. Command, Quantico, 1989-90; dep. ops. officer US European Command (USEUCOM), Stuttgart, Germany, 1990-91; chief of staff, dep. commdg. gen. Task Force Provide Comfort, 1991-92; dir. ops. Unified Task Force, Stuttgart, Somalia, 1992-93; commdg. gen. I Marine Expeditionary Force, 1994-96; dep. comdr. US Ctrl. Command (USCENTCOM), 1996-97, comdr., 1997-2000; spl. envoy to the Middle East US Dept. State, 2002—03; disting. sr. advisor Ctr. for Strategic & Internat. Studies, Washington, 2000—; pres. internat. ops. M.I.C. Industries, Inc., Reston, Va., 2006—07; exec. v.p. DynCorp International LLC, Falls Church, 2007—08; chmn. BAE Systems, Inc., 2009—; acting pres., CEO BAE Systems N.Am, 2009—. Bd. dirs. MHI Hospitality Corp., 2004—, McNeil Technologies Inc., 2004—, DynCorp International LLC, 2005—07, BAE Systems, Inc., 2009—. Co-author (with Tom Clancy & Tony Koltz): Battle Ready, 2004; co-author: (with Michael DeLong & Noah Lukeman) Inside CentCom: The Unvarnished Truth About the Wars in Afghanistan and Iraq, 2004; co-author: (with Tony Koltz) The Battle for Peace: A Frontline Vision of America's Power and Purpose, 2006. Roman Catholic. Office: BAE Systems North America 1601 Research Blvd Rockville MD 20850 Office Phone: 301-838-6000.*

ZINOBER, RICHARD NEIL, playwright, educator; MFA in creative writing, Columbia U., NYC, 1982. Prof. English Minn. State U., Moorhead, 1985—. Guest artist Kennedy Ctr. Summer Intensives, Washington. Author: (stage play) Seekers of the Light, Playscripts Inc., 2001 (winner, Ann White New Playwrights Contest, 1990), The House at the Edge of the World (Charles M. Getchell award, 1992), Once Loved (winner Porter Fleming Lit. Competition, 2004). Mem.: Assoc. Writing Programs. Office: Minn State Univ Moorhead 1104 Seventh Ave South Moorhead MN 56563 Office Phone: 218-477-2690. Office Fax: 218-477-2236. Personal E-mail: zinoberneil@yahoo.com. Business E-Mail: zinoberr@mnstate.edu.

ZINSER, TODD J., federal agency administrator; b. 1957; BA, No. Ky. U., 1979; MA, Miami U., Ohio, 1980. Dep. regional adminstr. Office of Labor Mgmt. Standards US Dept. Labor; spl.-agent-in-charge NY Region Office of Insp. Gen. US Dept. Transp., dep. asst. insp. gen. for investigations, asst. insp. gen. for investigations, 1996—2001, acting dep. insp. gen., 2000—01, dep. insp. gen., 2001—07, acting insp. gen., 2007; insp. gen. US Dept. Commerce, 2007—. Office: US Dept Commerce Herbert Clark Hoover Bldg 14th St & Constitution Ave NW 7898C Washington DC 20230 Office Phone: 202-482-4661. Office Fax: 202-482-0567. Business E-Mail: todd.j.zinser@oig.dot.gov.*

ZINTER, STEVEN L., state supreme court justice; m. Sandra Zinter; 2 children. Doctorate, Univ. So. Dakota, 1975, BS, 1972. Pvt. practice, 1978—86; state atty. Hughes County; cir. judge State of So. Dakota, 1987—97; presiding judge Sixth Judicial Cir., 1997—2002; judge SD Supreme Court, 2002—. Mem. Harry S Truman Found.; trustee So. Dakota Retirement Sys.; elect. pres. So. Dakota Corrections Commn. Mem.: ABA, S.D. Judges Assn. (past pres.), S.D. Bar Assn. Office: SD Supreme Ct 500 E Capital Ave Pierre SD 57501-5070*

ZIOLKOWSKI, ANDREW T., metal products executive; B, Indiana Univ., Pa.; MBA, St. Joseph's Univ. Mgmt. positions through v.p. bar & coil products bus. Carpenter Tech. Corp., 1989—. Office: Carpenter Tech Corp 2 Meridian Blvd Wyomissing PA 19610-1339 Office Phone: 610-208-2232. Business E-Mail: aziolkowski@cartech.com.*

ZIOLKOWSKI, JAN MICHAEL, medievalist educator, library director; b. New Haven, Nov. 17, 1956; s. Theodore J. and Yetta (Goldstein) Z.; m. Elizabeth Ann Hillenius; children: Saskia Elizabeth, Ada Margaret, Yetta Joy. AB summa cum laude, Princeton U., 1977; PhD, U. Cambridge, Eng., 1982; MA (hon.), Harvard U., 1987. Asst. prof. Harvard U., Cambridge, Mass., 1981-84, John L. Loeb assoc. prof. of the humanities, 1984-87, prof. medieval Latin and comparative lit., 1987—2002, Arthur Kingsley Porter prof. medieval Latin, 2002—; dir. Dumbarton Oaks Rsch. Libr. & Collection, Washington, 2007—. Author: Alan of Lille's Grammar of Sex, 1985, Nigel of Canterbury, Miracles of the Virgin Mary, 1986, Jezebel: A Norman Latin Poem, 1989, On Philology, 1990, Talking Animals: Medieval Latin Beast Poetry, 1993, Nigel of Canterbury, The Passion of St. Lawrence, 1994, The Cambridge Songs, 1994, 98, Obscenity: Social Control and Artistic Creation in the European Middle Ages, 1998, The Medieval Craft of Memory, 2002, Fairy Tales from Before Fairy Tales, 2006; editor Comparative Literature Studies. Pres. Internationales Mittellateiner Komitee, 2000—. Fellow Guggenheim Found., 1987-88, ACLS, 1986, Netherlands Inst. for Advanced Study, 2005—; Rome Prize fellow Am. Acad. in Rome, 1980-81; Marshall scholar, 1977-80. Mem. Medieval Acad. Am. (councillor 1991-94), Dante Soc. Am. (councillor 2004—), Am. Philol. Assn., Phi Beta Kappa. Office: Harvard Univ Classics 221 Boylston Hall Cambridge MA 02138 also; Dumbarton Oaks Rsch Libr & Coll 1703 32d St NW Washington DC 20007-2961 Office Phone: 617-496-6062. Business E-Mail: jmziolk@fas.harvard.edu.

ZIOLKOWSKI, RICHARD WALTER, electrical engineer, educator; b. Warsaw, NY, Nov. 22, 1952; s. William Walter and Alfreda (Smutek) Z.; m. Lea Anne Reynolds, May 30, 1981; children: Mira Beth, Cory David. BSc in Physics magna cum laude, Brown U., 1974; MS in Physics, U. Ill., 1975, PhD in Physics, 1980. Project engr. Lawrence Livermore Nat. Lab., Livermore, Calif., 1981-90; assoc. prof. Dept. Elec. and Computer Engring. U. Ariz., Tucson, 1990-96, prof., 1996—; John M. Leonis disting. prof. Litton Industries; with Coll. Optical Scis. Named Prof. of Yr. Tau Beta Pi, 1993, Prof. of Yr. Eta Kappa Nu, 1993, 98. Fellow IEEE (assoc. editor 1992-98); mem. Am. Phys. Soc., Internat. Radio Sci. Union (sec. 1994-96), Optical Soc. Am., Acoustical Soc. Am. Achievements include patent for Electromagnetic and other directed energy pulse launcher. Home: 2229 E 3rd St Tucson AZ 85719-5108

ZIOLKOWSKI, THEODORE JOSEPH, literature educator, writer; b. Birmingham, Ala., Sept. 30, 1932; s. Miecislaw and Cecilia (Jankowski) Z.; m. Yetta Bart Goldstein, Mar. 26, 1951; children: Margaret Cecilia, Jan Michael, Eric Josef. AB, Duke U., 1951, AM, 1952; student, U. Innsbruck, Austria, 1952-53; PhD, Yale U., 1957; DrPhil honoris causa (hon.), U. Greifswald, 2001. Instr., then asst. prof. Yale U., New Haven, 1956-62; assoc. prof. Columbia U., NYC, 1962-64; prof. Germanic langs. and lit. Princeton (N.J.) U., 1964-69, chmn., 1973-79, Class of 1900 prof. modern langs., 1969-2001, prof. comparative lit., 1975-2001, dean Grad. Sch., 1979-92, prof. emeritus, 2001. Vis. prof. Rutgers U., 1966, Yale U., 1967, 75, CUNY, 1971, Bristol U., 1987, U. Munich, 1992; vis. scholar U. Ctr. in Va., 1971, Piedmont U. Ctr., N.C., 1971; Dancy Meml. lectr. U. Montevallo, 1973; Christopher Longest lectr. U. Miss., 1979; Patten Found. lectr. Ind. U., 1980; vis. lectr. Österreichische Akademie der Wissenschaften, 1992; vis. lectr. Korean Ministry of Edn., 1996; chmn. N.Y. State Doctoral Evaluation Program in German, 1975-80; nat. rev. panel for U.S. Nat. Grad. Fellows Program, 1985-87, 91—; chmn. overseers vis. com. on German Harvard U., 1982-88; mem. selection com. for Bennett award, 1988; mem. German-Am. Acad. Coun., 1993-99; chmn. N.Y. State Humanities Screening Com., 1996; chmn. bd. German-Am. Ctr. for Vis. Scholars, 1997-99; forum assembly spkr. Brigham Young U.; mem. evaluation team Rosenzweig Zentrum of Hebrew U., Jerusalem, 1999; mem. search com. for chair in German, Bristol U., 1999; mem. search com. for dean Internat. U. Bremen, 1999-00. Author: Hermann Broch, 1964, The Novels of Hermann Hesse, 1965, Hermann Hesse, 1966, Dimensions of the Modern Novel, 1969, Fictional Transfigurations of Jesus, 1972 (James Russell Lowell prize MLA), Disenchanted Images, 1977, Der Schriftsteller Hermann Hesse, 1979, The Classical German Elegy, 1980, Varieties of Literary Thematics, 1983, German Romanticism and Its Institutions, 1990, Virgil and the Moderns, 1993, The Mirror of Justice, 1997 (Christian Gauss prize Phi Beta Kappa), Das Wunderjahr in Jena, 1998, The View from the Tower, 1998, The Sin of Knowledge, 2000, Berlin: Aufstieg einer Kulturmetropole um 1810, 2002, Hesitant Heroes, 2004, Clio the Romantic Muse, 2004 (Barricelli prize), Ovid and the Moderns, 2005 (Robert Motherwell award Dedalus Found.), Vorboten der Moderne: Eine Kulturgeschichte der Fruehromantik, 2006, Modes of Faith: Secular Surrogates for Lost Religious Belief, 2007, Minos and the Moderns: Cretan Myth in Twentieth-Century Literature and Art, 2008, Mythologisierte Gegenwart: Deutsches Erleben seit 1933 in antikem Gewand, 2008, Scandal on Stage: European Theatre as Moral Trial, 2009, Heidelberger Romantik: Mythos und Symbol, 2009; editor: Hermann Hesse, Autobiographical Writings, 1972, Hermann Hesse, Stories of Five Decades, 1972, Hesse: A Collection of Critical Essays, 1972, Hermann Hesse, My Belief: Selected Essays, 1974, Hermann Hesse, Tales of Student Life, 1976, Hermann Hesse, Pictor's Metamorphoses and Other Fantasies, 1982, Hermann Hesse, Soul of the Age: Selected Letters, 1891-1962, 1991, Friedrich Dürrenmatt, Selected Writings 2: Fictions, 2006; mem. editl. bd. Germanic Rev., 1962-95, Publs. MLA, 1971-75, Arbitrium, 1983-, 17th Century Studies, 1985-2005, Germanistik, 1987-, Jahrbuch für Internat. Germanistik, 1997-, World Literature Today, 1998-, Etudes Germaniques, 1998-, Publications of the English Goethe Society, 2003-09, Spectrum Lit./Comparative Studies, 2004-; mem. editl. bd. Princeton U. Press, 1972-75, trustee, 1982-95; translator (with Yetta Ziolkowski): The Poetics of Quotation (Herman Meyer) 1968, Hermann Hesse: A Pictorial Biography, 1975; contbr. over 180 articles and 400 revs. Decorated comdr.'s cross Order of Merit (Germany), 2000; recipient Howard T. Behrman award for disting. achievement in humanities, 1978, Wilbur Lucius Cross medal Yale U., 1982, Goethe Inst. gold medal, 1987, Henry Allen Moe prize in humanities, 1988, Festschrift Themes and Structures (ed. Alexander Stephan), 1997, Jakob-und-Wilhelm Grimm prize for German Studies, 1998, Humboldt Sr. Rsch. prize, 1998; Mellon Emeritus Faculty fellow, 2003; Fulbright rsch. grantee, 1958-59, grantee Am. Philos. Soc., 1959, NEH grantee, 1978, Guggenheim fellow, 1964-65, Am. Coun. Learned Socs. fellow, 1972, 76; resident fellow Bellagio Study Ctr., 1993. Mem. MLA (hon. life; exec. coun. 1976-77, pres. 1985), Acad. Lit. Studies, Am. Comparative Lit. Assn., Am. Acad. Arts and Scis., Assn. Lit. Scholars and Critics, Authors Guild, Am. Assn. Tchrs. German (hon. life), Yale Grad. Sch. Assn. (pres. 1974-76), Assn. Grad. Schs. (v.p. 1989-90, pres. 1990-91), Heinrich von Kleist Gesellschaft, Goethe-Gesellschaft, Novalis-Gesellschaft, Internat. Vereinigung für Germanistik (exec. coun. 1985-95, treas. 1990-95), Am. Philos. Soc. (councillor 1991-97), Göttingen Akademie der Wissenschaften, Austrian Akademie der Wissenschaften, Deutsche Akademie für Sprache und Dichtung, Inst. Germanic and Romance Studies London, Phi Beta Kappa. Home: 36 Bainbridge St Princeton NJ 08540-3902 Personal E-mail: tjziol@aol.com.

ZIPES, DOUGLAS PETER, cardiologist, researcher; b. White Plains, NY, Feb. 27, 1939; s. Robert Samuel Zipes and Josephine Helen Weber; m. Marilyn Joan Jacobus, Feb. 18, 1961; children: Debra, Jeffrey, David. BA cum laude, Dartmouth Coll., 1961, B of Med. Sci., 1962; MD cum laude, Harvard Med. Sch., 1964. Diplomate Internal Medicine 1970, Cardiovascular Disease 1972. Intern, medicine Duke U. Med. Ctr., Durham, NC, 1964—65, resident, cardiology, 1965—66, fellow, 1966—68; joined Ind. U. Sch. Medicine, Indpls., 1970, prof. medicine, 1976—94, disting. prof., medicine, pharmacology and toxicology, 1994—2007, disting. prof. emeritus, 2007—, dir., cardiology divsn. and Krannert Inst. Cardiology, 1995—. Bd. dirs. Inst. for Clin. Evaluation; cardiology adv. com NIH, 1991—94; mem. med. adv. bd. ABCNews-.com, 2000—; mem. dean's coun. Dartmouth Med. Sch., Ind. Med. Sch. Contbr. articles to profl. jours., chapters to books in medicine; founding editor-in-chief Jour. Cardiovascular Electrophysiology, founding editor Heart Rhythm, N.Am. Soc. Pacing and Electrophysiology/Heart Rhythm Soc., mem. of several editl. bds. of peer-reviewed jours. Past pres. Indpls. Opera. Recipient Sagamore of Wabash, Gov. of Ind., 2001, Disting. Alumnus award, Duke U. Med. Ctr., 2007. Master: Am. Coll. Cardiology (past pres., Disting. Scientist award 1996); fellow: Heart Rhythm Soc. (past pres., Disting. Scientist award 1995); mem.: Am. Bd. Internal Medicine (past chair), Assn. U. Cardiologists (past pres.), Cardiac Electrophysiology Soc. (past pres.), Argentine Cardiology Soc. (hon.), Am. Heart Assn. (Disting. Achievement award 1989, James B. Herrick award 1997, Cor Vitae award 2004), Assn. Am. Physicians, Am. Soc. Clin. Investigation. Home: 10614 Winterwood Carmel IN 46032-9688 Office: Krannert Inst Cardiology Rm E474 1801 N Capitol Ave Ste E400 Indianapolis IN 46202-1228 Office Phone: 317-962-0555, 317-962-0556. Office Fax: 317-962-0568. Business E-Mail: dzipes@iupui.edu.

ZIPF, JENNIFER E., marketing professional; b. Edison, NJ, Nov. 7, 1973; d. James and Patricia Zipf; BA in Journalism, Rider U., Lawrenceville, NJ, 1995. Asst. editor Quadrant Healthcom, Inc., Belle Mead, NJ, 1996, Philip Lief Group, Princeton, NJ, 1996—98; publs. specialist Rec. for Blind & Dyslexic, Princeton, 1998—99; assoc. editor, mktg. comm. Merrill Lynch Investment Mgrs., Plainsboro, NJ, 1999—2001, asst. v.p., e-business, 2001—04; mktg. comm. mgr. MarketingNPV, Princeton, 2004—08; dir., mktg. comm. Inspire, Princeton, 2008—. Participant, fundraiser Susan G. Komen Race for Cure, Princeton, 2000—06; vol. Friends of Homeless Animals, Princeton, 2002—05, SAVE, Princeton, 2007—; instr. NE Acad. Martial Arts, Mercerville, 2006—; trustee Lawrence Square Village II Bd., Lawrenceville, 2007—08; writer Winter Prefix Mag., 2007—; vol. Kerry/Edwards presdl. campaign, Princeton, 2004. Recipient Best Redesign award, APEX, 1999, Hon. Mention, NJ Pub. Rels. Soc. Am., 1999, Gold B-to-B Best E-mail Opt-in Campaign award, MarketingSherpa, 2006. Mem.: Mensa, Phi Sigma Tau, Pi Delta Phi, Omicron Delta Kappa. Democrat. Avocations: travel, kickboxing, music, writing, photography. Office Phone: 609-651-7274. Personal E-mail: jz117@comcast.net.

ZIPF, ROBERT EUGENE, JR., medical laboratory director, legal medicine consultant, pathologist; b. Sept. 18, 1940; s. Robert Eugene and Meriam (Murr) Z.; m. Nancy J. Gaskell, Sept. 11, 1965; children: Karin Lorene, Marjorie Kristine. BA, DePauw U., 1962; MD, Ohio State U., 1966. Diplomate Am. Bd. Pathology. Intern Miami Valley Hosp., Dayton, Ohio, 1966-67; dir. forensic pathology Duke U. Med. Ctr., Durham, NC, 1967-72; dir. radioisotope pathology Riverside Meth. Hosp., Columbus, 1974-78; dep. coroner, forensic pathologist Franklin County, Columbus, 1974-78; regional forensic pathologist State of N.C., Rocky Mount, 1978—; pres. R.E. Zipf, PA, Pathology Assocs., Rocky Mount, NC, 1978—2005. Clin. asst. prof. East Caroline U. Med. Sch., Greenville, N.C., 1979—; adj. prof. Atlantic Christian Coll., Wilson, N.C., 1980-89, dir. Sch. Med. Tech., 1983-89; dir. clin. and diagnostic labs., chief pathology Nash Gen. Hosp., Rocky Mount, 1978-2006; dir. forensic toxicology lab. Nash Health Care Sys., Rocky Mount, 1990-2000; cons. in field, v.p. Computerized Official Sys. Inc. 1986-2000, Founder Clintrac Pathology Computers. Contbr. articles to profl. jours. Trustee United Fund, 1979-84; active Mayor's Com. on Drug and Substance Abuse, 1987—; bd. dirs. NC Wesleyan Coll. Found., 2005—, Nash C.C., 2005—; advisor Zipf Charitable Trust and Fund, 1999—; mentor Nash-Rocky Mount Pub. Schs., 1980—. Maj. USAF, 1967—74, chief anatomic pathologist med. ctr. USAF, 1972, cons. USAF, 1972—74, surgeon gen. USAF, 1972—74. Fellow Am. Soc. Clin. Pathologist, Am. Acad. Forensic Scientists; mem. SMS (clin. adv. bd. 1988-91, lab. advisors bd. 1989-91, pres. advisor bd. 1990), Assn. Clin. Scientists, Am. Coll. Nuc. Medicine, N.C. Med. Soc., N.Y. Acad. Scis. (pres. Lab. Users Group 1988-90, 92), Nash County Med. Soc. (pres. 1995). Home: 120 Newby Ct Rocky Mount NC 27804-3322 Personal E-mail: rezpath@hotmail.com.

ZIPFEL, PAUL ALBERT, bishop; b. St. Louis; s. Albert and Leona (Rau) Zipfel. BST, Cath. U. Am., 1961; MA in Edn., St. Louis U., 1965. Ordained priest Archdiocese of Saint Louis, 1961, aux. bishop,

1989—96; ordained bishop, 1989; bishop Diocese of Bismarck, ND, 1996—. Roman Catholic. Office: Diocese of Bismarck PO Box 1575 420 Raymond St Bismarck ND 58502-1575 Office Phone: 701-223-1347. Office Fax: 701-223-3693.

ZIPPIN, CALVIN, epidemiologist, educator; b. Albany, NY, July 17, 1926; s. Samuel and Jennie (Perkel) Z.; m. Patricia Jayne Schubert, Feb. 9, 1964; children: David Benjamin, Jennifer Dorothy. AB magna cum laude, SUNY, Albany, 1947; ScD, Johns Hopkins U., Balt., 1953. Rsch. asst. Sterling-Winthrop Rsch. Inst., Rensselaer, NY, 1947-50, Johns Hopkins U., Balt., 1950—53; instr. biostats. Sch. Pub. Health, U. Calif., Berkeley, 1953-55; asst. to full rsch. biostatistician Sch. Medicine U. Calif., San Francisco, 1955-67, asst. prof. preventive medicine, 1958-60; post doctoral fellow London Sch. Hygiene and Tropical Medicine, 1964-65; prof. epidemiology U. Calif., San Francisco, 1967-91, prof. emeritus, 1991—. Vis. assoc. prof. stats. Stanford U., 1962; adv. WHO, 1969—; vis rsch. worker Middlesex Hosp. Med. Sch., London, 1975; com. mem. Am. Cancer Soc. and Nat. Cancer Inst., 1956—; faculty adviser Regional Cancer Centre, Trivandrum, India, 1983—; cons., lectr., vis. prof. in field. Co-author book, book chpts.; author or co-author papers primarily on biometry and epidemiology of cancer; editl. advisor Jour. Stats. in Medicine, 1981-86. Mem., alt. mem. Dem. Ctrl. Com., Marin County, Calif., 1987-96. Recipient Disting. Alumnus award SUNY, Albany, 1969, Lifetime Achievement and Leadership award Nat. Cancer Inst., 2003, also awards, fellowships and grants for work in cancer biometry and epidemiology. Fellow Am. Statis. Assn., Am. Coll. Epidemiology, Royal Statis. Soc. Gt. Britain; mem. Biometric Soc. (mem. internat. coun. 1978-81, pres. Western N.Am. region 1979-80), Calif. Cancer Registrars Assn. (hon.), Internat. Assn. Cancer Registries (hon.), B'nai B'rith (pres. Golden Gate lodge 1970-71, pres. Greater San Francisco unit 21 2003-06, internat. bd. govs. 2005—07, greater San Francisco Man of Yr., 2009), Phi Beta Kappa, Sigma Xi, Delta Omega. Office: Univ Calif Dept Epidemiology and Biostats San Francisco CA 94107 Office Phone: 415-514-8000. Business E-Mail: calvin.zippin@ucsf.edu.

ZIRBES, MARY KENNETH, retired minister; b. Melrose, Minn., Sept. 4, 1926; d. Joseph Louis and Clara Bernadine (Petermeier) Z. BA in History and Edn., Coll. St. Catherine, 1960; MA in Applied Theology, Sch. Applied Theology, Berkeley, Calif., 1976. Joined Order of St. Francis, Roman Cath. Ch., 1945. Tchr. Pub. Grade Sch., St. Nicholas, Minn., 1947-52; prin. Holy Spirit Grade Sch., St. Cloud, Minn., 1953-59, St. Mary's Jr. HS, Morris, Minn., 1960-62; coord. Franciscan Mission Team, Peru, South America, 1962-67, Franciscan Missions, Little Falls, Minn., 1967-70; dir. St. Richard's Social Justice Ministry, Richfield, Minn., 1971-80, Parish Community Devel., St. Paul, Mpls., Minn., 1980-85; councillor gen. Franciscan Sisters of Little Falls, 1960-62, 67-70; asst. dir. Renew-Archdiocese of St. Paul-Mpls., 1986-89; coord. Parish Social Justice Ministry-Archdiocese of St. Paul-Mpls., 1990-93; min. Franciscan Assocs., 1993—2003; leader of team on evangelical life Franciscan Sisters of Little Falls, 1994-96; ret., 2003. Co-developer Assn. of Pastoral Ministers, Mpls., St. Paul, 1979-81, Compañeros/Sister Parishes-Minn. and Nicaragua, 1984-89, Minn. Interfaith Ecology Coalition, 1989-92. Author: Parish Social Ministry, 1985, (manual) Acting for Justice, 1992. Organizer Twin Cities Orgn., Mpls., 1979-80; bd. dirs. Franciscan Sisters Health Care, Inc., Little Falls, 1990-93, Rice-Marion Residents Assn., St. Paul, 1991-92. Named Outstanding chair Assn. Pastoral Ministers, 1981; recipient Five Yrs. of Outstanding Svc. award Companeros, 1989. Mem. Assn. Pastoral Ministers (chair 1979), Audubon Soc., Minn. Call to Action, Com. on Peace, Justice and Integrity of Creation. Avocations: painting, birding, golf, reading.

ZIRKEL, RAYMOND ELLIOT, psychologist, educator; b. NYC, Feb. 23, 1959; s. Michael Meyer and Ruth Zirkel; 1 child, Jonathan. PhD in Psychology, Yeshiva U., Bronx, NY, 1998. Cert. sch. psychologist Dept. Edn. NY, 1987. Sch. psychologist NYC Dept. Edn., 1987—; supr. counselor tng. Westchester Day Sch. Summer Program, Mamaroneck, NY, 1997—; tchr. Temple B'nai Or, Morristown, NJ, 2001—.

ZIRNHELD, JENNIFER L., engineering educator, researcher; b. Buffalo, May 12, 1969; d. Mark D. McMahon and Carolyn V. Pfeil; m. Mark J. Zirnheld, May 22, 1993. BSEE, SUNY, Buffalo, 1993, MS, 1997, PhD, 2004. Lectr. SUNY, Buffalo, 1997—2004; co-prin., investigator, dep. dir. Energy Systems Inst., 2005—. Contbr. articles to profl. jours. Recipient Milton Plesur award, U. Buffalo Student Assn., 2000—01; Bergquist Doctoral fellow, SUNY, Buffalo, 1998—2002, James Clerk Maxwell Primex doctoral fellow, 2000—01. Mem.: IEEE (treas. 2000, newsletter editor 2000—, chair 2001—02), Am. Phys. Soc., Am. Soc. Engring. Edn., Eta Kappa Nu. Office: University of Buffalo 312 Bonner Hall Buffalo NY 14260 Business E-Mail: zirnheld@eng.buffalo.edu.

ZISCHKE, DOUGLAS ARTHUR, foreign service officer; b. Sioux Falls, SD, May 24, 1929; s. Arthur Gustav and Alice Minetta (Wedeking) Z.; m. Janice Mae Kuehnemann, June 8, 1957; children: Mark Douglas, Deborah Jan, Todd Lincoln. BS in Journalism cum laude, U. Wis., 1951, MS, 1952. Joined U.S. Fgn. Svc., 1957; tech. editor Forest Svc., Madison, 1955-57; asst. info. officer USIS, Montevideo, Uruguay, 1957-58, La Paz, Bolivia, 1958-59; asst. cultural affairs officer, br. pub. affairs officer Mexico, 1960-65; info. specialist Washington, 1965-67; pub. affairs officer Tegucigalpa, Honduras, 1967-69; dep. pub. affairs officer Buenos Aires, 1969-71; pub. affairs officer Guatemala City, Guatemala, 1971—74; assigned to U.S. Army War Coll., 1974-75; dep. pub. affairs officer Am. embassy Tehran, Iran, 1975-78; cultural coord. USICA, Washington, 1979-80; internat. cons., 1980-86; fgn. affairs advisor State Dept., 1986-98. Author monograph. Bd. dirs. Boy Scouts Am; dir. Lutheran Ch. 1973-74. Served with Signal Corps, AUS, 1953-55. Mem. Diplomatic and Consular Officers Ret. Home Phone: 703-779-0902.

ZISCHKE, MICHAEL HERMAN, lawyer; b. Yokahama, Japan, Dec. 30, 1954; s. Peter H. and Alice Marian (Oliver) Z.; children: Julia Carol, Jessica Marian; m. Nadin Sponamore, Sept. 30, 2006. BA magna cum laude, Dartmouth Coll., 1977; JD, U. Calif., Berkeley, 1982. Bar: Calif. 1982. Legis. asst. Congressman Bob Carr, Washington, 1977-79; assoc. Miller, Starr & Regalia, Oakland, Calif., 1982-87, McCutchen, Doyle, Brown & Enersen, Walnut Creek, Calif., 1987-91, counsel, 1991-93; ptnr. Landels Ripley & Diamond LLP, San Francisco, 1993—2000, Morrison & Foerster LLP, San Francisco, 2000—06, co-chmn. land use and environ. law practice group, 2003—06; ptnr. Cox Castle & Nicholson, LLP, 2007—. Lectr. land use issues U. Calif. Extension, 1988—2006, U. Calif. Davis Sch. Law, 1993—2001, U. Southern Calif. Law Sch., 1995—2006. Co-author: Land Use Initiatives and Referenda in California, 1990, Practice Pursuant to the California Environmental Quality Act, 1993, 2d edit., 2008; contbr. articles to profl. jours. Dir. Boys & Girls Clubs Oakland, 1988-2000, Child Care Law Ctr., 1998-2008. Mem. Calif. State Bar Assn. (exec. com. environ. law sect., 1995-2004), Calif. Bldg. Industry Assn. (select com. on industry litigation), Bar Assn. San Francisco. Democrat. Episcopalian. Office Phone: 415-262-5109.

ZISSIOS, PATRICIA ANN, principal; b. Hempstead, NY, Nov. 10, 1952; d. William Arnell and Loretta Woodie; m. Charles S. Zissios, Apr. 21, 1974; children: Stergios, Katerina. BS in Elem. Edn. and German cum laude, Longwood Coll., Farmville, Va., 1974; MEd in Adminstrn. and Supervision summa cum laude, George Mason U., Fairfax, Va., 1987, PhD in Adminstrn. and Supervision summa cum laude, 1994. Kindergarten-6th grade tchr., 1973—95; summmer sch. asst. prin., 1987; elem. prin. designee, 1989—91; adminstrv. asst. to assoc. supt. instrn., 1994—95; elem. asst. prin., 1996—98; elem. sch. prin. Lyles Crouch Traditional Acad., Alexandria, Va., 1998—. Part-time faculty mem. George Mason U., 1999—; presenter, cons., facilitator in field. Author: (monograph) An Oxford Experience, (book) The Legal Implications of Empowerment in Education as Theyh Specifically Relate to Site-Based Management, A Liability and Risk Management Instructional Manual for Site-Based Practitioners. Mem. steering com. Celebrate Fairfax/Millennius; active Crestwood Cmty. Resource Ctr.; mem. Vincent E. Reed's Prins. Leadership Inst., Washington; Pres. Springfield Inter-Svc. Club Coun.; bd. dirs. Springfield Cultural ARts Ctr. Recipient No. Va. Leadership award for pub. svc., Leadership Fairfax, 2001; named Citizen of Yr., Springfield Times, 2000, Educator of Yr., Am. Legion, 2003. Mem.: ASCD, Coun. Exceptional Children., Fairfax Assn. Elem. Sch. Prins., Va. Assn. Elem. Sch. Prins., Nat. Assn. Elem. Sch. Prins., Springfield C. of C., Phi Delta Kappa. Avocations: travel, reading. Office: Alexandria City Pub Schs Lyles-Crouch Acad 530 S St Asaph St Alexandria VA 22314 Business E-Mail: patricia.zissios@acps.k12.va.us.

ZITNAY, JILL M., educational consultant, educator; d. William S. and Nancy Ann Noga; m. Jeffrey Stanley Zitnay, Oct. 5, 1991; children: Joshua William, Jordan Kathryn. BS, So. Conn. State U., New Haven, 1990, MS, 2000. Spl. edn. tchr. Fairfield Pub. Schs., Conn., 1990—2003; reading cons. Orange Elem. Schs., Conn., 2004—. Creative Tchg. grants, Orange Elem. Schs., 2007. Mem.: ASCD, NCTE, Internat. Reading Assn., Nat. Staff Devel. Coun. Home: 34 Bee Mountain Rd Oxford CT 06478 Office: Turkey Hill Sch 441 Turkey Hill Rd Orange CT 06477 Personal E-mail: beanerr@sbcglobal.net. Business E-Mail: jzitnay@orange-ed.org.

ZITO, ALLISON ANN, textile weaver, member; b. Elizabeth, NJ, Oct. 26, 1960; d. Robert Joseph Zito and Kathleen Marie (Carriere) Mazzaccaro; m. Kevin Paul Kittredge, Oct. 24, 1992; 1 child, Brendan. Student, Moore Coll. Art, 1978-80; BFA, Phila. Coll. Art, 1984; student, Phila. Colls. of Textiles and Scis., 1992. Weaver illustrator Hoch Studios, Glenmore, Pa., 1975-85; tchr.fashion illustration Taylor Bus. Inst., Pomona, N.J., 1981; artist handweaver Allison Zito & Son, Art, Edn. & Environ. Svcs., Phila., 1984—; gallery dir. Mill Brook Art Gallery, Brownsville, Vt., 1986-88; exhibit preparator Balch Inst. for Ethnic Studies, Phila., 1988—, Mutter Mus., Phila., 1989-91, Nat. Mus. Am. Jewish History, Phila., 1990—; computer operator Neveling Card Stamping Co., Phila., 1989; conservator Carli Restorations, Phila., 1991; studio art tchr. U. Penn. Morris Arboretum, Phila., 2002—; prof. history architecture, fashion history, color theory, modern dance Harcum Coll., Bryn Mawr, Pa., 2004—. Art handler Phila. Mus. Art, 1992. Exhibited in group shows Del. Art Mus., Wilmington, 1989, Berkshire Mus., Pittsfield, Mass., 1990, Phila. Mus. Art, 1990, Nat. Mus. of Am. Jewish History, 1992, The State Mus. Pa., 1993, numerous juried and invitational exhibits, 1984—; contbg. artist Contemporary Phila. Artists, 1990. Pa. Coun. on Arts fellow, 1991, Craft, Visual Arts and Art Criticism fellow, 1993. Mem. Am. Craft Coun. Avocation: nature studies. Home and Office: 207 Edgemont Ave Ardmore PA 19003 Business E-Mail: allisonzitoandson@gmail.com. E-mail: artextiles@verizon.net.

ZITO, CHRISTINA IVINS, molecular biologist, educator; b. New Haven, Dec. 23, 1971; d. Roy Michael and Alma Maria Ivins; m. Gregory N. Zito, Sept. 14, 2001; children: Juliette Elizabeth, Cosette Emily. BA, Mt. Holyoke Coll., South Hadley, Mass., 1993; PhD, Yale U., New Haven, 2003. Postdoc. assoc. Yale U. Sch. Medicine, 2003—; adj. instr., biology Sacred Heart U., Fairfield, Conn., 2008—. Mem.: Nat. Postdoc. Assn., Assn. Women Sci. Independent. Achievements include research in signal transduction pathways in cancer. Office: Yale Univ Sch Medicine 310 Cedar St New Haven CT 06510 Business E-Mail: christina.zito@yale.edu.

ZITO, RAE NANETTE, retired elementary school educator; b. Salt Lake, Utah, May 27; d. Grant Ludlow Cope and Mara Ardell Swain; m. Robert Waldemar Zito, Dec. 18, 1959; children: Penni Rae, Angela Dawne, Robert Grant. BSc cum laude, U. Utah, 1959, MS in Elem. Edn., 1987, cert. in Gerontology, 1989, MPhil in Health Edn., 1993. Tchr. Elem. Sch. Murray Dist. Schs., Salt Lake City, 1958—59, Salt Lake (Utah) Dist. Schs., 1959—61, Granite Dist. Schs., Salt Lake City, 1961—99; ret. Vol. AARP, Salt Lake City, 1999—2005; bd. mem. Mt. Olympus Sr. Ctr. Hornaday, Utah, 2007—; bd. dirs. Women's State Legis. Coun., 2001—05; specialist family history ctr. LDS Ch., Salt Lake City, 2003—; mem. Speaking Women's health Com., 2003—. Recipient award, Utah State Legis., 1994; named Woman of Yr., Delta Kappa Gamma, 2004, Outstanding Vol., Retirement Inn, 1993; scholar, PTA, 1955, Delta Kappa Gamma, 1985. Mem.: Learning Disabilities Assn. Utah (pres. 2002—05). Democrat. Mem. Lds Ch. Avocations: bicycling, golf, reading, knitting. Home Phone: 801-277-1440; Office Phone: 801-910-2464. Personal E-mail: bzito@juno.com.

ZITO, ROBERT JOHN AMADEUS, lawyer; b. NYC, Sept. 11, 1956; s. Joseph J. and Phyllis A. (Esposito) Z.; m. Dana Sabin Cole, July 4, 1992. BA, Tulane U., 1978; JD, N.Y. Law Sch., 1981. Bar: N.Y. 1985, U.S. Dist. Ct. (so. and ea. dists.) N.Y. 1983, (no. dist.) 1993, U.S. Ct. Appeals (2nd Cir.) 1988, U.S. Ct. Appeals (9th Cir.) 2000, U.S. Tax Ct. 1984, U.S. Supreme Ct. 1988; ordained deacon Epis. Ch. of U.S., 2001; parish deacon, Ch. of the Incarnation, N.Y.C. Assoc. LaRossa Cooper, NYC, 1981-85, Spengler Carlson, NYC, 1985-90; ptnr. Zito & Assocs., NYC, 1990-91, Sullivan Donovan, NYC, 1991-93, Tanner Propp & Farber, NYC, 1993—98, Fischbein Badillo Wagner Harding, NYC, 1998—2003, Schiff Hardin, LLP, NYC, 2003—07, Carter Ledyard & Milburn LLP, NYC, 2007—. Lt. col. (ret.) N.Y. Guard, 1991-2001; editl. adv. bd., Episcopal New Yorker. Recipient Bklyn. Achievement award Bklyn. Dems., 1994; N.Y.S. Long and Faithful Svc. award, N.Y.G. Achievement Medal. Mem. ABA, N.Y. Bar Assn., Fed. Bar Coun., Columbian Coun., Ancient Chpt. RAM, Holland Lodge F & AM (past master), Knights Templar, the Most Venerable Order of the Hosp. of St. John of Jerusalem (officer brother, chair NY regional com.), Royal Order Merit Ho. of Savoy (knight). Republican. Episcopalian. Avocations: musical instruments, sailing. Office: Carter Ledyard & Milburn LLP 2 Wall St New York NY 10005 Office Phone: 212-238-8768. Business E-Mail: zito@clm.com.

ZITO, ROBERT THOMAS, pharmaceutical executive; b. Bayonne, NJ, Nov. 20, 1953; s. Thomas W. and Rose (Scarito) Z. BA in English, Fairfield U., Conn., 1975. Asst. sports editor Bridgeport Telegram, Conn., 1975-79; account exec. Hill and Knowlton, Inc., NYC, 1979-83; v.p. CN Comm., Rahway, NJ, 1983-87; mng. dir. advt. and comm. svcs. NY Stock Exch., 1987-90, exec. v.p., 1994—2004; v.p. corp. comm. Sony USA Inc. and Sony Software Corp., NYC, 1990—94; with Bristol-Myers Squibb, 2004—, sr. v.p. corp. and bus. comm., chief comm. officer. Owner Lotsa' Pasta, Inc., Woodbridge, NJ, 1982-87; cons. Arctic Sports Shops, Inc., Bridgeport, 1976-82; bd. dirs. HDC, Inc., Bayonne. Dir. youth basketball progs. YMCA, Trumbull, Conn., 1977; basketball coach Barlow HS, Redding, Conn., 1977; bd. mem. Bristol-Myers Squibb Found., St. Peter's Prep., FDNY Found., Cento Amici, Robert Wood Johnson U. Hosp. Recipient Ellis Island Medal of Honor, 1998. Mem. Nat. Sportscasters and Sportswriters Assn., Wisemen, PR Seminar. Office: Bristol Myers Squibb 345 Park Ave New York NY 10154-0037

ZITOUNI, IMED, research scientist; arrived in US, 2001, permanent resident, 2005; s. Ali and Radhia (Ben Yaala) Zitouni; m. Barbara Voinier, Sept. 11, 2000; 2 children. MEng in Computer Sci. with honors, Nat. Sch. Computer Sci., ENSI, Tunisia, 1995; MS in Computer Sci. with honors, U. Nancy 1, France, 1996, PhD in Computer Sci. with honors, 2000. Cert. profl. design software engr., Nat. Sch. Computer Sci., ENSI, 1995. Rschr., tchg. asst. U. Nancy 1, 1997—2000; r & d engr. Dialoca, Paris, 2000—01; sr. rsch. mem. tech. stuff Bell Labs./Alcatel-Lucent, Murray Hill, NJ, 2001—04; sr. rsch. scientist IBM Rsch., Yorktown Heights, NY, 2004—. Contbr. chapters to books, articles to profl. jours. Named Outstanding Rschr., US Citizenship and Immigration Svcs., 2005. Mem.: IEEE, Internat. Speech Comm. Assn., Assn. Computational Linguistics (info. officer spl. interest group 2006—). Achievements include design of call center applications using natural language call routing and spoken dialog systems; next generation media servers using SIP; invention of novel approaches in the fields of natural language processing, speech, and computational linguistics; first to in contributing to the improvement of speech and natural language understanding systems; system and method for semantic role labeling of high morphological text, improve the state of the art language modeling techniques; contribute to improvement of state of the art speech, machine translation and natural language understanding systems and improve natural language call routing techniques and spoken dialog applications; research in applying statistics and machine learning techniques for information extraction, distillation statistical machine translation and semantic search; use of machine learning techniques for health care data analytics; use of machine learning techniques and stochastic approaches for data analytics; patents in field. Avocations: music, travel, sports. Home: 16 Park Terrace White Plains NY 10603 Office: IBM Thomas J Watson Research Center Yorktown Heights NY 10598 Office Fax: 914-945-4490. Personal E-mail: imed.zitouni@gmail.com. Business E-Mail: izitouni@us.ibm.com.

ZITRIN, ARTHUR, physician; b. Bklyn., Apr. 10, 1918; s. William and Lillian (Elbaum) Z.; m. Charlotte Marker, Oct. 4, 1942; children—Richard Alan, Elizabeth Ann. BS, City Coll. N.Y., 1938; MS, N.Y. U., 1941, MD, 1945; certificate psychoanalytic medicine, Columbia, 1955. Diplomate: Am. Bd. Psychiatry and Neurology. Research fellow animal behavior Am. Museum Natural History, 1939-42; intern King County Hosp., 1945-46; resident psychiatry Bellevue Hosp., 1948-51; instr. physiology Hunter Coll., NYC, 1948-49; mem. faculty N.Y.U. Sch. Medicine, 1949-97, prof. psychiatry, 1967-97, prof. emeritus, 1997—; mem. staff Bellevue Hosp., NYC, 1951—, dir. psychiatry, 1955-68, N.Y.C. Dept. Hosps., 1962- 64; pvt. practice, 1949—; attending psychiatrist Univ. Hosp., NYC. Cons. psychiatrist Manhattan Va Hosp. Author papers in field. Served to capt., M.C. AUS, 1946- 48. Fellow Am. Psychiat. Assn. (life), N.Y. Acad. Medicine; mem. AMA, N.Y. Soc. Clin. Psychiatry (pres. 1966- 67), Am. Psychoanalytic Assn. (life), Sigma Xi, Alpha Omega Alpha. Home: 56 Ruxton Rd Great Neck NY 11023-1529 Office: 550 1st Ave New York NY 10016-6402 Office Phone: 212-683-1560. Personal E-mail: azitrin@aol.com.

ZITTEL-PALAMARA, KIMBERLEY, social worker, educator; married. BA, Houghton Coll., NY, 1992; MSW, SUNY, Buffalo, 1994, PhD, 2003. In home health care aid, NY, 1992; cert. social worker Dept. Edn., NY, 1994, NJ., 1995, NASW, 1996, lic. State Edn. Dept., NJ, 1997, masters social work 2004, cert. trauma and grief intervention trainer SUNY, Sch. Social Work, 1998, critical incident trauma trainer 1998, Nat. Bd. Cognitive Behavioral Therapist, 1998. Clin. asst. prof. SUNY, Sch. Dental Medicine, 2001—05, dir., 2001—05; asst. prof. Buffalo State Coll., 2005—. Bd. mem. Postpartum Resource Ctr. NY State, West Islip, 2007—. Contbr. articles to profl. jours. County com. mem. Dem. Party, Buffalo, 2004—08; ch. sch. bd. mem. St. Paul's Episcopal Cathedral, Buffalo, 2005—07; women's mentor Chapel Crosspoint, Amherst, NY, 2007—08; bd. dir. Postpartum Resource Ctr. NY, West Islip, 2007; chair Am. Dental Edn. Assn. Behavioral Sci. Sect., Washington, 2007—08; expert blogger WGRZ Channel 2 News, Buffalo, 2007—08. Recipient Geriat. Access Care award, 2005; named Social Worker of Yr., NASW, 2007; Treatment Fund grant, Nat. Found. Ectodermal Dysplasias, 2004, Access Oral Health Care grant, NIH, 2004—05, Postpartum Depression Care grant, Buffalo State Coll. Rsch. Found., 2006, Postpartum Depression Tng. grant, Ctrs. Devel. Human Svcs., 2007, Educating Child Protective Workers grant, 2008, Rsch. grant, 2008—. Mem.: Kappa Omega Chpt., Phi Alpha Honor Soc. (faculty advisor 2005). Office: Buffalo State Coll 1300 Elmwood Ave Buffalo NY 14222 Business E-Mail: zittelkm@buffalostate.edu.

ZITTRAIN, JONATHAN L., law educator; b. Pitts., Dec. 24, 1969; s. Lester and Ruth Zittrain. BS, Yale U., 1991; JD, Harvard U., 1995, MPA, 1995. Bar: Pa. 1995, DC 1996, US Ct. Appeals (DC cir.) 1996. Chief forum adminstr. Compuserve Info. Svc., 1984—86; editl. columnist Computer Shopper, 1986-90; program mgr. Microsoft Corp., Redmond, Wash., 1990; with US Dept. State, DC, 1991; staff US Senate Select Com. on Intelligence, DC, 1992, 94; law clk. US Ct. Appeals, DC, 1995; exec. dir., co-founder Berkman Ctr. for Internet & Society, Harvard Law Sch., Cambridge, Mass., 1997—2000, faculty co-dir., 2000—; lectr. law Harvard Law Sch., Cambridge, Mass., 1997—99, asst. prof., 2000—, Jack N. and Lillian R. Berkman asst. prof. for entrepreneurial legal studies, 2001—; prof., chair internet governance & regulation, dir. grad. studies, Oxford Internet Inst. Oxford U., 2005—. Author: The Future of the Internet - And How to Stop It, 2008; co-editor: Access Denied: The Practice and Policy of Global Internet Filtering, 2008; contbr. articles to profl. jours., chapters to books. Achievements include patents for state adaptation devices and methods for wireless devices; a system for facilitating communications over a network amoung participants and a moderator. Office: Berkman Ctr for Internet & Society Harvard Law Sch Baker House 1587 Massachusetts Ave Cambridge MA 02138 Business E-Mail: zittrain@law.harvard.edu.

ZITZER-COMFORT, CAROL, literature and language professor; children: Heidi Comfort, Joshua Comfort, Jacob Williams-Zitzer. PhD, Claremont Grad. U., Calif., 2003. Dir., student support svc. program Calif. State U. Poly., Pomona, 1993—2003; asst. prof. English CSU Long Beach, 2003—. Co-editor: (anthology) Through the Eye of the Deer. Co-chair 2008 internat. conv. Williams Syndrome Assn., Deerborn, Mich., 2007—08. Office: Calif State Univ Long Beach 1250 N Bellflower Blvd Long Beach CA 92831 Business E-Mail: ccomfort@csulb.edu.

ZIV, JONATHAN, cosmetic dentist; m. Jayne Ziv; children: Zak, Piper. BS in Biol. Scis., U. Calif., Irvine; grad., Las Vegas Inst. Advanced Dental Studies. Cert. in laser dentistry Esthetic Profl. Edn. Facility. Founder, dentist Ziv Studio for Smile Design, Agoura Hills, Calif. Spkr. in field. Pres. Habitat for Hollywood Beach; active Thousand Oaks/Westlake Village Regional C. of C., bd. dirs., Channel Islands Beach Cmty. Svcs. Dist., 2004—. Fellowship, Internat. Acad. Dental-Facial Esthetics. Mem.: ADA, Internat. Congress Oral Implantologists, Internat. Coll. Cranio-Mandibular Orthops., Acad. Gen. Dentistry, Calif. Dental Assn., American Acad. Cosmetic Dentistry. Office: Ziv Studio for Smile Design 5353 Reyes Adobe Rd Ste B Agoura Hills CA 91301 Office Phone: 818-991-0263, 800-576-4537.

ZIVIN, KARA, psychiatry professor, researcher; d. Justin Allen and Reni-Zoe Zivin. BA, Johns Hopkins U., Balt., 1997; MA, Johns Hopkins Sch. Advanced Internat. Studies, Washington, 1998; MS, Harvard Sch. Pub. Health, Boston, 2002; PhD, Harvard U., Cambridge, Mass., 2004. Post-doc. fellow Harvard Med. Sch., 2004—06; asst. prof. U. Mich. Med. Sch., Ann Arbor, 2006—; rsch. investigator Dept. Veterans Affairs, 2006—; treas. Health Policy Stats. Sect., Am. Statis. Assn., 2008—. Recipient New Investigator Poster award, NIMH, 2007; Pharm. Policy fellowship, Harvard Med. Sch., 2004—05, Thomas O. Pyle fellowship, 2005—06. Mem.: Am. Assn. Geriatric Psychiatry, Academy Health, Pi Sigma Alpha, Golden Key Nat. Honors Soc. Office: Univ Michigan Med Sch 4250 Plymouth Rd Box 5765 Ann Arbor MI 48109 Office Fax: 734-615-8739.

ZLATEVA, GERGANA P., pharmaceutical executive, director; b. Varna, Bulgaria, Sept. 1971; d. Peter L. Zlatev and Valentina G. Zlateva; m. Philippe H. Elghouayel; children: Arthur Eric Elghouayel, Paul Anrie Elghouayel. BA, Southern Ill. U., Carbondale, 1994, MPA, 1996; PhD, Fordham U., NYC, 2004. Programme mgr. UN Devel. Programme, NYC, 1996—97, Moscow, 1998, UNESCO, Moscow, 1999—2000; mgr., worldwide outcomes rsch. Pfizer, NYC, 2004—06, assoc. dir., outcomes rsch., 2006—07, dir., team leader, global outcomes rsch., 2007—. Cons. Interexperts Inc., NYC, 1997—. Contbr. articles to numerous profl. jours. (Best Practice award, Internat. Collaboration, ARVO, 2006, Editor's Choice Symposium, 2008), scientific papers. Class rep., Parents Assn. Browning Sch., NYC, 2007—. Recipient Best Poster award, European Congress ISPOR, Dublin, 2007, Lyrica Team award, Pfizer Global Med. and Global R & D, 2008; Tng. grant, US Agy. Internat. Devel., 1999—2000. Fellow: Winston Found. World Peace, Am. Acad. Ophthalmology; mem.: Internat. Health Economics Assn., Internat. Soc. Pharmacoepidemiology, Internat. Soc. Pharmacoeconomics and Outcomes Rsch. Achievements include establishing 1st Center for Social Partnership, Moscow; establishing 1st Center for Women Management, Komi Republic, Russia. Office: Pfizer Inc 235 E 42nd St New York NY 10017 Personal E-mail: gapp@nyc.rr.com. Business E-Mail: gergana.zlateva@pfizer.com.

ZLATKUS, LIZABETH H., insurance company executive; b. 1959; BS with distinction, Pa. State U. With Peat Marwick Mitchell & Co.; property, casualty ops. acctg. The Hartford Fin. Svcs. Grp., Inc., Conn., 1983, dir. disability grp., life bus., 1996—97, sr. v.p., 1997—99, head grp. benefits divsn., 1999—2000, exec. v.p. life ops., 2000, CFO life ops., 2003—06, co-COO life ops., pres internat. wealth mgmt. & grp. benefits, 2006—08, exec. v.p., CFO, 2008—. Bd. dirs. Hartford Action Plan on Infant Health; bd. advisors HP Fin. Svcs.; bd. visitors Pa. State U.; mem. Pres. Com. on Employment of People with Disabilities, 1999—; bd. dirs. LOMA, 2005—. Named one of Top 100 Women to Watch, Bus. Ins. mag., 2000, 2006, 8 Remarkable Women, Hartford Bus. Jour., 2008. Office: Hartford Fin Svcs Grp Inc One Hartford Plaza 690 Asylum Ave Hartford CT 06115 Office Phone: 860-547-5000. Office Fax: 860-547-2680. Business E-Mail: lizabeth.zlatkus@thehartford.com.

ZLATOFF-MIRSKY, EVERETT IGOR, violinist; b. Evanston, Ill., Dec. 29, 1937; s. Alexander Igor and Evelyn Ola (Hill) Z.-M.; m. Janet Dalbey, Jan. 28, 1976; children from previous marriage— Tania, Laura. B.Mus., Chgo. Mus. Coll., Roosevelt U., 1960, M.Mus., 1961. Mem. faculty dept. music Roosevelt U., Chgo., 1961-66. Founding mem., violinist, violist Music of the Baroque, 1971-2003. Violinist orch. Lyric Opera of Chgo., 1974-2003; concert master, pers. mgr., 1974-2003, violinist, violist, Contemporary Chamber Players U. Chog., 1964-82, solo violinist, Bach Soc., 1966-83; violist, violinist, Lexington String Quartet, 1966-81; rec. artist numerous recs., radio-TV and films; solo violinist appearing throughout U.S. Recipient Olive Ditson award Franklin Honor Soc., 1961 Mem. Nat. Acad. Rec. Arts and Scis. Republican. Roman Catholic. Home: 1600 Old Pecos Trail Santa Fe NM 87505 E-mail: jdzm@aol.com.

ZLOTCHEW, CLARK MICHAEL, Spanish educator; b. Jersey City, Oct. 14, 1932; s. Harry and Francine (Granoff) Z.; m. Marilyn Barbara Kocin, Dec. 26, 1965; children: Philip, Ethan, David. BS, NYU, 1957; MA, Middlebury Coll., 1966; PhD, SUNY, BInghamton, 1974. Asst. prof. Norwich U., 1966-68; instr. Spanish SUNY, Geneseo, 1970-74, asst. prof. Fredonia, 1975-78, assoc. prof., 1978-82, prof., 1982—2008, disting. tchg. prof., 2008—; project coord. program for Hispanic seasonal workers Bd. Cooperative Ednl. Svcs., Batavia, N.Y., 1974-75. Author: Estilo literario, Análisis y creacion, 1993, Libido into Literature: The "Primera Epoca" of Benito Perez Galdos, 1993, Voices of the River Plate: Interviews with Argentine and Uruguayan Writers, 1995, Alpha Teach Yourself Spanish in 24 Hours, 2000, 2nd edit., 2004, (as Cliff Garnett) Talon Force: Dire Straits, 2001, Spanish at Your Fingertips, 2007, Varieties of Magic Realism, 2007, Once Upon A Decades: TAles of Fifties, 2009; translator: Seven Conversations with Jorge Luis Borges, 1982, Falling Through the Cracks: Stories of Julio Ricci, 1989; (with others) Light and Shadows: Selected Poems of Juan Ramon Jimenez, 1987, The House At Isla Negra, 1988, The House in the Sand: Prose Poems by Pablo Neruda, 1990, 2004, Neruda At Isla Negra: Prose Poems by Pablo Neruda, 2001; contbr. articles to jours. Recipient SUNY Pres.'s award, 1988, Kasling Lectr. award, 1992. Mem. MLA, Am. Assn. Tchrs. Spanish and Portuguese, N.E. MLA, Academia Portena del Lunfardo (corr.), Inst. Internat. de Lit. y Cultura Hispanica, N.Y. State Coun. on Linguistics (sec. 1979), No. Chautauqua Torch Club (pres. 1990-91). Avocations: guitar, classical music, writing short stories. Home: 18 Westerly Dr Fredonia NY 14063-1606 Office: Suny Fredonia NY 14063 Business E-Mail: zlotchew@fredonia.edu.

ZLOTNICK, NORMAN LEE, lawyer; b. Bklyn., Nov. 2, 1947; s. Harry S. and Frances Zlotnick; m. JoAnn L. Zlotnick, Nov. 26, 1976; m. Sharon Harris, Mar. 12, 2000. BA in History, CCNY, 1969; JD, Rutgers U., 1972. Bar: N.J. 1972, U.S. Dist. Ct. N.J. 1972, U.S. Ct. Appeals (3d cir.) 1974, U.S. Supreme Ct. 1976, N.Y. 1990. Assoc. Perskie & Callinan, 1972-77; ptnr. Perskie, Bloom & Zlotnick, P.A., 1977-79, Bloom & Zlotnick, 1979-82, Biel, Zlotnick & Feinberg, P.A., Atlantic City, 1982—. Contbr. Rutgers-Camden Law Jour. Mem. ABA, ATLA, N.J. Bar Assn., N.Y. Bar Assn., Cape May County Bar Assn., Atlantic County Bar Assn. (N.J. Supreme Ct. spl. ethics master, Atlantic County civil case arbitrator, cert. civil trial atty.). Address: 20 Devon Dr Egg Harbor Township NJ 08234-7569 Office: 450 Tilton Rd Ste 120 Northfield NJ 08225 Office Phone: 609-344-1173. Business E-Mail: normanzlotnick@mbzflaw.com.

ZLOTOWSKI, MARTIN, psychologist; b. Lodz, Poland, Aug. 10, 1934; s. Pawel and Helen Zlotowski; m. Judith Ann Lifschitz, May 17, 1974; children: David, Steven, Laura. BA, NYU, 1955; MA, Mich. State U., 1958, PhD, 1960. Rsch. assoc. Grad. Sch. Pub. Health U. Pitts., 1960-61; rsch. assoc., lectr. Boston U., 1961-62; staff psychologist VA Hosp., Coatesville, Pa., 1962-65, unit chief, 1965-73; clin. dir. St. Mary Providence, 1966-70; assoc. prof. spl. edn. West Chester (Pa.) U., 1973—2003. Grad. coord., 1987-2000; dir. Counseling Assocs., Paoli, Pa., 1973-85, exec. dir., 1985—. Pres. Chester County Family Acad., 1999-2002, bd. trustees 2002-04; v.p. Victim Witness Svcs. Chester County, 1976-77. Fellow: Phila. Psychol. Assn., Phila. Soc. Clin. Psychologists (pres. 1978—79, sec. human svcs. ctr. 1982), Am. Orthopyschiat. Assn. (life); mem.: APA, Pa. Fedn. Coun. Exceptional Children (pres. Pa. divsn. behavior disorders 2000—04). Democrat. Jewish. Home: 241 Torrey Pine Ct West Chester PA 19380 Office Phone: 610-647-8270. Personal E-mail: martinzlot@comcast.net.

ZLOTY, PETER, ophthalmologist; b. Apr. 16, 1960; BS, Rensselaer Polytechnic Inst., Troy, NY, 1980; MD, Albany Med. Coll., Union Univ., 1984. Cert. Ophthalmology 1993. Intern, categorical diversified medicine Albany Med. Ctr. Hosp., resident, ophthalmology; fellowship in corneal and external disease Albany Med. Coll., NY, 1991; ophthalmologist Southeast Eye Clinic, Dothan, Ala.; dir., cornea and external disease and anterior segment surgery, Eye Ctr. South, Dothan. Spkr. in field. Published (articles concerning advances in glaucoma therapy, pterygium surgery, and infectious diseases of the eye), featured on Miracle Workers (ABC), 2006. Active mem. Mt. Gilead Baptist Ch. and enjoys participating in mission trips. Emergency room physician USN, 1985—88, Newport Naval Hosp. Fellow: Am. Acad. Ophthalmology; mem.: Am. Soc. Cataract and Refractive Surgeons, Sigma Xi Rsch. Soc. (assoc.). Office: Southeast Eye Clinic 102 Doctors Dr Dothan AL 36301-2911 also: Eye Ctr South 103 Creek Ridge Rd Dothan AL 36301 Office Phone: 334-794-1968. Business E-Mail: DrZolty@SoutheastEyeClinic.com.*

ZLOWODZKI, MICHAL PAWEL, surgeon, researcher; MD, U. Hamburg, Germany, 1999; PhD, Humboldt U., Berlin, 2001. Rsch. assoc. U. Miss., Jackson, 2001—02, Vanderbilt U., Nashville, 2002—03; rsch. mgr. Regions Hosp., St. Paul, 2003—04; rsch. fellow McMaster U., Hamilton, Ontario, Canada, 2004—05, 2006—07; surg. intern U. Minn., Mpls., 2005—06, orthopaedic surgery resident, 2007—. Cons. clin. study design Stryker GmBH, Kiel, Germany, 2007; editl. bd. mem. Jou. orthop. Trauma & Advance in Theory. Contbr. articles to profl. jours. Recipient Jacques Dupart Poster award, European Fedn. Nat. Assns. Orthopaedics, 2007, award for 1 of 10 best presentations, Orthop. Trauma Assn., 2007. Mem.: German Trauma Surgery Assn., European Soc. Biomechanics, European Rsch. Soc., Am. Soc. Biomechanics, Internat. Soc. Fracture Repair, Orthopadic Trauma Assn. Roman Catholic. Achievements include patents pending for bone plating system for hip fractures. Avocations: table tennis, weight lifting, triathons, music. Office: Univ Minn Dept Orthop Surgery 2450 Riverside Ave S Ste R200 Minneapolis MN 55403

ZOBEL, RYA WEICKERT, federal judge; b. Germany, Dec. 18, 1931; AB, Radcliffe Coll., 1953; LLB, Harvard U., 1956. Bar: Mass. 1956, U.S. Dist. Ct. Mass., 1956, U.S. Ct. Appeals (1st cir.) 1967. Assoc. Hill & Barlow, Boston, 1967-73, Goodwin, Procter & Hoar, Boston, 1973-76, ptnr., 1976-79; judge U.S. Dist. Ct. Mass., Boston, 1979—; dir. Fed. Jud. Ctr., Washington, 1995-99. Mem. Boston Bar Assn., Am. Bar Found., Mass. Bar Assn., Am. Law Inst. Office: US District Ct 1 Courthouse Way Boston MA 02210-3002

ZOBELL, KARL, lawyer; b. La Jolla, Calif., Jan. 9, 1932; s. Claude E. and Margaret (Harding) ZoB.; m. Barbara Arth, Nov. 22, 1968; children: Bonnie, Elizabeth, Karen, Claude, Mary. Student, Utah State U., 1949-51, Columbia U., 1951-52, AB, 1953, student of law, 1952-54; JD, Stanford U., 1958. Bar: Calif. 1959. Assoc., lawyer DLA Piper US LLP, Gray Cary Ware & Freidenrich and formerly Gray, Cary, Ames and Frye, San Diego, 1959-64, ptnr., lawyer, 1964—, chmn., 1989-90. Bd. dirs., founder La Jolla (Calif.) Bank and Trust Co.; v.p. bd. dirs. Geisel-Seuss Enterprises, Inc. Trustee La Jolla Town Coun., 1962-87, chmn. bd. trustees, 1967-68, pres. 1976-77, 80-81, v.p., 1986-87; trustee La Jollans Inc., 1964-80, founder, 1964, pres. 1965-68, 73-76, 78-79, Dr. Seuss Found., 1992—; mem. charter rev. com. City San Diego, 1968, 73; chmn. City of San Diego Planning Commn., 1988-93; trustee La Jolla Mus. Art, 1964-72, San Diego Mus. Contemporary Art, 1990-92; pres. 1967-70, bd. dirs Scripps Meml. Hosp. Found., 1980-84, bd. overseers, Stanford Law Sch., 1977-80, U. Calif., San Diego, 1974-76. Served to lt. USCG, 1954-57. Fellow Am. Coll. Trust and Estate Counsel; mem. ABA, Calif. Bar, La Jolla Beach and Volleyball Club (pres. 1982-90), La Jolla Beach and Tennis Club, Lambda Alpha. Republican. Home: Po Box 1 7585 Country Club Dr La Jolla CA 92037-3731 Office: DLA Piper US LLP 1200 Prospect St Ste 575 La Jolla CA 92037-3645 Office Phone: 858-638-6800. Business E-Mail: karl.zobell@dlapiper.com.

ZODY, JOHN C., legislative staff member; BS in Pub. Affairs, Ind. U., Bloomington, 1999. Prog. mgr. Ind. Dept. Commerce, 1999—2001; dep. dir. comm./planning Office of Govs. Frank O'Bannon & Joe Kernan, Ind., 2001—04; prog. mgr., dir. civic engagement Ivy Tech. Cmty. Coll., Bloomington, 2004—07; dist. dir, to congressman Baron Hill US House of Reps., 2007—09, chief of staff, 2009—. 8th Dist. regional field dir. Ind. Dem. Party, 2000. Democrat. Mailing: US House Reps 223 Cannon HOB Washington DC 20515 Office Phone: 202-225-5315. Office Fax: 202-225-6866.*

ZOE, RACHEL (RACHEL ZOE ROSENZWEIG), fashion stylist; b. NYC, Sept. 1, 1971; m. Rodger Berman. Grad., George Washington U., 1993. With YM Mag.; fashion stylist for various celebrities including Cameron Diaz, Kate Beckinsale, Jennifer Garner, Paris Hilton, Keira Knightley; fashion stylist to Nicole Richie, 2004—06. TV appearances The Simple Life, 2006, Project Runway, 2006; exec. prodr.: (TV series) The Rachel Zoe Project, 2008—.

ZOELLER, DAVID LOUIS, lawyer, bank executive; b. Indpls., Nov. 26, 1949; s. John Louis and M. Maxine (Snoderly) Z.; m. Wesley Anne Carlton, Aug. 14, 1971; children: Laura Anne, David Carlton. BA, So. Meth. U., Dallas, 1971; JD, Ind. U., 1974. Bar: Ind. 1974, US Dist. Ct. (so. dist. Ind.) 1974. Asst. sec., legal counsel Stokely-Van Camp Inc., 1974-83; legal mgmt. positions through exec. v.p., sec., gen. counsel Nat. City Corp., Cleve., 1983—. Mem. ABA, Ind. Bar Assn., Indpls. Bar Assn., Ohio Bar Assn., Cleve. Bar Assn., Am. Soc. Corp. Secs., Lawyers Coun. Fin. Svcs. Roundtable. Republican. Presbyterian. Office: Nat City Corp Nat City Ctr 1900 E 9th St Cleveland OH 44114-3484 Office Phone: 216-222-2000.

ZOELLER, DONALD J., lawyer; b. Queens Village, NY, Mar. 18, 1930; s. Henry Adolph and Marion Elizabeth (Brodie) Z.; m. Susan Josephine Campisi, Sept. 3, 1955; children— Paul Joseph, Jean Marie, Diane Marie AB, Fordham Coll., 1951; LL.B., Fordham Sch. Law, NYC, 1958. Bar: N.Y. 1959, D.C. 1967. Law clk. to judge U.S. Dist. Ct. (so. dist.) N.Y., NYC, 1958-59; assoc. Mudge Rose Guthrie Alexander & Ferdon, NYC, 1959-68, ptnr., 1968-95, exec. ptnr., 1991-95, chmn. exec. com., 1995; counsel Carter, Ledyard & Milburn, NYC, 1995-96, ptnr., 1997-98, of counsel, 1999—2003, ret., 2003. Adj. prof. law Fordham U. Law Sch., 1989—; lectr. in field. Contbr. articles to legal publs. Trustee Oyster Bay-East Norwich Bd. Edn., 2007—; v.p. Oyster Bay-East Norwich Sch. Bd. Edn.; 1st vice comdr. Korean War Veterans Assn., Nassau County Chpt.; mem. Am. Hegemony. 1st lt. US Army, 1951—53, Korea. Mem.: Bar Assn. City of NY. Republican. Roman Catholic. Avocations: skiing, swimming, tennis, reading. Office Phone: 516-922-7205. Business E-Mail: dzoeller@optonline.net. *Notable cases include: Matsushita Electric Indsl. Co. Ltd. et al vs. Zenith Radio Corp. et al, 475 U.S. 574, 89 L. edit. 2d 538, 106, s.ct. 1438.*

ZOELLER, GREG, state attorney general; m. Kerrie Turner; children: Gretchen, Katherine, Michael. JD, Ind. U., Bloomington, 1982. Bar: Ind., DC. Spl. asst. to US atty. gen. US Dept. Justice, 1988; legis. and exec. aide to Senator Dan Quayle, 1982; asst. to v.p. The White House, 1989—91; sr. counsel to Com. of Govt. Reform and Oversight US House of Reps., 1998; pres., dir. World Trade Ctr. of Ind., 1999; chief dep. to atty. gen., chief litig. divsn. and adv. svcs. State of Ind., 2001—09, atty. gen., 2009—. V.p. Ind. Coun. of World Affairs in 1992 US Del. to NATO, Brussels, 1992; adj. faculty mem. polit. sci. dept. Indiana U.-Purdue U. at Indpls. Former delegate Rep. Nat. Convention. Recipient Sagamore of the Wabash, 1988. Republican. Office: Office of Ind Atty Gen Ind Govt Ctr S 302 W Washington St Indianapolis IN 46204 Office Phone: 317-232-6201. Office Fax: 317-232-7979.*

ZOELLER, JACK CARL, diversified financial services company executive; b. Buffalo, Feb. 26, 1949; s. Ronald Carl and Margaret Lillian (Wademan) Z.; m. Kathryn Louise Helmke, Apr. 25, 1981; children: Andrew, Alexander, Charles (dec.). BS, U.S. Mil. Acad., 1970; M of Pub. Policy, Harvard U., 1972; M of Letters, Oxford U., Eng., 1974. Program budget officer Army Chief of Staff's Office, Pentagon, Washington, 1978-80; v.p. E.F. Hutton & Co., Inc., NYC, 1982; pres. E.F. Hutton Indemnity Group, NYC, 1983-85, Capital Risk Mgmt., Iselin, NJ, 1985-87; exec. v.p., bd. dirs. Comfed Mortgage Co., Lowell, Mass., 1987-88, pres., 1988-91, ComFed Savs. Bank, Lowell, 1990-91; chmn. chief exec. officer ComFed Bancorp., Cambridge, Mass., 1990-95; pres. The Zoeller Group, Washington, 1993-95. Bd. dirs. N.Am. Health Plans, Inc., Amherst, NY, 1995—99; pres. AtlantiCare Risk Mgmt. Corp., 1995—2004; chmn., CEO AtlantiCare, Inc., 1995—2004; pres. N.Am. Health & Life Ins., Barbados, 1996—2006; vis. rsch. prof. George Washington U., 2005—; pres., CEO Cordia Bancorp Inc, Washington, 2009—. Mem. exec. com. Lowell Devel. and Fin. Corp., 1989-91, class gift com. U.S. Mil. Acad., 1990-95; youth sports coach, 1990-96; Am. chmn. 750th Ann. Campaign Univ. Coll., Oxford, Eng., 1998-2002; parent group leader Maret Sch., Washington, 1998-2003; bd. dirs. Transcommunity FinCorp., Va., 2006-. Served to capt. US Army, 1970—80. Decorated Meritorious Svc. medals; Rhodes scholar, Oxford U., 1972. Mem. West Point Soc. N.Y. (bd. govs. 1985-87), West Point Soc. D.C., Am. Friends Univ Coll. Oxford, Inc. (v.p. 1999—), Fed. Nat. Mortgage Assn. (N.E. regional adv. bd. 1990-91), Assn. Am. Rhodes Scholars (bd. dirs. 2004—, treas. 2006-09), New Eng. Hist. Geneal. Soc., Soc. Mayflower Descs. Home and Office: 2810 31st St NW Washington DC 20008-3523 Home Phone: 202-342-5553. Personal E-mail: jackzoeller@yahoo.com.

ZOELLICK, ROBERT BRUCE, President of the World Bank, former federal agency administrator; b. Evergreen Park, Ill., July 25, 1953; s. William T. and Gladys Zoellick; m. Sherry Lynn Ferguson, June 28, 1980. BA with honors, Swarthmore Coll., 1975; M in Pub. Policy, Harvard U., 1981, JD magna cum laude, 1981; LittD (hon.), St. Joseph's Coll., 2002. Law clk. to Hon. Patricia M. Wald, US Ct. Appeals (DC Cir.), Washington, 1982-83; v.p., asst. to chmn. & CEO Fannie Mae, Washington, 1983-85; from dep. asst. sec. for fin. instns. policy, to counselor to sec. & exec. sec. US Dept. Treasury, Washington, 1985-88; counselor with rank under sec. US Dept. State, Washington, 1989-92, under sec. for econ. & agrl. affairs, 1991-92; dep. chief of staff, asst. to Pres. The White House, Washington, 1992-93; exec. v.p. housing & law Fannie Mae, Washington, 1993-97; Olin prof. nat. security US Naval Acad., Annapolis, Md., 1997-98; rsch. scholar Belfer Ctr. Sci. and Internat. Affairs Harvard U., Cambridge, Mass., 1999—2001; U.S. Trade Rep. Exec. Office of the Pres., Washington, 2001—05; dep. sec. US Dept. State, Washington, 2005—06; vice chmn. internat. The Goldman Sachs Group, Inc., NYC, 2006—07; pres. The World Bank Group, Washington, 2007—. Decorated Knight Comdr.'s Cross (for work on German unification, Germany); recipient Alexander Hamilton award US Treasury Dept., 1988, Disting. Svc. award US State Dept, 1992, Disting. Pub. Svc. medal Dept. Def., 2006-07. Mem. Phi Beta Kappa. Office: The World Bank Group 1818 H St NW Washington DC 20433 Office Phone: 202-458-2500.

ZOFFER, H. JEROME, business educator, dean; b. Pitts., July 23, 1930; s. William and Sarah Leah (Fisher) Z.; m. Maye Rattner, July 19, 1959; children: Gayle Risa, William Michael. BBA, U. Pitts., 1952, MA, 1953, PhD, 1956; CPCU, Am. Inst., Phila., 1954. Sales and mgmt. cons., 1952—60; instr. Sch. Bus. Adminstrn., U. Pitts., 1953—56; asst. prof. Sch. Bus. Adminstrn. U. Pitts., 1956—59, assoc. prof. Joseph M. Katz Grad. Sch. Bus., 1959—66, prof. Sch. Bus. Adminstrn., Grad. Sch. Bus., 1966—, chmn. dept. real estate and ins., 1958—60, dir. spl. studies, 1960—62, asst. dean acad. affairs, 1962—65, assoc. dean for adminstrn., 1965—68, dean Grad. Sch. Bus., 1968—96, dean emeritus, 1996—. Ford Found. fellow in applied math. U. Pa., Phila., 1961—62; mem. visitation com. Am. Assembly Collegiate Schs. of Bus., 1972—2000, mem. stds. com., 1974—78, mem. exec. com., 1975—87, chmn. accreditation rsch. com., 1974—84, v.p. bd. dirs., 1984—85, pres., 1985—86, chmn. Mid. State Evaluation Accrediting Teams, 1967—85. Author: The History of Automobile Liability Insurance Rating: 1900-1958, 1959; also monographs.; contbr. articles to profl. jours. Bd. dirs., v.p. Leadership Inst. for Community Devel., 1968-73, Allegheny chpt. Epilepsy Found. Am., 1971-77; bd. dirs. Pitts. Dist. Export Coun., 1974-77, Sch. Advanced Jewish Studies, 1976-79, Czech Mgmt. Ctr., 1989-2005, Travelers Aid Soc., Pitts., 2006-, Emerald Growth Fund, 1992-2006, Y2K Fund, 1995-2000, Emerald Bank Fund, 1998-2000, Emerald Tech. Fund, 2000-06, Oliver Realty Co., 1981-86, Penwood Saving and Loan Assoc., 1991-2000, Enterprise Corp., 1993-96, Eckstein Co., 1969-82, Penn Traffic Co., 1975-87, Red Bull Inns America, 1975-82; bd. govs. Internat. Ins. Seminars, Inc., 1968-77; pres. Temple Sinai Congregation, 1979-81; mem. festival bd. Three Rivers Art Festival, 1988-93; mem. steering com. Leadership Pitts., 1986-91; sec. Am. Jewish Com., 1993-95; bd. dirs. Student Cons. Project, U. Pitts., 1970-96, Consortium for Coop. and Competitiveness, 1986-96, Moral Force in the Workplace, 1986-96; investment com. United Jewish Fedn., 1992-95; sec.treas., bd. dirs. David Berg Found., 1995-. Named Man of Yr. in Edn., Vectors Pitts., 1986, Disting. Alumnus, 1989, U. Pitts.

Alumni Assn. Mem. Soc. Psychol. Study Social Issues, Mid. Atlantic Assn. Colls. Bus. Adminstrn. (pres. 1972-73), Am. Assn. Univ. Adminstrs. (exec. com. 1971-79, pres. 1975-77, dir. 1980-83, pres. found. 1983-95), Univ. Club (bd. dirs. 1988-94, sec. 1990-91, v.p. 1991-92, pres. 1992-93), Omicron Delta Gamma, Beta Gamma Sigma (pres. Beta chpt. 1964-68). Home: 220 N Bellefield Ave Ph 1201 Pittsburgh PA 15213-1468 Office: U Pitts Pitts Campus Katz Grad Sch Bus Pittsburgh PA 15260 Business E-Mail: zoffer@katz.pitt.edu.

ZOFKA, ADAM, civil engineer, educator; PhD, U. Minn., Twin Cities, 2007. Rsch. asst., dept. civil engring., U. Minn., 2002—07; asst. prof., dept. civil environ. engring. U. Conn., Storrs, 2007—. Office: Univ Conn 261 Glenbrook Rd Unit 2037 Storrs Mansfield CT 06269-2037 Office Fax: 860-486-2298. Business E-Mail: azofka@engr.uconn.edu.

ZOGBY, WILLIAM JOSEPH, history professor, management consultant; b. Utica, NY, Feb. 21, 1947; s. Joseph Reagan and Josephine Wasil Zogby; m. Janet Rushing Rushing, Feb. 9, 1980; children: Matthew Reagan, Elizabeth Rushing, William Tyler, Nathaniel Joseph. BA, U. Scranton, Pa., 1969; MA, Northeastern U., Boston, 1971; MBA, Syracuse U., NY, 1974. Prof. history Mohawk Valley C.C., Utica, 1989—. Bus. cons. Self-employed, New Hartford, NY, 1987—. Office: Mohawk Valley CC 1101 Sherman Dr Utica NY 13501 Business E-Mail: wzogby@mvcc.edu.

ZOGHBI, WILLIAM ANTOINE, cardiologist, educator; b. Beirut, Oct. 28, 1955; arrived in US, 1977; m. Huda El Hibri, Sept. 17, 1983; children: Roula Maya, Anthony William. BS, Am. U., Beirut, 1975; postgrad., Am. U., 1975-77; MD, Meharry Med. Coll., 1979. Diplomate Internal Medicine 1982, Cardiovascular Diseases Am. Bd. Internal Medicine, 1985. Intern, internal med. U. Tex. Med. Br. Hosps., Galveston, 1979-80; resident, cardiology Baylor Coll. Affiliated Hosps., Houston, 1980-82; fellow, electrocardiogram Baylor Coll. Medicine, Houston, 1982-85, instr., asst. prof., 1985-91, assoc. prof., 1991-98, prof. medicine, 1998—, dir., echocardiography rsch.; assoc. dir., echocardiography lab. Methodist DeBakey Heart Ctr., Tex., dir., Cardiovascular Imaging Inst. Tex.; William Williams Chair in Cardiovascular Imaging Methodist Hosp., Tex. Dir. medicine Meth Hosp., Houston, 1990—. Contbr. articles to profl. jours.; reviewer (of sci. jours.). Fellow: Coun. on Clin. Cardiology, Am. Coll. Cardiology (chmn. scientific sessions 2000, bd. trustee (five-year) 2002—07, bd. trustee 2008—09, treas.); mem.: Harris County Med. Soc., Tex. Med. Assn., Am. Heart Assn. (prog. com. 1991—94), Am. Soc. Echocardiography (v.p. 2006—07, pres.-elect 2007—08, pres. 2008—, bd. dirs.), Alpha Omega Alpha. Home: 6618 Sewanee St Houston TX 77005-3750 Office: Methodist Hosp 6550 Fannin St SM 677 Houston TX 77030-2717 also: Methodist Hosp 6550 Fannin Ste 1901 Smith Tower Houston TX 77030 Office Phone: 713-441-1100.

ZOGHI, MANOOCHEHR, civil engineering educator; b. Tehran, Iran, July 23, 1956; came to U.S., 1975; s. Farokh A. and Mahlegha Zoghi; m. Afsaneh Khorramshi-Bayat, Dec. 16, 1991; children: Shayan, Shervin. BS, U. Louisville, 1979, MEngring, 1981; PhD, U. Cin., 1988. Teaching asst. U. Louisville, 1979-80; teaching/rsch. asst. U. Cin., 1980-83; rsch./project engr. Lockwood Jones & Beals, Dayton, Ohio, 1983-86; asst. prof. U. Dayton, 1986-91, assoc. prof., 1991—. Mem. exec. com. Ohio Infrastructure Inst., 1987—, interim dir., 1995—; organizing com. Ohio River Valley Seminar, Ohio-Ky., 1991— Contbr. articles to profl. jours., chpts. to books. U. Dayton teaching fellow, 1988, Fund for Ednl. Devel. fellow, 1991, Earthquake Rsch. fellow, 1994. Mem. ASCE (chmn. geotech. com. 1987-96, v.p. Dayton sect. 1994-95, treas. 1992-94, pres. 1996-97), Am. Soc. Engring. Edn., Prestressed/Precast Concrete Inst. Achievements include development of Con/span bridges. Office: Univ of Dayton 300 College Park Ave Dayton OH 45469-0001 Home: 600 Schenck Ave Dayton OH 45419-3823

ZOHN, MARTIN STEVEN, lawyer; b. Denver, Oct. 22, 1947; s. William and Alice Zohn; m. Carol Falender, June 6, 1980; children: David Joseph, Daniel Robert. BA, Ind. U., 1969; JD, Harvard U., 1972. Bar: Calif. 1972, Ind. 1973, US Ct. Claims 1980, US Supreme Ct. 1980, US Ct. Appeals (9th cir.) 1981. Assoc. Cadick, Burns, Duck & Neighbors, Indpls., 1972-77, ptnr., 1977-80, Pacht, Ross, Warne, Bernhard & Sears, Inc., LA, 1980-86, Shea & Gould, LA, 1986-89, Proskauer Rose LLP, LA, 1989—. Adj. prof. U. SC Law Sch.; pres. Indpls. Settlements, Inc., 1977-79. Bd. dirs. Pub. Counsel, 2001—, treas., 05, sec., 06, vice chair, 07, chair 2008. Mem. Fin. Lawyers Conf. (mem. bd. govs. 2007, sec. 2008, v.p. 2009), LA County Bar Assn. (exec. com. prejudgment remedies sect. 1985-92, exec. com. bankruptcy sect. 2001—), Beverly Hills Bar Assn. (exec. com. bus. law sect. 1985-92, exec. com. bankruptcy sect. 2003—). Office Phone: 310-284-5648. Business E-Mail: mzohn@proskauer.com.

ZOI, CATHERINE RADFORD (CATHY ZOI), federal agency administrator; b. 1961; BS in Geology, Duke U., 1983; MS in Engring., Dartmouth Coll. Mgr. EPA; chief of staff environ. policy Washington, 1993—95; founding CEO NSW Sustainable Energy Devel. Authority, Sydney, 1996—99; asst. dir. gen. NSW EPA, Sydney, 1999—2003; group dir. Landis+Gyr Holdings (formerly Bayard Group), 2003—07; founding CEO Alliance for Climate Protection, 2007—09; asst. sec. for energy efficiency & renewable energy US Dept. Energy, Washington, 2009—. Office: US Dept Energy 1000 Independence Ave SW Washington DC 20585*

ZOIS, CONSTANTINE NICHOLAS ATHANASIOS, meteorologist, educator; b. Newark, Feb. 21, 1938; s. Athanasios Konstantinos and Asimina (Speros-Biekas) Zois; m. Elyse Stein, Dec. 26, 1971; children: Jennifer, Jonathan. BA, Rutgers U., 1961; MS, Fla. State U., 1965; PhD, Rutgers U., 1980. Draftsman Babcock and Wilcox Corp., Newark, 1956; designer Foster Wheeler Corp., Carteret, NJ, 1956; instr. Rutgers U., New Brunswick, NJ, 1961-62; grad. asst. Fla. State U., Tallahassee, 1962-65; rsch. meteorologist Nat. Weather Svc., Garden City, LI, NY, 1965-67; prof. Kean Coll. N.J., Union, 1967—. Founder meteorology program Kean Coll. N.J., Union, 1967—, chmn. all coll. promotion com., 1991—93; cons. Connell, Foley, Geiser, Roseland, NJ, 1986—88. Author, editor: Papers in Marine Science, 1971; author: Observation of the Newark NJ Nocturnal Heat Island and Its Consideration in Terms of a Physical Model, 1980, Dynamical and Physical Oceanography, 1988, Atmosphere Dynamics: Exercises and Problems, 1988, Climatology Workbook, 1988, Weather Map Folio, 1989; co-author: Outcomes Assessment at Kean College at NJ, 1992, Synoptic Meterology-Exercises and Readings, Vols. 1-3, 1995, Weather Folio, Vol. 2, NWS Map Anthology, 2003. Mem.: AAAS, N.J. Marine Scis. Consortium, N.Y. Acad. Scis. (vice chmn. atmospheric scis. sect. 1986—87, chmn. 1987—88, mem. adv. com. atmospheric sci. sect. 1988—), Am. Meteorol. Soc. (pres. N.J. chpt. 1980—81), Nat. Weather Assn., Phi Beta Kappa. Republican. Greek Orthodox. Avocations: guitar, banjo, fishing, baseball, snorkeling. Home: 2798 Carol Rd Union NJ 07083-4831 Office: Kean Coll of NJ Dept Meteorology Morris Ave Union NJ 07083-7117 Office Phone: 908-737-3693. *It is water that consecrates the atmosphere as a cathedral of wonderment, as it is water that incarnates the sea as an oasis of life.*

ZOLA, GARY PHILLIP, rabbi, historian; b. Chgo., Feb. 17, 1952; m. Stefani Paula Rothberg; children: Amanda Roi, Jorin Benjamin, Jeremy Micah, Samantha Leigh. BA in Am. History with distinction, U. Mich., 1973; MA in Counseling Psychology, Northwestern U., 1976; PhD in Am. Jewish History, Hebrew Union Coll., Cin., 1991. Ordained rabbi, 1982. Dir. informal edn. and youth activities Temple Israel, Mpls., 1973-74; regional youth dir., asst. camp dir. Olin-Sang-Ruby Union Inst., UAHC, Chgo., 1974-77; student pulpit B'nai Israel Congregation, Williamson, W.Va., 1978-79; mem. student pulpit Anshe Sholom Congregation, Olympia Fields, Ill., 1979-80, Columbus Hebrew Congregation, Columbus, Ind., 1981-82; rabbi for high holy days Chgo. Jewish Experience, Chgo., 1982-94; nat. dir. admissions Hebrew Union Coll.-Jewish Inst. Religion, Cin., 1982-89, nat. dean admissions and student affairs, 1989-91, nat. dean admissions, student affairs and alumni rels., 1991-98; exec. dir. Jacob Rader Marcus Ctr. Am. Jewish Archives at Hebrew Union Coll., Cin., 1998—; assoc. prof. Am. Jewish Experience Hebrew Union Coll. Jewish Inst. of Religion. Del. Emerging Leaders Conf., Am. Coun. for Internat. Leadership, 1989, 91; bd. dirs. Am. Jewish Com., Cin., 1982—, mem. exec. com., 1984—; bd. dirs. Hillel U. Cin., 1991-94, Jewish Fedn., Cin., 1993-95; pres. Greater Cin. Bd. Rabbis, 1993-95, Jewish Cmty. Rels. Coun., (bd. dir.,1994—); founding mem. Kehillah of Cin., Jewish Think Tank; pres. Martin Luther King Jr. Coalition Cin., 2003-05; chair Commn. for Commemorating 350 Years of Am. Jewish History. Author: Isaac Harby of Charleston, 1994; editor: Hebrew Union College--Jewish Institute of Religion--A Centennial History, 1875-1975, (Michael A. Meyer), 1992, Women Rabbis: Exploration and Celebration, 1996, The Dynamics of American Jewish History, 2003, A Place of Our Own: The Rise of Reform Jewish Camping, 2006, The Americaization of the Jewish Prayer Book, 2008; editor: The American Jewish Archives Jour., 1998—; contbr. numerous scholarly articles to profl. jours.; mem. editl. bd. Reform Judaism, Bd. dirs. ethics com. Jewish Hosp., Cin.; life mem. N.Am. Fedn. Temple Youth; active NCCJ. Mem. Ctrl. Conf. Am. Rabbis, Orgn. Am. Historians, Assn. Jewish Studies, So. Jewish Hist. Soc., Am. Jewish Hist. Soc., N.Am. Fedn. Temple Youth (life), Abraham Lincoln Bicentennial Commn. Academic Coun. Office: Hebrew Union Coll Jewish Inst Religion 3101 Clifton Ave Cincinnati OH 45220-2404

ZOLA, JOSHUA, psychologist; b. Middletown, NY, Oct. 26, 1974; s. John Charles and Rita Zola. BA in Psychology, Clemson U., SC, 1997; MA, Citadel - Grad. Coll., Charleston, SC, 2000, EdS in Sch. Psychology, 2000; postgrad., U. SC. Cert. sch. psychologist II SC. Dept. Edn., 2002, brain injury specialist Am. Acad. Cert. Brain Injury Specialists, 2007, substance abuse counselor Clemson U., 1997. Field rsch. coord. U. Oreg. Fed. Grant, Eugene, 1998—99, team leader; psychometrician L. Randolf Waid, Mt. Pleasant, SC, 1998—99; sch. psychologist Shrewbury Pub. Schs., Mass., 2000—02, Charleston County Sch. Dist., SC, 2002—, lead psychologist, traumatic brain injury team, 2007—. Author: (play) Last Days of Wonder Piggy and his Gang. V.p. Sigma Alpha Epsilon, Clemson, 1996—97, Students Against Drunk Driving, Great Barrington, Mass., 1992—93. Achievements include invention of graphic representation of academic progress system. Avocations: tennis, racquetball, kayaking, college football. E-mail: joshua_zola@charleston.k12.sc.us.

ZOLD, ROBERT KENNETH, educational administrator; b. Racine, Wis., Sept. 16, 1933; s. Joseph and Pearl Julian (Despins) Z.; m. Margaret Jean Oman, June 30, 1978; children— Kenneth, Kevin. B.S., U. Wis.-La Crosse, 1955; M.A., U. Iowa, 1961; Ph.D., U. Wis.-Madison, 1972. Tchr. Roosevelt Jr. High Sch., Cedar Rapids, Iowa, 1957-62; tchr., asst. prin. McKinley Jr. High Sch., 1962-66; prin. McKinley Middle Sch., Racine, 1966-84; asst. supt. pupil personnel services Racine Unified Schs., 1984—. Served with U.S. Army, 1955-57. Named Citizen of Yr. McKinley PTA Coun., 1981, 82, Prin. of Yr. Racine Unified Sch. Dist., 1982; named to Southeastern Wis. Hall of Fame, 1991; recipient Exec. Educator Top 100 Vet. Adminstrs. Am. award, 1989, State Task Force Sch. Records, 1986-89. Mem. Assn. Wis. Sch. Adminstrs. (pres. 1984—), Nat. Assn. Secondary Sch. Prins., Racine Adminstrs. Assn. (pres. 1980-82), Kiwanis, Phi Delta Kappa. Avocations: reading, traveling.

ZOLLA-PAZNER, SUSAN, hospital administrator, biologist, biomedical researcher; MD, U. Calif., San Francisco, PhD in Med. Microbiology, 1967. NIH postdoctoral fellow NYU Med. Ctr., 1967—69; dir., immunology rsch. lab. Veterans Affairs Med. Ctr., NYC, dir. rsch. AIDS ctr. U.S. chair U.S.-Japan Commn. on AIDS Rsch.; editorial bd. mem. AIDS Rsch. and Human Retroviruses, Cellular Immunity, Journ. Immunologic Methods. Author more than 240 scientific papers on cancer, AIDS and various human pathogens. Named one of The 50 Most Powerful Women in NYC, NY Post, 2007. Office: VET 18 18147N 423 E 23 St New York NY 10010

ZOLLAR, JAWOLE WILLA JO, artist, choreographer; b. Kansas City, Kans., Dec. 21, 1950; d. Alfred Jr. and Dorothy Delores Zollar; 1 child, Elizabeth Herron. BA in Dance, U. Mo., Kansas City, 1975; MFA in Dance, Fla. State U., 1979; PhD (hon.), Columbia Coll., Chgo., 2002. Faculty Fla. State U., Tallahassee, 1977-80, Nancy Smith Fichter prof. dance, 1997—; founding artistic dir. Urban Bush Women, Bklyn., 1984—; Worlds of Thought Resident Scholar Mankato State Univ., 1993—94; regents lectr., dept. dance, world arts and culture UCLA, 1995—96; vis. artist Ohio State Univ., 1996; Abramowitz Meml. lectr. MIT, 1998. Recipient NY Dance Performance award, 1992, 2006, Capezio award for outstanding achievement in dance, 1994, Doris Duke awad, Am. Dance Festival, 1997; named Outstanding Alumni, U. Mo., 1993, Regent's lectr. dept. dance and worlds culture, UCLA, 1995—96, Alumna of Yr., U. Mo., 1993, Fla. State U., Tallahassee, 1997; fellow John Simon Guggenheim Meml. Found., 2009; Choreography fellow, NEA, 1992, 1993, 1994, Wynn fellow in dance, US Artists, 2008. Mem.: Internat. Assn. Blacks in Dance, Assn. Am. Cultures. Office: Urban Bush Women # 4B 138 S Oxford St Brooklyn NY 11217 also: care IMG Artists 420 W 45th St Fl 6 New York NY 10036-3503 Office: Florida State Univ Dept of Dance PO Box 3062120 130 Collegiate Loop Tallahassee FL 32306-2120 Office Phone: 850-644-2525. E-mail: info@urbanbushwomen.org, jwjzollar@mac.com.*

ZOLLARS, SCOTTY M., library director; b. Wellington, Kans., Oct. 4, 1962; s. Elmore B. Zollars and Valera M. Zumbrun Zollars; m. Ruth E. Wagoner, Nov. 12, 1982; children: Johanan (Joe) M., Timothy R. BA, Coll. Ozarks, Point Lookout, Mo., 1986; MLS, Tex. Woman's U., Denton, 1996. K-12 libr. Lead Hill Sch. Dist., Ark., 1986—90, HS Spanish instr., 1986—90; asst. libr. dir. North Ark. Coll., Harrison, 1990—2000; dir. libr. svcs. Labette CC, Parsons, Kans., 2000—. Mem. Lions Club Internat., Parsons, 2001—; lector St. Patrick's Cath. Ch., Parsons, 2001—, eucharistic min., 2004—; trustee Parsons Pub. Libr., 2002—. Mem.: ALA, Kans. Libr. Assn. (chair, acad. libr. interest group 2006), Mountain Plains Libr. Assn., Lawrence County Ind. Hist. Soc. Avocations: genealogy, reading. Office: Labette CC Library 200 S 14th Parsons KS 67357 Office Fax: 620-421-1469. Business E-Mail: scottz@labette.edu.

ZOLLARS, WILLIAM D., freight company executive; b. 1947; BA, U. Minn., 1969. Various exec. positions with Eastman Kodak, 1970—94; sr. v.p. Ryder Integrated Logistics Ryder Sys., Inc., 1994—96; pres. Yellow Freight Sys., 1996-99; chmn., pres., CEO YRC Worldwide, Inc. (formerly Yellow Roadway Corp.), Overland Park, Kans., 1999—. Bd. dirs. Cigna Corp., Cerner Corp., Butler Mfg. Co. Trustee ProLogis Trust, Midwest Rsch. Inst.; bd. mem. Heart of Am. United Way, Civic Council of Greater Kans. City, Carlson Sch. Mgmt., Univ. Minn., NAM. Mem.: Am. Trucking Assn. (bd. mem.), Phi Beta Kappa. Office: YRC Worldwide Inc 10990 Roe Ave Overland Park KS 66211-1213

ZOLLER, KAREN ANN, library and art gallery director; b. East Cleveland, Ohio, May 16, 1956; d. Paul John and Sonia Ann Klodor. BA in Psychology summa cum laude, Case Western Res. U., 1978, MLS in Law Librarianship, 1981. Mgr. Booksellers, Beachwood, Ohio, 1982—87; cataloger, reference libr. Clara Fritzsche Libr., Notre Dame Coll., South Euclid, Ohio, 1988—92, interim libr. dir., 1992, libr. dir., 1993—, gallery dir., 1997—. Co-founder, bd. mem. Tolerance Resource Ctr. Notre Dame Coll., South Euclid, 1997—; presenter in field; established Eastern Ch. Resource Ctr., Notre Dame Coll., South Euclid, 1999—. Editor: On The Threshold of a New Century: The City of South Euclid, 1967-1999, 1999; compiler: source book Researching Grants on the Internet: A Resource Manual, 1999, mem. editl. bd.: Notre Dame Today, 2003—. Mem. steering com. Hillcrest Cmty. Connections, South Euclid, 2003—04; founding mem. South Euclid Cmty. Partnerships, 2005—; judge & coord. Notre Dame Coll. & Social Justice Essay Contest, 2009. Recipient Ameritech Partnership award, Ameritech, 1999, Pres.'s Outstanding Staff award, Notre Dame Coll., 2006, Pres.'s Appreciation award, 2008; N.E. Ohio Network grantee, Gund Found., 1998, mini-grant, Ohio Humanities Coun., 2005. Mem.: ALA, Phi Beta Kappa. Roman Catholic. Office: Clara Fritzsche Libr Notre Dame Coll 4545 College Rd South Euclid OH 44121 Business E-Mail: kzoller@ndc.edu.

ZOLLER, MICHAEL, otolaryngologist, head and neck surgeon, educator; b. New Orleans, July 21, 1947; s. Harry and Mildred (Daitch) Z.; m. Linda Kramer, Dec. 21, 1974; children: Rebecca, Jonathan. BS, U. New Orleans, 1971; MD, Tulane U., 1972. Resident in gen. surgery Jewish Hosp., St. Louis, Washington U. Sch. Medicine, 1972—74; resident in otolaryngology Mass. Eye and Ear Infirmary, Harvard U. Med. Sch., Boston, 1974—77; pres. Ear, Nose and Throat Assocs., Savannah, Ga., 1977—; chmn. eye, ear, nose and throat dept. Candler Hosp., 1996—98. Asst. clin. prof. otolaryngology, head and neck surgery Med. Coll. Ga., Augusta, 1982—96, clin. prof. otolaryngology, head and neck surgery, 2009, assoc. clin. prof. otolaryngology, head and neck surgery, 1996—2009, clin. prof. otolaryngology & head surgery; assoc. prof. surgery Mercer Med. Sch., 2000—09; dir. otology otoneurology dept. St. Joseph's Hosp., Savannah, 1994—; bd. dirs. Darby Bank and Trust, 2007—. Chmn. med. divsn. United Way, Savannah, 1990, chmn. profl. divsn., 1991, 94-2001, vice chmn. campaign, 2002, chmn. campaign, 2003, bd. dirs., 2002-07, vice chmn. bd. dirs., 2004-05, chmn. bd. dirs., 2005-2006; mem. allocation panel, 1997-2002; bd. dirs. Am. Cancer Soc., Savannah, 1993-2000, pres. Chatham County unit, 1996-97, chmn. bd., 1997-98; bd. dirs. Savannah Country Day Sch., 1993-97, chmn. ann. campaign, 1995-96; bd. dirs. St. Joseph's Candler Found., 2001-; pres. Savannah Jewish Fedn., 1991-93; active Savannah Jewish Fedn. Endowment Bd., 1995-99; mem. med. adv. bd. South Coll., 1996-2000; mem. parents coun. Washington U., St. Louis, 1997-2001, Tulane U., 2002-05, Tulane Med. Sch., 2005-06, Tulane Med. Alumni Assn, 2007-; bd. dirs. Leadership Savannah, 1996-98, Darby Bank & Trust, 2007-. Recipient Young Leadership award Savannah Jewish Fedn., 1985, Boss of Yr. award Savannah Jaycees, 1993, Celebrate Savannah award for outstanding contbns. to Savannah, Ga. Guardian, 1996; Harvard U. Med. Sch. fellow, 1976-77. Fellow: ACS; mem.: AMA, So. Med. Assn. (otolaryngology sec. 2006—07), Ga. Soc. Otolaryngology (pres. bd. trustees 1997—98, editor newsletter 1998—2001, Lester Brown Lifetime Achievement award 2005), Med. Assn. Ga. (mem. ho. of dels. 1990—2005, bd. dirs. 1995—2004, editl. bd. 2001—, Ga. Cup award 1993, Ayest-Wyeth Cmty. Svc. award 1996, Cmty. Svc. award 2001), 1st Dist. Med. Assn. (pres. 1987—88), Ga. Med. Soc. (pres. 1992, chmn. bd. trustees 1997, chmn. endowment fund 2004—, John B. Rabun Cmty. Svc. award 1995, Hero's award 2001), Am. Neurotology Soc., Am. Soc. Head and Neck Surgery, Am. Acad. Otolaryngology and Head and Neck Surgery (tonsils and adenoids com. 1996—99, sleep disorders com. 1996—2002, pediat. otolaryngology com. 2003—, equilibrium com. 2005—). Office: Ear Nose and Throat Assocs Savannah 5201 Frederick St Savannah GA 31405-4501 Personal E-mail: MZ47ent@aol.com.

ZOLLI, BARBARA TURK, museum director; BS in Art Edn., Mass. Coll. Art, Boston, 1965. Art tchr., Mass. and Pa., 1965—81; advt. sales cons., layout artist Venango Newspapers, Inc., Oil City, Pa., 1985—86; dir., mktg./pub. rels. Tweed Corp., Oil City, 1986—87; dir. Venango Mus. Art, Sci. and Industry, Oil City, 1987—89; mus. educator Drake Well Mus., Titusville, Pa., 1990—93, dir., 1993—. Presenter in field. Office: Drake Well Mus 202 Museum Ln Titusville PA 16354 Office Phone: 814-824-1147 ext. 102. Business E-Mail: bzolli@state.pa.us.

ZOLLINGER, DAN, engineering educator; b. Logan, Utah; m. Bonnie R. Zollinger; children: Eugene, Corey, Jessica, Heather, Mindy, Tyler. PhD, U. Ill., Champaign - Urbana, 1988. Lic. in profl. engring., Tex., 1990, Calif., 1990; registered Cement and Concrete Inst., Mexican Chpt. ACI, 2003. Lt. col. USAR, Phoenix, 1970—; prof. Tex. A&M U., Coll. Sta., 1988—; pres. Internat. Soc. Concrete Pavements, Columbia, Md., 2006—. Cons. CMS Engring. Group, Coll. Sta., 2003—08. Tchr. LDS Ch., Bryan, Tex., 1989—2008. Fellow: Am. Concrete Inst. Achievements include development of test method to measure aggregate Cote. Office: Tex A&M Univ 503e CE/TTI Bldg College Station TX 77845-3136 Business E-Mail: d-zollinger@tamu.edu.

ZOLOTOV, YURY ALEXANDROVICH, chemist; b. Vysokovskoe, Moscow region, Russia, Oct. 4, 1932; s. Alexander Georgievich Zolotov and Alexandra Mikhailovna Zolotova; m. Galina Alexeevna Ivanova, Apr. 19, 1959; children: Michael Yu, Maria Yu (dec.). Diploma Chemist, Moscow U., 1955; Candidate of Sci., Vernadskii Inst., Moscow, 1959, DSc, 1966; D (hon.), Kiev Nat. U., 1994. Cert. chemistry rschr. Jr. scientist Vernadskii Inst. Geochemistry and Analytical Chemistry, Moscow, 1958-62, sr. scientist, 1962-68, dep. dir., 1968-79, head lab. solvent extraction, 1972-89; dir. Kurnakov Inst. Gen. and Inorganic Chemistry, Moscow, 1989-99. Prof. chem. dept. Moscow U., 1978-89, head analytical chemistry divsn., 1989—. Author: Extraction of Chelate Compounds, 1968 (Mendeleev Chem. Soc. award 1969), Ion Chromatography in Water Analysis, 1988, Preconcentration of Trace Elements, 1990, Analytical Chemistry: Problems and Achievements, 1992, others; contbr. over 700 sci. papers to profl. jours.; 30 patents in field. Recipient USSR State prize, 1972, Russian State prize, 1991, 2000; co-recipient Austrian Soc. Analytical Chemistry, 1990; named Disting. Prof., Moscow U., 1999. Mem.: Royal Soc. Art and Sci. Göteborg, Mendeleev Russian Chem. Soc. (pres. 1991—95, Mendeleev Gold medal 1993), Russian Acad. Scis. (pres. sci. coun. analytical chemistry 1988—, full mem. 1987—), Japan Soc. Analytical Chemistry (hon.). Office: Kurnakov Inst 31 Leninskii Prospect 119991 Moscow Russia Office Phone: 78499 633-849. Business E-Mail: zolotov@igic.ras.ru.

ZOMBIE, ROB (ROBERT CUMMINGS), musician, filmmaker; b. Haverhill, Mass., Jan. 12, 1966; m. Sheri Moon, Oct. 31, 2002. Founding mem. White Zombie, 1985—96. Musician: (albums) (with White Zombie) Psycho-Head Blowout, 1986, Soul Crusher, 1987, Make Them Die Slowly, 1989, La Sexorcisto, 1992, Astro-Creep 2000, 1995, Supersexy Swingin' Sounds, 1996, (solo albums) Hellbilly Deluxe, 1998, American Made Music to Strip By, 1999, The Sinister Urge, 2001, Educated Horses, 2006, Zombie Live, 2007; prodn. asst. (TV series) Pee-wee's Playhouse, 1986, writer, dir. (films) House of 1000 Corpses, 2003, Halloween II, 2009, writer, dir., prodr. The Devil's Rejects, 2005 (Chainsaw award, 2006), actor Slither, 2006, writer The Haunted World of El Superbeasto, 2006. Office: 8491 Sunset Blvd Ste 215 West Hollywood CA 90069*

ZON, LEONARD IRA, pediatrics educator, researcher; b. Hartford, Conn. BS in Chemistry and Natural Sciences, Muhlenberg Coll., Allentown, Pa., 1979; MD, Jefferson Med. Coll., 1983. Diplomate Am. Bd. Internal Medicine; lic. physician, Mass. Rsch. asst. Jefferson Med. Coll., Phila., 1980-82; intern New Eng. Deaconess Hosp., Boston, 1983-84, from jr. to sr. resident in internal medicine, 1984-86; rsch. fellow Children's Hosp., Boston, 1987-90, founder, dir. Stem Cell Rsch. Program, Grousbeck prof. hematology/oncology; instr. Harvard Med. Sch., Boston, 1989-91, asst. prof. pediatrics, 1991—, mem. faculty grad. program biol. and biomed. scis., 1994—, prof. pediat. medicine, Children's Hosp. Boston; investigator Howard Hughes Med. Inst., 1993—. Guest faculty Okla. Health Scis. Ctr., 1993; lectr. in field. Contbr. articles to Am. Jour. Physiology, Jour. Clin. Microbiology, Lancet, Am. Jour. Medicine, Br. Jour. Haematology, Nature, Biotechniques, Molecular Cell Biology, Biology of Hematopoiesis, Jour. Biol. Chemistry. Recipient Hyman Menduke Rsch. awrd, 1983; Friends of the Farber fellow, 1987, Dana-Farber Cancer Inst. fellow, med. oncology, 1986-89; grantee NSF, 1978, NIH, 1980, 89—, Chalres H. Hood Found., 1990-92, Hoffmann-La Roche, 1991-94. Mem. AMA, ACP, Am. Soc. Clin. Oncology, Am. Soc. Hematology, Am. Fisheries Soc., Mass. Med. Soc., Inst. Medicine., Internat. Soc. for Stem Cell Rsch. (founder, past pres.), Am. Soc. for Cln. Investigation;fellow AAAS, Am. Acad. Arts & Scis. Achievements include research in hematopoiesis, development, genetics. Office: Childrens Hosp Boston 300 Longwood Ave Karp-7 Boston MA 02115 also: Howard Hughes Med Inst New Rsch Bldg Rm 7211 1 Blackfan Cir Boston MA 02115 Office Phone: 617-919-2069. Office Fax: 617-730-0222. E-mail: zpn@enders.tch.harvard.edu.

ZONA, LOUIS ALBERT, museum director; s. Patricia Zona; 1 child, Tace. BS in Edn. magna cum laude, Youngstown U., Ohio, 1966; MS in Edn., U. Pitts., 1969; DFA, Carnegie Mellon U., 1973. Asst. to dir. The Butler Inst. of Am. Art, Youngstown, 1980—81, exec. dir., 1981—, also chief curator; prof. art history Youngstown State U., 1970—, chmn. art dept., 1978-82. Adj. prof. art and museology Westminster Coll., 1976-80. Contbr. numerous articles to profl. publs. Recipient Gari Melchers medla Artists' Fellowship, NYC, 1996, Gov.'s award for the Arts in Ohio, 1990, Disting. Profl. Svc. award Ohio Steel Valley Art Tchrs. Assn., 1982. Office: Butler Inst Am Art Beecher Ctr 524 Wick Ave Youngstown OH 44502 Office Phone: 330-743-1711. E-mail: l_zona@butlerart.com.

ZONANA, VICTOR, lawyer, educator; b. Zagazig, Eqypt, Aug. 28, 1940; s. Isaac A. and Fortunee (Cohen Beyda) Z.; m. Mary Linda Haynie, Aug. 22, 1964; children: David A., Nancy B. Zonana Dickinson. BS in Econs., Hofstra U., 1961; LLB, NYU, 1964, LLM, 1966. Bar: N.Y. 1965. Assoc. Kaye, Scholer, Fierman, Hays & Handler, NYC, 1966-69; prof. NYU, 1969-80, adj. prof., 1981—, Charles S. Lyon vis. prof., 1994; dep. tax legis. counsel U.S. Dept. Treasury, 1975-76; cons. to asst. commr. IRS, 1975, office of chief counsel, 1994; counsel, ptnr. Kaye, Scholer, Fierman, Hays & Handler, NYC, 1980-87, Arnold & Porter, NYC, 1988—2001; prof. Bklyn. Law Sch., 1996—2002; prin. KPMG LLP, London, 2002—. Mem., chmn. adv. bd. NYU Tax Inst. Fellow Am. Coll. Tax Counsel; mem. ABA, N.Y. State Bar Assn. (co-chmn. com. on fgn. activities of U.S. taxpayers, chmn. com. on depreciation and investment credit, co-chmn. com. tax acctg. matters, com. tax policy). Office: KPMG LLP 8 Salisbury Sq London EC4Y 8BB England Home Phone: +44 (0)207 976 6964; Office Phone: +44 (0)207 694 1737.

ZONAY, THOMAS A., lawyer; b. 1963; BS; JD, Vt. Law Sch. Bar: Vt. 1988. Criminal def. lawyer Carrol, George & Pratt, Rutland, Vt.; ptnr. Ford & Zonay, P.C., Woodstock, Utah, 2000—. Mem.: Vt. Bar Assn. (pres. 2004—, mem. bd. mgrs.). Home: 37 Central St Woodstock VT 05091-1006 Office Phone: 802-457-1000. Office Fax: 802-457-1874. E-mail: tazonay@sover.net.

ZONIA, DHIMITRI, artist; b. St. Louis, June 12, 1921; s. Ligori and Polixenna Zonia; m. Margaret C. Wieland, July 11, 1927; children: Margaret E., Susan C., Carolynn L., Laura E. Ind. study, Italy and Eng., 1972. Editl. cartoonist Postmark Prague, 1984—86; editl. cartoonist illustrator Cry Justice Now, St. Louis, 1998—2000; staff mem. The Scene Newspaper, 2002—05. Vis. artist Albanian Nat. Gallery, Tirane, 2005. One-man shows include Tattershall Castle, London, 1982, Nat. Gallery Art, Tirana, Albania, 2001—05, Forest Pk. CC, St. Louis, 2004—05, exhibitions include Oak Grove Mauselium, 1972, Palais de Congress, Paris, 1976, Yamaha Corp., Madison Sq. Garden, NYC, 1977, Jewish Cmty. Wall Mural Ctr., 1978, Macdonnel Planetarium, St. Louis, 1978, Mo. Botanical Garden Poster Ltd. Edit., 1988, Polish Bi-ennial, Warsaw, 1992, Anheuser-Bush Breweries Employees Prints Ltd. Edit., 1992, St. Louis C.C., 2007, Christmas Cards, St. Anthony Hosp., St. Louis, Mo., 2006, Represented in permanent collections St. Bernadette Mus. Sacred Art, Albuquerque, Okla. Art Ctr., Oklahoma City Ark. Art Ctr., Little Rock, Albrecht Art Ctr., St. Joseph, Mo., Rapid City Art Ctr., SD, Butler Inst. Am. Art, Youngstown, Ohio, pvt. collections, Am., Europe, Japan, Australia, Galleria Kom Betare Te Artiva, Tirane, Albania, 2009, cover photo, Savvy Family mag., 2006; author: Art and Poetry, 2006; one-man shows include Concordia Publishing House Gallery, St. Louis, Mo., 2008, William Woods U., Fulton, Mo., 2008, Forest Pk. Coll., 2009, Invitational Exhibition, William Woods U., exhibitions include Surfing In Cosmos, Albania Nat. Gallery; author: DC Coloring Book, St. Louis CC; exhibitions include Planetaria, Praha, Czech Republic, 2002. Bd. govs. St. Louis Artists Guild, St. Louis, 1967. Recipient 1st prize for editl. art, Mo. Coll. Media Assn., 2002—05, 3d pl. award, 2006, Journalism award, ACLEU, 2006. Mem.: Soc. Ind. Artists (life; hon.). Mailing: 4680 Karamar Dr Saint Louis MO 63128 Office Phone: 314-487-8506. Personal E-mail: weizon@aol.com.

ZONIS, MARVIN, political scientist, educator; b. Boston, Sept. 18, 1936; s. Leonard and Clara (Barenberg) Z.; m. Lucy Salenger, Jan. 3, 1976; children by previous marriage-Nadia E. Leah; 1 stepdaughter, Brix E. Smith. AB, Yale U., 1958; postgrad., Harvard Grad. Sch. Bus., 1958-59; PhD, M.I.T., 1968; candidate, Inst. for Psychoanalysis, Chgo., 1977-85. Mem. faculty U. Chgo., 1966—, assoc. prof. and prof. behavioral scis., 1973-89—, prof. Grad. Sch. Bus., 1989—; dir. U. Chgo. (Center for Middle Eastern Studies), 1976-79; pres. Marvin Zonis and Assocs., Internat. Cons., 1991—. Cons. in field; chmn. com. on Middle East Am. Coun. Learned Socs.-Social Sci. Rsch. Coun., 1970-76; pres. Am. Inst. Iranian Studies, 1969-71; bd. dirs. CNA Fin. Corp. Author: The Political Elite of Iran, 1971, Khomeini, The Islamic Republic of Iran, and the Arab World, 1987, Majestic Failure: The Fall of the Shah, 1991, The East European Opportunity: The Complete Business Guide and Source Book, 1992; co-author The Kimchi Matters: Global Business and Local Politics in a Crisis Driven World, 2002; contbr. articles to profl. jours. Served with USAF, 1959-60. Recipient Quantrell award for excellence in teaching U. Chgo., 1979 Home: 4950 Chicago Beach Dr Chicago IL 60615 Office: U Chgo 5807 S Woodlawn Ave Chicago IL 60637-1515 Office Phone: 773-702-8753. Business E-Mail: marvin.zonis@chicagogsb.edu. *Psychoanalytic approaches to the study of political phenomena open new vistas to understanding as well as facilitating the design of U.S. policy.*

ZOOGMAN, NICHOLAS JAY, lawyer; b. NYC, Apr. 2, 1947; s. Morris William and Hannah (Stern) Z.; m. Carla Ganz, June 7, 1970; children: Sarah Elizabeth, Peter William. BA, NYU, 1967; MA, Harvard U., 1969, JD, 1973. Bar: N.Y. 1974, U.S. Dist. Ct. (so. and ea. dists.) N.Y. 1974, U.S. Ct. Appeals (2d cir.) 1975, U.S. Supreme Ct. 1979, U.S. Dist. Ct. (ea. dist.) Mich. 1988, U.S. Ct. Appeals (D.C. cir.) 1990, U.S. Ct. Appeals (6th cir.) 1993, U.S. Ct. Appeals (5th cir.) 1997. Assoc. Donovan Leisure Newton & Irvine, NYC, 1973-75; ptnr. Anderson Kill & Olick, NYC, 1976-2000; counsel Dickstein Shapiro LLP, NYC, 2000—05, ptnr., 2006—. Mem. ABA, N.Y. State Bar Assn., Assn. Bar City of N.Y., Phi Beta Kappa, Pi Sigma Alpha. Office: Dickstein Shapiro LLP 1633 Broadway New York NY 10019 Office Phone: 212-277-6500. Business E-Mail: zoogmann@dicksteinshapiro.com.

ZOOK, ELVIN GLENN, plastic surgeon, educator; b. Huntington County, Ind., Mar. 21, 1937; s. Glenn Hardman and Ruth (Barton) Z.; m. Sharon Kay Neher, Dec. 11, 1960; children— Tara E., Leigh A., Nicole L. BA, Manchester Coll., 1959; MD, Ind. U., 1963. Diplomate Am. Bd. Surgery, 1970, Am. Bd. Thoracic Surgery, 1970, Am. Bd. Plastic Surgery, 1972, Am. Bd. Plastic Surgery, Hand Surgery, 1989. Intern Meth. Hosp., Indpls., 1963-64; resident in gen. and thoracic surgery Ind. U. Med. Center, Indpls., 1964-69; resident in plastic surgery Ind. U. Hosp., Indpls., 1969-71, asst. prof. plastic surgery, 1971-73; asso. prof. surgery So. Ill. U., Springfield, 1973-75, prof. plastic surgery, 1975—2006, chmn. div. plastic surgery, 1973—2006, prof. emeritus of plastic surgery, 2006—. Mem. staff Meml. Med. Center, St. Johns Hosp., Springfield. Author of five books, contbr. over 100 articles to med. jours., contbr. to over 40 books. Mem. Ind. Nat. Guard 1963-71. Recipient Michael J. Caey Meml. Svc. award, McCaskey award, Mem. Assn. Acad. Surgery, Am. Soc. Plastic Surgery (sec. 1988-91, v.p. 1991-92, pres.-elect 1992-93, pres. 1993-94), Midwestern Soc. Plastic Surgery (pres. 1986-87), ACS, Sangamon County Med. Soc. (pres. 1987), Am. Cleft Palate Assn., Am. Assn. Plastic Surgery (trustee 1987-90), Plastic Surgery Rsch. Coun. (chmn. 1981), Am. Burn Assn., Ill. Surg. Soc., Am. Soc. Surgery Hand (coun.), Am. Bd. of Plastic Surgery (sec.-treas. 1988-91, chmn. 1991-92), Am. Soc. Aesthetic Plastic Surgery, Am. Soc. Surgery of Trauma, Assn. Acad. Chmn. Plastic Surgery (pres. 1986-87), Am. Surg. Assn., RRC for Plastic Surgery, Sangamo Club, Springfield Med. Club, Island Bay Yacht Club. Clubs: Sangamo, Springfield Med, Island Bay Yacht. Presbyterian. Office: Div of Plastic Surgery 747 N Rutledge St Springfield IL 62702-6700 Office Phone: 217-545-6314. Office Fax: 217-545-2588. E-mail: ezook@siumed.edu. *Do the best possible in all that is possible.*

ZOOK, RON, college football coach; b. Loudonville, Ohio, Apr. 28, 1954; m. Denise Baugh; children: Jacquelyn, Casey. BS in Comprehensive Sci., Miami U., Ohio, 1976. Football coach Orrville HS, 1976—77; defensive backs coach Murray State U. Racers, 1978—80; defensive coord. U. Cin. Bearcats, 1981—82, Kansas U. Jayhawks, 1983; defensive backs coach U. Tenn. Volunteers, 1984—86; defensive coord., asst. head coach Va. Poly. Inst. and State U. Hokies, 1987; defensive backs coach Ohio State U. Buckeyes, 1988—90; defensive coord., defensive backs coach U. Fla. Gators, 1991—93, spl. teams coord., nickelbackers coach, 1994, head coach, 2002—04; spl. teams coach Pitts. Steelers, 1996—98; defensive backs coach Kansas City Chiefs, 1999; defensive coord. New Orleans Saints, 2000—01; head coach U. Ill. Fighting Illini, 2005—. Active Am. Cancer Soc., Cunningham Children's Home, Urbana, Ill. Named Coach of Yr., Big Ten Conf., 2007, Divsn. I-A Nat. Coach of Yr., Nat. Football Found. and Coll. Hall of Fame, Inc., 2007. Office: Univ Ill Football Office 1402 S First St Champaign IL 61820 Business E-Mail: rzook@illinois.edu.

ZOON, KATHRYN CHRISTINE, biochemist; b. Yonkers, NY, Nov. 6, 1948; d. August R. and Violet T. (Pollock) Egloff; m. Robert A. Zoon, Aug. 22, 1970; children: Christine K., Jennifer R. BS, Rensselaer Poly. Inst., 1970; PhD, Johns Hopkins U., 1976. Rsch. chemist divsn. biochem. biophys. Bur. Biologics FDA, Bethesda, Md., 1980-84, rsch. chemist divsn. virology, 1984-88, rsch. chemist divsn. cytokine biology Ctr. Biologics, 1988—92, divsn. dir., 1989-92; dir. Ctr. Biologics Evaluation and Rsch., 1992—2003; dep. dir. Ctr. for Cancer Rsch. Nat. Cancer Inst., NIH, 2003—04; dep. dir. planning and devel. divsn. intramural rsch. NIAID, NIH, 2004—06, dir. divsn. intramural rsch., 2006—. Chmn. expert com. on biol. standardization WHO, 1997-98, 99, 2000, 01; mem. adv. com. of CMR, 2000-03; mem. adhoc expert on biology standardization WHO, 2004—; dir. NIH, NIAID, DIR; lectr. in field. Contbr. articles to rsch. in biol. chemistry to sci. jours.; sect. editor Jour. Interferon and Cytokine Rsch., 1980—. Bd. dirs. Found. Advanced Edn. Scis., 1996-2004, 1st v.p., 1999-03; mem. adv. bd. Def. Advance Rsch. Projects Agy., 1998-00, Inst. Medicine Nat. Acad. Sci., 2002-. Recipient Person of the Yr. award Biopharm, 1992, Pub. Svc. and Genetic Engrng. News award, 1995, Presdl. Meritorious Exec. Rank award, 1994, Grateful Patient award Nat. Assn. Cancer Patients, 1997, Rensselaer Alumni Assn. award, 1997, Sec.'s award for disting. svc. Dept. Health and Human Svcs., 2001, 03, Disting. Alumnus award Johns Hopkins U., 2003; NY State Regents fellow, 1970, Interferon rsch. fellow NIH, Bethesda, 1975-77, staff fellow, 1979-80. Mem. Am. Soc. Biochem. and Molecular Biology, Intenat. Soc. Interferon and Cytokine Rsch. (pres. elect 1998-99, pres. 2000-01), Internat. Assn. Biol. Standardization (mem. 1984—, v.p. 1996—, mem. adv. coun. 2000—), Inst. of Medicine. Roman Catholic. Office: NIAID/NIH Bldg 33 Rm 2NN05 10 Center Dr Bethesda MD 20892 Office Phone: 301-496-3006. Business E-Mail: kzoon@niaid.nih.gov.

ZOPF, EVELYN LANOEL MONTGOMERY, retired guidance counselor; b. Laurel, Miss., July 10, 1932; d. Arthur LaNoel and Ruby Lee (Lewis) Montgomery; m. Paul Edward Zopf, Aug. 5, 1956; 1 child, Eric Paul. MusB in Edn., U. So. Miss., 1953, MA, 1954. Guidance counselor U. So. Miss., 1953—54, U. Fla., 1954—56; tchr. New Orleans City Schs., 1956—57; pub. sch. music tchr., band dir., choral dir. Putnam County Schs., Fla., 1957—59; pvt. music tchr. voice, piano, clarinet and trumpet, 1953—61; substitute tchr. Guilford County Schs., 1959—93. Mem. arts series com. Guilford Coll., 1973—77; interim choir dir. New Garden Friends Meeting, 1961, chmn. music com., 1974—76; adviser to fgn. students, 1954—56, 1959—62; mem. First Internat. Congress on Quaker Edn. Com., 1987—88, Guilford Coll.'s Sesquicentennial Com., 1985—87; spkr. various religious and art groups. Vol. ARC, Boy Scouts Am.; active U. Fla. Union Bd., 1955—56; vol. com. worker NC dist. auditions Met. Opera, 1999—2001; precinct del. County Dem. Conv., 1977, 1979, precinct worker, 1980, campaign worker, 1980; bd. dirs. Greensboro Friends of Music, 1970—71; bd. dirs. Greensboro chpt. NC Symphony Bd., 1979—83; feeder bd. Guilford Coll. Friends of the Lib. Bd., 1993—94, exec. bd., 1994—95. Mem.: United Soc. of Friends Women (pres. 1979—81), Internat. Fellowship Quaker Women, Guilford Coll. Cmty. Chorus, Women's Soc. (dir. 1978—82), Guilford Coll. Arts Appreciation (v.p. 1980—81, pres. 1981—82), Guilford Gourmet Club, Phi Mu. Home: 815 George White Rd Greensboro NC 27410-3317

ZOPFI, EMMA G., elementary school educator; arrived in U.S., 1961; d. Gilberto L. and Maria B. Garcia; m. Charles W. Zopfi, Dec. 2, 1975; children: Charles W. Jr., Catherine Marie. BS in Bilingual Elem. Edn., U. Tex., El Paso, 1989. 2d grade tchr. North Loop Elem., El Paso, 1989—2000, 3d grade tchr., 2001—02, 4th grade tchr., 2002—. Gifted & talented tchr. North Loop Elem., El Paso, 2003—06; grade level rep. CEIC-North Loop Elem., 2005—; tchr. rep. Bel Air area Sci. Scope & Seq. Com. 4th grade, El Paso, 2005—06, El Paso, 2006—07; rep. Sci. Think Tank, 2006—07. Vol. Bel Air HS Theater, El Paso, 2001—02, Christo Rey Ch., El Paso, 2001—02. Named Tchr. of the Yr., YISD, 1998—99, 2002—03; grantee. Mem.: ATPE, State Tchr. Sci. Assn., Soc. for the Advancement of Chicanos in Sci. Assn. Avocations: sewing, crafts. Office: North Loop Elem 412 Emerson El Paso TX 79915 Business E-Mail: ezopfi@yisd.net.

ZOPP, ANDREA LYNNE, energy company executive, lawyer; b. Rochester, NY, Jan. 25, 1957; d. Reuben K. and P. Greta (Hurst) Davis; m. William E. Zopp, Jr., Oct. 7, 1989; children: Alyssa, Kelsey, William. BA cum laude, Harvard Coll., 1978; JD, Harvard U., 1981. Bar: Ill. 1981, U.S. Dist. Ct. (no. dist.) Ill. 1981, U.S. Ct. Appeals (7th cir.) 1982. Law clk. Hon. George N. Leighton, U.S. Dist. Ct., Chgo., 1981-83; asst. U.S. atty. U.S. Atty.'s Office, Chgo., 1983-86, dept. chief OCDETF, 1986-88, dep. chief criminal lit., 1988-90; ptnr. McDermott, Will & Emery, Chgo., 1990-91; chief narcotics prosecutions bur. Cook County State's Attys. Office, Chgo., 1991-92, first asst. state's atty., 1992—96; ptnr. Sonnenschein Nath & Rosenthal, 1997—2000; v.p., dep. gen. counsel Sara Lee Corp., 2000—03; sr. v.p., gen. counsel Sears, Roebuck & Co., Hoffman Estates, Ill., 2003—06; exec. v.p., chief human resources officer Exelon Corp., 2006—08, exec. v.p., gen. counsel, 2009—. Mem. Gov.'s Commn. on Capital Punishment, State of Illinois, 2000—; bd. dirs. Andrew Corp., 2005—07. Bd. dirs. Aux. Bd., Art Inst. Chgo., 1987-2000, Chgo. Regional Bd. of Jr. Achievement, 1991-95, Chgo. Area Project, 1992—. Fellow Leadership Greater Chgo., 1989-90; Kizzy Scholarship Fund award, 1991-92; named a Women of Achievement, The Anti-Defamation League, 2008 Fellow Am. Bar Found., Am. Coll. Trial Lawyers; Mem. ABA, Chgo. Bar Assn., Chgo. Inn of Ct., Cook County Bar Assn., Black Women Lawyers Assn., Leadership Greater Chgo. (bd. dirs.). Avocations: running, music, theater. Office: Exelon Corp 10 S Dearborn St 48th Fl PO Box 805398 Chicago IL 60680*

ZORE, EDWARD JOHN, financial services executive; b. Milw., July 5, 1945; s. Joseph F. and Marie A. Z.; m. Diane Widemshek, Aug. 19, 1967; children: Annemarie, Kathryn. BS in Econs., U. Wis., Milw., 1968, MS in Econs., 1970. With investment dept. Northwestern Mut. Fin. Network, Milw., 1969—, chief investment officer, 1990—98, CFO, 1995—98, exec. v.p. life and disability income ins., 1998—2000, pres., 2000—09, CEO, 2001—09, chmn., CEO, 2009—. Bd. trustees Northwestern Mut. Fin. Network, 2000—; bd. dirs. Manpower, Inc., 2000—. Republican. Roman Catholic. Office: Northwestern Mutual 720 E Wisconsin Ave Milwaukee WI 53202-4797

ZOREA, AHARON W., history professor; b. Houston, Mar. 5, 1969; s. Moshe Calberg and Rivka Chana Zorea; m. Debbi Anne Sander; children: Jacob Aharon Augustine, Jonah Charles Athanasius. BA, U. Alaska, Anchorage, 1991; MA, Purdue U., West Lafayette, Ind., 1993; PhD, St. Louis U., 2005. Asst. prof. history U. Wis., Richland Ctr., 2004—. Author: (history book) In the Image of God: A Christian Response to Capital Punishment. Home: 215 N Grove St Richland Center WI 53581 Office: Univ Wis Richland 1200 Hwy 14 W Richland Center WI 53581 Business E-Mail: aharon.zorea@uwc.edu.

ZORICK, NANCY LEE, artist, actress; b. Chgo., July 24, 1946; d. William Russel and Wilma Beatrice (Fithian) Noble; m. Peter Michael Zorick, Aug. 8, 1980. Student, Art Inst. Chgo., 1965-67, Second City Workshop, Chgo., 1967-68, Am. Acad. Art, 1971. Comml. artist Embosograph Display Co., Chgo., 1964-66, Stevens-Biondi-DiCiccio, Chgo., 1966-68. Illustrator: Making Weight, 1991, The Little Acorn, 1996; exhbns. include Fontana Arts Assn., Calif., 1988, Riverside County Art Exhbn., 1990; one woman art show Coachella Valley Mus., 2008; appeared in plays My Sweet Charlie, Chgo., 1968, Harold, Chgo., 1969, films include Medium Cool, 1968, Jackson County Jail, 1976, Outside Chance, 1978; appeared in commercial Tastee Freeze, 1969. Mem Des Arts, 1981, historian, 1983—85, parliamentarian, 1986—93, 1996—2006, pres., 1993—95, 2006—08. Recipient 1st place in Fine Arts, Nat. Date Festival, 1983, 2d place, Riverside Nat. Date Festival, 1993, 1996, 2001, 2007, Best of Show in Fine Arts, Des-Arts, 1988, 1st place, Des Arts, 1986, 1990, 1992—93, 1996—98, 2000—01, 2003—05, Best of Show in Fine Arts, Fontana (Calif.) Arts Assn., 1988; named to Taft Alumni Hall of Fame, Chgo., 2000. Avocations: teaching Sunday school, ballet, bookpals reading. Home: 51-555 Monroe St #31 Indio CA 92201 Personal E-mail: noblezorick@aol.com.

ZORILLA FULLAONDO, ENRIQUE, bank executive; BA, U. Iberoamericana; MBA, Northwestern U. CPA Universidad Nacional Autonoma de México. Account exec. corp. banking Banca Nacional de Mexico (Banamex), Mexico City, 1982, asst. v.p., 1985—88, Monterrey, 1988—91, sr. v.p. corporate and middle markets, North divsn., 1991—93, exec. v.p. North divsn., 1993—96, corp. dir. commercialization Mexico City, 1996—2006, head of commercial markets, 2006, CEO, 2006—. Sr. leadership com. Citigroup; bd. dirs. Seguros Banamex, Afore Banamex, Credito Familiar. Founder Diversity Com., Mexico. Office: Banamex Isabel la Católica 44 CP 06000 Mexico City Mexico*

ZORN, ELAYNE LESLEY, anthropologist, educator; b. NYC, Feb. 3, 1952; d. Sol Zorn and Sandra Gordon; 1 child, Gavriel Enrique Cutipa-Zorn. BFA in Textile Arts, Calif. Coll. Arts, Oakland, 1975; MA in Latin Am. Studies, U. Tex., Austin, 1983; MA in Anthropology, Cornell U., Ithaca, NY, 1987, PhD, 1997. Ethnologist Mus. Nat. Etnografia Folklore, La Paz, Bolivia, textile specialist, 1977—78; rsch. assoc. prin. rschr. U. Liverpool, England, 1991—92; vis. asst. prof. interdisciplinary writing Colgate U., Hamilton, NY, 1994—97, vis. asst. prof. anthropology, 1997—98; asst. prof. anthropology U. Ctrl. Fla., Orlando, 1998—2004, assoc. prof. anthropology, 2004—. Contbr. chapters to books, scientific papers. Treas. Soc. Latin Am. & Caribbean Anthropology, 2007—09. Scholar Ruta de Aprendizaje, PRAIA-La Paz,

2006; Small grant, Wenner-Gren Found. Anthrop. Rsch., 1994, fellowship, NEH, 1995. Fellow: Internat. Acad. Intercultural Rsch., Soc. Applied Anthropology; mem.: AAUW, SE Coun. Latin Am. Studies, Latin Am. Studies Assn., Fla. Folklore Soc., Fla. Acad. Scis., Bolivian Studies Assn. (bd. dirs. 2006—), Am. Anthrop. Assn., Textile Soc. America (rep. at large 1999—2001). Avocations: travel, reading, music. Office: Univ Ctrl Fla Dept Anthropology Orlando FL 32816-1361 Office Fax: 407-823-3498. Business E-Mail: ezorn@mail.ucf.edu.

ZORN, ERIC STUART, retail executive; b. Newark, Oct. 2, 1948; s. Arthur and Evelyn (Bernstein) Z.; m. Lois Karen Green, Nov. 29, 1979. Student, Fairleigh Dickinson Coll., Wayne, NJ, Upsala Coll., East Orange, NJ. Cash ops. supr. Vornado Inc., Garfield, N.J., 1966-69; corp. auditor Mangel Stores Corp., NYC, 1969-70; sr. v.p. Jamesway Corp., Secaucus, NJ, 1970; pres. Omnia Protective Services Inc., Ft. Lee, NJ, 1979, 1530 Owners Corp. (coop. bldg.), Ft. Lee; regional v.p. Wal-Mart Stores Inc., 1993—97, v.p. realty, 1997—99, sr. v.p. realty, 1999, pres. realty, 2003—05, exec. v.p. Wal-Mart Realty, 2005—. Mem. Internat. Mass Retailing Inst. (chmn. loss prevention group 1979-82), NJ Retail Mchts. Assn. (chmn.), Internat. Soc. Stress Analysts, Soc. Strategic Planning, Internat. Coun. Shopping Centers (trustee). Republican. Jewish. Office: Wal-Mart Realty 2001 SE 10th St Bentonville AR 72712-6489*

ZORN, JIM (JAMES ARTHUR ZORN), professional football coach, retired professional football player; b. Whittier, Calif., May 10, 1953; m. Joy Zorn; children: Rachael, Sarah, Danielle, Isaac. Attended, Cerritos Jr. Coll., Calif., 1971—72, Calif. State Poly. U., Pomona. Quarterback Seattle Seahawks, 1976—84, Green Bay Packers, 1985, Winnipeg Blue Bombers, Can. Football League, 1986, Tampa Bay Buccaneers, 1987; offensive asst., quarterbacks coach Boise State U. Broncos, 1989—91, offensive coord., 1992—94; quarterbacks coach U. Minn. Golden Gophers, 1995—96; offensive asst. Seattle Seahawks, 1997; quarterbacks coach Detroit Lions, 1998—2000, Seattle Seahawks, 2001—08; head coach Washington Redskins, 2008—. Active Med. Teams Internat., Pro Athletes Outreach. Named Am. Football Conf. Offensive Rookie of Yr., NFL, 1976; named to Seattle Seahawks Ring of Honor. Achievements include leading the NFL in: pass attempts, 1976, passes intercepted, 1976. Office: Washington Redskins Redskins Pk 21300 Redskins Pk Dr Ashburn VA 20147 Office Phone: 703-726-7000.*

ZORN, JOHN, composer, musician; b. NYC, Sept. 2, 1953; Band mem. Naked City, NYC, 1989—94; founder, mem. Masada, 1994—; founder & exec. prodr. Tzadik record label, NYC, 1995—. Numerous commissions including NY Philharm., Kronos Quartet, Am. Composers Orch., Bklyn. Philharm., Stephen Drury, Bayerische Staatsoper, WDR Orch. Köln. Major compositions include: Christabel, 1972, Conquest of Mexico, 1973, Mikhail Zoetrope, 1974, Lacrosse, 1977, Hockey, 1978, Fencing, 1978, The Book of Heads, 1978, Pool, 1979, Archery, 1979, Track & Field, 1980, Locus Solus, 1982, Sebastopol, 1983, Rugby, 1983, Cobra, 1984, Xu Feng, 1985, Godard, 1985, Spillane, 1986, Hu Die, 1986, Ruan Lingyu, 1987, Hwang Chin-ee, 1988, Cat O'Nine Tails, 1988, Quê Trân, 1988, For Your Eyes Only, 1989, Bézique, 1989, Torture Garden, 1990, Grand Guignol, 1990, Dead Man, 1990, Elegy, 1991, Leng Tch'e, 1991, Carny, 1992, Memento Mori, 1992, Kristallnacht, 1992, Absinthe, 1992, Angelus Novus, 1993, Masada, 1993-97, The Sand's Share, 1994, Redbird, 1995, Dark River, 1995, Aporias, 1995, Music for Children, 1996, Duras, 1996, Kol Nidre, 1996, Orchestra Variations, 1996, Etant Donnés, 1997, Shibboleth, 1997, Cycles du Nord, 1998, Rituals, 1998, The String Quartets, 1999, Cartoon S&M, 2000, Love, Madness & Mysticism, 2001, Hockey, 2002, Hemophiliac, 2002, Magick, 2004, Rituals, 2005, Mysterium, 2005, Moonchild, 2006, Astronome, 2006, Six Litanies for Heliogabalus, 2007, From Silence to Sorcery, 2007, The Stone, 2007, The Dreamers, 2008, Lucifer: The Book of Angels 10, 2008; composer for films: White & Lazy, 1986, She Must Be Seeing Things, 1987, Distribution of Lead, 1988, The Golden Boat, 1990, Maohgai, 1993, Hollywood Hotel, 1994, Zigrail, 1995, The Black Glove, 1997, Trembling Before G-d, 2001, Secret Lives: Hidden Children & Their Rescuers During WWII, 2002, Shaolin Ulysses, 2003, Invitation to a Suicide, 2004, Protocols of Zion, 2005, The Treatment, 2006; appears in films: Rising Tones Cross, 1985, Put More Blood Into the Music, 1987, The Revenge of the Dead Indians, 1993, Sabbath in Paradise, 1998, A Bookshelf on Top of the Sky: 12 Stories About John Zorn, 2002, Jack Smith & the Destruction of Atlantis, 2006. MacArthur fellow, John D. & Catherine T. MacArthur Found., 2006. Office: Tzadik PMB 126 200 E 10th St New York NY 10003 E-mail: info@tzadik.com.

ZORNOW, DAVID MERRILL, lawyer; b. NYC, Mar. 31, 1955; s. Jack and Marion (Gilden) Z.; m. Martha Malkin, July 21, 1985; children: Samuel Morris, Hannah Jane, Ethan Lewis. AB summa cum laude, Harvard U., 1976; JD, Yale U., 1980. Bar: NY 1981, DC 1988, US Ct. Appeals (3d cir.) 1982, US Dist. Ct. (so. dist.) NY 1983, US Ct. Appeals (2d cir.) 1984, US Dist. Ct. DC 1989, US Ct. Appeals (DC cir.) 1989, US Dist. Ct. (ea. dist.) NY 1993. Law clerk to Hon. Herbert J. Stern US Dist. Ct. NJ, Newark, 1980-82; assoc. Kramer Levin Kamin Nessen & Frankel, NYC, 1982-83; asst. US atty. So. Dist. NY US Atty.'s Office, NYC, 1983-87; assoc. ind. counsel Office Ind. Counsel-Iran/Contra Investigation, Washington, 1987-89; head NY white collar criminal def. practice Skadden, Arps, Slate, Meagher & Flom LLP, NYC, 1989—, ptnr., Global Head Litig., Controversy Practices, 2009—. Chmn. NYC Civilian Complaint Rev. Bd., 1994-96; vis. faculty Trial Advocacy Workshop Harvard Law Sch., Cambridge, Mass., 1988, Benjamin N. Cardozo Sch. Law; spkr. and writer on white collar crime issues. Contbr. articles to profl. publ. Mem. Fed. Bar Coun., Assn. Bar City NY, NY Coun. Def. Lawyers., Phi Beta Kappa. Office: Skadden Arps Slate Meagher & Flom LLP 4 Times Sq Fl 39 New York NY 10036-6595 Office Phone: 212-735-2890. Office Fax: 917-777-2890. E-mail: dzornow@skadden.com.

ZOROWSKI, CARL FRANK, engineering educator, academic administrator; b. Pitts., July 14, 1930; s. Stanley and Mary Josephine (Kozuch) Z.; m. Sarah Jane Crossley, Aug. 7, 1954 (dec. 1983); children: Kathleen Ann, Karl Alan, Kristine Alaine; m. Louise Parrish Lockwood, Apr. 13, 1985. BSME, Carnegie Inst. Tech., 1952, MSME, 1953, PhD, 1956. Instr. Carnegie Inst. Tech., Pitts., 1952-56, asst. prof., 1956-61, assoc. prof., 1961-62; prof. dept. mech. and aero. engring. N.C. State U., Raleigh, 1964-66; R.J. Reynolds Industries prof., 1966-97; assoc. dept. head, 1964-72; dept. head, 1972-79; assoc. dean acad. affairs Sch. Engring., 1979-85; dir. Integrated Mfg. Sys. Inst., 1986-92; dept. head, 1992-93; dir. Succeed/NSF Coalition, 1993-97; assoc. dean acad. affairs, 1993-94; R.J. Reynolds Industries emeritus prof., 1997—. Contbr. articles to profl. jours.; patentee in field. 2d lt. USAR, 1952-58. Recipient Rsch. award Sigma Xi, 1967. Fellow ASME (Richards Meml. award 1975), Fellow Am. Soc. Engring. Edn. (We. Electric award 1968); mem. Fiber Soc. (Achievement award 1970). Home: 103 Windyrush Ln Cary NC 27511-9758 Office: NC State U PO Box 7901 Raleigh NC 27695-0001 Home Phone: 919-851-3145. Personal E-mail: zorowski@mindspring.com. Business E-Mail: zorowski@eos.ncsu.edu.

ZORTHIAN, BARRY, communications executive; b. Kutahia, Turkey, Oct. 8, 1920; naturalized, US, 1930; s. Herbert Peter and Annaly (Markarian) Zorthian; m. Margaret Aylaian, June 6, 1948; children: Gregory Jannig, Stephen Arnak. BA, Yale U., 1941; LLB, N.Y. U., 1953; LLD (hon.), Ind. Inst. Tech., 1970. Bar: NY 1953. Newspaper reporter, 1936-42; newspaper and radio reporter, 1947-48; news and policy editor USIA, 1948-56, program mgr. Voice of Am., 1956-61; dep. pub. affairs. officer USIS, India, 1961-64; min.-counselor for info. Am. Embassy, Vietnam, 1964-68; v.p. Time, Inc., 1969-79, v.p. govt. affairs, 1974-79; pres. Time-Life Broadcast, 1969-73, Washington/Balt. Regional Assn., 1979-81; sr. v.p. Gray and Co., Washington, 1981-84; ptnr. Alcalde & Fay, Arlington, Va., 1984—. Bd dirs Am. Univ. Armenia, Armenian Gen Benvolent Union, Internat. Rsch. and Exchs. With USMC, 1942—46, col USMCR, 1946—73. Mem.: Marine Corps Res. Officers Assn., Washington Inst. Fgn. Affairs, Am. Fgn. Svc. Assn., Coun. Fgn. Rels., Congl. Country Club (Washington), Met. Club (Washington), Burning Tree Club (Washington), Century Assn. Club (N.Y.C.). Home: 4201 Cathedral Ave NW Apt 405E Washington DC 20016-4914 Office: Alcalde & Fay 2111 Wilson Blvd Ste 850 Arlington VA 22201-3051 Home Phone: 202-244-1984; Office Phone: 703-841-0626. Personal E-mail: barzor2@aol.com.

ZOSIKE, JOANIE FRITZ, theater director, actress, writer; b. Bklyn., July 6, 1949; d. Nathan and Gloria S. (Greenberg) Hieger; m. Godson Zosike. BA in Theatre, NYU, 1980. Actor The Living Theatre, NYC, 1990—. Co-dir. DADAnewyork; co-founder and co-dir. Action Racket Theatre, N.Y.C., 1998—; artist-in-residence Living Theatre Workshops (USA) Author: (stage prodns.) You Told Me That the Carousel Was Crystal, Frames, Inside, 12 Steps to Murder; author: (with Hanon Reznikov) And Then The Heavens Closed; actress (stage prodns.) Chisciotte, Not in My Name, Mysteries and Smaller Pieces, Utopia, Anarchia, Humanity, Body of God, I and I, Midsummer Night's Dream, Mother Courage, Maudie and Jane, Brunch at the Luther, (solo performances) All Right So I AM the Earth, Harpies Complex, Ereshkigal's Peg, Fritzgabriel Cabaret, Alen Mak Festival (Bulgaria), Festival des Politisches Liedes (Germany), (chapbook) The Character Poems, 2000, (films) Mass and Masses, Human Flesh; vocalist (radio show) Women on the Edge of Time; contbr. Between Ourselves: Letters Between Mothers and Daughters (edited by Karen Payne), Women in American Theatre (edited by Helen Krich Chinoy and Linda Walsh Jenkins); contbr. poetry and articles to artistic jours. Bd. dirs. N.Y.C. Peoples Life Fund; steering com. Theatres Against War. Mem. War Resisters League, New Yorkers Against the Death Penalty. Office: The Living Theatre 21 Clinton St New York NY 10009 Personal E-mail: jhiegerzosike@nyc.rr.com.

ZOSS, ABRAHAM OSCAR, chemical company executive; b. South Bend, Ind., Feb. 17, 1917; s. Harry and Fannie (Friedman) Z.; m. Betty Jane Hurwich, Dec. 24, 1939; children: Roger, Joel, Hope; m. Magda Szanto, May 26, 1978. BSChemE, U. Notre Dame, 1938, MS, 1939, PhD, 1941. With Gen. Aniline & Film Corp., Easton, Pa., 1941—47, from tech. mgr. to plant mgr. Linden, NJ, 1947—57; from mfr. mfg. adminstrn. to prodn. mgr. chem. divsn. Minn. Mining & Mfg. Co., St. Paul, 1957—60; v.p. Photek, Inc., West Kingston, RI, 1960—62; asst. corp. tech. dir. Celanese Corp., NYC, 1962—65, corp. tech. dir., 1965—66, corp. dir. comml. devel., 1966—69; v.p. corp. devel. Tenneco Chems. Inc., NYC, 1969—71, Universal Oil Products Co., Des Plaines, Ill., 1971—72; group v.p. Engelhard Industries divsn. Engelhard Minerals & Chem. Corp., Murray Hill, NJ, 1972—74, v.p. bus. devel., 1974—77; v.p. corp. devel. CPS Chem. Co., Inc., Old Bridge, NJ, 1977, dir., v.p., chief adminstrv. officer, 1978—84; pres. Bus. Devel. Internat., NJ, 1984—. Mem. field info. agy. Office Tech. Svc., Commerce Dept., Europe, 1946; tchg. asst. U. Notre Dame, 1939-41. Contbr. articles to profl. jours.; patentee in field. Active Met. Mus. Art., N.Y.C. Recipient Centennial Sci. award U. Notre Dame, 1965, accredited Profl. Chemist, 1980. Fellow AAAS, Am. Inst. Chemists; mem. AIChE, Am. Chem. Soc., N.Y. Acad. Scis., Soc. Chem. Industry, Soc. Chimie Industrielle (pres. Am. sect.), Chemists Club (N.Y.C.). Achievements include pioneering research in stereospecific polymerization. Home and Office: 333 Elmwood Ave Ste D538 Maplewood NJ 07040-2449 Home Phone: 973-762-5812; Office Phone: 973-762-5802. Personal E-mail: aozoss@aol.com.

ZOTALEY, BYRON LEO, lawyer; b. Mpls., Mar. 18, 1944; s. Leo John and Tula (Koupis) Z.; m. Theresa L. Cassady, Sept. 7, 1969; children: Nicole, Jason, Krisanthy. BA in Psychology, U. Minn., 1966; MATC, U. St. Thomas, St. Paul, 1968; JD, William Mitchell Coll. of Law, 1970. Bar: Minn. 1970, U.S. Dist. Ct. Minn. 1971, US Ct. Appeals (8th cir.) 1972, U.S. Supreme Ct. 1975. Pres. LeVander, Zotaley & Vander Linden, Mpls., 1970-99, Zotaley Law Offices, Ltd., Hopkins, Minn., 1999—. Arbitrator Minn. No Fault Panel, 1974—2009; cons. Marthe Properties, Mpls., 1980-90; pres. Theron Properties, Mpls., 1985—. Bd. dirs. Minn. Consumer Alliance, 1994-95; mem. adv. bd. Benilde-St. Margaret's Jr. H.s., 1993-95; bd. trustees St. Mary's Greek Orthodox Ch. Mpls., 1997-2005, 2008-, v.p., 1998, pres., 1999-2004, Chgo. Met. Coun., 2007-, Go America Archdiscoso Stewardship Commn., 2008-. Mem. ABA, ATLA, Minn. Bar Assn., Hennepin County Bar Assn., Minn. Trial Lawyers Assn. (chmn. Amicus Curiae com. 1980-87, bd. govs. 1982-93, mem. exec. com. 1987-89, emeritus, 1994—). Home: 5504 Parkwood Ln Edina MN 55436-1728 Office: 400 Wells Fargo Bank Bldg 1011 1st St S Hopkins MN 55343-9413 Office Phone: 952-933-5100. Fax: 952-933-9034.

ZOU, LINHUA, research scientist; s. Guangchang Zou and Qinxian Hu; m. Ying Ding, June 30, 1998; 1 child, Fangyu. BS, Northeastern U., Shengyang, Liaoning, China, 1988; MS, Inst. Precious Metals, Kunming, Yunnan, China, 1995; PhD, Ctrl. South U., Changsha, Hunan, China, 1999. Cert. univ. tchr. Ministry Edn. of People's Republic China, 2004. Asst. tchr. Kunming Metallurgy Coll., 1988—92; grad. rsch. asst. Inst. Precious Metals, Kunming, China, 1992—95, Ctrl. South U., Changsha, China, 1995—99; postdoctoral rschr. Tsinghua U., Beijing, 1999—2002; rsch. scientist Korea Inst. Materials Sci., Chang-Won, Kyung-Nam, Republic of Korea, 2002—03; assoc. prof. U. Sci. and Tech. Beijing, Beijing, 2004—06; postdoctoral rschr. U. SC, Columbia, 2006—07, U. Calif., LA, 2007—. Contbr. articles to profl. jours. Mem.: Am. Ceramic Soc., Sigma Xi. Achievements include displaying nanostructures inside the fiber cell wall of a bamboo culm; research in the microstructural or mechanical characterization ont he Cf/ZrC composite fabricated by RMI. Avocations: running, tennis. Home: 3180 Sawtelle Blvd #208 Los Angeles CA 90066 Office: Dept Materials Sci and Engring U Calif Los Angeles 405 Hilgard Ave Rm 3040 Los Angeles CA 90095-1595 Business E-Mail: lhzou@ucla.edu.

ZOU, QIYUE, systems engineer; s. Zhenfeng Zou and Ruixian Zhang. BS (hon.), 2001; MS in Elec. & Electronic Engring., Nanyang Technol. U., Singapore, 2003; MA in Math., 2008; PhD in Elec. Engring., U. Calif., LA, 2008. Rsch. engr. Nanyang Technol. U., Singapore, 2001—04; staff engr., comm. sys. Wilinx Corp., Carlsbad, Calif., 2008—. Contbr. scientific papers to profl. jours. Recipient Young Inventors award, Tan Kah Kee Found., 2001, Motorola Book prizes, Nanyang Technol. U., 2001. Mem.: IEEE Signal Processing Soc. (Young Author Best Paper award 2007). Home: 3777 Mentone Ave Apt 110 Los Angeles CA 90034

ZOU, TONG, electrical engineer; PhD, Vanderbilt U., Nashville, Tenn., 2004. Cert. reliability engr., Am. Soc. Quality, 2008. Engr. GE Energy, Greenville, SC, 2005—. Contbr. articles to profl. jours. Mem.: Sigma Xi. Office: GE Energy 300 Garlington Rd Greenville SC 29615

ZOU, YIYU, medical educator; b. Shenyang, Liaonning, China, June 15, 1955; s. Wenxin Qian and Shanqing Zou. PhD, Shenyang Coll. Pharmacy, China, 1990. Asst. prof. MD Anderson Cancer Ctr., Houston, 1996—2002, Albert Einstein Coll. Medicine, Bronx, NY, 2002—08, assoc. prof., 2008. Grant, NIH, 2006—09. Achievements include patents pending for; patents in field. Office: Albert Einstein Coll Medicine 1300 Morris Park Ave C626 Bronx NY 10461 Office Fax: 718-430-8663. Personal E-mail: yiyuzou@yahoo.com.

ZOUBAREFF, KATHY OLGA, actress, model; b. Hassalt, Belgium; d. Vladimir F. and Kataryna (Sarcov) Z. Grad. in TV acting, J.R. Powers Sch.-Model Agy.; BA in Polit. Sci., Wayne State U.; postgrad., Ann Parsley Sch. Dance, Clinton Twp., Mich., 1990-95, Mary Skiba Sch. Dance, 1995—; A in Gen. Studies, Drama, Macomb Community Coll.; fitness and nutrition cert., Internat. Corr. Schs. Ctr., Scranton, Pa.; voice studies, Ctr. for Creative Studies, Detroit, 1994—; drama studies, Wayne State U., 1994—; broadcasting studies, Macomb C.C., Warren, Mich., 2001. Cert. method actress Grad. Level 3, Dramatic Arts, Studies Mich. Ferndale. Benefits coord. physician group Wayne State U., 1990—96, 2007—08; office mgr. Univ. Orthopaedic Assocs. Detroit, P.C., 1996-98; with The Zoubareff Co., 1998—; actress, model One Source Talent. Actress, dancer, belly dancer, fashion, TV comml. and photog. model/film screen extra, Hawaiian Tropic Pageants; fragrance model Coty Fragrances, Celion Dion; swimsuit model Ujena; nat. spokesperson Dryell, Physique, Pantene, Oil of O'Lay, Vidal Sassoon, Cover Girl, Coca Cola, Marlboro, Nascar, Indy 400, others; voice over talent, Mae West look-alike; beauty cons. Olay, Cover Girl, Rimmell, London, Lee Jeans, Actress & Model, 2008, Ujena Team Leader, Mich., 2008. Presenter Prodns.-Plus Talent Mgmt., Bingham Farm, Mich., One Sq. Talent, Troy, NY, J.D. Prodn., Bloomfield Hills, Mich. Mem. Renaissance Ctr. Fashion Panel, Detroit, 1989-91, St. Clair Shores Players; contbg. Am. Film Inst., L.A., 2006 Avocations: art, drawing, exercise. Home: 38579 Delta Dr Clinton Township MI 48036-1711 Office: One Source Talent 3250 West Big Beaver Rd #520 Troy MI 48084 Office Phone: 586-243-0923. Personal E-mail: zoubareff@aol.com.

ZOULAS, SOTERIOS C., communications educator, consultant; s. Chris S. and Demetrula Zoulas; m. Grace Ann Sahagian, Sept. 17, 2006. BA, Boston U., 1966; MA, Assumption Coll., 1968. Tenured instr. and chair, comm. dept. Quincy Coll., Mass., 1991—2000; dir. comm. Brown U. Annenberg Inst., Providence, 1999—2004; assoc. prof. and chair, comm. arts dept. Eastern Nazarene Coll., Quincy, 2002—. Pres. Zoulas Comm., Sudbury, Mass., 1991—. Prodr.(writer and dir.): (film) (media award, ABC TV Network and nominated for an Emmy, 1981),: TV Talk Show, Radio Talk Program (Phillips award, Info. Radio Broadcast Program in New Eng.). Chair, Am. com. St. George Soc., Worcester, Mass., 2004—09; chair, fundraising com. Lowell Homeless Shelter, Mass.; sr. advisor East Boston APAC; com. mem. St. Spyridon Cathedral, Worcester, Mass.; pres. New Eng. Sch. Acupuncture, Watertown, Mass., 1992—93. Named Best Press Sec. in Mass. State Govt., State House Press Corps., 1990; Travel fellowship, Inst. Ednl. Leadership, 1984—85. Mem.: World Affair Coun., Nat. Comm. Assn., Pub. Rels. Soc. America. Greek Orthodox. Avocations: travel, reading, writing, working out. Office: Eastern Nazarene Coll 32 E Elm St Quincy MA 02170 Business E-Mail: soterios.c.zoulas@enc.edu.

ZOULLAS, DEBORAH DECOTIS, investment company executive; b. Salem, Mass., Nov. 13, 1952; d. John and Marie (Mahoney) DeC.; m. Nicholas B. Zoullas, Aug. 15, 1987. BA, Smith Coll., 1974; MBA, Stanford U., 1978. Analyst Morgan Stanley & Co. Inc., NYC, 1974-76, assoc., 1978-81, v.p. London, 1982-84, prin. NYC, 1985-87, mng. dir., 1988-95, adv. dir., 1996—; exec. v.p. Sotheby's Holdings, NYC, 1998—2000; dir. Sotheby's Holding Corp., NYC, 2000, Armor Holdings Inc., 2002—07. Co-chair spl. projects com. Meml. Sloan Kettering Cancer Ctr.; bd. mem. Henry St. Settlement. Mem. adv. coun. Stanford Grad. Sch. Bus., 2003-09; trustee Helena Rubinstein Found. Miller scholar Stanford U., 1978. Home: 160 E 72d St New York NY 10021

ZOUMALAN, RICHARD ABRAHAM, otolaryngologist; b. Encino, Calif., June 18, 1979; s. George and Bella Zoumalan. BS, U. Calif., LA, 2001; MD, Northwestern U., 2005. Physician NY U. Sch. Medicine, 2005—.

ZOURARAKIS, DEMETRIO PERIFERACHIS, natural resource scientist; b. Buenos Aires, Argentina, Mar. 2, 1952; s. Jorge Demetrio Zourarakis and Elena Periferachis, Jorge Periferachis and Palmira Angela Comerci; m. Joyce Carol Zourakis, July 13, 1945; 1 child, Zachary Alexander. BS, Universidad Nacional de Buenos Aires, 1977; MSc, Iowa State U., Ames, 1987; PhD, U. Ky., Lexington, 1992. Geog. info. sys. processing specialist divsn. conservation Ky. Dept. Natural Resources, Frankfort, 2000—04; remote sensing and geog. info. sys. analyst divsn. geog. info. Commonwealth Office Tech., Frankfort, 2004—. Adj. prof. dept. geography and geosciences U. Louisville, 1998—. J. Fielding Reed fellow, Potash and Phosphate Inst., 1988. Fellow: Soil and Water Conservation Soc. (mem. Ky. Bluegrass chpt.); mem.: Mensa, Gamma Sigma Delta, Sigma Xi (hon.). Home: 5011 Venetian Way Versailles KY 40383 Personal E-mail: demetrio.zourarakis@gmail.com. Business E-Mail: demetrio.zourarakis@ky.gov.

ZREDA, MAREK, science educator; BS, Warsaw U., Poland, 1986; MS, N.Mex Tech, Socorro, 1990, PhD, 1993. Asst. prof. hydrology U. Ariz., 1994—2000, assoc. prof. hydrology and assoc. prof. geology, 2000—. Asst. prof. geology U. Ariz., 1999—2000. Contbr. articles to profl. jours., chapters to books. Mem.: Am. Geophys. Union. Office: Univ Ariz Hydrology and Water Resources Dept Tucson AZ 85721

ZRNIC, REIKO LUKIC, physics educator; b. Belgrade, Serbia-Monteneg, Aug. 8, 1971; d. Slobodanka Mirovic, Vladimir Mirovic (Stepfather); m. Uros Zrnic; children: Luka, Kosta, Andreja. PhD, U. North Tex., Denton, 2003. Post doctarate U. North Tex., 2003—04, adj. prof., 2004—. Contbr. articles to profl. jour. Achievements include research in effects of substrate orientation on the spontaneous ordering of gaassb epilayers. Home: 310 Quiet Valley Coppell TX 75019 Office: Univ North Tex PO Box 311427 Denton TX 76203

ZSCHAU, JULIUS JAMES, lawyer; b. Peoria, Ill., Apr. 1, 1940; s. Raymond Johann Ernst and Rosamond Lillian (Malicoat) Z.; m. Leila Joan Krueger, Aug. 7, 1971; children: Kristen Elisabeth, Kimberly Erna, Kira Jamie White, Karla Johanna. BS, U. Ill., Champaign, 1964, JD,

1966; LLM, John Marshall Law Sch., 1978. Bar: Ill. 1966, Fla. 1975. Atty. Ill. Central Gulf R.R. Co., Chgo., 1966-68; assoc. Coin & Sheerin, Chgo., 1968-70, Snyder, Clarke et al, Waukegan, Ill., 1970-72; counsel Ill. Ctr. Corp., Chgo., 1972-74; v.p., gen. counsel, sec. Am. Agronomics Corp., Tampa, Fla., 1974-76; pres. Sorota & Zschau, Clearwater, Fla., 1976-90; shareholder Baynard, Harrell, Ostow & Ulrich PA, 1990-94, Johnson, Blakely, Pope, Bokor, Ruppel and Burns, Clearwater, 1994—2002, Pennington Moore Wilkinson Bell & Dunbar PA, 2002—. Bd. dirs. Attys. Title Ins. Fund, Inc., chmn. bd. dirs., 1994—95; chmn. com. on land trusts Fla. Bar, past chmn. Real Property, Probate and Trust Law sect., vice chair grievance com., 1985—87, chair leadership conf., 1987; chmn. Jud. Nominating Commn. of 6th Jud. Dist., 1991—94; chmn. jud. nominating com. Ct. Appeals (2d dist.). Mem. Pinellas County Exec. Com., Tampa Regional Planning Coun., 1988-92. Served to capt. USNR, 1962-92. Fellow: Am. Bar Found. (life); mem.: ABA (chmn. standing com. lawyers title guaranty funds 1991, chmn. land trust com., chmn. standing com. lawyers title guaranty funds 2004—07), Fla. Bar Found. (chmn. jud. nominations procedures com. 1992—93, legal aid to poor com.), Fla. Coun. Bar Assn. (past pres., past chmn. vol. bar liaison com.), Clearwater Bar Assn. (past pres.), Chgo. Bar Assn., Ill. Bar Assn., Am. Coll. Real Estate Lawyers (past chmn. condominium com.), Clearwater C. of C. (bd. govs., exec. com., past v.p.), Countryside Country Club. Republican. Home: 1910 Saddlehill Rd N Dunedin FL 34698-2437 Office: Julius J Zschau 1247 S Myrtle Ave Clearwater FL 33756-3469 Home Phone: 727-784-8490.

ZSCHAU, MARILYN, singer; b. Chgo., Feb. 9, 1944; d. Edwin Arthur Eugene and Helen Elizabeth (Kelly) Z.; m. Frans Baars, Sept. 2005. BA in Radio, TV and Motion Pictures, U. N.C., 1959; grad., Juilliard Sch. Music, 1965; studied opera theatre with Christopher West, studied voice with Florence Page Kimball, studied with John Lester. Toured with Met. Nat. Co., 1965-66; debut, Vienna Volksoper, in Die Tote Stadt, 1967, Vienna Staatsoper, in Ariadne auf Naxos, 1971; with N.Y.C. Opera in La Fanciulla del West, 1978; debut Royal Opera, covent Garden in La Boheme, 1982, Met. Opera, in La Boheme, 1985, La Scala, in Die Frau ohne Schatten, 1986; has toured and sung in many countries including S.Am., Japan, and Australia. Office: 4245 Wilshire Blvd Oakland CA 94602-3549 Home Phone: 510-336-9269; Office Phone: 510-484-7742. E-mail: marilynzschau@yahoo.com.

ZUBECK, JACQUELINE ANN (NINA ZUBECK), literature and language professor; b. Tucson, Ariz., Nov. 9, 1953; d. Richard Karl Zubeck and Joan Marie Gurka Zubeck; m. Nicholas Nichols, 1978 (div. 1985); m. Kevin O'Donoghve, 1991 (div. 1998); 1 child, Jon Thomas Nichols. BA, State U. NY, Purchase, 1990; MA, Rutgers, State U. NJ, NB, 1995, PhD, 1998. Cert. in paralegal Rockland CC, 1988. Vis. asst. prof. English Manhattan Coll., Riverdale, NY, 2001—07; vis. asst. prof. English & world lit. Coll. Mt. St. Vincent, Riverdale, 2007—; adminstr., tchr. Bard Coll. Clemente Course, 2000—05, tchr., 2007—. Seminar leader lit. & democracy NJ Coun. Humanities, Trenton, 2008—. Contbr. articles to profl. jours. Mem. Holy Myrrhbearers Women's Choir, Tappan, NY, 1997—2008. Reconsidering Flannery O'Connor fellowship, NEH, 2007. Mem.: MLA, Flannery O'Connor Soc., Don DeLillo Soc., Am. Lit. Assn. Russian Orthodox. Avocations: singing, hiking, sailing, wooden boat building. Office: Coll Mt Saint Vincent 6301 Riverdale Ave Bronx NY 10471 Personal E-mail: jacqueline.zubeck@gmail.com. Business E-Mail: jackie.zubeck@mountsaintvincent.edu.

ZUBERBIER, JO ANN, elementary school educator; b. Perryville, Mo., Mar. 8, 1936; d. Henry Herman and Marcella Mae (Koeneman) Schaefer; m. Orlan Gene Zuberbier, June 11, 1960; children: Todd Alan, Gregg Milo, Dawn Cheryl Zuberbier Flatt. BA magna cum laude, U. Wis., Green Bay, 1971. Cert. life tchr., Wis. Tchr. St. John's Luth. Sch., Red Bud, Ill., 1954-55, St. Paul's Luth. Sch., Mt. Prospect, Ill., 1956-61, Kennedy Elem. Sch., Green Bay, Wis., 1971-92, Christa McAuliffe Elem. Sch., Green Bay, 1992—97; ret., 1997. Vol. gen. ednl. devel./HS equivalency diploma tchr. St. Croix County Jail, Hudson, Wis. Mem. ASCD, NEA, Green Bay Edn. Assn., WEAC. Home: 1146 County Rd H New Richmond WI 54017-6125 Personal E-mail: jazubie@frontiernet.net.

ZUBERNIS, LYNN SMITH, psychologist, counselor; d. Kevlin Walter and Carol Luckins Smith; m. James J. Zubernis, June 25, 1983 (div. Mar. 1994); children: Emily Kevlin, Jeffrey James. BA in Psychology, Rosemont Coll., 1994; MA in Sch. Psychology, Bryn Mawr Coll., 1997, PhD in Clin., Devel. and Sch. Psychology, 2002. Cert. Sch. Psychologist Pa., 1997, lic. Psychologist Pa., 2005. Intern psychologist Marple Newtown Sch. Dist., Newtown Square, Pa., 1996—97, Child Study Inst., Bryn Mawr, Pa., 1996—98, St. Gabriel's Hall, Audubon, Pa., 1997—98; sch. psychologist Tower Hill Sch., Wilmington, Del., 1999—; intern psychologist Friends Hosp., Phila., 2000—01; therapist Penn Friends Behl Health, Phila., 2001—02; counselor St. Josephs U., Phila., 2002—, asst. dir., Counseling Ctr. Instr. West Chester State U., 1999, adj. prof., 2006; adj. Haverford Coll., 2000. Contbr. articles to profl. jours. Mem.: APA, Pa. Psychol. Assn., Delta Epsilon Sigma, Alpha Sigma Lambda. Avocations: writing, films. Office: St Josephs Univ Counseling Ctr 5600 City Ave Philadelphia PA 19131 Business E-Mail: lzuberni@sju.edu.

ZUBIETA, ALBERTO ALEMAN, construction executive; b. Panama City, Panama; Degree in indsl. engring., civil engring., Tex. A & M U. Adminstr. Panama Canal Commn., 1998—2000, Panama Canal Authority, 1998—. Recipient Fed. Engr. of Yr. award, ASCE, 1998, Personality 2001 award, Seatrade Orgn. Mem.: Young Profls. Assn. (Panama Chpt.), Panama Architects and Engrs. Assn., Panamanian Chamber of Constrn. (William Ross Medal 1992). Office: Panama Canal Authority PO Box 526725 Miami FL 33152-6725

ZUBIETA, JON ANDONI, chemistry professor; b. NYC, June 16, 1945; s. Francisco Zubieta and Anna Agirre; m. Susan Kay Jereb, Nov. 5, 1983; children: Chloe, Christa, Amy Kay, Jon Francisco. BS, Fordham U., Bronx, NY, 1966; PhD, Columbia U., NYC, 1971. Prof. Syracuse U., NY, 1990—2004, disting. prof., 2004—. Postdoc. fellow U. Sussex, Brighton, England, 1971—73; asst. prof. SUNY, Albany, 1973—80, assoc. prof., 1980—87, prof., 1987—90. Recipient Syracuse Sect. award, Am. Chem. Soc., 2004; fellow, Woodrow Wilson Found., 1966—67, grant, Nat. Inst. Health, 1975—90, 2002—03, NSF, 1985—. Fellow: Royal Soc. Chemistry; mem.: Am. Chem. Soc. Conservative. Roman Catholic. Achievements include research in solid state materials for catalysis; design of technetium & Trmenium based radiopharmaceuticals. Avocations: history, hiking. Office: Dept Chemistry Syracuse Univ Coll Pl Syracuse NY 13244 Office Fax: 315-443-4070. Business E-Mail: jazubiet@syr.edu.

ZUBIETA, MARIA JOSE, language educator; b. Montevideo, Uruguay, June 17, 1968; d. Carlos Manuel Zubieta and Maria Elena Rodrigo; m. Mario Michelena, July 21, 2001; 1 child, Sabrina Zubieta Michelena. PhD, U. Calif., Los Angeles, 2002. Bar: State of NJ. (ct. interpreter) 2008. Sr. lang. lectr. NYU, 2000—. Judiciary interpreter State NJ., Trenton, 2008—. Independent. Avocations: reading, movies, travel.

ZUBIK, DAVID ALLEN, bishop; b. Sewickley, Pa., Sept. 4, 1949; s. Stanley and Susan (Raskosky) Zubik. BA, Duquesne U., 1971, M in Edn. Adminstrn., 1982; grad., St. Mary Sem. and U., Balt. Ordained priest Diocese of Pitts., 1975, adminstrv. sec., 1987—88, adminstrv. sec. & master of ceremonies, 1988—91, dir. clergy personnel, 1991—95, assoc. gen. sec., chancellor, 1995—96, gen. sec., vicar gen., 1996—97, aux. bishop, 1997—2003, bishop, 2007—, Diocese of Green Bay, Wis., 2003—07; parochial vicar Sacred Heart Parish, Shadyside, Pa., 1975—80; vice-prin. Quigley Cath. HS, Baden, Pa.; ordained bishop, 1997. Bd. advisors U. St. Mary of the Lake Mundelein Sem., Chgo., 2004—07. Mem.: US Conf. Cath. Bishops (chmn. laity com. 2005—08, adminstrv. com., audit sub-com., nat. Adv. Coun.). Roman Catholic. Office: Diocese of Pitts 111 Blvd of the Allies Pittsburgh PA 15222 Office Phone: 412-456-3000.

ZUBRETSKY, JOSEPH M., insurance company executive; BSBA, Univ. Hartford. Ptnr. Coopers & Lybrand, 1990—96; exec. v.p., CFO Healthsource Inc., 1996—97; exec. v.p. bus. develop., CFO MassMutual Fin. Group, 1997—99; pres., CEO GAB Robins Group, 1999—2005; sr. v.p. fin., investments & corp. develop. UnumProvident Corp., 2005—07; exec. v.p., CFO, chief risk officer Aetna Inc., Hartford, Conn., 2007—. Office: Aetna Inc 151 Farmington Ave Hartford CT 06156*

ZUBRIN, JAY ROSS, surgeon; b. Phila., June 11, 1936; BS, Dickinson Coll., 1959; MD, Temple U., 1963. Diplomate Am. Bd. Surgery. Intern San Francisco Gen. Hosp., 1963-64; resident in gen. surgery U. Calif. Med. Ctr., 1964-69; pvt. practice; chief of staff Hoag Meml. Hosp. Presbyn., Newport Beach, Calif. Mem. ACS, AMA, Calif. Med Assn., Orange County Med. Assn. (pres. 2005-06). Office: Ste 601 351 Hospital Rd Newport Beach CA 92663-3500 Office Phone: 949-548-2264. Office Fax: 949-650-3606. Business E-Mail: JZubrin@hoaghospital.org.

ZUBROW, BARRY LEE, diversified financial services company executive; b. Feb. 19, 1953; s. Sol E. Zubrow; m. Jan Debra Rock, Apr. 12, 1986; 2 children. BA, Haverford Coll., 1975; MBA, U. Chgo., 1979, JD, 1980. Fin. mgmt. positions Goldman Sachs Group Inc., NYC, 1979—88, ptnr. through v.p., investment banking div., 1988—94, chief credit officer, 1994—99, chief adminstrv. officer, 1999—2004; pres. ITB LLC, 2004—08; chief risk officer J.P. Morgan Chase & Co., NYC, 2008—. Vice-chmn., lead ind. dir. Nuvelo Inc., 2004—07. Adv. on fiscal & policy matters NJ Gov. Jon Corzine; chmn. NJ Schools Construction Corp., 2006—07, NJ Schools Devel. Authority, 2007—; co-chmn. bd. managers Haverford Coll.; bd. dir. Pingry Sch., Juvenile Law Ctr., Phila.; past mem. vis. com. U. Chgo. Law Sch.; past vice-chmn. Liberty Sci. Ctr., NJ. Office: JP Morgan Chase & Co 270 Park Ave New York NY 10017*

ZUCARO, ALDO CHARLES, insurance company executive; b. Grenoble, France, Apr. 2, 1939; s. Louis and Lucy Zucaro; m. Gloria J. Ward, Oct. 12, 1963; children: Lucy, Louis, Faye. BS in Acctg, Queens Coll., NYC, 1962. C.P.A., N.Y., Ill. Ptnr. Coopers & Lybrand (and predecessor), Chgo. and NYC, 1962-76; exec. v.p., chief fin. officer Old Republic Internat. Corp., Chgo., 1976-81, pres., 1981—, CEO, 1990—93, chmn., CEO, 1993—. Pres., bd. dirs. Old Republic Life Ins. Co., Old Republic Life of N.Y., Old Republic Ins. Co., Internat. Bus. and Merc. Reassurance Co., Republic Mortgage Ins. Co., Old Republic Nat. Title Ins. Co., Home Owners Life Ins. Co. Editor: Financial Accounting Practices of the Insurance Industry, 1975, 76. Mem. AICPAs. Roman Catholic. Office: Old Republic Internat Corp 307 N Michigan Ave Chicago IL 60601-5311

ZUCK, ALFRED MILLER, public administration educator; b. East Petersburg, Pa., Aug. 27, 1934; s. Walter Newton and Mary (Miller) Z.; m. Geraldine Connelly, July 21, 1957; children: Susan, David. BA, Franklin and Marshall Coll., 1957; MPA, Syracuse U., 1958. Dir. fed. program Presdl. Commn. on Youth Opportunities, Washington, 1967-68; dir evaluation Employment and Tng. Adminstrn., Dept. Labor, Washington, 1968-70, dir adminstrn. and mgmt., 1970-75; comptroller U.S. Dept. Labor, Washington, 1975-77; exec. dir. Commn. on Exec., Legis. and Jud. Salaries, Washington, 1980; asst. sec. Dept. Labor, Washington, 1977-83, acting sec., 1981; asst. adminstr. EPA, Washington, 1983; exec. dir. Nat. Assn. Schs. of Pub. Affairs and Adminstrn., Washington, 1983-97; disting. prof. Am. U., Washington, 1996—2005, emeritus prof., 2005—. Pres. Internat. Inst. Adminstrv. Scis., Brussels, 1989-92, Am. Consortium for Internat. Pub. Adminstrn., Washington, 1984-89; bd. dirs. Pub./Pvt. Venture, Inc., Phila., 1984-90. Recipient Presdl. Disting. Exec. award Pres. of U.S., 1980; Disting. Alumni award Franklin and Marshall Coll., 1980. Fellow Nat. Acad. Pub. Adminstrn. (trustee 1989-95, chmn. bd. trustees 1993-95); mem. Phi Beta Kappa. Personal E-mail: alzuck@aol.com.

ZUCK, ROSEMARY, social worker, educator; b. Rochester, NY, Sept. 11, 1948; d. George Philip and Laura Zuck. BA in Math., Nazareth Coll., Rochester, 1970; MA in Edn., U. Rochester, 1974; MSW, Syracuse U., NY, 1996. LCSW N.Y., 2005; cert. tchr. math. grades 7-12 1974. Tchr., coord. math. East Rochester Pub. Schs., NY, 1970—97; program coord./sr. social worker upstate N.Y. chpt. Nat. MS Soc., Rochester, 1997—2002, dir. programs, 2002—04; social worker Unity Health Sys. -Edna Tina Wilson Living Ctr., Rochester, 2004—08; affiliate educator Aetna, 2006—. MS support group facilitator, Rochester, 1997—2008; mem. Rochester Effectiveness Partnership Provider Tng. and Alumni Study Group Partnership, 2001—03. Contbr. book. Mem. City-County Coun. for People with Disabilities Accessibility Com., Rochester, 1998—2001; co-chair and com. mem. Women's Workshop Planning Com. - A Workshop for Women Living with Disabilities and Chronic Illnesses, Rochester, 2001—04; pastoral visitor Rochester Gen. Hosp., 1987—90. Mem.: NASW, Rochester Threshold Choir, Finger Lakes Choral Festival, Rochester Oratorio Soc. Avocations: singing, gardening, reading, antiques, journaling. E-mail: rosemaryzuck@rochester.rr.com.

ZUCKER, ALEXANDER, physicist, researcher; b. Zagreb, Croatia, Aug. 1, 1924; came to U.S., 1939; s. William and Bertha (Klopfer) Z.; m. Joan-Ellen Jamieson, Nov. 28, 1953; children: Rebecca, Claire, Susannah. BA, U. Vt., Burlington, 1947; MS, Yale U., New Haven, 1948, PhD, 1950. Physicist Oak Ridge Nat. Lab., 1950-60, assoc. dir. electro-nuclear div., 1960—70, dir. heavy ion project, 1972—74, assoc. dir. phys. scis., 1973-88, acting lab. dir., 1988, assoc. dir. for nuclear techs., 1989-93; exec. dir., environ. studies bd. NAS-NAE, Washington, 1970-72; prof. physics U. Tenn., 1996—. Mem. U.S. del. to USSR on Peaceful Uses of Atomic Energy, 1963; Ford prof. physics U. Tenn., Knoxville, 1968-73; U.S. del. to Pugwash Conf., 1971; research coordination council Gas Research Inst., Chgo., 1978-85; com. Army manpower Nat. Research Council, Washington, 1982-83; adv. panel on technologies to reduce U.S. materials import vulnerability Office of Technology Assessment, Washington, 1982-85; council on energy engring. research Dept. of Energy, Washington, 1983—; industry, nat. lab. steel initiative White House, Washington, 1984 Editor Internat. Jour. Nuclear Sci. Applications, 1980—; cons. editor Ency. and Yearbook of Sci. and Tech. McGraw-Hill Pub. Co., 1989; mem. editorial bd. Science, 1981-82; contbr. articles to profl. jours. Pres. Oak Ridge Civic Music Assn., Oak Ridge Arts Coun.; bd. chair Ridgeview Psychiatric Hosp. Guggenheim fellow, 1966-67; Fulbright-Hays Research scholar, 1966-67 Fellow Am. Phys. Soc., AAAS, Sigma Xi; mem. ASME, Nat. Acad. Scis. (nuclear physics del. to People's Republic of China 1979), Internat. Union Pure and Applied Physics (mem.-at-large U.S. nat. com. 1976-78) Achievements include research in nuclear physics with heavy ions and protons; accelerators, especially cyclotrons; materials research programs, especially high-temperature materials and surfaces; nuclear power reactors, especially gas-cooled reactors; research reactor with ultra high neutron flux.

ZUCKER, ALFRED JOHN, English and history educator, academic administrator, historian; b. Hartford, Sept. 25, 1940; s. Samuel and Rose (Zucker) Z.; m. Sallie Lea Friedheim, Dec. 25, 1966; children: Mary Anne, John James Jr., James Patrick, Patrick Jonathan, Anne-Marie Kathleen, Kathleen Mary. AA, LA Valley Coll., 1960; AB in English, UCLA, 1962, AB in Speech, MA in English, 1962, MA in Speech, 1963, PhD, 1966; postgrad., U. So. Calif., Harvard U.; MA in history, Calif. State U., Long Beach, 2000, MA in Polit. Sci., 2004. Prof. English and history, chmn. div. humanities LA SW Coll., 1968-72; prof. English El Camino Coll., 1985—, LA Valley Coll., 1989—, chmn. dept. English, honors sponsor, 1997—. Contbr. articles to profl. jours. Mem. LA Coll. Dist. Senate, 1969—. Mem. AAUP, LA Coll. Tchrs. Assn. (dir.), Calif. Jr. Coll. Assn., Calif. Tchrs. Assn., World Affairs Coun., Calif. Scholarship Fedn., Mensa, KC, Gold Key, Phi Beta Kappa, Phi Delta Kappa (pres. UCLA chpt. 1966-67, v.p. 1967-68), Tau Alpha Epsilon, Phi Theta Kappa, Phi Alpha Theta, Phi Kappa Phi, Phi Delta Gamma. Office: 5800 Fulton Ave Van Nuys CA 91401-4062 Home: 1701 Simplicity Irvine CA 92620 Office Phone: 818-947-2586. Business E-Mail: zuckeraj@lavc.edu.

ZUCKER, ARTHUR, lawyer; b. Newark, July 31, 1958; s. Neal M. and Sylvia Zucker; m. Elyse Zucker; children: Neal, Jeremy, Todd. BA cum laude, U. Md., 1980; JD cum laude, Wash. Coll. Law, 1983. Bar: N.J. 1983, U.S. Dist. Ct. 1983, U.S. Tax Ct. (3d cir.), cert.: Supreme Ct. N.J. (criminal trial atty.). Asst. prosecutor Atlantic City Prosecutor Office, Mays Landing, N.J., 1984—87; asst. U.S. atty. U.S. Atty's Office, Newark, N.J., 1987—92; assoc. Cole, Schotz, Meisel et al., Hackensack, N.J., 1992—93; ptnr. Ferro Labella & Zucker, Hackensack, 1993—. Tchr. Seton Hall U., Newark, 1994—2000; NITA lectr. Nat. Inst. Trial Advocacy, 2002—03. Bd. mem. N.J. Homes, Wyckoff, 2004—. Mem.: N.J. State Bar Assn. Office: Ferro Labella & Zucker LLC 27 Warren St Hackensack NJ 07601 Office Fax: 201-489-5653. Business E-Mail: azucker@ferrolabella.com.

ZUCKER, DAVID F., former information technology executive; b. Wichita Falls, Tex., Aug. 8, 1962; s. Paul Zucker and Margaret Anne (Keating) Chisholm. BA in Econ., Princeton U., 1984; MBA, Harvard, 1988. Fin. analyst Goldman, Sachs & Co., NYC, 1984-86; exec. pub. ABC, Inc., Travel Agent Mag., NYC, 1988-90; mgr. current series programming ABC Entertainment, LA, 1991; dir. programming Eurosport, London, Paris, 1992-93; v.p. programming to exec. v.p. ESPN, Inc., Bristol, Conn., 1993-94; sr. v.p., managing dir. ESPN Internat., NYC, 1995—99; pres., CEO Diva Systems Corp., 1999—2000, Skillgames LLC, 2000—02; mng. dir. Walker Digital LLC, 2000—02; pres., COO Playboy Enterprises, Inc., 2002—03; pres., CEO Midway Games, Inc., 2003—08.

ZUCKER, JEFFREY A., broadcast executive; b. Homestead, Fla., Apr. 9, 1965; m. Caryn Stephanie Nathanson, 1996; children: Andrew, Elizabeth, Peter. BA in Am. History, Harvard Coll., 1986. Rschr., 1988 Olympic Games, Seoul, Korea NBC Sports, 1986—88; field prodr. NBC News, 1989; exec. prodr. Today, 1992—93, Now with Tom Brokaw and Katie Couric, NBC Nightly News with Tom Brokaw, 1993, Today, 1994—2000; pres. NBC Entertainment, 2000—03, NBC Entertainment, News and Cable Group, 2003—05; CEO NBC Universal TV, 2005—07; pres., CEO NBC Universal, 2007—. Exec. prodr.: (news segments) Russian coup, 1991, Persian Gulf War, 1991, 1993 and 1997 presdl. inaugurations, the bombing of Centennial Olympic Pk., 1996, 1996 and 2000 polit. conventions, Decision 2000; writer: The Games of the XXIV Olympiad (Emmy award, outstanding writing, 1988); supervising prodr.: "Senator Edward Kennedy" Today (Emmy award, outstanding interview, 1991); exec. prodr.: "California Fire" Now with Tom Brokaw and Katie Couric (Emmy award, outstanding coverage of a single breaking news story, 1993), "Tragedy in Rwanda" Now with Tom Brokaw and Katie Couric (Emmy award, outstanding background/analysis of a single current story, 1994), "The Brain" Now with Tom Brokaw and Katie Couric (Emmy award, outstanding informational or cultural program, 1994). Jewish. Office: NBC 3000 W Alameda Ave Burbank CA 91523-0002 also: NBC Universal 52nd Fl 30 Rockefeller Plz New York NY 10112*

ZUCKER, NORMAN LIVINGSTON, political science professor, writer; b. NYC, Aug. 1, 1933; s. George Meyer and Beatrice Lillian (Livingston) Zucker; m. Naomi Judith Flink, June 25, 1961; children: Sara, George. BA, Rutgers U., 1954, MA, 1956, PhD, 1960. Instr. polit. sci. Northeastern U., Boston, 1960-61, asst. prof., 1961-62, Tufts U., Medford, Mass., 1962-66; assoc. prof. U. R.I., Kingston, 1966-69, prof., 1969—. Cons. Select Commn. Immigration and Refugee Policy, 1980; manuscript cons. to pubs. Author: George W. Norris: Gentle Knight of American Democracy, 1966, The American Party Process, 1968, The Coming Crisis in Israel: Private Faith and Public Policy, 1973, The Guarded Gate: The Reality of American Refugee Policy, 1987, Desperate Crossings: Seeking Refuge in America, 1996; cons. editor: World Affairs, 1975—84, assoc. editor: Jour. Refugee Studies, 1987—90; mem. adv. bd. Forced Migration Rev., 2000—; contbr. articles and revs. to profl. jours., chapters to books. Grantee, Am. Philos. Soc., 1964; fellow, Found. Def. Democracies, 2003; Wurzweiler Found. grantee, 1963, Rockefeller Found. fellow in human rights, 1980. Mem.: AAUP, New Eng. Polit. Sci. Assn., Am. Polit. Sci. Assn. Office: U RI Dept Polit Sci Kingston RI 02881

ZUCKER, ROBERT A(LPERT), psychologist; b. NYC, Dec. 9, 1935; s. Morris and Sophie (Alpert) Z.; m. Martine Latil; children: Lisa, Alex, Eleanor; m. Kristine Ellen Freeark, Mar. 10, 1979; 1 child, Katherine. B.C.E., CCNY, 1956; postgrad., UCLA, 1956-58; PhD, Harvard U., 1966. Diplomate Am. Bd. Profl. Psychology (clin.); lic. psychologist, Mich. From instr. to asst. prof. psychology Rutgers U., 1963-68; from asst. prof. to assoc. prof. to prof. Mich. State U., 1968-94; prof. psychology in psychiatry and psychology U. Mich., 1994—, dir. Addiction Rsch. Ctr., 1994—, dir. substance abuse sect. Dept. Psychiatry, 1994—, faculty assoc. RCGD Inst. for Social Rsch., 1996—. Vis. prof. U. Tex., Austin, 1975; vis. rsch. prof. psychology in psychiatry U. Mich., 1990-91; vis. scholar Nat. Inst. Alcohol Abuse and Alcoholism, 1980; dir. clin. tng. Mich. State U., 1982-94; lectr. Nebr. Symposium on Motivation, 1986; cons. in field. Co-author, editor: Further Explorations in Personality, 1981, Personality and the Prediction of Behavior, 1984, The Emergence of Personality, 1987, Studying Persons and Lives, 1990, Personality Structure in the Life Course, 1992, The Development of Alcohol Problems: Exploring the Biopsychosocial Matrix of Risk, 1994, Alcohol Problems Among Adolescents: Current Directions in Prevention Research, 1995, Alcohol Problems and Aging, 1998, Multiproblem Youth: Intervention and Treatment, 2004; contbr. chpts. and articles to profl. publs. Bd. dirs. Nat. Coun. on Alcoholism-Mich., 1978-82; mem. Psychosocial Initial Rev. Group, Nat. Inst. Alcohol Abuse and Alcoholism, 1989-92; mem. HPRB study sect. Ctr. for Sci. Rev., NIH, 1998-2000. Recipient Fellow's award, Inst. Children Youth and Families, Mich. State U., 1993, Excellence in Clin. Rsch. award, Blue Cross-Blue Shield Mich. Found., 1997; grantee Method Extend Rsch. Time, NIH, 2003—. Fellow AAAS, APA (pres. addictions divsn. 50 1997-98), APS, Am. Orthopsychiat. Assn.; mem. Midwestern Psychol. Assn., Rsch. Soc. on Alcoholism (sec., bd. dirs. 2000-03, bd. dirs. 2007—), Polish Soc. Rsch. Addictions, Polish Soc. Psychiatrists (hon., named to Hall Fame 2007). Office: Univ Mich Addiction Rsch Ctr 4250 Plymouth Rd Ann Arbor MI 48109-2700 Office Phone: 734-232-0280. Business E-Mail: zuckerra@umich.edu.

ZUCKER, STANLEY HOWARD, special education educator; b. NYC, Aug. 9, 1947; s. Sidney and Sally Zucker; m. Randy E. Kogel, Aug. 23, 1970; children: Matthew Farrell, Gabrielle Pamela. BA, SUNY, Stony Brook, 1970; MS, Hofsta U., 1972; PhD, U. Mo., 1975. Cert. psychologist. Prof. Ariz. State U., Tempe, 1975—. Author: Multilevel Academic Survey Test, 1986, Curriculum-Based Evaluation: Teaching and Decision Making, 1993; editor Edn. and Tng. in Mental Retardation and Devel. Disabilities, 1987—. Fellow Am. Assn. Mental Retardation; mem. Coun. for Exceptional Children (pres. div. mental retardation 1983-84). Office: Ariz State U Spl Edn Program Tempe AZ 85287

ZUCKERBERG, MARK ELLIOT, Internet company executive, entrepreneur, programmer; b. Dobbs Ferry, NY, May 14, 1984; Attended, Harvard U. Co-founder, CEO Facebook, Inc., Palo Alto, Calif., 2004—. Named Media Achiever of Yr., Campaign Media Awards, 2007, Most Influential Person in High Tech. Industry, Agenda Setters, 2007, Best Start-up CEO, CrunchBase, 2007; named one of 50 Who Matter Now, Business 2.0, 2006, The 100 Most Influential People in the World, TIME mag., 2008, Top 25 Web Celebs, Forbes mag., 2007; named to 50 Most Interesting List, Creativity mag., 2008. Achievements include development of one of the most widely used networking websites among college and high school students throughout the US, Canada and Europe; being the youngest ever self-made billionarie. Office: Facebook Inc 156 University Ave Ste 300 Palo Alto CA 94301-1631

ZUCKER-FRANKLIN, DOROTHEA, internist, educator; b. Berlin, Aug. 9, 1930; came to U.S., 1949; d. Julian J. and Gertrude Zucker; m. Edward C. Franklin (dec.); 1 child, Deborah Julie. BA, CUNY, 1952, PhD in Sci. (hon.), 1996; MD, N.Y. Med. Coll., 1956. Diplomate Am. Bd. Medicine. Intern Phila. Gen. Hosp., 1956-57; resident in internal medicine Montefiore Hosp., NYC, 1957-59, postdoctoral fellow in hematology, 1959-61; postdoctoral fellow in electron microscopy NYU Sch. Medicine, NYC, 1961-63, asst. prof. medicine, 1963-67, assoc. prof., 1968-74, prof. medicine, 1974—; assoc. attending physician Bellevue Hosp., 1968-74, attending physician, 1974—. Assoc. attending physician Univ. Hosp., Tisch Hosp., 1968—74, attending physician, 1974—; cons. physician Manhattan VA Hosp., 1970—; meml. editl. bd. numerous publs., including Blood, 1963—76, 1980—86, Am. Jour. Pathology, 1979—, Ultrastructure Pathology, 1979—, Blood Cells, 1980, Am. Jour. Medicine, 1981—87, Hematology Oncology, 1982—, Jour. AIDS Rsch., 1987—, Hematopathology and Molecular Hematology, 1987—, others; meml. bd. reviewing editors Jour. Lab. and Clin. Medicine, 1990—; mem. hematology panel Health Rsch. Coun. City of N.Y., 1971—74; mem. pathology tng. com. Nat. Inst. Med. Scis., 1971—74; mem. allergy and immunology rsch. com. Nat. Inst. Allergy and Infectious Diseases, 1974—81; mem. U.S.-Israel Binat. Sci. Found., 1980—; mem. ad hoc promotion com. Harvard Med. Sch., 1981, 83; mem. blood products adv. com. FDA, 1981—86; mem. sci. adv. bd. and sci. rev. panel Israel Cancer Rsch. Found., 1982—90; mem. grant rev. panel VA AIDS Ctr., 1988—89; vis. fellow Assn. Claude Bernard, 1974—75. Co-author: The Physiology and Pathology of Leukocytes, 1962, Amyloidosis, 1986, Atlas of Blood Cells: Function and Pathology, 2 vols., 1981, 3d edit., 2003, Thrombopoiesis and Thrombopoietins: Molecular, Cellular, Preclinical and Clinical Biology, 1996; contbr. over 300 articles to profl. jours. Bd. dirs. Henry M. and Lillian Stratton Found., Inc., 1987-95. Named to Hall of Fame, Hunter Coll., 1977, Internat. Profl. and Bus. Women, 1994. Fellow: AAAS, N.Y. Acad. Scis.; mem.: NTLV and Related Viruses, Internat. Retrovirology Assn., N.Y. Soc. Study of Blood (chair program com. 1976—80, pres. 1981—82), N.Y. Soc. Electron Microscopists (program chair 1984, pres. 1984—85), Am. Soc. Cell Biology (program com. internat. congress 1976), Am. Soc. Exptl. Pathology, Am. Assn. Immunologists, Am. Acad. Arts and Scis., Reticuloendothelial Soc. (life; program com. 1974—76, nominating com. 1976—78, pres. 1984—85), Am. Soc. Physiology, Federated Socs. Exptl. Biology and Medicine, Am. Soc. Hematology (program com. 1973, edn. com. 1974—78, chair subcom. on leukocyte physiology 1977, chair subcom. on immunohematology 1984, com. on advanced learning resources 1986—, exec. coun. 1987—91, pres.-elect 1992, v.p. 1993, pres. 1994—95, chair adv. bd. 1996, com. on govt. affairs 2001), Am. Soc. Clin. Investigation, Am. Fedn. Clin. Rsch., Am. Assn. Physicians, Inst. Medicine NAS, Alpha Omega Alpha, Phi Beta Kappa. Office: NYU Med Ctr 550 1st Ave New York NY 10016-6402 Office Phone: 212-263-5634. Business E-Mail: dorothea.zucker-franklin@med.nyu.edu.

ZUCKERMAN, HARRIET, sociologist, educator; b. NYC, July 19, 1937; d. Harry and Anne D. (Wiener) Z; m. Robert K. Merton, 1993. AB, Vassar Coll., Poughkeepsie, NY, 1958; PhD, Columbia U., NYC, 1965. Asst. prof. sociology Columbia U., 1965-72, assoc. prof., 1972-78, prof., 1978-92, prof. emerita, 1993—; sr. rsch. scholar, 1993—; chmn. dept. Columbia U., 1978-81; v.p. Andrew W. Mellon Found., 1991-98, sr. v.p., 1998—. Vis. scholar Russell Sage Found., 1971—72, 1985—87; mem. adv. bd. Social Sci. Citation Index Inst. Sci. Info., 1972—98; dir. Ann. Revs., Inc.; trustee Am. Savs. Bank, 1978—83. Author: Scientific Elite: Nobel Laureates in the United States, 1977, rev. edit., 1996; co-editor: Toward A Metric of Science: The Advent of Science Indictors, 1978, The Outer Circle: Women in the Scientific Community, 1991; mem. editorial bd. Scientometrics, 1977-, Am. Jour. Sociology, 1972-74, 77-79, Am. Sociol. Rev, 1972-74, 87-91, Sci., 1985-86; contbr. articles to profl. jours. Bd. dir. Social Sci. Rsch. Coun., 1974-76, AAAS, 1980-84, Women's Forum, 1989-91; trustee Ctr. for Advanced Study in Behavioral Scis., 1976-88, 89-2001, 03—; mem. ednl. adv. bd. John Simon Guggenheim Meml. Found., 1986-93, mem. com. on selection, 1989-91. Woodrow Wilson fellow, 1958-59; Ctr. for Advanced Study in Behavioral Scis. fellow, 1973-74; Guggenheim fellow, 1980-81; Phi Beta Kappa vis. scholar, 1982-83; recipient Dean's award for Disting. Achievement Columbia U. Grad. Sch., 1998. Mem. Am. Philos. Soc. (councillor 1997-03, 2005—, v.p. 2006-,chmn. Class III membership com. 2002-05), Am. Acad. Arts and Scis. (chmn. class III membership com. 1991-94), Soc. Social Studies Sci. (pres. 1989-91), The Century Assn., Coun. on Fgn. Rels.

ZUCKERMAN, HERBERT LAWRENCE, lawyer; b. Newark, June 11, 1928; s. David and Adele Zuckerman; m. Janet Albert, Sept. 10, 1950; children: Julia, Elizabeth, William. BSBA, Lehigh U., 1949; JD, Rutgers U., 1953. Acct. Zuckerman & Black, Newark, 1949-56; pvt. practice law Newark, 1956-71; ptnr. Zuckerman, Aronson & Horn, Newark, 1971-81; ptnr., v.p. Sills Cummis, Newark, 1981-98, sr.counsel, 1998—. Bd. dirs. Am. Jewish Com., 1990—; vol. The Hospice, Glen Ridge, N.J., 1985-93. Fellow Coll. of Tax Counsel; mem. ABA, N.J. Bar Assn., Fed. Bar Assn., Essex County Bar Assn., Mental Health Assn. (bd. dirs. 1997-99), Mensa. Avocations: tennis, music, theater, opera, reading. Office: Sills Cummis 1 Riverfront Plz 13th Fl Newark NJ 07102-5400

ZUCKERMAN, JOSEPH D., orthopedist, surgeon; b. Bronx, NY, Jan. 25, 1952; s. Morris and Lee Zuckerman; m. Janet Rivkin, July 1, 1984; children: Scott, Matthew. BS, Cornell U., Ithaca, NY, 1973; MD, Med. Coll. Wis., Milw., 1978. Diplomate Am. Bd. Orthop. Surgery (mem.), 1986, Am. Bd. Orthop. Surgery (mem.), 1996. Intern and resident U. Wash., Seattle, 1978—83; fellow Brigham and Women's Hosp., Havard Med. Sch., Boston, 1983—84, Mayo Clinic, Rochester, Minn., 1984; vice chmn.dept. orthop surgery Hosp. for Joint Diseases, NYC, 1990—94, chmn. dept. orthop. surgery, 1994—97; Walter A.L. Thompson prof., chmn. dept. orthop. surgery N.Y.U. Med. Ctr. /Hosp. for Joint Diseases, 1997—. Co-author (editor): Comprehensive Care of Orthopaedic Injuries in the Elderly, 1990; co-author: Fractures and Dislocations.Hospital for Joint Diseases, 1995; co-editor: Fractures in the Elderly, 1998, A Comprehensive Review Text of Orthopaedic Surgery, 1999; co-author: Fractures of the Hip: A Practical Guide to Management, 1999. Recipient Clin. Rsch. award, Orthop. Rsch. and Edn. Found., 1987; fellow Mary and David Hoar fellowship in Musculoskeletal /Trauma Rsch., 1987. Mem.: Orthop. Rsch. Soc., Shoulder and Elbow Surgeons, Am. Acad. Orthop. Surgeons (pres. 2009—), Am. Orthop. Assn. (N. Am. traveling fellowship 1985), Alpha Omega Alpha. Office: Hosp for Joint Diseases 301 E 17th St New York NY 10003 Office Phone: 212-598-6674. Office Fax: 212-598-6793. E-mail: joseph.zuckerman@med.nyu.edu.*

ZUCKERMAN, MARC ABRAHAM, finance educator; b. NYC, May 30, 1951; s. Henry and Rela (Ast) Z.; m. Sue Carol Kezurer, Dec. 6, 1981; 1 child, Sam David. BA cum laude, CUNY, Bronx, 1973; MA, Columbia U., 1974; MBA, Manhattan Coll., 1984. Cert. mgmt. acct., treasury profl., credit executive. Dir. corp. credit Clinton Swan Clothes, NYC, 1978-80; dir. fin. Lord Jeff, Norwood, N.J., 1980-88; dir. corp. credit Bernard Chaus, Inc., Secaucus, N.J., 1988-89; asst. treas. Warnaco, Bridgeport, Conn., 1989; treas. Bernard Chaus, Inc., Secaucus, 1989-95; corp. contr. Precision Custom Coatings, Totowa, N.J., 1996-99; v.p. ops., CFO Triboro Quilt Mfg. Corp., 1999—. Pres. Meadowlands Fin. Group, 1991-95; adj. prof. fin. Contbr. articles to profl. jours. Pack com. mem. Ridgewood Boy Scouts Am., 1997-2000, treas. 1997-2000. Mem. Inst. Mgmt. Accts., Treas. Mgmt. Assn., Treas. Mgmt. Assn. N.J., Nat. Assn. Credit Mgmt., N.J. Corp. Treas. Mgmt. Assn. (treas. 1996-99), Nat. Apparel Mfrs. Credit Assn. (bd. dirs. 1993-95), Bergen Rockland Inst. Mgmt. Accts. (bd. dirs. 1996-97). Avocations: jogging, golf. Home: 153 Lincoln Ave Ridgewood NJ 07450-4105 Office: Triboro Quilt Mfg Corp 172 South Broadway White Plains NY 10605

ZUCKERMAN, MARVIN, retired psychologist; b. Chgo., Mar. 21, 1928; s. Eli and Sophia (Pilder) Z.; children: April B. Zuckerman Schanoes, Steven H. BA, NYU, 1949, PhD, 1954. Rsch. assoc. Inst. Psychiat. Rsch., Ind. U. Med. Ctr., 1956-59; asst. prof. psychology Bklyn. Coll., 1959-62; rsch. assoc. Albert Einstein Med. Ctr., Phila., 1963-69; prof. psychology U. Del., Newark, 1969—2002, prof. emeritus, 2002—, ret., 2002. Author: (with C.D. Spielberger) Emotions and Anxiety, 1976, Sensation Seeking: Beyond the Optimal Level of Arousal, 1979, Biological Bases of Sensation Seeking, Impulsivity and Anxiety, 1983, Psychobiology of Personality, 1991, 2d edit. 2005, Behavioral Expressions and Biosocial Bases of Sensation Seeking, 1994, Vulnerability to Psychopathology, 1999, Sensation Seeking and Risky Behavior, 2007. Fellow APA, Assn. Psychol. Sci.; mem. Internat. Soc. Study Individual Differences (past pres.). Home: 1500 Locust St Apt 4013 Philadelphia PA 19102-4326 Home Phone: 215-732-2408. Business E-Mail: zuckerma@udel.edu.

ZUCKERMAN, MARY ELLEN WALLER, marketing educator; b. Gainesville, Fla., Jan. 10, 1954; d. David Allen and Ruth Barbera (Ergood) Waller; m. Miron Zuckerman, Sept. 3, 1988; children: David Benjamin, Jonathan Michael. BA, Simmons Coll., 1976; MBA, Columbia U., 1982, PhD, 1987. Fgn. svc. officer U.S. Dept. of State, Washington and NYC, 1982-83; assoc. prof. SUNY, Geneseo, 1985—; rsch. fellow Gannett Found. Media Ctr., NYC, 1989-90. Vis. assoc. prof. McGill U., Montreal, Can., 1990-91. Author: Sources on the History of Women's Magazines 1792-1960, 1991, (with others) The Magazine in America, 1991; contbr. articles to profl. jours. NEH grantee, 1987; Spencer Found. fellow, 1992-95. Mem. Am. Mktg. Assn. (pres. Rochester, N.Y. chpt. 1991—, Eastern rep. 1989—), Am. Hist. Assn., Assn. for Consumer Rsch., Econ. and Bus. History Orgn., Orgn. of Am. Historians, Bus. History Conf., Berkshire Conf. on Women's History. Office: SUNY 206C Welles Geneseo NY 14454

ZUCKERMAN, MICHAEL, history professor; b. Phila., Pa., Apr. 24, 1939; s. Hyman and Henrietta Zuckerman; m. Sharon Ann Holt, June 27, 1986; children: Elizabeth, Helen; m. Diane Weitzman, June 12, 1966; children: Adam, Harman, Maria. PhD, Harvard U., Cambridge, Mass., 1967. Instr. U. Pa., Phila., 1965—84, asst. prof., assoc. prof., prof. history, 1984—. Author: (books) Peaceable Kingdoms, Friends and Neighbors, Almost Chosen People, Beyond the Century of the Child; contbr. articles. Pres. Powelton Village Civic Assn., Phila., 2008—09. Grantee fellow, NEH, 1972—73;, Woodrow Wilson Fellowship Found., 1961—62, 1964—65, Social Sci. Rsch. Coun., 1968, Guggenheim, 1977—78, Am. Coun. Learned, 1977—78, Fulbright, 1977—78, Rockefeller, 1978—79, Netherlands Inst. Advanced Study, 1997—98, Bellagio, 1998. D-Liberal. Jewish. Avocations: travel, theater. Home: 3207 Winter St Philadelphia PA 19104 Office: Univ Pa Dept History Philadelphia PA 19104 Home Fax: 215-573-2089. Business E-Mail: mzuckerm@history.upenn.edu.

ZUCKERMAN, MORTIMER BENJAMIN, publishing executive, real estate developer; b. Montreal, Ont., Can., June 4, 1937; arrived in US, 1961, naturalized, 1977; s. Abraham and Esther Zuckerman; m. Marla F. Prather, Sept. 27, 1996 (div. 2001); 1 child, Abigail. BA in Econs./Polit. Theory, with honors, McGill U., Montreal, 1957, LLB with honors, 1961; MBA with distinction, U. Pa. Wharton Sch. Bus., 1962; LLM, Harvard Law Sch., 1962. Sr. v.p., CFO Cabot, Cabot & Forbes, Boston, 1965—69; co-founder, chmn. bd. Boston Properties Co., 1970—, dir., 1997—; pres., chmn. bd. Atlantic Monthly Co., Boston, 1980—99; chmn., editor-in-chief US News & World Report, 1984—; chmn., co-pub. NY Daily News, 1993—2004, chmn., pub., 2004—. Lectr., then assoc. prof. Harvard U. Grad. Sch. Design, 1966—74; vis. lectr. city and regional planning Yale U., 1967—69; dir., mem. exec. com. Stride Rite Corp., 1970—83; dir. Property Capital Trust Co., 1979—80, RET Income Found., 1976—79; pub. interest dir. Fed. Home Loan Bank of Boston, 1972—73; dir. Havas Holdings, Inc., 1970—; mem. JP Morgan Nat. Adv. Bd., Internat. Inst. Strategic Studies, Washington Inst. Near East Policy. Founder Zuckerman Fellowships Harvard U., 2004—; pres. bd. trustees Sidney Farber Cancer Inst., Boston, 1980; trustee Meml. Sloan-Kettering, Aspen Inst., NYU, Hole in the Wall Gang Fund, Inc., Center for Comm.; dir. Partnership for NYC, Inc., NYC2012, Inc. Recipient Commandeur De L'Ordre des Arts et des Lettres, France, Lifetime Achievement Award, Guild Hall, Gold Medal, Am. Inst. Architecture; named one of Forbes' Richest Americans, 2006. Mem.: Coun. Fgn. Rels., Harmonie (NYC), Harvard Club (Boston, NYC). Office: NY Daily News 450 W 33rd St Fl 3 New York NY 10001-2681 also: US News & World Report 1050 Thomas Jefferson St NW Washington DC 20007-3817 also: Boston Properties 599 Lexington Ave Rm 1800 New York NY 10022-6030 Office Phone: 212-326-4013, 202-955-2000.*

ZUCKERMAN, PAUL HERBERT, lawyer; s. Max B. and Minnie (Mendelson) Z.; m. Sara Shiffman, Aug. 25, 1963; children: David Isaac, Daniel Mark. BS in Econs., Wharton Sch., U. Pa., 1957; MBA in Corp. Fin., NYU, 1964; JD, Bklyn. Law Sch., 1967. Bar: N.Y. 1968, U.S. Dist. Ct. (so. and ea. dists.) N.Y. 1975, U.S. Tax Ct. 1977, U.S. Ct. Appeals (2d cir.) 1972, U.S. Supreme Ct. 1973. Security analyst U.S. Trust Co., NYC, 1962-66; sr. security analyst CNA Mgmt. Rsch. Corp., NYC, 1966-71, mgr. dept. investment rsch., 1971-73; sole practice NYC, 1973—. Speaker and writer in field; radio, TV appearances. Served to lt. (j.g.) USN, 1957—60. Mem.: Wharton Bus. Sch., NYC Bar Assn. Office: 8th Fl 226 W 26th St New York NY 10001-6785 Office Phone: 212-367-1900. Office Fax: 212-255-6562. Business E-Mail: EstatesWillsTrusts@gmail.com.

ZUCKERMAN, RICHARD ENGLE, lawyer, educator; b. Yonkers, NY, Aug. 2, 1945; s. Julius and Roslyn (Ehrlich) Z.; m. Denise Ellen Spoon, July 14, 1968; children: Julie Ann, Lindsay Beth. BA, U. Mich., 1967; JD cum laude, Southwestern U., 1974. Bar: Calif. 1974, Mich. 1976, Nev. 1986, U.S. Dist. Ct. (ea. and we. dists.) Mich. 1977, U.S. Ct. Appeals (6th cir.) 1977, U.S. Ct. Appeals (9th cir.) 1982, U.S. Ct. Appeals (2d and 7th cirs.) 1994, U.S. Tax Ct. 1980, U. S. Supreme Ct. 1985, U.S. Ct. Appeals (4th cir.) 2001. Spl. atty. organized crime and racketeering sect. U.S. Dept. Justice, Detroit, 1974-77; sr. ptnr. Raymond, Rupp, Wienberg, Stone & Zuckerman, P.C., Troy, Mich., 1977-87, Honigman, Miller, Schwartz & Cohn, Detroit, 1987—, chair litigation dept., 1996—2002, also bd. dirs., 1999—2003. Adj. prof. Detroit Coll. Law, 1978—98, 2004—06; mem. Mich. Atty. Grievance Commn., 1995—2001, vice-chmn., 1999—2000, chmn., 2000—01; judicial qualification com. State Bar Mich., 2005—. Served to lt. USN, 1967-71, Vietnam. Mem. ABA (grand jury com. criminal justice sect., state bar com. on judicial qualifications, 2006), Fed. Bar Assn. (chmn. criminal law sect. Detroit chpt. 1985-90, bd. dirs. 1985-94, co-chair criminal def. com. 1990-95), Knollwood Country Club (West Bloomfield, Mich.), Std. Club (Detroit), Am. Inns Ct. (master of bench 1995-97), Tam O'Shanter Country Club. Republican. Jewish. Office: Honigman Miller Schwartz & Cohn 2290 First National Bldg Detroit MI 48226 Office Phone: 313-465-7618. Business E-Mail: rez@honigman.com.

ZUCKERMAN JACOBSON, HEIDI, museum director; MA, Hunter Coll. Asst. curator 20th-century art Jewish Mus., NYC; Phyllis Wattis curator MATRIX program Berkeley Art Mus., U. Calif., 1999—2005; dir., chief curator Aspen Art Mus., Colo., 2005—. Office: Aspen Art Mus 590 North Mill St Aspen CO 81611

ZUE, VICTOR W., engineering educator; ScD in Elec. Engring., MIT, Cambridge, Mass., 1976. Prof. elec. engring. and computer sci. MIT, Cambridge, dir., Computer Sci. and Artificial Intelligence Lab, Delta Electronics chair. Chair Info. Sci. and Tech. study group Defense Advanced Rsch. Projects Agency, US Dept. Defense, 1996—98. Contbr. articles to profl. jours. Fellow: Acoustical Soc. Am.; mem.: NAE, IEEE. Independent. Office: MIT Computer Sci and Artificial Intelligence Lab Stata Ctr, Bldg 32 32 Vassar St Cambridge MA 02139 Office Phone: 617-253-8513. Business E-Mail: zue@csail.mit.edu.

ZUGAZAGOITIA, JULIAN, museum director; b. Mexico City; arrived in U.S., 1999; Grad., l'Ecole du Louvre; PhD in Philosophy and Aesthetics, Sorbonne, Paris. Cons., spl. advisor to dir. Getty Conservation Inst., LA; dir. visual arts Spoleto Festival, Italy, 1997—99; asst. to the dir. Guggenheim Mus., NYC, 1999—2002; exec. dir. El Museo del Barrio, NYC, 2002—. Cultural attaché to Mexican del. UNESCO. Cultural corr.: Excélsior Newspaper. Recipient Chevalier des Arts et des Lettres, 2004. Office: El Museo del Barrio 1230 Fifth Ave New York NY 10029 Office Phone: 212-831-7272. Office Fax: 212-831-7927. Business E-Mail: directorsoffice@elmuseo.org.

ZUGHAIER, SUSU M., microbiologist, researcher, immunologist; d. Mahmoud Hamed and Maliha Abdul Zughaier; m. Mohammed Najdat Zohbe, July 9, 2000; children: Mariam M. Zohbe, Salma M. Zohbe. BSc in Lab. Medicine, Yarmouk U., Irbid, Jordan, 1986; diploma in Anaerobic Microbiology, London Coll. Medicine, 1991; MSc in Clin. Microbiology, U. Wales, 1995, PhD in Med. Microbiology and Immunology, 1999. Med. microbiologist Makassed Hosp., Jerusalem, 1986—94; postgraduate rschr. U. Wales Coll. Medicine, Cardiff, Wales, 1995—99; postdoctoral scientist Harvard Sch. of Medicine, Boston, 1999—2000; postdoctoral assoc. Emory U. Sch. Medicine, Atlanta, 2000—05, sr. rsch. scientist, 2005—09, rsch. asst. prof., 2009—. Dep. lab. dir. Makassed Hosp., Jerusalem, 1999—99; academic cons. Al-Quds U., Sch. of Pub. Health, Jerusalem, 1999—99. Contbr. articles to profl. jours. Grantee Welsh Scheme for Rsch. & Devel., Welsh Assembly, 1996 - 1999; Brit. Councel scholar, Brit. govt., 1990—91, 1994—95. Mem.: Am. Chemical Soc., Internat. Endotoxin and Innate Immunity Soc., Am. Soc. for Microbiology. Muslim. Achievements include discovery of differential activation of toll-like receptor 4 by endotoxins; patents for vaccine material; first Palestinian to establish anaerobic microbiology laboratory; first Palestinian to introduce local HIV testing. Avocations: reading, drawing, cooking, travel. Office Phone: 404-321-6111 ext. 17570. Business E-Mail: szughai@emory.edu.

ZUHDI, NAZIH, retired surgeon; b. Beirut, May 19, 1925; arrived in US, 1950, naturalized, 1960; s. Omar and Lutfiye (Atef) Z.; children by previous marriage: Omar, Nabil; m. Annette McMichael; children: Adam, Leyla, Zachariah BA, Am. U., Beirut, 1946, MD, 1950. Diplomate Am. Bd. Surgery, Am. Bd. Thoracic Surgery. Intern St. Vincent's Hosp., SI, NY, 1950-51, Presbyn.-Columbia Med. Ctr., NYC, 1951-52; resident Kings County SUNY Med. Ctr., NYC, 1952-56; fellow SUNY Downstate Med. Ctr., Bklyn., 1953-54; resident Univ. Hosp., Mpls., 1956, Okla. City, 1957-58, practice surgery specializing in cardiovasc. and thoracic, 1958-87, Nazih Zuhdi Transplant Inst. adminstr., 1985-99, ret., 1999; co-founder, chmn. labs. Mercy Heart and Rsch. Inst., 1958—65. Founder, chmn., dir., surgeon-in-chief Oklahoma Transplantation Inst. (renamed Nazih Zuhdi Transplant Inst., Aug., 1999) Bapt. Med. Ctr., 1984-99, chmn. dept. transplantation, Baptist Hosp., Okla. City, 1994-99; co-founder, chmn. Okla. Cardiovasc. Inst., Okla. City, 1983-84, Okla. Heart Ctr., Okla. City, 1984-85 Contbg. author Cardiac Surgery, 1967, 2d edit., 1972; contbr. articles to profl. jour.; developer numerous med. devices, techniques, rsch. and publs. on cardiopulmonary bypass, internal hypothermia, assisted circulation, heart surgery and transplantation of thoracic organs; developer heart-lung machines; designer, use of exptl. plastic bypass hearts; originator of clin. nonhemic primes of heart-lung machines producing total intentional hemodilution, at present, the universally accepted principle of cardiopulmonary bypass for partial and total body perfusion, use of banked citrated blood for surgical field blood loss replacement if needed beyond the cell-saver during open heart surgery, heart transplantation, and lung transplantation; researcher in cardiovasc. studies. Founder Islamic Ctr., Inc., Oklahoma City, 1985-1986; Internat. Bd. Vis., U. Okla., 1996-. Named to Okla. Hall of Fame, 1994. Fellow ACS; mem. AMA, NCCJ (Humanitarian award 1996), Am. Thoracic Soc., Okla. Thoracic Soc., So. Med. Assn., Okla. Med. Assn., Internat. Coll. Angiology, Am. Coll. Chest Physicians, Oklahoma City C. of C., Oklahoma County Med. Soc., Oklahoma City Clin. Soc., Okla. Surg. Assn., Oklahoma City Surg. Soc., Southwestern Surg. Congress, Am. Coll. Cardiology, Am. Soc. Artificial Internal Organs, Soc. Thoracic Surgeons (founding mem.), Am. Assn. for Thoracic Surgery, Internat. Cardiovasc. Soc., Okla. State Heart Assn., Osler Soc., So. Thoracic Surg. Assn., Lillehei Surg. Soc., Internat. Soc. Heart Transplantation, Dwight Harken's Founder's Group Cardiac Surgery, Westaby's Pioneers in Cardiac Surgery, Internat. Soc. Cardiothoracic Surgery (Japan, founding mem.), Am. Soc. Transplant Surgeons, Milestones of Cardiovas. Medicine of Am. Coll. Cardiology, Okla. City Golf and Country Club, Okla. Hall of Fame. Moslem. Achievements include first to use banked citrated blood for cardiopulmonary bypass for open heart surgery; origination of experimental leading to and first clinical non-hemic primes of heart-lung machines producing total intentional hemodilution, laid the foundation and opened the gateway for bloodless surgery for all patients. Personal E-mail: anz70@aol.com.

ZUICK, ERNEST RONALD, JR., career officer, advertising executive; b. San Bernardino, Calif., Nov. 2, 1935; s. Ernest Ronald Sr. and Catherine Louise (Leach) Z.; m. Johnnie Fern Lemons, Aug. 19, 1966. BA, Fresno State U., 1964, MA, 1968; MPA, Auburn U., 1974; postgrad., Air Command and Staff Coll., 1974, Air War Coll., 1982. Cert. tchr., Calif. Joined Calif. Air N.G., 1958, advanced through grades to col., 1984; advt. acct. exec., sports and polit. cartoonist Turlock (Calif.) Jour., 1956-62; advt. acct. exec. Fresno (Calif.) Bee, 1965-76; various assignments Calif. Mil. Dept., Sacramento, 1976-85, dir. legis., 1985-95, spl. projects dir., 1999—2001; dir. Media Svcs., 2001—04. Mem. ancillary staff Res. Forces Policy Bd., Office of Sec. of Def., 1982-95. Editor: Grizzly mag., 2002-04, 2005; contbr. articles to profl. jours. Mem. N.G. Assn. Calif. (pres. 1983-84). Avocations: writing, cartooning, video production.

ZUIDEMA, GEORGE DALE, surgeon, educator; b. Holland, Mich., Mar. 8, 1928; s. Jacob and Reka (Dalman) Z.; m. Joan K. Houtman, June 2, 1953; children: Karen Sue, David Jay, Nancy Ruth, Sarah Kay. AB, Hope Coll., 1949, D.Sc. (hon.), 1969; MD, Johns Hopkins U., 1953. Diplomate: Am. Bd. Surgery. Intern Mass. Gen. Hosp., 1953-54, asst. resident surgeon, then chief resident surgeon, 1954, 57, 58, 59; asst. prof. surgery, then assoc. prof. U. Mich. Sch. Medicine, 1960-64; prof. surgery, dir. dept. Johns Hopkins Sch. Medicine; also surgeon in chief Johns Hopkins Hosp., 1964-84; prof. surgery, vice provost med. affairs U. Mich., 1984-94. Cons. Walter Reed Army Med. Center, Sinai Hosp., Balt., Balt. City Hosp., Clin. Center of NIH; chmn. Study on Surg. Svcs. for U.S., 1970-75 Editor: (with O.H. Gauer) Gravitational Stress in Aerospace Medicine, 1961; (with G.L. Nardi) Surgery-A Concise Guide to Clinical Practice, 1961, 4th edit., 1982; (with R.D. Judge and F. Fitzgerald) Physical Diagnosis, 1963, 6th edit., 1997; (with W.F. Ballinger and R.B. Rutherford) Management of Trauma, 1968, 4th edit., 1985; (with L. Schlossberg) Atlas of Human Functional Anatomy, 1977, 4th edit., 1997, Shackelford's Surgery of the Alimentary Tract, 5th edit., 2001; editor Jour. Surg. Rsch., 1966-72, assoc. editor, mem. editl. bd., 1972—; mem. editl. bd. Surgery Ann., 1968-75, Surgery, 1970-97, co-editor in chief, 1975-97. Bd. dirs. Md. divsn. Am. Cancer Soc., 1964-68; trustee William Beaumont Hosp., Royal Oak, Mich., 1984-94, Hope Coll., Holland, Mich, 1987—. Capt. M.C., USAF, 1954-56. John and Mary R. Markle scholar academic medicine, 1961-66; recipient Henry Russell award U. Mich., 1963 Fellow ACS, Royal Coll. Surgeons Ireland (hon.); mem. Assn. Am. Med. Colls., Ctrl. Soc. Clin. Rsch., Soc. Univ. Surgeons, Am. Surg. Assn., So. Surg. Assn., Soc. Clin. Surgery, Soc. Vascular Surgery, Internat. Cardiovascular Surgery, Halsted Soc., Nat. Inst. Medicine, Assn. Acad. Surgeons (pres. 1967-69), Allen O. Whipple Soc., Coun. on Grad. Med. Edn., Ft. Del. Soc. (dir., 2006—), Del. Acad. Soc. (pres., 1994-1996, 2004—, dir., 1990—), Phi Beta Kappa, Tri Beta, Alpha Omega Alpha. Home and Office: 983 Willow View Ct Holland MI 49424-6615

ZUK, CARMEN VEIGA, psychiatrist; b. Buenos Aires, Mar. 5, 1939; arrived in USA, 1971, naturalized, 1979; d. Carlos and Carmen Villella Veiga; m. Gerald Harvey, May 7, 1974; children: Cary Elizabeth and Gabrielle Anne. MD, U. Buenos Aires, 1964, cert. psychiatry, 1969. Diplomate Am. Bd. Psychiatry and Neurology. Intern Med. Coll. Pa., Phila., 1974—75; resident in psychiatry Norristown State Hosp., Norristown, Pa., 1977—79; child psychiatry fellowship Med. Coll. Pa. and Ea. Pa. Psychiat. Inst., Phila., 1979—81; dir. child and adolescent unit Hosp. of Med. Coll. Ga., Augusta, 1981—83; dir. treatment team New Orleans Adolescent Hosp., 1983—85; assoc. Psychiatry Med. Group, Calif., 1985—86; mental health psychiatrist L.A. County Dept. Mental Health San Fernando Mental Health Svcs., 1986—88; psychiatrist-ptnr. So. Calif. Permanente Med. Group, Van Nuys, 1988—98, ptnr., 1988—98; staff psychiatrist Santa Clarita Child and Family Ctr., 1999—2002; ret., 2006. Asst. prof. dept. psychiatry Med. Coll. Ga., 1981-83; clin. asst. prof. dept. psychiatry and neurology Tulane U., 1983-85. Co-author: Psychology of Delusion, 2005; contbr. articles to profl. jours. Mem. AMA, Internat. Soc. for Adolescent Psychiatry. Avocations: reading, cooking, gardening, swimming, music. Home: 7620 Hollister Ave 219 Goleta CA 93117 Personal E-mail: carmenzuk@msn.com.

ZUK, GERALD HARVEY, psychologist, consultant; b. Chgo., Oct. 25, 1929; s. Albert and Gladys (Gross) Z.; m. Carmen Veiga, May 7, 1974; children: Cary and Gabrielle (twins). BA, L.A. State Coll., 1951; PhD, U. Chgo., 1955. Lic. psychologist, Calif. Asst. rsch. psychologist Inst. Child Welfare/U. Calif., Berkeley, 1955-56; clin. psychologist Pacific State Hosp., Pomona, Calif., 1956-57; chief psychologist St. Christopher's Hosp. for Children, Phila., 1957-61; assoc. dir., dir. tng. program dept. family psychiatry Ea. Pa. Psychiat. Inst., Phila., 1961-80; prof. dept. psychiatry, dir. family therapy program Med. Coll. Ga., 1981-83; clin. prof. dept. psychiatry and neurology Tulane U. Sch. Medicine, New Orleans, 1983-85; assoc. and dir. family therapy tng. program Beck Psychiat. Med. Group, Los Angeles County, 1985-86; pvt. practice Calif., 1986—. Cons. and presenter in field. Author: Family Therapy: A Triadic-Based Approach, 1972, 2d edit., 1981, Process and Practice in Family Therapy, 1975, 2d edit., 1986; co-author: The Psychology of Delusion, 2005; editor: Family Therapy Approaches for Adolescents, 1985; co-editor: Family Therapy and Disturbed Families, 1967; founding editor Internat. Jour. Family Therapy, 1979-86; mem. editl. bd. Family Process, Psychotherapy: Theory, Rsch. and Practice, Jour. Marriage and Family Counseling, Terapia Familiar; contbr. articles to profl. jours. Fellow APA. Avocation: classical music. Home and Office: Zuk Cons 7620 Hollister Ave # 219 Goleta CA 93117-2442 Personal E-mail: geraldzuk@msn.com.

ZUKERMAN, MICHAEL, lawyer; b. Bklyn., Oct. 3, 1940; s. Charles Morris and Gertrude Ethel Zukerman; m. Claire J. Goldsmith, June 25, 1961 (div. 1986); children: Steven, Amy; m. Elaine DeMasi, Nov. 21, 1986 (div. 1999); children: Jaclyn, Laura; m. Janey Alexander, Feb. 2, 2001. BS, U. Fla., 1961; LLB, St. John's U., 1964; LLM, NYU, 1966. Bar: NY 1965, Pa. 1983, U.S. Tax Ct. 1984. Credit analyst, loan officer Franklin Nat. Bank, 1964-66; assoc. Jaffin, Schneider, Kimmel & Galpeer, NYC, 1966-67; ptnr. Zukerman, Licht & Friedman and predecessors, NYC, 1967-79, Baskin & Sears, P.C., NYC, 1979-85, Graubard, Moskowitz, Dannett, Horowitz & Mollen, NYC, 1985-86, Gersten, Savage, Kaplowitz & Zukerman, NYC, 1986-89; of counsel Olshan, Grundman, Frome & Rosenzweig, NYC, 1990-95, Graham & James, NYC, 1995-2000, Bryan Cave LLP, 2000—03; exec. v.p. Brookhill Group, 1986-89; of counsel Sonnenschein Nath and Rosenthal, NYC, 2003—04, Warshaw Burstein Cohen Schlessinger & Kuh LLP, NYC, 2004—. Pres. First Ptnrs. Credit Corp., NYC, 1988—93; bd. dirs. Interjurist Ltd., Whitestone Realty Capital, LLC; mng. dir. Nat. Aspbergers Rsch. Found., 1993—, trustee, 2001—; lectr. in field; mem, bd. dirs. Programme Toy Sys., Watsaw Inc, 1984—93; mem, adv. bd. Metro Capital LLC. Contbr. articles to profl. jours. Trustee Temple Beth Torah, Melville, N.Y., 1972-80, YMHA Suffolk County, Hauppague, N.Y., 1980-85; bd. dirs. Dayton Mgmt. Corp., 1974-2001, Suffolk Jewish Cmty. Planning Bd., Hauppague, 1982-85, Congregation Bnai Elohim, 1994, 2nd v.p., 1995; co-chmn. bus. adv. coun. Town of Greenburgh, 1992. Mem.: ABA. Home: 915 Cherry Ln Valley Stream NY 11581-2722 Office: Warshaw Burstein Cohen Schlessinger & Kuh LLP 11th Fl 555 Fifth Ave New York NY 10016 Home Phone: 516-792-0220; Office Phone: 212-984-7836. E-mail: mzukerman@whitestonerealty.com.

ZUKERMAN, PINCHAS, concert violinist, violist, conductor; b. Tel Aviv, July 16, 1948; came to U.S., 1962; s. Yehuda and Miriam (Lieberman) Z.; m. Eugenia Rich, May 26, 1968 (div.); children: Natalia, Arianna; m. Tuesday Weld, 1985 (div.); m. Amanda Forsyth, Mar. 2004. Student, Juilliard Sch. Music, 1965-68; MusD (hon.), Brown U., 1989. Ind. concert violinist, 1968—. With impresario, Sol Hurok, 1967-76; condr., soloist English Chamber Orch., 1974, Mostly Mozart Festival, N.Y.C., 1975; guest condr., soloist Los Angeles Philharm., Boston Symphony, Chgo. Symphony, Pitts. Symphony, Phila. Orch., N.Y. Philharm.; music dir. South Bank Festival, London, 1978-80, St. Paul Chamber Orch., 1980-87, Nat. Arts Ctr. Orch., 1998—; prin. festival condr. Dallas Internat. Summer Music Festival, 1990-94; prin. guest condr. Dallas Symphony, 1993-95; toured with Isaac Stern; mem. trio with Daniel Barenboim and Jacqueline du Pre; (rec. artist) CBS, EMI, Philips Classics labels, RCA Victor Red Seal, BMG Classics. Winner Internat. Levintritt Competition, 1967, Medal of Arts, 1983, Isaac Stern award Nat. Arts Awards, 2002. Office: care Kirshbaum Demler & Assoc 711 W End Ave Apt 5KN New York NY 10025-6821 Business E-Mail: info@kirshdom.com.

ZULAUF, SANDER (SANDER WILLIAM ZULAUF), poet, educator, editor; b. Paterson, NJ, 1946; s. S. William Z. and Marion Ann Zulauf; m. Christianne, 1968 (div. 1976); 1 child, Scott; m. Madeline, 1979; stepchildren: Michael, Mary Beth. BA, Gettysburg Coll., 1968; MA, Ind. U., 1973. Tchr. Martin Luther King Sch., Paterson, NJ, 1968—69, Hanover Park Regional H.S., East Hanover, NJ, 1969-71; prof. County Coll. Morris, Randolph, NJ, 1973—. Editor, pub. Ars Poetica, Lake Hopatcong, N.J., 1996-99. Author: (poetry) Succasunna New Jersey, 1987, Living Waters, 2005, Where Time Goes, 2008; editor: The Poets of New Jersey: From Colonial to Contemporary, 2005, Jour. N.J. Poets, 1989—; founding editor Index Am. Periodical Verse, 1971—82. Sec.-treas. Forest South Homeowners Assn., Byram Twp., 1989—94, pres., 2004—; lay eucharistic min. St. Dunstan's Episcopal Ch., Succasunna, 1974—. Recipient Allen Ginsberg award, Poetry Ctr., Passaic, N.J., 1993, 2001, 2002, Excellence in Print award, Jour. N.J. Poets Pub. Radio's Poet and the Poem, 2002; named 1st Poet Laureate, Diocese of Newark, 1999—; grantee N.J. Arts Coun., 1992—93; fellow NEH, Princeton, 1987. Mem. Acad. Am. Poets, Poetry Soc. Am., Poets House, Kenneth Burke Soc., Thoreau Soc., Assn. Writers and Writing Programs, Skylands Writers and Artists Assn. (sec. treas. 1994-98, v.p. 1999-2000). Democrat. Episcopalian. Avocations: camping, boating, environmental preservation, gardening, travel. Home Phone: 973-347-1068; Office Phone: 973-328-5471. Personal E-mail: sanderzpoet@msn.com. Business E-Mail: szulauf@ccm.edu.

ZULEY, MARGARITA, radiologist, educator; Grad., U. Notre Dame; MD, U. Pitts. Resident & fellow U. Pitts.; assoc. prof. dept. radiology Magee-Women's Hosp. U. Pitts. Med. Ctr., dir. breast imaging. Office: Magee-Women's Hospital 300 Halket St Pittsburgh PA 15213 Office Phone: 412-641-5591. E-mail: zuleyml@upmc.edu.*

ZULFI, TASLEEM ELAHI (TASLEEM ELAHI QURESHI), broadcast executive, television personality; b. Shikoh A'abad, India, July 13, 1947; arrived in Saudi Arabia, 1950, arrived in Can., 1990; s. Naseem Elahi Qureshi; children: Noman, Nadia, Huda, Faryal. MA in Sociology, Karachi U., 1970; MA in English Lit., Am. U., Beirut, 1972. Tech. co-coord. aircraft maintenance Saudi Arabian Airlines, Jeddah Airport, 1969—89; v.p. PK Urdu TV Canada, 2000—, prodr., dir., show host, newscaster. Contbr. poetry to books and jours., articles to profl. Canadian jours., columns in newspapers. Recipient Excellence award for 20 yrs. profile and tech. svcs., Saudi Arabian Airlines, 1989, Excellence award for top class lit. creativity, Govt. Can., 1994. Mem.: NASA Planetary Soc. Achievements include being fluent in English, Arabic and Persian. Avocation: literature. Office: PK Urdu TV Canada 142 Oxford St Richmond Hill ON L4C 4L7 Canada Office Phone: 416-737-3458. Business E-Mail: zulfi@rogers.com.

ZULKER, CHARLES BATES, broadcasting company executive; b. Pleasantville, NJ, Dec. 20, 1926; s. William John and Virginia (Carr) Z.; m. Virginia Wright, June 24, 1949; children: Connie Lee, Timothy Scott Charles. Adminstrv. officer Princeton (N.J.) U., 1950-60; asst. mgr. Sta. WPEL, Montrose, Pa., 1960-65; gen. mgr. Sta. WCHR, Trenton, NJ, 1965—. Trustee Princeton Evang. Fellowship, 1973-83; bd. council Word of Life Internat., Schroon Lake, N.Y., 1974-82; mem. exec. bd. Upper Makefield Community Assn., 1972-79; deacon Westerly Rd. Ch., Princeton, 1999-2002. With U.S. Army, 1945-46. Mem. Wooden Canoe Heritage Assn. Am., Nat. Religious Broadcasters, Nat. Assn. Broadcasters, Squam Lakes Assn. (Holderness, N.H.). E-mail: czulker@nassaubroadcasting.com.

ZUMBRUNNEN, DAVID ARNOLD, engineering educator; b. Salt Lake City, Sept. 3, 1955; m. Elizabeth. B in Mech. Engring., U. Minn., 1977; MS in Mech. Engring., Purdue U., 1984, PhD in Mech. Engring., 1988. Registered profl. engr., Ind., SC. Co-founder NSF Ctr. Advanced Engring. Fibers and Films; asst. prof. mech. engring. Clemson U., SC, 1988—93, assoc. prof. mech. engring., 1993—97, prof. mech. engring., 1997—2003, Warren H. Owen-Duke Energy disting. prof. mech. engring., 2003—. Lt. USN, 1977—82. Presdl. Faculty Fellow The White House/NSF, 1992-97. Fellow: ASME; mem.: Am. Nuclear Soc., Polymer Processing Soc., Material Rsch. Soc., SPE, Am. Chem. Soc., AIChemE. Achievements include invention of structured materials formed by chaotic advection, chief technology officer of smart blending technology LLC. Office: Dept Mech Engring Clemson Univ Clemson SC 29634-0921 Business E-Mail: zdavid@clemson.edu, davez@smartblending.com.

ZUMETA, WILLIAM MARK, public policy educator; b. Trenton, NJ, Oct. 2, 1947; s. Bertram William and Ruth (Astbury) Z.; m. Terrea Dodge O'Rand, Jan. 4, 1975; children: Rebecca, Benjamin, Brian. BA, Haverford Coll., 1969; MPP, U. Calif., Berkeley, 1973, PhD, 1978. Dir. rsch. Southeastern Pa. Econ. Devel. Corp., Phila., 1971; program review and evaluation analyst Calif. Dept. Fin., Sacramento, 1972-75; vis. asst. prof. faculty commerce U. B.C., Vancouver, 1976-78; sr. rsch. assoc. Higher Edn. Rsch. Inst. UCLA, 1979-85; adj. prof. edn. Claremont (Calif.) Grad. Sch., 1983; asst. prof. Grad. Sch. Pub. Affairs U. Wash., Seattle, 1985-87, acting dean Grad. Sch. Pub. Affairs, 1988, assoc. prof. Grad. Sch. Pub. Affairs, 1987—99, prof. Evans Sch. Pub. Affairs, 1999—, assoc. dean Evans Sch. Pub. Affairs, 2001—05; faculty chair PhD program, 2008—; co-dir. Collaborative Rschrs. Edn. Scis. Tng. Program, 2009—. Cons. Higher Edn. Coord. Bd., Olympia, 1988-89, 92, 94, 2003, 08, Nat. Inst. Ind. Colls. and Univs., Washington, 1990, 92, NRC, 1987, 92, 94, 2001, NEA, 93, 94-2003, Calif. Higher Edn. Policy Ctr., 1993-97, Nat. Ctr. on Pub. Policy and Higher Edn., 1998-2002, sr. fellow, 2005-, Social Policy Rsch. Assocs., 1997-2000, WICHE, 1995-96, assoc. scholar U. Alban, 2004- Co-editor: Washington Policy Choices: 1990s, 1990; author: Extending the Educational Ladder, 1985; mem. editorial bd. Jour. of Pub. Adminstrn. Rsch. and Theory, 1990-93, 98-2005, Rev. of Higher Edn., 1991-94; contbr. more than 70 articles, reports to profl. publs. Vol. cons. to various community groups, L.A., 1978-85, Seattle, 1985—. Grantee Spencer Found., Chgo., 1980-81, Lilly Endowment, Indpls., 1981-82, 90-91, Pew Charitable Trusts, 1992-94, NSF, 1981-82, Rand, 1994, Sloan Found., 1998-2001, Hewlett Found., 2007, US Dept. Edn., 2009-. Fellow TIAA-CREF Inst., mem. Am. Soc. Pub. Adminstrn., Policy Studies Orgn., Assn. Pub. Policy and Mgmt. (nat. bd. 1997-2001), Assn. Study Higher Edn. (bd. mem. 2009-, pres. 2009-). Office: Univ of Washington Daniel J Evans Sch Pub Affairs Box 353055 Seattle WA 98195-0001 Office Phone: 206-543-0743.

ZUMPANO, CARLOS ANTONIO, lawyer; b. Hanover, NH, Mar. 21, 1974; s. Bernard Joseph and Rosa Maria (Canto) Zumpano; m. Monica P. Zumpano, Feb. 25, 2000; children: Daniella Rosa, Isabella Mia. AB cum laude, Harvard U., Cambridge, Mass., 1996; JD cum laude, U. Miami, Fla., 1999. Bar: Fla., U.S. Dist. Ct. (no., so. and mid. dists.) Fla. Assoc. Carlton Fields, PA, Miami, 1999—2002, Duane Morris LLP, Miami, 2002—04; shareholder Infante and Zumpano, PA, Coral Gables, Fla., 2005—06; mem. Infante, Zumpano, Hudson and Miloch, LLC, Coral Gables, 2006—. Trustee rep. Greater Miami C. of C., Trustee Infante, Zumpano, Hudson and Miloch, LLC. Harvey T. Reid scholar, U. Miami Sch. Law, 1996—99. Mem.: ABA, Dade County Bar Assn., Cuban Am. Bar Assn. Avocations: fishing, racquetball, boating.

ZUMPANO, LEONARD VINCENT, finance educator; b. NYC, Apr. 27, 1945; s. Edward Anthony and Frances Zumpano; m. Gale Brooke Koven, Dec. 27, 1975. B, Iona Coll., New Rochelle, NY, 1967; M, Pa. State U., University Pk., 1969, PhD in Economics, 1976. Asst. prof. fin. U. Ala., Tuscaloosa, 1975—81, assoc. prof. fin., 1981—86, assn. realtors chair real estate, 1985—, prof. fin., 1987—. Vis. scholar Nat. Assn. Realtors, Washington, 1989, 92; exec. dir. Ala. Real Estate Ctr., Tuscaloosa, Ala., 1996—2006; vis. prof. U. Pisa, Italy, 2004; exec. editor Jour. Housing Rsch., 2005—; editl. bd. Jour. Real Estate Rsch., 2008—. Contbr. articles to profl. jours. Mem. Rotary Internat., 2002—07. Recipient Tchg. Excellence award, Coll. Commerce, U. Ala., 1988, 1992, Faculty Excellence award, MBA, 2003. Mem.: Am. Real Estate & Urban Economics Assn., Soc. Indsl. & Office Realtors, Am. Real Estate Soc. Office: Univ Ala Dept Economics Tuscaloosa AL 35487 Business E-Mail: lzumpano@cba.ua.edu.

ZUMWALT, KENNETH WAYNE, assistant principal; b. Hope, Ark., Sept. 15, 1951; s. William Roy and Trula Faye Zumwalt; m. Retta Jackson Zumwalt, Dec. 22, 1973; children: Kenneth Wayne Jr., Meagan Lucyle. BE, So. Ark. U., Magnolia, 1973; EdM, Northeast La. U., Monroe, 1976. Biology tchr. Mt. Holly Schs., Ark., 1973—75; grad. asst. Northeast La. U., 1975—76; coach, physical edn. tchr. First Bapt. HS, Shreveport, La., 1976—80, dean students, 1980—84; coach, sci. tchr. Walton Jr. HS, Bentonville, Ark., 1984—90; biology tchr., coach Bentonville HS, 1990—93; asst. prin. Spring Hill Mid. Sch., Bentonville, 1993—. Named Coach Yr., Ark. Coaches Assn., 1977, 1993. Mem.: Ark. Assn. Mid. Level Edn., Ark. Adminstr. Assn., Fellowship Christian Athletes. Republican. Southern Baptist. Avocations: woodcarving, fishing, camping. Home: 6 Thursby Ln Bella Vista AR 72714 Office: Spring Hill Mid Sch 3400 Hwy 72 W Bentonville AR 72712

ZUMWALT, ROGER CARL, healthcare accreditation consultant; b. Eugene, Oreg., Oct. 26, 1943; s. Robert Walter and Jean Elaine (Adams) Z.; children: Kathryn Nicole Zumwalt DeWeber, Timothy Robert Zumwalt. Student, Boise State U., 1963—65; BA, We. Oreg. U., 1969; postgrad., U. Iowa, 1969—71; MA cum laude, Oreg. State U., 1973. Adminstr. Coulee Cmty. Hosp., Grand Coulee, Wash., 1973-75; exec. dir. Eastmoreland Hosp., Portland, Oreg., 1975—81, Cmty. Hosp., Grand Junction, Colo., 1981-97; pres., healthcare cons. accreditation Zumwalt Consulting, Salem, Oreg., 1997—; dir. adminstrv. svcs. divsn. SAIF Corp., Salem, 1998—2008. Chmn., bd. dirs. Alphabet House Pediat. Rehab. and Edn., 1998—2000, Castle Rock Med. Group, Inc., Denver, 1998—2003; part owner, chmn. bd. dirs. Castle Rock Med. Ctr., Colo., 1998—, N.W. Okla. Regional Med. Ctr. Cherokee, 2000; spkr. numerous local and nat. presentations, subjects including healthcare, hosp. mktg./success/costs, 1981—97; guest lectr. Mesa State Coll., 1992—98, Colo. Christian Coll., 1996—98. Newspaper columnist, 1973-75; contbr. articles, presentations to profl. publs. Commr. Multnomah County Health Care Commn., Portland, Oreg., 1978-81; health cons. Grant County Housing Auth., Grand Coulee, 1974-75; mem. pk. bd. City of Tigard, Oreg., 1976-78; caucus rep. Mesa County Rep. Party, Grand Junction, 1988; mem. adv. com., pres.'s office Mesa State Coll., Grand Junction, 1989; bd. dirs. Hospice of Grand Valley, Grand Junction, 1992-97, mem. devel. com., 1993-97, vice chmn. bd. dirs., 1994-97; bd. dirs. Grand Valley Hospice, 1992-96; comn. mem. Salem

Coalition on Youth Literacy, 2000—. Fellow Coll. Osteo. Healthcare Execs. (bd. dirs. 1985-88, pres. 1987, examiner 1989—, Disting. Svc. award 1989); mem. Am. Osteo. Healthcare Assn. (bd. dirs. 1987-98, treas. 1992-93, 1st v.p. 1994-95, 2d v.p. 1993-94, vice chairperson 1994-95, chmn. 1996-97, chairperson 1997-98, past chmn. 1998), Am. Osteo. Assn. (ex-officio mem. bd. dirs. 1996), Bur. Healthcare Facilities Accreditation (v.p. 1994, advisor 1995-98, accreditation cons. 1995—, accreditation surveyer 1978—, accreditation survey instr. 1994—), Joint Commn. on Am. Healthcare Orgn. (task force on small and rural hosps. 1994-98), Colo. Hosp. Assn. (bd. dirs. 1987-92), Mountain States Vol. Hosp. Assn. (bd. dirs. 1984-98, exec. com. 1991-98, v.p. 1993, vice chmn. bd. dirs. 1992-98), We. Coll. Ind. Practice Assn. (Medicine Mauls Measles com., fin. com. 1991-92), We. Colo. Health Care Alliance (bd. dirs. 1989-94, v.p. 1992, chmn. bd. dirs. 1993), Mesa County Mental Health Assn. (bd. dirs. 1988-89, 91-92), Grand Junction C. of C. (bd. dirs. 1991-93), Rotary (Grand Coolee, Wash. 1973-75, Portland 1975-81, Grand Junction 1981-98, Salem 1998—, chmn. fund raising com. 2000-01, bd. dirs. 2001-02), Western Oreg. U. Alumni Assn. (bd. dirs. 2006—, v.p. bd. dirs. 2006-07, pres.-elect 2007-08, pres., 2008-09, past pres. 2009), Masons, Shriners (pres. Grand Junction club 1989, bd. dirs. El Jebel 1986-90, 1st v.p. Western Colo. club 1989, pres. 1990-91), KC. Republican. Roman Catholic. Avocations: golf, camping, fishing, travel. Home and Office: 592 Meadowbrook Ln Stayton OR 97383-1465

ZUMWALT, ROSS EUGENE, forensic pathologist, educator; b. Goodrich, Mich., July 18, 1943; s. Paul Lawrence and Lila Ann (Birky) Z.; m. Theresa Ann Schar, Sept. 12, 1970 (div. Apr. 1988); children: Christopher Todd, Tenley Ann; m. Cheryl Lynn Willman, Sept. 4, 1988; 1 child, David Willman Zumwalt. BA, Wabash Coll., 1967; MD, U. Ill., 1971. Diplomate in anat. and forensic pathology Am. Bd. Pathology. Intern, resident in pathology Mary Bassett Hosp., Cooperstown, NY, 1971-73; resident in anat. and forensic pathology Southwestern Med. Sch., Dallas, 1973-76; asst. med. examiner Dallas County, Dallas, 1974-76; staff pathologist, dir. labs. Naval Regional Med. Ctr., Camp Lejeune, NC, 1976-78; dep. coroner Cuyahoga County, Cleve., 1978-80, Hamilton County, Cin., 1980-86; assoc. prof. pathology U. Cin. Sch. Medicine, 1980-86; prof. pathology U. N.Mex. Sch. Medicine, Albuquerque, 1987—; chief med. investigator Office of Med. Investigator, Albuquerque, 1991—; pres. Am. Bd. of Pathology, Tampa, 2000—01. Trustee Am. Bd. Pathology, Tampa, Fla., 1993-2004. Lt. comdr. USN, 1976-78. Fellow Am. Acad. Forensic Scis., Coll. Am. Pathologists; mem. AMA, Nat. Assn. Med. Examiners (bd. dirs. 1984-96, pres. 1995-96), Am. Soc. Clin. Pathologists, Am. and Can. Acad. Pathologists. Avocation: golf. Home Phone: 505-344-7480; Office Phone: 505-272-0710. Business E-Mail: rzumwalt@salud.unm.edu.

ZUNA, ROSEMARY ELIZABETH, pathologist; MD, Jefferson Med. Coll., Phila., 1972. Diplomate Am. Bd. Pathology, 1981. Pathologist U. Ark. Med. Sci., Little Rock, 1978—84, SUNY, Stony Brook, 1984—89, Cornell Med. Coll., NYC, 1989—96, U. Okla. Health Sci. Ctr., Okla. City, 1996—. Fellow: US and Can. Acad. Pathology, Coll. Am. Pathologists; mem.: Am. Assn. Cancer Rsch., Am. Soc. Cytopathology. Business E-Mail: rosemary-zuna@ouhsc.edu.

ZUNES, STEPHEN, political science professor, writer; b. Salisbury, NC, Nov. 5, 1956; s. John Athas and Helen (Karnes) Z.; m. Nanlouise Wolfe, May 23, 1987; children: Shanti, Kalila, Tobin. PhD, Cornell U., Ithaca, NY, 1989. Sr. scholar Inst. Global Security Studies, Seattle, 1992—95; prof. politics U. San Francisco, 1995—. Vis. prof. U. Puget Sound, 1993-94; speaker, cons. on U.S. Med. East rels. Contbr. articles to profl. and gen. publs. Rsch. grantee U.S. Inst. of Peace, 1990-91, Inst. for Global Security Studies, 1993—. Mem. Am. Polit. Sci. Assn., Internat. Studies Assn., Caucus for New Polit. Sci., Consortium on Peace Rsch., Edn. and Devel., Middle East Studies Assn. Avocations: folk music, wilderness recreation. Office: Univ San Francisco 2130 Fulton St San Francisco CA 94117 Business E-Mail: zunes@usfca.edu.

ZUNG, THOMAS TSE-KWAI, architect; b. Shanghai, Feb. 8, 1933; came to the U.S., 1937, naturalized, 1954; 1 child, Thomas Bates. Student, Drew U., 1950-51, Va. Poly. Inst., 1951-53, Columbia U., 1955-57; BArch, U. Mich., 1960; MS in Design Sci., Internat. Coll., 1982. Project arch. Edward Durell Stone, Arch., NYC, 1958, 60-65; arch. Cleve., 1967—. Pres. Buckminster Fuller, Sadao and Zung, Archs., 1979—; disting. sr. fellow Stanford U. Librs.; John Denver Windstar Found. Symposium spkr., Aspen, Colo., 2004. Author-editor: Buckminster Fuller, Anthology for the New Millennium; Discovery Channel: Dome Over Houston 2009; Mus. Contemporary Arts Chgo. 2009; Chgo. Am. Inst. Architects 2009; prin. works include City Cleve. Pub. Utilities Bldg., Cleve. State U. Geodesic Elongated Dome, Mayfran, Inc., Sawmill Creek Lodge, U. Akron Guzzetta Hall, Music, Speech and Theater Arts Ctr., Alumni Ctr. Bowling Green State U., U. Akron Master Plan-West, City of East Cleveland, Superior Euclid beautification plan, student recreation ctr. Bowling Green State U., Glenville Pub. Libr., campus bldg. Tex. Wesleyan Coll., recreation, health and phys. edn. bldg. Wittenberg U., Medina Res. Park Office, arena, health, phys. edn. complex U. Akron, Dyke Coll., Lima State Prison, Cleve. Children's Christian Home, State of Ohio Pre-Release Ctr. Cleve., Lorain-Grafton State Prison, Mayfield H.S., Asian Village Project, Cleve. Metroparks Tropical Rainforest Bldg., Student Union Wittenberg U., YWCA, Salem, Ohio, China Internat. Trade Ctr., People's Rep. China, additions to Cleve. Hopkins Internat. Airport, Ohio State U. Coll. of Dentistry-Postle Hall and Hist. Costume and Textile Mus., Master Plan Schreiner Coll. and Cailloux Student Ctr., Griffin Welcome Ctr., Master Plan Walsh Univ., Walsh Student Union, Columbus, Western Res. Psychiat. Hosp., Ohio, Trumbull State Prison, Ohio Dept. Transp. Prototypical Rest Stop Design; patentee in field. Trustee Pace Assn., 1970-73, Karamu House, 1974-80, Cleve. Inst. Music, 1979-86, Chinese Cultural Assn., 1980-84, Ohio Arts Coun., 1982-84; task force chmn. Greater Cleve. Growth Assn., 1970; mem. Coun. Human Rels., 1972, Leadership Cleve. Class '77; cubmaster local Boy Scouts Am., 1977-79; vestryman St. Christopher-by-River, 1980-83; bd. dirs. Buckminster Fuller Inst., 1983—, Pearl S. Buck Found., 1989-98, cons. arch. hist. house com.; mem. Adv. Coun. Aging, State of Ohio, 1997—2007; founder, pres. Bratenahl 100, 2006-; commr. VFW Cuyahoga County Vet. Svc., 2006-. With Signal Corps, U.S. Army, 1953-55. Decorated 5 medals; recipient Pub. Works award, State of Ohio, 1971, Design award, Korean Inst. Constrn. Tech., 1984, Ohio Valley ABC Design Excellence award, Wittenberg U. Student Union, 1989, Synergeticists N.E. Corridor award, 2005, Buckminster Fuller SNEC award, 2005, others; Disting. sr. fellow, Stanford U. Librs. Mem. AIA (dir. Cleve. chpt. 1980, Design award Cleve. chpt. 1972, Design award 1989), Am. Soc. Planning Ofcls., English Speaking Union (trustee 1972-75), Ohio Soc. Archs., Ohio Assn. Minority Archs. and Engrs. (trustee 1982-90), Hermit Club, City Club (dir. 1972-74, v.p. 1974), Rotary; Buckminster Fuller Inst. (bd. mem.). Office: Buckminster Fuller Sadao & Zung 1 Bratenahl Pl Cleveland OH 44108-1181

ZÚÑIGA, MARKOS MOULITSAS, political blogger, social activist; b. Chgo., Oct. 11, 1971; m. Elisa Batista, 2000; children: Aristotle, Elisandra. B in Philosophy, Journalism, and Polit. Sci., Northern Ill. U., 1996; JD, Boston U. Sch. Law, 1999. Founder, main author weblog Daily Kos, San Francisco, 2002—. Contbr. Brit. daily newspaper The Guardian, 2006; columnist The Hill, Newsweek; co-founder sports blog network SB Nation; fellow New Politics Inst. Author: Taking On the System: Rules for Radical Change in a Digital Era, 2008; co-author (with Jerome Armstrong): Crashing the Gate: Grassroots, Netroots, and the Rise of People-Powered Politics, 2006. Served with US Army, 1989—92. Named one of 100 Most Influential Hispanics, People en Español, 50 Most Important People on the Web, PC World; named to Northern Star Hall of Fame, Northern Ill. U., 2007, Forbe's Web Celeb 25. Democrat. Office: c/o Newsweek 251 W 57th St New York NY 10019

ZUNINO, NATALIA, psychologist; b. NYC, Nov. 23, 1937; d. Frank Anthony and Elizabeth (Delafield) Zunino; m. Philip Puschel, June 29, 1974 (div. 1978). BA, Mt. Holyoke Coll., Mass., 1959; MA, Columbia U., 1962, NYU, 1975, PhD, 1982. Rschr. Time-Life Books, NYC, 1962-67; sr. editor Harcourt Brace Jovanovich, NYC, 1967-80; staff psychotherapist Met. Ctr. for Mental Health, NYC, 1983-85; pvt. practice, 1984—; staff psychotherapist Washington Sq. Inst., NYC, 1984-87; supr. Met. Inst. Tng. in Psychoanalytic Psychotherapy, NYC, 1985—; supr., staff psychotherapist Eating Disorder Resource Ctr., NYC, 1986—2004; mem. faculty Ctr. for Study of Anorexia and Bulimia, NYC, 1987—96, supr., 1995—; psychotherapist family and couple treatment Inst. Contemporary Psychotherapy, NYC, 1988—90; participant intensive-extern program Family Inst. Westchester, Harrison, NY, 1990—94; participant Ea. Group Psychotherapy Tng. Program, 1997—98. Mem. intake com. Ctr. Study Anorexia and Bulimia, 1997—, exec. com., 2006—; adj. asst. prof. Coll. S.I., NY, 1984—86. Editor: Psychology: Its Principles and Applications, 1969, 8th edit. 1984, Sociology: The Study of Human Relationships, 1972, 2nd edit. 1977; contbr. articles to profl. jours. Mem. APA, Acad. for Eating Disorders, Nat. Eating Disorders Assn. Avocations: horseback riding, gardening. Home: 115 4th Ave #7G New York NY 10003-4909 Office Phone: 212-677-0804.

ZUNOUBI, MOHAMMAD R., engineering educator; m. Loyla Zunoubi; 1 child, Sepehr M. Degree, U. Ill., Urbana Champaign, 1999; PhD, Miss. State U., 1996. Assoc. prof. SUNY, New Paltz, 2001—. Recipient Provost Rsch. award, SUNY, 2005. Mem.: IEEE. Achievements include invented and designed a new type of dielectric resonator antenna. Office Phone: 845-257-3932. Business E-Mail: zunoubm@engr.newpaltz.edu.

ZUNZ, OLIVIER JEAN, history professor; b. Paris, July 19, 1946; s. Jean R. and Monique M. (Blin) Z.; m. Christine M. Crommen, July 3, 1970; children: Emmanuel, Sophie. Licence in history and geography, U. Paris X, 1968, M in History, 1969; Doctorat-ès-Lettres, U. Paris I, Panthéon-Sorbonne, 1982. Scientist Ctr. Nat. de la Recherche Scientifique, Paris, 1976-78; asst. prof. dept. history U. Va., Charlottesville, 1978-83, assoc. prof., 1983-88, prof., 1988-99, Commonwealth prof., 1999—. Vis. prof. Ecole des Hautes Etudes en Scis., Sociales, Paris, 1985—, Coll. France, 1997; dir. seminar for Coll. Tchrs. NEH, 1989, 92. Author: The Changing Face of Inequality: Urbanization, Industrial Development, and Immigrants in Detroit, 1980-1920, 1982, Making America Corporate, 1870-1920, 1990, Why the American Century?, 1998; editor, co-author: Reliving the Past: The Worlds of Social History, 1985; editor: Alexis de Tocqueville, Democracy in America (transl. A. Goldhammer), 2004; co-editor: (with David Ward) The Landscape of Modernity: Essays on New York City, 1900-1940, 1992, (with Leonard Schoppa and Nobuhiro Hiwatari): Social Contracts under Stress: The Middle Classes of America, Europe, and Japan at the Turn of the Century, 2002, (with Alan S. Kahan): The Tocqueville Reader: A Life in Letters and Politics, 2002; mem. editl. bd. Revs. in Am. History, 1990-98; contbr. articles, book revs. to profl. jours. Jr. fellow Mich. Soc. Fellows, 1973-76, John Simon Guggenheim Meml. Found. fellow, 1986-87; grantee U. Mich.-Ford Found. Population Devel. Fund, 1974-76, NSF, 1976-78, NEH, 1979-81, 84-87, Ford Found., 2004-07 Named Chevalier de L'ordre du Mérite, French Govt.; also recipient numerous rsch. grants. Mem. Am. Hist. Assn., Orgn. Am. Historians, The Tocqueville Soc. (pres. 2001—06). Home: 1368 Hilltop Rd Charlottesville VA 22903-1225 Office: U Va Corcoran Dept of History PO Box 400180 Randall Hall Charlottesville VA 22904-4180 Business E-Mail: oz@virginia.edu.

ZUO, QIUHAI KEN, engineering educator, researcher; b. Guannan, China, Oct. 18, 1965; s. FengJia Zuo and Guiying Liu; m. Yang Cao, Jan. 17, 1987; children: Heather C., David C. BS, SE U., Nanjing, China, 1984; MS, Xian U. Hwys., Xian, China, 1987; PhD, U. N.Mex, Albuquerque, 1995. Post-doctoral rsch. assoc. U. Ill., Urbana, 1995—97; mem. tech. staff Los Alamos Nat. Lab., N.Mex., 1997—2006; assoc. prof. U. Ala., Huntsville, 2006—. Contbr. articles to profl. jours. Recipient Excellence in Grad. Work in Mech. Engrng. Y.C. Hsu Meml. award, U. N.Mex, 1995, Def. Programs Excellence award, Dept. Energy, 2005. Mem.: ASME. Achievements include development of several advanced models for deformation, damage, and failure of materials. Office: Univ Ala Huntsville 301 Sparkman Dr Huntsville AL 35899

ZUPAN, MARK A., dean, economics professor; b. Rochester, NY, July 28, 1959; s. Janez and Maria (Močnik) Zupak; m. Carol Shuherk; children: Will, Walker. BA in economics, Harvard U., 1981; PhD in economics, MIT, 1987. Teaching fellow dept. economics Harvard U., Cambridge, 1983-86; asst. prof. to prof. economics Marshall Sch. Bus., U. So. Calif., 1987—97, assoc. dean masters programs; dean, prof. economics Eller Coll. Bus. and Pub. Adminstrn., U. Ariz., 1997—2004; dean Simon Grad. Sch. Bus., U. Rochester, NY, 2004—, prof. economics and pub. policy. Vis. prof. Amos Tuck Sch. Bus. Adminstrn., Dartmouth Coll.; mem. editl. bd. Pub. Choice, Jour. Bus. Economics, Rsch. in Law and Economics; bd. dirs. PAETEC Holding Corp., Constellation Brands, Inc., 2007—. Co-author: (with E.K. Browning) Microeconomic Theory and Applications, (with T. W. Gilligan, A. M. Marino) Microeconomic Cases and Applications; Contbr. articles to profl. journals. Mem. Phi Beta Kappa. Lodges: Rotary. Office: William E Simon Grad Sch Bus Adminstrn U Rochester CS-2202H Carol Simon Hall Rochester NY 14627-0107 Office Phone: 585-275-3316. Business E-Mail: mark.zupan@simon.rochester.edu.*

ZUPONCIC, VEDA HELEN, music educator, art director; b. Biwabik, Minn., Aug. 3, 1946; d. Herman Martin and Helen Bradach Zuponcic; 1 child, Gavriel Moshe Heine. MusB, Ind. U., Bloomington, 1967, MusM, 1968. Instr. Phila. Musical Acad., 1968—71; prof. music Rowan U., Glassboro, NJ, 1971—. Artistic dir. Hollybush Festival, Glassboro, 1982—90, Northern Lights Music Festival, Aurora, Minn., 2004—. Musician: European Debut Tour (Martha Baird Rockefeller grant, 1971), Americans from Moscow, The Romantic Piano, (performance) Alice Tully Hall debut, Debut in Great Hall of Moscow Conservatory. Home: 111 Munn Ln Cherry Hill NJ 08034 Office: Rowan Univ Dept Music Glassboro NJ 08028 Business E-Mail: zuponcic@rowan.edu.

ZURAWSKI, JEANETTE, rehabilitation services professional; b. June 30, 1951; Student, U. Wis., 1969-70, Portland CC, 1974-78; BS in Chemistry, Portland State U., 1981; MD, Oreg. Health Scis. U., 1985; postgrad. in Acupuncture, UCLA, 2000. Diplomate Am. Bd. Phys. Medicine and Rehab. Resident U. Kans. Med. Ctr., Kansas City, 1985-89; med. dir. rehab. svcs. North Miss Med. Ctr., Tupelo, 1989-97; pvt. practice Tupelo, Miss. Past mem. adv. com. Medicare Carrier; presenter in field; bd. dirs. Gilbert's Home Health Care Agy. Past chair pers. com., exec. bd. mem., co-chair fund raising com. Big Brothers/Big Sisters, Lee County, Miss. Mem. AMA, Am. Acad. Phys. Medicine and Rehab. (chairperson edn. com., mem. exec. coun. resident physician sect.), Am. Med. Women's Assn., Am. Bus. Women's Assn. (chair membership com., treas., recipient Woman of the Year), Miss. State Med. Assn., Assn. Acad. Physiatrists, Am. Med. Acupuncture Assn. (bd. eligible), Iota Sigma Pi. Home: 637 W Main St Tupelo MS 38804-3732

ZUREK, PATRICK JAMES, bishop; b. Wallis, Tex., Aug. 17, 1948; s. Arnold and Victoria Zurek. BS in Math. magna cum laude, U. St. Thomas, Houston; STB in Theology magna cum laude, U. St. Thomas, 1974; STL in Moral Theology magna cum laude, Inst. of Lateran U., 1976. Ordained priest Diocese of Austin, Tex., 1975; assoc. pastor St. Mary's Cath. Ch., Temple, Tex., 1976—79, St. Joseph's Cath. Ch., Bryan, Tex., 1979—82; founding pastor St. Thomas Aquinas Cath. Ch., College Station, 1982—92; pastor St. John Neumann Cath Ch., Austin, 1992—98; ordained bishop, 1998; aux. bishop Archdiocese of San Antonio, 1998—2008; bishop Diocese of Amarillo, Tex., 2008—. Mem.: Czech Am. Priests Assn. (pres., CEO 2002—), US Conf. Cath. Bishops. Roman Catholic. Office: Diocese of Amarillo Chancery Office 1800 N Spring St Amarillo TX 79117 Office Phone: 806-383-2243. Office Fax: 806-383-8452.

ZURIER, ROBERT BURTON, rheumatology educator; b. Passaic, NJ, Feb. 19, 1934; s. Milton and Lillian (Matzner) Z.; m. Catherine Elizabeth Miers, June 3, 1962 (dec. Apr. 21, 2007); 1 child, Adam Wheaton. BS, Rutgers U., 1955; MD, U. Tex. Southwestern Med. Sch., Dallas, 1962; MA (hon.), U. Pa., 1981. Intern, then resident in medicine Boston City Hosp., 1962-64; fellow in medicine St. Lukes Hosp., NYC, 1964-66; fellow in rheumatology NYU, 1970-73; pvt. practice internal medicine Holden, Mass., 1967-70; asst. prof. medicine U. Conn., Farmington, 1973-76, assoc. prof., 1976-80; prof., chief. rheumatology U. Pa., Phila., 1980-91; prof. medicine, dir. rheumatology div. U. Mass. Med. Ctr., Worcester, 1991—2006, prof. medicine, 2006—. Served to capt. USAR, 1956-68. Guggenheim Found. fellow, 1986. Mem. AAAS, Am. Coll. Rheumatology (master), Am. Soc. Clin. Investigation, Interurban Clin. Club (pres. 1989-90). Office: U Mass Med Ctr 55 Lake Ave N Worcester MA 01655-0002 Office Phone: 508-856-6246. Business E-Mail: robert.zurier@umassmed.edu.

ZURSTADT, WILLIAM JOHN, history professor; children: Claire, Anna. BA, Ind. U., Bloomington, 1976; BS, U. Southern Ind., Evansville, 1986; MS, Ind. State U., Terre Haute, 1988. History instr. Bethune-Cookman U., Daytona Beach, Fla., 2000—. Home: 347 S Orchard St Ormond Beach FL 32174 Office: Bethune-Cookman Univ 640 MM Bethune Blvd Daytona Beach FL 32114 Personal E-mail: willzurstadt@yahoo.com. Business E-Mail: zurstadtw@cookman.edu.

ZUSMAN, EDIE ELLEN, neurosurgeon; b. El Paso, Oct. 29, 1963; d. Sidney Harold and Sandra Phyllis Zusman; m. Stephen Roy Pratt, Feb. 17, 1991; children: Adam, Abby. BS, Northwestern U., 1985, MD, 1987. Diplomate Am. Bd. Neurol. Surgery, Nat. Bd. Med. Examiners. With U. Calif., San Francisco, 1993-94, clin. instr., 1994-97, molecular med. rsch. fellow, 1994-96; staff neurosurgeon Kaiser Permanent, Sacramento, 1997-99; asst. prof. U Calif. Davis Sch. Medicine, Sacramento, 1999—; dir. adult neurosurgery Sutter Neuroscience Inst., Sacramento. Mem. exec. com. Coun. State Neurol. Socs., 1997—; adj. asst. prof. neurol. surgery U. Calif., Davis; prin. investigator Ctr. for Biophotonics Sci. and Tech. Author: The Outcome Following Traumatic Spinal Cord Injuries, 1992; contbr. articles to profl. jours. Participant Habitat for Humanity, Oakland, Calif., 1997—. Mem. AMA, Am. Assn. Neurol. Surgeons (bd. dirs.), Congress Neurol. Surgeons, Calif. Assn. Neurol. Surgeons, Northwestern U. Alumni Assn., Women in Neurological Surgery (past pres.), Coun. of State Neurosurgical Soc., Am. Epilepsy Soc. Avocations: tennis, opera. Office: Sutter Neuroscience Med Group Ste 500 2800 L St Sacramento CA 95816 Office Phone: 916-454-6936. Business E-Mail: zusmane@sutterhealth.org.

ZUSMAN, RANDALL MARK, physician; b. Detroit, Apr. 10, 1948; s. Herman Hyman and Sarah Belle (Goldberg) Z.; children: Mara, Laura, Lisa, Todd. BSc in Chemistry, U. Mich., Ann Arbor, 1969; MD, Yale U., New Haven, 1973. Diplomate Am. Bd. Internal Medicine, Am. Bd. Cardiovasc. Disease. Clin. fellow in medicine Harvard Med. Sch., Boston, 1973-75; intern in medicine Mass. Gen. Hosp., Boston, 1973-74, jr. asst. resident in medicine, 1974—75, sr. resident in medicine, 1977, chief resident in medicine, 1978, clin. and rsch. fellow in medicine, 1979—80, asst. in medicine, 1980—84, dir. hypertension clinic, 1981—83, dir. hypertension divsn., 1982—89, dir. hypertension assocs., 1983—, assoc. physician in medicine, 1989—, physician, medicine, 2009—; clin. assoc. Nat. Heart, Lung and Blood Inst. NIH, Bethesda, Md., 1975-77; clin. fellow in medicine Harvard Med. Sch., Boston, 1977-78, rsch. fellow in medicine, 1979-80, instr. in medicine, 1978-79, asst. prof. medicine, 1980-93, assoc. prof. medicine, 1994—; cons. in internal medicine Mass. Eye and Ear Infirmary, Boston, 1980-83; dir. cardiac rehab. program Spaulding Rehab. Hosp., Boston, 1992-98; clin. specialist hypertension Am. Soc. Hypertension, 1999—; cons., cardiology, med. dept. Mass. Inst. Tech., Cambridge, 2001—. Assoc. editor: Prostaglandins, 1981-84, Clinical Research, 1981-83, Hypertension, 1983-88; editor elect: Clinical Research, 1983-84; editor: Clinical Research, 1984-89; mem. editl. bd.: (jours.) Jour. of Clinical Hypertension, Journal of Hypertension, 1990-93; mem. editl. adv. bd.: (jour.) Reviews in Contemporary Pharmacotherapy, 1996—; contbr. chpts. to books. Lt. commdr. USN, 1975-77. Fellow Am. Coll. Cardiology; mem. Am. Fedn. for Clin. Rsch. (pub. policy com. 1981-90, co-chmn. 1982, chmn. 83-84, chmn. 50th anniv. mem. campaign 1989-90), Am. Soc. Nephrology, Am. Heart Assn., Am. Soc. Hypertension. Jewish. Avocations: reading, travel, sports. Office: Mass Gen Hosp 15 Parkman St Boston MA 02114-3117 Office Phone: 617-726-7790.

ZUTAUT, STEVEN ERIC, systems analyst, application developer; s. James and Magdaline Zutaut. BS in Computer Sci./Chemistry, U. Ala., Huntsville, 1984, PhD in Materials Sci., 1993. Journeyman knowledge-based applications developer Minn., cert. internet application developer Oracle Corp., solution developer.net Microsoft Corp., developer for JavaTM 2 Platform Sun Microsystems, Inc. Assoc. systems analyst Unisys, Montgomery, Ala., 1984—87; knowledge engr. PEAKSolutions Corp., Bloomington, Minn., 1987—89; rsch. assoc. U. Ala., Huntsville, 1993—96; rsch. scientist Nichols Rsch. Corp., Huntsville, 1996—99; sr. cons. Computer Scis. Corp., Huntsville, 1999—2001; software developer (cons.) AEROTEK, Huntsville, 2001—02; sr. systems analyst III Teledyne Solutions, Inc., Huntsville, 2002—04; software developer (cons.) TEKSystems, Huntsville, 2005—06; software engr. Westar

Aerospace and Def. Group, 2006—. Contbr. articles to profl. jours. Mem.: IEEE, Assn. Computing Machinery. Home: 305 Dovington Dr Huntsville AL 35806-1680 Personal E-mail: sezutaut@msn.com.

ZUTHER, SIMONE MARGRIETHA, curator; b. Neuss, North Rhine-Westphalia, Germany, July 18, 1978; d. Gerd Gustav Johannes and Yvonne Helene Zuther. BA, Coll. William and Mary, Williamsburg, Va., 2000; MS, Pratt Inst., Bklyn., 2005; PhD student, Va. Commonwealth U., Richmond, 2005—. Mgr. Freundorfer Gallery, NYC, 2000—01; grad. asst. Pratt Inst., 2003—04; curatorial intern, dept. European art VMFA, Richmond, 2006—06, intern, office dir., 2007—08; grad. asst. and instr. Va. Commonwealth U., 2006—08; assoc. curator Nancy Rosen Inc., NYC, 2008—. Planning com. mem. New Scholars and New Ideas Symposium, Richmond, 2005—06; spkr. Pratt Inst. 5th Ann. Master' Student Symposium, Bklyn., 2006—06; presenter Grad. Student Assn. 10th Ann. Rsch. Symposium, Richmond, 2007; attendee Hamad Bin Khalifa Symposium Islamic Art, Doha, Qatar, 2007—07; spkr. Mid. Atlantic Symposium History Art, Wash., 2008. Fellowship, Paul and Fredrika Jacobs, 2007—08. Mem.: AAUW, Southeastern Coll. Art Conf., Coll. Art Assn., Am. Assn. Mus., Phi Kappa Phi. Home: 97 Clinton Ave # 3 Brooklyn NY 11205 Personal E-mail: zuthersimone@mac.com.

ZWANCH, ANDREW V., science educator; Instr. precision machining tech. Johnson Coll., Scranton, Pa., 1987—. Office: Johnson Coll 3427 N Main Ave Scranton PA 18508

ZWANGER, JEROME, physician; b. NYC, Apr. 4, 1923; m. Bernice E. Lomazov, May 22, 1955; children: Susan, Roberta (dec.), Melissa, Betsy. AB, U. Pa., 1943; MD, Chgo. Med. Sch., 1947. Diplomate Am. Bd. Radiology. Intern Wyckoff Heights Hosp., Bklyn., 1947-49; resident L.I. Coll. Hosp., Bklyn., 1949-52; practice medicine specializing in radiology; asst. dir. dept. radiology L.I. Coll. Hosp., NYC, 1953-54; radiologist L.I. Jewish Hosp., 1955-60; dir. radiology North Shore U. Hosp., Plainview, NY, 1961—, also bd. dirs. Asst. prof. clin. radiology SUNY, Stony Brook, 1974-80; governing bd. Nassau-Suffolk Health Systems Agy.; mem. N.Y. State Bd. Medicine, Bd. Profl. Med. Conduct N.Y. State Dept. Health. Mem. vis. com. Met. Mus. Art, Phila. Art Mus.; bd. overseers Sch. Arts and Scis., U. Pa. Fellow: Nassau Acad. Medicine (founding fellow, past pres.), Am. Coll. Radiology (councilor 1975—); mem.: AMA, Soc. for Breast Imaging, Am. Inst. Ultrasound in Medicine, L.I. Radiol. Soc. (past pres.), N.Y. State Radiol. Soc. (pres. 1986—87), Radiol. Soc. N.Am., Nassau County Med. Soc. (past pres.), Med. Soc. N.Y., U. Pa. Alumni Assn. (bd. overseers 1997). Office: 126 Hicksville Rd Massapequa NY 11758-5822

ZWASS, MAURICE S., medical educator; s. Samuel and Rosa Zwass; m. Jennifer Baisch, Sept. 3, 1995; children: Rachel H., Isabel F., Sofia G. MD, UC San Francisco, 1981. Prof. anesthesia and pediat. UCSF, San Francisco, 1988—2008, prof., 1988—. Business E-Mail: zwassm@anesthesia.ucsf.edu.

ZWASS, VLADIMIR, computer science and information systems educator; b. Lvov, USSR, Feb. 3, 1946; came to U.S., 1970, naturalized, 1979; s. Adam and Friderike (Getzler) Z.; m. Alicia Kogut, Apr. 24, 1977; 1 child, Joshua Jonathan MS, Moscow Inst. Energetics, 1969; MPhil, Columbia U., 1974, PhD, 1975. Mem. profl. staff IAEA, Vienna, 1970; asst. prof. computer sci. Fairleigh Dickinson U., Teaneck, NJ, 1975-79, assoc. prof., 1979-84, prof., 1984—, prof. computer sci. and mgmt. info. sys., 1990—, disting. prof. computer sci. and mgmt. info. sys., 1999—, Gregory Olsen Endowed chair and disting. prof. computer sci. and mgmt. info. sys., 2008—, chmn. com. computer sci., 1976—. Cons. U.S. Govt., Met. Life Ins. Co., Citibank, Diebold Group; seminar assoc. Columbia U., 1986—; speaker nat. and internat. meetings. Author: Introduction to Computer Science, 1981, Programming in Fortran, 1981, Programming in Pascal, 1985, Programming in Basic, 1986, Management Information Systems, 1992, Foundations of Information Systems, 1998; editor-in-chief: Jour. Mgmt. Info. Sys., 1983—, Internat. Jour. Electronic Commerce, 1996—, Advances in Mgmt. Info. Systems, —; contbr. articles to profl. jours. and publs., Ency. Britannica, N.Y. Times, chpts. to books. Columbia U. fellow, 1970-71; Helena Rubinstein Found. scholar, 1971-75; grantee USN, other agys. Mem. IEEE, Assn. Computer Machinery, Assn. for Info. Sys., Sigma Xi, Eta Kappa Nu. Home: 19 Warewoods Rd Saddle River NJ 07458-2712 Office: Sch Computer Sci and Info Sys Fairleigh Dickinson U Teaneck NJ 07666 Office Phone: 201-327-9239. Personal E-mail: zwass@fdu.edu.

ZWEBEN, STUART HARVEY, information scientist, educator, dean; b. Bronx, NY, Apr. 21, 1948; s. Max D. and Ruth (Schwartz) Z.; m. Rochelle T. Small, June 13, 1971; 1 child, Naomi. BS, CUNY, 1968; MS, Purdue U., 1971, PhD, 1974. Sys. analyst IBM Corp., Kingston, NY, 1969-70; asst. prof. Ohio State U., Columbus, 1974-80, from vice chmn. to acting chmn. computer sci. dept., 1982-84, assoc. prof., 1980-92, prof., 1992—, chmn., 1994—2005, assoc. dean academic affairs and adminstrn. Coll. Engring., 2006—. Pres. Computing Scis. Accreditation Bd., Stamford, Conn., 1989-91, v.p. 1987-89, sec., treas. 1986-87; sec.-treas. Fedn. on Computing in the U.S., Washington, 1992. Contbr. articles to profl. jours. Rsch. grantee NSF, 1981-83, 88-97, 2005-06, Army Rsch. Office, 1980-83, Dept. Edn., 1983-85, Applied Info. Tech. Rsch. Ctr., 1990-91, Honda R&D, 1998-2006, Dayton, Ohio, 2003-09; Equipment grant AT&T Bell Labs, 1984, 86-88. Fellow Accreditation Bd. Engring. and Tech., Inc. (computing accreditation commn. exec. com. 2001—09, vice chmn. ops., 2005-06, chair-elect, 2006-07, chmn., 2007—08, accreditation coun. chmn., 2009), Assn. for Computing Machinery (pres. 1994-96, v.p. 1992-94, coun. mem. 1982-88, chpt. bd. chmn. 1982-85, publications bd. 1988-92, fin. com. 1990-92, nominating com. chmn. 1999-2000, fellows com. chmn. 2003, constn. and bylaws chmn. 1988-92, Recognition of Svc. award 1980, 85, 87-88, Outstanding Contbn. award 1997, SIGSOFT Disting. Serv. award 2009); mem. AAUP, IEEE Computer Soc. (assoc. editor 1990-98), Computing Rsch. Assn. (bd. dirs. 1997-2004, Spl. Svc. award 2006), Coun. Sci. Soc. Presidents (sec. 1998), Columbus Tech. Coun. (Tech. Person of Yr. award 2000, Presdl. U. Disting. Sci. Alumnus, 2009). Avocations: sports, stamp collecting/philately. Office: Ohio State U Computer Scis 2015 Neil Ave Columbus OH 43210-1210 Office Phone: 614-292-9526. Business E-Mail: zweben@cse.ohio-state.edu.

ZWEIBEL, JOEL BURTON, retired lawyer; b. NYC, Feb. 7, 1935; s. Jacob and Ruth (Fleischner) Z.; m. Lynn Herzog (dec. Nov. 1984); children: Jane, Emily; m. Chrystine Marie Trichter. BBA magna cum laude, CCNY, Baruch Coll., 1955; LLB, Yale Law, 1958. Bar: NY 1959. Ptnr. Kaye, Scholer, Fierman, Hays & Handler, NYC, 1969-79, Gelberg & Kronovet, NYC, 1979-81, Kramer, Levin, Nessen, Kamin & Frankel, NYC, 1981-90, O'Melveny & Myers, NYC, 1990—2001, ptnr. in-charge N.Y. office, 1998—2000. Lectr. 2d Ann. Uniform Comml. Code Law Inst., 1968, Practicing Law Inst. Sr. Workout Officers Roundtable. Author: Creditors' Rights Handbook, 1980; co-author: Herzog's Bankruptcy, Forms and Practice, 6th edit., 1980; contbr. articles to profl. jours. Recipient award Bankruptcy and Reorgn. Divsn. Fedn. United Jewish Appeal, 1989. Mem. ABA, Assn. Bar City NY (chmn. com. on bankruptcy and corp. reorgn. 1981-84), Nat. Bankruptcy Conf. (chmn. com. on avoiding powers 1983-2000, mem. exec. com., treas. 1991-2000), Yale Law Sch. Alumni Assn. (bd. dirs. 2004-), Am. Coll. Bankruptcy (dir., regent 2d cir.), (co-founder, mem. steering com. execs. on campus program, Baruch Coll., CUNY, advisor prelaw soc. 2002-08). Avocations: art, theater, music, photography, tin whistle. Office: 570 Park Ave New York NY 10021 Personal E-mail: jbzweibel@aol.com.

ZWEIFEL, CLINT, state treasurer; b. Florissant, Mo. m. Janice Zweifel; 2 children. BA in Polit. Sci., U. Mo., St. Louis, 1996, MBA, 2001. State rep. Dist. 78 Mo. House Reps., 2002—09, com. assignments, appropriations, small bus. & tax policy; treas. State of Mo., 2009—. Democrat. Office: State Treasurer PO Box 210 Jefferson City MO 65102 Office Phone: 573-751-8533. Office Fax: 573-751-0343.*

ZWEIFEL, DAVID ALAN, newspaper editor; b. Monroe, Wis., May 19, 1940; s. Cloyence John and Uva Lorraine (Skinner) Z.; m. Sandra Louise Holz, Sept. 7, 1968; children: Daniel Mark, Kristin Lynn. BJ, U. Wis., 1962. Reporter The Capital Times, Madison, Wis., 1962-71, city editor, 1971-78, mng. editor, 1978-83, editor, 1983—. V.p. Simpson St. Free Press, 2001—; bd. dirs. Swiss Am. Ctr., Friends of Monona Terrace, Capital Times Co., Madison Newspapers Inc., William T. Evjue Charitable Trust. V.p. Alliance for Children and Youth, Madison, 1983—; bd. dirs. United Cerebral Palsy Dane County, Madison, 1984-91. Lt. U.S. Army, 1963-65; col. USNG, ret. Named Investigative Reporter of Yr. Madison Press Club, 1972; Disting. Journalism grad., U. Wis., 2003 Mem.: Soc. Profl. Journalists (Spl. Achievement award 1992, 1996), Wis. Freedom of Info. Coun. (pres. 1986—2000), Wis. AP (pres. 1987—88), Am. Soc. Newspaper Editors (com. freedom of info., Pulitzer Prize juror 2000, 2001), U. Wis. Alumni Assn., Wis. N.G. Assn. (trustee 1975—81), Elks. Avocations: running, bowling, book collecting. Home: 5714 Tecumseh Ave Monona WI 53716-2964 Office: The Capital Times PO Box 8060 Madison WI 53708-8060

ZWEIFEL, DONALD EDWIN, editor, lobbyist, consultant; b. LA, Nov. 30, 1940; s. Robert Fredrick and Eugenia Bedford (White) Z.; m. Donna Jean Croslin; 1 son, Phillip Matthew. Student, Orange Coast Coll., 1963-67, 90-92, U. Calif., Irvine, 1968-70, Western State U. Coll. Law, 1973, Irvine U. Coll. Law, 1974-75, Rancho Santiago Jr. Coll., 1988, Chapman U., 1993—97; grad., Aviation Ground Sch., 1990; student, USAF Air U., 1994—95, USAF Air. U., 2000—01. Cert. student pilot, registered lobbyist Calif. State Legislature, lic. general class Nat. Assn. for Amateur Radio, 2009. Devel. tech. Hughes Aircraft, Newport Beach, Calif., 1963-64; co-founder, station mgr. Sta. KUCI-FM, Irvine, Calif., 1970; owner, mgr. Zweifel Jaguar Car Sales and Svc., Santa Ana, Calif., 1975-76; pres. Zweifel & Assocs. Inc., Santa Ana, 1977-86, Zweifel South Coast Exotic Cars, Orange, Calif., 1987-96, ret., 1996; assoc. editor, cons. Compliance News Pub. Co., Long Beach, Calif., 1998—. Mem. small bus. coun. CalTrans, 2000—07; legis. com., small bus. adv. coun. Calif. Dept. Gen. Svcs., 2005—07; environ. air and water quality com. Associated Gen. Contractors, 2007—, mem. Regulatory and Environ. Task Force, Calif., 2007—. Co-author: Challenge 2000, Regaining the America's Cup, 1996; editor: (coll. textbook) The Dream Is Alive, Space Flight and Operations In Earth Orbit. Vol. emergency coord. emergency mgmt. divsn. Orange County Fire Authority, 1985-87, Navy Relief Soc., 1993, 1st. lt. CAP Squadron 88 Group VII, 1993-95, sr. programs officer, 1993-94, asst. transp. officer Calif. Wing Hdqrs., 1994-95, Group VII Facilities officer, 1994-95, 2000-02, squadron pers. officer, 1993-95, 2000-02, Calif. wing rep. to Orange County Vol. Orgns. Active in Disaster, ARC, 1994-95, Calif. wing vol. Office Emergency Svcs., Calif., 1994-96, 2000-21, grad. Squadron Leadership Sch., 1993, Wing Supply Officers Sch., 1995, squadron safety officer, pub. affairs officer, asst. aerospace edn. officer, 1998-2001; program coord. Young Astronaut Coun., 1989-90; cadet CAP, USAF aux., Long Beach, Calif., 1953-59; mem. Orange County Homeless Issues Taskforce, 1994-95, 1997-2000, Orange County Homeless Svc. Providers for the Reuse of Marine Corps Air Sta., Tustin, Calif., 1994-95; legis. com. Orange County Vets. Adv. Coun., 1998-2006; chmn. tech. rev. subcom. Marine Corps Air Sta., El Toro, Calif., 1998-2001; apptd. to CalEPA DTSC Adv. Group Mil. Base Closure, 1995-99, CalEPA Dept. Toxic Substances Control Adv. Group pro-bono cons., Orange County Citizen's Adv. Commn. and El Toro Local Redevel. Authority, 1996-2001; vol. mediator Victim-Offender Reconciliation program, 1995-96; restoration adv. bd. MCAS Tustin, 1994—, co-chair, 2003—; restoration adv. bd. MCAS, El Toro, Calif., 1994—, Freedom Com. Orange County; cmty. emergency response team City of Placentia, 2003—; homeless vets. com. United Vets. Orgn. Orange County; fed. advocate for Disabled Veteran Bus. Enterprise, 2004-; dir. Orange County Walk of Honor, 1998; disaster action team mem. ARC Orange County chpt., 2009-. With U.S. Army Nat. Guard, 1958—59. Recipient 6 certs. achievement Fed. Emergency Mgmt. Agy., 1989-96, 2 certs. appreciation CAP, 2 certs commendation, 1994, cert. appreciation Southwest Divsn. Naval Facilities Engring. Commd., 2000, Meritorious Svc. award, Calif. State Assembly Restoration Adv. Bd. Assemblyman John Campbell, 2001. Mem. Air Force Assn. (life; vice-chmn. civilian recruitment Calif. state membership com. 1988-91, v.p. govt. rels. Calif. 2006—, v.p. membership, Gen. Doolittle chpt. bd. dirs. 1987-89, 90-92, dir. Gen. Jimmy Doolittle chpt. 2005-08, Exceptional Svc. award Gen. Jimmy Doolittle chpt. 1988, 91, Calif. Meritorious Svc. award 1988, v.p. membership Gen. Curtis E. LeMay Orange County chpt. 2000-02, 2004, v.p. Aerospace Edn., Gen. Curt E. LeMay chpt. 2008-), Calif. Assn. Aerospace Edn. (fellow), Marine Corps Hist. Found. (life), Aerospace Edn. Found. (Gen. Jimmy Doolittle fellow 1988, Gen. Ira Eaker fellow 1989, Pres.'s award 1988), US Naval Inst., AIAA (Cert. of Appreciation 1989, LA chpt. hist. com. 1989), Gulf & Vietnam Vets. Strategic Studies Archives (cons., co-founder 1983—, dir.), Marine Corps League (assoc., capt. Heinsey detachment 2000-02), Confederate Air Force (col.1989), AmVets (nat. jr. coord. com. 2003-05, Calif. jr. coord. 2003-04, 2d vice comdr. dist. II, Dept. Calif 2003-04, 1st vice comdr. dist. 2004-05, 2d vice-comdr. post 18 2006-07, Govt. rels. liaison, dept. Calif., 2008, Dept. Calif. JROTC/ROTC awards coord., southern area, 2009-), Masons, Saddleback Master Chorale of Orange County. Avocations: sailing, travel, flying. Personal E-mail: dzweifel@sbcglobal.net.

ZWEIFEL, PAUL FREDERICK, retired physics professor; b. NYC, June 21, 1929; s. Fritz and Dorothy Mary Zweifel; m. Kathleen Anne McKay, Nov. 13, 1967; children: Christen Anne Whitten, Frederick Feza, Evan Rudolph, Kathryn Clements. BS, Carnegie Inst. of Tech., Pitts., Pa., 1948; PhD, Duke Univ., Durham, NC, 1949. Rsch. assoc., mgr. theoretical physics, consulting physicist GE Knolls Atomic Power Lab., Schenectady, NY, 1953—58; from assoc. prof. to prof. of nuc. engring. U. Mich., Ann Arbor, 1958—68; from prof. to univ. disting. prof. Va. Poly. Inst. and State U., Blacksburg, 1968—96; univ. disting. prof. emeritus Va. Poly. Inst. and State Univ., Blacksburg, 1996—. Cons. numerous orgns. including U.S. AEC, Oak Ridge, Argonne and Los Alamos Nat. Labs., 1958—88; vis. prof. numerous univs. including both U.S. and fgn. in Italy, Germany, Slovenia, Turkey; mem. numerous editl. bds. Translator opera supertitles; contbr. music articles, including opera program notes. Recipient E.O. Lawrence medal, US Govt. (Atomic Energy Commn.), 1972; Guggenheim fellowship, John Simon Guggenheim Found., 1974-75. Fellow: Am. Nuc. Soc., Am. Phys. Soc.; mem.: Fed. Am. Scientists (sec. 1956—59), Am. Math. Soc. Liberal. Episcopalian. Avocations: music, travel, bridge, flight instructor, sportswriter. Home and Office: 6820 Sahalee Cir Radford VA 24141 Personal E-mail: zweifel@alumni.duke.edu.

ZWEIFEL, RICHARD GEORGE, curator; b. LA, Nov. 5, 1926; s. Harold Charles and Kathleen Marguerite (Garland) Z.; m. Frances Ann Wimsatt, July 30, 1956; children: Matthew Karl, Kenneth Paul, Ellen Katrina. BA, UCLA, 1950; PhD, U. Calif., Berkeley, 1954. Mem. staff Am. Mus. Natural History, NYC, 1954-89, chmn. curator dept. herpetology, 1968-80, curator emeritus, 1989—; sci. attaché Gondwana, 1974-75. Served with AUS, 1945-46. Mem. Soc. Study Amphibious and Reptiles, Am. Soc. Ichthyologists and Herpetologists. Home: PO Box 16354 Portal AZ 85632-1354

ZWEIMAN, BURTON, allergist, immunologist, educator; b. NYC, June 7, 1931; s. Charles and Gertrude (Levine) Z.; m. Claire Traig, Dec. 30, 1962; children: Amy Beth, Diane Susan. AB, U. Pa., 1952, MD, 1956. Diplomate Am. Bd. Internal Medicine, Am. Bd. Allergy & Immunology. Intern Mt. Sinai Hosp., NYC; Hosp. U. Pa., Bellevue Hosp. Ctr. Hosp. U. Pa., Bellevue Hosp. Center, 1957-60; fellow NYU Sch. Medicine, 1960-61; mem. faculty dept. medicine U. Pa. Sch. Medicine, Phila., 1963—, prof. medicine, chief allergy and immunology divsn., 1975-98. Cons. U.S. Army, NIH; co-chmn. Am. Bd. Allergy and Immunology, 1979-81. Editor Jour. Allergy Clin. Immunology, 1988-93; editor Allergy and Asthma: Disease Management Center, 1998—, now med. editor; contbr. articles to med. jours. Served with M.C., USNR, 1961-63. Allergy Found. Am. fellow, 1959-61 Fellow ACP, Am. Acad. Allergy, Asthma and Immunology (past pres.); mem. Am. Assn. Immunologists, Am. Fedn. Clin. Rsch., Phi Beta Kappa, Alpha Omega Alpha. Office: PA Presbyn Med Ctr 518 Mutch Bldg 38th Market St Philadelphia PA 19104 Business E-Mail: bzweiman@mail.med.upenn.edu.

ZWERDLING, ALEX, language educator; b. Breslau, Germany, June 21, 1932; came to U.S., 1941, naturalized, 1946; s. Norbert and Fanni (Alt) Z.; m. Florence Goldberg, Mar. 23, 1969; 1 son, Antony Daniel. BA, Cornell U., 1953; postgrad. (Fulbright scholar), U. Munich, Germany, 1953-54; MA, Princeton U., 1956, PhD, 1960. Instr. English Swarthmore Coll., 1957-61; asst. prof. English U. Calif., Berkeley, 1961-67, asso. prof., 1967-73, prof., 1973-86, prof. English Berkeley, 1988—, chmn. grad. studies, 1985-86; univ. prof. George Washington U., 1986-88. Vis. prof. Northwestern U., 1977; dir. edn. abroad program U. Calif., London, 1996-98; mem. advanced placement exam. com. Ednl. Testing Svc., 1975-79; mem. fellowship panel Nat. Endowment for Humanities, 1977-82, 84-87, Nat. Humanities Ctr., 1989-90; fellow Ctr. for Advanced Study in Behavioral Scis., 1964-65. Author: Yeats and the Heroic Ideal, 1965, Orwell and the Left, 1974, Virginia Woolf and the Real World, 1986, Improvised Europeans: American Literary Expatriates and the Siege of London, 1998; mem. adv. com. PMLA, 1978-82. Recipient Berkeley citation U. Calif., Berkeley, 2003; Am. Coun. Learned Socs. fellow, 1964-65; NEH fellow, 1973-74; Guggenheim fellow, 1977-78; Woodrow Wilson Ctr. fellow, 1991-92, fellow Nat. Humanities Ctr., 1992-93. Mem. MLA (chmn. 20th Century Brit. lit. div. 1969-70, 85-86). Office: U Calif Dept English Berkeley CA 94720-1030

ZWERLING, GARY LESLIE, retired investment company executive; b. NYC, Aug. 6, 1949; s. Seymour Joseph and Evelyn Rhoda (Posner) Z.; m. Marierose Miraglia, Aug. 25, 1974; children: Cara Marisa, Craig Harris. BEngring., SUNY, Stony Brook, 1970; MBA, SUNY, Albany, 1972. V.p. Chase Manhattan Bank, NYC, 1972-78; ptnr. Goldman, Sachs & Co., NYC, 1978-96; ret., 1996. Trustee Babson Coll., United Jewish Appeal Fed. No. NJ; bd. overseers Mus. Jewish Heritage-A Living Meml. to the Holocaust; sec., bd. govs. NY chpt. Arthritis Found.; bd. dirs. Am. Fedn. Aging Rsch. Mem. Thoroughbred Owners and Breeders Assn., Nat. Thoroughbred Racing Assn. Jewish.

ZWICK, EDWARD M., director, producer, scriptwriter; b. Winnetka, Il., Oct. 8, 1952; s. Allen and Ruth Ellen (Reich) Z.; m. Lynn Liberty Godshall, Oct. 24, 1982. BA, Harvard U., 1974; MFA, Am. Film Inst., 1976. Editor, feature writer The New Republic, Rolling Stone, 1972-74; co-founder The Bedford Falls Co., 1985. Writer, prodr., dir.: (TV series) Family, 1976-80 (Humanitas prize 1980), (TV spl.) Spl. Bull., 1983 (Emmy award for outstanding drama spl. 1983, Dir. Guild award 1983, Writers Guild award 1983, Humanitas prize 1983), (films) The Seige, 1998, The Last Samurai, 2003, Defiance, 2008; dir.: (TV movies) Paper Dolls, 1982, Having It All, 1982, Extreme Close-Up, 1990, (films) About Last Night, 1986, Glory, 1989, Leaving Normal, 1992, Legends of the Fall (also prodr.), 1994, Courage Under Fire, 1996, Blood Diamond (also prodr.), 2006; prodr. Shakespeare in Love, 1998 (Oscar award for best picture, 1998, BAFTA award for best picture, 1999, Golden Satellite award for best picture, 1998), Traffic, 2000 (NY Film Critics Circle award for best picture, 2000, Golden Satellite award for best picture, 2000), I Am Sam, 2001, Women Vs. Men (TV movie), 2002, Abandon, 2002, Lone Star State of Mind (exec. prodr.), 2002; co-creator, exec. prodr.: (with Marshall Herskovitz) Thirtysomething, 1987-91 (Emmy award for outstanding drama series 1988), Dream Street, 1989, My So-Called Life, 1994-95, Relativity, 1996-97, co-creator, prodr. Once and Again, 2000; exec. prodr., writer (TV series) Quarterlife, 2008; author: Literature and Liberalism, 1975.*

ZWICK, KENNETH LOWELL, lawyer, director; b. Cleve., Oct. 30, 1945; s. Alvin Albert Zwick and Selma (Mack) Durbin; m. Ruth Winifred Epstein, June 21, 1969; children: Tara, Monica. BSME,BS in Mgmt., MIT, 1969; JD, Temple U., 1976. Bar: Pa. 1976. Engr. Raytheon Corp., Norwood, Mass., 1969-71; tech. mgr. On-Line Systems, Inc., Phila., 1971-76; staff atty. Mead Data Cen., Washington, 1976-83; dir. litigation support office U.S. Dept. Justice, Washington, 1983-88, dir. mgmt. programs office, 1988—. Recipient Presdl. rank award, 1994. Mem. ASME (assoc.). Democrat. Jewish. Home: 9316 Wescott Pl Rockville MD 20850-3452 Office: US Dept Justice 3140 Main Justice Bldg Washington DC 20530-0001 Home Phone: 301-251-0684; Office Phone: 202-514-4552. Business E-Mail: ken.zwick@usdoj.gov.

ZWICKY, BARBARINA EXITA, humanities educator, researcher; d. Fritz and Anna Margaritha Zwicky; 1 child, Christian Alexander Fritz. Diploma, Alliance Française, 1974; diploma in fashion design, Modeschule Brunn, Zurich, 1974, Adrian Teen Modeling Agency, 1980; AS, Pasadena City Coll., 1999, AA, 2000; BA, Pacific Oaks Coll., 2002, MA, 2005; D (hon.), Yorker Internat. U., 2007. Cert. nursing asst. Calif., 1990. V.p. Continental Enterprises, Pasadena, 1980—91; tchr. human devel. Pacific Oaks Coll., Pasadena, 2003—. Owner Barby's Baby Boutique, Monrovia, Calif., 1985—90. Bd. dirs. Arcadia Am. Little League, Calif., 2004, Fritz Zwicky Found., Switzerland; vol. Huntington Meml. Hosp., 1995, ARC, Pasadena, 2000; activist Rep. Party, Pasadena. Mem.: AAUW (mem. Evelyn Brandt Scholarship com. 2000—, chair pub. policy 2002—04), Matterhorn Young Swiss Club, Swiss Ladies Soc., United Swiss Soc. So. Calif., Omicron Mu Delta, Alpha Gamma Sigma (hon. bd. 1999). Republican. Avocations: skiing, art, literature, swimming. Home: 2065 Oakdale Ave Pasadena CA 91107 Personal E-mail: barbarinaz@aol.com.

ZWIENER, DAVID KENNETH, bank executive; b. 1954; BA, Duke U., Durham, NC; MBA in Fin. and Mktg., Northwestern U. Asst. treas. internat. ops. Kimberly Clark Corp., 1984—87; sr. v.p., treas. to exec. v.p. capital markets Heller Internat. Corp., 1987—93; CFO, exec. v.p. ITT Fin. Corp., 1993—95; exec. v.p., CFO Hartford Fin. Svcs. Group, Inc., 1995—2001, pres., COO property & casualty ops., 2000—07; mng. dir., co-head fin. inst. group The Carlyle Group, Washington, 2007—08; sr. exec. v.p., CFO Wachovia Corp., Charlotte, NC, 2008—. Office: Wachovia Corp 301 S Coll St Ste 4000 Charlotte NC 28288 Office Phone: 704-590-0000. Office Fax: 704-374-3425.*

ZWIEP, DONALD NELSON, mechanical engineering educator, department chairman; b. Hull, Iowa, Mar. 18, 1924; s. Daniel and Nellie (De Stigter) Z.; m. Marcia J. Hubers, Sept. 3, 1948; children: Donna J., Mary N., Joan L., Helen D. BSME, Iowa State Coll., 1948, MSME, 1951; DEng (hon.), Worcester Polytech. Inst., 1965. Registered profl. engr., Mass. Design engr. Boeing Airplane Co., 1948-50, sr. tool engr., summer 1953, summer faculty asso., 1955; asst. prof. Colo. State U., 1951-56, assoc. prof., 1956-57; cons. engr. aviation div. Forney Mfg. Co., 1956-57; prof., head dept. mech. engring. Worcester Polytech. Inst., 1957-88, acting head mgmt. engring., 1974-76, chmn. Mfg. Engring. Application Ctr., 1981-88, acting provost, v.p. acad. affairs, 1988-90, prof., dept. head emeritus, 1990—. Constrn. engr. U.S C.E., 1954; cons. engr., acting chief engr. J.J. Malir, Inc., 1956. Chmn. emeritus, bd. trustees James F. Lincoln Arc Welding Found., 1976—2006. Served as pilot USAAF, World War II, CBI; lt. col. USAFR; cons. and ednl. specialist. Fellow ASME (life, hon.; v.p. edn. 1972-74, pres. 1979-80); mem. ASME (hon.), Am. Soc. Engring. Edn. (life, pres. Colo. State U. chpt. 1954-55, treas. Rocky Mountain sect. 1955, nat. bd. dirs. 1974-75), Am. Assn. Engring. Socs. (chair coun. pre-coll. edn.), Am. Welding Soc., Soc. Mfg. Engrs., C. of C. of Orange City, Torch Club, Sigma Xi, Omicron Delta Kappa, Tau Beta Pi, Sigma Tau, Pi Tau Sigma. Home: 119 2d St SW Orange City IA 51041 Home Phone: 712-737-6837. Personal E-mail: dnzwiep@earthlink.net.

ZWIER, TIMOTHY S., chemistry professor; married. BS in Chemistry, Calvin Coll., 1977; PhD Chem. Physics, U. Colo., Boulder, 1981. Postdoctoral rsch. assoc. U. Chgo. James Franck Inst., 1981—83; asst. to assoc. prof. chemistry Calvin Coll., 1983—88; asst. prof. chemistry Purdue U., West Lafayette, Ind., 1988—93, assoc. prof. chemistry, 1993—97, prof. chemistry, 1997—. JILA vis. fellow, 1994—95; mem. planetary atmosphere review panel NASA, 2000, 03, 04; assoc. head dept. chemistry Purdue U., 2001—03, head dept. chemistry, 2004—; mem. combustion rsch. facility adv. bd. Sandia Nat. Labs., 2004—; mem. external adv. com. for rsch. corp. evaluation James Madison U., 2005—; lectr. in field. Co-editor: Internat. Revs. in Phys. Chemistry, 1998—2003; sr. editor: Jour. Phys. Chemistry, 2003—; mem. editl. bd. Molecular Physics, 2001—; contbr. articles to profl. jours. Named Faculty Scholar, Purdue U., 1999—2004; Alfred P. Sloan Rsch. fellow, 1989—91. Fellow: Am. Phys. Soc. (councilor-at-large divn. chem. physics 2002—05, Earle K. Plyler prize for Molecular Spectroscopy 2007); mem.: AAAS, Am. Astron. Soc., Am. Chem. Soc. Office: Purdue U Rm B155 Dept Chemistry 560 Oval Dr West Lafayette IN 47907-2084 E-mail: zwier@purdue.edu.

ZWIERLEIN, MARTIN WOLFRAM, physics professor; b. Hamburg, Germany, Nov. 5, 1977; s. Otto Zwierlein and Erika Elisabeth Zwierlein-Diehl. Diplome d'Etudes Approfondies en Physique Theorique, Ecole Normale Supérieure, Paris, 2002; PhD in Exptl. Atomic Physics, MIT, Cambridge, Mass., 2006. Rsch. assoc. U. Mainz, Germany, 2006—07; asst. prof. physics MIT, 2007—. Recipient Sofja Kovalevskaja-award, Alexander von Humboldt-Stiftung, 2006, Klung-Wilhelmy-Weberbank prize, Freie U. Berlin, 2007; rsch. fellowship, Alfred P. Sloan Found., 2008—. Mem.: European Phys. Soc., German Phys. Soc., Am. Phys. Soc. Achievements include discovery of high-temperature superfluidity in ultracold fermi gases; Bose-Einstein Condensation of molecules & fermion pairs; fermionic superfluidity with imbalanced spin populations. Office: MIT Rm 26-255 77 MA Ave Cambridge MA 02139 Office Fax: 617-253-4876. Business E-Mail: zwierlein@mit.edu.

ZWILICH, ELLEN TAAFFE, composer; b. Miami, Fla., Apr. 30, 1939; d. Edward Porter and Ruth (Howard) Taaffe; m. Joseph Zwilich, June 22, 1969 (dec. June 1979). MusB, Fla. State U., 1960, MusM, 1962; D Mus. Arts, Juilliard Sch., 1975; studies with Roger Sessions and Elliott Carter; MusD (hon.), Oberlin Coll., 1987, Converse Coll., 1994; LHD (hon.), Manhattanville Coll., 1991, Marymount Manhattan Coll., 1994, N.Y. New Sch., Mannes, 1995, Mich. State U., 2006. Francis Eppes disting. prof. Fla. State U., Tallahassee, 1999—. Composer in residence Santa Fe Chamber Music Festival, 1990, Am. Acad. Rome, 1990; first Composer's Chair, Carnegie Hall, 1995-99, Saratoga Chamber Music Festival, 2004. Premiere, Symposium for Orch., Pierre Boulez, N.Y.C., 1975, Chamber Symphony and Passages, Boston Musica Viva, Richard Pittman, 1979, 82. Symphony 1, Gunther Schuller, Am. Composers Orch., 1982; violinist Am. Symphony, N.Y.C., 1965-73; composer: Sonata in Three Movements, 1973-74; String Quartet, 1974; Clarino Quartet, 1977; Chamber Symphony, 1979; Passages (for Soprano and Chamber Ensemble), 1981; String Trio, 1982; Symphony 1:3 Movements for Orch., 1982 (Grammy nomination New World Records, 1987); Divertimento, 1983; Einsame Nacht, 1971; Emlekezet, 1978; Im Nebel, 1972; Passages for Soprano and Orch., 1982; Trompeten, 1974; Fantasy for Harpsichord, 1983; Intrada, 1983; Prologue and Variations, 1983; Double Quartet for Strings, Chamber Music Soc. of Lincoln Ctr., 1984; Celebration for Orch., Indpls. Symphony, John Nelson, 1984; Symphony #2 (Cello Symphony) San Francisco Symphony, Edo De Waart, 1985, Symphony #2 Louisville Orch. recording, L.L. Smith (Grammy nomination 1991); Concerto Grosso 1985, Handel Festival Orch., Steven Simon, 1986; Concerto for Piano and Orch., Detroit Symphony, Gunther Herbig, Marc-André Hamelin, 1986; Images for 2 Pianos and Orch., Nat. Symphony Orch., F. Machetti, 1987; Tanzspiel, Peter Martins N.Y.C. Ballet, 1987; Praeludium Boston chpt. AGO, 1987; Trio for piano, violin and cello; Kalichstein, Laredo, Robinson trio, 1987; Symbolon, Zubin Mehta and the N.Y. Philharm., Leningrad and Moscow (USSR), N.Y.C. (Koussevitsky Internat. Rec. award nominee 1990), 1988; concerto for trombone and orch. J. Friedman, Sir Georg Solti, Chgo. Symphony, 1989, concerto for trombone and orch. Christian Lindberg, James De Priest, Malmö Symphony, concerto for flute and orch. D.A. Dwyer, Seija Ozawa, Boston Symphony, 1990, quintet for clarinet and string quartet David Schiffrin, Chamber Music N.W., Lincoln Ctr. Chamber Mus. Soc., 1990; concerto for oboe and orch. John Mack, Christoph von Dohnanyi, Cleve. Orch., 1991; concerto for bass trombone strings, timpani and cymbals Chgo. Symphony Orch. Ch. Vernon, Daniel Barenboim, 1991; concerto for violin, violoncello and orch. Jaime Laredo, Sharon Robinson, Louisville Orch., L. Smith, 1991; Immigrant Voices Peter Leonard, St. Lukes Orch., N.Y. Internat. Festival ot the Arts Chorus, Ellis Island, 1991, concerto for flute and orch, D.A. Dwyer, J. Sedares, London Symphony Orch., 1992, Symphony # 3 (Grammy nominee 1993), J. Ling, N.Y. Philharmonic, 1993, concerto for bassoon and orch., Nancy Goeres, Lorin Maazel, Pitts. Symphony, 1993, concerto for horn and string Orch., David Jolley, Rochester Philharm., L.L. Smith., 1993, Fantasy for Orch., JoAnn Falletta, Long Beach Symphony Orch., 1994, American Concerto Doc Severinsen, J. Falletta San Diego Symphony, 1994, A Simple Magnificat, 1994, Triple Concerto Kalichstein, Laredo, Robinson Trio Zdenek Macal, Minn. Orch., 1995, for piano and orch., Peanuts Gallery, 1996, violin concerto, Pamela Frank, H. Wolff, 1997; String Quartet # 2, 1998, Emerson Quartet; Upbeat! 1998, Nat. Symphony Orch., conducted by Anthony Aibel, Symphony # 4 (orch., chorus, children's chorus) Mich. State U., L. Gregorian 2000, Lament for solo piano Carnegie Hall, 2000, Millenium Fantasy for Piano & Orch., J. Biegel, J. Cobos-Lopez, Cin. Symphony, 2000, Lament for Cello & Piano, Met. Mus., N.Y.C., 2000, Partita for Violin & String Orch., Carnegie Hall, 2001, One Nation, 2002, Openings for Orch., 2002 JoAnn Falletta Va. Symphony, Clarinet Concerto, D. Shifrin, Chamber Music Soc. of Lincoln Ctr., Buffalo Philharm, 2002, Episodes for Violin & Piano, Itzhak Perlman, 2003, Quartet for Oboe & Strings, Saratoga Festival, 2004, Rituals for 5 Percussionists and Orchestra, Iris Orchestra, Nexus, 2004, LUVN BLM, Calif. Ear Unit, 2005, Naxos Am. Classics, Violin Concerto and Rituals, M.Stern, Frank, 2005; New World Records: Music By Ellen Taaffe Zwilich; N.Y. Philharm. conducted by Zubin Mehta. Bd. dir. Copland Fund. Recipient Elizabeth Sprague Coolidge Chamber Music prize, 1974, Gold medal, G.B. Viotti, Vercelli, Italy, 1975, citation, Ernst von Dohnanyi, 1981, Pulitzer prize for music, 1983, Composers award, Lancaster Symphony Orch., Arturo Toscanini Music Critics award, 1987, Alfred I. DuPont award, 1991, Performing Arts award, Miami Ctr. Performing Arts, 2000, named, Musical Am. Composer of Yr., 1999, Key to the City Cinn., 2001; named Martha Baird Rockefeller Fund rec. grantee, 1977, 1979, 1982, Guggenheim fellow, 1981; named to, Fla. Artists Hall of Fame, 1994. Fellow: Am. Acad. Arts & Sci.; mem.: AAAL (Acad. award 1984), Guggenheim Found. (bd. dirs.), MacDowell Colony (bd. dirs.), Am. Fedn. Musicians (hon.; life), BMI Found. (bd. dirs.), Am. Music Ctr. (v.p. 1982—84, bd. dirs.). Office: Coll Music Fla State Univ Tallahassee FL 32306-1180 Office Phone: 850-644-4744. Office Fax: 850-644-2033.

ZWILLINGER, MARC J., lawyer; b. NYC; BA in Polit. Sci., magna cum laude, Tufts U., 1991; JD magna cum laude, Harvard U., 1994. Bar: Ill. 1994, DC 1996; Cert. Info. Systems Security Profl. Law clk. to Judge Mark L. Wolf US Dist. Ct. Dist. Mass., 1994—95; assoc. Kirkland & Ellis, Chgo., 1995—97; trial atty. computer crime & intellectual property sect., criminal divsn. US Dept. Justice, 1997—2000; ptnr. Kirkland & Ellis, Washington, 2000—03, head cyberlaw & info. security group, 2001—03; ptnr. Sonnenschein Nath & Rosenthal LLP, Washington, 2003—, chair firm info. security & internet enforcement practice group, 2003—. Office: Sonnenschein Nath & Rosenthal LLP Ste 600, E Tower 1301 K St NW Washington DC 20015 Office Phone: 202-408-9171. Office Fax: 202-408-9171. Business E-Mail: mzwillinger@sonnenschein.com.

ZWINGE, RANDALL JAMES HAMILTON See RANDI, JAMES

ZWISLOCKI, JOZEF JOHN, neuroscience educator, researcher; b. Lwow, Poland, Mar. 19, 1922; arrived in U.S., 1951; s. Tadeusz and Helena (Moscicki) Z.; m. Ruth Gerber, Oct. 29, 1945 (div. May 1954); m. Sylvia Claire Goldman, July 11, 1954 (dec. July 17, 1992); m. Jadwiga M. Morrison, Dec. 2, 1993. Diploma, Fed. Tech. Inst., Zurich, Switzerland, 1944, ScD, 1948; D honoris causa, U. Adam Mickiewicz, Poznán, Poland, 1991, Syracuse U., NY, 2004. Head electroacoustic lab. dept. otolaryngology U. Basel, Basel, Switzerland, 1945-51; rsch. fellow psychoacoustic lab. Harvard U., Cambridge, Mass., 1951-57; dir. Bioacoustic Lab. Syracuse U., 1958-63, founder, dir. Lab. of Sensory Communication, 1963-73, founder dir. Inst. for Sensory Rsch., 1973—84, prof. neurosci., 1984—88, disting. prof. neurosci., 1988—92, disting. prof. emeritus, 1992—; prof. communicative disorders dept. spl. edn. Syracuse U. Sch. Edn., 1982—92; rsch. prof. SUNY Health Sci. Ctr., Syracuse, 1967—. Affiliate prof. bioengring. L.C. Smith Coll. Engring., Syracuse U., 1986-92; Carhart Meml. lectr. Am. Auditory Soc., 1992; Richard C. Heyser Meml. lectr. Audio Engring. Soc., 2005; mem. exec. coun. Com. Hearing, Bioacoustics and Biomechanics, NRC, Washington, 1965-68, chmn., 1967-68; mem. rev. panel on communicative scis. NIH, Bethesda, Md., 1966-70, chmn., 1969-70; mem. Communicative Disorders Program Project rev. com. NIH, Bethesda, 1971-75; chmn. Bd. Sci. Advs. Ctr. Health Scis., U. Wis., Madison, 1975-78. Inventor acoustic ear simulator, acoustic bridge, several types of ear defenders; contbr. articles to profl. jours.; author: Auditory Sound Transmission: An Autobiographical Perspective, 2002, Sensory Neuroscience: Four Laws of Psychophysics, 2009. Recipient Faculty Rsch. award Syracuse chpt. Sigma Xi, 1973, Internat. Ctr. Ricerche e Studi Amplifon prize, 1976, Chancellor's citation for exceptional acad. achievement Syracuse U., 1980, Javits Neurosci. Investigator award NIH, 1984, Kwiek medal Acoustics Inst., A. Mickiewicz U., Poland, 1991, medal Acoustical Soc. Poland, 1991, Hugh Knowles prize Northwestern U., 1992, Life Achievement award, Am. Auditory Soc., 2007, Legend of Auditory Sci., Am. Acad. Audiology, 2006. Fellow Acoustical Soc. Am. (chmn. tech. com. on psychol. and physiol. acoustics 1962, 63, exec. coun. 1982-85, recipient 1st Bekesy medal 1985, chmn. long-range planning com. 1983-86, nominating com. 1986-87, mem. com. on tutorials 1988-91, com. on meetings 1988-91, chmn. spring meeting, 1989), Am. Speech and Hearing Assn., The Polish Inst. Arts and Scis. Am.; mem. NAS, Polish Acad. Scis., Internat. Soc. Audiology (v.p. 1967-72), Internat. Union of Physiol. Scis. (commn. on auditory physiology 1982-89), Internat. Union Pure and Applied Physics (Commn. on Acoustics 1982-89), Collegium Oto Rhino Laryngologicum Amicitiae Sacrum, Assn. for Rsch. in Otolaryngology (award of merit 1988), Am. Otol. Soc. (assoc.), Hearing Rsch. (editl. bd.). Avocations: skiing, tennis, trout fishing, inventions.

ZWISSLER, ALEXANDER, museum director; b. 1957; m. Jimmie Lee Zwissler. BA in Polit. Sci., U. Calif. Berkeley. Dir. cable TV and telephone co., England; exec. dir. Fort Mason Found., San Francisco, 1999—2006; exec. dir., CEO Chabot Space & Science Ctr., Oakland, Calif., 2007—. Sec. bd. dirs. Joint Powers Agy., 2007—. Office: Chabot Spce & Sci Ctr 10000 Skyline Blvd Oakland CA 94619 Office Phone: 510-336-7383.

ZWOYER, EUGENE MILTON, retired consulting engineering executive; b. Plainfield, NJ, Sept. 8, 1926; s. Paul Ellsworth and Marie Susan (Britt) Z.; m. Dorothy Lucille Seward, Feb. 23, 1946; children: Gregory, Jeffrey, Douglas. Student, U. Notre Dame, 1944, Mo. Valley Coll., 1944-45; BS, U. N.Mex., 1947; MS, Ill. Inst. Tech., 1949; PhD, U. Ill., 1953. Mem. faculty U. N.Mex., Albuquerque, 1948-71, prof. civil engring., dir. Eric Wang Civil Engring. Rsch. Facility, 1961-70; rsch. assoc. U. Ill., Urbana, 1951-53; owner, cons. engr. Eugene Zwoyer & Assocs., Albuquerque, 1954-72; exec. dir., sec. ASCE, NYC, 1972-82; pres. Am. Assn. Engring. Socs., NYC, 1982-84; exec. v.p. T.Y. Lin Internat., San Francisco, 1984-86, pres., 1986-89; owner Eugene Zwoyer Cons. Engr., 1989—2002; COO, treas. Polar Molecular Corp., Saginaw, Mich., 1990, exec. v.p., 1991-92; ret., 2002. Trustee Small Bus. Research Corp., 1976-80; trustee Engring. Info., Inc., 1981-84; internat. trustee People-to-People Internat. 1974-86; v.p. World Fedn. Engring. Orgns., 1982-85. Served to lt. (j.g.) USN, 1944-46. Named Outstanding Engr. of Yr. Albuquerque chpt. N.Mex Soc. Profl. Engrs., 1969, One Who Served the Best Interests of the Constrn. Industry, Engring. News Record, 1980; recipient Disting. Alumnus award the Civil Engring. Alumni Assn. at U. Ill., 1979, Disting. Alumnus award Engring. Coll. Alumni Assn., U. N.Mex., 1982, Can.-Am. Civil Engring. Amity award Am. Soc. Civil Engrs., 1988, Award for Outstanding Profl. Contbns. and Leadership Coll. Engring. U. N.Mex., 1989 Mem. AAAS, ASCE (dist. bd. dirs. 1968-71), NSPE, AFTRA, Am. Soc. Engring. Edn., Nat. Acad. Code Adminstrn. (trustee, mem. exec. com. 1973-79), Engrs. Joint Coun. (bd. dirs. 1978-79), Engring. Soc. Commn. on Energy (bd. dirs. 1977-82), Sigma Xi, Sigma Tau, Chi Epsilon. Home: 6363 Christie Ave Apt 1326 Emeryville CA 94608-1940 E-mail: eugenezwoyer@comcast.net.

ZYGOCKI, RHONDA I., oil industry executive; b. St. John's, Nfld., Can., July 1957; B. in Civil Engring., Meml. U. Nfld., 1980. Petroleum engr. Chevron Can. Resources, Calgary, gen. mgr. strategic bus. svcs., 1993—94, CFO, 1997—99; profit ctr. mgr. Chevron USA Prodn. Co., Houston, 1994—97; mgr. strategic planning Chevron Corp., San Ramon, Calif., 1999—2000, adv. to bd. chmn., 2000—01, v.p. health, environment & safety, 2003—07, corp. v.p. policy, govt. & pub. affairs, 2007—; mng. dir. ChevronTexaco Australia Pty. Ltd., Perth, 2001—03. Bd. dirs. Internat. Petroleum Industry Environ. Conservation Assn., Internat. Assn. Oil & Gas. Bd. dirs. Engrs. Without Borders, Tiger Woods Learning Ctr. Office: Chevron Corp 6001 Bollinger Canyon Rd San Ramon CA 94583-2324*

ZYROFF, ELLEN SLOTOROFF, information scientist, classicist, educator; b. Atlantic City, Aug. 1, 1946; d. Joseph George and Sylvia Beverly (Roth) Slotoroff; m. Jack Zyroff, June 21, 1970; children: Dena Rachel, David Aaron. AB, Barnard Coll., 1968; MA, The Johns Hopkins U., 1969, PhD, 1971; MS, Columbia U., 1973. Instr. The Johns Hopkins U., Balt., 1970-71, Yeshiva U., NYC, 1971-72, Bklyn Coll., 1971-72; libr., instr. U. Calif., 1979, 81, 91, San Diego State U., 1981-85, 94; prof. San Diego Mesa Coll., 1981-95; dir. The Reference Desk Rsch. and Pub. Rels. Svcs., La Jolla, Calif., 1983—; prin. libr. San Diego County Libr., 1985—2008. v.p. Archaeol. Soc. Am., Balt., 1970-71. Author: The Author's Apostrophe in Epic from Homer Through Lucan, 1971, Cooperative Library Instruction for Maximum Benefit, 1989; contbr. articles to profl. jours. Pres. Women's Am. ORT, San Diego, 1979-81, Zionist Orgn. of Am., San Diego dist., 1997-2000; mem. adv. bd. With Israel Now. Mem.: ALA (chair divsn. and roundtable coms. 1982—, coun. 2003—06, dir. grant programs 2006—), Libr. Congress Cataloging in Publs. Adv. Group, Assn. Jewish Librs., Am. Classical League, Calif. Libr. Assn. (assembly 1993—99, editor Calif. Librs. 1997—99, pres. mgmt. sect. 2000—01), Am. Philol. Assn., Toastmasters, Beta Phi Mu. Office: PO Box 12122 La Jolla CA 92039-2122

ZYWICKI, ROBERT ALBERT, retired electric power industry executive; b. Chgo., Sept. 23, 1930; s. Martin Albert and Margaret Irene (Mackowski) Z.; m. Barbara Joan Hagerty; children: Robert, Cheryl, Cindy, Carrie. B in Commerce, Northwestern U., 1966. Teller Chgo. Title and Trust Bank, Chgo., 1949-50; painter Getz Molding Co., Chgo., 1950-51; purchasing agt. Woodworker's Tool Works, Chgo., 1953-54; serviceman Addressograph Multigraph, Chgo., 1954-55; mem. Chgo. Fire Dept., 1955-62; v.p. Anixter Bros. Inc., Skokie, Ill., 1955-87; co-owner A-Z Industries, Northbrook, Ill., 1987—2003; ret., 2003. Served as cpl. U.S. Army, 1951-53. Mem. Am. Legion (comdr.). Republican. Roman Catholic. Avocations: thoroughbred horse racing, classical music, baseball card collecting, tennis. Home: 1330 Sprucewood Ln Deerfield IL 60015-4771 Personal E-mail: peter1330@comcast.net. *Love your family, respect your friends and co-workers, value your customers and suppliers. Always keep each in its proper perspective. Most of all, remember - love, value and respect are all two-way streets.*

ZYWICKI, TODD JOSEPH, law educator; b. McKeesport, Pa., Jan. 28, 1966; married. AB, Dartmouth Coll., Hanover, NH, 1988; MA in Economics, Clemson U., SC, 1990; JD, U. Va., Charlottesville, 1993. Bar: Ga. 1993. Law clk. Judge Jerry Smith, US Ct. Appeals Fifth Cir., Houston, 1993—94; atty. Alsont & Bird, Atlanta, 1994—96; prof. law Miss. Coll. Sch. Law, Jackson, Miss., 1996—98, George Mason U. Sch. Law, Arlington, Va., 1998—; dir., office policy planning FTC, Washington, 2003—04. Trustee Dartmouth Coll., 2005—. Chair, academic adv. coun. We The People in IMAX, Kansas City, Mo., 2003—08, McCormick-Tribuen Freedom Mus., Chicago, Ill., 2003—08; dir. and chair of academic adv. coun. Bill Rights Inst., Arlington, 2007—08; dir. and mem. adv. coun. Fin. Svcs. Rsch. Program, Washington, 2007—08. Searle Freedom Fellow, Searle Found., 2008, W. Glenn Campbell and Rita Ricardo-Campbell Nat. Fellow and the Arch W. Shaw Nat. Fellow, Hoover Instn., 2008—. Roman Catholic. Office: George Mason Univ Sch Law 3301 N Fairfax Dr Arlington VA 22201 Office Fax: 703-993-8088.

ZYWIEC SIDOR, DAVID ALBIN, bishop; b. Ea. Chgo., Ill., July 15, 1947; Ordained priest Order of Friars Minor Capuchin, 1974; ordained bishop, 2002; aux. bishop Vicariate of Bluefields, Nicaragua, 2002—. Roman Catholic. Office: Vicariate of Bluefields Apartado 8 Bluefields Zelaya Norte Nicaragua

Geographic Index

UNITED STATES

ALABAMA

Abbeville
Anderson, Ruth T. *retired air traffic controller*
Baker, Locy (Sonny) L. *state legislator*

Alabaster
McChesney, Robert Michael, Sr. *retired academic administrator*

Albertville
Walker, Phillip *finance company executive, insurance company executive*

Andalusia
Fuller, William Sidney *lawyer*

Anniston
Boyd, Barbara Bigsby *state legislator*
Bragg, Cheryl H. *museum director*
Fite, Lea *state legislator*
Huddleston, Tim *aerospace industry executive*
Klinefelter, James Louis *retired lawyer*

Arab
Black, Daniel Hugh *retired social studies educator*

Ashland
Ingram, Kenneth Frank *retired state supreme court justice*

Athens
Bebin, Martina *pediatrician, neurologist*
Glenn, Robert Kyle *academic administrator*
Lafevor, Kimberly Ann *human resources specialist, educator*
Smith, Patricia Crawford *elementary school educator*

Attalla
Saffels, Anna Wayne Brothers *retired mathematician, educator*

Auburn
Amacher, Richard Earl *retired literature educator*
Ball, Donald Maury *agronomist, consultant*
Bell, Leonard N. *science educator*
Chin, Bryan A. *materials engineer, educator*
Chizik, Gene *college football coach*
Clark, Janet Eileen *retired political science professor*
Cochran, John Euell, Jr. *aerospace engineer, lawyer, educator*
Crocker, Malcolm John *mechanical engineer, educator*
Cutchins, Malcolm Armstrong *aerospace engineer, educator, researcher*
Fortner, Nell *women's college basketball coach*
Galbraith, Ruth Legg *retired dean, home economist*
Govil, Narendra Kumar *mathematics professor*
Groccia, James Edward *education educator*
Hanley, Thomas Richard *engineering educator*
Hatfield, Donald Gene *retired art educator*
Heck, Ross *design educator, consultant*
Housel, David *emeritus athletic director*
Jaeger, Richard Charles *electrical engineer, educator, science association director*
Klesius, Phillip Harry *microbiologist, researcher*
Lebo, Jeff *men's college basketball coach*
Liu, Juncheng *research scientist*
Mao, Shiwen *engineering educator*
Miller, Wilbur Randolph *academic administrator*
Millman, Richard George *architect, educator*
Nane, Erkan *mathematics professor*
Park, Minseo *physicist, educator*
Sankar, Chetan Subramanian *management information systems educator*
Seroka, James Henry *social studies educator, academic administrator*
Sforzini, Richard Henry *aerospace engineer, educator*
Sorokulova, Iryna *microbiologist, educator*
Tolbert, Clinton Jame *army officer, machinist*
Turnham, Joe (Joseph R. Turnham) *political organization administrator*
Zallen, Harold *academic administrator, chemist*

Auburn University
Anderson, Christopher John *biology professor*
Carvalho, John *communications educator*
Clement, Prabhakar T. *engineering educator, researcher*
Eden, Mario Richard *engineering educator*
Evans, R. Lee *dean*
Gogue, Jay (G. Jay Gogue) *academic administrator*
Johnson, Peter Dexter, Jr. *mathematics professor*
Liao, Ming *mathematics professor*
MacEwan, Bonnie *librarian, dean*
Mosjidis, Jorge *agricultural studies educator, researcher*
Reddy, Munagala *agricultural studies educator*
Simmons, Karla Peavy *researcher, educator*
Strom, Paris Scott *education educator*

Bay Minette
Hollinger, Faron Lavaughn *school system administrator*

Bayou La Batre
Benjamin, Regina Marcia *physician, health facility administrator*

Bessemer
Collins, Patricia Ann *pastor, pastoral counselor*
Dunn, Priscilla *state legislator*
Garlikov, Patricia Moodie *education educator*
Hitchcock, Francesca Marie Oglesby *educator*
Stringfellow, Mary Willingham *mathematics educator*

Birmingham
Alexander, James Patrick *lawyer, educator*
Allen, Lee Norcross *historian, educator*
Allen, Maryon Pittman *former senator, clothing designer, journalist*
Allen, William Jere *minister*
Andrews, Gail *museum director*
Andrews, James R. *orthopedic surgeon*
Arnett, Donna K. *epidemiologist, educator*
Arnoletti, Juan Pablo *oncologist, educator*
Ayasoufi, Anahita *engineer, researcher*
Baker, David Remember *lawyer*
Baker, Robert Joseph *bishop*
Balch, Samuel Eason *lawyer*
Benditt, Theodore Matthew *humanities educator*
Bennett, Joe Claude *pharmaceutical executive*
Berte, Neal Richard *academic administrator*
Bittner, Vera *cardiologist*
Black, Kelley P. *microbiologist, educator*
Blan, Ollie Lionel, Jr. *retired lawyer*
Bloomer, Joseph Robert *physician, educator*
Bonatz, Ekkehard *hand surgeon*
Boomershine, Donald Eugene *bureau executive, development official*
Bottino, Marco Cicero *dentist*
Boyd, Gwendolyn Louise *anesthesiologist, educator*
Bradley, Laurence Alan *psychologist*
Braunewell, Karl-Heinz *neuroscientist*
Breitfeld, Philip Paul *pharmaceutical executive, oncologist*
Briggs, Dick Dowling, Jr. *physician, educator*
Bueschen, Anton Joslyn *physician, educator*
Carmody, Richard Patrick *lawyer*
Carruthers, Thomas Neely *lawyer*
Carter, Frances Tunnell (Fran Carter) *fraternal organization administrator*
Casazza, Krista *dietician, researcher*
Cates, Marshall E. *pharmacist, medical educator*
Caulfield, James Benjamin *pathologist, educator*
Chattopadhyay, Debasish *medical educator, researcher*
Chowdhury, Shafiul A. *research scientist*
Chung, Byung-Hong *retired biochemist*
Clark, William Northington *lawyer, retired military officer*
Clemmensen, Jon L. *communications educator*
Cohen, Ross Neil *lawyer*
Cohen-DeMarco, Gale Maureen *pharmaceutical executive*
Coleman, Brittin Turner *lawyer*
Coleman, Merika *state legislator*
Comer, Donald III *investment company executive*
Cooper, Karen René *health facility and nursing administrator*
Cooper, N. Lee *lawyer*
Corliss, Deane Kenworthy *lawyer*
Couch, Robert M. *real estate company executive*
Crocker, Carolyn Robertson *language educator*
Culpepper, Mary Kay *editor*
Deal, William Brown *medical school dean, physician, educator*
Dean, Joseph Oral, Jr. *retired pharmaceutical executive*
Denson, William Frank III *lawyer*
Diasio, Ilse Wolfartsberger *volunteer*
Diethelm, Arnold Gillespie *surgeon*
Donahue, Timothy Patrick *lawyer*
Donmoyer, Jay Frank *retired private school educator*
Dorsett, Lyle Wesley *religious studies educator*
Dugan, Byrdena DeeAnn *medical educator*
Ely, Bruce Peter *lawyer*
English, Laura Lynn *psychologist, educator*
Farley, Joseph McConnell *lawyer*
Ferniany, William (Isaac William Ferniany) *health system administrator*
Finley, Sara Crews *medical geneticist, educator*
Finley, Wayne House *medical educator*
Fintel, Marion Carson *biology professor*
Foft, John William *physician, educator*
Gaggar, Amit *medical educator, researcher*
Garner, Robert Edward Lee *lawyer*
Gavino, Alde Carlo Patdu *dermatologist*
George, Frank Wade *small business owner, antiquarian book dealer*
Givhan, Robert Marcus *lawyer*
Goldman, Jay *industrial engineer, educator, dean emeritus*
Goodrich, Thomas Michael *engineering and construction executive, lawyer*
Gorrie, M. Miller *construction executive*
Griffin, Eleanor *publishing executive, editor*
Grinney, Jay *health facility company executive*
Gross, Iris Lee *not-for-profit association executive*
Hahn, Beatrice H. *biomedical researcher, medical educator*
Hall, Robert Alan *construction company executive*
Hanson, Victor Henry, II, *newspaper publisher*
Harris, Aaron *management consultant*
Haskell, Wyatt Rushton *lawyer*
Hawley, Gregory H. *lawyer*
Hedden, William James *plastic surgeon*
Hendley, Dan Lunsford *retired bank executive*
Hilliard, Earl Frederick *Former United States Representative, Alabama, lawyer*
Hinton, James Forrest, Jr. *lawyer*
Houston, James Gorman, Jr. *retired state supreme court justice*
Hubbard, Ron *performing arts educator*
Huechtker, Edward Darrell *department chairman*
Hull, William Edward *theology studies educator*
Irons, William Lee *lawyer*
James, Donald M. *construction materials executive*
Jo, Young Gyun *nuclear engineer*
Johns, John D. *insurance company executive, lawyer*
Johnson, Wylie Pierson *electric utility executive*
Johnston, Carden *emergency physician, pediatrician, educator*
Jones, D. Paul, Jr. *lawyer, retired bank executive*
Jun, Ho-Wook *science educator*
Kennedy, Joe David, Jr., (Joey Kennedy) *editor*
Kimberly, Robert Parker *medical educator*
King, Alfreda L. *finance educator*
Korf, Bruce Richard *clinical geneticist, neurologist*
Kuhn, Kenneth August *electrical engineer, educator*
Lacy, Alexander Shelton *retired lawyer*
Laeger, Therese Roach *performing arts educator*
Langford, Larry P. *Mayor, Birmingham, Alabama*
Langum, David John *law educator, historian*
Lawhon, Sharon Leding *music educator, director*
Ledgerwood, Mikle Dave *language educator*
Lester, V. Markham *history professor*
Long, Deborah Joyce *lawyer*
Long, Thad Gladden *lawyer*
Lowman, John D., Jr. *physical therapist, researcher*
Marchase, Richard Banfield *cell biologist, educator, research administrator*
Markland, Alayne Denise *geriatrician, educator*
Mc Callum, Charles Alexander *academic administrator*
McKinley, Cameron Sharbel *elementary school educator*
Mc Millan, George Duncan Hastie, Jr. *lawyer, former state official*
McWhorter, Hobart Amory, Jr. *lawyer*
Meezan, Elias *pharmacologist, educator*
Mills, William Hayes *lawyer*
Miyagawa, Ichiro *physicist*
Mohon, Earlene Mann *counselor*
Molen, John Klauminzer *lawyer*
Monk-Tutor, Mary R. *pharmacist, educator*
Moorer, Douglass Charles *educator*
Morgan, Kathryn Diane *criminology educator*
Muturi, Ephantus J. *entomologist, researcher*
Nance, Marione E. *biology educator*
Nanda, Navin Chandar *cardiologist, educator*
Neal, Phil Hudson, Jr. *retired manufacturing executive*
Ness, Timothy John *anesthesiologist, researcher*
Newton, Alexander Worthy *lawyer*
Newton, Don Allen *economic development consultant*
Northen, Charles Swift III *retired bank executive*
Nunn, Grady Harrison *retired political science professor*
Omura, George Adolf *medical oncologist*
Oparil, Suzanne *cardiologist, educator, researcher*
Palmer, Robert Leslie *lawyer*
Pappas, Dennis G. *otolaryngologist*
Pasche, Boris Claude Roger *physician*
Pass, Robert *pediatrician*
Passey, George Edward *psychologist, educator*
Peeples, William Dewey, Jr. *mathematics professor*
Perry, Helen *medical/surgical nurse, secondary school educator*
Pijeaux, Lawrence J., Jr. *museum director*
Pittman, Constance Shen *endocrinologist, educator*
Pittman, James Allen, Jr. *endocrinologist, educator*
Pizitz, Richard Alan *retail executive, real estate company officer*
Pollick, G. David *academic administrator, philosopher*
Potter, John Leith *retired mechanical and aerospace engineer, educator, consultant*
Powell, Jerry W. *lawyer*
Powell, Larry *communications educator*
Powell, William Arnold, Jr. *retired bank executive*
Prichard, Mark Neal *virologist, educator*
Pryor, William Holcombe, Jr. *federal judge, former state attorney general, educator*
Rajendra, Anand Laxmikantrao *electrical engineer*
Rankin, Don *art educator, educator*
Reilly, Kevin Denis *computer scientist, educator*
Rich, Robert Regier *academic administrator, immunologist, medical educator*
Ritter, C. Dowd *diversified financial services company executive*
Robinson, Edward Lee *retired physics professor, consultant*
Rogers, Ernest Mabry *lawyer*
Roth, William Stanley *hospital foundation executive*
Rountree, Asa *lawyer*
Russell, Richard Olney, Jr. *retired cardiologist*
Sanchez, Fabian *dancer*
Sanderson, Ralph *medical educator*
Sansom, Dennis Lee *philosopher, educator*
Scarritt, Thomas Varnon *newspaper editor*
Schafer, James Arthur *physiologist*
Scripa, Rosalia *engineering educator, researcher*
Seitz, Karl Raymond *editor*
Selfe, Edward Milton *lawyer*
Sen, Bisakha Pia *performing arts educator*
Shawn, Gilbert R. *orthopedist, educator*
Shelton, Bessie Hunter *music educator, director*
Siegal, Gene Philip *pathology educator*
Simon, Cliff *design educator*
Singh, Satinder P. *medical educator, director*
Sirmans, Barbara C. *library director*
Sisiopiku, Virginia P. *civil engineer*
Sklenar, Herbert Anthony *industrial products manufacturing company executive*
Slive, Michael Lawrence *sports association executive, lawyer*
Small, Clarence Merilton, Jr. *lawyer*
Solomon, Gloria Lee *educational consultant*
South, Lisa *nursing educator*
Stabler, Lewis Vastine, Jr. *lawyer*
Stephens, James T. (J.T. Stepehens) *publishing executive*
Stephens, Jerry Wayne *librarian, director*
Stevenson, Edward Ward *retired otolaryngologist, surgeon*
Styslinger, Lee Joseph, Jr. *manufacturing executive*
Taub, Edward *psychology researcher*
Tonkery, Dan *Internet company executive*
Trigg, Jack Walden, Jr. *retired physician*
Trimmier, Charles Stephen, Jr. *lawyer*
Tucker, Thomas James *retired investment company executive*
Vance, Joyce White *prosecutor*
Velu, Sadanandan E. *science educator*
Vinson, Laurence Duncan, Jr. *lawyer*
Volanakis, John Emmanuel *immunologist, rheumatologist*
Vyazovkin, Sergey *chemistry professor*
Warburton, Reed Thomas *lawyer*
Weaver, Dennis Russell *lawyer*
Wells, Huey Thomas, Jr. *lawyer*
Westmoreland, Andrew *academic administrator*
Wheeler, Ruric E. *mathematics professor*
Whigham, Mark Anthony *computer scientist*
Whitaker, Elaine Emanuel *humanities educator*
Wilson, James Charles, Jr. *lawyer*
Wilson, Tracey L. *biology educator*
Wokman, Charles Thomas *language educator*
Wrinkle, John Newton *lawyer*
Wyatt, James Alexander III *lawyer*
Young, Carlton Joseph *abdominal transplant kidney and pancreas surgeon, educator*

Brewton
Baker, Alan *state legislator*

Brilliant
Franks, Gracie G. *elementary school educator*

Camden
Fendley, George W. III *lawyer*

Carbon Hill
Guin, James Kenneth (Ken Guin) *state legislator*

Chickasaw
Erwin, Sandra Kay *music educator*
French, Elizabeth Irene *retired biology professor, musician*

Citronelle
Surry, Melinda Owen *reading coach*

Clanton
Baughman, Bruce Prentiss *state agency administrator*
Tidwell, Betty Davenport *special education educator*

Clayton
Beasley, Billy *state legislator*

Coosada
Reynolds, Linda Ann *elementary school educator*

Crossville
Blessing, Maxine Lindsey *secondary school educator*

Cullman
Ivey, Mona Kay *secondary school educator, association administrator, consultant*

Cusseta
Bridges, DuWayne *state legislator*

Daphne
Curreri, Peter William *health facility administrator, consultant*
Jeffreys, Elystan Geoffrey *petroleum consultant*

Decatur
Julich, Nancy C. *secondary school educator*
Michelini, Sylvia Hamilton *auditor*
Miles, Mary Ellen *retired human resources specialist*

Smith, Trina *academic administrator*
Smith, Troy Alvin *aerospace research engineer*
Talley, Richard Woodrow *accountant*

Dothan
Baxley, Wade H. *lawyer*
Fleming, Jennie M *retired education educator*
Flowers, V. Anne *retired academic administrator*
Jones, Sandra Lee *retired dean*
Lord, Jacqueline Ward *retired accountant, photographer, artist*
Peterson, Roger *community bank executive, retired international investment banker, manufacturing executive, air force officer*
Phillips, Kenneth Edward *history educator, writer*
Shimoda, Nick Yoshinari *lawyer*
Thomas, Shannon Lawson *academic administrator, educator*
Williams, Claudia Baxter *retired media specialist, school librarian*
Wright, Burton *sociologist*
Zloty, Peter *ophthalmologist*

Eclectic
Tracy, Patricia Ann Koop *secondary school educator*

Elberta
Wilkinson, Edward Anderson, Jr. *retired military officer, manufacturing executive*

Enterprise
Parker, Ellis D. *retired military officer*

Eufaula
Conniff, Alexandra Acosta *secondary school educator*

Eva
Hudson, Rhonda Ann *science educator*

Evergreen
Jackson, Eula *nursing educator*
Joyner, Daphne *biology professor*

Fairfield
McCaslin, LaTanya *art educator*

Fairhope
Faust, Teddy Joe, Sr., (Joe Faust) *state legislator*
Norton, Margaret Sarah *retired insurance company executive*

Fayette
Estes, John Timothy *biology professor*

Florence
Barfield, Kenny Dale *religious organization administrator*
Cale, William Graham, Jr. *university administrator, environmental sciences educator, researcher*
Curtis, Mike *state legislator*
Foote, Avon Edward *web developer/producer, communications educator*
Hansen, Vagn Keith *political science educator, college administrator*
Johnson, Johnny Ray *retired mathematics professor*
Knight, Karen Anne McGee *artist, educator, educational research administrator*
Parker, Tina M. *lawyer*
Reynolds, Celia Robinson *academic librarian, educator*
Rhodes, Anthony H. *retired biologist*
Ruebhausen, David K. *theater educator*
Warren, David Harold *religious studies educator*

Foley
St. John, Henry Sewell, Jr. *utility company executive*

Fultondale
Taylor, Patricia Nail *mathematics and science educator*

Gadsden
Farr, Dwayne Louis *automotive executive*
Ford, Craig *state legislator*
Galliher, Blain *state legislator*
Grimm, James R. (Ronald) *management consultant*
Reynolds, Sharon Jones *elementary school educator*

Gardendale
McKay, Marie Conyers *librarian, writer*

Geneva
Beck, Warren Harris *state legislator*

Greensboro
Massey, James Earl *retired clergyman, educator*

Greenville
Longmire, Venus DeLoyse *minister*

Gulf Shores
Virden, Frank Stanley *naval officer*
Wallace, John Loys *retired aviation services executive*

Hamilton
Barnes, Judith Ann *director, educator*

Hanceville
Buckelew, Kathy *literature and language professor*
Davis, Robert Scott *history professor*
Fields, James C., Jr. *state legislator*
Holmes, Kristen Jones *academic administrator*

Hartselle
Coon, Elizabeth M. *artist*
Grantland, Ronald *state legislator*
Johnson, Loyd *agricultural engineer, researcher*
Slate, Joe Hutson *psychologist, educator*

Helena
Coulter, Fern Goshen *retired secondary school educator*

Hoover
Lanier, Mildred *finance educator*

Hueytown
Nelson, Susan Rhodes *media specialist, educator*

Huntsville
Abram, Stephen *librarian, writer*
Allan, Barry David *research chemist, government official*
Anwer, Khursheed Nadeem *research and development company executive*
Baird, James Kern *educator, consultant, academic administrator*
Ball, Mike A. *state legislator*
Bass, Clayton *museum director*
Battle, Thomas *Mayor, Huntsville, Alabama*
Bearden, Thomas Eugene *research scientist*
Benzle, Curtis Munhall *artist, educator*
Burko, Lior M. *physicist, educator*
Burrows, Shania Kay *civilian military employee*
Cachán, Manuel *Spanish language educator*
Cirtain, Jonathan W. *astrophysicist*
Costes, Nicholas Constantine *aerospace scientist, educator, retired government agency administrator*
Daussman, Grover Frederick *electrical engineer, consultant*
Edmonson, Brenda *ophthalmologist*
Elsamadicy, Abdalla Mousa *physics professor*
Freas, George Wilson, II, *computer scientist, consultant*
Gill, Glenda Eloise *theater educator*
Gillani, Noor Velshi *atmospheric scientist, researcher, educator*
Hall, Laura *state legislator*
Hawley, Harold Patrick *educational consultant*
Ho, Fat Duen *engineering educator*
Howard, Richard T. *aerospace engineer*
Ivy, Joan Carol *data processing executive*
Karbhari, Vistasp M. *engineering educator, researcher*
Kruja, Mira *music educator*
Lang, Sharon *historian*
Libutti, Frank *information technology company executive, retired military officer*
Lundquist, Charles Arthur *academic administrator*
Malm, Carl Elmer *minister, educator*
Norman, Ralph Louis *retired physicist, consultant*
Nwaneri, Sam O. *science educator*
Parker, Wayne, Jr. *insurance company executive*
Parnell, Thomas Alfred *physicist*
Pastrick, Harold Lee *aeronautical engineer*
Pittman, William Claude *electrical engineer*
Ratchford Merchant, Betty Jo *retired elementary school educator*
Richardson-Weninegar, Loretta Lynne *biologist, educator*
Sackheim, Robert Lewis *aerospace engineer, educator*
Schumann, J. Paul *retired federal agency administrator*
Schwinghamer, Mary Denise *veterinarian*
Smith, Robert Earl *space scientist*
Sovyanhadi, Yoedono *biology professor*
Stewart, Verlindsey Laquetta *accounting educator*
Su, Ching-Hua *materials scientist*
Sun, Yuzhi *mechanical engineer, researcher*
Turner, Mary Alice *curriculum specialist*
Vaughan, William Walton *atmospheric scientist*
Wang, Zhi Jian *aerospace engineer*
Wells, Buren Earl *computer engineer, educator*
Wieland, Paul Otto *environmental control systems engineer*
Williamson, Donald Ray *retired military officer*
Wright, John Collins *retired chemistry professor*
Zuo, Qiuhai Ken *engineering educator, researcher*
Zutaut, Steven Eric *systems analyst, application developer*

Irondale
Statnikov, Efim Smulevich *physicist, researcher*

Irvington
Collier, Spencer *state legislator*

Jacksonville
Bundrum, Kenneth Owen *lawyer, writer*
Chargois, Deborah Majeau *psychology professor, researcher*
Dunaway, Carolyn Bennett *retired sociology professor*
Goodwin, Debra Kay *science educator*
Harbor, Kingsley Okoro *communications and journalism educator, researcher*
Hubbard, William James *library director*
Skinner, Jauneth *graphic artist, educator*
Spector, Daniel Earl *historian, educator*

Jasper
Sparkman, Brandon Buster *educator, consultant, writer*
Sparks, Nicholas B. *lawyer*

Lafayette
Woody, Mary Florence *nursing educator, academic administrator*

Leeds
Drake, Owen *state legislator*
Wilson, Maggie Isabelle Lovell *secondary school educator*

Livingston
Cannon, Marsha A. *nursing educator*
Davis, Debbie Dawson *literature and language professor*
Green, Asa Norman *academic administrator*

Loachapoka
Schafer, Elizabeth Diane *historian, writer*
Schafer, Robert Louis *agricultural engineer, researcher*

Madison
Bogard, Eileen Judith *investor, retired small business owner, education administrator*
Brannan, Eulie Ross *educational consultant*
Jones, Christine Regina *secondary school educator*
Lee, Soojeong *music educator, soprano*
Morgan, John Derald *foundation director, electrical engineer, educator, writer, researcher*
Parlier, Greg H. *military officer, analyst, engineer, educator, researcher*
Petty, Margaret *elementary school educator*
Robertson, Glen A. *aerospace engineer*
Vo, Hieu N. *architect*

Marion
Cleveland, Willie Mae *elementary school educator*

Maylene
Copes, Marvin Lee *academic administrator*

Midfield
Daniels-Rogers, LaTausha *social sciences educator, entrepreneur*

Mobile
Abi-Saleh, Bernard S. *cardiologist*
Alsobrook, David Ernest *museum director, archivist, historian*
Armbrecht, William Henry III *retired lawyer*
Bahr, Alice Harrison *librarian*
Bonner, Josiah Robins, Jr., (Jo Bonner) *United States Representative from Alabama*
Braswell, Louis Erskine *lawyer*
Brogdon, Byron Gilliam *radiologist, educator*
Buskey, James E. *state legislator*
Butler, Charles Randolph, Jr. *federal judge*
Campbell, Stephen Frank *theology studies educator*
Castello, Sergio A. *economics professor*
Clark, Jack *retired health facility administrator*
Copeland, Lewis *principal*
Cox, Emmett Ripley *federal judge*
Crowell, Tangie Michelle *elementary school educator*
Donalson, Malcolm Drew *classics educator*
Edwards, Jack *former congressman, lawyer*
Ellzey, Wayne Ewell *retired accountant*
Foster, John Wade *microbiologist, educator*
Franks, Ronald Dwyer *dean, psychiatrist, educator*
Frye, Karen Ernst *surgeon*
Gaston, Henry Victor (Victor Gaston) *state legislator*
Giles, Rebecca McMahon *education educator*
Gordon, James O. *state legislator*
Graddick, Charles Allen *judge*
Granade, Callie Virginia Smith *federal judge*
Guarino, Anthony Michael *pharmacologist, educator, consultant, counselor*
Harris, Benjamin Harte, Jr. *lawyer*
Hart, Eric Mullins *consumer products company executive*
Helmsing, Frederick George *lawyer*
Holland, Lyman Faith, Jr. *lawyer*
Howard, Alex T., Jr. *federal judge*
Jones, Joseph Seymour *small business owner, poet*
Jones, Samuel L. *Mayor, Mobile, Alabama*
Kargleder, Charles Leonard *language educator*
Lipscomb, Oscar Hugh *archbishop emeritus*
Littleton, Jesse Talbot III *radiology educator*
McCleery, Winston Theodore *information technology executive*
Miller, Harrison Stewart *history professor*
Parsley, Brantley Hamilton *librarian*
Phan, Anh-Vu *adult education educator, researcher*
Pierce, Donald Fay *lawyer*
Ponnambalam, Ananthasekar *pediatrician, gastroenterologist*
Reeves, W. Boyd *lawyer*
Richelson, Paul William *curator*
Roddy, Harry Louis, Jr. *language educator*
Rodi, Thomas John *archbishop*
Rodning, Charles Bernard *surgeon*
Roedder, William Chapman, Jr. *lawyer*
Rummel, Harold Edwin *construction executive*
Scantlebury, Velma Patricia *surgeon*
Schenk, Joseph Bernard *museum director*
Shelley-Tremblay, John Fontaine *psychology professor*
Smith, Anne Sisson *private school educator*
Smith, Jesse Graham, Jr. *dermatologist, educator*
Spechalske, Frank Herman *retired educational administrator*
Suess, James Francis *retired clinical psychologist*
Thomason, Michael V.R. *retired history professor*
Varghese, Sakoorikal Lonappan *physicist, researcher*
Vitulli, William Francis *retired psychology educator*
Wisner, Pamela L. *social worker*

Monroeville
Estill, Donna Rae *literature and language professor, director*
Hudson, Wanda Meadows *finance educator*

Montevallo
Killian, Tammy Lee *theater educator, director*
Seagle, Mary Jane *educational association administrator*
Stephens, Scott *art educator*
Stoops, Rosa Maria *language educator*

Montgomery
Barton, James E., Jr. *state legislator*
Beasley, Jere Locke *lawyer*
Bennett, James Ronald *Labor Commissioner, Alabama*
Bolin, Michael F. *state supreme court justice*
Bristol, Caterina *music company executive*
Byrne, Bradley Roberts *lawyer*
Campbell, Maria Bouchelle *lawyer, consultant*
Canary, Leura Garrett *prosecutor*
Canfield, Greg *state legislator*
Carnes, Edward E. *federal judge*
Chapman, Beth Killough *Secretary of State, Alabama*
Clark, Eddie *psychology professor*
Cobb, Sue Bell *state supreme court chief justice*
Cornett, Lloyd Harvey, Jr. *retired historian*
Das, Sunil R. *computer scientist, educator*
Davis, Randy *state legislator*
Dees, Morris Seligman, Jr. *lawyer*
DeMarco, Paul J. *state legislator*
Dixon, Larry Dean *state legislator*
Dubina, Joel Fredrick *federal judge*
Dzata, Gladstone K. *biology professor*
Folsom, Jim, Jr., (James Elisha Folsom Jr.) *Lieutenant Governor of Alabama, former governor*
Graham, Betty Carol *state legislator, retired academic administrator*
Gravatt, Lincoln Edmund *history educator*
Greeson, Todd *state legislator*
Grimes, David G. III *state legislator*
Hamner, Reginald Turner *lawyer*
Harrison, John D. *state banking agency administrator*
Hester, Douglas Benjamin *lawyer*
Hester, Hortense *retired physical education educator*
Hilliard, Earl F. *state legislator, lawyer*
Hubbard, Mike *state legislator, political organization administrator*
Ivey, Kay Ellen *state treasurer*
Jinright, Charles W. *acting Mayor, Montgomery, Alabama*
Joan, Perl *nurse, educator*
Johnson, Mark Matthew *museum director, curator*
Kennedy, Kamela Denise *director*
Kerr, Kim *medical educator*
King, Andrea S. *secondary school educator*
King, Troy *state attorney general*
Kloess, Lawrence Herman, Jr. *retired lawyer*
Lawson, Thomas Seay, Jr. *lawyer, actor*
Leslie, Henry Arthur *lawyer, retired bank executive*
Lewis, Joseph Brady (Jay Lewis) *lawyer*
Li, Xiaolin *science educator*
Love, Jay *state legislator*
Lowder, Robert E. *bank executive*
Luce, Dena Lahue *university librarians*
Luna, Patricia Adele *marketing executive*
Maddox, Alva Hugh *retired state supreme court justice*
May, Cecil Richard, Jr. *academic administrator*
McElvy, James Douglas *lawyer*
McFadden, Frank Hampton *lawyer, former judge*
Miller, John Winfield *language educator, researcher*
Morton, Joseph *state official, school system administrator*
Munson, Edward Harry, Jr. *medical investigator*
Murdock, Glenn *state supreme court justice*
Northcutt, Robert F. *lawyer*
Owes, Jaunita *library director*
Pan, Chai-Fu *engineering educator*
Parker, Tom *state supreme court justice, lawyer*
Riley, Bob (Robert Renfroe Riley) *Governor of Alabama*
Rose, Shirley Kelly *retired language educator*
Sass, Neil Leslie *toxicologist*
Segall, Robert D. *lawyer*
Shaw, James Gregory (Greg) *state supreme court justice*
Smith, Patricia M. (Patti Smith) *state supreme court justice*
Steele, Rodney Redfearn *judge*
Stuart, Lyn (Jacqueline Lyn Stuart) *state supreme court justice*
Sullivan, Margaret M. *biologist, educator*
Tennimon, Dannie Earl *academic administrator, educator*
Wall, William Herbert *state coordinator student loan programs*
Washington, Kara Elizabeth *music educator*
Williamson, Donald Ellis *state agency administrator, public health service officer*
Wood, James Jerry *lawyer*
Woodall, Thomas A. *state supreme court justice*
Wortham, Joycelyn Foy *education specialist*

Moody
Brasher, Terrie Walker *secondary school educator*
Sublett, Sherry Lake *junior high school educator*

Mosul
Southern, Terry Keith *engineering executive*

Muscle Shoals
Thompson, Bradford *mathematics professor*

Normal
Batra, Ashok K. *physics professor, researcher*
Bhattacharjee, Sudip *engineering educator*
Nyochembeng, Leopold M. *plant pathologist, educator*
Qureshi, Halima Akhtar *economics professor*
Sajjala, Seshadri Reddy *agronomist*
Vaughn, Michael Oscar *history professor*
Walker, Lloyd T. *food scientist*

Northport
Burry-Stock, Judith Anne (Anne Burry) *education educator*
Stephens, Annabel Kuykendall *retired library and information scientist*

Opelika
Bandy, George C. *state legislator*
Jenkins, Richard Lee *manufacturing executive*
Samford, Yetta Glenn, Jr. *lawyer, director*
Smith-Sanders, Carol Ann *physical therapist, music therapist, psychologist*

Opp
Bundrick, Tracy Lee *engineering educator*

Orange Beach
Conrad, Marcel Edward *hematologist, oncologist, educator*

Ozark
Clouse, Steve *state legislator*

Point Clear
Holt, Thaddeus *lawyer*

Prattville
Gipson, H. Mac, Jr. *state legislator*

Rainsville
Huntley, Daphne White *lawyer*

Ramer
Napier, John Hawkins III *historian*

Rogersville
Oldham, Dewey Lindon (Spooner Oldham) *musician, songwriter*

Salem
Gibbons, Dona Alden Coe *electrical engineer, technical education coordinator*

Selma
Calhoun-Bates, Carolyn E. *social services administrator*
Carstarphen, Minnie Lee *library director*

Semmes
Dockery, Herbert Donald *health and rehabilitation company executive*
Fincher, Chad *state legislator*

Slocomb
Vikcers, Tom M. *secondary school educator*

Spanish Fort
van Aken, John Henry *retired marine engineer*

Talladega
Lanier, Anita Suzanne *musician, educator*

Theodore
Hollis, Julia Ann Roshto *critical care, medical, and surgical nurse*

Thomasville
Moore, Chester *engineering educator*

Thorsby
Pounders, Stephen C. *music educator*

Town Creek
Ford, Stephen Allyn *farmer, educator*

Troy
Anderson, Rod L. *protective services official*
Boothe, Alan C. *state legislator*
Davidson, Barry Sheldon *academic administrator, comparative and adult education educator*
Kline, John Alvin *distinguished professor of leadership*
Magrath, Christi Lee *biology professor*
Mitchell, Norma Taylor *history professor*
Moten, Sebrena R. *law educator*
Rinehart, James Forrest *political science professor, department chairman*
Schubert, Donna Clark *public relations educator, professional society administrator*
Stewart, Henry R. *library director*

Trussville
Jacobson, James Edmund *retired newspaper editor*
Spahn, James Francis *marketing professional*

Tuscaloosa
Adams, Hilda J. *English language educator*
Allen, Gerald *state legislator*
Appiah-Opoku, Seth *urban planner, educator*
Baklanoff, Eric Nicholas *economist, educator*
Bao, Ningzhong *chemical engineer*
Bentley, Robert J. *state legislator, dermatologist*
Cook, Camille Wright *retired law educator*
Cramer, Dale Lewis *retired economics professor*
Dixon, David Adams *chemistry professor, researcher*
Doughty, Julian Orus *mechanical engineer, educator*
England, Chris (Christopher John England) *state legislator*
Farahat, Medhat S. *researcher*
Fields, Ruth Kinniebrew *secondary and elementary educator, consultant*
Fish, Mary Martha *economics professor*
Gaddy, Kenneth C. *museum director*
Gibson, George Edward, Jr. *civil engineering educator, consultant, researcher*
Grant, Anthony *men's college basketball coach*
Grimes, Deborah Jeanne *library director*
Hocutt, Max Oliver *retired philosophy educator*
Hopkins, Martha Ann *artist*
Iran-Nejad, Asghar *psychology professor*
Jemison, Sandra J. *educational association administrator, educator*
Jennings, Thomas Steven *history professor*
Keeton, J. E. *retired psychiatrist*
Lumpkin, Thomas Riley *retired physician*
Mancini, Ernest Anthony *geologist, educator, researcher*
Mankey, Gary Jay *physics professor, director*
McFarland, James William *real estate company executive, consultant*
McNealey, Ernest *college president*
Metzger, Robert Melville *chemistry educator*
Moynihan, Gary Peter *industrial engineering educator*
Orcutt, Ben Avis *retired social work educator*
Osburn, Charles Benjamin *retired librarian, dean*
Pass, Charlotte Louise *literature educator, consultant*
Pieroni, Robert Edward *internist, educator, military officer*
Rand, Elizabeth Hartmann *psychiatrist*
Randall, Kenneth C. *dean, law educator*
Ray, Nelda Howton *financial consultant*
Ray, Paul Sukhamay *engineering educator, researcher*
Reinhart, Kellee Connely *journalist*
Saban, Nick (Nicholas Lou Saban) *college football coach, former professional football coach*
Sinclair, Robert Ewald *retired physician*
Smalley, Donna Wesson *lawyer, educator*
Smith, Ralph Harrison, II, *lawyer*
Taaffe, James Griffith *retired academic administrator, educator*
Taylor, Gary Kenneth *accountant, educator*
Thomas, Joab Langston *retired academic administrator, biologist, educator*
Walock, Michael James *research assistant*
Weeks, Lillian Durrett *law librarian*
Wilson, William Roberts, Jr., (Bob Wilson) *lawyer*
Witt, Robert E. *academic administrator*
Wright, Darrell Dean *educator*
Zumpano, Leonard Vincent *finance educator*

Tuscumbia
Black, Marcel *state legislator*

Tuskegee
Cheng, William I. *business educator*
Green, Elbert P. *retired academic administrator*
Jiang, Li *engineering educator*
Lester, Cynthia Yvette *engineering educator*
Powell, Nichole Larai *chemistry professor, researcher*
Rangari, Vijaya Kumar *chemistry professor, researcher*
White, Mildred Virginia *secondary school educator, retired counseling administrator*
Yehualaeshet, Teshome E. *microbiologist, educator*

Tuskegee Institute
Casimire-Etzioni, Athema Louise *veterinary pathologist*
Cooley, Fannie Richardson *counselor, educator*
Hill, Walter A. *agricultural sciences educator, researcher*
Kumar, Akshaya *research scientist, educator*
Nimmanapalli, Ramadevi *veterinarian, educator*
Siaway, Arthur T.G. *finance educator, educator*
Sumbry, Jo Ann *academic administrator, educator*
Triggs, Eldon Dale, II, *aerospace engineer, educator*

Vestavia
Nuckols, Frank Joseph *psychiatrist*

Warrior
Johnson, Barbara L. *retired municipal official*

ALASKA

Anchorage
Arnold, Robert Wendell *ophthalmologist*
Begich, Mark P. *United States Senator from Alaska, former mayor*
Berkowitz, Ethan A. *lawyer, former state representative*
Bothum, Mark Sumner *engineering educator*
Brown, Dean Naomi *state official, geologist*
Brown, Keith E. *lawyer*
Burgess, Timothy M. *federal judge, former prosecutor*
Burke, Marianne King *state agency administrator, finance executive, consultant*
Butler, Rex Lamont *lawyer*
Byrd, Milton Bruce *academic administrator*
Campbell, Craig E. *Lieutenant Governor of Alaska*
Cantor, James Elliot *lawyer*
Choudhury, Raj Deo *global energy industry executive*
Christen, Morgan *state supreme court justice*
Claman, Matthew W. *lawyer, acting Mayor, Anchorage*
Comeau, Carol Smith *school system administrator*
Craig, Robert Dean *historian, educator*
Cuddy, Daniel Hon *bank executive*
David, Edgecombe P. *theater educator*
De Lisio, Stephen Scott *lawyer, director, pastor*
Dutta, Utpal *engineering educator*
Ealy, Jonathan Bruce *lawyer*
Eastaugh, Robert L. *state supreme court justice*
Fabe, Dana Anderson *state supreme court justice*
Fleischer, Hugh William *lawyer*
Galloway, Christopher George *oncologist, director*
Gazaway, Barbara Ann *music and art educator*
Grahame, Heather H. *lawyer*
Grant, William Stewart *geneticist*
Hickel, Walter Joseph *retired investment company executive, foundation administrator, former United States Secretary of the Interior governor of alaska*
Higgins, Patti Carolyn *political organization administrator*
Hofseth, Pauline C. *realtor*
Kasmar, Marilyn Walsh *health facility administrator, nurse*
Katcher, Jonathon A. *lawyer*
Kendall-Miller, Heather *lawyer*
Kincaid, Karen Owers *nursing educator*
Lerman, Averil *lawyer, historian*
Loeffler, Karen Louise *prosecutor*
Mandsager, Richard *hospital administrator*
Maynard, Kenneth Douglas *architect*
Mills, William James, Jr. *orthopedist, surgeon, researcher*
Nielsen, Jennifer Lee *molecular ecologist, researcher*
Olofsson, John Arndt *engineering educator*
Parker, Walter Bruce *arctic research specialist, consultant*
Pepper Henry, James *museum director*
Peterson, Kim Moreau *biology professor*
Plant, Randall Leslie *otolaryngologist*
Porcaro, Michael Francis *advertising executive*
Rasmuson, Edward Bernard *banker*
Reed, Frank Metcalf *bank executive, director*
Riendl, Robin W. *wealth advisor LPL branch manager*
Roberts, John Derham *lawyer*
Ruedrich, Randy *political organization administrator*
Sandberg, Arlene *elementary school educator*
Schnell, Roger Thomas *small business owner, retired state official, military officer*
Schoen, John W. *biologist, educator*
Schwietz, Roger L. *archbishop*
Sellers, Sheila Renea *special education educator*
Shively, John Terry *cruise line executive*
Smithers, Paul T (Smithers T) *civil engineer, educator*
Stohl, Sharon Aline *art therapist*
Strid-Chadwick, Karen S. *musician, educator*
Strohmeyer, John *writer, retired editor*
Sturgulewski, Arliss *state legislator*
Sullivan, George Murray *transportation executive, consultant, retired mayor*
Thomas, Lowell, Jr. *writer, retired military officer, state senator*
Trevithick, Ronald James *underwriter*
Ulmer, Frances Ann *academic administrator, retired state official*
von der Heydt, James Arnold *federal judge*
Wilson, Heather Marie *biologist*
Winfree, Daniel Edward *state supreme court justice, lawyer*
Wolf, Dan C. *real estate company executive, broker*
Ziemba, Mary Rose *biology professor*

Auke Bay
Waldrip, Karen Marie *career planning administrator*

Bethel
Owen, Lauri J. *lawyer*
Turner, Kathy Ann *special education services professional, director*

Big Lake
Gillette, Muriel Delphine *nurse*

Chiniak
Griffin, Elaine B. *educator*

Dillingham
Bouker, Ina B. *elementary school educator*

Eagle River
Cotten, Samuel Richard *fisheries consultant, fisherman, former state legislator, consultant*
Dyson, Fred *state legislator*
Sparks, Jack Norman *dean*

Fairbanks
Beistline, Earl Hoover *mining consultant*
Bhatt, Uma Suren *meteorologist, educator*
Brigham, Lawson Walter *oceanographer, researcher*
Cahill, Catherine Frances *environmental scientist, educator*
Charles, Dexter N. *finance educator*
Cysewski, Stephen David *retired science educator*
Doran, Timothy Patrick *academic administrator*
Duffy, Lawrence Kevin *biochemist, educator*
Fathauer, Theodore Frederick *meteorologist*
Hamilton, Mark R. *academic administrator*
Hartman, Chris M. *science educator*
Irish, Joel David *anthropologist*
Jonaitis, Aldona Claire *museum director, art historian*
Jones, Stephen B. *academic administrator*
Kan, Rosalind J. *highway design engineer and language educator*
Kessel, Brina *ornithologist, educator, researcher*
Kettler, Donald Joseph *bishop*
Kleinfeld, Andrew J. *federal judge*
Knutsen, Deborah May *librarian*
Kramm, Gerhard *meteorologist, researcher*
Lawlor, Orion Sky *science educator*
Lin, Chuen-Sen *mechanical engineer, educator*
Lingle, Craig Stanley *glaciologist, educator*
Matusevich, Yelena *artist, educator*
Moelders, Carmen Nicole (Nicole Mölders) *science educator, researcher*
Mölders, Nicole *environmental scientist, educator*
Murkowski, Frank Hughes *former Governor of Alaska*
Nakoneczny, Michael Martin *artist*
Pippenger, Michael Kirk *economics professor, researcher*
Roederer, Juan Gualterio *retired physics professor*
Royer, Thomas Clark *oceanographer*
Shier, Juliet Marie *social studies educator*
Thompson, Daniel Emerson *vending machine service company executive*
Tilsworth, Timothy *retired environmental/civil engineering educator*
Zhang, Jing *science educator*

Fort Wainwright
McWilliams, Grant *osteopath*

Gakona
Ainsworth, Cynthea Lee *folklorist*

Girdwood
Trautner, John James *real estate executive*

Haines
Clarke, Jerrie *museum director, researcher*
Kaufman, David Graham *construction executive*

Homer
Beggs, Heather *museum director*

Juneau
Burnett, Jerry *state treasurer*
Burns, Edward James *bishop*
Butler, Jay C. *public health service officer*
Carpeneti, Walter L. *state supreme court justice*
Davis, Bettye Jean *state legislator*
Hogan, William (Bill Hogan) *state agency administrator, public health service officer*
Hovanec, Lorie *state banking agency administrator*
Johansen, Kyle *state legislator*
Kato, Bruce H. *curator*
Kelly, Timothy Donahue *former state legislator*
Kerttula, Beth *state legislator*
LeDoux, Larry *state official, school system administrator*
Parnell, Sean *Governor of Alaska, former state legislator*
Schorr, Alan Edward *librarian, publishing executive*
Shepard, Beatrice L. *retired microbiologist, historian*
Siddeek, M. S.M. *marine biologist, educator*
Smith, Charles Anthony *foundation administrator, director*
Sullivan, Daniel S. *state attorney general*
Thibodeau, Linda *state librarian*
Wilson, Peggy *state legislator*

Kodiak
Haakanson, Sven *museum director, anthropologist*
Jamin, Matthew Daniel *lawyer, judge*
Selby, Jerome M. *mayor*

Palmer
Burton, Jamin L. *music educator*
Lawler, Marita A. *therapist*
Ping, Chien-Lu *soil scientist, educator*
Young-Campbell, Laura L. *speech pathology/audiology services professional*

Soldotna
Jozwiak, Elizabeth Anna *biologist*
Moore, Hubert, Jr. *retired addictions counselor, consultant*

Valdez
Devens, John Searle *natural resources administrator*
Moore, Dawson *performing company executive, playwright*

Wasilla
Cole, Brad (Bradford Cole) *real estate broker*

Wrangell
Miller, Jennifer L. *elementary school educator, small business owner*
Smith, Kimmie Christine *small business owner*

ARIZONA

Amado
Criswell, Stephen *astronomer*

Anthem
Guerra, Aldo Benjamin *plastic and cosmetic surgeon*
Hagerty, George James III *former academic administrator, educator, consultant*

Arizona City
Landers, Patricia Glover *language educator*

Bisbee
Behney, Charles Augustus, Jr. *veterinarian*
Gustavson, Carrie *museum director*
Moreno, Patricia Frazier *lawyer*
Page, Deborah J. *accountant*

Buckeye
Brown, Kyle Daniel *elementary school principal*

Carefree
Mangouni, Norman *publishing executive*
Putney, Mark William *lawyer, utilities executive*
Wearly, William Levi *retired manufacturing executive*
Whittington, Thomas Lee *lawyer*

Casa Grande
McGillicuddy, Joan Marie *psychotherapist, consultant*

Cave Creek
Collins, Jack Adam *mechanical engineer*

Chandler
Angus, Patricia Jean *biology professor*
Braunisch, Henning *electronics engineer, researcher*
Brown, Brenda *library director*
Brunello-McCay, Rosanne *sales executive*
Casteel, Camille *school system administrator*
Dawson, Bennette Renee *psychologist*
Dunn, Boyd W. *Mayor, Chandler, Arizona, lawyer*
Kim, James Joo-Jin *electronics company executive*
Krabbenhoft, Jonna *psychologist*
Meieran, Eugene Stuart *materials scientist*
Penley, Larry Edward *former academic administrator, finance educator*
Pietambaram, Srinivas V. *engineer*
Powers, Ronald George *management consultant*
Wang, Jinlin *chemical engineer*
Williams, James Eugene *management consultant*
Winterer-Schulz, Barbara Jean *graphics designer, writer*
Zavala-Alarcon, Edgardo Donato *medical association administrator, director*
Zhang, (Mike) Tao *electrical engineer, researcher*

Chinle
Coor, Caren Barbara *art educator*
Hodson, William David *elementary school educator, consultant*

Chino Valley
Casey, Bonnie Mae *artist, educator*
Norton, Douglas Ray *former auditor general*
Walker, Winnetta Dorrean *social studies educator*

Clarkdale
Silvern, Leonard Charles *retired engineering executive*
Tod, Martha Ann *retired small business owner*

Coolidge
Schiller, Marjorie A. *special education professor*

Cottonwood
Groseta, Andy (Peter Andrew Groseta) *lobbyist*

Oneill, John Robert *library director*

Desert Hills
Evans, Carol Ann *reading specialist*

Flagstaff
Balda, Russell Paul *biologist, educator*
Bolin, Richard Luddington *industrial development specialist, consultant*
Breunig, Robert Glass *museum director*
Brumbaugh, David Scott *geophysicist, educator*
Cortner, Hanna Joan *retired political scientist, researcher*
Denham, Aaron Renfrew *anthropologist, educator*
Evans, Ronald Allen *lodging chain executive*
Lapsley, James Norvell, Jr. *minister, educator*
Millis, Robert Lowell *astronomer, science observatory director*
Neary, Daniel George *soil scientist*
Nelson, Emily Jane *conservationist*
Pickett, A. Dean *lawyer*
Price, Nicole Denise *literature and language professor*
Price, Peter Wilfrid *ecology educator, researcher*
Reese, Marilya Veteto *literature and language professor*
Scott, Louise H. *music educator*
Shoemaker, Carolyn Spellman *planetary astronomer*
Stevens, Lawrence Edward *ecologist, curator*
Trotter II, Robert Talbot *anthropologist, educator*
Wilburn, Nancy *accounting educator*
Wilcoxson-Ueckert, Catherine Ann *science educator, consultant*

Florence
Brahms, Katheryn Ann *early childhood educator*
Mosby, Nora Jane *music educator*

Fort Defiance
Morgan, Leon Terrell *environmental health services specialist*

Fort Huachuca
Sleeper, Nancy JoAnn *mental health services professional*

Fountain Hills
Berg, Madelaine R. *lawyer*
Erickson, Edward Grant *electrical engineer*
Israel, Robert Allan *statistician*
Magazine, Cynthia Penrose *retired health care consultant*
Tyl, Noel Jan *retired vocalist, astrologer, writer*
Wright, C. T. Enus *former academic administrator*

Gilbert
Berman, Steven *Mayor, Gilbert, Arizona*
Kenney, Thomas Frederick *retired broadcast executive*
Ring, Jack *systems engineer, educator*

Glendale
Almstead, Sheila Louise *art gallery owner*
Arias, Hugo Rubén *chemist, biochemist, researcher, educator*
Bai, Haowei *aerospace engineer and scientist*
Brown, Jason Andrew *science educator*
Cacciatore, Joanne *thanatologist and social worker*
Cotton, Sally Jean *retired music educator*
Doan, Shane *professional hockey player*
Eyres, Beth Kathleen *literature educator*
Flanigan, Sean *education educator, coach*
Gretzky, Wayne Douglas *professional hockey coach, retired professional hockey player*
Gutierrez, Michael Edward *elementary school educator, department chairman*
Heathcotte, Toby Fesler *retired educator, writer*
Honsa, Vlasta *retired librarian*
Jovanovski, Ed *professional hockey player*
Mahrous, Hisham *pharmacist, educator*
Maloney, Don *professional sports team executive, retired professional hockey player*
McNatty, Danny *pharmacist*
Milne, Karen Louise *retired science educator*
Montague, Michelle Louise *geologist, educator*
Moss, Douglas G. *professional sports team executive*
Porter, Kevin *professional hockey player*
Scruggs, Elaine M. *Mayor, Glendale, Arizona*
Smelser, Philip Sidney *history educator*
Teague, Robert Cole *physician*

Gold Canyon
Johnson, Charles Foreman *architectural firm executive*

Goodyear
Brunk, Samuel Frederick *oncologist*
Carlson, Norman A. *retired federal agency administrator*
Eppen, Gary Dean *business educator*
McBride, Janet Marie *small business owner*
Nixon, Daniel Walker *oncologist, researcher*
Privette, Louise Judith *school psychologist*

Green Valley
Bachman, David Christian *orthopedic surgeon*
Brewington, Arthur William *retired English language educator*
de Soto, Ernest Frank *artist, writer*
Fateley, William Gene *chemist, educator, inventor*
Ford, Neville F. *clinical pharmacologist*
Hanson, John M. *structural engineer, consultant*
Lusk, Harlan Gilbert *national park superintendent, business executive*
Moser, Robert Harlan *internist, educator, writer*
Pike, George Harold, Jr. *religious organization administrator, clergyman*
Ragan, James Thomas *communications executive*
Reichlin, Seymour *endocrinologist, educator*
Smith, Raymond Lloyd *former university president, consultant*

Hereford
Hirth, John Price *metallurgical engineering educator*

Schenk, Quentin Frederick *retired social work educator, psychologist, mayor*
Seeland, Arthur David *bishop*

Holbrook
Lawson, Michael J. *history and anthropology educator*
O'Hop, Suzanne Elizabeth *educator*
Solomonson, Michael *performing arts, department chairman*

Kingman
Basinger, Richard Lee *lawyer*
Ramadan, Mohamed Ibrahim *psychiatrist*
Rebik, James Michael *otolaryngologist*

Lake Havasu City
Mahan, James E. *archivist, educator*

Lakeside
Seely, Dennis M. *secondary school educator*

Laveen
Meneses (Gonzales), Diana Marina *history professor*

Marana
Davidson, Gilbert *city manager*
Evarts, Caren Goodin *music educator, recording artist, performer, pianist*
O'Shaughnessy, James Patrick *lawyer, consultant*
Steckler, Larry *publishing executive, writer*

Maricopa
Kimball, Bruce Arnold *soil scientist*

Mesa
Ahearn, Geraldine *medical/surgical nurse, writer, poet*
Bateman, Heather L. *biology professor*
Baxter, Gene Kenneth *mechanical engineer, engineering company executive*
Biekert, Russell George *engineering educator, consultant*
Cooley, Jack Crain *cardiovascular surgeon*
Cox, Heidi Pinkerton *pediatric surgeon*
David, Susan Holcombe *child and family therapist*
DeRosa, Francis Dominic *chemical company executive*
Doyle, Matthew Brian *computer graphics designer*
Dutson, Lyn *theater educator*
Duvall, Debra *school system administrator*
Garlick, William Steven *retired biology professor*
Gottry, Steven Roger *communications executive, scriptwriter*
Hausel, William Dan *economic geologist, martial artist, public speaker, artist, writer*
Janik, Joseph S. *pediatrician*
Jastrzembski, Tiffany S. *psychologist*
Kronenfeld, Michael Reed *medical librarian*
Linxwiler, Louis Major, Jr. *retired finance company executive*
Luth, William Clair *geochemist, retired research manager*
Murphy, Edward Francis *sales executive*
Nelson, Scott Bruce *psychologist*
Nganje, William Evange *finance educator*
Phelps, Norris D. *biology professor*
Pollack, Daniel H. *real estate company executive*
St. Cyr, Margaret Ann (Peggy St. Cyr) *writer*
Schneider, Rebecca *librarian*
Shovkovy, Igor Andriyovich *physicist, researcher*
Singhal, Avinash Chandra *engineering administrator, educator*
Skoldberg, Phyllis Linnea *musician, educator*
Smith, Scott *Mayor, Mesa, Arizona, business, financial and legal consultant*
Wilson, Thomas H. *museum director*
Wolf, Heather *library director*

Oracle
Mueller, Timothy I. *psychiatrist*
Rush, Andrew Wilson *artist*

Oro Valley
Abbassian, Assad *urologist*
Haller, Archibald Orben *sociologist, educator*

Page
Hoodenpyle, Sandra Kay *elementary school educator*

Paradise Valley
Lorenzen, Robert Frederick *ophthalmologist*
Russell, Paul Edgar *electrical engineering educator*
Sharma, Virender *medical educator, director*
Targovnik, Selma E. Kaplan *dermatologist*
Tubman, William Charles *lawyer*
Tyner, Neal Edward *retired insurance company executive*
Unruh, James Arlen *bank executive*
Weinberger, Arnold *retired electrical engineer*

Patagonia
La Noue, Terence David *artist, educator*

Payson
Hershberger, Robert Glen *architect, educator*
Salomon, Marilyn *artist*
Stephenson, Larry Kirk *geography educator, financial planner*

Peoria
Bailey, Claudia Jean *artist, retired librarian*
Gould, Dorothy Mae *executive secretary, soprano*
Jenkins, Carol Anne *educator*
Nelson, Mary Kathryn *bilingual counselor, small business owner, real estate and insurance agent, artist*
Nicchi, Vincent, Jr. *cardiologist*
Schindler, William Stanley *retired public relations executive*
Willard, Garcia Lou *artist*
Willis, Edward Oliver *management consultant, state agency administrator*

Phoenix
Adkerson, Richard C. *mining executive*
Agudo, Mercedes Engracia *psychiatrist*
Allen, John Rybolt L. *chemist, biochemist*
Allen, Robert Eugene Barton *lawyer*
Altiere, Lauren M. *music educator, consultant*
Altmann, Jon Christopher *research and development company executive*
Anders, Gary C. *economics professor*
Andersen, Ib *performing company executive*
Anderson, Lawrence Ohaco *federal judge, lawyer*
Atkinson, Joseph Matthew *lawyer*
Baier, Maria *Councilwoman*
Baker, William Dunlap *lawyer*
Bakker, Thomas Gordon *lawyer*
Bales, W. Scott *state supreme court justice*
Ballinger, James K. *museum director*
Barbosa, Leandro Mateus *professional basketball player*
Beauchamp, David George *lawyer*
Bee, Timothy S. *state legislator*
Begam, Robert George *lawyer*
Bennett, Kenneth R. *state official, former state senator*
Bennett, Peter Howard *retired medical researcher*
Berch, Rebecca White *state supreme court justice, lawyer*
Berry, JoAnn I. *psychologist*
Birk, David R. *lawyer, electronics executive*
Birnbaum Reed, Barbara Irene *psychologist*
Bivens, Donald Wayne *lawyer, political organization administrator*
Bodney, David Jeremy *lawyer*
Boldin, Anquan *professional football player*
Breland, Sandy Ann *broadcast executive, director*
Brewer, Jan (Janice Kay Brewer) *Governor of Arizona*
Broomfield, Robert Cameron *federal judge*
Brown, Jack A. *state legislator, rancher, real estate broker*
Burke, Timothy John *lawyer*
Byrnes, Eric James *professional baseball player, radio, television personality*
Campbell, Cloves C., Jr. *state legislator*
Canby, William Cameron, Jr. *federal judge*
Cappelli, Gregory W. *investment banker, Education Company Executive*
Carpenter-Olney, Tami Anne *Spanish elementary language educator*
Carroll, Earl Hamblin *federal judge*
Cartwright, James William (Bill Cartwright) *professional basketball coach, retired professional basketball player*
Case, David Leon *lawyer*
Chambliss, Linda R. *obstetrician, consultant*
Charlton, John Kipp *pediatrician*
Chavez, Nelba R. *state and former federal agency administrator*
Church, Steve *electronics executive*
Coghill, William Thomas, Jr. *retired lawyer*
Cohen, Jon Stephan *lawyer*
Cole, Daniel John *anesthesiologist, educator*
Comus, Louis Francis, Jr. *lawyer*
Conant, Paul Allen *lawyer*
Cook, Michael David *academic administrator, director*
Cornella, Jeffrey Lynn *surgeon*
Covey, Donald David *school system administrator*
Crosatti, Lorenzo *research scientist*
Crozier, Scott A. *lawyer*
da Fonte, Mauro Valente *medical educator*
David, Christian Rubi *language educator*
Davies, David George *lawyer, educator*
Dawson, John Joseph *lawyer*
Derdenger, Patrick *lawyer*
Dewane, John Richard *retired manufacturing executive, small business owner*
DiCiccio, Sal *Councilman*
Dino, Gerald Nicholas *bishop*
Donovan, Timothy R. *lawyer*
Doto, Irene Louise *statistician*
Duyck, Kathleen Marie *poet, musician, retired social worker*
Eckstein, David Mark *professional baseball player*
Edelstein, Charles Bruce *investment banker, education company executive*
Edens, Gary Denton *broadcast executive*
Edwards, Vicki Ann *director, consultant*
Ehmann, Anthony Valentine *lawyer*
Ellison, Cyril Lee *literary agent, retired publishing executive*
Elms, Susan *music educator*
England, Robert (Bob) *city health department administrator, epidemiologist*
Everroad, John David *lawyer*
Falck, David Phillip *lawyer, utilities executive*
Farmer, Kenneth Lloyd, Jr. *health system administrator, retired military officer*
Feldberg, Harley *marketing professional*
Feldman, Jeremy Phillip *pulmonologist*
Fellows, Gerald Lee *lawyer*
Fenzl, Terry Earle *lawyer*
Fitzgerald, Larry Darnell, Jr. *professional football player*
Flejter, Wendy L. *geneticist, director*
Fleming, Patricia V. *state legislator*
Francis, Philip L. *retail executive*
Frank, Tim *engineering educator*
Frehner, Patricia Ann *education educator, consultant*
Freyermuth, Clifford L. *structural engineering consultant*
Gaines, Corey *professional basketball coach*
Gaines, Francis Pendleton III *judge*
Galbut, Martin Richard *lawyer*
Gallagher, Michael L. *lawyer*
Garcia, Ernest G. *audiologist, technologist*
Gentry, Alvin *professional basketball coach*
Gibson, Kirk Harold *professional baseball coach, retired professional baseball player*
Giedt, Bruce Alan *paper company executive*
Gillette, Robert J. *aerospace transportation executive*
Giltner, Phil (F. Phillips Giltner III) *food distributing executive*
Goddard, Terry *state attorney general*
Goldstein, Stuart Wolf *lawyer*
Gomez, David Frederick *lawyer*
Goodyear, Frank H(enry), Jr. *museum director*
Goorman, Brad *financial consultant*
Gordon, Phillip Bruce *Mayor, Phoenix*
Grant, Merwin Darwin *lawyer*
Graves, Rod *professional sports team executive*
Grimwood, Helen Perry *lawyer*
Grumbles, Benjamin H. *state official, former federal agency administrator*
Haberman, Iidia W. *literature and language professor*
Halford, Sharon Lee *academic administrator, educational consultant*
Halpern, Barry David *lawyer*
Hamada, Rick *electronics executive*
Hardwick, Catherine R. *lawyer*
Haren, Dan (Daniel John Haren) *professional baseball player*
Harrison, Mark I. *lawyer*
Hawkins, Jasper Stillwell, Jr. *architect*
Hawkins, Michael Daly *federal judge*
Hay, John Leonard *lawyer*
Hayden, William Robert *lawyer*
Hicks, William Albert III *lawyer*
Hill, Grant *professional basketball player*
Hinch, A.J. (Andrew Jay Hinch) *professional baseball coach*
Hoecker, Thomas Ralph *lawyer*
Holaday, Barbara (Bobbie) Hayne *writer*
Hooper, Daniel Lee *music educator, composer*
Horne, Thomas Charles *state official, school system administrator*
Howard, William Matthew *arbitrator, lawyer, writer*
Hudson, Karen G. *special education educator*
Huelster, Jeffery James *social studies educator*
Humble, William *state agency administrator, public health service officer*
Huntwork, James Roden *lawyer*
Hurwitz, Andrew D. *state supreme court justice*
Isom, Robert D., Jr. *air transportation executive*
Itkin, Robert Jeffrey *lawyer*
Jakubczyk, John Joseph *lawyer*
James, Charles E., Jr. *lawyer*
Jason, Philip Caplan *psychiatrist*
Jirauch, Charles W. *lawyer*
Johnson, Christopher D. *lawyer*
Johnson, Elizabeth Misner *health services executive*
Johnson, Michael *councilman*
Johnson, Mystie L. *obstetrician, gynecologist, department chairman*
Jones, Eddie *architect*
Kamins, Edward *electronics executive*
Kant, Robert S. *lawyer*
Karnas, Fred G., Jr. *poverty and homeless specialist*
Kerr, Steve (Stephen Douglas Kerr) *professional sports team executive, retired professional basketball player*
Khan, Mohammed Yousuf *physician, consultant*
King, Robert L. *foundation and former academic administrator*
Klahr, Gary Peter *retired lawyer*
Klausner, Jack Daniel *lawyer*
Klos, Siobhán Lydia *theater director*
Knoller, Guy David *lawyer*
Kurn, Neal *lawyer*
Kyl, Jon Llewellyn *United States Senator from Arizona*
LaPointe, Gregory Vincent *psychologist*
Laufer, Nathan *cardiologist*
LaVoy, Christopher Alan *lawyer*
Leach, John F. *editor, director, journalist, educator*
Lee, Barbara S. *special education educator*
Lee, Wontae *environmental engineer, researcher*
Leinart, Matthew Stephen *professional football player*
Lemieux, Claude *retired professional hockey player*
Lemon, Leslie Gene *retired diversified financial services company executive, lawyer*
Levetown, Robert Alexander *lawyer*
Lewis, Orme, Jr. *real estate company executive, land use adviser*
Long, Michael Alan *musician, writer*
Loscher, Tricia Diane *curator, director*
Lovely, Randy *editor-in-chief*
Lovett, William Lee *surgeon*
Lubin, Stanley *lawyer*
Majerle, Daniel Lewis *professional basketball coach, retired professional basketball player*
Malhotra, Ashish *medical researcher*
Maneshni, Bahman *economics professor*
Marsh, Patricia A. *business educator*
Martin, Dean *state treasurer*
Martinez-Conde, Susana *neurologist, researcher*
Martori, Joseph Peter *lawyer*
Mast, Gregory Lewis *lawyer*
Masters, Jonathan Edward *clinical psychologist*
Mattox, Claude *councilman*
McAuliffe, Daniel Joseph *lawyer*
McCain, Cindy (Cindy Lou Hensley McCain) *philanthropist, wholesale distribution executive*
McConnell, Albert Lynn *dean of education*
McKellips, Gordon Wayne, Jr. *lawyer, land developer*
McMillan, Lee Richards, II, *lawyer, mining executive*
McNamee, Stephen M. *federal judge*
McRae, Hamilton Eugene III *lawyer*
Meyer, Hermann Belton Perrin *retired neonatologist, health facility administrator, bioethicist*
Mitchell, Robert D. *lawyer*
Mitchell, Wayne Lee *retired health administrator*
Mondry, Lawrence N. *automotive executive*
Moran, Robert F. *retail executive*
Moyer, Alan Dean *retired newspaper editor*
Moyes, Jerry C. *transportation executive, professional sports team executive*
Mullen, Daniel Robert *finance company executive*
Nash, Steve *professional basketball player*
Neely, Peggy *councilwoman*
Newman, Donald Lynn *psychologist, consultant*
Nowakowski, Michael *Councilman*
Olmsted, Thomas James *bishop*
Olsen, Alfred Jon *lawyer*
O'Steen, Van *lawyer*
Patel, Vimla L. *research scientist*

Pelander, John *state supreme court justice*
Peralta, Everett Figueroa *college professor, department chairman*
Perry, Lee Rowan *retired lawyer*
Pershad, Ashish *cardiologist*
Petitti, Michael Joseph, Jr. *lawyer*
Phillips, Steve *electronics executive*
Pietzsch, Michael Edward *lawyer*
Pillalamarri, Seshasayi *computer scientist and engineer, researcher*
Pitman, Jim *professional sports team executive*
Placenti, Frank Michael *lawyer*
Platt, Warren E. *lawyer*
Pondexter, Cappie *professional basketball player*
Price, Charles Steven *lawyer*
Pullen, Randy *political organization administrator*
Quirk, Kathleen L. *mining executive*
Rathwell, Peter John *lawyer*
Reed, Wallace Allison *anesthesiologist*
Refo, Patricia Lee *lawyer*
Rekate, Harold Louis *neurosurgeon*
Reynolds, Andrew *psychologist*
Richardson, Jason Anthony *professional basketball player*
Richardson, Judy McEwen *investment banker, consultant*
Richardson, Mary L. *psychotherapist*
Rister, Gene Arnold *humanities educator*
Rivera, Jose de Jesus *lawyer*
Roberts, Christopher Wayne *psychologist, educational consultant*
Robertson, Samuel Harry III *transportation safety research engineer, educator*
Roof, Sally Jean-Marie *library and information scientist, educator*
Rose, David L. *lawyer*
Rotellini, Felecia A. *state banking agency administrator*
Rudolph, Gilbert Lawrence *lawyer*
Ryan, Michael D. *state supreme court justice*
Sadowski, Raymond *electronics executive*
Salmon, Matt *Former United States Representative, Arizona, communications executive*
Sanchez, Steven M. *financial executive*
Sanders, Barry R. *lawyer*
Sarver, Robert G. *professional sports team owner*
Schiffner, Adrienne Anita *art historian, educator*
Schiffner, Charles Robert *architect*
Schilling, Curt (Curtis Montague Schilling) *retired professional baseball player*
Schrader, Susan Rae *elementary school educator*
Schroeder, Mary Murphy *federal judge*
Schwartz, Eric Alexander *biomedical researcher, educator*
Sherk, Kenneth John *lawyer*
Shishov, Michael *rheumatologist*
Short, Dean C., II, *lawyer*
Sidora-Arcoleo, Kimberly Joan *nursing educator*
Silverman, Alan Henry *lawyer*
Silverman, Barry G. *federal judge*
Sima, Chao *biologist, researcher*
Simes, Michael Louis *lawyer*
Simplot, Tom *Councilman*
Slager, Donald W. *waste management executive*
Snow, G. Murray *federal judge*
Sperling, John Glen *educational services company executive*
Stahl, Richard G. C. *journalist, editor*
Steckler, Phyllis Betty *business owner*
Stern, Richard David *investment company executive*
Storey, Norman C. *lawyer*
Stoudemire, Amare Carsares *professional basketball player*
Strand, Roger Gordon *federal judge*
Swafford, Leslie Eugene *physician assistant, consultant*
Taurasi, Diana Lurena *professional basketball player*
Taylor, Elizabeth Jane *investment advisor, real estate company and marketing executive*
Tennen, Leslie Irwin *lawyer, consultant*
Thompson, Terence William *lawyer*
Tritle, Bradley *health facility administrator*
Tyus, Gordon *graphics designer, educator*
Ulrich, Paul Graham *lawyer, writer, editor*
Upson, Donald V. *retired corporate financial executive*
Vallee, Roy A. *electronics executive*
Van Fleet, David Dominic *management educator*
Von Hoff, Daniel Douglas *oncologist, researcher*
Wait, Scott D. *neurosurgeon*
Wall, Donald Arthur *lawyer*
Webb, Brandon (Tyler Webb) *professional baseball player*
Weisenburger, Theodore Maurice *retired judge, poet, educator*
Welker, Kristina Diane *psychotherapist*
Welts, Rick *professional sports team executive*
Wheaton, Marilyn *musician*
White, Danny Levius *counselor, consultant, educator*
White, Edward Allen *electronics executive*
Wilenchik, Dennis I. *lawyer*
Williams, Quinn Patrick *lawyer*
Williams, Thelda *Councilwoman*
Willocks, Robert Max *retired librarian*
Wilson, Adrian (Adrian Lemar Wilson) *professional football player*
Winthrop, Lawrence Fredrick *judge*
Wirken, Charles William *lawyer*
Wolf, G. Van Velsor, Jr. *lawyer*
Wright, Richard Oscar III *pathologist, educator, clinical ethicist*
Wu, Xu *communications educator*
Yarnell, Michael Allan *mediator, arbitrator, law educator*
Yzaguirre, Raul Humberto *civil rights leader*
Zerella, Joseph T. *retired pediatric surgeon*
Zidich, John M. *publishing executive*
Zillmer, John J. *waste management administrator*

Pinetop

Gilbert-Tiegs, Marion Ann *gifted and talented educator, consultant*

Portal

Zweifel, Richard George *curator*

Prescott

Beatty, Jametha Ann *communications educator*
Bieniawski, Zdzislaw Tadeusz Richard *engineering educator, writer, consultant*
Blaess, Donna Adele *psychotherapist, educator, counseling administrator*
Chesson, Eugene *retired civil engineering educator, consultant, volunteer*
Cook, K. L. *literature educator*
Edmondson, William Brockway *retired foreign service officer*
Forth, Kevin Bernard *beverage distributing industry consultant*
Garcia-Buñuel, Luis *neurologist*
Garvey, Daniel Edward *foundation administrator, educator*
Glidden, Moses *language educator*
Ivanova, Dorothea *physics professor, researcher*
Kahne, Stephen James *systems engineering educator, engineering company executive, academic administrator*
Langellier, John *museum director*
Masotti, Louis Henry *real estate educator, consultant*
Newton, Ray C. *university official*
Sagman, Arthur M. *radiologist*
Sanderson, John Lewis *financial advisor*
Sandum, Allan Ira *retired biology educator*
Semon, Warren Lloyd *information scientist, educator*
Slominski, Elena Gregoryevna *mathematics educator*

Prescott Valley

Shelley, Bonnie J. *retired voice educator*

Quartzsite

Michel, Verlyn Lyle *mayor, consultant*

Rio Rico

Lowell, J(ames) David *geological consultant, cattle rancher*

Rio Verde

Culligan, John Austin *thoracic surgeon*
Harding, John Hibbard *retired insurance company executive*
Ramsey, David Selmer *retired health facility administrator*
Scott, Louis Edward *advertising executive*
Vanselow, Neal Arthur *retired academic administrator, internist*

Safford

Kaliher, Michael Dennis *historian, librarian*

Sahuarita

Albertson, Paulette Smith *music educator*

San Luis

Kryger, Jerri Renee *elementary school educator*

Scottsdale

Afsary, Cyrus *artist*
Arora, Sandeep *cardiologist*
Baker, Edward Martin *engineering and industrial psychologist*
Ballinger, Charles William *sanitary engineer, consultant*
Bassett, Joyce *dentist*
Breus, Michael J. *psychologist*
Brown, Frederick Lee *health facility administrator*
Brown, Shirley Margaret Kern (Peggy Brown) *interior designer*
Bruhn, John Glyndon *retired university provost and dean*
Buri, Charles Edward *lawyer*
Calise, Nicholas James *lawyer*
Carpenter, Peter Rockefeller *retired bank executive*
Crawford, Robert F. *lawyer*
Dahl, Mark Victor *dermatologist, educator*
Doede, John Henry *investment company executive*
Everett, James Joseph *lawyer*
Farley, James Newton *retired manufacturing executive, electrical engineer*
Ferree, John Newton, Jr. *fundraising specialist, consultant*
Fowler, R. Stuart *gynecologist*
Freedman, Stanley Marvin *manufacturing executive*
Friedland, Jack Arthur *plastic surgeon*
Friesen, Oris Dewayne *software engineer, historian*
Garfield, Ernest *bank executive, consultant*
Gookin, Thomas Allen Jaudon *civil engineer*
Gregory, Robert Erb *surgeon*
Grenell, James Henry *retired manufacturing company executive*
Grier, James Edward *hotel executive, lawyer*
Haas, Ingrid Elizabeth *physician*
Hamilton, Rita *library director*
Harrison, Nedra Joyce *surgeon*
Hathaway, Peter S. *corporate financial executive*
Hill, Louis Allen, Jr. *retired dean, civil engineer, consultant*
Hilton, Steven J. *real estate executive*
Hinni, Michael L. *otolaryngologist*
Hittner, George J. *lawyer*
Howard, William Gates, Jr. *electronics company executive*
Hu, Rusheng *research scientist*
Huizingh, William *former accounting educator*
Hutchison, Stanley Philip *retired lawyer*
Inman, William Peter *lawyer*
Jarman, Beth S. *president FarSight group, author, former cabinet secretary, educator, consultant*
Jayaraman, Ganapathi Subramaniam *healthcare industry executive*
Jenkins, Charles Franklin *educator*
Jesky, T. J. *pharmaceutical products executive*
Joseph, Gregory Nelson *media critic, writer, actor, advocate*
Khandheria, Bijoy K. *cardiologist*
Kinsinger, Jack Burl *chemist, educator*
Kiyosaki, Robert Toru *investor, entrepreneur, author*
Krupp, Clarence William *lawyer, health facility administrator*
Land, George Ainsworth *philosopher, consultant, writer*
Lane, W. James *Mayor, Scottsdale, Ariz., airline executive, CPA*
Lasys, Joan *medical/surgical nurse, educator*
La Vista, Frank William *writer, educator*
Leonard, George Edmund *bank executive, credit manager, marketing professional*
Levine, Stanley Walter *chemical company executive*
Lindgren, D(erbin) Kenneth, Jr. *retired lawyer*
Lloyd, Eugene Walter *retired construction company executive*
Lloyd-Lee, Beverly *interior designer*
Lord, Robert James *lawyer*
Lowry, Edward Francis, Jr. *lawyer*
Magenta, Muriel *artist*
Marks, Merton E. *lawyer, international arbitrator, mediator, consultant*
Mediate, Rocco *professional golfer*
Meyers, Marlene O. *retired hospital administrator*
Mikhael, Joseph *hematologist*
Milanovich, Norma JoAnne *training services executive*
Mireau, Jennifer Lyn *band director, gymnastics coach*
Morrison, James William, Jr. *lobbyist, government agency administrator, consultant*
Mutz, Steven *astronomer, educator*
Northey, William Thomas *microbiologist, educator*
Orford, Robert Raymond *physician, consultant*
Overgaard, Cordell Jersild *lawyer, rancher, director*
Parish, James Michael *medical educator*
Parsons, Bob (Robert R. Parsons) *entrepreneur, domain register and web host company executive*
Peshkin, Samuel David *retired lawyer*
Phillips, Wanda Charity *secondary school educator, writer*
Quayle, Dan (James Danforth Quayle) *former Vice President of the United States*
Quayle, Marilyn Tucker *wife of former United States Vice President, lawyer*
Quigley, Jerome Harold *management consultant*
Rethore, Bernard Gabriel *manufacturing and mining company executive, consultant*
Reznick, Richard Howard *pediatrician*
Roarke, Michael Charles *medical educator, nuclear medicine physician*
Samson, Allen Lawrence *investor, retired bank executive*
Sanderson, David R. *physician*
Schleifer, Thomas C. *management consultant, author, lecturer*
Schrader, Carol Ann *artist, painter*
Sengupta, Partho P. *cardiologist, educator*
Sheridan, Donald Charles *orthopedist, hand surgeon*
Smith, David Burnell *lawyer, state legislator*
Stambaugh, Armstrong A., Jr. *restaurant and hotel executive*
Stone, Alan Jay *retired academic administrator*
Stott, Brian *software company executive, consultant*
Strock, James Martin *author, speaker, executive educator, sustainability leadership development*
Taylor, James C. *writer*
Timmons, Evelyn Deering *pharmacist*
Trimble, Thomas James *retired utilities executive, lawyer*
Underwood, Paul Lester *cardiologist*
Vairo, Robert John *insurance company executive*
Valdivieso, Angelica *physical therapist*
Walker, Richard K. *lawyer*
Walsh, Edward Joseph *food products and cosmetics executive*
Washburn, Jerry Martin *accountant, corporate executive*
Watkins, Eugene Leonard *surgeon, educator*
Weaver, Linda Marie *pharmacist, education educator*
Williams-De Silva, Lisa Annette *small business owner, adult nurse practitioner*
Winkler, Sheldon *dentist, educator*
Wojcik, Martin Henry *not-for-profit executive*
Woods, Duane C. *waste management executive*
Yost, William Albert *speech and hearing science professor*

Sedona

Briney, Allan King *retired radiologist*
Catterton, Marianne Rose *occupational therapist*
Coleman, M.L. (Michael Lee) *artist*
Dansby, John Walter *retired oil industry executive*
Hawkins, David Ramon *psychiatrist, writer, researcher, spiritual teacher*
Metzner, Richard Joel *psychiatrist, psychopharmacologist, educator*
Sasmor, James Cecil *publishing representative, educator*

Sells

Ostrum, Robert F. *orthopaedic surgeon*

Show Low

Pershing, Robert George *retired telecommunications industry executive*

Sierra Vista

Bates, Norman Walter *literature educator, department chairman*
Bordelois, Martha *language educator*
Mutchler, J.C. *history professor*
Ponder, Herman *geologist*
Sizemore, Nicky Lee *computer scientist*
Smith, Barbara Jane *computer scientist, educator*

Sun City

Arbogast, Susan D. *nursing educator*
Black, Robert Frederick *retired gas industry executive*
Buchman, Elwood *internist, former pharmaceutical executive, director*
Davies, Percy (Pete) Charles *mechanical engineer*
Erickson, Richard Ames *physicist, emeritus educator*
Hamilton, Ronald Ray *minister*
Joyce, Jeffrey *research scientist, consultant*
Keesling, Karen Ruth *lawyer*
Oppenheimer, Max, Jr. *foreign language educator, consultant*
Reynolds, John Francis *insurance company executive*
Thompson, Betty Jane *retired small business owner*
Williams, William Harrison *retired librarian*

Sun City West

Berkenkamp, Fred Julius *management consultant*
Bowkett, Gerald Edson *editorial consultant, writer*
Brown, Ruth Geisler *retired electronics engineer*
Schrag, Adele Frisbie *business education educator*
Stevens, George Richard *business consultant, public information officer*

Sun Lakes

Dean, Charles Thomas *industrial arts educator, academic administrator*
Glein, Richard Jeriel, Sr. *lawyer*
Hall, Barbara Louise *interior designer, artist*
Sharpless, Joseph Benjamin *retired county official*
Thompson, Loring Moore *retired academic administrator, writer*

Surprise

Bradford, Mariah *elementary school educator, consultant*
Burns, Clare Marie *retired elementary school educator*
Clark, Lloyd *historian, writer, educator*
Hayes, Ray, Jr. *lawyer*
Hosmer, Eileen Gaylord *special education educator*
Lazar, Max Seymour *retired pharmaceutical company executive*
Miller, James Rumrill III *finance educator*
Rosenbaum, Mary Louise *elementary school educator*

Tempe

Abedinpour, Siamak *electrical engineer*
Alford, Terry L. *materials scientist, educator*
Anand, Suresh Chandra *physician*
Andrews, Steven R. *lawyer*
Anselin, Luc E. *research scientist, educator*
Arkfeld, Louraine C. *judge*
Barfoot, Charles Howard *theology studies educator*
Barnaby, Hugh James *engineering educator*
Bauer, Ernst Georg *physicist, researcher*
Berman, Neil Sheldon *retired chemical engineering professor*
Black, John Arthur, Jr. *electrical engineer, computer scientist, publisher*
Bryan, Glynis A. *corporate financial executive*
Burg, Barry Richard *history educator, writer*
Cao, Yu *engineering educator, researcher*
Carpenter, Ray Warren *materials scientist, engineering educator, materials engineer*
Chiriac, Victor Adrian *aerospace engineer, researcher*
Choi, Seokheun *research scientist*
Crnic, Keith A. *psychology professor, department chairman*
Crow, Michael M. *academic administrator*
Crowe, Barbara J. *recreational therapist, educator*
Crown, Timothy A. *information technology executive*
Curtiss, Roy III *life sciences professor*
Denhardt, Robert B. *political science professor, director*
DeSerpa, Allan C. *economics professor*
Duncan, Kate Corbin *art historian, educator*
Dustman, Patricia (Jo) Allen *elementary school educator, consultant*
Duvernay, Jennifer *librarian*
Emerson, Charles LeRoy *religious studies educator*
Ericksen, Linda E. *computer science educator*
Erickson, Dennis *college football coach, former professional football coach*
Fabricius, William Van *psychology professor*
Fafitis, Apostolos *engineering educator, researcher*
Fennessy, Richard A. *information technology executive*
Ferry, David Keane *electrical engineering educator*
Fu, Yue *electrical engineer*
Gabbard, Ralph Barnhart *user services officer*
Gaffney, John T. *lawyer*
Gordon, Leonard *social sciences educator*
Goronkin, Herbert *physicist*
Grimm, Nancy Beth *research ecologist*
Grimm, Russ *professional football coach, retired professional football player*
Haggerson, Nelson Lionel, Jr. *education educator*
Hallman, Hugh *Mayor, Tempe, Arizona*
Happel, Stephen Kent *business educator, dean*
Hechter, Michael Norman *sociologist*
Hendrickson, Suzanne Bader *language educator*
Herbots, Nicole *retired physics professor*
Hickson, Robin Julian *mining company executive*
Hölldobler, Berthold Karl *zoologist*
Iverson, Peter James *historian, educator*
Jacobs, Mark *biology professor, dean*
Jagos, Vic Bruce *history professor*
Jang, Jin-Wook *electronics engineer*
Johanson, Donald Carl *physical anthropologist*
Johnson, Stephen L. *lawyer, transportation executive*
Juvet, Richard Spalding, Jr. *chemistry professor*
Karády, George György *electrical engineering educator, consultant*
Kaufman, Herbert Mark *finance educator*
Kerr, Derek J. *transportation executive*
Kirby, J. Scott *air transportation executive*
Knox, Robert Lee *economics professor*
Lacroix, Zoé *engineering educator, researcher*
Lakefield, Bruce R. *air transportation executive*
Laybourne, Stanley *computer technology company executive*
Lee, Tae-Woo *aerospace engineer, researcher, educator*
Lei, Lei *biology professor, researcher*
Li, Wei *social sciences educator*
Lombardi, Eugene Patsy *retired conductor, musician, educator*
MacKinnon, Stephen R. *Asian studies administrator, educator*
Mahajan, Subhash *electronic materials educator*
Maienschein, Fred *retired physicist*
Matheson, Alan Adams *law educator*

McCartney, Martha Rogers *physics professor*
McKelvy, Michael John *chemist, research scientist*
Menjivar, Cecilia *social sciences educator*
Metros, Mary Teresa *librarian*
Metz, Eric D. *professional sports agent*
Milke, Linda Jean *elementary school educator*
Mittelstaedt, Robert E., Jr. *dean*
Montgomery, Douglas Carter *industrial engineering educator*
Moore, Carleton Bryant *geochemistry educator*
Myint, Soe Win *geographer, educator*
Nelson, Kelly *anthropologist, educator*
O'Clair, Katherine Clemens *library and information scientist*
O'Neil, Michael Joseph *opinion survey executive, marketing research consultant*
Page, Robert Eugene, Jr. *biology professor*
Panchanathan, Sethuraman *computer science educator*
Pany, Kurt Joseph *finance educator, consultant*
Parent, Annette Richards *freelance writer, artist*
Parker, Doug (William Douglas Parker, W. Douglas Parker) *air transportation executive*
Pettit, George Robert *chemist, educator, cancer researcher*
Ponce, Fernando Agustin *physics professor*
Poste, George Henry *biology professor, former pharmaceutical company executive*
Prescott, Edward C. *economist, educator*
Raby, William Louis *writer, consultant*
Reckers, Philip Merle *accountant, educator*
Richard, Thelma Shinn *literature and language professor*
Rivers, Patrick A. *education educator, researcher*
Rowley, Beverley Davies *sociologist*
Roy, Asim *business educator*
Sampson, David Arthur *research scientist*
Schiff Berman, Paul *dean, law educator*
Schmidt, Sherrie *library director, dean*
Schneller, Eugene Stewart *health administration and policy educator*
Sendek, Herb *men's college basketball coach*
Shock, Everet *biochemist, educator*
Simon, Sheldon Weiss *political science professor*
Skromme, Brian J. *engineering educator*
Smith, Harvey Alvin *mathematics professor, consultant*
Smith, V. Kerry *economics professor*
Spritzer, Ralph Simon *lawyer, educator*
Strom, Robert Duane *psychologist, educator*
Tabbara, Hadi *director, researcher*
Thor, Linda M. *college president*
Traynor, Kirsten Shoshanna *research scientist*
Turner, Billie Lee, II, *geographer, educator*
Turner Thorne, Charli *women's college basketball coach*
Uttal, William R(eichenstein) *psychology and engineering educator, research scientist*
Vanden Heuvel, Michael John *literature educator*
van der Leeuw, Sander Ernst *archaeologist, educator*
VanderMeer, Philip R. *history professor*
Vannela, Raveender *biotechnologist, environmental scientist*
Vasileska, Dragica *electrical engineer, educator*
Vittal, Vijay *electrical engineer, educator*
Volek, Emil *educator*
Warner, Kurt (Kurtis Eugene Warner) *professional football player*
Weigend, Guido Gustav *geographer, educator*
Whisenhunt, Ken *professional football coach*
Zhou, Ding-Wei *mechanical engineer, researcher*
Zucker, Stanley Howard *special education educator*

Thatcher
Bapat, Madhuri R. *physics educator*
Jordahl, Patricia Ann *music educator, theater director*
McCarthy, Michael Scott *biology professor, publishing executive*
Morris, David *science educator*
Raines, Ken S. *literature and language professor*
Wilton, Marilyn Jean Mueller *literature and language professor*

Tsaile
Mayer, Margaret Ann *environmentalist, educator*
Vecenti, Gene Ortizio Juanajillo Altitzar *educator*

Tuba City
Hozie, William Charles *social sciences professor*

Tubac
Chilcote, Samuel Day, Jr. *trade association administrator*

Tucson
Abelt, Ralph William *bank executive*
Ablin, Richard Joel *immunologist, educator*
Aiello, Antonio J. *education educator*
Alberts, David Samuel *physician, pharmacologist, educator*
Alfie, Fabian Roberto *language educator*
Allred, Kendall S. *emergency physician*
Allvin, Paul G. *communications educator*
Alpert, Joseph Stephen *cardiologist, educator*
Amhowitz, Harris J. *lawyer, educator*
Angel, James Roger Prior *astronomer*
Appleton, Clyde Robert *music educator*
Arnell, Walter James William *engineering educator, consultant*
Aurand, Charles Henry, Jr. *music educator*
Axinn, George Harold *rural sociology educator*
Babcock-Parziale, Judi L. *medical researcher, psychology professor*
Baca, Damian *language educator*
Bainton, Denise Marlene *lawyer*
Baker, Victor Richard *geologist, hydrologist, researcher, research scientist, educator*
Bandurski, Bruce Lord *retired ecologist, environmental scientist*
Banerjee, Bhaskar *gastroenterologist, medical educator*
Barrett, Bruce Richard *physics professor*
Barrette-Mozes, Susan Jean *counselor, psychotherapist*
Bartlett, David Carson *state legislator*
Barton, Stanley Faulkner *retired management consultant*
Basefsky, Mitchell *public information officer*
Bayly, Bruce Jeremy *mathematics professor*
Beattie, Bruce Robert *economics professor*
Becker, Gary J. *radiologist, health science association administrator*
Ben-Asher, M. David *physician*
Bernstein, Carol *molecular biologist*
Betteridge, Frances Carpenter *small business owner, retired lawyer, mediator*
Blackman, Lee L. *lawyer*
Block, Michael Kent *economics and law professor, former government official*
Bloembergen, Nicolaas *physicist, researcher*
Bodinson, Holt *conservationist*
Bootman, J. Lyle *dean, pharmacy educator*
Bradley, Gilbert Francis *retired bank executive*
Brammer, J. William, Jr. *judge, lawyer*
Breiger, Ronald Louis *social sciences educator*
Brescia, Michael M. *historian, educator*
Brubaker, Galen Wayne *engineering educator*
Brusca, Richard Charles *biologist, researcher, educator, administrator*
Butcher, Russell Devereux *writer, photographer*
Cain, Vernon *retired diversified financial services company executive*
Campbell, Mary Kathryn *chemistry professor*
Carleton, Willard Tracy *retired finance educator*
Carmona, Richard Henry *health facility administrator, former Surgeon General of the United States*
Celania-Fagen, Elizabeth *school system administrator*
Chandler, Vicki L. *biologist, educator, director*
Christiano, Thomas Dominic *law educator*
Chung, Gunhui *hydrologist, researcher*
Chutkow, Lee Robinson *retired physician*
Coan, Richard Welton *psychologist, educator*
Coleman, Jane Candia *writer, English educator*
Conant, Howard Somers *artist, educator*
Cook, William Howard *architect*
Cooper, Corinne *communications consultant, lawyer*
Cooper, Jean Saralee *retired judge*
Corrigan, James John, Jr. *pediatrician, dean, educator*
Cortés-Torres, Mayra E. *language educator*
Crist, William Miles *academic administrator, pediatrician, educator*
Crooks, Roselyn June *artist, writer*
Cuello, Joel L. *biosystems engineer, professor*
Cunniff, Christopher M. *pediatrician, educator*
Dadante, Elizabeth Frances *history educator, cognitive coach*
Dalen, James Eugene *cardiologist, educator*
Davenport, Sandra *cultural organization administrator, eldercare specialist*
Deming, Alison Hawthorne *writer, poet, academic administrator*
De Young, David Spencer *astrophysicist, educator*
Diáz, Elena R. *community health nurse*
Dobbs, Dan Byron *lawyer, educator*
Dohm, James M. *aerospace scientist*
Donoghue, John Charles *application developer, consultant*
Dredge, Jill Ann *artist*
Dunn, Floyd *biophysics and biomedical engineering professor*
Dyer-Raffler, Joy Ann *retired special education diagnostician, educator*
Effken, Judith A. *nursing educator*
Elger, William Robert, Jr. *accountant*
Enright, Paul Lewis *pulmonologist*
Erickson, Robert Porter *genetics researcher, educator, clinician*
Esposito, Joseph Louis *lawyer*
Ewy, Gordon Allen *cardiologist, researcher, educator*
Fajardo, Sarah Elizabeth Johnson *financial consultant*
Falco, Charles Maurice *physicist, researcher*
Fan, Paula *music educator*
Fay, Mary Anne *retail executive*
Feldman, Stanley George *lawyer*
Feng, Changjian *biochemist, chemist*
Ferebee, Susan Shepherd *psychology professor*
Fishkind, William J. *ophthalmologist*
Fleming, Sean *science educator*
Foley, Louise *medical educator, retired military officer*
Francesconi, Louise L. *defense equipment manufacturing company executive*
Fredericksen, Dick Hartman *retired computer programmer*
Fritts, Harold Clark *botanist, educator*
Froman, Sandra Sue *lawyer*
Fulcher, Claire E *psychotherapist, organization consultant*
Gabitov, Ildar *mathematics professor*
Gaither, William Samuel *civil engineering executive, consultant*
Gantz, David Alfred *law educator, academic administrator*
Garner, Girolama Thomasina *retired educational administrator, educator*
Gerba, Charles Peter *microbiologist, educator*
Girardeau, Marvin Denham *physics professor*
Glueck-Rambaldi, Mary Audrey *retired psychiatric and mental health nurse*
Goldfarb, Robert Paul *neurological surgeon*
Goldman, Steven *cardiologist, researcher*
Goshima, Kaoru Ruth *surgeon, educator*
Graham, Anna Regina *pathologist, educator*
Grana, William A. *orthopedist, surgeon*
Grand, Marcia *civic worker*
Grand, Richard D. *lawyer*
Greenfield, Russell Howard *physician, educator*
Gruhl, James *energy scientist, artist*
Guerin, Charles Allan *museum director, artist*
Hall, Henry Kingston, Jr. *chemistry professor*
Haney, Robert Locke *retired insurance company executive*
Harcleroad, Fred Farley *higher education administrator, consultant*
Harris, David Thomas *immunology educator*
Hattery, Robert Ralph *radiologist, educator*
Hawke, Robert Francis *dentist*
Haynes, Caleb Vance, Jr. *geology and archaeology educator*
Hays, James Fred *geologist, educator*
Heller, Frederick *retired mining executive*
Hellon, Michael Thomas *tax specialist, political organization worker*
Herrnstadt, Richard Lawrence *American literature educator*
Heywood, Stanley John *educator*
Hildebrand, John G(rant) *neuroscientist, educator*
Hill, Henry Allen *physicist, researcher*
Horne, William McHenry *finance educator*
Houser, Harold Byron *epidemiologist*
Howell, Wanda H. *dietician, educator*
Hubbard, William Bogel *planetary sciences educator*
Hull, Herbert Mitchell *botanist, researcher*
Hunter, Leslie Gene *history educator*
Ingram, Charles Owen *priest, educator*
Jeffe, Sidney David *automotive executive, engineer*
Jefferies, John Trevor *astrophysicist, director*
Jerez, Marco A. *language educator*
Jeter, Wayburn Stewart *retired microbiologist, educator*
Johnson, John Gray *retired university chancellor*
Jones, Frank Wyman *management consultant, director, mechanical engineer*
Jurkowitz, Lisa Amy *language educator*
Kaltenbach, C(arl) Colin *dean, educator*
Kany, Judy C(asperson) *retired state senator*
Karkoschka, Erich *planetary science researcher, writer*
Katakkar, Suresh Balaji *hematologist, oncologist*
Kearney, Joseph Laurence *retired athletic conference administrator*
Kellogg, Frederick *historian*
Kerwin, William James *electrical engineering educator, consultant*
Khouzam, Rami Nadim *physician*
Kicanas, Gerald Frederick *bishop*
King, James Edward *retired museum director, consultant*
Kischer, Clayton Ward *human embryologist, educator*
Knight, Robert E. *museum director*
Kohler, Sigurd H. *retired physics professor*
Kohloss, Frederick Henry *retired engineer*
Kozolchyk, Boris *law educator, consultant*
Krell, Rebecca Dawn *music educator*
Kuklin, Susan Beverly *lawyer, librarian, educator*
Lammers, Mark Edward *music educator, musician*
Larwood, Laurie *psychologist, artist*
Lauer, Tod Richard *astronomer*
Leon, Luis R. *surgeon*
Levenson, Alan Ira *psychiatrist, physician, educator*
Lewis, Wilbur H. *educational management consultant*
Likins, Peter William *retired academic administrator*
Lomawaima, Hartman H. *museum director*
Lomicka, William Henry *investor*
Longan, George Baker III *real estate company executive*
Lunine, Jonathan Irving *astronomer, educator*
Macleod, Hugh Angus McIntosh *optical science educator, physicist, consultant*
Marcialis, Robert Louis *planetary astronomer*
Marcus, Frank Isadore *cardiologist, educator*
Marri, Pradeep Reddy *research scientist*
Marshall, Robert Herman *retired economics professor*
Martin, June Johnson Caldwell *journalist*
Massaro, Toni Marie *retired dean, law educator*
Mc Donald, John Richard *lawyer*
McNulty, Terence Patrick *metallurgist, consultant*
Meehan, Michael Joseph *lawyer*
Megdal, Sharon B. *water resource educator, consultant*
Mendelson, Neil H. *microbial geneticist, educator*
Menick, Frederick J. *plastic surgeon*
Mense, Allan Tate *research and development engineering executive*
Mercker, Mary Alice *aviation school administrator*
Mikesell, Elizabeth Bremond *foundation administrator*
Miller, Leslie Beth *judge*
Miller, Sean *men's college basketball coach*
Mills, Jan-Ruth *history professor*
Mims, Nathalia Regina *music educator*
Mishra, Sudib Kumar *research scientist*
Modica, Robert I., IV, *humanities educator*
Morgan, Wayne Joseph *medical educator, medical association administrator*
Morrow, James Franklin *lawyer*
Moten, Darlene *elementary school educator*
Mould, Jeremy Richard *astronomer*
Mullen, Rod *nonprofit organization executive*
Nelson, Edward Humphrey *architect*
Neugebauer, Marcia *physicist, researcher*
Nikolich-Zugich, Janko *biomedical scientist, educator*
Noonan, James C. *lawyer, mediator, arbitrator*
Nord, Myrtle Selma *writer, researcher*
Ogilvie, T(homas) Francis *marine engineering educator*
O'Leary, Thomas Michael *lawyer*
Oleshko, Vladimir P. *physical chemist, nanoscience researcher*
Orr, Ethan *non-profit organization executive*
Pace, Thomas M. *lawyer*
Palacios-Fest, Manuel Roberto *geologist, paleoecologist*
Pant, Ravi *research scientist*
Parthasarathy, Sairam *pulmonologist*
Patchett, P. Jonathan *science educator*
Pedersen, Arlene *web design company executive*
Peeler, Stuart Thorne *oil industry executive, consultant*
Pelletier, Kenneth R. *behavioral physician, educator, author*
Peters, Charles William *nuclear energy industry executive*
Peterson, John Kenneth *elementary school educator*
Pitpitan, Consuelo Lopez *pharmacist, educator*
Ponoroff, Lawrence *dean, law educator, consultant*
Popson, Lucy (Maria D. Popson) *elementary school educator*
Portney, Paul Rogers *dean*
Powell, Winona *music educator*
Powers, Linda Sue *biophysicist, educator, biomedical engineer*
Prewitt, Charles Thompson *geochemist*
Rabuck, Donna Fontanarose *English writing educator*
Ralstin, Monte Robert *musician, director*
Reed, H. Owen *retired music educator*
Reff, Steven M. *economics educator*
Reitan, Ralph Meldahl *clinical neuropsychologist, former educator*
Rieke, Marcia J. *astronomer, educator*
Riggs, Lew *foundation executive*
Riley, Mark Richard *biochemical engineer, educator*
Roemer, Elizabeth *retired astronomer, educator*
Rogers, Lee Frank *radiologist*
Rose, Carol Marguerite *law educator*
Rousos, Linda *language educator*
Russell, Findlay Ewing *physician*
Samet, Dee-Dee *lawyer*
Schimberg, Barbara *organizational development consultant*
Schorr, S. L. *lawyer*
Schulz, Renate Adele *German studies and second language acquisition educator*
Schwartz, Gary E. *psychologist, educator*
Schwebel, Milton *psychologist, educator*
Seaman, Arlene Anna *retired musician*
Seay, Suzanne *financial planner, educator*
Seehausen, Richard Ferdinand *architect*
Shahidullah, Mohammad *medical researcher, educator*
Shelton, Robert Neal *academic administrator, physics professor, researcher*
Shropshire, Donald Gray *hospital executive*
Slack, Donald Carl *agricultural engineer, educator*
Smerdon, Ernest Thomas *engineering educator*
Smith, David Wayne *retired psychologist, educator*
Snyder, Richard Gerald *research scientist, administrator, educator, consultant*
Soren, David *archaeologist, educator, writer, filmmaker*
Spaeth, Jan Mills *jury consultant*
Staubitz, Arthur Frederick *retired lawyer, health products executive*
Stitt, Mari Leipper *poet*
Stoffle, Carla Joy *university library dean*
Stoops, Mike *college football coach*
Strong, John William *lawyer, educator*
Sweeney, Joseph Dudley *law educator, political organization worker*
Tang, Esther Don *real estate developer, consultant, social worker*
Thal, Sergio Gustavo *cardiologist, director, medical educator*
Thompson, Raymond Harris *retired anthropologist, educator*
Thompson, Rodger Irwin *astrophysicist, educator*
Thomson, Donald Arthur *education educator*
Thorpe, Jason M. *non-profit organization director*
Thurman, Robert Kenneth *retired military officer*
Tifft, William Grant *retired physics professor, scientist*
Tindall, Robert Emmett *lawyer, educator*
Tirrell, John Albert *organization executive, consultant*
Troxell, Mary Theresa (Terry Troxell) *geriatrics services professional*
Tuchi, Ben Joseph *retired finance educator*
Tuller, Markus *geophysicist, educator*
Underwood, Jane Hainline Hammons *anthropologist, educator*
VanEtten, Hans D. *plant pathologist, educator*
Venkata, Subrahmanyam Saraswati *engineering educator, researcher*
Vincent, Deborah *nursing educator*
Voorakaranam, Ram *optics scientist*
Walker, Ronald Hugh *foundation administrator*
Walkup, Robert E. *Mayor, Tucson*
Wallach, Leslie Rothaus *architect*
Waterbury, Deborah Kay *minister*
Weil, Andrew Thomas *physician, educator*
Weiss, Stephen M. *lawyer*
Whitaker, Ewen Adair *retired astronomer*
White, Herbert Spencer *library and information scientist, educator, dean*
Wickham, John Adams, Jr. *retired army officer*
Williams, Joy *writer*
Willoughby, Stephen Schuyler *mathematics professor*
Wolfe, Brian Thomas *music educator*
Wong, Simon S. *environmental health scientist, educator*
Woolfenden, James Manning *nuclear medicine physician, educator*
Wright, George Thaddeus *humanities educator*
Yocum, Harrison Gerald *horticulturist, botanist, educator, researcher*
Zheng, Wenxin *gynecologist, pathologist*
Ziolkowski, Richard Walter *electrical engineer, educator*
Zreda, Marek *science educator*

Wickenburg
Brooks, Donna Jean *retired counselor, educator*
Daniel, James Richard *corporate financial executive*

Wikieup
Brattstrom, Bayard Holmes *biology professor*

Williams
Calley, Tranquil Hudson *retired travel consultant, educator, counselor*

Winkelman
Wilson, Maren *anthropologist, educator*

Young
Burke, Karen A. *medical/surgical nurse*

Yuma
Anderson, John Albert *physician*

Hodson, Roy Goode, Jr. *retired logistician*
Hossler, David Joseph *lawyer, educator*
Houggard, Santa Carol Hall *family nurse practitioner, consultant*
Hudson, John Irvin *retired career officer*
Martínez, Martha C. *language educator*
McCarthy, Sherri Nevada *psychologist, educator, educational consultant*
Norton, Dunbar Sutton *economic developer*
Smith, Jimmie Dee *lawyer*

ARKANSAS

Arkadelphia
Bradshaw, Joseph Earl *chemistry professor*
Dunn, Charles DeWitt *academic administrator*
Elrod, Ben Moody *academic administrator*
Grant, Daniel Ross *retired academic administrator*
Graves, John William *historian*
Handiboe, Mary Ellen *theater educator*
Johnson, Trina Lynn *special education educator*
Nelson, Leon *retired data processing professional*
Pemberton, Barbara Butler *religious studies educator*
Wiebers, Todd *psychology professor*
Woodall, Peggy Keaton *special education educator*

Ashdown
Finley, John Cyrus III *lawyer, judge*

Batesville
Carius, Robert Wilhelm *mathematics professor, retired military officer*
Harkey, John Norman *retired judge*
Lankford, George Emerson III *social sciences educator*
McNamee, Kathleen Metzger *academic administrator*

Beebe
Knapp, Stephen John *language educator*
Russ, Ronald Steven *librarian*
Sites, Jerry *agricultural studies educator*

Bella Vista
Medin, Myron James, Jr. *city manager*

Benton
Krueger, Marlo Bush *retired lawyer*

Bentonville
Agwunobi, John Oderah *retail executive, former federal agency administrator*
Castro-Wright, Eduardo *retail executive*
Chambers, Susan (M. Susan Chambers) *retail executive*
Cornell, Brian Christian *retail executive*
Curran, Patricia A. *retail executive*
Dach, Leslie Alan *retail executive, former public relations company executive*
Dobbs, Johnnie C., Jr. *retail executive*
Duke, Mike (Michael Terry Duke) *retail executive*
Fleming, John E. *retail executive*
Ford, Rollin L. *retail executive*
Gearhart, Jeffrey J. *retail executive, lawyer*
Hefner, Linda P. *retail executive*
Holley, Charles Murphy, Jr. *retail company executive*
Hubbard, Mary Miller *literature and language professor*
Hyde, Thomas D. *retail executive, lawyer*
McKenna, Margaret Anne *foundation administrator, former academic administrator*
McMillon, Doug (Carl Douglas McMillon) *retail executive*
Mora, Alberto J. *retail executive, lawyer*
Ohm, Seong K. *consumer products company executive*
Peerson, Michael B. *pharmacist, director*
Pogue, William Reid *retired astronaut, foundation administrator, aerospace scientist, consultant*
Quinn, Stephen F. *marketing executive*
Schoewe, Thomas M. *retail executive*
Scott, Lee (Harold Lee Scott Jr.) *retail executive*
Simon, William S. *retail executive*
Sinclair, Jack L. *retail executive*
Spragg, Gregg E. *retail executive*
Trius, Vicente *retail executive*
Tuthill, John G. *academic administrator*
Walton, Jim Carr *bank executive*
Walton, (Samuel) Rob(son) *discount department store chain executive*
Weir, Rita Mary *retail executive*
Westling, John T. *retail executive*
Whaley, Steven P. *retail executive*
Young, Wanda *marketing executive*
Zorn, Eric Stuart *retail executive*
Zumwalt, Kenneth Wayne *assistant principal*

Blytheville
Slowik, Richard Andrew *air force officer*
Thomasson, Emily *mathematics educator*

Cabot
Arbeene, Michael James *entrepreneur, business consultant*
Tackett, Viti Lee *writer*

Camden
Gunnels, Robert D. *academic administrator*
Owen, Larry Gene *academic administrator, educator, electronics engineer, consultant*

Carlisle
Glover, Bobby L. *state legislator*

Cedarville
Whitaker, Ruth Reed *state legislator, retired publishing executive*

Conway
Baker, Gilbert R. *state legislator*
Burris, Debra L. *physics professor*
Courtway, Thomas C. *academic administrator, former state legislator*
Friedman, William H. *engineering educator*
Harlan, Mary Hope *education educator, department chairman*
Harris, Marjorie Jane *religious studies educator*
Hatcher, Joe Branch *management consultant*
Horton, Joseph Julian, Jr. *economics and finance educator*
Hutchinson, Bruce D. *filmmaker, educator*
Johnson, James Douglas (Jim Johnson) *lawyer*
Leffler, Jean Riise *religious organization administrator*
McNew, Bennie Banks *retired finance educator*
Meadors, Allen Coats *academic administrator, educator*
Monty, Julie Anne *language educator*
Spatz, Kenneth Chris(topher), Jr. *statistics educator*
Ziegler, John Alan *historian, political scientist, educator*

Deer
Vance, Sue Ann *musician, educator*

Earle
Swift, Peggy Lynette *elementary school educator*

El Dorado
Arn, Nancy Lynn *library director*
Barnes, Harry Francis *federal judge*
Cossé, Steven A. *lawyer, oil industry executive*
Fitzgerald, Kevin Gerard *oil industry executive*
Nolan, William C., Jr. *oil industry executive*
Wood, David M. *oil industry executive*

Fayetteville
Agee, Eve *anthropologist*
Amy, Apon Weathers *science educator*
Bajwa, Sreekala G. *agricultural engineer, educator*
Barnes, Jeffrey K. *curator*
Bell, Debbie McCulley *science educator*
Brooks, Mary Elizabeth *bank executive*
Brown, Avert Hayden *animal scientist, educator*
Brown, Connell Jean *retired animal science educator*
Broyles, Frank (John Franklin Broyles) *athletic director, retired college football coach*
Candido, Joseph Dominic *literature and language professor*
Chakhalian, Jak *physics professor*
Cochran, Robert Brady *literature and language professor*
Costrell, Robert Michael *economist*
Epley, Lewis Everett, Jr. *lawyer*
Fink, William James *retired surgeon*
Fosu, Ignatius *communications educator*
Gaddy, James Leoma *chemical engineer, educator*
Gearhart, G. David *academic administrator, education educator*
Hajihashemi, Mohammad Reza *engineer*
Joon Jin, Song *mathematics professor, statistics professor*
Kellogg, David Wayne *agricultural studies educator, researcher*
Kester, Charles Melvin *lawyer*
Kester, Cheryl L. *management consultant*
Kim, Jeong-Hwan *research scientist*
Kim, Jin Woo *engineering educator*
Kohler, Peter Ogden *retired academic administrator, internist, educator*
Kunets, Vasyl Petrovych *research scientist*
Levine, Daniel Blank *classical studies educator*
Malone, David Roy *public fund consultant retired educational association administrator, director*
Malshe, Ajay P. *engineering educator*
Mc Gimsey, Charles Robert III *anthropologist*
Murchison, Gayle Minetta *music educator*
Musick, Gerald Joe *retired entomology educator*
Nance, Cynthia Eleanor (Cyndi Nance) *dean, law educator*
Parker, Lee Bryan *retired physician*
Petrino, Bobby *college football coach*
Rardin, Ronald L. *engineering educator*
Schoppmeyer, Martin William *education educator*
Schoppmeyer, Martin William, Jr. *school system administrator*
Setia, Pankaj *management educator*
Smith, Lavenski Roy *federal judge*
Smith, Robert Victor *academic administrator, educator*
Steele, Kenneth Franklin, Jr. *hydrologist*
Venkatesh, Viswanath *information systems professional, educator, consultant*
White, John Austin, Jr. *engineering educator, retired academic administrator*
Wilkins, Charles L. *chemist, educator*
Wilson, Charles Banks *artist*
Yang, Jie *electrical engineer, researcher*
Yoon, Hargsoon *engineering educator*

Fort Smith
Bailey, Donald Keith *music educator, composer, musician*
Colbert, Alice Taylor *history professor*
Cooper, Richard F. *lawyer*
Davidson, Robert A. *trucking executive*
Hembree, Hugh Lawson III *diversified holding company executive*
Horton, William Gene *lawyer*
Lee, Arthur Carson *geologist*
Meadors, C. Brian *lawyer*
Momand, Elizabeth Blanton *singer, music educator*
Norin, Lori Ann *communication educator*
Siler, Dennis James *literature and language professor*
Snider, James Rhodes *radiologist*
Van Arsdale, Dennis G. *librarian*
Zacharella, Alexandra *music educator, director*

Gravette
Hendren, Kim *state legislator*

Greenwood
Walters, Bill *retired state senator*

Harrison
Holtslander, Dorothy Brock *counselor, educator, author, reporter*

Heber Springs
Rawlings, Paul C. *retired government official*
Stroud, Peggy *secondary school educator*

Helena
Roscopf, Charles Buford *lawyer*

Hope
Freeman, Thomas Bruce (Tom Freeman) *social studies educator*

Hot Springs
Drake, Joshua *lawyer*
Farris, Jefferson Davis *university administrator*
Kamel, Hosam Kamal *medical educator, researcher, geriatrician*
Miller, Gary C. *lawyer*
Pelton, Elois Bleidt *retired physical education educator*
Selix, Karen Elizabeth *writer, artist, vocalist*

Hot Springs National Park
Schnipper, Don Martin *lawyer*

Hot Springs Village
Philpott, Larry La Fayette *retired horn player*
Smith, Preston *retired minister, small business owner*

Jefferson
Bagnyukova, Tetyana Volodymyrivna *biologist*
Hotchkiss, Charlotte Evans *veterinarian, researcher*
Leakey, Julian Edwin Arundell *toxicologist, researcher*
Wolff, George Louis *biomedical researcher*

Jonesboro
Bookout, Paul *state legislator*
Deacon, John C. *lawyer*
Elkins, Francis Clark *historian, educator, director*
Jones, Kenneth Bruce *surgeon*
Pearce, Amy R *psychology professor*
Rowe, William Johnston, Jr. *dentist*
Smith, Eugene Wilson *retired academic administrator, education educator*

Lavaca
Kincade, John C. *science educator*

Little Rock
Allen, H(enry) William *lawyer*
Altes, Robert Dennis (Denny) *state legislator*
Anand, Kanwaljeet Singh *pediatrician, researcher*
Anderson, Philip Sidney *lawyer*
Arnold, Morris Sheppard *federal judge*
Ashcraft, Carolyn *state librarian*
Banks, Alicia *elementary school educator*
Bass, Evelyn Elizabeth *elementary school educator*
Bates, Jonathan R. *hospital administrator*
Beebe, Mike D. (Michael Dale Beebe) *Governor of Arkansas, former state attorney general, lawyer*
Bell, Richard Eugene *agricultural products executive, state official*
Bird, Samuel N. *judge*
Boe, Myron Timothy *lawyer*
Bowen, William Harvey *bank executive, lawyer*
Braithwaite, Wilfred John *retired physics professor*
Britt, Billy Jean *retired elementary school educator, economic education specialist*
Broadway, Shane *state legislator*
Brown, Larry Douglass *research consultant, writer*
Bruce, Thomas Allen *physician, educator*
Bryles, Steve M. *state legislator*
Burchfield, Jessie Wallace *law librarian*
Calloway, Billie Jean *retired educator*
Campbell, Gilbert Sadler *surgeon, educator*
Capps, John Paul *state legislator*
Casciano, Daniel Anthony *biologist, educator*
Chapman, Alger Baldwin *financial services company executive, lawyer*
Cheek, James Richard *ambassador*
Chiang, Chia-Chu *computer scientist, educator*
Chilcote, Lugean Lester *retired architect, researcher*
Coleman, Marshia Adams *social sciences educator*
Corbin, Donald L. *state supreme court justice*
Cross, J. Bruce *lawyer*
Daniels, Charlie L. *Secretary of State, Arkansas*
Danielson, Paul E. *state supreme court justice*
Darsey, Jerome Anthony (Jerry) *chemistry professor, consultant*
Davis, Suanna Jeanette *mezzo-soprano, retired music educator*
Dillard, William, II, *department store chain executive*
Duke, Jane W. *prosecutor*
Elbein, Alan David *medical science educator*
Elliott, Joyce *state legislator*
Emanuel, Peter D. *medical educator, director*
Eubanks, Gary Leroy, Sr. *lawyer*
Ferguson, Alesia C. *medical educator*
Fiser, Debra H. *pediatrician, educator, dean*
Ford, Scott T. *telecommunications industry executive*
Franks, Candace Ann *state banking agency administrator*
Freeman, James I. *retail department store company executive*
Fribourgh, James Henry *retired university administrator*
Gardner, Jeffrey R. *communications executive*
Garner, Terri *library and museum director*
Gealt, Michael A. *environmental microbiologist, educator*
Geffken, Carolyn D. *special education educator*
Goddard, H. Wallace *family life professor*
Good, Mary Lowe *investment company executive, educator*
Greenberg, Paul *editor*
Gunter, James Houston, Jr. *state supreme court justice*
Gunter, Russell Allen *lawyer*
Halter, Bill (William A. Halter) *Lieutenant Governor of Arkansas*
Halverson, Paul Kenneth *state agency administrator, public health service officer*
Hannah, James *state supreme court chief justice*
Hart, Ronald Wilson *radiobiologist, educator, toxicologist, business adviser*
Haught, William Dixon *lawyer, writer*
Hinson, Jack Allsbrook *research toxicologist, educator*
Hoover, Paul Williams, Jr. *lawyer*
Huang, Guoliang *science educator*
Hussman, Walter E., Jr. *publishing executive*
Imber, Annabelle Clinton *state supreme court justice*
Jansen, G. Thomas *dermatologist*
Julian, Diana *state official, school system administrator*
Karabacak, Tansel *physics professor, researcher*
Kaushal, Gur Prasad *biochemist, educator*
Kaza, Greg John *economist, educator*
Khanal, Ramesh C. *animal scientist, researcher*
Ledbetter, Calvin Reville, Jr., (Cal Ledbetter) *political science professor, legislator*
Lemke, Judith A. *lawyer*
Levy, Eugene Pfeifer *architectural firm executive, architect*
Light, Jo Knight *stockbroker*
Lipe, Linda Bon *lawyer*
Lucy, Dennis Durwood, Jr. *neurologist, educator*
Mahabhashyam, Sai Rajesh *application developer*
Massey, Richard N. *lawyer, telecommunications industry executive*
May, Ronald Alan *lawyer*
McDaniel, Dustin *state attorney general*
Mehta, Jawahar Lal *cardiologist*
Miller, Brian Stacy *federal judge*
Mulkey, Jack Clarendon *retired library director*
Murphey, Arthur Gage, Jr. *law educator*
Nelson, Edward Sheffield *lawyer, retired utilities executive*
Nunn, Patarica Dian *poet*
O'Brien, Mark Stephen *pediatric neurosurgeon*
Olden, Kevin William *medical researcher*
Parkhurst, Ted A. *publishing executive*
Patil, Naveen *preventive medicine physician*
Pennington, Jodie A. *education outreach educator*
Plummer, Ellen *museum director*
Portis, Charles McColl *reporter, writer*
Prince, David Cannon *lawyer*
Raney, Miriam Day *actress*
Raza, Asim *psychiatrist*
Recken, Stephen Louis *history professor*
Schroeder, Paul J., Jr. *lawyer*
Selz, Nan *museum director*
Sherman, William Farrar *lawyer, former state legislator*
Shoffner, Martha Ann *state treasurer*
Smith, G. Richard *psychiatry educator*
Smith, Griffin *executive editor*
Smith, Susan *bank executive*
Sotomora-von Ahn, Ricardo Federico *pediatrician, educator*
Stockburger, Jean Dawson *lawyer*
Stodola, Mark Allen *Mayor, Little Rock, Arkansas, former prosecutor*
Sugg, Barney Alan *academic administrator*
Suva, Larry John *orthopedic researcher*
Tarasenko, Olga *biologist, educator*
Taylor, Anthony Basil *bishop*
Terry, William Leake *lawyer*
Trice, William Henry III *lawyer*
Truemper, John James, Jr. *retired architect*
Truex, Dorothy Adine *retired university administrator*
Turner, Todd *political organization administrator, lawyer*
Ursery, Frederick Stanley *lawyer*
Vinikas, Vincent *historian, educator*
Waters, Zenobia Pettus *retired finance educator*
Webb, Doyle L. *political organization administrator, former state legislator*
Weiss, Richard A. *state official*
Whiteside, Charles B. III *investment company executive*
Wills, Elana Cunningham *state supreme court justice*
Witherspoon, Carolyn Brack *lawyer*
Wright, Susan Webber *federal judge*
Xi, Jinxiang *engineering educator, researcher*
Yanoviak, Stephen Paul *ecologist, educator*
Yoder, R. Paul *literature and language professor*
York, John Lyndal *medical educator*

Lowell
Thompson, Kirk *transportation executive*

Magnolia
Clark, James R. *secondary school educator, director*
Davis, La'Tricia Danyelle *administrative assistant*
Mallory, Kathleen Norris Brown *literature and language professor*
Terry, Robert Arthur *literature and language professor, director*

Malvern
Dodd, Jerry Lee *lawyer*
Faris, Steve *state legislator*

Marion
Lodor, Marci Ann *dietitian*

Maumelle
Bayrak, Coskun *computer scientist, researcher, educator*

Mena
Eddleman, Floyd Eugene *retired language educator*

Monticello
Babin, Claude Hunter *history professor*
Ball, William Kenneth *lawyer*
Vincent, Angelia Annette *librarian*

Montrose
Bates, Jimmy W. *secondary school educator, director, minister*

Mountain Home
Baker, Robert Leon *military officer*

North Little Rock
Herron, Ronald Leroy *aeronautical engineer, educator*
Komoroski, Richard Andrew *medical sciences educator, spectroscopy researcher*
Patty, Claibourne Watkins, Jr. *lawyer*
Robbins, Dorothy Ann *retired foreign language educator*
Welch, Morgan E. *lawyer*

Palestine
Taylor, Barbara Mae Helm *artist, educator*

Paragould
Crandall, Elizabeth Diane *science educator, microbiologist*

Perryville
McCallister, Carolyn G. *secondary school educator*

Pine Bluff
Engle, Carole Ruth *aquaculture economics professor*
Long, Edward Arlo *management consultant, retired manufacturing executive*
Scott, Vicki Sue *retired school system administrator*
Sims, David Lloyd *lawyer*
Strode, Joseph Arlin *lawyer*
Walker, Richard Brian *chemistry professor*

Pocahontas
Moss, Linda Elaine *science educator*

Rogers
Balfe, Robert Cramer III *lawyer, former prosecutor*
Bledsoe, Cecile H. *state legislator*
Goff, Deborah Oleta *elementary school educator*

Rose Bud
Spradley, Pamela Claire *art educator*

Russellville
Inch, Morris Alton *theology educator*
Jenkins, Ellen Janet (Jan) *history professor*
Morris, Lois Lawson *retired education educator*

Salem
Harber-Hurtt, Lisa Lynn *art educator*

Scranton
Uzman, Betty Ben Geren *retired pathologist*

Searcy
Frazier, Allen Wayne *finance educator*
Gastineau, Zane D. *engineering educator, department chairman*
Harris, Julie E. S. *history professor*
Hobby, Kenneth Lester *psychology professor*
Hughes, Teresa Lee *lawyer, educator*
Hughes, Thomas Morgan III *circuit judge*
Love, Joli Gibbs *language educator*
Province, Dennis *chemistry professor*
Willmore, Catherine Bernadette *pharmacist professor, research scientist*
Wood, Michael B. *principal*
Yecke, Cheri Pierson *educational researcher, administrator, policymaker, writer*

Sherwood
Cantu, Jennifer St. John *gifted and talented educator*

Siloam Springs
Himes, Jonathan Bryant *literature and language professor*
Martin, Bobby C. *graphics designer, educator*
Wubbena, Jan Helmut *music professor*

Springdale
Holman, L. Charlene *elementary school educator*
Leatherby, Dennis *food products executive*
Minkel, Justin *elementary school educator*
Rosenschein, Guy Raoul *pediatric and visceral surgeon, airline pilot*
Strong, B. Jean *writer, publisher*
Tollett, Leland Edward *food products executive*
Tyson, John H. *food products executive*
Van Bebber, David L. *food products executive, lawyer*

State University
Allen, Marti Lu *museum director*
Brady, John E. *men's college basketball coach*
Cave, Eric Macdonald *philosopher, educator*
Guha, Gauri Shankar *economics professor*
Hannigan, Robyn E. *science educator, researcher*
Milner, Clyde A., II, *historian*

Stuttgart
Layne, Allen *historian, educator*
Moldenhauer, Karen Ann Kuenzel *agriculturist, educator*

Texarkana
Petty, Marsha *chemistry educator*
Stroud, John Fred, Jr. *judge*

Walnut Ridge
Gore, Kenneth Wendell, Jr. *religious studies educator*
Wheeless, Charlotte Ann *science educator*

Ward
Gray, Janet Faye Walker *science educator*

Warren
Claycomb, Hugh Murray *lawyer, writer*

Widener
Crumbly, Jack *state legislator*

CALIFORNIA

Agoura Hills
Barker, Wiley Franklin *surgeon, educator*
Canatsey, Ken *nurse*
Chagall, David *journalist, writer*
Currie, Malcolm Roderick *retired aerospace and automotive executive, research scientist*
deCiutiis, Alfred Charles Maria *oncologist, television producer*
Fox, Stuart Ira *physiologist*
Gilbert, Jane H. *health science association administrator*
Gressak, Anthony Raymond, Jr. *sales executive*
Hancock, Lani Jane *artist*
Kurland, Stanford L. *mortgage company executive*
Lingl, James Peter *lawyer, mediator*
Stagg, Enid *educational consultant*
Ziv, Jonathan *cosmetic dentist*

Alameda
Asomugha, Nnamdi *professional football player*
Bartalini, C. Richard *judge*
Blackmore, Peter *computer company executive*
Cable, Thomas Lee (Tom Cable) *professional football coach*
Cho, Myeong-Je *plant biologist, researcher*
Davis, Al (Allen Davis) *professional football team executive*
Doerr, Robert Douglas *psychologist, educator, artist, mediator*
Earle, Sylvia Alice *research biologist, oceanographer*
Garcia, Jeff (Jeffrey Jason Garcia) *professional football player*
Griffith, Saul *engineering innovations inventor*
Lechler, Shane (Edward Shane Lechler) *professional football player*
Lu, Hong Liang *telecommunications industry executive*
McFadden, Darren *professional football player*
Robinson, Joanne Adele *retired secondary school educator, volunteer*
Russell, JaMarcus *professional football player*
Stonehouse, James Adam *lawyer*
Whorton, M. Donald *physician, epidemiologist*
Wu, Shuning *statistician*

Alamo
Liggett, Lawrence Melvin *vacuum equipment manufacturing company executive*
Madden, Palmer Brown *lawyer*
Schreiber, John T. *lawyer*
Shiffer, James David *retired utilities executive*
Whalen, John Sydney *management consultant*

Albany
Kahlon, Talwinder Singh *research scientist*
Mills, Nicholas John *biology educator*

Alhambra
Determan, John David *lawyer*
Duke, Donald Norman *publishing executive*
Im, Jaemo *research scientist*
Sussman, Steven Yale *preventive medicine and psychology educator*
Suzuki, Bob H. *retired academic administrator*

Aliso Viejo
Blum, Scott Allen *Internet company executive*
Cohen, Sasha (Alexandra Pauline Cohen) *ice skater*
Dutile, Robert Arthur *information technology manager*
Hamersley, M. Robert *environmental microbiologist professor*
Harder, Wendy Wetzel *communications executive*
Kister, Henry Z. *chemical engineer*
La Marca, Jeffry Peter *language educator, consultant*
Morrison, Patricia B. *former electronics executive*
Purdy, Alan MacGregor *financial executive*
Schultz, E. Eugene, Jr. *information security engineer*
Srikumar, Ramakrishnan *microbiologist, researcher*
Steuert, Douglas Michael *engineering and construction management company executive*
Williams, James Dale *language educator, researcher*

Alpine
Oliverio, Ponzio *protective services official, educator*
Roberts, Dwight Loren *engineer, writer*

Alta Loma
Klein, Henry *lawyer*
Straka, Laszlo Richard *retired publishing consultant*

Altadena
Coles, Donald Earl *retired engineering educator*
Mkryan, Sonya *geophysicist, educator, research scientist*

Anaheim
Abreu, Bobby (Bob Kelly Abreu) *professional baseball player*
Browne, Autumn Lee *theater educator and director, actress*
Carlyle, Randy *professional hockey coach, retired professional hockey player*
Figgins, Chone (Desmond DeChone Figgins) *professional baseball player*
Fuentes, Brian Christopher *professional baseball player*
Getzlaf, Ryan *professional hockey player*
Giguere, Jean-Sebastien *professional hockey player*
Glazer, Sidney *physician, director*
Gobar, Alfred Julian *retired economic consultant, investor, educator*
Goodspeed, Kathryn Ann *pre-school educator*
Guerrero, Vladimir Alvino *professional baseball player*
Hedican, Bret *professional hockey player*
Hunter, Torii Kedar *professional baseball player*
Jolley, Weldon Bosen *surgery educator, research executive*
Kazmir, Scott (Edward) *professional baseball player*
Koivu, Saku *professional hockey player*
Lano, Charles Jack *retired financial executive*
Lee, Donna Jean *retired nurse*
Matallana, Lynne *patient advocacy association administrator*
McNulty, James Francis *engineering executive*
Moreno, Arturo (Arte Moreno) *professional sports team executive, former advertising executive*
Murray, Bob (Robert Frederick Murray) *professional sports team executive, former professional hockey player*
Niedermayer, Scott *professional hockey player*
Nonis, David *professional sports team executive*
Palfenier, David *food products executive*
Pringle, Curt *Mayor, Anaheim, California*
Reagins, Tony *professional baseball team executive*
Schulman, Michael *professional sports team executive, lawyer*
Selanne, Teemu *professional hockey player*
Unan, George Vincent *adult education educator*

Angwin
Andrianarijaona, Vola Masoandro *physics professor, researcher*
Kurtz, Robert Walden *theology, philosophy, mathematics studies educator, pastor, writer*
Vance, Rodney *film producer, writer*

Antelope
Nenov, Ivo P. *mathematical and software researcher*

Antioch
Stamm, Barbara Marie Anderson *elementary school educator, interior designer*

Apple Valley
Jackson, Betty Eileen *music and elementary school educator*

Aptos
Bohn, Ralph Carl *educational consultant*
Coe, Virginia L. *literature and language educator*
Epperson, Willia Anderson (Skip Epperson) *theater educator, department chairman*
Griffin, James Bernard, Jr. *application developer, educator*
Heron, David Winston *librarian*
Miura, Masako Kusayanagi *retired dermatologist*
Nicholson, Joseph Bruce *real estate developer*
Robles, Félix *retired language educator, dean*
Trounstine, Philip John *communications consultant, online publisher*
White, Elizabeth Nichole *lab administrator, educator*

Arcadia
Anderson, Holly Geis *health facility administrator, educator, commentator*
Belnap, David F. *journalist*
Burbano, Arturo A. *process engineer*
Jemelian, John Nazar *management consultant*
Matsuura, Kenneth Ray *counseling administrator*
Sathyavagiswaran, Lakshmanan *pathologist, county official*
Trussell, R(obert) Rhodes *environmental engineer*
Ulrich, Peter Henry *banker*
Yen, Wen-Hsiung *language and music professional, educator*

Arcata
Black, Jeffrey M. *professor (wildlife)*
Dengler, Lori *science educator*
Grafman, Lonny *engineering educator, editor*
Land-Weber, Ellen *photography professor*
McCrone, Alistair William *retired academic administrator*
Wang, Rui *dean, educator*

Arleta
Kelley, Frances A. *occupational therapist, consultant*

Aromas
Fleischman, Paul *children's author*

Arroyo Grande
Benedict, Lawrence Neal *foreign service officer*
Hoffmann, Jon Arnold *retired aeronautical engineer*
Lagomarsino, Robert John *former congressman*
Saari, David John *retired law educator*
Willis, Ralph Walker *retired firefighter*

Atascadero
Colamarino, Katrin Belenky *lawyer, consultant*
Locke, Virginia Otis *writer*
Rios, Evelyn Deerwester *columnist, musician, artist, writer*

Atherton
Baran, Paul *computer executive*
Barker, Robert Jeffery *financial executive*
Coleman, Robert Griffin *geology educator*
Eggers, Alfred John, Jr. *research corporation executive*
Ferris, Robert Albert *lawyer, venture capitalist*
Fried, John H. *chemist*
Gill, Stephen Paschall *retired physicist, mathematician*
Goodman, Sam Richard *electronics executive*
Hooper, Mark Scheller *electrical engineer, educator*
Lowry, Larry *engineering company executive*
Lynch, Charles Allen *investment company executive, director*
Morel-Seytoux, Hubert Jean *civil engineer, educator*

Atwater
LiWang, Andy *research scientist, educator*

Auburn
Blaney, Suzanne Avery *artist, writer*
Henrikson, Donald Merle *forensic pathologist*
Hess, Patrick Henry *chemist, researcher*
Miller, Susan L. *social services administrator*
Rothwell, Elaine B. *artist*

Azusa
Adams, Jim J. *minister and higher education administrator*
Aguilar, Gladys Maria *counselor, educator*
Alam, Maksudul M. *chemical engineer*
Conover, Roger B. *economics professor*
Estrada-Lee, Christine *psychologist*
Griesinger, Emily Ann *literature and language professor*
Harrell, Shelley Renee *school librarian*
Miyake, Stephanie Ann *psychology professor, director, marriage and family therapist*
Pacino, Maria Antonieta *education educator, department chairman*
Parham, Thomas David *education educator*
Rojas-González, Marcela *language educator*

Bakersfield
Asher, Curtis Martin *librarian*
Bernard, Alexander *protective services official*
Burns, Sarah Chloe *historian, educator*
Chidgey, Guy Clement *marketing executive*
Enriquez, Carola Rupert *museum director*
Fiedler, Joseph Robert *mathematician, educator*
Flachmann, Michael Charles *English language educator*
Frazier, Jo Frances *religious organization administrator, writer*
Huerta, Dolores Clara (Dolores Fernández) *labor union administrator*
Kegley, Jacquelyn Ann *philosophy educator*
Lai, Mun Sim (Nicole Lai) *economics professor*
McAlister, Michael H. *architect*
McBride, Todd *biology professor, department chairman*
Meyers, Christopher *humanities educator, consultant*
Osterkamp, Dalene May *psychology educator, artist*
Provencio, Roberto Enrique *music educator and minister*
Reep, Edward Arnold *artist*
Sharma, Sanjiv *cardiologist*
Sio, Jimmy Ong *embryologist*
Zarra, Ernest Joseph III *secondary school educator, researcher*

Baldwin Park
Driskill, James Lawrence *minister*

Banning
Gladden, Garnett Lee *psychologist, healthcare consultant, educator*

Bayside
Cocks, George Gosson *retired chemical microscopy professor*

Beaumont
Youngren, Delvana Hope *secondary school educator*

Bellflower
Henry, Harold M. *obstetrician, gynecologist, maternal-fetal medicine*
Lee, Paul Yue-Yan *surgeon*
Maples, Karen Elizabeth *obstetrician, gynecologist*

Belmont
Renwick, Stephen P. *engineer*

Belvedere
Hugenberg, Patricia Ellen Petrie *product designer*

Belvedere Tiburon
Fishman, Robert Allen *retired neurologist, educator, department chair*
Hoffman, Julien Ivor Ellis *pediatrician, cardiologist, educator*
McFarland, Ronald George (Ron) *composer, music educator, musician*
Rayner, Arno Alfred *investment company executive, consultant*
Rosenthal, Robert Jon *newspaper editor, journalist*
Stotter, Lawrence Henry *lawyer*
Williams, Robin *actor, comedian*

Benicia
Nelson, Elmer Kingsholm, Jr., (Kim Nelson) *political scientist, educator, writer, mediator, consultant*
Szabo, Peter John *investment company executive, mining engineer, financial planner, lawyer*

Berkeley
Agogino, Alice Merner *computer scientist, mechanical engineer, educator*
Akerlof, George Arthur *economics professor*
Alesander, Terry Pink *museum director*
Alhadeff, David Albert *economics professor*
Alivisatos, Armand Paul *chemist, educator*
Alter, Robert Bernard *literature educator, critic*
Anderson, William Scovil *classics educator*
Arguedas, Cristina Claypoole *lawyer*
Arkin, Adam Paul *biology professor*
Attwood, David Thomas *physicist, researcher*
Auerbach, Alan Jeffrey *economist, educator*
Baack, Lawrence James *energy executive, history professor*
Bagdikian, Ben Haig *journalist, educator*
Bajcsy, Ruzena Kucerova *computer science educator*
Barrett, Reginald Haughton *wildlife management educator*
Bazian, Hatem Ahmad *religious studies educator, consultant*
Bell, Alexis T. *chemical engineer, educator*
Bellah, Robert Neelly *sociologist, educator*
Benedict, Burton *retired museum director, anthropologist*
Berdahl, Paul Hilland *physicist*
Berger, Stanley Allan *mechanical and biomechanical engineering educator*
Bergman, Robert George *chemist, educator*
Bern, Howard Alan *biologist, researcher, science educator*

Berring, Robert Charles, Jr. law educator, librarian, association administrator
Birgeneau, Robert Joseph academic administrator, physicist, researcher
Bloom, Robert language educator
Blume, James Beryl investment advisor
Bogy, David B(eauregard) mechanical engineering educator
Booth, Stephen Walter language educator
Botchan, Michael R. molecular biologist, biochemist
Boyarin, Daniel social studies educator
Boyle, Joanne women's college basketball coach
Bragg, Robert Henry physicist, researcher
Brandes, Stanley Howard anthropology educator, writer
Brocchini, Ronald Gene architect
Brooke, Tal (Robert Taliaferro) writer
Browne, G.M. Walter Shawn journalist, publisher
Buckland, Michael Keeble librarian, educator
Budinger, Thomas Francis radiologist, educator
Budnitz, Robert Jay nuclear scientist
Buell, Evangeline Canonizado advocate
Buxbaum, Richard M. lawyer, educator
Byron, Don musician, composer
Cairns, Elton James chemical engineering professor, consultant
Calendar, Richard Lane biochemistry educator
Callenbach, Ernest retired writer, editor
Campbell, Tom law and business professor, former dean, congressman
Campion, Edmund Joseph composer, educator
Cantor, Rusty Sumner artist
Cardwell, Kenneth Harvey architect, educator
Caron, David Dennis lawyer, educator
Casida, John Edward toxicology and entomology professor
Cerny, Joseph III chemistry professor, retired dean, director
Chatterjee, Sourav statistician, educator
Chen, Lu neurobiologist, biology professor
Chetin, Helen Campbell writer
Chew, Geoffrey Foucar physicist
Chiang, John Chun Hong science educator
Chihara, Charles Seiyo philosophy educator
Chirurg, James Thomas financial holding company executive
Choper, Jesse Herbert law educator, dean
Chorin, Alexandre Joel mathematician, educator
Christ, F. Michael mathematics professor
Chua, Leon O. electrical engineering and computer science educator
Chytry, Josef V. humanities educator
Clarke, John physics professor
Cohen, Lawrence anthropologist, writer
Collier, David political science professor
Concus, Paul mathematician, educator
Costa, Gustavo Italian studies scholar
Daftari, Inder Krishen physicist, researcher
Day, Lucille Lang museum administrator, educator, writer
Diamond, Marian Cleeves neuroscientist, educator
Dornfeld, David Alan engineering educator
Dowall, David Edmund social sciences educator
Dudley, Anna Carol singer, voice educator
Dunlop, Neil computer scientist, department chairman
Dynes, Robert C. physics professor, former academic administrator
Eisenbud, David mathematics professor
Ennals, Robert J. research scientist
Enoch, Jay Martin optometrist, research scientist, educator
Fabe, Marilyn film arts educator
Firestone, Richard B. nuclear scientist, researcher
Fleiszig, Suzanne Mariane Janete optometry educator
Fleming, Graham Richard chemistry educator
Fowler, Thomas Kenneth physicist
Fréchet, Jean chemistry professor
Frede, Dorothea Aline philosopher, educator
Frei, Heinz Markus research scientist
Friedland, Gerald computer scientist, researcher
Fuerstenau, Douglas Winston mineral engineering educator
Fung, Inez Y. science educator
Gaillard, Mary Katharine physicist, educator
Garrison, William Louis civil engineering educator
Genn, Nancy artist
Gilbert, Neil Robin social work educator, writer, consultant
Gillespie, Rosemary science professor, museum director
Ginger, Ann Fagan lawyer
Glaser, Donald Arthur physicist
Gluss, Brian mathematician, statistician, engineer, systems expert
Goldberg, Evgueni computer scientist
Goldhaber, Gerson astrophysicist, researcher
Gombocz, Erich Alfred biochemist
Gray, Paul Russell academic administrator, electrical engineering educator
Green, David nonprofit organization administrator
Grigoropoulos, Costas mechanical engineering educator
Grossman, Bonnie art gallery director
Grossman, Elmer Roy pediatrician
Gumbs, Pam pharmacist
Hakansson, Nils Hemming economist, educator
Halbach, Edward Christian, Jr. law educator
Haley, George Patrick lawyer
Hall, Bronwyn Hughes economics educator
Haller, Eugene Ernest materials scientist, educator
Harris, Michael Gene optometrist, lawyer, educator
Hartman, Robert Leroy artist, educator
Hartshorne, Robert (Robin Hartshorne) mathematics professor
Hasegawa, Yoko educator
Hass, Robert Louis poet, literature educator
Hearst, John Eugene retired chemistry professor, consultant, researcher
Heathcock, Clayton Howell chemistry educator, researcher
Helson, Henry Berge publisher, retired educator
Herr, Richard history professor
Hertelendy, Paul critic, writer, poet
Higgins, Paul Andrew Twistington research scientist
Hinshaw, Stephen P. psychology professor, department chairman
Hoffman, Darleane Christian chemistry professor
Hollinger, David Albert historian, educator
Hoskins, Roger Allen geneticist
Hritonenko, Victoria microbiologist
Hsu, Chieh Su applied mechanics engineering educator, researcher
Hu, Chenming engineering educator
Ivey, Susan Lee health services researcher, educator
Jackson, J(ohn) David physicist, researcher
Janmohmed, Abdul Raheman language educator
Javey, Ali engineering educator
Jones, Vaughan Frederick Randal mathematician, educator
Joyce, Rosemary Alexandria anthropology educator, department chairman
Kadish, Sanford Harold law educator
Kane, Sharad Ramchandra retired physicist
Karabel, Jerome Bernard sociologist, educator
Karp, Richard Manning computer science educator
Kastenberg, William Edward engineering professor, former academic administrator
Kay, Herma Hill law educator
Kay, Paul de Young linguist
Keasling, Jay D. chemistry professor, research scientist
Kerth, Leroy T. physics professor
Kindblad, Nina Claire educational therapist
King, Cary Judson III chemical engineer, educator, academic administrator
King, Nicole molecular biologist, educator
Kirch, Patrick Vinton anthropology educator, archaeologist
Kirz, Janos physicist
Klaus, Peggy Louise consultant, communication and leadership coach
Klein, Spencer Robert physicist
Klinman, Judith Pollock biochemist, educator
Kluger, Richard writer, editor
Knox, Helene Margrethe poet, editor
Ko, Seung Hwan research scientist
Kohwi-Shigematsu, Terumi research scientist
Kremen, Claire conservation biologist, educator
Kunanbaeva, Alma B. history educator
Kuriyan, John science educator, researcher
Kurtzman, Ralph Harold, Jr. biochemist, researcher, consultant
Lakoff, George linguistics professor
Lee, Ronald Demos demographer, economist, educator
Lee, Yuan Tseh retired chemistry professor
Leitmann, George mechanical engineer, educator
Leonard, Thomas C. librarian, dean
Lesser, Wendy editor, writer, consultant
Lester, William Alexander, Jr. chemist, educator
Letiche, John Marion economist, educator
Levine, Michael Steven science educator
Lewis, Edwin Reynolds biomedical engineering educator, academic administrator
Lidicker, William Zander, Jr. zoologist, educator
Ligon, Ethan Andrew agricultural studies educator
Linn, Marcia Cyrog education educator
Linn, Stuart Michael biochemist, educator
Lipps, Jere Henry biology and geology professor
Litwack, Leon Frank historian, retired educator
Lloyd, Elisabeth Anne philosophy educator
Ma, Fai mechanical engineering educator
Ma, L. Eve Armentrout television producer, director, educator
Majumdar, Arunava mechanical engineer, educator
Mandelstam, Stanley physicist
Manga, Michael earth science educator, geophysicist
Marcy, Geoffrey W. astronomer, physicist, educator
Markowitz, Samuel Solomon chemistry professor
Marletta, Michael A. biochemistry educator, researcher
Maslach, Christina psychology professor
Matsumura, Vera Yoshi pianist
McFadden, Daniel Little economist, educator
McKenzie, Jean Hazel academic librarian
McLaughlin, Sylvia Cranmer volunteer, environmentalist
McNulty, John Kent lawyer, educator
McPhail-Geist, Karin Ruth secondary school educator, musician
Meador, Ross DeShong lawyer
Meza, Juan C. mathematician, computer scientist
Middlekauff, Robert Lawrence historian, educator, academic administrator
Miller, William Hughes theoretical chemist, educator
Mitra, Mautusi biologist
Miyasaki, George Joji artist
Monismith, Carl Leroy civil engineering educator
Montgomery, Mike men's college basketball coach
Moore, C. Bradley chemistry professor
Moore, Calvin C. mathematics professor, academic administrator
Moran, Rachel law educator
Morris, John William, Jr. metallurgy educator
Moskowitz, Joel M. psychologist, researcher
Muir, William Ker, Jr. political science professor
Muller, Richard Stephen electrical engineer, educator
Murgia, Charles E. retired classicist
Myers, Miles Alvin educational association administrator, researcher
Nader, Laura anthropologist, educator
Nemeth, Charlan Jeanne psychology educator
Norgaard, Richard Bruce ecological economist, educator, consultant
Odermatt, Diana B. development consultant
Onishi, Lisa chemical engineer, researcher
Orbison, James Archer, Jr. cardiologist, surgeon
Ott, David Michael engineering company executive
Pagni, Patrick John mechanical engineering science educator, safety engineer, researcher
Palmer, Stephen E. psychology professor
Partridge, Loren Wayne art historian, educator
Perlmutter, Saul astrophysicist, educator
Perry, Dale Lynn chemist
Petiet, Carole Anne psychologist
Pigford, Thomas Harrington nuclear engineering educator
Pines, Alexander chemistry educator, researcher, consultant
Pister, Karl Stark engineering educator
Polak, Elijah engineering educator, computer scientist
Pollan, Michael author, journalist, professor
Powell, James L. economics professor
Power, Mary Eleanor biology professor
Prausnitz, John Michael chemical engineer, educator
Pugsley, Michael Kenneth cardiac pharmacologist, research scientist
Purcell, Alexander Holmes entomologist, educator
Quigley, John Michael economist, educator
Quinn, Nigel William Trevelyan research scientist
Raphael, Steven P. dean, political science professor
Rasmussen, John Oscar nuclear research scientist
Rauch, Irmengard linguist, educator
Rausser, Gordon C(lyde) agricultural and resource economics educator
Raymond, Kenneth Norman chemistry professor, researcher
Reich, Robert Bernard political economics educator, former United States Secretary of Labor
Reid, Frances Evelyn Kroll freelance/self-employed cinematographer, film director, communications executive
Reiman, Amanda E. social sciences educator
Remer, Lillian Gladys public health researcher
Rex, Walter Edwin III humanities educator
Rhodes, John Lewis mathematics professor
Richards, Mark A. dean, earth and planetary science professor
Richmond, Hugh Macrae English language educator
Rine, Jasper geneticist, educator
Ring, Bonnie psychologist, consultant, priest
Rippe, Lynn E. portfolio manager
Ritchie, Robert Oliver materials science educator, department chairman
Romanowicz, Barbara geology and geophysics professor
Romer, David economics professor
Rosenthal, Bernard Michael small business owner
Rundall, Thomas Gene medical educator
Ruzer, Lev Solomon lab administrator, researcher
Sadoulet, Elisabeth economics professor
Saraph, Prasad Vaman research scientist, industrial engineer
Sastry, Sosale Shankara electrical engineer, computer scientist, dean, educator
Scheiber, Harry N. law educator, historian
Schekman, Randy W. molecular biology administrator, biochemist
Schoenfeld, Alan Henry mathematics education professor, researcher
Scotchmer, Suzanne Andersen economics professor
Scott, Eugenie Carol science foundation director, anthropologist
Seil, Fredrick John retired neuroscientist
Seligman, Brad lawyer
Selz, Peter Howard art historian, educator
Sen, Koushik science educator
Séquin, Carlo H. computer science educator
Sessler, Andrew Marienhoff physicist
Shaheen, Susan Alison research faculty
Shannon, Thomas Frederic German language educator
Shugart, Howard Alan physicist, researcher
Sikder, Abdur R. information technology executive, director
Simon, Horst D. computer scientist
Simpson, David William artist, educator
Sinclair, Alistair science educator, researcher
Slezkine, Yuri history professor
Smith, Alan Jay computer science educator, consultant
Smith, Otto J. M. electrical engineering educator
Smolensky, Eugene economics professor
Smoot, George Fitzgerald III astrophysicist
Somorjai, Gabor Arpad chemist, educator
Spiller, Pablo Tomas economics and public utilities educator
Stagaman, David John priest, theology educator
Stapp, Henry Pierce physicist
Staubus, George Joseph finance educator
Steigmann, David John professor
Steiner, Herbert Max physics professor
Sternberg, Hilgard O'Reilly geographer, educator
Stoller, Claude architect
Strauss, Herbert Leopold chemistry professor
Sulloway, Frank Jones social sciences educator, historian
Susskind, Teresa Gabriel publishing executive
Tansman, Alan language educator
Taylor, John Lockhart retired municipal official
Teeguarden, Dennis Earl forest economist, educator
Tempelis, Constantine Harry immunologist, educator
Thompson, Anthony Wayne metallurgist, educator, consultant
Thorner, Jeremy W. biology professor
Tirrell, Matthew V. engineering educator, department chairman
Tjian, Robert Tse Nan biochemistry educator, medical institution administrator
Townes, Charles Hard physics professor
Traynor, J. Michael retired lawyer
Trilling, George Henry physicist, researcher
Valentine, James William paleontologist, educator, writer
Varian, Hal Ronald economics professor
Veklerov, Eugene mathematician, computer scientist, educator
Vojta, Paul Alan mathematics professor
Wake, Marvalee Hendricks biology professor
Waters, Alice L. executive chef, restaurant owner, writer
Weir, Margaret sociologist, political science professor
Westheimer, Gerald optometrist, educator
Whaley, Katharine Birgitta chemistry professor
White, Richard Manning electrical engineering educator
Wieczorek, John Richard application developer, systems analyst
Wiegel, Robert Louis consulting engineering executive
Wilensky, Harold L. political science professor, sociologist, researcher
Williamson, Oliver Eaton business economics and law professor
Wilt, Fred biology professor
Winkelstein, Warren, Jr. physician, educator
Wiser, Ryan research scientist
Wolf, Joseph Albert mathematician, educator
Wolfinger, Raymond Edwin retired political science professor
Wolfram, Charles William law educator
Woodhouse, Thomas Edwin lawyer, trust company administrator
Worrell, Frank Clayton psychology professor
Wunderer, Cornelia Beatrix aerospace scientist
Yang, Peidong material science researcher
Yeung, Ronald Wai-Chun engineering educator, researcher
Yoo, John Choon law educator, former federal agency administrator
Yu, Bin statistician, educator
Zhang, Hui researcher
Zimring, Franklin E. lawyer, educator
Zwerdling, Alex language educator

Beverly Hills

Abrams, J.J. (Jeffrey Jacob Abrams) television producer, scriptwriter
Adams, Amy (Amanda Jessica Adams) actress
Adamson, Andrew film producer, film director, scriptwriter
Affleck, Casey actor
Ahmanson, Howard F., Jr. philanthropist
Alba, Jessica actress
Alberghetti, Adriana literary agent
Allen, Joan actress
Allen, Ted television personality
Allen, Tim (Timothy Allen Dick) actor, comedian
Alter, Gary plastic and reconstructive surgeon, urologist
Ambrose, Lauren (Lauren Anne D'Ambruoso) actress
Amron, David M. plastic surgeon
Anderson, Loni Kaye actress
Anderson, Paul Thomas film director, film producer, scriptwriter
Anderson, Wes (Wesley Wales Anderson) film director
Apatow, Judd scriptwriter, television and film producer
Arnold, Tom actor, comedian, television producer
Arquette, David actor
Azaria, Hank actor
Bacon, Kevin actor
Badgley, Penn actor
Baldwin, William actor
Bale, Christian actor
Ball, Alan screenwriter
Bao, Katherine Sung pediatric cardiologist
Baron Cohen, Sacha (Ali G, Borat) actor, comedian
Barrymore, Drew actress
Bartkowiak, Andrzej cinematographer
Basinger, Kim (Kimila Ann Basinger) actress
Bay, Michael Benjamin film director
Bell, Zoë stunt-woman, actress
Benjamin, Andre Lauren (Dre, André 3000) vocalist, actor
Berger, Adam Internet company executive
Bergman, Nancy Palm real estate investment company executive
Biel, Jessica actress, model
Bierko, Craig actor
Billick, Brian Harold sportscaster, former professional football coach
Black, Jack (Thomas Black) actor
Blanchett, Cate (Catherine Elise Blanchett) actress
Blumenfeld, Eli lawyer
Bonham-Carter, Helena actress
Bordy, Michael Jeffrey lawyer
Bosworth, Kate actress
Breslin, Abigail Kathleen actress
Brockovich-Ellis, Erin legal researcher
Broderick, Matthew actor
Brody, Adam Jared actor
Brokaw, Norman Robert talent agency executive
Brolin, Josh actor
Brown, Paul J. travel company executive
Burnett, Carol actress, comedienne, singer
Burns, Marvin Gerald lawyer
Buscemi, Steve actor
Caliendo, Frank comedian, actor
Carrere, Tia (Althea Rae Duhinio Janairo) actress
Castellaneta, Dan (Daniel Louis) actor
Caster, Andrew Ian ophthalmologist
Catz, Boris endocrinologist, educator
Cera, Michael actor
Chan, Jackie actor, film director
Chase, David (David DeCaesare) scriptwriter, television director and producer
Cho, John actor
Christensen, Hayden actor
Clark, Marcia Rachel former prosecutor
Clarkson, Patricia actress
Coates, Anne V. film editor
Cody, Diablo (Brooke Busey-Hunt) scriptwriter
Coen, Ethan film director, writer
Coen, Joel film director, writer
Collette, Toni actress, singer
Congdon, Amanda actress, web video blogger, writer
Connelly, Jennifer actress
Conrad, Lauren Katherine television personality, apparel designer
Cook, Dane (Dane Jeffrey Cook) comedian, actor
Cooper, Bradley actor
Corwin, Stanley Joel book publisher
Covitz, Carl D. investment company executive, federal and state official
Cox Arquette, Courteney actress
Cranston, Bryan Lee actor
Croll, Tony cinematographer, television director
Crudup, Billy actor
Cryer, Jon actor
Crystal, Billy actor, comedian
Cusack, Joan actress
Cusack, John actor
Daly, Carson Jones television personality

Daniels, Jeff *actor, playwright*
Danson, Ted (Edward Bridge Danson III) *actor*
Delany, Dana (Dana Welles Delany) *actress*
Denman, David *actor*
Dennings, Kat (Katherine Litwack) *actress*
Depp, Johnny *actor*
Dern, Bruce MacLeish *actor*
Deschanel, Zooey *actress*
DeVito, Danny Michael *actor, film director*
Diamond, Jason Brett *plastic surgeon*
Diaz, Cameron *actress*
Diaz, John *plastic surgeon*
Diesel, Vin (Mark Vincent) *actor*
Dion, Celine *musician*
Donaldson, Michael Cleaves *lawyer*
Dorff, Stephen *actor*
Duhamel, Josh (Joshua David Duhamel) *actor*
Eastwood, Clint (Clinton Eastwood Jr.) *actor, film director*
Eisner, Michael Dammann *investment and former entertainment company executive*
Elfman, Jenna (Jennifer Mary Butala) *actress*
Elizabeth, Shannon (Shannon Elizabeth Fadal) *actress*
Epps, Omar *actor*
Evans, Louise *investor, retired psychologist*
Fallon, Jimmy Thomas *actor, talk show host*
Faris, Anna May *actress*
Farrow, Mia *actress*
Favreau, Jon *actor, film director, film producer*
Fein, William *ophthalmologist*
Fergie, (Stacy Ann Ferguson) *singer*
Ferguson, Craig *actor, television personality*
Ferrell, Will (John William Ferrell) *actor*
Ferretti, Dante *display designer*
Fey, Tina (Elizabeth Stamatina Fey) *actress*
Fisher, (Donald) Garth *plastic surgeon*
Flaum, Marshall Allen *television producer, writer, director*
Flockhart, Calista *actress*
Fox, Megan Denise *actress*
Foxx, Jamie (Eric Bishop) *actor, comedian*
Fraser, Brendan *actor*
Frey, David S. *cosmetic dentist*
Friedman, Robert Lee *film company executive*
Gabler, Elizabeth Brand *film company executive*
Gaghan, Stephen *scriptwriter, film director*
Gambrell, Thomas Ross *investor, retired physician, surgeon*
Garth, Jennie *actress*
Gassner, Dennis *production designer*
Gershon, Gina *actress*
Goldsmith, Bram *banker*
Gooding, Cuba, Jr. *actor*
Gossett, Louis, Jr. *actor*
Grant, Michael Ernest *educational administrator, management educator*
Graves, Peter *actor*
Grazer, Brian *film company executive*
Greenberg, Jill *photographer*
Greenberg, Richard *playwright*
Greer, Judy Evans *actress*
Grenier, Adrian *actor*
Griffin, Kathy *comedienne, actress*
Groban, Josh *vocalist*
Groening, Matthew (Abram) *writer, cartoonist*
Haley, Jackie Earle *actor, film director*
Harmon, Angie Michelle (Angie Sehorn) *actress*
Harris, Neil Patrick *actor*
Hart, Matthew J. *hotel and recreation executive*
Hartnett, Josh *actor*
Harvey, Steven Patrick (Steve Harvey) *comedian, actor*
Hathaway, Anne *actress*
Hayes, Sean (Sean Patrick Hayes) *actor, comedian*
Heasley, Thomas Allen *composer, musician*
Heaton, Patricia *actress*
Hefter, Lee *chef*
Hewitt, Jennifer Love *actress, singer*
Hill, Chandra *Internet company executive*
Hill, David *broadcast executive*
Hill, Jonah *actor*
Hilton, (William) Barron *hotel executive*
Hines, Cheryl *actress*
Hirsch, Emile *actor*
Hoffman, Dustin *actor*
Hogan, Steven L. *lawyer*
Holmes, Katie (Katherine Noelle Holmes) *actress*
Hooper, Tom *film and television director*
Hopper, Dennis *actor, writer, photographer, film director*
Horvitz, Louis J. *television director*
Howard, Ron *film director*
Hudlin, Reginald Alan *broadcast executive, film director, writer*
Hunter, Holly *actress*
Huston, Anjelica *actress*
Iglesias, Enrique (Enrique Miguel Iglesias Preysler) *singer*
Imperioli, Michael *actor*
Isaacs, Cheryl Boone *marketing executive, consultant*
Jaffe, F. Filmore *lawyer, retired judge*
Jaffe, Stephen Singer *media specialist*
Janney, Allison *actress*
Jarrahnejad, Payam *plastic surgeon*
Jeong, Jae Hoon *physician*
Johnson, Dwayne Douglas (The Rock) *actor, former professional wrestler*
Johnson, Magic (Earvin Johnson Jr.) *professional sports team and development company executive, retired professional basketball player*
Jolie, Angelina *actress*
Jones, Tommy Lee *actor*
Jordan, Glenn *film, television and theater director*
Josephson, Nancy *talent agency executive*
Judd, Ashley *actress*
Kadz, Bruce B. *plastic surgeon*
Kamrava, Michael M. *reproductive endocrinologist*
Kardashian, Kim (Kimberly Noel Kardashian) *apparel retailer, television personality*
Karpman, Harold Lew *cardiologist, educator, writer*
Kattan, Chris Lee *actor*
Kaufman, Charlie *scriptwriter*
Kaufman, Robert *lawyer*
Kavner, Julie *actress*
Keaton, Diane *actress*
Keener, Catherine *actress*
Keitel, Harvey *actor*
Kelly, Minka *actress*
Kenny G, (Kenneth Gorelick) *musician*
Kerkorian, Kirk *investor, former motion picture company executive, consultant*
Khan, Chaka (Yvette Marie Stevens) *singer*
King, Regina *actress*
Klein, Arnold William *dermatologist*
Klein, Frederick Christophe (Frederick Christophe Klein) *actor*
Klum, Heidi *model, actress*
Knight, Theodore Raymond (T.R. Knight) *actor*
Koechner, David *actor*
Kotler, Robert *cosmetic surgeon*
Kozberg, Joanne Corday *public affairs consultant*
Kunis, Mila (Milena Markivna Kunis) *actress*
Kurtz, Swoosie *actress*
Lahti, Christine *actress*
Lake, Ricki (Pamela) *talk show host, actress*
Lane, Diane *actress*
Langella, Frank *actor*
Lansbury, Angela Brigid *actress*
Laurie, Hugh *actor*
Lawrence, Martin *actor, comedian*
LeBlanc, Matt (Matthew Steven LeBlanc) *actor*
Leguizamö, John *actor, comedian*
Leigh, Jennifer Jason (Jennifer Leigh Morrow) *actress*
Lemmons, Kasi *actress, film director*
Leonard, Robert Sean *actor*
Levinson, Barry L. *film director*
Li, Linda (Linda Jian-Yuh Li) *plastic surgeon*
Limato, Edward Frank *talent agent*
Linney, Laura *actress*
Liotta, Ray *actor*
Liu, Lucy *actress*
Lloyd, Christopher *actor*
Lond, Harley Weldon *editor, publishing executive*
Lord, Marjorie *actress*
Loughlin, Lori *actress*
Lovitz, Jon *actor, comedian*
Lowe, Rob *actor*
MacLaine, Shirley *actress*
Madonna, (Madonna Louise Veronica Ciccone) *singer, actress, producer*
Maher, Bill (William Maher Jr.) *television personality and producer, comedian*
Malhotra, Neil *computer game company executive*
Mann, Leslie *actress*
Mann, Michael Kenneth *film director, producer*
Marks, Howard *computer game company executive, information technology executive*
Marshak, Harry *plastic surgeon*
Marshall, Penny (C. Marshall, Carole Penny Marshall) *director, actress*
Martin, Steve *actor, comedian*
McAdams, Rachel *actress*
McCarthy, Jenny *actress*
McDermott, Dylan *actor*
McG, (Joseph McGinty Nichol) *television producer, film director*
Mendelsohn, Daniel *writer, humanities professor*
Mendes, Eva *actress*
Messing, Debra *actress*
Miller, Sienna *actress*
Minnillo, Vanessa Joy *news correspondent*
Moelleken, Brent Roderick Wilfred *plastic surgeon*
Mol, Gretchen *actress*
Moore, Julianne (Julie Anne Smith) *actress*
Moore, Mandy (Amanda Leigh Moore) *actress, singer*
Morgan, Tracy *actor, comedian*
Morton, Samantha *actress*
Mullally, Megan *actress*
Murphy, Brittany *actress*
Myers, Mike *actor, scriptwriter, film producer*
Nassetta, Christopher J. *hotel executive*
Nassif, Paul S. *facial plastic and reconstructive surgeon*
Newman, Jeanne *lawyer*
Nimoy, Leonard *actor, director*
Nixon, Cynthia *actress*
Norton, Edward *actor*
Novak, Maximillian Erwin *retired English literature professor*
Oldman, Gary *actor*
Olmos, Edward James *actor*
Omidi, Michael M. *plastic surgeon*
Opri, Debra Ann *lawyer*
Ordon, Andrew Paul (Drew Ordon) *plastic surgeon*
Ormond, Julia *actress*
Ortega, Kenny *television director, choreographer*
Pacino, Al (Alfredo James Pacino) *actor*
Pantoliano, Joe *actor*
Parker, Mary-Louise *actress*
Parker, Sarah Jessica *actress*
Patric, Jason *actor*
Patton, Antwan Andre (Big Boi) *rap artist, singer*
Paxton, Bill *actor, film director*
Peet, Amanda *actress*
Perlman, Jon Arthur *plastic surgeon*
Perlman, Ron (Ronald Francis Perlman) *actor*
Perrineau, Harold *actor*
Pezzullo, Ralph Michael *writer, playwright*
Pfeiffer, Michelle *actress*
Phillippe, Ryan *actor*
Pinkett-Smith, Jada *actress*
Pitt, Brad *actor*
Platt, Oliver *actor*
Plummer, Christopher (Arthur Plummer) *actor*
Poehler, Amy *comedienne, actress*
Polanski, Roman *film director, writer, actor*
Posey, Parker *actress*
Prinze, Freddie, Jr. *actor*
Procter, Emily Mallory *actress*
Pulliam, Keshia Knight *actress*
Quaid, Dennis *actor*
Quinn, Patricia K. *international television consultant, co-producer*
Ramer, Bruce M. *lawyer*
Rapino, Michael *music company executive*
Reiner, Carl *director, actor, writer*
Reiner, Rob *film director, actor*
Rey, Robert M. *plastic surgeon*
Reynolds, Burt *actor, film director*
Reynolds, Ryan Rodney *actor*
Rhames, Ving (Irving) *actor*
Rhys Meyers, Jonathan *actor*
Ricci, Christina *actress*
Richter, Andy *actor*
Rimes, LeAnn *country music singer*
Rinsch, Maryann Elizabeth *occupational therapist*
Rivers, Joan (Joan Alexandra Molinsky) *entertainer*
Rose, Jessica Lee *actress*
Rosen, Richard A. (RicK Rosen) *agent*
Ross, Tracee Ellis (Tracee Joy Silberstein) *actress, model, fashion editor*
Rossellini, Isabella *actress, model*
Roth, Eric *screenwriter*
Rudd, Paul *actor*
Rudolph, Maya *actress, comedienne*
Ruffalo, Mark *actor*
Rush, Geoffrey *actor*
Russell, Keri *actress*
Ryder, Winona (Winona Laura Horowitz) *actress*
Salz, James Joseph *medical association administrator*
Samberg, Andy *actor*
Sandler, Adam *actor*
Sands, Kevin B. *cosmetic dentist*
Schaff, Manya *foundation administrator*
Schiff, Gunther Hans *lawyer*
Schneider, Charles Ivan *newspaper executive*
Schulian, John (Nielsen Schulian) *screenwriter, author*
Scott, Ridley *film director*
Seacrest, Ryan (Ryan John Seacrest) *television and radio personality, entrepreneur*
Sedgwick, Kyra *actress*
Segel, Jason Jordan *actor*
Seidel, Joan Broude *securities dealer, investment advisor*
Sevigny, Chloë *actress*
Shanley, John Patrick *playwright, screenwriter*
Sherak, Thomas Mitchell (Tom Sherak) *motion picture association executive*
Sherman, Robert B(ernard) *composer, lyricist, screenwriter*
Sherwood, (Karen) Kehela *broadcast executive*
Short, Martin *actor, comedian, film critic*
Shue, Elisabeth *actress*
Siciliano, Rocco Carmine *cultural institute executive*
Silverman, Sarah *comedian, actress*
Simmons, Gene (Chaim Witz, Gene Klein) *musician*
Simmons, J.K. (Jonathan Kimble Simmons) *actor*
Sinise, Gary *actor*
Siragusa, Tony (Anthony Siragusa) *sportscaster, retired professional football player*
Slade, Bernard *playwright*
Smith, Jaclyn *actress*
Smith, Will (Willard Christopher Smith Jr.) *actor, film producer*
Smith, Yeardley *actress*
Sobelle, Richard E. *lawyer*
Sommers, Stephen *film director, producer, scriptwriter*
Sonnenfeld, Barry *director, cinematographer*
Sorvino, Paul *actor*
Spade, David (David Wayne Spade) *actor*
Spelling, Tori (Victoria Davey Spelling) *actress*
Stamos, John *actor*
Steenburgen, Mary *actress*
Stefani, Gwen Renee *singer*
Stern, Leonard Bernard *television and motion picture production company executive*
Stern, Sandor *film director, writer*
Stewart, Kristen Jaymes *actress*
Stewart, Patrick *actor*
Strauss, Ricky *film company executive, producer*
Sutherland, Kiefer *actor*
Swank, Hilary *actress*
Swayze, Patrick *actor, dancer*
Switzer, Barry *sportscaster, retired professional football coach*
Sykes, Wanda *comedienne, actress*
Symone, Raven (Raven-Symoné Christina Pearman) *actress, singer*
Tabak, Steven William *cardiologist*
Tambor, Jeffrey *actor, theater director, educator*
Tamkin, Curtis Sloane *real estate development company executive*
Tatum, Channing *actor*
Taylor, Christine *actress*
Theron, Charlize *actress*
Thirlby, Olivia *actress*
Thompson, Emma *actress*
Tierney, Maura *actress*
Torn, Rip (Elmore Rual Torn Jr.) *actor, theater director*
Traugott, Peter S. *television producer, broadcast executive*
Travolta, John *actor*
Tucci, Stanley *actor*
Turner, Kathleen *actress*
Tyler, Liv *actress*
Underwood, Blair *actor, television producer*
Van Sant, Gus (Gus Greene Van Sant Jr.) *film director*
Van Zandt, Steven *actor, musician, radio personality*
Vardalos, Nia *actress, screenwriter*
Vaughn, Vince *actor*
Ventimiglia, Milo Anthony *actor*
Wachowski, Andy *film director*
Wachowski, Larry *film director*
Walker, William Tidd, Jr. *investment banker*
Weaver, Sigourney (Susan Alexandra Weaver) *actress*
Wellins, Cori *literary agent*
Whaley, Frank *actor*
White, Betty *actress, comedienne*
White, Meg(an) (Martha) *musician, vocalist*
Whitford, Bradley *actor*
Wiczyk, Modi *media company executive*
Wilkinson, Tom *actor*
Wilson, Owen *actor*
Winthrop, John *wines and spirits company executive*
Witt, Alicia *actress*
Wolper, David Lloyd *motion picture and television executive*
Woods, James *actor*
Yuan, Robin Tsu-Wang *plastic surgeon*
Zahn, Steve *actor*

Big Bear Lake
Mix, Jill Kaye *secondary school educator, artist*

Big Pine
Reynaud-Roepke, Suzanne *psychologist*

Bishop
Klinger, Robert Charles *ecologist*

Bloomington
Lawrence, William, Jr. *retired elementary school educator*
Ojo-Amaize, Emmanuel Ade *immunologist*

Blythe
Wells, James Wayne *retired secondary school educator*

Bodega Bay
Clegg, James Standish *physiologist, biochemist, educator*
Sorensen, Linda *lawyer*

Bolinas
Harris, Paul *sculptor*

Bonita
Deane, Debbe *psychologist, journalist, editor, consultant*

Borrego Springs
Strong, John Oliver *plastic surgeon, educator*

Brawley
Kinder, Joseph Donald *retired principal*

Brea
Hewitt, Hugh *editor, writer, radio talk show host*
Oh, Tai Keun *business educator, consultant*
Painchaud, Phillip Andre *metrologist*
Vargas, Louis F. *marketing executive, author, speaker*

Brentwood
Albers, Lucia Berta *land developer*

Brisbane
Daniels, Caroline *information services executive*

Buellton
Porter, Bruce Jackman *computer engineer, application developer, portfolio manager, civil engineer*

Burbank
Akil, Mara Brock *television writer and producer*
Aviv, Oren R. *film company executive*
Ballew, Pat *elementary school educator*
Beard, Frank *musician*
Berwick, Frances *broadcast executive*
Bird, Andy *film company executive*
Bower, Richard James *minister*
Branch, Michelle (Michelle Jaquet DeSevren Branch) *musician*
Brandis, Bernardine *lawyer*
Braverman, Alan N. *lawyer*
Bublé, Michael *singer*
Caouette, David Paul *public relations executive*
Chase, Debra Martin *film producer*
Clapton, Eric *musician, singer*
Cohen, Polly *film company executive*
Cook, Richard W. (Dick Cook) *film company executive*
DeGeneres, Ellen Lee *actress, comedienne, talk show host*
Diggs, Taye (Scott Diggs) *actor*
Dreyfuss, Richard Stephan *actor*
Facinelli, Peter *actor*
Fishburne, Laurence *actor*
Fleishman, Susan Nahley *entertainment company executive*
Franco, James *actor*
Gibbons, Billy F. *musician*
Glavin, Edward P. *television producer*
Hill, Dusty *musician*
Horn, Alan F. *film company executive*
Howard, James Newton *composer*
Iger, Bob (Robert Allen Iger) *entertainment company executive*
Jonas, Joseph Adam *singer*
Jonas, Kevin (Paul Kevin Jonas II) *singer*
Jonas, Nicholas Jerry *singer, actor*
Joseff, Joan Castle *manufacturing executive*
Jovovich, Milla (Natasha Militza Jovovich) *model, actress*
Kroll, Sue (Susan A. Kroll) *film company executive*
Kwan-Rubinek, Veronika *broadcast executive*
Lakshmi, Padma *actress, television host, model*
Lamas, Lorenzo *actor, director*
Lang, K. D. (Katherine Dawn Lang) *country music singer, composer*
Leno, Jay (James Douglas Muir Leno) *talk show host, comedian, writer*
Lindelof, Damon Laurence *television producer, scriptwriter*
Marinelli, Janice *broadcast executive*
Matlin, Marlee Beth *actress*
McGraw, Tim *country music singer*
McLoughlin, Hilary Estey *broadcast executive*
McPherson, Stephen *broadcast executive*
Meyer, Barry Michael *motion picture executive*
Michel, Donald Charles *editor*
Millan, Cesar *television personality*
Miller, Clifford Albert *merchant banker*
Moore, Ryan Natalie *creative director*
Murphy, Peter E. *corporate financial executive*
Newman, Thomas *composer*
Nielsen, Kenneth Ray *academic administrator*
Ostroff, Dawn T. *broadcast executive*
Petty, Tom (Thomas Earl Petty) *musician, composer*

Ponty, Jean-Luc violinist, composer, producer
Rainwater, Carol Jean psychology communication professor
Raulinaitis, Pranas Algis electronics executive, consultant
Rawlinson, Joseph Eli foundation administrator, lawyer
Remini, Leah actress
Renner, Andrew Ihor surgeon
Rhimes, Shonda producer, director, writer
Ringwald, Molly actress
Rivera, Miluka actress, journalist, poet
Robinov, Jeff (Jeffrey Stephen Robinov) film company executive
Roth, Peter broadcast executive
Sanz, Alejandro (Alejandro Sánchez Pizarro) singer
Schlaerth, John Burr oncologist, gynecologist
Shuler, Dennis W. entertainment company executive
Silver, Joel film producer
Staggs, Thomas O. entertainment company executive
Stewart, Rod (Roderick David Stewart) singer
Sweeney, Anne M. cable television company executive
Tarrant, Alison broadcast executive, marketing professional
Weiskopf, Wanda mezzo soprano, writer, poet
Wonder, Stevie (Steveland Hardaway Judkins, Stevland Morris) musician
Zhao, Chonghao neurologist, educator
Zimmer, Hans Florian composer
Zucker, Jeffrey A. broadcast executive

Burlingame
Anders, George Charles journalist, writer
Corcoran, Elizabeth Anne journalist
Cotchett, Joseph Winters lawyer, writer
McCloskey, Pete (Paul Norton McCloskey Jr.) lawyer, former congressman
Rosenfield, Lorne King plastic surgeon
Schwantes, Robert Sidney international relations executive
Villavicencio, José Antonio secondary school educator
Wright, Ian M. automotive executive, electrical engineer

Calabasas
Asscher, Jean-Claude electronics executive
Bhatnagar, Atul telecommunications industry executive
Desoer, Barbara Jean mortgage company executive
Dreier, R. Chad (Robert Chad Dreier) construction and mortgage company executive
Geckle, Timothy J. lawyer
Ginsberg, Errol telecommunications industry executive
Goldfield, Emily Dawson finance company executive, artist
Hawkins, John N. education educator, writer
McLaughlin, Thomas Keith diversified financial services company executive
Nicholson, Larry T. construction executive
Samuels, Sandor Eli lawyer, diversified financial services company executive
Sieracki, Eric P. diversified financial services company executive
Tarr, Ralph William lawyer, former federal government official
van Schoonenberg, Robert G. lawyer, consumer products company executive

California City
Flakes, Susan playwright, screenwriter, non-fiction writer, hotel reviewer, theater director

Calimesa
Zimmermann, Muriel Madeline retired biology professor

Calistoga
Savage, Michael John Kirkness oil industry, performing arts company executive and winegrower

Camarillo
Bowman, Bruce art educator
Bryan, Bob Charles professional tennis player
Bryan, Mike Carl professional tennis player
Cobb, Shirley Ann Dodson public relations consultant, journalist
David, Marie M. pre-school educator
Epperson, Stuart W. religious raido broadcaster
Gigas, Gunter George retired physicist, physician
Mihalopoulos, Catherine Elizabeth art educator
Moffett, Kenneth Lee superintendent
Rush, Richard R. academic administrator
Smith, David Michael financial planner
Sullivan, Michael Evan investment company executive
Truman, Ruth Dixon administrator, writer, lecturer, consultant
Wakelee, Daniel William academic administrator

Cambria
Gray, Thomas Stephen writer
Harden, Marvin artist, educator
Morse, Richard Jay human resources and organizational development specialist, consultant

Campbell
Browne, Sylvia (Sylvia Shoemaker) spiritual medium, writer
Levy, Salomon mechanical engineer
Ross, Hugh Courtney electrical engineer
Vincent, David Ridgely financial consultant

Canoga Park
Lederer, Marion Irvine cultural administrator
Taesch, Richard Edmund music educator

Canyon Country
Alvarez, Neisy Virginia physician assistant
Catalani, Richard William forensic specialist, writer
Rivero, Luis Raul aerospace physician, military officer

Canyon Lake
Sparks, Dale Boyd allergist, health facility administrator

Capistrano Beach
Sears, Jim (James M. Sears) pediatrician
Sears, William pediatrician

Capitola
Jackson, Kingsbury Temple educational and financial consultant

Cardiff
Juskalian, Lee J. former government official

Cardiff By The Sea
Epstein, Robert psychologist, consultant

Carlsbad
Benjamin, Theresa Mary retired psychotherapist
Chopra, Deepak preventive medicine physician, writer
Crooke, Stanley Thomas pharmaceutical executive
Farah, Tawfic Elias political scientist, educator
Ghiu, Silvana Melania Stefania process and development engineer
Gillis, Christine Diest-Lorgion retired certified financial planner, stockbroker
Golden, Paula Englander psychology social work and addiction educator, consultant
Hanscom, Eric Alan lawyer
Howard, Robert Staples newspaper publisher
Kauderer, Bernard Marvin retired naval officer, consultant
Kim, Kyehee environmental engineer, consultant
Kizer, Kenneth Wayne physician, executive, educator
Langland, Olaf Elmer retired dental educator
Mezzullo, Louis Albert lawyer
Prakash, Thazha Purathiyath research scientist, chemist
Ritchie, Doris Lee executive secretary
Steele, Charles Glen retired accountant
Stenbit, John Paul former federal agency administrator
Wilson, Donald Grey engineering management consultant
Wollam, Jean Farr retired diplomat

Carmel
Aurner, Robert Ray, II, retail development executive
Barton, Hugh Perry bank executive
Bohannon-Kaplan, Margaret Anne non-profit organization executive, lawyer
Chung, Kyung Cho Korean history specialist, writer, educator
de Vos, Paula Francesca finance company executive, investment advisor, consultant
Dobey, James Kenneth banker
Freed, Sharon Lou retired principal
Hamilton, Lyman Critchfield, Jr. telecommunications industry executive
Hobbs, C. Fredric artist, filmmaker, writer
Jacobs, Ralph, Jr. artist
Koeppel, Gary Merle publishing executive, art gallery owner, writer
Mollman, John Peter publishing executive
Reamy, Michaelin marriage and family therapist, educator, consultant
Smith, Gordon Paul management consultant
Weitzman, Ronald Alfred psychology professor

Carmel Valley
Kasson, James Matthews electronics executive
Wolfe, Maurice Raymond retired museum director, educator

Carmichael
Friedman, Mary Kathleen secondary school educator
Hellmuth, William Frederick economics professor
Ryan, Gretchen Margarete Frieda art educator
Speir, Marcia Ann retired accountant
Throner, Guy Charles, Jr. aerospace engineering executive, scientist, inventor, consultant

Carpinteria
Hansen, Robert William artist, educator
Li, Winston Zai-Yang language educator
Morgan, Alfred Vance management consulting company executive
Rau, Margaret E. writer
Schmidhauser, John Richard retired political science professor, former congressman

Carson
Arena, Bruce professional soccer coach
Beckham, David (Robert Joseph) professional soccer player
Buehlmann, Urs K. engineering educator, researcher
El-Ahraf, Amer M. health facility administrator, educator
Heiser, James S. manufacturing executive
Hirsch, Gilah Yelin artist, writer
Jones, Matthew G. mathematics professor
Mantravadi, Murty V. retired optics scientist
Paige, Dorothy Billiard consultant-academic coach
Palmer, Beverly Blazey psychologist, educator
Siegel, Neil Gilbert computer engineer, consultant
Suchenek, Marek Andrzej computer science educator
Zimmerer, Kathy Louise museum director

Castaic
Holmes, Dale Arthur optics scientist

Castro Valley
Evans, Robert William psychologist, theologian
Morrison, Glenn Leslie minister
Scherrer, Deborah King computer scientist, educational association administrator
West, Doyle Thomas retired music educator
Wycoff, Charles Coleman writer, retired anesthesiologist

Castroville
Rhoades, Mark Matthew risk management consultant, educator

Cathedral City
Berry, Ester Lorée vocational nurse
Jackman, Robert Alan retail executive

Century City
Ward, David Schad scriptwriter, film director

Cerritos
Lee, Jhemon Hom physician
Zhang, Lianfeng chemical engineer

Channel Islands
Steinorth, Christina Enni psychotherapist, author

Chatsworth
Becerra Ibanez Pelliza, Julio C. psychologist, consultant
Gunn, Stanley Veerin retired engineer
Nalbandian, Ruben engineering company executive
Strieby, B. Lorraine artist

Chico
Cummings, Anne Alexandra retired writer
Hornaday, Richard H. artist, retired educator
Jacobs, Douglas Bram law educator, attorney
Livingston, Myran Jay author, film writer, director and producer
Ritter, Dale William obstetrician, gynecologist
Roth, Ronald Lee engineering educator
Smith, Valene Lucy anthropologist, educator
Zingg, Paul Joseph academic administrator

Chino Hills
Fisher, Teresa Marie psychologist, forensic specialist
Lipinsky, Daren H. lawyer
Ofner, William Bernard investor, speechwriter
Wood, Terri Lynn secondary school educator

Chula Vista
Blankfort, Lowell Arnold newspaper publisher
Capehart, Bonnie language educator
Cohen, Elaine Helena pediatrician, cardiologist, educator
Cox, Cheryl Mayor, Chula Vista, California
Hollowell, Daria Mae social sciences educator
Nelson, Carl Alfred author, international business educator, Former Captain USN
Russom, James Rayford minister
Schrauzer, Gerhard Norbert science educator, researcher
Sullivan, Patrick Allen strategic management educator

Citrus Heights
Daves, Sandra Lynn poet, lyricist
Leisey, Donald Eugene learning materials executive

City Of Commerce
Plamann, Alfred A. wholesale distribution executive

City Of Industry
Calderon, Ronald Steven state legislator
Padilla, James G. paralegal
Roski, Edward P., Jr. real estate developer, professional sports team executive

Claremont
Ackerman, Gerald Martin art historian, consultant, author
Alexander, John David, Jr. college administrator
Ansell, Edward Orin lawyer
Atlas, Jay David philosopher, consultant, linguist, educator
Bekendam, Carol Helen psychologist
Benjamin, Beverly Paschke retired education educator
Benjamin, Karl Stanley artist, educator
Bennett, William John (Bill Bennett) radio personality, former United States Secretary of Education
Bettison-Varga, Lori academic administrator, geologist, educator
Blitz, Mark philosopher
Borcherding, Thomas Earl economist
Boucquey, Thierry literature and language professor
Burdekin, Richard Charles Keighley economics professor
Burns, Richard Dean historian, educator, writer
Coleman, Courtney Stafford mathematician, educator
Coleman, Monica Anita theology studies educator
Csikszentmihalyi, Mihaly psychology professor
Davis, Nathaniel humanities educator
Deese, E(thel) Helen retired literature and language professor
Dym, Clive Lionel engineering educator
Ferguson, Cleve Robert lawyer, educator
Forti, William Bell manufacturing executive
Gann, Pamela Brooks academic administrator
Halpern, Diane F. psychology educator, professional association executive
Hansch, Corwin Herman chemistry professor
Henriksen, Melvin mathematician, educator
Hoopes, Laura L Mays biology professor
Huang, Hao H. music educator, department chairman
Jaffa, Harry Victor political philosophy educator emeritus
Johnson, Jerome Linné cardiologist, educator
Keil, Manfred Werner economics professor
Kennedy, Brian T. think-tank executive
Kerchner, Charles Taylor educator
Klawe, Maria Margaret academic administrator, engineering and computer science educator
Kury, Bernard Edward lawyer
Lasswell, Marcia Lee psychologist, educator
Lerner, Jesse filmmaker
Lipman-Blumen, Jean public policy and organizational behavior educator
Lofgren, Charles Augustin historian, educator
Martin, Jay Herbert psychoanalyst, literature professor, political science professor
Martonosi, Susan E. mathematics professor
McKirahan, Richard Duncan classics and philosophy educator
Molinder, John Irving engineering educator, consultant
Monson, James Edward electrical engineer, educator
Moreno, William A. museum director
Moss, Myra Ellen (Myra Moss Rolle) philosophy educator
Myhre, Janet statistician, educator, consultant
Nelson, Mark D. music educator, arts education administrator
Neumann, Harry philosophy educator
O'Kelly, Crystal Kathleen secondary school educator, television producer
Oxtoby, David William academic administrator, chemistry professor
Petropoulos, Jonathan George history professor
Phillips, John Richard engineering educator
Phillips, M. Ian physiologist, educator
Pippenger, Nicholas John mathematician, Computer Scientist Researcher Educator
Platt, Joseph Beaven former college president
Pray, Ralph Emerson metallurgical engineer
Rachlin, Nathalie language educator
Rankaitis, Susan artist
Rossum, Ralph Arthur political science professor
Sanders, James Alvin retired minister, retired religious studies educator
Schellhorn, Henry mathematics professor
Schroerlucke, Leslie Jean music educator
Skandera Trombley, Laura Elise academic administrator, literature educator
Steinmetz, Wayne Edward chemistry educator
Stokes, Anne Dorothy retired educational association administrator
Strauss, Jon Calvert retired academic administrator
Tang, Yao Liang medical educator, researcher, surgeon
Tao, Ran economics professor, researcher
Wachtel, Albert writer, educator
Wall, Helena M. historian, educator
Wheeler, Geraldine Hartshorn historian, writer
Woodress, James Leslie, Jr. language educator
Young, Howard Thomas foreign language educator

Clayton
Bower, Fay Louise academic administrator, nursing educator
Rainey, William Joel lawyer

Clovis
Contreras, Carlos Arturo retired history professor
Engle, Margarita writer, poet
Kawashima, Hope Nozomi musician
Miner, Craig Alan special education educator
Shields, Allan Edwin writer, educator, photographer
Turner, Eugene Andrew manufacturing executive
van der Paardt, Tamara Ann music educator
Von Prince, Kilulu Magdalene retired occupational therapist, sculptor

Coachella
Trover, Ellen Lloyd lawyer, rancher, art dealer

Coalinga
Frame, Ted Ronald lawyer
Tincher, Chris Michael history professor

Colfax
Deaderick, John F. actor, educator

Colma
Papakonstantino, Stacy language educator

Colton
Allen, Blair Hamilton writer, poet, artist, editor, photographer

Colusa
Carter, Jane Foster agricultural industry executive

Compton
Drew, Sharon Lee sociologist
Wang, Charles Ping engineering executive

Concord
Accatino, Steven C. instrumental music educator, orchestra conductor
Amies, Christopher Jude medical products executive
Blair, Virginia Devoto music educator
Borson, Daniel Benjamin lawyer, educator
Broadbent, Amalia Sayo Castillo graphic arts designer
Moyal, Maurice lawyer, former accounting and business law educator
Tkachuk, Andrei engineering company executive
Turnbull, Thomas Leigh social studies educator, secondary school educator
Uremovich, Michael Elliot transportation company executive

Corona
Chambers-Belida, Candace R. radio personality, writer, television producer, educator
Chao, Allen Y. pharmaceutical executive
Everett Nollkamper, Pamela Irene writer, educator
Haynes, Moses Alfred physician
Holt, Chifra dancer, educator, choreographer
Lincoln, Tami Marie art educator
Nolan, Steve Mayor, Corona, California
Silva, A. R. surgeon, educator
White, Joy Mieko retired communications executive
Wood, Brenda Jean pastor, evangelist

Corona Del Mar
Allen, Russell G. lawyer
Britten, Roy John biophysicist
Fabricant, Jill Diane technology company executive

Karson, Burton Lewis *musician, educator*
O'Brien, John William, Jr. *management consultant*
Tobis, Jerome Sanford *physician*
Yeo, Ron *architect*

Coronado
Herman, Stephen Charles *lawyer*
Herring, Charles David *lawyer, educator*
Hubbard, Donald *marine artist, writer*
Mock, David Clinton, Jr. *internist*
Raushenbush, Walter Brandeis *retired law educator*
Sack, Edgar Albert *electronics company executive*
Smith, Albert Cromwell, Jr. *investment company executive, writer*

Corte Madera
Mindel, Laurence Brisker *restauranteur*
Tate, John William *consumer products company executive, former food products executive*

Costa Mesa
Anderson, Jon David *lawyer*
Berkompas, Susan K. *theater director*
Brady, John Patrick, Jr. *electronics educator, consultant*
Caldwell, Courtney Lynn *lawyer, real estate consultant*
Daniels, James Walter *lawyer*
Faridi, Abbas M. *physics professor*
Giannini, Valerio Louis *investment banker*
Guerra, Arnold III *physics professor*
Harley, Halvor Larson *bank executive, lawyer*
Hazewinkel, Van *manufacturing executive*
Jones, H(arold) Gilbert, Jr. *lawyer*
Kiang, Assumpta (Amy Kiang) *brokerage house executive*
Marshall, Ellen Ruth *lawyer*
McCarthy, Mary Ann *counselor, educator*
Mooradian, George T. *lawyer*
Muller, Jerome Kenneth *photographer, art director, editor*
Ortlund, Anne (Elizabeth Anne Ortlund) *writer, musician*
Samet, Jack I. *lawyer*
Schaaf, Douglas Allan *lawyer*
Triggs, Ray Ellis, Jr. *history educator*
Williams, William Corey *theology educator, consultant*

Coto De Caza
Bezar, Gilbert Edward *retired aerospace company executive, volunteer*
Kishel, Patricia Gunter *management consultant, writer*

Cottonwood
Stewart, John Norman *scenic artist*

Covina
Baker, Elenora Frances *retired elementary school educator*
Nguyen, Loc H. *social services administrator*
Paulson, Raymond Arnold *science engineering executive*

Crescent City
Carter, Neville Louis *geophysicist, educator*
Owen, Thomas Sumner *lawyer*

Cromberg
Kolb, Ken Lloyd *writer*

Culver City
Alwash, Mohamad Ali *mathematics professor, researcher*
Arceneaux, Edgar *artist*
Brooks, James L. *film producer, director*
Brooks, Mel *film producer and director, actor, scriptwriter*
Chaffin, Ceán *producer*
Cherry, Debra Lynn *clinical psychologist*
Duncan, Michael Clarke *actor*
Fincher, David *film director and producer*
Gordon, Florence Irene *graphics designer, illustrator*
Grant, Joan Julien *artist*
Jacobs, Betty Jane Lazaroff *communications educator*
Kaufman, Richard Stuart *conductor*
Lee, Ang *film director*
Leve, Alan Donald *electronics executive*
Maltzman, Irving Myron *psychology professor*
Mark, Laurence Maurice *film producer*
Marshall, Garry K. (Garry Kent Marsciarelli) *film producer, director, writer*
Muller, Jenny Helen *physician, psychiatrist*
Netzel, Paul Arthur *fundraising management executive, consultant*
Nicholas, Frederick M. *lawyer*
Ochoa, Ruben *artist*
Pascal, Amy Beth *film company executive*
Phoenix, Joaquin Raphael *actor*
Pierstorff, Erik *biomedical engineer*
Roberts, Virgil Patrick *lawyer, judge*
Simmons, Kimora Lee (Kimora Lee Perkins) *apparel designer, television personality, model*
Taylor, Regina *actress*
Thomas, Geraldine Hoge *elementary school educator*
Van Galder, Valerie *marketing executive*
Vollack, Lia *broadcast executive*
Wick, Douglas *producer*

Cupertino
Bernhardt, Richard Bruce *electronic company executive*
Bregman, Mark *information technology executive*
Cook, Timothy D. *computer company executive*
Cooperman, Daniel *computer company executive, lawyer*
Courville, Arthur F. *lawyer*
DeSouza, Francis *software company executive*
Fadell, Tony (Anthony M. Fadell) *computer company executive*
Fletcher, Homer Lee *librarian*
Gong, Yihong *research and development company manager*
Haskell, Barry Geoffry *computer engineer, researcher*
Ive, Jonathan *information technology executive, product designer*
Jelinch, Frank Anthony *lawyer*
Jobs, Steve (Steven Paul Jobs) *computer company executive*
Johnson, Ron *computer company executive*
Knapp, George Griff Prather *retired insurance executive*
Merdinger, Charles John *civil engineer, educator, military officer, academic administrator*
Mueller, Gerhard Gottlob *retired financial accounting standard setter, educator*
Oppenheimer, Peter *computer company executive*
Papermaster, Mark D. *computer company executive*
Patton, Marilyn Dilworth *english and literature educator*
Podolny, Joel M. *academic administrator, management educator, former dean*
Salem, Enrique T. *information technology executive*
Schiller, Philip W. *computer company executive*
Serlet, Bertrand *information technology executive*
Svalya, Phillip Gordon *lawyer*
Tamaddon, Sina *information technology executive*
Tetsuro, Motoyama *electronics engineer*
Thompson, John Wendell *information technology executive*
Wildman, Iris J. *retired law librarian*

Cypress
Cully, Joseph Andrew *hazard substance scientist*
Guzman, Indira Rita *information science educator, researcher*
Hu, Houchun Harry *research scientist*
Mosqueda-Ponce, Therese *counselor, professor*
Olschwang, Alan Paul *lawyer, crossword and variety puzzle author*

Daly City
Batlin, Robert Alfred *retired newspaper editor*
Dunlap, Robert William *internist, cardiologist, educator*
Kennedy, Gwendolyn Debra *artist, scriptwriter, playwright*
Mobley, Clarence Fowler *retired civil engineer*
So, Samuel Cho Yee *therapeutic radiological physicist, physician*

Dana Point
Blacketer, James Richard *artist*
Fisher, Delbert Arthur *pediatric endocrinologist, educator, retired health facility administrator*
Kramer, Kathryn Leslie *film director, educator*
Mallory, Frank Linus *lawyer*
Walker, Doris Isaak *writer, historian, educator*

Danville
Bergsten, James Robert *computer technology architect*
Candland, D. Stuart *lawyer*
Cross, Christopher T. *educational association administrator, consultant*
Gold, Anne Marie *library consultant*
Harks, Helene Louise *elementary school educator*
Monheit, Molly Jane *artist*
Pescatore, Christopher *cosmetic dentist*
Winer, David M. *computer software company executive, software developer, blogger*

Darwin
Palazzo, Robert Paul *lawyer, accountant*

Davis
Alston, Julian Mark *agricultural studies educator*
Ardans, Alexander Andrew *veterinarian, educator, lab administrator*
Barbour, Michael G(eorge) *botanist, educator, ecologist, consultant*
Biggart, Nicole Woolsey *management educator, former dean*
Blodgett, Harriet *retired language educator*
Bodine, Sue Carol *medical educator*
Brault, Aaron Cole *science educator*
Bruch, Carol Sophie *law educator*
Bryant, Brenda K. *psychologist, educator*
Brynda, Marcin Artur *chemist, researcher*
Bunch, Richard Alan *writer, educator, poet, philosopher*
Burtis, Kenneth C. *biochemist, educator*
Cahill, Thomas Andrew *physicist, researcher*
Calderon de la Barca Sanchez, Manuel *physicist, educator*
Cameron, A. Colin *economics professor*
Cardiff, Robert Darrell *pathology educator*
Carroll, Patrick Eamonn *social sciences educator*
Cech, Joseph J., Jr. *biology professor*
Chancellor, William Joseph *agricultural engineering educator*
Chaudhari, Abhijit Jayawant *research scientist*
Cheney, James Addison *civil engineering educator*
Choi, Hongsoo *research scientist*
Cole, Kimberly Ree *music educator, musician*
Conn, Eric Edward *plant biochemist*
Coss, Richard Gerrit *psychology professor*
Currall, Steven C. *dean, management educator*
Day, Howard Wilman *geology educator*
Dehesh, Katayoon *science educator*
Enders, Allen Coffin *anatomy educator*
Engebrecht, JoAnne *biology professor, department chairman*
Epstein, Emanuel *plant physiologist*
Fadley, Charles Sherwood *research scientist, educator*
Fannjiang, Albert *mathematician, educator*
Feeney, Floyd Fulton *law educator*
Fuhs, G(eorg) Wolfgang *environmental research manager*
Gardner, Murray Briggs *pathologist, educator*
Gates, Bruce Clark *chemical engineer, educator*
Groth, Alexander Jacob *political science professor*
Gubler, Walter Douglas *plant pathologist, educator*
Halsted, Charles Hopkinson *internist*
Hess, Charles Edward *environmental horticulture educator*
Hoffman, Michael Jerome *humanities educator*
Hong, Kyung Hwa *research scientist*
Hoynes, Hilary Williamson *economics professor, researcher*
Iacovelli, John Chesley *performing arts educator*
Imwinkelried, Edward John *law educator*
Jensen, Hanne Margrete *pathologist, educator*
Johnson, Kevin Raymond *dean, law educator*
Jones, Edward George *neuroscientist, educator*
Jungerman, John Albert *physics professor*
Kado, Clarence Isao *molecular biologist*
Katehi, Linda P.B. *academic administrator, engineering educator*
Kauzlarich, Susan Mary *chemistry educator, researcher*
Knoepfler, Paul *cell biologist*
Kowalczykowski, Stephen Charles *biochemist, biophysicist, microbiologist, cellular and molecular biologist, educator*
Kraft, Rosemarie *dean, educator*
La Mar, Gerd Neustadter *retired chemistry professor*
Langley, Charles Hunt *geneticist, educator*
Lavernia, Enrique Jose *materials science and engineering educator, dean*
Lazzara, Michael James *literature and language professor*
Liu, Kai *physics professor*
Lucas, William John *science educator*
Major, Clarence Lee *writer, painter, poet, educator*
Mangun, George R. *psychology professor, director*
Marino, Miguel Angel *engineering educator*
Mason, William A(lvin) *psychologist, educator, researcher*
Maurer, Frank W., Jr. *land trust administrator*
McHenry, Henry Malcolm *anthropologist, educator*
Medellin-Azuara, Josue *environmental scientist*
Modjtahedi, Bagher *economist, educator*
Morgan, Maggie *costume designer, design educator*
Morisseau, Christophe Henri Pierre *entomologist, researcher*
Moyle, Peter Briggs *marine biologist, educator*
Mukherjee, Amiya K. *metallurgy and materials science educator*
Müller, Hans-Georg *statistician*
Murphy, Terence Martin *biology professor*
Musolf, Lloyd Daryl *political science professor, educational association administrator*
Navrotsky, Alexandra *geophysics educator*
Ortiz, Pablo *composer*
Palmer, Philip Edward Stephen *radiologist*
Perschbacher, Rex Robert *law educator*
Poulos, Joan Graham *lawyer*
Pritchard, William Roy *former university systems administrator*
Qualset, Calvin O. *agronomist, educator*
Rappaport, Lawrence *plant physiology and horticulture educator*
Rhode, Edward Albert *veterinary medicine educator, veterinary cardiologist*
Richman, David Paul *neurologist, educator, researcher*
Ronald, Pamela C. *plant pathologist, educator*
Rooks, George Malcolm *writer, educator, small business owner*
Rost, Thomas Lowell *retired botany educator*
Schank, Jeffrey Charles *science educator, researcher*
Schoener, Thomas William *ecologist, educator*
Scott, Thomas Wallace *entomologist, director*
Sergueeva, Alla Vladimirovna *materials scientist, researcher*
Shackelford, James Floyd *materials science educator, researcher*
Sharrow, Marilyn Jane *library administrator*
Siegler, Richard Louis *pediatric nephrologist, educator*
Sillman, Arnold Joel *physiologist, educator*
Simonton, Dean Keith *psychology professor*
Smith, Michael Peter *social sciences educator, researcher*
Spindler, George Dearborn *anthropologist, educator, writer*
Springer, Sally Pearl *university administrator*
Stern, Judith Schneider *nutritionist, researcher, educator*
Stevens, Robert David *librarian, educator*
Stroeve, Pieter *chemical engineering researcher and educator*
Tanno, John W. *university librarian*
Tchobanoglous, George *civil engineering educator*
Terning, John *physics professor, researcher*
Torrance, Robert Mitchell *comparative literature educator*
Tracy, Craig Arnold *mathematics educator*
Turcotte, Donald Lawson *geophysical sciences educator*
Vanderhoef, Larry Neil *biology professor, former academic administrator*
Waddington, Raymond Bruce, Jr. *language educator*
Wallender, Wesley William *engineering professor*
Walters, Richard Francis *computer science educator*
Wang, Shih-Ho *electrical engineer, educator*
Williamson, Alan Bacher *literature educator, poet, writer*
Willis, Frank Roy *historian, educator*
Wu, Lin L. *retired botanist, ecologist, educator*
Wydick, Richard Crews *lawyer, educator*
Yilma, Tilahun Daniel *virologist, veterinarian, educator, researcher*
Zavortink, Thomas James *retired biology professor*
Zhu, Xiangdong *physics professor*

Del Mar
Farquhar, Marilyn Gist *cell biologist, pathologist, educator*
Iverson, Gilbert Michael *retired immunologist*
Kenyon, Kern E. *retired oceanographer*
Marcus, Larry David *broadcast executive*
Morton, Frederic *author*
Quinn, Katherine Sarah *psychologist*
Seitman, John Michael *arbitrator, mediator, lawyer*
Wilkinson, Eugene Parks *nuclear engineer, director*

Delano
Salmassi, Sadegh *physician*

Denair
Hale, Lois J. *retired mathematics educator*

Desert Hot Springs
Laws, Maurice Wesley *set decorator, museum exhibit designer*
Zarres, Sharon L. *marriage and family therapist, health facility administrator*

Diablo
Burnison, Boyd Edward *lawyer*

Diamond Bar
Chih, Luke *music educator, conductor*
Knox Rios, Delilah Jane *lawyer*
Mirisola, Lisa Heinemann *program supervisor*
Snoop Dogg, (Calvin Broadus) *vocalist, actor*

Dove Canyon
Bird, Brian Rex *writer, producer television/film*

Downey
Bessman, Alice Neuman *internist, educator*
Hackney, Jack Dean *physician*
Meysenburg, Mary Ann *principal*
Orozco, Jorge *rehabilitation hospital administrator*
Perry, Jacquelin *orthopedist, surgeon*
Robles, Darline P. *school system administrator*
Todd, Margaret Donnellan *library director*

Duarte
Chu, David Z.J. *surgeon, oncologist, research scientist*
Figlin, Robert Alan *hematologist, oncologist*
Grannis, Frederic Winslow, Jr. *thoracic surgeon*
Reckamp, Karen *medical educator*
Riggs, Arthur D. *health facility administrator, research scientist*
Smith, Steven Sidney *molecular biologist*
Williams, Lawrence Ernest *physicist*

Dublin
Woodson, Roderick Kevin *sportscaster, football coach, retired professional football player*

East Palo Alto
Bates, William III *lawyer*
Schelling, Donald Lawrence *lawyer*

Edwards
Liu, Chi Tsieh *aerospace scientist, researcher*
Spinelli, Christopher John *military officer*

Edwards AFB
Fritz, Matthew T. *pilot*

El Cajon
Graf, Sheryl Susan *lawyer*
Ishmael, Wanda Shutt *psychology educator*
Jammo, Sarhad Yawsip Hermiz *bishop*
Melahaji, Jalal Assad *science educator*
Russell, Anne M. *editor-in-chief*
Thomas, Esther Merlene *elementary and adult education educator*
Tuttle, Sandia Lou DeWaide *literature and language educator*

El Cerrito
Burger, Edmund Ganes *architect*
Crompton, Louis William *English literature educator*
Herzberg, Dorothy Crews *retired secondary school educator*

El Dorado Hills
Alexander, Candice M. *sales executive*
Bartlett, Robert Watkins *metallurgist, educator, consultant*
Sparks, Robert Dean *medical administrator, gastroenterologist*
Tierney, Kevin Allen *elementary school educator*

El Monte
Last, Marian Helen *public administration*

El Segundo
Abdul-Jabbar, Kareem (Lew Alcindor, Lewis Ferdinand Alcindor) *professional basketball coach, retired professional basketball player*
Barram, David J. *information technology executive, former federal agency administrator*
Brown, Lorraine Ann *founder, event coordinator, minister*
Bryant, Kobe *professional basketball player*
Buettner, Douglas John *physicist, astronautical engineer, director*
Buss, Jerry (Gerald Hatten Buss) *professional sports team owner*
Bynum, Andrew *professional basketball player*
Churchill, Bruce B. *broadcast executive*
DeBuck, Donald G. *computer company executive*
Doyle, Patrick T. *broadcast executive*
Eckert, Robert A. *consumer products company executive*
Farr, Kevin M. *consumer products executive*
Fisher, Derek Lamar *professional basketball player*
Gasol, Pau *professional basketball player*
Gieselman, Jon *advertising executive*
Guyardo, Paul *broadcast company executive*
Harwick, Wayne Thomas *economist*
Hsia, Irene Yee *electrical engineer*
Hunter, Larry Dean *broadcast executive, lawyer*
Kilpatrick, Frank Stanton *marketing executive*
Kim, Sung Jin *computer engineer*
Kupchak, Mitchell *professional sports team executive, retired professional basketball player*
Laphen, Michael W. *computer services company executive*
Lee, Anne Lim *electrical engineer*
Macskassy, Sofus Attila *computer scientist, educator*
Mende, Howard Shigeharu *mechanical engineer*
Milton-Jones, DeLisha *professional basketball player*
Muhlbach, Robert Arthur *lawyer*

Musk, Elon *aerospace transportation executive*
Nguyen, Tien Manh *technical executive*
Nissenson, Allen Richard *physician, educator*
Normile, Robert J. *lawyer, consumer products company executive*
Odom, Lamar Joseph *professional basketball player*
Palkovic, Michael W. *broadcast executive*
Pontual, Romulo *broadcast executive*
Pruetz, Adrian Mary *lawyer*
Smith, Milan Dale, Jr. *federal judge*
Thiry, Kent J. *health products executive*
Treat, John Elting *entrepreneur*
Whitney, Richard K. *health products executive*

Elk Grove
Forbes, Kenneth Albert Faucher *retired urological surgeon*
Tran, Lien *military officer*
Vang, Timothy Teng *religious organization administrator*

Emeryville
Bangs, Richard Johnston *publishing executive, explorer*
Bird, Brad (Phillip Bradley Bird) *film director, writer, animator*
Catmull, Edwin Earl *film company executive, computer graphics engineer*
Chang, Ying-Lan *technologist*
Doctor, Pete *animator, film director, scriptwriter*
Fields, Howard Lincoln *neurologist, physiologist, educator*
Houghton, Michael *geneticist*
Lasseter, John Alan *film company executive, computer animator*
Masri, Merle Sid *biochemist, consultant*
O'Dea, Patrick J. *food products executive*
Penhoet, Edward E. *retired foundation administrator, former biochemicals company executive, former dean*
Peterson, Bob III *animator, film director, scriptwriter*
Renton, Hollings C. *health products executive*
Robb, Walter *food products executive*
Stanton, Andrew *animator, film director, film producer, scriptwriter*
Tori, Christopher Dante *psychology professor*
White, Raymond Leslie *geneticist*
Witbrodt, Jane Ann *medical researcher*
Zwoyer, Eugene Milton *retired consulting engineering executive*

Encinitas
Deets, Dwain Aaron *retired aerospace technology executive*
Hale, David Fredrick *biotechnology executive*
Lougeay, Denruth Colleen *clinical psychologist, educator*
Shields, Patricia Allene *retail executive*

Encino
Friedman, George Jerry *aerospace engineering executive*
House, Karen House Milburn *nursing consultant*
Ingels, Marty *agent, broadcast executive*
Irmas, Audrey Menein *not-for-profit developer*
Joy, Alexa *small business owner, artist, educator*
Knuth, Eldon Luverne *engineering educator*
Lambirth, Timothy A. *attorney*
Lesavoy, Malcolm Alan *plastic surgeon*
Parrott, Dennis Beecher *retired insurance industry executive*
Rose, I. Nelson *lawyer, educator*
Shire, David Lee *composer*
Silva, Carole *elementary school educator*
Smith, Selma Moidel *lawyer, composer*
Westmore, Michael George *make-up artist, writer*
Willard, Fred *actor*

Escalon
Barton, Gerald Lee *farming company executive*

Escondido
Bakko, Orville Edwin *retired health facility administrator*
Briggs, Edward Samuel *naval officer*
Carlson, Mary Lou *elementary school educator, sister*
Damsbo, Ann Marie *psychologist*
Devine, Walter Bernard *naval architect, marine engineer*
Ghandhi, Sorab Khushro *electrical engineering educator*
Guinn, Stanley Willis *retired lawyer*
Linzey, Verna May *minister, writer*
McCarberg, Bill Harold *physician*
Newman, Barry Ingalls *retired bank executive*
Sanders, Adrian Lionel *retired educational consultant*
Walker, Patricia Ann *special education educator*

Eureka
Bowker, Lee Harrington *sociologist, educator, writer*
Kramer, Erik Daniel *physics professor*

Fair Oaks
Betts, Barbara Lang *lawyer, real estate agent, rancher*
Haugen, David Lee *surgeon*
Hutton, Essex Clark, Sr. *adult education educator*
Potter, George Kenneth *artist*
Weston, Louanne C. *marriage and family therapist*

Fairfax
Kadoyama, Margaret *museum educator, management consultant*

Fairfield
Chen, William T. *plastic surgeon*
Dabeck, Donna *nursing administrator*
Edson, William Alden *retired electrical engineer, researcher*
Forssell, Linda Lee *secondary school educator, illustrator*
Kirkorian, Donald George *retired academic administrator*
Mary, Diane Bradley *elementary school educator, secondary school educator*
Ornellas, Maile Louise *filmmaker, educator*
Schunke, Hildegard Heidel *accountant*
Spake, Reuben Michael *mathematics professor, researcher*
Williams, Lena Rose *academic administrator*

Fallbrook
Freeman, Harry Lynwood *retired accountant*
Hamilton, Robert *retired corporate financial executive, councilman*
Ragland, Jack Whitney *artist*

Felicity
Istel, Jacques Andre *Mayor, Felicity, California*

Fillmore
Orozco, Marc Peter *secondary school educator*

Folsom
Bahbah, Amr G. *application developer, consultant*
Ettlich, William F. *electrical engineer*
Ewing, Russell Charles, II, *physician*
Haga, Enoch John *retired computer educator, writer, editor*
Peck, Ellie Enriquez *retired state administrator*
Ritzi-Marouf, Viviane Cosette *language educator, department chairman*
Smith, Candy *economics professor*
Textor, Alice Middle *political science professor*
Yang, Dan *marketing executive, researcher*

Fontana
Higgins, Rosemarie Lorraine *librarian*
Nuaimi, Mark N. *Mayor, Fontana, California*

Fort Bragg
Gjerde, Rosalie Carolyn *music educator, conductor*

Foster City
Alton, Gregg H. *pharmaceutical executive, lawyer*
Denny, James M. *pharmaceutical and former retail executive*
Karnazes, Elizabeth Marie Barnson *lawyer, photojournalist travel agency owner*
Krikorian, Blake *entrepreneur, consumer electronics company executive*
Liang, Yu *biomedical researcher*
Liu, Leonard *software services company executive*
Lucier, Gregory Thomas *medical technology executive*
Lucio, Antonio J. *finance company executive*
Lutvak, Mark Allen *computer company executive*
Martin, John C. *pharmaceutical company executive*
Milligan, John F. *information technology executive*
Pollitt, Byron H., Jr. *finance company executive, former retail executive*
Sommer, Kenneth *finance company executive*
Tretton, Jack *electronics executive*
Yan, Martin *celebrity chef*

Fountain Valley
Armstrong, Jeffrey Lee *oceanographer*
Carter, John Frederick *missionary educator*
Crecelius, Daniel Neil *history professor*
de Jong-Pombo, Teresa Maria *concert pianist, educator*
Einstein, Stephen Jan *rabbi*
Montgomery, Thom Mathew *health program administrator, counselor*
Smith, Marie Edmonds *real estate agent, property manager*
Treadway-Dillmon, Linda Lee *actress, stuntwoman, dancer, dispatcher, athletic trainer*
Warwick, Randall James *biology professor, writer*
Wilhite, Steve *automotive executive*
Worden, Mark K. *multimedia designer, educator*

Fowler
Bowman, Joseph Paul *protective services official, writer, retired military officer*

Frazier Park
Edwards, Sarah Anne *social worker, psychologist*

Fremont
Alsborg, Thomas C. *electronics executive*
Bagley, James W. *semiconductor equipment company executive*
Blank, Thomas *theater educator*
Bray, Richard Daniel *librarian*
Brown, Michael Gene *vice principal*
Chao, Kwang-Chu *chemical engineer, educator*
Chen, Wai-Kai *electrical engineering and computer science educator, consultant*
Chien-Hale, Elizabeth *lawyer*
Engelbart, Douglas C. *engineering executive*
Grant, Alan J. *business executive, educator*
Hofacket, Jean *library director*
Hsu, Gloria *piano educator*
Huang, Robert T. *electronics executive*
Jensen, Paul Edward Tyson *business educator, consultant*
LaRose, Katherine Stencel *music educator*
Le, Thuy Trong *nuclear engineer, educator*
Lemon, Deborah *literature and language professor, dancer*
Leung, Simon *lawyer, electronics executive*
Murai, Kevin M. *electronics executive*
Newberry, Stephen G. *semiconductor equipment company executive*
Peebles, Lucretia Neal Drane *education educator*
Polk, Dennis *electronics executive*
Rangavajhula, Krishna *mechanical engineer, educator*
Smith, Bernald Stephen *retired pilot*
Stinnett, Terrance LLoyd *lawyer*
Tang, John *network technician, information scientist, educator*
Venturini, Judith Anne *education educator*
Wasserman, Robert *Mayor, Fremont, California*
Wu, James Chen-Yuan *aerospace engineering educator*
Yamamoto, Masako *music educator, director*
Yang, Di *systems administrator*
Zhu, Sha *materials engineer*
Zimmer, George A. *men's apparel executive*

Fresno
Autry, Alan *Former Mayor, Fresno, California, film company executive, actor, former professional football player*
Berman, Richard P. *lawyer*
Burnett, Lynn Barkley *health science educator*
Chang, Sidney H. *history professor*
Contreras, Luis A. *literature and language professor*
Corless, Dorothy Alice *nursing educator*
Dackawich, S. John *sociology educator, academic administrator*
Dauer, Donald Dean *investment company executive*
Epperson, Robert Dale *farmer*
Garrison-Finderup, Ivadelle Dalton *writer, educator*
Genini, Ronald Walter *retired history educator*
Girvin, Shirley Eppinette *retired elementary school educator, journalist*
Gordus, Andrew George *ecotoxicologist*
Gruet, Karin *chemistry professor*
Harris, Breck Anthony *business educator, writer, researcher*
Hunter, Timothy *industrial technology educator*
Joseph, James William *political scientist, consultant, educator*
Kauffman, George Bernard *chemistry professor*
Lagle, John Franklin *retired lawyer*
Lambe, James Patrick *lawyer*
Lanter, Lanore *writer, educator*
Martinez, Carlos *museum director*
McConnell, Charles Prescott *retired science educator*
Misakian, Jo Ellen Priest *school librarian*
Monaghan, Kathleen M. *art museum director*
Nakamoto, Tokumasa *science educator*
Patnaude, William Eugene *architect*
Pings, Anthony Claude *architect*
Reinhardt, LeRoy Jacob *lawyer*
Riggs, Krista Dyonis *music educator, librarian*
Ryan, Judy *literature and language professor*
Shmavonian, Gerald S. *political organization administrator*
Siroky, Allen James *history professor*
Smith, Richard Howard *banker*
Steinbock, John Thomas *bishop*
Swearengin, Ashley *Mayor, Fresno, California*
Tellier, Richard Davis *management educator*
Tudman, Cathi Graves *elementary school educator*
Wang, Zhi *environmental scientist, educator*
Warwick, Tanya C. *neurologist, educator, researcher*
Waters, Rosemary R. *biology professor*
Wilson, James Ross *communications educator, broadcast executive*
Winslow, Norman Eldon *small business owner*
Xiong, Tousu Saydangnmvang *minister, theology studies educator*

Fullerton
Atallah, Youssef Chahine *environmental scientist*
Ayala, John L. *retired librarian, dean*
Bjorklund, Nancy Basler *history professor*
Choi, John U. *periodontist, educator*
Clymer, John *electrical engineer, educator*
de Rios, Marlene Dobkin *medical anthropologist, psychotherapist*
Donoghue, Mildred Ransdorf *education educator*
Druon, Michele Valentine *language educator*
Farka, Mira *economics professor, financial consultant*
Fischer, Robert Blanchard *academic administrator, researcher*
Foote, Paul Sheldon *business educator, administrator, consultant*
Frizell, Samuel *law educator*
Frost, Jacqueline Beth *cinematographer, educator*
Garrett, Scott T. *medical products executive*
Horn, Michael H. *biologist*
Jensen, Robert Russell *dean, consultant*
Johnson, Carolyn Elizabeth *librarian*
Ketter, Charles David *theater educator, director*
Khalifa, Sherif Hussein *economics professor*
Kwon, Young D. *engineering educator, researcher*
Lewandoski, Robert Henry *editor, publisher*
Loupe, Leleua Laurita *history professor*
Lundegard, Paul *geologist, consultant*
Miller, Arnold *electronics executive*
Nolan-Riegle, Mary Catherine *biology professor*
Praitis, Irena *literature and language professor*
Puente, Henry *communications educator*
Sadrudin, Moe *humanitarian organization executive*
Shapiro, Mark Howard *physicist, educator, dean*
Sheridan, Christopher Frederick *human resources executive*
Smith, Ephraim Philip *academic administrator*
Steinmeyer, Robert Jay *retired lawyer*
Suceava, Bogdan Dragos *mathematics professor, writer*
Sugarman, Michael *physician, rheumatologist*
Tehrani, Fleur Taher *electrical engineer, educator, researcher*
Tiwari, Binod *civil engineer*
Woyski, Margaret Skillman *retired geology educator*
Zeballos, Abel *theater educator, make-up artist, consultant*

Garberville
Nyokka, Suzette *artist, natural health educator*

Garden Grove
Cochrum, Ellen Joan *language educator*
Dalton, William J. *Mayor, Garden Grove, California*

Gardena
Martin, Melissa Carol *radiological physicist*
Shelby, Carroll Hall *automotive designer*

Gilroy
Borton, George Robert *retired airline captain*
Wu, Wayne Wen-Yau *artist*

Glen Ellen
Berkland, James Omer *geologist*
Hurlbert, Roger William *information technology executive*

Glendale
Brestle, Daniel J. *corporate financial executive*
Cobey, Virginia Branum *artist, actress, art collector*
Cross, Richard John *bank executive*
Daly, Ann Michelle *broadcast executive*
de Grassi, Leonard *art historian, educator*
Drayman, John *Mayor, Glendale, California*
Ereshefsky, Larry *scientific officer, executive, psychopharmacology educator, consultant*
Figueira-McDonough, Josefina *emeritus professor of justice studies*
Filosa, Gary Fairmont Randolph, II, *film and television producer*
GLobe, Anne *film company executive*
Harris, John J. *food products executive*
Hoffman, Donald M. *lawyer*
Hughes, Bradley Wayne *storage company executive*
Jacobson, Nina R. *film producer, former company executive*
Jones, William Allen *retired lawyer*
Katzenberg, Jeffrey *film company executive*
Kay, Alan C. *computer scientist, nonprofit organization executive*
Kazanjian, Phillip Carl *lawyer, educator*
Landau, Annette Henkin *writer, librarian*
Levy, Murray *business educator*
MacDonald, Laurie *film company executive*
Martinetti, Ronald Anthony *lawyer*
Michelson, Lillian *librarian, researcher*
Parkes, Walter F. *film company executive*
Prager, Dennis *radio talk show host*
Reppen, Kyra E. *Internet company executive*
Shou, Sharon Louise Wikoff *vocational rehabilitation counselor*
Snider, Stacey *film company executive*
Sotelo, Eduardo (El Piolín) *radio personality*
Stevens, Steve J. *lawyer*
Stewart, Julia A. *food service executive*
Weaver, Dave *Councilman*

Glendora
Starobin, Nancy *photographer*

Gold River
Andrew, John Henry *lawyer, writer*

Goleta
Everhart, Thomas Eugene *retired academic administrator, engineering educator*
Gilbert, Richard Keith *biology professor, researcher*
Nahra, Lynda J. *bank executive*
Zuk, Carmen Veiga *psychiatrist*
Zuk, Gerald Harvey *psychologist, consultant*

Granada Hills
Aller, Wayne Kendall *psychologist, educator, computer company executive, property manager*
Lehtihalme, Larry K. (Lauri Lehtihalme) *financial planner*
Silver, Vanessa Marie *educational therapist, consultant*

Granite Bay
Hartmann, Frederick Howard *retired political science professor*
Kemper, Dorla Dean Eaton (Dorla Dean Eaton) *real estate broker*

Grass Valley
Cheney, Margaret *writer, retired editor*
Ely, Parry Haines *dermatologist, educator*
Suri, Jasjit S. *research scientist*
Sutton, John Paul *lawyer*
Washington, Allyn Jarvis *writer*

Greenbrae
Blatt, Morton Bernard *medical illustrator*
Bonapart, Alan David *lawyer*
Eisenberg, Peter David *internist, oncologist*
Freedman, Albert Z. *publishing executive*
Parnell, Francis William, Jr. *otolaryngologist*
Poulos, Stanley *plastic surgeon*
Rosbe, Kristina W. *pediatric otolaryngologist, surgeon*
Teller, Pauline Ivancovich *artist*
Tyng, Anne Griswold *architect*

Gualala
Ring, Alice Ruth Bishop *retired preventive medicine physician*

Guerneville
Mannino, J. Davis *psychologist, educator, author*

Gustine
Ramirez, Nola Marie *librarian*

Hacienda Heights
Dodson, Arleen Cecilia *language educator*

Half Moon Bay
Lambert, Frederick William *lawyer, educator*
Lu, Adolph *physicist, researcher*
Robertson, Abel L., Jr. *pathologist*

Happy Camp
Black, Barbara Ann *publisher*
Brown, Barbara Black *publishing company executive*

Hawthorne
Fila, John Charles *psychoanalyst*

Hayward
Bachicha, Joseph Alfred *physician, educator*
Beck, Edward William *lawyer*
DeVaro, Jed *economics professor*
Duncan, Doris Gottschalk *information systems educator*

Fajilan, Ann *theater educator*
Garcia, Melva Ybarra *counseling administrator, educator*
Garcia, Richard Amado *history professor, writer*
Helgren, Erik B. *physics professor*
Henig, Gerald S. *history professor*
Jordahl, Kathleen Patricia (Kate Jordahl) *photographer, educator*
Kwon, Myoung-ja Lee *retired academic librarian*
Lauzon, Carol *science educator*
McKenzie, Brian Bruce *finance educator*
Paz, Marcelo *literature and language professor*
Rees, Norma S. *academic administrator*
Reevy-Manning, Gretchen Maria *psychologist, educator*
Reichman, Henry Frederick *history educator*
Shannon, Patricia D. *theology studies educator*
Staudohar, Paul David *economics professor, labor arbitrator*
Weiss, Jessica *history professor*
Wong, Wanda Yuk-Wa *graphics designer, educator*

Healdsburg
Castellini, Mary Mercer *author*
Eade, George James *retired military officer, researcher*
Flores-Deras, Ever J. *counseling administrator*
Keane, Douglas *chef*
Myers, Robert Eugene *writer, educator*
Vedros, Neylan Anthony *microbiologist, educator*

Hemet
Berger, Lev Isaac *physicist, researcher*
Clark, Harold L. *technology company executive, consultant*
Culverwell, Albert Henry *historian*
Frances, Carol *economics professor*
Mata, David Joseph *physician*
Monk, Sharon Anne *special education educator*

Hercules
Richards, Gerald Thomas *lawyer, educator, writer*
Tyson, Kathleen Hayhurst *educational association administrator*

Hermosa Beach
Chi, Lois Wang *retired biology professor, research scientist*
Kokalj, James Edward *retired aerospace administrator*
Wickwire, Patricia Joanne Nellor *psychologist, educator*

Hesperia
Fisher, Richard Paul *chemist*

Highland
Fangerow, Kay Elizabeth *nurse*
MacQueen, Cherie K. *interior designer, artist, retired newscaster, retired sportscaster*
Miller, R. Warburton *psychologist, farmer*
Tacal, Jose Vega, Jr. *retired public health official, veterinarian*

Hillsborough
Keller, John Francis *retired food products executive, mayor*
Mitchell, Bruce Tyson *lawyer*
Westerfield, Putney *management consulting executive*

Hollister
Miller, Alisa Dorothy Norton *artist*

Hollywood
Batt, Anthony *Internet company executive*
Berryman, Guy *musician*
Brooks, Lila *animal rights activist*
Buckland, Jon *musician*
Burke, Cheryl *dancer*
Champion, Will *musician*
Cintron, Alan *Internet company executive*
DioGuardi, Kara *songwriter, producer*
Fisher, Joel Marshall *political scientist, educator, wine consultant*
Goldman, Tyler *Internet company executive, lawyer*
Greenwood, Colin Charles *musician*
Greenwood, Jonathan Richard Guy (Jonny Greenwood) *musician*
Luti, Anthony Ngula *lawyer*
Lynne, Shelby (Shelby Lynn Moorer) *country singer*
Martin, Chris *singer*
Melchior, Ib Jorgen *scriptwriter, author, film director*
Miles, Joanna *actress, playwright, director*
O'Brien, Edward John *musician, vocalist*
Parks, Robert Myers *appliance manufacturing company executive*
Salzman, David Elliot *entertainment industry executive*
Selway, Phillip James *musician*
Will.i.am, (William James Adams Jr.) *rap artist*
Yorke, Thom (Thomas Edward Yorke) *singer*

Hopland
Jones, Milton Bennion *retired agronomist*

Hughson
Hailey, Kathleen Wilson *elementary school educator*

Huntington Beach
Baroni, Michael L. *lawyer*
Bohr, Keith *Mayor, Huntington Beach, California*
Burson, Thomas Daniel *retired aerospace executive*
Carter, Henrietta McKee *music educator, department chair*
Coerper, Gil *Councilman, Huntington Beach, California*
De Massa, Jessie G. *media specialist*
Foose, Chip *automotive designer, television personality*
Garofalo, David P. *publishing executive, former mayor*
Garrels, Sherry Ann *lawyer*
Goldman, Henry Howard *management consultant*
Herron, Harriette A. *retired occupational health nurse*
Horowitz, Jed H. *plastic surgeon, reconstructive surgeon*
Houck, Aleda Jean *dean*
Jensen, Dennis Lowell *lawyer*
Leveton, Ian Sinclair *civil engineer*
Macdonald, R. Fulton Smith *venture developer, business executive, educator, consultant*
Martin, Wilfred Wesley Finny *psychologist, property owner and manager*
McKay, David E. *mathematics professor*
McKnight, Robert B., Jr. *sporting goods manufacturing executive*
Ramphal, Julie Frances *retired secondary school educator*
Sward, Andrea Jeanne *information and computer scientist, musician*
Winterowd, Walter Ross *language educator*

Huntington Park
Gaines-Page, Rena L. *science educator*

Idyllwild
Jones, William Lee, Jr. *psychologist, educator*

Imperial
Cormier, Judy Ann *literature and language professor*
Plascencia, Jose J. *social worker, consultant*

Imperial Beach
Gerlach, Murney *foundation administrator, historian, educator*
Merkin, William Leslie *retired lawyer*

Indian Wells
Jennings, Richard Milburn *resort developer*
Kelley, John Paul *communications consultant*
McDermott, Thomas John, Jr. *lawyer*
Reuben, Don *lawyer*

Indio
Garra, Raymond Hamilton, II, *marketing executive*
Houghton, Robert Charles *secondary school educator*
Zorick, Nancy Lee *artist, actress*

Inglewood
Barrett, Ronald Keith *psychology educator, consultant, researcher*
Dorr, Lawrence Douglas *orthopedic surgeon*
Sludikoff, Stanley Robert *publisher, writer*

Irvine
Ahmanson, Roberta Green *philanthropist*
Aigner, Dennis John *economics professor, consultant*
Aitken, Ashleigh E. *lawyer*
Alexopoulos, Nicolaos George *electrical engineer, educator, dean*
Alspach, Philip Halliday *manufacturing executive*
Arthur, David *research scientist*
Ayala, Francisco José *geneticist, educator*
Baldwin, Kenneth Milton *biology professor*
Barsamian, Harut *computer scientist, consultant*
Bartkus, Richard Anthony *magazine publisher*
Bastiaanse, Gerard C. *lawyer*
Baumgartner, Anton Edward *automotive sales professional*
Bic, Zuzana *medical educator*
Bollens, Scott Alan *urban planner, educator*
Bose, Swaraj *ophthalmologist, educator*
Boyd, Carolyn Patricia *history professor*
Brandt, Eric K. *corporate financial executive*
Bras, Rafael Luis *dean, engineering educator*
Broadhurst, Norman Neil *food products executive*
Bullock, James Steven *physics professor*
Burton, Michael Ladd *anthropology educator*
Butts, Carter Tribley *social sciences educator*
Carew, Thomas James *neuroscientist, educator*
Carson, Juli Christine *art educator*
Catrakis, Haris John *science educator*
Chelapati, Chunduri Venkata *civil engineering educator*
Chemerinsky, Erwin *dean, law educator*
Cho, Zang Hee *physics professor*
Chong, Arthur *lawyer*
Christensen, Becky Vanderhoof *lawyer*
Chronley, James Andrew *real estate executive*
Clark, Bruce Robert *geologist, consultant*
Clayman, Ralph Victor *urologist, medical educator, dean*
Clegg, Michael Tran *genetics educator, researcher*
Crawford, Susan Jean *federal judge*
Danziger, James Norris *political science professor*
Detrano, Robert *medical educator*
Drake, Michael V. *academic administrator, ophthalmologist, educator*
Druffel, Ellen R.M. *research scientist, educator*
Duckles, Sue Piper *pharmacologist, educator*
Dull, David A. *lawyer*
Duncan, Greg John *economics researcher*
Dzyaloshinskii, Igor Ekhielievich *physicist*
Elsasser, Gary *computer company executive*
Fahim, Amr *electrical engineer*
Feldman, Martha Sue *political scientist, educator*
Feldstein, Paul Joseph *management educator*
Feliciano, Cynthia *social sciences educator*
Finlayson-Pitts, Barbara Jean *chemistry professor*
Fisker, Henrik *automobile designer and company executive*
Fleischer, Everly Borah *academic administrator, department chairman*
Folkenflik, Robert *retired literature and language professor*
Friedenberg, Richard Myron *radiologist, physician, educator*
Fulton, Kenneth Ray *professional association administrator*
Garb, Paula Jean *humanities educator, researcher*
Gibson, Patrick Daniel *accountant, historian*
Grabowski, Richard Joseph *lawyer*
Graham, John Lawrence *finance educator, writer*
Greenberger, Ellen *psychologist, educator*
Grossman, Barbara Robinson *marriage and family therapist*
Guo, Yifan *electronics engineer, educator*
Gupta, Sudhir *immunologist, educator*
Hansen, William D. *former federal agency administrator*
Henry, Valerie *mathematics professor*
Herzog, Dennis Neil *psychologist, supervisor*
Hine, Robert V. *historian, educator*
Hoffman, Donald David *cognitive and computer science educator*
Horne, Terry *publishing executive*
Huang, Wendy Wan-Juoh *lawyer*
Hubbell, Floyd Allan *internist, educator*
Huff, C(larence) Ronald *sociologist, criminologist, educator*
Ingram, Douglas Stephen *lawyer*
Jamshidipour, Yousef *bank executive, economist, financial advisor*
Jeliazkov, Ivan *economics professor*
Jones, Joie Pierce *physicist, acoustician, writer, educator*
Jorion, Philippe *education educator*
Kaneko, Tadashi S. *engineer, researcher*
Kang, Sukhee *Mayor, Irvine, California*
Karlovic, Martin Stephen *marketing executive, electrical engineer*
Khalifeh, Ala F. *research and development company researcher*
Kraemer, Kenneth Leo *architect, urban planner, educator*
Krom, Beth *former Mayor, Irvine, California*
Kuppermann, Baruch D. *ophthalmologist, educator*
Kwon, Young Jik *bioengineering researcher and educator*
Lampert, Seymour *retired mechanical engineering educator, consultant*
Leonard, Karen Isaksen *anthropology professor*
Lesonsky, Rieva *editor-in-chief*
Leung, Simon *artist*
Li, Peter Wai-Kwong *mathematics professor*
Lowe, Kathlene Winn *lawyer*
Luce, R. Duncan (Robert Duncan Luce) *psychology professor*
Maas, Korey Devlin *religious studies educator*
Maradudin, Alexei A. *physics professor*
Matros, Richard K. *insurance company executive*
McEligot, Archana Jaiswal *epidemiologist, educator*
McGregor, Scott A. *broadband communications company executive*
McLaughlin, Calvin Sturgis *biochemistry professor*
McWilliams, Roger Dean *physicist, researcher*
Meiselbach, James Vincent *mechanical engineer, educator*
Miller, Crystal Ann *respiratory therapist*
Mirnajafizadeh, Seyed Ali *engineering educator, researcher*
Molloi, Sabee *medical educator*
Morhaime, Mike *video game company executive*
Mu, Mingquan *meteorologist*
Munoff, Gerald J. *university librarian*
Mussey, Joseph Arthur *health and medical product executive*
Nelson, Edward Lee *biomedical researcher, educator*
Nie, Qing *mathematics professor*
Nowick, Arthur Stanley *metallurgy and materials science educator*
Noymer, Andrew *medical educator, researcher*
Osborne, Burl *retired publishing executive*
Ovens, David *food service executive, marketing professional*
Parker, Ian *science educator*
Penner, Reginald Mark *chemistry professor*
Peterson, Jeffrey V. *construction executive*
Phalen, Robert Franklynn *environmental scientist*
Policano, Andrew J. *dean, finance educator*
Power, Francis William *newspaper publisher*
Pritt, Stacy L. *veterinarian*
Pyott, David Edmund Ian *pharmaceutical executive*
Qin, Yufen *immunologist, researcher*
Qu, Qi *communications engineer*
Quilligan, Edward James *retired obstetrician, gynecologist, educator*
Ramzy, Ibrahim *medical educator*
Rankin, James *finance company executive*
Ray Chaudhuri, Samit *civil engineer, researcher*
Re, Joseph R. *lawyer*
Rooklidge, William Charles *lawyer*
Rose, Irwin A. (Ernie) *biochemist, educator*
Rowland, Frank Sherwood *chemistry professor*
Rumbaut, Rubén G., Sr. *social sciences educator*
Ruyter, Nancy Lee Chalfa *dance educator*
Rynn, Nathan *physics professor, consultant*
Saari, Donald Gene *mathematician, department chairman, economist*
Samueli, Henry *electrical engineer, educator, professional sports team executive*
Schonfeld, William Rost *political science professor*
Schwegler, Armin *language educator*
Seller, Gregory Erol *marketing executive, consultant, writer*
Sexton, Jared *African American studies professor*
Shojaeian, Parvin *research scientist, educator*
Siegel, Barry *journalist, writer, literature educator*
Silverman, Louis E. *information technology executive*
Simmons, Peter A. *medical researcher*
Sirignano, William Alfonso *aerospace and mechanical engineer, educator*
Sklansky, Jack *electrical and computer engineering educator, researcher*
Smoot, Skipi Lundquist *psychologist*
Snyder, Rick (Richard D. Snyder) *computer company executive*
Specter, Richard Bruce *lawyer*
Sperling, George *psychologist, educator*
Stack, Geoffrey Lawrence *real estate developer*
Stern, Jean *museum director*
Sunshine, Steven H. *lawyer*
Tachner, Leonard *lawyer*
Tang, Shao-Jun *biologist, educator*
Ting, Albert Chia *biomedical engineer, researcher*
Uhlaner, Carole Jean *political science professor*
Utts, Jessica Marie *statistician, educator*
Vandell, Kerry Dean *real estate consultant, educator, director, finance educator*
Wenzel, Lari Bea *psychologist*
Werlin, Lawrence B. *obstetrician, gynecologist, reproductive endocrinologist*
White, Stephen Halley *biophysicist, educator*
Wickramasinghe, Hemantha Kumar *electrical engineer, physicist*
Wilderson, Frank B. III *performing arts educator, writer*
Wilentz, Amy *literature educator*
Windsor, Adrian Sharon *real estate broker, literature and language professor*
Wine, Mark Philip *lawyer*
Wintrode, Ralph Charles *lawyer*
Wolken, Matthew J. *mechanical engineer, educator*
Won, Kwang Woong *chemical engineer*
Wong, Brian Jet-Fei *surgeon*
Wong, Nathan Donald *medicine and epidemiology researcher, educator*
Workman, Jerome James, Jr. *chemist*
Yamamoto, Lisa Maria *music educator*
Yazdi, Ahmad *computer scientist, researcher*
Yehezkel, Shaul *orthodontist*
Yousefi'zadeh, Homayoun *science educator*
Zhang, guohao (Gary) *electronics engineer*
Zheng, Weian *mathematics professor*

Irwindale
Zavala, Gabino *bishop*

Jamul
Newmeyer, Robert J. *lawyer*

Joshua Tree
Hope, Harry Joe (Joeseph) *retired corporate communications specialist, writer*

Keene
Rodriguez, Arturo Salvador *labor union official*

Kelseyville
Berry, John Joseph *educational administrator*

Kensington
Appelman, Evan Hugh *retired chemist*
Connick, Robert Elwell *retired chemistry professor*

Kentfield
Blum, Joan Kurley *retired fundraising consultant, copy editor and graphics designer*
Edgar, James Macmillan, Jr. *management consultant*
Fitzpatrick, Mary Patricia *language educator, writer*
German, Donald Frederick *physician*
Halprin, Anna Schuman (Mrs. Lawrence Halprin) *dancer*

Kingsburg
Olson, Maxine Louise *artist, lecturer*

La Canada
Paniccia, Patricia Lynn *journalist, writer, lawyer, educator*

La Canada Flintridge
Baines, Kevin Hays *astronomer, planetary scientist*
Byrne, George Melvin *physician*
Costello, Francis William *lawyer*
Macmillan, Robert Smith *electronics engineer*

La Crescenta
Baldwin, Alec (Alexander Rae Baldwin III) *actor*
Riccardi, Vincent Michael *pediatrician, educator, entrepreneur*

La Habra
Chase, Cochrane *advertising agency executive*

La Honda
Jahn, Thomas M. *medical educator*

La Jolla
Adamson, John William *hematologist*
Akiskal, Hagop Souren *psychiatric researcher, educator*
Al-Delaimy, Wael *medical educator*
Anthony, Harry Antoniades *retired city planner, architect, educator*
Antin, David *poet, critic*
Asmus, John Fredrich *physicist*
Atkinson, Richard Chatham *academic administrator, cognitive scientist*
Backus, George Edward *theoretical geophysicist*
Baouendi, M. Salah *mathematics professor*
Bardwell, Wayne Allen *psychologist, director*
Bardwick, Judith Marcia *management consultant*
Barshop, Bruce A. *science educator*
Bavasi, Peter Joseph *sports management executive*
Beebe, Mary Livingstone *curator*
Berger, Wolfgang H. *oceanographer, educator, geologist*
Beutler, Bruce A. *biology professor, researcher*
Blantz, Roland C. *nephrologist, educator*
Boger, Dale L. *chemistry professor*
Bokoch, Gary Michael *immunology research scientist*
Branscomb, Lewis McAdory *physicist, researcher*
Brenner, David Allen *academic administrator, medical educator*
Brenner, Sydney *molecular biologist, researcher*
Bromirski, Peter Donald *marine geophysicist, physical oceanographer*
Buchholz, Debby *lawyer*
Burbidge, E. Margaret *astronomer, educator*
Burbidge, Geoffrey *astrophysicist, educator*
Cain, William Stanley *experimental psychologist, educator, researcher*
Carethers, John Michael *physician, gastroenterologist, researcher*
Carmichael, David Burton *physician*
Chang, William Shen Chie *electrical engineering educator*
Chau, Pao C. *engineering educator*
Chien, Shu *physiology and bioengineering educator*

Cobble, James Wikle *chemistry professor*
Coburn, Marjorie Foster *psychologist, educator*
Colbert, James, Jr. *academic administrator, educator, pharmacist*
Cole, Michael *psychology professor*
Copley, David C. *publishing executive*
Cortes, Jorge *engineering educator*
Counts, Stanley Thomas *retired military officer, retired electronics executive*
Coutts, Richard David *surgeon*
Crutzen, Paul Josef *research meteorologist, chemist*
Csordas, Thomas John *anthropologist, educator*
Dandan, Randa Hilal *pharmacologist, researcher*
Dang, Qun *pharmacologist*
Daniels, Lori B. *cardiologist*
Davidow, Jeffrey *think-tank executive, former ambassador*
Davies, Hugh Marlais *museum director*
de Callafon, Raymond *engineering educator*
DeFanti, Thomas Albert *retired distinguished professor*
Dimsdale, Joel Edward *psychiatry educator*
Drake, Hudson Billings *aerospace and electronics executive*
Edelman, Gerald Maurice *biochemist, neuroscientist, educator*
Edgington, Thomas S. *pathologist, molecular and vascular biologist, educator*
Encalada, Sandra *biologist*
Evans, Ronald M. *microbiologist, educator*
Fantino, Edmund *psychology professor*
Farson, Richard Evans *psychologist*
Feher, George *biophysicist, educator*
Foley, L(ewis) Michael *real estate company officer*
Fowler, James H. *political science professor*
Fowler, Raymond Dalton *psychologist, educator*
Freedman, Jonathan Borwick *journalist, writer, educator*
Freedman, Michael Hartley *mathematician, educator, researcher*
Fukuda, Minoru *cancer research scientist*
Fung, Yuan-Cheng Bertram *bioengineering educator, writer*
Gabay, Janis T. *literature and language educator*
Gardner, Humphrey Athelstan Roy *pathologist*
Garland, Cedric Frank *epidemiologist, educator*
Geckler, Richard Delph *retired metal products executive*
Gere, Cathy *history professor*
Gilbert, James Freeman *geophysics educator*
Ginsberg, Mark H. *biomedical scientist, physician*
Golomb, Beatrice Alexandra *physician, medical researcher*
Goltz, Robert William *retired dermatologist*
Gordon, Roger Hall *economics educator*
Graham, Ronald Lewis *mathematician*
Grinstein, Benjamin *physicist, researcher*
Guillemin, Roger C.L. *physiologist, academic administrator*
Hamburger, Robert N. *pediatrician, educator, consultant*
Harilal, Sivanandan S. *physicist, researcher*
Harris, Philip Robert *management and space psychologist*
Harris, T. George *editor*
Havis, Allan Stuart *playwright, theatre educator*
Haxo, Francis Theodore *marine biologist*
Heeb, Mary Jo *biochemist, researcher*
Hendrickson, David Norman *chemistry professor*
Hofmann, Alan Frederick *biomedical researcher, educator*
Horner, Anthony Adam *pediatrician, educator*
Hougie, Cecil *retired science educator, retired hematologist*
Hunter, Tony (Anthony Rex) *molecular biologist, educator*
Imana, Jorge Garron *artist*
Intriligator, Kenneth *physicist, educator*
Itano, Harvey Akio *biochemistry educator*
Ivanov, Andrey V. *atmospheric chemist researcher*
Jacobson, Gary Charles *political science professor*
Järvinen-Pasley, Anna (Maaria Anna) *neuroscientist, researcher*
Johnson, Gayle Ann *cardiology nurse*
Jones, Kenneth Lyons *pediatrician, birth defects researcher*
Jorgensen, Judith Ann *psychiatrist, educator*
Kadonaga, James Takuro *biochemist*
Kalichman, Michael *neuropathologist*
Karten, Harvey Jules *neurosciences educator*
Katinsky, Steven B. *communications company executive*
Kay, Steve A. *dean, molecular biologist, educator*
Kennel, Charles Frederick *atmospheric physics professor, academic administrator, government official*
Kirchheimer, Arthur E(dward) *lawyer, business executive*
Kluender, Robert E. *linguist, educator*
Kolodner, Richard David *biochemist, educator, director*
Kono, Dwight *medical educator*
Kooyman, Gerald Lee *physiologist, researcher*
Korn, Bobby *ophthalmologist, educator*
Kozarich, John Warren *biochemist*
Krishnamurthy, Ramanarayanan *chemistry professor, researcher*
Kutas, Marta *psychologist, educator*
Lakshmana, Madepalli Krishnappa *neuroscientist*
Langacker, Ronald Wayne *linguistics educator*
Latz, Michael I. *marine biologist, educator*
Lerer, Seth *literature professor, writer*
Lerner, Richard Alan *chemistry educator, scientist*
Levy, Ralph *engineering executive, consultant*
Levy, Thomas Evan *anthropologist, educator*
Liddington, Robert C. *biomedical researcher, educator*
Lieber, Richard Louis *biomedical engineering scientist, educator*
Lipton, Stuart Arthur *neuroscientist*
Liu, Bao *engineering educator*
Liu, Shumo *molecular biologist*
Liu, Zhaowei *engineering educator*
Lowy, Andrew M. *oncologist, surgeon*
Ma, Wenxue *medical scientist*
MacRae, Ian John *medical educator, researcher*
Makhluf, Huda A. *research scientist*
Mandler, George *psychologist, educator*
Mandler, Jean Matter *psychologist, educator*
Margolin, Frances Mongin *clinical psychologist, educator*
Marti, Kurt *chemistry professor*
Martin, James John, Jr. *systems analyst, retired research and development company executive*
Masters, Guy *science educator*
Mayer, James Hock *lawyer, mediator*
McCammon, James Andrew *chemistry professor*
McDonald, Marianne *classicist*
Mendoza, Stanley Atran *pediatric nephrologist, educator*
Micciancio, Daniele *computer scientist*
Miller, David R. *academic administrator*
Milstein, Laurence Bennett *electrical engineering educator, researcher*
Molina, Mario Jose *physical chemist, educator*
Moossa, A. R. *surgeon, educator*
Morello, Candis Marguerite *pharmacist, educator*
Morgan, Neil *editor, journalist, writer*
Morgens, Warren Kendall *retired lawyer*
Mundt, Arno J. *oncologist, department chairman*
Nahavandi, Amir Nezameddin *retired engineering firm executive*
Nakamura, Robert Motoharu *pathologist*
Nicolaou, Kyriacos Costa (K. C. Nicolaou) *chemistry professor*
Nyhan, William Leo *pediatrician, educator*
Olafson, Frederick Arlan *philosophy educator*
Oldham, Sean Michael *medical educator, consultant*
Oreskes, Naomi *science historian*
Patton, Stuart *biochemist, educator*
Penner, Stanford Sol *engineering educator*
Pfeiffer, Phyllis Kramer *publishing executive*
Pound, Glenn Simpson *university dean*
Pratt, George Janes, Jr. *psychologist author*
Quinton, Paul Marquis *physiologist, educator*
Rahimi, Babak *literature and language professor*
Rahman, Yueh-Erh *biologist*
Rajasekar, Arcot *computer scientist*
Ramirez, Michael P. *editorial cartoonist*
Rapaport, Samuel I. *educator, physician*
Richman, Douglas Daniel *medical virologist, educator, internist*
Ride, Sally Kristen *physics professor, research scientist, retired astronaut*
Ries, Andrew *dean, educator*
Rinaker, Samuel Mayo, Jr. *retired utilities executive*
Rotenberg, Manuel *physics professor*
Rothschild, Richard E. *astrophysicist*
Rubenstein, Howard S. *physician, writer*
Rubin, Lewis Joseph *physician, researcher*
Rubinstein, Kim *theater educator*
Rudakov, Dmitry L. *research scientist*
Ruoslahti, Erkki *cell biologist, cancer researcher*
Sandwell, David *geophysicist, educator*
Schatz, Richard A. *cardiologist*
Scheffler, Immo Erich *molecular biologist, educator*
Schmid-Schoenbein, Geert Wilfried *biomedical engineer, educator*
Schneider, Benjamin *psychology professor, consultant*
Schneider, Gerald L. *plastic surgeon*
Schooley, Robert T. *medical educator*
Schottlaender, Brian E.C. *university librarian*
Schroeder, Julian Ivan *biology professor*
Schwartz, Donald A. *finance educator*
Seminoff, Jeffrey Aleksandr *ecologist, educator*
Shakespeare, Frank *ambassador*
Sham, Lu Jeu *physics professor*
Sharpless, K. Barry *chemist, educator*
Sherman, Irwin William *biological sciences educator, academic administrator*
Shu, Frank Hsia-San *physics professor, research scientist, educator*
Shuler, Kurt Egon *chemist, educator*
Silver, Dee Edward *physician, neurologist*
Singer, Robert *plastic surgeon*
Sirotin, Nicole Ashley *physician*
Snyder, Lisa *social worker, consultant*
Somerville, Richard Chapin James *atmospheric scientist, educator*
Starr, Ross Marc *economist, educator*
Steinberg, Daniel *biomedical scientist*
Sullivan, Robert S. *college dean*
Tan, Eng Meng *immunologist, biomedical researcher*
Taur, Yuan *physicist, researcher*
Teirstein, Paul Shepherd *cardiologist, educator*
Terras, Audrey Anne *mathematics professor*
Thompson, Charlotte Ellis *pediatrician, educator, writer*
Thompson, Steve Charles *engineer*
Topol, Eric Jeffrey *academic administrator, cardiologist, educator, geneticist*
Truksa, Jaroslav *molecular biologist*
Tsien, Roger Yonchien *chemist, cell biologist*
Tsuang, Ming Tso *psychiatrist, educator*
Tsuji, Frederick Ichiro *biochemist, molecular biologist*
Vallbona, Marisa *public relations counselor*
Van Dine, Vance *investment banker*
Van Lint, Victor Anton Jacobus *physicist*
Waddy, Lawrence Heber *writer*
Walker, Richard Hugh *orthopaedic surgeon*
Wallach, Nolan R. *mathematician, consultant*
Wang, Lei *biochemist*
Watson, Kenneth Marshall *physics professor*
West, John Burnard *physiologist, educator*
Whaley, Storm Hammond *retired federal agency administrator*
Wilkie, Donald Walter *retired biologist, aquarium administrator*
Wilkins, Floyd, Jr. *retired lawyer*
Wilson, Bonnie Jean *lawyer, educator, investor*
Wolynes, Peter Guy *chemistry researcher, educator*
Wong, Chi-Huey *chemistry professor*
Wood, Samuel H. *science company executive, physician, scientist*
Wright, Andrew *English literature educator*
Wulbert, Daniel Eliot *mathematician, educator*
Yoshimura, Kei *oceanographer*
Zeidler, James Robert *electrical engineer, researcher*
Zentella, Ana Celia *retired language educator*
Zhang, Dong-Er *medical educator*
Zhou, Quansheng *medical researcher*
ZoBell, Karl *lawyer*
Zyroff, Ellen Slotoroff *information scientist, classicist, educator*

La Mesa
Canzoneri, Lois H. *retired church musician*
Hansen, Grant Lewis *retired, aerospace executive*
Schmidt, James Craig *retired bank, savings and loan association executive*

La Mirada
Burke, Peggy A. *education educator*
Edwards, John Kent *religious studies educator, minister*
Hayward, Douglas J. *religious studies educator*
Kuld, Paul *retired biology professor*
Mumford, Lawrence R. *composer, educator*
Stangl, Walter David *science educator*
Weathers, Matthew *educator*

La Palma
Levy, Elaine Ann *music educator*

La Puente
Chico, Darlene Ehrich *elementary school educator*
Pleitez, Concepcion Maria *elementary school educator*
Ver Kuilen, Marion Jane *retired instructional aide*
Vetter, Lawrence Anthony *art educator, consultant*

La Quinta
Hoston, Germaine Annette *political science professor*
Mathre, Lawrence Gerhard *minister, federal agency administrator*
Pitkin, Roy Macbeth *retired obstetrician, educator*
Puente, Maria Luz *bilingual educator*

La Verne
Fleck, Raymond Anthony, Jr. *retired academic administrator*
Gelm, Richard Joseph *political scientist, educator*
Morgan, Stephen Charles *academic administrator*
Mosley, Shane *boxer*
Pollock, Donald *communications educator, filmmaker*
Rossum, Constance *management and marketing educator, consultant*

Ladera Ranch
Nguyen, Monique M. *optometrist, educator*
Skidmore, Michelle Marie *elementary school educator, principal*

Lafayette
Davies, Paul Lewis, Jr. *retired lawyer*
Dethero, J. Hambright *banker*
Edwards, Aura C. *political organization worker, volunteer*
Freeman, Tom M. *lawyer*
Kang, Isamu Yong *retired nuclear medicine physician*
Krueger, Robert Edward *mechanical engineer, manufacturing executive*
Lewis, Sheldon Noah *technology consultant*
Lichterman, Martin *history professor*
Morehouse, Valerie Jeanne *librarian*
Nolan, Janiece Simmons *retired health system administrator, consultant*
Romanowski, Bill (William Thomas Romanowski) *nutrition company executive, retired professional football player, actor*
Sherrer, Charles William *lawyer, writer*

Laguna Beach
Anderson, Elizabeth Carmal (Bette Anderson) *librarian, writer*
Arnold, John David *management counselor*
Barr, Ronald Jeffrey *dermatologist, pathologist*
Bent, Alan Edward *political science professor*
Darrow, Paul Gardner *painter, printmaker, cartoonist, illustrator*
Fry, Edward Bernard *retired education educator*
Hanauer, Joe Franklin *real estate company officer*
Simons, Barry Thomas *lawyer*
Toliver, Harold Earl *retired English language professional*

Laguna Hills
Banuelos, Betty Lou *rehabilitation nurse*
Beard, Ronald Stratton *lawyer*
DeGrave, Douglas Michael *lawyer*
Hammond, R. Philip *chemical engineer*
Reinglass, Michelle Annette *lawyer, mediator, arbitrator*
Rossiter, Bryant William *chemistry consultant*

Laguna Niguel
Cooper, Roger Merlin *information technology executive, federal agency and school system administrator*
Pollock, John Phleger *retired lawyer*
Reimer, Nona Brinkman *biology professor*
York, James Orison *retired real estate executive*

Laguna Woods
Badgley, John Roy *architect*
Hussey, William Bertrand *retired diplomat*
Leonard, Elizabeth Adney *social worker*
McClure, Hal H. *film producer*

Lagunitas
Holman, Arthur Stearns *artist*

Lake Arrowhead
Fitzgerald, John Charles, Jr. *investment banker*

Lake Elsinore
Young, Patricia Janean *speech pathology/audiology services professional*

Lake Forest
Bukaty, Raymond M. *lawyer*
Coyne, John F. *computer company executive*
Earhart, Donald Marion *management consultant, health care company executive*
Higby, Lawrence M. *medical products executive*
Larsen, Robert Ray *healthcare executive, surgeon*
Pardun, Thomas E. *telecommunications industry executive*
Schroeder, John A. *systems engineering consultant, educator*
Warren, Rick (Richard Duane Warren) *minister, writer*

Lake Isabella
Fraser, Eleanor Ruth *radiologist, administrator*

Lake View Terrace
McCraven, Eva Stewart Mapes *health service administrator*
Troyer, Verne *actor*

Lakewood
Gelb, Arthur Franklin *pulmonologist, educator*
Lestmann, Phillip Edward *mathematics educator, analyst and computer programmer*

Lancaster
Dumas, Louise Isabelle *elementary school educator*
Holley, Susan L. *psychologist*
Jones, Betty Ann *retired elementary school educator*
Khanal, Sanjaya *cardiologist, educator*
Kim, Gloria Seunghee *music educator, singer, director*
Suzuki-Laitila, Junko Kianna *biology professor*
Zamudio, Celia Isabel *language educator*

Larkspur
Greenberg, Myron Silver *lawyer*
Ramos, Charles Joseph (Joe Ramos) *wealth management consultant*
Ratner, David Louis *retired law educator*
Strunk, Brian L. *medical educator*

Lawndale
Robinson, Mary Beth *educational administrator*

Lemoore
Krend, William John *secondary school educator*
Rogers, Joel *biology professor*

Lincoln
Chong, Vernon *retired surgeon, military officer*
Dorn, Mary Ann *retired auditor*
Helzer, James Dennis *retired health facility administrator*
Johnson, Ursula Anne *artist*
Patten, Thomas Henry, Jr. *retired educator, personnel director*
Rockwell, Don Arthur *retired psychiatrist*

Littlerock
Haas, Sir Russell *ambassador*

Live Oak
Spilman, Janet Lynne *special education educator*

Livermore
Alder, Berni Julian *physicist, researcher*
Beller, Harry R. *microbiologist, chemist, researcher*
Chernov, Alexander Alexandrovich *physicist, researcher*
Cook, Robert Crossland *chemist, researcher*
Cowgill, Donald Franklin *physicist*
Hallquist, John O. *engineering company executive*
Hooper, Edwin Bickford *physicist*
Karr, Thomas John *research physicist*
Kidder, Ray Edward *physicist, consultant*
King, Ray John *electrical engineering educator, engineering company executive*
Leith, Cecil Eldon *retired physicist*
Malkin, Alexander J. *biophysicist*
Nellis, William J. *physicist*
Nuckolls, John Hopkins *physicist, researcher*
Raymond, Kristy Lynn *language educator*
Remington, Bruce A. *physics researcher*
Rescigno, Thomas Nicola *theoretical physicist*
Santer, Benjamin David *atmospheric scientist*
Seward, James Pickett *internist, educator*
Tarter, Curtis Bruce *physicist, science administrator*
Trebino, Rick Peter *physicist*
Tripodes, James G. *nuclear safety and environmental regulatory affairs professional*
Zalk, David Mark *industrial hygienist, EHS manager occupational health researcher*

Livingston
Foster, Ron *agricultural products supplier and executive*

Lodi
Reinold, Christy Diane *school counselor, consultant*

Loma Linda
Bailey, Leonard Lee *surgeon*
Bull, Brian Stanley *pathologist, educator*
Carter, Ronald *academic administrator*
Chan, Philip J. *medical educator*
Chinnock, Richard *pediatrician, educator*
Coggin, Charlotte Joan *cardiologist, educator*
Condon, Stanley Charles *gastroenterologist*
Herrmann, Paul C. *physician, chemist*
Lee, Sean S. *dentist, researcher*
Llaurado, Josep G. *nuclear medicine physician, researcher*
Lohman, Everett III *medical educator, director*
Longo, Lawrence Daniel *physiologist, obstetrician, gynecologist, educator*
Mohan, Subburaman *biochemist, educator*
Molnar, Violet *mental health nurse*
Ojogho, Okechukwu N. *surgeon, educator*
Schwab, Ernest Roe III *physiology educator, researcher, academic administrator*
Singh, Pramil Nand *epidemiologist, educator*
Slater, James Munro *radiation oncologist*

Strother, Allen *biochemical pharmacologist, researcher*
Sun, Shu-Wei (Richard Sun) *science educator*
Tanyi, Ruth A. *family practice nurse practitioner, lifestyle diseases consultant*
Taylor, Barry Llewellyn *microbiologist, educator*
Wareham, Ellsworth Edwin *cardiothoracic surgeon, educator*
Williams, Paul Allen *biomedical engineer, researcher*
Wood, Virchel Edgar *orthopedist, surgeon, educator*

Lomita
Sartoris, Joseph Martin *bishop emeritus*

Lompoc
Belisle-Foreman, Karen *music educator*
Means, James Andrew *retired engineer*
Wagner, Geraldine Marie *nursing educator, consultant*

Long Beach
Alexander, F. King *academic administrator*
Amouzegar, Mahyar *dean, systems analyst*
Barron, (Mary Lou) Slater *artist, retired educator*
Baruah, Bipasha *social sciences educator*
Brown, Roxanne (Jerene Roxanne Brown) *sales executive*
Burnett, Ella M. Glenn *education educator*
Calhoun, John R. *lawyer*
Chapman, Lisa Ann *financial planner*
deAlbuquerque, Joan Marie *conductor, music educator*
Deukmejian, George *lawyer, Former Governor, California*
Dillon, Michael Earl *mechanical engineering executive, educator*
Duran, Matias Martin *retired adult education educator*
Elston, Joan Wilma *adult education educator, real estate agent*
Engelhardt, James F. *theater educator*
Engle, Robert Irwin *music educator, translator*
Fenton, Gayle B. *academic administrator*
Fiebert, Martin Stephen *psychology professor*
Fischler, Sandy Lynn *charitable and informational organization executive*
Fleming, Jane Williams *retired elementary school educator, writer*
Foster, Robert G. (Bob Foster) *Mayor, Long Beach, California*
Fradella, Henry F. *law educator*
Halili, Antonio Marquez *facilities maintenance mechanic*
Haller, Howard Edward *investment banker, real estate developer, filmmaker*
Hancock, John Walker III *banker*
Higginson, John *retired career officer*
Hinton, Marie-Laure *language educator, researcher*
Hsu, John C. *system, aerospace mechanical engineer*
Hu, Chi Yu *retired physicist, educator*
Jeynes, William Hettich *education educator, religious organization administrator, minister*
Killian, Thomas J. *engineering educator*
Kumar, Rajendra *electrical engineering educator*
Kwaan, Jack Hau Ming *retired physician*
Lathrop, Irvin Tunis *retired dean*
Macer, George Armen, Jr. *orthopedic hand surgeon*
Mandolini-Pesaresi, Massimo *classicist, educator*
Marks, Melvin I. *physician, educator, hospital administrator, consultant*
Mathieu, Susan Leifer *recreational therapist, educator*
McGaughey, Charles Gilbert *retired biochemist*
Metzger, Vernon Arthur *management educator, consultant*
Molina, Joseph Mario (Mario Molina) *medical administrator*
Monson, Dan *men's college basketball coach*
Moon, Hojin *statistician, educator*
Murray, John Patrick *education educator*
Myers, Robert *museum director*
Nagai, Chikako *social sciences educator*
Nishino, Hitoshi *physics professor*
Philpott, Lindsey *civil engineer, researcher, educator*
Proust, Joycelyn Ann *retired librarian*
Ross, Melvin Lee *history professor*
Sassoon, Catherine *pulmonologist, educator*
Sato, Eunice Noda *former mayor, consultant*
Schmidt, Eleanore *library director*
Schroeder, Arnold Leon *mathematics professor*
Schubel, Jerry Robert *marine scientist educator, dean*
Schultz, Gary David *lawyer*
Sciortino, Antonella *engineering educator*
Sidhwa, Frank N. *engineering executive*
Smeal, Kemp Leslie *psychotherapist, musician*
Springer, Wilma Marie *retired elementary school educator*
Toma, Ramses Barsoum *food science and nutrition educator*
Tsang, Chit-Sang *engineering educator*
Tucker, Marcus Othello *judge*
Walker, Linda Ann *financial planner*
Wise, George Edward *lawyer*
Worcester, Howard Lester *internist*
Wu, Sing-Yung *physician, researcher*
Yousef, Fathi Salaama *communications educator, management consultant*
Zitzer-Comfort, Carol *literature and language professor*

Los Alamitos
Aberman, Harold Mark *veterinarian*

Los Altos
Alexander, Kathryn Jean Macaulay (Kay) *retired art curriculum writer, consultant*
Aryanfar, Farshid *electrical and electronics engineer*
Bergrun, Norman Riley *aerospace executive*
Green, George Reite *psychologist*
Hahn, Harold Thomas *physical chemist, chemical engineer*
Hickman, Martha Whitmore *writer*
Kaiman, Sarah *retired physician*
King, Chi-Yu *research scientist*
Larson, Carol S. *foundation administrator, lawyer*
Mackey, Sean Charles *anesthesiologist, electrical engineering consultan*
Miller, Thormund Aubrey *lawyer*
Nivison, David Shepherd *language educator, philosopher*
Oh, Kyung Suk (Dan Oh) *electrical engineer*
Peterson, Victor Lowell *aerospace engineer, consultant*
Yang, Roxana Hwu *lawyer, investor*

Los Altos Hills
Gibbs Stayte, Patricia Leigh *social sciences educator, researcher*
Sharpe, Roland Leonard *structural engineer, consultant*

Los Angeles
Aberbach, Joel David *political science professor, writer*
Abrams, Norman *retired law educator, former academic administrator*
Adams, Thomas Merritt *lawyer*
Adell, Hirsch *lawyer*
Adler, Erwin Ellery *lawyer*
Adler, Fred Peter *retired electronics company executive*
Affleck, Ben *actor*
Agnew, John A. *science educator*
Agus, David Bernard *oncologist, researcher, medical educator*
Akhtari, Massoud *medical educator*
Alarcón, Arthur Lawrence *federal judge*
Alkalay, Arie L. *neonatologist*
Alkon, Ellen Skillen *physician*
Allen, Michael John Bridgman *language educator*
Allen, Sharon *accounting firm executive*
Allen, Walter Recharde *sociology educator*
Allen, William Richard *retired economist*
Allred, Gloria Rachel *lawyer*
Allums, Henriene *elementary school educator*
Alpers, Edward Alter *history professor*
Alvarez, Rodolfo *sociology educator, consultant*
Alves, Rodney Almeida *lawyer, consultant*
Anawalt, Patricia Rieff *anthropologist, researcher*
Anderson, Joshua E. *lawyer*
Anderson, Martin Mathew *pediatrician, educator*
Angeloff, Dann Valentino *brokerage house executive*
Aniston, Jennifer *actress*
Annaud, Jean-Jacques *film director, producer, scriptwriter*
Ansell, Benjamin Jesse *physician*
Ansley, Julia E. *retired elementary school educator, poet, writer*
Apt, Charles *artist*
Apt, Leonard *pediatric ophthalmologist*
Apuzzo, Michael Lawrence John *neurological surgeon*
Archerd, Army (Armand A. Archerd) *columnist, retired commentator*
Armenian, Haroutune Krikor *science educator*
Armstrong, Lloyd, Jr. *academic administrator, physics professor*
Arnett, Will *actor*
Aronoff, Vera *law librarian*
Aronzon, Paul S. *lawyer*
Artest, Ron (Ronald William Artest Jr.) *professional basketball player*
Arthur, John M. *editor*
Ashforth, Alden *musician, educator*
Askanas-Engel, Valerie *neurologist, educator, researcher*
Austen, Karl Ramsdell *lawyer*
Avenaim, Jerry *commercial photographer*
Avidan, Alon Y. *physician*
Axelrod, Jeremiah Borenstein *writer, educator*
Azad, Susan Stott *lawyer*
Azen, Stanley Paul *medical educator*
Bacharach, Burt *composer, conductor*
Baehr, Jason *philosopher, educator*
Bahr, Ehrhard *Germanic languages and literature educator*
Bakaly, Charles George, Jr. *lawyer, mediator*
Baker, Craig J. *surgeon, department chairman*
Baker, Dylan *actor*
Baker, Robert Frank *molecular biologist, educator*
Balaski, Belinda L. *actress, educator, writer, artist, photographer*
Banerjee, Utpal *biology professor, research scientist*
Bangalter, Thomas *recording industry executive, musician*
Banks, Elizabeth *actress*
Banks, Tyra (Tyra Lynne Banks) *television personality, retired model*
Barberopoulou, Aggeliki *geophysicist, educator*
Bardem, Javier *actor*
Barker, Bob (Robert William Barker) *television personality*
Barone, Sherry Joy *test engineer*
Barren, Bruce Willard (HRH The Duke de Serres) *merchant banker*
Barrett, Jane Hayes *lawyer*
Barrios, Jarrett Tomas *civils rights organization executive, former state legislator*
Barron, Stephanie *curator*
Barton, Alan Joel *lawyer*
Bassett, Angela Evelyn *actress*
Bates, Kathy *actress*
Bates, Marcia Jeanne *information scientist educator*
Baum, Michael Lin *lawyer*
Baumann, Richard Gordon *lawyer*
Baumbach, Noah *screenwriter*
Baumgarten, Ronald Neal *lawyer*
Baxter, Frank Edward *United States Ambassador to Uruguay, former brokerage executive*
Bazargan-Hejazi, Shahrzad *medical researcher*
Beart, Robert W., Jr. *colon and rectal surgeon, educator*
Begley, Ed, Jr. *actor*
Bekey, George Albert *computer scientist, educator*
Bell, Drake (Jared Drake Bell) *actor, singer*
Bell, Kristen *actress*
Bell, Lee Phillip *television personality, producer*
Bell, William J., Jr. *television producer*
Bender, Charles William *lawyer*
Bendiksen, Oddvar Olav *aerospace engineer, educator*
Bendix, Helen Irene *lawyer*
Benedict, Diane *theater educator, director*
Bening, Annette *actress*
Bennett, Charles Franklin, Jr. *biogeographer, educator*
Bennett, Fred Gilbert *lawyer*
Bennington, Chester Charles *singer*
Bennis, Warren Gameliel *business administration educator*
Benson, Michael *marketing executive*
Benson, Sidney William *chemistry researcher*
Berk, Blair *lawyer*
Berman, David Albert *pharmacologist, educator*
Berman, Geoffrey Louis *diversified financial services company executive*
Berman, Myles Lee *lawyer*
Berns, Marla C. *museum director*
Bernstein, Sol *cardiologist, educator*
Berry, Halle Maria *actress*
Berry, Stephen Joseph *reporter*
Bhaumik, Mani Lal *physicist*
Bibicoff, Hillary Sue *lawyer*
Bice, Scott Haas *dean, law educator*
Biele, Hugh Irving *retired lawyer*
Biggs, Jason *actor*
Billig, Franklin Anthony *retired chemist*
Bilson, Rachel *actress*
Binder, Gordon M. *venture capitalist*
Birge, Bettine *history professor*
Black, Keith Lanier *neurosurgeon, educator*
Blahd, William Henry *nuclear medicine physician, director*
Blair, Selma (Selma Blair Beitner) *actress*
Blake, Charles E. *minister, bishop*
Blencowe, Paul Sherwood *lawyer, private investor*
Bloom, Alan *lawyer*
Bloom, Claire *actress*
Blue, Violet (Ada Mae Johnson) *blogger*
Bodkin, Henry Grattan, Jr. *lawyer*
Boehm, Barry William *computer science educator*
Bogen, George *endodontist, educator*
Boles, Richard Gregory *clinical geneticist, researcher*
Bonesteel, Michael John *lawyer*
Bonner, Robert Cleve *lawyer*
Bookheimer, Susan Yost *neuropsychologist*
Borenstein, Daniel Bernard *psychiatrist, educator*
Borkowski, George Myron *lawyer*
Borneman, John Paul *pharmaceutical executive*
Bottjer, David John *earth science and biology educator*
Bourdon, Robert Gregory *musician*
Bowa, Larry (Lawrence Robert Bowa) *professional baseball coach, retired professional baseball player*
Boxer, Lester *lawyer*
Boyajian, Timothy Edward *public health officer, educator, consultant*
Boyd, Malcolm *minister, writer*
Boyer, Paul Delos *biochemist, educator*
Boyle, Barbara Dorman *film company executive*
Boyle, Kevin Richard *lawyer*
Bradley, Lawrence D., Jr. *lawyer*
Bradshaw, Murray Charles *musicologist, educator, composer*
Branca, John Gregory *lawyer, consultant*
Brand, Michael *museum director*
Bratton, Bill (William Joseph Bratton) *police chief*
Braun, Harland W. *lawyer*
Braxton, Toni *singer, actress*
Brendel, Bettina *abstract artist*
Brenneman, Amy *actress*
Brent, Gregory *endocrinologist, educator*
Breslow, Lester *public health physician, educator*
Bressan, Paul Louis *lawyer*
Breuer, Stephen Ernest *religious organization administrator, consultant*
Broad, Eli *foundation administrator, art collector*
Brody, Adrien *actor*
Brolin, James (James Brunderlin) *actor*
Brown, Deborah Ellen *gifted and talented educator, writer*
Brown, Dustin *professional hockey player*
Bryan, Greyson *lawyer*
Bryson, Louise Henry *retired broadcast executive*
Buffett, Jimmy (James William Buffett) *vocalist, songwriter, writer*
Buffington, Gary Lee Roy *safety engineer, construction executive*
Bugliosi, Vincent T. *lawyer, writer*
Burch, Robert Dale *lawyer*
Burcham, David W. *academic administrator, law educator*
Burke, Michael S. *corporate financial executive*
Burke, Robert Bertram *lawyer, political scientist, lobbyist*
Burnett, Charles *film director, screenwriter, producer*
Burnett, T-Bone (Henry John Burnett) *music producer, musician*
Burrows, James *television and motion picture director, producer*
Burton, Brian Joseph (Danger Mouse) *sound recording engineer, musician*
Burton, Tim (Timothy William Burton) *film director, film producer*
Bush, Wesley G. *aerospace transportation executive*
Butcher, Larry L. *neuroscientist, educator*
Butler, James Robertson, Jr. *lawyer*
Byrd, Christine Waterman Swent *lawyer*
Byrnes, James Bernard *museum director, consultant*
Caine, Sir Michael (Maurice Joseph Micklewhite, Jr.) *actor*
Caldwell, Nikki *women's college basketball coach*
Camby, Marcus D. *professional basketball player*
Cannon, Reuben *casting company executive, film producer*
Cantu, Roberto *social sciences educator*
Capron, Alexander Morgan *lawyer, educator, bioethicist*
Caram, Eve La Salle *language educator, writer*
Cardenas, Tony *councilman*
Caren, Jeffrey F. *cardiologist, educator*
Carleson, Lennart A(xel) E(dvard) *mathematics professor*
Carmona, Victor Daniel *biology professor*
Carnicke, Sharon Marie *theater director, educator, theater specialist*
Carolla, Adam *actor, radio personality, film producer, scriptwriter*
Caroompas, Carole Jean *artist, educator*
Carr, Willard Zeller, Jr. *retired lawyer*
Carrey, Jim *actor*
Carrey, Neil *lawyer, educator*
Carroll, Pete *college football coach*
Carter, Chris *producer, director*
Casillas, Jacqueline Nieto *hematologist, oncologist, educator*
Castro, Leonard Edward *lawyer*
Cates, Gilbert *television and film producer, theater director*
Caywood, KayDee *special education educator*
Cecere, Domenico *homebuilding company executive*
Cee-Lo, (Thomas DeCarlo Callaway) *singer*
Chadwick, William Jordan *lawyer*
Chaiken, Stacie Rae *writer, performer, theater director, educator*
Champagne, Duane Willard *sociology educator*
Champlin, Charles Davenport *television personality, critic, writer*
Chan, David Ronald *tax specialist, lawyer*
Chandor, Stebbins Bryant *pathologist*
Chang, Cyndie Marie *lawyer*
Chang, Henry C. *library administrator*
Chang, Jane P. *chemical engineering educator*
Chang, Tom Shio *min ophthalmologist*
Chapman Collins, Janice *school system administrator*
Charney, Dov *apparel executive*
Chavez, Michael Robinson *photojournalist*
Chazen, Stephen I. *oil industry executive*
Cheadle, Donald Frank *actor*
Chedid, John George *bishop emeritus*
Cheeseboro, Margrit *retired economics educator*
Chen, Tony Dong *lawyer*
Cheng, Hong *library and information scientist*
Cherry, James Donald *pediatrician*
Chhetri, Dinesh Khatri *surgeon, educator*
Chiate, Kenneth Reed *lawyer*
Cho, Eung-Rae (Brian) *bank executive*
Chopra, Inder Jit *endocrinologist*
Christol, Carl Quimby *lawyer, political science professor*
Christopher, Warren Minor *lawyer, former United States Secretary of State*
Chu, Morgan *lawyer*
Chugal, Nadia *dental educator, director*
Clark, Burton Robert *sociologist, educator*
Clark, Dick *performer, producer*
Clark, Edward *bishop*
Clark, R(ufus) Bradbury *lawyer, director*
Clarke, Peter *communications and health educator*
Clayburgh, Jill *actress*
Clemente, Carmine Domenic *anatomist, educator*
Coates, Thomas Duane *pediatrician, hematologist, educator*
Cohen, Cynthia Marylyn *lawyer*
Cohen, S(tephen) Marshall *philosophy educator*
Colacurcio, Michael J. *English professor*
Cole, Carolyn *photojournalist*
Cole, K.C. *journalist, writer*
Coleman, Charles Clyde *physicist, educator*
Colletti, Ned Louis, Jr. *professional sports team executive*
Collier, Charles Arthur, Jr. *lawyer*
Comai, Lucio *biology professor*
Cong, Jason Jingsheng *computer scientist, educator, consultant, researcher*
Conklin, Jeffrey L. *medical educator, director*
Connor-Dominguez, Billie Marie *retired science information professional*
Contreras-Sweet, Maria *bank executive*
Cook, Ian Ainsworth *psychiatrist, researcher, educator*
Cooley, Steve *prosecutor*
Cooper, Chris *actor*
Cooper, Michael Jerome *professional basketball coach, former professional basketball player*
Cooper, Robert E. *lawyer*
Cooper, Stephen F. *management consultant, film company executive*
Copeland, Stewart *composer, musician*
Cora, Cat *chef*
Cordasco, Kristina M. *medical researcher, educator*
Cordova, Richard D. *hospital administrator*
Corley, Constance *social worker, professor*
Corman, Roger William *film director*
Cornwall, John Michael *physics professor, consultant*
Corrigan, Timothy *interior designer, former advertising executive*
Corwin, Norman *scriptwriter, film producer, film director*
Coupe, James Warnick *lawyer*
Cowan, Louis Geoffrey *communications educator, writer*
Coyne, Joseph Francis, Jr. *lawyer*
Crabtree-Ireland, Duncan *lawyer*
Craig, Daniel *actor*
Crawford, Chace *actor*
Crockett, Donald Harold *composer, music educator*
Cruise, Tom (Thomas Cruise Mapother IV) *actor*
Cruz, Penélope *actress*
Cuadra, Carlos Albert *library and information scientist, consultant*
Cummings, Jeffrey L. *neurologist, educator*
Curran, Darryl Joseph *photographer, educator*
Currie, Janet M. *economics professor*
Currier, Jesse *cardiologist*
Curtiss, Thomas, Jr. *lawyer*
Cushman, John C. III *real estate company executive*
Custen, Barbara S. *library director*
Cyrus, Billy Ray *country music performer, actor*
Czer, Lawrence S.C. *internist*
D'Accone, Frank Anthony *music educator*
Daldry, Stephen *theater director, film director*
Daley, Melita *psychiatrist, director*
Daly, Robert Anthony *international relief organization, former professional sports team and film company executive*
Daly, Timothy *actor*

Damasio, Antonio R. *psychology and neurology professor, researcher*
Damasio, Hanna *psychology and neuroscience professor, researcher*
Daniels, John Peter *lawyer*
Dano, Paul Franklin *actor*
Danoff, Dudley Seth *surgeon, urologist*
Danziger, Bruce Edward *structural engineer*
Darby, Michael Rucker *economist, educator*
Darden, Christopher Allen *lawyer, writer*
Davidson, Ezra C., Jr. *obstetrician, gynecologist, academic administrator, educator*
Davis, Baron *professional basketball player*
Davis, Gray (Joseph Graham Davis) *lawyer, former governor*
Davis, LaVan *actor*
Davis-Fernandes, Tina Denise *secondary school educator, coach*
Dawson, Rosario *actress, singer*
Day, Richard Hollis *economics educator*
Dayton, Sky *telecommunications company executive*
De Brier, Donald Paul *lawyer, oil industry executive*
Decker, Richard Jeffrey *lawyer*
Dee, Ruby (Ruby Dee Davis) *actress, writer, film director*
Dekmejian, Richard Hrair *political science professor*
De La Hoya, Oscar *retired boxer*
Delson, Brad Phillip *musician*
Del Toro, Benicio (Benicio Monserrate Rafael del Toro Sánchez) *actor*
Delugach, Albert Lawrence *journalist*
Demoff, Marvin Alan *lawyer*
Denari, Neil M. *architectural firm executive, educator*
Denham, Robert Edwin *lawyer*
Dennehy, Brian *actor*
DePamphilis, Donald Michael *finance professor*
dePaolis, Potito Umberto *food company executive*
de Passe, Suzanne *record company executive*
De Robertis, Edward M. F. *research scientist, educator*
Detels, Roger *epidemiologist, retired dean*
Deville, Jaime Gerardo *medical educator*
Dewey, Donald Odell *dean, academic administrator*
Dhir, Vijay K. *engineering educator*
Diamond, Stanley Jay *lawyer*
Dienes, Louis Robert *lawyer*
Dillon, Kevin *actor*
Dinel, Richard Henry *lawyer*
Dinklage, Peter *actor*
Dodd, Jan Eve *lawyer*
Domingo, Plácido (José Plácido Domingo Embil) *tenor, conductor, opera company director*
Don, Manuel *medical researcher*
Donaldson, Roger *film director, film producer*
Donner, Neal Arvid *educator*
Dorfman, William M. (Bill Dorfman) *dentist*
Dorman, Albert A. *engineering executive, consultant, architect*
Dotolo, Vinny *chef*
Downey, Robert, Jr. *actor, singer*
Dows, David Alan *emeritus chemistry professor*
Dr. Dre, (Andre Ramelle Young) *rap musician, record producer*
Driver, Minnie *actress*
Drooyan, Richard E. *lawyer*
Dr. Phil, (Phillip Calvin McGraw) *psychologist, television personality*
Dubeau, Louis *medical educator, researcher*
Duel, Barry P. *urologist, pediatrician*
Dummett, Clifton Orrin *dentist, educator*
Dunkel Schetter, Christine *psychology educator*
Dunleavy, Mike (Michael Joseph Dunleavy Jr.) *professional basketball coach*
Duranti, Alessandro *anthropology professor*
Duritz, Adam *musician*
Durnil, John Michael *civil rights organization executive*
Dutta, Shantanu *dean*
Dworsky, Daniel Leonard *architect, educator*
Dwyre, William Patrick *journalist*
Eatman, Louis Perkins *lawyer*
Eckhart, Aaron *actor*
Edelman, Scott Alan *lawyer*
Edgerton, Bradford Wheatly *plastic surgeon*
Edwards, Marion *broadcast executive*
Efron, Zac *actor, singer*
Elderkin-Thompson, Virginia *Neuropsychologist*
Electra, Carmen (Tara Leigh Patrick) *actress*
Ellenbogen, Richard *plastic surgeon*
Elrod, Lu *music professor emerita, actress*
Elswit, Robert *cinematographer*
Engel, Jerome, Jr. *neurologist, neuroscientist, psychiatry professor*
Engel, William King *neurologist, educator*
Enstrom, James Eugene *epidemiologist*
Eo, SuRak *plastic surgeon, educator*
Epstein, Marsha Ann *public health physician*
Erdos, Joanna E. *school counselor, secondary school educator*
Ervin, Gary W. *aerospace transportation executive*
Escarce, José J. *medical educator*
Eskin, Eleazar *science educator*
Espinosa-Jeffrey, Araceli Marie *neurobiologist*
Es-Said, Omar Salim *metallurgy educator*
Etheridge, Melissa Lou *singer, lyricist*
Ettenger, Robert Bruce *physician, pediatric nephrologist*
Ezaki, Motoko *literature and language professor*
Faber, George Donald *retired communications executive*
Fairbank, Robert Harold *lawyer*
Fairey, Shepard *printmaker*
Fanselow, Michael Scott *psychology professor*
Farmer, Robert Lindsay *lawyer*
Farnham, Katherine A. *recording artist*
Farrell, David Michael *musician*
Farrell, Joseph *film producer and company executive, financial analyst*
Fathpour, Sasan *optical engineer, researcher*
Feig, Stephen Arthur *pediatrician, hematologist, oncologist, educator*
Feigen, Brenda S. *lawyer, film producer, writer*
Fein, Ronald Lawrence *lawyer*
Feinberg, David T. *hospital administrator*
Feldman, Larry Robert *lawyer*
Feldman, Lewis G. *lawyer*
Feldman, Robert C. (Bob) *public relations executive*
Felker, Patti C. *lawyer*
Felton, Lewis Peter *engineering educator*
Feniger, Susan *chef, television personality, writer*
Fenning, Lisa Hill *lawyer, mediator, retired judge*
Ferrell, Bruce Allen *medical educator*
Ferrera, America Georgine *actress*
Feshbach, Seymour *psychology professor*
Feuerstein, William Michael *application developer*
Fickett, Edward Hale *architect, educator, arbitrator*
Field, Sally Margaret *actress*
Field, Ted (Frederick) *film company and former recording industry executive*
Fielding, Jonathan Evan *county health department administrator, pediatrician*
Fields, Bertram Harris *lawyer*
Fincher, Edgar Franklin *dermatologic surgeon*
Finegold, Sydney Martin *infectious disease and microbiology researcher*
Finnegan, Michael J. *lawyer*
Firstenberg, Jean Picker *retired film institute executive*
Fischer, Alfred George *geology educator*
Fischer, Jenna (Regina Marie Fischer) *actress*
Fisher, Isla Lang *actress*
Fisher, Ruth E. *lawyer*
Fitzgerald, Tikhon (Lee R. H. Fitzgerald) *bishop*
Fleming, Andrew Macdonald *film director*
Fleming, Arthur Wallace *physician, surgeon*
Fletcher, Louise *actress*
Fodor, Peter Bela *plastic surgeon, educator*
Foley, Martin James *lawyer*
Follick, Edwin Duane *law educator, dean, chiropractor*
Fonarow, Gregg Curtis *cardiologist, educator*
Fonda, Jane *actress*
Fonkalsrud, Eric Walter *pediatric surgeon, educator*
Forness, Steven Robert *educational psychologist*
Forrester, James Stuart *cardiologist, medical educator*
Forte, Will (Orville Willis Forte IV) *actor, scriptwriter*
Fossum, Louis Eric *theater educator, writer*
Foster, Sutton *actress*
Foust, Lawrence L. *lawyer*
Fragner, Matthew Charles *lawyer*
Francis, Merrill Richard *lawyer*
Freehling, Allen Isaac *rabbi*
Freier, Elliot G. *lawyer*
Friedlander, Saul *historian, educator*
Frolov, Alexander *professional hockey player*
Fujie, Holly J. *legal association administrator, lawyer*
Fulco, Armand John *biochemist*
Gabriel, Ronald Samuel *child neurologist*
Galton, Stephen Harold *lawyer*
Gampel, Elaine Susan *investment company executive, consultant*
Ganas, Perry Spiros *physicist*
Ganz, Patricia Anne *medical educator, physician*
Garbacz, Gregory A. *lawyer*
Garban, Hermes J. *biomedical researcher, educator*
Garcetti, Eric *councilman*
Gardner, Joseph Lawrence *editor, writer*
Garofalo, Ellyn S. *lawyer*
Gasson, Judith C. *molecular biologist, research scientist*
Gatti, Richard A. *medical geneticist, educator*
Gatz, Margaret *psychology professor, department chairman*
Gazzale, Bob *film institute executive*
Gehry, Frank Owen *architect*
Geller, Kenneth Allen *otolaryngologist*
Geller, Stephen Arthur *pathologist, educator*
Geoffrion, Arthur Minot *management scientist*
Geragos, Mark John *lawyer*
Gere, Richard *actor*
Gest, Howard David *lawyer*
Gewertz, Bruce Labe *surgeon, educator*
Ghez, Andrea Mia *astronomy and physics educator*
Gianopulos, Jim *film company executive*
Giffin, Margaret Ethel (Peggy Giffin) *management consultant*
Gilliam, Franklin D., Jr. *dean, political science professor*
Gilman, John Joseph *research scientist*
Gilroy, Tony *scriptwriter, film director*
Ginsberg, David *medical educator*
Girardi, Thomas Vincent *lawyer*
Glaser, Patricia L. *lawyer*
Glasgow, Istiharoh *art administrator*
Glaspy, John *hematologist and oncologist, cancer researcher*
Goda, Keisuke *research scientist*
Goedde, Alan George *financial company executive*
Goff, Phillip Atiba *psychology professor, consultant*
Goin, Marcia Kraft *physician*
Gold, Victor J. *dean, academic administrator, law educator*
Goldberg, Robert B. *molecular biologist, educator*
Goldman, Allan Bailey *lawyer*
Goldman, Donald Aaron *lawyer*
Goldman, Ronald L.M. *lawyer*
Goldsman, Melvin Saul *lawyer*
Golleher, George *food company executive*
Gomez, Diana L. *professional society administrator, engineer*
Gondry, Michel *film director*
Gong, William C. *pharmacist, educator*
Goodman, Max A. *lawyer, educator*
Gordon, Basil *retired mathematics professor*
Gordon, Malcolm Stephen *biology professor*
Gordon-Levitt, Joseph Leonard *actor*
Goren, Edward Gerald (Ed Goren) *broadcast executive*
Gorman, Joseph Gregory, Jr. *lawyer*
Gorney, Roderic *psychiatrist, educator*
Gosling, Ryan (Ryan Thomas Gosling) *actor*
Gothold, Stuart Eugene *school system administrator, education educator*
Gottfried, Ira Sidney *management consulting executive*
Govan, Michael James *museum director*
Graham, Heather *actress*
Grammer, Kelsey *actor*
Graves, Anna Marie *lawyer*
Gray, John L. *museum director*
Green, Trent Jason *sportscaster, retired professional football player*
Green, William Porter *lawyer*
Greenberg, Barry Michael *talent executive*
Greenberg, Gordon Alan *lawyer*
Greuel, Wendy Jane *city official*
Griffin, Blake Austin *professional basketball player*
Grinnell, Alan Dale *neuroscientist, educator*
Grobe, Charles Stephen *lawyer, accountant*
Grody, Wayne William *physician, educator*
Guarnieri, Roberta Jean *elementary school educator, consultant*
Gubera, Jon Christien *secondary school educator*
Guerrero, Daniel G. *sports association administrator*
Guevara, Ramon Emmanuel *epidemiologist*
Gugino, Carla *actress*
Guider, Elizabeth Grier *editor*
Guo, Wei *research scientist*
Gurfein, Peter J. *lawyer*
Gutierrez, Carlos Miguel *former United States Secretary of Commerce, former grocery manufacturing company executive*
Gutierrez, Mary Alice *pharmacist, educator*
Guzy, Peter Michael *cardiologist, educator*
Gyllenhaal, Maggie *actress*
Haas, Mark *pathologist*
Hachamovitch, Rory *cardiologist, consultant*
Hack, Bruce *computer game and music company executive*
Hackman, Gene (Eugene Alden Hackman) *actor*
Hahn, Janice *councilwoman*
Hahn, Joseph *disc jockey, video director*
Hakim, Sam *finance educator, consultant*
Halberstadter, David *lawyer*
Haley, Roslyn Trezevant *educational program director*
Halkett, Alan Neilson *lawyer*
Halloran, John Alan *information technology executive*
Hamilton, Patricia Rose *art dealer*
Hamm, Catherine *travel editor*
Han, Xinhai *research scientist*
Hanks, Tom *actor, film producer, director*
Hannah, David H. *metal products executive*
Hansell, Dean *lawyer*
Hanson, John J. *retired lawyer*
Harber, Philip *preventive medicine physician, educator*
Harberger, Arnold Carl *economist, educator*
Hardison, Kadeem *actor*
Harkness, Nancy P. *lawyer*
Harper, Hill (Frank Harper) *actor*
Harrelson, Woody *actor*
Harris, Godfrey *public policy consultant*
Harrison, Rick E. *pediatrician*
Harrison, William Burwell, Jr. *retired diversified financial services company executive*
Hart, Melissa Joan *actress*
Hartenstein, Eddy W. *publishing executive, former electronics executive*
Hartke, Stephen Paul *composer, educator*
Hartsough, Gayla Anne Kraetsch *management consultant*
Harvey, PJ (Polly Jean Harvey) *singer*
Hateley, J. Michael *human resources executive*
Havel, Richard W. *lawyer*
Hawley, Philip Metschan *retired retail executive, management consultant*
Hayek, Salma *actress*
Hayes, Timothy Kai *language educator*
Haywood, L. Julian *cardiologist, educator*
He, Haihong *accounting educator*
Hecht, Joel Randolph *oncologist*
Hedley, Mary Lynne *biopharmaceutical executive*
Hefner, Hugh Marston *editor-in-chief*
Heigl, Katherine Marie *actress*
Heinke, Rex S. *lawyer*
Heller, Philip *lawyer*
Hellwarth, Robert Willis *physicist, researcher*
Hemminger, Pamela Lynn *lawyer*
Henderson, Brian Edmond *preventive medicine physician, educator, former dean*
Henkel, Kathy *composer*
Henley, Don *singer, drummer, songwriter*
Henriksen, Eva Hansine *retired anesthesiology educator*
Henson, Taraji Penda *actress*
Herrmann, Christian, Jr. *medical educator*
Herscher, Uri David *academic administrator, history educator, rabbi*
Herschman, Harvey Roy *medical educator, researcher*
Hextall, Ron *professional sports team executive, former professional hockey player*
Highberger, William Foster *lawyer*
Hill, Bonnie Guiton *consulting company executive*
Hill, Millicent E. *English educator*
Hilton, Perez (Mario Armando Lavandeira Jr.) *celebrity gossip blogger*
Hinojosa, Lynard Chris *lawyer*
Hirai, Denitsu *surgeon*
Hirsch, Judd *actor*
Hoang, Duc Van *pathologist, educator*
Hobbs, Pamela *communications educator, retired lawyer*
Hockney, David *artist*
Hoffman, Philip Seymour *actor*
Hoi, Samuel Chuen-Tsung *academic administrator*
Holbrook, Hal (Harold Rowe Holbrook Jr.) *actor*
Hollander, Sidney *computer systems engineer*
Holliday, Thomas Edgar *lawyer*
Hollihan, Thomas Andrew *communications educator*
Holscher, Mark Charles *lawyer*
Holt, James Franklin *retired numerical analyst, scientific programmer analyst*
Holtzman, Robert Arthur *lawyer*
Hooks, Rosie Lee *museum director, actor, filmmaker*
Hooper, Patric *lawyer*
Hopkins, Bernard *professional boxer*
Horovitz, Adam Keefe (Adrock, King Ad-Rock) *musician*
Houk, Kendall Newcomb *chemistry professor*
Hounsou, Djimon Gaston *actor*
House, John William *otolaryngologist*
Houston, Ivan James *insurance company executive*
Hovanessian, Shahen Alexander *electrical engineer, educator, consultant*
Howland, Ben *men's college basketball coach*
Hsiao, Cheng *economics educator*
Hubbard, John Randolph *retired academic administrator, diplomat*
Hubbell, Wayne Lester *ophthalmologist, chemist, educator*
Hudson, Kate *actress*
Hudson, Orlando Thill *professional baseball player*
Hufstedler, Shirley Mount *lawyer, former United States Secretary of Education*
Huizar, Jose *councilman*
Hull, LeAnne von Neumeyer *public relations and communications executive, research consultant, writer*
Hundley, Norris Cecil, Jr. *historian, educator*
Hurd, Gale Anne *film producer*
Hurt, William *actor*
Husar, Linda S. *lawyer*
Hutchins, Joan Morthland *manufacturing executive, farmer*
Hyde, Manly Richard *thoracic surgeon*
Hyman, Ursula H. *lawyer*
Ice-T, (Tracy Marrow) *rap artist, actor*
Ignarro, Louis J. *pharmacology educator*
Inaba, Carrie Ann *choreographer, dancer*
Ingersoll, Raymond Vail *geologist, educator*
Inman, James Russell *claims consultant*
Intriligator, Michael David *economist, educator*
Irani, Ray R. *oil, gas and chemical company executive*
Ireland, Kathy *actress, apparel designer*
Irwin, Michael Ray *psychology professor, researcher*
Irwin, Philip Donnan *lawyer*
IsHak, Waguih William *psychiatrist*
Itoh, Tatsuo *engineering educator*
Jackman, Hugh *actor*
Jackson, Alan Jay *prosecutor*
Jackson, Joshua Carter *actor*
Jackson, Philip Douglas *professional basketball coach*
Jackson, Samuel L. *actor*
Jacobson, Marcus J. *retired mechanical engineer*
Jacobson, Sidney *editor*
Jacoby, Neil Herman, Jr. *astronautical scientist, engineer, consultant*
Jadvar, Hossein *nuclear radiologist, biomedical engineer*
Jalali, Behnaz *psychiatrist, educator*
Jamieson, Beth D. *medical educator, director*
Jarrin, Jaime Leonardo *sportscaster, broadcast executive*
Jelliffe, Roger Woodham *cardiologist, pharmacologist*
Jensen, David Gram *management consultant*
Jobe, Frank Wilson *orthopedic surgeon*
Johansson, Scarlett *actress*
Johnson, Cage Saul *hematologist, educator*
Johnson, E. Eric *insurance company executive*
Johnson, Earl, Jr. *retired judge, author*
Johnson, Jeffrey M. *private equity company executive, former publishing executive*
Johnson, Jonathan Edwin, II, *lawyer*
Johnson, Kym *dancer*
Jones, January *actress*
Jones, Quincy *producer, composer, arranger, conductor, trumpeter*
Jones, Sir Tom (Thomas Jones Woodward) *singer*
Jordan, Robert Leon *lawyer, educator*
Jordan, Thomas Hillman *geophysicist, educator*
Joseph, George *insurance company executive*
Kagan Bierman, Ivy *lawyer*
Kahane, Jeffrey Alan *conductor, pianist, music director*
Kahn, Matthew E. *economics professor*
Kalis, Murray *advertising agency executive, writer*
Kalish-Weiss, Beth Isaacs *psychologist, psychoanalyst, consultant*
Kamine, Bernard S. *lawyer*
Kang, Alvin *bank executive*
Kanoff, Mary Ellen *lawyer*
Kanter, Sandra May *lawyer*
Kaplan, Isaac Raymond *chemistry professor*
Kaplan, Mark Vincent *lawyer*
Kaplan, Nadia *writer*
Kaplan, Robert Malcolm *health researcher, educator*
Kar, Saibal *cardiologist*
Karlan, Beth Young *gynecologic oncologist*
Karp, Harvey Neil *pediatrician*
Karst, Kenneth Leslie *law educator*
Kassner, Michael Ernest *materials science educator, researcher*
Katz, Roger *pediatrician, allergist, immunologist, educator*
Katzenstein, Andrew M. *lawyer*
Katzin, Carolyn Fernanda *nutritionist, consultant*
Kaul, Sanjay *cardiologist*
Kaunitz, Jonathan Davidson *physician*
Keenan, Edward L. *linguist, educator*
Keith, David *symphony orchestra conductor*
Kelley, David E. *producer, writer*
Kelly, Arthur Paul *physician*
Kelly, Henry Ansgar *language educator*
Ken, Susanto Suwarno *engineer*
Kendell, Ken *music educator*
Kennedy, George *actor*
Keyes, Cheryl L. *musician, educator*
Keyes, Geoffrey Robin *plastic surgeon*
Kidman, Nicole *actress*
Kieffer, George David *lawyer*
Kiley, Anne Campbell *lawyer*
Kim, Jeongbin John *mechanical engineering educator*
Kim, Kwang-Jin *medical educator*
Kim, Min Jung *bank executive*
Kim, Yong Jin *economics educator*
King, Bryan Harry *neuropsychiatrist, medical educator and researcher*
Kirkland, John C. *lawyer*
Kirsch, Claudia Françoise *radiologist*
Kivelson, Margaret Galland *physicist*
Klauss, Kenneth Karl *composer, music educator*
Klein, Deborah L. *lawyer*

Kleingartner, Archie *dean, educator, academic administrator*
Kleinrock, Leonard *computer scientist*
Kline, Richard Stephen *communications and public affairs executive*
Klinger, Marilyn Sydney *lawyer*
Klitzner, Thomas S. *pediatric cardiologist*
Klunder, Jack D. *publishing executive*
Knott, Jack H. *dean, political science professor*
Kobashigawa, Jon Akira *internist, cardiologist, researcher, educator*
Koepp, David *screenwriter*
Koga, Rokutaro (Rocky Koga) *physicist*
Kollatz-Florido, Rebecca Lynn *music educator*
Kolve, V. A. *English literature educator*
Kopitar, Anze *professional hockey player*
Koules, Oren D. *film producer, professional sports team executive*
Kramer, Barry Alan *psychiatrist, educator*
Krause, Peter *actor*
Krieger, Ellie *chef, dietitian, TV personality*
Krupka, Robert George *lawyer*
Krupp, Edwin Charles *astronomer*
Kuehl, Hans Henry *electrical engineering educator*
Kupferman, Steven Barry *oral & maxillofacial surgeon*
Kuroda, Hiroki *professional baseball player*
Kutcher, Ashton (Christopher Ashton Kutcher) *actor*
Kveton, Kyle *lawyer*
Kyles, Cedric Antonio (Cedric the Entertainer) *comedian, actor*
LaBonge, Tom *councilman*
La Force, James Clayburn, Jr. *economist, educator*
Langan, Kenneth J. *lawyer*
Lange, Jessica Phyllis *actress*
Lanham, Richard Alan *retired English language educator, literary critic*
Lappen, Chester I. *lawyer*
Larkin, Thomas Ernest, Jr. *investment management company executive*
Larry the Cable Guy, (Daniel Lawrence Whitney) *comedian, radio personality*
Larter, Ali (Alison Elizabeth Larter) *actress*
Lasorda, Tommy (Thomas Charles Lasorda) *retired professional baseball team manager*
Latham, Joseph Al, Jr. *lawyer*
Lauerhass, Ludwig, Jr. *history professor*
Lauridsen, Morten Johannes *composer, music educator*
Lawler, Jean Marie *lawyer*
Lawrence, Sanford Hull *physician, immunochemist, author*
Layne, Jonathan K. *lawyer*
Layton, Harry Christopher *art director*
Lazarus, David *journalist*
LeBeau, Mary Delle *dancer, educator, writer*
Lee, Stan (Stanley Martin Lieber) *cartoon publisher, writer*
Legohn, Lisa Marie *vocational school educator*
Lehrer, Robert Irving *medical educator*
Lekovic, Gregory Punisa *surgeon, lawyer*
LeMay, Harry Adrian *artist, educator*
LeMoyne, Robert *biomedical engineer*
Lennox, Annie *rock musician*
Leoni, Téa (Elizabeth Tea Pantaleoni) *actress*
Leslie, Lisa DeShaun *professional basketball player*
Lesser, Joan L. *lawyer*
Letterman, David *talk show host, producer, comedian, writer*
Letwin, Leon *law educator*
Leung, Frankie Fook-Lun *lawyer*
Levin, Harvey Robert *reporter, television producer, lawyer*
Levine, Marci Robyn *lawyer*
Levine, Michael *public relations executive, author, television and radio personality*
Levine, Pamela *film company executive*
Levine, Philip *classics educator*
Levine, Raphael David *chemistry professor*
Levine, Robert Arthur *economist, educator, policy writer*
Levinsohn, Peter *film company executive*
Levy, Seth David *lawyer*
Lewis, Claudia *film company executive*
Lewis, Karla R. *metal products executive*
Lhuillier, (Diane) Monique *apparel designer*
Li, Yong-Gang Frank *research scientist, educator*
Lichter, Linda *lawyer*
Liebling, Debbie (Deborah Liebling) *film company executive*
Lienert, James M. *oil industry executive*
Liman, Doug *film director, film producer*
Lindholm, Dwight Henry *lawyer*
Linkletter, Arthur Gordon *radio and television broadcaster*
Linsk, Michael Stephen *real estate company executive*
Linton, Mike *marketing executive*
Lionnet, Francoise *French and comparative literature educator*
Lipshutz, Gerald S. *medical educator, researcher*
Lipsig, Ethan *lawyer*
Litewka, Albert Bernard *entertainment executive*
Livanos, Alexis C. *aerospace transportation executive*
Lizarraga, David C. *non-profit community development corporation administrator*
Ljubimov, Alexander V. *molecular biologist, cell biologist, researcher*
Lombardi, Dean *professional sports team executive*
London, Andrew Barry *film editor*
Long, Gregory Alan *lawyer*
Long, Justin Jake *actor*
Lopez, George *actor, comedian*
Lopez, Jennifer *actress, singer, dancer*
Lovato, Demi (Demetria Devonne Lovato) *actress*
Lozano, Monica Cecilia *publishing executive*
Lu, Jia Grace *physicist, electrical engineer, educator*
Lyder, Courtney Harvey *dean, nursing educator*
Lynch, Beverly Pfeifer *education and information studies educator*
Lyons, James Richard *research scientist*
MacAlpin, Rex Nere *physician, educator*
Macavinta-Tenazas, Gemorsita *physician*
MacLachlan, Kyle *actor*
MacLaughlin, Francis Joseph *lawyer*
Macy, William H. *actor*
Mager, Artur *retired aerospace executive*
Maharaj, Davan R. *editor*
Mahmoodzadegan, Navid A. *investment banker*
Mahony, Roger Michael *cardinal, archbishop*
Malkin, Michelle *columnist, political commentator*
Malkovich, John *actor*
Maloney, Robert Keller *ophthalmologist, medical educator*
Man, Lawrence Kong *architect, art dealer, entrepreneur*
Mancino, Douglas Michael *lawyer*
Manella, Nora Margaret *judge*
Manelli, Donald Dean *scriptwriter, film and television producer*
Manheim, Camryn *television and film actress*
Marciano, Georges G. *apparel executive*
Marciano, Maurice *apparel executive*
Marciano, Paul L. *apparel executive*
Marder, John Adam *lawyer*
Margo, Rod David *lawyer*
Markland, Francis Swaby, Jr. *biochemist, educator*
Marmorstein, Victoria E. *lawyer*
Marrow, Deborah *foundation administrator*
Marsden, James Paul *actor*
Marshall, Mary Jones *civic worker*
Martin, Roland S. *journalist, former editor*
Martin, Russell (Nathan Coltrane Jeanson), Jr. *professional baseball player*
Martinez, Miguel Acevedo *urologist, consultant, lecturer*
Martinez, Vilma Socorro *lawyer*
Martins, David *medical researcher*
Masterson, Mary Stuart *actress*
Mathias, Alice Irene *business management consultant*
Matise, John J. *investment company executive*
Matlock, David Louis *obstetrician, gynecologist, reconstructive surgeon*
Matthews, Dave *singer, musician*
Maxson, Robert E. *biology professor*
Maxworthy, Tony *mechanical and aerospace engineering educator*
May, Rabbi Meyer H. *museum director*
McBride, Danny R. *actor*
McCabe, Edward R. B. *hospital administrator, educator, physician*
McCarthy, Paul *artist*
McCourt, Jamie *professional sports team executive*
McCurdy, Deborah K. *pediatric rheumatologist*
McFadden, P. Michael *physician, surgeon*
McGagh, William Gilbert *financial consultant*
McGough, James John *psychiatrist*
McGregor, Judith Ann *education educator*
McKinney, Virginia Elaine Zuccaro *educational administrator*
McKinzie, Carl Wayne *lawyer*
McKnight, Carl Phillip *psychologist*
McLane, Frederick Berg *lawyer*
McLaren, Mary *film company executive*
McLurkin, Thomas Cornelius, Jr. *lawyer*
McNevin, Christopher J. *lawyer*
McQueen, Justice Ellis (L. Q. Jones) *actor, television director*
McSavaney, Raymond S. *photojournalist*
Meaders, Donald W. *lawyer*
Medak, Peter *film director*
Medearis, Miller *lawyer*
Melby, Donna D. *lawyer*
Melnick, Michael *geneticist, educator*
Mendel, Jerry Marc *electrical engineering educator*
Mendez Ashla, Mario *neurologist, educator, internist*
Mentzer, Roslyn *academic administrator*
Mesereau, Thomas Arthur, Jr. *lawyer*
Meshki, Hamed *lawyer*
Messick, Andrew *marketing executive*
Metzger, Robert Streicher *lawyer*
Meyer, Bruce D. *lawyer*
Meyer, Michael Edwin *lawyer*
Meyer, Nick *film company executive*
Mezger, Jeffrey T. *construction executive*
Midler, Laurence H. (Larry) *lawyer, real estate company executive*
Mihan, Richard *retired dermatologist*
Milano, Alyssa *actress*
Milchan, Arnon *film producer*
Millard, Neal Steven *lawyer, educator*
Miller, Lee Todd *pediatrician, educator*
Miller, Milton Allen *lawyer*
Milliken, Mary Sue *chef, television personality, writer*
Mills, Linda A. *aerospace transportation executive*
Min, Soo Bong *bank executive*
Mishra, Shri Kant *neurologist, educator, neuroscientist*
Mitsuyasu, Ronald T. *physician, researcher, medical educator*
Mobasser, Anthony *cosmetic dentist*
Modabber, Zia F. *lawyer*
Moe, Stanley Allen *architect, consultant*
Mollins, Gregg J. *metal products executive*
Mondino, Bartly J. *ophthalmologist*
Montoya, Velma *economist, consultant*
Moore, Wesley Sanford *vascular surgeon*
More, Philip Harvey Birnbaum *business administration educator*
Morgan, Jean Elizabeth *plastic surgeon*
Morisky, Donald E. *director, medical educator*
Moriuchi, K. Derek *secondary school educator*
Morrissey, J. Richard *lawyer*
Morrow, Winston Vaughan *financial executive*
Mosk, Richard Mitchell *judge*
Motykie, Gary *plastic surgeon*
Moxley, John Howard III *internist*
MoY, Ronald Leonard *dermasurgeon*
Muldaur, Diana Charlton *actress*
Muntz, Eric Phillip *aerospace and mechanical engineering educator, consultant*
Murdock, David H. *food products executive*
Murphy, Eddie *actor, comedian*
Murphy, (Frances) Elaine *musician, harpist, flutist*
Murray, Anthony *lawyer*
Murray, Chad Michael *actor*
Murray, Terry (Terence Rodney Murray) *professional hockey coach*
Mussina, Michael Cole (Mike Mussina) *retired professional baseball player*
Myers, Hector *psychology professor, department chairman*
Nachshin, Robert Jay *lawyer*
Nadler, Gerald *management consultant, educator*
Naik, Vinayak Shashikant *research scientist*
Nathanson, Theodore Herzl *aeronautical engineer, architect*
Nathwani, Bharat N. *pathologist, educator*
Navab, Mohamad *cardiologist, educator*
Nazarian, Sam *hotel executive, film producer*
Needleman, Jack *education educator, researcher*
Negro, Mary Joan *art educator*
Neiter, Gerald Irving *lawyer*
Nelson, Barbara J. *public policy professor, former dean*
Nelson, Howard Joseph *geographer, educator*
Neufeld, Elizabeth Fondal *biochemist, educator*
Neuheisel, Rick (Richard Gerald Neuheisel, Jr.) *college football coach*
Neuwirth, Bebe (Beatrice Neuwirth) *dancer, actress*
Newhart, Bob (George Robert Newhart) *entertainer*
Newman, Michael Rodney *lawyer*
Newman, Richard G. *engineering company executive*
Newman, William I. *geophysicist, astrophysicist, educator*
Ng, Kim (Kimberly J. Ng) *professional sports team executive*
Nicholas, William Richard *lawyer*
Nicholson, Jack *actor*
Nielsen, Leslie *actor*
Nishi, Gregg K. *surgeon, educator*
Nobe, Ken *chemical engineering professor*
Noble, Ernest Pascal *pharmacologist, biochemist, educator, psychiatrist*
Noce, Walter William, Jr. *hospital administrator*
Nochimson, David *lawyer*
Nordlinger, Stephanie G. *lawyer*
Nuechterlein, Keith H. *psychology professor*
Obert, Jeanne L. *alcohol/drug abuse services professional, director*
O'Boyle, Christina *science educator*
O'Brien, Robert Charles *lawyer*
O'Brien, Thomas Peter *lawyer, former prosecutor*
Ochoa, Arthur J. *lawyer, hospital administrator*
O'Connell, Kevin *lawyer*
O'Connell, Taaffe Cannon *actress, publishing executive*
Odell, John Stephen *political scientist*
Ogilvie, Lloyd John *clergyman*
Oh, Soon Young *researcher*
O'Hurley, John *actor*
Okrent, David *engineering educator*
Olah, George Andrew *chemist, educator*
O'Leary, Prentice Lee *retired lawyer*
Olian, Judy D. *dean, management educator*
Oliver, Carl Russell *science educator*
Oliver, Dale Hugh *lawyer*
Olsen, Ashley Fuller *actress, apparel designer*
Olsen, Jørn *epidemiology educator, researcher*
Olsen, Mary-Kate *actress, apparel designer*
Olson, Ronald Leroy *lawyer*
O'Neal, Tatum *actress*
O'Neil, Harold Francis *psychologist, educator*
O'Neill, Kevin *men's college basketball coach*
Oppenheim, Charles B. *lawyer*
Oppenheimer, Randy (Mark Randall Oppenheimer) *lawyer*
Ordin, Andrea Sheridan *lawyer*
Orme, Antony Ronald *geography educator*
Osborne, Danny *psychologist, researcher*
Osment, Haley Joel *actor*
Oster, Marcia Rebecca *mental health services professional*
Owen, Clive *actor*
Owen, Michael Lee *lawyer*
Owens, Stephen Thomas *lawyer*
Ozcan, Aydogan *electrical engineer, educator*
Pagden, Anthony Robin *political science professor, historian, writer*
Pakbaznia, Ehsan *electrical engineer*
Palevsky, Max *industrialist, director*
Palmer, James F. *aerospace transportation executive*
Palmer, Keke (Lauren Keyana Palmer) *actress*
Palmieri, Victor Henry *lawyer, director, investment advisor*
Paltrow, Gwyneth *actress*
Panish, Brian Joseph *lawyer*
Parent, Mary Campbell *film company executive*
Parente, Robert Bruce *electrical engineer, consultant*
Park, Daeyoung *engineer, researcher*
Park, Lee (Lee Parklee) *artist*
Parker, Candace Nicole *professional basketball player*
Parks, Bernard *councilman*
Parks, Michael Christopher *journalist, educator*
Parmelee, Arthur Hawley, Jr. *pediatric medical educator*
Parsky, Gerald Lawrence *lawyer*
Parsons, Terence Dwight *linguist, educator*
Pascotto, Alvaro *lawyer*
Pasich, Kirk Alan *lawyer*
Patrick, Robert *playwright*
Paulson, Richard John *obstetrician, gynecologist, educator*
Pearl, Judea *computer scientist, educator*
Pecora, Vincent Pitt *English educator*
Penn, Sean *actor*
Perlis, Michael Fredrick *lawyer*
Perloff, Joseph Kayle *cardiologist, educator*
Perrine, Richard Leroy *environmental engineer, educator*
Perron, Edward Adrian *lawyer*
Perry, Jan *Councilwoman*
Perry, Katy (Katheryn Elizabeth Hudson) *singer*
Perry, Matthew *actor*
Perry, Ralph Barton III *lawyer*
Pervan, Nenad Neno *theater educator*
Pesta, Ben W., II, *lawyer, writer*
Peterson, Kurt C. *lawyer*
Petrocelli, Daniel M. *lawyer*
Pfaelzer, Mariana R. *federal judge*
Phillips, Keith Wendall *minister*
Phillips, Stacy D. *lawyer*
Phillips, Todd *film director, film producer*
Pi, Edmond Hsin-Tung *psychiatry educator*
Pierre, Juan *professional baseball player*
Piller, Charles Leon *journalist*
Pinto, Freida *actress*
Pircher, Leo Joseph *lawyer, director*
Pisano, Jane G. *museum administrator*
Pittman, Amanda Nelson *music educator*
Piven, Jeremy *actor*
Poitier, Sidney *actor, film director*
Pompeo, Ellen *actress*
Porter, Theodore Mark *history educator*
Porter, Verna Louise *lawyer*
Portman, Natalie *actress*
Powell, James Lawrence *educational association administrator, museum director, geologist*
Power, John Bruce *lawyer*
Prakash, Surya G.K. *chemistry educator*
Pressly, Jaime Elizabeth *actress*
Prewitt, Jean *not-for-profit organization executive*
Price, Frederick Kenneth Cercie *minister*
Prins, Robert Michael *medical educator*
Pritchett, Philip Lentner *physicist, researcher*
Provda, Lois M. *psychologist, educator*
Provencio, Marla *marketing executive*
Pugsley, Robert Adrian *law educator*
Puliafito, Carmen Anthony *dean, ophthalmologist, healthcare executive*
Pullman, Bill *actor*
Qiao, Jian-Hua *pathologist, researcher*
Que Hee, Shane Stephen *environmental health educator*
Quinlan, Catherine *library director*
Quinn, John B. *lawyer*
Quinn, John J. *lawyer*
Quinn, Tom *communications executive*
Racine, Scott H. *lawyer*
Raeder, Joachim *geophysicist*
Raja, Rajalingam *immunologist, educator*
Ramanathan, Rangasamy *pediatrician*
Ramer, Lawrence Jerome *corporation executive*
Ramirez, Manny (Manuel Aristides Ramirez) *professional baseball player*
Ramo, Simon *retired engineering executive*
Ramos, Francisco *language educator*
Ramos, Jorge *newscaster*
Rao, Narsing A. *ophthalmologist, pathologist, educator*
Rasmussen, Robert Kenneth *dean, law educator*
Rath, Howard Grant, Jr. *lawyer*
Ratzenberger, John Deszo *actor, writer, film director*
Raven, Bertram H(erbert) *psychology professor*
Ray, Charles *sculptor*
Reed, Irving Stoy *electrical engineer*
Reisler, Emil *biochemist, educator, dean*
Reiss, Howard *chemistry professor*
Reiter, Robert E. *urologist, educator*
Renwick, Edward S. *lawyer*
Resnick, Lynda *corporate financial executive*
Resnick, Stewart Allen *diversified company executive*
Reyes, Ed P. *councilman*
Rice, Peter *broadcast executive*
Rice, Thomas Howard *healthcare educator*
Rich, Alan *music critic, writer*
Richardson, John Vinson, Jr. *library and information science professor*
Richland, Kent Lewis *lawyer*
Richman, Michael F. *thoracic surgeon, consultant*
Rickles, Donald Jay *comedian, actor*
Riff, Lawrence P. *lawyer*
Riggen, Patricia *film director, film producer*
Rigole, Rose Hickman *lawyer*
Rimoin, David Lawrence *medical geneticist*
Rishwain, James Michael, Jr. *lawyer*
Rivera, John Zarate *director*
Roberts, Emma Rose *actress*
Roberts, Julia Fiona *actress*
Roberts, Sidney *biological chemist*
Robitaille, Luc *professional sports team executive, retired professional hockey player*
Rock, Chris *actor, comedian*
Roeder, Richard Kenneth *business owner, lawyer*
Roeser, Andy *professional sports team executive*
Rogen, Seth *actor*
Rong, Yue *environmental services administrator*
Rosenbaum, Arthur L. *ophthalmologist*
Rosenberg, Alan *actors guild executive*
Rosenberg, Joan I. *psychologist, educator*
Rosenbloom, Paul Simon *computer scientist*
Rosendahl, Bill *councilman*
Rosenfeld, John Lang *geology educator*
Rosenthal, Sol *lawyer*
Rosett, Arthur Irwin *lawyer, educator*
Ross, Bruce Shields *lawyer*
Ross, Marion *actress*
Roth, Tim *actor*
Rothenberg, Alan I. *lawyer, professional sports association executive*
Rothman, Tom (Thomas Edgar Rothman) *film company executive*
Rourke, Mickey (Philip Andre Rourke Jr.) *actor*
Rouse, Richard Hunter *historian, educator*
Roussey, Robert Stanley *accountant, educator*
Rouze, Jeffrey Alan *real estate executive*
Roven, Alfred Nathan *surgeon*
Rowell, Victoria *actress*
Roy-Burman, Pradip *molecular biology and virology educator*
Rubin, Robert Terry *psychiatrist, researcher, educator*
Rubin, Stanley Creamer *television producer, film producer*
Rubinstein, Moshe Fajwel *engineering educator*
Rush, Herman E. *television executive*
Ruskin, Joseph Richard *actor, director*
Rustand, Kay *lawyer*
Ruthberg, Miles N. *lawyer*
Ryan, Meg (Margaret Mary Emily Ann Hyra) *actress, film producer*
Saban, Haim *investment company executive, television producer*
Sachs, George *biology professor, physician*
Sadraie, Hamid Reza *civil engineer, researcher*
Safonov, Michael George *electrical engineering educator, consultant*

Sager, Kelli L. *lawyer*
Sahai Srivastava, Soma *neurologist, educator*
Sahimi, Muhammad *engineering educator*
Salazar, Alexander *bishop*
Salicki, Roman *commercial photographer*
Saltzman, Joseph *journalist, educator, television producer*
Salusky, Isidro B. *pediatric nephrologist, educator*
Samet, Jonathan Michael *epidemiologist, educator*
Sample, Steven Browning *academic administrator*
Sandhofer, Catherine *psychology professor*
Sanditz, Lisa *painter*
Sankar, Raman *pediatric neurologist*
Santaolalla, Gustavo *musician, composer, record producer*
Santelli, Robert *museum director, historian*
Sargent, Margaret Holland *portrait artist, actress, writer*
Sarma, Radha J. *cardiologist, educator*
Sarnat, Bernard George *plastic surgeon, educator, researcher*
Sarnoff, Thomas Warren *television executive*
Saxe, Deborah Crandall *lawyer*
Schallert, William Joseph *actor*
Scheibel, Arnold Bernard *psychiatrist, educator, research director*
Schelbert, Heinrich Ruediger *nuclear medicine physician*
Schiff, Richard *actor*
Schill, Michael H. *dean, law educator*
Schlesinger, Adam *musician*
Schneider, Edward Lewis *medicine educator, research administrator*
Schneider, Paul Leonard *internist*
Scholtz, Robert Arno *electrical engineering educator*
Schott, Robert W. (Bob Schott) *film producer, actor, film director*
Schultz, Louis Michael *advertising agency executive*
Schwartz, Robert M. *lawyer*
Schwarz, Ernst Ruediger *cardiologist, researcher*
Scott, Robert Lane *chemist, educator*
Scott-Thomas, Kristin *actress*
Scuderi, Rob *professional hockey player*
Seal, (Seal Henry Olusegun Olumide Adelo Samuel) *musician*
Sears, David O'Keefe *psychology professor*
Seeman, Melvin *sociologist, educator*
Selby, Robert Rick *surgeon*
Selleck, Tom *actor*
Serkis, Andy *actor*
Seto, Theodore Paul *lawyer, educator*
Settles, F. Stan, Jr. *engineering educator, manufacturing executive*
Sewell, William George III *electronics engineer, writer*
Shackleford, Gregory M. *cancer researcher, molecular and cell biologist, educator*
Shacter, David Mervyn *lawyer*
Shafipour, Pouya *physician, dermatologist*
Shagan, Steve *scriptwriter, film producer*
Shah, Prediman K. *cardiologist, educator*
Shaheen, Robert Joseph *bishop*
Shaiman, Marc *composer, arranger, orchestrator*
Shank, Russell *librarian, educator*
Shapiro, Robert L. *lawyer*
Shaw, Brian K. *professional basketball coach, retired professional basketball player*
Shearer, Derek Nocross *political science professor, diplomat, academic administrator*
Sheehan, Lawrence James *lawyer*
Sheller, John Willard *lawyer*
Shelton, Samantha *psychologist*
Shemin, Richard Jay *cardiothoracic surgeon, educator*
Sherrell, John Bradford *lawyer*
Sherwood, Arthur Lawrence *lawyer*
Shi, Songtao *dentist, educator*
Shiba, Wendy C. *lawyer*
Shideler, Ross Patrick *literature and language educator, writer, translator, poet*
Shieh, John Ting-chung *economics professor, department chairman*
Shields, William Donald *physician, educator*
Shinoda, Michael Kenji *musician, artist*
Shivkumar, Kalyanam *cardiologist, consultant*
Shook, Jon *chef*
Shortz, Richard Alan *lawyer*
Shostak, S. Richard *lawyer*
Shuger, Debora Kuller *humanities educator*
Shultz, John David *lawyer*
Shuster, Alvin *journalist, reporter*
Shyamalan, M. Night (Manoj Nelliyattu Shyamalan) *film director*
Siegel, Michael Elliot *nuclear medicine physician, educator*
Siegel, Stuart Elliott *pediatric oncologist, educator*
Siemens, Reynold (Rene Siemens) *lawyer*
Silbergeld, Arthur F. *lawyer*
Silverman, Ben *broadcast executive, television producer*
Silverman, Debora Leah *history professor*
Silverstein, Suzanne *art therapist*
Silverton, Nancy *chef*
Simmons, Donna Marie *neuroscientist, histotechnologist, neuroendocrine anatomist, researcher*
Simpson-Wentz, Ashlee Nicole *singer*
Sinay, Joseph *retail executive*
Sinbad, (David Adkins) *actor, comedian*
Singer, Martin Dori *lawyer*
Singh, Bedi Ajay *film company executive*
Sisko, Diane *film producer*
Sitrick, Michael Steven *public relations executive*
Skaggs, David L. *orthopedist, educator*
Sklar, Richard Lawrence *political science professor*
Skotheim, Robert Allen *retired academic administrator, educator*
Slamon, Dennis Joseph *research scientist*
Sloan, Harry Evans *film company executive*
Sloan, Sheldon Harold *lawyer*
Small, Stacy H. *luxury travel company executive, former magazine editor*
Smart, Amy *actress*
Smiley, Tavis *television talk show host, writer*
Smith, Greig Louis *councilman*
Smith, Laurence *social sciences educator*
Snider, Darryl *lawyer*
Snow, Brittany *actress*
Snyder, Zack *film director*
Sobieski, Leelee (Liliane Rudabet Gloria Eslveta Sobieski) *actress*
Sofroniew, Michael Victor *medical educator*
Solis, Oscar Azarcon *bishop*
Song, Yongyi *librarian*
Sonnenfeld, Albert *retired French literature and comparative literature educator, food historian*
Sorvino, Mira *actress*
Spogli, Ronald Paul *private equity form executive, former ambassador*
Springsteen, Bruce (Bruce Frederick Joseph Springsteen) *musician, singer*
Squire, Molly Ann *organizational psychologist*
Stahl, Nick *actor*
Stamm, Alan *lawyer*
Stamp, Terence Henry *actor*
Stanton, Robert James, Jr. *geologist, educator*
Stanton, Russ W. *editor-in-chief*
Starr, Kevin *librarian, educator*
Statham, Jason *actor*
Steh, Bill Drago *neuropsychologist*
Stein, Laurence Jay *lawyer*
Stellwagen, Robert Harwood *biochemistry professor*
Stenstrom, Michael Knudson *civil engineering educator*
Stephens, Loren M. *publishing executive, writer, film producer*
Stephens, Philip John *chemistry professor*
Stephenson, Gary Van *aerospace engineer*
Sterling, Donald T. *real estate mogul, professional sports team owner*
Stevenson, Robert Murrell *music educator*
Stickler, Stephen H. *photographer*
Stiehm, E. Richard *pediatrician, educator*
Stinehart, William, Jr. *retired lawyer*
Stockwell, Robert Paul *linguist, educator*
Stone, Marla Susan *history professor*
Straatsma, Bradley Ralph *ophthalmologist, educator*
Streep, Meryl (Mary Louise Streep) *actress*
Streeter, Oscar Edward, Jr. *radiation oncologist*
Streisand, Barbra Joan *singer, actress, film director*
Strick, Jeremy *curator, museum director*
Strong, Gary Eugene *university librarian*
Strong, George Gordon, Jr. *lawyer, management consultant*
Strong, Pamela Kay *material and process engineer*
Sugar, Ronald D. *aerospace transportation company executive*
Sulentic, Robert E. *real estate company executive*
Sullivan, Stuart Francis *anesthesiologist, educator*
Sun, Brian A. *lawyer*
Svehlak, Steven Andrew *plastic surgeon*
Swamikannu, Xavier *environmental engineer, state official*
Sweeney, Paul W., Jr. *lawyer*
Swofford, Beth *agent*
Szego, Clara Marian *cell biologist, educator*
Taati, Poopak *media director*
Tabachnick, Norman Donald *psychiatrist, educator*
Tachdjian, Raffi *pediatrician*
Tao, Terence Chi-Shen *mathematics professor*
Tardio, Thomas A. *public relations executive*
Taylor, Charles Ellett *biologist, educator*
Tellem, Arn *media company executive, agent*
Tellem, Nancy Reiss *broadcast executive*
Telles, Cynthia Ann *psychologist*
Territo, Mary C. *health facility administrator, hematologist, educator*
Thicke, Alan *actor*
Thomas, Rob (Robert Kelly Thomas) *singer, songwriter*
Thome, Jim *professional baseball player*
Thompson, Richard Frederick *psychologist, neuroscientist, educator*
Thomson, William Ennis *music theorist, author*
Thoren-Peden, Deborah Suzanne *lawyer*
Thorne, Richard Mansergh *physicist*
Thornton, Al *professional basketball player*
Tigue, William Bernard *adult education educator*
Tiles, Neal *broadcast executive*
Timlin, Robert J. *judge*
Tirador, Gabriel *insurance company executive*
Title, Gail Migdal *lawyer*
Tobisman, Stuart Paul *lawyer*
Todd, Michael Cullen *sculptor, painter*
Tolstrup, Kirsten *cardiologist, educator*
Toman, Mary Ann *federal official*
Tomlin, Lily *actress*
Tongson, Karen *language educator*
Torre, Joe (Joseph Paul Torre) *professional baseball team manager*
Torres, Cynthia Ann *marketing professional*
Treister, George Marvin *lawyer*
Trembly, Cristy *television executive*
Trento, Alfredo A. *thoracic surgeon, educator*
Trenton, Patricia Jean *art historian*
Tribble, Denise Hall *registrar*
Trimble, Stanley Wayne *hydrologist*
Tritle, Lawrence Alan *history professor*
Trivedi, Abhishek *application developer*
Trope, Sorrell *lawyer*
Troy, Nancy J. *art history educator*
Trygstad, Lawrence Benson *lawyer*
Tsotsis, Theodore Thomas *engineering educator*
Turner, Ralph Herbert *sociologist, educator*
Turturro, John *actor*
Udvar-Hazy, Steven F. *leasing company financial executive*
Udwadia, Firdaus Erach *engineering educator, consultant*
Ukropina, James R. *lawyer*
Ullman, Tracey *actress, singer*
Umberg, Thomas John *lawyer*
Underwood, Carrie Marie *singer*
Urena-Alexiades, Jose Luis *electrical engineer*
Urzhumov, Yaroslav Aleksandrovich *application developer, researcher*
Utley, Nancy *film company executive*
Uva, Joe *broadcast executive*
Valli, Frankie (Francis Castelluccio) *singer*
Van Buren, Abigail (Jeanne Phillips) *columnist, educator*
van Dam, Heiman *psychoanalyst*
Van de Kamp, John Kalar *lawyer*
Vanderveen, R. Pete (Randall L. Vanderveen) *dean, pharmacist, educator*
Varat, Jonathan D. *law educator, dean*
Veasey, Pamela Renea *television producer*
Vega, William A. *psychiatrist, educator*
Veitch, Jonathan *academic administrator*
Ver Steeg, Donna Lorraine Frank *nurse, sociologist, educator*
Villablanca, Jaime Rolando *neuroscientist, medical educator*
Villaraigosa, Antonio Ramon *Mayor, Los Angeles*
Vizcaino, Jose Luis Pimental *professional baseball coach, retired professional baseball player*
Vo, Ashley *medical association administrator*
Vojdani, Aristo *medical association administrator, researcher*
von Kalinowski, Julian Onesime *lawyer*
Vredevoe, Donna Lou *academic administrator, microbiologist, educator, biomedical researcher*
Wagar, Elizabeth Ann *microbiologist, director*
Wagner, Christian Nikolaus Johann *materials engineering educator*
Wagner, Darryl William *lawyer*
Wagner, William Gerard *dean, information scientist, consultant, physicist, investment manager*
Wakimoto, Roger Masao *meteorology educator, researcher*
Walcher, Alan Ernest *lawyer*
Walden, Dana *broadcast executive*
Walden, Olga Ascher *music educator*
Waldinger, Roger *social studies educator*
Walendowski, George Jerry *accounting and business educator*
Walken, Christopher *actor*
Walker, Raymond John *physicist*
Walsh, Kate *actress*
Ward, John James *bishop emeritus*
Warren, Robert Stephen *lawyer*
Wasser, Dennis Matthew *lawyer*
Wasser, Laura Allison *lawyer*
Waterman, Christopher *dean*
Waterman, Michael Spencer *mathematics and biology professor*
Waterston, Sam *actor*
Watson, Karol Elizabeth *internist, educator*
Watts, Emma *film company executive*
Watts, Naomi *actress*
Wayne, June Claire *artist*
Wayte, Alan (Paul) *lawyer*
Weatherup, Roy Garfield *lawyer*
Weiner, Perrie M. *lawyer*
Weiss, Kenneth R. *newswriter*
Weiss, Martin Harvey *neurosurgeon, educator*
Weiss, Walter Stanley *lawyer*
Welch, Lloyd Richard *electrical and communications engineer, educator, consultant*
Wesson, Herb J. *councilman*
West, Charles David *chemistry professor*
Westerfield, Randolph W. *finance educator, former dean*
Weston, John Frederick *business educator, consultant*
Wexler, Robert *academic administrator*
Whalen, Lucille *retired academic administrator*
Whitaker, Forest *actor*
White, Brett *real estate company executive*
White, Jennifer Elizabeth Belk *corporate training specialist*
White, Robert Joel *lawyer*
Whitten, Charles Alexander, Jr. *physics professor*
Whybrow, Peter Charles *psychiatrist, educator, director, author*
Wilcox, Rand Roger *psychology professor*
Wilkinson, Alan Herbert *nephrologist, educator*
Williams, Harold Marvin *lawyer, retired foundation, academic and federal agency administrator*
Williams, Kenneth Scott *entertainment and advertising company executive*
Williams, Michelle *actress*
Williams, Norma Jean *lawyer*
Williams, Richard Thomas *lawyer*
Williams-Paisley, Kimberly *actress*
Willner, Alan Eli *electrical engineer, educator*
Wilson, Chandra Danette *actress*
Wilson, Ed *broadcast executive*
Wilson, Miriam Geisendorfer *retired physician, educator*
Wilson, Patrick Joseph *actor*
Wincor, Michael Z. *psychopharmacology educator, clinician, researcher, director*
Winters, Barbara Jo *musician*
Withers, Hubert Rodney *radiotherapist, radiobiologist, educator*
Witherspoon, Reese (Laura Jean Reese Witherspoon) *actress*
Wong, James Bok *economist, chemical engineer, technologist, consultant*
Wood, Evan Rachel *actress*
Wood, James Nowell *foundation administrator, retired museum director*
Wood, Nancy Elizabeth *psychologist, educator*
Woodley, David Timothy *dermatology educator*
Woodley, Shailene Diann *actress*
Woodruff, Fay *paleoceanographer, geological researcher*
Woodsome, Edwin Valentine, Jr. *lawyer*
Woolf, Nancy Jean *neuroscientist, educator*
Wright, Byron T. *physicist, researcher*
Wright, Edward Leonard *astronomy educator*
Wright, Kenneth Brooks *lawyer*
Wright, Mary Ellen *theater educator*
Wu, George H. *federal judge*
Wu, Vivian Y. *finance educator*
Wyle, Noah *actor*
Yamaguchi, Dean Takao *medical educator, researcher*
Yamauchi, Paul Steven *dermatologist, researcher*
Yamini, Daniel *plastic surgeon*
Yang, Allen S. *medical educator*
Yang, Debra Wong *lawyer, former prosecutor*
Yari, Bob *film company executive, producer*
Yazdani, Shahram *pediatrician*
Yen, Teh Fu *civil and environmental engineering educator*
Yiu, Samuel Chi-Hung *ophthalmologist, researcher*
York, Michael (Michael York-Johnson) *actor*
Yortsos, Yannis C. *petroleum engineer, educator, dean*
Young, Ronald Frederick *neurosurgeon*
Yslas, Stephen Daniel *lawyer*
Yu, John Sun *neurosurgeon, immunologist*
Zaller, John Raymond *political science professor*
Zeitlin, Maurice *sociology educator*
Zellweger, Renée *actress*
Zelmanowitz, Julius Martin *mathematics professor, academic administrator*
Zelon, Laurie Dee *judge*
Zeltzer, Lonnie K. *pediatrician, educator*
Zemeckis, Robert L. *film director*
Zeng, Fan-Gang *neuroscientist*
Zhang, Lin *research scientist*
Ziffren, Kenneth *lawyer*
Zine, Dennis P. *councilman*
Zou, Linhua *research scientist*
Zou, Qiyue *systems engineer*

Los Banos
Yoshizumi, Donald Tetsuro *dentist*

Los Gatos
Allan, Lionel M. *director for-profit and non-profit companies, Legal and Business Advisor*
Carson, Sol Kent *artist, educator*
Hastings, Reed (Wilmot Reed Hastings Jr.) *film rental company executive, former education association administrator*
Hurtak, James J. *social scientist, consultant*
McLaughlin, Glen *financial services company executive*
Mintz, Marilyn D. *artist, writer*
Ohanjanian, Ruzanna *clinical psychologist*
Rachlin, Jeanne-Marie *mathematics educator*
Rosenheim, Donald Edwin *electrical engineer*
Sonkusale, Sahcin Ramrao *electrical engineer*
Waydo, Stephen *aeronautical engineer, researcher*

Los Olivos
Knowles, Elizabeth Pringle *museum director*

Los Osos
Kreitzer, David Martin *artist*
Kreitzer, Jacalyn Bower *vocalist, educator*

Lower Lake
Garcia, Beatrice Maude *social worker, director*
Hodgkin, John E. *pulmonologist*

Lynwood
Dove, Donald Augustine *city planner, educator*
Sitomer, Alan Lawrence *literature and language educator*
Sterling, Arthur James *retired legal assistant*

Madera
Curry, Cynthia J. R. *geneticist*

Magalia
Haard, Norman Frederick *retired chemistry professor, editor*

Malibu
Almond, Paul *film director and producer, scriptwriter, novelist*
Baskin, Otis Wayne *business educator*
Bedrosian, Edward *retired electrical engineer*
Benton, Andrew Keith *academic administrator, lawyer*
Bush, Kristian *musician*
Cihak, Herbert Earl *law librarian, educator*
Davenport, David *lawyer, educator, academic administrator*
Davis, Stephen Darrel *biology professor, researcher*
DeMieri, Joseph L. *retired bank executive*
Dominguez, Sylvia Margarita *electrical engineer, researcher*
Factor, Max III *arbitrator, mediator*
Harris, Ed (Edward Allen Harris) *actor*
Hunt, Valerie Virginia *electrophysiologist, educator*
Kim, Rebecca *social sciences educator*
Kirkland, Geoffrey Alan *motion picture production designer*
Kubena, Randall L. *physicist*
Langford, Michèle K. *language educator*
Larson, Edward John *history and law professor*
Liu, David Shiao-Kung *research scientist, consultant*
Lorenzi, Paola *literature and language professor, writer*
Marshall, Donald Glenn *English language and literature educator*
Martin, Karen Lynn Matthews *biology professor*
McCall, Elizabeth Kaye *columnist, consultant, writer*
Morgenstern, Leon *surgeon*
Nelson, Grant Steel *law educator*
Nettles, Jennifer *singer*
Pepper, David M. *scientist, educator*
Phillips, Ronald Frank *academic administrator*
Srinivasa, Narayan *research scientist*
Starr, Kenneth Winston *dean, law educator, lawyer*
Warder, Michael Young *academic administrator*
Wilson, James Quinn *public policy professor*

Manhattan Beach
Allmon, Michael Bryan *accountant, financial consultant*
Blanton, John Arthur *architect, writer*
Maisel, David *entertainment company executive*
McQuillin, Richard Ross *management consultant*
Rae, Matthew Sanderson, Jr. *lawyer*

Manteca
Talmage, Kenneth Kellogg *consumer products company executive*
Tonn, Elverne Meryl *pediatric dentist, dental benefits consultant, forensic odontologist*

Marina
Shane, William Whitney *astronomer*

Marina Del Rey
Bennett, Joel Herbert *construction executive*
Deelman, Ewa *computer scientist, educator*
Dexheimer, Henry Phillip, II, *insurance agency executive*
Gold, Carol Sapin *international management consultant, speaker, writer*
Gregg, Lucius Perry, Jr. *aerospace executive*
Jeffrey, John Orval *Internet company executive, lawyer*
Lindheim, Richard David *broadcast executive, director*
Neuman, Clifford *computer scientist, educator*
Parks, D. Gene *gynecologist*
Rimer, John Thomas *language educator, academic administrator, writer*
Stebbins, Gregory Kellogg *foundation executive*
Stevens, William Grant (Grant Stevens) *plastic surgeon*
Stoker, David Allen *plastic surgeon*
Swartout, William R. *mathematician, educator, director*
Watkins, Robert G *surgeon*
Will, Peter Milne *computer and robotics research executive*

Martinez
Tong, Siu Wing *computer programmer*

Mckinleyville
Berry, Glenn *artist, educator*
Emenhiser, JeDon Allen *retired political science professor, dean*
Peithman, Roscoe Edward *physicist, educator*
Walker, Dennis Kendon *retired botany professor*

Mendocino
Eckert, Rinde *composer, librettist*
Feehan, Christine *writer*
Masterson, William A. *retired judge*

Menifee
Balow, Irving Henry *retired education educator*
Roark, Robert Cameron *insurance agent*
Uhl, Suzanne M. *educator*

Menlo Park
Allen, Matthew Arnold *physicist*
Altman, Drew E. *foundation executive*
Bales, Royal Eugene *retired philosophy educator*
Bechtolsheim, Andy (Andreas von Bechtolsheim) *information technology executive*
Bernstein, Lawrence R. *inorganic chemist, pharmaceutical chemist*
Bourne, Charles Percy *information scientist, educator*
Brest, Paul A. *foundation administrator, law educator*
Brodsky, Stanley Jerome *physics educator, consultant*
Bukry, John David *geologist*
Byers, Brook *venture capitalist, investor*
Bynum, Gretchen Luepke *geologist*
Carlson, Curtis R. *electronics research industry executive*
Chao, Howard H. *lawyer*
Chapin, June Roediger *education educator*
Cohn, Robert Greer *literary arts educator*
Collins, Nancy Whisnant *foundation administrator*
Compton, Kevin R. *venture capitalist, professional sports team executive*
Crawford, Roy Edgington III *lawyer*
Crosley, David Risdon *chemical physicist*
Davies, Paul Lewis III *venture capitalist*
Doerr, John (L. John Doerr III) *venture capitalist*
Doppalapudi, Rupa S. *cytogeneticist*
Dorfan, Jonathan Mannie *physicist, researcher*
Drell, Persis Sydney *physicist*
Drell, Sidney David *physicist, arms control and national security specialist*
Dubinsky, Donna L. *information technology executive*
DuMaine, R. Pierre *bishop emeritus*
Dyer, Charles Arnold *lawyer*
Eslambolchi, Hossein *communications executive*
Fenton, Noel John *venture capitalist*
Fetterman, David Mark *anthropologist, educator, evaluator*
Fisher, Ora T. *lawyer*
Giancarlo, Charles H. *investment company executive, former computer systems network executive*
Gordon, William Bingham (Bing Gordon) *venture capitalist, former software marketing executive*
Grimes, Michael D. *investment banker*
Harris, Edward Day, Jr. *physician*
Hearst, William Randolph III *lawyer, former newspaper publisher*
Heller, Esther A. *writer, educator*
Hildreth, Edward Wesley (Wes Hildreth) *geologist*
Hockett, Christopher Burch *lawyer*
Honey, Richard Churchill *retired electrical engineer*
Jaros, John A. *physics professor*
Jarrold, William *computer scientist*
Joy, Bill (William Nelson Joy) *venture capitalist, former computer software company executive*
Karel, Steven *lawyer*
Kaufman, Christopher Lee *lawyer*
Kelly, Daniel Grady, Jr. *lawyer*
Kennelly, Dennis L. *lawyer*
Kirk, Cassius Lamb, Jr. *retired lawyer, investor*
Kovachy, Edward Miklos, Jr. *psychiatrist, consultant*
Kramlich, C(harles) Richard (Dick) *venture capitalist*
Kuwabara, James Shigeru *research hydrologist*
Labiosa, William Bruce *civil engineer, researcher*
Lane, Laurence William, Jr. *retired ambassador, publisher*
Lanzone, Jim *Internet company executive*
Levenson, Milton *chemical engineer, consultant*
Lucas, Donald Leo *investor*
Madison, James Raymond *lawyer*
Mankinen, Edward A. *geologist, researcher*
Marks, Michael E. *electronics executive*
Marquardt, David F. *venture capitalist*
Mathews, Irimpan Ittoop *macromolecular crystallographer*
McDonald, Warren George *accountant, mortage company, savings and loan association executive, consultant*
Mendelson, Alan Charles *lawyer*
Messmer, Harold Maximilian, Jr., (Max Messmer) *consulting company executive*
Michael, Andrew Jay *geophysicist*
Mill, Theodore *chemist, researcher*
Moritz, Michael J. *venture capitalist*
Neumann, Peter Gabriel *computer scientist*
Nicholas, Keri *real estate agent*
Nordlund, Leif Niklas Dennis *research scientist*
Okarma, Thomas Bernard *biotechnology company executive*
Patterson, Anna *information technology executive*
Penzias, Arno Allan *astrophysicist, information scientist, researcher*
Perkins, Tom (Thomas James Perkins) *venture capital company executive*
Radlo, Edward John *lawyer, mathematician*
Ratcliff, Blair Norman *physicist*
Ravilisetty, Padmanabha Rao *research scientist*
Richter, Burton *physicist, educator*
Roberts, George R. *investment banker*
Saifer, Mark Gary Pierce *pharmaceutical executive*
Schmidt, Chauncey Everett *banker, director*
Scholes, Myron S. *financier, former law and finance educator*
Sharma, Bhavender Paul *biotechnologist*
Singh, Kuldev *medical educator*
Smith, Marshall Savidge *foundation executive*
Taft, David Dakin *chemicals executive*
Taylor, Richard Edward *physicist, researcher*
Thatcher, Wayne *geophysicist*
Vane, Sylvia Brakke *anthropologist, writer*
VanHook, Tracie Lynnette *small business owner*
Waddell, M. Keith *consulting company executive*
Westcott, Brian John *manufacturing executive*
White, Cecil Ray *librarian, consultant*
Winick, Herman *physicist, educator*
Yang, Joseph *lawyer*

Merced
Albano, Valerie Dawn *biology professor*
Amussen, Susan Dwyer *history professor*
Davila, Lilian P. *research scientist*
Kallmann, Marcelo *science educator*
Lashley, Lenore Clarisse *lawyer*
Near, Delia Mary *librarian*
Shirley, Kahlert *literature and language professor*
Tomlinson-Keasey, Carol Ann *academic administrator*
Yanagi, Cary *science educator*

Mill Valley
Adessa, Lori *music educator*
Coulter, Catherine (Jean Catherine Coulter Pogany) *writer*
D'Amico, Michael *architect, urban planner*
Dillon, Richard Hugh *librarian, author*
Hargrave, Sarah Quesenberry *consulting company and training executive*
Leslie, Jacques Robert, Jr. *journalist*
Mumford, Christopher Greene *corporate financial executive*
Nemir, Donald Philip *lawyer*
Padula, Fred David *filmmaker*
Premo, Paul Mark *oil industry executive*
Schiff, Jan Pedersen *conductor, voice educator*
Schreyer, Chara *foundation administrator, art collector*
Schwartzbach, M. Gerald *lawyer*

Milpitas
Agarwal, Nipun *materials scientist*
Allen, Irma M. *adult education educator*
Chiu, Peter Yee-Chew *physician*
Dai, Guang-ming George *optics scientist*
Harari, Eli *computer company executive*
Hasler, William Albert *electronics executive*
Roddick, David Bruce *construction company executive*
Talwalkar, Abhi Y. (Abhijit Y. Talwalkar) *computer company executive*
Zheng, Min *engineer*

Mission Hills
Wilkerson, Gerald Eugene *bishop*

Mission Viejo
Lake, Jane Burford *retired special education educator, hypnotherapist, small business owner*
Ruben, Robert Joseph *lawyer*
Sganga, John B. *retired furniture holding company executive*
Tuohey, Conrad Gravier *lawyer*

Modesto
Brown, Candy Lee *elementary school educator*
Jensen, Ronald D. *podiatrist*
Jones, Mary Cunningham *music educator*
Khanna, Kanwal *rheumatologist*
Kushar, Kent *information technology executive*
Mitchell, Joan LaVerne *research scientist*
Moe, Andrew Irving *veterinarian*
Nicholson, Coy Lee *language educator, writer*
Ridenour, Jim *Mayor, Modesto, California*
Robinson, Tonya Louise *nursing educator, director*
Sawicki, Geraldine *social studies educator*
Whiteside, Carol Gordon *foundation executive*

Moffett Field
Berenji, Hamid Reza *research scientist, educator*
Chaban, Galina M. *research scientist*
Chen, Bin *materials scientist*
Colombano, Silvano Pietro *aeronautical engineer, researcher*
D'Angelo, Gennaro *research scientist, educator*
Dholakia, Geetha Ramaswamy *physicist, researcher*
Goebel, John Henry *physicist, researcher*
Heere, Karen R. *astrophysicist*
Horikawa, Daiki *aerospace scientist*
Kittel, Peter *research scientist*
Li, Jun *materials scientist, researcher*
Lissauer, Jack Jonathan *astronomy educator*
Makeev, Maxim A. *physicist*
Mattioda, Andrew Lige *chemist, researcher, space scientist*
Sharma, Surendra Prasad *technical manager, scientist*
Srivastava, Ashok Narain *computer scientist, consultant*
Statler, Irving Carl *aerospace engineer*
Worden, Simon Pete *science administrator, career military officer*

Mojave
Melvill, Michael W. *aircraft company executive, experimental test pilot*
Rutan, Burt (Elbert Leander Rutan) *aircraft designer, aircraft company executive*
Witt, Stuart O. *aerospace transportation executive*

Monrovia
Andary, Thomas Joseph *biochemist, researcher*
Edwards, Kenneth Neil *chemical engineering executive*
Fannin, Daniel Paul Clark *information systems executive*
Kimnach, Myron William *botanist, horticulturist*

Montague
Downs, Floella McIntyre *retired ferry pilot, instructor, flight examiner*
Ryan, Daberath *chemistry professor*

Montclair
Haage, Robert Mitchell *retired history professor, cultural organization administrator*

Montecito
Burford, Jerrad Dalon *corporate financial executive, writer*
Meghreblian, Robert Vartan *manufacturing executive, physicist*
Purl, O. Thomas *retired electronics company executive*
Wheelon, Albert Dewell *physicist*

Monterey
Boger, Dan Calvin *science professor, consultant*
Brown, Gerald G. *operations research specialist, educator*
Butler, Jon Terry *computer engineering educator, researcher*
Cornish, Bonita Clark *retired secondary school educator*
Denning, Peter James *computer scientist, engineer*
Duran, June Clark *legal research company executive*
Fargues, Monique P. *electrical engineer, educator*
Garcia, Richard John *bishop*
Gaver, Frances Rouse *lawyer*
Goldstein, Kenneth F. *entertainment and publishing company executive*
Hanlon, James Allison *confectionery company executive*
Hensel, Nayantara Diana *finance educator*
Kolar, Ramesh *technologist, educator*
Langland, Rolf H. *meteorologist*
Looney, Robert Edward *economist, educator*
Maier, William Bryan, II, *physics professor*
Matthews, David Fort *career officer*
McNelley, Terry R. *engineering educator*
Opperman, Rosanna Resendez *vice principal*
Owen, Guillermo *mathematician, educator*
Peet, Phyllis Irene *art historian, women's studies educator*
Read, Robert Richard *mathematical statistics educator*
Reneker, Maxine Hohman *librarian*
Rice, Joseph Aubrey *physics professor, researcher*
Ruehsen, Moyaa *political science professor, consultant*
Ryan, Sylvester Donovan *bishop emeritus*
Schrady, David Alan *civilian military employee, educator*
Thompson, William Travis *physicist*
Vu, Bruce Thanh *aerospace engineer, educator*
Whittington, E. Michael *museum director*

Monterey Park
Grasse, Wanda Gene *lawyer, writer*
Smith, Betty Denny *county official, administrator, fashion executive*
Stankevitz, Diane Lynn *athletic trainer*
Stapleton, Jean *journalism educator*
Wilson, Linda *librarian*

Moorpark
Kessner, Dolly Eugenio *music educator, concert pianist*
Viviani, Fabio *chef*

Moraga
Allen, Richard Garrett *healthcare educator*
Bennett, Randy *men's college basketball coach*
Gerber, Nicholas *investment advisor, entrepreneur*
Gorsch, Robert E. *literature and language professor, department chairman*
Malary, Claude Rheal *language educator*
Scott, Christina Lynn *psychology professor*
Thier, Herbert David *director, retired academic administrator*
Tom, Randolph L. *corporate financial executive, lawyer*

Moreno Valley
Bajor, Renee Allyson *special education educator*
Batey, William H., II, *Mayor, Moreno Valley, California*
Marshall, Debra Lynn *secondary school educator*
McLaughlin, Veronica *psychologist*
Phillips-Brown, Exa *educator*

Morgan Hill
Freimark, Robert (Bob Freimark) *artist*
Kuster, Robert Kenneth *semi-retired scientist*

Morro Bay
LaLanne, Jack (François Henri LaLanne) *physical fitness specialist, entrepreneur*

Moss Beach
Glauthier, T. J. *management consultant*

Moss Landing
Bellingham, James Gladen *marine technologist, researcher*
Breaker, Laurence Coates *oceanographer, educator*
Brewer, Peter George *ocean geochemist*
Clague, David A. *geologist*
Lange, Lester Henry *mathematics professor*
Williams, Phyllis Eleanor *retired educator*

Mount Shasta
Stienstra, Stephani Ann *editor, writer*

Mountain View
Abel, Elizabeth Ann *dermatologist*
Baker, Mitchell *computer software developer, foundation administrator*
Bills, Robert Howard *political party executive*
Blackwell, Trevor *Internet company executive*
Bloch, Joshua J. *software designer*
Brilliant, Larry (Lawrence Brent Brilliant) *preventive medicine physician, entrepreneur*
Brin, Sergey Mihailovich *information technology executive*
Brown, Shona L. *Internet company executive*
Buchheit, Paul *computer programmer, entrepreneur*
Campbell, William V. *computer company executive*
Cerf, Vinton Gray *information technology executive*
Chu, Wai C. *engineer, researcher*
Cook, Scott David *computer software company executive*
Coughran, William M., Jr. *information technology executive, researcher*
Denzel, Nora Manley *information technology executive*
Di Muccio, Mary-Jo *retired librarian*
Drummond, David C. *information technology executive, lawyer*
Engeström, Jyri *Internet company executive*
Eustace, Alan *information technology executive*
Fried, Benjamin Cecil *Internet company executive*
Golden, Neville Hylton *pediatrician*
Golub, Ben *Internet company executive*
Graham, Paul *Internet company executive, writer*
Halvorsen, Per-Kristian *software company executive, former educator, researcher*
Healy, Jodi *library services manager*
Hoagland, Albert Smiley *electrical engineer, researcher*
Hoffman, Reid *Internet company executive*
Huang, Charles *computer game company executive*
Huang, Kai *computer game company executive*
Isaacs, Nicholas Stephen *music educator, director*
Jing, Tong *electrical engineer*
Johnson, Conor Deane *mechanical engineer*
Jonaris, George G. *electrical and computer engineer*
Kobza, Dennis Jerome *architect*
Koopmans, Chris *telecommunications industry executive*
Koponen, Petteri *Internet company executive*
Kraw, George Martin *lawyer, writer*
Lamport, Leslie B. *computer scientist*
Lewin, Dan'l *computer software company executive*
Livingston, Jessica *Internet company executive*
Masonis, Todd *Internet company executive*
Mayer, Marissa Ann *information technology executive*
Nash, Horace Lyons *lawyer*
Page, Larry (Lawrence E. Page) *information technology executive*
Pan, Junfeng *application developer, researcher*
Pasahow, Lynn Harold *lawyer*
Perrella, Anthony Joseph *electronics engineer*
Pichette, Patrick *information technology company executive*
Price, Penry *advertising executive*
Qureishi, A. Salam *computer company executive*
Reicher, Dan William *information technology executive, former federal agency administrator*
Ring, Cameron *Internet company executive*
Rubin, Andrew E. (Andrew E. Rubin) *technology product developer*
Schickli, Jeanne Hlavka *virologist, researcher*
Schmidt, Eric Emerson *information technology executive*
Showalter, Mark Robert *astronomer*
Smarr, Joseph *Internet company executive*
Spang-Hanssen, Henrik Stakemann *lawyer, researcher*
Sumner, Kelly *computer game company executive*
Tan, Chade-Meng *application developer, educator*
Tang, Paul C. *medical administrator, educator*
Tyabji, Hatim Ahmedi *computer systems company executive*
Vaillant, Jean-Luc *Internet company executive*
Warren, Richard Wayne *obstetrician, gynecologist*
Weiner, Jeff *Internet company executive*
Woodside, Dennis *information technology executive*

Murrieta
Geffe, Philip Reinhold *electrical engineer, consultant*
Lake, Bruce Meno *physicist*
Miller, Stephen Herschel *surgeon, educator*
Rose, Norma Louise *retired human services manager*
Yates, Ronald Eugene *newspaper editor, educator, author, journalist*

Napa
Ali, Yusuf *research and development company executive*
Battisti, Paul Oreste *retired municipal official*
Cahill, Richard Frederick *lawyer*
Chiarella, Peter Ralph *vintner*
Hess, Donald Marc *diversified financial services company executive*
Kanaan, Samer Azzam *cardiothoracic surgeon*
Rosselli, Denise Louise *literature and language professor, department chairman*

Shin, Ernest Eun-Ho *physicist, educator, researcher*
Stauffer, Thomas Michael *university president*
Thomas, William Scott *lawyer*
Zimmermann, John Paul *plastic surgeon*

National City
Beauchamp, Miles Philip *editor, columnist, consultant*
Becerra, David *language educator*
Caruana, Sean David *education educator*

Nevada City
Chalpin-Fleitas, Susan Gail *environmental health specialist, forester*

Newark
Gupta, Anju *risk management consultant*
Thissell, James Dennis *physicist*

Newbury Park
Bleiberg, Leon William *surgeon, podiatrist*
Fisk, Charles John *meteorologist, researcher, consultant*
Knutzen, Robert *health science association administrator, educator*
Lindsey, Joanne M. *flight attendant, poet*

Newhall
Stone, Susan Foster *mental health services professional*

Newport Beach
Aiello, William Philip *plastic surgeon*
Alvarado, John *computer game engineer*
Arnott, Robert Douglas *investment company executive*
Baskin, Scott David *lawyer*
Batniji, Rami K. *facial plastic surgeon*
Belic Weiss, Zoran *artist, design educator, director*
Bennett, Bruce W. *retired construction executive, civil engineer*
Bissell, George Arthur *architect*
Blankenship, Edward G. *architect*
Borges, Fredrick Mario *lawyer*
Brant-Zawadzki, Michael *radiologist, director*
Bren, Donald L. *real estate company executive*
Brown, Giles Tyler *history professor, lecturer*
Bruggeman, Terrance John *corporate financial executive*
Butera, Barclay *interior designer*
Casey, Thomas Clark *retired trust company executive, investment advisor*
Cheever, Sharon Ann *insurance company executive, lawyer*
Chiu, John Tang *physician*
Connolly, John Earle *surgeon, educator*
Cote, Brian E. *financial executive*
Daniel, Rollin Kimball *plastic surgeon*
Duncan, John Alexander *lawyer*
El-Erian, Mohamed A. *investment company executive*
Fargo, Brian *computer game company executive*
Fawcett, John Scott *real estate developer*
Fehner, Michael Richard *lawyer*
Fielding, Roy Thomas *software scientist*
Findley, Matthew *computer game company executive*
Frederick, Dolliver H. *investment banker*
Fries, Arthur Lawrence *life and health insurance broker, disability claim consultant*
Gilchrist, Richard Irwin *real estate developer*
Goldstein, Michael Gerald *lawyer, director*
Gross, Bill (William H. Gross) *investment company executive, financial analyst*
Grover, Sanjay *plastic surgeon*
Harlan, Nancy Margaret *lawyer*
Haussmann, Trudy Diane *financial planner*
Heinrichs, Harvey L. *plastic surgeon, educator*
Herron, J. Jay *lawyer*
Hueston, John Charles *lawyer*
Kenney, William John, Jr. *real estate developer*
Kolyer, John McNaughton *materials scientist, retired chemist*
Koontz, Dean Ray *writer*
Kraus, John Walter *former aerospace engineering company executive*
Lambros, Val (Vasilios S. Lambros II) *plastic surgeon*
Landau, Martin *actor*
Lee, Kyehyung *systems engineer*
Marcoux, Carl Henry *former insurance company executive, writer, historian*
Matteucci, Dominick Vincent *real estate developer*
Mc Culloch, Samuel Clyde *history professor*
Millar, Richard William, Jr. *lawyer*
Morris, James T. *insurance company executive*
Nolan, Christopher Aloysius III *real estate developer, architect, music promotion*
Pace, Peter *former Chairman of the Joint Chiefs of Staff, management consultant*
Parks, Fredrick Scott *systems engineer*
Paul, Malcolm David *plastic and reconstructive surgeon*
Prince, Thomas E. *bank executive*
Rinehart, Charles R. *savings and loan association executive*
Schnapp, Roger Herbert *lawyer, consultant*
Seify, Hisham *plastic surgeon, researcher*
Shonk, Albert Davenport, Jr. *advertising executive*
Spitz, Barbara Salomon *artist*
Steinberg, Leigh William *sports agent*
Thorp, Edward Oakley *investment management company executive*
Tran, Khanh T. *insurance company executive*
Turner, Jana L. *real estate company executive*
Wade, Michael Robert Alexander *import/export company executive*
Wallis, Mary Camilla *civic leader*
Wentworth, Diana von Welanetz *author*
Wentworth, Theodore Sumner *lawyer*
Whittemore, Paul Baxter *psychologist*
Yoder, Michael G. *lawyer*
Zubrin, Jay Ross *surgeon*

Newport Coast
Evanoff, George C. *retired consumer products company executive*
Pavony, William H. *financial and management consultant*
Swan, Peer Alden *public utility executive*

Norco
McNeal, Phyllis Paulette *parole agent*
Morrison, James V. *biology professor*

North Hills
Deets, Richard M. *secondary school educator, consultant*
Fujikawa, Denson Gen *neurologist, researcher*
Iacocca, Lee (Lido Anthony) *venture capitalist, retired automotive executive*
Thannickal, Thomas Chacko *neurophysiologist, researcher*

North Hollywood
Ajalat, Sol Peter *lawyer*
Boulanger, Donald Richard *financial services executive*
Campos, Luis *puzzle writer*
Chang, Wung *academic administrator, investment advisor, educator*
de la Houssaye, Brette Angelo-Pepe *electrical engineer, researcher, educator*
English, Diane *television producer, writer, communications executive*
Fanning, Dakota *actress*
Holmes, Michael *performing arts company executive, educator*
McMartin, John *actor*
Smothers, Tom *actor, singer*
Thomson, John Ansel Armstrong *biochemist*
Toplitt, Gloria H. *music educator, actress, vocalist*
Totton, Carl Allen, II, *psychologist*
Toussieng, Yolanda *make-up artist*
Vasilyeva, Anna *artist, writer*
Wadsworth, Steve *Internet company executive*

North Tustin
Dean, William Evans *aerospace engineer, engineering company executive, consultant*

Northridge
Ackerman, David Scott *finance educator*
Afifi, Marianne H. *dean*
Akbarzadeh, Alireza *physicist*
Avsharian, Roupen *prosecutor, academic administrator*
Bassler, Robert Covey *artist, educator*
Boberg, Dorothy Kurth *author*
Bostrom, Sandra Janine *music educator*
Bouguarche, Ahmed *language educator, researcher*
Bradshaw, Richard Rotherwood *engineering executive*
Cartwright, Nancy *actress, television producer*
Covrig, Vicentiu *finance educator*
Dart, John Seward *journalist, editor*
Dudgeon, Steven Robert *biology professor*
Duran, Karin Jeanine *librarian*
Falk, Heinrich Richard *humanities and theater educator*
Finley, Mary Margaret *librarian*
Gehart, Diane Rebecca *marriage and family therapist, educator*
Gunther, Richard Edward *operations management professor, consultant*
Jackiewicz, Edward Louis *geographer, educator*
Kabo, J. Michael *mechanical engineering educator*
Logan, Lee Robert *orthodontist, department chairman*
Luedders, Jerry Duane *music educator, academic administrator*
Madelian, Vergine *biology professor*
Mehler, Ronald W. *science educator*
Mitchell, James Andrew *education educator*
Mitchell, Rie Rogers *psychologist, counselor, educator*
Nama, Adilifu *educator*
Omatsu, Glenn *Asian American studies professor*
O'Sullivan, Donal *educator*
Palerm, Cesar C. *electrical engineer, researcher*
Parker, David Miller *history professor, retired advertising executive*
Perez, Pamela Lindsey *language educator*
Reagan, Janet Thompson *psychologist, educator*
Rowlands, Kathleen Dudden *education educator*
Runquist, Lisa A. *lawyer*
Sefton, James Edward *history professor*
Smathers, James Burton *medical physicist, educator*
Stark, Martin J. *international management consultant*
Swenson, Patricia J. *literature and language professor*

Norwalk
DeMichele, Anna Tina *music educator*
Ernest, Roger Craig *language educator*
Haas, John Henry *history professor*
Jaime, Jennie H. *literature and language professor*
Kouns, Alan Terry *writer, consultant*
Solomon, Namala *economics professor*

Novato
Bibeault, Donald Bertrand *corporate turnaround executive, investor*
Bredesen, Dale Eric *neurologist, director*
Criswell, Eleanor Camp *psychologist*
Doris, Robert J. *computer video company executive*
Habiger, Dave *computer video company executive*
Lane, Michele Jeanne *special education educator*
McAllister, Todd *biomedical engineer*
McNamara, John Stephen *artist, educator*
Minogue, Robert Brophy *retired nuclear engineer*
Patterson, W. Morgan *college president*
Spinrad, Michael Irwin *social studies educator*
Yap, Clarence *biotechnology executive*

Oak Hills
Whiting, Gary Brian *design educator*

Oak Park
Vinson, William Theodore *lawyer*

Oak View
Tennant, John Randall *management consultant*

Oakdale
Saletta, Mary Elizabeth (Betty Saletta) *sculptor*

Oakland
Alexander, Stewart A. *political organization worker*
Ames, Bruce Nathan *biochemistry and molecular biology professor*
Beasley, Bruce Miller *sculptor*
Berry, Phillip Samuel *lawyer*
Bibel, Debra Jan *medical scientist, editor, artist*
Bouska Lee, Carla Ann *nursing and healthcare educator*
Brindis, Ralph *cardiologist, consultant, medical educator*
Brock, Theresa Jean (Terry) *retired elementary school educator*
Brust, David *physicist*
Bryant, Arthur H. *lawyer*
Buttimer, Jessica *consumer products company executive, marketing professional*
Cannady, Walter Jack *lawyer*
Carwell, Hattie Virginia *health physicist*
Cary, Alice Shepard *retired physician*
Cheaney, Calbert Nathaniel *professional sports team executive, retired professional basketball player*
Cherry, Lee Otis *scientific institute administrator*
Coaston, Shirley Ann Dumas *librarian*
Cohan, Christopher J. *professional sports team owner*
Cordileone, Salvatore Joseph *bishop*
Dailey, Garrett Clark *publisher, lawyer*
DeFazio, Lynette Stevens *dancer, choreographer, violinist, actress, educator*
Dellums, Ronald Vernie *Mayor, Oakland, California, retired congressman*
Deming, Willis Riley *retired lawyer*
De Vos, George Alphonse *psychologist, anthropologist*
Diaz, Sharon *education administrator*
DiMaggio, Debbi *realtor*
Duran, Claudio E. *composer, writer*
Ellis, Monta *professional basketball player*
Feusner, James *oncologist, director*
Fleming, Jayne Elizabeth *lawyer*
Fogarty, Lori *museum director*
Foley, Jack (John Wayne Harold Foley) *poet, writer, editor-in-chief*
Garciaparra, Nomar (Anthony Nomar Garciaparra) *professional baseball player*
Geren, Bob (Robert Peter Geren) *professional baseball manager*
Green, David Edward *retired librarian, priest, translator*
Greer, Sandra Charlene *academic administrator, chemistry professor*
Griffin, Betty Jo *elementary school educator*
Gruber, Ronald P. *plastic surgeon, researcher*
Hafey, Joseph Michael *retired health association executive*
Haiman, Franklyn Saul *writer, communications educator*
Halvorson, George Charles *healthcare insurance company executive*
Hargrave, Charles R. *nonprofit organization supervisor*
Harken, Alden Hood *thoracic surgeon*
Harris, Larry *professional basketball coach*
Haskell, Arthur Jacob *retired water transportation executive*
Heinrich, Daniel J. *chemicals executive*
Heminger, Steve *city official*
Herring, Bernard Duane *physician*
Horning, Robert Eugene *artist, educator*
Howatt, Sister Helen Clare *human services administrator, director, retired school librarian*
Iribarren, Carlos *epidemiologist*
Jackson, Stephen *professional basketball player*
Jensen, D. Lowell *federal judge*
Ji, Jun *engineering company executive*
Johnson, Kenneth F. *lawyer*
Kazan, Steven *lawyer*
Killebrew, Ellen Jane (Mrs. Edward S. Graves) *cardiologist, educator*
Knauss, Donald R. *consumer products company executive*
Kohn, Steven M. *lawyer*
Lancaster, Kathy *insurance company executive*
Lebda, Douglas R. *Internet company executive*
Lee, Ella Louise *librarian, educator*
Lee, Jong Hyuk *accountant*
Lee, Low Kee *electronics engineer, consultant*
Linford, Rulon Kesler *physicist, electrical engineer*
Macmeeken, John Peebles *foundation executive, educator*
Maggette, Corey Antoine *professional basketball player*
Magloire, Alix J. (Magloire) *internist*
McKinney, Judson Thad *broadcast executive*
Melchert, James Frederick *artist, educator*
Mullin, Christopher Paul *professional sports team executive, retired professional basketball player*
Nelson, Donald Arvid (Nellie Nelson) *professional basketball coach*
Newsome, Randall Jackson *judge*
Ng, Lawrence Ming-Loy *pediatrician*
Parker, Melissa Bernice *advertising executive*
Penzien, Joseph *structural engineering educator*
Preston, Elizabeth A. *psychologist*
Price, Gary *librarian*
Quinby, William Albert *lawyer, arbitrator, mediator*
Reese, Charles Woodrow, Jr. *lawyer, real estate developer*
Richmond, Mitchell James *professional sports team executive, retired professional basketball player*
Rowell, Robert *professional sports team executive*
Roy-Burman, Arup *pediatrician*
Rubin, Rhea Joyce *library consultant*
Safka, Jim *information technology executive, investment services company executive*
Schacht, Henry Mevis *writer, consultant*
Schell, Farrel Loy *transportation engineer*
Schrag, Peter *editor, writer*
Sheldon, Marianne Buroff *history professor*
Singh, Amandeep *emergency physician*
Smith, Christopher Allen *operations executive, financial executive*
Stein, Laura *lawyer, consumer products company executive*
Stetler, Russell Dearnley, Jr. *investigator*
Sutter, Elouise C. *retired art educator*
Terry, Keith *performing company executive, dancer, body musician*
Trachtenberg, Elizabeth Anne *geneticist, researcher*
Vichinsky, Elliott P. *pediatrician, director*
Wallis, Eric G. *lawyer*
Westergren, Timothy Brooks *music company executive*
Widener, Mary Lee *non-profit financial executive*
Williams, Carol H. *advertising executive*
Woo, Janice *librarian*
Wood, James Michael *lawyer*
Wood, Larry (Mary Laird) *journalist, writer, public relations executive, educator, environmental consultant*
Yamaguchi, Kristi Tsuya *ice skater*
Yudof, Mark George *academic administrator, law educator*
Zschau, Marilyn *singer*
Zwissler, Alexander *museum director*

Occidental
Rumsey, Victor Henry *electrical engineering educator emeritus*

Oceanside
Curtin, Thomas Lee *ophthalmologist*
Daniel, Susan Qualls *secondary school educator*
Garfin, Louis *retired actuary*
Hoff, Bernadine Ryan *management consultant*
Jennex, Murray Eugene *engineering educator, consultant*
Klaas, Nicholas Paul *management consultant*
Lange, Clifford Elmer *retired librarian*
L'Annunziata, Michael Frank *chemist, nuclear scientist, consultant*
Lyon, Richard *retired mayor, military officer*
Miller, Donald Eugene *retired air traffic controller*
Montgomery, Michael Davis *research and development company executive, real estate investor*
Netsiri, Chaiyapoj *research scientist, consultant*
Sullivan, Patrick James *lawyer*
Taverna, Rodney Elward *financial services company executive*
Wood, Jim *mayor, Oceanside, California*
Yurist, Svetlan Joseph *mechanical engineer*

Ojai
Griffin, John Lawrence *psychology professor*
Shagam, Marvin Hückel-Berri *private school educator*

Olivehurst
Green, Tim M. *mathematics educator*

Ontario
Chavez, Virginia *bilingual counselor*
Dastrup-Hamill, Faye Myers *city official*
Hanner, Jean P. *retired state civil servant*
Kloepfer, Marguerite Fonnesbeck *writer*
Leon, Paul S. *Mayor, Ontario, California*
Myers, Christopher D. *bank executive*

Orange
Ahlquist, John B. *application developer*
Alkire, Michael T. *anesthesiologist, researcher*
Amin, Alpesh N. *internist*
Banning, Donna Rose *art educator*
Barb Mingo, Arturo *romance literature and languages educator*
Batchelor, James Kent *lawyer*
Batra, Anjan S *medical educator*
Bauer, Bruce F. *retired aerospace engineer*
Berman, Michael Leonard *gynecologic oncologist*
Borghei, Peyman *medical researcher*
Bota, Daniela Annenelie *neurologist, educator*
Brown, Tod David *bishop*
Busby, Nita June *small business owner*
Chang, Jae Chan *hematologist, oncologist, educator*
Christian-Brougham, Ruby Rosalie *psychology professor*
Crumley, Roger Lee *surgeon, educator, otolaryngologist*
Dearden, John Duncan *aircraft manufacturing executive*
de Souza, Marcela *educator*
DiSaia, Philip John *obstetrician, gynecologist, radiology educator*
Djalilian, Hamid *neurosurgeon, director*
Evans, Gregory Randolph Dean *plastic surgeon, educator*
Finley, David Scott *surgeon*
Flores, Cirilo *bishop*
Fruehauf, John Paul *oncologist, director*
Gatcliffe, Troy Antony *gynecologic oncologist, researcher*
Goodwin, Scott Craig *interventional radiologist*
Hoyt, David Butler *surgeon, department chairman*
Kenney, John William III *chemistry educator*
Kobayashi, Mark Robert *plastic surgeon, educator*
Kraft, Arthur *dean*
Liao, Solomon *geriatrician, educator*
Lott, Ira Totz *pediatric neurologist*
Luong, Dominic *bishop*
Machan, Tibor Richard *college professor, newspaper columnist*
McFarland, Norman Francis *bishop*
Morgan, Beverly Carver *pediatrician, educator*
Muhonen, Michael Gordon *neurological surgeon*
Najm, Wadie I. *geriatrician, educator*
Pare, Laura *neurosurgeon, educator*
Post, Barbara J. *retired mathematics educator*
Rotunda, Ronald Daniel *law educator, consultant*
Rowen, Marshall *radiologist*
Saremi, Farhood *radiologist*
Simjee, Aisha *ophthalmologist, educator*

Smith, Ronald Edward *ophthalmologist*
Smith, Vernon Lomax *economist, educator*
Steiner, Ronald Lee *lawyer, educator, director*
Stephen, Berens *artist, educator*
Stevens, Cherita Wyman *social sciences educator, writer*
Tamiko, Washington Suzette *theater educator*
Tuggle, Francis Douglas *entrepreneur, consultant, management educator, scientist*
Vaziri, Nosratola Dabir *internist, nephrologist, educator*
Williams, Danna Beth *reading specialist, educator*
Williams, Patricia Sue *agricultural studies educator*
Wirth, Garrett Andrew *plastic surgeon*
Wright, William Grandfield *biology professor*
Yu, Jen *medical educator*
Zetin, Mark I. *psychiatrist*

Orangevale
Gibson, Gordon Ronald *chemist*
Meigel, David Walter *retired career officer, musician*

Orinda
Counelis, James Steve *education educator*
Hetland, John Robert *law educator*
Trowbridge, Thomas, Jr. *mortgage company executive*

Oroville
Gantt, Ileana Maria *language educator*
Manera, Rose Ellen *music educator, elementary school educator*

Oxnard
Alexy, Kimberly E. *investment company executive*
Holden, Thomas E. *Mayor, Oxnard, California*
Kirschbaum, Alan Ira *air force officer, systems integration specialist*
O'Connell, Hugh Mellen, Jr. *retired architect*
Sands, Velma Ahda *lawyer*
Tolmach, Jane Louise *community activist, municipal official*

Pacific Grove
Davis, Robert Edward *retired communications educator*
Elinson, Henry David *artist, language educator*
Epel, David *biologist, educator*
Ericson, Jon Meyer *academic administrator, language educator*
Somero, George Nicholls *biology educator*
Sproule, James Michael *communications educator, writer*
Tanguy-Tracey, Sheila Anne *artist, poet*

Pacific Palisades
Beck, John Christian *physician, educator*
Cale, Charles Griffin *lawyer, real estate and corporate financial company executive*
Caster, Jacqueline Jacobs *not-for-profit executive*
Chesney, Lee Roy, Jr. *artist*
Claes, Daniel John *physician*
Diehl, Richard Kurth *retail executive, consultant*
Flattery, Thomas Long *lawyer, administrator*
Goodman, John *actor*
Griver, Jeanette A. *psychologist, consultant*
Hagenbuch, Rodney Dale *finance educator, consultant*
Herman, Elvin E. *retired consulting electronic engineer*
Hoffenberg, Marvin *retired political science professor*
Hubbs, Donald Harvey *foundation executive*
Humphreys, Robert Lee *advertising executive*
Jennings, Marcella Grady *rancher, investor*
Jones, Edgar Allan, Jr. *lawyer, arbitrator, educator*
Kaufer, Shirley Helen *artist, painter*
Kirkgaard, Valerie Anne *marketing company partner, media group executive, radio host, producer, writer, consultant*
Longaker, Richard Pancoast *retired political science professor, academic administrator*
Mulryan, Henry Trist *mining executive, consultant*
Outcalt, David Lewis *academic administrator, mathematics professor, consultant, musician*
Perloff, Marjorie Gabrielle *literature educator*
Rachelefsky, Gary Stuart *medical educator*
Ritter, Jason *actor*
Share, Richard Hudson *lawyer*
Snowhook, Ann Laferty *social services administrator*

Pacifica
Latham, Benjamin Erwin *music educator*
Petersen, Roland *artist, printmaker*

Pacoima
Alarcón, Richard *councilman*

Palm Desert
Adelman, Bayla Ann *occupational therapist*
Ayling, Henry Faithful *editor, consultant, journalist, poet*
Bantz, Jody Lenore *psychologist*
Baxter, Betty Carpenter *life coach, consultant*
Budzinsky, Armin Alexander *investment banker*
Epstein, Marvin Morris *retired construction company executive*
Goldberg, Martin Stanford *retired lawyer*
Hook, John Burney *investment company executive*
Ponder, Catherine *clergywoman*
Sausman, Karen *zoological park administrator*
Stenhouse, Everett Ray *clergy administrator*

Palm Springs
Arnold, Stanley Norman *management consultant, educator*
Carnase, Thomas Paul *graphics designer, consultant*
Conover, Robert Warren *retired librarian*
Ellsworth, Frank L. *not-for-profit executive*
Gerard, James Wilson *publishing consultant*
Hammond, Michael *museum director*
Jones, Milton Wakefield *publisher*
Kimberling, John Farrell *retired lawyer*
Nash, Steven Alan *museum director, curator, art historian*
Nelson, K. Bonita *literary agent*
O'Neill, Michael James *retired special education educator*
Petermann, Hans Jürgen *research scientist*
Scott, Walter, Jr. *business consultant*
Stearns, Robert Leland *curator*
Wlaschin, Ken *cultural organization administrator, writer*
Wouk, Herman *writer*

Palmdale
Anderson, R(obert) Gregg *real estate company executive*
Kilanowski, Dana Marcotte *historian, writer, filmmaker, archaeologist*
Phillips, Ruthanne *special education administrator*
Yore, Joseph N. *communications executive*

Palo Alto
Abrams, William F. *lawyer*
Adamson, Geoffrey David *reproductive endocrinologist, surgeon*
Agassi, Shai *alternative energy company executive, former application developer*
Amdahl, Gene Myron *computer company executive*
Andersen, Torben Brender *optical researcher, astronomer, software engineer*
Banerjee, Prith *computer company executive, computer engineering professor*
Barford, Lee Alton *computer scientist*
Baron, Frederick David *lawyer*
Baum, Brandon *lawyer, educator*
Bennett, Alan Jerome *electronics executive, physicist*
Bensch, Klaus George *pathology educator*
Benton, Lee F. *lawyer*
Bertaccini, Edward J. *anesthesiologist, educator*
Bianchini, Gina L. *Internet company executive*
Bocian, Peter *computer company executive*
Bohman, Bryan *anesthesiologist, hospital administrator*
Bradley, Donald Edward *lawyer*
Bradley, Todd (Richard Todd Bradley) *computer company executive*
Bratkovsky, Alexander Mikhailovich *physicist*
Breyer, James W. (James William Breyer) *venture capitalist*
Brodell, Anne Rayne *psychotherapist, consultant*
Brown, David Randolph *electrical engineer*
Bush, Barbara Pierce *not-for-profit executive, volunteer, former first daughter*
Card, Stuart Kent *psychologist, researcher*
Cashion, Susan *retired performing arts educator*
Cassidy, Sukhinder Singh *venture capitalist, former information technology executive*
Chaturvedi, Nalin A. *aerospace engineer, researcher*
Chen, Stephen Shi-hua *pathologist, biochemist*
Climan, Richard Elliot *lawyer*
Cohen, Karl Paley *nuclear energy consultant*
Commons, George W. *plastic surgeon*
Dawes, Christopher *hospital administrator*
de Waal Malefyt, Rene *immunologist*
Diamond, Diana Louise *editor, journalist*
Dillman, Linda M. *computer company executive, former retail executive*
Donatelli, David *computer company executive*
Dubin, Anne *medical educator*
Ebersman, David A. *Internet company executive*
Fattal, David *physicist*
Feldman, Boris *lawyer*
Flanagan, Robert Joseph *economics professor*
Flaum, Keith Avery *lawyer*
Flaxman, Jon E. *computer company executive*
Fordis, Jean Burke *lawyer*
Fries, James Franklin *internal medicine educator*
Fruchterman, James Robert, Jr. *computer company and not-for-profit executive*
Furbush, David Malcolm *lawyer*
Gaither, James C. *lawyer*
Galel, Susan Alpert *transfusion medicine physician*
Gorman, Maureen J. *lawyer*
Grantham, Donald *computer company executive, former computer systems network executive*
Greco, Joseph A. *lawyer*
Gubins, Samuel *publishing executive*
Guertin, Timothy E. *medical products executive*
Halluin, Albert Price *lawyer*
Hays, Marguerite Thompson *nuclear medicine physician, educator*
Heneveld-Story, Christy Jean *educational researcher*
Hinman, Harvey DeForest *lawyer*
Hiscox, Frank S. *lawyer*
Hoak, Jonathan S., Sr. *lawyer*
Hodge, Philip Gibson, Jr. *mechanical and aerospace engineering educator*
Holman, Halsted Reid *physician, educator*
Holston, Michael Joseph *lawyer, computer company executive*
Horngren, Charles Thomas *finance educator*
Huberman, Bernardo A. *physicist*
Hurd, Mark Vincent *computer company executive*
Ivey, Thomas J. *lawyer*
Jain, Vivek *electronics and communication engineer, researcher*
Jeng, Michael Raymond *medical educator*
Johnson, Noble Marshall *research scientist*
Joshi, Vyomesh I. *computer company executive*
Kanumuri, Sandeep *communications engineer, researcher*
Kim, Wan Hee *engineering educator*
King, Kenton J. *lawyer*
Klein, Robert Nicholas, II, *real estate developer*
Knoles, George Harmon *history educator*
Laurie, Ronald Sheldon *lawyer*
Lee, Gordon *plastic surgeon, educator*
Lesjak, Catherine A. *computer company executive*
Lipsick, Joseph Steven *research scientist, medical educator*
Livermore, Ann Martinelli *computer company executive*
Lo, Yee On *composer*
Lobdell, Frank *artist*
Loewenstein, Walter Bernard *nuclear energy industry executive*
Lyons, Cathy *computer company executive*
Marina, Neyssa *pediatrician, educator*
Maritz, Paul *computer software company executive*
Martin, Robert Bruce *chemistry professor*
McAniff, Richard *computer software company executive*
McCall, Jennifer Jordan *lawyer*
McCormick, Steven J. *foundation administrator*
Mendenhall, Michael *computer company executive*
Michels, Dirk *lawyer*
Mitchell, Beverly Shriver *hematologist, oncologist, educator*
Moll, John Lewis *retired electronics engineer*
Mommsen, Katharina *retired literature and language professor, foundation administrator*
Moore, Cassandra Chrones *policy analyst*
Moos, Rudolf H. *psychologist, researcher*
Morris, Arlene Myers *biopharmaceutical company executive*
Moskovitz, Dustin Aaron *Internet company executive, entrepreneur, application developer*
Mott, Randy (Randall D. Mott) *computer company executive*
Neal, Stephen Cassidy *lawyer*
Nichols, William Ford, Jr. *foundation, health science association administrator, educator*
Nishar, Dipchand (Deep Nishar) *Internet company executive*
Nopar, Alan S. *lawyer*
Nuchi, Lior O. *lawyer*
O'Donnell, John Setel *energy executive*
Ohayon, Maurice Moyses *medical educator, director*
Perez de Alonso, Marcela *human resources specialist, information technology executive*
Perl, Martin Lewis *physicist, educator, chemical engineer*
Petkanics, Donna M. *lawyer*
Pizzo, Philip A. *dean, pediatrician, educator*
Quate, Calvin Forrest *engineering educator*
Radcliffe, Mark Flohn *lawyer*
Ressi, Adeo (Adeo Gregory Ressi di Cervia) *Internet company executive*
Ricardo-Campbell, Rita *retired economist educator*
Robison, Shane V. *computer company executive*
Roos, John Victor *lawyer*
Rose, Jessica *medical educator*
Sager, Philip Travis *pharmaceutical executive, cardiologist, researcher*
Salvatierra, Oscar, Jr. *transplant surgeon, urologist, educator*
Sandberg, Sheryl Kara *Internet company executive*
Sanders, William John *research scientist*
Saxena, Arjun Nath *physicist*
Schafer, Ronald William *electrical engineering educator*
Schendel, Stephen Alfred *surgeon, educator*
Schmidt, Cyril James *librarian*
Schrier, Stanley Leonard *hematologist, educator*
Schurman, David Jay *orthopedic surgeon, educator*
Scitovsky, Anne Aickelin *economist, researcher*
Sculley, John *investment company executive, former computer company executive*
Seethaler, William Charles *high technology manufacturing executive*
Sherlock, Phyllis Krafft *psychologist*
Shetty, Jay K. *research and development company executive, researcher*
Shi, Qin *lawyer, technologist*
Shuer, Lawrence Mendel *neurosurgery educator, dean*
Silverman, Norman Henry *cardiologist, educator*
Skoll, Jeffrey S. *philanthropist, former Internet company executive*
Sledd, Robert C. *food products executive*
Sleep, Norman H. *geophysics educator*
Smith, Glenn A. *lawyer*
Smith, Julie Ann *pharmaceutical executive*
Sonsini, Larry W. *lawyer*
Spohn, Nor Rae *computer company executive*
Staprans, Armand *electronics executive*
Strober, Samuel *immunologist, educator*
Sudhof, Thomas Christian *molecular genetics educator*
Tansey, Richard J. *research scientist*
Taylor, John Joseph *nuclear engineer, researcher*
Tiffany, Joseph Raymond, II, *lawyer*
Urquhart, John *medical researcher, educator*
Weiss, Leonard *mathematician, consultant, writer*
Westphal, Lynn Marie *obstetrician, gynecologist*
Whitaker, Urban George, Jr. *educational consultant, former dean*
Wojcicki, Esther Denise *journalist, educator*
Wong, Y(ing) Wood *real estate investment company executive, real estate development company executive, venture capital investment company executive*
Wu, Lin *cardiologist, researcher*
Yang, Jianhua Joshua *materials scientist, researcher*
Zuckerberg, Mark Elliot *Internet company executive, entrepreneur, programmer*

Palos Verdes Estates
Abbott, A. Dwight *retired astronautical engineer*
DeLuce, Richard David *lawyer*
Lazzaro, Anthony Derek *academic administrator*
Paulikas, George Algis *retired physicist*
Raue, Jorg Emil *electrical engineer*
Seide, Paul *civil engineering educator*
Smith, Stephen Randolph *aerospace executive*
Yarbrough, Allyson Debra *electrical engineer*

Palos Verdes Peninsula
Alkon, Paul Kent *language educator*
Christie, Hans Frederick *retired utilities executive*
Grant, Robert Ulysses *retired manufacturing executive*
Leone, William Charles *retired manufacturing executive*
Manning, Christopher Ashley *finance educator, consultant*
Mirels, Harold *aerospace engineer*
Slayden, James Bragdon *retired retail executive*
Slusser, Robert Wyman *aerospace transportation executive*
Thomas, Claudewell Sidney *psychiatrist, educator*
Van Der Meulen, Joseph Pierre *neurologist*
Wilson, Theodore Henry *retired electronics executive, aerospace engineer*

Panorama City
Bass, Harold Neal *pediatrician, medical geneticist*
Fleisher, Arthur A., II, *physician*
Janis, Elinor Raiden *artist, educator*
Lieberthal, Allan Stuart *pediatrician, educator*
Lugg, Marlene Martha *immunization coordinator, health information systems specialist, health planner*
Sue, Michael Alvin *allergist*

Paradise
Barr, Donald Roy *statistics and operations research educator, statistician*

Pasadena
Allen, Clarence Roderic *geologist, educator*
Andersen, Richard Alan *physiologist*
Andreetto, Marco *research scientist*
Arnold, Frances Hamilton *chemistry educator*
Baltimore, David *microbiologist, educator, former academic administrator*
Barish, Barry C. *physics professor, researcher*
Barnes, Charles Andrew *physicist, researcher*
Bass, Deborah Simone *engineering company executive*
Beer, Reinhard *atmospheric scientist*
Bejczy, Antal Károly *research scientist and facility administrator*
Bertani, Lillian Elizabeth Teegarden *biologist, researcher, educator*
Bishop, Robert Calvin *pharmaceutical company executive*
Blake, Geoffrey Allen *chemistry professor*
Bogaard, William Joseph *mayor, lawyer, educator*
Boochever, Robert *federal judge*
Bosley, Edward Richmond *historical site administrator*
Boxe, Christopher Shawn *research scientist*
Bradley, James Edwin *religious studies educator*
Breckinridge, James Bernard *optical scientist*
Bridges, William Bruce *electrical engineer, educator, researcher*
Brogden-Stirbl, Shona Marie *writer, researcher*
Brotman, Richard Dennis *counselor*
Buck, Jonathan Frederick *lawyer*
Bugga, Ratnakumar Venkata *electrochemist, researcher*
Byun, Sung Hun *research scientist*
Caine, Stephen Howard *data processing executive*
Call, Merlin Wendell *lawyer*
Calleton, Theodore Edward *lawyer, educator*
Capponi, Agostino *research scientist*
Carroll, Sean M. *physicist*
Chahine, Moustafa Toufic *atmospheric scientist*
Chameau, Jean-Lou *academic administrator*
Chan, Sunney Ignatius *retired chemistry educator*
Chang, Eng-Pi *materials scientist*
Childs, Billy *composer*
Chui, Talso C. P. *research scientist*
Clauser, Francis H. *applied science educator*
Coleman, Max Laurence *biogeochemist, educator, director, research scientist, lab administrator*
Cutri, Roc Michael *research scientist*
D'Angelo, Robert William *lawyer*
Davidson, Robert C., Jr. *manufacturing executive*
Dervan, Peter Brendan *chemistry professor*
Diallo, Laura Mann Willis *finance company executive, consultant*
Dickinson, Michael Hughes *physiologist, biotechnologist*
Dimitrius, Jo-Ellan *trial consultant*
Douglas, Kimberly *university librarian*
Dressler, Alan Michael *astronomer*
Dubovitsky, Serge *engineering educator, researcher*
Duxbury, Thomas *planetary scientist*
Eisenstein, James P. *physicist, educator*
Elachi, Charles *aerospace engineer*
Ellis, Richard Salisbury *astronomer, educator*
Ellner, Carolyn Lipton *non-profit organization executive, dean, consultant*
Elowitz, Michael *molecular biologist, educator*
Fernandez, Ferdinand Francis *federal judge*
Fisher, Raymond Corley *federal judge*
Frautschi, Steven Clark *physicist, researcher*
Fredericks, Ward Arthur *venture capitalist*
Freedman, Wendy Laurel *astronomer, educator, director*
Freeman, Ralph Carter *investment banker, management consultant*
Fu, Lee-Lueng *oceanographer*
Gill, Gene *artist*
Gillespie, Harry Robinson *management consultant*
Gilman, Richard Carleton *retired academic administrator*
Giorgini, Jon *aerospace scientist*
Glovsky, Myron Michael *medical educator*
Goldreich, Peter Martin *astrophysics and planetary physics educator*
Goldschmidt, Walter Rochs *anthropologist*
Golombek, Matthew Philip *research scientist, planetary geologist*
Goodstein, David Louis *physics professor*
Goodwin, Alfred Theodore *federal judge*
Gorsuch, Richard Lee *psychologist, educator, minister*
Gray, Harry Barkus *chemistry professor*
Greenhall, Charles August *mathematician*
Gregory, Timothy Peter *historian, consultant*
Grotzinger, John Peter *paleontologist, educator*
Grubbs, Robert Howard *chemistry professor*
Haight, James Theron *lawyer*
Hall, Cynthia Holcomb *federal judge*
Halsted, Margo *music educator, carillonneur*
Harvey, Joseph Paul, Jr. *orthopedist, educator*
Hernandez, Enrique, Jr., (Rick Hernandez) *security firm executive*
Hicklin, Ronald Lee *music production company executive*
Hitlin, David George *physicist, researcher*
Holzmann, Gerard Johan *computer science researcher*
Horak, Jan-Christopher *filmmaker, educator, curator*
Hornung, Hans Georg *aeronautical engineering educator, science administrator*
Hou, Thomas Yizhao *mathematician*
Houman, Owhadi *mathematician*
Huang, Alice Shih-hou *biologist, educator, virologist*

Hunt, Gordon *lawyer*
Hunt, Hazel Analue Stanfield *retired accountant*
Hunter, Milton *construction company executive, retired career military officer*
Jennings, Paul Christian *civil engineering educator, academic administrator*
Jo, Chulsu *theologian*
Johnson, Barbara Jean *retired judge, lawyer*
Jones, Jennifer *actress*
Kaplan, Gary *executive recruiter*
Kim, Joo Hyeon *astronomer*
Kitaev, Alexei *physics and computer science professor*
Knowles, James Kenyon *applied mathematician, educator*
Koch, Christof *microbiologist, educator, engineering educator*
Konishi, Masakazu *neuroscientist, educator*
Kozinski, Alex *federal judge*
Kresa, Kent *manufacturing executive, retired aerospace executive*
Lake, Kevin Bruce *medical association administrator*
Ledyard, John Odell *economics professor, consultant*
Leeson, Peter J., IV, *lawyer*
Lingenfelter, Sherwood Galen *academic administrator, retired anthropologist*
List, Ericson John *environmental engineering science educator, consultant*
Logan, Francis Dummer *retired lawyer*
Lopes, Rosaly Mutel Crocce *astronomer, planetary geologist*
Losh, Samuel Johnston *engineering administrator*
Marcus, Rudolph Arthur *chemist, educator*
Markley, William C. *lawyer*
Marlen, James S. *chemical, plastics and building materials manufacturing company executive*
Marsano, Joseph D. *physicist*
Martin, Craig Lee *engineering company executive*
Massey, Richard *astrophysicist*
Matthews, Mildred Shapley *retired editor*
Mc Carthy, Frank Martin *oral surgeon, educator*
Mc Koy, Basil Vincent Charles *theoretical chemist, educator*
Menefee, John William III *cinematographer, film producer*
Meyerowitz, Elliot Martin *biology professor*
Miller, Susan Calabrese *lawyer, consumer products company executive*
Mosher, Sally Ekenberg *lawyer, musician*
Mueth, Joseph Edward *lawyer*
Murray, Richard M. *engineering educator*
Myers, R(alph) Chandler *lawyer*
Nackel, John George *health venture capital executive*
Nelson, Dorothy Wright *federal judge*
Ng, Dominic *bank executive*
Nguyen, Hien Trong *astrophysicist, researcher*
Norton, Karen Ann *accountant*
O'Brien, Grace Wilhelmina Ehlig *genealogical consultant, psychologist, retired educational administrator, writer*
O'Bryant, Daniel R. *consumer products company executive*
Omery, Anna *nursing administrator*
Opel, William *medical research administrator*
Orphan, Victoria Jeanne *science educator*
Ortiz, Michael *engineering educator*
Ouchi, Masami *astronomer*
Owen, Ray David *biology professor*
Paez, Richard A. *federal judge*
Palfrey, Thomas Rossman *economics professor, political science professor*
Parker, Jeffrey Scott *systems engineer, researcher*
Parr, James Allan *literature professor*
Pashgian, M. Helen *artist*
Phillips, Robert *engineering educator, researcher*
Pieri, David C. *research scientist*
Pikov, Victor *physiologist*
Pinsky, Drew (David Drew Pinsky) *television personality, psychotherapist*
Politzer, Hugh David *physicist, educator*
Revel, Jean-Paul *biology professor*
Roberts, John D. *chemist, educator*
Robinson, Roger *actor, director*
Rothemund, Paul W.K. *research scientist*
Rutledge, David B. *electrical engineer, educator*
Ryan, Margaret Amy *chemist, researcher*
Rymer, Pamela Ann *federal judge*
Sabersky, Rolf Heinrich *mechanical engineer*
Sackmann, Inge-Juliana *astrophysicist*
Sandage, Allan Rex *astronomer*
Sarani, Siamak *aerospace engineer*
Sargent, Wallace Leslie William *astronomer, educator*
Schmidt, Maarten *astronomy educator*
Schneider, Tapio *environmental scientist, educator*
Schwarz, John Henry *theoretical physicist, educator*
Scudder, Thayer *anthropologist, educator*
Seinfeld, John Hersh *chemical engineering professor*
Sengupta, Anita *aerospace engineer, researcher*
Shaw, Anthony *pediatric surgeon, retired educator*
Shaw, R. Daniel *anthropology professor*
Shim, Changsub *research scientist*
Shimada, Katsunori *retired electrical engineer*
Short, Elizabeth M. *internist, educator, retired federal agency administrator*
Shum, Matthew *social sciences educator*
Smith, Howard Russell *manufacturing executive, director*
Smith, Michael Robert *electro-optical engineer, physicist*
Solis, Carlos *lawyer*
Song, Seok Goo *geophysicist*
Spilker, Linda Joyce *aerospace scientist*
Staehle, Robert L. *foundation executive*
Steiner, Greg *Internet company executive*
Sternberg, Paul Warren *biologist, educator*
Stevens, Roy W. *sales and marketing executive*
Stone, Edward C. *physicist, researcher*
Sullivan, William Francis *lawyer*
Sun, Xiankai *research scientist*
Supatto, Willy *research scientist*
Talukder, Ashit *research scientist*
Tashima, Atsushi Wallace *federal judge*
Tombrello, Thomas Anthony, Jr. *physics professor*
Tsurutani, Bruce Tadashi *physicist*
Varshavsky, Alexander Jacob *molecular biologist, educator*
Vogt, Rochus Eugen *physicist, researcher*
Waldorf, Gregory *Internet company executive, venture capitalist*
Wardlaw, Kim A. McLane *federal judge*
Warren, Neil Clark *Internet company executive, psychologist*
Wasserburg, Gerald Joseph *geology and geophysics educator*
Watkins, John Francis *management consultant*
Watson, Noel G. *construction executive*
White-Thomson, Ian Leonard *retired mining executive*
Williams, Bradley Bennett *historian*
Winbush, Olga Joyce *education educator, consultant*
Wood, Lincoln Jackson *aerospace engineer*
Wyatt, Joseph Lucian, Jr. *lawyer, writer*
Yariv, Amnon *electrical engineering educator, research scientist*
Yeomans, Donald Keith *astronomer*
Yin, Peng *computer scientist*
Yohalem, Harry Morton *lawyer*
Zewail, Ahmed Hassan *chemistry and physics educator, consultant, editor*
Zwicky, Barbarina Exita *humanities educator, researcher*

Paso Robles
Boxer, Jerome Harvey *accountant, management consultant, vintager*
Brown, Benjamin Andrew *retired journalist*
Gerstung, Estella Rose Baker *literature professor*
Judd, Dennis Paul *history professor*

Pauma Valley
Lewis, Gerald Jorgensen *judge*

Pearblossom
Goldman, Gary Steven *computer scientist, consultant*

Pebble Beach
Dallmann, William Charles *speech educator, writer*
Getreu, Sanford *retired city planner*
Mortensen, Gordon Louis *artist, printmaker*
Sullivan, James Francis *university administrator*

Penn Valley
McDonald, Douglas Robert *retired non profit agency executive*
Nix, Barbara Lois *real estate broker*
Sands, Sharon Louise *graphics designer, artist*
Whitsel, Richard Harry *retired biologist, entomologist*

Penngrove
Haslam, Gerald William *writer, educator*

Petaluma
Archer, Richard Joseph *lawyer*
Bailey, Preston Edward *music educator*
Gervais, Cherie Nadine *small business owner*
Pronzini, Bill John (William Pronzini) *writer*
Skalagard, Hans Martin *artist*
Spiegelman, Art *writer, cartoonist*
Thomas, Nancy Hinckley *special education educator*

Piedmont
Montgomery, Theodore Ashton *physician*
Putter, Irving *retired French language educator*
Reich, Stanley Benjamin *radiologist, medical educator*
Welch, John *computer game company executive*

Pinedale
Falcone, Patricia Jeanne Lalim *investor, foundation administrator*

Pittsburg
Gustafson, Sally Ann *counselor, cosmetologist, educator*
Williams-Thierry, Elizabeth A. *financial planner, consultant*

Placentia
Klapthor, James *broadcast media executive*

Placerville
Leland, Kathryn Ann *literature and language professor*
Maxfield, John Edward *retired university dean*

Playa Del Rey
Baker, Robert M.L., Jr. *academic administrator, research scientist*
Hite, Janet Sue *retired elementary school educator*
Lewis, Carl (Frederick Carlton Lewis) *retired Olympic track and field athlete*
McNeill, Daniel Richard *writer*
Mishelevich, David Jacob *medical products executive*
Weir, Alexander, Jr. *chemical engineer, consultant*

Pleasant Hill
Ashby, Denise Stewart *speech educator, communications consultant*
Bastrenta, Brigitte Elisabeth *school administrator*
Dixon, Martha Lee *anatomist, physiologist, educator*
George, Brian Thomas *historian*
Hollister, Arthur Clair, Jr. *epidemiologist, consultant, retired public health service officer*
Mikolavich, Daniel Keith *literature and language professor, consultant*
Nelson, Bette Sturr *secondary school educator*
Nelson, Douglas Swede Raymond *sheriff*
Okosi, Nsikak Paulinus *physics professor*
Rodriguez, John M. *physics professor*
Shahbazi, Shahbaz *finance and business educator*

Pleasanton
Askanas, Mark S. *lawyer*
Balmuth, Michael A. *retail executive*
Bond, David F. *food products executive*
Burd, Steven A. *food service executive*
Call, John G. *corporate financial executive*
Ching, David T. *food products executive*
Cribb, Gary L. *retail executive*
Denavit, Jacques *retired physicist*
Dietz, Diane M. *marketing executive*
Edwards, Robert L. *corporate financial executive*
Everette, Bruce L. *retail executive*
Ferber, Norman Alan *retail executive*
Fine, Marjorie Lynn *lawyer*
Gordon, Robert Allen, Jr. *food service executive, lawyer*
Jackson, Russell M. *food service executive*
LeHocky, Mark *retail executive, lawyer*
Liu, Wei-Min *statistician, director*
Novak, Randi Ruth *systems engineer, computer scientist*
Opperwall, Stephen Gabriel *lawyer*
Plaisance, Melissa C. *consumer products company executive*
Renda, Larree M. *retail executive*
Roshong, Dee Ann Daniels *dean, educator, counselor*
Shachmut, Kenneth Michael *retail executive*
Stallings, Charles Henry *retired physicist*
Stern, David R. *retail executive*
Tidwell, Jerry *retail executive*
Van Dreser, Merton Lawrence *ceramics engineer*
Weiss, Robert Stephen *medical manufacturing company operating executive*
Wright, Donald P. *retail executive*

Point Richmond
Edginton, John Arthur *lawyer*
Herron, E. Patricia *retired judge*

Pomona
Abedini, Kamran *management consultant*
Ambrose, William Wright, Jr. *dean, educator, academic administrator*
Aurilia, Antonio *physicist, researcher*
Bhandari, Subodh *engineering educator*
Bidlack, Wayne Ross *nutritional biochemist, toxicologist, food scientist*
Callaway, Linda Marie *special education educator*
Chalkiadakis, Fanourios *electrical engineer, educator*
Chung, Eunice P. *pharmacist, educator*
Dobbs, Steven Kent *aerospace engineer, educator*
Gambone, Joseph Charles *medical educator, consultant*
Gupta, Eric K. *pharmacist, educator*
Hargis, Barbara Picasso *artist*
Holmes, Louis Ira *retired physician assistant, educator, photojournalist*
Huang, Ying *medical educator*
Khasawneh, Fadi T. *medical educator, researcher*
Lee, Myong Jae *educator*
Li, Mingheng *engineering educator*
Lin, Lianlian *management educator*
Loo, Dennis *social sciences educator*
Lou, Yiming *chemical engineer*
Mezey, Robert *poet*
Morsberger, Robert Eustis *English language educator*
Nguyen, Megan *pharmacist, educator*
Nise, Norman S. *engineering educator*
Rodriguez, Jose L. *neurosurgeon, educator*
Rothman, Elliott *Mayor, Pomona, California*
Selco, Jodye Isabel *chemistry professor*
Teague, Lavette Cox, Jr. *systems educator, consultant*
Tomiyasu, Kiyo *retired consulting engineer*
Torres, Norma *state legislator*
Turner, Howard *engineering educator, consultant*
Venketaraman, Vishwanath *microbiologist, immunologist, educator*
Wohlcke, Anne Elizabeth *historian, educator*

Port Hueneme
Schneider, Arthur Paul *retired videotape and film editor, author*

Port Hueneme Cbc Base
Nichols, Gina Lynn *archivist, writer*

Porterville
Benander, Kathryn Marie *literature and language professor*
Hargis, Jay Jackson *history professor*
Kusserow, James *music educator*
Neal-Parker, Shirley Anita *obstetrician, gynecologist*

Portola Valley
Carnochan, Walter Bliss *retired humanities educator*
Fogarty, Thomas James *surgery educator*
Garsh, Thomas Burton *publisher*
Graham, William James *packaging company executive*
Hafkenschiel, Joseph Henry, Jr. *retired cardiologist*
March, James Gardner *social sciences educator*

Poway
Conant, Kim Untiedt *retired elementary school educator*
Farrell, Peter Craig *health care company executive*
Hunt, George Wayne *real estate appraiser*
Sirangelo, Mark N. *aerospace transportation executive*

Quartz Hill
McAllister, Bruce Richard *art educator*

Quincy
Hall, Anthony Elmitt *agriculturist, physiologist*

Ramona
Hoffman, Wayne Melvin *retired airline official*
Marquez, Alfredo C. *federal judge*
Newman, Malane L. *computer graphics designer, cartoonist, illustrator, computer graphics designer, educator*

Pordon, William Philip *music educator*
Yoldas, Bulent Erturk *materials scientist, educator*

Rancho Cordova
Hendrickson, Elizabeth Ann *retired secondary school educator*

Rancho Cucamonga
Alvarez, Tirso Reyes, Jr. *engineer*
Cosand, Diana Jeanne *biology professor*
Kurth, Donald James, Jr. *Mayor, Rancho Cucamonga, California, medical educator*
Stewart, Howard L. *engineering educator*
Tirado, Victoria *language educator*

Rancho Dominguez
Janura, Jan Arol *apparel manufacturing executive*

Rancho Mirage
Atiba, Joshua Olajide Oluwabunmi *internist, philanthropist, oncologist, educator, pharmacologist*
Blixseth, Timothy *real estate developer*
Chuang, Tsu-Yi *dermatologist, epidemiologist, educator*
Cone, Lawrence Arthur *medical educator*
Fromm, Erwin Frederick *retired insurance company executive*
Lange, Gary F. *psychotherapist, educator*
Leydorf, Frederick Leroy *lawyer*
Leydorf, Mary Malcolm *physician, writer*
Misa, Kenneth Franklin *management consultant*
Pais, Claudette Rachel *former horse breeder, political consultant*
Pierno, Anthony Robert *lawyer*
Shaeffer, Charlie Willard, Jr. *cardiologist*
Sheldon, Deena Lynn *television camera operator, film producer*
Shen, Alfred C. *neurosurgeon*
Stone, Richard Alan *medical educator*

Rancho Palos Verdes
Allbee, Sandra Moll *real estate broker*
Booth, Doris Palmer *biology professor*
Chlebowski, Rowan Thomas *oncologist, educator*
Curtis, Carole Ortale *executive recruiter, consultant*
Douglass, Craig Bruce *computer technology executive*
Dunlop, Laurence James *religious studies educator*
Haile, Lawrence Barclay *lawyer*
Kwan, Benjamin Ching Kee *ophthalmologist*
Loether, Herman John *sociologist, educator*
Mac Innes, David Harold *artist, small business owner*
MacInnes, Margaret E. *retired art educator*
Neilan, Aidan Joseph *radiologist*
Petak, William John *systems management educator*
Schimmenti, John Joseph *lawyer*
Yassin, Robert Alan *museum director, curator*

Rancho Santa Fe
Affeldt, John Ellsworth *retired physician*
Arledge, Charles Stone *former aerospace executive, entrepreneur*
Best, Jacob Hilmer, Jr. *retired hotel chain executive*
Byrd, Betty Rantze *writer*
Carr, David Turner *physician*
Cuatrecasas, Pedro Martin *research biochemist, educator*
Haddad, Gabriel G. *pediatrician, educator*
Jordan, Charles Morrell *retired automotive designer*
Nadler, Henry Louis *pediatrician, educator, geneticist*
O'Driscoll, Margaret Millar (Peggy O'Driscoll) *real estate broker*
Rockoff, S. David *radiologist, physician, educator*
Ruiz, Ramón Eduardo *history professor*
Step, Eugene Lee *retired pharmaceutical executive*
Woolley, Roger Swire *lawyer*

Rancho Santa Margarita
Berta, Melissa Rose *mathematics professor*
Bunkis, Juris *plastic surgeon*
Hoppe, Dorothe Anna *chemistry educator*
Lawson, Thomas Cheney *marketing executive*
Parth, Frank R. *consulting company executive, educator*
Shusterman, Neal Douglas *writer, scriptwriter*

Randsburg
Ramirez Gelpi, Ana Sofia *language educator, consultant*

Redding
Lund, Harold Emerson *mathematics professor*
Matenaer, Tegwin A. *artist, retired educator, consultant*
Renard, Ronald Lee *allergist*
Wertz, Carol R. *education educator*

Redlands
Bricker, Lauren Weiss *architectural historian*
Burgess, Larry Eugene *library director, historian, educator*
Clopine, Gordon Alan *consulting geologist, educator*
Gonzalez, Olga Carreras *language educator*
Goto, Toshiko *retired art educator*
Kohli, Gurmander Singh *plastic surgeon*
Lu, Hongwei *literature and language professor*
Pick, James Block *business professor, writer*
Roberts, Katharine Adair *retired bookkeeper*
Ryan, Jason K. *finance educator*
Scott, Eric *paleontologist, educator*
Skomal, Edward Nelson *aerospace company executive, electromagnetic environments consultant*
Skoog, William Arthur *retired oncologist*

Redondo Beach
Brodsky, Robert Fox *aerospace engineer, educator, author*
Freeland, Pete *aerospace transportation executive, consultant, actor*

Grollman, Julius Harry, Jr. cardiovascular and interventional radiologist
McWilliams, Margaret Ann home economist, educator, writer
Richards, Denise actress
Sloan, Michael Dana information systems specialist, management consultant

Redwood City
Adelman, Barnet Reuben management consultant
Bell, Frank Ouray, Jr. lawyer
Block, Keith computer software company executive
Burkhardt, Roger information technology executive
Calvin, Allen David psychologist, educator
Coddington, Clinton Hays lawyer
Cremer, Jay Theodore, Jr. research scientist
Daley, Dorian Estelle lawyer, computer software company executive
Danielson, David Robert information technology manager, consultant
Deng, Shiming engineer
Deresinski, Stanley C. epidemiologist
Fredericson, Michael physiatrist
Grandsaert, John Leo judge
Gunderson, Robert Vernon, Jr. lawyer
Iverson, Charles physics professor
Kurian, Thomas computer software company executive
Lee, V. Paul entertainment software company executive
McLaughlin, David Michael lawyer
Mockapetris, Paul V. computer scientist, information technology executive
Palmer, Pamela Pierce anesthesiologist
Pape, Glenn Michael lawyer, retired financial planner
Parameswaran, Rupa software security developer
Penner, Susanne Mary communications executive
Phillips, Charles E., Jr. computer software company executive
Pleasants, John F. electronics executive
Polese, Kim software company executive
Poole, Will computer company executive
Powers, Matthew Douglas lawyer
Probst, Lawrence F. III interactive software/gaming executive
Riccitiello, John S. interactive software and gaming executive, venture capitalist
Rottler, Juergen computer software company executive
Rozwat, Charles computer software company executive
Schappert, John Conrad computer software company executive
Sim, Judith marketing executive
Spangler, Nita Reifschneider volunteer
Tyson, Laura D'Andrea economics professor, former dean
Wang, Chen Chi electronics, real estate and diversified financial services company executive
Wilhelm, Robert Oscar lawyer, civil engineer
Winters, Vernon Michael lawyer

Redwood Shores
Catz, Safra Ada computer software company executive
Ellison, Larry (Lawrence Joseph Ellison) computer software company executive
Epstein, Jeffrey Emanuel computer software company executive
Henley, Jeffrey O. computer software company executive

Redwood Valley
Speed, Cynthia Agnes retired mathematics professor

Reedley
Dick, Henry Henry minister
Jones, Steven D. academic counselor

Reseda
Banks, Carol T. elementary school educator
Hoover, Pearl Rollings nurse
Mirzaei, Shahnam engineering educator

Rialto
Elliott, Susan Donise secondary school educator
Robertson, Carey Jane musician, educator

Richmond
Arnon, Stephen Soulé physician, research scientist
Corbin, Rosemary MacGowan former mayor
Dolberg, David Spencer lawyer
Hommeltoft, Sven Ivar chemist
Jenkins, Everett Wilbur, Jr. lawyer, writer, historian
Onisko, Bruce Charles mass spectroscopist
Qiu, Zhijun engineer, researcher
Sibitz, Michael William school system administrator
Wessel, Henry photographer
Windham, Gayle C. epidemiologist

Ridgecrest
Bennett, Harold Earl physicist, optics researcher
Miears-Cutsinger, Mary Ellen artist, gallery owner
St-Amand, Pierre geophysicist

Rio Vista
Azarnoff, Daniel Lester pharmaceutical executive, consultant

Riverside
Bailey-Serres, Julia N. geneticist, educator
Balandin, Alexander A. electrical engineer, educator
Barkin, Kenneth David history professor
Bartnicki-Garcia, Salomon microbiologist, educator
Beckage, Nancy E. physiologist, educator, entomologist
Bell, Helen Lavin artist
Beni, Gerardo electrical engineer, educator
Blair, Scott Craig physics professor
Bricker, Neal S. physician, educator
Brinkerhoff, Dericksen Morgan art historian, educator
Calfee, Robert Chilton psychologist, educator
Chamberlain, Willard Thomas retired metal products executive
Chronister, Eric L. chemistry professor, department chairman
Coffey, Michael David plant pathologist, educator
Darling, Scott Edward lawyer
Day, Renee Noelle special education and secondary school educator
Ellstrand, Norman Carl plant genetics, conservation and evolution educator
Fairbairn, Daphne Janice biology professor
Fontana, Sandra Ellen Frankel special education educator
Gaffney, M. Mason economics professor
Green, Jonathan William museum director, educator, artist, writer
Griffin, Keith Broadwell retired economics professor
Grimm, Reinhold humanities educator
Hayashi, Cheryl biologist, educator
Head, Randolph Conrad history professor
Heiting, James Otto lawyer
Hille, Russ biochemist, educator
Jackson, Ruth Moore university librarian
James, Etta (Jamesetta Hawkins) recording artist
Jung, Timothy Tae Kun otolaryngologist
Khayer, Mohammad Abul electrical engineer, researcher
Khoury, Sarkis Joseph professor, consultant
Koo, Bonjun environmental scientist, educator
Kroeger, Dennis Michael school system administrator
Kuang, Shilong mathematics professor
Lee, Raejin music educator, soprano
Loveridge, Ronald Oliver Mayor, Riverside, California
MacDougall, Diana E. interpreter, educator, social sciences educator
Maclaughlin, Douglas Earl physicist, educator
Mancilla, Faustina Ramirez retired psychologist
McHughen, Alan geneticist, educator
Minot, Stephen writer
Page, Albert Lee soil science educator, researcher
Parke, Ross Duke psychology professor
Peterson, Arthur Laverne foundation administrator
Petrinovich, Lewis Franklin psychologist, educator
Pogorelov, Nikolai physicist, researcher
Rabenstein, Dallas Leroy chemistry professor
Rainey, Susan J. school system administrator
Ratliff, Louis Jackson, Jr. mathematics professor
Robert, Bates D. archaeologist, educator
Rosenthal, Robert psychology professor
Ross, Delmer Gerrard historian, educator
Rudolph, Conrad medieval art history educator
Russo, Marisa Natalina educational consultant
Salzman, Michele Renee historian, educator
Schoeller, Wolfgang Wilhelm chemistry educator
Shapiro, Victor Lenard mathematics professor
Shouse, Peter John soil scientist, researcher
Smith, Elden Leroy recreational vehicle and manufactured housing company executive
Snyder, Henry Leonard historian, educator, writer
Sokolsky, Robert Lawrence journalist
Su, Kenneth C. H. gynecologist
Suyenaga, Elsie Sakae retired elementary school educator
Tinianow, Dan Eric communications educator
Turk, Austin Theodore social studies educator
Van Gundy, Seymour Dean plant pathologist, educator
White, Clara Jo small business owner, consultant
White, Timothy Peter academic administrator

Rocklin
Bowen, Brenda Denise literature and language professor
Dwyer, Darrell James finance company executive
Erickson, William Lawrence academic administrator
Haley, James Brian dean
Herzog, Nathan Braden professor, consultant
Stanley, Elizabeth Kathryn music educator

Rohnert Park
Babula, William dean, writer
Byrne, Noel Thomas sociologist, educator
Rank, Nathan biologist, educator
Steiner, John Michael sociologist, educator
Wautischer, Helmut philosophy educator

Rolling Hills Estates
Bellis, Carroll Joseph surgeon, educator
Conrad, Paul Francis cartoonist
McCreight, Louis retired materials scientist

Rosemead
Adler, Robert L. lawyer, utilities executive
Craver, Theodore F., Jr. utilities and energy executive
Featherstone, Diane L. utilities executive
Gault, Polly L. utilities executive
House, Cecil R. utilities executive
Jin, Jing Yi photographer, film director
Parsky, Barbara J. utilities executive
Scilacci, W. James, Jr. utilities executive
Yazdi, Mahvash utilities executive

Roseville
Carmen, Robert G. insurance company executive
Dodds, Larry D. insurance company executive
Gerth, Donald Rogers retired university president, educator
Liu, Davis physician, writer
Murray, Michael gynecologist, department chairman
Netto, Paul V. critical care nurse
Rebok, Douglas E. insurance company executive, accountant
Smith, Kaye Train artist
Yates, Coleen Denise special education educator

Ross
Giovinco, Joseph non profit agency administrator, writer
Godwin, Sara writer
Nicholson, William Joseph energy and environmental consultant

Rowland Heights
Chou, George Kechung architect, civil engineer, small business owner, urban planner

Running Springs
Liddle, Sidney George retired mechanical engineer, researcher
Marcus, John Richard lawyer

Rutherford
Staglin, Garen Kent computer services company executive, venture capitalist

Sacramento
Abdur-Rahim, Shareef (Julius Shareef Abdul-Rahim) professional basketball coach, retired professional basketball player
Acree, G. Hardy airport executive
Ailman, Christopher J. investment company executive
Albertson, Timothy E. physician, educator
Aldrich, Thomas Albert former brewing executive, consultant
Amaral, David G. neuroscientist, educator
Amezcua, Esther Hernandez elementary school educator
Ashburn, Roy state legislator
Baccigaluppi, Roger John agricultural products executive
Barankin, Joseph Paul director, consultant
Beckon, William Nelson environmentalist
Bell, Wayne S. lawyer, state agency official
Belshé, Kimberly state agency administrator, public health service officer
Betts, Bert A. retired treasurer, accountant
Bleckley, Jeanette A. lawyer
Bogren, Hugo Gunnar radiology educator
Bornstein, Julie Ilene state agency administrator
Bowen, Debra Lynn Secretary of State, California, former state legislator
Braden, Charles Goetzman III theater educator
Brotman, Martin health care services executive, gastroenterologist
Brown, Jerry, Jr., (Edmund Gerald Brown Jr.) state attorney general, former mayor, governor
Brown, Lawrence George prosecutor
Burks, Rocky Alan disability access manager and consultant
Burton, Randall James lawyer
Bustamante, Cruz M. former lieutenant governor
Callahan, Consuelo Maria federal judge
Callahan, Edward J. dean
Carr, Gerald Francis language educator
Carril, Pete (Peter J. Carril) professional basketball consultant
Chamie, Karim urologist
Chapman, Michael William orthopedist, educator
Chesbro, Wesley state legislator
Chick, Laura Newman state official, former city official
Clover, Haworth Alfred elementary school educator, historian
Cochran, Roger toxicologist, consultant
Covin, David L. retired political science professor
Crawford, Robert Lawrence mathematics professor
Crimmins, Philip Patrick retired metallurgical engineer, lawyer
Cunningham, Mary Elizabeth (Mary Cunningham-Lusby) physician
Day, James McAdam, Jr. lawyer
Dear, Joseph Albert pension fund administrator
Dell, Cheryl Elbright publishing executive
de Vere White, Ralph urologist, educator
Donald, Paul James otolaryngologist
Drachnik, Catherine Meldyn recreational therapist, artist, counselor
Flamm, Melvin Daniel, Jr. cardiologist
Forsyth, Raymond Arthur civil engineer, consultant
Franz, Jennifer Danton public opinion and marketing researcher
Friedman, Morton Lee retired lawyer
Fry, Patrick insurance company executive
Fung, Maxwell Alexander medical educator
Garamendi, John R. Lieutenant Governor of California, former state legislator
Gardner, Jerry Lee financial consultant
Gilbert, William McBeath physician, perinatologist
Hales, Robert Ernest psychiatrist, educator
Henson, Glenda Maria newswriter
Hernandez, James, Jr. criminal justice educator
Hinks, Lyle Allen special education educator
Horton, Mark B. state agency administrator, public health service officer
Houpt, James Edward lawyer
Huh, Joan lawyer
Hunter, Patricia Rae (Tricia Hunter) state official
Jackson, Richard Joseph epidemiologist, educator, pediatrician, preventive medicine physician
Jimenez, Regina Ann librarian
Johnson, Kevin Maurice Mayor, Sacramento, retired professional basketball player
Jones, Lial A. museum director
Kalish, Nancy psychology professor
Karsiere, Sarma art educator
Katranis Fotopoulos, Kathy Ekaterini Christou ancient language educator, social sciences educator
Katzberg, Richard Wier radiologist, researcher
Kelso, J(ohn) Clark law educator, consultant
Kerri, Kenneth Donald civil engineering educator
Khatri, Vijay Pranjivan surgeon, researcher, educator
Kon, Alexander A. pediatrician, educator
Kuehl, Sheila James state board member
Lara, Primo medical educator
Laslett, Lawrence J. physician, educator
Lathi, Bhagawandas Pannalal retired electrical engineering educator
Lawson, Kara professional basketball player
Leake, Sherrill Ann psychologist
Lim, Alan Young plastic surgeon
Lin, Lily Koo ophthalmologist
Lionakis, George architect
Lloyd, William C. III ophthalmologist
Lockyer, Bill (William Lockyer) state treasurer
Loewy, Erich H. bioethicist educator
Low, Reginald Inman cardiologist
Luo, Zairen transportation engineer
Lynch, Peter John retired dermatologist
Madera Uribe, Jose de Jesus bishop emeritus
Majesty, Melvin Sidney psychologist, consultant
Makker, Sudesh Paul physician
Maloof, Gavin Patrick professional sports team executive
Maloof, Joseph professional sports team owner
Manson, H. Craig (Harold Craig Manson) law educator, former federal agency administrator, former judge
Marin, Rosario state agency administrator, former federal agency administrator
Masuyama, Kazue literature and language professor
Maverakis, Emanual dermatologist, educator
Maxwell-Jolly, David state agency administrator, public health service officer
Mazzaferro, James Joseph music educator
McCann-Lawson, Kim theater educator, director
McDonald, Kelly Kristin engineering educator
McGrath, William Arthur arbitrator, mediator, lawyer, real estate broker
Mendez, John Anthony federal judge
Merayyan, Saad M. engineering educator
Miguel, Caio F. psychology professor
Moulds, John F. judge
Myrrdin, Terry A. state agency administrator
Nagy, Stephen Mears, Jr. physician, allergist
Natarajan, Arutselvan chemistry professor, researcher
Nehring, Ron political organization administrator
Newland, Chester Albert public administration educator
Nice, Carter conductor
Nichols, Mary D. state official, former federal agency administrator
Nocioni, Andres Marcelo professional basketball player
O'Connell, Jack T. state official, school system administrator
Olson, Steven Arthur orthopaedic surgeon
Ozcelik, Hakan finance educator
Palermo, Joseph Anthony history professor
Palmer, William Joseph accountant
Pang, Jing engineering educator
Parker, Elizabeth Rindskopf dean, law educator
Partovi, M. Hossein physics professor, department chairman
Petrie, Geoffrey Michael professional sports team executive, retired professional basketball player
Phipps, Shawn Christopher occupational therapist
Piper, Jami Kathleen music educator, composer, musician
Piskoti, Carol Lee art educator
Pomeroy, Claire dean, academic administrator, medical educator
Pruitt, Gary B. publishing company executive
Purdy, James Aaron medical physics professor
Quinn, Francis Anthony bishop emeritus
Rab, George T. pediatric orthopedic surgeon
Rainwater, Eric composer, music educator
Reynolds, Jerry Owen professional sports team executive
Richardson, Michael physics professor, department chairman
Roberts, Paul Dale state agency administrator, writer
Robinson, Muriel Cox psychiatrist
Rosenberg, Dan Yale retired plant pathologist
Schmidt, Steve (Stephen E. Schmidt) public relations executive
Schwarzenegger, Arnold Alois Governor of California
Scott, Jack Alan academic administrator, former state senator
Scott, McGregor W. lawyer, former prosecutor
Sherwood, Robert Petersen retired social sciences educator
Shewry, Sandra telehealth company executive
Shriver, Maria Owings former news correspondent
Sill, Melanie editor-in-chief
Singh, Amrik literature and language professor
Soto, Jaime bishop
Stausboll, Anne pension fund administrator
Swatt, Stephen Benton communications executive, consultant
Takanikos-Quiñones, John Nicholas history professor
Taylor, Joseph Evans law educator
Taylor, Walter Wallace retired lawyer
Thomas, John professional sports team executive
Torres, Art former political organization administrator, former state legislator
Tract, Larry Scott construction management consultant
Trujillo, Nicholas Lee science educator
Trzyna, Thaddeus Charles academic institution administrator
Van Camp, Brian Ralph judge
von Friederichs-Fitzwater, Marlene Marie researcher
Walsh, Denny Jay reporter
Wang, Ta-Chen economics professor
Warriner, Kristin Palmquist retired public school educator
Wasserman, Barry L(ee) architect
Weigand, William Kenneth Bishop Emeritus
Westphal, Paul professional basketball coach
Whisenant, John professional basketball coach
Williams, Arthur Cozad retired broadcasting executive
Wolfman, Earl Frank, Jr. surgeon, educator
Wolkov, Harvey Brian oncologist, researcher
Wun, Ted medical educator
Yee, Leland Y. state legislator
Young, Heather M. academic administrator, nursing educator
Zaidi, Emily Louise retired elementary school educator
Zhang, Du engineering educator
Zhou, Kecheng mathematics professor
Zusman, Edie Ellen neurosurgeon

Saint Helena
Kostow, Christopher chef
Seavey, William Arthur lawyer, vintner

Sone, Hiro *chef, restaurant owner, writer*
Yates, Donald Alfred *retired literature educator*

Salida
Bawiec, John C. *real estate broker*

Salinas
Castro, Robert *pediatrician, educator*
Hoffman, Steven *museum administrator*
Jeffries, Russell Morden *communications company official*
Mettee-McCutchon, Ila *municipal official, retired military officer*
Puckett, Richard Edward *artist, former recreation executive*
Ryder, Edward Jonas *geneticist*
Stevens, Wilbur Hunt *accountant*

San Andreas
Cretan, Donna *neonatal nurse, consultant*

San Anselmo
Chiaverini, John Edward *construction company executive*
Noel, James Anthony *religious studies educator, minister*
Truett, Harold Joseph, III, (Tim) *lawyer*

San Bernardino
Baluyut, Pearlie Rose Salaveria *art educator*
Barnes, Gerald Richard *bishop*
Brown, Jack H. *supermarket company executive*
Brown-Jensen, William Ellis *psychologist*
Burgess, Michael (Robert Reginald) *librarian, writer*
De Haas, David Dana *emergency physician*
Del Riego, Rutilio J. *bishop*
Kakihara, Yuichiro *mathematics professor*
Kaufman, James Corey *psychologist, researcher*
Legutki, Gregg *project specialist*
Martinez, Benjamin Ray *security firm executive, public relations executive, retired military non-commissioned officer*
Michaelis, Kenneth A. *biology professor*
Morris, Patrick J. *Mayor, San Bernardino, California*
Nam, Sang Seok *special education educator*
Paul, Margaret Lee *psychologist*
Robinson, James Sidney *public health service officer*
Terrell, Charles Shaul, Jr. *educational administrator*
Willis, Harold Wendt, Sr. *real estate developer*

San Bruno
Browne, Kathryn Williams *education educator*
Chen, Steve Shih *Internet company executive*
Edwards, Kassandra Bennett *psychotherapist, consultant*
Grove, Steve *Internet company executive*
Hurley, Chad Meredith *Internet company executive*
Mangano, Dennis Thomas *science educator, director*

San Carlos
Eberhard, Martin *automotive executive, electronics engineer*
Eby, Michael John *marketing research and technology consultant*
Lund, Victor L. *healthcare company executive*
Vanderryn, Jack *environmental services administrator*

San Clemente
Betts, Andres Betkowsky *anesthesiologist*
Clark, Earnest Hubert, Jr. *tool company executive*
Kim, Edward William *ophthalmic surgeon*
Konney, Paul Edward *health products executive, lawyer*
Petruzzi, Christopher Robert *business educator, consultant*
Renk, Pamela Jean *counselor, psychotherapist, small business owner*
Wolfram, Thomas *physicist, educator*

San Diego
Achar, Suraj Arthur *medical educator*
Adams, Loretta *marketing executive*
Afuwape, Samuel A. *research scientist*
Afzali, Abdi *alumni association administrator, infosystems specialist*
Albright, Thomas D. *science foundation director, educator, researcher*
Allen, P. Blake *lawyer*
Altman, Steven *education company executive, academic administrator*
Altman, Steven R. *telecommunications executive*
Alving, Amy Elsa *information technology executive*
Anderson, Paul Maurice *electrical engineering educator, researcher, consultant*
Anello, Michael M. *federal judge*
Astroth, Margo Foltz *mental health nurse, nurse psychotherapist*
Atayee, Rabia Samady *pharmacist, educator*
Auld, Robert Henry, Jr. *biomedical engineer, educator, consultant, writer*
Ballinger, Charles Edwin *educational association administrator*
Barrett, Kim Elaine *medical educator*
Barrow, Deborah *library director*
Basmadjian, Edward *marine biologist*
Batchelder, David H. *investment advisory firm executive*
Bates-Romeo, Delores Alvenia *music educator, consultant*
Baxter, Robert Hampton *insurance company executive*
Beck, Niels Johannes *mechanical engineer*
Befort, Carlene Mae *music educator*
Bell, Robert Jeffrey *lawyer*
Benirschke, Kurt *retired pathologist, educator*
Bernstein, Sanford Irwin *biology professor*
Bhargava, Valmik *biomedical engineer, researcher*
Bigby, Timothy D. *medical educator*
Bird, Lynne Marie *geneticist*
Black, Bud (Harry Ralston Black) *professional baseball manager*
Bloom, Floyd Elliott *internist, neuroscientist*
Blum, Edward James *history professor*
Boggs, William S. *lawyer*
Bot, Adrian Ion *immunologist*
Bowie, Peter Wentworth *judge, educator*
Brandes, Raymond Stewart *historian, educator, dean*
Breen, Stephen P. *editorial cartoonist*
Brody, William Ralph *academic administrator, radiologist, educator*
Brom, Robert Henry *bishop*
Brooks, John White *lawyer*
Browne, John Robert *education and African studies educator, educational consultant*
Brownlie, Robert William *lawyer*
Burgin, George Hans *computer scientist, educator*
Buska, Sheila Mary *chief financial officer, columnist, writer*
Butcher, Bobby Gene *retired military officer*
Butterfield, Alexander Porter *air transportation executive, former federal official*
Buyuksonmez, Fatih *environmental engineer, researcher*
Cady, Joseph Howard *management consultant*
Campbell, Ian David *opera company director*
Cannon, Gary Curtis *lawyer, publishing executive*
Cantor, Charles Robert *biochemistry professor*
Cao, Zhiheng *engineer*
Cartwright, Derrick *museum director*
Casas, Veronica *microbiologist, educator*
Chambers, Henry George *orthopedic surgeon*
Chaudhri, Javade *lawyer, utilities executive*
Chavez, Gilbert Espinoza *bishop emeritus*
Chen, Kun-Mu *electrical engineering educator*
Clark, Kevin Bradford *biologist*
Cohn, Marjorie F. *law educator, legal association administrator*
Cole, Kevin *dean, law educator*
Comrie, Sandra Melton *human resources executive*
Conroy, Stephen J. *economics professor, consultant*
Corbett, Luke Robinson *lawyer*
Covey, Dana Curtis *military officer, orthopaedic surgeon*
Crump-Pace, Jacqueline Anita *music educator*
Crutchfield, Susan Ramsey *neurophysiologist*
Dahlberg, Kenneth C. *engineering executive*
Darmstandler, Harry Max *retired military officer*
De Angelis, Flavio *electrical engineer, researcher*
DeMaio, Carl *councilman*
DeMaria, Anthony Nicholas *cardiologist, educator*
Doherty, Joni K. *neurologist, educator*
Dollarhide, Mary C. *lawyer*
Doppelt, Roy Martin *lawyer*
Dorne, David J. *lawyer*
Downing, David Charles *retired minister*
Dulbecco, Renato *biologist, educator*
Dunlop, Marianne *retired language educator*
Durrant, Barbara Susan *reproductive physiologist*
Ecker, Joseph R. *plant molecular and cellular biologist*
Eckhart, Walter *molecular biologist, educator*
Edmonds, Jason Lemuel *art educator, writer*
Edmonds, Jim (James Patrick Edmonds) *professional baseball player*
Edwards, Darrel *psychologist, researcher, philosopher*
Eigner, William Whitling *lawyer*
El-Khamy, Mostafa *electrical engineer, researcher*
Emerald, Marti *councilwomen, reporter*
Emerick, Robert Earl *retired sociologist, educator*
Estrada, Jaime Olalde *language educator, department chairman*
Faulconer, Kevin *councilman*
Felsinger, Donald E. *utilities corporation executive*
Fernandes, Kathleen *systems analyst*
Flettner, Marianne *opera administrator*
Fricke, Martin Paul *science company executive*
Friedman, Arthur Daniel *electrical engineer, computer scientist, investment company executive, educator*
Friedman, Paul Jay *retired radiologist*
Frye, Donna *councilwoman*
Fu, Peilin *engineering educator*
Gage, Fred H. *neuroscientist, educator*
Galst, Carey Jo *biologist, educator*
Gardella, Duane MacIntyre *set designer, educator*
Gates, Antonio *professional football player*
Gazell, James Albert *public administration educator*
Ge, Sheng *research scientist, educator*
Gengor, Virginia Anderson *retired financial planning executive, educator*
Georgeson, Jacquelyn J. *audiologist, director*
Gerber, Robert Scott *lawyer*
German, Randall Michael *materials scientist, educator*
Getis, Arthur *geography educator*
Gilbertson, Oswald Irving *marketing executive*
Giles, Brian Stephen *professional baseball player*
Gloria, Todd *councilman*
Golding, Brage *university president*
Golding, Susan G. *former mayor*
Goldstein, Mark Kingston Levin *information technology executive, researcher*
Gomez, John Hamilton *lawyer*
Gonzalez, Adrian *professional baseball player*
Gordon, Robert Lee *economics professor*
Greenberg, Barry H. *cardiologist, medical educator*
Grier, Terry B. *school system administrator*
Gupta, Madhu Sudan *electrical engineering educator*
Haddad, Jiryes Michael *language educator*
Hagarty, Mark *lawyer*
Hager, Michael W. *museum director*
Hales, Alfred Washington *mathematics professor, consultant*
Harbola, Upendra *physicist*
Hardin, Sally Brosz *dean, nursing educator*
Harris, Jeffrey Paul *otolaryngologist*
Hauck, James Pierre *scientist*
Hawkins, Rey *shop owner, educator*
Heidrich, Robert Wesley *lawyer*
Henne, Andrea Rudnitsky *business educator*
Herrera, Fernando A. *physician*
Hewitt, Karen Peckham *prosecutor*
Horgan, Santiago *surgeon*
Hua, Guogang *engineer*
Hudzinski, Leonard Gerard *social sciences educator, researcher*
Hueso, Ben *councilman*
Hunt, Barnabas John *priest, religious organization administrator*
Hutcheson, S. Douglas *telecommunications industry executive*
Idos, Margarita de Leon *elementary school educator*
Inchiosa, Mario Emil *physicist*
Ingle, John Ide *dental educator*
Insogna, Anthony M. *lawyer*
Jacobs, Ginger Elaine *lawyer*
Jacobs, Gustaaf Bernardus *mathematician, mechanical engineer, aerospace engineer*
Jacobs, Irwin Mark *communications executive*
Jacobs, Paul E. *communications company executive*
Jagoda, Barry Lionel *communications executive, writer*
Jamali, Hamadi *research and development company executive*
Jamieson, Stuart William *surgeon, educator*
Jarman, Tracy *fire chief*
Jenkins, Scott Alan *oceanographer*
Jessen, Bart Andrew *toxicologist*
Jeste, Dilip Vishwanath *psychiatrist, researcher*
Jing, Zhigang *electrical engineer*
Kahn, Bruce S. *obstetrician, gynecologist*
Kane, Christopher J. *urologist, educator*
Kang, Seung Hyuk *materials scientist, electronics engineer*
Kaplan, George Willard *urologist*
Kasbeer, Stephen Frederick *retired university official, investor*
Kellogg, Huston Glenn *pediatrician, medical educator*
Kessler, Armin M. *retired pharmaceutical company executive*
Kim, Choll W. *spine surgeon*
Kim, Namsoo *electrical engineer*
Klinedinst, John David *lawyer*
Koka, Prasad S. *biomedical researcher*
Korneitchouk, Igor *music educator, composer*
Kung, Faith Hilda *pediatrician, educator*
Lam, Carol Chien-Hua *lawyer*
Lane, Gloria Julian *foundation administrator*
Lane, Sylvia *economist, educator*
Lang, Linda A. *food service executive*
Langenberg, Bret James *surgeon*
Larom, David Lee *engineering educator*
Larson, Arvid Gunnar *electrical engineer*
Larson, Mark Devin *communications executive*
Lathrop, Mitchell Lee *lawyer*
Lauer, Len J. *telecommunications industry executive*
Lavine, Joel Edward *physician, medical educator*
Lechner, Roger A. *monsignor*
Lee, Christian C. *pharmacist, researcher*
Lee, Ki Dong *communications engineer*
Levine, Harvey Robert *lawyer*
Levy, Jerome *dermatologist, retired military officer*
Lewis, Shirley Jeane *retired therapist, educator*
Liang, Lei *composer*
Lightner, Sherri *councilwoman, mechanical engineer*
Livshitz, Boris *research scientist*
Lundy-Slade, Bettie B. *retired electronics worker*
Lyons, Mary E. *academic administrator*
Macchione, Nick *city health department director*
Madhavan, Murugappa Chettiar *economics professor*
Madireddi, Mallareddy *physiologist*
Maloney, Ellen Claire *elementary school educator*
Markowitz, Harry Max *finance and economics educator*
Maurer, Lawrence Michael *retired acting school administrator, educator*
McBrayer, Sandra L. *educational director, homeless outreach educator*
McCoy, Lilys D. *lawyer*
McGinnis, Robert E. *lawyer*
McKeown, Mary Margaret *federal judge*
Mc Kinnon, Clinton Dan *aerospace transportation executive*
McMahon, Gerald Lawrence *lawyer*
Mebane, Julie S. *lawyer*
Merriman, Shawne DeAndre *professional football player*
Mestechkin, Mikhail Markovich *retired mathematics physicist*
Minteer, Daniel C. *lawyer*
Mittermiller, James Joseph *lawyer*
Mollica, Joseph A. *pharmaceutical executive*
Mooney, Patricia Kathryn *business owner, video producer, writer, philanthropist*
Moorad, Jeff *professional sports team executive*
Moore, Linda A. *art dealer, curator*
Myers, Douglas George *zoological society administrator*
Nahm, Walter K. *dermatologist, researcher*
Nelson, Kadir *illustrator, artist*
Noel, Craig *performing arts company executive, producer*
Nordhoff, Henry Louis (Hank Nordhoff) *biotechnology company executive, investor*
Nosseir, Nagy Sabet *engineering educator*
Novotny, Thomas Edward *healthcare educator, consultant*
Nyiri, Joseph Anton *sculptor, art educator*
O'Brien, Jack George *artistic director*
Oldham, Maxine Jernigan *real estate broker*
Olshevsky, George *editor*
Overton, Marcus Lee *performing arts association administrator, actor, writer*
Padmanabhan, Santhosh *research scientist*
Padovani, Roberto *communications executive*
Pagan, Keith Areatus *music educator, academic administrator*
Page, Eric J. *physics professor*
Paget, John Arthur *mechanical engineer*
Panetta, Joseph Daniel *biotechnologist, director*
Parthemore, Jacqueline Gail *internist, educator, hospital administrator*
Pathan, Nuzhat *medical researcher*
Payne, Margaret Anne *lawyer*
Peffer, Rodney Gene *philosopher, educator*
Pfiffner, Patrick Meehan *musician, educator*
Pharies, Stephen Andrew *lawyer*
Pitt, William Alexander *cardiologist*
Plotkin, Allen *aerospace engineer, educator*
Plourd, Christopher John *lawyer, consultant*
Porras, Jess *special education educator*
Pray, Ralph Marble III *lawyer*
Prior, Mark William *professional baseball player*
Pugh, Richard Crawford *lawyer, educator*
Rady, Ernest S. *thrift and loan association executive*
Rains, Cameron Jay *lawyer*
Rasih, Buu-Van AjareyaJemir *language and culture expert*
Rasochova, Lada *research scientist*
Rastetter, William H. *biotechnology company executive*
Ray, Albert *physician, educator*
Reid, Robert Tilden *medical association administrator, internist*
Reimann, Joachim Oskar Ferdinand *psychologist, public health researcher*
Reinhard, Christopher John *merchant banker, venture capitalist, biotechnologist, director*
Resnik, Robert *medical educator*
Rice, Clare I. *electronics company executive*
Riedy, Mark Joseph *finance educator*
Rivers, Philip *professional football player*
Robinson-Zañartu, Carol A. *psychology professor, department chairman*
Rodenberg, Johanna Kristine *education educator, consultant*
Rohatyn, Dennis *philosopher, educator*
Roizen, Michael F. *anesthesiologist, medical educator, writer*
Rolland, Alain P. *pharmaceutical executive*
Roseman, Charles Sanford *lawyer*
Rosen, Mark Daniel *chemist*
Rosenberg, Donald Jay *communications company executive, lawyer*
Ross, John, Jr. *cardiologist, educator*
Roth, Jonathan David *pharmacist, researcher*
Rowe, Peter A. *columnist*
Rowson, Sebastian *engineering executive*
Ruane, James Edward, Jr. *engineering executive*
Rubin, Stuart Harvey *computer science educator, researcher*
Russo, Anthony Joseph *public relations professional*
Ruth, Dianne *personal growth and prosperity coach, holistic counselor*
Sabbagh, Marwan Noel *physician, researcher*
Saito, Frank Kiyoji *import and export firm executive*
Salvador, Mari Lyn C. *museum director*
Sammartino, Janis Lynn *federal judge*
Sanders, Jerry *Mayor, San Diego, former social services executive*
Sauer, David Andrew *librarian, writer*
Savall, Brad M. *pharmaceutical executive, researcher*
Schaechter, Moselio *microbiology educator*
Schallhorn, Steven *ophthalmologist*
Schilz, Jodye Lynn Dickson *history professor*
Schmale, Neal E. *utilities company executive*
Schmidt, Joseph David *urologist*
Schon, Isabel *library science specialist, educator*
Scorcioni, Ruggero *research scientist*
Scorgie, Kathryn *education educator*
Scott, Douglas Edward *lawyer*
Scott, Richard Malachi *psychologist*
Seau, Junior (Tiana Baul Seau Jr.) *professional football player*
Sejnowski, Terrence Joseph *science educator*
Seo, Dongwon *communications engineer, design scientist*
Shah, Hemang J. *systems engineer*
Shapiro, Philip Alan *lawyer*
Sharma, Satish Kumar *engineering educator*
Shashkin, Pavel Nikolayevich *biochemist*
Shedroff, Sharon D. *psychologist, anthropologist, researcher, consultant*
Sheldon-Morris, Tiffini Anne *clinical psychologist, consultative examiner*
Shepherd, Bruce P. *lawyer*
Shippey, Sandra Lee *lawyer*
Shneour, Elie Alexis *biophysicist, researcher, historian*
Sidner, Robert Brown *museum director*
Simpson, William *information technology manager, consultant*
Skwara, Erich Wolfgang *writer, poet, critic, literature educator*
Smith, A.J. *professional sports team executive*
Smith, Steven Ray *law educator*
Snell, Mark A. *utilities executive*
Song, Jane Inyoung *lawyer*
Sopp, Mark W. *corporate financial executive*
Spanos, Alexander Gus *construction and professional sports team executive*
Spence, Jean Louise *biology professor, researcher*
Spira, Patricia Goodsitt *retired association executive*
Sproles, Darren Lee *professional football player*
Squire, Larry Ryan *neuroscientist, psychologist, educator*
Stahovich, Marcia *nurse*
Stambaugh, Larry G. *strategic business consultant*
Steen, Paul Joseph *retired broadcasting executive*
Stein, Franklin Joseph *music educator*
Stoessinger, John George *political science professor*
Talamini, Mark A. *surgeon, department chairman*
Tayman, Jeff *retired economics professor*
Teagle, Rachel *museum director*
Thompson, David Renwick *federal judge*
Thompson, Gordon, Jr. *federal judge*
Thorud, Jeffrey Scott *lawyer, legal studies director*
Tom, Lawrence *technology executive*
Tomlinson, LaDainian *professional football player*
Tozer, William Evans *entomologist, educator*
Treger, Marjorie Mae *theater director, educator*
Turner, B. Russell *tax accountant, financial planner, real estate broker*
Turner, Norv (Norval Eugene Turner) *professional football coach*
Uribe, Jennie Ann *elementary school educator*
Urquhart, Bruce *government agency administrator, engineering educator*
Vaida, Florin *statistician, educator*
Vandegriff, Kim Denise *biochemist*
van der Geer, Peter *biochemist, educator*
Van Tassel, Lowell Thomas *mathematics professor*

Vega, Carolyn Jane *elementary educator, consultant, writer*
Venkataraman, Satchi *engineering educator*
Verma, Inder M. *biochemist*
Vitek, Reg(inald) A. *lawyer*
Wagner, Sandra M. *lawyer*
Wallace, Candy *culinary association administrator*
Wallace, J. Clifford *federal judge*
Wamba, Kolo *physicist*
Wawrytko, Sandra Ann *humanities educator*
Weaver, Michael James *lawyer*
Weber, Stephen Lewis *academic administrator*
Weeks, John Robert *geographer, social studies educator*
Weldele, Edda Hilda Temoche *language educator*
Wertheim, Robert Halley *national security consultant*
West, James Harold *finance company executive*
Westwick, John Keirn *molecular cell biologist*
Wiesler, James Ballard *retired banker*
Wilson, Darcy Benoit *science association director*
Wilson, John Human III *museum director, art historian*
Winfield, Dave (David Mark Winfield) *professional sports team executive, sportscaster, retired professional baseball player*
Wing, Thomas M. *military officer, systems engineer*
Winner, Karin E. *editor*
Withee, Diana Keeran *art historian, art dealer, educator*
Wolfe, Deborah Ann *lawyer*
Young, Tony *councilman*
Zhou, Bo *systems engineer*

San Dimas

Deliman, Robert Michael *surgeon*
Flores, Frank Cortez *public health researcher, educator, administrator*
Mori, Allen Anthony *retired academic administrator*

San Fernando

Salkin, Barbara Ruth *social worker*
Shannon, George Raymond *gerontologist, educator*

San Francisco

Abbas, Abul K. *pathologist, educator*
Abbott, Barry Alexander *lawyer*
Abbott, Richard Lee *physician*
Abramson, Norman *retired engineering educator, electronics executive*
Adams, Lisette *Sheriff*
Adelson, Jay Steven *Internet company executive*
Adkins, Mark *publishing executive*
Adler, Nancy Elinor *psychologist, educator*
Affeldt, Jeremy David *professional baseball player*
Alberts, Bruce Michael *cell biologist, former foundation administrator*
Aldrich, Michael Ray *library curator, health educator*
Alesi, Tommy *musician*
Alioto-Pier, Michela *city supervisor*
Alpert, Bernard Stephen *plastic surgeon, educator*
Alyesh, Jason R. *writer*
Amend, William John Conrad, Jr. *physician, educator*
Anderson, Chris W. *editor-in-chief*
Anderson, Edward Virgil *lawyer*
Anderson, R. John *apparel executive*
Appleman, Nate *chef*
Aragon, Sergio R. *chemistry professor*
Arnold, Lauren *art historian, writer*
Atkins, Howard Ian *bank executive*
Atrouni, Marwan *dentist*
August-deWilde, Katherine *banker*
Avalos, John *city supervisor*
Aweeka, Francesca Teresa *pharmacist, educator*
Azarinfar, André *dentist*
Babcock, Jo *artist, educator*
Bainton, Dorothy Ford *pathologist, educator*
Baker, Joy Doreen *art educator, artist*
Bancel, Marilyn *fund raising management consultant*
Bancroft, James Ramsey *lawyer*
Banks, Michelle *lawyer, retail executive*
Barbagelata, Robert Dominic *lawyer*
Barcon, Barbara L. *utilities executive*
Barlow, William Pusey, Jr. *accountant*
Barondes, Samuel Herbert *psychiatrist, educator*
Bartels, Dennis M. *museum director*
Baskin, Laurence Seth *pediatrician, educator*
Batterman, Boris William *physicist, educator, academic administrator*
Bauch, Thomas Jay *financial consultant, retired lawyer, apparel executive*
Bauerlein, Monika *magazine editor*
Baxter, Marvin Ray *state supreme court justice*
Baysinger, Kara *lawyer*
Bea, Carlos Tiburcio *federal judge*
Beall, Dennis Ray *artist, educator*
Beaulieu, Richard Joseph *pediatric nurse practitioner*
Bechtel, Riley Peart *engineering company executive*
Bechtel, Stephen Davison, Jr. *retired engineering company executive*
Becker, David Kenneth *pediatrician, educator*
Bee, Robert Norman *banker*
Behrens, M. Kathleen *medical researcher*
Beinfield, Harriet *medical association administrator*
Beitel, Karl *researcher*
Bell, C. Gordon *computer architect and engineer, entrepreneur, researcher*
Benet, Leslie Zachary *pharmacologist, educator*
Benezra, Neal *museum director, curator*
Benioff, Marc *Internet company executive*
Bennett, James Patrick *lawyer*
Bensinger, David August *dentist, dean*
Bereuter, Douglas Kent *foundation administrator, former congressman*
Berning, Paul Wilson *lawyer*
Bernstein, Gerald William *management consultant, researcher*
Bernstein, Harold Seth *pediatric cardiologist, molecular geneticist*
Berzon, Marsha S. *federal judge*
Bettinger, Walter W., II, *investment company executive*
Bibbins-Domingo, Kirsten Beatrice *internist*
Bikle, Daniel David *research physician*
Bitterman, Mary Gayle Foley *foundation executive*
Blackburn, Elizabeth Helen *molecular biologist*
Bleich, Jeffrey Laurence *lawyer, educator*
Blohm, Kenneth E. *lawyer*
Bocobo-Balunsat, Dalisay *librarian, journalist*
Bodenheimer, Thomas Siegmund *physician, educator*
Boles, Roger *otolaryngologist*
Bondoc, Rommel *lawyer*
Borowsky, Philip *lawyer*
Bostwick, James Stephen *lawyer*
Botvinick, Elias H. *nuclear medicine physician, researcher, medical educator*
Bourne, Henry R. *pharmacology professor, department chairman, researcher*
Boutros, George F. *investment banker*
Boven, Douglas George *lawyer*
Bracken, Thomas Robert James *real estate investment executive*
Brand, Jeffrey S. *dean, law educator*
Brandel, Roland Eric *lawyer*
Bratton, Christopher Alan *academic administrator, videographer, art educator*
Breaux, Jimmy *musician*
Brevig, Eric *special effects expert, executive*
Briscoe, John *lawyer*
Bronstein, Phil *publishing executive*
Brook, Michael Morris *cardiologist, educator*
Brosnahan, James Jerome *lawyer*
Brown, Donald Wesley *lawyer*
Browner, Warren Seth *hospital administrator, internist, educator*
Browning, James Robert *federal judge*
Bruen, James A. *lawyer*
Bryant, Allison S. *obstetrician, educator*
Buchanan, John Edward, Jr. *museum director*
Buckmaster, Jim *online community bulletin board company executive*
Bull, Henrik Helkand *architect*
Buncke, Gregory M. *plastic surgeon*
Buntic, Rudy F. *plastic surgeon*
Burchard, Esteban Gonzalez *physician, educator*
Burlingame, Alma Lyman *chemist, educator*
Burns, Brian Patrick *lawyer*
Burton, John L. *political organization administrator, retired state legislator*
Burton, Joseph M. *lawyer*
Burtt, Ben *sound designer, director, editor*
Bushee, Ward III *editor*
Cabraser, Elizabeth Joan *lawyer*
Caldwell, Dalton *Internet company executive, application developer*
Calhoun, John Joseph (Jack) *retail executive*
Callahan, Patricia R. *bank executive*
Callan, Terrence A. *attorney*
Campbell, Jeffrey C. *health products executive*
Campos, David *city supervisor, lawyer*
Canales, James Earl, Jr. *foundation president*
Caniparoli, Val William *choreographer, dancer*
Carpenter, Steven A. *Internet company executive*
Carr-Ruffino, Norma *management educator*
Cartmell, Nathaniel Madison III *lawyer*
Cary, Stephen *educational consultant*
Casey, Bernard J. *lawyer*
Chambers, Henry F. *epidemiologist, educator*
Chan, Iris S. *bank executive*
Chapman, William B. *lawyer*
Chatterjee, Kanu *cardiologist, educator*
Chen, Zhigang *physics professor*
Cherny, Robert Wallace *historian, educator*
Chin, Ming W. *state supreme court justice*
Chin, Sue Soone Marian (Suchin Chin) *artist, photojournalist*
Chin-Hong, Peter Vincente *medical educator*
Chiu, Cynthia S. *ophthalmologist, educator*
Chiu, David *city supervisor, lawyer*
Chou, Fang-yu *science educator*
Chu, Carmen *city supervisor*
Chung, Eric C. *lawyer*
Church, Gwynne D. *pediatrician, educator*
Clements, John Allen *physiologist*
Clever, Linda Hawes *physician*
Clifford, Geraldine Joncich *retired education educator*
Clowes, John Howard *lawyer*
Cluff, Lloyd Sterling *earthquake geologist*
Cobbs, Price Mashaw *social psychiatrist*
Coburn, Lawrence *Internet company executive*
Cohen, Bram *web programmer*
Cohen, Fred Ehrenkranz *biophysics professor*
Cohn, Cindy A. *lawyer*
Cohn, Kathleen Mandry *writer*
Coleman, Thomas Young *lawyer*
Cominos, Dion Nicholas *lawyer*
Coombe, George William, Jr. *lawyer, retired bank executive*
Coppola, Francis Ford *film director, film producer, scriptwriter*
Cornehl, Jarrod *dentist*
Corrigan, Carol A. *state supreme court justice*
Corrigan, Robert Anthony *academic administrator*
Costa-Zalessow, Natalia *foreign language educator*
Coughlin, Shaun R. *research scientist, medical professor*
Cranston, Mary Bailey *lawyer*
Crawford, J. Brooks *ophthalmologist, educator*
Crawford, Michael Howard *cardiologist, educator, researcher*
Cruse, Allan Baird *mathematician, computer scientist, educator*
Curran, Mary *lawyer*
Dachs, Alan Mark *investment company executive*
Dachs, Lauren Bechtel *non-profit organization executive*
Dae, Michael W. *cardiologist, medical educator, researcher*
Daly, Chris *city supervisor*
Danoff, Eric Michael *lawyer*
Darbee, Peter A. *utilities executive*
Darling, Cynthia Lee *research professor*
Darney, Philip Dempsey *gynecologist, educator*
Davidson, Keay *newswriter*
Davis, Roger Lewis *lawyer*
Dean, Lloyd H. *insurance company executive*
Deicken, Raymond Friedrich *neuropsychiatrist, neuroscientist*
Delgado, Eliana *orthopedic surgeon*
Dell, Robert Michael *lawyer*
Dellas, Robert Dennis *retired investment banker*
DeMuro, Paul Robert *lawyer*
Dennehy, Raymond Leo *philosopher, educator*
DeRisi, Joseph L. *biochemist, educator*
des Jardins, Traci *chef, restaurant owner*
Desmond-Hellmann, Susan *academic administrator, former medical products manufacturing executive*
Diab, Mohammad *orthopedic surgeon*
Dickinson, Eleanor Creekmore *artist, educator*
Dickinson, Wade *oil industry executive, educator*
Dill, Kenneth Austin *pharmaceutical chemistry educator*
Dodge, Geoffrey A. *information technology executive, former publishing executive*
Dolby, Ray Milton *electrical engineer, company executive*
Dolev, Jacqueline *physician, researcher*
Dolinko, Robert A. *lawyer*
Dorman, David W. *management consultant, former telecommunications industry executive*
Dorsey, Jack *software architect*
Doucet, David *musician*
Doucet, Michael *musician, songwriter*
Dracup, Kathleen Anne *dean, nursing educator*
Draper, William Henry III *venture capitalist*
Dryden, Robert Eugene *lawyer*
Dubreuil, Francis W. *lawyer*
Dufty, Bevan *city supervisor*
Dugoni, Arthur A. *dean emeritus, orthodontics educator*
Durdik, Paul A. *lawyer*
Durie, Daralyn J. *lawyer*
Duscha, Julius Carl *journalist*
Dwyer, Carrie Elizabeth *lawyer, investment company executive*
Edelman, Brad *computer game company executive*
Edwards, Robin Morse *lawyer*
Egan, Patricia Jane *foundation administrator, retired director*
Eggers, Dave *fiction writer, magazine editor*
Ekman, Paul *psychologist, educator*
Ellis, Linda *archaeologist, director*
El-Sayed, Ivan Homer *otolaryngologist, researcher*
Elsbernd, Sean R. *city supervisor*
Emunah, Renee *drama therapist, professor*
Epstein, Charles Joseph *pediatrician, geneticist, biochemist, educator*
Epstein, John Howard *dermatologist*
Erskine, John Morse *surgeon*
Esserman, Laura Jean *oncologist, educator*
Estes, Carroll Lynn *sociologist, educator*
Facchini, Francesco Stefano *internist, researcher, nephrologist, researcher*
Falk, Jerome B., Jr. *lawyer*
Farmer, Diana Lee *pediatric surgeon*
Farrington, Gregory C. *museum director, former academic administrator*
Feachem, Richard George Andrew *health science association administrator*
Feldman, Mitchell Dean *medical educator*
Feldman, Robert Paul *lawyer*
Fergus, Gary Scott *lawyer*
Ferriero, Donna M. *pediatric neurologist*
Fessel, Walford Jeffrey *rheumatologist*
Field, John Louis *architect*
Figueredo, Jorge L. *human resources specialist*
Finberg, James Michael *lawyer*
Finberg, Laurence *pediatrician, educator, dean*
Finck, Kevin William *lawyer*
Fischer, David Joseph *ambassador*
Fisher, Donald G. *retail executive*
Fisher, Doris *retail executive*
Fisher, Kathleen V. *lawyer*
Fisher, Martin J. *not-for-profit executive*
Fisher, Robert Morton *foundation and academic administrator*
Fletcher, William A. *federal judge, educator*
Floum, Joshua R. *finance company executive, lawyer*
Fogarty, James P. *retail executive, corporate financial executive*
Folberg, Harold Jay *lawyer, educator, dean, mediator*
Folkman, David H. *retail, wholesale and consumer products consultant*
Fong, Kevin Murray *lawyer*
Foster, David Scott *lawyer*
Foster, Elyse *cardiologist, educator*
Foster, Kenneth J. *art association administrator*
Foster-Barber, Audrey Elizabeth *neurologist, educator*
Fox, Mitchell B. *publishing executive*
Fox, Steve *editor-in-chief*
Freeman, Matt *advertising executive*
Frenkel, Val S. *environmental engineer*
Freund, Fredric S. *real estate broker and manager*
Frick, Oscar Lionel *pediatrician, educator*
Frieden, Ilona Josephine *pediatric dermatologist*
Friedman, Gary *plastic surgeon*
Friedman, K. Bruce *lawyer*
Friedman, Suzanne *holistic medical practitioner*
Friese, Robert Charles *lawyer*
Fuller, James William *financial planner*
Garchik, Leah Lieberman *journalist*
Garcia, Carlos *school system administrator*
Gardner, Sue *Internet company executive, journalist*
Garg, Akash *Internet company executive*
Garvey, Joanne Marie *lawyer*
Gascón, George *police chief*
Gekelman, Diana *dentist, dental educator, researcher*
Gellin, Gerald Alan *dermatologist*
Gemello, John Michael *economics professor, consultant, academic administrator*
George, Ronald M. *state supreme court chief justice*
German, William *newspaper editor*
Getto, Ernest John *lawyer*
Gibbard, Ben *singer, musician*
Gillette, Frankie Jacobs *retired savings and loan association executive, federal agency administrator, social worker*
Giudice, Linda Carmen *obstetrician, gynecologist, biochemist, reproductive endocrinologist*
Gockley, David (Richard David Gockley) *opera company director*
Gold, Herbert *author*
Goldschlager, Nora Fox *internist, cardiologist, educator*
Goldstein, David Baird *energy executive, physicist*
Goldstine, Stephen Joseph *art educator*
González, Arturo J. *lawyer*
Gonzalez, Matt *lawyer*
Goodby, Jeffrey *advertising agency executive*
Goode, Erica Tucker *internist*
Goode, Joe *performing company executive*
Goodman, Daniel F. *ophthalmologist*
Goodwin, David B. *lawyer*
Gordon, Andrew K. *lawyer*
Gore, Al (Albert Arnold Gore Jr.) *former Vice President of the United States*
Gossman, Bill *Internet company executive*
Gravelle, Stephanie *Internet company executive*
Graysmith, Robert *political cartoonist, author*
Green, Lawrence Winter *public health educator*
Greenblatt, Ruth Martha *medical educator, researcher*
Greene, Warner Craig *medical educator, administrator*
Greenspan, Deborah *dental educator*
Greenspan, Francis S. *physician*
Greenspan, Louise Catherine *pediatrician*
Greenwald, Glenn *columnist, lawyer*
Gresham, Zane Oliver *lawyer*
Grodsky, Gerold Morton *biochemistry professor*
Gruenert, Dieter C. *geneticist, educator*
Grumbach, Melvin Malcolm *pediatrician, educator*
Guggenheim, Davis *film and TV director, producer*
Guggenhime, Richard Johnson *lawyer*
Guttentag, Lucas *advocate, lawyer*
Haas, Raymond P. *lawyer*
Habelitz, Stefan F. *research scientist, educator*
Haber, Scott R. *lawyer*
Hafner, Katie *reporter*
Hagenbuch, John Jacob *investor*
Hale, Cecil *communications and business educator*
Hale, Victoria G. *chemist, pharmaceutical executive*
Hammergren, John H. *health products executive*
Hamsayeh, Niloufer G. *dentist*
Hanahan, Douglas *biochemist, educator*
Hansen, Carol Louise *literature and language professor*
Hansen, Marka *retail executive*
Haraf, William S. *state banking agency administrator*
Hare, Julia *educational psychologist, author, consultant*
Harris, Kamala D. *prosecutor*
Harriss, Cynthia Therese (Cynthia Therese Clarke) *retail executive*
Harvey, Kent M. *utilities executive*
Hastings, Edward Walton *theater director*
Havel, Richard Joseph *physician, educator*
Havian, Eric R. *lawyer*
Hawgood, Sam *dean, pediatrician, medical educator*
Hazard, Geoffrey Cornell, Jr. *law educator*
Hedberg, Gail Elizabeth *registered veterinary technician, consultant*
Heilbron, David Michael *lawyer, arbitrator, mediator*
Hellman, F(rederick) Warren *investor*
Henderson, Isaac Craig *oncologist, researcher*
Henson, Ray David *law educator, consultant*
Hernandez, Gary A. *lawyer*
Hernandez, Jennifer Lynn *lawyer*
Hertz, Betti-Sue *curator, art gallery director*
Hewitt, Conrad W. *former commissioner, accountant*
Heyda, Pamela *elementary school educator*
Heyman, Melvin Bernard *pediatric gastroenterologist*
Heyneman, Donald *parasitology and tropical medicine educator*
Hickerson, Glenn Lindsey *leasing company executive*
Higashida, Randall Takeo *radiologist, neurosurgeon, medical educator*
Highman, Bruce James *lawyer*
Hills, Austin Edward *vineyard executive*
Hilton, Stanley Goumas *lawyer, educator, writer*
Hirsch, (William) Reece *lawyer*
Hirst, Karen L. *actor, singer, theater educator*
Hisert, George Arthur *lawyer*
Hodgson, John Graeme *medical researcher*
Hoffman, William Yanes *plastic surgeon, educator*
Hofmann, John Richard, Jr. *retired lawyer*
Holden, Frederick Douglass, Jr. *lawyer*
Horton, Jonathan Charles *neuroscientist, neuro-ophthalmologist*
Hotchkiss, Ralf David *engineer, educator*
Howard, Carl *retired lawyer*
Hoyt, David A. *bank executive*
Hsu, Chi-yuan *nephrologist, researcher*
Hubbell, Robert B. *lawyer*
Huhs, John I. *international lawyer*
Hui, Jonathan Wing Yan *engineer*
Hwang, Helen *orthodontist*
Ikeda, Clyde Junichi *plastic and reconstructive surgeon*
Ikuta, Sandra Segal *federal judge*
James, George Barker, II, *financial executive*
James, Thomas Larry *chemistry professor*
Jampolis, Melina Beth *internist, physician nutrition specialist*
Jan, Lily Yeh *physiology, biochemist*
Jarvis, Donald Bertram *judge*
Jeffery, Clara *magazine editor*
Jennings, Jim *architect*
Jiang, Xiangning *neuroscientist*
Johns, Christopher P. *utilities executive*
Johnson, Alexander D. *biochemist, molecular biologist, educator*
Johnson, Chalmers *educational association administrator, retired political science professor*
Johnson, Matilee Howard *retired headmistress*
Johnson, Randy (Randall David Johnson) *professional baseball player*
Jones, Stanton William *management consultant*

Jonsen, Albert R(upert) *medical ethics educator*
Jorgensen, Blake J. *apparel company executive, former Internet company executive*
Julian, Paul C. *health products executive*
Julius, David *biochemist*
Juster, Kenneth Ian *lawyer*
Justice, William J. *bishop*
Kahle, Brewster *communications executive*
Kan, Yuet Wai *hematologist, educator*
Kapor, Mitchell David *application developer, foundation administrator*
Katzung, Bertram George *pharmacologist*
Kavanaugh, David Henry *entomologist, educator*
Kaymen, Amelia *dermatologist*
Keker, John Watkins *lawyer*
Kelley, Michael Garhart Roosevelt *historian, educator, writer*
Kelly, J. Michael *lawyer*
Kelly, James Anthony *priest*
Kelly, Roberto Conrado (Bobby Kelly) *professional baseball coach, retired professional baseball player*
Kennard, Joyce L. *state supreme court justice*
Kennedy, Raoul Dion *lawyer*
Kern, Brad D. *lawyer*
Kertzman, Mitchell E. *former software company executive, venture capitalist*
Kessler, David Aaron *medical educator, writer, former federal agency administrator, dean*
Khatri, Sikandar Khan *engineering educator*
Kidner, Frank L. *retired history professor*
Kim, David Woojin *plastic surgeon, educator*
Kimber, Richard B. *Internet company executive*
King, Alonzo *artistic director, choreographer*
King, Talmadge E. *physician*
Kingdon, Mark *computer software company executive*
Kinsell, Jeffrey Clift *investment banker*
Kitundu, Walter *sound artist, instrument designer, composer*
Klammer, Joseph Francis *retired management consultant*
Kline, Howard Jay *cardiologist, educator*
Kneen, Simon *apparel executive*
Knoll, John *visual effects supervisor*
Kochetkova, Maria *dancer*
Koda-Kimble, Mary Anne *pharmacologist, educator, dean*
Koeppel, John A. *lawyer*
Koffel, Martin M. *engineering company executive*
Kolkey, Daniel Miles *former judge, lawyer*
Koo, John Ying Ming *psychiatrist, dermatologist*
Kovacevich, Richard Marco (Dick Kovacevich) *bank executive*
Kozloff, Lloyd M. *dean, microbiologist, educator*
Krevans, Rachel *lawyer*
Kriegstein, Arnold *neurologist, educator*
Kriken, John Lund *architect*
Krippner, Stanley Curtis *psychologist*
Krishnan, Suneeta *epidemiologist, educator*
Kroenert, Rob *Internet company executive, marketing professional*
Kuhl, Paul Beach *lawyer*
Kumar, Deept *information technology manager*
Kunwar, Sandeep *neurosurgeon*
Kunz, Heidi *healthcare company executive*
La Farge, Timothy *retired plant geneticist*
Lam, Peter *orthodontist*
Lamberson, John Roger *insurance company executive*
Lane, Fielding H. *retired lawyer*
Laret, Mark R. *hospital administrator*
LaRiva, Gloria *labor union administrator, advocate*
Larrabee, Matthew Lloyd *lawyer*
Larson, John William *lawyer*
Lattanza, Lisa *orthopedist, consultant*
Le, Caroline M. *dentist*
Leap, Emily *dancer, acrobat*
Leard, Lorriana E. *medical educator*
LeBuhn, Gretchen *biology professor*
Lee, Charles K. *plastic surgeon, educator*
Lee, Pamela Anne *bank executive, accountant, financial analyst*
Lee, Richard Diebold *lawyer, educator*
Lee, Samuel Sangwon *civil, environmental and agricultural engineer*
Lehane, Christopher S. *political consultant*
Lenk, Edward C. (Toby) *retail executive*
Leshy, John David *lawyer, solicitor, educator*
Lessard, Etienne *medical physicist, researcher, consultant*
Lester, W. Howard *retail executive*
Levi, Nick *dentist*
Levine, Alison *entrepreneur, leadership development consultant, adventurer*
Leviton, Alan Edward *curator*
Levy, Jay A. *medical educator*
Levy, Richard D. *bank executive*
Lewis, Hilda Present *academic administrator, educator*
Lincecum, Timothy LeRoy *professional baseball player*
Lindstrom, Kent J. *Internet company executive*
Lisberger, Stephen G. *physiologist, educator*
Little, Jan Nielsen *lawyer*
Livermore, Samuel Morgan *lawyer*
Livsey, Robert Callister *lawyer*
Lomong, Lopez (Lopepe Lomong) *Olympic track and field athlete*
Loughlin, Michael J. *bank executive*
Low, Randall *internist, cardiologist*
Lowell, Frederick K. *lawyer*
Lucas, Adam Ronald *science educator*
Lucas S.J., Thomas Martin *art and architecture professor*
Lucia, Marilyn Reed *physician*
Luft, Harold S. *health economist*
Lustig, Lawrence Robert *medical educator*
Lynn, Paul *health facility administrator*
Lyon, David William *retired research executive*
Maa, John *surgeon*
Maas, Corey S. *plastic surgeon*
MacNeil, Justin W. *lawyer*
Magowan, Peter Alden *professional sports team and retail executive*
Mahadevan, Uma *physician*
Mahmoodi, Hamid *engineer*
Mahoney, David L. *former pharmaceutical wholesale and healthcare management company executive*
Mahoney, Michael James *investment company executive*
Maier, Peter Klaus *lawyer*
Maly, Michael Kip *lawyer*
Mann, Bruce Alan *lawyer, investment banking executive*
Manning, Jerome Alan *retired lawyer*
Mar, Eric Lee *city supervisor, college professor*
Markoff, John *reporter*
Márquez-Magaña, Leticia Maria *biology professor*
Marshall, Grayson William, Jr. *materials scientist, biomedical engineer, health sciences educator, dentist*
Marshall, Patrick C. *lawyer*
Marston, Michael *economist, consultant*
Martel, John Sheldon *lawyer, writer, musician*
Marten, Timothy James *plastic surgeon*
Martin, Fred *artist, academic administrator*
Martinetto, Joseph R. *investment company executive*
Martinez, Belinda *health insurance company executive*
Martinez, Leo *dean, law educator*
Mason, Dean Towle *cardiologist*
Masters, Joseph *lawyer, engineering company executive*
Mathias, Robert S. *pediatric nephrologist*
Mattern, Douglas James *think-tank executive*
Matthews, Gilbert Elliott *investment banker*
Matthews, Philip Richard *lawyer*
Maxwell, Sophenia (Sophie) *city supervisor*
Mayer, Ronald Wesley *psychology professor*
McAninch, Jack Weldon *urological surgeon, educator*
McClintock, Jessica *fashion designer*
McCollam, Sharon L. *retail executive*
McCormick, Frank *research scientist, biology professor*
McCracken, Harry *journalist*
McFadden, Nancy Elizabeth *utilities executive*
McGegan, Nicholas *conductor*
McGettigan, Charles Carroll, Jr. *investment banker*
McGinnis, Christopher *travel correspondent, editor*
McGinnis, James Landon *lawyer*
McGuire, Kathleen Alison *conductor*
McManis, Dena Edwy *psychologist, consultant*
Mellor, Robert E. *building materials company executive, lawyer*
Mendlin, Ronald C. *employment specialist, writer*
Merrick, Fred Harold *retired marine engineer*
Merzenich, Michael *neuroscientist, educator*
Miller, Arthur Joseph *neurophysiology and craniofacial biology researcher*
Miller, Bruce Lawrence *neurologist, educator*
Miller, Carol A. *pediatrician, educator*
Miller, Walter Luther *scientist, pediatrician, educator*
Miller, William Napier Cripps *lawyer*
Minar, Paul G. *interior designer, consultant*
Minnick, Malcolm David *lawyer*
Mirkarimi, Ross *city supervisor*
Mitchell, Theodore Reed *educational association administrator, former academic administrator*
Modjtabai, Avid *bank executive*
Monteith, Matthew *photographer*
Mooney, Brian Joseph *lawyer*
Moreno, Carlos R. *state supreme court justice*
Moris, Lamberto Giuliano *architect*
Morrissey, John Carroll, Sr. *lawyer*
Mosavian, Parisa *dentist*
Mostov, Keith Elliot *cell biologist, educator*
Mullenweg, Matt(hew) (Charles) *software developer, blogger*
Mullin, Hadley (Mary Hadley Mullin) *private equity firm executive*
Munson, Alexander Lee *management consultant*
Muren, Dennis E. *special effects expert*
Murphy, Glenn T. *retail executive*
Murray, Kathleen Anne *lawyer*
Mustacchi, Piero *preventive medicine physician, educator*
Nash, Jill *communications executive*
Neaman, Elliot Yale *history professor*
Needham, Tristan *mathematics professor*
Needleman, Jacob *philosophy educator, writer*
Nelson, Paul Douglas *lawyer*
Neukom, William H. *professional sports team executive, lawyer*
Newmark, Craig Alexander *Internet company executive*
Newsom, Gavin Christopher *Mayor, San Francisco*
Neylan, Thomas Coogan *psychiatrist*
Nguyen, Ann Cac Khue *pharmaceutical and medicinal chemist*
Niederauer, George H. *archbishop*
Nobuhara, Kerilyn *medical educator*
Noonan, John T., Jr. *federal judge, educator*
Nye, Margaret Bien *middle school educator*
Odgers, Richard William *lawyer*
Okeke, Christian Nwachukwu *law educator*
Olds, John Theodore *banker*
Olson, Robert Howard *lawyer*
Oman, Mark C. *bank executive*
Omer, Selma *biochemist, educator*
Ousterhout, Douglas Kenneth *plastic surgeon*
Owen, Marc E. *health products executive*
Owsley, John Quincy, IV, *plastic surgeon, educator*
Palmer, Venrice Romito *lawyer, educator*
Pantell, Robert Howard *pediatrician, educator*
Park, Hyun *lawyer, utilities executive*
Patel, Bharat *financial executive*
Paterson, Richard Denis *corporate financial executive*
Patterson, James (Jim) *economist, writer*
Patti, Marco Giuseppe *surgeon, educator*
Paxton, Jay L. *lawyer*
Peck, Art *retail executive*
Penny, Brad (Bradley Wayne Penny) *professional baseball player*
Perlman, David *journalist*
Perry, E. Lynn *lawyer*
Peterlin, Boris Matija *physician*
Petrakis, Nicholas Louis *epidemiologist, medical researcher, educator*
Pfeffer, Patrick *architect*
Phillips, Theodore Locke *radiologist, educator*
Phoenix, Bethany Joyce *healthcare educator*
Pickett, Donn Philip *lawyer*
Poitras, Gilles Lee *librarian*
Policy, Carmen A. *professional sports team executive*
Popofsky, Melvin Laurence *lawyer*
Pottruck, David Steven *private equity firm executive*
Pringle, Paul C. *lawyer*
Pringle, Robert Bernard *lawyer*
Pritzker, John A. *leisure services executive*
Privett, Stephen A. *academic administrator, priest*
Prusiner, Stanley Ben *neurologist, educator, biochemist*
Ptacek, Louis John *medical educator, medical researcher*
Quinn, John Raphael *archbishop emeritus*
Raffin, Thomas Alfred *physician, educator, venture capitalist*
Randall, Janet Ann *biology professor, researcher*
Rankin, Katherine Pollock *psychology professor, researcher*
Ratum, Cecilia Bangloy *retired psychologist*
Razak, Arisika *social studies educator, department chairman*
Redberg, Rita Fran *cardiologist*
Reding, John Anthony, Jr. *lawyer*
Reed, Doug *Internet company executive*
Reijo Pera, Renee A. *reproductive science director, educator*
Renteria, Edgar Enrique *professional baseball player*
Rhein, Kevin A. *bank executive*
Rheingold, Ted *Internet company executive*
Rice, Denis Timlin *lawyer*
Rice, Dorothy Pechman *medical economist*
Richards, Norman Blanchard *lawyer*
Richtel, Matt (Theron Heir) *reporter, cartoonist*
Rienhoff, Hugh *venture capitalist, physician, geneticist*
Righetti, David Allen (Dave Righetti) *professional baseball coach, retired professional baseball player*
Ristow, Brunno *plastic surgeon*
Rivlin, Gary *writer, reporter*
Robbins, Elizabeth *pediatric hematologist, oncologist*
Robertson, Merle Greene *art historian, academic administrator*
Robinson, Ralph W. *lawyer*
Rock, Arthur *venture capitalist*
Rogan, Richard A. *lawyer*
Rogers, T. Gary *apparel company executive, former food products company executive*
Rosedale, Philip E. *computer software company executive*
Rosen, Moishe *religious organization founder*
Rosen, Sanford Jay *lawyer*
Rosenberg, Rand L. *utilities executive*
Rosenberg, Richard Morris *banker*
Rosenfeld, Robert A. *lawyer*
Rosenheim, Daniel Edward *journalist, television news director*
Rosenstein, Barry *hedge fund manager*
Rosenthal, Philip *gastroenterologist*
Rosinski, Edwin Francis *medical educator*
Ross, Jeffrey S. *lawyer*
Rowland, John Arthur *lawyer*
Royer, Kathleen Rose *pilot*
Rudolph, Abraham Morris *pediatrician, educator*
Runnicles, Donald *conductor*
Rusher, William Allen *writer, commentator, columnist*
Russell, Sabin *newswriter*
Russoniello, Joseph Pascal *prosecutor, lawyer*
Rutherford, George Williams III *public health association administrator, educator*
Ryan, Kevin Vincent *lawyer, former prosecutor*
Sachs, Marilyn Stickle *writer, editor, educator*
Sadée, Wolfgang *pharmacy educator*
Saeger, Rebecca *advertising executive*
Safreno, Casey *investment banker*
Sage-Gavin, Eva Marie *retail executive*
Sakamoto, Katsuyuki *retired academic administrator, psychologist, educator*
Sanchez, Freddy (Frederick Phillip Sanchez) *professional baseball player*
Sanders, Joel Steven *lawyer*
Sansweet, Stephen Jay *journalist, writer, marketing executive*
Sasaki, Robert J. *financial services executive*
Satin, Joseph *language educator, retired dean*
Satre, Derek Davies *psychologist, researcher*
Saunders, Joseph W. *finance company executive*
Saunders, Sally Love *poet, educator*
Savage, Mark Randall *lawyer*
Sawaya, George F. *obstetrician, gynecologist, educator*
Schenkkan, Dirk McKenzie *lawyer*
Schickman, Mark Isaac *lawyer*
Schioldager, Amy Lee *investment company executive*
Schleier-Smith, Johann *Internet company executive*
Schmidt, Robert Milton *preventive medicine physician, educator, medical association administrator*
Schramm, Darrell G.H. *literature and language professor*
Schroeder, Steven Alfred *medical educator*
Schuberth, John M. *surgeon*
Schwab, Charles Robert, Jr., (Chuck Schwab) *investment company executive*
Seabolt, Richard L. *lawyer*
Seebach, Lydia Marie *physician*
Seeger, Laureen E. *lawyer, health products executive*
Serota, Gilbert Ross *lawyer*
Shackley, Douglas John *fire alarm company executive*
Shah, Premal *non-profit microloan company executive*
Shank, J. William *art conservator*
Sharkey, Tina *Internet company executive*
Shaw, Richard Eugene *cardiovascular researcher*
Shen, David *orthodontist*
Shepherd, John Michael *lawyer*
Sherr, Elliott Harold *neurologist, researcher*
Shiffman, Michael A. *lawyer*
Shorenstein, Walter Herbert *commercial real estate development company executive*
Shorenstein Hays, Carole *theater producer*
Shostak, Linda E. *lawyer*
Shushkewich, Kenneth Wayne *structural engineer*
Silk, Thomas *lawyer*
Silverstein, Richard *advertising agency executive*
Simini, Joseph Peter *accountant, financial consultant, writer, former educator*
Simmons, Sabrina L. *apparel executive*
Simon, John R. *utilities executive*
Singer, Allen Morris *lawyer*
Siniscalco, Gary Richard *lawyer*
Skaggs, Sanford Merle *lawyer*
Slipsager, Henrik C. *building services company executive*
Smegal, Thomas Frank, Jr. *lawyer*
Smith, Bernard Joseph Connolly *retired civil engineer*
Smith, David Elvin *physician*
Smith, Lloyd Hollingsworth *physician*
Smith, Patrick (Patrick Santosuosso) *columnist, pilot*
Snow, Tower Charles, Jr. *lawyer*
Snyder, Darin W. *lawyer*
Soberon, Presentacion Zablan *state bar administrator*
Soh, Chunghee Sarah *anthropology educator*
Soifer, Scott Jay *pediatrician*
Solo, Ashu M. G. *engineer, researcher*
Somsouk, Ma *gastroenterologist*
Sonneborn, William Charles *diversified financial services company executive*
Spanier, Joshua *advertising agency executive, director*
Sparks, Thomas E., Jr. *lawyer*
Speidel, John Joseph *public health professional, educator*
Speight, Joycelyn *oncologist*
Spivey, Bruce E. *ophthalmologist, educator, health facility administrator*
Spratt, Randall N. *healthcare services and information technology executive*
Sproul, John Allan *retired utilities executive*
Stahr, Celia Suzanne *art historian, educator*
Stamper, Robert Lewis *ophthalmologist, educator*
Starcher, Diana L. *bank executive*
Staring, Graydon Shaw *lawyer*
Stephens, Elisa *college president*
Stermer, Dugald Robert *designer, writer, illustrator, consultant*
Stewart, Richard Edwin *insurance consulting company executive*
Steyer, Thomas Fahr *hedge fund manager*
Stoller, Marshall *urologist, educator*
Stone, Issac (Biz Stone) *application developer, consultant*
Stoppelman, Jeremy *Internet company executive, entrepreneur*
Story, Joan H. *lawyer*
Strawbridge, William J. *healthcare educator*
Street, Paul Shipley *lawyer*
Strober, Jonathan Bret *neurologist, educator*
Stromberg, Ross Ernest *lawyer*
Strother, James M. *lawyer*
Stump, David James *philosopher, educator*
Stumpf, John Gerard *bank executive*
Su, Hua *medical educator*
Sugarman, Myron George *lawyer*
Sugarman, Paul William *lawyer*
Suh, Sang Won *medical educator*
Sullivan, Robert Edward *lawyer*
Taekman, Michael Seymour *neurological surgeon*
Takemoto, Steven Kan *medical educator*
Tanagho, Emil Abdelsayed *urologist, eductor*
Tantum, James Kent *artist, publisher*
Tarnoff, Peter *federal agency administrator, consultant*
Tasooji, Michael B. *retail executive*
Taylor, William James (Zak) *lawyer*
Templeton, Brad *information technology executive, software engineer, entrepreneur*
Ternar, Mine Y. *artist, educator*
Terr, Lenore Cagen *psychiatrist, writer*
Thayer, M. Patricia *lawyer*
Thiel, Peter Andreas *hedge fund manager*
Thompson, Patrick S. *lawyer*
Tihan, Tarik *pathologist, educator*
Tintiangco-Cubales, Allyson Goce *social studies educator*
Tolstedt, Carrie L. *bank executive*
Tomasson, Helgi *performing company executive, dancer, choreographer*
Tomer, Britta *orthodontist, educator*
Torme, Margaret Anne *public relations executive, management consultant*
Torvalds, Linus Benedict *application developer*
Tricaro, Robert Collet *biologist, editor, poet, educator*
Tripp, Alan H. *educational association administrator, consultant*
Trott, Mena *application developer*
Trounson, Alan Osbourne *state agency administrator, embryologist*
Tseng, Greg *Internet company executive*
Turek, Paul John III *construction executive*
Uba, Alan Keith *pediatrician, educator*
Uri, George Wolfsohn *accountant*
Urick, James R. *dentist*
Uskokovic, Vuk *research scientist*
Vail, Thomas Parker *orthopaedic surgeon*
Varanasi, Venu Gopal *biomedical researcher*
Varma, Madhulika G. *colon and rectal surgeon*
Vars, John *Internet company executive*
Vazquez-Azpiri, A. James *lawyer*
Veaco, Kristina *lawyer*
Vega, Frank J. *publishing executive*
Venning, Robert Stanley *lawyer*
Vidwans, Smruti Jayant *microbiologist*
Volberding, Paul Arthur *academic physician*
Volpe, Peter Anthony *surgeon*
Wald, Peter Allen *lawyer*
Walker, Vaughn R. *federal judge*

Walla, Chris *musician, music producer*
Walter, Peter *biochemist*
Wang, Ignatius Chung *bishop emeritus*
Wang, William Kai-Sheng *law educator*
Ware, Billy *musician*
Warner, Harold Clay, Jr. *banker, investment company executive*
Warner, Rollin Miles, Jr. *economics educator, real estate broker*
Way, E(dward) Leong *pharmacologist, toxicologist, educator*
Weber, Arnold I. *lawyer*
Weihrich, Heinz *management educator*
Weinberg, Doron *lawyer*
Weiner, Michael W. *neuroscientist, researcher, educator*
Weinstein, Philip *neurosurgeon, educator*
Werdegar, Kathryn Mickle *state supreme court justice*
Wernick, Sandra Margot *meeting event planner and public relations executive*
Wescott, William Burnham *oral maxillofacial pathologist, educator*
White, Julie M. *bank executive*
Whitehead, David Barry *lawyer*
Wilcke, Sam Lewis *financial analyst, consultant*
Wild, Nelson Hopkins *lawyer*
Williams, Cecil *minister*
Williams, Evan *Internet company executive*
Winblad, Ann *investment company executive*
Woeber, Kenneth Alois *physician*
Wolaner, Robin Peggy *Internet and magazine publisher*
Wolford, Richard G. *food products executive*
Wolters, Paul John *medical educator*
Wonder, John Walder *classicist, educator*
Wong, Ray L. *lawyer*
Wood, Robert Warren *lawyer*
Woo Ho, Doreen Woo *bank executive*
Wyatt, Tom (John Thomas Wyatt) *apparel executive*
Wyle, Frederick S. *lawyer*
Xu, Jay Jie *museum director*
Yalamanchi, Ramu *Internet company executive*
Yamanaka, Shinya *stem cell scientist, educator*
Yellen, Janet Louise *bank executive*
Ying, Weihai *biomedical researcher, educator*
Yost, Nicholas Churchill *lawyer*
Young, Bryant Llewellyn *lawyer*
Young, Douglas Rea *lawyer*
Zellerbach, William Joseph *retired paper company executive*
Zhang, Yu *medical researcher*
Zippin, Calvin *epidemiologist, educator*
Zunes, Stephen *political science professor, writer*

San Gabriel
Chen, John Calvin *retired psychiatrist, educator*
Shao, Zhenhua *electrical engineer, consultant*
Tomich-Bolognesi, Vera *educator*

San Jose
Alire, Camila A. *dean emerita, librarian, educator*
Alldis, Phung *language educator, director*
Arvizu, Charlene Sutter *elementary school educator*
Bazzi, Samer *software developer, consultant*
Belluzzo, Rick E. (Richard) *information technology and former computer software company executive*
Bermudes, Louis David *construction executive*
Blake, Rob *professional hockey player*
Boac, Thelma Blantucas *principal*
Bordenyuk, Andrey *laser scientist*
Bostrom, Susan L. *marketing executive*
Boyle, Dan *professional hockey player*
Bronson, Joseph R. *manufacturing executive*
Butler, David J. *newspaper editor*
Calderoni, Frank A. *computer company executive*
Campos, Nora *Councilwoman*
Carey, Peter Kevin *reporter*
Carges, Mark Thomas *Internet company executive*
Cedolini, Anthony John *psychologist*
Chambers, John Thomas *computer systems network executive*
Chandler, Mark D. *computer systems network executive, lawyer*
Chase, Joy Doris *librarian*
Cheechoo, Jonathan *professional hockey player*
Chirco, Judy *Councilwoman*
Chizen, Bruce R. *computer software company executive*
Cho, Yushin *computer scientist*
Chu, Kansen *councilman*
Chuang, Alfred Sze *information technology executive*
Cobb, William C. (Bill Cobb) *Internet company executive*
Constant, Pete *councilman*
Contos, Paul Anthony *engineer, investment consultant*
Dalis, Irene *mezzo soprano, performing arts association administrator*
Danopoulos, Constantine P. *political science professor*
D'Arrigo, Stephen, Jr. *agricultural company executive*
Dennison, Ronald Walton *engineer*
Denver, Thomas HR *lawyer*
Donahoe, John Joseph, II, *Internet company executive*
Edmonds, Charles Henry *retired publisher*
Elfrink, Wim *computer company executive*
Emmett, Brian *software developer*
Estabrook, Reed *artist, educator*
Fitzgerald, Timothy Kevin *writer, political organizer*
Friess, Peter *museum administrator*
Fusco, Jack A. *energy executive*
Gallo, Joan Rosenberg *lawyer*
Gilliss, David *finance educator*
Gong, Zhenxiang *application developer*
Grandison, Tyrone Wilberforce André *systems administrator*
Guthrie, Laura D. *energy executive, human resources specialist*
Ha, Kiet Tuan *hospital administrator*
Hall, Robert Emmett, Jr. *investment banker, realtor*
Hamill, Patrick James *physics professor, environmental scientist*
Hanasaki, Philip Toshifusa *communications educator*
Haycock, Kenneth Roy *academic administrator, educator, consultant*
Hernández, Fernando Vargas *lawyer*
Hernandez, Jo Farb *museum director, curator, professor, consultant*
Herrera, Rose A. *councilwoman*
Hill, Richard S. *manufacturing executive*
Ho, Chungwu *mathematics professor*
Hughes, Daniel David *performing company executive*
Hutton, Carole Leigh *not-for-profit executive, former newspaper editor*
Huynh, Minh Quan *physician*
Ibarra, Rufino H. *science educator*
Iben, Icko Eric Timothy *electrical engineer*
Iglesias, Don *school system administrator*
Inani, Anand *manufacturing executive, director*
Jacobson, Michael R. *lawyer, Internet company executive*
Jamison, Gregory John *professional sports team executive*
Jiang, Lijun *mechanical engineer*
Jiang, William Yuying *business educator, consultant, researcher*
Jin, Hailin *computer scientist*
Justice, Richard J. *computer company executive*
Kalra, Ash *councilman*
Kim, Jong-Shik *soil microbiologist, researcher*
Koo, Yido *electronics executive*
Krane, Susan *museum director, curator*
Kumar, Sailesh *network technician, researcher*
Lee, Sung-Chang *mechanical engineer*
Lehman, Tobin J. *research scientist*
Lendl, Jennifer Lynn *psychologist*
Li, Mike Peng *technologist*
Liccardo, Sam T. *councilman*
Light, Jane Ellen *library director*
Lippe, Philipp Maria *neurosurgeon, academic administrator, educator*
Liu, Derek *Internet company executive*
Lloyd, Robert L. *computer systems network executive*
Loiacono, John P. *information technology executive*
Loventhal, Milton *writer, playwright, lyricist*
Lynch, Kevin *computer software company executive, application developer*
Madra, Satbir Singh *materials researcher, mechanical engineer*
Maekawa, Koji Ogura *technology company administrator*
Makasyuk, Igor *physicist, consultant*
Malloy, Tom *computer company executive*
Marleau, Patrick *professional hockey player*
Masters, Gary *dancer, choreographer*
McDowell, Jennifer *sociologist, composer, playwright*
McLellan, Todd *professional hockey coach*
McManis, James *lawyer*
Mitchell, David Walker *lawyer*
Morelos-Zaragoza, Robert Henry *communications engineer*
Mou, Bo *philosopher, educator*
Nabokov, Evgeni *professional hockey player*
Nahat, Dennis F. *performing company executive, choreographer*
Narayen, Shantanu *computer software company executive*
Nava, Elizabeth M. *history professor*
Near, Timothy *theater director*
Nelson, Lionel M. *otolaryngologist*
Nguyen, Madison *councilwoman*
Nguyen-Wong, Khanh-Hoa Thi *literature and language professor*
Norrington, Lorrie M. *Internet company executive*
Okerlund, Arlene Naylor *academic administrator, writer*
Oliverio, Pierluigi *councilman*
Omidyar, Pierre M. *Internet company executive*
Parkin, Stuart Stephen Papworth *materials scientist, physicist*
Pausa, Clements Edward *electronics company executive*
Pham, Christopher Hoang *application developer, educator*
Pillai, Hari *electronics executive*
Pinnell, Sabrina L. *political science professor*
Pond, Randy *computer company executive*
Poyadue, Florene Stewart *nurse, foundation administrator*
Prasad, Neil A. *telecommunications industry executive, computer company executive*
Pyle, Nancy *Councilwoman*
Rathore, Jitendra S. *chemist*
Reed, Charles Rufus (Chuck Reed) *Mayor, San Jose, California, lawyer*
Rodgers, T(hurman) J. *semiconductor company executive*
Roelandts, Willem P. *data processing executive*
Rosenblum, Frank Michael *civil engineer, consultant, surveyor*
Rothblatt, Donald Noah *urban and regional planner, educator*
Rushdi, Ahmad A. *systems engineer*
Sajjadi, Hamed *otolaryngologist*
Shao, Otis Hung-I *retired political science professor*
Sherman, Craig *Internet company executive*
Silver, Steven David *science educator*
Silverman, Josh *communications executive*
Sola, Jure *electronics executive*
Stein, Arthur Oscar *retired pediatrician*
Stein, John C. *lawyer*
Stevens, David Alec *medical educator*
Stewart, Denise Margaret *ESL educator, consultant*
Stutzman, Thomas Chase, Sr. *lawyer*
Sueltz, Patricia C. *information technology executive*
Swan, Robert H. *Internet company executive*
Tanaka, Richard Koichi, Jr. *architect, planner*
Thompson, Jan Newstrom *art historian, educator*
Thornton, Joe *professional hockey player*
Togasaki, Shinobu *computer scientist*
Tretz, Christophe Robert *electrical engineer*
Trousdale, Stephen Richard *newspaper editor*
Tully, Mac *publishing executive*
Tyler, Michael Robert *lawyer*
Wallace, Richard P. *computer company executive*
Wang, Fei *research scientist*
Warnock, John Edward *computer company executive*
Warrior, Padmasree Y. *computer systems network executive*
Whitmore, Jon Scott *academic administrator, play director*
Wilson, Douglas Frederick *professional sports team executive, retired professional hockey player*
Wrede, Robert Clinton, Jr. *mathematician, educator*
Yang, Stanley *computer company executive*
Yu, Weider D. *engineering educator*
Zaro, Brad A. *research and development company executive, biologist*
Zhu, Lin *engineer*

San Juan Bautista
Nutzle, Futzie (Bruce John Kleinsmith) *artist, writer, animator*

San Juan Capistrano
Barreto, Hector V., Jr. *not-for-profit organization executive, former federal agency administrator*
Ealy, Cynthia Pike *artist, real estate agent*
Graves, Patrick Lee *lawyer*
Suzuki, Yasuhiko *retired law educator*
Wyland, Mark *state legislator*
Zalta, Edward *otolaryngologist, physician*

San Leandro
Dolgin, Stephen Mark *secondary school educator, retired social worker*
Sawyer, Malcolm James, Jr. *religious studies educator*
Zeller, Scott L. *psychiatrist*

San Luis Obispo
Anderson, Warren Ronald *electrical engineering educator*
Baker, Warren J(oseph) *university president*
Bing, Qu *engineering educator*
Daly, John Paul *lawyer*
Dowell, David Ray *library administrator*
Fernando, Raymond H. *chemistry professor, consultant*
Fisher, Eric O'Neill *economist*
Hafemeister, David Walter *physicist*
Hsu, John Yu-Sheng *computer scientist, educator*
Jamieson, James Bradshaw *foundation administrator*
Mann, Nancy Jean *biology professor*
Pinkel, Donald Paul *pediatrician*
Pohl, Jens Gerhard *architecture educator, director*
Self, Brian P *engineering educator*
Shlaudeman, Harry Walter *retired diplomat*
Suhr, Moon Ja Minn *dance educator*
Sullivan, Thomas James *retired manufacturing company executive*
Taufik, Taufik *electrical engineer, educator*

San Luis Rey
Williams, Elizabeth Yahn *poet, writer, educator, lawyer*

San Marcos
Anover, Veronica *language educator*
Barnes, Howard G. *communications executive, film producer*
Gentile, Robert Dale *optometrist, consultant*
Houk, Benjamin Noah *performing company executive, choreographer*
Jackson, Russell Eric *psychology professor*
Kagan, Stephen Bruce (Sandy Kagan) *corporate financial executive*
Kumar, Chetan *entrepreneur, educator*
Mohamed, Jabari *language educator*
Purdy, Alan Harris *biomedical engineer*
Rolle-Rissetto, Silvia *foreign languages educator, writer, artist*
Scaduto, Provvidenza *language educator*
Sepinwall, Alyssa *history professor*
Velasco, Martha *literature and language professor*
Zhang, Xiaoyu *science educator*

San Marino
Galbraith, James Marshall *lawyer, corporate executive*
Grantham, Richard Robert *financial consultant*
Hong, Kurt *nutritionist, director*
Lashley, Virginia Stephenson Hughes *retired computer science educator*
Martin, Olivia Jean *social studies educator*
Mortimer, Wendell Reed, Jr. *retired judge*
Murdoch, John *museum director*
Sadun, Alfredo Arrigo *neuro-ophthalmologist, scientist, educator*
Sherwood, Midge *writer*
Tomich, Lillian *lawyer*
Zall, Paul Maxwell *language educator, consultant*

San Mateo
Chabra, Anand *public health physician, epidemiologist*
Douglass, Donald Robert *banker*
Fu, Dan *information technology manager*
Gómez, Martín *library director*
Helfert, Erich Anton *management consultant, writer, educator*
Huxley, Mary Atsuko *artist*
Johnson, Charles Bartlett *corporate financial executive*
Johnson, Gregory Eugene *diversified financial services company executive*
Johnson, Rupert Harris, Jr. *diversified financial services company executive*
Johnson, Victoria L. *library director*
Kennedy, W(ilbert) Keith, Jr. *retired electronics executive, transportation executive*
Kim, Joseph Ho *engineering educator*
Lewis, Kenneth Allan *diversified financial services company executive*
O'Reilly, Terence John *lawyer*
Pileggi, Jennifer Wendy *lawyer, transportation services executive*
Sisson, Kathy B. *chef*
Stotlar, Douglas W. *transportation executive*
Sutherland, Vanna Rae *psychiatrist*
Tobisawa, Hiroshi *computer game company executive*
Tsujimoto, Kenzo *computer game company executive*
Tyle, Craig S. *lawyer, investment company executive*
Van Kirk, John Ellsworth *retired cardiologist*
Washington, Robin L. *pharmaceutical executive*
Zander, Edward J. *retired communications executive*

San Pablo
Murphy, Thomas Patrick *science educator, researcher*

San Pedro
Gaines, Frank, Jr. *retired management consultant*
Gaines, Jerry Lee *retired secondary school educator*
Hamai, James Yutaka *manufacturing executive*
Ingerson, Nancy Nina Moore *special education educator*
McCarty, Frederick Briggs *electrical engineer, consultant*
Simmons, William *retired aerospace engineer, research and development company executive*

San Quentin
Hanna, Nessim *marketing educator*

San Rafael
Adcock, Muriel W. *special education educator*
Amada, Gerald *retired psychotherapist*
Bass, Carl *computer software company executive*
Brubeck, David Warren *musician*
Busterud, John Armand *lawyer, consultant*
Chilvers, Robert Merritt *lawyer*
Coelho, Vania R. *biology professor*
Cortés, Antonio Luis *lawyer*
Djordjevich, Miroslav-Michael *bank executive*
Douglas, James *construction engineering educator*
Drexler, Kenneth *lawyer*
Faden, Glenn *application developer*
Fink, Joseph Richard *academic administrator*
Finkelstein, James Arthur *management consultant*
Friesecke, Raymond Francis *health company executive, president*
Greene, John Clifford *dentist, retired dean*
Gryson, Joseph Anthony *orthodontist*
Hart, John *writer*
Hinners, Billy *computer software company executive*
Hoffman, Charles Louis *physician*
Keegan, Jane Ann *insurance executive, consultant*
Lucas, George Walton, Jr. *film director, producer, scriptwriter*
Malifrando, Frank *healthcare executive, theater producer, consultant, film producer, international real estate investor, publisher*
Manny, Carter Hugh, Jr. *architect, retired foundation administrator*
Morgan, Michael Brewster *publishing executive*
Payne, David L. *bank executive*
Pomerantz, Martin Arthur *astronomer, educator, physicist*
Santana, Carlos *musician*
Thelen, Phyllis B. *artist*
Thomas, Mary Ann McCrary *counselor, school system administrator*
Tosti, Annette Brewer *artist*
Turner, William Weyand *writer*

San Ramon
Badruzzaman, Ahmed *nuclear scientist, educator*
Beebe, Lydia I. *oil industry executive, lawyer*
Bethancourt, John E. *oil industry executive*
Breber, Pierre R. *oil industry executive*
Garten, David Burton *lawyer*
Gass, John D. *oil industry executive*
Haynes, William James, II, *lawyer*
Humphrey, Mark A. *oil industry executive*
James, Charles Albert *lawyer, oil industry executive*
Kalicki, Jan H. *economist, political scientist, energy executive*
Kirkland, George L. *oil industry executive*
Laymon, Joe W. *human resources specialist*
Litman, Robert Barry *physician, writer, television and radio commentator*
McDonald, John W. *oil industry executive*
O'Reilly, David J. *oil industry executive*
Pate, R. Hewitt (Robert Hewitt Pate III) *lawyer, oil industry executive*
Pryor, Jay R. *oil industry executive*
Schofield, James Roy *computer programmer*
Schuttish, Thomas R. *oil industry executive, lawyer*
Siegele, Paul K. *oil industry executive*
Su, George Shenghui (Sheng-Hui Su) *chemist, medical researcher, educator*
Taylor, Charles A. (Chuck Taylor) *oil industry executive*
Vatannia, Shahla *mechanical engineer*
Watson, John S. *oil industry executive*
Wirth, Michael K. (Mike Wirth) *oil company executive*
Yarrington, Patricia E. *oil industry executive*
Zygocki, Rhonda I. *oil industry executive*

Sand City
Coile, Russell Cleven *electrical engineer, consultant*

Sanger
Patton, Jack Thomas *family practice physician*

Santa Ana
Aitken, Wylie A. *lawyer*
Amoroso, Frank *retired communication system engineer, consultant*
Bowers, Cherie Lynn *mathematics professor*
Boyd, Larry C. *information technology executive, lawyer*
Brusic, Ken *editor-in-chief*
Capizzi, Michael Robert *lawyer, former prosecutor*
Connell, Bruce F. *plastic surgeon*
DeGiorgio, Kenneth D. *lawyer, insurance company executive*
Digorgio, Kenneth *lawyer*
Dillard, John Martin *lawyer, pilot*
Donchey, Sheryl Diane *theater educator*

Elo, Jeffrey A. *oral and maxillofacial surgeon*
Gilmore, Dennis J. *insurance company executive*
Guilford, Andrew John *federal judge*
Humes, William D. *information technology executive*
Katz, Tonnie *newspaper editor*
Kelly, James Patrick, Jr. *retired engineering executive*
Kennedy, Parker S. *finance company executive*
Klassen, Margreta *clinical counseling psychologist, educator*
Kropp, William Rudolph *physicist*
Laurance, Dale R. *oil company executive*
Lawson, Barbara Slade *elementary school educator, artist*
Martinez, Rueben *entrepreneur*
McMahon, Frank V. *insurance company executive*
Micic, Miodrag *chemist, researcher*
Monié, Alain *information technology executive*
Myers, Marilyn Gladys *pediatric hematologist, oncologist*
Patel, Paresh *application developer*
Piszel, Anthony S. (Buddy Piszel) *mortgage company executive*
Pulido, Miguel Angel *Mayor, Santa Ana, California*
Roberts, Hilda R. *business educator*
Salem, Karen E. *information technology executive*
Schaefer, Ronald Dean *secondary school educator*
Spierkel, Gregory M. *information technology executive*
Sporty, Lawrence Douglas *psychiatrist*
Storer, Maryruth *law librarian*
Stotler, Alicemarie Huber *federal judge*
Tanaka, Richard I. *computer company executive*
Torrez, Caroline Herminia *human resources specialist, director, actress, musician, singer, dancer*
Washburn, Lawrence Robert *manufacturing executive*

Santa Barbara

Abbott, Horace Porter *English literature educator*
Ackerman, Marshall *publishing executive*
Aldisert, Ruggero John *federal judge*
Allaway, William Harris *retired academic administrator*
Altus, Grace Merriman Thompson *psychologist*
Athanassakis, Apostolos N. *classics educator*
Avery, Robert Logan *ophthalmologist*
Awramik, Stanley Michael *geology educator*
Awschalom, David Daniel *physics professor*
Badash, Lawrence *science history educator*
Bartlett, James Lowell III *investment company executive*
Behrens, June Adelle *writer*
Behrman, Richard Elliot *pediatrician, dean*
Birnir, Bjorn *mathematics professor, director*
Bischel, Margaret DeMeritt *physician, consultant*
Boehm, Eric Hartzell *information technology executive*
Boyan, Norman J. *retired education educator*
Braun, David A(dlai) *lawyer*
Brilliant, Ashleigh Ellwood *cartoonist, writer*
Brodhead, James E(aston) *actor, writer*
Brown, J'Amy Maroney *journalist, media consultant, investor*
Bruch, John Clarence, Jr. *engineer, educator*
Bunton, Clifford Allen *chemist, educator*
Burgee, John Henry *architect*
Caldwell, David Orville *physics professor*
Campagna, Jason Adam *anesthesiologist*
Cappello, A. Barry *lawyer*
Chafe, Wallace LeSeur *linguist, educator*
Christman, Arthur Castner, Jr. *science advisor, consultant*
Coffin, Dwight Clay *retired grain company executive*
Comanor, William S. *economist, educator*
Conley, Philip James, Jr. *retired air force officer*
Crowell, John C(hambers) *geology educator, researcher*
Curry, Thomas John *bishop*
Davidson, Roger H(arry) *political science professor*
Del Chiaro, Mario Aldo *art historian, archaeologist, etruscologist, educator*
Dunne, Thomas *geology educator*
Earl, Jennifer Suzanne *sociologist, educator*
Eguchi, Yasu *artist*
Emmeluth, Bruce Palmer *investment company executive, venture capitalist*
Erasmus, Charles John *anthropologist, educator*
Erickson, Robert Allen *English literature educator*
Evans, Anthony Glyn *materials scientist, educator*
Evans, Thomas Edgar, Jr. *title insurance agency executive*
Feigin, Joel *composer, educator*
Feinberg, Larry J. *museum director, curator*
Fingarette, Herbert *philosopher, educator*
Fisher, Steven Kay *neurobiology educator*
Freudenburg, William R. *sociology educator*
Gallo, Marta Irene *retired literature and language educator*
Gartrell, David Christian *archivist*
Giddings, Steven B. *physics professor*
Göllner, Marie Louise *musicologist, retired educator*
Gordon, Helen Heightsman *language educator, publishing executive, writer*
Gravitz, Herbert L. *clinical psychologist, writer*
Gross, David Jonathan *physicist*
Gunner, Michael Richard *real estate manager, hotel executive*
Gurven, Michael Douglas *anthropologist*
Heeger, Alan Jay *physicist, educator*
Hoffmeister, Gerhart *German language educator*
Holdrege, Barbara A. *religious studies educator*
Holly, Dianne Jean *costume designer, educator*
Horne, Marilyn Berneice *mezzo-soprano*
Howorth, David *producer, director*
Hubbard, Arthur Thornton *chemist, educator*
Hutterer, Karl Leopold *museum director*
Jackson, Beverley Joy Jacobson *columnist, educator*
Janelle, Donald G. *geographer, researcher*
Ji, Chen *science educator*
Jiang, Yong *materials scientist*
Jochim, Michael Allan *archaeologist*
Johnson, Brenda L. *university librarian*
Jordan, Mary Ann *research biologist*
Jovanoviè, Lois *medical researcher*
Jullien, Dominique M. *literature and language educator*
Kanjo, Kathryn *museum director*
Kendler, Howard H(arvard) *psychologist, educator*
Kohn, Roger Alan *surgeon*
Kohn, Walter *physicist, retired educator*
Kramer, Edward John *materials engineering educator*
Kroemer, Herbert *electrical engineering educator*
Kruger, Kenneth Charles *architect*
Kryter, Karl David *retired research scientist*
Kydland, Finn E. *economics professor*
Laris, Katherine Elizabeth *theater director, educator*
Lomeli, Francisco A. *language educator, department chairman*
Lopus, Manu *biologist*
Macdonald, Ken Craig *geophysicist*
Mahlendorf, Ursula Renate *literature educator*
Marshall, Philip James *astrophysicist*
Mathews, Barbara Edith *gynecologist*
Mayer, Richard Edwin *psychology professor*
McCoy, Lois Clark *retired social services administrator, county official, editor*
McGee, James Sears *historian, educator*
McMeeking, Robert Maxwell *mechanical engineer, educator*
Minc, Henryk *mathematics professor*
Mitra, Sanjit Kumar *electrical and computer engineering educator*
Morse, Daniel E. *biochemistry educator, science administrator*
Norris, Virginia Oakley *secondary school educator*
Nyborg, Vanessa Marie *psychologist, researcher, educator*
Obern, Vivian Marie Hapeman *volunteer*
O'Dowd, Donald Davy *retired university president*
Orfalea, Paul James *investment company executive, former printing company executive*
Peck, Abraham *editor, media consultant, educator*
Pei, Yi *electronics engineer, researcher*
Pilafian, Christopher *choreographer*
Pilgeram, Laurence Oscar *biochemist*
Poulsen, Henrik Nørskov *research scientist*
Prezelin, Barbara Berntsen *science association director, educator*
Pyron, Nona Faye *music educator, director*
Ramsay, William Charles *writer, composer*
Ray, Charles Dean *neurosurgeon, spine surgeon, bioengineer, inventor*
Reed, Frank Fremont, II, *retired lawyer*
Reich, Norbert Otto *biochemist, educator*
Rickels, Laurence Arthur *foreign language educator*
Rock, David Peter *history professor*
Rose, Mark Allen *humanities educator*
Russell, Jeffrey Burton *historian, educator*
Samuel, Charles E. *virologist, biochemist, educator*
Schneider, Edward Lee *botanist, researcher*
Schultz, Arthur Warren *retired communications executive*
Sensiper, Samuel *electrical engineer*
Simons, Stephen *mathematics professor, researcher*
Sinsheimer, Robert Louis *retired academic administrator, educator*
Steckel, Julie Raskin *psychotherapist, lecturer, consultant*
Suh, Wonsuk Warren *radiation oncologist*
Theofanous, Theofanis G. *engineering educator, consultant*
Tilton, David Lloyd *savings and loan association executive*
Tucker, Shirley Lois Cotter *botanist, educator*
Von Weizsäcker, Ernst Ulrich *environmental scientist, dean*
Vos, Hubert Daniel *investor*
Weidemann, Celia Jean *social sciences educator, management consultant, financial consultant*
White, Robert Stephen *retired physics professor*
Wilkins, Burleigh Taylor *philosophy educator*
Witherell, Michael S. *physicist, educator*
Wittenstein, George Juergen *retired surgeon, retired educator*
Wollman, Glenn David *physician, medical guide*
Yang, Henry T.Y. *academic administrator, educator*
You, Sukkyung *research faculty*
Ziegler, R. W., Jr. *lawyer, consultant*

Santa Clara

Alexanderson, Gerald Lee *mathematician, educator, writer*
Baker, Robert J. *computer company executive*
Benson, Jon H. *information technology executive*
Beveridge, Crawford W. *information technology executive*
Bhagat, Nancy *marketing executive*
Bolin, Christopher *software security company executive*
Bray, Tim(othy) (William) *computer company executive, software developer*
Bruce, Isaac Isidore *professional football player*
Bryant, Andy D. *computer company executive*
Bryant, Diane M. *information technology executive*
Bucklin, Christine B. *information technology executive*
Chan, Shu-Park *electrical engineering educator*
Culbertson, Leslie S. *computer company executive*
Cundy, Kenneth Charles *pharmaceutical executive*
Dafforn, Geoffrey Alan *biochemist*
Davis, George S. *manufacturing executive*
DeWalt, David G. *software company executive*
Dham, Vinod K. *Indo-US venture capitalist company executive*
Dillon, Adrian T. *financial executive*
Dillon, Michael A. (Mike) *lawyer, information technology executive*
Dolich, Andrew Bruce *professional sports team executive*
DuChene, Todd Michael *lawyer*
Fowler, John *information technology executive*
Gadre, Anil *information technology executive*
Glancy, Dorothy Jean *lawyer, educator*
Goodchild, Lester Francis *higher education educator*
Gope, Dipanjan *computer engineer*
Goyal, Shalabh *electronics engineer*
Green, Rich *information technology executive*
Hall, William Spencer *software engineer*
Halla, Brian L. *electronics executive*
Halloran, Jean M. *human resources specialist*
Harris, David M. *information technology executive*
Hayn, Carl Hugo *physics professor, priest*
Heel, Joe *information technology executive*
Hofstetter, Jane Robinson *artist, educator*
Holt, William M. *computer company executive*
Hopkinson, Shirley Lois *library and information scientist, educator*
Hsieh, Marina Cing *lawyer, educator*
Huang, Jen-Hsun *electronics executive*
Iyar, Subrah S. *information technology executive*
Kalinovsky, Tatiana *writer*
Kamal, Abu Hena M. *electrical engineer, researcher*
Karas, Timothy *library director*
Kim, Yongtae *accounting educator*
Klosinski, Leonard Frank *mathematics professor*
Le, Son Minh *philosophy educator*
Lee, Chan-Yun *physicist, process engineer, educator*
Lee, Hyung Jai *material scientist*
Lehman, Michael Evans *information technology executive*
Li, Lihong *Internet company researcher*
Lin, Frank C. *computer company executive*
Locatelli, Paul Leo *academic administrator*
MacGowan, Bill *information technology executive*
Maloney, Sean M. *electronics company executive*
McCabe, Eugene *information technology executive*
McCloughan, Scot G. *professional sports team executive*
McGrath, Patrick Joseph *bishop*
McNealy, Scott Glenn *information technology executive*
Miller, Dan *information technology executive*
Moore, Gordon E. *electronics executive, researcher*
Morgan, James C. *retired manufacturing executive*
Nassif, Nabil *engineering executive, director*
Nordlund, Donald Craig *lawyer, electronics executive*
Ostwald, Venice Eloise Varner *librarian, educator, minister, writer*
Otellini, Paul Stevens *electronics company executive*
Papadopoulos, Gregory Michael *information technology executive*
Papay, Lauri Louise *mathematics professor*
Parden, Robert James *engineering educator, management consultant*
Pattanayak, Deva Narayan *engineering company executive*
Perlmutter, David (Dadi) *computer company executive*
Pinto, Mark R. *manufacturing executive*
Polden, Donald *dean, law educator*
Ranjan, Rahul *engineer, researcher*
Robel, Chuck (Charles J. Robel) *computer software company executive*
Ryan, Peter *computer systems network executive*
Schapp, Rebecca Maria *museum director*
Schwartz, Jonathan Ian *information technology executive*
Scott, Edward William, Jr. *retired computer company executive & philanthropist*
Sewell, D. Bruce (Bruce Sewell, Durward Bruce Sewell) *lawyer*
Shaw, Jane Elizabeth *electronics company executive, retired pharmaceutical company executive*
Simmons, Janet Bryant *writer, publishing executive*
Singletary, Mike *professional football coach, retired professional football player*
Smith, Alex (Alexander Doug Smith) *professional football player*
Smith, Stacy J. *computer company executive*
Sodhani, Arvind *computer company executive*
Solomon, Darlene J.S. *electronics executive*
Spikes, Takeo *professional football player*
Splinter, Michael R. *manufacturing executive*
Staples, Nathan Charles *biology professor*
Stern, Hal *information technology executive*
Sullivan, William P. *electronics executive*
Sutphin, Brian *information technology executive*
Sweeney, Joseph J. *lawyer, manufacturing executive*
Tremblay, Marc *information technology executive*
Troccoli, Mariano *physicist, researcher, entrepreneur*
Van Den Hoogen, Ingrid *information technology executive*
Vu, Quat Thuong *electrical engineer*
White, Ian *information technology executive*
Willis, Patrick L. *professional football player*
Worrall, Robert *information technology executive*
Yang, Cary *engineering educator*
Yen, David *information technology executive*

Santa Clarita

Boyer, Carl III *not-for-profit developer, retired mayor, municipal official*
Feldman Nebenzahl, Bernardo *composer, educator*
Goodrick, Dell Ariel *dentist*
Lavine, Steven David *academic administrator*
Mays, Kenneth Robert *music educator*
Neunhoffer, Steven Charles *protective services official*
Perrault, Penni Marilyn *elementary school educator*
Sturges, Sherry Lynn *recording industry executive*
Varner, William *religious studies educator*
Walker, Robert F. *social studies educator*

Santa Cruz

Basu, Dilip Kumar *history professor, film company executive, director*
Blumenthal, George *academic administrator, astronomy and astrophysics professor*
Brown, George Stephen *physics professor*
Bunnett, Joseph Frederick *chemist, educator*
Carson, Benjamin Leeds *composer, educator*
Cheung, Yin-Wong *economics professor*
DeWald, Celeste *museum director*
Dominguez, Virginia Rosa *anthropologist*
Epps, Harland Warren *astronomy educator, optical design consultant*
Faber, Sandra Moore *astronomer, educator*
Garcia-Luna-Aceves, J.J. *education educator*
Griggs, Gary Bruce *oceanographer, geologist, educator, director*
Hankamer, Jorge *linguistics educator*
Huskey, Harry Douglas *information and computer science educator*
Kahn, Philippe *telecommunications industry executive, entrepreneur*
Kang, Sung-Mo (Steve Kang) *electrical engineering educator*
Kobayashi, Nobuhiko Paul *materials scientist, professor*
Kubby, Joel *electrical engineer, educator*
Langenheim, Jean Harmon *biologist, educator*
Lasar, Matthew *History Instructor*
Lay, Thorne *geosciences educator*
Leicester, Henry Marshall, Jr. *literature and language professor*
Leikin, Anatole *music educator*
Margon, Bruce Henry *astrophysicist, educator*
Max, Claire Ellen *physicist*
Noller, Harry Francis, Jr. *biochemist, educator*
Pettigrew, Thomas Fraser *social psychologist, educator*
Roby, Pamela Ann *sociologist, educator*
Sands, Matthew Linzee *physicist, researcher*
Seligmann, William Robert *lawyer, author*
Shaffer, Scott A. *biology professor, researcher*
Shi, Chao *research scientist*
Shorenstein, Rosalind Greenberg *internist*
Smith, M(ahlon) Brewster *retired psychologist, educator*
Steel, Virginia (Ginny Steel) *university librarian*
Stevens, Stanley David *historian, researcher, retired librarian, archivist*
Stormes, John Max *systems analyst*
Stuart, Joshua M. *biology professor*
Walsh, Carl E. *economics professor*
Wang, Xin *computer engineer, researcher*
Weiner, Claire Zundell (CZ Cameron) *theatrical director*
Wiberg, Donald Martin *electrical engineering educator, consultant*
Widom, Harold *mathematician, educator*
Williams, Quentin Christopher *geophysicist, educator*
Wipke, W. Todd *chemistry professor*
Woosley, Stanford Earl *astrophysicist*
Xin, Wang *researcher*
Young, Allan Peter *physics professor*

Santa Maria

Arnold, Stephen L. *systems engineer*
DeLaurier, Roger Darren *conservator, director*
Isaacson, Robert Anton *language educator, researcher*
Moret, Jeanine *film educator*

Santa Monica

Aaron, David L. *diplomat, author*
Akerman, Malin Maria *actress*
Alpern, Harvey L. *cardiologist*
Angel, Steven *musician*
Berman, Gail *former film company executive, media company executive*
Besson, Nicole Marie Archambault *speech pathology/audiology services professional*
Bilchik, Anton Joel *surgeon*
Blankley, Tony *public relations executive, columnist, radio personality*
Bratt, Benjamin *actor*
Bruckheimer, Jerry Leon *producer*
Bush, William Glenn *manufacturing company executive, engineer*
Cameron, James *film director, screenwriter, producer*
Campbell, Douglas Allen *landscape architect, consultant*
Chapman Holley, Shawn Snider *lawyer*
Cole, Gary Michael *actor*
Constan, Sandy *marketing and advertising executive*
Cooper, Jay Leslie *lawyer*
Cowan, Jeffrey Wrubel *lawyer*
Craig, Stuart N. *film production designer*
Curran, Leigh *actress, playwright*
Davis, Paul Kensil *strategic planner*
DeLonge, Thomas Matthew, Jr. *musician*
Dixon, Lloyd S. *economist*
Ellickson, Phyllis Lynn *political scientist*
Eminem, (Marshall Mathers III) *rap artist*
Falco, Edie *actress*
Ferrell, Conchata Galen *actress, performing arts educator*
Friedman, Monroe *psychologist, educator, consultant, editor, writer*
Geiser, Thomas Christopher *lawyer, insurance company executive*
Giuliano, Armando Elario *surgical oncologist, educator, author*
Goldman, Charles A. *science administrator*
Gray, Laura B. *psychology professor, counselor*
Greenberg, Sarah *film company executive*
Griffith, Huw *advertising executive*
Gritton, Eugene Charles *nuclear engineer, director*
Grossman, Marshall Bruce *lawyer*
Handler, Chelsea Jane *comedian, television personality*
Handzlik, Jan Lawrence *lawyer*
Hannigan, Alyson *actress*
Heimbuch, Babette E. *bank executive*
Heller, Lawrence Howard *lawyer*
Hinerfeld, Robert Elliot *lawyer*
Hirschhorn, Jason *Internet company executive*
Huffington, Arianna *columnist, writer, editor*
Intriligator, Devrie Shapiro *physicist*
Iovine, Jimmy *recording industry executive*
Jain, John Kumar *medical educator, health facility administrator*
Jones, Michael *Internet company executive*
Kanouse, David Earl *research and development company executive*
Kawamoto, Henry Katsumi, Jr. *plastic surgeon*
Kayton, Myron *engineering company executive*
Keeler, Emmett Brown *research mathematician*
Kelly, Brian *computer game company executive, accountant, lawyer*
Kennedy, David *musician*
Kennedy, Kathleen *film producer*
Kotick, Robert Andrew *computer software company executive*
Kurtzman, Joel Allan *economist*
Kuzmanovic, Jane Violet *academic administrator*

Lady Gaga, (Stefani Joanne Angelina Germanotta) *singer*
Lempert, Robert Jay *Policy Analyst Educator*
Levin, Barry Raymond *rare book dealer, film producer*
Levin, Gerald M. (Jerry Levin) *former media and entertainment company executive*
Levin, Marvin Eugene *lawyer*
Louis-Dreyfus, Julia *actress*
Malphus, Edward Wilson *pediatric gastroenterologist*
Mancuso, Frank G. *entertainment and communications company executive*
Mandelbaum, Bert Roland *orthopedist*
Masterson, Lisa M. *gynecologist, obstetrician*
Masucci, Michael James *artist*
Mayne, Thom *architect*
McGinley, John C. *actor*
McGlynn, Elizabeth A. *health policy analyst*
McGuire, Michael Francis *plastic surgeon*
McNall, Bruce *film producer, former professional sports team executive*
Meester, Leighton (Leighton Marissa Claire Meester) *actress*
Meier, Steven W. *orthopedist, surgeon, consultant*
Milken, Michael R. *think-tank executive, philanthropist*
Morgan, Kermit Johnson *lawyer*
Moses, Samuel B. *certified public accountant, consultant*
O'Connor, Edward Joseph *neurologist*
Oppenheim, William L. *pediatric orthopedist*
Ovitz, Michael S. *communications executive*
Palmatier, Malcolm Arthur *editor, consultant*
Parker, William Howard *obstetrician-gynecologist*
Patel, Chandra Kumar Naranbhai *communications executive, educator, entrepreneur, researcher*
Peña, Michael Anthony *actor*
Porter, Verna R. *neurologist, educator*
Resnick, Jeffrey I. *plastic surgeon*
Rich, Michael David *think-tank executive, lawyer*
Rifkin, Arnold *film company executive*
Risman, Michael *lawyer, real estate developer, broker*
Rosensweig, Daniel L. *video gaming company executive*
Salveson, Melvin Erwin *management sciences corporation chief executive, educator*
Schaeffer, Leonard David *health insurance company executive*
Schultz, Victor M. *physician*
Scott, Jill *poet, musician*
See, Carolyn *English language educator, writer, book critic*
Seyfried, Amanda Louise *actress*
Shannon, Molly Helen *actress*
Shearmur, Alli *film company executive*
Sherman, Zachary *civil engineer, aerospace engineer, consultant*
Singer, Frederick Raphael *medical researcher*
Smith, James Patrick *economist*
Smith, Michael S. *interior designer, furniture designer*
Sonnenfeld, Stefan *film editor*
Soodik, Lynn *lawyer*
Soule, Howard R. *medical association administrator*
Spacek, Sissy (Mary Elizabeth Spacek) *actress*
Spooner, Sharon Nau *pediatric ophthalmologist*
Stern, Walter Eugene *neurosurgeon, educator*
Stiehm, Judith Hicks *political scientist*
Summer, Donna (La Donna Adrian Gaines) *singer, songwriter, actress*
Tamblyn, Amber Rose *actress*
Taylor, James Vernon *musician*
Teitelbaum, Steven *plastic surgeon*
Teleki, Stephanie *policy analyst*
The Edge, (David Howell Evans) *musician*
Thomson, James Alan *think-tank executive*
Timbaland, (Timothy Z. Mosley) *recording industry executive, rap artist*
Tinsley, Jeffrey *Internet company executive*
Tompkins, Ronald K. *retired surgeon, educator*
Tunney, John Varick *lawyer, former United States Senator from California*
Valentine, Dean *film producer*
Van Natta, Owen Thomas *Internet company executive*
Wachs, Martin *urban planning educator, author, consultant*
Wang, Jeffrey C. *surgeon*
Watson, Doc (Arthel Lane Watson) *vocalist, guitarist, banjoist, recording artist*
Weber, Bruce *photographer, filmmaker*
Weden, Margaret *research and development company executive*
Weitzman, Howard L. *lawyer, former film company executive*
Wexler, Haskell *film producer*
Willard, Atom (Adam Willard) *musician*
Wolf, Charles, Jr. *economist, educator*
Zarem, Harvey Alan *plastic surgeon*

Santa Paula
Broughton, Margaret Martha *mental health nurse*
Edwards, Samuel Roger *retired internist*
Lattimore, Steven *classicist, educator*

Santa Rosa
Aman, Reinhold Albert *philologist, writer*
Andriano-Moore, Richard Count *retired military officer, secondary and elementary school educator*
Biderman, Charles Israel *diversified financial services company executive*
Callum, Myles *magazine editor, writer*
Cohn, Joseph David *surgeon*
Farrell, Thomas Joseph *insurance company executive, consultant*
Fruiht, Dolores Giustina *artist, educator, poet*
Gleason, Ken Bell *historian, educator, journalist*
Gorin, Susan *Mayor, Santa Rosa, California*
Grundy, Richard David *engineer*
Hales, Raleigh Stanton, Jr. *retired mathematics professor, academic administrator*
Jackson, Jess S. *vintner*
Klim, James D. *dentist*
Lewis, Alvin Edward *pathology educator*
Lieberman, Sharon L. *retired psychology professor*
Marougi, Salam D. *engineering educator*
McAvoy, John Martin *plastic surgeon*
Monk, Diana Charla *small business owner*
Person, Evert Bertil *retired newspaper and radio executive*
Rider Stevenson, Jane *artist, educator*
Rosaschi, Jim *librarian*
Schwartz, Marine Lenore *humanities educator*
Smith, Betty L. *small business owner, educator*
Wagner, Harold A. *retired gas industry executive*
Walsh, Daniel Francis *bishop*
Webb, Charles Richard *retired university president*
Yatsenko, Nikolai Afanasyevich *physics researcher, educator*
Ziemann, George Patrick *bishop emeritus*
Zimmer, Richard *anthropologist, educator*

Santa Ynez
O'Grady, Barbara Vinson *retired community health nurse, administrator*

Saratoga
Barna, Lillian Carattini *school system administrator*
Greenleaf, John Edward *human research consultant*
Houston, Joseph Brantley, Jr. *optical instrument company executive*
Konnyu, Ernest Leslie *former congressman*
Liccardo, Salvador A. *lawyer*
Reagan, Joseph Bernard *retired aerospace executive, management consultant*
Rollo, F. David *healthcare company executive, cardiologist*
Syvertson, Clarence Alfred *management consultant, engineer*

Sausalito
Apatoff, Michael John *entrepreneur*
Berkman, William Roger *lawyer, retired major general army*
Brand, Stewart *editor, writer, multimedia designer*
Gordon, Robert Eugene *lawyer*
Jepsen, Mary Lou *information technology executive*
Keeffe, Emmet Britton *medical educator*
Ornish, Dean *medical association administrator and educator*

Scotts Valley
Cassidy-Eagle, Erin Lynne *social science researcher, director*
Crandell, Kenneth James *management consultant, entrepreneur*
Hudson, William L. *lawyer, electronics executive*
Luczo, Stephen James *computer hardware company executive*
Pletsch, Marie Eleanor *plastic surgeon*

Seal Beach
Denson-Low, Wanda K. *lawyer, aerospace transportation executive*
Matz, Sean Cormick *electrical engineer*
Pipes, Doris Perry *secondary school educator, consultant*

Seaside
Anderson, David Louis *academic administrator, history professor*
Krasnyanskaya, Elena *language educator*
May, James Harvey *communications educator*
Tringali, Maria Rosaria *language educator*
Zielina, Maria C. *literature and language professor*

Sebastopol
Greiner, Robert Philip *lawyer, real estate broker*
Griggs, Lewis Brown *executive producer, speaker, trainer*
Omi, Philip Nori *retired forestry professor*
O'Reilly, Tim *computer book publishing company executive, open sourcer advocate*
Rappaport, Stuart Ramon *lawyer*
Sabsay, David *retired library director*

Sepulveda
Yano, Elizabeth Martin *epidemiologist, researcher*

Sherman Oaks
Beck, Glenn *radio personality, commentator*
Clark, Susan (Nora Goulding) *actress*
Crump, Gerald Franklin *retired lawyer*
Douglas, Michael Kirk *actor, film director, film producer*
Drudge, Matt (Matthew Nathan Drudge) *journalist, celebrity blogger*
Eisenkop, Scott *oncologist*
Elfman, Danny *composer*
Ferguson, Lisa Beryl *accountant*
Fogerty, John Cameron *musician, composer*
Handel, Neal *plastic surgeon, researcher, educator*
Howard, Alison Koi *singer, music licensing consultant, lyricist*
Howe, Daniel Walker *historian, educator*
Jordan, Bonnie *television producer*
Joyce, Stephen Michael *lawyer*
Merritt, Jean *consulting firm executive, psychotherapist*
Mersel, Marjorie Kathryn Pedersen *lawyer*
O'Neill, Sallie Boyd *educational consultant, sculptor, small business owner*
Platus, Libby *journalist, art educator, sculptor, artist*
Reiner, Thomas Karl *manufacturing executive, engineering scientist*
Stein, Kira D. *psychiatrist*
Taylor, Elizabeth (Dame Elizabeth Rosemond Taylor) *actress*
Yasnyi, Allan David *communications company executive*

Signal Hill
Adler, Jeffrey D. *political consultant, crisis management expert*
Vandament, William Eugene *retired academic administrator*

Simi Valley
Blackwood, (R.) Duke *library and museum director*
Davenport, Alfred Larue, Jr. *manufacturing executive*
Eberhard-Neveaux, Christine *aviation and dispute resolution executive*
Erzinger, Kathy McClam *credential nurse educator*
Lewis, Richard B. *manufacturing and logistics executive*

Snelling
Jones, Mabel Bennett *retired history professor*

Solana Beach
Agnew, Harold Melvin *physicist*
Gildred, Theodore E. *former diplomat, real estate developer*

Solvang
Roberts, Monty *horse trainer, writer*

Sonoma
Beckmann, Jon Michael *publishing company executive*
Emery, John Edward *plastic surgeon, vintner*
Fellows, Alice Combs *artist*
Hobart, Billie *retired education educator*
Markey, William Alan *health facility administrator, consultant*
Muchmore, Robert Boyer *engineering executive, consultant*
Obninsky, Victor Peter *lawyer*

Sonora
Chandler, Edwin Russell *clergyman, writer*
Clarke, Paula Katherine *anthropologist, researcher, social studies educator*
Duensing, Lennie *medical association administrator*
Wheeler, Elton Samuel *financial executive*

Soquel
Cureton, Glen *pharmaceutical executive*
Tomash, Erwin *retired computer company executive*

South Lake Tahoe
Triano, Carolyn P. *special education educator*

South Pasadena
Askin, Walter Miller *artist, educator*
Echeveste, John Anthony *public relations consultant*
Finnell, Michael Hartman *mining executive*
Fuller, Kathy J. *special education educator, consultant, researcher*
Girvigian, Raymond *architect*
Kopp, Eugene Howard *communications and electrical engineer, consultant*

South San Francisco
Andre, Patrick *biologist, director*
Barbour, Robin McDaid *research scientist, director*
Hull, Cordell William *engineering, construction, and project management executive, investor*
Humphrey, Patrick Paul *pharmacologist*
Hurst, Deborah *pediatric hematologist*
Lee, Leonard S. *health facility administrator*
Schenk, Dale Bernard *pharmaceutical executive, neuroscientist*
Shi, Yining *biotechnologist*
Soriot, Pascal *pharmaceutical executive*
Su, Zheng *statistician*
Walsh, J. Michael *wholesale distribution executive*

Spring Valley
Love, Michael *secondary school educator*
Madigan, William Charles *literature and language professor, consultant*
Siddiqui, Razia Sultana *retired psychotherapist, educator*

Stanford
Abrams, Herbert LeRoy *radiologist, educator*
Alderkamp, Anne-Carlijn *environmental scientist*
Allen, Richard Vincent *international business consultant, former national security advisor*
Anderson, Theodore Wilbur *statistics educator*
Andreopoulos, Spyros George *writer*
Aoki, Masahiko *economics educator*
Archer, Cristina Lozej *research scientist*
Ardehali, Reza *cardiologist*
Arrow, Kenneth Joseph *economist, educator*
Aziz, Khalid *petroleum engineering educator*
Baer, Thomas M. *optical engineer*
Baker, Keith Michael *history professor*
Baldwin, Robert Lesh *biochemist, educator*
Bandura, Albert *psychologist, educator*
Baumard, Philippe Nicolas *strategic management educator*
Bejerano, Gill *engineering educator*
Berek, Jonathan Samuel *surgeon, gynecologic oncologist, writer*
Berg, Paul *biochemist, educator*
Bienenstock, Arthur Irwin *physicist, educator, federal official*
Blau, Helen Margaret *pharmacology educator*
Block, Steven Michael *biophysicist, educator*
Boaler, Jo *education educator*
Boskin, Michael Jay *economics professor*
Boudart, Michel *chemical engineer, consultant, educator*
Boxer, Steven G. *physical chemistry educator*
Brauman, John I. *chemist, educator*
Briggs, Winslow Russell *plant biologist, educator*
Brock-Utne, John *medical educator*
Brodsky, Jay Barry *medical educator*
Brody, Richard Alan *political science educator, researcher*
Brooks, Helen Bousky *literature and language professor, performing arts educator*
Brunger, Axel Thomas *biophysicist, researcher, educator*
Bryk, Anthony S. *educational association administrator*
Bube, Richard Howard *retired materials scientist, educator*
Byers, Tom H. *management science and engineering educator*
Cai, James J. *biologist, researcher*
Campbell, Allan McCulloch *bacteriology educator*
Cannon, Robert Hamilton, Jr. *aerospace engineering educator*
Cao, Linyou *research scientist*
Casper, Gerhard *law educator, retired academic administrator*
Chase, Robert Arthur *surgeon, educator*
Chertow, Glenn M. *internist, nephrologist, researcher*
Clarke, Michael F. *oncologist, educator*
Cohen, Albert *musician, educator*
Cohen, Stanley Norman *geneticist, educator*
Cohen, William *law educator*
Collman, James Paddock *chemistry professor*
Cook, Karen S. *sociologist, professor*
Cork, Linda Katherine *veterinary pathologist, educator*
Cox, Donald Clyde *electrical engineering educator*
Dally, William J. *computer science educator*
Damon, William Van Buren *developmental psychologist, educator, writer*
Darling-Hammond, Linda *education professor*
Davis, Jennifer *engineering educator, researcher*
Dekker, George Gilbert *literature professor, writer, former academic administrator*
Derksen, Charlotte Ruth Meynink *librarian*
Diamond, Larry *political scientist*
Djerassi, Carl *writer, retired chemistry professor*
Donaldson, Sarah Susan *radiologist*
Duffie, Darrell *finance educator*
Duus, Peter *retired historian*
Egbert, Peter Roy *ophthalmologist, educator*
Ehrlich, Paul Ralph *biology professor*
Eisner, Elliot W. *education educator*
Elliott, David Duncan III *science company executive*
Enthoven, Alain Charles *economist, educator*
Eustis, Robert Henry *design company executive, mechanical engineer*
Evers, Williamson Moore (Bill Evers) *education policy analyst, former federal agency administrator*
Falkow, Stanley *microbiologist, educator*
Farquhar, John William *physician, educator*
Fearon, William *cardiologist*
Feigenbaum, Edward Albert *retired computer science educator*
Felstiner, John *literature educator, translator*
Fetter, Alexander Lees *theoretical physicist, educator*
Fingar, Thomas (Charles Thomas Fingar) *political science professor, former federal official*
Fire, Andrew Z. *pathologist, geneticist, educator*
Fisher, George Albert, Jr. *internist, oncologist*
Fleishman, Lazar *literature educator*
Franklin, Marc Adam *law educator*
Fratkin, Eugene *research scientist*
Fredrick, Douglas Robert *pediatric ophthalmologist*
Friedman, Lawrence M. *law educator*
Fuchs, Victor Robert *economist, educator*
Galli, Stephen Joseph *biomedical researcher*
Gambhir, Sanjiv Sam *nuclear medicine physician, educator*
Garber, Alan Michael *internist, educator, economist*
Gelpi, Albert Joseph *language educator, department chairman, critic*
George, Tracy I. *pathologist, educator*
Glynn, Peter Winston Gunnar *engineering educator*
Goodman, Stuart B. *medical educator*
Gosling, John Arthur *education educator*
Gould, William Benjamin, IV, *law educator*
Granovetter, Mark *sociology educator*
Grossman, Arthur R. *science educator, researcher*
Grousbeck, Harold Irving *professional sports team owner, management educator*
Grundfest, Joseph Alexander *law and business educator*
Guilleminault, Christian *neurologist*
Hall, Robert Ernest *economics professor*
Hammer, Gregory Benson *anesthesiologist, pediatrician, educator*
Hanawalt, Philip Courtland *biology professor, researcher*
Hanrahan, Patrick M. *computer scientist*
Hansen, Peter Reinhard *economics professor*
Hanson, Victor Davis *historian, educator, writer*
Harbaugh, Jim (James Joseph Harbaugh) *college football coach, retired professional football player*
Harbaugh, John Warvelle *geologist, educator*
Harbury, Pehr A.B. *biochemist, educator*
Harrison, Robert Pogue *literature educator*
Harrison, Walter Ashley *physicist, researcher*
Hecker, Siegfried Stephen *metallurgist*
Henderson, Victor Warren *behavioral and geriatric neurologist, epidemiologist, researcher, educator*
Hennessy, John L. *academic administrator*
Henriksen, Thomas Hollinger *researcher*
Hesselink, Lambertus *electrical engineering and physics educator*
Hickman, Bert George, Jr. *economist, educator*
Hillard, Paula J. Adams *gynecologist, educator*
Hlatky, Mark Andrew *cardiologist, researcher*
Holloway, Charles Arthur *public and private management educator*
Horowitz, Mark A. *electrical engineering and computer science educator*
Horwitz, Ralph Irving *internist, epidemiologist, educator, former dean*
Hossein-Babaei, Faraz *research scientist*
Hoxby, Caroline Minter *economics professor*
Huang, Kerwyn Casey *engineering educator*
Hunt, Sharon Ann *cardiologist*
Iglehart, Donald Lee *engineering educator*
Inkeles, Alex *sociology educator*
Jackson, Matthew O. *economics professor*
Jardetzky, Oleg *retired medical educator, researcher*
Jeong, Min-Wook *electrical engineer*
Joffe, Josef *editor, columnist*
Joss, Robert L. *dean, business educator*
Kailath, Thomas *electrical engineer, educator*
Kamil, Michael *education educator*
Karlan, Pamela Susan *law educator*
Katznelson, Laurence *medical educator, researcher*
Kays, William Morrow *academic administrator, mechanical engineer*
Keller, Joseph Bishop *mathematician, educator*

Keller, Michael Alan *librarian, musicologist*
Kelman, Mark Gregory *law educator*
Kennedy, David Michael *historian, educator*
Kennedy, Donald *environmental scientist, educator, editor*
Keren, Kinneret *biophysicist*
Khosla, Chaitan S. *chemical engineer*
Kim, Na Young *physicist*
Kino, Gordon Stanley *electrical engineering educator*
Klausner, Michael David *law educator*
Klemperer, Simon Louis *geophysicist, educator*
Knuth, Donald Ervin *computer sciences educator*
Koller, Daphne *computer scientist*
Kornberg, Roger David *biochemist, structural biologist*
Kramer, Larry *dean, lawyer, educator*
Krasner, Stephen David *political science educator, former federal agency administrator*
Krensky, Alan Michael *pediatrician, educator*
Kruger, Paul *nuclear civil engineering educator*
Krumboltz, John Dwight *psychologist, educator*
Kurz, Mordecai *economics professor*
Lai, Tze Leung *mathematician, educator*
Lambers, James Vincent *mathematician, researcher, petroleum engineer*
Laughlin, Robert B. *academic administrator, physics professor*
Lazear, Edward Paul *economics professor*
Lehman, I(srael) Robert *biochemist, educator*
Lemley, Mark Alan *law educator*
Lessig, L. Lawrence III *law educator, writer*
Levin, Jonathan *economics professor*
Levy, Ronald *medical educator, researcher*
Lewis, John Wilson *political science professor*
Liang, Chunlei *mechanical engineer, researcher*
Linehan, John H. *engineering educator, biomedical engineer*
Little, William Arthur *physicist, researcher*
Liu, Tai-Ping *mathematics professor*
Loftis, John (Clyde), Jr. *language educator*
Long, Sharon Rugel *molecular biologist, educator*
Longaker, Michael T. *plastic surgeon, educator*
Lorenz, Hermann Peter *plastic surgeon*
Ludwig, Francis Leonidas *retired engineering educator*
Lyman, Richard Wall *foundation and academic administrator, historian*
Macovski, Albert *electrical engineer, educator*
Mansour, Tag Eldin *pharmacologist, educator*
Mark, James B. D. *surgeon, educator*
Marmor, Michael Franklin *ophthalmologist, educator*
Martin, Joanne *social sciences educator*
Martin, Richard Peter *classics educator, consultant*
McAdam, Douglas John *sociologist, educator, director*
McCarthy, John *computer scientist, educator*
McCarty, Perry Lee *civil and environmental engineering educator*
McClelland, James Lloyd *psychologist, educator, cognitive neuroscientist*
McDonald, John Gregory *financial investment educator*
McKinnon, Ronald Ian *retired economics professor*
Mc Lure, Charles E., Jr. *economist, consultant*
Mc Namara, Joseph Donald *researcher, retired protective services official*
McQuillen, Michael Paul *neurologist, educator*
Meng, Teresa H. *electrical engineer, educator*
Mignot, Emmanuel *medical researcher*
Milgram, R. James *mathematics professor*
Milgrom, Paul Robert *economics educator*
Miller, D. Craig *cardiovascular surgeon*
Miller, William Frederick *research and development company executive, educator, financial consultant*
Moerner, William Esco *physical chemist, educator*
Momeni, Arash *plastic surgeon*
Montgomery, David Bruce *marketing educator*
Moore, Tirin *neuroscientist, educator*
Morton, John M. *surgeon, consultant*
Negrin, Robert S *medical educator*
Nelson, W. James *biology professor, researcher*
Noll, Roger Gordon *economist, educator*
Oberhelman, Harry Alvin, Jr. *surgeon, educator*
Osheroff, Douglas Dean *physics professor, researcher*
Ott, Wayne Robert *environmental engineer*
Parkinson, Bradford Wells *astronautical engineer, educator*
Parsonnet, Julie *medical educator*
Paté-Cornell, Marie-Elisabeth Lucienne *engineering educator*
Perreau Guimaraes, Marcos *medical researcher*
Perry, William James *engineering educator, former United States Secretary of Defense*
Petersilia, Joan *law educator, criminologist*
Petrosian, Vahé *astrophysicist, educator*
Pfeffer, Jeffrey *business educator*
Plummer, James D. *electrical engineering educator, dean*
Prasad, Manika *geophysicist, researcher*
Quake, Stephen R. *physics professor, researcher*
Raisian, John *think-tank executive, economist*
Ramsaur, Michael F. *lighting designer*
Reddy, Vadiyala Mohan *cardiothoracic surgeon*
Reitz, Bruce Arnold *cardiac surgeon, educator*
Rhode, Deborah Lynn *law educator*
Rice, Condoleezza *political science professor, former United States Secretary of State*
Riggs, Henry Earle *academic administrator, engineering educator*
Robbins, Robert Clayton *surgeon*
Robert, Herfkens John *medical educator*
Roberts, Donald John *economics, business professor, consultant*
Robinson, Paul Arnold *historian, educator, writer*
Romer, Paul Michael *economics professor*
Rosenberg, Saul Allen *oncologist, educator*
Ross, John *physical chemist, educator*
Rossing, Thomas D. *physics professor*
Rothwell, Geoffrey Scott *economics educator*
Rubenstein, Edward *physician, educator*
Rumsfeld, Donald Henry *former United States Secretary of Defense*
Sag, Ivan A. *linguist, educator*
Sagan, Scott *political science professor*
Saha, Mitul *engineer*
Salehi, Ahmad *research scientist*
Salti, Ramzi *literature and language professor*
Schatzberg, Alan Frederic *psychiatrist, researcher*
Scott, Kenneth Eugene *lawyer, educator*
Scott, Matthew Peter *biology educator*
Seelig, Tina L. *entrepeneurship program director, educator*
Selfridge-Field, Eleanor *educator*
Shapiro, Lucy *molecular biology educator*
Shaqfeh, Eric Stefan G. *engineering educator*
Shatz, Carla J. *biology professor, researcher*
Sheehan, James John *historian, educator*
Shenker, Stephen *physics professor*
Shooter, Eric Manvers *retired neurobiology professor, consultant*
Shortliffe, Linda Marie Dairiki *urology educator, researcher*
Shulman, Lee S. *former educational association administrator*
Shultz, George Pratt *economics professor, former United States Secretary of State*
Siekierski, Maciej M. *curator*
Silbergleit, Alexander *physicist, mathematician*
Skirboll, Stephen Lance *neurosurgeon*
Skogstad, Philipp Leo *engineering company executive, director*
So, Samuel Kai Sum *surgeon, researcher*
Sofaer, Abraham David *lawyer, former federal judge, educator, consultant*
Sokol, Eric Russell *urogynecologist, reconstructive surgeon, educator*
Solomon, Edward Ira *chemistry professor, researcher*
Spence, Andrew Michael *former dean, finance educator*
Springer, George Stephen *mechanical engineering educator*
Stamey, Thomas Alexander *urologist, educator*
Stansky, Peter David Lyman *historian, writer, retired professor*
Steele, Charles Richard *biomedical and mechanical engineering educator*
Steele, Shelby *writer, educator*
Steinberg, Gary K. *neurosurgeon, educator*
Stone, William Edward *academic administrator, consultant*
Street, Robert Lynnwood *civil, mechanical and environmental engineer*
Strober, Myra Hoffenberg *education educator, consultant*
Sturrock, Peter Andrew *space science and astrophysics educator*
Suppes, Christine Johnson *publishing executive*
Susskind, Leonard *physicist, educator*
Sweeney, James Lee *engineering educator*
Tam, See-Ying Sebastian *biomedical researcher, consultant, entrepreneur*
Taylor, John Brian *economist, educator*
Theriot, Julie *microbiologist, medical educator*
Thompson, George Albert *geophysicist, educator*
Tiller, William Arthur *retired science educator, scientific researcher*
Tomlin, Claire J. *aeronautical engineer, educator*
Traugott, Elizabeth Closs *linguist, educator, researcher*
Trost, Barry Martin *chemist, educator*
Ullman, Jeffrey David *computer scientist, educator*
Valantine, Hannah A. *cardiologist, educator*
van Benthem, Johan Franciscus Abraham Karel *philosophy, mathematics and computer science educator*
VanDerveer, Tara *women's college basketball coach*
Van Horne, James Carter *economist, educator*
Vincenti, Walter Guido *aeronautical engineer, emeritus educator*
Wagoner, Robert Vernon *astrophysicist, educator*
Walt, Martin *physicist, educator*
Wen, Xian-Huan *hydrogeologist*
White, Robert Lee *electrical engineer, educator*
Whitney, Rodger Franklin *academic administrator*
Whyte, Richard Ian *surgeon*
Wojcicki, Stanley George *physicist, researcher*
Wolff, Tobias (Tobias Jonathan Ansell Wolff) *writer, English professor*
Yanofsky, Charles *retired biology professor*
Yao, Yuan *mathematician, researcher*
Yuen, Richard Joseph *university dean*
Zare, Richard Neil *chemistry professor*
Zarins, Christopher Kristaps *surgeon, educator*
Zhou, Ping *physical engineer*
Zimbardo, Philip George *psychologist, educator, writer*

Stevenson Ranch

Krainin, Julian Arthur *film director, producer, cinematographer, writer*
Wick, Mitchell A. *physician*

Stinson Beach

Metz, Mary Seawell *retired foundation and academic administrator*

Stockton

Acoba, Valerie Lee *performing arts educator*
Blaire, Stephen Edward *bishop*
Blodgett, Elsie Grace *elementary school educator, small business owner, property manager*
Camacho, Manuel *language educator*
Cobb, Judy Lynn *elementary school educator*
DeRicco, Lawrence Albert *retired college president*
DeRosa, Donald V. *academic administrator*
Ford, Shirley Griffin *science educator, pharmacist*
Ford, William Herschel *science educator*
Freeman, Nina Rebecca *psychologist*
Gertler, Fred *librarian, dean*
Gilbertson, Philip *academic administrator*
Guo, Xin *medical educator, researcher*
Hackley, Carol Ann *public relations educator, consultant*
Hawbaker, A. Craig *librarian*
Herrin, William E. *economics professor*
Johnston, Ann *Mayor, Stockton, California*
Knudsen, Robert L. *physiologist, educator*
Knudsen, Sondra Lynna *psychology professor*
Krise, Thomas Warren *academic administrator, literature and language professor, retired military officer*
Limbaugh, Ronald Hadley *retired historian, cultural organization administrator*
Matuszak, Alice Jean Boyer *pharmacy educator*
Michailoff, Ian Robert *real estate broker, land use planner*
Murphy, Jeremiah T. *professional sports team, construction executive*
Nagai, Nelson Kei *economics professor, history professor*
Parish, William Henry *lawyer*
Plovnick, Mark Stephen *business educator*
Post, Gerald V. *business educator*
Ren, Jianhua *education educator*
Samoshin, Vyacheslav Vladimirovich *chemistry professor, science educator, researcher*
Singleton, Marvin Ayers *state legislator, otolaryngologist*
Sorby, Donald Lloyd *retired dean*
Stoner, Harry David-Foxe *science educator*
Taylor, Francis Michael *auditor, municipal official*
Trager, Lorinda Adele *finance educator, legal association administrator*
Whiteker, Roy Archie *retired chemistry professor*
Whittington, Robert Bruce *retired publishing company executive*
Wilcox, Helena Marguerita (Helena Rita Wilcox) *music educator*
Wong, Patricia M.Y. *library director*
Yamashita, Kenneth Akira *library administrator, librarian*

Studio City

Barrett, Dorothy *performing company executive*
Boyett, Joan Reynolds *performing company executive*
Childs, Erin Therese *psychotherapist*
Delnik, Alexander *engineering executive, consultant*
Esposito, Jennifer *actress*
Gold, Arnold Henry *judge*
Hight, Jeremy James *artist, writer*
Hudson, Jennifer *singer, actress*
Kenney, H. Wesley, Jr., (Harry Wesley Kenney Jr.) *television producer and director*
King, Carole (Carole Klein) *lyricist, singer*
Laba, Marvin *management consultant*
La Cava, Donald Leon *communications executive*
Lasarow, Marilyn Doris *artist, educator*
Leonard, Herman *photographer*
Meenan, Alan John *clergyman, theology studies educator*
Parish, James Robert *writer, cinema historian*
Silverman, Bruce Gary *advertising executive, consultant*
Smart, Jean *actress*
Weiner, Sandra Samuel *critical care nurse, consultant*

Summerland

Cannon, Louis Simeon *journalist, writer*

Sun City

Schmoll, Edith Margaret *music educator*

Sun Valley

Cinnamon, William III *elementary and special education educator*
Mayhue, Richard Lee *dean, minister, writer*
Miller, Flemon Marshall *public works manager*

Sunnyvale

Baldwin, Penny *Internet company executive, marketing professional*
Balogh, Aristotle N. *information technology executive*
Banerjee, Sourav *mechanical engineer, researcher*
Bartz, Carol Ann *Internet company executive*
Bradford, Joanne K. *Internet company executive*
Brozek, Tomasz *research scientist*
Butterfield, Stewart *Internet company executive*
Callahan, Michael John *lawyer*
Chang, William Zhi-Ming *research scientist*
Cheng, Jun *chemist*
Claflin, Bruce L. *software company executive*
Das, Sandipan Kumar *research scientist*
Doluca, Tunc *electronics executive*
Ensminger, Dale *retired mechanical and electrical engineer*
Fake, Caterina *Internet company executive*
Filo, David *Internet company executive*
Flaherty, Lauren Patricia *marketing executive*
Goo, Jung-Suk *semiconductor company research engineer*
Guan, Xiang *electrical engineer*
Hawkins, Jeff *information technology company executive*
Johnson, Kevin *information technology executive, former computer software company executive*
Kispert, John H. *information technology executive*
Kraft, Reiner *information technology manager*
Kriens, Scott Gregory *information technology executive*
Lanaro, Clara Marrama *music educator, writer*
Leong, Chia Ken *mechanical engineer*
McCoy, Thomas M. *information technology executive*
McReynolds, Stephen Paul *lawyer*
Mehta, Swati *electrical engineer, researcher*
Meyer, Dirk (Derrick R. Meyer) *information technology executive*
Morse, Timothy R. *Internet company executive*
Nerurkar, Shailesh B. *research scientist*
Oei, Lok S. *digital communications systems and DSP engineer, researcher*
Orr, Dominic P. *information technology company executive*
Petersen, Kurt Edward *electrical engineer, researcher, entrepreneur*
Ratchev, Boris A. *high technology executive*
Rivet, Robert J. *semiconductor company executive*
Rubin, Gary Andrew *entrepreneur, computer engineer*
Rubinstein, Jonathan J. *communications executive, former computer company executive*
Ruiz, Hector de Jesus *information technology executive*
Rusch, Thomas William *manufacturing executive*
Sartain, Libby *Internet company executive*
Schneider, Hilary A. *Internet company executive*
Schwartz, Eleanore Anita *retired elementary school educator, small business owner*
Shanbhag, Abhijit G. *semiconductor company executive*
Steele, Elisa Anne *Internet company executive, marketing professional*
Sundberg, Carl-Erik Wilhelm *telecommunications executive, researcher*
Vig, John *electronics engineer, consultant*
Wehde, Albert Edward *lawyer*
Weinberg, William Henry *chemical engineer, physicist, educator*
Xie, Liang *application developer*
Zhang, Chi *engineer*

Sunol

Rebello, Marlene Munson *speech pathologist, consultant*

Sunset Beach

Pridham, Thomas Grenville *retired microbiologist*

Susanville

Brown, Rosanna Maria Nelson *library director*

Sutter Creek

Sanders, Elizabeth Anne Weaver (Betsy Sanders) *management consultant, coach, writer*

Sylmar

Foster, Dudley Edwards, Jr. *musician, educator*
Froelich, Beverly Lorraine *foundation administrator*
Kamangar, Nader *physician, pulmonologist, director, researcher, educator*
Koretz, Ronald Lee *medical educator*
Pursley, Mark R. *philosopher, educator*
Tutor, Ronald N. *construction executive*
Wong, Andrew L. *rheumatologist, educator*

Tarzana

Hansen, Robert Clinton *electrical engineer, consultant*
Jones, Dean Carroll *actor*
Lantz, Kenneth Eugene *consulting firm executive*
Lauter, James Donald *retired stockbroker*
Lindley, Charles Alexander *aerospace engineer, consultant*
Richman, Peter Mark *actor, painter, writer, film producer*
Smith, Mark Lee *architect*
Zeitlin, Herbert Zakary *college administrator, educational consultant, writer*

Tehachapi

Mitchell, Betty Jo *publishing executive, writer*
Smith-Thompson, Patricia Ann *public relations consultant, educator*
Sprinkle, Martha Clare *elementary school educator*

Temecula

Chung, Hee M. *retired nuclear scientist*
Keenan, Retha Ellen Vornholt *retired nursing educator*

Templeton

Abernathy, Shields B. *allergist, immunologist, internist*
Girolo, Nella Sue *retired voice educator*

The Sea Ranch

Baas, Jacquelynn *museum director, art historian*
Carter, Richard Duane *management educator*
Hayflick, Leonard *cell biologist, biogerontologist, microbiologist, educator, writer*

Thousand Oaks

Babaeizadeh, Saeed *research scientist*
Baek, Kwang-Hyun *research scientist*
Birren, James Emmett *research and development company executive*
Bonanni, Fabrizio *medical products executive*
Bradway, Robert *medical products executive*
Brogden, Stephen Richard *library director*
Dussault, Isabelle *medical researcher*
Eisenberg, Paul Richard *cardiologist, consultant, educator*
El Fattah, Yousri M. *computer scientist*
Farshidi, Ardeshir B. *cardiologist, educator*
Flanagan, Thomas James *medical products executive*
Fulton, Michael L. *optical company executive, researcher*
Gentile, Joseph F. *lawyer, educator*
Green, David Brian *chemistry educator*
Gregory, Calvin *real estate investor*
Hudson, Barbara *writer, actor*
Kroeger, Chad *musician*
Kroeger, Mike *musician*
Kuelbs, John Thomas *lawyer*
Lieberman, Judith L. *retired special education educator*
Loren, Sophia *actress*
McNamee, Brian *medical products executive*
Miller, Elizabeth Joan *artist, guidance counselor*
Morrow, George J. *medical products executive*
Newman, Paul Richard *physicist*
Peake, Ryan *musician*
Perlmutter, Roger *medical products executive*
Pincus, Howard J. *geologist, engineer, educator*
Remmele, Richard L., Jr. *research scientist, director*
Rooney, Mickey (Joe Yule Jr.) *actor*
Savarin, Cecile Geraldine *science administrator*
Scott, David J. *lawyer, medical products executive*
Sharer, Kevin W. *medical products executive*
Solomon, David Harris *geriatrician, educator*
Wolff, Stuart *online real estate executive*
Zhang, Zhongqi *chemist*

Tiburon

Stotter, Ruth *retired college program director*
Tobin, James Michael *lawyer*

Widman, Gary Lee *lawyer*

Toluca Lake
Costner, Kevin *actor*
Merchant, Roland Samuel, Sr. *retired health facility administrator, educator*
Nunez, Oscar *actor*
Ragan, Ann Talmadge *media and production consultant, actor*

Tomales
Oman, Doug *healthcare educator*

Topanga
Curedale, Robert A. *industrial designer*
Waldron, Jill Genevieve *retired language educator*

Torrance
Anderson, Marilyn Wheeler *English language educator*
Bae, Bonho *electrical engineer*
Brass, Eric Paul *internal medicine and pharmacology educator, academic administrator*
Bryan, Sharon Ann *lawyer*
Budoff, Matthew Jay *cardiologist*
Carlson, Terrance L. *lawyer, aerospace transportation executive*
Cummings, Anne *language educator*
Daar, Eric Steven *medical educator*
Dauphine, Christine E. *surgeon*
Emmanouilides, George Christos *physician, educator*
Enright, Stephanie Veselich *investment company executive, financial consultant*
Grigsby, Alice Burns *librarian*
Grzesik, Jan Alexander *electronics engineer, mathematician*
Hahn, Elliott Julius *lawyer*
Hammer, Terence Michael *physician*
Hansen, James Edward *medical educator, researcher*
Ibe, Basil Obijiaku *biochemist, educator*
Isenberg, Sherwin Jay *pediatric ophthalmologist*
Ismail, Alexandre *diversified technology and manufacturing company executive*
Kalantar-Zadeh, Kamyar *pediatrician, nephrologist*
Kim, Keehoon *cybernetic scientist*
Kopple, Joel D. *medical educator, researcher*
Kuc, Joseph A. *research scientist*
Lentz, James E. III *automotive executive*
Lieberman, Robert Arthur *physicist*
Marston, Douglas Robert *engineering educator*
Mason-Lipton, Holli Marie *pathologist, educator*
Mendel, John W. *automotive executive*
Moore, Christopher M. *lawyer*
Nachef, Joanna Medawar *performing company executive*
Omari, Bassam O. *cardiothoracic surgeon*
Petillon, Lee Ritchey *lawyer*
Rajfer, Jacob *urologist, educator*
Rogers, Howard H. *retired chemist*
Romanov, Volodymyr Alexeevich *computer science educator, researcher, computer science educator, researcher*
Scarlata, Ronald Alan *theater educator, director*
Stabile, Bruce Edward *surgeon*
Sugra, Cynthia Mariel *marketing executive*
Swerdloff, Ronald S. *physician, educator, researcher*
Tanaka, Kouichi Robert *hematologist, educator*
White, Rodney *surgeon*
Wise, Joyce Kathryn *nursing educator*
Zartman, Charleen Therese *physical education educator*

Tracy
Kiggins, Mildred L. *marketing professional*

Truckee
Todd, Linda Marie *nutrition researcher, circulation facilitator, financial consultant, pilot*

Tujunga
Ancu, Edward Florin *veterinarian*
Corea, Chick (Armando Corea) *pianist, composer*
Loehwing, Lord Rudi Charles *film producer, director, publicist, radio broadcasting executive, journalist*

Tulare
Hefflefinger, Clarice Thorpe *real estate broker*

Turlock
AbuKhalil, Asad *political science professor*
Ahlem, Lloyd Harold *psychologist*
Burns, James Wesley *academic administrator, researcher, consultant*
Lee, Virginia Fern *community volunteer*
Parker, John Carlyle *retired librarian and archivist, editor*
Regalado, Samuel *history professor*
Shirvani, Sir Hamid *architect, educator, philosopher, writer, university president*
Werling, Robert Lewis *law educator*

Tustin
Cruzen, Matt Earl *research biochemist*
Herdeg, Howard Brian *retired physician*
Hester, Norman Eric *chemical company technical executive, chemist*
Madory, Richard Eugene *lawyer*
Neutel, Joel *medical educator, director*
Schilling, Frederick Augustus, Jr. *geologist, consultant*
Zahrowski, James J. *orthodontist*

Twain Harte
Kinsinger, Robert Earl *property company executive, educational consultant*

Twentynine Palms
Clemente, Patrocinio Ablola *secondary school educator*
Panter, Nicole Olivieri *film educator, writer, film critic*

Ukiah
McClintock, Richard Polson *dermatologist*

Newell, Barbara Ann *coatings company executive*

Union City
Mo, Jianwei *research scientist*
Muñoz, Eduardo Rafael *elementary school educator*

Universal City
Baker, Bridget *broadcast executive*
Bromstad, Angela *broadcast executive*
Chavira, Ricardo Antonio *actor*
Cross, Marcia *actress*
Golper, John Bruce *lawyer*
Graboff, Marc J. *broadcast executive*
Huffman, Felicity (Flicka Huffman) *actress*
Kay, Christopher K. *travel company executive, lawyer*
Langley, Donna *film company executive*
Linde, David *film company executive*
Longoria, Eva (Eva Longoria Christopher, Eva Longoria Parker) *actress*
Madison, Paula *broadcast executive*
Menendez, Belinda *broadcast executive*
Merkerson, S. Epatha *actress*
Meyer, Ron *film company executive*
O'Brien, Conan *talk show host, writer, performer*
Quinto, Zachary John *actor*
Reitman, Ivan *film director, producer*
Rocco, Nikki *film company executive*
Sheridan, Nicollette *actress*
Silberling, Bradley Mitchell *film director*
Spielberg, Steven Allan *film director, producer*
Wolf, Dick (Richard A. Wolf) *television producer*
Zigler, Vivi *broadcast executive, marketing professional*

Upland
Cullen, Robert John *financial planner, investment advisor*
Jordan, Charles Wesley *retired bishop*

Valencia
Blake, Laurence *dean, educator*
Faris, Mary *medical researcher, director*
Ferry, Frank *mayor, Santa Clarita, California, principal*
Kersels, Martin *conceptual artist*
Smith, Ishmael Wadada Leo (Wadada Leo Smith) *musician, composer*

Vallejo
Brown, Earl Kent *historian, minister*
Davis, William Albert *parks director*
Foushee-Higgs, Rosa *elementary school educator, artist*
Paine-Clemes, Bunny Lee *humanities educator*
Toms, Kathleen Moore *nurse*
Towne, Sarah Patton *physician*
Wilson, Carrie Lee Stroud *principal*

Valley Ford
Mulkern-Kolosey, Sandy Kathleen *college counselor, educator, realtor*

Valley Springs
Anema-Garten, Durlynn C. *communications educator, counseling administrator, writer*

Valley Village
Barkin, Elaine Radoff *composer*
Davis, Edmond Ray *lawyer*
Diller, Phyllis (Phyllis Ada Driver Diller) *actress, writer*

Van Nuys
Arabian, Armand *arbitrator, mediator, lawyer*
Becker, Frawley *writer, dialogue director, location manager*
Crawford, Marvin Leonard, Sr. *retired school system administrator*
Dea, Fay Suey *counselor, educator*
Graham, Roger John *photography and journalism professor*
Nakamura, Lawrence T. *microbiologist, educator*
Zucker, Alfred John *English and history educator, academic administrator, historian*

Venice
Alf, Martha Joanne *artist*
Beery-Polglase, Penelope (Pixie) *education educator*
Eliot, Alexander *writer*
Eversley, Frederick John *sculptor, engineer*
Johnson, Cheryl *small business owner*
Museth, Ken *application developer, educator*
Padilla, Mario René *literature educator, writer*

Ventura
Abul-Haj, Suleiman Kahil *pathologist*
Armstrong, Dianne Owens *retired language educator*
Barber, Jerry Randel *retired medical device company executive*
Bierly, Shirley Adelaide *communications executive*
Bowles, Walter Donald *economist, educator*
Gaynor, Joseph *chemical engineer, management consultant*
Koch, Gerd Hermann *artist, educator*
Naurath, David Allison *engineering psychologist, researcher*
Sanchez, Tomas David *history professor*
Stauffer, Jeffery Dean *education educator*
Villaveces, James Walter *allergist, immunologist, consultant*

Victorville
Augustine-Carreira, Jacqueline *communications educator*
Davis-Butros, Tracy L. *history professor*
Kildal, Lori Ann *dean*
Sedeño, Eugene Raymond *electronics engineer, consultant*
Truelove, Terry N. *nursing educator*
Yochem, Barbara June (Runyan) *sales executive, lecturer*

Villa Park
Britton, Thomas Warren, Jr. *retired management consultant*
Hawe, David Lee *manufacturing consultant, venture capitalist*

Visalia
Crowe, John T. *lawyer*
Gray, Kris Diane *nursing consultant, forensic specialist*
Howell, Dave *geographer, educator*
Porterfield-Pyatt, Chaumonde R. *music educator, advocate*
Riegel, Byron William *ophthalmologist*
Sense, Edgar H. *language educator*

Vista
Cavanaugh, Kenneth Clinton *retired real estate consultant*
Ferguson, Margaret Ann *tax specialist, consultant*
Hawk, Tony *professional skateboarder*
Linhart, Letty Lemon *editor*
Olson, Linda Ann Salmonson *minister*
Wright, Kirby Michael *writer, editor*

Walnut
Johnson, Keith Liddell *management consultant, retired chemicals executive*
Kelkar, Vaibhav *chemical engineer*
McKee, Catherine Lynch *lawyer, educator*

Walnut Creek
Brown, William E. *retail executive*
Carson, Jay Wilmer *pathologist, educator*
Cassidy, John Joseph *hydraulic and hydrologic engineer*
Collen, Morris Frank *retired medical administrator, physician, consultant, researcher*
Elliott, Margaret S. *science educator*
Gershony, Gary *cardiologist*
Ginsburg, Gerald J. *lawyer, management consultant*
Grandi, Lois A. *theater director, choreographer, actor*
Hanschen, Peter Walter *lawyer*
Hanson, Robert Duane *engineering educator*
Hassid, Sami *architect, educator*
Henshaw, Guy Runals *management consultant*
Kyrpides, Nikos C. *biologist*
Lilly, Luella Jean *retired academic administrator*
Mackay, Patricia McIntosh *psychotherapist*
Man, Pang Ling *retired psychiatrist*
McCauley, Bruce Gordon *financial consultant*
Merrill, Richard James *retired educational director*
Ogilby, Barry Ray *lawyer*
Ostrander, Willis Frederick *retired real estate appraiser*
Pagter, Carl Richard *lawyer*
Reimann, Arline Lynn *artist*
Saavedra, Charles James *banker*
Seaborg, David Michael *evolutionary biologist*
Stupak, Ronald Joseph *dean, management educator, researcher, author, consultant*
Walston, Roderick Eugene *federal official*
Yu, Wei *economist, researcher*

Watsonville
Brown, Alan Charlton *retired aeronautical engineer*
Dorey, William G. *construction executive*

Weed
Schaefer, M. Elaine *music educator, conductor*

Weimar
Kerschner, Lee R(onald) *academic administrator, political scientist, educator*

West Covina
Cheng, Bridget *agricultural products executive*
Ebiner, Robert Maurice *lawyer*
Galen, Albert John *retired lawyer*
McHale, Edward Robertson *retired lawyer*
Torres, Esteban Edward *former congressman, trade association administrator*

West Hills
Abdo, Lynda Lee *art director*
Cheney, Anna Marie Jangula *retired medical/surgical nurse*
Geeting, Joyce Ann *musician, educator*

West Hollywood
Brace, Frederic F. (Jake Brace) *retired air transportation executive*
Braverman, Alan Michael *Internet company executive*
Cage, Nicolas (Nicolas Coppola) *actor*
Cole, Natalie Maria *singer*
Cyrus, Miley (Destiny Hope Cyrus, Hannah Montana) *actress, singer*
de Rossi, Portia *actress*
Duvall, Robert (Robert Selden Duvall) *actor*
Fein, Irving *television and motion picture executive*
Foster, Jodie (Alicia Christian Foster) *actress, film director, producer*
Franklyn, Audrey Pozen *talent promoter, television personality*
Goodwin, Ginnifer *actress*
Grey, Brad *film company executive*
Harden, Marcia Gay *actress*
Harper, Robert *actor*
Holloway, Josh *actor*
Huntsberry, Frederick D. *film company executive*
Jackson, Randy *music producer, television personality, musician*
Jbara, Gregory *actor*
McDormand, Frances *actress*
Pacquiao, Manny (Emmanuel Dapidran Pacquiao) *boxer*
Pine, Chris Whitelaw *actor*
Powell, Amy Ruth *film company executive*
Presley, Priscilla (Pricilla Ann Wagner, Priscilla Beaulieu Presley) *actress*
Routh, Brandon *actor*
Ryan, Amy *actress*

Sackett, Barnard (Barney) *actor, film producer, director, scriptwriter*
Sacks, David O. *Internet company executive, film production company executive*
Schreiber, Liev (Isaac Liev Schreiber) *actor*
Stein, Ben (Benjamin Jeremy Stein) *television personality, writer, lawyer, economist*
Stipe, Michael *musician, film producer*
Tarantino, Quentin Jerome *film director, scriptwriter*
Thornton, Billy Bob *actor, film producer*
Tomei, Marisa *actress*
Trachtenberg, Michelle *actress*
Washington, Kerry *actor*
Wright Penn, Robin *actress*
Zombie, Rob (Robert Cummings) *musician, filmmaker*

West Los Angeles
Bohn, Paul Bradley *psychiatrist, psychoanalyst*

West Sacramento
Anderson, William Wallace *financial executive*
Glaholt, William Edward *information technology manager*
Hakala, Nila Virginia *primary school educator*
Lehman, Peggy W. *oceanographer*
Liu, Fu-Tong *biomedical researcher, dermatologist*

Westlake Village
Belote, Lewis Rogers III *accountant*
Berkowitz, Steven *Internet company executive*
Borenstein, Lorna M. *information technology executive*
Caligiuri, Joseph Frank *retired engineering executive*
DeLorenzo, David A. *food products executive*
Lereah, David Alan *economist*
Long, W. Michael *Internet company executive*
Munson, John Backus *computer scientist, retired data processing executive*
Pingitore, Regina *psychologist, researcher*
Power, J.D., III, (James David Power III) *marketing executive*
Richardson, Leatrice Joy *artist*
Seymour, Jeffrey Alan *governmental relations consultant*
Smyth, Glen Miller *management consultant*
Strote, Joel Richard *lawyer*
Troxell, Lucy Davis *management consultant*

Westminster
Le, Anh Quang *mathematics professor*
Luong, Khanh Vinh Quoc *nephrologist, researcher*
Mattar, Mary Anne Y. *biology professor*
Pitts-Cutler, Melissa Anne *counselor, social worker*

Westwood
Sull, Wonhee *telecommunications industry executive*

Whittier
Arenowitz, Albert Harold *psychiatrist*
Cruz, Denis J. *elementary school educator*
Ekenel, Mahmut *civil engineer, researcher*
Kirsch, Scott Douglas *family practice physician, director*
McKenna, Jeanette Ann *archaeologist*
Mikalson, Barbara G. *economics professor*
Prewitt, Dezzie Allen *economics professor*
Prickett, David Clinton *physician*
Ross, Ami L. *insurance and finance company executive*
Weismiller, Eleanor Kovacs *library director*

Willits
Handley, Margie Lee *manufacturing executive*

Wilmington
Hands, Eric William *civil and electrical engineer researcher*

Wilton
Abraham, Bondi Corinne *artist*
Harrison, George Harry, III, (Hank Harrison) *publishing executive, author*

Windsor
Bradley, Matthew Joseph *engineering company executive*
Matkin, Judith Conway *product designer*

Winnetka
Roberts, Teri Alane *finance educator, volunteer*

Woodland
Bauer, Cynthia Renae *nurse*
Butler, Patricia *psychiatric and mental health nurse, educator, consultant*
Squires, Richard Felt *research scientist*

Woodland Hills
Berry, Barbara Cochran *education educator, writer*
Berry, Carol Ann *insurance company executive*
Brandewie, Richard Anthony *laser and optics consultant*
Capezza, Joseph C. *health insurance company executive*
Clarey, Patricia T. *health insurance company executive, former state official*
DeSantis, Richard A. *lawyer*
Doi, Roy Hiroshi *retired biochemist, educator*
Dompe, Rudy F. *literature and language professor*
Ennis, Thomas Michael *management consultant*
Feiman, Thomas E. *investment company executive*
Gellert, Jay M. *health and medical products executive*
Goldston, Mark R. *Internet company executive*
Greaves, Roger F. *health and medical products executive*
Jason, Sonya *writer*
Latona, Valerie Ann *editor-in-chief*
Mayhew, Karin D. *health and medical products executive*
McArthur, Steven B. *Internet company executive*
McCluggage, Kerry *film and television executive*
Morishita, Akihiko *trading company executive*

Mroz, Erik Shane *lawyer*
Mund, Geraldine *judge*
O'Connor, Brian D.A. *music educator, French horn musician*
Pettit, John W. *health facility administrator*
Phoenix, David D. *special education educator*
Pregerson, Harry *federal judge*
Ross, Robert K. *foundation administrator, physician*
Scheff, Jonathan H. *health and medical products executive*
Sivori, John P. *health and medical products executive*
Tiano, Linda V. *lawyer, insurance company executive*
Windrum, Ken *communications educator*
Woys, James E. *health and medical products executive*
Zeitlin, Eugenia Pawlik *librarian, educator, writer*

Woodside
Blum, Richard Hosmer Adams *foundation administrator, educator, writer*
Gates, Milo Sedgwick *retired construction company executive*
McCown, George E. *venture banking company executive*
Potter, Myrtle Stephens *healthcare consulting company executive, retired pharmaceutical executive*

Yorba Linda
Esparza, Karen Ann *history educator*
Lunde, Dolores Benitez *retired secondary school educator*
Lynch, Frank Thomas *aeronautical engineer, consultant*
McCune, Brenda L. *lawyer*
Naftali, Timothy J. *library director, historian, educator, writer*
Porcello, Leonard Joseph *engineering research and development executive*
Stavropoulos, Rose Mary Grant *community activist, volunteer*

Yountville
Keller, Thomas A. *chef*

Yreka
Hamilton, John Bruce *biologist*
Smith, Vin *editor, small business owner, writer*

Yuba City
Dhillon, Davinder Pal Singh *pulmonologist*
Kemmerly, Jack Dale *retired state official*
Leverett, Dawn R. *disability education consultant*
Price, Ardythe Bernadeane *registered nurse*
Sheppard, Lisa Marie *psychologist*

Yucaipa
Adams, Matthew Cavanaugh *physics professor*
Crise, Robert D., Jr. *mathematics professor*
Gomez, Louis Salazar *college president*
Lardy, Leonard Anthony *English educator*

COLORADO

Alamosa
Garcia, Castelar Medardo *lawyer*

Arvada
Bert, Carol Lois *retired educational assistant*
Chiou, Cary Tsair *environmental scientist, hydrologist*
Eickhoff, Theodore Carl *infectious disease physician, epidemiologist*
Krohnfeldt, Gretchen Ann *secondary school educator, genealogist*
Laidig, Eldon Lindley *financial planner*
Mullineaux, Donal Ray *geologist*
Powers, Christopher Sheridan *science educator, web site designer*
Schrier, Robert William *physician, educator*
Yamamoto, Kaoru *emeritus psychology professor*

Aspen
Berkeley, Edward *opera company director, music educator*
Hayes, Mary Eshbaugh *editor, writer*
Heyman, Juliane Marion *retired history educator, language educator*
Manosevitz, Martin *psychologist*
Newman, Ruth Gallert *psychologist*
Soldner, Paul Edmund *artist, ceramist, educator*
Zuckerman Jacobson, Heidi *museum director*

Aurora
Altiere, Ralph J. *dean, pharmacy educator*
Arend, William Phelps *medical researcher*
Balasubramaniam, Vivek *pediatrician, educator*
Battaglia, Frederick Camillo *physician*
Biester, Doris J. *hospital administrator*
Bjugstad, Kimberly Beret *neuroscientist, educator*
Connick, Elizabeth *medical educator, researcher*
Cowee, John Widmer *retired university chancellor*
Crawford, E. David *urologist, surgeon, researcher*
Crowley, Thomas James *psychiatry educator*
Degruy, Frank V. III *physician*
Deitrich, Richard Adam *pharmacology educator*
Dooley, J. Gordon *food scientist*
Doze, Maureen Adele (Maureen Adele Mee) *social studies educator*
Eckel, Robert H. *endocrinologist, educator*
Fennessey, Paul Vincent *pediatrics and pharmacology educator, researcher*
Furuta, Glenn Tsuyoshi *physician*
Galinkin, Jeffrey *pediatric anesthesiologist*
Gault, Paul Ryan *air transportation executive*
Golightly, Larry K. *pharmacist, educator*
Grace, William Pershing *petroleum geologist, real estate developer*
Green, Larry Alton *physician, educator*
Grover, Theresa R. *pediatrician, educator*
Haas, Robert Lance *surgeon, consultant*
Hamrick, Eliza Carney *secondary school educator, consultant*
Hughes, Christopher Adam *conductor, educator*
Jenkins, Herman Arthur *otologic educator, otolarynologist*
Johnston, Richard Boles, Jr. *pediatrician, educator, biomedical researcher*
Jones, M. Douglas, Jr. *pediatrician, educator*
Kappy, Michael Steven *pediatrics educator*
Katz, Michael Jeffery *lawyer*
Kingdom, Todd T. *otolaryngologist, educator*
Klaus, Charlotte S. *finance company executive, director*
Koyle, Martin Allan *surgeon, educator*
Krugman, Richard David *pediatrician, academic administrator, educator*
La Rosa, Francisco Guillermo *pathologist, researcher, educator*
Leehey, Maureen A. *neurologist, researcher*
Lindenfeld, JoAnn *physician, educator*
Lochmiller, Kurtis L. *real estate entrepreneur*
Mandell, Mercedes Susan *anesthesiologist, educator*
Mikulich Gilbertson, Susan Kay *science educator*
Morrow, Caroline Donovan *retired social worker*
Nelson, Marvin Ray *retired life insurance company executive*
Nichols, Clyde Richard *minister, consumer products company executive*
Nora, Audrey Hart *physician*
Nuffer, Monika *pharmacist, educator*
O'Donnell, Colin I. *statistician, researcher*
Olson, Allison W. *social studies educator*
Patel, Vikas *orthopedist, educator*
Razzaghi, Hamid *molecular biologist, researcher*
Ridgway, Eli Chester *medical educator*
Ringel, Steven Peter *neurology educator*
Ritchie, Coy Doyle *management consultant*
Rivera, Susan Frances *elementary school educator*
Rosich, Rayner Karl *physicist*
Rothman, Micol Sara *medical educator*
Said, M. Sherif A. *pathologist, consultant*
Schmitt, Barton Douglas *pediatrician, educator*
Seeds, Nicholas Warren *neuroscience educator, researcher*
Serkova, Natalie Julia *medical educator, researcher*
Sheffield, Nancy *city agency administrator*
Shore, James H(enry) *psychiatrist*
Tauer, Ed *Mayor, Aurora, Colorado*
Ton, Paul *investor, educator*
Weedin, James Frank *biology professor, researcher*
Wilson, Shandra Sheppard *urologist*
Younoszai, Adel K. *pediatrician, director*

Basalt
Shipp, Dan Shackelford *lawyer*

Bayfield
Collins, William Leroy *retired telecommunications engineer*
Horton, Frank Elba *academic administrator, geographer, educator*
Korns, Leota Elsie *writer, mountain land developer, insurance broker*

Bellvue
Candelora, Deborah Michael *engineer, sculptor*

Beulah
Anderson, Ronald Delaine *education educator*

Black Hawk
Rodgers, Frederic Barker *judge*

Boulder
Amadei, Bernard Paul *civil engineer, not-for-profit developer, educator*
Andrews, John T. *geophysicist, educator*
Banerjee, Arghya *aerospace engineer, researcher*
Barbosa, Francisco Javier *history professor*
Barnes, Frank Stephenson *electrical engineer, educator*
Barry, Roger Graham *climatologist, educator*
Beale, Paul Drew *physics professor*
Beer, Francis Anthony *political science professor emeritus*
Beylkin, Gregory *mathematician*
Bintliff, Barbara Ann *library director, law educator*
Bock, S. Allan *physician, educator*
Bolomey, Roger Henry *sculptor*
Borko, Hilda *education educator*
Bourne, Lyle Eugene, Jr. *psychology professor*
Bowman, Deborah Lynn *psychologist, educator*
Brand, Charles Macy *history professor*
Burns, Daniel Hobart *management consultant*
Byerly, Radford, Jr. *science administrator*
Cai, Huaqing *meteorologist*
Carlson, Lawrence Evan *mechanical engineering educator*
Carrigan, Jim R. *arbitrator, mediator, retired judge*
Cech, Thomas Robert *chemistry professor, former medical association administrator*
Chappell, Charles Franklin *meteorologist, consultant*
Charteris, Frances I.A. *art educator, artist*
Chu, Xinzhao *science educator, researcher*
Clark, Melvin Eugene *chemical company executive*
Coel, Margaret Speas *writer*
Coffey, Michael Thomas *physicist*
Collins, Jim *management researcher, author*
Colwell, James Lee *humanities educator*
Conti, Peter Selby *astronomy educator*
Cooper, Owen Roger *atmospheric scientist*
Cornell, Eric Allin *physics professor*
Corotis, Ross Barry *civil engineer, educator, academic administrator*
Cowell, James Andrew *language educator*
Cumalat, John *physics professor*
Datta, Subhendu K. *mechanical engineer, educator*
Deaktor, Darryl Barnett *lawyer*
DePuy, Charles Herbert *chemist, educator*
Diaz, Henry F. *retired meteorologist*
Diky, Vladimir *chemist, researcher*
DiStefano, Philip P. *academic administrator*
Dryer, Murray *physicist, educator*
Dudhia, Jimy *atmospheric scientist*
Dye, James Eugene *retired research scientist*
Eriksson, Stefan *space scientist*
Fenster, Herbert Lawrence *lawyer*
Fifkova, Eva *behavioral neuroscience educator*
Fiflis, Ted James *lawyer, educator*
Fink, Robert Russell *music educator and theorist, retired dean*
Fleming, Rex James *meteorologist*
Flowers, William Harold, Jr. *lawyer*
Garstang, Roy Henry *astrophysicist, educator*
Getches, David Harding *lawyer, educator, dean*
Gleeson, Todd Timothy *dean, biology professor*
Glover, Fred William *information scientist, director, educator*
Goeldner, Charles Raymond *retired business educator*
Golden, Joseph Hilary *meteorologist*
Gosling, John Thomas *space plasma physicist, researcher*
Greenawald, Glenn Dale *social studies trainer, curriculum developer, researcher*
Greenberg, Edward Seymour *political science professor*
Guild, Nancy Ann *biology professor*
Gupta, Vijay K. *hydrologist, educator*
Hall, Joan Lord *literature and language educator*
Hall, John Lewis *physicist, researcher*
Hanna, William Johnson *electrical engineering educator*
Harvey, Lewis O., Jr. *psychology professor, department chairman*
Hauser, Ray Louis *engineer, researcher, entrepreneur*
Hayes, Deborah *musicology educator, college administrator*
Hayes, Richard Johnson *association executive, retired lawyer*
Healy, Alice Fenvessy *psychology professor, researcher*
Hermann, Allen Max *physics professor*
Herring, Jackson Rea *physicist*
Hess, John Warren *professional society administrator*
Hill, David Allan *electrical engineer*
Hill, Mary C. *hydrologist*
Hofmann, David John *atmospheric science researcher, educator*
Holdsworth, Janet Nott *women's health nurse*
Hoover, Stewart Mark *religious studies educator*
Hunt, Alan James *biophysicist*
Hynes, James Thomas *chemist, educator*
Iatridis, Asimakis D. *lawyer, educator*
Jenkins, Christopher J. *research scientist*
Jessor, Richard *psychologist, educator, director*
Jin, Deborah *physicist, educator*
Jin, Xiaoying *software technical lead, electrical and computer engineer, researcher*
Johnson, Maryanna Morse *business owner*
Joy, Edward Bennett *electrical engineer, educator, consultant*
Kato, Shuji *chemist, researcher*
Kaye, Evelyn Patricia (Evelyn Patricia Sarson) *author, publisher, travel expert*
Keister, Jay Davis *musicologist, educator*
Kelso, Alec John (Jack Kelso) *anthropologist, educator*
Kenney, Belinda Jill Forseman *information technology executive*
Killeen, Timothy Laurence *aerospace scientist, science administrator*
Kim, Sudook A. *materials engineer, researcher*
Kim, Tae-Hyung *engineering educator*
Kintsch, Walter *retired psychology professor*
Knoelker, Michael T.F. *science observatory director*
Krarti, Moncef *engineer*
Lamping, Jennifer *economics professor*
Langer, Steven *human resources specialist, consultant, psychologist*
Leland, Harry Valentine *retired biologist*
LeMasurier, Wesley Ernest *geology educator, researcher*
Limerick, Patricia Nelson *history professor*
Low, Boon Chye *physicist*
Lu, Chungu *meteorologist, researcher, educator*
Mahanthappa, Kalyana Thipperudraiah *physicist, researcher*
Maley, Samuel Wayne *electrical engineering educator*
Matrosov, Sergey *senior research scientist*
McFarland, Robert Bruce *physician*
Mehalchin, John Joseph *entrepreneur, finance company executive*
Meier, Beverly Joyce Loeffler *science educator, consultant*
Meier, Mark Frederick *research scientist, educator, artist, small business owner*
Melicher, Ronald William *finance educator*
Minger, Terrell John *public administration and natural resource institute executive*
Mooney, William Piatt *actor*
Moses, Raphael Jacob *lawyer*
Motte, Warren F., Jr. *literature and language professor*
Mycielski, Jan *retired mathematics professor*
Nehls, Richard Charles *lawyer*
Nesbitt, David John *physics and chemistry professor*
Norris, David Otto *educator*
O'Brien, Elmer John *librarian, educator*
Pace, Norman R. *science educator, microbiologist*
Paulson, Archie Miller *geophysicist, educator*
Peters, Max Stone *chemical engineer, educator*
Peterson, Courtland Harry *law educator*
Phelps, Arthur Van Rensselaer *physicist, consultant*
Podhajsky, Ronald J. *biomedical engineer, researcher*
Porzak, Glenn E. *lawyer*
Princeton, Joy Carol *retired nursing educator*
Purvis, John Anderson *lawyer, educator*
Reitsema, Harold James *aerospace engineer*
Roellig, Leonard Oscar *physics professor*
Sable, Barbara Kinsey *retired music educator*
Sanders, Lucinda (Lucy Sanders) *information technology organization executive*
Sani, Robert LeRoy *chemical engineering professor*
Schneider, Vivian I. *psychologist, researcher*
Schulz-Heik, R. Jay *medical researcher*
Sheldon, Sara A. *museum director, writer*
Smith, Ernest Ketcham *electrical engineer*
Smythe, William Rodman *physicist, researcher*
Snow, Theodore Peck *astrophysics educator*
Snyder, Howard Arthur *aerospace engineering educator, consultant*
Sodal, Ingvar Edmund *retired electrical engineer, science administrator*
Song, Won Jay *electrical engineer, educator*
Southwick, Charles Henry *zoologist, educator*
Staehelin, Lucas Andrew *cell biology professor emeritus*
Stanton, William John, Jr. *marketing educator, author*
Steuben, Norton Leslie *lawyer, educator*
Stevens, Glenn H. *lawyer*
Tarpeh-Doe, Linda Diane *retired controller*
Tatarskii, Valerian Il'Ich *physics researcher*
Timmerhaus, Klaus Dieter *chemical engineering professor*
Tolbert, Bert Mills *biochemist, educator*
Toomre, Juri *astrophysicist, educator*
Trenberth, Kevin Edward *atmospheric scientist*
Vacek, Jaroslav *chemist, researcher*
Van Guilder, Gary Preston *medical researcher*
Volkamer, Rainer Martin *physicist, researcher, aerospace scientist*
Walker, Deward Edgar, Jr. *anthropologist, educator*
Washington, Warren Morton *meteorologist*
Wertheimer, Marilyn Lou *librarian, educator*
Widmann, R L. *literature and language professor*
Williams, James Franklin, II, *dean, librarian*
Yarus, Michael *biologist, educator*
Yee, Sienho *law educator*
Yin, Hang *chemistry professor*
Zable, Jack Louis *mechanical engineer, educator*

Breckenridge
Mosher, Joyce Devlin *literature and language professor*

Brighton
Wagner, Samuel Albin Mar *state agency administrator*

Broomfield
Andreiev, Yura (George) *electronics engineer*
Baker, Charles E. *lawyer*
Berte, Lucia Marie *quality management professional, consultant*
Boulos, Paul Fares *civil and environmental engineer*
Bressler, Marcus Nathan *engineer, consultant*
Crowe, James Quell (Jim) *communications executive*
Hayes, John A. *packaging company executive*
Hobbs, John Neil *communications executive*
Hoover, R. David *packaging company executive*
Marr, James Joseph *venture capitalist*
Parker, Bobby Douglas *radio broadcaster, photographer, educator*
Patel, Sunit *telecommunications industry executive*
Seabrook, Raymond J. *corporate financial executive*
Williams, John James, Jr. *architect*
Yount-Baxley, Kathleen Ann *psychologist*

Buena Vista
Scott, Gerald Wesley *retired American diplomat*

Canon City
Cochran, Susan Mills *research librarian*

Carbondale
Cowgill, Ursula Moser *biologist, educator, environmental consultant*

Castle Rock
Albright, Jeffrey R. *pharmaceutical executive*
Cooper, Kathryn Dupuy *musician, educator*
Hendrick, Hal Wilmans *human factors educator*
Wolfer, Dale *retired music educator*

Centennial
Bryan, A(lonzo) J(ay) *retired service club official*
Dineen, Bonnie R. *social studies educator*
Frame, Roger Everett *school psychologist*
Goughnour, Roy Robert *civil engineer, educator, director*
Greenberg, Elinor Miller *director, consultant*
Lessey, Samuel Kenric, Jr. *foundation administrator*
Udevitz, Norman *publishing executive*
Wilks, Dana Lyn *protective services official, writer*

Cherry Hills Village
Conroy, Mary Elizabeth *history professor*
Stapleton, Katharine Hall (Katie Stapleton) *commentator, writer*
Tisdale, Douglas Michael, Sr. *lawyer*
Van Loucks, Mark Louis *venture capitalist, financial planner*

Clark
Mayer, Frank Charles *math/science educator*

Colorado Springs
Abbott, Gina *municipal government executive*
Abeeluck, Akheelesh Kumar *physicist, researcher*
Adams, Bernard Schroder *retired college president*
Adams, Deborah Rowland *lawyer*
Adnet, Jacques Jim Pierre *astronautical and electrical engineer, consultant*
Ansorge, Iona Marie *musician, educator, real estate agent*
Baldvins, Lynn Ann *medical/surgical nurse, army officer*
Ballantyne, Arnold Paul *economist, educator*
Barber, Michael J. *cardiologist, educator*
Barton, Ruth *retired language educator*
Beard, Amanda *Olympic swimmer*
Blake, Esther Jean *retired elementary school educator*
Bowen, Clotilde Marion Dent *retired military officer, psychiatrist*
Brooks, Glenn Ellis *political science professor, educational association administrator*
Brosman, Catharine Savage *retired language educator, poet*
Caruana, Patrick Peter *retired military officer*

Celeste, Richard F. *academic administrator, retired ambassador, Former Governor, Ohio*
Chandler Mills, Leah *theater educator*
Cheek, Joey *Olympic athlete*
Clay, Bryan Ezra *Olympic track and field athlete*
Cockrille, Stephen *art director, business owner*
Colangelo, Jerry John *professional sports team executive*
Corry, Charles Elmo *geophysicist, not-for-profit developer*
Coughlin, Natalie *Olympic swimmer*
Cramer, Owen Carver *classics educator, department chairman*
Deeny, Raymond M. *lawyer*
Dobson, James Clayton *evangelist, psychologist, author*
Durham, Robert L. *psychology professor*
Evans, Paul Vernon *retired lawyer*
Farrer, Claire Anne Rafferty *anthropologist, educator*
Ferguson, Jackson Robert, Jr. *astronautical engineer*
Fielden, C. Franklin III *early childhood education consultant*
Glenn, Shannon Lea *music educator*
Hanifen, Richard Charles Patrick *bishop emeritus*
Haskins, Thomas Marston III *lawyer*
Heim, Werner G(eorge) *biology educator*
Hilberry, Jane Elizabeth *literature and language professor*
Howard, Larry Bruce *forensic scientist*
Jiang, Hong *language educator*
Johnson, Melody Jacqueline *tax professional*
Killian, George Ernest *retired educational association administrator*
Klipping, Robert Samuel *geophysicist*
Kraemer, Sandy Frederick *lawyer*
Kwan, Michelle Wing *professional figure skater*
Lamborn, Douglas L. *United States Representative from Colorado*
Laubhan, Matt *engineering educator*
Lokken, Steven Lee *chiropractor, internist, nutritionist*
Lomas, Clara A. *educator, researcher*
Madsen, Karen F. *retired elementary school educator*
May-Treanor, Misty *Olympic athlete*
McChesney, Jean Angeline *community health nurse*
McDade, Roberta Clark *secondary school educator*
Miller, Paula J. *library director*
Miller, Zoya Dickins *civic worker, consultant*
Millman, Robert A. *lawyer*
Moore, Donald L. *finance educator*
Morris, Steven Lynn *engineering consultant, retired military officer*
Murphy, Jane Holt *history professor*
Noyes, Richard Hall *bookseller*
Peirsol, Aaron *Olympic swimmer*
Phelps, Michael *Olympic swimmer*
Pickle, Joseph Wesley, Jr. *religious studies educator*
Raintree, Shawn *museum administrator, former insurance company executive*
Renuart, Victor Eugene, Jr., (Gene Renuart) *career military officer*
Rivera, Lionel *Mayor, Colorado Springs, Colorado*
Robran, Conrad John *retired education educator*
Sargent, Walter Harriman, II, *lawyer*
Schmidt, Bob *psychologist*
Schultz, Richard Dale *national athletic organization executive*
Sciorsci, Adam Q. *sales executive*
Scott, Carla Anne *musician, educator*
Scott, Stephen *composer, musician, educator*
Sheridan, Michael John *bishop*
Shockley-Zalabak, Pamela Sue *academic administrator*
Simmons, George Finlay *retired mathematics professor*
Stanley, David John *research and development company executive*
Stansbry, Michael David *set designer, educator*
Steinhoff, Lynnette Kay *special education educator*
Strickland, Sylvia Raye *social worker*
Theobald, Rebecca Bayless *geographer, educator*
Thor, Paul Viets *computer science educator*
Torres, Dara *Olympic athlete*
von Dassanowsky, Robert *literature and film professor, writer, producer*
Walsh, Kerri Lee *Olympic athlete*
Wariner, Jeremy *Olympic track and field athlete*
Watts, Linda K. *language educator*
Watts, Oliver Edward *engineering company executive*
Weslin, Anna Therese *clinical nurse specialist, dance consultant*
Willis, Frank Edward *retired air force officer*
Wynn, Thomas Grant *anthropologist, educator*
Yaney, George *retired history professor*
Yanney, Patrick Steven *human resources specialist*

Columbine Valley

Gagin, Lawrence Vincent *ceramics engineer, consultant*

Conifer

Boese, Michelle Lynne *accountant, consultant*

Cripple Creek

MacKell, Jan *historian, writer*

Delta

Lowell, Lauretta Jane *craftsman, poet*

Denver

Accurso, Frank Joseph *physician, educator*
Ahern, Arleen Fleming *retired librarian*
Alvarado, Linda G. *construction executive*
Amore, Shirley C. *library director*
Anderson, Benjamin Olney *surgeon*
Anderson, John David *architect*
Anderson, William (Albion), Jr. *management consultant*
Annandale, George William *engineer*
Anthony, Carmelo *professional basketball player*
Appel, Alicia Lynn *medical educator*
Argent, Lawrence *artist, educator*
Arguello, Christine Marie *federal judge*
Aro, Edwin Packard *lawyer*
Ash, Jason Stuart *biology teaching assistant*
Austin, H(arry) Gregory *lawyer*
Axelrod, Evan M. *psychologist, educator*
Bader, Gerald L., Jr. *lawyer*
Baer, Richard N. *lawyer, telecommunications industry executive*
Bain, Donald Knight *lawyer*
Balle, James Christian *systems engineer*
Banks, Britt D. *lawyer*
Barber, Patricia Louise *nurse practitioner*
Bartlit, Fred Holcomb, Jr. *lawyer*
Bender, Michael Lee *state supreme court justice*
Benson, Bruce Davey *academic administrator, oil and gas company executive*
Benton, Auburn Edgar *lawyer*
Berry, Robert Worth *lawyer, retired military officer, educator*
Bess, Charles Wayne *lawyer*
Billups, Chauncey *professional basketball player*
Blatter, Frank Edward *travel company executive*
Blitz, Stephen M. *lawyer*
Blum, Gary Bernard *lawyer*
Boasberg, Tom *school system administrator*
Boggs, Gil *principal ballet dancer*
Bondelevitch, David Joseph *film music editor*
Boyer, William Joseph *food products executive*
Brady, Brian T. *physicist, educator*
Brady, William John, Jr. *lawyer*
Brakken, William *construction executive*
Breeskin, Michael Wayne *lawyer*
Brega, Charles Franklin *lawyer*
Briggs, Steve Clement *lawyer*
Brimmer, Philip A. *federal judge*
Brown, Keith Lapham *retired ambassador*
Brownson, Jacques Calmon *architect*
Bruce, Teresa Mary *lawyer, educator*
Buckstein, Caryl Sue *writer*
Buescher, Bernard A. (Bernie Buescher) *state official, air transportation executive*
Bufe, Charles Glenn *geophysicist, researcher*
Burrows, Bertha Jean *retired academic administrator*
Butler, David *lawyer*
Byyny, Richard Lee *former academic administrator, physician, educator*
Cadman, Bill Lee *state legislator*
Cain, Douglas Mylchreest *lawyer*
Calonge, Bruce Nedrow (Ned Calonge) *public health service officer*
Campbell, William J. *lawyer*
Carbone, Rocco William III *elementary school educator*
Carlson, Erik B. *lawyer*
Carlson, Robert Ernest *freelance writer, architect, lecturer*
Carroll, Terrance D. *state legislator, lawyer*
Case, Steve (Stephen M.) *healthcare investment company executive, former media and entertainment company executive*
Castro, Obdulia *language educator, researcher*
Chapman, Rex *professional sports team executive, retired professional basketball player*
Chaput, Charles J. *archbishop*
Cheris, Elaine Gayle Ingram *business owner*
Chu, Roderick Gong-Wah *educational association administrator*
Clark, Phillip R. *lawyer*
Clevenger, Jeffrey Griswold *mining company executive*
Clinch, Nicholas Bayard III *small business owner*
Coats, Nathan B. *state supreme court justice*
Cobban, William Aubrey *paleontologist*
Cochran, John Howard *plastic and reconstructive surgeon*
Cohen, Andrew *news analyst, lawyer*
Conley, James Douglas *auxiliary bishop*
Considine, Terry *real estate company executive*
Coombe, Bob (Robert D.) *academic administrator*
Cooper, Paul Douglas *lawyer*
Cope, Thomas Field *lawyer*
Corriere, Jules *playwright, theater director*
Crystal, Darren *Internet company executive, application developer*
Cuba, Stanley L. *government official*
Curiel, Tyler Jay *immunologist, educator*
Dance, Francis Esburn Xavier *communication educator*
Daniel, Wiley Young *federal judge*
Dantley, Adrian *professional basketball coach, retired professional basketball player*
Dauer, Edward Arnold *law educator*
Davis, R. Steven *lawyer, telecommunications industry executive*
Dean, James Benwell *lawyer*
Decker, Peter Randolph *rancher, retired state official*
Delin, Geoffrey Norman *hydrologist*
Dempsey, Stanley (Howard Stanley Dempsey) *lawyer, mining and investment company executive*
Deutsch, Harvey Elliot *lawyer*
Dinarello, Charles A. *medical educator*
Dorr, Robert Charles *lawyer*
Dowdle, Patrick Dennis *lawyer*
Downey, Tom *museum director, former lawyer*
Drake, Sylvie (Jurras) *theater critic*
Duffy, William J. *lawyer*
Dunham, Joan Roberts *administrative assistant*
Durairaj, Vikram David *plastic surgeon*
Eaton, Gareth Richard *chemistry professor, dean*
Ebel, David M. *federal judge*
Eckstein, Max *law educator, director*
Edelman, Joel *health facility administrator*
Ehret, Josephine Mary *retired microbiologist researcher*
Eid, Allison Hartwell *state supreme court justice*
Eid, Troy A. *lawyer, former prosecutor*
Eklund, Carl Andrew *lawyer*
Elston, Frank *law educator, consultant*
Emmet, Thomas Addis, Jr. *college administrator, consultant*
Eppler, Jerome Cannon *investment advisor*
Euteneuer, Joseph John *communications executive*
Faatz, Jeanne Ryan *councilwoman*
Fails, Thomas Glenn *geologist*
Farber, Steven W. *lawyer*
Fay, Richard James *mechanical engineering executive, educator*
Featherstone, Bruce Alan *lawyer*
Felter, Edwin Lester, Jr. *judge*
Finney, Barbara Ann *biology professor*
Foote, Adam *professional hockey player*
Frangas, K. Jerry *state legislator*
Fredmann, Martin *ballet company artistic director, educator, choreographer*
Frevert, Donald Kent *hydraulic engineer*
Friesen, Robert Hattan *anesthesiologist*
Fuller, Robert Kenneth *architect, urban designer*
Gabow, Patricia Anne *internist, health facility executive*
Garcia, June Marie *librarian*
Gehres, James *retired lawyer*
Gellan, Kebede Gobena *literature and language, international law professor*
Giambi, Jason Gilbert *professional baseball player*
Glanz, Jason *epidemiologist, researcher*
Glendinning, Stewart *food products executive*
Glunz, Gregory *engineer*
Goebel, Karey Lyn *marketing professional, director*
Golitz, Loren Eugene *dermatologist, pathologist, medical association administrator*
Gorsuch, Neil McGill *federal judge, lawyer*
Graham, Pamela Smith *artist, educator*
Grant, Patrick Alexander *lawyer*
Grant, William West III *banker*
Green, Jersey Michael-Lee *lawyer*
Grover, Frederick Lee *cardiothoracic surgeon*
Guber, Myles Stuert *surgeon*
Guy, Mary Ellen Johnston *political science professor*
Haddon, Harold Alan *lawyer*
Hale, Allan L. *lawyer*
Hall, Larry Dean *utilities executive, lawyer*
Hall, Richard Murray, Jr. *finance executive, consultant*
Harris, Dale Ray *lawyer, arbitrator, mediator*
Heinrich, Christoph *curator*
Hejduk, Milan *professional hockey player*
Hendrix, Lynn Parker *lawyer*
Hickenlooper, John W. *Mayor, Denver*
Hobbs, Gregory James, Jr. *state supreme court justice*
Hoffman, Murray Stanley *internist, educator, cardiologist*
Hogan, Curtis Jule *labor union administrator, industrial relations specialist, consultant*
Holme, Richard Phillips *lawyer*
Hopfenbeck, George Martin, Jr. *lawyer*
Houghtaling, Walter Nicholas *lawyer*
Houtsma, Peter C. *lawyer*
Hylbert, Paul W. *construction executive*
Irwin, R. Robert *lawyer*
Jacobs, Paul Alan *lawyer*
Jarles, Ruth Sewell *education educator*
Jennett, Shirley Shimmick *health facility administrator*
Jestrab, Frank F. *retired lawyer*
Johnson, Candice Elaine Brown *pediatrician, educator*
Johnson, Walter Earl *geophysicist*
Johnston, Gwinavere Adams *public relations consultant*
Jones, Dwight D. *state official, school system administrator*
Jones, Richard Michael *lawyer*
Jones, Stephanie Lee *biologist, ornithologist, botanist*
Joseph, Fred J. *state banking agency administrator*
Juárez, José Roberto, Jr. *law educator, former dean*
Judd, Joel Stanton *state legislator, lawyer*
Kahn, Edwin Sam *lawyer*
Kappler, John W. *microbiology educator*
Karl, George *professional basketball coach*
Karsh, Philip Howard *retired advertising executive*
Kassan, Stuart S. *rheumatologist*
Katz, Martin Jonathan *law professor*
Keep, Marcus Floyd *neurosurgeon*
Keithley, Roger Lee *judge*
Kendig, Lynne E. *physician*
Kennedy, Cary *state treasurer*
Kern, Jerome H. *consulting firm executive*
Kerrigan, J. Michael *psychologist*
Kerwin, Mary Ann Collins *lawyer*
Kim, Fernando J. *urologist, director*
Kintzele, John Alfred *lawyer*
Knight, Greg *professional sports team executive*
Kosnett, Michael J. *medical toxicologist*
Krell, Frank-Thorsten *zoologist, researcher*
Krendl, Cathy Stricklin *lawyer*
Krikos, George Alexander *pathologist, educator*
Kroenke, E. Stanley *real estate developer, professional sports team owner*
Kruger, Paula *telecommunications industry executive*
Kundert, Judy A. *writer and publisher*
Kuppireddi, Sireesh *computer scientist*
Labrecque, Joseph *application developer*
Labuda, Jeanne *state legislator*
Lacroix, Pierre *professional sports team executive*
LaGanga, Linda Rose *health facility administrator, educator, researcher*
LaMendola, Walter Franklin *technology business executive, educator*
Larsen, Gary Loy *physician, researcher*
Larson, Randall J. *energy executive*
Larson, Ruth Elaine *elementary school educator*
Lazarus, Jeremy A. *psychiatrist*
Lefly, Dianne Louise *research psychologist*
Leung, Donald Y. M. *pediatric allergist*
Lewis, Evan Larson *urologist*
Lewis, Jerome A. *petroleum company executive, investment banker*
Leydon, Debra Jean *food products executive*
Lin, Eugene *radiologist, nuclear medicine physician*
Lin, Hai *chemistry professor*
Livingston, Johnston Redmond *manufacturing executive*
Low, Andrew M. *lawyer*
Low, John Wayland *lawyer*
Lucero, Carlos *federal judge*
Luna, Sheryl Alison *literature and language professor*
Lutz, John Shafroth *lawyer*
Lyons, James M. *lawyer*
MacDonald, Lunden Eschelle *language educator*
Macey, William Blackmore *oil industry executive*
MacGregor, George Lescher, Jr. *freelance/self-employed writer*
Mackey, Pamela Robillard *lawyer*
Madole, Richard Frank *geologist, consultant*
Major, Alice Jean *lawyer*
Mandarich, David D. *real estate corporation executive*
Marquess, Lawrence Wade *lawyer*
Marrack, Philippa Charlotte *immunologist, researcher*
Martin, Kenyon *professional basketball player*
Martin, Richard Jay *medical educator*
Martinez, Alex J. *state supreme court justice*
Mathis, Karen J. *lawyer, legal association administrator*
Mauro, Richard Frank *retired lawyer, investment company executive*
McCabe, John L. *lawyer*
McCall, Laura *education educator, writer*
McCandless, Bruce, II, *aerospace engineer, retired astronaut*
McCollum, Marianne *pharmacist, educator, medical researcher*
McConnell, John *environmental activist, founder of Earth Day*
McDermott, Sandra *national park administrator*
McGihon, Anne Lee *state legislator, lawyer*
McIntosh, Carolyn Leigh *lawyer*
McIntyre, Robert C., Jr. *surgeon, critical care consultant*
McMichael, Donald Earl *lawyer*
McMorris, Jerry *transportation company, sports team executive*
McWilliams, Robert Hugh *federal judge*
Meeks, Patricia Lowe *literature and language educator, consultant*
Mehler, Philip S. *internist*
Meiklejohn, Alvin J., Jr. *state legislator, lawyer, accountant*
Meister, Ryan Edward *marketing executive*
Mencer, Sue (Constance Suzanne Mencer) *former federal agency administrator*
Menke, Sean E. *air transportation executive*
Merker, Steven Joseph *lawyer*
Miller, Gale Timothy *lawyer*
Miller, Robert Nolen *lawyer*
Milliken, John Gordon *research economist*
Mitchem, Allen P. *lawyer*
Mizel, Larry A. *housing construction company executive*
Mogg, Jimmy W. *gas industry executive*
Moorcroft, William Herbert *retired bio-psychologist, educator, researcher*
Moore, Gregory L. *editor*
Morin, Christopher Joseph *vascular surgeon*
Morrison, Kendra Ann *environmental scientist*
Mueller, Edward A. *telecommunications industry executive*
Mullarkey, Mary J. *state supreme court chief justice*
Murane, William Edward *lawyer*
Murphy, Sister Lillian *sister, not-for-profit organization executive*
Myhren, Trygve Edward *communications company executive*
Nelson, Sarah Milledge *archaeology educator*
Nemiro, Beverly Mirium Anderson *author, educator*
Nenê, (Maybyner Rodney Hilario) *professional basketball player*
Newberry, Elizabeth Carter *greenhouse and floral company owner*
Newcom, Jennings Jay *lawyer, director*
Newman, Kimberly Eileen *adult education educator*
Nicholson, Will Faust, Jr. *bank executive*
Norton, Gale Ann *lawyer, former United States Secretary of the Interior*
Oakes, Terry Louis *resident real estate broker*
O'Brien, Barbara *Lieutenant Governor of Colorado*
O'Brien, Richard T. *mining executive*
O'Connor, Thomas C. *energy executive*
Ogard, Karen *investment advisor, financial planner*
Ogsbury, James Stanley III *neurosurgeon, educator*
Olsen, M. Kent *lawyer, educator*
Ormes, Jonathan Fairfield *astrophysicist, researcher, educator*
Osberg, Gregory John *mobile video company executive, former publishing executive*
Osman, Lee R. *lawyer*
Owen, Elizabeth Marie *art historian, educator*
Padilla, Alexandre *economics professor*
Palmer, David Gilbert *lawyer*
Papantoni Kazakos, Titsa *engineering educator*
Parikh, Chirag R. *physician scientist*
Payne, Stanley E. *mathematics professor*
Pearlman, David Samuel *allergist*
Petkun, Richard Michael *lawyer*
Petty, Thomas Lee *internist, educator*
Piché, Gregory Russell *lawyer*
Plummer, Ora Beatrice *nursing educator, consultant*
Pomerantz, Marvin *thoracic surgeon*
Pommer, John (Jack Pommer) *state legislator*
Porfilio, John Carbone *federal judge*
Porreco, Richard Patrick *physician*
Pozner, Larry S. *lawyer, educator*
Price, David W. *physician, educator, reseachrer*
Price, David William *physician, educator, researcher*
Price, Kathleen McCormick *editor, writer*
Purcell, Scott *Internet company executive, publishing executive*
Rael, Henry Sylvester, Sr. *retired health administrator, financial and management consultant*
Rainer, William Gerald *cardiac surgeon*
Refaeli, Yosef *biology professor*
Rench, Stephen Charles *lawyer*
Reshotko, Eli *aerospace engineer, educator*
Rice, Nancy E. *state supreme court justice*
Ritter, Bill (August William Ritter Jr.) *Governor of Colorado, former prosecutor*
Rodriguez, Juan Alfonso *information technology executive*
Rothman, Paul A. *publishing executive*
Rothrock, Lindsey Nichole *lawyer*

Rovira, Luis Dario *state supreme court justice*
Rubin, Cathy Ann *secondary school educator*
Sacco, Joe *professional hockey coach, retired professional hockey player*
Saltz, Howard Joel *newspaper editor*
Samuels, Donald L. *lawyer*
Scheid, Steven L. *investment company executive*
Schrenk, Gary Dale *foundation executive*
Schwartz, David A. *genetics, environmental sciences and pulmonology medicine physician, former federal agency administrator*
Seawell, Donald Ray *lawyer, performing company executive*
Sharp, Lewis Inman *museum director, curator*
Sheeler, Jim *journalist, educator*
Sheeran, Michael John Leo *priest, academic administrator*
Shepherd, John Frederic *lawyer*
Sherman, Greg *professional sports team executive*
Shwayder, Elizabeth Yanish *sculptor*
Singleton, William Dean *publishing executive*
Skaggs, David Evans *state official, former congressman*
Slotta, Oliveann Davis *mathematics educator, consultant*
Smith, David B. *geochemist, researcher*
Smith, Dwight Morrell *chemistry professor, academic administrator*
Smyth, Ryan *professional hockey player*
Snee, Lawrence Warren *geologist*
Snyder, Charles Royce *sociologist, educator*
Sparks, George *museum administrator*
Sparks, John Wesley *physician*
Staelin, Earl Hudson *lawyer*
Stamm, Carol Ann *obstetrician, gynecologist*
Steefel, David Simon *lawyer*
Street, Huston Lowell *professional baseball player*
Sullivan, William E. *wholesale distribution executive*
Suthers, John William *state attorney general*
Swinburn, Peter *brewery company executive*
Szefler, Stanley James *pediatrics and pharmacology educator*
Taylor, Edward Stewart *obstetrician, educator*
Taylor, Teresa A. *telecommunications industry executive*
Thomasch, Roger Paul *lawyer*
Thornton, Roland *telecommunications industry executive*
Tierney, Bill *university athletic coach*
Tracy, Jim (James Edwin Tracy) *professional baseball manager*
Tregemba, Robert D. *telecommunications industry executive*
Troutman, George William *geologist*
Trueblood, Harry Albert, Jr. *oil industry executive*
Tulowitzki, Troy Trevor *professional baseball player*
Tymkovich, Timothy Michael *federal judge*
Ulrich, Theodore Albert *lawyer*
Waak, Patricia Ann *political organization administrator*
Wagner, Judith Buck *investment firm executive*
Walker, Samuel David *lawyer*
Wang, Cecilia Chiacheh Low *internist, educator*
Warkentien, Mark *professional sports team executive*
Washington, Reginald Louis *pediatric cardiologist*
Weatherley-White, Roy Christopher Anthony *surgeon, consultant*
Weber, Matthew George *lawyer*
Welch, Alex *Internet company executive, application developer*
Wheeler, Malcolm Edward *lawyer, educator*
White, Joyce Louise *librarian*
Williams, Michael Anthony *lawyer*
Wimett, Lynn Cathy *educational association administrator, director*
Witold, Kaczanowski *painter, sculptor*
Wohlgenant, Richard Glen *lawyer, director*
Woodward, Jackie *marketing professional*
Woodward, Lester Ray *lawyer*
Wunnicke, Brooke *lawyer*
Yost, Dan *telecommunications industry executive*
Zimet, Carl Norman *psychologist, educator*

Dillon
Dugan, Michael Joseph *former career officer, health agency executive*
Follett, Robert John Richard *publisher*

Dolores
Rice, Wayne *artist, educator, small business owner*

Durango
Balas-Whitfield, Susan *artist*
Burnham, Bryson Paine *retired lawyer*
Foster, James Henry *advertising and public relations executive*
Korb, Julie *biology professor*
Lee, Nathan K. *theater educator, director*
Lehmer, Erin M. *biology professor*
Van Mols, Brian *publishing executive*
Zeller, Christopher Lee *preservation archaeologist*

Edwards
Prather, William Ronald *medical association administrator*

Englewood
Bailey, Champ *professional football player*
Barnes, David G. *data processing company executive*
Bennett, Robert R. *telecommunications company executive*
Bracken, Charles H.R. *communications executive*
Case, Paul Watson, Jr. *communications executive*
Clark, Ranjana B. *financial services company executive*
Dawkins, Brian Patrick *professional football player*
Dodge, R. Stanton *energy executive*
Dvorak, Bernard G. *communications executive*
Fillmore, Joseph H. *physiatrist*
Flowers, David J. *corporate financial executive*
Fordyce, Michael *rehabilitation hospital administrator*
Fries, Michael T. *communications executive*
Gertz, David Lee *homebuilding company executive*
Gold, Christina A. *data processing company executive*
Han, Bernard L. *communications executive*
Hardy, Wayne Russell *insurance and investment broker*
Jordan, LaMont *professional football player*
Keesling, Ruth Morris *foundation administrator*
Kelly, Jason Lincoln *radiologist*
Knize, David Maurice *plastic surgeon*
Maffei, Gregory B. *media company executive, former computer software company executive*
Malone, John C. *media company executive*
Markowski, Elizabeth M. *lawyer*
McDaniels, Josh *professional football coach*
Moskowitz, David K. *lawyer*
Nolan, Mike *professional football coach*
Olcer, Nuri Yelman *engineering researcher, educator*
Orton, Kyle *professional football player*
Polland, Anthony Travis *engineering company executive, director*
Rowe, Mike (Michael Gregory Rowe) *television personality*
Schleyer, William T. *cable company executive*
Shah, Manish Harikant *plastic surgeon*
Stockdale, Stewart A. *data processing company executive*
Tanabe, Charles Y. *lawyer*
Whiteneck, Gale *medical researcher*
Xanders, Brian *professional sports team executive*

Estes Park
Ojalvo, Morris *civil engineer, educator*
Ryder, Susan R. *elementary school educator*
Varilek, Julie *music educator*
Webb, Richard C. *engineering company executive*

Evans
Geisendorfer, Nancy Kay *mathematics educator*

Evergreen
Dobbs, Gregory Allan *journalist*
Haun, John Daniel *petroleum geologist, educator*
Heyl, Allen Van, Jr. *geologist*
Jackson, William Richard *entrepreneur*
Prichard, Vincent Marvin *lawyer*

Falcon
Jackson, Kathlynn L. *special education educator, behavior specialist*
Meek, Lisa K. S. *intervention coordinator, psychotherapist*

Federal Heights
Adams, Judith Ann *school nurse practitioner*

Fort Collins
Aboellail, Tawfik A. *pathologist, educator*
Abt, Steven R. *civil engineer, educator*
Adiku, Samuel Godfried Kwasi *soil scientist*
Baldwin, Lionel Vernon *retired university president*
Bamburg, James Robert *biochemistry professor*
Barbezat, Eugene LaVar *retired computer engineer, military officer*
Bartels, Randy A. *science educator, researcher*
Bloemen, Crystal Lynn *secondary school educator*
Borch, Thomas *chemistry professor*
Chappell, Barbara Kelly *retired child welfare consultant*
Chong, Edwin K. P. *engineering educator*
Chorpenning, H. R. III *minister*
Cochenour, Donnice *academic librarian*
Collett, Jeffrey Lee, Jr. *environmental scientist, educator*
Culver, Roger Bruce *astronomer, educator*
Dik, Bryan J. *psychology professor, consultant*
Douglas, Aaron Jack *economist, researcher*
Eddy, Gladys Louise *retired educational administrator*
Estep, Donald Joseph *mathematician, educator*
Evans, Norman Allen *retired civil engineering educator*
Ewing, Jack Robert *accountant*
Fausch, Kurt Daniel *fisheries ecologist, educator*
Fixman, Marshall *chemist, educator*
Follett, Ronald Francis *soil scientist*
Frank, Anthony A. (Tony Frank) *academic administrator*
Glantz, Michelle Medora *biology professor*
Goodrich, Laurie R. *veterinarian, educator*
Grandin, Temple *industrial designer, science educator*
Harper, Judson Morse *retired university administrator, consultant, educator*
Huffman Proctor, Jeremy Werner *literature and language professor*
Jacobs, Peter Alan *artist, educator*
Jaouen, Stephen H. *construction executive, educator*
Jin, Song *environmental scientist*
Johnson, Donald Edward, Jr. *lawyer*
Johnson, Robert Britten *geology educator*
Kaufman, Harold Richard *mechanical engineer, physics educator*
Keim, Wayne Franklin *retired agronomist, geneticist*
Kennedy, George Alexander *classicist, educator*
Kinnison, Robert Wheelock *retired accountant*
Kurosu, Michio *science educator*
Laituri, Melinda J. *science educator*
Lumb, William Valjean *veterinarian*
Maciel, Gary Emmet *chemistry professor, researcher*
Mader, Douglas Paul *research administrator*
Maher, Thomas George *academic administrator, producer, media educator*
Matthies, Frederick John *civil and environmental engineer*
May, Stephen James *communications educator, writer*
Mc Clellan, William Monson *retired library director*
McComb, David Glendinning *history professor*
Mielke, Paul William, Jr. *statistician, consultant*
Morgan, George Arthur *psychologist*
Mortvedt, John Jacob *soil scientist, researcher*
Murphy, Robert James *language educator, consultant, pianist, pipe organ performer*
Narayanasamy, Prabagaran *research scientist*
Newman, Steven Earl *horticulturist, educator*
Noh, Yoo-Jeong *research scientist*
Pagano, Rosario *staff scientist*
Palmer, Ross Howard *veterinarian, educator*
Peterson, Gary Andrew *agronomics researcher*
Phemister, Robert David *veterinary medical educator*
Rash, John Edward *medical educator*
Ray, Steven Billy *lawyer*
Rhyan, Jack C. *pathologist*
Richardson, Everett Vern *hydraulic engineer, educator, administrator, consultant*
Roesner, Larry August *civil engineer*
Rolston, Holmes III *theology studies educator, philosopher*
Rubin, Binyamin *aerospace engineer*
Santoni, Brandon Gerad *engineering educator, researcher*
Savage, Eldon Paul *retired environmental health educator*
Schaffer, Robert W. (Bob Schaffer) *former congressman*
Schlup, Philip *research scientist*
Schumm, Stanley Alfred *geologist, educator*
Schwartz, Allen R. *lawyer*
Sedei Rodden, Pamela Jean *psychologist, director*
Seidel, George Elias, Jr. *zoology educator*
Shaner, Dale L. *weed scientist*
She, Chiao-Yao *physics professor, researcher*
Skagen, Susan K. *biologist*
Stephens, Graeme Leslie *meteorologist, educator*
Stoaks, Ralph Duval *entomologist, educator, retired biotechnologist*
Theobald, David Martin *ecologist, educator*
Thurai, Merhala *research scientist*
Treaster, Melba Mauck *retired educational consultant and educator*
Venayagamoorthy, Subhas Karan *civil engineer, educator*
Vonder Haar, Thomas H. *meteorology educator*
Wang, Tian *immunologist, educator*
Wood, John Louis *chemistry professor*
Yust, David E. *artist, educator*
Zhang, Shu-xin *neuroscientist*

Fountain
Hazlett, David Lawrence *social studies educator*

Frisco
Helmer, David Alan *lawyer*
Janes, Donald Wallace *biologist, educator, academic administrator, consultant*

Fruita
Harvey, Barbara Lou *special education educator*
McCorkle, Anne Frances *social studies educator*

Georgetown
Stern, Mort(imer) P(hillip) *communications educator, editor, reporter, consultant*

Glenwood Springs
Jaffrey, Ira *oncologist, educator*
Kelley, Robert Daryl *retired biology professor, mathematics professor*
Ketzenbarger, Gary C. *speech educator, director*
Wadyko, Michael Anthony *historian, educator*

Golden
Ahn, Kwang-Soon *materials scientist, researcher*
Arora, Manohar Lal *engineering educator*
Baron, Robert Charles *publishing executive*
Bettinghaus, Erwin Paul *research scientist*
Bickart, Theodore Albert *university president emeritus*
Chouinard, Karen Reiko *elementary school educator*
Christensen, Robert Wayne *oral maxillofacial surgeon, minister*
Ciobanu, Cristian V. *engineering educator*
Coors, Peter Hanson *brewery company executive*
DeSanto, John A. *physicist, educator, mathematics professor*
Dickenson, Eric Reyvell Velázquez *engineering educator*
Dickinson, Carol Rittgers *art historian, cconsultant, writer*
Ding, Shi-You *energy executive, researcher*
Fude, Liu *research scientist*
Gordon, Douglas H. *literature and language educator*
Grossman, Terry Alan *medical association administrator, director*
Hamm, Nathaniel Paul *engineering educator*
Kim, Jin Young *materials scientist*
Kopel, David Benjamin *lawyer*
Krauss, George *metallurgist*
Mohagheghi, Ali *chemical engineer*
Nozik, Arthur Jack *research physical chemist*
Olson, Marian Katherine *management consultant*
Pegis, Anton George *retired language educator*
Petrick, Alfred, Jr. *economist, educator*
Phillipson, Donald E. *lawyer*
Sattel, Daniel *geophysicist*
Scales, John Alan *physics professor*
Scoggins, M. W. (Bill Scoggins) *academic administrator*
Shayer, Zeev *research scientist, educator*
Skokan, Catherine *engineering educator*
Sloan, Earle Dendy, Jr. *chemical engineering educator*
Suryanarayanan, Siddharth *electrical engineer, educator*
Taylor, Philip Craig *physics professor*
Trefny, John Ulric *retired college president*
Van Kirk, Craig William *petroleum engineer, educator*
von Roedern, Bolko Graf *energy executive, researcher*
Weimer, Robert Jay *geology educator, energy consultant, civic leader*
Wickesser, Thomas A. *finance company executive*
Wyman, Charles Ely *biotechnologist, research director, chemical engineer*
Yeatts, Frank Richard *retired physics professor*
Zhang, Yong *physicist, researcher*
Zimmer, Larry William, Jr. *sports announcer*

Grand Junction
Bishop, Tilman Malcolm *state legislator*
Bragdon, Lynn Lyon *library administrator*
Bruch, Julie *linguistics and language professor*
Coffin, Kelly Faye *nurse, educator*
Fay, Abbott Eastman *history professor*
Hoagland, Christina Gail *occupational therapist, industrial drafter*
Markham, Frank Bell *business educator*
Morton, Louis George *retired social sciences educator*
Rybak, James Patrick *retired engineering educator*
Schulte, Steven C. *history professor*
Waggoner, Heather E. *theater educator*

Greeley
Banerjee, Rashida *special education educator*
Bond, Richard Randolph *retired foundation administrator*
Chaudhuri, Jayati *librarian*
Cook, Donald Evan *pediatrician, educator*
Crandall, James L. *communications educator*
Downey, Matthew T. *history professor, writer*
Hawthorne, Barbara L. *anthropologist, educator*
Jackson, Paul Howard *minister*
Linde, Lucille Mae (Lucille Jacobson) *motor-perceptual specialist*
Malde, Melissa *singer, educator*
Miller, Diane Wilmarth *retired human resources director*
Murray, Robert Patrick *musician, educator*
Perl, Don A. *literature and language professor*
Rittner, Linda *educational consultant, director*
Szczyrba, Igor Nicholas *mathematical physicist, consultant*

Greenwood Village
Abbott, William J. *broadcast executive*
Arvizu, Dan Eliab *mechanical engineer*
Benson, Robert Craig III *business consultant*
Blank, Alan Robert *lawyer*
Capellas, Michael D. *information technology executive*
Chico, Beverly Ann *history professor, humanities educator*
Davis, Tracy A. *lawyer*
Dewald, Bruce Wayne *lawyer*
Elway, John Albert *professional sports team executive, retired professional football player*
Haliw, Jerome Michael *civil engineer*
Imhoff, Walter Francis *retired investment banker*
Lidstone, Herrick Kenley, Jr. *lawyer*
Money, David R. *lawyer, information technology executive*
Neiser, Brent Allen *foundation executive, public affairs and personal finance speaker, consultant*
Poe, Robert Alan *lawyer*
Rairdon, James Lee *paralegal, educator*
Ramsey, John Arthur *lawyer*
Schlapbach, David *lawyer*
Wadhams, Richard Ivory (Dick Wadhams) *policitcal organization administrator*
Wall, Phil *information technology executive*

Guffey
Szeliga, Victoria I. *retired social studies educator*

Gunnison
Gelwicks, James M. *retired communications educator*

Henderson
Reibold, Dorothy Ann *accountant, researcher*

Highlands Ranch
Brierley, James Alan *biohydrometallurgy consultant*
Cherno, Melvin *humanities educator*
Harris, Douglas Clay *retired newspaper executive*
Maucec, Marko *nuclear engineer, researcher*
Rogers, Benjamin Talbot *mechanical engineer, consultant*
Vosbeck, Robert Randall *architect*

Howard
Hopkins, Donald J. *retired lawyer*

Jefferson
Maatsch, Deborah Joan *manufacturing executive*

La Junta
Keith, RuAnn Rae *humanities educator*

Lafayette
Dowling, Thomas Allan *retired mathematics professor*
McNeill, William *environmental scientist*
Mehl, Albert L. *pediatrician, poet, composer*
Thornbury, John Rousseau *radiologist, physician*

Lake George
Norman, John Barstow, Jr. *graphics designer, educator*

Lakewood
Armstrong, William L. *former senator*
Axley, Hartman *retired estate planner, underwriter*
Barrett, Michael Henry *civil engineer*
Brownson, Sue McPherson *music educator*
Drendel, Gary *environmental scientist*
Eikleberry, Lois Schillie *physician*
Guyton, Samuel Percy *retired lawyer*
Hadley, Marlin LeRoy *financial planner, consultant*
Humphrey, Charles Edward, Jr. *lawyer*
Isely, Henry Philip *association and business executive, integrative engineer, writer, educator*
Knott, William Alan *library director*
Kulkarni, Kishore Ganesh *economics professor, consultant*
Lu, Paul Haihsing *mining engineer, geotechnical consultant*
Martinen, John A. *travel company executive*
McBride, Guy Thornton, Jr. *college president emeritus*

Nichols, Vicki Anne *financial consultant, librarian*
Orullian, B. LaRae *retired bank executive*
Peters, Julie Anne *writer*
Reed, Joan-Marie *special education educator*
Wilcox, Mary Marks *retired Christian education consultant, educator*
Winters, Richard Allen *mineral economist*

Laporte
Riba, Shirley *artist*

Limon
Richards, Ann Adair *psychologist*

Littleton
Asbjörnson, Kevin Donald *musician, small business owner*
Battilega, John A. *research and development company executive*
Cabell, Elizabeth Arlisse *psychologist*
Day, Susan Marie *music educator, composer*
Ergen, Charles W. (Charlie Ergen) *communications executive*
Erickson, William Hurt *retired state supreme court justice*
Forstot, Stephan Lance *ophthalmologist*
Keats, Donald Howard *composer, educator*
Keogh, Heidi Helen Dake *advocate*
Kullas, Albert John *management consultant, systems engineer*
Lode, Trygve Tennyson *entrepreneur, actor*
Marion, John Martin *instructional technology educator*
Meyer, Milton Edward, Jr. *retired lawyer, artist*
Mosier, Cheryl Angeline *secondary school educator, consultant*
Newell, Michael Stephen *finance company executive, protective services consultant*
Nimz, Timothy J. *museum director*
Paull, Richard Allen *geologist, educator*
Rolater, J. Rick *science association director*
Scrabeck, Jon Gilmen *retired dental educator*
Spalding, Robert Steele, II, *systems administrator*
Sutton, Robert Edward *investment company executive*
Vail, Charles Daniel *veterinarian, consultant*

Livermore
Tkachev, Sergey Nikolayevich *geophysicist*

Lone Tree
Grant, Nancy C. *dentist*
Morrow Campbell, Juliette Michelle *lawyer*
Spelts, Richard John *lawyer*
Spisak, John Francis *corporation executive*

Longmont
Coleman, Bud *choreographer, educator*
Davies, David Huw *electronics and engineering company executive*
Dierks, Richard Ernest *veterinarian, academic administrator*
Moats, Louisa Cook *educational consultant, researcher*
Newman, Dean Gordon *community volunteer*
Nordgren, Ronald Paul *retired engineering educator, researcher*
Rayback, Cynthia Ann *educational association administrator*
Salberg, Anne Scholberg *retired librarian*
Watkins, John Goodrich *psychologist, educator*

Louisville
Bluestein, Eve *plastic surgeon*
Bravo, Adele *elementary school educator*
Lipson, David Samuel *geologist*
Maddock, Jerome Torrence *library and information scientist*
Pneuman, Linda Jackson *retired physician*
Schonbrun, Michael K. *senior housing developer and operator*
Syed, Yasser Fouad Khaderi *electrical engineer*

Loveland
Armstrong, David Michael *biology professor*
Balsiger, David Wayne *television director, writer, television producer, television director, researcher*
Clark, Roger Earl *lawyer*
Fleischer, Gerald Albert *industrial engineer, educator*
Rodman, Alpine C. *arts and crafts company executive, photographer*
Schmitt, Roberta J. *psychologist, educator*

Mead
Jones, Beverly Ann Miller *nursing administrator, retired patient services administrator*

Montrose
Boice, Judith Lynette *physician, writer, educator*
Kontny, Vincent L. *rancher, retired engineering executive*
Modrell, Corey John *educator*
Radovich, Donald *painter, illustrator, retired art educator*

Monument
Klazura, Gerard E. *retired meteorologist*
McIver, Deborah Kay *tax specialist, entrepreneur, small business owner*
Posey, Carolyn Ann *secondary school educator*
Rokke, Ervin Jerome *military officer, academic administrator*

Morrison
Bowen, Peter Geoffrey *business educator, arbitrator*
Lutsky, Sheldon Jay *financial and marketing consultant, writer*

Nederland
Sutton, Philip D(ietrich) *psychologist, educator*
Thomas, Daniel Foley *retired diversified financial services company executive*

Niwot
Duerden, John H. *apparel executive*

Northglenn
Hemlock, Roberta Leigh *veterinary technician*
Kappler, Karen L. *musician, educator*

Norwood
Reagan, Harry Edwin III *lawyer*

Parachute
Leonard, Betsy Ann *director, writer*

Parker
Smartt, Richard A. *museum director*

Penrose
Hilderbrand, Richard L. *science association director, consultant*

Peterson AFB
Webster, William G., Jr. *career military officer*

Pine
Jones, David Milton *economist, educator*

Pueblo
Barnett, Janet Heine *mathematics professor*
Becker, Charles A. *adult education educator*
Deasy, Irene M. *retired protective services official*
Divelbiss, Maggie (Margaret G. Divelbiss) *museum director*
Farley, Thomas T. *lawyer*
Farwell, Hermon Waldo, Jr. *parliamentarian and speech educator*
Furman, Jane Christine *art educator*
Greenlaw, Roger Lee *interior designer*
Humes, James Calhoun *lawyer, communications consultant, writer, educator*
Occhiato, Michael Anthony *municipal official*
Rawlings, Robert Hoag *newspaper publisher*
Sisson, Ray L. *retired dean, author*
Tafoya, Arthur Nicholas *bishop*
Turner, Dorothy Jean *school librarian*

Ridgway
Lathrop, Kaye Don *nuclear scientist, educator*

Saguache
Sanchez, Karla Ann *language educator*

Salida
Hubicki, Frederick R. *artist*

Sedalia
Cooley, Andrew Lyman *computer company executive*

Snowmass
Lovins, Amory Bloch *physicist, energy consultant*

Snowmass Village
DiBiaggio, John A. *university president*
Strand, Curt Robert *hotel executive*

Springfield
Wessler, Melvin Dean *farmer, rancher*

Steamboat Springs
Moylan, James Joseph *lawyer*
Potter, William Bartlett *diversified financial services company executive*

Sterling
Jacquelyn, Rae Mathis *graphics designer, educator*
Mitchell, Stacy Marie *medical transcriptionist*
Walsh, Shari M. *literature and language educator*

Superior
Middlebrooks, Eddie Joe *environmental engineer*
Olatunji, Thabiti Shawki (Reverend Thabiti) *executive director, motivational speaker, advisor, educator*

Thornton
Johnson, Michael *principal*

Towner
Fees, Ruth Anna *secondary school educator*

Trinidad
Tamez, Lorraine Diane *writer, nurse*

U S A F Academy
Cummings, Russell Mark *aerospace engineer, educator*
Galema, Joseph M. *music director*
Lu, Yalin *physicist*
Merchant, P. Glenn, Jr. *military officer, physician*

Vail
Bevan, William Arnold, Jr. *emergency physician*
Kelton, Arthur Marvin, Jr. *real estate developer*
Millett, Peter J. *orthopedist*
Philippon, Marc Joseph *orthopaedic surgeon*

Walden
Ary, Bonnita Ellen *registrar, federal official*

Wellington
Grant, Lewis O. *agricultural products executive, meteorology educator*

Westminster
Bennani, Farah *biology professor*
Dockerty, Katherine *librarian, educator*
Heideman, Anthony Jon *history professor*
Kopperud, Marilyn Sue *music educator*
Scott, Gregory Kellam *former state supreme court justice, lawyer*
Udall, Mark *United States Senator from Colorado*
White, John David *composer, author*
Zhang, Li Larry *engineer, researcher, educator*

Wheat Ridge
Fleischaker, Gordon Henry, Jr. *pediatrician*
Hockenberry, E'Rena *music educator*
Morriss, Frank *writer, educator*

Windsor
DiFalco, John Patrick *lawyer, arbitrator*
Downey, Arthur Harold, Jr. *lawyer, mediator*
Mayer, Victor James *geologist, educator*

Wolcott
Flacke, Joan Wareham *physician, anesthesiologist, educator*

Woodland Park
Marcantel, Keith Bernard *school psychologist, educator*

Woody Creek
Jenkins, Robert Berryman *real estate developer*

CONNECTICUT

Ansonia
Dvoretzky, Israel *dermatologist*
Kerpa, Gary J. *computer science consultant*

Avon
Griggs, Julie Hinds *foundation administrator*
Harrison, Thomas Flatley *lawyer, environmental consultant*
Lerer, René *health services company executive*
Mazur, Edward John, Jr. *financial planner*

Bethany
Bell, Wendell *sociologist, educator, futurist*
Niederman, James Corson *retired internist, educator*

Bethel
Kurfehs, Harold Charles *real estate executive*
Shepard, Jean Heck *retired publishing consultant*
Tomasko, Edward A. *financial planner*

Bethlehem
Collins, Mother Augusta *agronomist*

Bloomfield
Cordani, David M. *insurance company executive*
Cornell, Robert Witherspoon *retired mechanical engineer*
Cronin, Daniel Anthony *archbishop emeritus*
De Maria, Anthony John *electrical engineer*
Foster, Benjamin, Jr. *educational administrator*
Hermann, Robert Jay *former manufacturing executive, consultant*
Mamlok, Walter Joseph *music educator, musician*
Nelson-Kauffman, Wendy *history educator*
Rendock, Mary Kay *elementary school educator*
Tortorello, Nicholas John *public opinion and market research company executive*

Bolton
Reyna, Magdalena Bessy *writer*

Branford
Rothberg, Jonathan M. *medical products executive, researcher*
Whitaker, Thomas Russell *English literature educator*

Bridgeport
Abdelsayed, George Gabriel *gastroenterologist*
Atweh, Nabil A. *surgeon, department chairman*
Bowen, Patrick Harvey *lawyer, consultant*
Choi, Young J. *pathologist, educator*
Coba-Loh, Claudine Jean *psychology professor*
Hendricks, Edward David *educator, consultant, speaker, trainer*
Lobdell, David Hill *retired pathologist*
London, Samuel Gene, Jr. *history professor*
Lori, William Edward *bishop*
Macdonald, Karen Crane *occupational therapist, geriatrics services professional*
Maher, Kathy *museum director*
Maiocco, Kenneth Joseph *dermatologist*
Maloney, Maureen Murphy *social sciences educator*
Mcpherson, Craig A. *cardiologist, educator*
Moss, Jeremy Ethan *dermatologist*
Pagano, Celeste Ann *retired realtor, social services coordinator*
Psarras, Mary Auten *language educator, tax specialist*
Richard, Ellen *theater executive*
Salam, Adil *pulmonary critical care physician*
Shiff, Alan Howard William *judge*
Syed, Rizvi Sajjad Haider *engineering educator, researcher*
Trefry, Robert J. *health facility administrator*

Bristol
Barnes, Carlyle Fuller *manufacturing executive*
Barnes, Wallace *manufacturing executive*
Berman, Chris *sportscaster*
Bodenheimer, George *broadcast executive*
Brown, Hubie (Hubert Jude Brown) *sportscaster, retired professional basketball coach*
Edwards, Herman Lee *sportscaster, former professional football coach*
Gammons, Peter *columnist, commentator*
Gruden, Jon David *sportscaster, former professional football coach*
Jackson, Mark *sportscaster, retired professional basketball player*
Knight, Bobby (Robert Montgomery Knight) *sportscaster, retired men's college basketball coach*
Lieberman-Cline, Nancy *sportscaster, former professional basketball coach and player*
Lobo, Rebecca *sportscaster, retired professional basketball player*
Mashburn, Jamal *sportscaster, retired professional basketball player*
Melrose, Barry James *studio analyst, former professional hockey coach and player*
Rose, Jalen *sportscaster, retired professional basketball player*
Smith, Emmitt (Emmitt James Smith III) *sportscaster, retired professional football player*
Theismann, Joe (Joseph Robert Theismann) *sportscaster, retired professional football player*
Van Gundy, Jeff *sportscaster, former professional basketball coach*
Vina, Fernando *sportscaster, retired professional baseball player*
Vitale, Dick *sportscaster, commentator*
Wallace, Rusty *sportscaster, retired race car driver*
Walsh, John A. *broadcast executive, editor*
Walton, William Theodore, III, (Bill Walton) *sportscaster, former professional basketball player*

Broad Brook
Kement, Isabella Viniconis *retired construction company executive*

Brookfield
Cohen, Mark Steven *dentist*
Oderwald, Susan *professional society administrator*

Brooklyn
McIlvane, Edward James *stained glass artist, educator*

Canaan
Beizer, Lance Kurt *retired priest, lawyer*
Thorne, Francis *composer*

Canton
Richardson, Dana Roland *technology consultant*

Canton Center
Humphrey, Samuel Stockwell *town official, physicist*

Centerbrook
Grover, William Herbert *architect*

Chaplin
Chatel, Regina G. *educational association administrator*
Wood, Wendy Deborah *filmmaker*

Cheshire
Eppler, Richard Andrew *chemical engineer, educator, consultant*
Ross, Michael Frederick *judge, lawyer*
Rowland, Ralph Thomas *retired architect*

Chester
Frost-Knappman, (Linda) Elizabeth *publishing executive, editor, writer*

Clinton
Douglas, Hope M. *psychotherapist, forensic specialist*

Colchester
Bartkowski, Kathleen Susan *musician*
Nikirk, Susan Silva (Susan Silva) *minister, writer, dancer, consultant*

Colebrook
McNeill, William Hardy *retired historian, writer*

Columbia
Stockmal, Henry F., Jr. *retired principal*

Cos Cob
Bruder, George Frederick *retired lawyer*
Murphy, R. Blair *management consulting company executive*

Coventry
Dimmock, Virginia Ellen *literature and language educator, consultant*
Hayes, Julia Moriarty *retired science educator*

Cromwell
Barber, William Joseph *economist, educator*
Günther-Stirn, Dagmar Dorothea *retired social sciences educator*
Izzo, Lucille Anne *sales representative*

Danbury
Anderson, Alan Reinold *real estate company and computer security firm executive, consultant*
Angel, Stephen F. *chemicals executive*
Arbitelle, Ronald Alan *retired elementary school educator*
Bassett, Robert Andrews *lawyer*
Belsky, Joseph L. *endocrinologist*
Breedlove, James T. (Jim Breedlove) *lawyer*
Cappiello, David J. *state legislator*
Collar, Emilio, Jr. *information systems consultant*
Hasskarl, Mark P. *library director*
Hawkes, Carol Ann *academic administrator*
Jennings, Alfred Higson, Jr. *music educator, actor, singer*
Leebens, Patricia Kay *psychiatrist*
Mann, Richard O. *public relations consulting company executive*
Moskowitz, Stanley Adam *finance company executive*
Nelson, Willie Hugh *musician, lyricist*
Pszota, Gabor *physics educator*
Reynolds, Jean Edwards *publishing executive*
Sawyer, James S. *chemicals executive*
Tolor, Alexander *psychologist, educator*
Yamin, Dianne Elizabeth *judge*

Darien
Becker, Ralph Edward *broadcast executive, consultant*
Brooke, Avery Rogers *publisher*

Charron, Paul Richard *consultant, former retail executive*
Dordelman, William Forsyth *food company executive*
Frey, Dale Franklin *financial investment company executive, manufacturing company executive*
Kaynor, Sanford Bull *lawyer*
Lim, Ralph Wei Hsiong *academic administrator*
McKim, Paul Arthur *management consultant, retired gas industry executive*
Michalski, Paul Peter *lawyer*
Prince, Kenneth Stephen *lawyer*
Rucci, Joseph J., Jr. *lawyer*
Schiff, Peter David *investment advisor, economist*
Sprole, Frank Arnott *retired pharmaceutical executive, lawyer*
Workman, Sharon Joy *journalist*

Dayville
Funk, Michael S. *food products executive*
Spinner, Steven L. *food products executive*

Deep River
Nidzgorski, Barbara Helen *gifted and talented educator, puppeteer*

Derby
Katz, David Lawrence *preventive medicine physician, researcher*
McEvoy, Sharlene Ann *law educator*

East Hampton
Tucceri, Clive Knowles *writer, science educator, consultant*

East Hartford
Barredo, Rita M. *auditor*
Dardas, Zissis *research scientist*
Lautzenheiser, Barbara Jean *insurance company executive*
Michels, H. Harvey *physicist*
Smith, Edmund Johnston *middle school educator*
Staroselsky, Alexander *mechanical engineer, materials scientist*

East Lyme
Mylari, Banavara L. *retired chemist*

Easton
Enos, Randall *cartoonist, illustrator*
Lorenz, Lee Sharp *cartoonist*
Maloney, John Joseph *writer*
Meyer, Alice Virginia *state official*

Enfield
Del Vecchio, Claudio *retail executive*
Doty, Victoria Skower *middle school educator*

Essex
Hieatt, Constance Bartlett *English language educator*
Miller, Elliott Cairns *retired bank executive, lawyer*
Miller, Walter Neal *insurance company consultant*
Thompson, George Lee *retail executive, consultant*

Fairfield
Baron, Shari Ann *academic administrator*
Beccalli-Falco, Ferdinando *manufacturing executive*
Begor, Mark W. *energy executive*
Bhatia, Karan Krishna *lawyer, former federal official*
Block, Joel Warren *geologist, educator*
Bolze, Stephen *energy executive*
Booth, George Keefer *corporate financial executive*
Bornstein, Jeffrey S. *energy executive*
Bryan, Barbara Day *retired librarian*
Bubencik, John William, II, *civil engineer, consultant, transportation engineer*
Burd, Robert Meyer *hematologist, oncologist, educator*
Caruso, Daniel F. *lawyer, judge, former state legislator*
Cassidy, Kathryn A. *diversified financial services company executive*
Cooper, L.E. Butck, Jr. *bank executive, lawyer, writer*
Daley, Pamela *diversified services, technology and manufacturing company executive*
Denniston, Brackett Badger III *lawyer*
Dineen, John C. *health products executive*
Dorn, Nancy Patricia *lobbyist, former federal official*
Falconi, John J. *diversified financial services company executive*
Fiddes, James William *biology professor*
Fitzsimons, Shane *diversified financial services company executive*
Fujimori, Yoshiaki *diversified financial services company executive*
Garwood, Jeff R. *diversified financial services company executive*
Guise, David Earl *architect, educator*
Hamilton, Gretchen Worley *retired public relations executive, management consultant*
Heintzelman, Daniel C. *diversified financial services company executive*
Henson, Daniel S. *marketing executive*
Hewett, Wayne M. *diversified financial services company executive*
Immelt, Jeffrey Robert *diversified technology and services company executive*
Ireland, Jay *diversified financial services company executive*
Ishrak, Omar S. *diversified financial services company executive*
Janki, Daniel C. *corporate financial executive*
Johnsen, Walter Craig *manufacturing executive*
Kaff, Albert Ernest *reporter, writer*
Klee, Ann Renee *lawyer*
Kleine, Herman *economist*
Kudlow, Lawrence Alan (Larry Kudlow) *financial news correspondent, economist*
Laopodis, Nick *finance educator*
Laxer, Richard *diversified financial services company executive*
Li, Cindy *academic librarian*
LoMonaco, Martha Schmoyer *theater educator, director*
Loth, Peter *mathematics professor*
Luther, David Byron *management consultant*
Lynch, John F. *human resources specialist*
Maxwell, Carole Ann *director*
Miles, Leland Weber *retired academic administrator*
Miller, Frederick Edwin, Jr. *history professor, government agency administrator*
Miller, Jamie S. *corporate financial executive*
Morehouse, Sarah McCally *retired political science professor*
Neal, Michael A. *diversified technology and services company executive*
Newton, Lisa Haenlein *philosopher, educator*
O'Connell, Edmond J. *chemist, educator, chemist, consultant*
Orris-Modugno, Michele Marie *public relations, marketing and advertising consultant*
Peters, Susan P. *human resources specialist*
Pressman, Ronald R. *manufacturing executive*
Reiner, Gary M. *diversified technology and services company executive*
Rice, John G. *diversified technology and services executive*
Samuels, John *lawyer*
Schauenberg, Trevor A. *corporate financial executive*
Schweikert, Timothy J. *industrial equipment company executive*
Sherin, Keith S. *corporate financial executive*
Stanton, Robert Alan *orthopaedic surgeon*
Stockton, Dmitri Lysander *diversified financial services company executive*
Ury, Frederic Stephen *lawyer*
Vachon, Mark L. *manufacturing executive*
Wales, Gwynne Huntington *retired lawyer*
Walker, Jonathan J. *art educator*
Wanchoo, Vishal K. *electromedical equipment company executive*
Whyte, Bruce Lincoln *management executive, Marketing Consultant*
Worrell, Brian *manufacturing executive*
Zavras, Eugenia T. *parasitologist, educator*
Zerella, Joseph A. *endodontist*

Falls Village
Cronin, Robert Lawrence *painter*
Purcell, Mary Louise Gerlinger *retired adult education educator*

Farmington
Bluestein, Paul A. *physician, insurance company executive*
Bronner, Felix *physiologist, biophysicist, educator, painter*
Burstone, Charles *dental educator, researcher*
Deckers, Peter John *surgeon, former dean*
Donaldson, James Oswell III *neurologist, educator*
Fortinsky, Richard Harold *medical educator*
Grafstein, Joel M. *lawyer*
Grant-Kels, Jane Margaret *dermatologist, educator*
Grunnet, Margaret Louise *retired pathologist, educator*
Herbert, Mickey *insurance company executive*
Hussain, Naveed *neonatologist & pediatrician*
Kaplan, Andre Albert *physician*
Lang, Jason M. *psychology professor*
Laurencin, Cato Thomas *biomedical engineer, orthopaedic surgeon, dean*
Liebowitz, Neil Robert *psychiatrist*
Mazzocca, Augusta D. *surgeon*
McCawley, Austin *psychiatrist, educator*
Melekote, Swathanthra Kumar *education educator*
Michaud-Daniel, Didier *manufacturing executive*
Nash, Judith Kluck *mathematics professor*
Nichols, Frank C. *dental educator*
Osborn, Mary Jane Merten *biochemist, educator*
Reeves, John Drummond *retired English language professional, writer*
Robinson, Peter J. *retired dean, periodontal educator, pathologist*
Rosinski, David J. *cardiovascular parfusionist*
Rothfield, Lawrence I. *microbiology educator*
Rothfield, Naomi Fox *physician*
Runowicz, Carolyn Dilworth *gynecologist, oncologist, researcher*
Scaniffe, Joseph Albert *anesthesiologist, consultant*
Shoemaker, William Joseph *neuroscientist*
Trani, John M. *former consumer products company executive*
Treggor, Josef Philip *music educator, composer, researcher*
Wand, Martin *ophthalmologist, educator*
White, William B. *medical educator, researcher*

Gaylordsville
Dunn, Virginia *artist*

Glastonbury
Bailey, Barbara *library director*
Cassotto, Mary Lou Grace *counselor, educator, librarian*
Fiszel, Geoffrey Lynn *investment banker, advisor*
Singer, Paul Richard *retired ophthalmologist*

Goshen
Kaplan, Theodore Norman *insurance company executive*

Greens Farms
Deford, Frank *sportswriter, commentator, writer*

Greenwich
Alonzo, Martin Vincent *mining and aluminum company executive, investor, financial consultant*
Applegarth, Paul Vollmer *investment and development executive*
Asness, Clifford Scott *hedge fund executive*
Atkins, Ronald Raymond *lawyer*
Ball, John Fleming *advertising and film company executive*
Ballard, Eugene G. *insurance company executive*
Bara, Jean Marc *finance and communications executive, artist*
Bedrosian, Gregory Ronald *investment banker*
Berkley, William Robert *insurance holding company executive*
Blumberg, Joel Myron *cardiologist*
Bonheim, Nelson Alfred *gastroenterologist, educator*
Brandrup, Douglas Warren *lawyer*
Brant, Peter M. *publishing executive, real estate developer*
Breeden, Richard C. *investment company executive, former federal agency administrator*
Carmichael, William Daniel *management consultant, educator*
Clements, Robert *insurance executive*
Coleman, Joel Clifford *lawyer*
Davenport, Lee Losee *physicist*
Davidson, Thomas Maxwell *corporate financial executive*
Dettmer, Robert Gerhart *retired beverage company executive*
Ewald, William Bragg, Jr. *writer, consultant*
Fleming, Martin *economist, strategist*
Foley, Thomas Coleman *investment company executive, former ambassador*
Ford, William E. *investment company executive*
Friedman, Stephen James *private equity firm executive, federal official*
Fuller, Theodore *retired insurance executive*
Ganek, David Kent *hedge fund manager*
Gelfman, Robert William *retired lawyer*
George, Cynthia Coulter *lawyer*
Gover, Alan Shore *lawyer*
Grant, Ronald Alfred *psychiatrist, pastoral counselor, psychoanalyst*
Halvorsen, Ole Andreas *hedge fund manager*
Hanson, Janet Tiebout *investment company executive*
Henkelmann, Thomas *chef*
Hewitt, Dennis Edwin *financial executive*
Hoberman, Mary Ann *author*
Jones, Paul Tudor, II, *hedge fund manager*
Kessler, Murray S. *consumer products company executive*
Kneeland, Michael J. *rental company executive*
Kovner, Kathleen Jane *civic worker, portrait artist*
Krauser, Robert Stanley *healthcare executive*
Kucic, Joseph Banrer *banker, management consultant, industrial engineer, network engineer, information security specialist*
Lampert, Edward S. *hedge fund manager*
Lederman, Ira Seth *insurance company executive, lawyer*
Macaulay, William Edward *financial executive*
Mandel, Stephen F., Jr. *hedge fund manager*
Matthaei, Gay Humphrey *interior designer*
Maxwell, Charles Thoburn *energy analyst*
May, William Frederick *manufacturing executive*
Moore, John Plunkett Dennis *publisher*
More, Douglas McLochlan *lawyer*
Mullen, Anthony J. *special education educator*
Nemser, Earl Harold *lawyer*
Nevin, Crocker *investment banker*
Nimetz, Matthew *lawyer, investment company executive*
Owens, Bill (William Forrester Owens) *investment company executive, former governor*
Pados, Frank John, Jr. *investment company executive*
Paul, Roland Arthur *lawyer*
Paulson, Paul Joseph *advertising executive*
Perless, Ellen *advertising executive*
Perless, Robert L. *sculptor*
Plummer, William B. *rental company executive, former publishing executive*
Rudy, Kathleen Vermeulen *small business owner*
Schneider, John Arnold *investor*
Schoonmaker, Samuel Vail III *lawyer*
Schwed, Roger E. *lawyer, rental company executive*
Selby, Leland Clay *lawyer*
Srere, Benson M(ortimer) *communications executive, consultant*
Sternberg, Betty J. *school system administrator*
Sternlicht, Barry Stuart *investment company executive, former hotel executive*
Stockman, David Alan *investment banker, former US Representative from Michigan*
Storms, Clifford Beekman *lawyer*
Tarantino, Dominic A. *retired professional services firm executive*
Tournillon, Nicholas Brady *investment company executive*
Van Houten, Leonard Erskine *consulting engineer*
von Braun, Peter Carl Moore Stewart *finance company executive*
Wallach, Magdalena Falkenberg (Carla Wallach) *writer*
Wyman, Ralph Mark *multifamily office firm executive*

Groton
Ebbin, Syma Alexi *environmental scientist, educator*
English, James Fairfield, Jr. *former college president*
Gai, Moshe *physics professor*
Galbraith, Marian *elementary school educator*
Kennedy, Evelyn Siefert *foundation and textiles executive*
Prakash, Chandra *chemistry educator*
Shumway, Sandra Elisabeth *shellfish biologist*
Swindell, Archie Calhoun, Jr. *statistician, consultant*
Wallach, Morton L. *scientist*

Guilford
Chatt-Ellis, Allen Barrett *psychologist, neuroscientist*
Colish, Marcia Lillian *history professor*
Dubin, Brock Thomas *lawyer*
Morgan, Leon Alford *retired utilities executive*
Ogletree, Thomas Warren *retired religious studies educator*
Pease, David Gordon *artist, educator*
Shelton, Darlene *psychologist, consultant*
Stevens, Lydia Hastings *community volunteer*

Hamden
Cline, John Carroll *psychologist*
Cooley, Francis Rexford *dean*
Dahl, Robert Alan *political science professor*
Forman, Charles William *religious studies educator*
He, Xiaohong *finance educator*
Ibbotson, Roger G. *financial educator*
Jansson, Maija *text editor*
Kagan, Donald *historian, educator*
Laskin, Alexander V. *Investor Relations Educator*
Margulies, Martin B. *lawyer, educator*
McClellan, Edwin *literature educator*
Nuland, Sherwin *surgeon, writer*
Oddi, Marie Caporale *educational administrator*
Schwartz, Douglas *public opinion poll director*
Sheikh, Aamer *accounting educator*
Valone, David Andrew *history professor*
Weinstein, Stanley *Buddhist studies educator*

Hartford
Abrahams, Ronald *pharmacist*
Alfano, Charles Thomas, Sr. *lawyer*
Anthony, Julian Danford, Jr. *lawyer*
Antonucci, Carl Anthony *library director, educator*
Ayer, Ramani *insurance company executive*
Bellemare, Alain M. *manufacturing executive*
Berall, Frank Stewart *lawyer*
Bertolini, Mark T. *insurance company executive*
Bieluch, William Charles *judge*
Bilston, Sarah Rosemary *novelist, college professor*
Blumberg, Phillip Irvin *law educator*
Blumenthal, Richard *state attorney general*
Bombara, Beth Ann *insurance company executive*
Bousbib, Ari *manufacturing executive*
Bowler, J. Thomas, Jr. *manufacturing executive*
Bronzino, Joseph Daniel *electrical engineer*
Brown, William M. *manufacturing executive*
Brubaker, Laurie *insurance company executive*
Bryant, Vanessa Lynne *federal judge, lawyer*
Butler, Gregory B. *lawyer, utilities executive*
Bysiewicz, Susan *Secretary of State, Connecticut*
Cain, George Harvey *lawyer, association administrator*
Campbell, Timothy R. *insurance company executive*
Carter, David George, Sr. *academic administrator*
Casazza, William James *insurance company executive, lawyer*
Casey, Coleman Hampton *lawyer*
Chênevert, Louis R. *manufacturing executive*
Chesman, Michael Richard *lawyer*
Coleman, George A. *school system administrator*
Cornell, James K. *diversified financial services company executive*
Curran, Ward Schenk *economist, educator*
Darnis, Geraud *manufacturing executive*
David, George Alfred Lawrence *manufacturing executive*
DiNardo, Nancy *political organization administrator*
Doucette, John J. *manufacturing executive*
Drake, Eileen *manufacturing executive*
Duffy, James Desmond *neopsychiatrist, palliative care physician*
Dworkin, Paul Howard *pediatrician*
Eshoo, Barbara Anne Rudolph *non-profit administrator*
Fedele, Michael Christian *Lieutenant Governor of Connecticut, computer company executive*
Fisher, Sheila Marie *literature and language professor*
Flaschen, Evan Daniel *lawyer*
Frost, James Arthur *former university president*
Galvin, J. Robert *state agency administrator, public health service officer*
Garabedian, Todd Evan *lawyer*
Geisler, James E. *manufacturing executive*
Giannaros, Demetrios Spiros *state legislator, economist, educator*
Gill, Charles D. *lawyer*
Godfrey, Robert Douglas *state legislator, lawyer*
Gould, Bruce Elliott *physician, academic administrator, educator*
Graziano, Richard J. *publishing executive*
Gunderson, Gerald Axel *economics professor*
Hamilton, Hugh Basil *minister*
Hammer, Alfred Emil *artist, educator*
Hay, Leroy E. *school system administrator*
Hayes, Gregory James *manufacturing executive*
Hazell, Naedine *editor*
Healy, Christopher *political organization administrator*
Hess, David P. *manufacturing executive*
Jahiel, Rene Ino *physician*
Jones, James Fleming, Jr. *academic administrator, language educator*
Kaimowitz, Jeffrey Hugh *librarian*
Katz, Joette *state supreme court justice*
Kedderis, Pamela Jean *academic administrator*
Killian, Robert Kenneth, Jr. *judge, lawyer*
Klimek, Joseph John *physician, educator*
Kreczko, Alan James *lawyer, insurance company executive*
Lauter, Paul *literature and language educator*
Leonhardt, Clifton Andrew *lawyer, public information officer*
Lloyd, Alex *lawyer*
Lotstein, James Irving *lawyer*
Louden, Wm. Bruce *lawyer*
Lyon, James Burroughs *lawyer*
Macaluso, Christie A. *bishop*
MacDonald, Anne *insurance company executive*
Mansell, Henry J. *archbishop*
Mardinly, Susan J. *musician, music educator*
Margulies, Beth Zeldes *state attorney general*
Mathias, Michael G. *insurance company executive*
Mattson, Ingrid *theology studies educator, religious organization administrator*
McGreevey, Greg *insurance company executive*
McHale, David R. *utilities executive*
McLachlan, C. Ian (Charles McLachlan) *state supreme court justice*
McQuade, J. Michael *manufacturing executive*
McQuillan, Mark K. *state official, school system administrator*
Meyer, J. Edward *state legislator*
Morin, Jared W. *computer scientist, educator, technologist*
Nappier, Denise L. *state treasurer*
Newman, Jon O. *federal judge*
Nicaise, Olivier Jean-Charles *chemistry professor*
Noel, Don Obert, Jr. *retired editor, columnist*

Norcott, Flemming L., Jr. *state supreme court justice*
O'Connor, Kevin James *lawyer, former federal agency administrator*
O'Donnell, Edward Francis, Jr. *lawyer*
Olivier, Leon J. *utilities executive*
O'Connor, Kevin J. *lawyer, former federal agency administrator*
Pach, Peter Barnard *columnist, editor*
Palmer, Richard N. *state supreme court justice*
Paul, Jeremy Ralph *dean, law educator*
Pepe, Louis Robert *lawyer, educator*
Peters, Ellen Ash *retired judge*
Pitkin, Howard F. *state banking agency administrator*
Ramanan, Sundaram V. *internist, hematologist, oncologist*
Rell, Jodi (Mary Jodi Rell) *Governor of Connecticut*
Reynolds, Scott Walton *academic administrator*
Richter, Donald Paul *lawyer*
Riggio, Milla C. *language educator, researcher*
Rogers, Chase Theodora *state supreme court chief justice*
Rosenberg, Ronald J. *radiologist, director*
Ryan, David Thomas *lawyer*
Sargent, Joseph Denny *insurance executive*
Schechter, Neil Lawrence *pediatrician, educator*
Scully, John Carroll *life insurance marketing research company executive*
Sorokin, Ethel Silver *lawyer*
Squatrito, Dominic J. *judge*
Strasser, Kurt Albert *law educator, researcher, author*
Sundaram, V. Ramanan *hematologist, educator*
Talbott, Susan Lubowsky *museum director, curator, arts administrator*
Tancredi, James J. *lawyer*
Taylor, Allan Bert *lawyer*
Vertefeuille, Christine Siegrist *state supreme court justice*
Vogt, Erik Michael *philosophy professor*
Voigt, Richard *lawyer*
Walters, John C. *insurance company executive*
Williams, Ronald A. *health insurance company executive*
Winter, Miriam Therese (Gloria Frances Winter) *nun, religious studies educator*
Wright, Douglass Brownell *retired judge, lawyer*
Wright, Elease *insurance company executive*
Zarella, Peter T. *state supreme court justice*
Zempsky, William Todd *physician*
Zlatkus, Lizabeth H. *insurance company executive*
Zubretsky, Joseph M. *insurance company executive*

Hebron
Kauffman, Scot R. *medical supply company executive*

Higganum
de Brigard, Emilie *anthropologist, consultant*

Ivoryton
Bendig, William Charles *editor, artist*
Osborne, John Walter *historian, educator, author*

Kent
Friedman, Frances *public relations executive*

Lakeville
Cook, Charles David *international lawyer, arbitrator, consultant*
Estabrook, Robert Harley *journalist*
Jerome, John James *lawyer*
Jones, Ronald David *retired lawyer*
Lipton, Lester *ophthalmologist, entrepreneur*

Ledyard
Chiang, Albert Chinfa *polymer chemist*
Harwood, Harold James, Jr. *biochemist*

Litchfield
Booth, John Thomas *private investor*
Fiederowicz, Walter Michael *lawyer*
Fields, Catherine K. *museum director*
Fishman, Mitchell Steven *lawyer*
Kennedy, Susan Orpha *physical education educator, consultant, sports official*
Martin, R. Keith *business and information systems educator, consultant*
Phillips, Kevin Price *political historian, writer*
Sherva, Dennis G. *retired investment company executive*

Lyme
Bloom, Barry Malcolm *research and development company executive, consultant*
LaForge, Mary Green *artist, educator*
Purcell, Bradford Moore *publishing company executive*

Madison
Anderson, G. Ernest, Jr. *retired education educator*
Cohen, Gordon S. *health products executive*
Egbert, Emerson Charles *retired publisher*
Golembeski, Jerome John *manufacturing executive*
Kay, Herbert *retired energy executive*
Kilbourne, Edwin Dennis *virologist, educator*
Pauley, Barbara Anne *author, educator*
Snell, Richard Saxon *anatomist*
Stevenson, Robert Edwin *microbiologist, consultant*

Manchester
Galasso, Francis Salvatore *materials scientist*

Mansfield Center
DiBenedetto, Anthony Thomas *engineering educator*

Mashantucket
Hatcher-White, Kimberly *museum director*

Meriden
Crespi, Tony David *psychologist*
Curran, Louis Jerome, Jr. *choral master*
Horton, Paul Chester *psychiatrist*
Lee, Henry C. *forensic scientist*
Shapiro, Philip Edwin *dermatologist, dermatopathologist, educator*
Tamburine, Jean Helen *sculptor, painter, illustrator*

Middlebury
Keggi, Kristaps J. *orthopedist, educator*
Phillips, Walter Mills III *psychologist, educator*

Middletown
Bohan, Lawrence Stewart *retired insurance company executive*
Bonin, John Paul *economics professor*
Buel, Richard Van Wyck, Jr. *retired history professor, editor, writer*
Coryell, May M. *language educator*
Fusco, George Matthew *retired military officer, engineer*
Gallarotti, Giulio M. *political science professor*
Gillmor, Charles Stewart *historian, researcher, educator*
Gruen, Lori *philosopher, educator*
Klare, Diane G. *librarian*
Linton, Fred Ernest Julius *mathematics professor, publishing executive*
Maltese, George John *mathematics professor*
Mark, Peter A. *history professor*
Meyer, Priscilla Ann *literature and language professor*
Miel, Jan *humanities educator*
Miller, Richard Alan *retired economist, educator*
Naegele, Janice Rae *science educator*
Pomper, Philip *historian, educator*
Reed, Joseph Wayne *American studies educator, artist*
Rockwood, Irving E., Jr. *publisher*
Roth, Michael S. *academic administrator, historian*
Scheibe, Karl Edward *psychology professor*
Schwarcz, Vera *historian, poet, educator*
Sengupta, Atanu *research scientist*
Slotkin, Richard Sidney *literature educator*
Wensinger, Arthur Stevens *literature and language professor, writer, translator*

Milford
Berchem, Robert Lee, Sr. *lawyer*
Bowie, William Thompson *chemist, educator*
Fagan, Alanna *artist, printmaker*
Friedman, Lloyd N. *medical educator*
Henderson, Albert Kossack *publishing and food products executive, consultant*
Hogan, John W., Jr. *lawyer*
Krall, Vita *psychologist*
Lee, Sin Hang *pathologist, educator*
Muth, Eric Peter *optician, consultant*
Perry, Dean M. *biologist*
Schwartz, Richard Edward Derecktor *retired sociologist, educator*

Monroe
Kranyik, Elizabeth Ann *secondary school educator*

Moodus
Cumming, Robert Emil *editor, writer*

Mystic
Ballard, Robert Duane *marine geologist*
Talbot, Suzanne Davidson *psychologist*
Teeson, Douglas H. *museum director*
Thompson, Robert Allan *aerospace engineer*

Naugatuck
Flannery, Joseph Patrick *manufacturing executive, director*
Mannweiler, Mary-Elizabeth *painter*
Sasso, Ruth Maryann *retired educator*

New Britain
Chung, Inkie *language educator*
Czajkowski, Eva Anna *aerospace engineer, educator*
Klonoski, Edward D. *academic administrator*
Lundgren, John F. *consumer products company executive*
Mulcahy, Daniel G. *education educator*
Murphy, Christopher S. *United States Representative from Connecticut, former state senator*
Naoumov, Viatcheslav I. *mechanical and aerospace engineer, educator*
Pearl, Helen Zalkan *lawyer*
Penniman, Clayton *biology professor*
Shen, Xiaoping *geography educator*
Stathos, Lifteria K. *retired educational association administrator*

New Canaan
Ackerman, Sigurd Howard *psychiatrist*
Allen, Joseph Henry *retired publishing company executive*
Bisbee, Gerald Elftman, Jr. *investment company executive*
Burns, Ivan Alfred *grocery products and industrial company executive*
Burns, John Joseph, Jr. *financial and insurance holding company executive*
Cohen, Richard Norman *insurance executive*
Coughlin, Francis Raymond, Jr. *surgeon, educator, lawyer*
Crossman, William Whittard *retired wire cable and communications executive*
Dean, Robert Bruce *architect*
Despres, Louise Fay *secondary school educator*
Ferro, Guy (Gaetano Ferro) *lawyer*
Fredericks, Jeanne Maria Judson *literary agent*
Grace, Julianne Alice *retired investor relations executive*
Hugo, Norman Eliot *retired plastic surgeon, educator*
Kamerschen, Robert Jerome *retired senior business executive, private investor, consultant*
Klenk, Rosemary Ellen *pediatrician, educator*
Kovatch, Jak Gene *artist*
MacEwan, Nigel Savage *retired merchant banker*
McIvor, Donald Kenneth *retired petroleum company executive*
McKeough, Susan Anne *elementary school educator*
Nichols, Ralph Arthur *retired lawyer*
Papp, Laszlo George *retired architect*
Pike, William Edward *retired banking executive*
Risom, Jens *furniture designer, consultant, manufacturing executive*
Steinmetz, Richard Bird, Jr. *lawyer*
White, Richard Booth *management consultant*
Wiechmann, Eric Watt *lawyer*

New Haven
Abramson, Arthur Seymour *linguistics educator, researcher*
Adair, Robert Kemp *physicist, educator*
Akkoyunlu, Mustafa *physician, scientist*
Albrecht, Alice *research scientist*
Alexander, Bruce Donald *real estate executive, educator*
Alexander, Elizabeth *poet, English language educator*
Alonzo, Suzanne Henson *ecologist, educator*
Alpern, Robert J. *dean, medical educator*
Altice, Frederick L. *epidemiologist, director*
Altman, Sidney *biology professor*
Anderson, Carl Albert *fraternal organization administrator, lawyer, dean*
Anderson, John Fredric *science administrator, entomologist, researcher*
Andiman, Warren Alan *epidemiologist, educator*
Andrews, Donald Wilfrid Kao *economics professor*
Aronson, Peter Samuel *physiologist, researcher*
Bagley, Constance Elizabeth *lawyer, educator*
Bailey, William Harrison *artist, educator*
Baker, Deanna Louise *technologist*
Balay, Robert Elmore *editor, librarian*
Baltay, Charles *physicist, educator*
Baltimore, Robert Samuel *pediatrician, epidemiologist*
Behling, Paul Lawrence *lawyer, educator*
Benfer, David William *hospital administrator*
Berland, Gretchen K. *medical educator, filmmaker*
Birnbaum, Irwin Morton *educational consultant, lawyer*
Blake, Ruth Elaine *geophysicist, educator*
Blatt, Sidney Jules *psychology professor, psychoanalyst, investigator*
Bloom, Harold *humanities educator, writer*
Bloomer, Kent Cress *architecture educator*
Bloomgarden, Gary Michael *neurosurgeon*
Borroff, Marie *English language educator*
Bowering, Gerhard *religious studies educator*
Boyer, James Lorenzen *internist, educator*
Bracken, Paul *political science professor*
Braverman, Irwin Merton *dermatologist, educator*
Brenzel, Jeffrey *dean*
Briggs, Derek Ernest Gilmor *science educator*
Brilmayer, R. Lea *lawyer, educator*
Brown, Thomas Huntington *neuroscientist*
Brownell, Kelly David *psychologist, educator*
Bugbee, Gregory Joseph *soil scientist, researcher*
Burt, Robert Amsterdam *lawyer, educator*
Burtness, Barbara Ann *medical educator, oncologist*
Bynum, Terrell Ward *humanities educator, consultant*
Cabranes, José Alberto *federal judge*
Calabresi, Guido *federal judge, educator*
Carter, Stephen Lisle *law educator*
Casten, Richard Francis *physicist, educator*
Cha, Charles *surgical oncologist, hepatobiliary surgeon*
Chhieng, Cheung David *pathologist, educator*
Clark, Elias *law educator*
Clark, Katerina *literature and language professor*
Coe, Michael Douglas *retired anthropologist*
Cohen, Lawrence Sorel *internist, educator*
Collins, William F., Jr. *neurosurgery educator*
Comer, James Pierpont *psychiatrist, educator*
Curran, Lisa M. *environmental scientist, educator*
Curtis, Jeptha P. *cardiologist, educator*
Daly, Radley Hutchinson *retired academic administrator*
Dannehy, Nora R. *prosecutor*
Dardik, Alan *surgeon, educator*
Days, Drew S. III *lawyer, educator*
Del Negro, John Thomas *lawyer*
De Rose, Sandra Michele *psychotherapist, coach, educator, administrator*
Dimock, Wai Chee *literature and language professor*
Donoghue, Michael John *biologist, educator, museum director*
Dorsey, Peter Collins *federal judge*
DuBois, Arthur Brooks *physiologist, educator*
Dubrow, Ro D. *public health service officer, educator*
Duke, Steven Barry *law educator*
Duncan, James S. *engineering educator*
Durham, John H. *prosecutor*
Dyson, William R. *state legislator*
Ehrenkranz, Richard Allan *pediatrician*
Ellickson, Robert Chester *law educator*
Ember, Carol R. *anthropology educator, writer*
Ember, Melvin Lawrence *anthropologist, educator*
Errante, Steven James *lawyer*
Fassler, Margot Elsbeth *music educator, religious studies educator*
Feldman, Grace A. *music educator*
Fischer, Michael John *computer science educator*
Fiss, Owen M. *law educator*
Fleming, Gregory James *law educator, former diversified financial services company executive*
Floch, Martin Herbert *physician*
Forget, Bernard G. *hematologist, educator*
Foster, Roger Sherman, Jr. *surgeon, educator, health facility administrator*
Fuchs, Elinor *theater critic, playwright, educator*
Funai, Edmund F. *gynecologist*
Gastwirth, Donald Edward *lawyer, literary agent*
Gauthier, Jacques Armand *geologist, educator, curator*
Gendler, Tamar Szabo *philosopher, educator*
Genel, Myron *pediatrician, educator*
Gent, Martin P.N. *agricultural scientist*
Gerow, Aaron *performing arts educator*
Gilbert, Creighton Eddy *art historian*
Gildea, Brian Michael *lawyer*
Girvin, Steven Mark *physicist, researcher, academic administrator*
Goffart, Walter André *history professor*
Goodrich, Isaac *neurosurgeon, educator*
Graetz, Michael J. *law educator*
Grauer, Jonathan Newman *orthopedist, educator*
Gray, Margaret *dean, nursing educator*
Greene, Liliane *literature and language educator, editor*
Grey, Margaret *nursing educator*
Gross, Ian *academic pediatrician, neonatologist*
Gusberg, Richard Jefferson *surgeon, educator*
Hacker, Jacob Stewart *political science professor, author*
Hallo, William Wolfgang *literature and language professor, writer*
Hamilton, Andrew D. *academic administrator, chemistry professor*
Hansmann, Henry Baethke *law educator*
Harries, Karsten *philosophy educator, researcher*
Harrison, Henry Starin *real estate appraiser, educator, entrepreneur*
Hayden, Dolores *author, educator*
Hayes, Jonathan *psychologist*
Heister, Carla Gayle *librarian*
Henderson, Timothy John *history educator*
Heninger, George Robert *psychology professor, researcher*
Hickey, Leo Joseph *museum curator, educator*
Hollander, John *humanities educator, poet*
Horwich, Arthur L. *biologist, educator*
Hostetter, Margaret K. *pediatrician, medical educator*
Howe, Roger Evans *mathematician, educator*
Hsiao, Allen L. *physician, educator*
Humphrey, David Aiken *painter, printmaker, educator*
Huwiler, Joan P. *public relations executive, consultant*
Igarashi, Peter *nephrologist, educator, nephrologist, researcher*
Jacob, Deirdre Ann Bradbury *manufacturing executive, finance educator, consultant*
Jatlow, Peter I. *pathologist, medical educator, researcher*
Johnson, Lester Fredrick *artist*
Johnson, Marcia K. *psychology professor, department chairman*
Johnstone, Quintin *law educator*
Jordt, Sven-Eric *pharmacologist, researcher*
Jorgensen, William L. *chemistry educator*
Kalyanpur, Arjun *radiologist*
Kalyvas, Stathis N. *political science professor, director*
Kashgarian, Michael *pathologist, educator*
Kastan, David Scott *literature educator, writer*
Kawano, Tsutomu *medical researcher*
Kazdin, Alan E. *psychology professor*
Kevles, Daniel Jerome *historian, educator, writer*
Kiernan, Benedict Francis *historian, educator*
Kim, Jung H. *medical researcher, educator*
Kim, Young Shin *psychiatrist, educator*
King, Robert Alan *psychiatrist, educator*
Krause, Peter James *pediatrician, researcher, educator*
Krumholz, Harlan Marc *cardiologist, internist, educator*
Kushlan, Samuel Daniel *internist, educator, hospital administrator*
Lamar, Howard Roberts *academic administrator, historian*
Lampert, Rachel *cardiologist, educator*
Langbein, John Harriss *lawyer, educator*
Lange, Fabian *economics professor*
LaPalombara, Joseph *political science educator, industrial management educator*
Leffell, David Joel *dermatologist, surgeon, writer, photographer, medical school administrator, educator*
Leo, Martha E. *advocate, counselor*
Levin, Rick (Richard Charles Levin) *academic administrator, economist*
Levine, Robert John *internist, medical educator, ethicist*
Lord, George deForest *language educator*
Lord, Ruth *researcher, writer, philanthropist*
Lytton, Bernard *urology educator*
Manley, Lawrence G. *literature educator*
Marcus, Ruth Barcan *philosopher, educator, writer, lecturer*
Margulis, Gregory A. *mathematics and science professor, researcher*
Marks, Lawrence Edward *psychologist, educator*
Marmor, Theodore Richard *political science professor, writer*
Mayhew, David Raymond *political science professor*
McClatchy, J. D. *editor, writer, educator*
McDermott, Drew Vincent *computer science educator*
McPartland, James *research scientist*
Meier, George Henry *vascular surgeon*
Mendelsohn, Robert *educator*
Mercurio, Mark R. *pediatrician, educator*
Meyers, Amy *museum director*
Miller, I. George *physician, educator, researcher*
Moczydlowski, Edward Gerard *biologist, researcher*
Modd, Lawrence R. *surgeon*
Monteiro, Antónia *biology professor*
Moore, Peter Bartlett *biochemist, educator*
Mostaghimi, Mehdi *economist, educator*
Mostow, George Daniel *mathematics professor*
Musto, David Franklin *medical researcher, educator, historian, consultant*
Narendra, Kumpati Subrahmanya *electrical engineer, educator*
Nelson, Alondra R. *social sciences educator*
Newick, Craig David *architect*
Novick, Peter J. *cell biologist, educator*
Okerson, Ann Shumelda Lillian *librarian*
Oster, Sharon M. *dean, management educator*
Pan, Baocheng *biophysicist, researcher*
Patrizio, Pasquale *reproductive endocrinologist, andrologist, and infertility specialist*
Patterson, Lee *language educator*
Patwa, Huned S. *neurology educator*
Pauls, David *human geneticist, researcher*
Paveza, Gregory J. *dean*
Pelli, Cesar *architect*

Persing, John Arthur *surgeon*
Phillips, Caryl *writer*
Phillips, Peter Charles Bonest *economist, educator, researcher*
Pieribone, Vincent Allen *medical researcher, educator*
Pollard, Thomas Dean *cell biologist, educator*
Pospisil, Leopold Jaroslav *anthropologist, law educator*
Post, Robert Charles *dean, law educator*
Priest, George L. *law educator*
Prochaska, Alice *historian, librarian*
Prown, Jules David *art historian, educator*
Quint, David Louis *literature and language professor*
Rakic, Pasko *neuroscientist, educator*
Ranis, Gustav *economist, educator*
Rawson, Claude Julien *literature and language professor*
Redmond, Donald Eugene, Jr. *neuroscientist, educator*
Reed, Mark Arthur *research scientist, educator*
Reynolds, Jock *artist, curator, art gallery director*
Risch, Harvey A. *epidemiologist, educator*
Roberts, Kurt Eric *medical educator, director*
Robinson, Dorothy K. *lawyer*
Robinson, Fred Colson *language educator*
Rosazza, Peter Anthony *bishop*
Rose, Aron D. *ophthalmologist, educator*
Rose-Ackerman, Susan *law and political economy educator*
Rosenbluth, Frances McCall *political scientist, educator*
Roth, Harold *architect*
Rothman, James Edward *cell biologist, educator*
Russett, Bruce Martin *political science professor*
Ryder, Robert Winsor *medical epidemiologist*
Salovey, Peter *academic administrator, psychology professor*
Sammons, Jeffrey Leonard *foreign language educator*
Sartorelli, Alan Clayton *pharmacologist, educator*
Sasaki, Clarence Takashi *surgeon, educator*
Saunders, Martin *chemistry educator, researcher*
Savoye, Mary *dietician, researcher*
Schmitz, Oswald Joseph *biology professor*
Schowalter, John Erwin *child and adolescent psychiatry educator*
Schuck, Peter Horner *lawyer, educator*
Schultz, T. Paul *economics professor*
Scoutt, Leslie M. *medical educator*
Seashore, Margretta Reed *physician, educator*
Semmel, Stuart *historian*
Shapiro, Eugene David *pediatrician, epidemiologist, educator*
Shaw, Albert Cheng-gin *medical educator, researcher*
Shiller, Robert James *economist*
Siegel, Reva B. *law educator*
Silberschatz, Abraham (Avi Silberschatz) *computer scientist, educator, researcher*
Silbert, Jonathan E. *judge*
Simon, John Gerald *law educator*
Skowronek, Stephen Lee *political scientist, educator*
Smith, Brian Richard *hematologist, oncologist, pathologist*
Smith, John Edwin *philosophy educator*
Snowden, Frank Martin III *history professor*
Sommer, Miriam Goldstein (Mimi G. Sommer) *writer, photographer*
Speth, James Gustave *dean, environmental studies educator, lawyer*
Spiegel, Matthew *finance educator*
Srihari, Vinod Hiremagalur *psychiatrist*
Stack, Gary Edward *medical educator*
Stahl, Richard Sheldon *surgeon*
Stapleton, James Francis *lawyer*
State, Matthew W. *cell biologist, neuroscientist, educator*
Steitz, Joan Argetsinger *biochemistry professor*
Steitz, Thomas A. *science educator*
Stepto, Robert Burns *literature and language professor*
Stern, Robert *psychiatrist*
Stevens, Joseph Charles *psychology professor*
Stith-Cabranes, Kate *law educator*
Stokes, Susan C. *political science professor*
Strauss, John Steaven *psychiatrist, educator*
Stuehrenberg, Paul Frederick *librarian*
Sullivan, Shaun Stuart *lawyer*
Summers, William Cofield *science educator*
Sussman, Henry Stephen *literature and language professor*
Sutterlin, James Smyrl *political science professor, researcher*
Swensen, David Frederick *investment advisor*
Thakur, Vinay V. *research scientist*
Thaw, David Bernard *law educator*
Tinetti, Mary E. *geriatrician, educator*
Tirro, Frank Pascale *music educator, composer, writer*
Trumble, Angus A. G. *curator, writer*
Turner, Frank Miller *historian, educator*
Underdown, David Edward *historian, educator*
Urry, Meg (C. Megan Urry) *physics professor*
Vermeire, Jon J. *research scientist*
Volkmar, Fred Robert *psychiatrist, educator, director*
Waggoner, Paul Edward *agricultural scientist*
Wagner, Allan Ray *psychology professor*
Walker, Walter Dray, Jr. *lawyer*
Walker, John Mercer, Jr. *federal judge*
Wallerstein, Immanuel *sociologist*
Wandycz, Piotr Stefan *historian, educator*
Webster, Tashonna *health services researcher*
Weiss, Robert M. *urologist, educator*
Werner, Volker Ralph *physics professor*
Williams, Tom *college football coach*
Winroth, Anders *historian, educator*
Winter, Jay Murray *history professor*
Winter, Ralph Karl, Jr. *federal judge*
Wolf, Werner Paul *physicist, researcher*
Yeargan, Michael *scenic designer*
Yeazell, Ruth Bernard *English language educator*
Zaret, Barry Lewis *cardiologist, medical educator*
Zedillo Ponce de León, Ernesto *economics professor, former president of Mexico*
Zelitch, Israel *retired scientist*
Zito, Christina Ivins *molecular biologist, educator*

New London
Asselin-Connolly, John Thomas *lawyer*
Carpenter, Bruce William *information technology manager, director*
Clarke, Florence Dorothy *minister, educator*
Dr. Zapalska, Alina M. *economics professor*
Dunne, Michael William *research and development company executive*
Higdon, Leo Ignatius, Jr., (Lee Higdon) *academic administrator*
Paxton, Frederick S. *history professor*
Reardon, Robert Ignatius, Jr. *lawyer*
Schoenberger, Steven Harris *physician, research consultant*
Tassinari, Melissa Sherman *teratologist, developmental toxicologist*
Urbanetti, John Sutherland *internist, consultant*

New Milford
Fabricand, Burton Paul *physicist, researcher*
Jeyapalan, Jey K. *civil engineer*

Newington
Anderson, Kathryn Parks *music educator*
Chiarenza, Frank John *language educator*
Cohen, Fern K. *music educator*
Reynolds, Patricia Jean *psychiatric social worker, songwriter*

Newtown
Coates, John Peter *technical executive*
Cole, Richard John *marketing executive*
Cottingham, Robert *artist*
Forger, Robert Durkin *retired professional association administrator*
Sanetti, Stephen Louis *lawyer*

Niantic
Butler, Jonathan Putnam *architect*
Deakyne, William John *library director, musician*
Douglas, Robert Gordon, Jr. *physician*

Norfolk
Jessup, Philip Caryl, Jr. *retired lawyer*
O'Malley, John Patrick *dean*

North Branford
Blum, John Morton *retired historian*
Gasparine, Barbara Ellen *elementary school educator*
Ingram, George *manufacturing executive*
Mead, Lawrence Myers, Jr. *retired engineering executive*

North Haven
Apter, David Ernest *political science and sociology professor*
Herzenberg, Arvid *physicist, researcher*
Hogan, James Carroll, Jr. *public health administrator, research biologist*
Hudson, Richard L. *retired adult education educator, minister*
Moeller, Judith Stone *reading educator, consultant*

North Stonington
Svengalis, Kendall Frayne *law librarian, publishing executive, educator, writer*

Northford
Gregan, Edmund Robert *landscape architect*
James, Virginia Stowell *retired elementary and secondary school educator*

Norwalk
Alvey, Brian *blogger*
Baylis, Robert Montague *investment banker, charity director*
Bays, John Theophanis *consulting engineer*
Brown, William Terrel *psychology professor, educational consultant*
Cammaker, Sheldon Ira *lawyer*
Carlucci, David R. *information technology executive*
DeCesare, Donald E. *broadcast executive*
Falsone, Jack Joseph *physician*
Fish, James *healthcare administrator*
Gold, Richard N. *management consultant*
Guzzi, Anthony J. *construction executive*
Hammer, Warren *chiropractor*
Harris, Holton Edwin *plastics machinery manufacturing executive*
Herring, Jennifer E. *museum administrator*
Hudson, Thomas Richard, Jr. *hedge fund manager*
Johnson, Robert James *psychology educator*
Johnston, Catherine Viscardi *former magazine publisher*
Littman, Edward *physician*
MacInnis, Frank T. *construction and holding company executive, securities trader*
Nelson, Paula Morrison Bronson *retired reading specialist*
Nightingale, William Joslyn *management consultant*
Perry, Charles Owen *sculptor*
Piper, Thomas Laurence III *banker*
Pompa, Mark A. *construction executive*
Reilly, Edward Arthur *lawyer*
Soper, Jeannine *real estate agent*
Tropin, Kenneth G. *hedge fund manager*
Walker, Kellye L. *lawyer*
Yeosock, Michael Michael *funeral director, civil engineer*
Zimmerman, Lawrence A. *printing company executive*

Norwich
Cote, Michael Richard *bishop*
Pudlo, Steven Edward *computer technician*
Ringel, Faye Joyce *retired literature educator*

Oakville
Carroll, Constance Marie *pianist, music educator*

Old Greenwich
Dixon, John Morris *magazine editor*
Lorefice, Laurence Santo *psychiatrist*
Robertson, Dawn H. *former retail executive*

Old Lyme
Andersen, Jeffrey W. *museum director*
Carey, William Michael, Jr. *research physicist, engineer*
Fairfield-Sonn, James Willed *management educator, consultant*
Willauer, George Jacob *American literature educator*

Old Saybrook
Geer, Lois Margaret *music educator*
Gilmore, Clarence Percy *editor-in-chief, writer*
Norcia, Stephen William *advertising executive*
Phillips, William E. *advertising agency executive*
Smith, David Clark *research scientist*

Orange
Davies, Richard Warren *lawyer*
Davis, David Brion *historian, educator*
Liu, Chuanju *orthopedist, educator*
Powers, Timothy H. *electric power industry executive*
Zitnay, Jill M. *educational consultant, educator*

Oxford
Hayes, Arthur Hull, Jr. *physician, clinical pharmacology educator, medical school dean, business executive, consultant*

Pawcatuck
Gitzendanner, Robert *manufacturing engineer, director*
Gnanaraj, Joseph Sathiya *senior scientist*

Plainfield
Brown, Philip Henry *psychiatric social worker*

Plainville
Chase, Peter *library director*
Glassman, Gerald Seymour *metal products executive*
Perkins-Banas, Melissa Veronica *neuropsychologist*

Plantsville
Roy, Ralph Lord *clergyman*

Pomfret Center
Sweatt, Ermelinda Espinola *retired mathematics educator*

Prospect
Powell, Raymond William *financial planner, school administrator*

Putnam
Day, John Anthony, Jr. *pulmonologist*

Redding
Begell, William *publisher*
Kobak, James Benedict *management consultant*
Poulos, Christopher *literature and language educator*
Quinn, Andrew Peter, Jr. *lawyer, retired insurance company executive*

Ridgefield
Benton, Suzanne *sculptor, mask ritualist, printmaker, painter*
Brewster, Carroll Worcester *former academic administrator*
Bucha, Paul William *real estate consultant, management consultant, policy advisor*
Busacca, Carl Alan *chemist*
Hammel, Heidi B. *physicist, researcher, astronomer*
Hilbrich, Lutz *physician, pharmaceutical executive*
Ingram, Samuel William, Jr. *retired lawyer*
Levine, Paul Michael *paper company executive, consultant*
McConnell, John Edward *retired electrical engineering company executive*
Mesznik, Joel R. *investment banker*
Ramírez-Montagut, Mónica *curator*
Taylor, Edwin R. *music director*
Yang, Jianfei *immunologist*

Riverside
Coulson, Robert *retired professional society administrator, arbitrator, writer*
Deering, Allan Brooks *retired soft drink company executive*
Geismar, Richard Lee *communications executive*
Powers, Claudia McKenna *state legislator*

Rocky Hill
Decker, Robert Owen *history professor, clergyman*
Wilson, Karen Lynn *esthetician*

Salisbury
Dresser, James van Benschoten *retired management consultant*
Kilner, Ursula Blanche *genealogist, educator, writer*

Sandy Hook
Rosenblatt, Stephen Paul *marketing and sales promotion company executive*

Sharon
Gordon, Nicholas *broadcast and performing arts executive*
Johns, Jasper *artist*
Learsy, Raymond J. *private investor*
Lisle, Laurie *author*
Tucker, Alan David *publisher*

Shelton
Aferzon, Mark *otolaryngologist*
DeLucia, David Ralph *psychologist*
Kantrowitz, Jonathan Daniel *publishing executive, educator, lawyer*
Spivack, Barney S. *physician*

Simsbury
Eisenmann, Carl D. *lawyer*
Long, Michael Thomas *lawyer, manufacturing executive*
Osborne, Louise *publishing executive*
Roberts, Celia Ann *librarian*

Somers
Blake, Stewart Prestley *retired ice cream company executive*

South Glastonbury
Schroth, Peter William *lawyer, management, educator*

South Kent
Baker, John Milnes *architect*
Keehner, Michael Arthur Miller *investment banking executive*
Samartini, James Rogers *retired appliance company executive*

South Windsor
Baretta, Marsha Motyl *elementary school physical education educator*
Mulé, Lisa Nystrom *speech pathology/audiology services professional*
Murtha, Roger Gerry *music educator*
van Dokkum, Jan *electric power industry executive*

Southbury
Atwood, Edward Charles *economist, educator*
Foxworth, Johnnie Hunter *retired state agency administrator*
Hopf, Frank Rudolph *retired dentist*
Rorick, William Calvin *portrait artist, retired librarian*
Russell, Allan David *lawyer*
Welton, Sharon Marie *food service executive*

Southington
Bagwell, Carol Tessier *special education educator, consultant*
Byeff, Peter David *hematologist, oncologist*

Southport
Cutler, Kenneth B., Jr. *dermatologist, educator*
Damson, Barrie Morton *oil and gas exploration company executive*
Fignar, Eugene Michael *finance company executive, lawyer*
Herzog, John E. *numismatist*
Twiname, John Dean *minister, human services administrator*
Wilbur, E. Packer *investment company executive*
Yach, Derek *epidemiologist, health policy analyst*

Stafford Springs
Guglielmo, Anthony *state legislator*

Stamford
Allott, Anthony J. *packaging industry executive*
Babson, Jane Frances *artist, writer*
Bainton, J(ohn) Joseph *lawyer*
Barker, James Rex *water transportation executive, director*
Bostin, Marvin Jay *hospital and health services consultant*
Brasser, William J. *finance company executive*
Burns, Ursula M. *copier company executive*
Burston, Richard Mervin *marketing executive*
Burton, David K. *lawyer*
Burton, Robert Gene *printing company executive*
Buzzard, James A. *paper, packaging and chemical company executive*
Caldwell, Philip *retired automobile manufacturing and finance company executive*
Cary, William H. (Bill Cary) *finance company executive*
Cassidy, Denis Andrew *artist, architect*
Certilman, Steven Andrew *lawyer*
Chang, Ted T. *chemist*
Chilton, Richard L., Jr. *hedge fund manager*
Chomnycky, Paul Patrick *bishop*
Cohen, Steven A. *hedge fund manager*
Colthup, Norman Bertram *retired spectroscopist*
Cook, Colin Burford *psychiatrist*
Dell, Warren Frank, II, *management consultant*
Della Rocco, Kenneth Anthony *lawyer*
Dolan, Thomas J. *printing company executive*
Dunbar, Kwamie O. *economics professor, director*
Duncan, Thomas Webb *media executive*
duPont, Augustus Irénée *lawyer*
Dupont, Ralph Paul *lawyer, educator*
Engel, Gerald L. *engineering educator*
Erichson, Robert B. *hematologist, oncologist*
Faraci, John Vincent, Jr. *paper company executive*
Fast, Eric Carson *manufacturing executive*
Fernandez, Manual A. *information technology consulting executive*
Firestone, James A. *printing company executive*
Frank, Laura Jean *computer scientist*
Gladstone, Herbert Jack *manufacturing executive*
Glassman, Hilary E. *lawyer, communications executive*
Gold, Steven Michael *lawyer*
Goldsmith, Donna *sports entertainment company executive*
Goodhue, Peter Ames *obstetrician, gynecologist, educator*
Gross, Ronald Martin *forest products executive, consultant*
Handler, Evelyn *former academic administrator*
Horrigan, D. Gregory *packaging products executive*
Hudson, Harold Jordon, Jr. *retired insurance executive*
Jason, J. Julie *portfolio manager, writer, lawyer*
Karp, Steve *agent*
Keane, Margaret *bank executive*
Klein, Neil Charles *physician*
Koproski, Alexander Robert *real estate company executive*
Krutter, Forrest Nathan *lawyer*

Lane, Hana Umlauf *editor*
Leader, Leonard *lawyer*
Lesko, Newland A. *paper company executive*
Levitan, Gutman *research and development company executive, communications engineer*
Liu, Don H. *lawyer, printing company executive*
Losten, Basil Harry *bishop emeritus*
Mac Donald, Michael C. *printing company executive*
Macurdy, John Edward *bass*
Malloy, Dannel Patrick *Mayor, Stamford, Connecticut*
Martin, John K. *communications executive*
Martin, Murray D. *manufacturing executive*
McCarrick, Edward R. *publishing executive*
McGrath, Richard *lawyer*
McKenna, Matthew Morgan *lawyer*
Mc Kinley, John Key *retired oil company executive*
McMahon, Robert Matthew *corporate financial executive*
Monahan, Michael *manufacturing executive*
Monson, Robert Joseph *education educator*
Montross, Franklin, IV, (Tad Montross) *reinsurance company executive*
Mulcahy, Anne Marie *copier company executive*
Mulrooney, Melissa Hutchens *museum director*
Munera, Gerard Emmanuel *manufacturing executive*
Nazemetz, Patricia M. *printing company executive*
Nitowsky, Harold Martin *physician, educator*
Novikova, Tatyana *music educator*
O'Meara, Vicki A. *lawyer*
Pansini, Michael Samuel *financial analyst, tax specialist*
Pappas, Alceste Thetis *consulting company executive, educator*
Perle, Eugene Gabriel *lawyer*
Pickel, Alan Scott *lawyer*
Ressel, Teresa Mullett *diversified financial services company executive, former federal agency administrator*
Robins, Robert Sidwar *political science professor, department chairman*
Rose, Richard Loomis *lawyer*
Rosenstock, Arthur Richard *plastic surgeon, educator*
Shanman, James Alan *lawyer*
Sherman, Mickey (Michael Sherman) *lawyer*
Silver, R. Philip *packaging products executive*
Simon, Scott *neurosurgeon, director*
Skidd, Thomas Patrick, Jr. *lawyer*
Smith, Rodger Field *financial executive*
Staab, Diane D. *lawyer*
Teitell, Conrad Laurence *lawyer, writer*
Thompson, Fred *public relations executive, former medical association administrator*
Vandebroek, Sophie Verdonckt *printing company executive*
Walker, Jay Scott *media company executive*
Walsh, Kevin P. *energy executive, financial services executive*
Walsh, Thomas Joseph *ophthalmologist*
Weitzel, William Conrad, Jr. *lawyer*
Wilderotter, Maggie (Mary Agnes Wilderotter) *software company executive, former cable television executive*
Willkie, Wendell Lewis, II, *lawyer*
Yarish, Charles *biology professor, researcher*

Stonington
Cole, Richard A. *retired lawyer*
Elliott, Inger McCabe *apparel designer, textiles executive, consultant*
Simmons, Robert Ruhl *former congressman*

Storrs
Diaby, Moustapha *operations research educator*
Edsall, Randy Douglas *college football coach*
Kiene, Susan Maria *psychologist*
Mueller-Westerhoff, Ulrich Theodor *retired chemistry professor*
Peters, Thomas Joseph *computer scientist, mathematician*
Shah, Farhed *economics educator*

Storrs Mansfield
Adelson, Jill Lynn *assistant professor, educational research consultant*
Auriemma, Geno *women's college basketball coach*
Azimi, Fakhreddin *history professor*
Baldwin, Carlita Rose *minister*
Barnes-Farrell, Janet Lorraine *psychologist*
Bartram, Ralph Herbert *physicist*
Basu, Joysurya *technologist, researcher*
Baxter, Donald Leon Murray *education educator*
Brown, Richard David *history professor*
Bzymek, Zbigniew Marian *engineering educator*
Calhoun, Jim *men's college basketball coach*
Caner, Daniel Folger *classicist, history professor*
Cazel, Fred A., Jr. *history professor*
Charters, Ann *literature educator*
Chazdon, Robin Lee *botanist, educator*
Chiu, Wilson K. S. *engineering educator*
Coons, Ronald Edward *historian, educator*
Devereux, Owen Francis *retired metallurgy educator*
Do, Cuong M. *research scientist*
Eisdorfer, Assaf *finance educator*
Franklin, Brinley *library director*
Ghosh, Chinmoy *finance educator*
Goldich, Terri Jean *curator*
Grasso, Domenic *civil engineering educator*
Gross, Robert Alan *history professor*
Harel, Ofer *statistician, educator*
Harty, Leanne Kennedy *museum director*
Hogan, Michael J. *academic administrator*
Holsinger, Kent Eugene *biology professor, educator*
Irizarry, Guillermo B. *language educator*
Islam, Muhammad M. *theoretical physicist*
Katz, Leonard *psychology professor, researcher*
Kenny, David A. *physics professor*
Kerr, Kirklyn M. *academic administrator, veterinarian, pathologist*
Kessel, Quentin Cattell *physicst, educator*
Kim, Jeong-Ho *engineering educator*
Klemens, Paul Gustav *physicist, researcher*
Laufer, Hans *developmental biologist, educator*
Leach, Colin Wayne *psychology professor*
MacDonald, John Thomas *school system administrator*
Marcus, Harris Leon *materials science educator*
McEachern, William Archibald *economics educator*
Michaels, Claire Farley *psychology educator*
Moynihan, William Trumbull *educator*
Mulkey, Daniel K. *research scientist*
Narayan, Sumit *research assistant*
Nicholls, Peter J. *academic administrator*
Orringer, Nelson Robert *Spanish and comparative literature educator*
Petrovic, Kimberly Ann *nursing researcher, educator*
Pitkin, Edward Thaddeus *aerospace engineer, consultant*
Rajasekaran, Sanguthevar *computer science educator*
Reed, Howard Alexander *retired historian, educator*
Reifsnider, Kenneth Leonard *metallurgist, educator*
Rickards, John Patrick *psychology professor*
Rimland, Lisa Phillip *writer, composer, lyricist*
Rohner, Ronald Preston *anthropology educator, psychologist*
Rose, Dale A.J. *performing arts educator*
Ross, Stephen L. *economics professor*
Schulthess, Cristian P. *chemistry professor*
Shapiro, Eve Ilana *medical researcher*
Simons, Doreen Lee *language educator, researcher*
Stwalley, William Calvin *physics and chemistry professor*
Tucker, Edwin Wallace *law educator*
Turchin, Peter *biology professor*
Wachman, Murray *retired mathematics professor*
Wang, Fei *pharmacist, educator*
Willis, Brian G. *chemistry professor*
Woods, David G. *dean*
Zofka, Adam *civil engineer, educator*

Stratford
Blair, Sylvia H. *project engineer*
Feinberg, Dennis Lowell *dermatologist*
Giordano, Kathryn M. *psychology educator*
Jonas, Tina Westby *helicopter manufacturing company executive, former federal agency administrator*
Linder, Anthony *marketing executive*
Mahoney, Maurice Jeremiah *medical educator*
O'Rourke, James Louis *lawyer*
Pino, Jeffrey P. *manufacturing executive*

Suffield
Bianchi, Maria *critical care specialist, acute care nurse practitioner, consultant*
Hanzalek, Astrid Teicher *public information officer, consultant*

Taconic
Medvecky, Patricia *retired elementary school educator*

Terryville
Block, Fran *library media specialist*

Thomaston
Mühlanger, Erich *ski manufacturing company executive*

Torrington
Gradowski, Kristine Shepard *language educator*
Kathuria, Nirmal Bhatia *psychiatrist*
Lippincott, Walter Edward *law educator*
Rolfe, Ellen Mary *retired music educator*
Wall, Robert Anthony, Jr. *lawyer*

Trumbull
Bernstein, Larry Howard *clinical pathologist*
Lang, James Richard *software designer, magician*
Norcel, Jacqueline Joyce Casale *educational association administrator*
Watson, Donald Ralph *architect, dean, writer, artist*

Uncasville
Thibault, Mike *professional basketball coach*

Vernon Rockville
Courtney, Joe (Joseph D. Courtney) *United States Representative from Connecticut*
Marmer, Ellen Lucille *pediatrician, cardiologist*

Voluntown
Caddell, Foster *artist*

Wallingford
Firestone, Raymond Armand *chemist*
Frisch, Michael Jay *computer scientist*
Hartz, Richard Allen *research scientist*
Kryger, Meir *medical educator, researcher*
Lauttenbach, Carol *artist*
Lelas, Snjezana *pharmacologist, researcher*
Loeffler, Martin H. *electronics executive*
Norwitt, Richard Adam *manufacturing executive*

Washington
Brimelow, Peter *journalist*
Leab, Daniel Joseph *history professor*

Washington Depot
Levine, Laurence Brandt *investment banker*

Waterbury
Carrington, Virginia Gail (Vee) *marketing professional, consultant*
Chabria, Shiven B. *physician, educator*
DeCesare, Joyce Shiel *retired guidance counselor*
DeFrancesco, Mark Stephen *physician*
Donahue, Linda Wheeler *retired humanities educator, writer*
Dost, Mark W. *lawyer*
Dudrick, Stanley John *surgeon, research scientist, educator*
Flaherty, Billie S. *lawyer, chemicals executive*
Garsten, Joel Jay *gastroenterologist*
Harper, Barbara Clara *educational program administrator, counselor*
Lang, Christine JoAnn *middle school educator*
Lipshaw, Jeffrey Marc *lawyer, chemicals executive, educator*
Lum, Johnny *physician assistant, consultant*
MacLeod, Glen Gary *language educator*
Martone, Eric Anthony Domenic *history educator*
McSweeney, J. Emmett *library director*
Moon, Lloyd N. *chemicals executive*
Pape, William James, II, *newspaper publisher*
Renda, Joseph L. *nephrologist, educator*
Rogerson, Craig Allan *manufacturing executive*
Shivery, Charles W. *utilities executive*
Silbert, Jonathan E. *ophthalmologist, educator*
Sullivan, William J. *state supreme court justice*
Swiech, Alan M. *human relations executive*
Upson, Thomas Fisher *judge, retired state senator, lawyer*
Zasada, Mary Eileen *nursing administrator*

Waterford
Commire, Anne *playwright, writer, editor*
Hinkle, Janet *financial analyst*
Hinkle, Muriel Ruth Nelson *naval warfare analysis company executive*
Morgan, John Richard *writer, publishing executive*
Pierson, Anne Bingham *physician*
Weidenbaum, Rhoda Sussman *history educator, researcher*

West Cornwall
Estern, Neil Carl *sculptor*
Simont, Marc *artist*

West Hartford
Bonee, John Leon III *lawyer*
Braus, Ira L. *music educator, researcher*
Bullock, Karen *social sciences educator*
Calip, Roger *writer, educator*
Chase, Carol Johnson *mathematics educator*
Collins, Alma Jones *language educator, writer*
Doran, James Martin *retired food products company executive*
Ealy, Nicholas *language educator*
Einfeldt, Teri Lynn *cultural organization administrator*
Faude, Wilson Hinsdale *museum director, consultant*
Gitterman, Alex *social work educator*
Glasser, Joseph *management consultant, educator*
Gould, Laurence Ira *physicist*
Hall, Robert Stevens *retired dentist*
Harrison, Walter Lee *university president*
Herzog, Brigitte *retired lawyer*
Jepsen, Jane Barry *secondary school educator*
Keller, Dorothy Bosch *art educator*
Malone, Thomas Francis *academic administrator, meteorologist*
Markham, Claire Agnes (M. Clare Markham) *retired chemistry educator, consultant*
McAuliffe-Curnias, Susan Eileen *secondary school educator*
Neace, William Phillip *psychology professor, consultant*
Raffay, Stephen Joseph *manufacturing executive, director*
Reid, Pamela Trotman *college president, psychology professor*
Silver, Herbert *physician*
Sullivan, Kevin B. *museum administrator, former lieutenant governor, state legislator*
Sumukadas, Narendar *finance educator*
Tonkin, Humphrey Richard *academic administrator, educator*
Visconti, Joseph B. *contractor, small business owner*
Wolman, Martin *lawyer*

West Haven
Collura, Michael Anthony *chemical engineer, educator*
Corraro, Dominic J. *language educator*
Dausey, David James *program analyst*
Deck, Richard Allen *political scientist, consultant, writer, volunteer*
Haley, George Thomas *marketing educator*
Kyriakides, Tassos Constantino *biostatistician*

West Redding
Sinha, Bikash Kumar *mechanical engineer, researcher*

West Simsbury
Evans, Meg *psychologist*
Rockas, Leo *English educator*

Weston
Aibel, Howard James *arbitrator, mediator*
Bleifeld, Stanley *sculptor*
Diforio, Robert George *literary agent*
Falber, Harold Julius *marketing professional*
Fredrik, Burry *theater producer, director*
Kilty, Jerome Timothy *playwright, theater director, actor*
Murray, Stephen James *lawyer*
Murray, Thomas J. *advertising executive*
Thompson, N(orman) David *insurance company executive*
Zimmerman, Bernard *investment banker*

Westport
Barberi, Robert Obed *lawyer*
Blau, Barry *marketing professional, financial consultant*
Breitbarth, S. Robert *manufacturing executive*
Carr, Cynthia *lawyer*
Chernow, Ann Levy *artist, educator*
Clausman, Gilbert Joseph *retired medical librarian*
Cohen, Eric I. *lawyer*
Cramer, Allan P. *lawyer*
Dalio, Raymond Thomas *hedge fund manager*
Davidson, JoAnn W. *retired elementary school educator*
Daw, Harold John *lawyer, director*
Defeo, Ronald M. *machinery manufacturing executive*
Demakis, Louise Ward *archivist historian, writer*
Donaldson, James Neill *banker*
Fisher, Leonard Everett *artist, educator, writer*
Fried, Burton Theodore *lawyer*
Gans, Eugene Howard *cosmetic and pharmaceutical company executive, consultant*
Hall, Andrew J. *oil industry executive*
Hayden, Vern Clarence *financial planner*
Heyman, Ronnie Feuerstein *lawyer*
Hotchner, Aaron Edward *author*
Kelly, Paul Knox *investment banker*
Kramer, Sidney B. *publishing executive, literary agent, lawyer*
Lewis, Margaret Mary *marketing professional*
MacCormack, Charles Frederick *international relief organization executive*
Manley, John Frederick *political scientist, educator*
Margolis, Emanuel *lawyer, educator*
McCormack, Donald Paul *newspaper consultant*
McKane, David Bennett *business executive*
Mioli, Joseph S. *state legislator*
Ogintz, Eileen *travel writer*
O'Keefe, John David *brokerage house executive*
Razzano, Pasquale Angelo *lawyer*
Ready, Robert James *finance company executive*
Reilly, Nancy (Anne Caulfield Reilly) *painter*
Riordan, Thomas J. *manufacturing executive*
Rudd, Nicholas *investor, consultant*
Sacchetta, Pasquale Joseph *financial services executive*
Sacks, Herbert Simeon *psychiatrist, educator, consultant*
Sheiman, Ronald Lee *lawyer*
Siff, Marlene Ida *artist, designer*
Smith, Peter Wolfgang *physicist, artist*
Solum, John Henry *flutist, educator, author, advocate for arts*
Stewart, Martha Kostyra *entrepreneur, lecturer, author*
Walton, Alan George *venture capitalist*
Warner, Kerstin Julianna *gifted and talented educator*
Widman, Phillip C. *machinery manufacturing executive*
Wolson, Craig Alan *lawyer*
Wussler, Robert Joseph *broadcast executive, media consultant*

Willimantic
Barbuto, Leah M. *early childhood and technology educator, consultant*
Brodie, Ellen Faith *theater educator, director*
Jennings, Julianne *cultural organization administrator*
Mitchell, Homer *marketing executive*
Peterson, Elizabeth Holly *art association administrator*

Willington
Zhang, Heng *research scientist, educator*

Wilton
Adams, Thomas Tilley *lawyer*
Brown, James Thompson, Jr. *operations research specialist, information scientist*
Burki, Arde A. *retired military officer*
Davis, Joel *publisher*
Duke, Robert Dominick *lawyer*
Fricke, Richard John *lawyer*
Hawley, Frank Jordan, Jr. *venture capital executive*
Healy, James Casey *lawyer*
Kaskell, Peter Howard *professional society administrator, lawyer*
Nickel, Albert George *advertising agency executive*
Pethley, Lowell Sherman *retired management consultant*
Poundstone, Sally Hill *library director*
Radin, Alan Mervyn *physician*
Seitz, Nicholas Joseph *editor, journalist*
Ziegler, William Alexander *lawyer*

Windsor
Auten, Arthur Herbert *history professor*
Ferraro, John Francis *corporate executive*

Windsor Locks
Hoffman, Lee D. *prosecutor*

Wolcott
Cordone, Kathleen Ann *media specialist*

Woodbridge
Alvine, Robert *industrialist, entrepreneur, world business leader, philanthropist, business owner*
Dupré, Louis *retired philosopher, educator*
Ecklund, Constance Cryer *French language and literature educator*
Haering, Margaret Elaine *lawyer*
Kleiner, Diana Elizabeth Edelman *art historian, educator, academic administrator*
Mason, John Wayne *psychoneuroendocrinologist, retired medical educator*
Zeller, Michael Edward *physicist, researcher*

Woodbury
Feskoe, Gaffney Jon *management consultant*
Giuliano, Rosemary E. *lawyer*
O'Brien, Bonnie Jeanne *counseling administrator*
Skinner, Brian John *geologist, educator*

Woodstock Valley
Allaby, Stanley Reynolds *clergyman*

DELAWARE

Bear
Hudson, Kelly Marie *music educator*
Yannul, Edward *chemical engineer, writer*

Bethany Beach
Jacobsen, Julia Mills *educational administrator*

Dagsboro
Hanna, Anne Marie *artist*

Wallach, Harold Charles *health policy and health services research administrator, educator*

Dover

Amick, Steven Hammond *state legislator, lawyer*
Armstrong, Anthony Michael *political science professor*
Britt, Maisha Dorrah *protective services official*
Bullock, Jeffrey W. *state official*
Coyle, Kevin Francis *planner*
Danberg, Carl Christian *state agency administrator, former state attorney general*
Denn, Matthew P. *Lieutenant Governor of Delaware*
Ennis, Bruce Clifford *retired lawyer*
Hankoua, Bertrand Bachaumond *molecular biologist, educator*
Hoff, Samuel Boyer *political scientist, educator*
Jones, Geraldine Ann Johnson *secondary school educator*
Jones-Potter, Velda *state treasurer*
Kim, Dae Ryong *management information systems educator*
Lowery, Lillian M. *state official, school system administrator*
Markell, Jack A. *Governor of Delaware*
Pongsree, Saharat Oak *economics professor*
Ridgely, Henry duPont *state supreme court justice*
Rubino, Joelle L. *physical therapist, athletic trainer*
Smyth, Joel Douglas *newspaper executive*
Taylor, Suzonne Berry Stewart *real estate broker*
Thomas Rattay, Karyl *state agency administrator, public health service officer*
Wasfi, Sadiq Hassan *chemistry professor*
Wilson, Clealyn Bullock *elementary school educator*

Georgetown

Fiedler, Clarence Wesley *psychologist*

Greenville

DeWees, Donald Charles *security firm executive*
McDonough, Kenneth Lee *pharmaceutical company medical administrator*
Miller, Duane King *health and beauty care company executive*
Parets, Paul L. *music educator*
Reynolds Cooch, Nancy D. *sculptor*
Rocek, Jan *retired chemist*
Stone, F. L. Peter *lawyer*

Harrington

Bulischeck, Anita Marie *guidance counselor, special education educator*

Hockessin

Croyle, Barbara Ann *health facility administrative executive*
Igwe, Godwin Joseph *chemical engineer*
Mitchell, Peter Kenneth *educational consultant*
St. Clair, Jesse Walton, Jr. *retired savings and loan association executive*
Ulmer, William H., Sr. *dentist*
Valbuena-Briones, Angel Julian *retired language educator, author*
Yasik, Christine Marie *literature and language educator*

Laurel

Lydic, Garrett Walton *elementary school educator*
Selby, Cora Norwood *retired elementary school educator*

Lewes

Beaufait, Frederick W(illiam) *retired engineering educator*
Costigan, Constance Frances *artist, educator*
Donovan, James Francis *retired school system administrator*
Fried, Jeffrey Michael *health care administrator*
Little, R. Donald *real estate entrepreneur*
Spence, Sandra *retired trade association administrator*
Warden, Richard Dana *government labor union official*

Middletown

Hall, Peter Michael *physics professor, electronics engineer*

Milford

Konowitz, Herbert Henry *retired textile company executive*

Milton

Carrow, Milton Michael *law educator*

New Castle

Almquist, Don *illustrator, artist*
Cansler, Leslie Ervin *retired newspaper editor*
Doberstein, Audrey K. *college president*
O'Donnell, Christine T. *political commentator, marketing consultant*
Price, Leon R. *elementary school educator*
Sanderson, Devon Lee *elementary school educator*
Shafer, Yvonne *theater educator, writer*
Williamson, Sandra Kaye *education educator*

Newark

Abrams, Burton A. *economics professor*
Aristigueta, Maria Pilar *public relations executive, educator*
Bailey, Daniel Carl *higher education administrator*
Barteau, Mark Alan *chemical engineering and chemistry educator*
Beris, Antony Nicolas *chemical engineer, educator*
Bilinsky, Yaroslav *political scientist*
Boncelet, Charles George *engineering educator*
Breslin, Nancy Ann *photographer, educator*
Breslin, Wynn Boin *artist*
Brown, Hilton *artist, educator*
Buma, Takashi *electrical engineer, educator*
Burmeister, John Luther *chemistry professor, consultant*
Butkiewicz, James Leon *economics professor, researcher, consultant*
Byrne, John Michael *energy and environmental educator*
Campbell, Linzy Leon *molecular biology researcher, educator*
Chajes, Michael Joseph *civil engineer, educator*
Chen, Jingguang G. *chemical engineer, educator*
Colton, David Lem *mathematician, educator*
Cornell, Howard Vernon *ecology educator*
Day, Robert Androus *literature and language professor, retired library director, editor, publisher*
Dempsey, Kandie *medical researcher, director*
DeVivo, Sal J. *newspaper executive*
DiRenzo, Gordon James *sociologist, psychologist, educator*
Dursun, Derya *environmental engineer, researcher*
Elson, Charles Myer *law educator*
Frassetto, Michael *history professor*
Gantzer, Mary Lou *medical products executive*
Gardner, Timothy Joseph *surgeon, educator*
Green, Jerry M *biologist, weed scientist*
Halio, Jay Leon *language educator*
Harker, Patrick Timothy *academic administrator, systems engineer, educator*
Homer, William Innes *art history educator, expert, writer*
Jackson, Marvin Dennis *retired journalism educator, writer*
Kee, Chandra A. *psychiatrist, director*
Kennedy, Gerald L. *toxicologist, researcher*
Korber, Louise Ann *artist*
Krishnan, Palaniappa *agricultural engineering educator*
Kwansa, Francis A. *educator*
Lathrop, Thomas Albert *language educator, publisher*
Lemole, Gerald Michael *surgeon*
Luke, David Russell *mathematician, educator*
Ma, Xu *engineer, researcher*
Mangone, Gerard J. *international maritime law educator*
Mason, Charles Eugene *entomologist, educator*
McNutt, John Glenn *educator*
Murray, Richard Bennett *retired physics professor*
Neal, James Preston *state senator, project engineer*
Nomura, Jason T. *emergency physician*
Quintus, John Allen *English professor*
Rowe, Charles Alfred *artist, graphics designer, educator*
Russell, Thomas William Fraser *chemical engineer, educator*
Sandler, Stanley Irving *chemical engineering educator*
Sawyer, John Edward *management educator*
Sparks, Donald Lewis *soil chemistry educator*
Szeri, Andras Z. *engineering educator*
Thibault, Bruno *literature and language professor*
Turkel, Gerald Michael *social sciences educator*
Tynan, William Douglas *psychologist*
Vinson, Jack Roger *mechanical engineer, educator*
Weintraub, Stanley *arts and humanities educator, writer*
Wolters, Raymond *historian, educator*
Woo, S. B. (Shien-Biau Woo) *retired state official, physicist, educator*
Zhang, Yuhong *mechanical engineer, researcher*

Rehoboth Beach

Stokes, Richard Francis *lawyer*

Rockland

Cosgrove, Howard Edward, Jr. *utilities executive*
Rubin, Alan A. *pharmaceutical and biotechnology consultant*

Wilmington

Alonso, Caridad *elementary school educator*
Ambro, Thomas L. *federal judge*
Anton, David L. *research and development company executive, biotechnologist, researcher*
Baron, Stuart *academic administrator, art educator, artist*
Baumann, Julian Henry, Jr. *lawyer*
Baxter, Beverley Veloris *economic association administrator, educator*
Berger, Carolyn *state supreme court justice*
Biden, Beau (Joseph Robinette Biden III) *state attorney general, lawyer*
Bills, David G. *chemicals executive*
Bloom, David Andrew *communications operations director*
Borel, James Calvin *chemical company executive*
Bounds-Seemans, Pamella J. *artist*
Cecala, Ted Thomas, Jr. *banker, accountant*
Chehi, Mark *lawyer*
Cohen, Betsy Z. *bank executive*
Connelly, Thomas M., Jr. *chemicals executive*
Copeland, Tatiana Brandt *accountant*
Dadmarz, Kewmars Ebrahim *physician, educator*
Daniello, John D. *political organization administrator*
Darko, Denis F. *research scientist, physician*
Diemer, Russell Bertrum, Jr. *chemical engineer, educator*
DiLiberto, Richard Anthony, Jr. *lawyer*
Emmert, Richard Eugene *retired industrial and professional association executive*
Euganeo, Kathleen *radiologic technologist, educator*
Feingold, Ellen *pediatrician, medical writer*
Fenton, Wendell *lawyer*
Finkelstein, Jesse Adam *lawyer*
Fisher, Linda J. *consumer products company executive, former federal agency administrator*
Fredrick, Susan Walker *tax company manager*
Freeh, Louis Joseph *consulting firm executive, former FBI director*
Frelick, Robert Westcott *physician, consultant*
Fullerton, Ann Elizabeth *retired biology educator*
Gaiber, Maxine *museum director*
Genetta, Ann H. *psychologist, neuropsychologist*
Gilmore, Clare Mae *writer*
Goodmanson, Richard R. *chemicals executive*
Green, James Samuel *lawyer*
Gulyas, Diane H. *manufacturing executive*
Halfpenny, Geoffrey *museum director*
Harcke, Howard Theodore *diagnostic radiologist*
Hartzell, Charles R. *science foundation director, cell biologist, biochemist*
Herdeg, John Andrew *lawyer*
Hewitt, Cynthia A. *financial consultant, stockbroker*
Higgins, Roxanne Snelling *educational consultant*
Holliday, Chad (Charles O. Holliday Jr.) *chemicals executive*
Holtzman, Arnold Harold *chemical company executive*
Hsia, Judith Ann *physician*
Ikeda, Satoshi *thoracic and cardiovascular surgeon*
Jacobs, Jack Bernard *state supreme court justice*
Jaycox, Gary Delmar *research scientist, writer*
Jezl, Barbara Ann *retired chemist, automation consultant*
Johnston, William David *lawyer*
Jolles, Janet K. Pilling *lawyer*
Jordan, Kent A. *federal judge*
Kaiser, Mary Agnes *chemist, chemical company executive*
Keating, Mimi Y. *chemist*
Keefer, Jeffrey L. *chemicals executive*
Kirkpatrick, Andrew Booth, Jr. *lawyer*
Kissa, Erik *retired chemist, consultant*
Klayman, Barry Martin *lawyer*
Kneavel, Ann Callanan *humanities educator, communications consultant*
Koch, Carl Mark *retired environmental engineering executive*
Kristol, Daniel Marvin *retired lawyer*
Kullman, Ellen Jamison *chemicals executive*
Kwolek, Stephanie Louise *chemist, researcher*
Lassen, John Kai *financial instruments executive*
Linderman, Jeanne Herron *priest*
Lockhart-Videtto, Elizabeth Mary *music educator, director*
Malatack, James Jeffrey *pediatrician, liver transplant specialist*
Malooly, William Francis *bishop*
Mand, Martin Gary *financial executive*
Marcali, Jean Gregory *retired chemist*
McLeer Free, Laureen Dorothy *drug development and pharmaceutical professional*
Mekler, L. Arlen *lawyer, chemist*
Messina, Charles *artist*
Miller, Christopher John *statistician*
Miranda-Evans, Valetta Lee *social worker, human services manager*
Netta-Turner, Denise *nurse*
Nichols, George Leon, Jr. *minister*
Nolen, Samuel Augustus *lawyer*
Parshall, George William *chemist, researcher*
Parsons, Donald Francis *judge*
Paschetto, John J. *lawyer*
Pell, Sidney *epidemiologist*
Peterson, Russell Wilbur *environmental services administrator, Former Governor, Del*
Phillips, Joyce A. *insurance company executive*
Pizarro, Christian *surgeon, department chairman*
Porter, John Francis III *banker*
Reed, Thomas James *law educator*
Rice, Danielle *museum director*
Rogoski, Patricia Diana *corporate financial executive*
Rose, Selwyn H. *chemicals executive*
Roselle, David Paul *retired academic administrator, mathematician, educator*
Ross, Thomas Stuart *political organization administrator*
Roth, Jane Richards *federal judge*
Sager, Thomas Lauck *chemical company executive, lawyer*
Salinger, Frank Max *lawyer*
Saltarelli, Michael Angelo *bishop*
Saruk, Michael *dermatologist, educator*
Schacter, Bernice Zeldin *biotechnology consultant, researcher*
Seidenstat, Paul *retired economics professor*
Semple, James William *lawyer*
Shah, Udayan Kanaiyalal *surgeon*
Shipley, Samuel Lynn *advertising and public relations executive*
Sippel-Wetmore, Frances Marie *microbiologist, retired business owner*
Spruance, Halsey *museum director*
Stapleton, Walter King *federal judge*
Stargatt, Bruce M. *lawyer*
Steele, Myron Thomas *state supreme court chief justice*
Struthers, Ric (Richard K. Struthers) *bank executive*
Sullivan, Lawrence Matthew *lawyer*
Teng, Renli *pharmacologist, director*
Tumas, Michael B. *lawyer*
Uffner, Michael S. *automotive executive*
Waisanen, Christine M. *lawyer, writer*
Ward, Rodman, Jr. *lawyer, director*
Waritz, Richard Stefan *toxicologist, researcher*
Wasson, Ellis Archer *history educator*
Weisenfeld, Carol Ann Trimble *marketing executive, consultant*
Williams, Richmond Dean *library consultant and appraiser*
Wilson, Samuel Earl *anesthesiologist*
Winslow, Helen Littell *lawyer*
Zahralddin-Aravena, Rafael Xavier *law educator*

Winterthur

Bowman, Leslie Greene *museum director*

DISTRICT OF COLUMBIA

Bolling AFB

Green, Charles Bruce *career military officer, surgeon*

Fort McNair

Raines, Edgar Frank, Jr. *historian*

Pentagon

Lynn, William James III *federal agency administrator*

Washington

Aaronson, David Ernest *lawyer, educator*
Abbey, Robert Vernon (Bob Abbey) *federal agency administrator*
Abbott, Alden Francis *lawyer, federal official*
Abbott, Jim (James Anthony Abbott) *advocate, retired professional baseball player*
Abbott, Sherburne Bradstreet *federal official*
Abedin, Huma M. *federal official*
Abell, Richard Bender *federal judicial officer, lawyer*
Abercrombie, Neil *United States Representative from Hawaii*
Abizaid, John Philip *investment company executive, retired military officer*
Able, Edward H. *association executive*
Abraham, Spencer (Edward Spencer Abraham) *consulting company executive, former United States Secretary of Energy*
Abramowitz, Michael *museum program director*
Abrams, David B. *nonprofit organization director, former federal agency administrator*
Abrams, Edgar M. (Mac Abrams) *legislative staff member*
Abrams, Elliott *former federal official*
Acheson, David Campion *retired lawyer, policy analyst, writer*
Acker, Joseph G. *science association director*
Ackerman, Gary Leonard *United States Representative from New York*
Ackerson, Nels J(ohn) *lawyer*
Ackil, Josh *lobbyist*
Adams, A. John Bertrand *public affairs consultant, director*
Adams, Frances Grant, II, *lawyer*
Adams, Michelle T. *legislative staff member*
Adams, Robert Edward *journalist*
Adams-Campbell, Lucile L. *epidemiologist, oncologist, educator*
Adamson, Jeremy E. *library director*
Adamson, Terrence Burdett *lawyer*
Adelstein, Jonathan Steven *federal agency administrator, former commissioner*
Aderholt, Robert B. *United States Representative from Alabama, lawyer*
Adler, Howard Bruce *lawyer*
Adler, John Herbert *United States Representative from New Jersey, former state legislator*
Agrast, Mark David *lawyer*
Aguilar, Luis A. *commissioner*
Aguillen, Dean *lobbyist*
Aguirre, Eduardo, Jr. *United States Ambassador to Spain and Andorra*
Ahlgren, James David *oncologist*
Ahmed, Akbar S. *religious studies educator*
Ahmed, Atif Ali *pathologist*
Ahouse, Daniel J. *legislative staff member*
Ain, Sanford King *lawyer*
Akaka, Daniel Kahikina *United States Senator from Hawaii*
Akerson, Daniel Francis *private equity firm executive, former telecommunications industry executive*
Akin, Todd (William Todd Akin) *United States Representative from Missouri, former state legislator*
Albee, Luke S. *legislative staff member*
Alberg, James L. *lawyer*
Albrecht, Kathe Hicks *art historian, visual resources manager*
Albrecht, Ralph P. *lawyer*
Albright, Madeleine Korbel *consulting firm executive, political science professor, former United States Secretary of State*
Aldock, John Douglas *lawyer*
Aleinikoff, Thomas Alexander *dean, law educator*
Alexander, Adele Logan *history professor*
Alexander, Clifford Joseph *lawyer*
Alexander, Joseph Kunkle, Jr. *physicist*
Alexander, Lewis Suverkrop *federal official, economist*
Alexander, Rodney M. *United States Representative from Louisiana*
Alexander, Stacey Anne *legislative staff member*
Ali, Russlynn *federal agency administrator*
Alito, Samuel Anthony, Jr. *United States supreme court justice*
Allbaugh, Joe M. (Joseph Marvin Allbaugh) *consulting firm executive, former federal agency administrator*
Allegra, Francis M. *federal judge, retired federal official*
Allen, Bernadette *United States Ambassador to Niger*
Allen, Jeanne *educational association administrator*
Allen, Thad William *career military officer*
Allen, Tom (Thomas Hodge Allen) *trade association administrator, former United States Representative from Maine*
Alleyne, Sir George A.O. *public health administrator, educator*
Allgeier, Peter Frederick *federal official*
Allison, Herbert Monroe, Jr. *federal agency administrator, former mortgage company executive*
Almquist, Katherine J. *federal agency administrator*
Alper, Jill *political consultant*
Alperovitz, Gar *author, educator*
Alster, Tina S. *dermatologist, educator*
Alterman, Eric Ross *journalist, writer, English professor*
Altmire, Jason *United States Representative from Pennsylvania*
Altschul, Alfred Samuel *airline executive*
Alvarez, Scott G. *lawyer*
Alvillar-Speake, Theresa *federal agency administrator*
Alward, Ruth Rosendall *nursing consultant*
Alwood, Edward McQueen *author, journalist, professor*
Amaral, Johnny A. *legislative staff member*
Ambrose, Myles Joseph *lawyer*
Ameri, Goli *federal agency administrator*
Ames, Frank Anthony *musician, film producer*
Amos, James F. *career military officer*
Anderson, Frederick Randolph, Jr. *lawyer, educator*
Anderson, James E. *lawyer*

Anderson, John Bayard *lawyer, former United States Representative from Illinois*
Anderson, Norman B. *health science association administrator, psychologist, educator*
Anderson, Thomas D. *lawyer, former prosecutor*
Anderson-Lee, Michelle D. *legislative staff member*
Andres, Gary *lobbyist*
Andrés, José *chef*
Andrew, Joseph Jerald *lawyer*
Andrews, Bruce *lawyer, former automotive executive*
Andrews, Mark Joseph *lawyer*
Andrews, Robert Ernest *United States Representative from New Jersey, lawyer*
Andril, David T. *lawyer*
Anthony, Stephen Pierce *lawyer*
Anthony, Virginia Quinn Bausch *medical association executive*
Anuzis, Andrius A. *legislative staff member*
Aoki, Steven *federal agency administrator*
Appel, Peter H. *federal agency administrator*
Apple, Daina Dravnieks *federal agency administrator*
Apple, James Glenn *lawyer, educator*
Apple, Martin Allen *science executive and educator*
Arana, Marie *editor, writer*
Aranoff, Shara Louise *federal official*
Archambault Gillette, Jodi *federal official*
Archer, Glenn LeRoy, Jr. *federal judge*
Arcuri, Michael Angelo *United States Representative from New York*
Arenas, Gilbert *professional basketball player*
Arend, Anthony Clark *social studies educator, academic administrator*
Arkilic, Galip Mehmet *mechanical engineer, educator*
Arlook, Ira Arthur *advocate, communications executive*
Armstrong, Alexandra *financial planner*
Arndt, Richard Tallmadge *writer, consultant, cultural administrator*
Arnez, Nancy Levi *educational leadership educator*
Arnold, William Edwin *health advocate, consultant*
Arnovitz, Benton Mayer *editor*
Aronica, Joseph J. *lawyer*
Asbill, Henry W. (Hank Asbill) *lawyer*
Ascensão, João Luis Afonso *physician, researcher, educator*
Aschheim, Joseph *retired economist, educator*
Asfaw, Abay *economist, consultant, research scientist*
Ashcroft, John David *lobbyist, law educator, former United States Attorney General*
Ashktorab, Hassan *molecular biologist*
Ashley, Wiley Ross III *federal agency administrator*
Asike, Joseph Ike *philosopher, educator*
Asker, James Robert *magazine editor*
Åslund, Anders *economist*
Asselbaye, Amy Brinkmeyer *legislative staff member*
Ates, Katherine A. (Kerry Ates) *legislative staff member*
Atkin, James *legislative staff member*
Atkinson, Caroline *economist*
Atkinson, Robert David *think tank administrator, economic policy analyst*
Atlas, Liane Wiener *writer*
Attridge, Daniel F. *lawyer*
Atwood, James R. *lawyer*
Atwood, Susan Jennifer *institute administrator*
Aulisi, Edward Fiore *neurosurgeon*
Austin, Lisa A. *legislative staff member*
Austin, Lloyd J. III *career military officer*
Austin, Roy L. *United States Ambassador to Trinidad & Tobago*
Austria, Steve *United States Representative from Ohio, former state senator*
Avil, Richard Daniel, Jr. *lawyer*
Axelrod, David M. *federal official*
Axelrod, Jonathan Gans *lawyer*
Ayalde, Liliana *United States Ambassador to Paraguay*
Ayer, Donald Belton *lawyer*
Ayers, Stephen Thomas *architect*
Ayres, David T. *lobbyist*
Ayres, Mary Ellen *federal official*
Azcuenaga, Mary Laurie *lawyer*
Babbitt, Bruce Edward *lawyer, former United States Secretary of the Interior*
Babbitt, Randy (Jerome Randolph Babbitt) *federal agency administrator, former pilot*
Babby, Ellen Reisman *educational association executive*
Babby, Lon S. *lawyer*
Baca, Joe *United States Representative from California*
Bachmann, Michele *United States Representative from Minnesota, former state legislator*
Bachus, Spencer T. III *United States Representative from Alabama, lawyer*
Backstrom, Nicklas (Lars Nicklas Backstrom) *professional hockey player*
Bacon, Kenneth J. *mortgage company executive*
Bacon, Sylvia *judge, educator*
Badillo, Alejandro *lawyer*
Bae, Insoo *science educator*
Baer, Donald Aaron *public relations executive*
Baer, Kenneth S. *federal official, communications executive*
Baer, Michael Alan *political scientist, educator*
Baer, William J. *lawyer*
Bagnoli, David Christopher *architect*
Bailey, Pamela Giles *trade association administrator*
Bainum, Peter Montgomery *aerospace engineer, consultant*
Bair, Sheila Colleen *federal agency administrator*
Baird, Brian N. *United States Representative from Washington*
Baker, David Harris *lawyer*
Baker, Dean *economist, think-tank executive*
Baker, Howard Henry, Jr. *lawyer, former US Senator from Texas, White House chief of staff*
Baker, James Edgar *federal judge, educator*
Baker, Meredith Attwell *commissioner*
Baker, P. Jean *lawyer, mediator*
Baker, Richard Hugh *lobbyist, former congressman*
Baker, Roger W. *federal agency administrator*
Balcombe, Jonathan Peter *animal advocate*
Baldrate, Brian Christopher *lawyer*
Baldwin, Tammy *United States Representative from Wisconsin, lawyer*
Baldyga, Leonard J. *retired diplomat, consultant*
Ball, Markham (Robert Ball) *lawyer, arbitrator, educator*
Ball, William Lockhart III *lobbyist, former civilian military employee*
Balzer, Marjorie Mandelstam *anthropology educator, editor*
Bandler, Donald Keith *international consultant, former ambassador*
Bandows Koster, Janet *science association director*
Bangura, Abdul Karim *academic administrator, researcher, scientist*
Bank, Rita M. *lawyer*
Banks, Richard Charles *ornithologist*
Banks, Vanita M. *lawyer*
Bansal, Preeta D. *federal official, lawyer*
Barber, Ben Bernard Andrew *journalist*
Barbosa, Rubens Antonio *former ambassador*
Barcella, Ernest Lawrence, Jr. *lawyer*
Barclay, George N. *lawyer*
Barker, Constance S. *commissioner*
Barlow, Michelle L. *legislative staff member*
Barnes, Donald Michael *lawyer*
Barnes, Frederic Wood, Jr. *journalist, political analyst*
Barnes, Mark James *lawyer*
Barnes, Melody C. *federal official*
Barnet, Robert Joseph *cardiologist, philosopher*
Barnett, Helaine M. *legal association administrator, lawyer*
Barnett, Robert Bruce *lawyer*
Barnett, Thomas Overton *lawyer, former federal agency administrator*
Barnette, Curtis Handley *retired metal products executive, lawyer*
Barno, David W. *think-tank executive, retired military officer*
Barofsky, Neil M. *federal agency administrator, former prosecutor*
Barone, Michael D. *political correspondent, writer, editor*
Barr, Michael S. *federal agency administrator, law educator*
Barrasso, John Anthony *United States Senator from Wyoming, orthopedic surgeon*
Barrett, Barbara McConnell *United States Ambassador to Finland*
Barrett, James Gresham *United States Representative from South Carolina*
Barron, Jerome Aure *law educator*
Barrow, John Jenkins *United States Representative from Georgia, lawyer*
Barry, Dennis M. *lawyer*
Barry, Marion Shepilov, Jr. *city councilman, former mayor*
Barry, Paul H. *utilities executive*
Barshefsky, Charlene *lawyer, former federal official*
Barth, Richard C. *federal agency administrator*
Bartheld, Elizabeth L. *legislative staff member*
Bartlett, Doyle *lobbyist*
Bartlett, Roscoe G. *United States Representative from Maryland*
Bartlett, Steve (Harry Steven Bartlett) *former congressman, mayor*
Bartnoff, Judith *judge*
Barton, Joe Linus *United States Representative from Texas*
Barton, R. Joseph *lawyer*
Barton, Robert Leroy, Jr. *judge, educator*
Baruah, Sandy K. (Santanu Kumar Baruah) *former federal agency administrator*
Barusch, Ronald Charles *lawyer*
Basham, W. Ralph *federal agency administrator*
Baskerville, Lezli *educational association administrator*
Baskin, Roberta *television correspondent*
Bateman, Paul William *federal agency administrator*
Bates, John D. *federal judge*
Batini, Nicoletta *economist, educator*
Batshaw, Mark Levitt *pediatrician, director*
Battista, Robert James *federal official, lawyer*
Battle, Michael A. *lawyer, former federal agency administrator, prosecutor*
Battles, Caroline Pelot *legislative staff member*
Baucus, Max Sieben *United States Senator from Montana*
Bauer, Gary Lee *political action committee executive*
Bauer, Robert F. *lawyer*
Bauerly, Cynthia Leora *commissioner, lawyer*
Bauleke, Howard Paul *legislative staff member, lawyer*
Baum, Lynne Miriam *lawyer*
Baumann, Linda Adriene *lawyer*
Bayh, Birch (Birch Evans Bayh Jr.) *lawyer, former senator*
Bayh, Evan (Birch Evan Bayh III) *United States Senator from Indiana*
Bayly, John Henry, Jr. *judge*
Beach, Gineen Bresso *federal agency administrator*
Beall, Julianne *librarian*
Bean, Melissa *United States Representative from Illinois*
Beard, Daniel P. *legislative staff member*
Beard, Jean-Louise *legislative staff member*
Bea Roberts, Barbara Ann *legal secretary*
Becerra, Xavier *United States Representative from California, lawyer*
Beck, Andrew C. *federal agency administrator*
Becker, Brenda L. *medical products executive, former federal official*
Becker, David M. *federal agency administrator, lawyer*
Becker, Mary Louise *political scientist*
Becker, Tim *legislative staff member*
Beckström, Rod Allen *internet security company executive, former federal agency administrator*
Beckwith, Edward Jay *lawyer*
Beddow, Thomas F. *lobbyist*
Beers, Rand *federal agency administrator, former think-tank executive*
Beeton, Jonathan *legislative staff member*
Begala, Paul Edward *political scientist, educator, television personality*
Beghe, Renato *federal judge*
Behan, Kathleen A. (Kitty Behan) *lawyer*
Behney, Clyde Joseph *health science association administrator, researcher*
Beier, David *medical products executive*
Beinart, Peter Alexander *editor, journalist*
Beiro Farabow, Sara *lawyer*
Beliveau, Emmett S. *federal official*
Bell, Ford Watson *museum association administrator*
Bell, Stephen Robert *lawyer*
Beller, Herbert N. *lawyer*
Bellinger, John B. III *lawyer, former federal official*
Bellows, Keith Adams *editor-in-chief, writer*
Belson, James Anthony *Senior Judge, DC Court of Appeals*
Benczkowski, Brian Allen *legislative staff member, lawyer*
Bender, David Ray *retired library association executive*
Benjamin, Daniel *federal agency administrator*
Benjamin, Georges Curtis *medical association administrator, emergency physician, consultant*
Benner, C. Jonathan *lawyer*
Bennet, Michael Farrand *United States Senator from Colorado*
Bennett, Alexander Elliot *lawyer*
Bennett, Barry P. *legislative staff member*
Bennett, Robert F. *United States Senator from Utah*
Bennett, Robert Stephen *lawyer*
Bennett, Stephen *medical association administrator*
Benoit, Marilyn B. *psychiatrist, consultant*
Benson, David C. *mortgage company executive*
Bentsen, Kenneth E., Jr. *lobbyist, former United States Representative from Texas*
Ben-Veniste, Richard *lawyer*
Benzing, Sarah Ruth *legislative staff member*
Berardini, Christopher F. *legislative staff member*
Berdahl, Robert Max *history professor, association and former academic administrator*
Berendzen, Richard *astronomer, educator, author*
Berenson, Bradford A. *lawyer*
Beresford, Douglas Lincoln *lawyer*
Berg, Patricia Elene *molecular biologist*
Berger, Sandy (Samuel Richard Berger) *financial consulting firm executive, former national security advisor*
Bergmann, Barbara Rose *economics professor*
Bergner, Jane Cohen *lawyer*
Bergreen, Timothy S. *legislative staff member*
Bergren, Eric *legislative staff member*
Berkley, Shelley (Rochelle Levine Berkley) *United States Representative from Nevada, lawyer*
Berlack, Evan Raden *lawyer*
Berlin, Kenneth *lawyer*
Berman, Howard Lawrence *United States Representative from California, lawyer*
Berman, Michael S. *lobbyist, lawyer*
Berman, Wayne L. *lobbyist*
Bernabei, Lynne Ann *lawyer*
Bernanke, Ben Shalom *chairman board of governors of the Federal Reserve System*
Bernardi, Roy A. (Romolo Albert Bernardi) *lobbyist, former federal agency administrator*
Berner, Frederic George, Jr. *lawyer*
Bernhardt, David Longly *lawyer, former federal agency administrator*
Bernhardt, W. Bret *legislative staff member*
Bernstein, Jared *federal official, economist*
Bernstein, Mitchell Harris *lawyer*
Bernstock, Robert F. *postal service executive*
Bernthal, Frederick Michael *research association executive*
Berrington, Craig Anthony *lawyer*
Berry, John *federal official, former zoological park administrator*
Berry, Marion *United States Representative from Arkansas*
Berry, Matthew *federal agency administrator*
Bersin, Alan Douglas *federal official, former county official*
Bertin, Margaret A.H *museum administrator*
Besen, Stanley Martin *economist*
Best, Judah *lawyer*
Betancourt Lopez, Antonio L. *association executive*
Beyrle, John R. *United States Ambassador to Russia*
Bezner, Mark *United States Charge d'Affaires for Palau*
Bial, Joseph J. *lawyer, consultant*
Biche, Peter *professional sports team executive*
Biden, Jill Tracy Jacobs *Second Lady of the United States, literature and language professor*
Biden, Joe (Joseph Robinette Biden Jr.) *Vice President of the United States, former United States Senator from Delaware*
Bielamowicz, Steven A. *otolaryngologist, educator*
Bierly, Eugene Wendell *meteorologist, science foundation director*
Bierman, James Norman *lawyer*
Biesenbach-Lucas, Sigrun *language educator, consultant*
Biggert, Judith Borg *United States Representative from Illinois, lawyer*
Bilbray, Brian Patrick *United States Representative from California*
Bilirakis, Gus Michael *United States Representative from Florida, lawyer*
Billington, James Hadley *librarian, historian*
Binder, Lisa B. *former bank executive*
Bingaman, Jeff (Jesse Francis Bingaman Jr.) *United States Senator from New Mexico*
Birman, Igor *legislative staff member*
Birnbaum, Norman *writer, humanities educator*
Birnbaum, S. Elizabeth (Liz Birnbaum) *federal agency administrator, lawyer*
Birnkrant, Henry Joseph *lawyer*
Bishop, Clyde *United States Ambassador to the Marshall Islands*
Bishop, James Dodson *lawyer, mediator*
Bishop, Robert *United States Representative from Utah*
Bishop, Sanford Dixon, Jr. *United States Representative from Georgia, lawyer*
Bishop, Timothy H. *United States Representative from New York*
Bjornstad, Jeff *legislative staff member*
Black, Barry C. *chaplain, retired military officer*
Black, Duncan Bowen *political blogger*
Black, Stephen Franklin *lawyer, writer*
Blackburn, Marsha *United States Representative from Tennessee*
Blackburne-Rigsby, Anna *Associate Judge, DC Court of Appeals*
Blackman, Sir Courtney Newlands *diplomat*
Blackwelder, Brent Francis *environmentalist*
Blackwell, Ken (John Kenneth Blackwell) *former state official, former mayor*
Blackwill, Robert Dean *lobbyist, former federal agency administrator*
Blahous, Charles Paul (Chuck Blahous) *former federal official*
Blair, Dennis Cutler *Director of National Intelligence, retired military officer*
Blair, James Pease *freelance photographer*
Blair, Robert Allen *lawyer*
Blake, Robert Orris, Jr. *federal agency administrator*
Blakely, Robert T. *financial executive*
Blalack, K. Lee *lawyer*
Blanchard, Bruce *civil engineer, consultant*
Blanchard, Charles Alan *lawyer*
Blanchard, Denise *legislative staff member*
Blanchard, James Johnston *lawyer, former Governor of Michigan*
Blanco, Cesar *legislative staff member*
Blazek-White, Doris *lawyer*
Blitzer, Wolf *journalist, news correspondent*
Bloch, Susan Low *law educator*
Block, John Rusling *former United States Secretary of Agriculture*
Block, Lawrence J. *federal judge*
Bloomfield, Sara J. *museum director*
Blumenfeld, Jeffrey *lawyer, educator*
Blumenthal, William *lawyer*
Blunt, Matt (Matthew Roy Blunt) *lobbyist, former Governor of Missouri*
Blunt, Roy D. *United States Representative from Missouri*
Blustein, Gideon D. *legislative staff member*
Boardman, Joseph H. *rail transportation executive*
Boaz, David Douglas *foundation executive*
Boccieri, John A. *United States Representative from Ohio, former state senator*
Bock, Paul S. *legislative staff member*
Bockorny, David A. *lobbyist*
Bodde, Peter William *United States Ambassador to Malawi*
Bodine, Susan Parker *lawyer, former federal agency administrator*
Bodner, John, Jr. *lawyer*
Boehm, Steven Bruce *lawyer*
Boehner, John Andrew *United States Representative from Ohio*
Boerckel, Winfield A., Jr. *legislative staff member*
Bogard, Lawrence Joseph *lawyer*
Bogdanovich, Michele L. *legislative staff member*
Boggs, George Robert *educational association administrator*
Boggs, George Trenholm *lawyer*
Boggs, Thomas Hale, Jr. *lobbyist, lawyer*
Bohigian, David Steele *federal agency administrator*
Boland, Christopher Thomas, II, *lawyer*
Bolar, Lucas J. *legislative staff member*
Bolden, Charles Frank, Jr. *federal agency administrator, retired astronaut, retired military officer*
Bolino, August Constantino *economics professor*
Bollinger, Lori *economist*
Bolton, John Robert *lawyer, former ambassador*
Bomar, Mary Amelia *federal agency administrator*
Bond, Christopher Samuel (Kit Bond) *United States Senator from Missouri, lawyer*
Bonds, Anita *political organization administrator*
Bonfiglo, Joseph *legislative staff member*
Bonicelli, Paul J. *federal agency administrator*
Bonior, David Edward *former congressman, educator*
Bonlender, Brian N. *legislative staff member*
Bono Mack, Mary Whitaker *United States Representative from California*
Bonosaro, Carol Alessandra *professional society and retired federal agency administrator*
Bonvillian, William Boone *lawyer*
Bonyun, Sean C. *legislative staff member*
Booker, Salih *human rights organization executive*
Boorstin, Robert Olsan *Internet company executive, political consultant*
Booth, Donald E. *United States Ambassador to Zambia*
Boozman, John *United States Representative from Arkansas*
Bordallo, Madeleine Zeien (Mrs. Ricardo Jerome Bordallo) *Delegate to United States House Representative from Guam*
Bordonaro, Molly *United States Ambassador to Malta*
Boren, David Daniel *United States Representative from Oklahoma*
Borenstein, David Gilbert *internist, writer, rheumatologist*
Borg, Joseph Philip *securities association administrator, lawyer*
Born, Brooksley Elizabeth *retired lawyer*
Borntrager, Randy *legislative staff member*
Borsari, George Robert, Jr. *lawyer, commentator*
Borzi, Phyllis Corinne *federal agency administrator*
Boskey, Bennett *lawyer*
Boss, Lenard Barrett *lawyer*
Bost, Eric M. *United States Ambassador to South Africa*
Bostic, Raphael William *federal agency administrator, educator*
Boston, Daniel T. *lobbyist*
Boswell, Eric J. *federal agency administrator*
Boswell, Leonard L. *United States Representative from Iowa*

Boucher, Rick (Frederick Carlyle Boucher) *United States Representative from Virginia, lawyer*
Boulware, Mark *United States Ambassador to Mauritania*
Bourke, Jaron *legislative staff member*
Bourne, Peter Geoffrey *physician, educator, writer*
Boustany, Charles W., Jr. *United States Representative from Louisiana, surgeon*
Bowden, Aisha L. *elementary school educator*
Bowen, David *legislative staff member*
Bowker, David William *lawyer*
Bowman, John E. *federal agency administrator*
Bowser, David G. *legislative staff member*
Boxer, Barbara *United States Senator from California*
Boyd, April S. *federal agency administrator*
Boyd, F. Allen, Jr. *United States Representative from Florida, farmer*
Boyd, Thomas Marshall *lawyer*
Braden, Gregory C. *lawyer*
Bradfield, Michael *lawyer*
Bradlee, Ben (Benjamin Crowninshield Bradlee) *publishing executive, retired editor-in-chief*
Bradley, David G. *publishing executive*
Bradley, John A. *career military officer*
Bradtke, Robert A. *United States Ambassador to Croatia*
Brady, Kevin Patrick *United States Representative from Texas*
Brady, Robert A. *United States Representative from Pennsylvania*
Brailer, David J. *federal agency administrator*
Brain, Charles M. (Chuck Brain) *lobbyist*
Brainard, Lael S. *economist, writer*
Braley, Bruce *United States Representative from Iowa*
Branche, Christine M. *federal agency administrator, epidemiologist*
Brand, Adam G. *legislative staff member, lawyer*
Brandell, Jim (James F. Brandell) *legislative staff member*
Branton, Brian E. *legislative staff member*
Brasseux, Barnaby L *federal agency administrator*
Brauchli, Marcus Walker *editor*
Braverman, Jordan *columnist*
Brazeal, Aurelia Erskine *former ambassador*
Brazile, Donna L. *political strategist*
Brecher, Mitchell Fredrick *lawyer*
Bregman, Arthur Randolph *lawyer, educator*
Breitman, Richard David *historian, educator, writer*
Brennan, John Owen *federal official, former technical solutions company executive*
Brennan, Joseph Edward *federal official, former United States Representative from Maine*
Brenner, Janet Maybin Walker *lawyer*
Brenner, Joel F. *federal agency administrator*
Bresnahan, Pamela Anne *lawyer, mediator, arbitrator*
Bretzfelder, Deborah May *retired museum staff member*
Breuer, Lanny Arthur *federal agency administrator, lawyer*
Brewster, Robert Charles *diplomat, consultant*
Breyer, Stephen Gerald *United States supreme court justice*
Brickman, Blake *legislative staff member*
Bridges, Jerry *federal agency administrator, accountant*
Briggs, Kerri Layne *state official, school system administrator*
Bright, Bobby Neal, Sr. *United States Representative from Alabama, former mayor*
Brimmer, Andrew Felton *economist, consultant*
Brimmer, Esther Diane *federal agency administrator*
Brinkman, William Frank *federal agency administrator, physicist*
Broad, Molly Corbett (Margaret Corbett Broad) *educational association administrator*
Brobeck, Stephen James *consumer advocate*
Brock, Gregory E. *editor*
Broder, David Salzer *journalist, writer*
Brody, Peter Martin *lawyer*
Broglio, Timothy Paul Andrew *archbishop*
Bromwich, Michael Ray *lawyer*
Bronstein, Alvin J. *lawyer*
Brooks, Arthur C. *think-tank executive*
Brooks, Jane K. *real estate agent, educator*
Brooks, Renana Esther *clinical psychologist, business and political consultant, researcher*
Broome, Darryl (James Darryl Broome) *legislative staff member*
Broome, David *federal official*
Brophy, Stephen J. *legislative staff member*
Brosnan, Carol Raphael Sarah *retired art association administrator*
Brougher, Kerry *curator*
Broun, Elizabeth *art historian, curator*
Broun, Paul Collins, Jr. *United States Representative from Georgia, physician*
Brower, Charles Nelson *lawyer, judge*
Brown, Barbara Berish *lawyer*
Brown, Barry (Barrington Lee Brown) *legislative staff member*
Brown, Campbell (Alma Dale Campbell Brown) *newscaster*
Brown, Corrine *United States Representative from Florida*
Brown, Cynthia *legislative staff member*
Brown, Dana A. *federal agency administrator*
Brown, Gayleatha Beatrice *United States Ambassador to Benin*
Brown, Harold *former United States Secretary of Defense*
Brown, Henry E., Jr. *United States Representative from South Carolina*
Brown, James W. *legislative staff member*
Brown, Janice Rogers *federal judge, former state supreme court justice*
Brown, John Patrick *publishing executive, financial consultant*
Brown, Laurel *legislative staff member*
Brown, Laurence G. *federal agency administrator, physician*
Brown, Laurence George *medical director*
Brown, Lester Russell *research and development company executive*
Brown, Lisa (Elizabeth Merrill Brown) *lawyer*
Brown, Mary Patrice *federal agency administrator*
Brown, Michael D. *Shadow Senator to US Congress from DC*
Brown, Michael DeWayne *consulting firm executive, former federal agency administrator*
Brown, Nathan Jude *political scientist, educator*
Brown, Pamela Wedd *artist*
Brown, Preston *lawyer*
Brown, Sherrod Campbell *United States Senator from Ohio, former congressman, former state official*
Brown, Thomas L. *legislative staff member*
Brownback, Samuel Dale *United States Senator from Kansas, lawyer*
Browne, Richard Cullen *lawyer*
Brownell, Mark David *legislative staff member*
Browner, Carol Martha *federal official, consulting firm executive*
Brownfield, William R. *United States Ambassador to Colombia*
Browning, Steven Alan *United States Ambassador to Uganda*
Brubaker, Joel L. *legislative staff member*
Bruce, Carol Elder *lawyer*
Bruce, Estel Edward *lawyer*
Bruce, Stephanie Robin *geriatrician*
Bruck, Nicholas *economist, educator*
Bruemmer, Russell John *lawyer*
Bruggink, Eric G. *federal judge*
Brunsvold, Brian Garrett *lawyer, educator*
Bruzelius, Nils Johan Axel *journalist*
Bryson, William Curtis *federal judge*
Brzezinski, Zbigniew *political science professor, former national security advisor*
Buchan, Douglas Charles *gas industry executive, government agency administrator*
Buchanan, Michael Dee *legislative staff member*
Buchanan, Vern (Vernon G. Buchanan) *United States Representative from Florida*
Buck, Jennifer Cooney *federal agency administrator*
Buck, Leon C., Jr. *legislative staff member*
Buckles, Tony J. *legislative staff member*
Buckley, Jeremiah Stephen *lawyer*
Buckley, Mary A. *dancer*
Buckner, Jason L. *legislative staff member*
Buffon, Charles Edward *lawyer*
Bui, Hung H. *lawyer*
Buis, Tom (Thomas Paul Buis) *alternative energy advocate, former labor union administrator*
Bulir, Ales *economist*
Bunch, Lonnie III *museum director*
Bunn, Shelia *legislative staff member*
Bunning, Jim (James Paul David Bunning) *United States Senator from Kentucky, retired professional baseball player*
Burchfield, Bobby Roy *lawyer*
Burck, William Anthony *lawyer*
Burger, Anna B. *labor union administrator*
Burgess, Michael Clifton *United States Representative from Texas*
Burgess, Ronald L., Jr. *federal agency administrator, career military officer*
Burgin, Walter Hotchkiss, Jr. *retired academic administrator*
Burk, Susan Flood *ambassador*
Burka, Robert Alan *lawyer*
Burke-Ables, Kim S. *biology educator*
Burks, Elizabeth Hurley *legislative staff member*
Burnett, Arthur Louis, Sr. *judge*
Burnham, David Bright *writer, educator*
Burnley, James Horace, IV, *lawyer, former United States Secretary of Transportation*
Burns, Conrad Ray *former senator*
Burns, David Mitchell *writer, musician, retired diplomat*
Burns, Stephen Gilbert *lawyer*
Burns, William Joseph *federal agency administrator, former ambassador*
Burr, Richard M. *United States Senator from North Carolina, former congressman*
Burris, James Frederick *federal healthcare administrator, educator*
Burris, Roland Wallace *United States Senator from Illinois, former state attorney general, former state controller*
Burrus, William Henry *labor union administrator*
Burt, Jeffrey Amsterdam *lawyer*
Burtless, Gary Thomas *economist, consultant*
Burton, Bill *federal official*
Burton, Dan L. *United States Representative from Indiana*
Burton, Douglas *interior designer*
Burton, Robert Arnold *lawyer*
Busby, David *lawyer*
Busching, Mark *legislative staff member, lawyer*
Buser, Carolyn Elizabeth *adult education educator*
Bush, Lynn Jeanne *federal judge*
Butler, Caron (James Caron Butler) *professional basketball player*
Butler, Mary K. *prosecutor*
Butler, Michael Francis *lawyer*
Butler, Paul William *lawyer*
Butler, Rhett *legislative staff member*
Butterfield, George Kenneth, Jr. *United States Representative from North Carolina, former state supreme court justice*
Butts, Cassandra Quin *lawyer*
Buyer, Stephen Earle *United States Representative from Indiana, lawyer*
Byrd, Robert Carlyle *United States Senator from West Virginia*
Cabral, Anna Escobedo *former federal agency administrator*
Cabrera, Cesar B. *United States Ambassador to Mauritius and Seychelles*
Cabrera, Orlando Jose *lawyer*
Cadogan, Rene Felipe *counseling administrator, educator*
Cafferty, Jack *news anchor*
Calamaro, Raymond Stuart *lawyer*
Calder, Kent Eyring *political science professor, federal agency administrator*
Calhoun, Noah Robert *retired oral maxillofacial surgeon, educator*
Caliguiri, Laura M. *federal agency administrator*
Calingaert, Michael *non-profit organization executive*
Callahan, Robert J. *United States Ambassador to Nicaragua*
Callaway, Clifford Wayne *physician*
Callender, Clive Orville *surgeon*
Callery, T. Grant (Grant Callery) *lawyer*
Calvani, Terry *lawyer*
Calvert, Ken *United States Representative from California*
Calvert, Sandra L. *psychology professor*
Cameron, Donald B., Jr. *lawyer*
Camp, David Lee *United States Representative from Michigan, lawyer*
Campbell, Jane Louise *senator to chief staff, former mayor*
Campbell, John B. T. III *United States Representative from California, former state senator*
Campbell, Kurt M. *federal agency administrator*
Campbell, Nancy Duff *lawyer*
Campbell, Neil D. *legislative staff member*
Campos, Laura M. *legislative staff member*
Campos, Roel Clark *lawyer, former commissioner*
Cantor, Eric Ivan *United States Representative from Virginia, lawyer*
Cantwell, Maria E. *United States Senator from Washington*
Cao, Joseph (Anh Cao) *United States Representative from Louisiana, lawyer*
Capito, Shelley Moore *United States Representative from West Virginia*
Caplin, Mortimer Maxwell *lawyer, educator*
Capps, Lois Ragnhild Grimsrud *United States Representative from California, former school nurse*
Caprara, Anne M. *legislative staff member*
Capuano, Michael Everett *United States Representative from Massachusetts, lawyer*
Carbonell, Ana *legislative staff member*
Cardin, Benjamin Louis *United States Senator from Maryland, former congressman*
Cardoza, Dennis A. *United States Representative from California*
Carey, Sarah Collins *lawyer*
Carfine, Kenneth E., Jr. *federal agency administrator*
Carhart, Homer Walter *retired research scientist*
Carleton, Ronnie P. *legislative staff member*
Carlisle, Linda Elizabeth *lawyer*
Carmack, Terry *legislative staff member*
Carmen, David M. *lobbyist*
Carmody, Carol Jones *transportation executive, former federal agency administrator*
Carnahan, Russ (John Russell Carnahan) *United States Representative from Missouri, lawyer*
Carneal, George Upshur *lawyer*
Carney, Christopher Paul *United States Representative from Pennsylvania, political science educator*
Carpenter, Ted Galen *political scientist*
Carper, Thomas Richard *United States Senator from Delaware, former governor*
Carr, Carolyn Kinder *art gallery director, museum director*
Carr, Christopher M. (Chris Carr) *legislative staff member*
Carr, Lawrence Edward, Jr. *lawyer*
Carr, Robert M. *former United States Representative, Michigan, lawyer*
Carr, William B., Jr. *retired judge*
Carrión, Adolfo, Jr. *federal official, former city official*
Carroll, Jeffrey C. *legislative staff member*
Carson, André D. *United States Representative from Indiana, marketing specialist*
Carson, Johnnie *federal agency administrator, former ambassador*
Carstensen, James *legislative staff member*
Carter, Ashton Baldwin *federal agency administrator*
Carter, Barry Edward *law educator*
Carter, John Rice *United States Representative from Texas, lawyer*
Carter, William Joseph *lawyer*
Cartwright, James E. *career military officer*
Caruso, Guy *federal agency administrator*
Cary, George S. *lawyer*
Casey, George William, Jr. *career military officer*
Casey, Kathleen L. *commissioner*
Casey, Robert Patrick, Jr., (Bob Casey) *United States Senator from Pennsylvania*
Cashen, Henry Christopher, II, *lawyer, government agency administrator*
Cassell, Samuel James *professional basketball coach, retired professional basketball player*
Casserly, James Lund *lawyer*
Cassidy, Bill (William Cassidy) *United States Representative from Louisiana, former state senator*
Cassidy, Gerald *lobbyist, lawyer*
Cassidy, Robert Charles, Jr. *lawyer*
Castagnetti, David A. *lobbyist, political strategist*
Castle, Anne *federal agency administrator, lawyer*
Castle, Michael N. *United States Representative from Delaware, lawyer*
Catoe, Bette Lorrina *pediatrician, educator*
Caulfield, John *United States Charge d'Affaires for Venezuela*
Causey, C. Chad *legislative staff member*
Cehelsky, Marta *scientific organization executive*
Centanni, Steve *national news correspondent*
Centilli, Douglas *legislative staff member*
Chabot, Elliot Charles *lawyer*
Chabot, Herbert L. *federal judge*
Chadwick, Kirsten Ardleigh *lobbyist*
Chaffetz, Jason *United States Representative from Utah, former corporate communications executive*
Chamberlain, John Loomis III *retired pediatrician, educator*
Chamberlin, Wendy J. *think-tank executive, former ambassador*
Chambers, Glen R. *legislative staff member*
Chambers, Hilarie *legislative staff member*
Chambliss, Saxby (Clarence Saxby Chambliss) *United States Senator from Georgia*
Chamot, Dennis *science policy executive*
Champlin, Steven M. *lobbyist*
Chan, Wing-Chi *cultural consultant and organization administrator, musicologist*
Chandler, Ben (Albert Benjamin Chandler III) *United States Representative from Kentucky, former state attorney general*
Chandler, Carrol H. (Howie Chandler) *career military officer*
Chandler, James Phillip III *law educator*
Chandler, Peter H. *legislative staff member*
Chandler, Shana M. *legislative staff member*
Chandrasekaran, Rajiv *editor, writer*
Chang, Sam Hsien-Cheng *lawyer*
Chanin, Michael Henry *lawyer*
Chanin, Robert Howard *lawyer*
Chao, Daniel S. *legislative staff member*
Chao, Elaine Lan *former United States Secretary of Labor*
Chaplin, Peggy Louie *lawyer*
Chapman, George Bunker *biology professor*
Chapman, Stuart (Christopher S. Chapman) *legislative staff member*
Chase, Thomas Newell *neurologist, researcher, educator, entrepreneur*
Chatoor-Koch, Irene *child psychiatrist*
Chaudhry, Asif J. *United States Ambassador to Moldova*
Chavarria, Adam *federal agency administrator*
Chavez-Thompson, Linda *political organization administrator, retired labor union administrator*
Chellaraj, Rajkumar *federal agency administrator*
Cheney, Lynne Vincent *humanities educator, writer, former Second Lady of the United States*
Cheng, Tsung O. *cardiologist, educator*
Cheng, Xiuzhen *engineering educator*
Chertoff, Michael *consulting firm executive, lawyer, former United States Secretary of Homeland Security*
Chester, Alexander Campbell III *physician*
Chevat, Benjamin *legislative staff member*
Chiang, Peter K. *science administrator*
Chiarelli, Peter W. *career military officer*
Childers, Travis Wayne *United States Representative from Mississippi, former real estate agent*
Chiles, Lisa *federal official*
Chiller, Matthew R. *legislative staff member*
Chilton, Bart (Bartholomew Hamilton Chilton) *commissioner*
Chin, Curtis S. *federal agency administrator*
Chiu, Arthur Oi-Shui *pathologist, toxicologist*
Chocola, Chris (Joseph Christopher Chocola) *political organization executive, former United States Representative from Indiana*
Choi, Woon Gyu *economist*
Chopko, Mark E. *lawyer*
Chopra, Aneesh Paul *federal official*
Chorba, Timothy A. *lawyer, former ambassador*
Choukas-Bradley, James Richard *lawyer, musician*
Chrisler, Tamara E. *federal official*
Christian, Adrienne *legislative staff member*
Christian, Betty Jo *lawyer*
Christian, Ernest Silsbee, Jr. *lawyer*
Christian-Christensen, Donna Marie *Delegate to United States House Representative from Virgin Islands*
Christopherson, Charles (Chuck) Richard, Jr. *Sub Cabinet Official*
Chu, David S.C. *federal agency administrator, economist*
Chu, Judy May *United States Representative from California, former state agency administrator*
Chu, Steven *United States Secretary of Energy, physics professor*
Chuang, Tze-Jer *mathematician*
Chun, Shinae *federal agency administrator*
Churchill, John Hugh *college academic administrator*
Chwastyk, Christopher D. *legislative staff member*
Cianchette, Peter E. *United States Ambassador to Costa Rica*
Ciccoella, Charles S. (Chick) *federal agency administrator*
Cicerone, Ralph John *foundation administrator, research scientist*
Cino, Maria *political organization administrator, former federal agency administrator*
Cipolla, Vin *foundation administrator, entrepreneur*
Cizik, Rev. Richard L. *lobbyist, minister*
Clapper, James R., Jr. *federal agency administrator, retired military officer*
Clapton, Charles M. (Chuck Clapton) *legislative staff member*
Clark, Dick *former senator, ambassador, foreign affairs specialist*
Clark, John F. *federal agency administrator*
Clark, Julia L. Akins *lawyer*
Clarke, Jerome T. *legislative staff member*
Clarke, Yvette Diane *United States Representative from New York*
Clavel, Lise *legislative staff member*
Clay, William Lacy, Jr. *United States Representative from Missouri*
Clayton, Carol A. *lawyer*
Clayton, Michael F. *lawyer*
Cleaver, Emanuel, II, *United States Representative from Missouri, former mayor, minister*
Clement, Paul Drew *lawyer, former federal agency administrator*
Clemente, Rosa Alicia *journalist, advocate*
Clevenger, Raymond Charles III *federal judge*
Clewell, Beatriz Chu *director, researcher*
Clift, Eleanor *journalist, writer*
Clifton, James K. (Jim Clifton) *consulting company executive*
Cline, William Richard *economist, educator*
Clinton, Hillary Rodham (Hillary Diane Rodham Clinton) *United States Secretary of State, former United States Senator from New York, former First Lady of United States*
Cloud, John Albert, Jr. *United States Ambassador to Lithuania*
Clough, G. Wayne (Gerald Wayne Clough) *museum administrator, former academic administrator*
Clyburn, James Enos (Jim Clyburn) *United States Representative from South Carolina*

Clyburn, Mignon L. *commissioner*
Coady, David Patrick *economist, educator*
Coats, Daniel Ray *lawyer, former ambassador, Former United States Senator, Ind*
Cobb, Ty *lawyer*
Cobbs, Nicholas Hamner *lawyer, judge*
Coble, John Howard *United States Representative from North Carolina, lawyer*
Coburn, Tom (Thomas Allen Coburn) *United States Senator from Oklahoma*
Cochran, Kelvin James *federal agency administrator*
Cochran, Robert A. *legislative staff member*
Cochran, Thad (William Thad Cochran) *United States Senator from Mississippi*
Coffey, Matthew B. *senior advisor to industry*
Coffina, Scott A. *lawyer*
Coffman, Callie M. *legislative staff member*
Coffman, Mike (Michael H. Coffman) *United States Representative from Colorado, former state official*
Cogman, Don V. *public relations executive*
Cohen, David S. *federal agency administrator, lawyer*
Cohen, Eliot Asher *political scientist*
Cohen, Howard *lobbyist*
Cohen, Jeffrey M. *legislative staff member*
Cohen, Larry *labor union administrator*
Cohen, Louis Richard *lawyer*
Cohen, Mary Ann *federal judge*
Cohen, Michael *educational association administrator*
Cohen, Steve (Stephen Ira Cohen) *United States Representative from Tennessee, former state legislator*
Cohen, William Sebastian *consultant, former United States Secretary of Defense*
Cohn, Sherman Louis *lawyer, educator*
Cole, Jason *legislative staff member*
Cole, John Pope, Jr. *lawyer*
Cole, Johnnetta Betsch *museum director, former academic administrator*
Cole, Lorraine *women's association executive*
Cole, Ray *lobbyist*
Cole, Robert Theodore *lawyer*
Cole, Tom (Thomas Jeffrey Cole) *United States Representative from Oklahoma*
Coleman, Bernell *physiologist, educator*
Coleman, William Thaddeus, Jr. *lawyer, former United States Secretary of Transportation*
Collamore, Thomas Jones *corporate financial executive*
Collea, Joseph Vincent *perinatologist, educator*
Collender, Stanley E. *communications executive, columnist*
Colley, Mark Douglas *lawyer*
Collins, Daniel Francis *lawyer*
Collins, James Franklin *retired ambassador*
Collins, John M. *legislative staff member*
Collins, Michael E. *legislative staff member*
Collins, Rob W. *legislative staff member*
Collins, Robert Ellwood *surgeon*
Collins, Susan Margaret *United States Senator from Maine*
Collinson, Dale Stanley *lawyer*
Collipriest, Mary Jane *legislative staff member*
Colson, Earl Morton *lawyer, educator*
Colton Skolnick, Judith A. *artist*
Colvin, John O. *federal judge*
Comas, Daniel L. *manufacturing executive*
Combs, Roberta *political organization president CEO*
Comerford, Cristeta *chef*
Compton, Mary Beatrice Brown *public relations executive, writer*
Comstock, Robert Francis *lawyer*
Conaway, Mike (K. Michael Conaway) *United States Representative from Texas*
Condeluci, Laura *legislative staff member*
Condrell, William Kenneth *lawyer*
Coneway, Peter Richard *United States Ambassador to Switzerland and Liechtenstein*
Connaughton, Jeffrey J. *legislative staff member*
Connelly, Warren E. *lawyer*
Conner, Frank M. (Rusty) III *lawyer*
Connolly, Gerald E. *United States Representative from Virginia*
Connor, Chuck *federal agency administrator*
Connor, Jeffrey C. *legislative staff member*
Connor, Michael Lee *federal agency administrator*
Conrad, Kent (Gaylord Kent Conrad) *United States Senator from North Dakota*
Conrad, Robin S. *lawyer*
Conroy, Amy *museum director*
Conway, James Terry *career military officer*
Conway, Kellyanne *political strategist, pollster*
Conyers, John, Jr. *United States Representative from Michigan*
Cook, Bryson Leitch *lawyer*
Cook, Elisebeth Collins *lawyer, former federal agency administrator*
Cook, Frances D. *management consultant*
Cook, Frederick B. *United States Ambassador to Central African Republic*
Cook, Harry Clayton, Jr. *lawyer*
Cook, Mary Ann *adult education educator*
Cook, Michael Harry *lawyer*
Cooke, Benson George *counseling psychologist, psychology professor, consultant*
Cooper, Byron Stanley *internist, educator*
Cooper, Charles *legislative staff member*
Cooper, Charles Justin *lawyer, former federal agency administrator*
Cooper, Ginnie *library director*
Cooper, James Hayes Shofner (Jim Cooper) *United States Representative from Tennessee, lawyer*
Cooper, Ronald Stephen *lawyer*
Copher, Michael A. *legislative staff member*
Copps, Michael Joseph *commissioner*
Cordes, Joseph John *economics professor, director*
Coreth, Joseph Herman *investment advisor*
Corker, Bob (Robert Phillips Corker Jr.) *United States Senator from Tennessee*
Corn-Revere, Robert *lawyer*
Cornyn, John III *United States Senator from Texas*
Corr, William V. (Bill Corr) *federal agency administrator, lobbyist*
Corso, John Anthony *management consultant, educator*
Cortese, Alfred William, Jr. *lawyer, consultant*
Corts, Paul Richard *educational association and former federal agency administrator*
Cosgrove, John Patrick *editor*
Costa, Jim *United States Representative from California*
Costello, Jerry F., Jr. *United States Representative from Illinois*
Coston, William Dean *lawyer*
Cothron, Tony L. *career military officer*
Coughlin, Daniel P. *chaplain*
Coulter, Ann Hart *writer, political columnist, lawyer*
Couper, William *bank executive*
Courson, John A. *lobbyist*
Covucci, George E. *lawyer*
Cowan, Edward *journalist, editor*
Cox, Ana Marie *writer, former political blogger*
Cox, John W. *federal agency administrator*
Cox, M. Carolyn *lawyer*
Cox, Rebecca Gernhardt *air transportation executive*
Cox, Robert Haymes *lawyer*
Cox, Warren Jacob *architect*
Coyne, Patrick Joseph *lawyer*
Craft, Robert Homan, Jr. *lawyer*
Craig, Gregory Bestor *lawyer*
Craig, John Charles *educational consultant*
Craig, John Tucker *economist, consultant*
Cramer, Bud (Robert Edward Cramer Jr.) *lobbyist, former United States Representative from Alabama*
Crandall, Frank B. *marine biologist, engineer*
Crane, Edward Harrison III *think-tank executive, financial analyst*
Crapo, Michael Dean *United States Senator from Idaho, former congressman, lawyer*
Cravens, Michael J. *legislative staff member*
Crawford, Brian C. *legislative staff member*
Crawford, George C. *lobbyist*
Crawford, Hunt Dorn, Jr. *retired military officer, educator, diplomat*
Crawford, Lester Mills, Jr. *scientic consultant, former federal agency administrator*
Crawford, Stephen *think tank manager*
Crawford-Mason, Clare Wootten *television producer, journalist*
Creighton, Patrick J. *legislative staff member*
Crenshaw, Albert Burford *retired journalist*
Crenshaw, Ander *United States Representative from Florida, lawyer*
Cretz, Gene A. *United States Ambassador to Libya*
Crocker, Chester Arthur *diplomat, federal agency administrator*
Crocker, Thomas Edward *lawyer*
Crosby, William Duncan, Jr. *lawyer*
Cross, Gerald Marion *federal agency administrator*
Cross, Meredith B. *lawyer*
Cross, Terry M. *career military officer*
Crowley, Jeffrey S. *federal official*
Crowley, Joseph *United States Representative from New York*
Crowley, Philip J. (P.J. Crowley) *federal agency administrator*
Cruden, John Charles *federal agency administrator, lawyer*
Crump, John *lawyer*
Crutchfield, Danielle M. *federal official*
Cubeta, Paul Marsden *English literature educator*
Cuellar, Henry *United States Representative from Texas, lawyer*
Culberson, John Abney *United States Representative from Texas, lawyer*
Culbertson, James B. *United States Ambassador to The Netherlands*
Cullen, Frank W. *legislative staff member*
Cullison, Thomas R. *career military officer*
Culp, H. Lawrence *manufacturing executive*
Culvahouse, Arthur Boggess, Jr. *lawyer*
Cumber, Sada *United States Special Envoy to the Organization of the Islamic Conference*
Cummings, Elijah E. *United States Representative from Maryland*
Cummings, Frank *lawyer*
Cunningham, James Blair *United States Ambassador to Israel*
Cunningham, Paul G. *legislative staff member*
Cunningham, Peter *federal agency administrator*
Curris, Constantine William *educational association administrator*
Curry, Thomas J. *federal official*
Curtin, Jeremy *federal agency administrator*
Curtin, Peter J. *lawyer*
Curtis, Debbie *legislative staff member*
Cusick, Robert Irwin *federal official, lawyer*
Cutler, Bernard Joseph *editor-in-chief, writer*
Cutter, Stephanie *federal official*
Cylke, Frank Kurt *librarian*
Czarnecki, Karen M. *legislative staff member*
D'Agostino, Thomas Paul *federal agency administrator*
Dahlkemper, Kathy (Kathleen A. Dahlkemper) *United States Representative from Pennsylvania*
Dailey, John Revell *museum director, retired military officer*
Dale, Adrianne Marie *information technology executive, consultant*
Daley, Henry J. *lawyer*
Dallavecchia, Enrico *mortgage company executive*
Dalley, George Albert *legislative staff member, lawyer, consultant*
Daly, George Garman *dean*
Damelin, Harold D. *lawyer, former federal agency administrator*
Damich, Edward John *federal judge*
Dana, Jonathan M. *lawyer*
Dang, Hai-Anh Hoang *economist, consultant*
D'Aniello, Daniel A. *investment company executive*
Daniels, Stephen M. *government official*
Danilovich, John J. *investment company executive, former ambassador*
Danon, Steve S. *legislative staff member*
Danziger, Raphael *political scientist, researcher*
Darden, William Horace *federal judge*
Datri, James Edmund *advertising association executive, lawyer*
Davidson, Daniel Ira *lawyer*
Davidson, Daniel Morton *lawyer*
Davidson, Donetta Lea *federal agency commissioner, former state official*
Davidson, Eugene Abraham *biochemist, educator, academic administrator*
Davidson, Jo Ann *political organization administrator, state legislator*
Davidson, Tom William *lawyer*
Davies, J. Clarence (Terry Davies) *author, consultant*
Davis, Anselm G., Jr. *federal agency administrator*
Davis, Artur Genestre *United States Representative from Alabama, lawyer*
Davis, Cameron *federal agency administrator, environmentalist*
Davis, Danny K. *United States Representative from Illinois*
Davis, Donald Ray *entomologist*
Davis, Geoff *United States Representative from Kentucky*
Davis, Lance Alan *foundation administrator, research and development executive, metallurgical engineer*
Davis, Lincoln *United States Representative from Tennessee*
Davis, Lula Johnson *legislative staff member*
Davis, Michele Aileen *federal agency administrator, former mortgage company executive*
Davis, Randy Lee *soil scientist*
Davis, Robert Nolan *federal judge, educator*
Davis, Susan A. *United States Representative from California*
Davis, Thomas M., III, (Tom Davis) *former United States Representative from Virginia*
Davis, William E. *lawyer*
Davison, Calvin *retired lawyer*
Dawley, Edward Armistead III *language educator*
Dawson, Horace Greeley, Jr. *former diplomat, government official*
Dawson, Howard Athalone, Jr. *federal judge*
Dawson, Mimi Weyforth *public policy consultant*
Day, Carol R.T. *nursing educator, director*
Day, Doris (Doris von Kappelhoff) *singer, actress*
Day, Gordon W. *electrical engineer*
Day, Lincoln Hubert *demographer, educator, documentary filmmaker*
Day, Mary Louise *volunteer*
Dayzie, LaDaniel *military officer*
Deal, Jill B. *lawyer*
Deal, Nathan J. *United States Representative from Georgia, lawyer*
Deal, Timothy *association executive, former diplomat*
Dean, Howard Brush III *former Governor of Vermont*
Dean, John F. *federal judge*
Dean, Robert J. *funeral director*
Dearborn, Rick A. *legislative staff member, former federal agency administrator*
de Baca, Luis C. *federal agency administrator*
Debele, Bekele *water resources specialist*
Debevoise, Eli Whitney, II, *federal official, lawyer*
De Borchgrave, Arnaud *editor, writer, lecturer*
DeCesare, Michael J. *legislative staff member*
Decheine, Robert B. *legislative staff member*
Deckelbaum, Nelson *lawyer*
Decker, Brett M. *bank executive*
DeCoster, Mark Allen *research biochemist*
Deeb, Mary-Jane *editor, educator, librarian*
Deese, Brian C. *federal official*
Deese, Pamela McCarthy *lawyer*
DeFazio, Peter Anthony *United States Representative from Oregon*
DeFrancis, Suzanne Cox *international relief organization executive, former federal agency administrator*
DeFrank, Thomas Michael *journalist*
De Gette, Diana Louise *United States Representative from Colorado, lawyer*
DeGioia, John J. *academic administrator*
DeGraffenreidt, James H., Jr. *gas company executive*
deKieffer, Donald Eulette *lawyer*
Delahay, John N. *orthopedist, surgeon*
Delahunt, William D. *United States Representative from Massachusetts*
Deland, Michael Reeves *attorney-at-law, disability and environmental consultant*
DeLauro, Rosa L. *United States Representative from Connecticut*
Delbanco, Suzanne F. *human services administrator*
DeLeon, Patrick Henry *legislative staff member, lawyer*
de Leon, Sylvia A. *lawyer*
Delgado, Patricia Coufal *legislative staff member*
Delio, Ilia *theology studies educator*
Dell'Orto, Daniel Joseph *lawyer*
Dembling, Paul Gerald *lawyer, former government official*
DeMuth, Christopher Clay *think-tank executive*
Denison, Mary Boney *lawyer*
DeParle, Nancy-Ann Min *federal official, former private equity firm executive*
DePass, Michelle J. *federal agency administrator*
Derse, Anne E. *United States Ambassador to Azerbaijan*
Desai, Mehul J. *physician, director*
Deshmukh, Vivek R. *neurosurgeon, medical educator*
de Souza Briggs, Xavier N. *federal official, sociology professor, writer*
Deutsch, Jeremy *legislative staff member*
Deutsch, Peter R. *former congressman*
Devine, Tad (Thomas A. Devine) *media consultant*
DeWaal, Caroline Smith *education and advocacy organization executive, lawyer*
Dezenhall, Eric B. *management consultant, writer*
Diaz, Eduardo *cultural organization administrator*
Diaz-Balart, Lincoln *United States Representative from Florida, lawyer*
Diaz-Balart, Mario *United States Representative from Florida*
Dick, Steven J. *historian*
Dicks, Norman De Valois *United States Representative from Washington*
Dienelt, John F. *lawyer*
Diercks, Walter Elmer *lawyer*
Dieter, Robert J. *United States Ambassador to Belize*
DiGanci, Todd T. *financial regulatory service executive*
diGenova, Joseph E. *lawyer*
Di Lella, Alexander Anthony *biblical studies educator*
Dillin, John Woodward, Jr. *retired editor, reporter*
Dillon, Jennifer O'Malley *political organization administrator*
Dillon, Patrick (Michael Patrick Dillon) *federal official*
Dillon, Veronica *publishing executive, lawyer*
Dillon, Wilton Sterling *anthropologist, foundation administrator*
Dimino, Joseph Thomas *archbishop emeritus*
Dingell, John David *United States Representative from Michigan*
Dinger, Larry M. *United States Charge d'Affaires to Myanmar (Burma)*
Dinh, Viet D. *law educator*
DiPerna, Frank Paul *photographer, educator*
Disheroon, Fred Russell *lawyer*
Dixon, Debra A. *legislative staff member*
Dixson, Diane Elizabeth *library congress docent retired,acquisitions librarian, tax preparation business owner visitors service office retired senior acquisitions librarian, financial counselor*
Dizard, Wilson Paul, Jr. *international affairs consultant, educator*
Dobrozsi, Jeffrey J. *legislative staff member*
Dodaro, Gene (Eugene Louis Dodaro) *federal official*
Dodd, Christopher John *United States Senator from Connecticut*
Doggett, Lloyd Alton, II, *United States Representative from Texas, retired judge*
Dolan, Michael William *lawyer*
Dolder, Nancy S. *legislative staff member, judge*
Dole, Bob (Robert Joseph Dole) *lobbyist, lawyer, retired United States Senator from Kansas*
Dolin, Mitchell F. *lawyer*
Domenech, Edgar A. *federal agency administrator*
Dominguez De Marty, Idalia T. *legislative staff member*
Domning, Daryl Paul *paleontologist, educator*
Donahue, Thomas Reilly *trade union official*
Donald, Admiral Kirkland H. *military officer, federal agency administrator*
Donar, Erin *legislative staff member*
Donatelli, Frank J. *lobbyist, lawyer*
Donegan, Charles Edward *lawyer, educator*
Donilon, Thomas E. *federal official, lawyer*
Donley, Michael Bruce *civilian military employee*
Donnelly, Joseph Simon *United States Representative from Indiana, lawyer*
Donohoe, Cathryn Murray *journalist*
Donohue, Joyce Morrissey *biochemist, toxicologist, dietician, educator*
Donohue, Kenneth M. *federal agency administrator*
Donohue, Tom J. (Thomas Joseph Donohue) *business association administrator*
Donovan, Garrett H. *legislative staff member*
Donovan, George Joseph *transportation executive, consultant*
Donovan, Joseph Richard, Jr. *United States Consul General in Hong Kong*
Donovan, Shaun L. *Secretary of Housing and Urban Development*
Doolittle, Jesse William, Jr. *lawyer*
Doran, Charles Francis *political scientist, consultant*
Doran, Lynn Lanz *finance educator, director*
Dorfman, Marc *lawyer*
Dorgan, Byron Leslie *United States Senator from North Dakota*
Dorn, James Andrew *editor*
Dorn, Jennifer Lynn *professional association executive, former federal agency administrator*
Dornatt, Rochelle S. *legislative staff member*
Dorsey, David Byard *non-profit executive*
Doty, James Robert *lawyer*
Dougherty, Jude Patrick *philosopher, educator, dean*
Douglas, Derek *federal official*
Douglas, Leslie *investment banker*
Douglass, Madonna Cynthia *legislative staff member*
Douthat, Ross Gregory *editor, columnist, writer*
Dowd, John Maguire *lawyer*
Dowd, Maureen *columnist*
Dowley, Joseph Kyran *lawyer*
Downey, Mortimer Leo III *consulting firm executive, former transportation executive*
Downey, Thomas Joseph *lobbyist, former congressman*
Downie, Leonard, Jr. *publishing executive, retired editor, professor*
Downie, Richard Duncan *government agency administrator, retired military officer*
Downs, Anthony *economist, real estate consultant*
Downs, Clark Evans *lawyer*
Downs, Glen Alan *legislative staff member*
Downs, Thomas Michael (Tom Downs) *transportation executive*
Doyle, Michael F. (Mike) *United States Representative from Pennsylvania*
Drapeau, Mark David *defense contractor*
Dreier, David Timothy *United States Representative from California*
Drew, Elizabeth *commentator, journalist, writer*
Dribinsky, Leonard *lawyer*
Driehaus, Steven L. *United States Representative from Ohio*
Droms, William George *finance educator, investment advisor*
Duberstein, Kenneth Marc *lobbyist, former White House chief of staff, management consultant*
DuBester, Ernest William *federal agency administrator*
DuBois, Joshua *minister, federal official*
DuBois, Raymond Francis, Jr. *former civilian military employee, former marketing professional*
Ducic, Ivica *medical educator*

Duckworth, Tammy (Ladda Tammy Duckworth) *federal agency administrator, military officer*
Dudas, Jon W. *lawyer, former federal agency administrator*
Dudley, Susan Elaine *federal official*
Duemling, Robert Werner *diplomat, museum director*
Duff, James C. *lawyer*
Duffey, Joseph Daniel *academic administrator*
Duffy, Beau *legislative staff member*
Duffy, Michael F. *federal agency administrator*
Dugan, John Cunningham *federal agency administrator, lawyer*
Duke, Elaine Costanzo *federal agency administrator*
Duke, Elizabeth A. (Betsy Duke) *federal official, former bank executive*
Dunbar, Leslie Wallace *writer, consultant*
Duncan, Arne *Secretary of Education, former school system administrator*
Duncan, Jeffrey S. *legislative staff member*
Duncan, John Dean, Jr. *lawyer*
Duncan, John J., Jr. *United States Representative from Tennessee*
Duncan, Thomasenia P. *federal official*
Dunn, Adam Troy *professional baseball player*
Dunn, Anita Babbitt *federal official, political communications specialist*
Dunn, James Milton *retired religious organization administrator*
Dunn, Joseph A. *federal agency administrator*
Dunn, Michael V. *commissioner*
Dunn, Timothy J. *United States Chief of Mission for Netherlands Antilles and Aruba*
Dunne, Patrick W. *federal agency administrator, retired military officer*
Dunton, James Raynor *publisher*
Du Pont, Pierre Samuel, IV, *former Governor of Delaware, lawyer*
Durbin, Dick (Richard Joseph Durbin) *United States Senator from Illinois*
Durfee, Harold Allen *philosophy educator*
Durney, Michael Cavalier *lawyer*
Durnil, Gordon Kay *lawyer, arbitrator, diplomat*
Dutro, John Thomas, Jr. *geologist, paleontologist*
Dwyer, Maureen Ellen *lawyer*
Dye, Rebecca Feemster *commissioner*
Dyer, Cynthia (Cindy Dyer) *federal agency administrator, former prosecutor*
Dyk, Timothy Belcher *federal judge*
Dyke, Charles William *retired army officer*
Dykema, Richard T. (Rick Dykema) *legislative staff member*
Dyson, Michael Eric *religious studies educator, writer*
Eads, George Curtis *senior consultant*
Eagleburger, Lawrence Sidney *public policy advisor, former United States Secretary of State*
Earll, Jerry Miller *internist, educator, endocrinologist*
Eastment, Thomas James *lawyer*
Easton, John Jay, Jr. *lawyer*
Easton, John Q. *federal agency administrator, former educational association administrator*
Eaton, William A. *United States Ambassador to Panama, former federal agency administrator*
Ebrahim, Shahul Hameed *health science association administrator*
Echaveste, Maria *lobbyist, former federal official*
EchoHawk, Larry *federal agency administrator, lawyer, former state attorney general*
Eckberg, William Robert *biologist, educator, researcher*
Eckenhoff, Edward Alvin *health facility administrator, educator*
Eddy, Julie *legislative staff member*
Edelman, Marian Wright *not-for-profit developer, lawyer*
Edelman, Peter Benjamin *lawyer, educator*
Eden, Guinevere F. *neurologist, educator*
Edmisten, Jane Moretz *lawyer, educator*
Edmonds, Kenneth A. *legislative staff member*
Edwards, Bob (Robert Alan Edwards) *radio news anchor*
Edwards, Chet (Thomas Chester Edwards) *United States Representative from Texas*
Edwards, Donna F. *United States Representative from Maryland, former foundation administrator*
Edwards, Harry Thomas *federal judge*
Edwards, Mickey (Marvin Henry Edwards) *think-tank executive, former congressman*
Edwards, Willarda V. *medical association administrator, internist*
Effron, Andrew S. *federal judge*
Efimba, Robert *engineering educator, consultant*
Efros, Ellen Ann *lawyer*
Eggenberger, Andrew Jon *retired federal agency administrator*
Eggleston, W. Neil *lawyer*
Egolf, David A. *physics professor*
Ehlers, Vernon James *United States Representative from Michigan*
Ehrenhaft, Peter David *lawyer*
Eigler, Friederike *literature and language professor*
Ein, Daniel *allergist*
Eisenberg, Pablo Samuel *non-profit organization executive*
Eisner, Howard *engineering executive, educator*
Eizenstat, Stuart Elliot *lawyer, former federal agency administrator*
Elcano, Mary S. *international non-profit organization executive, lawyer*
Elfin, Mel *magazine editor*
Elias, Thomas Sam *botanist, author*
El Khadem, Hassan Saad *chemistry professor, researcher*
Eller, Joseph Burton, Jr. *federal agency administrator*
Ellett, Ted (E. Tazewell Ellett) *lawyer*
Ellicott, John LeMoyne *lawyer*
Elliott, Daniel Robert III *federal agency administrator, lawyer*
Elliott, Emerson John *education consultant, policy analyst*
Elliott, Thomas Michael *retired association executive, educator, consultant*
Ellis, Courtenay *lawyer*
Ellis, Jacqueline A. *legislative staff member*
Ellis, Jennifer Lynn *thoracic surgeon*
Ellison, Keith Maurice *United States Representative from Minnesota, former lawyer*
Ellsworth, Brad (Bradley Ellsworth) *United States Representative from Indiana, former police officer*
Elmendorf, Douglas William *federal official, economist*
Elmendorf, Steven A. *lobbyist*
Elmer, Brian Christian *lawyer*
Elrod, Eugene Richard *lawyer*
Elsasser, Glen Robert *journalist*
Elwood, Patricia Cowan *city official, political scientist, consultant*
Emanuel, Rahm Israel *White House Chief of Staff, former United States Representative from Illinois*
Emely, Mary Ann *association executive*
Emerson, Jo Ann H. *United States Representative from Missouri*
Emge, Kirk J. *electric power industry executive, lawyer*
Emperado, Mercedes Lopez *librarian*
Engel, Eliot Lanze *United States Representative from New York*
Engler, John M. *manufacturing executive, former governor*
English, Charles Lewis *United States ambassador to Bosnia and Herzegovina*
English, Richard Allyn *sociologist, educator*
Englund, Julie Irene *academic administrator*
Ensenat, Donald Burnham *lawyer, former ambassador*
Ensign, John Eric *United States Senator from Nevada*
Entman, Robert Mathew *communications educator, consultant*
Enzi, Michael Bradley *United States Senator from Wyoming, accountant*
Epifani, Lisa Eyonne *federal agency administrator, lawyer*
Epps, Roselyn Elizabeth Payne *pediatrician, educator*
Epstein, Anthony Charles *judge*
Epstein, Gerald Lewis *technology and security policy analyst*
Epstien, Jay Alan *lawyer*
Erdmann, Charles Edgar (Chip Erdmann) *federal judge, former state supreme court justice*
Erdtmann, Frederick J. *physician, retired military officer*
Ereli, Joseph Adam *United States ambassador to Kingdom of Bahrain*
Eribo, Broderick E. *microbiologist, educator*
Erickson, Chris *counselor, educator*
Erickson, Nancy *federal official*
Ericsson, Sally Claire *not-for-profit consultant*
Ernst, Mark A. *federal agency administrator, former financial services company executive*
Ershler, William Baldwin *biogerontologist, educator*
Esau, Laurie *legislative staff member*
Escobar, Jennifer Van Der Heide *legislative staff member*
Eshkevari, Ladan *nursing educator*
Eshoo, Anna Georges *United States Representative from California*
Eskew, Carter *public relations executive*
Espy, Mike (Alphonso Michael Espy) *lawyer, former United States Secretary of Agriculture, former United State Representative from Mississippi*
Estabrook, Joseph Walter *bishop*
Estefan, Nabil *finance and business executive*
Estopinán, Arturo A. *legislative staff member*
Etheridge, Bob (Bobby Ray Etheridge) *United States Representative from North Carolina*
Etzel, Ruth Ann *pediatrician, epidemiologist, educator*
Evans, David C. *lawyer*
Evans, Donald Louis *think-tank executive, former United States Secretary of Commerce*
Evans, Joan M. *federal agency administrator*
Everett, Ralph Bernard *think-tank executive*
Ewing, Kenneth Patrick Ky *lawyer*
Faden, Alan Ira *neurology educator*
Faherty, Robert Louis *publishing executive*
Fahey, John M., Jr. *magazine and book publishing executive*
Fahmy, Nabil *ambassador*
Fairbanks, Richard Monroe III *lawyer, educator, retired ambassador*
Fairchild, Scott M. *legislative staff member*
Faleomavaega, Eni Fa'auaa Hunkin *Delegate to United States House Representative from American Samoa*
Fannin, Paul Robert *United States Ambassador to the Dominican Republic*
Fanning, Fred Eldridge *public administrator*
Farr, Judith Banzer *retired literature educator, writer, lecturer*
Farr, Sam *United States Representative from California*
Farrell, Diana *federal official*
Farrell, Michael W. *Senior Judge, DC Court of Appeals*
Farris, Amanda *federal agency administrator*
Farrow, Elizabeth Oliver *public and government relations consultant*
Farrow, Frank *think-tank executive*
Fassler, Jess C. *legislative staff member*
Fattah, Chaka *United States Representative from Pennsylvania, former state legislator*
Faulkner, Douglas L. *federal agency administrator*
Faux, Jeff (Geoffrey Peter Faux) *economist, writer*
Favreau, Jonathan *speechwriter*
Fazio, Vic (Victor Herbert Fazio Jr.) *lobbyist, lawyer, former congressman*
Feather, Karen M. *legislative staff member*
Fedders, John Michael *lawyer*
Feder, Judy *political science professor*
Feder, Samuel L. *lawyer*
Fedoroff, Nina Vsevolod *research scientist, consultant, educator*
Feeley, William F. *federal agency administrator*
Feffer, Gerald Alan *lawyer*
Feil, Michael Bruce *statistician*
Feinberg, Kenneth Roy *federal official, lawyer*
Feingold, Russell Dana *United States Senator from Wisconsin, lawyer*
Feinstein, Deborah L. *lawyer*
Feinstein, Dianne *United States Senator from California*
Feith, Douglas Jay *lawyer, former federal agency administrator*
Feld, Karen Irma *journalist, commentator, speech professional*
Feldman, Clarice Rochelle *lawyer*
Feldman, Elliot Jay *lawyer*
Feldman, Eric *legislative staff member*
Feldman, Michael *public relations executive*
Feliciano, Carmen M. *legislative staff member*
Felix, Larry R. *federal agency administrator*
Fell, James Carlton *traffic safety research and evaluation executive, consultant*
Feltman, Jeffrey David *federal agency administrator, former ambassador*
Fennell, Stephen A. *lawyer*
Fenty, Adrian M. *Mayor, Washington, DC*
Ferguson, Lewis Hamilton III *lawyer*
Ferguson, William, Jr., (Bill Ferguson) *lobbyist*
Ferren, John Maxwell *Senior Judge, DC Court of Appeals*
Ferris, Charles Daniel *lawyer, former government official*
Fertel, Marvin S. *civil engineer*
Feulner, Edwin John, Jr. *think-tank executive*
Fichtner, Jason J. *federal agency administrator*
Fiedler, Marc *lawyer, advocate*
Field, Andrea Bear *lawyer*
Fielding, Fred Fisher *lawyer*
Fields, Stuart Howard *labor relations specialist*
Fields, Wendy Lynn *lawyer*
Filner, Bob (Robert Filner) *United States Representative from California*
Findley, S. Brenna *legislative staff member*
Fine, Glenn Alan *federal agency administrator*
Fineberg, Harvey Vernon *health science association administrator*
Fineman, Howard David *columnist, writer, news correspondent*
Finkel, Eugene Jay *lawyer*
Finkle, Jeffrey Alan *professional association executive*
Finney Brody, Perry *legislative staff member*
Fiorina, Carly (Cara Carleton Sneed Fiorina) *think-tank executive, former computer company executive*
Firestone, Charles Morton *lawyer, educator*
Firestone, Nancy B. *federal judge*
Fischer, Elizabeth (Betsy) *television producer*
Fischer, Peter C. *legislative staff member*
Fishbein, Thomas Marlon *general surgeon, transplant surgeon*
Fishburne, Benjamin Postell III *lawyer*
Fishel, Andrew S. *managing director*
Fisher, Alice Stevens *lawyer, former federal agency administrator*
Fisher, Bart Steven *lawyer, educator, investment banker*
Fisher, Benjamin Chatburn *lawyer*
Fisher, John R. *Associate Judge, DC Court of Appeals*
Fisher, Miles Mark, IV, *education and religious studies educator, minister*
Fisher, Robert Dale *stockbroker, retired naval officer*
Fishman, Ira *sports association executive, lawyer*
Fitzmyer, Joseph Augustine *theology studies educator, priest*
Fitzpatrick, James Franklin *lawyer*
Flagg, Ronald Simon *lawyer*
Flake, Jeff *United States Representative from Arizona*
Flanagan, Michael Patrick *former congressman, lawyer*
Flanigan, Timothy Elliott *lawyer, former federal official*
Flannery, Ellen Joanne *lawyer*
Fleischman, Aaron I. *lawyer*
Fleisher, Eric Wilfrid *retired foreign service officer*
Fleming, Denis, Jr. *legislative staff member*
Fleming, John Calvin, Jr. *United States Representative from Louisiana, physician*
Fletcher, Lee *legislative staff member*
Flournoy, Michèle A. *federal agency administrator, former think-tank executive*
Flügelman, Máximo Enrique *financier, composer*
Foer, Franklin *editor*
Fogarty, Kevin C. *legislative staff member*
Foley, April H. *United States Ambassador to Hungary*
Foley, James B. *federal official, former ambassador*
Foley, Maurice B. *federal judge*
Fong, Ivan Kenneth *lawyer, former health products executive*
Fong, Phyllis Kamoi *federal agency administrator, lawyer*
Forbes, James Randy *United States Representative from Virginia*
Ford, Ann K. *lawyer*
Ford, Carl W., Jr. *consulting firm executive, former federal agency administrator*
Ford, Christopher Ashley *federal official, lawyer*
Ford, Harold Eugene, Jr. *law educator, former United States Representative from Tennessee*
Ford, Randall W. (Randy Ford) *legislative staff member*
Fore, Henrietta Holsman *federal agency administrator*
Forese, James John *investment company executive*
Forester, John Gordon, Jr. *lawyer*
Forkan, Patricia Ann *foundation executive*
Fornace, Albert J., Jr. *medical researcher*
Forrest, Herbert Emerson *lawyer*
Fortenberry, Jeffrey Lane *United States Representative from Nebraska*
Fortuno, Victor M. *lawyer*
Foscarinis, Maria *lawyer*
Foss, Clive Frank Wilson *history professor*
Foster, Bill (George William Foster) *United States Representative from Illinois, physicist*
Foster, C(harles) Allen *lawyer*
Foust, Robert Schmertz *political science professor*
Fowler, Elizabeth J. *legislative staff member*
Fox, J. Charles *federal agency administrator, environmentalist*
Fox, J. Edward (James Edward Fox Jr.) *federal agency administrator*
Fox, Nancy *legislative staff member*
Fox, Sam *United States ambassador to Belgium, manufacturing executive*
Foye, Randy *professional basketball player*
Fraker, Ford M. *United States Ambassador to Saudi Arabia*
Franco, Omar *government agency administrator*
Francois, Francis Bernard *retired professional society administrator, lawyer, transportation consultant*
Frank, Barney (Barnett Frank) *United States Representative from Massachusetts*
Frank, Richard Asher *lawyer, health products executive*
Frank, Theodore David *lawyer*
Franken, Al (Alan Stuart Franken) *United States Senator from Minnesota, political commentator, comedian, writer*
Franklin, Barbara Hackman *investment company executive, former United States Secretary of Commerce*
Franklin, Paige Elizabeth *literature and language professor*
Franks, Trent *United States Representative from Arizona*
Franzen, Byron T. (John Franzen) *media specialist*
Fraser, William M. III *career military officer*
Fraulino, Philip Samuel *telecommunications industry executive*
Freedman, Jay Weil *lawyer*
Freeman, Charles W., Jr., (Chas Freeman) *writer, former ambassador*
Freeman, Peter A. *dean*
Freis, James H., Jr. *federal agency administrator, lawyer*
Frelinghuysen, Rodney P. *United States Representative from New Jersey*
Frey, Bridgett *legislative staff member*
Frias, Michael J. *legislative staff member*
Fricke, Heinz *conductor*
Fried, Bruce Merlin *lawyer*
Fried, Daniel *ambassador, former federal agency administrator*
Frieder, Gideon *computer scientist, educator*
Friedman, Alan Jacob *educational association administrator, former museum director*
Friedman, Daniel Mortimer *federal judge*
Friedman, Gregory H. *energy administrator*
Friedman, Robert Sidney *political science professor*
Friedman, Thomas Loren *foreign correspondent, writer*
Friedrich, Dabney Langhorne *lawyer, commissioner*
Friedrich, Matthew Wilhelm *lawyer, former federal agency administrator*
Friend, William L. *retired engineering/construction industry executive*
Frost, Martin, III, (Jonas Martin Frost III) *lawyer, former congressman*
Frum, David *columnist*
Frumin, Alan Scott *parliamentarian*
Fu Claffe, Lily *lawyer*
Fudge, Marcia Louise *United States Representative from Ohio, former mayor*
Fuentes, Jennice *legislative staff member*
Fugate, Craig (William Craig Fugate) *federal agency administrator*
Fukuyama, Francis *political scientist, educator*
Fulgham, Alonzo L. *federal agency administrator*
Fuller, Edwin Daniel *hotel executive*
Fulton, Scott Colton *lawyer*
Furchtgott-Roth, Harold Wilkes *economist, consultant*
Furgurson, Ernest Baker, Jr., (Pat Furgurson) *writer*
Furman, Jason L. *federal official, economist*
Fusco, Aurilla Marie *director*
Futey, Bohdan A. *federal judge*
Futrell, Mary Alice Hatwood *dean, education association administrator*
Gaa, Willy C. *ambassador*
Gable, Edward Brennan, Jr. *lawyer*
Gabre-Madhin, Eleni Zaude *economist, researcher*
Gaffney, Glenn A. *federal official*
Gage, John *labor union administrator*
Gaibler, Floyd D. *federal agency administrator*
Gaillard, William Davis *physician*
Gainer, Terrance William *protective services official*
Gainey, Kathleen M. *career military officer*
Gainsborough, Jenni *advocate*
Gajarsa, Arthur J. *federal judge*
Galante, Carol J. *federal agency administrator, former home construction company executive*
Gale, Joseph H. *federal judge*
Gallagher, Michael David *lawyer, former federal agency administrator*
Gallas, Philip S. *lawyer*
Gallegly, Elton William *United States Representative from California*
Gallo, Anthony Ernest *playwright, theatrical artistic director, economist*
Gallo, Kenneth A. *lawyer*
Galston, William Arthur *political scientist, educator*
Gambatesa, Donald Anthony *federal agency administrator*
Gandhi, Natwar M. *city official*
Garcia, Frances *federal official, accountant*
Garcia, Jorge Mance *cardiologist*
Gardiner, Kent A. *lawyer*
Gardner, Janice Bradley *federal agency administrator*
Gardner, William Albert, Jr. *pathologist, medical products executive*
Garfinkel, Renée Efra *psychologist*
Garland, Merrick Brian *federal judge*
Garland, Sara G. *legislative staff member*
Garr, Sally D. *lawyer*
Garre, Gregory G. *law educator, former federal agency administrator*
Garrett, Scott (E. Scott Garrett) *United States Representative from New Jersey, lawyer*
Garrett, Theodore Louis *lawyer*
Garris, Charles Alexander *mechanical engineer, educator*

Garrish, Theodore John *lawyer*
Garthoff, Raymond Leonard *retired diplomat, diplomatic historian*
Gartzke, Dana G. *legislative staff member*
Garver, Lori Beth *federal agency administrator*
Garvey, Janet E. *United States Ambassador to Republic of Cameroon*
Gary, Lawrence Edward *social work educator*
Garza, Alexander Gerard *federal agency administrator, emergency physician*
Garza, Deborah A. *lawyer, former federal agency administrator*
Gaspard, Patrick H. *federal official, former labor union administrator*
Gastwirth, Joseph Lewis *statistician, educator*
Gates, Robert Michael *United States Secretary of Defense, former academic administrator*
Gavrilis, James *military officer*
Gazzola, Robert Allen *lawyer*
Gebhardt, Debra *legislative staff member*
Geduldig, Sam *lobbyist*
Gehrig, Leo Joseph *retired surgeon*
Geisel, Harold Walter *federal agency administrator*
Geithner, Timothy Franz *United States Secretary of the Treasury*
Geller, Kenneth Steven *lawyer*
Genachowski, Julius *federal official*
Geniesse, Robert John *lawyer*
Gensler, Gary S. *federal agency administrator*
George, Warren S. *labor union administrator*
Gerard, Jack N. *trade association administrator*
Gerber, Joel *federal judge*
Gerety, Tom R. *former academic administrator, lawyer, educator, philosopher*
Gerlach, Jim (James William Gerlach) *United States Representative from Pennsylvania*
Germond, Alice Travis *political organization administrator*
Gerson, Michael John *journalist*
Gerson, Stuart Michael *lawyer*
Gerstell, Glenn Steven *lawyer*
Gessaman, Donald Eugene *retired government executive*
Gfoeller-Volkoff, Tatiana C. *United States Ambassador to Kyrgyzstan*
Ghafari, Yousif Boutrous *United States Ambassador to Slovenia*
Giallorenzi, Thomas Gaetano *optical engineer*
Giambastiani, Edmund Peter, Jr. *retired military officer*
Giannini, Margaret Joan *pediatrician, federal agency administrator*
Gibbs, Lawrence Blair *lawyer*
Gibbs, Robert L. *White House press secretary*
Giblin, Vincent J. *labor union administrator*
Gideon, Kenneth Wayne *lawyer*
Gidley, J. Mark *lawyer*
Gierke, Herman Fredrick, III, (Sparky Gierke) *federal judge*
Giesta, Maria E. *legislative staff member*
Gifford, Rufus (John Rufus Gifford) *political organization administrator*
Giffords, Gabrielle *United States Representative from Arizona, former state senator*
Gilchrist, Robin *federal agency administrator*
Giles, Cynthia J. *federal agency administrator, environmentalist*
Gillespie, Ed (Edward Walter Gillespie) *lobbyist, former political organization administrator*
Gillibrand, Kirsten Rutnick *United States Senator from New York, lawyer*
Gillingham, Robert Fenton *economist, consultant*
Gilman, Benjamin Arthur *former congressman, lawyer*
Gilmore, Dee D. *legislative staff member*
Gilmore, James Stuart III *lawyer, former governor*
Gingrey, Phil (John Phillip Gingrey) *United States Representative from Georgia*
Gingrich, Newt (Newton Leroy Gingrich) *writer, former United States Representative from Georgia*
Ginsberg, Benjamin L. *lawyer*
Ginsberg, Daniel Brian *civilian military employee*
Ginsburg, Douglas Howard *federal judge*
Ginsburg, Martin David *lawyer, educator*
Ginsburg, Paul B. *health facility administrator*
Ginsburg, Ruth Bader *United States supreme court justice*
Giordano, Nick (Nicholas P. Giordano) *lobbyist*
Girard, James Emery *chemistry professor*
Giusti, Luis E. *gas industry executive*
Givhan, Robin Deneen *journalist*
Glancz, Ronald Robert *lawyer*
Glass, Brent D. *museum director*
Glasscock, Stacey *legislative staff member*
Glassman, Leonard M. *radiologist*
Glauber, Joseph *federal agency administrator, economist*
Glazer, Charles Louis *United States Ambassador to El Salvador*
Glazewski, Timothy M. *legislative staff member*
Gleklen, Jonathan Ian *lawyer*
Glendening, Parris Nelson *former governor, political science educator*
Glenn, Jerome Clayton *futurist, director*
Glick, Leslie Alan *lawyer*
Glickman, Stephen H. *judge*
Glynn, Edward F., Jr. *lawyer*
Gnehm, Edward W., Jr. *ambassador*
Godec, Robert F. *United States Ambassador to Tunisia*
Goeke, Joseph Robert *federal judge, lawyer*
Goel, Anish *foreign affairs officer, chemical engineer*
Goelzer, Daniel Lee *non-profit corporation administrator*
Goesl, Andrew L. *legislative staff member*
Goewey, David W. *lawyer*
Goff, James Franklin *physicist, consultant*
Gohmert, Louis Buller, Jr., (Louie Gohmert) *United States Representative from Texas, former judge, lawyer*
Gokcigdem, Murat T. *legislative staff member*
Gold, Martin B. *lobbyist, lawyer*
Gold, Peter Frederick *lawyer*
Gold, Richard M. *lobbyist, lawyer*
Goldberg, Fred T., Jr. *lawyer*
Goldberg, Jolande Elisabeth *law librarian*
Goldberg, Jonah Jacob *political columnist*
Goldberg, Seth A. *lawyer*
Goldberg, Stanley Joshua *federal judge*
Goldgeier, James *social sciences educator*
Goldscheider, Frances K. *sociologist, educator*
Goldsmith, Barry Richard *lawyer*
Goldsmith, Stephen *investment company executive, former mayor*
Goldstein, Allan Leonard *biochemist, educator*
Goldstein, Frank Robert *lawyer*
Goldstein, Michael B. *lawyer*
Golodner, Jack *labor association official, consultant*
Gomez, Gabriella Cecilia *federal agency administrator*
Gonzalez, Breann C. *legislative staff member*
Gonzalez, Charles A. *United States Representative from Texas*
Gonzalez, Emilio T. *federal agency administrator*
Goodlatte, Bob (Robert William) *United States Representative from Virginia, lawyer*
Goodman, Alfred Nelson *lawyer*
Goolsbee, Austan Dean *federal official, economics professor*
Goosby, Eric Paul *ambassador, epidemiologist*
Gordon, Bart (Barton Jennings Gordon) *United States Representative from Tennessee, lawyer*
Gordon, David F. *consulting firm executive, former federal agency administrator*
Gordon, Philip H. *federal agency administrator, political scientist*
Gordon, Robert *federal official*
Gore, Elizabeth M. *legislative staff member*
Gorelick, Jamie Shona *lawyer*
Gormley, William T. *dean, political science professor*
Gorn, Janet Marie *government official*
Gorrell, J. Warren, Jr. *lawyer*
Gottemoeller, Rose Eilene *federal agency administrator*
Gottfried, Keith Evan *lawyer*
Gottschalk, Thomas A. *lawyer, retired automotive executive*
Gould, Tessa A. *legislative staff member*
Gould, W. Scott (William Scott Gould) *federal agency administrator*
Gover, Kevin *museum director, former federal agency administrator*
Graber, Richard William *United States Ambassador to Czech Republic, lawyer*
Gradison, Bill (Willis David Gradison Jr.) *non-profit corporation administrator, former United States Representative from Ohio*
Graefe, Frederick H. *lawyer*
Graham, Donald Edward *publishing company executive*
Graham, John H., IV, *association executive*
Graham, Jonathan P. *lawyer*
Graham, Lindsey Olin *United States Senator from South Carolina*
Grandi, Edward *medical association administrator*
Grandmaison, J. Joseph *federal agency administrator*
Granger, Kay *United States Representative from Texas*
Grant, Carl N. *communications and sales executive*
Grant, Paula DiMeo *lawyer, mediator, nursing educator*
Grapin, Jacqueline G. *economist*
Grappo, Gary Anthony *United States Ambassador to Oman*
Grassley, Chuck (Charles Ernest Grassley) *United States Senator from Iowa*
Gration, Scott (Jonathan Scott Gration) *diplomat, retired military officer*
Graves, Samuel B., Jr. *United States Representative from Missouri, state legislator*
Gray, Edward Wesley *lawyer*
Gray, Lyons *federal agency administrator, former state representative*
Gray, Mary Wheat *statistician, lawyer*
Gray, Sheila Hafter *psychiatrist, researcher*
Gray, William Herbert III *consulting firm executive, Former United States Representative, Pennsylvania*
Grayson, Alan Mark *United States Representative from Florida, lawyer*
Greaux, Cheryl Prejean *federal agency administrator*
Green, Al *United States Representative from Texas*
Green, Donald Hugh *lawyer*
Green, Gene (Raymond Eugene Green) *United States Representative from Texas*
Green, Madeleine F. *educational association administrator*
Green, Mark Andrew *United States Ambassador to Tanzania, former congressman*
Green, Mike *professional hockey player*
Green, Thomas Charles *lawyer*
Greenberg, Milton *political science professor*
Greenberg, Stanley B. *political strategist, pollster*
Greenberger, Marcia Devins *lawyer*
Greene, David *reporter*
Greene, William P., Jr. *federal judge*
Greenert, Jonathan W. *career military officer*
Greenhalgh, Paul *academic administrator*
Greenlee, Kathy Jo *federal agency administrator*
Greenspan, Alan *consulting firm executive, former Chairman of the Board of Governors of the Federal Reserve System*
Gregg, Judd Alan *United States Senator from New Hampshire, former Governor of New Hampshire*
Gregory, David Michael *journalist, news correspondent*
Gregson, Wallace C., Jr., (Chip Gregson) *federal agency administrator, retired military officer*
Gresham, Dana Grant *federal agency administrator*
Grieco, Jeffrey Joseph *federal agency administrator*
Griffenhagen, George Bernard *trade association executive*
Griffin, Christine M. *federal official*
Griffin, Kelly Ann *public relations executive, consultant*
Griffin, Paul L. *publishing executive, fraternal organization administrator*
Griffith, Lanny *lobbyist, lawyer*
Griffith, Parker *United States Representative from Alabama, former state senator*
Griffith, Thomas Beall *federal judge*
Grigsby Queen, Sharlyn Ann *human resources specialist*
Grijalva, Raul *United States Representative from Arizona*
Grimes, Darrell Jay *microbiologist*
Grimes, John Grayson *federal agency administrator*
Grimes, Ronald Jay *legislative staff member*
Groff, Peter C. *federal agency administrator, former state legislator*
Gross, Charles R. *prosecutor*
Gross, David Andrew *federal official, lawyer*
Gross, Kenneth Andrew *lawyer*
Gross, Patrick Walter *information technology executive*
Grossman, Claudio M. *dean, law educator*
Grosvenor, Gilbert Melville *journalist, educator, publishing executive*
Grove, Brandon Hambright, Jr. *diplomat*
Groves, Robert Martin *federal agency administrator*
Grubisich, Tom *web editor*
Gruenberg, Martin J. *federal agency administrator, lawyer*
Grumet, Jason Seth *environmental policy adviser*
Grunfeld, Ernie *professional sports team executive, retired professional basketball player*
Grunwald, Mandy *media consultant*
Guhathakurta, Madhulika *astrophysicist*
Gulland, Eugene D. *lawyer*
Gumpert, Gunther *artist*
Gunderson, Brian F. *federal official*
Gunn, Will A. *lawyer, retired military officer*
Gurdon, Hugo *editor-in-chief*
Gustafson, David Douglas *federal judge*
Guthrie, Brett (Steven Brett Guthrie) *United States Representative from Kentucky, former state senator*
Guthrie, Priscilla Elizabeth *federal agency administrator*
Gutierrez, Luis V. *United States Representative from Illinois*
Gutman, Harry Largman *lawyer, educator*
Gutman, Stanley Theodore (Huck Gutman) *legislative staff member, literature and language professor, educator*
Guttman, Egon *law educator*
Guyton, Clara L. *librarian*
Guzy, Carol *photojournalist*
Guzzo, Joseph L. *legislative staff member*
Gwaltney, Corbin *publishing executive, editor*
Haas, Kate (Katherine L. Haas) *legislative staff member*
Haave, Carol A. *federal agency administrator*
Hackett, Susan J. *legal association administrator, lawyer*
Hagel, Lawrence B. *federal judge*
Hager, Jenna (Jenna Welch Bush) *language educator, writer, volunteer, former first daughter*
Hagner, John D. *lawyer*
Haines, Harry Allen *federal judge*
Halbert, Gary L. *lawyer*
Hale, David M. *federal agency administrator, former ambassador*
Hale, Janet S. *accounting firm executive, former federal agency administrator*
Hale, Robert Fargo *federal agency administrator*
Hale, Sarah C. *legislative staff member*
Haley, Roger Kendall *librarian*
Hall, John Joseph *United States Representative from New York, musician*
Hall, Keith D. *federal agency administrator*
Hall, Ralph Moody *United States Representative from Texas*
Hallgren, Richard Edwin *meteorologist*
Hallman, Linda D. *foundation administrator*
Hallmon, Phyllis G. *legislative staff member*
Halloran, Michael James *lawyer*
Halperin, Morton H. *political scientist*
Halperin, Samuel *education and training policy analyst*
Halpern, James S. *federal judge*
Halvorson, Deborah DeFrancesco (Debbie Halvorson) *United States Representative from Illinois, former state legislator*
Halvorson, Newman Thorbus, Jr. *lawyer*
Ham, Debra Newman *historian, educator*
Hamdar, Samer Hani *civil engineer, educator*
Hamilton, Christina Langelier *legislative staff member*
Hamilton, Lee Herbert *think-tank executive, former United States Representative from Indiana*
Hamilton, Samuel D. *federal agency administrator, biologist*
Hamlisch, Marvin Frederick *composer, conductor, musician, entertainer*
Hampton, Thomas E. *state banking agency administrator*
Hamre, John J. *think-tank executive, former federal agency administrator*
Hand, John Oliver *museum curator*
Hand, Lloyd N. *lawyer*
Handel, Mark David *atmospheric scientist, sports official*
Hanlon, William R. *lawyer*
Hannan, Timothy Hale *economist*
Hansen, Christopher W. *trade association administrator*
Hansen, Jennie Chin *nursing educator, association executive*
Hansen, Joseph T. *labor union administrator*
Hansen, Kenneth *lawyer*
Hanson, Alan R. *legislative staff member*
Hanzlik, Rayburn DeMara *lawyer*
Harbert, Karen Alderman *think-tank executive, former federal agency administrator*
Harbour, Pamela Jones *commissioner, lawyer*
Harden, Krysta L. *federal agency administrator*
Harding, Fann *retired scientist, administrator*
Harding, Frances M. *federal agency administrator*
Harding, Justin *legislative staff member*
Hare, Phil (Philip G. Hare) *United States Representative from Illinois*
Harkin, Tom (Thomas Richard Harkin) *United States Senator from Iowa*
Harlem, Susan Lynn *librarian*
Harley, Derek N. *legislative staff member*
Harlow, Larry (Bryce Larimore Harlow) *lobbyist, former federal official*
Harman, Charlie (Charles E. Harman Jr.) *legislative staff member*
Harman, Jane *United States Representative from California*
Haro, Steven M. *legislative staff member*
Harper, Bill (William Harper) *legislative staff member*
Harper, Edwin Leland *corporate financial executive, manufacturing executive*
Harper, Emery Walter *lawyer*
Harper, Gregg *United States Representative from Mississippi, lawyer*
Harper, Keith M. *lawyer*
Harper, Mary Annie *legislative staff member*
Harrington, Anthony Stephen *consulting firm executive, former ambassador*
Harris, Don Victor, Jr. *lawyer*
Harris, Jeffrey *lawyer*
Harris, Leslie *think-tank executive, lawyer*
Harris, Ondray T. *federal agency administrator*
Harris, Scott Blake *lawyer*
Harris, Seth David *federal agency administrator*
Harris, Steven Brown *non-profit corporation administrator, lawyer*
Harrison, Earl David *lawyer, real estate company officer*
Harrison, Randolph *legislative staff member*
Hart, Christopher Alvin *federal agency administrator*
Hart, Elizabeth *legislative staff member*
Hart, Jack Steven *lobbyist, lawyer, accountant*
Harter, Donald Harry *neurologist, medical educator*
Hartig, Rachel Mildred *literature and language professor, writer*
Hartley, Gregg L. *lobbyist*
Hartman, Michael Ross *lawyer*
Hartman, Patrick James *mechanical engineer, researcher*
Hartmann, Christopher M. *legislative staff member*
Hartmann, Robert Sankey *health facility administrator, not-for-profit fundraiser*
Harvey, Eleanor Jones *museum curator*
Harvey, John Collins, Jr. *career military officer*
Haslach, Patricia M. *ambassador*
Haslem, John Arthur *financial economist, educator*
Hasselmo, Ann Hayes Die *executive recruiter, psychologist, academic administrator, consultant, educator*
Hassett, Joseph Mark *lawyer*
Hastert, Dennis (John Dennis Hastert) *Former United States Representative from Illinois*
Hastings, Alcee Lamar *United States Representative from Florida, retired judge*
Hastings, Doc (Richard Norman Hastings) *United States Representative from Washington*
Hastings, Douglas Alfred *lawyer*
Hatch, Orrin Grant *United States Senator from Utah*
Hathaway, John G. *federal agency administrator, retired military officer*
Haurek, Alex *legislative staff member*
Hausfeld, Michael D. *lawyer*
Havens, Charles William III *retired lawyer*
Hawke, John Daniel, Jr. *lawyer, former federal official*
Hawks, T.A. (Thomas Allen Hawks) *legislative staff member*
Hawley, Edmund S. (Kip Hawley) *federal agency administrator*
Hawley-Bowland, Carla *career military officer*
Hay, Austin (George A. Hay) *actor, artist, pianist, writer*
Hayes, Daniel Fleming *oncologist, educator*
Hayes, David John *federal agency administrator, lawyer*
Hayes, Mark *legislative staff member*
Haynes, Leonard L. III *federal agency administrator, director*
Haynes, R. Michael *lawyer*
Head, Robert H. *legislative staff member*
Heddell, Gordon S. *federal agency administrator*
Hedgepeth, Ryan K. *legislative staff member*
Hedges, Harry George *retired computer scientist*
Heelan, Patrick Aidan *philosophy educator*
Heffernan, James Vincent *lawyer*
Hefferon, Thomas Michael *lawyer*
Height, Dorothy I. *former foundation administrator*
Heil, David J. *legislative staff member*
Heinrich, Martin T. *United States Representative from New Mexico*
Heintz, John Edward *lawyer*
Heintz, Paul *legislative staff member*
Heinz Kerry, Teresa (Maria Teresa Thierstein Simoes-Ferreira) *foundation administrator*
Helal, Gamal *interpreter, diplomat*
Helfer, Michael Stevens *lawyer*
Helgerson, John Leonard *federal agency administrator*
Heller, Jack Isaac *lawyer*
Heller, John Roderick III *lawyer, corporate financial executive*
Helm, Lewis Marshall *communications executive*
Helms, Robert Brake *economist*
Henderson, Douglas Boyd *lawyer*
Henderson, Karen LeCraft *federal judge*
Henke, Michael John *lawyer, educator*
Henke, Robert Joseph *federal agency administrator*
Henke, Tracy Ann *lobbyist, former federal agency administrator*
Henkin, Robert Irwin *neuroscientist, internist, nuclear medicine physician, medical products executive*
Henriquez, Sandra Brooks *federal agency administrator*
Henry, Charles Jay *library and information scientist*
Hensarling, Jeb *United States Representative from Texas*
Herbst, John Edward *federal agency administrator, former ambassador*
Herger, Walter William, Jr. *United States Representative from California*

Herman, Anthony *lawyer*
Hernandez, Israel *former federal agency administrator*
Hershey, Robert Lewis *mechanical engineer, management consultant*
Hersman, Deborah Anne Plummer *federal agency administrator*
Herzog, Richard Barnard *lawyer*
Herzstein, Robert Erwin *lawyer*
Hess, John H. III *legislative staff member*
Hess, Michael Edward *federal agency administrator*
Hess, Stephen *political scientist, writer*
Hevel, Gary Francis *public information officer, consultant*
Hewitt, Emily Clark *federal judge, minister*
Hewitt, Paul Buck *lawyer*
Heyman, David F. *federal agency administrator*
Hiatt, Fred *editor, journalist*
Hickok, Gene (Eugene Welch Hickok) *lobbyist, former federal agency administrator*
Hiebert, Ray Eldon *writer, educator*
Higgins, Bradford R. *federal agency administrator*
Higgins, Brian *United States Representative from New York*
Higgins, James Henry III *marketing executive*
Higgins, Paul John *career military officer*
Higgins, Richard Brendan *bishop*
Hightower, Dennis Fowler *federal agency administrator*
Hill, Anna E. *legislative staff member*
Hill, Baron Paul *United States Representative from Indiana*
Hill, Christopher Robert *United States Ambassador to Iraq*
Hill, Daniel O. *federal agency administrator*
Hill, David R. *lawyer, former federal agency administrator*
Hill, Edwin D. *labor union administrator*
Hill, Greg *legislative staff member*
Hilleary, Van (William Vanderpool Hilleary) *former congressman, lawyer*
Hills, Carla Anderson *lawyer, former United States Secretary of Housing and Urban Development*
Hills, Roderick M. *lawyer, former government official*
Hills, Stephen P. *publishing executive*
Hilton, Alison *art historian, educator*
Himes, Jim (James A. Himes) *United States Representative from Connecticut, former nonprofit organization executive*
Hinchey, Maurice D. *United States Representative from New York*
Hinden, Stanley Jay *newspaper editor*
Hines, Barbara Bealor *communications educator, director*
Hinojosa, Rubén *United States Representative from Texas*
Hinz, Jean *legislative staff member*
Hirschhorn, Eric Leonard *lawyer*
Hirschmann, Susan B. *lobbyist*
Hirsh, John Campion *literature and language professor*
Hisey, David C. *mortgage company executive*
Hitchens, Christopher Eric *columnist, writer*
Hjalmarsson, Erik *economist*
Hoagland, Richard Eugene *United States Ambassador to Kazakhstan*
Hobbs, J. Timothy, Sr. *lawyer*
Hobelman, Carl Donald *lawyer*
Hochberg, Fred Philip *bank executive, former dean*
Hochman, Nathan Joseph *lawyer, former federal agency administrator*
Hodes, Paul William, II, *United States Representative from New Hampshire, lawyer*
Hodge, Linda M. *former educational association administrator*
Hodges, Heather M. *United States Ambassador to Ecuador*
Hodges, Robert H., Jr. *federal judge*
Hoeflich, Scott J. *legislative staff member*
Hoekstra, Peter *United States Representative from Michigan, manufacturing executive*
Hoffa, James Phillip *labor union administrator*
Hoffinger, Adam Steven *lawyer*
Hoffman, E. Leslie *lawyer*
Hoffman, Eric P. *medical geneticist, educator*
Hoffman, Joel Elihu *lawyer*
Hoffman, Richard Bennett *court administrator*
Hoffmann, Sandra Ann *economist, researcher*
Hogan, Cynthia C. *federal official, lawyer*
Hogan, Felicity *artist*
Hogen, Philip Nere *federal agency administrator, lawyer*
Hoglander, Harry R. *federal official*
Holden, Tim (Thomas Timothy) *United States Representative from Pennsylvania*
Holder, Eric Himpton, Jr. *United States Attorney General*
Holder, Nicholas *legislative staff member*
Holdren, John Paul *federal official, physicist, educator*
Holland, Joy *health care facility executive*
Hollingsworth, Joe Gregory *lawyer*
Hollins, Hunter *museum administrator*
Hollis, Sheila Slocum *lawyer*
Holmes, Mark V. *judge*
Holmstead, Jeffrey Ralph *lawyer, former federal agency administrator*
Holt, Rush D. *United States Representative from New Jersey*
Holtz-Eakin, Douglas J. *economist, former federal official*
Honda, Michael M. (Mike Honda) *United States Representative from California*
Hong, Y. Mark *urologist*
Hope, William Duane *retired zoologist, curator*
Horahan, Edward Bernard III *lawyer*
Horn, Charles M. *lawyer*
Horn, Marian Blank *federal judge*
Horne, David L. *federal agency administrator*
Horowitz, Herbert Eugene *retired diplomat*
Horowitz, Philip Martin *lawyer*
Hotez, Peter Jay *parasitologist, educator*
House, W(illiam) Michael *lobbyist, lawyer*
Houston, Kate *federal agency administrator*
Howard, Glen Scott *lawyer, consultant*
Howard, Jack *industrial relations specialist, consultant*
Howard, Jeffrey Hjalmar *lawyer*
Howard, Muriel A. *educational association administrator, former academic administrator*
Howard, Roscoe Conklin, Jr. *lawyer, former prosecutor*
Howe, Fisher *management consultant, retired foreign service officer*
Howell, Beryl A. *lawyer, commissioner*
Howell, Mary L. *multi-industry company executive*
Hoyer, Steny Hamilton *United States Representative from Maryland*
Hoyt, Robert F. *lawyer*
Hsiao, Juei-chen *language educator*
Huang, Margaret *human rights advocate*
Huband, Frank Louis *educational association executive director, electrical engineer, lawyer*
Huberman, Richard Lee *lawyer*
Huddleson, Edwin Emmett III *lawyer*
Hudson, Kathy *microbiologist, geneticist, educator*
Hudson, Michael Craig *political science professor*
Hufbauer, Gary Clyde *economist, lawyer, educator*
Huge, Harry *lawyer*
Hughes, Elizabeth R. (Beth Hughes) *lawyer*
Hughes, Ellen Roney *historian, curator, educator*
Hughes, Kent Higgon *economist*
Hughes, Marija Matich *law librarian*
Hughes, Miriam K. *United States Ambassador to Micronesia*
Hughes, Thomas Lowe *foundation executive*
Hugya, John A. *legislative staff member*
Hulon, Willie T. *federal agency administrator*
Hume, Brit (Alexander Britton Hume) *journalist*
Hume, Cameron R. *United States Ambassador to Indonesia*
Humphrey, Connie J. *legislative staff member*
Hungate, Joseph Irvin III *government executive*
Hunnicutt, Charles Alvin *lawyer*
Hunt, Earl Stephen *federal agency administrator*
Hunt, Wayne Robert, Sr. *non-profit organization executive*
Hunter, Caroline C. *commissioner, lawyer*
Hunter, Duncan Duane *United States Representative from California, military officer*
Huntsman, Jon Meade, Jr. *United States Ambassador to China, former Governor of Utah*
Hurd, H. Scott *federal agency administrator, epidemiologist*
Husband, Shelley H. *legislative staff member*
Huso, Ravic R. *United States Ambassador to Laos*
Hussain, Syed Taseer *biomedical researcher, educator*
Hussain, Taseer S. *science educator*
Huston, John Wilson *military officer, historian*
Hutchinson, James S. (Jamie Hutchinson) *lawyer*
Hutchison, Claude B., Jr. *federal agency administrator*
Hutchison, Kay Bailey (Kathryn Ann Bailey Hutchison) *United States Senator from Texas*
Hutt, Peter Barton *lawyer*
Hutter, Paul J. *federal agency administrator, lawyer*
Huttler, Stephen B. *lawyer*
Hyder, Rebecca J. *legislative staff member*
Hyman, Lester Samuel *lawyer*
Ickes, Harold McEwen *public relations executive, former federal official*
Iezzi, Carmen K. *trade association administrator, director*
Ifft, Edward Milton *government official*
Ignagni, Karen Marie *lobbyist*
Ihnen, Jeffrey L. *lawyer*
Iklé, Fred Charles *former federal agency administrator, policy advisor, defense expert*
Indyk, Martin Sean *think-tank executive, former ambassador*
Inglis, Bob (Robert Durden) *United States Representative from South Carolina*
Ingols, Adam *federal agency administrator*
Ingram, Thomas J. *legislative staff member*
Inhofe, James Mountain *United States Senator from Oklahoma*
Inouye, Daniel Ken *United States Senator from Hawaii*
Inslee, Jay Robert *United States Representative from Washington*
Insulza, José Miguel *international organization official, former Chilean government official*
Ipatov, Sergei Ivanovich *mathematician, astronomer*
Irion, Mark S. *lobbyist, management consultant*
Irvine, Mary M. *legislative staff member*
Irving, Alfred S., Jr. *judge*
Irving, Susan Jean *government executive*
Irving, Thomas L. *lawyer*
Isaac, Alan G. *economics professor*
Isaacs, Claudine Janet Diana *internist*
Isaacson, Walter Seff *think-tank executive, writer*
Isakowitz, Mark W. *lobbyist*
Isakowitz, Steven Jeffrey *federal agency administrator, aeronautical engineer*
Isakson, Johnny (John Hardy Isakson) *United States Senator from Georgia*
Isbell, David Bradford *lawyer, educator*
Ishimaru, Stuart Jon *commissioner, lawyer*
Iskandar, Harris *attache*
Israel, Steven Jay *United States Representative from New York*
Issa, Darrell E. *United States Representative from California*
Ives, Stephen Bradshaw, Jr. *retired lawyer*
Iwry, J. Mark *lawyer*
Jablon, Ann M. *legislative staff member*
Jackson, Darryl W. *lawyer, former federal agency administrator*
Jackson, Jeanine E. *United States Ambassador to Burkina Faso*
Jackson, Jesse Louis, Jr. *United States Representative from Illinois*
Jackson, John Howard *lawyer, educator*
Jackson, Lisa Perez *federal agency administrator*
Jackson, Rhonda Ann *legislative staff member*
Jackson Lee, Sheila *United States Representative from Texas*
Jacob, Gregory F. *federal agency administrator*
Jacobs, Alonzo *federal agency contracting officer*
Jacobs, David Ernest *environmental health scientist*
Jacobs, Janice Lee *federal agency administrator, former ambassador*
Jacobs, Julian I. *federal judge*
Jacobs, Madeleine *professional society administrator, writer*
Jacobsen, Hugh Newell *architect*
Jacobson, David Edward *lawyer*
Jacobson, Michael Faraday *consumer advocate, writer*
Jacobson, Richard Lee *lawyer, educator*
Jacobson, Tracey Ann *United States Ambassador to Tajikistan*
Jafari, Beth *legislative staff member*
Jakes, J. Michael *lawyer*
James, David W. *federal agency administrator*
James, Otteson Roger *finance educator*
Jamison, Antawn Cortez *professional basketball player*
Janes, William Sargent *real estate company executive*
Jankowsky, Joel *lobbyist, lawyer*
Jarmon, Charles *social sciences educator, dean*
Jarrett, H. Marshall (Howard Marshall Jarrett) *federal agency administrator, lawyer*
Jarrett, Valerie Bowman *federal official*
Jaskowiak, Mark M. *federal agency administrator*
Jaspersen, Frederick Zarr *economist*
Jawad, Said Tayeb (Said Tayeb Djawad) *ambassador, commentator, writer*
Jecklin, Lois Underwood *art corporation executive, consultant*
Jee, Justin Soonho *government official*
Jeffery, Reuben III *federal agency administrator*
Jeffress, William Horace, Jr. *lawyer*
Jeffrey, James Franklin *United States Ambassador to Turkey*
Jenkins, Bonnie Denise *ambassador*
Jenkins, Loren B. *broadcast executive, publisher, writer*
Jenkins, Lynn M. *United States Representative from Kansas*
Jennings, Chris *lobbyist*
Jennings, Kevin Brett *federal agency administrator*
Jensen, John Bradford *economics professor*
Jenson, William G. *federal agency administrator*
Johanns, Michael Owen *United States Senator from Nebraska, former United States Secretary of Agriculture*
Johns, Christopher George *editor-in-chief, photojournalist*
Johnson, Brenda LaGrange *United States Ambassador to Jamaica*
Johnson, Broderick D. *lawyer, lobbyist*
Johnson, David M. *mortgage company executive, former insurance company executive*
Johnson, David Timothy *federal agency administrator*
Johnson, Donald Crandall *United States Ambassador to Republic of Equatorial Guinea*
Johnson, Eddie Bernice *United States Representative from Texas*
Johnson, Eric *legislative staff member*
Johnson, Eric H., Sr. *special education services professional*
Johnson, Harvey E., Jr. *federal agency administrator, retired military officer*
Johnson, Jace *legislative staff member*
Johnson, James A. (Jim Johnson) *investment company executive*
Johnson, Jeh Charles *lawyer*
Johnson, Jennifer J. *federal official*
Johnson, Joel *lobbyist*
Johnson, Katie *federal official*
Johnson, Kristina M. *federal agency administrator, former academic administrator*
Johnson, Nancy Lee *former congresswoman*
Johnson, Oliver Thomas, Jr. *lawyer*
Johnson, Philip McBride *lawyer*
Johnson, Ralph Raymond *lobbyist, retired ambassador*
Johnson, Richard Kent *publishing executive*
Johnson, Samuel (Sam Johnson) *United States Representative from Texas*
Johnson, Sheila Crump *entrepreneur*
Johnson, Timothy Peter *United States Senator from South Dakota*
Johnson, Timothy Vincent *United States Representative from Illinois, lawyer*
Johnston, Alan Cope *lawyer*
Johnston, Gerald Samuel *physician, educator*
Johnston, Kimberly D. *legislative staff member*
Jolly, Thomas R. *lawyer, lobbyist*
Jonas, John Francis *lawyer*
Jonas, Richard Andrew *medical educator*
Jones, A. Elizabeth *corporate communications specialist, former federal agency administrator*
Jones, Aidan Drexel *lawyer*
Jones, Allen, Jr. *lawyer*
Jones, Ashley *legislative staff member*
Jones, Boisfeuillet, Jr., (Bo Jones) *publishing executive*
Jones, Brian (William Brian Jones) *public affairs executive*
Jones, Brian Wesley *lawyer*
Jones, Deborah K. *United States Ambassador to Kuwait*
Jones, Diane Auer *educational association administrator, former federal agency administrator*
Jones, George Washington, Jr. *lawyer*
Jones, Hal S. *publishing executive*
Jones, James Logan, Jr. *National Security Advisor, retired military officer*
Jones, James Robert *former White House chief of staff, ambassador, congressman*
Jones, Jeffrey Allen (Jeff Jones) *men's college basketball coach*
Jones, John Melvin *US Ambassador to Guyana*
Jones, Judith Miller *director*
Jones, Kelsey A. *law educator, law administrator*
Jones, Kevin R. *federal agency administrator*
Jones, Michael D. *lawyer*
Jones, Stanley Boyd *retired researcher*
Jones, Van *federal official, lawyer*
Jones, Walter Beaman, Jr. *United States Representative from North Carolina*
Joo, Douglas D.M. *video production and aviation executive*
Jordan, Jim (James D. Jordan) *United States Representative from Ohio, former state legislator*
Jordan, Robert Elijah III *lawyer*
Jordan, V. Craig *endocrine pharmacologist, educator*
Jose, Pedro A. *physician*
Joseph, Meg (Margaret Joseph) *legislative staff member*
Josten, R. Bruce *lobbyist*
Joyce, Anne Raine *editor*
Joyner, Christopher *legislative staff member*
Joyner, Christopher Clayton *international relations educator*
Jurith, Edward Howard *federal official*
Justesen, Tracy Ralph *federal agency administrator*
Kabalkin, Barry E. *lawyer*
Kabel, Robert James *lawyer, political organization administrator*
Kadis, Averil Jordan *retired librarian*
Kafka, Gerald Andrew *lawyer*
Kagan, Elena *federal agency administrator, former dean*
Kagan, Robert William *foreign policy commentator, historian*
Kagen, Steven L. *United States Representative from Wisconsin, physician*
Kahlow, Barbara Fenvessy *statistician*
Kahn, Charles N., III, (Chip Kahn) *lobbyist*
Kahn, Michael *stage director*
Kahn, Thomas S. *lawyer*
Kahn, Walter Kurt *engineering and applied science educator*
Kaidanow, Tina S. *federal agency administrator, former ambassador*
Kaiser, Michael M. *performing arts center executive*
Kalasinsky, Victor Frank *chemist*
Kalfoglou, Andrea Lynn *medical educator, researcher*
Kalil, Tom *federal official*
Kaludis, George *management consultant, publishing executive, educator*
Kamalidiin, Saïs Telmeth *music educator*
Kamber, Victor Samuel *political consultant*
Kamras, Jason *mathematics educator*
Kamwangamalu, Nkonko Mudipanu *language educator*
Kane, Robert *energy executive*
Kang, Eugene *federal official*
Kanjorski, Paul Edmund *United States Representative from Pennsylvania, lawyer*
Kanner, Marty (Martin B. Kanner) *lobbyist*
Kanovsky, Helen Renee *lawyer*
Kanter, Martha J. *federal agency administrator*
Kantor, Mickey (Michael Kantor) *lawyer, former United States Secretary of Commerce*
Kao, Timothy Wu *civil engineering educator*
Kapikian, Catherine Andrews *artist*
Kaplan, Elaine D. *lawyer*
Kaplan, Gilbert B. *lawyer*
Kaplan, Paul A. *lawyer*
Kaplan, Stephen *federal official*
Kaplan, Steven *lawyer*
Kapp, Robert Harris *lawyer*
Kappaz, Michael H. *engineering and energy executive*
Kappel, Brett Guthrie *lawyer, lobbyist*
Kappes, Stephen R. *federal agency administrator*
Kappler, Ann M. *lawyer, finance company executive*
Karpinski, Gene Brien *political organization executive*
Karsner, Andy (Alexander Armand Karsner) *federal agency administrator*
Karvelas, Dave (David M. Karvelas) *legislative staff member*
Kashkari, Neel Tushar *federal agency administrator*
Kasold, Bruce Edward *federal judge, lawyer*
Kass, Benny Lee *lawyer*
Kass, Leon Richard *humanities educator*
Kassiday, Joel David *legislative staff member*
Katich, Steve J. III *legislative staff member*
Kato, Ryozo *ambassador*
Katyal, Neal Kumar *federal agency administrator, law educator*
Katz, Daniel E. *legislative staff member*
Katz, Ira R. *psychiatrist, mental health services administrator*
Katz, John W. *lawyer, state official*
Katz, Sherman E. *lawyer*
Katzen, Jay Kenneth *retired diplomat, state legislator, government agency administrator*
Katzen, Sally *lobbyist, lawyer, educator*
Katzman, Scott H. *lawyer*
Kaufman, Joshua Jacob *lawyer*
Kaufman, Ronald C. *lobbyist*
Kaufman, Ted (Edward E. Kaufman) *United States Senator from Delaware*
Kaufman, Thomas Frederick *lawyer, educator*
Kauzlarich, Richard Dale *retired ambassador, political scientist, consultant*
Kavanaugh, Brett Michael *federal judge*
Kazin, Michael *historian, writer*
Keaney, Thomas Addis *academic administrator, management consultant, military officer*
Kearney, Stephen Michael *federal agency administrator*
Keating, Francis Anthony, II, *Former Governor, Oklahoma, lawyer*
Keefe, Maura *legislative staff member*
Keelen, Matt *lobbyist*
Keeley, Robert Vossler *retired academic administrator, ambassador*
Keenan, Nancy *pro-choice association executive*
Keeney, John Christopher *lawyer*
Keeney, John Christopher, Jr. *lawyer*
Keiser, Andy (Andrew J. Keiser) *legislative staff member*
Keisler, Peter Douglas *lawyer, former federal agency administrator*
Keith, James *United States Ambassador to Malaysia*
Kelley, Colleen M. *labor union administrator*
Kelley, David Christopher *philosopher*
Kelliher, Joseph Timothy *commissioner*
Kelly, Brian J. *editor*

Kelly, Craig A. federal agency administrator, former ambassador
Kelly, Franklin Wood museum curator, educator
Kelly, Suedeen G. commissioner
Kelly, Thomas J., Jr. lawyer
Keltz, Ilean K. military officer
Kemp, Geoffrey Thomas Howard political scientist, consultant
Kendall, Peter Landis television news executive
Kendall, Quintin C. federal agency administrator
Kendrick, John Whitefield economist, educator, consultant
Kenlaw, Jessie professional basketball coach
Kennan, Stephanie Ann senior policy advisor
Kennard, Mary Elizabeth lawyer
Kennard, William Earl private equity firm executive, former federal agency administrator
Kennedy, Anthony McLeod United States supreme court justice
Kennedy, Brian Vincent federal agency administrator
Kennedy, Ethel Skakel philanthropist
Kennedy, Ambassador J. Christian United States Special Envoy for Holocaust Issues
Kennedy, Katherine freelance/self-employed media consultant
Kennedy, Patrick Francis federal agency administrator, former ambassador
Kennedy, Patrick Joseph, II, United States Representative from Rhode Island
Kennedy, Richard Odell physician
Kennedy, Ted (Edward Moore Kennedy) United States Senator from Massachusetts
Kennedy, Victoria Reggie lawyer, not-for-profit executive
Kenney, Kristie Anne United States Ambassador to the Philippines
Kent, Jill Elspeth entrepreneur, art appraiser, lawyer
Kent, M. Elizabeth lawyer
Kepplinger, Gary L. lawyer
Kerlikowske, R. Gil (Richard Gil Kerlikowske) federal official, former police chief
Kern, John Worth III Senior Judge, DC Court of Appeals
Kern, Paul John retired military officer
Kerr, T. Michael federal agency administrator
Kerry, Cameron Forbes lawyer
Kerry, John Forbes United States Senator from Massachusetts
Kerwin, Cornelius Martin academic administrator, educator
Kesselman, Marc L. federal agency administrator
Ketchum, James Roe curator
Ketchum, Richard Gardner financial regulatory service executive
Keyser, Timothy Kent legislative staff member
Khuzami, Robert S. federal agency administrator, lawyer
Kienitz, Roy Warren federal agency administrator
Kies, Kenneth J. lobbyist, lawyer
Kiko, Philip George lawyer
Kilberg, William Jeffrey lawyer, director
Kildee, Dale Edward United States Representative from Michigan
Kilgore, Edwin Carroll retired federal agency administrator
Kilgore, Peter George trade association executive, lawyer
Killefer, Nancy consulting firm executive, former federal agency administrator
Killgore, Andrew Ivy former ambassador
Kilpatrick, Carolyn Cheeks United States Representative from Michigan
Kilroy, Mary Jo United States Representative from Ohio, former county official
Kim, Heungsoo research scientist
Kim, Mikyong Minsun education educator
Kim, Sukhan lawyer
Kim, Sung United States Special Envoy for the Six-Party Talks
Kim, Wan J. lawyer, former federal agency administrator
Kimbell, Abigail R. federal agency administrator
Kimes, Don Mark artist, educator
Kimmitt, Robert Michael lawyer, former federal official
Kim-Renaud, Young-Key linguist, educator
Kincaid, Trevor legislative staff member
Kind, Ronald James United States Representative from Wisconsin, lawyer
King, Colbert Isaiah columnist
King, Crystal A. legislative staff member
King, Elizabeth Lee federal agency administrator
King, Larry (Lawrence Harvey Zeiger) broadcaster, radio personality
King, Michael M. chemistry professor, department chairman
King, Sophia Atlee legislative staff member
King, Steve United States Representative from Iowa
King, Warren R. Senior Judge, DC Court of Appeals
Kingham, Richard Frank lawyer
Kingston, Jack United States Representative from Georgia
Kinney, George Patrick broadcast engineering executive
Kiplinger, Knight Austin journalist, publishing executive
Kirch, Darrell Gene medical association administrator, former dean
Kirincich, John G., Jr. legislative staff member
Kirk, Artemis G. university librarian
Kirk, Donald journalist
Kirk, Mark Steven United States Representative from Illinois
Kirk, Ronald federal official, former mayor
Kirkpatrick, Ann L. United States Representative from Arizona, lawyer
Kirkpatrick, Laird Clifford dean, law educator
Kirsanow, Peter N. federal agency administrator
Kirsch, Laurence Stephen lawyer
Kiser, Chérie R. lawyer
Kissel, Peter Charles lawyer
Kissell, Larry (Lawrence Webb Kissell) United States Representative from North Carolina, former social studies educator
Kittrell, Steven Dan lawyer
Kittrie, Nicholas international lawyer, writer
Klain, Ronald Alan federal official, former investment company executive
Klarfeld, Peter James lawyer
Klawiter, Donald Casimir lawyer
Klein, Charlotte Feuerstein art consultant
Klein, Franz J. physics professor
Klein, Roger A. lawyer
Klein, Ronald Jay United States Representative from Florida, lawyer
Klemm, Hans G. United States Ambassador to Timor-Leste
Klessig, Margaret J. legislative staff member
Klimchuk, James Andrew astrophysicist, researcher
Kline, John Paul United States Representative from Minnesota
Kline, Thomas R. lawyer
Klobuchar, Amy Jean United States Senator from Minnesota, lawyer
Klose, Kevin broadcast executive
Klotz, Frank G. career military officer
Klug, Christopher Aaron physicist
Knapp, Richard Maitland association executive
Knapp, Steven academic administrator
Kneedler, Edwin S. federal agency administrator
Knight, Athelia Wilhelmenia journalist
Knight, Bruce Irving federal agency administrator
Knight, Linda K. financial company executive
Knowles, Jeffrey D. lawyer
Knox, Wendy legislative staff member
Knutson, Karen Y. legislative staff member
Koffel, William E. science association director, fire protection engineer
Koh, Harold Hongju federal agency administrator, former dean
Koh, Howard Kyongju federal agency administrator, former academic administrator
Kohl, Herbert H. United States Senator from Wisconsin, professional sports team owner
Kohl, Jennifer D. legislative staff member
Kohn, Donald L. federal official, economist
Kohn, Stephen Martin lawyer
Kohr, Howard A. lobbyist
Kohut, Andrew research center executive
Kojm, Christopher A. political science professor
Kolasky, William Joseph, Jr. lawyer
Kolb, Charles Chester foundation administrator
Kolb, Charles Edward Mealey think-tank executive, lawyer, former federal offical
Kolb, Ingrid (Ingrid Ann Christner Kolb) federal agency administrator
Kollar-Kotelly, Colleen federal judge
Kolodner, Robert M. federal agency administrator, health information technology executive
Komarov, Andrei M. biophysicist, educator, research scientist
Kondracke, Morton Matt journalist, commentator
Koonin, Steven Elliot federal agency administrator, physicist, educator
Korb, Donald L. lawyer
Korn, David pathologist, educator
Kornicker, Louis Sampson museum curator
Korologos, Tom Chris former ambassador
Koromilas, Alec J. legislative staff member
Korth, Fritz-Alan lawyer
Koshalek, Richard museum director, former academic administrator
Kosiak, Steven Michael federal official
Kosinski, Dorothy M. museum director
Koski, James E. legislative staff member
Kosmas, Suzanne M. United States Representative from Florida, former real estate company executive
Kostelnik, Michael Charles commissioner, retired military officer
Kotz, H. David (Harold David Kotz) federal agency administrator
Kouters, Angela M. legislative staff member
Kovach, Ildiko Maria chemistry professor, researcher
Kovacic, William Evan commissioner, law educator
Kovar, Peter A. federal agency administrator
Koziol, John Craig (Craig Koziol) federal agency administrator, career military officer
Krahe, Julia Louise legislative staff member
Kramer, Andrew Michael lawyer
Kramer, David J. federal agency administrator
Kramer, Noël Anketell Associate Judge, DC Court of Appeals
Kramer, William David lawyer
Krasnow, Erwin Gilbert lawyer
Kratovil, Frank Michael, Jr. United States Representative from Maryland, lawyer
Krauthammer, Charles columnist, editor
Kravis, Marie-Josée Drouin economist
Krebs, Rockne artist
Kreig, Andrew Thomas trade association executive
Krenik, Edward D. lobbyist
Krieger, William C. legislative staff member
Kriesberg, Simeon M. lawyer
Kringen, John A. federal agency administrator
Kris, David S. federal agency administrator
Kristol, William (Bill Kristol) political analyst, editor
Kroener, William Frederick III lawyer
Kroupa, Diane Lynn federal judge
Krueger, Alan B. federal agency administrator, economics professor
Krueger, Anne economist
Krulfeld, Ruth Marilyn anthropologist, educator
Krumholtz, Jack lobbyist
Krump, Gary Joseph marketing executive, lawyer, judge
Krupnick, Dan legislative staff member
Kulski, Julian Eugeniusz architect, writer
Kumar, Manmohan Singh international monetary fund manager, researcher
Kunder, James R. federal agency administrator
Kundra, Vivek federal official
Kurtzman, Howard Steven psychologist
Kushner, Gary Jay lawyer
Kutler, Alison L. lawyer
Kuttner, Robert Louis editor, writer, columnist
Kyhos, Thomas Flynn lawyer
Kyriakopoulos, Irene economist, educator
Kyriakopoulos, Nicholas engineering educator
Labbok, Miriam Harriet physician, educator
Lackey, Gerald Francis management consultant
Lackey, Miles M. legislative staff member
Lagon, Mark P. former federal agency administrator
LaHaye, Beverly religious organization administrator
LaHood, Ray H. Secretary of Transportation, former United States Representative from Illinois
Lake, Anthony political science professor, former national security advisor
Lake, William Truman lawyer
Lamb, Brian Patrick broadcast executive
Lambert, Charles (Chuck) federal agency administrator
Lambert, Jeremiah Daniel lawyer, educator
Lambert, Steven Charles lawyer
Lamberth, Royce C. federal judge
Lambro, Donald Joseph columnist
Lamken, Jeffrey A. lawyer
Lamm, Carolyn Beth lawyer
Lamont, Thomas R. civilian military employee, lawyer
Lance, Alan George federal judge, former state attorney general
Lance, Leonard United States Representative from New Jersey, former state legislator
Landefeld, Steven federal agency administrator
Landrieu, Mary Lorretta United States Senator from Louisiana
Landry, Brock R. lawyer
Lane, Bruce Stuart lawyer
Lane, Charlotte R. Commissioner, United States International Trade Commission, lawyer
Lane, Jeff A. legislative staff member
Lane, John Dennis lawyer
Lane, William C. lobbyist
Langevin, James R. (Jim Langevin) United States Representative from Rhode Island, former state official
Langfeld, Stanley Chaitt government executive
Lanier, Cathy L. police chief
Lapidus, Lawrence Searle lawyer
Laporte, Gerald Joseph Sylvestre lawyer
Lappin, Harley G. federal agency administrator
Lardner, George, Jr. journalist, writer
Lardy, Nicholas Richard economist, educator
Laredo, James surgeon, educator
Largent, Steven Michael telecommunications industry executive, former congressman, retired professional football player
Laro, David federal judge
Larroca, Raymond G. lawyer
Larsen, Richard Ray (Rick Larsen) United States Representative from Washington
Larson, Alan Philip former federal agency administrator
Larson, Charles W., Jr. United States Ambassador to Latvia
Larson, John Barry United States Representative from Connecticut, insurance company executive
Larson, Judy L. museum director, curator
Laskawy, Philip Alan mortgage company executive, retired accounting and management consulting firm executive
Lastowka, James Anthony former federal agency administrator, lawyer
Latham, Patricia Horan lawyer
Latham, Patricia S. physician
Latham, Peter Samuel lawyer
Latham, Tom United States Representative from Iowa
Latham, Weldon Hurd lawyer
Latimer, Katharine Ruth lawyer
Latta, Robert Edward (Bob Latta) United States Representative from Ohio
Laudato, George A. federal official
Lauerman, William medical educator
Laughlin, Felix B. lawyer
Laughlin, James Harold, Jr. lawyer
Launius, Roger D. museum administrator
Lavelle, Joseph P. lawyer
Lavine, Henry Wolfe lawyer
Lavine, Thelma Zeno philosophy educator
Lavoy, Peter Rene federal official
Law, Steven James lawyer, former federal agency administrator
Lawler, William E. III lawyer
Lawrence, Frederick M. dean, law educator
Lawson, Donna Yvette special education educator
Lawson, Jennifer broadcast executive
Lawson, Peter H. lobbyist, automotive executive
Laxminarayan, Ramanan economist
Lazarus, Arthur, Jr. lawyer
Lazarus, Kenneth Anthony lawyer
Leahy, Patrick Joseph United States Senator from Vermont
Leamer, Laurence Allen writer
Leavandosky, Stacey E. legislative staff member
Le Baron, Joseph Evan United States Ambassador to Qatar
Leckey, Dolores R. religious organization administrator, writer
Ledley, Robert Steven biophysicist
Lee, Barbara Jean United States Representative from California
Lee, Christopher J. United States Representative from New York, former manufacturing executive
Lee, Debra Louise cable television company executive
Lee, Gwendolyn B. educational association administrator
Lee, Nicole C. human rights advocate
Lee, Ronald Derek lawyer
Leeds, Charles Alan publishing executive
Leff, Deborah foundation administrator
Leffall, LaSalle Doheny, Jr. surgeon, educator
Lefkowitz, Jay United States Special Envoy for Human Rights in North Korea
Legro, Patrice museum director
Lehman, Donald Richard physicist, educator, academic administrator
Lehmberg, Robert Henry retired research physicist
Lehrman, Margaret McBride broadcast executive, television producer
Leibach, Dale William government relations and public affairs executive
Leibold, Arthur William, Jr. lawyer
Leibowitz, Jon commissioner, department chairman
Lelyveld, Gail Annick actress
LeMieux, George S. United States Senator from Florida, lawyer
Lemnios, Zachary J. federal agency administrator, electrical engineer
Lendsey, Jacquelyn L. foundation administrator
Lenhardt, Thomas A. military officer
LeoGrande, William Mark political science professor, writer, dean
Leonard, Joe, Jr. federal agency administrator
Leonard, Robert J. lobbyist
Leone, Katherine C. legislative staff member
Leopold, Patrick R. legislative staff member
Leshner, Alan Irvin science administrator
Lessin, Lawrence Stephen hematologist, oncologist, educator
Lettow, Charles Frederick federal judge
Leubsdorf, Carl Philipp publishing executive
Levett, Todd A. government agency administrator
Levey, Stuart A. federal agency administrator
Levin, Carl Milton United States Senator from Michigan
Levin, Edward M. lawyer
Levin, Michael legislative staff member
Levin, Sander Martin United States Representative from Michigan, lawyer
Levine, Felice J. educational association administrator
Levine, Henry David lawyer
Levinson, Daniel Ronald federal agency administrator, lawyer
Levinson, Lawrence Edward lawyer
Levinstein, Mark Steven lawyer, educator
Levy, Gregg H. lawyer
Levy, Mark Irving lawyer
Lew, Ginger Ehn federal agency administrator, lawyer
Lew, Jack (Jacob Joseph Lew) federal agency administrator
Lewin, John Calvert medical association administrator
Lewis, Anne McCutcheon architect
Lewis, Charles Jeremy (Jerry Lewis) United States Representative from California
Lewis, Charles Joseph journalist
Lewis, Eleanor Roberts lawyer
Lewis, Guy A. prosecutor
Lewis, John Robert United States Representative from Georgia
Lewis, Lorraine former federal agency administrator
Lewis, Mark K. lawyer
Lewis, Muffy (Lucille Miraim Lewis) legislative staff member
Lewis, Prudence Fox Christian science practitioner
Lewis, Robert David Gilmore retired editor
Lewis, Roger Kutnow architect, educator, author
Lewis, William Henry, Jr. lawyer
Lewis, Wilma Antoinette federal agency administrator
Lewris, Basil J. lawyer
Li, Li research scientist
Libin, Alexander Viktorovich psychologist, researcher, writer
Lichtblau, Eric journalist
Lichtenstein, Elissa Charlene legal association executive
Lidinsky, Richard A., Jr. commissioner
Lieber, Robert James political science professor
Lieberman, Joe (Joseph Isadore Lieberman) United States Senator from Connecticut
Liebeskind, Richard lawyer
Liebman, Jeffrey B. federal official, economist
Liebman, Wilma B. federal agency administrator
Lierman, Terry L. legislative staff member
Lightfoot, Karen legislative staff member
Limbaugh, Mark A. lobbyist, former federal agency administrator
Lincoln, Blanche Lambert United States Senator from Arkansas
Linde, Jason P. legislative staff member
Lindemann, Adam communications executive
Linder, John E. United States Representative from Georgia, dentist
Lindsey, Seth Mark lawyer
Lipinski, Daniel United States Representative from Illinois
Lipnic, Victoria Ann federal agency administrator
Lippert, Mark William federal official
Lippincott, Joan K. library director
Lipscomb, Sara D. federal agency administrator
Liptak, Adam lawyer, reporter
Lira, José A. legislative staff member
Litt, Robert S. lawyer
Littig, Lawrence William psychologist, educator
Little, Corey legislative staff member
Littler, Diane Scullion marine biologist
Liu, Michael Minoru Fawn lobbyist, former federal agency administrator
Livingood, Wilson S. protective services official
Livingston, Bob (Robert Linlithgow Livingston Jr.) lobbyist, former United States Representative from Louisiana
Livingston, Donald Ray lawyer
Livingston, Douglas Mark lawyer
Livingston, Robert Gerald historian, journalist
Lizardo, Thomas Charles legislative staff member
Llorens, Hugo United States Ambassador to Honduras
Lo, Shyh-Ching pathologist
Locke, Gary Faye Secretary of Commerce, former Governor of Washington
Locker, Raymond Duncan editor
Lockhart, Joe (Joseph P. Lockhart) public relations firm executive, former White House press secretary
Locklear, Arlinda Faye lawyer
Loebsack, Dave United States Representative from Iowa, former political science professor
Loepere, Carol Colborn lawyer
Lofgren, Zoe United States Representative from California

Lofthus, Lee J. *federal agency administrator*
Loftus, Carroll Michael (Michael Loftus) *lawyer*
Logan, Lara *news correspondent*
Logan, Paul Ellis *language educator, consultant*
London, Herbert Ira *think-tank executive, humanities educator*
Longnecker, David Eugene *anesthesiologist, educator*
Loots, James Mason *lawyer*
Lopatin, Alan G. *lawyer*
Lorell, Beverly H. *medical products executive, consultant*
Lott, Trent *lobbyist, former United States Senator from Mississippi*
Lourie, Alan David *federal judge*
Love, Reggie *federal official*
Lovelace, Telly *legislative staff member*
Loveng, Jeffrey R. (Jeff Loveng) *legislative staff member*
Low, Daniel L. *lawyer*
Lowe, Mary Frances *federal official*
Lowell, Abbe David *lawyer*
Lowenstein, James Gordon *former diplomat, international consultant*
Lowery, Clay *lobbyist, former federal agency administrator*
Lowery, William David (Bill Lowery) *lobbyist, former congressman*
Lowry, Charles Bryan *librarian, dean*
Lu, Christopher P. *federal official*
Lubar, Jeffrey Stuart *journalist, trade association executive*
Lubchenco, Jane *federal agency administrator, marine ecologist*
Lubic, Benita Joan Alk *travel company executive*
Lucas, James Walter *federal official*
Ludwig, Eugene Allan *financial consulting firm executive*
Luetkemeyer, Blaine *United States Representative from Missouri*
Lugar, Dick (Richard Green Lugar) *United States Senator from Indiana*
Lujan, Ben Ray, Jr. *United States Representative from New Mexico, former state official*
Lujan, Manuel, Jr. *think-tank executive, former United States Secretary of the Interior, retired congressman*
Lummis, Cynthia Marie *United States Representative from Wyoming, former state official, lawyer*
Luna, Luis A. *federal agency administrator*
Lundsager, Margrethe (Meg Lundsager) *federal official*
Lungren, Daniel Edward *United States Representative from California, former state attorney general*
Lungren-McCollum, Kelly *legislative staff member*
Lupo, Raphael V. *lawyer*
Luque, Nancy *lawyer*
Lurensky, Marcia Adele *lawyer*
Lurie, Nicole L. *federal agency administrator, former health science association administrator*
Luskin, Robert David *lawyer*
Lustig, M. Bruce *rabbi*
Lute, Douglas E. *federal official, career military officer*
Lute, Jane Holl *federal agency administrator, retired military officer*
Luttwak, Edward Nicolae *academic administrator, policy and business consultant, senior advisor*
Luxton, Jane Charlotte *lawyer*
Lybecker, Martin Earl *lawyer*
Lydon, Kathleen *legislative staff member*
Lydon, Timothy *legislative staff member*
Lyles, David S. *legislative staff member*
Lynch, Christopher W. *legislative staff member*
Lynch, Michael Lee *legislative staff member*
Lynch, Stephen F. *United States Representative from Massachusetts*
Lynn, D. Joanne *physician, researcher*
Lyon, Andrew Bennet *economist*
Lyons, Dennis Gerald *lawyer*
Lyons, Mona *lawyer*
Mabus, Raymond Edwin, Jr. *civilian military employee, former Governor of Mississippi*
MacBeth, Angus *lawyer*
Macedo, Pedro Buarque de *physics professor, researcher*
Machen, Ronald C. *lawyer*
Macias, Linda C. *legislative staff member*
Mack, Connie, IV, *United States Representative from Florida*
Mack, David L. *think-tank executive, former federal agency administrator*
Mack, Julia Cooper *retired judge*
Macleod, John Amend *lawyer*
Macomber, John D. *investment company executive*
Macomber, Marshall C. *legislative staff member*
Maddaloni, Martin J. *retired labor union administrator*
Madden, Thomas James *lawyer, educator*
Madras, Bertha Kalifon *federal official, neuroscientist, researcher*
Maffei, Daniel B. *United States Representative from New York, former investment company executive*
Magary, Adam J. *legislative staff member*
Magee, Charles Thomas *international consultant, retired diplomat*
Magielnicki, Robert L. *lawyer*
Magner, Timothy J. *federal agency administrator, educator*
Magnuson, Rachel *legislative staff member*
Magrath, C. Peter *academic administrator, educational association executive*
Mahler, Jason M. *legislative staff member*
Mahoney, Maureen E. *lawyer*
Mak, I. Tong *biologist, educator*
Makhlouf, Hala R. *pathologist, educator*
Malcolm, Ellen Reighley *political advocacy association administrator*
Malek, Frederic Vincent *finance company executive*
Malet, David Samuel *social sciences educator*
Malley, Claudia *publishing executive*
Mallon, Thomas *writer*
Maloney, Carolyn Bosher *United States Representative from New York*
Maloney, Drew *lobbyist*
Mamantov, Andrew *chemist*
Mamaux, Lale M. *legislative staff member*
Manatt, Charles Taylor *lawyer*
Mancuso, Mario *lawyer, former federal agency administrator*
Mandel, Harold George *pharmacologist, educator*
Manderson, Easton L. *orthopedist, surgeon*
Maness, Theodore E. (Ted Maness) *legislative staff member*
Manfreda, John J. *federal agency administrator*
Mangano, Philip F. *federal agency administrator*
Manger, William, Jr. *federal agency administrator*
Mangogna, Richard Frederick *federal agency administrator*
Mani, Inderjeet *computer scientist, educator*
Maniscalco-Theberge, Mary Elizabeth *surgeon, medical educator*
Mann, Oscar *retired physician, internist, educator*
Mann, Thomas Edward *political scientist*
Manning, Michael J. *lawyer*
Manning, Timothy W. *federal agency administrator*
Mansfield, Edward Patrick, Jr. *advertising executive*
Manthei, John Richard *lawyer*
Mantyla, Karen *distance learning consultant*
Manzanares, J. Robert *Permanent United States Representative to the Organization of American States*
Manzullo, Donald A. *United States Representative from Illinois, lawyer*
Maples, Michael D. *federal agency administrator, career military officer*
Maran, Stephen Paul *astronomer*
Marantis, Demetrios J. *federal official*
Marchant, Kenny *United States Representative from Texas*
Marchio, Sam *legislative staff member*
Marcuss, Rosemary Daly *economist*
Marcuss, Stanley Joseph *lawyer*
Marder, Michael V. *philosopher, educator*
Margeton, Stephen George *law librarian*
Margo, Adair *art association administrator, art gallery owner*
Margolis, Doris May Rosenberg *editor, writer*
Margolis, Lawrence Stanley *federal judge*
Marincola, Elizabeth Mark *nonprofit executive*
Markey, Betsy (Elizabeth Helen Markey) *United States Representative from Colorado*
Markey, Edward John *United States Representative from Massachusetts*
Marks, Herbert Edward *lawyer*
Marks, Ronald Anthony *communications industry executive*
Marmolejos, Poli A. *federal agency administrator*
Marquardt, R. Niels *United States Ambassador to the Comoros and Madagascar*
Marques, Christine Schon *political organization administrator*
Marquez, Mercedes M. *federal agency administrator*
Marr, Phebe Ann *retired historian, educator*
Marrett, Michael McFarlene *chaplain*
Marriott, John W. III *hotel executive*
Marriott, John Willard, Jr. *lodging and senior living executive*
Marshall, Alison Buell *lawyer*
Marshall, Capricia Penavic *federal official*
Marshall, Jim (James Creel Marshall) *United States Representative from Georgia*
Marshall, John Lindsay *medical educator*
Marshall, Joshua Micah *publisher, blog writer, columnist, editor, political journalist*
Marshall, Margaret Blair *thoracic surgeon*
Marshall, William III *think-tank executive*
Marston, Christopher M. *federal agency administrator*
Marston, Michelle Presson *legislative staff member*
Martella, Roger Romulus, Jr. *lawyer, former federal agency administrator*
Martin, Carmel M. *federal agency administrator*
Martin, David Alan *lawyer, law educator*
Martin, David Briton Hadden, Jr. *lawyer*
Martin, Guy *lawyer*
Martin, Jay (Robert Joseph Martin) *legislative staff member*
Martin, Thomas Stephen *lawyer*
Martin, William R. (Billy Martin) *lawyer*
Martinez, Herminia S. *economist, banker*
Martinez, Kathleen M. (Kathy Martinez) *federal agency administrator*
Martinez-Fonts, Alfonso *federal agency administrator*
Maruyama, Warren H. *federal official, lawyer*
Marvel, Kevin Boyd *professional society administrator, astronomer*
Marvel, L. Paige *federal judge*
Marventano, David *engineering and construction management company executive*
Mason, David Marion *commissioner*
Massa, Eric J.J. *United States Representative from New York, retired military officer, former congressional aide*
Massimino, Julia A. *legislative staff member, lawyer*
Masters, Edward Eugene *association executive, former foreign service officer*
Mastromonaco, Alyssa *federal official*
Matheson, James David (Jim) *United States Representative from Utah*
Mathews, Jessica Tuchman *think-tank executive, former federal official, columnist*
Mathieu, Gail Dennise *United States Ambassador to Namibia*
Matsui, Doris Okada *United States Representative from California*
Mattoo, Aaditya *economist*
Mattoon, Daniel J. *lobbyist*
Maxwell, Mary Beth *labor advocate*
May, Stephen *writer, federal official, historian*
May, Timothy James *lawyer*
Mayer, Haldane Robert *federal judge*
Mayers, Daniel Kriegsman *lawyer*
Mayo, George Washington, Jr. *lawyer*
Mayo, John W. *finance educator*
Mayopoulos, Timothy J. *lawyer, mortgage company executive*
Mayorkas, Alejandro N. *federal agency administrator, lawyer*
Mays, Janice Ann *lawyer*
Mazer, Roslyn A. *federal official, lawyer*
Mazo, Mark Elliott *lawyer*
Mc Afee, William *government official*
McAvoy, Susan A. *legislative staff member*
McBee, Steve *lobbyist*
McBee, Susanna B. *freelance journalist*
McBride, Jonathan Evans *governance consultant, director*
McBride, William R. *legislative staff member*
McCabe, Brian *political strategist*
McCain, John (John Sidney McCain III) *United States Senator from Arizona*
McCann, Clifton Everett *lawyer*
McCann, John Michael *performing arts company professional*
McCann, Tim *legislative staff member*
McCannell, Christopher *legislative staff member*
McCarron, Douglas J. *labor union administrator*
McCarter, Katherine Sauter *association executive*
McCarthy, Carolyn *United States Representative from New York*
McCarthy, Dennis M. *federal agency administrator, retired military officer*
McCarthy, Kevin *United States Representative from California, former state legislator*
McCarthy, Regina (Gina McCarthy) *federal agency administrator*
McCarty, Mary Colleen *legislative staff member*
McCaskill, Claire C. *United States Senator from Missouri*
McCaul, Michael T. *United States Representative from Texas*
McClellan, Mark B. *former federal agency administrator*
McClellan, Scott *consulting company executive, former White House press secretary*
McClintock, Peter L. *federal agency administrator*
McClintock, Tom (Thomas Miller McClintock II) *United States Representative from California, former state senator*
McClung, Gwendolyn *soil microbiologist*
McClure, Frederick Donald *lawyer*
McClure, William Pendleton *lawyer*
McCollum, Betty *United States Representative from Minnesota*
McConnaughey, Flip *legislative staff member*
McConnell, Mitch (Addison Mitchell McConnell) *United States Senator from Kentucky, lawyer*
McConnell, Nicholas Stillwell *lawyer*
McCormick, David Harold *federal agency administrator*
McCormick, Walter Bernard, Jr. *trade association administrator*
McCormick, William Paul *United States Ambassador to New Zealand and Samoa*
McCotter, Thaddeus George *United States Representative from Michigan*
McCoy, Jerry Jack *lawyer*
McCreary, Robert J. *legislative staff member*
McCrery, Jim (James Otis McCrery) *lobbyist, former United States Representative from Louisiana*
McCue, Susan M. *communications executive*
McCullough, Mary T. (Terri McCullough) *legislative staff member*
McCurdy, David Keith *trade association administrator, former congressman*
McCutchen, Tammy Dee *lawyer, former federal agency administrator*
McDaniels, William E. *lawyer*
McDavid, Janet Louise *lawyer*
McDermott, James A. *United States Representative from Washington, psychiatrist*
McDiarmid, Robert Campbell *lawyer*
McDonald, Ed *legislative staff member*
McDonnell, Erin M. *lawyer*
McDonough, Denis *federal official*
McDowell, Robert Malcolm *commissioner*
McEldowney, Nancy Eileen *United States Ambassador to Bulgaria*
McElroy, Tucker Sprague *mathematician, consultant, statistician*
McElveen, Junius Carlisle, Jr. *lawyer*
McElveen-Hunter, Bonnie *international relief organization executive*
McEntee, Gerald W. *labor union administrator*
McFarland, Stephen George *United States Ambassador to Guatemala*
McFaul, Daniel F. *legislative staff member*
McGahn, Donald F., II, *commissioner, lawyer*
McGann, C. Steven *United States Ambassador to Fiji, Nauru, Kiribati and Tonga and Tuvalu*
McGee, James D. *United States Ambassador to Zimbabwe*
McGee, James M. *federal agency administrator*
McGinley, Matthew S. *legislative staff member*
McGinnis, James Michael *physician*
McGinnis, Patricia Gwaltney *non-profit organization executive*
McGovern, James P. *United States Representative from Massachusetts*
McGovern, Michael B. *lawyer*
McGrath, Kathryn Bradley *lawyer*
McGrath, Kevin Michael *military analyst, civilian military employee, researcher*
McGrath, Raymond J. *lobbyist, former congressman*
McGuire, Jack (John F. McGuire) *international relief organization executive*
McGuire, Patricia A. *lawyer, academic administrator*
McGuirl, Marlene Dana Callis *law librarian, educator*
McGurn, William Joseph *speechwriter, editor*
McHale, Judith A. *federal agency administrator, former broadcast executive*
McHale, Paul F., Jr. *lawyer, former United States Representative from Pennsylvania*
McHenry, Patrick Timothy *United States Representative from North Carolina*
McIntyre, Mike (Douglas Carmichael McIntyre II) *United States Representative from North Carolina*
Mc Kay, Emily Gantz *civil rights and nonprofit professional*
McKay, Kenneth K. *political organization administrator*
McKee, Margaret Jean *federal agency administrator*
McKeever, Joseph Francis III *lawyer*
McKenney, Kerry B. *legislative staff member*
McKeon, Howard Phillip (Buck McKeon) *United States Representative from California*
McKinley, P. Michael (Peter Michael McKinley) *United States Ambassador to Peru*
McKinney, David Duane *museum director, architectural historian*
McLarty, Mack (Thomas F. McLarty III) *leasing company executive, former White House chief of staff*
McLaughlin, John J. *broadcast executive, television producer, journalist, political commentator*
McLucas, William Robert *lawyer, former federal agency administrator*
McMahon, Francine *publishing executive*
McMahon, Michael E. *United States Representative from New York, former city councilman*
McMahon Hawkins, Patricia *United States Ambassador to Togo*
McMorris-Rodgers, Cathy *United States Representative from Washington*
McMullen, Ronald *United States Ambassador to Eritrea*
McMurray, Claudia Anne *federal agency administrator, lawyer*
McNamara, Michael T. *lawyer, lobbyist*
McNerney, Jerry (Gerald M. McNerney) *United States Representative from California, engineer*
McNulty, Paul J. *lawyer, former federal agency administrator*
Mc Pherson, Harry Cummings, Jr. *lawyer*
McPherson, James E. *legal association administrator, former judge, retired military officer*
McPherson, Peter (M. Peter McPherson) *educational association administrator, former publishing executive*
McQueary, Charles E. (Chuck McQueary) *federal agency administrator*
McQueen, Lynn *public health service officer, information scientist, administrator*
McQuillan, Laurence Joseph *communications consultant, educator*
McReynolds, Mary Armilda *lawyer*
McSlarrow, Kyle E. *lobbyist, former federal agency administrator*
McSweeny, Dorothy Pierce *art association administrator*
Meachum, Pete (Charles Peterson Meachum) *legislative staff member*
Mead, Christopher *lawyer*
Mead, Kenneth Minor *lawyer, former federal agency administrator*
Means, Thomas Cornell *lawyer*
Mecher, Greg *legislative staff member*
Mederos, Carolina Luisa *public policy consultant*
Meek, Kendrick B. *United States Representative from Florida*
Meese, Ed (Edwin Meese III) *law and public policy educator, former United States Attorney General*
Meggers, Betty Jane *anthropologist, researcher*
Mehlman, Bruce P. *lobbyist, lawyer, formal federal agency administrator*
Mehri, Cyrus B. *lawyer*
Mehta, Prakash H. *lawyer*
Meijer, Paul Herman Ernst *physicist, educator*
Meisburg, Ronald Edward *federal agency administrator, lawyer*
Melamed, Arthur Douglas *lawyer*
Melancon, Charles *United States Representative from Louisiana*
Meléndez de Santa Ana, Thelma *federal agency administrator*
Melendy, David Russell *newscaster, reporter*
Mellman, Mark Steve *public opinion researcher*
Mellor, John Williams *economist, consultant*
Meloy, Sybil Piskur *retired lawyer*
Melson, Kenneth E. *federal agency administrator, lawyer*
Melton, Carol A. *communications executive*
Meltzer, Daniel J. *lawyer, law educator*
Memmott, Scott A. *lawyer*
Menaker, Frank H., Jr. *lawyer*
Menarchik, Douglas Edward *federal agency administrator*
Mencher, Bruce Stephan *judge*
Mendelsohn, Martin *lawyer*
Mendez, Victor M. *federal agency administrator*
Mendoza, Julie C. *lawyer*
Menendez, Robert (Bob Menendez) *United States Senator from New Jersey*
Mercado, Moses C. *lobbyist*
Mermoud, J. Frank *United States Special Representative, Commercial and Business Affairs*
Meron, Daniel *lawyer*
Merow, James F. *federal judge*
Merrell, Jesse Howard *writer*
Merrifield, Dudley Bruce *finance educator, federal official*
Merrigan, John A. *lobbyist, lawyer*
Merrigan, Kathleen Ann *federal agency administrator*
Merrill, Susan L. *financial regulatory service executive, lawyer*
Merski, Richard P. *insurance company executive*
Messina, Jim (James A. Messina) *federal official*
Metwalli, April Beeman *legislative staff member*
Metz, Craig Huseman *lawyer*
Metz, Thomas Frederic *career military officer*
Meyer, Dennis Irwin *lawyer*
Meyer, Paul *information technology executive*
Meyerhoff, Andrea Nikki *former federal agency administrator, biodefense executive, medical educator*
Meyers, Wayne Marvin *microbiologist, physician*
Meyerson, Adam *foundation administrator*
Mica, John L. *United States Representative from Florida*
Michaels, Patrick Joseph *climatologist*
Michaelson, Martin *lawyer*
Michalak, Michael Walter *United States Ambassador to Vietnam*

Michaud, Michael Herman *United States Representative from Maine*
Michel, Bob (Robert Henry Michel) *lobbyist, former United States Representative from Illinois*
Michel, Paul Redmond *federal judge*
Michnich, Marie E. *health policy analyst, consultant, educator*
Middleton, Victoria J. *legislative staff member*
Migliore, Marcus Charles *lawyer*
Mikulski, Barbara Ann *United States Senator from Maryland*
Mikva, Laurie I. *lawyer*
Milam, William Bryant *senior policy scholar, former ambassador*
Miles, David Michael *lawyer*
Miles, Veryl Victoria *dean, law educator*
Miller, Aaron David *political scientist, writer*
Miller, Andrew Pickens *lawyer*
Miller, Anthony Wilder (Tony Miller) *federal agency administrator*
Miller, Brad (Ralph Bradley Miller) *United States Representative from North Carolina*
Miller, Brian David *federal agency administrator*
Miller, Candice S. *United States Representative from Michigan*
Miller, Chris J. *legislative staff member*
Miller, Christine Odell Cook *federal judge*
Miller, Debra Lynn *political scientist*
Miller, Ewing Harry *retired architect*
Miller, Gary G. *United States Representative from California*
Miller, George III *United States Representative from California*
Miller, H. Todd *lawyer*
Miller, James Forrest *lawyer*
Miller, James N., Jr. *federal agency administrator*
Miller, James W. (Jim Miller) *federal agency administrator*
Miller, Jeanne-Marie Anderson (Mrs. Nathan J. Miller) *language educator, academic administrator*
Miller, Jeff *United States Representative from Florida*
Miller, John *federal agency administrator, former news correspondent*
Miller, John T., Jr. *lawyer, educator*
Miller, Laura Ariane *lawyer*
Miller, Margery *psychologist, educator, speech pathology/audiology and mental health services professional, university administrator, academic administrator*
Miller, Marshall Lee *lawyer*
Miller, Scott Eugene *legislative staff member*
Miller, William Green *former ambassador*
Millian, John C. *lawyer*
Milligan, Robert S. *business association administrator*
Mills, Karen Gordon *federal agency administrator, venture capitalist*
Milman, Natalie Bordelon *education educator*
Milovanovic, Gillian Arlette *United States Ambassador to Republic of Mali*
Min, James B. *legislative staff member*
Mineta, Norman Yoshio *consulting firm executive, former United States Secretary of Commerce and Transportation*
Minnick, Walter Clifford *United States Representative from Idaho, former building materials company executive*
Minow, Nell *financial analyst, editor*
Minton, Mark C. *United States Ambassador to Mongolia*
Mirvahabi, Farin *lawyer*
Mishel, Lawrence *think-tank executive, economist, researcher*
Mishkin, Barbara Friedman *lawyer*
Mishra, Lopa *gastroenterologist, educator*
Mishra, Prachi *economist*
Missar, Charles Donald *retired librarian*
Mitchell, Andrea *journalist, television news anchor*
Mitchell, George John *diplomat, former United States Senator from Maine*
Mitchell, Harry E. *United States Representative from Arizona, former state legislator*
Mitchell, Peter J. *legislative staff member*
Mitchell, Stephen Ray *dean, rheumatologist*
Mitchell, Todd (James Todd Mitchell) *legislative staff member*
Mitchelson, Mary Sue *federal agency administrator, lawyer*
Mizroch, John F. *lawyer, former federal agency administrator*
Mobley, Dawn Kelly *legislative staff member*
Moe, Kari J. *legislative staff member*
Moe, Richard Palmer *lawyer*
Moeller, Philip D. *commissioner*
Mohrman, Kathryn J. *academic administrator*
Moler, Elizabeth Anne *utilities executive*
Molinari, Susan *lobbyist, former congresswoman*
Moller, Patricia Newton *United States Ambassador to Burundi*
Mollohan, Alan Bowlby *United States Representative from West Virginia*
Mombouli, Serge *ambassador*
Mondello, Lisette McSoud *legislative staff member, former federal agency administrator*
Monroe, Loren *lobbyist*
Montanez-Johner, Nancy *federal agency administrator*
Montano, Gloria I. *legislative staff member*
Montgomery, Edward Bruce *federal official, former dean, economics professor*
Montgomery, John A. *physicist*
Mooney, Marilyn *lawyer*
Moore, Barbara C. *fraternal organization administrator*
Moore, Bob Stahly *communications executive*
Moore, Dale *lobbyist, former federal agency administrator*
Moore, Dennis *United States Representative from Kansas*
Moore, Donald Emerson III *zoological park administrator, curator, wildlife biologist*
Moore, Gregory T. *civil rights association executive*
Moore, Gwendolynne S. (Gwen Moore) *United States Representative from Wisconsin*
Moore, Jacquelyn Cornelia *retired labor union administrator, editor*
Moore, Kimberly Ann *federal judge*
Moore, Powell Allen *former federal agency administrator*
Moore, Robert Madison *food products executive, lawyer*
Moore, Roderick W. *United State Ambassador to Montenegro*
Moore, Steven E. *legislative staff member*
Moorman, William A. *federal judge, retired career military officer*
Morales, Hector Elias, Jr. *ambassador, former bank executive*
Moran, Ellen *federal agency administrator*
Moran, Jerry *United States Representative from Kansas*
Moran, Jim (James Patrick Moran Jr.) *United States Representative from Virginia, stock broker*
Morehouse, David Frank *geologist*
Morell, Michael J. *federal agency administrator*
Moreno, Jaime *professional soccer player*
Moreno, Luis Alberto *bank executive*
Moriarty, James Francis *United States Ambassador to Bangladesh*
Morin, Jamie Michael *civilian military employee*
Morris, Brad *legislative staff member*
Morris, Lee C. *federal agency administrator*
Morris, Martin W. *legislative staff member*
Morris, Melanie R. *legislative staff member*
Morrison, Brendan *professional hockey player*
Morrison, Richard Thane *federal judge*
Morrison, Thomas Allen *retired military officer, lawyer, dean*
Morrissey, Patricia A. *federal agency administrator*
Morse, M. Howard *lawyer*
Morton, John Templeton *federal agency administrator*
Moses, Alfred Henry *lawyer, writer, diplomat*
Moskowitz, Jedd I. *legislative staff member*
Mostoff, Allan Samuel *lawyer, consultant*
Mosychuk, Susan *legislative staff member*
Motevalli, Vahid *engineering educator*
Moy, Edmund C. *federal agency administrator*
Mozena, Dan W. *United States ambassador to Angola*
Mroczka, Victor Stanislaw *lawyer*
Muckenfuss, Cantwell Faulkner III *lawyer*
Mueller, Robert Swan III *FBI director*
Mueller, Sharon Lee (Sherry Mueller) *educational organization executive*
Mujica, Barbara Louise *language educator, writer*
Mullen, Mike (Michael Glenn Mullen) *Chairman of the Joint Chiefs of Staff*
Muller, Steven *international studies educator, academic administrator*
Mulloy, Patrick Aloysius *lawyer*
Mulvaney, Sean R. *federal agency administrator*
Muñoz, Cecilia *federal official, civil rights advocate*
Muñoz, Leo R. *legislative staff member*
Munson, Alden V., Jr. *federal official*
Munson, Lester *legislative staff member*
Munter, Cameron *United States Ambassador to Serbia*
Murat, William M. *legislative staff member*
Murguia, Janet *non-profit organization administrator*
Murkowski, Lisa Ann *United States Senator from Alaska*
Muro, Steve L. *federal agency administrator*
Murphy, Betty Southard *lawyer*
Murphy, Edward Joseph *government agency administrator*
Murphy, Frances M. *federal agency administrator*
Murphy, Gerard Norris *trade association executive*
Murphy, Joseph Albert, Jr. *lawyer*
Murphy, Ryan *legislative staff member*
Murphy, Scott (Matthew Scott Murphy) *United States Representative from New York*
Murphy, Terence Roche *lawyer, international trade executive*
Murphy, Timothy F. *United States Representative from Pennsylvania*
Murphy, Timothy P. *federal agency administrator*
Murray, Alan Stewart *publishing executive*
Murray, Christopher Charles III *architect*
Murray, Liz *legislative staff member*
Murray, Patty (Patricia Lynn Murray) *United States Senator from Washington*
Murray, Robert Fulton, Jr. *physician*
Murry, Harold David, Jr. *lawyer*
Murtha, John Patrick, Jr. *United States Representative from Pennsylvania*
Mushnick, Ashley *legislative staff member*
Mussa, Michael L. *economist, educator*
Mwenda, Kenneth Kaoma *legal association administrator, consultant*
Myers, James R. *lawyer*
Myers, Mindy *legislative staff member*
Myles, Marianne Matuzic *United States ambassador to Cape Verde*
Myrick, Gary *legislative staff member*
Myrick, Sue Wilkins *United States Representative from North Carolina, former mayor*
Nabors, Robert Lee, II, *federal official*
Nacht, Michael Leonard *federal agency administrator, political science educator*
Nader, Ralph *advocate, lawyer, writer*
Nadler, Jerrold Lewis *United States Representative from New York, lawyer*
Nagle, Thomas W. *legislative staff member*
Naím, Moisés *editor-in-chief*
Nakayama, Granta Yoneo *lawyer, former federal agency administrator*
Nannes, Michael Edward *lawyer*
Napolitano, Grace Flores *United States Representative from California*
Napolitano, Janet Ann *Secretary of Homeland Security, former Governor of Arizona*
Nardi Riddle, Clarine *chief staff, lawyer*
Narisetti, Raju *editor*
Nash, James Lee *poet, security official*
Nash, John Davidson, Jr. *economist*
Nason, David George *financial consulting firm executive, former federal agency administrator*
Nason, Nicole R. *National Highway Traffic Safety Administrator, United States Department of Transportation*
Nass, Sharyl Jeanne *medical educator*
Natarajan, Githa *elementary school educator*
Natividad, Irene *women's rights advocate*
Natonski, Dave *legislative staff member*
Natsios, Andrew Stephen *diplomat, former federal agency administrator*
Nazareth, Annette LaPorte *lawyer, former commissioner*
Neal, Richard Edmund *United States Representative from Massachusetts, former mayor*
Nebeker, Frank Quill *Senior Judge, DC Court of Appeals*
Neimark, Sheridan *lawyer*
Nelson, (Earl) Ben(jamin) *United States Senator from Nebraska, former governor, lawyer*
Nelson, Bill (Clarence William Nelson) *United States Senator from Florida*
Nelson, Charles J. *academic administrator, diplomat, consultant*
Nelson, Douglas Thomas *lawyer*
Nelson, Karen *legislative staff member*
Nelson, Terry A. *public relations executive*
Nemeroff, Michael Alan *lawyer*
Nesbitt, Wanda L. *United States Ambassador to Cote d'Ivoire*
Ness, Andrew David *lawyer*
Nesti, Leon J. *orthopedist, educator*
Nethercutt, George Rector, Jr. *lawyer, consultant, former congressman*
Nethery, John Jay *government official, military officer*
Neugebauer, Dale *legislative staff member*
Neugebauer, Randy (Robert R. Neugebauer) *United States Representative from Texas*
Neureiter, Norman P. *science association director*
Neville, J. Gabriel *legislative staff member*
Neville, Leonora Alice *history professor*
Newberry, Edward J. *lawyer*
Newkirk, Thomas Charles *lawyer*
Newman, Pauline *federal judge*
Newman, Sherryl Hobbs *former district secretary*
Nicely, Olza M. (Tony) *insurance company executive*
Nicholson, Jim (Robert James Nicholson) *lawyer, former United States Secretary of Veterans Affairs, former ambassador*
Nicholson, Kristin E. *legislative staff member*
Nicholson, Leslie A. *federal agency administrator*
Nicholson, Marvin, Jr. *federal official*
Nickles, Peter *state attorney general*
Nickson, Julie L. *legislative staff member*
Nicolson, Dan Henry *retired plant taxonomist*
Niemeier, Charles D. *non-profit corporation administrator, accountant*
Nightingale, Elena Ottolenghi *pediatric geneticist, academic administrator, educator*
Nigro, Louis J., Jr. *United States Ambassador to Republic of Chad*
Nilsson, Kent R. *federal agency administrator*
Nims, Arthur Lee III *federal judge*
Nirenberg, Darryl D. *lawyer*
Niskanen, William Arthur, Jr. *economist, retired think-tank executive*
Nitze, William Albert *government official, lawyer, not-for-profit developer, energy executive*
Noble, John W. *legislative staff member*
Noe, Adrianne *museum administrator*
Nolan, John Edward *lawyer*
Nolan, Robert B. *United States Ambassador to Lesotho*
Nolan, Stephen James *United States ambassador to Republic of Botswana*
Nordhaus, Robert Riggs *lawyer*
Nordlinger, Gerson *investor*
Norland, Richard Boyce *United States Ambassador to Uzbekistan*
Norquist, David L. *federal agency administrator*
Norquist, Grover Glenn *economist*
Norris, Jackie *federal official, history educator*
Norton, Eleanor Holmes *Delegate to United States House Representative from District of Columbia, lawyer, educator*
Norton, Susan E.S. *museum director*
Norwalk, Leslie V. *federal agency administrator*
Norwood, Deborah Anne *law librarian*
Novak, Michael (John) *religion educator, author, editor*
Novascone, Todd *legislative staff member*
Novick, Robert T. *lawyer*
Novitch, Mark *physician, retired pharmaceutical executive*
Nsouli, Talal Mounir *physician, allergist, immunologist*
Nugent, Rachel A. *economist*
Nuland, Anthony C. J. *lawyer*
Nunes, Devin *United States Representative from California*
Nunn, Sam (Samuel Augustus Nunn Jr.) *think-tank executive, former United States Senator from Georgia, lawyer*
Nussle, Jim (James Allen Nussle) *former United States Representative from Iowa*
Nwagbaraocha, Joel Onukwugha *academic administrator, educator*
Nye, Glenn Carlyle III *United States Representative from Virginia*
Oates, Jane *federal agency administrator*
Obama, Barack Hussein, Jr. *44th President of the United States*
Obama, Michelle LaVaughn Robinson *First Lady of the United States, former hospital administrator*
Oberholtzer, Lydia S. *economist, consultant*
Obering, Trey (Henry A. Obering II) *federal agency administrator, career military officer*
Oberly, Kathryn Anne *judge*
Oberstar, James Louis *United States Representative from Minnesota*
Obey, David Ross *United States Representative from Wisconsin*
O'Black, Sean *legislative staff member*
Oblinger, Diana G. *educational association administrator*
O'Brien, Danny *legislative staff member*
O'Brien, Lawrence Francis, III, (Larry O'Brien) *lobbyist, lawyer*
Obsitnik, Vincent *United States Ambassador to Slovakia*
O'Connell, David M. *academic administrator, priest*
O'Connell, Dawn C. Myers *legislative staff member*
O'Connor, Gail *legislative staff member*
O'Connor, Karen *political science professor, researcher, writer*
O'Connor, Tom *corporate executive, management consultant*
O'Dell, Douglas V., Jr. *federal agency administrator, retired military officer*
Odle, Robert Charles, Jr. *lawyer*
O'Donnell, Amy L. *legislative staff member*
O'Donnell, Patrick Emmett *lawyer*
O'Donnell, Tom *legislative staff member*
Oehme, Wolfgang Walter *landscape architect*
Oertel, Yolanda Castillo *pathologist, educator*
Ogden, David William *federal agency administrator*
O'Grady, Richard T. *science administrator*
Oh, Jung Eun Jen *transportation executive, researcher*
Ohanian, Bernard Jay *writer, editor*
O'Hara, Sabine U. *academic administrator, dean, economist, educator*
Ohl, Joan Eschenbach *federal agency administrator*
Ohring, George *meteorologist*
Okun, Deanna Tanner *federal official*
Oldham, Cheryl A. *federal agency administrator*
Olding, Michael *plastic and reconstructive surgeon*
Olender, Jack Harvey *lawyer*
Olesko, Kathryn Mary *historian*
Oliver, LeAnn Michelle *government official*
Olmstead, Cecil Jay *lawyer*
Olson, Pamela Faith *lawyer, former federal agency administrator*
Olson, Pete *United States Representative from Texas, former congressional aide*
Olson, Richard Gustave *United States Ambassador to the United Arab Emirates*
Olson, Theodore Bevry (Ted Olson) *lawyer, former federal agency administrator*
Olver, John Walter *United States Representative from Massachusetts*
O'Malley, Ann S. *research scientist*
Omole, Duncan Wambogo *information scientist, corporate communications specialist*
O'Neil, Thomas Francis III *lawyer*
O'Neill, Brian Dennis *lawyer*
O'Neill, Maura Louise *legislative staff member, environmentalist*
O'Neill, Michelle *federal agency administrator*
O'Neill, Molly Ann *federal agency administrator*
O'Neill, Terry Anne *feminist organization executive, lawyer*
O'Neill, William Patrick *lawyer*
Onek, Joseph Nathan *lawyer*
Oosterhuis, Paul William *lawyer*
Opfer, George Joseph *federal agency administrator*
Oppenheimer, Franz Martin *lawyer*
Oran, Elaine Surick *physicist*
Ord, Keith J. *finance educator*
Ornstein, Norman Jay *political scientist, columnist*
O'Rourke, P.J. (Patrick Jake O'Rourke) *writer, political satirist, journalist*
Orszag, Peter Richard *federal official, economist*
Ortiz, Manuel *lobbyist*
Ortiz, Solomon Porfirio, Sr. *United States Representative from Texas*
Ortner, Donald J. *biological anthropologist, educator*
Osicka, Teresa D. *health economist, consultant*
Osnos, David Marvin *lawyer, director*
Ososanya, Esther Titilayo *engineering educator*
Ostendorff, William Charles *federal agency administrator, career military officer*
Ostrov, Jerome *lawyer*
O'Sullivan, Stephanie L. *federal agency administrator*
O'Sullivan, Terence M. *labor union administrator*
Otero, Maria *federal agency administrator, former international development executive*
Otis, Bud (Harold F. Otis) *legislative staff member*
Ottaway, David Blackburne *journalist*
Ourisman, Mary M. *United States Ambassador to Barbados and the Eastern Caribbean*
Oursler, Tara Linnehan *legislative staff member*
Outlaw, Wanda Cecelia *priest*
Ouyang, Xiaomei O. *corporate financial executive*
Ovechkin, Alexander *professional hockey player*
Overby, Charles L. *foundation administrator*
Overdahl, James A. *economist*
Overman, Dean Lee *lawyer, investor, writer*
Owen, Henry *former ambassador, consultant*
Owen, Michael *federal agency administrator*
Owen, Roberts Bishop *lawyer, arbitrator*
Owens, Stephen Alan (Steve Owens) *federal agency administrator, lawyer*
Oxford, Vayl *federal agency administrator*
Oxley, Michael Garver *lawyer, former United States Representative from Ohio*
Ozden, Caglar *economist*
Pacelle, Wayne *animal rights organization administrator*
Pachter, Marc *retired museum director*
Padilla, Christopher Alan *lobbyist, former federal agency administrator*
Pagano, Edward *legislative staff member*
Page, John Martin, Jr. *economist*
Page, Robert Wesley *engineering and construction company executive, federal official*
Paige, Kathleen K. *naval officer*
Painter, William Hall *law educator*
Paliwal, Dinesh C. *electronics executive*
Pallone, Frank, Jr. *United States Representative from New Jersey, lawyer*
Palmer, Christopher E. *lawyer*
Palmeter, N. David *lawyer*
Pals, Tony Mitchel *public relations executive, director*
Palumbo, Benjamin Lewis *public relations executive, consultant*
Pan, Florence Y. *judge*
Pan, Qing *statistician, educator*

Rockefeller, Edwin Shaffer lawyer
Rockefeller, Jay (John Davison Rockefeller IV) United States Senator from West Virginia
Rocque, Vincent Joseph lawyer
Rode, Meredith Eagon artist, educator
Rodgers, Ronald L. federal agency administrator, lawyer
Rodley, Carol Ann United States Ambassador to Cambodia
Rodriguez, Ciro Davis United States Representative from Texas
Rodriguez, Jorge Jacinto psychiatrist
Rodriguez, Rosemary E. former municipal official, federal agency administrator
Roe, Jamie A. legislative staff member
Roe, Phil (David Phillip Roe) United States Representative from Tennessee, former vice-mayor
Roemer, Timothy John United States Ambassador to India, former United States Representative from Indiana
Rogan, Elizabeth A. professional society administrator
Rogan, Michael P. lawyer
Rogers, Desiree Glapion federal official, former insurance company executive
Rogers, Edward Maurice, Jr. lobbyist, lawyer
Rogers, Harold Dallas (Hal) United States Representative from Kentucky
Rogers, Hayden legislative staff member
Rogers, Judith Ann Wilson federal judge
Rogers, Mike (Michael J. Rogers) United States Representative from Michigan
Rogers, Mike D. United States Representative from Alabama
Rogers, Thomasina Venese commissioner
Rogoff, Peter M. federal agency administrator
Rohner, Ralph John lawyer, educator, dean
Rohrabacher, Dana T. United States Representative from California
Rojer, Olga Elaine German studies educator, translator
Rolando, Fredric V. labor union administrator
Romeo, Peter John lawyer
Romer, Christina Duckworth federal official, economist
Romer, Roy R. educational association administrator, former Governor of Colorado
Rooney, Daniel M. United States Ambassador to Ireland, professional sports team executive
Rooney, Tom United States Representative from Florida, lawyer
Rope, William Frederick educator
Roper, Wayne R. legislative staff member
Rosch, John Thomas (Tom) commissioner, lawyer
Rose, Charles P. lawyer
Rose, George Andrew Internet information systems specialist
Rose, James McKinley, Jr. lawyer, government official
Rose, Jonathan Chapman lawyer
Rosebush, James Scott financial services company executive, former government official
Rosen, Gerald Robert editor
Rosen, Jeffrey Adam lawyer
Rosen, Jeffrey Matthew law educator, journalist
Rosenau, James Nathan political scientist, educator, writer
Rosenbaum, Sidney J. (Jerr Rosenbaum) legislative staff member
Rosenberg, Chuck (Charles P. Rosenberg) lawyer, former prosecutor
Rosenberg, Ruth Helen Borsuk lawyer
Rosenberg, Simon think-tank executive
Rosenblatt, Jason Philip literature and language professor
Rosenblatt, Peter Ronald lawyer, former ambassador
Rosenbloom, David Harry political science and law educator
Rosenbloom, H(arry) David lawyer
Rosenfeld, Arthur F. federal official, lawyer
Rosenkrantz, Steven Jay lawyer
Rosenthal, Douglas Eurico lawyer
Rosenthal, Steven Siegmund lawyer
Ros-Lehtinen, Ileana Carmen United States Representative from Florida
Rosman, Michael E. lawyer
Ross, Annie Lee minister, counselor
Ross, Douglas lawyer
Ross, Malcolm minerals consultant
Ross, Mike United States Representative from Arkansas
Ross, Stanford G. lawyer, government official
Ross, Terence P. lawyer
Rossides, Eugene Telemachus lawyer, writer
Rotberg, Eugene Harvey investment banker, lawyer
Rothenberg, Stuart political scientist, columnist
Rother, John association executive, lawyer
Rotherham, Andrew J. educational association administrator
Rothkopf, Arthur J. business association executive
Rothkopf, David Jochanan consulting firm executive, former federal agency administrator
Rothman, Steven R. United States Representative from New Jersey
Rothrock, John G. legislative staff member
Rothstein, Barbara Jacobs federal judge
Rothstein, Paul Frederick lawyer, educator
Rotunda, Donald Theodore public relations consultant
Roubideaux, Yvette federal agency administrator
Roughead, Gary career military officer
Rouse, Cecilia Elena federal official, economics and public affairs professor
Rouse, Peter M. federal official
Rouson, Vivian Reissland alcohol/drug abuse services professional, consultant, journalist
Rouvelas, Emanuel Larry lawyer
Rovelstad, Mathilde V(erner) retired library and information scientist, educator
Rowden, Marcus Aubrey lawyer, retired government agency administrator
Rowe, Leslie V. United States Ambassador to Papua New Guinea, Solomon Islands & Vanuatu
Rowe, Richard Holmes lawyer
Roybal-Allard, Lucille United States Representative from California
Royce, Ed (Edward Randall Royce) United States Representative from California
Roycroft, Howard Francis lawyer
Rubenstein, David M. investment company executive
Rubenstein, Lisa V. medical association administrator, educator
Ruckert, Kyle legislative staff member
Ruckman, Roger Norris pediatric cardiologist
Ruddy, Frank lawyer, retired ambassador
Rudolph, Kimberly legislative staff member
Ruehle, Charles Joseph pathologist, military officer
Ruemmler, Kathryn H. lawyer, former prosecutor
Rufe, Roger T., Jr. federal agency administrator
Ruiz, Vanessa Associate Judge, DC Court of Appeals
Rule, Charles Frederick (Rick) lawyer
Runge, Jeffrey William former federal agency administrator
Ruoff, Janis Kaye human services administrator
Ruppersberger, Charles Albert, III, (Dutch) United States Representative from Maryland
Rush, Bobby L. United States Representative from Illinois
Ruskin, Robert Sterling educational association administrator
Russell, Cathy (Catherine M. Russell) federal official
Russell, Clara B. information technology manager
Russell, Robert A. legislative staff member
Russell, William Joseph educational association administrator
Russin, Jonathan lawyer, consultant
Russo, Martin A. lawyer, lobbyist, former congressman
Rutherford, Boyd Kevin political organization administrator, former federal agency administrator
Rutkin, Amy B. legislative staff member
Rutstein, David W. lawyer, food products executive
Ruttenberg, Charles Byron lawyer
Ruttinger, George David lawyer
Ruwe, Robert Paul federal judge
Ryan, Anthony William federal agency administrator
Ryan, David Alan systems analyst
Ryan, Edward A. lawyer, hotel executive
Ryan, James (Jimmy) lobbyist, diversified financial services company executive
Ryan, Margaret A. federal judge
Ryan, Paul United States Representative from Wisconsin
Ryan, Robert Kevin legislative staff member
Ryerson, Paul Sommer lawyer
Ryn, Claes Gösta political science professor
Sabagh, Denyse lawyer
Sablan, Gregorio Camacho (Gregorio Kilili Camacho Sablan) Delegate from the Northern Mariana Islands
Sacher, Steven Jay lawyer
Sadosky, Cora Susana mathematician, educator
Sáenz, Albert William theoretical physicist, researcher, consultant
Safir, Peter Oliver lawyer
Safire, William journalist, foundation administrator
Sagely, Matt (Christopher Matthew Sagely) legislative staff member
Saidi, Reza engineering educator
Sajery, Algene T. legislative staff member
Sakai, James K. legislative staff member
Salamon, Linda Bradley retired English literature scholar
Salazar, John Tony United States Representative from Colorado
Salazar, Ken (Kenneth Lee Salazar) Secretary of the Interior
Salem, George Richard lawyer
Salisbury, Dallas L. researcher, director
Saltzburg, Stephen Allan law educator, consultant
Salyer, Stephen Lee educational program administrator
Sambi, Pietro archbishop
Sampas, Dorothy Myers retired government official
Samper, Cristián museum director
Sampson, Sara Ann law librarian, educator
Sams, Ronald F. career military officer
Samuelson, Drey legislative staff member
Samuelson, Kenneth Lee lawyer
Samuelson, Robert Jacob journalist
Sánchez, Linda T. United States Representative from California
Sánchez, Loretta United States Representative from California
Sanchez-Way, Ruth Dolores public health administrator
Sandalow, David Blake federal agency administrator
Sanders, Bernard (Bernie Sanders) United States Senator from Vermont, former congressman
Sanders, Robin Renee United States Ambassador to Nigeria
Sanderson, Janet Ann United States Ambassador to Haiti
Sandlin, Stephanie Herseth United States Representative from South Dakota, lawyer
Sandman, James Joseph lawyer
Sandy, John A. legislative staff member
Sanger, David E. news correspondent
Sant, Roger W. retired energy executive
Santorum, Rick (Richard John Santorum) lawyer, former United States Senator from Pennsylvania
Santos, Leonard Ernest lawyer
Sarbanes, John Peter Spyros United States Representative from Maryland, lawyer
Sarros, P. Peter diplomat, consultant
Sartori, Michael A. lawyer
Sarukhan, Arturo ambassador
Satcher, Daraka E. (Dok) legislative staff member
Satter, David Arnold author, journalist
Saunders, Flip (Philip D. Saunders) professional basketball coach
Saunders, Harold Henry foundation administrator
Scalia, Antonin Gregory United States supreme court justice
Scalia, Eugene lawyer
Scalise, Steve (Stephen Joseph Scalise) United States Representative from Louisiana, former state legislator
Scanlon, Terrence Maurice think-tank executive
Schafer, Jacqueline Ellen federal agency administrator
Schakowsky, Janice United States Representative from Illinois
Schall, Alvin Anthony federal judge
Schapiro, Mary L. federal agency administrator
Schauer, Mark Hamilton United States Representative from Michigan
Schaumber, Peter Carey federal agency administrator
Schechter, Geraldine Poppa hematologist
Scheck, Barry C. legal association administrator, educator
Scheffman, David Theodore economist, management educator, consultant
Scheinberg, Phyllis F. federal agency administrator
Scheunemann, Randy (Randall J. Scheunemann) lobbyist
Schiappa, David S. legislative staff member
Schieffer, Bob newscaster
Schieffer, J(ohn) Thomas (Tom) United States Ambassador to Japan, former professional baseball team executive
Schiff, Adam Bennett United States Representative from California, lawyer
Schiffer, Lois Jane lawyer
Schiliro, Philip M. federal official
Schiller, Vivian L. broadcast executive, former Internet company executive
Schlesinger, B. Frank architect, educator
Schley, Wayne Arthur political scientist, consultant
Schlick, Austin C. lawyer
Schloegel, Scott P. legislative staff member
Schloss, Howard Monroe financial regulatory service executive
Schlosser, Lisa chief information officer
Schmidt, Jean United States Representative from Ohio
Schmidt, Susan journalist
Schmidt, William Arthur, Jr. lawyer
Schneider, Carol Geary educational association administrator
Schneider, Cynthia Perrin former ambassador, political science professor
Schneider, Mark political science professor
Schneider, Mark Lewis foreign policy executive, retired government agency administrator
Schneider, Matthew Roger lawyer
Schock, Aaron Jon United States Representative from Illinois, former state legislator
Schoelen, Mary Jeanette federal judge
Schoettle, Enid C.B. federal agency administrator
Schofield, Regina Brown foundation administrator, former federal agency administrator
Schor, Laurence lawyer
Schorr, Lisbeth Bamberger policy analyst
Schrader, Kurt United States Representative from Oregon, former state senator
Schram, Martin Jay journalist
Schreiber, Sara legislative staff member
Schreiber Hughes, Lisa Bobbie United States Ambassador to Suriname
Schubert, Brian legislative staff member
Schulman, Melissa A. lobbyist, former legislative staff member
Schumer, Chuck (Charles Ellis Schumer) United States Senator from New York
Schwartz, Allyson Y. United States Representative from Pennsylvania
Schwartz, Daniel C. lawyer
Schwartz, Eric Paul federal agency administrator
Schwartz, Michael legislative staff member
Schwartz, Norton A. career military officer
Schwartz, Victor Elliot lobbyist, lawyer, educator
Schwartzman, Andrew Jay lawyer
Schwebel, Stephen Myron arbitrator, mediator, legal advisor
Schwelb, Frank Ernest Senior Judge, DC Court of Appeals
Schwinger, David lawyer
Sclafani, Susan K. educational consultant, former federal agency administrator
Scoblic, J. Peter magazine editor
Scolese, Christopher J. federal agency administrator
Scott, Charneta Claudetta psychologist, educator
Scott, David Albert United States Representative from Georgia
Scott, James L. dean, emergency physician, educator
Scott, Makeda legislative staff member
Scott, Robert Cortez United States Representative from Virginia, lawyer
Scott, Stephanie D. city official
Scott, Thomas Jefferson, Jr. lawyer, electrical engineer
Scovel, Calvin L. III federal agency administrator
Scowcroft, Brent former national security advisor, retired military officer
Scrivner, Ellen M. psychologist
Scully, Thomas A. lawyer, former federal agency administrator
Seats, Peggy Chisolm public affairs executive
Sebelius, Kathleen Gilligan Secretary of Health and Human Services, former Governor of Kansas
Seche, Stephen A. United States Ambassador to Yemen
Seeba, John M. federal agency administrator, accountant
Sega, A. Christopher lawyer
Sega, Ronald Michael civilian military employee, former dean
Segal, Scott H. lawyer, lobbyist
Segal, Theodore D. lawyer
Segraves, Jamie Nicole language educator
Seidman, Ellen Shapiro lawyer, former federal agency administrator
Seifert, Jeffrey W. political scientist, researcher
Seims, La Rue K. public health service officer
Selib, Jonathan legislative staff member
Selig, William Paul advocate
Selingo, Jeffrey J. editor, reporter
Sellin, Theodore diplomat, consultant
Selva, Paul Joseph career military officer
Semas, Philip Wayne editor
Semo, Joseph lawyer
Sensenbrenner, Frank James, Jr. United States Representative from Wisconsin
Sentelle, David Bryan federal judge
Sepúlveda, John U. federal agency administrator
Sequeira, Leon R. federal agency administrator
Serrano, José Enrique United States Representative from New York
Sessions, Jeff (Jefferson Beauregard Sessions III) United States Senator from Alabama, former state attorney general
Sessions, Pete (Peter Anderson Sessions) United States Representative from Texas
Sessions, William Steele lawyer, former FBI director
Sessoms, Allen Lee academic administrator, physicist, educator, retired diplomat
Seum, Jack F. legislative staff member
Sevart, Daniel Joseph lawyer
Severino, Roberto language educator, academic administration executive
Sexton, Edmund M. federal agency administrator
Shackelford, Lottie Holt political organization administrator
Shadegg, John Barden United States Representative from Arizona
Shadow, Ruby L. Wesley nursing educator, administrator, researcher
Shaffer, Benjamin Scott surgeon
Shafroth, Frank H., Jr. legislative staff member
Shah, Rajiv Jana federal agency administrator
Shales, Thomas William television and film critic, writer, journalist
Shambaugh, David Leigh political scientist, educator, writer
Shanahan, Sheila Ann pediatrician, educator
Shanks, Hershel editor, writer
Shanmugam, Victoria Kate medical educator
Shannon, Donald Hawkins retired editor
Shannon, Thomas A., Jr. federal agency administrator
Shapiro, Andrew Joseph federal agency administrator
Shapiro, Howard M. lawyer, former prosecutor
Shapiro, Jeffrey A. legislative staff member
Shapiro, Robert Jacob economic advisory firm executive
Shapiro, Walter Elliot columnist
Shappert, Gretchen C.F. lawyer, former prosecutor
Sharkey, Andrew G. III science association director
Sharkey, Robert Emmett lawyer
Sharp, James E. lawyer
Sharp, Philip Riley think-tank executive, former congressman
Shaw, Michael mortgage company executive
Shaw, Rhod lobbyist
Shaw, Russell Burnham writer, journalist
Shaw, William Frederick statistician
Shay, Albert W. lawyer
Shea-Porter, Carol United States Representative from New Hampshire, social worker
Shear, Natalie Pickus conference and event management executive
Shedd, David R. federal official
Sheehan, Neil reporter, writer
Shelby, Richard Craig United States Senator from Alabama
Shelton, Jim (James H. Shelton) federal agency administrator, former educational association administrator
Shelton, William L. career military officer
Shen, Patrick P. lawyer
Shenon, Philip journalist
Sher, Susan S. lawyer, federal official
Sherali, Zeadally engineering educator
Sherer, Samuel Ayers lawyer, urban planner, consultant
Sherman, Bradley James United States Representative from California
Sherman, Jonathan Henry lawyer
Sherman, Wendy Ruth consulting firm executive, former federal agency administrator
Sherzer, Harvey Gerald lawyer
Shields, Christopher Andrew website director
Shields, Christopher D. legislative staff member
Shimkus, John Mondy United States Representative from Illinois
Shinseki, Eric Ken Secretary of Veterans Affairs, retired military officer
Shooshan, Alyssa legislative staff member
Shrier, Adam Louis investment company executive, consultant
Shrinsky, Jason Lee lawyer
Shukla, Deepshikha research scientist
Shulman, Douglas H. federal agency administrator
Shulman, Stephen Neal lawyer
Shust, Diane Marie educational association administrator, lawyer, educator
Siddique, Akhtar finance company executive
Siegel, Frederic Richard geology educator
Siegel, Lloyd Harvey architect, real estate developer, consultant
Siegel, Robert Charles broadcast journalist
Siegel, Robert Steven internist, oncologist, educator
Siggins, Robert G. legislative staff member
Sikorski, Gerry lobbyist, lawyer, former congressman
Silber, David Elliot clinical psychologist, educator
Silva, Peter S. federal agency administrator, civil engineer
Silver, Harry R. lawyer
Silvers, Damon Abraham lawyer
Simko, Jan English, foreign language and literature educator
Simmons, Ronnie (Elias R. Simmons) legislative staff member
Simon, Gary Leonard internist, educator
Simons, Carol Lenore magazine editor
Simons, Paul E. United States Ambassador to Chile
Simpson, Melissa M. federal agency administrator
Simpson, Michael K. United States Representative from Idaho
Sims, Joe lawyer
Sims, Ronald Cordell federal agency administrator

Sinel, Norman Mark *lawyer*
Singer, Daniel Morris *lawyer*
Singer, Maxine Frank *retired biochemist, science association director*
Singleton, Harry Michael *lawyer*
Sippel, Serra *advocate*
Sires, Albio *United States Representative from New Jersey, former state legislator*
Sison, Michele Jeanne *United States Ambassador to Lebanon*
Sivasubramanian, Kolinjavadi Nagarajan *neonatologist, educator*
Sjoblom, Thomas V. *lawyer*
Skancke, Nancy J. *lawyer*
Skelly, Thomas P. *federal agency administrator*
Skelton, Ike (Isaac Newton Skelton IV) *United States Representative from Missouri*
Skeris, Robert Alexander *theology and church music educator*
Skinner, Richard L. *federal agency administrator*
Skinner, Robert Earle, Jr. *civil engineer, engineering executive*
Skol, Michael *counter-money laundering consultant*
Skolnik, Merrill I. *electrical engineer*
Slater, Rodney Earl *lobbyist, lawyer, former United States Secretary of Transportation*
Slater, Valerie A. *lawyer*
Slaughter, Anne-Marie *federal agency administrator, former dean*
Slaughter, Louise McIntosh *United States Representative from New York*
Sloan, Clifford M. *lawyer, former publishing executive*
Sloan, Melanie Togman *lawyer, former prosecutor*
Slocombe, Walter Becker *lawyer, former federal official*
Sly, Ridge Michael *pediatrician, allergist, immunologist, educator*
Smalley, Robert Manning *retired diplomat*
Smith, Abbie Oliver *college administrator, educator*
Smith, Adam *United States Representative from Washington*
Smith, Adrian M. *United States Representative from Nebraska, real estate agent*
Smith, Amy D. *legislative staff member*
Smith, Bradley W. *legislative staff member*
Smith, Christopher Henry *United States Representative from New Jersey*
Smith, Cori Elizabeth *legislative staff member*
Smith, Daniel B. *federal official*
Smith, Daniel Clifford *lawyer*
Smith, Dean *communications advisor, arbitrator*
Smith, DeMaurice Fitzgerald *sports association executive, lawyer*
Smith, Edward M. *labor union administrator*
Smith, Esther Thomas *communications executive*
Smith, George Vinal *librarian*
Smith, Gordon Harold *lobbyist, former United States Senator from Oregon*
Smith, Jeffrey Hartman *lawyer*
Smith, Jessie P. Dowling *retired social services administrator*
Smith, John B. *publishing executive*
Smith, Kingston Earl *lawyer*
Smith, Lamar Seeligson *United States Representative from Texas*
Smith, Lee Elton *surgery educator, retired military officer*
Smith, Loren Allan *federal judge*
Smith, Patricia Grace *federal official*
Smith, R. Jeffrey *national investigative correspondent*
Smith, Robin L. *television personality, psychologist, writer*
Smith, Roy Philip *judge*
Smith, Russell Louis *lawyer*
Smith, Stephen Grant *journalist*
Smith, T. DeWitt, Jr. *religious organization administrator*
Smith, Tefft Weldon *lawyer*
Smith, William *legislative staff member*
Smith, William A. *legislative staff member*
Smith, William S., Jr. *education association administrator*
Smolen, Robert L. (Bob Smolen) *federal agency administrator, retired military officer*
Smyth, Paul Burton *lawyer*
Snowbarger, Vince *former congressman*
Snowe, Olympia J. *United States Senator from Maine*
Snyder, Charles Robert *United States Senior Representative on Sudan*
Snyder, Jed C. *foreign affairs specialist*
Snyder, Vic *United States Representative from Arkansas, physician*
Sobel, Clifford M. *United States Ambassador to Brazil*
Solarz, Stephen Joshua *former congressman*
Solis, Hilda Lucia *Secretary of Labor, former United States Representative from California*
Sollers, Joseph Sedwick III *lawyer*
Solomon, Elinor Harris *economics professor*
Solomon, Eric *federal agency administrator*
Solomon, Richard Harvey *think-tank executive*
Solomon, Sean Carl *geophysicist, lab administrator*
Solomons, Mark Elliott *lawyer, art dealer, entrepreneur*
Sommers, Jill Elaine *commissioner*
Sommers, Mark *lawyer*
Sonnenfeldt, Helmut *former government official, educator, consultant, writer*
Sorokowski, Andrew Dennis *lawyer, historian*
Sotomayor, Sonia *United States supreme court justice*
Sottile, James *lawyer*
Souder, Mark Edward *United States Representative from Indiana*
Souders, Patrick J. *legislative staff member*
Sours, David A. *legislative staff member*
Sozan, Michael L. *legislative staff member*
Space, Zack (Zachary T. Space) *United States Representative from Ohio*
Spaeder, Roger Campbell *lawyer*
Spagnoletti, Robert James *lawyer, former attorney general*
Spagnolo, Samuel Vincent *internist, pulmonary specialist, educator*
Spayd, Elizabeth Terry (Liz Spayd) *editor*
Spear, Scott Lawrence *plastic surgeon*
Spear, Susan *legislative staff member*
Speckhard, Daniel V. *United States Ambassador to Greece*
Specter, Arlen *United States Senator from Pennsylvania*
Spector, Melbourne Louis *retired foreign service officer*
Spector, Phillip Louis *lawyer*
Speier, Jackie (Karen Lorraine Jacqueline Speier) *United States Representative from California, former state senator*
Spellings, Margaret LaMontagne *former United States Secretary of Education*
Spencer, Alan C. *legislative staff member*
Sperling, Godfrey, Jr. *retired journalist*
Speth, Andrew D. *legislative staff member*
Spieler, Jeff *public health service officer*
Spillane, Robert Richard *school system administrator*
Spira, Michael *legislative staff member*
Spiro, Peter M. *legislative staff member*
Spitzer, Marc Lee *commissioner, former state legislator*
Splete, Allen Peterjohn *educational association administrator, educator*
Spooner, David M. *federal agency administrator, lawyer*
Spratt, John McKee, Jr. *United States Representative from South Carolina, lawyer*
Sproat, Edward F., III, (Ward Sproat) *federal agency administrator*
Spurgeon, Dennis Ray *federal agency administrator, former manufacturing executive*
Srinivasan, Sri *lawyer*
Staats, Elmer Boyd *foundation executive, former government official*
Stabenow, Deborah Ann *United States Senator from Michigan, former congresswoman*
Stackley, Sean Joseph *civilian military employee*
Stadtler, Walter Edward *diplomat*
Staley, Michael *legislative staff member*
Stallings, Tommy Ray *legislative staff member*
Stampley, Stephen M. *legislative staff member*
Stanislaus, Mathy V. *federal agency administrator, environmental lawyer, chemical engineer*
Stanko, Joseph C. *lawyer, lobbyist*
Stanley, Elizabeth G. *legislative staff member*
Stanley, Jean-Daniel *geoarchaeologist*
Stanton, Gregory Howard *lawyer, educator*
Stanton, Matt *lobbyist, beverage company executive*
Staples, George McDade *Director, Fgn Serv, United States Department State, former ambassador*
Stark, Fortney Hillman (Pete Stark) *United States Representative from California*
Starr, Dorothy Anne *retired psychiatrist*
Starr, Judson Wilmarth *lawyer*
Stayin, Randolph John *lawyer*
Steadman, John Montague *Senior Judge, DC Court of Appeals*
Stearns, Clifford Bundy *United States Representative from Florida*
Steele, Ana Mercedes *retired federal agency administrator*
Steele, Michael S. *political organization administrator, former lieutenant governor*
Steen, Ellen *lawyer*
Steensgaard, Anthony Harvey *federal agency administrator*
Steiger, William R. (Bill Steiger) *federal agency administrator*
Steigman, Andrew L. *academic dean*
Steinberg, James Braidy *federal agency administrator*
Stelzer, Irwin Mark *economist*
Stenholm, Charles Walter *lobbyist, former congressman*
Stent, Angela E. *political scientist, educator, director*
Stephan, Robert B. *federal agency administrator*
Stephanopoulos, George Robert *political reporter*
Stephens, Kathleen (D. Kathleen Stephens) *United States Ambassador to South Korea*
Stephenson, Barbara J. *United States Ambassador to Panama*
Stephenson, Sherry Madeline *trade economist*
Stephenson, Thomas F. *United States Ambassador to Portugal*
Stepp, Mary Ann *medical educator*
Sterlin, Shrita D. *legislative staff member*
Stern, Alan (Sol Alan Stern) *science administrator, astrophysicist, researcher*
Stern, Andrew L. (Andy Stern) *labor union administrator*
Stern, Carl Leonard *retired news correspondent, federal official, educator*
Stern, Elizabeth Espin *lawyer*
Stern, Gerald Mann *lawyer*
Stern, Marcus A. *journalist*
Stern, Paula *international trade consultant*
Stern, Samuel Alan *lawyer*
Stetson, Jane Watson *political organization administrator*
Stevens, David H. *federal agency administrator*
Stevens, Herbert Francis *lawyer, educator*
Stevens, John Paul *United States supreme court justice*
Stevens, Paul Schott *lawyer*
Stevens, Roberta A. *librarian*
Stevenson, Zollie Julius, Jr. *former school system and government agency administrator, consultant*
Stewart, David Pentland *lawyer, educator*
Stewart, Karen Brevard *federal agency administrator, former ambassador*
Stich, Roberta Lynn *not-for-profit fundraiser, social worker*
Stiff, Linda E. *federal agency administrator*
Stock, Stuart Chase *lawyer*
Stockman, Jennifer Blei *political organization administrator*
Stockton, Paul Noble *federal agency administrator*
Stoddard, Andrew T. *legislative staff member*
Stolberg, Sheryl Gay *journalist*
Stoll, Richard Giles *lawyer*
Stoltz, Joe *federal official*
Stone, Florence Smith *film presenter, festival producer, consultant*
Stone, Roger David *environmentalist*
Stonesifer, Patty (Patricia Q. Stonesifer) *former foundation administrator*
Stottlemyer, Todd A. *business association executive*
Stouck, Jerry *lawyer*
Straley, Tina H. *mathematics association director*
Strand, Margaret N. *lawyer*
Strange, Sharon Louise *special education educator, musician*
Strasburg, Stephen *professional baseball player*
Strauss, Paul *Shadow Senator to US Congress from DC*
Strautmanis, Michael (Michael A. Strautmanis) *federal official*
Strickland, Thomas L. *federal agency administrator, former insurance company executive*
Strickling, Lawrence E. (Larry Strickling) *federal agency administrator*
Strokoff, Sandra L. *lawyer*
Stromberg, Clifford Douglas *lawyer*
Stromberg, Jean Wilbur Gleason *lawyer*
Strong, Mark Tuthill *botanist*
Stroup, Richard L. *lawyer*
Struble, Wayne T. *legislative staff member*
Struelens, Michel Maurice Joseph Georges *political science professor, consultant*
Strum, Philippa *political science professor, researcher*
Stuart, Sandi *lobbyist*
Stucky, Scott Wallace *federal judge, lawyer*
Studds, Colin Eastman *ecologist, researcher*
Stuntz, Linda Gillespie *lawyer, former federal agency administrator*
Stupak, Bart (Bartholomew Thomas Stupak) *United States Representative from Michigan, lawyer*
Styles, Angela Barbee *lawyer, former federal official*
Suboleski, Stanley C. *federal agency administrator, mining engineer*
Suh, Rhea S. *federal agency administrator*
Sulick, Michael J. *federal agency administrator*
Sullivan, Brendan V., Jr. *lawyer*
Sullivan, James M. *hotel executive*
Sullivan, John A. *United States Representative from Oklahoma*
Sullivan, John J. *lawyer, former federal agency administrator*
Sullivan, Mark J. *federal agency administrator*
Sullivan, Martin Edward *museum director*
Sullivan, Michael J. *lobbyist, former prosecutor*
Sullivan, Michael J. *labor union administrator*
Sullivan, Timothy *lawyer*
Sullivan, William Michael, Jr. *lawyer*
Summers, Larry (Lawrence Henry Summers) *federal official, economist, former United States Secretary of the Treasury*
Sumwalt, Robert Llewellyn III *federal agency administrator, pilot*
Sundermeyer, Michael S. *lawyer*
Sundquist, Don *lobbyist, former governor*
Sunshine, Robert A. *federal official*
Susman, Louis B. *United States Ambassador to the United Kingdom, retired investment banker*
Sutley, Nancy Helen *federal official*
Sutphen, Mona K. *federal official*
Sutter, Eleanor Bly *retired diplomat*
Sutton, Betty *United States Representative from Ohio, lawyer*
Sutton, William G., Jr., (Woody Sutton) *federal agency administrator, retired military officer*
Svoboda, Patricia Helen *art historian*
Swan, James C. *United States Ambassador to Djibouti*
Swankin, David Arnold *lawyer, consumer products company executive*
Swart, Susan *federal official*
Sweeney, John Joseph *labor union administrator*
Sweeney, Margaret Mary *federal judge*
Swendiman, Alan Robert *lawyer*
Swift, Stephen Jensen *federal judge*
Swimmer, Ross Owen *federal official*
Swindell, Russell A., II, *legislative staff member*
Swonger, Chris *lobbyist, beverage company executive*
Swygert, Haywood Patrick *law educator, retired academic administrator*
Symington, W. Stuart, IV, (William Stuart Symington IV) *United States Ambassador to Rwanda*
Sypolt, Jennifer Lynn *legislative staff member*
Szabo, Joseph Clark *federal agency administrator*
Szymanski, Patrick Joseph *lawyer*
Taavila, Pia Seija *literature and language professor*
Tabb, Vandoster Langford, Sr. *retired military officer*
Tacha, Athena *sculptor, artist, educator*
Taft, William Howard, IV, *lawyer*
Tagen, Julie *legislative staff member*
Tagliabue, Paul John *lawyer, retired national football league commissioner*
Tahir-Kheli, Shirin *federal official*
Talbott, Strobe *think-tank executive*
Tallent, Stephen Edison *lawyer*
Talley, Vernon Andrew *museum administrator*
Tameron, Alexis C. *legislative staff member*
Tangherlini, Daniel Mark *federal agency administrator*
Tanielian, Matt *lobbyist*
Tanner, John S. *United States Representative from Tennessee, lawyer*
Tannon, Jay Middleton *lawyer*
Tanous, Peter Joseph *investment advisor*
Tantillo, Andrew M. *legislative staff member*
Tapella, Robert Charles *federal official*
Tapscott, Ed *professional sports team executive*
Taronji, Jaime, Jr. *lawyer*
Tarplin, Linda E. *lobbyist*
Tarplin, Richard J. *lobbyist, former federal agency administrator*
Tarullo, Daniel K. *federal official, law educator*
Tate, Daniel Clyde, Jr. *lobbyist, former legislative aide*
Tate, Rosemary *special education educator*
Tate, Sheila Burke *public relations executive*
Tateishi, Peter *legislative staff member*
Tatel, David Stephen *federal judge*
Taub, Robert G. *legislative staff member*
Taubman, Nicholas Frank *United States Ambassador to Romania*
Taubman, Philip M. *editor*
Tauscher, Ellen O'Kane *federal agency administrator, former United States Representative from California*
Taylor, Gene (Gary Eugene Taylor) *United States Representative from Mississippi*
Taylor, Nancy Elizabeth *lobbyist, lawyer*
Taylor, Ralph Arthur, Jr. *lawyer*
Taylor, William B., Jr. *United States Ambassador to Ukraine*
Tchen, Christina M. (Tina Tchen) *federal official, lawyer*
Teague, Harry *United States Representative from New Mexico*
Teague, Randal Cornell, Sr. *lawyer*
Teare, Richard Wallace *retired foreign service officer*
Tedeschi, George *labor union administrator*
Tedesco, Mark J. *career military officer, physician*
Teehee, Kimberly Kay *federal official*
Tefft, John F. *United States Ambassador to Georgia*
Teichler, Stephen Lin *lawyer*
Teitelbaum, Donald Gene *United States Ambassador to Ghana*
Temko, Stanley Leonard *lawyer*
Tenenbaum, Jeffrey S. *lawyer*
Tenpas, Ronald Jay *lawyer, former federal agency administrator*
Terpstra, A. Ellen *federal agency administrator*
Terris, Bruce Jerome *lawyer*
Terry, Adam *legislative staff member*
Terry, James Philip *federal agency administrator*
Terry, John Alfred *Senior Judge, DC Court of Appeals*
Terry, Lee Raymond *United States Representative from Nebraska, lawyer*
Terwilliger, George James III *lawyer, former federal agency administrator*
Terzian, Grace Paine *communications executive*
Terzian, Philip Henry *journalist*
Tester, Jon(athan) *United States Senator from Montana, former state legislator, farmer*
Tetelman, Alice Fran *small business owner*
Tetreault, Paul R. *theater director, museum administrator*
Teuber Moore, Terri *legislative staff member*
Teufel, Hugo III *former lawyer, federal agency administrator*
Tharp, Roland Geoge *psychology professor*
Tharpe, Don I. *foundation administrator*
Theodore, Eustace D. *educational association administrator, consultant*
Thomas, Bill (William Marshall Thomas) *Former United States Representative from California*
Thomas, Brian C. *legislative staff member*
Thomas, Clarence *United States supreme court justice*
Thomas, Ritchie Tucker *lawyer*
Thomas, Scott E. *lawyer, former commissioner*
Thomas-Greenfield, Linda *United States Ambassador to Liberia*
Thomas-Razza, Constance *retired elementary school educator*
Thomasson, Dan King *newspaper executive, columnist*
Thompson, Bennie G. *United States Representative from Mississippi*
Thompson, Bernida Lamerle *principal, consultant, educator*
Thompson, Christopher *legislative staff member*
Thompson, Darrel L. *legislative staff member*
Thompson, Glenn W., Jr. *United States Representative from Pennsylvania, former health facility administrator*
Thompson, Horace A., III, (Topper Thompson) *commissioner, lawyer*
Thompson, John III *men's college basketball coach*
Thompson, Mike (C. Michael Thompson) *United States Representative from California*
Thompson, Phyllis D. *Associate Judge, DC Court of Appeals, lawyer*
Thompson, Ryan D. *legislative staff member*
Thompson, Terry Lamar *orthopedist, educator*
Thompson, Tommy (Thomas George Thompson) *lawyer, former United States Secretary of Health and Human Services*
Thomsen, Linda Chatman *lawyer, former federal agency administrator*
Thorington, Richard Wainwright *biologist*
Thornberry, Mac (William McClellan Thornberry) *United States Representative from Texas*
Thornburgh, Dick (Richard Lewis Thornburgh) *lawyer, former United States Attorney General*
Thorne, David Hoadley *United States Ambassador to Italy and San Marino*
Thornton, D. McCarty (Mac) *lawyer*
Thornton, Michael B. *federal judge*
Thorson, Eric Mines *federal agency administrator*
Thune, John Randolph *United States Senator from South Dakota*
Tiahrt, Todd (W. Todd Tiahrt) *United States Representative from Kansas, former state senator*
Tidball, M. Elizabeth Peters *physiologist, educator*
Tiede, Tom Robert *journalist*
Tiedemann, Charles Welch (Chad) *lawyer*
Tierney, John F. *United States Representative from Massachusetts, lawyer*
Tighe, William (Bill Tighe) *legislative staff member*
Tijerino, Jose A. *foundation administrator*
Tillman, Judith R. *federal agency administrator*
Timken, William Robert, Jr. *United States Ambassador to Germany, former manufacturing executive*
Timmons, William Evan *retired consulting firm executive*
Tipre, Dnyanesh Nishikant *pharmacist, researcher*
Titus, Alice Costandina (Dina Titus) *United States Representative from Nevada, former state legislator*
Tobias, Andrew Previn *columnist, educator*
Tobias, Robert Max *labor leader, lawyer*

Todaro, Peter M. *lawyer*
Toedtman, James Smith *journalist, editor*
Toensing, Victoria *lawyer*
Tolchin, Martin *journalist, writer*
Toll, Steven J. *lawyer*
Tom, Willard Ken *lawyer*
Tomberlin, Michael *legislative staff member*
Tomlinson, Alexander Cooper *investment banker, consultant*
Tompkins, Hilary Chandler *lawyer*
Tompkins, Joseph Buford, Jr. *lawyer*
Toner, Michael E. *lawyer, former FEC commissioner*
Tonkin, Leo Sampson *educational association administrator*
Tonko, Paul David *United States Representative from New York, former state agency administrator*
Tonsager, Dallas P. *federal agency administrator*
Toomey, Daniel E. *lawyer*
Toretsky, Jeffrey A. *physician, researcher, educator*
Towns, Edolphus (Ed Towns) *United States Representative from New York*
Townsend, Brian Douglas *paralegal*
Townsend, John Michael *lawyer*
Townsend, Marjorie Rhodes *aerospace engineer, engineering executive*
Tracey, Peter Lake *lawyer*
Trachtenberg, Stephen Joel *political science professor, former academic administrator*
Trafford, Abigail *columnist, editor, writer, public speaker*
Trager, Michael David *lawyer*
Train, Russell Errol *environmentalist*
Trasviña, John David *federal agency administrator*
Treiber, Adam Mark *lawyer*
Trevena, Anthony *legislative staff member*
Triay, Inés R. *federal agency administrator*
Trisco, Robert Frederick *church historian, educator*
Trooboff, Peter Dennis *lawyer*
Trost, Robert Patrick *economist*
Troyer, Thomas Alfred *lawyer*
Trumka, Richard Louis *labor union administrator*
Truscott, Carl Joseph *security firm executive, former federal agency administrator*
Tsacoumis, Stephanie *lawyer*
Tsongas, Niki (Nicola S. Tsongas) *United States Representative from Massachusetts, former dean*
Tucker, Jonathan Brin *political scientist*
Tucker, Marna S. *lawyer*
Tucker, Stefan Franklin *lawyer*
Tuerk, William F. *federal agency administrator, lawyer*
Tuohey, Mark Henry III *lawyer*
Turner, James Hilton, Jr. *lawyer*
Turner, Jim (James W. Turner) *lawyer, former United States Representative from Texas*
Turner, John Andrew *economist*
Turner, Michael R. *United States Representative from Ohio*
Turtell, Neal Timothy *librarian*
Tyner, Lee Reichelderfer *lawyer*
Ucko, David Alan *science foundation official*
Udall, Thomas S. (Tom) *United States Senator from New Mexico*
Uehlein, Edward Carl, Jr. *lawyer*
Upton, Frederick Stephen *United States Representative from Michigan*
Urbancic, Frank Charles, Jr. *United States Ambassador to Cyprus*
Urbina, Ricardo Manuel *judge*
Urey, Richard *legislative staff member*
Urschel, Joe *museum director, former news executive*
Utley, Jon Basil *think-tank executive, journalist*
Vaccarello, Janine *museum administrator*
Vacketta, Carl Lee *lawyer, educator*
Vakerics, Thomas Vincent *lawyer*
Valachovic, Richard William *medical association administrator*
Valentine, Steven Richards *lawyer*
Valenzuela, Arturo Arms *political science professor, writer, consultant*
Van Antwerp, Robert L., Jr. *career military officer*
Vandaele, Bart *chef*
Vanderver, Timothy Arthur, Jr. *lawyer*
Van Hollen, Christopher, Jr. *United States Representative from Maryland*
Van Scoyoc, Stu (H. Stewart Van Scoyoc) *lobbyist, lawyer*
Van Tine, Kirk Kelso *lawyer, former federal agency administrator*
van Voorst, Carol *United States Ambassador to Iceland*
Vardaman, John Wesley *lawyer*
Variyam, Jayachandran N. *economist*
Varney, Christine Anne *federal agency administrator, lawyer*
Vasquez, Juan Flores *federal judge*
Vasquez, Vivian *education educator*
Vaught, Laura E. *legislative staff member*
Veatch, Robert Marlin *philosopher, researcher*
Vela, Moe (Moises Vicente Vela Jr.) *federal official, communications executive*
Velázquez, Nydia Margarita *United States Representative from New York*
Ventimiglia, Vincent J., Jr. *consulting firm executive, former federal agency administrator*
Verma, Richard R. (Rahul Verma) *federal agency administrator, lawyer*
Verner, James Melton *lawyer*
Veroneau, John K. *lawyer, former ambassador*
Verrill, Charles Owen, Jr. *lawyer*
Verrilli, Donald B., Jr. *federal agency administrator, lawyer*
Vershbow, Alexander Russell (Sandy Vershbow) *federal agency administrator, former ambassador*
Verveer, Melanne S. *ambassador*
Verveer, Philip L. *lawyer*
Verville, Elizabeth Giavani *federal official*
Vest, Charles Marstiller *engineering educator, former academic administrator*
Vickers, Michael G. *federal agency administrator*
Vickery, Raymond Ezekiel, Jr. *international business consultant, lawyer*
Videnieks, Barbara J. *legislative staff member*
Viers, Hillary Wicai *legislative staff member*
Vigilance, Pierre *state agency administrator, public health service officer*
Villarreal, June Patricia *retired sales executive*
Vilsack, Tom (Thomas James Vilsack) *Secretary of Agriculture, former Governor of Iowa*
Vine, Howard A. *lobbyist, lawyer*
Vines, Jim (James K.) *lawyer, former prosecutor*
Violante, Patricia *translator, language expert, writer, interpreter*
Visclosky, Peter John *United States Representative from Indiana, lawyer*
Vitter, David Bruce *United States Senator from Louisiana, former congressman*
Vittone, John Michael *federal judge*
Voeten, Erik *political scientist, educator*
Vogel, Alex N. *lobbyist, lawyer*
Vogel, Jon *political organization executive*
Voinovich, George Victor *United States Senator from Ohio*
Vojcic, Branimir R. *engineering educator, consultant*
Volcker, Paul Adolph *economist, former Chairman of the Board of Governors of the Federal Reserve System*
Voll, John Obert *history professor*
Volner, Ian D. *lawyer*
Voorhees, Theodore, Jr. *lawyer*
Wade, David Eckels *legislative staff member*
Wagner, Ann Louise *United States Ambassador to Luxembourg, former political organization executive*
Wagner, Annice McBryde *Senior Judge, DC Court of Appeals*
Wagner, Curtis Lee, Jr. *judge*
Wagner, Martha Jo *lawyer*
Wahlquist, Brent T. *federal agency administrator*
Wainstein, Kenneth L. *lawyer, former prosecutor*
Walcott, John L. *communications executive*
Wald, Douglas L. *lawyer*
Wald, Patricia McGowan *retired federal judge*
Wald, Robert Lewis *lawyer*
Walden, Greg *United States Representative from Oregon*
Walker, Audrey Thayer *clinical social worker, psychotherapist*
Walker, David Alan *finance educator*
Walker, John Stanley *legislative staff member*
Walker, Kristin *legislative staff member*
Walker, Mark Alan *legislative staff member*
Walker, Matthew Vincent *legislative staff member*
Walker, Robert Smith *lobbyist, former United States Representative from Pennsylvania*
Walker, Ryan P. *legislative staff member*
Wall, Christopher Read *lawyer*
Wallace, Don, Jr. *law educator*
Wallace, Kim N. *federal agency administrator*
Wallace, Richard Edward, Jr. *lawyer*
Wallace, Robert Bruce *lawyer, educator*
Walles, Jacob *Consul General in Jerusalem*
Walsh, Bridgett (Mary Bridget Walsh) *legislative staff member*
Walsh, George William *publishing company executive, editor, author*
Walsh, James Thomas (Jim Walsh) *lobbyist, former United States Representative from New York*
Walsh, Jennifer Fitzgerald *legislative staff member*
Walsh, John *television show host, missing children and victims' rights advocate*
Walsh, Michael J. *lawyer*
Walter, Elisse Barbara *commissioner*
Walter, Sheryl Lynn *lawyer*
Walters, John P. *think-tank executive, former federal official*
Walther, Steven T. *commissioner, lawyer*
Walton, Reggie Barnett *federal judge*
Walz, Tim (Timothy J. Walz) *United States Representative from Minnesota, former social science educator*
Wamp, Zachary Paul *United States Representative from Tennessee*
Wang, John Cheng Hwai *communications engineer, researcher*
Wang, Zhaoyang *engineering educator*
Ward, David *educational consultant, former educational association administrator, academic administrator*
Ward, Nancy L. *federal agency administrator*
Ward, Stephen D. *legislative staff member*
Warner, John William *lawyer, former United States Senator from Virginia*
Warner, Mark Robert *United States Senator from Virginia, former governor*
Warren, David Liles *educational association administrator*
Warsh, Kevin Maxwell *federal official*
Wartell, Sarah Rosen *think-tank executive*
Wartman, Steven A. *medical association administrator*
Washburn, Eric *lobbyist*
Washington, Eric T. *judge*
Washington, Linda Jacobs *federal agency administrator*
Wasko-Flood, Sandra Jean *artist, educator*
Wasserman-Schultz, Debbie *United States Representative from Florida*
Wasshausen, Dieter Carl *botanist*
Waters, Jennifer Nash *lawyer*
Waters, Maxine *United States Representative from California*
Watkins, Stanley *legislative staff member*
Watkins, Yelberton R. (Yebbie Watkins) *legislative staff member*
Watson, Arthur Dennis *federal official*
Watson, Diane Edith *United States Representative from California*
Watson, Harlan L(eroy) *federal agency administrator, physicist, economist*
Watt, Melvin Luther *United States Representative from North Carolina, lawyer*
Watts, J. C. (Julius Caesar Watts Jr.) *lobbyist, former United States Representative from Oklahoma*
Waxman, Henry Arnold *United States Representative from California*
Waxman, Seth Paul *lawyer*
Way, Kristi *legislative staff member*
Wayne, Stephen J. *government educator, writer*
Weaver, John *political strategist*
Weaver, Reg(inald) *educational association administrator*
Webb, Jim (James Henry Webb Jr.) *United States Senator from Virginia*
Webb, Nate *legislative staff member*
Webber, Richard John *lawyer*
Weber, Deanne *health science association administrator*
Weber, Vin (John Vincent Weber) *lobbyist, former United States Representative from Minnesota*
Webre, Septime *performing company executive, choreographer*
Webster, Douglas Wayne *federal agency administrator, management consultant*
Webster, William Hedgcock *lawyer, federal agency administrator*
Wedgwood, Ruth *law educator, international affairs expert*
Weedman, Daniel Wilson *astronomy educator*
Wehner, Peter Hermann *political scientist, former federal official*
Weich, Ronald Harris *federal agency administrator*
Weidenfeld, Edward Lee *lawyer*
Weidenfeld, Sheila Rabb *television producer, writer*
Weigel, George Shillow, Jr. *theologian*
Weigel, Kenneth George *lawyer*
Weinberg, Thomas *legislative staff member*
Weiner, Anthony David *United States Representative from New York*
Weiner, Robert Neil *lawyer*
Weiner, Robert Stephen *federal agency administrator*
Weiner, Stephen Francis *academic administrator, communications educator*
Weingarten, Randi *labor union administrator, lawyer*
Weingarten, Reid H. *lawyer*
Weingold, Marjorie Nassau *retired special education educator*
Weinhold, Linda Lillian *psychologist, researcher*
Weinman, Howard Mark *lawyer*
Weinstein, Harris *lawyer*
Weinstein, Kenneth N. *federal government administrator*
Weinstein, Kenneth R. *think-tank executive*
Weinstein, Mark Jay *opera general director*
Weintraub, Ellen L. *commissioner*
Weintraub, Sidney *economist, educator*
Weisgall, Jonathan Michael *lawyer*
Weiss, Charles, Jr. *educator*
Weiss, Daniel *legislative staff member*
Weiss, Mark Anschel *lawyer*
Weiss, Rick *reporter*
Weissman, William R. *lawyer*
Weitz, William F. (Bill Weitz) *legislative staff member*
Welch, Peter F. *United States Representative from Vermont, former state legislator*
Wellen, Robert Howard *lawyer*
Wellinghoff, Jon *commissioner*
Wells, Barry Leon *United States Ambassador to The Gambia*
Wells, Thomas B. *federal judge*
Wenner, Charles Roderick *lawyer*
Werner, Sharon *legislative staff member, lawyer*
Wertheim, Mitzi Mallina *information technology executive*
Wertheimer, Fredric Michael *public policy advocate*
West, Gail Berry *lawyer*
West, J. Robinson (Robin West) *petroleum finance company executive, former government official*
West, Robert MacLellan *science educator, consultant*
West, Togo Dennis, Jr. *lawyer, former United States Secretary of Veterans Affairs*
West, Tony (Derek Anthony West) *federal agency administrator, lawyer*
Westerlund, Li *law educator*
Westfall, Sandra Sobieraj *journalist*
Westmoreland, Lynn A. *United States Representative from Georgia*
Wexler, Robert *United States Representative from Florida*
Weymouth, Katharine Bouchage *publishing executive*
Whalen, Laurence J. *federal judge*
Wheeler, Douglas Paul *conservationist, state agency administrator, lawyer*
Wheeler, Sharon *legislative staff member*
Wheeler, Thomas Craig *federal judge*
Wheeler, Thomas Edgar *private equity executive*
Whelan, Andrew T. *legislative staff member*
Whelan, Roger Michael *lawyer, educator*
Wherry, Robert Allen, Jr. *federal judge, lawyer*
Whitaker, Mark Theis *broadcast executive, editor*
White, Dorinda *legislative staff member*
White, John Arnold *physics professor, research scientist*
White, John D. *legislative staff member*
White, Robert Edward *think-tank executive*
White, Robert Mayer *meteorologist*
White, Scott *federal agency administrator*
White, Sharman Lynell *lawyer*
White, Stanley V. *legislative staff member*
Whitehead, Kimberly B. *lawyer*
Whitehouse, Sheldon *United States Senator from Rhode Island, former state attorney general*
Whitehurst, Grover Jay (Russ Whitehurst) *psychologist, former federal agency administrator*
Whitener, Jeanette (Jeanette Penny Forcash Whitener) *legislative staff member*
Whiteside, Ruth A. *federal agency administrator*
Whitesides, John Lindsey, Jr. *aerospace engineering educator, researcher*
Whitfield, Edward (Wayne) *United States Representative from Kentucky*
Whiting, Richard Albert *lawyer*
Whitman, Shawn R. *legislative staff member*
Whitney, Benson K. *United States Ambassador to Norway*
Whitt, John J. *legislative staff member*
Whittemore, Edward Reed, II, *poet, retired educator*
Whitworth, Horace Algernon *mechanical engineer*
Whitworth, William A. *magazine editor*
Wiarda, Iêda Siqueira *political sicence educator*
Wicker, Roger Frederick *United States Senator from Mississippi*
Wieringa, Jeffrey A. *federal agency administrator, military officer*
Wiese, John Paul *federal judge*
Wilensky, Gail Roggin *economist, researcher*
Wiley, Richard Emerson *lawyer*
Wilhelm, John W. *labor union administrator*
Wilhoit, Gene *educational association administrator*
Wilkins, David Horton *United States Ambassador to Canada, former state legislator*
Wilkins, William J. *lawyer*
Wilkinson, Beth Ann *lawyer, former mortgage company executive*
Wilkinson, Ronald Sterne *science administrator, historian, environmentalist*
Wilkinson, Winston *federal agency administrator, lawyer*
Will, George Frederick *editor, journalist, commentator*
Williams, Aaron S. *federal agency administrator*
Williams, Anthony Allan (Tony Williams) *lobbyist, former mayor*
Williams, Armstrong *radio and television show host, political commentator*
Williams, B. John, Jr. *retired federal agency administrator, lawyer*
Williams, Carolyn Hastings *lawyer*
Williams, Clarence *legislative staff member*
Williams, Darlene F. *federal agency administrator*
Williams, David B. *legislative staff member*
Williams, E. Faye *lawyer, political organization executive, health products executive*
Williams, Earl Patrick, Jr. *retired editor, freelance writer*
Williams, Eddie Nathan *retired think-tank executive*
Williams, Ella Marilyn *mathematics educator*
Williams, James A. *labor union administrator*
Williams, James A. *federal agency administrator*
Williams, Jimmy (James F. M. Williams) *lobbyist*
Williams, Juan *news correspondent*
Williams, Karen Hastie *lawyer*
Williams, Lisa M. *legislative staff member*
Williams, Mary Ellen Coster *federal judge*
Williams, Michael J. *mortgage company executive*
Williams, Stephen Fain *federal judge*
Williams, Steven A., Jr. *environmental services administrator, former federal agency administrator*
Williams, Terrance Reynolds *architecture educator*
Williams, Tiffani Vivienne *lawyer*
Williams, Tonya *legislative staff member, lawyer*
Williamson, Clint (John Clint Williamson) *ambassador*
Williamson, Edwin Dargan *lawyer, former federal official*
Williamson, Irving A. *federal official*
Williamson, Thomas Samuel, Jr. *lawyer*
Willis, Arlene M. *legislative staff member*
Willman, David *investigative journalist*
Willner, Ann Ruth *political scientist, educator*
Willner, Dorothy *anthropologist, educator*
Wilson, Charles A., Jr. *United States Representative from Ohio, funeral director*
Wilson, Charles Nesbitt *lobbyist, former United States Representative from Texas*
Wilson, D. Edward, Jr. *lawyer*
Wilson, Frances C. *career military officer*
Wilson, Joe (Addison Wilson) *United States Representative from South Carolina, former senator, lawyer*
Wilson, John Silvanus, Jr. *federal agency administrator*
Wilson, Michael Moureau *lawyer, physician*
Wimmer, Kurt A. *lawyer*
Wine, L. Mark *lawyer*
Winfrey, Carey Wells *journalist, editor*
Winland, Thomas W. *lawyer*
Winston, David *political strategist, columnist*
Winston, Michael Russell *historian*
Winter, Douglas E. *lawyer, writer*
Winter, Melissa E. *federal official*
Winter, Thomas Swanson *publishing executive*
Wintrol, John Patrick *lawyer*
Wise, Bob (Robert Ellsworth Wise Jr.) *educational association administrator, former governor, congressman*
Wise, Lorraine E. *educational consultant*
Withers, John Lovelle, II, *United States Ambassador to Albania*
Witorsch, Philip *internist, educator*
Witt, James Lee *management consultant, former federal agency administrator*
Witte, Eric *legislative staff member*
Wittes, Janet Turk *statistician*
Wittman, Randy Scott *professional basketball coach*
Wittman, Robert J. *United States Representative from Virginia, former state legislator*
Wixon, Henry N. *lawyer*
Wogaman, John Philip *retired minister and educator*
Wolanin, Thomas Richard *federal agency administrator, educator*
Wolf, Frank Rudolph *United States Representative from Virginia, lawyer*
Wolfe, Sidney Manuel *physician*
Wolfensberger, Donald *political scientist, columnist*
Wolff, Candida (Candi Wolff) *lawyer, former federal official*
Wolff, Elroy Harris *lawyer*
Wolff, Otto J. *federal agency administrator*
Wolfowitz, Paul Dundes *former President of the World Bank*
Wolin, Neal Steven *federal agency administrator*
Woloshin, Douglas *lawyer*
Wolpe, Howard Eliot *former Congressman, political scientist*
Wolski, Victor J. *federal judge, lawyer*
Womack, Todd *legislative staff member*
Wood, James *magazine editor, literary critic*
Wood, John F. *lawyer, former prosecutor*
Wood, Michael M. *United States Ambassador to Sweden*
Woodall, Samuel Roy, Jr. *lawyer*
Woodall, William Robert *legislative staff member*

Woodward, Bob (Robert Upshur Woodward) *editor, writer*
Woofter, Vivien Perrine *interior designer, consultant*
Woolley, Leslie Ann *legislative staff member*
Woolsey, Lynn C. *United States Representative from California*
Woolsey, R. James (Robert James Woolsey) *lawyer, former CIA director*
Work, Charles Robert *lawyer*
Work, Robert O. *civilian military employee, retired military officer*
Wormmeester, Justin T. *legislative staff member*
Worsley, James Randolph, Jr. *lawyer*
Worthy, K(enneth) Martin *retired lawyer*
Wortley, George Cornelius *lobbyist, former United States Representative from New York*
Wright, Frank *artist, educator*
Wright, Ron *legislative staff member*
Wu, Frank H. *law educator, journalist*
Wyatt, John *legislative staff member*
Wybensinger, Netonis (Tonnie Wybensinger) *legislative staff member*
Wyden, Ron(ald) (Lee) *United States Senator from Oregon*
Wynn, Albert Russell *lobbyist, former United States Representative from Maryland*
Wyss, John Benedict *lawyer*
Yablon, Jeffery Lee *lawyer*
Yamamoto, Donald Yukio *United States Ambassador to Ethiopia*
Yambrusic, Edward Slavko *lawyer, consultant*
Yannucci, Thomas David *lawyer*
Yarmuth, John Allan *United States Representative from Kentucky*
Yarowsky, Jonathan R. *lawyer, lobbyist*
Yarwood, Bruce *health science association administrator*
Yates, John Melvin *United States Special Envoy for Somalia*
Yen, Hope S. *journalist, lawyer*
Yerkes, David Norton *architect*
Yingling, Edward L. *banking association executive*
Yock, Robert John *federal judge*
Yoder, Ronnie A. *judge*
Yonkura, Raymond *legislative staff member*
Young, Bill (Charles William Young) *United States Representative from Florida*
Young, Darlene H. *information system security officer*
Young, David *legislative staff member*
Young, Donald Edwin *United States Representative from Alaska*
Young, Todd Dean *legislative staff member*
Young, William H. *labor union administrator*
Youniss, James *psychology professor*
Yovanovitch, Marie L. *United States Ambassador to Armenia*
Yulish, Charles Barry *retired energy and environmental consultant, public relations executive*
Zabel, Matthew L. *legislative staff member*
Zamore, Michael Seth *legislative staff member*
Zane, Phillip Craig *lawyer*
Zarate, Juan Carlos *former federal official*
Zarnikow, Eric R. *federal agency administrator*
Zarychta, William Alex *aviation medical officer, physician assistant*
Zaucha, Jerome J. *lawyer*
Zax, Leonard A. *lawyer*
Zechman, Edwin Kerper, Jr. *medical facility administrator*
Zeidman, Fred S. *civic leader, corporate financial executive*
Zeidman, Philip Fisher *lawyer*
Zelman, Susan Tave *broadcast executive, former state official, school system administrator*
Zentay, John H. *lawyer*
Zhu, Tingju *environmental scientist*
Zients, Jeffrey D. *federal official*
Zierden, Don *professional basketball coach*
Ziglar, James W. *govt. official, investment banker, corporate, lawyer, educator*
Zikmund, Barbara Brown *minister, religious organization administrator, educator*
Zimmerman, Edwin Morton *lawyer*
Zimmerman, Ryan Wallace *professional baseball player*
Zinser, Todd J. *federal agency administrator*
Zody, John C. *legislative staff member*
Zoeller, Jack Carl *diversified financial services company executive*
Zoellick, Robert Bruce *President of the World Bank, former federal agency administrator*
Zoi, Catherine Radford (Cathy Zoi) *federal agency administrator*
Zwick, Kenneth Lowell *lawyer, director*
Zwillinger, Marc J. *lawyer*

FLORIDA

Alachua
Gaines, Weaver Henderson *lawyer*
Schneider, Richard T(heodore) *optics scientist, researcher, engineer*
Yang, Li-Xia *biomedical researcher, scientist, educator*

Altamonte Springs
Hoogland, Robert Frederics *lawyer*
Kaplan, Judith Helene *manufacturing executive*
O'Connor, Sean M. *diversified financial services company executive*

Amelia Island
Adelman, Robert Paul *retired construction executive, lawyer*
Freeman, Neal Blackwell *communications corporation executive*
Schiebler, Gerold Ludwig *pediatrician, educator*

Anna Maria
Hoffmann, Carl Konrad *retired lawyer*

Apopka
Carlson, Donna Marie *elementary school educator*
Fiorenza, Veronica Eve *pre-school educator*

Arcadia
Cline, Adrian H. *academic administrator*
Hall, Miles Lewis, Jr. *lawyer*
Spangler, Colleen Ann *marketing professional*
White, Will Walter III *public relations consultant, writer*

Atlantic Beach
Gartland, Alice Johnson *artist*
Walker, Richard Harold *pathologist, educator*

Aventura
Fishel, Peter Livingston *finance company executive*
Garcia, Marc Anthony *diplomat*
Kliger, Milton Richard *diversified financial services company executive*
McKenna, Peter Dennis *lawyer*
Rosenbluth, Morton *periodontist, educator*
Schwartz, Gerald *public relations and fundraising agency executive*
Wolfenson, Azi U. *electrical, mechanical and industrial engineer, consultant*

Avon Park
Markel, Tanna Michelle *design educator*

Bartow
Etheredge, Edward Ezekiel *retired surgeon*
Kincart, Robert Owen *technological executive*
Meuser, Fredrick William *retired church administrator, historian*

Bascom
Brooten, Kenneth Edward, Jr. *lawyer, author, writer, rancher*
Hart, James Whitfield, Jr. *retired public relations executive, lawyer*

Bay Harbor Islands
Solomon, Michael Bruce *lawyer*

Bay Pines
Jewell, Vanessa Yoder *surgical physician assistant*
Law, David Hillis *physician*

Belle Glade
Grear, Effie Carter *principal*

Belleair Beach
Fuentes, Martha Ayers *playwright*

Belleair Bluffs
Alexander, Christina Anamaria *translator, performing company executive*

Belleview
Savage, Sherelyn Sue *secondary school educator*

Big Pine Key
Fleischer, Roland Edward *art history professor*

Boca Grande
Marini, Robert Charles *environmental engineering executive*

Boca Raton
Agler, Richard Dean *rabbi*
Alpert, Martin Jeffrey *chiropractic physician*
Anderson, Roxanna Marion *psychology professor*
Arden, Eugene *retired university provost*
Asaduzzaman, Abu S. *computer scientist*
Ayyanathan, Kasirajan *biology professor*
Barry, Barbara Rosamond *music educator, writer*
Beber, Robert H. *lawyer, diversified financial services company executive*
Bolge, George Stephen *museum director*
Braisted, Mary Jo *elementary school educator*
Breakstone, Robert Albert *information technology and consumer products company executive, consultant*
Brehm, Patricia Christman *principal*
Brown, Charles E. *consumer products company executive*
Buchbinder, Ligaya H. *dermatologist*
Buckstein, Mark Aaron *lawyer, mediator, educator*
Burganger, Judith *concert pianist*
Calabrese, Carlo *naturopathic physician*
Clarke, Kenneth Kingsley *retired electronics executive*
Collins, Robert Arnold *literature and language professor*
Comment, Anna Mae *retired principal*
Cowen, Edward S. *lawyer, consultant*
Dickenson, Katharine Horn *historic preservationist*
Diffine, Suzanne Michele *language educator*
Dopkins, Leonard A(rnold) *accountant*
Dorfman, Allen Bernard *international management consultant*
Dunhill, Robert *advertising executive*
Ellis, Martin F. *computer company executive*
Fagien, Steven *ophthalmologist, consultant*
Faulkner, John Samuel *physicist, educator*
Feinman, Ronald *social sciences educator*
Foreman, Barbara Blatt *healthcare facility administrator*
Freedman, Howard Martin *financial planner*
Friedland, Michael Lawrence *dean, medical educator*
Gallaher, Ryan M. *engineering company executive, director*
Garcia, Elisa Dolores *lawyer*
Garelick, Martin *retired transportation executive*
Garrod, Kenneth J. *orthopedist, surgeon*
Godofsky, Stanley *lawyer*
Goldstein, Jerome Charles *retired professional society administrator, otolaryngologist, surgeon*
Gortz, Albert W. *lawyer*
Gracin, Hank *lawyer*
Gralla, Eugene *natural gas company executive*
Grimaldi, David *financial advisor*
Hampton, Benjamin Bertram *brokerage house executive*
Handel, Morton Emanuel *film company executive, management consultant*
Harris, S. Buddy *architect, interior designer*
Haugen, Christine *plastic surgeon*
Hecht, William David *retired accountant*
Iacobucci, Edward E. *air transportation and former software company executive*
Jackson, Stephanie A. *communications educator, consultant*
Jahanzeb, Mohammad *oncologist, hematologist*
Jarvis, Mike *men's college basketball coach*
Jessup, Jan Amis *arts volunteer, writer*
Johr, Robert Henry *dermatologist*
Joskow, Jules *economic research company executive*
Keyes, Daniel *author*
Kitzes, William Fredric *lawyer, advocate, researcher*
Kollander, Patricia *history professor*
Krouse, Rodger Russell *investment company executive*
Langbort, Polly *retired advertising executive*
Leary, William James *educational association administrator, educator*
Lerner, Theodore Raphael *dentist*
Lichtstein, Daniel M. *dean, internist*
Lin, Yukweng M. *engineer, educator*
Louda, J. William *chemist, biochemist, educator*
Luechtefeld, Monica *consumer products company executive*
Maguire, Kim D. *retail executive*
Makowski, Christopher *marine biologist, educator*
Man, Daniel *plastic surgeon*
Marcus, Andrea Candace Sills *lawyer*
Martin, James Russell *lawyer*
McFarland, Thomas *English literature educator*
McQueen, Scott Robert *broadcast executive*
Miller, Eugene *business educator, consultant*
Mitchell, Carmencita C. *literature and language professor*
Mussenden, Georg Antonio *electronics engineer*
Newman, Michael D. *retail executive*
Odland, Steve *consumer products company executive*
Párkányi, Cyril *chemistry educator*
Parra-Davila, Eduardo *surgeon, educator*
Pasternack, Stefan Alan *psychiatrist, psychoanalyst*
Pellen, Rita M. *associate dean*
Penhollow, Tina Marie *health science researcher, educator*
Raines, Deborah A. *neonatal/perinatal nurse specialist, educator, nursing researcher, consultant*
Rebel, Amy Louise *elementary school educator*
Reinstein, Joel *lawyer*
Richman, Joseph Herbert *retired public health service officer*
Ripps, Harris *ophthalmologist, educator*
Roddick, Andy Stephen *professional tennis player*
Roselli, Richard Joseph *lawyer*
Rothberg-Blackman, June Simmonds *retired nursing educator, psychotherapist*
Rubin, Chuck (Carl Rubin) *consumer products company executive*
Samuels, William Mason *physiology association executive*
Schechterman, Lawrence *lawyer, chef, business consultant*
Shah, Bimal *financial advisor, small business owner*
Shalom, Galit *psychologist*
Shusterman, Richard Marc *philosophy educator*
Sigel, Marshall Elliot *financial consultant*
Silver, Barry Morris *lawyer*
Smith, Dawn Mercedes *assistant dean*
Smith, Yoshimi O. *lawyer*
Snyder, Patricia Ann *chemistry professor*
Spagnuolo, Louis D. *banker*
Sperry, Len Thomas *psychiatrist and preventive medicine educator*
Strother, Judith Dianne Banks *linguistics educator*
Tennies, Robert Hunter *headmaster*
Tomasso, Anthony *banker*
Vanderlinde, Daisy *consumer products company executive*
Wang, Xin *engineering educator*
Weiner, Howard Marc *physician*
Weissbach, Herbert *biochemist, researcher*
Wolf, Jerome L. *lawyer*
Xie, Zhixiao *research scientist, educator*
Yoder, Patricia Doherty *public relations executive*
Zaitz, Cynthia Louise *creativity, music, theatre and dance educator*

Bokeelia
Donlon, Josephine A. *diagnostic and evaluation counseling therapist, educator*

Bonita Springs
Becker, Richard Charles *retired academic administrator*
Borchers, Janet Marise *elementary school educator, school counselor*
Costley, Gary Edward *food company executive*
Crutcher, Michael Bayard *lawyer, retired consumer products company executive*
Dignan, Thomas Gregory, Jr. *retired lawyer*
Elliott, Donna Louise *artist*
Gillis, James R. *consumer products company executive*
Hastings, Vivien N. *lawyer*
Johnson, Franklyn Arthur *academic administrator*
Kopf, George Michael *retired ophthalmologist*
Liebman, Phyllis Janice *volunteer, educator*
Powell, Robert Ellis *mathematics professor, dean*
Rainey, Barbara White *insurance company executive*
Sargent, Charles Lee *manufacturing executive*
Tuchman, Alan *consumer products company executive*

Boynton Beach
Allison, Dwight Leonard, Jr. *investor*
Altman, Allan *lawyer*
Bartholomew, Arthur Peck, Jr. *accountant*
Bernstein, Edwin S. *judge*
Chalal, Joseph B. *orthopedist, surgeon*
Glickman, Franklin Sheldon *dermatologist, educator*
Goldenberg, George *retired pharmaceutical executive*
Hochberg, Lois J. *retired school psychologist*
Hughes, Richard G. *principal, consultant*
Jacobs, Wendy *editor, realtor*
Jensen, Reuben Rolland *former automotive company executive*
Klein, Bernard *publishing executive*
Lessard, Raymond William *bishop emeritus*
McNair, Russell Arthur, Jr. *lawyer*
Pataky, Paul Eric *ophthalmologist*
Stolzberg, Mark Elliott *psychologist*
Warga, Jack *mathematician, educator*
Warshaw, Stanley Irving *federal official, consultant*

Bradenton
Alex, Elizabeth Robins *retired adult education educator, retired preschool director*
Anderson, Ruth McClendon *nursing educator*
Barnebey, Kenneth Alan *food products executive*
Beall, Robert Matthews, II, *retail executive*
Blanchard, Leonard Albert *writer, consultant, educator*
Brenner, Frank *lawyer*
Brunk, William Edward *astronomer*
Carnes, James Edward *retired electronics executive*
Diana, John Nicholas *physiologist*
Driscoll, Constance Fitzgerald *education educator, writer, consultant*
Engelman, Melvin Alkon *retired dentist, dental products executive*
Gauthier, Norman Leonidas *retired biology professor*
Gedeon, Peter Ferenc *photographer, director*
Grieneisen, Jeff *literature and language professor*
Haas, Tommy (Thomas Mario Haas) *professional tennis player*
Harris, Judith Ann White *occupational health nurse, educator*
Hashmi, Sajjad Ahmad *finance educator, dean*
Miller, Cory D. *science educator*
Mosca-Focht, Marlene *biology professor*
Price, Edgar Hilleary, Jr. *manufacturing executive, consultant*
Ruffner, Courtney Judith *literature and language professor*
Rutstein, Stanley Harold *apparel retailing company executive*
Seavers, Dean S. *security firm executive*
Shapiro, Richard Michael *lawyer*
Stewart, Priscilla Ann Mabie *art historian, educator*
Vereb, Teresa B. *psychiatrist*
White, Dale Andrew *journalist*
Wolf, John M. Jack *adult education seminar consultant*

Brandon
Stephens, Robert David *environmental engineering executive*

Brooksville
Brown-Waite, Virginia (Ginny Brown-Waite) *United States Representative from Florida*
Cario, Jeffrey Peter *lawyer*
Chamberlain, Daniel Robert *retired college president*
McBride, Tamera Shawn Dew *geologist*

Cape Canaveral
Carrick, Frederick Robert *neurologist, researcher*

Cape Coral
Bradley, Jean Irene *elementary school educator*
Burch, Jim *Mayor, Cape Coral, Florida*
Graham, Dorothy E. *elementary school educator*
Hopkins, Lee Bennett *writer, educator*
Martin, Benjamin Gaufman *ophthalmologist*
Stuart, Robert *container manufacturing executive*
Vilardi, Charles Ronald *principal*

Casselberry
Pantuso, Vincent Joseph *food service consultant*

Cedar Key
Starnes, Earl Maxwell *retired urban and regional planner, architect, educator*

Celebration
Johnson, Derrick M. *information technology executive*
Schroeder, James White *retired lawyer*

Clearwater
Bailey, Robin Keith *medical educator*
Baker-Bowens, Helen L. *administrative assistant, genealogy researcher*
Barry, Joyce Alice *dietician, consultant*
Bauwin, Roberta Elizabeth *counselor, director*
Campbell, Martha Etheredge *dean, educator*
Chisholm, William DeWayne *retired contractor*
Crites, Richard Ray *financial planner, finance company executive, investment advisor*
Dutkowsky, Robert M. *computer company executive*
Halsey, Jean Michele *nursing educator*
Howells, Jeffrey P. *computer company executive*
Kiehl, E. Robert *manufacturing executive, consultant*
Knoop, Maggie Pearson *language educator*
Lovik, Eric Gordon *academic administrator, director*
Maxwell, Richard Anthony *retail executive*
Osbourn, Joseph A. *information technology executive*
Peterson, James Robert *engineering psychologist*
Pope, Fred Wallace, Jr. *lawyer*
Raymund, Steven A. *computer company executive*
Sebring, Marjorie Marie Allison *former home furnishings company executive*
Slade, Roy *artist, college president, museum director*
Smith, Marion Pafford *retired avionics company executive*
Spiegel, Colleen *electric power industry executive*
Tragos, George Euripedes *lawyer*
Turley, Stewart *retired retail company executive*
Vetter, David R. *lawyer*
Weidemeyer, Carleton Lloyd *lawyer*

Zinkan, Jeffrey Patrick *real estate analyst*
Zschau, Julius James *lawyer*

Clermont
Ortiz Aponte, Sally *retired literature and language professor*
Sides, I. Ruth S. *retired music educator*

Clewiston
Osceola, Tina *museum director*

Cocoa
Bottesch, James Jonathan *research scientist, director*
Mihai, Florin Marius *language educator*

Cocoa Beach
Quinn, John Collins *publishing executive, editor*
Webb, Garfield *art educator*

Coconut Creek
Ramirez, Monica E. *science educator, dean*
Romero, Dora Y. Marron *language educator*

Coconut Grove
Softness, John *public relations executive*
Stuzin, James M. *plastic surgeon*
Tein, Michael *lawyer*

Cooper City
Kelly, Brian J. *media specialist*
Maugere, Dennis Paul *historian, educator*

Coral Gables
Balzebre, Anthony Francis, Sr. *real estate developer, investor*
Banks, Russell *financial planner, consultant*
Beylin, Andrey *physics professor*
Brandt, Frederic Sheldon *dermatologist*
Brownell, Edwin Rowland *retired banker, civil engineer, land surveyor*
Buell, Rodd Russell *lawyer*
Burini, Sonia Montes de Oca *apparel manufacturing and public relations executive*
Clay, Cynthia Joyce *writer, editor-in-chief*
Coe, Jack Martin *lawyer, consultant*
Cole, Todd Godwin *management consultant transportation*
Dady, Robert Edward *lawyer*
de Graaf, Melissa Jenny *music educator*
Einspruch, Norman Gerald *physicist, engineering educator*
Fitzgerald, John Thomas, Jr. *religious studies educator*
Galang, M. Evelina *literature and language professor*
Giancaspro, James *engineering educator, researcher*
Gould, Taffy *Internet company executive, real estate executive*
Graham, H. Dillon III *lawyer*
Green, Stephanie *lawyer*
Hernandez, Eugenio *lawyer*
Hertz, Arthur Herman *communications executive*
Hirschberg, Joseph Gustav *physicist, educator*
Klock, Joseph Peter, Jr. *lawyer*
Landon, Robert Kirkwood *philanthropist*
Lane, Christina M. *curator, educator*
Leblanc, Roger Maurice *chemistry professor*
Lomonosoff, James Marc *marketing professional*
Lucà-Moretti, Maurizio *research scientist, nutritionist*
Mantell, Murray I. *engineering educator*
Marcelin, Louis Herns *sociologist, educator*
Matta, Fabio *structural engineer, educator*
Miville, Nina DeCario *management consultant, educator*
Moss, Ambler Holmes, Jr. *lawyer, educator, former ambassador*
Murai, Rene Vicente *lawyer*
Negueruela-Azarola, Eduardo *linguist, educator*
Nunez-Portuondo, Ricardo *investment company executive*
Owens, Michael Howard *otolaryngologist*
Peebles, R. Donahue *real estate company executive*
Perez, Josephine *psychiatrist, educator*
Pérez Damera, Myra M. *lawyer*
Saleh, Anis Nouhad *lawyer*
Sandoval, Arturo *jazz musician*
Shalala, Donna Edna *academic administrator, former United States Secretary of Health and Human Services*
Siegel, Jeanne Hinton *occupational health nurse practitioner, educator*
Spivey, Donald *history professor*
Tien, James M. *dean, engineering educator, consultant*
Van Vliet, Carolyne Marina *physicist, researcher*
Weiner, Morton David *banker, insurance agent*
White, Patricia Denise *dean, law educator*
Wolf, Aizik Loft *neurosurgeon*
Wong, Kau-Fui Vincent *engineering educator, educator*

Coral Springs
Autry, Herman Allen, Sr. *lobbyist, writer, music executive*
Becker, Benjamin *professional tennis player*
Brill, Janet Bond *nutritionist, educator*
Burg, Ralph *art association executive*
Miller, Karl Frederick *insurance professional*
Vasquez, William Leroy *business educator, consultant*

Crawfordville
Brumby, James Remley, III, (Knox Brumby) *retired priest*
Simmons, Sharon Ritchey *counselor*

Crestview
Scott, George Gallmann *accountant*

Dade City
Barnes, Andrew Earl *former newspaper executive*
Brennan, Thomas Emmett *lawyer*
Burdick, Glenn Arthur *physicist, engineering educator*

Dania Beach
Spieler, Richard Earl *oceanographer, educator*

Davie
Abrams, Lendell Arlington *biology professor*
Ambris, Everiste *social worker, educator*
Arena, Paul Thomas *marine biologist, educator*
Branly, Rolando M. *astrophysicist, educator*
Henning, Dan *former professional football coach*
Ireland, Jeff *professional sports team executive*
Kang, Taeheon *dentist*
Lenchus, Joshua David *physician, pharmacist*
Long, Jake *professional football player*
Myers, Debbie *graphics designer, educator*
Obenauf, Steven D. *microbiologist, educator*
Parcells, Bill (Duane Charles Parcells) *professional sports team executive, retired professional football coach*
Pennington, Chad (James Chadwick Pennington) *professional football player*
Porter, Joseph Eugene (Joey Porter) *professional football player*
Richmond, Gail Levin *law educator*
Roddy, Christopher *academic administrator, educator*
Sparano, Tony *professional football coach*
Stackhouse, Daniel J. *science educator*
Taylor, Jason Paul *professional football player*
Upadhiaya, Umesh Chandra *engineer, consultant*
Walkinshaw, Nicole M. *performing arts educator*
Wang, Xiao *language educator*

Daytona Beach
Amick, William Walker *golf course architect*
Atherholt, Wayne David *museum director*
Barker, Robert Osborne (Bob Barker) *mediator, retired educator*
Bower, Roger Harrison *endocrinologist, director*
Bronson, Oswald Perry, Sr. *religious organization administrator, clergyman*
Cardwell, Harold Douglas, Sr. *retired rehabilitation services professional*
Castrale, Nicole *professional golfer*
Creamer, Paula *professional golfer*
Del Rosario, Romeo Rey *lawyer*
Dineen, Martin Kevin *urologist*
Duma, Richard Joseph *epidemiologist, microbiologist, pathologist, physician, researcher, educator*
Duval, Cynthia *art historian, museum administrator, curator, consultant*
Ekpo, Efremfon Frank *physicist, researcher*
Evans, Marsha Johnson *ladies professional golf association commissioner, retired military officer*
France, Brian Z. *sports association executive*
Green, Betty Nielsen *education educator, consultant*
Harris, Christy Franklin *lawyer*
Hartsell, Horace Ed *college president*
Helfrick, Albert Darlington *electronics engineering educator, consultant, department chairman*
Inkster, Juli *professional golfer*
Jang, Jeong *professional golfer*
Kerr, Cristie *professional golfer*
Kim, Mi Hyun *professional golfer*
Kruse, Marylin Lynn *retired language educator*
Libby, Gary Russell *museum director emeritus, writer*
Lincicome, Brittany *professional golfer*
Lynn, Evelyn Joan *state legislator*
Miyazato, Ai *professional golfer*
Neitzke, Eric Karl *lawyer*
Niemann, Judith A. *vocalist, educator*
Ochoa, Lorena *professional golfer*
Pak, Se Ri *professional golfer*
Picott, Jerry Lee, Jr. *music educator*
Poitier, Constance Rena *music specialist, educator*
Prammanasudh, Stacy *professional golfer*
Pressel, Morgan *professional golfer*
Regnier, Nancy Mae *medical educator*
Sanzenbacher, Richard *humanities educator*
Scott, John Brooks *retired research and development company executive*
Seenith, Sivasundaram *mathematician, educator*
Sen, Shukdeb *biology professor*
Smith, Garvin *economics professor*
Steinhauer, Heidi Marie *manufacturing engineer, educator*
Steinhauer, Sherri *professional golfer*
Tribble, Dennis Anthony *pharmaceutical executive*
Tseng, Yani *professional golfer*
Vasilaros, Steven Thomas *lawyer*
Webb, Karrie *professional golfer*
West, Carolyn Christensen *literature and language professor*
Whitworth, Kathrynne Ann *professional golfer*
Wie, Michelle Sung *professional golfer*
Yang, Thomas *electrical engineer, educator*
Zenkovsky, Betty Jean *modern languages educator*
Zurstadt, William John *history professor*

DeLand
King, Camille Tessitore *psychology professor*
Libby, Wendy B. *academic administrator*

Debary
Coble, Alicia Sharon *retired elementary and secondary school educator*

Deerfield Beach
Brown, Colin *automotive executive*
Gambino, S(alvatore) Raymond *lab administrator, educator*
Johnson, Mary Margaret Dickens *governmental and commercial researcher, contract management educator, consultant*
King, Don *boxing promoter*
Laser, Charles, Jr. *oil company executive*
Lenoff, Michele Malka *lawyer*
Martin, Dianna Luise *retired school administrator*
Panitz, Daniel R. *inventor, scientist, composer, psychologist, minister*
Ruga, Wayne *architect*
Schwarz, Susan Bowers Young *piano teacher*
Siegel, Steven L. *finance company executive, consultant*
Solomon, Barry J. *human services administrator, consultant*

Deland
Blais, Michael Roland *retired urologist*
Caccamise, Genevra Louise Ball (Mrs. Alfred E. Caccamise) *retired librarian*
Coolidge, Edwin Channing *chemistry professor*
Dascher, Paul Edward *dean, accounting educator*
Freeman, Ronald Eugene *environmental engineer*
Goldberg, Paul Bernard *gastroenterologist, clinical researcher*
Langston, Paul T. *dean, composer, music educator*
Markham, Reed B. *speech communication professor*
Sharpe, Virginia Deegan *educational consultant*
Wright, Jane Lanier *school librarian*

Delray Beach
Belizon, Avraham *colon and rectal surgeon, researcher*
Charyk, Joseph Vincent *retired satellite telecommunications executive*
Chavin, Walter *biological sciences educator, researcher*
Ehrlich, Geraldine Elizabeth *management consultant*
Ellsweig, Phyllis Leah *retired psychotherapist*
Hardiman, Joseph Raymond *security firm executive*
Hegstrom, William Jean *retired mathematics professor*
Leeds, Susanne *special education educator, writer*
Levinson, Harry *psychologist, educator*
Reichart, Stuart Richard *lawyer*
Richardson, R(oss) Fred(erick) *insurance company executive, consultant*
Rippeteau, Darrel Downing *retired architect*
Rosenfeld, Steven Ira *ophthalmologist*
St. George, Elaine *art educator*
Salsberg, Arthur Philip *publishing executive*
Simon, Albert *retired physicist, engineer, educator*
Smith, Robin Debra *primary school educator*
Sparrow, Kathleen Gail *retired secondary school educator*
Stewart, Patricia Carry *foundation administrator*
Templeton, Chelneca (Chelly Templeton) *education educator*
Zarwyn, Berthold *physicist, consultant*

Deltona
Bondinell, Stephanie *counselor, academic administrator*

Destin
Burns, Jurate *library director*
Deel, Frances Quinn *retired librarian*
Havens, Jason Edward *lawyer*
O'Brien, Gregory Michael St. Lawrence *academic administrator*
Robinson, Wilkes Coleman *retired federal judge*

Doral
Badia, Alejandro *orthopedist*
Brioso-Mesa, Maureen Diane *mental health services professional*
Heuer, Robert Maynard, II, *opera company executive*
Levermore, Monique A. *psychologist, educator*

Dover
Pearson, Walter Donald *editor, columnist*
Scholtes, Linda Marie *elementary school educator*

Dunedin
Klingbiel, Paul Herman *retired information scientist*
O'Dea, J. David *psychologist, educator*
Rosa, Raymond Ulric *retired banker*
Tapley, Earl Mays *retired college dean*

Dunnellon
Dixon, W(illiam) Robert *retired psychologist*

Eagle Lake
Farr, Ausonia Ann *special education educator*

Eglin AFB
Jones, George W. *museum director, military officer*
Vail, Thomas Leighton *military officer*

Elfers
Milana-Panopoulos, Maria *artist, model*

Ellenton
Edson, Herbert Robbins *retired foundation and hospital executive, military officer*

Englewood
McCall, Gene William *conservator, sculptor, artist, furniture designer*
Richard, Edward H. *manufacturing executive, retired municipal official*
Sanders, W(illiam) Eugene, Jr. *retired internist*
Simis, Theodore Luckey *investment banker, information technology executive*
Van Leuven, Robert Joseph *lawyer*

Estero
Brown, Theodore Lawrence *chemistry professor*
Brown, William Robert *trade association administrator, consultant*
Morgan, Dennis Richard *lawyer*
Routh, Donald K(ent) *psychologist, educator*

Eustis
Chorosinski, Eugene Conrad *writer, poet, author*
King, Robert Howard *marketing professional*

Fernandina Beach
Barlow, Anne Louise *pediatrician, medical researcher*
Britt, David Van Buren *retired educational communications executive*
Kurtz, Myers Richard *retired hospital administrator*
Smeeton, Thomas Rooney *government affairs consultant*

Fort Lauderdale
Acosta, Lydia M. *library director*
Adams, Nancy R. *nurse, retired military officer*
Adams, S.C. Chase *lawyer, writer, speaker, radio and television commentator, financial consultant*
Baldanza, Ben (Basil Ben Baldanza) *air transportation executive*
Barre, Steven Craig *lawyer*
Beach, Cecil Prentice *librarian*
Benavides, Sandra *pharmacist, educator*
Bogenschutz, J. David *lawyer*
Bolanos, Michael Templeton *media production executive*
Bunnell, George Eli *lawyer*
Burleigh, A. Peter *ambassador*
Bustamante, Nestor *lawyer*
Cannon, Robert Eugene *library director*
Cantwell, John Walsh *advertising executive*
Carroll, Chris *marketing executive*
Carter-Miller, Jocelyn *educational services company executive, former retail executive*
Carter Pereira, Claudine Renee *forensic specialist*
Cavendish, Kim L. Maher *museum administrator*
Crawford, Claire Cressman *volunteer, educator*
Cuc, Alexandru *psychology professor*
Das, Sudip Kumar *pharmaceutical scientist*
Dressler, Robert A. *lawyer*
Droege, Marcus *medical educator, researcher*
Edmund, Norman Wilson *educational researcher*
Esiobu, Nwadiuto *biotechnologist, educator*
Faraone, Antonio *electronics executive*
Ferrando, Jonathan P. *lawyer, automotive executive*
Fine, Howard Alan *management consultant*
Fischler, Abraham Saul *retired academic administrator, educator*
Fleisher, Jay M. *medical educator*
Franz, William Mathew *lawyer*
Gagnon Blodgett, Michelle Dawn *psychologist*
Galvis, J. Alberto *architect, educator*
Glick, Richard Stephen *internist, rheumatologist*
Goldberg, Alan Joel *lawyer*
Gonzalez, Jose Alejandro, Jr. *federal judge*
Greenberg, Howard *publishing executive*
Gunzburger, Suzanne Nathan *municipal official, social worker*
Haliczer, James Solomon *lawyer*
Hanbury, George Lafayette, II, *academic administrator*
Hargrove, John Russell *lawyer*
Hartley, Bruce A. *psychologist, educator*
Hilburn, Dawn *special education educator*
Hills, John Merrill *educational association administrator, consultant, public relations executive, researcher*
Hinson, Robert William *advertising executive, consultant*
Hirsch, Jeffrey Allan *lawyer*
Huizenga, Wayne (Harry Wayne Huizenga) *entrepreneur, professional sports team owner*
Itkin, Ivan *nuclear scientist, mathematician*
Jackson, Michael J. *automotive retail company executive*
Jarvis, Robert Mark *law educator*
Jotcham, Thomas Denis *marketing communications consultant*
Kjellmark, Eric William, Jr. *management consultant, performing company executive*
Krause, Roy G. *office staffing firm executive*
Kuehne, Benedict P. *lawyer*
Leach, Ralph F. *banker*
LeRoy, Miss Joy *model, apparel designer*
Li, Wei *computer scientist*
Lichtinger, Moises *obstetrician, gynecologist*
Litman, Donna Carol *law educator*
Littman, Marlyn Kemper *information scientist, educator*
Lodwick, Gwilym Savage *radiologist, educator*
Mahan, Mary Hoyle *retired physical educator*
Markus, Robert Michael *retired journalist*
Maroone, Michael E. *automotive executive*
Maucker, Earl Robert *editor, publishing executive*
Meeks, William Herman III *lawyer*
Moss, Stephen Bruce *lawyer*
Muza, Jay Phillip *oceanographer, educator, paleontologist*
Nyce, John Daniel *lawyer*
O'Brien, Patrick T. *lawyer*
O'Connor, James E. *waste management executive*
Parker, Sasha Smilka *medical educator, nurse, consultant*
Picazio, Kim Lowry *lawyer*
Polish, Sheldon S. *lawyer*
Pollinger, Teresita A. *multi-cultural resource educator*
Prosperi, David C. *social sciences educator*
Randi, James (Randall James Hamilton Zwinge) *magician, educator*
Ray, Raymond B. *federal judge*
Rojas, Jesus Jon *health products executive, researcher*
Roush, Robert Warren *electrical engineer, director*
Rubinson, Howard Alan *physician*
Russell, Terrence Joseph *lawyer*
Sanders, Dale R. *lawyer*
Schneider, Ursula Wilfriede *author*
Seiler, Jack P. *Mayor, Ft. Lauderdale, Florida, prosecutor*
Seltzer, Barry S. *federal judge*
Shaw, Andrea Elizabeth *literature and language professor, director*
Shen, Michael Yue-Hua *cardiologist*
Sherr, Brian J. *lawyer*
Shoemaker, William Edward *corporate financial executive*
Short, Michael J. *automotive executive*
Spangler, David Sheridan *composer, director, creative arts educator, writer*
Spungin, Charlotte Isabelle *retired secondary school educator, writer*
Stephan, John *finance educator*
Sullivan, Edward Delano *lawyer, investor*
Thayer, Charles James *investment banker*
Tristano, Antonio Gino *medical researcher*
Turner, Hugh Joseph, Jr. *lawyer*
Uchin, Robert Allen *dean, endodontist*
Velez, Ines *oral pathologist, educator*

Venkatachalam, Kallidaikurichi *biochemist, educator, researcher*
Webster, Ernest Wesley *musician, educator*
West, Allen *retired military officer, civilian military employee*
Whitmore, Douglas Michael *physician*
Williamson, William Paul, Jr. *journalist*
Winner, Paul Kevin *medical educator, researcher*
Wright, Blandin James *lawyer*
Yang, Rou-Ling *entomologist*

Fort Myers

Barbour, William Rinehart, Jr. *retired book publisher*
Beever, James William III *biologist*
Blanchard, Richard Emile, Sr. *retired management services executive, consultant*
Colasurd, Richard Michael *retired lawyer*
Colgate, Doris Eleanor *sailing school owner, administrator*
Curtin, Constance O'Hara *language educator, writer*
Curtin, David Yarrow *chemist, educator*
Danneffel-Mandelkorn, Mary Beth *nursing consultant*
Edmonds, Scott A. *apparel executive*
Fauerbach, Michael *physics professor*
Goodell, Warren Franklin *retired academic administrator*
Gorovoy, Mark S. *physician*
Goyak, Elizabeth Fairbairn *retired public relations executive*
Guo, Dahai *science educator*
Halloran, William Frank *English educator*
Haug, Warren R. *research and development consultant*
Horecker, Bernard Leonard *retired biochemistry professor*
Lamach, Bernard D. *professional engineer, county commissioner*
Lounsbury, David Arthur *protective services official, educator*
Mandelkorn, Robert Marc *ophthalmologist*
Medvecky, Robert Stephen *lawyer*
Meng, Gunter Richard *retired surgeon*
Miller, Kathleen Fairbrother *librarian*
Moeschl, Stanley Francis *electronics and electrical engineer, management consultant*
Rice, J. Jeffrey *lawyer*
Robertson, Mary Amos *mathematics educator*
Sappenfield, Charles Madison *architect, educator*
Schnackenberg, F. Richard *science educator, department chairman*
Schoonover, Jack Ronald *senior judge*
Schwartz, Carl Edward *artist, printmaker*
Stanley, Bruce McLaren, Sr. *lawyer*
Sturgis, Kathy Ann *lawyer*
Taylor, Kenneth Brooks *retired marketing executive*
Tinker, Thomas Eaton *retired headmaster*
Trudnak, Stephen Joseph *landscape architect*
Vavrina, Charles Laurel *art director*
Wendeborn, Richard Donald *retired manufacturing executive*
Wilder, Lynn K. *education educator*

Fort Pierce

Alvarez, Camila *literature and language educator*
Calvert, David Victor *soil science educator*
Conklin, Howard Lawrence *lawyer*
Jefferson, Zanobia Bracy *artist, educator*
McMullian, Anke Hilde *agricultural studies educator*
Pino, Veronica Woodard *humanities educator*
Rice, Mary Esther *biologist*
Schwenger, Wilbur John *mathematics educator*
Swenson, Ada Perez *artist*
Widder, Edith Anne *biologist*

Fort Walton Beach

Hicks, Patricia J. *secondary school educator*
Lord, William *retired electrical engineer*
Moran, Kimberly Dianne *secondary school educator, artist*
Register, Annette Rowan *literature educator*
Williams, Bethtina Qubré *minister*

Gainesville

Acholonu, Wilfred W., Jr. *clinical pharmacy specialist, educator*
Agresti, Alan *statistics educator*
Anderson, Timothy J. *chemical engineering distinguished professor*
Babb, Florence Evelyn *anthropologist, educator*
Baigorria, Guillermo Antonio *meteorologist, researcher*
Balabanian, Norman *electrical engineering educator*
Barber, Charles Edward *publishing executive, journalist*
Batich, Christopher David *biomedical engineer, educator*
Baz, Maher Afif *internist, educator, medical director lung transplant program*
Behnke, Marylou *pediatrician, educator*
Berns, Kenneth Ira *physician*
Besch, Emerson Louis *physiologist, educator, retired dean*
Blanch, Paul Bradford *biomedical engineer, researcher*
Boothroyd, Herbert J. *insurance company executive*
Boyes, Patrice Flinchbaugh *lawyer*
Briggs-Simmons, Karen Elaine *bankruptcy firm executive*
Brown, Myra Suzanne *university librarian*
Brown, William Samuel, Jr. *communication sciences and disorders educator*
Bryan, Robert Armistead *academic administrator, educator*
Bullivant, Keith *modern German literature educator*
Butler, Amanda *women's college basketball coach*
Bzoch, Kenneth Rudolph *speech and language educator, department chairman*
Cabrera, Victor Elias *environmental engineer, researcher*
Cantliffe, Daniel James *horticulture educator*
Capehart, Barney Lee *industrial and systems engineer, educator*
Carlson, David Edward *jounalism educator, journalist, consultant*
Chambers, Robert Hunter III *academic administrator, consultant, historian, educator*
Chiara, Toni *physical therapist*
Conrad, Joseph Henry *animal nutrition educator*
Conway, M. Margaret *political science professor, consultant*
Copeland, Edward Meadors III *surgeon, educator*
Courtenay, Walter Rowe, Jr. *biology professor, researcher*
Cousins, Robert John *nutritional biochemist, educator*
Criser, Marshall M. *lawyer, retired academic administrator*
Cristescu, Nicolaie Dan *engineering educator*
Curta, Florin *historian, educator*
Czarnecka-Verner, Eva *molecular biologist, educator*
Dahlgren, Robert Lawrence *social studies educator*
Delfino, Joseph John *environmental engineering sciences educator*
Denardo, Scott Jeffrey *cardiologist*
DesForges, Deborah Waln *music educator*
Dewsbury, Donald Allen *psychologist*
Dharnidharka, Vikas R. *pediatrician*
Dilcher, David Leonard *paleobotany educator, researcher*
Dinculeanu, Nicolae *mathematician, educator*
Dolan, Teresa A. *dean, educator, researcher*
Donovan, Billy (William John) *men's college basketball coach*
Dougherty, Molly Crocker *nursing educator, researcher*
Drago, Valeria *neurologist, researcher*
Drummond, Willa Hendricks *neonatologist, educator, information technology executive*
Dunn, William A., Jr. *cell biologist, educator*
Favini, Paul Furey *costume designer, educator*
Forrester, Sheila Mary *music educator, composer*
Forsmark, Chris E. *medical educator*
Fossum, Jerry George *electrical engineering educator*
Freund, Gerhard *retired medical educator*
Gentry, Robert Bryan *humanities educator, writer*
Gets, Lispbeth Ella *retired educational administrator*
Good, Michael Lowell *anesthesiologist, educator, dean*
Greer, Melvin *medical educator*
Gridley, Kelly Elizabeth *biotechnologist, researcher*
Grobman, Arnold Brams *retired biology educator, academic administrator*
Hahn, David Worthington *engineering educator*
Hanrahan, Robert Joseph *chemist, educator*
Harrison, Faye Venetia *anthropologist, educator, writer*
Heflin, Martin Ganier *diplomat, political scientist*
Heilman, Kenneth Martin *neurologist, educator*
Herzog, Roland W. *medical educator*
Hiers, Richard Hyde *lawyer, educator, writer*
Hollien, Harry Francis *communications engineer*
Hornberger, Robert Howard *retired psychologist*
Hoy, Marjorie Ann *entomology educator*
Hozic, Aida Arfan *political science professor*
Huang, Emina Hui-na *surgeon, educator*
Hulvey, S. Yumiko *literature educator*
Isaacs, Gerald William *retired agricultural engineering educator, consultant*
Jaeger, Ina Claire *music educator, violinist*
Jarzen, David MacArthur *research scientist*
Jerry, Robert Howard, II, *dean, law educator*
Jia, Huanguang *health scientist, researcher*
Jin, Bumsub *researcher*
Keesling, James Edgar *mathematics professor*
Kelly, Kathleen S(ue) *communications educator*
Khargonekar, Pramod Prabhakar *engineering educator*
Kirkland, Nancy Childs *secondary school educator, consultant*
Kraft, John *dean, management educator*
Krohn, Marvin D. *dean, educator*
Kumar, Pradeep *physics professor, researcher*
Kurzweg, Ulrich Hermann *engineering science educator*
Kushner, David Zakeri *musicologist*
Law, Mark Edward *electrical engineer, educator*
LeVeen, Robert Frederick *radiologist*
LeVine, Ann Marie *medical educator, director*
Levy, Julie Kay *veterinarian, educator*
Lin, Jenshan *engineering educator*
Liner, James *literature and language professor*
Link, William Allen *history educator*
Lowe, John Thomas, Jr. *church and concert musician*
Lowenstein, Ralph Lynn *university dean emeritus*
Lundgren, Tord *dental educator, researcher*
Lynn, Romrell John *medical educator*
Machen, James Bernard *academic administrator*
Magnusson, Ingvar *periodontist, educator*
Mann, Rajinder *entomologist, researcher*
Maple, Marilyn Jean *educational media coordinator*
Marshall, Kevin A. *director*
Maurer, Virginia Gallaher *law educator*
Mazzaferri, Ernest Louis *endocrinologist, educator*
Merz, Kenneth M., Jr. *chemistry professor*
Meyer, Urban *college football coach*
Micha, David Allan *chemistry and physics professor*
Milanich, Jerald Thomas *archaeologist, writer, curator*
Mills, Jon *dean emeritus, law educator*
Mitchell, William John *mathematics educator*
Modell, Jerome Herbert *anesthesiologist, educator*
Moore, John Hartwell *anthropology educator, consultant*
Mubarak, Kamal K. *pulmonologist, intensivist*
Nagy, Rebecca Martin *museum director*
Nair, Ramachandran P.K. *agroforestry educator, researcher*
Neiberger, Richard Eugene *pediatrician, nephrologist, educator*
Neims, Allen Howard *pediatrician, educator, dean, researcher*
New, Melvyn *retired literature and language professor*
Nguyen, Ru *entomologist*
Nicoletti, Paul Lee *retired veterinarian, educator*
O, Kenneth Kyongyop *engineering educator*
O'Donnell, Bernard Joseph, Jr. *lawyer*
Ohrn, Nils Yngve *chemistry and physics educator*
Oliver, Robert Bruce *retired investment company executive*
Oppenheimer, David Gray *botanist, educator*
Oren, Ido *political science professor*
Parker, Karen F. *sociology educator*
Patre, Parag *research scientist*
Paul, Ouida Fay *music educator*
Peck, Merton Joseph *economist, educator*
Pepine, Carl John *physician, educator*
Pereira, Roberto M. *entomologist*
Perry, Vernon G. *research scientist, educator*
Peters, Jorg *professor*
Pfaff, William Wallace *medical educator*
Phillips, Winfred Marshall *academic administrator, professor, mechanical engineer*
Pleasants, Julian McIver *history educator, summer school director*
Portier, Kenneth Michael *statistics educator*
Price, Mary Kathleen *law librarian, educator*
Probert, Walter *retired law educator*
Puckett, Ruby Parker *food service executive, writer, dietician*
Purcifull, Dan Elwood *retired plant virologist, educator*
Quesenberry, Kenneth Hays *agronomy educator*
Resnick Carswell, Sarah Jacqueline *registrar*
Rhoton, Albert Loren, Jr. *neurosurgeon, educator*
Riffee, William H. *dean, pharmacy educator*
Rosser, Charles J. *chemistry professor*
Rowland, Neil E. *psychology professor, department chairman*
Roy Choudhury, Kaushik *materials scientist*
Rubin, Melvin Lynne *ophthalmologist, educator*
Russell, Judith *librarian, dean*
Sabin, John Rogers *physics professor*
Sah, Chih-Tang *electrical and computer engineering educator*
Samuels, Warren Joseph *retired economics professor*
Saucerman, Alvera Adeline *elementary school educator*
Schelske, Claire L. *limnologist, educator*
Schmidt-Nielsen, Bodil Mimi (Mrs. Roger G. Chagnon) *retired physiologist, educator*
Schmitz, Andrew *agricultural studies educator*
Seale, James Lawrence, Jr. *agricultural studies educator, trade association administrator, researcher*
Selmore, Dametria Suzanne *actor*
Shabana, Yasser M. *plant pathologist professor, research scientist*
Shanklin, Douglas Radford *physician*
Sherif, S. A. *engineering educator*
Shugan, Steven Mark *finance educator*
Silva, Julie *social sciences educator*
Silverstein, Janet Hope *pediatrician, educator*
Singley, John Edward, Jr. *retired environmental scientist, consultant*
Slavickas, Rimas Anthony *electrical engineer, educator, researcher*
Small, Parker Adams, Jr. *pediatrician, educator*
Smith, David Thornton *lawyer, educator*
Smith, Haywood Clark, Jr. *astronomer, educator*
Smith, Matthew Denman *ecologist*
So, Franky *engineering educator*
Somma, Louis A. *biologist*
Spreen, Thomas H. *agricultural studies educator*
Stall, William M. *weed scientist, educator*
Stehouwer, Donald J. *neuroscientist*
Suzuki, Howard Kazuro *retired anatomist, educator*
Tebow, Tim (Timothy Richard Tebow) *student athlete*
Teitelbaum, Philip *psychologist*
Teixeira, Arthur Alves *food engineer, educator, consultant*
Thomas-Houston, Marilyn Miller *anthropologist, educator*
Thompson, John Griggs *mathematician*
Thorn, Charles Behan *physics professor*
Thrall, Grant Ian *geography educator, software developer-consultant*
Tisher, Charles Craig *nephrologist, educator, former dean*
Tonelli, Adriano R. *cardiologist*
Toskes, Phillip Paul *gastroenterologist, educator, researcher*
Tuli, Sonal *medical educator*
Tumlinson, James H. III *agriculturist*
Uhrig, Robert Eugene *nuclear engineer, educator*
Ulanowicz, Robert Edward *science educator*
Ulmer, Gregory Leland *literature and language professor*
Uryasev, Stan *science educator*
Valladares, Maria Elena *language educator*
Van Alstyne, W. Scott, Jr. *lawyer, educator*
Verstegen, John P.L. *theriogenologist, educator*
Viessman, Warren, Jr. *professor emeritus*
Vincent, Heather Ketelaar *physiologist, educator*
Vincent, Kevin Robert *physician, educator*
von Mering, Otto Oswald *anthropology educator*
Wachsman, Eric D. *engineering educator*
Wagner, Mary *medical educator*
Walsh, Katherine Jean *physician*
West-Olatunji, Cirecie *science educator*
Wharton, Arthur Emrie *pharmacist, director*
Wheat, Myron William, Jr. *cardiothoracic surgeon*
Wheeler, Bruce C. *engineering educator*
Wing, Elizabeth Schwarz *museum curator, educator*
Wingard, John Reid *medical educator*
Yamamoto, Janet Kazuko *science educator*
York, E. Travis *retired academic administrator*
York, Vermelle Cardwell *retired real estate broker and developer*
Yu, Simon Shyi-Jian *entomologist, educator*
Yuan, Zhen *biomedical researcher*
Zhou, YiLi *physician*

Gonzalez

Plischke, Le Moyne Wilfred *chemist, researcher*

Graceville

Kinchen, Thomas Alexander *college president*

Gulf Breeze

French, Jere Stuart *landscape architect*
Menzer, Robert Everett *retired toxicologist, educator*

Gulfport

Carroll, Charles Michael *music educator*

Haines City

Clement, Robert William *retired air force officer*

Hallandale

Braverman, Stanley Deems *ophthalmologist*
Vaserstein, Ludmila *music educator*

Hallandale Beach

Duffy, Earl Gavin *hotel executive*
Geller, Bunny Zelda *poet, writer, publisher, sculptor, artist*

Harbour Heights

Nash, Ruth S. *foundation administrator*

Heathrow

Argirion, Michael *editor*
Darbelnet, Robert Louis *automobile association executive*

Hernando

Keyser, Frank Ray, Jr. *lawyer, Former Governor, Vermont*
Manhold, John Henry *dental educator, consultant*

Hialeah

Arrarás, Maria Celeste *newscaster, journalist*
Browne, Donald Victor *broadcast executive*
Gallego, Jose Miguel *special education educator*
Laffitte-Reguera, Mary E. *finance executive*
Lester, Timothy M. *music educator, vocalist*
Robaina, Julio *mayor, state representative*
Sosa, Jorge Luis *surgeon*

Highland Beach

Frager, Albert S. *retired food products executive*
Upbin, Hal J. *consumer products company executive*

Hillsboro Beach

Marshall, Jo Taylor *social worker*
O'Connell, Richard (James) *English literature educator, poet*

Hobe Sound

Casey, Edward Paul *manufacturing executive*
Caspersen, Finn Michael Westby *diversified financial services company executive*
Houser, Constance W. (Connie Houser) *writer, artist*
Mark, Marsha Yvonne Ismailoff *artistic director*
Markoe, Frank, Jr. *lawyer, health facility administrator*
Parker, H. Lawrence *retired investor, rancher, investment banker*

Holiday

Peterson, George Folke *retired insurance company executive, writer*

Hollywood

Barnes, Gregory *media specialist, educator*
Clark, Deborah A. *secondary school educator*
Constantinescu, Alex R. *pediatrician, nephrologist*
Duffner, Lee R. *ophthalmologist*
Gonzalez, Fredi *professional baseball manager*
Isenberg, Abraham Charles *shoe manufacturing company executive*
Lutchman, Eva *middle school educator*
Moore, Victoria *artist*
Phillips, Gary Stephen *lawyer*
Rogovin, Lawrence H. *lawyer*
Scott, Mimi Koblenz *psychotherapist, actress, journalist, playwright*
Sofman, Michael S. *dermatologist*
Sundel, Martin *management consultant, psychologist, educator*

Holmes Beach

Dunne, Nancy Anne *retired social services administrator*
Kaiser, Albert Farr *manufacturing executive*

Homestead

Ireland, Patricia *lawyer*
Roberts, Larry Spurgeon *biological science educator, zoologist*
Willner, Eugene Burton *food and liquor company executive*

Howey In The Hills

Jeppesen, Richard Ferrill *real estate developer*

Hurlburt Field

Wurster, Donald C. *career military officer*

Hutchinson Island

Welch, Martha Lynn *environmentalist, educator*

Hypoluxo

DeBow, Jay Howard Camden *public relations executive*

Indialantic

Pavlakos, Ellen Tsatiri *sculptor*
Preece, Betty P. *electrical engineer, educator*
Scrivener, Lois Doing *retired principal, educator*

Indian Harbor Beach

Scanlon, Charles Francis *retired military officer, writer, publisher*

Indian River Shores

Wiegner, Edward Alex *financial and energy executive*

Indian Rocks Beach

DeLucia, Gene Anthony *government administrator, computer company executive*

Inverness
Barrow, Sally Settle *retired media specialist, librarian*
Crouse, John Oliver, II, *journalist, publisher*
Holland, Brett *psychologist*

Islamorada
Gates, Richard Daniel *retired manufacturing executive*

Jacksonville
Adams, Scott Leslie *accountant*
Aldana, Philipp Roque *neurosurgeon*
Aleschus, Justine Lawrence *retired real estate broker*
Ansbacher, Barry Barnett *lawyer*
Anthony, Yancey Lamar *minister*
Appel, Laurence Bruce *lawyer, retail executive*
Armitage, Faye *medical researcher*
Barrett, J. Lynn *literature and language professor*
Beattie, Donald A. *aerospace scientist, consultant*
Berquist, Thomas H. *radiologist, educator*
Beytagh, Francis X. *law educator*
Bickett, Brent B. *insurance company executive*
Bishop, William *Councilman*
Bodkin, Lawrence Edward *inventor, essayist, research and development company executive, consultant*
Bosworth, William Posey *physician, physical education educator*
Boyer, Tyrie Alvis *lawyer*
Bradford, Dana Gibson, II, *lawyer*
Brown, Reginald L. *Councilman*
Bryan, Joseph Shepard, Jr. *lawyer*
Bullock, Bruce Stanley *lawyer, mediator*
Cagle, Margaret Broughton *retired parochial school educator*
Carpenter, JoAnn Deakin *history professor*
Cavendish, Michael Robert *lawyer*
Chambers, Jack Allen *application developer, educator*
Chen, Lei-Shih *healthcare educator*
Cheshire, William Polk, Jr. *neurologist*
Clark, Richard *Councilman*
Clarke, Joseph Calvitt III *retired history professor*
Clarkson, Charles Andrew *real estate investment executive*
Cobb, James E. *lawyer*
Coker, Howard Coleman *lawyer*
Commander, Charles Edward *lawyer, real estate consultant*
Corrigan, Michael *Councilman*
Coxe, Henry M. III *lawyer*
Craft, Mary Faye *public relations executive, consultant, television producer*
Crescimbeni, John R. *Councilman*
David, Thompson Stuart *religious studies educator*
Davis, Craig Anderson *school system administrator, educator*
Davis, Daniel *Councilman*
Davis, Fred *journalist, educator*
Delaney, John Adrian *academic administrator*
Delaney, Kevin Francis *retired military officer, consultant*
Del Rio, Jack *professional football coach, former professional football player*
Edwards, Fred Hayden *cardiologist*
Edwards, Marvin Raymond *investment counselor, economical consultant*
Ejimofor, Cornelius Ogu *political scientist, educator*
Elsafty, Adel *engineering educator*
Erasmus, David B. *pulmonologist, consultant*
Evens, Ronald Paul *biotechnologist, consultant*
Farnell, Robert Henry, II, *lawyer*
Fernandez, Ileana Barbara *musician, educator*
Fisak, Brian *psychology professor*
Fitzsimmons, Ellen Marie *lawyer*
Foley, William Patrick, II, *insurance company executive*
Folk, David Wilbur *occupational health and safety administrator*
Fussell, Ronnie *Councilman*
Gabel, George DeSaussure, Jr. *lawyer*
Gaffney, Johnny A.
Galeone, Victor Benito *bishop*
Gerkens, Henry H. *trucking executive*
Godfrey, John Munro economic *consultant*
Graham, Arthur (Art) *Councilman*
Halil, Susan Terrell *dental hygienist*
Hartman, Frederick Cooper *retired biochemist*
Hartmann, Frederick William *newspaper editor*
Hill, James Clinkscales *federal judge*
Holt, Ray *Councilman*
Holt, Torry *professional football player*
Homsley, Denise Louise *music educator*
Howard, Marcia Morales *federal judge*
Hughes, Carolyn Wright *elementary school educator, director*
Hyde, Kevin *Councilman*
Israel, Kimberly Held *lawyer*
Jaffe, Barbara Gefen *finance company executive*
Jamrich, John Xavier *retired university administrator*
Johnson, Glorious J. *Councilwoman*
Jones, David Marshall *school librarian, director*
Jones, Warren A. *Councilman*
Jones-Drew, Maurice Christopher *professional football player*
Joost, Stephen C. *Councilman*
Jordan, Deborah Ann *theater educator, director*
Kelso, Linda Yayoi *lawyer*
Kennedy, Lee A. *financial services company executive*
Kent, John Bradford *lawyer*
Khan, Marty Z. *academic administrator*
Killea, Michael F. *lawyer*
Kinne, Frances Bartlett *academic administrator*
Kneller, Michael K. *transportation services executive*
Kusumoto, Fred *cardiologist, director*
Lange, Lori Jean *science professor, researcher*
Lee, E. Denise *Councilwoman*
Lee, Hwa-Wei *librarian, educator, consultant*
Lehmbeck, John Pierce *journalist, writer*
Leissring, Malcolm Arthur *neuroscientist, educator*
Lynch, Peter L. *retail executive*
Lyon, Wilford Charles, Jr. *insurance executive*
Mack, Jeannette Ana *medical technician*
Mai, Martin *nephrologist, consultant*
Main, Edna Dewey (June Main) *education educator*
Main, James L. *lawyer*
Mass, Myron Frank *allergist, immunologist*
Mazur, John M. *orthopedist, educator*
McBurney, Charles Walker, Jr. *state representative, lawyer*
McCarthy, Daniel Anthony *biology professor*
Mc Carthy, Edward, Jr. *retired lawyer*
McGovern, Jay *aeronautical engineer, consultant*
McKinney, James Clayton *electronics executive, electrical engineer*
Melton, Howell Webster, Sr. *federal judge*
Mendoza, William A. *physics professor*
Milton, Joseph Payne *lawyer*
Monsky, John Bertrand *investment company executive*
Mooradian, Arshag Dertad *internist, educator*
Moreno-Aspitia, Alvaro *physician, researcher*
Morgan, William Newton *architect, educator*
Moseley, James Francis *lawyer*
Mueller, Edward Albert *retired transportation engineer*
Munoz, Oscar *corporate financial executive*
Nussbaum, Bennett L. *food products executive*
Nussbaum, Michael Scot *physician, medical educator*
Olin, Marilyn *secondary school educator*
Olney, Robert Caldwell *pediatrician, researcher*
Osborn, Marvin Griffing, Jr. *educational consultant*
Otto, Elizabeth Hall *education educator*
Page, Willis *conductor*
Parmelee, John H. *communications educator*
Payne, Timothy D. *information technology executive*
Pelton, Margaret Marie Miller *retired art educator, academic administrator, artist*
Peter, Jack E. *museum administrator*
Portell, Keith S *application developer, consultant*
Pratt-Dannals, Ed *school system administrator*
Quirk, Raymond R. (Randy Quirk) *insurance company executive*
Radisky, Derek Charles *biomedical researcher, educator*
Reams-Johnson, Ansa *history professor*
Redman, Don *Councilman*
Reid, William Hill *mathematics professor*
Rinaman, James Curtis, Jr. *lawyer*
Rine, Rose Marie *physical therapist, educator*
Rogers, Linda L. *middle school educator*
Rood, John Darrell *real estate developer, former ambassador*
Sadowski, Peter T. *lawyer*
Sands, Michael Lee *infectious diseases physician*
Scanlon, George Patrick *transportation services executive, accountant*
ScarborougH, Marion Nichols *nutritionist, recreational facility executive*
Schlesinger, Harvey Erwin *judge*
Schultz, Frederick Henry *investor, former government official*
Scott, Kamela Koon *psychologist, educator*
Shad, Arthur (Art) *councilman*
Sheppard, William J. *lawyer*
Sheridan, Alice Virginia *photographer, educator*
Shula, Mike (Michael John Shula) *professional football coach, former college football coach*
Sifford, Charlie (Charles Luther Sifford) *professional golfer*
Siragusa, Daniel *radiologist, educator*
Smith, David A. *medical services executive*
Smith, Gene *professional sports team executive*
Snyder, John Joseph *bishop emeritus*
Stanley, Helen Camille *composer, musician*
Stein, Keith Lance *health system administrator*
Stewart, Sandra Kay *music educator*
Stinson, Alan Lynn *insurance company executive*
Talley, Nicholas Joseph *medical educator, research scientist, physician*
Tjoflat, Gerald Bard *federal judge*
Tomlinson, William Holmes *management educator, retired military officer*
Tripodi, Tony *retired social worker, dean, editor, writer*
Vane, Terence G., Jr. *finance company executive, lawyer*
Vasana, Susan (Chun-Ye) *engineering educator*
Vincent, Norman Fuller *broadcast executive*
Ward, Michael J. *rail transportation executive*
Weaver, Dianne Jay *lawyer*
Webb, Jack D. *Councilman*
White, Edward Alfred *lawyer*
Woodward, Timothy Andre *gastroenterologist*
Yarborough, Clay *Councilman*

Jacksonville Beach
Mahorner, James G. *lawyer*
McWilliams, John Lawrence III *lawyer*
Saltzman, Irene Cameron *consumer products company executive*

Jasper
Rehberg, Shirley M. *literature and language professor*

Jensen Beach
Dahn, Conney Colley *special education educator*
Lowrie, Jean Elizabeth *librarian, educator*
Peterson, David Frederick *retired government agency administrator*
Skrupky, Elaine Charlotte *art educator*

Juno Beach
Hay, Lewis III *utilities executive*
Knapp, George M. *lawyer*
Litchfield, R. Wade *energy executive*
Nelson, Bruce (Murray Bruce Nelson) *former consumer products company executive*
Robo, James L. *utilities executive*
Tancer, Edward F. *lawyer, utilities executive*
Terwillegar, Jane Cusack *retired librarian, educator*

Jupiter
Baum, Herbert Merrill *consumer products company executive*
Click, David Forrest *lawyer, investment advisor*
Ernst, Calvin Bradley *retired vascular surgery educator*
Eskandarian, Edward *advertising executive*
Feinberg, Herbert *wine company executive*
Garfinkel, Harmon Mark *retired specialty chemicals company executive*
Gerson, Irwin Conrad *advertising executive*
Jacobson, Jerry Irving *biophysicist, theoretical physicist, medical researcher*
Lasmezas, Corinne Ida *neuroscientist, researcher*
Migliaro, Marco William *electrical engineer*
Philippe, Bois Roger Jean *science educator, researcher*
Solomon, Stephen L. *lawyer*
Vanatta, Bob *athletic administrator*
Vazquez, Miguel Angel *literature and language professor*
Weissmann, Charles *molecular biologist, educator*
Wolff, Edward Alvin *electronics engineer*
Zelnick, Ronald Stuart *surgeon*

Kennedy Space Center
Amador, José Jorge *computer engineer, researcher*

Key Biscayne
Cardozo, Arlene Rossen *writer*
Cardozo, Richard Nunez *marketing professional, educator, entrepreneur*
de la Cruz, Carlos *wholesale distribution executive*
de la Cruz, Rosa *art collector*
Evans, Peter Kenneth *advertising executive*
Klarreich, Sue Friedman *education administrator, consultant*
Loisel, Gerard Roland *marine biologist, educator*
Pope, John Edwin *editor, columnist*
Ross, Marilyn J. *language and communications educator*

Key Largo
Daenzer, Bernard John *insurance company executive, consultant*
Hawkins, Frank Nelson, Jr. *investor relations consultant, writer*
Lynn, James Thomas *insurance company executive, lawyer, former United States Secretary of Housing and Urban Development*
Mattson, James Stewart *lawyer, environmental scientist, educator*

Key West
Klimowich, Edward John *architecture educator*
MacDougall, Peter *retired lawyer*
Mathews, Harry Burchell *poet, writer, educator*
McIntosh, Jon Charles *illustrator, graphics designer, painter*

Keystone Heights
Ohanian, Mihran Jacob *nuclear engineer, educator, dean, researcher*

Kissimmee
Gowda, Narasimhan Ramaiah *financial consultant*
Haynes, Ulric St. Clair, Jr. *retired dean*
McCann, Jean Friedrichs *artist, educator*
Roberds, Richard Mack *professor emeritus*
Schonauer, Lisa Lynn *music educator*
Severance, Jeri-Lynne White *elementary school educator*
Spears, Glenna Ellen *psychologist*

Lady Lake
Akins, Zane Vernon *agricultural products executive*
Granger, Robert Alan *mechanical and aerospace engineering educator*
Langevin, Thomas Harvey *retired educational association administrator, consultant*
Pflum, William John *retired physician*

Lake Alfred
Kender, Walter John *horticulturist, educator*
Nageswara Rao, Madhugiri *research scientist*

Lake Buena Vista
Biggar, Jim (James Biggar) *hotel executive*
Garfield, Randy Alan *marketing executive*

Lake City
Cummings, Charles Michael *finance educator*
Gay, John Marion *retired federal agency administrator, financial analyst*
Irwin, Byron *management executive*

Lake Helen
Finn, Stephen Martin *media producer, venture capitalist*

Lake Mary
Bachmann, Bill *photographer*
DiPaolo, Peter Thomas *engineering executive, educator*
Koser, Gary Richard *civil engineer*
Silver, Elaine Terry *lawyer*
Strang, Stephen Edward *editor*
Swonger, Thomas K. H., Jr. *insurance company executive*

Lake Placid
Adams, Herbert Ryan *publishing executive, retired minister*

Lake Suzy
Ogan, Russell Griffith *real estate broker*

Lake Wales
Connor, John Thomas, Jr. *portfolio manager*
Luing, Gary Alan *financial management educator*
Mc Call, Julien Lachicotte *banker*

Lake Worth
Asher, Kathleen May *communications educator*
Carlisle, Ervin Frederick *university provost, educator*
Heessel, Eleanor Lucille Lea *retired state agency administrator*
Liang, Lee Z. *biology professor*
Ramos, Carlos F. *physics educator*
Rudayeva, Yelena *biology educator*
Saffir, Leonard *public relations executive*
Willis, Clayton *broadcaster, government official, educator, arts consultant*
Wilson, William J. *language educator*

Lakeland
Attaway, John A., Jr. *lawyer*
Barnett, Hoyt R. (Barney Hoyt) *supermarket company executive*
Bawek, Paul D. *theater educator, director, actor*
Chapman, Angela Marie *science educator*
Cooper, James Russell *retired law educator*
Cotton, Rickey Allen *literature and language professor, department chairman*
Crutchfield, Drucella *language educator*
Davis, Joseph H. *theology studies educator*
Fettke, Steven M. *religious studies educator*
Garrott, Frances Carolyn *architectural engineer*
Giles, Barbara M. *political science professor*
Grossman, David Alan *finance educator*
Hatten, William Seward *manufacturing executive, consultant*
Jacobson, Barbara Dinger *music educator*
Jenkins, Howard M. *supermarket executive*
Jones, Todd *retail executive*
Kottke, Bruce A. *internist*
MacDonald, Susan Priest *media specialist, writer*
Mahr, Aaron Lee *government agency administrator*
Mallison, Craig T. *research scientist*
Meads, Walter Frederick *communications executive, consultant, writer*
Moseley, Lisa Lent *counseling administrator*
Mutz, Oscar Ulysses *manufacturing and distribution executive*
Phillips, David P. *grocery company executive*
Reich, David Lee *library director*
Rogers, James Gordon, Jr. *art educator*
Sheppard, Albert Parker, Jr. *retired computer science educator*
Stark, Bruce Gunsten *artist*
Stetson, Daniel Everett *museum director*
Taylor, Cheryl Meagan *pre-school administrator*
Washington, Gloria Dunn *secondary school educator*
Wendel, John Fredric *lawyer, consultant*

Lakewood Ranch
Domonkos, Leslie S. *history professor, researcher*
Fetterman, James Charles *lawyer*
Piper, Mark Harry *retired banker*

Land O Lakes
Loewe, Barbara *speech educator, theater educator, humanities educator*
McGrew, Kelly Calhoun *training services executive, systems engineer*
O'Connell, Carmela Digristina *appraisal executive, consultant*
Wilkinson, Denise V. *psychologist*

Largo
Brown, Warren Joseph *physician*
Bush, Debra W. *occupational health nurse*
Grove, Jeffrey Scott *family practice physician*
Hamlin, Robert Henry *public health service officer, educator, management consultant*
Hasen-Sinz, Susan Katherine *state agency administrator, actress*
Hult, Catherine Day *lawyer*
Inserra, Lisa *radio producer, educator*
Krolick, Merrill A. *cardiologist*
Ristow, George Edward *neurologist, educator*
Seidel, Richard L. *artist*
Shillinglaw, Gordon *retired finance educator*
Stover, Brian Allan *advertising executive, marketing professional*

Lauderdale By The Sea
Kennedy, Beverly (Kleban) Burris *financial advisor, television and radio personality*
Wynne, Brian James *retired professional society administrator*

Lecanto
Goss, Richard Henry *lawyer*
Wheatley, Deborah A. *music educator*

Leesburg
Austin, Robert Eugene, Jr. *lawyer*
Fechtel, Vincent John *legal administrator*
Genzen, Gary Carl *retired minister*
Greata, Joanne Dixon *educational consultant*
Jones, Marcia Lynn *meteorologist, educator*
Moore, Wistar *cardiovascular surgeon*
Morse, Barbara Jeanne *library director*
Osborne, Glenna Jean *health facility administrator*

Lighthouse Point
Gauthier, Doreen Ann *librarian*
Hampares, Katherine James *retired foreign language educator*

Lithia
Kulkarni, Kavita-Vibha Arun *chemist*
Richmond, Nancy Mason *retired state agency administrator*

Longboat Key
Dalgleish, Stuart McNaught *retired manufacturing executive*
Dorsey, Eugene Carroll *former foundation and communications executive*
Hazan, Marcella Maddalena *writer, educator, consultant*
Howell, Robert S. *retired pathologist*
McCollough, Newton Clark III *orthopaedic surgeon*
Morse, Marvin Henry *retired judge*
Stapleton, Harvey James *physics professor*

Longwood
Bernabei, Raymond *management consultant*
Campbell, David A. *secondary school educator*

Cirello, John *utility and engineering company executive*
Gasperoni, Emil, Sr. *realtor, real estate developer*
Smyth, Joseph Patrick *retired military officer, physician*
Tomasulo, Virginia Merrills *retired lawyer*

Loxahatchee
Russell-Tyson, Pearl Leonie *elementary school educator*
Wisnicki, Jeffrey Leonard *plastic surgeon*

Lutz
Corbitt, Doris Orene *retired real estate agent, dietician*
Cualing, Hernani Del Mundo *physician, researcher*
Ellis, Leslie Elaine *psychotherapist*
Kolb, Richard Maurice *sports writer, sportscaster*
Miller, Bonnie Sewell *marketing professional, writer*
Wester, J. Meredith *lawyer*

Madison
Hiss, Sheila Mary *librarian*
Molnar, Greg Robert *science educator*
Paulk, David Mitchell, II, *religious studies educator*

Maitland
DeWahl, Duncan Comrie *stockbroker*
Nelson, Stephen D. *music educator*
Wilder, Charles David *lawyer*

Marathon
Wiecha, Joseph Augustine *language educator*

Marco Island
Cooper, Thomas Astley *bank executive*
Guerrant, David Edward *retired food company executive*
Kelly, Robert Donald *management consultant*
Kerstetter, Wayne Arthur *law educator*
Moore, Faye Halfacre *jewelry manufacturer*
Sundberg, Ruth Dorothy *hematologist, educator*

Marianna
Dunkle, J. Robert *humanities educator*

Melbourne
Banerjee, Bonny *computer scientist*
Barua, Dilip Kumar *engineer educator*
Brown, Seymour R. *retired lawyer*
Buchanan, Richard Kent *electronics company executive*
Bush, Mark Bennett *ecologist, educator*
Cacciatore, S. Sammy *lawyer*
Catanese, Anthony James *academic administrator*
Cavallucci, Eugene S. (Gene Cavallucci) *lawyer*
Choi, Youngsik *engineering educator*
Evans, Arthur Forte III *real estate developer*
Fulton, Charles Thomas *mathematics professor*
Grenevicki, Lance Francis *surgeon*
Hament, Andrew Stanton *lawyer*
Hancock, Monte Floyd, Jr. *computer scientist*
Harms, Eric A. *science educator*
Koenig, Harold Paul *management consultant, ecologist, evangelist, writer*
Lakshmikantham, Vangipuram *mathematics professor*
Lance, Howard L. *communications executive, industrial engineer*
Laposata, Joseph Samuel *army officer*
Magee, Thomas Henry *radiologist, educator*
Michalski, Thomas Joseph *writer, political activist, retired city planner, developer,*
Nelson, Gordon Leigh *chemist, educator*
Patterson, Gordon M. *history professor*
Pocoski, David John *cardiologist*
Renee, Cheryl *literature and language professor*
Simokaitis, Frank Joseph *military officer, lawyer*
Trefry, John H. III *chemical oceanographer, educator*
Turner, Niescja E. *physics professor*
Ward, William Francis, Jr. *real estate investment broker*
Weaver, Lynn Edward *academic administrator, consultant, editor*

Merritt Island
Roub, Bryan R(oger) *electronics executive*

Miami
Abess, Leonard, Jr. *bank executive*
Abitbol, Carolyn Larkins *pediatrician, nephrologist, educator*
Addy, Dawn Emerson *adult education labor educator*
Albini, Thomas A. *ophthalmologist*
Alexandrakis, George *physics professor*
Allen, Charles Norman *television, film and video producer*
Alperin, Stanley I. *writer, editor, consultant*
Alvarez, Carlos *Mayor, Miami-Dade, Florida*
Alvarez, Cesar L. *lawyer*
Amos, Betty Giles *food service executive, accountant*
Anderson, Terence James *law educator*
Anwar, Shadab *hydrologist, researcher*
Arango, Penelope Corey *psychologist, consultant*
Arison, Micky *cruise line company executive, professional sports team owner*
Arison, Shari *investment company executive*
Arminio, Michael, Jr. *science educator*
Arnold, David Jack *surgeon, educator*
Arsht, Adrienne *lawyer, broadcast and bank executive*
Asensio, Juan A. *medical association administrator*
Astigarraga, Jose I(gnacio) *lawyer*
Auerbach, Ethel Louise *retired healthcare facility administrator*
Baena, Scott Louis *lawyer*
Baker, Thomas J., Jr. *plastic surgeon*
Bandstra, Emmalee S. *physician, pediatrician, researcher, educator*
Banks, Marcus (Arthur Lamarcus III) *professional basketball player*
Bannard, Walter Darby *artist, critic*
Banya, Kingsley *dean*
Barkett, Rosemary *federal judge*
Barry, Dave *columnist, writer*
Batcheller, Joe Ann *entrepreneur*
Baumberger, Charles Henry *lawyer*
Beasley, Michael Paul *professional basketball player*
Beck, Morris *allergist*
Becker, Steven Richard *beverage corporation executive*
Beckham, Walter Hull, Jr. *law educator*
Beckwitt, Richard *construction executive*
Bello, Milagros *art historian, educator*
Beltre-Sanchez, Provi *psychology professor*
Benyunes, Abraham Joseph *pediatrician*
Bergmann, Elizabeth Helene *dance educator, arts administrator*
Berman, Bruce Judson *lawyer*
Bernstein, Jeffrey Ian *economics educator, consultant*
Bianchi, Laura *physiologist, educator*
Birns, Ira Michael *corporate financial executive*
Birsh, Arthur Thomas *publishing executive*
Black, Creed Carter *newspaper executive*
Black, Roy *lawyer*
Blechman, Wilbur Jordan *medical educator*
Block, Norman Louis *oncologist, educator*
Bloom, Mark David *lawyer*
Blumberg, Edward Robert *lawyer*
Bluntzer, Elena C. *real estate company executive*
Bogusky, Alex *advertising executive*
Borkan, William Noah *electronics executive, biomedical engineer, entrepreneur*
Braman, Norman *automotive and former sports team executive*
Brodie, Steve Jeffrey *lawyer*
Buergel, Roger M. *curator, art historian, educator*
Burke, Geórge William III *surgery educator*
Burke, Redmond Paul *cardiologist, surgeon*
Burnett, Henry *lawyer*
Bush, Gregory Wallace *director*
Cabrera DeBuc, Delia *medical researcher, educator*
Campos, Michael *medical educator*
Capraro, Franz *accountant*
Carbonell, Josefina G. *healthcare company executive, former federal agency administrator*
Cardenas, Alberto R. *lawyer, lobbyist*
Carraway, Kermit *cell biologist, educator*
Castro, Jose Guillermo *infectologist, educator*
Cenziper, Debbie *journalist*
Chen, JiuHua *physicist, geophysicist, educator, materials scientist*
Chernow, Bart *critical care physician*
Chidsey, John W. *food service executive*
Chiron, Harlan S. *orthopedic surgeon, educator*
Chisholm, Martha Maria *dietitian*
Clark, Ira C. *hospital administrator, educator*
Clarke, Peter John *computer scientist, educator, educational consultant*
Clarkson, John G. *academic administrator, ophthalmologist*
Clemence, Cheryl Lynn *systems administrator*
Colon, Ennio M. *pediatrician*
Connor, Terence Gregory *lawyer*
Cooper, Johnnie Edward, Jr. *advocate*
Cotayo, Charles *journalist, critic, film producer*
Coton, Carlos David *finance manager*
Cristol, A. Jay *federal judge*
Culbertson, William W. *ophthalmologist, educator*
Culmer, Leome Frances *volunteer*
Damian, Carol Esposito *art educator, director*
Dammann, W. Paul *oceanographer*
David, Christopher Mark *lawyer*
Davis, Edward Bertrand *retired federal judge, lawyer*
DeChurch, Stephanie J. *pediatrician*
Dede, Mehmet Ismet Can *robotics researcher, educator*
De Sena, Ferdinando *composer, educator*
Diaz, Manny (Manuel Alberto Diaz) *Mayor, Miami, Florida*
Dienstag, Cynthia Jill *lawyer*
Donelan, Mark Anthony *physicist*
Dorion, Robert Charles *entrepreneur, investor*
Duchesne, Carlos A. *epidemiologist, military officer*
Dunn, Richard M. *lawyer*
Dursum, Brian A. *museum director, art educator*
Eaton, Joel Douglas *lawyer*
Eftekhari, Nasser *physiatrist*
Ehrlich, Morton *marketing executive, management consultant*
Elsas, Louis Jacob, II, *physician, educator*
Engel, Tala *lawyer*
England, Arthur Jay, Jr. *lawyer, former state justice*
Epstein, Gary M. *lawyer*
Escalon, Maricer *medical educator*
España, Lourdes Maria *mathematics professor*
Espinoza, Luis Alberto *medical educator, researcher*
Essen, Richard Joel *lawyer*
Fain, Richard David *cruise line executive*
Falco-Leshin, JoAnna M. *literature and language professor*
Farrell, Patrick *photographer, photojournalist*
Fatovic, Robert Dean *lawyer*
Feito, Jose *architect*
Felton, Sandra Haley *special education educator*
Fine, Rana Arnold *chemical and physical oceanographer*
Fleming, Joseph Z. *lawyer*
Floyd, Suzanne Elvira Izzo *music educator*
Fontanals-Cisneros, Ella *art association administrator, information systems specialist*
Fraser, Douglas Malcolm *career military officer*
Freeman, Lewis Bernard *forensic accountant, lawyer*
Freshwater, Michael Felix *hand surgeon, educator*
Freshwater, Shawna Marie *neuropsychologist, clinical psychologist, cognitive neuroscientist*
Frigo, James Peter Paul *industrial hardware company executive*
Frost, Phillip *pharmaceutical executive, dermatologist*
Fuerst, Michael *finance educator, researcher*
Fukata, Masayuki *gastroenterologist, hematologist*
Furst, Alex Julian *thoracic and cardiovascular surgeon*
Galatas, Ruth Ann *musician, publishing executive, educator*
Gang, Robert C. *lawyer*
Garcia, Joe *not-for-profit fundraiser*
Gebhard, Ralf Erich *anesthesiologist*
Ghai, Gauri L. *statistician, educator*
Gibson, William Shepard *retired insurance company executive*
Ginsberg, Myron David *neurologist*
Goldschmidt, Clermont Pascal J. *medical educator, cardiologist, dean*
Goldstein, Adam M. *cruise line executive*
Gong, Edmond Joseph *lawyer*
Gonzalez, Eddie *advertising executive*
Goodman-Milone, Constance B. (Connie Goodman-Milone) *writer*
Graves, Palmer *chemistry professor*
Green, Barth *neurosurgeon*
Greenleaf, Walter Franklin *lawyer*
Greer, Pedro Jose, Jr., (Joe Greer) *dean*
Gross, Leslie Jay *lawyer, real estate broker, investment banker*
Grossman, Robert Louis *lawyer*
Gyllenhaal, Anders *editor*
Haith, Frank James, Jr. *men's college basketball coach*
Hall, Andrew Clifford *lawyer*
Hampton, Mark Garrison *architect*
Hanrahan, Daniel J. *cruise line executive*
Hare, Joshua Michael *cardiologist, educator*
Harmon, Monica Renee *music educator*
Harper, Thomas Wayne *ophthalmologist*
Harrison, Stanley L. *editor, educator, writer*
Hartz, Steven Edward Marshall *lawyer, educator*
Heggen, Arthur William *insurance company executive*
Hershberger, Ray E. *cardiologist, educator*
Highsmith, Shelby *federal judge*
Hildenbrand, Susan Elaine *education educator*
Himburg, Susan Phillips *dietician, educator*
Hochstein, Leonard Mark *plastic surgeon*
Hoffman, Joel M. *museum director*
Hoffman, Larry J. *lawyer*
Houlihan, Gerald John *lawyer*
Howell, Ralph Rodney *pediatrician, geneticist, educator*
Humphrey, Christine M. *lawyer*
Ibarguen, Alberto *foundation administrator, former publishing executive*
Ibberson, Amy Kristen *musician, director*
Ichii, Hirohito *surgeon, educator*
Ishmael, Annesa Fazeela *elementary school educator*
Istifan, Jamil *language educator*
Iver, Robert Drew *dentist*
Jacobson, Leonard I. *psychologist, educator*
Jhabvala, Farrokh *lawyer*
Jimenez, Marcos Daniel *former prosecutor*
Juanes, (Juan Esteban Aristizábal Vásquez) *musician*
Kahn, Jack Merrill *television producer*
Kaiser, Robert Mark *geriatrician, educator*
Kanet, Roger Edward *political science professor*
Kaplan, Betsy Hess *retired school board member*
Karayalcin, Cem *economics professor*
Kasbar, Michael J. *energy executive*
Katz, Sandra *educational consultant, psychologist, educator*
Kerstetter, Kathleen Marie *music educator*
Kessler, Kenneth Michael *cardiologist*
Khan, Ahmad Arshan *engineer, researcher*
Khurana, Seema Rani *osteopath, educator*
Kim, Hee Kee *medical researcher*
Kislak, Jean Hart *art director*
Klein, Russell B. *fast food company executive, marketing professional*
Klonarides, Geraldine *education educator*
Kosel, Tiffany *advertising executive*
Kowalska, Maria Teresa *research scientist, educator*
Kurlansky, Paul Alan *cardiovascular and thoracic surgeon*
Labbie, Andrew Scott *pediatric urologist, surgeon*
Landsberg, David A. *publishing executive*
Landy, Burton Aaron *lawyer*
Landy, Howard Jay *medical educator*
Lawrence, David, Jr. *journalist, early childhood advocate*
Leatherman, Stephen Parker *geologist, educator, writer*
Lefley, Harriet Phillips *psychologist, educator*
Lehman, Douglas Kent *librarian*
Leibowitz, Mark Alan *lawyer*
Lemberg, Louis *cardiologist, educator*
Levine, Jay Alan *cardiologist*
Levine, Robert Jeffrey *lawyer*
Lew, John I. *surgeon, educator*
Lew, Salvador *radio station executive*
Lipoff, Norman Harold *lawyer*
Lippman, Marc Estes *oncologist, educator, medical researcher*
Loria, Jeffrey H. *sports team executive*
Lynch, Dennis O. *law educator, former dean*
Macias, Michael *research scientist*
Macken, Jodi *real estate company executive*
Madurga, Gonzalo F. *performing company executive, actor, singer, director*
Magrath, Kathleen Barry *retired municipal official*
Maidique, Modesto Alex *engineering educator, former academic administrator*
Makki, Shamila *project manager engineer, researcher*
Mallery, Charles Henry *college associate dean, biology educator*
Marcus, Stanley *federal judge*
Margolis, Gwen *former state legislator*
Martinez, Walfrido (Wally Martinez) *lawyer*
Martinez-Fraga, Pedro J. *lawyer*
Mayfield, Max (Britt Mayfield) *meteorologist*
McCabe, Robert Howard *college president*
McLaughlin, Margaret Brown *adult education educator, writer*
Medvin, Nadeen Beth *psychologist, consultant*
Mehta, Eileen Rose *lawyer*
Meltzer, Brad *writer*
Mena, Daniel *lawyer, arbitrator*
Menéndez Cambó, Patricia *lawyer*
Messiah, Sarah Elizabeth *medical researcher*
Michel, Jesse Steven *psychology professor*
Miller, Stuart A. *construction executive*
Moody, Jacqueline Elaine *music educator*
Morgan, Andrew Wesley *artist, educator*
Mudd, John Philip *lawyer*
Muench, Karl Hugo *clinical geneticist*
Murphy, Timothy James *lawyer*
Nachwalter, Michael *lawyer*
Nahab, Fatta B. *neurologist, educator*
Nahmad, Albert H. *manufacturing executive*
Nahmad, Michel Henry *thoracic surgeon*
Neu, Charles Eric *historian, educator*
Neuman, Susan Catherine *public relations and marketing consultant*
Neville, Holly Leigh *pediatrician, surgeon*
Newton, Terry Fernando *health facility specialist, writer*
Nguyen, Dao Minh *thoracic surgeon, director*
Noonan, John Gerard *bishop emeritus*
Norris, Timothy Jon *lawyer*
Nuernberg, William Richard *lawyer*
Nunez-Lawton, Miguel G. *financial analyst*
O'Brien, Christopher Blackburn *gastroenterologist, director*
Omohundro, William Addison *research marketing executive*
O'Neal, Jermaine *professional basketball player*
O'Neill, William Walter *dean, cardiologist, educator*
Orlin, Karen J. *lawyer*
Orro, Margarita B. *language educator*
Osinski, Martin Henry *healthcare consultant*
Page, Larry Keith *neurosurgeon, educator*
Panthaki, Zubin Jal *medical educator, plastic surgeon*
Papy, Charles C. III *lawyer*
Parks, Arva Moore *historian*
Patrie, Cheryl Christine *elementary school educator*
Paulson, Michael George *foreign language educator*
Pavlow, Shara Toursh *professor, medical administrator*
Pearse, Damien D. *neuroscientist, consultant*
Penick, John E. *educator*
Perez, Jorge M. *real estate developer*
Pericak-Vance, Margaret A. *medical geneticist, educator, health facility administrator*
Perkel, Robert Simon *photojournalist, educator*
Persoff, Myron Mayer *plastic surgeon*
Pfeiffer, Mary Louise *artist, educator*
Pham, Si Mai *cardiothoracic surgeon*
Pilafian, Audrey Kalenian *music educator*
Pimentel, Armando *energy executive*
Pomeranz, Felix *accounting educator*
Porter, Charles King *advertising executive*
Porter, Wayne Randolph *dermatologist*
Poston, Rebekah Jane *lawyer*
Pratt, John Patrick *lawyer*
Procop, Gary W. *microbiologist, educator, physician*
Quentel, Albert Drew *lawyer*
Raez, Luis Estuardo *physician*
Raffel, Leroy B. *real estate developer*
Ramirez, Hanley *professional baseball player*
Rao, Cv *medical educator*
Rawl, Arthur Julian (Lord of Cursons) *corporate director, retail executive, consultant, accountant, writer*
Richton, Samuel M. *pediatric endocrinologist*
Ricordi, Camillo *surgeon, researcher*
Riley, Patrick James *professional sports team executive*
Riley, Terence *curator, architect*
Rodríguez, Agustín Alejo Román *bishop emeritus*
Rodriguez, Irmina Bestard *science educator*
Rodriguez, Josefa Nieves *special education and language educator*
Rodriguez, René F. *orthopedic surgeon*
Rogers, Jim (James Beeland Rogers Jr.) *retired investment company executive*
Rosenberg, Mark B. *academic administrator*
Rossi, Anthony Fred *cardiologist*
Rossman, Stephen F. *lawyer*
Rothstein, Ronald *professional basketball coach*
Rubell, Donald *gynecologist, hotel executive, art collector*
Rubin, Steven D. *lawyer*
Russell, James Webster, Jr. *retired editor, columnist*
Sadjadi, Masoud *science educator*
Saldana, Alfonso Manuel *lawyer*
Salvaneschi, Luigi *real estate developer, management consultant, educator*
Samole, Myron Michael *lawyer, management consultant*
Samson, David P. *professional baseball team executive*
Sanchez, Danmary *research scientist*
Sanchez, Manuel *retired social services administrator, writer*
Sanchez, Robert E. *corporate financial executive*
Sanders, Lee Michael *medical association administrator, educator*
Santiago, Raymond *library director, educator*
Saralegui, Cristina Maria *Spanish language television personality, journalist*
Savage, James Francis *retired editor*
Schafer, Marie *nurse, educator*
Schally, Andrew Victor *endocrine oncologist, researcher*
Schriesheim, Chester Arthur *management educator*
Schulman, Carl *surgeon, educator*
Schulman, Clifford A. *lawyer*
Scott, Troy M. *microbiologist, director*
Scully, Sean Patrick *orthopaedic surgeon, educator*
Sears, John Patrick *lawyer*
Selin, Ivan *entrepreneur*
Shannon, Randy Lannard *college football coach*
Sheremata, William A. *neurologist, educator*
Sherman, Beatrice Ettinger *hotel executive*
Shusterman, Nathan *underwriter, financial consultant*
Siegel, Paul *judge*
Sirvén, José E. *lawyer*
Skolnick, S. Harold *lawyer*
Skyler, Jay S. *medical educator, consultant*
Slice, Kimbo (Kevin Ferguson) *mixed martial arts fighter*

Smeltzer, Debra Jean *botanist*
Smiddy, William Earl *ophthalmologist*
Smith, Stanley Bertram *clinical and anatomic pathologist, allergist, immunologist*
Sonberg, Steven *lawyer*
Sonnett, Neal Russell *lawyer*
Spoelstra, Erik *professional basketball coach*
Stebbins, Paul H. *energy executive*
Steinbaum, Bernice *art dealer*
Struhl, Theodore Roosevelt *surgeon*
Suarez, Mildred *speech pathology/audiology services professional, educator*
Swaminathan, Sethuraman *pediatrician, cardiologist*
Swienton, Gregory T. *transportation company executive*
Taddeo, Annette *language services professional*
Teicher, Morton Irving *social worker, anthropologist, educator*
Thaller, Seth Ray *plastic surgeon*
Thomas, Isiah Lord III *men's college basketball coach, retired professional basketball player*
Thornburg, Frederick Fletcher *lawyer executive, educator*
Thorpe, Marion Dennis, Jr. *former state agency administrator*
Tice, Dianne Lisa *social services administrator*
Tifford, Arthur W. *lawyer*
Traurig, Robert Henry *lawyer*
Underwood, Joseph Warren *athletic trainer, educator, actor*
Upshaw, Anthony N. *lawyer*
Van Wyck, George Richard *insurance company executive*
Vasquez, Jennifer *marketing and public relations executive, researcher*
Vazquez, America *language educator*
Vento, M. Thérèse *lawyer*
Veziroglu, Turhan Nejat *mechanical engineering educator, researcher*
Vogt-Lowell, Robert W. *pediatric cardiologist*
Wade, Dwyane (Dwyane Tyrone Wade Jr.) *professional basketball player*
Walkley, Mary L. *voice and music educator*
Walton, Rodney Earl *lawyer, historian*
Wang, Michael Y. *neurosurgeon*
Wax, William Edward *photojournalist*
Weed, Donald T. *otolaryngologist, educator*
Weiner, Lawrence *lawyer*
Weinger, Steven Murray *lawyer*
Weinstein, Alan Edward *lawyer*
Wheeler, Steve Dereal *neurologist*
Wilson, Thomas Strong, Jr., (Tam Wilson) *judge*
Wing, James David *lawyer*
Wolfson, Aaron Howard *radiation oncologist, educator*
Woolworth, Eric S. *professional sports team executive*
Yaziji, Hadi *lab administrator*
Young, Mark Philip *allergist*
Zack, Stephen Neal *lawyer*
Zaydon, Thomas John, Jr. *plastic surgeon*
Zeydel, Diana S. C. *lawyer, former professional ballet dancer*
Zhu, Yifu *physics professor*
Zubieta, Alberto Aleman *construction executive*

Miami Beach
Agatston, Arthur Stephen *cardiologist, educator*
Bredemeier, Mary Elizabeth *counselor, educator*
Camber, Diane Woolfe *association president*
Cohen, Philip Herman *accountant*
Cubiñá, Silvia Karman *museum director, curator*
Foote, Gwendolyn Sue *educator, artist*
Gagner, Michel *surgeon, educator*
Howard, Melvin *financial executive*
Justiniani, Federico Roberto *internist, educator*
Kalsner-Silver, Lydia *psychologist*
Katz, Brian Jeffrey *dermatologist*
King, Sky V. *librarian*
Koffler, Karen *internist*
Lanzkron, Rolf Wolfgang *manufacturing executive*
Lopera, Gustavo Adolfo *cardiologist, electrophysiologist*
Mandy, Stephen Howard *dermatologist, educator*
Palamara, Sherry A. *psychologist*
Rosenhaus, Drew *professional sports agent*
Ryce, Donald Theodore, Jr. *lawyer*
Sackner, Marvin Arthur *physician*
Shaw, Jon Angus *psychiatrist*
Todd, Christopher Michael *marketing executive, consultant*

Miami Gardens
Conley, James W. *English and language arts educator*
Ersek, Gregory Joseph Mark *lawyer*
Light, Alfred Robert *law educator*
Medina-Pascu, Isabel M. *academic administrator*
Robinson, Beatriz Gonzalez *academic administrator*

Miami Lakes
Graham, Bob (Daniel Robert Graham) *former United States Senator from Florida*

Miami Shores
Cremades, J. Gualberto *psychology professor*
Diener, Betty Jane *business educator*
Esposito, Luigi Gennaro *educator*
Estevez, Felipe de Jesús *bishop*
Favalora, John Clement *archbishop*
Fernández, Gilberto *bishop emeritus*
Missick, Lamont S. *literature and language professor*

Miami Springs
Neasman, Annie Ruth *health facility administrator*

Milton
Leddy, Amanda Collier *music educator*

Miramar
Catalano, Carl Philip *small business owner*
Florio, Donamarie Rose *secondary school educator*
Stewart Simpson, Donnamay Angela *interior designer*

Monticello
Burkart, Arnold Emil *music educator*

Montverde
Revis-Pyke, Robin Lynn *director*

Mount Dora
Crone, Eugene N. *addictions specialist, retired educator*
Hensinger, Margaret Elizabeth *real estate, horticultural and agricultural advertising and marketing executive*
Kirton, Jennifer Myers *artist*
Shepp, Judith Rosser *retired elementary school educator*
Trundle, W(infield) Scott *publishing executive newspaper, lawyer*

Mulberry
Bowman, Hazel Lois *retired English language educator*

Naples
Adams, John Marshall *lawyer*
Anderson, John Thomas *lawyer*
Askins, Wallace Boyd *manufacturing executive*
Berman, Robert S. *marketing consultant*
Blevins, Charles Russell *publishing executive*
Blumenberg, Robert Murray *retired surgeon, educator*
Bradley, Charles MacArthur *retired architect*
Brinker, Thomas Michael *retired finance company executive*
Bruce, Jackson Martin, Jr. *lawyer*
Butler, Frederick George *retired drug company executive*
Caldwell Portenier, Patty Jean Grosskopf *advocate, educator*
Capelle-Frank, Jacqueline Aimee *writer*
Carneiro, Ronaldo Dos Santos *surgeon*
Carrick, Lee *retired dermatologist*
Clapp, Roger Howland *retired publishing executive*
Clarke, John Patrick *retired newspaper publisher*
Cobb, Brian Eric *broadcast executive*
Cox, Joe Bruce *lawyer*
Crehan, Joseph Edward *lawyer*
Delano, Victor *retired naval officer*
de Saint Phalle, Thibaut *investment banker, consultant*
Dobranski, Bernard *dean, law educator*
Dorio, Martin Matthew, Jr. *real estate company executive, investor*
Doub, William Offutt *lawyer*
Dykstra, David Allen *business broker*
Eldridge, David Carlton *art and antique appraiser*
Ericson, Roger Delwin *lawyer, forest resource company executive*
Faison, William Franklin, II, *lawyer, retired manufacturing corporation executive*
Frantzen, Henry Arthur *retired investment company executive*
Frazer, John Howard *tennis association and retired manufacturing executive*
Gade, Marvin Francis *retired paper company executive*
Gardner, George Victor *lawyer*
Garratt, Reginald George *electronics executive*
Gaskins, William Darrell *ophthalmologist*
Gehring, David Austin *cardiologist, physician, health facility administrator*
Gelfand, Neal *oil industry executive*
Gilman, John Richard, Jr. *retired management consultant, sculptor*
Goldman, Joel J. *retired lawyer*
Goldman, Ralph Frederick *research physiologist, educator*
Greene, David *surgeon, researcher*
Hall, Beverly Barton *librarian*
Hansen, Claire V. *financial executive*
Heindl, Phares Matthews *lawyer*
Hogg, Virginia Lee *retired medical educator*
Hutson Councell, Janet Kern *retired small business owner, retired educator*
Jones, Philip Howard *broadcast journalist*
Kirby, Charles William, Jr. *dancer, choreographer*
Kley, John Arthur *banker*
Kozitka, Richard Eugene *retired consumer products company executive*
LaRusso, Anthony Carl *company executive, lecturer, consultant*
Leitner, Alfred *retired mathematical physicist, educator, educational film producer*
Lewis, Gordon Gilmer *golf course architect*
Lickhalter, Merlin *architect*
Liebenson, Gloria Krasnow *retired interior design executive, freelance writer*
Lowery, William Herbert *lawyer*
Ludwig, Richard Joseph *small business owner*
Madigan, Joseph Edward *financial executive, director, consultant*
Mahalawich, Anne Mary *retired mathematics educator*
Marienthal, George *telecommunications industry executive*
Marino, William Francis *telecommunications industry executive, consultant*
Martinuzzi, Leo Sergio, Jr. *banker*
Mavrides, Elaine *retired mental health services professional, social worker*
Meyers, Christine Laine *marketing and media executive, consultant*
Mills, Dorothy Jane (Dorothy Z. Seymour, Dorothy Seymour Mills) *writer, editor, consultant*
Moore, Oliver Semon III *publishing executive, consultant*
Myers, Robert Jay *retired aerospace executive*
Newsome, Gary D. *hospital operations company executive*
Norton, Elizabeth Wychgel *retired lawyer*
Ordway, John Danton *retired pension fund administrator, lawyer, accountant*
Peck, Bernard Sidney *lawyer*
Penniman, Nicholas Griffith, IV, *retired newspaper publisher*
Petersen, David L. *lawyer*
Pfister, Raymond Lawrence *otolaryngologist*
Portenier, Walter James *aerospace engineer*
Randall, Neil Warren *gastroenterologist*
Riggs, Fletcher Eugene *economist, consultant*
Root, Stanley William, Jr. *retired lawyer*
Rowe, Herbert Joseph *retired trade association executive*
Salentine, Thomas James *pharmaceutical executive*
Sampson, John Eugene *food products executive, consultant*
Schoen, William Jack *finance company executive*
Schwartz, Stephen Gregory *ophthalmologist*
Scott, Richard Lynn (Rick Scott) *investment company executive, former health and medical products company executive*
Seavey, Christopher Gordon *psychotherapist, alcohol/drug abuse services professional*
Sekowski, Cynthia Jean *health products executive, medical consultant*
Silvestri, Vito Nicholas *communications educator*
Slaff, Allan Paul *military officer, academic administrator, educator, entrepreneur*
Smith, Numa Lamar, Jr. *lawyer*
Sowman, Harold Gene *ceramics engineer, researcher*
Strauss, Jerome Manfred *lawyer, bank executive*
Suziedelis, Vytautas A. *retired engineering corporation executive*
Swanson, Donald Frederick *retired food company executive*
Synnott, William Raymond *retired management consultant*
Temple, Donald *retired allergist, dermatologist*
Thomas, Gary Lynn *information technology executive*
Vickrey, Robert Remsen *artist*
von Arx, Dolph William *food products executive*
Wedel-Cowgill, Millie Redmond *secondary school, performing arts, communication and education educator*
Westman, Carl Edward *lawyer*
White, Roy Bernard *performing arts association administrator*
York, Tina *painter*

Neptune Beach
Chambers, Ruth Coe *writer*
Mantle, Raymond Allan *lawyer*
Perniciaro, Charles Vincent *dermatologist, educator, entrepreneur*

New Port Richey
Brice, Jeanine Lynn *associate dean*
Day, Peter Rodney *geneticist, educator*
Johnson, Henry Eugene III *middle school educator*
Lake, Victor Hugo *former manufacturing company executive*
Maysilles, Daniel Bruce *pharmaceutical services executive*
Miller, Harvey William *retired military officer*
O'Farrell, Mark Theodore *religious organization administrator*
Plant, John Maxime *educator*
Summers, Horace Kenneth *biology professor*

New Smyrna Beach
Shaffer, Joye Coy *reading specialist*

Newberry
Thornton, J. Ronald *technology consultant*

Niceville
Litke, Donald Paul *acquisition executive, retired military officer*
Lopez Morgan, Maria Helena *literature and language professor*
Warren, J. Richard *editor, retired humanities educator*

Nokomis
Dodderidge, Ann Thornberry *real estate agent*
Novak, Joyce Keen *artist, secondary school educator*
Novak, Robert Louis *civil engineer, pavement management consultant*

North Fort Myers
Miller, William Charles *lawyer*

North Lauderdale
Dunham, Laura *elementary school educator*

North Miami
Downs, Antonie *librarian*
Ferro, Alejandro F. *obstetrician, gynecologist*
Martinez, Raul L. *public relations executive*
Plotkin, Sharon Lee *protective services official, educator*

North Miami Beach
Abbo, Bill *dentist, educator*
Castro, Angel *accountant, author, educator*
Sorosky, Jeri P. *academic administrator*
Soto, Jose Antonio *family medicine physician*

North Palm Beach
Brophy, Gilbert Thomas *lawyer*
Dreyfoos, Alexander W., Jr. *investor, research scientist*
Gaudieri, Alexander V.J. *art historian, museum director, educator*
Hayman, Richard Warren Joseph *conductor*
Higgins, Jay F. *diversified financial services company executive*
Kaplan, Muriel Sheerr *sculptor*
Nicklaus, Jack William *professional golfer, sports apparel executive*
Sieving, Charles E. *energy executive, lawyer*
Stall, John A. *energy executive*

Ocala
Brown, Warren Donald *adult education educator, retired police officer*
Capps, Ken Bryant *chemistry professor*
Cecil, Joseph Terry *education educator*
Cunha, Tim *biological researcher, entrepreneur*
Ettinger, Penny A. *medical/surgical nurse*
Hodges, William Terrell *federal judge*
Hornick, Susan Florence Stegmuller *artist, secondary education educator, fine arts educator, curriculum specialist, retired*
Hudson, Ann Elizabeth *music educator*
Massa, Conrad Harry *retired religious studies educator*
McClea, Robin Muse *museum director, painter*
Mishkin, Michael Lawrence *psychologist, educator*
Ray, Ruth Alice Yancey *retired rancher, real estate developer*
Rollerson, Corey L. *professional basketball coach*
Sostilio, Robert Francis *office equipment marketing consultant*
Strait, William Robert *computer technician*
Tait, Patricia Ann *secondary school educator*
Tesmer, Nancy Ann Stutler *retired librarian*

Odessa
Lawson, Mary Carolyn *elementary and middle school educator*

Okahumpka
Branham, Joseph Morhart *biologist, educator*

Okeechobee
Bishop, Sid Glenwood *union official*

Oldsmar
Brunner, George Matthew *management consultant, retired manufacturing executive*
Gambone, Victor, Jr. *internist, geriatrician*
Thompson, Mack Eugene *historian, educator*

Opa Locka
Ajhar, Edward A. *astrophysicist, dean*
Sample, Althea Merritt *retired secondary education educator, conductor*
Thevenin, Rose Carine *history professor*

Orange Park
Hunt, J(ulian) Courtenay *artist*
Miller, Martin Eugene *management labor negotiator, lobbyist*
Rice, Ronald James *hospital administrator*
VonGruenigen, Christine Michelle *microbiologist, educator*

Orlando
Adubato, Richard Adam (Richie Adubato) *sportscaster, former professional basketball coach*
Ahlers, Glen-Peter, Sr. *law library director, educator, consultant*
Allison, Anne Marie *retired librarian*
An, Linan *engineering educator*
Arkin, J. Gordon *lawyer*
Ashe, Diane Davis *psychology professor, sport psychology consultant*
Atwell, George Michael *composer, conductor, musician*
Badhwar, Vinay *thoracic surgeon, researcher*
Baker, Peter Mitchell *science association director, laser scientist*
Beckner, Cynthia Byrd *music and elementary school educator*
Bevc, Frank Peter *electrical engineer*
Birmele, Michele Nan *biologist*
Boreman, Glenn David *electrical engineer*
Breazeale, Will *pilot, military officer*
Brouillard, Robert Paul *maintenance planning manager*
Brownlee, Thomas Marshall *manufacturing executive*
Brumby, Andrew M. *lawyer*
Capraun, Lynn W. *chairperson respiratory care*
Carter, Glenn Arnold *academic administrator, consultant*
Carter, Vince *professional basketball player*
Chacon, Delia C. *secondary school educator*
Chow, Lee *physics professor*
Christiansen, Patrick T. *lawyer*
Clem, Alexander Murphree *lawyer*
Comfort, Iris Tracy *writer*
Connolly, Joseph Francis, II, *academic administrator, government consultant*
Courtright, Paul Eric *lawyer*
Cramer, Stephen John *paramedic, educator*
Davis, H. Alan *retired airline captain, consultant*
Dawson, Leslie Naryne *quality assurance professional*
deBeaubien, Hugo H. *lawyer*
DeCampli, William Michael *surgeon, researcher*
Deo, Narsingh *computer scientist, educator*
DeVos, Richard Marvin, Sr. *professional sports team owner, former network marketing company executive*
Dieker, Lisa A. *special education educator*
Dorleus, Joseph Alphonse Raoul *electronics engineer*
Dorsey, Norbert M. *bishop emeritus*
Dunn, William Bruna III *journalist*
Dyer, John Hugh, Jr., (Buddy Dyer) *Mayor, Orlando, Florida, lawyer*
Eagan, William Leon *lawyer*
Ewing, Patrick Aloysius *professional basketball coach, retired professional basketball player*
Fawsett, Patricia Combs *federal judge*
Fine, Terri Susan *political science professor*
Flinchbaugh, David Edward *physicist*
Flitsiyan, Elena S. *physicist, physics educator*
Forbes, Daniel Merrill *minister*
Forbes, Wanda Iris *nurse*
Fornaro, Robert L. *air transportation executive*
Fottler, Myron David *health services educator*
Frey, Louis, Jr. *lawyer, federal official*
Fritz, Jim *professional sports team executive*
Gangitano, James J. *lawyer*
Gao, Xingbo *engineering educator*
Garcia, Martha *language educator*
Gerber, Daniel J. *lawyer*
Gidel, Robert Hugh *real estate investor*
Gilbert, Suzanne E. *lawyer*
Goings, Everett Vernon (Rick) *consumer products company executive*

Port Orange
Collyer, Robert B. *retired trade association administrator*
Johnson, Susan F. *elementary school educator*
Mc Collister, John Charles *writer, minister, educator*
Millar, Gordon Halstead *mechanical engineer, agricultural products executive*

Port Richey
Fry, Ronald Sylvan *music educator, director*
VanMeer, Mary Ann *publishing executive, writer, webmaster*

Port Saint Lucie
Augelli, John Pat *geographer, educator, writer, consultant, rancher*
Christensen, Patricia *Mayor, Port St. Lucie, Florida*
Guglielmino, Lucy Margaret Madsen *education educator, researcher, consultant*
Guglielmino, Paul Joseph *educator*
LaHowchic, Nicholas John *consulting company executive*
Lambert, George Robert *lawyer, realtor*
Rothschild, Mary Ann *music educator*

Punta Gorda
Bailey, F. Lee (Francis Lee Bailey) *lawyer*
Cushman, Jaclyn Ellen *musician, director*
Fullman, Robert Louis *metallurgy consultant*
Haswell, Carleton Radley *banker*
Hollinshead, Ariel Cahill *oncologist, educator, researcher*
McDaniel, Norwood Allan *insurance broker*
O'Neal, Lyman Henry *biology educator*
Ott, Walter Richard *information technology executive, writer*
Pollard, Herschel Newton *artist, psychologist*
Presley, Brian *investment company executive*
Smith, Charles Edwin *computer science educator*

Quincy
Rittman, Benita Griffin *psychologist*

Reddick
Corwin, Joyce Elizabeth Stedman *construction company executive*
Romanski, Joyce Marie *secondary school educator, small business owner, instructor*

Riverview
Alvarez, Jorge *application developer*

Riviera Beach
Berliner, Hans Jack *retired computer scientist*
Schmidt, Thomas Charles *biomedical engineer, researcher*

Rockledge
Anderson, Robert Aeiker *college administrator*

Rotonda West
Durham, Olga Kalapaca *retired art educator, volunteer*

Royal Palm Beach
Cutler, Jonathan M. *podiatrist*

Ruskin
Chase, Don *reading and English teacher*
Dickson, Tim *music educator, marina general manager*

Safety Harbor
Dail, Joseph Garner, Jr. *retired judge*

Saint Augustine
Brady, James Joseph *labor arbitrator*
Couture, Sister Diane Rhea *sister, artist, educator*
Goldthwait, John Turner *emeritus humanities educator*
Harper, Robert Walter III *museum director*
Harvey, William Royal *physiologist, educator*
Henderson, Hazel *economist, writer*
Jurgens, Julie Graham *mathematics professor*
Lidh, Todd *literature and language professor, department chairman*
Lund, Frederick Henry *aerospace and electrical engineer*
Nolan, Joseph Thomas *journalism educator, communications consultant*
Poland, Richard Clayton *law educator*
Proctor, William Lee *state legislator, academic administrator*
Reeher, James Irwin *minister*
Sappington, Sharon Anne *retired school librarian*
Sorkin, Robert Daniel *psychologist, industrial engineer, educator*
Troemel, Jean Wagner-Willhite *artist*
Voguit, Steve George *humanities educator*
Wilkes, Delano Angus *architect*
Zacharias, David Alan *biotechnologist, educator*

Saint Cloud
Everett, Woodrow Wilson *electrical engineer, educator*

Saint Leo
Hammond, Bruce Ray *academic administrator, consultant, communications educator*
McTague, John J. *history professor*
Neuhofer, Mary Dorothy *archivist, librarian*
Ondrovic, Leo E. *medical researcher, educator*
Persky, David William *lawyer*
Van Kampen, Doris J. *librarian, educator*
Vicas, Astrid *philosopher, educator*

Saint Petersburg
Alexander, Forbes I.J. *electronics executive*
Allaster, Stacey *sports association executive*
Bairstow, Frances Kanevsky *arbitrator, mediator, educator*
Baker, Rick (Richard M. Baker) *Mayor, St. Petersburg, Florida*
Battaglia, Anthony Sylvester *lawyer*
Belich, John Patrick, Sr. *journalist, private investigator*
Bert, Theresa M. *science educator, researcher*
Betzer, Susan Elizabeth Beers *physician, geriatrician*
Brightman, Ross I. *biology professor*
Brooker, Jewel Spears *literature educator*
Bruni, Joseph Vincent, Jr. *protective services official, educator*
Bryant, Timothy Clark *investment brokerage executive*
Buckspan, Randy Jay *plastic surgeon*
Burrell, Pat (Patrick Brian Burrell) *professional baseball player*
Cardenas-Valencia, Andres Manuel *chemical engineer, researcher*
Carfora, Joan C. *elementary school educator*
Carlson, Jeannie Ann *writer*
Chabrier, Christina Ferree *literature and language professor*
Chang, Yenhui *geneticist, director*
Chapin, Lloyd Walter *academic administrator*
Chipman, Marion Walter *retired judge*
Chrobak, Nicholas James *military officer*
Collins, Carl Russell, Jr. *industrial engineer*
Connelly, David O'Brien *museum administrator, journalist*
Coraggio, James Thomas *educational researcher, measurement consultant*
Corty, Andrew P. *publishing executive*
Crawford, Carl Demonte *professional baseball player*
Davis, Christopher J. *management consultant, educator*
DeGregory, Lane *journalist, features writer*
D'Elia, Christopher Francis *marine biologist, educator, academic administrator*
Dementieva, Elena *professional tennis player*
Dinsdale, Carol Ellen *special education educator*
Dukes, Lyman Lee III *special education professor*
Emerson, William Allen *retired investment company executive*
Empric, Julienne H. *literature educator, consultant*
Engel, John Jacob *communications executive*
Escarraz, Enrique III *lawyer*
Fleming, William Sloan *energy and computer company executive*
Freeburg, Richard Gorman *financial derivatives company executive*
Freeman, Corinne *financial analyst, retired mayor*
Garza, Matthew Scott (Matt Garza) *professional baseball player*
Gilbert, Gordon Joel *neurologist, electroencelographer*
Ginn, Ronn *architect, environmental planner, general contractor*
Glass, Roy Leonard *lawyer*
Godbold, Francis Stanley *investment banker, security firm executive*
Grossman, Mindy *retail executive*
Haiman, Robert James *editor, journalist, educator, media consultant, expert witness, critic*
Higham, Frederick A. *lawyer*
Honein, Berthe *music educator*
Huber, Liezel *professional tennis player*
Hurley, John Kenneth *real estate company and merchant banking executive*
Jacob, Bruce Robert *law educator*
James, Thomas A. *investment company executive*
Janney, Oliver James *lawyer*
Janus, Nancy *human development professor*
Jenkins, Robert Norman *reporter, editor*
Jordan, William Reynier, Sr. *retired therapist, poet*
Kent, Allen *library and information sciences professor*
Kubiet, Leo Lawrence *media consultant*
Kuznetsova, Svetlana *professional tennis player*
Lang, Joseph Hagedorn *lawyer*
Lemoi, Brian André *religious organization administrator, religious studies educator, writer*
Linask, Kersti K. *medical educator*
Linhart, Joseph Wayland *retired cardiologist, educational administrator*
Longoria, Evan Michael *professional baseball player*
Lousberg, Peter Herman *former lawyer*
Lynch, Robert Nugent *bishop*
Macauley, Karen Elizabeth *nursing administrator, emergency nurse practitioner*
MaCris, Jack Achilles *surgeon*
Maddon, Joe (Joseph John Maddon) *professional baseball manager*
Main, Timothy L. *electronics company executive*
Mann, Sam Henry, Jr. *retired lawyer*
Matecki, Paul L. *lawyer*
Mayhall, Clifford Wesley *lawyer*
Meese, George Philip Elman *literature and rhetoric professor, consultant*
Meyer, Robert Allen *finance educator*
Mikals-Adachi, Eileen B. *translator, educator*
Mills, William Harold, Jr. *construction executive*
Mondello, Mark T. *electronics executive*
Moody, Lizabeth Ann *lawyer, educator*
Mussett, Richard Earl *city official*
Myskina, Anastasia *professional tennis player*
Naimoli, Vincent Joseph *diversified financial services company executive*
Naughton, James Martin *journalist*
Notaro, Gerald Anthony *university librarian*
Osterman, Lisa Ellen *geologist, researcher*
Patterson, Eugene Corbett *retired editor, publishing executive*
Paver, Robert L. *lawyer*
Pena, Carlos Felipe *professional baseball player*
Petty, M. S. Marty *publisher*
Petty, Marty *publishing executive*
Pittman, Robert Turner *retired newspaper editor*
Pizana, Orlando Akhiem *communications educator*
Raymond, Lisa *professional tennis player*
Robinson, Chester Hersey *retired dean*
Root, Allen William *pediatrician, educator*
Rosenblum, Martin Jerome *ophthalmologist*
Rosenblum, Zina Michelle Zarin *psychology professor, marketing professional, researcher*
Schloder, John E. *museum director*
Sharapova, Maria *professional tennis player*
Smith, Betty Robinson *retired elementary school educator*
Southworth, William Dixon *retired education educator*
Tash, Paul Clifford *editor, publishing executive*
Upton, B.J. (Melvin Emanuel Upton) *professional baseball player*
Wallach, Stanley *medical educator, consultant, administrator*
Wedding, Charles Randolph *architect*
Young, June Hurley *elementary school educator, writer*
Zacur, Richard Aaron *lawyer*
Zimmer, Donald William *former professional baseball coach, professional baseball manager, retired professional baseball player*

Saint Petersburg Beach
Garnett, Stanley Iredale, II, *utilities executive, lawyer*
Hurley, Frank Thomas, Jr. *realtor*
Mason, Phillip Howard *aircraft company executive, retired military officer*

Saint Teresa
Grubbs, Ralph Dean *marine biologist*

San Antonio
Beverland, Jack Edwin *retired retail executive, folk artist*

Sanford
Capps, James Leigh, II, *lawyer, military officer*
Davis, Darrell L. *retired automotive executive*
Dickison, Alexander Kane *physical science educator*
Drewry, Marcia Ann *physician*
Fitzgerald, J. Patrick *philosopher, educator, film producer*
Mena, Michele M. *counselor, therapist*
Scott, Mellouise Jacqueline *retired media specialist*
Shub, Harvey Allen *surgeon*
Vienneau, Laurence Edward, Jr. *art educator*

Sanibel
Ball, Armand Baer *former association executive, consultant*
Crown, David Allan *criminologist, educator*
Hasselman, Richard B. *retired rail transportation executive*
Rothschild, Donald Phillip *retired lawyer, arbitrator*
Trevor, Alexander Bruen *information technology consultant*

Sarasota
Allen, Charles Franklin *music educator*
Atwell, Robert Herron *academic administrator*
Aull, Susan *physician*
Bailey, Robert Elliott *financial executive*
Balliett, John William *entrepreneur, real estate company executive*
Beck, Robert Alfred *hotel executive, educator*
Benowitz, June Melby *historian, educator*
Blucher, Paul Arthur *lawyer*
Bowers, Charles Richard *surgeon*
Brandhorst, Wesley Theodore *retired library and information scientist*
Bushey, Alan Scott *retired insurance holding company executive*
Carstens, Charlene B. *composer, music educator*
Cavanagh, Denis *gynecologist, obstetrician, gynecological oncologist, educator*
Christ-Janer, Arland Frederick *college president*
Church, Martha Eleanor *retired academic administrator*
Clark, Eugenie *zoologist, educator*
Cleland, Sherrill *college president*
Culkin, Charles Walker, Jr. *retired trade association administrator*
Cummings, Martin Marc *physician, educator, academic administrator*
Daoust, Donald Roger *pharmaceutical executive, microbiologist, cosmetics executive*
De Gennaro, Richard *retired library director*
Derr, Frederick Mueller *civil engineer*
Deutsch, Sid *biomedical engineer, educator*
Doenecke, Justus Drew *history professor*
Dryce, H. David *accountant, consultant*
Dungy, Kathryn R. *humanities educator*
Ehrlich, Bernard Herbert *lawyer, trade association administrator*
El Shahawy, Mahfouz *internist, cardiologist, educator*
Faron, Sally Rogers *performing arts association administrator, consultant*
Fendrick, Alan Burton *advertising consultant*
Fitzgerald, Keith *state legislator, political science professor*
Freeman, Richard Merrell *retired lawyer*
Garland, Richard Roger *lawyer*
Gordon, Sanford Daniel *economics professor*
Greenfield, Robert Kauffman *retired lawyer*
Hanson, Virginia A. *human services administrator*
Heiser, Rolland Valentine *former army officer, foundation administrator*
Heitler, George *lawyer*
Herb, Frank Steven *lawyer*
Honner Sutherland, B. Joan *advertising executive*
Hughes, Allen *music critic*
Huppe, Alex *public relations executive*
Iverson, Robert Louis, Jr. *retired internist, physician*
Jacobson, Melvin Joseph *mathematician, educator*
Jelks, Mary Larson *retired pediatrician*
Jellison, Brian D. *manufacturing executive*
Jones, Sally Daviess Pickrell *writer*
Jones, Tracey Kirk, Jr. *retired minister, educator*
Knickerbocker, Robert Platt, Jr. *lawyer, consultant*
Landis, Edgar David *business consultant*
Lengyel, Alfonz *art history, archeology and museology educator*
Long, Robert Radcliffe *fluid mechanics engineer, educator*
Mahadevan, Kumar *marine life administrator, researcher*
Marino, Eugene Louis *publishing executive, director*
Masters, John Christopher *psychologist, educator*
Mattran, Donald Albert *management consultant, educator*
McCarthy, Brian Nelson *real estate developer*
McCollum, John Morris *tenor*
McFarlin, Diane Hooten *publisher*
McMaster, Gloria (Gloria Bugni Juhn) *mezzo-soprano, educator*
Metzger, Sidney *retired communications engineer*
Michalson, Gordon E., Jr. *academic administrator*
Middleton, Norman Graham *social worker, psychotherapist*
Miller, Peggy Gordon Elliott *retired academic administrator*
Miranda, Carlos Sa *food products company executive*
Mohl, Norman David *dental educator*
Montrose-Graem, Douglass *poet-painter, music-man, museum director, bank executive*
Morris, Gordon James *financial company executive, consultant*
Morrow, William Earl *retired government official, law educator*
Mullane, John Francis *pharmaceutical executive*
North, Marjorie Mary *writer*
O'Malley, Thomas Anthony *gastroenterologist, internist*
Phillips, Howard William *investment banker*
Pierce, Richard Harry *oceanographer*
Proffitt, Waldo, Jr. *newspaper editor*
Raimi, Burton Louis *lawyer*
Retzer, Mary Elizabeth Helm *retired librarian*
Runge, Paul E. *ophthalmologist, educator*
St. John, Terri *secondary school educator*
Scanlon, Janice Lynn *retired gifted and talented educator*
Schlegel, John Frederick *management consultant, personal trainer*
Schmalzried, Marvin Eugene *financial consultant*
Shulman, Arthur *communications executive*
Snyder, Lee Daniel *historian, educator*
Sparrow, Carol Sweeney *music educator*
Stevens, Elisabeth Goss (Mrs. Robert Schleussner Jr.) *writer, graphic artist*
Stewart, Donald George *musician, composer, music industry executive*
Stickler, Daniel Lee *health care management consultant*
Tachna, Ruth C. *retired lawyer*
Taplin, Winn Lowell *historian, retired federal agency administrator*
Torrey, Richard Frank *retired utilities executive*
Tucci, Steven Michael *health facility administrator, physician, recording industry executive*
Vasilaki, Linda Boozer *music educator*
Venit, William Bennett *electrical products company executive, consultant*
Wadsworth, Dyer Seymour *minerals executive*
Weeks, Albert Loren *writer, educator, journalist*
Wendlandt, Dorothea Schnepf *artist, writer*
West, Bob *pharmaceutical executive*
Wetenhall, John *museum director*
Zahn, Carl Frederick *museum program director, photographer, graphics designer*

Satellite Beach
Loney, Mary Rose *former airport administrator, aviation industry consultant*

Sea Ranch Lakes
Gore, George Henry *lawyer*

Sebastian
Eddy, Elsbeth Marie *retired government official, statistician*
Lagin, Neil *landscape designer, consultant*

Sebring
Hixon, Andrea Kaye *health science association administrator*
Littlewood, Douglas Burden *brokerage house executive*
McCollum, James Fountain *lawyer*
Parrett, Janelle Swilley *secondary school educator*
Schumacher, Cynthia Jo *retired elementary and secondary education educator*
Sherrick, Daniel Noah *real estate broker*

Seminole
Carrere, Charles Scott *judge, educator*
Evans, Thomas Passmore *management consultant*

Shalimar
Burke, Kelly Howard *retired military officer, entrepreneur*

Silver Springs
Tillis, Mel *entertainer, songwriter*

Singer Island
Gad, Lance Stewart *investment advisor, lawyer, private investor*

South Daytona
Fernández, Lianne *elementary school educator, consultant*

South Miami
Ballen, Ann E. *ophthalmologist*
Keedy, Christian David *lawyer*
Rossi, Patricio *radiologist*

Spring Hill
Mathia, Mary Loyola *parochial school educator, nun*
Vanderburg, Paul Stacey *insurance executive, consultant*
Wood, Shelton Eugene, Jr. *education educator, minister, consultant*

Stuart
Ankrom, Charles Franklin *landscape architect, consultant*
Bowdish, James L.S. *lawyer*
Bush, Harriet *psychologist*
Gary, Willie E. *lawyer*

Gilbert, Glenn Gordon *retired linguistics educator*
Grieve, William Roy *psychologist, educator, educational administrator, researcher*
Kirkpatrick, Harold (Kirk) Wayne *telecommunications industry executive*
Maldonado, Carlos Manuel *surgeon*
Moran, Michael E. *urologist*

Sugarloaf

Greenberg, Linda Garrett *education educator, volunteer, singer*

Summerfield

Gates, Elena Miranda *language educator*
Heflin, Jimmie Lee *elementary school educator*
McNulty, Carrell Stewart, Jr. *retired manufacturing executive, architect*
Swanson, David Henry *retired economist, educator, consultant*

Sun City Center

Chapman, Lenora Rosamond *day care provider, social service organization director*
Petersen, Carolyn Ashcraft *retired psychologist*
Willard, Louis Charles *retired librarian*

Sunny Isles Beach

Edelcup, Norman Scott *management and financial consultant*
Harezi, Ilonka Jo *medical technology research executive*

Sunrise

Adams, Nelson L. III *obstetrician, gynecologist*
Cohen, Alan Phillip *professional sports team executive, former pharmaceutical executive*
DeBoer, Peter *professional hockey coach*
Goldenberg, Felix *retired electrical engineer, researcher*
Maken, Sonny *real estate company executive, developer*
Sexton, Randy J. *professional sports team executive*
Stillman, Cory *professional hockey player*
Yormark, Michael *professional sports team executive*

Tallahassee

Anderson, Theresa Ann *science educator*
Aurell, John Karl *lawyer*
Baggett, Fred W. *lawyer*
Barnett, Martha Walters *lawyer*
Bartlett, Richard Adams *historian, writer, retired history professor*
Bellenot, Steven *mathematics educator, consultant*
Benton, Robert Tyrie, II, *judge*
Bert, Clara Virginia *retired secondary school educator, administrator*
Blair, Maudine *psychotherapist, communications executive, management consultant*
Bowden, Bobby (Robert Cleckler Bowden) *college football coach*
Bowen, Paul L. *information systems and accounting educator*
Browning, Kurt S. *Secretary of State, Florida*
Brueckheimer, William Rogers *social sciences educator*
Brunson, Jeana *museum director*
Buck, Thomas Randolph *retired lawyer, diversified financial services company executive*
Bye, Raymond Erwin, Jr. *academic administrator*
Canady, Charles Terrence *state supreme court justice, former congressman*
Carson, Leonard Allen *lawyer*
Carter, Tina A. *educator*
Cavanagh, James Ellsworth, Jr. *medical educator*
Charity, Linda B. *state banking agency administrator*
Choppin, Gregory Robert *chemistry professor*
Clifford, Dorothy Ring *journalist*
Cockrell, Wilburn Allen *archaeologist*
Coldiron, A. E. B. *language educator*
Coloney, Wayne Herndon *civil engineer*
Cooper, Martha H. *costume designer, educator*
Corzine, Jennifer Jean *music educator*
Crist, Charlie (Charles Joseph Crist Jr.) *Governor of Florida, former state attorney general*
Cronin, Jerome Joseph, Jr. *marketing educator, consultant*
Cui, Ming *social studies educator*
Curtin, Lawrence N. *lawyer*
Dadisman, Joseph Carrol *retired newspaper executive*
Dalban-Canassy, Matthieu *mechanical engineer*
Davis, John Dwelle *psychology professor*
Deeb, Larry Charles *pediatric endocrinologist, epidemiologist*
De Forest, Sherwood Searle *agricultural engineer, products executive*
Doffek, Pamala Jean *library director*
DuVal, Emily H. *biology professor, researcher*
Elsner, James Brian *meteorologist, educator*
Ervin, Charles Phifer, Jr. *education educator, retired military officer*
Ervin, Robert Marvin *lawyer*
Fielding, Raymond Edwin *writer, communications educator*
Ford, Ann Suter *family practice nurse practitioner, consultant*
Fulkerson, Laurel *humanities educator*
Gievers, Karen A. *lawyer*
Gilmer, Penny Jane *biochemist, educator*
Gilmer, Robert *mathematics professor*
Gleeson, Thomas Alexander *retired meteorologist*
Golden, Leon *classicist, educator*
Goldstein, Julia Sonia *librarian*
Gor'kov, Peter (Lev Petrovich) *biomedical engineer*
Grable, Bettye Ann *communications educator*
Greer, Jim *political organization administrator*
Grimes, Stephen Henry *retired state supreme court justice*
Gunter, William Dawson, Jr., (Bill Gunter) *insurance company executive, consultant*
Halpern, Paul G. *retired history professor*
Hamilton, Leonard *men's college basketball coach*
Hammer, Marion Price *association executive*
Hanley, Deborah Elizabeth *meteorologist, wildland firefighter*
Harper, Robert Augustus *lawyer*
Hayek, Saleh *engineer, researcher*
Hercule, Hantz C.P. *physician, research scientist*
Hernandez, Jose Yolando Balagtas *surgeon*
Hernandez, Minerva Cuadrante *physician, consultant*
Herrick, Nathan *biologist*
Herz, Werner *retired chemistry professor*
Hogan, Dexter L. *football coach*
Holcomb, Lyle Donald, Jr. *retired lawyer*
Holcombe, Randall Gregory *economics professor*
Houlihan, Gerri Paige *choreographer, educator*
Hu, Xiaolong Bill *environmental scientist, educator*
Hunt, John Edwin *insurance company executive, consultant*
Hunt, Mary Alice *retired humanities educator*
Islam, Tanveerul *engineering educator*
Jeong, Allan C. *education educator*
Johnson, Kelly Overstreet *lawyer*
Johnson, Margaret Anderson *writer, publishing and agricultural products executive*
Kandimalla, Karunya Kumar *pharmacist, educator*
Kercheval, Alec Norton *mathematician*
Kerns, David Vincent *lawyer*
Kim, HeeMin *political science professor*
Kimel, Jacob Daniel *physics professor*
Kirwin, Thomas F. *prosecutor*
Kitchen, E.C. Deeno *lawyer*
Kohout, Ladislav Jan *computer science educator*
Labarga, Jorge *state supreme court justice, lawyer*
Laird, Doris Anne Marley *retired humanities educator, musician*
Laird, William Everette, Jr. *economics professor*
Lambert, Nathaniel M. *researcher*
Leiber, Justin *philosophy educator, writer*
Lewis, R. Fred *state supreme court justice*
Lick, Dale Wesley *educational leadership educator, mathematician*
Lu, Junjie *molecular biologist*
Madsen, Clifford Kimball *music educator, therapist*
Maguire, Charlotte Edwards *retired pediatrician*
Marks, John R. III *mayor, Tallahassee, Florida, lawyer*
Marshall, Alan George *chemistry and biochemistry educator*
McClure, Charles Robert *library and information science educator, consultant*
McCollum, Bill (Ira William McCollum Jr.) *state attorney general, former congressman*
McCord, Guyte Pierce, Jr. *retired judge*
McMahon, Darrin Michael *history professor*
Mele, Alfred R. *philosophy educator*
Mesev, Victor *geographer, educator*
Meyer-Baese, Uwe *engineering educator*
Miles, Rebecca *urban planner, educator*
Miller, Gregory R. *retired prosecutor*
Miller, Morris Henry *lawyer*
Minnick, Bruce Alexander *lawyer*
Mooney, Krista Michele *academic administrator*
Morgan, Lucy Ware *senior correspondent, journalist*
Nam, Charles Benjamin *demographer, sociologist, educator, writer*
Nasser, Joseph Yousef *public safety administrator, consultant*
Navon, Ionel Michael *mathematics professor*
Nichols, Eugene Douglas *mathematics professor*
Nwabuzor, Augustine M. *global strategy educator, consultant*
Olcese, James Michael *neuroscientist, educator*
Oliver, Andrea LaKaye *history professor*
Onokpise, Oghenekome Ukrakpo *agronomist, educator, forester, geneticist*
Palladino-Craig, Allys *museum director, educator*
Pariente, Barbara J. *state supreme court justice*
Park, Jin Gyu *research scientist*
Perry, James E.C. *state supreme court justice*
Phipps, Benjamin Kimball, II, *lawyer*
Pla, Arthur James *school system administrator*
Plendl, Hans S. *retired physicist, editor*
Polston, Ricky L. *state supreme court justice*
Quince, Peggy A. *state supreme court chief justice*
Rahman, Saleh Mahmudur *medical educator*
Rai, Amitabh Shambhu *humanities educator*
Reardon, Robert C. *retired psychology professor*
Reichert, Philip E. *health science association administrator*
Reid, Sue Titus *law educator*
Rikvold, Per Arne *physicist, educator*
Ring, Judith A. *state librarian*
Robson, Donald *physics professor*
Rogers, Nancy Marie *music educator*
Sanchez, Robert Francis *journalist*
Schepkin, Victor D. *biophysicist*
Schlottmann, Pedro U. J. *physics professor*
Schrieffer, John Robert *physics professor, science administrator*
Semrau, Sue *women's college basketball coach*
Shih, Chiang *mechanical engineer, educator*
Simpson, Larry Dean *lawyer*
Sink, Adelaide Alexander *state official*
Sink, Alex *state treasurer*
Smith, Eric J. *state official, school system administrator*
Spooner, Donna *management consultant*
Standley-Burt, Nancy Vilma *retired psychologist, educator*
Standridge, Charles Robert *engineering educator, consultant*
Stipanovich, John McKager (Mac Stipanovich) *lobbyist, lawyer*
Strickland, Delphene Coverston *judge*
Sutterfield, J. S. *engineering educator*
Taylor, Gary *literature and language professor*
Terry, Anne Curtis *lawyer, writer*
Thagard, Norman E. *astronaut, physician, engineer, educator*
Thompson, Daniel Ray *statistician, consultant*
Thompson, Gregory Lee *social sciences educator*
Thompson, Jean Tanner *retired librarian*
Thurman, Karen L. *political organization administrator, former congresswoman, lobbyist*
Toran, Eric James *physical therapist, director*
Trujillo, Evelyn Franquiz *language educator, consultant*
Turnbull, Marjorie Reitz *educational consultant, state legislator*
Viamonte Ros, Ana M. *state agency administrator, public health service officer*
Waas, George Lee *lawyer*
Waas, Harriet Issner *elementary school educator*
Walker, Karen D. *lawyer*
Webster, Peter David *judge*
Weidner, Donald J. *dean, law educator*
Wetherell, Thomas Kent *academic administrator*
Wiedegreen, Eric Albert *interior designer, educator*
Williams, Charles D. *radiologist*
Wu, Tien-Shuenn *engineer, researcher, consultant*
Yerg, Beverly Johnson *retired physical education educator, researcher*
Yu, Ming *engineering educator, researcher*
Zachert, Martha Jane *retired librarian*
Zaiser, Kent Ames *lawyer*
Zimmerman, Kenneth Jay *humanities educator*
Zwilich, Ellen Taaffe *composer*

Tamarac

Galipault, Lorraine D. *adult education educator*
Krause, John L. *retired optometrist*
Thaung, U *journalist*

Tampa

Acs, Geza *medical educator, surgical pathologist*
Adams, Rex M. *health products executive, former telecommunications executive*
Afield, Walter Edward *psychiatrist, health facility administrator, educator*
Albritton, Arthur Dallas *lawyer*
Albritton, Brian (A. Brian Albritton) *prosecutor*
Alexander, William Olin *retired finance company executive*
Alstott, Michael Joseph (Mike Alstott) *retired professional football player*
Andersen, Jc *physical therapist, director*
Anton, John Peter *philosopher, educator*
Ash, William Mason *physicist, consultant*
Barbas, Stephen Michael *lawyer*
Barber, Ronde (Jamael Oronde Barber) *professional football player*
Barkin, Marvin E. *lawyer*
Barness, Lewis Abraham *physician*
Barron, Elizabeth Lee *librarian*
Barton, Bernard Alan, Jr. *lawyer*
Baumann, Martin F. *former finance company executive*
Bedgood, Alvin J. *information technology manager, director*
Bedke, Michael A. *lawyer*
Berg, Charles G. *health products executive*
Berne, Patricia Higgins *psychologist, writer, educator*
Binford, Jesse Stone, Jr. *chemistry professor*
Bishopric, Karl *insurance company executive, retired investment banker, real estate company executive, advertising executive*
Black, Caroline Kapusta *lawyer*
Boutros, Linda Nelene Wiley *medical/surgical nurse*
Bowman, Janet *media specialist*
Boyce, H. Worth *gastroenterologist, educator*
Branch, Mary Fletcher Cox *secondary school educator*
Branch, William Terrell *urologist, educator*
Brault, Rose *healthcare administrator, educator*
Brown, Troy Anderson, Jr. *retired electric power industry executive*
Campbell, Richard Bruce *lawyer*
Campbell, Ron *professional sports team executive*
Carnahan, Robert Paul *civil engineer, educator, researcher, consultant*
Castor, Kathy *United States Representative from Florida*
Christian, Terry Clifton *lawyer*
Coats, Janet S. (Janet Weaver) *editor*
Coleman, Rodney Albert *political scientist, consultant*
Corcoran, Clement Timothy III *lawyer, mediator, retired judge*
Cowell, Bruce Craig *biology educator, aquatic ecologist*
Culp, Faye Berry *state legislator*
Cury, Bruce Paul *lawyer, magistrate, educator*
Davidson, Charles Thomas *lawyer*
Davis, Helen Gordon *retired state senator*
Davis, Jim *lawyer, former congressman*
DeBoskey, Dana Stephens *psychologist, consultant*
de Quesada, Alejandro Manuel *film and museum consultant, writer*
DeVane, Mindy Klein *financial planner*
Diehr, Beverly Hunt *lawyer*
Doliner, Nathaniel Lee *lawyer*
Dominik, Mark *professional sports team executive*
Dubey, Rajiv *engineering educator*
Duda, Vaclav *social studies and biology educator, artist*
Dvorchik, Barry H. *pharmaceutical executive*
Eddy, Colette Ann *aerial photography studio owner, photographer*
Eichberg, Rodolfo David *physiatrist, educator*
El-Hadidy, Bahaa *information scientist, educator, consultant*
Ferree, Patricia Ann *quality assurance professional*
Flom, Edward Leonard *retired metal products executive*
Forsythe, Robert Elliott *economics professor*
Freedman, Sandra Warshaw *former mayor*
Friedlander, Edward Jay *journalist, educator*
Fung, Chi-Keung Victor *music educator, researcher*
Gallagher, Scott Farrell *surgeon, researcher*
Garrett, Howard Leon *lawyer*
Genshaft, Judy Lynn *academic administrator, psychologist, educator*
Gerhard, H. John *orthopaedic surgeon, retired military officer*
Germroth, Peter *biologist, educator*
Ghosh, Debarati *biology professor, researcher*
Gilbert, Leonard Harold *lawyer*
Gilbert-Barness, Enid F. *pathologist, educator*
Gonzalez, Joe Manuel *lawyer*
Grammig, Robert James (Bob Grammig) *lawyer*
Greenfield, George B. *radiologist*
Greenwald, Daniel Paul *plastic surgeon*
Gunn, Lee Delton, IV, *lawyer*
Gurrie, Christopher Timothy *speech educator, director*
Hall, Lawrence O'Higgins *computer science educator*
Hamilton, William F. *lawyer*
Hanford, Agnes Rutledge *retired investment advisor*
Hekkanen, Steve *psychology professor*
Helmick, Frank G. *career military officer*
Hernandez, Gilberto Juan *accountant, auditor, management consultant*
Hoffmann, Michael *neurologist*
Horvath, Michael J. *economics professor*
Howey, John Richard *architect, writer*
Howlett, Lee Ann *medical librarian, writer*
Huang, Jimin *civil engineer, consultant*
Hudson, Sherrill W. *energy executive*
Humphries, J. Bob *lawyer*
Hunter, Delroy M. *finance educator*
Hunter, Larry Lee *retired electrical engineer*
Iorio, Pam *mayor, Tampa*
Islam, Arif *educational association administrator, researcher*
Jacobson, Howard Newman *obstetrics and gynecology educator, researcher*
Jamieson, Michael Lawrence *lawyer*
Jennewein, James Joseph *architect*
Johnson, Randall Clyde *mortgage company executive*
Jones, Franklin Ross *education educator*
Joseph, Babu *chemical educator*
Kandel, Abraham *computer scientist*
Kasturi, Rangachar *electrical engineer, educator*
Kazem, Ismail *radiation oncologist, educator, health facility administrator*
Keach, Michael Andrew *library and information scientist*
Kimmel, Ellen Bishop *psychologist, educator*
Kirby, Russell Stephen *epidemiologist, geographer, researcher*
Knox, Michael Dennis *medical educator, research center administrator*
Koren, Edward Franz, Jr. *lawyer*
Kruschwitz, Walter Hillis *retired physics educator*
Kucera, Stephen D. *biology professor*
Lafferty, Barbara A. *finance educator*
Lane, Robin R. *lawyer*
LaRussa, Rudy G. *lawyer*
Lashley, Keith Livingstone *architect, educator*
Laurino, Joseph Philip *chemistry professor, consultant*
Lawton, Brian R. *professional sports team executive*
Lebouitz, Martin Frederick *diversified financial services company executive, consultant*
Lecavalier, Vincent *professional hockey player*
Leftwich, Byron Antron *professional football player*
Leopold, Blake *music educator*
Leto, Sharon Ann *secondary school educator, consultant*
List, Alan *medical educator*
Lockhart, Jorge Luis *urologist, educator*
Loewy, Michael *economics professor*
Loiselle, Joan Brenda *elementary school educator, art educator*
Lu, Jian John *engineering educator*
Luddington, Betty Walles *retired media specialist*
Lynch, Michael Joseph *criminologist, educator*
Ma, Wen-Xiu *mathematician, educator*
Macferran, Ernest Leslie *mechanical engineer*
Mahmoud, Hisham *research scientist*
Martin, Dean Frederick *retired chemistry professor*
Martin, Gary Wayne *lawyer*
Martinez, Bob *former federal official, former governor*
Matulich, Erika *marketing educator*
McAdams, John Pope *lawyer*
McDevitt, Sheila Marie *retired lawyer, energy executive, business consultant*
McIlwain, Harris H. *physician, researcher*
Meisels, Gerhard George *academic administrator, chemist, educator*
Mitchell, Mozella Gordon *language educator, minister*
Moore, Janet L.S. *music educator, dean*
Morrill, Donald *dean, director*
Morris, Kendall Francis *psychology professor*
Morris, Raheem *professional football coach*
Mulholland, Jason Christopher *lawyer*
Muroff, Lawrence Ross *nuclear medicine physician, educator*
Mushinsky, Henry R. *biology professor*
Nagera, Humberto *psychiatrist, psychoanalyst, educator, writer*
Nord, Walter Robert *business administration educator, researcher, consultant*
O'Brien, Mary Ellen Christina *artist, educator*
Odierno, Raymond T. *career military officer*
Okogbaa, Geoffrey Obitor *engineering educator*
Older, Jay Justin *ophthalmic plastic surgeon*
Olson, Eric Thor *career military officer*
Olson, Robert Eugene *physician, biochemist, educator*
O'Neill, Albert Clarence, Jr. *lawyer*
O'Neill, Robert E. *prosecutor*
Orlowski, James Phillip *pediatrician*
Ostrenko, Wit *museum administrator*
Owen, Chuck *composer, music educator*
Palmer, Denise E. *publishing executive*
Pankau, Barbara Ropes *lawyer*
Pasetti, Louis Oscar *retired dentist*
Pauly, Jennifer L. *director, graphics designer*
Pedowitz, Robert Alan *orthopaedic surgeon, researcher*
Pellett, Jon Michael *lawyer*
Pendyala, Ram Mohan *civil engineering educator*
Perry, James Frederic *philosophy educator, writer*
Petraeus, David Howell *career military officer*
Pfeiffer, Eric Armin *psychiatrist, gerontologist, writer*
Phan, Manh-Huong *materials scientist*
Pinjari, Abdul R. *assistant professor*
Platt, Jan Kaminis *former county official*
Plays, Dana *film director, educator*
Powers, Pauline Smith *psychiatrist, educator, researcher*
Prewett, Matthew Scott *research scientist*
Price, Douglas Armstrong *chiropractor*

Ranganathan, Nagarajan *engineering educator*
Rentos, Peter George *medical educator*
Robinson, John William, IV, *lawyer*
Ross, Mark Allen *engineering educator, consultant*
Rossignol, Jean-François Armand *research scientist, medical educator*
Rowlands, David Thomas *pathology educator*
Russell, Diane Elizabeth Henrikson *career counselor*
Rydberg, Marsha Griffin *lawyer*
Saba, Hussain Ismail *hematologist, researcher*
St. Louis, Martin *professional hockey player*
Sanberg, Paul Ronald *medical educator*
Sanchez, Mary Anne *retired secondary school educator*
Sarbacker, Donald LeRoy *economics professor*
Sbramaniam, Chitra P. *educational consultant*
Schiesser, Heath *health products executive*
Schueler, John R. *newspaper executive*
Schumacher, Margaret Lynn *not-for-profit fundraiser, director*
Sexton, Wade J. *oncologist, educator*
Shenefelt, Philip David *dermatologist*
Shephard, Bruce Dennis *obstetrician, educator, medical writer*
Sigety, Charles Birge *investment company executive*
Silbiger, Martin L. *radiologist, educator, dean*
Skvoretz, John Vincent *sociologist, educator*
Smith, David John, Jr. *plastic surgeon*
Smith, William Reece, Jr. *lawyer*
Sopher, Vicki Elaine *appraiser*
Spellacy, William Nelson *obstetrician, gynecologist, educator*
Spielberger, Charles Donald *psychologist, educator*
Stamkos, Steven *professional hockey player*
Studer, William Allen *security consultant, retired military officer*
Sullebarger, John Thompson *internist, cardiologist, educator*
Susanin, Timothy Scott *lawyer, health products executive*
Szonntagh, Eugene L. *chemical engineer, educator, chemist, historian, archaeometrist, organologist*
Tan, Jun *psychology professor, researcher*
Tanguay, Alex *professional hockey player*
Taub, Theodore Calvin *lawyer*
Tebbi, Cameron K *hematologist, oncologist*
Thomas, Gregg Darrow *lawyer*
Thomas, Wayne Lee *lawyer*
Tocchet, Rick *professional hockey coach, retired professional hockey player*
Tran, Thomas L. *health products executive*
Tully, Darrow *newspaper publisher*
Tunstall, Graydon Allen *history professor, professional society administrator*
Turner, Stephen Park *philosopher, sociologist, educator*
Unhjem, Michael Bruce *lawyer*
Vale, Fernando Luis *medical educator*
Vesely, David Lynn *medical educator, research scientist*
Volicer, Ladislav *physician, educator*
Wagner, Frederick William (Bill Wagner) *lawyer*
Waller, Edward Martin, Jr. *lawyer*
Watkins, Joan Marie *retired osteopath, physician*
Watson, Roberta Casper *lawyer*
Weinberg, Morris (Sandy Weinberg) *lawyer*
Weiner, Irving Bernard *psychologist*
Weizmann, Maria Pia *associate dean*
Whatley, Jacqueline Beltram *lawyer*
Wilson, Charles Reginald *federal judge*
Winslow, Kellen Boswell, II, *professional football player*
Wolfson, Jay *medical educator, consultant, lawyer*
Yerrid, C. Steven *lawyer*
Zaworotko, Michael John *chemistry professor*
Zhu, Yiliang *research scientist, educator*

Tarpon Springs
Crismond, Linda Fry *public relations executive*
Georgiou, Ruth Schwab *retired social worker*
Leisner, Anthony Baker *publishing company executive*

Tavares
Gross, Paul Allan *health products executive*
Kaiser, Robert Lee *retired engineering executive*

Temple Terrace
Crispell, Brian Lewis *history professor, dean of students*
Kashdin, Gladys Shafran *painter, educator, volunteer*

Tequesta
Swets, John Arthur *psychologist, researcher*

The Villages
Dupies, Donald Albert *retired civil engineer*
Graham, David Bolden *food products executive*
Mirkin, Gabe Baron *physician, medical educator, writer, radio personality*

Tierra Verde
Gaffney, Thomas Francis *principal*
Stewart, John Murray *bank executive*

Titusville
Duffy, John Charles *psychiatrist, educator, consultant*
Fuller, Joseph Patrick *economics professor*
O'Sullivan, Patricia Ann *principal, writer*
Rivenbark, Christine Klemenz *science educator, researcher*
Schau, Harvey Charles *physicist*
Stewart, David Witherington *business consultant*

Treasure Island
Dunn, Craig Andrew *entertainer, conductor, writer, composer, educator*

Trenton
Aderholt, David A. *state official*

University Park
Compain, Rita *librarian*
Walker, Jane Stewart *small business owner, publishing executive, educator*

Valparaiso
Merritt, Phyllis June *music educator, director*

Valrico
McCrystal, Jennifer Cross *elementary school educator*
Palmer, Louis Thomas *pathologist*

Velrico
Newman, Phyllis *retired counselor, therapist, hypnotist*

Venice
Abernathy, George Thomas *cardiologist, consultant*
Asp, William George *librarian*
Barritt, Evelyn Ruth Berryman *nurse, educator, dean*
Belok, Carol Jean *nurse, alcohol/drug abuse services professional*
Bluhm, Barbara Jean *communications agency executive*
Clarke, Edward Owen, Jr. *lawyer*
Cool, Kim Patmore *editor, publishing and retail executive*
Delaney, Robert Finley *retired columnist, political sociologist, lecturer*
Dewane, Frank Joseph *bishop*
Dodderidge, Richard William *retired marketing executive*
Feldmann, Edward George *pharmaceutical chemist, pharmacologist*
Felker, Ouida Jeanette Weissinger *special education educator*
Finlay, Susan Sparling *education educator*
Gooding, Charles Thomas *psychologist, educator, retired academic administrator*
Harlow, Joan Beverley Hiatt (Joan Hiatt Harlow) *writer*
Hrachovina, Frederick Vincent *retired osteopathic physician*
Miller, Allan John *retired lawyer, oil industry executive*
Nevins, John Joseph *bishop emeritus*
Seiler, Charlotte Woody *retired education educator*
Tausan, Carol A. *music educator*

Vero Beach
Ahrens, William Henry *architect*
Anderson, Raymond Quintus *diversified company executive*
Bennett, Jack Franklin *oil industry executive*
Beran, Denis Carl *publisher*
Bewkes, Eugene Garrett, Jr. *investment company executive, consultant*
Bigler, Harold Edwin, Jr. *retired investment company executive*
Chavez, Joseph *finance educator*
Christopher, Robert Paul *retired physical medicine physician*
Conway, Earl Cranston *business educator, retired manufacturing company executive, educator*
Crosby, John Griffith *investment banker*
Ferrell, Catherine K. *sculptor, painter*
Fish, Mardy *professional tennis player*
Fisher, Andrew *retired management consultant*
Freeman, Donald Wilford *real estate developer, horse breeder*
Gedeon, Lucinda Heyel *museum director*
Geiman, J. Robert *lawyer*
Higgs, John H. *lawyer*
Hilker, Robert Reuben John *medical educator, researcher, administrator, consultant*
Holloman, Marilyn Leona Davis *lobbyist, non profit administrator*
Ingwersen, Martin Lewis *water transportation executive*
Janicki, Robert Stephen *retired pharmaceutical executive*
Jonason, Pauline Marie *retired art educator*
Leonsis, Ted *media and professional sports team executive*
McCrystal, Ann Marie *community health nurse, administrator*
McNamara, Francis Joseph, Jr. *retired foundation executive, lawyer*
McNamara, John J(oseph) *advertising executive, writer*
Reed, Sherman Kennedy *chemicals executive, consultant*
Riefler, Donald Brown *financial consultant*
Schwarz, Berthold Eric *psychiatrist*
Snook, Stover Hoffman *retired social sciences educator*
Spivak, Alvin A. *retired public relations executive*
Standish, John Spencer *textile manufacturing company executive*
Ughetta, William Casper *lawyer, manufacturing executive, director*
Wilcox, Harry Wilbur, Jr. *retired manufacturing executive*

Viera
Nessel, Edward Harry *swimming coach*

Village Of Golf
Allen, Robert Eugene *retired telecommunications industry executive*
Birle, James Robb *investor*
Sutter, William Paul *lawyer*

Weeki Wachee
Davis, Larry Michael *air force officer, healthcare manager, consultant*
Finney, Roy Pelham, Jr. *urologist, surgeon, inventor*

Wellington
Behren, Robert Alan *lawyer, accountant*
Cohen, Edward *civil engineer*

Wesley Chapel
Mendelsohn, Louis Benjamin *financial analyst*
Revelle, Donald Gene *manufacturing and health care company executive, consultant*
Tucker, Robert C., Jr. *materials scientist, consultant*

West Palm Beach
Ackerman, David P. *lawyer*
Addison, Ferguson Lofton Lightbourne *retired bank executive*
Baker, Dina Gustin *artist*
Beall, Kenneth Sutter, Jr. *lawyer*
Beasley, James W., Jr. *lawyer*
Bergmann, Arthur M. *writer, retired journalist, retired county official*
Bernhardt, Marcia Brenda *mental health counselor*
Brown, Paul A. *medical services executive*
Brumback, Clarence Landen *physician*
Castiglione, Anita *pianist, music educator*
Chahine, Elias B. *pharmacist, educator*
Chimney, Michael John *aquatic biologist and limnologist, consultant*
Chopin, L. Frank *lawyer*
Colitz, Carmen Maria Helena *veterinarian, educator*
Cooney, Gail Austin *medical association administrator*
Coyle, Dennis Patrick *lawyer, retired utilities executive*
Damsel, Charles H., Jr. *lawyer*
Dye, Thomas Roy *political science professor*
Floyd, Raymond Loran *professional golfer*
Furlaud, Richard Mortimer *pharmaceutical executive*
Gildan, Phillip Clarke *lawyer*
Gold, Bela *economist, educator*
Gonzalez, Faustino Agustin *preventive medicine physician, director*
Hale, Marie Stoner *performing company executive*
Hardin, Luther *academic administrator, former state legislator*
Harper, Mary Sadler *wealth advisor and relationship manager*
Henry, Thornton Montagu *lawyer*
Herrick, John Dennis *financial planner, consultant, retired food products executive*
Hill, Thomas William, Jr. *lawyer, educator*
Hunter, Michael *publishing executive*
Jenkins, Ruben Lee *chemicals executive*
Johnson, Martin Allen *publishing executive, artist*
Karmelin, Michael Allen *financial executive*
Kelley, Craig I. *lawyer, educator*
Kendall, Carla P. *school system administrator, mathematician*
Kessler, Ronald Borek *journalist, writer*
Koslow, Stephen Hugh *health science association administrator, pharmacologist, neuroscientist*
Kulok, William Allan *entrepreneur, venture capitalist*
Lamb, Kevin Thomas *lawyer*
Lane, Matthew Jay *lawyer*
Levin, Ronald Mitchell *geriatrician*
Li, Zhongwei *hydrologist*
Link, Scott J. *lawyer*
Livingstone, John Leslie *accountant, economist, management consultant, educator*
Loring, Arthur *lawyer, diversified financial services company executive*
Lynch, Edward J. *small business owner, contractor*
Marshall-Beasley, Elizabeth *landscape architect*
Moore, George Crawford Jackson *lawyer*
Mrachek, Lorin Louis *lawyer*
Newmark, Emanuel *ophthalmologist*
Nolan, Richard Thomas *clergyman, educator*
Ogden, John Clifton III *environmental scientist, director*
Passy, Charles *writer*
Pietro, Kathleen C. *environmental scientist*
Pingpank, Robert Charles *retired mathematics educator*
Pottash, A. Carter *psychiatrist, hospital executive*
Rakip, Anne Marie *psychology professor*
Robinson, Raymond Edwin *conductor, music educator, writer*
Ronan, William John *management consultant*
Roshkind, Robin *divorce lawyer*
Ross, Edward Joseph *architect*
Royce, Raymond Watson *lawyer, rancher, citrus grower, investor*
Rukeyser, M.S., Jr. *television consultant, writer*
Schneider, Lisa A. *lawyer*
Siegel, Philip Harris *finance educator*
Spillias, Kenneth George *lawyer*
Stashenko, Vetaley *anatomist, educator*
Strolla, Cory C. *lawyer*
Thomashow, Steven Roy *military and intelligence officer*
Vilchez, Victoria Anne *lawyer*
Whitfield, Graham Frank *orthopedic surgeon*
Zeller, Ronald John *lawyer*

Weston
Alexander, Cynthia Louise *psychologist, educator*
Berry, Becky *music educator*
Blandon, Elizabeth Rose *lawyer*
Firgau, Conchita *artist*
Galvez-Jimenez, Nestor *neurologist*
Ghoniem, Gamal M. *urologist*
Gómez Martinez, Juan Carlos *senior executive and consultant*
Gordon, Lori Heyman *psychotherapist, author, educator*
Holtzman, Gary Yale *retired diversified financial services company executive*
Lazar, Marioara *psychiatrist*
Malave, Andres *pharmacologist, educator*
Marino, Dan (Daniel Constantino Marino Jr.) *sportscaster, retired professional football player*
Williams, Ricky (Errick Lynne Williams) *professional football player*

Wewahitchka
de Abreu, Sue *elementary school educator*

Windermere
Hahn, Dowon *pharmaceutical researcher, educator*
Lewis, Joseph *investor, real estate development company executive*
Rudzik, Lynne A. *musician, educator*
Westbrook, Clinton Howard *retired military petty officer, protective services official*

Winter Garden
Gillet, Pamela Kipping *special education educator*

Winter Haven
Bennett, Samuel *elementary school educator*
Boully, LaJuan Bonnie *minister, religious studies educator*
Burns, Arthur Lee *architect*
Cloud, Linda Beal *retired secondary school educator*
Cover, Norman Bernard *retired electronic data processing administrator*
Goodman, Karen Lacerte *retired financial services executive*
Grierson, William *retired agriculturist*
Johnson, Gordon Selby *consulting electrical engineer*
Okun, Neil Jeffrey *vitreoretinal surgeon*
Schepis, Anthony Joseph *artist, educator*
Scott, Sherry J. *psychologist*

Winter Park
Ackert, T(errence) W(illiam) *lawyer*
Alfond, Theodore B. *retired shoe company executive*
Baker, James L., Jr. *plastic surgeon, educator*
Bloodworth, Velda Jean *librarian, educator*
Blossey, Erich Carl *chemistry professor*
Builder, J. Lindsay, Jr. *lawyer*
Cavenaugh, Jennifer Jones *theater educator, department chairman*
Cook, Jo Ann Likins *psychologist*
Dempsey, Bernard Hayden, Jr. *lawyer*
Federle, Michael *publishing executive*
Granberry, Edwin Phillips, Jr. *safety engineer, consultant*
Hadley, Ralph Vincent III *lawyer*
Haendiges, Anne R. *retired marriage and family therapist*
Heinle, Richard Alan *lawyer*
Helms, Roger D. *lawyer*
Jontz, Jeffry Robert *lawyer*
Kittleson, Henry Marshall *lawyer*
Kolin, Irving Seymour *psychiatrist*
Leslie, John William *public relations and advertising executive*
Matulich, Serge *accounting educator, writer*
McKean, Thomas Wayne *retired dentist, military officer*
Merrill, Harvie Martin *retired manufacturing executive*
Morgan, Mary Ann *lawyer*
Murray, Susan Lyons *library director*
Rock, Charles Patrick *economics professor, researcher*
Rogers, Rutherford David *librarian*
Rooks, Linda *writer*
Seymour, Thaddeus *language educator*
Siry, Joseph Vincent *environmentalist, educator*
Smetanka, Sally S. *small business owner*
Starr, Martin Kenneth *management educator*
Swann, Richard Rockwell *lawyer, banker*
Troutman, Holmes Russell *lawyer*
Vila, Adis Maria *lawyer, educator, business government executive*
Wallace, Curtis Wilbern, Jr. *music director, organist*
Whitworth, Hall Baker *forest products company executive*
Wilson, Cecil Bruce *internist*
Wilson, Robley Conant, Jr. *language educator, editor, writer*
Wrancher, Elizabeth Ann *retired music educator, opera singer*

Winter Springs
Hall, Gene Christian (Chris Hall) *coach, educator*
McNeal, Mary Kay *secondary school educator*
San Miguel, Sandra Bonilla *social worker*
Smyth, Michael P. *archaeologist, educator*

Zephyrhills
Barron, Ilona Eleanor *elementary school educator, consultant*
Shea, Bernard Charles *retired pharmaceutical executive*
Walton, Shirley Dawn *retired medical technician*

GEORGIA

Acworth
Oloni, Anthony Olushegun *medical association administrator, director*
Salerno, John C. *biochemist*
Whitmore, Michael Raymond *science educator*

Albany
Ansari, Mohammed Ishaque *economics professor*
Bryant, Thedis W. *academic librarian*
Calhoun, Roy *school librarian*
Elufiede, Babafemi Olayiwola *social sciences educator*
Forsyth, Rosalyn Moye *middle school educator*
Gassel, Elizabeth Marie *literature and language professor*
Grey, Charles Robert *literature and language professor*
Johnson, Debra Pope *education educator*
King, Hanh *literature and language educator*
Liu, May Sumei *biology professor*
Marbury, Ritchey McGuire III *engineering executive, surveyor*
Marshall, Cindy Lou *science and social studies educator*
May, Michael *chemistry professor*
McLaughlin, LaVerne Laney *library director*
Melton, Maurice K. *history professor*
Moises, Alfonso Arturo *communications educator*
Seo, Seong S. *chemistry professor, researcher*
Stallworth, Charles Derotha, Jr. *psychologist*
Willis, Jakie Arleta *elementary and secondary educator*

Alma
Murphy, Kenny R. *finance educator*

Alpharetta
Adams, Kenneth Francis *automotive executive*
Bolton, Robin Jean *artist, painter*
Brands, James Edwin *medical products executive*
Bridges, Alan Lynn *physicist, researcher, application developer*
Bunker, Kimberly LeAnn *critical care nurse, emergency nurse practitioner*
Chatlen, Stanley Lee *transportation executive*
Filliat, Elizabeth Hartley *retired secondary school educator*
Michele, Chrisette (Chrisette Michele Payne) *singer*
Orr, Zellie *entrepreneur, educator, writer, researcher*
Wind, Alan Michael *history educator*
Winegar, Albert Lee *computer company executive*
Yeatman, Henry Clay *mechanical engineer*

Americus
Adler, Brian Ungar *language educator, director*
Barnetson, Katherine Olson *nursing educator*
Capitan, William Harry *university president emeritus*
Hooks, George Bardin *state legislator, insurance company executive*
Huffman, Charles M. *psychology professor*
Isaacs, Harold *history professor*
Reckford, Jonathan Thomas More *nonprofit organization administrator*
Shapiro, Paul D. *sociologist, educator*

Andersonville
Boyles, Frederick Holdren *historian*

Athens
Aaron, Ira Edward *retired educator*
Adams, Michael Fred *academic administrator, political scientist, educator*
Algeo, John Thomas *association executive, retired educator*
Allsbrook, Ogden Olmstead, Jr. *retired economics professor*
Bacon, Charles Wilson *mycologist, educator, research scientist*
Baile, Clifton A. *biologist, researcher*
Basawa, Ishwar V. *Statistics Professor*
Bennetzen, Jeffrey L. *molecular biologist*
Berdanier, Lynne *science educator*
Brackett, Benjamin Gaylord *retired physiology and pharmacology educator*
Brooks, Linda Marie *humanities educator*
Buck, Peter *musician, guitarist*
Carlson, Ronald Lee *law educator*
Chaffin, Verner Franklin *lawyer, educator*
Chu, Chung Kwang *medicinal chemistry professor*
Clute, Robert Eugene *political science professor*
Correa-Diaz, Luis Alberto *language educator*
Covington, Michael Aaron *computation linguist*
Donovan, James M. *librarian, anthropologist*
Dunham, Richard E. III *lighting and set designer, consultant, educator*
Dunn, Delmer Delano *political science professor*
Eiland, William U. *museum director*
Ellington, Charles Ronald *lawyer, educator*
Fameree, Randall Joseph, II, *physiologist, educator*
Fink, Conrad Charles *journalist, communications executive, consultant*
Fox, Mark *men's college basketball coach*
Garbin, Albeno Patrick *sociology educator*
Golembiewski, Robert Thomas *management consultant, educator*
Hellerstein, Walter *lawyer*
Herbert, James Arthur *retired art educator, artist, filmmaker*
Hinton, Arthur, Jr. *microbiologist*
Huszagh, Fredrick Wickett *lawyer, information technology executive, educator*
Hutchinson, Amelia M. *literature and language professor*
Jackson, Lori Lee *elementary school educator*
Johnson, Loch Kingsford *political science educator, researcher*
Johnson, Michael Kenneth *chemistry professor*
Kaufman, Glen Frank *art educator*
Kellough, J. Edward *political science professor, department chairman*
Klein, Jared Stephen *linguist, educator*
Krasnostchekova, Elena Alexander *literature and language educator*
Kretzschmar, William Addison, Jr. *language educator*
Kurtz, Paul Michael *law educator*
Kushner, Sidney Ralph *molecular genetics and biochemistry educator*
Lauth, Thomas P. *dean, political science professor*
Law, John Harold *biochemistry educator*
Mayo, John Arthur *microbiologist, researcher, educator*
McBee, Mary Louise *state legislator, academic administrator*
McCutcheon, Steven Clifton *ecological and environmental engineer, hydrologist*
Melton, Wayne Charles *real estate executive*
Menke, Richard *literature and language professor*
Miller, Herbert Elmer *accountant*
Miller, Ronald Baxter *language educator, writer*
Mills, Mike *musician*
Nelson, Stuart Owen *agricultural engineer, researcher, educator*
Nicewarner, Metta Lee *library director, artist*
Nichols, William Curtis *psychologist, educator, marriage and family therapist, consultant*
Oliveri, Michael Steven *art educator*
Olsen, Richard James *artist, educator*
O'Toole, Laurence Joseph *public administration and policy educator, researcher*
Outcalt, Kenneth W. *ecologist, researcher*
Paul, William Dewitt, Jr. *retired art educator, collector, artist*
Pollack, Robert Harvey *psychology professor*
Poss, C. Thomas *ancient language educator*
Potter, William Gray, Jr. *university librarian*
Puckett, Elizabeth Ann *law librarian, educator*
Rasmussen, Todd C. *hydrologist, educator*
Reitz, Elizabeth J. *anthropologist, educator*
Richt, Mark *college football coach*
Rittenberry, Harold W., Jr. *sculptor*
Roberts, Ken *electrical engineer, director*
Roellig, Dawn M. *research scientist*
Schaefer, Henry Frederick III *chemistry professor*
Schleyer, Paul von Ragué *chemistry educator*
Smagorinsky, Peter *education educator*
Smith (Cavanagh), Susan Carlton *artist, illustrator, sculptor*
Soloski, John *journalism and communications educator*
Stufken, John *statistician, educator*
Sullivan, Patricia Lynne *political science professor*
Sumichrast, Robert T. *dean, business educator*
Tolley, Edward Donald *lawyer*
Tyler, David Earl *veterinary medical educator*
Waters, John Caldwell *historic preservation professor*
Wessler, Susan R. *biologist, educator*
White, Rebecca Hanner *dean, law educator*
Williams, Susan Michelle *veterinarian, educator*
Winship, Michael P. *history professor*
Yang, Charles Qi-Xiang *chemistry educator, researcher, consultant*

Atlanta
Aaberg, Thomas Marshall, Sr. *academic administrator*
Aaron, Hank (Henry L. Aaron) *professional baseball team executive*
Abbott, Gay O. *bank executive*
Abdel-Khalik, Said Ibrahim *nuclear and mechanical engineering educator*
Abney, David P. *delivery service executive*
Abrams, Harold Eugene *lawyer*
Addison, Abby Ayer *middle school educator*
Affonso, Dyanne D. *dean*
Ahearn, Donald G. *microbiologist, consultant, researcher*
Aiken, Vernoy Fred *government agency administrator*
Aka, Ebenezer Osita *urban planner, educator, researcher, consultant*
Albee, Robert Bruce *gynecologist, endoscopic laser surgeon*
Albert, Marv *sportscaster, program director*
Albert, Ross Alan *lawyer*
Alexander, Cecil Abraham *academic administrator, consultant, retired architect*
Alexander, Kent B. *lawyer*
Alexander, Miles Jordan *lawyer*
Allan, Alexander R.C. (Sandy Allan) *food products executive*
Alleyne, Mark Dacosta *communications educator, journalist*
Allison, Stuart Anthony *chemistry professor, researcher*
Altman, Robert *lawyer*
Amanpour, Christiane *news correspondent*
Ames, William Francis *mathematician, educator*
Anderson, Garret *professional baseball player*
Anderson, Gloria Long *chemistry professor*
Anderson, John *professional hockey coach, retired professional hockey player*
Anderson, Richard H. *air transportation executive*
Anthony, Barbara Cox *foundation administrator*
Antonino, Lauren Slepin *lawyer*
Arias, Ileana *psychiatrist, educator*
Armstrong, Sarah Madden *beverage company executive*
Arroyo, F. Thaddeus *telecommunications industry executive*
Ashizawa, Annette Eiko *epidemiologist, researcher*
Bahl, Roy Winford *economist, educator, consultant*
Bailey, Stephanie B.C. *public health service officer*
Bainbridge, Frederick Freeman III *architect*
Baird, Marianne Saunorus *critical care clinical nurse specialist, administrator*
Baker, Thurbert E. *state attorney general*
Bakewell, Peter John *history educator*
Baldwin, Dee M. *nursing educator*
Bankoff, Joseph R. *art center administrator*
Bao, Gang *biomedical engineer, educator*
Barke, Richard P. *political science professor*
Barker, William Daniel *hospital administrator*
Barkley, Charles Wade *sportscaster, retired professional basketball player*
Barnes, David A. *delivery service executive*
Barnett, Crawford Fannin, Jr. *internist, educator, cardiologist, travel medicine specialist*
Barr, Robert Laurence, Jr., (Bob Barr) *lawyer, former United States Representative from Georgia*
Barrow, Daniel Louis *neurosurgeon*
Bassett, W. Randall *lawyer*
Bastian, Edward H. *air transportation executive*
Bayne, Katie J. (Katherine J. Bayne) *marketing executive*
Beazer, Brian C. *construction executive*
Becker, Mark Paul *academic administrator, statistician, educator*
Beckham, Walter Hull III *lawyer*
Beerman, Joel I. *lawyer, chemical manufacturing company executive*
Belkin, Steven *professional sports team executive*
Bell, Thomas Devereaux, Jr. *real estate company executive*
Bellamy, Ivory *elementary school educator, consultant*
Bellanca, Joseph Paul *engineering construction executive*
Benario, Herbert William *classicist, educator*
Benham, Robert *state supreme court justice*
Bennington, Geoffrey Peter *language educator, writer*
Benveniste, Lawrence M. *dean*
Berkelhamer, Jay Ellis *pediatrician*
Berryman, Robert Mogabgab *systems engineer*
Besser, Richard Eric *pediatrician, federal agency administrator*
Bevington, Paula Lawton *principal*
Bibby, Mike *professional basketball player*
Bifulco, Frank P. *marketing executive*
Birch, Stanley Francis, Jr. *federal judge*
Bird, Wendell Raleigh *lawyer*
Bisher, James Furman *journalist, writer*
Blackmon, Douglas A. *newspaper reporter, writer*
Blake, Elizabeth K. *lawyer*
Blake, Frank (Francis Stanton Blake) *consumer products company executive, lawyer*
Blalock, Rebecca A. *information technology specialist*
Blank, A(ndrew) Russell *lawyer*
Blum, Terry Christine *management educator, former dean*
Blumenthal, Daniel Sender *medical educator*
Blystone, Lawrence K. *machinery and equipment company executive*
Boden, Scott David *orthopedic surgeon, spine surgeon, educator*
Bolch, Carl Edward, Jr. *oil industry executive, lawyer*
Bonds, John Wilfred, Jr. *lawyer*
Booth, Gordon Dean, Jr. *lawyer*
Borek, Lois Brewer *physiologist, educator*
Borovikov, Valery *research scientist*
Bostic, James E., Jr. *paper company executive*
Bowden, Henry Lumpkin, Jr. *lawyer*
Bowers, W. Paul *utilities executive*
Bradley, Rebekah *healthcare educator, lab administrator*
Brandenburg, David Saul *gastroenterologist, educator*
Brandes, Johann Christoph *oncologist*
Branson, Bernard M. *medical association administrator, director*
Braswell, Robert M. *state banking agency administrator*
Bratton, James Henry, Jr. *lawyer*
Brecher, Armin George *lawyer*
Breeden, Mimi *bank executive*
Bremer, Karen Ingrid *food service executive*
Bremner, James Douglas *psychiatrist, researcher, education educator*
Brigham, Kenneth Larry *medical educator*
Brock, John F. *beverage company executive*
Brooks, Durado *health science association administrator, oncologist*
Brown, Carlton E. *academic administrator*
Brown, Lorene B(yron) *retired library educator*
Brown, William Virgil *internal medicine educator*
Brutto, Daniel J. *delivery service executive*
Bryant, Gregory Alexander *bishop*
Burns, Thomas Samuel *history professor*
Burrows, Nilka Rios *epidemiologist*
Byrne, Granville Bland III *lawyer*
Cadenhead, Alfred Paul *lawyer*
Cagle, Casey *Lieutenant Governor of Georgia*
Campbell, Ann-Marie *retail executive*
Campbell, Michael H. *air transportation executive*
Capra, C. Monica *science educator*
Carbonell, Joaquin R. III *telecommunications industry executive, lawyer*
Carey, Gerald John, Jr. *research institute director emeritus, former air force officer*
Carey, Matthew *consumer products company executive*
Carley, George H. *state supreme court justice*
Carp, Daniel Allen *air transportation executive, former consumer products company executive*
Carpenter, David Allan *lawyer*
Carrico, Paul D. *chemical company executive*
Carter, Dudley Rochelle *lawyer*
Carter, Jimmy (James Earl Carter Jr.) *39th President of the United States*
Carter, Rosalynn Smith (Eleanor Rosalynn Smith Carter) *former First Lady of the United States*
Carter, Stephen M. *telecommunications manufacturing industry executive*
Chancy, Mark A. *bank executive*
Charles, Sally Allen *financial consultant*
Chasen, Sylvan Herbert *data processing executive, financial planner*
Cherkaoui, Mohammed *aerospace engineer, educator*
Chiang, Tze I. *economist, researcher, consultant*
Chilivis, Nickolas Peter *retired lawyer*
Cilella, Mary Winifred *director*
Cilella, Salvatore George, Jr. *museum director*
Circeo, Louis Joseph, Jr. *research scientist, civil engineer*
Ciucci, Joseph A. *lawyer*
Clancy, Andrew Nelson *biology professor*
Clark, Wendy *advertising executive*
Clarke, Thomas Hal *lawyer*
Clearo, Kellie Anne *internist, pharmacist, psychiatrist*
Cleland, Max (Joseph Maxwell Cleland) *former United States Senator from Georgia*
Cobb, Kim M. *science educator*
Codner, Mark Allen *plastic surgeon*
Cohen, Ezra Harry *lawyer*
Cohen, George Leon *lawyer*
Cohen, Lori G. *lawyer*
Cohen, N. Jerold *lawyer*
Coles, Charlton J. *psychologist, educator*
Collins, Doug (Paul Douglas Collins) *sportscaster, former professional basketball coach*
Conboy, Kevin Patrick *lawyer*
Connelly, Terrence John, Sr. *broadcast executive*
Cook, Philip Carter *lawyer*
Cooper, Gerald Rice *clinical pathologist*
Cooper, Jerome Maurice *architect*
Cooper, William A. *cardiothoracic surgeon, medical educator*
Cooper-Ruspoli, Annie Nataf *psychiatrist, director*
Copenhaver, John Barns *not-for-profit executive, lawyer*
Corr, James Vanis *furniture manufacturing executive, accountant*
Costello, John H. III *business and marketing executive*
Coughlin, Steven Scott *epidemiologist*
Cox, Bobby (Robert Joe Cox) *professional baseball manager*
Cox, Kathy *state official, school system administrator*
Cox, Nancy Jane *microbiologist*
Cox, Shanna Nakia *research scientist*
Cramer, Howard Ross *geologist, environmental consultant*
Crawford, Aaron Jamal (Jamal Crawford) *professional basketball player*
Cressler, John David *electrical engineering educator*
Croft, Terrence Lee *lawyer, mediator, arbitrator*
Crow, Tim *consumer products company executive*
Crump-Caine, Lynn *management consultant, former food service executive*
Curtis, J. Vaughan *lawyer*
Daley, Sharon R. *human resources specialist*
Dalton, John Joseph *lawyer*
Darden, Claibourne Henry, Jr. *marketing research professional*
Darden, George Washington, III, (Buddy Darden) *lawyer, former United States Representative from Georgia*
Davis, Aimee Slaughter *social studies educator*
Davis, Benjamin Alando *lawyer*
Davis, D. Scott (D. Scott Davis) *delivery service executive*
Davis, Erroll Brown, Jr. *academic administrator, former utilities executive*
Davis, Frank Tradewell, Jr. *lawyer*
Davis, Lawrence William *radiation oncologist*
Davis, Michael *medical educator*
Davis, Stephen H. *food service executive, marketing professional*
Dawson, Robert G. *telecommunications industry executive*
Day, Diane Elaine *science educator, researcher*
Deane, Richard Hunter, Jr. *former federal judge, lawyer*
DeAngelo, Joseph J. *consumer products company executive*
Dearman, Andrew J. III *utilities executive*
Deason, Stephen Earl *computer company executive*
Declercq, Nico Felicien *research scientist*
de Heer, Walter A. *physics professor*
DeLong, Mahlon R. *neurologist, educator*
del Valle, Yamille Ellend *engineer, researcher*
Denny, Richard Alden, Jr. *retired lawyer*
DeRodes, Robert P. *information technology executive*
De Rosa, Christopher Thomas *biomedical researcher*
de Sousa Sheppard, Dalila *history professor*
de Waal, Frans B.M. *biologist, psychology professor*
Dhamala, Mukesh *physics professor*
Dhawan, Saurabh *physician, educator*
Dickinson, Robert Earl *atmospheric scientist, educator, retired science administrator*
Diedrich, Richard Joseph *architect*
Dierker, David F. *bank executive*
Dietz, William Harry *pediatrician*
Dimitroff, Thomas G., Jr. *professional sports team executive*
Din-Dzietham, Rebecca L.P. *cardiologist, educator*
Dobes, William Lamar, Jr. *dermatologist, educator*
Dobrzyn, Janet Elaine *quality assurance professional*
Domby, Arthur H. *lawyer*
Donis, Ruben *federal agency administrator, researcher, virologist*
Dorfman, Richard *bank executive*
D'Orsi, Carl Joseph *medical educator, radiologist, researcher*
Dotson, Albert *not-for-profit fundraiser*
Douglas, J. Alexander M. (Sandy) *beverage company executive*
Douglas, John Lewis *lawyer*
Douglas, John Simonton, Jr. *cardiologist, educator*
Douglas, Seymour Bentley *finance company executive, director*
Douglas, William W. *food products executive*
Dowling, Roderick Anthony *investment banker*
Driver, Walter W., Jr. *lawyer*
Dudley, Rick (Richard C. Dudley) *professional sports team executive, retired professional hockey player*
Duffey, William Simon, Jr. *federal judge, former prosecutor*
Dunlevie, Steven S. *lawyer*
Dupri, Jermaine *recording industry executive, music producer*
Durrett, James Frazer, Jr. *retired lawyer*
Dutt, Kamla *medical educator*
Eaddy, Felton Eugene *literature and language educator*
Ebersole, W. Daniel *state treasurer*
Eckl, William Wray *lawyer*
Edmondson, J.L. (James Larry Edmondson) *federal judge*
Edwards, Stephen Allen *lawyer*
Egan, Michael Joseph *retired lawyer, state legislator*
Ellingwood, Bruce Russell *structural engineer, educator*
Elliott, Lester Franklyn *plastic surgeon*
Ellis, Barbara Ann *microbiologist, epidemiologist*
Ellis, James O., Jr. *nuclear energy industry executive, retired military officer*
El-Sayed, Mostafa Amr *chemistry professor*
Enstrom, Tobias *professional hockey player*
Erera, Alan *engineering educator*
Erving, Julius (Winfield), (II) *business executive, retired professional basketball player*
Evans, Orinda D. *federal judge*
Everhart, Sue *political organization administrator*
Faber, Olaf Ulrich *structural engineer*
Fajardo, Geroncio Cagigas *epidemiologist*
Falk, Henry *pediatrician, epidemiologist, researcher*
Family, Fereydoon *physicist, researcher*
Fanning, Thomas Andrew *utilities executive*
Fayard, Gary P. *beverage company executive*
Fenton, Kevin Andrew *epidemiologist, educator*
Ferdinand, Keith C. *cardiologist*
Finan, Irial *beverage company executive*
Finnerty, Terry P. *lawyer*
Fivush, Robyn *psychology professor, department chairman*
Flanders, Karen *consumer products company executive*
Flannery, James William *performing arts educator, theater director and producer, singer*
Flax, Hugh *dentist*
Fleming, Julian Denver, Jr. *lawyer*
Fleming, Stephen Richard *finance company executive, investor*

Fletcher, Kathy Jordan *music educator*
Foege, William Herbert *public health administrator, educator*
Ford, Sandra Elizabeth *state agency administrator, public health service officer*
Forney, Larry J. *chemical engineer, educator*
Forry, Robert H. *lawyer*
Forte, Judy *parks director*
Fortin, Raymond D. *lawyer, bank executive*
Foulke, Edwin Gerhart, Jr. *lawyer, former federal agency administrator*
Fowler, Bruce Andrew *toxicologist, researcher, public health service official*
Fox, Mary Frank *sociology educator, researcher*
Fox, Robert E., Jr. *library director*
Franklin, Robert Michael, Jr. *academic administrator, theology studies educator*
Franklin, Shirley Clarke *Mayor, Atlanta*
Fratello, Mike (Michael Robert Fratello) *sportscaster, former professional basketball coach*
Freedman, Louis Martin *dentist*
Freeman, Brenda *broadcast executive*
Freeman, Thomas E. *bank executive*
Frey, Teryl Kenneth *biology professor, virologist*
Frias, Jaime Luis *retired pediatrician, clinical geneticist, educator*
Fridovich-Keil, Judith Lisa *molecular biology researcher, educator*
Frieden, Thomas R. *federal official, epidemiologist*
Frumkin, Howard *epidemiologist, educator*
Galina, Brenda Moss *museum director*
Gallagher, Thomas C. *diversified manufacturing executive*
Gambrell, David Henry *lawyer*
Ganaway, George Kenneth *psychiatrist, psychoanalyst, educator, researcher*
Ganesh, Thota *research scientist*
Garland, LaRetta Matthews *psychologist, nursing educator*
Garrett, Michael D. *utilities executive*
Gary, Kenneth J. *lawyer*
Gaudet, Matthew C. *lawyer*
Gay, Robert Derril *behavioral health consultant*
Gayle, Helene D. *pediatrician, public health service officer*
Gearon, John Michael, Jr., (Michael Gearon) *professional sports team owner, communications executive*
Genberg, Ira *lawyer*
Gephardt, Dick (Richard Andrew Gephardt) *consulting company executive, former United States Representative from Missouri, lawyer*
Gerakitis, Richard *lawyer*
Gershenhorn, Alan *delivery service executive*
Gibbons, Gary Hugh *cardiologist, educator*
Giddens, Don Peyton *engineering educator, researcher*
Gilligan, Bob *energy executive*
Girth, Marjorie Louisa *lawyer, educator*
Glaser, Arthur Henry *lawyer, mediator*
Glover, Renée Lewis *city official*
Goldstein, Elliott *retired lawyer, director*
Gomes, Matthew Trainor *lawyer*
Gonzalez, Ruben Rene *biochemist, researcher, educator*
Gonzalez-Ruiz, Julio *literature and language educator*
Goodman, Seymour Evan *computer science and international studies educator, researcher, consultant*
Goodman, Sherryl Hope *psychology professor*
Gordon, Frank Jeffrey *medical educator*
Gordon, Helen Tate *program assistant, nurse*
Gorman, Stephen E. *air transportation executive*
Grady, Kevin E. *lawyer*
Green, Holcombe Tucker, Jr. *investment company executive*
Greer, Bernard Lewis, Jr., (Ben Greer) *lawyer*
Gregory, Mel Hyatt, Jr. *retired insurance company executive*
Gregory, Wilton Daniel *archbishop*
Grossniklaus, Hans E. *ophthalmologist, educator*
Groton, James Purnell *lawyer, arbitrator*
Grumet, Priscilla Hecht *fashion specialist, consultant, writer*
Guerra, Larry Cacao *engineer, researcher*
Guldiken, Rasim Oytun *research scientist*
Gupta, Sanjay *neurosurgeon, educator, medical correspondent, journalist*
Gutman, Julie Rae *pediatrician*
Guyton, Robert A. *cardiothoracic surgeon, medical educator*
Gwynn, Anthony Keith (Tony Gwynn) *sportscaster, retired professional baseball player*
Hakes, Jay Edward *library director, former federal agency administrator*
Hall, Wilbur Dallas, Jr. *medical educator*
Hallen, Barry *philosopher, educator*
Halter, Hank *air transportation executive*
Handel, Karen *Secretary of State, Georgia*
Hao, Chunhai *pathologist, researcher*
Harkey, Robert Shelton *retired lawyer*
Harris, Clifford Joseph, Jr., (T.I., Tip Harris) *rap artist*
Harrison, Clifford *chef, small business owner*
Harrison, David Glenn *medical educator, cardiologist*
Harrison, George Brooks *engineer, researcher, retired military officer*
Hartfield-Méndez, Vialla *language educator*
Hasson, James Keith, Jr. *lawyer, educator*
Hatch, Helen Davis *architect*
Hatcher, Charles Ross, Jr. *surgeon, health facility administrator*
Hatcher, James A. *lawyer*
Hauenstein, Glen W. *air transportation executive*
Hawks, Barrett Kingsbury *lawyer*
Hay, Peter Heinrich *law educator*
Hays, Richard R. *lawyer*
He, Feng *environmentalist, consultant*
Healy, Bridget M. *lawyer*
Helmick, Charles Gardiner III *epidemiologist*
Helms, My Nga *physiologist, researcher*
Henry, Ronald James Whyte *academic administrator, physicist, educator*
Henry, Thomas Reid *education educator, researcher*
Hess, Dennis William *chemical engineering educator*
Hester, Thomas Roderick, Jr. *plastic surgeon, educator*
Higginbotham, Eve Juliet *ophthalmologist, educator, dean*
Hildreth, William Bartley *finance educator, consultant*
Hill, Allen Edward *delivery service executive*
Hill, Scott A. *stock exchange executive*
Hill, Tyrone *professional basketball coach, retired professional basketball player*
Hilliard, Robert Glenn *insurance company executive, lawyer*
Hinchey, John William *lawyer*
Hines, Preston Harris *state supreme court justice*
Hinkel, Daniel Farris *lawyer, writer, investment company executive*
Hinson, H. Douglas *lawyer*
Hobby, Scott M. *lawyer*
Hodges, Dewey Harper *aerospace engineer, educator*
Hodges, Helen Frishe *nurse, professor*
Hoff, Gerhardt Michael *lawyer, insurance company executive*
Hogan, John Donald *retired college dean, finance educator*
Holland, George Edison, Jr., (Ed) *lawyer, utilities executive*
Holly, Timothy Arnold *security firm executive*
Honaman, J. Craig *health facility administrator*
Honoré, Russel L. *retired military officer*
Hopkins, Donald Roswell *public health physician*
Hopkins, John David *lawyer*
Hopkins, Linton *chef*
Horford Reynoso, Alfred Joel (Al Horford) *professional basketball player*
Hoskyns, William A. *dentist*
Howard, Ayanna MacCalla *electrical and robotics engineer, educator*
Howard, Harry Clay *lawyer*
Howell, Arthur *lawyer*
Hug, Carl Casimir, Jr. *pharmacology and anesthesiology educator, medical ethics educator*
Hull, Frank Mays *federal judge*
Hung, Chin-Cheng *artist, educator*
Hunstein, Carol *chief justice*
Hussey, Kent J. *consumer products company executive*
Huynh, Boi Hanh *physics professor, researcher*
Hyland, Gregory E. *manufacturing executive*
Ide, Roy William III *lawyer*
Igietseme, Joseph Ugbodaga *biomedical researcher, educator*
Isdell, Neville (Edward Neville Isdell) *retired beverage company executive*
Israili, Zafar Hasan *pharmacologist, educator*
Izard, John *lawyer*
Jackson, Geraldine *entrepreneur*
Jackson, Robert Benton, IV, *environmental engineer*
Jameson, Louis Norwood (L. Norwood 'Woody' Jameson) *lawyer*
Janney, Donald Wayne *lawyer*
Jayaraman, Sundaresan *science educator*
Jeffery, Geoffrey Marron *medical parasitologist*
Jenkins, Albert Felton, Jr. *lawyer*
Johanson, Marie A. *physical therapist, educator*
Johnson, Benjamin F(ranklin) III *lawyer*
Johnson, F. Ross (Frederick Ross Johnson) *international management advisory company executive*
Johnson, Joe Marcus *professional basketball player*
Johnson, John H. *lawyer*
Johnson, Marsha Sampson *utilities executive*
Johnson, Paul *college football coach*
Jones, Chipper (Larry Wayne Jones Jr.) *professional baseball player*
Jones, Glower Whitehead *lawyer*
Jordak, John A., Jr. *lawyer*
Joseph, Pamela A. *bank executive*
Joung, Yeun-Ho *research and development company executive*
Judd, George R. *wholesale distribution executive*
Jurkiewicz, Maurice John *surgeon, educator*
Kachur, Stephen Patrick *health science association administrator*
Kahn, Bernd *radiochemist, educator*
Kalafut, George Wendell *retired distribution company executive, retired naval officer*
Kalogeropoulos, Andreas P. *cardiologist*
Kaminshine, Steven J. *dean, law educator*
Kamio, Michiya *research scientist*
Karp, Herbert Rubin *neurologist, educator, geriatrician*
Katz, Joel Abraham *lawyer*
Kaufman, Mark David *lawyer*
Kaufman, Mark Stuart *lawyer*
Kauten, James Richard *cardiothoracic surgeon*
Kaywood, Sam K., Jr. *lawyer*
Keiller, James Bruce *clergyman, dean*
Kelley, Brian P. *beverage and former relocation services company executive*
Kelly, Geoffrey J. *lawyer, beverage company executive*
Kelly, James Patrick *lawyer*
Kennedy, Dorian Bruce *lawyer*
Kennedy, James Cox *publishing and media executive*
Kenney, James Stevenson *engineering educator, consultant*
Kent, Muhtar *beverage company executive*
Kent, Philip I. *broadcast executive*
Keough, Donald Raymond *investment and former beverage company executive*
Kernis, Jay *broadcast executive*
Kessler, Richard Paul, Jr. *lawyer*
Ketchum, Mark D. *consumer products company executive*
Keyserling, Harry L. *pediatric infectious disease physician, researcher*
Khandelwal, Madhur *architectural firm executive*
Khoury, Kenneth F. *lawyer, air transportation executive*
Khoury, Muin J. *geneticist, epidemiologist*
Kidd, Jane V. *political organization administrator, former state legislator*
Kilgore, Cada T. III *lawyer*
Killorin, Robert Ware *lawyer*
Kim, Yoon Jo *mechanical engineer, researcher*
King, Debra Gray *cosmetic dentist*
King, Linda Orr *museum director, consultant*
King, Preston Theodore *social sciences educator, writer, political philosopher*
King, Spencer Bidwell III *cardiologist, educator, medical educator*
Kingsbury, Michael Bryant *organist, retired elementary and secondary school educator*
Kirby, C. Eugene, Jr. *bank executive*
Kirchner, Eric W. *delivery service executive*
Kitchens, William H. *lawyer*
Klein, Jonathan *broadcast executive*
Klippel, John H. *medical association administrator, physician*
Kloer, Philip Baldwin *journalist*
Klughart, Toni Anne *musician, singer, educator*
Knapp, Charles Boynton *economist, former university president, educator*
Kneisel, Edmund M. *lawyer*
Knowles, Marjorie Fine *law educator, dean*
Kohler, James J. *medical researcher*
Koplan, Jeffrey Powell *academic administrator, epidemiologist*
Kovalchuk, Ilya *professional hockey player*
Krebs, John W. *research scientist*
Krishnamurthy, Ramesh Saligrama *environmental scientist, researcher*
Kubina, Pavel *professional hockey player*
Kuehn, Kurt P. *delivery service executive*
Kuklenyik, Zsuzsanna *chemist, researcher*
Kung, Lisa *lawyer*
Kuntz, Marion Lucile Leathers *classicist, historian, educator*
Kushner, Howard I. *public health and history of medicine educator*
Lackland, Theodore Howard *lawyer*
LaDuke, Bettie *academic administrator*
Lally, John Patrick *investment company executive*
Lamberth, James A. *lawyer*
Lamberth, Rebecca M. *lawyer*
Landau, Michael B. *law educator*
Landon, James Henry *lawyer*
Laney, James Thomas *former ambassador, educator*
Lapu-Bula, Rigobert *cardiologist, medical educator, researcher*
Latham, John L. *lawyer*
Leach, Karen Kay *lawyer*
Leet, Alan C. *lawyer*
Leonard, David Morse *lawyer*
Lester, Charles Turner, Jr. *lawyer*
Levy, David Ruben *advertising and broadcasting executive*
Lewcock, Ronald Bentley *architect, educator*
Lewis, Earl *academic administrator*
Lewis, Lonzy James *Physics And Atmospheric Sciences Professor*
Lewis, Stephen E. *lawyer*
Li, Hong *language educator*
Liebmann, Seymour W. *construction executive, consultant*
Lilienfeld, Scott Owen *psychology educator*
Lim, Sung Kyu *computer scientist, educator*
Lin, Ming-Chang *physical chemistry professor, researcher*
Linch, Keth *commercial real estate and partnership lawyer*
Linkous, William Joseph, Jr. *lawyer*
Lipshutz, Robert Jerome *lawyer, former government official*
Litman, Seth Adam *lawyer*
Lobb, William Atkinson *financial services executive*
Lockhart, Dennis P. *bank executive*
Loewy, Robert Gustav *aerospace executive, engineering educator*
Looby, Brian William *lawyer, lobbyist*
Loveland, L. Joseph, Jr. *lawyer*
Lowe, Derek (Derek Christopher Lowe) *professional baseball player*
Lower, Robert Cassel *lawyer, educator*
Lu, Hanchao *humanities educator, writer*
Lubin, Michael Frederick *physician, educator*
Luce, Richard *university librarian*
Luce, Willard Ray *historian, director*
Luckovich, Michael Edward *cartoonist*
Lunsford, Mike (Michael Cameron Lunsford) *Internet company executive*
Lynn, David G. *biology and chemistry professor*
Macenczak, Lee Andrew *air transportation executive*
Mackay, Gregory James *plastic surgeon*
Madisetti, Vijay Krishna *electrical engineer, educator*
Mahaley-Johnson, Hosanna *school system administrator*
Malhotra, Naresh Kumar *marketing educator*
Malveaux, Suzanne *news correspondent*
Mandock, Randal Lee Nicholas *geophysicist, professor*
Mani, Ramesh G. *physicist*
Marohn, William D. *consumer products company executive*
Marshall, John Treutlen *lawyer, educator*
Martin, C. Alan *utilities executive*
Martin, David Edward *health sciences educator*
Marvin, Charles Arthur *law educator*
Massey, Charles Knox, Jr. *advertising agency executive*
Massey, Denise McLain *theology studies educator*
Matschullat, Dale Lewis *lawyer*
May, Sheldon W. *chemistry professor*
Mayberg, Helen Susan *neurologist, educator*
McAlpin, Kirk Martin *lawyer*
McCann, Brian Michael *professional baseball player*
McCann, Martin Bruce *civil engineer*
McCarthy, Ian J. *construction executive*
McCauley, Linda A. *dean, nursing educator*
McClure, Teri Plummer *lawyer, delivery service executive*
McCord, Clinton D., Jr. *oculoplastic surgeon*
McCrary, Charles D. *utilities executive*
McDavid, Sara June *librarian*
McDevitt, John *delivery service executive*
McDonald, L. Clifford *epidemiologist*
McDowell, David Lynn *mechanical engineering educator*
McFall, John *performing company executive*
McIntire, Larry Vern *biomedical engineering educator*
McLean, James Albert *artist, educator*
McLouth, Nathan Richard (Nate McLouth) *professional baseball player*
McNeill, Thomas Ray *lawyer*
Meachum, Daniel Ray *lawyer*
Meador, Kimford Jay *neurologist, researcher*
Meadors, Marynell *professional basketball coach*
Mecke, William Moyn *public information officer*
Medows, Rhonda M. *state agency administrator, public health service officer*
Meier, Gayle M. *library director*
Meindl, James Donald *electrical engineering educator, academic administrator*
Melton, Harold D. *state supreme court justice*
Mercer, John T.W. *lawyer*
Merkel-Moran, Christa Ilse *investor, linguist, educator*
Merkle, Sarah Lynn *research scientist*
Metters, Richard *finance educator*
Mezencev, Roman *arms control expert, consultant, translator*
Mialon, Sue *economics professor*
Mickens, Ronald Elbert *mathematician, physics professor*
Mildenhall, Jonathan *beverage company executive*
Miller, Douglas Linn *lawyer*
Miller, Joseph (Buzz) *lobbyist, nuclear energy industry executive*
Miller, Zell Bryan *former senator, governor*
Milton, Micah H. *medical researcher*
Minneman, Kenneth Paul *pharmacology educator*
Mize, Gerald L., Jr. *lawyer*
Mobley, John Homer, II, *lawyer*
Moeling, Walter Goos, IV, *lawyer*
Moeller, Joseph W. *forest products company executive, former chemicals executive*
Mones, Stuart Matthew *lawyer*
Moon, Kyoung-sik *research scientist*
Moore, Rodney Gregory *lawyer*
Morris, Douglas Claude *cardiologist, educator*
Muller, Edward Robert *energy executive, lawyer*
Mullin, Bernard James *media consultant*
Murphy, Douglas A. *cardiothoracic surgeon*
Murray, Janet Horowitz *humanities educator, multimedia designer*
Muth, Richard Ferris *economics professor*
Mutombo, Dikembe (Dikembe Mutombo Mpolondo Mukamba Jean Jacque Wamutombo) *retired professional basketball player*
Nagel, Jeffrey A. *energy executive*
Nagel, Vernon J. *chemicals and electronics executive*
Nahai, Foad *plastic surgeon, educator*
Nahmias, David E. *prosecutor*
Namnoum, Anne Brawner *obstetrician, gynecologist*
Namnoum, James Daniel *plastic surgeon*
Nana, Georges *language educator*
Neil, Robert F. *broadcast executive*
Nemeroff, Charles Barnet *neurobiology and psychiatry educator*
Newport, D. Jeffrey *psychiatrist, researcher*
Newton, Floyd Childs III *lawyer*
Nix, Jerry W. *automotive executive*
Norman, Albert George, Jr. *lawyer*
Nunn, Donald Ray *plastic surgeon*
O'Brien, Soledad *news anchor*
Odujebe, Oladapo A. *toxicologist, educator, emergency physician*
O'Kelley, William Clark *federal judge*
Oliker, Vladimir *mathematician, educator*
O'Regan, Ruth *oncologist, educator*
Owens, Christine M. *delivery service executive*
Owens, Laura Lewis *lawyer*
Pan, Yi *computer science educator*
Papapolymerou, John *engineering educator*
Parker, Dan *human resources executive*
Parker, John R., Jr. *food products executive, lawyer*
Parks, John Scott *pediatric endocrinologist*
Parsons, Leonard Jon *marketing educator, consultant*
Partlett, David F. *dean, law educator*
Patel, Pragna *epidemiologist*
Patterson, Dennis M. *bank executive*
Paul, Ketema Nnamdi *neuroscientist, educator*
Payne, William Porter (Billy Payne) *investment company executive*
Peacock, George Rowatt *retired life insurance company executive*
Pelypenko, Elizabeth *lawyer*
Peponis, John *architect, educator*
Perdue, George (Sonny Perdue) *Governor of Georgia*
Perera, Unil A.G. *physics educator, researcher*
Persons, (W.) Ray (W. Ray Persons) *lawyer, legal association administrator*
Peterson, George P. (Bud Peterson) *academic administrator*
Petrik, Michael Thomas *lawyer*
Petrovic, Bojan *nuclear engineer, educator*
Phillips, Barry *lawyer*
Pickering, Larry Kenneth *pediatrician, researcher*
Pike, Larry Samuel *lawyer*
Pilcher, James Brownie *lawyer*
Pindle, Arthur Jackson, Jr. *philosopher, researcher*
Podewils, Laura Jean *epidemiologist, researcher*
Polhamus, Barbara *behavioral scientist*
Polk, James Ray *journalist*
Pottle, Steven L. *lawyer*
Price, Edward Warren *retired aerospace engineer*
Price, Mark (William Mark Price) *professional basketball coach, retired professional basketball player*
Pu, Calton *computer scientist*
Pulgram, William Leopold *architect, space designer*
Puskas, John Daniel *cardiothoracic surgeon, medical educator*
Quatrano, Anne *chef, restaurant owner*
Quittmeyer, Peter Charles *lawyer*
Raby, Kenneth Alan *lawyer, retired military officer*
Rafuse, Nancy E. *lawyer, director*

Rahmani, Amir R. *research scientist*
Ramalingam, Suresh S *oncologist*
Ramesh, Balasubramaniam *science educator*
Ramsey, Ira Clayton *retired petroleum industry executive*
Raper, Charles Albert *retired management consultant*
Ratcliffe, David M. *utilities executive*
Raymond, Usher, IV, (Usher) *singer, actor*
Reed, Glen Alfred *lawyer*
Reed, James Whitfield *internist, educator, endocrinologist*
Reed, William R., Jr. *bank executive*
Reeder, Joe Robert *lawyer, former federal official*
Reese, Audrey Maria *music educator*
Reinhardt, Daniel Sargent *lawyer*
Remar, Robert Boyle *lawyer*
Ressler, Kerry *psychiatrist, educator*
Reynolds, Douglas R. *history professor*
Rhodes, Thomas Willard *lawyer*
Riccio, Felix *professional sports team owner*
Ridley, Clarence Haverty *retail executive*
Riggs, Gregory Lynn *lawyer*
Roberts, Edward Graham *librarian*
Robinson, J. Patrick *consumer products company executive*
Rodgers, Michael Owen *civil engineer, educator*
Rogers, C. B. *lawyer*
Rogers, DeWitt Ralph *lawyer*
Rogers, William H., Jr. *bank executive*
Rojas, Carlos *literature and language educator*
Rojas, Mauricio *research scientist, educator*
Roseborough, Teresa Wynn *lawyer*
Rothbaum, Barbara Olasov *psychologist, educator*
Rouhani, Shahrokh *civil engineering environmental educator, consultant*
Rousseau, Ronald William *chemical engineering educator, researcher*
Rucchin, Steve *professional hockey player*
Rusche, Mark C. *lawyer*
Rushdie, Sir Salman (Ahmed Salman Rushdie) *writer, educator*
Rust, George S. *physician, educator*
Salant, Richard Frank *mechanical engineer, educator*
Salbu, Steve *dean, business educator*
Salmon, Daniel Aryeh *public health policy fellow*
Sams, Louise S. *broadcast executive, lawyer*
Sander, John L. *broadcast executive*
Sanders, Carl E. *lawyer, former Governor of Georgia*
Sands, Jeff Michael *medical educator*
Sanfilippo, Fred Paul *academic administrator, medical educator, pathologist*
Sarpong, Kwabena Dua *biology professor*
Saslow, Debbie L. *cancer control specialist, director*
Satcher, David *public health service officer, former Surgeon General of the United States*
Schoen, Scott Alan *corporate executive*
Schroder, Jack Spalding, Jr. *lawyer*
Schuchat, Anne *federal agency administrator*
Schuerholz, John Boland, Jr. *professional baseball executive*
Schulte, Jeffrey Lewis *lawyer*
Schulze, Horst H. *hotel company executive*
Schuster, Gary Benjamin *academic administrator, chemistry professor*
Scott, Donald Lavern *city manager, librarian, former army officer*
Seffrin, John Reese *health science association administrator, educator*
Shah, Nikhil L. *urologist, surgeon*
Shams, Alicia Marie *microbiologist*
Shapiro, George Howard *retired lawyer*
Shapiro, Michael Edward *museum director*
Shinohara, Minoru *engineering educator*
Siffel, Csaba *medical epidemiologist*
Singh, Narendra *cardiologist, researcher, medical educator*
Sizemore, Michael Maynard *architectural firm executive*
Slaughter, Sandra Ann *management educator*
Sloan, Mary Jean *retired media specialist*
Smith, Edward Kendrick *lawyer*
Smith, Jeffrey Michael *lawyer*
Smith, Joanne *marketing executive*
Smith, Joe (Joseph Leynard Smith) *professional basketball player*
Smith, Richard F. *financial services company executive*
Smith, Robert A. *medical association administrator*
Smith, Robert Boulware III *vascular surgeon, educator*
Smith, Roland C. *food service company executive*
Smith, Sidney Oslin, Jr. *lawyer*
Snarey, John Robert *psychologist, educator*
Snyder, Robert Lyman *materials scientist, educator*
Somerhalder, John W., II, *energy executive*
Spain, Jim C. *environmental engineer, educator*
Spano, Robert *conductor, music director*
Speed, Bonnie Anne *museum director*
Spiegel, John William *banker*
Spillett, Roxanne *social services administrator*
Spitznagel, John Keith *retired microbiologist, immunologist, physician*
Sprecher, Jeffrey C. *commodities exchange executive*
Stacey, Weston Monroe, Jr. *nuclear engineer, physicist, educator*
Stallings, Ronald Denis *lawyer*
Stayton, William Ralph *psychologist, educator*
Stein, Douglas Warren *lawyer*
Steinberg, James Paul *infectious diseases physician, educator*
Steinhaus, John Edward *retired anesthesiologist, educator*
Stephan, Paula Elizabeth *economics professor, academic administrator*
Stephenson, Mason Williams *lawyer*
Stevens, Judy A. *epidemiologist*
Stillwagon, Gary Bouldin *radiation oncologist*
Stockton, David A. *lawyer*
Stoffel, Robert E. *delivery service executive*
Stormont, Richard Mansfield *hotel executive*
Stowe, Zachary Neil *psychiatrist, researcher*
Suciu, James N. *sales executive*
Sullivan, Louis Wade *medical educator, former United States Secretary of Health & Human Services*
Sullivan, Timothy E. *bank executive*
Sun, Qunhui *research scientist*
Sund, Rick (Richard W. Sund) *professional sports team executive*
Sweeney, Neal James *lawyer*
Swift, Frank Meador *lawyer*
Taliaferro, Sumayah Jamila *dermatologist*
Tanteh, Victor Nkangami *information technology educator*
Tatum, Beverly Daniel *academic administrator, writer, psychology and education educator*
Taylor, Andrew T., Jr. *radiologist, educator*
Taylor, George Kimbrough, Jr. *lawyer*
Taylor, Leslie M. *theater educator*
Taylor, Mark *former lieutenant governor*
Taylor, Roger Dale *lawyer*
Taylor, Susan L. *former magazine editor, philanthropist*
Terwilliger, J. Ronald *real estate company executive*
Thacker, Stephen Brady *medical association administrator, epidemiologist*
Thattassery, Emil George *cardiologist*
Thomas, Lizanne *lawyer*
Thompson, Hugh P. *state supreme court justice*
Thompson, Philip C. *lawyer, investment advisor, private equity fund manager, educator, journalist*
Thompson, Shirley Williams *mathematics professor*
Thrower, Randolph William *lawyer*
Thuesen, Gerald Jorgen *industrial engineer, educator*
Tighiouart, Mourad *statistician, researcher*
Tillman, Mary Norman *urban affairs consultant*
Tiwari, Tejpratap S. P. *epidemiologist*
Toledo, Andrew Anthony *obstetrician, gynecologist*
Tomé, Carol Buchenroth *consumer home products company executive*
Toner, Michael F. *journalist*
Toomey, Kathleen Elizabeth *federal agency administrator*
Torok, Ken *delivery service executive*
Travis, Robert M. *lawyer*
Tripodi, Joseph V. *beverage company executive*
Turner, Ted (Robert Edward Turner III) *retired broadcast company executive, philanthropist*
Udoff, Eric Joel *diagnostic radiologist*
Ulicny, Gary R. *rehabilitation center executive*
Vaccarino, Viola *professor medicine*
Vachon, Reginald Irenee *mechanical engineer*
Valk, Henry S(nowden) *physicist, researcher*
VanWoerkom, Jack A. *lawyer, consumer products company executive*
Varner, Chilton Davis *lawyer*
Vazirani, Vijay V. *science educator*
Vazquez, Javier Carlos *professional baseball player*
Velásquez, Lucía E. *language educator, researcher*
Verrill, F. Glenn *advertising executive*
Vigtel, Gudmund *retired museum director*
Vogel, Victor Gerald *medical educator, researcher*
Volentine, Richard J., Jr. *lawyer*
Vuola, Olli *engineering company executive*
Waddell, Don *professional sports team executive*
Wagner, James Warren *academic administrator, engineering educator*
Wald, Michael Leonard *public relations executive*
Wallace, Gladys Baldwin *retired librarian*
Wallace, Julia Diane *editor*
Wallace, Peter Marsden *radio personality and producer, commentator, writer*
Walton, Jim *broadcast executive*
Ward, Elizabeth *medical association administrator, director*
Ward, Horace Taliaferro *federal judge*
Waring, George Oral III *ophthalmologist, surgeon*
Weathers, Dwight Ronald *dental educator*
Weathersby, Michael Nelson *lawyer*
Weed, Roger Oren *rehabilitation services professional, educator*
Weiss, Jay M(ichael) *psychologist, educator*
Wellon, Robert G. *lawyer*
Wells, James M. III *bank executive*
Welp, Herrad Susanne *language educator*
Wenger, Nanette Kass *cardiologist, medical researcher, educator*
Weyand, Cornelia Maritta *medical educator*
White, Perry Merrill, Jr. *orthopedic surgeon*
Whitley, Joe Dally (Joe Dally Whitley) *lawyer*
Wickliffe, Charles Walton *cardiologist*
Wilkins, Dominique (Jacques Dominique Wilkins) *professional sports team executive, retired professional basketball player*
Wilkinson, Keith D. *biochemist, educator*
Williams, Bob *professional sports team executive*
Williams, Ifor R. *immunologist, director*
Williams, Neil, Jr. *retired lawyer*
Williamson, R. Mark *lawyer*
Willis, Sharon J. *music educator, director*
Wilmer, Mary Charles *artist*
Wilson, Brent Lawrence *lawyer, mediator*
Wilson, James Hargrove, Jr. *lawyer*
Wilson, Lawrence Joseph *chemist, researcher*
Wilson, Michael W. *academic librarian, educator*
Winer, Ward Otis *mechanical engineer, educator*
Winograd, Audrey Lesser *retired advertising executive*
Wolff, Phillip Mark *psychology professor*
Womack, Christopher C. *utilities executive*
Woo, Dong Hyuk *graduate research assistant*
Wood, L. Lin, Jr. *lawyer*
Woodard, Diane E. *music educator*
Woodson, Mike *professional basketball coach*
Wren, Frank *professional baseball team executive*
Wright, Peter Meldrim *lawyer*
Wu, De Ting *mathematics professor, researcher, writer*
Wylly, Barbara Bentley *volunteer*
Yaccarino, Linda *telecommunications industry executive, marketing professional*
Yancey, Asa G., Sr. *physician, educator*
Yates, Jerome William *scientific administrator, researcher*
Yoganathan, Ajit Prithiviraj *biomedical engineer, educator*
Young, Andrew Jackson, Jr. *consulting firm executive, former mayor, former United States Representative from Georgia*
Young, Charles Edward *former academic administrator*
Yount, Kathryn Mary *science educator*
Yuan, Jiahui *electronics engineer, researcher*
Yun, Jaeseok *research scientist*
Zadeh, Javad Hamadani *mathematics professor*
Zaghloul, Yasser A. *research and development company executive*
Zarama, Luis Rafael *bishop*
Zboray, Ronald John *history educator*
Zealey, Sharon Janine *lawyer*
Zhitnik, Alexei *professional hockey player*

Auburn
Hutchinson, Leslie Julian *preventive medicine physician*

Augusta
Albo, Daniel *surgeon, researcher*
Atteberry, Linda Rose *surgeon, retired military officer*
Baker, Carleton Harold *physiology educator*
Baker, Philip Steven *dentist, educator*
Barab, Patsy Lee *nutritionist, realtor*
Barnard, Druie Douglas, Jr. *former congressman, bank executive*
Bhatia, Jatinder J. S. *pediatrician*
Bittner, James Graham *surgeon*
Borke, James L. *medical educator*
Carroll, James Edwin *child neurologist, researcher*
Chamberlain, Sherman *gastroenterologist, educator*
Chandler, Arthur Bleakley *pathologist, educator*
Copenhaver, Deke *Mayor, Augusta-Richmond, Georgia*
Craig, Cynthia Mae *mathematics professor*
Cresci, Gail *surgeon, educator, nutritionist*
Davis, Minnie P. *minister*
Dodani, Sunita *physician, educator*
Dyer, James Harold, Jr. *language educator*
Fincher, Ruth Marie Edla *medical educator, dean*
Gamboa, Gloria Mabel *plastic surgeon, educator*
Gillespie, Edward Malcolm *hospital administrator*
Given, Kenna Sidney *surgeon, educator*
Glaser, Nancy Jane *museum director*
Hall, James Randal *federal judge*
Hepburn, Iryna Sophia *physician*
Hooks, Vendie Hudson III *surgeon*
Horuzsko, Anatolij *medical researcher*
Hyder, James Davis, Jr. *lawyer*
Jackson, Rosa M. *retired elementary school educator*
Jenks, Charles Evan *social sciences educator*
Johnson, William Michael *physician*
Kapuku, Gaston Kakota *medical educator*
Kumar, Vijay *urologist, researcher*
Kutlar, Ferdane *genetics educator, researcher*
Lapp, Carol Anne *oral biology educator*
Lee, Gregory Price *neuropsychology educator*
Logan, Betty Mulherin (Elizabeth Carson Logan) *human services specialist*
Londono, Martinez Jimmy *dentist*
Luxenberg, Malcolm Neuwahl *ophthalmologist, educator*
Meyers, Nicholaus *music educator*
Nesbit, Robert Raymond, Jr. *surgeon*
Nzeh, Okoroafor Ogbajie *director*
Ownby, Dennis Randall *pediatrician, allergist, educator, researcher*
Prisant, Louis Michael *cardiologist, educator*
Raja, Dayal Davis *endocrinologist*
Rempala, Grzegorz A. *mathematician, statistician, educator*
Rogers, Michael Bruce *orthodontist*
Ryan, James Walter *physician, researcher*
Schmidt, Buffie *finance educator*
Schultz, Nancy Jansson *artist*
Swenson, Gabriel J. *biology professor*
Talledo, Oscar Eduardo *medical educator*
Ustun, Celalettin *hematologist, educator, bone marrow transplant specialist*
William, W. Brackett *dentist, educator*
Wood, Lisa Godbey *federal judge, former prosecutor*
Woodhurst, Robert Stanford, Jr. *architect*
Wray, Betty Beasley *allergist, immunologist, pediatrician*

Austell
Anderson, Barbara Allen *alcohol/drug abuse services professional, archivist*
Halwig, J. Michael *allergist*
O'Rear, Clarence Michael *engineering company executive*
Pope, Jacqueline Privette *music educator*
Scott, Yvonnie Michelle *special education educator, diagnostician, paralegal*
Tissue, Mike *medical educator, respiratory therapist*

Avondale Estates
Bastin, Clinton *retired chemical engineer, nuclear scientist*
Rouse, Jacqueline Anne *historian, educator*

Bainbridge
Kuhn-Hancock, Lori Ann *performing arts educator, director*
LaFace, Betty *language educator, consultant*
Leggett, Carol Griffis *biology professor*
Miley, Jenna Yvonne *education educator, consultant*

Ball Ground
Tucker, Robert Dennard *health care products executive*

Barnesville
Anderson, Nancy Dixon *librarian*
Borders, Michael William *psychology professor*
Freeman, Angelia Brown *poet*
Hollingsworth, Edna Diane *librarian*
Parsons, Gail PaT *history professor*
Schmude, Richard Willis, Jr. *chemistry professor*

Bartow
Cason, Cedric Lee *religious studies educator*

Baxley
Williams, David Alfred *elementary school music specialist*
Williams, Sonia Kay *retired secondary school educator*

Big Canoe
Bendelius, Arthur George *engineering firm executive*

Blairsville
Stainback, Susan Bray *professor emeritus*

Blakely
Teal, Teresa *mathematics professor*

Brooklet
Warrick, Kimberley Kaye *language and social studies educator*

Brunswick
Fowler, Mary A. *administrative assistant*
LeMieux, Jeffery Alan *art educator*
Mihal, Sandra Powell *research scientist*
Patrick, Connie L. *federal agency administrator*
Riner, Deborah Lillian *mental health services professional*

Buford
Byrd, Larry Donald *behavioral pharmacologist*
Jondahl, Terri Elise *supply chain management, distribution and manufacturing executive*
Smith, Rebecca L. *musician*

Calhoun
Boykin, Frank H. *textiles executive*
Lorberbaum, Jeffrey S. *textiles executive*
Lucke, James T. *textiles executive*
Orfield, Robert Allen *special education director*
Perillo, Salvatore J. *lawyer*

Canton
Alexander, Constance Joy (Connie Alexander) *stone sculptor*
Angulo, Charles Bonin *foreign service officer, lawyer*
Frady, Rita R. *music educator, information technology manager*
Hamby, Ira Ben III *elementary school educator*
Jones-Kelner, Barbara Teryl *music educator*
Wilson, Brian Andrew *computing performance consultant, educator, writer, editor*
Yarbrough, Kathryn Davis *public health nurse*

Carnesville
Royston, Pamela Jean *special education educator*

Carrollton
Blair, John *language educator, director*
Gowens, Greg *science educator, small business owner*
Kelley, Patricia *marketing representative*
Larkin, Martha Jane *higher education educator*
Luken, Paul Clement *social studies educator*
MacKinnon, Aran Stuart *history professor*
Sethna, Beheruz Nariman *academic administrator, educator, management consultant*
Stone, Sandra Smith *sociologist, academic administrator, researcher*
Trotman Scott, Michelle Frazier *special education educator*
Williams, Mary Eleanor Nicole *retired writer*

Cartersville
Hopkins, Seth M. *museum director*
Swanson, William Fredin III *manufacturing executive*

Cataula
Averill, Ellen Corbett *retired secondary education science educator, administrator*

Clarkesville
Dowden, Thomas Clark *telecommunication executive*

Clarkston
Aliff, John Vincent *biology professor*
Barrow, Ellen *librarian, educator*
Charania, Barkat *real estate consultant*
Kahiga, Mundia James *economics professor*
Okafor, Martin Okechukwu *physics professor, educational consultant*
Peiffer, Jerri Ann *lab administrator, educator*

Claxton
Hagan, Christina M. *psychologist*
Price, Jennifer Leigh *social studies educator*

Cleveland
Edwards, John Carver *retired archivist*

College Park
Dollar, Creflo A. *minister, religious organization administrator*
Oliver-Warren, Mary Elizabeth *retired library science educator, library and information scientist*
Patterson, P(ickens) Andrew *lawyer*

Columbus
Amos, Daniel Paul *insurance company executive*
Amos, Paul Shelby *insurance company executive*
Amos, Paul Shelby, II, *insurance company executive*
Anthony, Richard E. *bank executive*
Baker, Janet *insurance company executive*
Bhandary, Madhusudan *statistician, educator*
Brinkley, Jack Thomas *lawyer, former United States Representative, Georgia*
Butler, Charles Thomas *museum director, curator*
Carr, Leila S. *bank executive*

Chan, Philip *retired dermatologist, military officer*
Cloninger, Kriss III *insurance company executive*
Cox, Kermitt L. *insurance company executive*
Daniels, Michael J. *economics professor, consultant*
Davis, Rebecca C. *insurance company executive*
Duncan, Frances Murphy *retired special education educator*
Friou, Phillip J. (Jack Friou) *insurance company executive*
Golden, Joseph David *music educator*
Graver, Steven F. *costume designer, educator*
Harbison, Ed *state legislator, broadcast journalist, motivational speaker*
Hart, Angela *insurance company executive*
Hatcher, Samuel F. *lawyer, diversified financial services company executive*
Hiatt, Florence Ellen *musician*
Janke, Kenneth S., Jr. *insurance company executive*
Jeffery, William Jeremy *insurance company executive*
Johnson, Walter Frank, Jr. *lawyer*
Kirkland, Ronald E. *insurance company executive*
Laney, John Thomas III *federal judge*
Langston, Vicky C. *economics professor*
Loudermilk, Joey M. *lawyer, insurance company executive*
Manuel, Kimberly Ann *design educator*
Newtson, Richard L. *sociologist, educator*
Norah, Patricia Ann *retired music educator*
Ottman, Bob *insurance company executive*
Patrick, James Duvall, Jr. *lawyer*
Peavy, Thomas Ostine *retired psychology professor, retired education educator*
Poydasheff, Robert Stephen *lawyer*
Pringle, David L. *insurance company executive*
Riggsby, Dutchie Sellers *education educator*
Rogers, Ralph A., Jr. *insurance company executive*
Shields, Gerald W. *insurance company executive*
Simmons, Lynda Teel *nurse, healthcare executive*
Simpson, Minnie Peach *interior designer*
Smyre, Calvin *state legislator*
Tillman, Audrey Boone *insurance company executive*
Tipton, James D. *retired military officer, education educator*
Wells, Kelly L. *media specialist*
Wetherington, Jim *Mayor, Columbus, Georgia, former protective services official*
White, Lisa L. *diversified financial services company executive*
White, Teresa Lynne *insurance company executive*
Wooten, Joel Orba, Jr. *lawyer*

Conyers
Grider, Rhonda Patriece *elementary school educator, writer*

Covington
Norwood, Brandi Aisha *middle school educator*
Sigh, Robert Virgil *public health physician*

Cumming
French, James Thomas *real estate broker*

Dahlonega
Formica, Sarah P. *physics professor*
Murray, Heather M. *history professor*
Thornton, Anita Lyn *family nurse practitioner*
Torres-Calderon, Alvaro Martin *language educator*
Williams, Linda Stallworth *literature and language professor*

Dallas
Gilbert, Martha W. *literature and language educator*
Jackson, Cynthia Williford *special education educator*

Dalton
Smith, Janet Susannah *literature and language educator, department chairman*

Dawsonville
Jorgensen, Alfred H. *retired information technology educator*

Decatur
Barnett, Rebecca Lynn *communications executive*
Beckemeyer, Elizabeth Frances *biology professor*
Bryant, Erika Knight *mathematics educator*
Dillingham, William Byron *literature educator, author*
Hagood, Susan Stewart Hahn *dietician*
Hamilton, Frank Strawn *musician, composer, educator*
Henderson, Ralph Hale *physician*
Hinman, Alan Richard *public health physician, epidemiologist*
Ioachimescu, Octavian Cosmin *medical educator*
Jones, Debbie Jo *finance educator*
Keaton, Mollie M. *elementary school educator*
Kelly, Karen Deloris *addiction counselor, administrator*
Kiss, Elizabeth *academic administrator, philosophy educator*
Knight, Walker Leigh *publishing executive, minister*
MacEwen, Sally *ancient language educator*
Manley, Frank *language educator, writer*
Mc Intosh, James Eugene, Jr. *interior designer*
Mobley, Barbara Jean *former state legislator, lawyer*
Pepperdene, Margaret Williams *English educator*
Polensek, Sharon Hartman *speech pathology/audiology services professional*
Rodgers, Richard Malcolm *management accountant*
Rosenberg, Mark L. *health facility administrator*
Shaw, Jeanne Osborne *editor, poet*
Showers Johnson, Violet Mary-Ann Iyabo *history professor*
Terry, Elizabeth Hudson *personal care industry executive, realtor*
Wheelan, Belle S. *educational association administrator*
Williams, Rita Tucker *lawyer*

Demorest
Rogers, Elizabeth (Betty) Carlisle *educator, consultant*

Schick, Barbara Jean *medical technician, educator*

Dillard
Aldridge, Melvin Dayne *engineering educator*

Doraville
Wempner, Gerald Arthur *engineering professor*

Douglasville
Smith, Stephanie Renae *middle school educator*
Walker, Pam *biology educator*

Dublin
Clark, Gail Brooks *educational association administrator*
Giannini, A. James *psychiatrist, educator, researcher, author*
Sapp, Peggy G. *pastor, editor, writer, speech professional*
Shuman-Riley, Brenda *literature and language educator*

Duluth
Beck, Andrew H. *farm equipment manufacturing executive*
Brody, Aaron Leo *food and packaging consultant*
Chandler, Elizabeth Brannen *lawyer*
Colwell, Gene Thomas *engineering educator*
Cothrun, Thomas Keith *secondary school educator*
Guillory, Barbara Ann *elementary school educator*
Kimmich, Madeline P. *business operations consultant*
Kuper, Debra E. *manufacturing executive, lawyer*
Lupton, Stephen D. *lawyer*
McCracken, William Henry *retired mining executive*
Moss, Shad Gregory (Bow Wow, Lil' Bow Wow) *rap artist*
Pratt, Bonnie *science educator*
Reed, Ralph Eugene, Jr. *political consultant, former political organization administrator*
Richenhagen, Martin H. *manufacturing executive*
Sloan, Donnie Robert, Jr. *lawyer*

Dunwoody
Askew Cain, Peggy *elementary school educator, consultant*
Callison, James W. *retired lawyer, air transportation executive*
Roddy, Kathleen *literature and language professor*

East Point
Bridgewater, Herbert Jeremiah, Jr. *radio personality*

Eatonton
Digby, Pamela Annette *elementary school educator*

Evans
Feldman, Elaine Bossak *medical nutritionist, educator*
Little, Robert Colby *physiologist, educator*
Owen, Shaun Sonia *elementary school educator, small business owner, consultant*
Rowland, Arthur Ray *librarian*
Zachert, Virginia *retired psychologist*

Fairburn
Holyfield, Evander *professional boxer*
Martin, Terry Malone *assistant principal*
Milam, Lynne Morgan *special education educator*
Williams, Pedelaphe *education educator*

Fayetteville
Addison, Maria José *literature and language professor*
Cokuslu, Lynda Elizabeth McCord *medical assistant*
De Revere, David Wilsen *retired professional society administrator*
Neal, Joan Burkes *retired librarian*
Turnipseed, Barnwell Rhett III *journalist, broadcaster, public relations consultant*

Flintstone
Ragon, Robert Ronald *clergyman*

Flowery Branch
Abraham, John *professional football player*
Blank, Arthur M. *professional sports team and retired lumber company executive*
Coll, Edward Girard, Jr. *university president*
Elam, Jason *professional football player*
Gonzalez, Tony (Anthony David Gonzalez) *professional football player*
Kilinski, April Conley *language educator*
McKay, Richard James *professional sports team executive*
Monroe, Melrose *retired bank executive*
Ryan, Matt (Matthew Thomas Ryan) *professional football player*
Smith, Mike *professional football coach*
Turner, Michael *professional football player*

Fort Benning
Gittins, Timothy Lee *military officer*
Hanner, Z. Frank *museum director*
Kotwal, Russ Steven *military officer, physician*

Fort Gaines
Chaffin, LaVerne *music educator*

Fort Gordon
Goksel, Tamer *oral surgeon, director*
Whittemore, Ronald Paul *hospital administrator, retired army officer, nursing educator*

Fort Oglethorpe
Christensen, Brian Duaine *education educator*

Fort Stewart
McCarthy, Dorothy A. (Landers) *educator*
Warner, Christopher Hugh *psychiatrist*

Fort Valley
Mahitab, Frank *librarian, director*
Williams, Barbara B. *retired music educator*

Yadav, Anand Krishna *biotechnologist, educator*

Franklin Springs
Benson, Jennifer Lester *communications executive*
Mann, Frank *physics professor*

Gainesville
Burd, John Stephen *retired academic administrator, music educator*
Coakley, Deirdre *columnist, writer*
Frank, Mary Lou Bryant *psychologist, educator*
Jones, David Leland *music educator*
Jones, William Benjamin, Jr. *retired electrical engineering educator*
Lee, Kathleen Mary *health facility administrator, nursing executive*
Lynn, Lois E. *finance educator*
May, Sterling Randolph *biology professor, department chairman*
Mills, Hugh Milton, Jr. *retired college president*
Nichols, Dana *literature and language educator*
Pinson, Vicki Faye *music educator, director*
Young, Douglas Parker, Jr. *social studies educator*

Greensboro
Campbell, Charles Alton *transportation executive*
Copelan, Ann Hanson *artist, psychologist*

Griffin
Bunnell, David Paul *library director*
Doyle, Michael Patrick *microbiologist, educator, director*
Henderson, Gloria Mason *retired literature and language professor*
Marshall, Allen Wright III *communications executive, financial consultant*
Shockley, Carol Frances *psychologist, psychotherapist*

Grovetown
Monassar, Hisham M.A. *language and linguistics educator*

Hartwell
Rushing, Tonnie Austin Page *musician, educator*

Hephzibah
Albarado, Rebecca Hill *elementary school educator*
Smith, Charles Joe, Sr. *music educator*

Hiawassee
Davis, Nighta J. *photographer, artist*

Hinesville
Etheridge, James Ralph *history professor*
Inman, Mitchell, II, *marketing educator*
Smith, Barbara *bank executive*

Hoschton
Sneed, Larry Allan *history professor*

Ila
Greene, Sheree' Jeane *elementary school educator, consultant*

Jackson
Beasley, Anita Claire *reading specialist, consultant*

Jasper
Keating, Thomas Patrick *health care administrator, educator*
Ledford, Shirley Louise *practical nurse*
Marger, Edwin *lawyer*
Wiltse, James Cornelius *retired electrical engineer*

Jeffersonville
Hawthorne, Sarah Beck *reading educator*

Jekyll Island
Norton, Terry M. *veterinarian, director*

Jonesboro
Galvin, John Rogers *retired army officer, law educator*
Harris, Queen Wiggs *mathematician, educator*
Mahone, Antonio *elementary school educator*
Perez, Maritza E. *special education educator*
Tanks, Ashley *legislative staff member*
Vaughn, Rosalyn Mae *academic administrator*

Kennesaw
Chen, Ming *design educator*
Hansen, Jon *librarian*
Huang, Yuling *art historian, educator*
McCoy, R. Wesley *biology educator*
Paterson, Paul Charles *retired private investigator, security consultant*
Siegel, Betty Lentz *president emeritus*
Simon, Robert *language educator*
Thompson, Eva M. *humanities educator*
Vladimirov, Katya *history professor*
Williamsen, Dannye Sue *personal development educator, publisher, ordained minister*
Yifru, Dawit Desalegn *environmental scientist*

Kingsland
Barlow, Paula C. *nurse*
Huygens, Remmert William *architect*

Lagrange
Barber Knoll, Kim *performing arts educator, department chairman*
Copeland, Robert Bodine *internist, cardiologist*
Hudson, Charles Daugherty *insurance executive*
West, John Thomas *retired surgeon*

Lake Park
Tucker, Glenn Gorham *retired educational administrator*

Lawrenceville
Bannick, Janice Carol *automotive dealerships executive*

Brannon, Ronald Roy *retired minister*
Fetner, Robert Henry *radiobiologist*
Folds, Frank Elliott *music educator*
Harris, Melba Iris *elementary and secondary school educator, state agency administrator*
Isola, Oluwabusuyi Olabode *real estate broker, educator*
Pursell, David P. *chemistry professor*
Rawson, Harve E. *psychologist, writer*
Schoen, Marc Alan *pension and employee benefits executive*
Swanson, Lynnette Sue *special olympics coordinator, special education educator*
Wall, Clarence Vinson *state legislator*

Leesburg
Hilley, Mary Kay *music educator*

Lilburn
Bendelius, Bonnie Sue *elementary school educator*
Neumann, Thomas William *archaeologist*

Lithonia
Baxter, Gene Francis *chemical researcher, consultant*
Johnson, Henry C. (Hank Johnson) *United States Representative from Georgia, lawyer*
McKinney, Cynthia Ann *former United States Representative from Georgia*

Loganville
McGonigle, Terry L. *theater educator, consultant*

Lookout Mountain
Dennison, William D. *interdisciplinary educator*

Lovejoy
Onukwuli, Francis Osita *computer scientist, secondary school educator, mathematician*

Mableton
Reeves, Denise Moseley *dancer, educator*
Rowe, Bonnie Gordon *music company executive*

Macon
Ambrose, Andy *museum director*
Anderson, Robert Lanier III *federal judge*
Bubacz, Monika *science educator*
Cook, Charlotte C. *psychologist*
Dantzler, Deryl Daugherty *lawyer, educator, dean*
Davis, David Scott *academic administrator, chemistry professor*
Dunwody, Eugene Cox *architect*
Elliott, Richard Laurence *psychiatrist, educator*
Floyd, Daisy Hurst *dean, law educator*
Franklin, Roosevelt *minister*
Glance, Jonathan Carlyle *literature and language professor, director*
Hails, Robert Emmet *retired aerospace engineer, manufacturing executive, military officer*
Harvey, James Mathews, Jr. *public relations administrator*
Hershner, Robert Franklin, Jr. *judge*
Huffman, Joan Brewer *history professor*
Jones, Frank Cater *retired lawyer*
Kitchens, William Charlie *accountant*
Klingelhofer, Eric Charles *history professor, archaeologist*
Lauterbach, Edward Charles *psychiatric educator*
Leonard, Michael Steven *industrial engineering educator*
Mulholland, Sean *economics professor*
Phillips, John Taylor *judge*
Pilcher, Christie W. *retired special education educator*
Robinson, Joe Sam *neurosurgeon, educator*
Robinson, W. Lee *lawyer*
Savage, Randall Ernest *journalist*
Scheetz, Allison Paige *medical educator*
Seale, James Paul *medical educator, researcher*
Shomaker, Andrea Kay *secondary school educator*
Steeples, Douglas Wayne *retired university dean, consultant, researcher*
Weaver, Jacquelyn Kunkel Ivey *artist, educator*
Young, Henry E. *tissue engineering medical educator*
Zalups, Rudolfs Karlis *medical educator, director*

Madison
DuBose, Charles Wilson *lawyer*

Marietta
Asgill, Austin Blanshard *electrical engineer, educator*
Atkins, Robert Wayne *engineering educator, consultant*
Bentley, Fred Douglas, Sr. *lawyer*
Bernal, Barbara V. *engineering educator*
Berryhill, Henry Lee, Jr. *retired geologist*
Braun, Michael Rene *lawyer*
Carnes, James Donald *real estate manager*
Clarkson, Lawrence William *air transportation executive*
Cochrane, J. La Juana *psychology professor*
Downs, Claudia Peery *special education educator*
Dudley, Gary Edward *psychologist*
Hellrung, Stephen Andrew *lawyer*
Hill, Stephen A. *pharmaceutical executive*
Houston, Dorothy Middleton *elementary school educator*
Kelly, William Watkins *retired educational association executive*
Kim, Sung Hee *engineering educator*
Laframboise, Joan Carol *middle school educator*
Lahtinen, Silja Liisa *artist*
Mahle, William T. *pediatric cardiologist, educator*
Manning, Judith Hubert *state legislator, real estate company executive*
McKenzie, Kay Branch *public relations executive*
Miles, Thomas Caswell *mechanical engineer*
Mutisya, Elizabeth M. *pharmaceutical executive*
Nowland, James Ferrell *lawyer*
Opre, Thomas Edward *retired editor, film company executive*
Overstreet, Regina Nix *mathematics educator*

Patterson, Philip Edward *engineering educator*
Petit, Parker Holmes *health care corporation executive*
Powell, Richard Lynn *lawyer*
Ranu, Harcharan Singh *biomedical scientist, administrator, orthopaedic biomechanics educator*
Roach, Carole Hyde *music educator*
Sampath, Ramanathan *chemical engineer, educator*
Sanner, George Elwood *electrical engineer*
Scheible, David W. *paper company executive*
Schell, Norman Barnett *preventive medicine physician, consultant*
Shpuza, Ermal *architecture educator*
Sigler, Paulette Terry *music educator*
Slomanski, Rev. Patricia Parker *minister*
Smith, Baker Armstrong *management executive, lawyer*
Smith, George Thornewell *retired state supreme court justice*
Spann, George William *management consultant*
Wenk, Michael Scott *environmental services administrator*

Martinez
Colborn, Gene Louis *anatomy educator, researcher*
Nesbitt, Robert Edward Lee, Jr. *physician, educator, research scientist, writer, poet*

Maysville
Leach, Claudia Rylee *media specialist, educator*

Mc Rae
Allen, Annette *minister*

Mcdonough
Mauney, Brandi Savage *special education educator*
Wilson, Russell Edward *music educator*
Yang, Bong-Jun *research scientist*

Milledgeville
Bailey, Anne J. *history professor*
Caldwell, Ann B. *music educator*
Engerrand, Doris Dieskow *retired business educator*
Mizelle, Nancy Batson *education educator, consultant*
Ragan, Charlotte Ann *music educator*
Skinner, Marilynn Kearnes *finance educator*
Tolbert, Patti McClure *music educator*
Vess, Deborah Lynn *history professor*
Wang, Huaihyu *philosopher, educator*

Milton
Tomaszewski, Richard Paul *market representation executive*

Morganton
Brathovde, James Robert *chemistry professor*

Morrow
Totty, Totty Okoro *soccer coach*

Moultrie
Collum, Rick Daniel *lawyer*
Cox, Carol Yvonne *counselor*
McCall, John Clark, Jr. *interior designer*

Mount Berry
Gregoire, Vincent Maric-Luc *language educator*
Mew, Thomas Joseph, III, (Tommy) *artist, educator*
Taylor, Ronald D. *mathematics professor*

Newnan
Barron, Thomas Willis *real estate broker*
Culbreth, Lucretia Joy *science educator*
Drake, W. Homer, Jr. *federal judge*
Krach, Dale James *science educator, athletic trainer*

Norcross
Chell, Beverly C. *retired media company executive, lawyer*
Cramer, James Perry *management strategist, author, educator*
Granger, Philip Richard *minister*
Greene, Don Howard *product designer*
Koman, Alan James *lawyer, educator*
Metz, Robert C. *media company executive*
Nuyan, Seyhan *control engineer*
Rubright, James Alfred *paperboard and packaging company executive*
Wagner, Robert Earl *retired agronomist*

Oakwood
Phillips, Ernie Howard *music educator*

Oxford
Galle, Jeffrey Wayne *literature and language professor, academic administrator*
Sitton, Claude Fox *newspaper editor*

Peachtree City
Day, Annette J. *music educator*
Ebneter, Stewart Dwight *utility industry management consultant*
Nix, Kemie Richards *educational association administrator, editor*
Roobol, Norman Richard *chemistry professor, consultant*

Perry
Jackson, Rutha Mae *pastor, military reserve officer, secondary school educator*

Pine Mountain
Bishop, Michael *writer*
Callaway, Howard Hollis *resort executive, former congressman*

Powder Springs
Creighton, Peggy Milam *media specialist, writer*

Reidsville
Dees, Louise Mitchell *language educator*

Richmond Hill
Dasher, Donna Shearouse *music educator*

Rincon
Purcell, Ann Rushing *state legislator, human services manager*

Ringgold
Muerth, Cherie Anne *retired social worker*

Robins AFB
Head, William Pace *historian, educator*
Wolfe, Sarah Catharine *curator*

Rock Spring
Spivey, Karen *nursing educator*
Walters, Michael W. *social sciences educator*

Rome
Bushnell, Brandon DuBose *orthopedist*
Davis, Susan Lynn *musician, educator*
Doyle, James Donald, Jr. *librarian*
Murphy, Harold Loyd *federal judge*

Roopville
Huckeba, Emily Causey *retired elementary school educator*

Roswell
Abernathy, Robert E. *health products executive*
Bauer, Joanne B. *health products executive*
Birmingham, Richard Gregory *lawyer*
Crawford, Mark E. *psychologist*
Feldman, Joel Martin *retired judge*
Gottung, Lizanne C. *health products executive*
Hill, Donald Dee *management consultant, educator, writer*
Ludacris, (Chris Bridges) *musician, actor*
McCloud, Melody T. *obstetrician, gynecologist, surgeon, media consultant, health care strategist*
Nilsen, Arthur Christian *lawyer*
Rogers, Richard Hilton *hotel executive*
Siepi, Cesare *opera singer*
Spencer, Jan B. *health products executive*

Saint Marys
Berry, Stephen L. (Steve Berry) *writer, lawyer*
Hall, Lois Bremer *secondary school educator, volunteer*

Saint Simons Island
Bell, Ronald Mack *university foundation administrator, consultant*
Douglas, William Ernest *retired commissioner*
Taylor, Philip Raymond *lawyer*
Thau, William Albert *lawyer*
Turbidy, John Berry *investor, management consultant*
Williamson, Richard Hall *federal agency administrator*

Sandy Springs
Eckert, Michael Joseph *television and technology executive*
Owen, Robert Hubert *lawyer, real estate broker*

Savannah
Aja-Herrera, Marie *fashion designer, educator*
Andrus, Jennifer Gail *otolaryngologist, surgeon, educator, educational consultant*
Berry, Jack K. *lawyer*
Boland, John Kevin *bishop*
Booth, Edmund A., Jr. *prosecutor*
Bose, Himangshu S. *cell biologist, educator*
Bowman, Catherine McKenzie *lawyer*
Cannon, Major Tom *retired special education educator*
Cartledge, Raymond Eugene *retired paper company executive*
Cebula, Richard John *economist, educator*
Chong, Bruce Simon *dean, broadcast executive*
Clemmons, John B. *bank executive, director, retired mathematics educator*
Coffey, Thomas Francis, Jr. *retired writer*
Craib, Kenneth Bryden *research and development company executive, physicist, economist*
Deen, Paula H. *television personality, restaurant owner, chef*
DeVaro, John Michael *ophthalmologist*
Dickey, David Herschel *lawyer, accountant*
Dirlam, David Kirk *education educator*
Dodge, William Douglas *risk management consultant*
Edenfield, Berry Avant *federal judge*
Fertig, Barbara Conway *history professor*
Fetterman, James William, Jr. *medical educator*
Fishburne, John Ingram, Jr. *retired obstetrician/gynecologist, educator*
Forbes, Morton Gerald *lawyer*
Gaines, Marion Saulsbury *accounting educator*
Hales, Kevin Joseph *history professor, researcher*
High, Steven Samuel *museum director*
Kincaid, Scott Edward *pharmacist, educator*
Klein, Benjamin Daniel Berrigan *medical educator, consultant*
Krahl, Enzo *retired surgeon*
Lancaster, Christopher Scott *science educator*
Leighton, Richard Frederick *retired dean*
Lindley, James Gunn, Jr. *neurosurgeon*
Lombardo, Joseph T. *aerospace transportation executive*
Martin, Grace Burkett *psychologist*
McCracken, Eugene Luke *lawyer*
Morris, Tony Ray *literature and language professor, writer*
Mukhtar, Mohamed Haji *social sciences educator*
Mustafa, Mohamad *engineering educator*
Otter, John Martin III *retired television advertising consultant*
Polite, Evelyn C. *retired elementary school educator, evangelist*
Postell, Cindy Deborah *secondary school educator*
Rowan, Richard G. *former academic administrator*
Rozantine, Gayle Stubbs *psychologist*
Sanders, James Grady *biogeochemist*
Saripalli, Lalitha Devi *biologist, educator*
Schultz, Lucinda D. *music educator*
Searcy, William Nelson *lawyer, director*
Shin, Jong-Yeob *aerospace scientist*
Singh, Harpal *research scientist*
Smith, David Lee *retired editor*
Smith, Elizabeth Mackey *retired financial consultant*
Spitz, Seymour James, Jr. *retired fragrance company executive*
Sprague, William Wallace, Jr. *retired food company executive*
Stanton, Kamille Stone *literature and language professor*
Stillwell, Walter Brooks III *lawyer*
Tackett, Kimberly Lynn *pharmacist, educator*
Tan, Yong *electronics engineer*
Tessema, George *mathematician, educator*
Thomas, Dwight Rembert *writer*
Thomson, Audrey Shire *volunteer*
Wallace, Paula S. *academic administrator*
Walter, Paul Hermann Lawrence *chemistry professor*
Yagami, Kazuo *historian*
Zoller, Michael *otolaryngologist, head and neck surgeon, educator*

Sea Island
Revoile, Charles Patrick *lawyer*

Sky Valley
Geer, Ronald Lamar *mechanical engineer, consultant, retired oil industry executive*
Wilkinson, Albert Mims, Jr. *lawyer*

Smoke Rise
Dees, Julian Worth *retired academic/research administrator*

Smyrna
Atkins, William Austin, Sr., (Bill Atkins) *former state legislator*
Jeffords, Keith (Kelland Keith Jeffords Jr.) *plastic surgeon*
Lnenicka, Wade Sheridan *purchasing agent, councilman, consultant*
Parikh, Priti P. *food scientist*
Seigler, Michael Edward *lawyer, librarian*

Snellville
Blankenship, Colleen Marie-Krick *secondary school educator, writer*
Dodd, Violet M. *nursing educator, dance therapist, counselor*

Social Circle
Penland, John Thomas *retired import/export and development company executive*

Springfield
Guggino, Nelson Maurice *secondary school educator*

Statesboro
Adhikari, Dharma Nanda *journalist, writer, educator*
Bartels, Jean Ellen *nursing educator*
Edenfield, Gerald M. *lawyer*
Fitzmorris, Kari Beth *medical educator*
Franklin, James Burke *lawyer*
Hamilton, Ann Hollingsworth *library director*
Henry, Nicholas Llewellyn *public administration educator*
James, Harris Kelly *science educator, department chairman*
Kwan, Yin Ling Eva *music educator*
Lloyd, Margaret Ann *psychologist, educator*
Mitchell, Wilfrid Bede *librarian, library association executive*
Piltner, Reinhard *engineering educator*
Skewis, Charles Arthur *librarian*
Sturges, Diana *medical educator*
Tootle, Kathleen Maloof *special education educator*
Vlcek, Brian L. *engineering educator*
Wilson, LeVon Edward *lawyer, educator*
Yang, Bill Z. *economics professor*

Stockbridge
Collins, Oliver Jack *military officer, secondary school educator*
Friedman, Robert Barry *neurosurgeon*

Stone Mountain
Bacon, Louis Albert *retired consulting civil engineer*
Brown, Rhonda Jean *special education educator*
Fairweather, Daniel Edward *music educator*
Gotlieb, Jaquelin Smith *pediatrician*
Jones, Ellen *elementary school educator*
Nerem, Robert Michael *engineering educator, consultant*
Reichert, Leo Edmund, Jr. *biochemist, department chairman, endocrinologist*

Summerville
Perry, Alan Eugene *literature and language educator, department chairman*

Suwanee
Cox, Albert Harrington, Jr. *retired economist*
Smith, Kimberly M. *assistant principal, educational consultant*
Wilson, Duane Bubba Regan *secondary school educator*

Swainsboro
Sapp, Gena Johnson *secondary school educator*
Watt, (Arthur) Dwight, Jr. *computer programming and microcomputer specialist*
Wilkes, Elaina B. *psychologist*

Sylvania
Harper, Michael Christopher *music educator*

Tallapoosa
Abney, Martha McEachern *music educator*

Temple
O'Dell, Connie Vincent *special education educator*

Thomaston
Adams, Cynthia Ann *librarian, media specialist, language educator*
Hardy, Christina Brown *dean*
Thomas, Joan E. *music educator*

Thomasville
Deese, George E. *food products company executive*
Tillinghast, Nancy *library director*

Tifton
Anderson, William F. *research scientist*
Dorminey, Henry Clayton, Jr. *allergist*
Haywood, Mary Gwendolyn *music educator*
Hubbard, Robert K. *soil scientist*
Lewis, Wallace Joe *entomologist, researcher*
McGruder, Larry *history professor*
Reinhardt, George Robert *lawyer*

Toccoa
Maypole, John Floyd *real estate company executive*

Toccoa Falls
Brock, Dorothy Dixon *psychologist, psychology professor*
Gardner, Donna Rae (Donna Rae Diehl) *education educator*

Trion
Robinson, Wynnelle Ann *counseling administrator*

Tucker
Das, Jagdish Chander *engineer, consultant*
Stewart, Connie Ward *retired academic administrator*
Streeb, Gordon Lee *diplomat, economist*

Tyrone
Bernard, Sallie *non-profit organization executive*

Union City
Malcolm, Gloria J. *small business owner*
Riley, Francena *nurse, retired non-commissioned officer*

Valdosta
Bailey, Hugh Coleman *academic administrator*
Beal, John M. *surgeon, medical educator*
Blanton, Vallye J. Jean *educator*
Dodd, Roger J. *lawyer*
Gunter, Philip Lee *special education educator, dean*
Halter, Henry James, Jr., (Diamond Jim Halter) *retail executive*
Morgan, Joe Leland *physician, psychiatrist*
Nikolov, Ivan P. *economics professor*
Pollock, Michael E. *mathematics educator, football coach, director*
Sinnott, John Patrick *lawyer, educator*
Whitehead, Jane Katharine *archaeologist, educator*

Vidalia
Fountain, Edwin Byrd *minister, librarian, poet*

Villa Rica
Blevins, Ernest Everett *genealogist, researcher, historian, preservationist*
McKibbin, William Alex *artist*

Waco
House, Janyce Elaine *science educator*
House, Myron Wade *retired professor & special collections librarian*

Waleska
Moore, George David *physics professor, researcher*
Naylor, Susan Embry *music educator*

Warner Robins
Bunn, Dumont C. *academic library director, educator, consultant*
Childs, Vivian L. *retired principal*
Cox, Lorna Diane *medical technician, director*
DePriest, C(harles) David *engineering executive, retired military officer*
Gayton, Johnny Lee *ophthalmologist, recreational facility executive, educator*
Gibson, John Robert *software engineer*
Merk, P. Evelyn *retired librarian*
Nugteren, Cornelius *air force officer*

Watkinsville
Meers, Suzanne *biology professor*
Tate, Curtis E., Jr. *management educator*
Wright, Robert Joseph *lawyer*

Waycross
Keeler, Margaret Alexandra Sandy *history professor*

Waynesboro
Byrd, Rebecca L. *science educator*

Whitesburg
Noell, Beverly Ann *music educator*

Williamson
Huckaby, Scott Allan *science educator, geologist*

Winder
Ouzts, Karl Claybourne *history educator*

Winston
Simon, Ted *toxicologist*

Woodbine
Konetzni, Albert H., Jr. *career officer*

Woodstock
Austin, John David *retired financial executive*
Barthlow, Michelle Jones *science educator*

Colgan, George Phillips *real estate developer and appraiser*
Collins, David Browning *religious institution administrator*
Hudson, Roy Davage *retired pharmaceutical executive*
Olton, Patricia McKinley *media specialist*
Soh-Harbin, Julie *music educator*

Young Harris

Cox, Cathy *academic administrator, former state official*
March, Boyd Lee *dean, political science professor, researcher*
Richardson, Vernal Edward *retired music educator*
Wolfersteig, Eloise Smith *retired music educator*
Wolfersteig, Robert Frederick *retired musician*

HAWAII

Aiea

Anderson, Brooks Doran, II, *geologist, consultant*

Camp H M Smith

Keating, Timothy J. *career military officer*

Ewa Beach

Butler, Debra Yvonne *special education educator, small business owner*
Croddy, Eric *translator*

Haleiwa

Shigemasa, Teresa *mental health services professional, educator*

Hana

Stevens, Muriel Kauimaeole Lee *retired elementary school educator*

Hawaii National Park

Swanson, Donald Alan *geologist*

Hilo

Besio, Kathryn Jean *performing arts educator*
Binder, Philippe-Michel *physicist, educator*
Crosby, Michael P. *science administrator*
Kenoi, William P. *Mayor, Hilo, Hawaii*
Kojima, Sheri S. *high school business educator*
Ornellas, Lorraine B. (Lori Ornellas) *small business owner*
Pezzuto, John Michael *dean, pharmacology educator*
Pezzuto, Mimi *pharmacist, educator*
Tripathi, Savarni *plant pathologist*
Vesper, Karl Hampton *business and mechanical engineering educator*

Holualoa

Scarr, Sandra Wood *retired psychology educator, researcher*

Honolulu

Acoba, Simeon Rivera, Jr. *state supreme court justice, educator*
Ahina, Leilani *psychologist*
Aiona, James R., Jr. *Lieutenant Governor of Hawaii*
Akiba, Lorraine Hiroko *lawyer*
Akinaka, Asa Masayoshi *lawyer*
Ariyoshi, George Ryoichi *lawyer, business consultant, former governor*
Ashraf, Kazi K. *architecture educator*
Baker, Tammy Hailiopua *theater educator*
Bender, Byron Wilbur *linguistics educator*
Bennett, Mark J. *state attorney general*
Bess, Henry David *management professor*
Betts, Barbara Stoke *artist, educator*
Betts, James William, Jr. *financial analyst, consultant*
Bitterman, Morton Edward *psychologist, educator*
Bloede, Victor Carl *lawyer, consultant, director*
Blust, Robert *linguist, educator*
Boas, Frank *retired lawyer*
Brady, Stephen R. P. K. *physician*
Bronster, Margery S. *retired state attorney general, lawyer*
Callies, David Lee *lawyer, educator*
Case, James Hebard *lawyer*
Castle, Alfred *administrator, executive*
Cazimero, Robert *musician*
Chapman, Duane Lee (Dog Chapman) *bail enforcement agent, television personality*
Char, Vernon Fook Leong *lawyer*
Chen, Wai-Fah *civil engineering educator*
Ching, Chauncey Tai Kin *agricultural studies educator, economist*
Cho, Lee-Jay *social scientist, demographer*
Clifton, Richard Randall *federal judge*
Cook, Bryan G. *education educator*
Cotlar, Morton *organizational scientist, educator*
Cowan, Stuart Marshall *lawyer*
Cox, Richard Horton *civil engineering executive*
Curb, Jess David *medical educator, researcher*
Dang, Marvin S.C. *lawyer*
Deaver, Phillip Lester *lawyer*
Devens, Paul *retired lawyer*
DeWeert, Michael James *technologist*
Diamond, Milton *anatomy and reproductive biology educator*
Doane, W. Allen *water transportation executive*
Duffy, James Earl, Jr. *state supreme court justice*
Duhamel, Solange *marine biologist*
Englert, Peter *academic administrator, director*
Finucane, Melissa Lucille *research scientist*
Fischer, Joel *social work educator*
Fitz-Patrick, David *endocrinologist, educator*
Flowers, Robert Swaim *medical educator, surgeon*
Fok, Agnes Kwan *retired cell biologist, educator*
Fong, Bernard W.D. *physician, educator*
Fong, Peter C. K. *lawyer, judge*
Forbis, Deborah Anne *history professor*
Franz, Charles Norman *radar and communication scientist*
Fukino, Chiyome Leinaala *state agency administrator, public health service officer*
Fukumoto, Leslie Satsuki *lawyer*
Fullmer, Daniel Warren *former psychologist, educator*
Gay, E(mil) Laurence *lawyer*
Gee, Chuck Yim *dean*
Gelber, Don Jeffrey *lawyer*
Ghasemi Nejhad, Mehrdad N. *mechanical engineering educator*
Gobush, Kathleen Schuyler *ecologist*
Godbey, Robert Carson *lawyer*
Goldstein, Sir Norman *dermatologist*
Goodhue, William Walter, Jr. *pathologist, military officer, educator*
Goto Sabas, Jennifer *legislative staff member*
Greenwood, M.R.C. *academic administrator, biologist, nutrition educator*
Griffin, Dominic B. III *state banking agency administrator*
Gubler, Duane J. *virologist, educator, researcher*
Guerrero, Reuben Castro *oncologist, internist*
Hack, Randolph C. *advocate, counselor, educator*
Haight, Warren Gazzam *investor*
Halloran, Richard Colby *writer, reporter, communications executive, editor*
Hamada, Harold Seichi *civil engineer, educator*
Hamamoto, Patricia *state official, school system administrator*
Hanabusa, Colleen W. *state legislator, lawyer*
Hannemann, Mufi *Mayor, Honolulu*
Hawke, Bernard Ray *planetary scientist, researcher*
Hays, Ronald Jackson *career officer*
Hazlett, Mark A. *lawyer*
Hefner, Carl J. *anthropology educator*
Heller, Ronald Ian *lawyer*
Herbig, George Howard *astronomer, educator*
Hey, Richard Noble *marine geophysicist*
Higgins, Christina Michael *applied linguist*
Hipp, Kenneth Byron *lawyer*
Hirai, Craig Kazuo *accountant*
Hirono, Mazie Keiko *United States Representative from Hawaii, former lieutenant governor*
Ho, Reginald Chi Shing *medical educator*
Hoffmann, Kathryn Ann *humanities educator*
Hook, Ralph Clifford, Jr. *business educator*
Hoonchamlong, Yuphaphann *literature and language professor*
Hue, Nguyen Van *soil scientist, chemist, educator*
Ihrig, Judson La Moure *chemist*
Ingersoll, Caroline Yee *director*
Inouye, Lorraine R. *state legislator*
Jarjees, Ekhlass A. *entomologist*
Johns, Timothy E. *museum director*
Jordan, Amos Azariah, Jr. *foreign affairs educator, retired military officer*
Jube, Sandro Lacerda Ramos *biotechnologist, researcher*
Kadohiro, Jane K. *nurse, educator, consultant*
Kaholokula, Joseph Keaweaimoku *psychologist health disparities researcher*
Kaiser, Ralf I *chemistry professor*
Kamemoto, Fred Isamu *retired zoologist*
Kane, Thomas Jay III *surgeon, educator*
Katayama, Robert Nobuichi *retired lawyer*
Kawamura, Georgina K. *state treasurer, finance company executive*
Keil, Klaus *geology educator, consultant*
Keith, Kent Marsteller *academic administrator, motivational speaker, lawyer, writer*
Kelley, Richard Roy *hotel executive*
Kennedy, Faye *retired social worker, author*
Keogh, Richard John *firearms and explosives consultant*
Khan, Mohammad Asad *geophysics educator, retired minister, former senator of Pakistan*
Kim, Albert Sechurl *civil engineer, educator*
Kim, Gregory Robert *lawyer, entrepreneur*
Kim, Ji-Yeon *developmental psychologist*
Kim-Rupnow, Weol Soon *education educator*
Kipnis, Kenneth *philosopher, educator*
Kobayashi, Donald Rikio *biologist*
Koide, Frank Takayuki *electrical engineering educator*
Kubo, Edward Hachiro, Jr. *prosecutor*
LaBelle, Thomas Jeffrey *research executive, academic administrator*
Lacy, John Robert *lawyer*
Lau, Constance H. (Connie Lau) *electric power industry executive*
Lau, H. Lorrin *obstetrician, gynecologist*
Lau, William Kienki *medical educator*
Lebedev, Konstantin Vladimirovich *oceanographer, researcher*
Lee, Dale W. *lawyer*
Lee, Willes K. *political organization administrator*
Lee, Yeu-Tsu Margaret *surgeon, educator*
Lilly, Michael Alexander *lawyer, writer*
Lingle, Linda *Governor of Hawaii*
Liu, Clark C. K. *engineering educator, director*
Louie, David Mark *lawyer*
Lu, Caixia *television director, language educator*
Ma, Alan Wai-Chuen *lawyer*
Ma, Tianwei *engineering educator*
Mandel, Morton *molecular biologist*
Masunaga, David K. *mathematics professor*
Mau-Shimizu, Patricia Ann *lawyer*
McMackin, Greg *college football coach*
Miller, Richard Sherwin *law educator*
Misawa, Mitsuru *finance educator*
Mochida, Paula T. *library director*
Moon, Ronald T.Y. *state supreme court chief justice*
Moore, Willis Henry Allphin *history educator*
Morris, Joseph Wesley *physician assistant*
Morrison, Charles Edward *think-tank executive*
Muranaka, Jami *biology educator*
Nakata, Gary Kenji *lawyer*
Nakayama, Paula Aiko *state supreme court justice*
Nasky, H(arold) Gregory *lawyer*
Ning, Cynthia Yumei *language educator*
Nishimura, Pete Hideo *oral surgeon*
Niyekawa, Agnes Mitsue *foreign language professor*
Noguchi, Hideo *insurance company executive*
Nordyke, Eleanor Cole *demographer, researcher, public health nurse*
Okinaga, Lawrence Shoji *lawyer*
O'Neill, Charles Kelly *marketing professional, retired advertising executive*
Owen, Cathy Hesse *nanotechnology company executive*
Paige, Glenn Durland *political scientist, educator*
Palia, Aspy Phiroze *marketing educator, researcher, consultant*
Parsa, Fereydoun Don *plastic surgeon*
Pedersen, Paul Bodholdt *psychologist, educator*
Pickens, Alexander Legrand *retired education educator*
Pinckney, Neal T. *psychologist, retired educator*
Plourde, William E. *secondary school educator*
Pollock, Gale Susan *career military officer*
Potts, Dennis Walker *lawyer*
Prevedouros, Panos D. *engineering educator, consultant*
Ramler, Siegfried *foundation administrator, researcher*
Rapson, Richard L. *history professor*
Reber, David James *lawyer*
Recktenwald, Mark E. *state supreme court justice*
Robinson, Robert Blacque *foundation administrator*
Rosenblum, Richard Mark *utilities executive*
Sagawa, Yoneo *horticulturist, educator*
Saiki, Patricia *federal agency administrator, congressman*
Saint Georges Chaumet, Eric *electronics engineer*
Sakamoto, Norman Lloyd *state legislator, civil engineer*
Sakamoto, Ronald Rikio *lawyer, construction executive*
Sato, Glenn Kenji *lawyer*
Schatz, Brian E. *political organization administrator, environmentalist, former state legislator*
Schatz, Irwin Jacob *cardiologist, educator*
Schweizer, Niklaus R. *German educator*
Seff, Karl *zeolite chemist, chemistry educator*
Sharma, Santosh Devraj *obstetrician, gynecologist, educator*
Shay, Roshani Cari *political science professor and healthcare professional*
Shimotsu, Ryan *biomedical engineer*
Shinagawa, Satoru *language educator*
Shiroma, Wayne A. *engineering educator*
Silva, Clarence Richard *bishop*
Silva, Mary Barnes *retired elementary school educator*
Simonds, John Edward *retired newspaper editor*
Soifer, Aviam *dean, law educator*
Solidum, James *finance and insurance executive*
Sparks, Robert William *retired publishing executive*
Staats, Arthur W. *psychology professor*
Steinmann, John Colburn *architect*
Stephan, John Jason *historian, educator*
Sugiki, Shigemi *ophthalmologist, educator*
Suh, Dae-Sook *political science professor*
Sumida, Gerald Aquinas *lawyer*
Swanson, Richard William *retired statistician*
Takumi, Roy Mitsuo *state legislator*
Tiwari, Atul *chemist, researcher*
Tjarks, Mark Damon *playwright, literature and language professor*
Uejo, Colleen Misaye *elementary school educator*
Vargas, Roger Irvin *entomologist, ecologist*
Vidal, Alejandro Legaspi (Andy Vidal) *architect*
Wang, Jaw-Kai *bioengineering educator*
Wellein, Marsha Diane Akau *military educator, director*
White, Emmet, Jr. *retirement community administrator*
White, Gary Richard *electrical engineer*
Wilson, William Hall, Jr. *retired telecommunications executive*
Withy, Kelley *medical educator*
Woo, Vernon Ying-Tsai *lawyer, real estate developer*
Yee, Alfred Alphonse *structural engineer, consultant*
Yee, Florence *library director*
Yeh, Raymond Wei-Hwa *architect, educator*
Yew, David *physician, director*

Kaaawa

Maris, Margaret Atma *psychotherapist, educator*

Kahului

Domingo, Cora Maria Corazon Encarnacion *minister*
Osgood, Christopher Mykel *radio sales manager*
Tolliver, Dorothy *library director*
Yamamoto, Irwin Toraki *editor, publishing executive*

Kailua

Tavares, Samantha *psychologist, educator*
Tubbs, Mary S. *curriculum coordinator*
Wright, John Cotton *archivist, consultant*

Kailua Kona

Diama, Benjamin *retired secondary school educator, composer, writer*

Kalaheo

Ragone, Carol Diane *horticulturist, ethnobotanist*

Kamuela

Adkins, Sean Michael *electrical, computer science and optical engineer*
Morgan, Andrew Lane *urologist, educator*

Kaneohe

Amioka, Wallace Shuzo *retired petroleum company executive*
Ashley, Elizabeth *dean, educator*
Coberly, Margaret *psychologist, educator*
Downing, Hazel Lawrence *nursing educator*
Dye, Stephen *physics professor*
Feagai, Hobie Etta *family practice nurse practitioner, educator*
Fisette, Scott Michael *landscape and golf course architect*
Ko, Seung Kyun *international relations educator, consultant*
Lewis, Mary Jane *film producer, director, scriptwriter*
Maeshiro, Mitzi (Mikilani) *literature and language educator*
Vincent, Thomas James *retired manufacturing executive*
Young-Pohlman, Colette Lisa *music educator*

Kapaa

Veylanswami, Satguru Bodhinatha *head of religious order*

Kapaau

McFee, Richard *electrical engineer, physicist*
Ralston, Joanne Smoot *public relations executive*

Kapolei

Zabanal, Eduardo Olegario *lawyer*

Kihei

Burns, Richard Gordon *retired lawyer, writer, consultant*
Galesi, Deborah Lee *artist*

Kilauea

Caspillo, Carol A. *retired secondary school educator*

Koloa

Donohugh, Donald Lee *physician*

Kula

Rohlfing, Frederick William *lawyer, retired judge, political scientist*

Lahaina

Percy, Helen Sylvia *physician*

Laie

Jonassen, Jon Tikivanotau Michael *political science professor, musician*
Miller, Ronald Mellado *education educator*
Richardson, Timothy Wayne *language educator*
Weber, Michael F. *physics professor*

Lihue

Lai, Waihang *art educator*

Makawao

Huff, Harriet *artist, educator*
Tanner, Barbara Ann *pediatrics nurse*

Mililani

Camery, John William *computer engineer*
Gardner, Sheryl Paige *gynecologist*
Hunkele, Lester Martin III *retired federal agency administrator*
Magee, Donald Edward *retired national park service administrator*
Okita, George Torao *retired pharmacologist*

Paia

Loomis, James Cook *mathematician, cyberneticist, writer, educator, navigator*

Pearl City

Fujita, James Hiroshi *history educator*

Pearl Harbor

Willard, Robert F. *career military officer*

Tamc

Uyehara, Catherine Fay Takako (Yamauchi) *physiologist, educator, pharmacologist*

Waianae

Bourke-Faustina, Marlene Frances *music educator*

Waikoloa

Calvert, Delbert William *retired energy executive*
Copman, Louis *radiologist*

Wailuku

Goldsmith, Stephen Ernest *lawyer*

Waipahu

Chang, Walter Tuck, Sr. *draftsman, real estate agent, religious studies educator*
Reyes, Arturo Pacheco *civilian military employee*

IDAHO

Aberdeen

Erickson, Charles *agronomist*
Krehbiel, Jennifer Nell *art educator*
Liu, Keshun *food chemist*

Boise

Aitken, Paul Arthur *composer, conductor*
Andrus, Cecil Dale *academic administrator, former United States Secretary of the Interior*
Appleton, Steven R. *electronics executive*
Armstrong, Richard *state agency administrator*
Bahnson, Paul Richard *finance educator*
Bell, Maxine Toolson *state legislator*
Benson, Kenneth Victor *manufacturing executive, lawyer*
Bieter, David H. *Mayor, Boise, Idaho*
Black, Pete *retired state legislator, educator*
Boren, Robert Reed *communications educator*
Brownson, Mary Louise *counselor, educator, artist*
Burdick, Roger S. *state supreme court justice*
Carlile, Thomas E. *paper company executive*
Cleary, Edward William *retired diversified forest products company executive*
Craig, Hemmens *law educator, director*
Crane, Ron G. *state treasurer*
Ditali, Akram *manufacturing executive*
Driscoll, Michael Patrick *bishop*
Durcan, D. Mark *engineering executive*
Eggert, Rudolph J. *engineering educator*
Eismann, Daniel T. *state supreme court chief justice*
Foster, Ronald C. *electronics executive*
Geston, Mark Symington *lawyer*
Gowler, Vicki Sue *editor-in-chief*
Grambo, Isaac *art educator*
Guha, Bhaswati *economics professor*
Hart, Richard LaVerne *retired college dean*

Herbert, Kathy J. *retail executive*
Holt, Isabel Rae *radio program producer*
Horton, Joel D. *state supreme court justice*
Hunter, Forrest Walker *lawyer*
Ilett, Frank, Jr. *trucking executive, educator*
Ingram, Cecil D. *accountant, state legislator*
Jones, James Thomas *state supreme court justice, former state attorney general*
Jones, Warren Eugene *state supreme court justice*
Kirklin, Vance Lane *software company executive*
LaRocco, Larry *former congressman*
Lazare, Michael *principal*
Leroy, David Henry *lawyer*
Lewis, Roderic W. *electronics executive, lawyer*
Little, Brad *Lieutenant Governor of Idaho, former state legislator*
Lojek, Helen Heusner *associate dean*
Maloof, Giles Wilson *academic administrator, educator, author*
McDevitt, Charles Francis *retired judge, lawyer*
McDougall, Duane C. *manufacturing executive*
McGown, John, Jr. *lawyer*
McLuskie, Ed *communications educator*
Meyer, Christopher Hawkins *lawyer*
Morgan, Barbara R. *science educator, former astronaut*
Moss, Thomas E. *prosecutor*
Nadelson, Sandra G. *nursing educator*
Nelson, Thomas G. *federal judge*
Osguthorpe, Richard D. *science educator*
Otter, Butch (C. L. Otter, Clement Leroy Otter) *Governor of Idaho, former United States Representative from Idaho*
Overgaard, Willard Michele *retired political scientist*
Papic, Milorad *electrical engineer, researcher*
Park, William Anthony (Tony Park) *lawyer*
Petersen, Chris *college football coach*
Pfouts, Ralph William *economist, consultant*
Plew, Mark G. *archaeologist, educator*
Pound, Kathleen Last *elementary school educator*
Saltzer, Jerome Howard *computer science educator*
Sather, John Henry *biologist, educator, dean*
Semanko, Norman M. *political organization administrator*
Shurtliff, Marvin Karl *lawyer*
Slaughter, Richard Arthur *political scientist, economist, educator*
Sloan, Nina *language educator*
Trott, Stephen Spangler *federal judge*
Wasden, Lawrence *state attorney general*
Washington, Dennis R. *contracting company executive*
Wilson, Jack Fredrick *retired federal government official*
Woods, Jean Frahm *science educator*
Ysursa, Ben T. *Secretary of State, Idaho*
Zarges, Thomas H. *engineering executive*

Caldwell
Angresano, James *political economics professor*
Hendren, Robert Lee, Jr. *academic administrator*
Hoover, Robert Allan *university president*
Kerrick, David Ellsworth *lawyer*

Coeur D' Alene
Clabby, Michael *computer graphics designer, educator*
Dahlgren, Dorothy *museum director*
Finney, Andrew W. *academic administrator*
Jain, Sachin *medical educator*
Reed, Scott W. *lawyer*
Wheeler, Dennis Earl *mining company executive, lawyer*

Donnelly
Ferensowicz, Michael Jay *real estate company executive*

Eagle
Chung, Caleb *inventor, toymaker, toy company executive*
McCahill, Barry Winslow *public relations executive*

Gooding
Larson, Lynn Wood *artist, musician*

Hailey
Dolas, Evelyn Ann *poet, musician*
Hogue, Terry Glynn *lawyer*
Roark, Keith (R. Keith Roark) *lawyer, political organization administrator*

Harrison
Carlson, George Arthur *artist*

Idaho Falls
Barbe, Betty Catherine *marketing professional, retired financial analyst*
Bruemmer, David Jonathan *robotics engineer*
Castle, Lyle William *dean*
Chang, Gray S. *nuclear engineer, consultant*
Gaffner, Vernon *dentist*
Gertman, David I. *research scientist*
Gray, Catherine Jean *librarian*
Hopkins, C. Timothy (Tim Hopkins) *lawyer*
Jue, Jan-Fong *materials scientist*
King, Ronald Amos *federal official, retired communications professional*
Lee, Glenn Richard *medical association administrator, educator*
Oh, Chang *chemical engineer, consultant*
Redden, George Dean *geochemist*
Riemke, Richard Allan *nuclear engineer*
Rydalch, Ann *federal agency administrator, former state senator*
Sharpe, Phil *nuclear scientist*
Thorsen, Nancy Dain *retired real estate broker*

Inkom
Ambrose, Tommy W. *chemical engineer, engineering executive*

Jerome
Rice, Melissa Ann *mathematics educator*

Kamiah
Mills, Lawrence *lawyer, business and transportation consultant*

Ketchum
Holland, Robert James *retired lawyer*
Mazzola, Chris *dentist*
McElhinny, Wilson Dunbar *banker*
Nalen, Craig Anthony *federal agency administrator*
Parry, Janet *retired health facility administrator*
Stennett, William Clinton (Clint) *state legislator, entrepreneur*
Ziebarth, Robert Charles *management consultant*

Kimberly
Owings, Vickie Ann *librarian*

Lewiston
Tait, John Reid *lawyer*

Meridian
Looney, Daniel Stephen *artist*
McKague, Shirley *state legislator*
Swalin, Richard Arthur *scientist, company executive*

Moscow
Abdel-Rahim, Ahmed *engineering educator*
Aston, D. Eric *engineering educator*
Bathurst, Pamela *music educator*
Cole, Douglas Gene *biochemist, educator*
Daley-Laursen, Steven B. *academic administrator, dean, environmental scientist, educator*
DeShazer, James Arthur *biological engineer, educator, research administrator*
Fischer, Jerome M. *rehabilitation services professional*
Goetschel, Roy Hartzell, Jr. *mathematician, researcher*
Hrdlicka, Patrick J. *chemistry professor*
Leithart, Peter James *theologian*
Mead, Phillip Gunn *architect, educator*
Miller, Maynard Malcolm *geologist, educator, geoscience institute director, former state legislator*
Renfrew, Malcolm MacKenzie *chemist, educator*
Roberts, Lorin Watson *botanist, educator*
Shreeve, Jean'ne Marie *chemist, educator*
Stumpf, Bernhard Josef *physicist, educator*
Top, Eva Maria *science educator*

Mountain Home
English, Brian Patrick *social studies educator*

Nampa
Bowes, A. Wendell *religious studies educator*
Rotz, Carol *retired theology studies educator*

Ola
Farr, Reeta Rae *special education administrator*

Parma
Sharkey, (John) Mick *biology educator*

Pocatello
Bennett, Byron Lee *chemistry professor, researcher*
Frazier, Timothy Howard *art educator*
Guo, Ruiling *medical librarian, educator*
Jackson, Allen Keith *retired museum administrator*
Jacobsen, Richard T. *mechanical engineering educator*
Lawson, Jonathan Nevin *academic administrator, educator*
May, Matthew P. *chemist*
Naidu, D. Subbaram *electrical engineer, educator*
Nye, W. Marcus W. *lawyer*
Olson, Gary Andrew *academic administrator, English language professor*
Owens, Christopher Taft *pharmacist, educator*
Piel, John A. *education educator*
Piland, Neill Finnes *health services economist, researcher, educator*
Robinson, Evelyn Etta *principal*
Smith, Norman Randy *federal judge*
Stucki, Margaret Elizabeth *painter, writer*

Post Falls
Chojnowski, Peter Edward *philosopher, educator*
Hasalone, Annette Leona *radio personality, research and development company executive*
Owsley, Frederick Mark *plastic surgeon*

Potlatch
Severns, Karen S. *family court services administrator*

Rathdrum
Dickinson, Linda Mary *web designer, graphics designer, art educator*

Rexburg
Barrus, Charles LaMar, Jr. *music educator*
Coates, Lawrence G. *history professor*
Ivers, John Joseph *language educator, dean*
Kumferman, Edwin C. *literature and language professor*
Pearson, Fred Ross *healthcare educator, consultant*
Weyland, Jack Arnold *physics educator, writer*

Rigby
Henry, Esther Kaye *secondary school educator*

Rogerson
Boss, Marylin Jeanette *elementary school educator*

Sagle
Groth-Marnat, Gabrielle *counselor*

Sandpoint
Bird, Forrest M. *retired medical inventor*
Daarstad, Erik *cinematographer*
Glock, Charles Young *retired sociologist, writer*

Shelley
Fleming, Chris K. *literature and language educator*

Sun Valley
Cassell, William Comyn *retired college president*
Pesch, LeRoy Allen *physician, educator, health and hospital consultant, business executive*
Stewart, John Todd *economist, consultant*

Twin Falls
Berry, L. Clyel *lawyer*
Cowger, Shari Ann *music educator*
Gentry, James Robert *education educator*
Ricketts, Virginia Lee *historian, researcher*
Selelyo, Pat *biology professor*
Wright, Frances Jane *educational psychologist*

ILLINOIS

Abbott Park
Abad-Zapatero, Celerino *crystallographer, researcher*
Ashley, Richard W. *pharmaceutical executive*
Freyman, Thomas C. *pharmaceutical executive*
He, Yupeng *virologist, cell biologist*
Hui, Yu-Hua *pharmaceutical researcher*
Liepmann, Holger A. *pharmaceutical executive*
Martin, Ruth L. *pharmacologist*
Nemmers, Joseph M., Jr. *pharmaceutical executive*
Schumacher, Laura J. *lawyer, pharmaceutical executive*
White, Miles D. *pharmaceutical executive*

Addison
Cherif, Abour Hachmi *biology and science educator*
Christopher, Doris K. *consumer products company executive*
McDonald, David Eugene *transportation operator*
Medjo Me Zengue, Mary *library director*

Alden
Tayloe, David T., Jr. *pediatrician*

Alexander
Eck, Gail Ann *elementary school educator*

Algonquin
Dooley, Meeghan Elizabeth *music educator*
Shaw, Cecelia *retired chef*

Anna
Srinivasaraghavan, Jagannathan *forensic psychiatrist*

Argonne
Abrikosov, Alexei Alexeyevich *physicist*
Aliberti, Gerardo *nuclear engineer*
Ban, Stephen Dennis *gas industry executive*
Chang, Yoon Il *nuclear engineer*
Derrick, Malcolm *physicist*
Gaffney, Jeffrey Steven *chemistry researcher*
Jellinek, Julius *scientist*
Kumar, Romesh *chemical engineer*
Lawson, Robert Davis *theoretical nuclear physicist*
Li, Wei *research scientist*
Lindert, Eric Alton *operations research specialist, small business owner*
Ma, Shengqian *research scientist*
Mancini, Derrick Charles *physicist*
Reimer, Paul E. *physicist*
Ruscic, Branko M. *chemist, researcher*
Schriesheim, Alan *science administrator*
Sizyuk, Valeryi *physicist*
Sumant, Anirudha *materials scientist, researcher*

Arlington Heights
Blomquist, Ernest Richard III *lawyer*
Giannini, Evelyn Louise *retired library consultant*
Griffin, Jean Latz *college instructor, writer, publisher*
Halbert, Keith *air transportation executive*
Lampinen, John A. *newspaper editor*
Li, Norman N. *chemicals executive*
Placek-Zimmerman, Ellyn Clare *school system administrator, educator, consultant*
Placik, Otto Joseph *plastic surgeon*
Ruder, John Regan *physician*
Smith, Norman Obed *retired physical chemist, educator*
Telleen, Judy *counselor*

Aurora
Daugherty, Patricia Ann *retired elementary school educator*
O'Donnell, Mickie Louise *religious educator*
Pappas, Margene *retired music educator*
Ross, Kristen Ann *school system administrator*
Weisner, Tom *Mayor, Aurora, Illinois*

Barrington
Amatangelo, Kathleen Driscoll *interior designer, educator*
Burrows, Brian William *retired research and development company executive*
Carter, Jeanie *performing company executive*
Chung, Joseph Sang-hoon *economics professor*
Hybels, Bill *Pastor*
Karlin, Gary Lee *insurance executive*
Lee, William Marshall *lawyer*
Murphy, Robert *executive recruiter, consultant*
Nadig, Gerald George *retired manufacturing executive*
Ross, Frank Howard III *management consultant*
Stephens, Norval Blair, Jr. *marketing consultant*
Verschoor, Curtis Carl *author, consultant*
Wyatt, James Frank, Jr. *lawyer*

Batavia
Bardeen, William Allan *research physicist*
Bhat, Pushpalatha C. *physics professor, researcher*
Darve, Christine *mechanical engineer*
Jonckheere, Alan Mathew *physicist*
Malik, Sudhir *physics professor*
Oddone, Piermaria Jorge *physicist*
Raja, Rajendran *physicist*
Rakhno, Igor *physicist*

Belleville
Braxton, Edward Kenneth *bishop*
Fietsam, Robert Charles *accountant*
Gale, Neil Jan *Internet company executive, computer scientist, consultant*
Gossage, Roza B. *lawyer, educator*
Grandberry-Edwards, Vera Lynn *elementary school educator*
Hess, Frederick J. *lawyer*
Hilgenbrink, Robert J. *academic administrator*
Jones, Donald Leigh *retired music educator*
Loehring, Brian Todd *social studies educator, department chairman*
Pounds, Regina Dorothea *writer*
Ripplinger, George Raymond, Jr. *lawyer*
Schlarman, Stanley Girard *bishop emeritus*
Shim, Sang Koo *mental health services professional*
Wittenbrink, Boniface Leo *priest*

Belvidere
Mc Nelly, Frederick Wright, Jr. *psychologist*

Berwyn
Hudik, Martin Francis *hospital administrator, educator, consultant, writer*

Bloomingdale
Flaherty, John Joseph *quality assurance company executive*
Roskam, Peter James *United States Representative from Illinois, former state legislator, lawyer*

Bloomington
Blackburn, John D. *insurance company executive*
Bolen, Charles Warren *university dean*
Bridges, Roger Dean *historian*
Brown, Jared *theater director, educator, writer*
Brunner, Kim M. *insurance company executive, lawyer*
Callahan, Christopher John *literature and language professor, interpreter*
Chrisman, Jay W. *cosmetic dentist*
Curry, Alan Chester *actuary*
Dietz, William Ronald *corporate management professional*
Laurenti, Joseph Luciano *language educator, writer*
Lindberg, Sandra D. *theater educator, director, actor*
Mead, Walter Bruce *retired political science professor*
Merwin, Davis Underwood *newspaper executive*
Olson, Rue Eileen *retired librarian*
Pana, Elisabeta *finance educator*
Pannell, Thierry Edgard *engineer, information technology manager*
Prandi, Julie Diane *retired literature and language professor*
Rust, Edward Barry, Jr. *insurance company executive, lawyer*
Rutrough, James E. *insurance company executive*
Skillrud, Harold Clayton *minister, retired bishop*
Switzer, Jon Rex *architect*
Trefzger, Richard Charles *surgeon*
Vayo, David Joseph *composer, music educator*

Bolingbrook
Gelin-Rodriguez, Maureen T. *psychologist*
Malicay, Manuel Alaban *physician*
Mell, Patricia *dean*
Price, Theodora Hadzisteliou *mental health services professional*
Sabau, Carmen Sybile *retired chemist*

Bourbonnais
Dalton, Martha Gomer *music educator*
McClure, Thomas Edward *lawyer*
Monts, Stephen Lee *retired chemistry professor*
Reams, Max Warren *geology educator, researcher*
Spruce, Sara Elizabeth *education educator*
Vance, David A. *information systems educator*

Brookfield
Rabb, George Bernard *zoologist, conservationist*
Wojciechowski, Sheila *zoological park administrator*

Buffalo Grove
Dunn, Jonathan *orthopedist, surgeon*
Kuennen, Thomas Gerard *journalist*

Burr Ridge
Bottom, Dale Coyle *marketing executive, director, management consultant*
Decker, Richard Knore *lawyer*
Rosenberg, Robert Brinkmann *information technology executive*
Wyatt, Robert Odell *journalism educator*

Cahokia
Schwemmer, Gabrielle *academic administrator, coach*

Calumet City
Muñoz, Romeo Solano *audio visual curator*
Oyeyemi, Olusola Olayinka *lawyer*
Pickel, Joyce Kiley *psychologist*
Scullion, Annette Murphy *lawyer, educator*

Carbondale
Anterola, Aldwin M. *biochemist, educator*
Asoh, Derek Ajesam *information scientist, educator*
Baker, Clora Mae *business educator*
Bauner, Ruth Elizabeth *library director*
Carlson, David Harold *library director, dean*
Che, Dunren *science educator*
Clemons, John Robert *lawyer*
Cole, Brad *mayor*
Dahlen, Michael F. *lawyer*
Dai, Chifeng *economics professor*
Davenport, Susan Gail *music educator, director*
Deng, Saiying *finance educator*
Dixon, Billy Gene *academic administrator, educator*
Duram, Leslie Aileen *geographer, educator*

Farhang, Kambiz *engineering educator*
Gertsman, Elina *art educator*
Headrick, Todd Christopher *mathematical statistician, educator*
Kawewe, Saliwe Moyo *social work educator, researcher*
King, Sheryl S. *animal scientist, educator*
Koc, Rasit *ceramics engineer, educator*
Kohler, Christopher Carl *zoology professor*
Lee, Mark Richard *lawyer, educator*
LeFebvre, Eugene Allen *zoology educator, ecologist*
Lowery, Christopher M. *men's college basketball coach*
Ma, Xingmao *environmental engineer, educator*
Mahajan, Ajay *engineering educator*
Malkin, Marjorie J. *recreational therapist, educator*
McKinnies, Richard Charles *radiation therapist, assistant professor*
Neuman, Edward George *mathematician, educator*
Oyana, Tonny J. *geoscientist, educator*
Panchapakesan, Subrahmanian *mathematics professor*
Poshard, Glenn (Glendal W. Poshard) *academic administrator, former congressman*
Preece, John Earl *plant and soil science educator*
Primont, Daniel *economics professor*
Rose, Gregory Mancel *neurobiologist*
Sasse, Mary Hawley *retired language educator, editor*
Sutton, David E. *anthropologist, educator*
Tolley, Luke *chemistry professor*
Trescott, Paul Barton *economics professor*
Tsige, Mesfin *physicist*
Wang, Lichang *chemistry professor*
Xiao, Dong *research scientist*

Carol Stream
Armerding, Hudson Taylor *retired college president, consultant*
Back, Robert Wyatt *investment company and pharmaceutical executive, consultant*
Bemis, Mary Ferguson *magazine editor*
Cole, Kevin John *science educator*
Franzen, Janice Marguerite Gosnell *magazine editor*
Janssen, Carron Joyce *music educator*
Larson, Ward Jerome *lawyer, retired banker*

Carrollton
Strickland, Hugh Alfred *lawyer*

Carterville
Krapf, Keith Alan *science educator*
Seagle, Mike *theater educator*

Carthage
Aanenson, Marian Ham *medical educator*
Glidden, John Redmond *lawyer*

Cary
Irey, Robin Elizabeth *performing company executive, performing arts educator*

Centralia
Sickmeyer, Kent A. *agricultural studies educator*
Williams, Virginia Lee *finance educator*

Champaign
Althaus, Scott L. *political science professor*
Baillargeon, Renee *psychology professor*
Baker, Jack Sherman *retired architect*
Balbach, Harold Edward *environmental scientist*
Batzli, George Oliver *ecology educator*
Boubekri, Mohamed *architecture educator*
Boyle, Francis Anthony *law educator*
Brighton, Gerald David *retired finance educator*
Buschbach, Thomas Charles *geologist, consultant*
Carmen, Ira Harris *political scientist, educator*
Cook, Paul Franklin *veterinarian, educator*
Cutcher-Gershenfeld, Joel E. *dean, professor*
Davis, James Henry *retired psychology educator*
DeBrock, Larry *dean, economics professor*
Douglas, George Halsey *language educator, writer*
Dulany, Donelson Edwin, Jr. *psychology professor*
Eriksen, Charles Walter *psychologist, educator*
Fang, Er *finance educator*
Farmer, Helen Sweeney *psychology professor*
Fredrickson, L(awrence) Thomas *composer*
Freedman, Philip *internist, educator*
Getz, Lowell Lee *zoology educator*
Gold, Paul Ernest *psychology and behavioral neuroscience educator*
Guttenberg, Albert Ziskind *planning educator*
Hackbarth, Dirk *finance educator*
Hager, Lowell Paul *biochemistry educator*
Harleman, Kathleen Towe *museum director*
Herman, Richard H. *academic administrator*
Hurd, Heidi M. *humanities and law educator*
Ikenberry, Stanley Oliver *education educator, director, former university president*
Irwin, David E. *psychology professor, department chairman*
Kim, Hyunjoo *research scientist*
Kim, Michael Kyong-il *professor, architect*
Kindt, John Warren *lawyer, educator*
Korst, Helmut Hans *mechanical engineer, educator*
Kotoske, Roger Allen *artist, educator*
Krause, Harry Dieter *law educator*
Kroner, Fred L. *journalist*
Levin, Geoffrey Arthur *botanist*
Maggs, Peter Blount *lawyer, educator*
Mamer, Stuart Mies *lawyer*
McConkie, George Wilson *education educator*
McConnell, William Stewart *application developer*
McGlathery, James Melville *retired foreign language educator*
McKay, JoAnn *retired musician, composer*
Melka, Tomi *language educator, historian*
Meyer, August Christopher, Jr. *broadcast executive, lawyer*
Moore, Jerry Jay *sales executive, retired archaeologist*
Nowak, John E. *law educator*
Okazawa, Hiromi *school librarian*
Perry, Kenneth Wilbur *finance educator*
Rebeiz, Constantin Anis *plant biochemist, lab and foundation administrator, educator*
Richardson, Selma Katherine *retired library and information scientist*
Riley, Robert Bartlett *landscape architect*
Ruan, Lian Jin *library director*
Ruggles, D. Fairchild *writer*
Schoenfeld, Hanns-Martin Walter *accounting educator*
Semonin, Richard Gerard *retired state official*
Smith, Bruce P. *dean, law educator*
Summerfield, Gale *director, educator*
Tao, Zhining *environmental scientist*
Tettegah, Sharon Yvonne *university professor*
Triandis, Harry Charalambos *psychologist, educator*
Turquette, Atwell Rufus *logician*
Watson, Jessica Lewis *writer*
Watts, Emily Stipes *retired English language educator*
Watts, Robert Allan *publisher, lawyer*
Weber, Bruce *men's college basketball coach*
Wolfram, Stephen *physicist, computer company executive*
Xiao, Zhijie *economics educator*
Zook, Ron *college football coach*

Charleston
Coutant, Mary McElwee *retired editor*
Dey, Suhrit K. *mathematician, researcher*
Faires, Joel Brooks *music educator*
Leddy, Michael *english educator*
Linton, David A. *astronomer, educator*
Rives, Stanley Gene *retired academic administrator*
Swartzbaugh, Dorothy Stoeppelwerth *middle school educator*
Thornburgh, Daniel Eston *retired university administrator, journalism educator*
Weidner, Robert Wright *retired musician, musicologist, educator*

Chatham
Post, Alan Richard *lawyer*

Chebanse
McLaughlin, Barbara Lyn *elementary school educator*

Chester
Welge, Donald Edward *food manufacturing executive*

Chicago
Abecassis, Michael *medical educator*
Abelson, Herbert Traub *pediatrician, educator*
Abrams, Charles B. *chemistry professor*
Abrams, Lee Norman *lawyer*
Achatz, Grant (Grant Sherman Achatz Jr.) *chef*
Acker, Ann E. *lawyer*
Adelman, Pamela Bernice Kozoll *education educator*
Adelman, Stanley Joseph *lawyer*
Adelman, Steven Herbert *lawyer*
Ailey, Sarah Herrink *nursing educator*
Ajayi, Murphy M. *sculptor, educator*
Akhter, Shahab A. *Cardio Thoracic Surgeon*
Aksikas, Jaafar *social sciences educator*
Alaraj, Ali *neurosurgeon*
Albrecht, Ronald Frank *retired anesthesiologist*
Alcantara, Anita Luisa *community arts administrator*
Alexander, Ann *lawyer*
Alexander, Kenneth Ross *scientist, educator*
Allen, Armstead *educator*
Allen, Belle *management consulting firm and communications executive*
Allen, Henry Sermones, Jr. *lawyer*
Allen, Thomas Draper *lawyer*
Allen, Thomas R. *alderman*
Allen-Meares, Paula G. *academic administrator, social work educator*
An, Howard S. *physician, educator*
Andersen, Burton Robert *immunologist, educator, medical historian*
Anderson, John Leonard *academic administrator, chemical engineering educator*
Anderson, Karl Stephen *retired journalist*
Anderson, Kimball Richard *lawyer*
Andersson, Gunnar Bengt Johan *orthopedist, educator*
Andolino, Rosemarie S. *transportation executive*
Andreoli, Kathleen Gainor *nurse, educator, dean*
Angst, Gerald L. *lawyer*
Anthony, Donald Barrett *engineering executive*
Anthony, Michael Francis *lawyer*
Antler, Steven David *manufacturing executive, economics professor*
Antonio, Douglas John *lawyer*
Anvaripour, M. A. *lawyer*
Anzia, Joan Meyer *psychiatrist*
Appel, Nina Schick *law educator, dean, academic administrator*
Arnold, Daniel *religious studies educator*
Aronson, Virginia L. *lawyer*
Arruda, Jose *nephrologist*
Ash, J. Marshall *mathematician, educator*
Ashley, Mary V. *biology professor*
Ashton, Rick James *librarian*
Aspen, Marvin Edward *federal judge*
Athas, Gus James *lawyer*
Aubin, Barbara Jean *artist*
Austin, Carrie *alderwoman*
Avery, Robert Dean *lawyer*
Ayers, Bill (William Charles Ayers) *education professor, writer*
Babcock, Lyndon Ross, Jr. *environmental engineer, educator*
Babcock, Sandra L. *lawyer, educator*
Babjak, Patricia M. *medical association administrator*
Bach, Bernard R., Jr. *orthopedist, educator*
Badel, Julie *lawyer*
Baer, John Richard Frederick *lawyer*
Bailey, Robert, Jr. *advertising executive*
Bailey, Robert Converse *epidemiologist, anthropologist, educator*
Baines, Harold Douglass *retired professional baseball player, baseball bench coach*
Baird, Douglas Gordon *law educator, dean*
Baird, James *lawyer*
Bajich, Milena Tatic *psychologist*
Bakay, Roy Arpad Earle *neurosurgeon, educator*
Baker, Bruce Jay *lawyer*
Bakris, George L. *nephrologist, educator, clinical researcher, hypertension specialist*
Balasa, Florin *software engineer, mathematician*
Balasi, Mark Geoffrey *architect*
Balcer, James A. *alderman*
Baldwin, DeWitt Clair, Jr. *physician, educator*
Baldwin, Shaun McParland *lawyer*
Balzekas, Stanley, Jr. *museum director*
Banisadr, Ghazal *science educator, researcher*
Banks, William J.P. *alderman*
Banoff, Sheldon Irwin *lawyer*
Barden, Larry A. *lawyer*
Barner, Sharon Ruth *lawyer*
Barnes, Brenda C. *food products executive*
Barnhart, Mary C. *health facility administrator*
Baron, Joseph Mandel *hematologist*
Baroody, Fuad *pediatrician, educator*
Barr, John Robert *retired lawyer*
Barr, Sanford Lee *dentist*
Barron, Harold Sheldon *lawyer*
Barron, Howard Robert *lawyer*
Barron, John *editor*
Bart, Susan Therese *lawyer*
Bartholomay, William C. *insurance brokerage company and professional sports team executive*
Barton, John Joseph *obstetrician, gynecologist, administrator, educator, researcher*
Bartter, Brit Jeffrey *investment banker*
Bashwiner, Steven Lacelle *lawyer*
Bast, Joseph L. *research organisation director*
Basu, Anirban *medical educator*
Bates, Zeline Kelly *media specialist, director*
Battle, Stephanie *literature and language professor*
Batu, Vedat *senior water resources engineer*
Bauer, Karen *music educator*
Bauer, William Joseph *federal judge*
Bauman, Jerry L. *dean, pharmacy researcher, educator*
Bayless, Rick *chef*
Beale, Anthony *alderman*
Beam, Craig Allen *biomedical researcher, educator, director*
Beck, Philip S. *lawyer*
Becker, Gary Stanley *economist, educator*
Becker, Michael Allen *internist, rheumatologist, educator*
Beem, Jack Darrel *retired lawyer*
Beestrum, Molly A. *school librarian, educator*
Beilinson, Alexander A. *mathematics professor*
Belden-Adams, Kris K. *journalist, educator*
Bell, Carl Compton *psychiatrist, researcher*
Bell, Graeme I. *biochemistry and molecular biology educator*
Bell, James A. *aerospace transportation executive*
Bellows, Laurel Gordon *lawyer*
Bendok, Bernard R. *neurosurgeon, researcher*
Bennington, Thomas Francis *lawyer, county official*
Bensinger, Peter Benjamin *consulting firm executive*
Benson, Al Bowen III *oncologist, educator*
Benson, Irene M. *nurse*
Benson, Moses, Jr. *retired education services specialist*
Bentley, Carol Ligon *retired library and information scientist*
Benzon, Honorio Tabal *anesthesiologist*
Berens, Mark Harry *lawyer*
Berenzweig, Jack Charles *lawyer*
Berger, Miles Lee *land economist*
Berger, Robert Michael *lawyer*
Berghoef, Henry R. *investment company executive*
Bergonia, Raymond David *venture capitalist*
Berkoff, Adam T. *lawyer*
Berkoff, Mark Andrew *lawyer*
Berkowitz, Sean M. *lawyer*
Berlin, Lawrence Norman *science educator*
Berman, Arthur Leonard *state legislator*
Bernardin, Thomas L. *advertising executive*
Bernatowicz, Frank Allen *management consultant*
Bernstein, Charles Bernard *lawyer*
Bernstein, H. Bruce *lawyer*
Berolzheimer, Karl *retired lawyer*
Bess, Ronald W. *advertising executive*
Bettman, Suzanne S. (Sue Bettman) *lawyer*
Betz, Hans Dieter *theology studies educator*
Bevington, David Martin *English literature educator*
Bickerstaff, Bernie (Bernard Tyrone Bickerstaff Sr.) *professional basketball coach*
Bicknell-Hentges, Lindsay Pugh *psychology professor*
Bidwell, Charles Edward *sociologist, educator*
Bigelow, Chandler III *publishing executive*
Bigg, Susan Jeanette *educational consultant*
Biggs, Robert Dale *Near Eastern studies educator*
Bindenagel, James Dale *university executive*
Binion, Celious *retired parochial school educator*
Bird, Andrew *musician*
Birnbaum, Barry William *special education educator*
Bixby, Frank Lyman *retired lawyer*
Bleiweiss, Shell J. *lawyer*
Block, Neal Jay *lawyer*
Block, Philip Dee III *retired investment company executive*
Blount, Michael Eugene *lawyer*
Bluhm, Neil Gary *real estate company executive*
Bobins, Norman R. *bank executive*
Boccara, Nino *physicist*
Bodenstein, Ira *lawyer*
Boehnen, Daniel A. *lawyer*
Boggs, Joseph Dodridge *pediatric pathologist, educator*
Bogolub, David Louis *physician*
Boho, Dan L. *lawyer*
Bona, Jerry Lloyd *mathematician, educator*
Bondra, Peter *professional hockey player*
Bonow, Robert Ogden *cardiologist, educator*
Borenstine, Alvin Jerome *search company executive*
Bosowski, Edward M. *manufacturing executive*
Bowe, William J(ohn) *lawyer*
Bowen, Stephen Stewart *lawyer*
Bower, Glen Landis *judge, lawyer*
Bowles, Graham Elliot *chef*
Bowman, Barbara Taylor *early childhood educator*
Bowman, James Edward *pathologist, educator*
Bowman, Scotty (William Scott Bowman) *professional sports team executive, retired professional hockey coach*
Bowman, Stan *professional sports team executive*
Boyer, Bruce A. *law educator, director*
Boyer, John William *history professor, dean*
Boykin, Richard Renarda *lawyer, former legislative staff member*
Boykins, Michael L. *lawyer*
Bradley, Milton Obelle *professional baseball player*
Brake, Cecil Clifford *retired diversified manufacturing executive*
Bramnik, Robert Paul *lawyer*
Brandt, William Arthur, Jr. *consulting executive*
Braun, Phillip A. *finance educator*
Brauner, Daniel *geriatrician, educator, rheumatologist*
Brawner, Cynthia D. *elementary school educator*
Brice, Roger Thomas *lawyer*
Bridges, Cynthia Elaine *music educator*
Briggs, Jennifer K. *literature and language professor*
Brinkman, John Anthony *historian, educator*
Brizzolara, Charles Anthony *lawyer, director*
Bro, Ruth Hill *lawyer*
Brodsky, William J. *stock exchange executive*
Bromley, Richard *lawyer*
Brooker, Thomas Kimball *oil industry executive*
Brookins, Howard, Jr. *alderman*
Brown, Alan Crawford *lawyer*
Brown, Elizabeth McCarthy *social services administrator*
Brown, Gregory K. *lawyer*
Brown, Jeremy Earle *advertising executive*
Brown, Matthew S. *lawyer*
Brown, Peter C. *video game company executive, former movie theater company executive*
Brown, Richard Holbrook *library director, historian, researcher*
Browne, Bliss Williams *social welfare administrator*
Browning, Don Spencer *religious educator*
Bruner, Philip Lane *arbitrator, mediator*
Bryan, Ashley F. *children's book author, illustrator*
Bryant, Fred Boyd *psychology professor*
Bucksbaum, John *real estate company executive*
Bucksbaum, Matthew *real estate investment trust company executive*
Buehrle, Mark Alan *professional baseball player*
Bujak, Denise A. *accountant, insurance company executive*
Bulger, Brian Wegg *lawyer*
Buniak, Raymond *educational professional*
Burget, Gary Crites *plastic surgeon*
Burke, Anne M. *state supreme court justice*
Burke, Edward Michael *alderman*
Burke, Thomas Joseph, Jr. *lawyer*
Burkhardt, Edward Arnold *rail transportation executive*
Burnett, Walter, Jr. *alderman*
Burns, James B. *prosecutor*
Burroughs, Margaret Taylor Goss *artist*
Burton, Barbara K. *medical geneticist, pediatrician, educator*
Busey, Roxane C. *lawyer*
Bush-Joseph, Charles A. *orthopedist*
Buttin, Barbara M. *oncologist, educator*
Bynoe, Peter Charles Bernard *investment banker, lawyer*
Byther-Smith, Ida W. *social services administrator*
Cabay, Robert John *physician, dentist, author, researcher*
Cafferty, Pastora San Juan *education educator*
Calabresi, Steven G. *law educator*
Callahan, Michael R. *lawyer*
Campbell, Brian Wesley *professional hockey player*
Campbell, Tracy M. *dermatologist*
Campbell Lee, Sally Ann *academic administrator, director*
Camper, John Jacob *writer, academic administrator*
Canelli, Florencia *physics professor*
Canning, John Anthony, Jr. *private equity firm executive*
Card, Deborah R. *orchestra administrator*
Cardenas, George A. *alderman*
Carey, Charles P. *mercantile exchange executive*
Carlin, Dennis J. *lawyer*
Carlson, LeRoy Theodore, Jr. *telecommunications industry executive*
Carlson, Walter Carl *lawyer*
Carlton, Dennis William *economics professor*
Caro, William Allan *physician, educator*
Carothers, Isaac Sims (Ike Carothers) *alderman*
Carpenter, David William *lawyer*
Carr, Jeffrey W. *lawyer, manufacturing executive*
Carr, Walter Stanley *lawyer*
Carreira, Domingo Jose *structural engineer*
Carroll, William Kenneth *lawyer, educator, psychologist, theologian*
Carson, Thomas Lee *philosopher, educator*
Cascino, Anthony Elmo, Jr. *lawyer, insurance company executive*
Case, Donni Marie *investment company executive, consultant*
Case, Gregory C. *insurance company executive*
Cassens Weiss, Debra Sue *professional association administrator, publishing executive*
Castillo, Mario Enrique *artist, educator*
Castillo, Ruben *federal judge*
Ceko, Theresa C. *lawyer, educator*
Celesia, Gastone Guglielmo *neurologist*
Cesario, Robert Charles *marketing executive*
Chafetz, Barry Richard *lawyer*
Chan, Lawrence Siu-Yung *dermatologist, educator*
Chandler, Kent, Jr. *lawyer*
Chanyungco, Delly Yangco *dean*
Charbel, Fady Toufic *neurosurgeon, educator*
Charrow, Joel *pediatrician, geneticist, educator, director*
Chatfield, Lloyd C. *lawyer*
Chatterton, Robert Treat, Jr. *reproductive endocrinology educator*
Chauhan, Vyjayanti *biology educator*
Chemers, Robert Marc *lawyer*
Cherney, James Alan *lawyer*

Chester, Stephen John *religious studies educator*
Chinniah, Nim *academic administrator*
Chizewer, David J. *lawyer*
Chlewicki, Lukasz Krzysztof *immunologist, educator*
Choi, Kyong Mee *composer, musician, educator*
Choldin, Marianna Tax *librarian, educator*
Chomicz, Thomas E. *lawyer, consultant*
Chowdhury, Masud H. *computer engineer, educator*
Christianson, Stanley David *finance company executive*
Chromizky, William Rudolph *accountant*
Chubinskaya, Susan *biochemistry professor, researcher, scientist*
Chudnovsky, Alexander *engineering educator, consultant*
Chung, Paul Myungha *mechanical engineer, educator*
Chunprapaph, Boonmee *physician, educator*
Cicero, Frank, Jr. *lawyer*
Citera, Peter M. *mortgage company executive*
Clark, Frank M. *utilities executive*
Clark, Gerda Margarete *special education educator*
Clark, Michael A. *lawyer*
Classen, Timothy J. *finance educator*
Clayton, Mona M. *accountant*
Clemens, Richard Glenn *lawyer*
Cline, William Chambers *automotive executive*
Clinton, Edward Xavier *lawyer*
Cloonan, James Brian *investment company executive*
Coase, Ronald Harry *economist, educator*
Cochran, Willie B. *alderman*
Coe, Fredric L. *internist, educator, researcher*
Coffey, Susanna Jean *artist, educator*
Cohan, Ryan *composer, pianist*
Cohen, Frederick H. *lawyer*
Cohen, Mark S. *orthopedist, medical educator*
Cohen, Russell *gastroenterologist*
Cohen, Ted *philosopher, educator*
Cohler, Bertram Joseph *psychologist, educator*
Cohn, Stanley Alan *cell biology educator*
Cohran, Valeria *pediatrician, educator*
Cole, Brian Jared *orthopedist, educator*
Cole, Thomas Amor *lawyer*
Collen, John *lawyer, educator*
Colon, Bartolo *professional baseball player*
Colon, Rey *alderman*
Comaroff, Jean *anthropologist, educator*
Comiskey, Michael Peter *lawyer*
Compagnon, Odile Anne *architecture educator*
Congalton, Christopher William *lawyer*
Conklin, Thomas William *lawyer*
Conway, Michael Maurice *lawyer*
Cook, Edwin H., Jr. *psychiatrist, educator*
Cook, John Q. *plastic surgeon*
Cooper, Charles Gilbert *cosmetics executive*
Copeland, Edward Jerome *lawyer*
Corley, Arlicia *science educator*
Cornelious, Vida *marketing executive*
Costello, Ellen M. *bank executive*
Costello, John William *lawyer*
Cox, Allan James *management consultant*
Coyne, Jerry Allen *ecologist, educator*
Craine, Thomas Knowlton *not-for-profit developer*
Crane, Barbara Bachmann *photographer, educator*
Crane, Christopher M. *utilities executive*
Crane, Edward M. *lawyer*
Crane, Sir Peter Robert *botanist, geologist, paleontologist, educator*
Crane, R.H. *poet*
Craven, George W. *lawyer*
Cremin, Susan Elizabeth *lawyer*
Cressey, Bryan Charles *venture capitalist*
Cronin, James Watson *physicist, researcher*
Crossan, John Robert *lawyer*
Crown, Lester *manufacturing executive*
Crull, Jan, Jr. *lawyer, investment banker, consultant*
Csar, Michael F. *lawyer*
Cudahy, Richard D. *federal judge*
Cullen, Charles Thomas *historian, librarian*
Cummings, Andrea J. *lawyer*
Cummings, Daniel *lawyer*
Cunningham, Robert James *lawyer*
Cuno, James *museum director*
Curry, Raymond Howard *physician*
Curwen, Randall William *retired journalist, editor*
Cusac, Anne-Marie *journalist, educator*
Cusack, John Thomas *lawyer*
Custer, Charles Francis *lawyer*
Czestochowski, Joseph Stephen *administrator, publisher, investor*
Dabrowski, Edward John *television technical director*
Daley, Michael Joseph *lawyer*
Daley, Richard Michael *Mayor, Chicago*
Daley, Vi *alderwoman*
Daley, Vincent Raymond, Jr. *real estate company executive, consultant*
Daley, William Michael *diversified financial services company executive, former United States Secretary of Commerce*
Dam, Kenneth W. *law educator, former federal agency administrator*
D'Amato, Anthony *law educator*
Dan, Bernard W. *brokerage house executive, former commodities exchange executive*
Dancewicz, John Edward *investment banker*
Daniel, T. *mime performer, theater director, choreographer*
Dardai, Shahid Moinuddin *computer science educator*
Dart, Thomas J. *protective services official*
Davidson, Michael H. *cardiologist, researcher*
Davies, Christa *insurance company executive*
Davis, Addie L. *mathematics educator*
Davis, Henry E. *psychologist*
Davis, Muller *lawyer*
Davis, Scott Jonathan *lawyer*
Dawson, Caron *medical and legal consultant*
Dawson, Michael C. *political science professor*
Dayal, Vijay Shanker *physician, educator*
De Armas, Frederick Alfred *foreign language educator*
Debus, Allen George *historian, educator*
Dechene, James Charles *lawyer*
DeCoursey, Thomas Eric *physiologist, educator*
Dee, Ivan Richard *book publisher*
Deitrick, William Edgar *lawyer*
Della Valle, Craig J. *orthopedist, medical educator*
Del Negro, Vincent Joseph (Vinny Del Negro) *professional basketball coach*
Delp, Wilbur Charles, Jr. *lawyer*
DeMay, Richard Mac *pathologist*
Dembowski, Peter Florian *foreign language educator*
D'Emilio, John *humanities educator, writer*
DeMoss, Jon W. *insurance company executive, lawyer*
Dempsey, Mary A. *library commissioner, lawyer*
Dempster, Ryan (Scott) *professional baseball player*
Deng, Luol *professional basketball player*
Dent, Thomas G. *lawyer*
Desjardins, Claude *physiologist, dean*
D'Esposito, Julian C., Jr. *lawyer*
Deutsch, Thomas Alan *ophthalmologist, educator, dean*
Devine, Richard A. (Dick DeVine) *lawyer, former prosecutor*
Diamond, Seymour *physician*
Dias Griffin, Anne *investment advisor*
Diefendorf, Jeanenne Marie *travel company executive*
Dilley, Kimberley Jo *pediatrician, educator*
Ditelberg, Joshua L. *lawyer*
Dix, Rollin C(umming) *mechanical engineering educator, consultant*
Dixon, Sharon Denise *alderwoman*
Dockterman, Michael *lawyer*
Doherty, Brian Gerard *alderman*
Dolan, Thomas Christopher *professional society administrator*
Dold, Robert Bruce *journalist*
Domanskis, Alexander Rimas *lawyer*
Dondanville, Patricia *lawyer*
Doniger, Wendy *history of religions educator*
Donlevy, John Dearden *lawyer*
Donohue, Craig S. *mercantile exchange executive*
Donohue, Richard Harney *lawyer*
Dorman-Rodriguez, Deborah *insurance company executive, lawyer*
Dow, Robert Michael, Jr. *federal judge*
Dowell, Pat *alderwoman*
Downham, Max C. *medical association administrator*
Downs, Robert K. *lawyer*
Draft, Howard Craig *advertising executive*
Dreher, Melanie Creagan *dean, nursing educator*
Drinfeld, Vladimir Gershonovich *mathematician, educator*
Drymalski, Raymond *lawyer*
D'Souza, Rohit Michael *diversified financial services company executive*
Du, Pan *biomedical researcher, educator*
DuCanto, Joseph Nunzio *lawyer, educator*
Duffy, Terrence A. *mercantile exchange executive*
Dulcan, Mina K. *psychiatrist, educator*
Dumanian, Gregory A. *surgeon*
Dunagan, Deanna *actress*
Duncan, John Patrick Cavanaugh *lawyer*
Dunea, George *nephrologist, educator*
Dunn, Edwin Rydell *lawyer*
Dupree, Candice *professional basketball player*
Durburg, Jack E. *real estate company executive*
Durchslag, Stephen P. *lawyer*
Dwivedi, Yogesh *science educator*
Dye, Jermaine *professional baseball player*
Dyer, Colin *real estate services executive*
Easterbrook, Frank Hoover *federal judge*
Eastman, Charmane I. *medical researcher*
Eaton, Maja Campbell *lawyer*
Ebert, Roger Joseph *film critic*
Edelstein, Teri J. *art educator, director, consultant*
Edlis, Stefan T. *plastics company executive*
Egan, Kevin James *lawyer*
Eggert, Russell Raymond *lawyer*
Eimer, Nathan Philip *lawyer*
Elden, Gary Michael *lawyer*
Elliott, William John *clinical pharmacology educator*
Elshtain, Jean Bethke *social sciences educator*
Elson, John S. *law educator*
Enenbach, Mark Henry *community action agency executive, educator*
Engeland, Christopher G. *neuroscientist, educator*
Epstein, Lee Joan *political science and law professor*
Erens, Jay Allan *lawyer*
Ernest, J. Terry *ocular physiologist, educator*
Espat, N. Joseph *surgeon*
Esrick, Jerald Paul *lawyer*
Evanich, Kevin Reese *lawyer*
Evans, Charles L. *bank executive*
Fagan, Shawn Francis *investment company executive*
Fahner, Tyrone C. *lawyer, former state attorney general*
Farina, Dennis *actor*
Farman, Gerrie P. *research scientist*
Farrakhan, Louis (Louis Eugene Walcott) *religious organization administrator*
Fazio, Peter Victor, Jr. *lawyer*
Feder, Robert *columnist*
Fedorova, Elena Albertovna *finance company executive, consultant*
Feingold, Daniel Leon *anesthesiologist, consultant*
Feinstein, Fred Ira *lawyer*
Feitler, Robert *shoe company executive*
Feldman, Matthew R. *bank executive*
Fellows, Jerry Kenneth *lawyer*
Felsenthal, Steven Altus *lawyer*
Fennell, Frank L. *literature and language professor, dean*
Fenton, Clifton Lucien *investment banker*
Ferguson, James Richard *lawyer, educator*
Ferguson, Stanley Lewis *lawyer*
Fernandez, Geno *insurance company executive*
Fernandez, James *anthropology educator*
Fernandez, John J. *orthopedist*
Fetridge, Bonnie-Jean Clark *civic volunteer*
Fetridge, Clark Worthington *publishing executive*
Fetzer, April M. *orthopedist*
Few, Julius Warren, Jr. *surgeon*
Filip, Mark Robert *lawyer, former federal agency administrator*
Filus, Lidia Z. *mathematics professor, researcher*
Findlay, Donald Cameron *lawyer, former federal agency administrator, insurance company executive*
Fine, Neil A. *surgeon*
Finke, Robert Forge *lawyer*
Finnegan, Sheila *lawyer*
Fioretti, Robert William *lawyer*
Fish, Ronda *realtor*
Fisher, Eugene *marketing professional, community leader*
Fisher, Lester Emil *retired zoo administrator*
Fisher, Randy *finance educator*
Fitzgerald, Patrick J., Jr. *prosecutor*
Fitzgerald, Robert Maurice *retired financial and bank executive*
Fitzgerald, Thomas Robert *state supreme court chief justice*
Fitzpatrick, Sheila Mary *historian, educator*
Flaherty, Emalee Gottbrath *pediatrician*
Flaum, Joel Martin *federal judge*
Fleming, Richard H. *finance executive*
Flores, Manuel *alderman*
Fogel, Robert William *economist, historian, educator*
Forman, Gar *professional sports team executive*
Fort, Jeffrey C. *lawyer*
Fortmann, Patrick *literature and language professor*
Foudree, Bruce William *lawyer*
Foudy, Julie Maurine *retired professional soccer player, Olympic athlete*
Foulkes, Toni *Alderwoman*
Fowler, Martin *software engineer, consultant*
Fowles, Sylvia Shaqueria *professional basketball player*
Fox, Paul T. *lawyer*
Francuch, Paul Charles *broadcast journalist*
Franklin, Richard Mark *lawyer*
Frederick, John Eugene *science educator*
Frederick, Thomas James *lawyer*
Frederiksen, Marilynn C. *physician*
Freed, Karl Frederick *chemistry professor*
Freehling, Daniel Joseph *lawyer, consultant*
Freeman, Lee Allen, Jr. *lawyer*
Freeman, Leslie Gordon *anthropologist, educator*
Freeman, Louis S. *lawyer*
Freeman, Susan Tax *anthropologist, educator, culinary historian*
Friedman, Lawrence Milton *lawyer, finance company executive*
Friedman, Michael *surgeon*
Froehle, Bryan Thomas *professor, director*
Fross, Roger Raymond *lawyer*
Fukudome, Kosuke *professional baseball player*
Fukui, Yoshio *engineering educator*
Funk, Carla Jean *library association director*
Furcon, John Edward *management and organizational consultant*
Furlane, Mark Elliott *lawyer*
Gabric, Ralph J. *lawyer*
Gadus, Peg *pastoral associate*
Gaggini, John Edmund *lawyer*
Gal, Susan *anthropologist, educator*
Galante, Jorge Osvaldo *orthopedic surgeon, educator*
Gallucci, Robert Louis *foundation administrator*
Gamoran, Reuben *candy company executive*
Gand, Gale *chef, restaurateur*
Gangopadhyaya, Asim *physics professor, department chairman*
Garanzini, Michael J. *academic administrator, priest*
Garber, Samuel B. *lawyer, retail executive*
Garcia-Siller, Gustavo *bishop*
Gardner, Chris(topher) *securities trader, entrepreneur*
Gardner, Howard Alan *travel company executive, writer, editor*
Garman, Rita B. *state supreme court justice*
Garrigan, Kristine Ottesen *English literature educator*
Gatti, Alberta *language educator, director*
Gavin, John Neal *lawyer*
Gavrilova, Natalia S. *demographer*
Gecker, James M. *lawyer*
Geller, Laurence S. *hotel executive*
Gelman, Andrew Richard *lawyer*
Genson, Edward Marvin *lawyer*
George, Francis Eugene Cardinal *cardinal, archbishop*
Georges, Mara Stacy *lawyer*
Georgiadis, Margaret Hastings (Margo Georgiadis) *private equity firm executive, former finance company executive*
Geraldson, Raymond I., Jr. *lawyer*
Gerber, Dean N. *lawyer*
Gerber, Diane *plastic surgeon*
Gerdes, Neil Wayne *library director, educator*
Gersh, Deborah Louise *lawyer*
Gerstein, Mark Douglas *lawyer*
Gervais, Mark G. *physical education educator*
Gettins, Peter Gregory Wolfgang *biology professor*
Gevorgyan, Vladimir *science educator, researcher*
Geyer, Michael *history professor*
Ghazzal, Zouhair *history professor, researcher*
Giangreco, Mark *sportscaster, director*
Giblin, Nan J. *psychologist, educator*
Gibson, McGuire *archaeologist, educator*
Giesen, Richard Allyn *business executive*
Gill, Phupinder *mercantile exchange executive*
Gillis, Ruth Ann M. *utilities executive*
Ginsburg, Allen J. *lawyer*
Giordani, Tania *mathematician, educator*
Gislason, Eric Arni *academic administrator, chemistry professor*
Gitelman, Darren Ross *neurologist, educator*
Gittler, Michelle S. *physiatrist*
Glass, Ira *radio producer, radio personality*
Glasser, James J. *retired leasing company executive*
Glassroth, Jeffrey *internist, educator*
Glieberman, Herbert Allen *lawyer*
Goedert, Raymond Emil *bishop emeritus*
Goetz, Christopher Graves *neurologist, educator*
Golan, Stephen Leonard *lawyer*
Gold, Allan Harold *architect, structural engineer, educator*
Goldberg, Arnold Irving *psychoanalyst, educator*
Goldberg, Edward Jay *orthopaedic surgeon*
Goldblatt, Stanford Jay *lawyer*
Goldin-Meadow, Susan *psychology professor*
Goldring, Norman Max *marketing professional*
Goldsmith, John Anton *linguist, educator*
Goldstein, William A. *investment counsel*
Golomb, Harvey Morris *hematologist, oncologist, educator*
Goltsiker, Aleksandr Davydovich *research scientist*
Gomberg, Paul *philosopher, educator*
Gomer, Robert *chemistry professor*
Gonzalez, William G. *healthcare advisor*
Goodman, Steven Michael *conservation biologist*
Gorbien, Martin John *medical educator, geriatrician*
Gordon, Howard Lyon *advertising and marketing executive*
Goss, Howard S(imon) *financial executive*
Gossett, Dana Rigsby *gynecologist, director*
Gossett, Philip *musicologist*
Gottschall, Joan B. *judge*
Gould, John Philip *economist, educator*
Graber, Doris Appel *political scientist, writer, editor*
Graber, Thomas M. *orthodontist, researcher*
Gralen, Donald John *lawyer*
Grant, Delvin A. *management information systems educator, researcher*
Grant, Robert McQueen *humanities educator*
Grant, Robert Nathan *lawyer*
Gray, Hanna Holborn *historian, educator*
Greenbaum, Lewis *lawyer*
Greenberg, Bernard *retired entomologist*
Greenberg, Richard T. *lawyer*
Greenberger, Paul Allen *allergist, immunologist, educator*
Greene Johnson, Willetta *physics professor*
Gregory, Stephanie Ann *hematologist, educator*
Griffin, Kenneth C. *hedge fund manager*
Grogger, Jeffrey *economics professor*
Grossi, Deann Christine *biology professor*
Grossman, Robert Mayer *lawyer*
Grove, David L. *stock exchange executive*
Grund, David Ira *lawyer*
Grynsztejn, Madeleine *museum director, curator*
Guillen, Ozzie (Oswaldo Jose Barrios Guillen) *professional baseball manager*
Gulati, Martha *health facility administrator, cardiologist*
Gundeti, Mohan Saheb *urologist, educator*
Gupta, Mahesh P. *psychology professor*
Guthman, Jack *lawyer*
Gutstein, Solomon *lawyer*
Guy, Buddy *blues guitarist*
Hackl, Donald John *architect*
Haffner, Charles Christian III *retired printing company executive*
Hagan, Kate (Kathryn T. Hagan) *library director, editor*
Hagin, Joseph Whitehouse, II, *aircraft maintenance company executive, former federal official*
Hahn, Arthur W. *lawyer*
Hahn, Yoon Sun *pediatric neurosurgeon, educator*
Hairston, Leslie *alderwoman*
Hallinan, Joseph Thomas *writer*
Halpern, Jack *chemist, educator*
Hamada, Robert S(eiji) *dean, economist, entrepreneur, educator*
Hambrick, Ernestine *retired colon and rectal surgeon*
Hamm, Mia (Mariel Margaret Hamm) *retired professional soccer player*
Hammond, Celeste M. *law educator*
Hamp, Eric Pratt *linguist*
Han, Euna *economist, researcher*
Hankewych, Jaroslaw J. *museum administrator*
Hannah, Wayne Robertson, Jr. *lawyer*
Hannay, William Mouat III *lawyer*
Hansen, Carl R. *management consultant*
Hanson, Floyd Bliss *mathematician*
Hanson, Mark S. *bishop*
Hanson, Ronald William *lawyer*
Hardaway, Ernest, II, *oral and maxillofacial surgeon, public health service officer*
Hardgrove, James Alan *lawyer*
Harford, Barney *travel company executive*
Harmon, Teresa Wilton *lawyer*
Harrington, Carol A. *lawyer*
Harrington, James Timothy *lawyer*
Harris, Donald Ray *lawyer*
Harris, Gerald David *surgeon*
Harris, Gregory Scott *state legislator*
Harris, Michelle A. *alderwoman*
Harris, Mildred Clopton *clergy member, educator*
Harris, Shirley *elementary, secondary and adult education educator*
Harrison, Holly A. *lawyer*
Harrold, Bernard *lawyer*
Hart, William Thomas *federal judge*
Hartz, Michael O. *lawyer*
Harvey, Allison Charmaine *chemist*
Harvey, Ronald Gilbert *research chemist*
Hast, Adele *historian, editor, writer*
Hast, Malcolm Howard *biomedical scientist, educator*
Hasten, Joseph Erwin *bank executive*
Hatsopoulos, Nicholas G. *biomedical researcher, educator*
Hayes, Alice Bourke *academic administrator, biologist, researcher*
Hayes, David John Arthur, Jr. *legal association executive*
Hayes, M. M.M. *publishing executive*
Hayner, Donald *editor-in-chief*
Hayward, Thomas Zander, Jr. *lawyer*
Head, Louis Rollin, II, *surgeon*
Heatwole, Mark M. *lawyer, director*
Heckman, Charles Jackson, II, *medical educator*
Heckman, James Joseph *economist, educator*
Heineman, Natalie *civic worker*
Heinemann, Allen W. *rehabilitation psychologist*
Heinz, John Peter *lawyer, educator*
Heinz, William Denby *lawyer*
Heisler, Quentin George, Jr. *lawyer*

Heisley, Michael E., Sr. *manufacturing executive, professional sports team owner*
Heller, Stanley J. *lawyer, physician, educator*
Hellman, Samuel *radiologist, educator*
Helman, Robert Alan *lawyer*
Helmholz, R(ichard) H(enry) *law educator*
Heltne, Paul Gregory *researcher, museum director*
Hemingway Hall, Patricia *health insurance company executive*
Hemond, Roland A. *professional baseball team executive*
Henning, Joel Frank *lawyer, writer*
Henrick, Michael Francis *lawyer*
Herald, J. Patrick *lawyer*
Herbert, William Carlisle *law educator*
Herbst, Arthur Lee *obstetrician, gynecologist*
Herbst, Walter Brown *industrial designer*
Herron, David A. *stock exchange executive*
Hershow, Ronald C. *epidemiologist, educator*
Hess, Sidney J., Jr. *lawyer*
Hickey, Jerome Edward *investment company executive*
Hildebrand, Roger Henry *astrophysicist, physicist*
Hill, Carlotta H. *physician*
Hill, Shepard W. *air transportation executive*
Hilliard, David Craig *lawyer, educator*
Hilliker, Donald Beckstett *lawyer*
Hillocks, George, Jr. *language educator, researcher*
Hiltz, Kenneth A. *corporate restructuring company executive*
Hilzinger, Matthew F. *utilities executive*
Himmelfarb, John David *artist*
Hinkelman, Ruth Amidon *insurance company executive*
Hinrichs, Charles A. *paper company executive*
Hirano, Ikuo *gastroenterologist*
Hirsh, Bobbe *lawyer, accountant*
Hirt, Jane *editor*
Hlavacek, Roy George *publishing executive*
Hobson, Mellody *investment company executive*
Hodes, Scott *lawyer*
Hofer, Roy Ellis *lawyer*
Hoff, John Scott *lawyer*
Hoffman, Richard Bruce *lawyer*
Hoffman, Valerie Jane *lawyer*
Hofman, David *physics professor*
Hofrichter, David Alan *management consultant*
Holabird, John Augur, Jr. *retired architect*
Holaday Royster, Lynn Christine *academic administrator, educator*
Holinger, Lauren Drake *surgeon*
Hollandsworth, Todd Mathew *sportscaster, retired professional baseball player*
Hollis, Donald Roger *management consultant*
Homburger, Thomas Charles *lawyer*
Hong, Philip Young P. *social worker, educator*
Hong, Seungpyo *science educator*
Honig, George Raymond *pediatrician*
Hoogenboom, Carol Annette *clinical neuropsychologist*
Hoplamazian, Mark Samuel *hotel executive*
Horwich, Allan *lawyer*
Hoskins, Richard Jerold *lawyer*
Hossa, Marian *professional hockey player*
Hou, Wanqiu *immunologist, microbiologist*
Howe, Jonathan Thomas *lawyer*
Howell, R(obert) Thomas, Jr. *lawyer, former food company executive*
Hubbard, Robert Louis, Jr. *religious studies educator*
Huberman, Ron *school system administrator*
Huckman, Michael Saul *neuroradiologist, educator*
Hucles, Angela Khalia *professional soccer player*
Huebner, Jeff *art journalist, freelance writer*
Huggins, Lois M. *human resources specialist, consumer products company executive*
Hughes, John Russell *neurologist, educator*
Hummel, Gregory William *lawyer*
Hung, Wu *art historian, educator*
Hunt, Craig A. *lawyer, paper company executive*
Hunt, Richard *sculptor*
Hunter, Tony *publishing executive*
Huttenlocher, Janellen *psychology educator, psychologist*
Hwang, Yujong *information scientist, educator*
Idol, Anna Catherine *magazine editor*
Inan, Zabrin *psychiatrist*
Inojosa, Franklin *music educator*
Inwang, Rosie L. *education educator*
Iqbal, Zafar Mohd *biochemist, molecular biologist, pharmacologist, cancer researcher, toxicologist, consultant*
Ismail, Tarek *lawyer*
Ivankovich, Anthony D. *anesthesiologist, educator*
Iyer, Kishore *transplant surgeon*
Jablonski, David *science educator*
Jachino, Daneen L. *legal administrator*
Jackson, Rev. Jesse Louis *civil rights activist, clergyman*
Jackson, Sandra (Sandi Jackson) *alderwoman*
Jacob, Mary Jane *curator*
Jacobs, Joshua J. *orthopaedic surgeon*
Jacobson, Marian Slutz *lawyer*
Jacoby, John Patrick *lawyer*
Jaconetty, Thomas Anthony *lawyer*
Jacover, Jerold Alan *lawyer*
Jager, Melvin Francis *lawyer*
Jahns, Jeffrey *lawyer*
Jakubowski, Thaddeus Joseph *bishop emeritus*
Jameson, James Larry *dean, educator, internist, endocrinologist*
Janecek, Lenore Elaine *healthcare and benefits specialist, consultant*
Jaskot-Inclan, Maria *theater director, educator*
Jegen, Sister Carol Frances *religious studies educator*
Jennings, Jonathan Scott *lawyer*
Jensen, Donald Milton *hepatologist*
Jezuit, Leslie James *manufacturing executive*
Jilhewar, Ashok *gastroenterologist*
Johnson, Barbara Elaine Spears *retired education educator*
Johnson, Bradford R. *endodontist, researcher*
Johnson, Garrett Bruce *lawyer*
Johnson, Gary Thomas *cultural organization and museum administrator*
Johnson, Janet Helen *literature educator*
Johnson, Richard Fred *lawyer*
Johnson, Timothy Patrick *health and social researcher*
Jones, Emil III *state legislator*
Jones, Sharon Elaine *cultural organization administrator, lawyer*
Jones, Tony *academic administrator*
Judge, Bernard Martin *retired editor, publishing executive*
Junewicz, James J. *lawyer*
Kadanoff, Leo Philip *physicist, educator*
Kadish, Alan Howard *internist, educator, researcher*
Kaegi, Walter Emil *history professor*
Kahana, Madelyn D. *pediatric anesthesiologist*
Kahrilas, Peter James *medical educator, researcher*
Kallick, David A. *lawyer*
Kalver, Gail Ellen *dance company executive, musician*
Kamin, Carol *medical educator*
Kamin, Kim *law educator*
Kaminsky, Richard Alan *lawyer*
Kamyszew, Christopher D. *film executive, educator, curator*
Kane, Francis Joseph *bishop*
Kane, Patrick *professional hockey player*
Kane, Sunanda Vinayak *internist, gastroenterologist*
Kang, Soo Yun *art historian, educator*
Kao, Johnny *radiologist, oncologist*
Kaplan, Howard Gordon *lawyer*
Kaplan, Morton A. *political science professor*
Kasule, Ssebunya Edward *political science professor*
Kataria, Tripti Caday *anesthesiologist*
Katz, Avrum Sidney *lawyer*
Katz, Mark Harold *urologist*
Kaufman, David J. *lawyer*
Kavey, Rae-Ellen Webb *pediatric cardiologist*
Kawitt, Alan *lawyer, arbitrator*
Ke, Yunbo *medical educator, researcher*
Kearney, John Walter *sculptor, painter*
Keenan, Barbara Byrd *professional society administrator*
Keenan, James George *classics educator*
Keiderling, Timothy Allen *chemistry educator, researcher*
Keith, Louis Gerald *medical educator*
Kellman, Barry S. *law educator, consultant*
Kelly, Arthur Lloyd *investment company executive*
Kelly, Jerry Bob *social services administrator*
Kerbis, Gertrude Lempp *architect*
Kern, Gerould W. *publishing executive, editor*
Kerr, Michael H. *stock exchange executive, lawyer*
Kerwin, Brian P. *lawyer*
Key, Steven *professional basketball coach*
Khalili, Mahmoud *physics professor*
Khan, M. Wasiullah *academic administrator*
Khuntia, Anjana (Annie Khuntia) *pediatrician, educator*
Kikoler, Stephen Philip *lawyer*
Kilbride, Thomas L. *state supreme court justice*
Kilpatrick, Sarah J. *obstetrician, gynecologist, educator*
Kim, Mi Ja *dean, academic administrator*
Kim, Michael Charles *lawyer*
Kim, Song-Jung *physiologist*
Kindzred, Diana *communications company executive*
King, Andre Richardson *architectural graphic designer*
King, Sharon Louise *retired lawyer*
Kinney, James M. (Jim Kinney) *real estate company executive*
Kiriakos, Thomas Sam *lawyer*
Kirsner, Joseph Barnett *physician, educator*
Kissel, Richard John *lawyer*
Kite, Steven B. *lawyer*
Kittle, Charles Frederick *surgeon*
Klatt, Wayne Roy *editor, writer*
Klenk, James Andrew *lawyer*
Klinger, Steven J. *paper company executive*
Knappenberger, Paul Henry, Jr. *science museum director*
Knight, Alrick Clauson, Jr. *language educator*
Knight, Christopher Nichols *lawyer*
Knight, Cranston S. *history professor*
Knuepfer, Robert Claude, Jr. *lawyer*
Kobs, James Fred *direct marketing consultant*
Koernig, Stephen K. *marketing professional, educator*
Kolek, Robert Edward *lawyer*
Konrad, Beth *professor, consultant*
Kopelman, Ian Stuart *lawyer*
Kornick, Michael *chef*
Kotsay, Mark Steven *professional baseball player*
Kozak, John W. *lawyer*
Kraft, Sumner Charles *physician, educator*
Kramer, Andrea S. *lawyer*
Krashesky, Alan *newscaster*
Krasnykh, Olga P. *Organic Medicinal Chemist Researcher*
Krent, Harold J. *dean, law educator*
Kriegshauser, John *architecture educator*
Krishnamurthy, Kathiravan *research assistant professor engineer*
Kriss, Robert J. *lawyer*
Krivkovich, Peter George *advertising executive*
Kroll, Barry Lewis *retired lawyer*
Kroot, Jason M. *lawyer*
Kroszner, Randall Scott *economics professor, former federal official*
Krueger, Bonnie Lee *editor, writer*
Krueger, Herbert William (Bert Krueger) *lawyer*
Kuiken, Todd Alan *medical researcher, rehabilitation services professional, educator*
Kulczycki, John Jacob *retired historian*
Kullberg, Duane Reuben *accounting firm executive*
Kunda, Dolores A. *marketing executive*
Kuner, Charles *retired secondary school educator*
Lal, Anil *health facility administrator*
Landerholm, Elizabeth Jane *early childhood education educator*
Landes, William M. *law educator*
Landow-Esser, Janine Marise *lawyer*
Landsberg, Lewis *endocrinologist, medical researcher, former dean*
Lane, Lona *alderwoman*
Laner, Richard Warren *lawyer*
Lange, Yvonne *cell biologist, educator*
Larson, Allan Louis *political scientist, educator, lay worker*
Larson, Nancy Celeste *information technology manager*
Latimer, Kenneth Alan *lawyer*
Lauderdale, Diane S. *epidemiologist, educator*
Laumann, Edward Otto *sociology educator*
Laurino, Margaret *alderwoman*
Lavey, Martha *performing company executive*
Lazar, Ludmila *concert pianist, music educator*
Learner, Howard Alan *lawyer*
Lee, Gyungho *engineering educator*
Lee, Raphael Carl *plastic surgeon, biomedical engineer*
Lee, Simon *orthopedist*
Leeper, Mary Ann *health science association administrator*
Lefco, Kathy Nan *law librarian*
Leff, Alan Richard *medical educator, researcher*
Leighton, George Neves *retired judge*
Leinenweber, Harry D. *federal judge*
Lenihan, Dermot Patrick *public health administrator*
Lerner, Alexander Robert *insurance company executive*
Lerner, Wayne M. *hospital administrator*
LeRoy, Spencer III *lawyer*
Letts, Tracy *actor, playwright*
Levandowski, Barbara Sue *education educator*
Levar, Patrick J. *alderman*
Leventhal, Bennett Lee *psychiatry and pediatrics educator, academic administrator*
Levi, John G. *lawyer*
Levin, Charles Edward *lawyer*
Levin, Jack S. *lawyer*
Levin, Lawrence Daniel *lawyer*
Levmore, Saul *dean, law educator*
Levy, Donald Harris *chemistry professor*
Levy, Peter A. *lawyer*
Levy, Susan C. *lawyer*
Lewis, Aylwin B. *food service executive, former retail executive*
Lewis, Charles B. *lawyer*
Li, An *medical educator*
Liao, Shutsung *biochemist, molecular oncologist*
Licari, Frank William *dentist, educator*
Lichter, Terry *neurosurgeon, neuro-oncologist*
Lieb, Peter *lawyer*
Liebenow, Franklin Eastburn, Jr. *English literature educator*
Liggio, Carl Donald *lawyer*
Lilly, Ted (Theodore Roosevelt Lilly) *professional baseball player*
Lima, Victor Osvaldo *economist, educator*
Lin, James Chih-I *biomedical and electrical engineer, educator*
Lin, Jie *engineering educator, researcher*
Linden, Henry Robert *chemical engineer, researcher*
Lipinski, Ann Marie *academic administrator, former publishing executive*
Liptay, Michael Justin *surgeon*
Litwin, Burton Howard *lawyer*
Liu, Ben-chieh *economist*
Lochbihler, Frederick Vincent *lawyer*
Lockwood, Gary Lee *lawyer*
Loesch, Katharine Taylor *communications educator, theater educator*
Loesch, William R. *lawyer*
Logemann, Jerilyn Ann *speech pathologist, educator*
Lona, Marie A. *lawyer*
Long, Jacqueline Flint *classicist, educator*
Longworth, Richard Cole *journalist, writer*
Looman, James R. *lawyer*
Lopez, Joseph R. *lawyer*
Lorch, Kenneth F. *lawyer*
Lorch, Robert K. *corporate financial executive*
Lorenz, Hugo Albert *retired insurance executive, consultant*
Lorys, Jan M. *museum director*
Lotocky, Innocent Hilarion *bishop emeritus*
Lovejoy, Paul Robert *lawyer, air transportation executive*
Low, David D., Jr. *real estate company executive*
Lowe, Mira *editor*
Lowe, Sandra Elveta *psychologist*
Lowenkron, Barry Frederick *foundation administrator, former federal agency administrator*
Lowinger, Frederick Charles *lawyer*
Lowry, James Hamilton *management consultant*
Lubawski, James Lawrence *businessman and consultant*
Lubin, Donald G. *lawyer*
Lucas, Robert Emerson, Jr. *economist, educator*
Luchins, Daniel Jonathan *psychiatrist*
Lufrano, Michael Richard *lawyer*
Luhrmann, Tanya Marie *anthropology educator, writer*
Lumbsch, Helge Thorsten *curator*
Lurain, John Robert III *gynecologist*
Lurie, Ann LaSalle *foundation administrator*
Lurie, Paul Michael *lawyer*
Luscombe, George A., II, *lawyer*
Lusk, Peggy June *retired counseling administrator*
Lussier, Yves A. *biomedical researcher, medical educator, physician*
Lutter, Paul Allen *lawyer*
Luttig, J. Michael (John Michael Luttig) *aerospace transportation executive, former federal judge*
Lyerla, Bradford Peter *lawyer*
Lyle, Freddrenna M. *alderwoman*
Lyne, Timothy Joseph *bishop emeritus*
Lynn, Nicholas J. *lawyer*
Macaulay, Susan Jane *lawyer, educator*
MacCarthy, Terence Francis *lawyer*
MacDougal, Gary Edward *corporate board member, foundation trustee*
Mack, Alan Wayne *interior designer*
Madara, James Lee *dean, pathologist, educator, epitheliologist, CEO*
Madden, John *professional hockey player*
Madigan, John William *publishing executive*
Madigan, Lisa *state attorney general*
Madigan, Michael Joseph *state legislator, political organization administrator*
Madsen, Dorothy Louise (Meg) *writer*
Maesen, William August *development consultant*
Magoon, Patrick Michael *hospital administrator*
Mahaffey, John Christopher *medical association executive*
Mahani, Mohammad Shadbakht *engineering educator*
Maher, John M. *lawyer*
Mahowald, Mary Briody *humanities educator*
Makinen, Marvin William *biophysicist, educator*
Malinowski, Arthur Anthony *lawyer, arbitrator*
Malkin, Cary Jay *lawyer*
Malkinson, Frederick David *dermatologist, educator*
Malovany, Howard *lawyer, food products executive*
Manafzadeh, Saeed *engineering educator, director*
Mancoff, Neal Alan *lawyer*
Manning, Amy B. *lawyer*
Manning, Frederick James *insurance company executive*
Mansfield, Karen Lee *lawyer*
Mansueto, Joseph Daniel *publishing executive*
Manz, John R. *bishop*
Manzo, Edward David *lawyer*
Martin, Arthur Mead *lawyer*
Martin, Ionis Bracy *artist, educator*
Martin, Kristin Emily *librarian*
Martin, Laura Keidan *lawyer*
Mascherin, Terri Lynn *lawyer*
Mason, Gregory Wesley, Jr. *secondary school educator*
Mason, Terry *city health department administrator, urologist*
Mason, William *opera company director*
Mateles, Richard Isaac *biotechnologist*
Matesky, Elisabeth Anne *international solo violinist, educator, composer, arranger*
Mathew, James M. *immunologist, educator*
Matis, Nina B. *lawyer*
Matthei, Edward Hodge *architect*
Maves, Michael Donald *medical association executive*
Maxwell, Sarz *psychiatrist, educator*
May, Aviva Rabinowitz *music educator, musician, linguist*
Mayer, Raymond Richard *business administration educator*
Mayer, Susan E. *dean, political science professor*
Mayo, Cora Louise *educator*
McCallister, Richard Anthony *business consulting company executive*
Mc Carter, John Wilbur, Jr. *museum executive*
McCarthy, Patrick M. *surgeon*
McCaul, Joseph Patrick *chemical engineer*
McClain, Shawn *chef*
McCloskey, Deirdre Nansen *economics and history educator*
McCloskey, Michael *social sciences, psychology, and sociology educator*
McClure, James Julius, Jr. *lawyer, former city official*
McConnell, E. Hoy, II, *advertising and public policy executive*
McCormick, David Loyd *toxicologist, researcher, educator*
McCracken, Thomas James, Jr. *lawyer*
McCrank, Lawrence J. *dean, university librarian*
McCue, Judith W. *lawyer*
McCullagh, Grant Gibson *retired architect*
McCullough, Richard Lawrence *advertising executive*
McCurry, Margaret Irene *architect, furniture and interior designer, educator*
McDermott, John H. *lawyer*
McDermott, Raymond, Jr. *physician*
McDonald, Anne Leggett *mathematics professor*
McDonald, Peter D. *air transportation executive*
McDonald, Theresa Beatrice Pierce (Mrs. Ollie McDonald) *church official, minister*
McDonald, Thomas Alexander *lawyer*
McDonough, John F. *professional sports team executive*
McElheny, Josiah G. *sculptor*
McGinn, Bernard John *theologian, educator*
McGowan, Michael Jeremy *lawyer*
McGrail, Jeane Kathryn *artist*
McHugh, Miles William *corporate financial executive*
McKee, Keith Earl *manufacturing technology executive*
McKenzie, Robert Ernest *lawyer*
McKinney, Megan *writer*
McKittrick, William Wood *lawyer*
McKoy, June Marcia *medical educator, researcher, lawyer*
McLaren, Richard Wellington, Jr. *lawyer*
McLaughlin, T. Mark *lawyer*
McLean, Ian P. *utilities executive*
McMath, Lula Wray *retired elementary school educator, realtor*
McNally, Andrew, IV, *publishing executive, director*
McNeill, G. David *psychologist, educator*
McNerney, James, Jr., (W. James McNerney) *aerospace transportation executive, former manufacturing executive*
McVisk, William Kilburn *lawyer*
Meadow, William Lee *medical educator*
Mearsheimer, John Joseph *political science professor*
Meccia, Francis (Frank) Anthony *physician assistant*
Mehlman, Mark Franklin *lawyer*
Mehta, Rajendra G. *research scientist, educator*
Meisels, Samuel J. *education educator*
Meissner, Laurel G. *insurance company executive*
Melamed, Leo *global consulting firm executive*
Melbinger, Michael S. *lawyer*
Mell, Richard F. *alderman*
Mellott, Ann L. *hematologist, oncologist*
Melnick, Jane Fisher *writer, educator, photographer*
Melton, David Reuben *lawyer*
Menchetti, David Barry *lawyer*
Mendelsohn, David Edward *lawyer*
Mendelsohn, Janis S. *pediatrician, educator*
Metcalf, James S. *manufacturing executive*
Metz, Charles Edgar *radiology educator*
Meyers, Kenneth Raymond *telecommunications industry executive*

Miceli, William Cyril, Sr. *director*
Michaels, Randy (Benjamin Homel) *multimedia company executive*
Michaels, Richard Edward *lawyer*
Migala, Lucyna J. *journalist, broadcast executive, artistic director*
Mikells, Kathryn Ann *air transportation executive*
Mikva, Abner Joseph *lawyer, retired judge*
Miller, Brad (Bradley Allen Miller) *professional basketball player*
Miller, Irving Franklin *chemical and biomedical engineer, academic administrator, educator*
Miller, Kenneth W. *lawyer*
Miller, Ronald Stuart *lawyer*
Miller, Stephen Ralph *lawyer*
Millichap, Joseph Gordon *neurologist, educator*
Millikan, Keith William *surgeon, educator*
Miner, Thomas Hawley *entrepreneur*
Minges Wols, Heather Ann *biology professor*
Minichello, Dennis *lawyer*
Minkowycz, W. J. *mechanical engineering educator*
Minneste, Viktor, Jr. *retired engineering executive*
Minow, Josephine Baskin *civic volunteer*
Minow, Newton Norman *lawyer, educator*
Mirza, Leona Lousin *elementary school educator, director*
Mirza, Mansha Parven Qamar Husain *public health service officer, consultant*
Mitchell, Lee Mark *private equity investor, executive*
Mitts, Emma *alderwoman*
Montgomery, Charles Barry *lawyer*
Montgomery, Charles Howard *retired bank executive*
Montgomery, William Adam *lawyer*
Moore, Joseph Arthur *alderman, lawyer*
Moore, Patrick J. *paper company executive*
Morales-Pita, Antonio Evaristo *economics professor*
Morency, Paula J. *lawyer*
Morgan, Anita L. *academic librarian*
Morgan, Betsy Stelle *lawyer*
Morgan, Donna Evensen *lawyer*
Morgan, Elaine R. *hematologist, oncologist, medical educator*
Morris, Rebecca *painter*
Morrison, Portia Owen *lawyer*
Morrow, Richard Martin *retired oil company executive*
Moseley Braun, Carol Elizabeth *food products executive, former United States Senator from Illinois*
Mosena, David R. *museum administrator*
Moss, Gerald S. *medical educator*
Motherway, Nicholas J. *lawyer*
Muehleisen, Ralph T. *architectural engineer, educator*
Muller, Kurt Alexander *lawyer*
Muñoz, Ricardo *alderman*
Murata, Tadao *engineering and computer science educator*
Murdock, Charles William *lawyer, educator*
Murphy, Kevin M. *economics professor*
Murphy, Michael Emmett *retired food company executive*
Murphy, Patricia M. *art gallery director*
Murray, Daniel Richard *lawyer*
Muti, Riccardo *conductor, music director*
Myers, Lonn William *lawyer*
Myerson, Roger Bruce *economist, educator*
Nachman, James Burt *pediatric hematologist-oncologist*
Nadler, Judith *library director*
Nahrwold, David Lange *surgeon, educator*
Naithani, Rajesh *oncologist*
Nakata, Cheryl *finance educator*
Nam, Ellis K. *orthopedist*
Nambu, Yoichiro *physics professor*
Narahashi, Toshio *pharmacology educator*
Nash, Jessie Madeleine *journalist, science writer*
Natarus, Burton F. *lawyer, former city alderman*
Nault, William Henry *publishing executive*
Nayar, Ritu *pathologist, educator*
Neff, David M. *lawyer*
Neithercut, David J. *real estate company officer*
Nelson, Harry Donald *telecommunications executive*
Neumeier, Matthew Michael *lawyer, educator*
Newlin, Charles Fremont *lawyer*
Newman, Bruce Ira *marketing professional*
Newman, Steven B. *hematologist, oncologist*
Nicholas, Ralph Wallace *anthropologist, educator*
Nicholson, Greg Powell *orthopedist*
Nickell, Jake *internet retail executive, apparel designer*
Nicklin, Emily *lawyer*
Niebylski, Dianna C. *Latin American and comparative literature professor*
Nielsen, Nancy H. *health organization executive, medical educator*
Niffenegger, Audrey Anne *artist, writer*
Nijman, Jennifer T. *lawyer*
Nitikman, Franklin W. *lawyer*
Njoku, Mary Gloria *psychology professor, researcher*
Nobles-Knight, Dolores *pharmacist, educator*
Noel, Carol Adele *music educator, opera singer*
Noesen, Darlene Dorothy *mathematics educator*
Noll, Kenneth Eugene *air resources engineering educator*
Nord, Henry J. *transportation executive*
Nordland, Gerald *museum administrator, historian, consultant*
Nordli, Douglas R. *neurologist*
Norgle, Charles Ronald, Sr. *federal judge*
Northcut, Terry Brumley *social sciences educator*
Notz, John Kranz, Jr. *arbitrator, mediator, retired lawyer*
Novak, John G. *construction executive*
Novak, Mark *lawyer*
Novich, Neil S. *metals distribution company executive*
Novotny, David Joseph *lawyer*
Nowacki, James Nelson *lawyer*
Nowak, Patricia Cari *lawyer*
Nygren, William C. *investment company executive*
O'Brien, James Phillip *lawyer*
Ocasio, Billy *state official, former alderman*
O'Connell, John Bernard, Jr. *medical educator, department chairman*
O'Connor, Patrick J. *alderman*
Odishoo, Sarah A. *literature and language professor, writer, poet*
Oehme, Reinhard *physicist, researcher*
Oesterle, Eric Adam *lawyer*
O'Hagan, James Joseph *lawyer*
O'Leary, Joseph P. *energy executive*
Olian, Robert Martin *lawyer*
Oliver, Harry Maynard, Jr. *retired brokerage house executive*
Olivo, Frank J. *alderman*
Olopade, Olufunmilayo Falusi (Funmi Olopade) *geneticist, educator, oncologist, hematologist*
O'Loughlin, Kathleen T. *dental association administrator*
Olsen, Edward John *geologist, educator, curator*
Olsen, Rex Norman *trade association executive*
Olson, Jack Conrad, Jr. *geriatrician*
Olson, Steven Thomas *medical researcher*
O'Malley, John Daniel *lawyer, educator, banker*
O'Neil, Michael C. *lawyer*
O'Reilly, Heather Ann *Olympic athlete*
Orpett, Mitchell A. *lawyer*
Osborn, William A. *investment company executive*
O'Toole, William George *lawyer*
Padberg, Helen Swan *violinist*
Pahl Schuette, Elfriede *pediatric transplant cardiologist*
Pallasch, Magdalena Helena (Mrs. Bernhard Michael Pallasch) *artist*
Paller, Amy S. *pediatric dermatologist, educator*
Pallmeyer, Rebecca Ruth *judge*
Palmer, John Bernard III *lawyer*
Palmer, Robert Towne *lawyer, bank executive*
Paloian, John R. *printing company executive*
Paprosky, Wayne G. *orthopedist*
Parent, Angele *research scientist*
Park, Thomas Joseph *biology researcher, educator*
Parker, Bonita M. *civil rights organization executive*
Parr, Virginia Helen *retired librarian*
Partridge, Mark Van Buren *lawyer, author, professional speaker, educator, mediator*
Pascal, Roger *lawyer*
Patrick, Dan *sportscaster*
Patterson, Carly *singer, former Olympic gymnast*
Paul, Ronald Neale *management consultant*
Pavalon, Eugene Irving *lawyer*
Paxson, John *professional sports team executive, retired professional basketball player*
Peavy, Jake (Jacob Edward Peavy) *professional baseball player*
Pedersen, Peer *lawyer*
Pelton, Russell Meredith *lawyer*
Peltzman, Sam *economics professor*
Pensler, Jay Michael *plastic surgeon, educator*
Peponis, Harold Arthur *insurance agent, portfolio manager*
Perambakam, Supriya *medical educator*
Perez, William D. (Bill Perez) *candy company executive, former sports apparel company executive*
Perzek, Philip John *lawyer*
Petersen, Donald Sondergaard *lawyer*
Peterson, Kenneth Allen, Jr. *lawyer*
Peterson, Ronald Roger *lawyer*
Pflaum, Steven F. *lawyer*
Phillips, Frank m. *orthopedic surgeon*
Phillips, Frederick Falley *architect*
Phillips, Gene Daniel *language educator*
Pilcher, James Eric *physicist*
Pincus, Theodore Henry *public relations executive*
Piniella, Lou (Louis Victor Piniella) *professional baseball team manager*
Pippin, Robert B. *philosopher, educator*
Pizer, Howard Charles *sports and entertainment executive*
Plotkin, Manuel D. *management consultant, educator, former corporate executive, government official*
Plotnik, Arthur *writer, columnist*
Plouffe, David *political strategist*
Poethig, Eunice Blanchard *clergywoman*
Poggenpohl, Teresa Loyola *marketing executive*
Pohl, Timothy R. *investment company executive, lawyer*
Pollak, Lisa *radio producer*
Pope, John A. *alderman*
Porowski, Anne M. *management consultant*
Posner, Kathy Robin *retired communications executive*
Posner, Richard Allen *federal judge*
Postiglione, Corey M. *artist, critic, educator*
Power, Joseph Aloysius, Jr. *lawyer*
Poznanski, Andrew Karol *pediatric radiologist*
Preckwinkle, Toni *alderwoman*
Prendergast, Brian *psychologist, educator*
Presser, Stephen Bruce *lawyer, educator*
Preuss, Daphne *geneticist, biology professor*
Price, Charles T. *lawyer*
Price, Paul L. *lawyer*
Primm, Earl Russell III *publishing executive*
Prinz, Richard Allen *surgeon*
Pritzker, Penny Sue *investor*
Pritzker, Thomas Jay *hotel executive*
Prochnow, Douglas Lee *lawyer*
Pugh, Carla M. *surgeon, educator*
Purcell, Philip James *investment company executive*
Putterman, Allen Michael *surgeon, oculofacial plastic surgeon*
Quaini, Duane C. *lawyer*
Quenneville, Joel *professional hockey coach*
Quinlan, Thomas J. III *printing company executive*
Rabin, Joseph Harry *marketing research company executive*
Rabineau, Phyllis *museum administrator*
Raby, Theri Greigo *health facility administrator, internist*
Racker, Darlene Katie *cardiovascular anatomist, electrophysiologist*
Rafeyan, Roueen *psychiatrist, educator*
Ragan, Charles Ransom *lawyer*
Ramsey-Goldman, Rosalind *physician*
Rankin, James Winton *lawyer*
Raphaelson, Joel *retired advertising agency executive*
Rappaport, Richard J. *lawyer*
Raskin, Richard D. *lawyer*
Ratner, Gerald *lawyer*
Ravanas, Philippe Claude Dominique *management educator, consultant*
Reardon, John E. *broadcast executive*
Reboyras, Ariel E. *alderman*
Redish, Martin Harris *law educator*
Reece, Beth Pauley *chaplain*
Reed, Keith Allen *lawyer*
Reed, Rondi *actress, theater director*
Reich, Allan J. *lawyer*
Reicin, Ronald Ian *lawyer*
Reidy, Daniel Edward *lawyer*
Reiffel, Leonard *physicist, consultant*
Reilly, Anne Huedepohl *university educator, researcher*
Reilly, Brendan *alderman*
Reilly, Robert Frederick *investment banker*
Reinsdorf, Jerry Michael *professional sports team owner, real estate company executive, accountant, lawyer*
Reiter, Michael A. *lawyer, educator*
Reitman, Jerry Irving *advertising agency executive*
Relias, John Alexis *lawyer*
Remini, Robert Vincent *historian*
Replogle, Robert Lee *cardiovascular and thoracic surgeon*
Resnick, Donald Ira *lawyer*
Reum, James Michael *lawyer*
Reyes, Victor H. *lawyer*
Reyna, Claudio *retired professional soccer player*
Reynolds, Ruth Carmen *school administrator, secondary school educator*
Rhind, James Thomas *lawyer*
Rice, Linda Johnson *publishing executive*
Rice, William Edward *journalist*
Rich, S. Judith *public relations executive*
Richard, Howard M. *lawyer*
Richman, John Marshall *lawyer, food products executive*
Richman, Lawrence I. *lawyer*
Ricketts, Thomas *investment company executive*
Rieser, Richard M., Jr. *banker*
Rikoski, Richard Anthony *electrical engineering executive*
Riley, Benjamin Robertson *engineering educator*
Riley, James B., Jr. *lawyer*
Rios, Alexis Israel *professional baseball player*
Ritchie, William Paul *lawyer*
Rizzello, Joseph Samuel *stock exchange executive*
Rizzo, Ronald Stephen *lawyer*
Roberson, Carolyn A. *counseling administrator*
Roberts, Jo Ann Wooden *school system administrator*
Roberts, John Charles *law educator*
Robertson, Anne Walters *music educator, music historian*
Robertson, Donna Virginia *architect, educator, dean*
Robertson, William Wright, Jr. *orthopedist, educator*
Robinson, June Kerswell *dermatologist, educator*
Rodriguez, Richard L. *transportation executive*
Rogers, Eugene Jack *retired medical educator*
Rogers, John W., Jr. *investment company executive*
Roitberg, Ben Zion *neurosurgeon, educator*
Roizman, Bernard *virologist, educator*
Romeo, Anthony Albert *orthopedic surgeon*
Rooney, John Edward *communications company executive*
Rooney, Matthew A. *lawyer*
Roper, Harry Joseph *lawyer*
Ropski, Gary Melchior *lawyer*
Rosales, Veronica *language educator*
Rose, Derrick Martell *professional basketball player*
Rosen, George *economist, educator*
Rosen, Rhoda *museum director*
Rosen, Steven Terry *medical professor, oncologist, hematologist*
Rosenberg, Aaron Glen *orthopedist, educator*
Rosenbloom, Lewis Stanley *lawyer*
Rosenfeld, Howard H. *lawyer*
Rosenson, Robert Sidney *cardiologist, researcher*
Rosner, Jonathan Lincoln *physicist, researcher*
Rosner, Robert *astrophysicist, educator*
Ross, Michael Neil *publishing executive*
Ross, Sharon Marie *communications educator*
Rosseau, Gail L. *neurosurgeon, educator*
Rovner, Ilana Kara Diamond *federal judge*
Rowan, Thomas Bernard III *political science professor*
Rowe, John William *utilities executive*
Rowley, Janet Davison *physician*
Roy, David Tod *literature educator*
Roy, Kevin *newscaster*
Rublee, Dale Allan *researcher*
Ruder, David Sturtevant *lawyer, educator, former federal agency administrator*
Rudnick, Lewis G. *lawyer*
Rugai, Virginia A. (Ginger Rugai) *alderwoman*
Rundio, Louis Michael, Jr. *lawyer*
Rupert, Donald William *lawyer*
Russell, Thomas R. *medical association administrator*
Russo, Gilberto *engineering educator*
Rutkoff, Alan Stuart *lawyer*
Rutledge, Edward K. *mortgage broker*
Ruxin, Paul Theodore *lawyer*
Ryan, Thomas F. *lawyer*
Ryan, William Arthur *mechanical engineer*
Rynkiewicz, Stephen Michael *journalist*
Rzepnicki, Tina L. *social sciences educator*
Sabatini, Lawrence *bishop emeritus*
Sabelli, Hector Carlos *psychiatrist, neuropharmacologist, writer*
Sadikot, Ruxana T. *internist, educator*
Sagraves, Rosalie *pharmacy practice educator, former dean*
Salah, Greg *marketing executive*
Salant, Talya *medical researcher*
Salopek, Paul F. *reporter, foreign correspondent*
Samuelson, Peter A. *management consultant*
Sanders, J. Ted *academic administrator, former educational association administrator*
Sanders, Jacquelyn Seevak *psychologist, educator*
Sanders, Richard Henry *lawyer*
Sandler, Richard H. *pediatric gastroenterologist*
Santangelo, Mario Vincent *retired dentist*
Saps, Miguel *pediatrician, gastroenterologist*
Sarwark, John Francis *orthopaedic surgeon, educator*
Sathy, Anup *lawyer*
Saunders, George Lawton, Jr. *lawyer*
Savage, Terry *television personality, journalist, stockbroker*
Sawyier, Michael Tod *lawyer, director*
Scarse, Olivia Marie *cardiologist, consultant*
Schaaf, Linda Ann *nurse, educator*
Schaffner, Howard Sheldon *lawyer*
Schaffner, Karen Ann (Karen Field) *real estate broker*
Schanwald, Steve *professional sports team executive*
Scharf, Stephanie A. *lawyer*
Scheiber, Stephen Carl *psychiatrist*
Scheiner, David Lawrence *internist*
Scheppach, Tracey L. *communications media company executive*
Schieser, Hans Alois *education educator*
Schiller, Donald Charles *lawyer*
Schilsky, Richard Lewis *oncologist, researcher*
Schimberg, A(rmand) Bruce *retired lawyer*
Schink, James Harvey *lawyer*
Schink, Julian C. *oncologist, director*
Schmidt, John R. *lawyer*
Schmitt, Natalie Crohn *theater educator*
Schmitz, Jeffrey Michael *performing arts educator*
Schneider, Robert Jerome *lawyer*
Schonfeld, Dan *educator*
Schopf, William Grant *lawyer*
Schornack, John James *accountant*
Schoumacher, Bruce Herbert *lawyer*
Schriver, John T. III *lawyer*
Schrock, Charles A. *energy executive*
Schroeder, Douglas Fredrick *architect*
Schroeder, James W., Jr. *otolaryngologist*
Schroeder, Walter Andreas *physics professor*
Schubert, William Henry *curriculum studies educator*
Schueppert, George Louis *financial executive*
Schulte, David Michael *investment banker*
Schulter, Eugene C. *alderman*
Schulz, Keith Donald *corporate lawyer, writer*
Schumann, William Henry III *corporate financial executive*
Schwab, Joel Gerson *pediatrician, educator*
Schwab, Stephen Wayne *lawyer*
Schwartzberg, Joanne Gilbert *physician*
Schwertfeger, Timothy R. *investment company executive*
Sciarra, John J. *obstetrician, gynecologist, educator*
Scogland, William Lee *lawyer*
Scommegna, Antonio *obstetrician, gynecologist, educator*
Scriven-Young, David Joseph *lawyer*
Seal, Robert A. *library director*
Seaman, Scott M. *lawyer*
Seeler, Ruth Andrea *pediatrician, educator*
Segerstrale, Ullica Christina *social sciences educator, researcher*
Selander, Larry *lawyer*
Selman, Russell Bertram *lawyer, department chairman*
Seminack, Richard Stephen *bishop*
Senior, Donald Paul *religious organization administrator*
Senior, Richard John Lane *linen and uniform services executive*
Sennet, Charles Joseph *lawyer*
Sennett, Michael *lawyer*
Sergi, Vincent A.F. *lawyer*
Serritella, James Anthony *lawyer*
Serritella, William David *lawyer*
Sha, Beverly E. *medical educator*
Shafiro, Valeriy *audiologist, educator*
Shah, Anil R. *plastic surgeon*
Shaikh, Sabina Lee *economist, educator*
Shanahan, Betty *professional society administrator*
Shankman, Stewart A. *psychologist, educator*
Shapiro, Keith J. *lawyer*
Shapiro, Stephen Michael *lawyer*
Shapo, Marshall Schambelan *lawyer, educator*
Shaver, Joan Louise Fowler *dean, women's health nurse*
Shaw, John M. *oncologist*
Shebel, Heather A. *editor*
Sheean, Patricia M. *nutritionist, educator*
Sheffield, Jeffrey T. *lawyer*
Sheinkop, Mitchell *orthopedist, surgeon, educator*
Sherman, Ian Matthew *lawyer*
Sherman, Jeremy P. *lawyer*
Shields, Thomas Charles *lawyer*
Shields, Thomas William *surgeon, educator*
Shikanov, Sergey *urologist*
Shiller, Helen *alderwoman*
Shore, Richard M. *radiologist, educator*
Short, Marion Priscilla *neurogenetics educator*
Sibener, Steven Jay *chemistry educator*
Sidle, Douglas M. *medical educator*
Siegler, Mark *internist, educator*
Silverman, Michael J. *lawyer*
Silverman, Ross O. *lawyer*
Silverstein, Jonathan Charles *surgeon, researcher*
Simmons, Adele Smith *foundation executive, former educator*
Simmons, Barbara *nursing educator, director*
Simon, John Bern *lawyer*
Simons, Helen *school psychologist, psychotherapist, educator*
Simpson, Dick Weldon *political science educator*
Sive, Rebecca Anne *public relations executive*
Skiko, Marla *communications executive*
Skinner, Samuel Knox *lawyer, retired transportation executive, former United States Secretary of Transportation*
Slansky, Jerry William *investment company executive*
Sloan, Robert Hal *computer science educator*
Smale, Stephen *mathematics professor*
Small, Richard Donald *travel company executive*
Smedinghoff, Thomas J. *lawyer*
Smith, Adrian Devaun *architect*

Smith, Arthur B., Jr. *lawyer*
Smith, Earl Charles *nephrologist, educator*
Smith, Ed H. *alderman*
Smith, Joanne C. *health facility administrator*
Smith, Lewis J. *medical educator, researcher*
Smith, Mary Ann *alderwoman*
Smith, Mary L. *lawyer*
Smith, Michael Cremin *neurologist, director*
Smith, Raymond Thomas *anthropology educator*
Smith, Sam *columnist, writer*
Smith, Stan Vladimir *economist, finance company executive*
Smolen, Lee M. *lawyer*
Snider, Rowe Winston *lawyer*
Snyder, Edward Adams *dean, economics professor*
Socol, Michael Lee *obstetrician, gynecologist, educator*
Solis, Daniel S. *alderman*
Solovy, Jerold Sherwin *lawyer*
Solow, Michael Barry *lawyer*
Sonderby, Susan Pierson *federal judge*
Song, David *plastic surgeon, medical educator*
Soriano, Alfonso Guilleard *professional baseball player*
Sorosky, Sheldon M. *lawyer*
Soto, Geovany *professional baseball player*
Southwell, Donald G. *insurance company executive*
Spaeth, Virginia Ann *biology professor*
Sparberg, Marshall Stuart *gastroenterologist, educator*
Spargo, Benjamin H. *renal pathologist, educator*
Spargo, R. Clifton *literature and language professor*
Spector, David M. *lawyer*
Spellmire, George W. *lawyer*
Spergel, Irving Abraham *social worker, researcher*
Spiotto, James Ernest *lawyer*
Sprayregen, James H.M. *lawyer, former diversified financial services company executive*
Sproger, Charles Edmund *retired lawyer*
Stack, Paul Francis *lawyer*
Stack, Stephen S. *manufacturing executive*
Staller, John Edward *archaeologist, anthropologist, educator*
Stallworth, Stanley B. *lawyer*
Stamler, Jeremiah *medical professor, researcher*
Standberry, Herman Lee *school system administrator, educational consultant, corporate executive*
Stanhaus, James Steven *lawyer*
Starkman, Gary Lee *lawyer*
Stayner, Leslie Thomas *epidemiologist*
Stead, James Joseph, Jr. *security firm executive*
Stearns, Neele Edward, Jr. *investment company executive*
Steinberg, Morton M. *lawyer*
Steinberg, Rubin *retired art educator, artist*
Steinberg, Salme Elizabeth Harju *academic administrator, historian*
Steiner, Donald Frederick *biochemist, physician, educator*
Steinfeld, Manfred *furniture manufacturing executive*
Stephan, Thomas *physicist, researcher*
Stephens, Richard *aerospace transportation executive*
Stern, Carl William, Jr. *management consultant*
Sternstein, Allan J. *lawyer*
Stevens, Stanley M. *lawyer*
Stevenson, Adlai Ewing III *lawyer, former United States Senator, Illinois*
Steves Keiser, Susan *bank executive*
Stewart, Donald M. *college president*
Stigler, Stephen Mack *statistician, educator*
Stillman, Nina Gidden *lawyer*
Stinton, Dale A. *real estate association executive*
Stirling, James Paulman *investment banker*
Stone, Bernard Leonard *alderman, vice mayor*
Stone, James Leland *surgical neurologist, educator*
Stone, Neil Joseph *cardiologist, educator*
Stone, Steven Michael *sports announcer, former baseball player*
Stone, Susan A. *lawyer*
Strassner, Howard Taft, Jr. *obstetrician, educator*
Straus, Francis Howe *pathologist, educator*
Strauss, Bernard S. *geneticist, educator*
Stroscio, Michael Anthony *physicist, researcher*
Suarez, Ray (Regner Suarez) *alderman*
Sugar, Joel *ophthalmologist*
Sulkin, Howard Allen *academic administrator*
Sullivan, Barry *lawyer, educator*
Sullivan, Marcia Waite *lawyer*
Sullivan, Peggy *librarian, consultant*
Sullivan, Thomas Patrick *lawyer*
Surendra, Basti *ophthalmologist, educator*
Sviokla, John Julius *technology consultant*
Swagel, Phillip L. *economics professor, former federal agency administrator*
Swanson, Don Richard *university dean*
Swartzman, Daniel *lawyer, educator*
Swibel, Steven Warren *lawyer*
Swiger, Elinor Porter *lawyer*
Swinand, Andrew *advertising executive*
Swonk, Diane Catherine *economist*
Sykes, Alan O'Neil *lawyer, educator*
Szerlag, Chester Theodore *health care executive*
Szuchet, Sara *biochemist, educator*
Tabin, Julius *lawyer, physicist*
Tague, John Patrick *air transportation executive*
Talbot, Pamela *public relations executive*
Tallchief, Maria *former ballerina*
Tallon, Dale *professional sports team executive*
Tanna, Angelo Peter *ophthalmologist, educator, researcher*
Tatar, Arnold Marshall *internist, educator*
Taub, Richard Paul *social sciences educator*
Telfer, Margaret Clare *internist, hematologist, oncologist*
Tellez, Claudia *hematologist, oncologist, educator*
Tezcur, Gunes Murat *political science professor*
Tharp, Michael D. *medical educator*
Theobald, Edward Robert *lawyer*
Thomas, Barbara L. *not-for-profit executive*
Thomas, Frederick Bradley *lawyer*
Thomas, J. Regan *plastic surgeon, educator*
Thomas, Latasha R. *alderwoman*
Thomas, Robert R. *state supreme court justice*
Thomas, Ronald L. *science educator, director*
Thomas, Stephen Paul *lawyer*
Thompson, George Fletcher *editor, publishing executive*
Thompson, James Robert, Jr. *lawyer, former governor*
Thompson, JoAnn *Alderwoman*
Tigerman, Stanley *architect, educator*
Tilton, Glenn F. *air transportation executive*
Tipsord, Michael L. *insurance company executive*
Tobin, Craig Daniel *lawyer*
Toews, Jonathan *professional hockey player*
Toig, Randall Marc *obstetrician, gynecologist*
Tolan, Patrick Henry *psychology educator*
Topel, Robert *economics professor*
Topinka, Judy Baar *state official, political organization worker*
Toriumi, Dean Michael *facial, plastic and reconstructive surgeon, educator*
Townsend, Katherine *psychologist, educator*
Trio, Edward Alan *lawyer, accountant*
Trost, Eileen Bannon *lawyer*
Trotter, Charlie *chef*
Trotter, Cortez *city official, former fire commissioner*
Truran, James Wellington, Jr. *astrophysicist, educator*
Truskowski, John Budd *lawyer*
Tryban, Esther Elizabeth *lawyer*
Tsay, Ruey Shiong *business and statistics educator*
Tunney, Thomas M. *alderman, restaurant owner*
Turilli, M. Louise *lawyer*
Turner, Michael Stanley *astrophysics professor, researcher, science administrator*
Turow, Scott F. *writer, lawyer*
Tyler, W(illiam) Ed *finance company executive*
Tyson, Kirk W. M. *management consultant*
Uhlig, Harald *economics professor*
Umans, Alvin Robert *manufacturing executive*
Umbdenstock, Richard J. *medical association administrator*
Underwood, Robert Leigh *venture capitalist*
Ungaretti, Richard Anthony *lawyer*
Urayama, Shiro *internist*
Urban, Jeff *food products executive*
Uretz, Robert Benjamin *biophysics educator, university dean*
Usiskin, Zalman Philip *mathematics educator*
Valerio, Joseph Mastro *architectural firm executive, educator*
Valle, Rafael F. *obstetrician, gynecologist, educator*
Valukas, Anton Ronald *lawyer, former prosecutor*
Van Den Hende, Fred J(oseph) *human resources executive*
Van Gorp, Jon D. *lawyer*
Van Hoene, William, Jr. *lawyer, utilities executive*
Van Zandt, David E. *dean, law educator*
Vartanian, A. John *otolaryngologist, researcher*
Vassallo, Brett Joseph *gynecologist, surgeon*
Vaughan, Douglas Eugene *medical association administrator, department chairman*
Verma, Nikhil *orthopedist*
Veverka, Donald John *lawyer*
Vezeau, Timothy J. *lawyer*
Vick, Linda H. *biology professor*
Videnovic, Aleksandar *medical educator*
Vie, Richard Carl *insurance company executive*
Vigneswaran, Wickii Thambiah *cardiothoracic surgeon, educator*
Villa-Flores, Javier *history professor*
Vitullo, Dolores *cardiologist, director*
Vogelzang, Jeanne Marie *professional society administrator, lawyer*
Vojcanin, Sava Alexander *lawyer*
Von Klan, Laurene *museum administrator*
von Ohlen, Robert Charles *lawyer*
von Rhein, John Richard *music critic, journalist, writer*
Voris, Harold K *curator*
Vrablik, Edward Robert *import/export company executive*
Waddell, Frederick H. (Rick Waddell) *finance company executive*
Wagner, Annette M. *dermatologist, surgeon*
Wagner, Susan Laurene *elementary gifted education educator*
Waguespack, Scott *Alderman*
Wakschlag, Milton Samuel *lawyer*
Walberg, Herbert John *psychologist, educator, consultant*
Walsh, Matthew M. *construction executive*
Walton, Robert Lee *plastic surgeon*
Walton, Surrey Max *educator*
Wander, Herbert Stanton *lawyer*
Wang, Albert James *violinist, educator*
Wang, Ting *biomedical researcher*
Ward, Jonathan P. *investment banker*
Ward, R. Parker *cardiologist, educator*
Wasan, Darsh Tilakchand *academic administrator, chemical engineer, educator*
Wasson, Jeffrey *music educator*
Wayne, Jeffrey D. *surgeon*
Webb, Dan K. *lawyer*
Weber, Hanno *architect*
Weber, Kathleen M. *sports medicine physician, orthopedist*
Weber, Richard Martin *theology studies educator*
Webster, James Randolph, Jr. *physician*
Weese-Mayer, Debra Ellyn *pediatrician, educator*
Weigand, Robert Eugene *university educator*
Weinberg, David B. *investor*
Weinberg, Walter S. *lawyer*
Weiner, Gerald Arne *stockbroker*
Weinfurter, Daniel Joseph *business services executive*
Weinstein, Robert A. *physician, medical educator, director, medical researcher*
Weis, Jody P. (J.P. Weis) *police superintendent*
Weiss, John Robert *lawyer*
Weiss, Steven Allan *lawyer*
Weissbluth, Marc *pediatrician, educator*
Weissenberger, Glen *law educator, former dean*
Weissman, Michael Lewis *lawyer*
Welsh, Kelly Raymond *lawyer, investment company executive*
Werner, Raymond J. *lawyer*
Wershil, Barry Kent *pediatrician*
Westbrook, Brian Collins *professional football player*
Westerberg, Gary W. *lawyer*
Weston, Roger Lance *investment manager*
Wham, David Buffington *secondary school educator*
Wheater, Ashley C. *former dancer, performing company executive*
Whitaker, Eric E. *academic administrator, former state agency administrator*
White, C. Vanessa *director*
White, Henry F., Jr. *legal association administrator, retired military officer*
White, Linda Diane *lawyer*
Whitington, Peter Frank *pediatric hepatologist, educator*
Whitney, Kent R.E. *securities trader*
Whitney, Patrick Foster *design educator*
Wicks, Sheila M. *hospital administrator, research scientist, educator*
Wied, George Ludwig *physician*
Wier, Patricia Ann *publishing executive, consultant*
Wigdor, Harvey Alan *dentist, educator*
Wille, Lois Jean *retired editor*
Williams, Ann Claire *federal judge*
Williams, Frederick Tyrone *entrepreneur, pastor*
Williams, Marsha C. *travel company executive*
Williams, Philip Copelain *obstetrician, gynecologist*
Williams, Richard Lucas III *electronics executive, director, lawyer*
Williams, Stephanie F. *oncologist*
Williamson, Richard Salisbury *lawyer, former ambassador*
Willoughby, William Franklin, II, *retired physician, scientist, military officer*
Winfrey, Oprah *television talk show host, actress, television producer*
Winstein, Bruce Darrell *physics professor*
Wirtz, Rocky (W. Rockwell Wirtz) *professional sports team executive, beverage company executive*
Wise, William Jerrard *lawyer*
Witcoff, Sheldon William *lawyer*
Wolf, Charles Benno *lawyer*
Wolf, Neal Lloyd *lawyer*
Wolf, Stephen M. *consumer products company executive, former air transportation executive*
Wolfe, David Louis *lawyer*
Wolfson, Warren D. *dean, law educator, former judge*
Wong, Thomas Tang Yum *engineering educator*
Wood, Diane Pamela *federal judge*
Wood, Mark D. *lawyer*
Wood, Patrick Henry III *former commissioner*
Woodford, Peter C. *lawyer*
Wright, Jeremiah Alvesta, Jr. *retired minister*
Wright, Judith Margaret *law librarian, educator, dean*
Wrigley, William, Jr., (Bill Wrigley Jr.) *candy company executive*
Wyndewicke, Kionne Annette (Annette Johnson Moorer) *retired secondary school educator*
Wynne, Martha Ellen *psychology professor*
Xu, Yang *engineering educator*
Yamada, Tohru *biologist, educator, researcher, director*
Yamamoto, Hisashi *chemistry professor*
Yang, Benson Pin-Sheng *neurosurgeon*
Yartz, Frank Joseph *retired professor, author*
Yeager, Mark Leonard *lawyer*
Yelin, David B. *lawyer*
Yellen, David N. *dean, lawyer*
Yu, Anthony C. *religion and literature educator*
Yu, Clement Tak *educator, researcher, consultant*
Yudkowsky, Rachel *medical educator*
Zagar, Robert John *psychologist, researcher*
Zagel, James Block *federal judge*
Zagel, Margaret Maxwell *lawyer*
Zalewski, Michael R. *alderman*
Zambrano, Carlos Alberto *professional baseball player*
Zelenka, H. Dayle Kendall *librarian*
Zell, Samuel *real estate company executive, publishing executive*
Zellner, Arnold *economics, econometrics and statistics professor*
Zhang, James Xuejie *healthcare educator*
Zhiglo, Andrey *research scientist*
Zhou, Ping *research scientist*
Zhou, Xiaofeng *biomedical researcher, medical geneticist*
Zimmer, Robert Jeffrey *academic administrator, mathematician, educator*
Zonis, Marvin *political scientist, educator*
Zopp, Andrea Lynne *energy company executive, lawyer*
Zucaro, Aldo Charles *insurance company executive*

Chicago Heights
Barrett, Reuben Edward *biology professor*
Reed, Scott C. *musician, educator, writer*
Rohwedder, Christopher *elementary school educator*

Cicero
Casey, Craig F. *physics professor*
Paprocki, Thomas John *bishop, lawyer*

Cissna Park
McCullough, Edward L. *artist, educator*

Clarendon Hills
Moritz, Donald Brooks *mechanical engineer, consultant*

Coal City
DiGiusto, Elaine Bessie *science educator*

Colchester
Combs, William Lee *history professor emeritus*

Country Club Hills
McClelland, Helen *music educator*

Crystal Lake
Anderson, Lyle Arthur *retired manufacturing executive*
Haas, Sheila Jean *secondary school educator*
Plinske, Kathleen A. *educational association administrator associate vice president*
Rozovics, Michelle Janeen *lawyer*
Schaefer, Mary Ann *health facility administrator, consultant*
Thoms, Jeannine Aumond *lawyer*
Wade, Edwin Lee *lawyer, writer*

Danville
Hantz, Charles Anthony *humanities educator*

Darien
Kulkarni, Bidy *reproductive endocrinologist, biomedical researcher, consultant*

Decatur
Bradshaw, Billy Dean *retired retail executive*
Cabrera, Eduardo C. *literature and language professor*
Hawkin, Evyonne *social studies educator*
Koucky, John Richard *metallurgical engineer, manufacturing executive*
Mayfield, Peggy Lee *counselor, educator*
Mills, Steven R. *agricultural company executive, accountant*
Rice, John D. *agricultural products executive*
Smith, David James *lawyer*
Woertz, Patricia Ann *agricultural company executive, retired oil company executive*

Deerfield
Ahlbrandt, Robert Alan *pharmaceutical executive*
Amundson, Joy A. *pharmaceutical and health products executive*
Ben-Shir, Rya Helen *medical librarian*
Blanchard, Eric Alan *lawyer*
Blaylock, Stanley B. *retail executive*
Boyd, Joseph Don *diversified financial services company executive*
Carbonari, Bruce A. *consumer products company executive*
Chawla, Sona *consumer products company executive*
Dammerman, Dennis Dean *finance company executive*
Davis, Robert M. *medical products executive*
Feil, Kimberly Lynn *marketing executive*
Fratt, Steven D. *humanities educator*
Gershteyn, Yefim *application developer, researcher*
Gochnauer, Richard Wallis *consumer products company executive*
Green, Dana I. *retail executive, lawyer*
Harris, Dana Michelle *religious studies educator*
Heiman, Marvin Stewart *finance company executive*
Heller, Matthew A. *psychology professor*
Ho Pao, Chrystal L. *biology professor*
Lezak, Carol Spielman *communications executive, editor, writer, design consultant, medical librarian*
Lichtenstein, Susan R. *lawyer, medical products executive*
McNally, Alan G. *retail executive*
Meyer, Mara Ellice *special education educator, consultant, academic administrator*
Miquelon, Wade D. *retail executive*
Omtvedt, Craig P. *consumer products executive*
Parkinson, Robert L., Jr. *medical products executive, health facility administrator*
Pugh, Bryan *retail company marketing executive*
Quinn, Donal *diagnostic equipment company executive*
Reich, Victoria J. *consumer products company executive*
Rentas, Angelo George *biology professor, director*
Riedl, George J. *retail executive*
Roche, Mark A. *lawyer, consumer products company executive*
Rudolphsen, William M. *retail executive*
Sanner, John Harper *retired pharmacologist*
Scott, John Joseph *lawyer*
Shakno, Robert Julian *hospital and social services administrator*
Wagner, Mark A. *retail executive*
Wasson, Gregory D. *retail executive*
Watts, Colin F. *retail executive*
Wesley, Norman H. *consumer products company executive*
Wilson, Stephen Ray *fertilizer manufacturing company executive*
Wrobbel, Karen *education educator, consultant*
Zavada, Jeffrey J. *retail executive*
Zywicki, Robert Albert *retired electric power industry executive*

Dekalb
Bennett, (Cecil) Jack(son) *biology professor*
Bukonda, Ngoyi K. Zacharie *health care management educator*
Chitwood, Judith *performing arts educator*
Cosenza, Glenda Lee *music educator*
Crosser, Carmen Lynn *marriage and family therapist, social worker, consultant*
Fehrenbach, Heide *historian, educator*
Gately, Kathryn *theater educator*
Gelman, Alexander *theater director, educator*
Goldenberg, William Bruce *musician, educator*
Gunkel, David J. *communications educator*
Hamilton, David Arnold *retired librarian*
Henry, Beverly Weidinger *dietician, educator*
Kevill, Dennis Neil *chemistry professor*
Kimball, Clyde William *physicist, researcher*
Leang, Kheang *language educator*
Li, Lan *educator*
Monat, William Robert *university official*
Moorman, Ted *finance educator*
Nissen, Christopher Karl *educator*
Peters, John G. *academic administrator, political scientist*
Phares, Dee Anna *literature and language professor*
Ryan, Timothy Andrew *literature and language professor*
Shernoff, David Jordan *psychology professor*
Slotsve, George Aaron *economist, educator, consultant*
Stahl, Norman A. *literature and language professor, department chairman*

Thomas, Lynne M. academic librarian, researcher, blogger
Troyer, Alvah Forrest agricultural products executive, horticulturist
Un, Kheang political scientist
Walzer, Norman Charles retired economics professor
Yoo, Young Zo materials scientist, researcher
Zhou, Shengde science educator, researcher

Des Plaines
Banach, Art John retired graphic artist
D'Anca, John Arthur psychotherapist, educator
Fortman, Fred J. professional society administrator
Frank, James S. automotive executive
Henrikson, Arthur Allen political cartoonist, educator
Johnson, Peter E. plastic surgeon
Kaczor, Diane L. marketing professional, researcher
Lee, Margaret Burke college president, language educator
McClure, Matthew K. secondary school educator
Page, Helen (Lyn) Bard Ward literature educator
Quintanilla, Antonio Paulet retired physician, educator
Sampson, David Allan insurance association executive, former federal agency administrator
Wilson, Elizabeth M. medical association administrator
Winfield, Michael D. engineering company executive

Dixon
Atchley, Charles E. physics professor
Huber, Marianne Jeanne art dealer and appraiser

Downers Grove
Ahmadzadeh, Azita chemical engineer
Allin, Edgar Francis retired anatomist
Bastian, Robert W. otolaryngologist
Bowen, Christopher Frank library director
Brekke, Stewart Ernest retired chemistry and physics educator
Bruesch, John R. social studies educator, department chairman
Dahdal, Wafa Y. pharmacologist, educator
Fraleigh, Christopher J. food products executive
Hart, Brett J. lawyer, food products executive
Hornish, Ronald Frederick music educator
Hubbard, Lincoln Beals medical physicist, consultant
Jacklin, William Thomas retired county official, educator
Kent, Geoffrey travel company executive
Klausner, Eytan A. pharmacist, educator
McGarr, Frank James retired federal judge, consultant
Morgan-Grenville, George S. travel company executive
Nelson, Paul D. podiatrist
Nolan, James W. food products executive
Rembos, Steven podiatrist
Richardson, Brent Earl otolaryngologist
Tack, Lois Catherine biochemist, researcher
Yeager, David P. transportation executive

Du Quoin
Ibendahl, Jean Ayres retired elementary and secondary educator

Dundee
Carlini, James management consultant

East Peoria
Bell, Lori (Lorelei Junot) library director, library and information scientist
Mellendorf, Kenneth Ernest physicist, researcher
Pope, Kitty library director
Wadsworth Walker, Cherilee music educator

East Saint Louis
Thomas, Mary Lee property manager
Wright, Katie Harper educational administrator, journalist

Edwardsville
Anop, Lenora-Marya violinist, music educator
Barnett, Eric B. museum director
Claudson, William Dolan music educator
Dietrich, Suzanne Claire communications consultant, researcher, museum director
Douglas, Thomas John finance educator
Hawkins, Deborah Anne lawyer
Karanovich, Frances Ann Bridger education educator, retired superintendent, consultant
Madison, Grace Lenore retired medical/surgical nurse, psychologist, educator
Malone, Robert Roy artist, educator
McCullough, Theresa Marie pharmacist, director
Newland, Pamela Kay nursing educator
Norris, Sandra Love occupational therapy assistant
Rikli, Donald Carl lawyer
Schultz, Norbert J. retired music educator
Stranc, Cathleen L. music educator
Watson, George William, Jr. science educator

Effingham
Fatheree, Joseph G. information technology educator

Elburn
Hansen, H. Jack management consultant

Elgin
Almen, Lowell Gordon clergy, church official
Beyer, Karen social worker
Braaten, Laurie J. religious studies educator
Del Genio, Irina L. dean
Freeman, Corwin Stuart, Jr. estate and financial consultant
Lodding, Dean W. dentist
Mao, Ruixuan (Rick Mao) dean
Robinson, Lois Hart retired public relations executive
Rogers, Carleton Carson, Jr. trade show and convention executive

Elk Grove Village
Alden, Errol R. medical association administrator
David, Tayloe T., Jr. pediatrician, medical association administrator
Jan, Chwu-Ching Hwang environmental chemistry consultant

Elmhurst
Angadiath, Jacob bishop
Banich, Francis Edward surgeon
Blain, Charlotte Marie internist, educator
Boggs, William Norman, Jr. marketing professional, educator
Choyke, Phyllis May Ford (Mrs. Arthur Davis Choyke Jr.) management executive, editor, poet
Eckhardt, Richard Dale retired physician, educator
Evrard, Marilyn L. oncologist, internist
Ferraro, John Ralph chemist, researcher
Ford, Russell Clarke philosopher, educator
Jaramillo, Andres lab administrator, researcher
Lee, Nancy C. religious studies educator
Lyster, Michael T. oncologist, hematologist
Niziolek, Alice academic administrator
Parker, James John engineer, marketing professional
Pruter, Margaret Franson editor
Rosi, David R. internist, oncologist, hematologist
Stanger, John Goodman literature and language professor, archivist
Valcarenghi, Ivan dentist
Weiger, Alan W. theater director, educator
Willis, Kathleen A. librarian

Elmwood Park
Spina, Anthony Ferdinand lawyer
Tiesenga, Marvin Francis surgeon

Elsah
Ritter, Joseph Michael chemistry professor, dean

Eureka
Edge, Rhea Arlene dean
Fulop, Ann psychology educator
Hearne, George Archer academic administrator
Staudenmeier, William John, Jr. sociology professor
Tookey, Keith R. computer science professor

Evanston
Achenbach, Jan Drewes engineering scientist
Allred, Albert Louis chemistry professor
Anderson, Kenneth Paul nephrologist, administrator
Arrington, Michael Browne foundation administrator
Awad, Issam Abdullah neurosurgeon, educator
Backman, Vadim biomedical engineer, educator
Belytschko, Ted engineering educator
Bethel, Kathleen Evonne librarian
Bishop, David Fulton retired library administrator
Bitner, John Howard lawyer
Bloomer, William David radiologist, oncologist, educator
Bobco, William David, Jr. consulting engineering company executive
Borcover, Alfred Seymour journalist
Boyang, Liu research scientist
Boye, Roger Carl academic administrator, journalism educator
Braithwaite, Susan Shapiro endocrinologist, educator
Brazelton, William Thomas chemical engineer, educator, dean
Brendler, Charles Burgess urologist, educator
Bro, William Price medical association administrator
Brown, James Allison anthropology educator
Cantor, Daniel Adam theater educator
Carr, Stephen Howard materials engineer, educator
Carroll, Peter James history professor
Chambers, Anthony LaRoyce psychologist, educator
Chernev, Alexander marketing educator, researcher
Christian, Richard Carlton dean, former advertising agency executive
Christiano, Lawrence Joseph economist, educator
Conger, William Frame artist, educator
Corey, Gordon Richard financial advisor, former utilities executive
Crawford, James Weldon psychiatrist, educator, administrator
Crawford, Susan library director, educator, editor, writer
Cvetanovic, Ivana medical educator, editor
Dallos, Peter John neurobiologist, educator
Danilov, Victor Joseph museum administrator, educator, writer
Daskin, Mark Stephen engineering educator
Dranove, David Stuart business educator, economist, consultant
Eagly, Alice Hendrickson social psychology educator
Eberley, Helen-Kay opera singer, recording industry executive, poet
Fenninger, Leonard Davis medical educator, consultant
Fessler, Raymond R. metallurgical engineering consultant
Fisher, Andrew Taylor computer software developer
Fitzgerald, Pat college football coach
Fong, Yuk-fai economist, educator
Frederick, Lewis Dunbar chemistry professor
Frey, Donald Nelson industrial engineer, educator, retired manufacturing executive
Gaiha, Vishnu Das cardiologist
Galvin, Kathleen Malone communications educator
Ghiglione, Loren Frank journalism professor
Gibbons, Reginald poet, literature and language professor
Gibbons, William Reginald, Jr. poet, writer, translator, editor
Goldberg, Erwin biochemistry educator
Good, Andrew Evans obstetrician
Gordon, Julie Peyton foundation administrator
Gordon, Robert James economics professor
Gourianova, Nina art and literary historian
Griffith, Jeanne Ballard retired medical illustrator
Griswold, Wendy sociologist, educator
Grunsfeld, Ernest Alton III architect
Hall, Bruce A. music educator
Hayford, Charles W. historian, educator
Hedges, Larry V. educator
Hemke, Frederick L. music educator
Hine, Darlene Clark history educator, administrator
Hoffman, Brian M. chemistry professor
Hughes, Edward F. X. healthcare educator, preventive medicine physician
Hughes, Susan L. gerontologist, researcher
Hurter, Arthur Patrick economist, educator
Ibers, James Arthur chemist, educator
Jacobs, Donald P. finance educator
Jacobs, Norman Joseph publishing executive
Jain, Dipak Chand dean, marketing educator, consultant
Jang, Joon I. physicist
Jerome, Joseph Walter mathematics professor
Jones, Robert Russell retired magazine editor
Kalai, Ehud economist, researcher, educator
Kalogera, Vassiliki (Vicky Kalogera) physics professor
Kan-Walsh, Karen Chih Pah music educator
Karaikovic, Eldin surgeon, educator
Kath, William Lawrence mathematics professor
Keer, Leon Morris engineering educator
Kertész, Imre writer
Kimbrough, Lorelei retired elementary and secondary school educator
Klein, William Lee neurobiology professor, researcher
Kliphardt, Raymond A. engineering educator
Koh, Jason orthopedic surgeon
Kotler, Philip marketing educator, writer
Krizek, Raymond John engineering educator, consultant
Kuenster, John Joseph editor
Kujala, Walfrid Eugene musician, educator
Kuzmanic, Ana design educator
Lamb, Robert Andrew molecular biologist, virologist, educator
Lambert, Joseph Buckley chemistry professor
Larson, Paul William public relations executive
Lewis, Charles A. foundation administrator
Lewis, Dan Albert education educator
Li, Shifeng technologist
Macsai, John retired architect
Marks, Tobin Jay chemistry educator
Matkowsky, Bernard Judah mathematician, educator
Matzkin, Rosa Liliana economics professor
McCarron, John Francis editor
Menke, Allen Carl retired manufacturing executive
Messersmith, Phillip B. biomedical engineer, educator
Mills, Edwin Smith economics professor
Mirkin, Chad A. chemistry professor
Morrison, John Horton lawyer, arbitrator
Murphy, Gordon John electrical engineer, educator
Mustoe, Thomas Anthony physician, plastic surgeon
Nechin, Herbert Benjamin lawyer
Novak, Giles Anthony astrophysicist
Novales, Ronald Richards zoologist, educator
Oakes, Robert James physics and astronomy professor
Oh, John Kie-Chiang political science professor, academic administrator
Olmstead, William Edward mathematics professor
Olson, Gregory Bruce materials science and engineering educator, academic director
Orsi, Robert religious studies educator
Ottino, Julio Mario engineering educator
Otwell, Ralph Maurice retired newspaper editor
Packman, Aaron Ian environmental engineer, educator
Palloni, Alberto Bruno social sciences educator
Peters, Gordon Benes retired musician
Peterson, Lance Robert physician
Piper, Robert Johnston retired architect, urban planner
Power, Peggy Ann elementary school educator
Prince, Thomas Richard accountant, educator
Pritchard, Sarah Margaret library director
Rasio, Frederic Armand astrophysicist
Reiss, Lenore Ann language educator, retired secondary school educator
Rielly, John Edward educational association administrator
Robertson, David Alan museum director, educator
Rosenthal, Todd set designer
Ruggero, Mario Alfredo physiologist, educator
Schapiro, Morton Owen academic administrator
Schluter, Robert Arvel physicist
Schwartz, Neena Betty endocrinologist, educator
Scott, Walter Dill management educator
Seidman, David N(athaniel) materials scientist, engineer, educator
Sener, Stephen Francis oncologist, surgeon
Severini, Thomas Alan statistician, educator
Shapiro, Anna D. theater director
Shenkar, Robert science educator, researcher
Sheridan, James Edward history professor
Silverman, Richard Bruce chemist, biochemist, educator
Smith, Spencer Bailey engineering and business educator
Spier, Kathryn Elizabeth economist, educator
Sprang, Milton LeRoy obstetrician, gynecologist, educator
Stern, Louis William marketing educator, consultant
Stoddart, J(ames) Fraser chemistry professor, researcher
Stumpf, David Allen pediatric neurologist
Taflove, Allen electrical engineer, educator, researcher, consultant
Tanner, Martin Abba statistician, educator
Thomas, Eugene social worker
Thrash, Patricia Ann retired educational association administrator
Traisman, Howard Sevin retired pediatrician
Tybout, Alice Marie educator
Van Ness, James Edward electrical engineering educator
Wang, Sona venture capitalist
Warren, Todd engineering educator, retired computer company executive
Weber, Arnold Robert academic administrator
Weertman, Johannes materials science educator
Weertman, Julia Randall materials engineering educator
Weisbrod, Burton Allen economist, educator
Weiss, Kevin Barton epidemiologist, medical association administrator
Wessels, Bruce W. materials scientist, educator
Whinston, Michael D. economics professor
Wilkinson, Anne Marie mathematics professor
Wills, Garry historian
Wright, John classics educator
Wu, Tai Te biological sciences and engineering educator
Youngman, Owen Ralph newspaper executive, educator
Zaslow, Eric Gallant mathematics professor
Zelinsky, Daniel mathematics professor
Zimmerman, Mary Alice performing arts educator, director, playwright

Evergreen Park
Wigsmoen, Susan Catania elementary school educator

Fairview Heights
Cox, A. Courtney prosecutor, lawyer
Walter, Arenstein Alan environmental services administrator

Flora
Shrum, John equal rights officer

Flossmoor
Cary, William Sterling retired church executive
Garrison, Ray Harlan lawyer
Parker, Eugene Newman retired physicist, educator

Fox River Grove
Abboud, Alfred Robert banker, investor, consultant, director

Frankfort
Burhoe, Brian Walter automotive executive

Franklin Park
Simpson, Michael retired metals service center executive

Freeport
Giaimo, Paul Sebastian English and philosophy educator
Setterstrom, James Robert agricultural studies educator
Vogt, Lorna Corrine retired librarian, small business owner
Weaver, Michael Glen pharmacist

Galena
Alexander, Barbara Leah Shapiro clinical social worker
Bezkorovainy, Anatoly medical educator, retired biochemist
Gallagher, Lynn social sciences educator
Sipiera, Paul P., Jr. foundation administrator, retired geology and astronomy professor

Galesburg
Coatney, Louis Robert librarian, historian
Edi, Eric political science professor, consultant
Gold, Penny Schine history professor
Gupta, Madan Lal cardiologist
Hamilton, Konrad M. history professor
Haywood, Bruce retired academic administrator
Hellenga, Robert Riner language educator, writer
Kehoe, Peter Herbert optometrist
Leath, Cheryl Lynn retired pre-school educator, poet, painter
McAndrew, Francis Thomas psychology professor
Miller, Michael D. mathematics educator
Mustain, Douglas Dee lawyer
Polay, Bruce musician, conductor, educator
Schroth, Stephen Timothy education educator, researcher
Schwartzman, Peter David environmental scientist, educator
Scotton, Carol Robinson economist, educator
Taylor, Roger Lee academic administrator, lawyer
Tourlentes, Thomas Theodore retired psychiatrist

Galva
Swatos, William Henry, Jr. priest, sociologist

Geneva
Lazzara, Dennis Joseph orthodontist
Mehta, Vishal M. orthopedist
Tyler, Lloyd John retired lawyer

Genoa
Cromley, Jon Lowell lawyer

Glen Carbon
Lazerson, Earl Edwin retired academic administrator
Lin, Steven An-Yhi economics professor

Glen Ellyn
Anderson, Barbara Jean biology professor
Baloun, John Charles retired wholesale distribution executive
Barrett, Carolyn Hernly manufacturing executive
Conti, Paul Louis management consulting company executive
Cook, Joann Catherine computer professor
Dieter, Raymond Andrew, Jr. physician, thoracic general and vascular surgeon
Emano, Dennis Jose Marmol associate professor
Evans, Margarita Sawatzky retired voice educator, academic administrator
Georgalas, Robert Nicholas English language educator
Greer, Julianna Patterson health and human services executive

Kapoor, Jagdish R. (Jack Kapoor) *marketing educator, writer*
Marszalek, Elizabeth A. *computer graphics designer, educator*
Mooring, F. Paul *physics editor*
Neurauter, Elizabeth Strain *secondary school educator*
Nunamaker, Susan Sun *mathematics professor*
O'Connell, Daniel James *lawyer*
Poromanska, Margarita Kirilova *environmental scientist, educator*
Sandrok, Richard William *lawyer*
Slusar, Linda *library and information scientist*
Ulrich, Werner *retired lawyer*
Venezia, Anthony D. *multimedia designer*
Wu, Jane Jiajing *history professor, consultant*

Glencoe
Cohen, Melanie Rovner *lawyer*
Hollins, Mitchell Leslie *lawyer*
Isaacs, Roger David *public relations executive*
Milloy, Frank Joseph, Jr. *surgeon*
Nebenzahl, Kenneth *rare book and map dealer, author*
Silver, Ralph David *financial planner*
Siske, Regina *artist*

Glendale Heights
Cook, Doris Marie *retired accountant, educator*

Glenview
Brady, Sharon *engineering executive*
Brunner, Robert E. *engineering executive*
Bruns, Nicolaus, Jr. *retired agricultural products executive, lawyer, educator*
Casas, Laurie Ann *plastic surgeon*
Corley, Jenny Lynd Wertheim *elementary school educator*
Dul, John A. *lawyer, electronics executive*
Eck, Robert J. *electronics executive*
Farber, Isadore E. *psychologist, educator*
Flaum, Russell M. *engineering executive*
Franklin, Lynne *corporate communications specialist, writer*
Gerstner, Robert William *structural engineering educator, consultant*
Gillis, Marvin Bob *retired chemical executive, consultant*
Golsby, Stephen W. *pharmaceutical executive*
Gresh, Philip M. *engineering executive*
Haddad, Steven L. *orthopaedic surgeon*
Haebich, Arthur T. *retired thoracic surgeon*
Hafner, Arthur Wayne *author, information scientist, academic librarian*
Hagy, James C. *lawyer*
Hansen, Thomas J. *engineering executive*
Hickey, John Thomas *retired electronics executive*
Hindman, Craig A. *engineering executive*
Hough, Winston *artist*
Hunt, Lawrence Halley, Jr. *lawyer*
King, Billie Jean Moffitt *retired professional tennis player*
Knox, James Edwin *lawyer*
Kropp, Ronald D. *engineering executive*
Letham, Dennis J. *wholesale company executive*
Levin, Donald Robert *business and finance executive, motion picture producer, professional sports team owner*
Mallory, Robert Mark *controller, retired finance company executive*
Marmet, Gottlieb John *lawyer*
Martel, Roland M. *engineering executive*
Mukoyama, James Hidefumi, Jr. *security firm executive*
Olson, Roy Arthur *retired government official*
Panarese, William C. *civil engineer*
Parry, David C. *engineering executive*
Rorig, Kurt Joachim *chemist, science association director*
Santi, E. Scott *engineering executive*
Speer, David Blakeney *chemicals executive*
Sutherland, Allan C. *engineering executive*
Underwood, Catherine H. *healthcare association administrator*
Van Zelst, Theodore William *civil engineer, engineering company executive*
Wooten, James H., Jr. *lawyer, engineering executive*
Zentmyer, Hugh J. *engineering executive*

Godfrey
Kessler, William Eugene *retired healthcare executive*
King, Ordie Herbert, Jr. *oral pathologist*
McDaniels, John Louis *retired mathematics professor*
Parton-Stanard, Susan *music educator, voice educator, musician*

Granite City
Cowan, Robert Randall *science educator*
Rarick, Philip Joseph *lawyer, retired state supreme court justice*

Grayslake
Bates, Ben *ceramics engineer, educator*
Bronner, Gwethalyn JeTaun *art association administrator, director*
Coykendall, Mark Alan *biology professor, department chairman*
Hopkins, Leslie Huntress *humanities educator, choreographer*
Turska, Joanna *music educator*

Great Lakes
Bienek, Diane Rose *research scientist*

Greenville
Filby, Ivan Leonard *management educator*
Junod, Daniel August *podiatrist*
Stampfli, Leonard Thomas *music educator, department chairman*

Gurnee
Bedore, Lenora T. *elementary school educator*
Hall, Terry *accountant*
Sommerlad, Robert Edward *environmental research engineer*

Hanover
Bleveans, John *lawyer*

Harrisburg
Maring-Sims, Mila L. *biology professor*
McKinstry, Glenn Allen *secondary school educator*

Harwood Heights
Rudel, Barbara Elizabeth *elementary school educator*

Hazel Crest
Freed, Melvyn Norris *retired educational association administrator, writer*
Williamson, Wayne C. *internist, geriatrician*

Herrin
Gauto, Nelson Fernando *plastic surgeon, consumer products company executive*

Herscher
Cessna, Katrina J. *music educator, composer*

Highland Park
Cohen, Burton David *food service executive, lawyer*
Fortnow, Lance Jeremy *computer scientist, educator*
Greenblatt, Miriam *writer, editor, educator*
Harris, Thomas L. *public relations executive*
Hobson, Stephen Gilbert *conductor, music educator*
Karol, Nathaniel H. *lawyer, consultant*
Korzenski, Robert M. *manufacturing executive*
Miller, Albert J. *cardiologist, internist*
Nelson, Richard David *lawyer*
Pattis, S. William *publishing executive*
Reed, Jan Stern *lawyer*
Rivkin, William B. *physicist*
Rudo, Milton *retired manufacturing executive*
Rutenberg-Rosenberg, Sharon Leslie *retired journalist*
Schindel, Donald Marvin *retired lawyer*
Slavick, Ann Lillian *retired art educator*
Slavsky, David Bruce *academic administrator, educator*
Stein, Paula Jean Anne Barton *hotel real estate company executive, broker*
Tobin, Calvin Jay *retired architect*
Uhlmann, Frederick Godfrey *securities trader*
Wolfson, Ouri *computer scientist*

Highwood
Brown, Lawrence Haas *retired banker*

Hillside
Savic, Jelena *mathematics educator*

Hines
Joehl, Raymond Joseph *surgeon, consultant*

Hinsdale
Bardfield, Steven *orthopedist*
Brueschke, Erich Edward *physician, researcher, educator*
Chassin, Eric *orthopedist*
Chudik, Steven *orthopedist*
Collins, Michael J. *orthopedist*
Daley, Robert *orthopedist*
Dederick, Robert Gogan *economist*
Durkin, Michael C. *orthopedist*
Dworsky, Brad *orthopedist*
Fox, David Wayne *banker*
Gilligan, William J. *orthopedist*
Kaminsky, Manfred Stephan *physicist*
Kirincic, Marie *orthopedist*
Kuhlman, Geoffrey S. *orthopedist*
Lorenz, Mark A. *orthopedist*
Louis, Steven *orthopedist*
Mehuron, William Otto *retired federal official*
Norton, John W., Jr. *chemical engineer, educator*
Shiffman, Kenneth *orthopedist, surgeon*
Trksak, Paul M. *orthopedist*
Unikel, Eva Taylor *interior designer*
Vargo, Robyn *orthopedist, surgeon*
Whitney, William Elliot, Jr. *advertising agency executive*
Wiet, Richard James *otolargynologist*
Zindrick, Michael R. *orthopedist*

Hoffman Estates
Austin, Karen A. *retail executive*
Coe, Nick *retail executive*
Collins, Michael D. *retail executive, accountant*
Crowley, William C. *retail executive*
de Bruin, Jerry Mark *retail executive*
Dziezak, Judie D. *lawyer*
Freidheim, Scott J. *retail executive*
Froman, John W. *retail executive*
Gerstein, Richard *marketing and retail company executive*
Harker, William R. *lawyer*
Israel, Craig M. *retail executive*
Johnson, W. Bruce *retail executive*
Lee, Gregory A. *human resources specialist*
McCullough, Gary E. *education company executive*
Moore, Douglas T. *retail executive*
Pearlman, Michelle *retail executive*
Peterson, Susan Carl *secondary school educator, gifted and talented educator*
Reed, Stuart C. *retail executive, former communications executive*
Snyder, Mark A. *marketing executive*
Trieb, Guenther *retail executive*
Winckler, Alicia Jean *human resources vice president*

Homewood
Schillings, Denny Lynn *retired history professor, educational and grants consultant*

Hoopeston
Hicks, Carol Ann *small business owner, educator*

Huntley
Balk, Alfred William *journalist*

Indian Head Park
Bamberger, Mary Ann *archivist, consultant*
Johnson, (Mary) Anita *physician, medical association administrator*

Ingleside
D'Andrea, Dana M. *medical/surgical nurse, lawyer*

Itasca
Duncan, Sam K. *retail executive*
Gallagher, J. Patrick, Jr. *insurance company executive*

Jacksonville
Anderson, Michael R. *elementary school educator, writer*
Findley, Paul *former congressman, author, educator*
Gallas, Martin Hans *librarian*
Green, Melinda Ann *psychologist, educator, research scientist*
Hardin, Susan Jean *social studies educator, department chairman*
Jerry, E. Claire *history professor, communications educator*
Johns, Beverley Anne Holden *special education administrator*
Kasper, Carol L. *biology professor*
Mathews, Jack Sherman *foundation administrator, retired insurance company executive*
Wells, Winston Raymond *political science professor*

Joliet
Easton, Kenneth Glenn *retired utilities executive*
Heeneman, Cheryl Lynn *biology professor*
Imesch, Joseph Leopold *bishop emeritus*
Manning-Smith, Kelly Ann *dean of students*
Reed, Brian Alan *school system administrator*
Rig, Alvin Manuel *pathologist, educator*
Sartain, James Peter *bishop*
Taylor, Jeffrey Scott *lawyer*
Thompson, Gregory Lynn *secondary school educator*
Tokatlioglu, Theresa Diaz Lopez *elementary school educator*
Williams, Jennifer Ann *public relations executive*
Yarrow, William Paul *literature and language professor*
Zhou, Ling-Yi *psychology professor*

Justice
Casselle, Corene *pre-school educator*

Kankakee
Crady, Paula Gannon *secondary school educator*
Smith, Joanne Genevieve *nursing educator*

Kenilworth
Bott, Harold Sheldon *accountant, management consultant*
Cook, Stanton R. *media company executive*
Feng, Paul Yen-Hsiung *lawyer, chemist*
Weaver, Clifford Lee *retired lawyer, winery owner*
Weaver, Donna Rae *winery executive*

Kildeer
Muffoletto, Mary Lu *retired educational association administrator, editor*

Kingston
Gherity, James Arthur *economics professor*

La Grange
Hoisington, Steven H. *industrial engineer*
Kerr, Alexander Duncan, Jr. *lawyer*
Kohlstedt, James August *lawyer*
Mehlenbacher, Dohn Harlow *civil engineer, consultant*
Sessions, Joan T. *administrator, educator*
Smith, Arthur Edward, Jr. *lawyer*

La Grange Park
Bradley, Harry A. *professional society administrator*
Butler, Margaret Kampschaefer *retired computer scientist*
Perkins, William H., Jr. *retired finance company executive*

Lake Barrington
Worrell, Sharyn Dianne Kelley *volunteer, retired flight attendant*

Lake Bluff
Crotty, John T. *investment advisor*
Griem, John Michael *management consultant*
Ochsner, Othon Henry, II, *importer, restaurant critic*
Sweetser, Marie-Odile Gauny *retired language educator*

Lake Forest
Angelo, Jerry *professional sports team executive*
Begley, Christopher B. *pharmaceutical executive*
Brewer, Paul Huie *advertising executive, artist, portrait painter*
Carroll, Barry Joseph *manufacturing and real estate executive*
Carter, Donald Patton *retired advertising executive*
Coleman, Kristin M. *lawyer*
Cutler, Jay *professional football player*
Emerson, William Harry *retired lawyer*
Feinberg, Jeffrey Enoch *religious studies educator, writer*
Forte, Matt *professional football player*
Hamilton, Peter Bannerman *manufacturing executive, lawyer*
Hammar, Lester Everett *retired manufacturing executive*
Hester, Devin *professional football player*
Howard, John Lawrence *lawyer*
Jadin, Ronald L. *wholesale distribution executive*
Jones, Gordon Kempton *dentist, retired military officer*
Keyser, Richard Lee (Dick Keyser) *wholesale distribution executive*
Knight, Lester B. *healthcare company executive*
Lambert, John Boyd *chemical engineer, consultant*
Leemputte, Peter G. *manufacturing executive*
Levy, Nelson Louis *immunologist, educator, surgeon*
Loux, P. Ogden *distribution company executive*
Marinelli, Rod *professional football coach*
McCoy, Dustan Elwood *manufacturing executive, lawyer*
Mohr, Roger John *retired advertising agency executive*
Morell, William Nelson, Jr. *retired foreign trade association executive, government agency administrator*
O'Mara, Thomas Patrick *manufacturing executive*
Pace, Orlando Lamar *professional football player*
Palmer, Ann Therese Darin *lawyer*
Peterson, Donald Matthew *insurance company executive*
Romans, Donald Bishop *manufacturing executive*
Ryan, James T. *wholesale distribution executive*
Salter, Edwin Carroll *retired pediatrician*
Schulze, Franz, Jr. *critic, educator*
Seaman, Irving, Jr. *banker*
Sherrill, Gregg M. *automotive executive*
Sikorovsky, Eugene Frank *retired lawyer*
Smith, Lovie *professional football coach*
Stecko, Paul T. *packaging company executive*
Swift, Edward Foster III *investment banker*
Terrasse, Anthony P. *plastic surgeon*
Trammell, Kenneth R. *automotive executive*
Urlacher, Brian Keith *professional football player*
Wardell, David A. *lawyer, automotive executive*
Weston, Arthur Walter *chemist, consultant, retired chemicals executive*
Wilbur, Richard Sloan *medical association administrator, physician*
Ysasi-Diaz, Gloria *wholesale distribution executive*

Lake In The Hills
Franks, David Brian *lawyer*
Shirazi, Eman Ali *dentist*

Lake Villa
Anderson, Milton Andrew *chemicals executive*

Lake Zurich
Krolopp, Rudolph William *retired industrial designer, consultant*
Schultz, Carl Herbert *real estate developer*

Lemont
Anitescu, Mihai *computer scientist, mathematician*
Doebert, Sandra L. *school system administrator*
Marx, Kenneth R. *music educator*

Libertyville
Bramhall, Robert Richard *management consultant*
Bush, Eugene Nyle *retired pharmacologist, pharmacist*
Forester, Thomas H. *portfolio manager, investment advisor*
Grote, Jonathan *chemist, researcher*
Jeyaraj, Arulsaravana *electronics engineer*
Maczulski, Margaret Louise *marketing professional*
Rassas, George James *bishop*
Thiruppukuzhi, Srikanth Vankeepuram *electronics engineer*
True, Raymond Stephen *editor, writer*

Lincoln
Bi, Shuwei *management information systems educator*
Eack, Cynthia A. *science educator, department chairman*
Franz, Karin *humanities educator*
Kurka, Robert Charles *minister, educator*
Mangano, Mark J. *religious studies educator*

Lincolnshire
Criglar, Melinda L. *retired dancer, educator*
Erickson, James Clifford III *anesthesiologist, educator*
Fradin, Russell P. *human resources company executive, former computer company executive*
Keller, Robert J. *consumer products company executive*
Michalik, John James *legal association administrator*
Simes, Stephen Mark *pharmaceutical executive*

Lincolnwood
Alexander, Cyrus A. *lawyer, arbitrator*
Bodi, Sonia Ellen *library director, educator*
Carroll, Howard William *state legislator*
DeBock, Cynthia Marie *archivist, researcher*
Glenner, Richard Allen *dentist, dental historian*
Kamensky, Marvin *lawyer*
Lebedow, Aaron Louis *consulting company executive*
Martin, Siva *lawyer*

Lindenhurst
Eron, Madeline Marcus *psychologist*
Theis, Peter Frank *engineering executive*

Lisle
Al-Banna, Ayham *architect*
Arnold, Catherine Leona Stein *nutritionist, educator, department chairman, researcher*
DeGreve, Luann *library assistant director*
Flock, Maryann *musician, director*
Krehbiel, Frederick August, II, *electronics executive*
Krehbiel, John H., Jr. *electronics company executive*
Kroll, Mark Alan *librarian*
Morrison, Delmar R. *chemical engineer*
Ruyle-Hullinger, Elizabeth Smith (Beth Ruyle) *municipal financial advisor, consultant*
Skweres, Thomas W. *sales executive, advertising executive, public relations executive, investor, entrepreneur*
Slark, Martin P. *electronics executive*
Thierer, Mark A. *retail executive*
Ware, George Henry *botanist*

Litchfield
Talley, Hayward Leroy communications executive

Lockport
Bentley, Stephen James psychologist, coach

Lombard
Ahlstrom, Ronald Gustin artist
Anderson, Phyllis Reinhold management consultant
Cisneros, Laura E. internist, hematologist, oncologist
Harris, Jeff M. waste management executive
Henkin, Robert Elliott nuclear medicine physician
Holgers-Awana, Rita Marie electrodiagnosis specialist
McCoy, Jeanie Shearer analytical chemist, consultant

Long Grove
Ausman, Robert K. surgeon, research and development company executive
Obert, Paul Richard lawyer, manufacturing executive

Loves Park
Dixon, John James retired music educator
Saporito-Hines, Lucille Ann special education educator

Lyons
Gordon, Mark Harry education professor

Machesney Park
Vaughn, Linda Marie municipal official

Macomb
Bauerly, Ronald John marketing educator
Boley, Mark S. physicist, mathematician
Brice, Lee L. history professor
Dexter, Donald Harvey surgeon, educator
Drea, John Thomas academic administrator, consultant
Hayes, Paul Robert retired field and clinical experiences coordinator
Hopper, Stephen Rodger hospital administrator
Karlowicz, Sarah Hanks musicologist
Key, Barclay Taylor history professor
Knod, Edward M., Jr. finance educator
Kouassi, Gilles Kouame chemistry professor, researcher
Lindner, Reinhard W education educator
Siddiqi, Mohammad A. journalist, educator
Voss, David Albert mathematics professor
Walker, Tammie Leigh music educator

Mahomet
Mashbern, William Allen minister, retired religious organization administrator

Maple Park
Carter, Ethel Ilene secondary school educator

Marengo
Franks, Herbert Hoover lawyer

Maryville
Bonneville, Richard Briggs retired gas industry executive
Stark, Patricia Ann psychologist

Mascoutah
Setterlund, Tina A.M. music educator

Matteson
Chatman, Gloria Lynn art educator

Mattoon
Bagger, Edward Duke James retired performing arts educator
Black, Todd Ronald music educator
Francis, Sue humanities educator
Hunzinger, Brenda C. biology professor
Phipps, John Randolph retired army officer

Maywood
Albain, Kathy S. oncologist
Aranha, Gerard V. surgeon
Barbato, Anthony L. hospital administrator, medical educator
Biller, Jose neurologist, educator
Flanigan, Robert Charles urologist, educator
Gianopoulos, John George obstetrician
Hatch, David A. urologist
Ludwig, Logan T. dean, consultant
Miele, Lucio physician, medical researcher, pharmacologist
Moran, John Francis cardiologist
Nand, Sucha medical educator
Origitano, Thomas Charles neurological surgeon
Samarel, Allen Mark physician, biochemistry and cell biology educator
Schultz, Richard Michael biochemistry educator, researcher
Shoham, David A. epidemiologist, educator
Sizemore, Glen William medical educator
Stiff, Patrick Joseph internist, hematologist, oncologist, educator
Varma, Niraj cardiologist, physiologist, researcher
Warpeha, Raymond Leonard surgeon, educator
Wheeler, John S., Jr. urologist

Mc Gaw Park
Bernardo, Angelito Alday nephrologist, medical products executive

Mchenry
Chamberlain, Charles James railroad labor union executive

Melrose Park
Banerji, Manatosh oncologist, hematologist
Bernick, Carol Lavin consumer products company executive
Boswell, Gina R. cosmetics executive
Klein, Lloyd William cardiologist, researcher
Rossof, Arthur Harold internal medicine educator
Schmidt, Gary P. lawyer, personal care industry executive
Shanes, Jeffrey Glenn cardiologist
Wechter, Clari Ann manufacturing executive

Moline
Allen, Samuel R. farm equipment manufacturing executive
Badmos, Adebayo Yekeen engineering educator, researcher
Cleaver, William Lehn lawyer
Doerder, Lowell E. mathematics professor
Field, James M. farm equipment manufacturing executive
Harwood, Richard D. science educator
Jenkins, James Robert lawyer, manufacturing executive
Johnson, Mary Lou lay worker, educator
Kasinger, Thomas Paul music educator
Lane, Robert W. farm equipment manufacturing executive
Mack, Michael J., Jr. farm equipment manufacturing executive
McFarland, David Alexander literature and language professor
Pearce, Jay Thomas history educator
Penn, J. B. economist, former federal agency administrator
Schwiebert, Deborah Johnson marketing executive
Taylor, Byron Keith industrial engineer

Monmouth
Cordery, Stacy A. history professor, writer

Morris
Rooks, John Newton lawyer

Morton
Andrews, Cynthia Kay librarian
Sutter, Elaine Joyce elementary school educator

Morton Grove
McKenna, Andrew, Jr. political organization administrator, printing company executive

Mossville
Clary, Wendy Anne principal
Silver, Ronald G. chemical engineer, researcher
Son, Youngjin mechanical engineer

Mount Carroll
Akar, Joseph G. medical educator

Mount Prospect
Catizone, Carmen A. health science association administrator, secretary
Eliason, Birdell painter, educator
Martin, David Julian medical association administrator
Sayers, Gale computer company executive, retired professional football player
Ullman, Christopher Charles school librarian, educator

Mount Vernon
Hall, Sharon Gay retired language educator, artist
Harvey, Morris Lane lawyer
LeMay, Nicholas K. broadcast executive
Withers, W. Russell, Jr. broadcast executive

Mundelein
Berg, Nancy Jeanne music educator
Kwon, Ho-Youn sociologist, researcher

Naperville
Arzoumanidis, Gregory G. chemist
Besanko, Bruce H. retail executive
Broad, Matthew lawyer
Bufalino, Vincent John cardiologist, medical administrator
Burken, Ruth Marie utilities executive
Caliendo, Stephen Maynard political science professor
Cholkeri-Singh, Aarathi gynecologist, surgeon
Crawford, Raymond Maxwell, Jr. management consultant
Desch, Theodore Edward retired insurance company executive, lawyer
Dombeck, Harold Arthur insurance company executive
Finzer, Carolyn Lauing artist
Folk, Frank Anton surgeon, educator
Fritz, Roger Jay management consultant
Gilmore, Brenda René literature and language educator, theater director
Jack, Zachary Michael performing arts educator
Katai, Andrew Andras chemical company executive
Kreipke, Merrill Vincent civil engineer, consultant
Kucera, Jane chemical engineer
Lanham-Murray, Nickole Cynthia theater educator
Larson, Mark Edward, Jr. lawyer, educator, financial planner
Larson, Roy journalist, retired publishing executive
McCallum, Gerald Christopher clinical psychologist
Miller, Charles E. gynecologist
Nash, Donald Gene retired federal investigator, economist
Nieto, Lou food products executive
Nortell, Bruce lawyer
Penisten, Gary Dean entrepreneur
Porumbescu, Doina Roxana psychologist, educator
Pullen, Robert W. telecommunications industry executive
Sellers, Gregory Jude physicist
Sherren, Anne Terry chemistry professor
Stall, Alan David manufacturing executive
Strobel, Russ M. gas industry executive, lawyer
Sukumar, Narayanasami research scientist
Tan, Li-Su Lin accountant, insurance company executive, consultant, registered investment advisor representative
Thacker, Robert George (Bob Thacker) marketing executive
Tibble, Douglas Clair lawyer
Vanagas, Rimantas Andrius (Ray Vanagas) entrepreneur, real estate developer, real estate company executive
VerHoven, Victoria voice educator
Vora, Manu Kishandas chemical engineer, consultant
Wilde, Harold Richard college president

Nashville
Karmeier, Lloyd A. state supreme court justice

New Lenox
Field, Robert Edward lawyer
Heffernan, Debra Jane administrator
Turner, Thomas J. engineering company executive

Niles
Beton, John Allen communications company executive
Renner, Jacqueline Marie industrial and wholesale supply company executive
Roepenack, Dwight Elmer public health service officer

Normal
Alferink, Larry Allen psychology professor
Bender, Paul Edward lawyer
Bowman, Clarence Alvin (Al Bowman) academic administrator
Brown, Lauren Evans zoologist, researcher, educator
Devinatz, Victor Gary industrial relations specialist, educator
Goodwin, Stephen Arthur marketing educator
Hattangady, Dipti Shashidhar Jyoti microbiologist, educator
Hoy, Jessica De May language educator
Huff, Cynthia Anne English educator
Kim, In-Sop speech professional, educator
Koch, John Michael music educator, singer
Lind, Nancy Susan political science professor
Lord, Timothy Charles philosophy educator
MacMinn, Richard Dean finance educator
Mockford, Edward Lee biologist, educator
Payne, James Earl economics professor, dean
Segelcke, Elke literary scholar
Shields, John Charles literature educator
Suh, Kyoungwon science educator, researcher
Throckmorton, Peter Eugene retired organic chemist, consultant
Titus, Janet Catherine psychologist, researcher
Trouille, Mary Seidman foreign language educator
Vetere, Michael J. III theater educator

Norridge
Petrakis, Myron Titos retired mechanical engineer

North Chicago
Chedid, Antonio pathologist, educator, researcher
Gall, Eric Papineau internist, educator
Hawkins, Richard Albert medical educator, administrator
Khraisat, Ahmad internal medicine, adult cardiovascular medicine
Kim, Yoon Berm immunologist, educator
Kosson, David Steven psychology professor
Loga, Sanda physicist, researcher
Nair, Velayudhan pharmacologist, educator, academic administrator
Schneider, Arthur Sanford medical educator
Sierles, Frederick Stephen psychiatrist, educator
Singh, Sarabjeet cardiologist

Northbrook
Afterman, Allan B. accountant, educator, financial consultant, researcher
Ben-Arie, Ronit Peleg elementary school educator
Brune, Catherine Spearman insurance company executive
Civgin, Donald E. insurance company executive
Clarey, John Robert executive recruiter, consultant
Cripe, Frederick F. insurance company executive
Cruikshank, John W. III insurance agent
Cucco, Ulisse P. retired obstetrician, gynecologist
Di Spigno, Guy Joseph industrial psychologist, international management consultant
Dubin, Arthur Detmers retired architect
Edelson, Ira J. venture capitalist
Feibel, Frederick Arthur financial consultant
Gratalo, John, Jr. banker, small business owner
Greffin, Judith insurance company executive
Griffiths, Robert Pennell banker
Kahn, Sandra S. psychotherapist
Keehn, Silas retired bank executive
King, Robert Charles biologist, educator
Lapin, Harvey I. lawyer
Levenfeld, Milton Arthur lawyer
Levy, Arnold S(tuart) real estate company executive
Mayes, Michele Coleman insurance company executive, lawyer
Metz, Adam S. real estate company executive
Moser, Larry Edward marketing professional
Newman, Lawrence William financial executive
Perelman, Jeffrey E. real estate company executive
Pesmen, Sandra (Mrs. Harold William Pesmen) journalist, educator
Richardson, Joseph J., Jr. insurance company executive
Roche, Michael J. insurance company executive
Rosemarin, Carey Stephen lawyer
Ruebenson, George E. insurance company executive
Sernett, Richard Patrick lawyer
Sorenson, Steven P. insurance company executive
Sudbrink, Jane Marie sales and marketing executive
Wajer, Ronald Edward management consultant
Walker, Joan H. insurance company executive
Warchol, Judith Marie small business owner
Wilson, Thomas Joseph insurance company executive

Northfield
Broos, Carol Linville music educator
Carlin, Donald Walter retired food products executive, consultant
Firestone, Marc food products executive, lawyer
Hadley, Stanton Thomas manufacturing executive, director, lawyer
Mamet, David Alan playwright, scriptwriter
Rosenfeld, Irene B. food products company executive
Shabica, Charles Wright retired geologist, earth science educator
Shillestad, John Gardner diversified financial services company executive
Smeds, Edward William retired food company executive
Stepan, Frank Quinn chemicals executive
Stepan, Frank Quinn, Jr., (F. Quinn Stepan Jr.) chemical company executive
Vilim, Nancy Catherine advertising executive
West, Mary Beth food products executive

Northlake
Haack, Richard Wilson retired police officer

O Fallon
Brown, Jessie Marquita elementary information specialist

Oak Brook
Alvarez, Ralph food products executive
Barnes, Karen Kay lawyer
Bensen, Peter J. food products executive
Biedron, Theodore John publishing and advertising executive
Carroll, Anja Morrisson marketing professional, food service executive
Christian, Joseph Ralph physician
Congalton, Susan Tichenor lawyer, business executive
Coudreaut, Dan chef
Daly, Patrick F. real estate executive, architect
DeLorey, John Alfred printing company executive
Dillon, Mary N. food products executive
Dmowski, W. Paul obstetrician, gynecologist, educator, endocrinologist, researcher
Fenton, Tim food service executive
Fields, Janice L. food service executive
Floersch, Richard R. food service executive, human resources specialist
Golden, Neil B. marketing executive
Goodwin, James E. (Jim Goodwin) retired air transportation executive
Hoffmann, Joan Carol retired academic dean
John, Richard C. enterprise development organization executive
Klinger, Gail Greaves art educator, illustrator
McKenna, Andrew James wholesale distribution, printing company executive, sports association executive
Nelson, Robert Eddinger retired management consultant
Peckenpaugh, Robert Earl investment advisor
Proud, Dayna public relations executive
Ring, Leonard M. lawyer, writer
Santona, Gloria lawyer, food products executive
Serry, Cyrus medical educator
Skinner, James A. food products executive
Thompson, Don food products executive
Wells, Karen food service company executive

Oak Forest
MacMullen, Nancy Jane critical care nurse, department chairman

Oak Lawn
elZein, Chawki Fayez pediatrician, surgeon
Hayani, Ammar pediatrician, director
Jachna, Joseph David photographer, educator
Laird, Jean Elouise Rydeski (Mrs. Jack E. Laird) author, adult education educator

Oak Park
Adelman, William John retired academic administrator, industrial relations specialist
Bedrossian, Ursula Kay Kennedy editor
Burnette, Mark C. librarian
Cannon, Patrick Francis public relations executive
Clark, John Peter III engineer, consultant
Devereux, Timothy Edward advertising executive
Heitzman, Frank Edward architect
Johnson, Porter Wear physics professor emeritus
Matsuda, Takayoshi surgeon, educator, biomedical researcher
Schubert, Blake H. lawyer
Senese, Suzanne Marie art and music educator, performance artist
Sengpiehl, Paul Marvin lawyer, retired state official
Shaw, Leroy Robert retired language educator, writer
Thomas, Malayilmelathethil minister, English language educator
Venerable, Shirley Marie retired gifted and talented educator

Oakbrook Terrace
Gruft, James Harris physiatrist, educator
Keller, Dennis James management educator
Taylor, Ronald Lee academic administrator

Oakland
Eriksen, Barbara Ann writer, researcher

Olive Branch
Shumaker, Jarod Kyle music educator

Olney
Jones, Carmen Rose social sciences educator

Oregon
Haynes, Gary Allen photojournalist, editor

Orland Park
Burfeind, Betty Ruth retired secondary school educator, coach
Evans, Wayne obstetrician, perinatologist
Gorman, John Robert bishop emeritus

Oswego
Johnson, Dawn Sundene chemistry educator

Riccio, Angela *science educator*
Schneider, Glen Walter *music educator, director*
Weinstein-Blackman, Ellen Donna *school psychologist*

Ottawa
Ballowe, James *writer, educator*
Thornton, Edmund B. *philanthropist*

Palatine
Albanese, Jim *electrical engineer*
Bank, Martin Lee *finance company executive, director*
Dittburner, Carl Michael *architect, educator*
Durian, Geoffrey P. *mathematics professor*
Edstrom, James A. *academic librarian*
Hernandez, Ana Lucia *language educator*
Hershenhorn, Robert Gene *bank executive*
Hull, Elizabeth Anne *retired English language educator*
McDonald, Andrew J. *bishop emeritus*
Middleton-Kaplan, Richard Edward *literature and language professor*
Neeley, Henrietta Nance *music school administrator*
Pohl, Frederik *freelance/self-employed writer*
Spinner, Lee Louis *accountant*
Styer, Denise Marie *psychologist*
Victor, Michael Gary *lawyer, physician*
Wilcox, C. Jayne *chemistry professor*
Zamarin, Ronald George *lawyer*

Palos Heights
Powell, Patricia Lynn *education and special education educator*

Palos Hills
Stratton, Pauline A. *retired elementary school educator, alderman*

Palos Park
Walther, Daniel Joseph *historian*

Paris
Essinger, Susan Jane *special education educator*
Hiddle, Susan K. *musician, educator*

Park Forest
Billig, Etel Jewel *theater director, actress*
Cribbs, Maureen Ann *artist, educator*
Dalke, Carl D. *school system administrator, consultant*
Goodrich, John Bernard *consultant*
Orr, Marcia *primary school educator, consultant, director*
Pryor, Vikki Lynn *lawyer*
Sullivan, Patricia Marie *elementary school educator*
Wheeler, Michael Joseph *protective services official, educator*
Williams, Jack Raymond *retired civil engineer*

Park Ridge
Albert, Elizabeth Franz (Mrs. Henry B. Albert) *investor, artist, conservationist*
Barber, Edward Bruce *medical products executive*
Bitran, Jacob David *internist*
Campbell, Bruce Crichton *hospital administrator*
Carr, Gilbert Randle *retired railroad executive*
Delany, Jim (James Edward Delany) *sports association administrator, lawyer*
Hegarty, Mary Frances *lawyer*
Kenney, John Patrick *dentist*
Lampert, Joan *school system administrator*
LaRue, Paul Hubert *retired lawyer*
Novey, Donald W. *physician, health facility administrator*
Pannke-Smith, Peggy *president*
Russell, William Steven *finance executive*
White, John Vincent *surgeon, consultant*

Pearl City
Kostallari, Adrian A. *language educator*

Peoria
Alkhouli, Osama Mohammad *engineer*
Arnold, Rebecca Leigh *theater educator*
Banwart, Sidney C. *human resources executive*
Bertschy, Timothy L. *lawyer*
Buda, James B. *lawyer, manufacturing executive*
Burritt, David B. *manufacturing executive*
Chamberlain, Joseph Miles *retired astronomer, educator*
Corpuz, Laura Balatbat *library coordinator*
de Alarcon, Pedro Antonio *pediatric oncologist, educator*
Eller, Fred Joseph III *entomologist*
Elmore, Donita Lynn *social studies educator*
Fukuchi, Ken-ichiro *medical educator, researcher*
Geiss, Roger William *pathologist, medical educator*
Guzman, Gregory G. *retired history professor*
Heiple, James Dee *retired state supreme court justice*
Hindi, Riyadh *engineering educator, researcher*
Hojilla-Evangelista, Milagros Parker *research chemist and scientist*
Jenky, Daniel Robert *bishop*
Katz, Seth Robert *literature and language professor*
Kelly, Grace Dentino *secondary school educator*
Labeda, David Paul *microbiologist*
Lavin, Richard P. *manufacturing executive*
Levenick, Stuart L. *manufacturing executive*
Lewer, Joshua J. *economics professor*
Liu, Shuangbiao (Jordan) *mechanical engineer*
Lu, Yufeng *engineering educator*
Malinowski, Aleksander *engineering educator*
Masi, Alfonse Thomas *medical educator*
Meriden, Terry *physician*
Mongkolrattanothai, Kanokporn *medical educator*
Oberhelman, Douglas Ray *tractor company executive*
Opdenbosch, Patrick *mechanical engineer, researcher*
Owens, James W. (Jim Owens) *manufacturing executive*
Parsons, Donald James *retired bishop*
Parsons, Richard Hugo *lawyer*
Pearl, Richard H. *surgeon*
Perrilles, Angela Terese *physical therapist*
Rapp, Edward J. *manufacturing executive*
Richerson, James J. *museum administrator, consultant*
Saxon, Randall Lee *pastor, author, educator*
Vittecoq, Gerard R. *manufacturing executive*
Williams, John Alexander *history professor*
Wright, Gina A. *voice educator*
Wunning, Steven H. *manufacturing executive*

Peoria Heights
Grebner, Bernice Prill *author, astrological counselor*

Petersburg
Hallmark, Donald Parker *retired museum director, educator*

Pinckneyville
Cawvey, Clarence Eugene *retired physician*

Plainfield
Chakrabarti, Subrata Kumar *offshore research engineer*
Matlock, B. Jane *science educator*
Schinderle, Robert Frank *retired hospital administrator*

Princeton
Collins, N. Dana *art gallery owner, consultant, retired art educator*

Prospect Heights
Byrne, Michael Joseph *manufacturing executive*
Jenkins, Marlys J. *special education educator*
Lynch, William Thomas, Jr. *advertising executive*

Quincy
Auluck, Nitin *educator*
Mallory, Troy L. *accountant*
Reynolds, Judith Amy *nutritionist, animal scientist, consultant, educator*
Straub, Sunny L. *retired elementary school educator*
Tomczak, Patricia Ann *dean, archivist*
Tyer, Travis Earl *librarian, consultant*

Red Bud
Light, David Mark *retired librarian, retired musician*

Richton Park
Pierce, Mary E. *retired elementary school educator, public relations consultant*

River Forest
Coe, Donald Kirk *retired academic administrator*
Davlin, Mary Clemente *literature and language professor, dominican sister*
Goetz-Sota, Germaine Helen *theatre and speech educator, department chairman*
Jackson, William Vernon *Latin American studies and library science educator*
Johnson, Arvid C. *dean*
Keberlein Gutierrez, Douglas Robert *history professor*
Mason, George Robert *retired surgeon, educator*
O'Meara, Thomas Franklin *priest, educator*
Rodgers, Jan A. *social work educator*
Steinmann, Andrew E. *theology studies educator*
Weldon, Clodagh *theology studies educator*
Wolfe, Regina Wentzel *business ethics educator*

River Grove
Jeans, Mary Millicent *educational association administrator*
McNamara, Dennis K. *art educator*
Stein, Thomas Henry *social sciences educator*

Riverside
Van Cura, Joyce Bennett *librarian*

Riverwoods
Douglas, Bruce Lee *oral and maxillofacial surgeon, occupational and geriatric health educator, consultant*
Gold, Deidra D. *lawyer*
Guthrie, Roy A. *finance company executive*
Hochschild, Roger C. *finance company executive*
Kirby, Emily Baruch *psychologist, writer, academic administrator*
Mandel, Karyl Lynn *accountant*
McNamara Corley, Kelly *lawyer*
Nelms, David W. *finance company executive*
Offereins, Diane M. *finance company executive*
Vollen, Robert Jay *lawyer*

Robbins
James, Marie Moody *clergywoman, musician, vocal music educator*

Robinson
Mallard, Carrie Charlene *science educator*
Rahman, Gaziur *finance educator*
Wolven, Ann Reed *literature and language professor, journalist*

Rochester
Butcher, Mark William *science educator*
Myers, Phillip Ward *retired otolaryngologist*

Rock Island
Blackmer, Michelle A. *women's health nurse, educator*
Goebel, Catherine Carter *art history professor, department chairman*
Horstmann, James Douglas *retired academic administrator*
Rafferty, Genevieve Kennedy *social service agency administrator*
Vivian, Kim *language educator*
Wallace, Franklin Sherwood *lawyer, director*

Rockford
Albert, Janyce Louise *human resources specialist, retired business educator, banker, consultant*
Bienen, Henry Samuel *former academic administrator, political scientist, educator*
Bomgarden, Ryan D. *biotechnologist, educator*
Borling, John Lorin *military officer*
Clodius, Robert LeRoy *retired economist*
Cole, Richie Thomas *musician, composer, educator*
Doran, Thomas George *bishop*
Gieras, Jacek Franciszek *engineering educator, research scientist*
Gregory, Dola Bell *bishop, customer service administrator*
Heerens, Robert Edward *physician*
Homewood, Elizabeth Holmes Nash *elementary school educator*
Hoshaw, Lloyd *retired historian, educator*
Jacobi, Fredrick Thomas *newspaper publisher*
Johanson, John F. *gastroenterologist, researcher*
Johnson, Elizabeth Ericson *retired educator*
Johnson, Thomas Stuart *lawyer*
Kampfe, Doris Elaine *storyteller, folk artist, poet*
Kapala, Frederick J. *federal judge*
King-Sturdivant, Constance Maria *social services administrator*
Koch, Carol Sue *secondary school educator*
Morrissey, Lawrence *Mayor, Rockford, Illinois*
O'Donnell, William David *retired construction firm executive*
Olson, Stanley William *physician, educator, dean*
O'Neill, Arthur Joseph *bishop emeritus*
Pantaleo, Lea *biology professor*
Porterfield, Susan Azar *literature and language professor*
Pryor, Landon Scott *plastic surgeon*
Raymond, Jill M. *microbiologist, educator*
Reno, Roger *lawyer*
Roberts, James Brian *engineer*
Robinson, Donald Peter *musician, retired electrical engineer*
Steele, Carl Lavern *academic administrator*
Sytsma, David Allen *history professor, department chairman*
Tuite, Gerald Francis *lawyer, commercial real estate manager*
Walhout, Justine Simon *chemistry professor*
Walters, Mary Lynn *nursing educator*

Rockton
Bolger, Jacqueline E. *literature and language educator*
Pennell, Danny Joe *social worker*

Rolling Meadows
Carbonell, David *psychologist*
Giampietro, Wayne Bruce *lawyer*
Roti, Thomas David *judge*
Yang, Shing Lung Steven *antenna engineer*

Romeoville
Carey, John Patrick *broadcasting executive and educator*
Hoppe, Elizabeth Anne *philosopher, educator*
Streit, Michael K. *aeronautical engineer, educator*
Tucker, Vicky Rose *systems analyst, director*

Roscoe
Sears, Donna Mae *writer, illustrator*

Roselle
Hanrath, Linda Carol *librarian, archivist*

Rosemont
Blake, Norman Perkins, Jr. *computer company executive*
Good, William Allen *professional society executive*
Meinert, John Raymond *apparel executive, investment banker*
Nichols, Robert Hastings *lawyer*
Reyes, J. Christopher *food products distribution executive*

Rosiclare
Largent, Judy *library director*

Round Lake Beach
Harold, Kathleen T. *elementary school educator*
Harter, Jeremiah Steven *lawyer*

Rushville
Dohner, Russell Rowland *physician*

Saint Charles
Best, William Robert *internist, educator, dean*
Didier, James William *academic administrator, consultant*
LaHood, Julie Ann *small business owner*
Larsen, David Allen *educational consultant*
Malinowski, MaryEllen *photographer, artist*
Thorsen, Denise *language educator*

Savoy
Hoffmeister, Donald Frederick *zoologist, educator*
Sinclair, James Burton *retired plant pathology educator, consultant*

Schaumburg
Adrianopoli, Barbara Catherine *librarian*
Brown, Gregory Q. *communications executive*
Colberg, Linda *physical education educator*
Conrado, Eduardo *marketing executive*
Davis, Joseph Dean *librarian*
Delaney, Eugene A. *electronics executive*
Dore, Patricia Ann *psychologist*
Firsel, Lynne Marie *education educator*
Fitzpatrick, Edward J. *corporate financial executive*
Hill, Raymond Joseph *packaging company executive*
Jha, Sanjay K. *communications executive*
Lawson, A. Peter *lawyer*
MacDonald, William Burke *secondary school educator, consultant*
Marshall, John David *lawyer*
Moloney, Daniel M. *electronics executive*
Nehs, (William) Scott *lawyer*
Otis, James, Jr. *architect*
Soon-Shiong, Patrick *pharmaceutical executive*
Stilling, Mark *psychologist, professional football coach*
Tompson, Marian Leonard *professional society administrator*

Scott Air Force Base
Lichte, Arthur J. *career military officer*
McNabb, Duncan J. *career military officer*
Rondeau, Ann E. *career military officer*

Serena
Freese, Carolyn Lee *art educator*

Seymour
Carringer, Robert *film and language educator*

Shorewood
Heaphy, John Merrill *lawyer*

Skokie
Anthony, Carolyn Additon *librarian*
Bush, Gail *librarian, educator, writer*
Corley, William Gene *engineering research executive*
Fein, Roger Gary *judge*
Filler, Robert *chemist educator*
Guillermo, Linda *clinical social worker*
Hedien, Wayne Evans *retired insurance company executive*
Langguth, Margaret Witty *health facility administrator*
Siegal, Burton Lee *product designer, consultant, inventor*
Turowski, Gregory *plastic surgeon*

South Barrington
Kissane, Sharon Florence *writer, consultant, educator*
Murarka, Narayan P. *electronics engineer, engineering executive*

South Beloit
Dunbar, Ortus Lee *librarian*

South Holland
Anderson, Paul Martin *musician, educator*
Burton, Art T. *history educator*
Connolly, Carla Marie *librarian*
Larsen, Mary Ann Indovina *counselor, educator*
Perry, Joseph Nathaniel *bishop*

Spring Grove
Garrigan, Richard Thomas *finance educator, consultant, editor*
Mason, Janice M. *principal, director*

Springfield
Arnold, Damon Theodore *state agency administrator, public health service officer*
Beckwith, Peter Hess *bishop*
Bell, John Perry *minister, religious organization administrator*
Bhat, Shyam Khandige *psychiatrist, internist, educator*
Brozoski, Thomas J. *otolaryngologist, researcher*
Burkhardt, Barbara Ann *literature and language professor, writer*
Callahan, Charles Daniel *physiatrist, director*
Chan, Hei-Chi *mathematics professor*
Chriswell, Linda D. *special education educator*
Cobb-Myers, Janet Lea *music educator*
Coulson, Elizabeth Anne *physical therapist, educator, Illinois State Representative*
Craig, Ann *library director*
Cullerton, John James *state legislator*
Currie, Barbara Flynn *state legislator*
Davis, Jack *former congressman*
Davis, Monique D. (Deon Davis) *state legislator*
Dodge, Edward John *retired insurance company executive*
Evans, Charles H. *federal judge*
Everingham, Karen E. *museum association administrator*
Giannoulias, Alexi *state treasurer*
Godwin, John E. *hematologist, oncologist*
Hannig, Gary L. *state legislator, state legislator*
Harris, Donald Wayne *research scientist*
Harris, Linda C. *training services executive*
Heaton, Rodger A. *prosecutor*
Hicks, David Eric *retired sports association executive*
Holland, John Madison *retired family practice physician*
Jackson, Jacqueline Dougan *literature educator, writer*
Jefferson, Charles E. *state legislator*
Kerr, Gary Enrico *lawyer, educator, musician*
Khaund, Munindra *educational association administrator*
Klingler, Gwendolyn Walbolt *state representative*
Kocis, Janet Kay *elementary school educator*
Kosel, Renée *state legislator*
Kuhn, Kathleen Jo *accountant*
Laubersheimer, David E. *academic administrator*
LeBlang, Theodore Raymond *law educator, lawyer*
Londrigan, Thomas Foster *lawyer*
Martinez, Iris *state legislator*
Mathewson, Mark Stuart *lawyer, editor*
Mills, Richard Henry *federal judge*
Morse, Saul Julian *lawyer*
Munyer, Edward Arnold *zoologist*
Poole, Connie *medical librarian*
Poorman, Robert Lewis *retired academic administrator*
Quinn, Patrick *Governor of Illinois*
Reed, Robert Phillip *lawyer*
Reyman, Jonathan Eric *archaeologist, anthropologist, researcher*
Roberts, Ryan M. *librarian, educator, webmaster*
Ryan, Daniel Leo *bishop emeritus*
Saltsgaver, Carol Madeleine *mathematics professor*
Schroeder, Joyce Katherine *state agency administrator, research analyst*
Schroeder, Raymond Ernest *educational administrator*

Seney, Ronald Joe *speech educator, theater educator*
Simpson, William Arthur *insurance company executive*
Solis, Jorge A. *state banking agency administrator*
Styles, Bonnie W. *museum director, archaeologist*
Temple, Wayne Calhoun *historian, writer*
Travis, Lawrence Allan *accountant*
Van Meter, Abram DeBois *lawyer, retired banker*
Wehrle, Leroy Snyder *economist, educator*
White, Jesse *Secretary of State, Ill*
Woodson, Gayle Ellen *otolaryngologist*
Yaffe, Stuart Allen *physician*
Zook, Elvin Glenn *plastic surgeon, educator*

Sterling
Moran, Joan Jensen *physical education and healthcare educator*
Pace, Ole Bly III *lawyer*
Tóth, Peter Paul *physician, researcher*

Stoy
Rhoten, Kenneth Dale *writer*

Streamwood
Bailey, Robert Short *retired lawyer*

Streator
Tyne, Gerald Robert *history professor*

Sugar Grove
Ashfaq, Rizwana *biology professor*
Iacopetti, Rebecca *language educator*
Morrical, Art Andrew *communications engineer*

Summit Argo
Fleischman, Gregory Joseph *chemical engineer, researcher*
Trumbore, David C. *retired building materials executive. consultant*

Sycamore
Johnson, Yvonne Amalia *elementary school educator, consultant*
Stone, Van Courtright *not-for-profit developer*
Whisenhunt, Donald Wayne *retired historian, dean, educator*

Table Grove
Thomson, Helen Louise *artist*

Tamms
Vellella, Christopher A. *science educator*

Taylorville
Austin, Daniel William *lawyer*

Tinley Park
Freitag, Carol Wilma *political scientist*
John, Thomas *ophthalmologist*

Toledo
Prather, William C. III *lawyer, writer*

Ullin
Dillow, Rhonda L. *mathematics professor, department chairman*

University Park
Alozie, Emmanuel C. *writer, educator*
Casey, Diane Dates *dean*
Cook, Constance A. *management educator*
Hakala, Reino William *mathematician, educator*
Maimon, Elaine Plaskow *academic administrator*
Saber, Aheda Arafat *chemistry professor*

Urbana
Adesida, Ilesanmi *engineering educator, researcher, dean*
Andersen, Kenneth Eldon *speech communication educator, consultant*
Andrawes, Bassem *engineering educator*
Arnstein, Walter Leonard *retired historian*
Baer, Werner *economist, educator*
Baker, David Hiram *nutritionist, educator*
Barenberg, Ernest John *engineering educator, consultant*
Bateman, Paul Trevier *mathematician, educator*
Beak, Peter Andrew *chemistry professor*
Bennett, Scott Boyce *retired librarian, consultant*
Bergeron, Clifton George *engineer, educator*
Blahut, Richard Edward *electrical and computer engineering educator*
Bocchino, Robert Louis *research scientist*
Boulatov, Roman *chemistry professor*
Brewer, Douglas James *anthropology professor, museum director*
Brichford, Maynard Jay *archivist*
Brunet, Marie-Christine *engineering educator*
Buetow, Dennis Edward *physiologist, educator*
Burkholder, Donald Lyman *mathematician, educator*
Cann, Isaac *microbiologist, educator*
Carroll, Robert Wayne *mathematics professor*
Caulet, Adeline Marie *astronomer*
Chato, John Clark *mechanical and bioengineering educator*
Cheng, Keh-Yung *electrical engineering educator*
Chow, Poo *wood technologist*
Christians, Clifford Glenn *communications educator*
Cisse, Ibrahim *research scientist*
Coleman, Paul Dare *physics and electrical engineering educator*
Conry, Thomas Francis *mechanical engineering educator*
Crang, Richard Francis Earl *plant biologist, writer, research scientist*
Cunningham, Clark Edward *anthropology educator*
Daruka, Govind Prasad *engineering educator, researcher, small business owner, consultant*
Dash, Leon DeCosta, Jr. *journalist*
Dawson, Jeffrey Owen *forester, educator*
Delcomyn, Fred *physiologist, educator, neurobiologist*
Eden, James Gary *electrical engineer, physicist, educator, researcher*
Edgar, Jim *former governor*
Fang, Nicholas X. *engineering educator*
Feng, Albert *science educator, researcher*
Fernandez, Rocio Luz *civil engineer, researcher*
Frederick, Robert George *lawyer*
Gabriel, Michael *psychology professor*
Garcia, Marcelo Horacio *engineering educator, consultant*
Ghosh, Avijit *academic administrator, business educator, former dean*
Giles, Eugene *anthropology educator*
Gillette, Martha U. *neuroscientist*
Gove, Samuel Kimball *retired political science professor*
Granato, Andrew Vincent *physics professor, researcher*
Gropp, William Douglas *computer scientist, educator*
Grossman, Margaret Rosso *law educator*
Gruebele, Martin *chemistry and biophysicist professor*
Haile, H. G. *German language and literature educator*
Hall, William Joel *retired civil engineer, educator*
Ham, MyungJoo *computer scientist*
Hannon, Bruce Michael *engineering educator*
Hasegawa-Johnson, Mark Allan *electrical engineer, educator*
Heath, James Edward *retired physiology educator*
Heichel, Gary Harold *agronomist, educator*
Henderson, Robert Arthur *educator*
Hendrick, George *retired English language educator*
Henson, C. Ward *mathematician, educator*
Hess, Karl *engineering and science educator*
Hlongwa, Tholani *language educator*
Hoeft, Robert Gene *agricultural studies educator*
Holonyak, Nick, Jr. *electrical engineering educator*
Hoxie, Frederick Eugene *history professor*
Huang, Thomas Shi-Tao *electrical engineering educator, researcher*
Iben, Icko, Jr. *astrophysicist, educator*
Jacobson, Sheldon Howard *engineering educator*
Jones, Benjamin Angus, Jr. *retired agricultural engineering educator, science administrator*
Kaufman, Jerome Benzion *retired neurosurgeon*
Kaufman, Paula T. *university librarian*
Kaufmann, Urlin Milo *English literature educator*
Knobloch, Neil A. *education educator*
Korban, Schuyler S. *molecular plant geneticist*
Koshy, Susan *literature and language professor*
Krock, Curtis Josselyn *pulmonologist*
Kumar, Panganamala Ramana *electrical and computer engineering educator*
Langenheim, Ralph Louis, Jr. *geology educator*
Lasersohn, Peter Nathan *linguist, educator*
Lazarus, David *physicist, researcher*
Le, Hieu Khac *information technology executive, researcher*
Lee, Esther Kim *theater educator*
Leggett, Anthony James *physics professor, researcher*
Leon, Arturo Segundo *civil engineer, researcher*
Lieberman, Laurence *poet, educator*
Loui, Michael Conrad *engineering educator*
Love, Joseph LeRoy *history professor, former cultural studies center administrator*
Lu, Stephen Chih-Yang *engineering educator, researcher, consultant*
Luo, Nie *professor engineering physics*
Lüschen, Günther Rudolf Friedo *social sciences educator*
Maeda, Akio *educator*
Mainous, Bruce Hale *foreign language educator*
Makela, Jonathan James *engineering educator*
Makri, Nancy *chemistry professor*
Martinez, Todd J. *chemistry professor*
Maxwell, William Hall Christie *civil and environmental engineer, educator*
May, Walter Grant *chemical engineer, educator*
McKay, John Patrick *history professor*
Meyer, Richard Charles *microbiologist, educator*
Miley, George H. *nuclear and electrical engineering educator, plasma engineer, energy conversion scientist*
Mintel, Richard Walter *chemistry professor*
Moore, Jeffrey Scott *chemist, materials scientist, educator*
Murtha, Joseph Patrick *civil engineer, educator*
Nam, Min-Young *computer scientist*
Nanney, David Ledbetter *geneticist, educator*
Neogi, Natasha Anita *astronaut, educator*
Nettl, Bruno *anthropologist, musicologist, educator*
Nichols, J(ohn) Alden *retired history professor*
Novak, Michael *physician, otologist*
O'Brien, Nancy Patricia *librarian, educator*
Olson, Scott M. *civil engineer, educator*
O'Morchoe, Charles Christopher Creagh *anatomist, surgeon, educator*
Osborn, Howard A. *retired mathematics professor*
Park, Sung-Jin *chemist, educator*
Prussing, Laurel Lunt *mayor, economist*
Puri, Vandana *linguist, educator*
Ra, Hyungshim Yoo *biologist, researcher*
Rao, Nannapaneni Narayana *electrical engineer*
Reagan, Leslie Jean *history professor, writer*
Resek, Robert William *economist*
Rich, Robert F. *law and political science professor*
Rowland, Theodore Justin *physicist, educator, researcher*
Satterthwaite, Cameron B. *physics professor*
Schoeps, Karl Heinz Joachim *German language educator*
Seigler, David Stanley *botanist, educator, chemist*
Sivapalan, Murugesu *engineer educator, consultant*
Sligar, Stephen Gary *molecular biologist, educator*
Snoeyink, Vernon L. *civil engineer, educator*
Snyder, Lewis Emil *astrophysicist, educator*
Solberg, Winton Udell *historian, educator*
Some-Guiebre, Wen-Yam Esther *language educator*
Song, Xiaodong *geophysicist, seismologist*
Spitze, Robert George Frederick *agricultural studies educator*
Stallmeyer, James Edward *engineering educator*
Stillinger, Jack Clifford *language educator*
Suslick, Kenneth Sanders *chemistry professor*
Swenson, George Warner, Jr. *engineering educator*
Switzer, Robert Lee *biochemistry professor*
Talbot, Emile Joseph *French language educator*
Thies, Richard Leon *lawyer, director*
Thompson, Robert Lee *agricultural economist, educator*
Vaughn, Linda F. *musician, educator*
Wah, Benjamin Wan-Sang *electrical and computer engineering educator*
Wandelt, Benjamin Dan *physics and astronomy professor*
Wang, Shaowen *information scientist, geographer, educator*
Wang, Xinlei *science educator*
Warren, Pamela A. *psychologist*
Watson, Paula D. *retired librarian*
Weissinger, Thomas *librarian, educator*
Whitt, Gregory Sidney *evolution educator*
Wirt, Frederick Marshall *retired political scientist, educator*
Woese, Carl R. *biophysicist, microbiology educator*
Wolfe, Ralph Stoner *microbiology educator*
Wuebbles, Donald James *atmospheric scientist, educator*
Yazdani, Ali *physicist, researcher*
Yeung, Ann *music educator*
Zimmerman, Steven Charles *chemistry professor*

Vernon Hills
Cho, Yong Hyo *education educator, consultant*
Edwardson, John Albert *information technology executive*
Gambill, Mark J. *marketing executive*
Kim, Jung *physician, health facility administrator*
Kim, Sachiko O. *music educator*
Klein, Barbara A. *information technology executive*
Leahy, Christine A. *lawyer, information technology executive*
Morcott, Scott M. *physician, health facility administrator*
Powers, Anthony Richard, Jr. *educational sales professional*
Richards, Thomas Edward *information technology executive, former telecommunications industry executive*
Stevens, Jonathan J. *information technology executive*
Zamyatin, Alexander *medical researcher*

Villa Park
Antonelli, Joseph K. *musician, educator*
Ellingsen, Barbara Joyce *music educator*
Pittelko, Roger Dean *clergyman, theology studies educator*

Wadsworth
Ahmad, Moghisuddin *chemist, researcher*
Young, Susan Jean *music specialist*

Warrenville
Boardman, Robert A. *retired lawyer*
Covey, Steven K. *lawyer*
Johnson, Douglas Wells *lawyer*
Ustian, Daniel C. *trucking executive*
Yoon, Seong-Hoon *energy executive, researcher*

Washington
List, Gary Ray *chemist, consultant*

Waterloo
Hoffmann, Mary Jukich *voice educator*

Wauconda
Gotthardt, Mary Jane *school teacher*
Meehan, Jean Marie Ross *human resources, occupational health and safety management consultant*

Waukegan
Houle, Jeanne Larson *retired music educator*
Miller, Helen Elizabeth *art and adult education educator, artist*
Stone, Jed *lawyer*

West Chicago
Fortner, Michael R. *state legislator, physics professor*
Noonan, Josette Marie *music educator*
Paulissen, James Peter *retired pediatrician, county official*

West Frankfort
Gray, Kenneth J. *former congressman*
Williams, Joseph Scott *energy and natural resources company executive, former city commissioner*

Westchester
Berger, Richard A. *orthopedist*
Gordon, Ilene *food products executive*
Holmes, George B., Jr. *orthopedist*
Masterson, John Patrick *retired language educator*
Pavelka, Elaine Blanche *mathematics professor*
Webb, Emily *retired plant morphologist*
Zhang, Yejia (Zhang Yejia) *physiatrist*

Western Springs
Hanson, Heidi Elizabeth *lawyer*

Westmont
Baule, Steven Michael *superintendent*
Friedrich, Charles William *insurance agent*
Kuhn, Christine Marie *library director*
Lucas, Wes W. *relocation company executive*
Schefdore, Ronald L. *dentist*
Warner, H. Ty *entrepreneur, manufacturing executive*

Wheaton
Allen, Henry Lee *sociology educator, consultant*
Cook, Edward David *institute executive director*
Douglas, Cynthia *paraprofessional*
Juhl, Nicole Marie *secondary school educator*
Lawrence-Water, Bette Ann *community health leader*
Leston, Patrick John *judge*
Lim, Cheryl Cheon-Ae *music educator*
Litfin, Duane *academic administrator*
Martin, Marcia Gray *retired architecture educator, artist, designer*
Pak, John *plastic surgeon*
Schwanda, Tom *religious studies educator*
Talbot, Mark Ross *philosophy educator*
Thompson, Bert Allen *retired librarian*
Tucker, Beverly Sowers *library and information scientist*
Warner, William Kent, Jr. *religious organization administrator, consultant*

Wheeling
Keats, Glenn Arthur *manufacturing executive*
Long, Sarah Ann *librarian*

Willowbrook
Foley, Joseph Lawrence *sales executive*
Thomas, Leona Marlene *retired healthcare educator*
Walton, Stanley Anthony III *lawyer*

Wilmette
Albright, Townsend Shaul *brokerage house executive, consultant*
Anderson, J. Trent *retired lawyer*
Atkinson, Jeff John Frederick *lawyer, educator, writer*
Boyle, Antonia Barnes *writer, editor*
Brink, Marion Francis *trade association administrator*
Bunge, Jonathan Gunn *lawyer*
Cherry, Daniel Ronald *lawyer*
Citrin, Judith *counselor, artist, educator*
Coughlan, Gary Patrick *pharmaceutical executive*
Hansen, Andrew Marius *retired library director*
Hier, Daniel Barnet *neurologist*
Lopez, Tania *literature educator*
Miripol, Jerilyn Elise *poet, writer, writing therapist*
Monter, E. William *retired history professor*
Olson, Patricia Hagey *retired elementary school educator*
Schloss, Nathan *retired economist*
Smutny, Joan Franklin *academic director, educator*
Wadden, Richard Albert *environmental engineer, educator, science administrator, consultant*
Wentz, Pete (Peter Lewis Kingston Wentz III) *musician*
Wishner, Maynard Ira *retired finance company executive, lawyer*

Winfield
Sporer, Scott M. *orthopedist, surgeon*

Winnetka
Berner, Robert Lee, Jr. *lawyer*
Cole, Kathleen Ann *advertising executive, social worker*
Crowe, Robert William *lawyer, mediator*
Greenblatt, Ray Harris *lawyer*
Hales, Daniel B. *lawyer*
Hickman, Frederic W. *retired lawyer*
Klapperich, Frank Lawrence, Jr. *investment banker*
Ladd, David Scott *music educator*
McKee, Judith Nelson *elementary school educator, educational consultant*
McWhirter, Bruce J. *retired lawyer*
Plowden, David *photographer*
Quaal, Ward Louis *broadcast executive*
Rossi, Ennio C. *internist, educator*
Rubnitz, Myron Ethan *pathologist, educator*
Sick, William Norman, Jr. *technology company executive*
Thomas, John Thieme *management consultant*
Weber, John Bertram *architect*
Webster, David Macpherson *lawyer*

Woodridge
Farrug, Eugene Joseph, Sr. *retired lawyer*
Jandes, Kenneth Michael *retired superintendent of schools*
Kolek, Mary Eileen *principal*
Murray, Eileen K. *investment company executive*
O'Connor, William Michael *search company executive*
Puthenpurakal, Joseph Mathew *information technology executive*

Woodstock
Dorn, Diane M. *science educator*

Yorkville
Rytkonen, Katie *psychologist*

Zion
Akouris, Dianne *elementary school educator*
Hilyard, Nann Blaine *librarian*

INDIANA

Alexandria
Irwin, Gerald Port *physician*

Anderson
Bailey, Michael John *biology professor*
Bracken, Linda Darlene *medical/surgical nurse*
Carrell, Terry Eugene *manufacturing executive*
Chappell, Rebecca A. *music educator*
Clanin, Douglas Edward *editor, researcher*
Conrad, Harold August *retired religious pension board executive*
Nicholson, Dorothy Nelis *retired pre-school educator*
Nicholson, Robert Arthur *college president*
Scott, John Toner *retired lawyer*
Shively, Fredrick Harold *religious studies educator*
Shrock, Joel D. *history professor*

Angola
Cain, Tim J. *lawyer*

Deller, Jean A. *academic administrator*
Laker, Craig William *social sciences educator*
Lin, Ping-Wha *engineering educator, consultant*

Auburn
Johnson, George Axil III *television producer*

Avon
Alsop, Thomas Walter *secondary education educator*

Batesville
Classon, Rolf Allan *pharmaceutical company executive*
Soderberg, Peter H. *health products executive*

Bedford
Hunter, Harlen Charles *orthopedic surgeon*

Beech Grove
Day, N. Susie *councilwoman*

Bloomington
Anderson, Judith Helena *English language educator*
Arnove, Robert Frederick *education educator*
Assensoh, Akwasi Bretuo *historian, educator*
Barnes, A. James *dean*
Baude, Patrick Louis *law educator*
Becker, William Edward *economist, consultant*
Belth, Joseph Morton *retired business educator*
Bernhardt-Kabisch, Ernest Karl-Heinz *English and comparative literature educator*
Bonser, Charles Franklin *public administration educator*
Bornholdt, Laura Anna *academic administrator*
Brehm, Sharon Stephens *psychology professor, former academic administrator*
Brescia, William Fred, Jr. *development officer*
Brinkman, Paul Del(bert) *retired foundation administrator, journalist, educator*
Brown, Keith *musician, educator*
Bullard, Thomas Eddie *researcher*
Chaifetz, Marshal Lawrence *educational consultant, educator*
Chang, Fwu-Ranq *economics professor, researcher*
Chen, Yu *medical educator*
Choksy, Jamsheed Kairshasp *historian, religious scholar, humanities educator, language educator*
Clemmer, Wendy Renee Saffell *biochemist*
Conrad, Geoffrey Wentworth *archaeologist, educator*
Crean, Tom (Thomas Aaron Crean) *men's college basketball coach*
Cummings, Jack Alan *psychology professor*
Dalmau, Michelle *library and information scientist*
Das, Narayan Chandra *physicist, chemist, researcher*
Dunn, Jon Michael *logician, dean emeritus, consultant*
Effron, David Louis *conductor, performing company executive*
Eisenberg, Paul David *philosophy educator*
El-Shamy, Hasan M. *philosopher, educator*
Engs, Ruth Clifford *health educator, historian*
Franklin, Timothy A. *communications educator*
Gealt, Adelheid Maria *museum director*
Gest, Howard *microbiologist, educator*
Gouker, Jane Ann *music educator*
Graham, John David *dean, former federal agency administrator*
Guth, Sherman Leon (S. Lee) *psychologist, educator*
Hanson, Karen *philosopher, educator*
Hattin, Donald Edward *geologist, educator*
Hawley, Kimra *computer company executive*
Henson, Jane Elizabeth *information management professional, adult education educator*
Hertz, David Michael *literature and arts educator*
Hites, Ronald Atlee *chemist, educator*
Hustad, Thomas Pegg *marketing educator, association executive*
Jackson, Jason Baird *folklorist, director*
Jacobi, Peter Paul *journalism educator, writer*
Johnsen, Dawn E. *law educator, former federal agency administrator*
Johnson, Owen Verne *historian, educator*
Kallaur, Barbara *music educator*
Kauffman, Erle Galen *geologist, paleontologist*
Kiesgen, Paul *music educator*
Kuratko, Donald F. *entrepreneurial educator, consultant*
Lebano, Edoardo Antonio *foreign language educator*
Lee, Don Yoon *publishing executive, academic administrator, writer*
Leeper, Eric M. *economics professor*
Letsinger, Robert Lewis *chemistry professor*
McCraw, Michael *music educator*
McDonald, Susann Hackett *music educator*
McRobbie, Michael Alexander *academic administrator, computer scientist, educator*
Mechref, Yehia *biochemist, director*
Mehlinger, Howard Dean *education educator*
Meho, Lokman I. *library and information scientist, educator*
Mellencamp, John (John Cougar) *singer, lyricist*
Merino, Enrique *retired geochemistry professor*
Mickel, Emanuel John *foreign language educator*
Mobley, Tony Allen *foundation administrator, former dean, recreation educator*
Moore, Ward Wilfred *medical educator*
Murray, Haydn Herbert *geology educator*
Newman, Paul *linguist, educator*
O'Hearn, Robert Raymond *stage designer*
O'Meara, Patrick O. *political science professor*
Ortiz, Gerardo *physicist, researcher*
Ostrom, Elinor *political science professor, researcher*
Peebles, Christopher Spalding *anthropologist, educator, academic administrator*
Perkins, William Clyde *business educator*
Peters, Dennis Gail *chemist*
Peterson, M. Jeanne *historian, educator*
Phillips, Harvey G. *musician, performing arts educator*
Pollock, Robert Elwood *nuclear scientist*
Port, Robert Frederick *linguist*
Prosser, Franklin Pierce *computer scientist*
Puri, Madan Lal *mathematics professor*
Ransel, David Lorimer *history professor*
Reingold, David Ami *sociologist, educator*
Reinisch, June Machover *psychologist, educator, researcher*
Risinger, C. Frederick *social studies educator*
Robel, Lauren *dean, law educator*
Robinson, Jennifer Meta *senior lecturer, consultant*
Rosenberg, Samuel Nathan *French and Italian language educator*
Rudolph, Lavere Christian *library director*
Ruesink, Albert William *biologist, plant sciences educator*
Ryan, John William *academic administrator*
Saunders, W(arren) Phillip, Jr. *economics professor, consultant, writer*
Scheiber, Laura Lee *archaeologist, educator*
Schurz, Scott Clark *newspaper executive*
Serot, Brian David *physics professor*
Shapshay, Sandra Lynne *philosopher, educator*
Shen, Chun-Yen *mathematics professor*
Sinor, Denis *history professor, linguist*
Smith, Carl Bernard *education educator*
Smith, Daniel C. *dean, finance educator*
Smith, Janet Sue *systems process specialist*
Smith, Linda B. *psychology professor, department chairman*
Spera, Dominic Gregorio *music educator, writer*
Stoeltje, Beverly June *liberal studies educator*
Studwell, William Emmett *librarian, writer*
Taylor, Jill Bolte *neuroanatomist*
Temam, Roger M. *mathematician, educator*
Thorelli, Sarah V. *economist, researcher*
Valdman, Albert *language and linguistics educator*
von Furstenberg, George Michael *economics professor, researcher*
Ward-Steinman, David *composer, music educator, pianist*
Watson, Charles Schoff *psychology professor*
Watts, Edward Jay *history professor*
Webb, Charles Haizlip, Jr. *retired dean*
Webb, Lisa Michelle *regulatory affairs manager*
Weinberg, Eugene David *microbiologist, educator*
Wentworth, Jack Roberts *business educator, consultant*
Wigley, Diana Gail *respiratory therapist*

Bluffton
Brockmann, William Frank *retired health facility administrator*

Boonville
Campbell, Edward Adolph *judge, electrical engineer*

Bristow
James, Marion Ray *retired publishing executive, editor*

Brownstown
Robertson, Joseph Edmond *grain processing company executive*

Burlington
Roussakis, Peter Ellwood *minister, publisher*

Carmel
Burkett, Robert E., Jr. *lawyer, insurance company executive*
Cohen, Marlene Lois *pharmacologist*
DeHayes, Daniel Wesley *business educator*
Eden, Barbara Janiece *commercial and residential interior designer*
Frazer, Margaret L. *neurologist, director*
Goodwin, William Maxwell *financial executive, retired*
Husman, Catherine Bigot *retired insurance company executive, consultant*
Mahoney, Margaret Ellis *advertising executive*
McLaughlin, Harry Roll *architect*
Pickens, Robert Bruce *retired accountant*
Priestley, Jason (Jason Bradford Priestley) *actor*
Prieur, C. James *insurance company executive*
Rand, Leon *academic administrator*
Rychlak, Joseph Frank *psychologist, educator*
Shoup, Charles Samuel, Jr. *chemicals and materials executive*
Sukapdjo, Wilma Irene *language educator*
Walsh, John Charles *investment company executive, director*

Chesterfield
Fry, Meredith Warren *retired civil engineer*

Chesterton
Crewe, Albert Victor *physicist, researcher, artist*
Martino, Robert Salvatore *orthopedic surgeon*
Petrakis, Harry Mark *author*
Wiemann, Marion Russell, Jr., (Baron of Camster) *biologist, ambassador general*

Cicero
Howe, James Tarsicius *retired insurance company executive*

Columbia City
Gust, Korrine Marie *education educator*

Columbus
Abts, Henry William *retired banker*
Blackwell, Jean Stuart *manufacturing executive*
Boll, Charles Raymond *engine company executive*
Bowden, David *conductor*
Harrison, Patrick Woods *lawyer*
Herman, Alexis Margaret *former United States Secretary of Labor*
Izadian, Afshin *electrical engineer, researcher*
Linebarger, Thomas (Norman Thomas Linebarger) *manufacturing executive*
Miller, William Irwin *finance company executive*
Rose, Marya Mernitz *lawyer*
Satterthwaite, Tony *manufacturing executive*
Schmidt, Steven Jameson *library director*
Solso, Theodore M. *manufacturing executive*
Spector, Judith Ann *retired english educator*
Tucker, Thomas Randall *public relations executive*
Wall, John C. *manufacturing executive*
Ward, Patrick J. *manufacturing executive*
Williams, Robert Joseph *behavioral health services executive, psychologist*

Connersville
Brooks, Susan W. *lawyer, academic administrator, former prosecutor*
Newton, Cindy Lynn *middle school educator, media specialist*

Corydon
Kelty, Paul David *obstetrician, educator*
Miller, Judith Elaine *retired middle school educator, musician*

Crawfordsville
Barnes, James John *historian, educator*
Catlin-Legutko, Cinnamon *museum director*
Fisher, A. James *theater educator, director, actor*
White, Patrick E. *academic administrator*

Donaldson
Buchanan, Thomas Wayne *history professor*

East Chicago
Chukwulebe, Bernard Obioma *manufacturing executive, consultant*
Platis, Mary Lou *media specialist*

Elkhart
Carnall, Timothy W. *music educator*
Eddy, Darlene Mathis *poet, educator*
Free, Helen Murray *retired chemist consultant*
Gassere, Eugene Arthur *lawyer, investment company executive*
Lawson, William Hogan III *electrical motor manufacturing executive*
Mathias, Margaret Grossman *manufacturing company executive, leasing company executive*
Mischke, Frederick Charles *retired manufacturing executive*
Treckelo, Richard M. *lawyer*
Vite, Frank Anthony *realtor*

Evansville
Baker, Gloria Marie *artist*
Bone, Paul *literature and language professor*
Brill, Alan Richard *entrepreneur*
Dallinger, Carol J. *music educator*
Ellerbrook, Niel Cochran *gas industry executive*
Fiedler, Anne Hastings *music educator*
Gettelfinger, Gerald Andrew *bishop*
Harrison, Joseph Heavrin *lawyer*
Hayes, Philip Harold *lawyer*
Jennings, Stephen Grant *academic administrator*
Kimberling, Clark Hershall *mathematics professor, small business owner*
Koch, Robert Louis, II, *manufacturing company executive, mechanical engineer*
Muehlbauer, James Herman *manufacturing and distribution executive*
Reed, R. Douglas *music educator*
Roth, Carolyn Louise *art educator*
Shoulders, Patrick Alan *lawyer, educator*
Streetman, John William III *museum director*
Wallace, Paul J. *lawyer*

Fishers
Christenson, Le Roy Howard *missions mobilizer*
Shults, Anna *elementary school educator*
Thomas, John Arlen *pharmacologist, educator, science administrator*

Fort Wayne
Anderson, Kathleen Marie *lawyer*
Bacchus, Harold Mustapha *physician*
Bard, Gary G. *academic administrator, dean*
Boylan, Daniel H. *finance educator*
Busse, Keith E. *manufacturing executive*
Camara, Esperanca Maria *art historian, educator*
Carroll, Betty Jean *retired application developer*
Colvin, Sherrill William *lawyer*
D'Arcy, John Michael *bishop*
Flinspach, Joan L. *museum administrator*
Glick, Anna Margaret *real estate broker, consultant*
Gutreuter, Jill Stallings *financial consultant, planner*
Helmke, Paul (Walter Paul Helmke Jr.) *lawyer, former mayor*
Henry, Thomas C. *Mayor, Fort Wayne, Indiana*
Khamalah, Joseph N. *finance educator, researcher*
Klugman, Stephan Craig *newspaper editor*
Krull, Jeffrey Robert *library director*
Lee, Shuishih Sage *pathologist*
Lee, Timothy Earl *international agency executive, paralegal*
Logan, Thomas D. *lawyer*
Mahmoud, Aly Ahmed *electrical engineering educator*
Maiko, Saneta Morara *educator and director*
Marine, Clyde Lockwood *agricultural products supplier, consultant*
Moustafa Leonard, Karen *finance educator*
Njock Libii, Josué *mechanical engineer, educator*
Pope, Mark Andrew *lawyer, academic administrator*
Rassuli, Ali *economist, consultant*
Richardson, Joseph Hill *physician, medical educator*
Salam, Gohar Azam *physician, director*
Shuster, Kirk Steven *retired primary school educator*
Smith, Matthew Joseph *literature and language professor*
Streeter, Robert Davenport *electrical engineer, consultant*
Sutter, Richard C. *anthropologist, educator*
Tahmassebi, Daryoush *chemistry professor*
Tourkow, Joshua Isaac *lawyer*

Fortville
Horner, Sylvia Ann *minister, real estate broker*

Fowler
Weist, William Bernard *lawyer*

Frankfort
Borland, Kathryn Kilby *writer*
LeBlanc, John Keith *manufacturing executive*
Sayers Butler, Patricia Ann *secondary school educator*

Franklin
Colburn-Alsop, Sara Noelle *language educator*
Hamner, Lance Dalton *judge*
Nuwer, Henry Joseph (Hank Nuwer) *journalist, educator*

Gary
Lin, Tin-Chun *economics professor, director*
Morgan, Dorothy Ann *literature and language educator*
Needleman, Ruth Ann *social sciences educator*
Schoon, Kenneth James *science educator, writer*
Smith, Vernon G. *education educator, Indiana State Representative*
Strupeck, C. David *accounting educator*

Goshen
Meyer, Albert James *educational researcher*

Granger
Cook, Pamela Margaret *French educator*
Marino, Joseph Paul, Sr. *dean, chemist, researcher*
Morgan, Ardys Nord *school improvement consultant*

Greencastle
Belyavski-Frank, Masha *literature and language professor, linguist*
Bottoms, Robert Garvin *academic administrator, director*
Casey, Brian William *academic administrator, history professor*
Dittmer, John Avery *history professor*
Farber, Robert Holton *retired dean*
Phang, May *music educator*
Spicer, Harold Otis *retired English language educator, communications educator*
Weiss, Robert Orr *speech educator*

Greenfield
Coleman, Mark R. *research scientist*
Hunter, Robert Paul *pharmacologist, senior research scientist*

Greensburg
Mills, Linda Lou *media specialist*

Greenwood
Greenbaum, Larry Marc *rheumatologist*
Hagedorn, Alan Patrick *social studies educator*
Koch, Michael Oscar *urologist*
Van Valer, Joe Ned *lawyer, real estate developer*

Griffith
Luetschwager, Mary Susan *educational consultant*

Hammond
Capp, David A. *prosecutor*
Detmer, David *philosopher, educator*
Diamond, Eugene Christopher *lawyer, health facility administrator*
Fathizadeh, Masoud *engineering educator*
Hansen, Jack Winsor *musician, educator*
Marrero, Benjamin *electrical engineer, educator*
Mitra, Amlan *economics professor, researcher*
Napora, Robert Alan *physics professor*
Neff, Gregory Pall *mechanical engineer, educator*
Parashar, Neeti *physics professor, researcher*
Pierson, Edward Samuel *engineering educator, consultant*
Rowberg, Kathryn L. *chemistry professor*
Van Bokkelen, Joseph Scott *federal judge, former prosecutor*

Hanover
Aguilar-Monsalve, Luis Antonio *language educator, writer*
Batchvarova, Madlen Todorova *music educator, conductor*
Dalka, Laverne Barbara *language educator*
Fearnow, Mark Allen *theater educator, writer*
Katsov, Yefim *mathematics professor*
Nickels, Ruth Elizabeth *band director*

Hebron
Walker, Joyce L. *music educator*

Hobart
Arand, Frederick Francis *accountant, finance company executive*

Huntington
Spenner, Richard Lee *media specialist*

Indianapolis
Albrecht, Willard Harold *retired medical educator*
Albright, Terrill D. *lawyer*
Allen, David James *lawyer*
Allen, Stephen D(ean) *pathologist, microbiologist*
Anderson, Maxwell L. *museum director*
Applegate, Kimberly Elaine *radiologist*
Armitage, Robert Allen *lawyer, pharmaceutical executive*
Avery, Melissa J. *lawyer*
Badger, David Harry *lawyer*
Baetzhold, Howard George *retired language educator*
Bailey, Dustin A. *school system administrator, secondary school educator*
Baird, Carol Lynne *nursing educator*
Ballard, Gregory A. *Mayor, Indianapolis, retired military officer*
Banya, Santonino Ku'Caya *science educator*
Barcus, Robert Gene *retired educational association administrator*
Barman, Charles Roy *science educator*
Bateman, Paul C., Jr. *councilman*
Beckwith, Lewis Daniel *lawyer*
Beer, Lori A. *health insurance company executive*

Bein, Frederick L. geography educator
Bennett, Tony (Charles A. Bennett) state official, school system administrator
Bepko, Gerald Lewis retired academic administrator, law educator
Bird, Larry Joe professional sports team executive, retired professional basketball player
Bleher, Pavel M. mathematics professor
Blythe, James David, II, lawyer
Bodenhamer, David Jackson historian, educator
Boehm, Theodore Reed state supreme court justice
Boldt, Michael Herbert lawyer
Boling, Joseph Edward numismatist, retired military officer
Boor, Anthony W. electronics executive
Born, Samuel Roydon, II, retired lawyer, practicing mediator and arbitrator
Bowyer, Suzanne Louise pediatrician, educator
Boxer, Mark L. healthcare insurance company executive
Braly, Angela Fick health insurance company executive, lawyer
Bramble, Laura library director
Brandt, Ira Kive pediatrician, geneticist
Brater, Donald Craig medical educator, dean
Braun, Robert Clare retired association and advertising executive
Brenner, Mark Lee academic administrator, physiologist, educator
Bright, John J. medical researcher
Broome, Marion E. dean, nursing educator
Brown, Edwin Wilson, Jr. preventive medicine physician, educator
Brown, Frank Burch theology studies educator, writer
Brown, Randy L. human resources specialist, health insurance company executive
Brown, Vernon councilman
Broxmeyer, Hal Edward medical educator
Buechlein, Daniel Mark archbishop
Bull, Marilyn Jean pediatrician, educator
Buranello, Raymond Terrence quality assurance executive, chemist
Burgomaster, Frederick music director
Burr, David Bentley anatomy educator
Cain, Virginia J. councilwoman
Caine, Virginia A. city health department administrator
Caldwell, Jim professional football coach
Campo, Gabrielle Nicole social worker
Cannon, John III lawyer, insurance company executive
Cardwell, Jeff Councilman
Cardwell, Sue Webb psychology professor
Carlisle, Sheila A. judge
Catchings, Tamika Devonne professional basketball player
Cato, Mo M. professional soccer coach, educator
Cheng, Liang pathologist
Chiang, Alan Y. statistician
Chism, Lauren P. educational association administrator
Choplin, John M., II, lawyer
Christen, Arden Gale dental educator, researcher, consultant
Christian, Joe Clark medical genetics researcher, educator, medical genetics researcher, educator
Clark, Charles M., Jr. medical school administrator
Clark, J. Murray (Murray Clark) political organization administrator, lawyer
Cleary, Robert Emmet gynecologist, infertility specialist
Cliff, Johnnie Marie mathematics and chemistry professor
Cockrum, Bob councilman
Coleman, Edward councilman
Coleman, John Joseph III plastic surgeon, educator
Conley, Robert R. psychiatrist, educator
Connor, Ulla M. linguistics educator
Cowen, Carl C. mathematics professor
Crabb, David William medical educator, researcher
Cravens, Gary Dean information scientist, physician
Crow, Paul Abernathy, Jr. retired minister
Dai, Yuan-Shun education educator
Dale, Robert Howard Ingleby psychology educator
Dalsing, Michael Cletus surgeon, educator
Daly, Walter Joseph medical educator
Daniels, Mitchell Elias, Jr. Governor of Indiana, former federal official
Davis, Edgar Glenn healthcare executive, educator
DeVeydt, Wayne S. health insurance company executive
de Waal, Cornelis philosophy professor, editor
Dickson, Brent E. state supreme court justice
DiMeglio, Linda A. pediatrician, endocrinologist, researcher
Divita, James J. retired social studies educator, writer, researcher
Dorrel, Ruth editor
Drentlicher, David lawyer, educator, physician
Dressel, Barry museum director
Dunayevich, Eduardo pharmaceutical executive
Dunn, Lin professional basketball coach
Durell, Todd psychiatrist, medical researcher
Dutton, Stephen James lawyer
Dyken, Mark Lewis, Jr. neurologist, educator
Easter, Jeanmarie conservator
Einhorn, Lawrence Henry oncologist, medical educator
Elberger, Ronald Edward lawyer
Enright, William Gerald religious institute administrator
Evans, Jose M. Councilman
Everly, Jack conductor
Everson, Mark Whitty commissioner
Ewbank, Thomas Peters lawyer, retired banker
Farag, Sherif Shafik physician scientist, educator
Faulk, Marshall Williams retired professional football player
Fels, James Alexander lawyer, mediator
Fife, Rose Spitz educator
Fink, Daniel L. hospital administrator
Finley, Katherine Mandusic professional society administrator
Fisher, Gene Lawrence controller, accountant
Fitzgerald, Joseph Francis pediatric gastroenterologist
FitzGibbon, Daniel Harvey lawyer
Florestano, Dana Joseph architect
Floyd, James M., Jr. adult education educator
Fluegel, Brad M. health insurance company executive
Ford, Terrence Jerod (T.J. Ford) professional basketball player
Foster, Kennard P. magistrate judge
Foster, Richard Scott urologist, educator
Fridell, Jonathan Aaron transplant surgeon
Fruehwald, Kristin Gail lawyer
Funk, David Albert retired law educator
Furlow, Mack Vernon, Jr. retired chief financial officer, treasurer
Gaffney, Margaret Mary dermatologist, educator
Gantz, Richard Alan museum administrator
Garmel, Marion Bess Simon retired arts journalist
Gerdes, Ralph Donald fire safety consultant
Ghetti, Bernardino Francesco neuropathologist, educator
Gilliland, John Campbell, II, lawyer
Gilman, Alan B. restaurant company executive
Glasscock, Larry Claborn health insurance company executive
Gnat, Raymond Earl librarian
Goggins, William Christopher surgeon, director
Gooldy, Patricia Alice retired elementary school educator
Goulet, Kenneth R. health insurance company executive
Granger, Danny, Jr. professional basketball player
Gray, Monroe, Jr. councilman
Gregg, Stephen Thompson political scientist, consultant
Grosfeld, Jay Lazar surgeon, educator
Grossman, Peter Zigmund economics professor
Grube, F. William refining company executive
Gunderman, Richard B. medical educator
Gupta, Manju research scientist
Halum, Stacey Leigh otolaryngologist, researcher
Hamilton, David Frank federal judge
Hammons, Timothy A. lawyer
Hancock, Everett Brady retired periodontist
Handel, David Jonathan health facility administrator
Hansbrough, Tyler professional basketball player
Hansell, Richard Stanley obstetrician, gynecologist, educator
Harden, Anita Joyce nurse
Harden, Annette C. recreation director
Harris, Robert B. economics professor
Havlik, Robert John plastic surgeon
Hegel, Carolyn Marie farm owner and organization executive
Helveston, Eugene McGillis pediatric ophthalmologist, educator
Henderson, Ronald Sherman lawyer
Hovde, F. Boyd lawyer
Hsu, Andrew To-ming engineering educator
Hubbard, Allan Brooks chemical company executive, former federal official
Hughes, Charles E. III plastic surgeon
Hunter, Benjamin Councilman
Hurd, William Ward obstetrician, gynecologist
Hynes, Martin Dennis III pharmacologist, toxicologist
Irsay, James Steven professional football team owner
Irvine, Nicholas chemist
Irwin, Glenn Ward, Jr. medical educator, physician, academic administrator
Irwin, Marilyn M. librarian, educator
Jegen, Lawrence A. III law educator
Johnston, Cyrus Conrad, Jr. medical educator
Kalwara, Joseph John engineer
Kappes, Philip Spangler lawyer
Kaufman, Barton Lowell financial services company executive
Kemper, James Dee lawyer
Kerr, William Andrew lawyer, educator
Kessler, Marcia Lynn school psychologist
King, J. B. medical device company executive, lawyer
Kinney, Eleanor De Arman law educator
Kirkpatrick, Robert Hugh communications executive
Knebel, Donald Earl lawyer
Knoebel, Suzanne Buckner cardiologist, educator
Kohart, Mary Beth real estate company executive
Konger, Raymond Lloyd pathologist
Krasean, Thomas Karl retired historian
Kroenke, Kurt medical educator, researcher
Lacy, Andre Balz industrial executive
Lagat, Bernard Olympic track and field athlete
LaGrotto, Louisa middle school educator
Lawrence, William T. federal judge
Lechleiter, John C. pharmaceutical executive
Leganza, Cathleen Ann psychologist
Lemberger, Louis pharmacologist
Lewis, Dijuana K. insurance company executive
Lewis, Maggie councilwoman
Lewis, Randall J. healthcare insurance company executive
Lindseth, Erik Lars humanities educator
Lobley, Alan Haigh retired lawyer
Lofton, Thomas Milton lawyer
Lucchi-Riester, Elisa literature and language professor
Lugar, Thomas R. manufacturing executive
Lutz, Robert councilman
MacDougall, John Duncan thoracic surgeon
Mahern, Brian Councilman
Mahern, Dane councilman
Mahony, Susan pharmaceutical company executive
Malone, Barbara councilwoman
Malone, Jean Hambidge educational consultant
Manders, Karl Lee neurosurgeon
Manning, Peyton Williams professional football player
Mansfield, Angela councilwoman
Marinkovic, Serge Peter urologist, educator, surgeon
Mason, Thomas Alexander historian, educator, author
Mawardi, Osman Kamel retired plasma physicist
McCarthy, Kevin Bart lawyer
Mc Farland, H. Richard food products executive
McHenry, Janice councilwoman
McKeand, Patrick Joseph newspaper publisher, educator
McKinney, Dennis Keith lawyer
McKinney, E. Kirk, Jr. retired insurance company executive
McKinney, Larry J. federal judge
McQuillen, Michael J. Councilman
Mead, Susanah M. law educator
Miller, Cynthia S. healthcare insurance company executive
Minton-McNeill, Doris councilwoman
Mirsky, Arthur retired geologist, educator
Moelhman, Amy Jo social worker
Monroe, Judith A. state agency administrator, public health service officer
Moore, David Harry medical educator
Moriarty Adams, Mary Bridget councilwoman, human resources specialist
Morris, James Thomas former international organization official
Morrison, Timothy M. prosecutor
Morway, David S. professional sports team executive
Mourdock, Richard E. state treasurer
Murphy, Meissa Bleu music educator, behaviorist
Musgrave Moosbrugger, Megan literature and language professor
Najjar, Diana elementary school educator
Nass, Connie Kay state auditor
Neff, Robert Matthew lawyer, finance company executive
Newman, Norman Richard lawyer
Norins, Arthur Leonard dermatologist, educator
Nussbaum, Samuel R. healthcare insurance company executive, medical educator
Nytes, Jackie (M. Jacqueline Nytes) councilwoman
O'Brien, Jim professional basketball coach
Ochs, Sidney neurophysiology researcher, educator
Oliver, William councilman
O'Neil, Joseph pediatrician
Onochie, Florence N. accountant
Packer, C. Subah physiologist, educator
Padgett, Gregory Lee lawyer
Pande, Prakash Narain cardiologist, educator, consultant
Parker, Dan J. political organization administrator
Patchen, Jeffrey Hart museum director, music educator
Patrick, Danica Sue race car driver
Paul, Stephen Howard lawyer
Paul, Steven M. pharmaceutical executive
Pawaskar, Manjiri D. medical researcher
Peribere, Jerome A. agricultural products executive
Petersen, James L. lawyer
Peterson, Bart R. (Barton R. Peterson) pharmaceutical company executive, former mayor
Pfisterer, Marilyn councilwoman
Plowman, Lincoln councilman, protective services official
Poinsette, Donald Eugene engineering executive, management consultant
Polian, Bill professional football team executive
Ralston, Ronald Lee retired manufacturing tradesman
Reuben, Lawrence Mark lawyer
Reynolds, Robert Hugh lawyer
Rice, Derica W. pharmaceutical executive
Ripley, Judith G. state banking agency administrator
Robbins, N. Clay foundation administrator
Roberts, Gary Raymond dean, law educator
Roberts, William Everett lawyer
Robertson, Michael John internist, research scientist, educator
Rogers, Robert Ernest medical educator
Rokita, Todd Secretary of State, Indiana
Ross, Edward cardiologist
Roth, Lawrence Max pathologist, educator
Rovnyak, Steven Michael engineering educator
Rucker, Robert D. state supreme court justice
Russell, David Williams lawyer
Russell, Frank Eli retired newspaper publishing executive
Rutledge, Joanne retired artist consultant
Ryder, Henry Clay lawyer
Ryerson, Dennis R. editor
Sachs, Greg Alan preventive medicine physician
Sadove, Alan Michael plastic surgeon
Sanders, Bob (Demond Sanders) professional football player
Sanders, Joanne councilwoman
Santini, Gino pharmaceutical executive
Sassi, Brian A. health insurance company executive
Saxena, Romil pathologist, educator
Scales, Christine Councilwoman
Scaletta, Phillip Ralph III lawyer
Schaad, Dee Edwin art educator
Schlegel, Fred Eugene lawyer
Schmenner, Roger William business educator
Schmetzer, Alan David psychiatrist
Schmid, John A. musician, voice educator
Schroyer, Michael Kevin healthcare consultant, hospital executive
Scism, Daniel Reed lawyer
Shaheen, Greg A. sports association executive
Shepard, Randall Terry state supreme court chief justice
Shula, Robert Joseph lawyer
Simon, David real estate company officer
Simon, Herbert real estate developer, professional sports team owner
Simon, Melvin real estate developer, professional sports team owner
Skillman, Becky Sue Lieutenant Governor of Indiana, former state legislator
Slaymaker, Gene Arthur public relations executive
Slocum, Judith Ann retired elementary school educator
Smith, Curt think tank executive, journalist
Smith, Donald Archie religious business executive, consultant
Smith, James Warren pathologist, educator, microbiologist, parasitologist
Smith, Kent B. councilman
Sokolov, Richard Saul real estate company executive
Spanogle, Robert William marketing and advertising company executive, association administrator
Speedy, Mike councilman, real estate consultant
Stayton, Thomas George lawyer
Stern, Phyllis Noerager nursing educator
Stevens, Brad K. men's college basketball coach
Stewart, Paul Arthur pharmaceutical company executive
Stewart, Sandra Kay dean
Stitle, Stephen A. bank executive
Strain, James Arthur lawyer
Sullender, Joy Sharon retired elementary school educator
Sullivan, Frank, Jr. state supreme court justice
Sutton, Gregory Paul obstetrician, gynecologist
Swhier, Claudia Versfelt lawyer
Swindle, Ralph Wilson, Jr. research psychologist
Sykes, Linda Diane retired elementary school educator
Tabler, Norman Gardner, Jr. lawyer
Taskonak, Burak medical educator, dentist
Tatom, John Anthony economist
Tellman, William C. dentist
Tezanos-Pinto, Rosa Hispanic American literature educator
Thurston, Kathy Lynn paralegal
Tudor, Tamara theater educator
Turner, Charles Hall biomedical engineer, educator
Turner-Wright, Marie Annetta retired librarian
Vanausdall, John museum director
VanTyle, Jeanne Hawkins pharmacy educator, consultant
VanVoorhis, Rebecca Jane social sciences educator, consultant
Vaughn, Ryan councilman
Vereen, Robert Charles retired trade association administrator
Villers, Lynne M. curator
Vinatieri, Adam Matthew professional football player
Von Ah, Diane Marie nursing researcher, educator
Vorndran-Jones, MaCharri lawyer, chemist
Watanabe, August Masaru physician, educator, retired pharmaceutical executive
Watkins, Harold Robert minister
Watkins, Sharon Elizabeth minister, religious organization administrator
Watson, David E. toxicologist, consultant
Watts, John S., Jr. insurance company executive
Weber, George oncology and pharmacology educator, researcher
Wheldon, Dan (Daniel Clive Wheldon) race car driver
White, Eugene G. school system administrator
White, James Patrick law educator
Williams, Bernard Olympic athlete
Williams, Eric S. cardiologist, educator
Williams, Luida K. retired elementary school educator
Wilson, Richard Harry, Jr. congressional chief of staff
Wishard, Gordon Davis, Sr. lawyer
Wong, David T. biochemist, researcher
Woodring, DeWayne Stanley religious organization administrator
Woods, Jeffrey George economist, researcher
Woolling, Kenneth Rau vascular internist
Wright, David Burton retired newspaper publishing company executive
Wu, Min cell biologist, researcher, educator
Yao, Yongxue immunologist
Yovits, Marshall Clinton information scientist, educator, dean
Zipes, Douglas Peter cardiologist, researcher
Zoeller, Greg state attorney general

Jasper
Brenner, Raymond Anthony priest

Jeffersonville
Hoehn, Elmer Louis lawyer, state and federal agency administrator, educator, consultant
Reisert, Charles Edward, Jr. realtor, real estate developer
Sodrel, Michael Eugene former congressman, small business owner
Walburn, John Clifford retired mental health services professional

Kendallville
Tipton, Deborah Jo psychologist

Kokomo
Coppock, Janet Elaine retired mental health nurse
Maugans, John Conrad lawyer
Sarratore, Steven T. academic administrator
Stein, Eleanor Bankoff retired judge
Tucker, Katherine Louise elementary school educator
Wysong, Earl Edward sociologist, educator

Kouts
Miller, Sarabeth secondary school educator

La Porte
Bakwin, Edward Morris banker
Johnson, Bruce Ross elementary school educator
Morris, Leigh Edward former mayor, retired health facility administrator

Lafayette
de Branges de Bourcia, Louis mathematics professor
Emerick, William E. lawyer
Etzel, James Edward environmental engineering educator
Geddes, LaNelle Evelyn nurse, physiologist
Gustafson, Winthrop Adolph retired engineering educator
Hamdi, Hamid S. neurologist, neurorehabilitation specialist, consultant, researcher
Hardin, Lowell Stewart retired economics professor

Higi, William Leo *bishop*
Jischke, Martin C. *retired academic administrator*
Kanne, Michael Stephen *federal judge*
Langston, Edward Lee *physician, pharmacist*
Liley, Peter Edward *retired engineering educator*
McBride, Angela Barron *nursing educator*
McBride, John Kuhns *lawyer*
McCully, Thomas Richardson *lawyer*
Minor, Ronald Ray *minister*
Mobley, Emily Ruth *library director, educator, dean*
Osborn, John Robert *retired engineering educator*
Pipes, Robert Byron *mechanical engineer, educator*
Renzetti, Phyllis Jean *retired technical editor, paleontologist*
Scaletta, Helen Marguerite *volunteer*
Schönemann, Peter Hans *psychologist, educator*
Schweickert, Richard Justus *psychologist, educator*
Troutner, Joanne Johnson *director, consultant, secondary school educator*

Lagrange
Brown, George E. *judge, educator*
Schmidt, David Joseph *senior resource specialist, consultant*

Liberty
Pringle, Lewis Gordon *marketing professional, educator*

Lizton
King, Richard Gene *superintendent*

Madison
Gotts, Edward Earl *psychologist, researcher*
Grahn, Ann Wagoner *retired science administrator*
Jones, Richard Sheffield *veterans service officer*

Marion
Fisher, Pierre James, Jr. *physician*
Miller, Peter Karl *music educator*
Puffer, Keith Andrew *psychology professor*

Merrillville
Compton, Clyde D. *lawyer*
Gioia, Daniel August *lawyer*
Hightman, Carrie J. *lawyer, former telecommunications company executive*
Miller, Richard Allen *lawyer*
Nguyen, Thach Ngoc *cardiologist*
O'Donnell, Michael W. *energy company executive*
Reitmeister, Noel *planner, advisor, insurance agent, mortgage consultant*
Skaggs, Robert C., Jr. *utilities executive, lawyer*
Smith, Stephen P. *utilities executive*
Tlapa, Richard Joseph *retired priest*
Wang, Josephine L. Fen *physician*
Yu, Peter Legaspi *rehabilitation physician*

Michigan City
Saxton, Carolyn Virginia *museum director*
Varro, Barbara Joan *retired editor*
Wiegand, Elizabeth Grieger *musician, educator*

Middlebury
Corson, Thomas Harold *retired manufacturing executive*
Dickey, Lucy Jane *elementary school educator*
Guequierre, John Phillip *manufacturing executive*
Stiver, James Frederick *retired pharmacist, health physicist, administrator, scientist*

Mishawaka
Haley, David Alan *healthcare executive*
Kendall, Michael Jay *musician, educator*
Rubenstein, Pamela Silver *manufacturing executive*
Troyer, LeRoy Seth *architect*

Muncie
Ali, Mir Masoom *retired statistician, educator*
Amman, E(lizabeth) Jean *academic administrator*
Anderson, Stefan Stolen *retired banker*
Blume, Peter Frederick *museum director*
Cheng, Chu Yuan *economics professor*
Dolak, Fritz *librarian, information administrator*
East, David Harold *mathematics professor*
Fritz, Robert Karl *language educator*
Harris, Joseph McAllister *retired chemist*
Hedin, Eric Robert *physics professor*
Hendrix, Jon Richard *biology professor*
Henzlik, Raymond Eugene *zoophysiologist, educator*
Hoffman, Mary Catherine *retired nurse, anesthetist*
Hoke, Brady *college football coach*
Hudson, Kevin Roy *language educator*
Kelly, Eric Damian *lawyer, educator*
Lawhead, Victor Bernard *education educator*
Mackey, Elizabeth Jocelyn *music educator*
Mertens, Thomas Robert *biology professor*
Nanko, Raymond S. *physician*
Richter, Elizabeth Margot *music educator*
Roch, Lewis Marshall, II, *ophthalmic surgeon, medical entrepreneur*
Schaefer, Patricia *retired librarian*
Seymour, Richard Deming *technology educator*
Shawger, David C. *set designer, educator*
Smith, Gregory Butler *lawyer*
Stewart, Rita Joan *academic administrator*
Sundaram, Srinivasan *finance educator*
Suppe, Frederick *historian, educator*
Swartz, B. K., Jr., (Benjamin Kinsell Swartz Jr.) *archaeologist, educator*
Thornbro, William Graden *writer*
Turcotte, Elizabeth Anne *art educator*
Vayman, Anna *music educator*
Wise, Charles Davidson *science educator*
Xu, Renmei *engineering educator*
Yeamans, George Thomas *librarian, educator*
Yssel, Nina *special education educator*

Munster
Larson, Dean Roy *management consultant, educator*
Potempa, Philip Matthew *journalist, columnist, communications educator*
Wang, Xiuling *engineering educator*

Nashville
Wills, Katherine V. Tsiopos *language educator*

New Albany
Orth, Susan Lynn *judge*
Pieper, Michael Joseph *television producer, actor, talk show host*
Rea, Patrick Shaw *secondary school educator*
Riehl, Jane Ellen *education educator*
Stallard, Donna *art educator*

New Castle
Cole, Adelaide Meador *retired physical education educator*
Dye, Mary Jane *elementary school educator*
Pierce, Terry Jo *medical/surgical nurse*

Newburgh
Saum, Elizabeth Pape *community volunteer*

Noblesville
Wilson, Norman Glenn *church administrator, writer*

North Manchester
Onyeji, Benson Chinedu *political science professor*
Schilling, Heather Anne *education educator*
Shearer, Velma Miller *clergywoman*
Switzer, Jo Young *college president*

Notre Dame
Ackermann, Carl *finance educator*
Arnold, Peri Ethan *political scientist*
Bartell, Ernest *economist, educator, priest*
Blakey, G. Robert (George Robert Blakey) *law educator*
Bloomer, W. Martin *classicist, educator*
Brey, Mike *men's college basketball coach*
Bruns, Gerald L. *English literature educator*
Burish, Thomas Gerard *academic administrator, psychology professor*
Coleman, Robert Randolf *art educator*
Crosson, Frederick James *retired dean, humanities educator*
Davis, Stacy Nicole *religious studies educator*
Despres, Leo Arthur *sociologist, anthropologist, educator, academic administrator*
D'Souza-Schorey, Crislyn *biology professor*
Eberhard, Kathleen Marie *psychology educator, researcher*
Fraser, Malcolm James, Jr. *biology professor*
Frohne, Mary Victoria *physicist, educator*
Gribble, Richard Edward, Jr. *priest, educator*
Hager, Kristin Margaret *biology professor*
Hallinan, Maureen Theresa *sociologist, educator*
Herdt, Jennifer A. *theology studies educator*
Hosle, Vittorio Giovanni *philosopher, educator*
Huber, Paul William *biochemistry professor, researcher*
Incropera, Frank Paul *mechanical engineering educator*
Jenkins, John I. *academic administrator*
Jensen, Richard Jorg *biologist, educator*
Juan, Anton Manauis *director/playwright, senior professor*
Kogge, Peter Michael *computer scientist, educator*
Kominkiewicz, Frances Bernard *social worker, educator, director*
Kulpa, Charles F. *microbiologist, educator*
Kwon, Dae Kun *civil engineer, researcher*
Langan, Jeffrey Joseph *political science professor*
Lanzinger, Klaus *language educator*
Loving, Charles Roy *museum director, curator*
MacCormack, Sabine Gabriele *history educator*
Malloy, Edward Aloysius *academic administrator*
McElroy, Jerome Lathrop *economics professor*
McGraw, Muffet *women's college basketball coach*
McInerny, Ralph Matthew *philosopher, educator, writer*
Meisel, Dan *chemist*
Merz, James Logan *electrical and materials engineering educator, researcher*
Mirowski, Philip Edward *economics professor*
Newton, Nell Jessup *dean, law educator*
Noble, Thomas Francis *history professor, department chairman*
Noll, Mark A. *history professor*
O'Hara, Patricia Anne *law educator, former dean*
O'Meara, Onorato Timothy *academic administrator, mathematician*
O'Rourke, William Andrew *literature and language professor, writer*
Perry, Catherine *language educator*
Pollard, Morris *microbiologist, educator*
Raymer, John David *literature and language professor*
Reilly, Frank Kelly *business educator*
Robinson, John Hayes *law educator*
Rodes, Robert Emmet, Jr. *law educator*
Scheidt, W. Robert *chemistry educator, researcher*
Schmitz, Roger Anthony *chemical engineer, educator, academic administrator*
Schoen, Suzanne *English educator*
Schuler, Robert Hugo *chemist, educator*
Shannon, William Norman III *college educator, food service executive*
Shephard, William Danks *physicist, educator*
Shrader-Frechette, Kristin *science educator*
Sloan, Phillip Reid *liberal studies educator*
Smith, James Ormal *engineering educator*
Sommese, Andrew John *mathematics professor*
Stadtherr, Mark A. *chemical engineer, educator*
Stamper, John W. *architecture educator, academic administrator*
Swarbrick, John Brian, Jr. *athletics director, lawyer*
Taccheri, Umberto *language educator*
Tan, Wanpeng *physicist*
Trozzolo, Anthony Marion *chemistry professor*
Valenzuela, Julio Samuel *sociologist, educator*
Walker, Clint B. *Russian language and literature educator*
Walshe, Aubrey Peter *emeritus political science professor*
Weigert, Andrew Joseph *sociology educator*
Weis, Charlie *college football coach*
Welch, Michael R. *sociologist, educator*
Woo, Carolyn Yauyan *dean*
Younger, Jennifer A. *university librarian*
Zachman, Randall Carrington *theology studies educator*

Oakland City
Spitler, Carolyn Elizabeth *music educator*

Pendleton
Kischuk, Richard Karl *insurance company executive*

Plainfield
Cavanaugh, Eric Maurice *lawyer*
Clark, Debra Elizabeth *music educator*
Fivel, Steven Edward *lawyer, communications executive*
Laikin, Robert J. *electronics executive*

Plymouth
Jurkiewicz, Margaret Joy Gommel *retired secondary school educator*
Merle, Patrick F. *communications educator*

Portage
Popp, Joseph Bruce *manufacturing executive*
Schroeder, Marvis Lynn *accountant, artist*

Princeton
Clem, Nancy Gayle *secondary school educator*

Rensselaer
Thiel, Robb G. *musician, director*
Thomas, Jerry Arthur *retired soil scientist*

Richmond
Howanitz, E. Paul *thoracic surgeon*
Murray, Kevin Dennis *surgeon*
Passet, Joanne Ellen *history professor, writer*

Rochester
Neff, Kathy S. *swimming and water safety educator*

Rockport
Davis, Karen Sue *hospital nursing supervisor*

Russiaville
Berry, Patricia A. *middle school educator*

Saint Mary Of The Woods
Cadwallader, Joyce Vermeulen *biology professor*
Wasmer, Donald J. *finance educator, director*

Saint Meinrad
Hagan, Harry *ancient language educator*

Santa Claus
Hoberg, Michael Dean *corporate financial executive, management analyst, educator*

Schererville
Galante, Gustavo E. *plastic surgeon*
Seward, John Edward, Jr. *insurance company executive*

Scottsburg
Burns, Paul D. *assistant principal*
Kho, Eusebio *surgeon*

Seymour
Aker, Julia Kathleen *library director*
Lewis, Judith Susanna *artist*
Norrell, Mary Patricia *nursing educator*
Pardieck, Roger L. *lawyer*
Paulson, James Marvin *retired engineering educator*

Shelbyville
Campbell, Wayne Edward *artist*
Lisher, James Richard *lawyer*
McNeely, James Lee *lawyer*

South Bend
Agbetsiafa, Douglas Kofi *financial and management consultant, economics professor, department chairman*
Bell, Wishart Bryan *music educator, conductor*
Bonham, Rebecca June *museum director, educator*
Carrington, Michael Davis *criminal justice and security consultant*
Davis, Glen Anthony *pediatrician*
Dowty, Alan Kent *political scientist, educator*
Harriman, Gerald Eugene *retired business administrator, economics professor*
Hellyer, Timothy Michael *protective services officer*
Horsbrugh, Patrick *architect, educator, environologist*
Hunt, Mary Reilly *organization executive*
Karns, Elizabeth A. (Libby Karns) *retired daycare administrator*
Larkin, Eugene David *artist, educator*
Manion, Daniel Anthony *federal judge*
Miller, Robert L., Jr., (Bob Miller) *federal judge*
Mooney, Elizabeth Kaatz *adult education educator*
Muniz, Jorge *composer, music educator*
Nilsen, Micheline Celestine *art historian, educator*
Reinke, William John *lawyer*
Ripple, Kenneth Francis *federal judge*
Seall, Stephen Albert *lawyer*
Shaffer, Thomas Lindsay *lawyer, educator*
Sheapentukh, Dmitry V. *history professor*
Shepherd, Terry Lynn *special education educator*
Shlapentokh, Dmitry Vladimir *history educator*
Skarbek, Denise Marie *music educator*
Spitzer, Bruce Alan *education educator*
Storin, Matthew Victor *retired editor*
Tinder, John Daniel *federal judge*
Trottier, Tracey *social studies educator*
van Inwagen, Peter Jan *philosophy educator*
Vogel, Nelson J., Jr. *lawyer*
Vrajitoru, Dana *engineering educator*
Yergler, Willard G. *orthopedist*

Spencerville
Clark, Donna M. *retired elementary school educator*

Terre Haute
Amlaner, Charles Joseph *ecologist, department chairman*
Badar, M. Affan *engineering educator*
Baker, Ronald Lee *folklore educator*
Bopp, James, Jr. *lawyer*
Britton, Louis Franklin *lawyer*
Chambers, Curtis Allen *clergyman, church administrator*
Chen, Ray Gow Hwei *artist, educator, department chair*
Cochrane, Phillip *mathematics professor*
Dando, William Arthur *academic administrator, geography and geology educator*
De Marr, Mary Jean *English language educator*
Frey, Susan M. *information specialist*
Goode, Gregory Justin *lobbyist*
Grcic, Joseph *philosophy educator*
Hunt, Effie Neva *retired dean, literature educator*
Leigh, Janis *clinician*
Malooley, David Joseph *electronics and computer technology educator*
Mehrens, Christopher Emile *musicologist, music librarian*
Papadopoulos, Peter Joseph *theater educator, playwright*
Roshel, John Albert, Jr. *orthodontist*
Steinbaugh, Robert P. *management and finance educator*
Thomas, Anne C. *nursing researcher, nurse practitioner*
Vincent, Richard C. *communications educator, researcher*
Vollmer, David L. *museum director*

Upland
Bade, Christopher *musician, educator*
Lay, Robert Franklin *religious studies educator*
Moore, John Morton *biology professor, consultant*
Ringenberg, William Carey *historian, minister*
Satterlee, Thom *literature educator, director*

Valparaiso
Cohen, Raymond *retired mechanical engineer, educator*
Cook, Addison Gilbert *chemistry professor*
Heckler, Mark Alan *academic administrator*
Katich, Janet *librarian*
Kobak, Alfred Julian, Jr. *obstetrician, gynecologist*
Maxin, Daniel *mathematics professor*
Mundinger, Donald Charles *retired college president*
Mundt, Marvin Glen *retired mathematics professor*
Parroquin, Rachel Rivers *language educator*
Peters, Howard Nevin *foreign language educator*
Schlender, William Elmer *management sciences educator*
Ziegler, Jennifer Anne *management consultant, educator*

Vincennes
Emison, Ewing Rabb, Jr. *lawyer*

Wabash
Ford, Richard Edwin *volunteer*
Scales, Richard Lewis *retired sales executive*

Walton
Chu, Johnson Chin Sheng *retired physician*

Warsaw
Binder, Jeffrey R. *medical products executive*
Dvorak, David C. *medical products executive, lawyer*
McGoldrick, John Lewis *medical products executive, lawyer*
Pfeiffer, Isobel Lorraine *education educator*
Throdahl, Mark Crandall *medical products executive*

West Lafayette
Abhyankar, Shreeram Shankar *mathematics professor*
Adelman, Steven Allen *chemist, educator*
Albright, Lyle Frederick *chemical engineering educator*
Amstutz, Harold Emerson *veterinarian, educator*
Ariyur, Kartik Balasubramanian *control systems engineer, researcher*
Avery, George H. *healthcare educator*
Barany, James Walter *industrial engineering educator*
Baumgardt, Billy Ray *professional society administrator, agriculturist*
Beering, Steven Claus *academic administrator, medical educator*
Belcastro, Patrick Frank *pharmacist, researcher*
Bergmann, Michael *philosophy professor*
Bertolet, Rodney Jay *philosophy educator*
Borowitz, Joseph Leo *pharmacologist, educator*
Brennan, Akiko Ohashi *language educator*
Broden, Thomas Francis III *French language educator*
Campanella, Osvaldo H. *biology professor*
Carlson, Gary Patrick *toxicologist, educator*
Carney, Thomas Quentin *academic administrator, educator, professional pilot*
Carvajal, M. Teresa *science educator*
Chang, Ching-jer *medicinal chemistry educator*
Chang, Karen C.K. *nursing educator*
Chien, Yili *economics professor*
Christian, John Edward *health science association administrator, educator*
Cicirelli, Victor George *psychologist*
Clifton, Christopher W. *researcher, educator*
Connor, John Murray *economics professor*
Contreni, John Joseph, Jr. *humanities educator*
Cooper, Arnold Cook *management educator, researcher*
Córdova, France Anne-Dominic *academic administrator, astrophysicist*
Corvalan, Carlos Maria *engineering educator*
Cosier, Richard A. *dean, finance educator*
Cox, Beverly E. *educational researcher, educator*
Cramer, William Anthony *biochemistry and biophysics researcher, educator*
Danielli-Garofalo, Donatella *mathematics professor*

Dasgupta, Anirban *statistician, researcher*
Davidson, James Daglish, Jr. *retired professor of sociology*
Dawuda, Alhassan *language educator*
Delleur, Jacques William *retired engineering educator*
Diamond, Sidney *chemist, educator*
Drnevich, Vincent Paul *engineering educator*
Dunning, John Barnard, Jr. *biology professor*
Dutta, Mohan *communications educator*
Edwards, Charles Richard *entomology and pest management educator*
Evans, Dennis Hyde *chemist, educator*
Farris, Paul Leonard *agricultural economist*
Ferruzzi, Mario G. *nutritionist, food scientist, educator*
Ford, Frederick Ross *retired university official*
Foster, Kenneth A. *economics professor*
Francis, Elaine J. *linguist, educator*
Geddes, Leslie Alexander *forensic engineer, educator, physiologist*
Givan, Robert *engineering educator*
Grace, Richard Edward *engineering educator*
Gruen, Gerald Elmer *psychologist, educator*
Hambrusch, Susanne E. *computer engineering educator*
Hearden, Patrick Joseph *history professor*
Holtvedt, Kristine June *performing arts educator, director*
Ichiyama, Dennis Yoshihide *art educator, educational association administrator*
Jackson, Mark James *engineering educator*
Jackson, Scott Allen *biology professor*
Jamieson, Leah H. *engineering educator, dean*
Janick, Jules *horticultural scientist, educator*
Jenkins, Jere H. *nuclear engineer, director*
Jeon, Ji-Hong *environmental and agricultural engineer, researcher*
Jevremovic, Tatjana *nuclear engineer, researcher*
Jiru, Teshome Edae *research scientist*
Johannsen, Chris Jakob *agronomist, educator, administrator*
Johnston, Clifford Thomas *soil and environmental chemistry educator*
Judd, William Robert *engineering geologist, educator*
Kadiyala, K. Rao *retired economics professor*
Kirksey, Avanelle *nutrition educator*
Labi, Samuel *civil engineering educator, researcher*
Ladisch, Michael R. *engineering educator*
Landgrebe, David Allen *electrical engineer*
Larson, John Lauritz *history professor*
Leary, James Francis *biomedical research scientist, educator, inventor*
Lechtenberg, Victor L. *agricultural studies educator*
Lee, Hanil *electrical engineer, researcher*
Lein, Clayton David *literature and language professor*
Le Master, Dennis Clyde *retired forester, economist, educator*
Lewellen, Wilbur Garrett *management educator, consultant*
Lin, Pen-Min *electrical engineer, educator*
Liu, Chunghorng Richard *engineering educator*
Loehman, Edna Tusak *economics professor*
Lord, Victoria Lynn *artist*
Luo, Xin *science educator*
Lyanda-Geller, Yuli B. *physicist*
Markee, Katherine Madigan *librarian, educator*
Marshall, Francis Joseph *aerospace engineer*
May, Robert E. *history professor*
Mc Bride, William Leon *philosopher, educator*
McMillin, David Robert *chemistry professor*
Moghadam, Valentine M. *sociology professor*
Morré, Dorothy Marie *nutrition educator, researcher*
Morrison, Harry *chemistry professor*
Moskowitz, Herbert *management educator*
Moyars-Johnson, Mary Annis *retired academic administrator*
Murray, Keith *educational association administrator*
Naik, Sameer Vijaykumar *mechanical engineer, educator*
Negishi, Ei-ichi *chemistry professor*
Nelson, Philip Edwin *food scientist, educator*
Nixon, Judith May *librarian*
Ohland, Matthew William *engineering educator, consultant*
Ohm, Herbert Willis *agronomy educator, agriculturist*
Overhauser, Albert Warner *physicist*
Painter, Matt *men's college basketball coach*
Peck, Garnet Edward *pharmacist, educator*
Perrucci, Robert *sociologist, educator*
Phillips, Terry LeMoine *investment advisor*
Pierret, Robert F. *electrical engineering educator*
Platt, Donald Oliver *literature and language professor*
Poulos, James Thomas *endocrinologist, educator*
Prabhu, Nagabhushana *industrial engineer, educator*
Rankine, Patrice D. *literature and language professor*
Reckowsky, Michael J. *academic administrator*
Ro, Byung Tak *accounting educator*
Rossmann, Michael George *biochemist, educator*
Rowland, Herbert *language educator*
Rutledge, Charles Ozwin *pharmacologist, educator*
Sadeghi, Farshid *engineering educator*
Salvendy, Gavriel *industrial engineer, educator*
Schendel, Dan Eldon *management consultant, finance educator*
Scholer, Sue Wyant *state legislator*
Schwartz, Richard John *electrical engineering educator, researcher*
Shaw, Stanley Miner *retired pharmacist, educator*
Shepson, Paul Bradford *chemistry professor*
Shertzer, Bruce Eldon *education educator*
Shin, Yung Chul *engineering educator*
Sojka, Paul E. *engineering educator*
Stob, Martin *retired physiology educator*
Svensson, Craig Karl *pharmaceutical sciences educator, dean*
Swensen, Clifford Henrik, Jr. *psychologist, educator*
Taber, Margaret Ruth *retired engineering technology educator*
Thomas, Marlin Uluess *industrial engineer, academic administrator, educator*
Thompson, Dorothea Kathleen *microbiologist*
Tyner, Wallace Edward *agricultural economics educator*
Varma, Arvind *chemical engineering educator, researcher*
Viskanta, Raymond *mechanical engineering educator*
Wankat, Phillip Charles *chemical engineering educator*
Wasynczuk, Oleg *electrical engineer, educator*
Weinstein, Michael Alan *political science professor*
Wendt, Oliver *special education educator*
Williams, Theodore Joseph *retired engineering educator*
Woodman, Harold David *historian, educator*
Yao, Bin *mechanical engineering educator*
Yeo, Yoon *biomedical engineer, educator*
Zheng, Wei *science educator*
Zwier, Timothy S. *chemistry professor*

Westfield

Bradbury, Betty Marie *retired history and music educator*
Hayashi, Tetsumaro *retired literature educator, writer, editor*

Westville

Serwatka, Judy Ann *computer and information systems educator*

Winamac

Ligocki, Gordon Michael *artist, educator*

Winona Lake

Davis, John James *religion educator*
Julien, Thomas Theodore *religious denomination administrator*

Zionsville

Hatfield, Tiffany Clellan *museum director and curator*

IOWA

Akron

Hultgren, Dennis Eugene *farmer, management consultant*

Albia

Jones, Betsy Lea *literature and language educator*

Alden

Oliver, Kerryn Hinrichs *music and religious studies educator*

Allison

Reese, Susan Marie *elementary school educator*

Altoona

Berkenes, Joyce Marie Poore *social worker, director*

Ames

Alumbaugh, JoAnn McCalla *magazine editor*
Anderson, Lloyd Lee *physiologist, educator*
Anderson, Robert Morris, Jr. *electrical engineer*
Barnes, Richard George *physicist, researcher*
Barton, Thomas J. *chemistry professor, researcher*
Baumann, Edward Robert *environmental engineering educator*
Benson, Neala Lawrence *volunteer*
Beran, George Wesley *veterinary microbiology educator*
Black, James Robert *industrial engineer*
Bonomi, Ferne Gater *public relations executive*
Briggs, Robert E. *veterinarian*
Buchele, Wesley Fisher *retired agricultural engineering educator*
Bugeja, Michael Joseph *director, educator, writer*
Chang, Carl K. *engineering educator*
Cleasby, John LeRoy *civil engineer, educator*
Clem, John Richard *physicist, educator*
Corbett, John Dudley *chemistry professor*
Cormicle, Larry W. *engineering educator*
Courteau, Joanna *foreign language educator*
Crabtree, Beverly June *retired dean*
Cravens, Hamilton *history professor*
Cross, Susan E. *psychologist, educator*
David, Herbert Aron *retired statistician, educator*
Davis, Wayne Pitman *public relations executive*
Dinnes, Dana L. *agronomist*
Ebbers, Larry Harold *education educator*
Fennelly, William (Bill Fennelly) *women's college basketball coach*
Fritz, James Sherwood *chemist, educator*
Fuller, Wayne Arthur *statistics educator*
Gautesen, Arthur K. *mathematics professor*
Geoffroy, Gregory L. *academic administrator, educator*
Greve, John Henry *veterinary parasitologist, educator*
Gschneidner, Karl Albert, Jr. *metallurgist, educator, editor, consultant*
Hallauer, Arnel Roy *geneticist*
Harl, Neil Eugene *economist, educator, lawyer, writer*
Hatfield, Jerry Lee *plant physiologist, agricultural meteorologist*
Hoffman, Elizabeth *academic administrator, economics professor*
Hogben, Leslie *mathematician*
Hong, Mei *chemistry professor*
Jackson, George Arthur *dean, educator*
James, Patrick *political science educator*
Jarecki, Marek Kazimierz *soil scientist, consultant*
Johnson, Lawrence Alan *cereal technologist, educator, administrator*
Kaufmann, Jeffrey Baer *finance educator*
Kim, Sang Hyoun *environmental engineer, researcher*
Kim, Sunghwan *civil engineer, researcher*
Kimura, Kayoko *veterinarian*
Kozak, John Joseph *provost, chemistry educator*
Kushner, Mark Jay *engineering and physics educator, dean*
Kusow, Abdi M. *social sciences educator*
Lando, Harry Alan *psychology educator*
Larsen, William Lawrence *engineering educator*
Larson, Sidner John *social sciences educator*
Levitas, Valery *mechanics and materials educator, researcher*
Lewis, Calvin Fred *architect, educator*
Lin, Zhiqun *science educator*
Lo, Chester C.H. *research scientist*
Lubberstedt, Thomas *plant pathologist, director*
Manatt, Richard *retired education educator*
Maxwell Dial, Eleanore *foreign language educator*
Mengeling, William Lloyd *retired veterinarian, virologist*
Mertins, James Walter *entomologist*
Monroe, John Warne *history professor*
Moore, Kenneth James *agronomist, educator*
Nair, Rajeev *engineering educator, researcher*
O'Berry, Phillip Aaron *retired veterinarian*
O'Boyle, Michael William *psychology educator*
Okiishi, Theodore Hisao *mechanical engineering educator*
Palermo, Gregory Sebastian *architect*
Randic, Milan *retired chemistry professor*
Randic, Mirjana *retired neurologist*
Reilly, Peter John *chemical engineer, educator*
Ross, Richard Francis *veterinarian, microbiologist, dean, educator*
Roth, James A. *medical educator, director*
Ruedenberg, Klaus *theoretical chemist, educator*
Sanders, Wallace Wolfred, Jr. *civil engineer*
Seifert, George *mathematician, educator*
Silet, Charles Loring Provine *emeritus literature and language professor*
Stabel, Judith R. *microbiologist*
Tang, Lie *agricultural engineer, educator*
Teas, Roy Kenneth *marketing educator*
Ten, Chee-Wooi *electrical engineer, researcher*
Topel, David Glen *agricultural studies educator*
Wegulo, Stephen Ngakhala *plant pathologist, researcher*
Wickert, Jonathan Adam *engineering educator*
Wilder, David Randolph *retired materials engineer*
Willham, Richard Lewis *zoology educator*
Xu, Min *research associate*

Ankeny

Keese, Jan *elementary school educator*
Myers, Robert J. *retail executive*
Weigel, Ollie J *dentist, former mayor*

Anthon

Herrick, Cynthia Jean *literature and language educator*

Atlantic

Johnson, Joan (Jan) Hope Voss *communications and public relations executive, photojournalist*

Bettendorf

Dittmer, Julie J. *nursing educator*
Dunn, Armond Russ Donald *science educator*
Greenhoe, David Stanley *performance artist, music educator*
Hartsuch, David *state legislator*
Heyderman, Arthur Jerome *engineer, civilian military employee*
Myatt, William Howard *theater educator, director, actor*
Schulz, Sally Ann *pastoral musician, conductor, educator*

Boone

Shirley, Donald Dean *appraiser*

Burlington

Hoth, Steven Sergey *lawyer, educator*
Koehler-Trickler, Sally Jo *illustrator*

Cambridge

Colvin, Thomas Stuart *agricultural engineer, farmer*

Cedar Falls

Blakesley, Kimberly Kay *art educator, consultant*
Buckholz, Christopher *music educator*
Chesnutt, Rod Martin *music educator*
Fanelli, Michael Paul *musician, educator, writer*
Ghosh, Arindam *engineering educator, researcher*
Gilgen, Albert Rudolph *retired psychologist, educator*
Hanson, Roger James *physics educator*
Jacobson, Ben *men's college basketball coach*
Licari, Michael J. *dean, political science professor*
Lindberg, Duane R. *bishop, historian*
Pecen, Recayi Reg *engineering educator*
Pedersen, Karen Sue *electrical engineer*
Posinasetti, Nageswara Rao *manufacturing engineering educator*
Power, Daniel Joseph *business educator*
Schnucker, Robert Victor *historian, educator*
Shepardson, Donald Eugene *history professor*
Siddens, Paul Jackson III *communication educator*
Skaine, James C. *retired communications educator*
Skaine, Rosemarie Keller *writer, publisher, consultant*
Taylor, Darrell Richard *art gallery director, artist*
van Wormer, Katherine Stuart *social work educator*
Waldron, Jennifer *science educator*

Cedar Rapids

Bahadur, Birendra *displays research specialist*
Baldwin, George Koehler *retired retail executive*
Chadick, Gary Robert *lawyer*
Davis, Michael A. *lawyer*
Dummermuth, Matt M. *prosecutor*
Eichhorn, Richard Gerard *economics professor*
Hansen, David Rasmussen *federal judge*
Houmes, Blaine V. *emergency physician*
Jones, Clayton M. *electronics company executive*
Keller, Eliot Aaron *broadcast executive*
Maikon, Marc Steven *podiatrist*
Melloy, Michael J. *federal judge*
Moore, Thomas *museum director, retired accountant*
Nassif, Shakeeb Joseph *performing arts educator*
Perkins, Marcus Matthew *special education educator*
Pitts, Terence Randolph *museum director, consultant*
Riley, Tom Joseph *lawyer*
Russell, Steve D. *elementary school educator*
Sauerman, Nancy *psychology professor*
Smith, Bruce Vaughn *electrical engineer*
Suiter, Jane *science educator*
Thompson-Stanton, Mary Jean *communications educator*
Underwood, Richard Lee *educator*
Wax, Nadine Virginia *retired bank executive*
Wilson, Robert Foster *lawyer*

Cherokee

Gordon, Roma Dianne *music educator*

Clear Lake

Broshar, Robert Clare *retired architect*
Brown, Robert Grover *engineering educator*
Enabnit, Ted *retired lawyer*

Clinton

Kearney, Michael John *banker*
Smith, Lauren Ashley *lawyer, clergyman, physicist, journalist*

Clive

Miller, Kenneth Edward *sociologist, educator*
Neis, Arthur Veral *healthcare and development company executive*

Coralville

Aly, Al Said *plastic surgeon, otolaryngologist*
Coulter, Charles Roy *lawyer*
Hobart, Thomas D. *lawyer*
Koprivnjak, Tomaz *microbiologist*
Thomas, Carole Lesniak *retired music educator*
Van Arendonk, Susan Carole *special education educator*

Council Bluffs

Alley, Mary Lou Vande Woude *retired medical/surgical nurse*
Kurt, Johnny Thomas *music educator*
Moeller, James Charles *writer, educator*

Creston

Dillenburg, Carolyn Eva Lauer *retired secondary school educator*

Davenport

Achs, Jack Horst *social studies educator*
Amos, Martin John *bishop*
Dcamp, Charles Barton *music educator*
Dettmann, David Allen *lawyer*
Eitrheim, Kristofer James *theater educator*
Findlay, Kim *museum administrator*
Foster, James Franklin *professional sports management executive*
Franklin, William Edwin *bishop emeritus*
Gildehaus, Thomas Arthur *manufacturing executive, museum director*
Herzig, Stella *reference librarian*
Holleran, Karen Elaine *literature and language professor*
Hudson, Celeste Nutting *education educator, consultant, reading clinic administrator*
Juckem, Wilfred Philip *manufacturing executive*
Opar, Michael E. *engineering educator, department chairman*
Roudebush, LaWanda Carpenter *library director*
Runge, Kay Kretschmar *library consultant*
Sheehey, Patricia Ann *secondary school educator*
Townsend, Julie Rae *artist, educator*
Woodruff, Theodore Sherman *economics professor*

Decorah

Christianson, John Robert *historian, educator*
Farwell, Elwin D. *minister, consultant*
Monson, Larry Lee *music educator*
Noble, Weston Henry *music educator*
Tejada, Rita María *literature and language professor*

Des Moines

Abel, Gregory E. *utilities company executive*
Appel, Brent Robert *state supreme court justice, lawyer*
Baker, David L. *state supreme court justice*
Begleiter, Martin David *law educator, consultant*
Bergman, Bruce E. *municipal official*
Bevilacqua, Nicholas J. *podiatrist, educator*
Brickman, Kenneth Alan *state agency administrator*
Brooks, Roger Kay *insurance company executive*
Bukta, Polly *state legislator*
Burn, Barbara Louise *literature and language educator*
Butler, Gayle *editor-in-chief*
Cady, Mark S. *state supreme court justice*
Carter, James Harvey *retired state supreme court justice*
Charron, Joseph Leo *bishop emeritus*
Clark, Craig Boyd *cardiologist*
Colloton, Steven M. *federal judge*
Conlin, Roxanne Barton *lawyer*
Corning, Joy Cole *retired state official*
Cownie, TM Franklin *Mayor, Des Moines*
Critelli, Nicholas *lawyer, barrister*
Crook, Charles Samuel III *lawyer*
Culver, Chet (Chester John Culver) *Governor of Iowa*
Deluhery, Patrick John *retired state official*
Devine, Michael Buxton *attorney, barrister, educator*
Duffy, Kathryn Ann Pohlmann *musicologist, educator*
Fisher, Thomas George *lawyer, retired media company executive*
Fitzgerald, Michael Lee *state treasurer*
Frederici, C. Carleton *lawyer*
Gaines, Ruth Ann *secondary school educator*
Gartner, Michael Gay *editor, baseball and television executive*

Graziano, Craig Frank *lawyer*
Griswell, J. Barry *insurance company executive*
Gronstal, Thomas B. *state banking agency administrator*
Habib, Shahid *medical association administrator*
Hansell, Edgar Frank *lawyer*
Harris, Charles Elmer *retired lawyer*
Hecht, Daryl L. *state supreme court justice*
Heiden, Cara *mortgage company executive*
Hill, Luther Lyons, Jr. *lawyer*
Hollingsworth, Laura L. *publishing executive*
Hunter, Linda Mason *author*
Jarvey, John Alfred *federal judge*
Jeffrey, Judy *state official, school system administrator*
Jensen, Dick Leroy *lawyer*
Judge, Patty Jean *Lieutenant Governor of Iowa, nurse*
Kelley, Bruce Gunn *insurance company executive, lawyer*
Kerr, William T. *publishing and broadcast executive*
Khots, Boris *mathematician, researcher*
Kiernan, Michael *political organization administrator*
Koehn, William James *lawyer*
Kruidenier, Elizabeth Stuart *lawyer*
Lacy, Stephen M. *publishing and broadcasting executive*
Larson, Jerry Leroy *state supreme court justice*
Lillis, Terry J. *insurance company executive*
Mauro, Michael Anthony *Secretary of State, Iowa*
Miller, Thomas J. *state attorney general*
Mitchell, Stuart *medical entomologist, consulting physician*
Nelson, Charlotte Bowers *retired public administrator*
Newton, Thomas *state agency administrator, public health service officer*
Norris, Glenn L. *lawyer*
Oren, Glenn M. *healthcare educator, consultant*
Pappajohn, John G. *venture capitalist*
Pates, Richard Edmund *bishop*
Peddicord, Roland Dale *lawyer*
Phelps, Mark *men's college basketball coach*
Poppe, Pamela J. *accountant*
Quirmbach, Herman Charles *state legislator*
Ramsden, Mary Catherine *substance abuse specialist*
Reece, Maynard Fred *artist, writer*
Schmett, Kim D. *lawyer*
Shaff, Karen E. *lawyer, insurance company executive*
Simpson, Lyle Lee *lawyer*
Smith, Diana Marie *business educator*
Smith, Neal Edward *former congressman, lawyer*
Sokol, David Lee *utilities company executive*
Song, Joseph *pathologist, educator*
Strawn, Matthew N. *political organization administrator*
Streit, Michael J. *state supreme court justice*
Ternus, Marsha K. *state supreme court chief justice*
Trout, Brett Joseph *lawyer*
Vaughan, Therese Michele *insurance educator*
Vestal, Allan W. *dean, law educator*
Walters, Clayton William *health facility administrator, rehabilitation services professional, consultant*
Walters, Ross A. *federal judge*
Washburn, Carolyn K. *editor-in-chief*
Wattleworth, Roberta Ann *physician*
Wegner, Mary *state librarian*
Whitaker, Matthew George *prosecutor*
Wiggins, David Stewart *state supreme court justice*
Witke, David Rodney *retired newspaper editor, consultant*
Wolle, Charles Robert *judge*
Zgarrick, David Paul *pharmaceutical executive*
Zimpleman, Larry Donald *insurance company executive*

Dubuque
Crahan, Jack Bertsch *retired manufacturing executive*
Dunker, Amy *music educator*
Eagleson, Gerald W. *neuroscientist, educator*
Enzler, Jerome Anthony *museum director*
Hammer, David Lindley *lawyer, writer, investor*
Hanus, Jerome George *archbishop*
Jorgensen, Gerald Thomas *psychologist, educator, lawyer*
Lathrop, Carolynne Sue *librarian*
Lee, Becky Glasson *education educator*
Meier, Joyce *education educator*
Muzinga, Laurent *finance educator*
Thompson, Melinda L. *theologian*

Earlham
Latham, Howard Douglas *school system administrator*

Eldridge
Downing, Paul R. *sports science educator*

Elk Horn
Conklin, Virginia Ruth *school librarian, educator*

Emmetsburg
Hoover, Thomas R. *secondary school educator*

Estherville
Ayres, Carol J. *music educator, director*
Dodge, Lynn Renee *mathematics professor*

Fairfield
Rogers, Benjamin Franklin *retired history professor*

Forest City
Biggs, Douglas Lee *historian, educator*
Fiebig, Jeremy Ray *theater educator*
Taylor, Kristín Jónína *musician, educator*

Fort Dodge
Naeve, Denise R. *music educator*

Fort Madison
Lorimer, Thomas Harold *minister*

Sodey, Angela Ann *gifted and talented educator*

George
Symens, Maxine Brinkert Tanner *retired marketing professional*

Glenwood
Campbell, William Edward *mental hospital administrator, psychologist, psychotherapist*

Grinnell
Adelberg, Arnold Melvin *mathematics professor, researcher*
Bonath, Gail Jean *Librarian*
Christiansen, Kenneth Allen *biologist, educator*
Kintner, Philip L. *history professor*
Michaels, Jennifer Tonks *foreign language educator*
Moyer, H. Wayne *political science professor*
Nyden, Tammy Marie *philosopher, educator*
Osgood, Russell King *academic administrator*
Rommereim, John Christian *music educator*
Walker, Waldo Sylvester *retired biologist, retired academic administrator*

Griswold
Blackburn, Leila Marie *pastor*

Harlan
Salvo, J. C. *lawyer*

Holstein
Soseman, Eleanor Douglass *volunteer*

Ida Grove
Snell, Bruce M., Jr. *judge*

Indianola
Dinesen, Tracy A. *language educator*
Ouderkirk, Mason James *lawyer*

Iowa City
Abboud, Francois Mitry *physician, educator*
Abdel-Malek, Karim A. *biomedical engineer, educator*
Addis, Laird Clark, Jr. *philosopher, educator, musician*
Albrecht, William Price *economist, educator, government official*
Ali, Saad *radiologist*
Anderson, Rachel L. *healthcare educator, researcher*
Andreasen, Nancy Coover *psychiatrist, educator, neuroscientist*
Aspel, Paulene Violette *retired language educator*
Atkins, Dianne L. *pediatrician, educator*
Atkinson, Kendall Eugene *mathematics professor*
Baker, Nancy L. *university librarian, educator*
Barkan, Joel David *political science professor*
Becker, Samuel Leo *retired communications educator*
Bell, Marvin Hartley *poet, language educator*
Bentz, Dale Monroe *retired librarian*
Bhattacharya, Debashish *environmental scientist, educator*
Bishara, Samir Edward *orthodontist*
Bonfield, Arthur Earl *law educator*
Boyd, Willard Lee *academic administrator, educator, lawyer, museum director*
Boyle, Linda Ng *engineering educator*
Bream-Rouwenhorst, Heather R. *pharmacist*
Brennan, Robert Lawrence *educational director, psychometrician*
Broffitt, James Drake *statistician, educator*
Brook, Stacey L. *economics professor*
Brophy, Patrick David *pediatrician, researcher*
Buckwalter, Joseph Addison *orthopedic surgeon, educator*
Burton, Donald Joseph *chemistry professor*
Christensen, Alan J. *psychology professor, department chairman*
Ciach, Grzegorz Jan *research scientist*
Clifton, James Albert *physician, educator*
Collins, Daniel W. *accountant, educator*
Cooper, Christopher S. *urologist, educator*
Cooper, Reginald Rudyard *orthopedic surgeon, educator*
Cornell, Robert Aaron *embryologist, educator*
Cowdery, John Stewart *physician*
Croft, Laurie Jane *social services administrator*
Dasgupta, Soura *engineering educator*
Densen, Paul Maximillian *retired health facility administrator*
Díaz-Duque, Ozzie Francis *literature and language professor*
Diekema, Daniel James *epidemiologist, educator*
Dietz, Frederick R. *orthopaedic surgeon*
Donelson, John Everett *biochemistry professor, molecular biologist*
Ertl, Wolfgang *German language and literature educator, artist*
Feldt, Leonard Samuel *academic administrator, educator*
Fellows, Robert Ellis *medical educator, researcher*
Ferentz, Kirk *college football coach*
Ferguson, Richard L. *educational association administrator*
Fethke, Gary C. *economics professor, former dean*
Folk, George Edgar, Jr. *environmental physiology educator*
Folsom, Lowell Edwin *language educator*
Frantz, Rita *dean, nursing educator*
Gallanis, Thomas P. *law educator*
Gelfand, Lawrence Emerson *historian, educator*
George, Weiner *medical researcher, director*
Geweke, John Frederick *economics professor*
Glenister, Brian Frederick *geologist, educator*
Gompper, David *composer, music educator*
Graham, Michael M. *nuclear medicine scientist, director*
Green, Peter Morris *classics educator, writer, translator*
Gronbeck, Bruce Elliot *communications educator*
Grose, Charles Frederick *pediatrician, epidemiologist*
Guentner, Wendelin Ann *literature and language professor*

Hammond, Harold Logan *oral and maxillofacial pathologist, retired educator*
Harper, Dennis Carlin *education educator*
Hawley, Ellis Wayne *historian, educator*
Hawtrey, Charles Edward *urologist, educator*
Heath, Richard *language educator*
Heistad, Donald Dean *cardiologist*
Hines, Norman William *law educator, retired dean*
Hogg, Robert Vincent, Jr. *mathematical statistician, educator*
Holland, Charles Joseph *lawyer*
Honey, Rex Dean *social sciences educator*
Hornsby, Roger Allen *classics educator*
Hovenkamp, Herbert *law educator*
Hunter, William Curt *dean, finance educator*
Huttner, Sidney Frederick *librarian*
Jepsen, David Andrew *retired counselor, educator*
Johnson, Chris Alan *ophthalmology educator*
Johnson, Nicholas *writer, lawyer, educator*
Jones, Carolyn C. *dean, law educator*
Jones, Catherine Clarissa *retired secondary school educator*
Joselson, Rachel *voice educator*
Kates, Kenneth P. *hospital administrator*
Kerber, Linda Kaufman *historian, educator*
Kerber, Richard E. *cardiologist*
Kessel, Richard Glen *zoology educator*
Kim, Chong Lim *political science professor*
Konety, Badrinath R. *surgeon, researcher*
Kopelson, Kevin *literature and language educator*
Kostina, Irina S. *language educator*
Kottick, Edward Leon *musician, educator*
Kramer, Paul Alexander *history professor*
Kurtz, Sheldon Francis *lawyer, educator*
Kwitek, Anne E. *medical educator*
Laronde, Michel Serge *language educator*
Laxmisan, Archana *medical researcher*
Lee, Ikjin *research scientist*
Leone, Leah Elizabeth *language educator*
Letendre, Donald E. *dean*
Levin, Irwin Paul *psychology professor*
Lickliter, Todd *men's college basketball coach*
Lim, Ramon (Khe-Siong Lim) *neuroscience educator, researcher*
Loewenberg, Gerhard *political science professor*
Lonngren, Karl Erik *electrical and computer engineering educator*
Lutgendorf, Philip *language educator*
Magboul, Magboul M. *anesthesiologist, educator*
Malanson, George Patrick *geography educator*
Mason, Edward Eaton *surgeon*
Mason, Sally Kay Frost *academic administrator, biology professor*
Mather, Roger Frederick *retired music educator, writer*
Maxson, Linda Ellen *biologist, educator*
Mazurkewycz, Christine A. *literature and language professor*
McCartney, David Farnham *archivist, educator*
McKee, Christopher Fulton *historian, educator*
Merrill, Christopher Lyall *writer*
Miller, Jordan D. *physiologist*
Montgomery, Rex *biochemist, educator*
Moritani, Toshio *radiologist, educator*
Morphew, Christopher Clark *education educator*
Morriss, Frank Howard, Jr. *pediatrics educator*
Muir, Ruth Brooks *alcohol/drug abuse services professional, consultant*
Myers, Virginia Anne *art educator*
Neumann, Roy Covert *architect*
Niebyl, Jennifer Robinson *obstetrician, gynecologist, educator*
Olin, William Harold *orthodontist, educator*
Park, Joon Bu *biomedical engineer, researcher, educator*
Patel, Virendra Chaturbhai *mechanical engineer, educator*
Percas-Ponseti, Helena *foreign language and literature educator*
Plapp, Bryce Vernon *biochemistry educator*
Preucil, Doris Bogen *music educator*
Prisinzano, Thomas Edward *chemistry professor, researcher*
Raeburn, John Hay *language educator*
Riesz, Peter Charles *marketing educator, consultant*
Riezman, Raymond *economics professor*
Robertson, Timothy Joel *statistician, educator*
Robillard, Jean Eugene *academic administrator*
Rothman, Paul B. *dean, medical educator*
Rushton, Gerard *geography professor, researcher*
Sandlow, Jay Ira *urologist, researcher*
Schulz, Rudolph Walter *university dean emeritus*
Siebert, Calvin D. *economist, educator*
Simon, J(ennings) Richard *psychologist, educator*
Sindt, Christine W. *medical educator*
Singer, Jane Bess *communications educator*
Skinstad, Anne Helene *psychologist, researcher*
Smith, Frederick M. *religious studies educator*
Smoker, Wendy Rue Kartinos *neuroradiologist, consultant, educator*
Snyder, Peter M. *medical educator, medical researcher*
Solbrig, Ingeborg Hildegard *retired literature educator, writer*
Spriestersbach, Duane Caryl *academic administrator, speech pathology/audiology services professional, educator*
Staggs, Susan Hettie *medical educator*
Stay, Barbara *zoologist, educator*
Stone, Gerald Lee *university administrator, educator, psychologist*
Titze, Ingo Roland *physics professor*
Trca, Randy Ernest *lawyer*
Tsalikian, Eva *physician, educator*
Van Beek, Edwin Jacques Rudolph *radiologist, researcher*
Vandenberg, Byron F. *cardiologist*
Weiner, George Jay *internist*
Williams, Richard Dwayne *physician, educator, urologist*
Wing, Adrien Katherine *law educator*
Wolf, Brian R. *orthopedist, educator*
Wunder, Charles C(ooper) *physiologist, biophysicist, educator*
Yao, Qingjiang *communications educator, researcher*

Zaheer, Asgar *medical educator*
Ziegler, Ekhard Erich *pediatrics educator*

Johnston
Oestreich, Dean *manufacturing executive*

Keokuk
White, John David *social sciences educator*

Lamoni
Casey, Michael S. *humanities educator*
Eppinger, Priscilla Elaine *religious studies educator*

Le Claire
Varney, Nils Roberts *neuropsychologist, researcher*

Madrid
Handy, Richard Lincoln *civil engineer, educator*

Maquoketa
Krum, Dee *secondary school educator*

Marion
Pate, Paul Danny *mayor*

Marshalltown
Brennecke, Allen Eugene *lawyer*
Davison, James A. *surgeon*
Thomas, David Llewellyn *physician*

Mason City
Collison, Jim *publishing executive*
Funkhouser, David Edward *lawyer*
Rodamaker, Marti Tomson *bank executive*
Winston, Harold Ronald *lawyer*

Mount Pleasant
Crane, Frederick Baron *retired music educator*

Mount Vernon
Cotton, Gregory Mark *librarian*
Gruber-Miller, John C. *humanities educator*
Teague, Craig M. *chemistry professor*

Muscatine
Askren, Stan A. *manufacturing executive*
Housh, E. William *manufacturing executive*
Lande, Roger Lee *lawyer*
Moorhead, Alan R. *internal auditor*
Nepple, James Anthony *lawyer*
Stanley, Richard Holt *consulting engineer*
Thomopulos, Gregs G. *consulting engineering company executive*

Nevada
Countryman, Dayton Wendell *lawyer*

New Providence
Reece, Marlene Williams *elementary school educator*

Newton
Padilla, Sue Ann *librarian*
Ponder, Marian Ruth *mathematics educator*
Ward, Doree Maxine *secondary school educator*

North Liberty
Brenneman, Tami K. *not-for-profit fundraiser*

Oelwein
Flaucher-Falck, Velma Ruth *retired special education educator*
McFarlane, Beth Lucetta Troester *retired mayor*

Orange City
Hancock, Albert Sidney, Jr. *engineering executive*
Josselyn-Cranson, Heather Rene *music educator*
Vander Aarde, Stanley Bernard *retired otolaryngologist*
Zwiep, Donald Nelson *mechanical engineering educator, department chairman*

Oskaloosa
Burrow, Nancy Kay *special education educator*
Burrow, Paul Irving *secondary school educator*
Gleason, Carol Ann *mental health nurse, educator*
Porter, David Lindsey *history and political science professor, writer*
Robbins, Janet Linda *language and citizenship educator*

Ottumwa
Brookhiser, Randall L. *aviation educator*
Ford, Ruston C. *language educator*
Krafka, Mary Baird *lawyer*
Lang, Janelle J. *accountant*
Luman, Richard Gordon *retired historian*
Miller-Meeks, Mariannette Jane *ophthalmologist*
Reed, Frank E., Jr. *finance educator*
Schindler, Fred H. *professor*

Panora
Hartman, James Austin *retired geologist*

Pella
Den Adel, Raymond Lee *classics educator*
Dout, Anne Jacqueline *manufacturing and sales company executive*
Sodd, Mary Jo *theatre educator*
Zaffiro, James J. *political science professor*

Peosta
Dilsizian, Rick Charles *retired computer science educator*
Doffing, Timothy J. *mathematics professor*

Pocahontas
Taylor, Sue Kay *science educator*

Polk City
Gaylor, James Leroy *biomedical research educator*

Sabula
McKone, Brenda Kay *elementary school educator, coach*

Sheldon
Eichmann, Harold D. *laboratory administrator*

Sioux Center
Vander Plaats, Gary Paul *accounting educator*

Sioux City
Andersen, Leonard Christian *former state legislator, real estate investor*
Ayi, Bertha Serwa *infectious disease specialist, internist*
Bennett, Michael L. *agricultural products executive*
Clovis, Samuel Harvey, Jr. *academic administrator*
Dye, Lana L. *music educator*
Hamilton, Ruth Milton Green *retired college administrator, consultant*
Hassenger, James Michael *writer, retired small business owner*
Madsen, George Frank *lawyer*
Nickless, Ralph Walter *bishop*
Nwanegbo, Edward *epidemiologist, researcher*
Oggel, Ynés M. *language educator, director*
Soens, Lawrence Donald *bishop emeritus*
Warnstadt, Jacqueline Rae *elementary school educator*

Sloan
Ullrich, Roxie Ann *special education educator*

Solon
Schneider, Robert *prosthodontist, educator*

Spirit Lake
Spriester, Rebecca Groen *librarian*

Storm Lake
Bochtler, Stanley Edwin *education educator*
Keeler, Paula A. *music educator, director*
Musel, Donna Sue *academic administrator*
Safley, Holli Ewoldt *music educator*

Toledo
Lyon, Norma Duffield *sculptor, agriculturist*

Walford
Brooks, Debra L. *healthcare executive, neuromuscular therapist, artist*

Washington
Buchholz, Lee William (Leroy William Buchholz) *retired music educator*

Waterloo
Alfrey, Marian Antoinette *retired education educator*
Johannsen, Sonia Alicia *retired small business owner*
Kober, Arletta Refshauge (Mrs. Kay L. Kober) *retired supervisor*
Mathys, Gordon D. *accountant, educator*
Mixdorf, Jon *science educator*

Waverly
Blair, Rebecca Sue *English educator*
O'Konski, Marjorie Katherine *music educator*
Schneider, Richard John *literature and language professor*

West Branch
Mather, Mildred Eunice *retired archivist*
Walch, Timothy George *library director*

West Burlington
Evans, James Richard *history professor*
Skeens, Lee Roy *psychology professor*

West Des Moines
Alberts, Marion Edward *retired physician*
Conner, William Bruce *facility engineer, consultant*
Gleason, Robert Lyle *financial analyst, realtor*
Goldsmith, Janet Jane *pediatric nurse practitioner*
Hockenberg, Harlan David *lawyer*
Hohmann, James E. *insurance company executive*
Johnson, John Paul *lawyer, judge*
Johnson, Shawn Machel *Olympic gymnast*
Lynch, David William *physicist, retired educator*
Matthews, Alexander *health facility administrator*
Myers, Mary Kathleen *publishing executive*
Owens, Fredric Newell *animal nutritionist, educator*
Power, Joseph Edward *lawyer*
Rosen, Matthew Stephen *retired botanist*
Thomas, Phelan R. *dentist*
Thompson, Gerald Everett *economics professor*
Tully, Robert Gerard *lawyer*

Windsor Heights
Beadel, Stephen Jay *author*

KANSAS

Abilene
Holt, Daniel D. *library director*

Arkansas City
Ewing, Dejon L. *communications educator*
Neal, Melinda K. *science educator*

Atchison
Lane, Elizabeth Ann *genealogist, researcher*
Newton, Lloyd Alfred *philosopher, educator*

Berryton
Schroer, Gene Eldon *lawyer*

Blue Rapids
Hood, Carol A. *music educator*

Caldwell
Struble, Thelma Pauline *elementary school educator*

Caney
Wilmoth, Marsha H. *elementary school educator*

Chanute
Dillard, Dean Innes *retired English language educator*
Fewins, David W. *marketing executive*
Froehlich, Conrad Gerald *museum director, researcher*
Harris, Tosca Dugan *academic administrator*
Watkins, Mark Charles Henry *finance educator*
Weilert, Mary E. *communications educator*

Chase
Stull, Evalyn Marie *artist*

Claflin
Burmeister, Paul Frederick *farmer*
Lewis, Robert V., Jr. *computer programmer*

Clearwater
Taverner, Pamela Johnson *secondary school educator*

Clifton
Compton, Doris Martha *lay worker*

Coffeyville
Nelson, Carolyn *auditor*

Colby
Dijanic, Angela A. (Rivenshield) *toxicologist, educator*

Concordia
Damman, Patrick Kelly *agricultural studies educator*
Leif, Todd R. *physics professor*

Copeland
Birney, Walter Leroy *religious administrator*

De Soto
Strubbe, Thomas R. *insurance industry executive*

Dodge City
Burke, Larry Keith *history professor*
Burns, Timothy Scott *welding instructor*
Gilmore, Ronald Michael *bishop*
Sewell, Carol Ann *artist*

El Dorado
Meyer, Ruth A. *mathematics professor*

Elbing
Templin, Noreen *finance educator*

Emmett
Byers, Walter *athletic association executive*

Emporia
Alshare, Khaled A. *information systems educator*
Aman, M. Robert *music educator*
Helbert, Michael Clinton *lawyer*
Phelps, Connie Lea *special education gifted educator*
Riegler, Roxane *language educator, researcher*
Sundberg, Marshall David *biology professor*
Walters, George Kauffman *retired business educator*

Fairway
O'Leary, Dennis Sophian *accrediting body executive*

Fort Leavenworth
Barker, Ray Todd *archivist, writer*
King, Curtis Steeble *history professor*
Mullis, Tony Randall *military history educator*
Stentiford, Barry Maxfield *education educator, military officer*

Fort Scott
Bailey, Ronda Wyckoff *literature and language professor*
Wassenberg, Evelyn M. *retired medical/surgical nurse, educator*

Garden City
Alam, A.N.M. Mahbub Ul *engineer, educator*
Loyd, Ward Eugene *lawyer*
Malik, Abid *psychiatrist*

Girard
Gayoso, Michael, Jr. *lawyer*

Goddard
Cundy, Amanda D. *psychologist*

Grantville
Hodges, Edna (Lee) Elizabeth *retired lawyer, educator*

Great Bend
Rittenhouse, Nancy Carol *elementary school educator*

Greeley
Fisher, William Ralph *retired geologist*

Halstead
Sigmund, Cynthia Marie *elementary school educator*

Hays
Arano, Kathleen *economics professor*
Bovee, David Steven *historian, educator*
Budig, Jeanette *special education educator*
Caprez, Judith V. *social worker, director*
Coyne, Patrick Ivan *physiological ecologist*
Mercer, Debbie K. *dean*
Nassif, Carrie *psychologist, educator*
Novototorov, Andrew *educator*
Tsereteli, Zurab *surgeon*

Haysville
Brown, Linda Carolyn *music educator*

Hillsboro
Kroeker, David Wayne *finance educator, coach*
Kyle, Richard Granville *history professor, religion educator*

Hope
Hottman, Geneva Rae *elementary school educator*

Hugoton
Schroeder, Eunice M. *library director*

Hutchinson
Baumer, Beverly Belle *journalist*
Bowman, Larry *chemistry professor*
Buzbee, Richard Edgar *retired newspaper editor*
Crater, Timothy Andrews *internist*
Kelly, Robert, IV, *library director*
Kerr, Dave *state official, marketing professional*
O'Neal, Michael Ralph *state legislator*
Orwoll, Christopher D. *museum administrator, military officer*
Swearer, William Brooks *lawyer*
Wendelburg, Norma Ruth *composer, educator, pianist*

Iola
Piazza, Tony *theater educator*
Toland, Clyde William *historic site director, lawyer*

Isabel
Brant, Dorris Ellen Stapleton *bacteriologist, music educator*

Junction City
Werts, Merrill Harmon *retired management consultant*

Kansas City
Albertini, David Fred *biomedical scientist, educator*
Anderson, Harrison Clarke *pathologist, educator, biomedical researcher*
Arakawa, Kasumi *physician, educator*
Atkinson, Barbara F. *academic administrator, dean, medical educator*
Berenbom, Loren David *cardiologist*
Drake, Kenneth David *geologist*
Duchene, David Arthur *urologist, educator*
Dunn, Marvin Irvin *physician*
Godwin, Harold Norman *pharmacist, educator*
Griebling, Tomas Lindor *urologist, educator*
Guenther, Sheldon *chiropractor, educator*
Holzbeierlein, Jeffery *medical educator*
Horvat, Rebecca Thayer *microbiologist, educator*
Hudson, Robert Paul *medical educator*
Huet, Raul *psychiatrist*
Jerome, Norge Winifred *nutritionist, anthropologist, educator*
Keleher, James P. *archbishop emeritus*
Kim, Samuel S. *endocrinologist, educator*
Kumm, Sharon Kay *critical care nurse*
Lancaster, Ronnie Lyle *psychologist*
Lawrence, Walter Thomas *plastic surgeon*
Lee, Kyo Rak *radiologist, educator*
Liu, Wen *biomedical engineer, researcher*
Lukert, Barbara P. *medical educator*
Lungstrum, John W. *federal judge*
Meyers, David George *internist, cardiologist, educator*
Minter, Karen Celeste *music educator*
Mohn, Melvin Paul *anatomist, educator*
Naima, Hasan A. *academic administrator, department chairman*
Naumann, Joseph Fred *archbishop*
Olofson, Tom William *technology company executive*
Penick, Elizabeth C. *psychologist*
Perez, Victor Manuel *physician, plastic surgeon*
Porter, Marty *museum director*
Rawitch, Allen Barry *medical educator, academic administrator*
Richards, Lorie Gage *occupational therapist, educator*
Schloerb, Paul Richard *surgeon, educator*
Shariati, Mehdi Sezavar *social sciences educator*
Smith, Peter Guy *neuroscience educator, researcher*
Thrasher, J. Brantley *urologist*
Vratil, Kathryn Hoefer *federal judge*
Warne, Alan M. *continuing education educator, consultant*
Waxse, David John *judge*
Xiao, Zhousheng *pharmacologist, bone biologist*

Kiowa
Conrad, Melvin Louis *biology professor*

Larned
Dodez, Diane M. *retired principal*

Lawrence
Adams, Craig David *environmental engineering educator*
Agrawal, Gail *dean, law educator*
Ammar, Raymond George *physicist, researcher*
Angino, Ernest Edward *retired geology and engineering educator*
Armitage, Kenneth Barclay *retired biology professor*
Audus, Kenneth L. *dean, pharmaceutical researcher*
Barnett, William Arnold *economics professor*
Benjamin, Bezaleel Solomon *structural engineer, educator*
Bial, Henry *theater educator*
Boyd, Beverly *English literature educator*
Briscoe, Mary Beck *federal judge*
Brundage, James Arthur *historian, educator*
Byers, George William *retired entomology educator*
Caminero-Santangelo, Marta Maria *literature and language professor*
Casad, Robert Clair *legal educator*
Chong, Kelly Haesung *sociologist*
Cienciala, Anna Maria *history professor*
Clowes, Edith W. *literature and language educator, consultant*
Cravens, Thomas E. *physics educator, researcher*
Crowe, William Joseph *librarian*
Darwin, David *engineering educator, consultant*
De George, Richard Thomas *philosophy educator*
Dickinson, Martin Brownlow, Jr. *law educator*
Dickinson, William Boyd, Jr. *media consultant*
Dreschhoff, Gisela Auguste Marie *physicist, researcher*
Eldredge, Charles Child III *art history educator*
Estep, Meredith E. *neuroscientist, educator*
Finneran, Lanell Rene *special education educator, drama therapist*
Frederickson, Horace George *retired academic administrator, humanities educator*
Gerhard, Lee Clarence *geologist, educator*
Givens, Richard Spencer *chemist, educator*
Grabow, Stephen Harris *architecture educator*
Gray-Little, Bernadette *academic administrator, psychology professor*
Gunn, James Edwin *language educator*
Hale, Richard Lee *magazine editor*
Hardin, Richard Francis *language educator*
Hardy, Saralyn Reece *museum director*
Haricombe, Lorraine *library director, dean*
Harvey, Douglas Scott *historian, educator*
Hemenway, Robert E. *history professor, former academic administrator*
Herlihy, Laura Hobson *anthropologist*
Himmelberg, Charles John III *mathematics professor, researcher*
Kelly, Mary Byrd *language educator*
Kim, ChangHwan *sociologist, educator*
Krishtalka, Leonard *paleontologist, educator, museum director, researcher*
Landgrebe, John Allan *chemistry professor*
Levin, Eve *history professor*
Lichtwardt, Robert William *mycologist*
Macpherson, Gwendolyn Lee *geochemist, educator*
Mangino, Mark Thomas *college football coach*
Manning, Danny (Daniel Ricardo Manning) *men's college basketball coach, retired professional basketball player*
Mattila, Edward Charles *music educator*
Mc Coin, John Mack *social worker*
Michener, Charles Duncan *entomologist, researcher, educator*
Miller, Timothy Alan *religion educator*
Mitscher, Lester Allen *chemist, educator*
Moore, Richard Kerr *electrical engineering educator*
Muirhead, Vincent Uriel *retired aerospace engineer*
Pasco, Allan Humphrey *literature educator*
Pasik-Duncan, Bozenna Janina *mathematics professor, researcher*
Pence, Ray *social studies educator*
Riffel, Laura Ann *director, special education educator*
Roskam, Jan *aerospace engineer*
Ryun, Jim (James Ronald Ryun) *former congressman*
Saleebey, Dennis *humanities educator*
Saul, Norman Eugene *historian, educator*
Schloss, John Vinton *biochemist*
Self, Bill *men's college basketball coach*
Shaffer, Harry George *retired economics professor*
Shankel, Delbert Merrill *microbiologist, biologist, educator*
Simons, Dolph Collins, Jr. *publishing executive, editor*
Simpson, Greg B. *psychology professor, department chairman*
Soberón Mainero, Jorge *former commission administrator, ecology researcher, educator*
Tacha, Deanell Reece *federal judge*
Takeyama, Akiko *anthropologist, educator*
Tsubaki, Andrew Takahisa *theater director, educator*
Tull, Pamela M. *public relations executive*
Turnbull, H. Rutherford III *lawyer, educator*
Tuttle, William McCullough, Jr. *history professor*
Van Vleck, Fred Scott *mathematician, educator, researcher*
Weber, Jennifer Lee *historian, educator*
Willhite, G. Paul *chemical engineer, petroleum engineer, educator*
Winter, Winton Allen, Jr. *lawyer, state legislator*
Woelfel, James Warren *philosophy and humanities educator*
Worth, George John *retired English literature educator*

Leavenworth
Crow, Michael P. *lawyer*

Leawood
Dykes, Archie Reece *finance company executive*
Epperly, Ted *physician, medical association administrator*
Garwood, Julie *writer*
King, Barbara Sackheim *travel company executive*
Mooney, Justin David *motel executive, consultant*
Vanatta, Chester B. *management consultant, educator*
Zell, Valerie *art historian, educator*

Lenexa
Amundson, Beverly Carden *retired artist*
Bona, Max *mechanical engineer, educator*
Cunningham, Paul George *minister*
Hackett, Jill M. *academic administrator*
Warenskjold, Dorothy *singer, educator*

Liberal
Devinney, Carroll Lynn *economics professor*
Hicks, Linda Reona *elementary school educator*
Richard, Loren Dru *bank executive*
Smothermon, Reba Maxine *elementary school educator*
Workman, Darin D. *music educator*

Lincoln
Crangle, Robert D. *lawyer, management consultant, entrepreneur*

Lindsborg
Ahlseen, Mark Jason *economics professor*
Homan, Delmar Charles *English educator*
LeGault, Gregory Lee *theater educator, playwright*
Lewis, Linda M. *humanities educator*
Pigge, Joyce A. *political science professor*

Logan
Manion, Kay Daureen *financial and office manager*

Louisville
Jabbar, Abdul *physician, educator, gastroenterologist*

Manhattan
Ahmed, A.S.M. Sabbir *nuclear engineer, physicist*
An, Soontae *communications educator*
Babcock, Michael Ward *economics professor*
Bai, Guihua *research scientist*
Barkley, Andrew Paul *economics professor*
Bhadriraju, Subramanyam Venkata *entomologist, consultant*
Chapes, Stephen Keith *immunologist, educator*
Coffman, James Richard *academic administrator, veterinarian, educator*
Durkee, William Robert *retired internist*
Erickson, Larry Eugene *chemical engineering educator*
Foerster, Bernd *architecture educator*
Gallagher, Richard Ray *engineering educator, dean*
Gould, Thomas HP *communications educator*
Hammaker, Robert Michael *chemist, educator*
Higham, Robin *historian, editor, publisher*
Hutchinson, Stacy Lewis *environmental engineer, educator*
Johnson, William Howard *retired agricultural engineer, educator*
Kaufman, Donald Wayne *research ecologist*
Kirkham, M. B. *plant physiologist, educator*
Klabunde, Kenneth J. *chemistry professor, researcher*
Lee, E(ugene) Stanley *engineering educator*
Lynch, Judith Arlene *academic administrator, director*
MacRitchie, Finlay *chemistry professor, consultant*
McCright, Paul R. *engineer, educator*
McKee, Richard Miles *retired agricultural studies educator*
Murray, John Patrick *psychologist, educator, researcher*
Myers, Richard Bowman *former Chairman of the Joint Chiefs of Staff*
Nafziger, Estel Wayne *economics professor*
Ollington, David McKenna *performing arts educator*
Patterson, Deb *women's college basketball coach*
Prins, Harald Edward Lambert *anthropologist, educator*
Richter, William Louis *social sciences educator*
Schmidt, David A. *engineering educator*
Schulz, Kirk H. *academic administrator*
Seaton, Edward Lee *editor, publishing executive*
Setser, Donald Wayne *chemistry professor*
Shanklin, Carol W. *dietician, educator*
Simons, Gale Gene *nuclear and electrical engineer, educator*
Sorensen, Christopher Michael *physics professor, researcher*
Stalheim-Smith, Ann *biology educator*
Stockli, Martin Peter *physics educator*
Swanson, Diane Loraine *business management and economics educator, researcher*
Thumm, Uwe *physics professor*
Tomich, John M. *biochemistry professor, science administrator*
Trussell, Alice J. *library director, department chairman*
Twiss, Page Charles *geology educator*
Walker, Charles Eugene *retired science educator*
Wesch, Michael *anthropology educator, cultural anthropologist, media ecologist*
Wysin, Gary Matthew *physics professor*

Mcpherson
Barber, Carla *museum association administrator*
Coppock, Doris Ellen *retired music and physical education educator*
Dickhudt, Gene Robert (Joe Dickhudt) *electrical engineer, college professor*
Hopkins, Kyle Darin *music educator, director*

Mission
Bonci, Andrew S. *chiropractor*
Bresky, Steven J. *agricultural products executive*
Churchill, James Garton *retired finance company executive*

Mission Hills
Rose, Stephen F. *columnist*

Neosho Falls
Bader, Robert Smith *biology and zoology educator, researcher*

North Newton
Ediger, Marlow *retired education educator*
Eitzen, David Stanley *sociologist, educator*
Pannabecker, Rachel K. *museum director, social sciences educator*
Sprunger, Keith L. *historian, educator*

Olathe
Anderson, Joshua M. *speech educator*
Colson, Judy C. *music educator*
Dodd, James B. *Internet executive*
Eichholz, Mark Joseph (Mick) *lawyer*
Fales, Jennifer Lea *family and consumer sciences educator*
Henning, Lillian Joyce *special education educator*
Kamberg, Mary-Lane *writer, journalist*
Kao, Min H. *manufacturing executive*
Kline, Phillip D. *prosecutor, former state attorney general*
Luetje, Charles Marion, II, *otolaryngologist*
McVey, Walter Lewis *retired lawyer, educator*
Monzon, Carlos Manuel *physician*
Peterson, Cynthia L. *communications educator*
Sattley, William Matthew *biology professor, researcher*
Stevens, Diana Lynn *elementary school educator*

Onaga
Dillinger, Susan Alice *instructor*

Overland Park
Alves, Paget L. *telecommunications industry executive*
Betts, Gene M. *telecommunications industry executive*
Blim, Richard Don *retired pediatrician, health facility administrator*
Burger, Henry G. *vocabulary scientist, anthropologist, writer*
Butrick, Charles W. *gynecologist*
Christian, Shirley Ann *journalist, author*
Churay, Daniel J. *lawyer*
Davis, Maureen *performing arts educator*
Diviney, Nancy Lynn *elementary school educator*
Ferrell, James Edwin *nuclear energy industry executive*
Follo, Judith E. *biology professor*
Gerke, Thomas A. *telecommunications industry executive, lawyer*
Gerlach, Carl R. *mayor, Overland Park, Kansas*
Ghahramani, Katie K. *associate professor*
Goetz, Kenneth Lee *cardiovascular physiologist, research consultant, writer*
Gray, Thomas Alva, Jr. *writer, retired protective services official*
Green, John Lafayette, Jr. *strategic planning executive, academic administrator*
Halloran, Rachelle *pre-school educator*
Hillen, James Joseph *language educator*
Hoare, Timothy Douglas *humanities educator*
Horen, Jeffrey Harry *statistician*
Karmeier, Delbert Fred *engineer, consultant, realtor*
Kem, Katherine Frances *urban planner*
Keplinger, Bruce (Donald Keplinger) *lawyer*
Landry, Mark Edward *podiatrist, researcher*
Morgan, William (Bill) *telecommunications industry executive*
Murray, Thomas Veatch *lawyer*
Noe, James Kirby *retired computer consultant*
Ostby, Frederick Paul, Jr. *meteorologist, retired government official, science administrator*
Patterson, James *telecommunications industry executive*
Paulsen, Ruth Ann *French and Spanish language educator*
Pribyl, Rick R. *English language educator*
Seitter, Julie E. *psychologist*
Shoemaker, Scott David *network consultant, educator*
Stanton, Roger D. *lawyer*
Stem, Carl Herbert *business educator*
Thompson, Mary Elizabeth *retired application developer*
Toussaint, Claudia S. *telecommunications industry executive, lawyer*
Velicer, Janet Schafbuch *retired elementary school educator*
Vratil, John Logan *state legislator*
Walker, H. Reed *lawyer*
Willsie, Sandra Kay *internist, educator*
Woods, Richard Dale *lawyer*
Wornall, Ilah Ruth (Ruthie Wornall) *publishing executive, educator*
Wunsch, Charles Robert *lawyer*
Zollars, William D. *freight company executive*

Oxford
Browning, Terri L. *secondary school educator*

Paola
Buntin, Sandra Lynn *music educator*

Parsons
Lomas, Lyle Wayne *agricultural research administrator, educator*
Walker, Robert R. *music educator*
Zollars, Scotty M. *library director*

Pittsburg
Beer, Pamela Jill Porr *writer, retired vocational school educator*
Lee, Earl Wayne *library science educator*
Morgan, Lyle Warner, II, *medical educator*
Muoghalu, Michael I. *finance educator*
Nettels, George Edward, Jr. *retired mining executive*
Trent, Darrell M. *ambassador, academic administrator, transportation executive*

Pleasanton
Earnest, Ola May *curator*

Prairie Village
Fairchild, Robert Charles *pediatrician*
Mainster, Martin Aron *ophthalmologist, educator*

Pratt
Hayden, (John) Michael *state official, former Governor of Kansas*
Loomis, Howard Krey *banker, director*

Russell
Harrington, Joan Kathryn *counselor*

Salina
Ackerman, Patricia Elizabeth *language educator*
Coakley, Paul Stagg *bishop*
Ferrell, Heather A. *museum director, curator*
Fitzsimons, George Kinzie *bishop emeritus*
Hale Carter, Mollie *bank executive*

Shawnee
Clifton, Thomas E. *academic administrator, minister*
Jordan, Nick M. *state legislator*
Mustard, Mary Carolyn *financial executive*
Poplau, Ronald W. *social studies educator*

Shawnee Mission
Badgerow, John Nicholas *lawyer*
Becker, David M. *lawyer*
Bell, Deloris Wiley *physician*
Braude, Michael *commodities trader, researcher*
Breen, Katherine Anne *speech and language pathologist*
Fleming, Michael O. *physician*
Flora, Jairus Dale, Jr. *statistician*
Gamet, Donald Max *appliance company executive*
Gates, Lawrence C. *political organization worker, lawyer*
Henley, Douglas E. *medical association administrator*
Johnson, Bradford McClure *financial consultant, investor*
Martin, Donna Lee *retired publishing company executive*
McEachen, Richard Edward *banker, lawyer*
Nulton, William Clements *retired lawyer*
Price, James Gordon *physician, educator*
Putman, Dale Cornelius *management consultant, lawyer*
Sader, Carol Hope *former state legislator*
Snyder, Willard Breidenthal *lawyer*
Starrett, Frederick Kent *lawyer*
Thomas, Christopher Yancey III *surgeon, educator*
Wagner, Robert Wayne *management consultant*

Stilwell
Hodgell, Murlin Ray *dean*

Tonganoxie
Torneden, Connie Jean *banker*

Topeka
Adkins, Amanda *political organization administrator*
Bayless, Kellis Matthew *biology professor*
Beier, Carol Ann *state supreme court justice*
Biles, Dan *state supreme court justice*
Bunten, William Daniel *retired banker*
Cantrell, Duane L. *retail executive*
Carlin, Sydney *state legislator*
Chinn, Jennie *museum director*
Cohen, Lauren Ann *psychologist*
Craw, Nicholas Wesson *motor sports association executive*
Cripe, Elizabeth Ann (Betty) *investment company executive*
Crow, Sam Alfred *judge*
Davis, Robert Edward *state supreme court chief justice*
Dennis, Dale M. *school system administrator*
Eberhart-Phillips, Jason *state agency administrator, public health service officer*
Elrod, Linda Diane Henry *lawyer, educator*
Findley, Troy Ray *Lieutenant Governor of Kansas, former state legislator*
Frahm, Sheila *association executive, academic administrator, former government official*
Garner, Jim D. *state official, lawyer*
Gordon, Lana G. *state legislator*
Griffin, Ronald Charles *law educator*
Hayse, Richard Franklin *lawyer*
Holmes, Carl Dean *state legislator*
Hoogenakker, Jim L. *literature and language professor*
Horst, Deena Louise *state legislator*
Johnson, Lee Alan *state supreme court justice*
Jones, Carlene P. *psychologist, educator*
Khan, Lori Marie *physical therapist*
Luckert, Marla Jo *state supreme court justice*
Marney, Brenda Joyce *reverend, computer programmer*
Marquardt, Christel Elisabeth *judge*
McFarland, William Joseph (Joe) *academic administrator*
McKinney, Dennis *state treasurer*
Menninger, William Walter *psychiatrist*
Monk, Carl Colburn *law educator, former legal association administrator*
Moore, William B. *energy executive*
Nuss, Lawton R. *state supreme court justice*
Parkinson, Mark Vincent *Governor of Kansas*
Posny, Alexa Emily *state official, school system administrator*
Prece, Paul M. *theater educator, department chairman*
Pruitt, Virginia Diane *literature and language professor*
Rogers, Richard Dean *federal judge*
Rosen, Eric S. *state supreme court justice*
Roy, William Robert *physician, lawyer, former congressman*
Rubel, Matthew Evan *retail executive*
Schmidt, Derek Larkin *state legislator*
Sheldon, Roy Albert *literature and language professor*
Six, Stephen N. *state attorney general, former judge*
Smith, Loran Bradford *political science professor*
Spencer, William Edwin *retired telecommunications industry executive, engineer*
Spohn, Herbert Emil *psychologist*
Stratton, Wayne Thomas *lawyer*
Thornburgh, Ron E. *Secretary of State, Kansas*
Thull, Tom (John Thomas Thull) *state banking agency administrator*
Varner, Charleen LaVerne McClanahan *nutritionist, educator, dietician*

Valley Center
Greenwood, Riley MacGregor *biology educator*

Westwood
Bodensteiner, David Carl *medical educator*

Wichita
Ayres, Ted D. *lawyer*
Badger, Ronald Kay *lawyer*
Bakken, Linda *Developmental And Social Psychology Professor*
Berner-Harris, Cynthia Kay *library director*
Betts, Donald, Jr. *state legislator*
Blakeslee, Donald J. *archaeologist, writer*
Bloom, Barry Theil *pediatrician, researcher*
Brewer, Carl *Mayor, Wichita, Kansas*
Brown, Wesley Ernest *federal judge*
Budnicki, Michael J. *nurse*
Cadman, Wilson Kennedy *retired utilities executive*
Da'Luz Vieira-Jones, Lorraine Christine C. *acupuncturist, researcher*
Dierks, Melinda Adair *science educator*
Docking, Thomas Robert *lawyer, former state lieutenant governor*
Dorr, Stephanie Tilden *psychotherapist*
Emami, Tooran *electrical engineer, researcher*
Feilmeier, Steve *corporate financial executive*
Gable, Wayne E. *lobbyist*
Gallardo, Cheryl K. *administrative assistant*
Gerber, Eugene John *bishop emeritus*
Guthrie, Diana Fern *nursing educator*
Gythiel, Anthony Paul *history professor*
Harstine, Stan D. *religious studies educator*
Hatteberg, Larry Merle *photojournalist*
Herr, Peter Helmut Friederich *sales executive*
Hittle, Lisa Lynn *musician, educator*
Holaday, Bonnie Jean *nursing educator*
Holden, Mark V. *lawyer*
Isakov, Victor Michael *mathematics educator and researcher*
Jackels, Michael Owen *bishop*
Johnson, Kevin Blaine *lawyer, educator*
Jones, Schuyler *museum director, anthropologist*
Kahn, Melvin A. *political science professor*
Kenned, Kermit Lee, Jr. *retired military officer*
Koch, Charles de Ganahl *industrial company executive*
McArthur, Tillian (Tilly McMac) *freelance/self-employed music educator, small business owner*
McDonnell, Patricia Joan *museum director*
McKee, George Moffitt, Jr. *retired civil engineer consultant*
Melgren, Eric Franklin *federal judge, former prosecutor*
Nassif, Bradley Louis *research scholar*
Nawrocki, Michael Alexander *veterinarian*
Park, Chan Hyung *cell biologist, physician*
Parker, Marietta *prosecutor*
Parks, Linda S. *lawyer*
Pottorff, Jo Ann *state legislator*
Sommer, James Steven *psychologist*
Stephenson, Richard Ismert *lawyer*
Unruh, Susan Marie *psychologist, educator*
Wilhelm, William Jean *civil engineering educator*
Winkler, Dana John *lawyer*
Yang, Shang-You *medical educator*

Winfield
Gray, Ina Turner *fraternal organization administrator*

KENTUCKY

Ashland
Ali, Arshad *cardiologist, medical researcher*
Beasley, Paul Wayland *academic administrator*
Georgas Flath, Mary Cat *biology professor*

Auburn
Buster-Kemplin, Katina Joy *educational consultant*

Barbourville
Wood, Andelys *literature and language professor*

Bardstown
Sutton, Brian K. *construction executive*

Bellevue
Carpenter, Woodrow Wilson *manufacturing executive, ceramics engineer*

Benton
Denial, Roy *editor, author*
Robichaud, Carolyn Wommack *retired secondary school educator*

Berea
Boggs, Bennett Gibson *academic administrator*
Cornette, Robert E. *pediatric nurse practitioner, educator*
Frazier, Joy A. *retired nurse*
Haddix, Susan Ann *secondary school educator*
Lamb, Irene Hendricks *medical researcher*

Bowling Green
Brett, Bolen Day *physics professor*
Cangemi, Joseph Peter *psychologist, consultant, educator*
Cheng, Chin-Min *environmental scientist*
Dahl, Darwin B. *educator*
Endres, Nikolai *literature educator*
Forrest, Dan *librarian*
Foster, Connie L. *librarian*
Haynes, Robert Vaughn *retired academic administrator, historian*
Holland, John Ben *clothing manufacturing company executive*
Huddleston, Joseph Russell *retired judge, mediator, arbitrator*
Li, Qi *science educator*
Navalta, James W. *physical education educator*
Pertusa, Inmaculada *language educator*
Slocum, Donald Warren *chemist, educator, researcher*
Spraker, John Stephen *mathematician, educator*
Watkins, Leslie M. *academic administrator*

Brandenburg
Bowen, Patricia Lederer *dental educator*

Brooksville
Dorton, Truda Lou *medical/surgical and geriatrics nurse*

Buckner
Kelley, Michael *internal medicine and pediatric physician*

Burlington
Kahmann, Sarah Stuber Blanken retired foundation administrator

Calvert City
Madison, Vicki DiAnne retired music educator

Campbellsville
Burch, John Russell, Jr. library director, historian, writer
Conner, Jeanette Jones retired elementary school educator
Creason, Larry Dean law educator
Foster, Joseph Darrol finance educator
Meece, Drewry retired education educator, minister
Parker, Jeanette psychology professor

Campton
Drake, David Lee electronics engineer

Catlettsburg
Nixon, Ronda Lynn paralegal

Cawood
Shepherd, William Michael music educator, musician

Columbia
Senters, Melinda history professor

Corbin
Barton-Collings, Nelda Ann retired political organization worker, bank executive, entrepreneur

Covington
Berg, Lorine McComis retired guidance counselor
Chambers, Lamar M. chemical company executive
Froesel, David W., Jr. medical products executive
Gemunder, Joel Frank healthcare company executive
Hausrath, David L. lawyer
Kobasuk, Mark G. lawyer, pharmaceutical executive
Littleton, Nan Elizabeth Feldkamp psychologist, educator
O'Brien, James J. manufacturing executive
Sloan, David B. lawyer

Crescent Springs
Chellgren, Paul Wilbur energy industry executive

Crestview Hills
Bryant, Gregory A. instructional technologist and designer, educator

Crestwood
Hanson, Richard Harris language educator
Roy, Elmon Harold minister

Cynthiana
Florence, Joyce Fritz mathematics professor

Danville
Allen, John Jay Spanish language educator
Anderson, David Anton economics professor
Bradshaw, Richard Albert historian, consultant
Breeze, William Hancock academic administrator
Holman, Deborah Young art educator
Johnson, Bruce Kenneth economics professor, department chairman
Levin, William Robert art historian
Montgomery, Henry Edward chemistry professor
Nickens, Harry Carl medical association administrator
Pappas, Marjorie L. library studies educator
Roush, John A. academic administrator

Eastwood
Snyder, Ronald R. lawyer

Edgewood
Dick, Barry Lee surgeon
Kalos, Alan V. health planning administrator

Elizabethtown
Buckles, Adrian Dale dean, educator
Lassanske, Donna J. nurse, educator
Rahman, Rafiq Ur oncologist, educator

Elkton
Manthey, Frank Anthony physician, director

Elsmere
Miller, Jackie Dean, I, genealogist, historian

Eubank
Karriker, Danny Allen small business owner, protective services official

Fedscreek
Bottom, Jean Bertrand media specialist

Florence
Gorman, Gayla Marlene Osborne consumer affairs executive
Robinson, William T. III lawyer

Fort Campbell
Griffin, Johnny Lee military officer
Gutheinz, Michael John military officer, lawyer

Fort Mitchell
Silvers, Gerald Thomas retired publishing executive

Fort Thomas
Hughes, William Anthony bishop emeritus
Yelton, Dianne Burgess secondary school educator

Fort Wright
Sullivan, Connie Castleberry artist

Frankfort
Bennett, Charles H. dean
Beshear, Steven Lynn Governor of Kentucky, lawyer
Carroll, Julian Morton state legislator, former Governor of Kentucky, lawyer
Conway, Jack W. state attorney general
Cunningham, Bill state supreme court justice
Fletcher, Winona Lee theater educator
Gibbons, Judith A. librarian
Grayson, Trey (C.M. Grayson) Secretary of State, Kentucky
Hacker, William D. state agency administrator, public health service officer
Hampton-Norphlet, Dantrea RayAnn librarian
Hecker, Margaret Prentice academic librarian
Hollenbach, Todd (L. J. Hollenbach IV) state treasurer
Holliday, Terry state official, school system administrator
Huebner, Ruth A. science educator, researcher
Lancaster, Susan Abramson education educator, consultant
Minton, John Dean, Jr. state supreme court chief justice
Mongiardo, Daniel (Frank Daniel Mongiardo) Lieutenant Governor of Kentucky, state senator, otolaryngologist
Obielodan, James Bolanle management information systems educator
Palmore, John Stanley, Jr. retired lawyer
Robertson, Steve political organization administrator
Schroder, Wil state supreme court justice
Scott, Will T. state supreme court justice
Sisney, Sherleen Sue secondary school educator
Stumbo, Gregory D. state legislator, former state attorney general
Trammell, Jerry Powell literature and language educator
Venters, Daniel Joseph state supreme court justice
Vice, Charles A. state banking agency administrator
Williams, Ellen C. lobbyist, political organization worker

Franklin
Law, Jerriann Marcella artist, poet, writer
Starks, Venessa G. retired elementary school educator

Georgetown
Arnson Svarlien, Diane translator, educator
Cairo, Michael political science professor
Caroland, William Bourne structural engineer
Drake, Albert Estern retired statistics educator, farming administrator
Hall, Sara Y. retired music educator
Klotter, James C. historian, educator
Livingston, Tracy biology professor
Patton, Mary Ritchie retired pediatric nurse practitioner, consultant
Wiseman, Frank L., Jr. chemistry professor

Glasgow
Fritsch, Jennifer Lynne middle school educator, artist
Whittaker, Bill Douglas minister

Grand Rivers
Young, Lucy Cleaver retired physician

Grayson
McDaniel, Charles J. art educator

Greenville
Walters, Sue Fox broadcast executive, accountant

Grethel
Hughes, Cindi Baker special education educator

Guston
Yundt, Betty Brandenburg elementary school educator

Hardin
Morrow, Bruce William academic administrator, management consultant

Hawesville
Curry, Michael Jason human resources specialist

Hazard
Cory, Cynthia Strong mathematics professor
Currie, Paul B. biology professor

Henderson
Logan, John A. III hospital administrator

Highland Heights
Foley, Sean P. construction executive, educator
Kenny, Gregory B. industrial equipment executive
Mittal, Banwari finance educator, entrepreneur

Hopkinsville
Neville, Thomas Lee food service company executive
Redmon-Holliday, Rose Marie secondary school educator

Independence
Hopgood, James F. anthropologist, educator

La Grange
Morgan, Mary Dan librarian

Lebanon
Cook, James veterinarian

Lexington
Al-Hasan, Majdi N. medical educator, researcher
Allison, Jonathan Mackinnon university professor, researcher
Anderson, James Wingo physician
Anderson, Terri Diane history professor
Arnold, J. Fred III cosmetic dentist
Aynsley, Richard Michael architect, researcher
Baker, Merl engineering educator
Ballard-Croft, Cherry medical educator, researcher
Bennett, Victoria Elizabeth rehabilitation nurse, dialysis nurse and technician
Boone, Megan E. engineer, director
Boyd, James Robert energy executive
Brennen, David A. dean, law educator
Brock, Carolyn Pratt chemist, educator
Brock, Louis Milton, Jr. engineering educator, researcher
Calipari, John Vincent men's college basketball coach
Calvert, C. Emmett former state agency administrator
Campbell, Charles Larry, Jr. cardiologist
Canales, Denise Niles software company executive
Carroll, John Sawyer educator, former newspaper editor
Chance, Kenneth Bernard, Sr. endodontist educator, academic administrator
Charnigo, Richard John, Jr. statistician, educator
Chi, Young-In science educator, researcher
Clawson, David Kay orthopedic surgeon
Coffman, Edward McKenzie retired history professor
Colbert, Marvin Jay retired internist, educator
Collins, Martha Layne academic administrator, former governor
Crooks, Peter Anthony professor, researcher, entrepreneur
Cross, Alvin Miller (Al Cross) journalist
Curlander, Paul Joseph technology executive
Davey, Diane Davis pathologist, educator
DeLuca, Patrick Phillip pharmacist, medical association administrator, educator
Diedrichs, Carol Pitts library dean
Donohue, Kevin D. computer engineer, educator
Drake, Vaughn Paris, Jr. electrical engineer
Ehmann, William Donald chemistry professor
Ettensohn, Frank Robert geologist, educator
Ferzacca, William retired education educator
Fleischman, Roger Alan medical educator, researcher
Fragneto, Regina anesthesiologist
Fryman, Virgil Thomas, Jr. lawyer
Gainer, Ronald William bishop
Gallaher, Art, Jr. university chancellor emeritus, anthropology educator
Garen, John Edward economics professor
Garman, Ray Fillmore occupational physician, director
Gedaly, Roberto surgeon, educator
Guskey, Thomas Robert education educator
Hagen, Michael Dale family physician educator
Hall, Harry H. agricultural economics educator
Hamilton-Kemp, Thomas Rogers organic chemist, educator
Hartsfield, James Kennedy, Jr. orthodontist, geneticist
Henrich, Sarah E. museum director
Herberth, Johann nephrologist, educator
Hillebrand, Evan Everett economist, educator
Hochstrasser, Donald Lee cultural anthropologist, community health and public administrator
Holsapple, Clyde Warren decision and information systems educator
Holsinger, James Wilson, Jr. cardiologist, physician
Hoven, Ardis Dee epidemiologist, medical educator
Huberfeld, Nicole Lauren healthcare educator
Huffman, Gerald P. science administrator, educator
Hultman, Charles William economics professor
Imhoff, Kathleen Ruth Tostrud library administrator
Isenhour, Kathleen Chaney special education educator
Jackson, Judy Faye academic administrator
Johnson, Jane Penelope freelance/self-employed writer
Justice, Laura L. dentist
Kelly, Timothy Michael newspaper publisher
Kern, Bernard Donald retired physicist
Kibler, William Benjamin orthopedist, surgeon
Kissling, Fred Ralph, Jr. publishing and insurance agency executive
Labianca, Giuseppe finance educator
Lai-Fook, Stephen Joseph retired science educator
Lain, Kristine Yoder medical educator
Larson, Jon S. lawyer
Lester, Roy David lawyer
Lewis, Robert Kay, Jr. fundraising executive
Lodder, Robert A. science educator
Lugo, Noemi G. voice educator
Male, Alan Thomas engineering educator, foundation administrator
Maloney, Doreen M. performing arts educator
Mason, Ellsworth Goodwin retired librarian
Matveeva, Elena Aleksandrovna microbiologist, biochemist, educator
Means, Robert Taylor, Jr. hematologist, educator, researcher
Miller, Pamela Gundersen retired mayor
Moliterno, David J. cardiologist, educator
Mostert, Paul Stallings retired mathematician
Mukherjee, Debabrata cardiologist, researcher
Newberry, Jim Mayor, Lexington, Kentucky
Noble, Mary C. state supreme court justice
Novak, Camille small business owner, consultant
Palli, Subba Reddy scientist, professor
Panayiotis, Zavos Michael retired medical educator
Partain, Gregory L. composer, educator
Paruchuri, Jithendra Kumar signal processing researcher
Pearson, Cheryl A. dentist
Pickens, Rupert Tarpley III French language educator
Piper, George Chilton lawyer
Puffer, James C. sports medicine physician, educator, medical association administrator
Randall, David Clark medical educator, researcher
Reed, Michael Robert agricultural economist
Reynolds, Eric William medical educator
Roberts, Kenneth Boyett pharmacy educator, former dean
Romanowitz, Byron Foster architect, engineer
Rous, Beth S. social studies educator, researcher
Saghaian, Sayed economics professor
Sandoval, Arturo Alonzo artist, educator
Santí, Enrico Mario humanities educator
Sekulic, Dusan P. science and engineering educator, researcher
Sexton, Robert Fenimore educational organization executive
Shawcross, John Thomas English educator
Shimojo, Masahito science educator
Sih, Andrew biologist, educator
Simon, Lisa travel association executive
Sineath, Timothy Wayne librarian, educator, dean
Smith, Charles Dennis neurologist, researcher
Stack, Steven J. emergency physician
Stempel, John Dallas international studies educator
Stilwell, William Earle III psychology educator, retired military officer
Straus, Robert behavioral sciences educator
Strup, Stephen Edward urologist, educator
Sun, LuZhe pharmacology educator, researcher
Svarlien, John E. classicist, educator
Thapar, Amul R. federal judge, former prosecutor
Thelin, John Robert historian, educator, researcher
Timoney, Peter Joseph veterinarian, educator, virologist, consultant
Todd, James Marion retired lawyer
Todd, Lee Trover, Jr. academic administrator, electrical engineer
Tribble, Joan Lucille (Joan Farnsley Tribble) retired literature and language professor, writer
Troedsson, Mats H.T. veterinarian
Turner, Sharon P. dean, dentist, educator
Varellas, Sandra Motte judge
Waid, Thomas Henry physician, researcher, educator
Walsh-Piper, Kathleen A. museum director
Wildasin, David E(arl) economics professor
Woodring, John Howell radiologist
Worell, Judith P. psychologist, educator
Zerhusen, James A. prosecutor

London
Keller, John Warren lawyer
Siler, Eugene Edward, Jr. federal judge

Louisville
Abramson, Jerry E. mayor, Louisville
Adams, Robert Waugh retired state agency administrator, economist, educator
Alpert, Brian oral surgeon, educator
Amin, Mohammad urology educator
Andrew, Lane N. medical researcher, educator
Andrews, Billy Franklin pediatrician, educator
Ansong, Miriam Adjoa pharmacist, educator
Aronoff, George Rodger medicine and pharmacology educator
Ballantine, John Tilden lawyer
Ballew, Laurie K. psychiatrist
Barnes, Brian Glen philosopher, educator, researcher
Barr, James Houston III lawyer
Barski, Oleg Aleksandrovich biochemist
Belanger, William Joseph chemist, consultant
Bloem, James H. managed health care executive
Bodduluri, Haribabu medical educator, researcher
Boggs, Danny Julian federal judge
Bosley, Gabriele W. language educator, director
Boykin, Gladys retired religious organization administrator
Bratton, Ida Frank retired secondary school educator
Breidenbach, Warren Conrad III plastic surgeon, hand surgeon
Brolick, Emil J. food products executive
Buell, Joseph F. surgeon, director
Callen, Jeffrey Phillip dermatologist, educator
Campbell, Christian Larsen lawyer, food service executive
Cantwell, Patricia A. guidance counselor
Carroll, Jean Gray retired mathematics educator
Carucci, Richard T. lawyer
Chagpar, Anees Bahadurali surgeon
Chen, James Ming dean, law educator
Chien, Sufan surgeon, educator
Choi, Namok education educator
Clover, Richard D. dean
Conner, Stewart Edmund lawyer
Dahl, Marilyn Gail psychotherapist
Dale, Judy Ries religious organization administrator, consultant
Danzl, Daniel Frank emergency physician
Das, Manabendra Nath mathematics professor
Datta, Susmita statistician, bioinformatician, educator
Daugherty, Kimberly academic administrator, educator
Davidson, Gordon Byron lawyer
Davis, Charles Raymond retired political scientist, educator
Deering, Ronald Franklin librarian, minister
DeMunbrun-Harmon, Donne O'Donnell retired family physician
Diaz, Paul J. health products executive
Dobbins, Joanne Jones microbiologist, educator
Draper, Charles William religious studies educator
Dudley, George Ellsworth lawyer
Early, Jack Jones foundation executive
Eaton, Roger food products executive
Eggeling da Encarnação, Luis Miguel computer scientist, research and development company executive
Eighmey, Douglas Joseph, Jr. hospital administrator
Elin, Ronald John pathologist, educator
Evans, Robert L. sports venue executive
Farman, Allan George radiologist, pathologist, educator
Fenner, Chris pastor, musician
Foulks, Gary Neal ophthalmologist, educator
Gall, Stanley Adolph immunologist, researcher
Garson, Arnold Hugh publishing executive
Gilfert, Justin Scott lawyer
Gilman, Sheldon Glenn lawyer
Gleis, Linda Hood physician
Goldstein, Irvin L. elementary school educator
Gowrishetty, Usha R. research scientist
Greaver, Joanne Hutchins mathematics educator, writer
Hardin, Carmen Marie music educator
Harkema, Susan medical researcher, director
Hasan, Hammam Adib education educator

Hathcock, Bonita Catherine (Bonnie Hathcock) managed health care company executive
Hayes, William Meredith pilot, retired military officer
Heiden, Charles Kenneth metal products executive, consultant, retired military officer
Helm, Cyril William physician, medical educator, researcher
Henry, Stephen Lewis retired lieutenant governor, orthopedic surgeon, educator
Herrington, Alice Elizabeth associate lawyer
Herrington, E. Paul III lawyer
Heyburn, John Gilpin, II, federal judge
Hickey, Bobby Ray underwriting assistant
Holt, Homer Anthony, Jr. urologist, educator
Houghton, David Jeffery neurologist, educator
Howard, Deanna Jean elementary school educator
Hu, Chuan cell biologist
Huber, Ruth social worker
Hughes Abramson, Lisabeth state supreme court justice
Hutti, Marianne Hopkins nursing educator
Ildstad, Suzanne T. transplant surgeon, immunologist, educator
Ivory, Bennie L. executive editor
Jenne, Sue Oak elementary school educator
Johnson, Alan Arthur physicist, educator, consultant
Jones, David A., Jr. insurance company executive
Jones, Frances Brooks lawyer, bank executive
Kantardzic, Mehmed M. engineering educator
Kaplan, Henry Jerrold ophthalmologist, educator
Kehrt, Bettie F. medical transcriptionist
Kelly, Thomas Cajetan archbishop emeritus
Klotz, Martin Gunter science educator
Koppel, Sheree Powers dean
Kragthorpe, Steve college football coach
Kuntz, Edward Lawrence healthcare executive
Kurtz, Joseph Edward archbishop
Kutz, Joseph Edward hand surgeon, educator
Landan, Henry Sinclair financial and business consultant
Lavelle, Charles Joseph lawyer
Lay, Norvie Lee law educator
Levinson, Stanley S. pathologist, educator
Lin, Ji-Tzuoh energy harvesting researcher
Lin, Stephen Houng Tze music educator
Lopez, Nelson theatre literature professor
Martin, Boyce Ficklen, Jr. federal judge
Martin, David Allen application developer, computer scientist
Martinez-Maldonado, Manuel academic administrator, dean, medical and science educator
Mather, Elizabeth Vivian healthcare executive
McCallister, Michael B. insurance company executive
McClain, Tim S. lawyer
McKim, Ruth Ann financial planner
McLeod, John Edmond history professor
Mellen, Francis Joseph, Jr. lawyer
Metzmeier, Kurt X. legal association administrator
Miller, Donald Max medical association administrator
Mohler, Richard Albert, Jr. academic administrator, theologian
Moore, Joseph Patrick medical researcher, educator
Mountz, Wade retired healthcare executive
Murray, James E. managed health care company executive
Musacchio, Marilyn Jean nurse midwife, educator
Nahata, Babu L. economics professor, researcher
Nasraoui, Olfa computer scientist, educator, electrical engineer
Neustadt, David Harold physician
Newell, Elizabeth Carolyn retired secondary school educator
Noland, Thomas Turley, Jr. managed healthcare company executive
Northern, Richard lawyer
Novak, David C. restaurant company executive
O'Brien, Kevin James museum director
Osborn, John Simcoe, Jr. lawyer
Parkins, Frederick Milton dental educator, dean
Pence, Stephen Beville lawyer, former lieutenant governor
Perez-Abadia, Gustavo A. medical educator
Pitino, Rick men's college basketball coach
Pottinger, Ronald Wayne food products executive
Ravindra, Kadiyala V medical educator, director
Richardson, James David surgeon
Riedman, Mary Suzanne lawyer
Ronald, Peter utilities executive
Rosky, Theodore Samuel insurance company executive
Rothstein, Laura law educator, former dean
Runyon, Keith Leslie lawyer, editor
Ruter, Ruth Evelyn elementary school educator
Sauk, John Joseph dean, educator
Schaefer, David A. dentist
Scott, David Albert biomedical researcher, dental educator
Scott, Ralph Mason retired radiologist, educator
Shields, Christopher Brian neurosurgeon
Shoemaker, Gradus Lawrence chemist, educator
Skees, William Leonard, Jr. lawyer
Stanton, Morris Duncan psychologist, researcher, dean
Sumanasekera, Gamini Udaya physics professor
Sumanasekera, Wasana Kumarihamy medical educator
Syed, Ibrahim Bijli medical educator, physicist
Talbott, Ben Johnson, Jr. lawyer
Talwalkar, Sameer S. pathologist, researcher
Tasman, Allan psychiatry educator
Taylor, Robert Lewis management educator
Terhune, Jerry David biology professor, researcher
Thompson, Kathy C. bank executive
Todoroff, Christopher M. lawyer, insurance company executive
Towles, Donald Blackburn retired publishing executive
Tran, Long Trieu industrial engineer
Tsai, Tsu-Min surgeon
Vadhanam, Manicka V. science educator
Varga, Paul C. beverage products executive
Venable, Charles L. museum director
Vish, Donald H. lawyer, writer, photographer
Waddell, William Joseph pharmacologist, toxicologist
Walz, Jeff (Jeffrey J. Walz) women's college basketball coach
Welsh, Sir Alfred John lawyer, investment advisor
Westberry, Robert Kent lawyer
Wiseman, Dennis R. science educator
Wright, Jeffrey A. biology, physics educator
Wright, Jesse Hartzell psychiatrist, educator
Yahyaoui, Nasr E. educational association administrator
Zahorik, Pavel psychology professor
Zimmerman, Gideon K. retired minister

Madisonville
Florea, Jeffrey Mark economics professor
Kington, Barry Clark investor, consultant
Parker, Faye C. elementary school educator
Price, Erica Hightower psychologist
Spain, Thomas B. retired state supreme court justice
Veazey, Doris Anne retired state agency administrator

Maysville
Quillen, Michael Duane biology professor

Middlesboro
Ahlstedt, Lisa Anne librarian

Midway
Juett, Beverly Willoughby biology professor

Morehead
Birriel, Jennifer Jean physics professor
Blair, Suanne Hower music educator
Caric, Ric Northrup educator
Dean, Lloyd retired high school counselor
Herron, James Dudley chemist, educator
Kiffmeyer, Thomas Joseph history professor
Klecker, Beverly McCauley academic administrator
Miller, Green Russell economist, educator
Pritchard, Elsie Tomlinson librarian

Mount Sterling
Aileen-Donohew, Phyllis Augusta educational consultant

Murray
Cox, James Ricky chemistry professor, researcher
Derting, Terry L. biology professor, researcher
Dunn, Randy J. academic administrator
Ferreyra, Rafael Andres agricultural and biological engineer, consultant, researcher
Guy, Sallie T. artist
Hassan, Seid Y. economics professor
Hill, Todd Edwin band director
Matlock, Pamela Durbin special education educator

Newport
Siverd, Robert Joseph lawyer

Nicholasville
Armstrong, Marcy Lynn literature and language educator
Midkiff, Dinah Lee retired elementary and middle school educator

Owensboro
Barrette, Craig Richard literature and language professor
Boswell, David E., Sr. state legislator
Caplan, Geralyn Marie biology professor
Hood, Mary Bryan museum director, painter
Matally, Moses minister
McRaith, John Jeremiah bishop
Moffett, Joe literature and language professor
Moore, Charles Edward lawyer, political organization administrator
Olssen, Jennifer Leigh elementary school educator
Thomas-Löwe, Christine L. small business owner

Paducah
Craig, Berry Franklin III history professor
Foreman, James Louis retired judge
Kirk, Terri G. library media specialist
Stice, Dwayne Lee broadcasting company executive, professional organist
Talbert, Debra Kaiser elementary school educator, artist

Paint Lick
Donaldson, Kathleen special education educator

Paintsville
Hovee, Mark John psychologist

Pewee Valley
Gill, George Norman newspaper publishing company executive

Pikeville
Hunter, Trudy Pearl surgical nurse
Mutter, Jennie secondary school educator, artist
Smith, Harold Hasken university administrator
Venters, Teresa Anne elementary school educator

Pippa Passes
Mitchell, Kossuth Mayer business educator

Prestonsburg
Bell, Daniel Edwin economics professor

Princeton
Bailey, William Anthony research scientist
Earnest, Melissa Webb education educator
Noffsinger, Nancy Leigh retired special education educator

Prospect
Aberson, Leslie Donald lawyer
Kehlbeck, Joseph H. software developer, consultant

Radcliff
Cole, Jessie Mae nursing assistant, freelance/self-employed writer

Richmond
Ballard, Michael Ray (Mickey Ballard) minister, music educator
Burch, John Russell retired military officer
Chenault, James Stouffer judge
Day-Lindsey, Lisa literature and language professor
Hall, Kathy health facility administrator
Houston, Robert Grant, Jr. economics professor
Huch, Ronald Kind historian, educator
James, Rob performing arts association administrator, consultant
Maumbe, Blessing Mukabeta finance educator
McQueen, Keven Darryl literature and language educator
Smith, Carla Anne music educator
Sweely, Gay Caryll art historian, educator
Whitt, Marcus Calvin marketing executive, public relations executive
Wright, John Daniel minister

Russellville
Harper, Shirley Fay nutritionist, educator, consultant, lecturer
Jukes, Jonathan H. school librarian

Scottsville
Secrest, James Seaton, Sr. lawyer

Shelbyville
Miller, Mary Helen retired state government administrator

Simpsonville
Burkhardt, Susanne M. elementary school educator

Somerset
Eastham, Donna Saunders interdisciplinary early childhood educator
Howard, Buford Philip biology professor
Sexton, Scotty Eugene music educator, gifted and talented educator
Watson, Rollin J. former academic administrator, educator, writer

Southgate
Glenn, Jerry Hosmer, Jr. retired language educator

Vanceburg
Phillips, Susan Diane secondary school educator

Versailles
Stober, William John, II, economics professor
Zourarakis, Demetrio Periferachis natural resource scientist

Wickliffe
Frueh, Deborah K.A. (Debi) artist, poet
Shadoan, William Lewis retired judge

Williamsburg
Bay, Mark Twitchell librarian
Blackmore-Haus, Margaret Ann athletic trainer, educator
Dzugan, Thomas chemistry professor
Pilant, Charles Alan history professor
Trickett, Dennis James psychology professor
Weaver, Susan Jeanne sociology educator

Wilmore
Hiatt, Robert Jeffrey religious studies educator
Pohl, Christine D. Christian ethics educator

Winchester
Book, John Kenneth (Kenny) retail store owner
Cantrell, Georgia Ann realtor
Snowden, Ruth O'Dell Gillespie artist

LOUISIANA

Alexandria
Bilotta, Warren Alexander economics professor
Freedman, Robert J. cardiologist, educator
Gootee, Christy Beck minister, educator
Hanley, Henry Gorman cardiologist
Herzog, Ronald Paul bishop
Mathews, Peggy Anne nurse
Miller, Elizabeth Ann mathematician, human services manager
Phillips, Virginia retired federal employee
Vanderslice, Stephen J. literature and language professor
Wesse, David Joseph higher education administrator, consultant

Amite
Parish, Richard Lee engineer, consultant

Baker
Baker, Otis McDowell small business owner
Baker, Yvonne Bell elementary school educator

Baton Rouge
Albagdadi, Fakhri Abdelkareem biology professor
Arceneaux, William historian, educator, association administrator
Arman, Ara civil engineering educator, dean
Banks, Willie Ivory educational administrator
Barbato, Michele engineering educator
Beard, Thomas Rex economics professor
Bedeian, Arthur George business educator
Bengtson, Richard Lee agricultural engineer, educator
Bensman, Stephen J. school librarian, researcher
Bernhard, James M., Jr. engineering executive
Besch, Everett Dickman veterinarian, dean emeritus, educator
Beyer, Horst Reinhard physicist
Blackman, John Calhoun, IV, lawyer
Bourdin, Blaise mathematics professor
Bray, George August internist, researcher, educator
Breaux, John Berlinger lobbyist, former senator
Brewer, Ralph Wright, Jr. lawyer, writer
Buchmann, Molly O'Banion choreographer, educator
Burns, Paul Yoder forester, educator
Byrd, Lidia Maria language educator
Caffey, Horace Rouse academic administrator, agricultural company executive
Calabrese, Michael Raphael manufacturing executive, lawyer, consultant
Caldwell, James David, Jr., (Buddy Caldwell) state attorney general
Camp, John Bliss journalist, television producer
Carman, Kevin R. oceanographer, educator
Casey, Robert Reisch lawyer
Cerise, Frederick P. academic administrator, former state agency administrator
Chan, Julia chemistry professor
Chancellor, Van women's college basketball coach
Chen, Peter Pin-Shan engineering, computer science educator, data processing executive
Cole, Luther Francis former state supreme court associate justice
Collier, John Robert chemical engineer, educator
Cooper, William James, Jr. history professor
Costonis, John J. law educator, former academic administrator
Cramer, Gail economist
Crawford, William Edward law educator
Crumbley, Donald Larry accounting educator, writer
Dardenne, Jay (John Leigh Dardenne Jr.) Secretary of State, La, former state legislator
Dasbach, Oliver T. mathematician, educator
Davis, Hall L., IV, funeral director
Dellinger, Harold Barrett Barry chemistry professor
DiBenedetto, Robert Lawrence retired obstetrician, retired gynecologist, retired insurance company executive
Diener, Peter astrophysicist
Doty, Gresdna Ann theatre historian, educator
Ducrest, John P. state banking agency administrator
Dugas, David Roy prosecutor
Elkins, Gary J. lawyer
Feldman, Martin engineering educator
Ferraioli, Brian K. engineering executive
Francois, M. Rony public health service officer
Gettys, Thomas Wigington medical researcher
Gibbons, William reproductive endocrinologist
Gikas, Carol Sommerfeldt museum director
Graphia, Gary P. lawyer
Grey, Emily Black lawyer
Gudi, Thirupathi computer scientist
Guidry, Jimmy public health service officer
Hamilton, John Maxwell university dean, writer
Hamilton, Rebecca L. state librarian
Hansel, William biology professor
Hardy, John Edward language educator, writer
Harper, Sandra Stecher academic administrator
Harris, Andres manager
Hobbs, Betty Juanita executive legal secretary
Holden, Melvin Lee Mayor-President, Baton Rouge, Louisiana
Hymel, L(ezin) J(oseph) lawyer, former prosecutor
Ingram, Donald Keith psychologist, gastroenterologist
Iqbal, Javed lab administrator
Irvine, Stuart Andrew religious studies educator
Jenkins, William L. academic administrator
Jindal, Bobby (Piyush Jindal) Governor of Louisiana, former United States Representative from Louisiana
Johnson, Joseph Clayton, Jr. lawyer
Johnson, Trent men's college basketball coach
Jolly, Jennifer L. education educator
Kang, Manjit Singh geneticist, plant breeder
Kastin, Abba Jeremiah endocrinologist, researcher
Kennedy, John Neely state treasurer
Khonsari, Michael M. mechanical engineering educator
Kight, Dawn Ventress technologist, consultant
King, Katherine Wright lawyer
Lacy, Fred engineering educator
Landolt, Arlo Udell astronomer, educator
Landrieu, Mitchell Joseph Lieutenant Governor of Louisiana
Lehner, Luis science educator
Leupin, Alexandre language educator
Levine, Alan state agency administrator
Li, Li physical education educator
Liu, Kam-Biu geography educator
Livesay, Thomas Andrew museum director, educator
Lombardi, John V. academic administrator, historian
Longwell, Harry J. retired oil industry executive
Lopez, Mandi J. veterinarian, scientist
Lott, Bret literature and language professor, writer
Lusk, Glenna Rae Knight librarian
Lusted, Dona Sanders music educator, consultant, organist
Madden, David author
Marks, Loren Dean psychology professor
Martin, Michael V. academic administrator, economics professor
Mathews, Sharon Walker performing company executive, secondary school educator
Maverick, Andrew William chemistry educator, researcher
Mc Cameron, Fritz Allen retired university administrator
McCoy, Wesley Lawrence musician, educator, conductor
Mc Glynn, Sean Patrick physical chemist, educator
McKay, Michael Wendell lawyer
Miles, Les (Leslie Edwin Miles) college football coach
Miller, Andrea Lynn communications educator
Moréteau, Olivier law educator
Mueller, Lisel writer, poet
Muench, Robert William bishop
O'Connell, Robert Francis physics professor
Oxley, James Grieve mathematics professor
Parks, James William, II, public facilities executive, lawyer

Pastorek, Paul G. *state official, school system administrator, lawyer*
Pike, Ralph Webster *chemical engineer, educator, academic administrator*
Pollock, David Daniel *biologist, educator, research scientist*
Prestage, James Jordan *consultant*
Pugh, George Willard *law educator*
Puyau, Francis Albert *retired radiology educator, physician*
Quartararo, Philip, Jr. *mathematics professor*
Raghavendra, Amar *systems engineer*
Rankin, Cliff (Clifton S. Rankin) *lawyer*
Rau, Ravi Prakash *physics professor, researcher*
Reeve, Thomas Gilmour *physical education educator*
Ricapito, Joseph Virgil (Giuseppe Ricapito) *literature educator*
Riedlinger, Stephen C. *federal judge*
Risinger, Beth N. *elementary school educator*
Robinson, James William *chemistry professor*
Rubin, Michael Harry *lawyer, educator*
Rutledge, Katherine Burck *artist*
Sandoz, George Ellis, Jr. *political science educator*
Sasek, Gloria Burns *English language and literature educator*
Seo, Dong Cheol *wetland biogeochemist, environmental chemist*
Shr, Mingdr *research scientist*
Singh, Vijay Pal *civil engineer*
Slaughter, Ralph *academic administrator*
Smith, Richard James *retired music educator*
Spearman, Diane Negrotto *art/special education educator*
Spencer, Fitzgerald *medical educator*
Stapp, Dan Ernest *retired lawyer, utilities executive*
Starkey, Bob (Robert G. Starkey) *women's college basketball coach*
Subudhi, Prasanta Kumar *agricultural studies educator*
Superneau, Duane William *geneticist, physician*
Sygula, Andrzej *chemist, researcher*
Tandberg, Gerilyn Gay *theater educator, retired costume designer*
Taylor, John McKowen *lawyer*
Thomas, Jeffrey Cone *financial executive, consultant*
Tipton, Kenneth Warren *retired agricultural administrator, researcher*
Traynham, James Gibson *chemist, educator*
Tumay, Mehmet Taner *geotechnical engineering educator, researcher, consultant*
Vallas, Paul G. *school system administrator*
Valsaraj, Kalliat Thazhathuveetil *chemical engineering educator*
Van Lopik, Jack Richard *geologist, educator*
Villere, Roger F., Jr. *political organization administrator*
Warner, Isiah Manuel *chemistry professor*
Weiss, Jack Meyar *academic administrator, law educator*
Whittington, Christopher L. *lawyer, political organization administrator*
Wisbar, Rebecca Kittok *lawyer*
Woods, R. Clive *electrical engineer, educator*
Xu, Feng *research scientist, educator*
Yarbrough, Martha Cornelia *music educator*
Younathan, Ezzat Saad *retired biochemistry educator*

Benton
Lynn, Jeff Wilson *history educator, farmer*

Bossier City
Brantley, Brenda Bradford *librarian*
Johnson, Russell W. *video editor*
Paris, Norma Jean *psychologist, educational consultant*

Boutte
Patricia, Pitre Agnes *media specialist*

Centerville
Dupre, Susan V. *science educator*

Chalmette
Mumphrey, J. Wayne *lawyer*

Chauvin
Chesney, Edward Joseph *marine biologist, educator*
Sammarco, Paul William *ecologist, researcher*

Choudrant
Lofton, Brenda M. *secondary school educator*

Coushatta
Wiggins, Mary Ann Wise *small business owner, educator*

Covington
Aaron, Shirley Mae *retired tax specialist*
Blossman, Alfred Rhody, Jr. *banker*
Doody, Louis Clarence, Jr. *retired accountant*
Maurin, James E. *real estate executive*
Metzner, David Mark *plastic and reconstructive surgeon*
Perez de la Mesa, Manuel Jose *swimming pool company executive*
Rice, Winston Edward *lawyer, priest*
Snyder, Charles Aubrey *lawyer*
Vercellotti, John Raymond *chemist, researcher*

Cut Off
Mestayer, Mary Frances *science educator*

Denham Springs
Ishler, Harold LeRoy, Jr. *retired physician*

Deridder
Mallory, Patricia Jody *museum curator*
Smith, Mabel Hargis *retired secondary school educator, musician*

Destrehan
Griffith, Steven Franklin, Sr. *lawyer, insurance agent*

Donaldsonville
Hambrick-Jackson, Kathe *museum director*
Watson, Stanley Ellis *clergyman, small business owner*

Doyline
Willis, Gladden Williams *retired pathologist, scientific photographer, tree farmer*

Dry Prong
McLain, Paul King *systems analyst*

Dubach
Straughan, William Thomas *structural engineering consultant, educator*

Eunice
Hernandez, Gloria Marie *mathematician, educator*
Vidrine, Malcolm Francis *biology educator*

Franklin
Fairchild, Phyllis Elaine *school counselor*
Rouly, Ellie Arceneaux *dancer, educator*

Frierson
Cobb, Kathleen Littlejohn *retired school administrator*

Gilbert
Bell, Wallace Edward *minister, insurance agent*

Gonzales
Kidd, Ruth Price *retired secondary school educator*

Grambling
Duckett, Rick *men's college basketball coach*
Favors, Steve Alexander *academic administrator*
Fields, Hall Ratcliff *retired finance educator*
King, Gennice Williams *librarian*
Laleh Parvaran, Parvin *communications educator*
Porter, Wilma Jean *retired educational consultant*

Hammond
Hemberger, Glen James *university band director, music educator*
Kirylo, James David *education educator, consultant*
Kraemer, Robert R. *health educator, researcher*
Lee, Sang Hyup *economics professor, researcher*
McFalls, Tiffany Beth *biology professor*
Merino, Dennis Iligan *mathematics educator, researcher*
Neuerburg, Kent M. *mathematics professor*
Ostarly-Ulfers, Lori Ann *history professor*
Parker, Clea Edward *retired university president*

Harvey
Simon, Keith R. *safety engineer, petroleum engineer, radio personality*

Houma
Babin, Regina-Champagne *artist, educator, musician, consultant*
Crochet, Jared John *research scientist*
Ponvelle, Brittany Gomez *elementary school educator*

Jackson
Kondrup, John Thomas *retired research scientist*

Jennings
Marcantel, Bernard Norman *lawyer, judge*

Kaplan
LeMoine, Frank Eugene *lawyer, judge*

Kenner
Carmon, Dominic *bishop emeritus*
Farber, George Allan *dermatologist, educator*
Scherich, Edward Baptiste *retired diversified company executive*

La Place
Fiffie Proctor, JoAnn *media and technology specialist*

Lacombe
Harlan, Jim *energy executive*

Lafayette
Angers, Winston Thomas *lawyer, publishing executive*
Appley, Alan J. *neurosurgeon*
Authement, Ray Paul *college president*
Barry, Mildred Castille *artist*
Boukadi, Fathi Hamda *petroleum engineer, researcher*
Brabant, Sarah Callaway *sociologist, educator*
Brasseaux, Carl Anthony *historian, educator, academic administrator, curator*
Cain, Judith Sharp *mathematics educator, consultant*
Carstens, Jane Ellen *retired library science educator*
Cravins, Donald R., Jr. *state legislator*
Dasgupta, Subrata *computer & cognitive science educator, director, writer*
Davidson, James Joseph III *lawyer*
Davis, William Eugene *federal judge*
Farshad, Fred F. *engineering educator*
Greco, Anthony Joseph *economics professor*
Groh, William C. *artist*
Guidry, Amy Michelle *artist*
Hail, Karen Lee *bank executive*
Honegger, Mark Andrew *language educator*
Jarrell, Charles Michael *bishop*
Judice, Marc Wayne *lawyer*
Lipstate, Linda *endocrinologist, educator*
Magidin, Arturo *mathematics professor*
Malinowski, Jerome Joseph *design educator*
Malone, Mike *dentist*
Marshak, Alan Howard *electrical engineer, educator*
McNeely, Jason Bryan *research scientist*
Menutis, Ruth Ann *small business owner*
Meza, Luis Alberto *internist, researcher*
Neuner, Frank X., Jr. *lawyer*
Raffel, Burton Nathan *novelist, poet, translator*
Roy, James Parkerson *lawyer*
Simon, Carmon Serena *biology educator*
Skinner, Michael David *lawyer, lobbyist, consultant*
Skinner, Sarah Jackson *economics professor*
Triche III, Charles Walter *librarian, director*
Wang, Hongqing *ecologist, educator*

Lake Charles
Batchelor, Karen Sue *music educator*
Belew, Barbara Jeanne *music educator*
Cook, Nancy J. *language educator*
Drez, David Jacob, Jr. *orthopedic surgeon, educator*
Ferguson, Clarence Edward *social sciences educator*
Fields-Gold, Anita *retired dean*
Gunderson, Clark Alan *orthopedic surgeon*
Kandalam, Anil K. *physicist, educator*
Lee, Brandi Gremillion *elementary school educator*
Levingston, Ernest Lee *engineering company executive*
Lines, Carol Fuqua *voice educator*
McNeill, Joseph Peele *librarian*
Mount, Willie Landry *state legislator*
Pace, (Audrey) Joy *theater educator*
Paris, Margaret G. *librarian*
Provost, Glen John *bishop*
Sawyer, Michael E. *library director*
Speyrer, Jude *bishop emeritus*
Walsh, Louise Jaquelyn *literature and language professor*

Leesville
Thompson, Darlene Bennett *realtor, musician*

Mandeville
Arrowsmith, Marian Campbell *elementary school educator, supervisor, educator*
Deano, Edward Joseph, Jr. *lawyer, state legislator*
Desper, Beatrice S. *obstetrician, gynecologist*
Ewen, Pamela Binnings *retired lawyer*
Landry, Joseph L., Jr. *retired affirmative action specialist*
Pittman, Jacquelyn *retired mental health nurse, nursing educator*
Treuting, Edna Gannon *retired nursing administrator, educator*

Many
Quarles, Mary Jo *school librarian, educator*

Marksville
Riddle, Charles Addison III *district attorney, former state legislator*

Marrero
Kushner, Frederick Gary *cardiologist, medical educator*
Love, Gayle Magalene *school system administrator*

Metairie
Brees, Drew (Drew Christopher Brees) *professional football player*
Burns, William Glenn *lawyer*
Bush, Reggie *professional football player*
Colon, Gustavo Alberto *plastic surgeon*
Colston, Marques *professional football player*
Crosby, Deborah Berry *artist*
Crosby, Marena Lienhard *retired academic administrator*
Dickerson, Lon Richard *library administrator*
Edisen, Clayton Byron *physician*
Falco, Maria Josephine *political scientist*
Farris, Patricia K. *dermatologist, educator*
Grimm, John Lloyd *marketing professional*
Grotkowski, Edward Michael *music educator, director*
Hannan, Philip Matthew *archbishop emeritus*
Harrington, Joey (John Joseph Harrington) *professional football player*
Hussain, Mohammed Ershad *finance educator, researcher*
Jacobs, Benjamin Franklin *cardiologist*
Loomis, Mickey *professional sports team executive*
Lourie, David E. *civil engineer, consultant*
Mirzai, Pirooz (Victor Mirzai) *architect, educator, consultant*
Myers, Iona Raymer *retired real estate property manager*
Nehrbass, Seth Martin *lawyer*
Nicoladis, Michael F. *engineering company executive*
Payton, Sean (Patrick Sean Payton) *professional football coach*
Rosen, Charles, II, *retired lawyer*
Roussos, Christopher Wayne *dental association administrator*
Sanderson, Christine Graves *literature and language educator*
Shockey, Jeremy Charles *professional football player*
Toups, Kim G. *language educator, department chairman*
Vilma, Jonathan Polynice *professional football player*
Wood, Jonathan Stuart *economist, educator*

Minden
Kemmerly, James Robert *obstetrician, gynecologist*

Monroe
Bhattacharjee, Joydeep *biology professor*
Cooksey, John Charles *ophthalmologist, former congressman*
Melder, Trevor F. *physics professor*
Parker, Tammy A. *economics professor*
Post, Glen Fleming III *telecommunications industry executive*
Profit, Loretha Spurs *retired elementary school educator*
Sartor, Daniel Ryan, Jr. *lawyer*
Smith, Pamela LaTrice *school psychologist*
Trapp, A. C. *retired music educator*
Wilson, Holly Lyn *social sciences educator, researcher*

Morgan City
Grant-Dupuy, Jennifer W. *music educator*

Morganza
Williams, Ella *healthcare educator*

Napoleonville
Maggio, Theresa Griffin (Terri Maggio) *librarian*

Natchitoches
Allen, Burt M. *music educator, director*
Derby-McDermott, Dennette S. *flutist, educator*
LeBreton, Marietta M. *history professor*
Wall, Jerry Leon *dean, management educator, university administrator*
Wolfe, George Cropper *retired private school educator, artist, writer*

New Orleans
Abaunza, Donald Richard *lawyer*
Acomb, Robert Bailey, Jr. *lawyer, educator*
Adriaan, St. Claire Marlin *elementary school principal*
Agrawal, Krishna Chandra *pharmacology educator*
Akundi, Murty Adinarayana *research scientist, educator*
Ali, Juzar *medical educator, director*
Alsobrook, Henry Bernis, Jr. *lawyer*
Andrews, E. Wyllys *archaeologist, educator*
Aymond, Gregory Michael *archbishop*
Balée, William L. *anthropology educator*
Barach, Jeffrey Alvan *management educator*
Barbee, Robert Wayne *cardiovascular physiologist*
Bardell, Derek D. *academic administrator*
Barry, Francis Julian, Jr. *lawyer*
Bart, Henry Leonard *biologist*
Beard, Elizabeth Letitia *physiologist, educator*
Beck, David Edward *surgeon*
Beer, Peter Hill *federal judge*
Beisenherz, Nona Kay *law librarian*
Bender, Thomas Benton, IV, *librarian*
Benjamin, Edward Bernard, Jr. *lawyer*
Bennett, James Toliver *pediatric orthopedist*
Berenson, Gerald Sanders *physician*
Bidima, Jean Godefroy *medical educator, researcher, Philosophy Professor*
Bieck, Robert Barton, Jr. *lawyer*
Bischof, Günter Josef *history professor*
Blakely, Edward James *city official, economics professor*
Blanchard, Terence *musician, composer*
Blonde, Lawrence *endocrinologist, director*
Boggs, Corinne Claiborne (Lindy Boggs) *Former United States Representative, La*
Bookhardt, Fred Barringer, Jr. *architect*
Botros, Fady T. *medical educator*
Boudreaux, Kenneth Justin *economist, educator*
Bower, Jeff *professional sports team executive*
Bowers, Cyril Y. *endocrinologist, educator*
Brennan, Ella *restaurant manager*
Brock, Cori M. *pharmacist, educator*
Brown, Jerry A. *federal judge*
Brumfield, William Craft *Slavic studies educator, photographer, writer*
Bryan, Amy *art educator, director*
Bullard, Edgar John III *museum director*
Carlson, Robert Marshall *health facility administrator*
Casellas, Joachim *art gallery executive*
Castaneda, Marco A. *economics professor*
Cheatwood, Roy Clifton *lawyer*
Childress, Steven Alan *law educator*
Chiu, Ernest Sai-Yun *plastic and reconstructive surgeon, educator*
Clement, Edith Brown *federal judge*
Cody, Wilmer St. Clair *educational policy consultant*
Cohn, Isidore, Jr. *surgeon, educator*
Colletti, Janet Sarradet *engineering educator*
Collins, Harry David *forensic, mechanical and nuclear engineer, claims consultant*
Combe, John Clifford, Jr. *lawyer*
Conroy, David Jerome *lawyer*
Conroy, Patrick *legal educator, department chairman*
Cook, Victor Joseph, Jr. *business educator, consultant*
Cornelius, Mary Lynn *entomologist*
Cospolich, James Donald *electronics executive, consultant*
Cowen, Scott S. *academic administrator*
Crumley, David Oliver *publishing executive, writer*
Crusto, Mitchell Ferdinand *lawyer, educator*
Cui, Yan *medical educator, researcher*
Culbertson, Richard Allen *healthcare educator, health facility administrator*
Daniels, Antonio Robert *professional basketball player*
DeFelice, Frances Radosta *retired restaurateur*
DeNisi, Angelo *dean*
Dennis, James Leon *federal judge*
Dong, Yan *biologist*
Dorris, Ronald *humanities educator, literature and language professor*
Du, Shanshan *anthropologist, educator*
Duggan, James Edgar *law professor and law librarian*
Easson, William McAlpine *psychiatrist, educator*
Echeverri, Margarita *researcher, educator*
Fabre, Shelton Joseph *bishop*
Fagaly, William Arthur *curator*
Filson, Ronald Coulter *architect, educator, dean*
Fisher, James William *pharmacologist, medical educator*
Flower, Walter Chew III *investment counselor*
Force, Robert *law educator*
Foti, Charles C., Jr. *lawyer, former state attorney general*
Fraiche, Donna DiMartino *lawyer*
Frohlich, Edward David *medical educator*
Frystak, Shannon Lee *historian, researcher*
Fuselier, Harold Anthony, Jr. *urologist, director, educator*
Gage, Anastasia Jessica *healthcare educator, researcher*
Gendusa, Charles Patrick *performing arts educator*

Goins, Richard Anthony *lawyer, educator*
Gordon, Joseph Elwell *university official, educator*
Gould, Harry J. III *neurology educator*
Griffin, Stephen M. *dean, law educator*
Gruber, J. Richard *museum director*
Guidry, Greg G. *state supreme court justice*
Hall, Gwendolyn Midlo *historian, educator*
Hardin, Harry S. III *lawyer*
Harris, Frances Flintroy *retired university administrator assistant, civic worker*
Hasselbach, Karlheinz *retired literature educator*
Healy, George William III *lawyer, mediator*
Herman, Michael F. *chemistry professor*
Higgins, Oleda Jackson *retired medical and surgical nurse*
Hill, James *medical educator, researcher*
Hobden, Jeffery Andre *medical researcher, educator*
Hoffman, Donald Alfred *lawyer*
Hollier, Larry Harold *vascular surgeon, hospital administrator, dean*
Hu, Jennifer J. *epidemiologist, researcher*
Hughes, Alfred Clifton *Archbishop Emeritus*
Hurley, Grady Schell *lawyer*
Hyslop, Newton Everett, Jr. *infectious disease specialist*
Incaprera, Frank Philip *internist*
Irons, Paulette Riley *state legislator, lawyer*
Jain, Prem C. *economics professor*
Jayawickramarajah, Janarthanan *chemistry professor*
Jenkins, James Stephen *internist*
Johnson, Bernette Joshua *state supreme court justice*
Jones, Philip Kirkpatrick, Jr. *lawyer*
Joshi, Virendra *medical educator*
Kahn, David M. *museum director*
Kalka, Morris *mathematics professor*
Kelly, Eamon Michael *economic development professor, retired university president*
Kern, Clifford Harold, Jr. *retired lawyer*
Kilroy, James Francis *humanities educator*
Kimball, Catherine D. *state supreme court chief justice*
Klingman, John Philip *architect, educator*
Knoll, Jeannette Theriot *state supreme court justice*
Kolinsky, Michael Allen *emergency physician*
Kruse-Jarres, Rebecca *medical educator*
Laborde, James Monroe *orthopedist*
Lagasse, Emeril *chef, restaurant owner, television show host, writer*
Lannes, William Joseph III *electrical engineer*
Lavie, Carl J. *cardiologist, researcher*
Legrand, Benjamin David *elementary school educator, consultant*
Lemann, Thomas Berthelot *lawyer*
Lesen, Amy E. *biology professor*
Letten, James B. *prosecutor*
Lichtveld, Maureen Yvette *medical educator, department chairman*
Liljeberg, Genevieve Brocato *artist*
Lind, Thomas Otto *barge transportation company executive*
Locke, William *retired endocrinologist*
Lodhi, Mahtab A. *social sciences educator*
Lowe, Robert Charles *lawyer*
Luza, Radomir Vaclav *retired historian, educator*
Lyons, Sue Ellen Landry Landry *private school educator, consultant*
Magnus, Jeanette H. *medical educator*
Manry, David L. *finance educator, consultant*
Mao, Zhiqiang *physics professor*
Marcus, Bernard *lawyer, arbitrator, mediator*
Martin, David Hubert *internist, epidemiologist, educator*
McAllister, James Anthony *literature and language professor*
McArthur, Janet Davis Penland *literature and language educator*
McCall, John Patrick *college president, educator*
McClay, Wilfred Mark *history educator, writer*
McGuire, James Horton *physics educator*
McMullan, Paul *cardiologist*
Melson, Lisa *psychology educator*
Millikan, Larry Edward *dermatologist*
Mislove, Michael William *mathematics educator, theoretical computer scientist*
Mitchell, Kenneth David *physiologist, educator*
Mitchell, Mary Niall *history professor*
Moely, Barbara E. *psychologist, educator*
Moffett, James Robert *mining executive*
Mogabgab, Rose-Warren Berryman *academic administrator, writer*
Moreno, Helena *newscaster*
Moulder, Peter Vincent *cardiovascular surgeon, educator*
Murrish, Charles Howard *oil and gas exploration compant executive*
Nagin, Ray C. (Clarence Ray Nagin Jr.) *Mayor, New Orleans*
Navar, Luis Gabriel *physiology educator, director, researcher*
Nichols, Ronald Lee *surgeon, educator*
Nuss, Daniel Wehrmann *surgeon, educator*
Ochsner, John Lockwood *thoracic-cardiovascular surgeon*
Okafor, Emeka (Chukwuemeka Noubuisi Okafor) *professional basketball player*
Okorn, Nchor Bichene *political science professor*
Olson, Richard David *psychology professor*
Osakwe, Christopher *lawyer, educator*
Ostendorf, Lance Stephen *lawyer, financial consultant, educator, importer exporter entrepreneur*
Pankey, George Atkinson *internist, educator, researcher*
Paolini, Gilberto *literature educator*
Paradise, Louis Vincent *education educator, dean*
Parsley, Ronald Lee *paleontology educator*
Paul, Chris *professional basketball player*
Perdew, John Paul *physics professor*
Perrons, Robert K. *engineer, researcher*
Phelps, Ashton, Jr. *newspaper publisher*
Pizer, Donald *author, educator*
Poesch, Jessie Jean *art historian*
Pope, John Marvin *journalist*
Poretto, Jodi *art dealer*
Porter, George Homer III *physician, medical foundation executive*
Prockop, Darwin Johnson *biochemist, medical educator*
Pullikuth, Ashok K. *research scientist*
Pyburn, Keith McBride, Jr. *lawyer*
Qian, Zhaoming *literature educator, critic*
Qiu, Meikang *engineering educator*
Query, Lance D. *dean, university librarian*
Raj, Madhwa Hg *healthcare educator*
Reck, Andrew Joseph *philosopher*
Reed, Willis *professional sports team executive*
Richardson, Donald Edward *neurosurgery educator*
Riddick, Frank Adams, Jr. *physician, healthcare administrator*
Rinker, Craig Wayne *minister, educator*
Rodriguez, Antonio Jose *lawyer*
Roesler, Robert Harry *media consultant*
Rosensteel, George Thomas *nuclear physicist, professor*
Ryu, Kisang *educator*
Sacks, Joel Gerald *ophthalmologist, educator*
St. Julien, Thais Mary *soprano, musician*
Salm, Steven J. *history professor*
Saloy, Mona Lisa *literature and language professor*
Schalow, Frank Hickey *philosopher, educator*
Schehr, Kevin John *art gallery owner*
Schnabel, Marta-Ann *lawyer*
Schnoebelen, Ian *chef*
Schulte, Francis B. *archbishop emeritus*
Scott, Byron *professional basketball coach, retired professional basketball player*
Sherry, Thomas Warren *ecologist*
Shinn, George *professional sports team owner*
Simmons, William Skip Bruce, Jr *science educator*
Simon, H(uey) Paul *lawyer*
Sloan, Dauphine de Montlaur *literature and language professor*
Sloan, Robert D. *energy executive, lawyer*
Smith, Juanita Bérard *lawyer, artist*
Snyder, Sharon Veta *management consultant, educator*
Steeg, Moise S., Jr. *lawyer*
Stojakovic, Peja *professional basketball player*
Strength, Catherine Bush *nursing educator*
Sullivan, Daniel Edmond *fundraising executive*
Summer, Warren R. *pulmonologist, director*
Surendran, Sankar *research scientist*
Susic, Dinko *physiologist*
Talley, Patrick A., Jr. *lawyer*
Tang, Jianwu *geochemist, researcher*
Tao, Jianmin *chemistry educator, researcher*
Tender, Gabriel Claudiu *neurosurgeon, consultant*
Threefoot, Sam Abraham *physician, educator*
Timmcke, Alan Edward *colon and rectal surgeon*
Tipler, Frank Jennings III *physicist*
Tou, Jen-sie Hsu *biochemistry educator*
Tracy, Richard E. *medical educator*
Traylor, Chet D. *state supreme court justice*
Trostorff, Danielle M. *lawyer*
Van Dyke, Russell Barrett *medical educator*
Vaudry, J. William, Jr. *lawyer*
Victory, Jeffrey Paul *state supreme court justice*
Waggonner, Joseph David III *architect*
Watson, James Raymond *education educator*
Weber, Hugh *professional sports team executive*
Weimer, John L. *state supreme court justice*
Weinmann, John Giffen *lawyer, ambassador*
West, David Moorer *professional basketball player*
Wiener, Jacques Loeb, Jr. *federal judge*
Wolfe, Richard Peel *lawyer*
Worley, Robert Bruce, Jr. *lawyer*
Zhu, Dongxiao *science educator*
Zimmerman, Robert S. *internist, endocrinologist*

New Roads
Hymel, Melissa K. *librarian*

Newllano
Boren, Lynda Sue *gifted education educator*

Opelousas
Lafleur, Kenneth Charles *ophthalmologist*
Underwood, Lorainne Ballard *literature and language educator*

Pearl River
Cantrell, Joseph Sires *chemistry professor*
Thiel, David Brian *physician assistant*

Pineville
Beall, Grace Carter *business educator*
Martin, W. Terry *librarian*
Quarles, Charles Leland *religious studies educator, researcher*
Thorn, Shannon H. *hospital administrator, consultant*
Thrasher, Fay C. *clinical psychologist*
Webb, Watts Rankin *surgeon*

Ponchatoula
Kuechmann, Christopher Robert *library director*
Kuhn, James Edward *judge*

Prairieville
Biri, Toni Roppolo *elementary school educator*
Brown, Robert Lawrence *research plant pathologist*

Rayne
Sha, Xueyan *agricultural studies educator*

River Ridge
Didriksen, Caleb H. III *lawyer*

Ruston
Carwile, Guy Winstead *architect, educator*
Davis, Despina *engineering educator*
de Mattos, Rudy *language educator*
Fang, Ji *electrical engineer*
Freasier, Aileen W. *special education educator*
Genov, Dentcho Angelov *engineering educator*
Hudnall, Jarrett, Jr. *management consultant, educator, marketing professional*
Liu, Don *researcher*
Nassar, Raja *statistics educator, researcher, consultant*
Saber, Aziz *engineering educator*
Sale, Tom S. III *financial economist*
Sarkar, Jayanta *economist, educator*
Thompson, Laura Ann Mobley *music educator*
Wasiuddin, Nazimuddin Mohammad *engineering educator*

Saint Martinville
Fournet, Patricia Sibley *retired secondary school educator*

Schriever
Jacobs, Sam Gallip *bishop*

Shreveport
Blondin, Joan *nephrologist educator*
Brannon, Guy Emilio *psychiatrist*
Bryant, J(ames) Bruce *lawyer*
Burton, George Aubrey, Jr. *accountant*
Butcher, Greg Q. *neuroscientist, educator*
Carmody, Arthur Roderick, Jr. *lawyer, director, author*
Carmouche, Paul J. *lawyer*
Chung, Jun *medical educator*
Conrad, Steven Allen *critical care and emergency physician, biomedical engineer, educator*
Cox, John Thomas, Jr. *lawyer*
Duca, Michael Gerard *bishop*
El-Haddad, Ghassan *nuclear medicine physician, researcher*
Glasgow, Dianne Britt *education educator, writer, consultant*
Glover, Cedric Bradford *Mayor, Shreveport, La*
Goodman, Robert Uhle *lawyer*
Hall, Amy Matthews *science educator*
Huang, Shile *biochemist, educator*
Hughes, Mary Sorrows *artist*
Jawahar, Ajay *neurosurgeon, educator*
Jones, Kenneth B., Jr. *surgeon*
Kendrick, Rhonda Lynn *poet, small business owner*
Lazarus, Allan Matthew *retired newspaper editor*
Mikaberidze, Alexander *history professor, researcher*
Misra, Raghunath Prasad *physician, educator*
Morelock, Jasmine Crawford *artist*
Parish, Roy Clayton *medical researcher*
Payne, Roy Steven *lawyer*
Pleasant, John Ruffin, Jr. *retired literature and language professor*
Powell, Thomas William *speech and language pathology educator*
Reddy, Pratap Chandupatla *cardiologist, educator, researcher*
Rodriguez, Juan *physics professor*
Shelby, James Stanford *surgeon, researcher*
Shemwell, Robert H. *federal judge*
Smith, Karen L. *elementary school educator*
Spaht, Carlos G., II, *mathematics educator*
Staats, Thomas Elwyn *neuropsychologist*
Stewart, Carl E. *federal judge*
Stucker, Fred Joseph *otolaryngology educator*
Sutton, G. Katherine Hallett *nurse*
Testerman, Traci L. *educator*
Timm, Donna Faye *librarian*
Vachharajani, Tushar Jitendra *nephrologist, researcher*
Wall, Simeon Heninger, Jr. *plastic surgeon*
Washington, Donald W. *prosecutor*
Wilson, John T. *pediatrics and pharmacology educator*

Sicily Island
Dale, Sam E., Jr. *retired educational administrator*

Slidell
Dabdoub, Paul Oscar *academic administrator*
Dearing, Reinhard Josef *curator, retired city official*
Fincher, Margaret Ann *retired secondary school educator*
McBurney, Elizabeth Innes *dermatologist, physician, educator*
Singletary, Alvin D. *lawyer*
Stuart, Charles Edward *electrical engineer, oceanographer*
Tewell, Joseph Robert, Jr. *retired electrical engineer*

Springhill
Morgan, Larry Ronald *minister*
Thomas, Faye Evelyn J. *elementary and secondary school educator*

Sulphur
Fuller, Betty Stamps *music educator*
Toniette, Sallye Jean *physician*

Thibodaux
Hebert, Frances Cynthia *music educator*
Hulbert, Stephen Thompson *academic administrator*
Soares, Luciana *music educator*

Tioga
Brandow, Stephen Jon *priest*

West Monroe
Ford, Mary Ann *secondary school educator*

Zachary
Price, Carol Leah *mathematics educator*
Rogillio, Kathy June *musician, director, small business owner, educator*

MAINE

Allagash
Hafford, Faye O'Leary *writer*

Alna
Beerits, Janet Penrose Robinson *sculptor*
Russell, Clifford Springer *economics, public policy, educator*

Andover
Kaltsos, Angelo John *electronics executive, educator, photographer*

Anson
Quimby, Janice Ann *minister*

Auburn
Clifford, Robert William *state supreme court justice*

Augusta
Baldacci, John Elias *Governor of Maine*
Cragin, Charles Langmaid *lawyer*
Davis, George Edward *internist*
Dunlap, Matthew Gordon *Secretary of State, Maine, former state legislator*
Finnegan, John Vianney *insurance company executive, risk management consultant, educator*
Gendron, Susan Ann *state official, school system administrator*
Gervais, Paul Nelson *foundation administrator, psychotherapist, writer, public relations executive*
Harvey, Brenda M. *state agency administrator*
Huntington, Thomas Gordon *hydrologist, researcher*
Johnson, Phillip Edward *lawyer*
Knutson, John *political organization administrator*
LaFountain, Lloyd P. III *state banking agency administrator*
Lemoine, David G. *state treasurer*
Martin, John Lewis *state legislator*
Mills, Janet Trafton *state attorney general, former state representative*
Mitchell, Elizabeth H. (Libby Mitchell) *state legislator*
Nickerson, John Mitchell *political science professor*
Phillips, Joseph Robert *museum director*
Randall, Richard J. *academic administrator*

Bangor
Ballesteros, Paula Mitchell *nurse*
Bickford, Meris J. *lawyer, bank executive*
Coffman, Michael S. *international organization official, ecologist*
Davis, Bruce Hewat *pathologist, researcher*
Erhardt, Niclas *finance educator*
Fletcher, Francis Stephen *marketing and management consultant*
King, Stephen Edwin *writer, scriptwriter*
MacTaggart, Terrence Joseph *education educator, researcher, former academic administrator*
Martin, Thomas Charles *pediatrician*
Merkel, Anne D. *science educator*
Pattenaude, Richard Louis *academic administrator, educator*
Rea, Ann W. *librarian*
Rich, Karen Verna Stonebridge *nursing educator*
Silver, Warren M. *state supreme court justice*

Bar Harbor
Coleman, Douglas *research scientist, educator*
Krevans, Julius Richard *academic administrator, internist*
Leiter, Edward Henry *cell biologist, researcher*
Petkov, Petko M. *geneticist, researcher*
Swazey, Judith Pound *academic administrator, science educator*

Bath
Galleher, Gay *psychologist*

Belfast
Griffith, Patricia King *journalist*

Biddeford
Ford, Charles Willard *medical educator*
Sandmire, David A. *biology professor*

Blue Hill
Katzer, James Robert *retired research scientist*

Boothbay
Kaplan, Fred *literature educator, biographer*

Brewer
Davis, William Edmund *retired education educator*

Brooklin
Schmidt, Klaus Dieter *marketing professional, management consultant, educator*

Brownfield
Kloskowski, Vincent John, Jr. *educational consultant, author, educator*

Brunswick
Fuchs, Alfred Herman *psychologist, educator*
Geoghegan, William Davidson *religion educator, minister*
Hodge, James Lee *German language educator*
King, Angus S., Jr. *former governor*
Kline, Katy *museum director*
Mills, Barry *academic administrator, lawyer*
Owen, H. Martyn *retired lawyer*
Peacher, Georgiana Melicent *poet, educator*
Sprague, Edward Auchincloss *retired professional society administrator, economist*

Bryant Pond
Conary, David Arlan *investment company executive*

Camden
Daly, Sean G. *bank executive*

Cape Elizabeth
Rich, John Hubbard, Jr. *retired news correspondent*

Cape Porpoise
Glasser, William Arnold *academic administrator*

Casco
Brown, Ronald Osborne *telecommunications and computer systems consultant*

Castine
Berleant, Arnold *philosopher*
Bernstein, Lester *editorial consultant*
Davis, Peter Frank *filmmaker, writer*

Kettis, Pär Axel *Swedish diplomat*
Wiswall, Frank Lawrence, Jr. *lawyer, educator*

Chebeague Island
Traina, Salvatore Albert *publishing executive*

Cumberland
Jamison, Elizabeth Alease *executive director*

Cumberland Foreside
Martin, Joseph Robert *retired corporate executive*

Dresden
Iserbyt, Charlotte Thomson *researcher, writer, educational consultant*
Turco, Lewis Putnam *writer, English educator*

East Boothbay
Eldred, Kenneth McKechnie *acoustician, consultant*
Gibson, Barry Joseph *editor*

Edgecomb
Carlson, Suzanne Olive *architect*

Ellsworth
Young, Lucia Patat *psychotherapist*

Falmouth
Cabot, Lewis Pickering *manufacturing company executive, art consultant*
Pierce, Philip Sargent *clinical psychologist*
Rohsenow, Warren Max *retired mechanical engineer, educator*
Toomey, Jeanne Elizabeth *animal activist*

Farmington
Barigar, Elizabeth Gayle *painter, art educator*
Frary, John Newton *history professor*
Kalikow, Theodora June *academic administrator*
Mathews, Linnea Koons *science educator, librarian*
Webster, Charles M. *political organization administrator*

Fort Fairfield
Shapiro, Joan Isabelle *lab administrator, medical/surgical nurse*

Fort Kent
Gauvin, Tony *entrepreneur, educator*

Fort Kent Mills
Paradis, Roger *history & folklore professor, researcher*

Freeport
Panish, Morton B. *retired physical chemist*

Fryeburg
Crane, Robert Kendall *engineering educator, researcher, consultant*

Gardiner
Dunbar, Robert Everett *writer, educator*

Georgetown
Chapin, Maryan Fox *civic worker*
Chapin, Richard *trustee*
Ipcar, Dahlov *artist, writer, illustrator*

Gorham
Kilroy, Wil *theater educator*
Whitten, Maurice Mason *chemistry professor*

Hallowell
Douglass, Neria Gay *state legislator, lawyer*

Hancock
Silvestro, Clement Mario *museum director, historian*

Harpswell
Ford, Elaine *english educator*

Harrington
Ray, Brittany E. *literature and language educator*

Hollis Center
Kaake, Norman Bradford *quality assurance professional*

Houlton
Michael, Hannigan Owen *biology educator*

Jefferson
MacKinnon, Victor Stuart *retired law educator*

Kennebunk
Damon, Edmund Holcombe *retired plastics company executive*

Kennebunkport
Featherman, Bernard *steel company executive*
Featherman, Sandra *retired academic administrator, political science professor*
Mulvihill, James Edward *periodontist, educator, health center administrator*
Picavet, Robert Clement *retired lawyer*

Kingfield
Silver, Sally *minister*

Kittery Point
Green, Edward Crocker *research scientist*

Lewiston
Aschauer, David Alan *finance educator*
Coleman, Laurel *geriatrician, internist*
Feintuch, Robert *painter*
Hansen, Elaine Tuttle *academic administrator*
Hodgkin, Douglas Irving *political science professor*
Semon, Mark David *physicist, researcher*
Singh, Abhay Kumar *psychiatrist, department chairman*
Speer, Richard Allan *library director*
Tardif, Donna Lynn *elementary school educator*
Wollman, Nathaniel *retired economics professor*

Long Island
Chassen-López, Francie R. *history professor*

Lubec
Hayes, Ernest M. *podiatrist*

Milbridge
Enslin, Theodore Vernon *poet*

Mount Desert
Crawford, Richard Bradway *biologist, biochemist, educator*
Elias, Merrill Francis *neuropsychology and neuroepidemiology researcher*

New Harbor
Fradley, Frederick Macdonell *retired architect*
Lyford, Cabot *sculptor*
Woolf-Wade, Sarah Jane *retired elementary school educator, writer*

New Vineyard
Smith, Frederick Orville, II, *agricultural products executive, retired military officer*

Newfield
Patten, Ronald James *university dean*

North Yarmouth
Fecteau, Rosemary Louise *educational administrator, consultant*

Ogunquit
West, Norman Ellsworth *artist*

Old Orchard Beach
Day, Marlene E. *elementary school educator*

Oquossoc
Hughes, William Frank *mechanical and electrical engineering educator*

Orono
Abedi, Ali *engineering educator*
Butterfield, Stephen Alan *education educator*
Clapham, William Montgomery *plant physiologist*
Cody, Howard Hugh *political science professor*
Cohn, Steven Frederick *sociology educator, consultant*
Crouch, Terrell Hunter *literature and language professor*
Dalton, Timothy John *economics professor*
Dewhurst, Timothy Bruce *mechanical engineer educator*
Goldstone, Sanford *psychologist, educator*
Hardy, Sandra E. *theater educator, director*
He, Zhongqi *chemist, researcher*
Jianhui, Yue *computer engineer, researcher*
Kearney, Adrienne Anne *economics professor*
Kennedy, Robert Alan *educational administrator*
Lin, Lin *research scientist*
Norton, Stephen Allen *earth sciences educator*
Rice, Edward Perry *secondary school educator*
Richard, Hollinger Vernon *archivist, historian*
Wiersma, G. Bruce *dean, forester, educator*

Orrs Island
Nelson, Robert Louis *lawyer*

Peaks Island
Bohan, Thomas Lynch *physicist, retired lawyer*

Penobscot
dePaolo, Ronald Francis *editor-in-chief, writer*

Portland
Alexander, Donald G. *state supreme court justice*
Altshuler, Kenneth Paul *lawyer*
Bjelic, Dušan Ilija *science educator*
Blair, Bonnie Kathleen *former professional speedskater, Olympic athlete*
Botman, Selma *academic administrator, political science professor*
Bradford, Carl O. *judge*
Chapkis, Wendy Lynn *women's studies educator, sociologist*
D'Abate, Richard *museum director, historian*
Dana, Howard H., Jr. *lawyer, retired state supreme court justice*
Dill, William Rankin *college president*
Edwards, Matthew William *systems engineer*
Glassman, Caroline Duby *state supreme court justice*
Glucksberg, Nadia *geologist, consultant*
Gorman, Ellen A. *state supreme court justice*
Graffam, Ward Irving *lawyer*
Hunt, David Evans *lawyer*
Ives, Samuel Clifton *minister*
Jones, Blair Anthony *lawyer*
Kayatta, William J., Jr. *lawyer*
Lancaster, Ralph Ivan, Jr. *lawyer*
LeBlanc, Richard Philip *lawyer*
Levy, Jon D. *state supreme court justice*
Lipez, Kermit V. *federal judge*
Malone, Richard Joseph *bishop*
Manuel, Peter Jay *poet, singer/songwriter, dramatist, language professor, librettist*
Masrani, Bharat B. *bank executive*
McAfee, Robert Elwood *retired surgeon*
McKusick, Vincent Lee *retired chief justice, arbitrator, lawyer, mediator*
Mead, Andrew M. *state supreme court justice*
Morgan, Patricia Ann *nursing educator*
O'Leary, Daniel E. *museum program director*
Pitegoff, Peter Robert *dean, law educator*
Reid, Rosemary Anne *insurance agent*
Saufley, Leigh Ingalls *state supreme court chief justice*
Sawyer, Dana Waide *religious studies educator*
Schwanauer, Francis *philosopher, educator*
Silsby, Paula D. *prosecutor*
Spalding, Tim *Internet company executive*
Stauffer, Eric P. *lawyer*
Summers, Charles E., Jr. *military officer, former state senator*
von Schack, Wesley W. *utilities executive*
White, Jeffrey Munroe *lawyer*
Wilkinson, Barbara J. *pediatrician, educator*
Zarr, Melvyn *lawyer, educator*

Presque Isle
Gentile, Caroline D. *adult education educator*

Raymond
Coughlan, Patrick Campbell *lawyer, mediator*

Rockland
Anne, Lois *artist, educator*
Collins, Samuel W., Jr. *retired judge*
Urbanelli, Lora *museum director*

Rockport
Goodwin, Doris Helen Kearns *historian, writer*

Sanford
Allan, Jonathan David *autograph dealer, pop culture historian, writer*

Scarborough
Clark, Gordon Hostetter, Jr. *physician*
Doermann, Humphrey *writer, consultant*
Sadik, Marvin Sherwood *art historian, consultant, retired museum director*
Shire, Donald Thomas *retired chemicals executive, lawyer*

Sidney
Gooldrup, Marjorie Shepard *music educator*

Skowhegan
Ross, James Owen *education educator, researcher*

South Bristol
Lasher, Esther Lu *minister*

South Freeport
Schwartz, Elliott Shelling *composer, writer, retired music educator*

South Portland
Thompson, Mark R. *museum director*
Thompson, Mark S. *electronics executive*
Wheeler, Hewitt Brownell *surgeon, educator*

Southport
Gibson, Edgar Thomas *retired surgeon, educator*

Southwest Harbor
Forbes, Peter *architect*

Spruce Head
Bird, John Adams *educational consultant*

Stockton Springs
Snyder, Arnold Lee, Jr. *retired military officer, research director*

Sullivan
Davis-Wexler, Ginia *singer, director*

Sumner
Rudd, David William *management consultant, chemical engineer*

Tenants Harbor
Bates, John Cecil, Jr. *lawyer*

Topsham
Arnold, Charles Burle, Jr. *retired physician*
Beckett, Kerrie J. *ecologist, researcher*
Wilson, Linda Smith *retired academic administrator*

Unity
Lynch, Donald Frederick *psychology professor*

Vinalhaven
Indiana, Robert (Clark) *artist*

Waterville
Adams, William D. *academic administrator*
Armstrong, Darlene L. *elementary school educator*
Bassett, Charles Walker *retired literature and language professor*
Easton, Thomas Atwood *writer, educator*
Fleming, James Rodger *science historian, educator*
Gilkes, Cheryl Louise Townsend *sociologist, educator, minister*
Laurence, Robert Lionel *chemical engineering professor*
Simon, David L. *art historian*

Wells
Carleton, Joseph George, Jr. *lawyer, state legislator*

Westbrook
Lee, Shepard *automobile dealership owner*

Wilton
O'Donnell, Patricia Eileen *art educator*

Windham
Ames, Ted *environmental scientist*
Diamond, G. William *state legislator*

Wiscasset
Leslie, Seaver *artist*

Yarmouth
Bischoff, David Canby *retired university administrator*
Grover, Mark Donald *software developer, town councilor, computer scientist*
Hart, Loring Edward *academic administrator*
Haynes, Peter Lancaster *retired utilities executive*

York
Haley, Priscilla Jane *printmaker*
Hallam, Beverly (Beverly Linney) *artist*
Smart, Mary-Leigh Call *civic worker*

MARYLAND

Aberdeen Proving Ground
Carrieri, Arthur Helmut *physicist, researcher*
Jones, Bruce Hovey *physician, researcher*
Kesavan, Jana *physicist, researcher*
Kuperman, Roman Gregory *toxicologist, ecologist*
Lenz, David E. *chemist, researcher*
Sagripanti, Jose-Luis *biomedical scientist*
Stuebing, Edward Willis *research scientist*
VanLandingham, Mark Reed *materials engineer*

Accokeek
Beddow, Richard Harold *retired judge*
Kutchi, Judith Ann *elementary school educator*

Adamstown
Munson, John Christian *acoustician*
Tidball, Charles Stanley *computer scientist, educator*

Adelphi
de Jong, Mark E. *academic librarian*
Kirwan, William English, II, *academic administrator, mathematics professor*
Nguyen, Lam Huy *electronics engineer*
Sutherland, Alan Roy *business educator*
Turner, Marvin Wentz *insurance company executive*
Zheleva, Tsvetanka Spassova *scientist*

Annapolis
Abels, Richard Philip *history professor, department chairman*
Andrews, Archie Moulton *retired federal official*
Battaglia, Lynne Ann *Judge, Maryland Court of Appeals*
Bontoyan, Warren Roberts *chemist, lab administrator*
Bowen, Linnell R. *director*
Branand, Claire Diane *advertising executive, writer*
Brann, Eva Toni Helene *philosophy educator*
Burt, Clarissa C. *literature and language professor*
Cheek, Graham Terry *chemistry educator, researcher*
Clagett, Virginia Parker *state legislator*
Clotworthy, John Harris *oceanographic consultant*
Correll, Francis David *physics professor*
Criscimagna, Ned Henry *engineer*
Dawson, Thomas Henry *engineering educator*
Doory, Ann Marie *state legislator*
Fowler, Jeffrey L. *academic administrator, career military officer*
Frosh, Brian Esten *state legislator, lawyer*
Fry, Virginia Milne *artist, poet*
Gavian, Peter Wood *venture capitalist, securities executive, securities analyst*
Greene, Clayton, Jr. *judge, Maryland Court of Appeals*
Halpern, Joseph Alan *physician*
Hammer, Jacob Myer *physicist, consultant*
Harmon, J. Scott *museum director*
Harris, Andrew Peter *state legislator*
Hite, William P. *labor union administrator*
Johnson, Bruce *engineering educator*
Kelley, Delores Goodwin *state legislator*
Kopp, Nancy Kornblith *state treasurer*
Kushner, Jack *physician executive*
Lillard, John Franklin III *lawyer*
Lombardo, David Domenic *human resources professor and consultant*
Marchant, Byron Frank *lawyer, foundation administrator*
Markman, Ronald *artist, educator*
McDonough, John Patrick *Secretary of State, Maryland*
Miller, John Grider *writer*
Miller, Richards Thorn *naval architect, engineer*
Miranda, Leopoldo *zoologist, director*
Mungan, Carl Edward *physics professor*
Nolan, Theresa A. *retired judge, mediator, arbitrator*
Nuesse, Celestine Joseph *retired university official*
O'Malley, Martin Joseph *Governor of Maryland, former mayor, lawyer*
O'Sullivan, Daniel W. *chemistry professor*
Pelura, James III *veterinarian, political organization administrator*
Perkins, Roger Allan *lawyer*
Poe, Luke Harvey, Jr. *lawyer*
Rogers, David Freeman *aerospace engineering educator*
Salem, Thomas Eric *electrical engineer, educator*
Schleicher, Nora Elizabeth *bank executive, treasurer, accountant*
Seep, Dorothy M. *music educator*
Shey, James *military officer*
Stern, Margaret Bassett *retired special education educator, author*
Trost, Carlisle Albert Herman *retired naval officer*
Turnbull, Susan W. *political organization administrator*
Weese, John Augustus *retired mechanical engineer*
Welch, Robert Bond *ophthalmologist, educator*
Williams, James Arthur *retired military officer, information technology executive*
Wolf, Alfred A. *physicist, educator*
Zarnoch, Robert Anthony *judge, lawyer, educator*
Ziegler, James F. *science educator*

Annapolis Junction
Koplow, Ellen Lori Saltzman *lawyer, brokerage house executive*

Arnold
Fitzgerald, Lynda P. *dancer, director*
Gagné, Doreen Frances *nurse practitioner, educator*

Green, John Cawley *lawyer*
Hepner, Donna Terese *art educator*
Lee, Yu-Jin *retired military physician*
Macaulay, Janice Michel *music educator, composer*

Ashton
Smith, Kent Ashton *information scientist, consultant*

Baldwin
Derwart, Gregory M. *non-profit executive*

Baltimore
Abadir, Peter M. *physician, educator*
Abrams, Rosalie Silber *retired state agency official*
Acharya, Soumyadipta *engineer, researcher, physician, researcher, educator*
Achuff, Stephen Charles *cardiologist*
Adams, Harold Lynn *retired architect*
Agre, Peter Courtland *medical institute executive, educator, researcher*
Ahuja, Nita *medical educator*
Alarcon, Cesar L *electrical engineer*
Allan, Janet D. *dean, nursing educator*
Allen, Ronald John *astrophysics educator, researcher*
Alsop, Marin *conductor, violinist, music director*
Amory, Reginald L. *civil engineer, educator*
Aneja, Alka *child psychiatrist*
Angelos, Peter G. *professional sports team executive, lawyer*
Appel, Lawrence John *physician, educator*
Appleby, Brian Stephen *psychiatrist*
Arrindell, Nicholas J. *academic administrator, educator*
Arsham, Hossein *operations research analyst*
Astrue, Michael James *commissioner, former pharmaceutical company executive*
Asuncion-Miller, Lana Martina *school psychologist*
Aucott, Susan Wright *medical educator, researcher*
Aumann, R. Karl *commissioner, former state official*
Aurelian, Laure *medical sciences educator*
Bahrami, Hossein *epidemiologist, physician*
Baker, Constance H. *lawyer*
Baker, R. Robinson *surgeon*
Baker, Timothy Danforth *physician, educator*
Baker, William Parr *lawyer*
Baldwin, Henry Furlong *banker*
Baldwin, John Wesley *history professor*
Baltzley, Patricia Creel *mathematics educator*
Bandaru, Veera Venkata Ratnam *research scientist, biomedical engineer*
Bardhan, Tridip K. *engineering educator, researcher*
Barnhill, Gregory Hurd *investment banker*
Barron, Henry B., Jr., (Brew) *energy executive*
Bartlett, James Wilson III *lawyer*
Battista, Stephen J. *marketing executive*
Baumgartner, William Anthony *cardiac surgeon*
Bealefeld, Frederick Henry III *police commissioner*
Beasley, Robert Scott *financial executive*
Beer, Michael *biophysicist, educator, environmentalist*
Bell, David Avrom *humanities educator*
Bell, Robert M. *Chief Judge, Maryland Court of Appeals*
Belzberg, Allan Joel *neurosurgery educator*
Bensmaia, Sliman J. *neuroscientist*
Berardesco, Charles A. *lawyer, energy executive*
Berkelman, Peter John *robotics researcher*
Berlage, Jan Ingham *lawyer*
Black, Betty Smith *psychiatrist*
Blakeslee, Wesley Daniel *lawyer, consultant, director*
Bleich, Sara *healthcare educator, researcher*
Bluh, Pamela M. *library associate director*
Blumenthal, Roger Scott *cardiologist*
Boardman, John Michael *mathematician, educator*
Bolger, Doreen *museum director*
Bollinger, Mary Elizabeth *immunologist*
Borders, William Donald *archbishop emeritus*
Boughman, Joann Ashley *dean*
Boyd, Amanda D. *elementary school educator*
Bradley, Wanda Louise *librarian*
Brady, Joseph Vincent *behavioral biologist, educator*
Brady, Thomas F. *energy executive*
Brant, Steven Ross *medical educator*
Brasic, James Robert *psychiatrist*
Brennan, Timothy John *economics professor*
Brenner, Joel I. *cardiologist, educator*
Brewer, Nevada Nancy *elementary school educator*
Brieger, Gert Henry *medical educator*
Bright, Margaret *sociologist*
Brock, Roslyn McCallister *civil rights association executive*
Broda-Hydorn, Susan *entomologist*
Brodie, Angela M. *biomedical researcher, educator*
Brodie, Menasha Jacob (Jay) *architect, city planner, government executive*
Brody, Eugene Bloor *psychiatrist, educator, editor*
Broholm, Collin Leslie *science educator*
Brookmeyer, Ronald *medical educator*
Brooks, Thomas V. *energy executive*
Brotman, Phyllis Block *advertising and public relations executive*
Brown, Anthony Gregory *Lieutenant Governor of Maryland, lawyer*
Brown, Richard A. *science educator*
Buccino, Daniel L. *psychotherapist, consultant*
Byun, Youngjoo *research scientist*
Canto-Soler, Valeria *medical educator, researcher*
Cao, Dengfeng *pathologist*
Caplan, Sharon M. *real estate company executive*
Carbine, James Edmond *lawyer*
Carlin, Paul Victor *legal association executive*
Carmi, Shlomo *mechanical engineering educator, research scientist*
Carney, Stephen Patrick *lawyer, retired insurance company executive*
Carrier, France *medical educator*
Carson, Benjamin Solomon *neurosurgeon*
Carver, Wendy Gage *elementary school educator*
Castellani, Rudolph Joseph *pathologist*
Catania, A(nthony) Charles *psychologist, educator*
Celnik, Pablo Ariel *neurologist*
Chakravarti, Aravinda *geneticist*
Chapelle, Suzanne Ellery Greene *history professor*
Chaudhry, Vinay *medical educator*
Cheskin, Lawrence J. *healthcare educator, director*
Childs, Barton *retired physician, educator*
Choudhury, Dipa *mathematician, educator*
Christopher-Stine, Lisa *rheumatologist*
Civiletti, Benjamin Richard *lawyer, former United States Attorney General*
Civin, Curt Ingraham *oncologist*
Clemens, Mark George *physiologist*
Cohen, Bernard A. *pediatric dermatologist*
Cole, John W. *neurologist*
Collins, John R. *energy executive*
Colmers, John M. *state agency administrator*
Colomer, Veronica *medical educator, researcher*
Colwell, Rita Rossi *microbiologist, former federal agency administrator, medical educator*
Connaughton, James Laurence *energy executive, former federal official*
Conway, Janet Donohue *surgeon*
Cook, J. Montgomery (Monty Cook) *editor*
Cooper, Jerrold Stephen *historian, educator*
Cooper, Joseph *political scientist, educator*
Cooper, Lisa Angeline *internist, medical educator*
Cooper, Matthew *surgeon, educator*
Coppel, Lawrence David *lawyer*
Costa, Paul Theodore, Jr. *lab administrator, researcher*
Craig, Nancy L. *molecular biologist, educator, geneticist*
Crawford, Fred Lee *public information officer*
Crowe, Thomas Leonard *lawyer*
Cullen, Kevin Joseph *oncologist, educator*
Czinn, Steven J. *pediatrician, department chairman*
D'Alfonzo, Samuel Donald *entrepreneur*
Dalrymple, Robert Anthony III *civil engineering educator*
Daniels, Ronald J. *academic administrator, law educator*
Dannenberg, Arthur Milton, Jr. *experimental pathologist, immunologist, educator*
Davidson, Nancy Ellen *oncologist*
Davis, Guy Donald *research scientist*
Dawkins, Stuart Earl *theater producer*
DeLateur, Barbara Jane *medical educator*
DePaulo, J. Raymond, Jr. *psychiatrist, researcher*
Desiderio, Stephen *molecular biology educator*
Deutsch, Robert William *physicist*
Devan, Deborah Hunt *lawyer*
DeVito, Mathias Joseph *retired real estate company executive*
DeVries, Donald Lawson, Jr. *lawyer*
DeWeese, Theordore L. *radiation oncologist*
Dewey, Joel Allen *lawyer*
Diaz-Starr, Lucía López *performing arts educator, singer*
Diba, Fantahun *biology professor*
DiBiagio, Thomas Michael *lawyer, former prosecutor*
Dickersin, Kay *researcher, educator*
Dickfeld, Timm-Michael *electrophysiologist, cardiologist, educator*
Dickinson, Jane W. *retired executive secretary, volunteer*
Dietz, Harry C. *pediatrician, educator*
Dixon, Sheila Ann *Mayor, Baltimore*
Dobs, Adrian Sandra *endocrinologist, educator*
Dover, George Joseph *pediatric oncologist*
Drachman, Daniel Bruce *neurologist, educator*
Dunn, Edward K., Jr. *banker*
Dunn, Jeffrey A. *lawyer*
Dutton, Richard P. *anesthesiologist, educator*
Eakle, A. Jonathan *medical educator, director*
Eberhart, Charles George *medical educator*
Eddington, Natalie Dawn *science educator, dean*
Eggleston, Peyton Archer *allergist, immunologist*
Eichhorn, Gunther Louis *chemist, researcher*
Eisenberg, Howard Michael *neurosurgeon*
Eisner, Jonathan David *lawyer*
Ekekwe, Ndubuisi *electronics engineer, researcher*
Elfenbein, Jessica I. *historian, educator*
Elias, Sarah Davis *retired English language educator*
El-Kamary, Samer S. *pediatrician, educator*
Ellenbogen, Henry Martin *investment company executive*
Ellin, Marvin *lawyer*
Ellis, Brother Patrick (H. J.) *academic administrator*
Epstein, Daniel Mark *poet, dramatist, biographer*
Erozan, Yener Sahir *pathologist, educator*
Etter, Paul Courtney *oceanographer*
Ettinger, David Seymour *oncologist*
Ezeugwu, Camellus O. *cardiologist, director*
Fahy, Brenda G. *medical educator, anesthesiologist*
Fakhraei, S. Hamid *economist, researcher*
Falk, Adam *dean, physics professor*
Fall-Dickson, Jane Murray *oncology nurse*
Feinberg, Andrew P. *medical geneticist, oncologist, educator*
Feldman, Leonard Samuel *medical educator*
Feller-Kopman, David *hospital administrator*
Fergenson, Arthur Friend *lawyer*
Fetting, Mark R. *finance company executive*
Finnerty, Joseph Gregory, Jr. *lawyer*
Finney, Jervis Spencer *lawyer, former prosecutor*
Fischer Walker, Christa Lynn *research scientist*
Fisher, Alan Hall *guidebook writer*
Fisher, Morton Poe, Jr. *lawyer*
Flacco, Joe (Joseph Vincent Flacco) *professional football player*
Fox, Harold Edward *obstetrician, researcher, gynecologist, educator*
Freeman, John Mark *pediatric neurologist*
Frenkil, Steven David *lawyer*
Friedman, Louis Frank *lawyer*
Fuentealba, Victor William *professional society administrator*
Galen, James Eugene *science educator*
Gall, Joseph Grafton *biologist, researcher, educator*
Gallagher, Michela *academic administrator, psychology professor*
Gallo, Robert Charles *research scientist*
Gamaldo, Charlene Edie *medical educator*
Ganem, Joseph Wilfred *physicist, writer*
Gansler, Douglas F. *state attorney general, former prosecutor*
Gately, Mark Donohue *lawyer*
Gauvey, Susan Kathryn *judge*
Georgiades, Christos *medical educator*
Gerson, Arlene C. *psychologist*
Gerstenblith, Gary *medical educator, cardiologist*
Giacconi, Riccardo *astrophysicist, educator*
Gibbons, Michael Louis *museum director, educator*
Gifford, Donald George *dean, law educator, consultant*
Gillece, James Patrick, Jr. *lawyer*
Gimenez, Luis Fernando *physician, educator*
Gindling, Thomas Henry (Tim Henry) *economics professor*
Ginsberg, Benjamin *political science educator*
Glassman, Jon David *aerospace executive*
Godenne, Ghislaine Dudley *physician, psychotherapist, educator*
Goldberg, Alan Marvin *toxicologist, educator*
Goldberg, Morton Falk *ophthalmologist, educator*
Goldman, Brian Arthur *lawyer, certified public accountant*
Goldman, Lawrence *biophysicist*
Goldman, Lynn Rose *medical educator*
Goldman, Meir *lawyer*
Goldman, Stuart Miles *podiatrist*
Goldstein, Jerri Irene *industrial engineer*
Golomb, George Edwin *lawyer*
Gonzales, Louise Michaux *lawyer*
Goodman, Steven N. *medical educator*
Goodman, William Richard *insurance adjusting company executive*
Goodrich, Michael Truman *computer science educator*
Gordis, Leon *physician*
Gorelick, David *medical educator*
Gorospe, Emmanuel Cruz *physician, medical researcher*
Gott, Vincent Lynn *physician*
Grabill, Vin *performing arts educator, department chairman*
Grasmick, Nancy S. *state official, school system administrator*
Gray, Frank Truan *lawyer*
Gray, Ronald H. *medical educator*
Green, Bert Franklin, Jr. *retired psychology professor*
Greenough, William Bates III *medical educator*
Greider, Carol Widney *molecular biologist*
Griffin, Diane Edmund *research physician, virologist, educator*
Griffith, Lawrence Stacey Cameron *cardiologist, educator*
Griffiths, Roland Redmond *biology educator*
Grossman, Allen Richard *poet, educator*
Grossman, Stuart Alan *oncologist, medical educator*
Guben, Jan K. *lawyer*
Guler, Osman *education educator, researcher*
Gupta, Yash P. *dean*
Hackerman, Willard J. *construction executive*
Haddon, Phoebe Anniese *dean, law educator*
Hafets, Richard Jay *lawyer*
Haig, Frank Rawle *physics professor, priest*
Han, Jaeho *electrical engineer, researcher*
Hanks, James Judge, Jr. *lawyer*
Harris, James Carol Overton, Jr. *psychiatrist, pediatrician*
Harvey, Alexander, II, *retired federal judge*
Hatef Naimi, Elham *medical researcher*
Hauser, Michael George *astrophysicist*
Hayden, Carla Diane *library director, educator*
Hayes, Dennis Courtland *civil rights association executive, lawyer*
Hecht, Alan Dannenberg *insurance executive*
Helfaer, Mark Allen *anesthesiologist*
Helm, Donald Cairney *geologist, retired engineer, educator*
Helrich, Martin *anesthesiologist, educator*
Henderson, Donald Ainslie *public health service officer*
Henderson, Lenneal Joseph, Jr. *political science professor*
Hess, Allan Duane *medical educator*
Hill, Martha N. *dean, community health nurse*
Hilton, Adriel Adon *researcher*
Himelfarb, Richard Jay *investment company executive*
Hirsh, Allan Thurman, Jr. *retired publishing executive*
Hirsh, Theodore William *lawyer*
Hody, Cynthia Ann *political science professor*
Hoffman, Elmer *surgeon*
Hofkin, Gerald Alan *gastroenterologist*
Hollinger, Paula Colodny *associate director*
Honemann, Daniel Henry *lawyer*
Hong Smith, Vicki YuKyung *ESOL educator*
Hopkins, Henry Holt *mutual fund attorney*
Howes, James Guerdon *communication and transportation executive*
Hsieh, Rebecca Tung *language educator, interpreter*
Huff, Aubrey Lewis *professional baseball player*
Hug, Richard Ernest *small business owner*
Huganir, Richard Lewis *neuroscientist, educator, researcher*
Huggins, Amy Branum *music educator*
Hulbert, Jarl O. *music educator*
Hungerford, David Samuel *orthopedic surgeon, educator*
Hurley, Robert W. *anesthesiologist, educator*
Hyle, Kathleen W. *energy executive*
Ihrie, Robert *oil, gas and real estate company executive*
Irwin, John Thomas *humanities educator*
Iverson, Kelly Hughes *lawyer*
Jackson, Stanley Edward *retired special education educator*
Jealous, Benjamin Todd *civil rights association executive, foundation administrator*
Jeffrey, Janofsky S. *psychiatrist, educator*
Johns, Richard James *physician, educator*
Johnson, Kenneth Peter *neurologist, researcher*
Johnson, Michael Paul *historian, educator*
Jones, Adam La Marque *professional baseball player*
Jones, John Martin, Jr. *lawyer*
Jones, Nicholas Patrick *engineering educator*
Judd, Brian Raymond *physicist*
Judson, Horace Freeland *history professor, writer*
Kalloo, Anthony *gastroenterologist, educator*
Kamanu, Uchemadu Chee *chemist*
Kandel, Nelson Robert *lawyer*
Kang, Jin U. *engineering educator*
Karni, Edi *economics professor*
Kass, Nancy *bioethicist, public health educator*
Kastor, John Alfred *cardiologist, educator*
Katz, Joseph Louis *chemical engineer, educator*
Kelemen, Mark David *cardiologist, hospital administrator*
Kelen, Gabor David *emergency physician*
Kennedy, James Aloysius Charles *investment company executive*
Kent, Edgar Robert, Jr. *investment banker*
Kent, Vicky P. *nursing educator*
Kerr, Douglas Anthony *neurologist, researcher*
Kerriem, Rasheed T. *human resources specialist, educator*
Kessler, Herbert Leon *art historian, educator, academic administrator*
Kessler, Irving Isar *epidemiologist, consultant*
Keutcha, Julienne Petnga *science educator*
Kim, Dong-Won *historian, educator*
Kimbrough, Natalie *history professor*
Kirkhart, Matthew Wayde *psychology professor*
Klejnot, Getha Jean *school nurse practitioner, music educator*
Klimantov, Alexius George *engineering executive*
Knapp, David Allan *pharmaceutical educator, researcher, former dean*
Koch, Edgar Frank *protective services official*
Kohn, Melvin L. *sociologist*
Konar, Shameek *corporate financial executive*
Krasna, Mark Jonathan *thoracic surgeon, researcher*
Kremen, Richard M. *lawyer*
Krolik, Julian Henry *astrophysicist, educator*
Kuo, Scot C. *engineering educator*
Labrique, Alain Bernard *epidemiologist, educator*
Ladenson, Paul *endocrinologist*
Landau, Barbara *neuroscientist*
Lawrence, Robert Swan *physician, educator*
Lawson, Edward Earle *neonatologist*
Lazar, John Edward *social services administrator, not-for-profit developer*
Lazarus, Fred, IV, *academic administrator*
Lazarus, Gerald Sylvan *dermatologist, educator, dean*
Lee, Steven Xavier *museum director, artist, educator and environmentalist*
Lee, Yuan Chuan *biology professor*
Lee, Yung-Keun *physicist, researcher*
Leffell, Mary Sue *educator*
Legum, Jeffrey Alfred *holding company executive*
Lemer, Andrew Charles *engineer, economist*
Levchenko, Andre *biomedical engineer, educator*
Levien, David Harold *surgeon*
Levin, Edward Jesse *lawyer*
Levine, Richard E. *lawyer*
Lewis, Ray Anthony *professional football player*
Li, Albert P. *cell biologist, toxicologist*
Liberto, Joseph Salvatore *retired bank executive*
Lidtke, Doris Keefe *retired computer science educator*
Lidtke, Vernon LeRoy *history professor*
Liebmann, George W. *lawyer*
Lima, João A.C. *cardiologist, educator*
Litrenta, Frances Marie *psychiatrist*
Littlefield, John Walley *geneticist, cell biologist, pediatrician*
Loeb, Stacy *physician*
Longo, Dan Louis *internist, researcher, oncologist*
Loucks, Allen Frazier *prosecutor, lawyer*
Lundy, Audie Lee, Jr. *lawyer*
Lurie, Jerald B. *lawyer*
Maccini, Louis John *economist, educator*
Macko, Richard Frank *medical educator*
MacPhail, Andrew B. *professional sports team executive*
Madden, Denis James *bishop*
Maguire, Brian J. *medical educator*
Manheimer, Eric *medical researcher*
Mann, Cindy *federal agency administrator, healthcare educator*
Manson, Paul Nellis *plastic surgeon, educator*
Mareiniss, Darren Peter *lawyer, physician*
Markakis, Nick (Nicholas William Markakis) *professional baseball player*
Marsh, Bruce David *geologist, educator*
Mason, Raymond Adams (Chip Mason) *diversified financial services company executive*
Massie, Maribeth Leigh *nursing educator*
McCarthy, Patricia Anne *reading educator*
McClain, Le'Ron De'Mar *professional football player*
McClung, A(lexander) Keith, Jr. *retired lawyer*
McDaniel, Mildred Gage *elementary school educator*
McGahee, Willis Andrew *professional football player*
McHugh, Paul R. *psychiatrist, neurologist, educator*
McMillan, Julia A. *pediatrician, educator*
McPartland, James Michael *academic administrator*
McPherson, Donald Paxton III *lawyer*
McWilliams, John Michael *lawyer*
Meeker, Alan Keith *biomedical researcher, educator*
Mehra, Mandeep Rajinder *cardiologist*
Melick, Clifford Francis *sociologist, researcher*
Meltzer, Arthur Adam *researcher*
Merritt, Betty L. *medical/surgical and mental health nurse*
Mezey, Esteban *internist, gastroenterologist, educator*
Migeon, Claude Jean *pediatrics educator*
Miller, Bill, III, (William Herbert Miller) *hedge fund manager*
Miller, Decatur Howard *lawyer*
Miller, Edward Doring *anesthesiologist, hospital administrator, dean*
Miller, Michael *physician, educator*
Millspaugh, Martin Laurence *real estate developer, consultant*
Mirski, Marek Alexander *anesthesiologist, educator*
Miser, Ann *retired government researcher*
Mixson, Archibald James *research scientist, internist, endocrinologist*
Mocko, George Paul *minister*

Moffitt, Robert Allen *economics educator*
Mogol, Alan Jay *lawyer*
Montaner, Silvia *medical educator, researcher*
Montgomery, Robert Avery *transplant surgeon*
Moon, Cheil *neuroscientist, researcher*
Moos, H. Warren *physicist, educator, astronomer, director*
Moser, Ann Boody *biochemist*
Motz, Diana Gribbon *federal judge*
Motz, John Frederick *federal judge*
Mountcastle, Vernon Benjamin *retired neuroscientist*
Muccie, Mary Rose *publishing executive*
Mydlack, Daniel James *filmmaker, educator*
Nahabedian, Maurice Y. *plastic surgeon*
Naqvi, Shahid Abbas *physicist, educator*
Nathans, Larry Allen *lawyer*
Nathanson, Harvey Charles *electrical engineer*
Nelkin, Barry David *oncology researcher and educator*
Nelson, Douglas W. *foundation administrator*
Nemphos, George J. *lawyer*
Neu, Alicia Mallare *pediatric nephrologist*
Newman, William Clifford *bishop emeritus*
Ngata, Haloti (Etuini Haloti Ngata) *professional football player*
Niemeyer, Paul Victor *federal judge*
Nilson, George Albert *lawyer*
North, Richard Boydston *neurological surgery educator*
Nuzzo, Jenniffer Bronwyn *epidemiologist*
O'Brien, Edwin Frederick *archbishop*
O'Carroll, Patrick P., Jr. *federal agency administrator*
Orman, Leonard Arnold *lawyer*
Ostrand-Rosenberg, Suzanne *immunology researcher*
Otal, Monica D. *music educator*
O'Toole, Tara Jeanne *medical educator, former federal agency administrator*
Paige, David Martin *pediatrician, educator*
Palmer, Jeffrey Bruce *physiatrist, researcher*
Panuska, Joseph Allan *retired academic administrator*
Park, Mary Woodfill *information consultant, librarian, writer*
Parsa, Cameron Farrokh *ophthalmologist, educator*
Pass, Carolyn Joan *dermatologist*
Passley, Josef Antonio *psychologist, educator, writer*
Pearlson, Godfrey David *psychiatrist, researcher, educator*
Pereira, Kevin *pediatrician, director*
Perez, Thomas Edward *state official, law educator*
Perler, Bruce Alan *vascular surgeon*
Permutt, Solbert *physiologist, physician*
Petri, Michelle *medical educator*
Phan, Phillip Hin Choi *business educator, consultant*
Philosophe, Benjamin *surgeon*
Pittenger, Arthur O., Jr. *mathematics educator*
Pittenger, David M. *aquarium administrator*
Plank, Kevin A. *apparel executive*
Plant, Albin MacDonough *lawyer*
Pollak, Mark *lawyer*
Pollin, Toni I. *endocrinologist, educator*
Posner, Gary Herbert *chemist, educator*
Potra, Florian Alexander *mathematics professor*
Powers, David V. *psychology professor, department chairman*
Pronovost, Peter J. *anesthesiologist, health facility administrator, medical educator*
Putzel, Constance Kellner *retired lawyer*
Quigley, Harry Alan *ophthalmologist, medical professor*
Quinn, Thomas Charles *medical researcher, educator*
Quiñones-Hinojosa, Alfredo *neurosurgeon, educator*
Rabin, Bernard M. *psychology professor*
Radding, Andrew *lawyer*
Radhakrishnan, Malathi *biologist, educator*
Ramirez Quintana, Jose Luis *research scientist*
Ranum, Orest Allen *historian, educator*
Raskin, Sarah Bloom *state banking agency administrator, lawyer*
Rayson, Glendon Ennes *internist, preventive medicine specialist, writer*
Reece, E. Albert *dean, obstetrician, gynecologist, perinatologist*
Reed, Ed (Edward Earl Reed Jr.) *professional football player*
Reiner, Van R. *museum administrator*
Reno, Russell Ronald, Jr. *lawyer*
Reynolds, William Leroy *lawyer, educator*
Rhodes, Sharyn S. *education educator, consultant*
Rice, Ray *professional football player*
Riess, Adam Guy *astronomer, educator*
Ripken, Cal (Calvin Edwin Ripken Jr.) *retired professional baseball player, sportscaster*
Robinson, Carrie *pastor*
Robinson, Florine Samantha *marketing executive*
Robinson, Sally Shoemaker *lay associate*
Rochlin, Paul R. *lawyer*
Rodowsky, Lawrence Francis *retired state judge*
Rogers, Brian Charles *investment company executive*
Rose, Noel Richard *immunologist, microbiologist, educator*
Roseman, Saul *biochemist, educator*
Rosenstein, Rod J. *prosecutor*
Rosenthal, William J. *lawyer*
Ross, Richard Starr *retired medical school dean, cardiologist, educator*
Rothenberg, Karen H. *law educator, former dean*
Rozanski, Mitchell Thomas *bishop*
Ruknudin, Abdul M. *health program administrator*
Rumbaugh, Jeffrey Arlin *neurologist, neuroscientist*
Russell, James William *neuroscientist*
Russell, Stuart Dean *cardiologist, educator*
Ryan, Timothy E. *publishing executive*
Rzepkowski, James Edward *energy executive*
Sack, George Henry, Jr. *molecular geneticist, internist*
Sadak, Diane Marie *director, performing arts educator*
Saini, Uma Arya *educational association administrator*
Salamon, Lester Milton *political science professor*
Sanders, Julius Ray *music company executive*
Savell, Catherine *humanities educator*
Schaefer, Robert Wayne *banker*
Scheeler, Charles P. *lawyer*
Schlaff, Barbara E. *lawyer*
Schochor, Jonathan *lawyer, educator*
Schoenrich, Edyth Hull *internist, preventive medicine physician*
Schultheis, Patricia Ann *writer, editor*
Scott, Frederick Isadore, Jr. *editor, management consultant*
Scriggins, Larry Palmer *lawyer, director*
Sensenig, Arthur Lloyd *economist, consultant*
Sham, James S.K. *medical educator*
Shamoo, Adil Elias *biochemist, educator*
Shamsuddin, AbulKalam Mohammed *medical educator*
Shapiro, Harry Dean *lawyer*
Sharfstein, Joshua Moses *federal agency administrator, pediatrician*
Shattuck, Mayo Adams III *utilities executive*
Shea, James L. *lawyer*
Shepherd, Kevin L. *lawyer*
Shiffman, Bernard *mathematician, educator*
Short, Alexander Campbell *lawyer*
Shuldiner, Alan Rodney *endocrinologist, educator*
Sidransky, David *molecular biologist*
Silbergeld, Ellen Kovner *epidemiologist, toxicologist, researcher*
Silverman, Ronald *plastic surgeon*
Silverman, Steven Donald *lawyer*
Simpkins, Cuthbert Ormond *surgeon, educator, writer*
Simpson, Elizabeth B. *medical association administrator, management consultant*
Simpson, Mildred Kathleen *health facility administrator*
Singh, Om V. *biotechnologist, researcher*
Sinha, Neeti *biophysicist, researcher*
Sirota, Wilbert H. *lawyer*
Slezak, Sheri *plastic surgeon*
Smith, Lisa J. *lawyer*
Smith, L.J. *professional football player*
Smith, Robert W., Jr., (Jay) *lawyer*
Smith, Seth Aaron *medical educator*
Snell, Steven Layne *lawyer, consultant*
Snyder, Solomon Halbert *neuroscientist, educator*
Somer-Greif, Penny Lynn *lawyer*
Sommer, Alfred *ophthalmologist, medical educator, researcher*
Sorkin, Alan Lowell *economist, educator*
Spence, Robert James *plastic surgeon*
Starfield, Barbara Helen *pediatrician, educator*
Stark, Walter J. *ophthalmologist, educator*
Stephens, Walter *language educator*
Stewart, Doris Mae *biology professor*
Stone, Precious *communications educator*
Storrs, Alexander David *astronomer*
Strauch, Eric David *surgeon*
Strull, Gene *technology consultant, retired manufacturing executive*
Suggs, Terrell (Terrell Raynonn Suggs) *professional football player*
Sutherland, Donald Sinclair *musician, educator*
Sykes, Melvin Julius *lawyer*
Tabb, Winston *library director*
Talalay, Paul *pharmacologist, educator*
Talbot, Donald Roy *management consultant*
Tamargo, Rafael J. *neurological surgeon, educator*
Tamminga, Carol Ann *neuroscientist*
Taylor, Frances O'Connell *lawyer*
Tchantchou, Flaubert *medical researcher*
Temirkanov, Yuri Khatuevich *conductor, music director*
Tenser, Beth Hillary *graphics designer, art director*
Terborg-Penn, Rosalyn Marian *historian, educator*
Teter, Eston Joe *musician, educator*
Thayer, Jonathan W. *energy executive*
Tiburzi, Paul A. *lawyer*
Trpis, Milan *vector biologist, educator*
Trujillo, J. Roberto *virologist*
Truong, Hoai-An *pharmacist, director*
Tucker, James L., Jr. *artist, educator*
Tyler, Ralph Sargent III *lawyer*
Vadakkumpadan, Fijoy *research scientist*
Valentine, April Sue *elementary school educator, department chairman*
Vogelstein, Bert *oncology educator*
Wachtel, Lee Elizabeth *psychiatrist, educator*
Wahl, Richard Leo *radiologist, educator, nuclear medicine physician, researcher*
Walker, Irving Edward *lawyer*
Walkup, John Timothy *psychiatrist, educator*
Wallace, Michael J. *energy executive*
Walsh, Patrick Craig *urologist*
Wang, Jian *medical researcher, educator*
Wasserman, Richard Leo *lawyer*
Weaver, Kenneth Newcomer *geologist, state agency administrator*
Weiner, Jonathan P. *health policy and management educator*
Weisfeldt, Myron Lee *cardiologist, educator*
Weiss, James Lloyd *cardiology educator*
White, Pamela Janice *lawyer*
White, Richard Lee *astronomer*
Wierman, John Charles *mathematician, educator*
Williams, Jerry Randall *radiation biologist*
Williams, Michael J. *philosopher, educator*
Williams, Robert Eugene *astronomer*
Wilson, Donald Edward *internist, educator, former dean*
Wilson, Thomas Matthew III *lawyer*
Winkelstein, Jerry Allen *retired pediatrician*
Winn, James Julius, Jr. *lawyer*
Wolman, M. Gordon *geography educator*
Wong, Dean *radiologist, educator*
Wong, Guang William *physiologist, educator*
Wood, Robert A. *pediatrician, allergist, educator*
Xing, Michael Mingzhao *endocrinologist, educator*
Yang, Vincent Wen-shan *gastroenterologist, educator, researcher*
Yau, King-Wai *neuroscientist, educator*
Young, Barbara *psychiatrist, educator, photographer, psychoanalyst*
Zaiman, Joel Hirsh *rabbi*
Zandi, Peter P. *medical educator*
Zerhouni, Elias Adam *former federal agency administrator, radiologist*
Zhu, Weidong *engineering educator*
Ziessman, Harvey A. *nuclear medicine physician, medical association administrator*
Ziff, Larzer *literature and language professor*
Zimmerman, Andrew *pediatrician, neurologist*

Bel Air

Alegi, Marc Patrick *middle school educator*
Helfrich, Cornelius David *lawyer*
Lu, David John *historian, writer*
Miller, Dorothy Eloise *education educator*
Miller, Max Dunham, Jr. *lawyer*
O'Bryon, James Fredrick *defense consultant*

Beltsville

Ahn, Heekwon *research biologist*
Basinger, William Daniel *computer programmer*
Bruckner, Daniel Raymond *history educator*
Chaney, Rufus L. *environmental scientist*
Luo, Yaguang *food scientist, researcher*
Merriam, Diane Louise *ESL educator*
Miller, Ted Robert *management consultant*
Murrell, Kenneth Darwin *microbiologist, parasitologist*
Schneider, Edwin Kahn *research scientist*
Tso, Tien Chioh *federal agency administrator, agronomist, researcher*
Wigand, Robert Charles, Jr. *retired civil engineer, retired aerospace engineer*
Young, Peter Robert *library director*

Berlin

Brodsky, Allen *retired biophysicist*
Hammond, Michelle *middle school educator*
Passwater, Barbara Gayhart *real estate broker*
Passwater, Richard Albert *biochemist, author*

Bethesda

Abdoo, Elizabeth A. *lawyer*
Adhya, Sankar L. *geneticist*
Adler, Robert S. *federal agency administrator*
Agardy, M. Tundi *marine biologist, director*
Aisenberg, Irwin Morton *retired lawyer*
Akhondi, Hossein *internist, researcher*
Aldridge, Edward Cleveland, Jr., (Pete Aldridge) *former federal agency administrator*
Alexander, Duane Frederick *federal agency administrator, pediatrician, researcher*
Allmon, Charles W. *investment advisor*
Allnutt, Robert Frederick *management consultant, lawyer*
Alter, Harvey J. *hematologist, educator*
Alving, Barbara *federal agency administrator, hematologist*
Ambs, Stefan *biochemist, researcher*
Anderson, George Kenneth *physician, retired military officer, foundation administrator*
Ansary, Cyrus A. *investment company executive, lawyer*
Appella, Daniel *chemist, researcher*
Arai, Andrew E. *cardiologist*
Ashwell, Jonathan D. *medical researcher*
Bachrach, Christine A. *federal agency administrator*
Baird, Bruce Allen *lawyer*
Banik, Sambhu Nath *psychologist*
Battey, James F., Jr. *federal agency administrator, neurologist*
Bauersfeld, Carl Frederick *lawyer*
Baum, Bruce J. *dentist, medical geneticist*
Beall, Robert Joseph *foundation executive*
Bebchick, Leonard Norman *lawyer*
Becker, Edwin Demuth *chemist, director*
Beecher, William Manuel *management consultant*
Bennink, Jack Richard *microbiologist, researcher*
Benson, Elizabeth Polk *art specialist*
Berg, Jeremy Mark *federal agency administrator, biochemist, researcher*
Berger, Robert Lewis *retired biophysicist*
Berman, Marshall Fox *lawyer*
Berquist, Carl Thomas *hotel executive, accountant*
Berzofsky, Jay A. *medical researcher*
Blackmore, John Thomas *historian, philosopher*
Bowsher, Charles Arthur *retired government official, financial executive*
Brady, John Norris *virologist, molecular biologist*
Brady, Roscoe Owen *neurogeneticist, educator*
Brooks, Philip J. *neurobiologist*
Brown, Paul Wheeler *neuroscientist*
Buetow, Kenneth H. *medical geneticist*
Burdeshaw, William Brooksbank *engineering executive*
Buscher, Leo F., Jr. *federal agency administrator*
Calhoun, Carol Victoria *lawyer*
Campbell, William Wesley *medical educator, department chairman*
Camphausen, Kevin A. *oncologist, researcher*
Cantor, Kenneth P. *epidemiologist, researcher*
Cao, Jie Jane *cardiologist, researcher*
Cassimatis, Emmanuel G. *educational association administrator, psychiatrist, educator*
Castelli, Alexander Gerard *accountant*
Celi, Francesco Saverio *geriatrician, endocrinologist*
Chan, Leighton *physiatrist, educator*
Chew, Emily Ying *epidemiologist, director*
Child-Olmsted, Gisèle Alexandra *retired language educator*
Chow, Carson C. *research scientist*
Choyke, Peter L. *radiologist, researcher*
Chronister, Gregory Michael *newspaper editor*
Citron, Bruce Alexander *geneticist, researcher*
Cleary, Robert Edward *government and public affairs educator*
Cleary, Timothy Finbar *professional society administrator*
Clore, G. Marius *biologist*
Cody, Thomas Gerald *management consultant, writer*
Cohen, Robert Abraham *retired physician*
Cohen, Sheldon Gilbert *physician, historian, immunologist*
Collins, Francis Sellers *federal agency administrator, geneticist*
Comey, James B., Jr. *aerospace company executive, lawyer, former federal agency administrator*
Conger, Lucinda *retired librarian*
Corn, Milton *dean, physician, consultant*
Cornish, Edward Seymour *magazine editor*
Cox, Kenneth Allen *retired lawyer, communications executive, consultant*
Cruz, Wilhelmina Mangahas *critical care physician*
Dahlberg, Gregory Robert *lobbyist*
Daniels, Michael Paul *lawyer*
Datiles, Manuel Bernaldes III *ophthalmologist, researcher*
Day, Robert Dwain, Jr. *foundation administrator, lawyer*
De Cherney, Alan Hersh *obstetrics and gynecology educator*
Dennin, Joseph Francis *former government official, lawyer*
de Vries, Margaret Garritsen *economist*
Dietrich, Robert Anthony *pathologist, consultant, medical association administrator*
Dignac, Geny (Eugenia M. Bermudez) *sculptor*
Di Paolo, Joseph Amedeo *geneticist*
Doroshow, James Halpern *federal agency administrator, oncologist*
Downey, Arthur Thomas III *lawyer*
Edwards, Virginia B. *editor, publishing executive*
Elliott, George Armstrong III *artist, journalist*
Emanuel, Ezekiel J. *oncologist, bioethicist*
English, William deShay *lawyer, director*
Ewing, Ky Pepper, Jr. *lawyer*
Fales, Henry Marshall III *chemist*
Faley, R(ichard) Scott *lawyer*
Farci, Patrizia *medical educator, researcher*
Farley, John Hall *medical educator*
Fauci, Anthony Stephen *federal agency administrator, allergist, immunologist*
Fee, Elizabeth *medical historian, administrator*
Feuerstein, Donald Martin *lawyer*
Fields, Richard Douglas *neuroscientist*
Fields, Stephen Timothy *environmental engineer*
Fine, Howard A. *medical researcher*
Fleming, Patricia Stubbs (Patsy Fleming) *artist*
Forster, Peter C. *construction executive*
Fradkin, Judith Elaine *endocrinologist, director*
Frank, Martin *physiologist, educator, medical association administrator*
Frank, Richard Sanford *retired magazine editor*
Fraumeni, Joseph Francis, Jr. *federal agency administrator, epidemiologist*
Freeman, Robert Charles *health scientist administrator*
Fukunaga, Masaki *medical researcher*
Gaarder, Marie *speech pathologist*
Gallin, John I. *federal agency administrator, medical researcher*
Gastwirth, Glenn Barry *medical association administrator*
Giaccone, Giuseppe *oncologist, researcher*
Glass, Roger I. *federal agency administrator, research scientist*
Goldstein, Murray *medical epidemiologist and research administrator*
Goldstein, Rise Belle *medical researcher*
Gonzalez, Frank J. *medical researcher*
Goodman, Wayne K. *psychiatrist, researcher*
Gottesman, Michael Marc *federal agency administrator, biomedical researcher*
Gottesman, Susan *federal agency administrator*
Grady, Patricia A. *federal agency administrator*
Grais, Alexandra *art appraiser, director*
Grau, John Michael *trade association executive*
Greenberg, Judith Horovitz *geneticist*
Greenwald, Peter *federal agency administrator, cancer prevention physician, epidemiologist, researcher*
Gress, Ronald E. *oncologist, medical researcher*
Guertin, Shawn M. *health facility administrator*
Gulley, James Leonard *internist, oncologist*
Guttmacher, Alan Edward *federal agency administrator, physician, educator*
Guttman, Helene Nathan *biomedical consultant, transpersonal counselor*
Hager, Gordon Lee *molecular biologist, researcher*
Hallett, Mark *neurologist, educator, researcher*
Hance, Kenneth William *immunologist, researcher*
Hannan, Myles *lawyer*
Harlan, Linda Carol *epidemiologist*
Harris, Curtis Craig *medical researcher*
Harris, Stanley S. *retired judge*
Harrop, William Caldwell *retired ambassador*
Harvey, John Collins *internist, educator*
Harvey, Larry K. *hotel executive*
Haseltine, Florence Pat *federal agency administrator, gynecologist, obstetrician*
Hausman, Steven Jack *health science association administrator*
Heath, Ralph D. *aerospace transportation executive*
Hejtmancik, James Fielding *medical researcher*
Helman, Lee J. *medical researcher*
Hemming, Val G. *retired dean, educator*
Herman, Edith Carol *journalist*
Herman, Mary Margaret *neuropathologist*
Highfill, Philip Henry, Jr. *retired language educator*
Hingson, Ralph W. *medical educator*
Hinnebusch, Alan Gerard *molecular geneticist*
Hodes, Richard J. *federal agency administrator, immunologist, researcher*
Holland, Steven M. *epidemiologist*
Holmberg, Ted *journalist, consultant*
Horne, Michael Stewart *retired lawyer*
Hrynkow, Sharon Hemond *federal agency administrator, neuroscientist, researcher*
Hsia, Chu Chieh *medical researcher*
Huebner, John Stephen *geologist*
Huntress, Wesley Theodore, Jr. *research scientist*
Hutchins, Michael *non-profit scientific society administrator, conservation biologist*
Hutton, John Evans, Jr. *surgeon, educator, retired military officer*
Insel, Thomas R. *federal agency administrator, psychiatrist*
Jackson, Michael John *retired physiologist, association executive*
Jacobson, Kenneth Alan *chemist, researcher*
Jaffe, Elaine Sarkin *pathologist, researcher*
Jaquish, Cashell Elizabeth *geneticist, director*
Jen, Jin *molecular biologist, researcher*

Johnson, Joyce Marie *psychiatrist, public health service officer, epidemiologist*
Johnson, Robert Louis *professional sports team owner, former broadcast executive*
Johnson, Thomas Dale *consultant and publishing executive*
Jonas, Gary Fred *healthcare executive*
Jones, Jack F. (John Franklin Jones Jr.) *federal agency administrator*
Josephson, Julian *writer*
Joy, Robert John Thomas *medical educator*
Joyce, Bernita Anne *retired federal agency administrator*
Kador, Peter Fritz *chemist*
Kapikian, Albert Zaven *physician, epidemiologist*
Karev, Georgiy Petrovich *application developer*
Kataoka, Tatsuki R. *pathologist, researcher*
Katz, Stephen Ira *federal agency administrator*
Kelly, Kathleen *medical researcher*
Kem, Richard Samuel *retired army officer*
Kempster, Norman Roy *journalist*
Kingsley, Mary Lee *writer, researcher, consultant, retired marketing executive*
Kington, Raynard Stuart *federal agency administrator*
Kirschstein, Ruth Lillian *federal agency administrator, retired physician*
Klee, Claude Blanc *medical researcher*
Knachel, Philip Atherton *librarian*
Koenig, Elizabeth Barbara *sculptor*
Korn, Edward David *biochemist*
Koroshetz, Walter J. *neurologist, educator*
Kotin, Robert Michael *biomedical researcher*
Kramer, Barnett Sheldon *federal agency administrator, oncologist*
Krantz, David S. *psychology educator, researcher*
Krause, Richard Michael *medical scientist, government official, educator, researcher*
Kruger, Gustav Otto, Jr. *retired oral surgeon, educator, department chairman*
Kubasik, Christopher E. *aerospace transportation executive*
Kuehl, W. Michael *medical researcher*
Kunos, George *pharmacologist*
Kutemeyer, Peter Martin *industrial engineering executive*
Kutty, Raghavakurup Krishnan *research scientist*
Laingen, Lowell Bruce *diplomat*
Landis, Story Cleland *federal agency administrator, neurobiologist*
Lane, H. Clifford *internist*
Larrabee, Donald Richard *publishing executive*
Larsen-Basse, Jorn *mechanical and materials engineering educator, researcher, consultant*
Lauer, Michael Solon *cardiologist, director*
Lebedev, Mikhail A. *neuroscientist*
Lee, Jongho *medical researcher*
Leitner, Wolfgang W. *research scientist*
Levine, Mark A. *endocrinologist*
Levine, Zachary Thomas *neurosurgeon*
Li, Qingdi Quentin *physician, research scientist, medical educator*
Libutti, Steven Kenneth *medical researcher*
Lichten, Michael J. *microbiologist, researcher*
Lichtenberg, Joseph David *psychiatrist*
Lindberg, Donald Allan Bror *federal agency administrator, library director, pathologist*
Linehan, William Marston *urologist, researcher*
Lipkin, Bernice Sacks *computer scientist, educator*
Lipman, David J. *medical association administrator, researcher*
Longacre, Lisa Schwartz *health scientist administrator*
Lowy, Douglas Ronald *oncologist, researcher*
Ludlow, Christy Leslie *speech pathologist, scientist*
Ludlow, Gregory *language educator*
Lumelsky, Nadya L. *medical researcher, director*
Lystad, Mary Hanemann (Mrs. Robert Lystad) *sociologist, writer*
Mackall, Crystal L. *medical researcher*
Maguire, Joanne M. *aerospace transportation executive*
Malech, Harry Lewis *immunologist, researcher*
Manasse, Henri Richard, Jr. *pharmaceutical executive*
Manolio, Teri A. *physician*
Marriott, Richard Edwin *hotel and contract services executive*
Martensen, Robert Lawrence *emergency physician, educator, historian, ethicist, writer*
Masnyk, Ihor Jarema *chemist, director*
Masur, Henry *internist*
Mateczun, John Matthew *career military officer*
Max, Edward Ellis *molecular biologist*
McClure, Brooks *management consultant*
McCurdy, Harry Ward *otolaryngologist*
Mc Gurn, Barrett *communications executive, writer*
McMurphy, Michael Allen *energy company executive, lawyer*
Meltzer, Paul S. *geneticist, researcher*
Merlino, Glenn T. *medical researcher*
Mishkin, Mortimer *neuropsychologist*
Mitchell, James B. *medical researcher*
Mock, Beverly A. *geneticist, researcher*
Mogel, William Allen *lawyer*
Moore, Thomas Hill *commissioner*
Morens, David Michael *epidemiologist, tropical medicine investigator*
Morgan, John Davis *government agency administrator, consultant*
Morrison, Bruce Andrew *federal official, public affairs consultant*
Mufson, Robert Allan *cell biologist*
Murayama, Makio *biochemist*
Murphy, Philip M. *biomedical researcher*
Murrett, Robert B. *federal agency administrator, career military officer*
Musil, Robert Kirkland *global environmental politics professor*
Nabel, Elizabeth Guenthner *federal agency administrator, cardiologist, researcher*
Nabel, Gary Jan *virologist*
Nasseripour, Mohammad Michel *artist, architect*
Nathan, Matthew Lincoln *career military officer, physician*
Neill, Denis Michael *management consultant*
Nelson, Ethelyn Barnett *civic worker*
Nelson, John Howard (Jack Howard Nelson) *journalist*
Nelson, William Eugene *lawyer*
Niederhuber, John Edward *federal agency administrator*
Nightingale, Stuart Lester *public health consultant*
Nord, Nancy Ann *commissioner*
North, William Haven *foreign service officer*
Northup, Anne Meagher *commissioner, former United States Representative from Kentucky*
Oberholtzer, J. Carl *pathologist, researcher*
Obrams, Gunta Iris *clinical research administrator*
Oddis, Joseph Anthony *health associations executive*
Ognibene, Frederick Peter *internist*
Olmsted, Jerauld Lockwood *telephone company executive*
Ostell, James M. *library and information scientist, biotechnologist*
Padgett, Nancy Weeks *retired law librarian, lawyer, consultant*
Pang, Lap-Yin *molecular biologist*
Park, Yikyung *epidemiologist, oncologist*
Parrish, Edgar L. *financial services executive*
Pastan, Ira Harry *medical researcher*
Paul, William Erwin *immunologist*
Penn, Audrey S. *federal agency administrator*
Perlin, Seymour *psychiatrist, educator*
Peterson, Charles Marquis *medical educator*
Pettigrew, Roderic I. *federal agency administrator, radiologist, researcher*
Phillips, Terence Martyn *immunologist*
Pickerell, James Howard *photojournalist*
Pinn, Vivian W. *federal agency administrator, pathologist*
Pipkin, James Harold, Jr. *lawyer*
Plant, Ewan P. *research scientist*
Pollard, Harvey B. *medical educator, neuroscientist*
Pommier, Yves Georges *medical researcher*
Purcell, Robert Harry *virologist, researcher*
Puri, Raj K. *medical researcher, director*
Quinnan, Gerald Vincent, Jr. *medical educator*
Rabson, Alan Saul *federal agency administrator, pathologist, educator*
Rapoport, Judith *psychiatrist*
Reed, Berenice Anne *cultural organization administrator, artist, educator*
Reed, Miriam Bell *legislative staff member*
Rennert, Owen Murray *pediatrician, geneticist, educator*
Reynolds, Herbert Young *internist*
Rice, Charles Lane *surgeon, educator*
Rice, Jerry Mercer *biochemist, consultant, pathologist*
Richardson, John *retired international relations executive*
Rider, Lisa G *pediatric rheumatologist, researcher*
Rockey, Sally Jean *federal agency administrator*
Rodgers, Griffin Platt *federal agency administrator, researcher*
Rosenbaum, Greg Alan *merchant banker, consultant*
Rosenberg, Steven Aaron *surgeon, medical researcher*
Rowell, Edward Morgan *retired foreign service officer, educator*
Ruffin, John *federal agency administrator, researcher*
Ruiz Bravo, Norka *federal agency administrator*
Saffiotti, Umberto *pathologist*
Salisbury, Franklin C., Jr. *foundation administrator*
Salmoiraghi, Gian Carlo *physiologist, educator*
Samelson, Lawrence Elliot *medical researcher*
SanGiovanni, John Paul *ophthalmic epidemiologist, eye and vision researcher*
Sarnoff, Lili-Charlotte (Lolo Sarnoff) *artist*
Saul, B. Francis, II, *bank executive, director*
Saunders, Charles Baskerville, Jr. *retired association executive*
Saville, Thorndike, Jr. *coastal engineer*
Saxinger, William Carl *microbiologist*
Scarpa, Antonio *federal agency administrator, physiologist, medical educator*
Schaeffer, Charles Perry *writer, editor*
Schechter, Alan Neil *medical researcher*
Schifter, Richard *lawyer*
Schlom, Jeffrey Bert *research scientist*
Schmidt, Raymond Paul *military officer, historian, government agency administrator*
Schrump, David Stuart *medical association administrator, researcher*
Shapeero, Lorraine G. *physician, researcher, educator*
Shaw, William J. *hotel executive*
Shevach, Ethan Menahem *physician*
Shlaes, John B. *foundation administrator*
Shortliffe, Edward Hance *internist, medical educator, computer scientist*
Shulman, Lawrence Edward *biomedical researcher, rheumatologist*
Sich, Jeffrey John *health education analyst*
Sieving, Paul A. *federal agency administrator, ophthalmologist, educator*
Silver, David *lawyer*
Simons-Morton, Denise G. *medical researcher*
Singer, Alfred *immunologist, researcher*
Singer, Dinah S. *federal agency administrator, immunologist, researcher*
Smoller, Bruce Melvyn *psychiatrist*
Sneiderman, Charles Alan *medical researcher*
Sobel, Mark Esar *pathologist, researcher*
Sokoloff, Louis *retired physiologist, neuroscientist*
Solomon, Henry *university dean*
Solomon, Robert *economist*
Song, Byoung-Joon *pharmacologist, biochemist*
Sorenson, Arne M. *hotel executive*
Spector, Eleanor Ruth *manufacturing executive*
Starkey, Russell Bruce, Jr. *energy executive*
Stetler-Stevenson, Maryalice *cytologist, director*
Stone, Jeremy Judah *professional society administrator*
Stover, Ellen L. *federal agency administrator, health scientist*
Stratton, Pamela *gynecologist*
Struyk, Raymond Jay *economist*
Sturtz, Donald Lee *surgeon, military officer, educator*
Sundaresan, Tharun *science educator*
Tabak, Lawrence A. *federal agency administrator, dentist*
Tanner, Bruce L. *aerospace transportation executive*
Tatusova, Tatiana A. *research scientist*
Taylor, Lindsay David, Jr. *health care executive, bank executive, federal agency administrator*
Tenenbaum, Inez Moore *federal agency administrator, former school system administrator*
Terragno, Paul James *information industry executive*
Thorgeirsson, Snorri Sveinn *medical researcher*
Tilley, Carolyn Bittner *information scientist*
Tracy, Thomas Miles *international health organization official*
Trus, Benes Louis *structural chemist*
Udey, Mark C. *dermatologist, researcher*
Ursano, Robert Joseph *psychiatrist*
van der Linden, Frank Morris *historian*
Van Dyke, Terry Ann *geneticist, researcher*
Vaughan, Martha *biochemist, educator*
Vest, George Southall *retired diplomat*
Volkow, Nora Dolores *federal agency administrator, medical researcher*
Vonderhaar, Barbara K. *medical researcher*
Vydelingum, Nadarajen Ameerdanaden *cell biologist, educator, researcher, health administrator*
Wagner, Cynthia Gail *editor, writer*
Wahl, Sharon Marie *immunologist*
Waldmann, Thomas Alexander *medical researcher, physician*
Walter, W. Edward *hotel and corporate financial executive*
Warren, Kenneth R. *federal agency administrator*
Wassermann, Eric M. *neurologist, department chairman*
Watanabe, Kazuhide *medical researcher*
Watashi, Koichi *medical educator, researcher*
Watson, Michael S. *medical geneticist, educator*
Webber, Derek *aerospace executive, space tourism entrepreneur*
Weinberger, Alan David *lawyer, business executive*
Weinstein, Lee S. *endocrinologist*
Weiss, George Herbert *senior scientist consultant*
Welch, John Kirtland *nuclear energy industry executive*
Wellems, Thomas E. *federal agency administrator*
Wells, Samuel Alonzo, Jr. *surgeon, educator*
Wiese, Wolfgang Lothar *physicist, researcher*
Williams, Marni Dianne *pharmacist*
Wiltrout, Robert H. *federal agency administrator, medical researcher*
Winters, Thomas Andrew *microbiologist*
Wise, Allen F. *health care company executive*
Witkop, Bernhard *chemist*
Wright, Pamela Ann *surgeon*
Wu, Carl *medical researcher*
Yamada, Kenneth Manao *cell biologist*
Yang, Key Paik *librarian, archivist*
Yewdell, Jonathan Wilson *cell biologist*
Yuspa, Stuart Howard *oncologist, researcher*
Zaghloul, Norann Amir *geneticist, research scientist*
Zielinski, Thomas C. *lawyer, insurance company executive*
Zierdt, Charles Henry *retired microbiologist*
Zoon, Kathryn Christine *biochemist*

Betterton
Kohl, Benjamin Gibbs *historian, educator*

Bowie
Baker, Marshina *physical education educator*
Bushnell, David Sherman *social psychologist, consultant*
Gourdine-Tyson, Natachia *CIO, ladiez legacy*
Hillsman, Joan Rucker *music educator*
Josyula, Darsana Purushothaman *computer scientist, educator*
LeCounte, Lola Houston *literature and language professor, educational consultant*
Lewis, Patricia Ann *music educator*
Littlefield, Roy Everett III *association executive, law educator*
Parr-Corretjer, Polly *singer, music educator*
Pearse, Warren Harland *obstetrician, gynecologist, medical association administrator*
Sengupta, Sunando *economics professor*
Staples, Lola Roebuck *healthcare educator*
Sterling, Richard Leroy *English and foreign language educator*
Stone, Edward Harris, II, *landscape architect*
Wardrip, Elizabeth Jane *retired librarian*

Boyds
Beach, Jeffrey E. *engineering educator, consultant*
Bu, Rulei *artist, educator*

Bozman
Wyatt, Wilson Watkins, Jr. *public relations executive, writer*

Brandywine
Richards, Madge Marie *business owner, professor, consultant, recruiter, professional fundraiser*

Brookeville
Zehner, Lee Randall *entrepreneur, chemist*

Brooklandville
Schlitz, Laura Amy *school librarian, writer*

Brooklyn
Young-Wilson, Brenda L. *special education educator*

Burtonsville
Hudson, Yvonne Morton *retired elementary school educator*
Kammeyer, Sonia Margaretha *real estate agent*

Cabin John
Townsend, John William, Jr. *physicist, retired federal agency administrator*

California
Powell, Melchior Daniel *educational administrator, lawyer*
Shoemaker, Cynthia Cavenaugh Jones *academic dean*

Calverton
DelSole, Timothy Michael *geophysicist, educator*
Hu, Zeng-Zhen *meteorologist*

Cambridge
Field, Tammy K. *civilian military employee*
Fisher, Thomas Richard *environmental scientist, educator*
Malone, Thomas Charleton *oceanography educator*
Tyagi, Punam *environmental services administrator*

Catonsville
Diggs, Carol Beth *marketing professional*
Groninger, Lowell *psychology professor*
Hubbard, Herbert Hendrix *lawyer*
Oden, Gloria *language educator, poet*

Centreville
Griffith, Alan Richard *retired banker*

Chestertown
Amos, James Lysle *photographer*
Clarke, Garry Evans *composer, academic administrator, musician*
Meima, Ralph Chester, Jr. *retired diplomat, real estate company executive*
Narita, Noriko *social studies educator*
Rather, Lucia Porcher Johnson *library administrator*
Shoge, Ruth Casandra *library director*
Wendel, Richard Frederick *economist, educator, consultant*

Cheverly
Miller, Mark Karl *journalist, editor*

Chevy Chase
Adler, James Barron *publishing executive*
Albright, Raymond Jacob *federal official*
Alexander, Arthur Jacob *economist*
Asher, Lila Oliver *artist*
Auerbach, Seymour *architect*
Bacon, Donald Conrad *writer, editor*
Baruch, Jordan Jay *retired management consultant*
Basa, Enikö Molnár *retired librarian*
Bisconti, Ann Stouffer *public opinion research company executive*
Bissinger, Frederick Lewis *retired manufacturing executive*
Broide, Mace Irwin *public information officer*
Bruno, Harold Robinson, Jr. *retired journalist, writer*
Cheng, David Keun *engineering educator*
Choppin, Purnell Whittington *science administrator*
Cline, Ruth Eleanor Harwood *translator*
Coerper, Milo George *lawyer, priest*
Cowen, Eugene Sherman *broadcast executive*
Croft, Joseph David *medical educator*
Curzan, Myron Paul *lawyer*
Cushwa, Patricia K. *commissioner*
Dufresne, Craig Roger *plastic surgeon, educator*
Emsellem, Helene *medical association administrator*
Ewing, Frank Marion *lumber company executive, real estate developer*
Feldman, Bruce Allen *otolaryngologist*
Fern, Alan Maxwell *art historian, retired museum director*
Fulwood, Isaac, Jr. *federal official*
Gildenhorn, Joseph Bernard *lawyer, real estate company executive, retired diplomat*
Goldstein, Lawrence Steven *medical professor and investigator*
Goodwin, Frederick King *psychiatrist*
Gottschall, Edward Maurice *editor, writer*
Hahn, Marc B. *physician, educator, former dean*
Hani, Antoine George *psychiatrist, psychoanalyst*
Harlan, William Robert, Jr. *internist, educator, researcher*
Hersh, Stephen Peter *psychiatrist, psycho-oncologist, chronic pain expert, educator*
Hunt, Frederick Talley Drum, Jr. *association executive*
Kandel, Eric Richard *neuroscience educator*
Khairalla, Eric William *plastic surgeon*
Kilborn, Peter Thurston *journalist, author*
Knable, Michael *medical researcher*
Kranking, Margaret Graham *artist, retired educator*
Kriegsman, Alan M. *arts critic*
Krupnick, Janice Lee *psychologist, psychotherapist, educator*
Lebow, Irwin Leon *communications engineering consultant*
Lyons, Jonathan Spencer *ophthalmologist*
Meltzer, Jack *retired dean*
Michaelis, Michael *management and technical consultant*
Mitchell, Cranston J. *commissioner*
Murphy, John Condron, Jr. *lawyer*
Noonan, Patrick Francis *conservation executive*
Norwood, Bernard *economist*
Norwood, Janet Lippe *economist*
Oudens, Gerald Francis *architect, architectural firm executive*
Pedersen, Wesley Niels M. *public relations and public affairs counselor*
Pirie, Robert Burns, Jr. *defense analyst*
Pogue, John Marshall *physician*
Pollard, Michael Ross *lawyer, health science association administrator*
Reilly, Edward Francis, Jr. *commissioner, former state senator*
Resnik, Harvey Lewis Paul *psychiatrist*
Rockwell, Theodore *nuclear engineer*
Sapin, Burton Malcolm *political science professor*
Shipler, David Karr *journalist, writer*
Shogan, Robert *news correspondent*
Short, Steve Eugene *engineer*
Sinclair, Rolf Malcolm *retired physicist*
Smith, Hedrick Laurence *journalist, television producer*

Toth, Robert Charles *retired journalist*
Zahl, Paul Francis Matthew *retired dean*

Clarksburg
Geem, Zong Woo *interdisciplinary scientist*

Clinton
Manchester, Robert W. *psychologist*
Sander, Clarence Ellis, Jr. *retired protective services official*
Whittington, Ralph Edward *retired curator, librarian*

Cockeysville
Barnes, Peter *retired federal official*
Bracey, Esi Eggleston *consumer products company executive, marketing professional*
Howard, Bettie Jean *retired surgical nurse*
Selway, Janet Small *family nurse practitioner*

Cockeysville Hunt Valley
Elkin, Lois Shanman *business systems company executive*
Whitehurst, William Wilfred, Jr. *management consultant*

College Park
Anandalingam, Gnanalingam *dean, management educator*
Anderson, John David, Jr. *aerospace engineer*
Ankem, Sreeramamurthy *science educator*
Antman, Stuart Sheldon *mathematician, educator*
Awad, Ehab *electronics engineer, computer engineer, researcher*
Barbe, David Franklin *electrical engineer, educator*
Barber, Benjamin R. *political scientist, educator*
Beasley, Maurine Hoffman *journalism educator, historian*
Benedick, Richard Elliot *diplomat*
Bennett, Reginald Wendell *microbiologist*
Betancourt, Roger Rene *economist*
Brill, Dieter Rudolf *physicist, educator*
Chodos, Alan *professional society administrator*
Chopra, Nikhil *systems engineer, researcher*
Colombini, Marco *biophysicist*
DeFries, Ruth S. *earth system scientist, researcher*
DeLoatch, Nicole T. *academic administrator*
Destler, I. M(ac) *political scientist, foreign policy writer*
Diener, Theodor Otto *plant pathologist, researcher*
Dieter, George Elwood, Jr. *academic administrator*
Dusold, Laurence Richard *chemist, computer specialist*
Dylla, H. Frederick *science administrator, physicist*
Egel, Andrew *education educator*
Elliot, Elisa Louise *microbiologist*
Epstein, Norman B. *psychologist, marriage and family therapist, educator*
Fanning, Delvin Seymour *soil science educator*
Farvardin, Nariman *engineering educator*
Fenselau, Catherine Clarke *chemistry professor*
Fetter, Steve *dean, physicist, educator*
Fink, Edward Laurence *communications educator*
Finkelstein, Barbara *education educator*
Fisher, Michael Ellis *physicist, chemist, educator, mathematician*
Frank, Howard *information technology educator, former dean*
Frese, Brenda S. *women's college basketball coach*
Friedgen, Ralph Harry *college football coach*
Fu, Michael C. *management science educator*
Gansler, Jacques Singleton *public policy educator*
Gates, Sylvester James, Jr. *physics professor, researcher*
Gaylin, Ned L. *psychologist, educator*
Gomery, Douglas *communications educator, writer*
Gopalan, Gaurav *aerospace engineer, researcher*
Gordon-Salant, Sandra *audiology educator*
Granatstein, Victor Lawrence *electrical engineer, educator*
Greenberg, Oscar Wallace *physicist, researcher*
Griem, Hans Rudolf *physicist, researcher*
Gu, Jie *research scientist*
Gupta, Ashwani Kumar *mechanical engineering educator*
Hakim, Toufic Maurice *educational association administrator*
Hall, William Sterling *psychology educator*
Hallett, Judith Peller *classical studies educator*
Haltiwanger, John C. *economics professor*
Hamilton, David Howard *mathematics professor*
Hassouneh, Munther A. *research scientist, educator*
Hill, Clara Edith *psychologist, educator*
Imig, David Gregg *professor practise, retired educational association administrator*
Ingold, Catherine White *academic administrator*
Johnson, Haynes Bonner *journalist, writer, commentator*
Johnson, Raymond Lewis *mathematician*
Just, Richard Eugene *economist, consultant, agriculturist, educator*
Kang, Kyeongpyo *transportation engineer, researcher*
Katz, Ronald Alan *dermatologist*
Kearney, Melissa Schettini *economics professor*
Kosco Cossard, Patricia Ann *school librarian*
Kundu, Mukul Ranjan *physics and astronomy professor*
Langenberg, Donald Newton *retired academic administrator, physicist*
Leathers, Howard *economics professor*
Levine, William Silver *electrical engineer, educator*
Lowell, Howard Parsons *archivist, federal agency administrator*
Lubkin, Gloria Becker *physicist*
Lucas, Henry Cameron, Jr. *information scientist, educator, writer*
Melngailis, John *physicist*
Mesgarani, Nima *electrical engineer, researcher*
Miller, Raymond Edward *computer science educator*
Minker, Jack *computer scientist, educator*
Montgomery, William Layton *musician, educator*
Mote, Clayton Daniel, Jr. *academic administrator, mechanical engineer, educator*
Murdoch, Amelia Clara *educational association administrator*
Nerlove, Marc Leon *economics professor*
Newcomb, Robert Wayne *electrical engineer educator*
O'Brochta, David A. *molecular biologist, researcher*
Odell, Stanley Jack *retired philosopher professor*
O'Hara, Michael M. *theater educator*
Olson, Charles Eric *economist*
O'Shea, Patrick Gerard *engineering educator, department chairman*
Oster, Rose Marie Gunhild *foreign language professional, educator*
Paik, Ho Jung *physics professor*
Panichas, George Andrew *language educator, critic, editor*
Pasch, Alan *philosopher, educator*
Petraitis, Karel Colette *lawyer*
Presser, Harriet Betty *social studies educator*
Presser, Stanley *social sciences educator, researcher*
Quester, George Herman *political science professor*
Quick, Edward Raymond *museum director, educator, curator*
Rabin, Herbert *physicist, educator, dean*
Rahman, Nurur *astrophysicist*
Richardson, W. C. *painter*
Rubin, Kenneth H. *psychology professor, writer*
Schelling, Thomas Crombie *economist*
Schwab, Susan Carroll *public policy educator, former federal official*
Shapiro, Debra L. *finance educator, consultant*
Shneiderman, Ben Abraham *computer science educator, writer*
Shoushtari, Amir H. *research scientist*
Sigall, Harold Fred *psychology professor*
Silverman, Joseph *chemistry professor*
Soergel, Philip Mark *history professor*
Soltan, Karol Edward *political science professor, director*
Spear, Richard Edmund *art history educator*
Stewart, Gilbert Wright *computer science educator*
Sundlof, Stephen Frederick *federal agency administrator, veterinarian*
Taylor, Leonard Stuart *engineering educator, consultant*
Thirumalai, Devarajan *physical sciences researcher, educator*
Tits, Andre Leon *electrical engineering educator*
Tomoya, Tatsuno *research scientist*
Turner, Mark Bernard *English language educator*
Vanderveen, John E. *nutritionist, federal agency administrator*
Veilleux, Sylvain *astrophysicist, educator*
Walters, William Ben *chemistry professor*
Weart, Spencer Richard *historian*
Weinstein, Allen *archivist*
Williams, Ellen D. *physics professor*
Wiseman, Donna L. *dean, education educator*
Yow, Deborah A. *athletic director*
Zen, E-an *research geologist, educator*
Zhu, Guangyu *computer scientist, researcher*

Columbia
Abel, Florence Catherine Harris *social worker*
Aiken, Robert B. *food products executive*
Armstrong, T. Paul *information technology executive*
Blackwell-Taffel, Camellia Ann *art educator, consultant*
Campbell-Alston, Deirdre Adina *anatomist, physiologist, researcher*
Carter, Karen Zepp *music educator, elementary school educator*
Closson, Walter Franklin *child support prosecutor*
Davis, Benjamin George *theologian, educator*
Davis, Janet Marie Gorden *secondary school educator*
Festa, (Al)Fred E. *chemicals executive*
Fisher, Dale John *retired chemist, medical investigator*
Giannopoulos, A.L. (Tom Giannopoulos) *information technology executive*
Gilbert, Douglas Brainerd *telecommunications industry executive*
Gregorie, Corazon Arzalem *operations research specialist*
Gross, Linda Maria *secondary school educator*
Gruhl, Andrea Morris *librarian*
Hyman, Lawrence Robert *psychiatrist*
Jani, Sushma Niranjan *pediatric psychiatrist*
Jones-Wilson, Faustine Clarisse *retired education educator*
Kearns, Ronald Edwin *music educator, performance artist*
Khare, Mohan *chemist, researcher*
Klein, Sami Weiner *librarian*
La Force, Hudson III *chemicals executive, former federal agency administrator*
Lok, Joan Mei-Lok *community affairs specialist, artist*
McCuan, William Patrick *philanthropist, real estate company executive*
Miller, Andrea R. *application developer, educator*
Mitchell, Helen Buss *philosophy educator*
Piou-Brewer, Magalie *psychotherapist, educator, small business owner*
Purcell, James Nelson, Jr. *international organization administrator*
Scornaienchi, Joan Webb *educational association administrator, consultant*
Strahlman, Richard Scott *pediatrician*
Straja, Sorin Radu *chemical engineer, mathematician, computer programmer*
Van Buiten, Robert D. *management consultant, career planner*
Whiting, Albert Nathaniel *former university chancellor*
Young, Donald Alan *former Federal Agency Administrator*

Crofton
Dey, Saikat *information technology manager*
Laurenson, Robert Mark *mechanical engineer*
Mahaffey, Redge Allan *movie producer, director, writer, actor, scientist, business executive*
Smith, Rebecca Anstine *harpist, educator*
Vranish, John Michael *electrical engineer, researcher*

Crownsville
Campbell, Walter Everett *adult education educator*
Irish, Leon Eugene *lawyer, non-profit organization executive, educator*

Cumberland
Frederick, Sharon L. *education educator*
Heckert, Paul Charles *sociologist, educator*
Riggs, Robert Meldrum *French educator*

Damascus
Styer, Joanne Louise *retired dietician*

Darnestown
Cohen, Sanford Irwin *physician, educator*

Dayton
Fischell, Robert Ellentuch *physicist*

Denton
Doster, Rose Eleanor Wilhelm *artist*
Miller, Frank Louis *school psychologist*

Derwood
Mealy, John Burke *clinical psychologist*
Mylonakis, Stamatios Gregory *artist, research scientist, retired lawyer*
Stadtman, Thressa Campbell *biochemist*

Dickerson
Duncan, Jack G. *lawyer*

District Heights
McDowell-Craig, Vanessa Dennise *supervisor, consultant*

Easton
Maffitt, James Strawbridge *lawyer*
Potter, Blair Burns *editor*
Rever, George Wright *psychiatrist, health facility administrator*
Shepard, William Seth *diplomat, writer*

Edgewater
Boehme, Jennifer *ecologist, oceanographer*
McCamy, Calvin Samuel *retired optics scientist*
Whaley, Beth Dowling *retired elementary school educator*

Elkton
Jasinski-Caldwell, Mary L. *insurance company executive*
Mayer, Margaret Ellen *medical coding specialist*
Xu, Ping *chemist*

Ellicott City
Benjamin, Thomas Edward *music educator, composer, conductor*
Bruley, Duane Frederick *academic administrator, consultant, engineer*
Cox, Pierre Napoleon *health and safety education consultant*
Estin-Klein, Libbyada *advertising executive, writer*
Loerke, William Carl *art historian, educator*
Marra Oram, Diana Marie *microbiologist, educator*
Pairo, Preston Abercrombie, Jr. *lawyer*
Singh, Narsingh Bahadur *chemist, researcher*

Emmitsburg
Merrill, Charles J. *language educator*
Tortora, Anne Halloran *music educator, director*

Forest Hill
Wolf, Martin Eugene *lawyer, educator*

Forestville
Moore, Virginia Bradley *librarian*

Fort George G Meade
Alexander, Keith B. *federal agency administrator, career military officer*
Nelson, Douglas J. *mathematician*
Robertson, Alonzo Morrell *lawyer, educator*
Schmitt, Robert Lee *computer scientist*

Fort Washington
Alexander, Gary R. *lawyer, state legislator, lobbyist*
Cameron, Rita Giovannetti *writer, publishing executive*
Caveny, Leonard Hugh *mechanical engineer, aerospace scientist, consultant*
Harrison, Ronnette *music educator, director*
Satterthwaite, George, II, *security firm executive*
Smoot, Burgess Howard *federal official*

Frederick
Belard, J-Louis Hubert *medical researcher*
Blumenthal, Robert P. *medical researcher*
Bobe, Gerd *medical researcher*
Butler, Jay *women's college basketball coach*
Byrd, R. Andrew *medical researcher*
Carlson, David Emil *physicist, researcher*
Colburn, Nancy Hall *medical researcher*
Course, Didier Jean *literature and language professor, writer*
Daniel, J. Christopher *health facility executive, family medicine physician, military officer*
De Jong, Marla J. *nurse, researcher*
DeVoe, Howard Josselyn *retired chemistry professor*
Dougherty, Jennifer P. *realtor*
Garver, Robert Vernon *retired research physicist*
Gordon, Rita Simon *civic leader, former nurse, educator*
Gudla, Prabhakar Reddy *research scientist*
Hanna, Michael George, Jr. *immunologist, pharmaceutical executive*
Henderson, Madeline Mary (Berry) *chemist, researcher, consultant*
Hogan, Ilona Modly *lawyer*
Hughes, Stephen H. *virologist, researcher*
Keefer, Larry Kay *medical researcher*
Kelsey, Ronald Grant *retired military officer, environmental engineer*
Le Grice, Stuart F.J. *senior investigator*
Lin, George *research and development company executive, biomedical researcher*
Malin, Howard Gerald *podiatrist*
Marquez, Victor E. *medical researcher*
McKee, Tawnya Carlene *research scientist*
McMahon, James Brislin *medical researcher*
Menotti-Raymond, Marilyn *geneticist, molecular biologist*
Merrill, Daniel A. *program manager*
Morrison, Deborah K. *medical researcher*
Oppenheim, Joost J. *allergist, immunologist, researcher*
Ortaldo, John R. *immunologist, researcher*
Perantoni, Alan O. *medical researcher*
Randall, Frances *technical writer*
Reynolds, Craig W. *research scientist*
Safavian, S. Rasoul *telecommunications industry executive*
Sharifi, Nima *oncologist, researcher*
Stern, Stephan Timothy *toxicologist, researcher*
Strathern, Jeffrey N. *medical researcher*
Tobin, Gregory John *biologist*
Trinchieri, Giorgio *medical researcher*
Weissman, Allan M. *medical researcher*
Whelihan, Alan Stuart *real estate developer, automotive executive*
Wlodawer, Alexander *medical researcher*
Young, Howard Alan *molecular biologist*
Zimmer-Galler, Ingrid E. *ophthalmologist, educator*

Friendship
Clagett, Diana Wharton Sinkler *museum docent*

Frostburg
Bauman, Jon Ward *retired music educator*
Horner, Ronald George *musician, educator*
Root, Edward Lakin *education educator, academic administrator*

Gaithersburg
Amis, Eric Jay *chemist, researcher, editor*
Beichl, Isabel M. *mathematician*
Bremenstuhl, David P. *elementary school educator*
Broderick, John Caruthers *librarian, educator*
Brodine, Charles Edward *physician*
Caplin, Jerrold Leon *health physicist*
Carasso, Alfred Sam *mathematician*
Caswell, Randall Smith *physicist*
Celotta, Robert James *physicist*
Chow, Laurence Chung-Lung *research scientist*
Clark, Charles Winthrop *physicist*
Cookson, Alan Howard *electrical engineer, researcher*
Coskuner, Orkid *research scientist, educator*
Costin, Gertrude-Emilia *toxicologist, director*
Currie, Lloyd Arthur *nuclear scientist, educator*
Decker, Amy *forensic specialist, researcher*
Delgado, Dwighd D(ubied) *electric power industry executive*
Fong, Jeffrey Tse-Wei *mechanical engineer*
French, Judson Cull *federal official*
Gerard, Gary Floyd *molecular biologist*
Gordon, Michael Robert *lawyer, state legislator*
Hall, Arthur Raymond, Jr. *retired minister*
Haque, Kashif Aziz *research scientist*
Hattrick-Simpers, Jason Ryan *materials scientist, researcher*
Hegyeli, Ruth Ingeborg Elisabeth Johnsson *pathologist, federal official*
Hertz, Harry Steven *government official*
Jacox, Marilyn Esther *chemist*
Jahanmir, Said *materials scientist, mechanical engineer*
Johnson, George H. *finance company executive*
Jurchescu, Oana Diana *research scientist*
Landel, Michel *food service and management company executive*
Laptev, Alexander Borisovich *physicist, researcher*
Lastra, Carlos Mariano *lawyer*
LaVan, David *engineering executive*
Levine, Robert Sidney *retired chemical engineer*
Lynn, Jeffrey Whidden *research physicist, educator*
McCann, Joseph Leo *lawyer, former government official*
McDowell, Donna Schultz *lawyer, educator*
Mighell, Alan Donald *physical chemist*
Nabors, Gary Scott *medical products executive*
Naylor, Phyllis Reynolds *writer*
Nedzelnitsky, Victor *electrical engineer, researcher*
Phillips, William Daniel *physicist*
Pierce, Daniel Thornton *physicist*
Polyakov, Sergey Vladimirovich *physicist, researcher*
Ramalingam, Murugan *researcher*
Ray, Charles Aaron *ambassador*
Reader, Joseph *physicist*
Rodgers, Mary Columbro *literature educator, writer, academic administrator*
Rosenblatt, Joan Raup *mathematical statistician*
Ruckman, Mark Warren *physicist*
Ruth, James Perry *financial planner*
Savransky, Vladimir M. *research scientist*
Schwartzberg, Allan Zelig *psychiatrist, educator*
Sengers, Johanna M. H. Levelt *physicist*
Song, Junfeng John *engineer, researcher*
Tarrio, Charles *physicist*
Weber, Alfons *physicist*
Werner, Samuel Alfred *physicist, educator*
Wineland, David J. *physicist*
Wright, Richard Newport III *retired engineering executive, engineering educator*

Galena
Hunsperger, Elizabeth Jane *art and design consultant, educator*

Garrett Park
Baldwin, Calvin Benham, Jr. *retired science administrator*
Elwood, William *medical educator*
Kornberg, Warren Stanley *journalist*

Germantown
Adamson, Richard Henry *pharmacologist*
Foulke, Judith Diane *health physicist*
Fountos, Barrett Nicholas *epidemiologist, researcher*

Hirsch, Roland Felix *chemist, educator*
Iqbal, Zafar *neuroscientist, biochemist, educator*
Kinniburgh, Alan James *not-for-profit administrator, molecular biologist*
Kronstadt, Jill *literature and language professor*
Lewis, Robert John Cornelius Koons *retired library director*
Naake, Joan Murray *English professor*
South, Gail *business and mathematics professor*
Stevceva, Liljana *medical educator, researcher*

Gibson Island
Forster, William Hull *management consultant*

Glen Arm
Blanton, Edward Lee, Jr. *lawyer*
Jackson, Theodore Marshall *retired oil industry executive*

Glen Burnie
Horine, Nelson Charles, II, *educator, educational administrator*
Mc Cabe, Gerard Benedict *retired library administrator*
Watts, Virginia Agnes *retired special education educator*

Glen Echo
Levinson, Peter Joseph *retired lawyer*

Glyndon
Renbaum, Barry Jeffrey *lawyer*

Greenbelt
Amato, Deborah Douglass *aerospace engineer*
Batchelor, David Allen *astrophysicist, educator*
Bernstein, Kenneth J. *secondary school educator*
Billingsley, Lance W. *lawyer*
Brennan, William Collins, Jr. *lawyer*
Chasanow, Howard Stuart *retired judge, mediator*
Danchi, William C. *astrophysicist*
Day, John H. *physicist*
Ericsson, Aprille Joy *aerospace engineer*
Fax, Charles Samuel *lawyer*
Ferguson, Frank Thomas *chemical engineer*
Gehrels, Neil (Cornelius A. Gehrels) *astrophysicist*
Jeong, Myeong-Jae *environmental scientist*
Kniffen, Donald Avery *astrophysicist, educator, researcher*
Kostiuk, Theodor *astrophysicist planetary scientist*
Kundu, Prasun Kumar *environmental scientist, physics professor*
Mather, John Cromwell *astrophysicist*
Matthews, Darryl R., Sr. *not-for-profit fundraiser*
McCarter, Sharondia Renee *elementary school educator*
Messitte, Peter Jo *federal judge*
Mumma, Michael Jon *research scientist*
Obamogie, Mercy A. *physician*
Rauscher, Bernard Joseph *astrophysicist*
Reupke, William Albert *engineer*
Rogers, Edward William *engineering company executive*
Schmidt, Joachim Matthias *research scientist*
Shen, Bo-Wen *research scientist*
Skillern, Gwendolyn D. *accountant*
Titus, Roger Warren *judge*
Weltz, Martin David *hematologist*
Wood, H(oward) John III *astrophysicist, astronomer*
Yang, Yuekui *atmospheric scientists*

Hagerstown
Berkson, Jacob Benjamin *lawyer, writer*
Clark, Ann Maureen *literature and language professor*
Feagin, James R.H. *librarian, director*
Harrison, Lois Smith *hospital executive, educator*
Harsh, Michael Gerard *social studies educator*
Higgins, M. Eileen *management consultant, educator*
Hull, Michele Lynn *music educator*
Jozik, Paul *physics professor*
Ksienski, Aharon Arthur *retired electrical engineer*
Moran, Suzannah *social sciences educator*
Munday, John Henry *chemist, physicist, educator*
Williams, Patricia C. *nursing educator*

Hampstead
Dotterweich, Patrick Timothy *social studies educator*

Hanover
DeLeaver, Douglas *retired protective services official, telecommunications industry executive, Law Enforcement Association Administrator*
Haque, Mohammed Nazmul *environmental engineer, researcher*
Henderson Hall, Brenda Ford *computer company executive*

Havre De Grace
Sweatman, Kelly *information technology executive*
Tabor, Pamela Dalton *elementary school educator, career planning administrator*
Wetter, Virginia Forwood Pate *broadcast executive*

Hollywood
Newhouse, Alan Russell *retired federal official*

Hunt Valley
Everton, Angus R. *lawyer*
Hiremath, Praveen S. *pharmaceutical executive, researcher*
Igusa, Jun-Ichi *mathematician, educator*

Hurlock
Shively, Bonnie Lee *pastor*

Hyattsville
Asongu, Januarius Jingwa *business executive*
Gillum, Richard Frank *epidemiologist*
Golden, Marita *literature educator, writer, foundation administrator*
Gonzalez, Joe Fred, Jr. *mathematical statistician, educator*
González Valer, Francisco *bishop*
Holley, Rev. Martin David *bishop*
Knestout, Barry Christopher *bishop*
Lovick, Norman *accountant*
O'Connor, Kevin Thomas *religious organization administrator*
Pritchett, Timothy Michael *physicist*
Ranjan, Priya *research scientist*
Spencer, Catherine Ellen *academic administrator*
Wuerl, Donald William *archbishop*

Indian Head
Bailey, Louella C. *music educator*

Jefferson
Beall, James Robert *toxicologist, consultant*

Joppa
Bates, Martha Copenhaver *elementary school educator*

Kennedyville
Schiff, Gary Stuart *academic administrator, educator, consultant*

Kensington
Chiazze, Leonard, Jr. *biostatistician, epidemiologist, educator*
Dauster, William Gary *lawyer, economist*
Ellwanger, Albert Thompson III *secondary school educator*
Forrest, Sidney *clarinetist, music educator*
Freeman, Ernest Robert *retired engineering executive*
Mavilio, Domenico *medical researcher, physician*
Oweiss, Ibrahim Mohamed *economist, educator*
Rosenthal, Alan Sayre *government official, lawyer*
Suraci, Charles Xavier, Jr. *retired federal agency administrator, air transportation executive, consultant*

La Plata
Bostwick, Catherine *psychologist*
Brantley, David H. *literature and language professor, department chairman*
Herdman-Fisher, Carolyn A. *music educator*
Johnson, Diane Jones *librarian*
Lauber, Kathleen P. *microbiologist, educator*
Layer, Marianne Elizabeth *literature and language professor, department chairman*
Martino, Paula L. *government agency administrator, art historian, educator*
Miklos, Athena Pauline *educator*
Montgomery, William E. *biology professor, department chairman*
Penick, Ann Clarisse *minister, counselor*
Stephanic, Barbara Jean *art historian, writer, curator, researcher*
Zinn, Michael Wallace *aerospace engineer*

Landover
Frederick, Amy L. *science administrator*
Levy, David Lawrence *retired lawyer, legal association administrator*
Luchs, Alison *curator, art historian*

Lanham
Cheng, Jian-Yu *mechanical engineer, researcher, application developer*
Degnan, John James III *physicist*
Freese, Rich *publishing executive*
Hughes, Catherine L. (Cathy Hughes) *broadcast executive, radio personality*
Ingraham, Cynthia Louise Johnson *educational consultant*
McClain, George Nelson *economist, lawyer*
Miller, Alwin Vermar *educational association administrator, consultant*

Lanham Seabrook
Barnes, Margaret Anderson *behaviorist/minister, statistician*

Largo
Ryan, Carol J. *educational administrator*

Laurel
Biermann, Paul Joseph *materials engineer*
Blewett, David T. *astrophysicist*
Boehmer, Jamie Layne *biologist, researcher*
Buffkins, LeRachel Harombe *small business owner*
Calvert, Richard John *medical researcher*
Dorsey, John Wesley, Jr. *retired academic administrator, economist*
Eaton, Alvin Ralph, Jr. *aeronautical and systems engineer, applied physics executive*
Hoffman, David John *physiologist, ecotoxicologist*
Hudson, Patrick Jay *engineer, educator*
Jones, Coletta L. *minister*
Land, Henry Bruce III *electronics engineer, researcher*
Levitt, Gerald Steven *engineering executive*
Maurer, Donald Eugene *mathematician*
McConnaughey, James Walter *economist*
Srinivasan, Rengaswamy *research scientist*
Weerackody, Vijitha *electrical engineer, researcher*
Williams, Barbara Ivory *retired educational researcher*

Laytonsville
Canapary, Herbert Carton *retired insurance company executive*

Lexington Park
Scanlan, Robert Dennis *systems analyst*

Linthicum
Ehrlich, Bob (Robert Leroy Ehrlich Jr.) *lawyer, Former Governor, Maryland*
Metzel, Alan Barry *manufacturing engineer*

Linthicum Heights
Skillman, William Alfred *consulting engineering executive*

Lothian
Messenger, Barbara Beall *artist*

Lusby
Eshelman, Ralph Ellsworth *historian, consultant, paleontologist*
Ladd, Culver Sprogle *secondary school educator*

Lutherville
Baramki, Theodore Atallah *gynecologist, reproductive endocrinologist*
Berg, Wendie *radiologist*
Chuck, Roy S. *surgeon*
Eisenberg, Joseph Martin *psychologist, consultant*
Elma, Bayani Borja *physician*
Freeland, Charles *lawyer, accountant*
O'Brien, Terrence P. *ophthalmologist, educator*

Lutherville Timonium
Auwaerter, Paul Gisbert *physician, educator*
Cappiello, Frank Anthony, Jr. *investment advisor*
Cedrone, Louis Robert, Jr. *retired critic*
Howell, Harley Thomas *lawyer*
Meyer, Jon Keith *psychiatrist, psychoanalyst, educator*
Park, Lee Crandall *psychiatrist, physician*

Madison
Hoffman, Alicia Coro *retired federal executive*

Manokin
Miles, Elizabeth Jane *social worker*

Marion Station
Handy, Mary Thomas *retired elementary school educator*

Middletown
Robinson, Daniel N. *psychology and philosophy professor*

Millersville
Culver, Catherine Marie *secondary school educator*

Mitchellville
Blasier, Cole *political scientist*
Brubaker, Lauren Edgar *retired minister*
Embree, Ainslie Thomas *history professor*
Griffen, Clyde Chesterman *retired historian*
Hammer, Jane Amelia Ross *advocate*
Heald, Morrell *humanities educator*
Kendall, Katherine Anne *social worker*
Marsh, Caryl Amsterdam *retired curator, psychologist*
Peretz, Don *political science professor*

Monkton
Parker, Robert M., Jr., (Bob Parker) *wine critic, writer*

Montgomery Village
Kushner, Lawrence Maurice *physical chemist, consultant*
Narum, David L. *parasitologist*

Mount Airy
Foley, Cornelia MacIntyre *retired artist*
Johnston, Josephine Rose *chemist*
Quarles, Steven Princeton *lawyer*
Spohn, William Gideon, Jr. *mathematician, retired musician*

New Market
Young, Russell Dawson *physicist, consultant*

North Bethesda
Chapman, Janet Carter Goodrich *economist, educator*
Edinger, Stanley Evan *clinical chemist*
Kreling, Barbara Bartholf *medical educator*
Moshman, Jack *statistical consultant*
Szabo, Daniel *federal official*

Ocean Pines
Crawford, Norman Crane, Jr. *academic administrator, consultant*
Fullerton, Jean Leah *retired language educator, researcher, census researcher*

Olney
Delmar, Eugene Anthony *architect*

Owings
O'Neill, Patricia Tydings *performing arts educator, language educator*

Owings Mills
Cameron, Cam (Malcolm G. Cameron III) *professional football coach*
Colussy, Dan Alfred *aviation executive*
Cymet, Tyler Childs *medical writer, researcher*
Harbaugh, John *professional football coach*
Heck, Albert Frank *retired neurologist*
Newsome, Ozzie *professional sports team executive*
Rose, Stephen *medical researcher*
Ryan, Judith W. *geriatrics nurse, educator*
Sanner, George Bradley *bank executive*
Smith, Troy *professional football player*

Parkton
Fitzgerald, Edwin Roger *physicist, researcher*

Parkville
Hill, Milton King, Jr. *retired lawyer*

Pasadena
Asti, Alison Louise *lawyer*
De Pauw, Linda Grant *historian, educator, writer*
Dubke, Marie E. *retired business educator*

Patuxent River
Stroup, Darryl Ray *systems engineer*

Pikesville
Rosen, Leslie Smith *humanities educator, director*
Sokol, Marian *medical association administrator*
Stein, Bernard Alvin *retail executive, consultant*
Wilson, Courtney B. *military officer, museum administrator*

Pomfret
Craley, Brian Scott *social sciences educator*

Poolesville
Noble, Pamela Lee *primatologist*

Port Deposit
Benjamin, Francis Ellis *analytical chemist, consultant*

Potomac
Bulger, Roger James *academic administrator*
Christian, John Kenton *publishing executive, marketing professional, consultant*
Cohen, Warren I. *historian*
Dickerman, Serafina Poerio *real estate broker, consultant*
Eaves, Maria Perry *realtor*
Fox, Arthur Joseph, Jr. *editor*
Fthenakis, Emanuel John *aerospace transportation and communications executive*
Gaston, Marilyn Hughes *physician, administrator, public health expert, author*
Hall, William Darlington *lawyer*
Hey, Nancy Henson *retired educational administrator*
Howe, Edmund Grant III *psychiatrist, educator*
Ingram, Richard Thomas *retired academic administrator, writer, consultant*
Karnow, Stanley *journalist, writer*
Keefe, Arthur Thomas III *non-profit fund raising executive*
Khachaturian, Zaven Setrak *neuroscientist*
Kuykendall, Crystal Arlene *educational consultant, lawyer*
Medin, A. Louis *computer company executive*
Medin, Julia Adele *mathematics professor, researcher*
Meyer, Lawrence George *lawyer*
Myers, Lawrence Stanley, Jr. *retired radiation biologist*
Navarro, Joseph Anthony *retired statistician, consultant*
Oertel, Goetz Kuno Heinrich *physicist, professional society administrator*
Owen, Harrison Hollingsworth *management consultant*
Penczner, Marius *media company executive*
Peter, Phillips Smith *lawyer*
Peters, Carol Beattie Taylor (Mrs. Frank Albert Peters) *mathematician*
Redding, Robert Ellsworth *lawyer*
Rhode, Alfred Shimon *retired finance educator*
Rosenberg, Sarah Zacher *retired cultural organization administrator*
Schmeltzer, Edward *lawyer*
Schwartz, Gregory John *international business lawyer, business and investments transactions specialist*
Shapiro, Richard Gerald *retail executive, consultant*
Sundick, Sherry Small *journalist, writer, poet*
Tressel, George Walter *television producer, science educator, consultant*
Troffkin, Howard Julian *lawyer*
Vadus, Gloria A. *scientific document examiner*
Walker, Charls Edward *economist, consultant*
Webster, Duane Ernes *retired librarian*
Williams, Peter MacLellan *nuclear engineer*
Wonnacott, Paul *retired economics professor*
Yerman, Anne Veronica *interior designer*

Prince Frederick
Beers, Richard H. *physics professor*

Princess Anne
Brockett, Ramona *criminologist, educator*
Brooks, Sharon Denise *librarian*
Chigbu, Paulinus *fisheries biologist, educator, research scientist*
Elobaid, Muna Elhag *computer instructor*
Khoza, Lombuso *science educator*
Malik, Malik B. *mathematics professor*
Nagoski, Marcelle *music educator*
Seabrook, Renita L. *criminal justice professor*
Sharma, Dinesh Kumar *management science educator*
Thompson, Thelma Barnaby *university president, classical languages educator*

Pylesville
Roth, George Stanley *biochemist, physiologist, researcher*

Queenstown
Corn, Morton *environmental engineer, educator*

Randallstown
Holt, John J. *mediator, arbitrator, retired human resources specialist*

Reisterstown
Broadbent, J. Streett *engineering executive*
Tirone, Barbara Jean *retired health insurance administrator*

Riverdale
Guetzkow, Daniel *technology company entrepreneur*
Passoa, Steven C. *entomologist*

Rockville
Abel, Dorothy B. *biomedical engineer*
Altmeyer, Mark P. *pharmaceutical executive*
Ashar, Hansraj G. *structural engineer, nuclear regulator*

Avery, Bruce Edward *lawyer*
Ayafor, Isaiah M. *education educator*
Banfield, William Gethin *physician*
Barbera, Mary Ellen *state appeals court judge*
Barker, Lewellys Franklin *medical association administrator*
Barkley, Brian Evan *lawyer, political consultant*
Barros, Colleen *federal agency administrator*
Bautista, Abraham Parana *immunologist*
Berryman, Richard Byron *lawyer*
Birns, Mark Theodore *physician*
Bough, Kristopher *pharmacologist*
Buchanan, John Donald *retired nuclear scientist*
Chiacchierini, Richard Philip *healthcare consultant*
Chiogioji, Melvin Hiroaki *retired federal official, entrepreneur*
Chretien, Paul Bernard *oncologist, medical researcher*
Clancy, Carolyn M. *internist, federal agency administrator*
Clark, Harry Westley *federal agency administrator*
Cline, Terry L. *federal agency administrator*
Cohan, June Elizabeth *small business owner*
Conroy, J. Michael *lawyer, judge*
Cornelius, Maria G. *financial advisor*
Crout, J. Richard *pharmacologist, researcher*
Davis, Beverly Watts *federal agency administrator*
De Jong, David Samuel *lawyer*
Dineen, Thomas G. III *securities regulator, writer*
Dragga, Patrick W. *lawyer*
Duke, Elizabeth M. *federal agency administrator*
Dunham, Bernadette Margaret *federal agency administrator, veterinarian*
DuPont, Robert Louis *psychiatrist, physician*
Edwards, Bert Tvedt *accountant*
Elespuru, Rosalie K. *molecular biologist and researcher*
Fink, Kenneth Stuart *physician, researcher*
Foreman, Todd Matthew *professional sports team owner, communications executive*
Frazier, Walter Ronald *real estate investment company executive*
Frye, Roland Mushat, Jr. *lawyer*
Galson, Steven Kenneth *federal official*
Garcia, Gregory T. (Greg Garcia) *federal agency administrator*
Gaunaurd, Guillermo C. *retired physicist, engineer, researcher*
Gluckstein, Fritz Paul *veterinarian, biomedical information specialist*
Goodman, Jesse *physician, director, public health facility administrator, research scientist*
Gray, Paulette Styles *federal agency administrator, biologist*
Griffith, Jerry Dice *energy executive, management consultant*
Haber, Margaret Wilson *informatics specialist, director*
Hamilton, Parker *library director*
Hare, John L. *literature and language professor*
Hepfer, Cheryl Lynn *lawyer*
Hewlett, Richard Greening *historian*
Jaczko, Gregory Bela *federal agency administrator, physicist*
James, Eric Robert *medical educator*
Johnson, Lenora *federal agency administrator, public health service officer*
Kadish, Richard L. *lawyer*
Kafka, Marian Stern *neuroscientist*
Karp, Ronald Alvin *lawyer*
Karson, Emile *lawyer*
Katz, Steven Martin *lawyer, accountant*
Kennedy, Roger George *museum program and parks director*
Kerxton, Alan Smith *lawyer*
Kim, Bong-Jo *molecular biologist, researcher*
Kimura, Tomohiro *biophysical and biochemical researcher*
Klein, Dale Edward *commissioner, engineering educator*
Kline, Raymond Adam *professional organization executive*
Klosson, Michael *public policy director*
Kohlmeier, Louis Martin, Jr. *newspaper reporter*
Kroner, Barbara L *epidemiologist*
Kruger, Jerome *materials science educator, consultant*
Kruger, Mollee Coppel *writer*
Landon, John Campbell *research and development company executive*
Leach, Berton Joe *medical educator*
LeCompte, Andrew C. *freelance/self-employed interpreter*
Lehman, Leonard *retired lawyer, consultant*
Lessenco, Gilbert Barry *retired lawyer*
Levenson, Bruce *professional sports team owner, communications executive*
Leventhal, Carl M. *neurologist, consultant, retired government agency administrator*
Levin, Alexander B. *mathematics professor*
Levitt, Mark Howard *sales executive*
Loyevsky, Mark Michael *biochemist, parasitologist, researcher*
Lyons, Peter B. *commissioner*
MacArthur, Diana Taylor *advanced technology executive*
Madle, Robert Albert *writer*
Malik, Waheed Ahmad *cardiologist*
Mallak, Craig T. *pathologist*
Marcuccio, Phyllis Rose *retired educational association administrator, editor*
McCann, S. Anthony *financial management consultant, former federal agency administrator*
McDonald, Capers Walter *biomedical engineer, manufacturing executive, entrepreneur, educator*
McLellan, Thomas (Andrew Thomas McLellan) *federal agency administrator, psychology professor*
McMurry, James Finley, Jr. *endocrinologist, researcher*
Medina, Eduardo Jose *language educator*
Menikoff, Jerry Alan *health facility administrator, law educator*
Miller, Claire Ellen *editor, educator, writer*
Miller, Kenneth Michael *electronics executive, director*
Morgan, William Bruce *naval architect*
Mummaneni, Padmaja *research scientist, educator*
Nelson, Kevin *statistician*
Niewiaroski, Trudi Osmers (Gertrude) *social studies educator*
Nithyanandan, Pallavi *research scientist*
O'Donnell, James Francis *retired health scientist administrator*
Oswald, Rudolph A. *economist*
Ovanesov, Mikhail V. *biophysicist, researcher, biomedical engineer*
Oyler, Anne *audiologist*
Parham-Hopson, Deborah *health programs administrator*
Pastor, Richard Walter *research chemist*
Peskowitz, Ed *professional sports team owner, communications executive*
Power, A. Kathryn *federal agency administrator*
Price, Simani Mohapatra *research scientist, director*
Proffitt, John Richard *information technology executive, educator, public official*
Provorny, Frederick Alan *lawyer, educator*
Psotka, Joseph *psychologist*
Ralph, Robert Alan *ophthalmologist, educator*
Rao, Potarazu Krishna *environmental consultant*
Renninger, Mary Karen *retired librarian*
Rice, Kenner Cralle *medicinal chemist*
Rodriguez-Cambero, Rafael Luis *project manager*
Rothenberg, Alan David *lawyer*
Ryan, Kevin William *virologist, clinical research administrator*
Sansalone, William Robert *biochemist, educator, biomedical researcher*
Sarma, Dandapantula Nandakumara *senior scientist*
Schindler, Albert Isadore *physicist, researcher*
Schwarz, Sidney Howard *rabbi*
Scully, Martha Seebach *speech and language pathologist*
Seagle, Edgar Franklin *environmental engineer, consultant*
Senger, Jeffrey M. *lawyer*
Slotta, Tracey *biology professor*
Smith, Hamilton Othanel *molecular biologist, educator*
Stansfield, Charles W. *educational administrator*
Suleiman, Orhan Hussein *radiological physicist*
Sullivan, Marian Toth *epidemiologist, researcher*
Svinicki, Kristine L. *commissioner*
Tabor, Edward *medical researcher*
Telesetsky, Walter *federal agency administrator*
Thompson, James Lee *lawyer*
Tomar, Richard Thomas *lawyer*
Toro, Jorge R. *dermatologist, researcher*
Torti, Frank Michael *federal agency administrator*
Um, Ki Sung *research scientist*
van Dyck, Peter Cuyler *federal agency administrator*
Venter, J. Craig (John Craig Venter, Craig Venter) *science foundation director, geneticist*
Wallenmeyer, William Anton *retired physicist*
Whitescarver, Jack Edward *federal agency administrator*
Williams, Robert C. *federal agency administrator*
Woodcock, Janet *federal agency administrator*
Yaes, Robert Joel *radiologist, educator*
Zaphiriou, George Aristotle *lawyer, educator*
Zinni, Anthony Charles *global defense company executive, retired military officer*

Royal Oak
Clizbe, John Anthony *psychologist, social services administrator*

Saint Leonard
Seifert, Betty L. *conservator, consultant*

Saint Marys City
Clifton, Lucille Thelma *author*
O'Brien, Jane Margaret *academic administrator*
Williams, Elizabeth Nutt *psychologist, educator*
Wilson, Bruce Matthew *literature and language professor*

Saint Michaels
Brown, Omer Forrest, II, *lawyer*
Feisel, Lyle Dean *retired dean, electrical engineer, educator*
Parnes, Stuart L. *museum director*
Peck, Charles Edward *retired construction and mortgage executive*
Trippi, Joe *media consultant*

Salisbury
Adkins, Sally D. *Judge, Maryland Court of Appeals*
Anderson, Eva Klauber *psychologist, educator*
Booker, Betty Mae *poet*
Cockey, Linda Essick *music educator*
Folger, William Michael *music educator*
Gorrow, Teena Ruark *education educator*
Kleiman, Gary Howard *broadcast, advertising and cellular communications consultant*
Kutchen, John E. *information technology manager*
Losonczy-Marshall, Marta Elizabeth *psychologist, educator*
O'Donnell, James Joseph *insurance company executive, economics professor*
Weer, Christy Harris *finance educator*
Wolter, John Amadeus *librarian, federal official*

Severna Park
Kumm, William Howard *energy products company executive*
Pumphrey, Janet Kay *editor, publishing executive*
Rheinstein, Peter Howard *healthcare company executive, physician, lawyer*
Schick, Edgar Brehob *language educator*

Shady Side
Devine, Donald J. *political science professor, consultant*

Sherwood Forest
Richards, Carol Ann Rubright *lecturer, retired editor, journalist*

Silver Spring
Altschul, b j *public relations counselor*
Aranya, Gwendalin Qi *painter, priest, educator, yoga instructor, reiki master*
Arvin, Linda Lee *counselor*
Arzayus, Krisa Murray *geochemist*
Bassett, William, Jr. *geospatial intelligence officer*
Bate, Marilyn Anne *psychologist*
Batra, Hitesh *research and development company executive*
Bauer, Norman James *retired education educator*
Beach, Bert Beverly *clergyman*
Beard, Lillian B. McLean *pediatrician, consultant*
Bennett, Carol(ine) Elise *retired reporter, actress*
Bergmann-Leitner, Elke S. *immunologist, researcher*
Berns, Peter Vernon *lawyer*
Biberman, Lucien Morton *retired physicist*
Borkovec, Vera Z. *literature and language professor*
Brandt, Carl David *research virologist*
Brog, David *former air force officer, consultant*
Buenconsejo, Joan *statistician*
Calvert, Gordon Lee *retired legal association executive*
Carter-Johnson, Jean Evelyn *management consultant*
Clark, Mizzell Phillips (Mitzi) *school librarian*
Coles, Anna Louise Bailey *retired dean, nurse*
Craig, Paul Max, Jr. *retired lawyer*
Davis, Marica Nanci Ella Riggin *retired artist*
de Zafra Atwell, Dorothea Elizabeth *retired government agency administrator*
Doherty, William Thomas, Jr. *historian, retired educator*
Dolan, Liz *multimedia company executive, marketing professional*
Doolan, Denise Louise *molecular biologist*
Drum, Bruce Alan *physicist*
Dunnigan, John H. *federal agency administrator*
Edwards, Kamala Doris *humanities educator*
Ehrlich, Charles David *physicist*
Eliot, John *psychologist, educator*
Erk, Frank Chris *biologist, educator*
Eydelman, Malvina *ophthalmologist*
Ganley, Charles James *federal agency administrator, internist*
Gilbert, Charles Richard Alsop *obstetrician, gynecologist, surgeon, educator*
Glickman, Albert Seymour *psychologist, educator*
Guzman, Martha Patricia *science educator*
Hamburg, Margaret Ann (Peggy Hamburg) *federal agency administrator, former public health administrator*
Hendricks, John S. *broadcast executive*
Heppner, Donald Gray, Jr. *immunology research physician, army officer*
Herbers, Tod Arthur *publisher*
Hsueh, Chun-tu *political scientist, educator, foundation administrator, historian*
Hudson, Ralph P. *physicist*
Jacobs, George *broadcast engineering consulting company executive*
Joyce, Stephen P. *hotel executive*
Kainz, Wolfgang *electrical engineer*
Kant, Gloria Jean *retired neuroscientist*
Kaplan, Marjorie *broadcast executive*
Khan, Mansoor A. *pharmaceutical science executive, director*
Kline, Jerry Robert *retired administrative judge, ecologist*
Koltnow, Peter Gregory *engineer, consultant*
Leeworthy, Vernon Robert *economist*
Lipstein, Robert A. *lawyer*
Maas, Joe (Melvin Joseph Maas) *retired federal agency administrator*
Maddy, Jim *museum association administrator*
Madison, Anne Conway *marketing, public relations professional*
Magill, Alan Jon *preventive medicine physician*
Makris, Margaret Lubbe *retired elementary school educator*
Mashin, Jacqueline Ann Cook *health facility consultant*
Mathis, Lisa *federal agency administrator*
Mlay, Marian *retired government official*
Mok, Carson Kwok-Chi *structural engineer*
Moon, Marilyn Lee *economist*
Mosholder, Andrew Donald *psychiatrist*
Noboa, Abdin I. *psychologist, educator*
Ohrt, Colin *pharmacologist, department chairman*
Papas, Irene Kalandros *English language educator, poet, writer*
Patton, Rebecca M. *nursing administrator*
Peiperl, Adam *sculptor, photographer*
Pisney, Raymond Frank *international consulting services executive*
Pollock, Martin L. *state agency administrator*
Rayburn, Carole Ann (Mary Aida) *psychologist, researcher, writer, consultant*
Reinhardt, John Edward *former international affairs specialist*
Rodgers, Johnathan *broadcast executive*
Rothberg, Morey David *historian, editor*
Sammet, Jean E. *computer scientist*
Sapienza, John Thomas *retired lawyer, director*
Scheuerman, William E. *academic administrator, political science professor*
Scipio, L. Albert, II, (Louis Albert Scipio II) *retired aerospace science engineering educator, historian*
Shalowitz, Erwin Emmanuel *civil engineer*
Shih-Carducci, Joan Chia-mo *food service executive, medical technologist, biochemist, writer, educator*
Shropshire, Walter, Jr. *biophysicist, pastor*
Simmons, Monika *microbiologist, researcher*
Sirken, Monroe Gilbert *statistician*
Smedley, Lawrence Thomas *retired organization executive*
Smith, Michael Bryan *civil engineer*
Snyder, Donald Ivandale *musician, educator*
Spinrad, Richard William *federal agency administrator, oceanographer*
Stover, Carl Frederick *foundation executive*
Striner, Herbert Edward *economist*
Supanich, Barbara Ann *physician*
Tobe, Barbara Gaines *information technology executive*
Vernon, Weston, III, (Wes Vernon) *broadcaster, writer, actor*
Waldrop, Francis Neil *physician*
Wang, Julian Xl *research scientist*
Ware, Thaddeus Van *retired government official*
Weinel, Pamela Jean *nurse consultant*
Whitmore, Frank Clifford, Jr. *retired geologist*
Whitten, Leslie Hunter, Jr. *writer, poet, reporter*
Williams, Paul *retired federal agency administrator*
Young, Jay Alfred *chemical safety and health consultant, editor, writer*
Zaslav, David M. *broadcast executive*

Simpsonville
Altschuler, Bruce Robert *research dentist*
Altschuler, Ruth Phyllis *realtor, secondary school educator*

Smithsburg
Gift, Edward Lee *history professor*

Solomons
Alves, C. Douglass, Jr. *museum director*
Harrington, John Vincent *retired communications executive, engineer, educator*
Miller, Thomas James *biology professor*
Roesijadi, Guritno *toxicology educator*

Sparks
Wilson, Alan D. *food products executive*

Sparks Glencoe
Carpenter, W. Geoffrey *lawyer, food products executive*

Spencerville
Whitaker, Joel *publishing executive, public official*

Springdale
Keith, Patricia *multi-media specialist*

Stevenson
DiSalvo, Diane *art administrator, director, curator*
Galbraith, Clotile Signora *psychology professor*
Hendler, Nelson Howard *physician, health facility administrator, director*
Hilgenberg, John Christian *retired corporate financial executive*
Hyman, Mary Bloom *science education programs coordinator*
Manning, Kevin James *academic administrator*
Stanley, Gregory V. *art educator*

Stevensville
Engel, Bradford Charles *educational association administrator, secondary school educator*
Keever, Kathy Jo Bertelsen *nurse midwife, educator*

Street
Spangler, Ronald Leroy *retired television and aircraft executive, automobile consultant*

Sudlersville
Covington, Donald Kingsley, Jr. *plywood sales executive*

Suitland
Assefa, Zelalem *research scientist*
Wilder, Elmon *retired university administrator*

Sunderland
Franklin, Jon Daniel *writer, journalist, educator*

Swanton
Cummins, Delmer Duane *academic administrator, historian*

Sykesville
Crist, Gertrude H. *civic worker*
Williams, Alice Noel Tuckerman *retired foundation administrator*

Takoma Park
Kranidis, Rita S. *educator*
Luna-Escudero-Alie, María-Elvira *language educator*
Miller, Kendra Danette *art services business owner*
Ndeumeni, Charles Dechateau *medical educator*
Ogora, Jane *university librarian*
Urciolo, John Raphael, II, *finance and real estate educator, developer*
Wagner, Marsden Grigg *medical educator, director*

Taneytown
Wisner, Gail Ann *media specialist*

Temple Hills
Ourisman, Mandell Jack *automotive executive*

The Kentlands
Moody, Mary Elizabeth *speech pathology/audiology services professional*

Thurmont
Schuettinger, Bruce Michael *conservator*

Timonium
Forrester, Alfred Whitfield *psychiatrist, educator*
Sagerholm, James Alvin *retired naval officer*
Zeren, Karl Joseph *dentist, educator*

Towson
Adams, Joseph Andrew *internist, health facility administrator, educator*
Ahearn, Elizabeth Lowe *performing arts educator, dance department chair*
Baker, Jean Harvey *history professor*
Caret, Robert Laurent *academic administrator*
Carney, Bradford George Yost *lawyer, educator*
Corcoran, Paul John *physician*
Douglas, Paul H. *university professor*
Fenton, Charles E. *lawyer*
Filmore, Jacquelyn V. *marketing professional*
Forrest, Juliet *dancer, choreographer, educator*
Gilliss, Edward Johnson *lawyer*

Ha, Phuoc Dai *physics professor*
Hairston, Joe A. *school system administrator*
Heaney, Steven *literature and language professor*
Huang, Joseph Chen-Huan *civil engineer*
Jothen, Michael Jon *music educator*
Kolagani, Rajeswari Moolathody *science educator*
Kues, Irvin William *financial planner*
Kurth, Lieselotte *foreign language educator*
Levin, Marguerite Baker *music educator*
Luchese, Diane *music educator*
Mangan, Michael D. *corporate financial executive*
McFalls, James C. *trombonist and music educator*
Murphy, Joseph F. *Judge, Maryland Court of Appeals*
Muuss, Rolf Eduard *retired psychologist, author*
Nelson, H. Wayne *gerontologist, advocate*
Passano, E. Magruder, Jr. *management consultant*
Pomykala, Joseph Steven *economics professor*
Proctor, Kenneth Donald *lawyer*
Ruppert, John Hutchins *sculptor*
Shah, Shirish Kalyanbhai *computer science, chemistry and environmental science educator*
Sills, Edward M. *pediatric rheumatologist*
Spodak, Michael Kenneth *forensic psychiatrist*
Tull, Willis Clayton, Jr. *retired librarian*

Tracys Landing
Smith, Elbert Benjamin *historian, educator*

Trappe
Anderson, Andrew Herbert *retired army officer*
Blades, G(ene) Granville *accountant*
Bowie, Norman Ernest *university official, educator*
Burns-Bowie, Maureen Elizabeth *sculptor*
Paul, James Caverly Newlin *law educator, retired dean*

Union Bridge
Hannah, Judy Challenger *private education tutor*

University Park
Beckenstein, Myron *journalist*

Upper Marlboro
Buffenbarger, R. (Robert) Thomas *labor union administrator*
Bune, Karen Louise *state agency administrator, legal assistant*
Greene, Monica Lynn Banks *psychologist*
Harrell, Glenn T., Jr. *judge*
Jones-Lukács, Elizabeth Lucille *physician*
Seibel, Charles Burgess *accountant, educator*

Waldorf
Raiman, Rosemary A. *advocate*
Wiggins, Stephen Edward *physician*

Walkersville
Welty, Sarah Osborn *secondary school educator*

West Bethesda
Scully, Roger Tehan, II, *lawyer*
Vogelgesang, Sandra Louise *writer, consultant, former ambassador*

West River
Atkinson, Dorothy Scott *retired accountant*

Westminster
Dulany, William Bevard *lawyer*
Erb, Betty Jane *retired real estate agent*
Konigsberg, Richard Lee *accountant*
Konigsberg, Robert Lee *retired electrical engineer*
Mian, Shabbir M. *physicist, educator*
Preston, Charles Michael *lawyer*
Saxton, Celeste Dawn *social studies educator, consultant*
Staples, Lyle Newton *lawyer*

Wheaton
Kaliner, Michael Aron *physician, researcher*
White, Martha Vetter *allergist, immunologist*

Woodbine
Mc Indoe, Darrell Winfred *retired nuclear medicine physician*
Uhl, Scott Mark *retired state agency administrator, consultant*

Woodstock
Hargadon, Michael T. *dentist*

Wye Mills
Knapp, Wesley Martin *ecologist*
Peterson, Richard Stewart *theater director*
Schnaitman, William Kenneth *retired finance company executive*
Tecce, Anita Mercedes *literature, language and theatre professor*

MASSACHUSETTS

Acton
Benz, Edward John, Sr. *clinical pathologist*
Conoby, Joseph Francis *chemist*
Evans, Robert, Jr. *economics professor*
Hicks, Walter Joseph *electrical engineer*
Judd, Michael W. *museum director*
Shah, Syed Faisal Ali *communications engineer*
Smith, Raoul Normand *computer science educator*
Ziegler, Robert George *psychiatrist, family therapist*

Agawam
Goodwin, Beverly Ann *elementary school educator*
Kantor, Simon William *chemistry professor*
Schilling-Nordal, Geraldine Ann *retired secondary school educator*

Allston
Mills, Daniel Quinn *business educator, consultant, author*

Amesbury
Heyman, Joseph Martin *gynecologist*

Amherst
Aelion, C. Marjorie *science educator*
Anber, Mohamed *research scientist*
Anderson, Ronald Trent *artist, educator*
Archer, Ronald Dean *chemist, educator*
Asker, Dalal *microbiologist, educator*
Backes, Ruth Emerson *counseling psychologist*
Baek, Sungmin *molecular biologist, researcher*
Baker, Lynne Rudder *philosophy educator*
Barker, Elizabeth E. *museum director, curator*
Benson, Lucy Wilson *historian, consultant*
Bentley, Richard Norcross *regional planner, writer, educator*
Berger, Seymour Maurice *social psychologist*
Black, Holly *writer*
Blair, Rhonda Louise *educator, actor*
Braun, Barry *kinesiologist*
Bricker, Phillip *philosopher, educator*
Brooks, A. Taeko *historian*
Bushouse, Brenda Kae *political science professor*
Cornish, Geoffrey St. John *golf course architect*
Daehler, Marvin William *psychology professor emeritus*
Donohue, Therese Brady *artistic director, choreographer, costume and set designer*
Fadeev, Alexander Y. *chemist, researcher*
Fink, Richard David *chemist, educator*
Franks, Lewis E. *electrical and computer engineering educator, researcher*
Gerstel, Naomi *social sciences educator*
Godfrey, Laurie Rohde *anthropologist, educator*
Goldstein, Joseph Irwin *materials scientist, educator*
Haas, Peter M. *political science educator*
Hallock, Robert Bruce *physics professor*
Hayashi, Robert Terry *educator*
Higginson, John Edward *history professor*
Hird, John A. *political science professor*
Holub, Robert Charles *academic administrator, language educator*
Jung-Lim, Lee *food scientist*
Kinney, Arthur Frederick *humanities educator, writer*
Klare, Michael Thomas *social sciences educator, director*
Larson, Joseph Stanley *environmentalist, educator*
Liebling, Jerome *photographer, educator*
Lupien, John Reilly *diplomat*
MacKnight, Carol Bernier *educational association administrator*
MacKnight, William John *chemist, educator*
Margulis, Lynn (Lynn Alexander) *evolutionist, educator*
Marx, Anthony W. *academic administrator*
May, Ernest Dewey *academic administrator, musician*
Metz, Ricardo Baer *chemistry professor*
Michael, Dietrich *biology professor*
Minear, Richard Hoffman *history professor*
Muschinski, Andreas *atmospheric physicist, educator*
Ni, Daiheng *engineering educator*
Oates, Stephen Baery *retired historian*
O'Hara, Patricia Bernadette *chemistry professor*
Palmer, John Derry *physiology educator*
Pollatsek, Alexander *retired psychology professor*
Prince, Gregory Smith, Jr. *retired college president*
Rabin, Monroe Stephen Zane *physicist*
Reed-Penttinen, Daphne Stevenson *artist*
Rexroth, Laura Jayne *conductor*
Romer, Robert Horton *physicist, researcher*
Romney, Patricia Ann *psychologist, educator*
Rossi, Alice S. *sociology educator, writer*
Sawyer, Eric Warren *composer, music educator*
Schafer, Gerald Lewis (Jay Schafer) *library director*
Schimmel, David M. *law educator*
Spratlan, Lewis *composer, educator*
Strickland, Bonnie Ruth *psychologist, educator*
Swift, Calvin Thomas *electrical and computer engineering educator*
Taubman, Jane Andelman *literature and language professor*
Taubman, William Chase *political science professor, writer*
Trumble, Paul *librarian*
Wills, David Wood *minister, educator*
Woodbury, Richard Benjamin *anthropologist, educator*
Wyman, David Sword *retired historian, educator*
Yarde, Richard Foster *art educator*
Zilberberg, Marya *epidemiologist, researcher*

Andover
Chao, Shirley Y.L. *food service executive*
Dyleski-Najjar, Debra *lawyer*
Govern, Frank Stanley *health facility and research administrator, healthcare educator, writer*
Jakes, William Chester *electrical engineer*
Yannalfo, Brett Conlon *bank executive*

Arlington
Junger, Miguel Chapero *retired acoustics researcher*
Keshian, Richard *lawyer*
Smialowski, Joseph A. *former mortgage company executive*
Stein, Miriam *social worker, training services executive*
Zimmer, Anna Held *retired social worker*

Ashfield
Gabriel, Peter Paul *business educator*

Ashland
Pettinella, Nicholas Anthony *corporate financial executive*
Sherr, Evan A. *biomedical engineer, consultant*

Auburn
Hurley, Joseph P. *science educator*
Mitchell, Karen Lee *special education educator, consultant*

Auburndale
Aronow, Saul *radiological physicist, consultant*
Drake, Elisabeth Mertz *chemical engineer, consultant*
Kibrick, Anne *retired nursing educator, dean*
Lindgren, Charlotte Holt *language educator*
Mark, Melvin *mechanical engineering educator, consultant*
Scheffler, Israel *philosopher, educator*

Ayer
Sizer, Theodore R. *education educator*

Babson Park
Genovese, Francis Charles (Frank) *economist, educator, editor-in-chief, writer*
Schlesinger, Leonard Arthur *academic administrator*
Tadepalli, Raghu *dean*

Barnstable
Paquin, Thomas Christopher *lawyer*
Perry, Blair Lane *lawyer*
Temkin, Robert Harvey *accountant*

Barre
Reno, Brad Jeffrey *political science educator*

Bedford
Dyer, Joseph Wendell *retired naval officer*
Fairhead, Rona *financial information company executive*
Greiner, Helen *mechanical engineer*
Jelalian, Albert V. *electrical engineer*
Payne, Harry Morse, Jr. *architect*
Shepley, Hugh *architect*
White, Alan Frederick *academic administrator*

Belchertown
Kitchell, Kenneth Francis, Jr. *classical studies educator*

Belmont
Benes, Francine M. *neuroscientist, psychiatrist*
Bingham, George Walter Chandler *retired sales executive*
Cohen, Bruce Michael *psychiatrist, educator, scientist, health facility administrator*
Coyle, Joseph Thomas *psychiatrist*
de Marneffe, Francis *psychiatrist, hospital administrator*
Dohanian, Diran Kavork *art historian, educator*
Forester, Brent Peter *psychiatrist*
Greer, Gordon Bruce *retired lawyer, writer*
Hanfling, Suki *social worker*
Hauser, George *biochemist, educator*
Lloyd, Boardman *investment company executive*
Lyon, Richard Harold *physicist, educator*
McCann, John Joseph *research scientist, consultant*
Merrill, Edward Wilson *chemical engineering professor*
Neumeyer, John Leopold *chemistry professor*
Onesti, Silvio Joseph *psychiatrist*
Pope, Harrison Graham, Jr. *psychiatrist, educator*
Raiffa, Howard *economics educator*
Reynolds, William Francis *mathematics professor*

Berlin
Lohr, Harold Russell *retired bishop*

Beverly
Ake, Margaret Sherrerd *finance educator*
Barger, Richard Wilson *hotel executive*
Eastman, W. Dean *secondary school educator*
Gangle, Rocco *philosopher*
Garner, Richard C. *research scientist*
Kozyrev, Vitaly A. *political science professor, consultant*
Lister, Graeme George *physicist, journalist*
Qin, Shu *materials scientist*
Smith, Derek Armand *information technology executive*

Billerica
Barnes, Shirley Moore *retired psychiatric social worker, genealogist*
Choi, Yong-Seok *device and materials scientist*
Gheith, Mohamed Ahmed *geology educator, consultant*
Kolb, Charles Eugene *research and development company executive*
KuLesza, Frank William *chemical engineer*
Oluwole, Oluwayemisi Oluwi *chemical engineer, researcher*
Wu, Xuanhui *electrical engineer*

Bolton
Devgun, Jas S. *environmental engineer*
Wintle, Suzanne *elementary school educator*

Boston
Abbott, William Saunders *lawyer*
Abby, Dean R. *academic administrator, director*
Aber, John William (Jack) *finance educator, consultant*
Ablow, Joseph *artist, educator*
Abrahm, Janet Lee *hematologist, oncologist, educator, palliative care specialist*
Abrams, Roger Ian *lawyer, educator*
Abularrage, Christopher Joseph *surgeon*
Abu-moustafa, Adel H. *medical educator, dean*
Adams, George Gabriel *mechanical engineering educator*
Adams, Jody *chef, restaurant owner*
Adelstein, S(tanley) James *radiologist, educator*
Adler, Dale Steven *internist, cardiologist*
Aeschliman, Michael David *education educator, writer*
Ahearn, Kevin J. *real estate broker*
Ainge, Danny Ray *professional sports team executive, retired professional basketball player*
Ainsley, P. Steven (Steve Ainsley) *publishing executive*
Aisenberg, Alan C. *physician, educator, researcher*
Ajemian, Marianne *lawyer*
Akins, Cary Willard *cardiac surgeon*
Albert, Martin Lawrence *behavioral neurologist, writer, educator, researcher*
Albright, Eric D. *medical librarian, director*
Alden, Vernon Roger *academic administrator*
Allen, Ray (Walter Ray Allen) *professional basketball player*
Allen, Tony *professional basketball player*
Alpert, Joel Jacobs *pediatrician, educator*
Altshuler, David Matthew *geneticist, endocrinologist*
Amaker, Tommy *men's college basketball coach*
Aman, Alfred Charles, Jr. *law educator*
Anderson, Ana Carrizosa *neurologist, educator*
Anderson, Kenneth Carl *physician, educator*
Anderson, William Stanley *neurosurgeon*
Angelo, E. Joanne *child, adolescent and adult psychiatrist*
Angelou, Maya (Marguerite Annie Johnson) *writer, actress*
Anissimova, Svetlana Vladimirovna *physicist, researcher*
Anselme, Jean-Pierre Louis Marie *chemist*
Antman, Elliott Marshall *cardiologist, educator*
Antman, Karen Hamm *oncologist, educator, dean*
Antonakes, Steven L. *state banking agency administrator*
Antonellis, Joseph C. *investment company executive*
Anversa, Piero *medical educator*
Aoun, Joseph E. *academic administrator, linguistics educator, researcher*
Apjohn, Nelson George *lawyer*
Appley, Mortimer Herbert *psychologist, retired academic administrator*
Aquilino, Daniel *banker*
Ardison, Matthew Tanner *physician assistant*
Aresty, Jeffrey M. *lawyer*
Armstrong, Rodney *librarian*
Aronson, Mark David *medical educator*
Ash, Barbara Lee *education and human services professor*
Ashok, Tara Devi S. *biology professor, researcher*
Atkinson, David *medical educator*
Audette, Joseph F. *medical educator, physician*
Auerbach, John M. *state agency administrator, public health service officer*
Auger, Jessie L. *elementary school educator*
Austen, W(illiam) Gerald *surgeon, educator*
Avorn, Jerry L. *epidemiologist, educator*
Azadzoi, Kazem M. *urologist, educator*
Bacevich, Andrew J. *international relations and history professor, writer*
Bacha, Emile A. *surgeon*
Bae, Donald S. *orthopedist*
Baicker, Katherine (Kate Baicker) *economics professor, former federal official*
Bailin, Michael Traherne *physician*
Baillieul, John Brouard *aerospace engineering and applied mathematics educator*
Balliro, Joseph James, Sr. *lawyer*
Bandipalliam, Prathap V. *oncologist, researcher*
Banks, Henry H. *orthopedist, educator, dean*
Barker, Edwin Bogue *musician*
Baron, Martin *editor*
Barouch, Dan Hung *physician, scientist, educator*
Barsky, Arthur Joseph III *physician, researcher*
Bates, David Westfall *internist, educator, medical researcher*
Baughman, Kenneth Lee *cardiologist, educator*
Bay, Jason Raymond *professional baseball player*
Beal, Robert Lawrence *real estate executive*
Becker, James Murdoch *surgeon, educator*
Beckett, Joshua Patrick *professional baseball player*
Beckwith, Jonathan Roger *geneticist*
Beggs, Alan Hendrie *geneticist, researcher*
Belkin, Michael *vascular surgeon*
Benacerraf, Baruj *pathologist, educator*
Benjamin, William Chase *lawyer*
Bennett, Richard Edward *lawyer*
Benneyan, James C. *research scientist*
Benz, Edward John, Jr. *hematologist, educator, health facility administrator*
Beranek, Leo Leroy *acoustical engineer, consultant*
Berger, Jerome Morris *communications executive*
Bergstresser, Daniel *economist, educator*
Bernhard, William Francis *thoracic and cardiovascular surgeon*
Bernstein, Edward *medical educator, director*
Berson, Eliot Lawrence *ophthalmologist, medical educator*
Berube, Brian A. *lawyer, chemicals executive*
Bines, Harvey Ernest *lawyer, educator, writer*
Binienda, John J., Sr. *state legislator*
Birmingham, Thomas F. *lawyer, former state legislator*
Bistrian, Bruce Ryan *internist, educator*
Black, Paul Henry *medical educator, researcher*
Black, Peter *neurosurgeon, educator*
Blacklow, Robert Stanley *internist, educator*
Blakely, Allison *history professor*
Blandford, Gaynor E. *academic administrator*
Blendon, Robert Jay *health policy educator*
Blinderman, Craig D. *physician*
Bodie, Zvi *finance professor, author*
Bodner, Randall Wayne *lawyer*
Boghosian, Bruce Michael *computational scientist, educator*
Bok, John Fairfield *retired lawyer*
Bokhari, Afshan *art educator, curator*
Bolman, R. Morton, III, (Chip Bolman) *surgeon, educator*
Bonauto, Mary *lawyer*
Boonma, Pruet *computer scientist*
Bornheimer, Allen Millard *lawyer*
Borus, Jonathan Frederick *psychiatrist, educator*
Boskin, Joseph *history professor*
Botsford, Margot *state supreme court justice*
Boudin, Michael *federal judge*
Bourque, Ray *retired professional hockey player*
Bower, Joseph Lyon *business administration educator*
Bowles, Ian A., Jr. *state official*
Boyd, David Preston *business educator*
Braunwald, Eugene *physician, educator*
Brecher, Kenneth *astrophysicist, educator*
Brenner, Barry Morton *physician*
Brenner, Gary Jay *medical association administrator*
Brenner, Michael Barry *rheumatologist, educator*

Brody, Richard Eric *lawyer*
Broitman, Selwyn Arthur *microbiologist, educator, assistant dean*
Bromberg, Lee Carl *lawyer*
Brooke, Peter A. *corporate financial executive*
Brown, Florence M. *endocrinologist, educator*
Brown, Margaret A. *lawyer*
Brown, Robert Arthur *academic administrator, chemical engineering professor*
Brown, Stephen Lee *retired insurance company executive*
Bruns, William John, Jr. *business administration educator*
Buchanan, Robert McLeod *lawyer*
Buchmiller, Terry Lynn *pediatrician, surgeon*
Bunker, Beryl H. *retired insurance company executive, volunteer*
Burleigh, Lewis Albert *lawyer*
Burnham, David Henderson *management consultant*
Burns, Thomas David *lawyer*
Bushari, Elad *real estate broker*
Busse, Paul Martin *oncologist, researcher*
Buxbaum, Robert C(ourtney) *internist*
Byer, David J. *lawyer*
Cabot, Louis Wellington *foundation trustee*
Cahill, Timothy P. *state treasurer*
Campion, Tracy *real estate broker*
Canavan, Christine Estelle *state legislator*
Canellos, George Peter *hematologist, oncologist, educator*
Capetillo-Ponce, Jorge Antonio *sociologist, educator*
Caplan, Louis Robert *neurologist, educator*
Caracoglia, Luca *civil engineer, educator*
Carey, John Andrew *investment company executive*
Carey, Martin Conrad *gastroenterologist, molecular biophysicist, educator, medical geneticist*
Carmany, George Walter III *finance company executive, consultant*
Carp, Jeffrey N. *lawyer, investment company executive*
Carroll, James Edward *lawyer*
Carter, Bob S. *neurosurgeon, educator*
Casadei, Gabriele *veterinarian, educator*
Castro Neto, Antonio Helio *physics professor*
Cavazos, Lauro Fred *medical educator, former United States Secretary of Education*
Celi, Leo Anthony G. *intensivist, infectious disease specialist, internist, informaticist, researcher*
Cellucci, Paul (Argeo Paul Cellucci) *lawyer, Former Governor of Massachusetts*
Chakrabarti, Supriya *space astrophysicist*
Chambers, Richard Wadsworth *theater educator*
Chandler, Harriette Levy *state legislator, management consultant, educator*
Chang, Shan Nan *education educator, academic administrator*
Chara, Zdeno *professional hockey player*
Chatzizisis, Yiannis S. *physician, researcher*
Chen, Ching-chih *information science educator, consultant*
Chen, Zheng-Yi *biologist*
Chiarelli, Peter *professional sports team executive*
Child, Christopher Challender *genealogist*
Cho, Sang Wan *physicist, researcher*
Chobanian, Aram *medical educator, cardiologist, former academic administrator*
Choo, Sin H. *neurosurgeon*
Christakis, Nicholas Alexander *internist, social scientist, educator*
Christen, William G. *epidemiologist, educator*
Christenson, Charles John *retired business educator*
Christopher, Irene *librarian, consultant*
Church, George McDonald *geneticist, educator, researcher*
Ciraulo, Domenic Anthony *psychiatrist, educator*
Cloonan, Michele V. *library director*
Coakley, Martha *state attorney general, former prosecutor*
Cobey, Frederick Carpinter *anesthesiologist*
Cody, Alan Morrow *financial consultant*
Coffin, John Miller *medical researcher, biology professor*
Cohen, Alan Barry *researcher, educator*
Cohen, Alan Seymour *internist*
Cohen, Lee Stuart *psychiatrist, educator*
Cohen, Rachelle Sharon *journalist*
Cohen, Robert Sonné *physicist, philosopher, educator*
Cohn, Andrew Howard *lawyer*
Cohn, Lawrence H. *cardiothoracic surgeon*
Collings, Robert Biddlecombe *judge*
Condrin, J. Paul III *insurance company executive*
Connolly, Thomas Edward *judge*
Connors, Jack, Jr., (John M. Connors, Jr.) *retired advertising executive*
Cordy, Robert J. *state supreme court justice*
Corless, Inge Baer *nursing educator and researcher*
Countryman, Gary Lee *retired insurance company executive*
Cowin, Judith Arnold *state supreme court judge*
Creedon, Geraldine *state legislator*
Creem, Cynthia Stone *state legislator, lawyer*
Crimlisk, Jane Therese *probation officer*
Cronin, Bonnie Kathryn Lamb *museum director*
Cronin, Philip Mark *lawyer*
Crosby, Steven Joseph *medical educator*
Curley, Robert Ambrose, Jr. *lawyer*
Curran, Michael J. *stock exchange executive*
Curtin, John Joseph, Jr. *lawyer*
Curtis, Marah A. *social worker, educator*
Cutrell, Charles C. III *lawyer*
Cypess, Aaron M. *endocrinologist*
Daffner, Kirk Reid *neurologist, researcher*
D'Agostino, Ralph Benedict *mathematician, statistician, educator, consultant*
Daley, George Quentin *hematologist, biomedical research scientist*
Daley, Paul Patrick *lawyer*
Daniels, Roanne Blythe *private equity firm executive*
Daniloff, Nicholas *journalist, educator*
Davidoff, Ravin *cardiologist*
Daynard, Richard Alan *law educator*
De Amicis, Don S. *lawyer*
DeBevoise, Charles Henry *lawyer*
de Burlo, Comegys Russell, Jr. *investment company executive, educator, retired treasurer*
DeCamp, Malcolm M., Jr. *thoracic surgeon*
Dedeoglu, Fatma *pediatrician, educator*
Delaney, John White *lawyer*
De Luca, Carlo John *biomedical engineer, educator*
Demidov, Vadim V. *biotechnologist, inventor, writer*
Demling, Robert Hugh *surgeon, researcher*
de Rham, Casimir, Jr. *lawyer*
DeSanctis, Roman William *cardiologist, educator*
Deshpandé, Rohit *business educator*
Diamandopoulos, Peter *philosophy professor*
DiCamillo, Curt Jonathan Gough *non-profit executive*
Dickie, Robert Benjamin *lawyer, educator*
Di Cola, Joan Barbara *lawyer*
Dienstag, Jules Leonard *dean, hepatologist, researcher*
Dillon, James Joseph *lawyer*
Dima, Ioana Maria *research scientist*
Dineen, John K. *lawyer*
Director, Stephen William *electrical and computer engineering educator, academic administrator*
Dluhy, Robert George *physician*
Dowd, Peter Jerome *public relations executive*
Drappatz, Jan *neuro-oncologist*
Drazen, Jeffrey Mark *medical educator*
Dreben, Raya Spiegel *judge*
Drew, J.D. (Jonathan David Drew) *professional baseball player*
Duda, Rosemary Bernadette *surgeon*
Dvorak, Harold Fisher *retired pathologist*
Dwyer, Johanna Todd *nutritionist, educator*
Ebb, Peter L. *lawyer*
Eckstein, Jens W. *venture capitalist, biotechnologist*
Eder, Esther Garcia *artist*
Eder, Joseph Paul, Jr. *physician*
Edmonds, Dean Stockett, Jr. *physicist, educator, director*
Edmondson, Amy Claire *management professor*
Egdahl, Richard Harrison *surgeon, educator, health science association administrator*
Egorina, Elena *medical researcher*
Eisenberg, Leon *psychiatrist, educator*
Eisenberg, Ronald Lee *radiologist*
Eisner, Sister Janet Margaret *college president*
El-Baz, Farouk *science administrator, educator*
Elfner, Albert Henry III *retired portfolio manager*
Eliopoulos, George Miltiades *epidemiologist*
Ellis, Franklin Henry, Jr. *surgeon, educator*
Engel, David Lewis *lawyer*
Engelman, Alan *medical educator*
Epler, Gary Robert *physician, author, educator*
Epstein, Arnold M. *medical educator*
Epstein, Theo N. *professional sports team executive*
Erban, John Kalil III *medicine educator, cancer specialist, researcher*
Essex, Myron Elmer *microbiologist and virology educator*
Estin, Hans Howard *retired investment company executive*
Estrada, Carlos R. *urologist*
Eurich, Richard Rex *lawyer*
Everett, Jonathan Jubal *lawyer*
Fallon, John A. *insurance company executive, physician*
Fan, Baojian *research scientist*
Fan, Xiaoduo *psychiatrist*
Farraye, Francis Anthony *gastroenterologist*
Fava, Maurizio *hospital administrator, researcher*
Faxon, David Parker *cardiologist*
Fazio, Sara *medical educator*
Federman, Daniel David *academic administrator, endocrinologist, educator*
Feeney, Mark *journalist*
Felson, David *epidemiologist, educator, rheumatologist*
Ferber, Richard Allen *neurologist, educator*
Fernandez, Manny (Emmanuel Fernandez-Lemaire) *professional hockey player*
Ferrer, Barbara *city health department executive director*
Field, Alison E. *medical educator*
Finegold, Barry R. *state legislator, lawyer*
Finegold, Maurice Nathan *architect*
Fink, Aaron *artist*
Finnegan, Neal Francis *retired banker*
Fiori, Dennis A. *museum director*
Firth, Everett Joseph *timpanist*
Fischer, Eric Robert *lawyer, educator*
Fischer, Mark Alan *lawyer*
Fishman, Robert A. *lawyer*
Fitzgerald, Warren Franklin *lawyer*
Flaherty, Alice Weaver *neurologist*
Fleisher, Gary Robert *pediatrician, educator*
Fletcher, Robert Hillman *medical educator*
Flier, Jeffrey S. *dean, endocrinologist*
Floor, Richard Earl *lawyer*
Fontanes, A. Alexander *insurance company executive*
Foote, Warren Edgar *neuroscientist, psychologist, educator*
Fortier, Albert Mark, Jr. *lawyer*
Foster, James J(ohn) *lawyer*
Fox, Donal *composer, jazz musician, pianist*
Fox, Francis Haney *lawyer*
Francis, Keith M. *graphics designer, artist*
Francona, Terry Jon *professional baseball manager, former professional baseball player*
Frank, Jason D. *lawyer*
Frank, Richard G. *healthcare educator*
Frank-Kamenetskii, Maxim D. *biomedical engineer*
Franko, Lawrence George *business educator/investment advisor*
Fraser, Donald C. *engineering executive, educator*
Fraser, Robert Burchmore *lawyer*
Freishtat, Harvey W. *lawyer*
Frigoletto, Fredric David, Jr. *physician*
Fuhlbrigge, Robert Conrad *pediatric rheumatologist, medical educator*
Gaff, Brian Michael *lawyer*
Galaburda, Albert Mark *neurologist, researcher, educator*
Galvin, William Francis *Secretary of the Commonwealth, Massachusetts*
Gants, Ralph D. *state supreme court justice*
Garber, Jeffrey Richard *endocrinologist*
Garnett, Kevin Maurice *professional basketball player*
Gary, Fireman D. *psychology professor*
Gates, Jonathan Dean *surgeon, educator*
Gaudreau, Russell A., Jr. *lawyer, educator*
Gault, Robert Mellor *lawyer*
Gawande, Atul A. *surgeon, writer*
Gay, Tyson *track and field athlete*
Gazelle, G. Scott *radiologist, researcher*
Gaziano, J. Michael *cardiovascular epidemiologist, geriatrician, educator*
Geha, Raif Salim *immunologist, allergist, pediatrician*
Gelb, Richard Mark *lawyer*
Gelman, Simon *anesthesiologist, educator*
Ghaemi, S. Nassir *psychiatrist, educator*
Gifford, Nelson Sage *finance company executive*
Gilbert McDonald, Patricia Kelly *director, educational publishing*
Gilchrist, Simon *economics professor*
Gill, Robert Tucker *lawyer*
Gilliland, Gary *oncologist, researcher*
Gilmartin, Raymond Vincent *management educator, former pharmaceutical company executive*
Gitlin, David *psychiatrist, director*
Giugliano, Robert Patrick *physician*
Glass, Milton Louis *retired manufacturing company executive*
Glass, Renée *educational health foundation executive*
Gleason, Daniel J. *lawyer*
Gleason, Jean Berko *psychology professor, researcher, author*
Glick, Thomas F. *history educator*
Glosband, Daniel Martin *lawyer*
Golby, Alexandra Jacqueline *neurosurgeon, educator*
Goldberg, Irving Hyman *molecular pharmacology and biochemistry educator*
Golden, Daniel *journalist*
Goldhaber, Samuel Zachary *cardiologist, educator*
Goldie, Sue J. *health service researcher*
Goldstein, Nathan *artist, writer*
Golub, Todd R. *research scientist*
Gonson, S. Donald *lawyer*
Goodman, Louis Allan *lawyer*
Goody, Joan Edelman *architect*
Goodyear, Laurie J. *physiologist, educator*
Gordon, Gregory Aaron *physician*
Gorton, Nathaniel M. *federal judge*
Gotham, Richard Ernest *professional sports team executive*
Gottfried, Michael R. *lawyer*
Gottlieb, Alice B. *dermatologist, rheumatologist*
Grant, Barbara Hurwitz *history educator*
Greco, Frank A. *physician, research scientist*
Green, Karen F. *lawyer*
Greenblatt, David J. *pharmacologist*
Gregory, Shawn Alen *cardiologist, physician, researcher*
Grenquist, Scott Anthony Francis *physicist, engineer*
Grillone, Gregory Angelo *otolaryngologist, educator*
Grinspoon, Steven Kyle *medical educator, director*
Groopman, Jerome *medical educator*
Grundfast, Kenneth Martin *otolaryngologist*
Guinan, Eva C. *hematologist, director*
Gura, Kathleen Marie *pediatric pharmacist, educator*
Halamka, John D. *emergency physician, information technology executive*
Hall, David *law educator, dean, department chairman*
Hall, Ferris M. *radiologist, educator*
Hall, Henry Lyon, Jr. *lawyer*
Halston, Daniel William *lawyer*
Halström, Frederic Norman *lawyer*
Hamersley, Gordon *food service executive*
Hamlin, Pam *marketing executive*
Hammond, Norman David Curle *archaeology educator, researcher*
Hamrah, Pedram *ophthalmologist, scientist*
Handly, Kevin J. *lawyer, educator*
Hanser, Suzanne Blottner *recreational therapist, department chairman*
Harrington, John Michael, Jr. *lawyer*
Harris, Mitchel Brion *orthopedist, surgeon*
Harris-Sharples, Susan Hoffman *education educator*
Hart, John William *religion and ecology educator*
Harvey, Christopher P. *lawyer*
Harvey, Mark Sumner *composer, educator, retired minister, musician*
Hasan, Masroor *transportation executive, consultant*
Haughton, Jonathan Haughton *economics professor, consultant*
Hayes, Andrew Wallace, II, *consumer products company executive*
Hayes, Robert Francis *lawyer*
Hayes, Robert Herrick *technology management educator*
Hayes, Samuel Linton III *business educator*
Hedley-Whyte, John *anesthesiologist, educator*
Hedlund, Ronald David *academic administrator, researcher, educator*
Heebner, Ken (George Kenneth Heebner) *portfolio manager*
Heier, Jeffrey S. *ophthalmologist, consultant*
Heigham, James Crichton *lawyer*
Heimann, David Isidore *computer engineer, educator*
Henderson, Rebecca Marta *economics professor*
Hendler, Gail Y. *medical librarian*
Hennessey, Robert Francis *bishop*
Henry, DeWitt Pawling, II, *literature educator, art association administrator, writer*
Henry, John William, II, *professional sports team executive*
Herndon, James Henry *orthopedic surgeon, educator*
Hershey, Nona *artist, printmaker, educator*
Herzlinger, Regina *economist, educator, writer*
Hettmer, Simone *hematologist, oncologist*
Hiatt, Howard H. *internist, educator*
Hickey, Paul Robert *anesthesiologist, educator*
Hieken, Charles *lawyer*
Hill, Richard Devereux *retired banker*
Hills, Patricia Gorton Schulze *curator, art historian*
Hintikka, Jaakko *philosopher, educator*
Hochberg, Fred *neurologist*
Hochedlinger, Konrad *biology professor, biomedical researcher*
Hoffman, Stanley Marc *composer, editor*
Hoffmann, Udo *radiologist, educator*
Holick, Michael Francis *nutritionist*
Hooley, Jay (Joseph L. Hooley) *investment company executive*
Hoort, Steven Thomas *lawyer*
Hopey, Christopher Edward *academic administrator*
Hoskins, William Keller *pharmaceutical executive, lawyer, mediator, arbitrator*
Hostetter, Amos Barr, Jr. *cable television executive*
Howe, Janice W. *lawyer*
Howley, Peter Maxwell *pathology educator*
Hoyt, Herbert Austin Aikins *television producer*
Hu, Chengcheng *biostatician, medical researcher*
Hubel, David Hunter *physiologist, science educator*
Huckaby, Sedrick Ervin *painter*
Hudson, Bradford Taylor *management educator*
Hudson, Dawn Emily *former food service company executive*
Hughson, Barry C. *performing arts association administrator*
Hunter, Durant Adams *executive search company executive*
Hutchinson, Bernard Thomas *ophthalmologist*
Iosifescu, Dan V. *psychiatrist*
Ireland, Roderick L. *state supreme court justice*
Ives, J. Atwood *financial executive*
Jacobs, Alice Kaufman *cardiologist, educator*
Jacobs, Charlie (Charles M. Jacobs) *professional sports team executive*
Jaeger, Gregg S. *physicist, engineer*
Jaff, Michael Ritt *osteopath, internist*
Jaguaribe, Maira Clodes *music educator*
Jain, Rakesh K. *chemical engineering and tumor biology educator*
James, Bill *baseball writer, statistician*
Jesse, Sandra L. *lawyer, insurance company executive*
Jeyapalan, Suriya *neurooncologist*
Jochum, Veronica *pianist*
Johnson, Abigail Pierrepont *investment company executive*
Johnson, Carol R. *school system administrator*
Johnson, Edward Crosby, III, (Ned Johnson) *investment company executive*
Johnston, Susan A. *lawyer*
Jones, Jeffrey Foster *lawyer*
Jordan, Alexander Joseph, Jr. *lawyer*
Julien, Claude *professional hockey coach*
Kaelin, William George, Jr. *oncologist*
Kafker, Frank A. *historian, educator*
Kahn, C. Ronald *research laboratory administrator*
Kahn, Shulamit *economics professor*
Kakkar, Rahul *cardiologist, researcher*
Kalkstein, Joshua Adam *lawyer*
Kang, Jing X. *medical researcher, educator*
Kanki, Phyllis Jean *pathobiology educator*
Kanter, Rosabeth Moss *management educator, consultant, writer*
Kaplan, Gary B. *psychiatrist, researcher*
Kaplan, Ilan Brett *brokerage house executive, researcher*
Kaplan, Karen *marketing and communications executive*
Kaplan, Robert Steven *management educator, investment banker*
Kaptchuk, Ted J. *writer, acupuncturist*
Karelitz, Robert N(elson) *lawyer*
Kariv, Ilona *molecular biologist, director*
Kassirer, Jerome Paul *medical educator*
Kaufmann, Patrick J. *business educator*
Kaye, Kenneth Marc *physician, educator, scientist*
Keating, Michael Burns *lawyer, educator*
Kehoe, William Francis *lawyer*
Keller, Stanley *lawyer*
Kelly, Edmund Francis *insurance company executive*
Kelly, Francis J. III *global marketing company executive*
Kelsey, Karl Timothy *medical educator*
Kennedy, Caroline Bouvier (Caroline Bouvier Kennedy Schlossberg) *foundation executive, writer, lawyer*
Kennedy, Joseph Patrick, II, *utilities executive, former United States Representative from Massachusetts*
Kenney, Raymond Joseph, Jr. *lawyer*
Kesari, Santosh *neurologist, oncologist, neuroscientist*
Kessel, Phil *professional hockey player*
Khan, Lurey *writer*
Khismatullin, Damir Borisovich *physicist, mathematician*
Kiang, Nelson Yuan-sheng *medical educator*
Kieran, Mark W. *pediatric oncologist*
Killingsworth, Cleve L., Jr. *insurance company executive*
Kim, Daniel *epidemiologist*
Kim, David Hanwuk *surgeon, orthopedist, researcher*
Kim, Ducksoo *radiologist, inventor, educator*
Kircher, Moritz Florian *radiologist, researcher*
Kirchick, William Dean *lawyer*
Kirsch, Robert L. *lawyer*
Kirschner, Marc Wallace *biochemist, cell biologist*
Kitz, Richard John *anesthesiologist, educator*
Klarman, Seth *hedge fund manager*
Kleiner, Fred Scott *art historian, archaeologist, educator, editor*
Kleinman, Ronald Ellis *pediatrician*
Klem, Christopher A. *lawyer*
Kline, Thomas Jefferson *foreign language educator*
Klotz, Charles Rodger *water transportation and investment company executive*
Knag, Paul Everett *lawyer*
Knepper, Ronald William *computer engineer, educator*
Kocher, Mininder Singh *pediatric orthopaedic surgeon, epidemiologist*
Kociubes, Joseph Leib *lawyer*
Koenen, Karestan *psychologist, educator*

Kolodny, Gerald M. *radiologist, director*
Komaroff, Anthony Leader *physician*
Kopelman, Leonard *lawyer*
Kornberg, Sir Hans Leo *biochemist, educator*
Kowalski, Gregory J. *engineering educator, researcher*
Kucherlapati, Raju *geneticist, educator*
Kukluk, Jacek *computer scientist*
Kumar, Vikram Sheel *information technology executive*
Kupper, Thomas S. *dermatologist, scientist, educator*
Kyriakos, Walid Elias *medical educator*
Lahiri, Jhumpa (Nilanjana Sudeshna) *writer*
Langer, Robert Martin *retired chemical engineering company executive, consultant*
Langwell, Dennis J. *insurance company executive*
Lapidus, Mariana *medical librarian*
Lasker, Morris E. *judge*
Last, Michael P. *lawyer*
Lataif, Louis Edward *dean*
Latif, Nasreen *finance educator*
Laufer, Marc R. *gynecologist*
Lawrence, Merloyd Ludington *editor*
Lawrence, Paul Roger *retired professor*
Lazar, Harold Lee *cardiothoracic surgeon*
Leaman, J. Richard, Jr. *paper company executive*
LeBoff, Meryl Susan *physician, medical educator*
Lee, Charles *cytologist*
Lee, David Stoddart *retired investment company executive*
Lee, I-Min *epidemiologist*
Lee, Jung Wan *Marketing Educator*
Lee, Thomas Henry *internist, cardiologist, healthcare executive*
Lee, William F. *lawyer*
Lehrer, Sherwin Sam *biochemist*
Leland, Timothy *retired newspaper executive*
Lemi, Adugna *economics professor*
Lepore, Ralph Thomas III *lawyer*
Le Quesne, Philip William *chemistry educator, researcher*
Lester, Jonathan Tyler *professional baseball player*
Levy, Stephen Raymond *venture capitalist*
Levy, Stuart B. *molecular biologist, educator, science administrator, researcher*
Liang, Marilyn G. *dermatologist*
Liao, James Kuang-Jan *cardiologist, educator*
Libby, Peter *cardiologist, medical researcher*
Licata, Arthur Frank *lawyer*
Lichtenstein, Alice Hinda *nutritional biochemist*
Light, Jay O. *dean*
Lin, Nancy U. *oncologist, educator*
Lindberg, Carter Harry *retired religious studies educator*
Little, John Bertram *radiologist, educator, researcher*
Litwin, Paul Jeffrey *lawyer*
Livingston, David Morse *internist, biomedical researcher*
Livingston, Frederic Holleyman *mechanical engineer*
Lockhart, Keith Alan *conductor, music director*
Loder, John Mark *lawyer*
Lodge, George C(abot) *business administration educator*
Loeffler, Jay Steven *physician, educator*
Logue, Ronald E. *investment company executive*
Loizou, Maria Jane *singer, librarian*
Looney, William Francis, Jr. *lawyer*
Loria, Martin A. *lawyer*
Loscalzo, Joseph *cardiologist, biochemist*
Loui, Psyche *medical educator*
Lowell, Mike (Michael Averett Lowell) *professional baseball player*
Lowenstein, Arlene Jane *nursing educator, health facility administrator*
Lowenstein, Nancy *occupational therapist, educator*
Lowry, Lois (Lois Hammersberg) *writer*
Lucchino, Lawrence *sports team executive, lawyer*
Ludwig, David S. *endocrinologist*
Luongo, C. Paul *public relations executive*
Lutchen, Kenneth R. *dean, biomedical engineer, educator*
Lynch, Barbara *chef, restaurant owner*
Lynch, Sandra Lea *federal judge*
Lyons, David Barry *philosophy and law educator*
Lyons, Paul Vincent *lawyer*
Macdonald, Peter J. *lawyer*
MacGillivray, Thomas E. *cardiothoracic surgeon*
MacLeish, Roderick, Jr. *lawyer*
Macomber, John D. *former construction executive*
Maffeo, Pino *chef*
Mahan, Susan Thayer *orthopedist*
Maisel, William Howard *cardiologist, internist*
Malchau, Henrik *orthopedist*
Malenka, Bertram Julian *physicist, researcher*
Malicki, Jarema *research scientist*
Malley-Morrison, Kathleen *psychology professor, researcher*
Malt, Ronald Bradford *lawyer*
Maltz, Allen P. *insurance company executive*
Mandelbrot, Didier A. *physician, internist, educator*
Mandell, James *health facility executive, urologist, educator*
Manekas, Jason Arthur *lawyer*
Manning, Peter Kirby *criminal justice educator*
Mansfield, Christopher Charles *lawyer*
Manson, JoAnn Elisabeth *endocrinologist*
Mantzoros, Christos Socrates *internist*
Marasco, Wayne A. *oncologist, educator*
Maratos-Flier, Eleftheria *physician, educator*
Marett, Louis J. *lawyer*
Markey, John K. *lawyer*
Marsh, Milton R.W. *composer*
Marshall, Margaret Hilary *state supreme court chief justice*
Martin, Gina Lynn *lawyer*
Martin, Joseph Boyd *neurologist, educator, retired dean*
Martin, Stanley Allen *lawyer*
Martinez, Victor Jesus *professional baseball player*
Maryniuk, Melinda Downie *medical educator, director*
Masi, Dale A. *social sciences educator, research and development company executive*
Mason, Charles Ellis III *magazine editor*
Mason, Herbert Warren, Jr. *religion and history educator, author*
Mason, Joel Bernard *internist, gastroenterologist*
Mason, Keira *anesthesiologist*
Matheson, Jean King *neurologist, educator*
Mathisen, Douglas J. *thoracic surgeon*
Matsuzaka, Daisuke *professional baseball player*
Matuschak, Mark G. *lawyer*
May, James Warren, Jr. *plastic surgeon*
May, Thomas J. *electric company executive*
Mayer, Robert J. *oncologist, gastroenterologist, educator*
Mayer, William P. *lawyer*
McArthur, John Hector *business educator*
McAuliffe, Rosemary *lawyer*
Mc Carthy, Joseph Michael *historian, educator*
McCormick, Marie Clare *pediatrician, educator*
McDougal, William Scott *urology educator*
McFarland Lord, Jenna *set designer, educator*
McGovern, Gail J. *international organization executive, former investment company executive*
McGovern, Patrick J. *communications executive*
McGowan, Francis X. *anesthesiologist, educator*
McLaughlin, Michael J. *lawyer*
McNeil, Barbara Joyce *radiologist, educator*
McNicol, Ewan *medical educator, director*
Meara, John Gerard *plastic surgeon*
Meehan, William Paul *pediatrician, educator*
Meisner, Mary Jo *foundation administrator, former newspaper editor*
Mela, Theofanie *physiologist*
Melnitchouk, Serguei *physician*
Mendillo, Jane Lisa *investment manager*
Menino, Thomas M. *Mayor, Boston*
Menna, Gilbert G. *lawyer*
Merk, Frederick Bannister *biomedical educator, researcher*
Merrill, Stephen *lawyer, consultant, Former Governor, New Hampshire*
Merton, Robert C. *economist, educator*
Meserve, William George *lawyer*
Meyerhardt, Jeffrey Abraham *internist, oncologist*
Miaoulis, Ioannis Nikolaos *museum director, mechanical engineer, educator*
Mihm, Martin Charles, Jr. *pathologist, educator*
Mikels, Richard Eliot *lawyer*
Milne, Christopher-Paul *medical association administrator*
Milstein, Richard Sherman *lawyer*
Milunsky, Aubrey *geneticist, pediatrician, educator*
Miner, Tracy A. *lawyer*
Minot, Winthrop Gardner *lawyer*
Mirabito, Anthony Jason *lawyer, educator*
Mitchell, Susan Lisa *geriatrician*
Mitchison, Timothy John *cell biologist, pharmacology educator*
Moellering, Robert Charles, Jr. *internist, educator*
Mongan, James John *healthcare system administrator*
Montgomery, John T. *lawyer*
Mooney, David Patrick *surgeon*
Mooney, Michael Edward *lawyer*
Moore, Paul D. *lawyer*
Moore, Richard Lawrence *structural engineer, consultant*
Moore, Richard Thomas *state legislator*
Morgan, James Philip *pharmacology and cardiology educator*
Moriarty, George Marshall *lawyer*
Moriarty, John *opera administrator, artistic director*
Morris, Gerald Douglas *newspaper editor*
Morton, Edward James *insurance company executive*
Moses, Marsha Anne *biochemist, researcher*
Mostafavi Abdolmaleky, Hamid *psychiatrist, researcher*
Motenko, Neil Philip *lawyer*
Moustakas, Theodore D. *engineering educator, researcher*
Mudge, Gilbert H., Jr. *cardiologist*
Mukamal, Kenneth J. *internist*
Muldoon, Robert Joseph, Jr. *lawyer*
Mundy, Patricia Wall *lawyer*
Murphy, George Francis *dermatopathologist, educator*
Murphy, Kathleen A. *diversified financial services company executive*
Musselman, Cecelia Anne *linguist, educator*
Myers, Jeff L. *surgeon*
Myers, Robert K. III *director, musician, composer*
Neely, Cam (Cameron Michael) *professional sports team executive, retired professional hockey player*
Nelson, Caleb P. *urologist, educator*
Newberg, Joseph H. *lawyer*
Newburger, Jane Wimpfheimer *pediatric cardiologist*
Nickole, Leonidas A. *performing arts educator, director*
Nissinen, Mikko Pekka *dancer, performing arts company executive, artistic director*
Nixon, Nicholas *photographer*
Nold, Carl Richard *museum administrator*
Noor, Jawwad *economics professor*
Norris, Lonnie Harold *dean*
Notopoulos, Alexander Anastasios, Jr. *lawyer*
Novack, Kenneth Joseph *lawyer*
Nunn, Martha Elizabeth *dental educator, director*
Nunnally, Allen C. *lawyer*
Nurko, Samuel *gastroenterologist, researcher*
Nuss, Roger Charles *otolaryngologist, director*
Oaklander, Anne Louise *medical educator*
Oates, William Armstrong, Jr. *investment company executive*
O'Brien, Thomas Francis *microbiologist, director*
O'Connell, Mary-Kathleen *lawyer*
O'Donnell, Thomas Lawrence Patrick *lawyer*
Odze, Robert D. *pathologist*
Oettgen, J. Peter *cardiologist, researcher*
O'Gara, Patrick Thomas *internist, cardiovascular physician*
Oh, William Kyu *oncologist*
O'Hern, Jane Susan *psychologist, educator*
Oken, Emily *physician, educator*
Olson, Cheryl Kay *public health consultant, educator*
Onderdonk, Andrew Bruce *microbiologist*
O'Neill, Philip Daniel, Jr. *lawyer, arbitrator, educator*
Onishi, Anna Tokiko *marketing professional*
Ono, Santa Jeremy *immunologist, educator, administrator*
Oringer, Kenneth M. *chef, restaurant owner*
O'Rourke, Maureen A. *dean, law educator*
Ortiz, David (David Americo Ortiz Arias) *professional baseball player*
Otu, Hasan Huseyin *medical researcher, educator*
Pallotta, Johanna Antonia (Johanna Stephen) *endocrinologist, educator*
Palmer, David Scott *political scientist, educator*
Papelbon, Jon(athan) (Robert) *professional baseball player*
Papisov, Mikhail I. *chemist*
Pappalardo, A. John *former prosecutor, lawyer*
Pardee, Arthur Beck *biochemist, educator*
Park, William H(erron) *financial services executive*
Park, William Wynnewood *law educator*
Parker, Jack *men's college hockey coach*
Parker, Olivia *photographer*
Partan, Daniel Gordon *lawyer, educator*
Patrick, Deval Laurdine *Governor of Massachusetts, lawyer*
Patterson, John de la Roche, Jr. *lawyer*
Pavlakis, Martha *medical association administrator, researcher*
Pearce, Elizabeth Niewoehner *endocrinologist, researcher*
Pearlman, Ronald Alan *lawyer, educator*
Peckham, John Munroe III *investment executive, author, lecturer*
Peckham, Thomas Elwood *lawyer*
Pedroia, Dustin Luis *professional baseball player*
Peirce, Georgia Wilson *public relations executive*
Pell, Anthony Douglas *financial management company executive*
Penney, Sherry Hood *academic administrator, consultant*
Perera, Lawrence Thacher *lawyer*
Perrault, Paul A. *bank executive*
Perrimon, Norbert Jean Paul *medical geneticist, educator*
Picker, Sebastián *artist*
Pienaar, Rudolph *biomedical researcher*
Pierce, Allan Dale *engineering educator, researcher, editor*
Pierce, Daniel Robert *lawyer*
Pierce, Paul Anthony *professional basketball player*
Pieretti, Rafael Vicente *urologist, pediatrician*
Pisani, Anthony Michael *architect*
Pitts, James Atwater *finance company executive*
Pline, Jennifer Alice *trust company executive*
Plotkin, Irving H. (Irving Herman Plotkin) *economist, consultant*
Plummer-D'Amato, Prudence *medical educator*
Pochi, Peter Ernest *physician*
Polito, Anthony Peter *law educator*
Polizzotti, Brian David *medical researcher*
Polyak, Kornelia *oncologist, researcher*
Pomahac, Bohdan *plastic surgeon, educator*
Pomeroy, Robert Corttis *lawyer*
Popeo, R. Robert *lawyer*
Porter, Jeffrey R. *lawyer*
Poussaint, Alvin Francis *psychiatrist, educator*
Powell, Benjamin *economics professor*
Preston, Jerome, Jr. *retired lawyer*
Prevost, Patrick M. *chemicals executive*
Pribaz, Julian Joseph *plastic surgeon, medical educator*
Price, Robert F. *lawyer*
Properzio, Paul J. *classicist, educator*
Psathas, George *sociologist, educator*
Purcell, Patrick Joseph *publishing executive*
Putnam, Thomas J. *library and museum director*
Quickel, Kenneth Elwood, Jr. *physician, medical center executive*
Rabkin, Mitchell Thornton *physician, educator, hospital administrator*
Radmanesh, Alireza *medical researcher*
Raish, David Langdon *lawyer*
Ramirez, Ramon Santo *professional baseball player*
Ramoni, Rachel Badovinac *medical educator*
Rao, Devulapalli Venkata *physics educator*
Rao, Sowmya R. *medical educator*
Rappaport, Carey Milford *electrical engineering educator*
Rathmell, James P. *anesthesiologist, educator*
Rauch, Paula *psychiatrist*
Reardon, Frank Emond *lawyer*
Recchi, Mark *professional hockey player*
Redo, Philip Lappano *broadcast executive*
Reese, C. Richard *data processing executive*
Reid-Cunningham, James *conservator*
Reinherz, Helen Zarsky *social worker, researcher*
Relman, Arnold Seymour *physician, editor, educator*
Remis, Robin E. *lawyer*
Remz, Sanford F. *lawyer*
Renehan, Richard William *lawyer*
Rennke, Helmut G. *pathologist, educator*
Resch, Edward J. *investment company executive*
Reynolds, Robert L. *investment company executive*
Rice, Jim (James Edward Rice) *sportscaster, professional baseball coach, retired professional baseball player*
Rich, Patricia R. *lawyer*
Richardson, Duncan W. *investment company executive*
Richardson, Martha (Marcie) Kirk *obstetrician, gynecologist*
Richmond, Alice Elenor *lawyer*
Ridker, Paul M. *cardiologist, medical educator*
Rigotti, Nancy *medical educator*
Riley, Laura E. *obstetrician, gynecologist*
Rivers, Doc (Glenn Anton Rivers) *professional basketball coach*
Robbins, David Lee *history professor, educator*
Roberts, Bronwyn L. *lawyer*
Robertson, Edwin Malcolm *psychology educator*
Robinson, Jeri *museum program director*
Rockoff, Mark Alan *pediatric anesthesiologist*
Rogers, Malcolm Austin *museum director, art historian*
Romney, Mitt (Willard Mitt Romney) *former Governor of Massachusetts*
Ronan, Laurence Joseph *internist, pediatrician*
Rondo, Rajon Pierre *professional basketball player*
Rosellini, Jay Julian *language educator*
Rosen, David Michael *public relations administrator, public affairs consultant*
Rosen, Harold *medical association administrator*
Rosen, Stanley Howard *humanities educator*
Rosenblatt, Michael *internist, dean, educator*
Rosengren, Eric S. *bank executive*
Rosman, Samantha L. *pediatrician, emergency physician*
Rosowsky, Andre *chemist, educator*
Ross, Elizabeth *advertising executive*
Rota, Marcello *medical educator*
Roth, Sanford Irwin *pathologist, educator*
Roubenoff, Ronenn *medical educator, researcher*
Rouzine, Igor M. *microbiologist, educator*
Royo, Sebastian *dean, finance educator*
Rudavsky, Dahlia C. *lawyer*
Rudman, Jeffrey B. *lawyer*
Russell, Paul Snowden *surgeon, educator*
Ruvkun, Gary B. *molecular geneticist*
Ryan, Allan Andrew, Jr. *lawyer, director, educator, writer*
Ryan, Amy E. *library director*
Ryan, Daniel Patrick *pediatrician*
Sachdeo, Amit *dentist, researcher*
Sachs, David Howard *surgeon, immunologist, educator*
Sadeghi-Nejad, Abdollah *pediatrician, educator*
Sahin, Mustafa *neurologist, educator*
Samet, Nachum *retired dental educator*
Samons, Loren J., II, *classicist*
Samuels, Martin Allen *neurologist*
Sanchez, Teresa *medical educator*
Santangelo, Susan L. *psychiatry professor*
Sargent, David Jasper *academic administrator*
Sargent, John *psychiatrist*
Sasani, Mehrdad *engineering educator*
Saunders, Donald Leslie *hotel executive, real estate developer*
Savard, Marc *professional hockey player*
Sawicki, Gregory *pulmonologist*
Sawyer, William C. *lawyer*
Scadden, David Thomas *hematologist, oncologist, research scientist*
Scanlon, Dorothy Therese *history professor*
Schlossman, Stuart Franklin *physician, educator, researcher*
Schlow, Michael *food service executive*
Schneeweiss, Sebastian *medical educator, pharmacoepidemiologist*
Schoenfeld, David Alan *statistician, educator*
Schouten, Ronald *psychiatrist, educator*
Schuppan, Detlef *medical educator, researcher*
Schutt, Russell K. *social studies educator, researcher*
Schwartz, Joel David *science educator*
Schwartz, John Henry *physician, educator*
Scollans, Carol G. J. *art educator*
Scott, Crouter *medical educator*
Scott, James Arthur *radiologist, educator*
Sears, John Winthrop *lawyer*
Seddon, Johanna Margaret *ophthalmologist, epidemiologist*
Seibel, Machelle Mayer *gynecologist, educator*
Seidman, Jonathan G. *geneticist, educator*
Seitter, Keith L. *professional society administrator, meteorologist*
Selkoe, Dennis Jesse *neurologist, researcher, educator*
Sellke, Frank William *cardiothoracic surgeon, researcher*
Shabestari, Khosrow Toutounchi (T. Shabestari) *research scientist*
Shackelford, George T. M. *curator*
Shaik, Shavali *medical researcher*
Shapiro, Eli *business consultant, educator, economist*
Shapiro, Sandra *lawyer*
Sharma, Prashant *physicist, educator*
Sharma, Ramaswamy *microbiologist, researcher*
Shay, Jonathan *psychiatrist, writer*
Sheehan, Gregory D. *lawyer*
Sheff, David *writer, editor*
Sheth, Kevin Navin *neurologist, researcher*
Shields, Lawrence Thornton *orthopaedic surgeon, educator*
Shilepsky, Nancy Sue *lawyer*
Shore, Miles Frederick *psychiatrist, educator*
Shulkin, Martin B. *lawyer*
Sigel, John D. *lawyer*
Silber, John Robert *retired academic administrator, law and philosophy educator*
Silbersweig, David Alan *physician*
Simmons, Sylvia Jeanne Quarles *academic administrator, educator*
Simons, D. Brenton *not-for-profit executive*
Singer, Steven D. *lawyer*
Singh, Ajay Kumar *nephrologist, educator*
Sinnott, William F. *lawyer*
Sirkin, Joel H. *lawyer*
Slack, Warner Vincent *medical educator, researcher*
Slavin, Peter L. *hospital administrator*
Sloan, Katherine (Kay Sloan) *college president*
Sloane, Carl Stuart *corporate executive, educator, management consultant*
Smith, Craig R. *lawyer*
Smith, Edwin Eric *lawyer*
Smith, Philip Jones *lawyer*
Smith-Doerr, Laurel A. *sociologist, educator*
Snyder, Richard Joseph *lawyer*
Soden, Richard Allan *lawyer*
Sodroski, Joseph G. *medical educator*
Solet, Maxwell David *lawyer*
Solomon, Caleb P. *editor*
Southard, William G. *lawyer*
Souza, Frederico Ferreira *radiologist*
Sparrow, Joshua D. *child psychiatrist*
Speer, Brownlow Main *lawyer*
Sperling, Reisa A. *neurologist, researcher*
Spiegel, Jeffrey H. *plastic surgeon*
Spieler, Emily A. *dean, law educator*
Spina, Francis X. *state supreme court justice*

Springer, Timothy Alan *health researcher, immunology educator*
Stachel, John Jay *physicist, researcher*
Stahl, Norman H. *federal judge*
Stair, Thomas Osborne *physician, educator*
Stallman, Richard Matthew *software developer*
Stanish, Heidi *science educator*
Stanley, Harriett Lari *state legislator*
Stanley, Harry Eugene *physicist, researcher*
Stecker, Michael S. *interventional radiologist*
Steere, Allen Caruthers, Jr. *physician, educator*
Steinberg, Laura *lawyer*
Stern, Donald Kenneth *lawyer*
Stevenson, Howard Higginbotham *business educator*
Stevenson, Lynne W. (Lynne Leslie Warner Stevenson) *cardiologist, educator*
Stewart, Elizabeth AnNella *gynecologist, researcher*
Stillwell, R. Newcomb *lawyer*
Stipho, Huda D. *dentist, educator*
Stobaugh, Robert Blair *professor emeritus*
Stone, Peter Howard *cardiologist, educator*
Storey, James Moorfield *lawyer*
Stossel, Thomas Peter *medical educator, researcher, director*
Streeter, Chris Conway *psychiatrist, educator*
Strominger, Jack Leonard *biochemist*
Strothman, Wendy Jo *literary agent*
Struhl, Kevin *molecular biologist, educator*
Stull, Donald LeRoy *architect*
Sugarman, Paul Ronald *lawyer, educator, academic administrator*
Sugumaran, Manickam *biology professor*
Sunstein, Bruce David *lawyer*
Surkin, Elliot Mark *lawyer*
Surman, Owen Stanley *psychiatrist*
Swartz, Katherine (B. Katherine Swartz) *economist, educator*
Swartz, Morton Norman *medical educator*
Swope, Jeffrey Peyton *lawyer*
Sykes, Megan *immunologist*
Szostak, Jack William *molecular biologist, educator*
Tabatabaei, Shahin *urologist, educator*
Tachado, Souvenir D. *medical educator*
Talarek, Nicolas *geneticist, researcher*
Tammaro, Kelly Ann *pharmacist, researcher*
Tang, Xiaolei *immunologist*
Tappé, Albert Anthony *architect*
Tarantino, Louis Gerald *lawyer, management consultant*
Tauro, Joseph Louis *federal judge*
Tavakkolizadeh, Ali *surgeon*
Taylor, Allen *nutritionist, educator*
Taylor, Thomas William *lawyer*
Teich, Malvin Carl *electrical engineering educator*
Teles, Flavia R.F. *clinical investigator, dental educator*
Tenner, Scott *physician, researcher*
Terrill, Ross Gladwin *writer, educator*
Theoharides, Theoharis Constantin *pharmacologist, physician, educator*
Thomas, Tim *professional hockey player*
Thompson, Christopher C. *gastroenterologist*
Thrall, James Hunter *radiologist, educator*
Thwin, Soe Se *medical researcher*
Tierney, Susan Fallows *consulting company executive, former federal agency administrator*
Tirella, Linda Grey *occupational therapist*
Tootell, Geoffrey Matthew Bemis *economist*
Torruella, Juan R. *federal judge*
Toth, Thomas Louis *medical educator, director*
Touster, Saul *law educator*
Trackman, Philip Charles *biochemist, researcher*
Tracy, Erin Elizabeth *obstetrician, gynecologist*
Trichopoulos, Dimitrios Vassilios *epidemiologist, educator*
Trier, Jerry Steven *gastroenterologist, educator*
Trimmier, Roscoe, Jr. *lawyer*
Tritos, Nicholas Angelos *internist*
Troupe, William Harold *lawyer*
Truta, Ioan *protective services official*
Tse, Marian A. *lawyer*
Tuchmann, Robert *lawyer*
Tuerck, David George *economist, educator*
Tullis, Gregory Earl *research scientist*
Turner, Christopher D. *pediatrician, director*
Twombly, Stephen Doane *magazine publisher*
Tworetzky, Wayne *cardiologist*
Tyson, Peter *editor-in-chief*
Udelson, James Eric *cardiologist, educator*
Vacanti, Joseph Philip *pediatric and transplant surgeon*
Vadivel, Nidyanandh *nephrologist*
Vaidya, Vishal S. *biologist, educator*
Vallet, Sonia *hematologist, researcher*
van Dam, Robert M. *epidemiologist, educator*
Van Etten, Richard A. *hematologist, researcher*
Varitek, Jason *professional baseball player*
Vassilev, Peter Mihailov *biomedical researcher*
Vaughan, Herbert Wiley *retired lawyer*
Vermilye, Peter Hoagland *banker*
Viguera, Adele Casals *psychiatrist, researcher*
Villalonga, Belen *finance educator, director*
Viswanathan, Akila *oncologist*
Volpe, Joseph John *pediatrician, neurologist, educator*
Volpe, MaryAnn Vitoria *pediatrician*
von Stackelberg, Katherine Ellen *environmental scientist, consultant*
Wagner, Billy (William Edward Wagner) *professional baseball player*
Wakefield, Timothy Stephen (Tim Wakefield) *professional baseball player*
Wakeling, William Michael *librarian, director*
Walek, David B. *lawyer*
Wall, Conrad III *lab administrator, researcher*
Wallace, Rasheed *professional basketball player*
Walrath, Patricia A. *state legislator*
Walsh, John Edward *political organization administrator, insurance company owner*
Walsh, Joseph Hayes *lawyer*
Walters, Kirk W. *bank executive*
Wang, Zhi *biomedical researcher*
Warab, Kristi *librarian*
Warth, James Arthur *physician, researcher*
Weiner, Stephen Mark *lawyer*
Weiss, Earle Burton *physician*
Weitzel, John Patterson *lawyer*
Werchniak, Andrew Eugene *dermatologist, educator*
Wermuth, Paul Charles *retired language educator*
Westling, Jon *university administrator*
Wheeler, W(illiam) Scott *composer, conductor, music educator*
White, Augustus Aaron III *orthopaedic surgeon*
White, Barry Bennett *lawyer*
White, Dennis J. *lawyer*
Whittemore, Anthony Dunster *vascular surgeon, chief medical officer*
Whitters, James Payton III *lawyer, educator*
Whouley, Michael J. *communications specialist, political strategist*
Wiesel, Elie *writer, educator*
Wiesner, David *illustrator, children's writer*
Wigglesworth, Margaret *real estate company executive*
Wilcox, Steven Alan *lawyer*
Willett, Walter Churchill *epidemiologist, educator*
Williams, Brown F *media specialist*
Williams, John Towner *composer, conductor*
Williams, Winfred W. *molecular biologist*
Wilson, Jack Martin *academic administrator, science educator*
Wilson, Rachel I. *neurobiologist, educator*
Winer, Eric P. *hematologist, oncologist, educator*
Winslow, Daniel B. *lawyer*
Wolf, Alice Koerner *state legislator, former mayor*
Wong, Richard Chi Kit *gastroenterology*
Wood, Malissa J. *cardiologist, educator*
Woodburn, Ralph Robert, Jr. *lawyer*
Woodlock, Douglas Preston *judge*
Woods, Ryan John *education director*
Woolf, Alan *pediatrician*
Wozniak, Janet *psychiatrist*
Wu, Fa Yueh *retired physics professor*
Wu, Jim S. *radiologist*
Wu, Julian K. *neurosurgeon*
Wu, Tung *curator, artist, art historian, educator*
Xie, Zhongcong *anesthesiologist, educator*
Xue, Yong *columnist, educator*
Yang, Youxin *research scientist*
Yaroslavsky, Anna *biophysicist, educator*
Youkilis, Kevin *professional baseball player*
Young, Laura *choreographer, educator*
Yuan, Junying *medical educator, researcher*
Yurko, Richard John *lawyer*
Zack, Arnold Marshall *lawyer, mediator, arbitrator, judge*
Zai, Adrian *medical researcher, director*
Zaleznik, Abraham *psychoanalyst, management specialist, educator*
Zannieri, Nina *museum director*
Zarutskie, Jennifer Anne *lawyer*
Zeitels, Steven Marc *surgeon, educator*
Zelen, Marvin *statistics educator*
Zobel, Rya Weickert *federal judge*
Zon, Leonard Ira *pediatrics educator, researcher*
Zusman, Randall Mark *physician*

Boxboro
Parmese, Gabriel J. *corporate financial executive*

Boxborough
Devor, Jonathan *application developer*

Boylston
Dixon, Anthony George *science educator*
Hanshaw, James Barry *pediatrician, educator*
Larson, Roland Elmer *health facility administrator*

Braintree
Driscoll, Megan *executive recruiter*
Hallenbeck, Rachel Kirsten *music educator, director*
Malloy, Ellen Ann *athletic trainer*
O'Malley, Sean Patrick Cardinal *cardinal, archbishop*
Sherman, Barnet *financial services executive*
Smyth, Peter Hayes *radio executive*
Watts, Kisha Mann *school system administrator, secondary school educator*

Bridgewater
Cochran, Michael G. *artist, educator*
Crowe, Margaret Isabella Roxburgh *history professor*
Dondero, Mary E. *artist, educator*
Heffernan, Peter John *state official*
Reynolds, Ronald Foster *science educator*
St. Aubin, Kendra Jane *Librarian*

Brighton
Dooher, John Anthony *bishop*
Lathi, Ellen S. *neurologist*
Valianti, Deborah L. *playwright*

Brockton
Carlson, Desiree Anice *pathologist*
Choquette, Keith Alan *psychologist*
Fennel, John Andrew *state attorney general*
Lyons, Paul Christopher *government geologist, educator*
Moore, Mary Johnson *retired community health nurse*
Sullivan, Brendan Paul *state official, consultant, communications educator*

Brookfield
Anderson, Theodore Robert *physicist, small business owner*
Couture, Ronald David *art association administrator, web site designer, consultant*

Brookline
Bander, Edward Julius *lawyer, librarian emeritus*
Barron, Ros *artist*
Binion, Rudolph *history professor*
Bourne, Katherine Day *journalist, educator*
Brenner, Robin E. *librarian*
Buchin, Jacqueline Chase *psychologist*
Bustros, Cyril Salim *archbishop*
Connolly, Thomas Francis *English language educator, theatre scholar*
Cromwell, Adelaide M. *sociology educator retired*
Epstein, Leslie *literature educator, writer*
Frankel, Ernst Gabriel *shipping and aviation business executive, educator*
Golan, Yoav *physician*
Goldsmith, Gary Norman *psychiatrist, psychoanalyst*
Jakab, Irene *psychiatrist*
Kliman, Sylvia Stern *communications executive*
Lipsitt, Don Richard *psychiatrist, educator*
Michopoulos, Aristotle V. *humanities educator, researcher*
Moon, John Ellis van Courtland *retired historian*
Nash, Leonard Kollender *retired chemistry professor*
Pal, Uday B. *engineering educator, consultant*
Pearlman, Justin D. *medical educator*
Ruthchild, Rochelle Goldberg *education educator*
Seltzer, Benjamin *neurologist, educator*
Slavin, Sumner Andrew *plastic surgeon*
Swirnoff, Lois *artist, educator*
Tyler, H. Richard *physician*

Burlington
Abkowitz, Stanley *research scientist*
Beamis, John Francis *pulmonologist*
Chen, Chau-Chyun *chemical engineer*
Cline, Jason Alexander *computer scientist*
Cosgrove, Garth Rees *neurosurgeon*
Hughes, Kevin Steven *surgeon*
Hurd, Joseph Kindall, Jr. *obstetrician, gynecologist*
McQuillen, Daniel Paul *infectious diseases physician, medical educator*
Mourtzinos, Arthur *urologist*
Nicholas, Lynn B. *medical association administrator*
Schoetz, David John, Jr. *colon and rectal surgeon, educator*
Shils, Jay Lawrence *neurologist, researcher*
Soto-Wright, Valena *gynecologist, director*
Sproull, Robert Fletcher *research and development company executive*
Wysopal, Chris *software company executive*
Yang, Ming *engineering company executive, researcher*

Buzzards Bay
Cirillo, Jeannine L. *pharmacist*
DiMassa, Diane D. *engineering educator*

Byfield
Baker, Charles Duane *business administration educator*
Kozol, Jonathan *writer*

Cambridge
Abadi, Abraham Albert *education educator*
Abelmann, Walter H. *internist, educator*
Afsaruddin, Asma *Arabic language educator*
Alberty, Robert Arnold *chemistry professor*
Alexander, Susan H. *lawyer, pharmaceutical executive*
Allen, Thomas John *business educator*
Allison, Graham Tillett, Jr. *political science professor, former federal agency administrator*
Alt, James Edward *political science professor*
Anderson, Stanford Owen *architect, architectural historian, educator*
Anderson, William Henry *psychobiology educator*
Angert, Esther Rita *biologist, researcher*
Ansolabehere, Stephen Daniel *political science professor*
Apostolakis, George E. *engineering educator, researcher*
Argon, Ali Suphi *mechanical engineering educator*
Armstrong, Robert C. *chemical engineer, educator*
Aronson, Michael Andrew *editor*
Arteta, Jorge *foreign language educator, consultant*
Arvind, *computer scientist, electrical engineer, educator, researcher*
Asani, Ali S. *foreign language and religious studies educator*
Athey, Susan Carleton *economics professor*
Bailyn, Bernard *historian, educator*
Bailyn, Lotte *psychologist, educator*
Bakanowsky, Louis Joseph *artist, architect, educator*
Banaji, Mahzarin Rustum *psychology educator*
Barger, James Edwin *physicist*
Barnet, Sylvan *English literature educator*
Barnhart, Cynthia *engineering educator, researcher*
Barro, Robert Joseph *economics professor*
Bartee, Thomas Creson *computer scientist, educator*
Bator, Francis Michel *economist, educator*
Battin, Richard Horace *aeronautical engineer*
Bebchuk, Lucian Arye *law and finance educator*
Beér, János Miklós *engineering educator*
Belcher, Angela *engineering educator*
Bell, Stephen P. *biology professor, researcher*
Berg, Howard C. *biology professor*
Berke, Neal S. *research and development company executive*
Berlowitz, Leslie *cultural organization administrator*
Berners-Lee, Sir Timothy John *inventor of world wide web, research scientist, writer*
Berzin, Isaac *chemical engineer*
Bilmes, Linda Jan *finance educator*
Bishop, Robert Lyle *retired economist, educator*
Bisognano, Maureen A. *medical association administrator*
Bizzi, Emilio *neurophysiologist, educator*
Blanchet-Fincher, Graciela Beatriz *physicist*
Bleichmar, Daniela *history professor*
Bleris, Leonidas *electrical engineer, researcher*
Bloom, Kathryn Ruth *public relations executive*
Blumberg, Paul N. *mechanical engineer, consultant*
Bobo, Lawrence D. *sociologist, educator*
Bochicchio, James *project coordinator*
Bolster, Arthur Stanley, Jr. *history professor*
Bomblies, Kirsten *molecular biologist, educator*
Bortnick, Rachel Anne *medical researcher*
Boyan, Justin Andrew *computer scientist*
Bradt, Hale Van Dorn *physicist, educator*
Brecher, Aviva *physicist, researcher*
Brooks, Rodney Allen *information technology executive, educator*
Browne, Janet *historian, educator*
Brusch, John Lynch *physician, educator, hospital administrator*
Brustein, Robert Sanford *literature and language professor, theater director, writer*
Bulovic, Vladimir *engineering educator*
Burke, Bernard Flood *physicist, researcher*
Burkle, Frederick Martin, Jr. *physician, educator*
Burns, R. Nicholas (Robert Nicholas Burns, Nick Burns) *international politics professor, former ambassador*
Burns, Virginia *social worker*
Cady, Blake *surgical oncologist*
Campbell, John Young *economics professor*
Campbell, Robert *architect, writer*
Canizares, Claude Roger *astrophysicist, educator*
Caplice, Christopher *engineering educator*
Carpenter, Daniel *political science professor*
Cassino, Peter Frank *music educator, musician*
Caves, Richard Earl *economist, educator*
Cestnick, Laurie L. *neuropsychologist, educator, scientist*
Chance, Kelly *geophysicist, educator*
Chandler, Fay Martin *artist*
Chatterjee, Sharmila *marketing educator*
Chen, Lincoln Chin-ho *medical educator*
Chernoff, Herman *statistics educator*
Chisholm, Sallie Watson *biological oceanography educator, researcher*
Chomsky, Noam (Avram Noam Choamsky) *linguistics and philosophy educator*
Ciarlo, David Michael *history professor*
Clark, George Whipple *physics professor*
Clarke, David R. *materials engineer*
Clay, Phillip L. *academic administrator*
Cogan, John Francis, Jr. *lawyer*
Colding, Tobias H. *mathematics professor*
Collier, Earl Miller, Jr. *biotechnology company executive*
Colton, Clark Kenneth *chemical engineering professor*
Connick, Harry, Jr. *musician, actor, vocalist, composer, lyricist*
Cooper, Richard Newell *economist, educator*
Corey, Elias James *chemistry professor*
Cott, Nancy F. *history professor, writer*
Covert, Eugene Edzards *aerospace engineer, aeronautics professor*
Cox, John Carrington *finance educator*
Craig, Albert M. *history professor, researcher*
Crandall, Stephen Harry *engineering educator*
Cummins, Christopher C. *chemistry professor*
Cutler, David M. *economics professor*
Dalgarno, Alexander *astronomy educator*
Damrosch, Leopold, Jr., (Leo Damrosch Jr.) *English educator*
Darnton, Robert Choate *library director, historian, educator*
Dawson, Steven Lee *radiologist, researcher*
de Fougerolles, Antonin Robert *research scientist*
Demirci, Utkan *medical educator*
de Neufville, Richard Lawrence *engineering educator*
Dennis, Jack Bonnell *computer scientist, educator*
Dershowitz, Alan Morton *law educator*
Deutch, John Mark *chemistry professor, former CIA director*
de Varon, Lorna Cooke *choral conductor*
de Weck, Oliver *engineering educator, researcher*
Dewey, Clarence Forbes, Jr. *engineering educator*
Díaz, Junot *writer, educator*
DiCamillo, Kate *writer*
DiStefano, Peter S. *pharmaceutical executive*
Djousse, Luc *epidemiologist, educator, medical researcher*
Dobriansky, Paula Jon *former federal agency administrator*
Dominguez, Jorge Ignacio *political scientist, educator*
Donahue, John David *federal agency administrator, educator*
Dowling, Timothy Edward *planetary science educator*
Drela, Mark *aeronautical engineer, educator*
Dresselhaus, Mildred Spiewak *physics and engineering professor*
Dudley, Richard Mansfield *mathematician, educator*
Dugundji, John *aeronautical engineer*
Dulac, Catherine *biology professor, researcher*
Dunsire, Deborah *pharmaceutical executive*
Dupree, Anderson Hunter *historian, educator*
Durant, John R. *museum director, educator*
Dussan V, Elizabeth B. *scientific advisor*
Dye, Nancy Schrom *academic administrator, historian, educator*
Dziewonski, Adam Marian *geologist, educator, science administrator, academic administrator*
Eagar, Thomas Waddy *metallurgist, educator*
Eagleson, Peter Sturges *civil and environmental engineer, educator*
Eckaus, Richard Samuel *economist, educator*
Edgerly, William Skelton *banker*
Edley, Christopher Fairchild, Jr. *dean, law educator*
Eggan, Kevin C. *molecular and cellular biology professor, researcher*
Egozy, Eran *video game development company executive*
Eisen, Herman Nathaniel *immunology researcher, medical educator*
Elkins, Caroline M. *history professor, writer*
Ellerman, Alfred Denny *economics professor*
Ellis, David Wertz *retired museum director, academic administrator, consultant, arbitrator*
Ellison, Glenn *finance educator*
Ellison, Peter Thorpe *anthropology professor*
Ellwood, David Tabor *dean, public policy educator*
Eltahir, Elfatih A.B. *engineering educator*
Emmens, Matthew W. *pharmaceutical executive*
Engell, James Theodore *language educator, department chairman*
Erikson, Raymond Leo *biology professor*
Fanger, Donald Lee *Slavic language and literature educator*
Fash, William Leonard, Jr. *anthropologist, educator, museum director*

Faust, Drew Gilpin (Catharine) *academic administrator, historian*
Fay, James Alan *mechanical engineering educator*
Fee, Michale Sean *science educator*
Feininger, Theodore Lux *artist*
Feldman, Joel J. *plastic surgeon*
Feldstein, Martin Stuart *economics professor*
Ferguson, Niall Campbell Douglas *history professor, writer*
Fink, Yoel *science educator, researcher*
Fischer, Kurt Walter *education educator*
Fischl, Bruce *neuroscientist, educator*
Fisher, Philip J. *English language and literature educator*
Fisher, Roger Dummer *negotiation expert, law educator*
Fleming, Ronald Lee *urban planner, consultant*
Flemings, Merton Corson *engineering educator, materials scientist*
Flier, Michael Stephen *Slavic languages educator*
Forbes, Kristin J. *economics professor, former federal official*
Forney, G(eorge) David, Jr. *retired electronics executive*
Forst, Edward C. *academic administrator, former diversified financial services company executive*
Foster, Charles Stephen *surgeon*
Fox, Maurice Sanford *retired molecular biologist, educator*
Francis, Carl A. *museum director, educator*
Frankel, Jeffrey Alexander *economist, educator*
Freitas, Mark R. *lawyer*
French, Anthony Philip *physicist, educator*
Freund, Robert *finance educator, consultant*
Frey, Daniel D. *engineering educator, researcher*
Frey, Frederick August *geochemist, researcher, educator*
Friedman, Benjamin Morton *economics professor*
Friedman, Jeffrey Robert *psychiatrist, educator*
Friedman, Jerome Isaac *physics professor, researcher*
Frisch, Rose Epstein *population sciences researcher*
Frosch, Robert Alan *retired automobile manufacturing executive, physicist*
Fryer, Roland Gerhard *economics professor*
Fu, Gregory Chung-Wei *chemistry educator*
Fudenberg, Drew *economics professor*
Fujimoto, James G. *electrical engineering educator*
Gagliardi, Ugo Oscar *systems software architect, educator*
Galakatos, Nick *pharmaceutical executive*
Gardner, Howard Earl *psychologist, educator, writer*
Garland, Carl Wesley *chemist, educator*
Gaskell, Ivan George Alexander De Wend *art museum curator, educator*
Gates, Henry Louis, Jr. *literature and language professor, historian*
Geller, Margaret Joan *astrophysicist, educator*
George, William Wallace (Bill George) *finance educator, former manufacturing executive*
Gergen, David Richmond *political science professor*
Gilbert, Daniel Todd *psychology professor*
Gilbert, Walter *molecular biologist, educator*
Giles, Robert Hartmann *journalist, educator*
Gingerich, Owen Jay *astronomer, educator*
Glauber, Roy Jay *physics professor*
Godfrey, Victoria *rental company executive, marketing professional*
Goentzel, Jarrod *information technology executive, director*
Goldberg, Marc Evan *healthcare venture capitalist*
Goldberg, Ray Allan *agriculturist, educator*
Goldman, Marshall Irwin *economist, educator*
Goldsmith, Jack Landman III *law educator, former federal agency administrator*
Goldstone, Jeffrey *physicist, educator*
Goodman, Alyssa Ann *astronomer, educator*
Goodman, Ellen Holtz *journalist*
Gordon, Roy Gerald *chemistry professor*
Goudey, Clifford A. *marine engineer, director*
Graessle, Dale Edward *astrophysicist*
Graham, Loren Raymond *historian, educator*
Graham, Patricia Albjerg *education educator*
Graham, William Albert *religious studies and history educator*
Gray, Paul Edward *academic administrator*
Greenblatt, Stephen Jay *literature and language professor, writer*
Greene, Frederick Davis, II, *chemistry professor*
Greenspan, Harvey Philip *applied mathematician, educator*
Griffith(-Cima), Linda G. *biomedical and chemical engineer*
Gross, Benedict H. *mathematician, educator, former dean*
Grossman, Alan D. *biology educator*
Grosz, Barbara Jean *dean, computer scientist, educator*
Grove, Timothy Lynn *geology educator*
Gruber, Jonathan H. *economist*
Gruen, Daniel M. *research scientist*
Guarente, Leonard P. *medical geneticist, educator*
Gusterson, Hugh P. *anthropology educator, writer*
Guthke, Karl Siegfried *language educator*
Hale, Patrick C. *engineering educator, director*
Halperin, Bertrand Israel *physics professor*
Hammonds, Evelynn Maxine *dean, history professor*
Han, Xinxin *chemist, researcher*
Hanan, Patrick Dewes *foreign language professional, educator*
Handlin, Oscar *historian, educator*
Hanken, James *biologist, educator, museum director*
Hansen, Kent Forrest *nuclear engineering educator*
Hart, Oliver D'Arcy *economics professor*
Harvey, Charles Franklin *hydrologist, educator*
Hastings, Daniel E. *aeronautical engineer, educator*
Hastings, John Woodland *biologist, educator*
Hatfield, Juliana *vocalist*
Hauser, John Richard *marketing and management science educator*
Hausmann, Ricardo *economics professor, director*
Havens, Leston Laycock *retired psychiatrist, educator*
Hax, Arnoldo Cubillos *management educator, industrial engineer*
Heaney, Seamus Justin *poet, educator*
Heimbach, Patrick *oceanographer*
Heineman, Benjamin Walter, Jr. *lawyer*
Helgason, Sigurdur *mathematician, educator*
Hernquist, Lars Eric *astronomer, educator*
Herr, Hugh Miller *biomechatronics researcher, educator*
Herschbach, Dudley Robert *chemistry professor*
Hewitt, Jacqueline N. *astronomy educator*
Hiaasen, Carl *writer, reporter*
Hirsch, Martin Stanley *internist, epidemiologist, researcher*
Hockfield, Susan *academic administrator, medical educator*
Holmstrom, Bengt R. *economics professor*
Holton, Gerald *physicist, educator, science historian*
Holtzman, Steven H. *pharmaceutical executive*
Horvitz, Howard Robert *biology professor, researcher*
Hostage, John Brayne Arthur *law librarian*
Howitt, Arnold Martin *academic administrator, educator*
Hubbard, Ruth *retired biology professor*
Huchra, John Peter *astronomer, educator*
Hughes, Libby *writer*
Hunt, Swanee Grace *public policy educator, former ambassador*
Hunter, Ian W. *engineering educator, researcher*
Hynes, Richard Olding *biology researcher, educator*
Iriye, Akira *historian, educator*
Ivanov, Yuri Anatoly *research scientist*
Izard, Véronique *psychologist, researcher*
Jackiw, Roman *physicist, researcher*
Jackson, Howell Edmunds *law educator, dean*
Jacoby, Henry Donnan *economist, educator*
Jaenisch, Rudolf *biologist, educator*
Jaffe, Arthur Michael *mathematician, physicist, educator*
Janes, Daniel E. *research scientist*
Jarosiewicz, Beata *neuroscientist*
Jencks, Christopher Sandys *sociologist, educator*
Jensen, Klavs Flemming *chemical engineering educator*
Johnson, Howard Wesley *retired academic administrator, finance company executive*
Jonas, Joan (Joan Amerman Edwards) *artist*
Joss, Paul Christopher *astrophysicist, atmospheric physicist, educator*
Kac, Victor G. *mathematician, educator*
Kagan, Jerome *psychologist, educator*
Kanwisher, Nancy G. *neuroscientist*
Kaplan, Benjamin *judge*
Kaplan, Justin *author*
Kaplow, Louis *law educator*
Kastner, Marc Aaron *physics professor, dean*
Kaufman, Andrew Lee *law educator*
Kaufman, Gordon Dester *theology studies educator*
Kaysen, Carl *economics professor*
Kazhdan, David *mathematician, educator*
Kazimi, Mujid Suliman *nuclear engineer, educator*
Keller, Evelyn Fox *philosophy of science professor*
Kelman, Herbert Chanoch *retired psychology professor*
Kelman, Steven Jay *education educator*
Keniston, Kenneth *psychologist, educator*
Kennedy, Duncan McLean *law educator*
Kennedy, Stephen Dandridge *economist, researcher*
Kerman, Arthur Kent *physicist, researcher*
Ketterle, Wolfgang *physics professor*
Keyfitz, Nathan *sociologist, demographer, educator*
Keyser, Samuel Jay *linguist, educator*
Khorana, Har Gobind *chemist, educator*
Khoury, Philip S. *academic administrator*
King, Gary *government studies educator*
King, William Bruce *retired lawyer*
Kirby, William C. *historian, former dean*
Kirchner, Leon *composer, pianist, conductor*
Klemperer, Willian *chemistry professor*
Knoll, Andrew Herbert *biology professor*
Kober, Jane *lawyer*
Koester, Helmut Heinrich *history professor*
Koh, Adrian Soo Jin *research scientist*
Kolachalama, Vijaya B. *mechanical engineer*
Koolhaas, Remment *architect, educator*
Kossak, Mitchell Scott *educator, director*
Kostant, Bertram *mathematician, educator*
Kraus, Rozann B. *performing company executive*
Kremer, Michael *economist, educator*
Kruger, Kenneth *architect*
Kugler, Maurice *economics professor*
Ladd, Charles Cushing III *civil engineer, educator*
LaGuardia, Cheryl M. *school librarian, writer*
Laiou, Angeliki Evangelos *history professor*
Lamberg-Karlovsky, Clifford Charles *anthropologist, archaeologist*
Lan, Fei *biologist, researcher*
Lander, Eric Steven *geneticist, molecular biologist, mathematician*
Langer, Robert Samuel, Jr. *chemical and biomedical engineering educator*
Langmuir, Charles Herbert *geology educator*
Lauder, George V. *marine biologist*
Lee, Barbara *political activist, foundation administrator*
Leiden, Jeffrey Marc *venture capitalist, molecular biologist, cardiologist*
Lenert, Andrej *research scientist*
Lenger, John Richard *journalism educator*
Lentz, Thomas W. *museum director, curator*
Levi, Herbert Walter *biologist, educator*
Lewin, Walter H.G. *physics professor*
Lewis, Henry Rafalsky *manufacturing executive*
Li, Yuexian *Research And Development Company Scientist*
Liberman, M. Charles *otolaryngologist, educator*
Lieber, Charles *chemistry professor, researcher, materials scientist*
Lieberman, Henry A. *research scientist*
Lieberson, Stanley *sociologist, educator*
Liebmann, Matthew Joseph *history professor*
Lim, Kok-Seong *medical researcher*
Lin, Lih-Ling *biologist, researcher*
Lindquist, Susan Lee *biology and microbiology professor*
Lipscomb, William Nunn, Jr. *retired chemistry professor*
Liskov, Barbara Huberman *software engineering educator*
Little, John Dutton Conant *management scientist, educator*
Liu, Xiong *atmospheric physicist*
Livingston, James Duane *physicist, researcher*
Lomon, Earle Leonard *physicist, educator, consultant*
London, Irving Myer *physician, educator*
Looker, Adam *chemist*
Losick, Richard M. *biology professor*
MacGillivray, Catherine Mary *histologist*
Magnanti, Thomas L. *management and engineering educator*
Mahoney, Kevin J. *lawyer*
Maiden, Barry *chef*
Maier, Charles Steven *history professor*
Malmstad, John Earl *literature and language professor*
Malone, Thomas W. *business educator, researcher*
Mandl, Robert *application developer*
Mankiw, Nicholas Gregory (Gregory Mankiw) *economics professor, former federal official*
Mansbridge, Jane Jebb *political scientist, educator*
Mansfield, Harvey C., Jr. *political science professor*
Marcus, Richard Sargon *research scientist*
Markey, Winston Roscoe *aeronautical engineering educator*
Marsden, Brian Geoffrey *astronomer*
Mathews, Joan Helene *pediatrician*
Matsui, Connie L. *pharmaceutical executive*
Mazlish, Bruce *historian, educator*
McCunney, Robert Joseph *physician*
McDonald, Christie Anne *literature and language professor, writer*
McElroy, Michael *physicist, researcher, educator*
McGarry, Frederick Jerome *civil engineering educator*
McMullen, Curtis T. *mathematics professor*
McNally, Richard James *clinical psychologist, educator*
Melcher, Jennifer *otolaryngologist, educator*
Melton, Douglas A. *molecular and cell biology educator*
Merrill, David *entrepreneur, researcher*
Meselson, Matthew Stanley *biochemist, educator*
Meyer, Dorothy Virginia *retired education educator*
Meyer, John Robert *economist, educator*
Milgram, Jerome H. *retired marine and ocean engineer, educator*
Milner, Richard Gerard *physicist*
Minow, Martha Louise *dean, law educator*
Minsky, Marvin Lee *mathematician, educator*
Moavenzadeh, Fred *engineering educator*
Monson, Ingrid *musicologist*
Mootha, Vamsi Krishna *biomedical researcher, educator*
Mora, Elizabeth *comptroller, academic administrator*
Moran, James Michael, Jr. *astronomer, educator*
Morgan, Marcyliena *sociologist, educator*
Morris, Robert Tappan *computer science educator, Internet company executive*
Moses, Joel *computer scientist, educator*
Mowatt-Larssen, Rolf *former federal agency administrator*
Mrowka, Tomasz *mathematics professor*
Mugane, John Muratha *literature and language professor*
Mullen, James C. *biotechnology company executive*
Murray, Cherry Ann *physicist, researcher, dean*
Myers, John *research scientist, consultant*
Narayan, Ramesh *astronomy educator*
Narayanamurti, Venkatesh *engineering educator, physics professor*
Narayanamurti, Venkatesh *engineering professor, former dean*
Nathanson, Larry *medical educator*
Necipoglu, Gülru *art history and architecture professor*
Negele, John William *physics professor, consultant*
Newey, Whitney K. *economist, educator*
Newman, Dava Jean *aerospace engineering educator, director*
Nocera, Daniel G. *chemistry professor*
Nordell, Hans Roderick *journalist, retired editor*
Nye, Joseph Samuel, Jr. *political science professor*
Ochsendorf, John *structural engineer, educator*
O'Connell, Richard John *geophysicist, educator*
Oettinger, Anthony Gervin *mathematician, educator*
Ogletree, Charles J., Jr. *law educator*
Olbert, Stanislaw *physicist*
O'Neil, Wayne *linguist, educator*
Oppenheim, Irwin *chemical physicist, educator*
Orchard, Robert John *theater producer, educator*
Orfield, Antonia Marie *optometrist, researcher*
Ortiz, Christine *engineering educator*
Owen, Edward Roger John (E. Roger Owen) *Middle Eastern studies professor, writer*
Padmanabhan, Bharani *neurologist, educator*
Page, David C. *biologist, educator*
Palestrant, Daniel *Internet company executive*
Pardue, Mary-Lou *biology professor*
Parker, Lisa Frederick *music educator, Dalcroze specialist*
Parker, Richard Davies *law educator*
Parlee, Mary Brown *psychology educator*
Patton, Bruce M. *law educator, management consultant*
Paul, William *physicist, researcher*
Penfield, Paul Livingstone, Jr. *electrical engineering educator*
Perdue, Peter C. *history professor*
Perelman, Leslie C. *academic administrator*
Perkins, Dwight Heald *economics professor*
Pesetsky, David Michael *linguist*
Petaev, Mikhail Ivanovich *senior geologist, researcher*
Petersen, Ulrich *geology educator*
Pilbeam, David Roger *paleoanthropology educator, curator*
Pillay, Srinivasan *psychology professor, consultant*
Pinker, Steven Arthur *psychology professor*
Pipes, Richard Edgar *historian, educator*
Plesch, Andreas *geologist, consultant*
Polenske, Karen Rosel *economics educator*
Porter, Roger Blaine *federal official, educator*
Porter, William Lyman *architect, educator*
Poterba, James Michael *economist, educator*
Pounds, William Frank *management educator*
Power, Samantha J. *public policy educator, writer*
Prinn, Ronald G. *atmospheric science educator*
Probstein, Ronald Filmore *mechanical engineering educator*
Purcell, Bill *academic administrator, former mayor*
Putnam, Robert D. *public policy professor*
Pytka, Stephen Milton *office equipment executive*
Ramme, Tina M. *biology professor, director*
Ramsey, Norman F. *physicist, researcher*
Randall, Lisa *physics professor*
Read, Russell *investment company executive*
Rehding, Alexander *musicologist*
Reif, L. Rafael *academic administrator, engineering educator*
Reimer, Bryan *research scientist*
Retsinas, Nicolas Paul *public policy educator, former federal official*
Rightmire, George Philip *anthropology educator*
Rigopulos, Alexander Peter *video game development company executive*
Ritvo, Harriet *historian*
Riva, Carlos *pharmaceutical executive*
Robinson, Allan Richard *oceanography educator*
Rogers, Peter Phillips *environmental engineer, educator, urban planner*
Rogoff, Kenneth Saul *economics professor*
Roos, Daniel *engineering educator*
Roozbehani, Mardavij *research scientist*
Rose, Robert Michael *materials engineering educator*
Rosenberg, Charles Ernest *historian, educator*
Rosovsky, Henry *economist, educator*
Rotberg, Robert Irwin *historian, political scientist, educator, academic administrator*
Rubin, Donald Bruce *statistician, educator, research and development company executive*
Rudolph, Larry *computer science educator, researcher*
Ruina, Jack Philip *electrical engineer, educator*
Russell, Kenneth Calvin *metallurgical engineering educator*
Sagan, Paul *information technology executive*
Samson, Leona D. *biological engineering educator, research center director*
Samuelson, Paul Anthony *economist, educator*
Sander, Frank Ernest Arnold *law educator*
Sanes, Joshua Richard *neurobiologist, researcher, educator*
Sankaranarayananan, Subramanian Krs *chemical engineer, researcher*
Sapers, Carl Martin *lawyer, educator*
Sapirie, Stephen Alan *international public health consultant*
Sapolsky, Harvey Morton *political scientist, educator*
Sauzier, Maria Consuela *psychiatrist, educator*
Schaub, Robert George *pharmaceutical executive*
Scherer, Frederic Michael *economics professor*
Schiller, Peter Harkai *biomedical engineering and physics educator*
Schlosser, C. Adam *hydrologist*
Schmalensee, Richard Lee *economics and management professor, former dean*
Schmittlein, David C. *dean, marketing professor*
Schrock, Richard Royce *chemistry professor*
Schuessler Fiorenza, Elisabeth *theology studies educator*
Scott, Hal S. *law educator*
Sen, Amartya Kumar *economist, educator*
Sevcenko, Ihor *history and literature professor*
Seyferth, Dietmar *chemist, educator*
Shapiro, David Louis *law educator*
Shapiro, Irwin Ira *physicist, researcher*
Shapiro, Jeffrey Howard *electrical engineering professor, consultant*
Sharp, Phillip Allen *biologist, educator*
Shavell, Steven M. *law educator*
Shinagel, Michael *dean, English literature educator*
Sidanius, James H. *psychology professor*
Silbey, Robert James *chemistry professor, researcher, consultant*
Simpson, W. James *literature and language professor*
Sims, Ezra *composer*
Sinha, Pawan *research scientist, educator, entrepreneur*
Skolnikoff, Eugene B. *political science professor*
Slive, Seymour *museum director, art educator*
Slosburg-Ackerman, Jill Rose *artist, educator*
Smida, Besma *engineering educator, researcher*
Smith, Amy B. *mechanical engineer, educator*
Smith, Henry Ignatius *engineering educator*
Smith, Kenneth Alan *chemical engineer, educator*
Smith, Merritt Roe *history professor*
Smith, Michael D. *dean, electrical engineering and computer science professor*
Snyder, James M., Jr. *political science professor, economics professor*
Soljacic, Marin *physicist, educator*
Sollors, Werner *literature and language educator*
Solow, Robert Merton *economist, educator*
Song, Xiangzhi *research scientist*
Spaepen, Frans August *physicist, educator*
Spelke, Elizabeth Shilin *psychology professor*
Staelin, David Hudson *electrical engineering educator, consultant*
Stauffer, John William *cultural historian*
Steadman, Stephen Geoffrey *physicist*
Stein, Jeremy Chaim *economics professor*
Steiner, Henry Jacob *law and human rights educator*
Steinfeld, Jeffrey Irwin *chemistry professor emeritus, writer*
Steins, Janet L. *librarian, consultant*
Stern, Joel N.H. *biochemist, researcher*
Stevens, Kenneth Noble *electrical engineer, educator*
Stewart, Charles Haines *political science educator*
Stiehl, Walter Dan *research scientist*
Stoddard, Roger Eliot *scholar*
Strandberg, Malcom Woodrow Pershing *physicist*
Stroock, Daniel Wyler *mathematician, educator*

Stuntz, William John *law educator*
Suh, Nam Pyo *mechanical engineering educator*
Sunstein, Cass Robert *law educator*
Suresh, Subra *materials engineer, educator*
Susskind, Lawrence Elliott *urban planner, mediator, educator*
Sussman, Joseph *engineering educator, researcher*
Tapscott, Stephen *literature educator*
Tarrant, Richard J(ohn) *classicist, educator*
Taubes, Clifford Henry *mathematician, educator*
Teevan, Jaime *application developer, researcher*
Telingator, Cynthia J. *psychiatrist, director*
Termeer, Henricus Adrianus *pharmaceutical executive*
Terry, James Layton, II, *research scientist*
Thaddeus, Patrick *physicist, researcher*
Thiemann, Ronald Frank *dean, religious studies educator*
Thompson, Dennis Frank *political science professor, consultant*
Ting, Samuel Chao Chung *physicist, researcher*
Tinkham, Michael *physicist, researcher*
Tobey, William Hayward *former federal agency administrator*
Todreas, Neil Emmanuel *nuclear engineering educator*
Tofighi Niaki, Aliassghar *research scientist*
Tomasiello, Alessandro *physicist*
Tomita, Masaru *engineering educator, researcher*
Tonegawa, Susumu *biology professor*
Toomre, Alar *applied mathematician, theoretical astronomer*
Triantafyllou, Michael Stefanos *engineering educator*
Tribe, Laurence Henry *law educator*
Trilling, Leon *aeronautical engineering educator*
Trumpbour, John *historian, researcher, director*
Tsai, Li-Huei *pathologist, researcher*
Tsitsiklis, John N. *electrical engineering and computer science educator*
Tucker, Louis Leonard *retired historical society administrator*
Ungar, Eric Edward *mechanical engineer*
Urban, Glen L. *management educator*
Urbanowski, Frank *publishing company executive*
Vagts, Detlev Frederick *law educator*
Valero, Henri-Pierre *research scientist*
Vander Velde, Wallace Earl *aeronautical and astronautical engineering educator*
Vanger, Milton Isadore *historian, educator*
Vargas, Julie S. *behaviorologist, educator*
Vendler, Helen Hennessy *literature educator, poetry critic*
Verba, Sidney *political science professor, retired library director*
Vernillet, Laurent *pharmacologist, researcher*
Vessot, Robert Frederick Charles *physicist, researcher*
Vogel, Ezra F. *sociology educator*
von Hippel, Eric Arthur *innovation educator*
Wacker, Warren Ernest Clyde *internist, educator*
Walker, Graham Charles *biology professor*
Walther, Philip *physicist, researcher*
Ward, John Milton *music educator*
Ware, Susan W. *historian*
Warren, Alvin Clifford, Jr. *law educator*
Warren, Elizabeth Ann *law educator*
Waters, Mary Catherine *sociology educator*
Watson, Nicholas James *literature and language professor*
Watts, Ross Leslie *finance educator*
Waugh, John Stewart *chemist, educator*
Weinberg, Robert Allan *biochemist, educator*
Weitzman, Arthur Joshua *language educator*
Weitzman, Martin L. *economics educator*
Welsch, Roy Elmer *statistician, educator*
Westervelt, Robert Moore *physics educator*
White, David Calvin *electrical engineer, educator, energy executive, consultant*
White, Shelby *art association administrator*
Whitesides, George McClelland *chemistry professor*
Whitlock, Charles Preston *former university dean*
Whitman, Robert Van Duyne *civil engineer, educator*
Widnall, Sheila Evans *aeronautical educator, former secretary of air force, university official*
Wiederschain, Dmitri *research scientist*
Wilcox, Maud *editor*
Wilczek, Frank Anthony *physics professor*
Williams, James Henry, Jr. *mechanical engineer, educator, consultant*
Willie, Charles Vert *social sciences educator*
Wilson, David Gordon *mechanical engineering educator*
Wilson, Edward Osborne *biologist, educator, writer*
Wilson, Robert Woodrow *radio astronomer*
Wirth, Peter *lawyer*
Wisse, Ruth R. *religious educator*
Wolfman, Bernard *lawyer, educator*
Wolk, Scott Joseph *astrophysicist*
Wolpert, Ann J. *library director*
Wones, Suzanne L. *academic librarian*
Woo, Kyu Sung *architect*
Wood, John Armstead *planetary scientist, geological sciences educator, artist*
Wood, Pamela Sharon *music educator, soprano*
Wozney, John M. *research scientist*
Wuensch, Bernhardt John *ceramic engineering educator*
Wurtman, Richard Jay *neuroscientist, educator, inventor*
Yannas, Ioannis Vassilios *polymer science educator*
Yau, Shing-Tung *mathematics professor*
Yea, Sehoon *consumer electronics industry executive, researcher*
Yergin, Daniel Howard *writer, consultant*
Yi, Wei *physicist*
Young, Laurence Retman *biomedical engineer, educator*
Zaldarriaga, Matias *cosmologist, physics professor*
Zeckhauser, Richard Jay *economist, educator*
Zinberg, Dorothy Shore *sociologist, educator*
Ziolkowski, Jan Michael *medievalist educator, library director*
Zittrain, Jonathan L. *law educator*
Zue, Victor W. *engineering educator*
Zwierlein, Martin Wolfram *physics professor*

Canton
Allen, Frances L. *marketing executive*
Bihldorff, John Pearson *hospital director*
Fuchs, Lawrence Howard *federal official, educator*
Judson, Arnold Sidney *management consultant*
Kelley, Irene W. *retired librarian, musician, artist*
Luther, Jon L. *food service executive*
Sawtelle, Carl S. *psychiatric social worker*
Travis, Nigel *food service executive*
Trupe, Mary-Ann *secondary school educator*

Carlisle
Drew, Philip Garfield *retired engineering company executive, consultant*

Carver
Baldo, Robert Voisine *elementary educator*
Neubauer, Richard A. *library science educator, consultant*

Centerville
Anderson, Gerald Edwin *retired utilities executive*
Condon, Ann Blunt *staff training and development*
Scherer, Harold Nicholas, Jr. *electric power industry executive*
Williams, Ann Meagher *retired hospital administrator*

Charlestown
Buckner, Randy L. *psychology professor, neuroscientist*
English, Todd *food company executive, chef*
Isselbacher, Kurt Julius *internist, educator*
Kegel, Kimberly B. *neurologist, educator*
Leaf, Alexander *preventive medicine physician, epidemiologist*
Nahmias, Yaakov *biomedical engineer*
Ntziachristos, Vasilis *radiology, bioengineering educator*
Orr, Bobby (Robert Gordon Orr) *retired professional hockey player, sports agent*
Potts, John Thomas, Jr. *physician, educator*
Raftery, Laurel A. *research biologist, educator*
Schneeberger, Eveline Elsa *pathologist, cell biologist, educator*
Sharma, Nutan *neurologist, educator*
Tanzi, Rudolph Emile (Rudy Tanzi) *neuroscientist, researcher, educator*
White, John P. *consulting firm executive, public policy educator*
Zamecnik, Paul Charles *oncologist, medical researcher*

Chatham
Cogan, Mary Hart *community activist, philanthropist*
Daly, Charles Ulick *foundation executive*
Gillies, Irene B. *library director*
O'Connell, Brian *community organizer, educator, writer*
Popkin, Alice Brandeis *lawyer*
Rhinesmith, Stephen Headley *leadership consultant*
Stout, Sharon Sparkes *elementary school educator, counselor*

Chelmsford
Ain, Aron J. *information technology executive*
Ain, Mark Stuart *information technology executive*
Bayat, Oguz *electrical engineer, educator*
Cleven, Carol Chapman *state legislator*
DiPillo, Patricia Anne *language educator, researcher*
Fulks, Robert Grady *computer company executive*
George, Peter *information technology executive*
Krishnan, Venkatarama *retired engineering professor*
Lacy, Paul *information technology executive*
Menitoff, Paul Alan *psychiatrist*

Chelsea
Burds, Jeffrey *history professor*
Gaetani, Kristina L. *art educator*
Jenkins, Alexander III *consumer products company executive, consultant*
Sutter, Diane *television executive*

Chestnut Hill
Altbach, Philip *director, educator*
Arndt, Kenneth Alfred *dermatologist, educator*
Batchelder, Samuel Lawrence, Jr. *retired corporate lawyer*
Beaton, Albert Eugene *education educator*
Bicks, Caroline *language educator*
Blanchette, Oliva *philosophy educator*
Boynton, Andrew C. *dean*
Cardona, Rodolfo *Spanish language and literature educator*
Dahlben, Salin Abraham *neuropsychiatrist*
Davarian, Baldwin L. *history professor*
Flax, Martin Howard *pathologist, retired educator*
Gaiser, Ted Joseph *academic administrator, minister*
Gottlieb, Marise Suss *epidemiologist*
Hachey, Thomas Eugene *British and Irish history educator*
Hebard, Barbara Adams *conservator*
Helmick, Raymond Glen *priest, educator*
Hyman, Albert Lewis *cardiologist, educator*
Kearney, Richard Marius *philosopher, educator, writer, poet*
Keenan, James F. *priest*
Kraus, Frederick Thier *pathologist*
Leahy, William Patrick *academic administrator, historian, educator*
Leone, Stephanie C. *history professor*
Mahoney, Kevin J. *social worker, educator*
Melnick, Rowell Shep *political scientist, educator*
Monan, James Donald *university chancellor*
Munnell, Alicia Haydock *economist*
O'Block, Robert Paul *management consultant*
Olufowote, James *communications educator*
Reed, James Eldin *historian, consultant, educator*
Resler, Michael *literature and language professor*
Spaziani, Frank *college football coach*
Sykiotis, Gerasimos *biomedical researcher, geneticist*
Taylor, E. Dennis *English language educator, editor*
Thier, Samuel Osiah *physician, educator*
Unver, M. Utku *economics professor*
Valette, Jean Paul *writer*
Valette, Rebecca Marianne *Romance languages educator*
Vance, Verne Widney, Jr. *retired lawyer*
York, Jerry *men's college hockey coach*

Clinton
Lanza, Robert Paul *medical scientist*
Russell, Kent dur *museum administrator*

Cohasset
Rabstejnek, George John *healthcare executive*
Wendorf, Richard Harold *library director, scholar*
Whipple, Jacqueline Conant *writer, media specialist*

Concord
Andrews, Joseph Lyon, Jr. *internist, pulmonologist, medical educator, writer*
Barney, Beverly Garrett *social worker, consultant*
Blackmer, Donald Laurence Morton *political scientist*
Boger, William Pierce III *ophthalmologist*
Caldwell, Desiree *museum director*
Coles, Robert *child psychiatrist, educator, writer*
Davidson, Frank Paul *retired macroengineer, retired lawyer*
Fowler, Charles Albert *electronics engineer*
Heinle, Beverly Diane *publishing executive*
Horwitz, Paul *physicist*
Ihara, Michio *sculptor*
MacNeill, Frederick Douglas *artist*
Parrish, Thomas Kirkpatrick III *marketing consultant*
Perkins, John Allen *lawyer*
Plummer, William Torsch *optical physicist*
Schiller, Pieter Jon *retired venture capital executive*
Villers, Philippe *mechanical engineer*
Weiss, James Michael *financial analyst, portfolio manager*

Cotuit
Ballou, Kenneth Walter *retired business executive, university dean*
Miller, Robert Charles *retired physicist*

Cummington
Wilbur, Richard Purdy *writer, educator*

Danvers
Dolan, John Ralph *retired electronics executive*
Haber, Frederic *lawyer*
Waite, Charles Morrison *food products executive*

Dartmouth
Connors, Robert Leo *city official*
de Sá, Maria Gloria *social sciences educator*
Larkosh, Christopher *language educator*
Souza, Kathleen Anne *middle school educator*
Sweeney, Shawna Elizabeth *political science professor, researcher*

Dedham
Fabiano, Mark G. *lawyer*
Ghosh, Asish *control engineer*
Lichtin, Norman Nahum *chemistry professor*
Magner, Jerome Allen *performing company executive*
Miner, Robert Matthew *orthodontist, educator*
Redstone, Shari Ellin *amusement company executive*

Dennis
Hunter, Elizabeth Ives-Valsam *museum director*

Dennis Port
Singer, Myer R(ichard) *lawyer*

Dorchester
Allen, Desser Lewis *retired elementary school educator*
Smith, Survilla Marie *social services administrator, artist, poet*

Douglas
Bachelder, Beverly Brandt *secondary school educator, assistant principal, director*

Dover
Aldrich, Frank Nathan *banker*
Bonis, Laszlo Joseph *consultant, executive, chemist*
Buyse, Marylou *pediatrician, geneticist, medical administrator*
Craver, James Bernard *lawyer*
Edwards, Carl Norman *lawyer*
Peirce, Bonnie *librarian*

Dudley
Downs, Lawrence Douglas *marketing educator, consultant*
Lambert, Paul Edward *history educator*

Duxbury
Schwartz, Edward Arthur *lawyer*
Wangler, William Clarence *retired insurance company executive*
Woods, Reginald Foster *management consulting executive*
Zachmann, William Francis *computer and communications industry market research company executive*

East Boston
Patinkin, Terry Allan *physician*

East Falmouth
Forte, Wesley Elbert *former insurance company executive, lawyer*

East Longmeadow
Skutnik, Bolesh J. *optics scientist, lay worker, lawyer*

East Orleans
Burkert, Robert Randall *artist*
Romey, William Dowden *geologist, educator*

Eastham
Birch, Eleanor Mansfield *management educator*
Tipton, Noel Martin, Jr. *musician, writer, composer*

Easthampton
Davis-Harris, Jeannette Gardrine *educator, historian*
Perkins, Homer Guy *manufacturing executive*

Edgartown
Rosenfeld, Walter David, Jr. *architect, writer*

Everett
Blake, Margaret Mary *director*

Fairhaven
Hotchkiss, Henry Washington *real estate broker, financial consultant*
Merolla, Michele Edward *chiropractor, broadcaster*

Fall River
Coleman, George William *bishop*
Corven, James M. *biology professor*
Medeiros, Antone Arruda *retired medical educator*
Wilner, Marion Leonard *art educator*

Falmouth
Brock, Nancy Jeanne *music educator, writer*
Litschgi, Richard John *computer manufacturing company executive*
McInnes, Donald Gordon *rail transportation executive*
Pedlosky, Joseph *geophysicist, educator*
Saunders, John Warren, Jr. *biology professor, consultant*

Fiskdale
Costello, Christine Ann *fine arts director, church organist*

Fitchburg
Ciottone, Judith Marino *chemistry professor*
Gim, Lisa *English professor*
Ifrim, Costin *electrical engineer, director*
Jareckie, Stephen Barlow *museum curator*
McKeon, John Joseph *economics professor*
Shemmeri, Thafur *pediatric dentist*
Williams, Ian *English literature professor*

Foxboro
Belichick, Bill (William Stephen Belichick) *professional football coach*
Brady, Tom (Thomas Edward Patrick Brady Jr.) *professional football player*
Caserio, Nick *professional sports team executive*
Dillon, Corey *professional football player*
Gostkowski, Stephen Carroll *professional football player*
Johnson, Thomas (Pepper Johnson) *professional football coach, retired professional football player*
Karelitz, Richard Alan *treasurer, lawyer*
Kraft, Robert K. *professional sports team executive*
Martin, Peter Gerard *computer technician, consultant, secondary school educator*
Mayo, Jerod *professional football player*
Moss, Randy Gene *professional football player*
Reese, Floyd *professional sports team executive*
Taylor, Fred *professional football player*

Framingham
Barron, Arnold S. *retail executive*
Bern, Murray Morris *hematologist, oncologist*
Butka, Paul C. *retail executive*
Cammarata, Bernard *retail executive*
Campbell, Donald G. *retail executive*
Campbell, Kristin A. *lawyer, retail executive*
Capobianco, Anthony G. *physician*
Castelli, William Peter *cardiovascular epidemiologist, educator*
Chande, Amee *retail executive*
Coiner, Maryrose C. *psychologist*
Crossley, Frank Alphonso *retired metallurgical engineer*
Dawicki, Doloretta Diane *analytical chemist, research biochemist, educator*
DeWerth, Gordon Henry *management consultant*
Doody, Joseph G. *retail executive*
Feldberg, Sumner Lee *retired retail executive*
Flanagan, Timothy James *academic administrator, criminal justice educator*
Flores, Greg *retail executive*
Gilbert, John F. *retail executive*
Goodman, Shira D. *retail office and business products executive*
Harrington, Joseph Francis *educational company executive, history educator*
Herrman, Ernie *retail executive*
Kannel, William Bernard *cardiovascular epidemiologist*
Klapholz, Henry *obstetrician, gynecologist, educator*
Komola, Christine T. *corporate financial executive*
Lesser, Richard G. *retired apparel executive*
Levy, Joseph Louis *publishing company executive*
Lindenmeyer, Peter W. *retail executive*
Lucci, Dorothy Ann *educational consultant, psychologist*
Mahoney, John J. *office supply company executive*
Matheus, Christopher John *computer scientist, researcher*
McCauley, Ann *lawyer, retail executive*
Meador, Charles Lawrence *management and systems consultant, educator*
Meyrowitz, Carol M. *retail executive*
Miles, Michael A., Jr. *retail executive*
Naylor, Jeffrey Gordon *retail executive*
Nivarthi, Raju Naga *anesthesiology educator*
Parneros, Demos *retail executive*
Rikleen, Lauren Stiller *lawyer*
Rossi, Jerome R. *retail executive*

Sargent, Ronald L. *retail office and business products executive*
Scaria, Abraham *molecular biologist, director*
Sherr, Richard *retail executive*
Starobin, Leslie Ann *art educator*
Sweetenham, Paul *retail executive*
Torres, Maryellen *marketing executive*
Tripathy, Nirmal K. *retail executive*
Vrabel, Joseph P. *lawyer*

Franklin
Benjamin, Bernard Edward *school system administrator, director*
Ferguson, Dennis Edward *musician, educator*

Gardner
Du Buske, Lawrence Michael *immunologist, rheumatologist*

Gloucester
Basile, Celestino *language educator*
Birchfield, John Kermit, Jr. *lawyer*
Fioravanti, Nancy Eleanor *retired banker*
Littlefield, Paul Damon *retired management consultant*
Sallah, Majeed (Jim) *retired real estate developer*
Socolow, Arthur Abraham *geologist*
Steele-Goetemann, Judith Ann *artist, gallery owner, educator*
White, Harold Jack *pathologist*

Grafton
Marino, Michelle S. *psychologist*

Granby
Ingham, Norman William *literature educator, genealogist*

Great Barrington
Curtin, Phyllis *music educator, dean, vocalist*

Greenfield
Young, Elizabeth V. *social worker*

Hanscom AFB
Crabtree, Peter *physicist, researcher*
Johnson, Charles L., II, *military officer*
Mailloux, Robert Joseph *physicist*
Rothman, Laurence Sidney *physicist*

Harvard
Barrie, Joseph Rollin *retired surgeon*

Harwich
Barton, Alice *physician, educator*
Caretti, Ann M. *school system administrator*
Diggs, Walter Whitley *health science facility administrator*

Harwich Port
Smith, Ralph Wesley, Jr. *retired federal judge*

Hatfield
Yolen, Jane *writer*

Haverhill
Bigelow, Peter *electronics executive*
DeSchuytner, Edward Alphonse *biochemist, educator*

Haydenville
Rupp, Sheron Adeline *photographer, educator*
Shallcross, Doris Jane *education educator*

Heath
Howland, Margaret E.C. *retired librarian*

Hingham
Allinson, Deborah Louise *economist*
Menzies, Ian Stuart *newspaper editor*
Riley, Robert Edward *financial services company executive*
Scarpa, Michael *former apparel executive*
Sullivan, Trudy (Gertrude Fulham Sullivan) *apparel company executive*
Zetcher, Arnold B. *apparel executive*

Holbrook
Crandlemere, Robert Wayne *engineering executive*

Holden
O'Neil, William Francis *academic administrator*

Holyoke
Clark, Lynn Laux *science educator*
Damon, Steven William *music educator*
Dearborn, Maureen Markt *speech and language clinician*
Dower-Gold, Catherine Anne *music history educator*
Murphy, Eileen Bridget *retired mathematics and computer science professor*
O'Leary, Mary Elizabeth *retired nursing educator, college dean*
Onu, Chukuemeka N. *chemistry professor, researcher*
Resnic, Burton S. *lawyer*

Hopkinton
Dacier, Paul T. *lawyer, information technology executive*
Goulden, David *information technology executive*
Liang, Jin *engineer, consultant*
Moran, Wendy Jacqueline *musician, educator*
Teuber, William J., Jr. *corporate financial executive*
Tucci, Joseph M. *information technology executive*

Hudson
Emer, Joel *computer engineer, educator*
Osoff, Jeffrey Arlin *media company executive*

Hull
Anderson, Timothy Christopher *educational association administrator*

Mathisen, Lauren J. *psychologist*
Medalie, Richard James *lawyer*

Hyannis
Attea, Paul J. *lawyer*
Campbell, Roy Niel *music educator*
Cochrane, Paul Hollis *general practice physician*
Segersten, Robert Hagy *lawyer, investment banker*

Ipswich
Getchell, Charles Willard, Jr. *lawyer, publisher, foundation executive*
Herrmann, Robert Lawrence *biochemist, educator*
Jennings, Frederic Beach, Jr. *economist, saltwater flyfishing guide*
Lombardo, Ann Marie *special education educator, writer, artist*
Londer, Yuri Y. *biochemist*
Roberts, Richard John *molecular biologist, consultant, research director*
Wilson, Doris H. *volunteer*

Jamaica Plain
Babcock, Gregory John *biotechnologist, director*
Enggasser, Justin L. *psychologist*
Pierce, Chester Middlebrook *retired psychiatrist, educator*
Valverde, Paloma *biochemist, educator*

Lancaster
Dugan, Maureen *biology educator, consultant*
Richards, Glenora *artist*

Lee
Thomas, Augusta Read *composer*

Leeds
Deane, James Garner *editor, conservationist*

Leicester
Statkus, Daryl Anne *literature and language professor*

Lenox
Collins, Oral Edmond *theology educator, archaeologist*

Lexington
Ackerman, Robert Wallace *private equity manager*
Bahcall, Safi R. *pharmaceutical executive*
Bailey, Fred Coolidge *retired engineering consulting company executive*
Balu, Sanjeev *pharacoeconomist*
Baron, Sheldon *research and development company executive*
Beusch, John Ulrich *engineer, researcher*
Brick, Donald Bernard *software company executive*
Brookner, Eli *electrical engineer*
Bussgang, Julian Jakub *electronics engineer, consultant*
Cazden, Courtney B(orden) *education educator*
Cohen, Saul G. *chemist, educator*
Collins, Allan Meakin *education educator*
Daltas, Arthur John *management consultant, software services manager*
Dinneen, Gerald Paul *electrical engineer, retired federal official*
Dionne, Gerald Francis *research physicist, educator, consultant*
Dougherty, Richard Hamlen *management and healthcare consultant*
Drouilhet, Paul Raymond, Jr. *retired science administrator, electrical engineer*
Fillios, Louis Charles *retired science educator*
Fray, Lionel Louis *management consultant*
Freed, Charles *engineering consultant, researcher*
Freitag, Wolfgang Martin *retired librarian*
Garing, Ione Davis *civic worker*
Goell, James Emanuel *electronics executive*
Grousbeck, Wycliffe *professional sports team owner, venture capitalist*
Hickey, Magali B. *chemist*
Huang, Robin K. *research scientist*
Kasputys, Joseph Edward *corporate executive, economist*
Keicher, William Eugene *electrical engineer*
Kennedy, X.J. (Joseph Kennedy) *writer*
Kent, Robert Brydon *law educator*
Kerekes, John Paul *electrical engineer*
Lehar, Joseph *science educator, director*
Levine, Janice R. *clinical psychologist*
McGirr, David William John *pharmaceutical executive*
Morrow, Walter Edwin, Jr. *electrical engineer, lab administrator*
Ott, John Harlow *museum administrator*
Papanek, Gustav Fritz *economist, educator*
Sandage, Bobby, Jr. *pharmaceutical executive*
Sheridan, Thomas Brown *mechanical engineering and applied psychology educator, researcher, consultant*
Silverman, Sam Mendel *physicist, lawyer*
Simon, Eckehard (Peter) *foreign language educator*
Smith, Robert Louis *construction company executive*
Wada, Yumiko *pharmacologist*
Waksman, Byron Halsted *immunologist, educator, medical association administrator*
Williams, Anthony *pharmaceutical executive*
Wilson, Wendy Scott *history educator*
Zayhowski, John J. *electrical engineer, researcher*
Zhang, Mei *pharmaceutical executive, researcher*

Lincoln
Bracken, (Myra) Jeanne Munn *librarian, writer*
Capasso, Nicholas John *curator, art historian, public art expert*
Gnichtel, William Van Orden *lawyer*
Kois, Dennis *museum director*
LeGates, John Crews Boulton *information scientist*

Longmeadow
Dovolani, Tony (Driton Dovolani) *dancer*
Ezrin, Myer *retired director*

Gallup, John Gardiner *retired paper company executive*
Katz, Barbara Stein *special education educator*
Keady, George Cregan, Jr. *judge*
Kenefick, Amy Laufer *nurse midwife, nurse practitioner, consultant*
Leary, Carol Ann *academic administrator*
Lemnios, Andrew Zachery *aerospace engineer, educator, researcher*
Lo Bello, Joseph David *bank executive*

Lowell
Abdelal, Ahmed T. *academic administrator, biology professor*
Altman, Albert *retired physicist*
Benjamin, Ann Cheryl *retired psychology professor*
Curtis, James Theodore *lawyer*
Das, Mitra *sociologist, educator*
Femia, John R. *science educator*
Karakashian, Aram Simon *physics professor*
Kaufman, Whitley Robert Peters *humanities educator*
Kegel, Gunter Heinrich Reinhard *physics professor, researcher*
Kheifets, Alexander *mathematics professor*
Kim, Byungki *engineering educator*
Lewis, Diane *educator*
Liakos, Effegenia *physiologist, educator*
Luo, Yan *engineering educator*
MacLean, John *professional hockey coach, former professional hockey player*
Marshall, Bridget *literature and language professor*
Martin, William Francis, Jr. *lawyer*
Meehan, Martin Thomas (Marty Meehan) *academic administrator, former congressman, lawyer*
Minkkinen, Arno Rafael *photographer, educator*
O'Donnell, Kathleen Marie *lawyer*
Pullen, David John *physicist, researcher*
Pyle, Jean L. *economist, consultant*
Sanborne, Erika L. *psychology professor*
Tandel, Sujit Kashinath *physicist, researcher*
Ting, John M. *dean, engineering educator*
Wakim, Fahd George *physicist, researcher*
Weitzen, Jay Allen *engineering educator*

Lynn
Berger, Harvey Robert *psychologist*
Chow, Humphrey Wai *mechanical engineer*
Copeland, Paul Michael *endocrinologist*
D'Entremont, Edward Joseph *application developer, educator*
Ryder, Edward Francis *secondary school educator*

Lynnfield
Kerrigan, Nancy *professional figure skater, retired Olympic athlete*
McGivney, John Joseph *lawyer*

Malden
Chester, Mitchell Dan *state official, school system administrator*
Guild, Richard Samuel *trade association management company executive*
Von Stein, Nicholas *political organization worker*

Manchester
Mack, Michael Edward *physicist*
Prout, Curtis *internist, educator*

Marblehead
Green, Richard John *architect*
Kennedy, Elizabeth Mae *musician*
McAndrews, Robert Kiernan *lawyer, social work educator*
Morton, Perry Williams *investment banker*
Peterson, Pam M. *museum director*

Marion
Landers, Donald Francis *mechanical engineer*

Marlborough
Bennett, C. Leonard *electrical engineer*
Johannes, Richard Scott *medical association administrator*
Murray, R. Scott *computer software company executive*
Norris, Richard Anthony *retired accountant*
Rayle, Heather Lynnette *chemist*

Marstons Mills
Martin, David Standish *education educator*
Martin, Susan Katherine *librarian*

Mashpee
Jamison, John L. *musician, educator*
Kilmartin, Joseph Francis, Jr. *information technology executive*
Wasiele, Harry W., Jr. *diversified electrical manufacturing company executive*

Mattapan
Messam, Leroy Anthony *accountant*
Walker, Dianne *dancer, performing company executive*

Mattapoisett
Mazer, Mike *cardiologist, retired nephrologist, artist*

Maynard
Lindsay, Leslie *packaging engineer*

Medfield
McQuillen, Jeremiah Joseph *distribution executive*

Medford
Abriola, Linda Marie *civil and environmental engineer*
Bacow, Lawrence Seldon *academic administrator, environmental scientist, educator*
Barwell, Nina *music educator*
Bedau, Hugo Adam *philosophy educator*
Berman, David *lawyer, poet*
Brunye, Tad T. *psychologist*

Caviness, Madeline Harrison *art history educator, researcher*
Centner, Ryan *sociologist, educator*
Chapra, Steven Christopher *engineering educator, endowed chair*
Conklin, John Evan *sociology educator*
Drezner, Daniel William *political science professor*
Elkind, David *psychology professor*
Fyler, John Morgan *language educator*
Goldberg, Pamela Winer *entrepreneur, educator*
Jacobs, Mary Lee *lawyer*
Kaiser-Lenoir, Claudia *literature and language professor*
Kumar, Krishna *chemistry professor*
Mazzotti, José Antonio *humanities educator, researcher*
Michalak, Jo-Ann *library director*
Miczek, Klaus Alexander *psychology professor*
Nasr, Vali Reza *international politics professor*
Oommen, Thomas *research scientist*
Pfaltzgraff, Robert Louis, Jr. *political scientist, educator*
Rubin, Alfred Peter *law educator, educator*
Salacuse, Jeswald William *lawyer, educator*
Sassaroli, Angelo *science educator, researcher*
Schneps, Jack *physics professor, department chairman*
Sternberg, Robert Jeffrey *dean, psychology professor, researcher*
Tu, Loring Wuliang *mathematics educator*
Wilson, Jonathan Michael *literature educator, writer*
Yi, Hyunmin *chemical engineer, educator*

Medway
Hoag, David Garratt *retired aerospace engineer*

Melrose
Desforges, Jane Fay *retired internist, hematologist, educator*

Methuen
Elya, John Adel *bishop emeritus*
McNaughton, William John *bishop emeritus*

Milford
Nassour, Jennifer A. *political organization administrator*

Milton
Corcoran, Robert Joseph *fundraising executive*
Frazier, Marie Dunn *speech professional, public relations executive, human resources specialist*
Randall, Lilian Maria Charlotte *museum curator*

Nantucket
Louderback, Peter Darragh *accountant, consultant*
Rauch, George Washington *lawyer, director*
Saperstein, Lee Waldo *mining engineering educator*

Natick
Adam, Gina E. *psychologist, researcher*
Arcidiacono, Steven *microbiologist*
Berglund, Larry Glenn *mechanical engineer, educator*
Dang, Pritpal S. *application developer*
Doona, Christopher J. *research chemist*
Edyvean, Walter James *bishop*
Elliott, Ray (J. Raymond Elliott) *biomedical device manufacturing company executive*
Forward, Frank D. *wholesale distribution executive*
Geller, Esther (Bailey Geller) *artist*
Gottlieb, Michael Norman *internist, educator, health facility administrator*
Grassia, Thomas Charles *lawyer, educator, writer*
Latanision, Ronald Michael *materials engineer*
LaViolette, Paul A. *former medical products executive*
Leno, Samuel R. *biomedical device manufacturing company executive*
McConnell, William F., Jr. *medical products executive*
Miller, George David *retired military officer, not-for-profit executive*
Nicholas, Peter M. *medical products executive*
Oulton, Donald Paul *lawyer*
Pokorny, Joseph Wenceslaus III *engineer*
Povich, Lon F. *wholesale distribution executive*
Pratt, Timothy *lawyer*
Rendell, Kenneth William *rare and historical documents dealer, consultant*
Sedo, Manuel Arturo *psychologist, researcher*
Sen, Laura J. *wholesale distribution executive*
Wallace, Elizabeth *medical/surgical nurse*
Zarkin, Herbert J. *wholesale distribution executive*

Needham
Bohnen, Michael J. *lawyer, foundation administrator*
Cogswell, John Heyland *retired telecommunications industry executive, financial consultant*
Cowell, Henry Richard *orthopaedic surgeon, journal editor*
Di Domenica, Robert Anthony *musician, composer*
Engels, Donald Whitcomb *history educator*
Grasso, James Anthony *public relations executive, educator*
Greenway, Hugh Davids Scott *journalist*
Karr, P. J. *education educator, writer*
Lain, David Cornelius *health scientist, researcher*
Miller, Richard Keith *academic administrator, engineering educator*
Osser, David Neal *psychiatrist, educator*
Rodman, Sumner *insurance company executive*
Ryan, Una Scully *health science association administrator, medical educator*

Needham Heights
Forman, Leonard P. *former publishing executive*
Gelfand, Jeffrey Alan *physician, educator*
Joseph, Nevil Elliot *application developer*
Salhany, Lucille S. (Lucy Salhany) *broadcast executive*

New Bedford
Benoit, Richard Armand *lawyer, retired police chief*

Bullard, John Kilburn *educational association administrator*
Matsumoto, Carolee Setsuko *researcher, education developer and administrator*
Smietana, Walter *educational research director*
Soares, Carl Lionel *quality assurance professional, metrologist*

Newburyport
Lessard, Arnold Fred *international business executive*
Robinson, Enders Anthony *geophysicist, educator, writer*
Robinson, Joyce McPeake *academic administrator, consultant*
Wilner, Eric Mark *radiologist*

Newton
Ardalan, Nader *architect*
Bagalay, John Earl *information technology executive, venture capitalist, consultant*
Baron, Charles Hillel *lawyer, educator*
Bassuk, Ellen Linda *psychiatrist*
Benner, Mary Wright *program director, the conference board*
Burlage, Dorothy Dawson *clinical psychologist*
Coquillette, Daniel Robert *lawyer, educator*
Dunlap, William Crawford *physicist*
Frankenheim, Samuel *retired lawyer*
Garcia, Eduardo *neurologist, consultant*
Glazer, Donald Wayne *lawyer, corporate financial executive, educator*
Glick-Weil, Kathy *library director*
Golomb, Dan S. *physical chemistry educator, consultant*
Isselbacher, Rhoda Solin *lawyer*
Klyosov, Anatole Alex *biochemist, researcher*
Marshall, Robert Lewis *musicologist, educator*
Matteson, Carol J. *academic administrator*
May, Harold Louis *retired surgeon, not-for-profit developer*
Parker, Jeff D. *operations research specialist*
Petrowski, Joseph H. *oil industry executive*
Sasahara, Arthur Asao *cardiologist, educator, researcher*
Steinberg, Roberta Gail *language educator*
Wahlberg, Mark *actor*
Weisz, Virginia Graves *law educator*
White, Burton Leonard *retired educational psychologist, writer, consultant*
Xiong, Renqiang *mechanical engineer, researcher*

Newton Center
Carter, Nick *academic administrator, minister*
Eichler, Marc *neurosurgeon*
Friedman, David Samuel *lawyer*
Garvey, John Hugh *dean, law educator*
Peck, Sheldon *orthodontist, educator, dental anthropologist*
Schuller, Gunther Alexander *composer*
Snyder, John Gorvers *lawyer*

Newton Highlands
Bricklin, Daniel *software designer, consultant*

Newtonville
Dews, P(eter) B(ooth) *retired pharmacology educator, physician*
Harris, Paul Lansley *education professor*
Mullen, Maureen Ann *social worker*
Polonsky, Arthur *artist, educator*

Newtown
Wilson, Paul Holliday, Jr. *lawyer*

North Adams
Bishoff, Robert Earl, Jr. *literature educator*
Gross, Marcia R. *library director, educator*
McConnell, Matthew Stephen *composer, educator*
Thompson, Joseph C. *museum director*
Thurston, Donald Allen *broadcast executive*

North Andover
Gelb, Harold Seymour *retired manufacturing executive, entrepreneur, consultant*
Jannini, Ralph Humbert III *electronics executive*
Keohan, Robert Daniel *literature and language educator, columnist*
Kravette, Ronald Irwin *professional athletics coach, educator*
Kurzweil, Raymond C. *computer scientist, entrepreneur*
Swallow, Kathleen Clinedinst *chemistry professor*

North Attleboro
Flynn, Kate Elizabeth *music educator, director*
Koussa, Harold Alan *insurance account executive*

North Chatham
Wilson, E. B. *manufacturing executive, consultant, writer*

North Chelmsford
Erkkila-Ricker, Barbara Howell *writer, photographer*
Kotelly, George Vincent *editor, writer, electrical engineer*
Noto, John *engineering executive*

North Dartmouth
Anderson, Michael Henning *finance educator*
Barrow, Clyde Wayne *social sciences educator*
Borim, Dario, Jr. *literature educator*
Fields, Keota *education educator*
Fisher, Elaine *art educator, photographer*
Hsu, Jong-Ping *physicist, educator*
Law, Frederick Masom *structural engineering firm executive, educator*
Rai, Bharatendra K. *statistician, educator*
Vasudevan, Gopala *finance educator*
Yoken, Mel B(arton) *language educator, writer, radio personality*

North Dighton
Cserr, Robert *psychiatrist, physician, hospital administrator*

North Easton
Lema, Karen Anne *special education educator*
Ohanyan, Anna *political science professor*
Varella, Hazel L. *historian, educator*

North Grafton
Costa, Lais Rosa Rodrigues *veterinarian, educator, medical researcher*
Herrmann, John *microbiologist*
Schwartz, Anthony *veterinary surgeon, educator, photographer*
Taeymans, Olivier N. *veterinarian, educator*

North Oxford
Carney, Roger Francis Xavier *retired military officer*

Northampton
Anastas, Jeane Wiener *social work educator*
Christ, Carol Tecla *academic administrator*
Dean, Dorothy G. *psychologist, social sciences educator, researcher*
Derr, Thomas Sieger *religion educator*
Donfried, Karl Paul *theologian, clergyman*
Ellis, Glenn W. *engineering educator*
Everett, Joyce E. *social sciences educator*
Fleck, George Morrison *chemistry professor*
Holbert, Kelly McKay *exhibition coordinator, art historian*
Kherdian, David *writer*
Naegele, Philipp Otto *musician, educator*
Newman, Lesléa *writer*
Piccinino, Rocco Michael *librarian*
Reinhardt, Nola *economics educator*
Robinson, Donald Leonard *social scientist, educator*
Rose, Peter Isaac *sociologist, writer, editor*
Santopietro, Albert Robert *lawyer*
Vaget, Hans Rudolf *language professional, educator*
Von Klemperer, Klemens *historian, educator*

Northborough
Cradler, Judith A. *science educator*
FitzGerald, Thomas Jeffrey *medical educator, department chairman*
Fulmer, Hugh Scott *physician, educator*
Lee, Sugjoon Joon *textile engineer, consultant*
Ou, Duan Li *chemist*
Wang, Jun *process engineer, materials scientist*
Yao, Wei-Dong *medical educator, researcher*

Norton
Crutcher, Ronald Andrew *academic administrator, music educator*
Mayer, Reinhard Albert *language educator*
Worthley, Harold Field *retired minister, educator*

Norwell
Brett, Jan Churchill *illustrator, author*
Case, David Knowlton *management consultant*
Mullare, T(homas) Kenwood, Jr. *lawyer*

Norwood
Berliner, Allen Irwin *dermatologist*
Fishman, Jerald G. *semiconductor executive*
Howell, Michael Dwight *physician, director*
Li, Chiang J. *pharmaceutical executive, physician scientist*
Sheingold, Daniel H. *electrical engineer*

Orange
Rivers, Robert Alfred *microwave company executive*

Orleans
Patterson, Elizabeth C. *choir director*
Rappaport, Margaret Mary Williams Ewing *psychologist, physician, writer, pilot, consultant*

Osterville
Schwarztrauber, Sayre Archie *former naval officer, maritime consultant*
Silk, Alvin John *management educator, consultant*

Oxford
Schur, Walter Robert *physician*

Paxton
Clarke, Edward Nielsen *engineering science educator*
Heslinga, Virginia *literature and language professor*

Peabody
Birdsall, Melinda R. *gynecologist*
Butz, Stefan Peter *science association director*
Dobbs, John McGregor *physicist, mechanical engineer*
Gordon, Bernard M. *computer company executive*
Irwin, Francis Xavier *bishop*
Lipman, Richard Paul *pediatrician*
Peters, Leo Francis *environmental engineer*
Southwick, Paul *retired public relations executive*

Pepperell
Holmes, Jean Louise *museum director, humanities educator*

Petersham
Chivian, Eric Seth *psychiatrist, environmental scientist, educator*

Pittsfield
Begley, Charlene *manufacturing executive*
Feigenbaum, Armand Vallin *systems engineer, information technology executive*
Guzzo, Jessica Ann *music educator*
Johnson, Rebecca L. *pathologist*
Kersten, Christian George *university administrator*
Rich, Philip Dewey *publishing executive*
Shammas, Nazih Kheirallah *environmental engineer, consultant, engineering educator*
Shanahan, Ellen C. *music educator*
Wenner, Gene Charles *arts management executive*
Wood, Elizabeth Ann *special education educator*

Plymouth
Baker, Peggy MacLachlan *cultural organization administrator, museum director*

Flood, H. Gay (Hulda Gay Flood) *editor, consultant*
Gregory, Dick *comedian, volunteer*
Lenard-Zabel, Ann Marie T. *psychologist, educator*
Staszesky, Francis Myron *electric power industry executive, consultant*

Prides Crossing
Crowley, Ann V. *lawyer*
Garcia, Adolfo Ramon *lawyer, director*

Provincetown
Collins, Larry Richard *artist, educator, art gallery director*
Giese, Graham Sherwood *oceanographer*
Hutchinson, Peter Arthur *artist*
Oliver, Mary *poet*
Wolfman, Brunetta Reid *education educator*

Quincy
Hall, John Raymond, Jr. *fire protection executive*
Hayes, Mary Dianne Wixted *lawyer*
Holway, David J. *labor union administrator*
Levin, Robert Joseph *food products executive*
Lippincott, Joseph P. *photojournalist, educator*
Moran, James Joseph, Jr. *insurance company executive*
Spangler, Arthur Stephenson, Jr. *psychologist*
Twining, Jonathan Emerson *biology professor*
Young, Richard William *chemicals executive*
Zoulas, Soterios C. *communications educator, consultant*

Randolph
Johnson, Laurence Michael *lawyer*
Manos, Sarantos John *physics educator*

Reading
Burbank, Nelson Stone *investment banker*
Frey, Joanne Alice Tupper *art educator*
Nordstrand, Nathalie Elizabeth Johnson *artist*
Ricci, Carla *psychologist*
Tuttle, David Bauman *electrical engineer*

Revere
Anthony, Sylvia *social welfare organization executive*
Paananen, Victor Niles *language educator*

Rochester
Teal, John M. *environmental scientist*

Rockland
Blethen, Sandra Lee *pediatric endocrinologist*
Dunne, Myra Schley *nurse, consultant*
Durant, Leigh-Ann Margaret *lawyer*
Tredway, Donald Ray *endocrinologist, educator*

Rockport
Bissell, Phil (Charles P. Bissell) *cartoonist*
Martin, Roger Hemenway *artist, educator*
Nicholas, Thomas Andrew *artist*
Wiberg, Lars-Erik *occupational compatibility consultant*

Roslindale
Spada, James *writer, photographer, publishing executive*

Roxbury
Peters, Alan *anatomy educator*
Simons, Elizabeth R(eiman) *biochemist, educator*

Sagamore Beach
Corn, Wanda Marie *retired fine arts educator*

Salem
Doran, Kathleen Brewer *dean, consultant*
Gozemba, Patrica Andrea *women's studies and English language educator, writer*
Jacobson, Joseph O. *oncologist, department chairman*
McLyman, Meghan *dance professor*
Monroe, Dan L. *museum director*
Moran, Philip David *lawyer*
Rabchenuk, Paul Thomas *lawyer*
Rhodes, Karin T. *language educator*
Staples, Mavis *singer*

Sandwich
Troy, Robert Sweeney, Sr. *lawyer*

Scituate
Wiley, David Nathan *biologist, researcher*

Sharon
Eiland, Howard Avery *literature educator*
Parker, Harry Lee *retired army officer, academic administrator*
Zenack, Les *mathematics professor*

Sheffield
Kaufman, Raun Kahlil *education center administrator, teacher*

Sherborn
Cushing, Steven *linguist, educator, writer, researcher, consultant*
Hancock, William Frank, Jr. *management consultant*
Kennedy, Chester Ralph, Jr. *retired state official, art director*

Shirley
Hoffmann, Micheal Joseph *theater director*

Shirley Center
Holden, Harley Peirce *retired archivist*

Shrewsbury
Falter, Robert Gary *real estate broker, educator*
Kranich, Margaret Mansley *artist*
Nixon, Eugene Ray *chemist, educator*
Onorato, Nicholas Louis *retired program director, economist*

Smith, Carolyn J(ane) Hostetter *psychologist, educator*
Watanabe, Mark David *pharmacist, educator*

Shutesbury
Abbott, Douglas Eugene *engineering educator*
Creed, Robert Payson, Sr. *retired literature educator*

Siasconset
Albani, Thomas J. *investor*

Somerville
Austill, Allen *dean emeritus*
Basáñez, Miguel Ebergenyi *political scientist, educator*
Berlet, John Foster *researcher*
Curwood, Steve *television producer, host*
Fitzpatrick, Terry *public radio reporter, producer*
Holmes, Lewis B. *pediatrician, medical geneticist*
Hume, Ellen Hunsberger *media analyst, educator, journalist*
Levy, Elliott Stuart *accounting educator*

South Boston
Boles, John P. *bishop emeritus*

South Dartmouth
Greene, William Caswell *investment company executive*
Mellberg, Leonard Evert *physicist*
Ward, Richard Joseph *university dean, educator, author*

South Hadley
Brownlow, Frank Walsh *literature and language professor*
Burns, Michael Thornton *historian, educator, farmer*
Creighton, Joanne Vanish *academic administrator*
Elleman, Barbara *editor*
Ewing Browne, Sheila *physical organic chemist, professor*
Farnham, Anthony Edward *language educator, department chairman*
Fisher, William Thomas *business administration educator*
Gundermann, Christian *language educator*
Hall, Lee *artist, educator, writer*
Horsnell, Margaret Eileen *retired historian*
Kaltenbach, Jane Couffer *biology educator*
Mullins, John Madison *educational consultant*
Townsend, Jane Kaltenbach *biologist, educator*
Van Handle, Donna *language educator*
Williamson, Kenneth Lee *chemistry professor*

South Hamilton
Nemeskal, Natalie Ann *massage therapist*

South Wellfleet
Blau, Monte *retired radiology educator*

South Weymouth
Young, Michael Chung-En *allergist, immunologist, pediatrician*

South Yarmouth
Tracey, William Raymond *international management consultant*

Southampton
Borowsky, Claude David *sports medicine physician*

Southborough
Kriegsman, Edward Michael *lawyer*
Lavin, Philip Todd *medical executive*
Mylotte, John Arnold *writer, educator*
Warren, John Coolidge *educational administrator*

Southbridge
Anderson, Ross Barrett *healthcare environmental services manager*

Springfield
Caprio, Anthony S. *academic administrator*
Crandall, Roger W. *insurance company executive*
Dibble, Francis Daniel, Jr. *lawyer*
Dupré, Thomas Ludger *bishop emeritus*
Engebretson, Douglas Kenneth *architect, interior designer*
Farkas, Paul Stephen *gastroenterologist*
Friedmann, Paul *surgeon, educator, research and development company executive*
Glavin, William Francis, Jr. *insurance company executive*
Habermehl, Lawrence LeRoy *philosophy educator*
Harnois, Veronica D'Urso *psychologist, educator*
Haskell, Heather R. *museum director*
Johnson, Robert Allison *life insurance company executive*
Kottamasu, Mohan Rao (K.V.R. Mohan Rao) *physician, health facility administrator*
Leslie, George J. *professor*
Liptzin, Benjamin *psychiatrist*
Maguire, Joseph F. *bishop emeritus*
McDonnell, Timothy Anthony *bishop*
McGee, William Tobin *internist*
Melconian, Linda Jean *state senator, lawyer, educator*
Miller, Leroy Paul, Jr. *language educator*
Neiman, Kenneth Paul *judge*
Oldershaw, Louis Frederick *retired lawyer*
Parke, David Alan *lawyer*
Petrone, William Francis *pediatrician, microbiologist, corporate executive*
Reese, Stuart Harry *insurance company executive*
Roellig, Mark D. *lawyer, insurance company executive*
Rollings, Michael Thomas *insurance company executive*
Romero, Ricardo Vicente *gastroenterologist*
Sarsynski, Elaine A. *insurance company executive*
Spencer, Estelle Heidi *library director*
Starr, David *editor, publisher*
Weiss, Ronald Phillip *lawyer*
Winn, Janice Gail *food products administrator*

Wronka, Joseph Michael *social policy analyst, human rights activist, educator*
Wurm, Alexander *physics professor*
Wyzik, Susan Aldrich *history professor*

Squantum
Robertson, Michael Swing *minister*

Sterling
Antonelli, Richard Christopher *pediatrician, educator*

Stockbridge
Kenny, Charles *orthopedist*
Moffatt, Laurie Norton *museum director, curator*
Shapiro, Edward Robert *psychiatrist, educator, health facility administrator, psychotherapist*

Stoughton
Gabovitch, Steven Alan *lawyer, accountant*
Hall, Roger Lee *musicologist, composer, educator*
Joseph, Anthony Barnett *psychiatrist*
Wedig, Christopher P. *environmental engineer*

Sudbury
Ames, Lois Winslow Sisson *social worker, educator, writer*
Aronson, David *artist, retired educator*
Campbell, Elaine Josephine *retired academic administrator, writer, critic*
Crooker, Nancy Uss *physicist, researcher*
Henderson, Ernest III *healthcare executive*
Lamont-Havers, Ronald William *retired physician, medical association administrator*
McCree, Paul William, Jr. *systems design and engineering company executive*
Meltzer, Donald Richard *retired treasurer*
Pitman, Ursula Wall *curator, educator*

Sunderland
Baritz, Loren *history professor*

Swampscott
Kaufman, William Morris *electrical engineer, consultant*

Taunton
Nunes, Anthony S. *language educator*
Ricciardi, Cynthia Booth *writer, researcher, educator*
Ricciardi, Louis Michael *brokerage house executive*
Ross, Murray David *psychologist*

Tewksbury
Black, Richard Bruce *corporate executive, consultant*
Faccini, Ernest Carlo *mechanical engineer*
Tabea, Emile Victor *health facility administrator*

Truro
Chaplin, Ansel Burt *lawyer*
Lazeren, Elizabeth *artist*
Preston, Malcolm *artist, art critic*

Uxbridge
Iannuccilli, Janet Ann *psychologist*

Vineyard Haven
Breuer, Joann Green *theater director*
Kimball, Julie Ellis *small press publisher, humorist, writer*
Schmetterer, Robert Allen *advertising executive*

Waban
Black, Eugene Charlton *historian, educator*
Rogoff, Jerome Howard *psychiatrist, psychoanalyst, forensic expert*
Schuntermann, Peter Paul *psychiatrist*
Shklar, Gerald *pathologist, periodontist, educator*

Wakefield
Fioravanti, Jeff *artist*

Waltham
Arena, Albert A. *museum director*
Bayone, Edward *finance company executive, educator*
Bensinger, James Robert *physicist*
Bernstein, Stanley Joseph *manufacturing executive*
Best, Lawrence C. *retired medical products executive*
Bohlen, Nina *artist*
Bok, Joan Toland *utilities executive*
Boykan, Martin *composer, music educator*
Brown, Edgar Henry, Jr. *mathematician, educator*
Burt, John D. *literature and language professor*
Campbell, Leland *marketing educator, consultant*
Cash, James Ireland, Jr. *retired business educator*
Casper, Marc Nolan *scientific instrument company executive*
Chang, Yu-Hui *composer*
Chory, John H. *lawyer*
Cox, Howard Ellis, Jr. *venture capitalist*
Dekkers, Marijn E. *electronics executive*
Epstein, Irving Robert *chemistry professor*
Faneuil, Edward J. *lawyer*
Farb, Thomas Forest *financial executive*
Fischer, David Hackett *historian, educator*
Fleming, Andrea L. *art educator, director*
Fleming, Samuel Crozier, Jr. *healthcare executive*
Foxman, Bruce Mayer *chemist, educator*
Friel, Robert F. *electronics executive*
Geng, Bolin *research scientist*
Goodheart, Eugene *literary critic*
Gumpertz, Werner Herbert *structural engineering company executive*
Hollister, Thomas J. *oil industry executive*
Hovsepian, Ronald W. *network management software company executive*
Jankowski, Paul Felix *history professor*
Kotchikian, Asbed *political science professor*
Krstansky, Adrianne Marie *actress, performing arts educator*
Landaw, Stephen Arthur *physician, educator*
Leach, Robert Ellis *orthopedist, surgeon, educator*
Levy, Elliott Stuart *accounting educator*
Lian, Bong H. *mathematics professor, department chairman*
Malis, Andrew Gary *telecommunications industry executive*
Manzi, Jim P. *investment company executive*
Marques, Nadejda *language educator, interpreter*
McCulloch, Rachel *economist, educator*
Metcalfe, Robert M. *venture capitalist, former science engineer, publishing executive, writer*
Nelson, Arthur Hunt *real estate company executive*
Newburg, David Stephen *biochemist*
Nichols, Guy Warren *retired institute and utilities executive*
Notkin, Leonard Sheldon *architect*
Nye, Dan *former internet company executive*
O'Connell, Jeanne *financial planner, insurance broker*
Pages-Rangel, Roxana *language educator*
Partenskii, Michael B. *science educator, researcher*
Reinharz, Jehuda *academic administrator, history educator*
Sachs, Murray *French language and literature educator, researcher*
Saxe, Leonard *social psychologist, educator*
Schrecker, John *historian, educator*
Sekuler, Robert William *science educator*
Shahrur, Husayn K. *finance educator*
Shepard, Donald Sloane *public policy research educator*
Simeonov, Simeon *computer scientist*
Slifka, Eric *oil industry executive*
Spack, Ruth Karten *literature educator*
Spoon, Alan Gary *venture capital company executive*
Stephens, Jay B. *lawyer, defense technologies company executive*
Storey, Mimi Ellis *lawyer*
Sullivan, Mary E. *retired secondary educator, former state legislator*
Swanson, William Henry *defense equipment manufacturing company executive*
Thamhain, Hans Jurgen *management educator*
Wajsgras, David C. *manufacturing executive*
Wawrzaszek, Susan V. *university librarian*
Whitfield, Stephen Jack *history educator*
Wilver, Peter M. *electronics executive, accountant*
Xue, Fei *epidemiologist*

Wareham
Nolan, Marilyn Ann *health facility administrator*

Watertown
Emerson, Charles P., Jr. *research scientist*
Erhardt, Peter *research scientist*
Joubert, Raymond Ernest *retired electrical engineer*
Kaloosdian, Robert Aram *lawyer*
Roosevelt, James, Jr. *insurance company executive, lawyer*
Stoddard, Anne Maher *biostatistician, researcher, educator*
Tompkins, Curtis Johnston *government agency administrator*
Young, Raymond Henry *lawyer*

Wayland
Brynjolfsson, Ari *nuclear physicist*
Dergalis, George *artist, educator*
Edelman, Stuart Edward *psychiatrist*
Huff, William Braid *retired publishing company executive*
Humphrey, Diana Young *fundraiser*
Moncure, Ashby Carter *surgeon, educator*

Webster
Fels, Gerald *insurance company executive*
Keller, David Martin *pediatrician*

Wellesley
Auerbach, Jerold S. *educator*
Baker, Charles D. *health insurance company executive*
Bidart, Frank *English educator, poet*
Birkerts, Gunnar *architect*
Bottomly, (H.) Kim *academic administrator, biology professor, researcher*
Burstein, Harvey *lawyer, educator*
Charpie, Robert Alan *physicist, researcher*
Clapp, Jennifer *lawyer*
Cummings, Cathleen Ann *art historian, educator*
DiCamillo, Gary Thomas *manufacturing executive*
Donato, Gary *political science professor*
Dougherty, Carol *humanities educator*
Gailius, Gilbert Keistutis *manufacturing executive*
Gerety, Robert John *microbiologist, researcher, pediatrician, pharmaceutical executive, drug developer*
Giddon, Donald B(ernard) *psychologist, educator*
Jacobs, Ruth Harriet *poet, playwright, sociologist, gerontologist*
Kato, Walter Yoneo *physicist*
Lefkowitz, Mary Rosenthal *ancient language educator*
Mistacco, Vicki E. *foreign language educator*
Morant, Ricardo Bernardino *psychology professor*
Murray, Joseph Edward *retired plastic surgeon*
Olsen, David Teng *performing arts educator*
Papageorgiou, John Constantine *management science educator*
Sangree, Walter Hinchman *social anthropologist, educator*
Silberman, Robert A. S. *lawyer*
Snitzer, Elias *physicist*
Stettner, Edward A. *political science professor*
Twitchell, Thomas Evans *neurologist, educator*
Weil, Thomas Alexander *retired electronics engineer*
Young, Delano Victor *cell biologist, pharmaceutical scientist, biochemist, educator*
Zhou, Li *medical researcher*
Zimmerman, Eve Kathleen *literature and language professor*

Wellesley Hills
Doorley, Thomas Lawrence III *management consultant*
Marcus, William Michael *rubber and vinyl products manufacturing company executive*
Peabody, Laura S. *lawyer, insurance company executive*
Tang, Jenny CC *music educator*

Wellfleet
Henry, Robert S. *art educator*
Limpitlaw, John Donald *publishing executive, clergyman*
Piercy, Marge *poet, writer*
Spaniol, LeRoy *retired psychologist*

Wenham
Barthold, Lauren Swayne *lay worker*
Flint-Ferguson, Janis Deane *English language and literature educator*
Mathewson, David *religious studies educator*
Schirer-Suter, Myron *library director*
Thuswaldner, Gregor *literature and language professor*

West Barnstable
Gautam, Virender *economics professor*
Martin, Kate M. *history professor*
Rapoza, Elizabeth *theater educator, playwright, director*

West Boylston
Perron, William Francis *retired protective services official*

West Brookfield
Higgins, Brian Alton *artist*

West Falmouth
Carlson, David Bret *retired lawyer*
Holz, George G., IV, *medical educator, research scientist*
King, Richard Hood *retired newspaper executive*

West Newton
Fox, John Bayley, Jr. *retired university dean*
Spitzer, Toba *rabbi*

West Roxbury
Ellenbogen, George *poet, educator*
Lovell, Francis Joseph *retired investment company executive*
Roach, Maureen S. *primary school educator*

West Springfield
Desai, Veena Balvantrai *obstetrician, gynecologist, educator*
Moore, Kelly Ann *secondary school educator*

West Tisbury
Howes, Ann M. *watercolor artist, cultural organization administrator, educator*
Méras, Phyllis Leslie *journalist*

Westborough
Catell, Robert Barry *gas industry executive*
Gionfriddo, Maurice Paul *aeronautical engineer, research and development company executive*
Jackson, Frederick Herbert *educational administrator*
Rekhi, Sandeep *geologist, physicist*
Reza, Shahed *electrical engineer*
Staffier, Pamela Moorman *psychologist*

Westfield
Aldrich-Jones, Jean Elizabeth *music educator*
Aquino, Gabriel *social sciences educator*
Buckmore, Alvah Clarence, Jr. *computer scientist, ballistician*
Cleaton-Ruiz, Christin *history professor*
Zayac, Linda Mary *sociologist, educator*

Westford
Alluè, Emilio Simeon *bishop*
Geary, Marie Josephine *art association administrator*
Haramundanis, Katherine Leonora *information scientist, writer, astronomer, science historian*
Nottenburg, Richard N. *former communications executive*

Weston
Barry, William Anthony *priest, writer*
Goldstein, Arthur Louis *retired utilities executive*
Higgins, Sister Therese *literature educator, former college president*
Katz, William Emanuel *retired chemical engineer*
Lashman, L. Edward *arbitrator, mediator, consultant*
Lin, Alice Lee Lan *physicist, researcher, educator*
Mannick, John Anthony *surgeon*
McDaniel, James Alan *lawyer*
Mc Innes, William Charles *priest, academic administrator*
Saad, Theodore Shafick *retired microwave company executive*
Tenney, Sarah G. *music educator*
Thomas, Roger Meriwether *lawyer*
Uhlir, Arthur, Jr. *retired electrical engineer, academic administrator*
Valente, Louis Patrick (Dan Valente) *financial planner, director*

Westport
Gormley, Robert John *retired publishing executive*

Westport Point
Fanning, William Henry, Jr. *computer specialist*

Westwood
Partnoy, Ronald Allen *lawyer*
Phillips, Marion Grumman *civic volunteer, writer*
Ragone, David Vincent *former university president*
Riley, Henry Charles *banker*
Smith, Denis Joseph *mathematics professor*

Whitinsville
Plaud, Joseph Julian *psychology educator*

Williamstown
Bell, Robert *literature educator*
Blair, Phyllis E. *artist*
Bolton, Roger Edwin *economist, educator*
Burns, Joan Simpson *writer, editor*
Canova, Jane E. *international education administrator*
Conforti, Michael Peter *museum director, art historian*
Cramer, Phebe *psychologist*
Crampton, Stuart Jessup Bigelow *physicist, researcher*
Dalzell, Robert Fenton, Jr. *historian, educator*
De Veaux, Richard Donald *statistician*
Dew, Charles Burgess *historian, educator*
Eusden, John Dykstra *theology studies educator, minister*
Fuqua, Charles John *retired classicist*
Graver, Suzanne Levy *English literature educator*
Hastings, Philip Kay *psychology professor*
Hill, Victor Ernst, IV, *retired mathematics professor, musician*
Kassin, Saul *psychology professor*
Morgan, Frank *mathematics professor*
Nolan, James Lawry, Jr. *sociologist*
Oakley, Francis Christopher *historian, educator*
Park, David Allen *physicist, researcher*
Pilachowski, David M. *library director*
Pistorius, George *language educator*
Robinson, Hobart Krum *management consulting company executive*
Rudolph, Frederick *history professor*
Scullin, Dorothy Dodworth *artist, writer*
Shainman, Irwin *musician, educator*
Sheahan, John Bernard *economist, educator*
Shepard, James Russell *literature and language professor*
Silva, Cesar Ernestro *mathematics educator*
Siniawer, Eiko Maruko *history professor*
Sprague, John Louis *management consultant*
Swift, Jane Maria *educational consultant, former governor*
Wagner, William G. *academic administrator*
Wobus, Reinhard Arthur *geologist, educator*

Wilmington
Devarajan, Siddharth *electronics engineer*
Lagace, Paul Alfred *aeronautical engineering educator*
Lang, Elvira Valentina *radiologist, educator, medical products executive*

Winchester
Blackham, Ann Rosemary *realtor*
Brennan, Francis Patrick *banker*
Ferrara, Lee *graphics designer, artist, educator*
Harris, Carole Ruth *education educator, researcher, consultant*
Irving, Gitte Nielsen *secondary school educator*
Jackson, Francis Joseph *research and development company executive*
Milburn, Richard Henry *physics professor*
Neuman, Robert Sterling *artist, educator*

Windsor
Leaf, Martin Norman *lawyer*

Winthrop
Brown, Patricia Irene *retired law librarian, lawyer*
Flockhart, Barbara Townsley *retired publishing executive*
Kearney, Eva M. *art educator*

Woburn
Andriano, Kirk Patrick *biotechnology executive*
Guo, Ling *musician, consultant*
Kang, Yun *pharmaceutical executive*
Lalgudi, Subramanian Natarajan *research scientist*
Mehra, Raman Kumar *aerospace and defense technology executive, automotion and control engineering researcher*
Perlovsky, Leonid Isaacovich *geophysicist, researcher*
Serfaty, Daniel *human systems engineer*

Woods Hole
Adams, Rex *dean*
Blake, James Alan *marine biologist, educator*
Cohen, Seymour Stanley *biochemist, educator*
Gagosian, Robert B. *chemist, educator*
Gifford, Prosser *retired library administrator*
Hart, Stanley Robert *geochemist, educator*
Hobbie, John Eyres *research scientist*
Inoué, Shinya *microscopy and cell biology scientist, educator*
Laster, Leonard *internist, gastroenterologist, academic administrator, educator, writer, researcher*
Limeburner, Richard *oceanographer, researcher*
Lough, Robert Gregory *oceanographer, researcher*
Melillo, Jerry M. *ecologist*
Newman, John Nicholas *naval architect educator*
Poag, Claude Wylie *geologist, researcher*
Prendergast, Robert Anthony *pathologist educator*
Rypina, Irina I. *oceanographer*
Saito, Mak *environmental scientist*
Shimomura, Osamu *chemistry professor*
Speck, William T. *former physician, health facility administrator*
Stanley, Rachel H. R. *oceanographer*
Steele, John Hyslop *marine scientist, oceanographic institute administrator*
Uchupi, Elazar *geologist, researcher*
Woodwell, George Masters *ecologist, conservationist*

Worcester
Akgul, Ferit Ozan *research scientist*
Ambros, Victor R. *geneticist, educator*
Amory, Francis Inman *social worker, educator*
Ayers, David C. *orthodontist, educator*
Bassett, John E. *academic administrator, language educator*
Bastien, Louis A. *literature and language professor*
Benjamin, Sheldon *psychiatrist, educator*

Benway, Gaelan Lee *sociologist, educator*
Berkey, Dennis Dale *academic administrator*
Bernhard, Jeffrey David *dermatologist, educator, editor*
Billias, George Athan *historian, educator*
Blount, F. Alexander *psychologist, director*
Brenneman, Betsey Jean *college librarian*
Candib, Murray A. *retail executive, consultant*
Chaudhury, Sujoy Krishna *research scientist*
Collins, Michael F. *academic administrator, medical educator*
Delorey, John Francis *music educator*
DiIorio, Alexander L. *biomedical engineer, director*
D'Lugo, Carol Clark *language educator*
Donnelly, James Corcoran, Jr. *lawyer*
Downs, Timothy John *environmental scientist, educator*
Drachman, David Alexander *neurologist*
Dunlap, Ellen S. *library administrator*
Dyer-Cole, Pauline *school psychologist, educator*
Edmonds, Regina Margaret *psychology professor*
Eppinger, Frederick H., Jr. *insurance company executive*
Felice, Marianne Elizabeth *pediatrician, educator*
Flotte, Terence Robin *dean, researcher, medical educator*
Greenberg, Nathan *accountant*
Hangen, Tona J. *history professor*
Harper, Doreen C. *nursing educator*
Hatfield, Renee S.J. *music educator*
Heman, Robert Jerome, Jr. *printing company executive, retired association executive*
Huang, Xinming *science educator*
Huber, J. Kendall *lawyer, insurance company executive*
Indic, Premananda *education educator, researcher*
Irwin, Richard Stephen *physician, scientist, educator*
Katz, Robert Nathan *ceramics engineer, educator*
Kearney, Kevin Robert *biochemist, educato, researcher*
Kerns, Christian Randolph *retired chemist*
Kirschner, Suzanne R. *psychology professor*
Koehler, Stephan A. *physics professor*
Kothare, Sanjeev Vithal *pediatrician*
Lamothe, Donat Romeo *music educator*
Lukes, Konstantina B. *Mayor, Worcester, Massachusetts, lawyer*
Luna, Elizabeth (Jean) *cell biologist, educator, researcher*
Malone, Joseph James *mathematics professor, researcher*
Mardilovich, Ivan P. *education educator, researcher*
Mathisen, Howard *psychologist, educator, minister*
McAvey, Marion Sheila *college professor, editor*
McCorison, Marcus Allen *librarian, cultural organization administrator*
McDaniels, Darryl (D.M.C.) *rap artist*
McFarland, Michael C. *academic administrator*
McManus, Robert Joseph *bishop*
Mello, Craig C. *molecular medicine educator, researcher*
Merken, Melvin *chemistry professor*
Mirick, John O. *lawyer*
Morse, Leonard J. *epidemiologist, public health service officer*
Newburger, Peter E. *hematologist, oncologist*
Parsons, Edwin Spencer *clergyman, educator*
Pitcher, Stephen M. *finance company executive, museum director*
Reilly, Daniel Patrick *bishop emeritus*
Savageau, Judith A. *epidemiologist, researcher*
Schmitt, Richard *philosopher, educator*
Schofield, Edmund Acton, Jr. *botanist, academic administrator, conservationist, writer*
Selin, Lisa K. *physician*
Stempsey, William Edward *medical philosopher*
Stutz, Cathleen Kinsella *education educator*
Swanson, Richard Sprague *oncologist, surgeon*
Uhl, Christopher Martin *lawyer*
van den Berg, Bert *biology professor, researcher*
Van Nostrand, Richard Charles *lawyer*
Vaughan, Alden True *history professor*
Vicuña, Maximo Quintiliano *retired language educator*
Wachholtz, Amy B. *psychologist, educator*
Welu, James A. *museum director*
Wilbur, Leslie Clifford *mechanical engineering educator*
Young, Stephen Bernard *urogynecologist, surgeon*
Zalosh, Robert Geoffrey *engineering educator*
Zeugner, John Finn *historian, educator, writer*
Zurier, Robert Burton *rheumatology educator*

Worthington

Bagg, Robert Ely *poet, educator, translator*
Schrade, Rolande Maxwell Young *composer, pianist, educator*

Wrentham

Bittenbender, Brad James *safety engineer*

Yarmouth Port

Gordon, Benjamin Dichter *pediatrician, health facility administrator, educator*
Hall, James Frederick *retired college president*
LeBaron, Francis Newton *retired biochemistry educator*
Stott, Thomas Edward, Jr. *retired engineering executive*
Weiner, Charles *historian, educator*

MICHIGAN

Ada

Lyall, Lynn *consumer products company executive*
Mason, James Hamilton *surgeon*
Mohr, Michael Arthur *lawyer*
Weiss, Joseph Joel *consulting company executive*

Adrian

Bleam, Sheri Reeves *communication educator, consultant*
Dodson, John Thomas *orchestra conductor*
Geyer, Richard Douglas *librarian, editor, poet*
Husband, Robert Wayne *retired, biology educator*
Lamprecht, Elizabeth Ann *mathematics professor*
McGuire, Sharon, Sr. *nursing educator*

Albion

Balke, Maureen A. *voice educator*
Lyons-Sobaski, Sheila A. *biology professor*
Myers, Perry W. *language educator*
Taylor, Lawrence Dow *geologist, educator*

Allegan

Gerl, Robert Raymond *psychologist, priest*

Allen Park

Bizon, Emma Djafar *management consultant*
Culpepper, Daunte *professional football player*
Cunningham, Gunther *professional football coach*
Hanson, Jason Douglas *professional football player*
Johnson, Calvin *professional football player*
Linehan, Scott Thomas *professional football coach*
Mayhew, Martin R. *professional sports team executive, retired professional football player*
Schwartz, Jim *professional football coach*
Stafford, Matt (John Matthew Stafford) *professional football player*

Allendale

Alexander, John K. *philosopher, educator*
Benjamin, Craig Gordon *history professor*
Gipson, Karen *physics professor*
Haas, Thomas Joseph *academic administrator, chemistry educator*
Murray, Diane Elizabeth *librarian*
Rayor, Diane Jill *classics educator*
Sun, Wanxiao *remote sensing educator*
Thogerson, Mark T. *biology professor, consultant*

Alma

Baleja, Gregory *marketing educator*
Beattie, Thomas Irving *physics professor*
Henry, David L. *political science educator, researcher*
Oemke, Mark Paul *biology professor, researcher*

Alpena

Hunter, Mark John *lawyer, photographer*
McLarney-Vesotski, Amber Renee *psychology professor*
Walchak, Karol Lynn *literature and language professor, department chairman*

Ann Arbor

Abrams, Gerald David *pathologist, educator*
Adams, James Charles *lawyer*
Adriaens, Peter *environmental engineer, consultant*
Agranoff, Bernard William *biochemist, educator*
Akcasu, Ahmet Ziyaeddin *nuclear engineer, educator*
Akerlof, Carl William *physics professor*
Akhoury, Ratindranath *physics professor, researcher*
Akil, Huda *neuroscientist, educator, researcher*
Akin, Cem *internist, allergist, medical researcher*
Allen, Geri A. *composer, pianist*
Allen, Layman Edward *law educator, research scientist*
Alterman, Eddie *editor-in-chief, writer*
Anderson, Austin Gothard *lawyer, consultant, academic administrator*
Annchild, Cynthia *educational consultant*
Ansbacher, Rudi *physician*
Arlinghaus, Sandra Judith Lach *mathematical geographer, educator*
Armstrong, Kenneth Howard *retail executive*
Arnedt, John Todd *psychologist, educator*
Ascione, Frank Joseph *dean, pharmacy educator*
Asso, Paolo *ancient language educator*
Atreya, Sushil Kumar *planetary-space science educator, astrophysicist*
Axelrod, Robert Marshall *political science and public policy educator*
Bacon, George Edgar *retired pediatrician*
Baker, Shan Ray *medical educator*
Baler, Blanche Kimoto *retired child psychiatrist*
Balkrishnan, Rajesh *education educator*
Barald, Katharine Francesca *developmental molecular neurobiologist, biochemist*
Barsan, William George *emergency physician*
Bartell, Lawrence Sims *chemist, educator*
Bates, Eric Randolph *physician, educator*
Bayatpur, Farhad *research scientist*
Beaubien, Anne Kathleen *librarian*
Beaver, Frank Eugene *critic, historian*
Becher, William Don *retired electrical engineer, educator, writer*
Beckley, Robert Mark *architect, educator*
Beeton, Alfred Merle *lab administrator, director, biologist, educator, environmentalist*
Behling, Charles Frederick *psychologist, educator*
Belcher, Louis David *marketing professional, retired mayor*
Bergin, Edwin Anthony *astrophysicist, educator*
Berguer, Ramon *medical educator*
Bhattacharya, Pallab Kumar *electrical engineering educator, researcher*
Bierbaum, Rosina M. *federal agency administrator*
Bierley, Mark Russell *retail executive*
Biro, Matthew *art educator, consultant*
Blinder, Seymour Michael *chemistry and physics professor, researcher*
Blome, Andrea *finance educator*
Bloom, David Alan *pediatric urology educator, department chairman*
Bloom, Jane Maginnis *emergency physician*
Blouin, Francis Xavier, Jr. *history professor*
Blum, James Marlow *medical educator, researcher*
Blumenthal, Jane Leonardi *library director*
Bolcom, William Elden *composer, educator, musician*
Bolling, Steven Fredric *cardiac surgeon, educator*
Bowdler, Anthony John *internist, educator*
Boxer, Laurence Alan *physician, research educator*
Brandon, David A. *food service executive*
Brick, Howard *historian*
Brown, Donald Robert *psychology professor*
Brown, Miranda Dympna *language educator*
Bruffett, Stephen L. *trucking executive*
Buckley, Francis J., Jr. *librarian*
Buesser, Anthony Carpenter *lawyer*
Burdi, Alphonse Rocco *anatomist*
Burns, Mark *engineering educator*
Cadigan, Kenneth Michael *science educator*
Cain, Albert Clifford *psychologist, educator*
Caminker, Evan H. *dean, law educator*
Carey, Thomas E. *medical educator, researcher*
Carlson, Bruce Martin *anatomist*
Carlson, Martha Diane *neurologist*
Carney, Thomas Daly *lawyer*
Casey, Kenneth Lyman *neurologist*
Chambers, Leigh Ross (Ross Chambers) *French and comparative language educator*
Chang, Chun-Shu *historian, educator, writer*
Charpie, John *medical educator*
Chervin, Ronald David *neurology educator*
Chey, William D *physician, researcher*
Chinnaiyan, Arul M. *pathologist, researcher*
Clark, John Alden *mechanical engineering educator*
Clark, Noreen Morrison *behavioral science educator, researcher*
Clemens, J. Quentin *urologist, educator*
Cochran, Kenneth William *toxicologist*
Cohen, Malcolm Stuart *economist*
Cole, David Edward *automotive executive, educator*
Collins, Susan Margaret *dean, political science professor*
Cooper, Edward Hayes *lawyer, educator*
Courant, Paul Noah *university librarian, economist, educator*
Coward, James Kenderdine *chemist*
Cowen, Roy Chadwell, Jr. *language educator*
Crippen, Gordon Marvin *chemist*
Curl, Rane Locke *chemical engineering educator, consultant*
Curley, Edwin Munson *philosophy educator*
Darlow, Julia Donovan *lawyer*
Daub, Peggy Ellen *library administrator*
Davis, Robert Leach *retired federal official*
Dawson, William Ryan *zoology educator*
Decker, Raymond Frank *chemicals and metal products executive*
Dekker, Eugene Earl *biochemistry educator*
Delbanco, Nicholas Franklin *language educator, writer*
Desai, Kashappa Goud *pharmaceutical executive, researcher*
DeVine, Edmond Francis *retired lawyer*
Diana, Joseph A. *retired foundation executive*
Dick, Macdonald, II, *pediatrician*
Dickinson, Chris John *gastroenterologist, director*
Didier, Elaine K. *library and museum director, educator*
DiMagno, Matthew J. *medical educator*
Dolan, Robert J. *dean*
Dominguez, Kathryn Mary *economist, educator*
Domino, Edward Felix *physician, clinical pharmacologist, educator*
Dormire, Sharon Lee *nurse, nursing educator*
Dougherty, Richard Martin *library and information science professor*
Doyle, Constance Talcott Johnston *physician, medical association administrator, educator*
Drach, John Charles *research scientist, educator*
Drake, John Warren *aviation consultant*
Driscoll, John C., Jr. *publishing executive*
Dunlap, Connie *librarian*
Dunnigan, Brian Leigh *historian, curator*
Duquette, Donald Norman *law educator*
Duren, Peter Larkin *mathematician, educator*
Eber, Robert Michael *dental educator, periodontist*
Eckstein, Peter Charles *retired labor union economist*
Eggertsen, John Hale *lawyer*
Eisenberg, Marvin Julius *retired art history educator*
Eisendrath, Charles Rice *journalism educator, farmer, consultant*
Eisenstein, Elizabeth Lewisohn *historian, educator*
Elder, James Tilford *dermatologist, educator*
El-Kattan, Ayman Fawzi *pharmacist, researcher*
Ellmann, Douglas Stanley *lawyer*
England, Anthony Wayne *engineering and science educator, dean*
Ewing, Rodney Charles *mineralogist, geology educator, materials scientist*
Fajans, Stefan Stanislaus *retired internist*
Farmer, Cheryl Christine *internist, industrial hygienist*
Farrand, William Richard *retired geology educator*
Faulkner, John Arthur *physiologist, educator*
Ferrell, Robert Hugh *historian, educator*
Fetters, Michael Derwin *medical educator, director*
Feuerwerker, Albert *historian, educator*
Fink, William Lee *ichthyologist, systematist*
Fisk, Lennard Ayres *physicist, researcher*
Fleming, Suzanne Marie *academic administrator, freelance/self-employed writer*
Foley, Daniel Ronald *retired personnel director, lawyer*
Ford, Betty Ann (Elizabeth Ann Ford) *former First Lady of the United States, health facility executive*
Forsyth, Ilene Haering *art historian*
Fox, David Alan *rheumatologist, immunologist*
Frey, William H. *demographer, educator*
Friedmann, Peretz Peter *aerospace engineer, educator*
Garcia-Guzman, Luis M. *research scientist, educator*
Garris, Michael Jack *lawyer*
Garton, Hugh J.L. *neurosurgeon, educator*
Gelehrter, Thomas David *medical educator, geneticist*
Gelman, Susan A. *psychology professor*
Ghannad Rezaie, Mostafa *research scientist*
Ghaziuddin, Mohammad *psychiatrist, educator*
Gibala, Ronald *metallurgical engineering educator*
Gikas, Paul William *medical educator*
Gilchrist, Brian E. *engineering educator, department chairman*
Gilman, Sid *neurologist*
Ginsburg, David *genetics educator, researcher*
Gloeckner, Phoebe Louise *cartoonist, author, illustrator*
Gray, Whitmore *lawyer, educator*
Grbic, Anthony *engineering educator*
Greenwood, Donald Theodore *retired aerospace engineering educator*
Gregerson, Linda Karen *poet, language educator, critic*
Griffin, Henry Claude *retired chemistry professor*
Gross, Barry H. *radiologist, educator*
Guy, Ralph B., Jr. *federal judge*
Hackett, Roger Fleming *historian, educator*
Haefner, Don Paul *retired psychology educator*
Harlow, Siobán D. *medical educator, consultant*
Hayes, John Patrick *electrical engineering and computer science educator, consultant*
He, Pingan *systems engineer*
Helvie, Mark Alan *radiologist, educator*
Hessler, David William *information and multimedia systems educator*
Hill, Bruce Marvin *statistician, educator*
Himle, Joseph Alan *social sciences educator*
Hinshaw, Ada Sue *nursing educator, former dean*
Hollenberg, Paul Frederick *pharmacology educator*
Holoshitz, Joseph *medical educator*
Horowitz, Samuel Boris *biomedical researcher, educational consultant*
House, Christopher *economics professor*
House, James Stephen *social psychologist, educator*
Humes, Harvey David *nephrologist, educator, director*
Hurvitz, Edward A. *physiatrist*
Hyzy, Robert Curtis *medical educator*
Izzo, Herbert John *language and linguistics educator, researcher*
Jackson, James Sidney *psychologist, educator*
Jackson, John Edgar *social scientist, educator, researcher*
Janko, Richard Charles Murray *humanities educator*
Jarrahi, Mona *engineering educator, researcher*
Johnston, Lloyd Douglas *social sciences educator*
Jones, Lawrence William *retired physicist*
Jonsson, Mattias *mathematics professor*
Joscelyn, Kent Buckley *lawyer*
Kahana, Alon *ophthalmologist, educator*
Kahn, Douglas Allen *law educator*
Kakarala, Madhuri *oncologist*
Kalbfleisch, John David *statistics educator*
Kaminski, Mark Stefan *medical educator*
Kamisar, Yale *lawyer, educator*
Kane, Gordon Leon *physics researcher and educator*
Kaplow, Julie B. *psychologist, educator*
Kapuscinski, Roman *business educator*
Kasapis, Christos *cardiologist*
Kaufman, Peter Bishop *biological sciences educator*
Kauper, Thomas Eugene *lawyer, educator*
Kelch, Robert Paul *former dean, pediatric endocrinologist*
Kelly, Raymond Case *anthropology educator*
Kennedy, David Boyd *foundation executive, lawyer*
Keppelman, Nancy *lawyer*
Keshamouni, Venkateshwar G. *medical educator*
Kesler, Stephen Edward *geology educator*
Ketefian, Shaké *nursing educator*
Kim, E. Han *financial economist, educator*
Kingdon, John Wells *political science professor*
Kirakosyan, Ara *research scientist*
Kitko, Carrie L. *medical educator*
Knott, John Ray, Jr. *language educator*
Kopelman, Raoul *chemist, physicist, educator*
Kopinski, Keith Lowell *art director, educator*
Kozma, Adam *electrical engineer*
Kramer, Elke *small business owner*
Krier, James Edward *law educator, writer*
Krimm, Samuel *physicist, researcher, educator, administrator*
Krisch, Alan David *physics professor*
Kubek, Anne Marie *retail executive*
Kucich, John Richard *English language educator*
Kuhl, David Edmund *nuclear medicine physician, educator*
Kumon, Ronald Edward *biomedical engineer, researcher*
Kurabayashi, Katsuo *engineering educator*
Lach, Alma Elizabeth *food and cooking writer, consultant*
Lawrence, Theodore S. *oncologist, educator*
Laycock, Harold Douglas *law educator, writer*
Lazarsfeld, Robert Kendall *mathematician, educator*
Leabo, Dick A. *retired statistics educator*
Lee, John Chaeseung *nuclear engineering educator*
Lee, Juseop *electronics engineer, researcher*
Lee, Theresa M. *psychology professor, department chairman*
Levine, John E. *pediatrician, director*
Levitsky, Melvyn *former ambassador*
Lichter, Paul Richard *ophthalmology educator*
Lin, Hai *physicist*
Lindsay, June Campbell McKee *communications executive*
Lok, Anna Suk-Fong *medical educator*
Longone, Daniel Thomas *chemistry professor*
Lorenzon, Wolfgang B. *physics professor, researcher*
Low, Malcolm James *research scientist*
Ludgate, Mathew William *medical educator*
Lupia, Arthur W. *political science educator*
Lyons, Harvey Isaac *mechanical engineering educator*
MacKinnon, Catharine Alice *lawyer, educator, writer*
Magee, John C. *surgeon, educator*
Marcus, Joyce (Joyce Marcus Flannery) *anthropology educator*
Maren, Stephen *neuroscientist, psychologist, educator*
Margolis, Philip Marcus *psychiatrist, educator*
Markel, Howard *physician, educator*
Markovits, Andrei Steven *political science professor*
Marshall, Ron *retail executive*
Martin, Claude Raymond, Jr. *marketing consultant, educator*
Martin, David Charles *materials science engineering educator*

Martin, William Russell *nuclear engineering educator*
McCarus, Ernest Nasseph *retired language educator*
McCormack, Terry R. *automotive executive*
McGuire, Richard (Mick McGuire) *retail executive*
McKenna, Barbara J. *clinical pathologist*
Menon, Ram Kumar *neurosurgeon, consultant*
Merchant, Juanita Lynne *gastroenterologist, educator*
Mersereau, John, Jr. *literature and language professor*
Merte, Herman, Jr. *mechanical engineering educator*
Meyer, John Frederick *engineering educator*
Meyers, Philip Alan *geochemistry educator, researcher*
Mian, Shahzad *ophthalmologist*
Miller, William Ian *law educator*
Mitchell, Edward John *economist, retired educator*
Mitchiner, James C. *emergency physician*
Mizruchi, Mark Sheldon *sociology professor, business administration professor*
Modell, Stephen Mark *medical researcher, educator*
Monto, Arnold Simon *epidemiology educator*
Moore, Thomas Edwin *biologist, educator, museum director*
Mounts, L. David *food service executive*
Moyer, Jeffrey S. *plastic surgeon, educator*
Munro, Donald Jacques *philosopher, educator*
Munson, David C. *computer engineer, educator, dean*
Napolitano, Lena Marie *surgeon, educator*
Nelson, Roy Jay *retired French educator*
Newman, Lisa Ann *surgical oncologist*
Nordman, Christer Eric *chemistry professor*
Nori, Franco Mauro *physicist, researcher*
Norton, Edward C. *economist, educator*
Nriagu, Jerome Okon *environmental geochemist*
Oakley, Deborah Jane *educator*
Oliver, William John *pediatrician, educator*
Omenn, Gilbert Stanley *academic administrator, internist, scientist*
Orringer, Jeffrey S. *dermatologist, educator*
Pan, Xiaoqing *materials scientist, educator*
Parkinson, William Charles *physics professor, researcher*
Parsons, Jeffrey Robinson *anthropologist, educator*
Parsons, Michael Gene *engineering educator*
Patil, Parag G. *neurosurgeon, educator*
Paul, Ara Garo *university dean*
Paxton, Tom *songwriter, entertainer, author*
Pedley, John Griffiths *archaeologist, educator*
Pehlke, Robert Donald *materials and metallurgical engineering educator*
Peng Chen, Hsiu-Hui *music educator*
Pescovitz, Ora Hirsch *health facility administrator, medical educator*
Petrick, Ernest Nicholas *mechanical engineer, researcher*
Petty, Elizabeth Marie *geneticist*
Pitt, Bertram *cardiologist, educator, consultant*
Platt, Jeffrey Louis *experimental surgeon, immunologist, pediatric nephrologist, educator*
Polverini, Peter J. *dean, dental educator*
Potempa, Kathleen M. *dean, nursing educator*
Powell, Kenneth Grant *aerospace engineering educator*
Powsner, Edward Raphael *physician*
Prahalad, C.K. *finance educator, corporate strategist*
Rabkin, Eric S. *English educator*
Radin, Margaret Jane *law educator*
Reed, John Wesley *lawyer, educator*
Reed, Joseph Duffield *ancient language educator*
Rees, Riley *medical educator*
Regan, Donald H. *law educator*
Richardson, Rudy James *toxicology and neurosciences educator*
Robbins, Jerry Hal *educational administration educator*
Roberts, J. Scott *psychologist, educator*
Rodríguez, María Isabel *literature and language professor*
Rodriguez, Rich *college football coach*
Roe, Byron Paul *physics professor*
Rogers, Bryan Leigh *dean, artist, educator*
Romani, John Henry *health science association administrator, educator*
Rosenthal, Amnon *pediatric cardiologist*
Ryan, Marianne Elizabeth *lawyer*
Sagher, Oren *neurosurgeon*
Sahiner, Berkman *science administrator, educator*
St. Antoine, Theodore Joseph *retired law educator, arbitrator*
Saitou, Kazuhiro *engineering educator*
Salant, Stephen Walter *economics professor, researcher*
Saltiel, Alan Robert *biochemist*
Sandalow, Terrance *law educator*
Saper, Joel R. *neurologist, educator*
Sasson, Comilla *medical researcher*
Scarnecchia, Suellyn *academic administrator, lawyer*
Scavarda, Donald Robert *composer, artist*
Schacht, Jochen Heinrich *biochemistry educator*
Schmitz, Philip Charles *editor, researcher*
Schottenfeld, David *retired epidemiologist, educator*
Schwenk, Thomas L. *physician*
Scott, Norman Ross *electrical engineering educator*
Scott, Rebecca J. *law and history educator*
Senior, Thomas Bryan A. *electrical engineering educator, researcher, consultant*
Shah, Rajal B. *pathologist*
Shanley, Thomas Patrick *medical educator*
Shapiro, Matthew David *economist, educator*
Shatz, Marilyn Joyce *psychologist, educator*
Sheldon, Ingrid Kristina *retired mayor, controller*
Shewach, Donna S. *pharmacologist, educator*
Shulman, Michael Eben *psychoanalyst, psychologist, consultant*
Simpson, A.W. Brian *law educator*
Skerlos, Steven John *engineering educator*
Sloan, Herbert Elias *physician, surgeon*
Smith, Daniel T. *retail executive*
Smith, Donald Cameron *retired preventive medicine physician*
Sobel, Alan *electrical engineer, physicist*
Solomon, Richard *pediatrician*
Sowers, MaryFran *epidemiologist, gynecologist, educator*
Stafford, Frank Peter, Jr. *economics professor, consultant*
Stanley, James Charles *vascular surgeon*
Stecke, Kathryn Elizabeth *operations management educator*
Steel, Duncan Gregory *engineering educator*
Stein, Eric *retired law educator*
Steward, James Christen *museum director, educator*
Strang, Ruth Hancock *pediatrician, cardiologist, priest, educator*
Strong, Douglas L. *health facility administrator*
Sullivan, Teresa Ann *law and sociology educator, academic administrator*
Suny, Ronald Grigor *political science professor, history professor*
Surovell, Edward David *real estate company executive*
Tanay, Emanuel *psychiatry professor, writer*
Taylor, Stephan F. *psychiatrist, educator*
Theut, C. Peter *lawyer*
Thoburn, Elisabeth Z. *humanities educator*
Thompson, Norman Winslow *surgeon, educator*
Thornton, Arland *sociologist, educator*
Thornton, Jonathan Mills *history professor*
Tkacheva, Olesya *political scientist*
Todd, Robert Franklin III *oncologist, educator*
Tomozawa, Yukio *retired physics professor*
Tosney, Kathryn W. *embryologist, biology educator*
Trautmann, Thomas Roger *history professor, anthropology educator*
Tsebelis, George *political science professor*
Turke, Paul William *pediatrician, anthropologist*
Ulaby, Fawwaz Tayssir *academic administrator, engineering educator*
Ulsoy, Ali Galip *engineering educator*
Van der Voo, Rob *geophysicist*
Vazquez, Delia M. *psychology professor, director*
Veltman, Martinus J.G. *retired physics educator*
Verrett, Shirley *soprano*
Vielmetti, Edward Marshall *webmaster*
Villaruel, Antonia M. *nursing educator*
Vining, (George) Joseph *law educator*
Waggoner, Lawrence William *law educator*
Waltz, Susan *political scientist, educator*
Warner, Kenneth E(dgar) *dean, public health educator, consultant*
Warren, Jane Carol *psychologist*
Webber, Bonny A. *educational consultant*
Weg, John Gerard *physician*
Wei, John Thomas *urologist, educator*
White, Dawn Roberta *energy executive*
White, James Boyd *law educator*
Whitman, Marina von Neumann *economist, educator*
Wicha, Max S. *oncologist, educator*
Williams, David R. *sociologist, educator, senior research scientist*
Williams, John Andrew *physiology researcher, educator*
Williams, Melvin Donald *anthropologist, educator*
Wilson, Richard Christian *engineering firm executive*
Withey, Jeffrey Howard *molecular biologist, researcher*
Wolf, Timothy Van de Wint *food products executive*
Wong, Sandra Lynn *oncologist, educator*
Woodroofe, Michael Barrett *mathematics and statistics professor*
Woolliscroft, James O. *dean, medical educator*
Wright, Steven Jay *environmental engineering educator, consultant*
Yagle, Andrew Emil *engineering educator*
Yang, Ralph Tzu-Bow *chemical engineer, educator*
Yen, Louis *research scientist*
Young, Edwin Harold *chemical and metallurgical engineering educator*
Young, Yin Lu *engineering educator*
Zhang, Youxue *geology educator*
Zhu, Ji *science educator*
Ziff, Robert Michael *engineering educator*
Zivin, Kara *psychiatry professor, researcher*
Zucker, Robert A(lpert) *psychologist*

Auburn Hills
Accavitti, Michael J. *automotive executive*
Beals, Randy S. *materials engineer*
Bembas, Catherine Hagan *literature and language professor*
Boag, Simon *automotive executive*
Brown, Kwame *professional basketball player*
Campi, John Paul *automotive executive*
Davidson, Karen W. *professional sports team executive*
Dumars, Joe III *professional sports team executive, retired professional basketball player*
Ebeid, Russell Joseph *glass manufacturing executive*
Etefia, Florence Victoria *retired school psychologist*
Ewasyshyn, Frank Joseph *automotive executive*
Farrar, Stephen Prescott *glass products manufacturing executive*
Fong, Peter L. *automotive executive*
Ford, Cheryl *professional basketball player*
Gasparovic, John J. *lawyer*
Gerson, Ralph Joseph *manufacturing executive*
Gordon, Ben *professional basketball player*
Gorlier, Pietro *automotive executive*
Hamilton, Richard Clay *professional basketball player*
Hill, Brian A. *professional basketball coach*
Knight, Jeffrey Alan *corporate financial executive*
Kuester, John *professional basketball coach*
Leese, Holly Elisabeth *lawyer, automotive company executive*
Mahorn, Rick (Derrick Allen Mahorn) *professional basketball coach, retired professional basketball player*
Malanga, Michael Thomas *research scientist*
Manganello, Timothy M. *auto parts company executive*
Manley, Michael *automotive executive*
Meyer, Deborah Wahl *automotive executive*
Nolan, Deanna Nicole *professional basketball player*
Ostfield, Alan *professional sports team executive*
Perry, Scott *professional sports team executive*
Press, Jim (James E. Press) *automotive executive*
Prince, Tayshaun Durell *professional basketball player*
Rae, Nancy Ann *automotive executive*
Smith, Katie (Katherine May Smith) *professional basketball player*
Unger, Susan J. *automotive executive*
Wallace, Ben *professional basketball player*
Wilson, Thomas S. *professional sports team executive*
Wu, Ming-Cheng *research scientist*

Bad Axe
Sullivan, James Gerald *small business owner*

Baroda
Reckline, Sigmund Joseph *publishing executive, editor*

Battle Creek
Baldwin, Susan Olin *commissioner, management consultant*
Bryant, John A. *food products executive*
Jenness, James M. *food products executive*
Mackay, David (A.D. David Mackay) *food products executive*
Matthews, Wyhomme S. *retired music educator, academic administrator*
Overton-Adkins, Betty Jean *foundation administrator*
Pilnick, Gary H. *food products executive, lawyer*
Speirn, Sterling K. *foundation administrator*
Wright, Judy A. *science educator*

Bay City
Boylan, Winnifred Padden *lawyer*
Hiner, John Patrick *newspaper editor*
Ludington, Thomas Lamson *federal judge*
Powers, David Louis *lawyer*

Belleville
Quigley, William G. *automotive supplier company executive*
Schaefer, James Theodore *writer, editor, educator*
Stebbins, Donald J. *car parts manufacturing company executive*
Wilson, David James *chemistry researcher, educator*

Benton Harbor
Binkley, David A. *human resources specialist*
Brown, Mark E. *manufacturing executive*
Fettig, Jeff M. *manufacturing executive*
Hopp, Daniel Frederick *lawyer, manufacturing company executive*
Templin, Roy W. *manufacturing executive*
Todman, Michael A. *manufacturing executive*

Berrien Springs
Agoki, George Sammy *engineering educator, director*
Bryson, Jeanette Patricia *literature and language professor, director*
Hamel, Lorie Ann *psychologist*
Lesher, William Richard *retired academic administrator*
Murray-Nseula, Marlene *educator*
O'Reggio, Trevor Evan *history professor*
Ritzenthaler, Beatriz Augusta *musician, educator*

Beulah
Auch, Walter Edward *security firm executive*
Edwards, Wallace Winfield *retired automotive executive*
Tanner, Helen Hornbeck *historian, consultant*

Beverly Hills
Castle, Maurice Emmett *orthopedist, surgeon*
Pardington, Mary Elizabeth *elementary school educator*

Big Rapids
Konovalov, Yuri *librarian, educator*
McLean, Roy L. *economics professor*
Ryan, Ray Darl, Jr. *academic administrator*
Westman, Craig Ellery *academic administrator*

Bingham Farms
Giles, Conrad Leslie *ophthalmic surgeon*
Goren, Steven Eliot *lawyer*

Birmingham
Auld, Frank *psychologist, educator*
Custer, Martha Lou *library director*
Edwards, Michael Gerard *physician*
Elsman, James Leonard, Jr. *lawyer*
Foxen, Richard William *manufacturing executive*
Hammami, Mouhanad *pediatrician*
Kienbaum, Thomas Gerd *lawyer*
Maxwell, Jack Erwin *manufacturing executive*
McCuen, John Joachim *columnist, educator, US military counterinsurgery and hybrid war consultant*
Sharf, Stephan *automotive executive*
Shields, Robert Emmet *merchant banker, lawyer*

Bloomfield Hills
Adams, Charles Francis *advertising and real estate company executive*
Banas, C(hristine) Leslie *lawyer*
Bauser, Nancy *social worker, disability life coach*
Berline, James H. *advertising and public relations executive*
Birnkrant, Sherwin Maurice *lawyer*
Bogas, Kathleen Laura *lawyer*
Brent, Robert Lewis *urologist*
Burnett, Patricia Hill *artist, educator*
Burstein, Richard Joel *lawyer*
Charla, Leonard Francis *lawyer, publishing executive*
Clippert, Charles Frederick *lawyer*
Coburn, Ronald Murray *ophthalmologist, surgeon*
Cook, Steven M. *lawyer, construction executive*
Cregg, Roger A. *construction executive*
Dawson, Stephen Everette *lawyer*
Dugas, Richard J., Jr. *construction executive*
Eller, Timothy R. *construction and real estate company executive*
Ellinghausen, James R. *construction executive*
Galante, Jerome Anthony *lawyer*
Googasian, George Ara *lawyer*
Haynes, Jeffrey Kennard *lawyer*
Jurkiewicz, Mary Louise *elementary school educator*
Kanter, Alan Michael *lawyer*
Kasischke, Louis Walter *lawyer*
Keane, Peter J. *construction executive*
Kirk, John MacGregor *lawyer*
Kurnick, Robert H., Jr. *automotive executive, lawyer*
Lapadot, Sonee Spinner *retired automobile manufacturing company official*
Ledwidge, Patrick Joseph *lawyer*
LoPrete, James Hugh *lawyer*
Mathog, Robert Henry *otolaryngologist, educator*
Mc Gehee, H. Coleman, Jr., (Harry Coleman McGhhe) *retired bishop*
Meyer, George Herbert *lawyer*
Norris, John Hart *lawyer, director*
O'Hara, John Paul III *orthopedic surgeon*
O'Shaughnessy, Robert T. *automotive executive*
Petruska, Steven C. *construction executive*
Pickard, William Frank *plastics company executive*
Poth, Stefan Michael *retired diversified financial services company executive*
Pulte, William J. *retired construction executive*
Rader, Ralph Terrance *lawyer*
Randall, Chandler Corydon *theologian*
Robinson, Jack Albert *retail executive*
Robinson, Logan Gilmore *lawyer*
Sandy, William Haskell *training and communication systems executive*
Simon, Evelyn *lawyer*
Smith, H(arold) Lawrence *lawyer*
Snyder, George Edward *lawyer*
Solomon, Mark Raymond *lawyer, educator*
Spradlin, Shane M. *lawyer, automotive executive*
Swift, Jonathan *television personality, educator*
Syme, Daniel Bailey *rabbi, institution executive*
Trojniak, Duane *marketing executive, consultant*
Weil, John William *technology management consultant*
Wittkopp, Gregory Mark *museum director*

Brighton
Clark, Robert Thomas *ophthalmologist*
McDonald, Patrick Allen *lawyer, educator, arbitrator*
Wallack, Rina Evelyn *lawyer*

Brooklyn
Vischer, Harold Harry *manufacturing executive*

Canton
Reed, Gary Brian *publishing executive*

Caro
Hile, Michele Vera *middle school educator*

Cass City
Althaver, Lambert Ewing *manufacturing executive*
Reeder, Mike Fredrick *materials engineer, consultant*

Charlevoix
Miles, David Loren *museum director*

Charlotte
Coirolo, Christina *writer, author representative*

Chassell
Spain, James Dorris, Jr. *biochemist, educator*

Cheboygan
Ostrowski, Stacey *athletic trainer, educator*

Chelsea
Weinreich, Gabriel *physicist, minister, educator*

Clawson
Smith, Paulette Weatherwax *secondary school educator*

Clinton Township
Holland, Ruby Mae *social welfare administrator*
Rybicki, Stephen (Steve Rybicki) *librarian*

Commerce Township
Thibideau, Carolyn C. *musician, educator*

Davison
West, Stacy Kathlena *athletic trainer*

Dearborn
Al-Tawil, Hashim M. *art educator, researcher*
Ameri, Anan *museum director*
Bakaj, Joseph *automotive executive*
Bannister, Michael E. *automotive executive*
Beyer, Roberta Bonnie *dean, education professor, writer, researcher*
Biegun, Stephen E. *automotive executive*
Booth, Lewis W.K. *automotive company executive*
Brown, James Ward *mathematician, educator, author*
Brown, Thomas K. (Tony Brown) *automotive executive*
Cairns, James Robert *mechanical engineering educator*
Cape, James Odies E. *fashion designer*
Chock, David P. *sustainability and environmental scientist, educator*
Cischke, Susan Mary *automotive executive*
Claerr, Thomas A. *language educator*
Czubay, Ken *automotive executive*
Daniel, Peter J. *automotive executive*
Day, Raymond F. *automotive executive*
Essenmacher, Alan J. *engineering educator, researcher*
Farley, James D. (Jim Farley) *automotive executive, marketing professional*

Fields, Felicia J. automotive executive
Fields, Mark automotive executive
Ford, Bill (William Clay Ford Jr.) automotive company executive
Ford, Elena (Elena Anne Ford-Niarchos) automotive industry executive
Ford, William Clay automotive and professional sports team executive
Fowler, Bennie W. automotive executive
Graziano, Robert automotive executive
Harris, John Fitgerald lawyer
Hazel, Darryl Barton automotive executive
Hinrichs, Joseph R. automotive executive
Hogan, Brian Joseph editor
Irving, Patrice Marie nursing educator
Kahn, Mark Leo arbitrator, educator
Kahveci, Nazli Eylem electrical engineer, researcher
Kiska, Timothy Olin communications educator, radio producer
Kuzak, Derrick M. automotive executive
Larionov, Igor (Igor Nikolayevich Larionov) retired professional hockey player
Leitch, David G. automotive executive, lawyer
Little, Robert Eugene engineering educator
Macfarlane, Ken automotive executive
Mascarenas, Paul A. automotive executive
Mays, J. C. automotive executive
Mooradian, Patricia museum administrator
Mulally, Alan R. automotive company executive, former aerospace company executive
Mulloy, Martin J. automotive executive
Narula, Chaitanya Kumar research scientist
Nelson, Alison R. lawyer
Ohtani, Hiroko automotive professional
Ojakli, Ziad S. lobbyist, automotive executive
Papazian, Dennis Richard retired historian, educator, commentator
Powell, Ronald Rowe retired library science educator
Rahman, Ahmad A. history professor, writer
Samardzich, Barb automotive executive
Samfilippo, Chris Martin finance educator, consultant
Schloss, Neil M. automotive executive
Schmidt, Gerhard automotive executive
Shanks, Robert L. automotive executive
Shen, Jie engineering educator
Spender, Philip G. automotive executive
Sviggum, Ingvar automotive executive
Tetreault, James automotive executive
Tomlinson, Mark C. professional society administrator
Wang, Shengquan science educator
Zhu, Qiang education educator

Dearborn Heights

Ghrist, Catherine Ann religious organization administrator
Johns, Diana secondary school educator
Jordan, Theresa Anne Rose language educator

Detroit

Abramson, Hanley Norman pharmacy educator
Abt, Jeffrey art educator, art historian, artist, writer
Abu-Soud, Husam M. science educator
Adeyinka, Adewale geneticist, director
Anderson, Gerard M. energy executive
Anderson, Moses Bosco bishop emeritus
Andrews, Caesar editor
Anger, Paul newspaper editor
Archer, Dennis Wayne lawyer, former mayor
Auner, Gregory medical educator
Babcock, Mike professional hockey coach
Banerjee, Amit cell and molecular biologist
Banko, Bernadette Illona advertising executive
Barclay, Kathleen S. automotive executive
Barra, Mary Teresa automotive industry executive
Barrett, Nancy Smith academic administrator
Bartlett, Mark R. insurance company executive
Bassett, Tina communications executive
Battah, Hammam Jamil civil engineer, utilities executive
Baugh, Reginald Franz otolaryngologist
Baytarian, P. Jeffrey not-for-profit fundraiser
Beal, Graham William John museum director
Beierwaltes, William Howard physiologist, educator
Berg, Terrence G. prosecutor
Bertuzzi, Todd professional hockey player
Besarab, Anatole internist
Bilstrom, Jon Wayne lawyer
Bing, David Mayor, Detroit, metal products executive, retired professional basketball player
Bluth, Martin H. medical association administrator
Borst, Walter G. automotive executive
Braid, Ralph M. economics professor
Brake, Willie Edward computer company executive, educator
Brown, Gloria Diane elementary school educator
Browning, Jonathan automotive executive
Burns, Lawrence D. automotive executive
Buttermore, John R. automotive executive
Cabrera, Miguel (Jose Miguel Cabrera) professional baseball player
Cacace, Anthony T. audiologist, educator
Calarco, N. Joseph theater educator
Calkins, Stephen lawyer, educator
Callahan, J(ohn) William (Bill Callahan) judge
Campbell, Margaret L. adult nurse practitioner, researcher
Candler, James Nall, Jr. lawyer
Charfoos, Lawrence Selig lawyer
Chasdi, Richard J. political science professor
Chou, Clifford Chi Fong research engineering executive
Clarke, Troy Allen automotive executive
Cleveland, Sandra D. nursing educator
Cockrel, Sheila M. Councilwoman
Cohen, Norton Jacob lawyer
Cole, Kenneth W. automotive executive, lobbyist
Collins, Barbara-Rose Councilwoman
Collins, Christopher Brian musician
Coombs, Martyn pharmaceutical executive
Corrigan, Maura Denise state supreme court justice
Cothorn, John Arthur lawyer
Covensky, Edith language educator, poet
Cowger, Gary L. automotive executive
Cox, Sean F. federal judge
Cranmer, Thomas William lawyer
Cyprus, Nicholas Stanley automotive executive, accountant
Darr, Alan Phipps curator, historian
Das, Shuvra engineering educator
Datsyuk, Pavel professional hockey player
Datta, Sudip finance educator
Dauch, Richard E. automotive executive
Day, Burnis C. artist, educator
Deason, Herold McClure lawyer
de Molina, Alvaro G. finance company executive, former bank executive
DeMoss, Lisa S. lawyer, insurance company executive
DeSilvio, David Michael history professor
Devellano, Jim (James Charles Devellano) professional sports team executive
DiChiera, David opera company director
Draper, Kris professional hockey player
Drescher, Dennis George biochemist, researcher
Drutchas, Gregory G. lawyer
Dudley, Arthur, II, lawyer
Dunn, William Bradley lawyer
Earley, Anthony Francis, Jr. utilities company executive, lawyer
Edmunds, Nancy Garlock federal judge
Edwards, Brian Francis Peregrine science educator
Elder, Jack S. urologist, educator
Elisevich, Kost neurosurgeon
Ellyn, Lynne energy executive
Elster, William Lawrence history professor
Engelhardt, Regina cosmetologist, artist, small business owner
Everett, Nancy C. automotive executive
Feikens, John federal judge
Filppula, Valtteri professional hockey player
Fleming, George Robert psychologist
Flores, Daniel Ernest bishop
Forster, Carl-Peter automotive executive
Frade, Peter Daniel chemist, educator, administrator
Francis, Edward D. architect
Franzen, Johan professional hockey player
Fussell, Karen Marie social worker, protective services official
Genest, Theresa Joan lab technician
Gettelfinger, Ronald A. labor union administrator
Gillum, Roderick D. automotive executive
Glowacki, David finance educator
Godzak, Roman Paul archivist
Goodman, Allen Charles economist, educator
Granderson, Curtis, Jr. professional baseball player
Gray, Herman B. hospital administrator
Groves, Odessa Marie science educator
Gueyser, Teresa N. school system administrator, lawyer
Gumbleton, Thomas John bishop emeritus
Gupta, Suraj Narayan physicist, researcher
Hampton, Verne Churchill, II, lawyer
Hancock, Daniel M. automotive executive
Harris, Steven Jay automotive executive
Hashimoto, Ken dermatologist, educator
Henderson, Fritz (Frederick A. Henderson) automotive executive
Heppner, Gloria Hill research administrator, educator
Hoffmann, Peter M. science educator, director
Holland, Ken professional sports team executive
Holmstrom, Tomas professional hockey player
Howbert, Edgar Charles lawyer
Huang, Yinlun science educator
Huber, Chester A., Jr., (Chet Huber) automotive executive
Hudgel, David William allergist, immunologist, educator
Hudson, Anne Laurie librarian
Hyde, Charles Keith historian, educator
Ilitch, Marian professional hockey team and food service executive
Ilitch, Michael professional hockey team and food products executive
Issa, Diane Christine special education educator, consultant
Jackson, Linda Shorter nutritionist, educator
Jarvis, James Nelson pediatrician, rheumatologist
Johnson, Lester Larue, Jr. artist, educator
Joost-Gaugier, Christiane Louise art history educator
Karmanos, Peter, Jr. computer company executive, professional sports team executive
Keith, Damon Jerome federal judge
Kelley, Mark Albert physician, educator, health products executive
Kempston-Darkes, Maureen automotive executive
Kennedy, Cornelia Groefsema federal judge
Kenyatta, Kwame councilman
Kessler, Philip Joel lawyer
Khalid, Imran physician
Koerner, Edward C. automotive executive
Koo, Winston medical educator, pediatrician
Krsul, John Aloysius, Jr. lawyer
Kruse, Ronia information technology executive
Kummler, Ralph H. chemical engineer, educator, dean
Kyff, Kimberly elementary school educator
LaNeve, Mark R. automotive executive, marketing professional
Lauckner, Jonathan J. automotive executive
Lawrence, John Kidder lawyer
Lee, Timothy Eby automotive executive
Lerner, Stephen Alexander microbiologist, physician, educator
Leuchtman, Stephen Nathan lawyer
Levine, Steven Richard neurology educator, medical facility administrator
Lewis, David Baker lawyer
Lewis, Richard Alan neurologist, educator
Leyland, Jim (James Richard Leyland) professional baseball manager
Lidstrom, Nicklas professional hockey player
Lieblein, Grace D. automotive executive
Lim, Henry Wan-Peng dermatologist
Lin, Ho-Sheng surgeon, educator
Lisak, Robert Philip neurologist, researcher, educator
Little, Laura Ann elementary school educator, art educator
Lockman, Stuart M. lawyer
LoRusso, Patricia M. medical educator, director
Low, James Thomas marketing educator
Lowery, Elizabeth A. automotive executive
Lu, Guozhen mathematics professor
Lupulescu, Aurel Peter medical educator, researcher, physician
Lutz, Robert Anthony (Bob Lutz) automotive executive
MacDonald, Douglas Andrew psychologist, educator
Madgett, Naomi Long poet, editor, publisher, educator
Maida, Adam Joseph Cardinal cardinal, archbishop
Maiese, Kenneth neurologist, neuroscientist
Maltby, Kirk professional hockey player
Mamat, Frank Trustick lawyer
Mari, Giancarlo obstetrician, gynecologist, educator
Marsh, Harold Michael anesthesiologist
Martin, Michael Thomas humanities educator, writer
Mayeed, Mohammed engineering educator, researcher
M. B., Sahana materials scientist, researcher
McArthur, Steven Francis psychologist, educator
McCarty, Darren professional hockey player
McKim, Samuel John III lawyer
McWhorter, Sharon Louise engineering executive, inventor, consultant
Mehta, Ruby pediatric gastroenterologist
Meier, Frederick Augustus physician, director
Menon, Mani urological surgeon, educator
Mika, Joseph John library and information scientist, educator
Miller, Bruce Abraham lawyer
Miller, Orlando Jack obstetrician, gynecologist, educator, geneticist
Millikin, Michael P. lawyer, automotive executive
Mittal, Sandeep neurosurgeon, director
Mooney, Dennis M. automotive executive
Moore, Juanita museum administrator
Moss, Leslie Otha homeland security specialist
Mueckenheim, Robert Carl literature and language professor
Muir, William F. finance company executive
Munkarah, Adnan R medical educator, department chairman
Murphy, Stephen Joseph III federal judge, former prosecutor
Nabozny, Heather professional sports team groundskeeper
Nathanson, Saul David oncologist, surgeon, educator
Newman, Andrea Fischer air transportation executive
Njus, David Lars biophysicist
Noland, Mariam Charl foundation executive
Nordstrom, Cheryl K. epidemiologist, researcher
Novak, Raymond Francis environmental services administrator, pharmacology educator
Ordonez, Magglio Jose professional baseball player
Orikri, Timothy UfuomaEfe landscape artist
Osgood, Chris professional hockey player
O'Sullivan, Nancy Louise immunologist, educator
Pan, Zhuo-Hua science educator
Pappas, Athina pediatrician, educator
Parry, Dale D. publisher, editor
Peck, William Henry curator, archaeologist, educator
Phillis, John Whitfield physiologist, educator
Pietrofesa, John Joseph psychologist, educator
Polanco, Placido Enrique professional baseball player
Polis, Nancy E. automotive executive
Powell, William E. automotive executive
Prasad, Ananda Shiva medical educator
Prihod, Kevin F. museum administrator
Rafalski, Brian professional hockey player
Rajlich, Vaclav Thomas computer science educator, researcher, consultant
Rashid, Frank Damian literature and language professor
Rathod, Mulchand mechanical engineering educator
Raymond, Richard Gerard, Jr. lawyer
Redman, Barbara Klug nursing educator
Reeves, Martha Councilwoman
Reilly, David N. (Nick Reilly) automotive executive
Reiss, Francis Ronald bishop
Reuss, Mark automotive executive
Rishi, Arun K. molecular biologist, educator
Rivin, Evgeny (Eugene) I. engineering educator, researcher, inventor, consultant
Rogers, Kenny (Kenneth Scott Rogers) professional baseball player
Rogers, Richard Lee academic administrator, educator
Romero, Roberto J. perinatologist, educator
Ronnick, Michele Valerie education educator
Rosen, Gerald Ellis federal judge
Ruckdeschel, John Charles health facility administrator
Ruden, Douglas Mark science educator
Ryan, James Leo federal judge
Ryu, Samuel surgeon
Salakhutdinov, Ildar physics professor, researcher
Samuelsson, Mikael professional hockey player
Sase, John Francis economist
Saxton, William Marvin lawyer
Schiffer, Charles Alan oncologist, educator
Schirmer, Barbara Rose special education educator, academic administrator
Schlichting, Nancy Margaret hospital administrator
Schreiber, Bertram Manuel mathematics professor
Schwartz, Alan Earl lawyer, director
Schweitzer, Vanessa Gayl otorhinolaryngologist
Sedler, Robert Allen law educator
Shade, George Henry, Jr. obstetrician, gynecologist, educator
Shapiro, Michael Bruce lawyer
Shi, Weisong computer scientist, educator
Skowronski, Nancy library director
Slatkin, Leonard Edward music director, conductor
Sloane, Bonnie Fiedorek pharmacology and cancer biology educator, researcher
Slym, Karl automotive executive
Small, Melvin historian, educator
Smith, Gary Richard technology educator
Smith, John F. automotive executive
Smith, S. Kinnie, Jr. lawyer
Smith, Wilbur Lazear radiologist, educator
Sobeck, Joanne L. social studies educator
Sokol, Robert James obstetrician, gynecologist, educator
Solomon, William B., Jr. lawyer, finance company executive
Sosne, Gabriel ophthalmologist, educator
Spanaki, Marianna V. neurologist, educator
Sparrow, Herbert George III lawyer, educator
Spurr, Stephen Josiah economics professor
Spyers-Duran, Peter librarian, educator
Ssemakula, Mukasa Emmanuel engineering educator
States, J. Christopher molecular biology educator, researcher
Stephens, Thomas G. automotive executive
Stewart, Melbourne George, Jr. physicist, researcher
Stuart, Brad professional hockey player
Szygenda, Ralph J. automotive executive
Tancer, Manuel E. psychiatrist
Taylor, Anna Diggs federal judge
Thelen, Bruce Cyril lawyer
Tinsley-Talabi, Alberta Councilwoman
Torres Cancel, Lourdes Ivelisse philosopher, educator
Tremblay, Diana D. automotive executive
Trent, Calvin R. city health department director
Trimpin, Sarah chemistry professor
Tyburski, James Gerard surgeon
Tzivion, Guri medical educator
Uberti, Joseph P. oncologist, educator
Valade, Alan Michael lawyer
Vander Heide, Richard Stuart pathologist, educator, research scientist
Vander Weg, John D. music educator
Van Slyke, Andrew James professional baseball coach, retired professional baseball player
Verlander, Justin Brooks professional baseball player
Vigneron, Allen Henry archbishop
Volz, William Harry lawyer, educator
Wale, Kevin E. automotive executive
Wang, Caisheng engineering educator
Washburn, Jarrod professional baseball player
Watson, JoAnn Councilwoman
Weaver, W(ayne) Douglas cardiologist, researcher, medical educator
Wexler, Raymond P. lawyer, automotive executive
Whitacre, Edward E., Jr. automotive executive, retired telecommunications industry executive
White, Gary A. automotive executive
White, Helene Nita federal judge
Whitehouse, Fred Waite endocrinologist, researcher
Wiener, Joseph pathologist, educator
Williams, Kevin W. automotive executive
Willis, Dontrelle (Wayne) professional baseball player
Wittlinger, Timothy David lawyer
Wolf, Barry geneticist, pediatric educator
Wolman, Jonathan Paley newspaper editor, journalist
Wong, Henry Keung dermatologist, educator
Wyrick, Jermaine Albert lawyer
Yaremchuk, Kathleen otolaryngologist, department chairman
Yee, Sandra Gayle Brown library director, dean
Young, Ray G. automotive executive
Yzerman, Steve (Stephen Gregory Yzerman) professional sports team executive, retired professional hockey player
Zemlicka, Jiri medical educator, researcher
Zetterberg, Henrik professional hockey player
Zhuo, Jia Long physiologist
Zuckerman, Richard Engle lawyer, educator

Dexter

Hanamey, Rosemary T. nursing educator
Zhang, Weiming engineer

Dollar Bay

Karpiak, Steven Thomas, Jr. retired social studies educator

Dowagiac

Dalton, Clyde biology professor

East Lansing

Abeles, Norman psychologist, educator
Abramson, Paul Robert political scientist, educator
Andersland, Orlando Baldwin retired engineering educator
Anderson, David Daniel retired humanities educator, writer, editor
Araujo, Luis Fernando Oliveira de economics professor
Austin, Sam M. physicist, educator
Baclawski, Diane Kay librarian, researcher
Baillie, Richard Thomas economist, educator
Bandes, Susan Jane museum director, educator
Benenson, Walter nuclear physics professor
Bromley, Stephen C. zoology educator
Brubaker, Robert Robinson microbiology educator
Bukovac, Martin John horticulturist, educator
Case, Eldon Darrel materials science educator
Chan, Christina chemical engineer, educator
Chivukula, R. Sekhar physics professor
Cibelli, Jose B. research scientist, educator
Crewe, Nancy Moe retired psychologist
Cross, Aureal Theophilus geology and botany educator
Cutts, Charles Eugene retired engineering educator
Dantonio, Mark college football coach
Dennis, Frank George, Jr. retired horticulture educator
Dewhurst, Charles Kurt museum director, curator, language educator
D'Itri, Frank Michael environmental research chemist
Donahue, Megan Elizabeth astrophysicist
Dow, Steven Benjamin social studies educator
Dye, James Louis retired chemistry professor
Fisher, Alan Washburn historian, educator

Flegler, Stanley Lewis *academic administrator, educator*
Foss, John Frank *mechanical engineering educator*
Freedman, Eric *journalist, educator, writer*
Gangur, Venu *medical educator*
Goodman, Erik David *engineering educator*
Gottschalk, Alexander *radiologist, educator*
Greenberg, Bradley Sander *communications educator*
Grotjohn, Timothy Allan *engineering educator*
Gulick, Peter Gregory *medical educator*
Hackel, Emanuel *science educator*
Haider, Syed Waqar *science educator*
Haka, Clifford Hughey *library director*
Harrison, Michael Jay *physicist, researcher*
Harrison, Tara Myers *veterinarian, educator, curator*
Hartmann, William Morris *physics educator*
Ilgen, Daniel Richard *psychology professor*
Izzo, Thomas (Tom Izzo) *men's college basketball coach*
Johnson, Clark Cumings *lawyer, educator, dean*
Jones, Brenda *Councilwoman*
Kalof, Linda Henry *sociologist, educator*
Kang, Jun-Koo *finance educator*
Kariagina, Anastasia *physiologist, educator*
Kirk, Edgar Lee *retired musician, educator*
Kirkpatrick, R(obert) James *geologist, educator*
Ladenson, Sharon *university librarian*
Lashbrooke, Elvin Carroll, Jr. *law educator, consultant, dean*
Linnemann, James Thomas *physics professor*
Luccock, Thomas Nelson *auditor, director*
Manderscheid, Lester Vincent *agricultural economics educator*
McMeekin, Dorothy *botanist, plant pathologist, educator*
Menchik, Paul Leonard *economist, educator*
Merchant, Suzy *women's college basketball coach*
Miracle, Gordon Eldon *advertising educator*
Mitra, Joydeep *electrical engineer, educator*
Monson, Carol Lynn *osteopath, psychotherapist*
Natoli, Joseph *language educator*
Noel, Mary Margaret *nutritionist, educator*
Perlstadt, Harry *medical sociology educator*
Perrin, Robert *writer, consultant*
Pervaiz, Mohammad Hassan *cardiologist*
Petrides, George Athan *ecologist, educator*
Pichler, Shaun *statistician, educator*
Preiss, Jack *biochemistry professor*
Press, Charles *retired political science professor*
Prestel, David Kirk *literature and language professor, department chairman*
Pysh, Joseph John *neurologist, neuroanatomist*
Rappley, Marsha D. *dean, physician, educator*
Rong, Yongwu *mathematician, researcher*
Rosenman, Kenneth D. *medical educator*
Rothert, Marilyn L. *dean, nursing educator*
Saul, William Edward *engineering educator*
Schmid, Alfred Allan *economist*
Schoenl, William James *history professor*
Sharkey, Thomas David *biochemist, educator*
Simon, Lou Anna Kimsey *academic administrator*
Snoddy, James Ernest *education educator*
Spagnuolo, Mark Mario *retired dentist*
Sparks, Harvey Vise, Jr. *physiologist*
Stapleton, James Hall *retired statistician, educator*
Strampel, William Derkey *dean, medical educator*
Tiedje, James Michael *microbiologist, ecologist, educator*
Tzitsikas, Helene *retired literature educator*
Wakoski, Diane *poet, educator*
Warrington, Willard Glade *retired university official*
Watson, Ralph Edward *internist, educator*
Wiley, David Sherman *sociologist, educator*
Wilkinson, William Sherwood *lawyer*
Wilson, R. Dale *marketing educator*
Winder, Clarence Leland *psychologist, educator*

Eastpointe
Backus, Joseph A. *mathematics educator*

Edwardsburg
Floyd, Alton David *cell biologist, consultant*
Moellenberndt, Scott D. *principal*

Elk Rapids
Thompson, Richard Thomas *academic administrator*

Escanaba
Weydt, Eric Charles *private school educator*

Fair Haven
Lenhausen, Georgia Rowena *secondary school educator*

Farmington
Ginsberg, Myron *computer scientist*
Gordon, Arnold Mark *state attorney general, arbitrator, educator*
Koziara, Michael *accountant, insurance company executive*
Penberthy, Stanley Josiah, Jr. *publisher*
Shaevsky, Mark *lawyer*
Subrahmanyam, Somashekar Ramachandran *mechanical engineer*
Werba, Gabriel *public relations consultant*

Farmington Hills
Blumberg, Seth N. *medical association administrator*
Bojrab, Dennis Issac *otologist, neurotologist, skull base surgeon*
Chapman, Gilbert Bryant, II, *physicist*
Dolan, Jan Clark *former state legislator*
Ellmann, Sheila Frenkel *investment company executive*
Fenton, Robert Leonard *lawyer, writer, film producer*
Fluharty, David Arthur *automotive manager, statistician, consultant*
Heiss, Richard Walter *retired bank executive, consultant, lawyer*
Hurd, Mary K. *civil engineer, writer*
Katzman, David *investment company executive*
Klausmeier, Herbert John *psychology professor*
Luby, Elliot Donald *psychiatrist, educator*
Meyer, Philip Gilbert *lawyer*
Plaut, Jonathan Victor *rabbi*
Purdy, Jan Rae *music educator*
Smith, Isabel Francis *financial planner*

Fennville
Kamman, Curtis Warren *retired ambassador*

Fenton
Gilbert, Ronald Rhea *lawyer*
Kruzan, James Brendan *financial planner*

Fife Lake
Knecht, Richard Arden *family practitioner*

Flint
Baird, Darryl Glenn *photographer, educator*
Iddings, Douglas Matthew *oncologist, researcher*
Knight, Suzanne Dee *literature and language professor*
Marcinkoski, Annette Marie *retired elementary school educator*
Marinucci, Ronald E. *history professor*
Simkani, Mehrdad *mathematics professor*
Simmons, Robert Randolph *principal*
Smith, Catherine Jean *artist, educator*
White, William Samuel *foundation executive*
Williams-Latnie, Veronica Myres *psychotherapist, social worker*

Flushing
Bain, William David *electronics engineer, writer*
Demankowski, Lisa Renee *architect, educator*

Frankfort
Foster, Robert Carmichael *banker*
Gerberding, Miles Carston *lawyer*
Storrer, William Allin *theater educator, consultant*

Franklin
Sax, Mary Randolph *speech and language pathologist*

Fraser
Veryser, Harry Cornelius *manufacturing executive, educator*

Gaylord
Cooney, Patrick Ronald *bishop*
Smith, Frank Earl *retired trade association administrator*

Glen Arbor
Wagner, Bruce Stanley *marketing professional*

Grand Ledge
Evert, Sandra Florence (Sandra Wheeler) *medical/surgical nurse, consultant*

Grand Rapids
Abadeer, Adel S *economics professor*
Abdel-Mageed, Aly S. *medical association administrator*
Adams, Celeste *museum director*
Adams, Dwayne Hurstle *religious studies educator, department chairman*
Adams, Joel Cameron *computer science educator*
Auwers, Stanley John *motor carrier executive*
Baker, Hollis MacLure *furniture manufacturing company executive*
Balog, C. Edward *academic administrator*
Barnes, Rosemary Lois *minister*
Barnes, Thomas John *lawyer*
Beals, Paul Archer *religious studies educator*
Becker, Robert Joseph *database consultant, application developer, educator, computer science specialist*
Beeke, Joel Robert *minister, educator, writer*
Bengtson, Bradley *plastic surgeon*
Brenneman, Hugh Warren, Jr. *judge*
Brinkmeyer, Scott S. *lawyer*
Byrne, James *insurance company executive*
Bytwerk, Randall Lee *communication educator*
Canepa, John Charles *banking consultant*
Carlotti, Ronald John *food scientist*
Currie, William G. *forest products executive*
Daniels, Joseph *neuropsychiatrist*
Davis, Henry Barnard, Jr. *retired lawyer*
Deems, Nyal David *lawyer, mayor*
Deppe, Dean Brian *theology studies educator*
DeVries, Robert K. *retired publisher, consultant*
Diekema, Anthony J. *college president, consultant*
Donahue, Dennis Donald *foreign service officer*
Dykstra, William Dwight *management executive, consultant*
Eidson, Dennis *retail executive*
Forzley, Gregory *physician, medical association administrator*
Glenn, Michael B. *forest products executive*
Greenfield, John Charles *biochemist, professional society administrator*
Gunnoe, Charles D. *history professor*
Haarsma, Deborah Joy Becker *physics professor*
Hackett, James P. *manufacturing executive*
Hall, William Wesley *lawyer*
Hammond, Dennis Clyde *plastic surgeon, educator*
Hawkins, Gregory *insurance company executive*
Heartwell, George K. *Mayor, Grand Rapids, Michigan*
Hoogenboom, Barbara Jo *physical therapist, educator*
Hooyenga, Judith Waara *lawyer*
Horn, Joyce Elaine *retired music educator*
Horn, Kimberly *insurance company executive*
Hruby, Norbert Joseph *former college president, educational consultant, playwright*
Hurley, Walter Allison *bishop*
Ingersoll, Patricia Lee *library director*
Jennette, Noble Stevenson III *lawyer*
Jones, Ora McConner *retired foundation administrator*
Jonker, Robert James *federal judge*
Karayil, Diljit Bahuleyan *physician, consultant*
Lee, Mary Esther *museum director*
Logie, John Hoult, Sr. *former mayor, lawyer*
Lubbers, Arend Donselaar *retired academic administrator*
Maupin, Karin Louise *secondary school educator*
McCallum, Charles Edward *lawyer*
Mears, Patrick Edward *lawyer*
Meijer, Hank *retail company executive*
Metzler, James Robert *musician*
Neff, Janet T. *federal judge*
Pichot, Michel *language educator, department chairman*
Pinheiro, John C. *historian, educator*
Quist, Gordon Jay *federal judge*
Reifler, David Martin *ophthalmologist*
Rumney, Helene Vosburgh *retired poet, peace activist*
Sadler, David G(ary) *manufacturing executive*
Secchia, Peter F. *forest products executive, former United States ambassador to Italy*
Sieger, Diana R. *foundation administrator*
Spaulding, Dan *public relations executive*
Sturken, Craig C. *retail executive*
Sytsma, Fredric A. *lawyer*
Tiemstra, John Peter *economics professor*
Vande Kopple, William John *literature and language professor*
Van Dyke, Michelle *bank executive*
VanScoy, Holly Carole *social and educational researcher*
Van Vugt, William E. *history professor*
Veazey, Richard Edward *accounting educator*
Verdier, David D'Ooge *ophthalmologist, educator*
Wendt, Vernon Earl *internist, cardiologist*

Grosse Ile
Smith, Veronica Latta *real estate company officer*
Stryker, Joan Copeland *retired obstetrician, gynecologist, educator*

Grosse Pointe
Amsden, Ted Thomas *lawyer*
Appleyard, Jennifer *allergist, immunologist*
Bryfonski, Dedria Anne *publishing executive*
Casey, Genevieve M(ary) *librarian, educator*
Hendrie, Janice Ellen *language educator*
Koo, Winston Wun Kwong *neonatologist, researcher, educator*
Marshall, Douglas William *health research administrator, educator*
Maurer, David Leo *lawyer*
Mengden, Joseph Michael *retired investment banker*
Moran, Justin Louis *retired management consultant*
Rosman, Howard S. *cardiologist, educator*
Ruffner, Frederick G., Jr. *book publisher*
Scarabelli, Tiziano Maria *molecular biologist, cardiologist, educator*
Wilkinson, Warren Scripps *manufacturing executive*

Grosse Pointe Farms
Thurber, Peter Palms *lawyer*

Grosse Pointe Park
Centner, Charles William *lawyer, educator*
Elsila, David August *editor*
Knapp, Mildred Florence *retired social worker*
Krebs, William Hoyt *industrial hygienist, health science association administrator*
Mogk, John Edward *law educator, association executive, consultant*

Grosse Pointe Shores
Burke, Thomas Joseph *civil engineer*
Holness, Gordon Victor Rix *engineering executive, mechanical engineer*
Sphire, Raymond Daniel *anesthesiologist, educator*

Grosse Pointe Woods
McWhirter, Glenna Suzanne (Nickie) *retired columnist*

Harbor Beach
Falkenberg, Mary Elaine *small business owner*

Harbor Springs
Smith, Wayne Richard *lawyer*

Harper Woods
Mitseff, Carl *lawyer*
Myhand, Cheryl *minister, educator*

Harsens Island
Woodford, Arthur MacKinnon *library director, historian*

Hastings
Jones, Kensinger *advertising executive, author, educator*

Herron
Elkie, Kimberly K. *medical editor*

Hesperia
Yob, Chuck (Charles Walter Yob) *political organization administrator*

Highland
Brown, Ray Kent *biochemist, physician, educator*

Hillsdale
Bachelder, Cheryl Anne *former food service company executive*
Brandon, James M. *theater educator*
Frudakis, Anthony Parker *sculptor, educator*
Pierson, Diana Lee *librarian, educator*

Holland
Albert, Stephen Wayne *information technology executive, manufacturing executive*
Catel, Mylène Jeanne *French educator, poet*
Gardner, Kevin Eugene *research scientist, director*
Garlough, William Glenn *marketing executive*
Gillmore, Jason George *chemistry professor*
Holmes, Jack Edward *political science professor*
Johnson, Freddie Lee III *history professor*
Kearns, Bobbi Lynn *music educator*
Murphy, Max Ray *lawyer*
Nakajima, Fumihito Andy *priest, educator*
Nieuwsma, Milton John *writer, journalist*
Nyenhuis, Jacob Eugene *academic administrator*
Swierenga, Robert *humanities educator, researcher*
Van Wylen, Gordon John *former college president*
Zuidema, George Dale *surgeon, educator*

Holly
Stolpin, William Roger *printmaker*

Holt
Smith, Betty W. *librarian*
Wood, Mary Elizabeth *retired secondary school educator, church musician*

Houghton
Abdelkhalik, Ossama *computer science educator, researcher*
Aleksandr, Sergeyev *engineering educator*
Burton, Andrew J. *ecologist, educator*
Elangovan, Shreehari *research scientist*
Hungwe, Kedmon Nyasha *education educator, researcher*
Kerfoot, W. Charles, Jr. *biology professor*
Lumsdaine, Edward *mechanical engineering educator, dean*
Miskioglu, Ibrahim *engineering educator*
Pandit, Sudhakar Madhavrao *engineering educator*
Pickens, James B. *science educator*
Utt, Glenn S., Jr. *retired medical products executive*

Howell
Watkins, Curtis WinthroP *artist*

Hudson
Kauffman, Janet *writer*

Idlewild
Wooley, Geraldine Hamilton *poet, writer*

Inkster
Bullock, Steven Carl *lawyer*

Jackson
Brunner, James Edwin *lawyer*
Farooq, Umar *mechanical engineer*
Feldmann, Judith Gail *language professional, educator*
Joos, David W. *energy executive*
Livesay, Jacqueline Ryder *music educator, choir director*
Marcoux, William Joseph *lawyer*
Nugent, Ted (Theodore Anthony Nugent) *musician, radio personality*
Popp, Nathaniel *archbishop*
Smith, Jeff M. *secondary school educator*
Webb, Thomas J. *utilities executive*
Whipple, Kenneth *utilities executive*
Wingblade, Loren Charles *social sciences educator*

Jenison
Wooster, Stephanie Lynne *art historian, artist*

Jerome
Dillon, Merton Lynn *historian, educator*

Jonesville
Corwin, Danny Willard *rehabilitation services professional, director*

Kalamazoo
Baas, Jane Thornbury *dancer, educator*
Badra, Robert George *theology studies and humanities educator*
Bennett, Arlie Joyce *clinical social worker*
Berkow, Jay *theater director*
Berto, Luigi Andrea *history professor*
Bradley, Paul Joseph *bishop*
Breisach, Ernst A. *historian, educator*
Bricker, Lee Alan *medical educator*
Bridenstine, James Aloysius *museum director*
Bridges, Cassandra Maddox *psychology professor*
Burns, James W. *education educator*
Carver, Norman Francis, Jr. *architect, photographer*
Curry, John Patrick *insurance company executive, management consultant*
Dahlinger, Martha Louise *elementary school educator*
Desmett, Don *art educator*
Desroches, Vincent *language educator*
Donovan, Paul V. *bishop emeritus*
Dybek, Stuart *language educator, writer*
Enslen, Richard Alan *federal judge*
Feinberg, Arthur Norman *medical educator*
Fischell, Tim Alexander *cardiologist*
Freedman, Lauren *education educator, consultant*
Gonzales, Andrea *biomedical researcher*
Gordon, Edgar George *retired lawyer*
Grantner, Janos L. *engineering educator*
Griffin, Monica Leigh *voice educator*
Grotzinger, Laurel Ann *librarian, educator*
Hartman, Curt *health products executive*
Hathaway, Richard B. *science educator, researcher*
Holmuhamedov, Ekhson Lukmanovich *biophysicist, biochemist*
Jamison, Frank Raymond *independent video producer, retired communications educator*
Jayasingh, Preetha *food scientist*
Katrovas, Richard *literature and language educator, director*
Kazanowski, Pawel *research and development scientist*
Lander, Joyce Ann *retired nursing educator, medical/surgical nurse*
Larrieu, Gloria Lynn *language educator*
Light, Christopher Upjohn *freelance/self-employed writer, photographer*
MacMillan, Stephen P. *health products executive*
Maier, Paul Luther *history professor, minister, writer*
Maloney, Paul Lewis *federal judge*
Marshall, Vincent de Paul *industrial microbiologist, researcher*
Mc Allister, Lester Belden *economics professor*

Munley, Patrick H. *psychologist, educator*
Murray, James A. *bishop*
Norris, Richard Patrick *museum director, historian, educator*
Nowicki, Stacy A. *library director*
Petersen, Anne C. (Cheryl Petersen) *foundation administrator, educator*
Port, Tamara Lynne *biology professor, writer*
Price, Kim Denise *counselor*
Ratner, Carl Joseph *opera stage director, baritone*
Rivara, Sara *language educator*
Rose, William N. (Bill Rose) *museum administrator*
Sauret, Martine *French educator*
Showalter, Shirley H. *former academic administrator*
Sinclair, Michael David *mathematics and science educator*
Straight, Bilinda *anthropologist, educator*
Van Slambrouck, John G. *lawyer*
Van Valey, Thomas Lee *sociologist, educator*
Yang, Li *computer scientist, educator*
Yehia, Sherif Abdel Aziz *civil engineer, educator*
Zinn, Donald Edward *biologist, researcher*

Kentwood
Kelley, DeVere Orin *media specialist*
Purchase-Owens, Francena *marketing professional, consultant, educator, scholar*
Roberts-Brown, Arlene Maria *executive assistant*
Yovich, Daniel John *chemist, educator*

Lake Angelus
Kresge, Bruce Anderson *retired physician*

Lake Orion
Berger, Laura Ann *dance studio owner*
Leonard, Jacquelyn Ann *retired elementary school educator*
Robinson, Marietta S. *lawyer*

Lansing
Baker, Frederick Milton, Jr. *lawyer*
Boyea, Earl Alfred, Jr. *bishop*
Brewer, Mark Courtland *political organization administrator*
Cavanagh, Michael Francis *state supreme court justice*
Cawthorne, Dennis Otto *lawyer*
Cherry, John D., Jr. *Lieutenant Governor of Michigan, former state senator*
Couto, C. Douglass *state agency administrator*
Cox, Mike (Michael A. Cox) *state attorney general*
Ewert, Quentin Albert *lawyer, consultant*
Fink, Joseph Allen *lawyer*
Flanagan, Michael P. *state official, school system administrator*
Foster, Joe C., Jr. *lawyer*
Franklin, James J. *librarian*
Granholm, Jennifer Mulhern *Governor of Michigan*
Harrison, Michael Gregory *judge*
Hathaway, Diane Marie *state supreme court justice*
Hess, Steven Charles *lawyer*
Hoffman, Philip Edward *legislative consultant*
Hoogendyk, Jacob William, Jr., (Jack Hoogendyk) *state legislator*
Kelly, Marilyn *state supreme court justice*
Kepros, John Paul *trauma surgeon*
Kleine, Robert J. *state treasurer*
Land, Terri Lynn *Secretary of State, Michigan*
Lobenherz, William Ernest *consumer products company executive, trade association administrator, lawyer*
Loepp, Daniel *insurance company executive*
Looyenga, Roger L. *insurance company executive*
Maio, Ronald Frank *emergency medicine physician*
Markman, Stephen J. *state supreme court justice*
Marvin, David Edward Shreve *lawyer*
McKeague, David William *federal judge*
Mengeling, Carl Frederick *bishop emeritus*
Nicholas, Caroline Jean *retired nurse, consultant*
Olszewski, Janet *state agency administrator, public health service officer*
Otten, Roberta Ann *theater and dance educator, choreographer*
Rogers, Paulleto *researcher, writer, delegate*
Rooney, John Philip *law educator*
Ross, Ken *state banking agency administrator*
Stockmeyer, Norman Otto *law educator, consultant*
Straus, Kathleen Nagler *academic administrator, educator*
Suhrheinrich, Richard Fred *federal judge*
Weiser, Ronald *political organization administrator, former ambassador*
Wise, Sharon *political organization administrator*
Yeutter, Clayton Keith *lawyer, former United States Secretary of Agriculture*
Young, Robert P., Jr. *state supreme court justice*

Lawrence
Applewhaite, Carlisle S. *special education educator, consultant*

Leland
Small, Hamish *chemist*
Soutas-Little, Robert William *mechanical engineer, educator*

Livonia
Bialosky, David L. *lawyer, automotive executive*
Budd, Jennifer Kathleen *literature and language educator*
Cantie, Joseph S. *automotive executive*
Gepford, Barbara Beebe *retired nutrition educator*
Gilbert, Daniel *professional sports team owner, mortgage company executive*
Hoffman, Barry Paul *lawyer*
Holtzman, Roberta Lee *French and Spanish language educator*
Istephan, Asaad A. *science educator*
Kujawa, Sister Rose Marie *academic administrator*
Lake, Peter J. *automotive executive*
Lunn, Steven *automotive executive*
Maibach, Ben C., Jr. *consumer products company executive*
Malalahalli, Jayalakshmi S. *history professor*
Malcolm, Mark M. *automotive executive*
Marchuk, Neil *automotive executive*
McHard, James Lorin *corporate financial executive, freelance/self-employed composer, writer*
Nelson, Troy Alan *music educator, church musician, assistant principal*
Plant, John Charles *automotive executive*
Steffen, Carolyn McKinnis *biology professor*
Taylor, Bonnita Kay *biology professor*
Uicker, Joseph Bernard *retired engineering company executive*
Valerio, Michael Anthony *diversified financial services company executive*

Ludington
Puffer, Richard Judson *retired college chancellor*

Macomb
Farmakis, George Leonard *retired education educator*

Madison Heights
Janke, Kenneth *investment consultant*
Peaslee, Robert Leon *metallurgical engineer, consultant*

Manistee
Broberg, Leonard Eliot *lawyer*
Trussell, Charles Tait *columnist*

Manistique
Jeffcott, Janet Bruhn *statistician, consultant*

Maple City
Duff, James George *retired finance company and automotive executive*

Marquette
Camerius, James Walter *marketing educator, corporate researcher*
Cotter, June Ann *special education educator*
Garland, James Henry *bishop emeritus*
Lehmberg, Z. Z. *educator*
Leuthold, Steven Michael *art educator*
Manning, Robert Hendrick *retired audio-visual services director, retired communications educator*
Osstyn, Randolph Beier *lawyer*
Sample, Alexander King *bishop*
Schmitt, Mark Francis *bishop emeritus*
Sotiropoulos, Carol Strauss *language educator*

Mattawan
Magrath, Shari Marie *healthcare educator*

Midland
Adams, Thomas Walton *corrections official*
Banholzer, William F. *chemical company executive*
Boxwell, Barbara P. *finance educator*
Burns, Stephanie A. *chemicals executive*
Bus, James Stanley *toxicologist*
Chao, Marshall *chemist*
Collins, James J. *epidemiologist*
Diegel, Betsy L. *research scientist, department chairman*
Dorman, Linneaus Cuthbert *retired chemist*
Fasone Holder, Julie *chemicals executive*
Frank, Timothy Charles *chemical engineer, researcher*
Freiwald, Gregory M. *chemical company executive*
Gambrell, Michael R. *chemicals executive*
Haller, Heinz *chemicals executive*
Hampton, Leroy *retired chemical company executive*
Kalil, Charles James *lawyer, chemicals executive*
Kepler, David E., II, *chemicals executive*
Kresge, Charles T. *chemicals executive*
Liveris, Andrew N. *chemical company executive*
Luptowski, Thomas Stephen *social sciences educator*
Meister, Bernard John *retired chemical engineer*
Merszei, Geoffrey E. *corporate financial executive*
Potts, Sandra *library director*
Robbins, Lanny Arnold *chemical engineer*
Rocks, Patti Temple *marketing executive*
Schmidt, William C. *retired chemicals executive*
Spaulding, William Ellis *finance educator, consultant*
Veurink, Gary R. *chemicals executive*

Milford
Bennur, Mallikarjuna *automotive executive*
Oliveri, Eugene Alfred *gastroenterologist*

Millington
Bickel, Elaine Carol *academic administrator*

Monroe
Darrow, Kurt L. *manufacturing executive*
Lipford, Rocque Edward *lawyer*

Mount Clemens
Robinson, Earl, Jr. *nanotechnologist, marketing, transportation executive, educator, retired air force officer*

Mount Pleasant
Dietrich, Richard Vincent *geologist, educator*
Doyle, Randall Jordan *history professor*
Lee, Roger Y. *engineering educator*
Lorenzen, Michael Gary *librarian, researcher*
Martin, Sue Ann *theater educator*
Mascolo-David, Alexandra *music educator*
Meixner, John B. *philosopher, educator*
Messick, Frederic Morton *librarian*
Mohanty, Dillip K. *chemistry professor, researcher*
Norris, Darcy Janelle *sign language teacher*
Nowak-Fabrykowski, Krystyna Teresa *early childhood education educator*
Oh-Lee, Justin DoHoon *psychology professor*
Petrick, Michael Joseph *journalism educator*
Peyrefitte, Ashton George, Jr. *meteorologist, educator*
Smallwood, Carol *writer*
Torgersen, Eric *literature and language professor*
Traines, Rose Wunderbaum *sculptor, educator*
Yelamarthi, Kumar *engineering educator*

Muskegon
Behrens, Holly Marie *finance educator, researcher*
McKendry, John H., Jr. *lawyer*
Nace, Doru *mathematics professor*
Nehra, Gerald Peter *lawyer*
Ohst, Wendy Joan *government agency administrator, educator*
Ross, Annette Lee *educational consultant*
Wible, Andy *philosopher, educator*

New Buffalo
Roemer, James Anthony *retired director*
Stassen, John Henry *retired lawyer*

Newport
Cerasuolo, Jennifer Lyn *preservationist*

Niles
Gibbs, Denis Laurel *radiologist*
Marshall, Gerald Francis *optical engineer, consultant, physicist*
Tenney, Jane Morris *real estate developer*

North Branch
Baker, Randy Thomas *social studies educator*
Stevenson, James Laraway *engineering company executive, electronics, computer and communications engineer, educator*

Northport
Schultz, Richard Carlton *plastic surgeon*
Scripps, Douglas Jerry *musician, educator, conductor*
Thomas, Philip Stanley *economist, educator*

Northville
Allen, Janet Louise *school system administrator*
Clawson, Curtis J. *manufacturing executive*
Davis, Lawrence Edward *church official*
Leavitt, Martin Jack *lawyer*
Nasr, Samya Z. *pediatric pulmonologist*
Porcher, Robert III *entrepreneur, retired professional football player*

Novi
Barr, David John *retired art educator*
Begley, Heidi Marie *nurse, entrepreneur*
Bullard, Willis Clare, Jr. *lawyer, public official*
Chadwick, Edward *insurance company executive*
Darke, Richard Francis *lawyer*
Hale, Daniel G. *lawyer, insurance company executive*
Hasler, Edward A. *automotive executive*
McElya, James S. *automotive executive*
Serenson, Lynn Ann *mathematics educator*
Smith, George Wolfram *physicist, researcher*
Swedish, Joseph *insurance company executive*

Oak Park
Coleman, Dorothy Charmayne *nurse*

Okemos
Berkman, Claire Fleet *psychologist*
Burnett, Jean B. *biochemist, educator*
Edwards, Caryn Louise *educational consultant, special education educator*
Huddleston, Eugene Lee *retired American studies educator*
Klunzinger, Thomas Edward *writer, actor, film director*
Solo, Robert Alexander *economist, educator*

Owosso
McKean, Sherry Lynn *neurodiagnostic technologist*
Schneider, Don (Charles Schneider) *museum administrator*

Oxford
Smith, Jay Lawrence *financial planning company executive*

Petoskey
Meengs, William Lloyd *cardiologist*
Nicholson, William Noel *clinical neuropsychologist*
Switzer, Carolyn Joan *artist, educator*

Pinckney
Britton, Clarold Lawrence *lawyer, consultant*

Plymouth
Berry, Charlene Helen *librarian, musician*
Martina, Carlo Jack *lawyer*
Vlcek, Donald Joseph, Jr. *food products executive, wholesale distribution executive, writer*

Pontiac
Andrews, Steven Nicholas *judge*
Hampton, Philip Michael *consulting engineering company executive*
Love, Sharon Irene *elementary school educator*
Pardee, Jeffrey Clark *county government official*
Riley, Mary Jane Stewart *secondary school educator*
Singh, Avinash *mechanical engineer*
Stein, Paul David *cardiologist*
Wang, Yucong *engineering executive*

Port Huron
Miller, Theresa L. *library director*
Rowark, Maureen *fine arts photographer*
Wu, Harry Pao-Tung *retired librarian*

Portage
Bergy, Dean H. *health products executive*
Brown, John Wilford *health products executive*
Fox-Smith, Andrew G. *health products executive*
Gregory, Ross *retired history professor, writer*
Hall, Curtis E. *lawyer, health products executive*
Schultheis, Ann Lucia *retired curriculum specialist*
Zhang, Charles C. *financial planner*

Redford
Karpinski, Huberta *library trustee*

Reed City
Rautiola, Norman A. *manufacturing executive*

Republic
Wixtrom, Donald Joseph *translator*

Richland
Atkinson, Arthur John, Jr. *pharmacologist, educator, consultant*

Riverview
Ward, George Edward *lawyer, law educator*

Rochester
Baker, Susan Gail *communication educator*
Cole, Natalie Bell *literature and language professor*
Cordes, Mary Kenrick *retired psychologist*
Goldberg, Andrew F.X. *biochemist, educator*
Guzik, Heather Jerrett *psychologist*
Haskell, Richard Edmund *engineering educator*
Hoffiz, Benjamin Theodore *literature and language professor*
Keller, Alison E. *library director*
Kraemer, Elizabeth Wallis *academic librarian*
McDonald, Gary C. *mathematics professor*
Packard, Sandra Podolin *education educator, consultant*
Reygaert, Wanda C. *medical educator*
Spears, James Richard *cardiologist*
Tepley, Norman *physics educator*
Youn, Anthony Sungjin *plastic surgeon*

Rochester Hills
Denton, Lawrence A. *automotive executive*
Minton, Henry Lee *psychology professor*
Unakar, Nalin Jayantilal *biological sciences educator*

Rockford
Grady, Kenneth Alan *lawyer, corporate secretary*

Romeo
Tsukamoto, Daniel *piano instructor, church organist*

Romulus
Yussouff, Mohammed *retired physicist, educator*

Roscommon
Giacobazzi, Frederic David *literature and language educator*

Rothbury
Fischer, Dorothy Virginia *retired small business owner*

Royal Oak
Britt, Stephen Thomas *medical educator*
Cook, Noel Robert *manufacturing executive*
Drenser, Kimberly *ophthalmologist*
Ernstoff, Raina Marcia *neurologist*
Fragomeni, James Mark *mechanical engineer, educator*
Grines, Cindy Lee *health facility administrator, cardiologist*
Hassan, Tarek S. *ophthalmologist*
Peters, Kenneth Michael *urologist, researcher*
Ryan, Jack *physician, retired hospital corporation executive*
Wagster, John Douglas *finance educator*
Wise, John Augustus *lawyer, director*

Saginaw
Chaffee, Paul Charles *newspaper editor, publisher*
Cistone, Joseph Robert *bishop*
Cline, Thomas William *real estate leasing company executive, management consultant*
Coughlin, Jeannine Marie *music educator*
Evans, Harold Edward *retired banker*
Hammel, Iriana Simona *geriatrician*

Saint Clair
Wittig, Carol Hill *special education educator*

Saint Clair Shores
Coleman, Fay *literature and language educator, director*
Hausner, John Herman *retired judge*

Saint Joseph
King, George Raleigh *retired manufacturing executive*
Moore, Melissa *professional society administrator*

Saline
Cornell, Richard Garth *biostatistics educator*
Cruden, Robert William *botany educator*
Jeffries, Charles Dean *microbiology educator, research scientist, dean*

Sanford
Wilmot, Thomas Ray *medical entomologist, educator*

Sault Sainte Marie
France, Jennifer Jean *lawyer, educator*
Stai, Deborah *biology professor, director*

Sebewaing
Corrion, Samantha Jae *music educator*

Shelby Township
Osuch, Debra K. *environmental engineer*

Sidney
Roy, Janice L. *mathematics professor*

Sodus
Handy, Virginia Mae *writer*

South Haven
LaRocque, Linda Lou *interior designer, educator, playwright*
Llorens, Merna Gee *elementary school educator, retired music educator*
Tyrrell, Cole Brooks *music educator*
Waxman, Sheldon Robert *lawyer*

South Lyon
Melkvik, Jennifer Kent *retired mathematics educator*

Southfield
Alapont, José Maria *automotive executive*
Andreoff, Christopher Andon *lawyer*
Barnett, Marilyn *advertising executive*
Bassey, Ronald D. *tax attorney*
Brackenbury, James M. *manufacturing executive*
Caponigro, Jeffrey Ralph *public relations counselor*
Clifford, Carolyn *news correspondent, reporter*
Darling, Robert Howard *lawyer*
Dawson, Dennis Ray *lawyer, manufacturing executive*
Ferguson, Roger Clark *computer science educator*
Fieger, Geoffrey Nels *lawyer*
Hentrel, Bobbie Kuykendall *elementary school principal*
Hettiarachchi, Chamil Hiroshan *civil engineer, educator*
Hotelling, Harold *economics professor, lawyer*
Ibrahim, Ibrahim Namo *bishop*
Katz, Robert L. *lawyer*
Kern, Michael L. III *corporate financial executive*
Larkin, Terrence B. *lawyer*
Levine, Robert-Bob Alter *biomedical researcher, educator*
Low, James William *lawyer*
Margolis, Sherry *newscaster*
Martin, Marcella Edric *retired community health nurse*
McKeen, Alexander C. *retired engineering executive, foundation administrator*
Miller, Nancy Ellen *computer scientist, consultant*
Monsell, Edwin *otolaryngologist, educator*
Morganroth, Mayer *lawyer*
Osborne, Marie-Angela *journalist*
Perez-Cruet, Mick Jorge (Miguelangelo Jorge Perez-Cruet) *neurosurgeon, educator*
Pieper, Daniel Roy *neurosurgeon*
Porter, Thomas W.B. *lawyer*
Ritchie, Alexander Buchan *lawyer*
Rossiter, Robert E. *manufacturing executive*
Salvatore, Louis R. *manufacturing executive*
Scott, Raymond E. *manufacturing executive*
Simoncini, Matthew J. *manufacturing executive*
Sliety, Mazin K. *engineering educator*
Song, Xubin *mechanical engineer, researcher*
Thurswell, Gerald Elliott *lawyer*
Timmons, Robbie *news anchor*
Toll, Sheldon Samuel *lawyer*
Torraco, Pamela Louise *psychotherapist*
Vandenberghe, James H. *manufacturing executive*
Vantsevich, Vladimir V. *engineering educator, director*
Weiner, Karen Colby (Karen Lynn Colby) *psychologist, lawyer*
Willingham, Edward Bacon, Jr. *ecumenical minister, administrator*

Southgate
Torok, Margaret Louise *insurance company executive*

Spring Arbor
Kuntzleman, Thomas *chemistry professor*
Moore-Jumonville, Kimberly *literature educator*

Spring Lake
Bussard, Janice Wingeier *retired secondary school educator*

Sterling Heights
Binno, Joseph Michael *retired state attorney general*
Forkan, Eveleen *counselor, educator, researcher*
Kelly, Nelson Allen *chemist, researcher*
Radzevich, Stepan Pavlovich *mechanical engineering educator*
Rizk, Maged *cardiologist, researcher*
Robatchka-Walters, Janice Marie *medical/surgical and critical care nurse*

Sturgis
Reiff, James Stanley *osteopathic physician, addictions and psychiatric physician, surgeon*

Sylvan Lake
Derdarian, Christine Anne *lawyer*

Taylor
DeMarie, Donald J., Jr. *consumer products company executive*
Leekley, John Robert *lawyer, consumer products company executive*
Manoogian, Richard Alexander *consumer products company executive*
Wadhams, Timothy *consumer products company executive*
Yaggi, W. Timothy *manufacturing executive*

Three Rivers
Boyer, Nicodemus Elijah *chemist, consultant*

Traverse City
Anderson, Carol Lynn *social worker, educator*
Drake, Daniel H. *thoracic surgeon*
Faulmann, Roger Ray *retired music educator*
Joshi, Ameet Vijay *engineering company executive, director*
Kubiak, Jon Stanley *lawyer, casino and hotel industry executive*
Leuenberger, Betty Lou *psychologist, educator*
Walker, Dorothea Leigh (Thea Walker) *art therapist, educator*
Weaver, Elizabeth A. *state supreme court justice*
Zimmerman, Paul Albert *retired academic administrator, minister*

Trenton
Sanak, Francene Elizabeth *librarian*

Trout Creek
Bruno, Judyth Ann *chiropractor*

Troy
Adderley, Terence Edward *human resources executive*
Alterman, Irwin Michael *lawyer*
Baker, Vernon G., II, *lawyer, automotive executive*
Branigan, Thomas Patrick *lawyer*
Camden, Carl T. *human resources company executive*
Castelli, Ralph Anthony, Jr. *lawyer*
Chalil, Joseph Mathew *sales executive, consultant, liver disease specialist, medical products executive*
Corona, George S. *recruiting company executive*
Craig, Jeffrey A. *automotive executive*
Cunningham, Gary H. *lawyer*
Donlon, James D. III *automotive executive*
Duffy, Michael Charles *physician, director*
Fritzsche, Hellmut *physics professor*
Haron, David Lawrence *lawyer*
Hilton, Michael E. *lawyer*
Koch, Albert Acheson *music distribution company executive, management consultant*
Kruse, John Alphonse *lawyer*
Lis, Daniel T. *lawyer*
Marshall, John Elbert III *foundation executive*
McClure, Charles G. *automotive executive*
Miller, Robert Stevens, Jr., (Steve Miller) *automotive parts company executive*
Navarro, Monica *lawyer*
Nefske, Donald Joseph *engineer*
O'Neal, Rodney *automotive company executive*
Park, Won Chan *mechanical engineer*
Pearce, Harry Jonathan *lawyer, manufacturing executive*
Rapson, Richard (Rip Rapson) *foundation administrator*
Schafer, Sharon Marie *anesthesiologist*
Sheehan, John D. *automotive executive*
Sherbin, David M. *lawyer*
Strome, Stephen *former music distribution company executive*
Thoms, David Moore *lawyer*
Weber, Mark R. *automotive executive*
Zoubareff, Kathy Olga *actress, model*

University Center
Bledsoe, David Martin *educator*
Byam, Brooks Philip *mechanical engineer, educator*
Clarey, Timothy Lee *geologist, educator*
Clark, Basil Alfred *language educator*
Elfakhani, Said M. *finance educator*
Faleski, Michael C. *physics professor*
Fogarty, Julia T. *language educator*
Gorte, Mary Curl *science educator*
Hill, Alan Gordon *sociologist, educator*
Kolar, Marek *economics professor*
Millikin, Marsha *finance educator*

Utica
Cooper, Lindsay D. *retired social studies educator*

Van Buren Township
Donofrio, John *lawyer*

Walled Lake
Gillespie, J. Martin *sales and distribution company executive*

Warren
Abd Elhamid, Mahmoud Hassan *engineer, researcher*
Binkowski, Don *retired judge, writer*
Caulk, David A. *engineering company executive, researcher*
Cutter, Jeffrey S. *music educator*
Deeb, Edward *food products executive*
Ferman, Martin A. *research and development company executive*
Halalay, Ion Cornel *research scientist*
Henning, Billie Harrold *retired speech educator*
Herbst, Jan Francis *physicist, researcher*
Kolakowski, Diana Jean *economic development director*
Samra, Nicholas James *bishop emeritus*
Schmieg, Steven Jeffrey *research and development company executive, researcher*
Teitge, Robert A. *medical association administrator*
Zavattieri, Pablo Daniel *research scientist, educator*

Waterford
Anderson, Peter Stanford *physics professor*
Gulda, Edward James *diversified financial services company executive*
James, William Ramsay *broadcast executive*
Pronovost, Amy Lynne *dancer, educator*
Randall, Karl W. *air transportation executive, lawyer*

Watervliet
Watkins, M(artha) Anne *family practice nurse practitioner*

Wayland
Stephenson-Bennett, Michelle Annette *music educator*

West Bloomfield
Barr, Martin *science educator, academic administrator*
Cox, Clifford Ernest *information systems consulting executive, former academic administrator*
Goldsmith, Arnold Louis *American literature educator*
Harwood, Julius J. *metallurgist, educator*
Lewis, Harold Allen *childcare company executive*
Mamut, Mary Catherine *retired entrepreneur*
Marx, Thomas George *economist*
Meyers, Gerald Carl *finance educator, retired automotive executive*
Morgan, Jane Hale *retired library director*
Rauwerdink, William Jay *accountant*
Simpson, Robert Lee *academic administrator, department chairman, biologist, educator*
Stern, Guy *German language and literature educator, writer*
Williamson, Marilyn Lammert *literature educator, academic administrator*

White Lake
Clyburn, Luther Linn *real estate broker, appraiser*

Whitehall
Squier, David Louis *manufacturing executive*

Williamston
Schab, Daniel J. *mathematics educator*

Wilson
Harris, Mary Lynn *science educator, consultant*

Wixom
Alpert, Daniel *broadcast executive*
Huff, Alvin Edward *retired engineer*
Welch, Cherie Lynn *healthcare educator*

Wyandotte
Pentiuk, Randall Alan *lawyer*

Wyoming
Couch, Katrina Denise *elementary school educator*

Ypsilanti
Barnes, James Milton *retired physics and astronomy professor*
Barr, John Monte *lawyer*
Benedek, Elissa Leah *psychiatrist*
Bhaganagar, Kiran *research scientist*
Block, Judith Florence *university librarian, distance education specialist*
Boone, Morell Douglas *information technology educator*
Cere, Ronald Carl *languages educator, consultant, researcher*
Ervin, Naomi Estalee *nurse, educator*
Evans, Gary Lee *communications educator, consultant*
Evett, Matthew *science educator*
Gillard, Montgomery *dermatologist*
Ilozor, Benedict Dozie *architect, researcher, facility manager, planner*
Khan, Zafar U. *engineering educator*
Lewis-White, Linda Beth *elementary school educator*
Li, Zhang *engineering educator*
Queen, Marla Frudden *psychologist*
Smith, Phil *medical educator, director*
Thueme, William Harold *secondary school educator, counselor, travel coordinator*
Tummala, V.M Rao *supply chain management and operations educator*
Van WIngerden, Daniel J. *retired physics professor*
Weinstein, Jay A. *social sciences educator, researcher*
Willis, Craig Dean *academic administrator*

Zeeland
Walker, Brian C. *manufacturing executive*

MINNESOTA

Ada
Sillerud, Arlen Roger *retired secondary school educator*

Afton
Robb, Babette *retired elementary school educator*

Alexandria
Capp, Cheryl L. *nurse, educator*
Lillestol, Jane Brush *educational consultant*
Scholer, Catherine Rochelle *language educator*

Apple Valley
Becker, Bruce Warren *music educator*

Arden Hills
Lahann, Jon Clifford *retired music educator*

Austin
Alcorn, Wallace Arthur *minister, writer*
Binder, Steven G. *food products executive*
Cavanaugh, James W. *lawyer*
Ettinger, Jeffrey M. *food products executive, lawyer*
Feragen, Jody H. *food products executive*
Rioux, Pierre August *psychiatrist*

Baxter
Tomonovich, Kristin L. *special education educator*

Bemidji
Bridston, Paul Joseph *strategic management consultant*
Conely, Patrice Erin *librarian*
Davgun, Satish K. *social sciences educator*
Gilbertson, Troy *criminology educator*
Kief, Paul Allan *lawyer*
Martinson, Ida Marie *retired medical/surgical nurse, physiologist*
Rogers, Patricia Louise *education educator, consultant, dean*
Sonsteng, Kathleen A. *education educator*

Bloomington
Ahmad, Kashif A. *science educator, researcher*
Bekrenev, Anatoliy *physicist*
Bigalk, Kristina *writing professor*
Buhrmaster, Robert C. *manufacturing executive*
Mooty, John William *lawyer*
Ouyang, Jun *electrical engineer, researcher*
Reutter, Michael A. *biology professor*
Sandok, Scott *economics educator, healthcare educator*
Smith, Henry Charles III *symphony orchestra conductor*
Wilhelm, Gary Bretz *physician*

Brainerd
Mickelson, Paul A. *biology professor, consultant*
Vig, Pradeep Kumar *geophysics educator*

Breezy Point
Anderson, Gail Marie *retired librarian*

Brooklyn Park
Paulus, Eugenia *chemistry professor*

Buffalo
Moon, James Russell *retired technology education educator*

Burnsville
Foss, Emma Thoren *retired social worker*
Lakin, James Dennis *allergist, immunologist, director*
O'Brien, Gerald James *utilities executive*

Caledonia
Dibert, Wendy Katherine *parochial school educator*

Cambridge
Van Alstine, Sharri Kay *music educator*

Chanhassen
Froemming, Herbert Dean *retired retail executive*
Prince, (Prince Rogers Nelson) *musician, actor*
Severson, Roger Allan *bank executive*

Chatfield
Opat, Matthew John *lawyer*

Circle Pines
Paisley, John *psychologist*

Cloquet
Belanger, Sharon Amling *special education educator*

Coleraine
Iwasaki, Iwao *engineering educator*

Collegeville
Díaz, Miguel H. *religious studies educator, writer*

Coon Rapids
Bordner, Patricia Anne *insurance agent, writer*
Klamm-Doneen, Kristin Irene *philosopher, educator*
McCarthy, Thomas Gregory *theater educator*
Vogel, Scott Charles *music educator*
Wilson, Sylvia Alyce *musician, educator*

Crookston
Balke, Victor Herman *bishop emeritus*
Elf, Pamela Kay *biology professor*
Hoeppner, Michael Joseph *bishop*
Killough, Alvin Lynard *psychology professor, consultant*

Detroit Lakes
Stowman, David L. *lawyer*

Duluth
Aufderheide, Arthur Carl *pathologist*
Balmer, James Walter *lawyer*
Burns, Richard Ramsey *lawyer*
Chee, Cheng-Khee *artist, educator*
Clarke, Margaret Jackson *physics professor, archivist*
Gallian, Joseph Anthony *mathematics professor*
Hodapp, William F. *literature and language professor*
Johnson, Arthur Gilbert *microbiology educator*
McKee, David Charles *neurologist*
Morath, Max Edward *entertainer, composer, writer*
Norberg-King, Teresa Joy *research aquatic biologist*
Pearce, Donald Joslin *retired librarian*
Rapp, George Robert (Rip) *geology and archeology educator*
Salmela, David Daniel *architect*
Schroeder, Fred Erich Harald *humanities educator*
Stauber-Johnson, Elizabeth Jane *retired elementary school educator*
Tadesse, Bedassa *economics professor, researcher*
Whiteman, Richard Frank *architect*
Worthing, Carol Marie *retired minister*

Eagan
Bauer, Kris *air transportation executive*
Becker, Michael J. *air transportation executive*
Bostock, Roy Jackson *investment company executive, air transportation executive*
Clemens, T. Pat *manufacturing executive*
Davis, David M. *air transportation executive*
Friedel, Jim *air transportation executive*
Griffin, J. Timothy *air transportation executive*
Haan, Philip C. *air transportation executive*
Hirst, Richard B. *air transportation executive, lawyer*
Knotek, Crystal *air transportation executive*
Matthews, Daniel B. *air transportation executive*
Rainey, Timothy J. *air transportation executive*
Roberts, Andrew C. *air transportation executive*
Wise, Theresa *air transportation executive*

East Gull Lake
Simons, John Nelson *surgeon, consultant*

Eden Prairie
Allen, Jared Scot *professional football player*
Arthur, Lindsay Grier *retired judge, editor, writer*
Brzezinski, Rob *professional sports team executive*
Childress, Brad *professional football coach*
De Bono, Luella Elizabeth *music educator*

Favre, Brett Lorenzo *professional football player*
Gernander, Barton Carl *lawyer*
Henningsen, Peter, Jr. *manufacturing executive*
Herkert, Craig R. *grocery retail and supply chain service company executive*
Higgins, Robert Arthur *electrical engineer, educator, consultant*
Hutchinson, Steve *professional football player*
Knickerbocker, Vicky Ann *sociologist, educator*
Knous, Pamela K. *wholesale distribution executive*
Lindbloom, Chad M. *transportation executive*
Murphy, Daniel J., Jr. *aerospace and defense manufacturing company executive, military officer*
Noddle, Jeffrey *retail and food distribution company executive*
Reha, Rose Krivisky *retired finance educator*
Satterlee, Scott A. *trucking executive*
Spielman, Rick *professional sports team executive*
Switz, Robert E. *telecommunications executive*
Van Helden, Peter J. *grocery company executive*
Wiehoff, John P. *trucking executive*
Williams, Kevin *professional football player*

Edina
Bagby, Robert L. *former investment company executive*
Bakken, Eric Allen *lawyer*
Barden, Robert Christopher *lawyer, psychologist, educator, writer*
Bisping, Bruce Henry *photojournalist*
Brown, Charles Eugene *retired electronics company executive*
Campbell, James Robert *retired bank executive*
Covington, Alec C. *retail executive*
Farah, Caesar Elie *retired language educator, historian*
Fenwick, Sheridan Mellon *psychologist, director*
Gottesman, Irving I. *psychologist, educator*
Kreiser, Frank David *real estate executive*
Lapadat, Paul *food products executive*
Leach, Bertram George *retired military officer, securities dealer*
Neff, Fred Leonard *lawyer*
Rucker, Richard Douglas, Jr. *emergency physician*
Schulze, Chad William *lawyer*
Tagatz, George Elmo *retired obstetrician, gynecologist, educator*

Elk River
McClure, Alvin Bruce *watchmaker*
Richardson, Mark P. *protective services official, educator*

Excelsior
Anderson, William Robert *retired pathologist educator*
Oliver, Edward Carl *state legislator, insurance company executive, small business owner*
Pfeifer, Polly Lee *elementary school educator*

Fairmont
Wolfgram, Kenneth Charles *retired agricultural engineer*

Falcon Heights
Jackson, Donna Cardamone *retired music educator*
Kreuter, Gretchen Von Loewe *academic administrator*

Faribault
Collins, Ruth Ann *special education services professional, director*

Farmington
Wurdeman, Lew Edward *Internet company executive, consultant*

Forest Lake
Skrip, Cathy Lee *psychologist*

Golden Valley
Hogan, Randall J. *manufacturing and electronics executive*
McMahan, Robert *pharmacist, director*
Schlichting, William Henry *lawyer, writer*
Spake, Mary Barbara *music educator*
Zabinski, Richard A. *pharmacist*

Good Thunder
Bothmann, Robert *librarian*

Goodridge
Hanson, Norma Lee *farmer*

Grand Marais
Hattery, Robert Wilber *political science educator*

Grand Rapids
Welch, Wayne Willard *educator*

Granite Falls
Alness, Mae Christine *retired medical/surgical nurse*

Harmony
Webster, Jeffrey Leon *graphic designer*

Hastings
McGovern, Jillaine *literature and language educator*

Hibbing
Calligan, William Dennis *retired life insurance company executive*
Carey, Jan *school librarian*

Hopkins
Young, Margaret Labash *librarian, information consultant, editor*
Zotaley, Byron Leo *lawyer*

Inver Grove Heights
Koenig, Robert August *minister, educator*

Kenyon
Peterson, Franklin Delano *lawyer*

La Crescent
Gelatt, Charles Daniel *manufacturing executive*

Lake Crystal
Pawlitschek, Donald Paul *management consultant*

Lake Elmo
Tomljanovich, Esther M. *retired judge*

Lake Lillian
Marquardt, Steve Robert *advocate*

Lakeland
Housley, Phil F. *coach, retired professional hockey player*

Lakeville
Kasella, Nancy E. *psychology educator*
Phinney, William Charles *retired geologist*
Setterholm, Jeffrey Miles *systems engineer*

Le Sueur
Yang, Mengyan *chemical engineer, research scientist*

Lindstrom
Messin, Marlene Ann *plastics company executive*

Little Falls
Perfetti, Robert Nickolas *educational consultant*
Stobb, Mary Jean *retired association administrator*

Long Lake
Lowthian, Petrena *academic administrator*

Madison
Husby, Donald Evans *engineering company executive*

Mahtomedi
Brainerd, Richard Charles *human resources executive, consultant, educator*

Mankato
Cherrington, Janet E. *religious studies educator, researcher*
Janc, John J. *language educator*
Kitsul, Pavel Ivanovich *mathematics professor, researcher*
Kunz, Alan Leonard *automotive executive, educator*
Levin, Daniel A. *law educator*
Longwell, Patricia Anne *language educator*
Park, Kwang Woo *financial planner, educator*
Purcell, Helen Duncan *sociologist, educator*
Purcell, Keith William *minister*
Salsbery, Meredith A. *legislative staff member*
Tomany, Maria-Claudia Christine *language educator, director*
Tung, Chia-chi *mathematics professor*

Maple Grove
Kirpes, Anne Irene *elementary school educator*
Oh, Allen James *lawyer*
Ones, Deniz S. *psychologist, educator*

Mapleton
John, Hugo Herman *natural resources educator*

Maplewood
Erhardt, Rhoda P. *occupational therapist*
Thomas, Cristina Urdaneta *chemical engineer, researcher*

Marshall
Ibrayeva, Elina *management, international business educator*
Pichaske, David Richard *language educator*
Varcoe, Jeffrey John *food service executive*

Mendota Heights
Bingham, Christopher *statistics educator*
Deans, Thomas Seymour *lawyer*
Frechette, Peter Loren *medical products executive*
Friedrichs, Terence Paul *special and gifted education teacher*
McMullin, Ernan Vincent *retired philosophy educator*

Minneapolis
Aamoth, Gordon M. *medical association administrator*
Ackerman, Eugene *biophysics professor*
Adams, John Stephen *geography educator*
Agyenkwah, Kennedy Seth *communications executive*
Alexander, Darsie *curator*
Almquist, Adrian K. *clinical cardiac electrophysiologist*
Alton, Ann Leslie *judge, lawyer, educator*
Anand, Inder S. *medical educator, director*
Anderson, Eric Scott *lawyer*
Anderson, John Edward *mechanical engineering educator*
Appel, William Frank *pharmacist*
Arnold, Douglas Norman *mathematician*
Atwood, John Brian *dean, political science professor*
Avella, Joseph Ralph *university professor*
Avgoustiniatos, Efstathios S. *chemical engineer, educator*
Bache, Robert James *physician, educator*
Baer, Timothy R. *lawyer, retail executive*
Bagan, Mark G. *grain exchange executive*
Baillie, James Leonard *lawyer*
Baldwin, Trista *playwright*
Balfour, Henry Hallowell, Jr. *medical educator, researcher, physician, writer*
Ballintine, Daniel John *lawyer*
Barnes, Nancy *editor-in-chief*
Bashiri, Iraj *Central Asian studies educator*
Berens, William Joseph *lawyer*
Berman, Walter S. *treasurer*
Berry, Susan A. *pediatrician, educator*
Berryman, Robert Glen *accounting educator, consultant*
Berscheid, Ellen S. *psychology professor, writer, researcher*
Bhavsar, Abdhish Raman *ophthalmologist, researcher*
Binger, Erika L. *foundation administrator*
Bizri, Hisham M. *filmmaker, educator*
Blewett, Lynn A. *healthcare educator*
Bonavia, Paul J. *energy executive*
Borger, John Philip *lawyer*
Boushek, Randy L. *insurance company executive*
Boyce, Karin R. *music educator*
Branson, Timothy E. *lawyer*
Brasket, Curt Justin *systems analyst*
Bress, Michael E. *retired lawyer*
Brink, David Ryrie *lawyer*
Brooker, Robert J. *biology professor*
Brosseau, Lisa M. *industrial hygienist, educator*
Brown, Carlyle *performing company executive, playwright*
Brown, Robert John *social sciences educator, consultant*
Bruininks, Robert H. *academic administrator, psychologist, educator*
Buchwald, Henry *surgeon, educator, researcher*
Burke, Richard T., Sr. *healthcare company executive, former professional sports team executive*
Burnet, Ralph W. *real estate company officer*
Burns, Matthew Kevin *psychology professor*
Busdicker, Gordon Gene *retired lawyer*
Cabrera, Orlando Luis *professional baseball player*
Caplan, Allan Hart *lawyer*
Carlson, Arne Helge *former governor*
Carlson, Thomas David *lawyer*
Carr, Peter William *chemistry professor*
Cattanach, Robert Edward, Jr. *lawyer*
Cecere, Andrew *bank executive*
Chahine, Iman Chafik *mathematics professor, director*
Champlin, Steven Kirk *lawyer*
Chavers, Blanche Marie *pediatrician, educator, researcher*
Chemberlin, Peg *minister, religious organization administrator*
Chipman, John Somerset *economist, retired educator*
Church, Timothy Robert *medical educator, researcher*
Ciresi, Michael Vincent *lawyer*
Clary, Bradley G. *lawyer, educator*
Clemence, Roger Davidson *landscape architect, educator*
Cohn, Jay N. *cardiologist, educator*
Cole, Phillip Allen *lawyer*
Connelly, Michael C. *lawyer, energy executive*
Constantine, Katherine A. *lawyer*
Cook, William M. *manufacturing executive*
Cope, Lewis *journalist*
Cowles, John, Jr. *publishing executive, women's sports promoter, civic activist*
Cracchiolo, James M. *diversified financial services company executive*
Craig, James Lynn *physician, health services administrator*
Crippen, John Raymond *museum director*
Crouch, Steven L. *mining engineer, dean*
Curler, Jeffrey H. *packaging manufacturing executive*
Dallas, H. James *medical products executive*
Danielson, James Walter *retired research microbiologist*
Davis, Richard K. *bank executive*
Davis-Blake, Alison *dean, management educator*
Davison, Mark L. *psychology, education professor*
DeForge, Anna *professional basketball player*
DiGangi, Frank Edward *academic administrator*
Dimond, Robert B. *food products executive*
Doty, David Singleton *federal judge*
Dragseth, Kenneth Allen *retired superintendent and educational consultant of schools*
Drake, Dallas Sumner *researcher*
Dunn, Brian J. *retail executive*
Durkin, G. Michael *food products executive*
Dworkin, Martin *retired microbiologist*
Dykstra, Dennis Dale *physiatrist*
Eck, George Gregory *lawyer*
Ellis, Gary *medical products executive*
Erdrich, Louise *writer, poet*
Erickson, Gerald Meyer *classical studies educator*
Fallon, Patrick R. *advertising executive*
Feldman, Kaywin *museum director, curator*
Feldman, Nancy Jane *insurance company executive*
Ferrari, Giannantonio *electronics executive*
Fetler, Paul *retired composer*
Finch, Frederick Earl *lawyer*
Finkelstein, Paul D. *personal care industry executive*
Firchow, Evelyn Scherabon *German language and literature educator, writer*
Firchow, Peter Edgerly *language professional, educator, writer*
Fisch, Robert Otto *medical educator*
Flanagan, Barbara *journalist*
Fletcher, Edward Abraham *engineering educator*
Flom, Gerald Trossen *lawyer*
Flynn Peterson, Kathleen A. *lawyer*
Francis, Michael R. *retail executive*
Freese, Andrew *neurosurgeon, educator*
Galambos, Theodore Victor *civil engineer, educator*
Gallagher, Gerald Raphael *venture capitalist*
Garon, Philip Stephen *lawyer*
Garton, Thomas William *lawyer*
Georgieff, Michael Kara *medical educator, researcher*
Gerberich, Susan Goodwin *epidemiologist, educator, medical researcher*
Gillom, Jennifer *professional basketball coach, retired professional basketball player*
Goldberg, Luella Gross *diversified financial services company executive*
Goldman, Allen Marshall *physics professor*
Goldstein, Richard Jay *mechanical engineer, educator*
Gomes, Ryan *professional basketball player*
Gorham, Eville *retired ecologist*
Gowrisankaran, Gautam *economist, educator*
Greener, Ralph Bertram *lawyer*
Griffith, John D. *retail executive*
Grimes, David Lynn *communications executive*
Gross, David J.F. *lawyer*
Grudzielanek, Mark James *professional baseball player*
Gruessner, Rainer W.G. *surgeon, educator*
Gudmundson, Barbara Rohrke *ecologist*
Gurvich, Vadim J. *chemist, director*
Guzina, Bojan B. *engineering educator*
Hadley, Katherine G. (Kit) *library director*
Haines, Stephen John *neurosurgeon*
Hale, James Thomas *retail executive, lawyer*
Hale, Roger Loucks *manufacturing executive, director*
Halley, James Woods *physics professor*
Hamel, Mark Edwin *lawyer*
Hampl, Patricia *writer, educator*
Hansen, Jo-Ida Charlotte *psychology professor, researcher*
Hansen, Robyn L. *lawyer*
Hanson, Arthur Stuart *physician, consultant*
Hanson, Samuel Lee *former state supreme court justice*
Harper, Donald Victor *retired transportation and logistics educator, consultant*
Harris, Ilene Barmash *researcher*
Harris, Morton Edward *mathematics educator*
Harris, Reuben Stewart *biology professor, researcher*
Harte, Christopher M. *publishing executive, investment manager*
Hartwell, Kimberly S. *telecommunications industry executive*
Hawkins, William A. III *medical products executive*
Haynsworth, Harry Jay, IV, *law educator*
Hays, Thomas S. *medical educator, researcher*
Hayward, Edward Joseph *lawyer*
Heffelfinger, Thomas Backer *lawyer, former prosecutor*
Heiberg, Robert Alan *lawyer*
Hellman, Geoffrey P. *philosopher, educator*
Helsene, Amy L. *lawyer*
Hemsley, Stephen J. *healthcare company executive*
Hendrixson, Peter S. *lawyer*
Herman, John Hughes *lawyer*
Hibbs, John Stanley *lawyer*
Hoffman, Michael J. *manufacturing executive*
Hoffmann, Thomas Russell *business management educator*
Holden, Susan M. *lawyer*
Horsch, Kathleen Joanne *social services administrator, educator, consultant*
Huntzicker, William Edward *journalism educator, writer*
Ibrahim, Hassan N. *nephrologist, educator*
Israni, Ajay *medical educator, researcher*
Jacob, Bernard Michel *architect*
Jacobs, Irwin Lawrence *diversified corporate executive*
Jarboe, Mark Alan *lawyer*
Jefferson, Al *professional basketball player*
John, Charles J. *public health service officer, educator*
Johnson, David Wolcott *psychologist, educator*
Johnson, John Warren *retired professional society administrator*
Johnson, Kenneth Harvey *veterinary pathologist*
Johnson, Lola Norine *retired advertising and public relations executive, educator*
Johnson, Margaret Ann (Peggy) *library administrator*
Johnson, Walter Heinrick, Jr. *retired educator, university administrator*
Johnson, Walter Kline *civil engineer*
Jones, B. Todd (Byron Todd Jones) *prosecutor*
Joseph, Marilyn Susan *gynecologist*
Joyce, Joseph M. *lawyer, retail executive*
Judson, Patricia Lynn *obstetrician, gynecologist, oncologist*
Junek, John C. *lawyer, finance company executive*
Kahn, David *professional sports team executive*
Kahn, Jonathan *law educator*
Kane, Robert Lewis *public health service officer, educator*
Kaplan, Sheldon *lawyer, director*
Katsiaficas, Diane *artist, educator*
Kaufman, Stephen Charles *ophthalmologist, clinician and surgeon*
Keenan, Joseph *retired medical educator, consultant, emergency physician*
Keene, Lonnie *lawyer*
Keets, John David, Jr. *insurance company executive*
Kelley, Douglas A. *lawyer*
Kelly, A. David *lawyer*
Kelly, Charles Harold *advertising executive*
Kelly, Richard C. *energy executive*
Kennedy, William Robert *neurologist, educator*
Keppel, William James *lawyer, educator, writer*
Keyes, Jeffrey J. *lawyer*
King, Lyndel Irene Saunders *museum director*
Kiresuk, Thomas Jack *psychologist, educator*
Kirtley, Jane Elizabeth *law educator*
Kjellstrand, Carl Magnus *physician, educator*
Klaas, Paul Barry *lawyer*
Knoke, David Harmon *sociology educator*
Koneck, John Michael *lawyer*
Korotkin, Fred *writer, philatelist*
Kozlak, Jodeen A. *retail executive*
Kratzke, Robert Arthur *oncologist, educator*
Kudrle, Robert Thomas *economist, educator*
Kumra, Sanjiv *psychiatrist, educator*
Kuncel, Nathan R. *psychology professor*
Kvalseth, Tarald Oddvar *mechanical engineer, educator*
Laing, Karel Ann *publishing executive*
Lambert, Robert Frank *electrical engineer, educator, consultant*
Lancaster, Peter McCreery *lawyer*
Larson, Sheryl Ann *social worker, researcher, writer*
Lavik, Bricker L. *lawyer*

Le, Thanh Trung *economics professor*
Lebedoff, David Miller *lawyer, writer*
Lebedoff, Jonathan Galanter *retired judge, mediator*
Legge, Gordon E. *psychology professor, department chairman*
Leon, Arthur Sol *research cardiologist, exercise physiologist*
Leppik, Ilo E. *neurologist, educator*
Lerner, Harry Jonas *publishing executive*
Leuchovius, Deborah *advocate, special education services professional, consultant*
Lewis, Stephen Richmond, Jr. *economist, educator*
Ligocki, Lawrence Francis *religious studies educator*
Lillehaug, David Lee *lawyer*
Lindell, Edward Albert *academic and religious organization administrator*
Lindgren, Jay Randolph *lawyer, former state senator*
Lindsay, Michael Anthony *lawyer*
Litman, Theodor James *medical educator*
Loh, Horace H. *pharmacology educator*
Loken, James Burton *federal judge*
Lougee, Wendy Pradt *university librarian, educator*
Lucke, Stephen P. *lawyer*
Lueck, Martin R. *lawyer*
Luepker, Russell Vincent *epidemiology educator*
Lumpkins, Robert L. *food products executive*
Mackay, Harvey B. *paper company executive, writer*
Magill, Frank J., Jr. *prosecutor*
Magnuson, Roger James *lawyer*
Maheshwari, Aditya V. *orthopedist, educator*
Mahoney, Kathleen Mary *lawyer*
Malmin, Cindy Lou *music educator*
Malmquist, Carl Phillip *psychiatrist*
Mammel, Russell Norman *retired food distribution company executive*
Mandel, Sheldon Lloyd *dermatologist, educator*
Mangia, Silvia *science educator*
Mansfield, William L. *manufacturing executive*
Marano, Thomas *finance company executive*
Maratsos, Michael Philip *psychology professor*
Marinello, Kathryn V. *human resources company executive*
Markus, Lawrence *retired mathematics professor*
Marshak, Marvin Lloyd *physicist, researcher*
Martenson, Edward Allen *theater manager*
Martin, Phillip Hammond *lawyer*
Martin, Roger Bond *landscape architect*
Martinson, Bradley James *lawyer*
Matheson, John H. *lawyer, educator*
Mauer, Joe *professional baseball player*
Maynard, Hugh M. *lawyer*
McConnell, Scott Rushton *educational psychology educator*
McDonald, John J., Jr. *lawyer*
McGunnigle, George Francis *lawyer, judge*
McKee, Tim *chef*
McLaren, Brian *pastor, Christian activist*
McLaughlin, Patrick J. *lawyer*
McNaron, Toni A.H. *literature and language educator, director*
Melendez, Brian *lawyer, political organization administrator*
Menge, David Maina *biomedical researcher*
Meshbesher, Ronald I. *lawyer*
Mikan, G. Mike *healthcare services company executive, corporate financial executive*
Miller, Alan M. *writer, educator, television host*
Mitau, Lee R. *lawyer, bank executive*
Moller, James Herman *pediatrician, educator*
Mondale, Joan Adams *wife of former Vice President of United States*
Mondale, Walter Frederick *former Vice President of United States, lawyer*
Monga, Manoj *medical educator*
Monroe, Craig (Keystone) *professional baseball player*
Montgomery, Lynn Marie *educational consultant*
Moor, Rob *professional sports team executive*
Morita, Norimasa *otolaryngologist, researcher*
Morneau, Justin Ernest George *professional baseball player*
Morrison, Fred LaMont *law educator*
Morrison, John Lewis *former food company executive, investor*
Mosley, Gregg Allen *microbiologist*
Mulligan, Donal L. *consumer products company executive*
Munsell, William A. *healthcare insurance company executive*
Murphy, Diana E. *federal judge*
Murphy, Joseph Edward, Jr. *broadcast executive*
Mwakabuta, Ndaga Stanslaus *electrical engineer*
Najarian, John Sarkis *surgeon, educator*
Narciso, Carmen Veronica *elementary school educator*
Nash, Elizabeth Hamilton *music and theater educator, vocalist, writer*
Nathan, Joseph Michael (Joe Nathan) *professional baseball player*
Nelson, Kenneth D. *bank executive*
Newman, Mari Alice *artist, architect, art designer*
Ni, Jessie H.-T. *research and development company executive, director*
Nicholson, Bruce J. *insurance company executive*
Nicholson, Hilton M. *telecommunications industry executive*
Noel, Franklin Linwood *judge*
Novak, Leslie Howard *lawyer*
Nyrop, Donald William *air transportation executive*
O'Brien, Patrick D. *telecommunications industry executive*
Oesterle, Stephen N. *medical products executive, cardiologist, educator*
O'Keefe, Thomas Michael *academic administrator*
Olson, James Richard *retired transportation executive*
Olson, John Richard *power industry electrician*
Opperman, Dwight Darwin *retired publishing company executive*
Oriani, Richard Anthony *metallurgical engineer, educator*
Ort, Shannon *lawyer*
Osterholm, Michael T. *epidemiologist, public health service officer*
Ostrem, Walter Martin *librarian, educator, consultant*
Ostrom, Don *retired political science professor*
Overmier, J. Bruce *psychology professor*
Page, Gregory R. *agricultural products and diversified services company executive*
Painter, Richard William *lawyer, educator*
Palmer, Deborah Jean *lawyer*
Palmore, Rick (Roderick A. Palmore) *consumer products company executive, lawyer*
Pambuccian, Stefan E. *cytologist, educator*
Parhi, Keshab Kumar *electrical and computer engineering educator*
Park, Eunsung *scientist, education educator*
Parran, Richard B., Jr. *telecommunications industry executive*
Parsons, Charles Allan, Jr. *lawyer*
Pate, Alexs Delaney *writer, educator*
Patterson, Steven Earl *chemistry professor, researcher*
Paulu, Frances Brown *retired international center administrator*
Payne, William Bruce *lawyer, director*
Penny, Timothy Joseph *former congressman*
Peterson, Adrian Lewis *professional football player*
Pfau, James Michael *lawyer*
Pfender, Emil *mechanical engineering educator*
Pflaum, Jeffrey D. *lawyer*
Phibbs, Clifford Matthew *surgeon, educator*
Plomondon, John Edmund *literature and language professor*
Pohlad, Robert C. *consumer products company executive*
Polly, David W., Jr. *surgeon*
Porter, Philip Wayland *geography educator*
Portoghese, Philip Salvatore *medicinal chemist, educator*
Powell, Deborah Elizabeth *pathologist, dean*
Powell, Ken (Kendall J. Powell) *consumer products company executive*
Pozen, Robert Charles *investment company executive*
Pratte, Robert John *lawyer*
Prestwich, Roger *educator*
Price, Joseph Michael *lawyer*
Quam, Lois *investment company executive, former health insurance company executive*
Quie, Paul Gerhardt *pediatrician, educator*
Radmer, Michael John *lawyer, educator*
Ramalho-Ahrndt, Maria Gabriela *art educator*
Rambis, Kurt (Darrell Kurt Rambis) *professional basketball coach, retired professional basketball player*
Raskind, Leo Joseph *law educator*
Rasmussen, Teresa J. *lawyer, insurance company executive*
Ratchye, Boyd Havens *lawyer*
Reich, Edgar *mathematics professor*
Reichgott Junge, Ember Darlene *broadcast commentator, retired state senator, lawyer, writer, radio personality*
Reini-Grandell, Lynette Eileen *literature and language professor, writer*
Reiss, Ira Leonard *retired sociology educator, writer*
Remmel, Rory Patrick *pharmacy educator*
Ridder, Par *former publishing executive*
Risch, Troy H. *retail executive*
Roe, Sharon Louise *architect, educator*
Rose, Thomas Albert *artist, educator*
Rosenbaum, James Michael *federal judge*
Rosenbaum, Robert A. *lawyer*
Rosenblatt, Cynthia Schaffer *lawyer*
Ross, Donald, Jr. *language educator, academic administrator*
Roth, Margaret Agnes *child development educator*
Rudelius, William *marketing educator*
Ruggles, Steven *science educator*
Ryan, Terry *professional sports team executive*
Rybak, R.T. *Mayor, Minneapolis*
Saeks, Allen Irving *lawyer*
Safley, James Robert *lawyer*
Salerno, Salvatore *medical educator*
Santana, Lymari Jeanette *lawyer*
Sawicki, Zbigniew Peter *lawyer*
Sawyer, Charles F. *lawyer*
Scallen, Thomas Kaine *broadcast executive*
Schreiner, John Christian *economics consultant, software publisher*
Schulze, Richard M. *retail executive*
Schutz, Ronald James *lawyer*
Scovanner, Douglas A. *retail executive*
Scully, Terrence J. *retail executive*
Seidel, Robert Wayne *science historian, educator*
Serrin, James Burton *mathematics professor*
Shapiro, Burton Leonard *dentist, maxillofacial pathologist, geneticist, educator*
Shifman, Mikhail *physicist*
Shively, William Phillips *political scientist, educator*
Shnider, Bruce Jay *lawyer*
Short, Marianne Dolores *lawyer*
Sidebottom, Charles Benton *engineering executive*
Sielaff, Timothy David *oncologist, department chairman*
Simonson, James S. *lawyer*
Sippel, William Leroy *lawyer*
Sisk, Gregory Charles *lawyer, educator*
Slettehaugh, Thomas Chester *retired art educator*
Smith, Bill *professional sports team executive*
Smith, Tubby *men's college basketball coach*
Sortland, Paul Allan *lawyer*
Sparby, David M. *energy executive*
Sparrow, Ephraim Maurice *engineer, educator*
Speedie, Marilyn Kay *microbiologist, dean, educator*
Spong, Douglas K. *public relations executive*
Spoor, William Howard *food products executive*
Stack, Jim *professional sports team executive*
Stageberg, Roger V. *lawyer*
Stauffer, William Moyer *medical educator, director*
Steen-Hinderlie, Diane Evelyn *social worker, musician*
Stein, Robert Allen *lawyer, educator, former legal association administrator*
Steinhafel, Gregg William *retail executive*
Stenwick, Michael William *retired internist, geriatrician, consultant*
Stephens, Lee-Ann Williams *elementary school educator*
Stern, Gary Hilton *bank executive*
Stern, Leo G. *lawyer*
Stevens, Simon *healthcare company executive*
Stoeri, William R. *lawyer*
Stouder, Robin Renee *academic administrator, realtor*
Struthers, Margo S. *lawyer*
Sullivan, Alfred Dewitt *academic administrator*
Sullivan, John L. *political science professor*
Sullivan, Michael Patrick *food service executive*
Sutherland, David E.R. *surgeon*
Svendsbye, Lloyd August *retired academic administrator, theologian, educator*
Swanson, David P. *lawyer*
Sweet, Robert Marten *urologic surgeon, medical simulation scientist/administrator*
Swickrath, Michael Jacob *research scientist*
Swiontkowski, Marc Francis *orthopedist*
Tanick, Marshall Howard *lawyer, educator*
Tatlock, Ann *writer*
Tesija, Kathee (Kathryn A. Tesija) *retail executive*
Thompson, Theodore Robert *pediatric educator*
Thormodsgard, Diane L. *bank executive*
Torgerson, Paul M. *prosecutor*
Toscano, James Vincent *medical foundation president*
Tracy, James Donald *historian, educator*
Tran, Nang Tri *research scientist, electrical engineer, entrepreneur*
Trestman, Frank D. *distribution company executive, director*
Trouten, Douglas James *journalist*
Trucano, Michael *lawyer*
Tuckson, Reed V. *physician, health insurance company executive*
Ugurbil, Kamil *radiologist, neuroscientist, educator*
Ulrich, Robert J. (Bob Ulrich) *retired retail executive*
Ulstrom, Robert A. *retired pediatrician*
Van Brunt, William A. *lawyer*
Vänskä, Osmo *conductor, music director*
Veblen, Thomas Clayton *management consultant*
Viso, Olga *museum director*
Vuchetich, John Patrick *psychiatrist*
Wahoske, Michael James *lawyer*
Wangberg, Larry W. *business consultant*
Ward, David Allen *sociology educator*
Warring, Douglas Franklin *education educator, psychologist*
Weir, Edward Kenneth *cardiologist, educator*
Weiss, Gerhard Hans *German language educator*
Weiss, Renee E. *accounting educator*
Welters, Anthony *health services executive*
Whelpley, Dennis Porter *lawyer*
White, Robert James *retired columnist*
Wichmann, David S. *health care services executive*
Wickesberg, Albert Klumb *retired management consultant*
Wiggins, Candice Dana *professional basketball player*
Wild, John Julian *surgeon, researcher, medical educator*
Wilks, David M. *energy executive*
Windhorst, John William, Jr. *lawyer*
Winer, Edward L. *lawyer*
Wippman, David *dean, law educator*
Wollenberg, Bruce Frederick *electrical engineering educator, consultant*
Woodman, Stewart *chef*
Woods, Robert Edward *lawyer*
Wright, Chris *professional sports team executive*
Wright, Herbert E(dgar), Jr. *geologist*
Wunsch, John D. *former bank executive, financial consultant*
Wurtele, Christopher Angus *paint and coatings company executive*
Yomba, Emmanuel *mathematician, researcher, physicist*
Young, Delmon Damarcus *professional baseball player*
Young, Lynda Jeanne *dental educator, director*
Younger, Judith Tess *law educator*
Yourzak, Robert Joseph *management consultant, educator, engineer*
Yuan, Jian-Min *epidemiologist*
Zapp, Kenneth Michael *engineering educator, department chairman*
Zelazo, Philip David *science educator*
Zlowodzki, Michal Pawel *surgeon, researcher*

Minnetonka
Anderson, Karen Jean *mayor, communications executive, researcher*
Boudreaux, Gail K. *insurance company executive*
Erlandson, Patrick J. *health products executive*
Gillies, Donald Richard *marketing and advertising consultant, educator*
Joly, Hubert Bernard *hotel and travel company executive*
Morisato, Susan Cay *actuary*
Nelson, Marilyn Carlson *hotel and travel company executive*
Penshorn, John S. *insurance company executive*
Pillsbury, George Sturgis *retired investment advisor*
Rivet, Jeannine M. *health insurance company executive*
Robbins, Orem Olford *insurance company executive*
Rogers, James Devitt *judge*
Sandy, Lewis Gordon *physician, healthcare executive*
Sperber, William Henry *microbiologist, writer*
Sussman, Bonnie Kaufman *art dealer, interior designer, consultant*
Sweere Komstadius, Lori *insurance company executive*
Tao, Li *application developer*
Wittcoff, Harold Aaron *chemist*

Moorhead
Buckley, Joan N. *retired literature and language professor*
Gargurevich, Eduardo *language educator*
Gee, Robert LeRoy *agriculturist, dairy farmer*
Heuer, Gerald Arthur *mathematician, educator*
Shoptaugh, Terry Lee *historian, archivist*
Smemo, Irwin Kenneth *history professor*
Strong, Judith Ann *retired chemist*
Zinober, Richard Neil *playwright, educator*

Morris
Hauger, Susan Mary *secondary school educator*
Johnson, Jane M.F. *soil scientist*
Kim, Jong-Min *education educator*
Ordway, Ellen *biologist, educator, entomologist, researcher*
Seggelke, Martin Heinrich *conductor, music professor*

Mounds View
Wang, Li *business director*

Nevis
Stibbe, Austin Jule *retired accountant*

New Hope
McDaniel, Randall Cornell *substitute teacher, retired professional football player*

New Ulm
Czer, Lawrence Joseph *literature and language professor*
LeVoir, John Marvin *bishop*

North Mankato
Lee, Chan H. *finance educator*
Solo, Joyce Rubenstein *volunteer*
Taylor, Glen A. *printing, direct mail and technology executive, professional sports team owner*

North Oaks
Engle, Donald Edward *retired rail transportation executive, lawyer*
Liu, Benjamin Young-hwai *engineering educator*
McDonald, Malcolm Willis *retired real estate company executive*

Northfield
Anderson, David R. *academic administrator*
Appleyard, David Frank *retired mathematics and computer science professor*
Christensen, Beth Elaine *music librarian*
Clark, Clifford Edward, Jr. *history professor*
Edwins, Jennifer *librarian*
Hawkins, Peggy Anne *veterinarian*
Immel, Cynthia Luanne *medical sales specialist*
Iseminger, Gary Hudson *philosophy educator*
Kucera, Karil J. *Ancient History Professor*
Levin, Burton *diplomat*
Lundergan, Barbara Keough *lawyer*
Mohrig, Jerry R. *chemistry professor, researcher*
Oden, Robert A., Jr. *academic administrator*
Olson, Deanna *school librarian*
Pomponio, Xun Z. *economics professor*
Schuster, Seymour *mathematician, educator*
Soule, George Alan *literature educator*
Sovik, Edward Anders *architect, consultant*
Steen, Lynn Arthur *mathematician, educator*
Thalhammer, Kristina Emma *political science professor*
Yandell, Cathy Marleen *language educator*

Oakdale
Russomanno, Frank P. *information technology executive*

Olivia
Cosgriff, James Arthur *physician*

Osseo
Anya, Adamma Chukwudi *special education educator*

Plymouth
Kahler, Herbert Frederick *manufacturing executive*
Kodali, Dharma Rao *engineering educator*
Mack, Richard L. *lawyer, software company executive*
Nagler, Lorna E. *apparel executive*
Prokopanko, James T. *agricultural products executive*
Saville, Derric James *lawyer*
Shadley, Robert D. *retired army officer*
Stranghoener, Larry W. *corporate financial executive*
Vieth, William Chapman *secondary school educator*
Willis, Bruce Donald *retired judge*

Prior Lake
Anderson, C. Wilson, Jr. *learning specialist*

Richfield
Anderson, Brad (Bradbury H. Anderson) *retail executive*
Ballard, Shari Lynn *retail executive*
Devlin, Barbara Jo *retired school district administrator*
Mayberry, Shawna *preventive medicine physician, educator*
Muehlbauer, James L. *retail executive*

Rochester
Abel, Martin D. *anesthesiologist*
Arnold, Phillip Gordon *plastic surgeon*
Asirvatham, Samuel J. *physician*
Bartholomew, Lloyd Gibson *physician*
Bartley, George B. *ophthalmologist, oculoplastic, surgeon*
Brewer, Jerry Dewayne *dermatologic surgeon, researcher*
Brown, Arnold Lanehart, Jr. *pathologist, educator, dean*
Charles, Erlichman *oncologist, educator*
Cicek, Muzaffer *medical researcher*
Cofield, Robert Hahn *orthopedic surgeon, educator*
Cortese, Denis A. *healthcare executive, medical educator*
Cullinane, Daniel Christopher *surgeon, educator*
Daly, Richard C. *director of heart transplantation*

Danielson, Gordon Kenneth, Jr. *cardiovascular surgeon, educator*
DeRemee, Richard Arthur *retired internist, educator, researcher*
Douglass, Bruce E. *physician*
Driscoll, David John *pediatric cardiologist*
Engel, Andrew George *neurologist*
Fervenza, Fernando C. *nephrologist, educator*
Forstrom, Lee Arthur *physician*
Frye, Robert Leo *medical educator, cardiologist*
Fye, W. Bruce III *cardiologist*
Garcia Franco, Carlos Enrique *thoracic surgeon*
Gervais, Sister Generose *hospital consultant*
Giannini, Caterina *neurologist, educator*
Gibbons, Raymond John *cardiologist*
Gloviczki, Peter *surgeon*
Goetz, Matthew P. *oncologist, educator*
Gorman, Colum Alphonsus *retired endocrinologist*
Haddy, Francis John *internist, educator*
Hammill, Stephen Charles *cardiologist, medical educator*
Hartmann, Lynn C. *physician, educator*
Hauri, Peter J. *psychology professor, researcher*
Herman, David Christopher *ophthalmologist, consultant*
Hiniker, LuAnn *management consultant, educator, researcher, grants consultant*
Hurley, Daniel L. *physician, consultant*
Inwards, David James *hematologist, educator*
Jensen, Michael Dennis *endocrinologist, researcher*
Johnson, Charles Daniel *radiologist*
Kantarci, Kejal *radiologist, researcher*
Kao, Pai Chih *clinical chemist*
Karpyak, Victor M. *psychiatrist, researcher*
Katipamula Malisetti, Rajini *hematologist*
Key, Jack Dayton *librarian*
Knopman, David S. *neurologist*
Kovtun, Irina V. *medical researcher, consultant*
Kyle, Robert Arthur *medical educator, hematologist*
Lange, Elizabeth Ann *retired librarian*
Li, James Tung Chieh *physician*
Loprinzi, Charles Lawrence *oncologist, educator*
Lou, Zhenkun *cell biologist, researcher*
Lucas, Alexander Ralph *child psychiatrist, educator, writer*
Maher, L. James III *molecular biologist*
Malkasian, George Durand, Jr. *obstetrician, educator*
McGoon, Michael Douglas *cardiologist, educator*
McGregor, Christopher George Aloysius *surgeon, educator, consultant*
Mrazek, David Allen *child and adolescent psychiatrist*
Naina, Harris V.K. *hematologist*
Neel, Harry Bryan III *surgeon, scientist, educator*
Nevling, Harry Reed *human resources consultant*
Nivatvongs, Santhat *colorectal surgeon*
Oh, Jae Kuen *cardiologist, consultant, medical educator, director*
Ordog, Tamas *research scientist, educator*
Orwoll, Gregg S.K. *lawyer*
Petersen, Ronald C. *neurologist, educator*
Phillips, Sidney Frederick *gastroenterologist, educator*
Piepgras, David G. *neurosurgeon, educator*
Pittelkow, Mark Robert *physician, dermatologist, educator, researcher*
Poland, Gregory A. *medical professor, researcher*
Riggs, Byron Lawrence, Jr. *physician, educator*
Rizza, Robert Allan *physician*
Robbins, Thomas Landau *researcher, editor*
Rogers, Roy Steele III *dermatologist, educator, dean*
Sanchez-Sotelo, Joaquin *surgery consultant*
Sartori-Valinotti, Julio *medical educator*
Schaff, Hartzell Vernon *surgeon*
Scott, John Paul *medical educator*
Seferian, Edward G. *medical educator*
Selcen, Duygu *physician*
Shampo, Marc Anthony *retired editor*
Siddiqui, Mustaqeem Ahmad *physician*
Siekert, Robert George *retired neurologist, educator*
Sim, Franklin H. *orthopedic surgery educator*
Sit, Arthur J. *ophthalmologist, researcher*
Stickler, Gunnar Brynolf *pediatrician*
Stockwell, Linda M. *principal*
Syed, Imran Shafi *cardiologist, consultant*
Tangalos, Eric G. *internist, geriatrician, educator*
Tescher, Ann Noreen *nurse*
Thomas, Randal J. *cardiologist*
Tindall, Donald James *biological chemistry educator*
Truty, Mark *surgeon*
Trzasko, Joshua Damon *research scientist*
Ward, Louis Emmerson *retired physician*
Warner, Mark A. *anesthesiologist*
Wass, C(harles) Thomas *anesthesiologist*
Whisnant, Jack Page *neurologist*
Wood, Douglas Lynn *medical educator*
Woods, John Elmer *plastic surgeon*
Xu, Shang-Zhi *toxicologist, director*

Rosemount
Aadland, Thomas Vernon *minister*

Roseville
El-Hilali, Oussama *application developer*
Gross, Alan Gerald *rhetoric educator*
Marten, Gordon Cornelius *agronomist, educator, federal agency administrator*
McMillan, Mary Bigelow *retired minister, volunteer*
Miller, Suzanne Marie *library director, educator*
Seagren, Alice *state official, school system administrator, former state legislator*

Saginaw
Stauber, Marilyn Jean *retired elementary and secondary school educator*

Saint Bonifacius
Gianoulis, George Christ *religious studies educator*
Grainger, Johnny Loujack *communications educator, consultant*

Saint Charles
Van Norman, Willis Roger *retired computer systems researcher, consultant*

Saint Cloud
Bruestle, Gregory J. *media specialist*
Burgeson, John C. *dean*
Hofsommer, Donovan Lowell *history professor*
Hossain, Md Mahbub *engineering educator*
Jha, Pranava K. *science educator*
Julstrom, Bryant Arthur *computer science educator*
Kinney, John Francis *bishop*
Motin, Susan Hubbs *school librarian*
Olagunju, Amos Omotayo *computer science educator, consultant, computer science educator, consultant*
Olson, Barbara Ford *physician*
Petzold, Mark Carl *electrical engineer, educator*
Prout, Robert Stephen *higher education consultant, law enforcement consultant*
Roiger, Deborah *physiologist, educator*
Russell, Patrick L. *psychology educator*
Sowada, Alphonse Augustus *bishop emeritus*
Specht-Jarvis, Roland Hubert *fine arts and humanities educator, dean*
Supanvanij, Janikan *finance educator*
Wentworth, Brenda Kathryn *theater educator*

Saint Joseph
Dillard, Leigh Williams *theater educator*
Fabres, Jose Antonio *educator*
Kirick, Daniel John *agronomist*
Lewis, Margaret *economics professor, director*

Saint Louis Park
Beecher, Lee Hewitt *psychiatrist*
Saliterman, Steven S. *internist, educator*

Saint Paul
Adler, Franklin Hugh *political science professor*
Agrimson, Erick Paul *physics professor*
Allison, John Robert *lawyer*
Alsop, Donald Douglas *federal judge*
Amidon, Paul Charles *publishing executive*
Anderson, G. Barry *state supreme court justice*
Anderson, Gordon Louis *foundation administrator*
Anderson, Paul Holden *state supreme court justice*
Armstrong, Chris R. *religious studies educator*
Backstrom, Niklas *professional hockey player*
Baker, Douglas M., Jr. *service industry executive*
Barnwell, Franklin Hershel *zoology educator*
Bell, Lawrence T. *lawyer*
Benet, Jay S. *insurance company executive*
Bressoud, David Marius *mathematics educator*
Brushaber, George Karl *academic administrator, minister*
Buckley, George W. *manufacturing executive*
Burton, Charles Victor *neurosurgeon*
Bute, Monte *social sciences educator*
Caine, Clifford James *educational administrator, consultant*
Campbell, Patrick D. *manufacturing executive*
Capello, Ernesto *history professor*
Carey, Ron *political organization administrator*
Cavert, Henry Mead *retired physician, educator*
Cheng, H. H. *soil scientist, agronomic and environmental science educator emeritus*
Clarke, Charles J. *insurance company executive*
Coleman, Christopher B. *Mayor, St. Paul, Minnesota*
Courtney, Eugene Whitmal *computer company executive*
Daly, Joseph Leo *law educator*
Davis, Margaret Bryan *paleoecology researcher, educator*
Debertin, Jay D. *energy and food products executive*
DeRouchie, Jason S. *ancient language educator*
Dietzen, Christopher J. *state supreme court justice*
Dybvig, Mary McIlvaine *educational consultant, psychologist*
Dykstra, Robert *retired education educator*
Eidman, Vernon Roy *agricultural economist, educator*
Ek, Alan Ryan *forester, educator*
Elde, Robert P. *dean, neuroscientist, educator*
Ettinger, Irwin R. *insurance company executive*
Fedorova, Nataliya Vasylivna *research scientist*
Fishman, Jay Steven *insurance company executive*
Fladung, Thom *editor-in-chief*
Fletcher, Chuck (George C. Fletcher) *professional sports team executive*
Flynn, Harry Joseph *archbishop*
Flynn, John Joseph *geographer, educator*
Foss, Richard John *bishop*
Fritze, Steven L. *service industry executive*
Fulton, Robert Lester *sociology educator*
Galvin, Michael John, Jr. *lawyer*
Garon, Jon M. *law educator, dean*
Gavin, Eileen A. *psychology educator*
Gehrke, Charles William *biochemistry professor*
Geis, Jerome Arthur *lawyer, educator*
Gildea, Lorie Skjerven *state supreme court justice*
Gilmore, Guy L. *publishing executive*
Gouin, Warner Peter *information technology consultant*
Greenwood, Stephen John *environmental engineer*
Hand, Mary Jane *artist, poet, educator*
Hanson, Tom *state treasurer*
Havlat, Martin *professional hockey player*
Heyman, William Herbert *financial services executive*
Hopper, David Henry *theologian, educator*
Hubbard, Stanley Stub *broadcast executive*
Huggins, Melanie *library director*
Huzar, Eleanor Goltz *historian, educator*
Janzen, Peter S. *lawyer, food products executive*
Johnson, John D. *energy and food products executive*
Johnson, Paul Oren *lawyer*
Jolly, Eric J. *museum director*
Kastelic, David Allen *lawyer, energy and food products executive*
Keillor, Garrison (Gary Edward Keillor) *writer, radio personality*
Keillor, Steven James *historian, educator*
Kelly, Patrick J. *lawyer*
Kennelly, Sister Karen Margaret *church administrator, nun, retired academic administrator*
Kiffmeyer, Mary *state legislator*
Kirwin, Kenneth Francis *law educator*
Kling, William Hugh *broadcast executive*
Kluempke, Patrick M. *energy and food products executive*
Knutson, Dan *food products executive*
Kommedahl, Thor *plant pathology educator*
Krop, Pamela Sue *lawyer*
Krupa, Sagar *environmental scientist, educator*
Larson, Thomas D. *energy and food products executive*
Lasansky, Leonardo *artist, educator*
Leighton, Robert Joseph *lawyer*
Leipold, Craig L. *professional sports team executive*
Leonard, Kurt John *retired plant pathologist, director*
Lofquist, Vicki L. *journalist*
Lynn, Tom *professional sports team executive*
MacLean, Brian W. *insurance company executive*
Magnan, Sanne *state agency administrator, public health service officer*
Magnuson, Eric J. *state supreme court chief justice*
Mammel, Mark Crawford *pediatrician, researcher*
Mather, Richard Burroughs *retired Chinese language and literature educator*
Maxa, Rudolph Joseph, Jr. *journalist*
Maxfield, Lori Rochelle *education educator*
McCormick, James Harold *academic administrator*
McKinnell, Robert Gilmore *retired zoologist, biology professor, geneticist*
McNiel, Elizabeth Ann *veterinarian, educator*
Meline, David W. *manufacturing executive*
Mennicke, David *music educator, director*
Meyer, Helen M. *state supreme court justice*
Michael, Alfred Frederick, Jr. *physician, medical educator*
Molnau, Carol L. *Lieutenant Governor of Minnesota*
Monson, Dianne Lynn *literacy educator*
Mulla, David Jamil *physicist*
Murphy, Kevin M. *state banking agency administrator*
Murray, Bill *actor, writer*
Nash, Nicholas David *retail executive*
Nerbonne, Julia Frost *environmentalist, educator*
Nienstedt, John Clayton *archbishop*
Nolan, Owen *professional hockey player*
Norton, Cynthia G. *biology professor*
Olson, Bettye Johnson *artist, retired educator*
Page, Alan Cedric *state supreme court justice*
Palmquist, Mark L. *energy and food products executive*
Pappas, Sandra Lee *state legislator*
Pawlenty, Timothy James *Governor of Minnesota*
Perry, James Alfred *environmental scientist, academic administrator, educator, consultant*
Phillips, Ronald Lewis *plant geneticist, educator*
Piché, Lee Anthony *bishop*
Pocius, Alphonsus Vytautas *physical chemist*
Policinski, Chris *food products executive*
Pratt, Jon *not-for-profit executive*
Pugh, Thomas Wilfred *lawyer*
Reardon, Jack Edward *economics professor*
Richards, Todd *professional hockey coach*
Ritchie, Mark *Secretary of State, Minnesota*
Rodríguez, Liliana Cristina *mathematics educator*
Rodriguez, Roberto Miguel *investment company executive, educator*
Rosenberg, Brian C *academic administrator*
Rossmann, Jack Eugene *psychologist, educator*
Rothmeier, Steven George *investment company executive*
Roy, Robert Russell *toxicologist*
Runge, Carlisle Ford *trade and environmental policy educator*
Sadowsky, Michael J. *microbiologist, educator*
Schmitz, John *energy and food products executive*
Schnitzer, Alan D. *lawyer*
Schwartz, Albert Truman *chemistry professor*
Senkler, Robert L. *insurance company executive*
Seymour, McNeil Vernam *lawyer*
Sisson, Bernice Belair *advocate*
Skillingstad, Constance Yvonne *social services administrator, educator*
Smith, Marschall Imboden *lawyer*
Snustad, Donald Peter *geneticist, educator*
Sonday, Arlene W. *educational consultant*
Spence, Kenneth F. III *lawyer, insurance company executive*
Starks, Daniel J. *medical technology and services executive*
Stibbe, Craig Jule *engineer*
Suh, Sangwon *environmental scientist, educator*
Swaiman, Kenneth Fred *pediatric neurologist, educator*
Swanson, Lori A. *state attorney general, lawyer*
Swanson, Susan Marie *children's book author, educator*
Thayanithy, Venugopal *biologist, geneticist, researcher*
Thompson, Mary Eileen *chemistry professor*
Thompson, Steven Bruce *music educator, director*
Van Pilsum, John Franklin *biochemist, educator*
von Geldern, James Robert *law educator*
Wagner, Mary Margaret *library and information scientist, educator*
Waters, Harry T., Jr. *theater educator, actor*
Weigelt, John August *surgeon*
Weiner, Carl Dorian *retired historian*
Westbrock, Leon E. *energy and food products executive*
Westermeyer, Joseph John *psychiatrist*
Wexler, Deborah Lee *physician*
Wiltz, James W. *medical products executive*
You, Yali *music educator*
Younoszai, Barbara B. *literature and language professor, researcher*
Zibell, Donald Fredrick *lawyer*

Saint Peter
Dille, Sarah Jane *theology studies educator*
Haeuser, Michael John *library administrator*
Jodock, Darrell Harland *minister, educator*
Maatman, Micah Joel *theater educator*
Mc Rostie, Clair Neil *economics professor*

Sartell
Morgan, Mary Jo *school system administrator*

Shakopee
Eibeler, Paul G. *former computer game company executive*
Eliason, Arlene F. *mathematician, educator*

Shoreview
O'Dea, Thomas Joseph *clinical engineer, medical physicist*

Stillwater
Asch, Susan McClellan *pediatrician*
Erwin, Raymond Maurice *secondary school educator*
Horsch, Lawrence Leonard *venture capitalist, corporate financial executive*

Thief River Falls
Anderson, Steven Keith *musical entertainer, writer*

Vadnais Heights
Polakiewicz, Leonard Anthony *foreign language and literature educator*

Virginia
Blyckert, Judith A. *engineering educator*
Knabe, George William, Jr. *pathologist, educator*

Waseca
Deike, Keith Lawrence *lawyer*
Frederick, Edward Charles *university official*

Waterville
Pettis, Patricia Amanda *secondary school educator, farmer*

Waubun
Christensen, Marvin Nelson *venture capitalist*

Wayzata
Bergerson, David Raymond *lawyer*
Blodgett, Frank Caleb *retired food company executive*
Feuss, Linda Anne Upsall *lawyer*
Heckt, Melvin Dean *lawyer*
Johnson, Sankey Anton *manufacturing executive*
Luthringshauser, Daniel Rene *manufacturing executive*
Palmer, Brian Eugene *retired lawyer*
Reutiman, Robert William, Jr. *lawyer*
Rich, Willis Frank, Jr. *banker*
Roth, Robert Paul *seminary educator, writer*
Schnobrich, Roger William *lawyer*
Skrowaczewski, Stanislaw *conductor, composer*
Sullivan, Austin Padraic, Jr. *retired diversified food company executive*
Waldera, Wayne Eugene *crisis management executive*

West Saint Paul
Cento, William Francis *retired newspaper editor*
Nightingale, Edmund Joseph *clinical psychologist, educator, consultant*

White Bear Lake
Bruhn, JoAnn Marie *radiologic technologist, writer, speaker*
Thinesen, Pamela Kay *biology faculty*

Willmar
Sheehan, William Patrick *psychiatrist, astronomer*

Winona
Beth, Sandra A. *library director*
Beyer, Mary Edel *primary education educator*
Haas, James Wayne *accountant*
Harrington, Bernard Joseph *Bishop Emeritus*
Hokanson, A. Drake *communications educator*
Holm, Joy Alice *goldsmith, psychology professor, artist*
Malone, Christopher John *statistician, educator*
Mayer, Kit *scenic designer, director*
Nasstrom, Roy Richard *educational consultant*
Oberton, Willard D. *industrial supply company executive*
Quinn, John Michael *bishop*
Rabuse, Lynne Marie *language educator*
Sefkow, Susan Bennett *psychology professor*
Valluri, Chandrasekhar (Chandu Valluri) *marketing and international business educator*

Winthrop
Leitheiser, Mark Steven *literature and language educator*

Woodbury
Beck, Warren Randall *retired glass technologist*
Bunch, William Franklin *retired music educator*
McGary, Carl Thomas *pathologist*

Worthington
Benton, Galen Lee *retired music educator*

MISSISSIPPI

Aberdeen
Aycock, Sharion *federal judge*
Davidson, Glen Harris *federal judge*

Ackerman
James, Lee J. *agriculture educator*

Alcorn State
Aceil, Sam *engineering educator*
Cuadra, Evelin J. *agricultural studies educator*
Wyatt, Helen J. *special education educator*
Yu, May Huang *librarian, educator*

Batesville
Carlson, George Clarence, Jr. *state supreme court justice*

Bay Saint Louis
Bernstein, Joseph *lawyer*
Hurlburt, Harley Ernest *ocean modeling and prediction scientist*

Biloxi
Brinsmade, Akbar Fairchild *chemical engineering consultant*
Gowdy, Marjorie E. *museum director*
Howze, Joseph Lawson Edward *bishop emeritus*
Love, James Sanford III *communications executive*
Morin, Roger Paul *bishop*

Booneville
Hawkins, Ricky Edward *engineering educator*
Russell, Belinda *education educator*

Brandon
Fargason, Patricia J. *psychologist*
Hall, Breda Faye Kimbrough Inman *counselor, educator*
Terrell, Elise I. *humanities educator*
Wand, Kimberly Joanne *assistant principal*
Wilson, Floyd *pathologist, educator*

Carriere
Stanton, Sylvia Doucet *artist, gallery owner*

Centreville
Nelson, Janie Rish *health facility administrator*

Clarksdale
Presley, Vivian Mathews *junior college administrator*

Cleveland
Boschert, Thomas Neville *historian, educator*
Meek, Ernest Carlysle *physics professor*

Clinton
Campbell, Edward Wesley *elementary school educator*
Durham, Carol Elise *musician, educator*
Gore, Samuel Marshall *art educator, sculptor*
Hataway, Michael Willis *graphics designer, educator*
Potts, James B. III *literature and language professor*
Randle, Jonathan Thomas *language educator*
Wilder, Brenda *music specialist*

Columbus
Adhikari, Dhruba Raj *mathematics professor, researcher*
Jones, Carol A. *nutritionist, artist*
Kantack, Catherine Margaret *retired music educator, international and bank broker*
Labensky, Sarah Ross *culinary educator*
Mahoney, Linda L. *education educator, consultant*
McClintock, Margaret Eleanor *finance educator*
Rood, Cynthia Hooper *landscape architect, consultant*
Segrest, Linda Hudson *music educator*
Summer, Emily Eugenia *artist, educator*
Traynham, Lurene Jones *retired secondary school educator*

Crystal Springs
Nixon, Brenda Joyce *elementary school educator, small business owner*

Decatur
Crenshaw, Phillip *history professor*

Diamondhead
Park, Richard A. *ecologist*
Simpson, W(ilburn) Dwain *physicist, communications executive*

Ellisville
Ross, Lisa Sims *special education educator*
Strickland, Carrie D *music educator*

Flora
Garbacz, Christopher *economist, researcher*

Florence
Anding, Robert Eugene *retired religion educator, minister*

Flowood
Byrd, Joyce Marie *dentist*
Das, Suman Kumar *plastic surgeon, researcher*
Verneuille, Kim R. *dean, educator*

Fulton
Ewing, John Arthur *biology professor*
Lowe, Robin Monaghan *language educator*
Miles, William Trice *state legislator*
Milner, Michelle Leaneatrice *biology professor, department chairman*
Nowicki, Kenneth Robert *physics professor*

Gautier
Block, Paul Conrad *registered respiratory therapist*
Feris, Alessandra Schmidt *music educator*
Moak, Rex R. *psychology educator*

Goodman
Diffey, Steven Dwayne *academic administrator, director*

Greenwood
Jones, Carolyn Ellis *retired employment agency owner*
Swayze, Charles J., Jr. *lawyer*

Grenada
Rummage, James Mark *history educator*
Thomas, Ouida Power *music educator*

Gulfport
Alston, Joanna *finance educator*
Egland, Katherine Tatum *educational consultant, director*
Harvey, Cathy Chance *literature and writing professor*
Lipscomb, Robert McBride *library director, educator*
Opel, Pamela Lynn *elementary school educator*
Phifer-Starks, Kim D. *paralegal, educator*
Phillips, Joy Lambert *lawyer, banker*
Swetman, Glenn Robert *literature and language professor, poet*
Thatcher, George Robert *banker, writer, columnist*
Topazi, Anthony J. *utilities executive*

Hattiesburg
Adelman, Michael Schwartz *lawyer*
Bass, Joby *geographer, educator*
Bedenbaugh, Angela Lea Owen *chemistry educator, researcher*
Buchanan, Randy *engineering educator*
Causey, Jana *science educator*
Chain, Bobby Lee *electrical contractor, former mayor*
Chambers, Douglas Brent *history professor*
Diket, Mary Read M. *academic administrator, educator*
Dunaway, Melissa Faye *pediatrics nurse*
Gunther, William David *academic administrator, economics professor*
Lucas, Aubrey Keith *retired university president*
Maung, Khin Maung *physics professor*
Mazher, Waseem *special education educator*
McNeese, Rose Marie *retired education educator*
Miao, Wujian *chemistry professor*
Mitchell, Geoffrey Scott *Spanish language educator*
Niroomand, Farhang *economics professor, researcher*
Noonkester, James Ralph *retired college president*
Reinshagen, Yolanda P. *elementary school educator*
Roy, Stephanie *academic administrator, educator*
Stockstill, David H. *musician, research historian, lecturer*
Vincent, Sharon Elaine *nursing educator*
Xue, Fei *communications educator*

Holly Springs
Moyo, Debayo R. *communications executive*

Indianola
Matthews, David *clergyman*

Itta Bena
Ikenga, Julius O. *biology professor, consultant*

Jackson
Ables, Jackson Henderson III *lawyer*
Ahmad, Hafiz Anwar *biology professor*
Allison, John S. *state banking agency administrator*
Ayensu, Wellington Kofi *biology professor*
Banks, Fred Lee, Jr. *former state supreme court justice, lawyer*
Barbour, Haley Reeves *Governor of Mississippi*
Barksdale, Rhesa Hawkins *federal judge*
Bell, Taunjah Patrease *research scientist*
Blair, William Dodd *engineering educator, director*
Bounds, Hank M. *school system administrator*
Bradley, Betsy *museum director*
Bryant, Phil *Lieutenant Governor of Mississippi*
Bynum, CeDric Darnell *professional baseball coach, elementary school educator*
Carden, Alan L. *hospital chaplain*
Carlisle, Peggy Jane *elementary school educator*
Carmichael, Sally W. *volunteer*
Chambers-Camper, Fransenna Ethel *special education educator*
Chandler, David A. *state supreme court justice*
Corlew, John Gordon *lawyer*
Cruse, Julius Major, Jr. *pathologist, educator*
Daniels, Patsy Jean *English professor*
Denault, Leo P. *energy executive*
deShazo, Richard Denson *medical educator, academic administrator*
Dickinson, Jess H. *state supreme court justice*
Drinkwater, William Wayne *lawyer*
Easley, Ray R. *seminary official, clergyman*
Fowler, Paul David *coach*
Freeman, Patricia Ann *economist, educator*
Frost, Joseph D. *theater educator*
Gardner, Bonnie Bowie *history professor*
Geissler, William Bennett *orthopaedic surgeon*
Graves, James E. *state supreme court justice, educator*
Hafter, Jerome Charles *lawyer*
Harisdangkul, Valee *physician*
Harkins, Patrick Nicholas III *lawyer*
Heitman, Elizabeth *healthcare educator, anesthesiologist*
Henegan, John C(lark) *lawyer*
Hood, Jim *state attorney general*
Hosemann, Delbert (C. Delbert Hosemann Jr) *Secretary of State, Miss.*
Houck, William Russell *bishop emeritus*
Houston, Jamie Giles III *lawyer, accountant*
Hughes, Byron William *oil industry executive*
Hughson, Michael Donald *pathologist, researcher, medical educator*
Hutchison, Mark Stevenson *lawyer*
Izevbigie, Ernest B. *biomedical researcher*
Jolly, E. Grady *federal judge*
Jones, Daniel Wayne *physician, medical educator*
Jordan, John W. *state official, school system administrator*
Kafoury, Ramzi M. *biology and environmental health educator, researcher*
Kennedy, Kristi D. *lawyer*
Kitchens, James W. *state supreme court justice*
Lamar, Ann Hannaford *state supreme court justice*
Langston, Rebecca McRae *lawyer*
Larsen, Samuel Harry *minister, educator*
Latino, Joseph Nunzio *bishop*
Lee, Tom Stewart *judge*
Leonard, J. Wayne *energy executive*
Lewis, Robert Edwin, Jr. *pathology and immunology educator, researcher*
Manning, R. Davis *physiologist, educator*
Marshall, Gailen Daugherty, Jr. *allergist, educator*
Martinez, Eduardo Vidal *lawyer*
Mayeaux, Anne Russell *education educator*
McAllister, Deuce (Dulymus Jenod McAllister) *professional football player*
McGuire, Sarah Lea *biology professor*
McIntyre, James G. *lawyer*
McLin-Bronson, Hattie Rogers *school system administrator*
Mitchell, Jerry *reporter*
Moll, George William *pediatrician, educator*
Molpus, Dick H. *investment company executive*
Montjoy, Richard Wilson, II, *lawyer*
Munera, Pedro Antonio *child and adolescent psychiatrist*
Muzny, Christina A. *infectious diseases physician*
Nix, J. Elmer *retired orthopedist, surgeon*
Penn, William M. *finance educator, consultant*
Pierce, Randy G. *state supreme court justice*
Porter, Scott E. *orthopedist*
Rajamohan, Kalluru R. *science educator, researcher*
Randolph, Michael K. *state supreme court justice*
Redmon, Cynthia Ann *poet, songwriter*
Reeves, Tate *state treasurer*
Remata, Suseela Reddy *environmental science educator, researcher*
Risley, Rod Alan *educational association administrator*
Roberts, Richard Charlton III *lawyer*
Sachs, Stephen Warren *music educator, director*
Savoie, Felix Henry III *orthopaedic surgeon*
Scanlon, Pat H. *lawyer*
Seivers, Lana C. *educational association administrator, former state official*
Smith, Carnice *music educator, director*
Smith, Richard J. *energy executive*
Smith, Sharman Bridges *state librarian*
Southwick, Leslie Harburd *federal judge, lawyer*
Sugg, Robert Perkins *retired judge*
Tchounwou, Paul Bernard *environmental health specialist, toxicologist, educator*
Thigpen, James Tate *oncologist, educator*
Thompson, Ed *state agency administrator, public health service officer, epidemiologist, educator*
Travis, Jay A. III *lawyer*
Uzodinma, Minta LaVerne Smith *retired nursing administrator, nurse midwife*
Vance, Ralph Brooks, Sr. *oncologist, educator*
Venegas-Pont, Marcia *physiologist, educator*
Waller, William Lowe, Jr. *state supreme court chief justice*
Waters, Guy Prentiss *theology studies educator*
Welch, W(alter) Scott III *lawyer*
White, Brad *political organization administrator*
Winter, William Forrest *Former Governor, Miss, lawyer*
Wooten, Kathy A. *finance educator, accountant*
Yanes, Licy Lorena *medical educator*
Yates, Anne Bridges *allergist, immunologist, educator*
Yedjou, Clement Guy *science educator, researcher*

Kosciusko
Cox, Howard Andrew *English educator*

Laurel
Lindstrom, Eric Everett *ophthalmologist*

Long Beach
Adan-Bante, Edith *mathematician, researcher*

Macon
Barge, Laura Inez *literature and language professor*

Madison
McDavid, John Sanford *lawyer*
Watts, Thomas Parrish *history educator, consultant*

Mayhew
Emerson, Tonsha Loranda *nursing educator*

Meridian
Marshall, John Steven *artist, educator, museum administrator*
Nabors, Steven Thomas *theater educator*
Thomas, Olin C. *secondary school educator*

Minter City
Mitchell, Patsy Malier *religious school founder, administrator*

Mississippi State
Cannayen, Igathinathane *agricultural engineer, educator*
Chi, Guangqing *demographer, educator*
Eksioglu, Burak *engineering educator*
Foglesong, Robert H. *academic administrator, career military officer*
Hopper, Peggy F. *education educator*
Jenkins, Johnie Norton *research geneticist, research administrator*
Kellermanns, Franz Willi *management consultant, educator*
Lowery, Charles Douglas *historian, dean, educator*
MacGown, Joe A. *entomologist, researcher*
Marcus, Alan I. *historian, educator*
Martin, Edward Curtis, Jr. *landscape architect, educator*
Rabideau, Peter Wayne *dean, chemistry professor, educator*
Rais-Rohani, Masoud *aerospace and engineering mechanics educator*
Reddy, Kambham Raja *botanist, educator*
Ruby, Roy Harris *academic administrator*
Silva, Juan Luis *food processing engineer, educator*
Stansbury, Rick *men's college basketball coach*

Monticello
Clyburn, Esmond Steve *secondary school educator*

Mooreville
Franks, Jamie (James R. Franks Jr.) *lawyer, political organization administrator*

Moorhead
Barr, Connie Buckels *finance educator, management consultant*
Corley, Barry James *agricultural studies educator, farmer*
Sanford, Kimberly Lynn *social sciences educator*
Stone-Street, Nancy Harrington *painter, printmaker, educator*

Morton
Cox, Marlina R. *social studies educator*

Moss Point
Bolton, Betty J. *medical/surgical nurse, poet*

Mound Bayou
Kamphefner, Pius *minister*
Robinson, Oliver Dale *counselor, pastor*

Natchez
Foster, Evaline L. *education educator, researcher*
Golden, Rolland Harve *artist*
James, Lula Bonds *science educator, small business owner, apparel designer*
Kirk, Susanne Smith *editor*
McLemore, Joan Meadows *librarian, consultant*
Posey, Clyde Lee *business administration and accounting educator*

Ocean Springs
Austin, Claude Lidell *retired surgeon*
Braumiller, Allen Spooner *gas industry executive, geologist*
Culberson, Gary Michael *hotel manager*
Jenkins, Lawanna *retired middle school educator*

Olive Branch
Carnall, George Hursey, II, *lawyer*
Leary, Frances Elizabeth Cooper *secondary school educator*

Oxford
Costner, Charles Lynn *retired civil engineer*
Greenlee, Jim Ming *prosecutor*
Gul, Waseem *research scientist*
Howorth, David Bishop *retired lawyer*
Keiser, Edmund Davis, Jr. *biologist, educator*
Knox, James Marshall *lawyer*
Landon, Michael de Laval *retired history professor*
Laurenzo, Frederick E. *retired history professor*
Moorhead, Sylvester Andrew *retired education educator*
Murthy, Narasimha S. *pharmaceutical scientist, researcher*
Scruggs, Richard F. (Dickie Scruggs) *lawyer*
Walton, Gerald Wayne *retired university official, retired university official*

Pascagoula
Wilkie, Barry James *manufacturing engineer*

Pass Christian
Henrion, Rosemary Provenza *psychotherapist, educator*
McCardell, James Elton *retired naval officer*

Pearl
Williams, Daniece H. *biology professor*

Perkinston
Tringle, Sarah Taylor *biology professor, department chairman*

Philadelphia
Duncan, Mark *prosecutor*

Picayune
Penton-Smith, Tammy L. *elementary school educator*

Poplarville
Foster, Delana Lynn *finance educator*

Raymond
Cook, Jeanne Wells *literature and language educator*
Flanders, Helen Juanita *school librarian, academic administrator*
Hilkert, Judith Rene *librarian*
Scifres, Denise Celia Le Blanc *historian, educator*

Saltillo
Hopkins, Betty Belinda *elementary school educator*

Scooba
Monk, Suzanne Renee *academic administrator*

Senatobia
Banham, Sandra Rodgers *language educator*

Shaw
Garner, Mable Tecola *health facility administrator*

Southaven
Butler, Elizabeth Rosanne *music educator, director*

Starkville
Balasubramanian, Suman *mathematician, educator*
Carino, Ricolindo L. *computer scientist, educator*
Eksioglu, Sandra Duni *industrial engineering educator*
Ford, Robert MacDonald III *architect, educator*
Mabry, Donald Joseph *retired academic administrator, history professor*
Mosley, Mary Nell H. *retired elementary school educator*
Topsakal, Erdem *science educator*

Stennis Space Center
Hou, Weilin (Will Hou) *oceanographer*
Mahoney, Kevin L. *oceanographer*

Stoneville
Stanturf, John Alvin, IV, *soil scientist, researcher*

Sturgis
Thomas, Charles Hill *geneticist, educator*

Sumrall
Downey, James Cecil *retired music and humanities educator*

Tougaloo
Ray, Larry L. *language educator*

Tupelo
Cleveland, Mary Heloise *elementary school educator*
Nash, Henry Warren *marketing educator*
Patterson, Aubrey Burns, Jr. *banker*
Witty, Thomas Ezekiel III *psychologist, researcher*
Zurawski, Jeanette *rehabilitation services professional*

Tylertown
Mord, Irving Conrad, II, *lawyer*

University
Al-Zoubi, Asem S. *science educator*
Beebe, Stephanie H. *speech pathology/audiology services professional*
Bradley, John Robin, Jr. *law educator*
Breazeale, Mack Alfred *research scientist, educator*
Chang, Yunhee *consumer economics professor*
Cheng, Alexander Hung-Darh *engineering educator, consultant*
Davis, Samuel Marion *dean, law educator, researcher*
Ding, Yan *engineering educator*
Dor, George W. K *music educator*
Duke, Stephen Oscar *physiologist, research scientist, educator*
Ervin, Elizabeth K. *engineering educator*
Field, Lester L., Jr. *historian, educator*
Guo, Gang *political science professor*
Gussow, Adam *literature and language professor*
Lowe, Rebecca *audiologist, educator*
Manson, Neil Alan *philosopher, educator*
Nutt, Houston Dale, Jr. *college football coach*
Panickar, Praveen *aeronautical engineer, researcher*
Sadana, Ajit *chemical engineer, educator*
Sam, Joseph *retired university dean*
Shughart, William Franklin, II, *economics professor, consultant*
Stolzenburg, Maribeth *research scientist*
Zhang, Yaoxin *engineer, researcher*

Utica
Marshall, Sophia S.L. *director*

Vicksburg
Bailess, Robert R. *lawyer*
Gong, Ping *ecologist, researcher*
Kuljaca, Ognjen *engineering educator, researcher*
Martin, William A. *environmental engineer, researcher*
Pace, Carol Rebecca *elementary school educator*

Waynesboro
Crager, Ginny Lee *gifted and talented educator*

Wesson
Ross, Thomas Albert *art educator*

Whitfield
Montgomery, John Harold *psychiatrist*

MISSOURI

Advance
Thomas, Rich L. *secondary school educator*

Anderson
Coble, Mary Gloria *protective services official, rancher*

Archie
Schulte, Troy Anthony *coach, director*

Arnold
Kasey, Arthur R. III *secondary school educator*
Porter, Kathy Lee *marriage and family therapist, minister*

Bakersfield
Barnes, Sandra Lynn *special education educator*

Ballwin
Ackerson, Charles Stanley *minister, educator, social worker*
Cornell, William Daniel *mechanical engineer*
Cowell, Kimberly *music educator*
Luberda, George Joseph *lawyer, educator*
Pallozola, Christine *not-for-profit executive*
Pierce, John Albert *retired medical educator*

Belton
Daggett, Kathleen *retired special education educator*
Hoye, Linda Lee *special education educator*
Taylor, Reginald L. *lawyer, consultant*

Bethel
Coonrod, Delberta Hollaway (Debbie) *retired educator, consultant*

Birch Tree
Holden, Janet L. *media specialist*

Blue Springs
Page, Leslie Andrew *retired consumer products company executive*
Washburn, Gladys Haase *retired church musician, educator, director*

Bolivar
Brown, Sandra L. *librarian, educator*
Fuhrman, C. Michael *religious studies educator*
Hooper, William Loyd *music educator, university administrator*
Kitchin, Robert Walter *chemistry professor, physics professor*
Malone, Kelly Scott *theology studies educator*
Miller, Brett *communications educator, consultant*
Smith, Sharina *marketing executive, writer*

Boonville
Cline-Denney, Dorothy May Stammerjohn *education educator, consultant*

Bosworth
Ireland, Betty Jean *retired principal, music educator*

Bowling Green
Bruce, Judith Esther *retired music educator, elementary school educator*
Carty, Elaine Smith *music educator*
Farris, Donald Herach *art educator*

Branson
Ford, Jean Elizabeth *retired language educator*
Ownby, Jerry Steve *landscape architect, educator*

Branson West
McCall, Charles Barnard *retired health facility administrator*
Zank, Virginia *retired literature and language professor, educational consultant*

Bridgeton
Andrews, William Frederick *manufacturing executive*
Hylla, Linda Kay *sister, social worker*
Kenison, Raymond Robert *fraternal organization administrator*

Brighton
Copus, Phyllis Lee *retired federal agency administrator*

Butler
Turner, Vicky Jo *music educator*

Canton
Gaither, Kimberly Ann *finance educator*
Li, Wei *psychology professor*

Cape Girardeau
Caragine, Louis Philip, Jr. *neurosurgeon*
Chan, Wai *mathematics professor*
Ghosh, Santaneel *physics professor*
Haynes, Joshua *legislative staff member*
Jeter Yanow, Cindie *communications educator*
Langenfeld, Mark E. *healthcare educator*
Limbaugh, Stephen Nathaniel, Jr. *federal judge, former state supreme court judge*
McManaman, Kenneth Charles *lawyer*
Sacha, Robert Frank *osteopath, educator*
Smallwood, Glenn Walter, Jr. *utility marketing management executive*
Snell, William E., Jr. *psychology professor, researcher*
Stepenoff, Bonnie Marie *history professor*
Suhr, Karl Friedrich *school librarian*

Carthage
Flanigan, Matthew C. *manufacturing executive*
Haffner, David S. *manufacturing executive*
Jett, Ernest Carroll, Jr. *lawyer*
McAfee, Diana Mae *media specialist, music educator*

Caruthersville
Puangsuvan, Somporn *surgeon, consultant*

Cassville
Cole, David A. *lawyer, political organization administrator*

Charleston
Cassell, Lucille Richardson *small business owner*

Chesterfield
Ashworth, Ronald Broughton *health facility executive, accountant*
Baker, Sandra Kay *music educator*
Canis, Randy Lawrence *lawyer, educator*
Carpenter, Will Dockery *chemicals executive*
Chambers, Jerry Ray *school system administrator, consultant*
Diamandis, Peter H. *foundation administrator, entrepreneur*
Gerard, Jules Bernard *law educator*
Hier, Marshall David *lawyer*
Kohnen, Carol Ann *librarian*
Morley, Harry Thomas, Jr. *real estate executive*
Qazi, Mujtaba A. *ophthalmologist*
Selfridge, George Dever *retired dentist, retired military officer*
Silber, Sherman J. *urologist, consultant*
Stork, Donald Arthur *advertising executive*
Williams, Luther Steward *research scientist*
Winter, William Earl *retired beverage company executive*
Wood, Donald Euriah *retired lawyer*

Chillicothe
Crouch, Frances Nadine *art educator*

Clayton
Kolker, Scott Lee *lawyer*
Mohan, John J. *lawyer*
Pain, George H. *lawyer*
Rupp, Joseph D. *metal products executive*
Tremayne, Eric Flory *lawyer*

Cleveland
Harper, Bill J. *floral designer, consultant, educator*

Clinton
Kelsay, David Roland *chemist*

Columbia
Almony, Robert Allen, Jr. *librarian*
Anderson, Mike *men's college basketball coach*
Anderson, Ralph Robert *endocrinologist, educator*
Bank, Barbara J. *sociology educator*
Barker, Alex W. *museum director, educator*
Barnes, Stephen L. *surgeon*
Beem, John Kelly *retired mathematician, educator*
Biddle, Bruce Jesse *social psychologist, educator*
Bien, Joseph Julius *philosophy educator*
Blevins, Dale Glenn *agronomy educator*
Brushwood, Mack Lewis *labor union administrator*
Burgoyne, Suzanne *theater educator, writer*
Caruthers, Janet *library director*
Churchill, Robert Joseph *radiologist, educator, dean*
Cogswell, James A. *library director*
Cogswell, Jim *library director*
Colwill, Jack Marshall *physician, educator*
Cowan, Nelson *cognitive psychologist, researcher*
Creighton, Donald Louis *mechanical engineer, consultant*
Cunningham, Milamari Antoinella *retired anesthesiologist*
Davis, Charles Nelson *journalism educator*
Deaton, Brady J. *academic administrator*
Decker, Wayne Leroy *meteorologist, educator*
Dessem, R. Lawrence *dean, law educator*
Easton, Stephen Douglas *lawyer, educator*
Eggers, George William Nordholtz, Jr. *anesthesiologist, educator*
Esbeck, Carl H. *law educator*
Forsee, Gary D. *academic administrator, former telecommunications industry executive*
Forte, Leonard Ralph *pharmacologist, educator*
Frisby, James Curtis *retired agricultural engineering educator*
Fulweiler, Howard Wells *language professional*
Greenlief, C. Michael *chemistry professor, director*
Guha, Suchismita *physics professor*
Gysbers, Norman Charles *counselor, educator*
Havens, Timothy C. *research scientist*
Hawthorne, Marion Frederick *chemistry professor*
Heflin, Colleen Marie *science educator*
Hensley, Elizabeth Catherine *nutritionist, educator*
Ho, Dominic KC *electrical engineering educator*
Hoard, Mary *psychologist*
Horner, Winifred Bryan *humanities educator*
Hossain, Maruf *research scientist*
Ikerd, John E. *retired economics professor*
Ingersoll, Christopher Glenn *toxicologist*
Islam, Naz E. *engineering educator, researcher*
James, Elizabeth Joan Plogsted *pediatrician, educator*
Johns, Williams Davis, Jr. *geologist, educator*
Kaiser, Edwin Michael *chemistry professor*
Kannan, Raghuraman *biochemist, educator*
Keown, Linda Jane *language educator*
Khojasteh, Ali *medical oncologist, hematologist*
Klippenstein, Brian *legislative staff member*
König, Peter *pediatrician, educator*
Kremer, Gary R. *museum director, historian, educator*
Loory, Stuart Hugh *journalist*
LoPiccolo, Joseph *psychologist, educator, author*
Manandhar, Gaurishankar *cell biologist, educator*
Mashhoon, Bahram *physicist, researcher*
McDaniel, Sue Powell *writer*
Men, Hongsheng *biologist, researcher*
Miller, Paul Ausborn *adult education educator*
Mitchell, Roger Lowry *retired agronomy educator*
Monson, Michael James *economist, consultant*
Moore, Mitchell Jay *lawyer, educator*
Morehouse, Lawrence Glen *veterinarian, educator, academic administrator*
Mullen, Edward John, Jr. *Spanish language educator*
Nikolai, Loren Alfred *accounting educator*
Nolph, Georgia Bower *physician*
Palaniappan, Kannappan *engineering educator*
Perry, Michael Clinton *internist, academic administrator, educator*
Phillips, Walter Ray *law educator*
Pinkel, Gary *college football coach*
Pinkerton, Marjorie Jean *retired librarian*
Pringle, Oran Allan *mechanical and aerospace engineering educator*
Randall, Douglas D. *biochemist, educator*
Randall, Linda Lea *biochemist, educator*
Reddy, Chada S. *toxicologist, researcher*
Roberts, R. Michael *animal scientist, biochemist, educator*
Rowlett, Ralph Morgan *archaeologist, educator*
Sable, Marjorie R. *social worker, educator*
Sanders, Keith Page *journalism educator*
Schuder, John Claude *retired biomedical engineer, educator*
Schwartz, Richard Brenton *English language educator, dean, writer*
Sengupta, Shramik *science educator*
Sethi, Yash Pal *radiologist, consultant*
Sharma, Krishna Kathribail *biochemist, educator*
Sowa, Grzegorz *pharmacologist, educator*
Stack, Frank Huntington *painter, retired art educator*
Stephenson, Hugh Edward, Jr. *retired surgeon*
Strickland, Arvarh Eunice *history professor*
Taft, William Howard *retired journalism educator*
Tarnove, Lorraine *medical association executive*
Tobias, Joseph Drew *pediatric anesthesiologist*
Twardowski, Zbylut Józef *nephrologist, educator*
Vale, Patrice J. *musician, consultant*
Von Holt, Lael Powers *psychotherapist, psychiatric social worker*
Wakefield, Mark Richard *urologist, educator*
Wanta, Wayne *communications educator*
Weisman, Gary Andrew *biochemist*
Westbrook, James Edwin *law educator*
Yanders, Armon Frederick *biological sciences educator, science administrator*
Yerram, Preethi *physician*
Yoon, So-Yeon *design educator*

Creve Coeur
Bockserman, Robert Julian *chemist*
Randle, Bernadette *musician, composer, graphics designer*

Cuba
Work, Bruce Van Syoc *small business owner, consultant*

Dexter
Ringer, John William *lawyer*

Doniphan
McCann, Lawrence Alton *music educator*

Earth City
Bulger, Marc *professional football player*

Eureka
Lindsey, Susan Lyndaker *zoologist*

Excelsior Springs
Mitchell, Earl Wesley *clergyman*
Schroeder, Horst Wilhelm *food products executive*

Farmington
Kellogg, Margaret *elementary school educator*

Fayette
Carter, John Jefferson *government educator, author*
Elliott, Dana Ray *biology professor, consultant*
Inman, Marianne Elizabeth *academic administrator*
Keeling, Joe Keith *religious studies educator, retired dean*

Fenton
Meyer, Joyce *television minister, author*
Sheble, Brian A. *psychologist, consultant, educator*

Ferguson
Chubb, Charles Ray *physicist, researcher*

Festus
Ducharme, Nicole Marie *endocrinologist*

Florissant
Ackley, Robert Arthur *mathematics educator, retired military officer*
Bommarito, Florence Ann *graphics designer, educator*
Conrad, Mary Trench *elementary school educator*
Kralemann, William Joseph *retired chemistry educator*
Sikora, Diana Marie *elementary school educator*
Tanphaichitr, Kongsak *rheumatologist, allergist, immunologist, internist*
Tomazi, George Donald *retired electrical engineer*

Forsyth
Klinefelter, Sarah Stephens *retired dean, broadcast executive*

Fort Leonard Wood
Collins, Pamela Marie *forensic specialist, educator*

Fredericktown
Sudmeyer, Alice Jean *art gallery owner*

Fulton
Hinchie, William Jules *nuclear engineer, director*
Jaeger, Theodore Bruce *psychology professor*
McClain, Cindy Dunstan *music educator*
Palmer, Kent Friedley *physics professor*

Gainesville
Sayles, Wayne Gerald *numismatist, writer, publisher*

Granby
Sparkman, Lyle Bruce *academic administrator, education educator*

Greenwood
Zeller, Marilynn Kay *retired librarian*

Hannibal
Faden, Regina *museum director*
Schafer, Bette Jane *education educator*

Hazelwood
Rajagopalan, Raghavan *medical researcher*

Hermann
Wilson, C. Daniel, Jr. *library director*

High Ridge
Karll, Jo Ann *retired judge, lawyer*

Hillsboro
Adkins, Gregory D. *higher education administrator*
Cummiskey, Raymond Vincent *academic administrator*
Everett, Gabrielle *history professor*
Loomis, Trish *literature and language professor*
Schuessler, Thomas Frederick *medical educator*

Holden
Martin, Laurabelle *property manager*

Hollister
Canfield, Cindy Sue *art educator*

Holt
Merrill, Donna *special education educator*

Humansville
Richler, Zenia H. *naturopath educator, health facility administrator*

Huntsville
Newbrough, Warren Wade *farmer*

Independence
Albano, Michael Santo John *lawyer*
Barker, Keith Rene *investment banker*
Devine, Michael J. *library and museum director, educator*

Evans, Margaret Ann *human resources administrator, business owner*
Francis, Mary Frances Van Dyke *small business owner, real estate company executive, retired editor*
Franklin, J. Richard *principal*
Johnson, Sharon Elaine *elementary school educator*
Lemon, Leslie Roy *radar meteorologist*
Lundy, Sadie Allen *small business owner*
Potts, Barbara Joyce *retired historic site director*
Shomin, Janet L. *paralegal*
Shover, Joan *retired secondary school educator*
Sturges, Sidney James *pharmacist, educator, investment and development company executive*
Tyree, Alan Dean *clergyman*

Jackson
Patrick, John *secondary school educator*

Jefferson City
Bandré, David George *lawyer*
Bartlett, Alex *lawyer*
Brandt, William Edmund *retired school system administrator*
Breckenridge, Patricia *state supreme court judge*
Carnahan, Robin *Secretary of State, Missouri*
Chapel, Nimrod T., Jr. *lawyer, government agency administrator*
Covington, Ann K. *lawyer, former state supreme court justice*
Deutsch, James Bernard *lawyer*
Donnelly, Margaret T. *state agency administrator, public health service officer, former state legislator*
Eivazi, Frieda *biology professor*
Fischer, Zel M. *state supreme court judge*
Gaydos, John Raymond *bishop*
Govang, Don C. *performing arts association administrator*
Greene, Debra Foster *history professor*
Griesheimer, John Elmer *state legislator*
Heermance, J. Noel *literature and language professor*
Kinder, Peter D. *Lieutenant Governor of Missouri, former state senator*
Koster, Chris *state attorney general, former state senator*
Markway, Barbara Gerth *psychologist, writer*
Mitten, L. Russell *lawyer, former telecommunications industry executive*
Nicastro, Chris L. *state official, school system administrator*
Nixon, Jay (Jeremiah Nixon) *Governor of Missouri*
Price, William Ray, Jr. *state supreme court chief judge*
Russell, Mary Rhodes *state supreme court judge*
Scott, Gary Kuper *retired academic administrator*
Smith, Lloyd Franklin *political organization administrator*
Stith, Laura Denvir *state supreme court judge*
Tackett, Natalie Jane *state administrator*
Teitelman, Richard B. *state supreme court judge*
Tettlebaum, Harvey M. *lawyer*
Walton Gray, Rochelle LaJoyce *state legislator*
Weaver, Richard J. *state banking agency administrator*
Wolff, Michael A. *state supreme court judge*
Zweifel, Clint *state treasurer*

Joplin
Daus, Arthur Steven *neurological surgeon*
Malzahn, Ray Andrew *chemistry professor, dean*
Nodler, Charles Edward, Jr. *archivist, history professor*
Wostal, Holly Ann *music educator*

Kansas City
Abdou, Nabih I. *physician, educator*
Acheson, Allen Morrow *retired engineering executive*
Alon, Uri S. *pediatrician, nephrologist*
Amerison, Janice Earline *special education educator*
Atkinson, David Neal *law educator*
Baisden, Eleanor Marguerite *retired airline compensation executive, consultant*
Baker, John Russell *utilities executive*
Baker, Ronald Phillip *service company executive*
Balloun, Joseph Eugene *lawyer*
Bass, Lee Marshall *food products company executive*
Beck, William G. *lawyer*
Beckett, Theodore Charles *lawyer*
Beihl, Frederick *retired lawyer*
Benton, William Duane *federal judge*
Bergman, Carla Elaine *hydrologist, consultant*
Berkley, Eugene Bertram (Bert Berkley) *envelope company executive*
Berkowitz, Lawrence M. *lawyer*
Bjerke, H. Scott *surgeon*
Blanton, W. C. *lawyer*
Bloch, Henry Wollman *diversified financial services company executive*
Boland, Raymond James *bishop emeritus*
Bowman, Pasco Middleton, II, *federal judge*
Brandmaier, Jeff *diversified financial services company executive*
Brous, Thomas Richard *lawyer*
Bugher, Robert Dean *professional society administrator*
Busby, Marjean (Marjorie Jean Busby) *retired journalist*
Carney, John Michael *professional football player*
Carroll, Gregory A. *museum director, educator, musician*
Carver, Terrence Wayne, Jr. *pediatrician, educator*
Cassel, Matt *professional football player*
Caulfield, Joan *director, educator*
Cheng, Kuang Lu *chemist, educator*
Chesser, Michael J. *gas and electric power industry executive*
Ching, Wai Yim *physics professor, researcher*
Churchman, Michael Steele Bright *educational consultant, educator*
Clarke, Milton Charles *lawyer*
Collins, Kathleen *academic administrator, art educator*
Courson, Marna B.P. *public relations executive*
Coveney, Raymond Martin, Jr. *geology educator*
Cozad, Rachael Blackburn *museum director*
Crain, Geralyn D. *dental educator*
Crawford, Randy M. *lawyer*
Cross, William Dennis *lawyer*
Danner, Kathleen Frances Steele *federal official*
Davis, John Charles *lawyer*
Davis, Richard Francis *city government official*
Deacy, Thomas Edward, Jr. *lawyer*
Deng, Hong-Wen *medical educator, researcher*
Dias, Jerry Ray *chemistry professor, researcher*
Diehl, James Harvey *church administrator*
Dimond, Edmunds Grey *medical educator*
Doan, Kirk Hugh *lawyer*
Drees, Betty *medical educator, dean*
Dwyer, William Michael *health care company advisor*
Egan, Charles Joseph, Jr. *lawyer, consumer products company executive*
Eick, J. David *dental educator, department chairman*
Eick, John David *materials engineer, educator*
Eubanks, Eugene Emerson *education educator, consultant*
Fincham, Jack Edwin *science educator*
Finn, Robert William *bishop*
Forstater, Mathew *economics professor*
Foster, Mark Stephen *lawyer*
Freeman, Frederick Roe *lawyer*
Friedlander, Edward Robert *pathologist*
Frisbie, Charles *retired lawyer*
Funkouser, Mark *Mayor, Kansas City, Missouri*
Geroe, Michael R. *lawyer*
Gibson, John Robert *federal judge*
Glass, David D. *professional sports team executive, retired retail executive*
Gorman, Gerald Warner *lawyer*
Gould, Charlene J. *dean, educator*
Gowin, Elijah *photographer*
Graebner, Carol F. *diversified financial services company executive, lawyer*
Graves, Todd Peterson *lawyer, former prosecutor*
Gray, Helen Theresa Gott *editor*
Greinke, Donald Zachary (Zach Greinke) *professional baseball player*
Gusewelle, Charles Wesley *journalist, writer*
Hagan, John Charles III *ophthalmologist*
Haley, Todd *professional football coach*
Hall, Donald Joyce, Jr. *consumer products company executive*
Hamilton, Richard Alfred *retired academic administrator, marketing executive*
Handley, Gerald Matthew *lawyer, educator*
Harper, Diane M. *medical educator, researcher*
Harris, Charlie J., Jr. *lawyer*
Haverty, Michael R. *rail transportation executive*
Heymach, George John III *physician, educator, health facility administrator, consultant*
Hillman, Trey (Thomas Brad Hillman) *professional baseball manager*
Hindman, Larrie C. *lawyer*
Hoenig, Thomas M. *bank executive*
Hoffmann, Donald *architectural historian*
Holcomb, George Whitfield *pediatrician, surgeon, educator*
Hong, Liang *dentist, educator*
Honley, Russell Loran *controller, accountant*
Johnson, Andrew T. *psychology professor*
Johnson, Larry (Larry Alphonso Johnson Jr.) *professional football player*
Johnson, Mark Eugene *lawyer*
Johnson, Richard Dean *pharmaceutical consultant, educator*
Johnston, John Steven *lawyer*
Jonas, Harry S. *medical education consultant*
Jones, Charles Calhoun *estate and business planning consultant*
Jung, Craig D. *food products executive*
Kaplan, Harvey L. *lawyer*
Katz, Milton S. *humanities educator*
Kays, David Gregory *federal judge*
Kemper, Jonathan McBride *banker*
Kilroy, John Muir *lawyer*
Kilroy, William Terrence *lawyer*
Kindred, Lynn Herbert *cardiologist*
Kirch, Donald Allen *writer, composer*
Kisslinger, Carl *geophysicist, educator*
Klamann, John Michael *lawyer*
Kobach, Kris William *law educator, former political organization administrator*
Koerner, Wendell Edward, Jr. *lawyer, mediator*
Kofler, Silvia Maria *writer, educator*
Krieg, Nancy Kay *social worker, poet, musician*
Krumlauf, Robert Eugene *neuroscientist, educator*
Langworthy, Robert Burton *lawyer*
Lawson, Melanie Kay *retired management administrator, early childhood consultant*
Lednicky, John A. *virologist, microbiologist*
Lee, Margaret Norma *artist*
Leitch, Christopher *museum director, artist*
Lenaghan, Michael John *association executive*
Lindsay, Twyla Lynn *music educator*
Litan, Robert Eli *lawyer, economist*
Lofland, Gary Kenneth *cardiac surgeon*
Londré, Felicia Mae Hardison *theater educator*
Long, Edwin Tutt *surgeon*
Lopez, Gerardo Isaac *movie theater company executive*
Magill, Kent B. *lawyer*
Martucci, William Christopher *lawyer*
Mast, Kande White *artist*
Matheny, Edward Taylor, Jr. *lawyer*
Mathur, Naresh Chandra *retired engineering educator*
McCallister, Ben D. *internist, cardiologist, educator*
McCollum, Clifford Glenn *college dean emeritus*
McDonnell, Thomas A. *information technology executive*
McGregor, Douglas Hugh *pathologist, educator*
McKelvey, John Clifford *mental health services professional*
McManus, James William *lawyer*
McPhee, Mark Steven *gastroenterologist, educator*
Medhi, Deepankar *computer science educator*
Mendenhall, Kathleen F. *art educator*
Milton, Chad Earl *lawyer*
Mobberley, James *music educator, composer*
Mobley, James Robert *dentist*
Molteni, Agostino *pathology educator*
Moore, Stephen James *lawyer*
Mordy, James Calvin *retired lawyer*
Muffly, Tyler *medical educator*
Murphy, John F. *lawyer*
Myers, Betty J. *retired music specialist*
Neaves, William Barlow *cell biologist, educator*
Nelson, Freda Nell Hein *librarian*
Newsom, James Thomas *lawyer*
Nguyen, Trung Hieu *internist*
Norris, Ruth Ann Fink *social worker*
Northrip, Robert Earl *lawyer*
O'Brien, James Edward *surgeon*
Oldani, Louis Joseph *literature educator*
Olitsky, Scott Eric *ophthalmologist*
Oliver, Thornal Goodloe *retired health facility administrator*
Parizek, Eldon Joseph *geologist, educator, dean*
Pelofsky, Joel *lawyer*
Piepho, Robert Walter *pharmacy educator, researcher*
Pioli, Scott *professional sports team executive*
Potter, George William, Jr. *mining executive*
Price, Charles H., II, *former ambassador*
Price, James Tucker *lawyer*
Prugh, William Byron *lawyer*
Pruitt, Stephen Wallace *finance educator*
Rada, David Charles *dermatologist*
Raghuveer, Geetha *pediatrician, educator*
Rasmus, John Charles *retired trade association administrator, lawyer, consultant*
Redfearn, Paul L. III *lawyer*
Reed, Michael John *dentist, dean, educator*
Reiter, Robert Edward *banker*
Reynolds, Jerry (Gerald A. Reynolds) *federal agency administrator*
Riggins, William G. *electric power industry executive*
Robb, Gary Charles *lawyer*
Robertson, Leon H. *management consultant, educator*
Roosa, Jan Bertorotta *psychologist, writer*
Rost, William Joseph *chemist*
Rowland, Landon Hill *diversified holding company executive*
Rudy, Paul *composer*
Sampson, William Roth *lawyer*
Schaffer, Sandra Sue *artist, educator*
Schwend, Richard Michael *orthopedist, educator*
Seligson, Theodore H. *architect, interior designer, urban planner*
Setser, Patricia A. *music educator*
Shaw, John W. *lawyer*
Sherburn, Rebecca Sue *voice educator*
Sizemore, William Christian *retired academic administrator, county official*
Slaughter, Rochelle Denise *elementary school educator*
Smith, Richard P. *dairy product company executive, lawyer*
Smyth, Russell P. *diversified financial services company executive, former food products executive*
Snelling, Troy Wayne *history educator*
Spalty, Edward Robert *lawyer*
Spielberg, Stephen Paul *pediatrician, medical educator, former dean*
Spigarelli, James L. *science administrator*
Starling, David L. *rail transportation executive*
Stevens, James Hervey, Jr. *retired financial planner*
Stoup, Arthur Harry *lawyer*
Stowers, James Evans, Jr. *investment company executive*
Suni, Ellen Y. *dean, law educator*
Surguchov, Andrei P. *biochemist, ophthalmologist, researcher*
Swaffar, Glenda Jean *director*
Thakre, Tushar P. *physician, scientist*
Thomas, Zach Michael (Zachary Michael Thomas) *professional football player*
Tio, Celina *chef*
Truog, William Edward III *pediatrician, educator, researcher*
Tyler, John Edward III *lawyer*
Van Dyke, Thomas Wesley *lawyer*
Vering, John Albert *lawyer*
Versfeld, Leon *lawyer*
Viani, James Laurence *retired lawyer*
Vogel, Arthur Anton *clergyman*
Walsh-Kelly, Christine Mary *pediatrician, educator*
Ward, R. Lawrence *lawyer*
West, Marc *information technology executive*
Whipple, Dean *federal judge*
Whisler, Joe B. *lawyer*
Whitener, William Garnett *dancer, choreographer*
Wilkinson, Ralph Russell *retired biochemistry educator, toxicologist*
Willy, Thomas Ralph *lawyer*
Wilson, Marc Fraser *art museum director*
Wirken, James Charles *lawyer*
Woods-Taylor, Cleora Lynesia *mathematics educator, consultant*
Woody, Teresa Ann *lawyer*
Woolley, Brian N. *lawyer*
Wright, Scott Olin *federal judge*
Wrobley, Ralph *lawyer*
Wyrsch, James Robert *lawyer, educator, writer*
Zieman, Mark *editor, publishing executive*

Kearney
Waltz, James Richard *physician*

Kingsville
Stimac, John Anthony *small business owner, poet, cartoonist, inventor*

Kirksville
Darmani, Nissar Ahmad *pharmacologist, educator*
Festa, Roger Reginald *chemist, educator*
Hanley, Mark Young *historian, educator, researcher*
Holman, Charles Raymond *osteopathic physician*
Ling, Huping *history professor*
Maldonado-Class, Joaquin *language educator*
Peterson, Donald Fred *physiologist, educator*
Quinn, John James *political science professor*
Rose, (M.) Lynn *history professor*

Knob Noster
Resch, Tonda Rae *language educator*

Lake Sherwood
Torbett, Gary Burl *retired telephone company executive*

Laurie
Currier, Mike *elementary school educator, writer*

Lebanon
Russell, Doug *manufacturing executive, former political organization administrator*

Lees Summit
Cil, Akin *orthopedic surgeon*
Foudree, Charles M. *financial consultant*
Henley, Joseph Oliver *manufacturing executive*
Korschot, Benjamin Calvin *retired investment company executive*

Liberty
Coleman, Ian David *music educator*
Haistings, Jeanine Lee *education educator*
Harriman, Richard Lee *performing arts administrator, educator*
Nore, Nano Ann *Art History Professor*
Samuel, Robert Thompson *optometrist*
Tanner, Jimmie Eugene *retired dean*

Mansfield
Cotrone, Janice Lynne *nursing consultant*

Marshall
Sayer, Ronald J. *composer, educator*

Marshfield
Frame, Susan S. *special education educator*
Knust, Daniel Max *lawyer*

Maryland Heights
Hahn, Mark A. *coach, educator*
Hall, Jeffrey H. *corporate financial executive*
Han, Xiao *computer scientist, researcher*
Holmes, Michael *health products executive*
Ignaczak, Edward B. *health products executive*
McNamee, Patrick *health products executive*
Paz, George *health products executive*
Porter, Douglas W. *health products executive*
Rey-Giraud, Agnès *health products executive*
Steward, David L. *technology company executive*

Maryville
Kharadia, Virabhai Chelabhai *economist, educator, researcher*
Kling, Carl Andrew *music educator*
Tennihill, Sally Kay *writer, music educator*

Mexico
Holman, Mark D. *secondary school educator*

Moberly
Agee, Patricia Ann *school librarian, director*
Donaldson, Daniel J. *minister, educator*
Fleming, David Avery *internist*
Koutz, Tarry Alvin *religious studies educator*

Mooresville
Totten, Tina Rosene *special education educator*

Mount Vernon
Shelton, Charity Faith *speach language pathologist*

Neosho
Allman, Ann Lowrance *counseling administrator*
Wallace, Richard Le Roy Wayne *language educator*
Weber, Margaret Laura Jane *retired accountant*
Williams, Bethia *education educator*

Nevada
Besaw, Jeanne Marie *school librarian*

O Fallon
Das, Sanjiv *mortgage company executive*
Gross, Stanley Merhl *chiropractor*

Oregon
Lynn, Brenda *physical education educator*

Overland
Clark, Maxine *retail executive*

Palmyra
Wosman, Brian D. *physical education educator, director*

Park Hills
Bayless, Alan Lee *finance educator*
Scheidt, Brian R. *geologist, educator*
Young, Shawn *education educator*

Parkville
Bohn, Beverly *computer science professor*
Noe, J. Mark *communications educator*
Schultis, Gail Ann *library director*

Pierce City
Cummings, Richard William *art educator*

Platte City
Jones, Jay Robert *music educator*
Kalin, D(orothy) Jean *artist, educator*

Point Lookout
Blake, John Tyler *literature and language professor*

Poplar Bluff
Nunnery, Pamela L. *literature and language educator*

Sievers, David secondary school educator
Smith, Terri C. accountant, educator
Wilson, Terrilyn Louella nursing educator
Young, William Webb military officer, aire warfare specialist, poet

Raymore
Fairlie, Jeffrey Scott engineering company executive
Spainhower, James Ivan retired college president

Richmond Heights
Shaich, Ronald M. food service executive

Riverside
Curry, Debbie Ann school librarian

Rogersville
Hover, Tryphena Machael music educator

Rolla
Adawi, Ibrahim Hasan physics professor
Alexander, Ralph William, Jr. physics professor
Bai, Baojun engineering educator
Banerjee, Arindam engineering educator
Carney, John F. III academic administrator
Cheng, Franklin Yih civil engineering educator
Datz, Israel Mortimer information systems specialist
Elrod, Cassandra C. finance educator
Grimm, Louis John mathematician, educator
Ingram, William Thomas III mathematics professor
Look, Dwight Chester, Jr. mechanical engineering educator, researcher
Mishra, Rajiv Sharan metallurgical engineer, educator
Mitchell, Owen Robert dean, electrical engineering educator
Samaranayake, V. A. science educator, director
Sin, Yong Wook researcher, educator
Stoecker, William Van physician, computer scientist
Switzer, Jay A(lan) chemistry educator
Venayagamoorthy, Ganesh Kumar electrical engineer, educator
Xu, Bin civil engineering researcher, educator
Yan, Dongming research scientist, educator
Zawodniok, Maciej Jan engineering educator

Saint Ann
Lema, Pickett Pat school system administrator

Saint Charles
Cannon, Douglas A. retail merchandising educator
Chilton, Kenneth Wayne former business research director, educator
Golik, Wojciech Ludwik mathematics professor, department chairman
Grooms, Pamela Gayle music educator
Gross, Charles Robert county official, former state senator, former bank executive
Hickenlooper, George Loening, Sr. playwright, educator
Hurst, Spencer Eugene literature and language professor, writer
Leavitt, Lynda professor
Rollings, Dale Linn lawyer
Tabaka, Sandra Lee retired medical/surgical nurse
Tretter, Sue Ann literature and language professor
Whaley, Michael Joseph history professor

Saint James
Stevens, Helen Jean music educator

Saint Joseph
Adkins, Kaye rhetoric and writing professor
Bogle, Deborah Confer education educator
Chilcote, Gary M. museum director, reporter
Kranitz, Theodore Mitchell lawyer
Malani, Ashok K. physician
Mockabee, M(arion) Eugene minister
Morris, Stephen philosopher, educator
Oldham, Terry L. museum director
Rachow, Sharon Dianne realtor
Saravanabhavan, Sheila education educator
Sischo, Lacey social studies educator
Taylor, Michael Leslie lawyer

Saint Louis
Abdul-Hafidh, Jamal educator
Achilefu, Samuel biomedical educator director
Agarwal, Banke gastroenterologist, educator
Agarwal, Ramesh Kumar aeronautical scientist, researcher, educator
Alford, Mark Gower physicist
Allen, Garland Edward historian of science, professor, writer
Alpers, David Hershel gastroenterologist, educator
Appleton, R. O., Jr. lawyer
Armstrong, Doug professional sports team executive
Armstrong, Theodore Morelock corporate financial executive
Arnold, Fred English lawyer
Arnold, John Fox lawyer
Arya, Bindu finance educator
Aylward, Ronald Lee lawyer
Bach, Richard Gordon internist, cardiologist, educator
Bachmann, John William security firm executive
Bacon, Bruce Raymond physician
Baernstein, Albert, II, mathematician, educator
Baker, Shirley Kistler academic administrator, university librarian
Baker, W. Randolph brewery company executive
Baldwin, Edwin Steedman lawyer
Ball, Dan H. lawyer
Ballinger, Walter Francis surgeon, educator
Balogh, María Teresa language educator
Barmann, Lawrence Francis historian, educator
Barmash, Pamela religious studies educator
Bascom, C. Perry retired foundation administrator, lawyer
Baum, Gordon Lee lawyer, non-profit organization administrator
Baum, M(ary) Carolyn occupational therapist
Baxter, Warner L. electric power industry executive
Bealke, Linn Hemingway banker
Beck, Lois Grant anthropologist, educator, author
Becker, David Mandel law educator, author, consultant
Becvar, Dorothy Stroh family therapist
Belshe, Robert epidemiologist, educator
Bender, Carl Martin physics professor, consultant
Benjamin, Brent R. museum director
Bennett, Edward Strachan optometrist
Berger, David Otto library director, educator
Bextermiller, Theresa Marie architect, computer engineer
Bhavsar, Neelima G. educator
Bickel, Floyd Gilbert III investment counselor
Bierut, Laura J. psychiatrist, educator
Binns, Walter Robert astrophysics researcher
Biondi, Lawrence academic administrator, priest
Bjerregaard, Preben cardiologist, educator
Black, Dale R. hotel and gaming company executive
Blalock, Kay J. history professor
Blanke, Richard Brian lawyer
Blankenship, Robert Eugene biochemistry educator
Blanton, Elizabeth Anne secondary school educator
Bodnar, John Charles lawyer
Boggs, Beth Clemens lawyer
Bonacorsi, Mary Catherine lawyer
Booth, Betty Jean retired daycare administrator, poet
Bornstein, Daniel E. history professor, religious studies educator
Boswell, C.B. plastic surgeon
Botteron, Kelly Nicole psychiatrist, educator
Bourne, Carol Elizabeth Mulligan biology professor, phycologist
Boyce, Gregory H. energy executive
Brandt, Keith E. plastic surgeon, educator
Branham, Gregory Harris facial plastic surgeon
Bregni, Simone language educator, researcher
Bretton, Randolph H. lawyer, researcher
Brewer, Eric professional hockey player
Brickler, John Weise lawyer
Bridgewater, Bernard Adolphus, Jr. retired retail executive
Bridwell, Keith Happ orthopedic surgeon
Brockhaus, Robert Herold, Sr. business educator, consultant
Browde, Anatole electronics company executive, consultant
Browman, David L(udvig) archaeologist
Brown, Bettye librarian, educator
Brown, Theodis (Ted), Sr. fire chief
Brudvig, Lars Andrew ecologist
Bruzzini, Kristen Blake biology professor, director
Bryant, Donald L., Jr. insurance and benefits company executive
Bryant, Ruth Alyne banker
Buggs, Dwayne Andre fine arts coordinator, music educator
Bullard, James B. bank executive
Burgess, James Harland physics professor, researcher
Burgin, Richard Weston writer, educator, editor
Burke, Thomas Michael lawyer
Burke, William neurologist
Bush, Harold K. literature and language professor
Byrnes, Christopher Ian engineering educator
Cain, James Nelson arts school and concert administrator
Calvert, Randall political scientist
Cann, C. J. librarian
Carlson, Robert James archbishop
Carp, Larry lawyer
Carpenter, Brian D. psychotherapist, educator
Carr, Gary Thomas lawyer
Casaregola, Vincent Gerard literature and language professor
Chaplin, Hugh, Jr. preventive medicine physician, educator
Checketts, Dave (David Wayne Checketts) professional sports team executive
Cheng, Steven Chih-nung nephrologist, educator
Chittooran, Mary M. education educator
Clark, Mark A. language educator, director
Clear, John Michael lawyer
Cloninger, Claude Robert psychiatrist, epidemiologist, educator, researcher
Colangelo, Carmon artist, printmaker, educator
Colletti, Ronald F. chemist, researcher
Concibido, Vergel C. research and development company scientist, plant geneticist, inventor
Constantino, John Nicholas medical educator, researcher
Copeland, Douglas Allen lawyer
Cornelius, Charles H. recruitment company executive
Cornfeld, Dave Louis lawyer
Cornfeld, Richard Steven lawyer
Correa-Perez, Juan Ramon andrologist, embryologist, researcher
Cosner, Raymond Robert aeronautical engineer
Costigan, Edward John retired investment banker
Cowsik, Ramanath physics professor
Crews, Michael C. energy executive
Crews, Terrell K. agricultural products executive
Crider, Robert Agustine international financier, protective services official
Crim, Courtney physician, educator
Crooks, Carol Yvonne power systems sales engineer
Cropf, Robert Allan department chairman
Cross, Dewitte Talmadge III radiologist
Cryer, Philip Eugene endocrinologist
Cullen, James D. lawyer
Curran, Michael Walter management scientist
Danforth, John Claggett lawyer, former ambassador, Former United States Senator, Missouri
Danforth, William Henry retired academic administrator, physician
Davidson, John professional sports team executive, former hockey analyst
Davis, Irvin advertising, public relations and broadcast executive
Davis, Mary Florence psychologist
DeBaun, Michael R. pediatrician, educator
DeVoto, Thomas C. lawyer
Dewald, Paul Adolph psychiatrist, educator
Dias, Konrad Joseph physical therapist, educator
Di Bisceglie, Adrian Michael pathologist, department chairman
DiPersio, John F. oncologist
Doody, Gregory L. lawyer, former energy executive
Dorwart, Donald Bruce lawyer
Dougherty, Charles Hamilton pediatrician
Dowd, Edward L., Jr. lawyer, former prosecutor
Downey, Michael Patrick lawyer
Drake, Francis Brett social studies educator, consultant
Dreessen, Chuck R. mathematics educator
Dreifke, Gerald Edmond electrical engineering educator
Dudukovic, Milorad P. chemical engineering educator, consultant
Duesenberg, Richard William lawyer
Duesenberg, Robert H. retired lawyer
Dugan, Timothy J. electrical engineer, rancher
Eckelkamp, Elizabeth Bremer literature and language professor
Eckstein, Julie healthcare administrator, former state agency administrator
Edison, Bernard Alan retired apparel executive
Elgin, Sarah Carlisle Roberts biology professor, researcher
Elliott, Howard, Jr. lawyer, gas industry executive
Elliott, Susan Spoehrer information technology executive
Ellis, Matthew James oncologist, educator
Engelhardt, Thomas Alexander editorial cartoonist
Epner, Steven Arthur computer consultant
Epstein, Robert Harry lawyer
Falk, William James lawyer
Fang, Hui research scientist
Faro, Albert pediatric pulmonologist
Farr, David N. electronics executive
Farria, Dione Marie radiologist, educator
Felthous, Alan Robert psychiatrist
Feng, Paul Chi-Chia metabolism chemist, biochemist
Ferguson, Gary Warren retired public relations executive
Fetter, Lee F. hospital administrator
Fitch, Coy Dean internist, educator
Fitch, Rachel Farr health policy analyst
Fleshman, James W. medical association administrator
Fletcher, Bill, Jr. political organization executive, activist
Flinn, Frank K. religious studies educator
Floyd, Richard D. historian, writer
Flye, M. Wayne surgeon, immunologist, educator, writer
Fogle, James Lee lawyer
Fondaw, Ronald Edward artist, educator
Fox, G. Richard lawyer
Fraley, Robert T. biotechnologist
Frandsen, Geralyn Marie nursing educator
Frank, Terrence Dooley diversified financial services company executive, director
Frater, John Lawrence medical educator
Freeman, Terrence Lyle engineering educator, consultant
Frey, Sharon Elizabeth internist, adult infectious disease physician
Frieden, Carl biochemist, educator
Friedlander, Michael Wulf physicist, researcher
Friedman, William Hersh otolaryngologist, educator
Fromm, Ronald A. apparel executive
Fryman, Bill information technology manager, educator
Galvin, Walter J. electrical equipment manufacturing executive
Gass, William H. writer, educator
Gauen, Patrick Emil news correspondent
George, Thomas Frederick academic administrator
Geslani, Gemma P. science educator, health researcher
Gfeller, Jeffrey D. psychologist, educator
Gibbons, Patrick Chandler physicist, researcher
Gibson, James Louis political science professor
Gillingham, John Rowley III history professor, writer
Gilster, Peter Stuart lawyer
Glaus, Troy Edward professional baseball player
Goldberg, Anne Carol physician, educator
Goldberg, Mark Paul neurologist
Goldblatt, Peter curator
Goldner, Jesse Alan law educator
Gordon, Brian G. history professor
Gordon, Jeffrey Ivan gastroenterologist, educator, molecular biologist, researcher
Graff, George Stephen aerospace transportation executive
Grant, Hugh agricultural products executive
Gray, Charles Elmer lawyer, rancher, investor
Green, Maurice molecular biologist, educator, virologist
Greenbaum, Stuart I. economist, educator
Greene, Khalil Thabit professional baseball player
Greenley, Beverly Jane lawyer, educator
Griggs, Leonard LeRoy, Jr. air transportation executive, consultant
Groneck, Daniel aerospace engineer
Grossberg, George Thomas psychiatrist, educator
Grubb, Robert L., Jr. neurosurgeon
Gruenberg, Gladys Walleman economics professor, arbitrator
Gruender, Raymond W. federal judge, former prosecutor
Guarigila, Dale A. lawyer
Guerri, William Grant lawyer
Gupta, Surendra Kumar chemicals executive
Haas, Daniel Louis structural engineer
Hackmann, Frank H. lawyer
Haines, Cindy D. physician, consultant
Hakkinen, Raimo Jaakko aerospace scientist
Hamilton, Jean Constance judge
Hammerman, Marc Randall nephrologist, educator
Handel, Peter H. physics professor
Handelman, Alice Samuels public relations professional, writer
Hansen, Charles lawyer
Hansman, Robert G. artist, educator
Harris, Whitney Robson lawyer, military officer, volunteer, educator
Hartley, Tom D. corporate financial executive
Harvey, David R. chemical company executive
Haskins, James Leslie mathematics professor
Hayman, Randy E. lawyer
Hegamin-Younger, Cecilia statistician, consultant, educator
Heiken, Jay Paul physician
Hendrickson, William Lee retired French language educator
Herbert, Kevin Barry John classics educator
Hermann, Robert Joseph bishop
Hermeling, Caroline L. lawyer
Herzog, Erik D. biology professor
Heuckeroth, Robert O. pediatrician, educator
Hickman, Clark Joseph education educator
Hirose, Keiko otolaryngologist, educator
Hirsch, Raymond Robert chemicals executive, lawyer
Hoft, Daniel Fredric immunologist, director
Holliday, Matt professional baseball player
Holmes, Nancy Elizabeth pediatrician
Holt, Glen Edward editor
Holtzer, Alfred Melvin chemistry professor
Holtzman, David Michael neurologist
Huestis, Jeffrey Charles academic administrator, dean
Hunt, Kevin J. food products executive
Hunter, Earle Leslie III retired professional association executive
Hurley, Andrew J. historian
Hyers, Thomas Morgan internist, biomedical researcher
Immel, Vincent Clare retired law educator
Inder, Terrie Eleanor pediatrician, educator
Inkley, John James, Jr. lawyer
Israel, Martin Henry astrophysicist, educator, academic administrator
Izuchukwu, John Ifeanyichukwu industrial and mechanical engineer
Jackson, Steven Rashad professional football player
James, James Edward music educator
James, William W. financial consultant
Janis, Larry Williard secondary school educator
Jaudes, Richard Edward lawyer
Jenkins, James Allister mathematician, educator
Joffrion, James L., Jr. pharmaceutical executive
Johnson, E. Perry lawyer
Joley, Lisa Annette lawyer, brewery company executive
Jordan, Julia Crawford secondary school educator
Kadan, Ohad finance educator
Kale, Sushant P. neurologist
Kamkwalala, Robert W. finance educator
Kariya, Paul professional hockey player
Kavadlo, Jesse literature and language professor
Kavanaugh, John Francis social sciences educator, director
Keffler, Karl Joseph private investor, lawyer, educator
Khomami, Bamin chemical engineer, educator
Kienstra, Kathleen O. radiation therapist professor, program director
Kimmey, James Richard, Jr. foundation administrator
King, Douglas R. museum administrator
King, Joseph, Jr. federal agency administrator
Klein, Ward M. consumer products company executive
Kling, S(tephen) Lee banker
Knoblauch-O'Neal, Christine Ann artist
Knutsen, Alan Paul pediatrician, immunologist, allergist
Koff, Robert Hess academic administrator, adult education educator
Kohn, Alan Charles lawyer
Kornblet, Donald Ross communications company executive
Kortenhof, Joseph Michael lawyer, educator
Kotrba, Camilla Anne dietician, consultant
Kouchoukos, Nicholas Thomas surgeon
Kraft, Carl David lawyer
Krukowski, Lucian philosopher, educator, artist
Kuhlmann, Fred Mark lawyer
Kwak, No Kyoon business administration educator
Lackey, Kayle Diann elementary school educator
Lai, H. Henry urologist
La Russa, Tony, Jr., (Anthony La Russa Jr.) professional baseball manager
Lasala, John M. cardiologist, medical educator
Lause, Michael Francis lawyer
Lawton, David Arthur literature and language professor
Lebowitz, Albert lawyer, writer
Leer, Steven F. mining executive
Leguey-Feilleux, Jean-Robert political scientist, educator
Lemons, Shelly L. history professor
Lents, Don Glaude lawyer
Le Vine, Victor Theodore retired political science professor
Lewis, Jeffrey E. dean, law educator
Lewis, Lawrence M. emergency physician, researcher
Lewis, Robert David ophthalmologist, educator
Ley, Timothy James hematologist, molecular biologist
Li, Ping pharmacologist, educator, researcher
Limbaugh, Stephen Nathaniel retired federal judge
Lindsey, Linda Lee sociology educator
Litz, Arthur retired judge
Llewellyn, Kathleen Marie language educator
Lock, Albert Larry, Jr. financial services company executive
Long, Christopher Howard professional football player
Lonsberg, John V. lawyer
López, Oscar R. language educator, researcher
Loughrey, Thomas James health and wellness professor
Lowenberg, David A. pharmaceutical executive
Lowenhaupt, Charles Abraham lawyer
Lubbock, James Edward retired writer, photographer, media consultant
Lucchesi, Lionel Louis lawyer
Ludmerer, Kenneth Marc medical educator
Lutz, John Thomas author
Lynch, Robert Martin lawyer, consultant
Lyons, Martin J., Jr. electric power industry executive

Macias, Edward S. *chemistry professor, dean, academic administrator*
MacInnis, Al *professional sports team executive, retired professional hockey player*
Mackinnon, Susan *plastic surgeon*
Madsen, Matthew J. *lawyer*
Mahan, David James *retired academic administrator*
Mahsman, David Lawrence *writer, church administrator*
Majerus, Philip Warren *physician*
Manary, Mark John *pediatrician*
Mandelstamm, Jerome Robert *lawyer*
Maposa, Sithokozile *nursing researcher*
Marti, Paul Edgar, Jr. *architect, educator*
Martin de Camilo, Jody Elizabeth *biology professor*
Mason, Philip John *geneticist*
Maurer, Frederic George III *bank executive*
Mazuski, John Edward *surgeon, researcher*
McCann, Melinda Camille *agricultural professional*
McCarter, Charles Chase *lawyer*
McCaslin, Sharon *librarian*
McDaniel, James Edwin *lawyer*
McKinnis, Michael Bayard *lawyer*
McNamee, Sister Catherine *educator*
McReynolds, Patricia Randolph *retired education educator*
Meehan, John Justin *lawyer*
Meissner, Edwin Benjamin, Jr. *retired real estate broker*
Merrell, James Lee *writer, minister*
Merrill, Charles Eugene *lawyer*
Messbarger, Rebecca Marie *literature and language professor*
Metcalfe, Elizabeth Brokaw *art educator*
Metcalfe, Walter Lee, Jr. *lawyer*
Meyer, David Alan *lawyer*
Michaelides, Constantine Evangelos *architect, educator*
Michenfelder, Albert A. *lawyer*
Middelkamp, John Neal *pediatrician, educator*
Miller, James Gegan *research scientist*
Miller, Judith Braffman *writer*
Mohanakumar, Thalachallour *medical educator, director*
Molina, Yadier B. *professional baseball player*
Momtahen, Amir Javad *radiologist*
Monroe, Thomas Edward *business and financial executive*
Monser, Edward L. *electronics executive*
Monteleone, Patricia L. *dean*
Moore, McPherson Dorsett *lawyer*
Moore, Terry Lynn *physician, researcher*
Morley, John Edward *physician*
Morris, John Carl *neurologist, educator, researcher*
Mowbray, Kevin D. *publishing executive*
Mulligan, Michael Dennis *lawyer*
Mumm, Steven Robert *geneticist, educator*
Murray, Andy *professional hockey coach*
Murray, Robert Wallace *chemistry professor*
Myerson, Robert J. *radiologist, educator*
Nagarkatti, Jai Prakash *chemical company executive*
Narayanan, Narayanan Narayanan *biologist, researcher*
Navarre, Richard A. *energy executive*
Neely, John Gail *otolaryngologist*
Neidorff, Michael F. *health care executive*
Nelson, D. Michael *gynecologist, educator*
Neville, James Morton *retired lawyer, consumer products company executive*
Newcomer, John Whitney *psychiatrist, researcher, educator*
Newman, Charles *lawyer*
Niblack, Tracey *social studies educator*
Nicholson, Pamela M. *rental and leasing company executive*
Noce, David D. *judge*
Norberg, Richard Edwin *physicist, researcher*
North, Douglass Cecil *economist, educator*
Nunley, Ryan M. *orthopaedic surgeon*
Oberlander, Michael I. *lawyer, consumer products company executive*
O'Connell, Daniel Craig *retired psychologist, educator*
Oh, Jung Hun *computer engineer*
O'Keefe, Michael Daniel *lawyer*
Oliver, George Charles *medical educator, cardiologist*
Olney, John William *psychiatry professor*
O'Malley, Kevin Francis *lawyer, educator, writer*
Orton, George Frederick *aerospace engineer*
Overall, Dianna *elementary school educator*
Owens, William Don *anesthesiology educator*
Ozawa, Martha Naoko *social work educator*
Pace, Charles *library director*
Palans, Lloyd Alex *lawyer*
Park, Young H. *dean*
Peacock, David A. *brewery company executive*
Pegg, Mark Gregory *historian, educator*
Peper, Christian Baird *lawyer*
Peters, Charles A. *electronics executive*
Peters, David Allen *mechanical engineering educator, consultant*
Petruska, Paul Eric *lawyer*
Phillips, Carl *poet, educator*
Phoenix, G. Keith *lawyer*
Piccinini, Gualtiero *philosopher, educator*
Pileggi, Annamaria *theater director, educator*
Piwnica-Worms, Helen M. *cell biologist, educator*
Pleau, Larry (Lawrence Winslow Pleau) *professional sports team executive*
Pollack, Joe *retired columnist, critic, writer*
Pollack, Seymour Victor *computer science educator*
Pope, Robert E(ugene) *fraternal organization administrator*
Prensky, Arthur Lawrence *pediatric neurologist, educator*
Price, Joseph Levering *neuroscientist, educator*
Pryor, David Bram *health science association administrator*
Pujols, Albert (Jose Alberto Pujols) *professional baseball player*
Purkerson, Mabel Louise *physician, physiologist, educator*
Quinn, Jeffry N. *chemicals executive, lawyer*
Raclin, Grier C. *lawyer, telecommunications industry executive*
Rainwater, Gary L. *electric power industry executive*
Randolph, Jennings, Jr., (Jay Randolph) *sportscaster*
Rank, Mark Robert *sociologist*
Rasche, Robert Harold *banker, retired economics educator*
Raven, Peter Hamilton *botanist, director*
Rednam, Krishna Rao Venkata *ophthalmologist*
Rendlen, Charles Earnest, III, (Sketch Rendlen) *federal judge, lawyer*
Revard, Stella Hill Purce *English literature educator*
Reynolds, Robert A., Jr. *electric distributor executive*
Rice, Patricia Jane *journalist*
Rice, Rose Ann M. *secondary school educator*
Riddle, Veryl Lee *lawyer*
Riew, K. Daniel *cervical spine surgeon*
Rigden, John Saxby *physicist*
Riley, Michael Robert *marketing and business development executive*
Ringkamp, Stephen H. *lawyer, educator*
Robbins, Arnie *editor*
Robertson, David *conductor, music director*
Rodin, Miriam B. *medical educator*
Roediger, Henry L. III *psychology educator*
Roodman, David A. *lawyer*
Rose, Albert Schoenburg *lawyer, educator*
Rosen, Adrienne *artist, educator*
Rosen, Fred *travel company executive*
Rosenbaum, Herbert Edwin *neurology educator*
Ross, Donald L. *rental and leasing company executive*
Roti Roti, Joseph Lee *scientist, educator*
Rowan, Steven William *history professor*
Rubenstein, Jerome Max *lawyer*
Ruland, Richard Eugene *literature educator, critic, historian*
Sabbert, Anne Ward *vision therapist, consultant*
Sachdeva, Ashutosh *pulmonologist, director*
Sachs, Alan Arthur *lawyer*
Sale, Merritt *classicist, educator, comparatist*
Salisbury, Robert Holt *political science professor*
Sansalone, Mary Jane *dean, structural engineer, educator*
Saunders, Alan Keith *professional football coach*
Savoie, Sean Michael *lighting designer, educator*
Schaal, Barbara Anna *evolutionary biologist, educator*
Scheffing, Dianne Elizabeth *special education educator*
Schlafly, Phyllis Stewart *writer*
Schmitz, Eloise E. *communications executive*
Schoch, Alexander C. *lawyer, energy executive*
Schoenhard, William Charles, Jr. *health system executive*
Schonfeld, Gustav *medical educator, researcher, administrator*
Schramm, Paul Howard *retired lawyer*
Schremp, Ted W. *communications executive*
Schvey, Henry I. *performing arts educator*
Schwartz, Alan Leigh *pediatrician, educator*
Schwarz, Egon *language educator, writer, critic*
Schweizer, Gregory Paul *music educator*
Scoggins, Rob *choreographer, director*
Searls, Eileen Haughey *retired lawyer, librarian, educator*
Sestric, Anthony James *lawyer*
Setser, Christie Elaine *auditor*
Shapiro, Larry J. *dean, educator, pediatrician*
Sherby, Kathleen Reilly *lawyer*
Shrauner, Barbara Wayne Abraham *electrical engineer, educator*
Shulkina, Tatyana *botanist, researcher*
Sibbald, John Ristow *management consultant*
Siegel, Barry Alan *radiologist*
Siemer, Paul Jennings *public relations executive*
Sita, Michael John *pharmacy educator*
Skarie, David P. *food products executive*
Skrainka, Alan Frederick *securities analyst*
Slay, Francis G. *Mayor, St. Louis*
Smit, Neil *telecommunications industry executive*
Smith, Arthur Lee *lawyer*
Smith, Kenneth Rupert, Jr. *neurosurgeon, educator*
Smith, L. Douglas *business educator*
Smith, Morton Edward *ophthalmology educator, dean*
Smith, Richard Jay *anthropologist, educator, dean*
Smoltz, John Andrew *professional baseball player*
Snively, David Frederick *agricultural products company executive, lawyer*
Snyder, William W. *corporate financial executive*
Softli, Tony *professional sports team executive*
Spagnuolo, Steve *professional football coach*
Spector, Gershon Jerry *otolaryngologist, educator, researcher*
Staines, Gail M. *academic administrator*
Stallings, Charles Kendall *music educator, composer*
Stearley, Robert Jay *retired packaging company executive*
Stenson, William Frederick *gastroenterologist*
Stewart, John Harger *music educator*
Stoecker, David Thomas *retired banker*
Stokes, Patrick T. *brewery company executive*
Stone, Christian Diaz *medical educator*
Stoneman, Mark L. *lawyer*
Stookesberry, Denise *musician, educator*
Stroup, John S. *high speed electronic industry executive*
Strunk, Robert Charles *physician*
Suen, Hon Chi *thoracic surgeon*
Sullivan, Steven R. *lawyer*
Sutera, Salvatore Philip *mechanical engineer, educator*
Sutherland, Mary (Marcus) *pianist, composer, conductor*
Swain, David O. *manufacturing executive*
Swearingen, Laura Colleen *music educator, director*
Swinson, Sara Hope *writer, artist*
Sykes, Charles E. *dean*
Tapp, Shelley Raye *marketing educator*
Taylor, Andrew C. *rental and leasing company executive*
Taylor, Jack Crawford *rental and leasing company executive*
Teasdale, Kenneth Fulbright *lawyer*
Telowitz, Marilyn Marie *English and social studies educator*
Temporiti, John J. *lawyer, former political organization administrator*
Ternberg, Jessie Lamoin *pediatric surgeon, educator*
Thach, Robert Edwards *biology educator, former dean*
Thacker, William D. *physics professor*
Thakor, Anjan V. *finance educator, consultant*
Tibi, Rigobert *seismologist, researcher*
Tiefenbrunn, Alan James *medical educator*
Tkachuk, Keith *professional hockey player*
Tollefsen, Douglas Meyer *medical educator*
Turner, Jonathan Shields *computer science educator, researcher*
Turner-Richard, Lana R. *musician, director, composer*
Tyler, William Howard, Jr. *advertising executive, educator*
Tyree, Donald Andrew *financial educator, department chairman*
Unanue, Emil Raphael *immunopathologist*
Underwood, Anthony Paul *lawyer*
Uraizee, Joya *literature and language professor*
van den Berg, Sara Jane *language educator*
Van Fleet, Lisa A. *lawyer*
Verbeck, Alison *librarian*
Voss, Thomas R. *electric power industry executive*
Wafapoor, Farzad *information technology executive, educator*
Wagner, Raymond Thomas, Jr. *lawyer*
Walker, Doretta Anita *director*
Walker Tucker, Dana *lawyer*
Walsh, David Joseph *pediatric neurologist, educator*
Walsh, Thomas Charles *lawyer*
Wang, Xue Min *biochemistry educator*
Wedner, H. James *physician, researcher*
Weidenbaum, Murray Lew *economist, educator*
Weiss, Charles Andrew *lawyer*
Weiss, Penny A. *political science professor, director*
Weiss, Robert Francis *retired academic and religious organization administrator, consultant*
Weixlmann, Joseph Norman, Jr. *language educator, academic administrator*
Weldon, Virginia V. *retired food products executive, pediatrician*
Wellman, Carl Pierce *philosophy educator*
Wells, W. David *lawyer*
Wheelock, Bryan King *lawyer, educator*
Whyte, Michael P. *genetics educator, researcher, director*
Wiggins, Dewayne Lee *financial executive*
Wilbanks, Donnie Jo *healthcare educator*
Wilkins, Addi L. *retired lay worker*
Wilkinson, Robert F. *lawyer*
Will, Clifford Martin *physicist, researcher, educator*
Williamson, Keith Harvey *lawyer*
Wilson, Edward Nathan *mathematician, educator*
Wilson, Richard K. *microbiologist, researcher*
Winer, Warren James *insurance executive*
Winter, Richard Lawrence *diversified financial services company executive*
Wolfard, Jason *basketball coach, educator*
Wolff, Frank Pierce, Jr. *lawyer*
Woolf, Steven Michael *artistic director*
Wrighton, Mark Stephen *academic administrator, chemistry professor*
Yaeger, Douglas Harrison *gas industry executive*
Yatskievych, George Alfred *curator, educator*
Yokoyama, Wayne Makoto *medical educator, researcher, rheumatologist*
Young, Paul Andrew *anatomist*
Young, Vernon Leroy *plastic surgeon, researcher*
Zar, David M. *research associate, consultant*
Zonia, Dhimitri *artist*

Saint Peters
Caples, Linda Griffin *retired secondary school educator*
Dubé, George *optical equipment company executive*
Huckshold, Wayne William *elementary school educator*
Long, Lydia Ann *literature and composition professor*
Poettker, Mary Therese *music educator*
Pring, Robert Bradford *banker, securities trader*
Ranner, Shanna *music educator*
Thornton, Girard B., Jr., (Jerry) *elementary school educator*
Wang, William Weiqi *physician*

Sedalia
Rice, James Briggs, Jr. *lawyer*

Smithville
Johnson, Darryl Thomas *communications educator*

Springfield
Abidogun, Jamaine Marie *education educator, researcher*
Allcorn, Terry Alan *principal, educator*
Amtower, Debra Lynn *nursing consultant*
Armstrong, Bill Howard *artist, educator*
Baird, C. Ronald *lawyer*
Bartee, Wayne C. *retired history professor*
Beisswenger, Drew (Donald Andrew Beisswenger) *music librarian*
Blake, Loretta L. *music educator*
Bodo, Bela *historian, educator*
Branstetter, Ann Dyche *psychology professor*
Burgess, Ruth Lenora Vassar *speech and language educator*
Burt, Larry W. *history professor, researcher*
Carlson, Thomas Joseph *Mayor, Springfield, Missouri*
Carson, George R. *history and religious studies educator*
Cassity, Michael David *music therapy educator*
Cavner, Nadia *investment company executive*
Champion, Norma Jean *state legislator, communications educator*
Christian, John Catlett, Jr. *lawyer*
Criswell, Charles H. (Harry Criswell) *analytical chemist, environmental and forensic consultant, executive*
Dinwiddie, Keith E. *industrial engineer*
Don, Tosh H. *mathematics professor*
Easley, June Ellen Price *genealogist*
Frizell, Michael *director*
Garrett, Dale Lee *football coach, educator*
Giglio, James Nicholas *humanities educator, writer*
Gill, Angela Sue *clinical psychologist*
Given, Mark *religious studies educator*
Glazier, Robert Carl *publishing executive*
Hamra, Sam F. *lawyer, restauranteur*
Hancock, Mel *former congressman*
Harris, Jane Marie *music educator*
Henslee, Gregory L. *automotive executive*
Heyboer, Jill L. *musician, educator*
Horny, Karen Louise *library administrator*
Hosmer, Craig William *lawyer, political organization administrator*
Jenkins, Bonnie Lee *music educator*
Johnston, James Vann, Jr. *bishop*
Jura, James J. *electric utility executive*
Kavanaugh, Rosa Jean *dean*
Kim, Kee S. *management consultant, educator*
Leibrecht, John Joseph *bishop emeritus*
Manke, Dale R. *finance educator*
Mathis, Alicia *biologist, department chairman*
Newman, Earl E. *transportation engineer, consultant*
Nugent, Pauline *ancient language educator*
Nunnally, Waverly Earl *religious studies educator, writer*
O'Block, Robert *association, publishing executive*
Parrish, John Edward *state appellate judge*
Pedigo, Justin B. *audiology services professional, media consultant*
Pratt, John S. *lawyer*
Reed, Peggy Anne *education educator*
Salley, C. DeWitt, Jr. *education educator, director*
Sanders, Bryan Howard *law educator, consultant*
Schaefer, Cheryl Plaster *physics professor*
Schnake, Richard Lane *lawyer*
Sherman, Ruth Todd *counseling administrator, educator*
Smith, Gregory Arnold *dean*
Spicer, Holt Vandercook *retired theater educator*
Stone, Allan David *retired economics professor*
Tenneson, Michael Gunnar *biology professor*
Thompson, Clifton C. *retired chemistry professor, academic administrator*
Toste, Anthony Paim *chemistry educator, researcher*
Trout, Jacob Eugene *religious studies educator*
Wilkins, Sharon Kay Ramsey *music educator, director*
William, Paul Griffin *theology studies educator*

Stockton
Hammons, Brian Kent *executive lawyer*

Sturgeon
Dawkins, Amy *artist*

Town And Country
Fagerberg, Roger Richard *lawyer*
Levin, Marvin Edgar *physician*

Trenton
Cowling, Linda Sue *literature and language professor*
Gentry, Shirley *music educator, writer*
Pushkarsky, Louis Paul *retired mathematics educator*

Troy
Bockhorst, Barbara Alice *retired secondary school educator*
Krumlinde, Georganna *media specialist*
Mills, Marsha Lee *retired secondary school educator*

Union
Boehmer, Ann *mathematics professor*
Cook, Judyth W. *computer science educator*
Henderson, Russell J. *history professor*

University City
Krejnik, Kelley *social studies educator*
Winter, David Ferdinand *electrical engineering educator, consultant*

Villa Ridge
Laskowski, Leonard Francis, Jr. *microbiologist*

Walker
Martin, Phillip Dwight *bank consulting company executive, mayor*

Warrensburg
Lewandowski, Joseph D. *social studies educator, dean*
Yousef, Mahmoud *mathematics professor, computer scientist, educator*

Warrenton
Dapron, Elmer Joseph, Jr. *communications executive*

Wentzville
Saran, Shailee *dietician*

West Plains
Dreckman, Dale P. *medical educator*

Wildwood
Drucker, Barry Jules *environmental health specialist*
Hapner, Barry Nathan *performing arts educator*
Truitt, William Harvey *private school educator*

Windyville
Condron, Barbara O'Guinn *philosopher, educator, academic administrator, writer*
Condron, Daniel Ralph *academic administrator, metaphysics educator*

Winona
Marshall, Lucille Ruth *retired mathematics professor*

Wright City
Mabrey, Rick *science educator*

MONTANA

Big Sky
Ryan, Raymond D. *retired steel and insurance company executive*
Strickler, Jeffrey Harold *pediatrician*

Bigfork
Harvey, Nancy Melissa *media specialist, art educator*
Wetzel, Betty Preat *writer*

Billings
Barnea, Uri N. *rabbi, conductor, musician*
Cochran, William Michael *librarian*
Dalthorp, George Carrol *lawyer*
DeRosier, Linda Scott *psychologist, educator*
Fagg, Russell *judge, lawyer*
Fried, Michael D. *mathematician, educator*
Glenn, Guy Charles *pathologist*
Kerr, Shauna Gay *secondary school educator*
Knapp, Howard Raymond *internist, clinical pharmacologist*
Larsen, Kimbert E. *journalist*
Larsen, Richard Lee *city manager, consultant, retired mayor, arbitrator*
Mahlke, Amy Gerilyn *pre-school teacher*
Mercer, William W. *prosecutor*
Peterson, Robyn Gayle *museum director*
Sample, Joseph Scanlon *foundation executive*
Schaffer, Deborah Beth *English language educator*
Sites, James Philip *lawyer*
Thomas, Sidney R. *federal judge*
Thompson, James William *lawyer*
Towe, Thomas Edward *lawyer*

Bonner
Smith, Annick *writer*

Boulder
Kelly, Mark *secondary school educator*

Bozeman
Al-Kaisy, Ahmed *engineering educator, researcher*
Bayramian, Andy James *physicist, chemist, researcher*
Biegel, Debra Jeanne *music educator*
Buonamici, April Graham *elementary school and music educator*
Christopher, John Chambers *counseling psychology educator*
Cokelet, Giles Roy *biomedical engineering educator*
Conover, Richard Corrill *lawyer*
Davis, Nicholas Homans Clark *finance company executive*
DeHaas, John Neff, Jr. *retired architecture educator*
Delaney, Kevin J. *research scientist*
Duffié, Mary Katharine *anthropologist, educator*
Gray, Philip Howard *former psychologist, writer, educator*
McLeod, Bruce Royal *electrical engineering educator, consultant*
Minton, Dwight Church *manufacturing executive*
Mortenson, Greg *not-for-profit fundraiser, writer*
Pardue, A. Michael *retired plastic and reconstructive surgeon*
Patten, Duncan Theunissen *ecologist educator*
Pugesek, Bruce H. *statistician*
Sanks, Robert Leland *environmental engineer, retired educator*
Schmidt, Victor Hugo *physics professor, researcher*
Schrag, Anne Michelle *ecologist*
Stanislao, Joseph *engineering educator, consultant*
Vick, Jeffrey Harrison *musician, educator*

Browning
McKay, Michael I. *biologist, researcher*

Butte
Alvarado, Arlene *educational association administrator*
Clark, Gloria A. *music educator*
Gilmore, W. Franklin (Frank) *academic administrator*
Ray, John Wallace III *political science professor*

Clancy
Ekanger, Laurie *retired state official, consultant*

Columbia Falls
Chisholm, Dean D. *lawyer*
Spade-Shenker, George Lawrence (George Shenker) *research scientist*

Crow Agency
Crow, Joseph Medicine (Joe Crow) *Native American chief, historian*

Cut Bank
Johnson, Liane *political organization administrator*

Dayton
Catalfomo, Philip *retired university dean*
von Volborth, Alex (Alexis) *geochemist, geological engineering educator*

Dillon
Krank, Sarah Cleland *humanities educator*

Eureka
Kessler-Hodgson, Lee Gwendolyn *actress, marketing company executive*

Glendive
Holas, Marcia *finance educator*
McDonough, Russell Charles *retired state supreme court justice*

Great Falls
Christiaens, Chris (Bernard Francis) *financial analyst, state legislator*
Hugg, Harold J. *music educator, director*
Knudson, Ruthann *environmental consultant, anthropologist, archaeologist*
Olszewski, Chris Michael *science educator, director*
Walker, Leland Jasper *civil engineer*
Warfel, Michael William *bishop*

Hamilton
Henley, Jack Carson *retired military officer*

Harlem
Brekke, Alan Lee *industrial engineer*

Havre
Jestrab, Carol A. *librarian*
Maristuen, Keith A. *lawyer*

Helena
Bohlinger, John C. *Lieutenant Governor of Montana, former state legislator*
Bullock, Steve *state attorney general*
Cooney, Michael Rodman *state legislator*
Cotter, Patricia O'Brien *state supreme court justice*
Goodwin, Annie M. *state banking agency administrator*
Horton, Travis B. *biologist*
Hunt, William Edward, Sr. *lawyer, retired state supreme court justice*
Jergeson, Greg *Public Service Commissioner, Montana*
Johnson, John Philip *geneticist, researcher*
Juneau, Denise *state official, school system administrator*
Kelly, Janet Lee *state treasurer*
Leaphart, W. William *state supreme court justice*
McCulloch, Linda Harman *state official, former school system administrator*
McDonald, Dennis *rancher, political organization administrator*
McGrath, Mike *state supreme court chief justice, former state attorney general*
Meadows, Judith Adams *law librarian, educator*
Morris, Brian *state supreme court justice*
Morrison, John Martin *lawyer, State Auditor Montana*
Nelson, James C *state supreme court justice*
Peterson, James Erling *state legislator*
Pettit, Lawrence Kay *university president*
Rice, Jim *state supreme court justice*
Schweitzer, Brian *Governor of Montana*
Thomas, George Leo *bishop*
Toole, Joan Trimble *financial consultant*
Warner, John Arnan *state supreme court justice*
Whiting-Sorrell, Anna *state agency administrator*

Kalispell
Vickers, Lee Louise *minister*
Voronina, Valeriya *language educator, consultant*
Warneke, Joel *physics professor, mining engineer*

Livingston
Cummins, Milla Lattan *library director*
Schell, William Joseph, IV, *industrial engineer*

Miles City
Coffman, Richard C. *retired protective services official*
Gerber, Robin *history and social sciences educator*

Missoula
Auge', Cynthia Riley *humanities educator*
Barnett, Mary Louise *elementary school educator*
Bitar, Samir I. *language educator*
Bowman, Jean Louise *lawyer, civic worker*
Brown, Firman Hewitt, Jr. *drama educator, theater director*
Brown, Perry Joe *dean*
Brown, Robert Munro *museum director*
Chung, Woodam *agricultural studies educator*
Dent, Larry A. *pharmacist, educator*
Dial, Kenneth Paul *biology professor*
Doherty, Steve *lawyer, state legislator*
Grieves, Forest Leslie *political science professor, department chairman*
Grimes, Mark Lindsay *medical educator, researcher*
Howe, Scott E. *information technology executive*
Jakobson, Mark John *retired physics professor*
Kittredge, William Alfred *humanities educator*
Lopach, James Joseph *political science professor*
Millin, Laura Jeanne *museum director*
Roy, Tom McKim *social worker*
Sears, James Walter *geologist, educator*
Stratton, Timothy Patrick *pharmacy educator*
Tonev, Thomas (Toma) V. *mathematics professor*
Willey, Charles Wayne *lawyer*

Monarch
Baker, David Warren *earth scientist*

Montana City
Shaver, James Porter *retired education educator, dean*

Pablo
Lambert, Lorelei Anne *nursing educator*

Polson
Lenau, Laura Arline *retired nursing educator*
Marchi, Jon *retired brokerage house executive, rancher, venture capitalist*
Turnage, Jean Allen *retired state supreme court chief justice*

Pony
Anderson, Richard Ernest *agricultural engineer, consultant, rancher*

Poplar
Abbott, Margaret Ann *literature and language professor*
Scheetz, Anita A. *library director*

Twin Bridges
Ruppel, Edward Thompson *geologist*

West Yellowstone
Shea, Paul *museum association administrator, curator*

Whitehall
Bernard, Donald Ray *retired law educator*

Wolf Point
Morin, JoyAnn Hauge *education educator*

NEBRASKA

Adams
Badeer, Henry Sarkis *physiology educator*

Arlington
Moskus, Jerry Ray *retired academic administrator*

Ashland
McLean, John Mac *museum director*

Bellevue
Evans, Cleveland Kent *psychology professor*
Hawkins, Mary Bess *academic administrator*
Jeffrey, Mark D. *psychologist, consultant*
Kayne, Jon Barry *academic administrator, psychologist*
Milone, Anthony Michael *bishop emeritus*
Muller, John Bartlett *academic administrator*
Youssef, Carolyn Magdy *finance educator*

Bennington
Burgher, Louis William *physician, educator, academic administrator*
Fleming, William Hare *surgeon*

Blair
Conlon, Thomas James *marketing executive*
Udey, Susan S. *accounting educator*

Boys Town
DiBacco, Nadine Louise *retired library director, photographer, writer*
DiBacco, T. Jay *financial services executive, retired military officer*
Lynch, Thomas Joseph *museum director*

Brady
Novacek, Jay McKinley *retired professional football player*

Broken Bow
Sennett, John O. *lawyer*

Chadron
Bump, Bevin B. *lawyer*
Butterfield, Charles H. *ecologist, educator*
Lecher, Belvadine (Belvadine Reeves) *museum curator*
Mays, Roger William *theater educator*
Polak, Sarah *museum association administrator, educator*
Winkle, William Allan *music educator*

Columbus
Schumacher, Paul Maynard *lawyer*

Crete
Muckel, Robert Dale *retired biology professor*
Wentworth, Christopher Dean *physics professor*

Dalton
Kandel, Sue Ellen *English language educator*

Dodge
Inman, Mitchell Lee, Jr. *accountant*

Elkhorn
Regan, Timothy James *grain company executive*

Fremont
Dunklau, Rupert Louis *financial planner, consultant*
Elsberry, James *retired music educator, director*
Regier, Bryan L. *music educator*

Grand Island
Black, Joe *museum director, curator*
Dendinger, William Joseph *bishop, former career officer*
Garrelts, Deborah Louise *psychologist, educator, educational consultant*

Harrison
Coffee, Virginia Claire *civic worker, former mayor*

Hastings
Dugan, Jim *physics professor*
Dungan, John Russell, Jr., (12th Viscount Dungan of Clane, Hereditary Prince of Fermoy and Arra) *anesthesiologist, health facility administrator*
Dux-Ideus, Sherrie Lee *school librarian, history educator*
Gompert, Daniel *electronics engineer, consultant*
McCarthy, David Bruce *minister*
Morris, Amy *biology professor*
Thorndike, Ann M. *microbiologist, educator*
White, George William *theater educator*

Holdrege
Hendrickson, Bruce Carl *life insurance company executive*

Kearney
Arrieta, Mariela *language educator*
Carlson, Kimberly Ann *biology professor*
Forster, Bruce Alexander *dean*
Fryda, Nicolas J. *biologist*
Hardesty, Larry Lynn *librarian*
Hayes, Suzanne K. *finance educator*
Hertner, John F. *biology professor, horse breeder*
Hoback, William Wyatt *biology professor*
Mena-Werth, Jose *physics professor*
Miller, Richard Lee *psychology professor, department chairman*
Rothenberger, Steven John *biology professor*
Schnoor, Neal Henry *music educator*
Snider, Daren *educator*
Tenkorang, Frank A. *economist, educator*
Ziebarth-Bovill, Jane K. *social sciences educator*

Kimball
Kinnison, Daniel E. *manufacturing engineer*

Lincoln
Allen, Edward Martin *religious studies educator*
Anderson, John Edwin *economics professor, consultant*
Asgarpoor, Sohrab *engineering educator*
Auld, James S. *educational psychologist*
Avery, William Paul *state legislator, political scientist, educator*
Bahar, Ezekiel *electrical engineering educator*
Bauer, Daryl L. *environmental services administrator*
Beam, Clarence Arlen *federal judge*
Beutler, Christopher John *mayor, Lincoln, Nebr., state legislator*
Birla, Sohan *food scientist*
Bradley, Richard Edwin *retired academic administrator*
Breed, Roger *state official, school system administrator*
Bruning, Jon Cumberland *state attorney general*
Bruskewitz, Fabian Wendelin *bishop*
Burba, George G. *research scientist*
Campbell-Grossman, Christie Kay *nursing educator*
Caramagno, Thomas Carmelo *English educator*
Collier, Nathan Morris *musician, educator*
Connolly, William M. *state supreme court justice*
Council, Brenda Joyce *state legislator*
Covalt, Victor E. III *lawyer, political organization administrator*
Crump, Linda R. *lawyer*
Curry, Dawne Yvette *history professor*
Dappen, Glen Eugene *retired biology professor*
Deegan, Mary Jo *sociologist*
Dierks, Merton Lyle *state legislator, retired veterinarian*
Digman, Lester Aloysius *management educator*
Dixon, Wheeler Winston *film and video studies educator, writer*
Dowben, Peter Arnold *physics professor*
Dunlap, Michael S. *student loan company executive*
Dyer, William Earl, Jr. *retired newspaper editor*
Eckhardt, Craig Jon *chemistry professor*
Edison, Allen Ray *electrical engineer, educator*
Edwards, Carolyn Pope *psychology professor*
Edwards, Donald Mervin *systems engineer, educator, dean*
Fahleson, Mark A. *lawyer, political organization administrator*
Fisher, Calvin David *food products executive*
Foster, John Edward *entomologist, educator*
Fuess, Scott M., Jr. *economics professor*
Gale, John A. *Secretary of State, Nebraska*
Gerrard, John M. *state supreme court justice*
Giesecke, Joan Ruth *librarian, dean*
Giles-Watson, Maura *educator*
Grew, Priscilla Croswell *academic administrator, geologist, educator, museum director*
Gruverman, Alexei *physicist*
Guthery, John M. *lawyer*
Hansen-Daberkow, Michelle Len *elementary school art educator*
Hanway, Donald Grant, Sr. *retired agronomist, educator*
Hardin, Martha Love Wood *civic leader*
Harms, John N. *state legislator*
Harwood, David M. *geologist, educator*
Havlicek, Kathy L. *family practice nurse practitioner, counselor, nurse, health facility administrator*
Hayden-Roy, Priscilla Ann *language educator*
Heavican, Michael G. *state supreme court chief justice*
Heineman, David Eugene *Governor of Nebraska*
Hoff, Michael C. *art educator*
Hoffmann, Richard John *biology professor, academic administrator*
Holguin, Adelina *biomedical researcher*
Holmes, Mary Anne *geologist, research scientist*
Jiang, Hong *engineering educator, researcher*
Johnson, Douglas Blaikie *lawyer*
Jones, Lee Bennett *chemistry professor, academic administrator*
Kern, Jeanne Rustemeyer Wood *retired secondary school educator*
Koch Johns, Patricia A. *theater educator*
Koszewski, Bohdan Julius *retired internist, medical educator*
Kren, Josef *physiology professor*
Landis, David Morrison *state legislator*
Lee, Sang M. *management educator*
Leinieks, Valdis *classicist, educator*
Lewis, Nancy M. *science educator*
Lichty, Warren Dewey, Jr. *lawyer*
Lundstrom, Gilbert Gene *bank executive, lawyer*
Mach, Jan Ellen Walkenhorst *literature educator, editor*
Magorian, James *poet, writer*
Massengale, Martin Andrew *agronomist, educator, university president*
McCormack, Michael *state supreme court justice*
McCutcheon, Allan Lee *statistics educator*
McVey, David Scott *veterinarian, director*
Mendola, Joseph Robert *philosophy professor, department chairman*
Mennard, Mike *literature and language professor*
Michels, Dale E. *physician*
Miller-Lerman, Lindsey *state supreme court justice*
Mulvaney, Mary Jean *retired physical education educator*
Munn, John *state banking agency administrator*
Narain, Ralph B. *biologist*
Nickerson, Kenneth Warwick *biology professor*

Olson, David Louis *management educator, researcher*
Osborn, Shane *state treasurer*
Osborne, Tom (Thomas William Osborne) *college athletic director, former United State Representative from Nebraska*
Osterman, John Carl *biology professor*
Pannier, Angela Kaye *science educator*
Pao, Yen-Ching *engineering educator, consultant*
Parkhurst, Jack Lee *theater educator*
Pelini, Bo *college football coach*
Perlman, Harvey Stuart *academic administrator*
Perry, Edwin Charles *lawyer*
Qingping, Tao *research and development company executive*
Rader, Benjamin Gene *history educator*
Rembolt, James Earl *lawyer*
Rosenow, John Edward *foundation executive*
Rowe, David Winfield *lawyer*
Sawyer, Robert McLaran *historian, educator*
Schaefer, Joann *public health service officer*
Schimek, DiAnna Ruth Rebman *state legislator*
Sebora, Terrence *finance educator*
Sellmyer, David Julian *physicist, researcher*
Seng, Coleen Joy *church administrator, director, former mayor*
Sheehy, Rick *Lieutenant Governor of Nebraska, former mayor*
Smith, Rosemary J. *biology educator, researcher*
Spaulding, William D. *psychologist, educator*
Splinter, William Eldon *agricultural engineering educator*
Spry, Leslie Allen *nephrologist, director*
Stange, James Henry *architect*
Stephan, Kenneth C. *state supreme court justice*
Stoddard, Robert H. *geography educator*
Sullivan, Robert Emmett *pediatric dentist, educator*
Tavlin, Michael John *real estate company and manufacturing executive*
Taylor, Stephen Lloyd *toxicologist, food scientist, educator*
Timm, Delmar C. *engineering educator, consultant*
Treves, Samuel Blain *geologist, educator*
Trimi, Silvana *finance educator*
Unthank, Michael George *architectural firm executive*
Urbom, Warren Keith *federal judge*
Vidaver, Anne Marie *plant pathology educator*
Voigt, David William *surgeon, director*
Wagner, Rod *library director*
Wiersbe, Warren Wendell *clergyman, writer, lecturer*
Willborn, Steven L. *dean, law educator*
Wilson, Charles Stephen *cardiologist, educator*
Woollam, John Arthur *electrical engineering educator, physics professor*
Wright, John F. *state supreme court justice*
Young, Dale Lee *banker*
Zaghloul, Abdel Rahman M. *electrical engineering educator, consultant, entrepreneur*
Zempleni, Janos *nutritionist, educator*
Zhang, Luwen *virologist*

Lyons
Rose, Dwight Dean *music educator*

Mc Cook
Watts, Susan Helene *theater educator*

North Platte
Haneline, Richard Dik *art educator*

Offutt AFB
Chilton, Kevin Patrick *career military officer*

Omaha
Achelpohl, Steven Edward *lawyer*
Agrawal, Sandeep K. *pharmacologist, educator*
Allen-Gipson, Diane S. *assistant professor, scientist*
Alnouti, Yazen M. *medical educator*
Baker, Gail *director, ESL educator*
Baltaro, Richard J. *pathologist, medical educator*
Bang, Michele Alene *protective services official*
Barker, Thomas B. *information technology executive*
Batcheler, Colleen *lawyer, food products executive*
Benson, John Alexander, Jr. *internist, educator*
Bergt, Gregory Paul *chemist, consultant*
Bernardi, John Vincent *librarian*
Bewtra, Chhanda *pathologist, educator*
Boamah-Wiafe, Daniel *geographer, researcher*
Bolles, Al *food products executive*
Bracciano, Alfred Gerald *medical educator, occupational therapist*
Brenneman, Rick Alan *conservation geneticist*
Brock, Barbara Louise *education educator*
Bucko, Raymond *anthropologist, educator*
Buffett, Warren Edward *entrepreneur, investment company executive*
Caggiano, Joseph *retired advertising executive*
Caporale, D. Nick *lawyer*
Casale, Thomas Bruce *medical educator*
Casey, Murray Joseph *physician, educator*
Chow, Joan K. *food products executive*
Creigh, James Carey *lawyer*
Cross, Walter Thomas *investment company executive*
Crouse, Jerry K. *energy company executive*
Curtiss, Elden Francis *archbishop emeritus*
Dahlk, Thomas Harlan *lawyer*
Daub, Hal (Harold John Daub Jr.) *lawyer*
Derrick, Deborah Ball *editor, writer*
De Santiago-Young, Dena Kalene *investment company executive, writer*
DeSimone, Edward Mario, II, *pharmacist, educator*
Diamond, Arthur Mansfield, Jr. *economics professor*
Dittrick, William G. *lawyer*
Duffy, Dennis J. *rail transportation executive*
Dvorak, Allen Dale *radiologist*
Eggers, James Wesley *executive search consultant*
Eikenberry, Angela M. *public administration professor*
Eisele, Charles R. *rail transportation executive*
Ellis, Lisa *legislative staff member*
Enarson, Cam Edwin *medical educator, dean*
Fahey, Mike *Mayor, Omaha*
Fellman, Richard Mayer *retired lawyer*
Felton, Melanie K. *special education educator*
Fennell, Madaline *elementary school educator*
Fernandes, Praveen Paul *psychiatrist, educator*
Foster, Betty Louise *secondary school educator*
Foster, Edward Terence, Jr. *engineering and technology educator, consultant*
Freeman, Thomas L. *medical educator*
Fritzsch, Bernd *comparative neuroembryologist*
Gambal, David *retired biochemistry educator*
Garvin, Kevin L. *surgeon, educator*
Gehring, John F. *food products executive*
Gleason, James Mullaney *lawyer, insurance company executive*
Godfrey, Maurice *biomedical scientist*
Gollan, John Lachlan *dean, medical educator*
Gottschalk, John E. *newspaper publishing executive*
Grewcock, Bruce E. *construction and mining executive*
Gupta, Vinod (Vin Gupta) *information database company executive*
Hachten, Richard Arthur, II, *healthcare system executive*
Hamann, Deryl Frederick *lawyer, bank consultant*
Hamburg, Marc D. *investment company executive*
Hardy, Jim, Jr. *food products executive*
Haselwood, Eldon LaVerne *retired education educator*
Hawaux, André J. *food products executive*
Hawks, Howard L. *energy executive*
Heckman, Gregory A. *food products executive*
Hedren, Paul Leslie *retired parks director, historian*
Hemmer, J. Michael *lawyer, rail transportation executive*
Hinder, Ronald Albert *surgeon, researcher*
Hodgson, Paul Edmund *surgeon, department chairman*
Hopkins, Charles L., III, (Hop Hopkins) *information technology executive, former federal agency administrator*
Howard, Woodward Randal *orthopedist*
Huq, Ziaul *finance educator, researcher*
Huurman, Walter William *pediatric orthopaedic surgeon, educator*
Imray, Thomas John *radiologist, educator*
Jensen, Sam *lawyer*
Johanningsmeier, Charles *literature and language professor*
Johnson, James David *concert pianist, organist, educator*
Joyner, John Brooks *museum director*
Khots, Dmitriy *data mining executive*
Khoynezhad, Ali *surgeon, educator*
Knight, Robert M., Jr. *rail transportation executive*
Knopp, Lisa *literature and language professor*
Knudsen, Doug *food products executive*
Koley, James L. *lawyer, corporate director*
Koraleski, John J. *rail transportation executive*
Korbitz, Bernard Carl *hematologist, consultant*
Leopold, Donald A. *medical educator*
Lieben, Thomas Geoffrey *lawyer*
Louis, Virgie Lee *retired secondary school educator*
Louisa, Angelo Joseph *social studies educator, researcher, writer*
Lucas, George J. *archbishop*
Lund, Jan Louise *art historian, educator*
Lynch, Thomas Gerald *surgeon, educator*
Mactier, Ann Dickinson *state agency administrator*
Margalit, Eyal *ophthalmologist, educator*
Mark, Wayne Joseph *lawyer*
Maurer, Harold Maurice *pediatrician*
Maydwell, Robert Mason, Jr. *social sciences educator*
McClish, Richard R. *transportation executive*
McCook, Jacqueline K. Heslop *food products executive*
Mew, Calvin Marshall *advertising executive*
Moglia, Joseph H. *brokerage house executive*
Mohiuddin, Syed Maqdoom *cardiologist, educator*
Mordaunt, Owen Glen *literature and language professor, director*
Munger, Charles T. *diversified company executive*
Murrin, Leonard Charles, II, *pharmacology educator, researcher*
Nailon, Regina Eileen *nurse*
Neary, Daniel P. *insurance company executive*
Newton, John Milton *academic administrator, psychologist, educator*
Ni, Jinlan *economics professor*
O'Brien, Richard L(ee) *physician, educator, academic administrator*
Olney, Gisele Celeste *engineering educator, consultant*
Oyinlade, A. Olu *sociologist, educator*
Pamies, Rubens John *dean*
Pasley, Anthony J. *history professor*
Perez, Peter Michael *food products executive*
Pipinos, Iraklis Ilias *surgeon*
Podariu, Iulia Anca *physics professor, researcher*
Porter, Thomas R. *cardiologist*
Pouw, King T. *food products executive*
Quandahl, Mark C. *lawyer, former political organization administrator*
Qureshi, Sajda *information scientist, educator*
Ranks, Anne Elizabeth *retired elementary and secondary education educator*
Reilly, Hugh Joseph *humanities educator, writer*
Reiser, Richard Scott *lawyer*
Ress, Patricia Colleen *editor, writer*
Riepe, Charleine Williams *secondary school educator*
Riley, William Jay *federal judge*
Rizzo, William Bradley *pediatrician, educator*
Rock, Harold L. *lawyer*
Rodkin, Gary M. *food products executive*
Rogan, Eleanor Groeniger *oncologist, educator*
Roskens, Ronald William *management consultant, retired academic administrator*
Rush, Michael F. *human services professor*
Sankaranarayanan, Jayashri *medical educator, researcher*
Sass, Rivkah K. *library director*
Schaefer, Barbara W. *rail transportation executive*
Schlessinger, Joel *dermatologist, researcher, entrepreneur*
Schropp, Tobin *lawyer*
Scott, Walter, Jr. *telecommunications industry executive*
Sharpe, Robert Francis, Jr. *lawyer, food products executive*
Shilling, Kay Marlene *psychiatrist*
Skoog, Donald Paul *retired pathologist, educator*
Smal, Luba Dmitrievna *lawyer*
Smith, Leo W., II, *museum director*
Sooriyaarachchi, Gamini Sarathchandra *oncologist, hematologist, educator*
Stageman, James Henry *physician*
Stecher, Joe W. *prosecutor*
Stenberg, Donald B. *lawyer*
Stephens, William Olen *humanities educator, consultant*
Stinson, Kenneth E. *construction and mining company executive*
Storm, Christopher *music educator*
Strawhecker, Paul Joseph *fundraising consultant*
Strom, Lyle Elmer *judge*
Teer, Diane *food products executive*
Tennison, Lynden *rail transportation executive*
Thorson, Alan Glen *surgeon*
Tunnicliff, David George *retired civil engineer*
Turner, Robert W. *rail transportation executive*
Upadhyaya, Prashant Kudigram *surgeon*
Vandenberg, Edward V. *geriatrician, educator*
Vinogradov, Serguei V. *medical educator*
Vosburg, Bruce David *lawyer*
Wang, Jue *veterinarian, educator*
Ward, Vernon Graves *retired internist*
Wells, Roger W. *lawyer*
Werner, Clarence L. *transportation executive*
Werner, Gregory L. *transportation executive*
West, Mary E. *telecommunications industry executive*
Wigton, Robert Swift *medical educator*
Williams, Steven L. *theater educator, director*
Wilson, Daniel Richard *anthropologist, physician*
Winter, Jimmy *entrepreneur, systems administrator*
Wunsch, James Stevenson *political science professor*
Wyatt, Todd A. *medical educator*
Young, James R. *rail transportation executive*
Zaiman, K(oichi) Robert *dentist*
Zepf, Thomas Herman *retired physics professor*
Zetterman, Rowen Kent *gastroenterologist, hepatologist, dean*

Papillion
Snelling, James Anthony *biology professor, technologist*

Peru
Long, Daryl Clyde *mathematics professor, science educator*

Plattsmouth
Fusaro, Ramon Michael *dermatologist, preventive medicine physician, researcher*
Hunt, Stephen Lynn *library director*

Scottsbluff
Alkire, Garry R. *dean*
Kabalin, John Nicholas *urologist*
Shoemaker, Troy *hazardous materials response team coordinator, fire captain*
Whitaker, William L. *physiologist, educator*
Wylie, Guy Stephen *psychologist, educator*

Sidney
Highby, Dennis *retail executive*
Millner, Thomas L. *retail executive*

Staplehurst
Harre, Alan Frederick *retired academic administrator*

Stromsburg
Waltman, Bob Ray *coach, educator*

Tekamah
Cooper, Velma J. *elementary school educator*

Waverly
Jensen, Daniel *history educator*

Wayne
DeBoer, Buffany Dawn *biology professor*

York
Carlock, Ruth Marie *librarian, educator*
Eckman, Steven William *academic administrator*
McNeese, Beverly Diane *language educator*
Ratliff, Ramona *librarian*

NEVADA

Boulder City
Schultheis, Adam John *music educator, consultant*
Spadafor, Christine J. *management consultant*
Stephenson, Arthur Emmet, Jr. *investment company executive*
Wyman, Richard Vaughn *engineering educator, company executive*

Carson City
Agosti, Deborah Ann *retired senior justice*
Alexander, Judy Lynne *investor*
Ayres, Janice Ruth *social services administrator*
Barmore, James Gilbert *museum director, curator*
Brant, James William *educational consultant, mathematician*
Burns, Dan W. *manufacturing executive*
Cherry, Michael A. *state supreme court justice*
Eftimoff, Anita Kendall *retired educational consultant*
Gibbons, Jim (James Arthur Gibbons) *Governor of Nevada, former United States Representative from Nevada*
Gibbons, Mark *state supreme court justice*
Hardesty, James W. *state supreme court chief justice*
Krolicki, Brian Keith *Lieutenant Governor of Nevada, former state official, state legislator*
Marshall, Kate *state treasurer*
Masto, Catherine Marie Cortez *state attorney general, former county official*
Miller, Ross James *secretary of state*
Parraguirre, Ronald David *state supreme court justice*
Pickering, Kristina *state supreme court justice*
Raggio, William John *state legislator, lawyer*
Rheault, Keith W. *state official, school system administrator*
Saitta, Nancy M. *state supreme court justice*
Springer, Charles Edward *retired judge*
Wang, Yang *research scientist*
Whitley, Richard *state agency administrator*
Wiener, Valerie *state senator, communications executive, writer*

Cold Springs
Turner VanLydegraf, Claudia Beth *writer, researcher*

Dayton
Clements, Linda L. *innovator materials engineer, educator, journalist*

Elko
Heller, Dean *United States Representative from Nevada, former state official*
Lesbo, Paula Mae *secondary education educator*
Lovell, Walter Benjamin *music educator, radio personality*

Ely
Alderman, Minnis Amelia *psychologist, educator, small business owner*
Daniels, Frank Emmett *mathematician, educator*

Gardnerville
Griffiths, Barbara Lorraine *psychologist, marriage and family therapist, writer*

Glenbrook
Goldsmith, Harry Sawyer *surgeon, educator*

Hawthorne
Funk, Gary A. *secondary school educator*

Henderson
Berns, Philip Allan *lawyer*
Bhakta, Ragini S. *pharmacist, educator*
Cohan, George Sheldon *advertising and public relations executive*
Duong, Hon-Vu Quang *ophthalmologist, educator*
Freyd, William Pattinson *not-for-profit fundraiser, director*
Gibson, James B. *mayor, Henderson, Nevada*
Gollard, Russell Patrick *hematologist*
Goode, John Martin *manufacturing executive*
Holmes, BarbaraAnn Krajkoski *retired secondary school educator*
Huang, Eugene Yuching *civil engineer, educator*
Johnson, Joan Bray *insurance company consultant*
Kapel, David Edward *academic administrator, researcher, education educator*
Kebede, Kebret Theodore *medical educator*
Keene, Richard Brian *school system administrator, educational consultant*
Kelley, Michael John *newspaper editor*
Marcovitz, Leonard Edward *retail executive*
Martin, Gale D. *adult education educator*
McNeal, Ralph LeRoy, Sr. *management consultant, financial executive*
Ogg, Wilson Reid *lawyer, retired judge, poet, curator, publishing executive*
Ryan, Shelli Ann *public relations executive*
Schwartz, Richard *retired lawyer*
Teemant, Melanie J. *middle school educator*
Thanki, Sandip G. *educator*
Trivelpiece, Alvin William *physicist, educator, consultant*
Van Noy, Terry Willard *health care executive*
Waples, Jan Susan (Klein Waples) *priest*
Wennerstrom, Arthur John *aeronautical engineer*
Wills, Robert Hamilton *retired publishing executive*

Incline Village
Strack, Harold Arthur *retired electronics executive, military officer, financial consultant, musician, writer*
Thompson, David Alfred *industrial engineer*

Indian Springs
Dvorak, DeLyle Dennis *music and early childhood educator, consultant*

Lake Tahoe
Chase, Shari *real estate company executive, broker*

Lamoille
Vaughan, Robert Oren *lawyer*

Las Vegas
Adelson, Sheldon Gary *hotel and gaming company executive*
Ahmad, Shamoon *hematologist, oncologist, consultant*
Alexander, John Bradfield *scientist, retired army officer*
Ananias, José *retired school system administrator*
Anderson, Dominica C. *lawyer*
Andolina, Nancy Jean *retired middle school educator, dancer, English and language arts educator*
Arce, Phillip William *hotel and casino executive*
Arell, Bobby Ray, Jr. *pharmaceutical executive, management consultant*
Arteaga, Deborah *educator*
Ashley, David B. *academic administrator, engineering educator*
Atwood, Charles L. *hotel and gaming company executive*
Aulner, Dwane *biology professor*
Bai, Billy *hospitality and tourism educator*
Baley, Virko *composer, conductor, pianist*
Barbagallo, Al T. *real estate company executive*
Barden, Don H. *real estate company officer*
Barker, James Michael *lawyer*

Barnes, H. Lee *English and creative writing educator, writer*
Bartolotta, Paul Wenzel *chef*
Beeman, Karl Joseph, Jr. *warehouse manager*
Berghel, Hal L. *columnist, inventor, consultant, lecturer, educator*
Bernhard, Peter C. *lawyer, state agency administrator*
Bernstein, Maureen Ann *theater educator, director*
Bigelow, Robert Thomas *aerospace transportation executive*
Blattner, Meera McCuaig *computer scientist, educator*
Boyd, William S. *hotel and gaming company executive*
Brammell, Stephen Harrison *lawyer*
Bridges, B. Ried *lawyer*
Broca, Laurent Antoine *aerospace scientist*
Brock, Holly Melinda *marketing professional*
Brower, Gregory A. *prosecutor, lawyer*
Browning, Laura Ellen *lawyer*
Burns, George E. *state banking agency administrator*
Bybee, Jay Scott *federal judge, former federal agency administrator*
Canfield, James *artistic director*
Capanna, Albert Howard *neuroscientist, neurosurgeon, lawyer, banker*
Chopelas, Anastasia *geophysicist, researcher*
Chung, Sue Fawn *educator, researcher*
Clayson, William S. *history professor*
Collins, Clarence *musician*
Consul, Vincent A. *lawyer*
Culp, Gordon Louis *consulting engineer, management consultant*
Curran, William P. *lawyer*
Danielson, Deborah Lee *financial analyst*
Das, Biswajit *electrical engineer, educator*
Delgado, Carlos *physics professor*
Derrick, William Dennis *retired physical plant administrator, consultant*
Douglas, Michael Lawrence *state supreme court justice*
Dufek, Janet S. *research scientist*
Duke, Edward Marion, III, (Mickey) *health facility administrator, consultant*
Duva-Mikhail, Donna Marie *financial executive*
Edualino, Emilio Quial *school educator*
Emerson, Shirley *retired professor counseling*
Erwin, Daniel Timothy *literature and language professor*
Faiss, Robert Dean *lawyer*
Feiner, Edward A. *architect*
Fertitta, Frank J. III *sports association and casino executive*
Fertitta, Lorenzo J. *sports association and casino executive*
Freeman-Clark, J. P. Ladyhawk *vicar, underwater exploration, security and transportation executive, model*
Gafford, Mary May Grimes *retired humanities educator*
Gardner, Grace Joely *writer, psychologist, consultant*
Garn, Susan Lynn *art educator*
Gaspar, Anna Louise *retired elementary school educator, consultant*
Gerdes, Denise M. *school librarian*
Gilchrist, Ann Roundey *medical/surgical nurse*
Goldblatt, Hal Michael *photographer*
Goodman, Oscar Baylin *Mayor, Las Vegas, lawyer*
Goodwin, John Robert *lawyer, educator, writer*
Gourdine, Jerome Anthony (Anthony Gourdine, Little Anthony) *musician*
Graebel, William Paul *engineering educator*
Gremse, David Albert *pediatrician, educator*
Griesche, Robert Price *hospital purchasing executive*
Gubler, John Gray *lawyer*
Guinan, Mary Elizabeth *academic administrator, public health service officer, physician, researcher*
Halkyard, Jonathan S. *entertainment industry executive*
Hall, Gene E. *education educator*
Hall, Zuladawn *music educator*
Hannon, Erin E. *psychology professor*
Hardie, George Graham *casino executive*
Herridge, Elizabeth *museum director*
Hilbrecht, Norman Ty *lawyer*
Hill, Judith Deegan *retired lawyer*
Hoepfner, Mark Thomas *surgeon*
Holloway, Robert Wester *radiochemist*
Hrabal, Antonin *physician, educator*
Hua, Fred Huizhong *materials scientist*
Huston, Joyce A. *entertainment and publishing company executive*
Isidori, Joe *chef*
Jabara, Michael Dean *real estate developer, former technology entrepreneur*
Jacobs, Gary N. *lawyer, hotel executive*
Jakopec, Carl Thomas *pharmaceutical executive*
Jalbert, Janelle Jennifer *entrepreneur, educator, social researcher*
Johnston, Sally Jo *dean, department chairman*
Kalb, Benjamin Stuart *television producer, director*
Kamer, Gregory Jay *lawyer*
Kardum, Karmen Ana *lawyer*
Kay, Kenneth Jeffrey *hotel executive*
Kennedy, Margaret Alexis *law educator, researcher*
Kline, Ronald Michael *pediatrician, hematologist*
Kurlinski, John Parker *physician*
Leven, Michael Alan *hotel and gaming company executive*
Lewis, Jerry (Joseph Levitch) *comedian*
Lieberman, Sam *political organization administrator*
Lledo, Haroldo Luis *geologist*
Loveman, Gary W. *hotel and gaming company executive*
Lowden, Sue *political organization administrator*
Luckett, Byron Edward, Jr. *chaplain, retired military officer*
Lumpkin, Libby *museum director*
Mackey, Barbara *museum association administrator, director*
Manley, Edward Harry, Jr. *food safety and management trainer, professional association administrator, food products executive, retired military officer*
Mansfield, Lorraine J. *lawyer*
Maravich, Mary Louise *realtor*
Marcella, Joseph *information scientist*
Martin, Myron Gregory *foundation administrator*
Martinez, Adriana *photographer*
Massier, Paul Ferdinand *mechanical engineer*
McCann, Biff (Raymond Biff McCann) *plastic surgeon*
McCaw, Craig Oliver *communications executive*
McNulty, James Francis, Jr. *lawyer, consultant*
Meiner, Sue Ellen Thompson *nurse, consultant, gerontologist, author, writer*
Mellor, Eli *diversified financial services company executive, writer*
Merrill, Wendy Jane *realtor*
Messenger, George Clement *engineering executive, consultant*
Miller, Robert Joseph *lawyer, former governor*
Miller, Stephen M. *economics professor*
Moonen, Rick *chef, restaurant owner*
Morgan, Richard J. *law educator, dean*
Moritz, Timothy Bovie *psychiatrist*
Moss, Gary Curtis *lawyer*
Muhlenbruck-Fleischer, Deborah Lynn *music educator*
Murren, James Joseph *hotel corporation executive*
Nathanson, Rebecca *education educator, law educator*
Neumann, Edward Schreiber *transportation engineering educator*
Nicholson, R. Stephen *former cultural organization administrator*
Noback, Richardson Kilbourne *medical educator*
Numrich, Richard *economics professor*
Olsen, Dennis E. *veterinarian, director*
Orgill, MaryKay *chemistry professor*
Palmieri, Frederick William *structural engineer*
Park, Sung Min *finance educator*
Pepe, Joseph Anthony *bishop*
Pierce, Thresia Korte (Tish Pierce) *primary school educator*
Polovina, Gina Bri-Anne *casino gaming company executive*
Pravica, Michael Gojko *education educator*
Primeau, Keith *professional sports team executive, retired professional hockey player*
Pro, Philip Martin *judge*
Ramos, Albert A. *electrical engineer*
Rapoport, Nancy B. *law educator*
Rawlinson, Johnnie Blakeney *federal judge*
Reynolds, Douglas D. *mechanical engineer, educator*
Root, Wayne Allyn *entrepreneur, television producer, writer*
Sadineni, Suresh Babu *research scientist*
Sanders, Charlotta Elisabeth *nuclear engineer, educator*
Satre, Philip Glen *casino entertainment executive, lawyer*
Schneiter, George Malan *professional golfer, real estate developer*
Serfas, Richard Thomas *architecture educator, urban planner, municipal official*
Shaw, Jeffrey William *gas industry executive*
Shuman, R. Baird *academic administrator, consultant, language educator, writer*
Sileo, Nancy M. *special education educator*
Sillerman, Robert F. X. *communications executive, banker*
Silverman, Elaine Ann *mathematics educator*
Singh, Sahjendra Narain *electrical engineering educator, researcher*
Smith, Jimmy Wayne, Sr. *forensic specialist*
Smith, Keith E. *hotel and gaming company executive*
Snyder, John Henry *computer science educator, consultant*
Solomon, Jack Avrum, Jr. *lawyer, automotive executive, art dealer*
Sorrell, Michael E. *consulting company and hospitality management executive*
Speck, Eugene Lewis *internist*
Stanley, Tim *information technology executive*
Stark, S. Daniel, Jr. *casino and gaming resort company executive*
Stein, David Eric *physicist, defense analyst, futurist, retired military officer*
Stein, Stephen *lawyer*
Sullivan, Christopher David *real estate broker, attorney*
Tanenhaus, David Spinoza *historian, educator*
Tate, Eleanor Ann *educational association administrator*
Wakefield, Marie A. *counselor, educational association administrator*
Walker, Gwendolyn Kaye *guest teacher elementary education*
Ward, David Christian *science association director*
Weeks, Gerald *psychologist, educator*
Wheeler, Darren Thomas *pathologist*
White, John Valery *dean*
Williams, Mary Irene *business education educator*
Willis, Tricia Lee *special education educator*
Wynn, Steve Alan (Stephen A. Wynn) *hotel and gaming company executive*
Yackira, Michael William *electric power industry executive*

Laughlin
Cameron, Robert Allen *geophysicist, educator*

Logandale
Smiley, Robert William, Jr. *investment banker*

Minden
Downer, Craig *ecologist*
Yu, John Junyao *mechanical engineer, researcher*

Nellis AFB
Malachowski, Nicole *pilot*

North Las Vegas
Ackerman, Allan Joesph *computer engineer, educator*
Brown, Angela Khristin *lab administrator, educator*
El-Husseini, Randa A. *physician*
Eliopulos, Tina Dawn Ann *language educator*
Janzen, Donna Lee (Bricker) *music educator, singer*
Manley, Audrey Forbes *retired academic administrator, pediatrician, military officer*
Montandon, Michael *Mayor, North Las Vegas, Nevada*
Neff, William *educator*
Roth, Kelly *choreographer, educator*
Talley, Brenda S. *performing arts center director, theatrical light designer*
Webber, Robert *medical researcher*
Williams, Richard L. *literature and language professor*
Wyckoff, Theri Lynne *education educator*

Pahrump
Lubbers, Alice Dianne *operating room nurse*

Reno
Adams, Kenneth Robert *gaming analyst, writer, historian, consultant*
Akiyama, Toshio *cardiologist, educator, researcher, director*
Aldrich, Gary O. *singer, educator*
Atkinson, Glen W. *retired economics professor*
Barone, Diane *social sciences educator*
Batchman, Theodore Earl *electrical engineering educator, researcher*
Bauer, Bruno Steven *plasma physicist*
Binns, James Edward *retired banker*
Bonaldi-Moore, Lorraine Kay *nursing educator*
Brunetti, Melvin T. *federal judge*
Calvo, Randolph Roque *bishop*
Carlson, Severin A. *lawyer*
Carr, James Russell *engineering educator*
Ceppos, Jerry (Jerome Merle Ceppos) *dean, former newspaper editor*
Chapman, Samuel Greeley *political science professor, criminologist*
Collier, Helen Vandivort *psychologist*
Coronella, Charles J. *chemical engineer, educator*
Crognale, Michael Anthony *medical educator, neuroscientist, consultant*
Crowley, Joseph Neil *political science professor, former academic administrator*
Cummings, Nancy *library director*
Cummings, Nicholas Andrew *psychologist*
Daniels, Ronald Dale *conductor*
Danko, George *engineering educator*
Davidson, Jane P. *art educator*
De Sa Kono, Denise Ann Rene *cultural organization administrator*
Dietrich, Dean Forbes *academic administrator*
Dillard, Robert Lee *academic administrator*
Evrenosoglu, Cansin Yaman *electrical engineer, educator*
Fadali, Mohammed Sami *engineering educator*
Ford, Victoria *retired public relations executive, writer, oral historian*
Frank, Lillian Gorman *human resources executive, management consultant*
Fuerstenau, M(aurice) C(lark) *metallurgical engineer*
Gifford, Gerald Frederic *retired science educator*
Glick, Milton Don *academic administrator, chemist*
Glotfelty, Cheryll *literature and language professor*
Goin, Peter Jackson *art educator*
Goodenow, Rew R. *lawyer*
Gundersen, Wayne Campbell *energy executive, consultant*
Gunes, Mehmet H *engineering educator*
Guneyi, Umit Ahmet *physician, consultant*
Hardy, Del *lawyer*
Harsh, Antoinette Mollett *investor*
Harvey, Robert Dale *physiologist and biophysicist, educator*
Hengstler, Gary Ardell *publisher, editor, lawyer*
Hibbs, Loyal Robert *lawyer*
Hill, Earl McColl *lawyer*
Hilts, Ruth *artist*
Hug, Procter Ralph, Jr. *federal judge*
Jacobson, Raymond Earl *electronics executive*
Kleinfeld, Erwin *mathematician, educator*
Kleppe, John Arthur *electrical engineer, educator, company executive*
Kurkul, Wen Wang *musician, educator, administrator*
Leland, Joy Hanson *retired anthropologist, researcher*
LoSasso, Vicki Rae *political organization worker, artist*
MacKintosh, Frederick Roy *oncologist*
Matthews, Thomas J. *game company executive*
McCarty-Puhl, J-Petrina *chemistry educator*
Middlebrooks, Deloris Jeanette *retired nursing educator*
Nevins, Marybeth Eleanor *anthropologist, educator*
Pagni, Albert Frank *lawyer*
Perry, Jean Louise *academic administrator*
Phaneuf, Ronald Arthur *physics professor*
Piercy, Earl *social sciences educator*
Pinson, Larry Lee *pharmacist, state agency administrator*
Pixley, John Seymour *immunology educator*
Ragavan, Anpalaki Jeyabalasinkham *software developer, researcher*
Ross, Robert Donald *library director*
Rubalcava, Micaela *education educator*
Sanders, Kenton Morris *medical educator*
Sandoval, Brian Edward *federal judge, former state attorney general*
Santos, Herbert Joseph, Jr. *lawyer*
Schweigert, Lynette Aileen *interior designer, consultant*
Scrimgeour, Gary James *writer, educator*
Shoen, Edward Joseph *transportation and insurance companies executive*
Small, Elisabeth Chan *psychiatrist, educator*
Svahn, John Alfred *federal agency administrator*
Taranik, James Vladimir *geologist, educator*
Tedford, Jack Nowlan III *construction executive, small business owner*
White, John, Jr. *lawyer*
Yan, Wei *science association director*

Ruby Valley
Hoover, William Graham *science educator*

Sandy Valley
Viscuglia, Jenny Lou *music educator*

Sparks
Bonham, Harold Florian *research geologist, consultant*
Holder, Harold Douglas, Sr. *investor, hotel executive*
Lagasse, Bruce Kenneth *retired structural engineer*
Trabitz, Eugene Leonard *aerospace company executive*
Yuhara, Makoto *mechanical engineer*

Winnemucca
Hesse, Martha O. *gas industry executive*
Smith, Jack N. *secondary school educator*

Yerington
Price, Judith Holm *educational psychologist*
Price, Thomas Munro *computer consultant, retired*
Scatena, Lorraine Borba *retired rancher, women's rights advocate, researcher*

NEW HAMPSHIRE

Amherst
Atwater, Verne Stafford *finance educator*
Johnson, Daryl Diane *painter*

Bartlett
Pomfret, David B. *medical educator, internist*

Bedford
Demers, Nancy Kae *nursing educator*
Hall, Pamela S. *environmental consulting services executive*
Steadman, David Rosslyn Ayton *corporate financial executive, director*

Bennington
Verney, Richard Greville *paper company executive*

Berlin
Doherty, Katherine Mann *librarian, writer*

Brentwood
Boozer-Blasco, Claudia Ruth *family and consumer resources educator*

Brookline
Hemming, Walter William *retired CPA and business executive*

Campton
Benton, Geraldine Ann *preschool owner, director*
Scrimshaw, Nevin Stewart *physician, nutritionist, educator*

Center Harbor
Shaw, Robert William, Jr. *management consultant, venture capitalist*

Center Sandwich
Booty, John Everitt *retired theology studies educator*

Chester
Volpe, Christopher Thomas *history educator*

Colebrook
Gueymard, Chris A. *research scientist*

Concord
Bagan, Merwyn *neurological surgeon*
Balla, Wesley G. *museum curator, historian*
Barry, Virginia M. *state official, school system administrator*
Bradley, Paula E. *former state legislator*
Broderick, John T., Jr. *state supreme court chief justice*
Brown, Tom Christian *newspaper publishing executive*
Buckley, Raymond Carl, II, *political organization administrator, former state legislator*
Clemons, Jane Andrea *state legislator*
Conboy, Carol Ann *state supreme court justice*
Cooney, Mary Ann *state agency administrator, public health service officer, community health nurse*
Cote, David Edward *state legislator*
Dalianis, Linda Stewart *state supreme court justice*
Delaney, Michael A. *state attorney general*
Denham, Robin Richardson *secondary school educator*
DiClerico, Joseph Anthony, Jr. *federal judge*
DiFruscia, Anthony R. *state legislator, lawyer*
Duggan, James E., Jr. *state supreme court justice*
Fitch, Orville Brewster, II, (Bud Fitch) *state official*
Foster, Linda Timberlake *state legislator*
Gardner, William Michael *Secretary of State, New Hampshire*
Gile, Mary Stuart *state legislator*
Haijin, Shi *research scientist*
Heard, Charles Wolfe *lawyer, consultant*
Hicks, Gary Ellis *state supreme court justice*
Hildreth, Peter C. *state banking agency administrator*
Howard, Jeffrey R. *federal judge*
Kacavas, John P. *prosecutor*
Kenney, Kimberly *elementary school educator*
Laplante, Joseph Normand *federal judge*
Larsen, Sylvia B. *state legislator*
Lynch, John H. *Governor of New Hampshire*
MacKay, James Robert *psychiatric social worker, mayor, educator*
Mevers, Frank Clement *state agency administrator, archivist*

Montero, José Thier *state agency administrator, public health service officer*
Norelli, Terie Thompson *state legislator*
Nowe, Ronald John *state legislator, small business owner*
Palm, Jessana *biology professor*
Pilliod, James P. *state legislator*
Potter, Fred Leon *lawyer, retired insurance company executive*
Provencher, Catherine A. *state treasurer*
Resnick, Kenneth *photography director*
Roberts, George Bernard, Jr. *management and government relations consultant, former state legislator*
Robinson, V. Gene (The Right Reverend V. Gene Robinson) *bishop*
Stadelmann, Wayne Karl *plastic surgeon*
Tolles, Bryant Franklin, Jr. *retired history and art history professor*
Uchida, Richard Y. *lawyer*
Vidaver, Robert Maxwell *medical educator*
York, Michael Charest *librarian*

Contoocook
Held, Wayne Edward *retired navy chief*
Wood, Richard Robinson *real estate company executive*

Derry
Craft, Katie Ann *health facility administrator*
Katsakiores, George Nicholas *state legislator, retired food service executive*
Willard-Wotring, Sheila Duram *retired English language and humanities educator*

Dover
Johnson, Verdenal Hoag *English language educator, art and copy editor, writer*
Parks, Joe Benjamin *entrepreneur visionary, state legislator*
Pelletier, Marsha Lynn *secondary school educator, poet*
Spires, Diane Hayes *music educator*
Wentworth, William Edgar *retired journalist*

Dublin
Hale, Judson Drake, Sr. *publishing executive, editor, writer*
Vecchiotti, Robert Anthony *management and organizational consultant*

Dunbarton
Kimball, Philip C. *professional society administrator*

Durham
Finkelhor, David *medical researcher, director*
Ford, Daniel (Daniel Francis Ford) *writer*
Gao, Mingchu *education educator*
Gittell, Ross Jacobs *economics and business and public policy educator*
Gould, Eliga H. *historian, educator*
Hapgood, Robert Derry *language educator*
Huddleston, Mark Wayne *academic administrator, political scientist, educator*
Kaufmann, Richard L. *physics professor*
Lofty, John Sylvester *English education and literature professor*
Loy, James Brent *education educator*
MacKay, Edward R. *academic administrator*
Pistole, Thomas Gordon *microbiology professor, researcher, department chairman*
Ramadanovic, Petar *literature and language professor, writer*
Ray, Ram Lakhan *civil engineer*
Simic, Charles *language educator, poet*
Straus, Murray Arnold *sociology educator*
Taylor, Robert Lawrence, Jr. *medical educator*
Thein, May-Win L. *mechanical engineer, educator*
Tisa, Louis S. *microbiologist, educator*
Tucker, Corinna Jenkins *social studies educator*
White, Christopher *engineering educator*
Young, Arthur Price *librarian, educator*

East Andover
Gould, Donald Everett *retired chemical company executive, consultant*

Epping
Whitesell, Ann Therese *elementary school educator*

Etna
Picoult, Jodi Lynn *writer*

Exeter
Kelley, Carolyn *biotechnology educator*
Richardson, Artemas P(artridge) *retired landscape architect*
Schubart, Caren Nelson *psychologist*
Thomas, Jacquelyn May *librarian*
Wicklein, John Frederick *journalist, educator*

Farmington
Panek, William Dominick *systems engineer executive*

Francestown
Milton, Peter Winslow *artist*

Franconia
Chen, Andrew Lawrence *orthopedist, surgeon, sports medicine specialist*
Schaffer, David Edwin *retired systems administrator*

Goffstown
Holden, Carol Helen *county official*
St. Pierre, Amada *psychologist, educator*
Wajenberg, Arnold Sherman *retired librarian, educator*

Goshen
Wright, Lilyan Boyd *physical education educator*

Grantham
Callahan, Barbara Grant *toxicologist, risk assessor*
Grimley, Robert Thomas *chemistry professor*
Hansen, Herbert W. *management consultant, educator*

Hampstead
Hargreaves, David William *retired communications company executive*

Hampton Falls
Sununu, John Henry *political organization administrator, former White House chief of staff, former governor of New Hampshire*

Hanover
Anthony, Denise L. *social sciences educator*
Beisswenger, Paul James *medical educator, researcher*
Bien, Peter Adolph *language educator, writer*
Boghosian, Varujan Yegan *sculptor, educator*
Bower, Richard Stuart *retired economist*
Brooks, H. Allen *architectural educator, author*
Chapman, Robert James *psychiatrist, educator*
Crory, Elizabeth Lupien *state legislator*
Daniell, Jere Rogers, II, *retired historian*
Danos, Paul *dean, accounting educator*
Doenges, Norman Arthur *retired classics educator*
Doyle, William Thomas *physicist, retired educator*
Ehrlich, David Gordon *film director, educator*
French, Kenneth Ronald *finance educator*
Gardner, Peter Jaglom *lawyer*
Garmire, Elsa Meints *electrical engineering educator, consultant*
Garthwaite, Gene Ralph *historian, educator*
Graves, Robert John *industrial engineering educator*
Green, Ronald Michael *bioethics educator*
Green, William R. *medical educator, researcher, dean*
Helble, Joseph John *dean, chemical engineer, educator*
Horrell, Jeffrey Lanier *library director*
Hoyt, Kendall *science educator*
Hughes, Howard Clark *psychology professor, researcher*
Isaacs, Robert Charles *retired lawyer*
Kennedy, Brian P. *museum director*
Kim, Jim Yong *academic administrator, preventive medicine physician*
Kleck, Robert Eldon *psychology professor*
Koop, C. Everett (Charles Everett Koop) *former Surgeon General of the United States, educator*
Kurtz, Thomas Eugene *retired mathematics professor*
Lamperti, John Williams *mathematician, educator*
Lipson, Jane Elizabeth Gotlieb *chemistry professor*
Logue, Dennis Emhardt *finance educator, writer, banker, consultant*
Lundquist, Weyman Ivan *lawyer*
Luxon, Thomas Hyatt *language educator, director*
Lyons, Gene Martin *political scientist, educator*
Mannix, Charles Raymond *law educator*
Mansell, Darrel Lee, Jr. *language educator*
Masters, Roger Davis *political scientist, toxicologist, educator*
McIlroy, M. Douglas *computer scientist, educator*
Montgomery, David Campbell *retired physics professor*
Oxenhandler, Neal *literature educator, writer*
Peart, David Ross *biology professor*
Pease, Donald Eugene *humanities educator, department chairman*
Queneau, Paul Etienne *retired metallurgical engineering educator*
Riley, Enrico *painter*
Rolett, Ellis Lawrence *cardiologist, educator*
Russell, Robert Hilton *Romance languages and literature educator*
Rutter, Jeremy Bentham *archaeologist, educator*
Scherr, Barry Paul *foreign language educator*
Sekula, David Joseph *lab administrator, researcher*
Sheldon, Richard Robert *retired literature and language professor*
Shewmaker, Kenneth Earl *history professor*
Slaughter, Matthew J. *economics professor, former federal official*
Spiegel, Evelyn Sclufer *biology professor*
Starzinger, Vincent Evans *political scientist, educator*
Swaine, Lucas *social sciences educator*
Weinstein, James Neil *orthopaedic surgeon*
Wright, James Edward *historian, educator, former academic administrator*

Henniker
Braiterman, Thea Gilda *economics professor, state legislator*

Jackson
Baker, Mary Jane *clinical social worker*

Keene
Baldwin, Peter Arthur *psychologist, educator, author, minister*
Bell, Ernest Lorne III *retired lawyer*
Bleam, Nancy Kay *physical education educator*
Cohen, Richard B. *grocery company executive*
Hackett, John Thomas *retired economist and financial executive*
Herold, Irene M.H. *academic librarian*
Jardine, Richard *mathematics professor*
Miller, Rita *die-casting company executive, personnel consultant*
Salcetti, Marianne *newswriter, educator*
Welkowitz, Walter *biomedical engineer, educator*

Laconia
Kenney, Kathleen *literature and language professor, department chairman*

Lebanon
Bernat, James Lawrence *neurologist, educator*
Bernstein, Henry H. *pediatrician, educator*
Brinckerhoff, Constance Elizabeth *medical educator, researcher*
Chertoff, Jocelyn D. *radiologist, department chairman*
Cohen, Jeffrey Allen *neurologist, educator*
DeLong, Peter *medical educator*
Emery, Virginia Olga Beattie *psychologist, researcher*
Fanciullo, Gilbert J. *physician, educator*
Ferrell, Richard Bradley *neuropsychiatrist*
Gallagher, John D. *anesthesiologist, educator*
Glass, Donald David *anesthesiologist*
Holmes, Gregory Lawrence *pediatrician, educator, neurologist*
Kantor, Stephen Richard *orthopedic surgeon*
Longnecker, Daniel Sidney *pathologist, researcher*
Mirza, Sohail K. *orthopedist, educator*
Munck, Allan Ulf *physiologist, educator*
Nugent, William C. *cardiothoracic surgeon*
Ou, Lo-Chang *physiology educator*
Oxman, Thomas Elliot *psychiatrist*
Plehn, Jonathan Freeman *internal medicine and cardiology educator*
Sateia, Michael John *psychiatrist, educator*
Shaker, Marcus Sidney *pediatrician*
Shu, Jennifer A. *pediatrician, writer*
Silberfarb, Peter Michael *psychiatrist, educator*
Skinner, Jonathan Snowden *economics educator*
Zayfert, Claudia *psychologist, educator*

Lincoln
Seltz, Jules M. *surgeon*

Litchfield
Darlington, David William *management consultant*

Littleton
Lucas, Kurt John *health facility director*
Merritt, Thomas Butler *lawyer*

Londonderry
Parten, Priscilla M. *medical and psychiatric social worker, educator*

Loudon
Moore, Beatrice *religious organization administrator*

Lyme
Cornwell, Gibbons Gray III *retired internist, educator*
Dwight, Donald Rathbun *publishing executive, corporate communications specialist*
McIntyre, Oswald Ross *physician*
Phetteplace, Gary *mechanical engineer*

Manchester
Christian, Francis Joseph *bishop*
DeFelice, Jonathan Peter *academic administrator, priest*
Dugan, Kevin F. *lawyer*
Gendron, Odore Joseph *bishop emeritus*
Gerry, Joseph John *bishop emeritus*
Haffer, Edward Anthony *lawyer*
Hood, James Calton *lawyer*
Ingraham, Alec *mathematics professor*
Jago, Barbara Jeanne *communications educator*
Kamen, Dean *biomedical engineer*
Lavery, Robert Michael *internist, cardiologist*
McCormack, John Brendan *bishop*
Middleton, Jack Baer *lawyer*
Reno, Stephen Jerome *former academic administrator*
Shaheen, Jeanne *United States Senator from New Hampshire, political scientist, former governor*

Meredith
Hatch, Frederick Tasker *research scientist*
Heald, Bruce Day *English and music educator, historian*
Lane, Sophia *art gallery director*
Lovett, Miller Currier *retired management educator, minister*

Merrimack
Gallup, Patricia *computer company executive*
Yannone, Ronald Matthew *systems engineer, researcher*

Milford
Morison, John Hopkins *casting manufacturing company executive*
Queeney, Deborah Ann *special education educator*

Milton
Edelman, Hendrik *library and information science professor*

Mirror Lake
Culleton, James Frederick *neurologist*
Phillips, Tyler Bradstreet *retired business executive*

Moultonborough
Patten, Betsey Leland *state legislator*

Nashua
Arthur, Rose Ann Horman *dean*
Bergeron, Paul Robert *city clerk*
Constantian, Mark Barbour *plastic surgeon, educator*
Dehner, Frederick Thomas *business administration and mathematics educator, retired military officer*
Egan, John Frederick *retired electronics executive*
Hahto, Sami K. *physicist*
Horn, Jennifer *former columnist, talk show host*
Knights, Edwin Munroe *pathologist*
Leech, John Warner *research scientist*
Lerch, Carol M. *mathematics professor*
Martel, Marci *mental health services professional*
Matarazzo, Maria C. *management educator, department chairman*
Perkins, George William, II, *financial services executive, film producer*
Pignatelli, Debora Becker *state official*
Rekart, Jerome Leo *science educator, researcher*
Siroty, William Charles *physician*

New Castle
Friese, George Ralph *retail executive*
Mapel, William Marlen Raines *retired bank executive*

New Durham
Quimby, Fred William *retired pathology educator, veterinarian*

New London
Anderson, Patrick D. *humanities educator*
Condict, Edgar Rhodes *manufacturing executive, minister*
Gepfert, Alan Harry *copywriter, finance educator, sculptor, management consultant*
Ourusoff, Nicholas *science educator*

Newmarket
Jernigan, David Bruce *men's college basketball coach*
McHose, Andre H. *industrial engineer*

Newport
Gayvoronsky, Ludmila *artist, educator*

North Hampton
Southworth, Robert Alexander, Jr. *education researcher, educator*
Taylor, Donald *retired manufacturing executive*

Orford
Karol, John J., Jr. *producer, filmmaker*
Martin, Allen *retired lawyer*

Ossipee
Bartlett, Diane Sue *counselor*

Peterborough
Cahill, George Francis, Jr. *physician, educator*
Eppes, William David *arts and humanities advocate*

Pittsfield
Pazdon, Melissa Joann *school psychologist*

Plaistow
Wilder, Dwight Safford *academic administrator*

Plymouth
Gorin, Stephen H. *social worker, educator*
Palmquist, Wendy Jean *psychology professor*
Vinogradova, Natalya *mathematician, educator*

Portsmouth
Abelson, Elias *lawyer*
Breen, Edward Deveaux *manufacturing executive*
Doleac, Charles Bartholomew *lawyer*
Hardy, Victoria Elizabeth *non profit administrator*
Harter, Hugh Anthony *foreign language educator*
Hopkins, Jeannette Ethel *book publisher, editor*
Krajeck, Amy Jo *literature and language educator*
Nylander, Jane Louise *museum director, educator, writer*
Tober, Stephen Lloyd *lawyer*
Volk, Kenneth Hohne *lawyer*
Wener, Brian D. *psychologist*
Yerdon, Lawrence J. *museum administrator*

Rindge
Birge, James *academic administrator*

Rochester
Dworkin, Gary Steven *insurance company executive*

Rye
Wilson, Ralph Sloan *retinal surgeon*

Salem
Simmons, Marvin Gene *retired geophysics educator*

Sanbornville
Berg, Warren Stanley *retired bank executive*

Silver Lake
Wilkins, David George *fine arts educator*

Sugar Hill
Miller, Bode (Samuel Bode Miller) *professional skier*

Sunapee
Springer, John Kelley *hospital administrator*

Tilton
Wolf, Sharon Ann *psychotherapist*

Walpole
Burns, Ken *documentary filmmaker*

Warner
Hunt, Everett Clair *engineering educator, researcher, consultant*

Waterville Valley
Saenger, Bruce Walter *consulting firm executive*

Wentworth
Bixby, Roland Maurice *writer, adult education educator*

West Chesterfield
Garinger, Louis Daniel *retired religion educator*

West Lebanon
Halperin, George Bennett *education educator, retired military officer*
Sox, Harold Carleton, Jr. *physician, educator, editor*

Wolfeboro
Baker, David Arthur *retired small business owner, manufacturing executive*
Bonin, Suzanne Jean *artist*
Bradley, Jeb E. (Joseph E. Bradley) *state legislator*

NEW JERSEY

Allendale
Ruth, Rodney *musician, music consultant, contractor, educator*

Allentown
Spreat, Susan Rogers *veterinarian*
Van Hise, Yvonne *librarian*

Annandale
Wu, Margaret *research scientist*

Atlantic City
Irvine, Robert *chef*
Jamieson, John Edward, Jr. *social services administrator, minister*
Knight, Edward R. *judge, psychologist, law educator*
Maddox, Odinga Lawrence, II, *head of religious order*

Atlantic Highlands
Levine, George Lewis *literature and language professor, critic*
Tice, George A(ndrew) *photographer*

Augusta
Martin, Richard L. *retired insurance executive*

Avenel
Berg, Louis Leslie *investment executive*

Avon By The Sea
Mataranglo, Robert Patrick *artist, educator*
Potter, Emma Josephine Hill *language educator*

Basking Ridge
Cleaves, Graham Robert *secondary school educator*
Conklin, Donald Ransford *retired pharmaceutical executive*
Craven, Pamela F. *lawyer*
D'Ambrosio, Louis J. *telecommunications industry executive*
Kim, Doh-Suk *electronics engineer*
Mason, Michael A. *telecommunications industry executive, former FBI agent*
Matthews, Craig Gerard *retired energy executive*
McAdam, Lowell C. *telecommunications industry executive*
Moden, Joleen *communications executive*
Morgan, Samuel P(ope) *physicist, applied mathematician*
Perez, Glad M. *marketing executive*
Ruesterholz, Virginia P. *telecommunications industry executive*
Schenker, Leo *retired utilities executive*
Schmidt, William Max *management consultant, marketing and business development executive*
Tamarelli, Alan Wayne *venture capitalist*

Bay Head
O'Brien, Robert Brownell, Jr. *banker, consultant, yacht broker, opera company executive, museum director*

Bayonne
Fitzpatrick, Harold Francis *lawyer*

Bayville
Atkins, Yvette *special education educator*
Tozer, Jean Frame *gifted and talented educator*

Bedminster
Bailye, John E. *software company executive*
David, Edward Emil, Jr. *electrical engineer, executive, management consultant*
Drewry, Don Neal *fire protection engineer*
Gardner, David John *communications executive, sound recording engineer*
Johnson, Garry D. *information technology executive*
Ripp, Joseph Allen *information technology executive*
Strigl, Dennis F. *telecommunications industry executive*

Belle Mead
Brown, Elizabeth Schmeck *fashion historian*
Dyer, Hugh Nelson III *management company owner*
Goodnick, Paul Joel *psychiatrist*
Sarle, Charles Richard *health facility executive*

Belleville
Salvini, Emil Robert *publishing executive, writer, historian*
Wagner, Rudolph Steven *ophthalmologist, educator*

Belmar
Downes, Laurence M. *gas industry executive*
Swett, Stephen Frederick, Jr. *artist, educator*

Belvidere
Walsh, John Alfred *retired social worker*

Bergenfield
Davidson, Marilyn Copeland *writer, musician, educator*

Berkeley Heights
Connell, Grover *real estate company executive*
Geusic, Joseph Edward *physicist*
Mac Rae, Alfred Urquhart *physicist, electrical engineer*
Momeni, Reza *plastic surgeon*

Bernardsville
Cooperman, Saul *retired educational administrator*
Dixon, Richard Wayne *retired communications company executive*
Flynn, Marie Cosgrove *retired portfolio manager, corporate financial executive*
Louria, Donald Bruce *retired medical educator*
Spofford, Sally (Hyslop) *artist*
Venezia, William Thomas *school system administrator, counseling consultant*

Blackwood
Getaz, Joan *library director*
O'Neal, Rondald Anson *finance educator*
Seeber, Fredrick Paul *emeritus physics professor*

Bloomfield
Bunin, Jeffrey Howard *management consultant*
Conta, Richard Vincent *actuary*
Lordi, Katherine Mary *lawyer*

Boonton
Bona, Frederick Emil *public relations executive*
Olimpio, Suzanne M. *psychologist*
Ward, Solveig Maria *marketing professional*

Bordentown
Zeitz, Joshua *history professor, writer*

Bound Brook
Shive, Richard Byron *architect*

Branchville
Murphy, Gregory E. *insurance company executive*

Brick
Kaufman, Nathan *oncologist*
Roache, Patrick Michael, Jr. *management consultant*

Bridgeton
Howell, James Burt III *retired agricultural products company sales consultant*

Bridgewater
Albrethsen, Adrian Edysel *metallurgist, consultant*
Bernson, Marcella S. *psychiatrist*
Chiu, George *information scientist*
Cohen, Marc *cardiologist, educator*
Dar, Yadunandan Lal *engineer*
Dreier, William Alan *lawyer*
Gallagher, Jerome Francis, Jr. *lawyer*
Hart, Karen Jean *special education educator*
Irace, Gregory *pharmaceutical executive*
Maynard, Kenneth Irwin *pharmaceutical executive, medical educator, researcher*
Patton, Diana Lee Wilkoc *artist, educator, illustrator*
Sethi, Shyam Sunder *management consultant*
Shun, Zhenming *statistician, director*
Sponzilli, Edward George *lawyer*
Weingast, Marvin *laboratory executive*
Wood, J(oshua) Warren III *lawyer, arbitrator, mediator*

Brookside
Fairchild, Samuel Wilson *retired federal agency administrator, manufacturing and financial services executive*

Browns Mills
Cha, Se Do *internist*
Clarke, Betty Ann *librarian, minister*
Di Nunzio, Dominick *educational administrator*
Moore, Roger Addison *pediatrician, anesthesiologist*

Budd Lake
Webb, John Gibbon III *lawyer*

Burlington
Cobb, Vanessa Wyvette *elementary school educator*
Haws, Elizabeth Anne *psychologist, director*
Kingsbury, Tom (Thomas A. Kingsbury) *retail executive*
Rowlette, Henry Allen, Jr. *social worker, counseling psychologist*
Tang, Paul C. *lawyer*

Butler
Kerler, Dov-Ber Boris *academic administrator*

Caldwell
Castano, Gregory Joseph *lawyer*
Kandel, Anatoly F. *economics professor, researcher*
Ryan, Joanne Winona *art administrator, artist, consultant, educator*
Savage, Joseph George *academic administrator*
Werner, Patrice (Patricia Ann Werner) *academic administrator*

Califon
Jeffers, Victoria Wilkinson *psychologist*
Rosen, Carol Mendes *artist*

Camden
Ances, I. G(eorge) *obstetrician, gynecologist*
Britt, Irene Chang *food products executive*
Brotman, Stanley Seymour *federal judge*
Christman, Michael F. *geneticist, biomedical researcher*
Conant, Douglas R. *food products executive*
Connolly, Sean *food products executive*
Driscoll, Jennifer Kay *food products executive*
Galante, Joseph Anthony *bishop*
Gordon, Walter Kelly *retired academic administrator, language educator*
Grazel, Regina M. *medical/surgical nurse*
Hillman, Noel L. *federal judge, former prosecutor*
Jean, Smith *biomedical researcher, director*
Kaden, Ellen Oran *lawyer, consumer products company executive*
Laskin, Lee B. *judge, state senator*
Linder, Maureen *food products executive, marketing professional*
Mazzoli, Linda Fabrizio *personal trainer, consultant, marketing professional*
Morrison, Denise M. *food products executive*
Owens, B. Craig *food products executive*
Parra, Raul O. *urologist, educator*
Parrillo, Joseph Edison, Jr. *allergist, immunologist, cardiologist*
Pomorski, Stanislaw *lawyer, educator*
Rajaram, Sri-Sujanthy *internist, educator*
Reardon, Nancy Anne *food products executive*
Ross, Steven Elliot *surgeon*
Simandle, Jerome B. *federal judge*
Soll, Jacob *history professor*
Solomon, Rayman Louis *dean, law educator*
Tan, LiQin *artist, educator*
Worrall, John Dennis *economics professor, consultant, writer*
Xue, Jinyu *physicist, medical specialist*

Cape May
Fox, Matthew Ignatius *publishing executive*
Kurkowski, David *marketing professional*
Savage, Maureen Walls *retired history professor*
Turner, Almon Richard *retired art historian, educator*

Cape May Court House
Cohen, Daniel Edward *writer*
Cohen, Susan Lois *writer*
Fineberg, Robert Alan *lawyer*
Hsu, Hsiu-hsiang *retired librarian*

Cape May Point
Fraser, Malcolm Cavanagh *former mayor*
Jordan, Joe J. *architect*

Cedar Grove
Mandel, Irwin Daniel *dentist*
Voynick, John S., Jr. *lawyer*

Cedar Knolls
Hariri, Robert Joseph *neurosurgeon, researcher*

Chatham
Brodkin, Adele Ruth Meyer *psychologist*
Earle, Jean Buist *finance executive*
Marconi, Dominic Anthony *bishop emeritus*
Meagher, James Proctor *editor*
Murphy, Joseph James *chiropractic physician*
Tepper, David Alan *hedge fund manager*
Zegas, Alan Lee *lawyer*

Cherry Hill
Batterman, Steven Charles *engineering mechanics and bioengineering professor, consultant*
Blakney, Juanita Mosley *psychotherapist*
Brooks, Gilbert L. *lawyer*
Bryan, Henry Collier *clergyman, retired secondary school educator*
Caldwell, Wesley Stuart III *lawyer, lobbyist*
D'Alfonso, Mario Joseph *lawyer*
Folkman, Benjamin *lawyer*
Fuentevilla, Manuel Edward *chemical engineer*
Goldberg, Jack *hematologist*
Gooden, Linda R. *aerospace transportation executive*
Gorenberg, Charles Lloyd *finance company executive*
Kole, Janet Stephanie *lawyer, writer*
Myers, Daniel William, II, *lawyer*
Pfeuffer, Robert John *musician*
Rochester, Andrew Lawrence *lawyer*
Rose, Joel Alan *legal consultant*
Rudman, Solomon Kal *magazine publisher*
Schelm, Roger Leonard *information systems specialist*
Swibinski, Edward Thomas *internist, endocrinologist, educator*
Werbitt, Warren *gastroenterologist, educator*

Chester
Albert-Vespignani, Kathleen M.G. *performing arts educator*
Lynch, Beverly Love *language educator*

Cinnaminson
Edwin, Robert *voice educator*

Cliffside Park
Samardzic, Veljko *engineering company executive, researcher*

Clifton
Burke, Bruce Lowell *consumer products company executive*
DiNicola, Robert J. *consumer products company executive*
Feinstein, Miles Roger *lawyer*
Giblin, Thomas Patrick *state legislator, labor union administrator*
Gries, Michael F. *consumer products company executive*
Lieb, L. Robert *lawyer*
Rodimer, Frank Joseph *bishop emeritus*
Serratelli, Arthur Joseph *bishop*
Shi, Qun *engineer*
Yau, Edward Tintai *toxicologist, pharmacologist*

Clinton
Hulse, Robert Douglas *biotechnologist*

Closter
Minikes, Neil Ira *pediatrician, allergist, immunologist*

Colts Neck
Crowder-Pagano, Linda Louise *special education educator*

Cranbury
Kimmich, Christoph Martin *former academic administrator, educator*
Testa, James A. *lawyer*
Yoseloff, Julien David *publishing company executive*

Cranford
Hrycak, Peter *retired engineering educator*
Jenssen, Warren Donald *microbiologist, consultant*
McCreedy, Edwin James *lawyer*
Mendelson, Joel Stuart *allergist, immunologist*
Russell, John Joseph *English educator*

Cream Ridge
Jacobs, Jim *actor, composer, librettist, playwright*

Cresskill
Pappachristou, Jennifer *psychologist*

Deal
Becker, Richard Stanley *music publisher*

Delanco
Lane, Carrie Belle (Hairston) *retired music educator*

Demarest
Dornfest, Burton Saul *anatomy educator scientist*

Dover
Derr, Debra Hulse *advertising executive, writer*

East Brunswick
Braun, Anna M. *music educator*
Daniel, Charles Timothy *transportation engineer, consultant*
Hurst, Gregory Squire *investment company executive, theater director and producer*
Johnson, Edward Elemuel *psychologist, educator*
Kaufman, Matthew *plastic surgeon*
Kirshner, Jacob *physician*
Meningall, Evelyn L. *retired educational media specialist*
Midlarsky, Elizabeth Ruth *psychologist, researcher, educator*
Milgraum, Sandy *surgeon, educator*
Wildnauer, Richard Harry *pharmaceutical executive*
Zatlin, Phyllis *language educator, translator*
Zaun, Anne Marie *lawyer*

East Hanover
Wen, Hong *pharmaceutical executive*

East Orange
Agarwal, Shashi Kant *cardiologist*
Fielo, Muriel Bryant *interior designer*
Hudson-Zonn, Eliza *nurse, psychologist*
Severe, Kim Lynette *psychologist*
Wright, Jameelah R. *pre-school educator*

East Rutherford
Carr, David *professional football player*
Cathey, Gertrude Brown *retired medical/surgical nurse*
Coughlin, Tom (Thomas Richard Coughlin) *professional football coach*
Frank, Lawrence *professional basketball coach*
Gilbride, Kevin *professional football coach*
Harris, Devin Lamar *professional basketball player*
Jacobs, Brandon *professional football player*
Kempner, Michael W. *public relations executive*
Kluge, John Werner *broadcast and advertising executive*
Lamping, Mark C. *professional sports team executive*
Manning, Eli (Elisha Nelson Manning) *professional football player*
Mara, John Kevin *professional sports team executive*
Pierce, Antonio *professional football player*
Reese, Jerry *professional sports team executive*
Robinson, Dennis R. *state agency administrator*
Snee, Christopher *professional football player*
Thorn, Rodney King *professional sports team executive, retired professional basketball player*
Tuck, Justin Lee *professional football player*
Umenyiora, Osi *professional football player*
Vanderweighe, Kiki (Ernest Maurice Vanderweighe III) *professional sports team executive, retired professional basketball player*
Vandeweghe, Ernest Maurice, III, (Kiki Vandeweghe) *professional sports team executive, retired professional basketball player*
Yi, Jianlian *professional basketball player*
Yormark, Brett D. *professional sports team executive*

Eatontown
Bouchard, Gilles *manufacturing executive*
Fritch, John Kenneth *civilian military employee*

Edgewater
Berliner, Barbara *retired librarian, consultant*
Pohan, Armand *transportation executive, professional hockey club executive, lawyer*
Teicher, Henry Earl *retired education educator*

Edgewater Park
Mednick, Sheldon Ira *pharmacist*

Edison
Alexander, John Charles *pharmaceutical executive, preventive medicine physician*
Biunno, Theresa *physical education educator*
Blanco, Virgil Harold *college professor, administrator*
Chen-Maxham, Li-Chan *soprano*
Garcia, Maria Luisa *biochemist, researcher*
Gizzi, Martin Sherman *neurologist, neurophysiologist*
Granuzzo, Nanette *language educator*
Kijowski, Rosemary Joan *small business owner, retired music educator*
Parisi, Angela I. *chemist*
Pedescleaux-Muckle, Gail *retired business analyst, writer, consultant, model*
Romaguera, Allan E. (Al Romaguera) *credit manager*
Roskoski, John *religious studies educator, coach*
Sapra, Puja *research scientist*
Thornton, Kirtley Elliott *psychologist*
Vercammen, Kenneth Albert *lawyer, prosecutor*
Winter, Robin Okner *health facility administrator*

Egg Harbor City
Earl, Donald W. *treasurer, executive secretary*
Farris, Vera King *former college president*

Egg Harbor Township
Carney, Michelle Catherine *assistant principal*
Lashman, Shelley Bortin *retired judge*
Robbins, Hulda Dornblatt *artist, printmaker*
Schreiber, Eileen Sher *artist*

Elizabeth
de la Viña-Sierra, Diana Maria *music educator*
Ferrara, Joseph Anthony, Sr. *vice principal*
Gellert, George Geza *food importing company executive*
Lucco, James Perry *writer*
Rauh, Linda Ann *rehabilitation services professional, counselor*
Sananman, Michael Lawrence *neurologist*
Yarasani, Venkatarama *chemist, researcher*

Elmwood Park
Kelsey, David H. *manufacturing executive*
Mangano, Louis *lawyer*
Weisberger, James David *hematopathologist*
White, H. Katherine *lawyer*

Englewood
Albee, Gloria *playwright*
Bloomenstein, Richard B. *plastic surgeon*
Boteach, Shmuley *rabbi, television personality, author*
D'Amico, Richard *plastic surgeon*
Elias, Steven *surgeon*
Fay, Toni Georgette *communications executive*
Frieden, Faith Joy *obstetrician*
Goldweit, Richard Scott *cardiologist*
Herman, Steven Douglas *cardiothoracic surgeon, educator*
Koons, Irvin Louis *graphics designer, consultant, marketing professional*
Minkoff, John *applied mathematics educator*
Puente, Tamagary *psychologist*
Rotondi, Nicholas John *automotive executive*
Schmidt, Ronald Hans *architect*
Shammash, Jonathan *medical educator*
Tobias, Geoffrey *otolaryngologist, plastic surgeon*
Wuhl, Charles Michael *psychiatrist*

Englewood Cliffs
Bartiromo, Maria Sara *financial news correspondent*
Burnett, Erin Isabelle *financial news correspondent*
Clift, Simon *consumer products company executive, marketing professional*
Faber, David *broadcast business news network correspondent*
Farrell, Patricia Ann *psychologist, educator, writer*
Hoffman, Mark *broadcast executive*
Lawrence, James A. *food products executive*
Master, Robert Jeffery *consumer products company executive, marketing professional*
Neis, Arnold Hayward *pharmaceutical company executive*
Polk, Michael B. *consumer products company executive*
Quick, Becky (Rebecca Quick) *financial news correspondent*
Saible, Stephanie Irene *editor-in-chief*

Ewing
Garrett, Leigh Ann *elementary school educator*
Kentengian, Isabel *language educator*
Taylor, James Stacey *philosopher, educator*

Fair Haven
McKissock, David Lee *retired manufacturing company executive*
Wyndrum, Ralph William, Jr. *communications consultant*

Fair Lawn
Greenberg, Edward *psychologist*
Namerow, David Mark *pediatrician*

Fairfield
Connell, William Terrence *lawyer, judge*
Fassel, Jim (James E. Fassel) *professional football coach*

Fanwood
Grallo, Richard Martin *research psychologist*

Far Hills
Glover, Lucas Hendley *professional golfer*

Farmingdale
Schluter, Peter Mueller *electronics executive*

Flanders
Huang, Jacob Chen-ya *physician, educator, city health official*
Kuzma, Deborah J. *vice principal, music educator*

Flemington
Buchsbaum, Peter A. *judge*
Kettler, Carl Frederick *airline executive*
Kiovsky, Douglas George *land use planner*
Lenagh, Thomas Hugh *lawyer, financial advisor*
Nowak, Jerry (Gerald C. Nowak) *music educator, Musician Writer Conductor*
Rushton, Alan R. *physician, medical researcher, historian*
Salamon, Renay *real estate broker*
Saylor-Castelgrant, Elizabeth Ann *educational association administrator*
Taylor, Duncan Paul *pharmacologist, researcher*

Florham Park
Bossen, Wendell John *retired financial planner*
Chase, Eric Lewis *lawyer*
Elias, John M. *lawyer*
Hardin, William Downer *retired lawyer*
Jotshi, Arun *operations research specialist*
Kahn, Richard *lawyer*
Kandravy, John *lawyer*
Laulicht, Murray Jack *lawyer*
Long, Stephen R. *lawyer*
Malone, Robert K. *lawyer*
Naimark, George Modell *marketing and management consultant*
Nittoly, Paul Gerard *lawyer*
O'Connell, Daniel Francis *lawyer*
O'Reilly, Gerard P. *engineering company executive*
Reid, Charles Adams III *lawyer*
Ridley, John A. *lawyer*
Rosenberg, Paul I. *lawyer*
Tallmadge, Mark Myron *lawyer*

Fords
Blond, Stuart Richard *magazine editor*

Fort Dix
Boyd, Larry Chester *colonel*

Fort Lee
Altomara, Rita Ecke *library director, writer*
Goldberg, Harry Finck *lawyer, business consultant*
Huang, Jianzhong *biomedical researcher*
Knopf, Claire *editor, writer*
Li, Tien-Shun *obstetrician, gynecologist, educator*
Lippman, William Jennings *investment company executive*
Mack, Earle Irving *former ambassador, real estate company executive*
Orman, Suze (Susan Lynne Orman) *news correspondent, writer*
Stuart, Carole *publishing executive*
Sugarman, Alan William *educational consultant*
Thomopoulos, Michael *music educator*
Weiss, Simona *retired paralegal*

Fort Monmouth
Leciston, David John *computer scientist*
Perlman, Barry Stuart *electrical engineer, researcher, director*
Poulos, Andrew, Jr. *protective services official, director*
Schwering, Felix Karl *electronics executive, researcher*
Thornton, Clarence Gould *electronics executive, civilian military employee*
Tse, Elizabeth Suet Hing *computer research engineer*

Franklin Lakes
Considine, John R. *pharmaceutical company executive*
Elkins, David V. *medical products executive*
Forlenza, Vincent A. *medical products executive*
Klepper, Kenneth O. *healthcare executive*
Ludwig, Edward J. *medical technology executive*
Moriarty, Thomas M. *lawyer*
Rubino, Richard J. *pharmaceutical executive*
Sherman, Jeffrey Scott *lawyer*
Snow, David B., Jr. *pharmaceutical executive*
Williams, Edward David *information technology management consultant*
Yi, Jizu *research scientist, educator*

Franklinville
Moyer, Mary A. *media specialist*

Freehold
Christ, Duane Marland *retired computer systems engineer*
Guadagno, Kimberly McFadden *county official, former prosecutor*
Jawidzik, Edward Mark *priest*
Krupp, John E. *social studies educator*

Galloway
Newell, Eric James *financial planner, retired insurance company executive*

Garfield
Herpst, Robert Dix *lawyer, optical materials company executive*

Gillette
Nathanson, Linda Sue *publishing executive, writer*

Glassboro
Blanck, Emily Vanessa *history professor*
D'Augustine, Robert *academic administrator, lawyer*
Flores, Eduardo Virgilio *physics professor*
Hasit, Cindi *literacy educator*
Heinzen, James Warren *history professor*
Holdcraft, Janet Rulon *school system administrator*
Hottle, Andrew D. *art historian*
Jorgensen, Donna W. *literature and language professor, department chairman*
Korieh, Chima J. *history professor*
Pillay, Gautam *chemical engineer, chemist, academic administrator*
Rosado, Maria Araya *anthropologist, educator*
Rusu, Adrian *engineering educator, director*
Savelski, Mariano J. *chemical engineer, educator*
Slater, C. Stewart *chemical engineering educator*
Wiltenburg, Joy *history professor*
Wright, William Cook *archivist, director*
Zuponcic, Veda Helen *music educator, art director*

Glen Ridge
Addison, Herbert John *consulting editor, writer*
Agnew, Peter Tomlin *employee benefit consultant*
Zbar, Lloyd Irwin Stanley *otolaryngologist, educator*

Glen Rock
Goldstone, Robert Allen *orthopaedic surgeon*
Keenaghan, Patricia Anne *principal, educator*
Mc Elrath, Richard Elsworth *retired insurance company executive*
Savoie, Brietta Dolores Giger *retired librarian*

Green Village
Swift, John Francis *retired health care advertising company executive*

Guttenberg
Boss, Jeffrey *banker*
Wright, Jane Cooke *oncologist, educator, consultant*

Hackensack
Agress, Harry, Jr. *radiologist, nuclear medicine physician*
Ahearn, James *columnist*
Alvarez, Manuel *hospital executive, medical educator and news correspondent*
Ashinoff, Robin *dermatologic surgeon*
Bhattacharyya, Pritish *hematologist, director*
Bronson, Meridith J. *lawyer*
Caminiti, Donald Angelo *lawyer*
Davies, Richard John *surgical oncologist*
Deener, Jerome Alan *lawyer*
Ferguson, John Patrick *health facility administrator*
Forman, Michael H. *lawyer*
Gardin, Julius Markus *cardiologist, educator*
Greenberg, Steven Morey *lawyer*
Gross, Peter Alan *epidemiologist, researcher*
Haines, Kathleen Ann *pediatrician, educator*
Hetherington, Robert Alexander *lawyer*
Kim, Richard Young Jin *plastic surgeon, educator*
Kimura, Yukiko *pediatric rheumatologist, educator*
Latimer, Stephen Mark *lawyer*
Mavrovic, Paul J. *information technology executive*
Mullin, Patrick Allen *lawyer*
Parisi, Cheryl Lynn *art educator*
Pecora, Andrew Louis *hematologist, oncologist*
Pero, Victoria *performing arts educator*
Rose, Arthur *lawyer*
Stagnaro-Green, Alex *medical educator*
Stein, Gary S. *lawyer, retired state supreme court justice*
Vort, Robert A. *lawyer*
Williamson, (Eulah) Elaine *elementary school educator*
Zucker, Arthur *lawyer*

Hackettstown
Holt, John R. *literature and language professor*
Iaione, Robin Jan *elementary school educator*
Kobert, Joel A. *lawyer*
Lamour, Kenol *artist, educator*
Singh, Harjit *medical educator, artist*
Van Campen, Stephen Bernard *executive recruiter, consultant*
Wiedemann, Charles Louis *dentist*

Haddon Heights
Weinberg, Ruthmarie Louise *special education educator, researcher*

Haddonfield
Baltake, Joe *film critic*
Baltake, Susan *marketing and communications professional*
Bauer, Raymond Gale *sales professional*
Capelli, John Placido *nephrologist, educator*
Fisher, George Ross III *physician, educator*
Gatti, Eugene Anthony *immunologist, pediatrician*
Iavicoli, Mario Anthony *lawyer*
Jensh, Ronald Paul *retired anatomist*
Spevak, Eric Scott *lawyer*

Hainesport
Sylk, Leonard Allen *manufacturing executive, real estate developer*

Haledon
Ishiguro, Hiroki *psychiatrist, geneticist, researcher*

Hamilton
Kilbourne, Claire Anne *retired gifted and talented education educator*
Sporn, Aaron Adolph *physician, educator*
Turnbull-Bruehl, Jo'Ann Hazel *special education educator*

Hammonton
Adetunji, Babatunde Abayomi *forensic psychiatrist*

Hampton
Nevins, Arthur Gerard, Jr. *lawyer*

Harrisonville
Stallone, George R. *neurophysiologist*

Hasbrouck Heights
Lieberman, Charles *economist*
Perham, Roy Gates III *industrial psychologist*

Haworth
Biesel, Diane Jane *editor, publishing executive*
Strum, Brian J. *real estate company officer*

Hawthorne
Clavijo, Pío *music educator, director*

Highland Park
Brudner, Harvey Jerome *physicist*
Fogiel, Max *publishing executive*
Kolodzei, Natalia A. *art association administrator, curator*
Safir, Ken *linguist, educator*
Spencer, Herbert Harry *structural engineer, researcher, computer analyst*

Highlands
Psuty, Norbert Phillip *marine sciences educator*

Hightstown
Darr, Walter Robert *financial analyst*
Elliott, Frank Nelson *retired college president*
Hunter, John Stuart *statistician, consultant*
Schorske, Carl Emil *historian, educator*

Hillsborough
Brodie-Colontino, Patricia *psychologist*
Sun, Wei *electrical engineer*

Hillsdale
Copeland, Lois Jacqueline *physician*

Hillside
Dickerson, Martin Lee *principal*
Wilson, Bertina Iolia *retired music educator*

Ho Ho Kus
Bryan, Thomas Lynn *lawyer, educator*

Hoboken
Bazil, Leon A. *science educator*
Bostwick, Randell Armour *retired food service executive*
Chassapis, Constantin *mechanical engineer, educator*
Choi, Chang-Hwan *science educator*
Fallah, M. Hosein *engineering management educator*
Fassoulis, Satiris Galahad *communications executive, director*
Fisher, Frank Thomas *engineering educator*
Griskey, Richard George *chemical engineering professor*
Halder, Raghunath *research scientist*
Matthews, Charles *school disciplinarian*
Nosonovsky, Michael *research scientist*
Raveché, Harold Joseph *academic administrator*
Roh, Heui-Seol *research scientist, educator*
Rothberg, Gerald M. *materials engineer, educator*
Savitsky, Daniel *retired structural engineer, educator*
Sommers, George R. *lawyer*
Tardiff, Jill Alexandria *publishing executive, photographer*
Ubell, Robert Neil *editor, educator, publishing executive, consultant*
Wakeman, Thomas Herbert III *civil engineer, regional administrator*
Widdicombe, Richard Palmer *librarian*
Xing, Yiping *electrical engineer, researcher*

Holmdel
Alferness, Rodney C. *physicist*
Bateman, Alan R. *municipal official*
Colmant, Andrew Robert *lawyer*
Doerr, Christopher Richard *research scientist*
Foschini, Gerard J. *electrical engineer*
Kane, Michael Joel *physician*
Kang, Inuk *research scientist*
Lang, Howard Lawrence *electrical engineer*
Levanda, Matthew *pharmacist, director*
Smith, Sibley Judson, Jr. *historic site administrator, educator*
Winzer, Peter J. *telecommunications industry executive, researcher*

Hopewell
Jaffe, Russell Merritt *pathologist, research director*

Irvington
Paden, Harry *municipal official*

Iselin
Dornbusch, Arthur A., II, *lawyer*
Ilinich, Oleg *chemist, researcher*
Liu, Xinsheng *chemist*

Jackson
Arminas, Scott Arnold *chemist, poet, writer*
Cohen, Walter Stanley *financial consultant*
Hagberg, Carl Thomas *financial executive*
Heck, Roberta M. *poet, writer*
Klostreich, Eva Tricules *educational association administrator*
Leveson, Irving Frederick *economist*
Tague, Charles Francis *retired engineering, real estate and construction company executive*
Wagner, Edward Kurt *publishing company executive*

Jersey City
Aschoff, Lawrence Michael (Mick) *computer information scientist*
Ashley, Willard Walden C., Sr. *minister*
Bulaong, Grace F. *library director*
Curran, Barbara A. *superior court judge*
D'Alessandro, Kathryn Carol *art educator*
DeCicco, John *law educator*
Filler, Ronald Howard *lawyer*
Fong, Kai Heng Elizabeth *psychologist*
Goldberg, Arthur *merchant banker, financial consultant, educator*
Greenberg, William Michael *psychiatrist*
Guarini, Frank Joseph *lawyer, real estate developer, former congressman*
Gurevich, Grigory *visual artist, educator, mime*
Healy, Jerramiah *Mayor, Jersey City, New Jersey*
Howard, Terrence Dashon *actor*
Klyatis, Lev Matusovich *test and reliability scientist*
Koster, Emlyn Howard *museum administrator, geologist, educator*
Laski, John N. *finance educator*
Mahood, Marie I. *counselor, educator*
Metallo, Frances Rosebell *mathematics professor*
Minnelli, Liza *singer, actress*
Nilsen, Martin John *lawyer*
Ott, Gilbert Russell, Jr. *lawyer*
Perhach, James Lawrence *pharmaceutical executive*
Peterson, George Anthony *psychologist, consultant*
Queen Latifah, (Dana Elaine Owens) *actress, musician*
Riotto, Joseph *finance educator*
Ross, John G. *educator*
Sangiuliano, Barbara Ann *tax director*
Scott-Allen, Cynthia *psychologist*
Smith, Frederick Augustus *librarian*
Soo Hoo, Tsung (Bill) Yao *security studies educator, consultant*
Tomczyk, Fredric John *brokerage house executive*
Turula, Joseph *lawyer*
Wangiwang, Julius Bolla *mathematics professor*
Warren, Maredia Delois *music educator*
Wolchuk, Roman *engineering educator*
Yoshimoto, Midori *art educator, director*

Kearny
Dunne, Frederick R., Jr. *lawyer*

Keasbey
Hari, Kenneth Stephen *painter, sculptor, writer*

Kendall Park
Hershenov, Bernard Zion *research and development company executive*
Nied, Stacey Jean *psychologist*

Kenilworth
Bertolini, Robert J. *pharmaceutical executive*
Covert, Theresa M. *treasurer*
Cox, Carrie S. *pharmaceutical executive*
Dodsworth, Roy W. *pharmaceutical executive*
Ehrenthal, Herb *health care company executive, marketing professional*
Greenlee, William John *chemist*
Hassan, Fred *pharmaceutical executive*
Jia, Yanlin *research scientist*
Neustadt, Bernard Ray *chemist*
Waskin, Hetty Anne *epidemiologist, director*

Keyport
McLeod, Robert E. *lawyer*

Kinnelon
Haller, Charles Edward *engineer, consultant*

Lake Hiawatha
Wyka, Tom *information technology manager*

Lake Hopatcong
Upadhya, Hiran S. *environmental engineer*

Lakewood
Appello, Patrick Paul *guitarist, lutenist, educator*
Bennett, Scott H. *history professor*
Doak, Nancy Ann *mathematics educator*
Forbes, Gordon Maxwell *sportswriter, retired commentator*
Houle, Joseph E. *mathematics professor*
Karol, Frederick John *retired industrial chemist*
Levine, Stephen M. *psychologist, educator, consultant*
Levovitz, Pesach Zechariah *rabbi*
Malamut, Myra Lewinter *music educator, director*
Marchese, Michael James, Jr. *radiation oncologist*
Pilgram, Suzanne *artist, educator*
Rader, Pamela J. *literature and language professor*
Williams, Barbara Anne *retired academic administrator*

Lambertville
Beyea, Jan Edgar *physicist*

Lanoka Harbor
Lake, William Robert *educator*

Laurel Springs
Roma, Aida Clara *artist*

Lawrenceville
Alig, Roger Casanova *physicist, engineer*
Brill, Michael Henry *physicist, editor*
Coleman, Wade Hampton III *management consultant, mechanical engineer, retired banker*
Cox, Teri Polack *public relations executive*
Gong, Linguo *science educator*
Hnasko, Amy Marie *primary school educator*
Jordan, Mildred Rice Loretta *education educator*
Lackie, Robert Jonathan *university librarian, educator, consultant*
Oram, Fern Amy *content director*
Rosenthal, Albert Lester *dermatologist, educator*
Rozanski, Mordechai *academic administrator*
Stein, Sandra Lou *educational psychology professor emerita*
Tharney, Leonard John *education educator, consultant*
Weaver, Charles Lyndell, Jr. *marketing executive, educational consultant*
Witte, Arnold Stewart *neurologist*

Lebanon
Barto, Susan Carol *writer*
Sabatino, Thomas Joseph, Jr. *lawyer, pharmaceutical executive*

Leonia
Deutsch, Nina *pianist, vocalist*
Dondysh, Victoria *pianist*
Kurtz, Anthony David *physicist*
Thiesfeldt, Sheila M. *artist, educator, small business owner*

Liberty Corner
Feeks, J. Michael *bank executive*

Lincoln Park
Sichuk, George *entrepreneur, creator and builder mental analyst, writer, atomic scientist, biochemist, physiologist, transcendental academic theologian*

Lincroft
Benham, Helen *music educator*
Ruiz Madas, Yesenia *educational counselor*
Ventola, Frances Ann *mathematics professor*
Zigo, Paul Edward *historian, educator*

Linden
Bukosky, Richard J. *allergist*
Dunn, John Mark *music educator, director*
Purves, Dennis Patrick *library director*

Linwood
Sutman, Frank Xavier *retired academic administrator, chemist, writer, educator*

Little Egg Harbor Township
Hoden, Virginia *technology educator*

Little Falls
Aregood, Richard Lloyd *editor*
Berra, Yogi (Lawrence Peter Berra) *former professional baseball player, coach, manager*
Fleming, Shane D. *plastic products company executive*
Luing, Larry Lee *educational administrator*
Margaritis, John Paul *advertising and public relations executive*
Shern, Stephanie Marie *investment company executive, accountant*

Little Ferry
Briggs, Alice *clinical child psychologist*
Dauber, Sheila *media specialist, school librarian*

Little Silver
Marcus, Abir A. *psychiatrist*
Schmidt, Daniel Edward, IV, *lawyer, arbitrator*

Livingston
Conde, Miguel A. *hematologist, oncologist*
Daman, Ernest Ludwig *mechanical engineer*
Ehrenkranz, Howard *dentist, educator*
Ingato, Robert Joseph *lawyer*
Leone, Joseph M. *finance company executive*
Pansini, Jill Anne *medical/surgical nurse, consultant*
Peek, Jeffrey M. *finance company executive*
Reilly, Christine L. *finance company executive*
Samojlik, Eugeniusz *medical educator, health facility administrator*
Wolfe, Jonathan W. *lawyer*

Lodi
Guillory, Ann Verrett *psychologist, educator, academic administrator*
Kelly, Mary Ann Therese *visual artist, educator*
McParland, Robert Patrick *literature educator, writer*
Vecchio, Maria Theresa *history professor*

Long Branch
Checton, John Burt *cardiologist*
Lagowski, Barbara Jean *writer, editor*
Luria, Martin Jay *endocrinologist*
Stewart, Georgiana Liccione *writer*

Lumberton
Campagnolo, Mary Frances *physician*
Friedberg, Thomas Harold *insurance company executive*

Lyndhurst
Prevoznik, Michael E. *lawyer*

Madison
Bazán-Figueras, Patricia *literature and language professor*
Benson, Peter *literature and language professor*
Brown, Paulette *lawyer*
Bull, Vivian Ann *retired academic administrator, educator*
Byrd, Stephen Fred *human resource consultant*
Culligan, Patrick John *obstetrician, urogynecologist, surgeon, researcher*
Demain, Arnold Lester *microbiologist, educator*
Dohlsten, Mikael *pharmaceutical executive, researcher*
Ellenbogen, Leon *nutritionist, biochemist, retired pharmaceutical executive*
Jennings, George Harold *psychology professor*
Jibilian, Gerald Arsen *lawyer, manufacturing corporation executive*
Lach, Eileen Marie *lawyer*
Naadimuthu, Govindasami *finance educator*
O'Brien, Mary Devon *communications executive, consultant*
Ochs, Peter Warren *religion educator*
Parker, Henry Griffith III *insurance executive*
Poussot, Bernard Jean *pharmaceutical executive*
Rosales Herrera, Raúl Joaquin *language educator*
Rosen, David M. *law educator*
Rubinstein, Ernest *librarian, educator*
Sawma, Gabriel M. *law educator*
Scrimgeour, Andrew David *library director*
Stein, Lawrence V. *lawyer*

Mahwah
Bear, Larry Alan *retired lawyer, educator*
Birnberg, Jack *financial executive*
D'Antonio, Lawrence *mathematics educator*
Gerstein, David Brown *manufacturing and professional sports team executive*
Gibbons, Robert Philip *management consultant, director*
Govindaluri, Srikrishna Madhumohan *management educator*
Hailparn, Diana Finnegan *psychotherapist, writer*
Harth, Marshall Stephen *psychology professor, psychotherapist*
Knight, Shirley Delores *librarian*
Lee, Reginald K. *orthopedist, researcher*
Martin, Sandra Hancock *language educator*
Padovano, Anthony Thomas *theologian, literature educator*
Rakotobe-Joel, Thierry *engineering educator, researcher, executive director*

Manalapan
Lin, Chiu-Tze *conductor, musician*
Stone, Fred Michael *lawyer*

Manasquan
Abate, John E. *electrical engineer, consultant*
Jones, Elizabeth Harding *real estate agent, retired elementary school educator*

Manchester
Madan, Deepak S. *engineering executive*

Maplewood
Fiorito, Frank Anthony *secondary educator*
Gilbert, Rose Bennett *journalist*
Johnson, Dewey, Jr. *retired biochemist*
Knight, Nathaniel *history professor*
Lally, Michael David *writer, actor*
Shuttleworth, Anne Margaret *psychiatrist*
Silverman, Martin Arnold *psychiatrist*
Tatyrek, Alfred Frank *retired chemist, environmental engineer*
Woods, Krystyna Janina *artist, pharmacist*
Zoss, Abraham Oscar *chemical company executive*

Margate City
Trocki-Videll, Cyla *psychiatrist, healthcare administrator*
Videll, Jared Steven *cardiologist*

Marlboro
Bass, David Steven *law educator, arbitrator, mediator*

Marlton
Cheney, Eleanora Louise *retired secondary school educator*
Clemens, David Allen *minister*

Martinsville
Baxter, Nancy *medical writer*
Raby, John Cornelius *secondary school educator*

Matawan
Amato, Vincent Vito *marketing and business consultant*
Gemelos, Michael S. *engineer, consultant*
Liggett, Twila C. *broadcast executive, educator*
Rivera-Dominguez, Alberto *mathematician, educator, mechanical engineer*
Thompson, Samuel D. *state legislator*
Wang, Shuangquan *research scientist*

Mays Landing
Gross, Michelle Bayard *dancer, educator*
LoBiondo, Frank A. *United States Representative from New Jersey*
McNeal, Jane Erskine *musician, educator*
Taggart, James Jeffrey *engineering educator*
Wilinski, Grant W. *dean*

Medford
Henderson, Rita Elizabeth *literary agent, journalist*
Hogan, Thomas Harlan *publisher*
Kang, Jie *healthcare educator*
Kaser, Richard Todd *communications executive*
Lawson-Ndu, Ovunda A. *emergency physician, surgeon*
Mayer, Joyce Harris *artist*
Micko, Alexander S. *corporate financial executive, educator, treasurer*
Sheffer, James Thomas *music educator*
Springer, Douglas Hyde *retired food products executive, lawyer*

Mendham
Hambleton, George Blow Elliott *retired management consultant*
Kirby, Allan Price, Jr. *investment company executive*
Pierson, Robert David *investor*
Tramutola, Joseph Louis *lawyer, educator*

Merchantville
Li, Christopher L. *epidemiologist, educator*

Metuchen
Arbeiter, Joan *artist, educator*
Bootkoski, Paul Gregory *bishop*
Cangemi, Michael Paul *accountant, author, consultant*
Demkovitz, Russell Bernard *deacon, cemetery director*
Hughes, Edward T. *bishop emeritus*
Macarin-Mara, Lynn *psychotherapist, consultant*

Middletown
Chiu, Angela Lan *architect, researcher*
Lundgren, Carl William, Jr. *physicist*
Meyler, William Anthony *financial analyst*
O'Neal, Susan *library director*
Shields, Patricia Lynn *educational broker, consultant*

Millburn
Bablin, Mark Edward *security administrator, mortgage consultant*
Diamond, Richard S. *lawyer*
Feng, Bo *biology professor*
Kuttner, Bernard A. *retired judge, lawyer, arbitrator*
Pace, Stephen Shell *artist, educator*

Milltown
Liebowitz, Larry Arnold *electroceramics materials engineer*

Millville
Caldwell, Linda E. *critical care nurse*

Monmouth Beach
Ginty, Karen *elementary school educator*
Herbert, LeRoy James *retired accounting firm executive*

Monmouth Junction
Kaminker, Marcia Kahn *physical therapist*
Kolan, Prakash Reddy *information technology manager*
Prestbo, John Andrew *editor, writer, journalist*

Monroe Township
Cushman, Helen Merle Baker *retired management consultant*
Stein, Florence Taub *retired social worker*
Sullivan-Szuts, Betty Anne *academic administrator, educator*
Treatman, Paul *retired school system administrator*
Wallach, Jacques Burton *pathologist, educator*
Zelin, Jerome *retired retail executive*

Montclair
Afzal-Khan, Fawzia *literature and language professor*
Bologna, Paul Andrew Xavier *biology professor, director*
Brock-Murray, Raymond *psychotherapist*
Campbell, Stewart Fred *foundation administrator, consultant*
Chemidlin, Michele Lynn *athletic trainer, consultant*
Chinard, Francis Pierre *physiologist, consultant physician, educator*
Cooke, Nicole *school librarian*
Craig, Mary Ann *music educator*
Delbourgo, Joëlle Lily *publishing executive*
Delgado, Ramon Louis *theater educator, author, director, playwright, lyricist*
Downie, Jeanine B. *dermatologist*
Du, Chunguang Charles *biologist, educator*
Dubrow, Marsha Ann *management consultant, musicologist*
Dufour, Josette Isabelle *language educator*
Eager, George Sidney, Jr. *electrical engineer, engineering executive*
Glasser, Stephen Andrew *publishing executive, lawyer*
Gollob, Herman Cohen *retired publishing executive*
Greenwald, Robert *public relations executive*
Hadzic, Gorica *literature and language educator*
Jones, Sylvia Calpurnia *investment company executive*
Kripalani, Lakshmi Assudomal *educator*
Lapp, Benjamin N. *history professor*
Luftglass, Murray Arnold *corporate financial executive*
Obydol-Alexandre, Kareen *literature and language professor*
Rosen, Allen David *plastic surgeon*
Straten, Roland *retired protective services company executive*
Walker, George Theophilus, Jr. *composer, music educator, pianist*
Zhang, Yanli *management consultant, educator*

Montvale
Claus, Eric *retail executive*
Falcon, Raymond Jesus, Jr. *lawyer*
Galgano, Brenda M. *corporate financial executive*
Haub, Christian W.E. *retail executive*
Lamach, Michael W. *diversified industrial company executive*
Politi, Beth Kukkonen *publishing services company executive*

Montville
Boudes, Pol Francis *pharmaceutical executive, researcher*
Heller, Hanes Ayres *lawyer*
Henn, Katherine A. *social studies educator*

Moorestown
Aziz, Tahira Hannan *psychologist*
Bennington, William Jay *management consultant*
Buckman, William H. *lawyer*
Cervantes, Luis Augusto *neurosurgeon*
Clark, Maryliz M. *retired minister*
Garrigle, William Aloysius *lawyer*
Hyland, William Francis *retired lawyer*
Mulligan, James Christopher *safety and environmental engineer and manager*
Myers, Christopher D. *defense company executive*
Saouaf, Sandra J. *immunologist, consultant*
Schwerin, Horace S. *marketing research consultant*

Morris Plains
Bennett, John Charles *former engineering and construction executive*
Capellos, Chris Spiridon *chemist*
Goldenberg, David Milton *experimental pathologist, oncologist*
Pluciennik, Thomas Casimir *lawyer, former assistant county prosecutor*
Spong, John Shelby *retired bishop, writer, columnist*

Morristown
Adams, Katherine Leatherman *lawyer, diversified technology and manufacturing company executive*
Adler, Kenneth R. *oncologist, hematologist*
Anderson, David J. *diversified technology and manufacturing company executive*
Aspero, Benedict Vincent *lawyer*
Boodey, Cecil Webster, Jr. *retired political science professor*
Bromberg, Myron James *retired lawyer*
Brown, Adriane McClenny *diversified technology and manufacturing company executive*
Butera, Virginia Fabbri *art gallery director, educator*
Call, Denise Hodgins *curator, artist*
Cameron, Nicholas Allen *manufacturing executive*
Coleman, James H., Jr. *lawyer, former state supreme court justice*
Colizza, Wayne Anthony *orthopaedic surgeon*
Cote, David M. *diversified technology and manufacturing company executive*
Cregan, Frank Robert *financial executive, consultant*
Deming, Frederick Wilson *retired economist, banker*
De Rosa, William Thomas *internist, hematologist, oncologist*
Fiel, Stanley Bruce *internist, pulmonologist, educator*
Finkel, Marion Judith *internist, pharmaceutical administrator*
Fradin, Roger Brent *manufacturing executive*
Gillen, James Robert *lawyer, insurance company executive*
Hastings, Mary Jane *minister*
Healey, Thomas J. *former government official, brokerage house executive*
Humick, Thomas Charles Campbell *lawyer*
Jacobs, Andrew Robert *lawyer*
Kearns, William Michael, Jr. *investment banker*
Kirby, Fred Morgan, II, *finance company executive*
Kirby, Jefferson W. *investment company executive*
Kittelberger, Larry E. *engineering executive*
Korf, Gene Robert *lawyer*
Koyce, Terence G. *communications educator*
Kramvis, Andreas Constantinos *chemicals company executive*
Lieberman, Lester Zane *engineering company executive*

Martelet, Francois R. *pharmaceutical executive*
Mertz, Francis James *university president*
Miller, Steven H. *museum director*
Murthy, N. Sanjeeva *physicist*
O'Grady, Dennis Joseph *lawyer*
Olcott, John Whiting *air transportation executive*
Parr, Grant Van Siclen *surgeon*
Personick, Stewart David *electrical engineer*
Pollock, Stewart Glasson *lawyer, state supreme court justice*
Prince, Leah Fanchon *lab administrator, executive secretary*
Prystauk, Elissa *artist*
Rogachefsky, Arlene Sandra *dermatologist*
Rogido, Marta Raquel *medical educator*
Rose, Robert Gordon *lawyer*
Ross, Thomas J., Jr. *personal financial adviser*
Smart, Frank Wilson *physician*
Sperber, Martin *pharmaceutical company executive, pharmacist*
Stanton, Patrick Michael *lawyer*
Timins, Julie Kelter *radiologist*
Weidenkopf, Thomas W. *human resources specialist*
Williams, Joseph Dalton *pharmaceutical executive*
Wolff, Derish Michael *economist*
Zaubler, Thomas Scot *psychiatrist, educator*

Mount Holly
Chatzidakis, Larry *state agency administrator, former state legislator*

Mount Laurel
Gray-Miceli, Deanna Lynn *geriatric nurse practitioner, educator, researcher*
Jones, Marian C. *music educator*
Klein, Gerhart Leopold *public relations executive*
Minkiewicz, Arlene French *computer scientist*
Verba, Linda *bank executive*

Mountain Lakes
Cook, Charles Francis *insurance executive*
Daniel, Royal Thomas III *lawyer, mechanical engineer, accountant*
Loomis, Rebecca C. *psychologist*
Wallace, MaryJean Elizabeth *science educator*

Mountainside
Helander, Robert Charles *lawyer, arbitrator, contributing editor*
Mansue, Amy *hospital administrator*
Vice, Susan F. *medicinal chemist*

Mullica Hill
Tosti, Susan Marie *educational consultant*

Murray Hill
Chandross, Edwin A. *chemist, consultant*
Chen, Jingdong *communications executive*
Ring, Timothy Michael *pharmaceutical executive*

Neptune
Aguiar, Adam Martin *chemist, educator*
Bediguian, Mariamig Jinx *operating room nurse*
Laraya-Cuasay, Lourdes Redublo *pediatrician, pulmonologist, educator*
Rice, Stephen Gary *pediatrician, sports medicine physician, educator*
Stumpf, Paul George *obstetrician-gynecologist*

Neptune City
DeValue, John M. *retired computer science educator*

Neshanic Station
Muckenhoupt, Benjamin *retired mathematics professor*

New Brunswick
Adickes, Sandra Elaine *language educator, writer*
Aisner, Joseph *oncologist, medical educator*
Alexander, Robert Jackson *economist, educator*
Anderson, James Doig *library and information science educator*
Awan, Ahmad Noor *civil engineer*
Bennett, Joan Wennstrom *biology educator*
Bertino, Joseph Rocco *oncologist, educator*
Bindra, Dilbir S. *pharmacist*
Biribauer, Richard Frank *lawyer*
Boyarsky, Andrew Harold *surgeon, educator*
Brilliant, Eleanor Luria *retired social work educator*
Bronner, Stephen Eric *political science professor*
Bunch, Charlotte *advocate*
Clauss-Ehlers, Caroline S. *psychologist, educator, journalist*
Coromilas, James *cardiologist*
Coscia, Anthony R. *state agency administrator, lawyer*
Day-Salvatore, Debra Lynn *medical geneticist*
Denda, Kayo *librarian*
Deyo, Russell C. *health products executive, lawyer*
Dhib-Jalbut, Suhayl S. *physician*
Dougherty, Neil Joseph *physical education educator, consultant*
Drachtman, Richard Allan *pediatrician, educator*
Ehrenfeld, David William *biology professor, writer*
Elias, Maurice Jesse *psychology educator*
Fisher, Hans *nutritional biochemistry educator*
Fisher, Helen E. *anthropologist, educator*
Foster-Cheek, Kaye I. *health products executive*
Friedrich, Gustav William *communications educator*
Gaunt, Marianne I. *university librarian*
Gibbon, Darlene G. *medical educator*
Gillette, William *historian, educator*
Glasser, Paul Harold *sociologist, educator, social worker, university administrator*
Goggins, Colleen A. *health products executive*
Golbe, Lawrence Ingram *neurologist*
Goldberg, Michael Ira *obstetrician, gynecologist*
Goldrich, Michael Seth *otolaryngologist*
Gorsky, Alex *pharmaceutical executive*
Greenberg, Douglas Stuart *dean, history professor*
Greenberg, Michael Richard *urban studies and community health educator*
Greenwald, Alfred Emanuel *retired cosmetic surgeon*
Grob, Gerald N. *historian, educator*
Haugerud, Angelique *professor of anthropology*
Heller, Bridgette P. *marketing executive*
Horowitz, Irving Louis *publisher, educator*
Jaluria, Yogesh *mechanical engineering educator, department chairman*
Jenkins, Alyce Mitchem *writer, educator*
Jenkins, Reese V. *historian, educator*
Johnson, James Turner *theology studies educator*
Joshi, Amit *research scientist*
Kantor, Paul *information scientist, educator*
Kaufman, Kenneth Roland *psychiatrist, educator*
Kenfield, John Fawcett III *art educator*
Kostis, John Basil *cardiologist*
Kulikowski, Casimir Alexander *computer scientist, engineer, educator*
Lachance, Paul Albert *food science educator, clergyman*
Laouar, Amale *immunologist, educator*
Larsen, Ralph S(tanley) *retired pharmaceutical executive*
Lepore, Frederick Everett *neurologist, educator*
Lesk, Michael E. *library and information science educator*
Leventhal, Elaine A. *internist*
Leventhal, Howard *health psychology educator, researcher*
Liu, Junfeng *statistician, educator*
Livingston, Lee Franklin *real estate consultant, financial consultant*
Lowry, Stephen Frederick *surgeon, educator*
Lustig, Graham *performing company executive*
Lu-Yao, Grace *epidemiologist*
Makhija, Mohan *nuclear medicine physician*
Mann, Richard Alan *physician, educator*
Maramorosch, Karl *virologist, educator*
Marker, Rhonda Joyce *librarian*
McCormick, Richard Levis *academic administrator*
McCoy, Sherilyn S. *pharmaceutical executive*
Mechanic, David *social sciences educator*
Miller, Lynn Fieldman *lawyer*
Mills, George Marshall *risk management consultant*
Mizrach, Bruce *economics professor*
Moreyra, Abel E. *medical educator*
Moss, Robert Allen *chemistry professor*
Nelson, Jack Lee *education educator*
Nissenblatt, Michael Jeffrey *medical oncologist*
Nosko, Michael Gerrik *neurosurgeon, educator*
O'Neill, William Lawrence *retired history professor*
Pandey, Ramesh Chandra *chemist, chemicals executive*
Perkins, Brian D. *consumer products company executive*
Pinals, Robert Stanton *physician*
Pitchumoni, Capecomorin Sankar *gastroenterologist, educator*
Raska, Karel Frantisek Julian, Jr. *pathologist, virologist, educator*
Reiss, Michael *medical oncologist, researcher*
Reock, Ernest C., Jr. *retired social studies educator, director*
Rhodes, Edward *political science professor*
Robock, Alan *meteorology professor*
Robson, Mark Gregory *agriculturist, educator*
Roth, Daniel B. *ophthalmologist, researcher*
Rowsell, Jennifer *literature and language professor*
Russell, Louise Bennett *economist, educator*
Salas, Max *pediatrician, educator*
Saltz, Amy *theater educator, director*
Saracevic, Tefko *information science educator*
Scanlon, Jane Cronin *mathematics professor*
Schneider, Stephen Harley *medical educator*
Scholz, Peter M. *surgeon, director*
Schrepfer, Susan R. *history professor, director*
Schuld, Susan Marie *performing arts educator*
Selby, Ronald M. *orthopedic surgeon*
Shapiro, Warren *anthropologist, educator*
Stanley, Jason *education educator*
Stauffer, George B. *dean, musician, historian, consultant*
Strauss, Ulrich Paul *chemist, educator*
Strawderman, William E. *statistics educator*
Strickland, Dorothy *education educator*
Tallia, Alfred F. *physician, educator*
Tanner, Daniel *education educator*
Tedrow, John Charles Fremont *soils educator*
Tiger, Lionel *social scientist, anthropology consultant*
Toby, Jackson *sociologist, educator*
Trivers, Robert L. *bioscience and anthropology educator, evolutionary biologist, sociobiologist*
Trooskin, Stanley Z. *surgeon*
Turshen, Meredeth *educator*
Upton, Arthur Canfield *experimental pathologist, educator*
Wailoo, Keith Andrew *historian, educator*
Weinstein, Melvin Phillip *physician educator*
Weldon, William Conrad *pharmaceutical executive*
Weng, George Jueng-Cious *engineering educator*
Whitener, Scott *music educator, researcher*
Yorke, Marianne *lawyer, real estate executive*

New Milford
Walsh, Joseph Michael *magazine distribution executive*

New Monmouth
Santos, Sharon Lee *parochial school educator*

New Providence
Bruch, Ruth E. *information technology executive*
Carapezzi, William R., Jr. *telecommunications industry executive, lawyer*
Chatterji, Debajyoti *retired manufacturing executive*
Del Tiempo, Sandra Kay *sales executive*
Dolch, Gary D. *health products executive*
Hirsch, Maxine K. *special education educator, councilman*
Kim, Jeong H. *telecommunications industry executive, communications engineer*
McCaffrey, Robert Henry, Jr. *retired manufacturing company executive*
McCarthy, G. Daniel *lawyer*
Morgan, Dennis R. *telecommunications industry executive*
Sniffen, Michael Joseph *hospital administrator*

New Vernon
Dugan, John Leslie, Jr. *foundation executive*
Kushen, Allan Stanford *retired lawyer, corporate executive*
McCormack, John Joseph, Jr. *insurance company executive*

Newark
Ahmed, Shaikh Sultan *cardiologist, educator*
Alexander, Mark C. *law educator, policy advisor*
Altenkirch, Robert A. *academic administrator*
Arias, David *bishop emeritus*
Armenante, Piero M. *chemical engineering educator*
Aron, Lester *lawyer*
Arwady, George E. *publishing executive*
Asatryan, Rubik *chemistry professor, researcher*
Ashley, Thomas R. *lawyer*
Askin, Frank *law educator*
Atluri, Vijayalakshmi *computer science educator*
Aubry, Nadine Nina *mechanical engineering educator*
Baer, Susan M. *airport executive*
Baker, Herman *medical educator, writer*
Bar-Ness, Yeheskel *electrical engineer, educator*
Barron, Kenny *musician*
Barry, Maryanne Trump *federal judge*
Bergen, Stanley Silvers, Jr. *retired academic administrator*
Bilgili, Ecevit Atalay *chemical engineer, researcher, assistant professor*
Bizub, Johanna *law librarian*
Blount, Susan L. *insurance company executive, lawyer*
Blumrosen, Alfred William *law educator*
Booker, Cory Anthony *Mayor, Newark, lawyer*
Brodeur, Martin *professional hockey player*
Brukh, Roman *engineer, educator, researcher*
Bruno, Rosemary Joan *lawyer*
Buck, Rebecca A. *museum administrator, registrar*
Byrd, Stephen C. *utilities executive*
Cahn, Jeffrey Barton *lawyer*
Carbone, Richard J. *diversified financial services company executive*
Carmel, Peter W. *neurosurgeon*
Cavanaugh, Dennis M. *federal judge*
Cheng, Mei-Fang *psychobiology educator, neuroscientist*
Cherniack, Neil Stanley *pulmonologist, educator*
Chukunta, Ndubuisi (Niki) Konyeaso Onuoha *literature and language professor*
Cicerchi, Eleanor Ann Tomb *not-for-profit fundraiser*
Colón, Melinda *lawyer*
Connolly, Mark W. *thoracic surgeon*
Connor, Holly Pyne *curator, art historian*
Contractor, Farok *business and management educator*
Cook, Stuart Donald *neurologist, educator*
Courter, James A. (Jim) *communications executive, former United States Representative, New Jersey*
Cowans, Jon *history professor*
Crawford, Marjorie E. *law librarian, educator*
Cruz, Manuel Aurelio *bishop*
Cummis, Clive Sanford *lawyer*
Cunningham, LeeAnn *assistant prosecutor*
da Cunha, Edgar Moreira *bishop*
Daniel, Carter Anderson *business communications educator, author*
Dauth, Frances Kutcher *journalist, editor*
Day, Edward Francis, Jr. *lawyer*
Debevoise, Dickinson Richards *federal judge*
Dee, Francis X. *lawyer*
Deutsch, Stuart Lewis *law educator, former dean*
Dhawan, Atam Prakash *engineering educator, dean*
Donahoo, James Saunders *cardiothoracic surgeon*
Donato, Gaetano Aldo *bishop*
Dorsa, Caroline D. *utilities company executive, former software company executive*
Edwards, Samuel Lawrence, II, *information technology executive, writer*
Elias, Patrik *professional hockey player*
Emrick, Mike (Doc Emrick) *sportscaster*
Evans, Hugh E. *pediatrician, educator*
Farmer, John Joseph, Jr. *dean, lawyer, former state attorney general*
Ferguson, Yale Hicks *political scientist, educator*
Fishman, Paul J. *lawyer*
Fleishman, Gregory D. *engineering educator*
Flesey, John Walter *bishop*
Foran, Margaret M. (Peggy Foran) *lawyer, financial services executive*
Freilich, Irvin Mayer *lawyer*
Friedland, Bernard *electrical engineer, educator*
Fuentes, Julio M. *federal judge*
Garde, John Charles *lawyer*
Garth, Leonard I. *federal judge*
Gibbons, John Joseph *lawyer, retired federal judge*
Gilman, Jane Piore *mathematician*
Givens, Theartis Tina Mansfield *primary school educator*
Goldman, Glenn *architect, educator*
Goldstein, Ira Morris *neurosurgeon*
Goldstein, Marvin Mark *lawyer*
Granick, Mark S. *plastic surgeon, medical educator*
Graycar, Adam *dean, former Australian government official*
Green, Stuart Paul *law educator*
Greenaway, Joseph Anthony, Jr. *judge*
Grier, Mark B. *diversified financial services company executive*
Hanesian, Deran *chemical engineer, environmental scientist, consultant, educator*
Haring, Eugene Miller *lawyer*
Hiltz, Starr Roxanne *sociologist, educator, writer, consultant, computer scientist*
Hobbs, Patrick Esmond *dean, law educator*
Hummel, Donald Keith *priest*
Iffy, Leslie *medical educator*
Izzo, Ralph *utilities executive*
Jackson, Nancy Lee *geography educator*
Janey, Clifford Bernard *school system administrator*
Järvi, Neeme *conductor, music director*
Jonas, Howard S. *communications executive*
Kennedy, Alyson *advocate, garment worker*
Kennedy, Leslie W. *criminal justice educator, former dean*
Kirmani, Jawad F. *neurologist, surgeon, researcher*
Kirschner, Marvin A. *retired endocrinologist*
Kott, David Russell *lawyer*
Kou, Victoria *medical educator*
Krasnoperov, Lev N. *chemistry professor*
Krovatin, Gerald *lawyer*
Lamoriello, Lou (Louis Anthony Lamoriello) *professional sports team executive*
Langenbrunner, Jamie *professional hockey player*
Langhorne, Richard Tristan Bailey *history professor*
Lanzerotti, Louis John *physicist*
Laperriere, Jacques (Joseph Hughes Laperriere) *professional hockey coach, retired professional hockey player*
La Rocco, Anthony P. *lawyer*
LaRossa, Ralph *utilities executive*
Lautenberg, Frank Raleigh *United States Senator from New Jersey*
Ledeen, Robert Wagner *neuroscientist, educator*
Leibovich, Samuel Joseph *biochemist*
Lemaire, Jacques *professional hockey coach*
Levis, William *utilities executive*
Lieb, Janice Rose *primary school educator*
Lillard, Michael *diversified financial services company executive*
Little, Alan Brian *gynecologist, educator*
Liu, Qinyue (Sherry Liu) *physician, consultant*
Lopriore, Richard P. *utilities executive*
Lorell, Jeffrey W. *lawyer*
Lynch, Jack *literature and language professor*
Mácal, Zdenìk *conductor, music director*
Maqsood, Ahsan *cardiologist, researcher*
Marhaba, Taha Farouk *engineering educator*
Marino, William J. *insurance executive*
McCarthy, Kathleen Jane *law educator, school librarian*
McDonnell, Charles James *bishop emeritus*
McGuire, William B(enedict) *lawyer*
McLean, David J. *lawyer*
Mehrberg, Randall Eric *lawyer, utilities executive*
Mendonca, David *engineering educator*
Mitchell, Jason Wayne *interventional radiologist*
Miura, Robert Mitsuru *mathematician, researcher, educator*
Moran, Eileen A. *utilities executive*
Myers, John Joseph *archbishop*
Nash, Alicia Lardé *application developer, physicist*
Newhouse, Mark William *publishing executive*
Nita, Gelu M. *physics professor, researcher*
Owen, William Franklin, Jr. *academic administrator, former research and development company executive*
Pagán, Gilberto, Jr. *psychologist*
Parise, Zach *professional hockey player*
Pego, Margaret M. *utilities executive*
Perez, John D. *lawyer*
Petillo, John J. *former academic administrator, priest*
Prestigiacomo, Charles Joseph *neurosurgeon, educator*
Price, Clement Alexander *historian, educator*
Price, Mary Sue Sweeney *museum director*
Pryor, Stefan I. *city manager, real estate developer*
Quinn, Kevin J. *utilities executive*
Raines, Tim (Timothy Raines) *baseball coach, retired professional baseball player*
Rao, I. Joga *mechanical engineer, educator*
Reichman, Lee Brodersohn *physician*
Reilly, William Thomas *lawyer*
Risinger, D. Michael *lawyer, educator*
Rittenhouse, Michele Raper *playwright, theater educator*
Robinson, Larry Clark *professional hockey coach, retired professional hockey player*
Rolston, Brian *professional hockey player*
Rosato, Anthony Dominick *mechanical engineer, educator*
Rothschild, Gita F. *lawyer*
Ryan, Lisa Kathleen *environmental and medical science educator*
Saadeghvaziri, Mohamad Ala *civil engineering educator*
Sabio, Dorothy *elementary school educator*
Santiago, Diana *music educator*
Schleifer, Steven J. *psychiatrist, educator*
Schweizer, Karl Wolfgang *historian, educator, author*
Selover, R. Edwin *lawyer, utilities executive*
Shanahan, Brendan Frederick *professional hockey player*
Siegal, Joel Davis *lawyer*
Sifri, Ziad C. *emergency physician, educator*
Simpson, Elbert C. *utilities executive*
Sommer, Bob (Robert G. Sommer) *public relations executive, lobbyist*
Spillers, William Russell *civil engineering educator*
Spruch, Grace Marmor *physics professor*
Steinbaum, Robert S. *publishing executive, lawyer*
Stephens, B. Consuela *minister, consultant*
Stevens, Scott *retired professional hockey player*
Stolberg, Victor *educator*
Strangfeld, John R., Jr. *diversified financial services company executive*
Tedesco, Barbara L. *dean, educator*
Tischman, Michael Bernard *lawyer*
Vajtay, Stephen Michael, Jr. *lawyer*
Vanderbeek, Jeffrey *professional sports team executive*
Verkhovsky, Boris *computer scientist, educator*
Vincenti, Gene A. *director, consultant*
Warren Ellison, Tasheaya L. *lawyer, director*
Weiss, Gerson *endocrinologist, educator*
Willse, James Patrick *editor*
Xiong, Hui *finance educator*
Zazzali, James R. *lawyer, retired state supreme court chief justice*
Zhou, Mengchu *engineering educator*
Ziavras, Sotirios George *computer and electrical engineer, educator*
Zuckerman, Herbert Lawrence *lawyer*

Newfield
Dreher, Frank H., Jr. *retired optician*

Newton
Boulware, Bobbie L. *music educator*
Cox, William Martin *lawyer, educator*
Hollander, Roslyn *artist, educator*

North Bergen
Archbold, Michael G. *consumer products company executive, former retail executive*
Gilbert, Stephen Alan *retired lawyer, organization executive*

North Brunswick
Bern, Ronald Lawrence *management consultant, writer*
Frenkiel, Richard Henry *retired systems engineer, consultant*
Marszalek, Wieslaw *electrical engineering educator*
Moon, Kathleen K. *language arts educator*

North Haledon
Latner, Selma *retired psychoanalyst*

North Plainfield
Dunbar, Holly Jean *communications executive, public relations executive*

Northfield
Margolis, Thomas Ira *vitreoretinal ophthalmologist*
Zlotnick, Norman Lee *lawyer*

Northvale
Di Mino, André Anthony *manufacturing executive, consultant*

Norwood
Murburg, Thelma D. *retired elementary school educator*

Nutley
Kong, Norman *chemist*
Marée, Kathleen Nancy *retired language educator*
Mostillo, Ralph *medical association administrator*
To, Stephen Edward *editor, writer*

ORADELL
Azmi, Hooman *neurosurgeon*

Oak Ridge
Kieren, Thomas Henry *management consultant & architectural photographer*

Oakland
Azar, Fred S. *biomedical engineer, strategic opportunities researcher*
Butterfield, Charles Edward, Jr. *educational consultant*
Guller, Irving Bernard *forensic and clinical psychologist, consultant, writer*
Keough, Daniel Emmet *retired magazine editor*
Reutty, Michele Marie *library director*

Ocean
Reich, Bernard *communications engineer*

Ocean City
Culbertson, Jane Young *statistician*
Hughes, William John *former congressman, diplomat*
Juliana, James Nicholas *manufacturing executive*
Kyriazis, Arthur John (Athanasios Ioannis Kyriazis) *lawyer, molecularbiologist, patent attorney*

Oceanport
Ruggeri, Dianne Ellen *music educator, band director*

Old Bridge
Nanton, Lisa Seeman *music educator*

Old Tappan
Lovitch, Joan *science educator, coach*

Oldwick
Sinfelt, John Henry *chemist*
Snyder, Arthur *publishing executive*

Oradell
Blakeslee, Edward Eaton *lawyer, insurance company executive*
Geisst, Charles Robert *finance educator*
Mavroudis, John M. *lawyer*
Mcglynn, Mary Aspinwall *artist, juror instructor*
Tong, Mary Powderly *retired mathematician, educator*

Paramus
Amato, Debra Jean *psychologist*
Bonnaffons, Ken J. *theater director, Professor ESL*
Chenoweth, Okey Everett *literature and language educator, writer, actor, director*
Fatica, Justin *youth minister, writer*
Hermance, Ronald E., Jr. *bank executive*
Highley, Robert S. *biology professor*
Hochstein, Martin Alan *endocrinologist*
Jacobs, Helen Nichols *artist*
Jenkins, Elaine *middle school educator*
Noguere, Suzanne *trade association administrator, poet*
Russell, Carol Ann Lamken *special education educator*
Saltzman, Jared *performing arts educator, lighting designer*
Tamburro, Peter James, Jr. *secondary school educator*

Park Ridge
Ciannella, Joeen Moore *small business owner*
Douglas, Elyse *automobile rental and leasing company executive*
Frissora, Mark P. *automobile rental and leasing company executive*
Giovannoli, Joseph Louis *entrepreneur, lawyer*
Zimmerman, J. Jeffrey *lawyer, automotive executive*

Parsippany
Cox, Melvin Monroe *lawyer*
Deones, Jack E. *lawyer, broadcast executive*
Ewan, David E. *lawyer*
Ferguson, Thomas George *retired healthcare advertising agency executive*
Garbarini, William Nicholas *pharmaceutical executive*
Gros, Simon Charles *travel company executive, former federal agency administrator*
Holmes, Stephen P. *hotel executive*
Hull, Anthony E. *real estate company executive*
Kunz, Thomas R. *real estate company executive*
Langrana, Anita *financial analyst, personal trainer*
Nelson, Ronald L. *travel services company executive, former film company executive*
Newman, Mark S. *electronics company executive*
Salerno, F. Robert *travel company executive*
Sclafani, Karen C. *lawyer*
Smith, Richard A. *real estate company executive*
Theiss, Richard Edward *electrical engineer, applications engineer*
Wasser, Marilyn J. *lawyer, real estate company executive*
Weisberg, Joseph Simpson *retired dean*
Winograd, Bernard B. *diversified financial services company executive*
Wyshner, David B. *travel company executive*

Passaic
Lindholm, Clifford Falstrom, II, *engineering executive, mayor*

Paterson
Alcala, Luisa Maria *psychologist*
DeFilippi, Vincent J(ohn) *cardiac surgeon*
Fields, Marvin Leon *secondary school educator*
Fink, David Leonard *surgeon*
Geschwendt, David *psychologist*
Kagan, Vladimir *furniture and interior designer*
Pou, Nelida (Nellie) *state legislator*
Richardson, Cynthia Teresa *music educator*
Torres, Jose (Joey) *mayor*

Peapack
Eddey, Gary Erwin *physician, administrator, educator*
Walsh, Philip Cornelius *retired mining executive*

Pennington
Bustin, George Leo *lawyer*
Calvo, Roque John *professional society administrator*
Cobb, Jeffrey William *psychologist*
Czach, Gabriela Bozena *personal care industry executive*
Donnelly, Gerard Kevin *marketing and retail executive*
Fong, Donald P. *psychiatrist*
Harkness, Joan Ann V. *retired health educator*
McBride, Anthony *pharmaceutical executive*
Nayeem, Akbar *chemist*
Sun, Jianxin *medical educator, researcher*
Townsend, Peggy (Stephanie G.) *headmaster*
Zhang, Hong (Rick) *design engineer, researcher*

Penns Grove
Reilley, James Clark *artist, cartoonist, retired small business owner*

Phillipsburg
Burke, John F. *retired surgeon*
Drago, Joseph Rosario *urologist, educator*

Piscataway
Amaral, Andre Renato Sales *education educator, researcher*
Balaguru, Perumalsamy *civil engineering educator*
Baykal-Gursoy, Melike *engineering educator*
Boile, Maria *transportation executive, educator*
Breslauer, Kenneth J. *science educator, researcher*
Chynoweth, Alan Gerald *retired telecommunications industry executive*
Cizewski, Jolie Antonia *physics professor, researcher*
Cohen, Morrel Herman *physicist, biologist, educator*
Colaizzi, John Louis *medical educator*
Conney, Allan Howard *pharmacologist, researcher*
Cosandey, Frederic *engineering educator, researcher*
Denhardt, David Tilton *molecular and cell biology educator*
Dill, Ellis Harold *university dean*
Ebright, Richard High *molecular biologist*
Essien, Francine B. *biologist, educator*
Glashausser, Charles Michael *physicist, researcher*
Goss, Mary E. Weber *sociology educator*
Gustafsson, Mary E. *lawyer*
Haladjian, Harry Haroutioun *psychologist*
Idol, James Daniel, Jr. *chemist, educator, inventor, consultant*
Ierapetritou, Marianthi G. *engineering educator*
Israel, Paul Bryan *editor, director*
Johnson, William Gessner *neurologist, educator*
Kilianski, Stephen *psychologist, educator*
Kim, Jin-Mo *finance educator*
Klein, Michael Tully *dean, chemical engineer, consultant*
Kosowsky, Arthur *physicist, educator*
Lacatus, Catalin *communications engineer*
Leath, Paul Larry *physicist, educator, former university official*
Lebowitz, Joel Louis *mathematical physicist, educator*
Leslie, Alan M. *psychology professor*
Li, Yanyan *mathematician, educator*
Lindenfeld, Peter *physics professor*
Lioy, Paul James *environmental health scientist*
Manowitz, Paul *biochemist, researcher, educator*
Mardikian, Jackie *medical librarian*
Matilsky, Terry Allen *astrophysicist, educator*
Mazurek, Monica Ann *engineering educator*
McKim, Kim S. *biology professor*
Menza, Matthew A. *psychiatrist*
Mihalef, Viorel *research scientist*
Mitchell, James Kenneth *geography educator*
Nachtigal, Patricia *lawyer*
Nowakowski, Richard Stanley *medical educator, director*
Ozel, Tugrul *engineering educator, researcher*
Pan, Long *chemist*
Pylyshyn, Zenon W. *science educator*
Ransome, Ronald D. *physics professor*
Robbins, Allen Bishop *physics professor*
Rosalsky, Barbara Ellen *artist, community health nurse*
Sahota, Amrik *medical researcher, educator, lab administrator*
Schiano, Greg *college football coach*
Shatkin, Aaron Jeffrey *biochemistry educator*
Sit, Ping-Fai *research scientist*
Smith, Bob *state legislator, lawyer*
Sopranzetti, Ben J. *finance educator, investment banker*
Stringer, C. Vivian (Charlene Vivian Stringer) *women's college basketball coach*
Tischfield, Jay Arnold *genetics educator*
Vieth, Wolf Randolph *chemical engineering educator*
Volfson-Doubova, Elena *psychiatrist, researcher*
Wadsworth, William Graham *biology professor, researcher*
West, Mark Otto *psychology professor*
Wielunski, Leszek Stanislaw *materials scientist*
Wininger, Michael T. *research scientist*
Witz, Gisela *research scientist, educator*
Younis, Ossama *research scientist*
Zhilina, Irina *language educator*
Zimmermann, Frank Martin *physicist, educator, research scientist*

Pitman
Cloues, Edward Blanchard, II, *lawyer*

Plainfield
Allen (Sup), Stuart *film and television company executive*
Da Rold, Joseph Hugh *library director, museum director*
Ellington II, Michael L. *lawyer*
Frost, David *retired biology professor, medical editor, consultant*
Limpert, John H., Jr. *fund raising executive*
Mazur, Thomas A. *music educator*
Ruiz, Pedro Javier *education educator*

Plainsboro
Baeckler, Virginia Van Wynen *librarian, writer*
Brolin, Robert Edward *physician, surgeon*
Chau, Wai Yip *surgeon*
Devine, Hugh James, Jr. *retired marketing executive*
Spiegel, Phyllis *public relations consultant, journalist*

Point Pleasant
Greene, Ellin *library service educator*

Pomona
Carracino, Christine *mathematics professor*
Fiedler, Marcia Stein *religious studies educator*
Fleck, Jessica I. *psychology professor*
Herath, Ajantha *education educator*
Jacobson, Kristin J. *literature educator*
Jones, Joseph E. *elementary school educator*
Latourette, Audrey Wolfson *law educator*
Lenard, Georgeann Terese *english educator*
Lester, David *psychology educator*
Lewis, Margaret E. *biology professor*
Lubenow, William Cornelius *historian, educator*
Mallett, Mark Edmund *theater educator*
Sharon, Yitzhak Yaakov *physicist, educator*
Wood, Roger Conant *biology professor, researcher*

Pompton Plains
Gummel, Hermann Karl *retired physicist, lab administrator*
Kettlewood, Bea Card *artist, retired educator*
Pischl, Adolph John *school administrator*
Shrem, Charles Joseph *metals corporation executive*

Port Norris
Canzonier, Walter Jude *shellfish aquaculturist*

Princeton
Aarsleff, Hans *linguistics educator*
Adler, Stephen Louis *physicist*
Altmann, Stuart Allen *biologist, educator*
Amosova, Olga *molecular biologist, consultant*
Anderson, Ellis Bernard *retired lawyer, pharmaceutical executive*
Anderson, Philip W. *physicist*
Armstrong, Richard Stoll *minister, educator, poet*
Arnheim, Juliette O'Neil *chemist, librarian, consultant*
Austin, Robert Hamilton *physics professor*
Balch, Stephen Howard *professional society administrator*
Bassler, Bonnie L. *molecular biologist*
Beitz, Charles R. *political scientist, educator*
Belshaw, George Phelps Mellick *bishop*
Bergman, Edward Jonathan *lawyer, educator*
Bergman, Richard Isaac *health information executive*
Bermann, Sandra Lekas *English language educator*
Bhadury, Punyasloke *molecular ecologist*
Billington, David Perkins *civil engineering educator*
Bishop, George Reginald, Jr. *foreign language educator*
Blinder, Alan Stuart *economist, educator*
Bodman, Richard Stockwell *telecommunications executive*
Bogan, Elizabeth Chapin *economist, educator*
Bogucki, Peter Ignatius *archaeologist*
Bombieri, Enrico *mathematician, educator*
Bowersock, Glen Warren *retired historian, educator*
Bramnick, Michael Richard *lawyer, energy executive*
Brombert, Victor Henri *literature educator, author*
Brooks, Peter (Preston) *literature educator, department chairman, writer*
Brown, Leon Carl *historian, educator*
Brown, Peter Robert Lamont *historian, history professor*
Bunnell, Peter Curtis *retired art educator, curator*
Burger, Leslie B. *library director, library association executive*
Campbell, Robert Emmett *retired health products executive*
Carr, Marcus Eugene, Jr. *internist*
Carter, Emily Ann *physical chemist, researcher, educator*
Carver, David Harold *retired pediatrician*
Cava, Robert J. *chemistry professor*
Cavanaugh, James Henry *health products executive, retired federal official*
Chaikin, Paul M. *physicist*
Chamberlin, John Stephen *investor, consumer products company executive*
Chang, Sun-Yung Alice *mathematics professor*
Cheiten, Marvin Harold *playwright, manufacturing executive*
Christman, Edward Arthur *physicist*
Christopherson, Elizabeth Good *foundation executive*
Coffey, Joseph Irving *political scientist, educator*
Connor, Geoffrey Michael *lawyer*
Cook, Michael Allan *social sciences educator*
Cooper, John Madison *philosophy educator*
Corngold, Stanley Alan *language educator, writer*
Corr, Donald Clayton *psychologist*
Craigie, James R. *consumer products and former sports equipment apparel company executive*
Crane, David W. *energy executive*
Crossley, Helen Martha *public opinion analyst, research consultant*
Davidson, Ronald Crosby *physicist, researcher*
Davies, Robert Abel III *consumer products company executive*
Dawes, Trevor A. *school librarian*
Debenedetti, Pablo Gaston *chemical engineering professor*
Deligne, Pierre René *mathematician*
Deming, James C. *history professor*
Desai, Kalpit Vikrambhai *biomedical engineer, researcher*
Dilkhin, Stanislav S. *research scientist*
Diller, Elizabeth E. *architect, educator, artist*
Dovey, Brian Hugh *health care products company executive, venture capitalist*
Drakeman, Lisa N. *biotechnologist*
Dreizin, Edward Leonid *physicist, researcher*
Duncan, Dianne Walker *elementary school educator*
Dyson, Freeman John *retired physics professor*
Engel, J. Mark *ophthalmologist*
Enquist, Lynn William *molecular biologist, educator*
Ermolaev, Herman Sergei *Slavic languages educator*
Fan, Jianqing *finance educator, director*
Fefferman, Charles Louis *mathematics professor*
Fisch, Nathaniel Joseph *physicist*
Fitch, Val Logsdon *physics professor*
Fleming, John Vincent *humanities educator*
Flexon, Robert C. *energy executive*
Florey, Klaus Georg *chemist, pharmaceutical consultant*
Ford, Andrew Laughlin *ancient language educator*
Ford, Jeremiah III *architect*
Fox, Mary Ann Williams *librarian*
Freeland, Clint *energy executive*
Fresco, Jacques Robert *biochemist, educator*
Friedberg, Aaron Louis *political science professor*
Ganoe, Charles Stratford *banker, consultant*
Gear, Charles William *computer scientist*
George, Thomas *artist*
Ghasemi, Seifi *chemicals executive*
Gibbons, Francis Clifford *lawyer, writer*
Gillham, John Kinsey *chemical engineering professor*
Giordmaine, Joseph Anthony *physicist*
Girgus, Joan Stern *psychologist, educator, director*
Glassman, Irvin *mechanical and aeronautical engineering educator, consultant*
Gmachl, Claire *electrical engineer, educator*
Goddard, Peter *academic administrator, mathematical physicist*
Goldston, Robert J. *research scientist*
Gordenker, Leon *political science professor*
Gould, James L. *biology professor*
Grabar, Oleg *retired art educator*
Grafton, Anthony Thomas *history professor*
Grant, Barbara Rosemary *research scientist*
Grant, Peter Raymond *biologist, researcher, educator*
Graves, Michael *architect, educator*
Gray, Nancy Wicklund *librarian, educator*
Grigger, Jane Elizabeth *earth science educator, photographer*
Grisham, Larry Richard *physicist*
Grossman, Gene M. *economics professor*
Grover, Gary James *pharmacologist*
Groves, John Taylor III *chemist, educator*
Gund, Gordon *venture capitalist, investment company executive*
Gunning, Robert Clifford *mathematician, educator*
Haberman, Shelby Joel *statistician, educator*
Halyo, Valerie *physics professor*
Harman, Gilbert Helms *philosophy educator*
Harvey, Norman Ronald *retired finance company executive*
Hekmatshoar, Bahman *research scientist*
Hermann, Janie L. *librarian*
Hillier, J(ames) Robert *architect*
Hochschwender, Karl Albert *international trade and government relations consultant*
Hodges, Neil *psychologist*
Hoebel, Bartley Gore *psychologist, educator*
Hollander, Robert B., Jr. *retired romance languages educator*
Hollander, Toby Edward *education educator*
Holt, Philetus Havens III *architect*
Howarth, William (Louis) *literature and language professor, writer*
Howell, David Luke *history professor*
Hynes, Samuel *language educator, writer*
Israel, Jonathan I. *history professor*
Itzkowitz, Norman *history professor*
Jeffers, Beverly Maynard *volunteer*
Jeffery, Peter Grant *musicologist, fine arts educator*
Jenkins, Edward Beynon *research astronomer*
Johnston, Robert Fowler *venture capitalist*
Jordan, William Chester *historian, educator*
Joyce, Carol Bertani *social studies educator*
Kahn, Eiko Taniguchi *artist*

Kahneman, Daniel *psychology professor*
Kang, Yibin *medical educator, researcher*
Kaplowitz, Karen (Jill) *lawyer, consultant*
Kateb, George Anthony *political science professor*
Katz, Stanley Nider *law educator*
Keeley, Edmund LeRoy *literature educator, writer, translator*
Keephart, Lydia Fabbro *lawyer, mediator*
Keevey, Richard Francis *federal and state official, educator*
Keller, Suzanne *sociologist, psychotherapist*
Kenen, Peter Bain *economist, educator*
Kenny, Jane M. *environmental and energy policy consulting executive*
Keohane, Robert Owen *political scientist, educator*
Khan, Sajid A. *management consultant, entrepreneur*
Knoepflmacher, Ulrich Camillus *literature educator*
Koepplin, Leslie W. *historian*
Kogan, Nathan *psychologist, consultant*
Kohli, Atul *political science professor*
Krugman, Paul Robin *economics professor, columnist, writer*
Kurtzer, Daniel Charles *public policy educator, former ambassador*
Lam, Sau-Hai (Harvey) *aeronautical engineering educator*
Landgraf, Kurt M. *educational association administrator*
Langlands, Robert Phelan *mathematician, educator*
Lavizzo-Mourey, Risa Juanita *medical foundation administrator*
Law, Stuart A., Jr. *lawyer*
Lazarus, Arnold Allan *psychologist, educator*
Lechner, Bernard Joseph *consulting electrical engineer*
Lee, Francis Y. *pharmacologist*
Leetmaa, Ants *environmental services administrator, educator*
Leonard, Naomi Ehrich *aerospace engineer, educator*
Lerner, Ralph *architect, university dean*
Levin, Simon Asher *mathematician, ecologist, educator*
Levine, Richard James *publishing executive*
Lewis, Bernard *retired social studies educator*
Lieb, Elliott Hershel *physicist, mathematician, educator*
Lippincott, Walter Heulings, Jr. *retired publishing executive*
Liu, Bede *electrical engineering educator*
Logue, Judith Felton *psychoanalyst, educator*
Long, Frank Wesley, Jr. *chemist*
Louka, Elli *lawyer, consultant*
Luchak, Frank Alexander *lawyer*
Lumpkin, John Robert *public health physician, state official*
Mahmoud, Adel A. *physician, molecular biologist, educator*
Maldacena, Juan Martin *physicist, researcher*
Malkiel, Burton Gordon *economist, educator*
Manabe, Syukuro *meteorologist*
Marks, James S. *public health service administrator*
Maskin, Eric Stark *economics professor*
Mauzerall, Denise L. *science educator*
McGowan, Angela Kay *public information officer*
Mc Pherson, James Munro *history professor*
McVicker, Charles Taggart *artist, educator*
Miller, George Armitage *psychologist, educator*
Mills, Bradford *merchant banker*
Mirzakhani, Maryam *mathematician*
Mittleberg, Eric Michael *pharmaceutical executive*
Moote, A. Lloyd *history professor*
Morris, Mac Glenn *advertising executive*
Mueller, Peter Sterling *psychiatrist, educator*
Mulchinock, David Steward *lawyer*
Muldoon, Paul B. *poet, educator*
Murakami, Eisuke *biochemist*
Murphy, J. Andrew (Drew Murphy) *energy executive, lawyer*
Nadeem, Tamer M. *research scientist*
Nash, John Forbes, Jr. *mathematician, researcher*
Nehamas, Alexander *philosophy educator*
Notterman, Daniel A. *pediatrician, educator*
O'Donnell, Laurence Gerard *retired managing editor*
Okounkov, Andrei *mathematics professor*
Onstott, Tullis *microgeologist, geology professor*
Opaits, Dmitry Florievich *research scientist*
Oppenheimer, Michael *physicist*
Orlanski, Isidoro *meteorologist, researcher*
Orphanides, Nora Charlotte *ballet educator*
Ostriker, Jeremiah Paul *astrophysicist, educator*
Paret, Peter *historian*
Paxson, Christina Hull *dean, economics and public affairs professor*
Pechen, Alexander *theoretical physicist, researcher*
Pfister, Marc *consumer products company executive, physician, researcher*
Pien, Howard *pharmaceutical executive*
Pimley, Kim Jensen *financial training consultant*
Poor, Harold Vincent *engineering educator*
Portes, Alejandro *sociologist, educator*
Potasek, Mary Joyce *physicist, researcher*
Powell, Warren B. *engineering educator*
Prevost, Jean Herve *civil engineer, educator*
Putukian, Margot *sports medicine physician*
Quandt, Richard Emeric *economics professor*
Ragan, John W. *energy executive*
Rampersad, Arnold *writer, literature educator*
Rauschenberger, Robert *psychologist, educator*
Rodgers, Daniel Tracy *historian, educator*
Rosenzweig-Lipson, Sharon Joy *pharmacologist*
Royce, Barrie Saunders Hart *physicist, researcher*
Rozman, Gilbert Friedell *sociologist, educator*
Rubin, Dorothy Molly *language educator, writer*
Russel, William Bailey *engineering educator*
Rutherford, Paul Harding *physicist*
Sandman, Peter M. *risk management consultant*
Schreyer, William Allen *retired finance company executive*
Scott, David Rodick *retired lawyer, educator*
Scott, Joan Wallach *historian, educator*
Seawright, James L., Jr. *sculptor, educator*
Seiberg, Nathan *physics professor*
Shapiro, Harold Tafler *economics professor, former academic administrator*
Shear, Theodore Leslie, Jr. *archaeologist, educator*
Shenk, Thomas Eugene *molecular biology educator, academic administrator*
Shimizu, Yoshiaki *art historian*
Sierocki, John Stanley *oncologist*
Sigal, Leonard H. *physician*
Sinai, Yakov G. *theoretical mathematician, educator*
Smith, Arthur John Stewart *physicist, researcher*
Soboyejo, Winston Oluwole *materials engineering educator, researcher*
Song, Zhen *electrical engineer, researcher*
Spiro, Thomas George *chemistry professor*
Stein, Elias M. *mathematician, educator*
Stengel, Robert Frank *engineering and applied science educator*
Sterzer, Fred *research physicist*
Stouffer, Ronald Jay *meteorologist*
Stout, Jeffrey Lee *religious studies educator*
Sullivan, Diane P. *lawyer*
Taylor, Edward Curtis *chemistry professor*
Taylor, Joseph Hooton, Jr. *radio astronomer, physicist*
Theivakumar, Jeyakumary Ruby *lawyer*
Tilghman, Shirley Marie *academic administrator, biology professor*
Tomlinson, W. John *physicist, researcher*
Torquato, Salvatore *materials scientist, chemistry professor*
Trainer, Karin A. *librarian*
Tsui, Daniel C. *electrical engineer, physicist*
Ueda, Atsuko *educator*
VanMarcke, Erik Hector *civil engineer, educator*
Villarini, Gabriele *geophysicist*
Voevodsky, Vladimir *mathematician*
von der Schmidt, Edward III *neurosurgeon, veterinarian*
Wallace, Walter L. *retired sociologist, educator*
Walter, Hugo Günther *humanities educator, poet*
Wang, Peiyuan *scientist*
Wei, James *chemical engineering professor, academic dean*
Weigert, Laura *history professor*
Weinman, Steven Alan *emergency nurse practitioner, educator, writer, health facility administrator*
Weiss, Renée Karol *editor, musician*
West, Charles Converse *retired theologian*
West, Cornel Ronald *humanities educator, writer*
Western, Bruce *sociologist, educator*
Westoff, Charles Francis *demographer, educator*
White, Barbara Ann *composer*
White, Morton Gabriel *philosopher, writer, historian, retired educator*
White, Roscoe Beryl *research physicist, educator*
Whitman, Christine Todd (Christie Whitman) *consulting firm executive, former federal agency administrator, former governor*
Wieschaus, Eric F. *molecular biologist, educator*
Wilentz, Sean *historian, educator, writer*
Wiles, Andrew J. *mathematician, educator*
Willig, Robert Daniel *economics professor*
Willingham, Warren Willcox *psychologist*
Wilmerding, John *art historian, educator, curator*
Witkin, Evelyn Maisel *retired geneticist*
Witten, Edward *mathematical physicist, educator*
Wood, Eric Franklin *earth and environmental sciences educator*
Yang, Hua *video coding expert*
Yao, Nan *educational association administrator*
Zakian, Virginia Araxie *molecular biology professor*
Zelizer, Viviana *sociologist, educator*
Ziolkowski, Theodore Joseph *literature educator, writer*

Princeton Junction
Amenta, Peter Sebastian *pathologist, dean*
Butorac, Frank George *librarian, educator*
Cohen, Florence Emery *retired financial services executive*
Mandel, Andrea Sue *packaging engineer*
Norback, Craig Thomas *writer*
Vahaviolos, Sotirios John *electrical engineer, researcher, engineering executive*

Rahway
Bloomfield, Daniel Mark *pharmaceutical executive*
Haupt, Richard M. *pharmaceutical executive*
Imbriglio, Jason E. *chemist, researcher*
Kaczorowski, Gregory John *biochemist, researcher, science administrator*
Truppo, Matthew David *biochemical engineer, researcher*
Xu, Jinyou *medical researcher*

Ramsey
Libin, Laurence Elliot *retired curator*

Randolph
Charm, Joel Barry *management consultant*
Chen, Kevin S. *management executive, consultant, educator*
Ghosh, Ajit Kumar *daycare administrator*
Goldman, Phyllis E. *psychology educator*
Strutin, Millard Desmond *surgeon*
Timbilla, James Abangah *entomologist, educator*
Whildin, Leonora Porreca *retired nursing educator*
Zelante, Thomas Andrew *lawyer*

Raritan
Fischer, Seth H.Z. *pharmaceutical executive*
Tortoriello, William Joseph *pharmaceutical executive*

Red Bank
Braddom, Randall Lee *physiatrist, educator*
Brown, Valerie Anne *psychotherapist, social worker, educator*
Carmody, Margaret Jean *retired social worker*
Clever, Marcia Sue *psychiatrist*
Etemad, Shahab *physicist, director*
Gutentag, Patricia Richmond *social worker, family counselor, occupational therapist*
Hertz, Daniel Leroy, Jr. *entrepreneur*
Hovnanian, Ara K. *real estate developer*
Hovnanian, Kevork S. *real estate developer*
Kazovsky, Leonid Gregory *electrical engineer, educator*
McWhinney, Madeline H. (Mrs. John Denny Dale) *economist, director*
Meyer, Robert Alan *management consultant*
Murphy, Philip D. *investment company executive, professional sports team executive*
Reinhart, Peter Sargent *lawyer*
Scaccia, Frank John *facial surgeon, otolaryngologist*
Smith, Kevin *film director, writer, actor*
Sorsby, James Larry *home building company executive*

Richwood
Robinette, Joseph Allen *playwright*

Ridgefield
Chmerkovskiy, Maksim *dancer*
Tracey, Matthew Sean *musician, educator*

Ridgefield Park
Cook, Steven *marketing executive*
Nagy, Christa Fiedler *biochemist*

Ridgewood
Baddoura, Rashid Joseph *emergency physician*
Brizzio, Mariano E. *thoracic surgeon, educator*
Clements, Lynne Fleming *marriage and family therapist, application developer*
Cutrona, Louis John, Jr. *computer system designer, neuroscientist*
Farrell, Gregory Alan *biomedical engineer*
Fox, Ingrid *curator*
Friedrich, Margret Cohen *guidance and student assistance counselor*
Hansmann, Ralph Emil *investment executive, director*
Harris, Micalyn Shafer *lawyer, arbitrator, mediator, educator, consultant*
Healey, Frank Henry *retired chemicals executive*
Kiernan, Richard Francis *publisher*
Kuiken, Diane (Dee) Marie *science educator*
Le May, Moira Kathleen *retired psychology educator*
Nachman, David Howard *lawyer*
O'Leary, Paul Gerard *retired insurance company executive*
Ostling, Richard Neil *journalist*
Seigel, Jonas Kearney *prosecutor*
Smethurst, E(dward) William, Jr. *investment banker*
Warner, John Edward *advertising executive*

River Edge
Gass, Manus M. *accountant, construction executive*

River Vale
Verebey, Karl Geza *toxicologist, pharmacologist, educator*

Riverdale
Bullough, John Frank *musician, educator*

Riverton
O'Brien, James Jerome *construction management consultant*
Rabil, Mitchell Joseph *lawyer*

Rivervale
Posamentier, Alfred Steven *retired mathematics educator, dean*

Rockaway
Steier, Audrey Keller *music educator*

Roseland
Bennett, John K. *lawyer*
Benson, James Bracken *lawyer, computer company executive*
Brody, Jane L. *lawyer*
Butler, Gary C. *computer company executive*
Byrne, Brendan Thomas, Sr. *former governor*
Cummis Sandlaufer, Deborah Gwen *lawyer*
Cutler, Laurence Jeffrey *lawyer*
Eakeley, Douglas Scott *lawyer*
Eichler, Burton Lawrence *lawyer*
Farber, Zulima V. *lawyer, former state attorney general*
Fuller, S(heri) Marce *energy executive*
Golden, Robert Charles *finance company executive*
Malafronte, Donald *health planning consultant*
Martone, S. Michael *computer company executive*
Mazie, David A. *lawyer*
McMahon, Edward Richard *lawyer*
Morrison, Debra Lynn *financial planner*
Panagides, John *pharmacologist*
Positan, Wayne John *lawyer*
Post, John N. *lawyer*
Reidy, Christopher R. *computer company executive*
Smith, Wendy Hope *lawyer*
Sugahara, Byron Masahiko *transportation executive*
Taylor, Lisa Deitsch *lawyer, arbitrator, mediator*
Vanderbilt, Arthur T., II, *lawyer*
Yun, Edward Joon *lawyer*

Roselle
Wilson, Arthur Theodore *education consultant*

Rutherford
Gerety, Peter Leo *archbishop emeritus*
Suarez, Sally Ann Tevis *health facility administrator, nurse, consultant*

Saddle Brook
Cohn, Albert Linn *lawyer*
Hickey, William V. *manufacturing executive*

Saddle River
Lasser, Gail Maria *psychologist, educator*
Noyes, Robert Edwin *publisher, writer*

Salem
Kates, Joan M. *art educator*

Scotch Plains
Klock, John Henry *lawyer*
Kraemer, Ira B. *symphony conductor*
Lipton, Bronna Jane *marketing communications executive*
Shaw, Alan *lawyer*

Sea Bright
Plummer, Dirk Arnold *chemical, electrical, and electronics engineer*

Sea Isle City
Ramsey, George Bernard *retired financial planner*
Tull, Theresa Anne *retired diplomat*

Secaucus
Austin, Ski *sports association executive*
Criqui, Robert J. *sports association executive*
Crovitz, Charles K. *former retail executive*
Crowley, Monica *political commentator*
Denenberg, David Scott *sports association executive, lawyer*
Hellmuth, Stephen M. *sports association executive*
Herndon, John Laird *accounting firm executive*
Koenig, William S. *sports association executive*
Larkin, Barry Louis *sportscaster, retired professional baseball player*
Liao, Paul Foo-Hung *electronics executive*
Payton, Gary Dwayne *sportscaster, retired professional basketball player*
Ratigan, Dylan *journalist, financial news correspondent*
Syms, Marcy *retail executive*
Webber, Chris (Mayce Edward Christopher Webber III) *sportscaster, retired professional basketball player*
Weil, Laura A. *apparel executive*
Weissmann, Arnie *editor-in-chief, travel writer*

Sewell
Brookins, Birdena *literature and language professor*
Crouse, Farrell R. *lawyer*
DePace, Nicholas Louis *physician*
Hallenbeck, Ralph Henry *retired educational administrator*

Shiloh
Garrison, John Raymond *organization executive*

Short Hills
Alesio, Steven W. *financial services company executive*
Austin, Danforth Whitley *media executive*
Chaiken, Bernard Henry *internist, gastroenterologist*
Gibson, William Lee *financial consultant*
Harwood, Jerry *market research executive*
Hauck, Walter S. III *financial services company executive*
Hazlehurst, Robert Purviance, Jr. *lawyer*
MacKinnon, Malcolm D(avid) *retired insurance company executive*
Mathew, Sara *corporate financial executive*
Mebane, William Black *controller, financial consultant*
Ogden, Maureen Black *state legislator*
Price, Michael F. *money management executive*
Robbins-Wilf, Marcia *educational consultant*
Schaefer, Charles James III *advertising executive, consultant*
Schaefer, Eleanor Montville *retired publishing executive*
Schirmeister, Charles F. *retired lawyer*
Siegfried, David Charles *retired lawyer*
Wharton, Lennard *engineering company executive*
Winter, Ruth Grosman (Mrs. Arthur Winter) *journalist*

Shrewsbury
Michaelson, Peter Lee *lawyer*
Rose, Michael Ian *plastic surgeon*

Sicklerville
Browna, Jo McIntyre *nurse*
Miller, Audrey Thornton *retired vice principal*
Simpson, Eugene Thamon *music educator, singer*

Skillman
Diaz, Teresita Perez *chemist*
Eiger, Richard William *retired publisher*
Rai, Sanjiv *research and development company executive, educator*
Tenenbaum, Bernard Hirsh *entrepreneur, educator*

Somerset
Armstrong, David Francis *environmental engineer, consultant*
Brophy, Joseph Thomas *computer company executive*
DeMonic, Betty Lee *music educator*
De Salva, Salvatore Joseph *retired pharmacologist, toxicologist*
Ilogu, Noel Obiajulu *physician*
Lichtig, Leo Kenneth *health economist*
Rosenberg, Seymour *psychologist, educator*
Staub, Carol Anne *artist*
Tracy, Janet Lynn *psychologist, consultant*
Tsou, Yu-Min *science administrator, chemistry researcher*
Wallfesh, Henry Maurice *communications executive, writer*

Somerville
Albin, Barry Todd *state supreme court justice*
Ferguson, Kevin P. *business development manager*
Fleischman, Joseph Jacob *lawyer*
Hutcheon, Peter David *lawyer*
Ligorano, Michael Kenneth *lawyer*
O'Brien, Walter John *retired artist management executive, writer*
Sivanesan, Sivaruban *mechanical engineer*

South Amboy
Ghezzi, Lawrence Victor *media specialist, educator*

South Orange
Bao, Xue-Ming *librarian, educator*
Gainsburg, Roy Ellis *publishing executive, researcher*
Hansell, Phyllis Shanley *nursing educator, administrator, researcher, consultant*
Hoffert, Eric Michael *application developer, information technology executive*
Holmes, Paul A. *academic administrator*
Leung, Edwin Pak-wah *social studies educator, researcher*
Loesch, Martha M. *academic librarian*
Long, Philip Lee *information systems executive*
Molesky, Mark *history professor*
Nowik, John David *musician, educator*
Talar, Anita Louise *university librarian*

South Plainfield
Kennedy, John William *engineering company executive*
Kwon, Ik Hyun *internist*

Southampton
Callaway, Ben Anderson *retired journalist*
O'Connor, Sheryl Broderick *retired literature and language educator*

Sparta
Bhattacharyya, Dev *information technology executive, consultant*
Jacobs-Quam, Vivien Marie *retired music educator*
McMeen, Elmer Ellsworth III *lay minister, musician, retired lawyer*
McMeen, Sheila Taenzler *retired lawyer*
Spence, Robert Leroy *publishing executive*

Spring Lake
De Pinies, Felix *retired physician*
D'Luhy, John James *investment banker*
Harrigan, John Thomas, Jr. *physician, obstetrician, gynecologist*
O'Connor, Francis X. *financial executive*

Springfield
Kerner, Michael Bernard *gastroenterologist*
Mamidwar, Sachin Sureshrao *medical products executive*
Mytelka, Arnold Krieger *lawyer*
O'Desky, Ilyse Hope *psychologist, educator*
Shilling, A. Gary *economist, consultant*
Weigele, Richard Sayre *police officer*

Stewartsville
Busch, Beverly Gail *English and literature educator, dean*

Stirling
Walsh, Peter Joseph *physics professor*

Stockton
Mahon, Robert *photographer*
Schoenherr, John (Carl) *artist, illustrator*

Stratford
Kosciuk, Mary C. *medical researcher, educator*
Levitas, Andrew Stephen *child psychiatrist, educator*

Succasunna
London, Fran *special education educator*

Summit
Baker, Alden *artist*
Caming, H. W. William *retired lawyer, consultant*
Carniol, Paul J. *plastic and reconstructive surgeon, otolaryngologist*
Duberstein, Joel Lawrence *internist, pulmonologist, educator*
Fuess, Billings Sibley, Jr. *advertising executive*
Fukui, Hatsuaki *retired electrical engineer, art historian*
Gerathy, E. Carroll *retired insurance company executive, real estate developer*
Greenberg, Rosalie *child psychiatrist*
Halperin, John Jacob *neurology educator, researcher*
Kenyon, Edward Tipton *lawyer*
Lewis, Donald Emerson *banker*
Lijoi, Peter Bruno *lawyer*
Lovett, Juanita Pelletier *clinical psychologist*
Macioce, Frank Michael *lawyer, financial services company executive*
Mueller, Paul Henry *retired bank executive*
Oppenheimer, John Jacob *allergist, immunologist*
Pfaltz, Hugo Menzel, Jr. *lawyer*
Phillips, James Charles *physicist, researcher*
Rosensweig, Ronald Ellis *chemical engineer, consultant*
Wang, Er-Jia *drug safety researcher*
Woller, James Alan *lawyer*
Zachary, Louis George *chemical company consultant*

Sussex
Puzio, Bonnie Jean *special education educator*

Swedesboro
Lovell, Theodore *electrical engineer, consultant*

Tabernacle
DiBella, Russell Thomas *federal investigator*

Teaneck
Alperin, Richard Martin *social worker, psychoanalyst*
Brownridge, Sonia Marie *language educator*
Brudner, Helen Gross *history professor, political science professor*
Cassimatis, Peter John *economics professor*
Connola, Donald Pascal, Jr. *management consultant*
Cowan, Wallace Edgar *retired lawyer*
D'Souza, Francisco B. *information technology executive, consultant*
Ehrlich, Ira Robert *mechanical engineering consultant*
Farrell, Mary Lupiani *education educator*
Fein, Lawrence Seth *investment advisor*
Feinberg, Robert S. *plastics company executive, marketing professional*
Goldfarb, Joel Peter *internist, gastroenterologist*
Gordon, Lois G. *language educator*
Holmes, Miriam H. *publisher*
Indick, Janet *sculptor*
Ladenheim, Jules Calvin *neurosurgeon*
Lafer, Fred Seymour *data processing executive*
Lichtenstein, Robert *education executive*
Lipsitz, Joshua Dan *psychologist, educator*
Mabli, Peter H. *history educator*
Meno, John Peter *religious organization administrator*
Murthy, Vadiraja Venkatesa *retired biochemist, researcher, educator*
Novogroder, Michael *pediatric endocrinologist*
Reid, Rufus Lamar *jazz bassist, composer*
Reinish, Gloria Brooks *electrical engineer, educator*
Scotti, Dennis Joseph *educator, researcher, consultant*
Stein-Smith, Kathleen *librarian, foreign language educator*
Tan, Alfredo Cheng *engineering educator, director*
Wallmann, Jeffrey Miner *author*
Warsawer, Harold Newton *real estate appraiser, consultant*
Weiss, Mitchell Joseph *librarian*
Wiener, Joel Howard *historian, educator*
Williams, John Alfred *educator, author*
Woerner, Alfred Ira *medical device manufacturer, educator*
Zwass, Vladimir *computer science and information systems educator*

Tenafly
Blank, Marion Sue *psychologist, educator*
Gerst, Paul Howard *physician*
Golomb, Frederick Martin *surgeon, educator*
Insana, Ron (Ronald Gerard Insana) *investment company executive, financial analyst*
Rudy, Dorothy Lucille *poet, educator*
Tall, Susan Porter *music educator*
Wechtler, Stephen Robert *library director*

Teterboro
Hagemann, Robert A. *health care company executive*
Mohapatra, Surya N. *laboratory executive*

Tinton Falls
Hoelzler, Michael Gebhard *veterinarian, surgeon*
Macdonald, Donald Arthur, Jr. *physician, surgeon*
Ostar, Allan William *educational consultant*
Priesand, Sally J. *rabbi*
Van Winkle, William *financial planner*

Titusville
Christopher, Klim *writer*
Cooper, Paul *retired mechanical engineer, director, researcher*
Girgis, Suzette *clinical pharmacologist, researcher*
Jain, Reema *pharmacist, pharmaceutical executive*
Manji, Husseini K. *pharmaceutical company executive, neuropsychopharmacologist*

Toms River
Bosley, Karen Lee Foley *language and communications educator*
Donaldson, Marcia Jean *lay worker*
Kanarkowski, Edward Joseph *data processing company executive*
Lauro, Dana *literature and language professor*
Tamm, Jayanti *writer*

Totowa
Peter, Samuel (Okon) *professional boxer*
Schady, Kathleen *pharmaceutical executive*

Trenton
Baron, Lisa Ann *environmental scientist*
Baroni, Bill (William E. Baroni Jr.) *state legislator*
Barry, Robert Christopher *environmental engineer*
Bigham, William J. *lawyer*
Blackburn, Audrey Peyton *lawyer*
Blake, Norma E. *library director*
Blando, James Douglas *research scientist*
Codey, Richard James (Dick Codey) *state legislator*
Corman, Randy *lawyer*
Corzine, Jon Stevens *Governor of New Jersey*
Cowen, Robert E. *federal judge*
Davy, Lucille E. *state official, school system administrator*
Demitry, Elpis Hope *retired music educator*
Donohue, Patricia Carol *academic administrator*
Fares, Louis George *surgeon, educator*
Fischer, Pamela Shadel *public relations executive*
George, Emery Edward *foreign language and studies educator, writer*
Gomez, William *orthopedist*
Green, Gerald B. *state legislator*
Greenberg, Morton Ira *federal judge*
Hoens, Helen E. *state supreme court justice*
Howard, Heather *state agency administrator*
Jasey, Neil N. *state banking agency administrator, retired lawyer*
Jones, Dale Edwin *public defender*
Jones, Sophia LaShawn *architect*
Kelly, Quentin Thorn *water and power company executive, writer*
LaVecchia, Jaynee *state supreme court justice*
Leipzig, Melvin *art educator*
Long, Virginia *state supreme court justice*
Marcus, Alan C. *public relations consultant*
Milgram, Anne M. *state attorney general*
Mohr, Daniel Reed *electronics engineer*
Obed, Leonora Rita Villegas *writer, educator*
Palmer, Douglas Harold *Mayor, Trenton, New Jersey*
Pruitt, George Albert *academic administrator*
Rabner, Stuart *state supreme court chief justice, former state attorney general*
Riccards, Michael Patrick *academic administrator*
Ritchey, Kenneth William *human services administrator*
Rivera-Soto, Roberto A. *state supreme court justice*
Rousseau, David R. *state treasurer*
Russell, Joyce Anne Rogers *retired librarian*
Scheiring, Michael James *college official*
Smallwood, Robert Albian, Jr. *retired secondary education educator*
Viscomi, Frank Joseph *pharmaceutical executive*
Vitale, Joseph F. *state legislator*
Wallace, John E. *state supreme court justice*
Wells, Nina Mitchell *Secretary of State, New Jersey*
Wilson, Tom *political organization administrator*
Zanna, Martin Thomas *physician*

Union
Adamson, Kunle Y. *economics professor, director*
Bottitta, Joseph Anthony *lawyer*
Castagna, Eugene A. *retail executive*
Cryan, Joseph P. *state legislator, political organization administrator*
DeMarco, Michael R. *history professor, writer*
Eisenberg, Warren *retail executive*
Feinstein, Leonard *retail executive*
Franklin, William George *manufacturing executive*
Kim, Youn-Suk Ernest *economist, educator*
Lederman, Susan Sturc *public administration professor*
Newman, Stephen Alexander *chemical engineer*
Norward, Josephine Norma *social work educator, consultant*
Pearlman, Bruce Allen *research scientist*
Rauch, Allan N. *lawyer*
Rogge, Rena Wolcott *librarian*
Shaw, Thomas M. *art historian, educator*
Shebitz, Daniela Joy *biology professor*
Temares, Steven H. *retail executive*
White, Robert Leslie Gordon, Jr. *aerospace transportation executive*
Zois, Constantine Nicholas Athanasios *meteorologist, educator*

Union City
Englese, Damon Joseph *director*

Upper Montclair
Chakraborty, Chandana *economics professor, department chairperson*
Gil, Eduardo *academic administrator*
San Vicente Portes, Luis *finance educator*
Tintle, Carmel Joseph *public relations executive*

Upper Saddle River
Cappitella, Mauro John *architect*

Vauxhall
Jacobs-Smith, Ruby Eudora *retired medical/surgical nurse, public health service officer*

Verona
Ayaso, Manuel *artist*

Vineland
Clinton, Lawrence Paul *psychiatrist*
Coant, Charles Ian *lawyer*
Schmid, Patti A. *library director*

Voorhees
Brahms, William Bernard *librarian, publisher, writer*
Glasofer, Eric David *allergist, immunologist, pediatrician, educator*
Lampert, S. Henry *retired dentist*
Leontiades, Milton *retired dean*
Litman, Bernard *electrical engineer, consultant*
Schneider, Orren *environmental engineer, researcher*
Schwartz, Bennett K. *dermatologist*
Siskin, Edward Joseph *engineering and construction company executive*
Somer, Robert A. *physician, educator*

Wall
Dugan, Mariellen *lawyer*
Height, Kelly A. *literature and language educator*
Monaco, Robert Anthony *radiologist*
Mudd, Mary Michaels *historian*
Nucciarone, A. Patrick *lawyer*
Sheprow, Matthew Warren *psychologist*

Wallington
Jarotski, Diane *guidance director*
Safira, Barabara *science educator*

Warren
Brundage, Maureen A. *lawyer, insurance company executive*
Cox, Robert C. *insurance company executive*
Degnan, John J. *insurance company executive, lawyer*
Feldman, Janie Lynn *psychologist*
Finnegan, John D. *insurance company executive*
Gerstman, Ned I. *insurance company executive*
Hennings, Dorothy Grant *education educator*
Knight, James P. *insurance company executive*
Krump, Paul J. *insurance company executive*
Maull, George Marriner *conductor, educator*
McElwee, Andrew Allison, Jr. *insurance company executive*
Morrison, Harold L., Jr. *insurance company executive*
O'Halloran, Patrick *psychologist*
O'Reilly, Michael *insurance company executive*
Raines, Marjorie D. *insurance company executive*
Robusto, Dino E. *insurance company executive*
Spiro, Richard Glenn *corporate financial executive*
Tomlinson, Janice Meyer *insurance company executive*
Ventantonio, James Bartholomew *lawyer*
Yang, Tsong-Toh (T.T.) *pharmacist, researcher*

Washington
Massimo, Anna Georgieva *medical educator*

Watchung
Michaelis, Paul Charles *engineering physicist executive*

Wayne
Babrowski, Claire Harbeck *retail executive*
Benedict, Theresa Marie *retired mathematics educator*
Bess, Alan L. *pharmaceutical executive, Physician Author*
Boire, Ron *retail executive*
Campanelli-Andreopoulos, Giuliana *economics professor*
Creasey, F. Clay *retail executive*
D'Andrea, Kathleen Claire *speech therapist*
Derby, Deborah *retail executive*
Friedman, Martin Burton *retired chemicals executive*
Garcia, Ofelia *art educator, administrator*
Geiger, David E. *engineer*
Gollance, Robert Barnett *ophthalmologist*
Heyman, Samuel J. *chemical manufacturing company executive*
Himmelstein, Jeffrey Alan *biology professor, researcher*
Pardo, Janette M. *archivist, librarian*
Rogoff, Paula Drimmer *English and foreign language educator*
Schwartz, David Jay *lawyer*
Speert, Arnold *academic administrator, chemistry educator*
Storch, Gerald L. (Jerry Storch) *retail executive*
Wise, Jeffrey Bruce *plastic surgeon, educator*

Weehawken
Hobson, Burton Harold *publishing executive*

West Caldwell
Dixon, Jo-Ann Conte *management consultant*
Page, Frederick West *retired business consultant*
Radest, Howard Bernard *clergyman, educator*
Schiff, Robert *healthcare consulting company executive*
Soderlind, Sterling Eugene *publishing executive, consultant*

West Deptford
Grasa, Gabriela Alexandra *chemist*

West Long Branch
Anderson, Sheri *theater educator*
Gaffney, Paul Golden, II, *academic administrator, retired military officer*
Gardner, Burdett Harmon *English language educator*
Lake, Elsa Taboada *retired language educator*
Lewandowski, Gary William, Jr. *psychology professor*
Zhang, Ying *science educator*

West Milford
Stelpstra, William John *minister*

West New York
Gruenberg, Elliot Lewis *electronics engineer and company executive*
Schmidt, Nancy Anne *psychotherapist*

West Orange
Atkins, Richard Bart *film and television producer*
Bornstein, Lester Milton *retired health facility administrator*
Brodkin, Roger Harrison *dermatologist, educator*
Casella, Anthony John *cardiologist*
De Lisa, Joel Alan *rehabilitation physician, research executive*
Gans, Bruce Merrill *physiatrist, educator, health facility administrator*
Gehl, Raymond Harold *psychiatrist, educator*
Ghali, Anwar Youssef *psychiatrist, educator*
Hill, George James *physician, educator*
Hwang, Karen *research scientist*
Jacobs, Fred M. *hospital administrator, former state agency administrator*
Jordan, Leo John *lawyer*
Kyle, Corinne Silverman *management consultant*
Langsner, Alan Michael *pediatric cardiologist*
Martin, Boston Faust *neurosurgeon*
McKinney, John Adams, Jr. *lawyer*
Richmond, Harold Nicholas *lawyer*
Rinsky, Judith Sue Lynn *foundation administrator, consultant, educator*
Rogal, Gary Jeffrey *cardiologist*
Samson, David *lawyer*
Whang, Matthew Ihn Seong *urologist*
Wylie, Glenn Richard *research scientist, educator*

West Paterson
Pataki, Andrew *bishop emeritus*
Skurla, William Charles *bishop*
Smith, Roy (R. Smith) *lawyer*
Varley, Herbert Paul *Japanese language and cultural history educator*

West Trenton
Farajollahi, Ary *health facility administrator*
Kennen, Jonathan Gary *ecologist*

Westfield
Bhagat, Phiroz Maneck *mechanical engineer*
Davoren, Steven Michael *marketing professional, psychologist*
Fitts, Leonard Donald *educational administrator*
Kean, Thomas H., Jr., (Thomas Howard Kean Jr.) *state legislator*
Simon, Martin Stanley *economist, consultant*

Westwood
Badalamenti, Anthony Francis *mathematician, researcher*
Cullen, Ruth Enck *reading specialist, elementary school educator*
Landzberg, Joel Serge *cardiologist*
Parish, J. Michael *lawyer, mutual fund executive, writer*

Wharton
Krosser, Howard S. *aerospace transportation executive*

Whippany
Ascione, Al Neil *electrical engineer, educator*
Vallee, Michelle Linda *pre-school educator*

Whitehouse Station
Anstice, David W. *pharmaceutical executive*
Clark, Richard T. *pharmaceutical company executive*
Deese, Willie A. *pharmaceutical executive*
Feingold, Mark Howard *lawyer*
Fiscus, Philip Wayne *underwriter*
Frazier, Kenneth C. *pharmaceutical executive, lawyer*
Graddick-Weir, Mirian *human resources specialist*
Kellogg, Peter Newman *pharmaceutical executive*
Kuhlik, Bruce Neil *lawyer*
McGuire, John Lawrence *pharmaceutical executive*
Scalet, J. Chris (James Christopher Scalet) *pharmaceutical executive*

Whiting
Foster, Eric Harold, Jr. *retail executive*
Willis, Ben *writer, artist*

Williamstown
Murashima, Kumiko *artist, educator*

Willingboro
Denslow, Deborah Pierson *primary school educator*
Ingerman, Peter Zilahy *systems analyst, consultant*

Wood Ridge
Micco, Vincent *banker*

Woodbridge
Barcan, Stephen Emanuel *lawyer*
Brown, Morris *lawyer*
Galkin, Samuel Bernard *orthodontist*
Gill, Raymond A., Jr. *lawyer*
Lepelstat, Martin L. *lawyer*
Seidman, Barbara R. *mathematics educator*

Woodbury
Donahue, Mary Lee *American English language professor, editor and author*
Doughty, A. Glenn *minister*

Woodcliff Lake
Pell, Elliott Louis *lawyer*

Woodland Park
Margulies, James Howard *editorial cartoonist*

Wyckoff
Gartner, Joseph John, II, *obstetrician, gynecologist*
Lavery, Daniel P. *management consultant*
Marcus, Linda Susan *dermatologist*
Munson, William Leslie *insurance company executive*

NEW MEXICO

Abiquiu
Howlett, Phyllis Lou *retired athletics administrator*

Alamogordo
Hayes, Randall *museum director*
Hobson, Suellen Ann Weber *retired elementary school educator*
Wills, Kimberly Kay *legal association administrator, educator*

Albuquerque
Adair, Kristin Lynn *computer scientist, director*
Adams, Mary Elizabeth *counselor, psychotherapist, writer*
Alexis, Tracy L. *project manager*
Alford, Steve (Steven Todd Alford) *men's college basketball coach*
Anaya, Rudolfo *writer, educator*
Anderson, Lawrence Keith *electrical engineer, consultant*
Andrews, Jonathan R. *electrical engineer, researcher*
Ardelean, Emil Valentin *mechanical engineer, researcher*
Aurbach, Robert Michael *legal executive, lawyer, consultant, photographer*
Baker, Chester Bird *agricultural economics professor*
Baker, Laura Kay *art gallery owner, writer*
Barry, Steve *sculptor, educator*
Baum, Carl Edward *electrical engineer, researcher*
Beach, Arthur O'Neal *lawyer*
Bell, Stoughton *computer scientist, mathematician, educator*
Berwick, Marianne *epidemiologist, educator*
Bova, Vincent Arthur, Jr. *lawyer, consultant, photographer*
Brown, Lee Kelvin *pulmonary, critical care and sleep medicine physician, researcher*
Burge, Mark R. *physician, educator*
Busani, Tito L. *research scientist, educator*
Byers, Steven N. *anthropologist, educator, computer professional*
Byrd, Wyatt *microbiologist, researcher*
Caplan, Edwin Harvey *retired dean, finance educator*
Cargo, David Francis *former Governor of New Mexico*
Caruso, Mark John *lawyer*
Chand, Hitendra S. *medical educator*
Chang, Barbara Karen *medical educator, director*
Chávez, Carmela Bernadette *lawyer, consultant*
Chavez, Martin Joseph *Mayor, Albuquerque, lawyer*
Chilton, Lance Alix *pediatrician*
Clark, Arthur Joseph, Jr. *mechanical engineer, retired electrical engineer*
Clarke, Gray B. *psychiatrist*
Clarke, Julia L. *library director*
Cole, Terri Lynn *organization administrator*
Colón, Brian S. *lawyer, political organization administrator*
Condie, Carol Joy *anthropologist, science administrator*
Conway, John E. *federal judge*
Croft, William Albert *linguistics educator*
Darbro, Nancy M. *nursing administrator*
Davidge, K. Genevieve *clinical social worker*
Davies, Thomas Mockett, Jr. *history professor*
Davis, Betty Bourbonia *real estate company executive*
de Gouvea, Raul *educator, consultant*
Deretic, Vojo Peter *cell biologist, educator*
Dickel, John Rush *physics professor*
Dorato, Peter *electrical and computer engineering educator*
Draper, Dorothy E. *middle school mathematics educator*
Dugan, Virginia Ruth *lawyer*
Duke, Wanda K. *artist*
Dutta Mazumdar, Rinita *social studies educator*
East, Daniel K. *small business owner*
Efremov, Anatoly Ivanovich *mechanical engineer, educator*
Eldredge, Jonathan DeForest *medical librarian, educator, social informaticist*
Emin, David *physicist*
Erickson, Sue Alice *health educator, consultant, nurse*
Everitt, Elizabeth M. *school system administrator*
Ewers, Robert Thomas *military officer*
Figueroa, Francisco Armando *aerospace defence executive, chief financial officer*
Flournoy, John Charles, Sr. *retired civilian military employee, officer*
Foster, Judi *interior designer, artist*
Fouratt, Gregory J. *prosecutor*
Freeman, Patricia Elizabeth *multi-media specialist, educational consultant*
Frias, Shirlee N. *elementary school educator*
Friberg, George Joseph *electronics company executive, entrepreneur*
Fry, Donald Edmund *surgeon*
Gahala, Estella Marie *writer, consultant*
Gander, John Edward *biochemistry educator*
Garcia, F. Chris *academic administrator, political scientist, educator*
Gibson, Ann L. *science educator, consultant*
Giller, Edward Bonfoy *retired government official, military officer*
Gordon, Larry Jean *sanitarian, environmental health consultant*
Graff, Pat Stuever *secondary school educator*
Green, Francis William *investment consultant, former missile scientist*
Hadas, Elizabeth Chamberlayne *editor*
Hall, Jerome William *research engineering educator*
Hannan, Barbara Ellon *philosophy educator, lawyer*
Hansen, Curtis LeRoy *federal judge*
Harden, Neva Ninette *writer, consultant*
Harris, David W. *academic administrator*
Harris, Fred R. *political scientist, educator, former United States Senator from Oklahoma*
Harris, Grant M. *biologist*
Hart, Frederick Michael *law educator*
Hartz, Harris L *federal judge*
Hayo, George Edward *management consultant*
Hopfinger, Anton Joseph *education educator, consultant*
Hovel, Esther Harrison *art educator*
Hsi, David Ching Heng *plant pathologist, geneticist, educator*
Hulsbos, Cornie Leonard *civil engineering educator*
Hutton, Paul Andrew *historian, educator, writer*
Ivnitski, Dmitri Markovich *bioelectrochemist*
Jaramillo, Mari-Luci *retired federal agency administrator*
Jayaweera, Sudharman K. *engineering educator, researcher*
Keleher, Michael Lawrence *lawyer*
Kempaiah, Prakasha *pathologist, researcher*
Knospe, William Herbert *medical educator*
Korman, Nathaniel Irving *research and development company executive*
Lambert, Jeffrey Scott *secondary school educator*
Lamphere, Louise *anthropology and women's studies educator*
Lang, Thompson Hughes *publishing executive*
Lange, Dale Lowell *language educator, researcher*
Lasater, W(illiam) Robert, Jr. *lawyer*
Lattman, Laurence Harold *retired academic administrator*
Lee, Sang-Joon *statistical professor*
Leeper, Ramon Joe *physicist*
Lewis, Linda Kathryn *librarian*
Lin, Henry C. *physician, researcher*
Lindeman, Robert Dean *medical educator, researcher, consultant*
Liotta, William A. *theater educator*
Long, Stephen Carrel Mike *lawyer*
Lopez, Nancy *sociologist*
Lucas, Spencer G. *paleontologist, curator, director*
Maddy, Coleen *editor*
Madrid, Patricia A. *former state attorney general*
Mapel, Douglas Wayne *epidemiologist, educator, pulmonologist, critical care specialist*
Martino, Sal *medical association administrator*
Martz, Clyde Ollen *retired lawyer*
Masefield, Oliver Leslie Peter *aerospace transportation executive, aerospace engineer*
May, Philip Alan *sociologist, educator*
Mays, G. Larry *criminal justice educator*
McCarthy, Denis M. *medical educator*
McCrady, Barbara Sachs *psychologist, educator*
Mock, Joan Bodet *music educator*
Nelson, Mary Carroll *artist, writer*
O'Brien, Daniel J. *lawyer*
Ofte, Donald *retired nuclear energy industry executive*
Omer, George Elbert, Jr. *retired orthopaedic surgeon, educator*
Orona, Joseph Ryan *information technology executive*
Orraj, Craig Allen *lawyer*
Ortiz, Patrick T. *lawyer*
Pabisch, Peter Karl *literature and language professor, humanities educator*
Parker, James Aubrey *federal judge*
Peña, Juan José *retired interpreter*
Phillips, John P. *neurologist, educator*
Pieper, John Albert *dean, educator*
Pirkl, James Joseph *industrial designer, educator, writer*
Polley, Richard Donald *microbiologist, chemist*
Priem, Richard Gregory *writer, executive*
Qi, Huaqing *special education educator*
Qualley, Charles Albert *art educator*
Raburn, Vern L. *air transportation executive, former Internet company executive*
Ramo, Roberta Cooper *lawyer*
Rayburn, William Frazier *obstetrician, gynecologist, educator*
Ré, Paul Bartlett *artist, writer, peace worker*
Rehder, Robert Richard *business management educator, management consultant*
Richter, Harvena *retired literature educator, poet*
Rivero, Dennis P. *orthopedist*
Robb, John Donald, Jr. *lawyer*
Roberts, Dennis William *retired construction executive*
Roehl, Jerrald J. *lawyer*
Roth, Paul Barry *dean, educator, emergency medicine physician*
Ruiz, Carlos Leon *nuclear scientist, physicist*
Rutherford, Thomas Truxtun, II, *state legislator, municipal official*
Salazar, John Paul *lawyer*
Sanchez, Robert Fortune *archbishop emeritus*
Sanchez, Victoria Wagner *science educator*
Schacht, Catherine Ann *musician, mezzo soprano*
Schmidly, David J. *academic administrator, biology professor*
Schuler, Alison Kay *lawyer*
Schwerin, Karl Henry *anthropology educator, researcher*
Scott, Bobby Randolph *biomedical researcher, writer*
Severs, William Floyd *actor*
Sheehan, Michael Jarboe *archbishop*
Shelnutt, John A. *physicist, researcher*
Silas, Pamala M. *professional society administrator*
Singer, Beverly R. *social sciences educator, film producer*
Sisk, Daniel Arthur *lawyer*
Sisson, Laurence P. *artist*
Slade, Lynn *lawyer*
Slate, Daniel Michael *economics professor*
Solimon, Ronald James (Ron Soliman) *museum administrator*
Spidle, Jake W. *history professor*
Stahl, Jack Leland *real estate company executive*
Sterba, Jeffry E. *energy executive*
Stevenson, Bradford Allen *management consultant*
Szasz, Ferenc M. *historian, educator*
Tchoumak, Adelina *corporate financial executive*
Truby, Betsy Kirby *artist, illustrator, photographer*
Tzamaloukas, Antonios Helias *nephrologist*
Uhlenhuth, Eberhard Henry *psychiatrist, educator*
Varela, Alan Mark *state agency administrator, lawyer*
Vigil, Charles J. *lawyer*
Vorobieff, Peter Vladimirovich *mechanical engineer, researcher*
Wade, Gaylia Suzanne *secondary school educator*
Waitzkin, Howard Bruce *internist, sociologist, educator*
Washburn, Kevin *dean, law educator*
Weh, Allen Edward *aviation executive*
Werder, Olaf H. *communications educator, researcher*
Westwood, Albert Ronald Clifton *management consultant, researcher*
White, Darren P. *protective services official*
Wild, Richard *music educator, musician*
Williams, Enid Roberta (Enid W. Troll) *psychologist, nurse*
Williams, Juanita Rosalie *artist*
Witkin, Joel-Peter *photographer, poet*
Wright, Cathy L. *museum director*
Yates, Harvey E. *oil industry executive, political organization administrator*

Arroyo Seco
McHenry, Jonathan Keith *artist*

Artesia
Jensen, Eric Reinhard *music educator*

Bayard
Foy, Thomas Paul *lawyer, retired state legislator, bank executive*

Bloomfield
Espinosa, Nancy Sweet *artist, anthropologist, curator*

Carlsbad
Christopherson, Ron *mathematics educator*
DeFeo, Dayna Jean *researcher*
Goad, Faith *nursing educator*
Pinching, Deborah Anne Odell *special education educator*

Cerrillos
Lutz, Nancy Cole *educational consultant*
Lutz, Raymond Price *retired industrial engineer, educator*

Clovis
Bradley, Walter D. *lieutenant governor, real estate broker*
Johnson, Janett *literature and language professor*

Corrales
Arkin, Michael Barry *lawyer, arbitrator, writer*
Campion, Kathleen Francis *lawyer, gifted and talented educator*
Eaton, Pauline *artist, educator*
Hooker, Van Dorn *architect, educator, artist*

Deming
Cilento-Foran, Deborah *lawyer, bank executive*

Dulce
Tiong, Tamra A. *elementary school educator*

Edgewood
Hamilton, Jerald *musician*

El Prado
Reading, Margery Schrock *psychology professor, artist*
Young, Jon Nathan *archaeologist*

Espanola
Fangyang, Shen *engineering educator*

Farmington
Anderson, Evelyn Louise *elementary school educator*
Carson, Theresa Ann *theater director*
Heil, Kenneth Del *retired botanist, consultant, researcher*
Mathers, Margaret *senior copy editor*
Perry, Mark Bradley *lawyer, minister*
Peterson Gerstner, Janet *English professor*
Schauer, Shelia I. *bank executive*
Titus, Victor Allen *lawyer*

Gallup
Cattaneo, Jacquelyn Annette Kammerer *artist, educator*
Edgewater, Virginia Lynn *language educator*
Fellin, Octavia Antoinette *retired librarian, historical researcher*
Wall, James S. *bishop*
Wilkins, Teresa J. *anthropologist, educator*

Grants
Barnes, Ina Jean *retired elementary educator*

High Rolls Mountain Park
Ellison, Luther Frederick *oil industry executive*

Hobbs
Connell, Linda Evans *literature and language professor*
Reagan, Gary Don *state legislator, lawyer*
Starling, Virginia R. *music educator, consultant*
Steinhaus, Richard Frederick *criminologist, educator*
Sumruld, Bill *history professor*

Hondo
Pawley, Ray L. *retired zoological park administrator, curator, conservationist*

Kirtland AFB
Degnan, James Henry *physicist*
Pham, Khanh Dai *aerospace engineer, researcher*

La Luz
Gonzales, Victor S. *principal*

Las Cruces
Barquet, Jesus Jose *literature and language professor, writer*
Bell, M. Joy Miller *financial planner, real estate broker*
Constantini, Louis O. *financial consultant, stockbroker*
Cruzado, Waded *academic administrator*
Ford, Clarence Quentin *mechanical engineer, educator*
Gale, Thomas Martin *university dean*
Genin, Joseph *engineering educator, researcher*
Heger, Herbert Krueger *education educator*
Huber, Wayne Carl *administrator, educator and artist*
Hunt, Darwin Paul *psychology professor*
Jacobs, Kent Frederick *dermatologist*
Jauregui, David Villegas *civil engineer, educator*
Kemp, John Daniel *biochemist, educator*
Kilmer, Neal Harold *application developer*
Laroche, Jacques M. *language educator*
Little, Karen J. *counselor*
Long, Richard Louis, Jr. *chemical engineer, educator*
Lopez, Carol Sue *artist*
Lutz, William Lan *lawyer*
Neves, Alexandra Moreira *language educator*
Nothom, Theodore John *professor*
Peterson, Robin Tucker *marketing educator*
Ramirez, Ricardo *bishop*
Reynolds, Collins James III *management consultant*
Reynolds, Terry Ray *curator, anthropologist, educator*
Richardson, Albert Edward *chemistry professor, researcher*
Salamanca-Riba, Susana Alicia *mathematics professor*
Schemnitz, Sanford David *wildlife biology professor*
Seger, Mark *molecular biologist*
Selden, Annie *mathematics professor*
Sohn, Hansuk *research scientist, educator*
Thode, Edward Frederick *chemical engineer, educator*
Tonn, Robert James *retired entomologist*
Tran, Son Cao *computer science educator*
Wang, Haobin *chemistry professor*
Wedel, Voleen *police official*
Whitford, Walter George *retired biology professor*
Williams, Susan L. *educator*
wwRupp, Michael Richard *immunologist*
Zakahi, Walter R. *dean, communications educator*
Zhang, Jie *engineering educator*
Zhang, Jinfa *geneticist, educator*

Las Vegas
Fries, James A. *academic administrator*
Gallegos, Gil Roman *engineering educator*
Howard, Leland William *writer*
Lbdell, David *art educator*
Lobdell, David *art educator*
Simpson, Dorothy Audrey *retired speech educator*

Lordsburg
Moralez, Joselyn Hope *special education educator*

Los Alamos
Anastasio, Michael R. *science administrator*
Atcher, Robert Whitehill *chemist, educator*
Baek, Seung-Ho *research scientist*
Balick, Lee K. *research scientist, researcher*
Bdzil, John B. *research scientist, educator*
Benjamin, Susan Selton *elementary school educator*
Beyerlein, Irene Jane *research scientist*
Blagoev, Krastan Blagoev *physicist, biophysicist*
Bronkhorst, Curt Allan *research scientist*
Brown, Lowell Severt *physicist, researcher*
Dai, Zhenxue *geologist, researcher, consultant*
Dienes, John Kalman *energy executive*
Dion, Heather M. *chemist, researcher*
Doggett, Norman A. *molecular biologist*
Dubey, Manvendra Krishna *environmental scientist*
Dudziak, Donald John *nuclear engineer, educator*
Dye, Robert Craig *research scientist*
Eads, Damian R. *open source software author*
Engelhardt, Albert George *physicist*
Friar, James Lewis *physicist*
Gibson, Benjamin Franklin *physicist*
Ginocchio, Joseph Natale *physicist*
Harlow, Francis Harvey *physicist, anthropologist, research scientist, artist*
Hosemann, Peter *materials scientist*
Janecky, David Richard *geochemist*
Judd, O'Dean P. *physicist*
Lamoreaux, Steve Keith Dutch *atomic physicist, consultant*
Leddy, Johna *electrochemistry educator*
Lee, Jung-Kun *materials scientist, researcher*
Lipnikov, Konstantin *mathematician*
Macek, Robert James *retired physicist*
Masse, William Bruce *archaeologist*
Mead, William Charles *physicist*
Mendius, Patricia Dodd Winter *retired editor, educator, writer*
Michaudon, André Francisque *physicist*
Mihaila, Bogdan *physicist*
Mihalas, Dimitri Manuel *astrophysicist, educator*
Misra, Amit *materials scientist, researcher*
Mitchell, Jeremy Neil *geologist, materials scientist*
Montgomery, David Scott *physicist, director*
Pack, Russell T. *retired theoretical chemist*
Picraux, Samuel Thomas *physicist, researcher*
Porch, William Morgan *physicist*
Ramsey, Margie *librarian*
Redondo, Antonio *physicist*
Schwarz, Ricardo B. *research scientist*
Selden, Robert Wentworth *physicist, consultant*
Shao, Lin *physicist, director*
Sharp, David Howland *physicist*
Smith, Fredrica Emrich *rheumatologist, internist*
Smith, James Lawrence *research physicist*
Souto, Francisco Javier *nuclear engineer, researcher*
Stauffer, Philip Henry *hydrogeologist*
Stoddard, Stephen Davidson *ceramics engineer, retired state senator*
Terrones, Guillermo *research scientist*
Thompson, Joe D. *physicist*
Thompson, Lois Jean Heidke Ore *psychologist*
Vrugt, Jasper Alexander *research scientist*
Wang, Moran *physicist*
Wang, Yuejian *research scientist*
Whalen, Daniel James *astrophysicist*
Willerton, Beverly Kay *mathematics educator*
Zhao, Yusheng *physicist*

Los Lunas
Jolly, Jeffrey Russell *musician, educator*
Melzer, Richard Anthony *historian, educator*

Lovington
Crutchfield, Carl Barry *lawyer*

Mayhill
Pastor, Stephen Daniel *chemistry professor, researcher, consultant*

Mesilla Park
Baker, Kevin D. *agricultural engineer*

Mora
Hanks, Eugene Ralph *real estate developer, rancher, forester, retired military officer, investor*

Moriarty
Cox, Darlene Beth *secondary school educator*
Moonwalker, Tu *minister, counselor, artist*

Penasco
Marx, Nicki Diane *sculptor, painter, jeweler*

Placitas
Hidy, George Martel *chemical engineer, engineering executive*
Schoen, Stevan Jay *lawyer*
Smith, Richard Bowen *retired national park superintendent*
Watson-Boone, Rebecca A. *dean, researcher, library and information scientist, educator*

Portales
Carr, Tracy A. *musician, educator*
Dal Porto, Mark Daniel *music educator*
Elder, Donald Cameron *history professor, broadcast executive*
Frost, Everett Lloyd *academic administrator, anthropologist*
Good, Kathie *special education educator, consultant, dean*
Hemley, David Dyson *finance educator*
Howard, Carolyn F. *elementary school educator*
Musonera, Etienne *finance educator, consultant*
Overton, Edwin Dean *retired campus minister, educator*
Paschke, Donald Vernon *music educator*
Varela, Manuel Francisco *molecular biologist, microbiologist, biochemist*
Walker, Melveta *librarian, director*
YSikes, Juanita Lou *art educator*

Raton
Carroll, William *publishing company executive*
Schmeits, Ronald L. *advocacy organization executive, bank executive*

Reserve
Wiley, James Dee *retired history and biology educator, national park service ranger*

Rio Rancho
Baehr, Karl Joseph *broadcasting executive*
Ives, John Milton *retired engineer*
Melendez, Robert F. *ophthalmologist*

Roswell
Anderson, Donald Bernard *oil industry executive*
Baldock, Bobby Ray *federal judge*
Buldra, Gina *physical therapist*
Gallagher, Bill *history professor*
Peterson, Dorothy Hawkins *artist, educator*
Rufe, Laurie J. *museum director*
Sutton, Ferron *engineering educator*
Tekut, Thomas Francis *chemistry professor*
Winslow, Sandra Eileen *financial manager, professor*

Ruidoso
Burns, Carla D. *science educator*

Ruidoso Downs
Smith, Jay S. *museum director*

Sandia Park
Greenwell, Ronald Everett *communications executive*
Rager, Rudolph Russell *retired lawyer*
Wilczynski, Janusz S. *manufacturing executive, retired physicist*

Santa Fe
Aarons, Stephen D. *lawyer*
Adams, Mark Kildee *lawyer*
Alfidi, Ralph Joseph *retired radiologist, educator, researcher, administrator*
Anderson, William Carl *former civilian military employee, lawyer*
Andrews, John Frank *editor, author, educator*
Bol, Marsha C. *museum director*
Brandt, Richard Paul *communications and entertainment company executive*
Burns, Scott *columnist*
Casey, Patrick Anthony *lawyer*
Cerny, Charlene Ann *director*
Chavez, Edward L. *state supreme court chief justice*
Cheetham, Alan Herbert *paleontologist*
Clyde, Larry Forbes *banker*
Cooper, Sandra Lenore *writer, artist*
Cordell, Linda S. *anthropologist, educator, museum director*
Cowan, George Arthur *chemist, bank executive, director*
Daniels, Charles Wesley *state supreme court justice, lawyer, educator*
Davis, Marcie L. *public health and human services consultant*
Denish, Diane D. *Lieutenant Governor of New Mexico*
Dirks, Lee Edward *newspaper executive*
Dodds, Robert James III *lawyer*
Dreisbach, John Gustave *investment banker*
Duhaime, Nina Lee *retired energy and research and development company executive*
Evans, Dick *artist*
Farber, Steven Glenn *lawyer*
Fisher, Robert Alan *laser physicist*
Franzen, Ulrich J. *architect*
Gaddes, Richard *former opera company director*
Garcia, Veronica C. *state official, school system administrator*
Gell-Mann, Murray *theoretical physicist, educator*
Giovanielli, Damon Vincent *physicist, consultant*
Gorski, Daniel Alexander *art educator, artist*
Groseclose, Everett Harrison *retired editor*
Guthrie, Catherine S. (Catherine S. Nicholson-Guthrie) *research scientist, consultant*
Hammer, Charles F. *retired chemistry professor*
Harroun, Dorothy Sumner *artist*
Herrera, Mary E. *Secretary of State, New Mexico*
Hoffmann, Louis Gerhard *immunologist, educator*
Howell, Vicky Sue *health data analyst*
Ice, Joyce *museum director*
Jonas, Chris *composer*
Jordan, James *psychotherapist, educator*
Justice, Jack Burton *retired lawyer, writer*
Kaman, Helen S. *retired aerospace engineer, artist*
Kaufman, Morris I. *mechanical engineer*
Kellner, Richard George *mathematician, computer scientist*
Kelly, Paul Joseph, Jr. *federal judge*
King, Gary K. *state attorney general*
Kingsmore, Stephen Francis *physician, research scientist*
Knight, Kenneth Hugh *conductor*
Kronberg, Philipp Paul *physicist, educator*
Lehmberg, Stanford Eugene *historian, educator*
Leon, Bruno *architect, educator*
Levine, Frances *museum director*
Lewis, James Beliven *state treasurer*
Lichtenberg, Maggie Klee *publishing executive*
Louck, James Donald *physicist, researcher*
Lynn, John Eric *nuclear physicist, researcher, consultant*
MacKay, Charles *opera company director*
Maes, Petra Jimenez *state supreme court justice*
McClaugherty, Joe L. *lawyer, educator*
Mercer, James Lee *management consultant*
Merrin, Seymour *computer company executive*
Miller, Dwight Richard *professional hair care industry executive, cosmetologist, consultant*
Momaday, Navarre Scott *writer, poet*
Mora, Pat *writer, speech professional*
Morrison, Malcolm Cameron *engineering management professional*
Newhall, Mary Anne *dancer, educator*
Nicholls, Anthony *biophysicist, software company executive*
Perroni, Carol *artist*
Peters, Margaret Annette *English language educator*
Pound, John Bennett *lawyer*
Richardson, Bill (William Blaine Richardson III) *Governor of New Mexico, former United States Secretary of Energy*
Robinson, Charles Wesley *boat design company executive*
Sabloff, Jeremy Arac *archaeologist*
Schiller, William Richard *surgeon*
Schwarz, Michael *lawyer*
Serna, Patricio *state supreme court justice*
Sloan, Jeanette Pasin *artist*
Smith, Philip Meek *science administrator, consultant*
Stolley, Richard Brockway *journalist*
Sturges, Molly *performing company executive, composer*
Sumner, Gordon, Jr. *retired military officer*
Thornburg, Garrett, Jr. *finance company executive*
Tinsley, Edward *small business owner, rancher*
Tisdale, Shelby Jo-Anne *museum director, consultant*
Vázquez, Martha Alicia *federal judge*
Verant, William J. *state banking agency administrator*
Vigil, Alfredo *state agency administrator*
Watkins, Stephen Edward *accountant, publishing executive*
Welch, Jasper Arthur, Jr. *security company executive, consultant*
Wertheim, John V. *lawyer, former political organization administrator*
West, Geoffrey B. *theoretical physicist, physics professor*
White, David Hywel *physics professor, researcher*
Williams, Ralph Chester, Jr. *physician, educator*
Williams, Stephen *anthropologist, educator*
Wilson-Segura, Channell Monique *secondary school educator*
Wolkoff, Eugene Arnold *lawyer*
Zlatoff-Mirsky, Everett Igor *violinist*

Seneca
Monroe, Kendyl Kurth *retired lawyer*

Silver City
Buhner, Stephen Harrod *research scientist*
Fritz, Scott *history professor*
Fryxell, David Allen *publishing executive*
Lopez, Linda Carol *social sciences educator*
Ortego, Gilda Baeza *library director, educator*
Snedeker, John Haggner *university president*
Tolar, Trinidad Uribe *education educator, director*
Toth, Bill D. *literature and language professor*

Socorro
Axen, Gary James *geology educator*
Bejnar, Thaddeus Putnam *law librarian*
Deng, Baolin *environmental engineering educator*
Fu, Song *science educator, researcher*
Hossain, Anwar M. *statistician, department chairman*
Lara-Martínez, Rafael *humanities educator*
Mukkamala, Srinivas *research scientist*
Simkin, Susan M. *retired astronomer*
Werbelow, Lawrence Glen *chemistry educator, researcher*

Sunspot
Keil, Stephen Lesley *astrophysicist*

Taos
Bolls, Imogene Lamb *English language educator, poet*
Brown, David Warfield *management educator, lawyer, academic administrator*
Garen, Kenneth Bruce *software designer, company executive*
Witt, David L. *curator, writer*

Tesuque
Bornstein, Paul *medical educator, biochemist*

Truth Or Consequences
Lederer, John Martin *retired aeronautical engineer*
Rush, Domenica Marie *health facilities administrator*

Zuni
Tsabetsaye, Jessica L. *science educator*

NEW YORK

Albany
Aceto, Vincent John *librarian, educator*
Acosta-Belén, Edna *literature and language professor*
Alessi, Robert Joseph *lawyer, real estate developer, pharmacist*
Armour-Garb, Bradley Philip *philosopher, educator*
Barsamian, John Albert *lawyer, arbitrator, criminologist, judge, educator*
Bassman, Ronald *psychologist*
Blount, Stanley Freeman *marketing educator*
Bonventre, Vincent Martin *lawyer, educator*
Brademas, John *retired academic administrator, former congressman*
Bradley, Edward James *state official, computer programmer and analyst*
Brcka, Jozef *physicist, researcher*
Brewer, Aida M. *state treasurer*
Cady, Nathaniel C. *biology professor, consultant*
Canestrari, Ronald J. *state legislator*
Carl, Allen Laurence *surgery educator*
Carmack, Robert Marquess *retired social sciences educator*
Carson, JoAnne *artist, educator*
Cavaliere, Ludovico Frank Roland *rheumatologist*
Chan, May Caroline *language educator*
Cogen, Richard M. *lawyer*
Cohn, Douglas Lloyd *veterinarian*
Cole, John Adam *insurance executive*
Cole, Richard *research scientist*
Corelli, John Charles *physicist, researcher*
Cortés-Vázquez, Lorraine *Secretary of State, New York*
Cuomo, Andrew Mark *state attorney general, former United States Secretary of Housing and Urban Development*
Daines, Richard F. *state health commissioner, former health services executive*
Davis, Paul Joseph *endocrinologist*
DeNuzzo, Rinaldo Vincent *pharmacy educator*
Devine, Eugene Peter *supreme court justice*
DiNapoli, Thomas Peter *state official, former state legislator*
Donohue, Mary O. *judge, former lieutenant governor*
Dushensky, Jacqueline Amelia *banker, educator*
Dutta, Saurav K. *accountant, educator*
Ebert, Loretta Caren *librarian*
Everett, James W., Jr. *lawyer*
Evoskevich, Paul Joseph *music educator*
Fanuele, Frank John *engineering executive, electrical engineer*
Farber, Martha J. (Marty Farber) *ophthalmologist, medical association administrator*
Fasullo, Michael Thomas *research scientist*
Finnessey, Samuel J., Jr. *lawyer*
Frank, Joachim *structural biologist, educator, biophysicist*
Gibbons, Vincent Paul *pediatric neurologist, educator*
Glenn, Linda MacDonald *social sciences educator, state attorney general*
Goldstein, Kenneth Scott *set designer*
Graffeo, Victoria A. *state appeals court judge*
Gruenthal, Michael *neurologist, department chairman*
Hass, Martha Ann *chemistry professor*
Heshmat, Hooshang *manufacturing executive*
Hoffmeister, Jana Marie *cardiologist*
Hogan, Michael F. *state official*
Howell, Robert Charles *philosopher, educator*
Hubbard, Howard James *bishop*
Huxley, Carole Frances Corcoran *former state official, school system administrator*
Hwang, Jeong-Hyon *computer scientist, educator*
Inomata, Akira *physics professor*
Jennings, Gerald D. (Jerry Jennings) *Mayor, Albany, New York*
Jones, Theodore T., Jr. *state appeals court judge*
Joris, Pierre *literature and language professor*
Joyce, William George, Jr. *transportation executive*
Kaloyeros, Alain Elie *engineering educator, researcher*
Kanwar, Vikramjit Singh *pediatrician, educator, oncologist*
Kennedy, William Joseph *novelist, educator*
Kennett, Ellen L. *lab administrator, pharmacist*
Kinal, Terrence *economics professor, consultant*
Koff, Howard Michael *lawyer*
Kranich, Laurence Joel *economics professor*
Langer, Judith Ann *psychologist*
Lenardon, Robert Joseph *classics educator*
Lepow, Martha Lipson *pediatric educator, consultant*
Levine, Howard Arnold *judge*
Ley, Ronald *psychologist, educator*
Lipetz, Ben-Ami *dean, information science educator*
Lynch, Patricia *lobbyist*
Magnus, P.D. *philosopher, educator*
Mannella, Carmen A. *research scientist*
Mason, Jerry *finance educator, consultant*
Meader, John Daniel *judge*
Mehta, Manish *surgeon*
Menges, Susan Debra Favreau *retired protective services official, management consultant*
Merrill, Andrea O. *music educator*
Metzger, Dennis W. *medical educator, immunologist, researcher*
Miles, Christine Marie *museum director*
Miner, Roger Jeffrey *federal judge*
Molho, Eric Steven *neurologist, researcher*
Mongin, Alexander Anatolievich *neuroscientist, educator*
Morga Bellizzi, Celeste *editor*
Mozhaev, Vadim *research scientist*
Nathan, Richard P(erle) *political science professor*
Novotny, F. Douglas *lawyer*
O'Connor, John Joseph, Jr. *academic administrator*
O'Keefe, Patrick William *research scientist*
Olmstead, Lucinda Sue *English professor*
Paterson, David Alexander *Governor of New York, former state legislator*
Philip, George Michael *academic administrator, former pension fund administrator*
Picotte, Susan Carroll *lawyer*
Pigott, Eugene F., Jr. *state appeals court judge*
Pinheiro, Joaquim Manuel Bernardino *pediatrician, educator*
Plowman, Travis S. *education educator, consultant*
Polimeni, John Matthew *economics professor*
Read, Susan Phillips *state appeals court judge*
Reese, William Lewis *philosophy educator*
Rinckey, Greg T. *state attorney general*
Ritter, Philip Wayne *library administrator*
Robbins, Cornelius (Van Vorse) *educational administration educator*
Rosenfeld, Harry Morris *editor*
Rosenkrantz, Daniel J. *computer science educator*
Rostow, Charles Nicholas *lawyer, educator*
Roy, Rob J. *biomedical engineer, anesthesiologist, educator*
rsch, Helmut V. B. *biology professor*
Schneider, Allan Stanford *biophysics, neuroscience and pharmacology educator, biomedical research scientist*
Sell, Stewart *pathologist, immunologist, educator*
Shapshay, Stanley M. *otolaryngologist, educator*
Sheehan, Deborah Hardick *lawyer*
Siegfried, Clifford A. *museum director*
Smith, Ada LaVerne *state legislator*
Smith, Malcolm A. *state legislator*
Smith, Rex William *journalist*
Smith, Robert Sherlock *state appeals court judge*
Steinbock, Bonnie *philosophy educator*
Steiner, David Milton *state official, school system administrator, former dean*

Stevens, Roy W. *microbiologist, researcher, photographer*
Straussman, Jeffrey *dean, political science professor*
Temple, Sally *neuroscientist, educator*
Tepper, Clifford *allergist, immunologist, educator*
Theroux, P. J. *sociologist, educator*
Treadwell, Alexander F. *foundation executive, former state official*
Tully, Mathew B. *lawyer*
Ungar, Barbara Louise *literature and language professor*
Van Slyke, Rosemary *retired tax specialist*
Veille, Jean-Claude *obstetrician, educator*
Verdile, Vincent Paul *dean, emergency physician*
Volker, Dale Martin *state legislator, lawyer*
Walton, James Farley *research and development company executive*
Wan, Shuangyi *research scientist*
Willard, Dan Edward *computer scientist, educator*
Winner, George Henry *lawyer, state legislator*
Yanas, John Joseph *lawyer, director*
Zambri, Melissa Marie *lawyer, educator*
Ziamandanis, Claire M. *language educator*
Zimmerman, Earl Abram *neurologist, educator*
Zimmerman, Joseph Francis *political scientist, educator*
Zimpher, Nancy Lusk *academic administrator*

Albertson
Berlin, Mark A. *lawyer*

Albion
Allamon, Karen Henn *minister*

Alden
Pajak, David Joseph *lawyer, consultant*

Alfred
Anderson, Martha G. *history professor*
Chambliss, Melvin C. *veterinarian, educator*
Eaklor, Vicki Lynn *history professor*
Higby, Wayne (Donald) *artist, educator*
Johnson, Carla Conrad *library dean*
Jonchhe, Yogendra B. *mechanical engineer, educator*
La Course, William Carl *glass science educator, researcher*
Newsome, William Brian *history professor*
Peterson, Thomas Virgil *religious studies educator*
Scheer, Joseph H. *artist, education educator*
Shelby, James Elbert *materials scientist, educator*
Smith, Mark Arthur *information scientist, educator*
Williams, John *engineering educator*

Alfred Station
Condrate, Robert Adam, Sr. *spectroscopy educator*

Amenia
Hale, Nathan Cabot *sculptor, artist, poet*

Amherst
Bharadwaj, Prem Datta *physics professor*
Brazeau, Gayle Ann *associate dean*
Butsch, John Lord *surgeon, educator*
Clark, Donald Malin *professional association executive*
Granger, Carl V. *physician, educator*
Jen, Frank Chifeng *finance and management educator*
Kryzan, Alice J. *retired lawyer*
Kurtz, Paul *philosopher, educator, writer, publisher*
Monte, Scott Vincent *medical researcher, director*
Shaw, David Tai-Ko *electrical and computer engineering educator, academic administrator*
Walsh, Laurie Ann *law educator*

Amityville
Citrano-Cummiskey, Debra Moira *chemist, network technician*
Imbert, Richard Conrad *insurance company executive, real estate developer*
Upadhyay, Yogendra Nath *physician, educator*

Amsterdam
Castro, Michael *oncologist*

Ancram
Blechman, R. O. *artist, filmmaker*

Ancramdale
Ditto, David Thomas *inventor, artist*
Weinstein, Joyce *artist*

Angola
Green, Gerard Leo *priest, educator*

Annandale On Hudson
Achebe, Chinua *writer, humanities educator*
Ashbery, John Lawrence *language educator, poet, playwright, art critic*
Botstein, Leon *academic administrator, conductor, historian*
Dougall, Jane *librarian*
LÊ, An-My *photographer, educator*
Morrow, Bradford *novelist, editor, educator*
Papadimitriou, Dimitri Basil *economist, educator, academic administrator*
Pfaff, Judy *artist*
Sandström, Sigrid *painter*
Sourian, Peter *writer, educator*

Apalachin
Linder, Fannie Ruth *psychotherapist, concert soprano*
Williamson, Mark Adam *science educator*

Arcade
Ezzo, David Albert *not-for-profit executive, anthropologist, educator*

Ardsley
Silman, Roberta Karpel *fiction writer, critic*
Tognino, John Nicholas *diversified financial services company executive*

Ardsley On Hudson
Lapine, Missy Chase *writer, chef*
Seaman, Alfred Barrett *journalist, writer*
Stein, Milton Michael *retired lawyer*

Armonk
Bakalar, Richard S. *physician*
Boies, David *lawyer*
Brown, Joseph Warner, Jr., (Jay Brown) *mortgage insurance company executive*
Daniels, Michael E. *information technology executive*
Greene, Jesse J., Jr. *computer company executive*
Iwata, Jon C. *computer company executive*
Kavanaugh, James J. *information technology executive*
Kelly, John E. III *information technology executive*
Kern, Franklin R. *information technology executive*
Loughridge, Mark *computer company executive*
O'Donnell, Daniel E. *lawyer, information technology executive*
Palmisano, Samuel J. *information technology executive*
Rometty, Ginny (Virginia Maria Rometty) *information technology executive*
Rosenberg, Michael *lawyer*
Schroeter, Martin J. *information technology executive*
Shaughnessy, Timothy S. *information technology executive*
Weber, Robert Carl *lawyer*
Wertheim, Ram D. *lawyer*

Astoria
Araki, Henry Angel *industrial designer*
DiGiovanni, Eleanor Elma *scaffold installation company executive*
Ethier, Scott *composer*
Francesa, Mike (Michael Patrick Francesa) *radio personality*

Attica
Morgan, Claire Marie *elementary school educator*
Rogers, Donald L. *music educator, department chairman, animal breeder*

Auburn
Bartolotta, Kristen *literature and language educator*
Coolican, Sharon *chemistry professor*

Aurora
Farnsworth, Beatrice Brodsky *history professor*

Averill Park
Blais, Christopher R. *social studies educator*
Haines, Walter Wells *retired economics professor*

Babylon
Brackett, Ronald E. *investment company executive, lawyer*
DaSilva, Lynn Judith *special education educator*
Herbst, Jane Elizabeth *school librarian*
Schnepp, Angela J. *secondary school educator*
Schwarz, Barbara Ruth Ballou *elementary school educator*

Baldwin
Aliano, Joy Caryl *retired elementary school educator*
Chopra, Samir *pharmaceutical and real estate company executive*

Baldwin Place
Kurian, George Thomas *publisher*

Baldwinsville
Pretzat, Julie *academic administrator, conductor*
Wilson, Harold Batting *retired treasurer*

Ballston Spa
Brown, Ifigenia Theodore *retired lawyer*
Westbrook, Jack Hall *metallurgist, consultant*

Barneveld
Hanna, Richard L. *construction executive*

Barrytown
Wilson, Andrew Murray *religious studies educator*

Batavia
Van Rees, Cornelius S. *lawyer*

Bath
BetzJitomir, Susan Marie *lawyer, educator, judge, policy analysis researcher*
White, Richard Thomas *radiologist*

Bay Shore
Benjaminson, Morris Aaron *microbiologist, director*
Williams, Tonda *entrepreneur, consultant*

Bayside
Avella, Tony *city councilman*
Bonous-Smit, Barbara *music educator, pianist, librarian*
Chugh, Om Parkash *mathematics professor, researcher, forensics specialist*
Ellerton, Sharon Speiser *biomedical researcher, science educator*
Gerus, John Patrick *portfolio manager, retired educator*
Kennedy, Mary Theresa *mental health services professional*
Madden, Joseph Daniel *trade association executive*
Miller, Albert *physician, researcher*
Mullany, Kevin Fergus *music educator, director*
Ohrenstein, Roman Abraham *economist, educator, rabbi*
Zinn, William *musician, composer*

Bayville
Calodny, Alan Lee *retired pharmacist*

Beacon
Rousseau, Christina Jeannie *elementary school educator*

Bedford
Bowman, James Kinsey *publishing executive, rare book dealer*
Chase, Chevy (Cornelius Crane Chase) *comedian, actor, writer*
Husted, William Armstrong *sales executive*
Palminteri, Chazz *actor*
Philip, Peter Van Ness *former trust company executive*
Tischler, Gary Lowell *psychiatrist, educator*

Bedford Corners
Singer, Craig *entrepreneur, inventor, executive*

Bedford Hills
Dublon, Dina *former bank executive*
Lustbader, Eric Van *writer*
Pappas, George Demetrios *retired anatomist, cell biologist, educator*

Belle Harbor
Re, Edward Domenic, Jr. *construction executive*

Bellerose
Stecher, Pauline *painter, educator*

Bellmore
Andrews, Charles Rolland *library administrator*
Lederman, Gary *dentist*

Bellport
Coonerty, Mary Elizabeth *special education educator*
Regalmuto, Nancy Marie *small business owner, consultant*
Schultheis, Edwin Milford *dean, business educator*
Townsend, Terry *publishing executive*

Bellvale
Murnion, William Edward *philosopher, theologian*

Bemus Point
Rollinger, Mary Elizabeth *retired school counselor, clinical director*

Bethel
Lawrence, Wade *museum director*

Bethpage
Conti, James Joseph *retired chemical engineer, educator*
Dolan, Charles Francis (Chuck Dolan) *media and entertainment company executive*
Dolan, James L. *communications executive*
Huseby, Michael P. *communications executive*
Ratner, Hank J. *broadcast executive*
Rutledge, Thomas M. *communications executive*
Schwartz, Jonathan D. *lawyer*
Seibert, Gregg George *communications executive, former investment company executive*

Big Flats
Keck, Donald Bruce *physicist*
Orsillo, James Edward *computer engineer, information technology executive*

Binghamton
Best, Robert Mulvane *insurance company executive*
Blackburn, Marcia C. *visual studies educator*
Bobinski, George S., Jr. *associate dean*
Brinker-Gabler, Gisela *literature educator*
Carrigg, James A. *retired utility company executive*
Catalano, George Dominic *engineering educator*
Choi, Janey *violinist, artist*
Coates, Donald Robert *geologist, educator*
Corley, Scott Anthony *history professor, academic service provider*
DeFleur, Lois B. *academic administrator*
Einhorn, Lois J. *rhetoric and communication professor, writer*
Eisch, John Joseph *research chemist, educator, writer, consultant*
Farrell, F. Thomas *mathematics professor*
Fowler, Mark L. *electrical engineer, educator*
Gaddis Rose, Marilyn *literature educator, translator*
Gouldin, David Millen *lawyer*
Greene, Kenneth Vincent *economics educator*
Hilton, Peter John *mathematician, educator*
Isaacson, Robert Lee *neurobehavioral scientist, educator*
James, Gary Douglas *biological anthropologist, educator, researcher*
Kadish, Gerald Edwin *history professor*
Klir, George Jiri *systems science educator*
Kowalik, Thomas Frederic *director community programs*
Lawrence, Karen Roseman *special education services professional, educator*
Lenzenweger, Mark Francis *psychologist, educator*
Levis, Donald James *psychologist, educator*
Little, Michael Alan *anthropology educator*
Madigan, Kathryn Grant *lawyer*
Masters, Stanley H. *economics professor*
Mazrui, Ali Al'Amin *political science professor, researcher*
Meador, John Milward, Jr. *dean, librarian*
Morello, Debra A. *dean*
Naslund, Howard Richard *geological science educator*
Peckham, Eugene Eliot *judge, lawyer*
Philips, George K. *parochial school educator*
Polachek, Dora Eisenberg *humanities educator*
Regenbogen, Adam *judge*
Scholtz, Andrew *music educator*
Sileo, Richard Nicholas *physics educator*
Skinner, Timothy Joseph *educator*
Sklar, Kathryn Kish *historian, educator*
Sonnenfeld, Gerald *microbiology and immunology educator*
Spanfelner, Deborah Calabro *college librarian*

Swain, Mary Ann Price *university official*
Taylor, Kenneth Douglas *stockbroker, finance and computer consultant, educator*
Terriquez-Kasey, Laura Marie *emergency nurse*
Valencia, Melanie Laine *music educator, performer*
Whittingham, M(ichael) Stanley *chemist*
Wildoner, Nancy Schamu *music educator, fine arts department chairman*
Zacks, Shelemyahu *mathematical sciences educator*

Bloomfield
Grasso, Jonathan *psychologist*

Blue Mountain Lake
Welsh, Caroline Mastin *museum director, curator, art historian*

Bohemia
Grandmaster Flash, (Joseph Saddler) *disc jockey*
Rudolph, Scott *pharmaceutical executive*

Brentwood
Burgess, John Thomas *physical education educator, consultant*
Cleland, Marshall Robert *nuclear scientist*
DeSario, James M. *art educator, photographer, writer*

Brewster
Ganguly, Adrish *materials engineer, researcher*
Nadel, Norman Allen *civil engineer*
Shepard, Lance Hastings *marketing professional, consultant, newscaster*
Stojakovic, Dejan *metallurgist, researcher*

Briarcliff Manor
Bernstein, Nadia Jacqueline *lawyer*
Bhargava, Rameshwar Nath *physicist*
Bingham, J. Peter *electronics research executive*
Bower, Thomas Michael *lawyer*
Cavalcanti, Dave Alberto Tavares *electrical engineer*
Loudig, Olivier Daniel *biochemist*
Pousada, Lidia *physician*
Read, John Conyers *non-profit company executive*
Sabia, Noreen Patricia *psychologist*
Wheeler, Margaret Jane *actress, soprano, voice educator*

Bridgehampton
Brennan, Paul *real estate broker*
Morabito, Enzo C. *real estate broker*
Saunders, Andrew *real estate company executive, real estate developer*

Brightwaters
Kavanagh, Eileen J. *librarian*
North, E(dward) Lee *retired writer, former aerospace company professional*

Brockport
Anand, Vishal *engineering educator*
Bowdler, Jane Maxon *mathematics educator*
Bucholz, Arden *historian, educator*
Cook, Laurie Boivin *biology professor*
Finley, Kay Thomas *chemistry professor, researcher*
Gemmett, Robert J. *dean, English language educator*
Hacker, Linda Wessels *librarian*
Leslie, William Bruce *history professor*
McGhee, Diane Baumann *dance instructor, consultant*
O'Brien, Kenneth Paul *historian, educator*
Ortiz, Joseph M. *literature and language professor, writer*
Rossi, Frank Dominick *language educator*
Sarrazin, Natalie Rose *music educator, researcher*
Tahar, Mohammed Zrendini *physics professor*
Tsubota, Stuart *biology professor*
Wakefield, Wanda Ellen *historian, educator, sports association executive*

Bronx
Abbott, Ira Richmond, III, (Rick) *pediatric neurosurgeon, educator*
Abdul, Raoul *music critic*
Adams, Alice *sculptor*
Afterman, Jean *professional sports team executive*
Ahmose, Nefertari A. *journalism educator*
Alcaide, Juan Abraham *literature and language professor*
Alderman, Elizabeth *pediatrician, educator*
Alvarez, Michael *librarian*
Andersen, Robin *media specialist, educator*
Antwi, Ebenezer Yaw *education educator*
Arroyo, Maria del Carmen *City Councilwoman*
Ask-Nanko, Lorraine Charlotte *music educator*
Bacarella, Flavia *artist, educator*
Baez, Maria *city councilwoman*
Balestra, Dominic J. *philosopher, educator*
Balka, Sigmund Ronell *lawyer*
Bark, Nigel Martyn *psychiatrist*
Barzilai, Nir Jacob *geriatrician, educator*
Behnken, William Joseph *artist, educator*
Berman, Stephen Leonard *mathematics and statistics educator*
Blaufox, Morton Donald *hypertension specialist, nuclear medicine physician, educator*
Block, Holly *museum director*
Bonelli, Vincent Francis *history professor*
Bowers, Francis Robert *educational consultant, literature educator*
Brakalova, Melkana Alexandrova *mathematician, researcher, educator*
Brandt, Lawrence Jay *internist, gastroenterologist, educator*
Brenner, Terence *mathematics professor*
Brent, Robert John *economics educator*
Bullaro, Grace Russo *literature, film and foreign language educator, critic*
Burnett, A.J. (Allen James Burnett) *professional baseball player*
Cano, Robinson Jose *professional baseball player*
Carter, Majora J. *urban planner*
Chamberlain, Joba *professional baseball player*

Chambers, Earle *epidemiologist, educator*
Chiang, I-Cheng Robert *science educator*
Cohen, Herbert Jesse *pediatrician, educator*
Cohen, Selma *retired librarian*
Cornfield, Melvin *lawyer, director*
Cosgrove, John Morgan *surgeon, department chairman*
Cruise, Keith R. *psychology professor*
Dam, Tarun *biomedical researcher, educator*
Damon, Johnny *professional baseball player*
Das, Ashoke Kumar *internist, consultant*
Das, Bhaskar Chandra *chemistry professor*
Dean, Nancy *literature educator, retired playwright*
DeAnda, Abelardo *thoracic surgeon, educator*
De Blasio, Maria P. *physician*
Deitrick, George Albert III *physician, surgeon*
Delgado-Lopez, Fernando *biochemist*
Diaz, Ruben, Jr. *city official*
Djukic, Aleksandra *medical educator, director*
Dolich, Barry H. *plastic surgeon, educator*
Drepaul, Loris Omesh *internist, infectious diseases physician*
Dunne, Kathleen Anne *structural engineer, educator*
Dutcher, Janice Jean Phillips *oncologist*
Ebose, Esokpan James *chemist*
Elkin, Jay S. *psychologist*
Engelke, Charles Edward *physics professor*
Fazal, Shafeek *assistant director*
Fine, Eugene Jonathan *nuclear medicine physician, educator*
Fisher, John Devens *cardiologist, educator*
Fishman, Yonatan *neuroscientist*
Flores, Guillermo *health science association administrator*
Font, Cecilio Rafael *retired biology educator, physician*
Foster, Helen Diane *city councilwoman, lawyer*
Frater, Robert William Mayo *surgeon, educator*
Freeman, Leonard Murray *radiologist, nuclear medicine physician, educator*
Garg, Madhur *oncologist*
Girardi, Joe (Joseph Elliot Girardi) *professional baseball manager, retired professional baseball player*
Goldfischer, Sidney Leo *pathologist, educator, dean*
Goldstein, Daniel J. *thoracic surgeon, medical educator*
Gonzalez, Angela E. *obstetrician, gynecologist*
Goodman, Robert L. *internist, epidemiologist, educator*
Goodman, Robert M. *biochemist, educator*
Goodrich, James Tait *neuroscientist, neurosurgeon*
Greenstein, Stuart Mark *surgical educator*
Gross, Susan *obstetrician, department chairman*
Gruson, Konrad *orthopedist, educator*
Guha, Sushovan *physician, researcher*
Haider, Quamrul *physics professor, researcher*
Hait, Gershon *pediatric cardiologist*
Hallett, Charles Arthur, Jr. *language educator, humanities educator*
Heagarty, Margaret Caroline *retired pediatrician*
Hermalyn, Gary Douglas *historian, publisher, educator*
Hilliard, Carol *nurse, educator, consultant, researcher*
Himmelberg, Robert Franklin *historian, educator*
Hinske, Eric Scott *professional baseball player*
Hobson, Rana Dirice *psychologist*
Hunt, George William *priest, magazine editor*
Jackson, Reggie (Reginald Martinez Jackson, Mr. October) *retired professional baseball player*
James, Gesille *librarian*
Jeter, Derek Sanderson *professional baseball player*
Kahn, Thomas *medical educator*
Kalnicki, Shalom *radiologist, educator*
Kalpana, Ganjam V. *biomedical researcher*
Kassoy, Hortense (Honey Kassoy) *artist, sculptor, painter*
Kaushik, Sashank *psychiatrist, researcher*
Keating, Tedd Michael *adult education educator*
Kennedy, Gary J. *psychiatrist*
Khan, Amir Maqbul *physician*
Khodakhah, Kamran *medical educator*
Kim, Soo G. *medical educator, lab administrator*
Kirsch, George Benson *history professor*
Kitt, Olga *artist*
Koppell, G. Oliver *city councilman, former NY State Atty. Gen., lawyer*
Koranyi, Adam *mathematics professor*
Korman, Barbara *sculptor*
Kornfeld, Robert Jonathan *playwright, photographer*
Koss, Leopold G. *pathologist, educator*
Lagares, Portia Octavia *music educator*
Laruccia, Stephen Dominic *academic administrator*
Lautin, Everett Marc *radiologist, educator*
Lee, Dong Hwan *business administration educator*
Levine, Randy Lewis *professional baseball team executive, lawyer*
Lienert, Christoph *physical education educator*
Lopez, Leo *cardiologist*
Macklin, Ruth *bioethics educator*
Matsui, Hideki *professional baseball player*
McClure, Margaret McNamara *psychologist, educator*
McShane, Joseph Michael *academic administrator, priest*
Melamed, Michal L. *epidemiologist*
Melman, Arnold *urologist*
Mendez, Ruben Policarpio *diplomat, educator, economist*
Menthena, Anuradha *research scientist*
Mitra, Sophie *economics professor*
Mittler, Diana (Diana Mittler-Battipaglia) *music educator, pianist*
Mueser, John Alan *elementary school educator*
Munch, Janet Butler *librarian*
New, Antonia S. *psychiatrist, educator*
Newman, Zelda Kahan *linguist*
O'Donnell, Brennan Patrick *academic administrator, literature and language professor*
Oertel, Michael *researcher, medical educator*
Oktay, Maja Hrzenjak *medical educator*
Owen, Randall P. *surgeon, researcher*
Padnos, Mark *library administrator, translator*
Palma, Annabel *city councilwoman*
Payson, Martin Saul *mathematics educator*
Peña, Tony (Antonio Francisco Peña) *professional baseball coach, retired professional baseball player*
Penella, Robert Joseph *ancient language educator*
Pettitte, Andy (Andrew Eugene Pettitte) *professional baseball player*
Piderit, John J. *educational consultant and author, former university president*
Posada, Jorge Rafael *professional baseball player*
Prabhu, Vrunda P. *mathematics professor*
Pranevicius, Mindaugas *anesthesiologist, educator*
Radel, Eva *pediatrician, hematologist*
Raman, Shankar *surgeon*
Ray, Carina *history professor*
Reeberg, Patricia Aldora *minister, entrepreneur*
Regan, Richard Joseph *political science professor, writer*
Rego, Simon Alexander *psychologist*
Reichgott, Michael Joel *medical educator, dean, physician*
Rhinehart, Alycia Celeste *principal*
Richman, Murray W. *lawyer*
Richman, Stacey Gayle *lawyer*
Rivera, Joel *city councilman*
Rivera, Mariano *professional baseball player*
Robinson, Gwendolyn Niema *elementary school educator*
Rodriguez, Alex (Alexander Emmanuel Rodriguez) *professional baseball player*
Rohan, Thomas E. *epidemiologist, educator*
Rolón, Rosalba *performing company executive*
Rose, Israel Harold *mathematics professor*
Rose, Susan Ann *psychology professor, consultant*
Rosenstreich, David Leon *medical educator, immunologist, allergist*
Rosenthal, Bernice Glatzer *history professor*
Rothstein, Anne Louise *academic administrator, educator*
Rubensky, Mitchell *band director*
Rubinstein, Arye *pediatrician, microbiologist, immunologist, educator*
Sabathia, C.C. (Carsten Charles Sabathia) *professional baseball player*
Sable, Robert Allen *gastroenterologist*
Safyer, Steven Michael *hospital administrator*
Sanchez-Silkman, Jennifer Christine *elementary school educator*
Schaller, George Beals *zoologist*
Schaumburg, Herbert Howard *neurology educator*
Schneider, Scott Michael *academic administrator*
Schramm, Vern L. *biochemist, educator*
Seabrook, Larry B. (Lawrence B. Seabrook) *city councilman, former state legislator*
Seltzer, William *statistician, social science administrator*
Senra, Jenny *psychologist*
Serrano, Helen *art educator*
Shafritz, David Andrew *physician, research scientist*
Shanklin, Elizabeth E. *secondary school educator*
Shapiro, David Joel *poet, art critic, educator*
Sheridan, Patrick Joseph Thomas *bishop emeritus*
Shinnar, Shlomo *pediatric neurologist, educator*
Singer, Robert H. *biology professor*
Spatt, Hartley Steven *humanities educator*
Spiegel, Allen Michael *dean, internist*
Spinka, William J. *art educator*
Spitzer, Adrian *pediatrician, educator*
Stadtmauer, David *judge*
Stein, Cy Aaron *oncologist, pharmacologist*
Stein, Ruth Elizabeth Klein *physician*
Steinbrenner, George Michael III *professional baseball team and shipbuilding company executive*
Steinbrenner, Hal (Harold Zeig Steinbrenner) *professional baseball team executive*
Strassberg, Barbara Esther *pediatrician, educator*
Swisher, Nick (Nicolas Thompson Swisher) *professional baseball player*
Tan, XiangLin *epidemiologist, researcher*
Tarver, Antonio Deon *professional boxer*
Teixeira, Mark Charles *professional baseball player*
Tong, Tommy R. *surgeon, pathologist*
Topyan, Kudret *finance educator*
Ultan, Lloyd *historian, educator*
Vacca, James *city councilman*
Van De Water, Thomas Roger *neuroscientist, educator*
Vaninsky, Alexander Yan *mathematician, educator, researcher, financial analyst, systems analyst*
Veith, Frank J. *vascular surgeon, researcher, educator*
Wabuda, Susan *historian, educator*
Wertheim, Mary Danielle *educational coordinator*
Whyte, Mary Christina *pediatrician*
Wylie-Rosett, Judith *dietician, educator*
Yalow, Rosalyn Sussman *biophysicist*
Yuan Gee, Ka Chuen Carol *school librarian*
Yunen, Jose R. *surgical intensivist, director, epidemiologist*
Zou, Yiyu *medical educator*
Zubeck, Jacqueline Ann (Nina Zubeck) *literature and language professor*

Bronxville

Bayens, Patrick James *religious studies educator*
Bent, John *otolaryngologist, educator*
Bertles, John Francis *physician, educator*
Biscardi, Chester *composer, educator*
Dodds, Jerrilynn D. *dean, art historian, lecturer, writer*
Doyle, Charlotte Lackner (Mrs. James J. Doyle) *psychology educator, writer*
Ellinghaus, William Maurice *communications executive*
Fuller, David Otis, Jr. *lawyer*
Hagendorn, William Hull *lawyer*
Lawrence, Karen R. *academic administrator, literature and language professor*
Lee, Clement William Khan *media consultant*
Lombardo, Philip Joseph *broadcasting company executive*
Longobardo, Guy *biomedical engineer, consultant*
Mills, Nicolaus *American studies educator, writer*
Peters, Sarah Whitaker *art historian, writer*
Pollin, Burton Ralph *language educator*
Rosenthal, Lucy Gabrielle *writer, editor, educator*

Brookhaven

Desiderio, Joseph Gerard *music educator*

Brooklyn

Abott, Michael Larry *physician*
Abrol, Sunil *thoracic surgeon, director*
Ackerman, Jacob Lewis *ophthalmologist*
Adachi, Masazumi *pathologist*
Al-Hafeez, Humza *minister, editor*
Al-Islam, Amir *social services administrator, educator*
Allison, Eric William *management consultant, historic preservationist*
Allison, Mary Ann *consulting company executive, writer, speaker*
Altura, Bella T. *physiologist, educator*
Altura, Burton Myron *physiologist, educator*
Armenakas, Anthony Emmanuel *aerospace engineering educator*
Asekoff, Louis S. *literature and language professor, director*
Astrow, Alan B. *oncologist, hematologist*
Austin, Denise *dietician*
Bandler, Martin *physician*
Barabash, Claire *lawyer, special education services professional, psychologist*
Barone, Frank C. *researcher and medical educator*
Barron, Charles *city councilman*
Bateman, Jason *actor*
Behm, Dutsi *physician*
Behzadan, Amir H. *engineering educator*
Bernard, Rev. A.R. *religious organization administrator*
Bielawa, Lisa *composer*
Birenbaum, Leo *retired engineering educator*
Biro, Laszlo *dermatologist*
Bishar, John Joseph, Jr. *utilities executive, lawyer*
Blake, Reginald Alexander *physics professor*
Block, Frederic *judge*
Bloomfield, David Charles *lawyer, educator, school district government official, not-for-profit public executive*
Bodis-Wollner, Ivan Gyorgy *neurologist, educator*
Boyko, Vladimir S. *physics professor, researcher*
Bradshaw, Thomas *playwright, educator*
Bressler, Robert Samuel *anatomy educator*
Brier, Pamela Sara *health facility administrator*
Brines, Seymour *psychotherapist, consultant, educator*
Brown, Evrick H. *medical educator*
Brown, Ronald K. *performing company executive, choreographer*
Bugliarello, George *academic administrator, educator*
Bullard, Thomas *theater educator, director*
Butt, Mohammad Zaman *internist, geriatrician, researcher*
Caggiano, Frank Joseph *bishop*
Campbell, Benton Jay *prosecutor*
Carswell, Lois Malakoff *botanical garden executive, consultant*
Catanello, Ignatius Anthony *bishop*
Chambers, William Edmond *writer*
Charton, Marvin *chemist, educator*
Childers, William P. *literature and language professor*
Choudhury, Deo Chand *physicist, educator, researcher*
Chung, Ping-Tsai *education educator*
Cisneros, Octavio *bishop*
Cohen, Carl I. *psychiatrist, educator*
Coplan, Jeremy David *psychiatrist, researcher*
Cracco, Roger Quinlan *neurologist, educator*
Daniels, Ellen Taxier *electrical advisor, computer engineer, educator*
D'Ayala, Marcus *surgeon*
Dealy, Michael Thomas *psychology educator*
D'Elia, Nicholas *secondary school educator*
Desmarais, Charles Joseph *museum director, writer*
Dilan, Erik Martin *city councilman*
DiMarzio, Nicholas Anthony *bishop*
Dinnerstein, Harvey *artist*
Dirisu, Afusat Olayinka *research scientist*
Donaldson, Stephen Reeder *author*
Donohue, Alfred F. *retired telecommunications supervisor*
Doretti, Mercedes *forensic anthropologist*
Edelheit, Abraham J. *history professor*
Enseki, Carol *museum director*
Erber, William Franklin *gastroenterologist*
Eugene, Mathieu *city councilman*
Faison, Seth Shepard *retired insurance broker*
Fani, Robert J. *gas industry executive*
Felder, Simcha *city councilman*
Fidler, Lewis A. *city councilman, lawyer*
Fischer, R.M. *sculptor*
Fischman, Myrna Leah *accountant, educator*
Flam, Jack Donald *art historian, educator*
Foronda, Elena Isabel *secondary school educator*
Forsberg, Suzanne *humanities educator*
Fox, Cynthia F. *journalist, writer*
Franco, Victor *theoretical physics educator*
Freilich, Gerald *mathematics professor*
French, Stephanie Taylor *grantmaking and philanthropy expert*
Friedman, Eli A. *nephrologist, educator*
Galatianos, Gus A. *computer company executive, consultant, real estate developer, educator*
Gamble, Cahtina Robyne *elementary school educator*
Garaufis, Nicholas G. *federal judge*
Garetz, Bruce Allen *physical chemist, educator*
Gentile, Vincent Joseph *city councilman, former state legislator*
Gerber, Donald Albert *medical educator*
Ghevariya, Vishal *internist*
Gianlorenzi, Nona Elena *art dealer, painter*
Gilmartin, MaryAnne *real estate development company executive*
Gioseffi, Daniela *poet, writer, playwright, critic*
Gisolfi, Diana (Pechukas) *art history educator*
Giusti, Robert John *pulmonologist, pediatrician*
Glasser, Israel Leo *federal judge*
Goncharov, Viktor *biochemist, researcher*
Gonsalves, Patricia E. *surgical nurse*
Gonzalez, Sara M. *city councilwoman*
Gordon, Michael *composer*
Grado, Angelo John *artist*
Greaves-Venzen, Gail-Ann G. *communications educator*
Green, William Larimore *physician*
Griffin, John Anthony *hedge fund manager*
Gulstone, Jacqueline *nurse*
Haber, Ira Joel *artist, educator*
Halley-Boyce, Jamesetta A. *hospital administrator*
Hammerschlag, Margaret Rosenblum *pediatrician, educator*
Hechtman, Howard *financial analyst*
Hendra, Barbara Jane *public relations executive*
Heron, Earl D. *communications executive*
Hill, Elizabeth Anne *academic administrator, lawyer*
Hoogenboom, Ari Arthur *retired history professor*
Hopkins, Karen Brooks *performing arts executive*
Hoyt, Ellen *artist, educator*
Huang, Yiwu *hematologist, oncologist, educator*
Ierardi, Eric Joseph *school system administrator*
Infante-Voelker, Josefina *literature and language professor, writer*
Jacobowitz, Israel Jacob *cardiothoracic surgeon*
Jacobson, Leslie Sari *biologist, educator*
Jones, Rudolph *minister*
Josephson, William Howard *retired lawyer*
Joy, Mark Kelly *physician*
Kamins, Barry Michael *lawyer*
Kanwar, Vivek Vik *law educator, consultant*
Kanza, Dominic *musician*
Kaplan, Jordan J. *management HRM educator*
Karmel, Roberta Segal *lawyer, educator*
Kazachkov, Mikhail *pediatric pulmonologist*
Kellman, Rona J. *psychologist*
Kemp, James William *graphic artist*
Kilanko, Oyenike Eunice *obstetrician, gynecologist*
Kim, Jin Ryoun *science educator*
Kinard-Wright, Judith Lauretta *elementary school educator, secondary school educator, special education educator*
King, Margaret Leah *history professor*
Klein, Laura Colin *publishing executive*
Korman, Edward Robert *federal judge*
Kriftcher, Noel N. *humanities educator, science director*
Krukowski, Jan *communications executive*
Kugler, Anne *medical educator*
Labianca, Dominick Anthony *chemist, educator*
Lakhi, Nisha Amarlal *obstetrician, gynecologist*
Lambert, Jeffrey Warren *special education educator, director*
Lang, David *composer*
Lange, Christopher Stephen *radiation biophysics professor*
Latif-Zade, Alisher *composer*
Laverty, Marilyn T. *public relations executive, media consultant*
Lazansky, Edward *artist, art educator*
Leamer, Robert Eldon *lawyer, hospital administrator*
Leary, Gordon *playwright, lyricist*
Lee, Spike (Shelton Jackson Lee) *film director and producer*
Lehman, Arnold Lester *museum director, art historian, educator*
Leung, Raymond W. *physical education educator*
Li, Xiangdong *science educator*
Lichstein, Edgar *cardiologist*
Lipson, Steven Mark *virologist, microbiologist, environmental scientist, educator*
Litto, Judith Cheryl *art educator*
Lobron, Barbara L. *speech educator, editor, photographer, writer*
Lockey, James Peter *public health service officer*
Lopate, Phillip *language educator, writer*
Loum, Anthony Webster *librarian*
Luka, Bishoy *pharmacologist, educator*
Macchiarola, Frank Joseph *academic administrator, educator*
MacKay, Malcolm *executive search consultant*
Mack-Harvin, Dionne L. *library director*
Mallory, Michael *art educator*
Mann, Roanne L. *federal judge*
Mansour, Gregory John *bishop*
Markowitz, Marty (Martin Markowitz) *city manager*
Martinez-Pons, Manuel *educational psychologist*
Matsumoto, Kiyo Ann *federal judge*
Mauskopf, Roslynn R. *federal judge, former prosecutor*
McSherry, J. Patrice *political science professor*
Mealy, Darlene *city councilwoman*
Medbury, Scot Daniel *botanical garden executive*
Miller, Greg *photographer*
Miller, Walter James *retired literature educator, writer*
Mirra, Suzanne Samuels *pathologist*
Mittman, Neal *nephrologist, medical educator*
Molina_Figueroa, Sintia E. *language educator*
Mook, Sarah *retired chemist*
Moran, Marissa J. *law educator*
Morris, Mark William *choreographer*
Najib, Jadwiga S. *pharmacist, educator*
Nazaire, Michel Harry *physician*
Nelson, Michael Chaim *city councilman*
Nemazie, Siamack *nephrologist, consultant*
Niesen, James Louis *theater director*
Nii, Yuko *artist*
Norstrand, Iris Fletcher *psychiatrist, neurologist, educator*
O'Farrill, Arturo *composer*
Ogle, Orrett E. *oral surgeon*
Okamoto, Yoshi *science educator*
Ortner, Everett Howard *magazine editor, writer*
Padovano, Anthony John *fine arts educator, artist*
Panwar, Shivendra Singh *education educator, researcher*
Parlamis, Michael Frank *civil engineer, construction executive*
Pearce, Eli M. *chemistry professor, academic administrator*
Pearlman, Ellen Lois *writer, filmmaker, critic, curator*
Pearsall, Otis Pratt *retired lawyer*
Peng, Yusheng *social sciences educator*
Peters, Mercedes *psychotherapist*
Piene, Chloe *artist, filmmaker*
Pitynski, Andrzej Piotr *sculptor*

Plotz, Charles Mindell *physician, educator*
Poludasu, Shyam Sunder *cardiologist*
Poser, Norman Stanley *law educator*
Price, Ely *dermatologist*
Purvin, Jack Mitchell *physician*
Raggi, Reena *federal judge*
Ranck, James Byrne, Jr. *neuroscience researcher, educator*
Ratner, Bruce C. *professional sports team owner, real estate developer*
Rauschenbusch, Stephanie *artist, educator, poet*
Recchia, Domenic M., Jr. *city councilman*
Reeves, William *language educator*
Reichel, Walter Emil *advertising executive*
Renner, Bernd *literature and language professor*
Reyna, Diana *city councilwoman*
Reynolds, Nancy Remick *writer, researcher, editor*
Richardson, Alfonso Austin *accountant, financial services executive*
Rogers, Michael Alan *writer*
Roker, Christopher A. *microbiologist, photographer*
Rosado, Rossana *publishing executive, editor-in-chief*
Rosario-Olmedo, Carmen Gloria *principal*
Rosenthal, Abigail Laura *philosophy educator*
Ross, Randolph Ernest *investor*
Roth, Robert *lawyer, journalist*
Rucker, Bronwyn *actress, writer, social worker*
Russell, Wayne Delano *activist, educator, poet*
Ryan, Leonard Eames *judge*
Salvodon-Stallings, Cynthia Judy *psychologist*
Sanford, David Boyer *journalist, editor*
Sansaricq, Guy A. *bishop*
Sanua, Marianne Rachel *historian, educator*
Savits, Barry Sorrel *surgeon*
Sawyer, Philip Nicholas *surgeon, educator, health science facility administrator*
Schaefer, Marilyn Louise *artist, writer, educator*
Schiffman, Gerald *microbiologist, educator*
Schwartz-Giblin, Susan Toby *neuroscientist, educator, dean emeritus*
Schwarz, Richard Howard *obstetrician, gynecologist, educator*
Schweikert, Edgar Oskar *dentist*
Schweikert, Mary Lou *elementary school educator*
Shalita, Alan Remi *dermatologist*
Sharma, Bhavneesh K. *internist, researcher*
Shaw, Kendall (George) *artist, educator*
Shcherbakova, Estella *chemist, mathematician, educator*
Shedrinsky, Alexander Mikchail *chemistry professor, conservator, consultant*
Shelov, Steven Patrick *pediatrician, educator*
Shivcharran, Jaigobin *secondary school educator, consultant*
Shulman, Abraham *otolaryngology educator, hospital administrator*
Siegel, Stephanie S. *mathematics professor*
Simons, Barbara *retired elementary school educator*
Singer, Eric T. *investment banker*
Skrobela, Katherine Creelman *music producer, data processing executive*
Snyder, Allegra Fuller *dancer, film director, educator*
Stewart, Kendall *city councilman, podiatrist*
Sullivan, Joseph Martin *bishop emeritus*
Swaminathan, Srividhya *literature and language professor*
Szenberg, Michael *economics professor, editor, consultant*
Tague, Gregory Frank *literature and language professor*
Taylor, Ian Logan *dean*
Thomas, Lucille Cole *librarian*
Thompson, Iola Pointer *choreographer, educator*
Toranzo, Nilsa Caridad *special education services professional*
Trager, David G. *federal judge*
Trefousse, Hans Louis *history professor*
Tsiklauri, Shalva *physics professor*
Tsygan, Leonid Iosifovich *civil engineer, writer*
Turitto, Gioia *physician*
Vann, Albert *city councilman, former state legislator*
Vidal, Maureen Eris *theater educator, actress*
Vitaliano, Eric Nicholas *federal judge*
von Rydingsvard, Ursula Karoliszyn *sculptor*
Wadgaonkar, Raj *biologist, director*
Weber, Michael A. *physician, researcher*
Wei, Xinzhou *engineering educator*
Weinstein, Jack Bertrand *federal judge*
Wexler, Joan G. *dean, law educator*
White, Suzanne Marie *medical educator*
Wiener, Hesh (Harold Frederic Wiener) *publishing executive, consultant*
Wilkow, Brian Richard *hospital administrator and clinician*
Wilson, Nancy Esther *social worker*
Wilson, Robert Warne *philanthropist*
Witherspoon, Maria Bernarda Pena *principal*
Wolf, Edward Lincoln *physicist, educator*
Wolfe, Ethyle Renee *academic administrator*
Wolintz, Arthur Harry *neurologist, ophthalmologist*
Wolitzer, Philip *accountant, educator*
Wrotten, Marylean *medical coordinator, counselor*
Yassky, David S. *City Councilman, Brooklyn, New York, lawyer*
Yokoshi, Yasuko *choreographer*
Zakanitch, Robert Rahway *artist*
Zhong, Jun *medical educator*
Zinnes, Alice Fich *artist, educator*
Zollar, Jawole Willa Jo *artist, choreographer*
Zuther, Simone Margrietha *curator*

Brookville
Hynes, Maureen Deirdre *cellist, conductor, teacher*
Swaner, Lynn E. *education educator*
White, Stephanie *computer science educator*

Brushton
Pietropaoli, Angelo Eugene *social studies educator, musician*

Buffalo
Alexandridis, Paschalis *chemical engineer, educator*
Ambrus, Clara Maria *physician*
Ambrus, Julian L. *physician, educator*
Andersen, Martha S. *biophysicist, researcher*
Anderson, Wayne Keith *dean, educator*
Aquilina, Suzanne *pediatric nurse practitioner, educator*
Bachman, Charles R. *literature and language professor*
Ballow, Mark *immunologist, educator*
Bang, Charles Douglas *minister*
Barber, Janice Ann *lawyer*
Bardos, Thomas Joseph *chemist, educator*
Bateman, Derek Robert *sociologist, educator*
Batt, Ronald Elmer *gynecologist, historian, biomedical research scientist*
Beckley, Carol *theater educator, set designer*
Beigel, Andrew Richard *education educator*
Berezney, Ronald *molecular biologist*
Bhattacharya, Arup B. *Homeopathy*
Blane, Howard Thomas *alcohol/drug abuse services professional, researcher*
Bobinski, George Sylvan *librarian, educator*
Bojinova, Emma D. *economics professor*
Boyar, Benjamin *music educator*
Brathwaite, Frank B. *education educator*
Brown, Byron William, Jr. *Mayor, Buffalo*
Brown, Lawrence Charles *lawyer*
Brydges, Thomas Eugene *lawyer*
Bucki, Carl Leo *judge*
Camhi, Rebecca Ann *librarian, writer*
Cao, Shousong *medical researcher, educator*
Cart, Stuart Edwin *air transportation executive, consultant*
Casey, David Michael *prosthodontist*
Chandel, Anil *endocrinologist*
Chang, Ching Ming (Carl) *engineering executive, mechanical engineer, educator, writer*
Churchill, Melvyn Rowen *chemistry professor*
Clarkson, Elisabeth Ann Hudnut *volunteer*
Coburn, Lewis Alan *mathematics professor*
Coffroth, Mary Alice *biologist, educator*
Cohen, Richard *philosopher, educator*
Coles, Robert Traynham *architect*
Collins, Christopher Carl *manufacturing executive*
Conte, Joseph Mark *literature and language professor*
Creaven, Patrick Joseph *pharmacologist*
Cropp, Michael W. *physician, insurance company executive*
Day, Donald Sheldon *lawyer*
Deshmukh, Hitesh *medical researcher*
Donahue, Richard P. *epidemiologist, educator*
Doren, Robert Alan *lawyer*
Dreishpoon, Douglas Scott *curator, art historian*
Duax, William Leo *biologist, researcher*
Eagan, John Gayle *business educator*
Ehrlich, Isaac *economist, educator, department chairman*
Ellis, Richard Emanuel *historian, educator*
Elm, Lloyd Martin, Sr. *science educator*
Flynn, Terrance Patrick *lawyer, former prosecutor*
Freedman, Maryann Saccomando *lawyer*
Fryer, Appleton *sales executive, diplomat*
Fuller, David Randall *musicologist*
Gao, Jiali *chemist, educator*
Gardner, Arnold Burton *lawyer*
Garrick, Laura Morris *biochemistry educator*
Gazzo, Arthur D., Jr. *history professor*
Genco, Robert Joseph *immunologist, periodontist, educator, scientist*
Germain, Pamela *health facility administrator, educator*
Gibson, Judith W. *retired psychotherapist*
Gill, Turner *college football coach*
Gingher, Merlene C. *occupational therapist, educator*
Glanville, Robert Edward *lawyer*
Goldberg, Neil Alan *lawyer*
Grasser, George Robert *lawyer, real estate developer, consultant*
Greene, Robert Michael *lawyer*
Grosz, Edward M. *bishop*
Haase, Elaine M. *microbiologist, educator*
Halbreich, Uriel Morav *psychiatrist, educator*
Halpern, Ralph Lawrence *lawyer*
Hauptman, Herbert Aaron *mathematician, educator, researcher*
Headrick, Thomas Edward *lawyer, educator*
Hetzner, Donald Raymund *forensic social scientist*
Hoffman, Faith Louise *social worker*
Houseknecht, Stephen *artist, educator*
Hui, Sek Wen *research biophysicist, educator*
Iggers, Georg Gerson *history professor*
Irwin, Robert James Armstrong *retired investment company executive*
Jackson-Forsberg, Eric M. *curator, educator*
Jacobs, Jeremy Maurice, Sr. *diversified financial services company and professional sports team executive*
Jiang, Juan *chemical engineer*
Judelsohn, Richard *pediatrician, consultant*
Jurasek, Barbara S. *language educator*
Kalman, Thomas Ivan *chemistry professor, researcher*
Karwan, Mark Henry *engineering educator*
Kesavadas, Thenkurussi *mechanical engineering educator, researcher*
Kmiec, Edward Urban *bishop*
Kristoff, Karl W. *lawyer*
Lamb, Charles Moody *political scientist, educator*
Leavitt-Noble, Kimberly A. *special education educator*
Leclaire, Joelle Julie *economics professor*
Lee, Jaekyung *education educator, researcher*
Lele, Amol Shashikant *obstetrician, gynecologist*
Lema, Mark Joseph *anesthesiologist, educator*
Lippes, Gerald Sanford *lawyer*
Lipsey, Stanford *newspaper publisher*
Lombardo Appleby, Linda Rose *music educator*
Lukasik, Daniel T. *lawyer*
Luo, Hong *professor*
Macomber, Debbie *writer*
Mahaney, Michael C. *library director*
Manning, Kenneth Alan *lawyer*
Marinaccio, Bridget C. *social sciences educator*
Martin, Margaret M. *artist, educator, Author*
McKee, Eliane *retired literature and language professor*
Mehltretter, Kathleen M. *prosecutor*
Meredith, Dale Dean *civil engineering educator*
Merini, Rafika *humanities and foreign languages educator, writer*
Meshlovitz, Mary E. *educational consultant, special education educator*
Miller, Ryan *professional hockey player*
Milligan, John Drane *retired historian, educator*
Mindell, Eugene Robert *surgeon, educator*
Mucci, Gary Louis *lawyer*
Mutua, Makau Wa *dean, law educator*
Naughton, John Patrick *cardiologist, educator*
Nolan, James Paul *internist, educator, researcher*
Numminen, Teppo *professional hockey player*
Odza, Randall M. *lawyer*
Oliver, Dominick Michael *business educator*
O'Loughlin, Sandra S. *lawyer*
Olsen, R. Nills *law educator, former dean*
Parks, Michael E. *art educator, department chairman*
Patel, Mulchand Shambhubhai *biochemist, researcher*
Paterson, Eleanor Cohen *language educator, director*
Pegels, C. Carl *management consultant, educator*
Peradotto, John Joseph *retired classics educator, editor*
Petropoulos, Michalis *research scientist*
Pietrzak, Ted S. *art gallery director*
Piver, M. Steven *gynecologic oncologist*
Pogrebnyak, Victor Alexandrovich *physicist, researcher*
Popat, Saurin Rajnikant *oncologist, surgeon*
Price, Justine D. *art educator*
Pridgeon, Anthony R. *science educator*
Privitera, Gregory Joseph *neuroscientist, educator*
Putnam, Susan K. *psychology educator*
Quinn, Larry (Lawrence Quinn) *professional sports team executive*
Rachlin, Lauren David *lawyer*
Rai, Ram C. *physics professor*
Regier, Darcy John *professional sports team executive*
Reismann, Herbert *engineer, educator*
Reitan, Paul Hartman *retired geologist, educator*
Rich, Robert E., Jr. *frozen foods company executive*
Roberts, John S. *process engineer, researcher*
Ross, Gary Earl *writing educator*
Ruckenstein, Eli *chemical engineering professor*
Ruff, Lindy *professional hockey coach*
Russo, Kelly Anne *secondary school educator*
Sahlem, James Robert *law librarian*
Salvi, Richard *psychologist, otolaryngologist, educator*
Schweitzer, Shannon Troy *lighting designer, design educator*
Segalla, Thomas Francis *lawyer*
Seitz, Mary Lee *mathematics professor*
Selman, Alan Louis *computer science educator*
Shapiro, Stuart Charles *computer scientist, educator*
Shick, Richard Arlon *finance educator*
Siedlecki, Peter Anthony *English language and literature educator*
Simpson, George True, II, *surgeon, educator*
Simpson, John Barclay *academic administrator*
Skerrett, I. Martha *cell physiology professor*
Skretny, William Marion *federal judge*
Smallwood, Sandra Denise *pastor, daycare administrator*
Springate, James Edward *pediatrician*
Srikrishnan, Thamarapu *cancer research scientist, biophysicist*
Starks, Fred William *chemicals executive*
Stojkovic, Dejan B. *physicist, educator*
Sullivan, Margaret M. *editor-in-chief*
Taub, Mary Louise *biochemist*
Townsend, Carol Agnes *artist, educator*
Triggle, David John *dean, pharmacist, consultant*
Trotter, Herman (Eager), Jr. *retired music critic*
Tsai, Christina W. *civil engineer, educator*
Tucker, Melvin Jay *education educator, researcher*
Twagilimana, Aimable *language educator, writer*
Urban, Henry Zeller *publishing executive*
Vanek, Thomas *professional hockey player*
Vanini, J. Tim *environmental educator, coach, consultant*
Vela, Diana *educational association administrator*
Vladutiu, Adrian O. *physician, educator*
Weber, Thomas William *chemical engineering professor*
Weinberg, Thomas Stephen *social sciences educator*
Whelley, Patrick Liam *geologist*
Wicher, Camille Phyllis *nursing administrator*
Wiesenberg, Russel John *statistician*
Wilding, Gregory Edward *statistician, educator*
Wilmers, Robert George *bank executive*
Wisbaum, Wayne David *lawyer*
Wiswall, Thomas S. *lawyer*
Wölck, Wolfgang Hans-Joachim *linguist, educator*
Woolverton, Diane Marie *literature language and education professor*
Wright, Dana Jace *retired emergency nurse practitioner*
Wu, Changxu *researcher, consultant*
Xu, Jinhui *engineering educator*
Yen, Tingfang *research scientist*
You, Youngjae *science educator, researcher*
Zarembka, Paul *economics professor*
Zawicki, Joseph Leo *science educator*
Zhuang, Jun *engineering educator, researcher*
Zieziula, Charmayne C. *education educator*
Zirnheld, Jennifer L. *engineering educator, researcher*
Zittel-Palamara, Kimberley *social worker, educator*

Buskirk
Johanson, Patricia Maureen *artist, architect, park designer*

Byron
Ruck, Rosemarie Ulissa *retired social worker, freelance/self-employed writer*

Cairo
Ludwig, Laura Lonshein *poet*

Camillus
Alvaro, Anthony Joseph *music educator*
Armani, Frank Henry *retired lawyer*
Jerge, Marie Charlotte *minister*
Thompson, Mary Cecilia *nurse midwife*

Campbell Hall
Greenly, Colin *artist*
Ottaway, James Haller, Jr. *newspaper publisher*

Canaan
Hooper, Ian (John Derek Glass) *retired marketing communications executive*
Pennell, William Brooke *lawyer*
Walker, William Bond *painter, retired librarian*

Canandaigua
Beal, Myron Clarence *osteopath*
Chapple, Thomas Leslie *lawyer*
Jorgensen, Mia Melody *archaeologist, educator*
Lowther, Frank Eugene *research physicist*
McGuire, David Robert *music educator, composer*
Principato, Amy *psychologist*
Wormer, Thomas Andrew *surgeon*

Canastota
Madle, Allen Geoffrey *economics professor*
Mirante, Thomas Anthony *retired secondary education educator*
Perkins, Eddie *retired professional boxer*

Canton
Auster, Nancy Eileen Ross *economics professor*
Fox, William Lloyd, Jr. *academic administrator, educator, minister*
Goldberg, Rita Maria *foreign language educator*
Nouryeh, Christopher *humanities educator*
Sullivan, Daniel F. *retired academic administrator, sociologist, educator*

Carle Place
McCann, Jim (James F. McCann) *consumer products company executive*

Carmel
Laporte, Cloyd, Jr. *retired lawyer, manufacturing executive*
Lowe, Edwin Nobles *retired lawyer*

Castile
Krolikowski, Gary E. *social sciences educator*

Catskill
Ferrara, Lorraine Mary *literature and language educator*
Philp, Richard Nilson *writer, editor, journalist, historian*

Cazenovia
Carlson, William Clifford *retired defense industry executive, military officer*
Shattuck, George Clement *retired lawyer*
Wyckoff, Sylvia Spencer *art educator, artist*

Cedarhurst
Lagnado, Jennifer M. *assistant principal*
Schonfeld, Esther Miriam *lawyer*
Taubenfeld, Harry S. *lawyer*

Centerport
Mallamo, J. Lance *museum director*
Stevens, Martin Brian *publisher*
Stratigos, William Narge *computer company executive*
Trotta, Ric Charles *aerospace transportation executive, consultant*
Yadeka, Theophilus Adeniyi *hospital administrator*

Central Islip
Boyle, E. Thomas *federal judge*
James, Sharon Ann *elementary school educator*
Morris, Jeffrey Brandon *law educator*
Platt, Thomas Collier, Jr. *federal judge*

Chappaqua
de Janosi, Peter Engel *research manager*
George, Jean Craighead *author, illustrator*
Laun, Louis Frederick *government official*
Romney, Richard Bruce *lawyer*

Charlton
Kekes, John *philosopher, educator*

Chatham
Light, Lisa *travel company executive*
Weiner, Jack H. *lawyer*
Yale, John Paul *computer systems developer*

Chautauqua
Jackson, Juanita Wallace *educational consultant*
Schmidt, Edward Craig *lawyer*

Chazy
Young, Eric Otis *soil scientist, researcher, agronomist*

Cheektowaga
Ganz, Howard *consumer products company executive*
Kipler, James Michael *musician, educator*
Wagle, A. Tina *education educator, researcher*

Cherry Creek
Lee, Tat-Sum *physician*

Cherry Valley
Humes, Graham *investment banker*

Chester
Amelar, Richard Daniel *urologist*
Mackerodt, Fred *public relations specialist*

Chestnut Ridge
Day, Stacey Biswas *physician, educator*

Chittenango
Cassell, William Walter *retired accounting operations consultant*

Churchville
Balch, Glenn McClain, Jr. *academic administrator, minister, writer*

Cicero
Pink, (Alecia Beth Moore) *singer*
Schiess, Betty Bone *priest*

Claverack
Barrett, William Gary *advertising and marketing executive*

Clifton Park
Hilts, Earl T. *lawyer, government official, educator*
Nair, Laura *retired music educator*
Valenti, Laurie M. *elementary school educator*

Clinton
Redfield, Robert Horace *mathematician, educator*
Ring, James Walter *physics professor*
Stewart, Joan Hinde *academic administrator*
Walker, Edward S., Jr. *political science professor, former ambassador*

Cobleskill
Braun, Mark Edward *urban studies professor*
Cronin, Thomas J. III *science educator*
Hunsinger, Todd W. *agricultural studies educator, researcher*
O'Hanlon, Carol Ann *minister*
Puciato, Kathleen *education educator*
Sanchez, Joanna Marie *communications educator*
Westervelt, Gayle Gaetano *physical education educator*
Zingale, Donald Paul *academic administrator, educator*

Cochecton
Berlind, Robert Elliot *artist, educator*

Cold Spring
Pugh, Emerson William *electrical engineer*

Cold Spring Harbor
Crosson, Helen M. *librarian, director*
DeOrsay, Paul *museum director*
Hannon, Gregory J. *biology professor, researcher*
MacKay, Robert Battin *museum director*
Sebat, Jonathan *geneticist, educator*
Stillman, Bruce *molecular biologist*

Commack
Cohen, Judith W. *retired academic administrator*
Kurtz, Joel Barry *finance executive*
Price, Amelia Ruth *not-for-profit foundation president, artist, small business owner*
Steindler, Walter G. *retired lawyer*

Conesus
Dadrian, Vahakn Norair *retired sociology educator*

Cooperstown
Bordley, James, IV, *surgeon*
Harman, Willard Nelson *malacologist, educator*
Henderson, Rickey Henley *retired professional baseball player, former professional baseball coach*
Mays, Willie Howard, Jr., (Say Hey Kid) *retired professional baseball player*
Peters, Theodore, Jr. *emeritus research scientist, consultant*
Resnick, Steven David *pediatric dermatologist, educator*
Sauer, Leonard Austin *retired medical researcher*

Copake
Johnson, Paul Edward *poet, writer*
Schneier, Edward Vincent *political science professor*

Corinth
Dingman, Carolyn *school librarian*

Corning
Behm, Forrest Edwin *retired glass manufacturing company executive*
Buechner, Thomas Scharman *artist, museum director, retired glass manufacturing company executive*
Dunbar, Deborah S. *instructor*
Flaws, James B. *technology executive*
Guzzy, Mary Elizabeth *humanities educator, director*
Hatton, Vincent Paul *lawyer*
Hauselt, Denise Ann *lawyer*
Miller, Roger Allen *physicist*
Neubauer, Dean Veral *statistician*
Spillman, Jane Shadel *curator, writer, researcher*
Swain, Kristin A. *museum director*
Volanakis, Peter F. *manufacturing executive*
Whitehouse, David Bryn *museum director*
Williams, Jimmie Lewis *chemist, researcher*
Wilson, Cecilia Ann *special education educator*
Yuen, Po Ki *engineering company executive*

Cornwall On Hudson
Cameron, Elsa Gerow *music educator*
Peirce, Karen Patricia *education educator*

Corona
Finkelpearl, Tom *museum director*
Jackson, Andrew Preston *library director*

Cortland
Anderson, Donna Kay *musicologist, educator*
Brush, Florence Clapham *kinesiologist, exercise physiologist, physical education educator*
McMahon, Joseph M. *economics educator*
Parks, Paul Joseph *curator, educator*
Taylor, Leland Baridon *lawyer*
Weaver, Wesley James III *literature and language professor*

Cortlandt Manor
Lupiani, Jennifer Lynne *school psychologist*

Coxsackie
Moyna, John Lawrence *priest*

Cranberry Lake
Glavin, James Edward *landscape architect*

Cross River
Lang, Robert Mays, Jr. *manufacturing and not-for-profit executive*
Thorn, Susan Howe *interior designer*

Croton Falls
Curtis, Frank R. *lawyer*
Jakes, John *author*

Croton On Hudson
Plotch, Walter *management consultant, fund raising counselor*
Wandel, Sharon Lee *sculptor*

Dansville
Dearing, Teresa Allison *librarian*

Deer Park
Saia, Robert Angelo *retired science educator*

Delhi
Tessier, Jack T. *biology professor*

Delmar
Button, Rena Pritsker *public relations executive*
FitzAlan-Howard, Bennett-Thomas Henry Robert *news analyst, consultant, political scientist, theologian*
Matuszek, John Michael, Jr. *environmental scientist, educator, consultant*

Derby
Cuomo, Rivers *singer, songwriter*
Pordum, Francis J. *supervisor, former state legislator, educator, marketing professional*

Dix Hills
Braun, Ludwig *retired engineering educator*
Mymit, Chuck W. *music educator, musician*
Somerville, Daphine Holmes *retired elementary school educator*

Dobbs Ferry
Anbinder, Paul *publishing executive, consultant*
Guggenheimer, Tobias Immanuel Simon *architect*
Juettner, Diana D'Amico *lawyer, educator*
Kraetzer, Mary C. *sociologist, educator, consultant*
Meyer, Mark Alan *lawyer*
Pesetsky, Bette *writer, educator*
Poian, Edward Licio *historian*
Postman, Robert Derek *dean, mathematics professor, writer*
Simon, Lothar *publishing executive*
Sutton, Francis Xavier *social services administrator, consultant*

Douglaston
Daily, Thomas Vose *bishop emeritus*

Dryden
Baxter, Robert Banning *insurance company executive*
Powell, Marsha *director, educator*

Dundee
Miller, Ronald K. *real estate broker, educator*

Dunkirk
Huels, Steven Mark *physicist, mathematician, astronomer*
Strychalski, Elizabeth Arlene *nanotechnologist, physicist, researcher*

East Amherst
Ennis, Carol Robbins *retired music educator*
Garver, Walter Raymond *artist*
Kirdani, Esther May *retired school counselor*
Raven, Ronald Jacob *education educator, researcher, consultant*
Watson, Stewart Charles *construction executive*

East Aurora
Keem, Michael Dennis *veterinarian*
Perry, Marion J.H. *English educator*
Woodard, Carol Jane *educational consultant*

East Greenbush
Chen, Zewu *optics scientist*
McConville, Edward Patrick *lawyer*
Morris, Margretta Elizabeth *conservationist*
Mucci, Patrick John *financial consultant, realtor, commercial loan broker*

East Hampton
Appelhof, Ruth Stevens *museum director, curator, art historian*
Bancheri, Louis P., Jr. *training specialist, retired educator*
Delson, Sidney Leon *architect*
DePersia, Gary R. *real estate company executive, broker*
Ehren, Charles Alexander, Jr. *lawyer, educator*
Garrett, Charles Geoffrey Blythe *physicist, consultant*
Hope, Judith H. *former political organization administrator*
Humphrey, Craig Reed *social studies educator*
Jaroff, Leon Morton *retired magazine editor*
Jaudon, Valerie *artist*
Karp, Harvey Lawrence *metal products executive*
Mencher, Stuart Alan *sales and marketing executive*
Nash, Edward L. *advertising executive*
Praetorius, William Albert, Sr. *artist, retired real estate company officer, retired advertising executive*
Scott, Rosa Mae *artist, educator*
Strassfield, Christina Mossaides *museum director, chief curator*
Threlkeld, Richard Davis *retired broadcast journalist*
Wainwright, Carroll Livingston, Jr. *retired lawyer*

East Islip
Edwards, Guy Paul *library director*

East Meadow
Adler, Ira Jay *lawyer*
Beyer, Norma Warren *secondary school educator*
Hyman, Montague Allan *lawyer, educator*

East Northport
Juliano, John Louis *lawyer*
Kehoe, Thomas J. *food products executive*
Schlam, Mark Howard *international marketing executive*

East Norwich
Busner, Philip H. *retired lawyer, judge*
Rosen, Meyer Robert *chemical engineer*

East Setauket
Badalamenti, Fred Leopoldo *artist, educator*
Petrey, Sandy *educator*
Simons, James Harris *hedge fund manager*

East Syracuse
Ali, Amer *mechanical engineer*
Oot, Michael P. *lawyer*

Eastchester
Giuliano, Robert Paul *pharmacist*
Kravath, Alan Wolfe *retired education evaluator*
Masucci, Carmine *retired electrical engineer*

Eden
Thomas, Jimmy Lynn *retired treasurer*

Elba
Kauffman, William Joseph *editor, writer*

Elma
Hawk, George Wayne *retired electronics company executive*

Elmhurst
Brown, Ronald Joseph *religious studies educator*
Chang, Sheng-Yen *Buddhist monk, educator*
Farrell, John Thomas *priest, educator*
Masci, Joseph Richard *physician*

Elmira
Burke, Rita Hoffmann *retired educational administrator*
Graham, David Richard *orthopedic surgeon*
Kelly, John J. *performing arts educator, director*
Leveen, Pauline *retired history professor, government professor*
Miran, Patricia Marie *art educator*
Reddick, Bryan DeWitt *academic administrator*
Smith, Martha C. *college librarian*

Elmont
Butera, Ann Michele *consulting company executive*
Cusack, Thomas Joseph *retired banker*

Elmsford
Demopoulos, Harry Byron *retired pathologist, pharmaceutical researcher*
Miranda, Robert Nicholas *publishing executive, director*
Panitz, Lawrence *physician*
Raymond, George Marc *city planner, educator*

Endicott
Chan, Benson *mechanical engineer*
Cocozzella, Peter *retired language educator*
Conlon, Michael James *literature and language professor*
Goodwin, Charles Hugh *technology education educator*
Markovich, Voya R. *information technology executive*
Matienzo, Luis J. *chemical engineer*

Fabius
Sweetland, Dale A. *former county official, former dairy farmer*

Fairport
Bartlett, Cody Blake *retired lawyer*
Chari, Krishnan *research scientist*

Far Rockaway
Epstein, Samuel Abraham *sales executive*
Helfgott, Samson *lawyer*
Ulrich, Eric A. *city councilman*

Farmingdale
Bandyopadhyay, Amitabha *engineering educator*
Chaskes, Stuart Jay *microbiologist, educator*
Dunne, John C. *bishop*
Goodstone, Michael S. *psychology professor, consultant*
Ibrahim, Ahmed Zaki *science educator*
Mason, James Eliot *energy executive, director*
Nolan, Peter John *physics professor*
Temple, Donald Edward *medical association administrator*

Fayetteville
Hadyk-Wepf, Sonia Margaret *artist, real estate manager*
Krathwohl, David Reading *retired education educator*
Pachter, Irwin Jacob *pharmaceutical consultant*

Fire Island Pines
Herregat, Guy-Georges Jacques *retired banker*

Fishkill
Brocks, Eric *ophthalmologist, surgeon*

Floral Park
Corbett, William John *lawyer, public relations executive, minister, consultant*
Curci, Paula *counseling educator, poet, radio personality*
Daloia, Rachel Rosemary *music educator*
Giuffré, John Joseph *lawyer*
Sottile, Kathleen M. *principal, music educator*

Flushing
Alcalay, Ammiel *literature and language professor, writer*
Baker, A. Harvey *psychology professor*
Beltran, Carlos *professional baseball player*
Beveridge, Andrew Alan *sociologist, educator, consultant*
Bird, Thomas Edward *foreign language and literature educator*
Carlson, Cynthia Joanne *artist, educator*
Cesarano, Michael Ferdinand *theater educator, actor*
Chang, Jason *artist, educator*
Dalal, Aman K. *infectious diseases specialist*
Delgado, Carlos Juan *professional baseball player*
Einhorn, Susan *theater educator, director*
Engel, Robert Ralph *chemist, educator, dean*
Farago, John Michael *law educator, consultant*
Feng, Ying *painter, educator*
Fichtel, Rudolph Robert *retired association executive*
Ghazarbekian, Sahak *retired international civil servant, United Nations consultant*
Goldenshteyn, Vladimir Lev *civil engineer*
Goldman, Norman Lewis *chemist, educator*
Goldsmith, Howard *writer, consultant*
Gonzalez, Tony *artist, educator*
Hart, Antonio Maurice *musician, educator*
Hernandez, Livan (Eisler Livan Carrera Hernandez) *professional baseball player*
Hon, John Wingsun *physician*
Hoyt, Marilyn Christine *science center executive*
Hu, Huping *biophysicist, lawyer*
Kaufmann, Hugo M. *economics professor, director*
Khalil, Andrea Flores *literature and language professor*
Kim, Mi Suk *medical educator*
Kim, Sun-Hae *retired medical/surgical nurse, writer, nurse midwife, physical therapist*
Kopp, Ilya Zinovij *engineer, educator, researcher*
Lonigan, Paul Raymond *language professional, educator*
Manuel, Jerry *professional baseball team manager*
Mendelson, Elliott *mathematician, educator*
Minaya, Omar *professional sports team executive*
Missick, Patricia Ann *secondary school educator*
Muehlbauer, Esther Indelman *biology professor*
Nussbaum, Michel Ernest *physician*
Pekar, Stephen F. *geologist, paleontologist, oceanographer*
Perez, Oliver *professional baseball player*
Putz, J.J. (Joseph Jason Putz) *professional baseball player*
Rabassa, Gregory *language educator, translator, poet*
Rahal, James Joseph, Jr. *medical educator*
Reddy, Boojala Vijay *biology professor*
Reyes, Jose Bernabe *professional baseball player*
Rodriguez, Francisco Jose *professional baseball player*
Rogers-Dillon, Robin *sociologist, educator*
Rotenberg, Susan A. *research scientist, educator*
Santana, Johan (Johan Alexander Santana Araque) *professional baseball player*
Schwartz, Estar Alma *lawyer*
Seeling, Joni M. *biology professor*
Sheffield, Gary Antonian *professional baseball player*
Shen, Ronger *artist, educator*
Smith, Charles William *social sciences educator*
Stahl, Frank Ludwig *civil engineer*
Stavisky, Toby Ann *state legislator*
Steinberg, Stephen *sociologist, educator, writer*
Stinson, Sara *anthropologist, educator*
Sungolowsky, Joseph *literature educator*
Torrence-Thompson, Juanita Lee *editor, public relations executive*
Tytell, John *literature educator, writer*
Washington, Mario R. *computer company executive*
Wilpon, Fred *professional sports team executive*
Winter, Amy *art historian, critic*
Wright, David Allen *professional baseball player*
Yeo, Kim Eng *artist*
Zinnes, Harriet Fich *poet, fiction writer, retired English educator, literary and art critic*

Fly Creek
Dusenbery, Walter Condit *sculptor*

Forest Hills
Barger, David J. *air transportation executive*
Barnes, Edward A. *air transportation executive*
Battaglia, Alex *air transportation executive*
Brooks, Martin *electronic media executive*
Buhks, Ephraim *college administrator, technology educator*
Eden, Alvin Noam *pediatrician, writer*
Flowers, Cynthia *investment company executive*
Henley, Arthur *writer, editor*
Katz, Melinda R. *city councilwoman, former state legislator*
Kra, Pauline Skornicki *French language educator*
Maruster, Robert Alan *air transportation executive*
Morgan, Jacqui *illustrator, painter, art educator, writer*
Polakoff, Abe *baritone*
Reis, Don *publishing executive*
Weber-Levine, Phyllis *secondary school educator*

Forestville
Adams, Lee Towne *lawyer*

Fort Drum
Youngs, Michael Theron, Jr. *non-commissioned officer*

Franklin Square
Indiviglia, Salvatore Joseph *artist, retired military officer*
Maffia, Jason *health services administrator*
Vanora, Jerome Patrick *lawyer*

Fredonia
Aghazadeh, Seyed-Mahmoud *finance educator*
Benton, Allen Haydon *biology professor*
Cox, Jonathan Andrew *mathematics professor*
Croxton, Jack Sanders *psychology professor, director, consultant*
Jarvis, Joseph Anthony *history professor*
McVicker, Jeanette *literature and language professor*
Stinson, John Jerome *literature and language professor*
Wescott, Howard Blakely *retired humanities educator*
Zlotchew, Clark Michael *Spanish educator*

Freeport
Berg, Alan *lawyer, arbitrator*
Ferentino, Sheila Connolly *psychologist, consultant*
Ledkovsky, Marina *retired Slavic languages and literature educator*
Mitchell, Alice Joyce Jones *retired secondary school educator, dietician*
Pullman, Maynard Edward *biochemist*

Fresh Meadows
Amram, Laura *psychiatrist*
Duckett, Lila Wheeler *retired language educator, writer*
Godfrey, Philip M. *plastic surgeon*
Greenberg, Robert Jay *law educator*
Ravinder, Ujwala *research scientist*
Vigoda, Paul Evan *secondary school educator*

Fulton
Dowd, Kenneth Robert *elementary school educator*

Gainesville
Drumma, Eric Matthew *elementary school educator*

Garden City
Bouchard, Wendy Ann Borstel *language educator*
Brett, Laurel *literature and language professor*
Calamari, Joseph August *legal educator*
Conlon, Brian Thomas *promotion executive*
Cook, George Valentine *lawyer, consultant*
Doucette, Mary-Alyce *computer company executive*
Douglas, Barry K. *plastic surgeon*
Einenkel, Robert Herbert *theater educator, actor, director*
Fishberg, Gerard *lawyer*
Freedman, Monroe Henry *lawyer, educator*
Harwood, Stanley *retired judge, lawyer, arbitrator, mediator*
Jenkins, Kenneth Vincent *literature educator, writer*
Kaplan, Joel Stuart *lawyer*
Klein, Arnold Spencer *lawyer*
Laureano, Mari *government agency administrator, writer*
McNair, Marcia L. *language educator, writer, editor*
Okoampa-Ahoofe, Kwame *language educator, historian*
Paterson, Basil Alexander *lawyer*
Persons, John Wade *lawyer*
Podwall, Kathryn Stanley *biology professor*
Prabhakar, Kumkum *biology professor*
Primeggia, Salvatore *sociologist, educator*
Riordan, Sean Patrick Josep *lawyer, educator*
Rosenberg, Lee *lawyer*
Russell, Stella Pandell *artist, author, educator*
Scott, Robert Allyn *academic administrator*
Sheinbaum, Marc X. *bank executive*
Shuart, James Martin *retired academic administrator*
Steuer, Michael *mathematics professor*
Wetherill, Linda Marie *musician, educator, performing arts association administrator*
Young, Yih-Jin *sociologist, educator*

Garden City Park
Radu, Bogdan *aerospace engineer*

Gardiner
Mabee, Carleton *historian, educator*

Garnerville
Chapman, Margaret Elizabeth *elementary school educator*

Garrison
Callahan, Daniel John *biomedical researcher*
Kaebnick, Gregory E. *editor, researcher*
Murray, Thomas Henry *bioethics educator, writer*

Geneseo
Beason, Robert Curtis *biologist, educator*
Cook, William Robert *history professor, religious studies educator*
Evans, Beverly Jean *literature and language professor*
Herzman, Ronald B. *literature and language professor*
Kelly, David Michael *poet, creative writing educator*
Mooney, Michael C. *academic administrator, coach*
Scalzo, Joseph *history professor*
Zuckerman, Mary Ellen Waller *marketing educator*

Geneva
Hrazdina, Geza *biochemistry educator*
Roelofs, Wendell Lee *biochemistry professor, consultant*
Vecchiotti, Tony V. *insurance agent*

Germantown
Farberman, Harold *conductor, composer*
Linney, Romulus *author, educator*

Getzville
Fujia, Shigeji *physics professor*

Ghent
Rao, Natti Sreerama *small business owner, consultant*

Glen Cove
Burnham, Harold Arthur *pharmaceutical executive, physician*
Hoynes, Louis LeNoir, Jr. *lawyer*
Mansi, Joseph Anneillo *public relations company executive*
Rothberg, Judith *elementary school educator, researcher*

Glen Head
Newmark, Marilyn *sculptor*
Stack, Edward William *diversified financial services company executive*

Glen Oaks
Hanoverian, Susan Michelle *lawyer*
Malhotra, Anil *psychiatrist, educator*

Glendale
Maltese, Serphin Ralph *state legislator, lawyer*

Glenford
Rieder, Naomi *artist*

Glenmont
Bellizzi, John J. *law enforcement association administrator, pharmacist, educator*

Glens Falls
Bartlett, Richard James *lawyer*
Mahoney, Mark *newspaper editor*
Setford, David F. *museum director*

Glenville
Anderson, Roy Everett *retired electrical engineer*

Glenwood
Chambers, Denning Jessyca *middle school educator*

Gouverneur
Kuehl, Alexander Edward *physician, health facility administrator, educator, writer*
Leader, Robert John *lawyer*

Grand Island
Hennigar, William Grant, Jr. *dentist*
Remson, Debra S. *music educator*

Great Neck
Appel, Gerald *investment advisor*
Arams, Frank Robert *electronics executive*
Bender, Bruce F. *book publishing executive*
Brownstein, Martin Herbert *retired dermatopathologist*
Christie, George Nicholas *economist, consultant*
Dines, David Michael *surgeon, educator*
Dines, Joshua S. *orthopedist, sports medicine physician*
Gabriel, Mordecai Lionel *biologist, educator*
Gold, Alan H. *plastic surgeon*
Goldman, Ira Steven *gastroenterologist*
Hurwitz, Johanna (Johanna Frank) *writer*
Jacobson, Marc Stephen *pediatrician, educator*
Jacono, Andrew A. *plastic surgeon*
Kahn, David *editor, author*
Kechijian, Paul *dermatologist, educator*
Marcus, Philip *associate dean*
Minkoff, Jack *retired economics professor*
Panes, Jack Samuel *publishing executive*
Samuel, Paul *retired cardiologist*
Scherr, Lawrence *internist, healthcare educator, historian*
Seckler, Bernard David *retired mathematics professor, translator*
Seidler, Doris *artist*
Shons, Alan Rance *plastic surgeon, surgical oncologist, educator*
Silber, Jeff Scott *physician, educator*
Wolff, Edward *physician*
Zaman, Kahkashan T. *psychologist*

Great River
Edwards, Christine E. *artist*

Greenfield Center
Bruchac, Joseph *writer, storyteller*

Greenlawn
Gorin, Brian A. *systems engineer*
Robinson, Kenneth Patrick *lawyer, electronics executive*

Greenport
Pedersen, Richard Foote *diplomat, academic administrator*
Watts, Harold Wesley *economist, educator*

Greenvale
Araoz, Daniel Leon *psychologist, educator*
Cordaro, Matthew Charles *energy and utility executive, educator*
Coutts, Robert B. *retired aerospace transportation executive*
Dircks, Phyllis Toal *language educator*
Halper, Emanuel B(arry) *lawyer, real estate developer, consultant, law educator, writer, real estate broker*
Krasnoff, Eric *health products executive*
Kusukawa, Akira *demographer, educator*
Manzari, Laura Lynn *law educator*
Regazzi, John James III *dean, publishing executive*
Senft, Mason George *musician*
Steinberg, David Joel *academic administrator, historian, educator*
Sugar, Joseph Robert *musician, conductor, educator*

Groveland
Battersby, Harold Ronald *retired anthropologist, archaeologist, linguist*

Guilderland
Nichols Randall, Barbara Lee *library director, educator*

Hamburg
Calkins, Evan *physician, educator*
Hargesheimer, Elbert III *lawyer*
Markulis, Henryk John *career military officer*
Wiltse, Peter Christian *lawyer*
Witt, Dennis Ruppert *mathematics educator*
Wolfe, Peter J. *retired performing arts educator*

Hamilton
Berlind, Bruce Peter *poet, educator*
Bien, Gloria *Chinese educator*
Dallal, Shawkat Jamil (Shaw Dallal) *law educator*
Edmonston, William Edward, Jr. *retired publishing executive, writer, psychology professor*
Hansen, Bruce C. *psychology professor*
Johnston, Michael (William) *political science educator, university administrator*
Knuth-Klenck, Deborah Jane *English and women's studies educator*
McIntyre, Lee Cameron *philosophy educator*
Moynihan, William J. *museum executive*
Parks, Beth *physics professor*
Pruitt, Nancy Louise *educator*
Roelofs, Lyle Dean *academic administrator, physics professor*
Rotter, Andrew Jon *history educator*
Tucker, Thomas William *mathematics professor*

Hampton Bays
Baker, Donald Gene *social sciences educator*
Bucicchia, Carolanne Stephanie *elementary school educator*
Jacobs, George Braun *neurosurgeon*
Wille, Rosanne Louise *educational consultant*

Hancock
DeLuca, Ronald *former advertising agency executive, consultant*
Senia, Grace Melanie *language and music educator*

Hannacroix
Schwebler, Stephen *retired chemist*

Harrison
Crawford, R. George *investment company executive, educator, filmmaker*
Hurley, Dean C. *bank executive, lawyer*
Kramer, Alan Sharfsin *lawyer*
Silverman, Amy Jocelyn *psychiatrist*
Strone, Michael Jonathan *real estate consultant, lawyer, art consultant*
Weinstein, Carol *psychiatrist*

Hartsdale
Chait, Maxwell Mani *physician*
Greenawalt, Peggy Freed Tomarkin *advertising executive*
Katz, John *investment banker*
Martin, Daniel Richard *pharmaceutical executive*
Pell, Arthur Robert *human resources specialist, consultant, writer*

Hastings On Hudson
Edelman, Paul Sterling *lawyer*
Goldstein, Alvin *lawyer*
Landau, Peter Edward *editor*
Reich, Herb *editor*
Rosch, Paul John *internist, educator*
Tarlov, Alvin Richard *foundation administrator, physician, educator*
Thornlow, Carolyn *law firm administrator, consultant*
Weinstein, Edward Michael *architect, consultant*

Hauppauge
Buckley, Robert Matthew *electrical engineer*
Doucette, David Robert *information technology executive*
Hausman, Howard *electronics executive*
Reid, Margaret Elizabeth *elementary and secondary school educator*
Rupp, Katherine M. *marketing executive*

Haverstraw
Alpert, Revell Judith *retired information technology executive*
Eidelman, Sharon (Sherry) R. *marriage and family therapist*

Hawthorne
Gong, Leiguang *computer scientist, researcher*
McClung, John Arthur *cardiologist*
Pianka, George *orthopedic surgeon*
Russell, Jim *application developer*
Taneja, Indu *medical educator, researcher*
Ward, Christopher *computer scientist, researcher*
Zadrozny, Wlodek W. *computer scientist*

Hempstead
Aaron, Merik Roy *financial executive, lawyer, judge, educator*
Berliner, Herman Albert *academic administrator, economist, educator, dean*
Callahan, Bill (William E. Callahan) *professional football coach*
Chaiken, MarthaLeah *psychology and biology scientist*
Coleman, Benjamin Joseph *music educator*
Condon, Martha Ann *ecologist, biologist*
Demleitner, Nora Verena *dean, law educator*
Faneca, Alan Joseph, Jr. *professional football player*
Freese, Melanie Louise *librarian, educator*
Galofaro, Manuel *language educator*
Goodhue, Thomas Wallace *Clergyman*
Heuermann-Nowik, Patricia Calhoun *theater director*
Karagozoglu, Ahmet *finance educator*
Levinthal, Beth Ellen (Kuby Levinthal) *museum director*
Mahon, Malachy Thomas, Sr. *lawyer, educator*
Masheck, Joseph Daniel *art critic, educator*
Ryan, Rex *professional football coach*
Sanchez, Mark *professional football player*
Schechtman, Saul *conductor*
Shafritz, Keith Michael *psychology professor*
Sharifov, Rovshan Chingiz *lawyer*
Sobel, Sabrina G. *chemistry professor*
Tannenbaum, Mike (Michael B. Tannenbaum) *professional sports team executive*
Washington, Leon *professional football player*
Waterman, Jason *pediatrician*
Wu, Michelle M. *dean, law educator*
Zagano, Phyllis *religious studies educator*
Zhou, Zuhan *literature educator*

Henrietta
Byfield, Bert A. *conservative humanitarian novelist*
Drummond, Malcolm McAllister *electronics engineer*

Herkimer
Gay, Douglas MacKenzie *pharmacologist*

Hewlett
Cohen, Lawrence Alan *health facility administrator*
Steinfeld, Philip Sheldon *pediatrician*

Hicksville
Kasimakis, Debra Ann *performing company executive*
Lieberman, Douglas Mark *lawyer*
Stein, Melvin A. *accountant*
Yen, Henry Chin-Yuan *computer systems programmer, software engineer, consulting company executive*

Highland Falls
Combs, Farah *ancient language educator*

Hillsdale
Lunde, Asbjorn Rudolph *lawyer*
Parmet, Herbert Samuel *historian, writer*

Holland
OBrien, Scott *entrepreneur*

Holley
Lepkowski, Suzanne Joy *language educator*

Hollis
Jairam, Khelanand Vishvaykanand *lawyer*

Homer
Gustafson, John Alfred *biology professor*

Honeoye Falls
Hillabrandt, Larry Lee *service industry executive*

Hopewell Junction
Ouyang, Xu *research and development company executive*
Sellingsloh, Hulda Knipling *retired artist*
Yin, Haizhou *computer scientist*
Yu, Haiping *research scientist*

Hornell
Hunter, John Orr *retired college president*
Pulos, William Whitaker *lawyer*

Horseheads
Clark, Judy Ann *elementary school educator*
Halm, Brian Thomas *technologist, educator*
Krauss, Patricia Richardson *educator*

Houghton
Congdon, Judy Ann *music educator*
Marcum, James Arthur *physiology and philosophy of science educator*

Howard Beach
Leiter, Samuel L. *theater educator*

Hudson
Agata, Burton C. *lawyer, educator*
Miner, Jacqueline *political consultant*

Hudson Falls
Leary, Daniel *artist*

Hunters Point
Lundgren, Richard John *real estate executive, city planner, preservationist*

Huntington
Anzalone, Robert S. *history professor*
Christiansen, Donald David *electrical engineer, publishing executive, consultant*
Connor, Joseph Robert *editor*
German, June Resnick *lawyer*
Hochberg, Ronald Mark *lawyer*
Hofmann, Jennifer *physician assistant, educator*
Joseph, Richard Saul *cardiologist, educator*
LaTourrette, James Thomas *retired electrophysics, electrical engineering and computer science educator*
Masear, Claude *music educator, musician*
Tucker, William P. *lawyer, writer*
Williams, Charles Theodore *language educator*

Huntington Station
Agosta, Vito *mechanical and aerospace engineering educator*
Stevens, Susan Seltenreich Cirillo *special education educator*

Williams, Una Joyce *retired psychiatric social worker*

Hurley
Smith, Lewis Motter, Jr. *retired advertising and direct marketing executive*

Hyde Park
Koch, Cynthia M. *library and museum director*
Ryan, L. Timothy *chef, educator, academic administrator*

Ilion
Vivacqua, Ritamarie Lillian *psychology educator*

Interlaken
Bleiler, Everett Franklin *writer, publishing company executive*

Inwood
Chernov, Yuriy D. *engineering executive*
Cohan, Delorie Rose *elementary music educator*

Irving
Greatbatch, Wilson *biomedical engineer*

Irvington
Carey, Edward John *utilities executive*
Jackson, Billy Ray *physical education educator*
Jackson, Thomas Gene *lawyer*
Sherman, Norman Mark *advertising agency executive*

Islandia
Christenson, Michael J. *management software technology company executive*
Handal, Kenneth V. *computer software company executive, lawyer*
McCracken, William E. *information technology executive*
Nugent, Alan F. *software company executive*
Pruzansky, Joshua Murdock *lawyer*
Swainson, John A. *software company executive*

Islip
Libert, Nancy Porta *retired elementary school educator*

Ithaca
Abrams, Meyer Howard *language educator*
Adler, Kraig (Kerr) *biology professor*
Alexander, Gregory Stewart *law educator*
Allmon, Warren D. *museum director, educator*
Ambegaokar, Vinay *retired physics professor*
Aneja, Rajindra *biotechnologist, consultant*
Ashdown, Susan P. *art educator*
Ayoub, Ali *agricultural and food scientist*
Azis, Iwan Jaya *economics educator*
Barbasch, Dan Mihai *mathematics professor*
Barcelo, John James III *law educator*
Barrett, Christopher B. *economics professor*
Bassett, William Akers *retired geologist, educator*
Bauman, Dale Elton *nutritional biochemistry professor*
Beer, Steven Vincent *plant pathologist, educator*
Ben Daniel, David Jacob *entrepreneurship educator, consultant*
Bramble, James Henry *mathematician, educator*
Briggs, Vernon Mason, Jr. *retired economics professor*
Butler, Thomas James *biochemist, researcher*
Clarkson, George Edward *theology educator, minister*
Clermont, Kevin Michael *law educator*
Colby-Hall, Alice Mary *language educator*
Confer, John L. *retired biology professor*
Cottrell, G. Walton *manufacturing executive*
Cramton, Roger Conant *lawyer, educator*
Crepet, William Louis *botanist, educator*
Csaki, Csaba *physicist*
Daouk, Hazem *finance educator*
Darlington, Richard Benjamin *retired psychologist, educator, researcher*
Datta, Ashim Kumar *engineering researcher and educator*
Davies, Peter John *plant physiology educator, researcher*
De Boer, Pieter Cornelis Tobias *mechanical and aerospace engineering educator*
Deinert, Herbert *German language, literature and history educator*
Dev, Chekitan *science educator*
Dhondt, André A. *zoologist, educator*
Dick, Richard Irwin *environmental engineer, educator*
Dietert, Rodney Reynolds *immunology and toxicology educator*
Dimitrova, Nora Mitkova *classics scholar*
Donahue, Steve *men's college basketball coach*
Dyckman, Thomas Richard *accountant, educator*
Earle, Clifford John, Jr. *mathematician*
Earle, Elizabeth Deutsch *biology professor*
Easley, David *economics professor*
Eastman, Lester Fuess *electrical engineer, educator*
Eddy, Donald Davis *language educator*
Ehrenberg, Ronald Gordon *economist, educator*
Eisner, Thomas *biologist, educator*
Emlen, Stephen Thompson *zoology educator*
Farnum, Cornelia Ellen *veterinarian, educator*
Feldman, Shelley *sociologist, director*
Ferri, Laurent *curator, educator*
Fick, Gary Warren *agronomist, educator*
Fonder, Mark Leslie *music educator*
Freed, Jack Herschel *chemist, educator*
Fuchs, W. Kent *engineering educator*
Ginsparg, Paul *physicist*
Gold, Michael Evan *law educator*
Goldsmith, Paul Felix *astronomy and physics professor*
Grippi, Salvatore William *artist*
Grubb, David Thomas *science educator, researcher*
Guckenheimer, John *mathematician*
Habicht, Jean Pierre *public health educator*
Hairston, Nelson George, Jr. *ecologist, educator*
Halpern, Bruce Peter *academic administrator, researcher, educator*
Hammer, David Andrew *nuclear science and engineering educator*
Hardy, Jane Elizabeth *communications educator*
Harriott, Peter *chemical engineering educator*
Haywood, Jennifer Sarah *music educator*
Hemmings, Madeleine Blanchet *retired, not-for-profit administrator, grant writer, public policy director, media consultant*
Henry, Susan Armstrong *biology professor, dean*
Herskowitz, Richard Julian *arts manager*
Hess, George Paul *biochemist, educator*
Hoffmann, Michael Peter *agricultural studies educator*
Hoffmann, Roald *chemist, educator*
Hohendahl, Peter Uwe *German language and literature educator*
Holowka, David A. *research scientist*
Hopcroft, John Edward *computer scientist, educator*
Howard, Scott Sheridan *research scientist*
Howarth, Robert W. *biology professor*
Howell, Debra Lynne *information technology executive*
Hull, Isabel Virginia *history professor*
Husa, Karel *composer, conductor, educator*
Jagendorf, André Tridon *physiologist*
Jarrow, Robert Alan *economist, educator*
Jeong, JongMin *systems administrator, researcher*
Jordan, Kurt Anders *archaeologist, educator*
Kadiyali, Vrinda *marketing & economics educator*
Kahn, Alfred Edward *economist, educator, government official*
Kahn, Lawrence Max *economics professor*
Kammen, Michael *historian, educator*
Kanbur, Ravi *economist*
Kennedy, Kenneth Adrian Raine *biological and forensic anthropologist*
Kennedy, Wilbert Keith, Sr. *agronomy educator, retired university official*
Kenney, Anne *university librarian*
Kessler, Andre *ecologist, educator*
Kingsbury, John Merriam *botanist, educator*
Kinoshita, Toichiro *physicist*
Kleinberg, Jon M. *computer scientist, educator*
Korf, Richard Paul *mycology educator*
LaCapra, Dominick Charles *historian, educator*
LaFeber, Walter Frederick *historian, educator, writer*
Laquatra, Joseph *humanities educator*
Lee, David Morris *physics professor*
Leibovich, Sidney *engineering educator*
Lengemann, Frederick William *retired physiology educator*
Lepage, Gerard Peter *physics educator*
Lesser, William Henri *marketing educator*
Linke, Simpson *electrical engineering educator*
Liu, Rui Hai *science educator*
Loucks, Daniel Peter *environmental systems engineer*
Lyons, Thomas Patrick *economics professor*
Maxwell, William Laughlin *retired industrial engineering educator*
McConkey, James Rodney *literature and language educator, writer*
McDougal, Stuart Yeatman *comparative literature educator, author*
McGuire, William *civil engineer, educator*
McLafferty, Fred Warren *chemist, educator*
Merrill, Andrea Tai *musician, educator*
Meyburg, Arnim Hans *transportation engineer, educator, consultant*
Mikus, Eleanore Ann *artist*
Mueller, Betty Jeanne *social work educator*
Nerode, Anil *mathematician, educator*
Nishii, Lisa *psychology professor*
Norton, Mary Beth *history educator, writer*
O'Connor, Stanley James *Asian studies educator*
Oliver, Jack Ertle *geophysicist, educator*
Onishi, Deidre *theater educator, director*
O'Rourke, Thomas Denis *civil engineer, educator*
Otani, Niels Fujio *electrical engineering educator*
Paau, Alan Shiukee *academic administrator, biotechnologist, educator*
Park, Roy Hampton, Jr. *advertising executive*
Parlange, Jean-Yves *environmental engineer, educator*
Pelto, Gretel H. *nutritional anthropologist, educator*
Perry, Margaret *librarian, writer*
Pikuz, Sergey *physicist, researcher*
Pohl, Robert Otto *physics professor*
Poleskie, Stephen Francis *retired art educator, artist, writer, publisher*
Pope, Stephen Bailey *mechanical engineer, educator*
Poppensiek, George Charles *retired veterinary scientist, educator*
Rader, Nancy Louise de Villiers *psychology professor, consultant*
Radzinowicz, Mary Ann *language educator*
Reyna, Valerie Frances *psychologist, educator, researcher*
Rhodes, Frank Harold Trevor *academic administrator, geologist*
Richardson, Robert Coleman *physics professor, researcher*
Rifkin, Deborah *music educator*
Roberts, E. F. *law educator*
Robinson, Franklin Westcott *museum director, art historian*
Rochon, Thomas Richard *academic administrator*
Rodríguez, Ferdinand *chemical engineer, educator*
Rogers, Michael Bruce *physics professor*
Rutzke, Corinne Johnson *research scientist*
Scheraga, Harold Abraham *retired physical chemistry professor*
Schneiderman, Anne Mercedes *lawyer, neurobiologist*
Schuler, Mary Callaghan *artist, educational association administrator*
Schwab, Stewart Jon *dean, law educator*
Schwartz, Donald Franklin *communication scientist*
Sethna, James Patarasp *physicist*
Seznec, Alain *dean, language educator*
Shepherd, Sean *composer*
Sherman, Paul W. *animal behavior educator*
Sherwin, Emily *law educator*
Shore, Richard Arnold *mathematics professor*
Silbey, Joel Henry *history professor*
Skorton, David Jan *academic administrator*
Smith, Julian Cleveland, Jr. *chemical engineering professor*
Smith, Robert John *anthropology educator*
Sukle, Robert J. *language educator*
Swieringa, Robert Jay *accounting educator, former dean*
Thomas, Jacob Earl *retired physicist*
Thomas, Louis Joseph *dean, management educator*
Thorbecke, Erik *economics professor*
Tiwari, Sandip *electrical and computer engineering educator*
Tomek, William Goodrich *agricultural economist*
Toorawa, Shawkat M. *social studies educator*
Trotter, Leslie Earl *operations research specialist, educator*
Urazghildiiev, Ildar R. *mathematician*
Vanek, Jaroslav *economist, educator*
Viele, Patricia Thompson *physics and astronomy librarian*
Walcott, Charles *neurobiology and behavior educator*
Waldman, Michael *economist, educator*
Walter, Michael Todd *engineering educator*
Wasserman, Robert Harold *biology professor*
Webb, Watt Wetmore *physicist, researcher*
Weinstein, Leonard Harlan *institute program director, educator*
Whitaker, Susanne Kanis *veterinary medical librarian*
Widom, Benjamin *chemistry professor*
Wikoff, Karin *school librarian*
Wills, Michael Stephen *nutritionist, quality assurance professional, photographer*
Wootton, John Francis *physiology educator*
Yu, Long-Xi *agriculturist, researcher*
Zall, Robert Rouben *food scientist, educator*
Zaslaw, Neal *musicologist*

Jackson Heights
Dacey, Paul *artist*
Imayeva, Olga Borisovna *artist*
Ryan, Judith Ann *dean*
Stevenson, Amanda (Sandy Stevens) *librettist, composer, songwriter*

Jamaica
Angione, Howard Francis *lawyer, retired editor*
Barjis, Joseph *computer scientist, educator*
Boghosian, Stella Maris *education educator*
Brondolo, Elizabeth *psychologist, educator*
Brown, Kenneth Lloyd *lawyer*
Bunshaft, Charles Edward *elementary school educator, consultant*
Cade, Walter III *artist, actor, musician, vocalist*
Chirico, Donna M. *psychologist, educator, researcher*
Cho, Seokhee *science administrator, director*
Chropufka, Mark A. *information technology executive, poet*
Coppa, Frank John *historian, educator*
DeBello, Joan Elizabeth *mathematics professor*
Desormeaux, Kent J. *jockey*
Edwards, Cynthia E. *principal*
Ekbatani, Glayol *language educator, director, writer*
Eltabib, Sarah *history professor*
Flake, Floyd Harold *former United States Representative from New York*
Galante, Thomas W. *library director*
Garcia-Febo, Loida *librarian*
Gati, William Eugene *architect, industrial designer, educator*
Geffner, Donna Sue *speech pathology/audiology services professional, audiologist, educator*
Holmes, Aliya E. *educational technology educator*
Kaplan, Carolyn Sue *elementary school educator*
Kemeny, M. Margaret *oncologist, surgeon, hospital administrator, educator*
Kinkley, Jeffrey C. *historian*
Lees, Francis *economics professor*
Meeks, Gregory Weldon *United States Representative from New York*
Merlino, Joseph P. *psychiatrist, director*
Morrill, Joyce Marie *social worker, educator, photographer*
Ostrovskii, Mikhail Iosifovich *mathematician*
Parmet, Robert David *historian, educator*
Pratt-Johnson, Yvonne Karen *education professor*
Ramlal, Derek *history professor, personal trainer*
Reitnauer, Andrew Richard *forensic specialist*
Roberts, Norm *men's college basketball coach*
Satyan, Shyama *ophthalmologist*
Sciame, Joseph *university administrator*
Sharma, Jayendra *pediatrician, cardiologist*
Simons, Michael A. *dean, law educator*
Traub, Barbara Gellis *law librarian*
Trombetta, Louis D. *medical educator, department chairman*

Jamestown
DJang, Arthur H.K. *pathologist, preventive medicine physician*
Idzik, Martin Francis *lawyer*
O'Brian, Jonathan D. *recreation director, story educator, language educator, educator*
Thompson, Birgit Dolores *civic worker, writer*

Jamesville
DeCrow, Karen *lawyer, educator, writer*

Jefferson
Sullivan, Jim *artist*

Jeffersonville
Craft, Douglas Durwood *artist*
Harms, Elizabeth Louise *artist*

Jericho
Beal, Carol Ann *lawyer*
Bertucelli, Robert Edward *accountant, educator*
Blau, Harvey Ronald *manufacturing executive*
Chaiet, Clifford Paul *lawyer*
Corso, Frank Mitchell, Jr. *business management and business consultant*
Edson, Andrew Stephen *public relations executive*
Kramer, Ronald J. *manufacturing executive*
Minicucci, Richard Francis *lawyer, former hospital administrator*
Rosen, Robert Arnold *management consultant, real estate owner, manager, developer, investor, farmer*
Sapan, Joshua Ward *cable television executive*
Schatkin, Andrew James *lawyer*
Shinners, Stanley Marvin *electrical engineer*

Jewett
Khanzadian, Vahan *tenor*

Johnson City
Bernardo, Aldo Sisto *retired foreign language educator*
McMillen, Marieta Louise *art educator*

Katonah
Bandon, William Edward III *lawyer*
Bashkow, Theodore Robert *electrical engineering consultant, former educator*
Bauman, Jonathan Hugh *psychiatrist*
Bergson, Henry Paul *professional society administrator, consultant*
Brownlee, Delphine *actress, musician*
Fry, John *magazine editor*
Giobbi, Edward Giacchino *artist*
McCauley, Gerard Francis *literary agent*
Morris, Stephen Burritt *marketing information company executive*
Simpson, William Kelly *curator, Egyptologist, educator*
Stillman, Michael Allen *dermatologist*
Wenglowski, Gary Martin *economist*

Kenmore
Elibol, Tarik *gastroenterologist, educator*
Gielow, Kathleen Louise *career planning administrator, special education educator, consultant*
Kenny, John Edward *computer analyst*
McLaughlin, Bernard Joseph *bishop emeritus*

Kew Gardens
Marshall, Helen M. *city official*
Reddick, Deirdre Shadeia *physician assistant*

Kinderhook
Glynn, Carlin (Carlin Masterson) *actress*

Kings Park
LaFantano, Elizabeth *music educator*

Kings Point
Butman, Boris S. *marine engineer, educator*
Stern, Marilyn *technical services, academic librarian*

Kingston
Clamar, Aphrodite J. *psychologist*
Davila, Elisa *language and literature educator*
Luke, Brian Thomas *theoretical chemist, researcher*
Tsirpanlis, Constantine N. *theology, philosophy, classics and history educator*

Lake Katrine
Konior, Jeannette Mary *retired elementary and secondary school educator*

Lake Luzerne
Goldstein, Manfred *retired management consultant*

Lake Placid
Pappalardo, Rosa Gloria *secondary school educator*
Reiss, Paul J. *academic administrator*
Rossi, Ronald Aldo *sports association administrator, Olympic athlete*

Lake Success
Handelsman, John Ellis *pediatric orthopedist, surgeon*
Lee, Brian Edward *lawyer*
Schlesinger, Irwin D. *neurologist*

Lakewood
Deppas, Louis Anthony *financial adviser*

Lancaster
Neumaier, Gerhard John *environmental services administrator, consultant*
Stoffel, Shelley L. *library media specialist*

Larchmont
Berridge, George Bradford *retired lawyer*
Bloom, Lee Hurley *lawyer, consultant, retired consumer products company executive*
Burkett, Bradford Charles *lawyer*
Cavanna, Dino Francesco *chemicals executive*
Greenwald, Carol Schiro *professional services marketing research executive*
Guttenplan, Joseph B. *biochemist, educator*
Hinerfeld, Norman Martin *manufacturing executive*
Hinerfeld, Ruth G. *civic organization executive*
Levi, James Harry *real estate executive, investment banker*
McSherry, William John, Jr. *lawyer, consultant*
Plumez, Jean Paul *advertising executive, consultant*
Rainier, Robert Paul *publisher, consultant*
Rockland, Lawrence Howard *psychiatrist, educator*
Siegel, Nathaniel Harold *sociology educator*
Sklarew, Robert Jay *biomedical research educator, consultant*
White, Thomas Edward *lawyer*
Zilberberg, Julie Marlene *social studies educator*

Latham
Bruno, Joseph L. *information technology executive, retired state senator*
Eisman, Glenn Alan *engineering educator*
Litchmore, Trevor Alexander *physician*
Schwartz, Robert William *management consultant*
Stallman, Donald Lee *environmental executive*
Wilkes, Brent Ames *management consultant*

Lawrence
Bursky, Herman Aaron *lawyer*
Henriquez, Allen *artist*

Levittown
Braverman, Lisa Rene *dean*
Massie, Clifford Michael *music company executive*

Lewiston
Dexter, Theodore Henry *chemist*
Moraca-Sawicki, Anne Marie *oncology nurse*

Lindenhurst
Boltz, Mary Ann *aerospace materials and travel company executive*
Kaufman, Susan Shiffman *psychologist*

Little Falls
Lowery, Kathleen Ann *elementary school educator*

Liverpool
Federico, Josephine A.M. *music educator*
Hamlett, James Gordon *electronics engineer, management consultant, educator*
Landers, Mary Dean J. *music educator*
Naum, Christopher John *fire protection, emergengy management, training consultant, educator, firefighter safety advocate*

Livingston Manor
Root, Stuart Dowling *lawyer, retired government agency administrator, banker*

Loch Sheldrake
Arnold, Richard Walter *academic librarian, artist*

Lockport
Carr, Edward Albert, Jr. *pharmacologist, educator, physician*
Lanham, Richard J. *oncologist, educator*
Penney, Charles Rand *lawyer, civic worker*

Locust Valley
Bentel, Frederick Richard *architect, educator*
Fairman, Joel Martin *retired broadcast executive*
Fletcher, Mary Lee *retired marketing professional*

Long Beach
Kasner, David A. *real estate consultant, investor*

Long Eddy
Hoiby, Lee *composer, concert pianist*

Long Island City
Coogan, Timothy Christopher, II, *history professor, researcher*
Heiss, Alanna *museum director*
Henrikson, C. Robert (Carl Robert Henrikson) *insurance company executive*
Lucca, Louis Anthony *academic administrator*
Madden, Steven *footwear designer*
Rosenfeld, Edward R. *apparel executive*
Viera, Lorraine *psychologist*
Westwick, Ed *actor*

Loudonville
Barbir, Karl K. *history professor*
Colesante, Robert J. *psychology professor, director*
Davies, Julian A. *philosopher, educator, archivist*
Doyle, Mathias Francis *academic administrator, political scientist, educator*
Fiore, Peter Amadeus *English educator, priest*
Karimi-Hakak, Mahmood *film director, educator*
McCaffery, Fran *men's college basketball coach*
Teepe, Christopher John *literature and language professor*
Toal, James Francis *academic administrator*

Lynbrook
Cangemi, Lisa Lynne *art director, graphics designer*
Good, Larry Irwin *gastroenterologist, educator*

Mahopac
Martone, Barbara *school psychologist*

Malverne
Van Bosse, Harold J.P. *orthopedic surgeon*

Mamaroneck
Halpern, Abraham Leon *psychiatrist*
Martin, Roger Harry *retired college president*
McEnroe, Patrick *former professional tennis player, sports commentator*
McLarnon, Mary Frances *neurologist*
Mizrahi, Abraham Mordechay *retired health products executive, pediatrician*

Manhasset
Bernstein, David *gastroenterologist*
Bosworth, Jay L. *radiation oncologist*
Brand, Oscar *folk singer, writer, educator*
Budman, Cathy Linda *psychiatrist, physician*
Burke, Alexander James, Jr. *publishing executive*
Calvin, Donald Lee *stock exchange official*
Carbon, Maren *research scientist*
Catanzaro, John N. *cardiologist*
Dabideen, Darrin *research scientist*
Doddamani, Sanjay *cardiologist, educator*
D'Olimpio, James Thomas *oncologist*
Esposito, Rick Anthony *thoracic surgeon*
Evans, Bob (Robert Evans) *publishing executive*
Foerst, John George, Jr. *retired fundraising executive*
Kandel, Anuj R. *surgeon*
Marchant, Donna *cardiologist, director*
Menzin, Andrew *gynecologist*
Milhorat, Thomas Herrick *neurosurgeon*
Ovadia, Marc *pediatric cardiologist, educator*
Pogo, Gustave Javier *cardiothoracic surgeon, educator*
Preston, Rob *editor-in-chief*
Rochelson, Burton L. *obstetrician*
Smith, Lawrence Gerard *dean, medical educator, health facility administrator*
Stevens, Thelma Kaplan *artist, educator*
Wachtler, Sol *lawyer, educator*
Weitzner, Steve *publishing executive*

Manlius
der Boghosian, Paula *retired computer business consultant*
Harriff, Suzanna Elizabeth Bahner *media consultant*
O'Reilly, Mary *environmental scientist, educator*
Vick, Dana James *physician*

Marcy
Rishel, Kenn Charles *school superintendent*

Maspeth
Baltakis, Paulius Antanas *bishop*

Massapequa
Faust, Naomi Flowe *education educator*
Pettersen, Kevin Will *investment company executive*
Pettersen, Kjell Will *securities trader, consultant*
Roberts, Kathleen Joy Doty *technology staff developer, educational consultant, supervisor*
Ruotolo, Charles J. *orthopedist, department chairman*
Turk, Elizabeth Ann *music educator*
Zwanger, Jerome *physician*

Massapequa Park
King, Peter Thomas *United States Representative from New York, lawyer*

Massena
Pollard, Fred Don *finance company executive, director*

Mattituck
Palumbo, Anthony Howard *lawyer*

Melville
Bergman, Stanley M. *health products executive*
Boehlke, Charles *industrial machinery company executive*
Breslawski, James P. *health products executive*
Brown, Peter Stewart *lawyer, electronics executive*
Copperman, Stuart Morton *pediatrician, educator*
Damadian, Raymond Vahan *biophysicist*
Ettinger, Michael Saul *lawyer*
Grayson, Gerald Herbert *economist, educator, arbitrator, writer*
Handelsman, Walt *cartoonist*
Hildebrand, John Frederick *columnist, educator*
Kissinger, Walter Bernhard *retired automotive executive*
Knight, Timothy P. *publishing executive*
Lane, Arthur Alan *lawyer*
Levin, Richard Louis *retired language educator*
Long, Michael J. *electronics executive*
Mancini, John *editor, publishing executive*
McMahon, John P. *electronics executive*
Mitchell, William Edmund *electronics executive*
Morris, M. Catherine *electronics executive*
Olesen, Robert Lind Ole *electrical engineer*
Paladino, Steven *health products executive*
Reardon, George Martin *lawyer*
Reilly, Paul J. *electronics executive*
Rossetti, George A. *editor, director*
Schmid, Charles Ernest *acoustical engineer, academic administrator*
Schoenfeld, Michael P. *lawyer*
Settle, Mark *information technology executive*
Sobol, Elise Schwarcz *music educator*
Taub, Jesse J. *electrical engineering researcher*
Waddell, John Comer *electronics executive*

Memphis
Woolson, Gloria Jean *education educator*

Mendon
Munson, Harold Lewis *education educator*

Merrick
Garfinkel, Lawrence Saul *academic administrator, television producer, educator*
Glogau, Lillian Flatow Fleischer Zeigen *retired educational administrator*
Harrison, Marjorie Freeman *secondary education educator, librarian*

Mexico
Halse, Frank Adams, Jr. *retired minister*

Middle Village
Crowley, Elizabeth S. *city councilwoman*

Middleburgh
Mau, Lisa Anne *special education educator*

Middletown
Bedell, Barbara Lee *journalist*
Kossar, Ronald Steven *lawyer*
Ojeda, Joseph A. *psychotherapist*
Paradies, Michele A. *biology professor*
Wright, Kathleen M. *literature and language professor*

Millbrook
Hall, Penelope Coker *editor, writer*
Likens, Gene Elden *biology and ecology educator*

Miller Place
Gresser, Mark Geoffrey *podiatrist*

Millerton
Hastings, Donald Francis *actor, writer*
Welsh, Donald Emory *publisher*

Mineola
Bartlett, Clifford Adams, Jr. *lawyer*
Brand, Donald Albert *medical researcher, educator*
Burakoff, Robert *gastroenterologist, educator*
Ente, Gerald *pediatrician*
Halloran, Daniel James *lawyer*
Harris, Henry William *physician*
Ilowite, Jonathan *pulmonologist*
Long, Graham E. *urban planner*
Lynn, Robert Patrick, Jr. *lawyer*
Martins, Jack M. *mayor*
Newman, Malcolm *mechanical and civil engineering consultant*
Niederman, Michael Steven *physician, educator*
Ortiz, Orlando *radiologist, department chairman*
Roberts, Jon *pulmonologist*
Schaffer, David Irving *lawyer*
Sher, Denise Linda *judge*
Yeh, James Kuen-Jann *nutritionist*
Zeldin, Lee M. *lawyer*

Monroe
Dierna, Joseph Biagio *construction company executive, land development consultant*
Fontana, John Arthur *employee benefits specialist*
Furman-Markowitz, Joanna Florence *dance educator*

Montauk
Butler, Thomas William *retired health and social services administrator*
Kahn, Richard Dreyfus *lawyer*

Montgomery
Feldman, Arlene Karp *special education educator, director*

Montrose
Reber, Raymond Andrew *chemical engineer*

Morrisville
Redmond, Rhonda Jean *psychologist*
Rusch, Lisa Marie *medical educator*
Scalzo, Christopher M. *entrepreneurship and business educator*
Turner, Linda Fay *finance educator*
Xu, Pei *agriculturist, educator*
Zbock, Jason Paul *mathematics professor*

Mount Kisco
Buglione, Anna Maria *pre-school educator*
Cameron, Daniel *internist, medical researcher*
Curran, Maurice Francis *lawyer*
Hayworth, Scott David *physician*
Kilbourn, Joseph A. *lawyer*
Kohlberg, James A. *venture capitalist*
Laster, Richard *biotechnologist, consultant*
Novak, Gregory *marketing professional*
Powell, Jeffrey Scott *endocrinologist*
Schneider, Robert Jay *oncologist*
Starobin, Michael *composer, orchestrator*
Zimmerman, Jean *lawyer*

Mount Sinai
Feinberg, Sheldon Norman *pediatrician, educator*
Kopp, Richard Edgar *electrical engineer*

Mount Vernon
Addesso, Angela Joyce *school system administrator*
Cammarosano, Joseph Raphael *economist, educator*
McBride, Susan Alyse *interior designer, consultant*
Rossini, Joseph *contracting and development corporate executive*
Scelsa, Joseph Vincent *sociologist, educator, dean*
Weisman, Richard Scott *lawyer*

Narrowsburg
Krause, Gloria Rose *music educator*

Nassau
Benamati, Dennis Charles *librarian, editor, consultant*

Nedrow
Lyons, Oren *Native American chieftain, conservationist*

Neponsit
Nicastri, Ann Gilbert *science educator*

Nesconset
Burns-Riviello, Michaela Aileen *social studies educator*
Laspina, Peter Joseph *computer resource educator*

New City
Esser, Aristide Henri *psychiatrist*
Zambri, Carla Nicole *psychologist*

New Hampton
Sinnard, Elaine Janice *painter, sculptor*

New Hartford
Anthony, Donald Charles *librarian, educator*
Boyle, William Leo, Jr. *educational consultant, retired academic administrator*
Weiss, Holly Anne *music educator, singer*

New Hyde Park
Blaufox, Andrew D. *medical educator*
Brock, William Alton *pediatric urologist*
Brun, Leslie Adolphe *investment advisor*
Esiason, Boomer (Norman Julius Esiason) *radio personality, sportscaster, retired professional football player*
Goilav, Béatrice Sarah *internist, educator*
Heller, Keith S. *surgeon*
Hyman, Abraham *electrical engineer*
Ilowite, Norman T. *pediatric rheumatologist*
Kamler, Kenneth Mark *microsurgeon*
Lehrer, Stanley *magazine publisher, editorial director, museum exhibitor*
Low, Frederick Emerson *language educator*
Mehta, Ashesh *neurologist*
Mittler, Mark A. *neurosurgeon*
Muscat, Joshua Ethan *epidemiologist*
Offner, Eric Delmonte *lawyer*
Palestro, Christopher J. *physician*
Pegalis, Steven E. *lawyer*
Richards, Bernard *investment company executive*
Schneider, Steven Jack *neurosurgeon*
Shanies, Stanley Alvin *cardiologist*
Sweetbaum, Marshall David *lawyer*
Weinbach, Arthur Frederic *retired computer company executive*

New Paltz
Brown, Peter David Gilson *German language educator*
Knapp, Ronald Gary *geography educator*
Lavallee, David Kenneth *chemistry professor, academic administrator*
Nyquist, Corinne Elaine *librarian*
Poskanzer, Steven Gary *academic administrator, lawyer*
Raskin, Jonathan D. *psychologist*
Schnell, George Adam *geographer, educator, retired demographer*

New Rochelle
Black, Page Morton *civic worker, vocalist, musician*
Branch, William Blackwell *playwright, producer, professor*
Buonanno, Elda *literature and language professor*
Cohen, Saul Bernard *retired academic administrator, geographer*
Donahue, Richard James *secondary school educator*
Eaton, Richard Gillette *retired surgeon, educator*
Gerardi, Paul *cardiologist, educator*
Gitler, Bernard *cardiologist, critical care specialist*
Johnson, John William, Jr. *business advisor*
Kumar, Anil *physician*
Lobach, Katherine S. *retired pediatrician*
Margolin, Harold *metallurgical educator*
Menzies, Henry Hardinge *architect*
Metz, Roxie Anne *art educator*
Morgan, Joseph Gerard *history professor*
Newsome, Frederick V. *medical educator*
Ong, Bruce Nelson *communication skills consultant*
Reddington, Mary Jane *retired secondary school educator*
Salamone, Frank Anthony *anthropology educator*
Saperstein, David *writer, film director, television personality*
Sommer, Jay *writer, literature and language educator*
Swire, Edith Wypler *music educator, violist, violinist*
Tassone, Gelsomina (Gessie) *metal products executive*
Thomson, Gerald Edmund *physician, educator*

New Windsor
Heinecke, John Kevin *military pilot, educator, researcher*
Mandel, Joel Emanuel *orthopedist*

New York
Aaron, Stewart D. *lawyer*
Abbatiello, Geraldine A. *geriatric nurse practitioner*
Abdel Dayem, Hussein Mahmoud *nuclear medicine physician, radiology educator*
Abdelnour, Gaby *diversified financial services company executive*
Abelson, Alan *columnist*
Abelson, Reed V. *reporter*
Abish, Cecile *artist*
Aboaf, Eric W. *diversified financial services company executive*
Aboulafia, Mitchell Stuart *liberal arts and philosophy educator*
Abrahams, Robert M. *lawyer*
Abramovich, Mark Nathan *entrepreneur, consultant*
Abramovitz, Robert *psychiatrist, director*
Abramowitz, Elkan *lawyer*
Abrams, Floyd *lawyer, educator*
Abrams, Muhal Richard *pianist, composer*
Abrams, Robert *lawyer, state attorney general*
Abruzzo, Joseph *media communications company executive, director*
Achinstein, Peter Jacob *philosopher, educator*
Ackman, William Albert *hedge fund manager*
Adams, Cindy *journalist*
Adams, David H. *cardiac surgeon, educator*
Adams, George Bell *lawyer*
Adams, John Brett *investment banker, pharmaceutical executive*
Adams, John Coolidge *composer, conductor*
Adams, Scott *cartoonist*
Adams, Yolanda Yvette *singer*
Addison, Linda Leuchter *lawyer, commentator, columnist*
Adichie, Chimamanda Ngozi (Amanda N.) *writer*
Adler, David A. *communications executive*
Adler, Edward I. *media and entertainment company executive*
Adler, Jerry *journalist, writer*
Adler, Margot Susanna *journalist, radio producer, correspondent, writer*
Adler, Norman Tenner *psychology educator, dean*
Adler, Stephen J. *editor-in-chief*
Adlersberg, Jay Ben *internist*
Adrian, Barbara (Mrs. Franklin C. Tramutola) *artist*
Adrian, Tobias *economist*
Agisim, Philip *advertising and marketing executive*
Agostinelli, Robert Francesco *investment banker*
Agranoff, Gerald Neal *lawyer*
Ahern, Patrick Vincent *bishop emeritus*
Ahmad, Jameel *civil engineer, researcher, educator*
Ahn, Jaimo *orthopedist, director*
Ahrens, Lynn *lyricist*
Ahrens, Mary Elizabeth *attorney*
Aidinoff, M(erton) Bernard *retired lawyer*
Ailes, Roger Eugene *broadcast executive*
Ainslie, Lee S. III *hedge fund manager*
Akin, Oguz *radiologist, educator*
Akinboboye, Olakunle Olaniran *cardiologist, educator*
Akon, (Aliaune Thiam) *singer*
Akselrad, Hal (Harold Eaton) *broadcast executive, lawyer*
Aksen, Gerald *arbitrator, mediator, lawyer*
Albee, Edward Franklin *playwright, writer*
Albert, Adrienne *real estate marketing executive*
Albert, Garett J. *lawyer*
Alda, Alan *actor, film director, scriptwriter*
Alden, Steven Michael *lawyer*
Alderson, Philip Otis *radiologist, educator*

Alecia, Suzanne Bussart *advertising executive*
Aleiner, Igor L. *physics professor*
Alemany, Ellen R. *bank executive*
Alessandrini, Gerard *playwright, theater director*
Alexander, Jane (Jane Quigley) *actress, theater educator, writer*
Alexander, Vologodskii *biophysicist*
Alexiades-Armenakas, Macrene Renee *dermatologist, scientist, researcher, educator, consultant*
Alexis, Andrew F. *dermatologist*
Alfano, Michael Charles *university administrator*
Alikhani, Zoubin *internist, molecular biologist, researcher*
Alizadeh, Kaveh *plastic surgeon, educator*
Allan, Col *editor-in-chief*
Allee, Debra Cole *environmental consultant*
Allen, Alice *communications and marketing executive*
Allen, Claxton Edmonds III *investment banker*
Allen, Herbert Anthony III *investment company executive*
Allen, Jeffrey C. *pediatric neurologist, educator*
Allen, Leon Arthur, Jr. *lawyer*
Allis, C. David *science educator*
Allison, James Patrick *immunology educator, medical association administrator*
Allyn, Susan M. *publishing executive, marketing professional*
Almon, Lorie *lawyer*
al-Nasser, Nassir Abdulaziz *ambassador*
Alpert, William Harold (Bill) *artist, painter*
Alschuler, Steven *public relations executive, writer, consultant*
Alter, Eleanor Breitel *lawyer*
Alter, Jonathan Hammerman *journalist*
Altfest, Lewis Jay *financial planner*
Altman, Lawrence Kimball *physician, journalist*
Altman, Roger Charles *investment company executive, former federal agency administrator*
Altman, Roy Peter *pediatric surgeon*
Altman, Stan *academic administrator, educator*
Alvarez, Antonio C., II, *restructuring company executive, former food products executive*
Alvarez, David (David Alvarez-Gonzalez) *actor, dancer*
Ambrosio, Anthony G. *broadcast executive*
Amdur, Martin Bennett *retired lawyer*
Amen, Robert M. *consumer products company executive*
Amerling, Richard *nephrologist, educator*
Ames, Richard Pollard *physician, educator, lecturer*
Ames, Roger *recording industry executive*
Amster, Linda Evelyn *newspaper executive, consultant*
Amsterdam, Anthony Guy *law educator*
Amsterdam, Mark Lemle *lawyer*
Anania, Vincent Jay *film director, educator*
Anastasi, William Joseph *artist*
Anaya, Raul *bank executive*
Ancier, Garth Richard *broadcast executive*
Anderer, Erich Gen *neurosurgeon*
Andersen, Holly Sue *cardiologist, educator*
Andersen, K(ent) Tucker *investment executive*
Andersen, Marianne Singer *psychologist*
Andersen, Mark *musician*
Anderson, Arthur Allan *management consultant*
Anderson, Bonnie S. *history professor, writer*
Anderson, David Poole *sportswriter*
Anderson, Dwight Walter *hedge fund manager*
Anderson, Fred D. *investment company executive, retired computer company executive*
Anderson, Jon *publishing executive, children's book author*
Anderson, Kathryn V. *developmental biologist, educator*
Anderson, Richard Theodore *trade association administrator, urban planner*
Anderson, Sunny *chef, television personality*
Andolsen, Alan Anthony *management consultant*
Andre, Michael (Kenneth Andre) *editor-in-chief*
Andree, Tim *advertising executive*
Andreotti, Lamberto *pharmaceutical executive*
Andrews, Gordon Clark *lawyer*
Andrias, Richard T. *judge*
Angel, Steven M. *sports association executive*
Angelson, Mark Alan *investment company executive, retired printing company executive*
Angland, Joseph *lawyer*
Antell, Darrick Eugene *plastic surgeon, educator*
Anthoine, Robert *lawyer, educator*
Anthony, William Graham *artist*
A.O., Leon Hertz *publishing executive*
Apa, Michael *cosmetic dentist*
Appel, Albert M. *lawyer*
Appel, Gerald Bernard *physician, nephrologist, educator*
Appel, Norman *ophthalmologist, educator, real estate and import/export company executive*
Appelbaum, Ann Harriet *lawyer*
Appelbaum, Paul Stuart *psychiatrist, medical educator, department chairman*
Aquila, Francis Joseph *lawyer*
Aquilino, Thomas Joseph, Jr. *federal judge, educator*
Arenson, Gregory K. *lawyer*
Arias, Ricardo Alberto *ambassador, lawyer*
Arkin, Alan Wolf *actor*
Arkin, Stanley S. *lawyer*
Arlander, Bodil M. *bank executive*
Arlen, Jennifer Hall *law educator*
Armani, Giorgio *fashion designer*
Armbrust, Joseph W., Jr. *lawyer*
Armen, Garo H. *research and development company executive*
Armenakas, Noel Anthony *medical educator*
Armitage, Karole *dancer, choreographer*
Arms, Anneli (Anna Elizabeth) *artist, educator*
Armstrong, Neil Alden *retired astronaut*
Armstrong, Richard A. *museum director, curator*
Arnaboldi, Nicole Sinek *investment company executive*
Arndt, Cynthia *educational administrator*
Arnell, Peter Eric *advertising executive, photographer, writer*
Arning, Mark E. *insurance company executive*
Arnold, Martin *editor, journalist*
Aron, Alan Milford *pediatric neurology educator*
Aronne, Louis J. *internist*
Aronson, Edgar David *venture capitalist*
Aronson, Jeffrey H. *private equity firm executive*
Aronstam, Neil Lee *media marketing firm executive*
Arouh, Jeffrey Alan *lawyer*
Arpaia, Donatella *restaurateur*
Arquit, Kevin James *lawyer*
Arrow, Allen H. *lawyer*
Arroyo, Martina *soprano*
Asakawa, Takako *dancer, choreographer, educator, director*
Ascheim, Tom (Thomas Eliot Ascheim) *publishing executive*
Ascherman, Jeffrey Alan *plastic and reconstructive surgeon*
Ashanti, (Ashanti Shequoiya Douglas) *vocalist*
Ashdown, Marie Matranga *writer, educator, cultural organization administrator*
Ashley, Dwayne *not-for-profit fundraiser*
Ashooh, Nicholas J. *insurance company executive*
Ashton, Dore *writer, educator*
Asner, Ed *actor*
Assael, Henry *marketing educator*
Astley, Amy Taran *editor-in-chief*
Aston, Sherrell Jerone *plastic surgeon, educator*
Aswady, Adiyatwidi Adiwoso *diplomat*
Ataeva, Aksoltan *diplomat*
Atkins, Peter Allan *lawyer*
Atlas, James Robert *editor, writer*
Atwood, Margaret Eleanor *writer*
Audet, Paul L. *diversified financial services company executive*
Aufses, Arthur Harold, Jr. *surgeon, educator*
Auslander, Mitchell J. *lawyer*
Auster, David L. *theatre executive*
Auster, Paul *writer*
Austin, Patti *singer*
Avery, Sean *professional hockey player*
Aviles, Alan D. *lawyer, insurance company executive*
Awad, George *bank executive*
Ax, Emanuel *pianist*
Axel, Richard *pathology and biochemistry educator*
Axelrod, Norman N *optical electro-optical and imaging consultant*
Axinn, Stephen Mark *lawyer*
Axthelm, Nancy *advertising executive*
Ayres, Charles *diversified financial services company executive*
Azenberg, Emanuel *theatrical producer*
Azria, Max *apparel executive*
Azzoli, Val *music company executive*
Bach, Thomas Handford *lawyer, investor*
Bachelder, Joseph Elmer III *lawyer*
Backstedt, Roseanne Joan *artist*
Bacon, Louis Moore *hedge fund manager*
Baden, Michael M. *pathologist, educator*
Badertscher, David Glen *law librarian, consultant*
Badgley, Mark *fashion designer*
Baer, Amy Bosley *film company executive*
Bagatelle, David Samuel *bank executive*
Bagger, Richard Hartvig *pharmaceutical executive*
Bagnall, Roger Shaler *history professor, director*
Baha, Christian J. *hedge fund manager*
Bahash, Robert J. *information technology executive*
Bahler, Gary M. *lawyer*
Bahlke, Conrad George *lawyer*
Bahr, Lauren S. *publishing executive*
Bailey, Colin Barry *curator*
Bailey, Glenda *editor-in-chief*
Bailey, Preston *Event Designer*
Bains, Leslie Elizabeth *banker*
Bair, Thomas J. *publishing executive*
Baird, Campbell Atkinson III *design educator*
Baird, Zoë *foundation administrator*
Baity, John Cooley *lawyer*
Baker, Daniel Clifton III *plastic surgeon, educator*
Baker, Deborah *editor, writer*
Baker, Elizabeth Calhoun *magazine editor*
Baker, Leslie David *actor*
Baker, Mark M. *lawyer, law educator*
Baker, Paul Raymond *historian, educator*
Bakhshi, Suneel *bank executive*
Balaban, Vivian *librarian, elementary school educator*
Baldacci, David *writer*
Baldessari, John Anthony *artist*
Balis, Janet *diversified media and merchandising company executive*
Ball, John Paul *publishing company executive*
Ballard, Charles Alan *investment banker*
Balmori, Diana *landscape designer*
Balogh, Mary *writer*
Bamberger, Michael Albert *lawyer, educator*
Ban, Ki-Moon (Ban Ki-Moon) *Secretary General of the United Nations, former South Korean government official*
Bancroft, Margaret Armstrong *lawyer*
Bandera, Natalia *finance company executive*
Banerjee, (Bimal) *artist, educator*
Banerji, Anirvan *economist, director*
Banikarim, Maryam *marketing executive*
Bank, Arthur *physician*
Banker, Amy Beth Cohen *artist, writer, educator, curator, actress, poet*
Banks, Jeffrey *fashion designer*
Bantom, Michael Allen *sports association executive*
Barandes, Robert *lawyer*
Barasch, Clarence Sylvan *lawyer*
Barasch, Mal Livingston *lawyer*
Barber, Dan *chef, restaurant owner*
Barber, Tiki (Atiim Kiambu Barber) *sportscaster, retired professional football player*
Barbour, Catherine Jean *actress, set designer, director, american mime*
Barchas, Jack David *psychiatrist, medical researcher, educator, behavioral molecular neurobiologist*
Bardach, Joan Lucile *clinical psychologist*
Bardos, Karoly *television and film educator, writer, director*
Bargmann, Cornelia I. *neuroscientist, science educator*
Barist, Jeffrey *lawyer*
Barker, Barbara Ann *ophthalmologist*
Barksdale, James Love *investment company executive*
Barnard, Kevin Francis *lawyer*
Barnet, Will *painter*
Barnet, Will *artist, educator*
Barnett, Gary (Gershon Swiatycki) *real estate company executive*
Barnett, LaShonda Katrice *writer, educator*
Barnett, Michael *professional sports team executive*
Barnett, Robert Joseph *social sciences educator*
Barnett, Vivian Endicott *curator*
Barney, Matthew *sculptor, filmmaker*
Barolini, Teodolinda *literary and cultural critic*
Barondess, Jeremiah Abraham *physician*
Barr, William Pelham *lawyer, former United States Attorney General*
Barrett, David A. *lawyer*
Barrett, Elizabeth Ann Manhart *psychotherapist, consultant, nursing educator*
Barrie, John Paul *lawyer, educator*
Barron, James Turman *journalist*
Barron, Susan *clinical psychologist*
Barr-Sharrar, Beryl *artist, art historian*
Barry, Dan *columnist*
Barry, Desmond Thomas, Jr. *lawyer*
Barry, Nancy Marie *bank executive*
Barry, Thomas Corcoran *investment advisor*
Barstow, David *journalist, investigative reporter*
Bart, Roger *actor*
Bartels, Steve *music company executive*
Bartholomew, Lincoln Edwin *physician*
Bartlett, Elizabeth Easton *interior designer*
Bartlett, Thomas A. *telecommunications industry executive*
Barton, Lewis *food products executive, consultant*
Bartow, Diane Grace *marketing professional, sales executive*
Baruch, Ralph M. *communications executive*
Barzilay, Judith Morgenstern *federal judge*
Baset, Salman Abdul *research scientist*
Bash-Polley, Stacy *diversified financial services company executive*
Bason, George R., Jr. *lawyer*
Basquin, Mary Smyth (Kit Basquin) *museum administrator*
Bassen, Ned Henry *lawyer*
Bastholm, Lars *interactive marketing executive*
Bastianich, Lidia Matticchio (Lidia Motika) *chef, food service executive*
Batali, Mario Francis *chef*
Batavia, Mitchell *physical therapist, educator*
Bateman, Paul T. *diversified financial services company executive*
Bates, Mason *composer, disc jockey*
Battle-Bey, Marva Smith *non-profit urban planning executive*
Bauer, Douglas F. *retired lawyer*
Bauer, Joel J. *surgeon, educator*
Bauer, Joy *nutritionist, consultant*
Bauer, Marion Dane *writer*
Baum, Stanley David *lawyer*
Baumgardner, John Ellwood, Jr. *lawyer*
Baumgarten, Sidney *lawyer*
Baumgartner, Brian *actor*
Baumol, William Jack *economist, educator*
Baumrin, Bernard Stefan Herbert *lawyer, educator*
Beal, M. Flint *neurologist*
Bearak, Barry Leon *journalist*
Beard, John *medical educator, researcher*
Bearman, Peter Shawn *social sciences professor*
Beason, Steve W. *computer company executive*
Beaton, Ann R. *educator*
Beattie, Ann *writer, educator*
Beattie, Richard Irwin *lawyer*
Beattle, E. Scott *cosmetics executive*
Beausoleil, Doris Mae *retired federal agency housing specialist*
Beaven, Richard *media strategy and marketing company executive*
Beck, Andrew James *lawyer*
Beck, Martha Ann *curator, director*
Becker, Brandon *lawyer, insurance company executive*
Becker, Helane Renée *financial analyst, company executive*
Becker, Susan Kaplan *management and marketing communication consultant, presentation coach, educator*
Beckman, Richard David *publishing and advertising executive*
Bederson, Benjamin *physicist, researcher*
Bedingfield, Natasha *singer*
Bednar, Rudy *television producer, director*
Beekman, William B. *lawyer*
Beerbower, John Edwin *lawyer*
Beeson, Ann *lawyer*
Beeson, Jack Hamilton *composer, educator, writer*
Begley, Louis *writer, lawyer*
Behar, Joy *television personality*
Behar, Richard *investigative journalist*
Behr, Alan Andrew *lawyer, writer, photographer*
Behrendt, John Thomas *lawyer*
Behrens, Kathleen *sports association executive*
Beim, Norman *playwright, actor, theater director, writer*
Beinecke, Candace Krugman *lawyer*
Beinecke, Frances G. *environmentalist*
Beinecke, Frederick William *investment company executive*
Beinecke, William Sperry *retired consumer products company executive*
Beldner, Steven *orthopedist, surgeon*
Beleson, Robert Brian *marketing executive*
Belgorod, Barry Miles *surgeon, educator*
Belknap, Norton *foundation administrator*
Belknap, Robert Lamont *literature educator*
Bell, David Arthur *retired advertising agency executive*
Bell, Hilari *writer, former librarian*
Bell, Jonathan Robert *lawyer*
Bell, Martin Allen *investment company executive*
Bell, Robin *interior designer*
Bell, Theodore Augustus, III, (Ted Bell) *writer, former advertising executive*
Bellanger, Serge René *bank executive*
Bellas, Albert Constantine *investment executive*
Beller, Gary A. *lawyer, former insurance company executive*
Belliveau, Gerard Joseph, Jr. *librarian*
Belson, Ken *reporter*
Belt, Bradley Deck *investment company executive, former pension fund administrator*
Belzer, Richard *actor, comedian*
Ben-Ami, Leora *lawyer*
Ben Amor, Yanis *microbiologist*
Benanti, Laura *actress*
Ben-Avi, Simon Stephen *biomedical researcher, educator*
Bender, Judith *journalist, editor*
Bender, Susan *financial advisor*
Bender, Susan L. *lawyer*
Bender, Thomas *historian, educator*
Bendet, Stacey *apparel designer*
Benenson, Joel R. *political consultant, pollster*
Benenson, Mark Keith *lawyer*
Ben-Haim, Zigi *artist*
Benioff, David *writer*
Benjamin, Harvey E. *lawyer, sports association executive*
Benjamin, Jeff *lawyer, pharmaceutical executive*
Benmosche, Robert H. *insurance company executive*
Bennack, Frank Anthony, Jr. *publishing company executive*
Bennett, James Marvin *consulting company executive*
Bennett, Paul B. *stock exchange executive*
Bennett, Scott Lawrence *lawyer*
Bensimon, Gilles *photographer*
Benson, Thomas Luther *academic administrator*
Bentley, Eric *writer, playwright, educator*
Beraka, George Joseph *plastic surgeon*
Berendt, John Lawrence *writer, editor*
Berenson, Alex *reporter, writer*
Berenstein, Alejandro *neuro-radiologist, educator*
Berg, Andrew N. *lawyer*
Berg, A(ndrew) Scott *writer*
Berger, Elizabeth H. *lobbyist*
Berger, George *lawyer*
Berger, Pearl *librarian, dean*
Berger, Stephen *finance company executive*
Berger, Thomas Louis *author*
Berghahn, Volker Rolf *history professor*
Bergman, Charles Cabe *foundation executive*
Bergman, Donald Arthur *endocrinologist, educator*
Bergmann, Peter George *lawyer*
Berke, Barry H. *lawyer*
Berkett, Neil *telecommunications industry executive*
Berkley, Seth Franklin *epidemiologist, international health specialist*
Berlin, Andrew Mark (Andy Berlin) *advertising agency executive*
Berlin, Heather Ayn *neuroscientist, philosopher, educator*
Berlinski, Milton R. *investment banking company executive*
Berman, Carol Wendy *psychiatrist*
Berman, Claire Gallant *freelance/self-employed writer*
Bernard, Claudie *literature educator*
Bernard, David George *retired management consultant*
Bernbach, John Lincoln *marketing professional*
Berndt, Andy *advertising executive*
Berne, Robert *academic administrator*
Berner, Andrew Jay *library director, writer*
Berney, Elizabeth A. *lawyer*
Bernsohn, Randall *construction executive, real estate developer*
Bernstein, Daniel Lewis *lawyer*
Bernstein, David William *lawyer*
Bernstein, Richard *financial analyst, investment advisor*
Bernstein, Richard Allen *food products executive*
Bernstein, Robert Jay *lawyer*
Bernstein, Robert M. *dermatologic surgeon*
Bernstein, Warren J. *lawyer*
Berry, John Nichols III *publishing executive, editor*
Berson, Anthony M. *oncologist*
Berstein, Robert Laurance *investment company executive*
Bertram, Paul Benjamin *language educator*
Beshar, Peter Justus *lawyer, insurance company executive*
Beshar, Robert Peter *lawyer*
Beslow, William S. *lawyer*
Bessey, Palmer Quintard *surgeon*
Bessler, Marc *surgeon, educator*
Best, Tony (Anthony J. Best) *diversified financial services company executive*
Best, Wanda *career planning consultant*
Besterman, Douglas *composer, orchestrator*
Bettis, Jerome Abram *sports commentator, retired professional football player*
Bettman, Gary Bruce *National Hockey League commissioner*
Betts, Katherine Hadley (Kate Betts) *editor*
Betts, Richard Kevin *political science professor*
Bevan, Ruth A. *political science professor, director*
Bewkes, Jeffrey Lawrence *multi media company executive*
Beyman, Jonathan Eric *investment company executive*
Bharara, Preet *prosecutor*
Bhargava, Peeyush *nuclear medicine physician*
Bhidé, Amarnath V. *business professor, writer*
Bholat, Omar *surgeon*
Bial, Deborah *educational association administrator*
Bialkin, Kenneth Jules *lawyer, director*
Bias, Val *foundation administrator*
Bickers, David Rinsey *dermatologist, educator, department chairman, health facility administrator*
Bicks, David Peter *lawyer*
Biddle, Flora Miller *art patron, museum administrator*
Biederman, Barron Zachary (Barry) *advertising agency executive*
Bienenstock, Martin J. *lawyer*
Biggs, John Herron *retired insurance company executive*

Biglari, Hamid *diversified financial services company executive*
Billows, Richard A. *history professor*
Binz-Scharf, Maria Christina *management consultant, educator*
Birch, Willie *artist*
Bird, Hector Ramón *child psychiatrist, psychoanalyst, educator*
Birkenhead, Thomas Bruce *theater producer, educator*
Birman, Joseph Leon *physics professor*
Birnbaum, Debra Gail *magazine editor*
Birnbaum, Edward Lester *lawyer*
Birnbaum, Sheila L. *lawyer, educator*
Birstein, Ann *writer, educator*
Bischoff, Theresa Ann *not-for-profit association executive*
Bishop, Susan Katharine *executive search company executive*
Bishop, Thomas Walter *French language and literature educator*
Bisignano, Frank J. *diversified financial services company executive*
Björk, (Björk Guðmundsdóttir) *singer, composer*
Black, Barbara Aronstein *legal history educator*
Black, Carole *broadcast executive*
Black, Cathie P. (Cathleen Prunty Black) *publishing executive*
Black, Henry Richard *physician*
Black, James Isaac (Jib) III *lawyer*
Black, Jerry Bernard *lawyer*
Black, Steven D. *diversified financial services company executive*
Blackman, Kenneth Robert *lawyer*
Blair, Dike *sculptor, painter*
Blair, William Granger *retired reporter*
Blair, William McCormick, Jr. *lawyer*
Blalock, Sherrill *investment advisor*
Blanc, Roger David *lawyer*
Bland, Frederick Aves *architect*
Blangiardi, Barbara *broadcast company executive, marketing professional*
Blank, Matthew C. *broadcast company executive*
Blankfein, Lloyd Craig *diversified financial services company executive*
Blasband, David *lawyer*
Blaser, Martin Jack *medical educator, researcher*
Blassberg, Franci J. *lawyer*
Blatt, Gregory R. *Internet company executive, lawyer*
Blau, Jeff T. *real estate company executive*
Blavatnik, Leonard *investment company executive*
Blazejowski, Carol Ann *professional sports team executive, retired professional basketball player*
Blechner, Mark Jacob *psychologist, educator*
Bledel, Alexis (Kimberly Alexis Bledel) *actress*
Bleser, Philip F. *diversified financial services company executive*
Blinder, Albert Allan *judge*
Blinken, Donald *ambassador, investment banker*
Blitzer, Andrew *otolaryngologist, educator, research scientist, writer*
Blivaiss, David Harvey *lawyer, accountant*
Blobel, Günter *cell biologist, educator*
Block, Dennis Jeffrey *lawyer*
Block, Francesca Lia *writer*
Block, Ned *philosopher, educator*
Bloom, Alfred Howard *academic administrator, educator*
Bloom, Martha Louise *artist, educator*
Bloomberg, Mike (Michael Rubens Bloomberg) *Mayor, New York City*
Bloomfield, April *chef*
Blue, Catherine Anne *lawyer*
Blum, Howard Robert *writer*
Blume, Judy *author*
Blumenthal, Sidney Stone *political columnist*
Boardman, D(ennie) Dixon *investment banker*
Boardman, Serena P. *real estate broker*
Bober, Lawrence Harold *retired banker*
Boccio, Frank M. *insurance company executive*
Bochner, Mel *artist*
Bockstein, Herbert *lawyer*
Boddewyn, Jean J. *RETIRED business educator*
Bodine, Susan H. *lawyer*
Bodley, Harley Ryan, Jr. *sportswriter, editor, announcer*
Boehner, Leonard Bruce *lawyer*
Boffey, Philip M. *journalist*
Bogart, Anne Dean *theater director, educator*
Bogdanos, Matthew F. *lawyer, reserve military officer, writer*
Bogdonoff, Morton David *internist, educator*
Bogen, Nancy *writer, English educator*
Boice, Craig Kendall *management consultant*
Bollinger, Lee Carroll *academic administrator, law educator*
Bologna, Anne *advertising executive*
Bolton, Roger *public relations executive*
Bond, Victoria Ellen *conductor, composer*
Bonfante, Larissa *classics educator*
Bonino, Fernanda *art dealer*
Bontecou, Lee *artist, sculptor*
Bookspan, Martin *broadcaster, writer*
Booth, Mitchell B. *retired lawyer*
Borchard, William Marshall *lawyer*
Borer, Jeffrey Stephen *cardiologist*
Borland, Virginia Ann *journalist, fiber company executive*
Borowitz, Sidney *retired physics professor*
Borras, Yolanda *music program administrator, educator, consultant*
Borrelli, John Francis *architect*
Bosl, George Joseph *physician, oncologist*
Bossert, Rex Thomas *editor-in-chief*
Bothmer, Dietrich Felix von *curator, archaeologist*
Botkin, Daniel Benjamin *biologist, environmental scientist, writer*
Boufford, Jo Ivey *health science association administrator, educator*
Boulhosa, Michael L. *lawyer*
Boullosa, Carmen *educator, writer*
Boulud, Daniel *chef, restaurant owner*
Bourgeois, Louise *sculptor*
Boutis, Tom *artist, painter, printmaker*
Bove, John Louis *chemistry and environmental engineering educator, researcher*
Bovin, Denis Alan *diversified financial services company executive*
Bowen, William Gordon *foundation administrator, economist*
Bowers, Brent *editor*
Bowers, John M. *labor union administrator*
Bowers, Patricia Eleanor Fritz *economist*
Bowers, William Charles *lawyer*
Bowles, Hamish *editor*
Box, C.J. *writer*
Boxer, Leonard *lawyer*
Boyd, Michael Alan *investment company executive, lawyer*
Boylan, Elizabeth Shippee *academic administrator, biologist, educator*
Bozeman, Beverley (Beverly B. Fuller) *dancer, singer, actress, choreographer, director*
Brabeck, Mary Margaret *dean, psychology professor*
Bracco, Lorraine *actress*
Brach, Richard S. *lawyer*
Bradbury, Ray Douglas *writer*
Bradford, Barbara Taylor *writer, journalist*
Bradley, Bill (William Warren Bradley) *investment company executive, former United States Senator from New Jersey, retired professional basketball player*
Bradley, E. Michael *lawyer*
Bradley, John Francis *diversified financial services company executive*
Bradley, Phillip Alden *lawyer, retail executive*
Bradshaw, Dove *artist*
Brady, Adelaide Burks *public relations agency executive, giftware catalog executive*
Brafman, Benjamin *lawyer*
Braham, Randolph Lewis *political science professor*
Brams, Steven John *political science professor*
Branch, Taylor *writer*
Bratten, Millie Martini *editor-in-chief*
Braudy, Susan Orr *writer*
Braun, Jeffrey Louis *lawyer*
Brauner, Gary Jules *dermatologist, cosmetic laser surgeon*
Braunstein, Douglas Lee *diversified financial services company executive*
Braverman, Robert Jay *management consultant, educator*
Brazinsky, Irv(ing) *chemical engineering educator, department chairman*
Brecker, Jeffrey Ross *lawyer, educator*
Breen, Thia *cosmetics company executive*
Breglio, John F. *lawyer*
Breinin, Goodwin M. *physician*
Bremmer, Ian *political scientist, writer*
Brendel, Alfred *concert pianist*
Brener, Richard *film company executive*
Brennan, Murray Frederick *surgeon, oncologist*
Brenneman, Gregory D. *private equity firm executive, former food service executive*
Brenner, Menachem *science educator*
Bresani, Federico Fernando *manufacturing executive*
Breslow, Esther May Greenberg *biochemistry professor, researcher*
Breslow, Ronald Charles *chemist, educator*
Breslow, Stephanie R. *lawyer*
Brett, Barry J. *lawyer*
Brett, Nancy Heléne *artist*
Brewer, Gale A. *city councilwoman*
Brien, Nick *advertising and marketing company executive*
Briggs, Patricia *writer*
Briley-Saebo, Karen Catherin *physics professor*
Brill, Paula Wolfe *radiologist, educator*
Brinkley, Alan David *historian, educator, former academic administrator*
Briskman, Louis Jacob *lawyer, broadcast executive*
Briskman, Robert David *engineering executive*
Britt, Glenn Alan *media company executive*
Britz Lotti, Diane Edward *investment company executive*
Brizel, Michael Alan *retail executive, lawyer*
Brizendine, Ellanor N. (Bodie) *headmaster*
Broad, William J. *science writer*
Broadwater, Douglas Dwight *lawyer*
Broatch, Robert E. *insurance company executive*
Brock, Charles Lawrence *lawyer, diversified financial services company executive*
Brod, Jon *Internet company executive*
Broder, Douglas Fisher *lawyer*
Brodie, Jonathan David *psychiatrist, educator*
Brodman, Michael Lewis *gynecologist, educator*
Brodsky, David Michael *lawyer*
Brody, Alan Jeffrey *investment company executive*
Brody, Jane Ellen *journalist, researcher*
Brody, Kenneth David *investment banker*
Brody-Lederman, Stephanie *artist*
Brokaw, Mark *theater director*
Bromage, Timothy G. *biological anthropologist, science educator*
Brome, Thomas Reed *retired lawyer*
Bronfman, Edgar Miles, Jr. *recording industry executive*
Bronstein, Hindy *research scientist*
Brooke, Beth *diversified financial services company executive*
Brooke, Linda Hundley *retired human resources specialist*
Brooks, David B. *editor, columnist*
Brooks, Deborah W. *foundation administrator*
Brooks, Gary *crisis management and family business consultant*
Brooks, Geraldine *writer, reporter, news correspondent*
Brosens, Frank Peter *hedge fund manager*
Brosnan, Timothy J. *sports association executive*
Brothers, Joyce Diane *television personality, psychologist*
Broude, Richard Frederick *lawyer, educator*
Broumand, Stafford R. *plastic surgeon*
Browdy, Joseph Eugene *lawyer*
Brown, Arthur Edward *physician*
Brown, Bobbi *cosmetics executive*
Brown, Carroll *retired diplomat, association executive, consultant*
Brown, Chris (Christopher Maurice Brown) *singer*
Brown, Clive Stuart *diversified financial services company executive*
Brown, Dan *writer*
Brown, Darrell James *publishing executive*
Brown, David *film producer, writer*
Brown, Edward James, Sr. *utilities executive*
Brown, Helen Gurley *editor-in-chief*
Brown, Jason Walter *neurologist, educator, researcher*
Brown, Jonathan *art historian, educator*
Brown, Joyce F. *academic administrator*
Brown, Loren H. *lawyer*
Brown, Paul M. *lawyer*
Brown, Ralph Sawyer, Jr. *retired lawyer*
Brown, Reneé M. *sports association executive*
Brown, Rita Mae *writer*
Brown, Robert Stephen, Jr. *physician*
Brown, Thomas K. *hedge fund manager*
Brown, Tina (Christina Hambley Brown) *journalist, television personality*
Brown, Trisha *dancer*
Browne, Arthur *newspaper editor*
Browning, Candace *investment company executive*
Brownwood, David Owen *lawyer*
Brozman, Andrew P. *lawyer*
Brucato, Robert Anthony *auxiliary bishop emeritus*
Bruce, Duncan Archibald *investor, writer*
Bruder, Harold Jacob *artist, educator*
Brumm, James Earl *lawyer, import/export company executive*
Brun, Henry *publishing executive*
Bruner, Jerome S. *law educator*
Bruni, Frank *restaurant critic*
Brunson, Curtis *communications systems company executive*
Brunswick, Ann Finkenberg *social psychologist, health researcher*
Brus, Louis Eugene *physical chemist*
Brust, John Calvin Morrison *neurologist, educator*
Brustein, Lawrence *finance company executive*
Bryan, Barry Richard *lawyer*
Bryan, Katherine Byram *healthcare executive*
Bryan, Stephen *music company executive*
Brymer, Chuck (Charles Edward Brymer) *advertising executive*
Buatta, Mario *interior designer*
Buchanan, Richard W. (Richard W. Buchanan) *sports association executive, lawyer*
Buchholz, Todd *journalist, social sciences educator, consultant*
Buck, Joe (Joseph Francis Buck) *sportscaster*
Buckles, Robert Howard *retired investment company executive*
Buckley, Christopher Taylor *editor, author*
Buckminster, Douglas E. *diversified financial services company executive*
Budd, Thomas Witbeck *lawyer*
Bujold, Lois McMaster *writer*
Bull, David *fine art conservator*
Bumiller, Elisabeth *journalist, writer*
Bundchen, Gisele *model*
Bunts, Frank Emory *artist*
Burak, H(oward) Paul *lawyer*
Burch, Tory *apparel designer*
Burden, Amanda Jay Mortimer *urban planner, city official*
Burgess, Clara Skipwith *retired principal*
Burgess, Lynne Anne *lawyer*
Burgheim, Richard *magazine editor*
Burgman, Dierdre Ann *lawyer*
Burgweger, Francis Joseph Dewes, Jr. *lawyer*
Burian, Peter *ambassador*
Burke, David *corporate and executive chef*
Burke, James Joseph, Jr. *investment banker*
Burke, Kevin *utilities executive*
Burnett, Mark *television producer*
Burns, Arnold Irwin *lawyer*
Burns, John F. *reporter*
Burns, M. Michele *management consulting firm executive*
Burns, Red *academic administrator*
Burrell, Lizabeth Lorie *lawyer*
Burroughs, Augusten (Christopher Robison) *writer*
Burrows, Kenneth David *lawyer*
Burrows, Michael Donald *lawyer*
Burrows, Stephen *apparel designer*
Burson, Harold *public relations executive, director*
Burstein, Danny *actor*
Burstein, Judd *lawyer*
Burstein, Lawrence C. *publishing executive*
Burstein, Nanette *film and television director, producer*
Burton, Eve Bradley *lawyer*
Burton, Peggy *advertising and marketing executive*
Burwell, Carter *composer*
Bushnell, Candace *columnist, writer*
Bushnell, George Edward III *lawyer*
Bussel, James Bruce *pediatrician, obstetrician, gynecologist, educator*
Butagira, Francis *ambassador*
Butler, David T. III *communications systems company executive*
Butler, Kerry *actress*
Butler, Samuel Coles *lawyer*
Butler, Vincent Paul, Jr. *internist, educator*
Buttenwieser, Lawrence Benjamin *lawyer*
Buttner, Jean Bernhard *diversified financial services company executive*
Buttrick, Harold *architect*
Butts, Calvin O. *pastor, academic administrator*
Butts, Hugh Florenz *physician, psychiatrist, psychoanalyst*
Butz, William Fortune *literature and language professor*
Buxton, Douglas Francisco *ophthalmologist, educator*
Byer, Diana *performing company executive*
Byowitz, Michael H. *lawyer*
Byrd, Debra Ann *actor, theater producer, performing company executive*
Byrne, David *musician, composer, artist, director*
Byrne, Gerard Anthony (Gerry) *publishing executive, consultant*
Byrne, Rhonda *television producer, writer*
Bystryn, Jean-Claude *dermatologist, educator*
Cagle, Jess *editor*
Cahn, Steven Mark *philosopher, educator*
Cailteux, Konrad Lee *lawyer*
Caine, Paul Jason *publishing executive*
Cajori, Charles Florian *artist, educator*
Calabrese, Rosalie Sue *management consultant, writer*
Calame, Kathryn Lee *microbiologist, educator*
Calbert, Michael M. *lawyer*
Caldwell, Leslie Ragon *lawyer, former prosecutor*
Calello, Paul *diversified financial services company executive*
Calero, Róger *advocate, editor, writer*
Calhoun, David L. *information and media company executive*
Califano, Joseph Anthony, Jr. *lawyer, former United States Secretary of Health Education and Welfare*
Calio, Nicholas E. *diversified financial services company executive, lobbyist*
Call, Neil Judson *management consultant*
Callahan, Don *diversified financial services company executive*
Callan, Erin M. *investment company executive*
Callo, Joseph Francis *writer*
Calotychos, Vangelis *literature and cultural studies, language professor*
Calpeter, Lynn Ann *broadcast executive*
Camacho, Philip Bruce *insurance company executive*
Cambria, Christopher C. *lawyer, communications systems company executive*
Camera, Nicholas J. *lawyer*
Cameron, Ewen *advertising executive*
Cammarata, Angelo *surgical oncologist*
Camp, Sharon L. *reproductive health organization administrator*
Campbell, George, Jr. *physicist, university administrator*
Campbell, Magda *retired child psychiatrist, researcher, educator*
Campbell, Mary Schmidt *dean*
Campbell, Naomi *model*
Campbell, Ronald Neil *retired graphics designer*
Campbell, Thomas P. *museum director, curator*
Campo, Carlos *apparel designer*
Campolattaro, Brian Nicholas *ophthalmologist, educator*
Campos, Fernando *entertainment editor*
Canada, Geoffrey *social welfare administrator, writer*
Canary, James Wayne *chemist, educator*
Cancro, Robert *psychiatrist, educator*
Canellos, Peter C. *lawyer*
Canetti, Alexandra *psychiatrist*
Canin, Ethan *writer*
Cannell, John Redferne *lawyer*
Canseco, Jose *retired professional baseball player*
Cantor, Richard Ira *physician, corporate health executive*
Cantrell, Lana *actress, lawyer, singer*
Cao, Yifang *research scientist*
Capalbo, Carmen *theater director, producer*
Caperton, Gaston (William Gaston Caperton III) *educational association administrator, former Governor of West Virginia*
Caponnetto, Marianne *information technology executive*
Cappellazzo, Amy *art appraiser, writer*
Cappuccio, Paul T. *lawyer, communications executive*
Capriati, Jennifer Maria *professional tennis player*
Caputo, Lisa Maria *diversified financial services company executive*
Caputo, Lucio *trade company executive*
Caraley, Demetrios James *political science professor, writer, publisher*
Carb, Stephen Ames *lawyer*
Cardile, Paul Julius *fine arts dealer*
Cardinale, Kathleen Carmel *retired health facility administrator*
Carell, Steve *comedian, actor*
Carelli, Thomas A. *sports association executive*
Carey, Chase (Charles G. Carey) *broadcast executive*
Carey, David *publishing executive*
Carey, Mariah *singer*
Carey, Peter Philip *writer, educator*
Carey, William Polk *investment banker*
Carlson, Ann Marie *choreographer, performance artist*
Carlson, Marvin Albert *theater educator*
Carlson, Tucker (Tucker Swanson McNear Carlson) *political analyst, writer, television host*
Carlucci, Paul V. *publishing executive*
Carman, Gregory Wright *federal judge*
Carmellini, Andrew *chef*
Carnell, Richard Scott *law educator*
Caro, Robert Allan *historian, writer*
Caroff, Phyllis M. *social work educator*
Carpenter, Michael A. *diversified financial services company executive*
Carr, Gladys Justin *publishing executive, editor, writer*
Carr, James T. *publishing executive*
Carroll, Tom *advertising executive*
Carroll, William Larkin *medical researcher*
Cartelli, Mary Anne *literature and language educator*
Carter, Graydon (Edward Graydon Carter) *editor-in-chief*
Carter, James Hal, Jr. *lawyer*
Carter, John Mack *publishing company executive*
Carter, Marshall Nichols *stock exchange executive*
Carter, Virgil R. *professional society administrator*
Carter, Zachary W. *lawyer*
Carucci, John A. *physician*
Casden, Andrew Michael *orthopedist*
Case, David Bartlett *internist, educator*
Case, Robert Brown *physician*
Casella, Cesare *chef, educator*
Casella, Jim *publishing executive*
Casey, Gerard William *retired food products executive, lawyer*
Casey, Susan *editor*
Casey, Thomas Jefferson *clean energy industry executive and entrepreneur, environmental activist*

Cashin, Richard Marshall, Jr. *diversified financial services company executive*
Castle, John Krob *merchant banker*
Castoro, Rosemarie *sculptor*
Castro, Jan Garden *writer, art educator, consultant*
Catalano, Robert Anthony *ophthalmologist, hospital administrator, writer*
Catsimatidis, John Andreas *retail executive*
Caulfield, Jerome Joseph *lawyer*
Cavallo, Jo Ann *language educator*
Cavanagh, Michael J. *diversified financial services company executive*
Cavenaugh, Matt *actor*
Cavuto, Neil Patrick *financial news correspondent*
Caws, Mary Ann *literature and language professor*
Cayea, Donald Joseph *lawyer*
Cayne, Neal Scott *surgeon*
Caytas, Ivo George *lawyer*
Cazala, Béatrice *pharmaceutical executive*
Cazeaux, Isabelle Anne Marie *retired music educator*
Cedarbaum, Miriam Goldman *federal judge*
Celentano, John E. *pharmaceutical executive*
Celmins, Vija *painter*
Cendali, Dale Margaret *lawyer*
Cenedella, Marc *Internet company executive*
Centrello, Gina *publishing executive*
Cephas, Derrick D. *bank executive, lawyer*
Cerfolio, Nina Estelle *psychiatrist, educator*
Chabot, John Anthony *surgeon*
Chaganti, Raju S. *geneticist, educator, researcher*
Chagnon, Kathleen *insurance company executive*
Chakravarti, Amitav *finance educator*
Chalfie, Martin *biology professor*
Chambrello, Michael R. *computer company executive*
Chan, Siu-Wai *materials science educator*
Chandrasekhar, Sujana S. *otologist, educator, neurotologist*
Chang, David *chef*
Chang, Laura *editor, journalist*
Chang, Marian S. *filmmaker, composer*
Chang, Mona Mei-Hsuan *computer programmer, analyst*
Chang, Nancy T. *pharmaceutical executive*
Chang, Ngee-Pong *physics educator*
Chang, Stanley *ophthalmologist*
Chang-Robbins, Joyce *diversified financial services company executive*
Chanos, James Steven *hedge fund manager*
Chao, James Si-Cheng *maritime executive*
Chapin, Julie Kurtz *lawyer*
Chapman, Georgina *apparel designer, actress*
Chapman, Herrick Eaton *historian, educator*
Chappell, John Charles *lawyer*
Chappell, Richard Lee *biology educator, neuroscientist*
Charash, Bruce D. *cardiologist, educator*
Charbonnet, Gabrielle *writer*
Charlton, Brittany Michelle *public health researcher*
Charon, Rita *internist, medical educator, writer*
Chatillon, Devereux *lawyer*
Chaudhry, Farooq A. *cardiologist*
Cheema, Faisal Habib *surgeon, researcher*
Cheh, Huk Yuk *electrochemist*
Chen, Chengjun Julian *physicist, engineering educator*
Chen, Elizabeth Shan Shan *research scientist*
Chen, Jessie *research scientist*
Chen, Jonathan M. *thoracic surgeon, educator*
Chen, Wesley *lawyer*
Chenault, Kenneth Irvine *finance company executive*
Cheney, Richard Eugene *public relations executive, psychoanalyst*
Cheng-Hopkins, Judy *international organization administrator*
Chenoweth, Kristin *actress*
Chermayeff, Ivan *graphics designer*
Cherryh, C. J. *writer*
Chesler, Evan Robert *lawyer*
Chesnutt, Jane *editor-in-chief*
Chestnut, Colette *broadcast executive*
Cheung, Raymond Yan Ling *pharmaceutical executive, director*
Chevray, Rene *engineering educator*
Chiang, Yung Frank *law educator*
Chiarchiaro, Frank John *lawyer*
Chiarello, Guy *diversified financial services company executive*
Chichilnisky, Graciela *scientist mathematician, economist, educator, writer*
Child, Lee (Jim Grant) *writer*
Childs, David M. *architectural firm executive*
Chin, Mel *sculptor*
Chin, Sylvia Fung *lawyer*
Chinn, Adam D. *diversified financial services company executive, lawyer*
Chinn, Yuen Yuey *art educator, painter*
Chirico, Emanuel *apparel executive*
Chiu, David Tak Wai *surgeon*
Choe, Won-Taek *neurologist, educator*
Choi, Susan *writer*
Chou, Ting-Chao *inventor, educator*
Chowdhury, Shoaib *engineer*
Christensen, Henry III *lawyer*
Christensen, Irene *artist*
Christensen, Kate *writer*
Christian, Leslie Kojo *ambassador*
Christopher, Maurine Brooks *foundation administrator, writer, editor*
Chromow, Sheri P. *lawyer*
Chubb, Sarah Caldecot *publishing executive*
Chung, Jung Git *retired aerospace engineer*
Church, Frank Forrester *minister, writer*
Church, Thomas Haden *actor*
Chused, Richard Harris *law educator*
Chutorian, Abe M. *pediatrician, educator*
Ciparick, Carmen Beauchamp *state appeals court judge*
Cisneros, Bettina Lynn *multimedia company executive, marketing professional*
Cisneros, Sandra *poet, short story writer, essayist*
Civiello, Mary *communications executive, journalist*
Clair, Bernard E. *lawyer*
Claire, Thomas Andrew *financial executive, consultant, educator, writer*
Clapp, Stephen Henry *violinist*
Clark, Howard Longstreth, Jr. *finance company executive, director*
Clark, James Joseph *lawyer*
Clark, Joan Hardy *retired journalist*
Clark, Mayree Carroll *investment company executive*
Clark, Robert Henry, Jr. *finance company executive*
Clark, Sheryl Diane *physician*
Clark, Wesley Kanne *investment company executive, retired military officer*
Clarke, Frank William *communications executive*
Clarke, Keith Charles *cartography educator*
Clary, Richard Wayland *lawyer*
Claster, Jill Nadell *academic administrator, history educator*
Clayton, Jon Kerry *insurance company executive*
Clayton, Joseph Paul *broadcast executive*
Cleary, Beverly Atlee (Mrs. Clarence T. Cleary) *writer*
Clemens, Rosemary A. *foundation and health facility administrator*
Clemente, Frank M., Jr. *civil engineer*
Cliff, Walter Conway *lawyer*
Clifford, Stewart Burnett *banker, director*
Clinton, Bill (William Jefferson Clinton) *42nd President of the United States*
Cloherty, Patricia M. *investment company executive*
Cloonan, Edward Thomas *insurance company executive*
Close, Chuck (Charles Thomas Close) *artist*
Close, Lanny Garth *otolaryngologist, educator*
Close, Michael John *property manager, lawyer*
Clow, Lee *advertising agency executive*
Coatsworth, John Henry *history professor, writer, dean*
Cobb, Henry Nichols *architect*
Coben, Harlan *writer*
Coddington, Grace *publishing executive*
Coe, Sue *artist, journalist*
Coen, Jessica *blog writer, editor*
Coffee, John Collins, Jr. *legal educator*
Coffey, Barbara Jane *psychiatrist*
Coffin, Anne Gagnebin *arts administrator, editor*
Cohen, Abby Joseph *diversified financial services company executive*
Cohen, Adam *reporter, lawyer*
Cohen, Alan L. *advertising executive*
Cohen, Alan M. *investment company executive, lawyer*
Cohen, Cora *artist*
Cohen, David Harris *neuroscientist, educator, academic administrator*
Cohen, Edmund Stephen *lawyer*
Cohen, Ezechiel Godert David *physicist, researcher*
Cohen, Harriet Newman *lawyer*
Cohen, Henry Rodgin (H. Rodgin Cohen) *lawyer*
Cohen, Howard A. *cardiologist*
Cohen, Joel Ephraim *biologist, educator, demographer*
Cohen, Jonathan Elliot *international human rights advocate*
Cohen, Joshua Robert *lawyer*
Cohen, Lyor C. *recording industry executive*
Cohen, Morton Norton *English educator, writer*
Cohen, Noel Lee *otolaryngologist, educator*
Cohen, Peter Anthony *investment company executive*
Cohen, Richard Martin *journalist*
Cohen, Robert Stephan *lawyer*
Cohen, Robin L. *lawyer*
Cohen, Seymour Martin *oncologist, hematologist, educator*
Cohen, Stephen Frand *political scientist, writer, historian, educator, commentator*
Cohn, Bertram Josiah *portfolio manager*
Cohn, Gary D. *diversified financial services company executive*
Cohn, Joshua D. *lawyer*
Cohn, Melissa Lynn *mortgage company executive*
Cohn, Theodore *management consultant*
Cole, Carolyn Jo *brokerage house executive*
Cole, Christopher A. *investment company executive*
Cole, Kenneth D. *apparel company executive*
Cole, Lewis George *lawyer*
Coleman, Charles Payson, Jr., (Payson Coleman) *lawyer*
Coleman, Charles Payson, III, (Chase Coleman) *hedge fund manager*
Coleman, Donald Jackson *ophthalmologist, educator*
Coleman, Gregory G. *Internet company executive, former magazine publisher*
Coleman, Jo-Ann S.E. *social worker*
Coleman, Morton *oncologist, educator*
Coleman, Stuart H. *lawyer*
Coleman, Sydney Reese *plastic surgeon, educator*
Colen, Helen Sass *plastic surgeon*
Colen, Stephen R. *plastic and reconstructive surgeon*
Coles, Joanna *magazine editor-in-chief*
Colette, S. *artist*
Colicchio, Tom *chef, food service executive*
Coll, John Peter, Jr. *lawyer*
Collazo, Salvador *lawyer*
Coller, Barry Spencer *internist, pathologist, hematologist, educator, department chairman*
Collesano, Stephen P. *insurance company executive*
Collins, Emilio *sports association executive*
Collins, Gail *journalist*
Collins, J. Barclay, II, *lawyer, oil industry executive*
Collins, Jackie (Jacqueline Jill Collins) *writer*
Collins, John *sports association executive*
Collins, John F. *lawyer*
Collins, Nancy Walbridge *historian, educator*
Collins, Richard Lawrence *editor*
Collinsworth, Cris *sportscaster, retired professional football player*
Colmes, Alan Samuel *political commentator, radio personality*
Comitas, Lambros *anthropologist, educator*
Compte, Maria Emilia *physician, educator, administrator*
Comstock, Beth (Elizabeth J. Comstock) *marketing executive*
Cona, Louis *publishing executive*
Conarroe, Joel Osborne *foundation administrator, editor, educator*
Conason, Robert *lawyer*
Conboy, Kenneth *lawyer, retired federal judge*
Concannon, Christopher R. *trading company executive*
Conelli, Maria Ann *museum director, art educator*
Connelly, Michael *writer*
Conniff, Richard *writer*
Connolly, John Joseph *publishing executive*
Connolly, John P. *corporate financial executive*
Connor, W(alter) Robert *foundation administrator, classicist, educator*
Conroy, Pat (Donald Patrick Conroy) *writer*
Consagra, Sophie Chandler *academic administrator*
Consolo, Faith Hope *real estate company executive*
Constantinides, Minas Spiros *otolaryngologist, plastic surgeon, educator*
Conston, Henry Siegismund *lawyer*
Conway, E. Virgil *financial consultant, lawyer*
Conway, Kevin *actor, performing company executive*
Conway, Richard Francis *investment company executive*
Cook, Blanche Wiesen *historian, educator, journalist*
Cook, Ian M. *consumer products company executive*
Cook, Michael Lewis *lawyer*
Cook, Richard A. (Rick Cook) *architect*
Cook, Stephen Lloyd *religious studies educator, writer*
Cooke, Lynne Catherine *curator*
Cooke, Phil *application developer*
Cooley, Thomas F. *dean, economics professor*
Cooney, Joan Ganz *broadcast executive, director*
Cooney, John Patrick, Jr. *lawyer*
Cooney, Michael J. *ophthalmologist*
Cooper, Anderson Hays *news correspondent, cable news anchor*
Cooper, Edith W. *investment company executive*
Cooper, Michael *reporter*
Cooper, Michael Anthony *lawyer*
Cooper, Rubin Seymour *pediatric cardiologist*
Cooper, Stephen Herbert *retired lawyer*
Coplan, Neil Lawrence *cardiologist*
Corbat, Michael Louis *diversified financial services company executive*
Corbin, Sol Neil *lawyer*
Corcoran, Barbara Anne *retired real estate company executive*
Corcoran, David *newspaper editor*
Corddry, Rob *comedian, actor*
Cordeiro, Peter Gabriel *plastic surgeon, medical educator*
Cornelio, Maria A. *language educator*
Cornelius, James Milton *pharmaceutical company executive*
Cornell, John Robert *lawyer*
Cornwell, Patricia Daniels *writer*
Corporon, John Robert *broadcast executive*
Corrigan, Edward Gerald *diversified financial services company executive*
Corsaro, Frank Andrew *theater director*
Cortese, Edward *marketing and public relations executive*
Cortez, Ricardo Lee *investment management executive*
Corwin, Leslie D. *lawyer*
Cory, Eleanor Thayer *composer, educator*
Costa, Francisco *fashion designer*
Costas, Bob (Robert Quinlan Costas) *sportscaster*
Cota, Christian *apparel designer*
Cotter, Holland *art critic, writer*
Cotton, Richard *lawyer*
Cottrell, Ted (Theodore John Cottrell) *professional football coach*
Coulter, David Alan *private equity firm executive*
Couric, Katie (Katherine Anne Couric) *newscaster, journalist*
Covello, Vincent Thomas *environmental science and medicine educator, foundation administrator*
Cowdell, Phil *media communications agency executive*
Cowin, Stephen Corteen *biomedical engineering educator, consultant*
Cox, Archibald, Jr. *investor*
Cox, Edward Finch *lawyer*
Cox, L. Kevin *human resources specialist*
Coyne, Nancy Carol *advertising executive*
Craft, Randal Robert, Jr. *lawyer*
Craig, Charles Samuel *marketing educator*
Craig, Edward Vincent *orthopedic surgeon, educator*
Craig, Elizabeth Coyne *marketing executive*
Craig, Pamela J. *management consulting firm executive*
Cramb, Charles W. *cosmetics executive*
Cramer, Douglas Schoolfield *broadcasting executive*
Cramer, Edward Morton *lawyer, music company executive*
Cramer, Jim (James J. Cramer) *financial information executive*
Crames, Michael J. *lawyer*
Crane, Benjamin Field *lawyer*
Crane, Charles Grant *financial analyst*
Crane, Stephen Charles *medical association executive*
Crapanzano, Vincent *anthropologist, educator, literary critic*
Crawford, Stephen S. *diversified financial services company executive*
Crews, Kenneth Donald *law educator, consultant, librarian, academic administrator*
Cribiore, Alberto *diversified financial services company executive*
Crist, Judith *film and drama critic*
Critchlow, Charles Howard *lawyer*
Croce, Arlene *critic*
Crocker, Elaine (M. Elaine Crocker) *investment company executive*
Crockett, Andrew Duncan *diversified financial services company executive*
Cromwell, Oliver Dean *investment banker*
Cross, Theodore Lamont *publisher, author*
Crouch, Stanley *writer, musician*
Crowdus, Gary Alan *film company executive*
Crown, Roberta Lila *artist, educator*
Crystal, James William *insurance company executive*
Crystal, Ronald G. *medical geneticist, educator*
Cucin, Robert Louis *plastic surgeon, lawyer*
Culhane, Stephen (David Stephen King Culhane) *lawyer*
Cullinan, Bernice Ellinger *education educator*
Cummins, Herman Zachary *physicist*
Cundiff, Victoria Anne *lawyer*
Cunha, Mark Geoffrey *lawyer*
Cunningham, Francis *artist*
Cunningham, Jennifer *lobbyist, consultant*
Cunningham-Rundles, Charlotte *physician, educator*
Cuomo, Mario Matthew *lawyer, former governor*
Cuozzo, Steven David *newspaper editor*
Curley, Thomas *newspaper executive*
Curren, Lois Clark *music company executive, television producer*
Curry, Ann *correspondent, anchor*
Curry, Jane Louise *writer*
Curtin, Jane Therese *actress, writer*
Curtis, Christopher Paul *writer*
Curtis, Paul James *mime, director*
Cushing, Charles R. *architectural firm executive*
Cutler, Bruce *lawyer*
Cutler, Stephen M. *lawyer, former federal agency administrator*
Cuttner, Janet *hematologist, educator*
Cyganowski, Melanie L. *federal judge*
Czajkowski, Jim (James Rollins, James Clemens) *writer*
Czepiel, Lori Anne *lawyer*
Dadakis, John D. *lawyer*
Dailey, Janet *writer*
Daintith, Stephen *publishing executive*
Dajani, Virginia *art association administrator*
Dales, Samuel *microbiologist, virologist, educator*
Dalton, Dennis Gilmore *retired political science professor*
Daltrey, Roger (Roger Harry Daltrey) *singer*
D'Amato, Alfonse Marcello *lobbyist, former United States Senator from New York*
d'Amboise, Jacques Joseph *former dancer, choreographer, educator, director*
D'Ambrosio, Ralph G. *communications systems company executive*
D'Amelio, Frank Anthony *pharmaceutical executive, former telecommunications industry executive*
Dana, F(rank) Mitchell *theatrical lighting designer*
Dancyger, Ida Flint *psychologist, educator*
D'Angelo, Charles H. *insurance company executive*
D'Angelo, Joseph Francis *publishing executive*
Danic, Robert Ian *application developer*
Daniel, David Ronald *management consultant*
Daniel, Samuel J. *hospital administrator, medical educator*
Daniels, Edward M. *small business owner, paralegal*
Daniels, Jennifer M. *lawyer*
Daniels, Randy A. *investment company executive, former state official*
Daniels, Susanne *broadcast executive*
Danishefsky, Samuel J. *chemistry professor*
Danitz, Marilynn Patricia *choreographer, video specialist*
Dannhauser, Stephen J. *lawyer*
Danto, Arthur Coleman *writer, philosopher, critic*
D'Antoni, Mike (Michael Andrew D'Antoni) *professional basketball coach*
Danziger, Lucy *editor*
D'Arezzo, David W. *retail executive*
Darling, Ronald Maurice (Ron Darling) *sportscaster, retired professional baseball player*
Darnell, James Edwin, Jr. *molecular biologist, educator*
Darnton-Hill, Ian *public health physician, nutrition consultant*
Darrell, Norris, Jr. *lawyer*
Darrow, Jill E(llen) *lawyer*
Dart, Leslee *public relations company executive*
Dash, Damon *recording industry executive, consumer products company executive*
Dassin, Lev L. *prosecutor*
Daum, Julie Hembrock *executive recruiter*
Dauman, Philippe P. *multimedia company executive*
Dave, Dhaval M. *economics professor*
Davenport, Tim *diversified financial services company executive*
David, Michael *theater producer*
David, Miles *marketing executive*
David, Reuben *lawyer*
David, Theoharis Lambros *architect, educator*
Davidovsky, Mario *retired composer*
Davidson, Anthony R. *education educator, consultant*
Davidson, Bruce *photojournalist*
Davidson, Donald William *advertising executive*
Davidson, Douglas E. *lawyer*
Davidson, George Allan *lawyer*
Davidson, Louise T. *editor*
Davidson, Paul *political economics educator, consultant*
Davidson, Robert Bruce *retired lawyer*
Davidson, Sheila Kearney *lawyer, insurance company executive*
David-Weill, Michel Alexandre *retired investment banker*
Davis, Christopher James *television producer*
Davis, Clive Jay *recording industry executive*
Davis, D. Lavelda *dean, academic administrator*
Davis, Evan Anderson *lawyer*
Davis, Florence Ann *foundation administrator, lawyer*
Davis, George Linn *banker*
Davis, Jessica G. *geneticist*
Davis, Karen *insurance company executive, educator*
Davis, Kimberly B. *bank executive*
Davis, Michael Steven *lawyer*
Davis, Morty (J. Morton Davis) *investment banker*
Davis, Owen Kidder *physician, reproductive endocrinologist*
Davis, Trayton M. *lawyer*
Davis, Viola *actress*

Dawson, Philip *history professor*
De, Prabal *finance educator*
De Angelis, Judy *anchorwoman*
Deaver, Jeffery (William Jefferies) *writer, former lawyer*
Debiec, Jacek *psychiatrist, research scientist, educator*
de Blasio, Bill *city councilman*
Debo, Vincent Joseph *lawyer, director, manufacturing executive*
Debrovner, Charles Howard *obstetrician, gynecologist, educator*
Debs, Richard A. *investment banker*
Decter, Midge *writer*
de Grazia, Victoria *historian, educator, writer*
DeGregorio, Carlo *social studies educator*
Delaney, Robert Vincent *former gas company executive, economic development consultant*
de Lange, Titia *research scientist, educator*
de la Renta, Oscar *fashion designer*
Delauney, Sophie *medical relief organization executive*
del Castillo, Graciana *economist, director*
Del Forno, Anton *classical guitarist, recording artist, composer, educator*
D'Elia, Valarie *travel writer and commentator*
Dellapina, John *sports association executive, writer*
Della Rocca, Steven *lawyer*
DelliBovi, Alfred A. *bank executive, former federal agency administrator*
Del Nunzio, Paula *real estate company executive*
DeLorenzo, Matt *editor-in-chief*
Del Pizzo, Joseph J. *urologist, educator*
Del Risco, Enrique A. *language educator*
Del Tufo, Robert J. *lawyer, former state attorney general*
Demarchelier, Patrick *photographer*
DeMarco, Jennifer C. *lawyer*
deMause, Lloyd *psychologist*
de Menil, Joy Alexandra *editor*
de Menil, Lois Pattison *historian, philanthropist*
DeMonte, Claudia Ann *artist, educator*
de Montebello, Philippe Lannes *retired museum director, art educator*
Demsey, John D. *cosmetics executive*
den Dikken, Marcel *language educator*
Denes, Agnes C. *environmental artist*
De Niro, Robert *actor, film producer and director, restaurant owner*
Denmark, Bernhardt *manufacturing executive*
Denmark, Florence Harriet Levin *psychology professor*
Denmark, Stanley Jay *orthodontist*
Denn, Morton Mace *chemical engineering educator*
Dennis, Diane Joy Milam *retired architect*
Dennis, Donna Frances *sculptor, art educator*
Dennis, Everette Eugene, Jr. *foundation executive, educator, writer*
Dennison, Lisa *auction house executive*
Denno, Deborah W. *law educator*
Denoon, David Baugh Holden *political economist, educator, consultant*
de Notaristefani, Carlo *pharmaceutical executive*
Denton, Nick *publishing executive*
DeNunzio, David Ames *investment banker*
DeOrchis, Vincent Moore *lawyer*
DePalma, Gina *chef*
DePreist, James Anderson *conductor*
D'Erasmo, Diane *bank executive*
de Ravel d'Esclapon, Pierre F. *lawyer*
Dermksian, George *cardiologist*
DeRoma, Nicholas John *lawyer, metal products executive*
Derow, Peter Alfred *publishing executive*
Derzaw, Richard Lawrence *lawyer*
Desai, Kiran *writer*
Desai, Vishakha N. *professional society administrator*
de St. Paër, Jerry Michael *insurance executive*
d'Escoto Brockmann, Miguel *President of United Nations General Assembly, priest*
De Sear, Edward Marshall *lawyer*
Desloge, Rosemary Byrne *otolaryngologist, educator*
Desmarais, John M. *lawyer*
Desmond, Laura *advertising executive*
Desnick, Robert John *human geneticist*
Detjen, David Wheeler *lawyer*
Deutsch, Ayala *sports association executive, lawyer, educator*
Deutsch, David Neil *investment banker*
Deutsch, Donny (Donald Jay Deutsch) *advertising executive, business commentator*
Deutsch, Irwin Frederick *lawyer*
Deutsch, Morton *psychologist, educator*
Deveraux, Jude *writer*
De Vido, Alfredo Eduardo *architect*
Devine, Jack *consulting firm executive, former federal agency administrator*
Devinsky, Orrin *neurologist, medical educator*
Devitre, Dinyar S. *tobacco company executive*
De Vivo, Darryl Claude *pediatrician, neurologist*
Devlin, Robert Manning *diversified financial services company executive*
DeVoe, David F., Sr. *publishing executive*
DeWoody, Beth Rudin *film producer*
Deyn, Agyness (Laura Hollins) *model*
Deyrmenjian, Liza (Liza D.) *fashion consultant, film producer*
Dial, Teresa A. (Terri Dial) *diversified financial services company executive*
Diamond, Bernard Robin *lawyer*
Diamond, Brian *lawyer*
Diamonstein-Spielvogel, Barbaralee *writer*
Diaz, Angela *pediatrician, educator*
Diaz-Cruz, Mario III *lawyer*
DiCarlo, Rosemary Anne *ambassador*
Dickens, Inez Elizabeth *city councilwoman, real estate executive*
Didion, Joan *writer*
Diercksen, John W. *telecommunications industry executive*
DiFebo, Valerie *advertising executive*
Di Fiore, Anthony *geneticist, educator*
Diggins, Peter Sheehan *arts administrator*
Diktaban, Theodore *plastic surgeon*
Diller, Barry *Internet company executive*
Diller, Matthew *dean, law educator*
Dillon, Matt *actor*
DiLorenzo, Louis Patrick *lawyer*
DiMaggio, Frank Louis *civil engineering educator*
DiMaio, Mary F. *pediatrician*
Di Meo, Dominick *artist, sculptor, painter*
DiMichele, Donna *medical educator, researcher*
Dimling, John Arthur *marketing executive*
Dimon, Jamie (James L. Dimon) *diversified financial services company executive*
Dion, Mark *installation sculptor, photographer*
Di Palma, Joseph Alphonse *investment company executive, lawyer*
DiPiazza, Samuel A., Jr. *finance company executive*
Disa, Joseph James *plastic surgeon*
DiSciullo, Alan Michael *lawyer*
Diskant, Gregory L. *lawyer*
Dixon, Wendy L. *pharmaceutical executive*
Dobbs, John Barnes *artist, educator*
Dobell, Byron Maxwell *magazine consultant*
Dobrinsky, Herbert Colman *university administrator*
Dobrof, Rose Wiesman *gerontology educator*
Doctoroff, Daniel L. *communications executive, former city manager*
Doctorow, E.L. (Edgar Lawrence Doctorow) *writer, English educator*
Doerfler, Ronald John *publishing executive*
Doherty, Thomas *publisher*
Dohle, Markus *publishing executive*
Dohrenwend, Bruce Philip *epidemiologist, social sciences educator*
Dolan, Timothy Michael *archbishop*
Dombroff, Robert Michael *lawyer*
Donnelly, John *publishing executive*
Donnelly, John L. *bank executive*
Donneson, Seena Sand *artist*
Donohoe, Noel B. *investment company executive*
Donovan, Anne *professional basketball coach*
Donovan, Maureen Driscoll *lawyer*
Donovan, Richard Edward *lawyer*
Donovan, Tara *sculptor*
Dooley, Douglas John *bank executive*
Dooley, Thomas E. *multimedia company executive*
Dooley, William N. *insurance company executive*
Dooner, John Joseph, Jr. *advertising executive*
Dopf, Glenn William *lawyer*
Dorfman, Howard David *pathologist, educator*
Dorkey, Charles E., III, (Trip Dorkey) *lawyer*
Dorman, Peter Fitzgerald *academic administrator, anthropologist, educator*
Dormann, Henry O. *magazine publisher*
Dorsen, Norman *lawyer, educator*
Dorsett, Burt *investment company executive*
Doty, Mark *poet*
Douglas, James McCrystal *lawyer*
Douglas, Peter Roderick *lawyer*
Douglas, Preston J. *lawyer*
Dowling, Danielle *writer*
Downey, Susan E. *plastic surgeon*
Doyle, Eugenie Fleri *pediatrician, cardiologist, educator*
Doyle, John *artistic director, designer*
Doyle, Joseph Anthony *retired lawyer*
Doyle, Lee *marketing and communications executive*
Draddy, James J. *stock exchange executive*
Drake, Laura *theater director, performer*
Draper, James David *art museum curator*
Dratch, Rachel *comedienne, actress*
Drayer, Burton Paul *hospital administrator, neuroradiologist*
Drebsky, Dennis Jay *lawyer*
Dreifus, Claudia *journalist, educator*
Drew, Ina R. *bank executive*
Drexler, Mickey (Millard Steven) *retail executive*
Dreyer, Benard Philip *pediatrician, educator*
Driver, Martha Westcott *literature educator, researcher, writer*
Drost, Marianne *lawyer, telecommunications industry executive*
Dru, Jean-Marie Paul *advertising executive*
Drucker, Richard Allen *lawyer*
Drum, Sydney Maria *artist*
Drury, Chris *professional hockey player*
Drzik, John P. *management consulting firm executive*
Duarte, Sergio de Queiroz *international organization official*
Dubbs, Thomas Allan *lawyer*
Duberman, Martin *historian, gay activist, educator*
Dubin, Glenn Russell *hedge fund manager*
Dubin, James Michael *lawyer*
Dubin, Louis M. *real estate company executive, entrepreneur*
Dubinsky, Brandon *professional hockey player*
Du Boff, Jill Bonnie Candise *sound effects artist, educator*
Dubois, Michel *anesthesiologist*
Dubuc, Nancy *communications executive*
Dubus, Andre III *writer*
Ducasse, Alain *chef*
Duch, Stephen *corporate financial executive*
Duchin, Peter Oelrichs *musician*
Duckett, Keith L. *insurance company executive*
Dudley, William C. *bank executive, economist*
Duersten, Althea L. *bank executive*
Duff, Hilary Ann *singer, actress*
Duff, John Ewing *sculptor*
Duff, William Brandon *lawyer*
Duffy, James Henry *writer, retired lawyer*
Duffy, W. Leslie *lawyer*
Dufresne, Wylie *chef, food service executive*
Dugan, James Connolly *lawyer*
Dugger, Celia Williams *journalist*
Duhon, Chris *professional basketball player*
Dukakis, Olympia *actress*
Duke, Anthony Drexel *retired sociologist, educator, philanthropist*
Dukmejian, Michael V. *publishing executive*
Du Mont, Nicolas *psychiatrist, educator*
Dungy, Tony *sportscaster, retired professional football coach*
Dunham, Wolcott Balestier, Jr. *lawyer*
Dunkelman, Loretta *artist*
Dunleavy, Kevin B. *investment company executive*
Dunn, James W. *communications systems company executive*
Dunn, Martin *editor-in-chief*
Duperreault, Brian C. *insurance company executive*
DuPuy, Bob (Robert A. DuPuy) *major league baseball executive*
Durkin, Dorothy Angela *university official*
Durkin, Patrick J. *private equity firm executive*
Dwek, Cyril S. *bank executive*
Dworetzky, Murray *retired physician, educator*
Dworkin, Ronald Myles *law educator*
Dylan, Bob (Robert Allen Zimmerman) *singer, musician*
Dyyon, Mario (LeRoy Frazier) *artist*
Eakins, William Shannon *lawyer*
Earl, Christopher D. *health products executive*
Earling, Debra Magpie *writer, educator*
Easton, Nina Jane *journalist*
Eaton, Richard Kenyon *federal judge*
Ebersol, Dick (Duncan Dickie Ebersol) *television broadcasting executive*
Eckert, Allan Wesley *writer*
Ecko, Marc (Marc Milecofsky) *apparel designer*
Eddleman, Keith Arnold *obstetrician-gynecologist*
Edelman, Judith H. *architect*
Edelman, Richard Winston *public relations executive*
Edelson, David Bick *diversified holding company executive*
Edelson, Gilbert Seymour *lawyer*
Edelstein, Barbara A. *radiologist*
Edgar, Harold Simmons Hull *legal educator*
Edlin, Richard A. *lawyer*
Edlow, Kénneth Lewis *security firm executive*
Edmiston, Mark Morton *publishing company executive*
Edsall, Thomas Byrne *reporter*
Edward, Jeffrey N. *diversified financial services company executive*
Edward, John (John Edward McGee Jr.) *spiritual medium, writer*
Edwards, Duncan *publishing executive*
Edwards, Harold Mortimer *mathematics professor*
Ehinger, Albert Louis, Jr. *securities trader*
Ehrenkranz, Joel S. *lawyer*
Eichenfield, Andrew Howard *pediatric rheumatologist*
Eichenwald, Kurt *writer*
Eichhorn, Guenther *publishing executive*
Einhorn, David M. *hedge fund manager*
Einiger, Carol Blum *investment company executive*
Eins, Stefan *artist, curator, science researcher, writer*
Einstein, Andrew J. *cardiologist, educator*
Einstein, Steven Henry *lawyer, investment banker*
Eisen, Robert L. *lawyer*
Eisenberg, Barbara Anne K. *lawyer*
Eisenberg, Herbert *lawyer*
Eisenman, Peter David *architect, educator*
Eisenstadt, G. Michael *diplomat, writer, educator, researcher*
Eisenthal, Kenneth B. *physical chemistry educator*
Eisert, Edward Gaver *lawyer*
Eisler, Susan Krawetz *advertising executive*
Eleta, Graciela (Graciela Eleta de Cacho) *broadcast company executive, marketing professional*
Elgert, Paul A. *cytotechnologist*
Elgort, Arthur *photographer*
Elinson, Jack *social sciences educator*
Elkin, Judith *lawyer*
Elkin, Michael S. *lawyer*
Ellenhorn, David N. *lawyer*
Ellig, Janice Reals *marketing professional, human resources specialist*
Elliot, Cameron Robert *lawyer*
Elliott, Missy (Melissa Arnette Elliot) *musician*
Elliott, Steven G. *bank executive*
Ellis, Lisa *music company executive*
Ellis, Rosemary *editor-in-chief*
Ellis, Ross *non-profit organization executive*
Ellroy, James *writer*
Elmer, Russell S. *diversified financial services company executive, lawyer*
El-Sadr, Wafaa Mahmoud *epidemiologist, medical educator*
Elsen, Jon *editor*
Elsen, Sheldon Howard *lawyer*
Emmerich, Adam Oliver *lawyer*
Emmerich, Toby *film company executive*
Emmerman, Michael N. *financial analyst*
Enders, Elizabeth McGuire *artist*
Engel, Amy J. *tobacco company executive*
Engel, Ralph Manuel *lawyer*
Engelhardt, Sara Lawrence *retired organization executive*
Englander, Israel A. *financier*
Engle, Robert F. *finance educator*
English, Joseph Thomas *psychiatrist, medical administrator*
English, Thomas Francis *lawyer*
Engstrom, Erik *publishing executive*
Ennis, Alan T. *cosmetics company executive*
Entwistle, Andrew John *lawyer, consultant*
Epling, Richard Louis *lawyer*
Epstein, Gerald N. *psychiatrist, educator*
Epstein, Melvin *lawyer*
Epstein, Michael Alan *lawyer*
Epstein, Stuart Joel *investment banker*
Ercklentz, Alexander Tonio *investment company executive*
Ercklentz, Enno Wilhelm, Jr. *lawyer*
Erdoes, Mary Callahan *bank executive*
Erikson, Robert S. *political science professor*
Erlanger, Bernard Ferdinand *biochemist, educator*
Erlenmeyer-Kimling, L. *psychiatrist, researcher*
Ernst, John Louis *management consultant*
Errico, Thomas *neurosurgeon, educator*
Erwitt, Elliott Romano *photographer, cinematographer*
Eschenbach, Christoph *conductor, musician, music director*
Essig, Jack *magazine publishing executive*
Esterow, Milton *publishing executive*
Estreicher, Samuel *lawyer, educator*
Ethan, Carol Baehr *psychotherapist, psychoanalyst*
Evangelisti, Joseph M. *bank executive*
Evanovich, Janet *writer*
Evans, Alfred Lee, Jr. *advertising executive*
Evans, Douglas Hayward *lawyer*
Evans, Greg *cartoonist*
Evans, John Thomas *lawyer*
Evans, Martin Frederic *lawyer*
Evans, Mary Johnston *corporate director*
Eveillard, Jean-Marie *finance company executive*
Ewing, John Harwood *professional math organization executive*
Faber, Neil *advertising executive*
Faber, Peter Lewis *lawyer*
Fabrikant, Geraldine *journalist*
Fager, Jeffrey *broadcast executive*
Fagin, Claire Mintzer *nursing administrator, educator*
Fahey, James Edward *brokerage house executive*
Fahey, Thomas *surgeon, educator*
Fahn, Stanley *neurologist, educator*
Fairchild, Megan *dancer*
Falcone, Philip Alan *hedge fund manager*
Falkenrath, Richard A. *protective services official*
Falt, Eric *government agency administrator*
Farah, Roger N. *retail company executive*
Farber, John J. *chemical company executive*
Farber, Michael *sportswriter*
Fargis, Paul McKenna *publishing executive, consultant*
Farley, Carole *soprano*
Farley, Katherine G. *real estate company executive*
Farley, Thomas A. *city health department administrator, epidemiologist, pediatrician*
Farley, Thomas W. *stock exchange executive*
Farrell, Herman D., Jr., (Denny Farrell) *state legislator*
Fascitelli, Michael Damon *real estate company executive*
Fasman, Zachary Dean *lawyer*
Fasnacht, Heide Ann *artist, educator*
Fass, Peter Michael *lawyer, educator*
Fastow, Jay N. *lawyer*
Fattori, Ruth A. *insurance company executive*
Favorule, Denise *publishing executive*
Fawbush, Andrew Jackson *lawyer*
Fawcett, Christopher Babcock *civil engineer, construction and water resources company executive*
Faxon, Roger *music company executive*
Fears, Linda *editor-in-chief*
Feder, Arthur A. *lawyer, association administrator*
Feder, Barnaby *reporter*
Feder, Benjamin *computer game company executive*
Feder, Saul E. *lawyer*
Feerick, John David *law educator*
Fehr, Donald M. *labor union administrator*
Feigelson, Jonathan *lawyer*
Feigen, Richard L. *art dealer, collector, writer*
Feiler, William S. *lawyer*
Feinberg, Stephen A. *hedge fund manager*
Feinberg, Wilfred *federal judge*
Feit, Glenn Martin *lawyer*
Feld, Eliot *dancer, choreographer, performing company executive*
Feldberg, Meyer *investment advisor, university dean emeritus*
Felder, Raoul Lionel *lawyer*
Felderman, Lenora I. *physician*
Feldman, Allan Roy *corporate development and marketing executive*
Feldman, Franklin *retired lawyer, printmaker*
Feldman, Ronald Arthur *sociologist, educator, social worker*
Feldman, Ruth *publishing executive*
Feldman, Stuart I. *Internet company executive*
Feldstein, Eric A. *former finance company executive*
Felman, Michelle *real estate investment company executive*
Feltus, Alan Evan *artist*
Fenchel, Gerd Hermann *psychoanalyst*
Feniger, Jerome Roland, Jr. *broadcast executive*
Fenley, Molissa *choreographer, performing company executive*
Fenster, Marvin *lawyer, retail executive*
Fensterstock, Blair Courtney *lawyer*
Ferber, Laurie R. *lawyer*
Ferber, Linda S. *museum director*
Feretic, Eileen Susan *editor*
Ferguson, Roger Walter, Jr. *finance company executive*
Fernandez, Charissa L. *educational association administrator*
Fernandez, Jose Walfredo *lawyer, department chairman*
Fernández, Teresita *sculptor*
Fernandez de Cordova, Sergio Alonso *advertising and publishing executive*
Ferraro, Geraldine Anne *attorney, former United States Representative from New York*
Ferriero, David S. *library administrator*
Ferrigno, Robert *writer*
Fertig, Howard *publishing executive*
Fetherston, Erin *apparel designer*
Feyer, Thomas *editor*
Field, Nikki E. *real estate broker*
Field, Patricia *apparel designer, stylist*
Field, Steven Philip *medical educator*
Fifty Cent, (Curtis James Jackson) *rap artist*
Figgie, Mark Phillips *surgeon*
Fili-Krushel, Patricia *media company executive*
Filimonov, Mikhail Anatolyevitch *investment company executive*
Filkins, Dexter Price *journalist*
Finan, Chris *foundation administrator, historian*
Findakly, Hani K. *investment company executive*
Fine, Drew S. *lawyer*
Fine, Jo Renée *management consultant*
Fine, Kit *philosophy educator*
Finel-Honigman, Irene Elizabeth *communications educator*
Finerman, Karen *investment company executive*
Fink, Laurence D. (Larry Fink) *investment company executive*
Fink, Matthew E. *neurologist*
Fink, Robert Steven *lawyer, writer, educator*
Finkelstein, James A. *media executive*
Finkelstein, Stuart M. *lawyer*

Finlay, Jonathan Lester pediatric oncologist, educator
Finley, John G. lawyer
Finley, Skip communications executive
Finn, Edwin Anthony, Jr. publishing executive
Finn, Peter public relations executive
Finn, Peter Michael broadcast executive
Finnerty, Joseph Gregory III lawyer
Fins, Joseph Jack internist, medical ethicist
Fiorato, Hugo conductor
Fiori, Pamela publishing executive, writer
Firestone, Louise lawyer
First, Michael Bruce psychiatrist, educator
Firth, Nicholas recording industry executive
Fischbach, Gerald D. science foundation director, neurobiology educator, former dean
Fischer, Avi medical educator
Fischer, Carl photographer, graphic designer, actor
Fischer, Mark David lawyer
Fishbein, Peter Melvin lawyer
Fisher, Edward Abraham cardiologist, educator
Fisher, Kenneth real estate company executive
Fisher, Laura Lani physician, educator
Fisher, Peter R. private equity firm executive, former federal agency administrator
Fisher, Robert I. lawyer
Fishman, Ellen Beth lawyer
Fishman, Fred Norman lawyer
Fishman, Steven T. psychologist
Fiske, Robert Bishop, Jr. lawyer, former prosecutor
FitzPatrick, Daniel M. trust company executive, lawyer
FitzPatrick, James A., Jr. lawyer
Fitzpatrick, Robert John museum director
Flaherty, Clementina Santi corporate communications specialist, writer
Flaherty, Pamela Potter bank executive
Flanagan, Steven physiatrist
Flannery, Kate actress
Flay, Bobby (Robert William Flay) chef, restaurateur
Fleischer, Ari (Lawrence Ari Fleischer) public relations executive, former White House press secretary
Fleischer, Arthur, Jr. lawyer
Fleischman, Albert Sidney (Sid Fleischman) writer
Fleischman, Barbara Greenberg public relations consultant
Fleischman, Edward Hirsh lawyer, consultant
Fleming, Renée L. opera singer
Flescher, Sharon art historian, educator
Fletcher, Anthony Lee lawyer
Fletcher, Harry George III curator and library director
Flinn, Michael de Vlaming investment company executive
Flint, Aili retired literature and language professor
Flint, George Squire lawyer
Flom, Joseph Harold lawyer
Florescue, Leonard George lawyer
Floret, Evelyn sculptor
Florin, Sharon artist
Florio, Thomas A. publishing executive
Flory, Marjorie Anne writer, editor
Flowers, J. Christopher (James Christopher Flowers) private equity firm executive
Fluhr, Howard consulting firm executive
Flumenbaum, Martin lawyer
Flynn, John J. museum curator
Flynn, Patrick Alex pediatric cardiologist
Flynn, Timothy P. accounting firm executive
Flynn, William Joseph insurance company executive
Fodor, Iris Elaine clinical psychologist, educator, psychotherapist
Fogel, Irving Martin consulting engineer
Fogelson, Susie marketing and broadcast executive
Fogler, Dan actor
Folio, James M. publishing executive
Foner, Eric historian, educator
Foner, Nancy anthropologist, educator, sociologist
Fontana, Thomas Michael television producer, scriptwriter
Forbes, Christopher (Kip Forbes) publisher
Forbes, Jim (James D. Forbes) investment banker
Forbes, Steve (Malcolm Stevenson Forbes Jr.) publishing executive
Forbes, Timothy Carter publishing executive
Ford, Eileen Otte (Mrs. Gerard W. Ford) modeling agency executive
Ford, Jack lawyer, news correspondent, news correspondent
Ford, Mark Patrick publishing executive
Ford, Ralph A. lawyer, moving and relocation company executive
Forden, Diane Claire magazine editor
Foreman, James K. risk management company executive
Foreman, Richard theater director, playwright
Forese, James Anthony diversified financial services company executive
Forrest, Katherine B. lawyer
Forstadt, Joseph Lawrence lawyer
Forstmann, Ted (Theodore J. Forstmann) private equity firm executive
Fosler, Gail D. economist
Foster, Carter curator
Foster, Craig Allen plastic surgeon
Foster, Richard Norman management consultant
Fotiades, George L. investment company executive
Foulkes, Llyn artist, educator
Fowler, Karen Joy writer
Fox, Arthur Charles cardiologist, educator
Fox, David lawyer
Fox, Keith publishing executive
Fox, Matthew actor
Fox, Michael J. (Michael Andrew Fox) actor
Fox, Paula writer
Fox, Robert Frederick, Jr. architect
Foxman, Ariel editor
Fragomen, Austin T. lawyer
France, Kim editor-in-chief
Frank, Elizabeth writer, educator
Frank, Gabriela Lena composer
Frank, Lloyd lawyer, director, retired chemicals executive
Frank, William Fielding computer company executive, consultant
Frankel, Adam B. lawyer
Frankel, Max retired journalist
Frankenthaler, Helen artist
Frankfort, Lew consumer products company executive
Franklin, Blake Timothy lawyer
Franks, Lucinda Laura journalist
Franks, Martin Davis broadcast executive
Frantz, Andrew Gibson endocrinologist, educator, dean
Frazier, Charles Robinson writer
Freda, Fabrizio cosmetics executive
Fredericks, Ivy Lindstrom investment banker
Fredericks, Wesley Charles, Jr. lawyer
Freed, Stanley Arthur retired museum curator
Freedman, Helen E. judge
Freedman, Jenna librarian
Freedman, Michael Leonard geriatrician, educator
Freeman, David John lawyer
Freeman, Harold Paul oncologist, educator, director
Freiberg, Steven J. diversified financial services company executive
Freilicher, Morton lawyer, educator
Freire, Maria C. medical association administrator
French, John III lawyer, director
French, Patrick writer
Frenkel, Jacob Aharon insurance company executive
Freudenheim, Milton B. journalist
Freund, Fred A. retired lawyer
Frey, Andrew Lewis lawyer
Fricklas, Michael David lawyer, broadcast executive
Fridson, Martin Steven finance company executive
Fried, Donald David lawyer
Fried, Linda Phyllis dean, medical educator
Fried, Richard L. lawyer
Friedberg, Barry Sewell investment banker
Friedenberg, Daniel Meyer investor, writer
Friedman, Adena T. stock exchange executive
Friedman, Alan Roy lawyer
Friedman, Arthur editor, educator
Friedman, Bart lawyer
Friedman, B(ernard) H(arper) writer
Friedman, George lawyer
Friedman, J. Roger publisher
Friedman, Jeff J. lawyer
Friedman, Jeffrey M. medical researcher, educator
Friedman, Richard Alan psychiatrist
Friedman, Robert Laurence investment company executive
Friedman, Samuel Selig lawyer
Friedman, Stephen J. dean
Friesner, Richard A. chemistry educator
Frischling, Carl lawyer
Frith, Michael Kingsbury artistic director, illustrator, writer, production company executive, actor
Frommer, William S. lawyer
Frost, David music producer
Frumkin, Joseph B. lawyer
Frumkin, William Ira cardiologist
Fry, Morton Harrison, II, lawyer
Frye, Clayton Wesley, Jr. finance company executive
Fu, Fang literature and language educator
Fuhrman, Susan H. academic administrator, education educator, researcher
Fung, Lance Michael curator, art gallery director
Funk, Mark Eugene medical librarian
Furman, Anthony Michael public relations executive
Furman, Roy Lance investment banker, theater producer
Fusaro, Peter C. environmental scientist, consultant
Fuster, Valentin cardiologist, educator
Futter, Ellen Victoria museum administrator
Fuzesi, Stephen, Jr. lawyer, communications executive
Fyfe, Joe painter
Gaborik, Marian professional hockey player
Gabrilove, Jacques Lester physician
Gadsden, Jeff Charles Frederick anesthesiologist, director
Gagosian, Larry Gilbert art dealer
Gaiman, Neil Richard novelist, comics writer, screenwriter
Galant, Paul S. bank executive
Galanter, Eugene psychologist, educator
Galanter, Marc psychiatrist, educator
Gallagher, Brian John lawyer
Gallagher, Mary Patricia pediatric endocrinologist, researcher
Gallay, Barbara travel company executive
Gallin, Pamela Frances pediatric ophthalmologist
Gallo, David scenic designer
Gallo, Martha Joan diversified financial services company executive
Gallo, William Victor cartoonist
Gallogly, Mark Timothy private equity firm executive
Galvis, Sergio J. lawyer
Gamble, Theodore Robert, Jr. investment banker
Gambs, Gerard Charles consulting engineer
Gandhi, Mayank financial analyst
Gandy, Sam neurologist, neuroscientist, educator
Gangwisch, James Edward assistant professor, researcher
Gans, Herbert J. sociologist, educator
Gant, Donald Ross investment banker
Ganz, David L. lawyer
Ganz, Howard Laurence lawyer
Garabedian, Paul Roesel mathematics professor
Garafola, Lynn dance critic, educator
Garbus, Martin Solomon lawyer
Garcia, Michael J. lawyer, former prosecutor
Garcia, Minerva Melinda human resources manager, director of diversity
Garcia, Nina publishing executive
Gardephe, Paul G. federal judge
Gardiner, E. Nicholas P. personnel director
Gardino, Vincent Anthony broadcast executive
Gardner, Richard Newton diplomat, lawyer, educator
Gardner, Stephen David lawyer, educator
Garfield, Leslie Jerome real estate executive
Garfinkel, Barry Herbert lawyer
Garland, David William law and sociology educator
Garodnick, Daniel R. city councilman, lawyer
Garrett, Robert investment banker, director
Garson, Andrew S. lawyer
Garson, Gary Wayne lawyer, diversified holding company executive
Gartner, Alan P. municipal official
Garvey, Richard Anthony retired lawyer
Garzon, Maria C. pediatric dermatologist
Gasman, Daniel E. retired history professor, writer
Gaspin, Jeffrey M. broadcast executive
Gatfield, Stephen J. advertising executive
Gatto, John Taylor educational analyst, public speaker
Gaudreau, Nicolas P. social worker, director
Gaughan, Eugene Francis lawyer, retired accountant
Gauster, Stephen Wilhelm lawyer, corporate financial executive
Gay, Peter historian, educator, writer
Gay, Richard communications executive
Gayen, Swapan Kumar physics professor, researcher
Gaynor, Mitchell oncologist, consultant
Gebbie, Kristine Moore medical educator
Geckle, Robert Alan manufacturing executive
Gehringer, Richard George publishing executive
Geier, Philip Henry, Jr. advertising executive
Geiser, Elizabeth Able publishing company executive
Geissbuhler, Stephan graphics designer
Gelb, Judith Anne lawyer
Gelb, Leslie Howard writer, lecturer, consultant
Gelb, Peter performing company executive
Gelband, Michael R. investment company executive
Geller, Robert James advertising executive
Gellert, Michael Erwin investment banker
Gellman, Barton David correspondent
Gelmann, Edward Paul oncologist, educator
Geltzeiler, Michael S. stock exchange executive, former publishing executive
Genden, Eric Michael otolaryngologist
Gender, Robert A. insurance company executive
Gendler, Ellen dermatologist
Geoghegan, Patricia lawyer
George, (Susan) Elizabeth writer
Gerard, Whitney Ian lawyer
Gerard-Sharp, Monica Fleur communications executive
Gerber, Robert Evan judge
Germano, Isabelle Margherita neurosurgeon
Germano, William Paul dean, former publishing executive
Gerner, Joan executive vice president
Gersh, Lisa broadcast executive, lawyer
Gerson, Alan J. city councilman, lawyer
Gersony, Welton Mark pediatrician, cardiologist, educator
Gerspach, John Charles diversified financial services company executive
Gerspach, Thomas Joseph lawyer
Gerst, Scott Richard radiologist, photographer
Gertler, Menard M. physician, educator
Gerzema, Mary advertising executive
Getnick, Neil Victor lawyer
Geurts, Tom Geerd real estate educator, consultant
Ghani, Cyrus lawyer
Ghesani, Munir radiologist
Ghilarducci, Teresa economist, educator
Ghnassia (Fortunato), Barbara counseling administrator
Ghosh, Amitav writer, educator
Ghost, Amanda (Amanda Louisa Gosein) music company executive, songwriter
Giamatti, Paul actor
Gianaris, Nicholas Vasil economics professor
Gianinno, Susan McManama advertising executive
Giannetti, Thomas Leonard lawyer
Giannini, Giancarlo actor, director, screenwriter
Giardina, Elsa Grace Vonna cardiologist, educator
Gibbons, Thomas Patrick (Todd Gibbons) bank executive
Gibbs, Linda I. city official
Giblin, James Cross writer, publishing executive
Gibson, Charles DeWolf newscaster
Gibson, Ralph H. (Ralph Holmes Gibson) photographer
Giffin, Emily Fisk writer
Gifford, Kathie Lee television personality, vocalist
Gifford, William C. lawyer, educator
Gigot, Paul Anthony editor
Gilbert, Alan T. conductor, music director
Gilbert, Elizabeth writer
Gilhart, Julie Lynn retail executive
Gill, E. Ann lawyer
Gill, Linda A. advertising executive
Gillers, Stephen law educator
Gillespie, George Joseph III lawyer
Gillespie, John Thomas retired university administrator
Gilligan, Carol psychologist, writer
Gilligan, Edward P. diversified financial services company executive
Gilligan, James F. psychiatrist, educator
Gillinson, Sir Clive Daniel music executive, former musician
Gilroy, Matt professional hockey player
Giniger, Kenneth Seeman publisher
Ginsberg, Hersh Meier rabbi, religious organization administrator
Ginsburg, Sigmund G. management and executive search consultant
Ginter, Valerian Alexius urban historian, educator
Ginzel, Andrew H. artist
Giordano, Bill A. psychotherapist
Giraldi, Robert Nicholas film director
Gissler, Sigvard Gunnar, Jr. journalist, educator, retired editor
Gitter, Max lawyer
Giuliani, Rudy (Rudolph William Louis Giuliani III) consultant, lawyer, former mayor
Gladwell, Malcolm writer
Glanzer, Murray psychology professor
Glasberg, H(erbert) Mark psychiatrist, educator
Glasberg, Scot Bradley plastic surgeon
Glaser, Daniel S. insurance company executive
Glaser, Milton graphics designer, illustrator
Glass, Philip composer, musician
Glass, Ronald Bernhard Jacob radiologist
Glassman, Alexander Howard psychiatrist, researcher
Glassman, Debra dentist
Glassman, Steven dentist
Glauber, Robert R. investment company executive, former financial regulatory service executive
Glaubinger, Lawrence David retired manufacturing company executive
Glekel, Jeffrey Ives lawyer
Glenn, William Henry diversified financial services company executive
Glesby, Marshall Jay physician, educator
Glickman, Robert Morris medical educator, former dean
Glickstein, Julie Sue pediatric cardiologist
Glickstein, Steven lawyer
Gliedman, Michael Seth sports association executive
Gliklich, Jerry physician, educator
Glowczewska, Klara Maria editor-in-chief, translator
Gluck, Carol history professor
Glusband, Steven Joseph lawyer
Gobin, Y. Pierre radiologist, educator
Gochberg, Thomas real estate investor, investment banker
Goddard, Donald Letcher writer, editor
Godfrey, Norman V. plastic surgeon
Godridge, Leslie V. bank executive
Godson, Godfrey Nigel molecular geneticist, educator
Goetz, Maurice Harold lawyer
Gogel, Donald J. investment company executive
Gokhale, Nachiket Hemant computer engineer, researcher
Golanski, Alani lawyer
Gold, Arnold P. neurologist
Gold, Jeffrey Mark investment banker
Gold, Martin Elliot lawyer, educator
Gold, Simeon lawyer
Gold, Stuart Walter lawyer
Goldberg, Beverly foundation administrator, consultant
Goldberg, Elkhonon medical association administrator, educator
Goldberg, Ira Jay internist, educator
Goldberg, Jay lawyer
Goldberg, Laurence investment banker
Goldberg, Nieca cardiologist, educator
Goldberg, Richard W. federal judge
Golden, Arthur F. lawyer
Golden, Daniel H. lawyer
Golden, Michael publishing executive
Golden, Thelma museum director, curator
Goldfarb, David investment company executive
Goldfarb, Donald industrial engineering educator
Goldfrank, Lewis Robert physician
Goldman, Charles Norton retired corporate lawyer
Goldman, George David psychologist
Goldman, Lawrence Saul lawyer
Goldman, Lee dean, cardiologist, educator
Goldman, Louis B. lawyer
Goldman, Martin Elliot cardiologist
Goldman, Peter Louis writer
Goldman, Steven M. lawyer, former commissioner
Goldmark, Peter Francis banker
Goldschmid, Harvey Jerome law educator, former commissioner
Goldschmidt, Charles advertising agency executive
Goldsmith, Clifford Henry retired consumer products company executive
Goldsmith, Merwin actor, theater director
Goldsmith, Stanley Joseph nuclear medicine physician, educator
Goldsmith, Willis Jay lawyer
Goldsmith-Thomas, Elaine film producer
Goldstein, Charles Arthur lawyer
Goldstein, Howard Sheldon lawyer
Goldstein, Howard Warren lawyer
Goldstein, Jeffrey Alan corporate financial executive
Goldstein, Linda C. lawyer
Goldstein, Marc surgeon, urologist, health facility administrator, educator
Goldstein, Marcia Landweber lawyer
Goldstein, Martin S. obstetrician, gynecologist, educator
Goldstein, Matthew academic administrator
Goldstein, Sandra Cara lawyer
Goldstone, Steven F. former consumer products company executive
Golick, Toby law educator, legal services administrator
Gollan, Douglas D. travel magazine editor-in-chief
Golomb, Susan L. literary agent
Golub, Harvey private equity firm executive
Golub, Steven J. investment company executive
Gomory, Ralph Edward foundation administrator, mathematician
Gonzalez, Luis J. librarian, educator
Goodale, James Campbell lawyer, television producer, columnist, educator
Goodale, Toni Krissel research and development company executive
Goodell, Roger Stokoe National Football League commissioner
Goodell, Timothy B. lawyer, oil industry executive
Goodman, Corey Scott neuroscientist, biotechnologist, educator
Goodman, Gary A. lawyer
Goodman, George Jerome Waldo (Adam Smith) writer, television journalist, consultant
Goodman, Michael B(arry) communications educator
Goodman, Roger Mark television director
Goodman, Roy Matz corporate financial executive, former state senator
Goodridge, Allan D. lawyer
Goodstein, Barbara insurance company executive
Goodwin, Beatrice nursing educator, consultant
Goodwin, Michael labor union administrator
Gott, Alan F(ranklin) lawyer
Gordon, Jeffrey Neil law educator
Gordon, Jennifer Lynn lawyer, law educator
Gordon, Leo Maury federal judge
Gordon, Linda history educator
Gordon, Mark actor, theater director, educator

Gordon, Marsha L. *dermatologist*
Gordon, Mary Catherine *writer*
Gordon, Stephen Louis *lawyer*
Gordon, Stuart A. *lawyer*
Gordon-Reed, Annette *law educator, historian*
Gorenstein, Ethan Ezra *psychologist, educator*
Gore Schiff, Karenna *nonprofit organization administrator, lawyer, writer*
Gorevan, Stephen Paul *engineer, department chairman*
Gorman, James P. *diversified financial services company executive*
Gorton, Mark Howard *information technology executive, entrepreneur*
Gosen, David *computer game company executive*
Gossett, Robert Francis, Jr. *merchant banker*
Gotbaum, Joshua *hedge fund manager*
Gottesman, David Sanford *investment company executive*
Gottesman, Noam *hedge fund manager*
Gotthoffer, Lance *lawyer*
Gotti, Victoria *columnist, writer, actress*
Gottlieb, Jerrold Howard *advertising executive*
Gotto, Antonio Marion, Jr. *dean, internist, medical educator*
Gotts, Ilene Knable *lawyer*
Gottschalk, Alfred *retired academic and museum administrator*
Gould, Harry Edward, Jr. *paper company executive*
Goulden, Joseph Chesley *author*
Goulianos, Konstantin *physicist, educator*
Gourevitch, David U. *private practice lawyer*
Gourguechon, Prudence Leib *psychoanalyst*
Grace, Nancy Ann *news correspondent, former prosecutor*
Grad, Frank Paul *lawyer, educator*
Graf, Peter Gustav *accountant, lawyer*
Grafstein, Bernice *physiology and neuroscience educator, researcher*
Grafton, Sue Taylor *writer*
Graham, Alma Eleanor *editor, writer, educational consultant*
Graham, Fred Patterson *news correspondent, journalist*
Graham, Philip Lamar *epidemiologist, physician*
Gramm, Phil (William Philip Gramm) *bank executive, former United States Senator from Texas*
Granger, Christopher *sports association executive*
Granger, David *editor*
Granito, Frank Henry III *lawyer*
Granoff, Gary Charles *lawyer, investment company executive*
Granoff, Jill *apparel executive*
Granstein, Richard David *dermatologist*
Grant, Alfred David *orthopaedic surgeon, educator*
Grasselli, Margaret Morgan *curator*
Grassi, Joseph F. *lawyer, mediator, arbitrator*
Grau, Marcy Beinish *real estate broker, former investment banker*
Grau, Shirley Ann (Mrs. James Kern Feibleman) *writer*
Graves, Adam *professional sports team executive, retired professional hockey player*
Graves, Earl G., Jr., (Butch Graves) *publishing executive*
Graves, Earl Gilbert *publishing executive*
Graves, Valerie Jo *advertising executive*
Gray, Bill *advertising executive*
Gray, James L. *investment company executive*
Gray, Jonathan David *real estate company executive*
Grayer, Jonathan *education company executive*
Grebow, Edward *finance company executive*
Greco, John A., Jr. *marketing executive*
Green, Alvin *lawyer, consultant*
Green, Dan *publishing executive*
Green, Dennis E. *professional football coach*
Green, George Joseph *publishing executive*
Green, Jane (Jane Green Warburg) *writer*
Green, Mark Joseph *lawyer, author*
Green, Michael Enoch *chemistry professor*
Green, Stephen Lawrence *real estate developer*
Green, Wayne Hugo *psychiatrist, psychoanalyst*
Greenawalt, Robert Kent *lawyer, educator*
Greenberg, Alex Michael *oral and maxillofacial surgeon*
Greenberg, David I. *tobacco company executive*
Greenberg, Ira George *lawyer*
Greenberg, Jack *lawyer, educator*
Greenberg, Jeffrey Wayne *private equity firm executive, former insurance company executive*
Greenberg, Peter S. *travel editor, news correspondent, writer*
Greenberger, Howard Leroy *lawyer, educator*
Greenblatt, Michael Noel *hospital administrator, primary care internist*
Greenblatt, Robert *broadcast company executive, producer*
Greenburg, Ross *broadcast executive, television producer*
Greene, Bernard Harold *lawyer*
Greene, Ira S. *lawyer*
Greene, Joshua *publishing executive, editor*
Greene, Richard H. *journalist, writer, policy analyst*
Greenfield, Lucille Jean *music educator, composer*
Greenfield, Stefani *entrepreneur*
Greengard, Paul *neuroscientist, educator*
Greenhill, Robert Foster (Bob Greenhill) *investment banker*
Greenland, Leo *advertising executive*
Greenspon, Robert Alan *lawyer*
Greenthal, Jill A. *investment banker*
Greenwald, Bruce Corman *finance educator*
Greenwald, Bruce Michael *pediatrician*
Greenwald, Julie *recording industry executive*
Greenwald, Martin *publishing company executive*
Greenwald, Sheila Ellen *writer, illustrator*
Greenwold, Mark *painter*
Gregor, Andrew, Jr. *corporate financial executive*
Gregorian, Vartan *foundation administrator*
Gregory, Jim (James Michael) *sports association executive, former professional sports team executive*
Gregory, Philippa *writer*
Greif, Michael *theatre director*
Greifeld, Robert *stock exchange executive*
Greiner, Stephen W. *lawyer*
Grenquist, Peter Carl *publishing executive, consultant*
Gribbin, D.J. (David James Gribbin IV) *investment company executive, former federal agency administrator*
Griefen, John Adams *artist, educator*
Griesa, Thomas Poole *federal judge*
Griffel, L. Michael *music educator, researcher*
Griffey, Anthony *tenor*
Griffin, Anne *political scientist, educator*
Griffin, Michael F. *lawyer*
Griffis, Fletcher Hughes *civil engineering educator, engineering executive*
Griffith, William R. *lawyer*
Griffiths, Sylvia Preston *physician, educator*
Grifo, James (Jamie) A. *obstetrician, gynecologist*
Grigely, Joseph Constantine, Jr. *artist, language educator*
Grignon, Perianne *trade association administrator, marketing professional*
Grillo, Kathleen M. *telecommunications industry executive*
Grisham, John (John Ray Grisham) *writer*
Grishina, Irina *science educator*
Griswold, William M. *museum director, curator*
Grody, Deborah *psychologist, director*
Grogan, John *writer, journalist*
Grohman, Michael D. *lawyer*
Gromada, Thaddeus V. *historian, academic administrator*
Gromek, Joseph R. *apparel executive*
Gropper, Allan Louis *judge*
Gross, Ari Michael *lawyer*
Gross, Christina *lawyer*
Gross, Jonathan Light *computer scientist, mathematician, educator*
Gross, Steven Ross *lawyer*
Grossman, Dan Steven *lawyer*
Grossman, Lawrence Kugelmass *former communications and advertising executive*
Grossman, Lev *journalist, writer*
Grossman, Melanie *dermatologist*
Grossman, Michael *economics professor*
Grossman, Robert Ivin *dean, neuroradiologist, scientist, educator*
Grubin, Sharon Ellen *lawyer, former federal judge*
Grubman, Allen J. *lawyer*
Grubman, Eric P. *sports association executive*
Gruen, Alison Brett *dermatologist*
Grueskin, William Steven (Bill Grusekin) *dean, educator, former editor*
Grune, Steven Bryan *publishing executive*
Grunebaum, Amos *obstetrician, gynecologist*
Grushkin, Jay D. *lawyer*
Gruzdeva, Natalia Mikhailovna *biologist, researcher*
Guberman, Josh *real estate company officer, real estate developer*
Gubert, Walter Alexander *diversified financial services company executive*
Guedry, James Walter *lawyer, retired manufacturing executive*
Guehenno, Jean Marie *international organization official*
Guernsey, Evelyn E. *diversified financial services company executive*
Guggenheim, Martin Franklin *lawyer, educator*
Guida, Robert Anthony *otolaryngologist, plastic surgeon*
Guiher, James Morford, Jr. *publisher, writer*
Gumbinner, Paul S. *advertising and executive recruitment agency executive*
Gumpert, Lynn *gallery director*
Gund, Agnes *retired museum administrator*
Gunn, Tim (Timothy M. Gunn) *apparel executive*
Gunning, Paul *advertising and marketing agency executive*
Guo, Xiang-Dong Edward *biomedical engineer, educator*
Gupta, Paul R. *lawyer*
Gupta, Rajat Kumar *management consultant*
Gupta, Sanjay *finance company executive*
Gure, Anna Valerie *retired social worker, consulting psychotherapist*
Gurevich, Alexander J. *lawyer, real estate developer*
Gurfein, Richard Alan *lawyer*
Gustafson, Albert Katsuaki *lawyer, engineer*
Gutfreund, John Halle *investment company executive, consultant*
Gutman, Henry B. *lawyer*
Gutman, Robert William *retired art educator*
Gutmann, Peter M. *economics professor*
Gutzwiller, Martin Charles *theoretical physicist, researcher*
Guzmán, Pilar *editor-in-chief*
Haacke, Hans Christoph Carl *artist, educator*
Haahr, Joan Gluckauf *English language educator*
Haas, Richard John *artist*
Haas, Thomas F. *marketing executive*
Haass, Richard Nathan *think-tank executive*
Haberman, Seth *advertising executive*
Habib, Ibrahim Wahby *computer engineer, educator*
Hackbarth, Steven Lyle *writer, educator, audio-visual specialist*
Hackett, George *editor*
Hackett, Kevin R. *real estate company executive, lawyer*
Hackett, Larry *editor*
Hackett, Veronica W. *real estate development company executive*
Haddad, Heskel Marshall *ophthalmologist, educator*
Haddad, Joseph, Jr. *pediatric otolaryngologist*
Hadjiangelis, Nicos Pavlos *medical educator, consultant*
Haegele, Patricia *publishing executive*
Haessle, Jean-Marie Georges *artist*
Haffner, Alden Norman *academic administrator*
Haffner, F. Kinsey *lawyer*
Haft, Adele J. *classicist, educator*
Haggerty, Luane Ruth Davis *theater director, actress, educator*
Hague, William Edward *writer*
Haig, Robert Leighton *lawyer*
Haight, David Hulen *ophthalmologist*
Hailey, V. Ann (Vera Ann Hailey) *retail executive*
Haines, Thomas Henry *biochemist, educator, researcher*
Haire, Jack *magazine publisher*
Hakala, Thomas John *private banker, financial planner, accountant*
Halaby, Samia Asaad *painter, educator, writer*
Halbreich, Kathy *museum director*
Hall, Alan *molecular biology educator*
Hall, Bryan H. *lawyer*
Hall, John Herbert *lawyer*
Hall, Peter W. *federal judge*
Hall, Thomas J. *lawyer*
Hallake, Marcello *lawyer*
Halliday, Joseph William *lawyer*
Halmi, Robert, Sr. *film, television producer*
Halper, Thomas *political science professor*
Halperin, Jonathan L. *medical school administrator*
Halpern, Merril Mark *retired investment banker*
Halsband, Frances *architect*
Halvey, John K. *lawyer*
Hamburg, Beatrix Ann *medical educator, researcher*
Hamburg, Charles Bruce *lawyer*
Hamburg, David A. *psychiatrist, foundation administrator*
Hamilton, Dorothy Cann *academic administrator*
Hamilton, Laurell Kaye *writer*
Hamilton Jackson, Marilyn J. *dancer, choreographer, educator*
Hamingson, Andrew Dean *theater director*
Hamm, David Bernard *lawyer*
Hammer, Bonnie *broadcast executive*
Hammett, Kirk Lee *musician*
Hammond, Lou Rena Charlotte *public relations executive*
Hammons, David *sculptor*
Hamoy, Carol *artist*
Han, Jefferson Y. *research scientist*
Hance, James Henry, Jr., (Jim Hance) *private equity firm executive, retired bank executive*
Handelsman, Lawrence Marc *lawyer*
Handforth, Mark *sculptor*
Handler, Arthur M. *lawyer*
Handler, Howard N. *music company executive, marketing professional*
Handler, Richard B. *investment company executive*
Handley, Siobhan A. *lawyer*
Hanisch, Toula *legal assistant*
Hanks, Kendyl T. *lawyer*
Hanley, William Herbert *professional society administrator*
Hann, Lucy E. *radiologist, educator*
Hanning, Barbara Russano *music educator*
Hannon, Gerard V. *lawyer*
Hansell, Saul Henry *reporter*
Hansen, James E. *physicist, meteorologist, federal agency administrator*
Hansen, Kristopher M. *lawyer*
Hanson, Jean Elizabeth *lawyer*
Hanson, Paula *sports association executive*
Hara, Eric *chef*
Haracz, Stephen M. *lawyer*
Harari, Saar *choreographer, dancer*
Harbison, James Wesley, Jr. *lawyer*
Hardin, Adlai Stevenson, Jr. *retired judge*
Hardin, Melora *actress*
Hardwick, Charles Leighton *pharmaceutical executive, former state legislator*
Hardy, John *artist*
Hargitay, Mariska Magdolina *actress*
Harkrider, John David *lawyer*
Harlow, Ruth *lawyer*
Harmon, James Allen *bank executive*
Harmon, Jane *theater producer*
Harpaz, Noam *medical educator*
Harper, Arthur Henry *investment company executive, former diversified technology and services company executive*
Harper, Gerard Edward *lawyer*
Harrell, Ray Evans *performing company executive, conductor, educator*
Harrington, Al (Albert Harrington) *professional basketball player*
Harris, Adam C. *lawyer*
Harris, Arlene *lawyer*
Harris, Charlaine *writer*
Harris, David Alan *not-for-profit organization executive*
Harris, David Henry *retired life insurance company executive*
Harris, Ethan S. *economist*
Harris, Joel B. (Joel Bruce Harris) *lawyer*
Harris, Julie (Ann) *actress*
Harris, Katherine Safford *speech and hearing educator*
Harris, Matthew Nathan *surgeon, educator*
Harris, Patricia E. (Patti Harris) *city official*
Harrison, Jordan *playwright*
Harrison, Kim *writer*
Harrow, Nancy (Mrs. Jan Krukowski) *editor, composer, singer*
Harry, Deborah Ann *singer*
Hart, Clare *information company executive*
Hart, Robert M. *lawyer*
Harter, Theo C. *music educator, composer*
Hartl, Roger *physician, researcher*
Hartman, Alan *investment company executive*
Hartman, Joan Edna *retired literature educator, dean, provost*
Hartnett, William M. *lawyer*
Hartwig, Maria *psychology professor*
Hartzell, Andrew Cornelius, Jr. *retired lawyer*
Harvey, David W. *humanities educator*
Hasday, Robert Joel *lawyer*
Haselmann, John Philip *management consultant*
Haskell, Barbara *curator*
Haskell, John Henry Farrell, Jr. *investment company executive*
Haslett, Jim (James Donald Haslett) *professional football coach*
Hass, Lawrence Joel *lawyer*
Hasselbeck, Elisabeth *television personality*
Hassell, Gerald L. *bank executive*
Hathaway, Gerald Thomas *lawyer*
Hatheway, John Harris *advertising agency executive*
Hatter, Richard Wayne *foundation administrator, artist*
Hauck, Marguerite Hall *broadcast executive*
Hauser, Francesca (Fran) *media communications executive*
Hauser, Gustave M. *media executive*
Hauser, Rita Eleanore Abrams *retired lawyer*
Havens, John Paul *diversified financial services company executive*
Hawke, Roger Jewett *lawyer*
Hawkins, Katherine Ann *hematologist, educator, lawyer*
Hayden, Raymond Paul *lawyer*
Hayes, Daniel Patrick *research scientist*
Hayes, Eddie (Edward W. Hayes) *lawyer*
Hayes, Ellen Louise *lawyer*
Hayes, Gerald Joseph *lawyer*
Hayes, John D. *diversified financial services company executive*
Haynes, Todd *film writer, producer, director*
Hays, Helen *museum program director*
Hays, Kathryn *actress*
Hazan, Scott L. *lawyer*
Head, Elizabeth *lawyer, arbitrator, mediator*
Headlam, Bruce *editor*
Headley, Mark J. *lawyer*
Healey, John Henry *orthopaedic surgeon, researcher*
Healy, J. Kevin *lawyer*
Hearn, George Henry *lawyer, water transportation executive*
Heartney, Eleanor *art critic*
Heaton, Eric *bank executive*
Hebert, Bliss Edmund *opera director*
Hebert, Jay Howell *lawyer*
Heekin, Jim (James Robson Heekin III) *advertising executive*
Heekin-Canedy, Scott H. *publishing executive*
Heffner, Richard Douglas *historian, educator, communications consultant, television producer*
Heim, Robert G. *lawyer*
Heimann, Gail *public relations executive*
Heimann, John Gaines *investment banker*
Heisler, Stanley Dean *lawyer*
Heitner, Kenneth Howard *lawyer*
Held, Huyler Clark *lawyer*
Heleniak, David William *diversified financial services company executive, lawyer*
Hellenbrand, Samuel Henry *lawyer*
Heller, Robert Martin *lawyer*
Hellerer, Mark R. *lawyer*
Heller Rouassant, Claude *ambassador*
Hellerstein, Rebecca *economist*
Helly, Dorothy Oxman *historian, educator*
Helm, Lenora Zenzalai *musician, educator*
Helms, Ed *comedian, actor*
Hemmerdinger, Dale (Henry Dale Hemmerdinger) *transportation executive*
Hemphill, Clara Jacobs *advocate*
Hemsing, Josephine Claudia *public relations executive*
Henchcliffe, Claire *neurologist, educator*
Henderson, Christopher *pathologist, educator, neuroscientist*
Henderson, Donald Bernard, Jr. *lawyer*
Henderson, Edward Drewry, Jr. *finance company executive*
Hendrickson, Wayne A(rthur) *biochemist, educator*
Hendry, Andrew Delaney *lawyer, consumer products company executive*
Henry, Daniel T. *diversified financial services company executive*
Henry, Emil William, Jr. *diversified financial services company executive, former federal agency administrator*
Henry, Lawrence Charles (Lonny Henry) *investment banker*
Henry, Sally McDonald *lawyer*
Henschke, Claudia Ingrid *physician, radiologist*
Henselmann, Caspar Gustav Fidelis *sculptor*
Hensle, Terry W. *pediatric urologist*
Hensley, Shuler *actor, vocalist*
Henze, William F., II, *lawyer*
Herbert, Bob *journalist*
Herbst, Todd L. *lawyer*
Herman, Darren *entrepreneur, marketing executive*
Herman, Dorothy (Dottie Herman) *real estate company executive*
Herman, Jerry *composer, lyricist*
Herman, Kenneth Beaumont *lawyer*
Herman, Stan *fashion designer*
Herman, Susan N. *legal association administrator, law educator*
Hernandez, Carlos Mauricio *diversified financial services company executive*
Hernstadt, Judith Filenbaum *city planner, real estate and broadcast executive*
Herr, Harry Wallace *medical researcher, educator, surgeon, urologist*
Herrera, Carolina *fashion designer*
Herrera, Paloma *dancer*
Herrmann, Lacy Bunnell *investment company executive, entrepreneur, venture capitalist*
Hersch, Dennis Steven *business executive, lawyer*
Hersh, Seymour Myron *journalist, writer*
Hershcopf, Gerald Thea *retired lawyer*
Hertzig, Margaret E. *psychiatrist*
Herz, Andrew Lee *lawyer*
Herzeca, Lois Friedman *lawyer*
Herzog, David L. *insurance company executive*
Herzog, David Lawrence *insurance company executive*
Herzog, Werner (Werner Stipetic) *film director*
Hess, John B. *oil industry executive*
Hess, Michael David *lawyer*
Hesse, Karen (Karen Sue Hesse) *writer, educator*
Hesselbein, Frances Richards *speaker, writer, editor*
Hessels, Jan-Michiel *stock exchange executive*
Hetfield, James *singer*
Hewitt, Vivian Ann Davidson (Mrs. John Hamilton Hewitt Jr.) *retired librarian*
Hewitt, William Joseph *lawyer*
Heyde, Martha Bennett *psychologist*
Hicks, Ken Carlyle *retail executive*
Hicks, Tyler Gregory *publishing company executive, writer*
Hidalgo, David Arthur *plastic surgeon*
Hiden, Robert Battaile, Jr. *lawyer*
Hielscher, Andreas Helmut *biomedical engineer*

Higgins, Christopher *professional hockey player*
Highstein, Jene Abel *sculptor*
Hilfiger, Tommy (Thomas Jacob Hilfiger) *apparel designer*
Hill, Alfred *law educator*
Hill, Gregory Paul *oil industry executive*
Hill, J(ames) Tomilson *investment banker*
Hill, Janine *foreign policy think-tank*
Hill, Marjorie Jean *health association administrator, psychologist*
Hill, Nancy *advertising association executive*
Hiller, John *Internet company executive*
Hilzinger, Kurt John *investment company executive*
Hindery, Leo Joseph, Jr. *investment company executive*
Hinton, Leslie Frank *publishing executive*
Hintz, Brad (Charles Brad Hintz) *financial services company executive*
Hinz, Theodore Vincent *architect*
Hippeau, Eric *publishing executive*
Hirokami, Junichi *conductor, former music director*
Hirsch, Edward Mark *language educator, poet*
Hirsch, Jules *physician, researcher*
Hirsch, Roseann Conte *publisher*
Hirschfield, Bradley *rabbi*
Hirschhorn, Kurt *pediatrics educator*
Hirschhorn, Rochelle *genetics educator*
Hirschorn, Michael W. *television producer, entertainment company executive*
Hirshman, Michele S. *lawyer, former prosecutor*
Hirshowitz, Melvin Stephen *lawyer*
Hjortsberg, William Reinhold *writer*
Ho, Betty Juenyü Yülin *retired musician, physiologist, educator*
Ho, David D. (Da-i Ho) *research physician, virologist, scientific organization director*
Hochberg, Mark Stefan *surgeon*
Hochman, Judith Sheryl *cardiologist, researcher*
Hochman, Richard H. *investment company executive*
Hochster, Howard S. *oncologist*
Hodge, Roger D. *editor*
Hoeflin, Ronald Kent *philosopher, writer*
Hoelz, André *biologist, researcher*
Hoffert, Martin Irving *aerospace scientist, educator*
Hoffman, Linda M. *chemist, educator*
Hoffman, Linda R. *social services administrator*
Hoffman, Lloyd Alan *plastic surgeon*
Hogan, Mary Beth *lawyer*
Hoge, Warren M. *editor*
Hoglund, Robert N. *utilities executive*
Hohn, Harry George *retired insurance company executive, lawyer*
Holland, Jimmie C. *psychiatrist, educator*
Holland, Michael Francis *investment company executive*
Holley, Steven Lyon *lawyer*
Holloway, Ralph Leslie *anthropology educator*
Holman, Bud George *lawyer*
Holquist, James Michael *literature educator, department chairman*
Holsenbeck, George Penn *tobacco company executive, lawyer*
Holstad, Christian *artist*
Holt, Peter Rolf *gastroenterologist, educator*
Holt, Sidney Clark *journalist*
Holtan, Tor *foundation administrator*
Holtz, Diane *retail executive*
Holtzman, Elizabeth *lawyer*
Holtzmann, Howard Marshall *lawyer, judge*
Holzer, Harold *museum and marketing executive, historian, writer*
Holzman, Eric *painter*
Holzman, Ian Ronald *pediatrician, educator*
Hong, Chung-Wha *advocacy organization director*
Hood, Donald Charles *academic administrator, psychologist, vision neuroscientist, educator*
Hooker, Wade Stuart *lawyer*
Hooper, Anthony C. *pharmaceutical executive*
Hopkins, Deborah C. *diversified financial services company executive*
Hopkinson, R. Ronald *lawyer*
Hoppenstein, Reuben *neurosurgeon, healthcare executive*
Hopson, Craig *chef*
Horan, Anthony J. *diversified financial services company executive*
Hormats, Robert David *economist, investment banker*
Horn, Karen Nicholson *investment company executive, former bank executive*
Horovitz, Len *internist, pulmonologist*
Horowitz, Steven Gary *lawyer*
Horsley, Heidi *psychologist, educator, radio personality*
Hort, Michael *art collector*
Hort, Susan *art collector*
Horvath, Robert G. *advertising executive*
Horyn, Cathy B. *editor*
Hoskins, William John *obstetrician, educator, gynecologist*
Hosseini, Khaled *writer*
Hostvedt, Anna *painter*
Hotchner, Holly *museum director, curator, conservator*
Hotz, Robert Lee *writer, editor*
Houghtlin, Robert G. *publishing executive*
Houser, Dan *computer game company executive*
Houser, Sam *computer game company executive*
Houston, Allan Wade *professional sports team executive, retired professional basketball player*
Houston, Whitney *singer*
Hovde, Carl Frederick *language professional, educator*
Hoving, Thomas *museum director, consultant, writer*
Howard, Bonnie *bank executive*
Howard, Mildred *sculptor*
Howard, Richard (Joseph) *poet, literary translator*
Howat, John Keith *retired museum executive*
Howe, Florence *literature educator, writer, publisher*
Howe, Louise R. *medical educator*
Howe, Richard Rives *lawyer*
Hoxter, Curtis Joseph *international economic advisor, public relations and communications executive*
Hoye, J.D. *foundation administrator*
Hoyt, Clark Freeland *editor, journalist*
Hricik, Lorraine E. *bank executive*
Hritz, George F. *lawyer*
Hruska, Alan J. *lawyer, filmmaker*
Hsu, Daphne T. *pediatrician, educator*
Hubbard, Glenn (Robert Glenn Hubbard) *dean, former federal official*
Huck, L. Francis *lawyer*
Hudes, Nana Brenda *marketing professional*
Hudis, Clifford Alan *internist, oncologist*
Hudson, Christopher John *publisher*
Huebner, Marshall Scott *lawyer*
Huet, Jean-Marc *pharmaceutical executive*
Huey, John Wesley, Jr. *editor*
Hughes, Denis M. *labor union administrator*
Hughes, Doug *theater director*
Hughes, Jeff *playwright, lyricist*
Hughes, Lisa Henriques *publishing executive*
Hughes, Richard P., Jr. *labor union administrator*
Hulbert, Richard Woodward *lawyer*
Hull, Cathy *artist, illustrator*
Hunt, Franklin Griggs *lawyer*
Hunter, Luke T. B. *biologist*
Hupper, John Roscoe *retired lawyer*
Hurd, Jeffrey J. *insurance company executive*
Hurley, Cheryl Joyce *book publishing executive*
Hurley, Lawrence Joseph *lawyer*
Hurlock, James Bickford *lawyer*
Huston, Barry Scott *lawyer*
Hutchings, Peter Lounsbery *retired insurance company executive, director*
Hutchins, Glenn H. *private equity firm executive*
Hutchins, Traver *publishing executive*
Hutton, G. Thompson *lawyer*
Hyde, David Rowley *lawyer*
Hyde, James *artist*
Hyman, Arthur *philosopher, educator*
Hyman, Bruce Malcolm *ophthalmologist*
Hyman, Earle *actor, educator*
Hyman, Jerome Elliot *lawyer*
Hyman, Joshua E. *pediatric orthopaedic surgeon*
Hyman, Morton Peter *private equity investment company executive*
Hynes, Patricia M. *lawyer*
Iacono, John *photographer*
Ianniello, Joseph R. *broadcast executive*
Iannuzzi, John Nicholas *lawyer, author, educator*
Icahn, Carl Celian *investor*
Ichel, David W. *lawyer*
Iglauer, Edith *writer, reporter*
Ikouebe, Basile *ambassador*
Ilacqua, Rosario Salvatore *securities analyst*
Ilchman, Warren Frederick *academic and foundation administrator, educator*
Iles, Greg *writer*
Ilkin, Baki *ambassador*
Ilse-Neuman, Ursula *curator*
Ilson, Bernard *public relations executive, writer*
Imber, Gerald *plastic surgeon*
Imparato, Anthony Michael *vascular surgeon, educator, researcher*
Imus, Don (John Donald Imus Jr.) *radio personality*
Incandela, Gerald Jean-Marie *artist*
Ingrassia, Lawrence *editor*
Ingrassia, Timothy J. *investment banker*
Innis, Niger *advocate, civil rights organization administrator*
Insel, Michael S. *lawyer*
Intriligator, Marc Steven *lawyer*
Ioachim, Harry L. *pathologist, educator*
Ireland, Patrick *artist*
Iriondo, Josu *bishop*
Irish, George Butler *media company executive*
Irvin, Michael Jerome *television personality, retired professional football player*
Isaacson, Steven Robert *surgeon*
Isay, Joshua D. *political consultant*
Isenberg, Steven Lawrence *literary association administrator, retired publishing executive*
Isom, O(ttis) Wayne *thoracic surgeon, educator*
Isquith, Fred Taylor *lawyer*
Issler, Harry *lawyer*
Iturbide, Graciela *photographer*
Jabs, Douglas Alan *ophthalmology professor, chairman, dean*
Jackson, Anne (Anne Jackson Wallach) *actress*
Jackson, Keith MacKenzie *retired sports commentator*
Jackson, Kenneth Terry *historian, academic administrator*
Jackson, Mark H. *lawyer, publishing executive*
Jackson, Mike *finance company executive*
Jackson, Robert *city councilman*
Jackson, Robert L. *literature and language professor*
Jackson, Stu *sports association executive, former men's college basketball coach*
Jacob, Edwin J. *lawyer*
Jacobs, Arnold Stephen *lawyer*
Jacobs, Dennis G. *federal judge*
Jacobs, Lawrence A. *media company executive, lawyer*
Jacobs, Marc *fashion designer*
Jacobs, Paul *lawyer*
Jacobs, Paul A. *music educator*
Jacobs, Philip M. *insurance company executive*
Jacobs, Robert Alan *lawyer*
Jacobs, Stacy *radiologist*
Jacobsen, Theodore H. (Ted H. Jacobsen) *labor union administrator, secondary school educator*
Jacobson, Jerold Dennis *lawyer*
Jacobson, Julius H., II, *vascular surgeon, writer*
Jacobson, Robert P. *insurance company executive*
Jacoby, Jacob *consumer psychology educator*
Jacoby, Robert Harold *management consulting executive*
Jacquette, Yvonne Helene *artist*
Jagger, Sir Mick (Michael Philip Jagger) *singer, musician*
Jallo, George Issa *physician*
James, Brian d'Arcy *actor*
James, Hamilton Evans (Tony James) *private equity executive*
James, Kate *diversified financial services company executive*
James, Letitia *city councilwoman, lawyer*
James, Robert Leo *advertising executive, director*
Jamison, Jayne *publishing executive*
Jamison, Judith *performing company executive, dancer*
Jan, Dominique Michel *surgeon, educator*
Janiak, Anthony Richard, Jr. *investment banker*
Janklow, Morton Lloyd *lawyer, literary agent*
Janney, Stuart Symington III *investment company executive*
Jannuzzi, Luigi *playwright, educator*
Janowitz, James Arnold *lawyer*
Jansky, Jeannette Jefferson *learning disabilities specialist*
Jarecki, Henry George *physician, financial planner*
Jariwala, Ashish *finance company executive*
Jarvik, Robert Koffler *biomedical research scientist*
Jasper, James Macdonald *writer, sociology educator*
Jasso, Guillermina *sociologist, educator*
Jassy, Everett Lewis *lawyer*
Javitt, Norman B. *medical educator, researcher*
Jay-Z, (Shawn Corey Carter) *music company executive, rap artist*
Jean, Wyclef *musician, recording industry executive*
Jeffrey, Robert (Bob) *advertising executive*
Jelks, Glenn William *plastic surgeon*
Jenkins, Paul *artist*
Jenner, Jesse Jacob *lawyer*
Jennings, Brian *sports association executive*
Jennings, Bruce *research institute director*
Jepson, Hans Godfrey *investment company executive, director*
Jervis, Robert *political science professor*
Jessell, Thomas M. *medical educator*
Jetter, Robert Bruce *plastic surgeon*
Jhabvala, Ruth Prawer *writer*
Jock, Paul F., II, *lawyer*
Joel, Richard Marc *academic administrator, law educator*
Joffe, Robert David *lawyer*
Johansen, Iris *writer*
Johnson, Betsey Lee *fashion designer*
Johnson, Brooke Bailey *broadcast executive*
Johnson, David J., Jr. *lawyer*
Johnson, Gus *sportscaster*
Johnson, Harold Earl *human resources specialist*
Johnson, Horton Anton *pathologist*
Johnson, J. Chester *corporate financial executive, consultant, writer*
Johnson, John H. *medical products executive*
Johnson, L. Oakley (Oakley Johnson) *insurance company executive*
Johnson, Peter James, Jr. *lawyer, legal analyst*
Johnson, Richard C. *editor*
Johnson, Ronald Lee *sports association executive, retired military officer*
Johnson, Thomas Stephen *retired banker*
Johnson, Valerie Lynne *pediatric nephrologist, educator*
Johnston, Charles D. *bank executive*
Johnston, Rita Rodin *lawyer*
Jonas, Ruth Haber *psychologist*
Jonas, Saran *neurologist, educator*
Jones, Alan Kent *investment company executive*
Jones, David *advertising executive*
Jones, David R. *not-for-profit executive*
Jones, Diana Wynne *writer*
Jones, Laurie Lynn *magazine editor*
Jones, Richard M. *broadcast executive*
Jones, (L.) Serene *academic administrator, theology professor*
Jones Reynolds, Star (Starlet Marie Jones) *television host, lawyer, former prosecutor*
Jong, Erica Mann *writer*
Joo, Eungie *curator*
Jordan, Tina *publishing association executive*
Jordan, Vernon Eulion, Jr. *lawyer*
Josefowicz, Leila Bronia *violinist*
Josell, Jessica (Wechsler) *public relations executive*
Joseph, Gregory Paul *lawyer*
Joseph, Leonard *lawyer*
Josephson, Jordan Stuart *otolaryngologist*
Josephson, Stephen C. *psychiatrist, educator*
Joskow, Paul Lewis *economist, educator*
Joyner, Alexandra Leigh *cell biologist*
Joynt, Stephen W. *financial services company executive*
Juceam, Robert E. *lawyer*
Judd, Karlan *composer*
Jung, Andrea *cosmetics company executive*
Jung, Doris *soprano*
Just, Gemma Rivoli *retired advertising executive*
Justin, Henry *real estate developer*
Kacker, Ashutosh *medical educator*
Kadel, Andrew Gordon *library director, priest*
Kaden, Lewis B. *diversified financial services company executive*
Kafin, Robert Joseph *lawyer*
Kagan, Julia Lee *magazine editor*
Kaggen, Lois Sheila *non-profit organization executive, advocate*
Kahan, Phyllis Irene *editor, writer, educator*
Kahn, Alan Edwin *lawyer*
Kahn, Norman *dental educator, pharmacologist*
Kahn, Wolf *artist*
Kailas, Leo George *lawyer*
Kaiser, Walter *language educator*
Kaish, Luise Clayborn *sculptor, painter, educator*
Kaish, Morton *artist, educator*
Kalajian-Lagani, Donna *publishing executive*
Kalik, Mildred *lawyer*
Kalik, Robert M. *financial services executive*
Kalikow, Peter Stephen *real estate developer, former transportation and publishing executive*
Kalish, Arthur *lawyer*
Kalish, Myron *lawyer*
Kallir, Jane Katherine *art gallery director, author*
Kallstrom, James K. *state official*
Kalsner, Stanley *pharmacologist, physiologist, educator*
Kalter, Albert *lawyer, educator*
Kamali, Norma *fashion designer*
Kamerman, Sheila Brody *social work educator*
Kamin, Sherwin *retired lawyer*
Kaminer, Ariel *editor*
Kamlot, Robert *performing arts executive*
Kan, Diana Artemis Mann Shu *painter, art educator, writer*
Kanakaredes, Melina *actress*
Kandarian, Steven A. *insurance company executive*
Kandel, Karen *actress*
Kandel, Myron *newscaster, columnist*
Kandel, William Lloyd *lawyer, arbitrator, mediator*
Kane, Susan *editor*
Kanick, Virginia *retired radiologist*
Kann, Peter Robert *retired publishing executive, journalist*
Kanter, Carl Irwin *retired lawyer*
Kanzer, Alan *lawyer*
Kapelman, Barbara Ann *hepatologist, gastroenterologist, educator*
Kapito, Robert S. *diversified financial services company executive*
Kaplan, Janice *editor*
Kaplan, Lawrence Jay *retired economist, educator*
Kaplan, Lewis A. *federal judge*
Kaplan, Mark Norman *lawyer*
Kaplan, Paul Michael *lawyer, educator*
Kaplan, Rick (Richard N. Kaplan) *broadcast executive*
Kapoor, Neera *optometrist, research scientist*
Kappas, Attallah *physician*
Karalekas, George Steven *advertising agency executive, political consultant*
Karan, Donna (Donna Faske) *fashion designer*
Karasu, T(oksoz) Byram *psychiatrist, educator, writer*
Karchin, Louis Samuel *composer, educator*
Kardon, Janet *museum director*
Karelis, Kathleen E. *lawyer, communications systems company executive*
Karl, Kurt Erskine *economist*
Karlgaard, Rich *publishing executive*
Karls, John Spencer *lawyer, accountant*
Karmali, Rashida A. *lawyer*
Karp, Brad S. *lawyer*
Karp, Martin Everett *management consultant*
Karp, Nolan Serge *plastic surgeon*
Karpel, Craig S. *journalist, editor*
Karsen, Sonja Petra *retired literature educator*
Kartiganer, Joseph *retired lawyer*
Kasi, Srinandan Ramamurthi *lawyer*
Kasirer, Suri *lobbyist*
Kaslow, Andrew J. *insurance company executive, human resources specialist*
Kassel, Catherine M. *community, maternal, and women's health nurse, consultant*
Kassel, Terry *human resources specialist*
Kassel, Virginia Weltmer *television producer, writer*
Katen, Karen L. *retired pharmaceutical company executive*
Kato, Tomoaki *surgeon*
Katsh, Salem Michael *lawyer*
Katz, Bruce Elliot *dermatologist*
Katz, Esther *historian, educator*
Katz, Gary *securities exchange executive*
Katz, Jerome Charles *lawyer*
Katz, Robert James *lawyer*
Katz, Ronald Scott *lawyer*
Katz, Stuart Z. *lawyer*
Katzman, John S. *educational organization executive*
Katzmann, Robert Allen *federal judge*
Katzowitz Shenfield, Lauren *philanthropy consultant*
Kauffmann, Stanley Jules *author*
Kaufman, Bel *author, educator*
Kaufman, David Marc *pediatric neurologist*
Kaufman, Elaine *restaurant owner*
Kaufman, Michele Beth *clinical pharmacist, educator, writer, editor, consultant*
Kaufman, Moisés *theater director, playwright*
Kaufman, Robert Max *lawyer, director*
Kaufman, Stephen Edward *lawyer*
Kaufman, Victor A. *broadcast and retired film company executive*
Kaufmann, Horacio Carlos *professor of neurology, medicine and pediatrics*
Kaufmann, Mark Steiner *banker, director*
Kaur, Harminder *language educator*
Kavaler, Thomas J. *lawyer*
Kavesh, Robert A. *economist, educator*
Kavoukjian, Michael Edward *lawyer*
Kaye, Joyce Rutter *publishing executive*
Kaye, Judith Smith *lawyer, retired state appeals court chief judge*
Kayser, Leo III *lawyer*
Kazemi, Farhad *political scientist, educator*
Kean, Hamilton Fish *lawyer*
Kean, Thomas Howard *retired academic administrator, former Governor of New Jersey*
Kearse, Amalya Lyle *federal judge*
Keathley, Wayne E. *hospital administrator*
Keegan, Peter W. *diversified holding company executive*
Keenan, John Fontaine *federal judge*
Keenan, Kerry *marketing and advertising executive*
Keenan, Michael Edgar *marketing professional*
Keene, Donald *writer, translator, language educator*
Keevil, Philip Clement *investment banker*
Kehret, Peg *writer*
Kelleher, Colm (Thomas Colm Kelleher) *diversified financial services company executive*
Kelleher, Kevin *music company executive*
Keller, Bill G. *executive editor*
Kellerman, Faye Marilyn *writer*
Kellerman, Jonathan Seth *writer, pediatric psychologist, educator*
Kelley, Darcy B. *biology professor*
Kelley, David Noel *lawyer, former prosecutor*
Kelley, Jacki *media communications agency executive, marketing professional*
Kelley, Mike *artist*
Kellogg, Clark *sportscaster*
Kelly, Alfred F., Jr. *diversified financial services company executive*
Kelly, Anastasia Donovan (Stasia Kelly) *lawyer, insurance company executive*
Kelly, Edward J., III, (Ned Kelly) *diversified financial services company executive*
Kelly, Patrick Joseph *neurosurgeon, educator*
Kelly, Raymond Walter *police commissioner*
Kelly, Robert P. *bank executive*
Kelly, Thomas Michael *lawyer*
Kelmenson, Leo-Arthur *advertising executive*

Keltner, Thomas Nethery, Jr. lawyer
Kende, Christopher Burgess lawyer, educator
Keneally, Kathryn Marie lawyer
Kennedy, Adrienne Lita playwright
Kennedy, David L. cosmetics company executive
Kennedy, David M. anthropologist, educator
Kennedy, Robert Francis, Jr. environmentalist, radio talk show host
Kennedy, Thomas Patrick financial executive
Kenney, Brian editor-in-chief
Kenney, John Joseph lawyer
Kenney, Robert J. lawyer
Keno, Leslie B. antiques dealer, appraiser
Kent, Deborah Warren hypnotherapist, consultant, lecturer
Kent, Linda Gail dancer
Kent, Susan library director, consultant
Kentridge, William visual artist
Kenyon, Sherrilyn writer
Kerman, Jules psychiatrist, educator
Kern, George Calvin, Jr. lawyer
Kerrey, Bob (Joseph Robert Kerrey) academic administrator, former United States Senator from Nebraska
Kerr Redniss, Andrea media agency executive, marketing and communications professional
Kersh, Candace L. lawyer
Kerwick, Colleen lawyer, actress
Kerz, Louise (Louise Hirschfeld) historian
Kessinger, Kevin M. diversified financial services company executive
Kessler, Eric broadcast executive
Kessler, Stuart accountant, financial planner
Ketterer, Gwyneth M. finance educator, retired private equity firm executive
Keys, Alicia (Alicia Augello Cook) singer
Khalil, Mounir A. librarian, educator
Khanna, Vikas chef
Kheradpir, Shaygan information technology executive
Khuri, Nicola Najib physicist, researcher
Khusid, Boris M. chemical physicist
Kid Rock, (Robert James Ritchie) singer
Kiernan, John S. lawyer
Kies, David M. lawyer
Kiessling, B. Robbins lawyer
Kiger, Kris advertising executive
Kilik, Jon film producer
Killian, John F. telecommunications industry executive
Kilmer, Val actor
Kilts, James M. diversified financial services company executive, former consumer products company executive
Kim, Chun Ki radiology and nuclear medicine educator
Kim, John Y. insurance company executive
Kim, Michael S. lawyer
Kim, Phillip physics professor
Kimball, John Devereux lawyer
Kimber, Karen Beecher ESL educator
Kind, Richard J. actor
Kindler, Jeffrey B. pharmaceutical company executive, lawyer
King, Alison lawyer
King, B.B. (Riley B. King) singer, guitarist
King, Edward Joseph clinical chemist, laboratory administrator
King, Gayle editor, radio and television personality
King, Henry Lawrence lawyer
King, Marcia Gygli artist
King, Stephen C. lawyer, commissioner, educator
King, Thomas physiologist, educator
Kinney, Gilbert Hart investor
Kinney, Jeff writer
Kinney, Stephen Hoyt, Jr. lawyer
Kins, Gloria public relations executive, photojournalist, writer, editor
Kinstler, Everett Raymond artist
Kinzler, Thomas Benjamin lawyer
Kirby, John Joseph, Jr. lawyer
Kirsch, Arthur William financial consultant
Kirsch, Donald financial consultant
Kirschbaum, Myron lawyer
Kirschner, Stuart Martin forensic specialist, psychology professor
Kissel, Howard William drama critic
Kistler, Darci Anna ballet dancer
Klapper, Richard H. lawyer
Klausen, Ray theatre set and television production designer, sculptor
Klausner, Peter L. lawyer
Kleber, Herbert David psychiatrist, educator
Kleckner, Robert George, Jr. retired lawyer
Klein, Calvin Richard fashion designer
Klein, Cynthia art appraiser
Klein, Donald Franklin psychiatrist, research scientist, educator
Klein, Eleazer lawyer
Klein, Harvey medical educator
Klein, Jason Evan publishing executive
Klein, Joe journalist, columnist, writer
Klein, Joel Irwin school system administrator
Klein, Martin I. lawyer
Klein, Steven photographer
Klein, T(heodore) E(ibon) D(onald) writer
Klein, William photographer, filmmaker
Kleinberg, Norman Charles lawyer
Kleinfeld, Klaus metal products executive, former electronics executive
Kleinzahler, August poet
Kleisner, Frederick J. hotel executive
Klemann, Gilbert Lacy, II, lawyer
Kliger, Jack publishing executive
Kliment, Robert Michael architect
Klimstra, David S. pathologist
Kline, Eugene Monroe lawyer
Kline, Kevin Delaney actor
Klinger, Alan Mark lawyer
Klinsky, Steven Bruce investor
Klipper, Mitchell S. retail executive
Klipstein, Robert Alan lawyer
Klores, Dan (Daniel Aaron Klores) public relations executive
Kluger, Jeffrey reporter, author
Knapp, Albert Bruce gastroenterologist
Knapp, Robert Charles retired obstetrics and gynecology educator
Knobler, Peter Stephen magazine editor, writer
Knoll, Monica not-for-profit organization administrator, marketing professional
Knowles, Alison artist
Kobak, James Benedict, Jr. lawyer, educator
Kobi, Daniel Casey lawyer
Kobrin, Lawrence Alan lawyer
Kobylarz, Erik Joseph neurologist, educator
Koch, David Hamilton chemical company executive
Koch, Ed (Edward Irving Koch) lawyer, former mayor
Koch, Stephen Bayard writer, language educator
Koegel, William Fisher lawyer
Koeltl, John George federal judge
Koen, Robert G. lawyer
Koeppel, Noel Immanuel financial planner, securities and real estate broker
Kohn, Immanuel lawyer
Kolata, Gina journalist, writer
Kolatch, Myron magazine editor
Kolker, Adam Ross plastic surgeon, educator
Kolodny, Edwin Hillel neurologist, geneticist, director
Komisar, Arnold otolaryngologist, educator
Koob, Charles Edward lawyer
Koons, Jeff artist
Kopelman, Richard Eric management educator
Kopenhaver, Patricia Ellsworth podiatrist
Koplik, Michael R. sales representation company executive
Koplovitz, Kay investment company executive
Kopp, Wendy educational association administrator
Koppelman, Chaim artist, educator
Koppelman, Dorothy Myers artist, consultant
Koral, Alan Max lawyer
Korein, Julius neurologist
Korenman, Sanders economics professor, researcher
Korf, Anthony composer, artistic director
Korins, David set designer
Kornberg, Alan William lawyer
Kornreich, Edward Scott lawyer
Korotkin, Michael Paul lawyer
Kors, Michael (Karl Anderson Jr.) fashion designer
Korsten, Susan Snyder mathematics educator
Kosofsky, Barry E. pediatric neurologist
Kostelanetz, Richard writer, media artist
Koster, Elaine publishing executive
Kostmayer, Peter Houston former congressman, community organization administrator
Koteff, Ellen editor
Kotlowitz, Dan lighting designer
Kotlowitz, Robert writer, editor
Kotuk, Andrea Mikotajuk public relations executive, writer
Kouliev, Eldar ambassador
Kourides, Ione Anne endocrinologist, researcher, educator
Kove, Miriam psychotherapist
Kovner, Bruce Stanley hedge fund manager
Kowalik, Trent Matthias actor, dancer
Kowalski, Michael J. retail products executive
Kozak, Harley Jane actress, writer
Kozik, Susan S. information technology executive
Kozinn, Allan music critic, reporter
Kozlowski, Cheryl M. fixed income analyst
Kramarsky, Werner H. art collector
Kramer, Linda Konheim curator, art historian
Kramer, Marc Z. publishing executive
Kramer, Orin Stuart hedge fund manager
Krane, Steven Charles lawyer
Krantz, Judith Tarcher novelist
Krasinski, John actor
Krasna, Alvin Isaac biochemist, educator
Kraus, Peter Steven investment company executive
Krauss, Herbert Harris psychologist
Kravis, Henry R. investment banker
Krebs, Carl F. architectural firm executive
Kreitzman, Ralph J. lawyer, mayor
Krell, David H. securities exchange executive
Krementz, Jill photographer, author
Kremins, Carolyn magazine publishing executive
Krens, Thomas museum administrator
Kressel, Henry venture capitalist
Kreuther, Gabriel chef
Krieger, Karl Hemingway cardiothoracic surgeon
Krieger, Sanford lawyer
Krill, Kay (Katherine Lawther Krill) apparel executive
Krimendahl, Herbert Frederick, II, investment banker
Krinsky, Carol Herselle art historian, educator
Krinsky, Robert Daniel consulting firm executive
Kristof, Nicholas Donabet journalist, columnist
Krivonos, Sergey pianist, educator
Kroeber, Karl language educator
Kroell, Devi accessories designer
Kroll, Sol lawyer
Krulwich, Terry Ann biochemistry researcher
Krupman, William Allan lawyer
Krupp, Fred D. lawyer, environmental services administrator
Kubek, Gary W. lawyer
Kubiak, Teresa Wojtaszek soprano
Kuby, Ronald Lawrence lawyer
Kuchta, Ronald Andrew museum director, editor, curator
Kuhbach, Robert Gerdes manufacturing executive
Kulish, Kiril Jacob actor, dancer
Kumalo, Dumisani Shadrack ambassador
Kumin, Maxine Winokur poet, writer
Kummel, Eugene H. advertising agency executive
Kunes, Richard W. cosmetics executive
Kuntz, Lee Allan lawyer
Kuntz, William Francis, II, lawyer, educator
Kuo, John Tsungfen geophysicist, educator, researcher
Kuperman, Robert Ian retired advertising agency executive
Kuppin, Sara postdoctoral fellow
Kurahara, Ted Naomi artist, educator
Kurman, Juta music educator
Kurnow, Ernest statistician, educator
Kurtz, Jerome lawyer, educator
Kurz, William Charles Frederick lawyer
Kurzweil, Edith social sciences educator, editor
Kurzweil, Harvey lawyer
Kushner, Brian Harris oncologist
Kushner, Jared Corey publishing executive, real estate developer
Kuttler, Judith Esther retired psychotherapist
Kya-Hill, Robert actor, educator
Kyriakou, Linda Grace communications executive
LaBarre, Dennis W. lawyer
Labunski, Stephen Bronislaw professional society administrator
LaBute, Neil scriptwriter, director, playwright
Lacamoire, Alex composer
Lachman, Marguerite Leanne real estate investment advisor
Lack, Robert Joel lawyer
Lacombe, Jacques conductor
Lacovara, Philip Allen lawyer
Lacy, Robinson Burrell lawyer
Ladjevardi, Hamid portfolio manager
Lafavore, Michael J. editor-in-chief
LaFayette, Reggie (Reginald A. LaFayette) political organization administrator
Lagani, Daniel publishing executive
Lagonegro, Dominick J. bishop
Lahita, Robert George immunologist
Lai, Charles museum director
Lai, W(ei) Michael retired engineering educator
Lakshmi-Ratan, Ramnath Ayyan marketing professional
Lalwani, Anil Kumar otolaryngologist
Lam, Derek apparel designer
Lamadrid, Carlos publishing executive
Lamb, Robert Boyden finance and management educator
Lamb, Wally writer
Lambert, Judith A. Ungar lawyer
Lamle, Hugh Roy investment advisor, consultant
Lamm, Donald Stephen literary agent
Lamm, Norman academic administrator, rabbi
Lammie, James Louis engineering executive, retired military officer
Lamont, Lansing journalist, writer, public affairs and trust executive
Lampen, Richard Jay lawyer, investment banker
Lamport, Anthony Matthew venture capitalist
Lanchner, Bertrand Martin lawyer, advertising executive
Landau, Sidney Ivan lexicographer
Lander, Bernard academic administrator, sociologist, clergyman
Landman, Jonathan editor
Landreth, Barbara Horan pediatrician, educator
Landrigan, Philip John epidemiologist
Landry, Donald William physician, educator, scientist
Lane, Jeffrey Bruce bank executive
Lane, Stewart F. theater owner, producer
Lang, George restaurateur
Langan, Richard F., Jr. lawyer
Lange, Phil C. retired education educator
Langer, Bruce Alden lawyer
Langer, David J. neurological surgeon
Langhammer, Fred H. cosmetics company executive
Lannamann, Richard Stuart executive search consultant
Lanyon, Ellen artist, educator
Lao, Joseph R. social sciences educator, researcher
Lapham, Lewis Henry editor, television personality, writer
Lapine, James Elliot playwright, director
Lappin, Jessica S. city councilwoman
LaQuaglia, Michael Patrick pediatric surgeon, neuroblastoma researcher
Laragh, John Henry physician, scientist, educator
Larberg, John Frederick retired social welfare executive, wine consultant, educator
LaRocca, Salvatore sports association executive
Larose, Lawrence Alfred lawyer
La Rossa, James Michael lawyer
Larsen, Jonathan Zerbe journalist
Lash, Stephen Sycle auction company executive
Lasker, Jonathan Lewis artist
Lasry, Marc hedge fund manager
Lasser, Joseph Robert investment company executive
Lataille, Ronald H. telecommunications industry executive
Latza, William D. lawyer
Lauder, Aerin Rebecca (Aerin Lauder Zinterhofer) cosmetics executive
Lauder, Evelyn H. cosmetics executive
Lauder, Jo Carole art association administrator
Lauder, Leonard Alan retired cosmetic and fragrance company executive
Lauder, Ronald Stephen investor
Lauder, William P. cosmetics executive
Lauer, Eliot lawyer
Lauer, Matt television personality
Laufer, Ira Jerome physician
Laufman, Harold surgeon, consultant
Lauren, Ralph fashion designer
Laurence, Jeffrey Conrad immunologist, educator
Laurents, Arthur playwright, theater director
Lavin, Howard S. lawyer
Lawlor, Norah public relations executive
Lawrence, Bryan Hunt investment company executive
Lawrence, Nina publishing executive
Lawrence, Robert Cutting III lawyer
Lawrence-Apfelbaum, Marc lawyer, broadcast executive
Lawson, Nigella cookbook writer, celebrity chef
Lawson, William otolaryngologist, educator
Lawson-Johnston, Peter Orman foundation executive
Lax, Peter David mathematician, educator
Layton, Donald Harvey diversified financial services company executive
Lazarcik, Gregor economist, educator, financial research company executive
Lazarus, Herbert pediatrician, educator
Lazarus, Shelly (Rochelle) advertising executive
Lazio, Rick (Enrico Anthony Lazio) diversified financial services company executive, former United States Representative from New York
Leahey, Lynn editor-in-chief
Leahey, Miles Cary economist
Leahy, John economist, educator
Leahy, Michael Joseph retired newspaper editor
Leary, Denis actor, comedian
Leaver, Marcus E. publishing executive
LeBlond, Richard Knight, II, banker
Lebovits, Gerald judge
Lechner, Alfred James, Jr. lawyer, former federal judge
LeClerc, Paul library director
LeCompte, Elizabeth theater director
Lederer, John A. retail executive
Lederman, Lawrence lawyer, writer, educator
Lederman, Stephanie medical association administrator
Ledger, William Joe obstetrician, gynecologist, educator
Le Dû, Jean-Luc Wine Shop Owner
Lee, David professional basketball player
Lee, Frances Helen editor
Lee, James Bainbridge, Jr. diversified financial services company executive
Lee, Jennifer journalist
Lee, Jerome G. lawyer
Lee, Kate literary agent
Lee, Sally A. editor-in-chief, publishing executive
Lee, Thomas F. art association administrator
Lee, Thomas H. private equity firm executive
Leech, Katharine (Kitty Leech) costume designer, educator
Leeman, Eve psychiatrist
Lees, Alfred William former magazine editor, writer, retired
Leet, Mildred Robbins social welfare administrator, consultant
Lefcourt, Gerald B. (Gerry Lefcourt) lawyer
Lefenfeld, Michael chemist, materials engineer
LeFevre, David E. lawyer, business executive
Lefferts, Gillet, Jr. architect
Leffler, Marvin foundation administrator, writer
Lefkovits, Albert Meyer dermatologist
Lefkowitz, David S. lawyer
Lefkowitz, Jay Philip state attorney general
Lefkowitz, Joel M. psychologist, educator
LeFrak, Richard Stone real estate developer
Legato, Marianne internist, educator
Legrand, Michel Jean composer
Lehane, Dennis writer
Lehman, Edward William social studies educator, researcher
Leibovitz, Annie photographer
Leibowitz, Herbert Akiba literature and language professor, writer
Leidheiser, Kathleen H. telecommunications industry executive
Leisure, Peter Keeton federal judge
Leiter, Al (Alois Terry Leiter) sportscaster, retired professional baseball player
Leitersdorf, Jonathan investment company executive
Leitman, I. Michael health facility administrator
Leive, Cindi (Cynthia M. Leive) editor-in-chief
Lekberg, Barbara sculptor
Lemann, Nicholas Berthelot dean, journalist
Lemarchand, Alain publishing executive
Lemon, Ralph choreographer
Lenobel, Jeffrey A. lawyer
Lents, Stacie performing arts educator
Leo, Jacqueline M. on-line publishing executive, former editor-in-chief
Leon, Martin Bert cardiologist, educator
Leonard, Edwin Deane lawyer
Lepor, Herbert urologist
Leppard, Raymond John conductor, musician
Lerer, Kenneth B. publishing executive, investor
Leritz, Lawrence R. choreographer, singer, dancer
Lerman, Bradley E. lawyer
Lerner, Marni Jo lawyer
Lerner, Martin museum curator
Lerner, Sandra artist
Lesesne, Carroll Boutell (Cap Lesesne) plastic surgeon
Lesk, Ann Berger lawyer
Lesser, Lori Ellen lawyer
Lessing, Brian Reid actuary
Lessing, Stephen M. investment company executive
Lessnau, Klaus-Dieter Karl pulmonologist, director, medical educator
Leubert, Alfred Otto Paul management consultant
Leung, Firman investment bank executive
Leung, Sandra pharmaceutical executive, lawyer
Levai, Pierre Alexandre art gallery executive
Leval, Pierre Nelson federal judge
Leven, Ann Ruth financial consultant
Levi, Isaac philosophy educator
Levi Caroti, Gisella lawyer
Levie, Joseph Henry lawyer, banker
Levin, Bernard physician
Levin, Frances R. psychiatrist, educator
Levin, Henry Mordechai economist, educator
Levin, Herbert retired diplomat, foundation administrator
Levin, Janna J. physicist, educator
Levin, Michael Joseph lawyer
Levin, Susan Bass state agency administrator, lawyer
Levine, Gail Carson writer
Levine, James Lawrence conductor, music director, pianist
Levine, Louis D. museum administrator, archaeologist
Levine, Naomi Bronheim academic administrator
Levine, Robert H. medical educator, psychiatrist
Levine, Robert Jay lawyer
Levine, Ronald Jay lawyer
Levine, Sherrie conceptual artist
Levinson, Carl E. bank executive
Levinson, Rascha psychotherapist
Levinson, Robert Alan textiles executive
Levinson, Warren Mitchell broadcast journalist
Levitan, David M(aurice) lawyer, educator
Levitan, Steve lawyer
Levitt, Arthur, Jr. investment company executive, former federal agency administrator
Levitt, Harry speech and hearing scientist
Levitz, Paul Elliot publishing executive
Levoy, Myron author
Levy, Albert physician

Levy, Builder *photographer*
Levy, Clifford J. *investigative journalist*
Levy, Jack *investment banker*
Levy, Joseph *physician, pediatric gastroenterologist*
Levy, Marguerite F. *psychology professor emerita*
Levy, Reynold *performing arts center administrator, retired telecommunications industry executive*
Levy, Stanley Herbert *lawyer*
Levy, Tara Walpert *advertising executive*
Lewin, Robert *lawyer*
Lewis, Alan James *foundation administrator, pharmacologist*
Lewis, Blair Seth *gastroenterologist*
Lewis, Jonathan Joseph *surgical oncologist, molecular biologist, educator, entrepreneur*
Lewis, Michael *writer, journalist*
Lewis, Robert E. *insurance company executive*
Lewis, William M. *diversified financial services company executive*
Lewis-Hall, Freda C. *pharmaceutical executive*
Lewy, Robert Max *physician*
Lewyn, Thomas Mark *lawyer*
Li, Tze-chung *lawyer, educator*
Li, Xiao Feng *research scientist*
Libby, Daniel M. *pulmonologist*
Libeskind, Daniel *architect*
Lichtenstein, Warren G. *hedge fund manager*
Licklider, Roy Eilers *political science educator*
Lieb, Richard Jay *investment banker*
Lieber, Robert C. *city official, former investment company executive*
Lieberman, Alan J. *paramedic, consultant*
Lieberman, Nancy Ann *lawyer*
Lieberman, Seymour *biochemist, educator*
Liebman, Pamela *real estate company executive*
Liebman, Theodore *architect*
Liebmann, Jeff S. *lawyer*
Liebowitz, Michael Robert *psychiatrist, educator*
Liebrandt, Paul *chef*
Liff, Zanvel A. *psychologist*
Lifton, Robert Kenneth *entrepreneur*
Ligh, Jonathan Kennard *ophthalmologist*
Liles, Kevin *music company executive*
Lilja, H. *chemist, educator*
Lil Wayne, (Dwayne Michael Carter Jr.) *rap artist*
Lima, Adriana Francesca *model*
Liman, Lewis Jeffrey *lawyer*
Limbaugh, Rush Hudson III *radio talk show host*
Limpe, Stephen T. *oil industry executive*
Lin, Grace *financial analyst*
Lincoff, Harvey Allen *ophthalmologist*
Lincoln, Edmond Lynch *investment banker*
Lindblad, Lisa *travel company executive, anthropologist, writer*
Linder, Bertram Norman *foundation administrator, horse breeder, actor*
Lindo-Fuentes, Hector *history professor*
Lindsay, George Peter *lawyer*
Lindsey, (Helen) Johanna *writer*
Lindsey, Robert J. *medical association administrator*
Lindstrom, Martin *marketing professional, writer*
Linhart, Jan *cosmetic dentist*
Link, Robert O., Jr. *lawyer*
Linker, Arthur S. *lawyer*
Lins, Pam *sculptor*
Linsky, Marty *education educator*
Linville, Judson C. *diversified financial services company executive*
Liodice, Robert D. *advertising executive*
Lipkin, Martin *medical scientist and educator*
Lipkin, Seymour *musician, conductor, educator*
Lipkin, W. Ian *epidemiologist, neurologist, educator*
Lipman, Ira Ackerman *security service company executive*
Lipper, Kenneth *investment banker, film producer, writer*
Lippman, Jonathan *chief judge*
Lippman, Sharon Rochelle *art historian and therapist, filmmaker*
Lipscomb, James Louis *lawyer, insurance company executive*
Lipsey, Robert Edward *economist, educator*
Lipsky, Pat *artist*
Lipton, Charles *public relations executive*
Lipton, James *television personality*
Lipton, Joan Elaine *advertising executive*
Lipton, Martin *lawyer*
Litman, Jack Theodore *lawyer*
Lituchy, Gregg *dentist*
Litvin, Joel M. *sports association executive, lawyer*
Lively, Blake Christina *actress*
Livingston, Debra Ann *federal judge, educator*
Livingston, Robert A. *manufacturing executive*
Llinás, Rodolfo Riascos *neuroscientist, researcher*
Lloyd, Jean *retired early childhood educator*
Lloyd, William Frederick *lawyer*
Lo, Anita M. *chef*
Loar, Peggy Ann *foundation administrator, museum administrator*
Lobenfeld, Eric Jay *retired lawyer*
Lobl, Herbert Max *lawyer, writer*
Lobo, Rogerio Arnaldo *obstetrician, gynecologist*
Lobrano, John D. *lawyer*
Lockhart, James Bicknell III *investment company executive, former federal agency administrator*
Lockwood, Molly Ann *communications company executive*
Lodge, Henry Sears *physician*
Loeb, Daniel Seth *hedge fund manager*
Loeb, John Langeloth, Jr. *investment counselor, consultant*
Loeb, John Nichols *physician, educator*
Loeb, Larry Morris *communications company executive*
Loengard, John Borg *photographer, editor*
Loft, Lloyd Mark *otolaryngologist*
Logan, Don *communications industry executive*
Logan, Kenneth Richard *lawyer*
Lohez, Dening Suzanne *electrical engineer*
Lohr, Steve *reporter*
Lombardi, Joseph J. *retail executive*
London, Nora *foundation administrator*
Loney, Glenn Meredith *theater educator*
Long, Charles *sculptor*
Longley, Marjorie Watters *newspaper executive*
Longobardi, David *executive vice president, chief content officer*
Loo, Marcus Hsieu-Hong *urologist, physician, educator*
Loomis, Carol J. *journalist*
Lopez, Ralph Ivan *pediatrics educator*
Lorber, Barbara Heyman *communications executive*
Lorch, Maristella De Panizza *writer, educator*
Lord, Marvin *apparel executive*
LoSchiavo, Linda Bosco *library director*
Lothian, James Robert *economist, educator*
Lotwin, Stanford Gerald *lawyer*
Lou, Liza *artist*
Louganis, Greg E(fthimios) *retired Olympic athlete, actor*
Loughlin, Gerald M. *pediatrician, educator*
Loughlin, Thomas G. *professional society administrator*
Love-Hassell, Esther Boyer *special education educator, consultant*
Lovell, Whitfield *artist*
Low, Ronald Bruce *hospital administrator*
Lowenberg, Marc Gregory *dentist*
Lowenfeld, Andreas Frank *law educator*
Lowenfels, Lewis David *lawyer*
Lowitt, Ian Theo *investment company executive*
Lowman, David B. *mortgage company executive*
Lowry, Glenn David *art museum director*
Lowy, George Theodore *lawyer*
Lubars, David Charles *advertising executive*
Lubetski, Edith Esther *librarian*
Lucas, Sylvie *ambassador*
Luce, William *playwright, librettist, screenwriter*
Ludden, David Ellsworth *history professor*
Lukes, Steven Michael *sociologist, educator*
Lukken, Walter L. *stock exchange executive, former commissioner*
Lumet, Sidney *film director*
Lunding, Christopher Hanna *lawyer*
Lundqvist, Henrik *professional hockey player*
Luntz, Maurice Harold *ophthalmologist*
Lupert, Leslie Allan *lawyer*
LuPone, Patti *actress*
Luria, Mary Mercer *lawyer*
Lurie, Alison *writer*
Lurie, Ranan Raymond *political cartoonist, artist, journalist*
Lusskin, Shari I. *psychiatrist, educator*
Lutnick, Howard William *brokerage house executive*
Luxenberg, Arthur Martin *lawyer*
Lyman, Peggy *artistic director, dancer, choreographer, educator*
Lynch, Carol *psychologist, minister*
Lynch, Gerard E. *federal judge*
Lynch, Kyle Thomas *lawyer*
Lynch, Richard J. *telecommunications industry executive, communications engineer*
Lyne, Susan Markham *Internet sales company executive, former multi-media company executive*
Lyon, Carl Francis, Jr. *lawyer*
Lyons, John Matthew *telecommunications industry, broadcast executive*
Lyons, Nick *retired publishing executive*
Lytton, William Bryan *lawyer, former manufacturing company executive*
Ma, Adrianna *private equity firm executive*
Ma, Yo-Yo *cellist*
Maas, Jane Brown *advertising executive*
Maas, Werner Karl *microbiology educator*
Macan, William Alexander, IV, *lawyer*
MacArthur, John Roderick C. G. (Rick MacArthur) *magazine publisher, journalist*
Maccioni, Sirio *restaurant manager*
MacCrate, Robert *lawyer*
Macer-Story, Eugenia Ann *writer*
MacFarlane, Seth Woodbury *television producer, scriptwriter*
MacGowan, Sandra Firelli *publishing executive, consultant*
Machon, Monika Maria *insurance company executive, lawyer*
Mack, John J. *diversified financial services company executive*
Mackay, Martin *pharmaceutical executive*
MacKinnon, Roderick *neuroscientist, educator*
Macklowe, Harry B. *real estate developer*
Macklowe, William S. *real estate company executive*
MacLeod, William Bentley *economics, law professor*
Maclin, Todd (Samuel Todd Maclin) *diversified financial services company executive*
Mac Low, Mordecai-Mark *astrophysicist*
MacNeil, Ian *theatrical set & costume designer*
MacRae, Cameron Farquhar III *lawyer*
Macris, Achilles O. *bank executive*
Macris, Michael *lawyer*
Maddaloni, Mark A. *toxicologist*
Madden, John J. *lawyer*
Madden, John Patrick *lawyer*
Madden, Michael Daniel *finance company executive*
Maddow, Rachel Anne *radio and TV personality, political activist*
Madhrira, Machaiah M. *nephrologist*
Madsen, Stephen Stewart *lawyer*
Mager, Ezra Pascal *investment company executive*
Magner, Marjorie J. (Marge Magner) *private equity firm executive*
Magramm, Irene *ophthalmologist*
Maguire, Gregory *writer*
Mahoney, Margaret Ellerbe *foundation executive*
Maia, Tiago Vaz *researcher*
Maidman, Richard Harvey Mortimer *lawyer*
Mailman, Stanley *lawyer*
Maitland, Guy Edison Clay *lawyer*
Makovsky, Kenneth Dale *public relations executive*
Malandrino, Catherine *apparel designer*
Maldonado-Bear, Rita Marinita *economist, educator*
Malernee, James Kent, Jr. *financial consultant*
Malgieri, Nick *food service executive, educator, chef, writer*
Malin, Irving *language educator, critic*
Malinowska-Sempruch, Kasia *director*
Malkin, Barry *film editor, consultant*
Malkin, Peter Laurence *lawyer, investor*
Malkin, Stanley Lee *neurologist*
Mallin, Joel *lawyer*
Mallis, Fern J. *fashion industry executive*
Mallow, Matthew J. *lawyer*
Manassah, Jamal Tewfek *electrical engineer, educator, management consultant*
Mandel, Carol Ann *university librarian*
Mandelbaum, Jay Philip *diversified financial services company executive*
Maneker, Morton M. *lawyer*
Manewitz, Mark Lee *lawyer*
Maney, Michael Mason *lawyer*
Manger, William Muir *internist, educator, writer, research scientist*
Manges, James Horace *investment banker*
Mann, Frank Bert *artist, educator*
Mann, Pamela A. *lawyer*
Manning, Dennis J. *insurance company executive*
Manoff, Richard Kalman *advertising executive, writer, public health service officer, consultant*
Mansouri, Lotfollah (Lotfi Mansouri) *retired performing company executive*
Mantel, Allan David *lawyer*
Manthorne, Katherine E. *art historian, educator*
Mapes, Glynn Dempsey *newspaper editor*
Marceau, Yvonne *ballroom dancer, educator*
Marcosson, Thomas I. *management consultant, advertising executive*
Marcus, Eric Robert *psychiatrist*
Marcus, Kenneth L. *federal official*
Marcus, Maria Lenhoff *lawyer, educator*
Marcus, Michael B. *mathematics professor*
Marcuse, Adrian Gregory *academic administrator*
Marder, Michael Zachary *dental educator, researcher*
Marenoff, Susan *museum director, former professional athletics manager*
Margalith, Helen Margaret *retired librarian*
Margolis, Mark Neal *actor*
Maria Antonella, Pelizzari *art history educator*
Mariani, Michael Matthew *lawyer*
Marin, Deborah B. *psychiatrist, educator*
Mariner, Jonathan D. *major league baseball executive*
Marino, Peter *architect*
Marino, Robin L. *multi-media company executive*
Mark, Mary Ellen *photographer*
Markel, Gregory Arthur *lawyer*
Marks, Paul Alan *oncologist, cell biologist, educator*
Marks, Ramon Paul *lawyer*
Marks, Theodore Lee *lawyer*
Mark-Viverito, Mellisa *Councilwoman*
Marlas, James Constantine *diversified financial services company executive*
Marrero, Victor *federal judge, lawyer*
Marriott, Michel *reporter*
Marron, Donald Baird, Sr. *venture capitalist*
Marsal, Bryan Paul *restructuring company executive*
Marsalis, Wynton *musician*
Marshall, Simone Verniere *psychologist, psychoanalyst*
Marshall, Tom *publishing executive*
Martell, Terrence F. *stock exchange executive*
Martin, Demetri (Demitri Martin) *comedian, scriptwriter*
Martin, Judith Sylvia *journalist*
Martin, Malcolm Elliot *lawyer*
Martin, Michael Townsend *sports association executive, marketing professional, consultant*
Martin, Ricky (Enrique Martin Morales IV) *vocalist, actor, producer, composer*
Martin, Rodney O., Jr. *insurance company executive*
Martinez, Lucy *lawyer*
Martínez-López, Carmen Leonor *management consultant, educator*
Martins, Peter *performing company executive, choreographer*
Marton, Tutzi *artist*
Martone, Patricia Ann *lawyer*
Marty, Alvin Leonard *retired economist, educator*
Marx, Owen Cox *lawyer*
Marx, Robert G. *orthopedic surgeon, educator*
Marzorati, Gerald *editor*
Masey, Jack *exhibition designer*
Masi, Jane Virginia *marketing and sales consultant*
Maslak, Peter George *hematologist*
Mason, Alexander Taylor *finance company executive*
Mason, Bobbie Ann *writer*
Mason, Christopher May *lawyer*
Mason, Marshall W. *theater director, educator, author*
Massad, Timothy G. *lawyer*
Masters, Blythe *bank executive*
Masters, Jon Joseph *corporate governance specialist, management consultant*
Masterson, James Francis *psychiatrist*
Mastrangelo, Matt *publishing executive*
Matarasso, Alan *plastic and reconstructive surgeon*
Matera, Cristina m *gynecologist, educator*
Materna, Joseph Anthony *lawyer*
Mathas, Theodore A. (Ted Mathas) *insurance company executive, lawyer*
Matheson, Linda *retired social worker*
Mathews, Michael Stone *investment banker*
Mathieson, Garrett Alfred *insurance brokerage executive*
Mathis, Catherine J. *publishing executive*
Mathisen, Harold Clifford *foundation administrator*
Matsuhisa, Nobuyuki *chef, restaurant owner*
Matters, Craig *editor*
Matteson, John Thomas *English educator, lawyer*
Matteson, William Bleecker *lawyer*
Matthews, Christopher John *political commentator, writer*
Matus, Wayne Charles *lawyer*
Matz, Alison Adler *publishing executive*
Maurer, Gilbert Charles *media specialist*
Maxfield, Guy Budd *lawyer, educator*
Maxmen, Mimi (Mary Elizabeth Maxmen) *costume and scenic designer*
Maxwell, Anders John *investment banker*
May, Gita *literature educator*
Mayer, Carl Joseph *prosecutor, lawyer, educator*
Mayer, Christopher *lawyer*
Mayer, Jane *journalist*
Mayer, Margery Weil *publishing executive*
Mayer, Rosemary *artist*
Mayer, Theodore V.H. *lawyer*
Mayer, William Emilio *investor*
Mayeux, Richard *hospital administrator, neurologist*
Maynard, John Rogers *language educator*
Maynard, Virginia Madden *foundation administrator*
Mayo, Paula *museum director*
Mayr-Harting, Thomas *ambassador*
Maysles, Albert H. *filmmaker*
Mazza, David S. *pediatric allergist, immunologist*
Mazzo, Kay *ballet dancer, educator*
Mazzola, Anthony Thomas *editor, graphics designer, consultant, curator*
Mazzola, John William *retired performing company executive, consultant*
Mazzucelli, Colette Grace Celia *author, educator*
McCabe, David J. *lawyer*
McCabe, Jim *Internet company executive*
McCabe, Mary F. *marketing professional*
McCaffrey, Judith Elizabeth *lawyer*
McCall, Anthony *filmmaker, conceptual artist*
McCall, H. Carl *financial services firm executive, former state official*
McCance, Sean E. *orthopedist*
McCarthy, Andrew *actor*
McCarthy, Cormac (Charles Joseph McCarthy) *writer*
McCarthy, Edith A. *pediatrician, educator*
McCarthy, Jonathan Paul *economist*
McCarthy, Joseph D. *advertising agency executive*
McCarthy, Joseph Gerald *plastic surgeon, educator*
McCarthy, Robert Emmett *lawyer*
McCartney, Scott *travel editor, columnist*
McCartney, Stella *apparel designer*
McCarty, V. K. *publishing executive, chaplain, librarian, editor*
McCaslin, Teresa Eve *human resources specialist*
McCaughey, Betsy (Elizabeth P. McCaughey) *health policy advocate, former lieutenant governor*
McCaw, Robert Bruce *lawyer*
McClelland, Shearwood Junior *orthopaedic surgeon*
McColgan, Ellyn A. *diversified financial services company executive*
McComb, William L. *apparel company executive*
McCormack, Richard Thomas Fox *diversified financial services company executive, former ambassador*
McCormack, Thomas Joseph *retired publishing executive, playwright*
McCormack, William J. *bishop emeritus*
McCrary, Eugenia Lester (Mrs. Dennis Daughtry McCrary) *civic worker, writer*
McCredie, James Robert *fine arts educator*
McCrie, Robert Delbert *prison reformer, editor, educator*
McCullough, Andrew Richard *physician*
McCullough, David *writer*
McDaniel, Raymond W., Jr. *financial information company executive*
McDermott, Alice *writer*
McDonald, Audra Ann *actress, vocalist*
McDonell, Terry *publishing executive, writer, editor*
McDowell, David Michael *psychiatrist, educator, researcher*
McDowell, Mary *bank executive*
McElhinney, James Lancel *artist, educator*
McEwen, Laura Ellen *publishing executive*
McFadden, Mary Josephine *fashion industry executive*
McFadden, Robert Dennis *reporter*
McFeely, William Drake *publishing company executive*
McGee, Hugh E. III *investment company executive*
McGinn, Eileen *public health service officer, researcher*
McGinn, Kevin B. *insurance company executive*
McGinnis, Arthur Joseph, Jr. *public relations executive*
McGonagle, Duncan Francis *mental health nurse, substance abuse counselor*
McGowen, Lorraine S. *lawyer*
Mc Gowin, William Edward *artist*
McGrath, Judy (Judith Ann McGrath) *broadcast executive*
McGrath, Michael G. *management consulting firm executive*
McGrath, Thomas John *lawyer, writer, film producer*
McGraw, Harold W., III, (Terry McGraw) *information company executive*
McGraw, Harold Whittlesey, Jr. *publishing executive*
McGraw, Nancy McCall *singer, theater producer*
McGuire, Maureen A. *marketing executive*
McGuire, Pierre *sports analyst, former professional hockey coach*
McGuire, Raymond J. *diversified financial services company executive*
McHale, John Joseph, Jr. *major league baseball executive, former professional sports team executive*
McInerney, Jay *writer*
McInerney, Thomas J. *Internet company executive*
McIntyre, Brian P. *sports association executive*
McKeefry, Mark *attorney, director*
McKenzie, Kevin Patrick *performing company executive*
McKinley-Haas, Mary *artist*
McKinnon, Floyd Wingfield *textile executive*
McKinnon, Paul *bank executive, human resources specialist*
McLane, Charles D., Jr. *metal products executive*
McLane, Derek *set designer*
McLaughlin, Joseph Michael *federal judge*
McLennan, Hamish *advertising executive*
McLeod, Mary S. *pharmaceutical executive*
McMahon, James Charles *lawyer*
McManus, Sean Joseph *broadcast executive*
McMillan, L. Londell *lawyer*
McMillan, Terry L. *writer, educator*
McMullan, Patrick *photographer*
McMullan, William Patrick III *investment banker*
McMurtry, Larry Jeff *writer*
McNally, Terrence *playwright*
McNamara, J. Donald (John Donald McNamara) *retired lawyer, business executive*
McNulty, James J. *futures exchange executive*

McPherson, Mary Patterson charitable foundation executive
McQuade, Eugene M. (Gene McQuade) diversified financial services company executive
McQuown, Judith Hershkowitz writer, consultant, financial planner
McTeer, Janet actress
McTiernan, Charles E., Jr. lawyer, energy executive
McWhinney, Deborah Doyle diversified financial services company executive
Meacham, Jon E. editor
Meachin, David James Percy investment banker
Mead, Daniel S. telecommunications industry executive
Mead, Lawrence Myers III political science educator
Meads, Mindy retail executive
Medina, Kate (Kathryn Bach Medina) associate publisher
Meehan, Sandra Gotham communications and creative consultant, writer
Meehan, Thomas writer
Mehler, Gordon lawyer, former federal prosecutor
Mehlman, Ken (Kenneth Brian Mehlman) public relations executive
Mehretu, Julie artist
Mehta, Linn Cary literature educator
Mehta, Zarin performing company executive
Meier, Diane Eve geriatrician, researcher, medical educator
Meier, Richard Alan architect
Meigs, James B. editor-in-chief
Meisel, Steven advertising photographer
Meiseles, Daniel sports association executive
Meller, Jose cardiologist
Mellins, Robert B. pediatrician, educator
Melloan, George Richard editor
Melone, Joseph James retired insurance company executive
Melton, Howell Webster, Jr. lawyer
Meltzer, Jay Ivan medical educator
Meltzer, Milton author
Mencher, Melvin journalist, educator
Mendez, Rosie city councilwoman
Mendoza, Roberto G., Jr. banker
Menicheschi, Edward John publishing executive
Mennin, Douglas Steven psychologist
Menschel, Robert Benjamin investment banker
Menton, Tanya Lia lawyer, educator
Menza, Claudia Marcella literary agent
Menzel, Idina actress, singer
Mergenthaler, Frank corporate financial executive
Meron, Theodor judge, educator, researcher
Merow, John lawyer
Merrell, Woodson C. integrative medicine specialist
Merrill, George Vanderneth lawyer, investment executive
Merriss, Philip Ramsay, Jr. banker
Mertens, Joan R. museum curator, art historian
Messer, Thomas Maria museum director
Messier, Jean-Marie corporate financial executive
Messier, Mark Douglas professional sports team executive, retired professional hockey player
Mestice, Anthony Francis Bishop Emeritus
Meyer, Danny restaurateur
Meyer, Karl Ernest retired journalist
Meyer, Stephenie writer
Meyer-Bahlburg, Heino F.L. psychology professor
Meyerhoff, Erich librarian, director
Meyers, Dale (Mrs. Mario Cooper) artist
Mezentsev, Alexandre Victor aerospace scientist, researcher
Miano, Louis Stephen arts advisor
Michaels, Al (Alan Richard Michaels) sportscaster
Michaels, Lorne television producer
Michaelson, Arthur M. lawyer
Michelassi, Fabrizio surgeon
Michelis, Michael Frank nephrologist
Michels, Robert psychiatrist, educator
Michelsen, Christopher Bruce Hermann surgeon
Michelson, Gertrude Geraldine retired retail executive
Michelson, Sarah choreographer
Middlesworth, William pediatric surgeon
Migiro, Asha-Rose international organization official
Migro, Asha-Rose international organization official
Mikumo, Akiko lawyer
Milch, David screenwriter, producer
Milch, Randal S. telecommunications industry executive, lawyer
Mildvan, Donna infectious diseases physician
Milicic, Darko professional basketball player
Millard, Wenda Harris multi-media company executive
Miller, Alan computer company executive, management consultant
Miller, Arthur Madden lawyer, investment banker, brokerage house executive
Miller, Barbara Kenton retired librarian
Miller, Charles Hampton lawyer
Miller, Corbin Russell investment company executive
Miller, Dennis comedian
Miller, Ernest Charles management consultant
Miller, Harvey R. lawyer, bankruptcy reorganization specialist
Miller, Harvey S. Shipley foundation trustee, philanthropist
Miller, Heidi Goldberg diversified financial services company executive
Miller, J. Allen lawyer
Miller, Jonathan F. investment company executive, former Internet company executive
Miller, Michael Campion lawyer
Miller, Michael Jeffrey editor, analyst
Miller, Neil Stuart advertising executive
Miller, Nicole Jacqueline fashion designer
Miller, Paul Samuel lawyer
Miller, Richard Kidwell artist, actor, educator
Miller, Robert advertising executive
Miller, Sam Scott lawyer
Miller, Sarah Gray editor-in-chief
Miller, Stephanie Katherine radio personality, comedian
Miller, Theodore Norman lawyer
Miller-Sydney, Audrey Yvonne music educator
Mills, William J. bank executive
Millstein, Ira M. lawyer, educator
Millstein, Lincoln media company executive
Milmoe, J. Gregory, Jr. lawyer
Milrod, Barbara psychiatrist
Milstein, Paul real estate developer
Mindich, Eric M. hedge fund manager
Minick, Michael publishing executive
Minkel, Herbert Philip, Jr. lawyer
Minkowitz, Martin lawyer, former state government official
Minskoff, Edward J. architectural firm executive
Minson, Arthur Internet company executive
Mintz, Douglas N. radiologist
Mintz, Norman Nelson investment banker, educator, retired academic administrator
Mir, Aleksandra artist
Miranda, Lin-Manuel actor, composer, lyricist
Mirenburg, Barry Leonard publishing executive, educator
Mirowski, Piotr medical researcher
Mirrer, Louise professional society administrator, former language educator
Mischka, James fashion designer
Miscik, Jami A. diversified financial services company executive, former federal agency administrator
Mishkin, Frederic Stanley economics professor, former federal official
Mishra, Bud science educator
Mitchell, Alison N. newspaper reporter, editor
Mitchell, Arthur dancer, choreographer, performing company executive, educator
Mitchell, Chris publishing executive
Mitchell, Mary Jenkins public health service officer
Mitchell, Patricia Edenfield broadcast museum administrator
Mitelman, Serge A. researcher
Miyake, Issey fashion designer
Mizrahi, Isaac fashion designer
Mnuchin, Alan Geoffrey investment banker
Modlin, Adam D. real estate company executive
Modlin, Howard S. lawyer
Moerdler, Charles Gerard lawyer
Moffat Salant, Marilyn physical therapist, educator
Mohler, Mary Gail magazine editor
Mohr, Jay Preston neurologist, educator
Molho, Emanuel publisher
Molinaro, Samuel L., Jr. diversified financial services company executive
Moline, Jacqueline occupational physician
Moloney, Thomas Joseph lawyer
Moltz, James Edward brokerage house executive
Momin, Shamim curator
Monaco, Julie bank executive
Monaghan, Craig Thomas automotive executive
Monaghan, Dominic actor
Monaghan, Michelle actress
Mone, Lawrence J. think-tank executive
Monk, Meredith Jane artistic director, composer, choreographer, filmmaker
Monk Kidd, Sue writer
Montalvo, Elba social services administrator
Moody-Adams, Michele Marcia dean, philosophy professor
Mooney, Richard Emerson writer
Moonves, Leslie broadcast executive
Moor, Kristian P. insurance company executive
Moore, Alma C. publishing executive, consultant
Moore, Ann S. publishing executive
Moore, Anne physician
Moore, Brian P. health care professional
Moore, Charles Hewes, Jr. manufacturing executive
Moore, Christopher writer
Moore, Jason theater director
Moore, Melissa J. diversified financial services company executive
Moore, Thomas A. lawyer
Moore, Thomas Ronald (Lord Bridestowe) lawyer
Morak, Glenn H. lawyer
Morales, Carlos M. lawyer
Moran, Martin Joseph fundraising company executive
Moran, Thomas J. insurance company executive
Morawetz, Cathleen Synge mathematician
Moreira, Marcio Martins advertising executive
Morgan, David Raymond financial consultant, retired bank executive
Morgan, Mary E. publishing executive
Morgan, Suann Lee information technology manager, consultant
Morgenthau, Robert Morris prosecutor
Morial, Marc Haydel civil rights association executive, former mayor
Morphy, James Calvin lawyer
Morreale, Joseph Constantino academic administrator, educator, economist, consultant
Morris, Dick columnist, political consultant
Morris, Doug (Douglas Peter Morris) recording industry executive
Morris, Maria R. insurance company executive
Morris, William Charles investor
Morrison, Briggs pharmaceutical executive
Morrison, Matthew actor
Morrison, Stacy Lynne editor
Morrissey, Michael Joseph finance executive
Morrow, Monica medical educator
Morse, David actor
Morse, Edward Lewis energy economist, director
Morse, Robert Parker investment company executive
Morse, Stephen Scott virologist, epidemiologist, immunologist, educator
Mortimer, Peter Michael lawyer
Mortimer, Tinsley Randolph apparel designer
Mortiz, Jacques obstetrician, gynecologist, educator
Morton, Andrew J. diversified financial services company executive
Morvillo, Robert Guy lawyer
Morwitz, Vicki Gail finance educator
Moses, Jeffrey Warren cardiologist, educator
Moskin, John Robert editor, writer
Moskin, Morton lawyer, director
Moskowitz, Ellen Hope lawyer
Moskowitz, Eva S. educational association administrator
Moskowitz, Randi Zucker nurse
Mosler, Bruce Elliot real estate company executive
Mosley, Walter Ellis writer
Moss, Adam editor-in-chief
Moss, Sara E. lawyer, cosmetics executive
Mosse, Peter John Charles financial services executive
Moss-Salentijn, Letty (Aleida) anatomist, educator
Mourning, Paul W. lawyer
Movshon, J. Anthony (Joseph Anthony Movshon) neuroscience educator
Mowshowitz, Abbe computer scientist
Moyers, Bill journalist, writer, former White House press secretary
Moyo, Dambisa economist, writer
Mucci, Richard L. insurance company executive
Muchnick, Richard Stuart ophthalmologist, educator
Mudd, Daniel H. investment company executive, former mortgage company executive
Mudick, Stephanie B. diversified financial services company executive, lawyer
Mueller, Thomas M. lawyer
Muir, Christopher Bryant financial analyst
Muir, Tom William chemistry professor
Mukasey, Marc L. lawyer
Mukasey, Michael Bernard lawyer, former United States Attorney General
Mukherjee, Sushmita science educator
Mulford, David Campbell finance company executive, former ambassador
Mullaney, Craig Michael writer
Mullaney, William J. insurance company executive
Mullen, Robert W. construction executive
Muller, Charlotte Feldman economist, educator
Muller, Jennifer choreographer, dancer
Muller, Scott William lawyer
Mulligan, Jeremiah T. lawyer
Mulligan, John J. tobacco company executive
Mumford, Robin Bruce foundation administrator, director, lighting designer
Mundell, Robert Alexander economist, educator
Mundheim, Robert Harry law educator
Munro, Alice Ann writer
Munroe, George Barber retired mining and manufacturing company executive
Murase, Jiro lawyer
Murdoch, Rupert (Keith Rupert Murdoch) multi media company executive
Murdock, Robert Mead curator
Muriel, Amador Cruz physicist
Murphy, Arthur William lawyer, educator
Murphy, Donna actress
Murphy, Helen recording industry executive
Murphy, James Edward public relations and marketing executive
Murphy, John B. portfolio manager
Murphy, John Vincent investment company executive
Murphy, Ramon J.C. (Ramon Jeremiah Castroviejo Murphy) pediatrician, physician, educator
Murphy, Richard William retired diplomat
Murphy, Rosemary actress
Murphy, Suzanne publishing executive
Murray, Brian publishing executive
Murray, Richard Maximilian insurance company executive
Muscato, Andrew lawyer
Musgrave, R. Kenton federal judge
Muskal, Tamar composer
Mutu, Wangechi collage artist, painter
Myer, Keats museum director
Myerberg, Marcia investment banker
Myers, Michelle publishing executive
Myers, Roberta A. (Robbie Myers) editor-in-chief
Myerson, Toby Salter lawyer
Myskowski, Patricia Lois dermatologist
Nabi, Stanley Andrew brokerage house executive
Nachamie, Mark Spencer cardiologist, educator
Nachtwey, James Alan photojournalist
Nadal, Kevin L. psychology professor, director
Nadler, David A. professional services executive
Nadler-Hurvich, Hedda Carol public relations executive
Naegle, Sue E. (Suzanne) broadcast executive
Naftalis, Gary Philip lawyer, educator
Naftolin, Frederick gynecologist, educator
Nahas, Gabriel Georges pharmacologist, educator, writer
Naidich, Thomas Paul neuroradiologist, educator
Naidoo, Loren Jay psychology professor
Nalder, Eric Christopher investigative reporter
Nally, Dennis Mathew finance company executive
Nance, Allan Taylor retired lawyer
Nantz, Jim (James William Nantz) sportscaster
Napolitano, Andrew P. lawyer, former judge
Naqvi, Nasir Hasnain psychiatrist, neuroscientist
Narayanan, Kumaran medical educator
Nass, Martin Leo psychology professor, psychologist
Nassau, Michael Jay lawyer
Nasser, Jacques private equity firm executive, former automotive company executive
Nasser, Jennifer Ann nutritionist, researcher, healthcare educator
Nath, Niharika biology professor
Nathan, Frederic Solis lawyer
Nathanielsz, Peter William physiologist
Natori, Josie Cruz (Josefina Almeda Cruz Natori) apparel designer
Nauman, Bruce artist
Navarra, Tova writer, artist
Nazem, Fereydoun F. venture capitalist, entrepreneur
Neal, James G. university librarian
Neal, Patricia actress
Nederlander, James Morton theater executive
Needham, George Austin investment banker
Neff, Daniel A. lawyer
Neff, Thomas Joseph search firm executive
Neidell, Martin H. lawyer
Neier, Aryeh author, human rights organization administrator
Neiman, LeRoy artist
Neiman, Richard H. state banking agency administrator
Neiman, Shirah prosecutor
Nelson, Anne media consultant, educator, writer
Nelson, Bill broadcast executive
Nelson, Jim editor-in-chief
Nelson, Kathy broadcast executive
Nelson, Martha Jane editor
Nemazee, Hassan investment banker
Neufeld, Peter J. lawyer
Neuger, Win Jay insurance company executive
Neumark, Liz entrepreneur
Neuwirth, Gloria S. lawyer
Neuwirth, Robert Samuel obstetrician, gynecologist, educator
Neveloff, Jay A. lawyer
New, Maria Iandolo pediatrician, educator
Newhouse, Jeffrey H. radiologist, educator
Newman, Charles Michael mathematician, physicist, educator
Newman, Diane publishing executive
Newman, Kenneth E. lawyer
Newman, Lawrence Walker lawyer
Newman, Randy singer, songwriter, musician
Newman, Thomas Rubin lawyer
Ney, Edward N. ambassador, advertising and public relations executive
Ne-Yo, (Shaffer C. Smith) singer
Nho, Shane Jay surgeon
Niccolini, Dianora photographer
Nicholas, Robert A. lawyer
Nicholas, Stephen J. orthopedic surgeon, sports medicine physician
Nicholaw, Casey theater director, choreographer
Nichols, Edie Diane real estate broker
Nickitas, Donna Marie nursing educator, researcher
Nickson, Robert Frazier film producer, educator
Nicol, Dominik writer, photographer
Niederauer, Duncan L. stock exchange executive
Niederhoffer, Roy Gary hedge fund manager
Niemeth, Charles Frederick lawyer
Niemiec, David Wallace investment company executive
Nieporent, Drew A. restaurant owner
Nigam, Hemanshu lawyer, Internet company executive
Nimer, Stephen David physician, leukemia researcher
Nimkarn, Saroj endocrinologist, researcher
Nimkin, Bernard William retired lawyer
Ninivaggi, Daniel A. lawyer, manufacturing executive
Niño, Deanna Hollye lawyer
Nirenberg, Louis mathematician, educator
Nisenholtz, Martin Abram telecommunications executive, educator
Niss, Barbara Joyce archivist
Nix, Kelsey I. lawyer
Nixon, Agnes Eckhardt television writer, producer
Noble, Kenneth Eric lawyer
Noble, Ronald Kenneth secretary general of Interpol
Nocera, Joseph columnist
Nogina, Elena Y. mathematics professor, researcher
Noonan, Peggy (Margaret Ellen Noonan) columnist, writer
Norell, Mark Allen paleontologist, curator
North, Charles Laurence poet, educator
North, Steven Edward lawyer, educator
Norton, Larry oncologist, researcher
Noth, Chris actor
Nottage, Lynn playwright
Novak, B.J. Manaly (Benjamin Joseph Novak) actor, television producer, scriptwriter
Novick, Barbara investment adviser
Novick, Nelson Lee dermatologist, internist, consultant, cosmetic dermasurgeon, writer
Novick, Richard Paul research scientist, public health institute administrator
Novitz, Charles Richard broadcast executive, reporter
Novogratz, Michael E. hedge fund manager
Novogrod, Nancy Gerstein editor
Nugent, Nelle theater, film and television producer
Nurse, Sir Paul M. academic administrator
Nusbacher, Gloria Weinberg lawyer
Nussenzweig, Michel Claudio immunologist, educator
Oakes, James history professor
Oates, Joyce Carol writer, educator
Oberfield, Sharon Elefant pediatric endocrinologist
Oberman, Michael Stewart lawyer
Obernauer, Marne securities company executive
Oberst, Conor Mullen singer, musician
Obler, Geri small business owner, artist, educator
Obogeanu, Madalina Maria reporter
Obolensky, Ivan investment banker, foundation administrator, writer
O'Brien, Clare lawyer
O'Brien, Michael J. lawyer, advertising executive
Och, Daniel S. hedge fund manager
Ochs, Carol Rebecca theologian, writer, theology studies educator, philosopher
O'Connor, Anahad S. journalist
O'Connor, Bridget investment company technology officer
O'Connor, Kevin computer programming executive
O'Connor, Rory pharmaceutical company executive, medical director
Odenweller, Robert Paul philatelist, trade association administrator, retired pilot
O'Doherty, Brian writer
O'Donnell, Mark Patrick writer, drama educator
O'Donnell, Norah news correspondent
Oechler, Henry John, Jr. lawyer
Oettgen, Herbert Friedrich physician
Offit, Morris Wolf investment company executive
Offit, Sidney writer, educator
Oglesby, Charles R. automotive executive
O'Grady, John Joseph III lawyer
O'Hara, Kelli singer, actress
Ohlemeyer, William S. lawyer
Ohlson, Douglas Dean artist, educator
Oinas, Valdar aerospace scientist
Okuhara, Tetsu artist, photographer
Okun, Herbert Stuart diplomat, educator
Okura-Marszycki, Mindy Emi editor
Olafsson, Olaf communications executive
Olbermann, Keith Theodore news analyst, sportscaster

Reno, Janet *former United States Attorney General*
Rescigno, Richard Joseph *editor*
Reses, Jacqueline Dawn *private equity firm executive*
Resika, Paul *artist*
Restani, Jane A. *federal judge*
Reuben, Gloria *actress, singer*
Reutter, Eberhard Edmund, Jr. *education and law educator*
Revenkova, Ekaterina *biologist, researcher*
Revesz, Richard Luis *dean, law educator*
Revkin, Andrew C. *writer, reporter*
Reyes, Diane S. *bank executive*
Reynard, Muriel Joyce *lawyer*
Reynolds, Harold Craig *sportscaster, retired professional baseball player*
Reynolds, James *management consultant*
Reynolds, Michael Timothy *lawyer*
Rheins, Carl Jeffrey *historian, educator*
Rhoads, Geraldine Emeline *editor, consultant*
Rhoden, Dwight *performing company executive, choreographer, dancer*
Rhodes, David *academic administrator*
Rhodes, Randi *radio personality*
Rhodes, Richard Lee *writer*
Rhodes, Samuel *violist, educator*
Rhodes, William Reginald (Bill Rhodes) *diversified financial services company executive*
Rhodes, Yorke E(dward) *organic chemist, educator*
Rhone, Sylvia Marie Miller *recording industry executive*
Rice, Barbara Lynn *stage manager*
Rice, Donald Sands *lawyer*
Rice, Joseph Lee III *lawyer*
Rice, Luanne *writer*
Rice, Susan Elizabeth *Permanent United States Representative to the United Nations*
Rice, Thomas Charles *lawyer*
Rich, Adrienne *poet*
Rich, Frank *journalist, writer*
Rich, Tracy Leon *lawyer, insurance company executive*
Richard, Stephen O. *sports association executive*
Richards, Cecile *healthcare network executive*
Richards, Craig Edward *academic administrator, educator*
Richards, David Alan *lawyer*
Richards, Keith *musician*
Richards, Michael *actor, comedian*
Richardson, Desmond *dancer*
Richardson, Richard Colby, Jr. *leadership and policy studies educator, researcher*
Richert, John Rolin *neuroimmunologist, educator*
Richieri, Kenneth A. *lawyer, publishing executive*
Richman, Daniel Charles *law educator*
Richman, Martin Franklin *lawyer*
Ridgway, Delissa Anne *federal judge*
Rieff, David Sontag *editor, critic*
Rielly, J(ohn) P. *oil industry executive*
Riesel, Sheila Ginsberg *lawyer*
Rifkind, Arleen B. *pharmacologist, researcher, educator*
Rifkind, Robert S. *lawyer*
Rigel, Darrell Spencer *dermatologist, educator, skin cancer researcher*
Riggio, Leonard *book store company executive*
Riggio, Stephen *book store company executive*
Rigolosi, Elaine La Monica *lawyer, educator*
Rihanna, (Robyn Rihanna Fenty) *singer, actress*
Rikon, Michael *lawyer*
Rikoon, Jonathan J. *lawyer*
Riley, Thomas Edward *lawyer*
Riley, William *wholesale distribution executive, writer, conservationist*
Ringel, Dean *lawyer*
Ringgold, Faith *artist*
Ripa, Kelly Maria *television personality, actress*
Ripert, Eric Frank *chef*
Ripert, Jean-Maurice *ambassador*
Ripka, Judith *jewelry designer*
Riss, Eric *psychologist*
Ritch, Kathleen *diversified financial services company executive*
Ritch, Robert Harry *ophthalmologist, educator*
Ritter, Ann L. *lawyer*
Rivera, Geraldo *television personality, journalist*
Rizkin, Iosif *retired systems, circuits, and computer scientist, writer*
Rizzi, Joseph Vito *banker*
Rizzuto, Katherine *publishing executive*
Robbins, John Clapp *management consultant*
Robbins, Lawrence M. *hedge fund manager*
Robbins, Tim (Timothy Francis Robbins) *actor, film director*
Robert, Jackson L. *education professor, literature and language professor*
Roberts, Burton Bennett *lawyer, retired judge*
Roberts, Francis Stone *advertising executive*
Roberts, Kevin *advertising executive*
Roberts, Nora (Eleanor Marie Robertson) *writer*
Roberts, Robin *newscaster*
Robertson, Andrew J. *advertising executive*
Robertson, Edwin David *lawyer*
Robertson, Hugh (Elihu F.) *lawyer*
Robertson, Jaquelin Taylor *architect, educator*
Robertson, Leslie Earl *structural engineer*
Robie, Daniel Cardigan *chemist*
Robins, Perry *dermatologist, educator, foundation administrator*
Robinson, Barbara Paul *lawyer*
Robinson, Irwin Jay *lawyer*
Robinson, James D. III *venture capitalist*
Robinson, Janet L. *publishing executive*
Robinson, Marilynne *writer*
Robinson, Nate (Nathaniel Robinson) *professional basketball player*
Robinson, Peter M. *business association executive*
Robinson, Richard *publishing executive*
Robinson, Roxana Barry *writer, art historian*
Robock, Stefan Hyman *retired economics professor*
Rocchi, Robin Henning *financial and automotive company executive*
Roche, Gerard Raymond *management consultant*
Rockefeller, David *banker*
Rocklen, Kathy Hellenbrand *lawyer*
Rockwell, David *architectural firm executive*
Rodewald, Heidi *musician, composer*
Rodin, Judith Seitz *foundation administrator, former academic administrator*
Rodriguez, Narciso *fashion designer*
Rodriguez, Vincent Angel *lawyer, director*
Roe, Bonnie Jean *lawyer*
Roeder, Robert Gayle *biochemist, molecular biologist, educator*
Roehrs, Christopher Scott *lawyer*
Roemer, Michael E. *insurance company executive*
Roethenmund, Otto Emil *finance company and bank executive*
Rogan, Brian G. *bank executive*
Rogers, Theodore Courtney *investment company executive*
Rogers, Theodore Otto, Jr. *lawyer*
Rogin, Gilbert Leslie *editor, author*
Rogoff, Tamar *choreographer*
Rohatyn, Felix George *diversified financial services company executive, former ambassador*
Roi, Alice (Roy Blumenthal) *apparel designer*
Roker, Al *newscaster*
Roland, J. Thomas *surgeon, researcher*
Roldan, Kenneth Arroyo *executive recruiter, lawyer*
Rolfe, Ronald Stuart *lawyer*
Rollins, Sonny (Theodore Rollins) *composer, musician*
Romano, John Francis *dermatologist*
Romans, John Niebrugge *lawyer*
Rome, Todd M. *air transportation executive*
Romero, Anthony D. *legal association administrator*
Romero, Raul Enrique *literature and language professor*
Romita, Mauro Charles *plastic surgeon*
Ronson, Mark Daniel *recording industry executive, disc jockey*
Rooney, Paul C., Jr. *retired lawyer*
Roosevelt, Theodore, IV, *investment banker*
Root, Nina J. *librarian, writer*
Rosaldo, Renato Ignacio, Jr. *cultural anthropology educator*
Rosand, David *art historian, educator*
Rose, Charlie (Charles Peete Rose Jr.) *television journalist*
Rose, Eric Allen *cardiothoracic surgeon*
Rose, Joanna Semel *volunteer*
Rose, Robert Neal *investment banker*
Rosell, Kurt F. *lawyer*
Rosen, Aby Jacob *real estate developer*
Rosen, Andrew W. *apparel executive*
Rosen, Jeffrey J. *lawyer*
Rosen, Michael N. *lawyer*
Rosen, Richard Lewis *lawyer, real estate developer*
Rosenbaum, Joan Hannah *museum director*
Rosenbaum, Michael A. *pediatrician, educator*
Rosenberg, Alan David *accountant*
Rosenberg, Alan Stewart *lawyer*
Rosenberg, Alex Jacob *art appraiser and dealer, educator*
Rosenberg, Marc Steven *lawyer*
Rosenberg, Robert Charles *housing corporation executive*
Rosenblatt, Lief Dov *hedge fund manager*
Rosenbloom, Daniel *investment advisor, lawyer*
Rosenblum, Jay Alan *neurologist*
Rosenblum, Scott S. *lawyer*
Rosenfeld, Isadore *cardiologist, educator*
Rosenfeld, Steven B. *lawyer*
Rosenfeld, Suzanne *pediatrician*
Rosenker, Mark Victor *former federal agency administrator*
Rosensaft, Menachem Zwi *lawyer, writer, foundation administrator*
Rosenshine, Allen Gilbert *retired advertising agency executive*
Rosenthal, Andrew Mark *newspaper editor*
Rosenthal, Howard Lewis *political science professor*
Rosenthal, Jacob (Jack Rosenthal) *foundation executive*
Rosenthal, Jane L. *film company executive*
Rosenthal, Larry W. *cosmetic dentist*
Rosenthal, Shirley Lord *cosmetics magazine executive, novelist*
Rosenzweig, Charles Leonard *lawyer*
Roskin, William A. *communications executive*
Rosner, Ingrid K. *pediatric allergist*
Rosput Reynolds, Paula Gail *insurance company executive*
Ross, Alex *music critic*
Ross, Barry C. *lawyer*
Ross, Brian Elliott *chief investigative correspondent*
Ross, Carne *international relations specialist, former diplomat*
Ross, Christopher Wade Stelyan *diplomat*
Ross, Diana *singer, actress, entertainer, fashion designer*
Ross, Jerrold *music educator*
Ross, Joseph Solomon *physician investigator*
Ross, Matthew *lawyer*
Ross, Norman Alan *publisher*
Ross, Stephen Michael *real estate company executive, professional sports team owner*
Ross, Wilbur Louis, Jr. *investment banker*
Rossen, Jordan *lawyer*
Rosset, Barnet Lee, Jr. *publishing executive*
Roth, Daryl *theater producer*
Roth, Kenneth *human rights advocate*
Roth, Michael I. *marketing executive*
Roth, Sol *rabbi*
Roth, Steven *real estate company executive*
Rothberg, Gerald *editor, publishing executive*
Rothberg, Glenda Fay Morris *lawyer*
Rothe, Desider J. *gynecologist-obstetrician*
Rothenberg, Jerome *writer, literature educator*
Rothenberg, Laraine S. *lawyer*
Rothenberg, Robert Philip *public relations counselor*
Rothfeld, Michael B. *theatrical producer, investor*
Rothman, David J. *historian, educator*
Rothman, Esther Pomeranz *social services administrator, psychologist*
Rothman, Henry Isaac *lawyer*
Rothschild, Amalie Randolph *filmmaker, producer, director, photographer*
Rothschild, Michael Alan *pediatric otolaryngologist, educator*
Rothwell, Timothy *pharmaceutical executive*
Roubini, Nouriel *economics professor*
Rouse, Christopher Chapman III *composer, educator*
Roven, Robert Bochner *cardiologist, educator*
Rover, Edward Frank *foundation administrator, lawyer*
Rovine, Arthur William *international arbitrator*
Rowen, Andrew S. *lawyer*
Rowland, Esther E(delman) *retired dean*
Rowland, Lewis Phillip *neurology educator, editor, clinical investigator*
Rowley, Cynthia *apparel designer*
Roy, Rachel *fashion designer*
Roye, David P., Jr. *pediatric orthopaedic surgeon*
Rozbruch, S. Robert *orthopedist, researcher*
Rozen, Jerome George, Jr. *entomologist, curator, professor, researcher*
Rozenberg, Lana *cosmetic dentist*
Rozencvaig, Perla *language educator*
Roznovschi, Mirela *law librarian, writer*
Ruben, Lawrence *real estate developer and company executive, lawyer*
Rubenstein, Howard Joseph *public relations executive*
Rubenstein, Joshua Seth *lawyer*
Rubenstein, Leonard *engineering company executive*
Rubin, Harry Meyer *software industry executive*
Rubin, Herbert *lawyer*
Rubin, Joel Edward *theatre consulting executive*
Rubin, Marilyn Marks *economics professor*
Rubin, Robert Samuel *investment banker*
Rubin, Theodore Isaac *psychiatrist, writer*
Rubinfien, Leo H. *photographer, writer*
Rubinstein, Aaron *lawyer*
Rubinstein, Javier H. *lawyer*
Rubinstein, Peter J. *rabbi*
Ruch, Barbara *Japanese literature and culture educator emerita*
Rucker, Kim K.W. *lawyer, cosmetics executive*
Rude, Eric John *public health service officer, researcher*
Rudel, Julius *conductor*
Rudenstine, David *law educator, former dean*
Rudenstine, Neil Leon *former academic administrator, educator*
Ruder, William *public relations executive*
Rudin, Scott *film and theatre producer*
Rudloff, Udo *surgeon, researcher*
Rudoff, Sheldon *lawyer*
Rudy, Bernardo *research scientist*
Rufeh, Mark *diversified financial services company executive*
Ruggiero, David Armand *neuroscientist*
Ruhanen, Troy *advertising agency executive*
Rumaker, Michael *writer, language educator*
Rupp, George Erik *international relief organization executive*
Rusch, Valerie Williams *thoracic surgeon*
Rusch, William Graham *religious organization administrator*
Ruscha, Edward *artist*
Rusmisel, Stephen Raymond *lawyer*
Russell, Stefanie Luise *dental educator*
Russo, Thomas Anthony *lawyer, former investment company executive*
Russotto, Paul *artist, educator*
Ruta, Thomas V. *professional sports team and accounting executive*
Rutcofsky, Barry *computer game company executive, lawyer*
Rutenberg, Michael Elliot *theater educator*
Rutkowski, Lawrence *lawyer*
Ruzal-Shapiro, Carrie B. *pediatric radiologist, educator*
Ryan, Lisa *lawyer*
Ryan, Regina Claire (Mrs. Paul Deutschman) *editor, literary agent*
Ryan, T. Timothy (Thomas Timothy Ryan Jr.) *securities industry association executive*
Sabel, Bradley Kent *lawyer*
Sacco, Ralph Lewis *neurologist*
Sachar, David Bernard *gastroenterologist, educator*
Sachar, Louis *writer*
Sachs, Jeffrey David *economist, educator*
Sack, Brian P. *bank executive, economist*
Sack, Robert David *federal judge, educator*
Sacks, Oliver Wolf *neurologist, writer*
Sadegh, Ali M. *mechanical engineering educator, researcher, consultant*
Sadick, Neil Scott *dermatologist*
Sadik-Khan, Janette I. *city manager, former federal agency administrator*
Sadove, Stephen Irving *retail executive*
Saeed, Faiza J. *lawyer*
Safra, Joseph *bank executive*
Saft, Stuart Mark *lawyer*
St. Germain, Jean Mary *medical physicist*
St. Martin, Charlotte *trade association administrator*
Salembier, Valerie Birnbaum *publishing executive*
Salgo, Peter Lloyd *internist, writer, anesthesiologist, journalist, commentator*
Salinger, J.D. (Jerome David Salinger) *author*
Salky, Barry A. *surgeon*
Salmans, Charles Gardiner *banker*
Salonen, Esa-Pekka *conductor, music director*
Salter, James *writer*
Salter, Mary Jo *poet*
Salvati, Edwardo A. *surgeon*
Salvatore, Diane J. *publishing executive*
Salzberg, Barry F. *accounting firm executive*
Salzer, James *biology professor*
Sampras, Pete *retired professional tennis player*
Sampson, Hugh Albert, Jr. *medical educator*
Sams, Jeremy *theater director, composer*
Samson, C. Michael A. *ophthalmologist*
Samuel, Selesnick H. *otolaryngologist, educator*
Samuels, Dorothy J. *journalist, writer*
Samuels, Leslie B. *lawyer*
Samuelsson, Marcus (Kasshun Tsegie) *food service executive*
Sanchez, Angel *apparel designer*
Sanders, Gina Susan *publishing executive*
Sandford, John (John Roswell Camp) *writer, journalist*
Sandler, Irving Harry *art critic, art historian*
Sandler, Lucy Freeman *art history educator*
Sanocki, Edward John, Jr. *lawyer*
Sanseverino, Raymond Anthony *lawyer*
Sansone, Guy *restructuring company executive*
Santelli, Rick *news correspondent, former financial executive*
Sanzone, Thomas J. *diversified financial services company executive*
Saphir, Richard Louis *pediatrician*
Sarachik, Myriam Paula Morgenstein *condensed matter physicist, educator*
Sarandon, Susan *actress*
Sareyan, Andy *publishing executive*
Sargent, Pamela *writer*
Sarkozy, Olivier (Pierre Olivier Sarkozy) *investment banker*
Sarnelle, Joseph R. *publishing executive*
Sarnoff, Ann M. *publishing executive, former sports association executive*
Sarnoff, Deborah Susan *dermatologist, educator*
Sarnoff, Richard *digital publishing executive*
Sasman, Irene Deak Handberg *publishing executive*
Sather, Glen Cameron *professional sports team executive, former professional hockey coach and player*
Satine, Barry Roy *lawyer*
Satlin, Lisa M. *pediatrician, educator*
Saul, Andrew M. *investment company executive*
Saul, Peter A. *artist, educator*
Saunders, Paul Christopher *lawyer*
Savage, Charles *reporter, news correspondent*
Savas, Emanuel S. *management educator, public official*
Savitz, David A. *epidemiologist*
Savran, David *theater educator*
Savrin, Louis *lawyer*
Sawers, Sir John *ambassador*
Sawyer, Diane *newscaster, journalist*
Sawyer, Linda *advertising executive*
Sawyers, Charles L. *oncologist, hematologist, educator*
Saxena, Brij B. *endocrinologist, biochemist, educator*
Scarborough, Chuck (Charles Bishop Scarborough III) *newscaster*
Scarborough, Joe (Charles Joseph Scarborough) *newscaster, former United States Representative from Florida*
Scarpelli, Bob (Robert) *advertising executive*
Sceusa, Nicholas A. *pharmacologist*
Schaab, Arnold J. *lawyer*
Schachter, Edwin Neil *pulmonologist, educator*
Schafer, Andrew I. *hematologist, department chairman*
Schafer, Charles J. *communications systems company executive*
Schaffer, Julie V. *pediatric dermatologist, researcher*
Schaffer, Seth Andrew *lawyer*
Schaffner, Bertram Henry *psychiatrist*
Schall, Ellen *dean, political science professor*
Schallert, Edwin Glenn *lawyer*
Schamus, James Allan *film producer and company executive, screenwriter*
Schapiro, Donald *lawyer*
Schapiro, Miriam *artist*
Scharf, Charles W. *diversified financial services company executive*
Schatz, Gary Stewart *marketing professional*
Schechner, Richard *theater director, educator*
Scheeder, Louis *theater producer, director, educator*
Scheiman, Eugene R. *lawyer*
Scheindlin, Raymond Paul *professor Hebrew literature*
Scheler, Brad Eric *lawyer*
Schell, J. Michael *metal products executive, lawyer*
Schenck, Will *publishing executive*
Schenk, Thomas *photographer*
Schenker, Gregg L. *real estate company executive*
Scher, Peter Lawrence *diversified financial services company executive, lawyer*
Scherre, Clare R. *diversified financial services company executive*
Schiano, Thomas Dominic *hepatologist, director*
Schick, Harry Leon *investment company executive*
Schick, Thomas *diversified financial services company executive*
Schiesel, Seth *reporter*
Schiff, David Tevele *investment banker*
Schiff, Howard Irwin *urologist*
Schiff, Nicholas D. *neurologist*
Schiffer, Stephen *philosopher, educator*
Schiffman, Daniel *lawyer, arts advocate*
Schirokauer, Conrad *history professor*
Schisgal, Murray *playwright*
Schizer, David Michael *dean, law educator*
Schizer, Zevie Baruch *lawyer*
Schlegel, Peter Niles *urologist, educator*
Schler, Michael Lawrence *lawyer*
Schlesinger, Sanford Joel *lawyer*
Schlesinger, Sarah Jane *medical educator, researcher*
Schlesinger, Stephen Cannon *foreign policy consultant*
Schley, William Shain *otolaryngologist*
Schlosser, Herbert S. *broadcasting company executive*
Schlosstein, Ralph L. *investment company executive*
Schmertz, Eric Joseph *lawyer, educator, commissioner*
Schmertz, Mildred Floyd *editor-in-chief, writer*
Schmidt, Benno Charles, Jr. *lawyer*
Schmidt, Joseph W. *lawyer*
Schmidt, William E. *editor*
Schmidt-Holtz, Rolf *music company executive*
Schmit, Timothy Bruce *musician*
Schmolka, Leo Louis *law educator*
Schnabel, Julian *artist, film director*
Schneider, David C. *bank executive*
Schneider, JoAnne *artist*
Schneider, Martin Aaron *photojournalist, ecologist, engineer, writer, artist, television director, filmmaker, public advocate, medical researcher, educator*
Schneider, Willys Hope *lawyer*
Schneiderman, Irwin *lawyer*
Schneier, Marc *rabbi*

Schnur, Jonathan *educational association administrator*
Schoenfeld, Jim *professional sports team executive, professional hockey coach*
Schoenhut, Frederick W. *stock exchange executive*
Schofield, Lorna Gail *lawyer*
Schonfeld, Irvin Sam *psychologist, educator*
Schoonmaker, Frances G. *education educator*
Schorer, Suki *ballet teacher*
Schotter, Andrew Roye *economics professor, consultant*
Schrade, Robert Warren *classical pianist, educator*
Schrager, Ian *hotel executive*
Schreiber, Brian T. *insurance company executive*
Schreiber, Pablo *actor*
Schreyer, Leslie John *lawyer*
Schroeder, Alice Davey *diversified financial services company executive, writer*
Schueller, Thomas George *lawyer*
Schueneman, Diane L. *diversified financial services company executive*
Schulhof, Michael Peter *electronics company executive*
Schulhofer, Stephen Joseph *law educator*
Schulhoff, Karen L. *information specialist*
Schulman, Amy Weinfeld *pharmaceutical company executive, lawyer*
Schulman, Dennis *clinical psychologist*
Schultz, Philip *poet*
Schulzrinne, Henning G. *computer science educator*
Schumacher, Harry Richard *lawyer*
Schumacher, Robert Denison *banker*
Schuman, Patricia Glass *publishing company executive, educator*
Schupak, Donald *merchant banker, lawyer, strategic planner*
Schupak, Leslie Allen *public relations company executive*
Schuster, Carlotta Lief *psychiatrist*
Schutte, Drew *publishing executive*
Schwab, Frank, Jr. *management consultant*
Schwab, George David *social sciences educator, writer*
Schwab, Harold Lee *lawyer*
Schwartz, Alan David *diversified financial services company executive*
Schwartz, Alan Victor *advertising executive*
Schwartz, Allan *cardiologist*
Schwartz, Anna Jacobson *economist*
Schwartz, Barry Fredric *lawyer, diversified holding company executive*
Schwartz, Bart *lawyer*
Schwartz, Gil (Stanley Bing) *broadcast executive, writer*
Schwartz, Herbert Frederick *lawyer*
Schwartz, Jordan M. *lawyer*
Schwartz, Marvin *lawyer*
Schwartz, Mischa *electrical engineering educator*
Schwartz, Renee Gerstler *lawyer*
Schwartz, Robert *finance educator*
Schwartz, Theodore H. *neurosurgeon*
Schwartz, Wallace L. *lawyer*
Schwartz, William *lawyer, educator*
Schwarz, David *retail executive*
Schwarz, Frederick A.O., Jr. *lawyer*
Schwarzkopf, Norman (Herbert Norman Schwarzkopf Jr.) *retired military officer*
Schwarzman, Stephen Allen (Steve Schwarzman) *private equity firm executive*
Sciame, Frank J. *real estate developer, construction executive*
Scieszka, Jon *children's author*
Sciutto, Jim *news correspondent*
Sclafani, Anthony Paul *plastic surgeon, educator, biomedical researcher*
Sclafani, Lisa *surgeon, educator*
Scofidio, Ricardo *artist, architect, educator*
Scott, Margaret Simon *retired mortgage broker*
Scott, Stanley DeForest *real estate company executive*
Scott, Susan Craig *plastic surgeon*
Scott, William Clement III *investor*
Scribner, Charles III *art historian, writer*
Sculco, Thomas Peter *surgeon*
Sealey-Laragh, Jean E. *emeritus medical educator, researcher*
Seaman, Alfred Jarvis *retired advertising agency executive*
Seary, Lawrence Anthony *cinematographer, television producer*
Secunda, Eugene *marketing professional, educator*
Sedaris, David Raymond *writer, comedian*
Seder, Sam (Samuel Lincoln Seder) *radio personality, comedian, writer*
Seeger, Pete *folk singer, songwriter*
Seelig, Jill *publishing executive*
Seely, Robert Daniel *cardiologist, medical association administrator*
Segal, Lore *writer*
Segal, Martin Eli *retired actuarial and consulting company executive*
Segal, Sheldon Jerome *biologist, educator, foundation administrator*
Seibel, Cathy *federal judge*
Seidelman, Susan *film director*
Seiden, Steven Arnold *executive search consultant*
Seidenberg, Ivan G. *telecommunications industry executive*
Seidler, Alan *composer, musician, music company executive*
Seidler, B(ernard) Alan *lawyer*
Seife, Charles *communications educator*
Seifert, Thomas Lloyd *lawyer*
Seiff, Eric A. *lawyer*
Seigel, Jerrold Edward *historian, writer*
Seigel, Stuart Evan *lawyer*
Selby, Cecily Cannan *dean, science educator*
Seldes, Marian *actress*
Selig, Bud (Alan Huber Selig) *Major League Baseball commissioner*
Selig, Karl-Ludwig *literature and language professor*
Seller, Jeffrey *theatre producer*
Sellers, Peter Hoadley *mathematician, educator*
Selver, Paul Darryl *lawyer*
Selznick, Brian *illustrator, writer*
Semple, Robert Baylor, Jr. *editor, journalist*
Sen, Kaustav *finance educator, consultant*
Sendax, Victor Irven *dentist, educator, dental implant researcher*
Sender, Adam D. *investment company executive, art collector*
Senor, Daniel Samuel *investment company and think-tank executive*
Senzel, Martin Lee *lawyer*
Serbaroli, Francis J. *lawyer, educator, writer*
Serchuk, Ivan *lawyer*
Serebrier, José *musician, composer, conductor*
Serota, James Ian *lawyer*
Serota, Susan Perlstadt *lawyer, educator*
Serra, Matthew D. *consumer products company executive*
Serra, Richard *sculptor*
Serulle, Yafell *medical researcher*
Serwer, Andy (Andrew E. Serwer) *editor, journalist*
Setrakian, Berge *lawyer*
Seward, George Chester *lawyer*
Sexton, John Edward *academic administrator, law educator*
Seymour, Everett Hedden, Jr. *lawyer*
Seymour, Karen Patton *lawyer, former prosecutor*
Seymour, Lesley Jane *editor-in-chief*
Shaffer Solovay, Susan *investment company executive*
Shafir, Robert S. *finance company executive*
Shah, Jatin Premanand *head and neck surgeon, educator*
Shah, Shamir *architect*
Shah, Vivek R. *publishing executive*
Shahn, Ezra *science educator*
Shain, Harold I. *publishing executive*
Shainwald, Sybil *lawyer*
Shankel, Lynne *conductor, composer*
Shannon, Careen Brett *lawyer, educator, writer*
Shannon, Kathleen E. *insurance company executive*
Shao, Qiuxia *literature and language professor*
Shapiro, Gary Evan *newspaper journalist*
Shapiro, Isaac *lawyer*
Shapiro, Louis A. *hospital administrator*
Shapiro, Mark S. *theme park company executive*
Shapiro, Marvin Lincoln *communications company executive*
Shapiro, Meryl *lawyer*
Shapiro, Michael *lawyer*
Shapiro, Neal *broadcast executive, television producer*
Shapiro, Robert Frank *investment company executive*
Shapiro, Steven R. *legal association administrator*
Shapiro, Theodore *psychiatrist, educator*
Shapley, Robert Martin *neurophysiology and perception educator*
Shargel, Gerald L. *lawyer*
Sharify, Nasser *librarian, educator, writer*
Sharkey, Catherine Moira *law educator*
Sharma, Deepak *bank executive*
Sharma, Deven *financial information company executive*
Sharma, Gaurav *finance company executive*
Sharma, Samin Kumar *internist, interventional cardiologist, educator*
Sharma, Vanshdeep *psychiatrist*
Sharp, J(ames) Franklin *finance educator, portfolio manager*
Sharpton, Al (Alfred Charles Sharpton Jr.) *minister, political activist, radio talk show host*
Shatter, Susan Louise *artist, museum administrator, educator*
Shattuck, Scott Harlan *performing company executive*
Shaw, David Elliot *computer scientist, hedge fund manager*
Shaw, L. Edward, Jr. *investment company executive, lawyer*
Shaw, Steven A. *information technology executive*
Shawn, Wallace *playwright, actor*
Shea, Edward Emmett *lawyer, educator, writer*
Shea, Martin M. *broadcast executive*
Shecter, Howard Lee *lawyer*
Shedlin, Gary Stephen *investment banker*
Sheehan, Michael Andrew *former protective services official, former federal agency administrator*
Sheehan, Robert C. *lawyer*
Sheehan, Susan *writer*
Sheekey, Kevin J. *city official*
Sheldon, Eleanor Harriet Bernert *sociologist, writer*
Shell, (Peterson) Juanita *psychologist, educator*
Shelley, Carole *actress*
Shen, Michael *lawyer*
Shen, Wei *performing company executive, choreographer*
Shenkman, Mark Ronald *investment and finance executive*
Shepard, Robert M. *lawyer, investment banker, engineer*
Shepard, Stephen Benjamin *journalist, educator, retired editor*
Shepard, Thomas Rockwell III *advertising executive*
Shepherd, Gillian Mary *physician*
Sheresky, Norman M. *lawyer*
Sherman, Arthur *theater educator, writer, actor, composer, sculptor*
Sherman, Eugene Jay *retired marketing professional, bank executive, economist*
Sherman, John Eric *plastic surgeon*
Sherman, Spencer E. *ophthalmologist*
Sherrod, Philip Lawrence *artist, composer, painter, poet*
Sherry, Lee Francis *literature and language professor*
Shick, Vicky *dancer, choreographer*
Shientag, Florence Perlow *lawyer*
Shier, Shelley M. *production company executive*
Shinder, Marcella Marie *marketing executive*
Shinkle, John Thomas *lawyer*
Shinnar, Reuel *engineering educator, consultant*
Shipley, Walter Vincent *retired bank executive*
Shires, Linda M. *English educator, writer*
Shmailo, Larissa *poet, director*
Shnayerson, Robert Beahan *editor, consultant*
Shohet, Zion *bank executive*
Shoket, Ann E. *editor-in-chief*
Shorter, James Russell, Jr. *lawyer*
Shortz, Will *puzzle editor*
Shoss, Cynthia Renée *lawyer*
Shreve, Anita *writer*
Shrum, Robert Matthew (Bob Shrum) *political strategist, educator, journalist*
Shulevitz, Uri *writer, illustrator*
Shuman, Earl Stanley *songwriter, music publisher*
Shupack, Jerome Leonard *dermatologist, educator*
Shutran, Richard *lawyer*
Shvo, Michael *real estate broker*
Shyer, John D. *lawyer*
Sibley, Jessica *publishing executive*
Sica, Frank Vincent *investment company executive*
Sicherer, Scott H. *pediatric allergist, researcher*
Sidamon-Eristoff, Anne Phipps *not-for-profit developer*
Sidamon-Eristoff, Constantine *lawyer*
Sidran, Miriam *retired physicist*
Siebert, John Weston *plastic surgeon*
Siebert, Muriel (Mickie) *brokerage house executive, retired bank executive*
Siegel, Edward M. *lawyer*
Siegel, Herbert Jay *communications executive, director*
Siegel, Jeffrey Norton *lawyer*
Siegel, Lucy Boswell *public relations executive*
Siegel, Marvin *newspaper editor*
Siegel, Randy *publishing executive*
Siegel, Stanley *lawyer, educator*
Siewert, Jake (Richard L. Siewert Jr.) *communications executive, former White House press secretary*
Siffert, John Sand *lawyer, educator, writer*
Sifton, Sam *editor*
Sigal, Elliott C. *pharmaceutical executive*
Sigal, Samuel Harold *gastroenterologist*
Sigal-Ibsen, Rose *artist*
Sigety, Cornelius Edward *real estate developer, director*
Siklos, Richard *reporter*
Silberberg, Richard Howard *lawyer*
Silberman, John Alan *lawyer*
Silbersack, John Walter *literary agent*
Silkenat, James Robert *lawyer*
Siller, Keith A. *neurologist, psychiatrist*
Siller, Stephen I. *lawyer*
Silva, Daniel Joseph *writer*
Silver, Adam *sports association executive*
Silver, Joan Micklin *film director, screenwriter*
Silver, Morris *economist, educator*
Silver, Nate *statistician, writer*
Silver, Richard Tobias *oncologist, educator, hematologist*
Silver, Sheldon *state legislator*
Silverberg, Michael Joel *lawyer*
Silverman, Al *editor*
Silverman, Allison *television producer, scriptwriter*
Silverman, Arthur Charles *lawyer*
Silverman, Eric F. *lawyer*
Silverman, Henry Richard *private equity firm executive*
Silverman, Moses *lawyer*
Silvers, Robert B. *editor*
Silvers, Sally *choreographer, performing company executive*
Silverstein, Larry A. *real estate developer*
Silverstein, Samuel Charles *cellular biology and physiology professor, researcher*
Silverstein, Scott A. *trading card company executive*
Simmons, John Derek *retired financial consultant*
Simmons, Joseph (Run Simmons, Rev Run) *musician*
Simmons, Peter Lawrence *lawyer*
Simmons, Sue *newscaster*
Simon, Eric Jacob *neuroscientist, educator*
Simon, Jacqueline Albert *political scientist, writer*
Simon, Ronald Charles *curator, educator*
Simone, Joseph R. *lawyer*
Simons, Albert III *lawyer*
Simpkins, Neil P. *investment and automotive company executive*
Simpson, Andrew J.G. *molecular biologist, researcher*
Simpson, Jessica Ann *singer, actress*
Sinclair, Daisy *communications executive*
Sinding, Steven William *political scientist*
Singer, Joy Daniels *journalist, consultant*
Singer, Niki *media consultant*
Singleton, Donald Edward *retired journalist*
Singleton, Ken *sportscaster, retired professional baseball player*
Sinsheimer, Warren Jack *lawyer*
Siraisi, Nancy Gillian *historian, writer, educator*
Sirkin, Michael S. *lawyer*
Sirlin, Alberto *physics professor*
Siskind, Arthur Michael *lawyer*
Siskind, Donald Henry *lawyer*
Sitarz, Anneliese Lotte *pediatrician, educator*
Sitomer, Sheila Marie *television producer and director*
Sittenfeld, Curtis *writer*
Sklyar, Adelina M. *lawyer*
Skolnik, Richard Alan *plastic surgeon*
Skyler, Edward Gabriel *city official*
Slacik, Claudia *bank executive*
Sladkus, Harvey Ira *lawyer*
Slavin, Rosanne Singer *textile converter*
Sleed, Joel *columnist*
Sleigh, Sylvia *artist, educator*
Slevin, Eileen T. *insurance company executive*
Sloan, Allan Herbert *journalist*
Sloan, Elaine Frank *librarian*
Sloane, Kathy *real estate broker*
Sloat, Richard Joel *artist*
Slomanson, Lloyd Howard *architect, musician, photographer*
Slone, Sandi *artist*
Slotnick, Barry Ivan *lawyer*
Sloujitel, Jacob Ben *mathematics professor, researcher*
Slusser, William Peter *investment banker*
Slutsky, Lorie A(nn) *foundation executive*
Small, George LeRoy *geographer, educator*
Small, Jonathan Andrew *lawyer, consultant*
Smigel, Irwin *dentist*
Smith, Barry Hamilton *foundation administrator, physician*
Smith, Brian D. *lawyer*
Smith, Carol A. *publishing executive*
Smith, Craig Richey *cardiothoracic surgeon*
Smith, Edward Paul, Jr. *lawyer*
Smith, Elizabeth A. (Liz Smith) *cosmetics company executive*
Smith, Gordon A. *diversified financial services company executive*
Smith, Hilary Cranwell Bowen *investment banker*
Smith, Ian K. *writer, columnist, physician*
Smith, Jason A. B. *lawyer*
Smith, Joseph Phelan *film company executive*
Smith, Kiki *artist*
Smith, Malcolm Bernard *investment company executive*
Smith, Malcolm Sommerville *bass vocalist*
Smith, Meredyth Hull *real estate broker*
Smith, Michael W. *physician, medical editor*
Smith, Patrick John *editor, writer*
Smith, Philip J. *performing arts organization administrator*
Smith, Phillips Guy *banker*
Smith, Raymond W. *investment banking executive*
Smith, Richard Mills (Rick) *former publishing executive*
Smith, Rick *foundation administrator*
Smith, Robert Everett *lawyer*
Smith, Robert Michael *sculptor, educator*
Smith, Shepard (David Shepard Smith Jr.) *newscaster*
Smith, Shirley *artist*
Smith, Warren Allen *writer, director, columnist*
Smoak, Evan L. *lawyer*
Smotrich, David Isadore *architect*
Smyth, Rich *publishing executive*
Snow, John William (Jack Snow) *investment company executive, former United States Secretary of the Treasury*
Snyder, Arlen Dean *actor*
Snyder, Jon David *dean*
Snyder, Leslie Crocker *lawyer*
Snyderman, Nancy *surgeon, journalist*
Sobbott, Susan *diversified financial services company executive*
Sobel, Howard D. *dermatologist*
Sochet, Mary Allen *psychotherapist, educator, writer*
Sockolow, Robbyn Ellen *pediatrician*
Softness, Barney *pediatrician, educator*
Softness, Donald Gabriel *marketing professional, manufacturing executive*
Sohm, Aldo *Sommelier*
Sohmer, Bernard *mathematics professor, administrator*
Solano, Henry L. *lawyer*
Solecki, R. Stefan *anthropologist, educator*
Solís, Marco Antonio *singer, composer*
Solomon, Andrew P. *lawyer*
Solomon, Howard *pharmaceutical executive*
Solomon, Terri Marcia *lawyer*
Solomonoff, Galia *architect*
Solomons, Gus, Jr., (Gustave Martinez) *choreographer, dancer, writer*
Solow, Sheldon H. *real estate developer*
Som, Peter M. *radiologist*
Son, Young K. *engineering educator*
Sonneman, Eve *artist*
Soocher, Stan *editor, lawyer*
Sorensen, Gillian Martin *United Nations official*
Sorensen, Ted (Theodore Chaikin Sorensen) *lawyer, former federal official*
Sorkin, David James *lawyer*
Sorkin, Ira Lee (Ike Sorkin) *lawyer*
Sorkin, Laurence Truman *lawyer*
Soros, George *hedge fund manager, entrepreneur, philanthropist*
Sorrenti, Mario *photographer*
Sorte, John Follett *investment firm executive*
Sorter, George Hans *accounting and law educator, consultant*
Sosnow, Lawrence Ira *health care company executive*
Soto, Claudio *medical educator*
Souham, Gérard *communications executive*
Soussloff, Andrew D. *lawyer*
Sovern, Michael Ira *law educator*
Soyer, David *cellist, music educator*
Spade, Kate (Katherine Noel Spade) *apparel designer*
Spar, Debora Lynn *academic administrator*
Sparkman, Robin Hamilton *editor*
Sparks, Nicholas *writer*
Spatafora, Marcello *ambassador*
Spatt, Robert Edward *lawyer*
Spear, Harvey M. *lawyer*
Spears, Britney *singer*
Spector, Jason A. *plastic surgeon, educator*
Spector, Nancy *curator*
Spelfogel, Evan J. *lawyer, educator*
Spellman Sweet, Julie T. *lawyer*
Spence, Sique (Mary Stewart Spence) *art dealer*
Spencer, Charles S. *anthropologist*
Spencer, Michael C. *lawyer*
Sperber, Alan B. *urologist*
Sperling, Gene B. *economist, former federal official*
Spero, Joan Edelman *foundation administrator*
Speyer, Jerry I. *real estate company executive*
Spielvogel, Sidney Meyer *retired investment banker*
Spier, Guy Selmar *investment advisor*
Spikol, Eileen *artist*
Spillane, Dennis Kevin *lawyer*
Spindler, James Andrew *not-for-profit executive*
Spinelli, Henry Michael *plastic surgeon*
Spinner, Marina A. *lawyer*
Springfield, Dempsey Stewart *physician, educator*
Sproule, Michael E. *insurance company executive*
Squeri, Stephen *diversified financial services company executive*
Squire, Walter Charles *lawyer*
Squires, John *publishing executive*
Srichai-Parsia, Monvadi Barbara *cardiologist, educator*

Srivastava, Rohit *real estate company executive, researcher*
Srulowitz, Marvin *lawyer*
Stacom, Darcy A. *real estate company executive*
Stacom, Tara Irene *real estate company executive*
Stade, George Gustav *humanities educator*
Stadler, Eva Maria *literature and language professor*
Stahl, Lesley Rene *news correspondent*
Stahl, Sandra Michelle *communications executive*
Stainrook, Harry Richard *photographer, retired bank executive*
Stakias, G. Michael *private equity*
Staley, Jes (James Edward Staley) *diversified financial services company executive*
Stanceu, Timothy Charles *federal judge*
Standard, Kenneth G. *lawyer*
Stang, Rolf Kristian *vocalist, educator, actor, advertising executive, writer*
Stanley, John Slusarski *art museum administrator*
Starer, Brian Douglas *lawyer*
Starr, Michael *lawyer*
Stecher, Esta E. *lawyer, investment company executive*
Steedman, Doria Lynne Silberberg *foundation administrator*
Steel, Danielle (Danielle Fernande Dominique Schuelein-Steel) *author*
Steel, George Robert *opera company director*
Steele, Claude Mason *academic administrator, psychology professor*
Steele, Mark A. *pediatric ophthalmologist*
Steglitz, Marc H. *museum administrator*
Steiger, Paul Ernest *editor-in-chief, journalist*
Stein, Alexander *psychoanalyst, consultant*
Stein, David Fred *investment company executive*
Stein, Elliot, Jr. *business executive*
Stein, Howard S. *retired banker*
Stein, Jared J. *theater director, educator*
Stein, Joel *physiatrist*
Stein, Marvin *psychiatrist, historian*
Stein, Richard Alan *cardiologist, educator*
Stein, Ronald J. *lawyer*
Stein, Stephen William *lawyer*
Steinberg, Arthur Jay *lawyer*
Steinberg, Debra Brown *lawyer*
Steinberg, Howard Eli *lawyer, diversified financial services company executive*
Steinberg, Jonathan S. *cardiologist, educator*
Steiner, Joshua Linder *private equity firm executive*
Steinglass, Peter Joseph *psychiatrist, educator*
Steinhardt, Michael H. *diversified financial services company executive*
Steinman, Ralph M. *medical educator*
Stelwagon, Jennifer Cooper *psychiatrist*
Stelzer, Paul *thoracic surgeon, educator*
Stengel, Richard *editor*
Stephenson, Alan Clements *lawyer*
Stephenson, Neal Town *writer*
Stepleton, James *composer*
Sterling, Robert Lee, Jr. *investment company executive*
Stern, David Joel *National Basketball Association commissioner*
Stern, Donald Allan *lawyer*
Stern, Fritz Richard *historian, educator*
Stern, Howard Allan *radio personality, television show host*
Stern, James Andrew *investment banker*
Stern, Jeffrey Ross *lawyer*
Stern, Leonard Norman *real estate developer, former pet supply manufacturing company executive*
Stern, Mitchell *broadcast executive*
Stern, Nathalie M. *pediatrician*
Stern, Robert Arthur Morton *architect, educator, writer*
Stern, Robert D. *publishing executive*
Stern, Roslyne Paige *magazine publisher*
Stern, Walter Phillips *investment company executive*
Stern, Yaakov *neuroscientist*
Sternman, Joel W. *lawyer*
Sterns, William S. III *lawyer*
Steuer, Richard Marc *lawyer*
Stevens, Rosemary Anne *medicine and public health historian, artist*
Steves, Gale C. *marketing professional, writer, editor-in-chief, publishing executive*
Stew, (Mark Stewart) *musician*
Stewart, E(dward) Nicholson *investment management executive*
Stewart, Ellen D. *theater producer*
Stewart, Geoffrey S. *lawyer*
Stewart, Jon (Jonathan Stewart Leibowitz) *television personality, comedian*
Stewart, Lynne F. *former lawyer*
Stiefel, Ethan *dancer, performing company executive, dean*
Stieg, Philip *neurosurgeon*
Stifelman, Michael D. *surgeon, director*
Stiglitz, Joseph Eugene *economics professor, former federal official*
Stillman, Charles Allen *lawyer*
Stimmel, Barry *cardiologist, internist, dean, educator*
Stimpson, Catharine Rosalind *literature educator, writer*
Stine, R. L. (Robert Lawrence Stine) *children's book author*
Sting, (Gordon Matthew Sumner) *musician, songwriter, actor*
Stock, Richard John *cardiologist*
Stolar, Charles J.H. *pediatrician, surgeon, educator*
Stoll, Neal Richard *lawyer*
Stoltzman, Richard Leslie *clarinetist*
Stone, Merrill Brent *lawyer*
Stone, Michael Howard *psychiatry educator*
Stoopler, Mark Benjamin *physician*
Storch, Arthur *theater director*
Stork, Gilbert *chemistry professor*
Störmer, Horst Ludwig *physicist, educator*
Stotsky, Adam *communications executive*
Stotzky, Guenther *microbiologist, educator*
Stoute, Stephen *marketing executive, entrepreneur*
Stover, Annette Birgit *advertising and public relations executive*
Strahan, Michael Anthony *sportscaster, retired professional football player*
Straka, Angeline C. *broadcast executive*
Straniere, Robert A. *lawyer, restaurant owner*
Straton, John Charles, Jr. *investment banker*
Stratton, John G. *telecommunications industry executive, marketing professional*
Straub, Chester John *federal judge*
Strauchen, James Arthur *medical educator, pathologist*
Strauss, Carolyn L. *former broadcast executive*
Strauss, Eric Jason *orthopedist*
Strauss, Peter L(ester) *law educator*
Strear, Joseph D. *public relations executive*
Streator, Edward *retired diplomat, management consultant*
Strianese, Michael T. *communications systems company executive*
Strickon, Harvey Alan *lawyer*
Stringer, Sir Howard *electronics company executive*
Stringer, Scott M. *city official, former state legislator*
Stroke, Hinko Henry *physicist, researcher*
Strom, Milton Gary *lawyer*
Stroman, Susan *choreographer, theater director*
Strome, Marshall *otolaryngologist, educator*
Strongwater, Allan *orthopedist, director*
Stroock, Mark Edwin, II, *public relations company executive*
Strout, Elizabeth *writer, educator*
Struve, Guy Miller *lawyer*
Stuart, Jill *apparel designer*
Stübgen, Joerg-Patrick *neurologist*
Stucky, Steven (Edward) *composer, conductor*
Studdard, (Christopher) Ruben *singer*
Studin, Jan *publishing executive*
Sturman, Deborah Muscha *attorney*
Sturtevant, Peter Mann, Jr. *television news executive*
Su, Edwin *orthopedist*
Sugihara, Kenzi *publishing executive*
Sui, Anna *fashion designer*
Sullivan, Andrew Michael *online journalist, editor, news blogger*
Sullivan, Dennis Joseph *bishop*
Sullivan, Hugh David *investment company executive*
Sullivan, Kathleen Marie *lawyer, educator*
Sullivan, Kenneth Wayne *engineer*
Sullivan, Martin J. *former insurance company executive*
Sullivan, Richard Joseph *federal judge*
Sultan, Mark R. *plastic surgeon*
Sulzberger, Arthur Ochs, Jr. *newspaper publisher*
Sunshine, Louise Mintz *real estate marketing executive*
Suskind, Ronald Steven *journalist, writer*
Susman, Sally S. *pharmaceutical executive, former cosmetics executive*
Sussman, Gerald *publishing company executive*
Sussman, Leonard Richard *foundation executive*
Sutton, Cece (Cecilia Stewart Sutton) *bank executive*
Sutton, Karen E. *museum director*
Suydam, John J. *lawyer*
Svenson, Charles Oscar *investment banker*
Swain, Laura Taylor *federal judge*
Swain, Robert *artist*
Swan, Philip George *librarian, educator, director, artist*
Sweed, Phyllis *publishing executive*
Swid, Stephen Claar *communications executive, director*
Swieca, Henry Alexander *hedge fund manager*
Swift, Ronnie Gorman *psychiatrist, educator*
Swig, Kent M. *real estate company executive*
Swistel, Daniel George *surgeon*
Sylla, Richard Eugene *economics professor*
Synnott, Aidan John *lawyer*
Sypher, Francis J. *writer, editor, educator*
Szalda, David Joseph *chemistry educator*
Szot, Paulo *baritone, singer, actor*
Szymanczyk, Michael E. *tobacco products executive*
Tabbal, Nicolas G. *plastic surgeon*
Taber, Kenneth W. *lawyer*
Tacopina, Joseph *lawyer*
Tagliaferri, Lee Gene *investment banker*
Taha, Assad M. *surgeon*
Tahari, Elie *fashion designer*
Tahbaz, Christopher K. *lawyer*
Tahir, Rabia *pharmacist, educator*
Takasu, Yukio *ambassador*
Takooshian, Harold *social psychology educator*
Talbot, Phillips *retired Asian affairs specialist*
Talese, Gay *writer, former journalist*
Tall, Alan R. *molecular biologist, educator*
Tallackson, Jeffrey Stephen *lawyer*
Talley, André Leon *editor-at-large*
Tallmer, Margot Sallop *psychologist, gerontologist, psychoanalyst*
Talmi, Yoav *conductor, composer*
Talmor, Mia *plastic surgeon*
Tamke, George William *venture capitalist*
Tan, Amy Ruth *writer*
Tan, Chin-Tuan *medical educator, engineering educator, consultant*
Tananbaum, Steven Andrew *investment consultant*
Tancredi, Laurence Richard *medical educator, psychiatrist*
Tanenbaum, Edward *lawyer*
Tanenbaum, William Alan *lawyer*
Tanenhaus, Sam *editor*
Tang, Terry *editor, lawyer*
Tangney, Michael J. *consumer products company executive*
Tannenbaum, Bernice Salpeter *national religious organization executive*
Tanner, Douglas Alan *lawyer*
Tanner, Harold *investment banker*
Tanner, Jonathan D. *educational association administrator*
Tanselle, George Thomas *language educator, foundation administrator*
Tapper, Jake *television journalist, news correspondent*
Taran, Leonardo *classicist, educator*
Tarde, Jerry (Gerard Tarde) *editor-in-chief*
Tarnoff, Jerome *lawyer*
Tarter, Fred Barry *advertising executive*
Tatum, Mark A. *sports association executive*
Taubman, Paul J. *diversified financial services company executive*
Tauke, Thomas Joseph *telecommunications company executive, former United States Representative from Iowa*
Taussig, Andrew Richard *investment banker*
Taylor, David J. *photographer*
Taylor, Diana Lancaster *investment company executive, former state official*
Taylor, Errol Bancroft *lawyer*
Taylor, Jean Ellen *mathematics professor, researcher*
Taylor, Jeffrey A. *lawyer, former prosecutor*
Taylor, John Read, Jr. *hedge fund manager*
Taylor, Lance Jerome *economics professor*
Taylor, Marilyn Jordan *architectural firm executive*
Taylor, Mildred D. *author*
Taylor, Paul B. *choreographer*
Taylor, Richard William *investment banker, portfolio manager*
Taylor, Terry R. *editor, educator*
Taymor, Julie *theater, film and opera director, designer*
Teague, Lettie *editor*
Tehrany, Armin M. *orthopedic surgeon, educator*
Teiman, Richard Barry *lawyer*
Teirstein, Alvin Stanley *physician*
Temkin, Ann *curator*
Tendler, David *investment company executive*
Tenenbaum, Ann G. *art association administrator*
Tenenbaum, Joseph *cardiologist*
Tenet, George John *investment company executive, former CIA director*
Tenke, Craig E. *neuroscientist, consultant*
Teplitzky, Jacky *real estate broker*
Tepper, Lynn Marsha *gerontologist, educator*
Terkelsen, Brian J. *entertainment marketing executive*
Terrell, J. Anthony *lawyer*
Terruso, Luigi Leonardo *artist, educator*
Terry, Frederick Arthur, Jr. *lawyer*
Testa, Michael Harold *lawyer*
Tetzeli, Rick *magazine editor*
Thal, Steven Henry *lawyer, consultant*
Thalacker, Arbie Robert *lawyer, director*
Thaler, David Solomon *research scientist, educator*
Thayer, Russell III *air transportation executive*
Thebner, Lisa Ilene *pediatrician*
Thoman, G. Richard *corporate financial executive*
Thomas, Brooks *publishing executive, director*
Thomas, Dorothy *indexing consultant, writer*
Thomas, Helen Amelia (Mrs. Douglas B. Cornell) *editor-in-chief, former White House correspondent*
Thomas, Jeremiah Lindsay III *lawyer*
Thomas, Roger Warren *lawyer*
Thompson, Donald Raymond *film producer, playwright*
Thompson, Fred Dalton *actor, former United States Senator from Tennessee*
Thompson, George Kennedy (Ken Thompson) *retired bank executive*
Thompson, Jewel Taylor *music educator*
Thompson, Lawrence Bigelow *lawyer*
Thompson, Paul Warwick *museum director*
Thompson, Timothy Lewis *lawyer*
Thompson, William Colridge, Jr., (Bill Thompson) *city official*
Thomson, Robert James *editor*
Thor, Brad *writer*
Thorne, Charles Hedges McKinstry *plastic surgeon*
Thorne, John Watson III *advertising and marketing executive*
Thorne, Nathan C. *investment company executive*
Thoyer, Judith Reinhardt *lawyer*
Threadgill, Henry *musician*
Thurm, David Aaron *publishing executive*
Tierney, James Edward *law educator, former state attorney general*
Tierno, Philip Mario, Jr. *microbiologist, educator, researcher*
Tiesi, Joseph A. *tobacco company executive*
Tighe, Mary Ann *real estate company executive*
Tilewick, Robert *lawyer*
Tillinghast, David Rollhaus *lawyer*
Tillman, Vickie A. *publishing executive, former financial information company executive*
Tilson, M(artin) David III *surgeon, scientist, educator*
Tilson Thomas, Michael *conductor, music director*
Timberlake, Justin Randall *singer*
Tipton, Jennifer *lighting designer*
Tisch, Andrew Herbert *diversified holding company executive*
Tisch, James Solomon *diversified holding company executive*
Tisch, Jonathan Mark *hotel company executive*
Tishman, Daniel R. *construction executive*
Tober, Barbara D. (Mrs. Donald Gibbs Tober) *editor*
Todd, Chuck (Charles David Todd) *news correspondent*
Todd, Ronald Gary *lawyer*
Tofel, Richard Jeffrey *non-profit publishing executive*
Toff, Nancy Ellen *book editor*
Tolbert, Bernard *sports association executive*
Tolchin, Joan Gubin *psychiatrist, educator*
Toledo, Isabel *apparel designer*
Toll, Barbara Elizabeth *art gallery director*
Tomasetti, Richard L. *structural engineer*
Tomashoff, Craig L. *magazine editor*
Tomkins, Calvin *writer*
Tomlinson, James Francis *retired news agency executive*
Tonchi, Stefano *editor*
Tong, Kaity *anchor*
Toobin, Jeffrey Ross *writer, legal analyst*
Tooker, George *painter, printmaker*
Toppeta, William John *insurance company executive, lawyer*
Toran-Allerand, C(laude) Dominique *neuroscientist, neurologist, educator*
Torreano, John Francis *painter, sculptor*
Torrenzano, Richard *public relations executive*
Tortolani, Anthony John *surgeon, educator*
Tortorella, John *professional hockey coach*
Tortorici, Peter *marketing executive*
Tosi, Laurence A. III *investment company executive*
Toulantis, Marie J. *former retail bookseller executive, consultant*
Toumey, Donald Joseph *lawyer*
Toussaint, Roger *labor union administrator*
Towbin, A. Robert *investment banker*
Townsend, Alair Ane *publishing executive*
Townsend, Chuck (Charles H. Townsend) *publishing executive*
Tozer, Elizabeth Farran *interior and floral designer*
Trabocchi, Fabio *chef*
Tracey, Dennis Henry III *lawyer*
Train, John *investment advisor, columnist*
Tramontine, John Orlando *retired lawyer*
Traverse, Lyn D. *not-for-profit fundraiser, communications executive*
Travis, Jeremy *academic administrator*
Travis, Tracey Thomas *retail executive*
Treadway, James Crispin Curran Corbett *lawyer, brokerage house executive, investor, federal official*
Treanor, William Michael *dean, law educator*
Treaster, Joseph B(land) *journalist*
Treitel, David Henry *aviation executive*
Trepper, Myron *lawyer*
Trestman, Robert Lee *psychiatrist, educator, administrator*
Trillin, Calvin *writer, journalist*
Trinkaus, John William *management educator*
Trotter, Lloyd G. *investment company executive, former diversified technology and services company executive*
Trujillo, Marc *painter*
Trujillo, Robert *musician*
Trump, Donald John *real estate developer*
Trump, Ivanka Marie *real estate company executive*
Tsao, Vivian J. *artist, educator*
Tscherny, George *graphics designer*
Tsividis, Yannis P. *electrical engineering educator*
Tsoucalas, Nicholas *federal judge*
Tuchman, Phyllis *critic*
Tuchmann, Eric P. *lawyer*
Tudor, Helen E. A. *materials engineer, consultant*
Tudryn, Joyce Marie *professional society administrator*
Tuft, Tom (Thomas Edwin Tuft) *investment banker*
Tuhrim, Stanley *physician, neurologist*
Tung, Ko-Yung *lawyer*
Turino, Gerard Michael *internist, educator*
Turitzin, John N. *entertainment company executive, lawyer*
Turk, Jon Branden *plastic surgeon*
Turley, James S. *corporate financial executive*
Turner, Alice Kennedy *editor*
Turner, Bracha *painter*
Turner, E. Deane *lawyer*
Turner, Kelli *diversified media and merchandising company executive*
Turner, Michael R. *energy executive*
Turner, Roger D. *lawyer*
Turo, Joann K. *psychoanalyst, psychotherapist, consultant*
Turro, Nicholas John *chemistry professor*
Turtil, Lawrence Charles *psychiatrist*
Tuschman, Bob *broadcast executive*
Tusiani, Joseph *foreign language educator, author*
Tusk, Bradley *communications specialist*
Tusk, Claude M. *lawyer*
Tuttle, Richard *artist*
Tutwiler, Margaret DeBardeleben *diversified financial services company executive, former stock exchange executive*
Twardus, Susan M. *artist, art gallery owner, display designer*
Tween, Douglas M. *lawyer, former prosecutor*
Tyner, McCoy (Alfred McCoy Sulaimon Saud Tyner) *jazz pianist, composer*
Tyson, Neil DeGrasse *astrophysicist, museum director*
Tzimas, Nicholas Achilles *orthopedic surgeon, educator*
Ubiñas, Luis Antonio *foundation president*
Uchitelle, Louis *journalist*
Ueberroth, Heidi J. *sports association executive*
Ulanoff, Lance *editor-in-chief*
Ule, Guy Maxwell, Jr. *stockbroker*
Ulrich, Lars *musician*
Umansky, Diane *editor*
Underberg, Mark Alan *lawyer*
Underhill, Paco *market research and consulting company executive, environmental psychologist*
Underwood, Joanna DeHaven *environmental services administrator*
Unger, David C. *journalist*
Unger, Peter Kenneth *philosophy educator*
Unger, Sydney Elliott *lawyer*
Unithan, Dolly *visual artist*
Unson, Cecilia G. *science educator, researcher*
Updike, Helen Hill *wealth manager*
Upright, Diane Warner *art dealer*
Upshaw, Dawn *soprano*
Uram, Gerald Robert *lawyer*
Urban, Amanda (Binky Urban) *literary agent*
Urban, Nina B.L. *psychiatrist, psychotherapist, researcher*
Uribe, Martin *economics professor*
Urowsky, Richard J. *lawyer*
Urroz-Rapold, Patricia Julia S. *retired diplomat, writer*
Vaccariello, Patrick *conductor*
Vachon, Christine *film producer*
Vachss, Andrew Henry *lawyer, writer, juvenile justice and child abuse consultant*
Valente, Peter Charles *lawyer*
Van Amstel, Louis *dancer*
van Ark, Bart (Hubertus Herman van Ark) *economist*
Vance, Cyrus Roberts, Jr. *lawyer*
Vanden Heuvel, Katrina *publishing executive, editor*
van der Klaauw, Wilbert H. *economics professor*
Van Nort, Sydney C. *school librarian, archivist*
Van Susteren, Greta Conway *newscaster, lawyer*
Varet, Michael A. *lawyer*
Vargas, Elizabeth *newscaster*

Zagat, Nina *publishing executive*
Zagat, Tim *publishing executive*
Zager, Steven Mark *lawyer*
Zagorin, Janet Susan *legal firm administrator, marketing professional*
Zahnd, Richard H. *sports association executive, lawyer*
Zaidi, Mone *endocrinologist, educator*
Zaitzeff, Roger Michael *lawyer*
Zakaria, Fareed Rafiq *editor, journalist*
Zalaznick, Lauren Jane *broadcast executive*
Zammit, Joseph Paul *lawyer*
Zand, Dale Ezra *business management educator*
Zannino, Richard F. *private equity firm executive, former publishing executive*
Zapata, Angel *pastor*
Zarb, Frank Gustave *private equity firm executive*
Zarghami, Cyma *broadcast executive*
Zarish, Janet Ann *art educator, director, actress*
Zaslow, Jeffrey Lloyd *journalist, columnist*
Zauderer, Mark Carl *lawyer*
Zawistowski, Stephen Louis *psychologist, educator*
Zedrosser, Joseph John *lawyer*
Zeichner, Joshua A. *dermatologist*
Zeleny, Milan *management systems scientist, economist*
Zelnick, Strauss *entertainment company executive*
Zenón, Miguel *musician*
Zeuschner, Erwin Arnold *brokerage house executive*
Zhuge, Jian *medical educator, researcher*
Ziegler, Richard Ferdinand *lawyer*
Zifchak, William C. *lawyer*
Zimand, Harvey Folks *lawyer*
Zimbalist, Michael *publishing executive*
Zimbler, Marc S. *plastic surgeon, director*
Zimmerman, Diane Leenheer *law educator*
Zimmerman, Elyn *artist*
Zimmerman, Kathleen Marie *artist*
Zimmett, Mark Paul *lawyer, educator*
Zinberg, David J. *lawyer*
Zinczenko, David *editor-in-chief*
Zinn, Keith Marshall *ophthalmologist, educator*
Zito, Robert John Amadeus *lawyer*
Zito, Robert Thomas *pharmaceutical executive*
Zitrin, Arthur *physician*
Zlateva, Gergana P. *pharmaceutical executive, director*
Zolla-Pazner, Susan *hospital administrator, biologist, biomedical researcher*
Zoogman, Nicholas Jay *lawyer*
Zorn, John *composer, musician*
Zornow, David Merrill *lawyer*
Zosike, Joanie Fritz *theater director, actress, writer*
Zoullas, Deborah Decotis *investment company executive*
Zubrow, Barry Lee *diversified financial services company executive*
Zucker-Franklin, Dorothea *internist, educator*
Zuckerman, Joseph D. *orthopedist, surgeon*
Zuckerman, Mortimer Benjamin *publishing executive, real estate developer*
Zuckerman, Paul Herbert *lawyer*
Zugazagoitia, Julian *museum director*
Zukerman, Michael *lawyer*
Zukerman, Pinchas *concert violinist, violist, conductor*
Zúñiga, Markos Moulitsas *political blogger, social activist*
Zunino, Natalia *psychologist*
Zweibel, Joel Burton *retired lawyer*

Newark
Biddle, Jane Lammert *retired English educator*

Newburgh
Adams, Barbara *literature and language professor, poet, writer*
Grossman, Stanley Lawrence *surgeon*
Joyce, Mary Ann *principal*
Sarro, Thomas John *biology professor*
Teutul, Paul John, Sr. *television personality, mechanic*

Newcomb
Chatzky, Herbert *music educator*

Niagara Falls
Askins, Arthur James *accountant, auditor*
Hawkins De Golier, Danielle *political activist*
Wos, Paul M. *music educator, infosystems specialist, educator*

Niagara University
Cowden Esq, Peter Alexander *education educator, consultant*
Melnik, Mikhail *economics professor*
Praetzel, Gary D. *dean*

Niskayuna
Arik, Mehmet *research and development company executive*
Asma, Evren *medical imaging researcher*
Happ, Harvey Heinz *electrical engineer, educator*
Huening, Walter Carl, Jr. *retired consulting application engineer*
Kostedt, William, IV, *engineer, researcher*
Laskaris, E(vangelos) Trifon *technologist, researcher*
Little, Mark M. *manufacturing executive*
Mangan, John Leo *retired electric power industry executive, international trade specialist*
Nichols, Albert Myron *retired minister*
Qu, Ronghai *electrical engineer*
Ruggiero, Eric John *mechanical engineer*
Sivasubramaniam, Kiruba Haran *engineer*
Srivastava, Alok M. *research scientist*
Suzuki, Akane *metallurgist*
Tangirala, Venkat E. *aerospace engineer, researcher*
Varanasi, Kripa Kiran *research scientist*
Wright, Theodore Paul, Jr. *political science professor*

North Babylon
Galligan, James *retired guidance counselor*

North Collins
Bowman, Georgianne *historian, reporter*

North Massapequa
Capone, Maryann *financial planner*

North White Plains
Erla, Karen *artist, painter, collagist, printmaker*

Northport
Adyanthaya, Rohit *ophthalmologist, researcher*
Allen, Marilyn Grace *school librarian*
Donenfeld, Kenneth Jay *investor relations consultant*
Graber, Mark L. *internist*
Hohenberger, Patricia Julie *fine arts and antique appraiser, consultant*
Lake-Bakaar, Gerond Vidal *gastroenterologist*
Reinertsen, Norman *retired air transportation executive*
Weaver, Eric James *educational administrator*

Norwood
Church, Richard Dwight *electrical engineer, scientist*

Nyack
Chien, Jennie *sculptor*
Cozart, Helen Ray *religious studies educator, educator*
Degenshein, Jan *architect, planner*
Flansburgh, John Conant *musician*
Hendin, David Bruce *literary agent, writer, numismatist, educator*
Karp, Peter Simon *marketing executive*
Linnell, John Sidney *musician*
Mann, Kenneth Walker *retired minister, psychologist*
Tirana, Bardyl Rifat *lawyer*
Widbin, Robert Bryan *theology studies educator*

Oakdale
Bertsch-Wells, Jane A. *theater educator*
Bouquet, Theresa F. *journalist, educator*
Jank, David A. *educator, researcher*
Miller, Rhoda *academic administrator*
Pope Robbins, Laura E. *librarian*
Sotelo-Dynega, Marlene *psychologist, professor*
Srinivasan, Raghavan *engineering educator*

Oakland Gardens
Costa, Philip Joseph *retired biology professor*
Lee, Duk Gyoo *civil engineer*
McGill, Georgia *theater educator, director*
Polak, Emil Joseph *history professor, researcher*

Oceanside
Zimmerman, Thomas Glenn *physician, educator*

Old Chatham
Severs, Charles A. III *lawyer*

Old Westbury
Boronico, Jess Stephen *management science educator, dean*
Dedkov, Eduard I. *medical educator*
Hegde, Narayan *language educator*
Hobson, Christopher Z. *literature and language professor*
O'Brien, Adrienne Gratia *communications educator*
Ostrander, Thomas William *retired investment banker*
Seelow, David D. *family therapist*
Watson, Denton L. *history professor*

Olean
Gates, Richard Wade *education educator*
McGovern-Scaturo, Diane Joan *psychotherapist*

Oneonta
Doughty, Amie A. *language educator*
Eluwawalage, Damayanthie *assistant professor, researcher, costume historian*
Freckelton, Sondra *artist*
Grimaldi, Richard Thomas, Jr. *meteorologist, educator*
Gruenhagen, Lisa M. *music educator*
Horner, Carl Matthew *chemistry professor*
Johnson, Richard David *retired librarian*
Larkin, F. Daniel *academic administrator, educator*
Malhotra, Ashok Kumar *philosophy educator*
Pietraface, William John *biology professor*

Ontario
Blackman, Lani Modica *copy editor*

Orangeburg
Basavarajappa, Balapal *medical researcher, educator*
DelliPizzi, AnnMarie *biology professor*
Dolgin, Ellen Ecker *English and gender studies professor*
Helpern, Joseph Alexander *biophysicist*
Levine, Jerome *psychiatrist, educator*
Nixon, Ralph Angus *psychiatrist, educator, research neuroscientist*
Rivet, Diana Wittmer *lawyer, farmer*
Yaragudri, Vinod K. *neuroscientist, researcher*

Orchard Park
Amborski, Leonard Edward *retired chemist*
Askew, Gloria Yarbrough *dietician*
Brandon, Russ *professional sports team executive*
Jauron, Dick (Richard M. Jauron) *professional football coach*
Lee, Richard Vaille *internist, educator*
Lynch, Marshawn Terrell *professional football player*
Owens, Terrell Eldorad *professional football player*
Santarpia, Susan Marie *psychologist*
Schobel, Aaron Ross *professional football player*
Sullivan, Mortimer Allen, Jr. *lawyer*
Urbanski, Jane F. *retired microbiologist*
Wilson, Ralph Cookerly, Jr. *professional football team executive*

Orient
Cochran, Judy Anne *psychiatric nurse practitioner*

Ossining
Dolmatch, Theodore Bieley *management consultant*
Galef, Sandra Risk *state legislator*
Gilbert, Joan Stulman *retired public relations executive*
Hall, H(erbert) Glen *lawyer*
Kelly, William Michael *investment company executive*
Maloney, William James *dentist, educator*
Robinson, Karen Vajda *dietician*
Sadan, Mark *photographer, film producer, artist*

Oswego
Bishop, Rand *retired humanities educator*
Davis, R. Deborah *education educator*
Fox, Michael David *retired art educator*
Friedman, Barry A. *social sciences educator*
Hockey, Christopher Lawrence *academic administrator*
Lewis, Tracy K. *Spanish language and Latin American studies educator, researcher in Guarani studies*
Macey, Kitty *costume designer, educator*
Malgieri, Lewis Joshua *psychologist, consultant*
Shore, Amy Elizabeth *performing arts educator, director*
Smiley, Marilynn Jean *musicologist*

Ovid
Scoles, Marie Y. *elementary school educator*

Owego
Zendle, Howard Mark *systems engineer*

Oyster Bay
Coates, Winslow Shelby, Jr. *lawyer*
Landrón, Ana *school psychologist*
Prey, Barbara Ernst *artist*
Schwab, Hermann Caspar *banker*
Smith, Pamela Rosevear *air transportation executive*
Walsh, Charles Richard *retired banker*

Ozone Park
Bellamy, Renee Adele *secondary school educator*
Joanidhi, Zhani *mathematician, educator*

Painted Post
Kirk, Connie Ann *writer*

Palisades
Broecker, Wallace S. *geophysicist, educator*
Burckle, Lloyd Henry *geologist, researcher*
Kellogg, Herbert Humphrey *metallurgist, educator*
Kent, Dennis V. *earth scientist, educator*
Lenton, Roberto Leonardo *environmental services administrator*
Purdy, G. Michael *observatory director*
Richards, Paul Granston *seismologist, geophysics educator*
Sanchez, Pedro Antonio *soil scientist, administrator*

Patchogue
Lombardo, Robin Ann *therapeutic recreation director, educator*
Marr, Robert Bruce *physicist, researcher*
McPherson, Sherry Lynn *social worker*

Pawling
Caplan, Ronald Mervyn *obstetrician, gynecologist*
Jones, James Earl *actor*
Lester, Helen Doughty *writer*

Pearl River
Bryant, Karen Worstell *financial advisor, investment company executive*
Kolb, Michael *chemist*
Meyer, Irwin Stephan *lawyer, accountant*
Riley, James Kevin *lawyer*
Skelly, Michael John *environmental engineer, consultant*
Verheijen, Jeroen Cunera *research scientist*

Peekskill
Black, Carolyn Rebecca *music educator*
Harte, Andrew Dennis *transportation company executive*
Lalor, Kieran *protective services official*

Pelham
Gaffney, Mark William *lawyer*
Hearle, Douglas Geoffrey *public relations consultant*
Tolliver, Lisa Marie *management consultant, educator*

Penfield
Chen, Alice W. *mycologist biomedical researcher*
Hamilton, Candis Lee *counselor*

Penn Yan
Mathewson, George Atterbury *retired lawyer*

Peru
Schwartz, Richard Frederick *electrical engineering educator*

Piermont
Berkon, Martin *artist*

Pittsford
Bernstein, Paul *retired academic dean*
Buzard, A. Vincent *lawyer*
Dunsky, Annie *artist*
Faloon, William Wassell *physician, educator*
French, Henry Pierson, Jr. *retired historian, educator*
Goldstein, David Arthur *biophysicist, educator*
Green, Martin Lincoln *retired medical products executive*
Hampson, Thomas Meredith *lawyer*
Herge, Henry Curtis, Jr. *information technology executive, consultant*
Hollingsworth, Jack Waring *mathematics professor*
Lever, O. William, Jr. *chemist*
Snyder, Donald Edward *finance company executive*
Sproull, Robert Lamb *retired academic administrator, physicist, director*
Steamer, Robert Julius *political science professor*
Stonehill, Eric *lawyer*
Thompson, Brian John *academic administrator, optics scientist, educator*
Turri, Joseph A. *lawyer*
Willett, Thomas Edward *lawyer*

Plainview
Kelemen, John *neurologist, educator*
Rich, Charles Anthony *hydrogeologist, consultant*
Sangesland, Odd Einar *mechanical engineer, consultant*
Snyder, Joel Bennett *engineering executive*
Stalzer, Frank Joseph *electronics company executive*

Plattsburgh
Bedworth, David Albert *health educator*
Bobbie, Gloria *anthropologist, educator*
Dawson, James Clifford *environmental science educator, geologist*
Jablonski, John E. *academic administrator, engineering educator*

Pleasant Valley
Becofsky, Arthur Luke *arts administrator, writer*
Ghedini, Gloria Maryann *language educator*
Marshall, Natalie Junemann *economics professor*
Vasti, Thomas Francis III *lawyer*

Pleasantville
Alston, Alyce C. *publishing executive, former diamond company executive*
Balaban, Anne *publishing executive*
Benton, Janetta Rebold *art historian, professor, writer*
Berner, Mary G. *publishing executive*
DeCaro, Shana *lawyer*
Dillon, Eva A. *publishing executive*
Eschweiler, Peter Quintus *planning consultant*
Grimes, Suzanne *publishing executive*
Kazakov, Sergey Victorovich *chemistry professor*
Knopf, Peter Martin *mathematics professor*
McCarty, Todd C. *publishing executive, former retail executive*
Meisel, Martin *retired English and comparative literature educator*
Mirakian-Escobar, Rachel Ann *language educator*
Northrop, Peggy *editor-in-chief*
Radin, Amy Janine *marketing executive, publishing executive*

Pocantico Hills
Humphrey, Jordan *theater producer*

Pomona
Haralick, Robert Martin *electrical engineering educator*

Port Chester
Ailloni-Charas, Dan *marketing executive*
Benoit, Mary *school librarian*
Rosenberg, William Mark *chef, restaurant owner*
Sayles, Eva *artist*

Port Jefferson
Ahmad, Arif *surgeon*
MacKinnon, Ann Laurie *retired elementary school educator*
Tovornik, Mary Rose *physical education educator*

Port Jefferson Station
Drucker, Matthew Douglas *secondary school educator*

Port Jervis
Healy, Julia Schmitt *artist, educator*
Martinez, Andres Manuel, Jr. *mathematics educator*

Port Washington
Andriola, Rocco F. *lawyer, diversified financial services company executive*
Candido, Arthur Aldo *publishing and distribution company executive*
Gordon-Tennant, Jennifer Jay *secondary school educator*
Jay, Frank Peter *retired writer, lexicographer, educator*
Leeds, Richard *computer marketing executive*
Rogatz, Peter *retired physician*
Roy, Ranja *mathematician, educator*
Rush, Curt Stefan *lawyer*
Ullman, Leo Solomon *lawyer*
van Schenkhof, Carol Dougherty (Carol Dovan) *soprano, educator*
Williams, George Leo *historian, retired secondary school educator, landmark director*

Potsdam
Andreescu, E. Silvana *chemistry professor*
Casper, Stephen Trevor *historian, educator*
Chin, Der-Tau *chemical engineer, educator*
Collins, Anthony G. (Tony Collins) *academic administrator*
Fanelli, Timothy C. *engineering educator, application developer*
Ha, Andrew Kwangho *education educator*
Hopke, Philip Karl *chemical engineering educator*
Islam, Muhammad Azadul *physicist, educator, researcher*
Kim, Eugene *education educator*
Krishnan, Sitaraman *engineering educator*
Matijevic, Egon *chemistry professor*
Qiu, Tong *engineering educator, consultant*
Rudiger, Lance Wade *secondary school educator*
Sazonov, Edward Stanislavovich *computer engineer, researcher*
Zanta, Carolyn A. *biology professor*

Poughkeepsie
Ardalan, Kavous *finance educator*
Bartlett, Lynn Conant *English literature educator*
Chu, Richard Chao-Fan *mechanical engineer*
Church, Jennifer *philosopher, educator*
Conklin, Donald David *academic administrator*
Coyne, Therese Anne *school librarian*
Daniels, Elizabeth Adams *English language educator*
Darrow, Emily M. *public relations executive, writer*
Deiters, Sister Joan Adele *psychoanalyst, nun, chemistry professor*
Dolan, Thomas Joseph *judge*
Glasse, John Howell *retired philosophy and theology educator*
Gregio, Marcus D. *literature and language professor*
Hansraj, Kenneth Karamchand *surgeon, research scientist*
Harmelink, Herman III *minister, writer, religious studies educator*
Hathaway, Richard Dean *retired language educator*
Heller, Mary Bernita *psychotherapist*
Hill, Catharine Bond (Cappy) *academic administrator, economics professor*
Johnson, M(aurice) Glen *political science professor*
Kim, David Sang Chul *publishing executive, evangelist, retired academic administrator*
Klingenberg, Beate *management educator, director*
Lang, William Warner *physicist*
Logue, Joseph Carl *electronics engineer, consultant*
Moore, Deborah Dash *religion educator*
Olsen, Barbara A. *literature and language professor, classicist, educator*
Opdycke, Leonard Emerson *retired literature and language educator, publishing executive, writer*
Padegs, Andris *electrical engineer, company executive*
Pisani, Michael Vincent *music educator*
Pohl, Michaela *historian, educator*
Qiu, Peipei *language educator*
Rosenblatt, Albert Martin *retired state appeals court judge*
Russell, Paul Elliott *literature and language professor*
Scileppi, John A. *psychologist, educator*
Sharp, Ronald Alan *language educator, writer, former dean*
Simons, Robert Edward *mechanical engineer, consultant*
Slade, Bernard Newton *electronics executive*
Stridsberg, Albert Borden (Paul Borden) *advertising consultant, editor, educator*
Tavárez, David Eduardo *anthropologist, educator*
VanBuren, Denise Doring *corporate communications executive*
Van Zanten, Frank Veldhuyzen *library director*
Vertullo, Christina A. *mathematics professor, director*
Willard, Nancy Margaret *writer, educator*
Wilson, Richard Edward *composer, music educator, pianist*

Pound Ridge
Darcy, Keith Thomas *finance company executive, educator, not-for-profit developer*

Preston Hollow
King, Steven *financial services consultant*

Purchase
Banga, Ajay *finance company executive*
Beraud, Jill *food products executive, marketing professional*
Black, Leon David *private equity firm executive*
Bodenrader, Andrew *academic administrator, educator*
Carey, Albert P. *retail sales professional*
Collins, Thom *museum director*
Compton, John C. *food products executive*
D'Amore, Massimo Fasanella *food products executive*
Ehrman, Lee *geneticist, educator*
Frost, Elizabeth Ann McArthur *physician*
Gioffre, Bruno Joseph *lawyer*
Goodman, Richard *food products executive*
Hanft, Noah Jonathan *lawyer*
Hartmann, Van Charles *literature and language professor*
Heuer, Alan J. *finance company executive*
Hilado, Tessa *beverage company executive*
Hund-Mejean, Martina *finance company executive*
Johnston, Hugh Francis *food products executive*
Joyce-Walter, Mary Ann *music educator, composer*
Kelly, Edmund Joseph *lawyer, investment banking executive*
Kelly, Joan *financial services company executive*
Kempczinski, Chris *marketing executive*
Magaziner, Elliot Albert *musician, conductor, educator*
Martin-Ruiz, Beatriz *music company executive*
Munro, Doug *musician, director*
Murdock, Wendy Jean *finance company executive*
Nooyi, Indra Krishnamurthy *food products executive*
Olstein, Robert A. *investment company executive*
Posner, Helaine J. *museum curator*
Rachlin, Harvey Brant *writer*
Schmitz, Robert Allen *executive, investor*
Schwarz, Thomas J. *academic administrator, lawyer*
Selander, Robert William *finance company executive*
Thompson, Larry Dean *lawyer, former federal agency administrator, food products executive*
Ughetta, James C. *lawyer*
Vardin, Patricia Anne *education educator*
Wachenheim, Edgar III *investment company executive*
Wallach, Kenneth L. *paper company executive*
West, Kazuko Ito *mathematics educator, department chair*
White, Michael Dennis *food products executive*

Queens
Ahmad, Dohra Khadija *psychology professor*
Comrie, Leroy G. *city councilman*
Gennaro, James F. *city councilman*
Gioia, Eric N. *city councilman, lawyer*
Liu, John C. *city councilman*
Sanders, James, Jr. *city councilman*
Sears, Helen *city councilwoman*
Vallone, Peter F. *city councilman, lawyer*
Weprin, David I. *city councilman, lawyer*

Queens Village
Megherian, Yefkin *sculptor*

Queensbury
De Pan, Harry McCarthy *retired surgeon*
Gallipeo, Paul *literature and language professor*
Mainwaring, Thomas Lloyd *transportation executive, director*

Quogue
Burkhardt, Ronald Robert *advertising executive, filmmaker, artist, writer*

Ravena
Coye, Mary P. *counselor*

Red Hook
Gudenzi-Ruess, Ida Carmen V. *music educator, artist*
Pastrana, Ronald Ray *theology studies educator, earth and space science educator, department chairman, psychotherapist, retired school system administrator*

Rego Park
Davidov, Ludmila G. *psychiatrist*
Lakah, Jacqueline Rabbat *political scientist, consultant*
Lowey, Nita Melnikoff *United States Representative from New York*
Robbins, Michael J. *cardiologist*

Remsenburg
Billman, Irwin Edward *publishing executive*

Rensselaer
Willis, John Patrick *chemist*

Rensselaerville
Fletcher, Raymond Russwald, Jr. *lawyer*

Rexford
Nitecki, Joseph Zbigniew *librarian*
Schmitt, Roland Walter *retired academic administrator*

Rhinebeck
Aarons, Jonas *arbitrator, mediator*
Crum, Albert B. *psychiatrist, consultant*
Ewald, Wendy Taylor *photographer, writer, educator*
Lesser, Elizabeth *not-for-profit organization administrator, writer*
Melley, Steven Michael *lawyer*
Sloane, Beverly LeBov *writer, instructor, consultant*

Richfield Springs
Walters, Marjorie Anne *interior designer, consultant*

Richmond Hill
Gintautas, Jonas *physician, scientist, administrator*
Posligua-Sinnott, Ketty *psychologist*

Ridge
Blume, Martin *physicist*

Riverdale
Glass, David Carter *psychologist, educator*
Klampfer, Lidija *medical educator*
Leylegian, John C. *engineering educator*
Silverman, Gordon *engineering educator*

Riverhead
Banfelder, Robert Joseph *award-winning novelist, lecturer and outdoors writer*
Orben, Jack Richard *investment company executive, director*
Pearson, John William *cardiologist*
Scherzer, Alfred L. *developmental pediatrician*

Rochester
Abu-Baker, Asim Mohammed *medical educator*
Adams, Carol H. *dean*
Adams, G. Rollie *museum executive*
Ader, Robert *psychology researcher*
Alling, Norman Larrabee *mathematics professor*
Ampadu, Paul *engineering educator*
Anderson, Kristin T. *educational association administrator, director*
Angerer, Lynne Musgrave *biologist, researcher*
Apostolakos, Michael John *medical educator, director*
Argetsinger, Gerald Scott *drama educator*
Aydelotte, Myrtle Kitchell *retired nursing administrator*
Bachison, Justine *customer service administrator*
Bajorski, Peter *statistician, educator*
Bannon, Anthony Leo *museum director*
Baumhaver, Judith Ford *surgeon*
Bennett, Kate *museum director*
Berman, Milton *history professor*
Berman, Robert L. *imaging company executive*
Bidlack, Jean Marie *pharmacologist, educator, researcher*
Black, Candace Regan *language educator*
Blanda-Holtzberg, Marianne Lourdes *education educator, consultant*
Bluhm, William Theodore *political scientist, educator*
Blumberg, Neil *hematologist, educator*
Boeckman, Robert Kenneth, Jr. *chemistry professor, researcher*
Bouyoucos, John Vinton *retired research and development company executive*
Bowen, William Henry *dental researcher, educator*
Braley, Oleta Pearl *community health nurse, writer*
Brody, Bernard B. *internist, educator*
Brooks, Bernard Peter *mathematics professor*
Buckley, Michael Francis *lawyer*
Burton, Richard Irving *orthopedist, educator*
Bushinsky, David Allen *nephrologist, educator, researcher*
Cain, Burton Edward *retired chemistry professor*
Campbell, Alma Jacqueline Porter *elementary school educator*
Carroll, Lorrie A. *psychologist*
Carstensen, Edwin Lorenz *retired biomedical engineer, biophysicist*
Caton, Scott Brenon *history professor*
Chen, Guangchun *medical researcher*
Chey, William Yoon *physician*
Chiarenza, Carl *art historian, critic, artist, educator*
Chiverton, Patricia Ann *nursing educator*
Cisney, Jennifer *photography and printing company executive, blogger*
Clark, Matthew Harvey *bishop*
Cohen, Ann Ellen *librarian*
Cohen, Jules *former dean, internist, educator*
Cohen, Nicholas *immunologist, educator*
Combs, Thomas *insurance company executive*
Conwell, Esther Marly *physicist, researcher*
Corsetti, James Pasquale *pathologist, medical educator*
Dannefer, William Dale *educator, dean*
Deci, Edward Lewis *psychologist, educator*
Destler, William W. *academic administrator*
Deveikis, John P. *radiologist*
Dobbs, Herbert Hotaling *automotive executive, consultant, research scientist, retired military officer*
Dolan, William A. *orthopedist, medical educator*
Dolin, Lonny H. *lawyer*
Doty, Robert William *neuroscientist, physiologist, educator*
Dreyfuss, Eric Martin *allergist*
Duarte, Francisco Javier *physicist, researcher*
DuBrin, Andrew John *management and behavioral sciences educator, writer*
Duffy, Robert John *Mayor, Rochester, New York*
Duke, Charles Bryan *electronics executive, physicist, educator*
Ebenhack, Ben Wright *not-for-profit company executive*
Eisenberg, Richard S. *chemistry professor*
Everett, Claudia Kellam *retired special education educator*
Fallesen, Gary David *journalist, lay worker, not-for-profit developer*
Faraci, Philip J. *imaging company executive*
Farmer, Richard Gilbert *academic physician, foundation administrator*
Fehn, Udo *geology educator*
Fenno, Richard Francis, Jr. *political scientist, educator*
Finkelstein, Jacob Noah *pediatrics and toxicology educator*
French, Lucia Ann *education educator, director*
Friedman, Eby G. *electrical engineer, educator*
Frisina, Robert Dana *neuroscientist, educator*
Frontz, Stephanie J. *librarian*
Gauldin, Robert L. *music educator, composer*
George, Nicholas *optics educator, researcher*
Ghazle, Hamad *medical educator, director*
Ghosh, Amitabha *engineering educator*
Gibbons, Susan Lynn *library director*
Goepp, Julius George Konrad *pediatrician, consultant*
Goldberg-Schaible, Jocelyn Hope Schnier *market research professional*
Golisano, B. Thomas (Tom Golisano) *financial services company and professional sports team executive*
Gordon, Dane Rex *philosophy educator, minister*
Graf, William E. *religious studies educator*
Griffin, Oliver *history professor*
Gunter, Thomas Edgar, Jr. *biophysicist, researcher*
Guo, Chunlei *science educator*
Guo, Hailong *immunologist, researcher*
Guzick, David S. *dean, educator*
Haag, Joyce P. *lawyer, imaging company executive*
Hall, Caroline Breese *pediatrician, educator*
Hanson, Karen Noble *financial holding company executive*
Harris, Diane Carol *merger and acquisition consulting firm executive*
Hauser, William Barry *historian, educator*
Haywood, Anne Mowbray *pediatrician, educator*
Hayzlett, Jeffrey Wayne *marketing executive*
Herbert, Andrew Mark *psychology professor*
Herminghouse, Patricia Anne *foreign language educator*
Hess, Benton Edward *music educator*
Hopkins, Thomas Duvall *economics professor*
Houde-Walter, Susan *optics scientist, educator*
Hu, Suxing *scientist*
Hurlbut, Robert Harold *health care services executive*
Huxlin, Krystel Raluka *neuroscientist, educator*
Hyman, Susan L. *pediatrician, educator*
Jacobs, Richard L. *secondary school educator, coach*
Jain, Manish *researcher*
Jean-Pierre, Pascal *oncologist, educator*
Jiang, Rulang *biomedical researcher, educator*
John, Susan V. *state legislator*
Johnson, Bruce Marvin *language educator*
Johnson, Timothy J. *social work educator*
Johnston, Frank C. *psychologist*
Jones, Ronald Winthrop *economics professor*
Joyce, John Joseph *language educator*
Joynt, Robert James *academic administrator, physician*
Judge, Jonathan J. *financial services company executive*
Kaidy, Mitchell *retired journalist, legislative staff member*
Kampmeier, Jack August Carlos *chemist, educator*
Kashyap, Randeep *surgeon*
Kende, Andrew Steven *chemist, educator*
Khorana, Alok Anand *oncologist, medical researcher*
Kirschenbaum, Howard *education educator*
Klinke, Louise Hoyt *volunteer*
Knauer, James Philip *physicist*
Knox, Robert Seiple *physicist, researcher*
Kondakov, Denis *research scientist*
Kozak, Jeffrey D. *engineering educator*
Krispinsky, David George *engineering educator*
Krober, Alfred *school librarian, director*
Kuby, Patricia J. *mathematics professor*
Kurdziel, Michael Thomas *engineering executive*
Kurlan, Roger *neurologist, educator*
Kurland, Harold Arthur *lawyer*
Kwok, Wingchi Edmund *medical physicist*
La Celle, Paul Louis *biophysics educator*
Laires, Fernando *concert piano educator*
Lake, Matthew *director*
Lamkin-Kennard, Kathleen A. *engineering educator*
Langstein, Howard Neil *plastic surgeon*
Lank, Edith Handleman *journalist, educator*
Lansky, Lewis *history professor*
Laties, Victor Gregory *psychologist, educator*
Law, Michael R. *lawyer*
Lebman, Robert Richard *social services administrator*
Lerner, Amy L. *engineering educator, researcher*
Lester, Howard Elliot *film company executive*
Levy, David Howard *research scientist*
Lichtman, Marshall Albert *hematologist, medical educator, research scientist*
Lindberg, Vern *physics professor*
Liptak, Gregory Stephen *pediatrician, educator*
Logigian, Eric L. *neurologist*
Long, John Broaddus, Jr. *economist, educator*
Lucas, Diane Marie *school librarian*
Lundback, Staffan Bengt Gunnar *lawyer*
Lyness, Jeffrey Marc *psychiatrist, educator*
Makous, Walter Leon *visual scientist, educator*
Marshall, Frederick J. *neurologist, educator*
Mavromatis, John *psychology professor*
McCarthy, Michael E. *protective services official, director*
McCrory, John Brooks *retired lawyer*
McDonald, Joseph Valentine *neurosurgeon*
Mc Kenzie, Lionel Wilfred *economist, educator*
McMeekin, Thomas Owen *dermatologist*
Meconi, Honey *musicologist, writer*
Mitchell, Lance Bernard *social worker*
Moore, Duncan Thomas *optics scientist, educator*
Moore, James Conklin *lawyer*
Morrison, Patrice Burgert *lawyer*
Moss, Arthur Jay *physician*
Nazarian, Lawrence Fred *pediatrician*
Ng, Yee Seung *physicist*
Niemi, Richard Gene *political science educator*
Niu, Greta Aiyu *language educator*
Nolan, Ted (Theodore John Nolan) *professional sports team executive, former professional hockey coach*
Nolasco, Lori D. *literature and language professor*
Notter, Robert H. *biomedical researcher, educator*
Oakes, David *statistician*
Oberdorster, Gunter *toxicologist, educator*
Ostrov, Gerald Martin *pharmaceutical executive*
Paauw, Scott H. *linguist, educator*
Pacala, Leon *retired professional society administrator*
Palermo, Anthony Robert *lawyer*
Paley, Gerald Larry *lawyer*
Palis, James *pediatrician*
Palvino, Jack Anthony *retired broadcasting executive*
Parker, Kathy P. *dean, nursing educator*
Parker, Kevin James *electrical engineer, educator, professor*
Payment, Kenneth Arnold *lawyer*
Pearson, Thomas Arthur *epidemiologist, educator*
Penwarden, Ann P *assistant director*
Phillips, Gordon Leigh, II, *oncologist*
Phillips, Harold John III *protective services official, consultant*
Pogal, Meredith A. *dentist*
Porsteinsson, Anton P. *medical educator, director*
Powers, James Matthew *neuropathologist, educator, researcher*
Price, Richard Edward *lawyer*
Primo, David Martin *political science professor*
Pryhuber, Gloria Salvini *pediatrician, educator*
Raimi, Ralph Alexis *mathematics professor*
Ravines, Patrick C. *conservator, researcher*
Regenstreif, S(amuel) Peter *political scientist, educator*
Remington, Royce Roger *design educator*
Ritchlin, Christopher Trevor *rheumatologist*
Rodgers, Suzanne Hooker *physiologist, consultant*
Rosenbaum, Richard Merrill *lawyer*
Rosenhouse, Michael Allan *lawyer, editor, consultant, columnist*
Rosner, Leonard Allen *lawyer*
Rothberg, Abraham *writer*
Samar, Vincent Joseph *lawyer*
Sammler, Anne Michelle *healthcare educator*
Santhanam, Kalathur S. V. *chemist, researcher*
Saunders, William Hundley, Jr. *retired chemist, educator*
Schneider, Sandra McEwen *emergency physician educator*
Seligman, Joel *academic administrator*
Shannon, Danielle *coach*
Sharma, Gaurav *imaging scientist, electrical engineer*
Sheppard, Luvon *art educator*
Sherman, Fred *biochemist, educator*
Shortell, Cynthia K. *vascular surgeon*
Shoulson, Ira *neurologist, pharmacologist, educator*
Sieg, Albert Louis *photographic company executive*
Singer, Alan Daniel *artist*
Siragusa, Charles J. *judge*
Sklarsky, Frank S. *manufacturing executive*
Sollecito, Larry A. *energy executive*
Sparks, Charles Edward *pathologist, educator*
Sparks, Janet Lindsay Dehoff *pathologist, educator*
Stewart, Sue S. *lawyer*
Stratton, John Alfred *electrical engineer, educator*
Suchman, Anthony Lee *physician, consultant*
Sussman, Paul I. *dentist*
Tantillo, Mary Darlene *nurse*
Thomson, William *economics professor*
Thorndike, Edward Harmon *physicist*
Tobin, Barbara Kay *minister*
Traub, Adam *librarian*

Tsouri, Gill R. *engineering educator, researcher, consultant*
Tyler, John Randolph *lawyer*
Utell, Mark Jeffrey *medical educator*
VanderLinden, Camilla Denice Dunn *telecommunications industry executive*
VanGelder, Kim E. *information technology executive*
Vernarelli, Michael Joseph *economics professor, consultant, academic administrator*
Vigdor, Justin Leonard *lawyer*
Vorobyev, Anatoliy Y. *research scientist*
Wagner, Aureen Pinto *psychologist, educator*
Waite, Stephen Holden *lawyer*
Wang, Sen *computer scientist, researcher*
Wayland-Smith, Robert Dean *retired banker*
Werren, John Haynes *biology professor*
White, Ann Marie *medical educator*
Williams, Marc Adrian *medical educator, scientist, researcher*
Williams, Thomas Franklin *physician, educator*
Wolsky, Jack *retired art educator*
Yip, Kwok Leung *physicist, researcher*
Zarrella, Ronald L. *retired pharmaceutical executive*
Zax, Melvin *psychologist, educator*
Zhu, Donghui *research scientist*
Zupan, Mark A. *dean, economics professor*

Rockaway Park
Charosh, Paul Carlin *information science educator, writer*

Rockville Centre
Beyer, Suzanne *advertising agency executive*
Daly, James Joseph *bishop emeritus*
Derbentli, Betty Ann *art educator, curator*
Fitzgerald, Janet Anne *philosophy educator, academic administrator*
Lewittes, Don Jordan *psychologist*
Libasci, Peter A. *bishop*
Lynch, Peter K. *education educator*
Murphy, William Francis *bishop*
Skelos, Dean George *state legislator*
Teyan, Frederick Gene *pediatrician*
Wcela, Emil Aloysius *bishop*

Rocky Point
Knapp, Craig Brian *musician, educator*

Rome
Anderson, Nora *retired nurse*
Simons, Richard Duncan *lawyer, retired judge*

Romulus
Ostrander, Robert Edwin *retired United Nations interregional advisor, petroleum company executive*

Ronkonkoma
Leventhal, Norman B. *entrepreneur*

Roosevelt
Walsh, Paul Henry *bishop*

Rosedale
Charles, William O. *electrical engineer*
Charrington, Karen Hillary *lawyer, consultant*

Rosendale
Trompetter, Amy Clemens *theater director*

Roslyn
Aptekar, Doris Mae Weinberg *psychotherapist, school psychologist, hypnotherapist*
Finke, Leonda Froehlich *sculptor, educator*
Greenberg, Steven M. *physician*
Hartman, Nancy Lee *physician*
Mazlen, Roger Geoffrey *internist, pharmacologist*
Robinson, Newell Bruce *cardiothoracic surgeon*
Rosen, Sarah Perel *social worker*
Shlofmitz, Richard Alan *cardiologist*
Shubin, Joanna *science educator*
Ulanoff, Stanley M. *communications executive*

Roslyn Heights
Faber, Adele *author, educator*
Guthart, Leo A. *electronics executive*

Rotterdam Junction
Cox, Paulyn Mae *retired elementary school educator*

Rouses Point
Weierstall, Richard Paul *retired pharmaceutical chemist*

Rushford
Devine, Stephen P. *minister, educator*

Rye
Barker, Harold Grant *surgeon, educator*
Capps, John Edward *lawyer, consumer products company executive*
Carey, John *judge*
Curtin, Brian Joseph *retired ophthalmologist*
Finnerty, Louise Hoppe *food products executive*
Franklin, Martin E. *consumer products company executive*
Greenwald, Gerald (Jerry Greenwald) *private equity group executive*
Harrington, Diane *librarian, writer*
Hurwitz, Sol *writer, consultant*
Kaufman, Shirona *cantor, educator*
Kaulakis, Arnold Francis *management consultant*
Ketchum, William Clarence *author, educator*
Lawi, David Steven *utilities executive, merchant banker*
Lehman, Lawrence Herbert *consulting engineering executive*
Megalli, Maguid Ramzi *retired health facility administrator, urologist*
Moore, Mechlin Dongan *communications executive, marketing consultant*
Nelson, Vita Joy *editor, publisher*
Newburger, Howard Martin *psychoanalyst*
Pearson, Nathan Williams *communications and investment executive*
Rolland, Peter George *landscape architect*
Sales, Mitzi S. *science educator*
Sollins, Susan *curator, television producer*
Waltz, Joseph McKendree *neurosurgeon, educator*
Wilmot, Irvin Gorsage *former hospital administrator, educator, consultant*

Rye Brook
Aquino, Joseph Mario *clinical psychologist*
Barasch, Richard A. *insurance company executive*
Berk, Alan S. *accountant*
Bryant, Gary Wayne *insurance company executive*
Kuntzman, Ronald *research and development company executive*
Mariam, Thomas Fred *public relations executive, radio producer*

Sag Harbor
Brody, Eugene David *investment company executive*
Brody, Jacqueline *editor*
Epstein, Jason *publishing company executive*

Sagaponack
Isham, Sheila *artist*

Saint Albans
Norfleet, Leontine Sandra *retired biologist*

Saint Bonaventure
Cellini, Alva V. *language educator, women's studies, translator*
Hunkins, Dalton R. *computer science professor*
Mazon, Margaret Fausold *language educator*
Tenglund, Ann M. *librarian*

Saint Huberts
Neilson, Winthrop Cunningham III *retired communications executive, financial consultant, photographer*

Saint James
Batule, Robert John *priest, writer*
Gambino, Richard Joseph *materials engineer, educator*
Kelly, Michael Joseph *academic administrator, consultant*
Maggipinto, V. Anthony *lawyer*

Saint Regis Falls
Gaggin, Warren William *personnel director, special education administrator*
O'Bryan, Margaret Sundberg *music educator*

Sanborn
Mezhir, James A. *law educator*
Michalak, Janet Carol *childhood education educator, coordinator*
Nowak (Jarosz), Linda Therese *special education educator, consultant*

Sands Point
Cohen, Ida Bogin (Mrs. Savin Cohen) *import/export company executive*
Lear, Erwin *anesthesiologist, educator*
Olian, JoAnne Constance *curator, art historian*
Wurzel, Leonard *retired candy manufacturing company executive*

Saranac Lake
Caguiat, Carlos Jose *health facility administrator, priest*
Kretser, Heidi Elizabeth *conservationist, researcher*

Saratoga Springs
Abrams, Kenneth Theodore *retired academic administrator*
Carovano, John Martin *retired not-for-profit developer*
Caruso, Adrienne Iorio *retired language educator*
Chen, Dung-Lan *librarian*
Dickinson, Richard Henry *accountant*
Ford, Dexter *retired insurance company executive*
Glotzbach, Philip A. *academic administrator, philosopher, educator*
Moran, Paul James *journalist, columnist*
Porter, David Hugh *musician, classicist, academic administrator, music educator*
Stake, Peter *artist, educator*
Wait, Charles Valentine *banker*

Saugerties
Falzano, Colleen *special education educator*

Sayville
Vigliotta, Margaret D. *retired secondary school educator, art educator, artist*

Scarsdale
Abbe, Colman *investment banker*
Angel, Dennis *lawyer*
Baruch Feldman, Caren Shein *psychologist*
Belasco, Steven Ronald *lawyer*
Beuchert, Edward William *lawyer*
Blitman, Howard Norton *construction executive*
Borg, Robert Frederic *civil engineer*
Bosses, Stevan J. *mediator, arbitrator*
Brilliant, Richard *art historian, educator*
Cohen, Irwin *economist*
Erbsen, Claude Ernest *retired journalist*
Gladstone, William Louis *accountant*
Glickenhaus, Sarah Brody *speech therapist*
Goodman, Jordan Elliot *journalist*
Graff, Henry Franklin *historian, educator*
Jacobs, Theodore Joseph *psychiatrist, educator*
Johnson, Boine Theodore *manufacturing executive, mayor*
Johnson, William Alexander *philosophy and theology educator, clergyman*
Kaufman, Robert Jules *communications consultant, lawyer*
Laufer, Leonard Justin *management consultant*
Lipman, Marvin Matthew *physician, medical educator, editor, writer*
Low, Murray *physiologist*
Mercando, Anthony Dominic *cardiologist*
Moser, Marvin *physician, educator, author*
O'Brien, Edward Ignatius *corporate financial executive, director, investor, lawyer*
O'Neill, Michael James *editor, author*
Paulin, Amy Ruth *civic activist, consultant, state legislator*
Porosoff, Harold *chemist, science administrator, research and development company executive*
Port, Lilly Bruck Lieb *retired advocate, columnist, commentator*
Rovit, Richard Lee *neurosurgeon*
Soley, Robert Lawrence *plastic surgeon*
Stamas, Stephen *not-for-profit administrator*
Topping, Audrey Ronning *photojournalist*
Topping, Seymour *writer*
Van Gundy, Gregory Frank *retired lawyer*

Schenectady
Ainlay, Stephen Charles *academic administrator, educator*
Barash, Eugene *research scientist*
Braslow, Nelson M. *insurance company executive*
Davis, Lewis Berkley *mechanical engineer*
DeLuke, Dean M. *oral surgeon*
Depan, Harry John *cardiothoracic surgeon*
Faidi, Waseem *research scientist*
Finks, Robert Melvin *paleontologist, educator*
Fleischer, Robert Louis *geology professor*
Frost, Robert Edwin *chemistry professor*
Goldmeer, Jeffrey S. *mechanical engineer, gas industry executive*
Hartkern, Danielle Anne *elementary school educator*
Heinegg, Peter *literature and language professor, writer*
Hull, Roger Harold *foundation and former academic administrator*
Huszar, Andrew Louis *school psychologist*
Kaplan, Ilene *social sciences educator*
Katz, Samuel *retired geophysics educator*
Levine, Sanford Harold *lawyer*
Lewis, Bradley Glenn *economics professor*
Lorang, George Joseph *special education educator*
Mancuso, J(ohn) James *librarian*
Oliker, David William *healthcare management administrator*
Philip, A. G. Davis *astronomer, educator, editor*
Pritchard, Mary D'Ercole *elementary school educator*
Ringlee, Robert James *retired consulting engineering executive*
Robb, Walter Lee *retired electric and management company executive, consultant*
Schenck, John Frederic *physician*
Steckler, Charles N. *theater educator*
Sternlicht, Beno *research and development company executive*
Szokody, Aniko *pianist, educator*
Tchako, Abraham *engineering educator*
Teff, Justin Samuel *lawyer*
Yu, Ting *research scientist*
Zeng, Kai *biomedical engineer*

Scotia
Buhrmaster, James R. *energy executive*
de la Rocha, Carlos A. *retired physician*

Scottsville
Williams, Henry Ward, Jr. *lawyer, writer*

Sea Cliff
Popova, Nina *retired dancer, choreographer, director*

Seaford
Bongiovi, Stephen *literature and language educator*
Furey, Raymond Joseph *lawyer*
González del Real, Rodolfo Antonio *language educator*
Setzler, William Edward *retired chemicals executive*

Selden
Busby, Robert Wilson *history professor*
Connors, William Francis, Jr. *academic administrator*
Schmitz, Michael *retired psychology professor*
West, Norman R. *history professor*

Seneca Falls
Norman, Mary Marshall *academic administrator, alcohol/drug abuse services professional, educator*

Shady
Malkine-Falvey, Fern Sylvie *writer, journalist, painter*

Sharon Springs
Pfau, Richard Anthony *retired university president*

Shelter Island
Moran, Daniel Thomas *dentist, poet*
Shaw, Alan Roger *finance educator, retired company executive*

Shelter Island Heights
Culbertson, Janet Lynn *artist*
Gage, Beau *artist*
Wolosoff, Bruce Germont *composer*

Shoreham
Fontana, Barbara *psychologist*

Shrub Oak
Vaccaro, Annette Andréa *music educator*

Sidney
Werner, David A. *paper company executive*

Skaneateles
Behrend, Donald Fraser *academic administrator, educator*
Garrett, Vicky P. *psychologist*
O'Connell, Sharon Kay *media specialist*
Vetrano, Anthony Joseph *foreign language and literature professor*
Veverka, Karen Elizabeth *music educator*

Skaneateles Falls
Shimer, Julie A. *health products executive*

Sleepy Hollow
Flynn-Connors, Elizabeth Kathryn *reporter, editor*
Melvin, Russell Johnston (Jay Melvin) *magazine publishing consultant*
Neill, Richard Robert *retired publishing executive*
Resnick, Adrienne Jo *clinical social worker, psychotherapist*
Schmidt, Klaus Franz *advertising executive*
Song, Yulin *physicist*

Slingerlands
Herman, Robert S. *former state official, economist, author, educator*
Ipsen, Carol Anne *psychiatrist, educator*
Jacobs, Karen Louise *musician, medical technician, educator*
Zacek, Joseph Frederick *historian, educator*
Zhu, Kehe *mathematician*

Smithtown
Mead-Haskins, Debra *educational consultant, academic administrator, educator*
Rockensies, John William *mechanical engineer*
Spellman, Thomas Joseph, Jr. *lawyer*
Tuzel, Suzanne L. *psychiatrist*

Snyder
Breverman, Harvey *artist*
Levine, George Richard *language educator*

Somers
Adkins, Rodney Carl *information technology executive*
Bauman, William Allen *pediatrician, educator, health systems consultant*
Bensen, Annette Wolf *graphic art company consultant*
Berisford, John L. *consumer products company executive*
Bronzo, Neal A. *consumer products company executive*
Cohn, Howard *retired magazine editor*
Concepcion, David *assistant principal*
Crawford, Victor L. *consumer products company executive*
Drewes, Alfred H. *consumer products company executive*
Foss, Eric J. *consumer products company executive*
Franks, Brent J. *consumer products company executive*
King, Robert C. *consumer products company executive*
Rapp, Steven M. *lawyer, consumer products company executive*
Reiman, Richard J. *lawyer*
Reznick, Steven Michael *orthopedic surgeon, educator*
Rubin, Samuel Harold *internist, consultant*
Sanford, Linda S. *information technology executive*

South Ozone Park
White, Thomas, Jr. *city councilman*

South Richmond Hill
Scheich, John F. *lawyer*

South Salem
Carpentieri, Carol Ellen *artist, educator*
Cowles, Frederick Oliver *lawyer*
Terman, Lewis Madison *retired electrical engineer, researcher, director*

South Setauket
Friedlander, Gerhart *nuclear chemist*
Poli, Kenneth Joseph *editor, writer, photographer*

Southampton
Brokaw, Clifford Vail III *investment banker*
Kapenhas-Valdes, Edna *hospital administrator*
Lopez, David *lawyer*
Moneypenny, Edward William *retail executive*
Platt, Jonathan James *lawyer*
Sheehy, Betty Jo *real estate company executive, investment advisor*
Sultan, Terrie Frances *museum director*
Swift, Mary Lou *art dealer, financial consultant*
Tuma, Mym *sculptor, painter, educator*

Sparkill
Dahl, Arlene *actress, writer, designer, cosmetics executive*

Spring Valley
Neal, Leora Louise Haskett *social services administrator*

Stamford
Bergleitner, George Charles, Jr. *investment banker*

Staten Island
Anderson, Robert Mapes *history professor*
Berci, Margaret Elizabeth *education educator*
Bruckstein, Alex Harry *internist, gastroenterologist, geriatrician*
Clark, Sylvia Dolores *business educator*
Fafian, Joseph, Jr. *management consultant*
Ferzli, George Salem *surgeon*
Foster, Paul *playwright*
Franzone, Eric Scott *psychologist*
Fusco, Jo Ellen *music educator*
Gaeta, Rosemarie *psychotherapist*
Gavrity, John Decker *retired insurance company executive*
Gelbein, Jay Joel *accountant*
Goodman, Robert Stanley *management educator*

Hensley, Donald Melton literature and language professor
Humphries, Edward Francis lawyer
Ignizio, Vincent city councilman
Israeli, Ron Samuel urologist
Lewis, Carla Susan psychology educator
Lo Re, Mary finance educator
Mbah, Emmanuel Mbah history professor
Meltzer, Yale Leon economist, educator
Molinaro, James P. city official
Newhouse, Donald E. newspaper publishing executive
Newhouse, Samuel Irving, Jr., (Si Newhouse Jr.) publishing executive
Oddo, James S. city councilman, lawyer
Okulewicz, Steven Charles geologist, educator
Pasciuto, Joseph Doria priest
Piegari, James A. psychologist
Popler, Kenneth behavioral health services administrator, psychologist
Porter, Darwin Fred writer
Prince, Andrew Steven lawyer, retired government agency administrator
Prince, Danforth publishing executive, journalist
Rizvi, Syed engineering educator
Sánchez, Margarita María science educator
Scherb, Richard John science educator
Sheka, Kedambady P. surgeon
Trogan, Roland Bernard composer, educator
Wilson, Van Ray secondary school educator
Winter, Steven internist, cardiologist
Xia, Ming political science professor
Yang, Song-Yu medical biochemist

Stony Brook
Alexander, John Macmillan, Jr. chemistry professor
Anderson, Michael Thomas mathematics professor, researcher, director
Andriola, Mary Repole neurologist, pediatrician
Aronoff, Mark H. linguistics educator, writer, consultant
Badalamente, Marie Ann orthopedist, educator
Baker, David A. obstetrician, gynecologist, educator
Bonner, Francis Truesdale chemist, educator, dean
Brandwein, Ruth Ann social welfare educator, social services administrator, writer
Broderick, Joan Eleanor psychologist, researcher
Brown, Gerald Edward physicist, researcher
Carr, Edward Gary psychology professor
Chiang, Fu-Pen mechanical engineering educator, researcher
Cochran, James Kirk dean, oceanographer, educator, geochemist
Corman, Marvin Leonard surgeon, educator
Dagum, Alexander B. plastic surgeon
Ebin, David Gregory mathematician, researcher, educator
Edelman, Norman Herman dean, medical educator, academic administrator
Filstrup, (E.) Christian library director, dean
Fine, Richard Nisan pediatrician, educator, dean
Fontanella, Luigi literature and language professor, writer
Fritts, Harry Washington, Jr. retired internist, educator
Gagnon, John Henry sociologist, educator
Gelato, Marie Catherine physician, clinical investigator, educator
Geller, Marvin Alan meteorology educator, researcher
Glass, Peter Stanley Abraham anesthesiologist, educator
Glimm, James Gilbert mathematician, educator
Goldfried, Marvin Robert psychology professor
Goldman, Vladimir Joseph physicist, researcher
Grim, Patrick Neal philosopher, educator, logician
Huang, Peisen Simon mechanical engineer
Hurst, Lawrence orthopedic surgeon
Ihde, Don philosopher, educator
Jaber, Rajaa physician, educator
Jasiewicz, Ronald Clarence anesthesiologist, educator, osteopath
Jonas, Steven preventive medicine physician, author
Kaler, Eric William academic administrator
Kuchner, Eugene Frederick neurosurgeon, neuroscientist, educator
Kulik, Igor Orestovich theoretical physics, researcher
Kuspit, Donald Burton art historian, critic, educator
Landman, Ursula N. anesthesiologist
Lauher, Joseph W. chemistry professor
Lawson, H(erbert) Blaine, Jr. mathematician, educator
Leakey, Richard Erskine paleoanthropologist, museum director
Lennarz, William Joseph research biologist, educator
Levinton, Jeffrey S. biology educator, oceanographer
Li, Baosheng physicist
Liang, Jerome Z. science educator
Liang, Jerome Zhengrong radiology educator
Lodge, Milton political science professor
Meliker, Jaymie R. medical educator
Meltzer, Donna medical educator
Meyers, Morton Allen radiologist, educator
Mignone, Mario B. language educator
Miller, Frederick pathologist
Milnor, John Willard mathematician
Monheit, Alan Goodman obstetrician, gynecologist
Olster, Stacey Michele literature and language professor
Pekarsky, Melvin Hirsch artist
Potapova, Irina A. cell biologist, educator
Rifkin, Barry R. dean, dental educator, researcher
Rohlf, F. James biologist, educator
Rosengart, Todd Kenneth cardiothoracic surgeon, researcher, neurosurgeon, consultant
Seifert, Frank C. thoracic surgeon
Shamash, Yacov dean, electrical engineering educator
Sherman, S. Murray neuroscientist, neurobiology educator
Shroyer, Kenneth Reed medical educator, department chairman
Silverman, Hugh J. philosophy educator
Simpson, Louis Aston Marantz language educator, writer
Sitharaman, Balaji biomedical engineer, educator
Sokal, Robert Reuven biology professor, writer
Stanley, Samuel Leonard, Jr. academic administrator, medical educator
Steigbigel, Roy Theodore epidemiologist, educator, research scientist
Stone, Arthur A. psychologist, researcher
Stone, Gaynell museum director, educator
Swanson, Robert Lawrence oceanographer, academic program administrator
Tanur, Judith Mark statistician, sociologist, educator
Tassiopoulos, Apostolos K. vascular surgeon
Tewarson, Reginald Prabhakar retired mathematics educator, consultant
Tucker, Alan Curtiss mathematics professor
Varadaraj, Kulandaiappan medical researcher, educator
Weidner, Donald J. geophysicist educator
Weisbrot, Deborah Marcia psychiatrist
White, Henry J. engineering educator, consultant
Williams, Peter C. medical association administrator
Wittpenn, John Ryder ophthalmologist, consultant
Zemanian, Armen Humpartsoum electrical engineer, mathematician

Stony Creek
La Grasse, Carol Winter property rights advocate, retired civil engineer

Suffern
Bierman, Mara-Lee language educator
Codispoti, Andre John allergist, immunologist
Mitchell, Shamika Ann literature and language professor

Sugar Loaf
Endico, Mary Antoinette artist

Syosset
Cordaro, Joanne human resources specialist, director
Kniffin, Paula Sichel insurance sales executive
Lee, Jong Pil mathematician, educator

Syracuse
Abaté, Charles Joseph engineering educator
Allis, Damian Gregory chemist, technologist, consultant
Arterian, Hannah R. dean, law educator
Badawy, Shawky Z.A. gynecologist, educator
Baker, Bruce Edward orthopedic surgeon, consultant
Baldwin, John Edwin chemistry professor
Baldwin, Robert Frederick, Jr. lawyer
Barclay, H. Douglas (Hugh Douglas Barclay) lawyer, legislator, diplomat
Basu, Subho social studies educator
Baxter, Andrew Thomas prosecutor
Becker, Lorne Arthur family physician
Bickford, Marion Eugene geologist, educator
Birkhead, Guthrie Sweeney, Jr. political scientist, dean
Boeheim, Jim college basketball coach
Braiman, Mark Stephen biomedical educator, researcher
Braungart, Richard Gottfried political scientist, educator
Broadnax, Walter Doyce former academic administrator, educator
Caldicott, Catherine V. medical educator, researcher
Cantor, Nancy academic administrator
Canute, Gregory William neurosurgeon
Caravan, Ronald L. music educator, composer
Carey, Robert J. medical educator
Carnes, Jeffrey Scott ancient language educator
Carter Grosso, Erika language educator
Chamorro Galán, María Gloria language educator
Choudhary, Madhuchhanda epidemiologist, educator
Cirando, John Anthony lawyer
Cohen-Cruz, Jan art educator, director
Colvin, Ruth Johnson literacy organization founder
Cooper, John Ambrose management consultant, marketing professional
Costello, Thomas Joseph bishop emeritus
Criss, Amy H.
Cunningham, Robert Joseph bishop
Cusato, Karen medical educator
DeFrancisco, John Anthony state legislator, lawyer
Dekaney, Elisa Macedo music educator, researcher
Eisele, Kathleen L. composition, literature educator
Elms, Ben actor, theater director
Emery, Robert Allan minister
Ende, Mark L. language educator
Fardad, Makan engineering educator
Fawcett, James Walter computer engineer, educator
Fitzgerald, Harold Kenneth social work educator, consultant
Fitzpatrick, James David lawyer
Forbes, Peter Edwin sculptor
Fortune, John B. medical educator
Freund, Deborah A. academic administrator
Gaal, John lawyer
García-Calderón, Myrna language educator
Gartner, Joseph Charles retired systems administrator
Gigante, Denise Mp chemistry professor
Givas, Thomas Peter lawyer
Gold, Joseph medical researcher
Graver, Jack Edward mathematics professor
Gray, Charles Augustus banker
Greenberg, Gerald R. language educator, dean
Hale, Sherrie LaFrance biology professor, researcher
Hallberg, Richard Lawrence cell biologist, molecular biologist
Hayes, David Michael lawyer
Heath, Patti art educator, musician
Higuchi, Hiroshi aerospace engineer, director
Hodge, Charles Joseph, Jr. neurosurgeon, educator
Honig, Arnold physics professor, researcher
Irwin, Peter C. not-for-profit fundraiser
Kadhikhaye, Sameer Pundlikrao engineer, researcher
Kalman, Melanie Beth nursing educator, researcher
Kane, Peter Bayard physician
Kaplan, Eugene Alken psychiatry professor, department chairman
Kim, Yong-Woo engineer, educator, consultant
King, Robert Bainton neurosurgeon, educator
Kriesberg, Louis sociologist, educator
La Graff, John Erwin engineering educator
Langdon, John W. history professor
Latham, Robert R., II, engineering educator
Lee, David Ames lawyer, banker
Luchsinger, John Francis, Jr. lawyer
Luft, Eric v.d. writer, educator, publisher
Malhotra, Yogesh information scientist, management educator, information technology executive, management consultant, engineer
Mansouri, Nazanin science educator
Marcoccia, Louis Gary accountant, academic administrator
Mathiason, John Roland political science professor, consultant
Mazur, Allan Carl sociologist, educator
McCabe, John B. emergency physician, health science association administrator
McCurn, Neal Peters federal judge
McLaughlin, Robert S. lawyer
Morris, Francis Lockwood computer scientist
Movileanu, Liviu physics professor
Moynihan, James Michael bishop
Murphy, Cornelius B., Jr., (Neil Murphy) academic administrator
Newman, David environmental services administrator, educator
O'Connor, Michael E. lawyer
Orentlicher, John video research educator, artist
Pardee, Otway O'Meara computer scientist, educator
Pearson, Gretchen Elaine college librarian
Philippone, David J. lawyer
Phillips, Paul Everard medical educator, rheumatologist
Pinsky, Roy David lawyer
Pooler, Rosemary S. federal judge
Powell, James Matthew history professor
Prettyman, John A. language educator
Prucha, John James geologist, educator
Rabuzzi, Daniel D. medical association administrator
Richardson, M. Catherine lawyer
Roberson, Michael Lee lawyer
Robinson, Joseph Edward geology educator, petroleum engineer, consultant
Romeu, Jorge Luis mathematics professor, writer
Salerno, Sister Maria advanced practice nurse, educator
Sanger, Joseph William cell biologist
Sargent, Robert George engineering educator
Scharoun, Susan L. psychologist, educator
Scheinman, Steven Jay dean, medical educator
Schiff, Eric Allan physics professor
Scott, Gary M. engineering educator, department chairman
Scullin, Frederick James, Jr. federal judge
Shields, William Michael biology professor, consultant
Smardon, Richard Clay landscape architect, environmental studies professor
Smith, Corinne Roth psychologist
Smith, Kenneth Judson, Jr. chemistry professor
Smith, Phillip H. biology professor, educational association administrator
Stam, David Harry librarian
Staples, Heidi L poet, writer
Sternlicht, Sanford literature educator, writer
Stevens, Richard Thomas neuroscientist, researcher
Streeten, Barbara Wiard ophthalmologist, medical educator
Suddaby, Glenn T. federal judge, former prosecutor
Szasz, Thomas Stephen psychiatrist, educator, writer
Teece, Mark A. chemistry professor
Thomas, Sidney fine arts educator, researcher
Thorin, Suzanne E. dean, university librarian
Verheyen, Peter David librarian, conservator
Waddy, Patricia A. art historian, retired architecture educator
Waggoner, Andrew composer
Wallerstein, Mitchel Bruce dean, political science professor
Walsh-Hunt, Linda Ann social worker, consultant, poet
Wiggins, James Bryan religion educator
Williams, William Joseph retired hematologist, educator
Wolff, Catherine Elizabeth opera company executive
Wolff, L. Thomas physician, educator
Yildirim, Yildiray finance educator
Zubieta, Jon Andoni chemistry professor

Tappan
Cardenas, Raul Rodolfo, Jr. engineering executive, educator, consultant
Fox, Muriel retired public relations executive

Tarrytown
Brownstein, Alan P. health foundation executive, consultant
Field, Barry Elliot internist, gastroenterologist
Garen, Daniel Joseph lawyer
Hyman, Leonard Stephen financial consultant, economist, writer
Osborne, Robin library and information scientist
Pollak, Martin Marshall lawyer, training company executive
Sullivan, Janet Nelson dermatologist, department chairman, health facility administrator
Teicher, Oren Jonathan trade association executive

Thornwood
Bassett, Lawrence C. management consultant

Tonawanda
Brunger, Eric Geoffrey social studies educator, coach
Drozdziel, Marion John aeronautical engineer
Haller, Calvin John banker
Rovison, John Michael, Jr. chemical engineer
Stall, Robert geriatrician

Troy
Ahlers, Rolf Willi philosopher, theologian
Baker, Kim Pearson education educator
Bennett, Kristin Paulette science educator
Berg, Daniel science and technology educator
Bergles, Arthur Edward mechanical engineering educator
Block, Robert Charles nuclear engineering educator
Boles, David Brian psychology educator
Chan, Wai Kin Victor engineering educator
Clemmons, Byard Quigg guidance counselor, prosecutor
Coppens, Marc-Olivier chemical engineer, educator
Cramb, Alan W. dean, engineering educator
Demertzoglou, Pindaro Epaminonda system administrator, clinical assistant professor
Dobry, Ricardo engineering educator
Dordick, Jonathan Seth chemical engineer, educator
Ehrlich, Henry Lutz biology professor
Ferris, James Peter chemist, educator
Fleming, Edwards A. engineering educator
Friedman, Gerald Manfred geologist, educator
Friedman, Sue Tyler technical publications executive
Gerhardt, Lester A. engineering educator, dean
Giaever, Ivar physicist
Gill, William Nelson chemical engineering professor
Glicksman, Martin Eden materials engineering educator
Goel, Anuj systems analyst, researcher
Hajela, Prabhat engineering educator, researcher
Hatami-Marbini, Hamed research scientist
Haviland, David Sands retired architectural educator, researcher, administrator
Hendler, James Alexander computer science educator, consultant
Holguin-Veras, Jose Ernesto transportation researcher
Hsu, Cheng decision sciences and engineering systems educator
Hull, Maria-Catherine engineering educator
Intes, Xavier research scientist
Jackson, Shirley Ann academic administrator, physicist
Jones, E. Stewart, Jr. lawyer
Kahl, William Frederick retired academic administrator
Kaye, Gordon Israel pathologist, educator, waste management consultant
Kilgallon, Susan Margaret architect, educator
LaMarche, George E. III lawyer
Lang, Valerie Anne educator
Lee, Moo-Yeal chemical engineer, researcher
Levinger, Joseph Solomon physicist, researcher
Littman, Howard chemical engineer, educator
Magdon-Ismail, Malik computer science professor
Mayo, Robert Raymond (Bob Mayo) university librarian
McDermott, Robert J. commissioner
Medicus, Heinrich Adolf physicist, researcher
Medicus, Hildegard Julie retired dentist, orthodontist, educator
Monahan, Martin J. social studies educator
Moore, James Alfred chemist, educator
Nagy, George education educator
Pezzolesi, Linda S.W. science educator
Sanderson, Arthur Clark engineering educator
Schechter, Stephen L. political scientist
Schowalter, Leo John physicist and educator
Schroeder, John physics professor
Shan, Yufeng research scientist
Sharfstein, Susan T. engineering educator
Shur, Michael electrical engineer, educator, consultant
Snyder, Patricia Di Benedetto theater director, producer
Welles, Wanda Lizak research scientist
Woods, John William electrical, computer and systems engineering educator, consultant
Zagorevski, Dmitri academic administrator
Zimmie, Thomas Frank civil engineer, educator

Tuckahoe
Thornton, Elaine Seretha oncology clinical nurse specialist

Tupper Lake
Welsh, Peter Corbett museum director, historian

Tuxedo Park
Dai, Wei biomedical researcher
Regan, Ellen Frances (Mrs. Walston Shepard Brown) ophthalmologist, educator
Zelikoff, Judith Terry medical educator, consultant

Uniondale
Berzow, Harold Steven lawyer
Biron, Martin professional hockey player
Dey, Chris professional sports team executive, entrepreneur
DiPietro, Rick professional hockey player
Duffy, James Raymond lawyer
Gordon, Scott professional hockey coach
Kotula, Michael Anthony lawyer
Lemle, Robert Spencer lawyer
Levy, Robert S. lawyer
Pratt, George Cheney law educator, retired judge
Sanchez, Laura Ann music educator
Snow, Garth professional sports team executive, former professional hockey player
Streit, Mark professional hockey player
Trottier, Bryan John professional sports team executive, former professional hockey player and coach
Wang, Charles B. professional sports team executive, former computer company executive
Weight, Doug professional hockey player

Upton
Aronson, Samuel science administrator
Baltz, Anthony John physicist
Bond, Peter Danford physicist

Chaudhari, Praveen *science administrator, materials physicist*
Choi, Jun-Ki *research scientist*
Cotlet, Mircea *research scientist*
Damazio, Denis Oliveira *research scientist*
Fowler, Joanna S. *chemist*
Goldhaber, Maurice *physicist, researcher*
Hamilton, Leonard Derwent *physician, molecular biologist*
Han, Wei-Qiang *research scientist*
Hanson, Albert LeRoy *physicist, engineer*
Harbottle, Garman *chemist*
Hendrie, Joseph Mallam *physicist, nuclear engineer*
Henn, Fritz Albert *psychiatrist*
Johnson, Peter David *physicist*
Lindenbaum, S(eymour) J(oseph) *physicist*
Lowenstein, Derek Irving *physicist*
Rau, Ralph Ronald *retired physicist*
Sakaguchi, Takao *physicist*
Setlow, Jane Kellock *biophysicist*
Setlow, Richard Burton *biophysicist, researcher*
Sherman, William Benjamin *research scientist*
Simos, Nikolaos *engineer, researcher*
Steinberg, Meyer *chemical engineer*
Tannenbaum, Michael J(ay) *physicist*
Wei, Xiangdong *physicist, researcher*
Weston, Ralph Emerson, Jr. *chemist*
Yoon, Won-Sub *materials scientist*

Utica
Andereck, Cynthia Perry *psychologist*
Antzelevitch, Charles *research and development company executive*
Boylan, Kristina A. *history professor*
Cardamone, Richard J. *federal judge*
Cattat, Vincent Joesph *retired education educator*
Dussault, Heather M.B. *electrical engineer, researcher*
Gifford, James J. *literature and language professor*
Jones, Daniel Keane *engineering educator*
Katz, David Raymond III *political science professor*
Lee, Hoseoup *engineering educator*
Liang, Yixiong *language educator*
Schweizer, Paul Douglas *museum director*
Stulmaker, Richard M. *retired social studies educator*
Vendetta, Constance Joan *language educator*
Wagner, Frederick Reese *retired language educator*
Zogby, William Joseph *history professor, management consultant*

Valhalla
Aronow, Wilbert Solomon *physician, educator*
Christesen, John D. *business educator*
Cohen, Martin Bruce *physician*
Del Guercio, Louis Richard Maurice *surgeon, educator*
De Nicola, Peter Francis *tax executive*
Fachnie, H(ugh) Douglas *film manufacturing company official*
Golombek, Sergio Gustavo *pediatrician, educator, neonatologist*
Hankin, Joseph Nathan *college president*
Iatropoulos, Michael John *health research executive, pathology educator*
Inchiosa, Mario Anthony, Jr. *pharmacologist*
Jenks, Eileen A. *academic administrator, real estate agent*
Kang, Jian *neuroscientist, educator*
Kline, Susan Anderson *internist, dean, educator*
Leone, Stephen Joseph *language educator, computer technician, consultant*
Lerner, Robert Gibbs *internist, hematologist, educator*
Liu, Delong *oncologist, hematologist*
Marks, Stephen J. *neurologist, educator*
McGoldrick, Kathryn Elizabeth *anesthesiologist, educator, writer*
O'Connell, Ralph Anthony *dean, psychiatrist, educator*
Palaniswamy, Chandrasekar *surgeon, researcher*
Parton, Lance A. *pediatrician, educator*
Quilley, John *medical educator, researcher*
Recchia, Fabio Anastasio *medical educator*
Reed, George Elliott *surgeon, educator, dean*
Safai, Bijan *physician, investigator*
Selman, Jay E. *neurologist*
Simpson, Sean *mathematics professor*
Weinstein, Arthur *rheumatologist, educator*
Williams, Gary Murray *pathologist, educator*
Yang, Yang-Ming *medical educator*

Valley Cottage
Bridgman, Art *choreographer, dancer*
Packer, Myrna *choreographer, dancer*

Valley Falls
Babbitt, Martha E. *retired science educator*

Valley Stream
Ellis, Bernice *financial planner, investment advisor*
Gustin, Mark Douglas *retired healthcare executive*

Verbank
Berry, Maryann Paradiso *minister*

Vestal
Adour, Colleen McNulty *artist, educator*
Donnelly, Mary Elizabeth *language educator*
Grinberg, Raul *internist*
Jones, Wayne Elfed, Jr. *chemist, researcher*
O'Connell, Patricia Ellen *musician, educator*
Oggins, Robin S. *history professor*
Weil, Joseph David *editor, writer*

Victor
Merkel, Paul Barrett *chemist, consultant*
Morris, G. Michael *science educator*
Mullin, Thomas J. *lawyer, food products executive*
Sands, Richard E. *food products executive*
Sands, Robert *food products executive*

Waddington
Babb, Harold *psychologist, educator*

Wadhams
Foley, Matthew William *electric power industry executive*

Wading River
Volonts, Marguerite Louise *music educator, singer*

Wainscott
Henderson, William Charles *editor*
Herzog, Arthur III *author*
Russo, Alexander Peter *artist, educator*

Walden
Miranda, Hermes *school counselor*
Murphy, Pamela Ann *musician, educator, actress*

Wallkill
Koch, Edwin Ernest *artist, interior designer*
Strauser, Susan Parkyn *performing arts educator, singer, professional soloist*

Wantagh
Berk, Adele L. *composer, music educator*
Blum, Melvin *chemical company executive, researcher*
Cahill, Kathleen J. *director*
Luchs, Jodi Ian *ophthalmologist*
Petris, Elli *bankruptcy case manager*
Smits, Edward John *historian, consultant*

Wappingers Falls
Hogan, Edward Robert *financial services executive*
Johnson, Jeh Vincent *architect*
Khare, Mukesh V. *information technology manager*
Puttlitz, Karl Joseph, Sr. *metallurgist*
Robinson, Paul David *literature and language educator*
Stabile, Patrice Christine *mathematics educator*

Warrensburg
Egan, Eric Omar *military officer, educator*

Warwick
Fletcher, Robert Alexander *artist, writer*
Linnéa, Sharon *writer, playwright*
Simon, Dolores Daly *copy editor*

Washingtonville
Casazza, Sharen *pediatrician*
Marcialis, Angelo Vincent *musician, educator*

Water Mill
Hagstrom, Jack Walter Carl Kling *retired pathology educator*

Waterford
Glavin, A. Rita Chandellier (Mrs. James Henry Glavin III) *lawyer*

Watertown
Coe, Benjamin Plaisted *retired state official*
McHugh, John Michael *United States Representative from New York*
Palmer, Ronald R *history professor*

Watervliet
Elrahman, O. Abd *environmental and transportation engineer, educator*
Kathe, Eric *mechanical engineer*

Watkins Glen
LaMoreaux, Kathleen Ann Warner *English educator*

Webster
Curtis, Deana A. *electronics executive, small business owner*
McWilliams, C. Paul, Jr. *engineering executive*
Powers, Richard Gerard *history educator*
Scherer, Marcia Joslyn *psychologist, researcher, educator*
Warford, Mark Kellison *language educator, consultant*
Zhang, Shengliang *materials scientist*

Wellsville
Tezak, Edward George *mechanics educator*

West Harrison
Boczko, Judd *urologist, educator*
Gutheil, Irene A. *social work educator, researcher*
Loranger, Steven R. *industrial manufacturing company executive*
Maffeo, Vincent Anthony *lawyer, director*
Ramos, Denise L. *corporate financial executive*
Reichelderfer, Brenda L. *manufacturing executive*

West Hempstead
Cantilli, Edmund Joseph *safety engineer, educator, translator, writer, consultant*
Chciuk-Celt, Alexandra M. *language educator*
Guggenheimer, Heinrich Walter *mathematician, educator*

West Islip
Cokinos, Stephan George *cardiologist*
Kaigh, Christopher Hamilton *psychologist*
Rifkin, Matthew D. *radiologist*

West Nyack
Fogelman, Rita Tavel *library director*
Pringle, Laurence Patrick *writer*

West Point
Beecher, Amanda I. *mathematics professor*
Chapman, Matthew A. *military officer, science educator*
Czajkoski, Christina Marie *language educator*
Dillon, Joel *military officer*
Gentile, Gian P. *history professor*
Hagenbeck, Franklin Lee *academic administrator, career military officer*
Hann, Ronald Koy *military officer, chemistry professor*

Keith, Bruce Edward *sociologist*
Reel, David Mark *curator, museum director*
Williams, Craig Stewart *organist, choirmaster, music educator, director*

West Seneca
Bidlack, Jerald Dean *manufacturing executive*
Humiston, Daniel J. *entrepreneur*

Westbury
Boes, Lawrence William *lawyer*
Greenberger, Roni Susan *elementary school educator*
Mondello, Joseph N. *political organization administrator*
Ross-Lee, Barbara *dean, educator*
Sandler, Gerald Howard *computer scientist, information technology executive, educator*

Westhampton Beach
Flood, Angela *interior designer, artist*
Ozero, Brian John *chemical engineer*

White Plains
Atnally, Edward Vincent *lawyer*
Baran, Xiaolei Yu *physician, psychiatry professor*
Barrera-Tobon, Carolina *language educator, researcher*
Berlin, Alan Daniel *lawyer, real estate company officer, consultant*
Bernard, Robert William *plastic surgeon*
Blass, John Paul *physician, biochemist*
Bodnar, Peter O. *lawyer*
Carlisle, Jay Charles, II, *lawyer, educator*
Carlucci, Joseph P. *lawyer*
Chase, Jenny Wei-Lang Kao *singer, music educator*
Culleton, James J. *lawyer, former prosecutor*
Davenport, Lindsay *professional tennis player*
Duncan, Bruce W. *hotel and retired real estate company executive*
Eil, Lois Helen *retired physician*
Estevez, Alvaro G. *biology professor, researcher*
Feder, Robert *lawyer*
Fisher, Jerome *apparel executive*
Flanigen, Edith Marie *materials scientist, consultant*
Fleischman, Alan Robert *medical educator, administrator*
Foster, John Horace *consulting environmental engineer*
Fowlkes, Nancy Lanetta Pinkard *social worker*
Freed, Arthur *civil engineer*
Gillingham, Stephen Thomas *financial planner*
Gofman, Alex J. (Alexander Gofman) *marketing executive, author*
Gottlieb, Lester M. *entrepreneur*
Greenawalt, William Sloan *lawyer*
Greenspan, Leon Joseph *lawyer*
Greenspan, Michael Evan *lawyer*
Haines, Daniel Webster *engineering consultant, educator*
Halpern, Philip Morgan *lawyer*
High, Kemba M. *special education educator*
Howse, Jennifer Louise *foundation administrator*
Jimenez, Frank R. *lawyer*
Katz, Michael *pediatrician, educator*
Kelly, Regina Fogel *lawyer*
Kirschenbaum, Ira H. *orthopedist*
Klein, Ross A. *hotel executive*
Landa, Howard Martin *lawyer, management consultant*
Leish, Kenneth William *retired publishing company executive*
Levine, Steven Jon *lawyer*
Lukaszewski, James Edmund *communications executive*
Machover, Carl *computer graphics designer, engineer, consultant*
Manville, Stewart Roebling *archivist*
Marano, Anthony Joseph *cardiologist*
Marino, Jane B. *library director*
Milone, Lydia A. *lawyer*
Moffat, Robert W., Jr. *information technology executive*
Morello, Daniel Conway *plastic surgeon*
Munich, Richard Lee *psychiatrist*
Munneke, Gary Arthur *law educator, consultant*
Narins, Rhoda S. *dermatologist, educator*
Null, William Seth *lawyer*
Ottinger, Richard Lawrence *dean emeritus, former congressman*
Park, John *Internet company executive*
Parker, Barrington D., Jr. *federal judge*
Parker, Everett Carlton *clergyman*
Payson, Martin F. *lawyer*
Pfeffer, Cynthia Roberta *psychiatrist, educator*
Prabhu, Vasant M. *corporate financial executive*
Rapp, Richard Tilden *economist, consultant*
Robinson, Nicholas Adams *law educator, department chairman*
Russo, Donna Lee *social worker*
Ryan, Robert Davis *lawyer*
Sacco, John Michael *accountant*
Schandler, Jon B. *hospital administrator*
Scott-Williams, Wendy Lee *library and information scientist*
Shamoian, Charles Anthony *psychiatrist, educator*
Sheehan, Timothy J. *lawyer*
Siegel, Kenneth S. *lawyer*
Slaughter, John Brooks *professional society administrator*
Sloan, F(rank) Blaine *retired law educator*
Smith, Gerard Peter *neuroscientist*
Steccato, Carl L. *lawyer*
Streisand, Robert L. *thoracic surgeon*
Szolnoki, John Frank *special education educator, administrator*
Trapp, Peter Jarl Rudolf *investment manager*
Underweiser, Irwin Philip *mining executive, lawyer*
Underwood, Steven Clark *financial services company executive*
van Paasschen, Frits *hotel executive*
Waterhouse, Lynette *mathematics educator*
Weisburger, John Hans *retired medical researcher*
Whittemore, Gail Farnsworth *law librarian*
Williams, Serena *professional tennis player, apparel designer*

Williams, Venus *professional tennis player*
Zuckerman, Marc Abraham *finance educator*

Whitesboro
Blake, Edward Stephens *secondary school educator*

Whitestone
Lodico, Cheryl Madeline *secondary school educator*
Wingate, Constance Blandy *retired librarian*

Williamsville
Ackerman, Philip Charles *gas industry executive*
Berner, Robert Frank *managerial statistics educator, administrator*
Cloudsley, Donald Hugh *retired library administrator*
Farrell, Mark G. *lawyer, judge*
Fortunato, Pat Deakin *fine artist*
Garton, Charles *classics educator*
Kim, Jung Taek *electrochemical engineer*
Levite, Laurence A. *publishing executive*
Metzger, Ernest Hugh *aerospace engineer, research scientist*
Neiman, Joseph Bruce *dermatologist, educator*
Ogra, Pearay L. *pediatrician, educator*
Pearson, Paul David *lawyer, arbitrator, mediator*
Perry, J. Warren *health facility administrator, educator*
Reisman, Robert E. *allergist, educator*
Rekate, Albert C. *physician*
Severo, Norman C. *retired statistics professor*
Zahn, Cindy Mae *dental educator*

Willsboro
Reuther, David Louis *retired children's book publisher, writer*

Windsor
Warner, Roberta Arlene *retired accountant, financial services executive*

Woodbury
Greenberg, Stephen Todd *plastic surgeon*
Guttenplan, Harold Esau *retired food company executive*
Heath, David Lewis *lawyer*

Woodhaven
Lipscomb, Thomas Heber III *media company executive*

Woodmere
Winick, Bernyce Alpert *artist, photographer*

Woodside
Hofmann, Herbert C. *diversified holding company executive*
Sfiroudis, Gloria Tides *library and information scientist, educator*

Woodstock
Banks, Rela *sculptor*
De Johnette, Jack *musician*
Godwin, Gail Kathleen *writer*
Lieberman, Josefa Nina *retired psychologist, writer*
Ober, Stuart Alan *investment advisor, writer*

Wyandanch
Fonseca, Alejandra *language educator*
Newman, Samuel *retired trust company executive*

Yonkers
Amicone, Philip A. *Mayor, Yonkers, New York*
Baumel, Herbert *violinist, conductor*
Botwinick, Michael *museum director*
Capodilupo, Elizabeth Jeanne Hatton *public relations executive, writer*
Holtz, Gilbert Joseph *steel company executive*
Hough, Barbara *library media specialist, educator*
Ismail, Jeanne *elementary school educator*
Johansen, Robert Joseph *consulting actuary*
Kilsch, Gunther H. *lawyer*
Kleman, Kimberly C. *editor-in-chief*
Liggio, Jean Vincenza *adult education educator, artist*
Lupiani, Donald Anthony *psychologist*
McKean, Kevin S. *publishing executive, writer*
Monegro, Francisco *alternative medicine consultant, psychology professor*
Philipps, Edward William *former banker, real estate appraiser*
Singer, Cecile Doris *bank executive, former state legislator*
Speirs, Greg *sports artist*
Torrese, Dante Michael *prosthodontist, educator*
Trentanelli, John Anthony *educational administrator*
Viola, Mary Jo *art history educator*
Westphal, Carol Jean *media specialist*

Yorktown Heights
Choi, Changhwan *operations research specialist*
Choi, Jong Hyuk *computer scientist*
Das, Koushik K. *industrial research manager*
D'Emic, Christopher Peter *chemical engineer, researcher*
Dennard, Robert Heath *engineering executive, scientist*
Gupta, Devendra *material scientist, engineer*
Hoffman, Alan Jerome *mathematician, educator*
Iyengar, Arun K. *computer scientist*
Joshi, Rajiv V. *information technology manager, researcher*
Kang, Sung Kwon *materials scientist, researcher*
Keyes, Robert W. *physicist, researcher*
Kim, Kyu-hyoun *electrical engineer, researcher*
Lang, Norton David *physicist*
Mayer, Gerard J. *physician*
Restle, Phillip J. *engineering company executive*
Salapura, Valentina *computer science educator*
Schiller, Barbara *retired special education educator*
Wade, James O'Shea *editor, writer*
Wynne, James J. *research scientist*
Zitouni, Imed *research scientist*

Youngstown
Alpert, Norman *chemical company executive*
Lamb, Charles F. *retired minister, educator*

NORTH CAROLINA

Advance
Cochrane, Betsy Lane *former state senator*
Guth, Caryl Joy *retired anesthesiologist*

Andrews
Fonda, Ronald Alan *epistemologist*
Marta, Dawn Reneé *psychologist*

Ararat
Marsh, Joseph Virgil *investment advisor, analyst, broker, consultant, research scientist*

Arden
Baker, Kerry Allen *management consultant*
Leacock, Rodney Owen *neurologist, educator*

Asheboro
Jones, David M. *zoological park administrator*
Sanders, William Eugene *marketing executive*

Asheville
Brown, David G. *academic administrator*
Cutright, Phillips *sociologist, educator*
Davis, Roy Walton, Jr. *lawyer*
Dickens, Charles Henderson *retired social sciences educator*
Elmore, Bruce Alexander, Jr. *lawyer*
Fedock, Barbara C. *primary school educator, consultant*
Fernandes, Jane K. *academic administrator, sign language professional*
Haynes, John Mabin *retired utilities executive*
Horwitz, Bertrand Nathan *finance educator*
King, Joseph Bertram *architect*
Latta, Diana Lennox *retired interior designer*
Lavelle, Brian Francis David *lawyer*
Letzig, Betty Jean *retired financial consultant*
Martin, Harry Corpening *lawyer, retired state supreme court justice*
Merrill, Deane Whitney, Jr. *education educator, consultant*
Merrill, Jonathan Alden *retired newsletter editor*
Meyerson, Seymour *retired chemist*
Mumpower, Carl III *councilman*
Mundt, Barry Maynard *management consultant*
Polite, Lettie Wilson *retired middle school educator, librarian*
Ponder, Anne *academic administrator*
Reidinger, Martin Karl *federal judge*
Rickman, Ellen Erwin *museum administrator*
Shuler, Heath (Joseph Heath Shuler) *United States Representative from North Carolina, retired professional football player*
Smith, James Finley *economist, educator*
Ter Horst, Jerald Franklin *public affairs counselor, former White House press secretary*
Thornburg, Lacy Herman *federal judge*
Tynes, Robert Dick *artist, educator*

Bakersville
Vesely, Pamela J. *social studies educator*

Bald Head Island
Smith, Allie Maitland *retired engineering educator*

Banner Elk
Hutcheson, James Sterling *retired physician, allergist*

Beaufort
Cullman, Hugh *retired tobacco company executive*
Waggett, Rebecca Jane *research scientist*

Belmont
Rishel, Tracy D. *finance educator, director*
Stamps, Leighton Elderkin *psychology educator*
Williams, David M. *theologian, educator*

Benson
Lunn, Ronald Alan *environmentalist*

Black Mountain
Belue, Janie A. *music educator*
Blackwell, Anna Nelle *medical educator, medical technician*
Dalton, Robert Edgar *retired mathematician, computer scientist*
Ingle, Robert P. *retail executive*

Boiling Springs
Cox, Tamara *language educator*
Lahaie, Scot *theater educator*
Qualls, Paula Fontana *religious studies educator*
Vanderburg, Timothy Warren *history professor*
Walker, Vickie Elaine *nursing educator*

Boone
Conrad, David Paul *business broker, real estate developer, retired food service executive*
Cox, Victoria Kathleen *humanities educator*
Frindethie, Martial Kokroa *literature and language professor*
Hill, Robert W. *psychology professor, director*
Hou, Guichuan *biology professor, director*
Johnson, Phillip Eugene *mathematics professor*
Lacy, Hollie Hutchison *musician, educator*
Martin, Vicki Joan *biology professor*
Mendel, Traci *composer, educator*
Mills, Susan Wilson *music educator*
Neff, Alice Elaine *costume designer*
Oelberg, Robert Nathan *landscape architect*
Sturgill, Brad *finance educator*
Udogu, E. Ike *social sciences educator, researcher*
Yaukey, Margaret Ann *art educator*

Brevard
Foster, Edward John *engineer physicist*
Phillips, Euan Hywel *publishing executive*

Bryson City
Miller, Gary H. *lawyer*

Buies Creek
Hight, H. K. *theater technical director*
Jonas, William Glenn, Jr. *religious studies educator, department chairman*

Burlington
Brennan, Michael W. *ophthalmologist*
Ellington, Beth Elder *librarian*
Holt, Bertha Merrill *state legislator*
King, David Paul *health services executive, lawyer*
Phillips, Ruth Ann *retired secondary school educator*
Powell, James Bobbitt *health facility administrator, pathologist*
Wilson, William Preston *retired psychiatrist*

Burnsville
Doyle, John Lawrence *artist*

Calabash
Strunk, Orlo Christopher, Jr. *psychology professor*

Camden
Hammond, Roy Joseph *reinsurance company executive*

Camp Lejeune
Kuhn, Michael A. *orthopedist*

Canton
Hand, Clelia *artist, art educator*
Roberts, Bill Glen *retired protective services official*

Cape Carteret
Mullikin, Thomas Wilson *mathematics professor*

Carrboro
Barbarin, Oscar Anthony *psychologist*
Dixon, Frederick Dail *architect*
Jones-Smith, Jessica Claire *dietician*
Prather, Donna Lynn *psychiatrist*

Carthage
Gebhardt, Robert Charles *lawyer*
Osmar, Christina *psychologist*

Cary
Bryant, Mynora Joyce *not-for-profit fundraiser*
Capps, Michael *video game company executive*
Conrad, Hans *materials science and engineering educator*
Dreyer, Duane Arthur *medical educator*
Goodnight, James H. *software company executive*
Goodwin, Barry Kent *economics educator*
Grubb, Gary S. *pharmaceutical executive*
Jingchun, Sun *research scientist*
Kennedy, Andrew Scott *nuclear medicine physician, educator*
Kung, Pang-Jen *materials scientist, electrical engineer*
Lawson, William, Jr., (B.J. Lawson) *medical products executive*
Martin, William Royall, Jr. *retired professional society administrator*
Montgomery, Charles Harvey *lawyer*
Slaattè, Howard Alexander *minister, philosophy educator*
Summers, Suzanne Frances Hemenway *elementary school educator*
Sundstrom, Mary Chary *psychologist*
Swanson, David C. *publishing executive*
Sweeney, Tim *computer game developer, programmer*
Taylor, David Wyatt Aiken *retired clergyman*
Timothy, David Harry *retired biology professor*
Vick, Columbus Edwin, Jr. *retired civil engineering design firm executive*
You, Taek H. *biology professor, researcher*

Cashiers
O'Connell, Edward James, Jr. *psychologist, educator, systems administrator, consultant*

Chapel Hill
Andrews, Richard Nigel Lyon *academic administrator, educator*
Atashili, Julius *epidemiologist*
Bailey, Herbert Smith, Jr. *retired publisher*
Baker, Edward L., Jr. *public health physician*
Ballard, David Eugene *anesthesiologist*
Baroff, George Stanley *psychologist, educator*
Barrett, Stephen *psychiatrist, educator, consultant*
Bender, Deborah E. *medical educator*
Benjamin, John Tabb *retired pediatrician*
Bennett, Peter Brian *medical researcher, educator*
Bernard, Stephen Alan *oncologist*
Binotti, Lucia *language educator*
Black, Stanley Warren III *retired economics professor*
Blouin, Robert A. *dean, pharmacy educator*
Boger, John Charles *law educator, dean*
Bowers, Thomas Arnold *journalism educator, dean*
Bowles, Erskine Boyce *academic administrator, former White House chief of staff*
Brooks, Frederick Phillips, Jr. *computer scientist, educator*
Brophy, Alfred Laurence III *law educator*
Brown, Frank *social sciences educator*
Brown, Michael L. *language educator*
Browning, Christopher R. *historian, educator*
Brummet, Richard Lee *retired accounting educator*
Buck, Richard Pierson *chemistry educator, researcher*
Burchinal, Margaret Ruth *statistician*
Bursey, Maurice M. *retired chemistry professor*
Buse, John Bernard *physician, educator*
Byrns, Ralph Truman *economics professor, writer*
Caldwell, Kia Lilly *humanities educator*
Callahan, Leigh Fleming *medical educator, researcher*
Campbell, Bobby Jack *academic administrator*
Campbell, Frances Alexander *psychologist*
Campion, Edmund Ronan *orthopedist, educator*
Carey, Lisa Anne *oncologist, educator*
Carroll, Roy *retired academic administrator*
Carson, Culley Clyde III *urologist, educator*
Chaney, Stephen Gifford *biochemistry and biophysics educator*
Chang, Paul Kuk Won *theology educator, researcher, pastor*
Clark, Arthur Watts *insurance company executive*
Cohen, Myron *epidemiologist*
Cole, Richard Ray *communications educator, former dean*
Collier, Albert M. *pediatrician, educator, director*
Conley, Patrick *clinic administrator*
Corrado, Michael Louis *law educator*
Cronenwett, Linda r. *dean, educator, hospital administrator*
Cummings, Sandra Eileen *medical products executive*
Davis, Butch (Paul Hilton Davis) *college football coach*
Davis, Morris Schuyler *astronomer*
Davis, Sarah Irwin *retired language educator*
Dean, James W., Jr. *dean, finance educator*
D'Ercole, Augustine Joseph *pediatrician, educator*
Dohlman, Henrik Gunnar *medical educator, department vice chairman*
Dowling, Dean Edward *information scientist, educator*
Drake, Amelia F. *otolaryngologist*
Drossman, Douglas Arnold *medical investigator, gastroenterologist, educator*
Drutz, David Jules *venture capitalist*
Egan, Thomas Michael *surgeon, educator*
Elbogen, Eric B. *psychologist, educator*
Escolar, Maria L. *pediatrician, educator*
Farber, Rosann Alexander *geneticist, educator*
Feduccia, J. Alan *biologist, educator*
Feins, Richard Harry *thoracic surgeon*
Fieleke, Norman Siegfried *economist, educator*
Fine, J(ames) Allen *insurance company executive*
Fitzpatrick, Whitfield Westfeldt *lawyer*
Fletcher, Suzanne Wright *epidemiologist, medical educator, editor*
Flora, Joseph M(artin) *language educator*
Fordham, Lynn Ansley *pediatric radiologist*
Forman, Donald T. *biochemist, educator*
Fowler, W. Craig *ophthalmologist, educator*
Frampton, Paul Howard *physics researcher, educator*
Frantz, Elman G. *pediatric cardiologist, surgeon*
Freedman, Irving Melvin *lawyer*
Ganley, Oswald Harold *retired director*
Garbutt, James C. *psychiatrist, educator*
Gherghe, Costin Marian *research scientist*
Gil, Karen M. *dean, psychology professor*
Godschalk, David Robinson *architect, urban development planner, educator*
Gold, Stuart Harrison *pediatrician*
Goldberg, Richard Miles *physician, medical oncologist*
Goldsmith, Lowell Alan *medical educator*
Gordon-Larsen, Penny *nutritionist, educator, researcher*
Goyer, Robert Andrew *pathology educator*
Gray, Virginia Hickman *political science professor*
Green, Paul Eliot, Jr. *retired optical engineer*
Greenwood, Robert Samuel *pediatric neurologist*
Greganti, Mac Andrew *physician, educator*
Gregory, Patricia Caroline *medical educator*
Grendler, Paul Frederick *historian, educator*
Griffiths, José-Marie *dean, library and information science educator*
Gura, Philip Francis *English and American literature educator*
Hadler, Nortin Marvin *rheumatologist, clinical investigator, educator*
Hamrick, Harvey J. *pediatrician*
Hardin, Paul III *law educator*
Hatchell, Sylvia R. *women's college basketball coach*
Henry, G. William *pediatrician*
Henson, O'Dell Williams, Jr. *retired anatomy educator*
Hines, Ian Neil *immunologist, educator*
Hirsch, Philip Francis *pharmacologist, educator*
Hulka, Jaroslav Fabian *obstetrician, gynecologist*
Hunt, Douglass *retired university official*
Hurwitz, Shepard Raphael *orthopaedic surgeon, educator*
Johnson, Lucie Jenkins *retired social worker*
Jones, Houston Gwynne *archivist, history professor*
Jones, Paul McDonald *distributed information researcher, educator*
Jones, W. S. (Steve Jones) *management educator, former dean*
Joyner, Leon Felix *university administrator, retired*
Kakoki, Masao *medical educator*
Kampov-Polevoi, Alexei Boris *psychiatrist, educator*
Kass, Emily *museum director*
Kaufman, David Gordon *medical educator*
Kindem, Gorham Anders *filmmaker, educator*
Klinefelter, Anne *law librarian, educator*
Kohn, Richard H. *historian, educator*
Krasno, Richard Michael *foundation executive, educator*
Latané, Bibb *social psychologist*
Lauder, Valarie Anne *editor, educator*
Lawrence, David Michael *lawyer, educator*
Lee, Kuo-Hsiung *medicinal chemistry professor*
Levine, Madeline Geltman *literature and language educator, translator*
Li, Wendan *literature and language professor, researcher*
Lich-Tyler, Stephen *economics professor*
Ligett, Waldo Buford *chemist*
Lochridge, Julie Deane *retired communications executive*
Loeb, Ben Fohl, Jr. *retired law educator*
Lohr, Jacob Andrew *pediatrician, educator*
Losh, Molly *science educator*
Lowman, Robert Paul *psychology professor, academic administrator*
Lundblad, Roger Lauren *biotechnology consultant*
Lysle, Donald T. *psychology professor, department chairman*
Macdonald, James Ross *physicist, researcher*
MacRae, Elizabeth (Elizabeth MacRae Halsey) *counselor, actor*
Magill, Samuel Hays *academic administrator, consultant*
Magnuson, Terry R. *geneticist, educator*
Marchionini, Gary Joseph *information science educator*
Margolis, David Michael *medical educator*
Maroni, Donna Farolino *biologist, researcher*
Martikainen, A(une) Helen *retired health specialist educator*
Mersini - Houghton, Laura *physicist, educator*
Merzbacher, Eugen *retired physics professor*
Messer, Jay James *environmental scientist*
Miller, C. Arden *physician, educator*
Moellering, John Henry *aviation maintenance company executive*
Moeser, James Charles *music educator, former academic administrator*
Moll, Stephan *medical educator*
Moore, Albert Cunningham *lawyer, insurance company executive*
Morrell, Dean Scott *pediatric dermatologist*
Mueller, Nancy Schneider *retired biology professor*
Munger, Michael Curtis *public policy educator*
Muss, Hyman Bernard *oncologist, educator*
Neff, Severine *music educator*
Nelson, Philip Francis *musicologist, consultant, conductor*
Nichol, Gene Ray, Jr. *law educator, former academic administrator*
Orthner, Dennis K. *social sciences educator, consultant*
Parr, Robert Ghormley *chemistry professor*
Patton, Lauren L. *dentist, researcher*
Peacock, Erle Ewart, Jr. *surgeon, lawyer, educator*
Pedersen, Lee G. *chemistry professor*
Pérez, Louis A., Jr. *history professor*
Perreault, William Daniel, Jr. *business administration educator*
Peterson, Herbert Bryson *obstetrician, gynecologist, educator*
Pfennig, David William *biology professor*
Pillsbury, Harold Crockett III *otolaryngologist*
Pisano, Etta D. *radiologist, educator*
Piven, Joseph *psychiatrist, educator*
Prange, Arthur Jergen, Jr. *psychology and psychiatry professor, neuroscientist*
Proffit, William Robert *orthodontics educator*
Pruett, James Worrell *librarian, educator, musicologist*
Rabil, Albert, Jr. *humanities educator*
Radding, Cynthia *historian, educator*
Ramsey, John Michael *chemistry professor, researcher*
Ravenel, Shannon *book publishing professional*
Reichart, Karaleah S. *anthropologist, educator*
Retsch-Bogart, George Z. *pediatric pulmonologist, surgeon*
Rezk, Naser Labeeb *biochemist, researcher*
Richman, Jack M. *social sciences educator*
Riess, Werner *ancient history and classics professor*
Riggs, Timothy Allan *museum curator*
Rimer, Barbara K. *dean, healthcare educator*
Roper, William Lee *dean, preventive medicine physician, administrator*
Ross, Coleman DeVane *accountant, insurance company executive*
Runyan, Desmond Kimo *medical educator, researcher*
Sanders, John Lassiter *retired academic administrator*
Schoonover, Brenda B. *ambassador*
Schoultz, Lars *political scientist, educator*
Schrock, Robert D., Jr. *retired orthopaedic surgeon, educator*
Selkirk, James Kirkwood *retired biochemist*
Sewright, Charles William, Jr. *mortgage banking advisory services company executive*
Shaheen, Nicholas J. *epidemiologist, educator*
Sheldon, George Frank *medical educator*
Sherman, Daniel James *art history professor*
Smith, Dean Edwards *retired men's college basketball coach*
Smith, Michael R. *dean, academic administrator*
Smith, Sidney Crawle, Jr. *cardiologist, educator*
Smithies, Oliver *geneticist, educator*
Sorenson, James Roger *public health educator*
Southern, Robert Allen *lawyer*
Sparling, Philip Frederick *medical educator*
Spencer, Elizabeth *writer*
Spencer, Roger Felix *psychiatrist, educator*
Stenberg, Carl W. III *public administration educator, dean*
Steponaitis, Vincas Petras *archaeologist, anthropologist, educator*
Stockman, James Anthony III *pediatrician*
Stouffer, George Andrew *cardiologist, educator*
Strauss, Albrecht Benno *retired language educator, editor*
Stumpf, Walter Erich *cell biology and pharmacology professor, researcher*
Summers, Sandra Lindemann *language educator*
Taft, Timothy Ned *orthopedist, surgeon, sports medicine physician*
Taylor, Michael E. *mathematics professor*
Terrenato, Nicola *archaeologist, researcher*
Thomas, Colin Gordon, Jr. *surgeon, medical educator*
Thorp, H. Holden *academic administrator, chemistry professor*
Thorp, John Mercer, Jr. *physician*
Tie, Jian-Ke *medical educator*
Tolley, Aubrey Granville *psychiatrist, health facility administrator*
Umminger, Bruce Lynn *government agency administrator, research scientist, educator, consultant*
Vargha, Rebecca Brogden *librarian, library association executive*

Visser, Robin *humanities educator*
von Allmen, Daniel *pediatric surgeon*
Watson, Harry L. *history professor, director*
Wegner, Judith Welch *lawyer, educator, dean*
Weinberg, Richard J. *medical educator*
Weiner, Timothy M. *pediatric surgeon*
West, Alisha Nicole *otolaryngologist, surgeon*
West, III, William Custis *retired ancient language educator*
White, Raymond Petrie, Jr. *dentist, educator, dean*
Whybark, David Clay *business educator, researcher*
Wilfert, Catherine M. *medical association administrator, pediatrician, epidemiologist, educator*
Williams, John N. *dean, dental educator*
Williams, Mark Edward *geriatrician*
Williams, Roy *men's college basketball coach*
Williamson, Joel Rudolph *humanities educator, writer*
Wilson, Frank Crane, Jr. *orthopedist*
Winfield, John Buckner *rheumatologist, educator*
Yow, Valerie Raleigh *historian, writer, counselor*
Zeisel, Steven H. *nutritionist, scientist, educator*
Zhang, Jian *physics professor, researcher*
Zhu, Hongtu *science educator*

Charlotte
Alphin, J. Steele *bank executive*
Al-Ruzzeh, Sharif *cardiothoracic surgeon*
Anderson, Gerald Leslie *finance company executive*
Armstrong, James David *editor, educator, minister*
Austin, Margaret Gibson *public relations executive*
Aycock, Hugh David *steel manufacturing company executive*
Aydin, Cemil *history professor*
Ayscue, Edwin Osborne, Jr. *lawyer*
Banks, Keith *bank executive*
Baronoff, Steven A. *bank executive*
Bass-Hollis, Cynthia Gibson *environmental services administrator*
Bauroth, Nancy Ann *journalist, former marketing executive*
Beams, Maliz *finance company executive*
Belk, Irwin *retail executive*
Belk, Thomas Milburn, Jr., (Tim) *apparel executive*
Bell, Raja *professional basketball player*
Bessant, Cathy (Catherine Pombier) *bank executive, marketing professional*
Blanchfield, Francis J., Jr. *lawyer*
Boe, Christopher Scott *education educator*
Bonnefoux, Jean-Pierre *choreographer, dancer*
Brackett, Martin Luther, Jr. *lawyer*
Brown, Larry (Lawrence Harvey Brown) *professional basketball coach*
Buchan, Jonathan Edward, Jr. *lawyer*
Buckley, Charles Robinson III *lawyer*
Bullock, Sharon King *biologist, educator*
Burnett, John Nicholas *retired chemistry educator*
Caulkins, Ann *publishing executive*
Chan, Yiumo *biochemist*
Chance, Gloria A. *bank executive*
Chandler, Tyson Cleotis *professional basketball player*
Clark-Claytor, Elizabeth B. *media specialist*
Clodfelter, Daniel Gray *state legislator, lawyer*
Coleman, Kent K. *science association director*
Conrad, Robert J., Jr. *federal judge*
Cooke, Steven John *chemical engineer, consultant, scientist*
Corvi, Carolyn *manufacturing executive*
Cosper, David P. *automotive executive*
Coss, Stephen K. *lawyer*
Craig, Depken II A. *economics professor*
Cramer, Robert W. *lawyer*
Crawford, Juanita Gatewood *nursing technician*
Crickenberger, Heather Marcelle *literature and language professor*
Cummings, Stephen Emery *investment banking executive*
Curlin, William George *bishop emeritus*
Darnell, David Clark *bank executive*
Delhomme, Jake Christopher *professional football player*
Diaw, Boris (Boris Diaw-Riffiod) *professional basketball player*
Dickson, Thomas Walter *textile company executive*
DiMicco, Daniel R. *manufacturing executive*
Dubois, Philip Leon *academic administrator, political scientist, educator*
Dunn, Jackson Thomas, Jr. *lawyer, educator*
Earnhardt, Dale, Jr. *race car driver*
Eaves, Felmont Farrell III *plastic surgeon*
Elanayar, Sunil K. *research and development engineer*
Eppes, Thomas Evans *advertising and public relations executive*
Eppley, Frances Fielden *secondary school educator, writer*
Erdman, David Williams *lawyer*
Ethridge, Mark Foster III *writer, publishing executive, consultant*
Ferebee, Stephen Scott, Jr. *retired architect*
Ferriola, John J. *manufacturing executive*
Finley, Glenna *writer*
Finucane, Anne M. *bank executive*
Fox, John *professional football coach*
Fretwell, Elbert K., Jr. *retired university chancellor, consultant*
Gage, Gaston Hemphill *lawyer*
Gambrell, Sarah Belk *retail executive*
Gantt, Harvey B. *architect, former mayor*
Goldfield, David *history professor, writer*
Goldstein, Stuart N. *lawyer*
Good, Lynn J. *energy executive*
Goolkasian, Paula A. *psychologist, educator*
Gordon, Jeff *race car driver*
Gorman, Peter C. *school system administrator*
Gotta, Joseph D. *music company executive*
Graham, Billy (William Franklin Graham) *evangelist*
Graham, Franklin (William Franklin Graham III) *evangelist, missionary*
Grigg, Eddie Garman *minister, educator*
Gross, Jordan Alan *professional football player*
Guelli, Pete *professional sports team executive*
Gunson, Douglas R. *lawyer*
Haines, Kenneth H. *sports television broadcasting and marketing executive*
Hall, James Bryan *gynecologist, oncologist*
Handy, John W. *shipping company executive, retired military officer*
Hankins, Irvin W. III *lawyer*
Hanna, George Verner III *lawyer*
Harris, Corey *blues musician*
Hatcher, James Gregory *lawyer*
Hauser, David L. *communications executive*
Hayes, Corlis Angela *communications educator, actor, director*
Higgins, Rod (Roderick Dwayne Higgins) *professional sports team executive, retired professional basketball player*
Horn, Carl III *retired federal judge, lawyer*
Huberman, Jeffrey Allen *architect*
Hunstad, Joseph Paul *plastic surgeon, educator*
Hurney, Marty *professional sports team executive*
Jackson, Gary Walker *lawyer*
Jacobs, Gordon Waldemar *surgeon, educator*
Jamil, Dhiaa M. *energy executive*
Janson, Julia S. *energy executive*
Jenkins, Benjamin P. III *bank executive*
Johnson, Constance Green *health facility administrator*
Johnson, Jimmie (James Kenneth Johnson) *race car driver*
Jones, Milton H., Jr. *bank executive*
Jordan, Carol Walker *librarian, educator*
Jordan, Michael Jeffrey *professional sports team executive, retired professional basketball player*
Jugis, Peter Joseph *bishop*
Kabengela, Lubambala Paul *engineering educator*
Kearney, Christopher J. *manufacturing executive, lawyer*
Kelley, Janet Godsey *lawyer*
Kelly, R. James *retail executive*
Kelly, Stanhope A. *bank executive*
Kistenberg, Cindy J. *communications educator, theater educator*
Kline, Phil *museum director*
Knox, Frances S. *lawyer*
Krawcheck, Sallie L. *diversified financial services company executive*
Kreimer, Michael Walter *financial planner, investment company executive*
Kuechle, Scott E. *manufacturing executive*
Laditka, Sarah Beth *healthcare educator*
Larsen, Marshall O. *manufacturing executive*
Lea, Scott Carter *retired packaging company executive*
Lee, Joseph William *sales executive*
Levine, Howard R. *retail executive*
Lewis, Kenneth D. *bank executive*
Lieving, Lori M. *psychologist, director*
Lilly, Kevin L. *lawyer, manufacturing executive*
Linda, Sickler Suda *music educator*
Linnert, Terrence Gregory *lawyer*
Lisenby, Terry S. *manufacturing executive*
Locke, Elizabeth Hughes *retired foundation administrator*
Lott, Hamilton, Jr. *manufacturing executive*
Macadam, Stephen E. *wholesale distribution executive*
Manly, Marc Edward *lawyer, energy executive*
Martin, James Grubbs *healthcare consultant, Former United States Representative, NC*
Massey, Walter Eugene *bank executive, retired academic administrator*
Mauney, Gary Vance *lawyer*
McAfee, Larry W. *chemistry educator*
McBryde, Neill Gregory *lawyer*
McClure, Howard Jean, Jr. *advocate*
McCoy, Michael D. *lawyer*
McCrory, Patrick *Mayor, Charlotte, North Carolina*
McFayden, Shannon W. *bank holding company executive*
McGill, John Knox *lawyer*
McKay-Wilkinson, Julie Ann *minister, marriage and family therapist*
Mehta, Kiran H. *lawyer*
Mercer, Evelyn Lois *retired counseling administrator*
Merrifield, Jeffrey S. *engineering company executive, former commissioner*
Milton, Michael Anthony *minister, writer*
Mohammed, Nazr *professional basketball player*
Monroe, Frederick Leroy *chemist*
Montag, Thomas K. (Thomas Kell Montag) *bank executive*
Montague, Edgar Burwell, III, (Monty Montague) *industrial designer*
Morgan, James H. *food services company executive, former investment company executive*
Moynihan, Brian T. *investment company executive, bank executive*
Mueller, Werner Heinrich *chemical company executive*
Muhammad, Muhsin, II, *professional football player*
Mullen, Graham Calder *federal judge*
Munroe, Jennifer *literature and language professor*
Murray, Cindy *bank executive*
Myers, Robert Manson *language educator, writer*
Nedzbala, Michael *lawyer*
Neel, Richard Eugene *economist, educator*
Noujaim, Fares Dourid *investment company executive*
O'Leary, Patrick J. *manufacturing executive*
Olson, William Charles *psychology professor*
Ozan, Erol *engineering educator, researcher*
Parrish, D. Michael *manufacturing executive*
Peacock, A(lvin) Ward *textile company executive*
Peppers, Julius (Frazier) *professional football player*
Peterson, Evonne Stewart *elementary school educator*
Prabha, Karan *lab administrator*
Preston, Margaret Mary V. *bank executive*
Price, Joe L. *bank executive*
Pyle, Gerald Fredric *geographer, educator*
Ragan, Robert Allison *private investment executive, financial consultant*
Ramaprabhu, Praveen *engineering educator*
Raper, William Cranford *lawyer*
Rawlins, Donald Ray *lawyer*
Rhue, Monika Rivera *archivist*
Roberts, David A. *manufacturing executive*
Roche, Cathy *energy executive*
Rogers, James Eugene (Jim Rogers) *energy executive*
Rolfe, Christopher C. *energy executive*
Rutkowski, Joseph A. *manufacturing executive*
Schafermeyer, Robert William *emergency physician, educator, health policy consultant*
Schnaper, Cara L. *diversified financial services company executive*
Schorr, Alvin Louis *social worker, educator*
Selig, Stefan M. *bank executive*
Shaw, Ruth G. *energy company executive*
Sherburne, Jane C. *lawyer, bank executive*
Shoffner, Robert L. III *economics professor*
Siegel, Samuel *metals company executive*
Sintz, Edward Francis *librarian*
Skains, Thomas E. *gas industry executive*
Slater, Charles James *construction company executive*
Smith, B. Scott *automotive executive*
Smith, Kenneth T. *retail executive*
Smith, O. Bruton *automotive company executive*
Smith, Stevonne Latrall (Steve Smith) *professional football player*
Smith, Wilburn Jackson, Jr. *retired bank executive*
Snyder, James C., Jr. *lawyer, consumer products company executive*
Spangler, Clemmie Dixon, Jr. *construction company executive*
Spiro, Robert Harry, Jr. *foundation and business executive, educator*
Steel, Robert King *bank executive, former federal agency administrator*
Sulg, Madis *manufacturing executive, entrepreneur*
Summa, Philip *lawyer*
Taylor, Harry *real estate broker*
Thames, Rick *publishing executive, editor-in-chief*
Thompson, Jocelyn Pharr *organist, director, educator*
Thompson, John Albert, Jr. *dermatologist*
Thompson, Ronald L. *finance company executive, former manufacturing company executive*
Thompson, Sydnor, Jr., (Charles William Sydnor Thompson Jr.) *lawyer, mediator, arbitrator*
Trent, B. Keith *lawyer, energy executive*
Turner, James Lee *energy executive*
Tyson, Cynthia Haldenby *academic administrator*
Valasquez, Joseph Louis *industrial engineer*
Van Allen, William Kent *lawyer*
Van Alstyne, Vance Brownell *management consultant*
Van Hoy, Philip Marshall *lawyer*
Veyera, Jeffrey Alan *bank executive*
Vinroot, Richard Allen *lawyer, mayor*
Walker, George W. C. *bishop*
Walker, Jewett Lynius *clergyman, church official*
Webster, Murray Alexander, Jr. *sociologist, educator*
Whitfield, Fred, Jr. *professional sports team executive*
Whitney, Frank DeArmon *federal judge, former prosecutor*
Williams, DeAngelo *professional football player*
Wood, William McBrayer *lawyer*
Woodward, James Hoyt *academic administrator, engineering educator*
Wright, Bonnie H. *middle school educator*
Wyche, James Ramage *lawyer*
Xie, Jiang *engineering educator*
Zheng, Naiquan Nigel *mechanical engineer, educator*
Zimmern, Emily Fairchild *museum director*
Zwiener, David Kenneth *bank executive*

Cherryville
Huffstetler, Palmer Eugene *lawyer*
Mayhew, Kenneth Edwin, Jr. *retired transportation executive*

Clemmons
Foxx, Virginia Ann *United States Representative from North Carolina, small business owner*
Jones, Marvin Lamar *histologist*

Clinton
Davis, William Maxie, Jr. *lawyer*
Griffin, Betty Lou *not-for-profit developer, educator*

Colerain
Stephens, William A. (Dean Stephens) *computer consultant*

Concord
Biffle, Greg *race car driver*
Edwards, Carl *race car driver*
Faw, Ernie M. *healthcare educator*
Franchitti, Dario *race car driver*
Howard, Vivian Amick *music educator*
Kahne, Kasey (Kenneth) *race car driver*
Kenseth, Matt Roy *race car driver*
Langford, Francis Page Johns *otolaryngologist*
Montoya, Juan Pablo *professional race car driver*
Peterson, Ralph E. *endocrinologist, researcher*
Smith, (Ollen) Bruton *sports association executive*

Conover
Jarrett, Dale (Arnold) *commentator, retired professional race car driver*

Cove City
Hawkins, Elinor Dixon (Mrs. Carroll Woodard Hawkins) *retired librarian*
Miller, Wendy A. *elementary school educator*

Cullowhee
Armfield, Terri Elaine *music educator, musician*
Barnes, Julia A. *mathematics professor*
Beam, Richard Squires *theater educator*
Catley, Kefyn *biology professor*
Coulter, Myron Lee *retired academic administrator*
Jensen, Donald A., Jr. *management consultant, educator*
Moss, Hollye K. *finance educator*
Rash, Ron *writer, educator*
Reed, Alfred Douglas *retired academic administrator*

Dallas
Blanton, Robert D'Alden *anthropologist, educator, history professor*
Conrad, Jamie Holleman *finance educator*
Easter, Willie, Jr. *artist, writer*
Neuman, Deborah *language educator*

Davidson
Cole, Richard Cargill *language educator*
Dixon, Stephanie Bell *elementary school educator*
Henkel, Herbert Ludwig *diversified industrial products company executive*
Klein, Benjamin Garrett *mathematics professor, consultant*
Palmer, Edward L. *psychologist, educator, writer*
Park, Leland Madison *retired librarian*
Ratchford, Joseph Thomas *science and technology policy educator, consultant*
Ross, Thomas Warren, Sr. *academic administrator, former judge*
Sprague, Raymond *music educator*

Denver
Gleasner, Diana Cottle *author*

Drexel
McCall, Maxine Cooper *publisher, minister, educator, writer*

Dublin
Herring, Robert Dewey *mathematics professor, physics professor*
Sellers, Ella Jo *literature and language professor*

Dunn
Wilson, Douglas Leonard *minister, educator*

Durham
Albala, David Mois *urologist, educator*
Aldrich, John Herbert *political science professor*
Amaya-Jackson, Lisa *psychiatrist*
Anderson, William Banks, Jr. *ophthalmology educator*
Andrews, Nancy Catherine *dean, pediatrician, hematologist, educator*
Anlyan, William George *surgeon, educator, academic administrator*
Anscher, Mitchell Steven *physician, educator*
Armstrong, Nancy *literature and language professor*
Asrani, Sanjay *ophthalmologist*
Auld, Skip (Hampton Auld) *library director*
Baker, Robert Flowers *lawyer, mediator and arbitrator*
Barker, Ben *chef, restaurant owner*
Barker, Karen *restaurant owner, chef*
Bartlett, Katharine Tiffany *law educator, former dean*
Bashore, Thomas Michael *cardiologist, educator*
Bates, Robert Hinrichs *political science educator*
Baxter, Stephen Bartow *retired historian*
Behn, Robert Dietrich *public policy educator, writer*
Bell, William (Bill) V. *Mayor, Durham, NC*
Bennett, Charles Lee *medical educator*
Berchuck, Andrew *gynecologic oncologist, educator*
Beresteanu, Arie *economist, educator*
Bernard, Pamela Jenks *lawyer*
Bettman, James Ross *management educator*
Birnbaum, Linda S. *federal agency administrator, toxicologist*
Blazer, Dan German, II, *psychiatrist, epidemiologist*
Blum, Jacob Joseph *physiologist, educator*
Bollinger, Ralph Randal *surgeon, researcher*
Bordley, William Clayton (Clay) *pediatrician, educator*
Borges-Neto, Salvador *radiologist, cardiologist, educator*
Bradford, William Dalton *pathologist, educator*
Bravender, Terrill (Terry) D. *pediatrician*
Breeden, Douglas Tower *finance educator, consultant, former dean*
Breland-Noble, Alfiee Matiese *psychologist, researcher*
Brodhead, Richard H. *academic administrator*
Brodie, Harlow Keith Hammond *psychiatrist, educator*
Brothers, Thomas *musicologist, educator*
Bryant, Robert Leamon *mathematics educator*
Buckley, Rebecca Hatcher *allergist, immunologist, pediatrician, educator*
Budd, Louis John *language educator*
Butters, Ronald Richard *language educator*
Califf, Robert McKinnon *cardiologist, educator*
Canada, Mary Whitfield *retired librarian*
Carrington, Paul DeWitt *lawyer, educator*
Carter, Calvin H., Jr. *materials engineer*
Case, Richard W. *sports association executive*
Casey, H(orace) Craig, Jr. *electrical engineering educator*
Cavazos, José Enrique *neuroscientist, neurologist*
Cayne, Bernard Stanley *editor*
Chang, Mou-Hsiung *mathematician*
Chang, Zheng *medical educator*
Christie, George Custis *lawyer, educator, writer*
Ciferri, Alberto *chemist, educator*
Clark, Robert Lewis, Jr. *mechanical engineer, consultant, dean*
Clay, Diskin *classical studies educator*
Cohen, Harvey Jay *geriatrician, hematologist, oncologist, educator*
Colton, Joel *historian, educator*
Colvin, O. Michael *medical association administrator, educator*
Conklin, George Henry *sociologist, educator*
Conover, Christopher James *health policy analyst, educator*
Cook-Deegan, Robert Mullan *physician, educator*
Coppridge, Alton James *urological surgeon*
Cox, James D. *law educator*
Crenshaw, James L(ee) *theology educator*
Crotty, Dominic *biomedical engineer*
Cushman, Ian *biomedical researcher*
Cutcliffe, David *college football coach*
Davis, Calvin De Armond *historian, educator*
Davis, Chuck *dance company executive, dancer*
Daw, Amy W. *music educator*

Dellinger, Walter Estes III law educator
Demott, Deborah Ann law educator
Dennis, Helen Oldham elementary school educator
Desjardins, Annick medical educator
Donatucci, Craig F. urologist, educator
Douglas, Pamela Susan physician, researcher, educator
Doyle, Gloria Thorpe secondary school educator
Echols, Laura Celeste psychologist, consultant
Edmond, John engineering company executive
Edwards, Christopher Levon medical association administrator
Eger, Joseph conductor
Elliot, Jeffrey M. political science professor, department chairman
Elmore, Susan A. pathologist
Eubanks, Mary biologist, anthropologist
Fairbank, John A. psychiatrist, educator
Falletta, John Matthew pediatrician, educator
Feaver, Peter Douglas political science educator, consultant, defense analyst
Fiske, Edward B. editor, journalist
Fitch, Robert D. orthopedic surgeon
Foreman, John William pediatrician, educator
Freedland, Stephen Jay urologist
Freedman, Sharon Fridovich opthalmologist
Fridovich, Irwin biochemistry professor
Friedman, Allan Howard neurosurgeon
Frothingham, Thomas Eliot pediatrician
Fulkerson, William hospital administrator, pulmonologist
Gainetdinov, Raul Radikovich pharmacologist, researcher
Garst, Jennifer oncologist
Georgiade, Gregory Stephen plastic surgeon, educator
Giannopoulos, Athina physician, surgeon
Gillham, Nicholas Wright geneticist, educator
Gillings, Dennis B. medical products executive
Gilliss, Catherine Lynch vice chancellor, dean, nursing educator
Goodwin, Frank Erik materials engineer
Grabowski, Henry George economics professor, director
Graffagnino, Carmelo neuroscientist, emergency physician
Gray jr, Leon Earl biologist, researcher
Greenfield, Joseph Cholmondeley, Jr. physician, educator
Gutman, Robert Allan nephrologist
Hammes, Gordon G. chemistry professor
Hammond, Charles Bessellieu obstetrician, gynecologist, educator
Hardaker, William Thomas orthopedist, director
Harrington, Robert A. cardiologist
Harrison, Dean Thomas medical educator
Havighurst, Clark Canfield law educator
Haynes, Barton Ford medical educator
Holder, Angela Roddey retired law educator
Holley, Irving Brinton, Jr. historian, educator
Holsti, Ole Rudolf political scientist, educator
Horowitz, Donald Leonard lawyer, arbitrator, political scientist, educator
Hotz, V. Joseph economics professor
Isaacs, Robert Eric neurosurgeon
Jakubs, Deborah university librarian
James, Sherman Athonia epidemiologist, educator
Jaszczak, Ronald Jack physicist, researcher, consultant
Jenkins, Richard Erik lawyer
Jennings, Robert Burgess experimental pathologist, medical educator
Jirtle, Randy medical educator, geneticist
Johnson, Davey (David Allen Johnson) professional baseball coach
Joklik, Wolfgang Karl biochemist, virologist, educator
Joseph, James Alfred retired ambassador, political scientist, educator
Kapadia, Anuj J. research scientist
Kashuba, Roxolana research scientist
Katz, Samuel Lawrence pediatrician, researcher
Keene, Jack Donald molecular genetics and microbiology educator
Keller, Thomas Franklin business administration educator
Kelley, Allen Charles economist, educator
Kiehart, Daniel P. biophysicist, educator
Kirkpatrick, John Paxton oncologist, educator
Kishnani, Priya Sunil medical geneticist
Koepke, John Arthur hematologist, clinical pathologist
Kort, Wesley Albert religious studies educator, writer
Krakowski, Jane actress
Krishnan, Krishnaswamy Ranga Rama R. psychiatry educator
Krzyzewski, Mike (Michael William Krzyzewski) college basketball coach
Kuniholm, Bruce Robellet academic administrator, educator
LaBean, Thomas Henry chemistry professor
Land, Kenneth Carl sociologist, educator, demographer
Lefkowitz, Robert Joseph biomedical researcher, educator
Levi, David F. dean, former federal judge
Levin, Lawrence Scott plastic surgeon
Lieberman, Rochelle Phyllis small business owner
Lifton, Walter M. psychology and education consultant
Lockhead, Gregory Roger retired psychology professor
Lopes, Renato Delascio cardiologist, researcher
Lyman, Gary Herbert epidemiologist, cancer researcher, educator
MacIntyre, Neil Ross, Jr. medical educator
Marcom, Paul Kelly oncologist
Masand, Prakash S. psychiatrist, researcher
Matchar, David B. physician, researcher
Maxwell, Richard Callender retired lawyer, educator
McCallie, Joanne P. women's college basketball coach
McClain, Paula Denice political scientist, educator
McMahon, John Alexander law educator
Mela, Carl Frederick marketing educator
Merson, Michael Howard public health physician, epidemiologist, educator
Meyer, Horst physics professor
Meyers, Eric Mark religion educator
Michener, James Lloyd medical educator
Mickiewicz, Ellen Propper political and social science educator
Mikhailov, Stepan Fedorovich physicist, researcher
Miller, David Sameul physiologist
Moore, Joy Jittaun dean
Moss, Marcia Lynn retired biochemist
Mudipalli, Anuradha biologist, researcher
Murphy, Thomas Miles pediatrician, educator
Nakarai, Charles Frederick Toyozo music educator
Newgard, Christopher B. medical educator
Nicandri, Gregg Thomas orthopedist
Nicolelis, Miguel A. L. neuroscientist, educator
O'Connor, Christopher M. cardiologist
Ohman, E. Magnus cardiologist, educator
Ostbye, Truls medical researcher, educator
Otterbourg, Robert Kenneth public relations consultant, writer
Parker, William education educator
Parkerson, George Robert, Jr. medical educator
Pearsall, George Wilbur materials scientist, mechanical engineer, consultant
Petroski, Henry engineering educator, writer
Pimm, Stuart L. ecology educator
Pizzo, Salvatore Vincent pathologist
Preminger, Glenn Michael urologist, surgeon
Prose, Neil Stuart pediatric dermatologist
Pruteanu-Malinici, Iulian research scientist
Putallaz, Martha psychologist, educator
Quin, Louis DuBose chemist, educator
Quinn, Jarus William physicist, former association executive
Randall, Dale Bertrand Jonas English language educator
Rao, Sunil V. cardiologist, educator
Raynor, Eileen Margolies otolaryngologist, educator
Reif, John Henry computer science educator
Richardson, Curtis John ecology educator
Robboy, Stanley J. pathologist, educator
Robertson, Horace Bascomb, Jr. retired law educator
Rorschach, Kimberly museum director
Rossiter, Alexander, Jr. publishing executive, author
Sampson, John Howard neurosurgeon, educator
Sanders, Donald Benjamin neurologist, educator
Scales, Jean Norris retired English language educator
Schwarcz, Steven Lance lawyer, educator
Scott, Anne Byrd Firor history professor
Shelburne, John Daniel pathologist
Sheppard, Blair H. dean, finance company executive, educator
Simons, Elwyn LaVerne physical anthropologist, primatologist, paleontologist, educator
Smith, Grover C(leveland) language educator
Smith, Peter K. cardiothoracic surgeon
Snyder, Denise nutritionist, researcher
Socolar, Joshua E. S. physics professor
Stacy, Mark Allen neurologist
Staelin, Richard business administration educator
Stanley, Carol Jones academic administrator, educator
Strauman, Timothy J. psychology professor, department chairman
Surwit, Richard Samuel psychology professor
Suslov, Vladimir Mikhaylovich physics professor, researcher
Svetkey, Laura Pat nephrologist
Swamy, Geeta K. obstetrician, gynecologist
Swanson, Jeffrey sociologist, researcher, educator
Syn, Wing-Kin gastroenterologist, hepatologist, researcher
Taekman, Jeffrey Marc anesthesiologist
Takahashi, Toku education educator, researcher
Talley, Joseph Eugene psychologist
Tcheng, James Enlou physician
Tedder, Thomas Fletcher immunology educator, researcher
Teng, Christina T. molecular biologist, researcher
Thompson, William Moreau radiologist, educator
Tigar, Michael Edward law educator
Tiryakian, Edward Ashod sociologist, educator
Treml, Vladimir Guy economist, educator
Ulshen, Martin Howard pediatric gastroenterologist, researcher
Van Deman, Barry Alan museum administrator
Vaslef, Steven Nicholas surgeon
Vaughan, Cathy Ann pharmacist
Vick, Marsha Cook writer, humanities educator
Vogel, Steven biologist, educator
Vredenburgh, James Joseph medical educator
Warner, Seth L. mathematician, educator
White, Kevin M. athletic director
Wilkins, Robert Henry neurosurgeon, editor, educator
Williams, George Walton language educator
Williams, Redford Brown medical educator
Williamson, Nancy E demographer
Wilson, Blake Shaw electrical engineer, researcher
Wilson, Joanne A.P. gastrenterologist, educator
Wolever, Ruth Q. psychologist, researcher
Xia, Jessie Qing research scientist
Yildirim, Huseyin engineering educator
Young, Terri L. ophthalmologist
Zenn, Michael Robert plastic and reconstructive surgeon
Zhang, Qingchun research scientist
Zhirnov, Victor physicist, researcher

Elizabeth City
Andrews, Alice K. librarian
Blackmon, Ronald H. biologist, science educator
Bluiett, Althea G. physics professor
Boyle, Terrence W. federal judge
Griffin, Gladys Bogues critical care nurse, educator
Khan, Sultana Ahmed medical educator, director
Nwala, Kingsley economics professor
Storie, Eric Duane science administrator
Williams, Rita Carroll protective services official, language educator, poet, librarian

Elkin
Casper, Rick D. literature and language professor

Ellerbe
Rankin, Pressley Robinson, Jr. physician

Elon
Buckmaster, Matthew Tobe musician, educator
Copeland, David communications educator
de Lama, Mayte language educator
Gang, Richard Philip theater educator
Powell, William Council, Sr. service company executive
Rubeck, Fredrick John performing arts educator
Tolley, Jerry Russell academic administrator
Yap, Alexander Y. educator, information systems, researcher, consultant

Fairmont
Spencer, Melissa Johanna psychotherapist, special education educator

Fairview
Brown, Gregory Neil academic administrator, forester, educator

Fayetteville
Ajani, Timothy T. language educator
Barnicle, Mary Anne music educator, piano accompanist
Barringer-Brown, Charletta Hope professor, educational consultant
Batts, Dorothy Marie clergywoman, educator, writer
Chavonne, Anthony G. Mayor, Fayetteville, North Carolina
Cui, Zhenlu mathematics professor
Curry, Virginia Frances retired language educator
Dandy, Roscoe Greer author, psychotherapist, educator, retired public health service officer
Farrior, Helen Hooks retired assistant principal
Flagg, Garrett Cortez communications educator
Greene, Walter Blair pediatric orthopedist
House, Terry C. engineering educator
Jansen, Michael John health facility administrator
Morley, James Thomas philosopher, educator
Rand, Anthony Eden state legislator, lawyer
Roe, Kathryn Jane elementary school educator
Soderberg, Herman Albert minister, educator
Townsend, William Jackson lawyer
Turner, Gwendolyn Marie band director, musician
Widdows, Marianne Shuta orchestra director

Fearrington Village
Cell, Gillian Townsend retired historian, educator

Flat Rock
Childress, Richard Thomas international business consultant, author
Weill, Hans medical educator

Fletcher
Seagle, J. Harold lawyer

Forest City
Watson, Tanya Parton school system administrator, director

Fort Bragg
Laney, Patricia Ann elementary school educator

Four Oaks
Jordan, Lyndon Kirkman physician

Franklin
Johnson, Herbert Alan historian, lawyer
Kinard, Cynthia Cochran artist writer poet

Franklinton
Elmore, Cenieth Catherine music educator

Gastonia
Bostic, Jerry Jackson principal
Burns, Judith O'Dell library assistant, educator
Crissman, Katherine Kolb counseling administrator
Fayssoux, Patricia Ann Paysour music educator
Lawson, William David III retired cotton company executive
McCall, Louise Callaham psychologist
Patterson, Elaine Wilcox art educator
Stott, Grady Bernell lawyer
Teem, Paul Lloyd, Jr. bank executive
Tippitt, Ann museum director
Wright, Wayne Kenneth retired federal agency statistician

Gerton
Whitt, Margaret Earley retired literature and language professor

Glendale Springs
Carter, Roy secondary school educator, coach

Goldsboro
Bass, Tara Thompson literature and language professor, director

Granite Falls
Humphreys, Kenneth King engineer, professional society administrator, educator

Greensboro
Allen, Jesse Owen III organizational behavior specialist
Barber, Elizabeth Anne education educator
Barnett, Sharron Hogan animal health technical director,paraseticides
Blackwell, William Ernest broadcast executive
Bolick, Ronnie Lee mechanical engineer
Bratton, Teresa Sue pediatrician
Brodie, Bruce Rogers cardiologist
Bullock, Frank William, Jr. lawyer, retired federal judge
Choplin, Melody L. manufacturing executive, educator
Clark, David McKenzie lawyer
Cummings, Candace S. lawyer, apparel company executive
Davis, Ferd Leary, Jr. law educator, consultant
Davis, Herbert Owen lawyer
Deere, James Dickson singer, pianist, music educator and writer
Diouf, Arona Ndoffene environmentalist, educator
Dobrogosz, Glenn D. museum director
Dollahite, David Curtis family science educator
Dugda, Mulugeta Tuji education educator
Eason, Robert Gaston psychology professor
Englar, John David finance educator, textiles executive, lawyer
Eromon, David Ighogboya electronics engineer, educator
Floyd, Jack William lawyer
Fonge, Fuabeh P. history professor
French, Lenny Sue middle school educator
Fujino, Michimasa aeronautical engineer
Gdanitz, Robert J. research scientist, educator
Gorden, Richard history faculty, associate director
Gumbiner, Kenneth Jay lawyer
Hammond, David Alan stage director, educator
Harris-Offutt, Rosalyn Marie counselor, consultant, mental health nurse, consultant, writer
Heil, John Eric theater educator
Helms-VanStone, Mary Wallace anthropology educator
Houston, Frank Matt dermatologist
Humburg, Patricia A. supervisor
Hunter, Bynum Merritt retired lawyer
Hunter, Phyllis Whitman history professor
Israel, Adrienne Manns history professor
Jellicorse, John Lee communications and theatre educator
Jin, Byoungho retail educator
Johnson, Marshall Hardy investment company executive
Johnson, Yvonne J. Mayor, Greensboro, NC
Kelkar, Ajit Dhundiraj mechanical engineer, educator
Knesel, Ernest Arthur, Jr. health facility administrator, chemicals executive
Koonce, Neil Wright lawyer
Levy, Michele Frucht literature and language professor
Locke, John R. music educator, director
Lou, Jianzhong chemical engineer, educator
Lowe, Kevin Brian finance company executive
Luecht, Richard M. psychology professor
Malveaux, Julianne Marie academic administrator, economist, writer
McGinn, Max Daniel lawyer
Melvin, Charles Edward, Jr. lawyer
Michalak, Sarah C. university librarian
Middleton, Herman David, Sr. retired theater educator
Miller, Don Maz literature and language professor
Moffett, Mondre musician, educator
Mohan, Ram Vasu engineering educator, researcher
Mozell, Herbert Lee mental health services professional
Nieman, Valerie Gail writer, language educator, journalist
Noble, Ralph C. animal scientist, department chairman
Obeng, Kofi science educator
Oliver, Donna H. academic administrator, former secondary school educator
Oliver, Terry James retired electronics engineer, communications engineer
Osteen, William Lindsay, Sr. federal judge
Osteen, William Lindsay, Jr. federal judge
Penley, Virginia Long social worker
Penninger, Frieda Elaine retired literature educator
Reece, Alton Davis, Jr. science educator
Revell, Henry, Jr. social services administrator, retired education educator
Ribar, David Christopher economics professor
Roberts, Jeffrey Owayne builder, renovator, consultant
Roberts, Kenneth Barry pediatrician
Rogers, William Raymond retired academic administrator, psychologist, educator
Ryan, John R. educational association administrator, former academic administrator, career military officer
Salam, A. F. economics professor
Schunk, Dale Hansen dean
Schweninger, Loren history professor
Schwenn, Lee William retired health facility administrator
Shaw, Robert Gilbert state legislator, food service executive
Shearer, Robert K. apparel executive
Sink, Harry Lee transportation executive
Sladek, Ronald John physics professor
Slaughter, James H. lawyer
Soles, William Roger insurance company executive, director
Staab, Thomas Robert consumer product company financial executive
Stocks, William L. federal judge
Sullivan, Patricia A. academic administrator
Swan, George Steven law educator
Venkateswarlu, Divi chemistry professor
Vestal, Richard D. biology professor
Wagoner, Anna Mills S. prosecutor
Wahlsten, Douglas psychology professor
Ward Black, Janet lawyer
Watson, Robert Winthrop poet
Wiseman, Eric C. apparel executive
Zopf, Evelyn LaNoel Montgomery retired guidance counselor

Greenville
Allison, Ron oncologist, researcher
Anderson, James Franciscous criminal justice educator
Babb, Joseph Dolby physician
Bearden, James Hudson university official
Beers, Burton Floyd historian, educator
Bjorkman, Sylvia Johnson psychologist
Carroll, Robert Graham physiologist, educator
Colombo, Michael Allen lawyer
Cunningham, Paul Raymond Goldwyn dean, medical educator
Daneri, Juan J. literature and language professor
Darby, F. Leonard theater educator

Dashiell, Carroll Vaughn, Jr. *musician, educator*
Deena, Seodial Frank *language educator*
Dickerson, Anne Elizabeth *educator*
Evans, Rand Boyd *psychologist*
Ferguson, Thomas Bruce, Jr. *cardiothoracic surgeon*
Flood, Joseph Patrick *environmental scientist*
Fraley, Todd *communications educator*
Gilham, Hanna Kaltenbrunner *writer*
Greenstein, Patricia *librarian, director*
Habal, Nizar *oncologist, surgeon, educator*
Howard, Malcolm Jones *federal judge*
Howell, John McDade *retired academic administrator, political scientist, educator*
Hu, Xiu-Hua *biomedical physicist, biomedical engineer*
Hughes, Ralph Eugene *management educator*
Jackson, Bobby Rand *minister*
Khuri, Soumaya Makdissi *mathematics professor*
Lee, Kenneth Stuart *neurosurgeon, educator*
Leggett, Donald Yates *academic administrator*
Lewis, Michael Justin *medical educator*
Lu, Qun *cell biologist, educator*
Moore, Charles Willard *music educator*
Newton, Edward R. *obstetrician, educator*
Painter, Jane A. *medical educator*
Palmer, Michael A. *history professor*
Parham, Peter Robertson *geologist*
Perkin, Ronald Murray *pediatrician, educator*
Phillips, Phil E. *professor, academic administrator*
Pleasant, James Carroll *mathematician, computer sciences educator*
Pories, Walter Julius *surgeon, educator*
Rheinhardt, Richard *ecologist, educator*
Romer, Frank E. *literature and language professor, department chairman*
Smith Canter, Lora Lee *special education educator*
Steinweg, Kenneth K. *medical educator, department chairman*
Stevens, John A. *classicist, educator*
Tahaney, Michael Hamilton *theatre professor, actor and director*
Twark, Jill E. *language educator*
Wallin, Leland Dean *artist, educator*
Waugh, William Howard *physician, research scientist*
Wilkerson, William Holton *banker*

Hampstead
Snyder, Clair Allison *banker*

Harrisburg
Economaki, Chris Constantine (Christopher Economaki) *publishing executive*

Hayesville
Turner, Lisa Phillips *human resources executive*

Henderson
Serafin, Donald *plastic surgeon, educator*

Hendersonville
Brittain, James Edward *science and technology educator, researcher*
Carney, Robert Arthur *restaurant executive*
Harris, James Braxton *retired humanities educator, freelance/self-employed writer*
Jefferson, Letitia Gibson *rehabilitation counselor*
Mitchell, William P. (Billy) *arbitrator*
Pierard, Richard Victor *history educator*
Roberts, James Allen *retired urologist, educator*
Snyder, William *library director*
Tatreau, (Dolores) Maxine *artist*
Trexler, Edgar Ray *minister, editor*
Weeks, Sandra Kenney *nursing administrator*

Hertford
Johnson, Donald Lee *retired agricultural materials company executive, product consultant*

Hickory
Ballenger, Thomas Cass *former congressman, retired plastics company executive*
Beasley, Diana F. *biology educator*
Dill, Karen Elizabeth *psychology professor, writer*
Drendel, Frank Matthew *cable company executive*
Johnson, Daniel *lawyer*
Lefler, Wade Hampton, Jr. *ophthalmologist*
Lynn, Tony Lee *import company executive*
Pasour, Katherine Meador *dean, educator*
Ratke, David C. *religious studies educator*
Sims, Janette Elizabeth Lowman *retired educational director*
Whiteley, Emily C. *biology professor*

High Point
Bardelas, Jose Antonio *allergist*
Carter, Kathleen Sharp *educational consultant, shop owner*
Chavis, Glenn Romero *retired historian, writer*
Corey, James William *political scientist, educator*
Draelos, Zoe Diana *dermatologist, consultant*
Fenn, Ormon William, Jr. *furniture company executive*
Kandt, Raymond S. *neurologist*
Palmer, Pamela Murrill *educator*
Pate, William Patrick *city manager*
Peoples-Marwah, Andrea Michelle *educational consultant, researcher*
Phillips, Stanley Davis (Dave) *United States Ambassador to Estonia*
Setzler, Mark H. *political science professor*

Highlands
Shaffner, Randolph Preston *shop owner, educator, writer, publisher*
Sheehan, Charles Vincent *investment banker*

Hillsborough
Johnston, William Webb *pathologist, educator*
Piper, Don Courtney *political scientist, educator*

Horse Shoe
Roskoski, Robert, Jr. *biochemist, educator, author*

Hudson
Council, Jimmy *director*

Huntersville
Atrak, Taisser M. *pediatrician, director*
Busch, Kyle *race car driver*
Gibbs, Joe Jackson *professional sports team executive, former professional football coach*
Headd, Kevin *investment advisor*
Logano, Joey *race car driver*
Tompkins, James Richard *retired special education educator*

Indian Trail
Brewer, James Timothy *music educator, director*

Jacksonville
Kimball, Lynn Jerome *historian*

Jefferson
Franklin, Robert McFarland *book publisher*
Mitchell, Patricia *finance educator, director*

Kannapolis
Mayfield, Jeremy (Allen) *race car driver*
Newman, Ryan Joseph *race car driver*
Stewart, Tony (Anthony Wayne Stewart) *professional race car driver*
Thigpen, Alton Hill *transportation executive*

Kings Mountain
Depew, Ellie *language educator, writer*

Kinston
Baker-Gardner, Jewelle *interior designer, business consultant*
Petteway, Samuel Bruce *college president*

Kitty Hawk
Sjoerdsma, Albert *research and development company executive*
Tucker, Don Eugene *retired lawyer*

Lake Junaluska
Goodgame, Gordon Clifton *retired minister*
Martinson, Jacob Christian, Jr. *academic administrator*
Stanton, Donald Sheldon *retired academic administrator*

Lake Toxaway
Raynolds, Elaine Spalding *sales executive, photojournalist*

Laurinburg
Sojka, Nickolas Joseph, Jr. *lawyer*

Leasburg
Treacy, Sandra Joanne Pratt *retired art educator, illustrator*

Lenoir
Bailey-Day, Kay Lynn *psychotherapist*
Caknipe, Christopher Howard *substance abuse services professional*
Warrick, Paul David *otolaryngologist*

Lexington
Carlton, Robbin Briley *elementary school educator*
Frontz, Leslie Kay *art educator*
Mabe, Walter Lee *music educator*
Snyder, James Eugene, Jr. *lawyer*

Liberty
Garner, M(ildred) Maxine *retired religious studies educator*

Lillington
Jewell, Eileen Kathryn *art educator*
Shull, Johnny Thomas *finance educator*

Littleton
Skinner, Sue Dossett *retired vocational director*

Louisburg
Miller, Brian Daniel *music educator, organist*

Lowell
Myers, Jeanette Moore *music educator, director*

Lumberton
Dent, Eric B. *management consultant*
Johnson, Judy Van *minister, educator*
Tolar, Anne Melton *minister, music educator*

Manteo
Crites, Tara Couch *psychology professor*

Marion
Burgin, Charles Edward *retired lawyer*

Mars Hill
Newton, Paul George *musician, retired librarian*
Payne, John Kenneth *acadmic administrator*
Sime, Donald Rae *retired business administration educator*

Matthews
Black, Albert George *English language educator*
Twisdale, Harold Winfred *dentist*

Mc Leansville
Miles, John Benjamin *lawyer*
Taggart, Christopher Scott *systems engineer*

Misenheimer
Stivers, Laura A. *religious studies educator*

Monroe
Casstevens, Charles Franklin, Jr. *music educator, minister*
Johnson, Sarah Smith *psychologist*
Kyle, John Emery *retired religious organization administrator*
Taylor, Jimmy Lynn *retired family practice physician, administrator*

Montreat
Hernandez, Horacio Antonio *literature and language professor*
Sprawls, Perry *biomedical engineer, educator*

Mooresville
Busch, Kurt Thomas *professional race car driver*
Castroneves, Hélio *race car driver*
Dixon, Scott (Ronald) *race car driver*
Johnston, James Wesley *retired consumer products company executive*
Mabry, Joseph M.(Mike), Jr. *consumer products company executive*
McCanless, Ross William *lawyer, retail executive*
Niblock, Robert A. *consumer home products company executive*
Petty, Richard *retired race car driver*
Turner, Michael G. *history professor*

Morehead City
Weber, Craig P. *meteorologist, newscaster*

Morganton
Carpenter III, Harry Everett *social sciences educator, history professor*
Hawkins, Seth C. *physician*
McGrady, C. Nadine *science educator*
Simpson, Daniel Reid *lawyer, mediator*
Styles, Naomi *biology professor*

Morrisville
Amelio, Bill (William J.) *computer company executive*
Harrison, Pete (Robert E. Harrison) *tobacco company executive*
Indursky, Mike *consumer products company executive, marketing professional*
Lopez, Rocio A. *chemist*
Shim, Woo Sub *research scientist*
Todd, Lori A. *toxicologist, professor*
Ward, Stephen M., Jr. *computer company executive*
Wiegerink, Robin L. *medical association administrator*

Mount Airy
Joyce-Norris, Elaine Rozelle *elementary school educator*
Woltz, Howard Osler, Jr. *retired metal products executive*

Mount Holly
Nutter, James Randall *management educator*

Mount Olive
Charles, Asselin *literature and language professor*
Hooks, Cheryl *art educator*
Raper, William Burkette *retired college president*
Ryberg, Susan Gribble *librarian*

Moyock
Prince, Erik D. *protective services company executive*

Murfreesboro
Wethington, Amy Rene *biology professor*
White, Martin Christopher *academic administrator*

Murphy
Bata, Rudolph Andrew, Jr. *lawyer*
Holcomb, Linda Laine *elementary school educator, director*
Jordan, Barbara Moore *retired psychiatrist*
Pezzella, Jerry James, Jr. *investment and real estate company executive*

Nags Head
Heinrich, Katharine Ann *gifted and talented educator*

Nashville
Penick, Angela Lucas *elementary school educator*

New Bern
Davis, James Lee *lawyer*
McKee, Francis John *medical association consultant, lawyer*
Moeller, Dade William *environmental engineer, educator*
Naumann, William Carl *consumer products company executive*
Overholt, Hugh Robert *lawyer, retired military officer*
Painter, Jack Timberlake *civil engineer*
Tolmich, Andrea J. *music educator, department chairman*
Whitehurst, Brooks Morris *chemical engineer*

Newland
Campany, Kay Hudkins *biology educator, assistant principal*

North Wilkesboro
Keener, Gaither McDonald, Jr. *corporate lawyer*
Stone, Larry Dean *consumer products company executive*

Pembroke
Curtis, Anthony R. *communications educator*
Gan, LooGeok Lydia *finance educator*
Power, June Lynn LaVoie *librarian*

Pfafftown
Wood, Stephen Wray *minister, educator, legislator*

Pine Knoll Shores
Graham, Gloria Flippin *dermatologist*

Pinehurst
Carroll, Kent Jean *retired naval officer*
Denton, Estelle Rosemary *retired federal agency administrator*
Huizenga, John Robert *nuclear chemist, educator*
Nordloh, David Joseph *literature and language professor, dean*
O'Loughlin, John Kirby *retired insurance executive*
Rees, Clifford Harcourt, Jr., (Ted Rees) *consulting company executive, retired trade association administrator, military officer*
Rhody, Ronald Edward *bank, communications executive*
Stevenson, Josiah, IV, *management consultant*

Pisgah Forest
Dixit, Ajit Suresh *chemicals executive, research scientist*

Pittsboro
Boyce, Emily Stewart *retired library and information scientist, educator*
Cotter, Michael William *retired ambassador*
Herman-Giddens, Marcia Edwina *physician associate*
Kachergis, Joyce W. *book designer*
Murdock, John Carey *economics professor, investor*
Richardson, Richard Judson *retired political science professor*

Raleigh
Agamloh, Emmanuel B. *systems engineer, consultant*
Allen, Barbara Kirkman *politcal organization administrator*
Allen, Steven Glen *economics and business professor*
Anderson, Norman Dean *science education educator, writer*
Aronson, Arthur Lawrence *retired veterinarian, toxicologist, educator, pharmacologist*
Ashmore, James Philip *minister, educator*
Aspnes, David Erik *physicist, researcher*
Bar, Roselyn R. *legal association administrator, executive secretary*
Barish, Charles Franklin *internist, gastroenterologist, researcher*
Barnhardt, Robert Alexander *retired dean*
Barrasso, Tom *professional hockey coach, retired professional hockey player*
Bateman, Angela Anderson *anesthetist*
Beatty, Kenneth Orion, Jr. *chemical engineer, educator*
Bennett, Betsy M. *museum director*
Bernholc, Jerzy *physicist, educator*
Bills, Jennifer Leah *lawyer*
Bitzer, Donald Lester *electrical engineer, educator, retired lab administrator*
Boone, Mary L. *library director*
Boyette, Richard T. *lawyer*
Brady, Edward Thomas *state supreme court justice*
Breidt, Fred *microbiologist*
Brind'Amour, Rod *professional hockey player*
Brisson, E. Carson *registrar*
Brooks, Jackie Daniel *social studies educator*
Brown, Robert Dale *wildlife science educator, dean*
Bruck, Robert Ian *education educator*
Burbridge, Michael Francis *bishop*
Burris, Craven Allen *retired college administrator, professor*
Burton, Troy *parks director, museum association administrator*
Cain, James Palmer *lawyer, former ambassador*
Carbonell, Ruben Guillermo *chemical engineering educator*
Carlton, Alfred Pershing, Jr. *lawyer*
Carter, Jean Gordon *lawyer*
Case, Charles Dixon *lawyer*
Chou, Wushow *retired computer scientist*
Clarke, Lewis James *landscape architect*
Clauberg, Martin *research scientist*
Cole, Erik *professional hockey player*
Cole, Kathryn Miller *psychologist, educator*
Cook, Maurice Gayle *soil science educator, consultant*
Cooper, Arthur Wells *retired ecologist, educator*
Cooper, Roy Asberry III *state attorney general*
Cotanch, Stephen Robert *physics educator*
Cowell, Janet *state treasurer*
Cox, David E. *application developer*
Craig, Lee A. *economics professor, consultant*
Cunningham, Michael *lawyer*
Dalton, Walter H. *lieutenant governor*
Daves, Linda *political organization administrator*
Davey, Charles Bingham *soil scientist, educator*
Davis, Egbert Lawrence III *retired lawyer*
Dolce, Carl John *education administration educator*
Doorn, Michiel Roelof Jan *environmental engineer, consultant*
Dornan, John Neill *public policy center professional*
Dorsett, James K. III *lawyer*
Dunphy, Edward James *science educator, crop extension specialist*
Eagles, Sidney Smith, Jr. *retired judge*
Eberly, Harry Landis *retired communications company executive*
Edens, Frank Wesley *physiologist*
Edmunds, Robert Holt, Jr. *state supreme court justice*
Edwards, Elizabeth (Mary Elizabeth Edwards) *lawyer, writer*
Ellis, Lester Neal, Jr. *lawyer*
Engel, Jeffrey P. *state agency administrator, public health service officer*
Farr, A. Celeste *communications educator*
Flournoy, William Louis, Jr. *retired landscape architect*
Foxe, Marye Anne *academic administrator*
Francis, Ron *professional sports team executive, retired professional hockey player*
Freeman, Franklin Edward, Jr. *government agency administrator*
Gailor, Frank Robert *lawyer*
Gardner, Robin Pierce *engineering educator*
Gordon, Morris Aaron *medical mycologist*
Gossman, Francis Joseph *bishop emeritus*
Gould, Christopher Robert *physics professor*
Hagan, Kay Ruthven *United States Senator from North Carolina*
Hardin, Eugene Brooks, Jr. *bank executive*

Hardin, James W. *botanist, educator, herbarium curator*
Hardison, Cynthia Ann Stoltze *retired hematologist, oncologist*
Hargrove, Wade Hampton *lawyer*
Hartford, Maureen A. *academic administrator*
Havlin, John Leroy *soil scientist, educator*
Havner, Kerry Shuford *civil engineering and solid mechanics educator, scientist*
Healey, Christopher Graham *engineering educator*
Hinton, David Owen *retired electrical engineer*
Hoch, Paul Frederick, Jr. *history educator*
Hodgson, Ernest *toxicologist, educator*
Holding, George E.B. *prosecutor*
Holton, William Coffeen *electrical engineering executive*
Howard, Kenneth B. *museum director*
Howell, Gary Wilbur *computer scientist, mathematician, consultant*
Hudson, Robin E. *state supreme court justice*
Hughes, Barbara Ann *dietician, public health administrator*
Hunt, James Baxter, Jr. *lawyer, former governor*
Hunt, Neal Kemp *state legislator, real estate company executive*
Imade, Lucky Osagie *political scientist, educator*
Jarrett, Polly Hawkins *retired secondary school educator*
Jessen, David Wayne *retired accountant*
Jing, Naihuan N. *mathematician*
Johnson, William Dean *electric power industry executive*
Jordan, John Richard, Jr. *lawyer*
Joyner, Gary Kelton *lawyer*
Kapp, Michael Keith *lawyer*
Kauffman, Terry *broadcast and communications educator, artist*
Khachatoorian, Haig Nmn *industrial designer, educator*
Kiec, Kate Smolko *literature and language professor*
Kinnaird, Eleanor Gates *state legislator, lawyer*
Kolbas, Robert Michael *electrical engineering educator*
Kuhler, Renaldo Gillet *retired museum director, medical illustrator*
LaMonte, Jennifer Adams Emnett *history professor*
Lancaster, H(arold) Martin *Former United States Representative, NC, academic administrator*
Larsen, Jamie Strauss *technical and professional writing educator, consultant*
Leak, Robert Edwards *economic development consultant*
Lee, Howard N. *educational association administrator*
Leonard, J. Rich *federal judge, educator*
Lilliston, Andrew Wilson, Jr. *lawyer*
Littleton, Isaac Thomas III *retired library director*
Loboa, Elizabeth Grace *biomedical engineer, educator*
Lowe, Sidney *men's college basketball coach*
Lucht, John Charles *management consultant, writer*
Malecha, Marvin John *architect, academic administrator*
Markoff, Brad Steven *lawyer*
Marshall, Elaine Folk *Secretary of State, NC*
Martin, John Charles *judge*
Martin, Mark D. *state supreme court justice*
Martin-Vega, Louis A. *dean, engineering educator*
Maurice, Paul *professional hockey coach*
McArthur, John R. *utilities executive, lawyer*
McKinney, Donald Lee *magazine editor*
McNish, Susan Kirk *retired lawyer*
Meek, Jerry (Gerald Francis Meek) *lawyer, former political organization administrator*
Meeker, Charles C. *Mayor, Raleigh, North Carolina, lawyer*
Millberg, John C. *lawyer*
Miller, Robert James *lawyer*
Mitchell, Burley Bayard, Jr. *lawyer*
Moon, Sangkil *finance educator*
Moore, Nancey Fay *history educator*
Moreland, Donald Edwin *physiologist*
Morrison, James Emerson *English language educator*
Mulhern, Mark F. *electric power company executive*
Murray, Raymond Le Roy *nuclear engineering educator*
Narayan, Jagdish *materials science educator*
Nelson, Larry A. *statistics educator, consultant*
Nepal, Neeraj *physicist, researcher*
Newby, Paul Martin *state supreme court justice*
Newman, Slater Edmund *psychologist, educator*
Niu, Steve *director*
Nutter, Susan K. *librarian, academic administrator*
Odum, Jeffery Neal *mechanical engineer*
Ogirri, Esther O. *Academic Librarian*
Padilla, Art *finance educator*
Pao, Chia-Ven *mathematics professor*
Parker, Sarah Elizabeth *state supreme court chief justice*
Parramore, Barbara Mitchell *education educator*
Parsons, William Jonathan *cardiologist*
Patterson, William S. *lawyer*
Pearsall, Samuel Haff III *ecologist, geographer, foundation administrator*
Perdue, Beverly Eaves *Governor of North Carolina*
Philbeck, John Heydt *lawyer*
Pittman, James Morris (Jack Pittman) *cartoonist, illustrator, character designer, consultant*
Poe, Terry Lynn *music educator*
Rahmani, Carol Hipp *retired school system administrator, psychologist*
Reeves, Ralph Bernard III *publishing executive*
Reynolds, C. Lewis, Jr. *materials scientist, educator*
Rhodes, Donald Robert *musicologist, educator, retired electrical engineer*
Riddle, John Marion *retired humanities educator*
Riviere, Jim Edmond *pharmacologist, toxicologist, educator*
Rizkalla, Sami *engineering educator*
Roach, Wesley Linville *lawyer, insurance executive*
Robinson, Charlotte Hill *artist*
Robinson, Prezell Russell *academic administrator*
Ruark, Gibbons *retired literature and language professor*
Rutherford, Jim *professional sports team executive*
Shea, Katherine Marie *physician, consultant*
Showalter, David Scott *teaching professor*
Simpson, Steven Drexell *lawyer*
Slaton, Joseph Guilford *social worker*
Slattery, Michael G. *humanities educator*
Sloan, O. Temple, Jr., (Temple Sloan) *automotive equipment executive*
Smetana, Frederick O. *aerospace engineer, educator, consultant*
Smith, Joseph A., Jr. *state banking agency administrator*
Smith, Lanty Lloyd *bank executive, lawyer*
Smith, Sherwood Hubbard, Jr. *retired electric utilities executive*
Sneed, Ronald Ernest *retired project engineer, educator*
Sorrell, Rozlyn *singer, actress, theater director, educator*
Sosower, Mark Lawrence *educator*
Spearman, Robert Worthington *lawyer*
Speer, Kevin Paul *surgeon*
Spruill, W. Murray *lawyer*
Staal, Eric *professional hockey player*
Stevens, Richard Yates *state legislator*
Stevenson, Denise L. *diversified financial services company executive, realtor, consultant*
Stroup, Richard Lyndell *economist, educator, writer*
Stuber, Charles William *retired genetics educator, researcher, director*
Sudhakar, Nori *materials scientist, researcher*
Suhr, Paul Augustine *lawyer*
Sun, Ying-Hsuan *research scientist*
Suter, Steven E. *veterinarian, educator*
Sutton, Ronnie Neal *state legislator, lawyer*
Swaisgood, Harold Everett *biochemist, educator*
Szulik, Matthew J. *information technology executive*
Tague, Fanella *language educator*
Taylor, Raymond Mason *lawyer, educator, former government official*
Terry, Stephen D. *mechanical engineer, educator*
Thompson Cornwall, Lonieta Aurora *music educator, consultant*
Timmons-Goodson, Patricia *state supreme court justice*
Torres, Talani *performing arts educator*
Tucker, Helen Welch *writer*
Turinsky, Paul Josef *nuclear engineer, educator*
Valois, Robert Arthur *lawyer*
Vepraskas, Michael J. *soil scientist, educator*
Vogel, Phyllis Jean *music educator*
Ward, Aaron *professional hockey player*
Watson, Kimberly *director, educator*
Wehring, Bernard William *nuclear engineering educator*
Weisel, Michael Lloyd *lawyer, educator*
Welch, Milton Lamont *literature and language professor*
Wesler, Oscar *retired mathematician, educator*
Wesley, Glen *retired professional hockey player*
Wetsch, John Robert *information scientist*
Wheeler, Lawrence Jefferson *museum director*
Whitehurst, Jim (James M. Whitehurst) *former air transportation executive*
Whitten, Jerry Lynn *chemistry professor*
Williams, Hugh Alexander, Jr. *retired mechanical engineer, consultant*
Windham, Donald Eric *bioinformatics analyst*
Xu, Le *engineer*
Yearwood, Douglas Lyman *legal association administrator, researcher*
Yim, Man-Sung *engineering educator, consultant*
Young, David *political organization administrator*
Youngman, Lola Jeanne *music educator*
Zelnak, Stephen P., Jr. *construction materials company executive*
Zorowski, Carl Frank *engineering educator, academic administrator*

Randleman
Jordan, Lillian B. *judge*

Research Triangle Park
Atkins, John L. III *architect*
Beach, Robert Henry III *economist, educator*
Bullock, Orren Russell, Jr. *research scientist*
Burris, John Edward *academic administrator, biologist, educator*
Connelly, Deirdre P. *pharmaceutical executive*
Everett, LaTonya Michelle *computer engineer*
Gavin, Norma Irene *medical researcher*
Haynes, Victoria Franchetti *science administrator*
Iiames, John Shepherd *geologist, researcher*
Meigs, Joseph Timothy *lawyer*
Raymer, James Howard *chemist, researcher*
Reynolds, Peter James *physicist*
Schrager, Mindy Rae *operations management specialist*
Stoker, Tammy Edwards *toxicologist, researcher*
Subramani, Velu *chemist, researcher*
Wani, Mansukhlal Chhaganlal *chemist*
Waters, Michael Dee *corporate scientific officer, consultant*
Welborn, Reich Lee *lawyer*
Whichard, Willis Padgett *lawyer, retired educator, judge*

Rich Square
Baugham, Samuel McCoy *actor, painter*

Rockwell
Cobb, Tyrus Raymond, Jr., (Ty Cobb) *retired engineer, retired military officer*

Rocky Mount
Evans, Emma *retired art educator*
Griffiths, Deborah Holmes *academic administrator*
Holmes, Marbeth Hunt *humanities educator*
Zipf, Robert Eugene, Jr. *medical laboratory director, legal medicine consultant, pathologist*

Rocky Point
MacAskill, Lloyd Edwin *systems analyst, consultant*

Rolesville
Patierno, Alycia Lynn *school psychologist*

Roseboro
Cobb, Katherine Simon *theater educator*

Rougemont
Holeman, Betty Jean *counseling administrator*

Roxboro
Gates, Rosalie Prince *history professor*

Rutherfordton
Crummie, Ann Vaughn *mental health services professional*

Salisbury
Candler, Faxon David *small business owner*
Crowe, John Albert, Jr. *surgeon*
Dougherty, Erin Brooke *costume designer, educator*
Freeze, Gary Richard *historian*
Hagy, David Lee *conductor*
Higbee, Dale (Strohe) *musician, retired psychologist*
Troxler, Willie Thomasene *retired elementary school educator*
Tseng, Howard Shih Chang *economics professor, investment company executive*
Turner, Willard Craig *academic administrator*

Sanford
Brown, Eva Everlean *business executive*
Harrington, Anthony Ross *radio announcer, educator*
Sodini, Peter J. *food service executive*
Watson, David Riddle *literature and language professor*

Sapphire
Lewis, William Headley, Jr. *manufacturing executive*

Seven Lakes
Reilly, David Henry *retired university dean*

Shelby
Gash, Chavis Dennord *coordinator*
Putnam, James Dean *secondary school educator*
Zamora, Bobbie Jean *literature and language professor*

Snow Hill
Stevens, JoAnn A. *textile, political leader, author, minister*

Southern Pines
Cardwell, Nina Fern *special education educator*
Funderburk, David Britton *Former United States Representative, NC, ambassador, consultant*
Owings, Malcolm William *retired management consultant*
Warren, Donald William *medical and dental educator*

Southern Shores
Aukland, Elva Dayton *retired biologist, educator*
Kegel, William George *mining company executive*

Southport
Pepper, Jeffrey Mackenzie *publishing executive*

Spindale
Day, Ashley Paris *biology professor*
Hoyle, Noelle L. *biology professor*
Tucker, Tom *science and invention writer, literature and language professor*

Spring Hope
Hildreth, James Robert *retired air force officer*

Statesville
Elliott, Carolyn Cole *secondary school educator, department chairman*
Flake, Mark Wayde *artist*
Johnston, Betty Parker *retired social service worker*
Redman, William Walter, Jr. *retired NC state senator, NC state utilities commissioner*

Supply
Pontious, Robert Ronald *literature and language professor*
Wescott, Joseph Warren, II, *academic administrator, education educator*

Swannanoa
Whittington, Lorin Dale *retired music educator*

Tabor City
Jorgensen, Ralph Gubler *lawyer, accountant*

Tarboro
Davis, Robert Christopher *law educator*
Hopkins, Grover Prevatte *lawyer*
Jordan, Michael J. *academic administrator*

Taylorsville
Ross, David Edmond *church official*

Thomasville
Johnson, Kathie Anne *hospital administrator*

Todd
Cole, Susan Stockbridge *retired theater educator*

Trinity
Walker, Kenneth Lynn *lawyer*

Tryon
Mellberg, James Richard *retired dental research chemist*

Valdese
Denison, Cynthia Lee *accountant, tax specialist*

Wake Forest
Johnson, Ben Sigel *music educator*
Kimrey, Karen Goss *secondary school educator*

Warrenton
Harrison-Jervay, Evelyn Yvonne *publishing executive*
Weddington, Elizabeth Gardner (Liz Gardner) *actress*

Waxhaw
Edwards, Irene Elizabeth (Libby Edwards) *dermatologist, educator, researcher*

Waynesville
Hale, Joe (Joseph Rice) *church organization executive*

Weaverville
Edwards, Otis Carl, Jr. *theology studies educator*

Welcome
Bowyer, Clint *professional race car driver*
Burton, Jeff Brian *race car driver*

Weldon
Barringer, Paul Brandon, II, *lumber company executive*

Wentworth
Evans, Jonathan Christopher *social worker*

West End
Krallinger, Joseph Charles *entrepreneur, consultant, writer*

Whispering Pines
Kuhn, Matthew *retired engineering company executive*

Wilkesboro
Bridgeford, Gregory M. *consumer products company executive*
Brown, Michael K. *retail executive*
Canter, Charles W. (Nick) *retail executive*
Hull, Robert F., Jr., (Bob Hull) *consumer products company executive*

Williamston
Denny, Brenda S. *art educator*

Willow Spring
Valvo, Barbara-Ann *lawyer, surgeon*

Wilmington
Alam, Shah *research scientist*
Boyle, Joseph Hugh *psychiatrist*
Conser, Walter Hurley, Jr. *religion and philosophy educator*
Fuller, Melvin Stuart *botany educator*
Gonzalez, Jorge Jose *medical educator*
Gray, Marilyn F. Grinwis *elementary school educator, music educator*
Herman, Russell Leland *mathematics, physics professor*
Jones, David Meredith *retired communications educator*
Kelley, Patricia Hagelin *geology educator*
McCauley, Cleyburn Lycurgus *lawyer*
Medlock, Donald Larson *lawyer*
Nice, Scott Dean *voice educator*
Puente, Antonio E. *psychologist, educator, scientist*
Seapker, Janet Kay *museum administrator, architectural historian, consultant*
Stanfield-Maddox, Elizabeth *language educator, writer, translator, library advocate*
Velders, Deborah *museum director*

Wilson
Kushner, Michael James *neurologist, consultant, educator*
Ladwig, Harold Allen *neurologist*
McCain, Betty Landon Ray *political party and state official*
Morris, Sharon Louise Stewart *emergency medical technician, paramedic*

Windsor
Bazemore, Naomi Smith *elementary school educator*

Wingate
Alston, Gregory Lloyd *pharmacist, educator*
Coleman, Gillis Byrns *religious studies educator, humanities educator*

Winston Salem
Adams, Alfred Gray *lawyer*
Adams, Reid C., Jr. *lawyer*
Adams, Thomas R. *tobacco company executive*
Allison, John Andrew, IV, *bank executive*
Applegate, William Brown *dean, researcher, medical educator*
Atala, Anthony John *surgeon*
Baillie, John (Nmn) *gastroenterologist*
Barnett, Richard Chambers *historian, educator*
Barnhill, Henry Grady, Jr. *lawyer*
Bible, Daryl N. *bank executive*
Blynn, Guy Marc *retired lawyer*
Boone, Derrick S., Sr. *finance educator*
Bourne, Henry Clark, Jr. *electrical engineer, educator, retired academic administrator*
Carlton, Capers Baity *secondary school educator, director*
Chaden, Lee A. *apparel and former food products executive*
Cherikh, Moula *business educator*
Chilson, John A. *lawyer, military officer*
Cook, Sharon Warren *social worker, educator*
Covey, Cyclone *history professor*
Davis, Linwood Layfield *lawyer*
Dean, Richard Henry *surgeon, educator*
Dos Santos, Patricia C. *chemistry professor*
Dyer, Raymond B. *diagnostic radiology physician*
Edwards, Charles Archibald *lawyer*
Ehle, John Marsden, Jr. *writer*

Eldridge, J. Charles *endocrinologist, educator, researcher*
Eliason, Russell Allen *retired judge*
Ellis, Thomas L. *neurosurgeon, educator*
Faccinto, Victor Paul *artist, gallery administrator*
Forrest-Carter, Audrey Faye *literature and writing professor*
Foy, Herbert Miles III *lawyer, educator*
Gaudio, Dino Joseph *men's college basketball coach*
Gentry, Jeffery S. *tobacco company executive*
Graham, William Thomas *lawyer*
Greason, Murray Crossley, Jr. *lawyer*
Grobe, Jim *college football coach*
Gunter, Michael Donwell *lawyer*
Hammon, John William, Jr. *medical educator, thoracic surgeon*
Hanes, Frank Borden *writer, former business executive, farmer*
Hanes, Ralph Philip, Jr. *network technician*
Harper-Harrison, Alfreda Denise *nursing educator, researcher*
Harrelson, Walter Joseph *minister, educator*
Hatch, Nathan Orr *academic administrator*
Hegde, Ashok *research scientist, educator*
Hendricks, J(ames) Edwin *retired historian, educator, consultant, author*
Henson, Christopher L. *bank executive*
Hill, Ivor Dennis *pediatrician, educator*
Holton, Walter Clinton, Jr. *lawyer*
Humphrey, Dudley *lawyer*
Ivey, Susan M. *tobacco company executive*
James, Francis Marshall III *anesthesiologist*
Jeevanantham, Vinodh *medical educator, researcher*
Jenkins, Barbara Alexander *pastor, overseer*
Jester, Jane Harris *school librarian*
Joines, Allen *mayor, Winston-Salem, North Carolina*
Kaur, Mandeep *dermatologist, educator*
King, Kelly S. *bank executive*
King, Roberta B. *lawyer*
King, Wayne Edgar *journalist, educator*
Kohut, Robert Irwin *otolaryngologist, educator*
Kritchevsky, Stephen Bennett *epidemiologist, educator*
Kuhar, Edward C., Jr. *religious studies educator*
Lambeth, Judy (E. Julia Lambeth) *tobacco company executive, lawyer*
Laxminarayana, Dama *geneticist, researcher, educator*
Lee, Sang Jin *materials scientist*
Leonard, R. Michael *lawyer*
Levine, Cynthia Oglesby *librarian*
Loeser, Richard Frank, Jr. *medical researcher, director*
Loughridge, John Halsted, Jr. *lawyer*
Ludolf, Marilyn Marie Keaton *lay worker*
Madjd-Sadjadi, Zagros *economics professor, consultant*
Margitić, Milorad R. *language educator, researcher*
Marks, Malculm Wernick *plastic surgeon, educator*
Maselli, John Anthony *food products executive*
May, Darlene Rae *language educator*
Maynard, Charles Douglas *radiologist*
Mclorie, Gordon Arthur *urologist, educator*
Mecimore, Charles Douglas *retired accounting educator*
Medlin, John Grimes, Jr. *banker, director*
Miller, Richard Harry *philosopher, educator*
Mokrasch, Lewis Carl *neurochemist, educator*
Moody, Dixon McGuire *radiologist*
Morant, Blake *dean, law educator*
Moser, Kenneth Allen *lawyer*
Murray, Nial Patrick *retired anesthesiologist educator*
Noll, Richard A. *apparel executive*
O'Donovan, Cormac A. *neurologist, educator*
Oldaker, Guy Brooklyn III *lawyer*
Oliver, Patricia *lawyer*
Osborn, Malcolm Everett *lawyer*
O'Steen, Wendall Keith *anatomist, neurologist, educator*
Patel, Ajay *finance educator*
Placilla, Christina Dawn *music educator*
Podgorny, George *emergency physician*
Powell, Bayard Lowery *oncologist, educator*
Preslar, Len Broughton, Jr. *hospital administrator*
Price, Henry Escoe *broadcast executive*
Quick, Elizabeth L. *lawyer*
Rauschenberg, Bradford Lee *retired museum program director*
Ray, Michael Edwin *lawyer*
Reinemund, Steven S. *dean, educator, retired food products executive*
Rights, Graham Henry *retired minister*
Rodgman, Alan *chemist, consultant*
Roth, Marjory Joan Jarboe *special education educator*
Sandridge, William Pendleton, Jr. *lawyer*
Sanford, Beverly Shaw *museum director*
Sawyer, John Wesley *retired mathematics and computer science educator, consultant*
Schollander, Wendell Leslie, Jr. *lawyer*
Schollander, Wendell Wes III *lawyer*
Schroeder, Thomas D. *federal judge, lawyer*
Schwartz, Robert Paul *pediatric endocrinologist*
Shapere, Dudley *philosophy educator*
Sharpe, Keith Yount *retired lawyer, writer*
Simon, Jimmy Louis *pediatrician, educator*
Singleton, Teresa *engineering educator*
Slaughter, Thomas Freeman *anesthesiologist, educator, physician*
Soliman, Elsayed Z. *cardiologist, educator*
Spach, Jule Christian *church executive*
Stein, Barry Edward *medical educator*
Stewart, Gwendolyn Johns *music educator*
Strickland, Robert Louis *retired retail executive*
Stroupe, Henry Smith *university dean*
Sutton, Lynn Sorensen *librarian*
Tatter, Stephen Bradley *neurosurgeon, educator*
Taylor, Daniel Russell, Jr. *lawyer*
Toole, James Francis *medical educator*
Vachharajani, Vidula T. *emergency physician*
Vaughan, Keith W. *lawyer*
Vaughn, Robert Candler, Jr. *lawyer*
Walker, George Kontz *law educator*
Walsh, Robert K. *law educator, former dean*
Wanders, Hans Walter *banker*
Weller, Robert Stephen *anesthesiologist*
Whittington, Stephen Lunn *museum director*
Wilson, Grover Gray *lawyer*
Winn, Albert Curry *clergyman*
Womble, William Fletcher *lawyer*
Yentzer, Brad A. *medical researcher*
Zagoria, Sam D(avid) *reporter, educator, federal agency administrator*
Zhang, Lei *physics professor*
Zhang, Zhu-ming *medical educator*

Winterville
Mayo, Calvin Jay *engineering executive*

Winton
Moore, Clemmie Archer *retired elementary school educator*

Woodland
Wilson, Lloyd Lee *registrar, educator*

Wrightsville Beach
Mc Ilwain, William Franklin *newspaper editor, writer*

Yanceyville
Webster, Hugh B. *accountant, former state legislator*

Youngsville
Burwell, Edith Brodie *retired elementary school educator*

Zebulon
Maness, Eleanor Palmer *researcher*
O'Neal, Cynthia Ann *lawyer*
Privette, Janet Brown *elementary school educator*
Ruffing, Anne Elizabeth *artist*

NORTH DAKOTA

Bismarck
Bruning, David Bruce *mathematics professor*
Camp, Gregory Scott *history professor*
Crothers, Daniel John *state supreme court justice*
Dalrymple, Jack *lieutenant governor*
Dwelle, Terry *state agency administrator, public health service officer*
Emineth, Gary *political organization administrator*
Hardy, Jayne Winifred *assistant professor theology*
Hildestad, Terry D. *energy executive*
Hilzendeger, Cori Lynn *principal*
Hoeven, John *Governor of North Dakota*
Jaeger, Al (Alvin A. Jaeger) *Secretary of State, North Dakota*
Kapsner, Carol Ronning *state supreme court justice*
Karls, Ken *foundation executive, former political organization administrator*
Karsky, Timothy J. *state banking agency administrator*
Klemin, Lawrence R. *state legislator, lawyer*
Knoll, Gloria Jean *music educator*
Maring, Mary Muehlen *state supreme court justice*
Moore, Sherry Mills *lawyer*
Murry, Charles Emerson *lawyer, federal official*
Nelson, Carolyn *state legislator*
Newborg, Gerald Gordon *retired state archives administrator*
Niksic, Gwen M. *biology professor*
Ott, Doris Ann *librarian*
Paaverud, Merlan E., Jr. *museum director*
Rettig, Pam *literature educator*
Sand, Duane *think-tank associate*
Sandness, Paul K. *lawyer, energy executive*
Sandstrom, Dale Vernon *state supreme court justice*
Sanstead, Wayne Godfrey *state official, school system administrator*
Schmidt, Kelly L. *state treasurer*
Stenehjem, Wayne Kevin *state attorney general, lawyer*
Strauss, David *political organization administrator, former legislative staff member*
VandeWalle, Gerald Wayne *state supreme court chief justice*
Zipfel, Paul Albert *bishop*

Bottineau
Roemmich, Dalonnes Kay *music educator*

Devils Lake
Rygg, Glenn *retired music educator*

Dickinson
Johnson, Bonnie Tunnicliff *History Instructor*
Laman, Barbara *retired literature and language professor*
Larson, Carl Frederick William *retired literature and language professor*
McGarva, Andrew Robert *psychology professor*

Ellendale
Schlieve, Hy C. J. *school administrator*

Fargo
Aquila, Samuel Joseph *bishop*
Brennan, Joseph Patrick *mathematician*
Bright, Myron H. *federal judge*
Bye, Kermit Edward *federal judge, lawyer*
Chinnam, Ratna Babu *industrial engineer, educator*
Friesner, Daniel *pharmacist, educator*
Herman, Sarah Andrews *lawyer*
Horvik, Lori Ann *theater educator, consultant*
Li, Kam Wu *mechanical engineer, educator*
Maocheng, Yan *research scientist*
Mathern, Tim *state legislator*
Meester, Holly *elementary school educator, music educator, sales executive*
Mistry, Bhargav Mangaldas *surgeon, director*
Pauley, Edward E. *museum administrator*
Phillips, Saul *men's college basketball coach*
Postema, Beth E. *librarian, director*
Reid, Michele M. *school librarian, dean*
Reitan, Daniel Kinseth *electric and computer engineering educator*
Riley, Thomas Joseph *anthropologist, academic administrator*
Rosenberg, Harry *biochemist, natural product chemist*
Ryan, Mark A. *museum staff member*
Schultz, Ed (Edward Andrew Schultz) *radio personality*
Sheridan, Mark A. *physiologist, educator*
Slator, Brian M. *computer scientist, educator*
Tallman, Dennis Earl *professor, research scientist*
Vinnakota, Bapeswara-Rao Venkata *engineering educator*
Williams, Michael James *lawyer*
Wrigley, Drew H. *prosecutor, lawyer*
Yates, Janet Kathleen *civil engineering educator*
Yoon, Jaewan *civil engineering educator*

Grand Forks
Aune, Adonica Schultz *education educator, consultant*
Baldwin, Gayle R. *religious studies educator*
Berger, Albert Isaac *historian, consultant*
Carlson, Edward C. *anatomy educator, cell biologist, department chairman*
Chalmers, Lynne *special education educator*
Davis, W. Jeremy *retired lawyer, dean*
Dennis, Steven Allen *financial consultant*
Gaul, Gerald *ophthalmologist*
Gjovig, Bruce Quentin *entrepreneur, consultant*
Glassheim, Eliot Alan *state legislator*
Handy-Marchello, Barb *history educator, researcher*
Haskins, James P. *finance educator, consultant*
Hoffmann, Mark R. *physical chemist, educator*
Huang, Luke Hanming *engineering educator*
Jackson, Jon *medical educator, consultant*
Ji, Yun *chemical engineer, researcher*
Jones, Arthur Frederick *art university administrator, educator*
Kellenbenz, Dave John *meteorologist*
Kelley, Robert Otis *academic administrator, anatomist*
Kozliak, Evguenii I. *chemistry professor*
Kulkarni, Manohar Ramchandra *mechanical engineer, educator*
Lim, Yeo H. *engineering educator*
Melvold, Roger Wayne *microbiologist, educator*
Myers, Bradley Kevin *lawyer, educator*
Nielsen, Forrest Harold *research nutritionist*
Nilles, Matthew L. *microbiology educator, researcher*
Nordlie, Robert Conrad *biochemistry educator*
Page, Sally Jacquelyn *university official, management educator*
Patton, Gregory Kenneth *management educator*
Rheude, Elizabeth Anne *music educator*
Russell, Sue Ann *clinical psychologist*
Sticca, Robert P. *surgeon*
Stolt, Wilbur A. *library director*
Swanson, Zona Luciel *retired elementary school educator*
Towne, Gary Spaulding *music educator*
Wakefield, Mary Katherine *medical association administrator, medical educator*
Widdel, John Earl, Jr. *lawyer*
Wogaman, George Elsworth *insurance company executive, financial consultant*
Wolfe, Eric Andrew *literature and language professor*
Yoshida, Glen Yoshio *otolaryngologist*
Zhang, Xiaodong *oceanographer, educator*

Hatton
Strand, Fred P. *mathematics educator*

Jamestown
Joy, Mark Stephen *history professor, department chairman*

Mandan
Bair, Bruce Blythe *lawyer*

Mayville
Brunsdale, Mitzi Louisa Mallarian *language educator, critic*
Champion, Kathleen Ann *mathematics professor*
Karaim, Betty June *retired librarian*
McMahon, Dalton Edward *history professor, social sciences educator, department chairman*
Skean, Mark Edgar *finance educator, consultant*

Minot
Allen, Warren George *college administrator*
Henderson, Liana Solorzano *language educator*
Iversen, David Stewart *librarian*
Srock, Marlene *elementary school educator*
Tollefson, Ben C. *state legislator, retired utilities executive*
Watne, Darlene Claire *county official*
Weinmann, Ronald Vincent *business educator*

Osnabrock
Monson, David Carl *state legislator*

Venturia
Kretschmar, William Edward *state legislator, lawyer*

Wahpeton
Donahe, Peggy Yvonne *gifted and talented educator, librarian, English elementary teacher*
Reubish, Gary Richard *English language educator*

Williston
Adducci, Joseph Edward *obstetrician, gynecologist*
Conway, Beverly E. *science educator*
Yockim, James Craig *foundation administrator*

OHIO

Ada
Alexander, Robert M. *political science professor*
Al-Olimat, Khalid Sulieman *electrical engineer, educator*
Baker, Kendall L. *academic administrator*
Estell, John K. *computer science and engineering educator, department chair*
Fenton, Howard Nathan III *lawyer, educator*
Freed, Catherine Carol Moore *education educator*
Jao, Feng *education educator*
Khorbotly, Sami *electrical engineer, educator*
Reza, Farhad *engineering educator*
Shen, Hui *engineering educator*
Srinivasa, Vemuru R. *engineering educator, researcher*
Wildman, Kenneth N. *professor emeritus of psychology*
Yoder, John-David Samuel *mechanical engineer*

Akron
Alexander, Anthony J. *electric power industry executive*
Allen, Philip Andrew *psychology professor*
Barker, Harold Kenneth *former university dean*
Bell, Samuel H. *federal judge, educator*
Belsky, Martin Henry *law educator, dean*
Bishop, Christy B. *lawyer*
Brake, Yvonne Marie *not-for-profit development director*
Brown, David Rupert *engineering executive*
Buzzelli, Charlotte Grace *special education educator*
Cadile, Pamela L. *chemist, sales planner*
Cherpas, Christopher Theodore *lawyer*
Collier, Alice Elizabeth Becker *retired social administrator, educational administrator*
Emmett, John Colin *retired inventor, consultant*
Fant, J. Clayton *classical studies professor*
Fei, Juntao *research scientist*
Fisher, James Lee *lawyer*
Fleming, Paul Daniel III *chemical physicist*
Garbrandt, Gail Elaine *political science professor, consultant*
Gent, Alan Neville *physicist, researcher*
Gil, Karen M. *medical researcher, director*
Gingo, Joseph Michael *chemicals company executive*
Grigg, Richard R. *energy executive*
Harvie, Crawford Thomas *lawyer*
Hopkins, Michael Patrick *obstetrician, oncologist, surgeon*
Jana, Sadhan C. *engineering educator, researcher*
Keegan, Robert J. *manufacturing executive*
Kennedy, Joseph Paul *chemist, researcher*
Kihn, Jean-Claude *automotive executive*
Knepper, George W. *historian, educator*
Kramer, Richard J. *manufacturing executive*
Lavin, Justin Paul, Jr. *obstetrician, gynecologist, perinatologist*
Liu, Liping *management consultant, educator*
Lombardi, Frederick McKean *lawyer*
Malone, Alicia Jane *minister, theologian*
Marsh, Richard H. *energy executive*
Martin, Jack *educational services company executive, former federal agency administrator*
McGuire, Robert A. *economics professor*
Moser, James Michael *medical educator*
Nelson, Michael Arnold *economics professor, department chairman*
Noble, Allen George *geography educator*
Olson, Byron Louis *biochemist, educator*
Pan, Ernian *engineering educator, researcher*
Phares, James Kenneth *retired electronics engineer*
Piirma, Irja *chemist, educator*
Plusquellic, Donald L. *Mayor, Akron, Ohio*
Ramsey, Sally Judith Weine *chemist, research and development company executive*
Reilly, Elizabeth Ann *law educator, dean*
Revay, Linda Ann *principal, educator*
Richert, Paul *law educator*
Ruocco, Joe *manufacturing executive*
Rzonzef, Michel *manufacturing executive*
Schrader, Alfred Eugene *lawyer*
Seiwald, Robert J. *retired inventor*
Smart, George M. *energy executive, former packaging company executive*
Srivatsan, Tirumalai Srinivas *engineering educator*
Stephens, Rachel De-Vore *finance company executive, educator*
Sterns, Harvey Leonard *psychologist, gerontologist*
Taylor, E. Jane *lawyer*
Tipping, Harry A. *lawyer*
Trotter, Thomas Robert *lawyer*
Vespoli, Leila L. *lawyer, energy executive*
von Spiegel, Janice Krieger *mathematics educator*
Weidknecht, Marcia E. *chemistry professor*
Wells, Darren R. *manufacturing executive*
West, Michael Alan *retired hospital administrator*
Williams, William Proctor *literature educator*
Wolfe, John Leslie *lawyer*

Alliance
Bergmann, Mark Allan *broadcast executive, educator*
Boehm, Patricia *music educator*

Amelia
Hayden, Joseph Page, Jr. *finance company executive*
Kahles, Cheryl Mary *elementary school educator*
Tracy, David James *chemist, consultant*

Amherst
Gerstenberger, Valerie *media specialist*

Ashland
Ford, Lucille Garber *economist, educator*
Moser, John Evan *history professor*
Seifert, Nancy Faye Eshelman *retired special education educator, consultant*
Waters, Ronald W. *theology studies educator, church administrator, pastor*
Watson, JoAnn Ford *theology studies educator*

Ashtabula
Carrel, Marianne Eileen *music educator*
Hornbeck, Harold Douglas *psychotherapist*
Morisue, Glenn T. *graphics designer*
Najafi, Mahmoud *mathematics professor*

Athens
Borchert, Donald Marvin *philosopher, educator*
Bruning, James Leon *academic administrator, educator*
Cooper-Chen, Anne *journalism educator, researcher*
Crowl, Samuel Renninger *retired dean, language educator*
Deguchi, Ayako *language educator*
Drabold, David Alan *physics professor, researcher*
Ehrlich, Philip *philosophy educator*
Grant, Anita H. *academic librarian*
Hazler, Richard John *counselor educator*
Hicks, Kenneth H. *science educator, researcher*
Kurz, David Bryan *web site designer*
Marks, Emilia Alonso *language educator, researcher*
Matthews, Jack (John Harold Matthews) *language educator, writer*
McDavis, Roderick J. *academic administrator*
McKerrow, Raymie E. *communications educator*
McNamara, John Regis *psychology educator*
Muhammad, Najee Emerson *education educator*
Nance, Richard Damian *geologist, consultant*
Patterson, Stephen M. *psychology professor*
Reisner, Andrew Douglas *psychologist*
Safran, Stephen Philip *educational program coordinator*
Sayrs, Elizabeth *music educator*
Scott, Charles Lewis *retired photojournalist*
Scott, Madeleine *performing arts educator*
Snow, Andrew P *communications educator, researcher*
Stempel, Guido Hermann III *journalism educator*
Thompson, Herbert George, Jr. *economics professor, consultant*
Ulbrich, David J. *history professor*
Uspenskiy, Vladimir Vladimirovich *mathematics professor*
Vedder, Richard Kent *economics professor*
Wen, Shih-Liang *mathematics professor*
Whealey, Lois Deimel *humanities scholar*
Wilhelm, David C. *venture capitalist*
Winters, Robert Louis *theater educator, consultant*
Wrage, William *retired language educator*

Aurora
Allen, Marc Kevin *emergency physician, educator*
Eakin, Thomas Capper *sports promotion executive*
Herington, Leigh Ellsworth *state legislator, lawyer*
Kirchner, James William *retired electrical engineer*
Lawton, Florian Kenneth *artist, educator*
Ross, Violet Bica *retired elementary school educator, psychologist*

Avon Lake
Douglas, Carolyn Grace *language educator*
Hrinczenko, Borys Walter *oncologist, hematologist, medical educator, medical researcher, consultant*
Lewis, Peter Benjamin *insurance company executive*
Newlin, Stephen Dore *chemicals executive*
Pascarella, Perry James *editor, writer*

Barberton
Kitto, John Buck, Jr. *mechanical engineer*
Vernacotola, Joseph N. *librarian*

Barnesville
Kelley-Hall, Maryon Hoyle *retired social worker*

Bath
Coyne, Thomas Joseph *economics and finance professor*

Bay Village
Sprague, Vicki L. *educational consultant*

Beachwood
Braverman, Herbert Leslie *lawyer*
Budish, Armond David *state legislator, lawyer, journalist*
Clegg, Christopher R. *lawyer*
Davis, Ben, Jr. *literature and language professor*
Demetriou, Steven J. *metal products executive*
Fufuka, Natika Njeri Yaa *retail executive*
Gatica, Norma *chemistry professor*
Krieger, Irvin Mitchell *retired chemistry professor*
Moskowitz, Roland Wallace *internist*
Pearlman, Samuel Segel *lawyer, educator*
Pruthi, Tarun *research scientist*
Robertson, Ned *dentist*
Stack, Sean M. *metal products executive*
Zambie, Allan John *retired lawyer*

Beavercreek
Notestine, Greg *dentist*
Pasupuleti, Venumadhav *information technology executive*

Bellaire
Kniesner, John Thomas *librarian*

Bellevue
Aigler, William Frank *lawyer*

Bellville
Hooker, James Todd *manufacturing executive*

Berea
Durst, Richard Wayne *academic administrator*
Gesink, Indira Falk *educator*
Jacques, Kevin *finance educator*
Kokinis, George *professional sports team executive*
Lewis, Jamal *professional football player*
Little, Richard Allen *mathematics professor, computer science educator*
Mangini, Eric *professional football coach*
Miller, Dennis Dixon *economics professor*
Quinn, Brady (Brady Tyler Quinn) *professional football player*
Winget, Jack B. *theater educator, director, actor*

Berlin Center
Haynali, Carolyn Ann *social services administrator*

Beverly
Sprague, Cathy L. *secondary school educator*

Bexley
Finley, Charles Edwin *communications educator*
Yashon, David *neurosurgeon, educator*

Bluffton
Dudley, Durand Stowell *retired librarian*
Rich, Ronald Lee *chemistry professor*

Boardman
Skinner, William Philip, Jr. *manufacturing executive*

Bowling Green
Berger, Bonnie G. *sport psychologist, educator*
Browne, Ray Broadus *popular culture educator*
Cartwright, Carol Ann *academic administrator*
Danilov, Evgeny *medical researcher, director*
Gabel, Rodney M. *communications disorders educator*
Grunden, Walter Eugene *history professor*
Guion, Robert Morgan *psychologist, educator*
Guthrie, Mearl Raymond, Jr. *business administration educator*
Hakel, Milton Daniel, Jr. *psychologist, educator, writer, consultant*
Hershberger, Andrew E. *art educator*
Kolla, Sri R. *engineering educator, researcher*
Leclair, Jacqueline Fairchild *musician, educator*
Lunde, Harold Irving *retired management educator*
McCaghy, Charles Henry *retired social sciences educator*
Newman, David Stefan *chemistry professor, consultant*
Ocvirk, Otto George *artist*
Park, Sung-Yeon *communications educator*
Umbarger, Gardner Thompson III *special education educator, researcher*
Varney, Glenn Herbert *finance educator*
Versteeg, Robert John *minister, actor, writer*
Zeilstra-Ryalls, Jill Helen *biology professor*

Bratenahl
Dunn, Horton, Jr. *organic chemist*
Jones, Trevor Owen *biomedical industry executive, management consultant*

Brecksville
Pappas, Effie Vamis *language educator, finance educator, writer, poet, artist*

Broadview Heights
Jergens, Maribeth Joie *school counselor*

Brookfield
Manos, Thomas G. *investment company executive*

Brookpark
Baumgartner, Kelli Ann Crews *aerospace engineer*
Heil, Michael Lloyd *military officer, academic administrator*

Brunswick
Sandvick, Janet Rose *history educator*

Bryan
Carrico, Virgil Norman *physician*
Shaffer, Wayne Eugene *lawyer*

Burton
Lynch, Deborah Ann *college administrator*

Cambridge
Barzda, Susan Marie *special education educator, music educator*
Zalenski, Amy Ralynn *athletic trainer, small business owner*

Canal Winchester
Roddy, Carol Lynn *library director*

Canfield
Scurich, Kelly Lemos *music director*
Weiss, Susan Ellen *adult nurse practitioner, educator*
Yurchekfrodl, Patricia *librarian*

Canton
Armentrout, Allison *literature and language professor*
Barnhart, Gene *lawyer*
Bell, Lee J. *lawyer*
Botean, John Michael *bishop*
Burkhart, William R. *lawyer*
Carpenter, Noble Olds *retired bank executive*
Esber, George S. *anthropologist, educator*
Griffith, James W. *manufacturing executive*
Howland, Willard J. *radiologist, educator*
Mann, John Martin *minister*
McFarren, Leland Cullen *educational association administrator, educator*
Nadas, John Adalbert *psychiatrist, educator*
Oliver, Kenton L. *library director*
Peck, Douglas Caton *dean, educator*
Pelanda, Raymond Victor *retired director*
Perry, Stephen A. *museum administrator, former federal agency administrator*
Puscas, Vasile Louis *bishop emeritus*
Schauer, Thomas Alfred *insurance company executive*
Starchman, Dale Edward *medical educator*
Swidarski, Thomas W. *manufacturing executive*
Timken, Ward J., Jr. *manufacturing executive*
Tippett, Andre *retired professional football player*
Trapani, John G., Jr. *philosophy professor*
Tyburski, Charles J. *lawyer*
Vazzano, Frank Paul *historian, educator*
Walker, James William *physics educator, freelance/self-employed writer*
Zimmerman, Gary Wayne *professional football player*

Cedarville
Firmin, Michael Wayne *psychology professor*
Grigorenko, Margaret Crook *education educator, consultant*
Humphreys, Donald Stephen Ray *academic administrator*
Mach, Thomas S. *history professor*
Moore, Julie L. *writer, director, poet*
Tuinstra, Timothy Ryan *engineering educator*
Wood, Michelle Gaffner *language educator*
Zavodney, Lawrence Dennis *mechanical engineer, educator*

Celina
Fanning, Ronald Heath *architect, engineer*

Centerburg
Reynolds, Don William *geologist*

Centerville
Appelbaum, Bernardine *cardiovascular nurse*
Giffen, Daniel Harris *lawyer, educator*

Chagrin Falls
Brophy, Jere Hall *manufacturing executive*
Brown, Jeanette Grasselli *retired director*
Heckman, Henry Trevennen Shick *retired steel executive*
Lingl, Friedrich Albert *psychiatrist*
Miller, John Robert *oil industry executive*
O'Neill, William M. (Bill O'Neill) *former appellate judge*
Shakley, Elaine M. *organist, department chairman*
Stec, John Zygmunt *retired real estate company officer*
Vail, Iris Jennings *civic worker*

Chardon
Kellis, Michael John *osteopathic physician*

Chesterland
Aster, Ruth Marie Rhydderch *business owner*

Chillicothe
Jayne, Cristina Marsh *retired elementary school educator*
Reiger, John Franklin *history professor, researcher*
Shahrestani, Hamid *economics professor*

Chippewa Lake
Javorek, Richard Alan *history educator, consultant*

Cincinnati
Abate, Anne Katherine *librarian, consultant, educator*
Adams, Edmund John *lawyer*
Agrawal, Dharma Prakash *engineering educator*
Aguirre, Fernando *food products executive*
Ahmad, Syed *surgeon*
Ahn, Chong Hyuk *engineering educator, researcher*
Albainy-Jenei, Stephen R. *lawyer*
Alexander, James Wesley *surgeon, educator*
Alexander, John Kurt *history professor*
Alexander, Wilma Jean *business education educator, management consultant*
Altug, Cetinkaya *oculo-plastic surgeon ophthalmologist*
Anand, Sam *engineering educator*
Anderson, James Milton *hospital administrator*
Anderson, Jerry William, Jr. *diversified financial services company executive, educator*
Anderson, Joan Balyeat *theology studies educator, minister*
Anderson, William Edward *electrical engineer*
Andritzky, Frank William *political science educator*
Anthony, Thomas Dale *lawyer*
Ashley, Lynn *social sciences educator, consultant*
Ates, Delories *retired counseling administrator*
Attee, Joyce Valerie Jungclas *artist*
Auyang, Grace Chao *education educator, consultant*
Bahlman, William Thorne, Jr. *retired lawyer*
Bahnfleth, William Parry *mechanical engineering consultant*
Bahr, Donald Walter *retired chemical engineer*
Baker, Dusty (Johnnie B. Baker Jr.) *professional baseball team manager, retired professional baseball player*
Baker, Raymond Charles *pediatrician, educator*
Balistreri, William Francis *pediatric gastroenterologist, educator*
Baron, Paul Andrew *research scientist*
Barrett, John F. *insurance company executive*
Bateman, Sharon Louise *corporate philanthropist*
Baughman, Robert Phillip *physician, educator*
Beary, John Francis III *rheumatologist, clinical pharmacologist, medical researcher, naval officer*
Benson, Cedric *professional football player*
Besier, James Louis *pharmacist, educator*
Betsky, Aaron *museum director*
Bilionis, Louis D. *dean, law educator*
Birmingham, Stephen *writer*
Bishop, George Franklin *political scientist, educator*
Bleznick, Donald William *Romance languages educator*
Bluestein, Venus Weller *retired psychologist, educator*
Boehne, Richard A. *newspaper company executive*
Bollen, Sharon Kesterson *artist, educator*
Bommireddy, Ramireddy *immunologist, researcher*
Boolchand, Punit *physics professor*
Boyd, Deborah Ann *pediatrician*
Brehm-Heeger, Paula *library director, library association executive*
Bridgeland, James Ralph, Jr. *lawyer*
Briggs, Henry Payson, Jr. *headmaster*
Briskin, Madeleine *oceanographer, paleontologist*
Brod, Stanford *graphics designer, educator*
Broderick, Dennis John *lawyer, retail executive*
Brown, Bruce *consumer products company executive*
Brown, Dale Patrick *retired advertising executive*
Brown, Daniel *curator, executive secretary*
Bruce, Jay A. *professional baseball player*
Bryant, Irene Melba *retired elementary school educator, artist*
Buchanan, Margaret E. *publishing executive*
Burke, Timothy Michael *lawyer, educator*
Butsch Kovacic, Melinda *epidemiologist, medical researcher*
Cabezas, Heriberto *chemical engineer, researcher*
Callinan, Tom *editor-in-chief*
Carmichael, Greg D. *bank executive*
Chalkley, Roger *mathematics professor*
Chatterjee, Jayanta *architecture and planning educator*
Chekour, Adam *interpreter, educator*
Chernus, Linda A. *psychoanalytic psychotherapy educator, social worker*
Chesley, Stanley Morris *lawyer*
Ching, Ho *surgeon*
Choo, Daniel *otolaryngologist, educator*
Christensen, Paul Walter, Jr. *retired gear manufacturing company executive*
Christenson, Gordon A. *law educator*
Chung, Eugene Sejin *cardiologist, director*
Ciani, Alfred Joseph *dean*
Cioffi, Michael Lawrence *lawyer*
Cissell, James Charles *lawyer*
Clark, Kenneth Edward *physiologist, educator*
Clay, Eric L. *federal judge*
Cobey, John Geoffrey *lawyer, consultant*
Cody, Thomas Gerald *retail executive, lawyer*
Coffaro, Steven C. *lawyer*
Cole, Thomas L. *retail executive*
Coles, Laveranues *professional football player*
Combs, Eric K. *lawyer*
Conaton, Michael Joseph *diversified financial services company executive*
Cook, Deborah L. *federal judge, former state supreme court justice*
Cordero, Francisco Javier *professional baseball player*
Cotton, Robin T. *pediatric otolaryngologist, surgeon*
Craft Davis, Audrey Ellen *writer, educator*
Crew, Spencer *museum administrator*
Cronin, Mick *men's college basketball coach*
Cruz, A. B., III, (Anatolio Benedicto Cruz III) *lawyer, multimedia company executive*
Cunningham, Margaret Gast *faculty member*
Cunningham, Pierce Edward *lawyer, city planner*
Curtin, Leah Louise *publisher, nurse, educator*
Daley, Clayton Carl, Jr. *consumer products company executive*
Daniel, J. Lovell *pediatrician, educator*
Daniels, Astar *artist*
Davis, Michael W. *theology studies educator*
de Courten-Myers, Gabrielle Marguerite *retired neuropathologist*
Dehner, Joseph Julnes *lawyer*
DeLong, Deborah *lawyer*
Desai, Deepak K. *lawyer*
De Witt, Jeanette Marie *physical therapist*
DeWitt, Thomas G. *pediatrician*
DeWitt, William O., Jr. *investor, professional sports team executive*
Diller, Edward Dietrich *lawyer*
Dillon, David Brian *retail grocery executive*
Dornette, W(illiam) Stuart *lawyer, educator*
Dougherty, David Francis *business process outsourcing executive*
Duffy, Virginia *minister*
Easley, Joanne L. *vocational evaluator*
Everson, Jean Watkins Dolores *librarian, media consultant, educator*
Faller, Susan Grogan *lawyer*
Farmer, Richard T. *uniform rental and sales executive*
Farmer, Scott D. *apparel executive*
Farrell, Pamela Christine *secondary school educator*
Fei, Lin *statistician*
Feinberg, Judith *physician, medical researcher, educator*
Fender, Kimber L. *library director, educator*
Fink, Jerold Albert *lawyer*
Francis, Marion David *consulting chemist*
Frenck, Robert W., Jr. *pediatrician, educator, epidemiologist*
Friedman, Penny *lawyer, not-for-profit developer*
Gaitonde, Krishnanath *urologist, educator*
Galloway, Lillian Carroll *modeling agency executive, consultant*
Gan, Subhadeep *mechanical engineer, researcher*
Gass, Margery Stoops *obstetrician, gynecologist*
Gates, Katherine A. *accountant, writer*
Geller, James Ian *pediatrician, oncologist*
Geracioti, Thomas Dino, Jr. *psychiatry, researcher*
Gerson, Myron Craig *cardiologist, researcher*
Gettler, Benjamin *lawyer, manufacturing company executive*
Ghia, Kirti N. *fluid mechanics engineer, aerospace educator*
Glendening, Everett Austin *architect*
Goetzman, Bruce Edgar *architecture educator*
Goodman, Bernard *physics professor*
Goodman, Stanley *lawyer*
Goodwin, John P. *consumer products company executive*
Gould, Michael *retail executive*
Greenberg, David Bernard *chemical engineering educator*
Greengus, Samuel *academic administrator, theology studies educator*
Griffin, Richard Allen *federal judge*
Grove, Janet E. *retail executive*
Hall, Ernest L. *electrical engineer, robotics educator*
Hall, Madelon Carol Syverson *retired elementary school educator*
Hanson, Amy *retail company executive*
Hantush, Mohamed M. *hydrologist, researcher*
Hardy, Thomas Cresson *insurance company executive*
Hardy, William Robinson *lawyer*
Harmon, Patrick *historian, retired editor, commentator*
Harris, Irving *lawyer*
Harrison, Donald Carey *academic administrator, cardiologist, educator*
Haswani, Dinesh K. *medical researcher*
Hawkins, Lawrence Charles *management consultant, educator*

Healey, Melanie Liddle *consumer products company executive, marketing professional*
Heimlich, Henry J. *physician, surgeon, educator*
Heldman, James Gardner *lawyer*
Heldman, Paul W. *lawyer, food service executive*
Hensgen, Herbert Thomas *medical technologist*
Hermanies, John Hans *retired lawyer*
Hess, Evelyn Victorine *medical educator*
Hill, Thomas Clark *lawyer*
Hiratzka, Loren F. *surgeon*
Hoefle, H. Frederick *lawyer*
Hoffheimer, Daniel Joseph *lawyer*
Hoguet, Karen M. *retail executive*
Holland, Edward J. *ophthalmologist, surgeon*
Holloman, J. Phillip *apparel executive*
Hom, David Brian *surgeon*
Hopkins, Jeffery P. *federal judge*
Hovanitz, Christine Anne *psychologist*
Huenefeld, Thomas Ernst *financial consultant, retired banker*
Idinopulos, Thomas Athanasius *religious studies educator, writer*
Inge, Thomas *pediatric surgeon*
Irwin, Miriam Dianne Owen *publishing executive, writer*
Järvi, Paavo *conductor, music director*
Jemison, Steven W. *lawyer, consumer products company executive*
Jensen, Elwood Vernon *biochemist*
Jobe, Alan Hall *pediatrician, educator*
Jocketty, Walt (Walter J. Jocketty) *professional baseball team manager, professional sports team executive*
Jone, Wen-Ben *computer scientist, researcher*
Jones, Nathaniel Raphael *lawyer, retired federal judge*
Joseph, Patricia Maxwell *pulmonologist, educator*
Joyce, David L. *air transportation executive*
Kabat, Kevin Thomas *bank executive*
Kamesar, Adam *literature educator*
Kari, Ross *bank executive*
Keck, Paul E., Jr. *psychiatrist*
Kelley, John Joseph, Jr. *lawyer*
Kelly, Brian *college football coach*
Kereiakes, Dean James *cardiologist*
Kessinger, Thomas Anthony *education and social studies educator, researcher, consultant*
Kethledge, Raymond Michael *federal judge*
Khurana Hershey, Gurjit *pediatrician, pulmonologist, educator*
Kindt, Monica V. *lawyer*
King, Margaret Ann *communications educator*
Kinman, Riley Nelson *engineering educator*
Kircher, Christopher *neurologist, consultant, medical researcher*
Klein, Jerry Emanuel *insurance and financial planning executive*
Knue, Paul Frederick *newspaper editor*
Koehl, Joerg *microbiologist, researcher, medical educator*
Kordons, Uldis *lawyer*
Krome, Frederic *editor*
Kronick, Susan D. *retail executive*
Kukielka, Gilbert Leon *physician*
Kuntz, Charles, IV, *neurosurgeon*
Kutcher, Louis Wm. *biology professor*
Kyle, Kimberly *lawyer*
Laffitte, Larry James *industrial organizational psychologist, consultant*
Lafley, A.G. (Alan George Lafley) *consumer products company executive*
Laney, Sandra Eileen *information technology executive*
Lang, Jackie Ann *nursing consultant*
Lawrence, James Kaufman Lebensburger *lawyer*
Lawson, Randall Clayton, II, *finance company executive*
Lehmann, Corinne E. *medical educator*
Levinson, Joseph E. *retired internist, rheumatologist, educator*
Lewis, Marvin *professional football coach*
Lichtin, Leon (Judah Leon Lichtin) *retired pharmaceutical educator*
Liggett, Stephen B. *pharmacologist, educator*
Lin, Ray Y. *science educator*
Lindberg, Charles David *lawyer*
Lindner, Carl H. III *insurance company executive*
Lindner, Carl Henry, Jr. *insurance company executive, professional sports team owner*
Lindner, Robert David *finance company executive*
Lindner, S(tephen) Craig *insurance company executive*
Lindsell, Christopher J. *statistician*
List, Teri L. *consumer products company executive*
Loggie, Jennifer Mary Hildreth *retired physician, educator*
Long, Phillip Clifford *retired museum director*
Longenecker, Mark Hershey, Jr. *lawyer*
Lower, Elyse E. *physician, educator*
Lucke, Robert Vito *investment company executive*
Luckner, Herman Richard III *interior designer*
Lundgren, Terry (Terrence J. Lundgren) *apparel company executive*
Mack, Chris *men's college basketball coach*
Madson, Philip Ward *engineering executive, consultant*
Majoras, Deborah Platt *consumer products company executive, former commissioner*
Malik, Punam *medical educator*
Mallory, Mark L. *Mayor, Cincinnati, former state legislator*
Maltz, Robert *surgeon*
Mann, David Scott *lawyer, former congressman*
Mantel, Samuel Joseph, Jr. *management educator, consultant*
Martin, John Bruce *chemical engineer*
Mattner, Jochen *medical educator, researcher*
Maxwell, Robert Wallace, II, *lawyer*
Mazlack, Lawrence Joseph *science educator*
McClain, William Andrew *lawyer*
McDonald, Douglass Wayne *museum administrator*
McDonald, Robert Alan (Bob McDonald) *consumer products company executive*
McGavran, Frederick Jaeger *lawyer*
McGeorge, Don W. *retail executive*
McGuff, Kevin *women's college basketball coach*
McMullen, W. Rodney *financial officer*
McMullin, Ruth Roney *retired publishing executive*
McMurray, James Scott *pediatric otolaryngologist*
Meal, Larie *chemistry professor, researcher, consultant*
Mechem, Charles Stanley, Jr. *retired broadcast executive*
Meisner, Patricia Ann *assistant principal*
Meister, Julia B. *lawyer*
Melcher, Sarah J. *theology studies educator*
Merrill, Walter Hilson *surgeon*
Meyers, Karen Diane *lawyer, educator*
Meyers, Pamela Sue *lawyer*
Mihaescu, Mihai *engineering educator, researcher*
Minai, Ali *engineering educator*
Mital, Anil *engineering educator*
Moeller, Jon R. *consumer products company executive*
Montavon, Victoria A. *university librarian, dean*
Moomaw, Sally Coup *education educator*
Morgan, Victoria *performing company executive, choreographer*
Morgan, William Richard *mechanical engineer*
Motch, Marjorie McCullough *service organization executive*
Mulvey, William J. *lawyer*
Munir, Muhammad *pain medicine physician, director*
Nakata, Akinori *epidemiologist, psychologist, researcher*
Nasrallah, Henry Ata *psychiatry researcher, educator*
Nebert, Daniel Walter *molecular geneticist, research administrator*
Nechemias, Stephen Murray *lawyer*
Nielsen, George Lee *architect*
Oberhaus, Geoffrey Luther *lawyer*
Ochocinco, Chad (Chad Javon Johnson) *professional football player*
Odeen, Philip A. *communications executive*
O'Hara, Sara Marie *radiologist*
O'Reilly, James Thomas *lawyer, educator, writer*
Otto, Charlotte R. *consumer products company executive*
Palmer, Carson *professional football player*
Parker, R. Joseph *lawyer*
Passerini, Filippo *information technology executive*
Pathak, Sanjeev *psychiatrist, researcher*
Pepper, John Ennis, Jr. *entertainment company executive, former consumer products company executive*
Perlman, Burton *judge*
Peterson, Randy *consumer products company executive, information technology professional*
Petrie, Bruce Inglis *lawyer*
Phillips, Brandon Emil *professional baseball player*
Phillips, Christopher *history professor, researcher*
Pilarczyk, Daniel Edward *archbishop*
Platow, Raphaela *museum director, curator*
Plevyak, Linda Huether *education educator, researcher*
Porembka, David Thomas *anesthesia and surgery educator*
Porter, Robert Carl, Jr. *lawyer*
Portman, Robert Jones *lawyer, former United States Representative from Ohio*
Poston, Daniel T. *bank executive*
Potoka, Karen *psychologist*
Prince, Susan Hukill *ancient language educator*
Pritchard, Marc S. *consumer products company executive*
Randolph, Leonard McElroy, Jr. *career officer*
Reardon, Martine *department store executive, marketing professional*
Rechnitzer, Haim Otto *religious studies educator*
Reichert, David *lawyer*
Reuter, Mark F. *lawyer*
Reynolds, Paul L. *lawyer, bank executive*
Rich, Robert Edward *lawyer*
Richardson, Eric W. *lawyer*
Ritschel, Wolfgang Adolf *medical educator, sculptor, artist*
Robinson, David M. *dentist*
Rogers, John Marshall *federal judge*
Rolen, Scott Bruce *professional baseball player*
Ross, Lori A. *lawyer*
Rucker, Fanon A. *lawyer*
Ruh, Michael A., Jr. *lawyer*
Russell, James Edward *physics professor*
Ruwe, Bradley N. *lawyer*
Sachse, Peter *retail executive*
Safdi, Alan V. *gastroenterologist, director*
Sallquist, Gary Ardin *retired minister, non-profit executive*
Samy, Ravi *otolaryngologist*
Sarembock, Ian Joseph *internist, cardiologist*
Sauer, Matthew James *history professor*
Schaefer, Frank William III *microbiologist, researcher*
Schafrik, Robert Edward *materials engineer, technology manager, information technologist*
Scheer, Brenda Case *architect, educator*
Schiff, John Jefferson, Jr. *finance company executive*
Schlotman, J. Michael *food products executive*
Schnurr, Dennis Marion *archbishop*
Schrier, Arnold *historian, educator*
Schuck, Thomas Robert *lawyer, farmer*
Shipley, Tony L(ee) *investor, software company executive*
Shirley, Edward D. *consumer products company executive*
Shore, Thomas Spencer, Jr. *retired lawyer*
Siegel, Robert M. *pediatrician, educator*
Siekmann, Donald Charles *accountant*
Silbersack, Mark Louis *lawyer*
Silberstein, Edward Bernard *nuclear medicine educator, oncologist, hematologist, researcher*
Singh, Sandeep *research scientist*
Sinha, Sunil K. *aerospace engineer, consultant*
Smarelli, David John *music educator, musician*
Smith, Leroy Harrington, Jr. *mechanical engineer, consultant*
Smith, Timothy W. *musician, educator*
Smittle, Nelson Dean *military analyst, artist*
Sommer, Scott William *control systems integrator manager*
Spicer, Emily Taylor *school system administrator*
Spohn, Dorothy M. *retired elementary school educator*
Stern, David Mark *dean, medical educator*
Stern, Noah J. *lawyer*
Stinson, Mary Florence *retired nursing educator*
Strauss, Arnold Wilbur *pediatrician, educator*
Sullivan, James F. *physicist, researcher*
Supp, Dorothy M. *medical educator, researcher*
Sutton, Jeffrey S. *federal judge*
Swank, Michael Lawson *orthopedist*
Swigert, James Mack *lawyer*
Talaska, Glenn *medical educator*
Ten Eyck, Dorothea Fariss *real estate agent*
Thompson, James E. *lawyer, food products executive*
Tobias, Paul Henry *lawyer*
Tobin, Duke *professional sports team executive*
Travis, Lawrence F. *law educator*
Trent, Judith Swanlund *communication educator*
Tsibulsky, Vladimir Lvovich *psychologist, researcher*
Tuuk, Mary *diversified financial services company executive*
Vander Laan, Mark Alan *lawyer*
Visscher, Marty Orrico *biomedical researcher*
Vogel, Cedric Wakelee *lawyer*
Volquez, Edinson *professional baseball player*
Wagner, Thomas Edward *academic administrator, educator*
Wales, Ross Elliot *lawyer*
Ward, Richard Leo *virologist*
Weber, Herman Jacob *federal judge*
Weeks, Steven Wiley *lawyer*
Wei, Heng *engineering educator*
Weinstein, Anna *music educator*
Weisenberger, Andrew *lawyer*
Weisman, Joel *retired engineering educator*
Wells Wulsin, Victoria *epidemiologist*
Welsh, George Franklin *plastic surgeon, educator*
Westbrook, Lynda A. *bank executive*
Wexler, Laura F. *cardiologist, academic administrator*
Wilson, Christopher J. *lawyer*
Winfrey, Marcellene S. *music educator, church musician*
Winkler, Henry Ralph *retired academic administrator, historian*
Wiot, Jerome Francis *radiologist*
Witten, Louis *physics professor*
Woods, Carol Smith *private school educator*
Woodside, Frank C. III *lawyer, educator, physician*
Worthen, Dennis Brent *researcher, educator*
Wray, Francis *biology professor*
Wright, Shane M. *corporate financial executive*
Wuebbling, Donald J. *lawyer, insurance company executive*
Wulker, Laurence Joseph *portfolio manager, educator, financial planner*
Wygant, Foster Laurance *art educator*
Wylie, Christopher Craig *biologist, educator*
Yun, Yeoheung *research scientist*
Zimmerman, James M. *lawyer*
Zola, Gary Phillip *rabbi, historian*

Circleville

Wentz, Mary H. *gifted and talented educator*
Wolford, Joanne M. *academic administrator, director*

Cleveland

Adamo, Kenneth Robert *lawyer*
Adams, Albert T. *lawyer*
Adams, H. Leslie *composer*
Adams, Kathryn Betts *social worker, educator*
Agayev, Nazim G. *mathematics professor*
Albano, Albert P. *Museum Association Administrator*
Aldrich, Ann *judge*
Anderson, Michael Robert *pediatrician, educator*
Angus, John Cotton *chemical engineering educator*
Arnold, Craig *manufacturing executive*
Arnold, James E. *pediatrician, educator*
Ashmus, Keith Allen *lawyer*
Austin, Arthur Donald, II, *lawyer, educator*
Awais, George Musa *obstetrician, gynecologist*
Bacon, Brett Kermit *lawyer*
Bajda, Andrew *finance educator*
Baker, Mark Early *radiology educator*
Baker, Saul Phillip *geriatrician, cardiologist, internist*
Ballou, Ronald Herman *supply chain management educator*
Banerjee, Amiya Kumar *biochemist*
Barksdale, Edward Metz, Jr. *pediatrician, educator*
Barsi, Stephen *research scientist*
Bause, George Stephen LoneRaven *anesthesiologist*
Bays, James C. *lawyer*
Bellamy, Gail Anne Ghetia *magazine editor, author, speaker*
Bergengren, Charles Lang *art educator*
Berger, Nathan Allen *medical educator, academic administrator*
Berick, James Herschel *lawyer*
Berman, Brian William *pediatrician, educator*
Bibb, Paul E., Jr., (Buck Bibb) *bank executive*
Binstock, Robert Henry *public policy educator, writer*
Blackwell, John *science educator*
Blazar, Kathleen Casteel *academic librarian, director*
Bodner, Donald Roger *urologist, medical educator*
Bogie, Kath *biomedical engineer*
Bolwell, Brian J. *oncologist, director*
Borowitz, Helen Osterman *art historian*
Boukis, Kenneth *lawyer*
Bowen, Richard Lee *architect*
Bowerfind, Edgar Sihler, Jr. *retired medical association administrator, internist, educator*
Boyd, Arthur Bernette, Jr. *surgeon, clergyman, beverage company executive*
Boyko, Christopher Allan *federal judge*
Brandt, John Reynold *editor, journalist*
Bravo, Kenneth Allan *lawyer*
Brennan, Maureen *lawyer*
Brentlinger, Paul Smith *venture capital executive*
Brody, Robert *dermatologist, educator*
Brooks, Elizabeth B. *rheumatologist, educator*
Brouhard, Ben Herman *hospital administrator, nephrologist*
Brown, Mike *professional basketball coach*
Brucken, Robert Matthew *lawyer*
Bruner, William Evans, II, *ophthalmologist, educator, researcher*
Buhrow, William Carl *religious organization administrator*
Burge, David Alan *lawyer, writer*
Burghart, James Henry *electrical engineer, educator*
Burke, Kathleen B. *lawyer*
Burke, Lillian Walker *retired judge*
Burns, Michael Kent *retired educator, chemical dependency counselor*
Burton, Gary *musician*
Calkins, Benjamin *lawyer*
Calkins, Hugh *foundation executive*
Callahan, Thomas James *lawyer*
Callesen-Gyorgak, Jan Elaine *special education educator*
Canepari, Bernard Louis *environmentalist, actor*
Carey, Paul Richard *biophysicist*
Carlsson, Bo Axel Vilhelm *economics professor*
Carrabba, Joseph A. *mining executive*
Carrol, Edward Nicholas *psychologist*
Carson, Van *lawyer*
Carter, E. Kennedy, Jr. *bank executive*
Castele, Theodore John *radiologist*
Cerone, David *academic administrator*
Cerqueira, Manuel DeCastro *nuclear medicine physician*
Chamis, Christos Constantinos *aerospace scientist, educator*
Chandra, Subodh *lawyer*
Charnas, Michael (Mannie) *investment company executive*
Chen, Shu Guang *neuroscientist, educator, pathologist*
Chiricosta, Richard Alan (Rick) *insurance company executive*
Christopher, William F. *metal products executive*
Church, James Michael *surgeon*
Chvetsov, Alexei V. *medical physicist, educator*
Cirincione, Ross Joseph *mathematician, educator*
Citardi, Martin Jason *medical educator*
Clark, Paul G. *bank executive*
Clarke, Charles Fenton *lawyer*
Coleman, Deborah Ann *lawyer*
Collin, Robert Emanuel *electrical engineering educator*
Collin, Thomas James *lawyer*
Colussi, Valdir Carlos *physicist*
Connor, Christopher M. *manufacturing executive*
Connors, Alfred Francis *internist, researcher*
Conrad, Robert David *broadcast executive, educator*
Cook, Susan J. *human resources specialist, manufacturing executive*
Cooper, Gregory Scott *epidemiologist, gastroenterologist, educator*
Copelan, Edward A. *medical educator*
Coquillette, William Hollis *lawyer*
Cowan, Dale Harvey *internist, lawyer*
Crosby, Fred McClellan *retail executive*
Crowl, Robert B. *bank executive*
Currivan, John Daniel *lawyer*
Cutler, Alexander MacDonald *manufacturing executive*
Cutler, Timothy Spence *music educator, composer*
Dampeer, John Lyell *retired lawyer*
Danco, Léon Antoine *management consultant, educator*
Dancyger, Ruth *art historian*
Daniel, Thomas Mallon *medical educator, researcher*
Daroff, Robert Barry *neurologist, educator*
Davis, Gainor Buckingham *museum administrator*
Davis, Pamela Bowes *pediatric pulmonologist, dean*
Deal, William Thomas *retired school psychologist*
Decker, John William *metal products executive*
de Groh, Kim K. *materials engineer, researcher*
Deissler, Robert George *fluid dynamics researcher*
Deissler, Robert J. *physicist*
DeKaser, Richard J. *bank executive*
Dell, Michael S. *pediatrician*
Dell'Osso, Louis Frank *neuroscience educator*
DeMetz, Kathleen Susan *lawyer*
Deming, David Lawson *art educator*
Demitrack, Thomas *lawyer*
DiCarlo, James Anthony *physicist*
DiSilvio, Marilena *lawyer*
Distelhorst, Garis Fred *trade association executive*
Djohan, Risal *plastic surgeon*
Dobyns, Brown McIlvaine *retired surgeon, educator*
Domeck, Brian C. *insurance company executive*
Douglas, Frank H., Jr. *insurance company executive*
Drake, Grace L. *retired state senator, cultural organization administrator*
Dunbar, Mary Asmundson *retired communications executive, investor relations and public relations consultant*
Duncan, Ed Eugene *lawyer*
Dunham, J. Andrew *bank executive*
Dunlap, Mark Evans *cardiologist*
Durand, Dominique M. *science educator*
Duvin, Robert Phillip *lawyer*
Edmonson, James Milton *museum director*
Edwards, William J. *prosecutor*
Egger, Terrance C.Z. *publishing executive*
Eiben, Robert Michael *pediatric neurologist, educator*
Ellis, Lloyd H., Jr. *emergency physician, art historian*
Ellison, Pamela Jean *science educator*
Emrick, Charles Robert, Jr. *lawyer*
Eng, Charis Eu Li *oncologist, geneticist*
Engelking, Tama Lea *language educator, department chairman*
Eustis, Joanne D. *university librarian*
Fabens, Andrew Lawrie III *lawyer*
Faiman, Charles *endocrinologist*
Fallon, Pat *artist, educator*
Fay, Regan Joseph *lawyer*
Fearon, Richard H. *manufacturing executive*
Federer, Roger *professional tennis player*
Ferry, Danny *professional sports team executive, retired professional basketball player*

Finn, Robert writer, educator
Fletcher, Robert retired lawyer
Flocke, Susan A. medical educator, director
Flynn, James O'Donnell statistician, educator
Flynn, Patricia M. director, special education and gifted and talented educator
Francis, Gary S. cardiologist, educator
Frate, Daniel J. bank executive
Friedman, Avery S. lawyer
Friedman, Harold Edward lawyer
Furman, Lydia M. pediatrician, educator
Futhey, Mike (Malcolm B. Futhey) labor union administrator
Gallagher, Lisa Marie music therapist
Gardner, Richard Kent retired librarian, editor, educator
Gary, Faye nursing educator
Gentile Sachs, Valerie Ann lawyer
Giannetti, Louis Daniel film critic, educator
Gibans, James David architect, consultant
Glaser, Robert Edward lawyer
Glazer, John Prescott psychiatrist
Glickman, Carl David banker
Goetz, Kenneth M. bank executive
Goffman, William mathematician, educator
Gold, Gerald Seymour lawyer
Goldberg, Susan editor
Goldberg, Victor M. orthopedist
Goldfarb, Bernard Sanford lawyer
Goldman, Steven Andrew plastic surgeon, educator
Goldstein, Marvin Emanuel aerospace scientist
Goler, Michael David lawyer
Gorman Koch, Colleen anesthesiologist, educator
Gorney, Jon L. bank executive
Gray, R. Benton lawyer
Grebenc, Jane bank executive
Greppin, John Aird Coutts philologist, editor, educator
Gries, Roger William bishop
Griffin, Brian Pius cardiologist
Groetzinger, Jon, Jr. lawyer, pharmaceutical executive, educator
Gross, Thomas S. manufacturing executive
Grossman, Mary Margaret retired elementary school educator
Grossman, Theodore Martin lawyer
Gubitosi-Klug, Rose Anne pediatrician
Gulick, James P. bank executive
Haaga, John R. radiologist
Hafner, Travis Lee professional baseball player
Haiman, Irwin Sanford lawyer
Hajj-Ali, Rula Adel rheumatologist, researcher
Harding, Clifford Vincent III medical educator
Hardy, Richard Allen mechanical engineer, engineering executive
Harris, Paul N. lawyer
Heman-Ackah, Yolanda Denise otolaryngologist, director
Henman, Tim retired professional tennis player
Hennessy, Sean P. corporate financial executive
Henry, Edward Frank retired data processing executive
Hermann, Robert Ewald retired surgeon
Hertzer, Norman Ray surgeon
Heuer, Arthur H. materials scientist, educator
Hisrich, Robert Dale business educator
Hochman, Kenneth George lawyer
Hoffman, Barbara G. filmmaker, educator
Hoffman, Gary Stewart rheumatologist
Hokenstad, Merl Clifford, Jr. social work educator
Horst, J. Robert lawyer
Horvitz, Michael John lawyer
Hrivnak, Mary Wilson educator
Hruby, Frank Michael musician, educator, critic
Huang, Alex Yee-Chen biomedical engineer, educator
Huang, David ophthalmologist, medical educator
Ilgauskas, Zydrunas professional basketball player
Isaacson, J. Harry medical educator
Jackson, Frank G. Mayor, Cleveland
Jacobs, Leslie William lawyer
James, LeBron Raymone professional basketball player
Jameson, J(ames) Larry chemical company executive
Janke, Ronald Robert lawyer
Jelinek, Gregory M. bank executive
Jensen, Kathryn Patricia (Kit Jensen) broadcast executive
Jenson, Jon Eberdt metal products executive
Jettke, Harry Jerome retired government official
Jorgenson, Mary Ann lawyer
Kahrl, Robert Conley lawyer
Kalina, Eunice Goldstein human services director
Kaltenbach, James Albert neurobiologist, educator
Kaouk, Jihad H. urologist
Kapadia, Samir R. cardiologist, educator
Karn, Jonathan molecular biologist, consultant
Karp, Marvin Louis lawyer
Kass, Lawrence hematologist, oncologist, educator
Katz, Lewis Robert law educator
Kelly, Jeffrey D. bank executive
Kenagy, David Neil pediatrician
Kestner, Robert Steven lawyer
Key, Helen Elaine accountant, educator, consulting company executive
Keys, L. Ken engineering educator
Khayat, Clark bank executive
Kiernan, Maureen art educator
Kilbane, Thomas Stanton lawyer
Kirsch, James F. materials executive
Klein, Eric Alan surgical oncologist, urologist
Klopman, Gilles chemistry professor
Knapp, Christian Jakob judge
Ko, Wen-Hsiung electrical engineering educator
Koenig, Jack Leonard chemist, educator
Kohn, Mary Louise Beatrice nurse
Kohn, William Irwin lawyer
Kolb, David Allen psychologist, educator
Komoroski, Len professional sports team executive
Kosar, Bernie Joseph, Jr. professional sports team executive, retired professional football player
Kovel, Terry Horvitz writer, antiques authority
Kowalski, Kenneth Lawrence physicist, researcher
Kramer, Edward George lawyer
Kumar, Ajay physician, director
Kumar, Mary Louise physician, educator
Lando, Jerome Burton macromolecular science educator
Lass, Jonathan Herschel ophthalmologist
Lathe, Timothy J. bank executive
Latimer, Bruce M. museum director, anthropologist, educator
Lawniczak, James Michael lawyer
Lawrence, Estelene Yvonne musician, transportation executive
Leavitt, Jeffrey Stuart lawyer
Lee, Jae-won communications educator, political campaign consultant
Lefferts, William Geoffrey internist, educator
Leiken, Earl Murray lawyer
Lenkoski, Leo Douglas retired psychiatrist, educator
Lennon, Richard Gerard bishop
Lennox, Heather lawyer
Lewine, Mark Saul anthropology professor
Lewis, John Francis lawyer
Liebson, Matthew Edward lawyer
Lietman, Steven Andrea physician
Lindsay, Bruce Duncan cardiologist
Linetsky, Tanya M. lawyer
Locke, Carl Eugene secondary school educator
Lopez, Nancy retired professional golfer
Lord, James Gregory organizational, community and philanthropic counsel
Lowe, James Allison lawyer, educator
Luke, Randall Dan retired manufacturing executive, lawyer
Lyons, Janis E. bank executive
Lytle, Bruce Whitney cardiovascular surgeon
Maciunas, Robert Joseph medical educator, researcher
Macklis, Roger Milton physician, educator, researcher
Madison, Robert Prince architect
Malangoni, Mark Alan surgeon, educator
Mandel, Jack N. manufacturing executive
Mann, C. Griffith curator
Manning, W. Robert, Jr. bank executive
Marcus, Randall Evan orthopaedic surgery educator
Markus, Richard M. judge, arbitrator
Matia, Paul Ramon lawyer
Mayland, Kenneth Theodore economist
Mayne, Lucille Stringer finance educator
Mays, MaryAnn neurologist
Mc Cartan, Patrick Francis lawyer
McCarthy, Mark Francis lawyer
McCartin, Joseph T. bank executive
McCollum, Delores LaRheine secondary school educator
McCrodden, Bruce A. bank executive
McCullough, Joseph retired academic administrator
McDonald, Mary Beth academic administrator
McFadden, John Volney retired manufacturing company executive
McGuire, Mark M. lawyer, manufacturing executive
McHale, Vincent Edward political science professor
McHenry, Martin Christopher physician, educator
McKee, Thomas Frederick lawyer
McLaughlin, Patrick Michael lawyer
Mehlman, Maxwell Jonathan law educator
Melsop, James William architect
Messinger, Donald Hathaway lawyer
Meyer, G. Christopher lawyer
Miller, Genevieve retired medical historian
Millisor, Kenneth Ray lawyer
Millstone, David Jeffrey lawyer
Minai, Omar Ahmad physician
Misra-Hebert, Anita Diana physician
Modic, Michael radiologist, educator
Moise, Claudia finance educator
Montague, Drogo K. urologist
Mooney, Beth bank executive
Moore, Karen Nelson federal judge
Moore, Kenneth Cameron lawyer
Morgenthaler, David Turner venture capitalist
Morikis, John G. manufacturing executive
Morris, Thomas William symphony orchestra administrator
Moutafakis, Nicholas James philosopher, educator
Murthy, Sudish C. thoracic surgeon
Myers, Stephen preventive medicine physician
Nanfito, Jacqueline literature and language professor
Naraine, Chameli bank executive
Neal, Carolyn V. librarian
Nelson, Sue Grodsky humanities educator, consultant
Neuhauser, Duncan vonBriesen medical educator
Newman, John M., Jr. lawyer
Nickerson, Gary Lee educational consultant
Nissen, Steven Evan cardiologist, researcher
Okada, Ronald Shig lawyer
O'Keefe, Francis Ronald lawyer
Olness, Karen Norma medical educator
O'Neal, Shaquille Rashaun professional basketball player
Palomo, Juan Martin dental educator, director, orthodontist
Parry, Michael not-for-profit fundraiser, singer, actor
Patel, Sanjay pulmonologist, educator
Payne, Michael Cordell medical researcher
Pekarek, Thomas substitute teacher
Penman, Robbie Mae volunteer, political organization worker
Perkovic, Robert Branko retired international management consultant
Perry, George Williamson lawyer
Pesek, Todd physician, director
Petschek, Rolfe George physics professor
Petterson, Gosta surgeon
Pianalto, Sandra bank executive
Pietrzen, Julie Lynn lawyer
Pike, Kermit Jerome cultural organization administrator
Pilla, Anthony Michael bishop emeritus
Piraino, Thomas Anthony, Jr. lawyer
Pistell, Timothy K. manufacturing executive
Pizot-Haymore, Fabienne language educator, translator
Podboy, Alvin Michael, Jr. law librarian, director
Pogue, Richard Welch lawyer
Pollock, Lawrence Ira (Larry Pollock) investment company executive
Pollock, R. Jeffrey lawyer
Post, Anthony Benjamin gastroenterologist, director
Pry, Carl G. bank executive
Pugh, David L. manufacturing executive
Putka, Andrew Charles lawyer
Quigney, Theresa Ann special education educator
Raaf, John Hart retired surgeon, educator, health facility administrator
Rains, M. Neal lawyer
Rawson, Robert H., Jr. lawyer
Remick, Scot Clifton oncologist, clinical investigator, educator
Renwick, Glenn M. insurance company executive
Rezai, Ali neurosurgeon, educator
Rhew, Perry James federal judge
Rice, Philip L. bank executive
Richlovsky, Thomas Andrew bank executive
Roberts-Mamone, Lisa A. lawyer
Rogers, Charles Edwin physical chemistry and polymer science professor
Roham, Masoud biomedical researcher
Roop, James John public relations executive
Rosenbaum, Jacob I. retired lawyer
Rothstein, Fred C. health facility administrator
Rowe, Robert C. bank executive
Rub, Timothy F. museum director
Ruben, Alan Miles law educator
Ruff, Robert Louis neurologist, physiologist, researcher
Saada, Adel Selim civil engineer, educator
Salomon, Roger Blaine retired language educator
Sande, Theodore Anton architect, educator, foundation executive
Sanislo, Paul Steve lawyer
Schader, Charles R. insurance company executive
Schauer, Philip R. surgeon
Schecter, William H. bank executive
Schreiber, Svetlana J. lawyer
Schuele, Donald Edward retired physics professor, dean
Schwartz, Michael academic administrator, sociology educator
Seifert, Shelley Jane bank executive
Seles, Monica retired professional tennis player
Shapiro, Fred David lawyer
Shrestha, Nabin K. physician, researcher
Sibley, Willis Elbridge anthropology educator, consultant
Sicherman, Marvin Allen lawyer
Sieg, Scott Frederick biology educator
Siemionow, Maria microsurgeon
Simson, Gary Joseph law educator
Slobozhanin, Lev Arkadievich fluid mechanics engineer, researcher
Smialek, James L. research scientist
Smith, Jerome not-for-profit developer, film producer, writer
Smith, Mark Anthony neuroscientist, educator
Snyder, Barbara Rook academic administrator
Sogg, Wilton Sherman lawyer
Solomon, Randall Lee lawyer
Soltis, Katherine editor
Sposet, Barbara Ann secondary school educator
Sridhar, Nigamanth engineering educator
Stanley, Hugh Monroe, Jr. lawyer
Stanton-Hicks, Michael D'Arcy anesthesiologist, pain medicine specialist
Starling, Randall Carson cardiologist, educator
Stauffer, Thomas George retired hotel executive
Stavitsky, Abram Benjamin immunologist, educator
Steinemann, Thomas L. ophthalmologist, educator
Stellato, Louis Eugene lawyer
Stepehnson, Andrew J. urologist
Stewart, Terry museum administrator
Stewart, William James cardiologist
Stokes, Louis lawyer, former congressman
Stone, James Merrill lawyer
Strimbu, Victor, Jr. lawyer
Stropki, John M., Jr. electric power industry executive
Strosaker, Robyn Heather pediatrician, educator
Stuhan, Richard George lawyer
Stulberg, Bernard Nathan orthopaedic surgeon, research scientist
Summers, William Lawrence lawyer
Swartzbaugh, Marc L. lawyer
Szarek, Stanislaw Jerzy mathematics professor
Talanow, Roland radiologist
Taw, Dudley Joseph sales executive, director
Taylor, Dawn M. biomedical engineer, educator
Taylor, Harris C. endocrinologist, consultant
Taylor, Steve Henry zoologist
Tengel, Jeffrey J. bank executive
Tetelman, Evan David dentist, educator
Thimmig, Diana Marie lawyer
Thomas, Dynda A. lawyer
Thomas, Felton, Jr. library director
Thomas, Richard Stephen construction executive
Thornton, Glenda Ann librarian
Threats, Travis T. speech-language pathologist
T'ien, James Shaw-Tzuu engineering educator
Tien, Norman C. dean, engineering educator
Tomashefski, Joseph Francis, Jr. pathologist, educator
Toomajian, William Martin lawyer
Triolo, Ronald J. research scientist, director
Tuzcu, Emin Murat cardiologist, educator
Updegraff, David music educator
Utian, Wulf Hessel gynecologist, endocrinologist
Varejao, Anderson Franca professional basketball player
Venkateshan, Prahalad Senior Financial Analyst
Videtic, Gregory physician
von Mehren, George M. lawyer
Waldeck, John Walter, Jr. lawyer
Waldo, Albert Leon cardiologist, educator
Wallach, Mark Irwin lawyer
Walsh, R. Matthew surgeon, gastroenterologist
Wang, Bingcheng oncologist, researcher
Warner, Carolyn G. musician, music educator
Washkewicz, Donald E. manufacturing executive
Watson, Richard Thomas lawyer
Webster, Leslie Tillotson, Jr. pharmacologist, educator
Wedge, Eric (Michael Wedge) professional baseball team manager
Weidenthal, Maurice David (Bud Weidenthal) academic administrator, journalist
Weiler, Jeffry Louis lawyer
Weir, Dame Gillian Constance musician
Weiss, Morry greeting card company executive
Weiss, Zev corporate financial executive
Wells, Lesley federal judge
Welser-Möst, Franz conductor, music director
Wertheim, Sally Harris director, academic administrator, dean, education educator, consultant
White, Gregory A. federal judge, former prosecutor
Whitney, Richard Buckner lawyer
Wiersma, Susan Renee pediatrician
Williams, Maurice (Mo Williams) professional basketball player
Williams, Wesley Montgomery medical researcher
Wilson, Jack aeronautical engineer
Wish, Jay Barry nephrologist, specialist
Wolinsky, Emanuel internist, educator
Wong, Margaret Wai lawyer
Wood, Kerry (Lee) professional baseball player
Workman, Deborah S. literature and language professor, director
Wykle, May L. dean, educator, researcher
Wynd, Christine Anne nursing service administration
Yan, Riqiang science educator
Yanoti, Timothy bank executive
Yao, Qingping rheumatologist
Yasick, Alison L. science educator
Yetman, Randall John plastic surgeon
Young, Henry Walthall, Jr. speech educator
Young, James Edward lawyer
Young, Jess Ray retired internist
Zahka, Kenneth George pediatrician, cardiologist, educator
Zaidat, Osama O. neurologist
Zhang, Amy Yanyun cancer and health services researcher
Zhang, Nengli research scientist
Zigmond, Richard Eric neuroscientist, researcher
Zoeller, David Louis lawyer, bank executive
Zung, Thomas Tse-Kwai architect

Cleveland Heights

Bidelman, William Pendry astronomer, educator
Challenger, Vicki Lee elementary school educator
Chilcote, Lee A. lawyer
Sandburg, Helga author
Zakaria, Asma neurologist

Columbia Station

Goll, Paulette Susan education educator

Columbus

Abaza, Ronney surgeon, director
Adelson, Edward physicist, educator, musician
Akins, Nicholas K. electric power industry executive
Alexander, Carl Albert materials engineer, educator
Alger, Chadwick Fairfax political scientist, educator
Allen, Hugh Daryl pediatric cardiologist, educator
Allen, Lois Arlene Height musician
Altan, Taylan engineering educator, director
Alutto, Joseph Anthony academic administrator, former dean, management educator
Anand, Jaideep management educator, consultant
Anderson, Betty Lise engineering educator
Artsimovitch, Irina science educator
Arvia, Anne L. bank executive
Baeslack, William, III, (Bud) engineering educator
Bailey, Daniel Allen lawyer
Baird, Leonard Lynn social scientist, educator, researcher, editor
Balasubramaniam, V. M. food scientist, educator
Balcerzak, Stanley Paul retired hematologist, oncologist, director, medical educator
Barlow-Ware, Jacqueline Sue music educator
Bartels, Robert Louis retired physical education educator, coach
Barth, Rolf Frederick pathologist, educator
Barthelmas, Ned Kelton brokerage house executive
Batisky, Donald Lee pediatrician, educator
Battersby, James Lyons, Jr. language educator
Beatty, Joyce state legislator
Beck, Paul Allen political science professor
Behrman, Edward Joseph biochemistry educator
Bell, Karen A. dean
Bemak, Frederic Paul psychology educator
Berlet, Gregory Charles surgeon
Berntson, Gary Glen psychiatry, psychology and pediatrics educator
Berry, William Lee business administration educator
Bhushan, Bharat mechanical engineer
Billings, Charles Edgar physician
Billman, George Edward physiologist, educator
Blackburn, John D(avid) lawyer, educator
Blomquist, Laura Louise Gavrelis academic librarian
Bloomfield, Clara Derber oncologist, educator, medical institute administrator
Blum, William George hematologist, clinical researcher educator
Bokhari, Shahid Hussain electrical engineer, educator
Booton, Gregory Charles geneticist, educator
Boyce, Kevin L. state treasurer
Boyle, Kevin Gerard historian, educator, writer
Branin, Joseph J. library director
Brantley, William Arthur dental educator, educator
Brodkey, Robert Stanley chemical engineering educator
Brooks, Richard Dickinson lawyer
Brown, Rowland Chauncey Widrig library and information scientist, consultant
Brubaker, Robert Loring lawyer
Brueggemeier, Robert W. dean, medical educator
Brunner, Jennifer Lee Secretary of State, Ohio, lawyer
Brustein, William Irving sociology educator
Buchenroth, Stephen Richard lawyer
Buchsieb, Walter Charles orthodontist, director

Budler, Joanne *library director*
Buehrer, Stephen *state legislator*
Buffington, C. A. Tony *nutritionist, educator*
Bullock, Joseph Daniel *pediatrician, educator*
Burgdoerfer, Stuart *retail executive*
Callstrom, Matthew Raymond *chemistry educator*
Campbell, Frederick Francis *bishop*
Carnahan, John Anderson *retired lawyer*
Carter, William H. *chemicals executive*
Chandler, Kathleen Leone *state legislator, former mayor, educator*
Chandrasekaran, Balakrishnan *computer scientist, educator*
Chappelear, Stephen Eric *lawyer*
Charles, Gerard *performing company executive, choreographer*
Chaudhari, Ajit Mohan Worthen *engineering educator, director*
Cheesman, Kerry Lee *biology educator, researcher*
Chen, Chun-Liang *oncologist*
Chesebrough, David E. *science association executive*
Chester, John Jonas *lawyer, educator*
Chisholm, Malcolm Harold *chemistry professor*
Chiu, Ing-Ming *biochemistry educator*
Chowdhury, Borun Dev *physicist*
Christoforidis, A. John *radiologist, educator*
Clark, K. Reed *medical geneticist, pediatrician*
Cole, Clarence Russell *college dean*
Cole, Ransey Guy, Jr. *federal judge*
Coleman, Michael Bennett *Mayor, Columbus, Ohio*
Commodore, Mike *professional hockey player*
Coopersmith, Jeffrey Alan *real estate developer*
Corbato, Charles Edward *geology educator, academic administrator*
Cordell, Philip Granvile *music educator, musician*
Cornwell, David George *biochemist, educator*
Corrigan, John Dudley *physiatrist*
Costin, Ovidiu *mathematics professor*
Coulson, Frank Thomas *humanities educator*
Coury, Daniel *pediatrician, educator*
Cox, Mitchel Neal *editor*
Craig, Hearcel F. *city councilman*
Cupp, Robert Richard *state supreme court justice, former state senator, attorney*
Curry, Timothy Jon *sociology educator*
Curtin, Michael Francis *publishing executive, writer*
Cvetanovich, Dan L. *lawyer*
Daab-Krzykowski, Andre *pharmaceutical and nutritional manufacturing company administrator*
Daehn, Glenn Steven *materials scientist*
Darling, George Curtis *minister, administrator*
Davis, Michael Walter *mathematics professor*
Davis, Steven A. *restaurant company executive*
Delisle, Deborah S. *state official, school system administrator*
Denlinger, David Landis *insect biology educator*
Desai, Anand *finance educator*
DeWine, Kevin *political organization administrator, former state legislator*
DiLorenzo, Carlo *pediatrician, gastroenterologist, educator*
DiMauro, Louis F. *physics professor, department chairman*
Dimmick, John W. *communications educator*
Duckworth, Winston Howard *researcher*
Dunlay, Catherine Telles *lawyer*
Duryee, Harold Taylor *insurance consultant*
Elliot, David Hawksley *geologist, educator*
Ellison, Edwin Christopher *surgeon, educator*
El-Sherbini, Magda A. *librarian, educator*
English, Carl L. *electric power industry executive*
Epstein, Arthur Joseph *physics and chemistry educator*
Everhart, Velma Vizedom *retired home economics educator, real estate agent*
Fahey, Richard Paul *lawyer*
Falcone, Robert Edward *surgeon*
Fan, Liang-Shih *chemical engineering educator*
Faure, Gunter *geology educator*
Fausey, Norman Ray *soil scientist*
Fawcett, Sherwood Luther *lab administrator*
Fay, Terrence Michael *lawyer*
Feng, Wu-chi *computer science educator*
Fenton, Robert Earl *electrical engineering educator*
Filliol, Olivier A. *manufacturing executive*
Fiorile, Michael J. *publishing executive*
Fisher, Lee I. *Lieutenant Governor of Ohio, former state attorney general*
Fishman, Steven S. *retail executive*
Foland, Kenneth A. *geological sciences educator*
Foster, Jim (James S. Foster) *women's college basketball coach*
Fraker, Theodore D'Eston, Jr. *cardiologist, educator*
Friedman, Avner *mathematician, educator*
Fry, Donald Lewis *physiologist, educator*
Frye, Richard Arthur *judge*
Gabbe, Steven Glenn *dean, obstetrician, gynecologist, educator*
Galantowicz, Mark Edward *cardiothoracic surgeon*
Gall, John Ryan *lawyer*
Ganschinietz, Deepa *elementary school educator*
Gee, Elwood Gordon *academic administrator*
Gibson, Rick J. *lawyer*
Gillmor, Karen Lako *state agency administrator, state legislator*
Ginther, Andrew J. *city councilman*
Glaser, Ronald *virologist, educator*
Glenn, John Herschel, Jr. *former senator, retired astronaut*
Golubitsky, Martin Aaron *mathematician, educator*
Graff, Harvey J. *history and humanities educator*
Gribble, Charles Edward *editor, language educator*
Griffith, Dennison W. *academic administrator, artist, educator*
Gross, James Howard *lawyer*
Grossberg, Michael Lee *theater critic, writer*
Grotenrath, Mary Jo *lawyer, writer*
Hahm, David Edgar *classics educator*
Hamilton, Ann Katherine *sculptor*
Hanawalt, Barbara Ann *British history educator, consultant*
Haque, Malika Hakim *pediatrician*
Hardymon, David Wayne *lawyer*
Harmon, Phillip Louis *lawyer*
Harris, Gene T. *school system administrator*
Harris, Ronald David *chemical engineer*
Hartmann, Susan M. *history professor*
Hasan, Ayesha *cardiologist, educator*
Hatler, Patricia Ruth *lawyer, insurance company executive*
Haubiel, Charles W., II, *lawyer, retail executive*
Herbst, Eric *physicist, astronomer, chemist*
Herron, Holly Lynn *critical care nurse, educator*
Herson, Lawrence J.R. *social sciences educator, consultant*
Higgins, Gloria C. *pediatrician*
Hildreth, James David *musician, educator*
Hilsheimer, Lawrence A. *insurance company executive*
Hitchcock, Charles L. *pathologist, educator*
Hitchcock, Ken *professional hockey coach*
Hobson, David Lee *consulting firm executive, former United States Representative from Ohio*
Hollenbaugh, H(enry) Ritchey *lawyer*
Holschuh, John David *federal judge*
Hopkins, Christiana *communications educator*
Houser, Donald Russell *mechanical engineering educator, consultant*
Howson, Scott *professional sports team executive*
Huber, Joan Althaus *sociology educator*
Hume, Elizabeth Valerie *science educator, department chairman*
Hutson, Jeffrey Woodward *lawyer*
Jackson, Alvin D. *state agency administrator, public health service officer*
Jackson, Leslie M. *psychology professor, researcher*
James, Donna Anita *consulting firm executive*
Janies, Daniel Andrew *biology educator*
Jarvis, Gilbert Andrew *humanities educator, writer*
Jeffries, Hasan Kwame *history professor*
Johnson, Mark Alan *lawyer*
Johnson, Martha Junk (Marty Johnson) *psychology professor*
Johnson, Neal Frederick *psychologist, educator*
Jolly, Daniel Ehs *dental educator*
Jones, Jeffrey Alan *physician, researcher*
Kapral, Frank Albert *microbiologist and immunology educator*
Keane, John B. *lawyer, electric power industry executive*
Kefauver, Weldon Addison *publishing executive*
Kennedy, Lawrence Allan *mechanical engineering educator*
Kern, Stephen Roger *history educator*
Kessel, John Howard *political scientist, educator*
Kidder, Robert (Charles Robert Kidder) *private equity firm executive, automotive executive*
Kim, Do Gyoon *biomedical researcher*
Kinzer, Allen Shawn *lawyer*
Koeppel, Holly Keller *electric power industry executive*
Kuehnle, Kenton Lee *lawyer*
Kuhn, Albert Joseph *language educator*
Laidlaw, William K. *not-for-profit developer*
LaLonde, Bernard Joseph *finance educator*
Lander, Ruth A. *medical association administrator*
Lanzinger, Judith Ann *state supreme court justice*
Lashutka, Gregory S. *mayor, lawyer*
Lee, Mei-Ling Ting *professor*
Lehiste, Ilse *retired language educator*
Leier, Carl Victor *internist, cardiologist*
Liston, Jefferson Edward *lawyer*
Long, Frederick *science educator*
Long, Sarah Elizabeth Brackney *physician*
Long, Teresa C. *city health department administrator*
Losinski, Patrick A. *library director*
Lott, John Alfred *chemist, educator*
Maciejunes, Nannette V. *museum director*
Mahoney, Kimberly Lynne *event and facility executive*
Mann, William Craig *lawyer*
Marrison, Benjamin J. *editor-in-chief*
Marsh, Clay Braden *pulmonologist, researcher*
Marsh, Fredrik *photographer*
Mason, Raymond E., Jr. *distributing company executive*
Mason, Steve *professional hockey player*
Matta, Thad Michael *men's college basketball coach*
Mayr, Nina A. *medical educator*
McCellon-Allen, Venita *utilities executive*
McConnaughey, George Carlton, Jr. *retired lawyer*
McConnell, John P. *metal products executive, professional sports team executive*
Mc Cormac, John Waverly *judge*
McCoy, Bernard Rogers *television anchor*
McCoy, John Bonnet *retired bank executive*
McCutchan, Gordon Eugene *retired lawyer, insurance company executive*
McDermott, Kevin R. *lawyer*
McKenna, Alvin James *lawyer*
McNealey, J. Jeffrey *lawyer, corporate executive*
Medeiros, Denis Michael *nutrition educator*
Mendell, Jerry R. *hospital administrator*
Mentel, Michael C. *city council president, lawyer*
Metrione, Lara *biomedical researcher*
Michael, Alan C. *dean, law educator*
Milford, Frederick John *retired research and development company executive*
Miller, A. Troy *city councilman, information technology executive*
Miller, Don Wilson *nuclear engineering educator*
Miller, Terry Alan *chemistry professor*
Miller, Terry Morrow *lawyer*
Miller, Wayne Clayton *academic administrator*
Minor, Robert Allen *lawyer*
Mirman, Joel Harvey *lawyer*
Modin, Fredrik *professional hockey player*
Moloney, Thomas E. *lawyer*
Moncrief, Jacqueline C. *retired state agency administrator*
Mone, Robert Paul *lawyer*
Moore, James L. III *counselor, educator*
Morris, Michael G. *electric power industry executive*
Morrison, Craig O. *chemicals executive*
Moul, William Charles *lawyer*
Moyer, Thomas J. *state supreme court chief justice*
Mueller, Charles Frederick *radiologist, educator*
Mueller, John Ernest *political science professor, dance critic*
Muller, Mervin Edgar *computer scientist, consultant, statistician, educator*
Murden, Robert A. *medical administrator, physician*
Nahata, Milap Chand *pharmacy educator*
Nash, Rick *professional hockey player*
Naylor, James Charles *psychologist, educator*
Needham, Glen Ray *entomology and acarology educator, researcher*
Nelson, Ardine *photographer*
Newman, Diana S. *foundation administrator, consultant, writer*
Newsom, Gerald Higley *astronomy educator*
Newton, William Allen, Jr. *pediatrician, pathologist*
Nigh, Joseph Aaron *lawyer*
Norris, Alan Eugene *federal judge*
Nwomeh, Benedict C. *pediatric surgeon*
Ockerman, Herbert W. *agricultural and international studies educator*
O'Connor, Maureen *state supreme court justice*
O'Donnell, Terrence *state supreme court justice*
Oman, Richard Heer *retired lawyer*
Osgood, Robert T., Jr. *architect, strategic planner*
Oxley, Margaret Carolyn Stewart *elementary school educator*
Özbay, Hitay *electrical engineering educator*
Ozguner, Fusun *engineering educator*
Pacht, Eric Reed *pulmonary and critical care physician*
Paley, Eileen Y. *city councilwoman, lawyer*
Paskett, Electra *epidemiologist, oncologist, educator*
Patmon, William Wesley III *lawyer*
Paxton, Pamela *social sciences educator*
Pease, William Stoess *physiatrist, educator*
Peca, Michael *professional hockey player*
Peterle, Tony John *zoologist, educator*
Peters, Leonard K. *environmental scientist*
Peterson, Gale Eugene *historian*
Petricoff, M. Howard *lawyer, educator*
Pfeifer, Paul E. *state supreme court justice*
Pfening, Frederic Denver III *manufacturing executive*
Phillips, James Edgar *lawyer*
Pitzer, Russell Mosher *chemistry educator*
Pizzuti, Ronald A. *real estate developer*
Poon, Christine A. *dean, business educator, retired pharmaceutical company executive*
Powers, Robert P. *electric power industry executive*
Priest, Michael b *professional sports team executive*
Pyatt, Leo Anthony *retired real estate broker*
Quigley, John Bernard *law educator*
Raabe, William Alan *tax writer, business educator*
Radnor, Alan T. *lawyer*
Ramaswamy, Bhuvaneswari *medical educator, researcher*
Ramey, Denny L. *bar association executive director*
Rapp, Robert Anthony *metallurgical engineering educator*
Rasmussen, Stephen Scott *insurance company executive*
Ray, Frank Allen *lawyer*
Reardon, John B. III *state banking agency administrator*
Rector, Susan Darnell *lawyer*
Redgrave, Martyn Robert *retail executive*
Reibel, Kurt *physicist, researcher*
Reiss, Steven *psychology professor*
Ress, Charles William *management consultant*
Ridgley, Thomas Brennan *lawyer*
Robinson, David *manufacturing executive*
Robol, Richard Thomas *lawyer*
Rogers, Nancy Hardin *law educator, former dean, former state attorney general*
Rosenstock, Susan Lynn *orchestra administrator*
Roth, Robert Earl *ecologist, educator*
Rund, Douglas Andrew *emergency physician*
Russell, Nas'Naga R. *illustrator*
Saad, Michael D. *lawyer*
St. Pierre, George Roland, Jr. *materials scientist, engineering executive, educator*
Saxbe, William Bart *lawyer, former United States Attorney General, former United States Senator from Ohio*
Sayers, Martin Peter *pediatric neurosurgeon*
Scanlan, James Patrick *philosophy and Slavic studies educator*
Schmid, Sigi *professional soccer coach*
Schmidt, Robert James, Jr. *lawyer*
Schuring, J. Kirk *state legislator*
Sebo, Stephen Andrew *electrical engineer, educator, researcher, consultant*
Sedmak, Daniel D. *academic administrator*
Selby, Diane Ray Miller *retired fraternal organization administrator*
Seoane-Vazquez, Enrique *research scientist*
Sestina, John E. *financial planner*
Shah, Kaushal J. *thoracic surgeon*
Shane, Peter Milo *law educator*
Sherrill, Thomas Boykin III *retired newspaper publishing executive*
Shinkel, Bernie (Bernard Albert Shinkel) *investment advisor*
Shore, Sheldon G. *chemist, educator*
Shroff, Ness *medical educator, researcher*
Sidman, Robert John *lawyer*
Silverberg, Alice *mathematician, educator*
Sims, Richard Lee *retired hospital administrator*
Singh, Rajendra *mechanical engineering educator, director*
Sites, Richard Loren *lawyer, educator*
Smidts, Carol *mechanical engineer, educator*
Smith, Gene *athletic director*
Smith, George Curtis *judge*
Smith, Philip John *industrial and systems engineering educator*
Soloway, Albert Herman *medicinal chemist*
Sood, Namita *medical educator*
Souba, Wiley William, Jr. *medical educator, researcher, dean*
Sowald, Heather Gay *lawyer*
Spoerry, Robert F. *manufacturing executive*
Stawicki, Stanislaw Peter *surgeon, medical researcher*
Stebbins, Barry Steven *educational technologist*
Stebenne, David Lawler *historian, educator*
Steinour, Stephen D. *bank executive*
Stephan, Alexander Friedrich *German language and literature educator*
Stephens, Thomas M(aron) *education educator*
Stern, Geoffrey *lawyer*
Stivers, Steve *state legislator*
Stratton, Evelyn Lundberg *state supreme court justice*
Strickland, Ted *Governor of Ohio, former United States Representative from Ohio*
Studer, William Joseph *library director*
Sully, Ira Bennett *lawyer*
Swarlis, Linda *library and information scientist*
Swift, David A. *lawyer*
Tadesse, Mesfin *botanist, biology professor, consultant, researcher*
Taggart, Thomas Michael *lawyer*
Tait, Robert E. *lawyer*
Takeshita, Oscar Yassuo *engineering educator*
Tarpy, Thomas Michael *lawyer*
Tavares, Charleta B. *city councilwoman*
Taylor, Benjamin Craig *orthopedist*
Taylor, Celianna Isley *information systems specialist*
Thompson, Harold Lee *lawyer*
Thompson, Lonnie G. *glaciologist, educator*
Thresher, Mark R. *insurance company executive*
Tiberi, Patrick Joseph *United States Representative from Ohio, former state legislator*
Tierney, Brian X. *utilities executive*
Titterington, Lynda Carol *biology professor, researcher*
Tomasky, Susan *electric power industry executive*
Trakas, James Peter *state legislator*
Trent, Elton Roger *educational assessment administrator, writer*
Tressel, Jim (James Patrick Tressel) *college football coach*
Triplehorn, Charles A. *entomologist, educator*
Turney, Sharen Jester *retail executive, cosmetics executive*
Tyack, Thomas Michael *lawyer*
Tyson, Priscilla R. *city councilwoman*
Vafai, Kambiz *mechanical engineering educator*
Virk, Subhdeep *psychiatrist*
Vogel, Thomas Timothy *surgeon, educator, lay worker*
Wadsworth, Jeffrey *research and development institute executive, metallurgist*
Wagner, Robert Walter *photographer, communications educator, film producer, consultant*
Wali, Mohan Kishen *environmental scientist, forester, educator*
Warden, Waldia Ann *retired retreat center administrator, director*
Warner, Charles Collins *lawyer*
Wasserman, Deborah L. *medical researcher*
Watson, John Allan *clergyman*
Weinhold, Virginia Beamer *interior designer*
Weinstein, Samuel *thoracic surgeon, pediatrician, researcher*
Weisberg, Herbert Frank *political science professor*
Welch, Dennis E. *electric power industry executive*
Wexner, Abigail *apparel executive*
Wexner, Leslie Herbert *retail executive*
Whipps, Edward Franklin *lawyer*
White, Ora Dade *educational consultant, writer, activist, counselor, community volunteer*
Wightman, Alec *lawyer*
Wigington, Ronald Lee *retired chemical information services executive*
Wilkinson, Deanna L. *social sciences educator*
Willcox, Roderick Harrison *lawyer*
Williams, James Case *metallurgist*
Williams, Susan Shidal *literature and language professor*
Willke, Thomas Aloys *academic administrator, statistician, educator*
Winters, Jane A. *nurse, educator*
Wiser, Vera Roubicek *psychologist*
Wojcicki, Andrew Adalbert *chemist, educator*
Wolfe, John F. *publishing executive*
Wood, Jackie Dale *physiologist, educator, researcher*
Yang, Yu-Ping *mechanical engineer*
Yeager, Nicholas D. *pediatrician, educator*
Yu, Chack Yung *pediatrics educator, molecular biologist*
Zakin, Jacques Louis *chemical engineering educator*
Zartman, David Lester *retired zoology educator, researcher*
Zweben, Stuart Harvey *information scientist, educator, dean*

Concord
Ulsenheimer, Dean *language educator*

Copley
Smith, Joan H. *retired women's health nurse, educator*
Weil, Edward David *chemist, researcher, consultant, inventor,*

Coshocton
Freund, Carol Louise *freelance staff development consultant*
McGinnis, Tammy Marie *health services manager*

Cuyahoga Falls
Barsan, Robert Blake *dentist*

Dayton
Ambalavanan, Siva *nephrologist, educator*
Battino, Rubin *retired chemistry professor*
Bauer, John-Jack J. *psychology professor*
Boice, Martha Hibbert *writer, publishing executive*
Brown, Gail Jones *physicist*
Buryachenko, Valeriy A. *research scientist*
Chin, Hong Woo *oncologist, educator, researcher*
Clark, Jim *labor union administrator*
Cooper, Thomas David *metallurgical engineer, consultant*
Curran, Daniel J. *academic administrator, sociologist, educator*
Daley, Robert Emmett *retired foundation executive*
DiSalvo, Debra Sue *gifted and talented educator*

Driesbach, Janice T. *museum director, curator*
Duval, Daniel Webster *electronics executive*
Eustace, Deogratias *civil engineer, educator*
Faruki, Charles Joseph *lawyer*
Finkelstein, Leo, Jr. *writer, communications executive, director, educator*
Forbis, Shalini G. *pediatrician, educator*
Furry, Richard Logan *lawyer*
Gaines, Elliot *communications educator*
Gillig, Paulette Marie *psychiatry educator, researcher*
Gregor, Clunie Bryan *geology educator*
Gregory, Brian *men's college basketball coach*
Hadley, Robert James *lawyer*
Hangartner, Thomas Niklaus *medical physicist, educator*
Harden, Oleta Elizabeth *literature educator, academic administrator*
Hitch, David Charles *surgeon*
Hoge, Franz Joseph *accounting firm executive*
Houpis, Constantine Harry *retired electrical engineering educator*
Huang, Hong-Hsin *engineering educator, researcher*
Huang, Shan Chun *physics educator*
Isaacson, Milton Stanley (Jim) *research and development company executive, engineer*
Jenefsky, Jack *wholesale company executive*
Jenks, Thomas Edward *lawyer*
Jeyaraj, Anand *information scientist*
Johnson, C. Terry *lawyer*
Joo, James Jinyong *mechanical engineering professor*
Kaylor, Douglas N. *library director*
Kazimierczuk, Marian Kazimierczuk *electrical engineer, educator*
Keane-Sexton, Maureen Bridget *literature and language educator*
Kirby, Tami Hart *lawyer*
Knapp, James Ian Keith *judge*
Lair, Vickie Sue *mathematics professor*
Lashley, William Bartholomew *county official*
Lasley, Thomas J., II, *education educator*
Laughlin, Richard T. *orthopedist, educator*
Lewyanvoon, Lok C. *science educator*
Lockhart, Gregory Gordon *prosecutor*
Loomis, John S. *engineering educator*
Macklin, Crofford Johnson, Jr. *lawyer*
Malhas, Faris Amin *engineering educator*
Massetti, Tony J. *computer services company executive*
Matheny, Ruth Ann *editor*
Mathews, David (Forrest David Mathews) *foundation executive, former United States Secretary of Health Education and Welfare*
McLin, Rhine Lana *Mayor, Dayton, Ohio, former state legislator*
Meister, Mark Jay *museum director, professional society administrator*
Meyer, David Gilbert *engineering educator*
Mitakides, Jane *corporate communications specialist*
Miyasaki, Donovan *philosopher, educator*
Mohler, Stanley Ross *preventive medicine physician, educator*
Monk, Susan Marie *pediatrician, educator*
Mossman, Douglas *psychiatrist, educator*
Mrozek, Lawrence James *educator*
Mues, Robert Leighton *lawyer*
Mukhopadhyay, Sharmila Mitra *materials engineer, educator*
Nixon, Charles William *retired acoustician*
Novak, Jason *music educator*
Nuti, William R. *computer services company executive*
O'Keefe, Linda Lee *physical education educator*
Parthasarathy, Triplicane Asuri *materials scientist*
Pascoe, John M. *pediatrician, educator*
Petzold, John Paul *judge*
Phillips, Chandler Allen *biomedical engineer, human factors engineer*
Reynolds, David Burkman *biomedical engineer, department assistant chair*
Ruegsegger, Donald Ray, Jr. *radiological physicist, educator*
Sableski, Thomas Lee *secondary school educator*
Saul, Irving Isaac *lawyer*
Schmitt, George Frederick, Jr. *materials engineer*
Senkov, Oleg N. *physicist, researcher, materials scientist*
Serrano Guerra, Damaris Elizabeth *language educator*
Shebilske, Wayne Lawrence *psychology professor, researcher*
Siddiqi, Munawar *anesthesiologist, consultant*
Singhvi, Surendra Singh *financial consultant*
Skinner, Thomas E. *physics professor*
Slade, R. Andrew *literature and language professor*
Snipe, Tracy David *political science professor*
Spokane, Robert Bruce *biophysical chemist*
Stalter, Ann Marie *nursing educator*
Stover, David S. *science educator*
Sudkamp, Thomas *science educator*
Swanson, Donald Roland *retired English literature and language educator*
Swartz Neuhardt, Sharen *lawyer*
Syed, Mubin Isaac *interventional radiologist, neuroradiologist*
Taft, Bob (Robert Alphonso Taft II) *former governor, educator*
Termuhlen, Paula *oncologist, surgeon*
Tilley, Terrence William *religious studies educator*
Todd, Dianna Kaye *nursing administrator, educator*
Vaughn, Noel Wyandt *lawyer*
Vice, Roy Lee *history professor*
Vukelich, Sharon Irene *aerospace engineer, consultant*
Wang, Bin *computer scientist, educator*
Wertz, Kenneth Dean *real estate company officer*
Wikstrom, Loretta Wermerskirchen *artist*
Wilson, Thomas H. *mathematics professor*
Wilson, William Campbell McFarland *gastroenterologist*
Winkler, Jonathan Reed *historian, educator*
Wischgoll, Thomas *engineering educator*
Wolff, Mitch *engineering educator, researcher*
Yeo, Yung Kee *physics professor*
Zoghi, Manoochehr *civil engineering educator*

Delaware
Arnold, Jay *retired engineering executive, educator*
Ciochetty, John Bryan *protective services official*
Fratantuono, Lee Michael *philatelist, educator*
Gardner, Bonnie Milne *theater educator, playwright*
Garner, Harvey Louis *computer scientist, engineering educator, consultant*
Hamre, Gary Leslie William *retired entrepreneur*
Huml, Donald Scott *manufacturing executive*
Iverson, Louis Robert *research ecologist*
Jin, Xudong *associate library director*
Kent, Conrad A. *education educator*
Lemke, Stacy J. *secondary school educator*
Schlichting, Catherine Fletcher Nicholson *librarian, educator*
Thomas, John Edward *educational consultant*
Vedder, Debra Scott *language educator*

Delta
Leavitt, Bradley S. *steelworker*
Miller, Beverly White *former college president, educational consultant*

Dillonvale
Stobbs, Richard D. (Dick Stobbs) *protective services official*

Dover
Haggis, Mary Ripley *nurse, genealogist*

Dublin
Barrett, George S. *health products executive*
Bird, Shelley *health products company executive, corporate communications specialist*
Calucci, Tony *performing arts educator*
Clark, R. Kerry (R. Kerry Clark) *health products executive*
Davids, Jody R. *information technology executive*
De Vore, Paul Warren *technology educator*
Duffy, Michael A., Jr. *health products company executive*
Henderson, Jeffrey W. *health products executive*
Jain, Vivek *health products company executive*
Jordan, Robert (Jay) L. *computer library service and research organization executive*
Kaufmann, Michael *health products executive*
Lynch, Michael A. *health products executive*
Morford, Craig S. *health products executive, former prosecutor*
Needham, George Michael *library consultant*
Rosenbaum, Mark E. *health products executive*
Schlotterbeck, David L. *health products executive*
Smith, K(ermit) Wayne *computer company executive*
Smith, Stephen Puntenney *plastic surgeon, educator*
Tenuta, Luigia *lawyer*
Troup, Gordon A. *health products executive*
Vassell, Gregory S. *electric utility consultant*
Walter, Robert D. *health products executive*
Wang, Andrew Hsing-Jen *marketing professional, information technology executive, journalist, librarian*
Watkins, Carole S. *human resources specialist, medical products executive*
Winstead, Dwight *medical products executive*

East Cleveland
England, Diana Whitten *elementary school educator*

East Palestine
Miller, Darren John *social worker*

Eastlake
Balester, Vivian Shelton *retired lawyer, consultant*
Suchanek, Wojciech Lukasz *materials scientist, researcher*

Eaton
Kisling, Fanny *counselor, educator*

Elyria
Dryden, Jonathan Norton *literature and language professor*
Mixon, Aaron Malachi III *medical products executive*
Myers, John T. *physical therapist, educator*
Robinson-Odom, June Frances Margaret A. *art educator*
Sanders, Phyllis May *musician*

Enon
Kankey, Roland Doyle *finance educator*

Euclid
Adrine-Robinson, Kenyette *writer, educator, poet, artist, photographer, percussionist*
Obloy, Leonard Gerard *priest*
Ramsey, Charles *retired government agency administrator*

Fairborn
Combs, Eric A. *social studies educator*
Goetz, Douglas Neil *contract management educator*

Fairfield
Allen, Lois Faye *art educator*
Benoski, James E. *insurance company executive*
Cimini, Eric Michael *lighting designer, director*
Gruenwald, James Howard *association executive, consultant*
Masanek, Michele *secondary school educator, soccer coach*
Moreland, Vicki Ann *education educator*
Stecher, Kenneth W. *financial corporation executive*

Fairview Park
Leickly, Portia Elaine *science educator*

Findlay
Armes, Roy V. *manufacturing executive*
Freed, DeBow *academic administrator*
Fry, Charles George *theologian, educator*
Gamba, Maria V. *international business, economics, finance educator*
Gupta, Shiv K. *finance educator*
Hanson, David Alan *music educator*
Hotaling, Cynthia Ann *nursing administrator, educator*
Kline, James Edward *lawyer*
Peters, Milton Eugene *retired educational psychologist*
Resseguie, James Lynn *theology educator*
Van Vorhis, Andrea Christine *literature and language professor*

Fostoria
Howard, Kathleen *computer company executive*

Fremont
Hill, Rebecca Baker *librarian*
Ziebold, Barbara M. *music educator*

Gahanna
Majtenyi, Steven Istvan *retired civil engineer, consultant*

Galena
Berggren, Ronald Bernard *surgeon, retired educator*

Galloway
Pelz, Carol E. *library director, consultant*

Gambier
Cho, Hyun Jai *physicist*
Leech, Charles Russell, Jr. *lawyer*
MacLeod, Wendy *playwright, performing arts educator*
Nugent, S. Georgia *academic administrator*

Garrettsville
Chattopadhyay, Sudipta *engineer*
Diskin, Michael Edward *consumer products and plastics company executive, construction executive*

Gates Mills
Enyedy, Gustav, Jr. *chemical engineer*
Reitman, Robert Stanley *management consultant, not-for-profit advisor*
van Heeckeren, Anna M. *biomedical researcher, veterinarian*
Veale, Tinkham, II, *retired chemicals executive, engineer*

Georgetown
Fite, Tom W. *retired mathematics educator, farmer*

Germantown
Fetzer, Ronald Charles *communications and business educator, consultant*
Lansaw, Charles Ray *rendering industry executive*

Girard
Madgar, Adam Jason *engineering company executive*

Glendale
Strom, Kristina Chase *writer, consultant*

Granville
Knobel, Dale Thomas *academic administrator, historian, educator*
Lisska, Anthony Joseph *humanities educator, philosopher*
Santoni, Ronald Ernest *philosophy educator*

Greenville
Thieme, Jean Louise *retired art association administrator*

Grove City
Kilman, James William *surgeon, educator*
Williams, Linda Dianne *retired music educator*

Groveport
Motts, Warren Earl *museum director*

Hamilton
Fein, Linda Ann *nurse anesthetist, consultant*
Munson, Richard Howard *horticulturist*
Werner, Laurie *science educator*

Harrison
Kocher, Juanita Fay *retired auditor*
West, Clark Darwin *pediatric nephrologist, educator*

Heath
Darst, David Earl *finance educator*

Hemlock
Johnson, George Warner *gifted and talented educator, consultant*

Highland Hills
Brathwaite, Ormond Dennis *chemistry professor*
Kharina, Nina Yurievna *science educator*

Hilliard
Cupp, David Foster *photographer, journalist*
McNutt, Suzanne Michaelene *music educator*
Pyles, Selma Broadway *music educator*
Rahal, Robert Woodward (Bobby Rahal) *automotive company and race car team executive, retired professional race car driver*

Hillsboro
Flum, Terry Eugene *biology educator*

Hiram
Tur, Clarisse *physicist*

Holland
Conlin, Thomas *conductor*
Matthews, Christian William, Jr. *minister*

Howard
Lee, William Johnson *lawyer*

Hubbard
Trucksis, Theresa A. *retired library director*

Hudson
Carducci, Judith Weeks Barker *artist, retired social worker*
Clark, Robert Phillips *editor, consultant*
Dowell, Michael Brendan *chemist*
Frank, John V. *foundation administrator*
Goheen, Janet Moore *counseling administrator, sales executive*
Lambacher, Kathleen Hartwell *retired education educator*
Merwin, John David *lawyer, former Governor of the Virgin Islands*
Webb, Darrell D. *retail executive*
White, David Lawrence *mechanical engineer, marketing professional*
Wooldredge, William Dunbar *health facility administrator*

Huron
Leser, Anne Elizabeth *education educator*
Saunders, Patrick Reed *history professor*

Independence
Chapa, Jeffrey *obstetrician, gynecologist*
Grabow, Raymond John *mayor, lawyer*
Kola, Arthur Anthony *lawyer*
Maser, Douglas James *legal and governmental operations lawyer*
Van Kirk, Robert John *nursing clinical manager, educator*

Ironton
Curry, Estella Roberta *education educator, school psychologist, consultant*
Thomas, Timothy Franklin *secondary school educator*

Jackson
Lewis, Richard M. *lawyer*

Jackson Center
Thompson, Wade Francis Bruce *manufacturing executive*

Johnstown
Fiedler, Karen E. *science curriculum coordinator*

Kent
Balan, Christine *special education educator*
Bedrosian, Wendy Kowalyk *pre-school educator*
Beer, Barrett Lynn *historian*
Bissler, Richard Thomas *mortician*
Breitbart, Yuri *computer scientist, educator*
Buttlar, Rudolph Otto *retired college dean*
Dahl, Peter Steffen *geologist, educator*
Evans, Melissa Rebecca *science educator*
Ference-Valenta, Mary Jean *osteopath, health facility administrator*
Gaston, Paul Lee *academic administrator, language educator*
Hassler, Donald Mackey, II, *English language educator, writer*
Henderson, James George *curriculum studies educator*
Kaplan, David Howard *geographer, educator*
Karpanty, Kimberly A. *choreographer, educator*
Kim, Junghyun Frannie *communications educator*
Koby, Geoffrey Stanhope *language and translation studies professor*
Kotun, Carol Ann *mathematics educator*
Manley, D. Mark *physics professor*
Marovitz, Sanford Earl *English language and literature educator*
M'Baye, Babacar *black literature educator*
Mitchell, Pamela R. *speech professional, educator*
Myers, R(alph) Thomas *chemist, educator*
Neal-Barnett, Angela Marie *psychology professor*
Reiss, Richard Arnold *theater director, actor*
Remley, R. Dirk *English educator, consultant*
Ryans, John Kelley, Jr. *marketing educator*
Scarnecchia, Timothy *history professor*
Shreve, Gregory Monroe *language educator, department chairman*
Sonnhalter, Carolyn Therese *physical therapist, consultant*
Timmons-Mitchell, Jane Christina *clinical psychologist, researcher, consultant, educator, entrepreneur*
Tuan, Debbie Fu-Tai *chemist, educator*
Varga, Richard Steven *retired mathematics professor*
Wakabayashi, Judy *translator, educator*
Was, Christopher A. *psychology professor*
Weber, Mark W. *library director, dean*
Williams, Christopher T. *history professor*
Williams, Donald R. *social sciences educator*
Zampini, Carmen C. *library director*

Kettering
Eubank, David Lynn *lawyer, consultant*
Kell, Joseph William *materials scientist*
Kent, Lawrence *retired association executive, education and mental health director*
Meckstroth, Wilma Jean *piano and organ educator, accompanist*
Porter, Walter Arthur *retired judge*

Kirtland
Armstrong, Mary Ogden *artist, graphics designer*
Santos, Rolando Aguilar *economics professor*

Lakeside Marblehead
Haering, Edwin Raymond *chemical engineering educator, consultant*

Lakewood
Greenman, Frederick F., Jr. *lawyer*
Kucinich, Dennis John *United States Representative from Ohio*

Pangrace, Ruth A. *history professor*
Sherry, Paul Henry *minister, religious organization administrator*

Lancaster
Katlic, John Edward *management consultant*
Libert, Donald Joseph *retired lawyer*
Lieber, Marla *secondary school educator*
Phillips, Edward John *consulting firm executive*
Varney, Richard Alan *health facility administrator*

Lebanon
Hartland, James Robert *retired minister*

Leetonia
Foreman, Gail Lynne *secondary school educator*

Lewis Center
Heinlen, Daniel Lee *alumni organization administrator, consultant*
Thomason, Sandra Lee *elementary school educator*

Lima
Bohle, Shannon Denise *archivist*
Derryberry, Glenn Hollis *judge*
Ignatieva, Maria *theater educator*
MacBenn, Joseph Vernon *director*
Page, Roger Allan *retired psychology professor*
Pranses, Anthony Louis *retired electric power industry executive*
Shafer, Scott L. *library director*

Lorain
Murrell, Jill Pongracz *music educator, director*
Quinn, Alexander James *bishop*

Loveland
Voluse, Charles Rodger III *retired education educator*

Lucasville
Reno, Ottie Wayne *former judge*

Lyndhurst
Dallas, Marie C. *retired psychology educator, consultant*
Guyuron, Bahman *plastic surgeon, educator*
Harper, Williard Flemmett *language educator*
Lipson, Renée Sue *organization development consultant*

Mansfield
Converse, Sandra *city finance director, financial planner*
Gibson, David Mark *biochemist, educator*
Gorman, James Carville *manufacturing executive*
Gregory, Deirdre Dianne *secondary school educator*
Gregory, Thomas Bradford *mathematics professor*
Houston, William Robert Montgomery *ophthalmologist, surgeon*
Pesec, David John *data systems executive*
Riedl, John Orth *retired university dean*
Sheridan, Mark William *mechanical engineer, financial planner*

Marblehead
Lis, David Joseph *priest*

Marietta
Abbott, Mary Ann *literature and language professor*
Fields, William Albert *lawyer*
Krawczyk, Carl Michal *history professor*
Montgomery, Jerry Lynn *retired education educator*
Putnam, Robert Ervin *chemist, consultant*
Torbett, David James *religion professor*
Wilbanks, Jan Joseph *retired philosopher*
York, James Farnsworth *engineering educator, retired chemical engineer*

Marion
Beery, Arthur *artist*
Blankenship, Betsy Lee *library director*
Thompson, Jo(an) *anthropologist*

Marysville
Hagedorn, James *landscape company executive*
Hamilton, Robert Otte *lawyer*

Mason
Clements, Michael Craig *health services consulting executive, retired renal dialysis technician*
Cuff, Virginia Evelyn *architectural firm executive, consultant*
Goldstein, Sidney *pharmacist*
Kohlhepp, Robert J. *apparel executive*
Lawson, Stephen C. *lab administrator*
Smith, C. LeMoyne *retired publishing executive*
Tracy, Allen Wayne *management consultant*

Massillon
Eckhart, Marylouise Christine Santilli *pre-school educator*
Vaughn, Lisa Dawn *physician, educator*

Maumee
Fallat, Dale William *lawyer*
Konopinski, Virgil James *retired safety engineer*
Marsh, Benjamin Franklin *lawyer*
Tuschman, James Marshall *lawyer*
Witherell, Dennis Patrick *lawyer*

Mayfield
Jarrett, Charles Elwood *lawyer, insurance company executive*

Mayfield Heights
Newman, Joseph Herzl *advertising executive, consultant*
Rankin, Alfred Marshall, Jr. *manufacturing executive*

Medina
Ballard, John Stuart *retired mayor, lawyer, educator*
Cooper, Allan D. *political science educator*
Pilat, Janet Louise B. Oberholtzer *adult education educator*
Skidmore, Tyler Lee *music educator*
Smith, Richey *manufacturing executive*
Sullivan, Frank C. *manufacturing executive*
Sullivan, Thomas Christopher *coatings company executive*

Mentor
Callsen, Christian Edward *health products executive*
Fiorello, Anthony James *biology professor*
Kaye, Christopher James *molding engineer*

Miamisburg
Byrd, James Everett *lawyer*
Louthain, James Allan *electrical engineer*
Perry, William Francis *nurse, educator*
Ringler, James M. *computer services company executive*
Suwyn, Mark A. *paper company executive*

Miamiville
Franz, (Iris) Vivian *dean, director*

Middleburg Heights
Shatila, Ahmad Hussain *surgeon, oncologist*

Middletown
Camara, Babacar *literature educator*
Carroll, Mike *steelworker*
Horn, David C. *lawyer*
Marine, Susan Sonchik *analytical chemist, educator*
McClain, Michael H. *writer*
Newby, John Robert *retired metallurgical engineer*
Rathman, William Ernest *retired lawyer, minister*
Turpin, Richard E. *sales executive*
Wainscott, James Lawrence *steel industry executive*

Milan
Henry, Joseph Patrick *chemicals executive*

Milford
Dattilio, Teri A. *chemist*

Morrow
Suddendorf, Matthew L. *band director*

Mount Healthy
Scheffel, Kenneth Paul *retired archivist*

Mount Vernon
Beal, Carrie D. *biology professor*
Dailey, Fred L. *former state agency administrator*
Madtes, Paul *biology professor*
Miller, Joyce Catherine *chemistry professor, research scientist*
Shriver, William Russell *secondary school educator*

Napoleon
Meekison, MaryFran *writer*
Wachtmann, Lynn R. *state legislator*

New Albany
Duggan, Thomas Patrick *management consultant*
Jeffries, Michael S. (Mike Jeffries) *apparel executive*
Stevens, Kenneth T. *retail executive*

New Concord
Schumann, Laura Elaine *conductor*

New Lexington
Harper, Toni Jane *secondary school educator*

New Philadelphia
Li, Hongshan *history professor*

Newark
Black, Boyd Carson *small business owner*
Brunell, Amy B. *psychology professor*
Busta, Paul Timothy *banker*
Federspiel, Howard M. *political science professor*
Lukco, Edward John *insurance company executive*
McConnell, William Thompson *bank executive*
Mencer, Jetta *lawyer*
Raykov, Ivan L. *mathematics professor*
Sharrock (Wrentmore), Anita Kay *information technology specialist*

Niles
Ruman, Renee *principal*

North Canton
Clevinger, Jennifer Amick *botanist*
Cooney, Sondra Miley *literature and language educator*
Deakins, Donald Eugene *biology professor*
Dettinger, Warren Walter *lawyer*
Dishong, Morris William *forensic specialist, nurse*
Di Simone, Robert Nicholas *radiologist, educator*
Fernandez, Kathleen M. *cultural organization administrator*
Fountain, Ronald Glenn *management consultant, corporate financial executive, entrepreneur, educator, investor*
Lynham, C(harles) Richard *manufacturing executive*
Norton-Smith, Thomas Michael *humanities educator*
Secrest, Beth Anne *accounting educator*

North Olmsted
Bluford, Guion Stewart, Jr. *engineering company executive*
Janson, Patrick *vocalist, educator, actor*
Semple, Jane Frances *health facility director*

North Ridgeville
Stewart, Arden Ruth *retired automotive executive*

North Royalton
Holliday, Walter William *architectural firm executive*

Norwalk
Mays, George Francis *small business owner*

Oak Harbor
Sievert, Vicki Lee *retired music educator*

Oberlin
Brown, John Lott *former university president, retired educator*
Carlton, Terry Scott *retired chemist, educator*
Colley, Susan Jane *mathematician, educator*
English, Ray *library administrator*
Kasper, Hirschel *economics educator*
Krislov, Marvin *academic administrator, lawyer, educator*
MacKay, Alfred F. *dean, philosophy educator*
Markowitz, Lawrence Peter *political science professor*
McGuire, Charles Edward *musicology educator*
Moore, Jane Ross *librarian, educator*
Rutstein, Sedmara Zakarian *concert pianist, educator*
Salter, Robin S. *immunologist, educator*
Taylor, Richard Wirth *retired political science professor*
Volk, Steven S. *history professor*
Wiles, Stephanie *museum director*
Zinn, Grover Alfonso, Jr. *retired religion educator*

Olmsted Falls
Faller, Dorothy Anderson *training services executive, consultant*

Orange Village
Jones, Susan Dorfman *real estate broker, writer*
Pace, Stanley Dan *lawyer*
Stauderman, Bruce Ford *advertising executive, writer*

Orrville
Harlan, Mary Ann *lawyer*
Hennell, Robert William III *secondary school educator*
Roncone, John Edward *health educator*
Smucker, Richard K. *food products executive*
Smucker, Timothy P. *food products executive*

Orwell
Strong, Marcella Lee *music specialist, educator*

Ottawa Hills
Bryant, Martin *automotive executive*
Levin, Marc S. *manufacturing company executive, lawyer*

Owensville
Seifert, Caroline Hamilton *community health nurse*

Oxford
Baird, Jay Warren *historian, educator*
Bergen, Doris *psychologist, educator*
Biran Weinberger, Mia *mental health educator*
Chung, Hsinglin Tracy *theater educator*
Crowder, Michael Wade *chemistry educator*
Dawisha, Adeed *political science professor*
Earhart, Eileen Magie *retired elementary school and child and family life educator*
Eshbaugh, W(illiam) Hardy *botanist, educator*
Ewing, Susan R. *artist, educator*
Fernandes, Joyce Juliana *science educator*
Forren, John Patrick *academic administrator, educator*
Frazier, Nishani *history professor*
Gordon, Gilbert *chemist, educator*
Harwood, Britton James *literature and language professor, department chairman*
Hedrick, Linnea S. (fka Dietrich) *retired art historian*
Hickey, R. James *botanist, educator*
Jaeger, Herbert *physics educator*
Marshall, Bryan William *educator*
McKinney, Mark *educator*
Miller, Norman Calvin *economist*
Miller, Robert James *education association administrator*
Morton, Yu Tong *electrical engineer, educator*
Pechan, Michael Joseph *physics professor, researcher*
Pratt, William Crouch, Jr. *literature and language professor, writer*
Rahman, Jacquelyn *language educator, researcher, director*
Rao, Dhananjai M. *engineering educator*
Rejai, Mostafa *political science professor*
Sanabria, Sergio Luis *architecture educator*
Sanders, Gerald Hollie *communications educator*
Sessions, Judith Ann *dean, university librarian*
Shriver, Edwin R. *psychologist*
Shriver, Phillip Raymond *academic administrator*
Smart, Leonard James, Jr. *science educator*
Ward, Roscoe Fredrick *engineering educator*
Wicks, Robert S. *museum director, educator*
Yamauchi, Edwin Masao *history professor emeritus*
Ziegler, Melanie McClure *social sciences educator*

Painesville
Davis, Barbara Snell *education educator*
Garwood, Barbara Ann *psychologist, educator*
LaTourette, Steven C. *United States Representative from Ohio*
Luhta, Caroline Naumann *airport manager, flight educator, museum administrator*
McQuaid, Kim *historian, educator, writer*

Parma
Chen, Chong *research scientist*
Kudrick, John Michael *bishop*
Moskal, Robert M. *bishop*
Musat, Katherine Gadus *retired music educator*
Petrus, Sally A. *elementary school educator*
Pitcher, Megan Louise *dancer, director*
Redles, David *history professor*
Romanovich, Patricia M. *parochial school educator*
Tener, Carol Joan *retired secondary school educator, consultant*

Pataskala
Ripley, Randall Butler *political scientist, educator*

Peninsula
Sigler, Theresa Jane *school system administrator*

Pepper Pike
Frazier, Arthur R. *political science professor, department chairman*
Martin, Aric Doyle *lawyer*
O'Neill, Katherine Templeton *journalist, former nursing educator, museum administrator*
Seaton, Jean Robarts *psychology educator*
Vail, Thomas Van Husen *retired publishing executive*

Perrysburg
Autry, Carolyn *artist, educator*
Baehren, James W. *lawyer*
Catalano, Dominic *art educator, illustrator*
Filippova, Daria Vladimirovna *private school educator*
Skiver, Stephen Allen *lawyer, physician*
Weaver, Richard L., II, *writer, educator, lecturer*
White, Edward C. *chemicals executive*
Williamson, John Pritchard *retired utilities executive*

Pickerington
Basinger, Ned Naden *farmer, educator*

Piqua
Retman, Deborah W. *biology educator*

Port Clinton
Ewersen, Mary Virginia *retired school system administrator, poet*
Woodson, Riley Donald *thoracic and cardiovascular surgeon, lawyer*

Portsmouth
Feight, Andrew Lee *history professor*
Gerlach, Franklin Theodore *lawyer*
Hamilton, Virginia Mae *mathematics professor, consultant*
Johnson, Janice E. *education educator, writer*
Spradlin, Patricia C. *literature and language professor*

Powell
Emanuelson, James Robert *retired insurance company executive*

Randolph
Pecano, Donald Carl *automotive manufacturing executive*

Ravenna
Turcotte, Margaret Jane *retired nurse*

Reynoldsburg
McDonald, Camille Ann *retail executive*

Richfield
Lewis, Sylvia Davidson *foundation executive*

Rio Grande
Cornelius, E. Ronald *engineering educator*
Hatfield, Barbara Scott *academic administrator*

Rocky River
Condon, George Edward *journalist*
Hosek, John Jude *planning organization executive*
O'Brien, John Feighan *investment banker*

Rootstown
Benshoff, Dixie L. *psychologist*
Bhatia, Deepak *pharmacist, educator*
Savickas, Mark Lee *psychology professor*
Sutariya, Vijaykumar Bhadabhai *medical educator*

Sagamore Hills
Miller, Susan Ann *retired school system administrator*

Saint Marys
Dickerson, Janice Eileen *music educator*
Kemp, Barrett George *lawyer*

Salem
Fehr, Kenneth Manbeck *retired computer company executive*
Madison, John Robert *surgeon*
Yates, Jacquelyn *political science professor*

Sandusky
Runner, Jack Charles *health facility executive*
Stacey, James Allen *retired judge*

Scio
Prusha, Jeffrey A. *elementary school educator*

Seven Hills
Stanczak, Julian *artist, educator*

Shaker Heights
Brachna, Gabor (Samuel) *elementary school educator*
Ludwig, L(owell) Mark *social studies educator*
Siegel, Robert *heat transfer engineer*
Solganik, Marvin *real estate executive*
Weinberg, Helen Arnstein *retired literature and art educator*

Sheffield Village
Herdendorf, Charles Edward III *oceanographer, limnologist, consultant*
Kolczun, Lee S. *lawyer*

Sidney
Leffler, Carole Elizabeth *retired women's and mental health nurse*
Menz, Robert L. *psychotherapist, minister*
Stevens, Robert Jay *magazine editor*

Silver Lake
Cantor, Arnold *labor relations official*

Solon
Bane, Glenice Gail *music educator*
Gallo, Donald Robert *retired literature educator*
Malik, Masroor Rasheed *engineering executive*
Rosen, Michael Joshua *surgeon*
Rosica, Gabriel Adam *retired manufacturing executive, electrical engineer*
Williams, Jeffery Lynn *secondary school educator, consultant, writer*

South Euclid
Zoller, Karen Ann *library and art gallery director*

Springboro
Saxer, Richard Karl *metallurgical engineer, retired military officer*

Springdale
Schreiner, Albert William *internist, educator*

Springfield
Cantrell, John L. *language educator*
Fleissner, Robert F. *retired English language educator*
Humphries, Jimmy *set designer, educator*
Kinnison, William Andrew *retired university president*
Lagos, James Harry *lawyer, small business owner*
Reed, Don Collins *philosopher, educator*
Smith, James Fitzpatrick *literature educator*
Stelzer, Patricia Jacobs *retired secondary school educator*
Taylor, Thomas Templeton *history professor*
Todd, Carol *music educator*
Welch, James M. *biology professor*

Steubenville
Conlon, Robert Daniel *bishop*
Levite, Bernard Lawrence *information scientist, educator*
Ottenweller, Albert Henry *bishop emeritus*
Rekowski, Lois Thompson *library director*
Sheldon, Gilbert Ignatius *bishop emeritus*

Stow
Castillo, Katherine Lynn *secondary school educator, business owner*

Streetsboro
Cielec, Greg J. *literature and language educator*

Strongsville
Blumer, Frederick Elwin *retired philosophy educator*
Cameron, David Ronald *entrepreneur, historian, researcher*
Pinkerton, Richard LaDoyt *retired management educator, writer*
Potter, David *sales executive*
Webb, Tara Yvette *music educator*
Yates, Patricia Lawrence *elementary school educator*

Sugar Grove
Dombrowski, Karen S. *social studies and education educator*

Sylvania
Burkhart, Craig Garrett *dermatologist, researcher*
Collins, Penny *graphics designer, illustrator*
Hountras, Peter Timothy *psychologist, educator*
Kujawa, Jean *economics professor*
Masten, Barbara Jean *education educator, department chairman*
Rutkowski, Sandra L. *library director*
Sampson, Earldine Robison *education educator*
Stockwell, Mary Elizabeth *history professor*

Terrace Park
Naylor, Paul Donald *retired lawyer*

Tiffin
Gridley, Mark Charles *psychologist*
Hillmer, Margaret Patricia *retired library director*

Toledo
Abron, James Arthur, Jr. *civil engineer, consultant, engineering educator*
Alby, Irene *theater educator, director*
Anspach, Robert Michael *lawyer*
Ashton, Dyrk Michael *performing arts educator*
Azad, Abdul-Majeed *materials scientist, educator*
Bacigalupi, Don *museum director*
Berendt, Emil Bohdan *economist*
Bjorkman, Jon Eric *astrophysicist, educator*
Blair, Leonard Paul *bishop*
Block, Allan James *communications executive*
Brockmyer, Jeanne H. *psychology professor*
Brown, Nancy J. *literature educator*
Bullerjahn, Anne *science educator*
Campbell, James *philosopher, educator*
Carr, James Gray *federal judge*
Chakraborty, Joana *physiologist, educator, science administrator*
Chambers, Virginia Anne *music educator*
Closius, Phillip J. *dean, law educator*
Comerota, Anthony James *vascular surgeon, biomedical researcher*
Convis, Gary L. *automotive parts company executive*
Dalrymple, Thomas Lawrence *retired lawyer*
Devine, John Martin *automotive parts company executive*
Dismukes, John P. *engineering educator*
Donnelly, Robert William *bishop emeritus*
Egan, Kevin J. *economics professor*
Ferguson Rayport, Shirley Martha *psychiatrist*
Finkbeiner, Carlton S. (Carty Finkbeiner) *Mayor, Toledo*
Gaillardetz, Richard Rene *religious studies educator, writer*
Geisler, Nathan David *financial consultant*
Girgis-Hanna, Mary Fahim *music educator*
Glaab, Charles Nelson *historian, educator*
Goodenday, Lucy Sherman *cardiologist, educator*
Griffith, Wendell Peter *chemistry professor*
Gutteridge, Thomas G. *academic administrator, arbitrator, consultant*
Hasan, Rashed A. *pediatrician, educator*
HassabElnaby, Hassan *accounting educator*
Heiney, Jake P. *orthopedist*
Heintz, Carolinea Cabaniss *retired home economist, educator*
Homolka, Linda Mary *radiographer, educator*
Hu, Xiche *chemistry professor*
Jackson, Reginald Sherman, Jr. *lawyer, educator*
Kaptur, Marcia Carolyn (Marcy Kaptur) *United States Representative from Ohio*
Konwinski, Jacqueline Marie Koralewski *secondary school educator*
Koo, Benjamin Hai Chang *structural engineer, educator*
Koskoski, Jarrod Francis *music educator*
Krull, Stephen Keith *lawyer*
Kunze, Ralph Carl *retired savings and loan association executive*
Lane, Richard Durelle *neuroscientist, educator*
Martin, Robert Edward *architect*
McSweeny, Austin John *psychology educator*
Mrak, Robert Emil *neuropathologist, educator*
Mulrow, Patrick Joseph *medical educator*
O'Connell, Maurice Daniel *lawyer*
Ormond, Paul A. *healthcare company executive*
Paquette, Jack Kenneth *management consultant, author, historian*
Pham, David Lan *secondary school educator, writer*
Phelps, Carmen Lanette *literature educator*
Pletz, Thomas Gregory *lawyer*
Potter, John William *federal judge*
Ray, Douglas Ellsworth *dean, law educator*
Rees, Michael A. *urologist*
Reichert, Christine Edwards *academic administrator*
Rejent, Marian Magdalen *retired pediatrician*
Romanoff, Marjorie Reinwald *retired education educator*
Romanoff, Milford Martin *retired building contractor*
Royhab, Ronald *journalist, editor*
Scoles, Clyde Sheldon *library director*
Shaikh, Bahu Sultan *physician, educator*
Sherry, Mark Dominic *educator, researcher*
Siddiqui, Fouzia *neurologist*
Slama, James T. *chemistry professor, researcher*
Springman, Richard Arthur *mechanical engineer, director*
Stepien, Carol Ann *molecular geneticist, fisheries educator*
Stierman, Donald John *geophysicist, educator*
Stroucken, Albert P. L. *consumer products company executive, former chemical company executive*
Sweetnam, James E. *automotive executive*
Talmage, Lance Allen *obstetrician, gynecologist, military officer*
Thaman, Michael H. *building material systems executive*
Trendel, Jill A. *pharmacist, educator*
Van Ness, Mary Beth *literature and language professor*
Vijh, Uma Parvathy *astrophysicist, researcher*
Wang, Leslie Tsun Chung *social sciences educator*
Webb, Thomas Irwin, Jr. *lawyer, director*
Weikel, Malcolm Keith *healthcare company executive*
Wicklund, David Wayne *lawyer*
Wolfe, Robert Kenneth *engineering educator*
Yost, James A. *automotive parts company executive*

Trotwood
Oluyitan, Emmanuel Funso *communications educator*

Troy
Platfoot, Christopher W. *systems administrator, information technology executive*
Puls, Sarah *marketing executive*
Puthoff, Mark Allen *lawyer*
Tipton, Clyde Raymond, Jr. *communications and resources development consultant*

Twinsburg
Murphy, Kathleen S. *science educator*

Uniontown
France, Dorothy Daniel *minister*
Taylor, Mary *state official*

University Heights
Cook, Alexander Burns *curator, artist, educator*
Eslinger, Kenneth Nelson *social sciences educator*
Langenfus, William Louis *philosopher, educator*
Milota, Marcella D. *librarian*
Murphy, Paul Regis, Jr. *business educator*
Seaton, Shirley Smith *academic administrator, consultant*

University Hts
Calkins, Lindsay Noble *economics professor*
Ford, Theron N. *education educator*

Upper Arlington
Bordelon, Carolyn Thew *elementary school educator*
Relle, Ferenc Matyas *chemist*

Urbana
Meyers, Marsha Lynn *retired social worker*
Phillips, Julieanne Appleson *history professor*

Vandalia
Scinto, Michael Jospeph *broadcast executive*

Vincent
Meek, Barbara Susan *retired elementary school educator*

Wadsworth
Aragon, Lynn D. *retired physician*
Furry, Benjamin K. *chemist*
Wilhelm, Cathy S. *elementary school educator*

Walton Hills
Wareham, L. Marie *elementary school educator*

Wapakoneta
Lusk Barlage, Mary Margaret *music educator*

Warren
Del Bene, Janet Elaine *chemistry educator*
He, Min *mathematics professor*
Nader, Robert Alexander *retired judge, lawyer*
Ross, Karen Lee Hromyak *retired school psychologist*
Rossi, Anthony Gerald *lawyer*
Ryan, Timothy J. *United States Representative from Ohio*

Warrensville Heights
Simmons, Clinton Craig *human resources executive*

Wauseon
Stutzman, Donna J. *minister*

Waverly
Cornish, Carol A. *media specialist*

Wellston
Loxley, Kathryn *retired elementary school educator*

West Chester
Mack, Mark Philip *chemical company executive*
Tanov, Romil R. *mechanical engineer, researcher*

Westerville
Brombacher, Bruce E. *mathematics educator*
Helvey, Edward Douglas *lawyer*
Kerr, Thomas Jefferson, IV, *academic administrator*
St. Pierre, Ronald Leslie *public health and medical educator, academic administrator*
Wilson, Edward Allyn *educational administrator*
Young, Sheldon Mike *lawyer, author*

Westlake
O'Brien, Thomas M. *travel company executive*
Rebholz, Andrew J. *hospitality company executive*
Schroth, Joyce Able *social worker*
Skulina, Thomas Raymond *lawyer*
Whitehouse, John Harlan, Jr. *systems software consultant, diagnostician*
Young, Mark R. *lawyer, hospitality company executive*

Wickliffe
Bauer, Joseph W. *lawyer, chemicals executive*
Cooley, Charles P. *chemicals executive*
Fisher, Nancy DeButts *library director*
Hambrick, James L. *chemicals executive*
Kidder, Fred Dockstater *retired lawyer*
Pevec, Anthony Edward *bishop emeritus*

Wilberforce
Onwudiwe, Ebere *humanities educator, writer*
Seleem, Suzanne *chemistry professor*

Willoughby
Baker, Charles Stephen *music educator*
Brass, Ernest H. III *financial planner*
Driggs, Charles Mulford *lawyer*
Eyman, Culver Francis III *social studies educator, department chairman*
Guy, Eleanor Bryenton *retired writer*
Krause, Marjorie N. *biochemist*
Krider, Margaret Young *art educator*
Linsenmeier, Carol Vincent *music educator*
Pennington, John Robert *biology educator, department chairman*

Wilmington
Alexander, J. Wynn *theater educator, director*

Wooster
August, Robert Olin *retired journalist*
Dehority, Burk Allyn *microbiology professor*
Geiser, Robert Neil *computer scientist*
Kennedy, Charles Allen *lawyer*
Krain, Matthew *political science professor*
Loess, Henry Bernard *psychology professor*
Lovato, Monica *boxer*
Schreiber, Clare Adel *journalist*
Steward, Larry G. *agricultural studies educator, consultant*
Zink, Harry A. *ophthalmologist*

Worthington
Aggarwal, Gaurav *engineer*
Bernhagen, Lillian Flickinger *retired school health consultant*
Compton, Ralph Theodore, Jr. *electrical engineering educator*
Fisher, Fredrick Lee *lawyer*
Minton, Harvey Steiger *lawyer*
Speck, Samuel Wallace, Jr. *federal official*
Vladem, Steven Allen *writer, film producer, motivational speaker*
Winter, Chester Caldwell *surgeon, educator, historian, writer*

Wright Patterson AFB
Banda, Siva S. *research scientist*
Boeckl, John J. *research scientist*
Carlson, Bruce *career military officer*
Cranston, Stewart E. *career officer*
Fernelius, Nils Conard *physicist*
Goltz, Mark Neil *environmental engineer*
Hager, Gordon Douglas *scientist, engineering educator*
Jackson, Jason M. *military officer, educator*
Meccia, Neil Rocco *health facility administrator, physician*
Metcalf, Charles David *museum director, retired military officer*
Palazotto, Anthony N. *aerospace engineering educator*
Tripp, Lloyd Dale *research scientist*

Wyoming
Cooley, William Edward *research scientist, consultant*

Xenia
Bigelow, Daniel James *aerospace executive*
Nutter, Zoe Dell Lantis *retired public relations executive*

Yellow Springs
Cawood, Albert McLaurin (Hap Cawood) *retired newspaper editor*
Seon, Yvonne *retired cultural educator, minister*
Trolander, Hardy Wilcox *engineering executive, consultant*
Webb, Paul *physiologist, educator, researcher, consultant*

Youngstown
Barr, Richard Gary *radiologist, chemist*
Bowers, Bege Kaye *literature and communications educator, academic administrator*
Brown, Steven Ray *language professional*
Camacci, Michael A. *real estate broker and developer, consultant*
Catoline-Ackerman, Pauline Dessie *small business owner*
Dunlap, Catherine Mary *clergywoman*
Edirisooriya, Gunapala *finance educator*
Estrin, Melvyn J. *computer products company executive*
Hudak, Cheryl C. *travel company executive*
Islam, A.K.M. Anwarul *civil engineer, consultant*
Itts, Elizabeth Ann Dunham *retired psychotherapist, consultant*
Jackson, Cryshanna A. *social sciences educator*
Mehra, Jagdish *economics professor*
Mettee, Howard Dawson *chemistry professor, consultant*
Miller, Kenneth Lee *counselor, educator*
Murry, George Vance *bishop*
Pavlik, Kelly (Robert) *boxer*
Pintar, Jennifer A. *healthcare educator*
Powers, Paul J. *manufacturing executive*
Redfern, Chris *political organization administrator, former state legislator*
Valenta, Janet Anne *substance abuse professional*
Yozwiak, Bernard James *retired mathematics educator, academic administrator*
Zona, Louis Albert *museum director*

Zanesville
Childers, Susan Lynn Bohn *special education educator, school system administrator, human resources and transition specialist, consultant*
Earhart, Margaret V. *social studies educator*
Giannandrea, Beatrice *language educator*
Holdren, Susan *literature and language professor, foundation administrator*
Marks, John R. *retired science educator*
McLaughlin, James Lee *musician, director*
Shepherd, James Leonard *biology professor*
Strahm, Mary Ellen *music educator*

OKLAHOMA

Ada
Anoatubby, Bill *Governor of The Chickasaw Nation*
Baker, Judith Ann *retired computer technician*
Daniel, Arlie V. *speech education educator*
Emrich, Paul M. *psychotherapist, educator*
Lu, Feng Hu *environmental scientist*
Parham, Betty Ely *credit bureau executive*
Schubert, Geri M. *psychotherapist*
Stafford, Donald Gene *chemistry professor*
Wilkin, Richard Thomas *geochemist*

Altus
Coakley, Toni M. *science educator*
Shelby, Karla Jane *music company executive, director*

Alva
Batalha da Conceicao, Jose Joao *chemistry professor, researcher*
Steed, Patricia L. *literature and language professor*

Ardmore
Dixon, Richard Arthur *botanist, educator, researcher*
Molander, Deborah Jean *special education educator*
Monteros, Maria *biochemist and plant breeder, educator*

Bartlesville
Baker-Morris, Kay *special education educator*
Berney, Rand C. *oil industry executive*
Doty, Donald D. *retired bank executive*
Hankinson, Risdon William *retired chemical engineer*
Rockey, Peggy Ann *pre-school educator*
Silas, Cecil Jesse *retired petroleum company executive*
Sweem, Billy Don *bishop, religious organization administrator*

Beaver
Hodges, Vivan Pauline *educator and consultant*

Bethany
Alexander, Patrick Byron *hospital administrator*
Arbuckle, Averil Dorothy (Cookie Arbuckle) *healthcare facility administrator*
Campbell Detrixhe, Dia D. *nursing educator*
Dorough, Carol *nursing educator*
Feisal, Marcia Moon *communications educator*
Leggett, James Daniel *bishop*
Murrow, Wayne Lee *retired communications educator, dean*

Bixby
McManus, Delana Ann *elementary school educator*
Walker, Jerald Carter *academic administrator, minister*

Bristow
Caudle, Letha Grace *secondary school educator*
Primeaux, Henry III *automotive executive, author, speaker*

Broken Arrow
Gaddis, Richard William *management educator*
Hong-Nam, Kyungsim Kay *education educator, consultant*
Huff, Melinda Louise *art educator*
Jones, Jp *graphics designer*
Muller, Patricia Ann *nursing administrator, educator*
Vargas, Traci Junelle *special education educator*

Chickasha
Hanson, Dan Lewis *music educator, entertainer, composer*

Claremore
Blakely, David *theater educator, playwright*
Heidlage, Patsy Jo *physical education educator*
Steidley, Juan Dwayne *lawyer, judge*
Wittenberg, Henry Taylor, Jr. *physician, surgeon*

Cleveland
Henry, Kathleen Marie *marketing executive*

Disney
Hamilton, Carl Hulet *retired academic administrator*

Duncan
Burum, Sharon *educator*

Durant
Adair, Aaron Lucas *theater educator*
Cunningham, James Grady *theater educator*
Gumm, Jay Paul *state legislator, association executive*
Hrncir, Theresa June *accounting educator*
Turner, Michael Dan *academic administrator*

Edmond
Adams, Donald E. *physiatrist*
Angel, Steven Michael *retired lawyer*
Bristow, Donald Gene *theater educator*
Chen, Wei R. *physics professor*
Currier, Susanne *economics professor*
Halverstadt, Donald Bruce *urologist, educator*
Hopwood, Howard Hoppy Perry *military officer*
Laughlin, Monique Myrtle Weant *mental health counselor, retired*
Lester, Andrew William *lawyer*
Lester, Richard Garrison *radiologist, educator*
Lewis, Gladys Sherman *university professor*
Loman, Mary LaVerne *retired mathematics professor*
Loving, Susan Brimer *lawyer, former state official*
Morishige, Teruo Ted *engineering educator*
Powell, Courtney Davis *lawyer*
Sibley, William Arthur *retired academic administrator, physics professor, consultant*
Wilson, Julia Ann Yother *lawyer*

Enid
Jones, Stephen *lawyer*
Marquardt, Shirley Marie *retired management consultant*
Taveggia, Thomas Charles *retired management consultant, educator*
Ward, Llewellyn Orcutt III *oil industry executive*

Fort Towson
Pike, Thomas Harrison *plant chemist*

Frederick
Evans, Michael D. *lawyer*
Stone, Voye Lynne *women's health nurse practitioner*

Grove
Trippensee, Gary Alan *retired aerospace executive*

Guthrie
Davis, Frank Wayne *lawyer*
Womack, Destiny Mary Louise *artist*

Hodgen
Brower, Janice Kathleen *library and information scientist*

Holdenville
Cook, Francile *retired library director*

Inola
Mullen, Deborah W. *elementary school educator*
Paul, Gary Wayne *music educator*

Jennings
Nixon, Arlie James *gas and oil company executive*

Kingfisher
Buswell, Arthur Wilcox *physician, surgeon*
Elsener, G. Dale *lawyer*

Konawa
Jabeen, Seema *internist*

Lamont
Covalt, Edna Irene *retired medical/surgical nurse*

Langston
Haysbert, JoAnn Wright *academic administrator*
Mambula, Charles J. *finance educator, consultant*
Showalter, Betsy S. *mathematics educator*

Lawton
Bonnell-Mihalis, Pamela Gay Scoggins *library director*
Carraher, Shawn Michael *investment company executive, management educator*
Davis, Ellen Marie *business educator*
Detweiler, Stanley Bruce *music educator*
Gagliardi, Charlotte Marie *music educator, secondary school educator*
Graves, Russell W. *social studies educator*
Heflin, James L. *communications educator*
Liontas-Warren, Katherine *art educator*
Mays, Quincey *art educator*
Moore, Roy Dean *retired judge*
Perez-Cruet, Jorge *geriatric psychiatrist, researcher*
Soylu, Ali *finance educator*
Sukar, Abdulhamid I. *economics professor*
Thomlinson, Vivian Aytes *literature and language professor*
Underwood, Kirsten Fedje *musician, educator*

Lookeba
Davis, Michael D. *principal, coach*

Maramec
Blair, Marie Lenore *elementary school educator*

Mcalester
Cornish, Richard Pool *lawyer*
Hanway, Wayne Edward *library director*

Mcloud
Goats, Debbie *elementary school educator*

Medford
Robbins, Frankie *civil engineer*

Midwest City
Cheek, Norma Jean *retired elementary school educator*
Gilbert, James Neil *science educator*
Harrell, Beverly Ellen *mathematics professor*
Wier, Leanne May *life sciences educator*

Moore
Chiles, Mary Jane *secondary school educator*
Lee, Myung Woo *accountant, financial secretary*

Mounds
Halsey, James Albert *entertainer, theater producer*

Muskogee
Hasler-Reid, Linda *elementary school educator*
Hinshaw, Marilyn L. *retired library director*
Kent, Bartis Milton *retired physician*
Robinson, Adelbert Carl *lawyer, judge*
Sperling, Sheldon J. *prosecutor*

Mustang
Wood, Jean Carol *poet, lyricist*

Newalla
Hixson, Janice Vee *music educator, composer*

Nichols Hills
Trost, Louis Frederick, Jr. *banker, financial planner*

Norman
AbuBakr, Samer *microbiologist, educator*
Affleck, Marilyn *retired sociology educator*
Altan, M(ustafa) Cengiz *mechanical engineering educator*
Ambrosini, Armand Anthony *music educator*
Apanasov, Boris N. *mathematics professor, researcher*
Berkowitz, Ari *medical educator, director*
Bert, Charles Wesley *mechanical and aerospace engineer, educator*
Biscoe, Belinda P. *academic administrator, psychologist*
Bluestein, Howard Bruce *meteorology educator*
Boren, David Lyle *academic administrator, former senator*
Bradford, Sam *student athlete*
Breen, Marilyn *mathematics educator*
Buchwald, Michael Carl *theater educator*
Campbell, John Morgan *retired chemical engineer*
Capel, Jeff III *men's college basketball coach*
Censky, Ellen Joan *curator, biologist, museum director*
Coale, Sherri *women's college basketball coach*
Commuri, Sesh *electrical engineer, educator*
Cowan, John James *physicist, astronomer, educator*
Dalbo, Vincent James *psychologist, researcher*
DeSpain, Matthew Stanley *history professor*
Diaz, Nina Isabel *industrial engineer*
Dille, John Robert *retired physician*
Dinh, Anh Viet *research scientist*
Dorrough, Vicki Lee *theater educator*
Droegemeier, Kelvin K. *meteorologist, educator*
Dunbar, Norah Ellen *communications educator*
Edwards, Roger *meteorologist, researcher*
Elkouri, Frank *law educator*
Fears, Jesse Rufus *historian, academic dean, educator*
Fedorovich, Evgeni *geophysicist*
Gollahalli, Subramanyam Ramappa *engineering educator*
Henderson, Arnold Glenn *architect, educator*
Henderson, George *educational sociologist, educator*
Hutchison, Victor Hobbs *biologist, educator*
Jones, Charlotte *director*
Kang, Thomas H.-K. *engineering educator*
Keppel, Ben *history professor*
Khoury, Naji *engineering educator*
Kondonassis, Alexander John *economist, educator*
Lamb, Peter James *meteorology educator, researcher, consultant*
Lee, Sul Hi *library administrator, dean*
Lester, June *library and information scientist, educator*
Levy, David William *history educator*
Lowitt, Richard *history professor*
Lura, Susan *librarian*
Mallinson, Richard Gregory *chemical engineering educator*
Mares, Michael Allen *ecologist, educator, Museum Association Administrator*
Masters, Anne *library director*
Miller, Claude Harold *communications educator*
Miller, Fred Heins *lawyer, retired educator*
Page, Rex L *computer scientist, educator, software consultant*
Pappas, James Pete *university administrator*
Perkins, Edward Joseph *political science professor, retired ambassador*
Ramseyer, Chris Charles Emil *engineering educator*
Risser, Paul Gillan *academic administrator, botanist*
Robertson, Lindsay Gordon *law educator*
Sasaki, Yoshi Kazu *meteorology educator, researcher*
Savage, William Woodrow, Jr. *historian, consultant, social sciences educator*
Sellars, Nigel Anthony *historian, writer*
Spurgeon, Jim D. *dentist*
Stoops, Bob *college football coach*
Strauss, Michael George *physics professor*
Trimble, Preston Albert *retired judge*
Tussing, Marilee Appleby *music educator*
Van Fleet, Connie Jean *library and information scientist, educator*
Van Horn, Richard Linley *academic administrator*
Weber, Jerome Charles *human relations educator, retired academic administrator*
Williams, Ronald L. *dentist*
Winters, Martha P. *history and language educator*
Wood, Betty Jean *conceptual artist, educator*
Zaman, Musharraf *civil engineering educator*
Zapffe, Nina Byrom *retired elementary school educator*
Zhai, Yan *education educator, researcher*

Nowata
Acebo, Ronnie Vic *literature and language educator, coach*

Ochelata
Hitzman, Donald Oliver *microbiologist*

Oklahoma City
Abid, Farida *neurologist, pediatrician*
Adams, Russell Lee *neuropsychologist*
Adelson, Kenneth I. *professional sports team executive*
Alaupovic, Alexandra Vrbanic *artist, educator*
Alaupovic, Petar *biochemist, educator*
Allbright, Karan Elizabeth *psychologist, consultant*
Andrews, Mitchell Dewayne *internist, dean, educator*
Aravindan, Natarajan *medical educator*
Askins, Jari *Lieutenant Governor of Oklahoma*
Bamgbola, Oluwatoyin Fatai *pediatric renal physician, researcher*
Barth, Danny *professional sports team executive*
Beltran, Eusebius Joseph *archbishop*
Bennett, Clayton Ike *professional sports team owner*
Beveridge, Norwood Pierson *law educator*
Binning, Bette Finese (Mrs. Gene Hedgcock Binning) *athletic association official*
Binning, Gene Barton *real estate company executive*
Blick, Kenneth Edward *clinical chemist, educator*
Bogardus, Carl Robert, Jr. *radiologist, educator*
Boston, Billie *costume designer, history educator*
Botch, Sabra Ruvera *biochemist*
Boutsen, Frank R. *healthcare educator*
Bozalis, John Russell *physician*
Branch, John Curtis *biology professor, lawyer*
Broach, Dana *psychologist, researcher*
Brooks, Scott William *professional basketball coach*
Broyles, Robert Herman *biochemistry and molecular biology educator*
Butnev, Viktor Yurievich *research scientist*
Carlisle, Jeffrey Deward *history professor*
Claflin, James Robert *pediatrician, allergist*
Coats, Andrew Montgomery *dean, lawyer, former mayor*
Colbert, Thomas *state supreme court justice*
Collins, William Edward, Jr. *aeromedical administrator, psychologist, researcher*
Comp, Philip Cinnamon *medical researcher*
Copeland, Kyle A. *physicist*
Cornett, Mick *Mayor, Oklahoma City*
Couch, James Russell, Jr. *neurology educator*
Court, Leonard *lawyer, educator*
Craig, George Dennis *economics professor, consultant*
Cruz-Rodz, Armando L. *chemistry professor*
Culkin, Daniel Joseph *urologist, educator, department chairman*
Cunningham, Madeleine White *microbiologist, immunologist*
Dailey, Patrick R. *health facility administrator*
DeGiusti, Timothy D. *federal judge*
Delaney, Peter B. *energy executive*
Dixon, Steven *energy executive*
Dubowski, Kurt Max *toxicologist, educator, consultant*
Durant, Kevin Wayne *professional basketball player*
Edmondson, Drew (William Andrew Edmondson) *state attorney general*
Edmondson, James E. *state supreme court chief justice*
Elder, James Carl *lawyer*
Escobedo, Marilyn Barnard *physician, educator*
Fallin, Mary Copeland *United States Representative from Oklahoma, former lieutenant governor*
Fenton, Elliott Clayton *lawyer*
Fernandez, Lisa *softball player*
Fiegel, Jacque R. *bank executive*
Filley, Warren Vernon *allergist*
Ford, Michael Raye *lawyer*
Forni, Patricia Rose *nursing educator*
Garrett, Sandy Langley *state official, school system administrator*
George, James Noel *hematologist, oncologist, educator*
Gilchrist, John Mark *otolaryngologist*
Gourley, James Leland *editor, publishing executive*
Granger, Brenda Ann *museum director*
Green, Jeff *professional basketball player*
Green, Vickie *music educator*
Greiner, Kenneth Donald, Jr. *retired management consultant, health facility administrator*
Halligan, James Edmund *retired academic administrator, retired chemical engineer, state legislator*
Halpin, Anna Marie *retired architect*
Hampton, Carol McDonald *priest, educator, historian*
Hampton, James Wilburn *hematologist, oncologist*
Hardeman, Carole Hall *education educator*
Hargrave, Rudolph *state supreme court justice*
Harley, John Barker *rheumatologist*
Harolds, Jay Alan *radiologist, nuclear medicine physician*
Hefner, William Johnson, Jr., (W. John Hefner Jr.) *oil and gas industry executive*
Henderson, J. Neil *medical anthropologist*
Henry, Brad (C. Brad Henry) *Governor of Oklahoma*
Henry, Robert Harlan *federal judge, former attorney general*
Hilger, Robyn *music educator*
Hoge, Margaret R. *art educator*
Holloway, William Judson, Jr. *federal judge*
Holmes, Ivan *political organization administrator*
Homsey, Joseph Richard, Jr. *lawyer*
Hood, Henry J. *lawyer, energy executive*
Hooper, Marie E. *history professor*
Hurst, Robert Evan *biochemist, educator*
Jackson, Wanda Lavonne *country western musician*
Jacobs, Eric J. *epidemiologist, researcher*
Johnson, Glen D., Jr. *educational association administrator*
Jones, Charles Edwin *historian, bibliographer, chaplain*
Jones, Gary *political organization administrator*
Jones, Tad *state legislator*
Kamm, Steven D. *physics professor*
Kasus-Jacobi, Anne *biochemist, cell biologist, researcher*
Kauger, Yvonne *state supreme court justice*
Keddissi, Jean I. *medical educator*
Kelley, Ed *editor-in-chief*
Kelly, Vicky Leloie *music educator*
Kerr, Lou C. *foundation administrator*
Komori, Naoka *neuroscientist, biochemist*
Kreth, Jens *medical educator*
Kriesel, Deanna *education educator*
Krstic, Nenad *professional basketball player*
LaMotte, Janet Allison *retired management consultant*
Lavender, Maxine Knight *special education educator*
Lavender, Robert Eugene *former state supreme court justice*
Lazzara, Ralph *cardiologist*
Legg, William Jefferson *lawyer*
Leonard, Timothy Dwight *federal judge*
Loftus, Christopher Miranda *neurosurgeon*
Lowe, Lyle Justin *lawyer*
Lynn, Thomas Neil, Jr. *retired medical center administrator, physician*
McCaffree, Mary Anne Wight *pediatrician, neonatal-perinatal specialist, educator*
McCampbell, Robert Garner *lawyer, former prosecutor*
McClellan, Mary Ann *pediatric nurse practitioner*
McClendon, Aubrey K. *energy executive*
McElvany, Rocky *state agency administrator*
McKee, Patrick Allen *physician*
McMillin, James Craig *lawyer*
McNall-Knapp, René Yvonne *pediatrician, educator*
McShan, William Michael *medical educator*
Meacham, Scott *state treasurer*
Mellott, Greg L. *film producer, writer, director*
Meyer, William H. *pediatrician, educator*
Miller, Herbert Dell *petroleum engineer*
Mold, James William *geriatrician, preventive medicine physician, educator*
Moler, Edward Harold *retired lawyer*
Morgan, Catherine Marie *psychologist, writer*
Moser, Eleanor T. Pendell *federal administrative law judge*
Murray, James William III *manufacturing executive, lawyer*
Murry, Donald Arvil *economics professor*
Mustion, Alan Lee *pharmacist*
Myers, Densel Lee *economics professor*
Nelon, Robert Dale *lawyer*
Oehlert, William Herbert, Jr. *cardiologist, administrator, educator*
Ogle, James David *lawyer*
Opala, Marian Peter *state supreme court justice*
Otto, Donald R. *museum director*
Ozer, Howard *oncologist, hematologist*
Paris, Lee Anne Hagewood *academic librarian*
Parke, David Wilkin, II, *ophthalmologist, educator, health facility administrator*
Paul, William George *lawyer*
Payne, Gareld Gene *vocal music educator, medical transcriptionist*
Peace, H. W., II, *small business owner, retired oil industry executive*
Perry, Steven L. *lawyer*
Plafker, Scott *medical educator*
Plummer, William Hamilton III *museum director, editor*
Poole, Richard William *economist*
Postier, Russell Glen *surgeon*
Presti, Sam *professional sports team executive*
Price Boday, Mary Kathryn *choreographer, small business owner, educator*
Rabadi, Meheroz Hoshang *neurologist, consultant*
Raj, Tilak D. *anesthesiologist, educator*
Reich, Richard Allen *bank executive*
Reif, John F. *state supreme court justice*
Reimer, Dennis J. *retired career military officer*
Resman-Targoff, Beth Holly *pharmacist, educator*
Rhoades, Everett Ronald *medical educator*
Rice, Andrew *state legislator*
Richels, John *energy executive, lawyer*
Richter, John Charles *prosecutor*
Ridley, Betty Ann *theology studies educator*
Rockett, D. Joe *lawyer, director*

Ross, William Jarboe *lawyer*
Rowland, Marcus C. *energy executive*
Ruffin, Richard A. *orthopedic surgeon*
Russell, David L. *federal judge*
Sanchez, Cindi Asbury *physical education educator*
Sanghera, Dharambir K. *biology professor*
Savage, Susan M. *Secretary of State, Oklahoma, former mayor*
Sawalha, Amr *medical educator*
Schroeder, Charles P. (Chuck Schroeder) *museum director*
Schroeder, David J. Dean *retired psychologist*
Schuster, E. Elaine *lawyer*
Shillingburg, Herbert Thompson, Jr. *dental educator*
Smith, (Carl) Michael *lawyer, former federal agency administrator*
Soderstrand, Michael Alan *mathematics professor, electrical engineer*
Spencer, Melvin Joe *retired health facility administrator, lawyer, consultant*
Springer, Karl *school system administrator*
Steinhorn, Irwin Harry *lawyer, corporate financial executive, educator*
Stewart, Robert D., Jr. *lawyer*
Stong, Roger Alan *lawyer*
Stringer, L. E. (Dean) *retired lawyer*
Taylor, Lyndon Clint *lawyer, energy executive*
Taylor, Steven W. *state supreme court justice*
Taylor-White-Grigsby, Queen Deloris *minister, consultant*
Thadani, Udho *physician, cardiologist*
Thomas, Etan *professional basketball player, poet*
Thompson, David *publishing executive*
Thompson, Mick *state banking agency administrator*
Towery, Curtis Kent *lawyer*
Triplett, E. Eugene *editor*
Tuggle, David W. *pediatric surgeon*
Vargo, Stephen Louis *travel company executive*
Walsh, Lawrence Edward *lawyer*
Watson, Brenda Bennett *insurance company executive*
Watt, Joseph Michael *state supreme court justice*
Weddington, Stacey Lee *not-for-profit developer*
Weigel, Paul Henry *biochemistry educator, researcher, consultant*
West, Eileen C. *general internal medicine physician, educator*
West, Lee Roy *federal judge*
Williamson, Marvel *dean, nursing administrator, sexologist, educator*
Winchester, James R. *state supreme court justice*
Wolraich, Mark Lee *pediatrician, educator*
Wong, Carson *surgeon, educator*
Woods, Harry Arthur, Jr. *lawyer*
Woods, Pendleton *college director, author*

Okmulgee
Mitcham, Julius Jerome *accountant*

Oologah
Thomas, Rick W. *school system administrator*

Park Hill
Yeager, Debra Lyn *science educator*

Pawhuska
Strahm, Samuel Edward *retired veterinarian*

Ponca City
Northcutt, Clarence Dewey *lawyer*
Raley, John Wesley, Jr. *lawyer*
Rice, Sue Ann *retired dean, psychologist*

Poteau
Long, Sheila Joan *academic administrator*

Ripley
Chlouber, Dale Edward *curator*

Roosevelt
Franks, Tommy Ray *retired military officer*

Sand Springs
Quinn, Art Jay *retired veterinarian, educator*

Sayre
Brooks, David Eugene *lawyer*
Clifton, E. Roxann *lab administrator*

Seminole
Hamm, Dawna R. *accountant, educator*
Helseth, David Carl *biology professor*
Jacomo, Tracy Wood *social sciences educator, consultant*
Kirk, Kelly D. *art educator, department chairman*
Koenig, Pamela *social sciences educator*

Shawnee
Pollei, Dane F. *museum director*
Sharp, Ron *secondary school educator*

Stillwater
Adams, Brant *music educator, director*
Allison, Robin W. *veterinarian, educator*
Basu, Arpita *dietician, educator*
Campbell, John Roy *animal science professor, academic administrator*
Case, Kenneth Eugene *industrial engineering educator*
Cooper, Donald Lee *physician*
Dabo, Sira Mady *science educator*
Darcy, Robert Emmett *political science and statistics professor*
Das, Sumanta Kumar *research scientist, educator*
DeLacerda, Melissa Griner *lawyer*
Doolen, J. Kevin *theater educator*
Dr. Eissa, Fahd Z. *toxicologist, educator*
Farr, Cheryl Ann *science educator, researcher*
Fischer, LeRoy Henry *historian, educator*
Giddens, Cheryl LeAnn *medical educator*
Gilliland, Stanley Eugene *dairy-food microbiology professor*
Grischkowsky, Daniel Richard *research scientist, educator*
Gundy, Mike *college football coach*
Hargis, V. Burns (Burns Hargis) *academic administrator, lawyer*
Hebert, Paulette R. *design educator*
Hoberock, Lawrence Linden *mechanical engineer, educator*
Hubbard, Todd Philip *aerospace scientist*
Jones, Edward John *literature and language professor*
Jones, Nigel R. *architect, educator*
Kim, Jaebeom *economics professor*
Leech, Robin *librarian*
Leuschen, Martin Leslie *engineer*
Lucas, Frank D. *United States Representative from Oklahoma*
Luebke, Neil Robert *philosophy educator*
Mansy, Khaled *engineering educator, architect*
Max, Elizabeth *english language educator*
Melancon, Celinda Reese *psychologist*
Mize, Joe Henry *industrial engineer, educator*
Rahnavard, Nazanin *engineering educator*
Rebek, Eric *entomologist, educator*
Senat, Joey *communications educator*
Sharda, Ramesh *management science-information systems educator*
Sherwood, Peter Miles Anson *chemistry educator*
Strathe, Marlene I. *academic administrator*
Thompson, David Russell *engineering educator, dean*
Waller, George Rozier, Jr. *retired biochemistry educator*
Wang, Ning Lian *geographer, educator*
Westhaus, Paul Anthony *retired physics professor*
White, Jeffery Lane *chemistry professor, researcher*

Stilwell
Doyle, Rhonda Gail *science educator*

Tahlequah
Duncan, Janice Marie *education educator*
Haskins, V. Lyle *retired academic administrator*

Tecumseh
Moser, Glenda Faye *media specialist*

Terlton
Bender, John Henry, Jr., (Jack Bender) *editor, cartoonist*

Tinker AFB
Goodman, Ernest Monroe *military officer*

Tonkawa
Allen, Bart W. *finance educator*

Tulsa
Angelini, Marcello *performing company executive*
Arrington, John Leslie, Jr. *lawyer*
Azar, J. J. *engineering educator*
Ball, Rex Martin *urban planner, architect*
Barker, John Roy *lawyer, gas industry executive*
Bell, Stephen Scott *engineering educator*
Bender, James J. *lawyer, oil industry executive*
Biolchini, Robert Fredrick *lawyer*
Blais, Roger Nathaniel *physics professor, academic administrator*
Bransford-Young, Angharad Ann *counselor, educator*
Bryant, Hubert Hale *lawyer*
Buckley, Thomas Hugh *historian, educator*
Buthod, Mary Clare *school administrator*
Chappel, Donald R. *petroleum pipeline company executive*
Chew, Pamela Christine *language educator*
Clement, Evelyn Geer *librarian, educator*
Cobbs, James Harold *engineer, consultant*
Collins, John Roger *transportation company executive*
Collins, Laura Jane *music educator, singer*
Cooper, Richard Casey *lawyer*
Cox, William Jackson *retired bishop*
Daniel, Samuel Phillips *lawyer*
Davis, Tamra S. *business educator*
Dinan, Curtis L. *gas industry executive*
Donaldson, Robert Herschel *university administrator, educator*
Dotson, George Stephen *retired oil industry executive*
Dugger, William Mayfield *economics professor*
Ekdahl, Richard William *educational association executive*
Farnsworth, David *language educator*
Farrell, John L., Jr. *lawyer, consultant, corporate financial executive*
Frey, Martin Alan *lawyer, educator*
Frizzell, Gregory Kent *federal judge*
Gabbard, Douglas, II, (James Gabbard) *judge*
Gaberino, John Anthony, Jr. *lawyer*
Gardner, Dale Ray *lawyer*
Garrison, Beverly Mustain *history professor*
Gentry, Bern Leon, Sr. *management consultant*
Gibson, John W. *gas industry executive*
Givens, Jack Rodman *lawyer*
Goodman, Jerry L(ynn) *judge*
Gregg, Elena *physics professor*
Haring, Robert Westing *newspaper editor*
Hartman, Roger D. *physics professor*
Hatfield, Jack Kenton *lawyer, accountant*
Hayden, Donald Eugene *retired emeritus English language educator*
Haynie, Tony Wayne *arbitrator, lawyer, mediator*
Hellman, Chan M. *psychology professor*
Helmerich, Hans Christian *oil industry executive*
Herr, Stephen Richard *environmental scientist, educator*
Holmes, Jerome A *federal judge*
Horkey, William Richard *retired oil industry executive*
Hoskison, Thomas Karl *medical educator*
Howard, Gene Claude *lawyer, retired state senator*
Huckin, William Price, Jr. *prosecutor*
Huntley, Julie *business educator*
Ingram, Charles Clark, Jr. *energy executive*
Johnson, Cornelius Raymond *lawyer*
Jurgensen, Monserrate *clinical nurse, consultant*
Kaiser, George B. *corporate financial executive*
Kaul, Rashmi *immunologist, educator*
Kern, Terry C. *judge*
Kneale, James C. *gas company executive*
Korstad, John Edward *biology professor*
Kronfeld, Edwin *natural gas company executive*
Kyle, David L. *gas industry executive*
LaBelle, Patti (Patricia Louise Holte) *singer, entertainer*
LaButti, Ronald Stephan *orthopedist*
Lamp, Jeffrey S. *minister, educator*
Latham, Sean *literature and language professor*
Lawhorn, Caron A. *gas industry executive*
Lewis, Patricia Mohatt (Patty) *special education educator*
Liu, Xiaofan Sophie *engineering educator*
Luks, Christi Patton *engineering educator*
Luthey, Graydon Dean, Jr. *lawyer, educator*
Madison, Eddie Lawrence, Jr. *public relations consultant, editor, writer*
Malcolm, Steven J. *petroleum pipeline company executive*
Marlar, Donald Floyd *lawyer*
McCullough, Robert Dale, II, *osteopath*
Neas, John Theodore *investment company executive*
Nedom, H. Arthur *petroleum consultant*
Nell, Gay *pre-school educator*
Nettles, John Barnwell *obstetrics and gynecology educator*
Norvell, John Edmondson III *retired neuroscientist, educator*
Nyikos, Stacy Ann *publishing executive*
Oliver, Georgianna White *technology consulting company executive*
O'Mealey, Jimmy Dee *finance educator*
O'Meilia, David E. *prosecutor, lawyer*
Osborn, La Donna Carol *clergywoman*
Owens, Jana Jae *entertainer*
Phillips, Mary Gutierrez *biology professor*
Say, Burhan *retired physician*
Seymour, Stephanie Kulp *federal judge*
Siddons, Jeffrey G. *school librarian*
Sowell, Laven *retired music educator*
Stewart, Mary Tomlinson *science educator, researcher*
Strecker, David Eugene *lawyer*
Suffolk, Randall *museum director, curator*
Swails, John Washington III *history professor, director*
Taylor, Kathryn L. *Mayor, Tulsa*
Thomas, Robert Eggleston *retired manufacturing executive*
Thompson, Scott L. *automotive executive*
Thornton, Charlie Mae *secondary school educator*
Trennepohl, Gary Lee *academic administrator, finance educator*
Upham, Steadman *academic administrator, anthropologist, educator*
Valero, Maria Teresa *photographer, art educator*
Weinstock Rad, Katheryn Louise *music educator*
Williams, John Horter *civil engineer, energy industry executive*
Williamson, Walter Bland *lawyer*
Wyant, Clyde W., Jr. *manufacturing executive*

Valliant
House, Janie Burdette *music educator*

Wagoner
Hadley, Charline A. *protective services official*

Weatherford
Blatnick, Tammy D. *nursing educator*
Craig, Viki Pettijohn *language educator*
Fitzgerald, Brad W. *engineering educator, consultant*

Wewoka
Rains, Mary Jo *banker*
Trimble, Vance Henry *retired newspaper editor*

Wilburton
Carey, Levenia Marie *counselor*

Yukon
Kang, Heesam *investment analyst, educator*

OREGON

Albany
Ares, Adrian *research scientist*
Oakley, Carolyn Le *state legislator, city manager, director*
Smith, Steve *pharmaceutical executive*

Arch Cape
Markham, John Charles *biologist*

Ashland
Abrahams, Sidney Cyril *physicist, crystallographer*
Bornet, Vaughn Davis *social sciences educator, historian, researcher*
Christianson, Roger Gordon *biology professor, department chairman*
Grover, James Robb *chemist, editor*
Harrison, Robert Thomas *history professor*
Hay, Richard Laurence *theater set designer*
Kreisman, Arthur *higher education consultant, retired humanities educator*
Kristina, Foltz *musician, educator*
Love, John M. *policy researcher*
May, Richard Lee *biologist, educator*
Mularz, Theodore Leonard *architect*
Quainoo, George Kow *physics professor, department chairman*
Rauch, Bill *performing company executive, theater director*
Risser, James Vaulx, Jr. *journalist, educator*
Rowland, Paul Stephen *psychology professor*
Severin, Ezra B. *musician*
Tikekar, Rahul Vasant *computer science educator*

Astoria
Haskell, Donald McMillan *lawyer*
LaMear, Arline Joan *librarian, writer*

Aurora
Ringle, Philip Hamilton, Jr. *lawyer*

Bandon
Handley, Louise Patricia *artist*
Lindquist, Louis William *artist, researcher, writer*

Beaverton
Azuma, Mitsuyoshi *pharmaceutical executive*
Bird, Lewis L. III *apparel executive*
Blair, Donald W. *apparel executive*
Carter, James C. *lawyer, apparel executive*
Clarke, Thomas E. *apparel executive*
Claycomb, Cecil Keith *biochemist, educator*
Denson, Charles D. *apparel executive*
DeStefano, Gary M. *apparel executive*
Dima, Smolyansky *marketing executive*
Duncan, Richard Fredrick, Jr. *retired secondary school educator, consultant*
Gilbert, Barrie *electronics engineer, director*
Hatfield, Tinker L. *architect, apparel and product designer*
Houser, Douglas Guy *lawyer*
Hubbard, Robert Lane *research scientist*
Jackson, Jeanne Pellegren *apparel executive, former investment company executive*
Kamenev, Boris V. *applications developer, materials scientist, metrologist, engineer, researcher*
Knight, Philip Hampson *apparel executive*
Leen, Todd Kevin *physicist*
Mc Cray, Ronald David *lawyer, apparel executive*
McKenney, Paul E. *application developer*
Monalisa, Mitali *application developer*
Parker, Mark G. *apparel executive*
Pond, Patricia Brown *library and information science educator*
Wang, Baoliang (Bob Wang) *applications scientist, researcher*

Bend
Connolly, Thomas Joseph *bishop emeritus*
Lemas, Noah *small business owner*
Moss, Patricia L. *bank executive*
Peters, Gerald Eugene, Jr. *dermatologist, surgeon*
Singletary, DeJuan Theresa *child and adolescent psychiatrist*
Thompson, Douglas C. *engineer*
Upp, Janeanne A. *museum administrator*
Vasa, Robert Francis *bishop*

Brookings
Kovach, Robin *environmental services administrator*
Maxwell, William Stirling *retired lawyer*

Canby
Sundquist, Leah Renata *military officer*

Cannon Beach
Greaver, Harry *artist*
Wismer, Patricia Ann *retired secondary school educator*

Central Point
Ingraham, Laura Anne *political commentator, radio talk show host*
Richardson, Dennis Michael *lawyer, educator*
Savage, Michael (Michael Alan Weiner) *radio personality, commentator*

Christmas Valley
Johnson, Mary Alice *magazine editor*

Clackamas
Thomas, Sonia *provider specialist, trainer*

Coos Bay
Gee, Nina Foran *retired journalist, elementary school educator, writer*
Hockman, Catherine *counselor, educator*

Corvallis
Anthony, Robert Gene *ecologist, educator, research scientist*
Baird, William McKenzie *chemical carcinogenesis researcher, biochemistry professor*
Byers, William D. *engineering executive*
Byrne, John Vincent *educational consultant*
Castle, Emery Neal *economist, educator*
Chambers, Kenton Lee *botany educator*
Chung, Woon-Gye *toxicologist, researcher*
Dalrymple, Gary Brent *research geologist*
Davis, John Rowland *academic administrator*
Drake, Charles Whitney *physicist*
Farber, Vreneli Regula *retired linguist*
Frakes, Rodney Vance *plant geneticist, educator*
Frohnmayer, John Edward *lawyer, writer*
Gillis, John Simon *retired psychologist, educator*
Gitelman, Alix I. *statistician, educator*
Hall, Don Alan *editor, writer*
Hawkes, Stephen James. *chemistry educator*
Headrick, Charlotte Jane *theater educator*
Henny, Charles Joseph *biologist, researcher*
Holman, Robert Alan *oceanography educator*
Kelbert, Anna *geophysicist*
Kovchegov, Yevgeniy V. *mathematics professor*
Lancaster, Stephen Thomas *science educator*
Lee, Shiwoo *engineering educator*
Lertsutthiwong, Monchai *research scientist*
McKinney, William Mark *retired geology educator*
Monkul, Mehmet Murat *geotechnical engineering researcher*
Morita, Richard Yukio *microbiology and oceanography educator*
Oldfield, James Edmund *retired nutrition educator*
Olson, Deanna Helen *ecologist, researcher*
Parks, Harold Raymond *mathematician, educator*
Petersen, Roger Gene *biometrician, educator*
Qian, Michael C. *science educator, consultant*
Riley, Michael *college football coach*
Riley, Mike *college football coach*
Rudinsky, Norma Leigh *English language educator, translator*
Salafsky, Susan Rebecca *ecologist*

Sapon-White, Richard E. *librarian*
Sarker, Mahfuzur Rahman *microbiologist*
Shen, Jianqiang *research scientist*
Stehr, Christian Peter *literature and language professor*
Tappeiner, II, John C. *forester, educator*
Temes, Gabor Charles *electrical engineering educator*
Temesgen, Hailemariam *statistician, educator*
Van Holde, Kensal Edward *biochemistry educator*
Verts, Lita Jeanne *academic administrator*
Waring, Richard Harvey *retired research scientist*
Waromg, Richard Harvey *ecologist, educator*
Westwood, Melvin Neil *horticulturist, pomologist*
Wilkins, Caroline Hanke *advocate, political organization worker*
Yeats, Robert Sheppard *geologist, educator*

Cottage Grove
Clark-Bourne, Kathryn Orpha *retired consul*

Culver
Siebert, Diane Dolores *author, poet*

Dayton
Anderson, Herbert Hatfield *lawyer, farmer*

Depoe Bay
Eaton, Leonard Kimball *retired architecture educator*

Eugene
Acker, Martin Herbert *psychotherapist, educator*
Aldave, Barbara Bader *lawyer, educator*
Bailey, Exine Margaret Anderson *soprano, educator*
Baker, Alton Fletcher III *editor, publishing executive*
Bascom, Ruth F. *retired mayor*
Bellotti, Mike *college football coach*
Bergquist, Peter *retired music educator*
Bichsel, Ruth J. *psychologist, educator*
Candee, Stephen M. *political science professor*
Cawood, Elizabeth Jean *public relations executive*
Cheng, Nancy Yen-wen *architecture educator*
Collas-Dean, Angela G. *retired state commissioner, small business owner*
Crasemann, Bernd *physicist, researcher*
Csonka, Paul L. *theoretical physicist, educator*
Deshpande, Nilendra Ganesh *physics professor*
Donnelly, Russell James *physicist, educator*
Doty, Angela *career planning administrator*
Edwards, Ralph M. *librarian*
Farrington, Marianne Patricia *choreographer, educator*
Frederick, Elizabeth Eleanor Tatum *watercolor artist, retired educator*
Freyd, Jennifer Joy *psychology professor*
Frohnmayer, David Braden *retired academic administrator*
Gall, Meredith (Mark) Damien *education professor emeritus, writer*
Graziano, Margaret A. *chaplain, recreational therapist, educational consultant, volunteer*
Griffith, Osbie Hayes *retired chemistry professor*
Hill, Terrell Leslie *chemist, researcher, biophysicist*
Hunt, Elizabeth Hope *psychologist*
Jenkins, Dennis L. *archaeologist, educator*
Jewell, Mark Laurence *plastic surgeon*
Khang, Chulsoon *economics professor*
Kimble, Daniel Porter *psychology educator*
Lariviere, Richard Wilfred *academic administrator, educator*
Lindholm, Richard Theodore *economics and finance educator*
Littman, Richard Anton *psychologist, educator*
Loescher, Richard Alvin *retired gastroenterologist*
Luu, Phan *engineering company executive*
Matthews, Brian W. *molecular biology educator*
Maurer, Robert Distler *retired industrial physicist*
Mazo, Robert Marc *retired chemistry professor*
Melnick, Robert *dean*
Miner, John Burnham *industrial relations educator, writer*
Moseley, John Travis *academic administrator, physicist, researcher*
Moses, Louis J. *psychology professor, department chairman*
Neville, Helen J. *psychology professor, neuroscientist*
Paris, Margaret L. *dean, law educator*
Pascal, C(ecil) Bennett *classics educator*
Pickett, Stephen Wesley *academic administrator, consultant*
Retallack, Gregory John *geologist, educator*
Roe, Thomas Leroy Willis *retired pediatrician*
Sanders, Jack Thomas *religious studies educator*
Scoles, Eugene Francis *lawyer, educator*
Starbuck, William Haynes *business management educator*
von Hippel, Peter Hans *chemistry professor, researcher*
Walters, Martha Lee *state supreme court justice*
Weatherhead, Andrew Kingsley *educator*
White, Patricia Marie *psychology professor, researcher*
Wilhelm, Kate (Katy Gertrude) *author*
Woolley, Donna Pearl *lumber company executive*
Youngquist, Walter Lewellyn *geologist, consultant*
Ziliak, James Patrick *economics educator*

Fall Creek
Light, Betty Jensen Pritchett *retired dean*

Florence
Ericksen, Jerald Laverne *retired science engineering educator*
Marble, Duane Francis *geography educator, researcher*
Van Horn, O. Frank *retired counselor, consultant*

Forest Grove
Burch-Pesses, Thomas Michael *music educator*
Fuiten, Helen Lorraine *small business owner*
Garcia, Sandra Pearl *language educator*
Nye, Tracy D. *psychologist*

Grants Pass
Murdock, Doris Dean *special education educator, program developer*
Smith, Barnard Elliot *management educator*

Gresham
Barnes, James Keener *retired history professor*
Cooke, Jackie (Jacqueline Marie Cooke) *elementary school educator*
Russell, Michael *chemistry professor*
Waagen, Linda Louise *elementary school educator*

Hillsboro
Dubrulle, Françoise M. *architect, painter, interior designer*
Kocharyan, Varuzhan *electrical engineer, educator, researcher*
Koh, Kwang-Jin *electrical engineer*
Kotlyar, Roza *research scientist*
Long, Men *computer engineer*
Mudanai, Sivakumar P. *research scientist*

Jacksonville
Enders, John *museum administrator, former journalist*
Hennion, Reeve Lawrence *communications executive*
O'Connor, Karl William (Goodyear Johnson) *retired lawyer*

John Day
Tuttle, Kenneth Lewis *retired engineering educator, consultant, researcher*

Joseph
Gilbert, David Erwin *academic administrator, physicist*

Keizer
Dmytryshyn, Basil *historian, educator*
Stevens, Sharon Cox *lawyer*
Stuivenga, Douglas R. *engineering educator*

Klamath Falls
Culler, David Earl *engineering educator, researcher*
Wendt, Richard L. *manufacturing executive*
Woodall, David Monroe *engineer, researcher, dean*

La Grande
Bush, Ken *theater educator*
Espinosa, Leandro *composer, conductor, educator*

Lake Oswego
Byczynski, Edward Frank *lawyer, corporate financial executive*
Gehrig, Edward Harry *electrical engineer, consultant*
Hutchens, Tyra Thornton *pathologist, educator*
Julien, Robert Michael *anesthesiologist, writer*
McKay, Laura L. *bank executive, consultant*
McPeak, Merrill Anthony *retired military officer, investor, company director*
Owen, Berniece Marie *law librarian, director*
Parrick, Gerald Hathaway *communications and marketing executive*
Rasmussen, Richard Robert *lawyer*
Wicklund, Lee Arthur *retired school system administrator*

Lebanon
Griswold, Elaine C. *nurse, consultant*

Lincoln City
Arant, Eugene Wesley *lawyer*

Lorane
Plésums, Guntis *architect, retired educator*

Lowell
Boyle, John Howard *history educator*

Madras
Ramsey, Jarold William *literature and language professor, writer*

Mcminnville
Nelson, Donna Gayle *state legislator*
Walker, Charles Urmston *retired university president*

Medford
Carter, William G. *lawyer*
Deatherage, William Vernon *lawyer*
De Boer, Sidney B. *automotive executive*
Dixon, Andrew Derart *retired academic administrator*
Entorf, Richard Carl *retired management consultant*
Franklin, Darlene Kay *elementary school educator*
Gill, Gudrun *retired language educator*
Schubert, Ruth Carol Hickok *artist, educator*
Shekhar, Stephen S. *obstetrician, gynecologist*
Straus, David A. *architectural firm executive*

Milton Freewater
Gipson, Stephen Richard *journalist, construction executive*
Piefer, Thomas R. *history educator*

Milwaukie
Sklovsky, Robert J. *naturopathic physician, pharmacist, educator*

Monmouth
Chong, Che *marketing executive*
Dunn, Doris Marjory *retired secondary school educator, volunteer*
Lee, Gordon *composer, educator*
Rector, John Lawrence *history professor*

Myrtle Creek
Atwater, James E. *chemist, chemical engineer*

Myrtle Point
Walsh, Don *engineer, consultant*

Newberg
Adams, Wayne Verdun *pediatric psychologist, educator*
Foster, Michael R. *engineering educator*
Johnson, Thomas Floyd *former academic administrator, educator*
Keith, Pauline Mary *artist, illustrator, writer*
Koler, Robert Donald *medical educator*
Warford, Patricia *psychologist*

Newport
Ferraro, Steven Peter *marine biologist, researcher*
Gilhooly, David James III *artist*
Goudy, Josephine Gray *social worker*
Morrow, James Thomas *energy executive*
Pavlish, Catherine Ann *language educator, writer*

North Bend
Hudson, Mary Anne *public health nurse*

Oakland
Lopez, Delia *real estate manager*

Oceanside
Wadlow, Joan Krueger *retired academic administrator, construction executive*

Oregon City
Bown, Jennifer Porter *biology professor*
Lounsbury, Steven Richard *lawyer*

Pendleton
Klepper, Elizabeth Lee *retired physiologist*
Muller, Michael *land use planner, educator*
Reese, Julie *museum director, association administrator*
Smiley, Richard Wayne *researcher*

Phoenix
Dodd, Darlene Mae *retired nurse, retired military officer*

Portland
Abel, William Edward *applied physicist, consultant*
Abravanel, Allan Ray *lawyer*
Adams, Sam *Mayor, Portland, Oregon*
Anastasiou, Harry *international peace and conflict studies professor*
Andresen, Michael Christian *biomedical research scientist*
Arthur, Michael Elbert *financial advisor, lawyer*
Atkinson, Patricia Anne Webster *economics professor*
Backlar, Byron *lawyer*
Bacon, Vicky Lee *lighting services executive*
Balkowiec, Agnieszka Zofia *science educator, researcher*
Ball, Melvyn *medical educator*
Barbeau, Monique Andrée *chef*
Bartlett, Thomas Alva *retired educational administrator*
Basci, Pelin *literature and language professor*
Bates, Doug *editor*
Beatty, John Cabeen, Jr. *judge*
Beckerman, James Gregg *cardiologist*
Beckham, Stephen Dow *history educator*
Beer, Tomasz M. *physician*
Bennett, William Michael *internist, educator, nephrologist*
Bentley-Quintero, Sarah Catherine *language educator*
Berentsen, Kurtis George *music educator, conductor*
Bhatia, Peter K. *editor, journalist*
Bierzychudek, Paulette F. *biology educator*
Blank, Eugene *pediatrician, radiologist, educator*
Bleich, Michael Robert *dean, nursing educator*
Bleiler, Steven A. *mathematician*
Blumenauer, Earl *United States Representative from Oregon*
Boutwell, Anne Dielschneider *artist, painter*
Bragdon, Paul Errol *retired academic administrator, educator*
Brenneman, Delbert Jay *lawyer*
Browne, Joseph Peter *retired librarian*
Bryant, Carmen Julia *missionary, educator*
Bunza, Linda Hathaway *editor, writer, composer, director*
Burchiel, Kim James *neurosurgeon*
Cable, John Franklin *lawyer*
Campbell, John Richard *pediatric surgeon*
Carter, John D. *metal products executive*
Casey, Daniel E. *psychiatrist, educator*
Cereghino, James Joseph *health facility administrator, neurologist*
Cheifetz, Hamilton *music educator*
Cherala, Ganesh *healthcare educator, researcher*
Christensen, John F. *psychologist, director*
Cohen, Norm *chemist, music historian*
Collins, Maribeth Wilson *retired foundation administrator*
Conkling, Roger Linton *management consultant, business administration educator, retired utilities executive*
Cook, Nena *lawyer*
Cooke, Roger Anthony *lawyer, manufacturing executive*
Crowell, John B., Jr. *lawyer, former government official*
Daneshmand, Siamak *urologist*
Detweiler-Bedell, Jerusha Beth *psychology professor*
Diver, Colin S. *academic administrator, educator*
Donegan, Mark *metal products executive*
Druker, Brian Jay *medical educator, researcher*
Dunn, Randall Lawson *judge*
Ebberts, Blaine Daniel *biologist*
Ebert, Leslie *artist*
Engelberg, Elaine A. *retired secondary school educator*
English, Stephen Francis *lawyer*
Epperson, Eric Robert *finance executive, film producer*
Epstein, Edward Louis *lawyer*
Erickson, Mike *transportation executive*
Faller, Thompson Mason *philosophy educator*
Fan, Lee Siu *professional-technical training educator, entrepreneur, business executive, management consultant*
Farner, Darla A. *artist*
Fawls, Maurita Therese *economics professor*
Fernandez, Rudy *professional basketball player*
Ferris, Kassim M. *patent lawyer*
Ferriso, Brian J. *museum director*
Feuerstein, Howard M. *lawyer*
Filip, Gregory Michael *forest pathologist*
Finley, Lewis Merren *financial consultant*
Fisher, Ann Lewis *judge*
Foley, Ridgway Knight, Jr. *lawyer, writer*
Fraunfelder, Frederick Theodore *ophthalmologist, educator*
Friesen, David Douglas *musician, educator, composer*
Furse, Elizabeth *Former United States Representative, Oregon, small business owner*
Gard, Gary Lee *chemistry professor, researcher*
Glanville, Jerry *college football coach, former professional football coach*
Goodson, Raymond Eugene *business educator, retired automotive executive*
Graber, Susan P. *federal judge*
Grady-Weliky, Tana Annette *psychiatrist, educator*
Gu, Danan *demographer*
Hacker, Thomas Owen *architect*
Hagel, Shawn R. *corporate financial executive*
Hagenstein, William David *forester, consultant*
Hanna, Harry Mitchell *lawyer*
Harnden, Edwin A. *lawyer*
Harris, Charles David *music educator*
Hatfield, Mark Odom *former senator*
Hayashi, Satomi *language educator*
Hays, Daniel J. *theater educator*
Hickcox, Leslie Kay *health education educator consultant*
Hinckley, Gregory Keith *software industry executive*
Hinkle, Charles Frederick *lawyer, educator*
Hirshon, Robert Edward *lawyer*
Hochstettler, Thomas John *academic administrator, historian*
Hoffman, Alice *writer*
Hudson, Jerry E. *foundation administrator*
Hunt, Barry L. *performing arts educator, director*
Hyun, Saang-Yoon *research scientist, consultant*
Jacob, Stanley Wallace *surgeon, educator*
Jarvis, Peter R. *lawyer*
Johnson, Virginia Macpherson *secondary school educator, consultant*
Johnston, David Frederick *lawyer*
Johnston, Virginia Evelyn *retired editor*
Jolles, Bernard *lawyer*
Jones, Robert Edward *federal judge*
Josephson, Richard Carl *lawyer*
Kalmar, Carlos *conductor, music director*
Kanter, Stephen *lawyer, educator, dean*
Kardon, Joshua R. *legislative staff member*
Katz, Vera *former mayor, college administrator, state legislator*
Kaufman, John Andrew *radiologist*
Kendall, John Walker, Jr. *internist, researcher, dean*
Kester, Randall Blair *lawyer*
Khalil, Mohammad Aslam Khan *environmental science, engineering and physics educator*
Kim, Sunghan *research scientist*
Klonoff, Robert Howard *lawyer, educator*
Kocaoglu, Dundar F. *engineering management educator, industrial engineer, civil engineer*
Koenenkamp, Rolf *physics professor*
Kohn, Melvin A. *state agency administrator, public health service officer*
Kohne, Heidi Ann *church musician*
Korb, Christine Ann *music therapist, researcher, educator*
Krol, Alfons *dermatologist, educator*
Lake, Joseph Edward *ambassador*
Lall, B. Kent *civil engineer, educator*
Larpenteur, James Albert, Jr. *retired lawyer*
Larson, Wanda Z. *writer, poet*
Larsson, William Dean *metal products executive*
Leavy, Edward *federal judge*
Leupp, Edythe Peterson *retired education educator*
Levi, Alexis *professional sports team executive, owner, agent*
Lincoln, Sandra Eleanor *retired chemistry professor*
Linstone, Harold Adrian *management consultant, educator*
Lopez, Stephanie Ann *elementary school educator, consultant*
Love, William Edward *lawyer*
Lundgren, Tamara L. *metal products executive*
Machida, Curtis A. *research molecular neurobiologist, molecular virologist, oral biologist, educator*
Maloney, Robert E., Jr. *lawyer*
Mandel, Gail *immunologist*
Martin, Kenneth E. *electrical engineer, consultant*
Matarazzo, Joseph Dominic *psychologist, educator*
Matarazzo, Ruth Gadbois *behavioral neuroscience and psychiatry professor emerita*
Maziarz, Richard Thomas *hematologist, educator*
McDowell, Michael J. *literature and language professor*
McGregor, Michael N. *writer, educator*
McMillan, Nathaniel (Nate McMillan) *professional basketball coach*
Menashe, Albert Alan *lawyer*
Merkley, Jeffery A. *United States Senator from Oregon*
Meyer, Paulette Ann *history professor*
Miller, Andre Lloyd *professional basketball player*
Miller, Larry G. *professional sports team executive*
Miller, William Richey, Jr. *lawyer*
Mooers, Christopher Northrup Kennard *physical oceanographer, educator*
Morgan, Douglas F. *public service educator*
Mosman, Michael W. *federal judge, former prosecutor*
Mowe, Gregory Robert *lawyer*
Murphy, Timothy E. *lawyer*
Myers, Hardy *former state attorney general*
Neavoll, George Franklin *writer*
Njoku, Scholastica Ibari *retired college librarian, writer*

Oden, Greg *professional basketball player*
O'Neil, Katherine Huff *lawyer*
O'Scannlain, Diarmuid Fionntain *federal judge*
Packard, Robert Goodale III *urban planner*
Pamplin, Robert Boisseau, Jr. *manufacturing company executive, minister, writer*
Parsons, Eric E. *insurance company executive*
Patterson, James Randolph *physician*
Pearson, David Petri *chemist*
Pierson, Wayne George *trust company executive*
Poehlein, Christian Heinrich *medical researcher*
Pomeroy, Naomi *chef*
Prasad, Shalini *electrical and communications engineer*
Pritchard, Kevin *professional sports team executive*
Redden, James Anthony *federal judge*
Reich, Jerome Mark *pulmonologist, consultant*
Richardson, Campbell *retired lawyer*
Richter, Peter Christian *lawyer*
Ritchie, David *communications educator, researcher*
Rosen, Steven O. *lawyer*
Rosencrantz, Lawrence *holding company executive, lawyer*
Rowe, Sandra Mims *editor*
Roy, Brandon Dawayne *professional basketball player*
Rutherford, William Drake *investment executive*
Ryan, John Duncan *lawyer*
Sandler, Alan Bart *oncologist*
Scott, John D. *pharmacologist*
Seymour, B(arbara) J(ean) *social worker*
Shangraw, Robert Edward *medical educator, researcher*
Sheard, Tim *science educator*
Shertz, Laurie *lawyer*
Simpson, Robert Glenn *lawyer*
Skopil, Otto Richard, Jr. *federal judge*
Smith, Carole *school system administrator*
Smith, Dennis B. *neurologist, educator*
Smith, Meredith Wood *political organization administrator*
Starr, Albert *thoracic surgeon, educator, research scientist*
Steiner, Kenneth Donald *bishop*
Steinman, Lisa Malinowski *English literature educator, writer*
Stickel, Frederick A. *publishing executive*
Stone, Richard James *lawyer*
Stott, Peter Walter *investment company executive*
Stowell, Christopher R. *performing company executive, choreographer, retired dancer*
Street, Terry M. *artist, educator*
Stueber, Nancy *museum director*
Sullivan, Donal D. *federal judge*
Sullivan, Edward Joseph *lawyer*
Sussman, Michael David *orthopedic surgeon*
Sutherland, Donald Wood *retired cardiologist*
Swanstrom, Lee Leray *surgeon*
Swenson, Constance Rae *lawyer*
Taylor, J(ocelyn) Mary *museum director, educator, zoologist*
Taylor, Robert Brown *physician, educator, writer*
Tiernan, Bob (Robert Tiernan) *political organization administrator, former state legislator*
Tobin, Allen Gerald (Jerry) *science educator*
Trimble, Anmarie *language educator, editor*
Tucker, Roy W. *lawyer*
Tuska, Jon *writer, publishing executive*
Underwood, Jan Marie *language educator*
Vanderslice, Ellen *architect, composer*
Van Hoomissen, George Albert *state supreme court justice*
Van Valkenburg, Edgar Walter *lawyer*
Vaughan, Thomas James Gregory *historian, writer*
Waggoner, James Clyde *lawyer*
Walker, Morgan Wailes *art educator*
Wall, Brian Raymond *forest economist, business consultant, researcher*
Watkins, Charles Reynolds *medical equipment company executive*
Watne, Donald Arthur *retired accountant, educator*
Weber, George Richard *financial and internet marketing executive, writer*
Weeks, Wilford Frank *retired geophysics educator, glaciologist*
Westbrook, Gary L. *neurologist*
Westwood, James Nicholson *lawyer*
White, Douglas James, Jr. *lawyer*
Wiens, Arthur Nicholai *psychology professor*
Wildin, Robert *medical geneticist*
Williamson, Charles Ready III *lawyer*
Wilson, Owen Meredith, Jr. *lawyer, mediator, arbitrator*
Wilson, William Harwell *psychiatrist, educator*
Wood, Cynthia Wilder *elementary school educator*
Wood, Marcus Andrew *lawyer*
Wooster, Rossitza Bouneva *economics professor*
Wrightman, Caroline Anne McGhee *nursing educator*
Wu, David *United States Representative from Oregon*
Yamayee, Zia Ahmad *engineering educator, dean*
Zalutsky, Morton Herman *lawyer*
Zerbe, Kathryn Jane *psychiatrist*

Prineville
Geisen, Michael *science educator*

Redmond
Dey, Charlotte Jane *retired community health nurse*

Roseburg
Ball, Char Lee Frances *retired special education educator*
Gugel, Merilynn Sue *artist*
Little, James Stewart *military officer*
Oliphant, Charles Romig *retired physician*

Salem
Balmer, Thomas Ancil *state supreme court justice*
Breen, Richard F., Jr. *law librarian, educator*
Brown, Eden Rose *lawyer*
Brown, Kate *state official, former state legislator*
Burdick, Ginny Marie *state legislator*
Butts, Edward Perry *civil engineer, environmental & water consultant*
Carter, Margaret Louise *state legislator*
Castillo, Susan *state official, school system administrator*
Clark, David Scott *law educator, consultant*
De Muniz, Paul J. *state supreme court chief justice*
Dubanevich, Keith Scott *lawyer*
Durham, Robert Donald, Jr. *state supreme court justice*
Gangle, Sandra Smith *arbitrator, mediator*
Gillette, W. Michael *state supreme court justice*
Haselton, Rick Thomas *lawyer*
Hunt, David G. *state legislator, coalition executive*
Kistler, Rives *state supreme court justice*
Kroger, John Richard *state attorney general, former prosecutor, law educator*
Kulongoski, Ted (Theodore Ralph Kulongoski) *Governor of Oregon, former state supreme court justice*
Linde, Hans Arthur *state supreme court justice*
Linder, Virginia Lynn *state supreme court justice*
Loftus, Ronald Phelps *literature and language professor*
Mainwaring, William Lewis *publishing company executive, author*
Mannix, Kevin Leese *lawyer*
Nafziger, James Albert Richmond *law educator*
Olbrantz, John Paul *museum director, art historian*
Peterson, Edwin J. *retired judge, mediator, educator*
Robertson, Marian Ella (Hall) *small business owner, handwriting analyst*
Scheppke, Jim *library director*
Tatman, David C. *state banking agency administrator*
Taylor, Janet R. *Mayor, Salem, Oregon*
Westlund, Ben (Bernard John Westlund II) *state treasurer*
Wu, Hekun Andre *music educator, director*

Sandy
Jensen, Judy Dianne *psychotherapist, consultant*
Rosier, David Lewis *retired investment banker*

Stayton
Gay, Larry Kenneth *artist, automotive executive, consultant*
Zumwalt, Roger Carl *healthcare accreditation consultant*

Summerville
Hopkins, Gerald Frank *trade association administrator*

Talent
MacMillen, Richard Edward *biological sciences educator, researcher*

The Dalles
Hayden, I. Jill *secondary school educator*

Tigard
DeRuntz, John A., Jr. *computer scientist*

Troutdale
Unis, Richard L. *judge*

Tualatin
Hick, Kenneth William *marketing executive*
Peters, Robert Wayne *small business owner*
Tongue, John Richard *orthopedist*
West, Michael G. *electric power industry executive*

Waldport
Smith, John William Hugh *civil engineer*

Welches
Merrill, William Dean *retired architect, medical facility planning consultant*

West Linn
Bohrer, Richard William *author, editor, educator*

Wilsonville
Gordon, John Charles *forestry educator*

Yachats
Robeck, Mildred Coen *retired education educator, writer*

PENNSYLVANIA

Abington
Anderson, Valerie B. *actress, writer*
Bildersee, Robert Alan *lawyer*

Acme
Boggs, Brenda Lee *religious studies educator, librarian*

Adrian
Hogg, Yvonne Marie *principal*

Akron
Dickinson, Margery Elsie *missionary, clinical psychologist*
Leithmann, David Edward *music educator*
Rupley, Lawrence A. *economics professor*

Aldan
Stegmuller, Agnes Leonore *physical education educator*

Aliquippa
Staby, Dorothy Louise *elementary school educator*

Allentown
Arangio, George A. *orthopedist, educator*
Balog, Ibolya *accountant*
Barraco, Robert Don *surgeon*
Barres, John O. *bishop*
Battle, Turner Charles III *art educator, educational association administrator*
Beltzner, Gail Ann *music educator*
Bennett, Siobhan L. (Sam Bennett) *small business owner*
Borger, Ann Work *computer and communications professional*
Brown, W(illiam) Douglas *lawyer*
Brunner, John Wilson *foreign language educator*
Coyle, Charles A. *marketing educator*
Cullen, Edward Peter *bishop emeritus*
Dearborn, Karen *performing arts educator, director*
Doughty, George Franklin *airport administrator*
Farr, Paul A. *electric power industry executive*
Gammon, Sally (Sara T. Gammon) *hospital administrator, physical therapist*
Gaylor, Donald Hughes *surgeon, educator*
Gewartowski, James Walter *retired electrical engineer*
Grey, Robert J. (Bob Grey) *lawyer, electric power industry executive*
Heitmann, George Joseph *business educator, consultant*
Hemerly, Dorothea M. *music educator, director*
Holt, Leon Conrad, Jr. *lawyer, chemicals executive*
Huck, Paul E. *chemicals company executive*
Hutton, William Michael *technology & consulting executive*
Jacobs, Michelle Munno *performing arts educator*
Jones, Stephen J. *lawyer, chemicals company executive*
Kocsis, James Paul *artist*
Liebhaber, Barbara *music educator*
Lovett, John Robert *retired chemical company executive*
Maffeo, Alphonse A. *anesthesiologist*
McGlade, John E. *chemicals executive*
Miller, James H. *electric power industry executive*
Osterweil, Ara Cybele *art educator*
Pavelich, Judith *retired secondary school educator*
Perry, Gregory J. *museum director*
Platt, William Henry *judge*
Saab, Deanne Keltum *real estate broker, appraiser*
Sacks, Patricia Ann *librarian, consultant*
Slimmer, David Allen *physics educator*
Smulian, John C. *obstetrician*
Spence, William H. *electric power industry executive*
Tjeltveit, Alan C. *psychology professor*

Allison Park
Ewalt, Henry Ward *lawyer*
Herrington, John David III *retired lawyer, director*
Howe, Eleanor B. *librarian, educator*
Jones, Carolyn Jane *minister*
LaDow, C. Stuart *financial consultant*
Rulis, Christopher C. *lawyer*
Toerge, Lynn *athletic trainer*

Altoona
Anthony, Bertha M. *minister*
Cutsforth-Huber, Bonnie Bridget *music educator, singer*
Gurman, Andrew William *orthopedist, educator*
Moffitt, Charles William *owner servello gallery art*
Tormey, Brian B. *environmental geomorphologist, aerial mapping consultant*

Ambler
Carey, Francis James *investment banker*
Kim, Junghoon *medical researcher, educator*
Veber, Daniel Frank *chemist, researcher*

Ambridge
Powell, Pamela Baker *education educator, minister*

Annville
Mecham, Mark Leonidas *music educator, department chairman*
Verhoek, Susan Elizabeth *botany educator*

Ardmore
Goodrich, Edward (Ned) Olin *surgeon, educator*
Honebrink, Ann Louise *gynecologist, educator*
Levy, Rochelle Feldman *artist*
Weiss, Marisa C. *breast cancer oncologist, non-profit breast cancer organization executive*
Zito, Allison Ann *textile weaver, member*

Ashland
Polyakov, Yuriy Sergeyevich *engineer, researcher*

Aspinwall
Eckert, Jean Patricia *elementary school educator*

Aston
DiMarco, David *mathematician, educator*
Kain, James P. *literature and language educator*

Atglen
Souders, Roberta Belshaw *literature and language educator*

Audubon
Williams, Lawrence Soper, Jr. *photographer*

Avondale
Friel, Daniel Denwood, Sr. *manufacturing executive*

Bakerstown
Beachley, Michael Charles *radiologist*

Bala Cynwyd
Corliss, John Ozro *zoology educator*
Dorwart, Bonnie Brice *historian, retired rheumatologist*
Garrity, Vincent Francis, Jr. *lawyer*
Glazer, William H. *real estate developer*
Hancock, Herbert Jeffrey (Herbie Hancock) *composer, pianist, publisher*
Manko, Joseph Martin, Sr. *lawyer*
Mattison, Priscilla Jane *lawyer*
Miller, L. Martin *accountant, financial planner*
Murphey, Murray Griffin *history professor*
Oswald, James Marlin *education educator, researcher*
Peret, Karen Krzyminski *health facility administrator*
Shepard, Geoffrey Carroll *insurance company executive*
Wiener, Thomas Eli *lawyer*

Bath
Ditty, Mary Dawn *secondary school educator*

Beach Lake
Chatlos, William Edward *management consultant*

Beaver
Strock, Robert S. *retired education educator*

Beaver Falls
Ancil, Ralph E. *economics educator*
Copeland, Robert Marshall *music educator, department chairman*
Miller, Albert Jay *retired library director*

Belle Vernon
Wapiennik, Carl Francis *manufacturing executive, planetarium and science institute administrator*

Bensalem
Carruthers, Catherine Douglas *surgeon*
Kang, Benjamin Toyeong *journalist, minister*
Long, Robert C. *retired military officer, management consultant*
Osterhout, Richard Cadwallader *lawyer*
O'Toole, Michael Anthony *academic administrator*
Rosskamm, Alan D. *retail executive*
Segal, Robert Martin *lawyer*

Bentleyville
Blasko, Barbara Ann *secondary school educator*

Berwick
Pasukinis, Cheryl Renee *elementary school educator*

Berwyn
Bluestone, Ellen Hope *literature, writing, and women's studies professor, writer*
Devlin, Thomas McKeown *biochemist, educator*
Fry, Clarence Herbert *retired retail executive*
Hambrecht, William R. *investment banking firm executive*
Huffaker, John Boston *lawyer*
Kauffman, Joel Mervin *retired chemistry educator, researcher, consultant, medical writer*
Seidel, Arthur Harris *lawyer*
Watters, Edward McLain III *lawyer*

Bethel Park
Florig, Patricia Stickle *music educator*
Korchynsky, Michael *metallurgical engineer*
Menees, Katherine Determan *retired parochial school educator*
Willard, John Gerard *communications executive, consultant, writer, educator*

Bethlehem
Agbeh, Anthony Odey *education educator, consultant*
Allen, Beatrice *music educator, pianist*
Aronson, Jay Richard *economics professor, researcher, academic administrator*
Barsness, Richard Webster *management educator, academic administrator*
Bartoli, Filbert J. *electrical engineer, educator*
Binford, Hilde Marga *music educator*
Cao, Huai-Dong *mathematician*
Caskie, Grace I. L. *statistics professor*
Chisholm, Darlene Chris *economics educator*
Christodoulides, Demetrios Nicolaou *electrical engineering educator*
Cordero, Lidia Estrada *psychologist, social worker*
Dent, Charles Wieder (Charlie Dent) *United States Representative from Pennsylvania*
Diggs, David B. *musician*
El-Aasser, Mohamed S. *engineering educator, academic administrator*
Gaeta, Jane *minister*
Gardiner, Keith Mattinson *engineering executive, educator*
Gast, Alice Petry *academic administrator, chemical engineering educator*
Guillon, Christophe *research scientist*
Gulick, Sean Paul Sandifer *geologist*
Hartmann, Robert Elliott *retired manufacturing executive*
Heindel, Ned Duane *chemistry professor*
Hemphill, Meredith, Jr. *retired lawyer*
Herman, Richard Gerald *research chemist, consultant, educator*
Kanofsky, Alvin Sheldon *physics professor*
Kim, Yong Wook *physicist, educator*
Koel, Bruce Edward *chemist, educator, researcher*
Kovalskiy, Andriy *research scientist*
Lyman, Charles Edson *materials scientist, educator*
Marsh, Robert Harry *chemicals executive*
Michopoulos, John George *civil engineer, researcher*
Mirro, John *engineering company executive*
Neti, Sudhakar *mechanical engineering educator*
Parmet, Harriet Abbey L. *literature educator*
Pavlock, Barbara R. *literature and language professor*
Pense, Alan Wiggins *metallurgical engineer, academic administrator*
Rambo, Kelly Clifford *lawyer*
Saeger, James Schofield *history professor, writer*
St. John, Anthony Paul *retired manufacturing executive*
Schattschneider, Doris Jean *retired mathematics professor*
Sengupta, Arup Kumar *engineering educator, researcher*
Smolansky, Bettie Moretz *sociology educator*
Smyth, Donald Morgan *chemistry professor, researcher*
Spillman, Robert Arnold *architect*
Steffen, Lloyd Howard *minister, religious studies educator*

Stella, John Anthony *financial executive*
Taggart, Bruce M. *library administrator*
Tan, Gang *engineering educator*
Terlaky, Tamás *mathematics educator*
Trautmann, Nancy E. *language educator*
Treisner, George Henry, Jr. *vocational educator, electrical contractor, financial advisor and tax consultant*
Voloshin, Arkady *mechanical engineering and mechanics educator*
Wetcher-Hendricks, Debra Elizabeth *social sciences educator*
Wu, S. David *dean, industrial and systems engineering educator*

Birdsboro
Dieffenbach, Lisa M. *music educator*

Blairsville
Stiffler, Erma Delores *minister, pastoral counselor, retired elementary school educator*

Bloomsburg
Bertelsen, Dale Alan *communications educator*
Brasch, Walter Milton *journalist, educator*
Decker, Mark Tingey *literature and language professor*
Defenbaugh, Nicole Lynn *communications studies professor*
Greene, Nathaniel Robert *physics professor*
Obiozor, Williams Emeka *special education educator*
Oman, Terina Louise *nursing educator*
Srinivasan, Avinash *science educator*
Trapane, Ruth *educator, artist*

Blue Bell
Agersborg, Helmer Pareli K. *pharmaceutical company executive, researcher*
Blazey, Douglas R. *lawyer*
Brownlowe, William Harold *engineer*
Chhatwal, Jagpreet *health economist*
Coleman, J. Edward (Ed Coleman) *information technology executive, former computer company executive*
Deschaine, Barbara Ralph *retired real estate broker*
Earl, Judy *microbiologist, educator*
Edwards, Joselle Elizabeth *performing arts educator*
Elliott, John Michael *lawyer*
Evans, John Derelc *marketing executive*
Giordano, Nicholas Anthony *brokerage house executive*
Gregson, Nigel Christopher *pharmaceutical executive, consultant*
Haugen, Janet B. *corporate financial executive*
Lazar, Stanley William *history professor*
May, Barbara *social sciences educator*
Raskin, Anna Viktorovna (Roper Raskin) *history professor*
Roden, Carol Looney *retired language educator*
Rounick, Jack A. *lawyer, clothing retail executive*
Sundheim, Nancy Straus *lawyer, computer company executive*
Swansen, Samuel Theodore *lawyer*
Venuti, Elaine M. *biology professor*
Wilson, H(arold) Fred(erick) *chemist, research scientist*

Boalsburg
Gardner, James Richard *retired pharmaceutical company executive, investor*
Gettig, Martin Winthrop *retired mechanical engineer*

Boyers
Shiloh, Allen *writer*

Boyertown
Fortes, Brenda Joyce *English language educator*
Lydic, Nadine K. *music educator*

Bradford
Frederick, Richard George *history professor*
Hopkins, Judy G. *literature and language educator*

Bridgeville
Marcinek, Cara A. *psychologist*
Moore, Daniel Edmund *psychologist, educator, retired educational administrator*

Bristol
Card, Wesley Roy *apparel and footwear company executive*
Kimmel, Sidney *apparel company executive, film producer*
McClain, John T. *corporate financial executive*
Murphy, Patrick Joseph *United States Representative from Pennsylvania*

Broomall
Fras, Christian Ivan *orthopedist*

Brownsville
Martin, Richard H. *principal*

Bryn Athyn
Henderson, Brian D. *history professor*

Bryn Mawr
Ackoff, Russell Lincoln *social systems designer, educator*
Anderson, Eric Edward *psychologist, consultant, healthcare executive, educator*
Baird, John Absalom, Jr. *retired academic administrator*
Bernstein, Eric Ferenc *dermatologist, educator*
Braha, Thomas I. *oil industry executive*
Brunt, Manly Yates, Jr. *psychiatrist*
Burciaga, Juan Ramon *physics professor*
Crawford, Maria Luisa Buse *geology educator*
Dudden, Arthur Power *historian, educator*
Eiser, Barbara J.A. *management consultant, executive coach*
Frank, Edward David, II, *history educator*
Frick, Benjamin Charles *lawyer*
Gaisser, Julia Haig *classics educator*
Godinez, Marye H. *anesthesiologist*
Goutman, Lois Clair *retired drama educator*
Harte, Tim *history professor*
Hegedus, L. Louis *chemical engineer, consultant, retired research and development company executive*
Hirsh, Sharon Latchaw *academic administrator, art history educator*
Huth, Edward Janavel *internist, educator, editor*
Krausz, Michael *philosopher, educator*
Lane, Barbara Miller (Barbara Miller-Lane) *humanities educator*
Lang, Mabel Louise *classics educator*
Levitt, Robert E. *gastroenterologist*
McAuliffe, Jane Dammen *academic administrator, religious studies and Islamic studies educator*
McCabe, Louise Beachboard *language educator*
Moyer, F. Stanton *financial executive*
Noone, Robert Barrett *plastic surgeon*
Pew, Robert Anderson *retired real estate and equipment leasing corporation officer*
Phillips, Stephen S. *lawyer*
Pietrzak, Rona *dean, director*
Porter, Judith Deborah Revitch *sociologist*
Roszkowski, Michael Joseph *psychologist*
Thompson, Geraldine Kelleher Richter *retired orthopedist*
Thompson, Wayne Wray *historian*
Vickers, Nancy J. *retired academic administrator*
Webber, John Bentley *orthopedic surgeon*

Buffalo Mills
Duppstadt, William Homer *retired botanist, educator, lay worker*

Bushkill
Garretto, Leonard Anthony, Jr. *insurance company executive*

Butler
Walsh, Joy Irene *literature and language educator*

California
Pokol, Albert Ronald *librarian*

Camp Hill
Brandow, Theo *architect*
Cardinale, Gerald P. (Jerry Cardinale) *retail executive*
Davis, Don P. *retail executive*
Donley, Douglas E. *retail executive*
Fazzolari, Salvatore D. *mining products executive*
Hall, Christopher S. *retail executive*
Johnston, Thomas McElree, Jr. *retired church administrator*
Keough, Philip J., IV, *retail executive*
Learish, John *retail executive*
Lester, Wilson A., Jr. *retail executive*
Mackin, Charles Philip, Jr. *lawyer*
Martindale, Kenneth Allen *retail executive*
Mastrian, James P. *retail executive*
Mazzolla, D. Patrick *healthcare services executive*
McGeary, Barbara Joyce *artist, educator*
Mead, James Matthew *insurance company executive*
Miller, Robert G. *drug store chain company executive*
Rugen, Karen *retail executive, corporate communications specialist*
Sammons, Mary Frances *retail executive*
Shirtliff, Bryan *retail executive*
Standley, John T. *retail executive*
Strassler, Marc A. *lawyer, retail executive*
Tokuhata, George K. *retired medical educator, epidemiologist, consultant*
Vitrano, Frank G. *retail executive*
Yates, James Arthur *plastic surgeon*

Canonsburg
Bresch, Heather M. *pharmaceutical executive*
Cashman, James E. III *engineering software company executive*
Coury, Robert J. *pharmaceutical executive*
Harvey, J. Brett *energy executive*
Mascetta, Joseph Anthony *principal*
Richey, P. Jerome *lawyer, energy executive*
Smith, Peter J. *engineering software company executive*
Southern, David W. *history professor*
Varney, Jolene *corporate financial executive*

Carlisle
Bowers, Teresa Marie *music educator*
Butler, William Elliott *lawyer, educator*
Crane, Conrad C. *history professor*
Darr, Jonelle Prether *librarian*
Durden, William G. *academic administrator*
Efird, Cynthia Grissom *academic administrator, former ambassador*
Fish, Chester Boardman, Jr. *retired editor*
Fox, Arturo Angel *Spanish language educator*
Laws, Kenneth L. *physics professor*
Long, Howard Charles *retired physics professor*
McConnaughay, Philip J. *dean, law educator*
Shrader, Charles Reginald *historian*
Vickery, Jon Livingstone *neurologist*

Catawissa
Gardner, Paula J. *psychologist*

Center Valley
Gambet, Daniel G(eorge) *academic administrator, minister*
Hojjat, Tahereh Alavi *economics professor*
Lewis, Anne M. *actress, educator*
Razze, Dennis *theater educator, director*
Risher, William Henry *cardiothoracic surgeon, educator*

Chadds Ford
Duff, James Henry *museum director, environmental services administrator*
Isakoff, Sheldon Erwin *chemical engineer*

Chalfont
Ashley, Kathleen Labonis *elementary school educator*
Wilson, Jean Louise *state legislator*

Chambersburg
Elias, Janilyn *student personnel director*
O'Connor, John Morris III *retired humanities educator*
Rumler, Robert Hoke *agricultural products executive, consultant, retired trade association administrator*

Charleroi
Lekse, William John *water transportation executive*

Cheltenham
Fleisher, Linda *medical researcher, director*
Weinstock, Walter Wolfe *systems engineer*

Chester
Bruce, Robert James *retired academic administrator*
Buck, Lawrence Paul *history professor, former academic administrator*
Harris, James Thomas III *college administrator, educator*
Huang, Zhongping *engineering educator*
Nicosia, Mark *engineering educator*
Nippert, Charles *engineering educator, department chairman*
Prewitt Diaz, Joseph O. *psychologist, educator*
Saad, Germaine H. *business management professor, researcher*
Thompson, Jayne Marie *literature and language professor*

Chesterbrook
Chou, John G. *lawyer*
Collis, Steven H. *corporate financial executive*
Cox, Karen Michelle *finance educator, computer company executive*
DiCandilo, Michael D. *corporate financial executive, accountant*
Gozon, Richard C. *pharmaceutical executive, retired paper distribution executive*

Cheyney
Bagley, Edythe Scott *theater educator*
Gaffin, Virgilette Nzingha *language educator, department chairman*
Mullaney, Beth Jo *school librarian*

Clairton
Mina, John Louis (Ivan Minea) *religious studies educator, archivist*

Clarion
Feroz, Raymond Felix *rehabilitation sciences professor*
Foreman, Thomas Alexander *dentist*
Goodman, Greg S. *education educator*
Trejos, Sandra Roxana *economics professor*

Clarks Green
Bourcier, Richard Joseph *retired French language and literature educator*
Kubic, Charles Richard *civil engineer*

Clarks Summit
Evans, Lynn Susan *financial planner*

Clearfield
Krebs, Margaret Eloise *publishing executive*
McCracken, Mark B. *county official*

Coatesville
Ainslie, George William *psychiatrist*

Cochranville
Sazegar, Morteza *artist*

Collegeville
Alesci, Salvatore *science association director*
Chambliss, Catherine Anne *psychologist, educator*
Ellison, Mark *chemistry professor*
Harris, Philip A. *chemist*
Mahady, Joseph Michael *pharmaceutical executive*
O'Neill, Heather Munro *economics professor*
Quinet, Elaine Marie *molecular biologist, researcher*
Sabatucci, Joseph P. *chemist*
Strassburger, John Robert *academic administrator*

Connellsville
Humbert, Kimberly Ramsay *secondary school educator*
Shearer, Linda Rae *English educator*

Conshohocken
Barry, Michael F. *chemicals company executive*
Naples, Ronald James *manufacturing executive*
Spaeth, Karl Henry *retired chemicals executive, lawyer*
Spiers-Lopez, Pernille (Pernille Lopez) *consumer products company executive*
Thompson, Pamela Padwick *public relations executive*

Coopersburg
Bednar, Charles Sokol *political science professor*
Siess, Alfred Albert, Jr. *engineering executive, management consultant*

Coplay
Norbeck, Jack Carl *library exhibitor*
Stockman, Kathleen Helen *elementary school educator*

Coraopolis
Beaver, William R. *sociology professor*
Kay, George Paul *environmental engineer*
Koepfinger, Joseph Leo *retired utilities executive*

Cranberry Township
Hart, Melissa Anne *former congresswoman*
Lorenz, John George *librarian, consultant*

Dallas
Betterly, Richard Douglas *historian, educator*
Filipiak, Stephen *web programmer, educator*
Liuzzo, Anthony L. *economic educator*
Rogan, Joseph P. *special education educator*

Danville
Blankenship, James Colegrove *cardiologist*
Maroon, Michele Senga *dermatologist*
Pierce, James Clarence *surgeon, educator*
Sidorov, Jaan Erik *physician, researcher*
Steele, Glenn Daniel, Jr. *oncologist, healthcare system executive*
Toms, Steven A. *neurosurgeon, researcher*

Darby
Eiser, Arnold Robert *physician executive, bioethicist, nephrologist, internist, medical educator*

Delta
Quesenbery, Erika Lynn *media specialist, curator*
Withrow, James A. *music educator*

Denver
Milner, Charles Fremont, Jr. *manufacturing executive*

Derry
Baltzer, Cynthia Louise *music educator*

Devon
Boehne, Edward George *banker*
Porter, Roger John *research and development company executive, neurologist, pharmacologist*
Quinn, Lois Marie *health service innovator*
Toth, Marian Davies *Teacher, Author Educational Administrator,*
Wilson, Malcolm Campbell *investment trust management executive*

Dillsburg
Jackson, George Lyman *retired nuclear medicine physician*

Dover
Butterfield, Andrea Christine *school system administrator*

Downingtown
Deb, Arun Kumar *environmental engineer*
Romanosky, LuAnn *elementary school educator*
Scheer, R. Scott *physician*
Sweeney, Sarina Marie *psychologist, consultant*
Wusinich, Joseph F. III *lawyer, educator*

Doylestown
Elliott, Richard Howard *lawyer*
Katsiff, Bruce *artist*
Manion, Tom *pharmaceutical executive*
Mishler, John Milton (Yochanan Menashsheh ben Shaul) *science educator, artist*
Solly, Richard Peter *music educator*
Thomas, Ellen Louise *school system administrator*

Dresher
Faust, Carrissima Washington *educational consultant*
Levicoff, Valerie Ann *music educator*

Drexel Hill
Benglian, Barbara Mason *music educator*
Martino, Michael Charles *entertainer, musician, actor*
Thompson, William David *minister, educator*
Tirado, Janet A. *advertising marketing and public relations communications executive*
Williams, W. Craig *prosecutor*

Duncansville
Shoaf, Frank Joseph *military officer*
Smith, D. Brooks *federal judge*

Dunmore
Marino, Thomas A. *lawyer, former prosecutor*
Timlin, James Clifford *bishop emeritus*

East Petersburg
Pedrow, Brenda M. *retired language educator*

East Stroudsburg
Che, Dongsheng *computer scientist, educator*
Kansfield, Norman J. *former seminary president*
Meyers, Ronald J. *literature and language professor*
Romano, Stephanie Anne *education educator, consultant*
Squeri, Lawrence *history professor*
Switzer, Sharon Cecile *language educator, researcher*
Waters, Faith H. *retired education educator*

Easton
Bellissimo, Mary E. *art educator*
Bose, Ajay Kumar *chemistry professor emeritus*
Brown, Robert Carroll, Jr. *lawyer*
Dougherty, Andrew *physics professor*
Ferri, James K. *science educator*
Grunberg, Robert Leon Willy *nephrologist, educator*
Holmes, Larry *retired professional boxer*
Hughes, Michael P. *principal*
Kincaid, John *political science professor, editor*
Lamb-Faffelberger, Margarete Barbara *foreign language educator*
McConlogue, Terence R. *protective services official*
McMahon, Elizabeth Wagner *mathematician, educator*
Milgrim, Roger Michael *lawyer*
Murphy, Bruce Allen *government and law educator, writer*
Schlueter, June Mayer *literature educator, writer*

Stull, Frank Walter *elementary school educator*
Sun, Robert Zu Jei *manufacturing company executive, inventor, educator*
Teboh-Ewungkem, Miranda Ijang *education educator*
Traldi, Lorenzo *mathematician, educator*
Trigiano, Lucien Lewis *physician*
Van Antwerpen, Franklin Stuart *federal judge*
Weiss, Daniel H. *academic administrator, former dean*

Edgemont
Davis, Scott Charles *music educator, political activist*

Edinboro
Bemko, Ihor Jurij Tadej *history professor*
Chompalov, Ivan Mihailov *social sciences educator*
Gendlin, Gerry *political science educator*

Eighty Four
Hardy, Joseph A., Sr. *wholesale distribution executive*
Magerko, Margaret Hardy (Maggie) *lumber company executive*

Elizabethtown
Brown, Dale Weaver *clergyman, theology studies educator*
Bucher, Christina *religious studies educator*
Dietz, William Dunfee, Jr. *elementary school educator*
Garber, Margaret Mary *elementary school educator*
Gordon, Laurie Anne *academic director*
Lobdell, Jared Charles *editor, educator*
Mead, Dana Gulling *literature and language professor*
Ritsch, Frederick Field *academic administrator, historian*
Sample, Frederick Palmer *former college president*
Wennberg, Hans-Erik *communications educator*

Elkins Park
Burnley, June Williams *secondary school educator*
Davidson, Abraham Aba *art historian, educator, photographer*
Erlebacher, Martha Mayer *artist, educator*
Esquenazi, Alberto *physiatrist*
Pak, Hyung Woong *community advocate*
Stinnett, Hester *art school administrator, educator*
Zelac, Ronald Edward *physicist*

Emlenton
Berg, Janice Carol *elementary school educator*

Emmaus
Bowers, Klaus D(ieter) *electronics executive, researcher*
Dorn, Jonathan Andrew *editor-in-chief*
Murcko, Mary *publishing executive*
Rodale, Ardath Harter *publishing executive*
Rodale, Maria *publishing executive*

Enola
Beatty, Robert Clinton *religious studies educator*

Ephrata
Reed, Galen K. *music educator*

Erdenheim
Schiff, Lawrence Alan *dentist*

Erie
Baker, Parris Jerome *humanities educator*
Brunner-Martinez, Kirstin Ellen *pediatrician, psychiatrist*
Burgoyne, Noel Jaeger *retired secondary school educator*
Cavanaugh, Terrence W. *insurance company executive*
Daly, Mary *college administrator*
Evans, Karen L. *education educator, director*
Ftorek, Robbie Brian (Robert Brian Ftorek) *professional hockey coach, retired professional hockey player*
Gauriloff, Larry Paul *biology professor, researcher*
Giannelli, Mariagrazi Licia *language educator*
Gilloteaux, Jacques Jean-Marie Anthime *cell biologist, researcher*
Glaser, Earleen R. *school librarian, archivist*
Gottschalk, Frank Klaus *real estate company executive*
Hagen, Thomas Bailey *business owner, former state official, retired insurance company executive*
Hay, Christine Marie *dancer, educator*
Jones, Darci *school librarian, director*
Kondylis, Philip Demetrios *colon and rectal surgeon*
Ludrof, Jeffrey A. *insurance company executive*
Mason, Gregg Claude *orthopedic surgeon, researcher*
Maxted, Lawrence Richard *librarian*
Michaelides, Doros Nikita *internist, medical educator*
Renkis, Alan Ilmars *plastics formulating company executive*
Staniunas Hopper, Jodi Ann *graphics designer, educator*
Su, Meng *science educator*
Sucha, George R. *education educator*
Tanous, James Joseph *lawyer, insurance company executive*
Trautman, Donald Walter *bishop*
Vanco, John L. *art museum director*
Welch, William James *journalist, educator*
Wise, Penelope M. *librarian*
Zelazny, Catherine *retired elementary school educator*
Zhao, Lin *engineering educator*

Evans City
Pagonis, William Gus *retired army general*

Everett
Barr, Tony *special education educator*
Whetstone, Joni Lee *music educator*

Export
Carter, Linda Whitehead *oncological nurse, educator*

Exton
Bertolino, Dean A. *lawyer*

Fairfield
Freund, John Richard *former English educator*

Fairless Hills
Frazier, Brett W. *waste management executive*

Fairview
Graziani, Linda Ann *secondary school educator*
Sorhannus, Ulf Mikael *biology professor*
Stern, Marilyn Jean *special education educator*

Fallsington
Foote, Kathryn Ann *music educator*

Fayetteville
Molitor, Graham Thomas Tate *lawyer*
Scarlata, Paul Anthony *oral surgeon*

Feasterville Trevose
Kats, Marina *lawyer*

Flourtown
Christy, John Gilray *diversified financial services company executive*
Cooke, Sara Mullin Graff *daycare provider, kindergarten educator, medical assistant*

Fogelsville
Huang, Tai-Yin *physics professor*

Ford City
Smits, Ronald Francis *retired language educator, poet*

Fort Washington
Hallman, Patricia L. *retired musician*

Franklin
Sauer, Mary Julia *special education educator*

Frazer
Baldino, Frank, Jr. *biopharmaceutical executive*
Pappert, Jerry (Gerald J. Pappert) *lawyer, former state attorney general*

Fredericksburg
Daubert, Harlan Aaron *music educator, director*

Fredericktown
Molinaro-Thompson, David Robert *secondary school educator*

Friedens
Shaffer, Brenda Joyce *minister*

Friendsville
Bjick, Suzanne Carter *psychologist*

Gaines
Beller, Martin Leonard *retired orthopaedic surgeon*

Gap
Burton, Mary Louise Himes *retired information technology executive*
Slater, Bruce *small business owner*

Garnet Valley
Chirinos, Julio Alonso *physician, researcher*

Gettysburg
Coughenour, Kavin Luther *career officer, military historian*
Hallberg, Budd Jaye *retired management consulting firm executive*
Harman, Troy D. *history professor*
Hendrix, Sherman Samuel *biology professor, researcher*
Riggs, Janet Morgan *academic administrator, psychology professor*
Roach, James Clark *retired federal agency administrator*
Sasnett, Kathleen Beth *theater educator, director*
Snively, Carolyn S. *ancient language educator, archaeologist*

Gibsonia
Benson, Stuart Wells III *lawyer*
Groves, Michael *banker*
Krause, Helen Fox *retired otolaryngologist*
Lichina, April Marie *elementary school educator*

Gladwyne
Acton, David *lawyer*
Booth, Harold Waverly *lawyer, finance company executive*
Cooney, Patricia Ruth *civic worker*
Geisel, Cameron Meade, Jr. *retired bank executive*
Kaye, Donald *internist, educator*
Morrison, Gail *internist, nephrologist, educator*
Patten, Lanny Ray *gas industry executive*
Silvers, Willys Kent *geneticist*

Glen Mills
Churchill, Stuart Winston *chemical engineering educator*
Goldberg, Morton Edward *pharmacologist*
Huang, Wenlin *research scientist*
Kaufman, Antoinette Dolores *information technology manager*
O'Tanyi, Theodore J., Jr. *retired biology professor*

Glenmoore
Fix, Irene M. *pianist*

Glenolden
Malykhina, Anna P. *medical educator*

Glenshaw
Vogrin, Joseph Edward III *lawyer*
Wilkes, John Michael *military officer, auditor*

Glenside
Block, Isaac Edward *professional society administrator*
Kleckner, Chris J. *theater educator*
Medel, Rebecca Rosalie *artist*
Mermelstein, Jules Joshua *lawyer, educator, commissioner*
Reiss, George Russell, Jr. *physician*
Thompson, Joan Hulse *political science professor*
Trueman, Carl Russell *theology studies educator*
Willig, Barbara Adele *music educator*

Grantham
Cornacchio, Rachel Ann *music educator*
Gulde, Katharine Haynes *musician, educator*
LaGrand, James B. *history professor*
Mark, Kenneth Dean *museum director, educator*
Patrick, Nancy J. *special education educator, researcher*

Greencastle
Scott, Leighton Reeves *interior designer, artist, writer*
Wertime, Timothy Ray *music educator*

Greensburg
Bosco, Anthony Gerard *bishop emeritus*
Brandt, Lawrence Eugene *bishop*
Demosky, Lou Anne *lawyer*
Duck, Patricia Mary *librarian*
Evanson, Paul John *utilities executive*
Ference, Edward W. *engineering executive, structural engineer*
Freidheim, Cyrus F., Jr. *former publishing and food products executive*
Gibson, Donald Elmer *sociologist, educator, writer*
Gounley, Dennis Joseph *lawyer*
Greenfield, Sayre Nelson *literature and language professor*
Honeygosky, Stephen R. *priest, educator*
Langer, Alois *biomedical engineer*
Neff, Mary Ellen Andre *retired elementary school educator*
Ramm, Douglas Robert *psychologist*

Greentown
Forcheskie, Carl S. *former apparel company executive*

Greenville
Morrill, Allen S. *library director*
Reinhart, Connie S. *academic administrator, educator*

Grove City
Dixon, James George III *literature and language professor, department chairman, theater director*
Fair, Mark C. *engineering educator*
Moser, Mary Ann *music educator, director*
Spradley, Garey B. *philosopher, educator, rancher, theologian*
Throckmorton, Warren *psychology professor, consultant*
Tinkey, Patricia A. *literature and language professor*
Trammell, Catherine Louise *language educator*

Hallstead
Remakus, Bernard Leo *physician, medical educator, writer, medical journalist*

Hanover
Davis, Ruth Carol *pharmacist, educator*
Kline, Donald *food company executive*

Harleysville
Geraghty, Paul D. *bank executive*
Salomon, Mark *chemist*
Smagalski, Carolyn M. *publishing executive, webmaster, director*

Harrisburg
Adams, Barbara *lawyer*
Angino, Richard Carmen *lawyer*
Bailey, Diandrea Michelle *rehabilitation services professional*
Bishop, Louise Williams *state legislator*
Boswell, James Aurthur, Jr. *English language educator*
Brown, John Walter *vocational education supervisor*
Cadieux, Roger Joseph *geriatrics services professional*
Cavanaugh, John C. *academic administrator, psychology professor*
Chernicoff, David Paul *osteopathic physician, educator*
Cockeram, Paul D. *humanities educator*
Corbett, Thomas Wingett, Jr. *state attorney general, lawyer*
Cortés, Pedro A. *Secretary of the Commonwealth, Pennsylvania*
Dennis, VanEngelsdorp *agriculturist*
Derk, Patricia Keach *retired secondary school educator*
Diehm, James Warren *lawyer, educator*
Dinniman, Andrew Eric *state legislator, international studies and history professor*
Fenstermacher, Joyce Doris *real estate agent and appraiser*
Fine, David R. *lawyer*
Fontana, Mark Allan *lawyer*
Franco, Barbara Alice *museum director*
Fulmer, Deborah Lee *education educator, oncological nurse*
Gilhooley, Antoinette (Toni Gilhooley) *retired protective services official*
Gleason, Robert A., Jr. *political organization administrator*
Gornish, Gerald *lawyer*
Gover, Raymond Lewis *retired newspaper executive*
James, Everette *state agency administrator*
Kane, Yvette *lawyer, judge*
Kaplan, Steven *state banking agency administrator*
Kelly, Robert Edward, Jr. *lawyer*
Knackstedt, Mary V. *interior designer*
Koones, Donald Gregory *associate dean, educator*
Kreidie, Marwan *human services administrator*
Lappas, Spero Thomas *lawyer*
Leighow, Jack (John C. Leighow, Jr.) *museum director*
Mahey, John Andrew *retired museum director*
McCord, Robert M. *state treasurer*
Meilton, Sandra L. *lawyer*
O'Brien, Dennis M. *state legislator*
Pileggi, Dominic F. *state legislator*
Pizzingrilli, Kim *state official*
Reider, Victoria A. *state banking agency administrator*
Rendell, Edward Gene *Governor of Pennsylvania, retired mayor, lawyer*
Rhoades, Kevin Carl *bishop*
Rooney, Terence Joseph (T.J.) *political organization administrator, former state legislator*
Rudy, Frank R. *pathologist*
Saylor, Thomas G. *state supreme court justice*
Scarnati, Joseph B. III *Lieutenant Governor of Pennsylvania, state legislator*
Schneider, Nina Michelle *nursing educator*
Sheldon, J. Michael *lawyer, educator*
Smith, Eric Ledell *historian*
Stanley, Edward Alexander *geologist, paleontologist, researcher, retired director, forensic specialist*
Sullivan, John Cornelius, Jr. *lawyer*
Warshaw, Allen Charles *lawyer*
West, James Joseph *lawyer*
Weston, R. Timothy *lawyer, government administrator*
Williams, Constance *state legislator*
Williams, Jewell *state legislator*
Wolfe, Gary Donald *commissioner, retired librarian*
Zales, Mary Clare *library director*

Hatfield
Jesberg, Robert Ottis, Jr. *educational consultant, science educator*
Shi, Hongjian *research scientist*

Haverford
Aronson, Carl Edward *pharmacology and toxicology educator*
Brown, William Hill III *lawyer*
Castillo Sandoval, Roberto *literature and language professor*
DiBerardino, Marie Antoinette *developmental biologist, educator*
Emerson, Stephen G. *academic administrator, oncologist, hematologist, educator*
Gollub, Jerry Paul *physics professor*
Gutwirth, Marcel Marc *literature educator*
Jilani, Saleha *economics assistant professor*
Kee, Howard Clark *religion educator*
Kitroeff, Alexander *history professor*
McGovern, Stephen John *political scientist*
Meyers, Mary Ann *foundation administrator, consultant, writer*
Noordergraaf, Abraham *biophysics educator*
Palmer, Richard Ware *retired lawyer*
Stiller, Jennifer A. *lawyer*
Stroud, James Stanley *retired lawyer*
Wernick, Richard Frank *composer, conductor, educator*
Williams, William Earle *artist, educator, curator*

Havertown
Crouse, Carol K. Mavromatis *elementary school educator*
Evarts, Mary H. *retired mathematics educator*
Hendrickson, Paul Joseph *journalist, writer, educator*
Wing, Kennard Thompson *educational organization official*
Wright, Cecilia Powers *gifted and talented educator*

Hazleton
Barletta, Louis *mayor*

Hershey
Berlin, Cheston Milton, Jr. *pediatrician, educator*
Bixler, Edward O. *psychiatrist, educator*
Buck, Michele G. *food products executive*
Caputo, Gregory Michael *internist, educator*
Collins, Christopher Michael *engineering educator*
Davis, Dwight *cardiologist, educator*
Eyster, Mary Elaine *hematologist, educator*
Fedok, Fred G. *plastic surgeon, educator*
Ghossaini, Soha Nadim *medical educator*
Hauck, Randy Milton *surgeon, educator*
Hopper, Anita Klein *molecular genetics educator*
Hufford, David J. *humanities educator*
Janicki, Piotr K. *anesthesiologist, educator*
Jones, Marshall Bush *education educator, researcher*
Kauffman, Gordon Lee, Jr. *surgeon, educator*
Krieg, Arthur Frederick *pathologist*
Lynch, Scott Alan *orthopedist, educator*
Madewell, John Edward *radiologist*
Marks, James Garfield, Jr. *dermatologist*
Naeye, Richard L. *pathologist, educator*
Ostrov, Barbara E. *physician*
Paz, Harold Louis *hospital administrator, internist, educator*
Pierce, William Schuler *cardiac surgeon*
Planas-Silva, Maricarmen Delia *cancer researcher*
Schuller, Diane Ethel *allergist, immunologist, educator*
Severs, Walter Bruce *pharmacology educator, researcher*
Sheaffer, Cristal S. *music educator*
Shope, Timothy Robert *medical educator*
Snyder, Burton Harold *lawyer*
Tan, Tjiauw-Ling *psychiatrist, educator*

Thomas, Patrick Robert Maxwell oncologist, educator, academic administrator
Uhde, Thomas Whitley psychopharmacology, psychiatrist
Undar, Akif research scientist, biomedical engineer, educator
Vesell, Elliot Saul pharmacologist, educator
Waldhausen, John Anton retired surgeon, editor
Wassner, Steven Joel pediatric nephrologist, educator
West, David J. food products executive
Zagon, Ian Stuart neuroscience and anatomy educator, researcher, inventor
Zelis, Robert Felix cardiologist, educator

Hollidaysburg
Adamec, Joseph Victor bishop
Bloom, Lawrence Stephen retired clothing company executive
McPhee, Norma Howatt publishing executive, author
Shuster, William (Bill Shuster) United States Representative from Pennsylvania

Homestead
Mandel, Herbert Maurice civil engineer

Honesdale
Barbe, Walter Burke education educator
Brown, Kent Louis, Jr. magazine editor

Horsham
Barzilay, Zvi real estate developer
Best, Franklin Luther, Jr. lawyer
Christian, Mildred Stoehr health products executive
Cohen, Michael R. health facility administrator, pharmacist
DeHoratius, Raphael Joseph rheumatologist
Harrison, Deborah Lynn accountant, consultant
Ippolito, Andrew science educator, photographer
Rassmann, Joel H. H. corporate financial executive
Sachs, Keith L. manufacturing executive
Toll, Bruce Elliot real estate developer
Toll, Robert Irwin home construction company executive

Hughesville
Kuhar, Deborah Ann librarian

Hulmeville
Jackson, Mary L. health services executive

Hummelstown
Biebuyck, Julien Francois physician, anesthesiologist, medical administrator, educator

Huntingdon
Kepple, Thomas Ray, Jr. college administrator
Mathur, Ryan social sciences educator
Rosell, Karen J. art history professor
Schettler, Paul D. chemistry professor

Huntingdon Valley
Godfrey, John Carl medicinal chemist
Gryminska, Teresa Lidia literature and language professor, interpreter
Holland, Burt S. statistics educator, consultant
Krzyzanowski, Richard L. lawyer
West, A(rnold) Sumner chemical engineer

Immaculata
Comber, George Thomas psychology professor

Indiana
Alkhatnai, Mubarak H. language educator
Al-Shammari, Hussam A. management educator
Atwater, Tony university president
Ciano-Federoff, Lynda psychologist, educator
Hood, Michael James theater educator, arts administrator
Hwang, Eun Jin education educator
Jalongo, Mary Renck educator
Maina, Joshua Y. electronics engineer, researcher
Mannard, Joseph Gerard history professor
Mc Cauley, R. Paul criminologist, educator
McCreary, Patrick theater educator, director
Miller, Vincent Paul, Jr. geography and regional planning educator
Nealen, Paul science educator
Reynolds, Virginia Edith sociologist, anthropologist, educator, artist
Sherwood, Kenneth W. language educator
Stoudt, Gary Scott mathematics professor

Irwin
Brown, Donald Clyde surgeon
Kuhn, Howard Arthur engineering executive, educator
Perich, Terry Miller retired secondary school educator

Jamison
Touhill, C. Joseph environmental engineer

Jefferson Hills
Smith, Leslie Edgar vocational school administrator

Jenkintown
Bales, John Foster III retired lawyer
Black, Thomas Donald retired religious organization administrator
Hidalgo, Alfreda Edith elementary school educator
Mason, John Murwyn, Jr. bank executive
Oh, Soojin Susan elementary school educator
Sadoff, Robert Leslie psychiatrist, educator

Jim Thorpe
Bickel, Jean Louise school librarian
Meneeley, Edward Sterling artist

Johnstown
Alcamo, Frank Paul retired principal
Dewey, Joseph Owen literature and language professor
Errett, Daniella K. Cope psychology professor
Frye, Randy L. finance educator
Kaharick, Jerome John lawyer
Kilpatrick, Stephen Timothy biology professor
McGrath, John Michael educator
Miloro, Protopresbyter Frank religious organization administrator, theology studies educator
Ondrejcak, Sally Suzanne psychotherapist
Smisko, Nicholas Richard bishop, educator

Kelton
Gulick, Walter Lawrence psychologist, educator, retired academic administrator

Kennett Square
Conard, Alfred Fletcher legal educator
Harrington, Anne Wilson medical librarian
Hennes, Robert Taft former management consultant, investment executive
Hinz, Carl Frederick, Jr. immunologist, educator
Landstrom, Elsie Hayes retired editor
Long, Kimberly A. biologist, educator
Martin, George (Whitney) writer
Orsini, James A. veterinarian, educator, author, surgeon, editor
Richardson, Dean Wheeler equine surgeon, veterinary educator
Smith, Virginia Eleanore psychologist, educator
van der Veur, Paul W. humanities educator

King Of Prussia
Burda, Steven financial analyst and manager
Clauson, Sharyn Ferne consulting company executive, educator
Davis, Charles Baldwin chemist
Filton, Steve G. corporate financial executive
Gallis, John Nicholas retired military officer, executive leadership training consultant
Gilbert, Bruce Rits lawyer
Goldsmith, Eleanor Jean retired hospital administrator
Greenberg, Lon Richard energy executive, lawyer
Gunn-Morton, Dawnell S. auditor
Helmetag, Diana music educator
Katolik, Leonid I. surgeon, educator
Lee, Robert engineer
Lubiniecki, Anthony Stanley microbiologist, researcher
Miller, Alan B. hospital management executive
Schumann, Paula M. L. writer
Souney, Paul Frederick pharmacist
Swank, Annette Marie software designer
Thorneloe, Kevin S. biologist
Turner, Peter biopharmaceutical company executive
Volpe, Ralph Pasquale retired insurance company executive
Walsh, John L. energy executive
Waterworth, Dawn Marie research and development company executive, director
Zajac, Matthew A. chemist

Kingston
Weisberger, Barbara artistic director, advisor, educator

Knox
Rupert, Elizabeth Anastasia retired dean

Kutztown
Gupta, Venu Gopal psychology professor
Meyer, Susan Moon speech pathologist, educator
Vasko, Francis Joseph mathematics professor
Watson, Carol Elizabeth education educator

La Plume
Boehm, Edward Gordon, Jr. college administrator, educator
Jennings, Patricia A. literature and language educator
White, Sara Kathryn literature and language professor

Lafayette Hill
Delacato, Janice Elaine special education educator, consultant
Eagleson, William Boal, Jr. banker
Edwards, JoAnn Louise human resources executive
Miller, Nancy Lois senior pastor

Lake Ariel
Petrosky, Michele Marie school librarian

Lake Harmony
Polansky, Larry Paul legal association administrator

Lancaster
Bell, Frances Louise medical technologist
Binkley, Luther John philosophy educator
Buchanan, Lovell entertainer
Burkholder, Michele Stawinski lawyer
Burlingame, Mark Wayne cardiothoracic surgeon
Carlisle, James Patton entrepreneur
Ebersole, Mark Chester emeritus college president
Fry, John Anderson academic administrator
Glick, Garland Wayne retired theological seminary president
Hanahoe-Dosch, Patricia language educator
High, S. Dale construction executive
Joseph, John historian, educator
Kelly, Robert Lynn advertising executive
Kneedler, (Alvin) Richard academic administrator
Lockhart, Michael D. manufacturing executive
Markley, Jill L. music educator
Matthews, Kelly E. chemistry professor
Maula, Mohammad Mojibul biology professor
Nast, Dianne Martha lawyer
Poser, Joan Rapps artist, writer
Rigas, John Nicholas lawyer
Schuyler, David P. historian, educator
Shaw, Charles Raymond journalist
Shelley, Leo Eugene retired librarian
Shenk, Lois Elaine Landis writer
Steiner, Robert Lisle retired language educator
Taylor, Ann writer, educator
Tien, Joy Garcia mathematics, human development counseling professor
Zimmerman, Donald Patrick lawyer

Langhorne
Caruso, Dominic J. pharmaceutical executive
Day, Melvin Sherman retired information and telecommunications company executive
Manyak, Michael John urologist, educator, researcher
Palladino, Christopher James social studies educator
Schoenstadt, Barbara Laison special education educator

Lansdale
Bierman, Arnold optometrist
Didden, Lynn Williams music educator
Fawley, John Jones retired banker
Geiger, Alexander lawyer
Hargens, Charles William III electrical engineer, consultant
Sensenig, David Martin retired surgeon
Strohecker, Leon Harry, Jr. orthodontist

Lansdowne
Geist, Lorraine Pinnelli music educator, director
Purcell, Mary Hamilton speech educator
Tolliver, Elkin, Jr. judge

Latrobe
Cardoso, Carlos M. metal products executive
Dur, Philip Alphonse retired shipbuilding executive, military officer
Greenfield, David W. lawyer
Gruber, Mark Francis priest, educator
Koehl, Jennifer biology professor
McLevish, Timothy R. food products executive
Porembka, Michael Richard assistant principal, supervisor
Quinlivan, Gary M. dean, educator
Towey, Jim (H. James Towey) academic administrator, former federal official

Lawrenceville
Kipferl, Christiana A. special education educator

Lehman
Felty, Wayne Lee chemist, educator
Williams, Thomas Alan high school guidance counselor, small business owner

Lemoyne
Custer, John Charles portfolio manager
Stewart, Richard Williams lawyer

Leola
Chatterjee, Hem Chandra electrical engineer

Levittown
Edson, Megan school librarian
Ferraro, Ronald Louis health facility administrator
Henshaw, Jonathan Cook retired manufacturing executive

Lewisburg
Candland, Douglas Keith psychology professor
Delgado-Morales, Manuel language educator
Edgerton, Mills Fox retired foreign language educator
Fernsler, John Paul lawyer
Hauck, William Edward retired education educator
Jump, Chester Jackson, Jr. clergyman, church official
Kochel, R. Craig geologist, educator
Mastascusa, Edward John electrical engineering educator
Mitchell, Brian Christopher academic administrator
Muller, Riana Ricci musician, educator
Neuman, Nancy Adams Mosshammer civic leader
Nottis, Katharyn E.K. educational psychologist, researcher
Payne, Michael David English language educator
Pizzorno-Simpson, Marie C. biology professor, department chairman
Siewers, Alfred Kentigern Karlson literature educator
Smith, Marguerite Irene gifted and talented educator

Lewistown
Levin, Allen Joseph lawyer

Ligonier
Mellon, Seward Prosser brokerage house executive
Pilz, Alfred Norman manufacturing executive
Vogelsang, Eric R. language educator, basketball and soccer coach

Limerick
Black, Jeffrey P. manufacturing executive

Lincoln University
Bradt, Donald James III political science professor
Major, Helen E. physics professor, researcher
Nelson, Ivory Vance academic administrator
Norris, JoAnne Wareham school counselor
Nwachuku, Levi Akalazu social sciences and behavioral studies educator
Van Dover, James Kenneth education educator
Venerable, Grant Delbert, II, chemist, educator, systems scientist
Williams, Willie, Jr. physicist, researcher

Lititz
Gingerich, Naomi R. emergency room nurse
Lehman, Richard William electrical engineer
Sandercox, Robert Allen academic administrator, minister

Lock Haven
Forbes, Edward John, III, (Ted Forbes) retired developmental psychologist, educator
Fulton, Tara Lynn library director, academic administrator
Jia, Dongdong nanoscience and physics educator
Lima, Sally Murphy education educator
Satya, Laxman D. history professor
Story, Julie Ann language educator

Loretto
Balough, Sandra A. library director
Jareb, Jerome history professor, researcher, retired
Langer, Marian biology professor

Lower Burrell
Croushore, James counseling administrator

Lower Gwynedd
Pendleton, Robert Grubb pharmacologist

Loysburg
Stuckey, Ellen Mae music educator

Lykens
Sultzbaugh, John Stephan retired historian, educator, researcher

Macungie
Rubin, Arthur Herman retired academic administrator

Malvern
Brennan, Jack (John Joseph Brennan) investment company executive
Cameron, John Clifford lawyer, health science association administrator
Dohan, Andrew H. lawyer
Espe, Matthew J. manufacturing executive
Ferran, Carlos finance educator
Flynn, James R. augusterian priest, school system administrator
Hallenbeck, Paul Leon medical researcher, director
McNabb, F. William, III, (Bill McNabb) investment company executive
Mulford, Richard Albert mechanical engineer, professional society administrator
Paul, Gerald D. electronics executive
Qiu, Robin G. adult education educator
Roggio, Bob retired manufacturing executive
Zandman, Felix electronics executive

Manns Choice
Braendel, Douglas Arthur hotel executive

Mansfield
DiMarco, Scott R. library director
Gaskievicz, Andrew history professor, department chairman
Keeth, William P. language educator
Maris, Robert C. biologist, educator
Monkelien, Sheryl L. music educator
Washington, Edward T. literature and language professor

Marion Center
Purdy, David Lawrence medical products executive

Marshalls Creek
Svoboda, Joanne Dzitko artist, educator

Martinsburg
Neff, Robert Wilbur academic administrator, educator, minister

Marysville
Trigilio, John Patricio pastor

Mc Elhattan
Garner, Charles William retired educational administration educator, consultant

Mc Keesport
House, Audrey Ann school librarian
Kessler, Steven Fisher lawyer
Micale, Frank Jude lawyer

Mc Murray
Langenberg, Frederick Charles manufacturing executive

Meadville
Adams, Earl William, Jr. retired economics professor
Helmreich, Jonathan Ernst history professor
Stewart, Anne Williams historian, writer, researcher

Mechanicsburg
Eakin, J. Michael state supreme court justice
Earle, Jane I. biologist, consultant
Harper, Diane Marie retired corporate communications specialist
Juditz, Lillian Mickley retired communications educator
Ortenzio, Robert A. health and medical products executive
Ortenzio, Rocco Anthony health products executive
Owen, Tony Quinn investment company executive, horse trainer
Page, William J. criminal justice educator

Media
Barnett, Samuel Treutlen consultant
Behbehanian, Mahin Fazeli surgeon
Bonnell, Allen Thomas college president emeritus, consultant
Bortner, Doyle McClean retired college dean
Bury, Lorraine secondary school educator
Durham, James W. lawyer
Emerson, Sterling Jonathan lawyer
Garrison, Walter R. engineering executive, director
Garvin, Florence Ward management consultant
Ginsberg, Robert E. philosophy educator, editor
Robertson, James Henry history professor
Sestak, Joe (Joseph A. Sestak Jr.) United States Representative from Pennsylvania, retired military officer
Voltz, Sterling Ernest physical chemist, researcher

Mendenhall
Reinert, Norbert Frederick *lawyer, retired chemicals executive*

Mercer
DaCosta, Caroline Lee *small business owner*

Merion Station
Burch, Francis Floyd *clergyman*
Gillman, Derek A. *museum director, academic administrator*

Middletown
Clark, Shirley Elizabeth *engineering educator*
Walters, Marian R. *research administrator*

Mifflinville
Farber, Phillip Andrew *retired biological and allied health sciences educator*

Milford
Le Guin, Ursula Kroeber *writer*

Milford Square
Sewell, Gloriana *music educator*

Millersville
Briola, Richard David *literature and language educator*
Dushkina, Natalia Mitkova *physicist, researcher*
Gaudry-Hudson, Christine M. *literature and French language professor*
Himmele, Persida *language educator, consultant*
Miller, Steven Max *humanities educator*
Rineer, Carla Mary *literature and language professor*
Shin, Duckhee *literature and language professor*

Millville
Gilmore, Stephen R. *retired ancient language educator*

Monaca
Haggerty, Denny C. *physics professor*

Monongahela
Yovanof, Silvana *physician*

Monroeville
Skolnick, Herbert *geologist*
Skolnick, Marilyn *civic worker*
Wagner, Greg William *computer scientist, educator*

Mont Alto
Doncheski, Michael A. *physics professor*

Montoursville
Huff, Carl Raymond *academic administrator*

Moon Township
Alstadt, Lynn Jeffery *lawyer*
Cellante, Donna L. *dean*
Eckman, Robin Jean *literature and language professor*
Elliott, Lisa J. *choreographer, educator*
Harold, Philip J. *political science professor*
Maurer, Cheryl *lab administrator, researcher*
Racic, Stanko *finance educator*

Mount Joy
Lodde, Gordon Maynard *health physics consultant*

Mount Pleasant
Collins, Frederick George *music educator, secondary school educator*
Dangelo, Eugene Michael *elementary school educator*
Morgan, Joyce Kaye *social worker*

Murrysville
Creenan, James William *lawyer*
Ferri, Karen Lynn *lawyer*
Yang, Wen-Ching *chemical engineer*

Myerstown
Zimmerman, Dennis Neal *psychologist*

Nanticoke
Bassham, Mia Wang *university librarian*
Eddy, Carl F. *engineering educator*
Emelett, Stephen John *physicist, researcher*
Kashatus, William Charles *history professor*

Narberth
Grenald, Raymond *architectural lighting designer*
Nathanson, Neal *virologist, epidemiologist, educator*
Newhall, John Harrison *retired business executive, management consultant*
Strom, Brian Leslie *internist, educator*

Nazareth
Farbod, Faramarz *political science professor*
Ferraro, Margaret Louise (Peg) *secondary school educator*

Nelson
Kyofski, Bonelyn Lugg *retired education educator*

New Alexandria
Sehring, Hope Hutchison *library science educator*

New Cumberland
Peters, Ralph Edgar *architectural firm and engineering executive*

New Freedom
Sedlak, Valerie Frances *retired English language and literature educator, academic administrator*

New Holland
Fanus, Pauline Rife *librarian*
Papadakis, Emmanuel Philippos *physicist, consultant*
Roesch, Clarence Henry *banker*
Sheaffer, M. P. A. *educator*
Wagner, Bradley Jeremiah *agricultural engineer*

New Hope
Cook, Geoff *Internet company executive*
Coyle, Diane Bonanomi *special education educator*
Ecker, Sidney Wolf *urologist, consultant*
Freyer, Victoria C. *fashion and interior design executive*
Hover, John Calvin, II, *banker*
Pelleymounter, Mary Ann *research scientist*
Raabe, Gerhard Karl *epidemiologist*

New Kensington
Gilley, Jennifer R. *librarian*
Parks, Shannon Lynn Isovitsch *civil engineer*
Ray, Siba Prasad *materials scientist, ceramics scientist*
Wallace, Henry Jared, Jr. *lawyer*
Zaidi, Mohammad A. *metal products executive*

New Milford
Cunningham, Mary Ann Michael *secondary school educator*

New Wilmington
Lind, Robin Anna-Karin *music educator*
Long, Kenneth Maynard *chemistry professor*
Pitman, Grover Allen *music educator*

Newtown
Bernstine, Daniel O'Neal *educational association administrator, law educator*
Booraem, Hendrik, V, *education educator, historian*
Brennan, Thomas John *city and state official, consultant, educator*
Franc, Frannie *science educator, consultant*
Godwin, Robert Anthony *lawyer*
Loughran, Richard David *history professor*
Morrill, Nancy Porter *management consultant*
Rao, Sudhakar *aerospace engineer, researcher*
Ross, Edwin William *rubber company executive*
Sheridan, John J. *musician, educator*
Strauss, John *literature and language professor*

Newtown Square
Bertolet, Caroline Lynne Georgeanne *special education educator, labor union administrator*
Bower, Ward Alan *management consultant, lawyer*
Cordes, Eugene Harold *retired pharmacy and chemistry educator*
DeLuca, Jennie M. *language educator*
de Rivas, Carmela Foderaro *retired psychiatrist, health facility administrator*
Kendall, Robert Louis, Jr. *lawyer*
Lawrence, Theodore *retired physician*
McDermott, William R. *information technology executive*
Pan, Yude *forest ecologist*
Perrone, Nicholas *engineering company executive*
Ranganathan, Natarajan *research and development company executive*
Reiley, T(homas) Phillip *consultant*
Staats, Dean Roy *retired reinsurance executive*
Swing, Elizabeth Sherman *education educator*

Norristown
Aman, George Matthias III *lawyer*
Colcher, Robert Ely *surgeon*
DeMedio, Kathleen Marie *chemistry educator*

North Wales
Calder, Robert Austin *preventive medicine physician, administrator*
Fletcher, William A. *pharmaceutical executive*
Gorby-Schmidt, Martha Louise *pharmacologist, researcher*
Kim, Peter Sungbai *pharmaceutical and research and development company executive, educator*
Marth, William S. *pharmaceutical executive*
Musliner, Thomas Allen *cardiologist, director*
Nguyen, Bach-Yen T. *medical association administrator*

North Warren
Carlson-Johnson, Michelle Ann *psychologist, consultant*

Northern Cambria
Fisher, Connie Marie *physical therapist*

Nottingham
Sweeney, Richard Edward *biomedical engineer, consultant*
White, Richard Edmund *human resources specialist*

Oakdale
Wire, Gary Lee *retired metallurgist*

Oaks
Marland, Alkis Joseph *leasing company executive, computer scientist, educator, financial planner*
Snyder, Jeffrey Scott *chiropractor*

Oil City
Clemente, Nancy Ellen *school librarian*

Orefield
Armor, John N. *chemical company scientist, consultant, research manager*

Orwigsburg
Mason, Joan Ellen *nurse*

Oxford
Bowden, Mark Robert *writer*
Cole, Charles Chester, Jr. *academic administrator*

Paoli
Brundage, Russell Archibald *retired data processing executive*
Burget, Dean Edwin, Jr. *plastic surgeon*
Denny, William Murdoch, Jr. *investment management executive*
Gotshall, Jan Doyle *financial planner*
Hardin, John Wesley *electronics executive*
Hermance, Frank S. *electronics executive*

Penn Run
Thibadeau, Eugene Francis *education educator, consultant*

Pennsburg
Hovanec, Julia Lynne *art educator*

Perkasie
Ohama, Gary Louis *dental ceramist*

Phila
Pahl, Jon F. *religious studies educator*

Philadelphia
Abel, Edwin George, III, (Ted Abel) *biologist, educator, researcher*
Abramowitz, Robert Leslie *lawyer*
Acker, Michael A. *thoracic surgeon, educator*
Ackerman, Arlene C. *school system administrator, education professor*
Adamany, David Walter *law and political science educator, former academic administrator*
Adams, Jonathan Craig *business immigration attorney*
Adawi, Nadia Sharon *business consultant*
Adler, Freda Schaffer *criminologist, educator*
Adler, Martin William *neuropharmacologist*
Ajzenberg-Selove, Fay *physicist, researcher*
Akers, David *professional football player*
Akiyama, Cliff *forensic science educator, criminologist, researcher, gang specialist, consultant*
Albert, Todd James *orthopedist*
Alexander, William Herbert *business educator, former construction executive*
Alford, Larry P. *university librarian*
Allen, Julian Lewis *pediatric pulmonologist, medical educator*
Allen, Keith *professional sports team executive*
Altschuler, Steven M. *health facility executive, pediatrician, gastroenterologist*
Ambrosini, Paul John *child psychiatry educator*
Ammon, Gary D. *lawyer*
Ances, Beau M. *neurologist*
Anders, Jerrold P. *lawyer*
Anderson, Rolph Ely *finance educator*
Angel, Marina *law educator*
Angelakis, Michael J. *communications executive*
Anjan, Chatterjee *neurologist, educator*
Arce, A. Anthony *psychiatrist, educator*
Armstrong, Clay *physiology educator*
Arnold, Anne Katrin *communication researcher, international development civil servant*
Asbury, Arthur Knight *neurologist, educator*
Asch, David Alan *economist, educator, healthcare educator*
Auten, David Charles *lawyer*
Auten, Donald R. *lawyer*
Avgiris, Catherine *financial executive*
Ayers, Randy *professional basketball coach*
Babbel, David Frederick *finance and insurance educator*
Bagley, Demetrius H. *urologist, educator, researcher*
Ballweg, Jean A. *pediatrician, educator*
Banerji, Ranan Bihari *mathematics professor*
Banse, Amy L. *communications executive, lawyer*
Barbour, John A. (Jack Barbour) *lawyer*
Barker, Clyde Frederick *surgeon, educator*
Barnett, Bonnie Allyn *lawyer*
Barnett, Jonathan *urban planner, educator, architect*
Baron, David A. *neuropsychiatric researcher, educator*
Barrett, John J(ames), Jr. *lawyer*
Bartlett, Allen Lyman, Jr. *retired bishop*
Bartlett, Scott Paul *plastic surgeon*
Baum, Stanley *radiologist, educator*
Beck, Aaron Temkin *psychiatrist, educator*
Beck, John Robert *pathologist, information scientist*
Beck, Stuart Edwin *lawyer*
Beck, Tracey Rae *museum director*
Becker, Lance B. *medical educator*
Ben-amos, Dan *Folklore Educator*
Bennett, Jean *ophthalmologist, educator*
Benson, Romona A. Riscoe *marketing executive, museum administrator*
Berg, Ivar Elis, Jr. *social science educator*
Berger, Harold *lawyer, electrical engineer*
Berger, Lawrence Howard *lawyer*
Berkley, Emily Carolan *lawyer*
Bernard, John Marley *lawyer, educator*
Bernheim, Daniel S. *lawyer*
Bernstein, Charles *poet, writer, educator*
Bershad, Jack R. *retired lawyer*
Bersoff, Donald Neil *lawyer, psychologist, educator*
Betancourt, Philip P. *art historian, archaeologist, educator*
Beyer, Gerald John *theology educator*
Bibbo, Marluce *physician, educator*
Biddle, Daniel R. *editor, reporter*
Bigelow, Douglas C. *otolaryngologist*
Bilgutay, Nihat Mustafa *engineering educator, associate dean*
Bing, Zhanyong *medical educator*
Black, Allen Decatur *lawyer*
Black, Creed C., Jr. *lawyer*
Blackwell, Jannie L. *councilwoman*
Blaszczyk, Regina Lee *historian, writer*
Blavat, Jerry (Gerald Joseph Blavat) *radio and television personality, actor*
Block, Arthur R. *communications executive, lawyer*
Blumberg, Baruch Samuel *research scientist, educator*
Blume, Fred *lawyer*
Blume, Marshall Edward *finance educator*
Blyn-LaDrew, Roslyn *language educator*
Boden, Guenther *endocrinologist*
Bogan, Arthur Eugene *archaeologist*
Bogdanoff, Charles Jay *lawyer*
Bogen, Daniel *engineering educator*
Boggia, Eugene Stephen *lawyer*
Bogutz, Jerome Edwin *lawyer, educator*
Bonovitz, Sheldon Michael *lawyer*
Bordogna, Joseph *engineering educator, former science foundation executive*
Bortnick, Newman Mayer *research chemist*
Boss, Amelia Helen *lawyer, educator*
Boucher, Brian *professional hockey player*
Bovaird, Brendan Peter *lawyer*
Bove, Alfred Anthony *medical educator*
Brady, Luther W., Jr. *radiation overlogist, educator*
Braham, William Walter III *architecture educator*
Brand, Elton Tyron *professional basketball player*
Breiner, David M. *architecture educator*
Bressler, Barry E. *lawyer*
Bricknell, Sarah M. *lawyer*
Bridges, Charles R. *cardiologist, surgeon*
Briere, Daniel *professional hockey player*
Brigham, David R. *museum director*
Brighton, Carl Theodore *orthopedic surgery educator*
Brinster, Ralph Lawrence *biologist, educator*
Briscoe, Jack Clayton *lawyer*
Brondeau, Pierre R. *chemicals executive*
Brookman, Marc D. *lawyer*
Brooks, John Samuel Joseph *pathologist, researcher*
Brown, Blondell Reynolds *councilwoman*
Brown, Denise Scott *architect, urban planner*
Brown, Ronald Terry *psychologist, educator*
Brown, William Yancey *museum administrator*
Browne, Stanhope Stryker *lawyer*
Brucker, Alexander J. *ophthalmologist, educator*
Brucker, Paul C. *academic administrator, physician*
Buccino, Ernest John, Jr. *lawyer*
Buchholz, Carl M. *lawyer*
Buckwalter, Ronald Lawrence *federal judge*
Bucky, Louis P. *plastic surgeon, educator*
Bucurescu, Gabriel *neurologist*
Budin, Beverly R. *lawyer*
Bura, John *bishop*
Burbank, Stephen Bradner *law educator*
Burke, Jim *chef*
Burke, Stephen B. *broadcast executive*
Burstein, Elias *physicist, researcher*
Butler, Marie Gladys *nursing educator*
Callahan, James Michael *physician, educator*
Calman, Robert Frederick *mining executive*
Calvert, Jay H., Jr. *lawyer*
Campbell, Robert Murray, Jr. *surgeon, researcher*
Capanna, Robert *educational association administrator, composer*
Caplan, Arthur Leonard *university program director, educator*
Cardoza, Tonya *women's college basketball coach*
Carey, Arthur Bernard, Jr. *editor, columnist*
Carle, Matt *professional hockey player*
Carrig, Kenneth J. *human resources specialist*
Carroll, Jack Adien *rehabilitation hospital administrator*
Carter, Jeff *professional hockey player*
Casale, Pasquale *urologist, consultant, researcher*
Casper, Charles B. *lawyer*
Castille, Ronald D. *state supreme court chief justice*
Chagares, Michael Arthur *federal judge*
Chang, Howard Fenghau *law educator, consultant*
Charkes, N. David *nuclear medicine physician, educator*
Charney, Natalie J. *behavioral health services professional, researcher, clinician*
Chen, Xiaoli *pathologist*
Chen, Yibai *mass spectrometrist*
Cherken, Harry Sarkis, Jr. *lawyer*
Childress, Scott Julius *medicinal chemist*
Chiou, Richard Y. *science educator, researcher*
Choi, Jongmoo Jay *finance educator*
Chrysikou, Evangelia G. *psychology professor*
Chung, Esther Kyunghi *pediatrician*
Clair, Angelina Theresa *principal*
Clark, Peter S., II, *lawyer*
Clark, William H., Jr. *lawyer*
Clarke, Darrell L. *councilman*
Clarke, Robert Earle (Bobby Clarke) *professional sports team executive, commentator*
Clauss, Peter Otto *lawyer*
Clearfield, Harris Reynold *physician*
Cohen, Akiva S. *neuroscientist, educator*
Cohen, David Louis *communications executive*
Cohen, David Walter *academic administrator, educator, periodontist*
Cohn, Mildred *retired biochemist, educator*
Coleman, Gerald Charles *judge, educator*
Coleman, Robert J. *lawyer*
Collings, Robert L. *lawyer*
Colman, Robert Wolf *hematologist, educator*
Colson, Rosemary *music educator*
Comisky, Hope A. *lawyer*
Connolly, Colm F. *lawyer, former prosecutor*
Conway, John W. *manufacturing executive*
Cooney, J(ohn) Gordon, Jr. *lawyer*
Cooper, Edward Sawyer *retired cardiologist, internist, educator*
Cooper, Frank G. *lawyer*
Cooper, Joel David *physician, medical educator*
Cortès, Luis *religious organization administrator*
Coulson, Zoe Elizabeth *retired consumer marketing executive*
Cox, Roger Frazier *lawyer*
Coyne, Charles Cole *lawyer*
Cramer, Harold *lawyer*
Crawford, James Douglas *lawyer*
Croisetiere, Jacques M. *chemicals executive*
Cross, Milton H. *lawyer*
Crumb, George Henry *composer, educator*
Cunningham, Jacqueline Lemmé *psychologist, educator, researcher*
d'Agostino, Peter *art educator*
Dai, Hai-Lung *physical chemist, researcher*
Dalembert, Samuel Davis *professional basketball player*
Dalton, David Robert *chemistry professor*
Daly, John M. *surgeon, educator*
Damsgaard, Kell Marsh *lawyer*
D'Angelo, Christopher Scott *lawyer*
D'Angio, Giulio John *radiologist, educator*
Dasgupta, Indranil *physician, educator*
Daskalaki, Irini *medical educator*

Daugherty, F(rancis) Mark *music educator, conductor, theater director*
Davidoff, Joanne Malatesta *multi-media specialist*
Davis, Allen Freeman *history professor, writer*
Dawid, Sister Doloretta *literature and language professor*
Days, Michael *editor*
DeBunda, Salvatore Michael *lawyer*
de Cani, John Stapley *retired statistician, educator*
Decherney, Peter *media educator*
Delaney, Terence (Terry) P. *oil industry executive*
Del Raso, Joseph Vincent *lawyer*
de Paulo, Craig J. N. *priest, philosopher, educator*
Deschler, Daniel Gert *otolaryngologist, educator*
De Simone, Louis Anthony *bishop emeritus*
Devlin, John Gerard *lawyer, writer*
Diaz, Nelson A. *lawyer*
Diaz, Romulo L., Jr. *lawyer*
Di Benedetto, C. Anthony *marketing educator*
DiCapua, Christopher *literature and language professor*
Dichter, Marc Allen *physician*
DiCicco, Frank J. *councilman*
DiIulio, John J., Jr. *political science professor*
DiLeo, Tony *professional sports team executive*
DiMarino, Anthony J., Jr. *gastroenterologist, educator*
DiPalma, Joseph Rupert *pharmacology educator, dean*
Dominici, Paul G. *emergency physician*
Donahue, Timothy J. *manufacturing executive*
Donner, Henry Jay *lawyer*
Donohue, James J. *lawyer*
Donohue, John Patrick *lawyer*
Dorfman, John Charles *lawyer*
Dormans, John Paul *surgeon, educator*
Doty, Richard L. *medical researcher*
Dougherty, Brian James *lawyer*
Dougherty Buchholz, Karen *systems administrator*
Drake, William Frank, Jr. *lawyer*
Dreher, Derick *museum director*
Driscoll, Deborah Anne *gynecologist, obstetrician*
Driver, Robert Baylor, Jr. *opera company director*
Dunphy, Fran *men's college basketball coach*
Efstratiades, Anastasius *lawyer*
Ehrlich, George Edward *rheumatologist, consultant*
Eisen, Howard Joel *internist, researcher*
Eisenstein, Toby K. *microbiology professor*
Eiswerth, Barry Neil *architect, educator*
Elliott, Homer Lee *lawyer*
Ellman, Norman Stephen *language educator*
Elsenhans, Lynn Laverty *oil industry executive*
Emery, Ray *professional hockey player*
Emmett, Edward Anthony *medical practitioner, government executive*
Engstrom, Paul F. *oncologist, medical educator*
Epps, JoAnne A. *dean, law educator*
Epstein, Jonathan A. *medical educator, researcher*
Eraslan, Hulya K. *finance educator*
Erdmann, James Bernard *educational psychologist*
Eskin, Bernard Abraham *obstetrics and gynecology educator, researcher*
Esser, Carl Eric *lawyer*
Evan, William Martin *sociologist, educator*
Fala, Herman Camillo *lawyer*
Farley, Richard John *architect, engineer*
Farren, Ann Louise *chemist, information scientist, educator*
Fegley, Kenneth Allen *systems engineering educator*
Feldman, Arthur M. *cardiologist*
Fernandez, Happy Craven (Gladys) *academic administrator*
Fickler, Arlene *lawyer*
Fiebach, H. Robert *lawyer*
Fielding, Allen Fred *oral and maxillofacial surgeon, educator*
Finkelstein, Joseph Simon *lawyer*
Finney, Graham Stanley *management consultant*
Fischer, Bruce G. *oil industry executive*
Fishbein, Martin *psychologist, educator*
Fisher, Aron Baer *physiology educator*
Fisher, Marshall Lee *operations management educator*
Fishman, Alfred Paul *physician*
Fitts, Donald Dennis *chemist, educator*
Fitts, Michael Andrew *dean, law educator*
Flanagan, Joseph Patrick, Jr. *retired lawyer*
Fleisher, Lee Alan *anesthesiologist, educator*
Floyd, Michael O'S. *retired lawyer*
Foa, Edna *psychologist, educator*
Forbes, Brian John *pediatrician, orthopedist*
Foster, Gary D. *psychologist*
Fox, Renée Claire *sociology educator*
Fox, Richard L. *lawyer*
Frank, Barbara Balis *gastroenterologist, educator*
Frank, George Andrew *lawyer*
Frankel, Francine Ruth *political science professor*
Friedberg, Joseph Stewart *surgeon*
Friedenberg, Frank K. *medical educator*
Friedman, Harvey Michael *infectious diseases educator*
Fritton, Karl Andrew *lawyer*
Fromm, Eli *engineering educator*
Frucher, Meyer S. (Sandy Frucher) *stock exchange executive*
Fuchs, Barry D. *hospital administrator*
Fuller, Charles H, Jr. *playwright*
Furth, John Jacob *molecular biologist, educator, pathologist*
Fusco, Richard *English literature educator*
Gagné, Simon *professional hockey player*
Gallagher, Rollin M. *psychiatrist, anesthesiologist*
Gallagher, William T. *lawyer, manufacturing executive*
Gamble, Kenneth *recording industry executive, music producer*
Ganley, Theodore *orthopedist*
Garcia, Fernando Uriel *pathologist, educator*
Garcia, Rudolph *lawyer*
Garonzik, Sara Ellen *stage producer*
Gausas, Roberta Elisabeth *oculoplastic and orbital surgeon*
Gavrin, Jonathan Robert *medical educator, internist*
Gearhart, John D. *obstetrician, gynecologist, medical educator, developmental geneticist*
Geifman-Holtzman, Ossie *health science association administrator*
Genkin, Barry Howard *lawyer*
Gerner, Edward William *medical educator*
Giammarco, Maurizio Mercedes *literature educator, director*
Gilberg, Kenneth Roy *lawyer*
Giles, James T. *lawyer, retired federal judge*
Girard-diCarlo, David Franklin *lawyer, former ambassador*
Girifalco, Louis Anthony *retired physics professor*
Givens, Janet Eaton *writer*
Glandt, Eduardo Daniel *chemical engineering educator*
Glass, Dennis Robert *insurance company executive*
Glick, John H. *oncologist, medical educator*
Glusker, Jenny Pickworth *chemist*
Godfrey, Joseph John *philosophy professor, priest*
Goldberg, Joseph *lawyer*
Goldberg, Mitchell Steven *federal judge*
Goldberg, Richard Robert *lawyer*
Gonzalez-Scarano, Francisco Antonio *neurologist, virologist*
Goode, W. Wilson, Sr. *minister, former mayor*
Goode, W. Wilson, Jr. *councilman*
Goodenough, Ward Hunt *anthropologist, educator*
Goodman, Gwen Ducat *museum director*
Goodman, Stephen Murry *lawyer*
Goon, Arthur David *academic administrator, educator*
Gopalan, Ram *finance educator*
Gordon, Anne Kathleen *editor*
Goschke, Linda Fry *artist*
Gough, John Francis *lawyer*
Gould, Claudia *museum director*
Govindaraj, Muthu *engineering educator*
Gowa, Andrew *investor, lawyer*
Grady, M. Sean *neurosurgeon*
Graffman, Gary *academic administrator, pianist, educator*
Granger, Randy William *art educator, consultant*
Grant, M. Duncan *lawyer*
Grazian, David *sociologist, educator*
Green, William Joseph, IV, (Bill Green) *councilman, lawyer*
Greenberg, Stephen Jay *lawyer*
Greenlee, William K. *councilman*
Greenstein, Jeffrey Ian *neurologist*
Grove, David Lavan *lawyer*
Guérin, Roch *systems engineer, educator*
Gueson, Emerita Torres *obstetrician, gynecologist*
Gupta, Rajiv Lochan *chemicals executive*
Gutmann, Amy *academic administrator, political science and philosophy educator*
Gyulai, Laszlo *psychiatrist, educator*
Hackney, (Francis) Sheldon *history professor, former academic administrator*
Hagan, Annmarie T. *insurance company executive*
Haimm, Neil Keith *lawyer*
Haines, Clifford E. *lawyer*
Haley, Vincent Peter *retired lawyer*
Haller, Mark H. *history professor, researcher*
Halpern, Eric Franklin *university publishing director*
Hameka, Hendrik Frederik *chemistry professor*
Hamels, Cole (Colbert Michael Hamels) *professional baseball player*
Hamilton, Stephen David Derwent *lawyer*
Hammond, Benjamin Franklin *microbiologist, educator*
Hanway, H. Edward *insurance company executive*
Hardiman, Thomas Michael *federal judge*
Harkins, John Graham, Jr. *lawyer*
Harmelin, Stephen Joseph *lawyer*
Harper, Christopher *journalist, educator*
Harris, Isiah, Jr. *former telecommunications industry executive*
Hart, Ann Weaver *academic administrator*
Harvey, Gregory Merrill *lawyer*
Harvey, John Adriance *psychologist, pharmacologist, researcher, educator*
Hatcher, Darien *retired professional hockey player*
Hayes, John Freeman *architect*
Heckert, Tom *professional sports team executive*
Hennigan, Michael J. *oil industry executive*
Henrich, William Joseph, Jr. *lawyer*
Herling, Irving Marc *internal medicine educator, cardiologist*
High, Katherine Ann *physician, researcher*
Hodges, Richard Andrew *museum director, archaeologist, educator*
Hoelscher, Robert James *lawyer*
Hogarty, Michael David *pediatrician*
Hojat, Mohammadreza *psychologist, psychological researcher*
Hoke-Scedrov, Bonnie Carol *music educator, soprano*
Holmgren, Paul *professional sports team executive, retired professional hockey player*
Homan, Richard V. *dean*
Hong, Riyehee *musician, litrugist, educator, researcher*
Hough, Melissa Ellen *curator, museum director*
Howard, David Miles *lawyer*
Howard, Ryan James *professional baseball player*
Hoxie, James A. *virologist, educator*
Huang, Liquan *molecular biologist, neuroscientist*
Huff, Leon A. *music producer, composer*
Humphreys, Tatyana *medical educator, director*
Hunter, James Austen, Jr. *lawyer*
Hynes, Virtner Gilmore *rehabilitation services professional*
Ibanez, Raul Javier *professional baseball player*
Iglewicz, Boris *statistician, educator*
Iguodala, Andre Tyler *professional basketball player*
Jackson, Harold *journalist*
Jacobs, Jonathan Mark *parliamentary consultant*
Jaffe, Eileen Karen *biochemist*
Jaron, Dov *biomedical engineer, educator*
Jarrett, Joseph Timothy *biochemistry educator*
Jemmott, Loretta Sweet *HIV/AIDS researcher, nursing educator*
Jessup, Mariell L. *cardiologist, educator*
Jiang, Pingjun *finance educator*
Jimenez, Sergio A. *internist, educator, rheumatologist*
Joglekar, Prafulla Narayan *information systems management educator, consultant*
Johnson, Philip Rudolph, Jr. *pediatrician, epidemiologist*
Johnson, Victor Lawrence *banker, director*
Jones, C. Darnell, II, *federal judge, law educator*
Jones, Curtis, Jr. *councilman*
Jones, Robert Jeffries *lawyer*
Jordan, Eddie Montgomery *professional basketball coach*
Joseph, Andrea Stein *pharmacist, educator*
Julian, Melanie Blair *voice educator*
Kadison, Richard Vincent *mathematician, educator*
Kahn, James Robert *lawyer*
Kaier, Edward John *lawyer*
Kaiser, Roy *performing company executive*
Kaji, Hideko *pharmacology educator*
Kalghatgi, Sameer *engineering educator*
Kamen, Leonard Bert *osteopath*
Kamp, R. Stephen *finance educator*
Kang, Ju-Seop *medical educator, consultant, medical researcher*
Kang, Yoogoo *anesthesiologist, educator*
Kapur, Drew K. *lawyer*
Kargbo, David M. *science & engineering educator*
Katherine, Robert Andrew *chemicals executive*
Kaufman, Russel Eugene *hematologist, oncologist*
Kazazian, Haig Hagop, Jr. *pediatrician, researcher, educator*
Keene, John Clark *lawyer, educator*
Kefalides, Nicholas Alexander *physician, educator*
Keidat, Edward E. *finance educator*
Keim, Donald Bruce *finance educator*
Kelley, Vincent J. *oil industry executive*
Kelley, William Nimmons *physician, educator, science administrator, dean*
Kelly, John P. (Jack Kelly) *councilman*
Kendall, Philip C. *psychologist, educator*
Kennedy, David William *otolaryngologist, medical administrator, educator*
Kenney, James F. *councilman*
Kessler, Alan Craig *lawyer*
Kimberly, John Robert *management educator, consultant*
Kinsella, Thomas *poet*
Klasko, Herbert Ronald *lawyer, educator, writer*
Klausner, Samuel Zundel *sociologist, educator*
Klein, Howard Bruce *lawyer, educator*
Klein, Julia Meredith *freelance journalist, editor*
Klein, Lawrence Robert *economist, educator*
Klein, Michael Elihu *physician*
Klein, Michael Lawrence *research chemist, educator*
Klein-Szanto, Andres J. P. *pathologist*
Kline, Thomas Richard *lawyer*
Klumpp, Thomas Russell *bone marrow transplant physician, educator*
Knauer, Georg Nicolaus *philologist*
Knoll, Michael Steven *law educator*
Knopp, Marvin Isadore *mathematics professor*
Knudson, Alfred George, Jr. *medical geneticist*
Koc, Lorraine K. *lawyer*
Kolb, Nancy Dwyer *museum director*
Kopp, Charles Gilbert *lawyer*
Koprowski, Hilary *microbiologist, educator*
Koretzky, Gary Alan *rheumatologist, educator*
Kormes, John Winston *lawyer*
Kraeutler, Eric *lawyer*
Krajewski, Joan L. *councilwoman*
Kresh, J. Yasha *cardiovascular researcher, educator*
Krott, Joseph P. *oil industry executive, comptroller*
Krueger, Dirk *economist, educator*
Ksansnak, James Edward *diversified financial services company executive, accountant*
Kujubu, Dean Akira *physician, educator*
Kupperman, Louis Brandeis *lawyer*
Kuritzkes, Michael S. *oil industry executive, lawyer*
LaCheen, Stephen Robert *lawyer*
LaFollette, Paul Sumner, Jr. *science educator*
Laguzzi, Carina *lawyer*
Lambertsen, Christian James *environmental physiologist, physician, educator*
Lang, Adam A. *computer engineer*
Lange, Beverly J. *pediatric oncologist*
Langer, Jill E. *radiologist, educator*
Larson, Donald Clayton *physics professor, consultant*
Lasher, Lori L. *lawyer*
Lavorgna, Gregory Joseph *lawyer*
Lawley, Alan *materials engineer, educator*
Lawson, John Quinn *architect*
Lazar, Mitchell Avery *physician, educator*
Ledwith, John Francis *lawyer*
Lee, Cliff (Clifton Phifer Lee) *professional baseball player*
Lee, David Inkoo *urologist*
Lee, Virginia M. -Y. *medical educator, health science association administrator*
Leech, Noyes Elwood *lawyer, educator*
Leist, Paul Thomas *neurologist, director*
Leiter, Robert Allen *journalist, editor, writer*
Lemanski, Larry Fredrick *medical educator, academic administrator*
Lent, John Anthony *journalist, educator*
Leonard, Thomas *lawyer*
Le Roux, Peter David *neurosurgeon*
Lesser, Bruce R. *lawyer*
Lester, Marsha I. *chemistry professor*
Leventhal, Lawrence Jay *rheumatologist, educator*
Levin, Murray Simon *lawyer*
Levinthal, Daniel Alan *management educator*
Levitt, Jerry David *medical educator*
Levy, Michael L. *lawyer*
Lewis, E(arl) B(radley) *artist, illustrator*
Lewis, Edward Ted *academic administrator*
Lewis, Frank Russell, Jr. *surgeon*
Lewis, John Hardy, Jr. *lawyer*
Leyva, Nick (Nicholas Tomas Leyva) *professional baseball coach*
Li, Weiye *ophthalmologist, educator, biochemist*
Liacouras, Peter James *academic administrator, lawyer, arbitrator, educator*
Liang, Ling L. *science educator*
Libonati, Michael Ernest *law educator, writer*
Lidge, Brad (Bradley Thomas Lidge) *professional baseball player*
Liebenberg, Roberta D. *lawyer*
Liebermann, Dan A. *cancer investigator, medical educator*
Liebman, Andrew Michael *management educator*
Lin, Liyong *physicist*
Lipman, Frederick D. *lawyer, educator, writer*
Lippa, Carol Frances *neurologist*
Litzky, Leslie Anne *pathologist, educator*
Loder, David E. *lawyer*
Lodish, Leonard Melvin *marketing educator, entrepreneur*
Logue-Kinder, Joan *public relations consultant*
Lombard, John James, Jr. *lawyer, writer*
Lonergan, Robert A. *lawyer, chemicals executive*
Long, Sarah Sundborg *pediatrician, educator*
Lubensky, Tom Carl *physics professor*
Ludwig, Edmund Vincent *federal judge*
Ludwig, Stephen *pediatrics and emergency medicine educator*
Luukko, Peter A. *professional sports team executive*
Lynam, Jim *professional basketball coach*
MacDonald, Brian P. *oil industry executive*
Magargee, W(illiam) Scott III *lawyer*
Magaziner, Henry Jonas *architect, writer*
Maginnis, Robert P. *bishop*
Mahmud, Jamal *psychiatrist*
Mair, Victor Henry *language and literature educator*
Maitin, Ian *physiatrist*
Malkowicz, Stanley Bruce *urologist*
Mallery, David *education leader, teacher seminars, consultant*
Malloy, Michael Patrick *lawyer*
Mancall, Elliott Lee *retired neurologist, educator*
Mancall, Jacqueline Cooper *library and information scientist, educator*
Mann, Theodore R. *lawyer*
Manuta, David Mark *chemist, consultant*
Mao, Weidong *communications engineer, technology executive*
Maqbool, Asim *pediatrician, gastroenterologist*
Marcotte, Paul John *neurosurgeon, educator*
Margo, Katherine Lane *family physician, educator*
Margolies-Mezvinsky, Marjorie *former congresswoman, political organization worker*
Marimow, William K. (Bill Marimow) *editor*
Marple, Dorothy Jane *retired church executive*
Martelli, Phil *men's college basketball coach*
Martinez, Pedro Jaime *professional baseball player*
Mathes, Stephen Jon *lawyer*
Mattoon, Peter Mills *lawyer*
Maxman, Susan Abel *architect*
McCabe, James J. *lawyer*
McCaffery, Seamus P. *state supreme court justice*
McConnell, Stephen John *lawyer*
McDade, Sean *market research company executive*
McFadden, Cori Erin *psychotherapist, educator*
McFadden, Joseph Patrick *bishop*
Mc Ghan, William Frederick *pharmacist, educator*
McHugh, James Joseph, Jr. *lawyer*
McKee, Lynn B. *human resources specialist, food products executive*
McKee, Theodore A. *federal judge*
McKeever, John Eugene *lawyer*
McLaren, Kyle *professional hockey player*
McLaughlin, Mary A. *Federal Judge*
McNabb, Donovan *professional football player*
McQuiston, Robert Earl *lawyer*
Meigs, John Forsyth *lawyer*
Meisel, Zachary Franklin *emergency physician, educator*
Meleis, Afaf Ibrahim *dean, nursing educator*
Melvin, John Lewis *physical and rehabilitation physician, educator, administrator*
Meropol, Neal J. *oncologist, researcher*
Mertins, Detlef *architect, educator*
Meucci, Olimpia *medical educator*
Meyer, Dianne A. *lawyer*
Michel-Kerjan, Erwann O. *finance educator*
Milbourne, Walter Robertson *lawyer*
Miller, Buffy *dancer*
Miller, Donna Reed *councilwoman*
Miller, Henry Franklin *lawyer*
Ming, Si-Chun *pathologist, educator*
Mistrano, Joseph *lawyer*
Mitchell-Boyask, Robin Norman *classics educator*
Miyamori, Keiko *artist*
Mochalin, Vadym N. *research assistant professor, consultant*
Mode, Charles J. *mathematician, educator*
Modla, Virginia Bordonaro *education educator*
Momjian, Arthur James *lawyer*
Montone, Kathleen T. *pathologist*
Morgan, Elizabeth K. *retired critical care nurse*
Morimoto, Masaharu *chef, television personality*
Morisey, A. Alexander *government agency administrator*
Mornhinweg, Marty *professional football coach*
Morris, Roland *lawyer*
Moskowitz, Robert Lawrence *biology professor*
Moss, Arthur Henshey *lawyer*
Moss, Roger William *historian, writer, administrator*
Moxon, Karen Anne *medical educator*
Moyer, Jamie *professional baseball player*
Mraovic, Boris *medical educator, researcher*
Muhammad, Mike *advocate*
Mulé, Ann C. *oil industry executive*
Muller, Ralph W. *hospital administrator*
Murabito, John M. *insurance company executive*
Muravchick, Stanley *anesthesiologist, educator*
Murray, Dwayne M. *fraternity organization administrator, lawyer*
Mustokoff, Michael Mark *lawyer*
Mutz, Diana C. *political science professor*
Nathanson, Katherine L. *medical geneticist, educator*
Nelson, Philip Charles *physics professor*
Neubauer, Joseph *food services company executive*
Nevels, James Edwin *investment company executive*
Newman, Bernie Sue *social worker, educator*
Newman, Libby *painter, printmaker, curator*
Newman, Sandra Schultz *lawyer, former state supreme court justice*
Newschaffer, Craig J. *epidemiologist, educator*
Nikonova, Elena Vladimirovna *physician, scientist*

Nowell, Peter Carey *pathologist, educator*
Nutter, Michael Anthony *Mayor, Philadelphia, former councilman*
Nygaard, Richard Lowell *federal judge*
O'Brien, Denis P. *utilities executive*
O'Connor, Charles Edward, Jr. *state government official, lawyer*
Offit, Paul Allan *pediatrician*
Oley, Jodi Dyan *lawyer*
Ominsky, Harris *lawyer*
O'Neill, Brian J. *councilman*
Onley, Sister Francesca *academic administrator*
Overton, Willis F. *psychology professor*
Owens, Robert W. *oil industry executive*
Owens, Rochelle *poet, playwright*
Ozmucur, Suleyman *economics professor, researcher*
Paddock, John (Alvin John Paddock) *professional sports team executive, former professional hockey coach*
Paglia, Camille *writer, humanities educator*
Pagliaro, James Domenic *lawyer*
Palmer, Russell Eugene *investment company executive, retired dean*
Paone, Peter *artist*
Pappas, Charles Nicholas III *dentist, educator*
Park, Chan Ho *professional baseball player*
Parks, J. Manly *lawyer*
Parry, Lance Aaron *publishing executive*
Parry, William DeWitt *lawyer and speech-language pathologist, speech pathology/audiology services professional*
Parveen, Zahida *medical educator, researcher*
Parvizi, Javad *orthopedist, educator*
Pasquariello, Patrick S., Jr. *pediatrician*
Pasternak, Jill Margot *radio producer, host, musician, educator*
Patrick, Ruth (Mrs. Ruth Hodge Van Dusen) *botany educator, curator*
Pavuk, Alexander *history professor*
Peachey, Lee DeBorde *biology professor*
Peck, Robert McCracken *naturalist, historian, writer*
Pedersen, Darlene Delcourt *publishing executive, writer, psychotherapist*
Pennoni, Celestino R. (Chuck Pennoni) *civil engineer, academic administrator*
Pepe, Frank A. *cell and developmental biology educator*
Perlman, Barry Steven *sociologist, educator*
Petrelli, Thomas J. *lawyer*
Petren, Carol Ann *lawyer, insurance company executive*
Phelps, Charlotte DeMonte *retired economics professor*
Piccoli, David Anthony *pediatrics educator*
Pien, Grace *medical educator*
Pillarisetti, Anand *mechanical engineer*
Piltz-Seymour, Jody Robin *ophthalmologist*
Pinto-Martin, Jennifer Anne *epidemiologist, educator*
Plimack, Elizabeth R. *oncologist*
Plosser, Charles Irving *bank executive, economics professor*
Pokotilow, Manny David *lawyer, educator*
Pomerantz, Nora E. *lawyer*
Ponte-Castañeda, Pedro *mechanical engineering educator*
Popovics, Sandor *civil engineer, educator, researcher*
Porat, M. Moshe *dean, management educator*
Porter, Andrew Calvin *dean, psychologist, educator*
Porter, Gerald Joseph *mathematician, educator*
Porter, Jill *journalist*
Potero, Valerie Jane *elementary school educator*
Potsic, William Paul *otolaryngologist, educator*
Price, Lara *professional sports team executive*
Price, Robert Stanley *lawyer*
Price, Vincent Edward *academic administrator, communications and political science professor*
Prischmann Gryniewicz, Deborah Anne *vocalist, educator*
Promislo, Daniel *lawyer, small business owner*
Pronger, Chris *professional hockey player*
Putnam, Alfred W., Jr. *lawyer*
Pyeritz, Reed Edwin *geneticist, educator, medical researcher*
Quann, Joan Louise *French language educator, real estate broker*
Quinn, John Albert *chemical engineering professor*
Quiñones-Sánchez, Maria D. *councilwoman*
Rabaté, Jean-Michel *literature and language professor*
Rachofsky, David J. *lawyer*
Rackow, Julian Paul *lawyer*
Rader, Daniel J. *cardiologist, educator*
Raghupathi, Ramesh *neuroscientist, educator*
Ramani, Girish *marketing educator, researcher*
Ramsey, Charles H. *police commissioner*
Ramsey, Natalie D. *lawyer*
Raymond, Fred Douglas III *lawyer*
Reardon, Siobhan A. *library director*
Rech, Lori Dillard *museum administrator*
Redeker, James Russell *lawyer*
Reed, Lowell A., Jr. *federal judge*
Reed, Michael Haywood *lawyer*
Reed, Sally Gardner *cultural organization administrator*
Reich, Abraham Charles *lawyer*
Reid, Andy (Andrew Walter Reid) *professional football coach*
Reinstein, Robert J. *law educator, former dean*
Reiss, John Barlow *lawyer*
Reiter, Joseph Henry *lawyer, retired judge*
Reitz, Curtis Randall *lawyer, educator*
Ren, Huizhen *language educator*
Rendell, Marjorie O. *federal judge*
Rescorla, Robert Arthur *psychology professor*
Richards, Mike *professional hockey player*
Rickels, Karl *psychiatrist, educator*
Rigali, Justin Francis Cardinal *cardinal, archbishop*
Rima, Ingrid Hahne *economics professor*
Rimel, Rebecca Webster *foundation administrator*
Ritchie, Wallace Parks, Jr. *retired surgeon, educator*
Ritter, Deborah Elizabeth *anesthesiologist, educator*
Roberts, Brian L. *communications executive*
Roberts, Carl Geoffrey *lawyer*
Roberts, Ralph Joel *telecommunications industry and cable broadcast executive*
Robertson, Thomas Sinclair *dean, marketing educator*
Rogers, Carmen Villegas *language educator*
Rogers, Carton (H. Carton Rogers III) *library director*
Rogers, Fred Baker *medical educator*
Rohan, Karen S. *insurance company executive*
Rollins, Jimmy (James Calvin Rollins) *professional baseball player*
Romano, David Gilman *archaeologist*
Romer, Daniel *university official, psychologist, educator*
Rorer, John Whiteley *publisher, consultant*
Rorke-Adams, Lucy Balian *pathologist, educator*
Rose, Jane A. *financial planner*
Rosenberg, Robert Allen *psychology professor*
Rosenbloom, Bert *marketing educator, consultant, writer*
Rosenbloom, Morey Stephen *lawyer*
Rosenstein, James Alfred *lawyer, mediator, negotiation facilitator*
Rosenthal, Edward Charles *management science educator*
Ross, Daniel R. *lawyer*
Rossi, John Patrick *retired history professor*
Rossman, Milton David *medical educator, director*
Roth Rogers, Sheryl Lynn *marketing professional*
Rubenstein, Arthur Harold *dean, internist, educator*
Rubesin, Steohen E. *radiologist*
Rubin, Benjamin Arnold *microbiologist, immunologist, medical educator, researcher*
Rubin, Stephen Curtis *gynecologic oncologist, educator*
Rudczynski, Andrew B. *academic administrator, medical researcher*
Ruggieri, Michael Raymond *pharmacologist, educator*
Rukhadze, Irma *neuroscientist*
Russakoff, Nina L. *lawyer*
Russo, Irma Haydee Alvarez de *pathologist*
Rutkowski, Duane Joseph *social studies educator*
Rybczynski, Witold Marian *architect, educator, writer*
Sachs, Katherine Stein *art historian*
Samuel, Asante T. *professional football player*
Samuel, Ralph David *lawyer*
Sankar, Pamela Lee *social sciences educator*
Satinsky, Barnett *lawyer*
Savitz, Samuel J. *actuarial consulting firm executive*
Sawallisch, Wolfgang *conductor*
Saylor, Peter M. *architect*
Scandura, Joseph Michael *neuroscientist, application developer*
Schatz, Philip *psychology professor*
Scher, Howard Dennis *lawyer*
Schiffman, Harold Fosdick *Asian language educator*
Schifter, Stephan Clay *retired finance educator*
Schmidt, Marc F. *neuroscientist, educator*
Schmuhl, Thomas Roeger *lawyer*
Schorling, William Harrison *lawyer*
Schotland, Donald Lewis *retired medical educator, neurologist*
Schultz, Richard M. *biology professor*
Schumacher, H(arry) Ralph *internist, rheumatologist, medical educator, researcher*
Schwaber, James Stephen *neuroscientist, director*
Schwartz, Donald F. *city health department administrator*
Schwartz, Gordon Francis *surgeon, educator*
Schwartz, J. Sanford *internist, educator*
Schwartz, Marshall Zane *pediatric surgeon*
Schweiker, Mark S. *former governor*
Scirica, Anthony Joseph *federal judge*
Scullion, Mary (Sister Mary Scullion) *nun, advocate*
Sebold, Russell Perry III *romance languages educator, writer*
Segal, Bernard Louis *cardiologist, educator*
Segal, Jonathan A. *lawyer*
Seiden, Michael V. *hospital administrator, physician*
Selles, Robert Hendrikus *retired actuary*
Senior, Timothy C. *bishop*
Servodidio, Thomas Gerard *lawyer*
Shaffer, Thomas H. *medical educator, consultant*
Shapiro, Norma Sondra Levy *federal judge*
Shapiro, Paula *retired maternal/women's health nurse*
Shaw, William J. *religious organization administrator*
Shay, Kathleen M. *lawyer*
Sheils, Denis Francis *lawyer*
Sheldon, Deborah Ann *music educator, consultant*
Shestack, Jerome Joseph *lawyer*
Shoemaker, Innis Howe *art museum curator*
Showalter, Michael *marketing executive*
Shure, Myrna Beth *psychologist, educator*
Sibolski, Elizabeth Hawley *academic administrator*
Siegel, Bernard L. *lawyer*
Siegel, Jeremy James *finance educator*
Sigman, Scott P. *lawyer*
Silberberg, Donald H. *neurologist*
Silberstein, Stephen David *health facility administrator, neurologist*
Silfies, Sheri *physical therapist, educator*
Simpson, Colleen Healy *lawyer*
Slaughter-Defoe, Diana Tresa *education educator, psychologist*
Slomsky, Joel Harvey *federal judge*
Sloviter, Dolores Korman *federal judge*
Slupianek, Artur *medical educator*
Smarkola, Claudia *education educator*
Smith, John Francis III *lawyer*
Smith, Lloyd *musician*
Smith, Rogers Mood *political scientist, educator*
Smith, Sharon A. *museum administrator*
Snelbecker, Glenn Eugene *psychologist, educator*
Snider, Edward Malcolm *professional sports team executive*
Sokol, Jason *historian*
Solano, Carl Anthony *lawyer*
Solomon, Phyllis Linda *social work educator, researcher*
Soroka, Stefan *archbishop*
Soroko, John J. *lawyer*
Soslau, Gerald *biochemistry professor*
Spaeth, Edmund Benjamin, Jr. *retired lawyer, retired law educator, former judge*
Spaeth, George Link *ophthalmologist, educator, writer*
Spandorfer, Merle Sue *artist, educator, writer*
Spiegel, Joseph *medical educator*
Spinner, Nancy Bettina *medical educator, director*
Spolan, Harmon Samuel *lawyer*
Staley, Kenneth Bernard *civil engineer*
Starr, Stephen *restaurant owner*
Stefanski, Edward A. *professional sports team executive*
Steinberg, Marvin Edward *orthopaedic surgeon, educator*
Steinberg, Robert Philip *lawyer*
Stevens, John *professional hockey coach, retired professional hockey player*
Stock, William August *lawyer*
Stone, Antoinette R. *lawyer*
Stonecipher, David A. *insurance company executive*
Stow, George *history professor*
Strasbaugh, Wayne Ralph *lawyer*
Strickler, Matthew M. *lawyer*
Stunkard, Albert James *psychiatrist, educator*
Sugrue, Thomas J. *history and social sciences professor*
Suh, Byungse *medical educator*
Sulyk, Stephen *archbishop emeritus*
Summers, Robert *economics professor*
Sutherland, L(ewis) Frederick *food products executive*
Suzuki, Jon Byron *medical educator, periodontist, microbiologist*
Sykes, David Terrence *lawyer*
Tahir-Kheli, Raza A. *physics professor*
Talerman, Aleksander *pathologist, educator*
Taney, Francis Xavier, Jr. *lawyer*
Taniguchi, Tadatsugu *biology professor, researcher*
Tannen, Richard Laurence *nephrology educator*
Tasco, Marian B. *councilwoman*
Taslidere, Ezgi *science educator*
Tavana, Madjid *science educator*
Taylor, Matthew A. *lawyer*
Tchou, Julia *surgeon, educator*
Testa, Joseph R. *geneticist, researcher, biologist*
Thomas, Daniel Edward *bishop*
Thomson, Michael J. *oil industry executive*
Tierney, Brian Patrick *publishing executive, former advertising and public relations executive*
Ting, Jan C. *political science professor, lawyer, consultant*
Toomey, David Charles *lawyer*
Torg, Joseph Steven *orthopaedic surgeon, educator*
Tourtellotte, Charles Dee *internist, rheumatologist, educator*
Tran, Judith Thuha *psychiatrist*
Trerotola, Scott Oakley *intervention radiologist, division chief*
Tritton, Thomas Richard *former academic administrator, biologist, educator*
Trodden, Mark *physicist*
Truant, Allan L. *medical educator, laboratory scientist, health science administrator*
Tsykalov, Eugene *neuroscientist, researcher*
Tuan, Kailin *management consultant, educator*
Tumola, Thomas Joseph *lawyer*
Tuttle, Karen Ann *violist, educator*
Tüzün, Erdem *neurologist, consultant*
Undieh, Ashiwel S. *science educator, department chairman*
Utley, Chase *professional baseball player*
Uzzo, Robert G. *physician, consultant*
Vadigepalli, Rajanikanth *engineering educator*
Vaira, Peter Francis *lawyer*
Vanarsdall, Robert Lee, Jr. *orthodontist, educator*
Van Decker, William Arthur *cardiologist*
Vazirani, Kavita *broadcast company executive*
Veitz, Sister Mary Frances *director*
Venturi, Robert *architect*
Verlin, Jonathan R. *secondary school educator*
Verna, Anna Cibotti *councilwoman*
Vetri, Marc *chef*
Vetter, Victoria L. *pediatric cardiologist, educator*
Vick, Michael (Michael Dwayne Vick) *professional football player*
Victorino, Shane Patrick *professional baseball player*
Virelli, Louis James, Jr. *lawyer*
Vitek, Vaclav *materials scientist*
Vogel, Warren *lawyer*
Wachter, Susan Melinda *finance educator*
Wajert, Sean Peter *lawyer*
Wales, Walter D. *physicist, researcher*
Wallace, Anthony Francis Clarke *anthropologist, educator*
Wallace, Emily Mitchell *writer, editor, educator*
Walter, William G. *consumer products company executive*
Wapner, Keith Leslie *orthopedic surgeon, educator*
Waskow, Arthur Ocean *theologian, educator*
Webb, Gary Douglas *cardiologist*
Webb, Helen *literature and language professor*
Webb, William Yerick *lawyer*
Webber, Ross Arkell *management educator*
Weesner, Anna *composer, music educator*
Weisberg, Morris L. *retired lawyer*
Weitz, Howard Hy *cardiologist, educator*
Weller, Elizabeth Boghossian *child and adolescent psychiatrist*
Whinnery, Peter B. *design educator*
Whitaker, Linton Andin *plastic surgeon*
White, Howard D. *information science educator*
Whiteside, William Anthony, Jr. *retired lawyer*
Wicks, Judy *restaurant manager*
Willet, E. Crosby (Everett Crosby Willet) *artist*
Willi, Steven Matthew *physician, educator, researcher*
Williams, Gerald Ross *orthopedist, surgeon*
Williams, R. Seth *lawyer*
Williams, Sankey Vaughan *health services researcher, internist*
Winey, Karen I. *engineering educator, researcher*
Wint, Dennis Michael *museum director*
Wittels, Barnaby Caesar *lawyer, writer*
Witty, Andrew *pharmaceutical executive*
Wolff, Deborah H(orowitz) *lawyer*
Wolfson, Marla R. *medical educator*
Won, Chang-Hee *science educator*
Woosnam, Richard Edward *venture capitalist, lawyer*
Wray, Matt *healthcare educator*
Wright, Minturn Tatum III *retired lawyer*
Wu, Hong *pathologist*
Wysocki, Charles Joseph *neuroscientist*
Xu, Yao L *marketing professional, consultant*
Yang, Shu *materials scientist*
Yanoff, Myron *ophthalmologist*
Yeo, Charles John *surgery educator*
Yilmazkuday, Hakan *assistant professor*
Young, Donald Stirling *clinical pathology educator*
Yousuff, Ajmal *engineering educator*
Zderic, Stephen Anthony *urologist, surgeon*
Zeleny, Dennis *oil industry executive, human resources specialist*
Ziegler, Donald Robert *cpa*
Zubernis, Lynn Smith *psychologist, counselor*
Zuckerman, Marvin *retired psychologist*
Zuckerman, Michael *history professor*
Zweiman, Burton *allergist, immunologist, educator*

Phoenixville

Hanlon, Barbara Jean *family and consumer sciences educator*
Lukacs, John Adalbert *historian, retired educator*

Pipersville

Block, Caryn S. *composer*
Ferrari, Robert Joseph *retired finance educator, bank executive*
McNutt, Richard Hunt *manufacturing executive*

Pitcairn

Rose, Robert Didier *neurophysiologist*
Wallace, Mark Alexander *social studies educator*

Pittsburgh

Adams, Craig *professional hockey player*
Aggarwal, Shushma *anesthesiologist, educator*
Ahluwalia, Ajit Singh *physician, educator*
Albert, Lorrie Kay *lawyer*
Allen, Rachel Lorey *lawyer*
Alonso, Laura Cristina *endocrinologist*
Amara, Susan *neuroscientist*
Ammerman, Robert Thompson *clinical psychologist*
Anoosh, Farhad *surgeon*
Arac, Jonathan *literature and language professor*
Aronson, Mark Berne *retired lawyer, advocate*
Arumugam, Darmindra Danaraj *research scientist*
Atthipalli, Gowtam *research scientist*
Baer, Max *state supreme court justice*
Balas, Egon *mathematician, educator*
Baldis, Sean R. *elementary school educator*
Baldwin, Cynthia Ackron *lawyer, former state supreme court justice*
Bardyguine, Patricia Wilde *dancer, performing company executive*
Barry, Herbert III *psychologist, educator*
Bartley, Burnett Graham, Jr. *oil industry executive*
Bartoletti, Stefano C. *radiologist*
Basinski, Anthony Joseph *lawyer*
Bates, Beverly Jo-Anne *artist, educator*
Beblo, Richard Vincent *research scientist*
Beck, Paul A. *lawyer*
Becker, Dorothy J. *pediatrician, educator*
Behrmann, Marlene *psychology professor, speech pathology/audiology services professional*
Belani, Chandra Prakash *oncologist*
Belda, Alain J. P. *metal products executive*
Berenato, Agnus McGlade *women's college basketball coach*
Bernt, Benno Anthony *entrepreneur, investor*
Biondi, Manfred Anthony *physicist*
Bissoon, Cathy *lawyer*
Block, John Robinson *newspaper publisher, editor-in-chief*
Bloom, Ron A. *federal official, labor union administrator*
Bloom, William Millard *furnace design engineer*
Bluestone, Charles D. *otolaryngologist*
Blumstein, Alfred *urban and public affairs educator*
Bobby, Theodore N. *lawyer, food products executive*
Bodine, William Beekman, Jr. *museum director*
Boninger, Michael Lee *physiatrist*
Booker, Daniel I. *lawyer*
Boston, John Robert *electrical engineer, researcher*
Boswell, William Paret *lawyer*
Bothner-By, Aksel Arnold *chemist*
Boyce, Doreen Elizabeth *foundation administrator, educator*
Brean, Richard Joseph *labor union administrator, lawyer*
Brosky, John G. *retired judge*
Brown, James Benton *lawyer*
Brownlee, David A. *lawyer*
Brumovsky, Pablo Rodolfo *neuroscientist*
Buchanan, Mary Beth *prosecutor*
Bunch, Charles E. *manufacturing executive*
Burger, Herbert Francis *retired advertising agency executive*
Bylsma, Dan *professional hockey coach, former professional hockey player*
Caginalp, Gunduz *mathematician, educator, researcher*
Cagney, William Robert *psychologist*
Candris, Laura A. *lawyer, mediator*
Carbo, Toni (Toni Carbo Bearman) *information scientist, educator*
Caritis, Steve Nick *obstetrician, gynecologist, educator*
Carr, Walter James, Jr. *research physicist, consultant*
Carty, Sally E. *endocrine surgeon*
Casasent, David Paul *electrical engineer, educator, data processing executive*
Caserio, Rebecca JoAnn *dermatologist, educator*
Cassidy, William Arthur *geology and planetary science educator*
Caushaj, Philip *surgeon*
Charap, Stanley Harvey *electrical engineering educator*
Cheever, George Martin *lawyer*
Chelly, Jacques E. *anesthesiologist*

Chieffe, Natalie *financial planner*
Cho, Sangyeun *engineer*
Choyke, Wolfgang Justus *physicist*
Christin, Nicolas *computer scientist, researcher*
Clack, Jerry *classics educator*
Cockerham, Kimberly Peele *ophthalmologist, educator*
Cohen, Bernard Leonard *physicist, researcher*
Cohen, Nelson P. *prosecutor*
Cohen, Sheldon *psychologist, psychology professor*
Cohill, Maurice Blanchard, Jr. *federal judge*
Cohon, Jared L. *academic administrator*
Colbert, Kevin *professional sports team executive*
Colen, Frederick Haas *lawyer*
Collins, Bobby McManus, II, *dental educator*
Collins, Terence James *chemistry professor*
Coltman, John Wesley *physicist*
Coney, Aims C., Jr. *lawyer, labor-management negotiator*
Connors, Eugene Kenneth *lawyer, educator*
Cowan, Barton Zalman *lawyer*
Cox, Richard James *information science educator*
Cranor, Lorrie Faith *science educator, researcher*
Crosby, Sidney *professional hockey player*
Crossely, Mary A. *dean, law educator*
Cubbage, Bobbie Danielle *pre-school educator*
Curry, Nancy Ellen *psychologist, psychoanalyst, educator*
Damianos, Sylvester *architect, sculptor*
Daniel, Robert Michael *lawyer*
Dato, Virginia Marie *public health physician*
Davis, Larry E. *academic administrator*
Davis, Lewis U., Jr. *lawyer*
Dawes, Robyn Mason *psychology professor*
Dawson, Mary Ruth *curator, educator*
DeGroat, William Chesney *pharmacology educator*
Demchak, William Stanton *bank executive*
Dempsey, Jerry Edward *retired service company executive*
Detre, Thomas *psychiatrist, educator*
DeTurk, Nanette *insurance company executive*
Diamond, Gustave *federal judge*
Dillavou, Ellen D. *thoracic surgeon*
Dixon, Jamie P., II, *men's college basketball coach*
Doft, Bernard Harvey *ophthalmologist*
Dohar, Joseph *pediatrician, educator*
Donnorummo, Bob Pepe *history professor, department chairman*
Doty, Robert Walter *lawyer*
Dougherty, Charles John *academic administrator*
Drennan, Robert D. *archeology educator, researcher*
Drescher, Seymour *historian, educator, writer*
Druckenmiller, Stanley Freeman *hedge fund manager*
Druzdzel, Marek Jozef *computer science educator, researcher*
Duffy, John *economics professor*
Dugan, John F. *lawyer*
Dunbar-Jacob, Jacqueline *dean, nursing educator, researcher*
Duncan, Steven Ray *pulmonologist, immunologist, educator*
Dunn, Kenneth B. *dean, economics professor*
Dutt, Varun *systems and software engineer*
Dzombak, David Adam *environmental engineering educator*
Eaton, Joseph W. *sociology educator*
Edelman, Harry Rollings III *engineering and construction company executive*
Ehrenwerth, David Harry *lawyer*
Ehrlich, Garth David *molecular biologist*
Emmerich, Werner Sigmund *physicist, educator*
Engel, John J. *electronics executive*
Epstein, Barbara A. *medical librarian*
Farrell, Mark Oliver *engineering educator*
Farrior, James *professional football player*
Favorini, Attilio Anthony *playwright, educator*
Fawcett, David B. III *lawyer*
Fedotenko, Ruslan *professional hockey player*
Feingold, David Sidney *microbiology and biochemistry educator, researcher*
Feller, Robert Livingston *chemist, art conservation scientist*
Feng, Rentian *biologist*
Fernstrom, John Dickson *pharmacology and nutrition researcher, educator*
Ferrara, Albert E. *corporate executive*
Fetkovich, John G. *physics professor*
Fienberg, Stephen Elliott *statistician*
Fireman, Philip *pediatrician, allergist, immunologist*
Fischer, Nora Barry *federal judge, lawyer*
Fischhoff, Baruch *psychologist, educator*
Fisher, Bernard *surgeon, educator*
Fisher, D. Michael *federal judge*
Fishman, Craig L. *lawyer*
Fitzgerald, Judith Klaswick *federal judge*
Flaherty, John Paul, Jr. *chief justice emeritus*
Flechtner, Harry Marshal *law educator*
Fleury, Marc-Andre *professional hockey player*
Flinn, Michael James *lawyer*
Fontes, Paulo A. *surgeon, educator*
Fortunato, Joseph *retail executive*
Frank, Alan I W *manufacturing executive*
Frank, Ronald William *lawyer*
Franklin, Kenneth Ronald *management consultant*
Frazer, Jendayi Elizabeth *political science professor, former federal agency administrator*
Friday, Gilbert Anthony, Jr. *pediatrician*
Friede, Samuel A(rnold) *healthcare executive*
Frolik, Lawrence Anton *lawyer, educator, consultant*
Gale, Robert Lee *retired literature educator, critic*
Gancas, Ronald S. *museum administrator, historian*
Garcia, Calixto Isaac *science educator*
Garraux, James D. *lawyer, metal products executive*
George, Carole A. *usability specialist*
Gerard, Leo W. *labor union administrator*
Gerjuoy, Edward *physicist*
Geskin, Larisa *dermatologist, researcher*
Gilman, Frederick Joseph *physicist*
Girnita, Alin Lucian *medical educator, researcher*
Goldberg, Mark Joel *lawyer*
Goldstein, Bernard David *environmental scientist, educator*
Goldstein, Donald Maurice *historian, educator*
Gollin, Susanne Merle *cell biologist, cancer researcher, geneticist*
Gonchar, Sergei *professional hockey player*
Goodish, John H. *metal products executive*
Gorge, John Anthony *health corporation executive*
Gormley, Kenneth Gerald *lawyer, educator*
Granato, Tony *professional hockey coach, retired professional hockey player*
Gray, Matthew Ian *performing arts educator, communications educator, consultant*
Gray, Robert C. *insurance company executive*
Greenspan, Jane Cutler *state supreme court justice*
Grossmann, Ignacio Emilio *chemical engineering educator*
Grünbaum, Adolf *philosophy educator, writer*
Guadagnino, Frank T. *lawyer*
Guerin, Bill *professional hockey player*
Gull, Dawn K. *lawyer*
Gulley, Joan Long *banker*
Gupta, Anil K. *philosophy professor*
Guter, Donald J. *law educator, former dean, career military officer*
Guyaux, Joseph C. *corporate financial executive*
Haas, Joanna E. *museum director*
Hackett, Mary J. *lawyer*
Haggerty, Gretchen R. *metal products executive*
Haley, Roy W. *electronics executive*
Hardesty, Robert Lynch *surgeon, educator*
Harper, Robert William *engineering educator*
Harrell, Edward Harding *wine festival executive*
Harris, Ann Birgitta Sutherland *art historian*
Harrison, James, Jr. *professional football player*
Harrold, Ronald Thomas *research scientist*
Harshman, Richard J. *metal products executive*
Harth, Sidney *musician, educator*
Hartman, Ronald G. *lawyer*
Hassey, L. Patrick *metal products executive*
Hatfull, Graham F. *microbiologist, educator*
Heath, David Clay *mathematics professor, consultant*
Heckler, Frederick Roger *plastic surgeon*
Heilman, Marlin Stephen *medical products executive*
Heitzenroder, David August *investment advisor, investment banker*
Hellman, Arthur David *law educator, consultant*
Hendrickson, Chris Thompson *civil and environmental engineering educator, researcher*
Heo, Jingu *research scientist*
Hernandez, William H. *chemical company executive*
Herrington, Howard Ray *artist*
Hershey, Dale *lawyer, educator*
Hill, John Howard *retired lawyer*
Hillenbrand, David M. *museum administrator*
Hillman, Henry Lea *investment company executive*
Hitt, Leo N. *lawyer, educator*
Hoburg, James Frederick *electrical engineering educator*
Holder, Gerald D., Jr. *dean*
Hollingsworth, Samuel Hawkins, Jr. *bassist*
Holmes, Santonio, Jr. *professional football player*
Honeck, Manfred *conductor, music director*
Hopey, Stephen Donald *journalist, educator*
Horwitz, Mara *medical educator*
Hounshell, David Allen *history professor*
Huntington, James Cantine, Jr. *retired equipment manufacturing company executive*
Huntington, Neal A. *professional sports team executive*
Huq, Mohammed Saiful *medical educator, director*
Ijiri, Yuji *finance educator*
Jacobson, Lewis A. *biology professor*
Janis, Allen Ira *retired physicist, educator*
Jannetta, Ann Bowman *retired history professor*
Jarrett, Fredric *surgeon, educator*
Jefferson, Joseph Murray *banker*
Jenkins, Frank *pathologist, educator*
Jenkins, Georgann Klaus *librarian*
John, Robert Hotchkiss *medical educator*
Johnson, Richard J. *bank executive*
Johnson, Robert Alan *lawyer*
Johnson, William R. *food products executive*
Jones, Craig Ward *retired lawyer*
Jordan, Angel Goni *electrical and computer engineering educator*
Jordan, Gregory B. *lawyer*
Joyce, Judith Marie *radiologist*
Jukes, D. E. *actor, theater director, educator*
Jung, Kwan-Jin *science association director*
Kahle, Charles F., II, *manufacturing executive, chemist*
Kanade, Takeo *science educator, director*
Kanal, Emanuel *radiologist*
Kapucu, Naim *researcher*
Karol, Paul J *chemistry professor, consultant*
Kassam, Amin B. *neurosurgeon, educator*
Kaye, Robin D. *pediatric radiologist, educator*
Kehwar, T. S. *physicist, educator*
Kennedy, Tyler *professional hockey player*
Kenrick, Charles William *lawyer*
Kerber, Frank John *retired diplomat*
Ketter, David Lee *lawyer*
Khetan, Sushil K. *chemist, researcher*
Khosla, Pradeep Kumar *engineering educator*
Kiger, Robert William *botanist, science historian, educator, researcher*
Kilkeary, Kevin P. *hospitality executive*
Kim, SeungJun *research scientist*
King, Elaine A. *curator, art historian, critic*
King, Robert Alan *lawyer*
Klatzky, Roberta Lou *psychologist, educator*
Kline, Gary R. *music educator*
Knox, Charles Graham *lawyer*
Kochanek, Patrick Michael *pediatrician, educator*
Koepsel, Richard Robert *engineering educator*
Kolmakov, German Valentinovich *physics professor, researcher*
Kondziolka, Douglas *neurosurgeon*
Kowalski Trakofler, Kathleen Madland *psychotherapist, researcher*
Krasik, Carl *lawyer, bank executive*
Kroboth, Patricia Dowley *dean, pharmacy educator*
Kunitz, Chris *professional hockey player*
Kupfer, David J. *psychiatry professor*
Kutka, J. James, Jr. *metal products executive*
LaJohn, Lawrence Anthony *research scientist*
Lam, Khee Poh *architecture educator, consultant*
Landreneau, Rodney J. *surgeon*
Larsen, Ronald L. *dean, information scientist, educator*
Lave, Judith Rice *economics professor*
LeBeau, Dick (Charles Richard LeBeau) *professional football coach*
Lee, W.P. Andrew *plastic surgeon*
Lego, Paul Edward *retired manufacturing executive*
Lehoczky, John Paul *statistics educator*
Lejeune, Miguel *engineering educator*
Lemieux, Mario *professional sports team executive, retired professional hockey player*
Leney, George Willard *retired consulting engineer*
Lenhart, Cheryl Hayes *nursing administrator, consultant*
Lennox, James G. *science educator*
Levine, Macy Irving *physician*
Lewis, David Alan *neuroscientist, psychiatrist, educator*
Li, Ching-Chung *electrical engineering educator*
Li, Hanna Wu *music educator*
Lin, Ridwan *neurologist*
Lippincott, Louise *museum director, curator*
Litman, Roslyn Margolis *lawyer*
Loewenstein, George F. *economics professor, psychology professor*
Lohr, David H. *metal products executive*
Lovett, Robert G. *lawyer*
Lugar, Gary Lance *librarian*
Lunsford, Lawrence Dade *medical educator*
Lyjak Chorazy, Anna Julia *retired pediatrician, retired health facility administrator*
Lyncheski, John E. *lawyer*
MacWhinney, Brian James *psychology professor*
Maher, James Vincent, Jr. *physics professor, academic administrator*
Mahone, Glenn R. *lawyer*
Malkin, Evgeni *professional hockey player*
Maly, Wojciech P. *engineering educator, researcher*
Marazita, Mary Louise *genetics researcher*
Mark, Scott M. *pharmacist, director, healthcare educator*
Masich, Andrew Edward *museum director, historian*
Matyjaszewski, Krzysztof *chemist, educator*
Mayer, George *materials scientist, chemist, consultant*
McAvoy, Bruce Ronald *engineer, consultant*
McCafferty, Leo Raymond *plastic surgeon*
McCallum, Bennett Tarlton *economist, educator*
McCartney, Robert Charles *retired lawyer*
Mc Dowell, John Bernard *bishop emeritus*
McDuffie, Keith A. *literature educator*
McGhee, Carl Andrew *lawyer*
McGough, Walter Thomas, Jr. *lawyer*
McGuire, Timothy William *economics and management educator, dean, information technology executive*
McLaughlin, Charlotte *bank executive*
McLaughlin, John Sherman *lawyer*
Mcmahon, Patrick J. *orthopedist*
Means, Dwight Bardeen, Jr. *financial consultant, educator*
Mehalik, Matthew M. *industrial engineer, educator*
Meisel, Alan *law educator*
Melani, Kenneth R. *insurance company executive*
Meltzer, Allan H. *economist, educator*
Mickle, Marlin Homer *electrical engineer, educator*
Miller, David William *historian, educator*
Miller, Ronald Lynn *director*
Miller, Rush Glenn, Jr. *library director*
Miller, William Charles *theological educator, anglican priest*
Milnes, Arthur George *electrical engineer, educator*
Milsom, Robert Cortlandt *banker, director*
Minnigh, Joel Douglas *library director*
Minshew, Nancy J. *neurologist, educator*
Mitchell, Ann Margaret *psychiatric nurse practitioner, educator*
Moore, Pearl B. *retired nursing educator*
Morehouse, David *professional sports team executive*
Morgan, M(illett) Granger *electrical engineering educator, researcher*
Morsi, Badie I. *engineering educator, researcher*
Mosesso, Vincent Nicholas, Jr. *emergency physician*
Mountz, James Michael *radiologist, educator, biomedical researcher*
Muder, Robert Richard *physician, epidemiologist*
Mullen, Charles Frederick *health educator*
Münck, Eckard *chemistry professor*
Murdoch, David Armor *lawyer*
Murdoch, Robert Whitten *lawyer*
Murray, John Edward, Jr. *academic administrator, law educator*
Murrin, Regis Doubet *retired lawyer*
Mutlu, Onur *research scientist*
Mutterperl, William Charles *lawyer, corporate financial executive*
Myers, Eugene Nicholas *otolaryngologist, educator*
Narasimhan, Priya *engineering educator*
Nash, David Reinthal *pediatrician*
Neel, John Dodd *cemetery executive*
Neuman, Charles P. *electrical and computer engineering educator*
Nichols, Larry *medical educator*
Nielsen, Paul Douglas *engineering executive, retired military officer*
Noll, Walter *mathematics professor*
Nolting, Daniel Lincoln *school librarian*
Nordenberg, Mark Alan *academic administrator, law educator*
Norris, James Harold *lawyer*
Ober, Russell John, Jr. *lawyer*
O'Connor, Edward Gearing *lawyer*
O'Donnell, William James *engineering executive*
Oh, Chang Kook *civil engineer, researcher*
Olson, Stephen M(ichael) *lawyer*
O'Neill, Paul Henry *former United States Secretary of the Treasury*
Orr, Terrence S. *dancer, ballet master, artistic director*
Oxendale, Roger A. *hospital administrator*
Packard, Rochelle Sybil *retired elementary school educator*
Palevsky, Paul Marc *nephrologist, educator*
Park, Jeong-Heon *electronics engineer, researcher*
Parness, Jerome *medical educator*
Parrette, Leslie Jackson *lawyer*
Partanen, Carl Richard *biology professor*
Paul, Robert Arthur *steel company executive*
Paulston, Christina Bratt *linguistics educator*
Peele, Pamela Bonifay *economics educator*
Pennell, Daniel Mark *researcher*
Perel, James Maurice *pharmacology and healthcare educator, researcher*
Perlmutter, David H. *physician, educator*
Perloff, Robert *psychologist, educator*
Peterman, Donna Cole *communications executive*
Peterson, Robert Scott *electrical engineer*
Pettit, Frederick Sidney *metallurgical engineering educator, department chairman*
Phillips, Larry Edward *lawyer*
Pilewski, Joseph Mark *medical and cell biology educator*
Pintauer, Tomislav *chemistry professor*
Pirris, Stephen Montgomery *neurosurgeon*
Pittner, John R *electrical engineer, researcher*
Plazek, Donald John *materials scientist, educator*
Plowman, Jack Wesley *lawyer*
Polamalu, Troy (Trou Aumua Polamalu) *professional football player*
Pollack, Ian Fredric *physician, researcher*
Post, Peter David *lawyer*
Price, John Roy, Jr. *financial executive*
Pudlin, Helen Pomerantz *lawyer*
Quinn, Brian Patrick *physics professor*
Radakovich, Daniel I. *communications executive, consultant*
Randolph, Robert DeWitt *lawyer*
Rao, Dittakavi N. *law librarian*
Rastogi, Priya *medical educator*
Rathke, Sheila Wells *strategic planning and marketing executive*
Ravenstahl, Luke R. *Mayor, Pittsburgh*
Ravi, R. *finance educator*
Raynovich, George, Jr. *retired lawyer*
Rebich, Lois J. *elementary school educator*
Reed, Douglas Scott *immunologist*
Reed, W. Franklin *lawyer*
Reichblum, Audrey Rosenthal *public relations and publishing executive*
Rescher, Nicholas *philosopher, author, educator*
Restivo, James John, Jr. *lawyer*
Rice, Edward G. *lawyer*
Roethlisberger, Ben *professional football player*
Rohr, James Edward (Jim Rohr) *bank executive*
Rolla, Maureen J. *museum director*
Rosenberg, Jerome Laib *chemist, educator*
Rosenberger, Bryan David *lawyer*
Ross, Eunice Latshaw *retired judge*
Ross, Madelyn Ann *academic administrator, newspaper editor*
Roth, Loren H. *psychiatrist*
Rubin, J. Peter *plastic surgeon*
Russell, John William *professional baseball team manager, retired professional baseball player*
St. Clair, Gloriana Strange *librarian, dean*
Salter, Russell David *medical educator, researcher*
Sashin, Donald *physicist, educator*
Satan, Miroslav *professional hockey player*
Scaife, Richard Mellon *publishing executive, philanthropist*
Schatten, Gerald Phillip *stem cell biologist, reproductive biologist, educator*
Schatzkamer, Laura *biology professor*
Schaub, Marilyn McNamara *theology studies educator*
Scheinholtz, Leonard Louis *lawyer*
Schmidt, Christopher C. *orthopedist*
Schott, Basil Myron *archbishop*
Schwartz, Andrew B. *neuroscientist, educator*
Schwendeman, Paul William *lawyer*
Segal, Frederick Leslie *lawyer*
Sekerka, Robert Floyd *physics and mathematics professor*
Servan-Schreiber, David *psychiatrist*
Shaw, Daniel Stephen *psychology professor, department chairman*
Sheon, Aaron *art historian, educator*
Shero, Ray (Rejean Shero) *professional sports team executive*
Shin, Sungjae *nutritionist*
Shribman, David Marks *editor*
Shuman, Joseph Duff *lawyer*
Shvedova, Anna Alexandrovna *nutrition research manager, consultant*
Sieg, Wilfried *philosophy educator*
Siker, Ephraim S. *anesthesiologist*
Silveira, Fernanda de Pinho *infectious diseases physician, educator*
Silverman, Arnold Barry *lawyer*
Simmons, Richard L. *surgeon*
Simon, Jacob Matthew *lawyer*
Simpson, Daniel H. *ambassador*
Sirbu, Marvin Alan *engineering educator*
Slivka, Adam *medical educator*
Smartschan, Glenn Fred *educational consultant*
Smith, Alan David *quantitative and natural sciences educator*
Smith, Kenneth J. *medical educator, researcher*
Sokolowski, Thomas William *museum director*
Sokulski, Gary A. *lawyer*
Spatt, Chester S. *finance educator*
Srinivasan, Soundararajan *engineer, researcher*
Staal, Jordan *professional hockey player*
Stack, Edward W. *retail executive*
Stahl, Laddie L. *engineering company executive*
Standish, William Lloyd *judge*
Star, Alexander *chemist, educator*
Starzl, Thomas Earl *physician, educator*
Stepanian, Steven Arvid, II, *lawyer, financial consultant*
Sterling, Thomas W. *metal products executive*
Stirewalt, John Newman *coal company executive*
Stoffer, David Stewart *mathematics educator*
Stout, Janet E. *microbiologist, director*
Strader, James David *lawyer*
Straub, Terrence D. *metal products executive*
Strauss, Robert Philip *economics professor*
Strollo, Patrick J., Jr. *medical educator, researcher*
Stroyd, Arthur Heister, Jr. *lawyer*
Surma, John P., Jr. *metal products executive*
Sussna, Edward *economist, educator*

Sweeney, Clayton Anthony *lawyer, business executive*
Talbot, Maxime *professional hockey player*
Talbott, Evelyn Eleanor *epidemiologist, educator*
Tao, Ran *immunologist, researcher*
Tarasi, Louis Michael, Jr. *lawyer*
Tarr, Joel Arthur *historian, educator*
Thase, Michael E. *psychiatrist*
Thiel, Glenn R. *finance educator*
Thomas, Paul D. *metal products executive, human resources specialist*
Thomason, Sarah Grey *linguistics educator*
Thuma, Holly Diane *performing arts educator*
Thurman, Andrew Edward *lawyer*
Todd, Debra *state supreme court justice*
Tomlin, Mike *professional football coach*
Tristram-Nagle, Stephanie Ann *research scientist, educator*
Trotter, Joe William, Jr. *history professor, writer*
Truitt, Gary R. *lawyer, insurance company executive*
Tuell, Steven Shawn *religious studies educator, minister*
Turner, Harry Woodruff *lawyer*
Turnshek, David Alvin *physics and astronomy professor, department chairman*
Ummer, James Walter *lawyer*
Vagt, Robert F. *foundation administrator, former academic administrator*
van Driel, Edwin Christiaan *theology studies educator*
Van Kirk, Thomas L. *lawyer*
Van Oss, Stephen A. *electronics executive*
Vater, Charles J. *lawyer*
Veeder, Peter Greig *lawyer*
Vidic, Radisav *engineering educator*
von Ahn, Luis *computer science educator, computer scientist*
Wabby, James Patrick *quality assurance professional, educator*
Wald, Niel *public health educator*
Waldeck, David H. *chemistry professor*
Waldo, Kurt *lawyer, metal products executive*
Wallenberger, Frederick T. *fiber scientist*
Walls Perry, J(oyce) Lorraine *elementary school educator*
Walton, James Mellon *investment company executive*
Walton, Jon David *lawyer, metal products executive*
Wang, Bing *medical educator*
Wannstedt, David Raymond *college football coach, former professional football coach*
Ward, Hines, Jr. *professional football player*
Warman, Guy Lee *lawyer*
Wartmann, Michael Rudi *chemical engineer, researcher*
Weidman, John Carl, II, *education and sociology educator, consultant*
Weingartner, Rudolph Herbert *philosophy educator*
Weis, Joseph Francis, Jr. *federal judge*
Werner, Jane *museum administrator*
Wessels, Daniel L. *lawyer*
West, Michael Davidson *English educator*
White, Robert Marshall *retired physicist, educator, government official, consultant*
Wholey, Mark H. *radiologist, director*
Widom, Michael *physicist, researcher*
Wilkinson, James Allan *lawyer, healthcare executive*
Wilson, Frances Helen *retired occupational therapist*
Wilson, Mark Lowell *philosopher, educator*
Wing, Jeannette Marie *computer science educator, consultant*
Winkleblack, Arthur B. *food products executive*
Winter, Peter Michael *anesthesiologist, educator*
Winter, William Joseph *bishop emeritus*
Winters, Sharon Beth *medical researcher, director*
Wipf, Peter *chemist*
Wohleber, Lynne Farr *archivist, librarian*
Woo, Savio Lau-Yuen *bioengineering educator*
Xie, Xiang-Qun Sean *pharmacist, educator*
Xu, Juan *medical researcher*
Yang, Wesley *lawyer*
Yonas, Howard *neurosurgeon, neuroscientist*
Young, Hugh David *physics professor, writer*
Zahler, Clara Tatar *music educator*
Zanardelli, John Joseph *healthcare organization executive*
Zeevi, Adriana *microbiologist, immunologist*
Zelevansky, Lynn *museum director*
Zelle, Boris Alexander *orthopedist, researcher*
Zhou, Chenming *research scientist*
Ziegler, Donald Emil *retired federal judge*
Zoffer, H. Jerome *business educator, dean*
Zubik, David Allen *bishop*
Zuley, Margarita *radiologist, educator*

Pittston
Kupetz, James Michael *mathematics professor*

Plymouth Meeting
Howitz, Konrad Theodor *biochemist*
Mannino, Edward Francis *lawyer, educator*
Nobel, Joel J. *biomedical researcher*

Pocono Summit
Yorke-Viney, Sally Anne *elementary school educator*

Port Matilda
Holt, Frieda M. *nursing educator, retired academic administrator*

Port Royal
Wert, Jonathan Maxwell, II, *management consultant*

Pottstown
Cross, Carole Ann *plastics engineer*
Hergert, Herbert Lawrence *retired consultant and chemist*
Holladay, Victor Mason *music educator*
Hylton, Thomas James *author*
Kensicki, Marybeth *literature and language professor*
Nestler, Patricia C. *English professor*
Trahan, Kelly *design educator*

Pottsville
Thomas, Mark P. *conductor, educator*

Presto
Moeller, Audrey Carolyn *retired energy company executive, corporate secretary*

Punxsutawney
Dinsmore, Roberta Joan Maier *library director*

Quakertown
Babb, Lisa Marie *physical education educator*

Quarryville
Harris, Robert Laird *minister, theology educator emeritus*

Radnor
Buck, James Mahlon, Jr. *venture capitalist*
Crawford, Frederick J. *insurance company executive*
Gadsden, Christopher Henry *lawyer, educator*
George, Marie Angelella *academic administrator*
Hemphill, James S. *investment management executive, financial advisor*
Paier, Adolf Arthur *management consultant*
Raju, T. Shantha *medical researcher*
Sicoli, Mary Louise Corbin *psychologist, educator*
Simon, David Frederick *lawyer*

Reading
Brightbill, David John *lawyer, former state legislator*
Chester, Mark Steven *finance educator*
Constantine, Andrew *conductor, music director*
DeMeo, Marybeth *literature and language professor*
Dietrich, Bruce Leinbach *museum administrator, astronomer, educator*
Fitzpatrick, Caroline *communications educator, director*
Garrison, Matthew Moore *artist, educator*
Hamwi, Bonnie L. *education educator, consultant*
Horacek, Constance Heller *graphic designer, educator*
Hornish, Sam, Jr., (Samuel Jon Hornish Jr.) *race car driver*
Kraras, Gust C. *hotel executive*
Lehman, John F., Jr. *private equity firm executive*
Mack, Sara Rohrbach *librarian, educator*
McCullough, Eileen (Eileen McCullough LePage, Elli McCullough) *financial consultant, writer, editor, educator*
McVey, Diane Elaine *accountant*
Moriarty, John Klinge *electrical engineer, consultant*
Pumariega, Andres Julio *medical administrator, educator, researcher*
Pumariega, JoAnne Buttacavoli *mathematics educator*
Rodgers, Lana Loretta Lusch *retired elementary school educator*
Roth, Ronald C. *museum director*
Russell, Brenda L. *psychology professor*
Shin, Dong-Hee *communication technology educator*
Shultz, Lois Frances Casho *nursing supervisor*
Weicker, Michelina Eva *biology professor, consultant*
Zervanos, Stamatis Michael (Stam Zervanos) *biology professor*

Rector
Smith, David A. *museum director*

Red Lion
Hartman, Charles Henry *transportation and not-for-profit executive, educator*

Renfrew
Meredith, Joanne Cusick *retired special education educator*

Richboro
Higginbotham, Kenneth James *finance company executive*
Maholic, Nancy L. *nurse*

Ridley Park
Walls, William Walton, Jr. *management consultant*

Riegelsville
Banko, Ruth Caroline *retired library director*

Rochester
Douglas, Elizabeth Asche *artist, musician, educator, writer*

Royersford
Krell-Morris, Cheri Lee *psychologist*

Rutledge
Senior, Robert Thomas *retired military officer*

Rydal
Boreen, Henry Isaac *computer company executive*
Fernberger, Marilyn Friedman *not-for-profit developer, consultant, volunteer*
Heebner, Albert Gilbert *retired economist, educator, bank executive*
Johnson, Waine Cecil *dermatologist, educator*

Sadsburyville
Gellman, Gloria Gae Seeburger Schick *marketing professional*

Saegertown
Ralph, NancyJo *retired music educator*

Saint Davids
Bertsch, Frederick Charles III *appraiser, finance company executive*
Boehne, Patricia Jeanne *foreign languages educator, department chairman*
Sheftel, Roger Terry *merchant banker*
Silverang, Kevin J. *lawyer*

Saint Marys
Johnson, J. M. Hamlin *manufacturing executive*

Saint Peters
Detterline, Milton E., Jr. *minister*

Sayre
Bentley, Dianne H. Glover *minister, consultant*
Moody, Robert Adams *neurosurgeon*

Schaefferstown
Skamangas, Anna Lynn *manufacturing executive, educator*

Schnecksville
Foulsham, Christopher *retired language educator*
Gerken, Joanne D. *literature and language professor*
Kiriposki, Marie *biology professor*
Labbiento, Julianne Marie *mathematics professor*
Riola, Patricia Anne *computer engineer, educator*
Schillow, Ned William *mathematics professor*

Scottdale
Lee, John Lawrence, Jr. *educational administrator*
Tavoularis, Marjorie Osterwise *psychiatrist*

Scranton
Arter, Patricia Sullivan *special education educator*
Blewitt, Thomas Michael *federal judge*
Carlson, Martin C. *prosecutor*
Comstock, Arthur *finance educator, consultant*
Conover, Willis M. *history professor*
Dawoody, Alexander R. *public administrator, policy assistant professor*
De Celles, Charles Edouard *theologian, educator*
Dougherty, John Martin *bishop*
Elvidge, Christina Marie *director*
Gubbiotti, Christine M. *lawyer*
Haggerty, James Joseph *lawyer*
Hinkle Maria, Lisa *photographer, educator*
Jaeger, Gale Albano *education educator*
Kocis, Robert A. *political science professor*
Lawhon, Patricia Patton *literature, language and writing professor*
Lynett, William Ruddy *publishing and broadcast executive*
Martino, Joseph F. *bishop*
McKenna, Ann K. *nutritionist, educator*
O'Malley, Carlon Martin *judge*
Parente, William Joseph *political science professor*
Passon, Richard Henry *retired academic administrator, language educator*
Rhiew, Francis Changnam *radiologist, physician*
Sethi, Arjinder P. S. *program director*
Stufft, Derry L. *education educator*
Turock, Jane Parsick *nutritionist*
Zwanch, Andrew V. *science educator*

Secane
Hudiak, David Michael *academic administrator, lawyer*

Selinsgrove
Henry, Geneive E. *chemistry professor*
Livingston, Valerie A. *art educator, consultant*
Tober, Nina *music educator, department chairman*

Sellersville
Alpert-Diani, Linda *psychologist*

Sewickley
Bly, James Charles, Jr. *finance company executive*
Bouchard, James Paul *metal products executive*
Jehle, Michael Edward *financial advisor, lawyer*
Kornetchuk, Elena *curator, art dealer*
Maurer, Richard Michael *investment company executive*
Swann, Lynn Curtis *management consultant, retired professional football player*
Woody, Carol Clayman *data processing executive*

Shippensburg
Abdurrahman, Abdulmajeed Mohamed *physics professor*
Bao, Julie Qiu *education professor*
Basler, Linda Gerber *retired elementary school educator*
Carey, Allison C. *sociologist, educator*

Shiremanstown
Nesbit, William Terry *small business owner, consultant*

Shohola
Reuder, Mary E(ileen) *retired psychology professor, retired statistician*

Sidman
Miller, Noelle Christine *librarian*

Silverdale
Carney, Shannon Maureen *small business owner, educator*

Sinking Spring
Bausher, Verne C(harles) *retired bank executive*

Slippery Rock
Colbert-Lewis, Sean C.D., Sr. *educator, consultant*
Cosgrove, Cornelius *composite and literature professor, middle state coordinator*
Gray, Colleen Gail *music educator*
Kefeli, Valentin Ilich *biologist, botanist, educator, researcher*
McIlvaine, Robert Morton *literature educator*
Nolen Holland, Nola *choreographer*
Payne, Ursula Octavia *choreographer, educator*
Peacock, Joan Sunita *literature and language professor*
White, Frederick *literature and language professor, researcher*

Solebury
Anthonisen, George Rioch *sculptor, artist*
Valentine, H. Jeffrey *legal association executive*

Souderton
Hoeflich, Charles Hitschler *banker*
Silvestri, George Joseph, Jr. *retired thermodynamics engineer*

South Park
Furman, L. Robert *principal, music educator*
Lotze, Barbara *retired physicist*

South Williamsport
Ogurcak, Janice L. *museum director, educator*

Southampton
Christakis, Alexander N. *finance company executive*
Gniewek, Debra Lyman *school librarian, consultant*
Lenox, Gina Marie *music educator*
Nathan, Dusty *journalist, shop owner*
Weil, Jeffrey George *lawyer*

Southeastern
Rassbach, Herbert David *marketing executive*

Spring House
Rosoff, William A. *lawyer*
van Steenwyk, John Joseph *healthcare plan consultant*

Spring Mills
Woodruff, Thomas Ellis *electronics consulting executive*

Springfield
Boyer, Harold Norman, Sr. *library director, educator*
Maclay, Donald Merle *retired lawyer*
Sing, Robert Fong *physician*

State College
Albright, Gifford Harry *retired architectural engineering educator, consultant*
Banks, Jeffrey Christopher *engineer, researcher*
Barnoff, Robert Mark *civil engineering educator*
Book, Edward Raymond *retired trade association administrator*
Brault, Gerard Joseph *French language educator*
Byrnes, Lisa T. *instructional designer*
Byrom, Fletcher Lauman *chemical manufacturing company executive*
Dupuis, Victor Lionel *retired curriculum and instruction educator*
Foderaro, Anthony Harolde *nuclear engineering educator*
Franklin, Paula Anne *artist, writer, psychologist*
Garrett, Steven Lurie *physicist*
Gillan, Garth Jackson *writer, retired philosopher, deacon, psychoanalytic psychotherapist*
Goldschmidt, Arthur Eduard, Jr. *retired educator, historian, writer*
Grimes, Dale Mills *physics and electrical engineering educator*
Haas, John C. *architect*
Hoffa, Harlan Edward *retired university dean, art educator*
Huck, John Lloyd *pharmaceutical executive*
Kirchner, Elizabeth Parsons *clinical psychologist*
Lamb, Robert Edward *retired diplomat, professional society administrator*
Madjid, A. Hamid *retired science educator*
McKeel, Lillian Phillips *retired education educator*
Olson, Donald Richard *mechanical engineering educator*
Phillips, Janet Colleen *retired educational association administrator, editor*
Pisciotta, Henry Andrew *librarian, researcher*
Porter, Richard James *real estate broker, art historian, actor, voice over artist*
Redford, Donald Bruce *historian, archaeologist*
Ren, Kailiang *materials scientist, educator*
Reutzel, Edward William *mechanical engineer*
Schmalstieg, William Riegel *retired Slavic languages educator*
Schmalz, Robert Fowler *geology educator*
Simpson, Stephen George *mathematician*
Subler, Edward Pierre *advertising executive*
Thompson, Stephen C. *research scientist*
You, Xiaoye *literature and language professor*

Steelton
Zimmerman, Connie Ann *public administrator*

Strasburg
Dunn, David W. *museum director*
Goss, Stephen D. *musician, educator*
Lindsay, George Carroll *former museum director*
Morton, D. Holmes *physician*

Stroudsburg
Finch, Alberta May *retired pediatrician*
Hunt, James Christopher *marine biologist, researcher*

Sugarloaf
Waldron, Theodore Charles *physician*

Summerdale
Pickel, Diane Dunn *education educator*

Sunbury
Cafiso, Bonna R. *retired language educator*
Ely, Donald J(ean) *retired clergyman, secondary school educator*
Weis, Robert Freeman *supermarket company executive*

Swarthmore
Bilaniuk, Oleksa Myron *physicist, researcher*
Carey, William Bacon *pediatrician, educator*
Chopp, Rebecca S. *academic administrator*
Devin, Lee (Philip) *consultant, dramaturg, author*
DuPlessis, Robert Saint-Cyr *history professor*

Elman, Gerry Jay *lawyer*
Field, Dorothy Maslin *minister*
Gilbert, Scott Frederick *biologist, educator, author*
Guardiola, Maria Luisa *literature and language educator*
Hopkins, Raymond Frederick *political science educator*
Keith, Jennie *anthropology educator, academic administrator, writer*
Krendel, Ezra Simon *systems and human factors engineering consultant*
Krizek, Edwin John *marketing professional*
Marecek, Jeanne *psychologist, educator*
McGarity, Arthur Edwin *engineering educator, researcher*
Mee, Erin B. *theater educator*
North, Helen Florence *classicist, educator*
Ostwald, Martin *retired classicist*
Pagliaro, Harold Emil *language educator*
Pasternack, Robert Francis *chemistry professor*
Pryor, Frederic L. *economist, educator*
Thornton, Edward Ralph *chemistry professor*

Swiftwater
Brooks, Joyce Maria *music educator*

Tamaqua
Cardimona, Kimberly Marie *language educator*

Telford
Boughter, Barbara B. *retired mathematics educator*

Thorndale
Gougher, Ronald Lee *retired language educator*
Hodess, Arthur Bart *cardiologist*

Titusville
Zolli, Barbara Turk *museum director*

Tobyhanna
Lapidus, Arnold *mathematician, educator*

Tower City
Adams, Susan L. *art educator*

Townville
Rudy, Elaine Kim *elementary school educator*

Turbotville
Brewer, Elizabeth Ann *elementary school counselor*

Union City
Thomas, Paul Milton *retired science educator*

Uniontown
Halfhill, Terry Ray *researcher, educator*

Unionville
De Marino, Donald Nicholson *federal agency administrator, diversified financial services company executive*
Pitts, Joseph R. (Joe Pitts) *United States Representative from Pennsylvania*

University Park
Acharya, Biswa Ranjan *biologist, researcher*
Allcock, Harry R. *chemistry professor*
Alley, Richard B. *geologist, educator*
Andrews, George Eyre *mathematics professor*
Antle, Charles Edward *statistics educator*
Aplan, Frank Fulton *metallurgical engineering educator*
Barlow, Jesse Louis *computer scientist, educator*
Barnes, Hubert Lloyd *geochemistry educator*
Blackadar, Alfred Kimball *meteorologist, educator*
Bose, Nirmal Kumar *electrical engineer, mathematics educator*
Brantley, Susan L. *geochemist, science association director*
Bressan, Alberto *mathematics professor*
Buskirk, Elsworth Robert *physiologist, educator*
Carlson, Toby N. *retired meteorologist*
Castleman, Albert Welford, Jr. *physical chemist, educator*
Chan, Moses Hung Wai *physicist, researcher*
Craig, Nathan Mc Donald *anthropologist, educator*
Davids, Norman *engineering educator, researcher*
DeChellis, Ed *men's college basketball coach*
Dutton, John Altnow *meteorologist, educator*
Eaton, Nancy Ruth Linton *librarian, dean*
Ebitz, David MacKinnon *art historian, educator, museum director*
Federoff, Nina V. *biology professor, federal official*
Garmire, Gordon Paul *astronomer, educator*
Garrison, Barbara Jane *chemistry professor*
Garud, Raghu *finance educator*
Grayson, Robert Larry *engineering educator, mining executive*
Griffin, Kimberly Anne *educator*
Grosholz, Emily Rolfe *philosopher, educator, poet*
Gul, Omer *chemist, researcher*
Hahm, Jong-in *science educator*
Halsey, Martha Taliaferro *Spanish language educator*
Hammes-Schiffer, Sharon *chemist, educator*
Heid, Mary Kathleen *mathematics educator*
Herr, Edwin Leon *educator, academic administrator*
Hosler, Charles Luther, Jr. *meteorologist, educator*
Howell, Benjamin Franklin, Jr. *geophysicist, educator*
Irwin, Mary Jane (Janie) *engineering educator*
Jackman, Lloyd Miles *chemistry professor*
Jain, Jainendra Kumar *physics professor*
Johnson, Kenneth Allen *biologist, educator*
Joyce, William Leonard *librarian*
Kasting, James Fraser *research meteorologist, physicist*
Kim, Ke Chung *entomology, systematics, and biodiversity educator, researcher*
Lima, Robert *language educator*
Mark, Melvin M. *psychology professor, department chairman*
Marks, Jonathan H. *law & bioethics educator*
Mayers, Stanley Penrose, Jr. *public health service officer, educator*
McKeown, James Charles *accounting educator, consultant*
Miller, Webb C. *computer scientist, biology professor*
Modest, Michael Fritz *mechanical engineering educator*
Muhlert, Jan Keene *art museum director*
Murphy, Kevin R. *psychology professor*
Nei, Masatoshi *biology professor*
Osseo-Asare, Kwadwo *engineering educator*
Paterno, Joe (Joseph Vincent Paterno) *college football coach*
Purao, Sandeep *engineering educator*
Ray, William Jackson *psychologist*
Richard, Thomas Lehman *agricultural engineer, educator*
Rolls, Barbara Jean *nutritionist, educator, director*
Roy, Rustum *citizen scientist*
Schuster, Stephan Christoph *biochemist, researcher*
Semouchkina, Elena *physicist, researcher*
Sen, Ayusman *chemistry professor*
Shane, Philip Barry *accounting educator*
Shapiro, Beth *biology professor*
Spanier, Graham Basil *academic administrator*
Stern, Robert Morris *psychologist, gastroenterology researcher*
Todd Copley, Judith A. *engineering educator*
Underwood, Robyn M. *medical researcher*
Vairo, Giampietro Luciano *professional athletic trainer*
Vannice, M. Albert *chemical engineering professor, researcher*
Vrentas, James Spiro *chemical engineering professor*
Wagener, Thorsten *hydrologist, educator*
White, William Blaine *geochemist, researcher*
Whitehead, Paul *law educator, former labor union administrator*
Winograd, Nicholas *chemist*
Wormley, David Neal *engineering educator*

Upper Black Eddy
Wechsler, Gil *lighting designer*

Upper Saint Clair
Raymond, Bruce Allen *retired surgeon, medical association administrator*

Valley Forge
Bogle, John Clifton (Jack Bogle) *investment company executive*
Dachowski, Peter Richard *manufacturing executive*
Erb, Robert Allan *physical scientist*
Guttentag, Jack Mark *economist, educator*
Kelly, Peter *energy executive*
Knauss, Robert H. *lawyer, oil industry executive*
LaBoon, Lawrence Joseph *human resources specialist, consultant*
Phelizon, Jean Francois *finance company executive*

Vandergrift
Aikins, Candace Sue *music educator, consultant*

Verona
Demmler, John Henry *retired lawyer*

Villanova
Alaways, LeRoy Ward *mechanical engineer, educator*
Beck, Robert Edward *computer scientist, educator*
Bergquist, James Manning *history professor*
Capolupo, Joan M. Novelli *counselor, educator*
DelTosto Brogan, Doris *dean, law educator*
Friend, Theodore Wood III *foundation executive, historian, writer*
Hanouna, Paul Emmanuel *finance educator*
Heitzmann, Ray *education educator, athletic coach*
Helmetag, Charles Hugh *foreign language educator*
Hu, Bangbo *social studies educator*
Johannes, John Roland *political science professor, dean*
Langran, Robert Williams *political scientist, educator*
Lucky, Crystal J. *educational consultant*
Maule, James Edward *law educator*
McLaughlin, Philip VanDoren, Jr. *mechanical engineering educator, researcher, consultant*
Meltzer, Gary Stephen *ancient language educator*
Mires, Charlene *historian, educator*
Murphy, John Francis *law educator, consultant*
Norton, Douglas Evatt *mathematician, educator*
Omran, Elsayed M. *language educator, consultant*
Petropoulos, Kostas *music educator*
Phares, Alain Joseph *physicist, researcher*
Poeta, Salvatore J. *literature and language professor*
Radhakrishnan, T. *engineering educator, educator*
Samanta, Biswanath *engineering educator*
Tomlinson, J. Richard *retired engineering services company executive*
Wright, Jay *men's college basketball coach*
Wu, Qianhong *engineering educator, researcher*
Yemelyanov, Konstantin *research scientist, educator*
Zhang, Yimin *researcher*

Wallingford
Adamiec, Jean Kraus *retired advertising executive*
Morrison, Donald Franklin *statistician, educator*
Severdia, Anthony George *chemistry researcher*

Warminster
Birnstiel, Charles *consulting engineer*
Bleam, Laura Jane *pediatrics nurse, educator*
Ciao, Frederick J. *school system administrator, educator*
Gamarnik, Moisey Yankelevich *solid state physicist*
Hull, Lewis Woodruff *manufacturing executive*
Leinweber, Bruce Kornblatt *obstetrician, gynecologist, educator*
Weaver-Stroh, Joanne Mateer *education educator, consultant*

Warrendale
O'Donnell, James V. *apparel executive*
Rumbaugh, Max Elden, Jr. *professional society administrator*
Schutt, David L. *engineering association executive*

Warrington
Sigety, Elizabeth Donnem *lawyer*
Ulmer, Gene Carleton *geochemist, educator*
Vosik, Wayne Gilbert *lawyer*
Ward, Hiley Henry *journalist, educator*

Washington
Forrest, Robert Gilliland *mathematics professor*
Haring-Smith, Tori *academic administrator*
Kastelic, Robert Frank *aerospace transportation executive*
Lerner, William C. *lawyer*
Longo, James McMurtry *academic administrator*

Washington Boro
Snyder, John Jacob *researcher*

Washington Crossing
Means, John Barkley *director, language educator*
Roche, Gail Connor *editor*

Wayne
Binder, David Franklin *lawyer, writer*
Carroll, Robert W. *retired management consultant*
Conde, Cristobal I. *computer company executive*
Coughey, Donna M. *bank executive*
DeBusk, Charles Richard *engineer, consultant*
Earley, Laurence Elliott *retired medical educator*
Etris, Samuel Franklin *trade association research consultant*
Fabbri, Anne R. *critic, curator*
Faust, Christa *writer*
Garrison, Guy Grady *librarian, educator*
Kalogredis, Vasilios J. *lawyer, healthcare management consultant*
Krutsick, Robert Stanley *retired science center administrator*
Newman, David John *chemist*
Patterson, Scott David *lawyer*
Ross, Roderic Henry *retired insurance company executive*
Schoff, Dennis L. *lawyer, insurance company executive*
Silbey, Victoria E. *lawyer*
Sims, Robert John *financial planner*
Tatta, Joseph *language educator*
Thelen, Edmund *research executive*
Wilson, Bruce Brighton *lawyer, retired transportation executive*
Yoskin, Jon William, II, *insurance company executive*
Yost, R. David (David Yost) *pharmaceutical executive*
Ziglar, William Larry *academic administrator, historian, religious studies educator*

Waynesboro
Coles, Robert Nelson, Sr. *religious organization administrator*
Cryer, Theodore Hudson *ophthalmologist, educator*
Kirk, Daniel Lee *retired physician, consultant*

Waynesburg
Maguire, Mildred May *retired chemistry professor*
Powers, Edward Lewis *theater educator*

Wernersville
Koenig, Robert Emil *clergyman*

West Chester
Albert, Kristen Ann *music educator*
Archbold, William Cornell, Jr. *lawyer*
Ballbach, John M. *wholesale distribution executive*
Blasiotti, Robert Vincent *accountant, consultant*
Brennan, Patricia Clark *financial planner*
Briselli, Carol *music educator*
Carter, Shawn David *protective services official*
Chu, Hung M. *finance educator*
Clarkin, John Francis *health care management executive*
da Costa, Virginia Marie *art educator*
Dobrzelewski, Jean-Christophe *music educator*
Dowdell, Crystal *assistant principal*
Falcone, James S., Jr. *chemistry professor*
Gadsby, Robin Edward *chemicals executive*
Griffith, Edward *judge*
Gunter, Cheryl Darcel *speech pathology/audiology services professional, educator*
Hanna, Colin Arthur *management consultant, political consultant*
Heaps, Marvin Dale *retired food services company executive*
Hipple, Walter John *language educator*
Lamb, William H. *lawyer, former state supreme court justice*
Li, Huimin *finance educator*
Loedel, Peter Henning *political science professor*
Mahoney, William Francis *editor, writer*
McFarland, Ann Louise *music educator*
Murray, Lawrence *management consultant*
Myrsiades, Kostas Yannis *literature educator*
Nicastro, Anthony Joseph *academic administrator, educator*
Pauly, Rebecca Mehl *foreign languages educator*
Ramanathan, Geetha *literature and language professor*
Rovine, Harvey *theater educator*
Scythes, James Michael *history professor*
Shaffer, Leigh S. *psychology professor*
Tartar Esch, Stacy *literature and language professor*
Teti, Louis Nicholas *lawyer*
Varricchio-Di Vito, Andrea *language educator*
Watts, Claire A. *retail executive*
Zandi, Mark M. *economist, financial consultant*
Zlotowski, Martin *psychologist*

West Conshohocken
Lenfest, Harold FitzGerald *former cable television executive, lawyer*
Mullen, Eileen Anne *human resources executive*
Odell, Herbert *lawyer*
Sager, Margaret E.W. *lawyer*
Saul, Ralph Southey *diversified financial services company executive*
Schneider, John K. *financial advisor*
Teillon, Louis Pierre, Jr. *lawyer*
Templeton, John Marks, Jr. *retired pediatric surgeon, foundation administrator*

West Grove
Allman, Margo Hutz *sculptor, painter*
Fuller, Jack Glendon, Jr. *retired plastics engineer*
Olson, Leroy Calvin *retired educational administration educator*
Snow, James Byron, Jr. *otolaryngologist, research administrator, educator*

West Mifflin
Ardash, Garin *mechanical engineer*
Lindenfelser, Rodger William *finance educator*
Rosko, Maryann A. *nurse*

West Point
Buckland, Barry Christopher *chemical engineer*
Grabenstein, John Douglas *pharmacist, military officer*
Greenwood, Susan Kay *biologist*
Renger, John Joseph *neurobiologist*
Schoepp, Darryle D. *pharmaceutical executive, researcher*
Sun, Li *chemist, researcher*
Webber, Andrea L. *research scientist*
Wise, L. David *toxicologist*

Wexford
Bossart, Paul Nathaniel, Jr. *geologist, geophysicist, consultant*
Rastogi, Anil Kumar *health products executive*
Roy, Suzanne Scully *reading specialist*
Stover, Richard L. *investor*

Whitehall
Mansell, Danny Eugene *construction executive*

Wilkes Barre
Casale, Alfred Stanley *thoracic and cardiovascular surgeon*
Feerick, John Paul *neurologist, researcher, military officer*
Hackett, Chris *entrepreneur*
Hao, Qian *accountant, educator*
Hayes, Wilbur Frank *retired biology professor*
Hepp, John Henry, IV, *historian, lawyer*
Horoszy, Albert John *mathematics educator*
Lindemann, George L. *gas industry executive*
Loomis, Richard Morgan *literature and language educator*
McHale, Maureen Bernadette Kenny *controller*
Mech, Terrence Francis *library director*
Murray-Galella, Suzanne *special education educator, consultant*
Nikam, Shivprasad *vascular and endovascular surgeon*
Schwartz, Roger Alan *judge*
Wenger, Diane E. *history professor*
Whitman, Brian E. *engineering educator*

Williamsport
Beaston, Lawrence Keith *literature and language professor*
Buckman, Debra Ann *science educator*
Carlucci, William Philip *lawyer*
Gorka, Sandra *information technology executive, educator*
Hintz, Harry W., Jr. *residential construction educator, contractor*
Hudock, Barbara Benner *financial consultant*
Kinley, Kenneth James *engineering educator*
Kule, Chris Edward *biology professor*
Martin, Thomas John *pediatrician, sports medicine physician*
McClure, James Focht, Jr. *federal judge*
McDonald, Peyton Dean *brokerage house executive*
Muir, Malcolm *federal judge*
Noviello, Donald *science educator*
Wozniak, Robert Andrew *architectural technology professor*

Willow Grove
Schiffman, Louis F. *management consultant*
Suer, Marvin David *architectural consultant*

Willow Street
Blevins, William Edward *management consultant*
Coleman, Ernest Albert *plastics and materials consultant*
Henderson, Joseph Ralston *educator*
Keiser, Paul Harold *retired hospital administrator*
Wesbury, Stuart Arnold, Jr. *health science association administrator, educator*
Yrigoyen, Charles, Jr. *retired church denomination executive*

Windber
Hu, Hai *biomedical researcher, director*

Woodlyn
Turso, Aimee Lynn *music educator*

Wyncote
Booker, Alvin Eugene *publishing executive, consultant*
Ehrenkrantz, Dan *rabbi*

Wyndmoor
Barrett, James Edward, Jr. *management consultant*
Brown, Gary Christian *ophthalmologist, director*
Mastovska, Katerina *chemist, researcher*
Pfeffer, Philip Elliot *biophysicist*
Strobaugh, Terence Philip, Jr. *molecular biologist, microbiologist*
Yadav, Madhav P. *chemist*

Wynnewood
Alter, Milton *retired neurologist*

Anyanwu, Chukwuma Uchenna *clinical pharmacist, biomedical researcher*
Benz, Robert L. *internist*
Clarke, John Rodney *surgeon*
Frankl, William Stewart *cardiologist, educator*
Marks, Gerald *surgeon, educator*
Robinson, Robert L. *retired diversified financial services company executive, lawyer*
Rosefsky, Jonathan Benensohn *pediatrician*
Rosen, Gerald Harris *physicist, consultant, educator*
Sanyour, Michael Louis, Jr. *diversified financial services company executive*
Shems, Estherina *retired child psychiatrist*
Sider, Ronald J. *theology educator, author*
Ying, Gui-shuang *ophthalmologist, educator*
Zhang, Li *medical researcher*

Wyomissing
Carlino, Peter M. *gaming company executive*
Genieser-DeRosa, Anya *psychologist*
Gordon, Mildred Harriet Gross *hospital executive*
Hildreth, Eugene A. *physician, educator*
Stevens, Anne L. *metal products executive, retired automotive executive*
Wilmott, Timothy J. *gaming company executive*
Ziolkowski, Andrew T. *metal products executive*

Yardley
Basil, Biju *psychiatrist, researcher*
Breitenfeld, Frederick, Jr. *retired educational consultant, broadcast executive*
Fraser, David William *epidemiologist*
Hunt, David Allen *organic chemist*
Makadok, Stanley *management consultant*
Marus, Robert *dentist*
Millner, Rachel Erin *psychology educator, occupational therapist*
Minter, Philip Clayton *retired communications company executive*
Tice, Jennifer S. *music educator*
Weaver, William Clair, Jr., (Mike Weaver) *human resources development executive*

York
Addison, Brian Michael *lawyer*
Alcon, Sonja L. *retired medical social worker*
Avillo, Philip J., Jr. *history professor*
Bartels, Bruce Michael *health facility administrator*
Bergren, Byron L. *retail executive*
Buzzendore, Robert L. *lawyer*
Day, Ronald Richard *retired financial executive*
Dzubak, Cora M. *educational association administrator*
Foster, Timothy Edward *educational association administrator*
Hodgson, Elizabeth *biology professor, consultant*
Hoffmeyer, William Frederick *lawyer, educator*
Horn, Russell Eugene *engineering executive, consultant*
Horn, Russell Eugene, Jr. *engineering executive*
Kennedy, Christopher Robin *ceramics engineer, director*
Knowlton, Warren D. *plastics company executive*
Lehr, Donald P. *psychology professor*
Livingston, Pamela A. *corporate image and marketing management consultant*
McGhee, James Hamill *theatre director, teacher, poet*
Phillips, Amy J. *lawyer*
Pucino, Carrie *critical care nurse*
Robert, Jephrey Lee *urban planner, musician*
Schanbacher, David Charles *lawyer*
White, Timothy Paul *brokerage house executive*
Wiles, William Wharton *retired federal government official*
Wills, Richard Andrew *materials handling equipment company executive*
Wise, Bret W. *chemical company executive*
Yeater, Kathleen Wecker *musician, educator*

Youngstown
Palmer, Arnold Daniel *professional golfer*

Youngwood
Shafert, Tim D. *science educator*

RHODE ISLAND

Barrington
Carpenter, Charles Colcock Jones *internist, educator*
Cicione, Giovanni D. *lawyer, political organization administrator*
Mihaly, Eugene Bramer *management consultant*
Moody, Marilyn Leavitt *retired special education educator*
Soutter, Thomas Douglas *retired lawyer*

Bristol
Bogus, Carl Thomas *law educator*
Danzberger, Alexander Harris *retired chemical engineer, consultant*
Guralnick, Lonnie J. *biology professor, dean*
Krech, Shepard III *anthropology educator, museum director*
Moffa, John L. *media specialist, director*

Charlestown
Huetteman, Susan Bice *writer*
Rohm, Robert Hermann *sculptor, educator*

Chepachet
Jubinska, Patricia Ann *ballet instructor, choreographer*

Cranston
Alston, Jametta O. *lawyer*
Blessing, George Patrick *psychologist*
Burge, David Russell *concert pianist, composer, educator*
Cayouette, Steven L. *state banking agency administrator*
Langlois, Michael A. *financial consultant*
Lisi, Deborah Jeanne *performance improvement coordinator*
Livingston, Carolyn Harris *music educator*
Papitto, Ralph Raymond *manufacturing executive*
Torelli, Anthony-Alexander *musician, conductor, educator*

Cumberland
Clemente, Alice Rodrigues *language educator*

East Greenwich
Dence, Edward William, Jr. *retired lawyer, bank executive*

Greenville
Lemons, James Stanley *history professor*

Harmony
Fogarty, Charles Joseph *former lieutenant governor*

Jamestown
Parks, A. Lauriston *lawyer*
Ullrich, Robert Albert *academic administrator*
Worden, Katharine Cole *sculptor*
Wright, Harrison Morris *historian, educator*

Johnston
Subramaniam, Shivan Sivaswamy *insurance company executive*

Kingston
Barnett, Stanley M. *engineering educator*
Caldwell, Naomi Rachel *library and information scientist, educator, writer*
Carothers, Robert Lee *academic administrator*
Dunson, Stephanie *literature and language educator, consultant*
Gilton, Donna Louise *library and information scientist, educator*
Hufnagel, Linda Ann *biology professor, researcher*
Kim, Yong Choon *philosopher, theologian, educator*
Lee, Kang-Won Wayne *engineering educator*
Martin, Lenore Marie *bioorganic researcher, educator*
Mazze, Edward Mark *marketing educator, consultant*
McCurdy, Karen *human development professor*
Molloy, David Scott, Jr. *labor relations educator*
Newman, Barbara Miller *psychologist, educator*
Petro, Nicolai *political science professor, consultant*
Shim, Minsuk Kim *education educator*
Smith, Jason Kemmitt *communications educator*
Sundlun, Bruce *former governor*
Turnbaugh, William Arthur *archaeologist, educator*
Zucker, Norman Livingston *political science professor, writer*

Lincoln
Barlow, August Ralph, Jr. *minister*
Marini, Kelly Jean *elementary school educator*
Marsden, Herci Ivana *classical ballet artistic director*

Little Compton
Caron, Wilfred Rene *retired lawyer*
Middendorf, J. William, II, *investment banker*

Middletown
Demy, Timothy James *retired military chaplain, professor*
Ellison, William Theodore *marine engineer*
Gibbs, June Nesbitt *state legislator*
Gontarz, Christopher Stanley *lawyer*
Jackson, John Edward *adult education educator, retired military officer*
Leighton, Charles Milton *retired specialty consumer products executive*

Narragansett
Bentley-Scheck, Grace Mary *artist*
Goos, Roger Delmon *retired mycologist*
Grear, Jason S. *ecologist*
Lohmann, Rainer *science educator*
Nixon, Scott West *oceanography science educator*
Pilson, Michael Edward Quinton *oceanography educator*
Stark, Dennis Edwin *private investor, retired bank executive and university administrator*
Stedman, Victoria *economics professor*

Newport
Antone, M. Therese *academic administrator, nun*
Carpenter, Stanley Dean MacDonald *military officer, educator*
Cowley, Robert William *editor, writer, editorial consultant*
Cutler, Laurence Stephan *architect, museum administrator, writer, advertising executive, educator*
Englander, Roger *television producer, director*
Gerety, Jane *academic administrator, nun*
Haas, William Paul *humanities educator, retired academic administrator*
Harrison, Brian Francis *engineer, researcher*
Hence, Jane Knight *architectural designer*
Johnson, William Carter *biology professor*
Malkovich, Mark Paul III *musician, performing company executive*
McConnell, David Kelso *lawyer*
Petro, Allison N. *language educator*
Raum, Mary Beth *performing arts educator*
Roos, Casper *actor*
Rous, Stephen Norman *urologist, educator*
Ruffa, Anthony Armand *mechanical engineer*
Sands, Harold Winthrop *banker, financial planner*
Woods, Donald E. *healthcare executive*

North Kingstown
Kullberg, Gary Walter *advertising agency executive*
Mellor, Kathy *English as a second language educator*
Morse, Barbara *mathematics educator*
Novich, Bruce Eric *chemicals executive*

North Providence
Stankiewicz, Andrzej Jerzy *physician, biochemistry educator*

North Smithfield
Gelineau, Louis Edward *bishop emeritus*

Pawtucket
Cheever, James Jefferson *counselor*
Crowley, James Patrick *hematologist, medical educator, immunologist*
Doyle, James E., II, *state legislator*
Doyle, James Ernest *mayor*
Glicksman, Arvin S(igmund) *radiation oncologist*
Goldner, Brian D. *toy company executive*
Hargreaves, David D. *toy company executive*
Hassenfeld, Alan Geoffrey *retired toy company executive*
La Bresh, Kenneth Albert *cardiologist*
McCool, Franklin Dennis *pulmonologist, researcher*
Orson, Barbara Tuschner *actress*
Thomas, Deb *toy company executive*
Verrecchia, Alfred Joseph *toy company executive*

Portsmouth
Bergstrom, Albion Andrew *retired military officer, educator*
Fontaine, David G. *librarian, education educator, consultant*
Needham, Richard Lee *magazine editor*

Providence
Abbotson, Susan Claire Whitfield *literature and language professor*
Ackerman, Felicia Nimue *philosophy educator, writer*
Adu-Gyamfi, R. Siisi *multi-industry company executive*
Ajello, Edith H. *state legislator*
Algiere, Dennis Lee *state legislator*
Alswang, Hope *museum director*
Anderson, James Alfred *cognitive science professor*
Archer, William M. *marketing executive*
Aronson, Stanley Maynard *physician, educator*
Avery, Donald Hills *metallurgist, educator*
Barbour, Brian *English professor*
Barnhill, James Orris *theater educator*
Berkelhammer, Robert Bruce *lawyer*
Biron, Christine Anne *medical science educator, researcher*
Blase, William A., Jr. *telecommunications industry executive*
Blasing, Mutlu Konuk *English language educator*
Block, Bartley Cavanough *biologist, educator*
Bohlen, Kenneth C. *multi-industry company executive*
Borts, George Herbert *economist, educator*
Bready, Richard Lawrence *manufacturing executive*
Breuer, Kenneth *engineering educator*
Buka, Stephen L. *epidemiologist, educator*
Bulman, John *lawyer*
Butler, John D. *multi-industry company executive*
Campbell, Lewis B. *multi-industry company executive*
Canning, Deborah *technology educator*
Caprio, Frank Thomas *state treasurer, lawyer*
Carcieri, Donald L. *Governor of Rhode Island*
Carlotti, Stephen Jon *lawyer*
Carpenter, Gene Blakely *crystallography and chemistry educator*
Chafee, Lincoln Davenport *political science professor, former senator*
Chlebus, Andrew J. *lawyer*
Cicilline, David N. *Mayor, Providence, Rhode Island*
Cladis, Mark S. *religious studies educator*
Cohen, Deborah Anne *historian*
Conley, Patrick T. *lawyer, educator, history professor, real estate developer, writer*
Connors, Daniel Paul *state legislator*
Cooper, Leon N. *physicist, researcher*
Corrente, Robert Clark *lawyer, former prosecutor*
Curran, Joseph Patrick *lawyer*
Dafermos, Constantine Michael *applied mathematics professor*
Dahlberg, Albert Edward *biochemistry professor*
Davis, Robert Paul *retired physician, educator*
DeGiorgis, Joseph Alan *medical educator*
Degroot, Leslie Jacob *medical educator*
de Leon, Cedric *sociologist, educator*
Demaria, Gerald C. *lawyer*
Demopulos, Harold William *lawyer*
Donahue, John Edward *physician*
Donnelly, Scott C. *manufacturing executive*
Donovan, Bruce Elliot *literature educator, dean*
Dowben, Robert Morris *physiologist, researcher*
Easton, J(ohn) Donald *neurologist, educator*
Enteman, Willard Finley *retired philosopher*
Espinosa, David *history professor*
Estrup, Peder Jan *physics and chemistry professor*
Fairbrother, Will *biology professor*
Faraone, Philip *organist, director, consumer products company executive*
Farmer, Susan Lawson *retired broadcast executive, former secretary of state*
Feldman, Allan Maurice *economist*
Feldman, Walter Sidney *artist, educator*
Ferguson, Simone D. *literature and language professor*
Fish, Lawrence Kingsbaker *bank executive*
Fishman, Bernard Philip *museum director*
Flaherty, Francis Xavier *state supreme court justice*
Fleming, Wendell Helms *mathematician, educator*
Fogarty, Edward Michael *lawyer*
Fornara, Charles William *historian, classicist, educator*
Freiberger, Walter Frederick *mathematics professor*
Frerichs, Ernest Sunley *religious studies educator*
Fritz, Gregory Kenneth *psychiatrist*
Gasbarro, Pasco, Jr. *lawyer*
Gerritsen, Hendrik Jurjen *physics professor, researcher*
Gifford, David R. *state agency administrator, geriatrician*
Gilchrist, James Manning *neurologist, researcher, educator*
Gilmore, Judith Marie *physician*
Gist, Deborah A. *state official, school system administrator*
Glicksman, Maurice *engineering educator, retired dean, provost*
Goldberg, Maureen McKenna *state supreme court justice*
Golden, Hal *artist, consultant*
Gould, Richard Allan *anthropologist, archaeologist, educator*
Grace, Richard John *history professor*
Gravenstein, Stefan *medical educator, director*
Green, Andrew *orthopedist, educator*
Greer, David Steven *dean, educator, physician*
Grossi, Linda Marie *elementary school educator*
Guggenheim, Frederick Gibson *psychiatrist, educator*
Hagopian, Jacob *federal judge*
Hamerly, Michael T. *librarian, historian*
Hamolsky, Milton William *retired physician*
Harleman, Ann *literature educator, writer*
Hazeltine, Barrett *electrical engineer, educator*
Head, James William III *geological sciences educator*
Heath, Dwight Braley *anthropologist, educator*
Hemmasi, Harriette Ann *university librarian*
Hennessey, James Vincent *physician, educator*
Heyman, Lawrence Murray *printmaker, painter*
Hobday, Debra J. *dean*
Hochberg, Leigh Robert *neurologist, neuroscience educator*
Hogan, Dennis Patrick *sociology educator*
Houston, Stephen D. *anthropologist, educator*
Howes, Lorraine de Wet *fashion designer, educator*
Hoy, Erik Alexander *plastic surgeon*
Intrator, Nathan *applied mathematician, researcher*
Jackson, Benjamin Taylor *retired surgeon, educator, health facility administrator*
Jacobson, Sandra A. *medical educator, physician*
Janis, Christine *biology professor*
Jones, Lauren Evans *lawyer*
Joukowsky, Artemis A. W. *private investor*
Kadin, Marshall Edward *hematopathologist, educator*
Kane, Agnes Brezak *pathologist, educator*
Keefe, David Lawrence *medical doctor & infertility specialist, biomedical researcher*
Kenna, George Anthony *pharmacist, researcher*
Kennedy, David William *academic administrator, law educator*
Khrushchev, Sergei Nikitich *engineering educator*
Kim, Jaegwon *philosophy educator*
Knopf, Paul Mark *immunologist*
Konstan, David *classics and comparative literature professor, researcher*
Kosterlitz, J. Michael *physics professor*
Kraemer, Michael Frederick *lawyer*
Kramer, Peter David *psychiatrist, educator*
Kushner, Harold Joseph *mathematics professor*
LaFrance, William Curt Phillip, Jr. *neuropsychiatrist, educator, medical researcher*
Lagueux, Ronald Rene *federal judge*
Landsberg, Greg *physicist*
Lanou, Robert Eugene, Jr. *physicist, researcher*
Lapczyk, Ireneusz *research and development company researcher*
Lawal, Taiwo Muniru *civil engineer*
Ledbetter, Beverly Elizabeth *lawyer*
Lesko, Leonard Henry *historian, educator, writer, publisher*
Levin, Frank S. *physicist, educator*
Lewis, David Carleton *medical educator, academic administrator*
Lipsey, Howard Irwin *lawyer, educator*
Liu, Paul Yu *plastic surgeon, educator*
Long, Beverly Glenn *retired lawyer*
López-Morillas, Frances (Mapes) *translator*
Lynch, Patrick C. *state attorney general*
Lynch, William Joseph *political organization administrator, lawyer*
Lysaght, Michael John *biomedical engineer, educator*
Maeda, John *academic administrator, graphics designer, artist, computer scientist*
Mandelbaum, David Ezra *pediatric neurologist*
Marinatto, John *sports association executive*
Marks, Sally Jean *historian, educator*
Marsh, Robert Mortimer *sociologist, educator*
Mastropietro, Gail *psychologist, consultant*
McAndrew, Thomas Joseph *lawyer*
McCann, Gail Elizabeth *lawyer*
McClure, Donald E. *mathematics professor, mathematical society executive*
Mc Donald, Charles J. *dermatologist, educator*
McElroy, Michael Robert *lawyer*
McIntyre, Jerry L. *lawyer*
Medvedovski, Eugene *ceramics engineer, researcher*
Merlino, Anthony Frank *orthopedist*
Miller, Ivan Wilfred *psychologist, educator*
Miller, Kenneth Raymond *biologist, educator*
Miller, Linda B. *political scientist*
Miranda, Robert *psychologist, researcher*
Mollis, A. Ralph *Secretary of State, Rhode Island, former mayor*
Mumford, David Bryant *mathematics professor*
Nacheman, Elinor Laurie *librarian*
Nelson, Jonathan M. *private equity firm executive*
Nieto Hernández, María de la Purificación *language educator*
Nurmikko, Arto Veikko *engineering educator*
O'Donnell, Terrence *lawyer, multi-industry company executive*
Oh, William *physician*
Olsen, Hans Peter *lawyer*
Pearce, George Hamilton *archbishop emeritus*
Pendergast, John Joseph III *lawyer*
Price, William Walley, Jr. *counselor, artist*
Pueschel, Siegfried M. *pediatrician, educator*
Putnam, Michael Courtney Jenkins *classics educator*
Putterman, Louis G. *economics professor*
Raaflaub, Kurt Arnold *classics educator*
Reilly, John B. *lawyer*
Rhodes, Ramona Lagiers *medical educator, researcher*
Ribbans, Geoffrey Wilfrid *language educator*
Richardson, Julie G. *private equity firm executive*
Richman, Jesse *ophthalmologist, researcher*
Richman, Marc Herbert *engineer, forensic specialist, educator*

Riordan, Cornelius *sociology educator, writer, consultant*
Risen, William Maurice, Jr. *chemistry educator*
Risica, Patricia *medical researcher, educator*
Roberts, Elizabeth H. *Lieutenant Governor of Rhode Island, former state legislator*
Robinson, William Philip III *state supreme court justice*
Rohr, Donald Gerard *history professor*
Roney, John M. *lawyer*
Rosenbaum, Randall *arts association administrator*
Rosenberg, Alan Gene *editor*
Rueschemeyer, Marilyn Schattner *sociology educator*
Saint-Amand, Pierre Nemours *humanities educator*
St. Florian, Friedrich Gartler *architect, educator*
Savage, John Edmund *computer science educator, researcher*
Schulz, Juergen *art historian, educator*
Scott, Jonathan P. *think-tank executive*
Selya, Bruce Marshall *federal judge*
Senerchia, Rory Elizabeth *language educator*
Sherman, Deming Eliot *lawyer*
Sherman, Merrill W. *bank executive*
Shu, Chi-Wang *mathematics professor, researcher*
Silverman, Joseph Hillel *mathematics professor*
Simmons, Ruth J. *academic administrator*
Steinbach, Meredith Lynn *writer, educator*
Stratt, Richard Mark *chemistry researcher, educator*
Stultz, Newell Maynard *retired political science professor*
Suttell, Paul Allyn *state supreme court justice*
Suuberg, Eric Michael *chemical engineering educator*
Sweeney, Patrick J. *medical educator*
Szostak, (M.) Anne *consulting firm executive, former bank executive*
Tang, Jay X. *physics professor*
Tobin, Thomas Joseph *bishop*
Tranghese, Michael A. *sports association executive*
Treaba, Diana Olguta *physician*
Triche, Elizabeth W. *epidemiologist, educator*
Vezeridis, Michael Panagiotis *surgeon, educator*
Viner-Brown, Samara I. *public health administrator*
Walecki, Wojciech Jan *physicist, engineer*
Webster, Thomas Jay *engineering educator*
Weiner, Jerome Harris *mechanical engineering educator*
Weinstock, Martin Arthur *dermatologist, epidemiologist, educator*
Weitberg, Alan Barry *physician, researcher, dean*
Wetle, Terrie Fox *gerontologist, educator, dean*
Wharton, Kristi Anna *biology professor*
Wideman, John Edgar *English literature educator, novelist*
Williams, David Owen *cardiologist*
Williams, Frank J. *retired state supreme court chief justice, historian, writer*
Wilmeth, Don Burton *theatre arts educator and historian, administrator, writer, editor, actor, director*
Wing, Edward Joseph *biomedical researcher, educator, dean*
Wood, Gordon Stewart *historian, educator, writer*
Wright, Carolyn D. *poet, literature and language professor*
Yates, Richard L. *multi-industry company executive*
Zhao, Lan *mathematics professor*
Zhou, Linda Hua *dermatologist, educator*
Zienowicz, Richard Joseph *plastic surgeon*

Riverside
Lekas, Mary Despina *retired otolaryngologist*
Rawlinson, Kenneth J. *dentist*
Schwegler, Nancy Ann *librarian, writer*
Thayer, Walter Raymond *retired internist*
Weisberger, Joseph Robert *retired state supreme court justice*

Rockville
Walker, Howard Ernest *lawyer*

Saunderstown
Leavitt, Thomas Whittlesey *retired museum director, educator*
Waters, Chris Harold *literature and language professor, poet*
Zaccaria, Mark Stuart *marketing professional*

Scituate
Neves, David *musician, educator*

Smithfield
Litoff, Judy Barrett *history professor*
Reedy, Walter Jay *history professor*
Simons, Kathleen A. *accountant, educator*
TEbaldi, Edinaldo *economics professor*

Tiverton
Kamm, Lewis *language educator*

Wakefield
Alexander, Jacqueline Peterson *retired librarian*
Boothroyd, Geoffrey *industrial and manufacturing engineering educator*
Frostic, Frederick Lee *strategic planning and defense policy consultant*
Leete, William White *retired artist*
Mason, Scott MacGregor *entrepreneur, inventor, consultant*
Moore, George Emerson, Jr. *geologist, educator*

Warren
Hedlund, Ellen Louise *administrator, educator*
Mehlman, Edwin Stephen *endodontist*

Warwick
Amante y Zapata, Joseph John *music professor*
Brown, Ann Eckert *artist, educator*
Hayes, Catherine Davis *elementary school educator*
Izzi, John *mathematics educator, writer, actor*
Kaiser, Audrey Kathleen *music educator*
Kelley, James Edward *actor, writer*
Losek, Darren Thomas *property manager, sales manager*
Madden, Cheryl Ann *history professor*
McNeil, Paul Joseph, Jr. *financial analyst*
Richards, Priscilla Ann *medical/surgical nurse*
Roque, Francis Xavier *bishop emeritus*

West Warwick
Carter, Wilfred Wilson *retired finance company executive, controller*

Westerly
Barnes, Chaplin Bradford *lawyer*
Crowley, Cynthia Warner Johnson *secondary school educator*

Woonsocket
Bodine, Chris W. *retail executive*
Brennan, Troyen A. *physician, retail pharmacy company executive*
Crowley, Rosa Quinonez *literature and language educator*
Denton, David M. *pharmaceutical executive*
Ferdinandi, V. Michael *retail executive*
Foulkes, Helena B. *pharmaceutical executive*
Frappier, Pearl Peters *retired bookkeeper*
Lankowsky, Zenon P. *lawyer, retail executive*
McGuigan, Stuart M. *pharmaceutical executive*
McLure, Howard A. *pharmaceutical executive*
Merlo, Larry J. *retail executive*
Rickard, David B. *retail executive*
Roberts, Jonathan C. *pharmaceutical executive*
Roszkowski, Joseph John *lawyer*
Ryan, Thomas Michael (Tom Ryan) *pharmaceutical company executive*
Sgarro, Douglas A. *retail executive, lawyer*
Wanebo, Harold J. *surgeon, educator*

SOUTH CAROLINA

Adams Run
Stewart, Shirley S. *retired elementary school educator*

Aiken
Bertsch, Paul M. *ecologist, director*
Bransome, Edwin Dagobert, Jr. *internal medicine educator*
Brisbin, I. Lehr, Jr. *retired research scientist*
Chelberg, Robert Douglas *military officer*
Dewberry, Raymond Allen *research scientist, combat engineer*
Dickson, Paul Wesley, Jr. *physicist*
Fadimba, Koffi Baana *mathematics professor*
Geyer, Andrew *literature and language professor*
Jefferson, Helen Butler *health protection technician*
Losey, Mary Haejung *music educator*
Porca, Sanela *economics professor*
Reid, Thomas F. *mathematics professor*
Rudnick, Irene Krugman *lawyer, educator, former state legislator*
Smith, Gregory White *writer*
Sykes, Richard Nesbit *retired history professor, department chairman*

Anderson
Bailey, Jake Schultz *volunteer, retired electrical engineer*
Chipman, Dennis Clarence, Jr. *forensic psychiatrist, consultant*
Kaiser, Louise Martin *elementary school educator*
Kline, George Louis *writer, translator, retired philosophy and literature educator*
Lummus, William Faulkner *retired physician*
Millwood, Kenneth Andrew *university librarian*
Palacios, Conny *language educator, writer*
Pryor, Betty Jo *biology professor*
Williford, Sandra Simmons *music educator*

Beaufort
Harvey, William Brantley, Jr. *lawyer, retired lieutenant governor*
Hunt, Rosemary Richardson *language educator*
Ivy, Conway Gayle *paint company executive*
Mauriocourt, Gregory *history professor*
Miller, Robert *retired military officer*
Pinkerton, Robert Bruce *mechanical engineer*
Saravo, Anne Cobble *clinical psychologist, mental health consultant*
Vido, Karen Phinney *education educator*

Bennettsville
Kinney, William Light, Jr. *editor, publishing executive*

Bluffton
Cann, Sharon Lee *retired health science librarian*
Croft, George T. *physicist*
Jerger, Edward William *engineering educator, dean*
Markwood, Stephen Ernest *Educational Consultant*
Pendley, William Tyler *military officer, educator*
Reuben, Alvin Bernard *communications and entertainment executive*
Staton, Joseph L. *marine biologist, educator*

Blythewood
Turfa, Arthur William *literature and language professor*

Camden
Pierce, Janis Vaughn *insurance executive, consultant*

Cayce
McElveen, William Lindsay *broadcast executive, educator*

Central
Sinnamon, Walter Bruce *college administrator, biology educator*

Charleston
Allen, Robert Johnson *plastic surgeon, educator*
Appleget, Terri Lynn *elementary school educator*
Ballenger, James C. *psychiatrist, researcher*
Barbour, John Richard *plastic surgeon*
Barickman, Donald *chef*
Barrett, Michael Baker *historian, educator*
Bass, Jack *journalism educator*
Bell, Norman Howard *retired endocrinologist, educator*
Benson, P. George *academic administrator, finance educator*
Boger, Heather Anne *research scientist*
Briggs, Patrick Ray *physics professor*
Brumgardt, John Raymond *museum director*
Cadwallader, Stephen Wayne *history and government educator*
Cantwell, Don *artistic director*
Carek, Donald J(ohn) *child psychiatry educator*
Carnell, Claude Mitchell, Jr. *academic administrator*
Chi, Angela *pathologist, educator*
Chiaramida, Salvatore *cardiologist, educator, health facility administrator*
Colomina-Garrigos, Maria D. *language educator*
Colwell, John Amory *physician*
Cooper, George, IV, *cardiologist, educator*
Cox, Walter Thompson III *lawyer, federal judge, educator*
Crawford, Fred Allen, Jr. *cardiothoracic surgeon, educator*
Daniell, Herman Burch *pharmacologist*
DiPiro, Joseph Thomas *dean, pharmacy educator*
Donnem, Sarah Lund *financial analyst, non-profit and political organization consultant*
Egelson, Pauline C. *director*
Fei, James Robert *engineering executive, consultant*
Fenno, Edward Thorndike *lawyer*
Frankel, Bruce Michael *neurosurgeon, researcher*
Freer, Robert Elliott, Jr. *lawyer*
Garnovskaya, Maria N. *medical educator, researcher*
Garr, David Ross *physician, educator*
Geentiens, Gaston Petrus, Jr. *former construction management consultant company executive*
Glassman, Armand Barry *physician, educator, scientist, administrator, pathologist*
Grant, J. Kirkland *lawyer, educator*
Grantham, Todd *philosopher, educator*
Greenberg, Charles Steven *hematologist*
Greenberg, Raymond Seth *academic and health facility administrator, educator*
Gross, Richard H. *surgeon, educator*
Guglielmone, Robert Eric *bishop*
Gunn, Morey Walker, Jr. *director music organist*
Gupta, Monika *nephrologist, researcher*
Haemmerich, Dieter *biomedical engineer*
Harold, Antony S. *biology professor*
Hulsey, Thomas C. *epidemiologist, researcher*
Jaffa, Ayad A. *medical educator, researcher*
Jaffe, Murray Sherwood *retired surgeon*
Jenkins, Pearl G. *retired secondary school educator, realtor*
Kahn, Ellis Irvin *lawyer*
Ketner, Linda *consulting company executive, civic worker*
Key, Lester Lyndon, Jr. *pediatrician, director*
Klaper, Martin Jay *lawyer*
Knackstedt, Lori Ann *research scientist*
Knapp, Keith Nathaniel *history professor*
Krause, James Stuart *psychology professor, director*
Lader, Philip *corporate director, lawyer, academic administrator, diplomat*
Leman, Robert Burton *cardiology educator*
Machowski, Liisa Ervin Sharpes *science educator*
Madory, James Richard *hospital administrator, retired military officer*
Malcolm, Robert James *psychiatrist, educator, clinical investigator*
Mallin, Robert *medical educator*
Maria, Bernard L. *pediatric neurologist*
Martin, Roblee Boettcher *retired cement manufacturing executive*
Martin, Thomas Rhodes *communications executive, writer, educator*
McConnell, Bright III *orthopaedic surgeon*
McCullough, Ralph Clayton, II, *law educator*
McCurdy, Layton *medical educator*
Meister, Howard Scott *marine biologist, educator*
Metcalf, John Stevenson *surgical pathologist, dermatologist*
Milliken, Garrett Wilson *psychology professor*
Mohr, Lawrence Charles *physician*
Newhard, James Michael Lloyd *medical educator*
Oates, James Caldwell *rheumatologist, physician, research scientist*
Osguthorpe, John David *otolaryngologist, educator*
Othersen, Henry Biemann, Jr. *surgeon, physician, educator*
Patrick, Charles William, Jr. *lawyer*
Peek, Pamela *language educator*
Pritchett, Samuel Travis *finance and insurance educator, researcher, consultant*
Reed, Carolyn E. *thoracic surgeon*
Reves, Joseph Gerald (Jerry Reves) *anesthesiology educator, dean*
Richardson, Anne Worsham *art gallery owner, artist*
Robinson, Neil Cibley, Jr. *lawyer*
Rollins, John Maxwell *business professor, disc jockey*
Rosa, John William *academic administrator, career military officer*
Rousseau, Paul Charles *geriatrician, palliative care physician, educator*
Sahn, Steven Alan *internist, educator*
Sanders, Alexander Mullings, Jr. *judge*
Scheman, L. Ronald *lawyer, author, bank executive*
Schreadley, Richard Lee *newswriter, retired editor*
Seaman, Sheila Lynne *librarian*
Simms, Lois Averetta *retired secondary school educator*
Simon, Kindra Lee *language educator, translator*
Sinisi, Kyle Scott *history professor*
Smith, J. Roy *museum director, education educator*
Smith, Todd D. *museum director*
Solomon, Kerry D. *ophthalmologist, surgeon, consultant*
Sparks, Donals L. *economics professor*
Strauch, Katina Parthemos *college librarian, publishing executive*
Stuart, Robert Kenneth *internist, hematologist, oncologist, educator*
Swenson, Cynthia Cupit *psychologist, educator*
Thompson, David Bernard *bishop emeritus*
Tolliver, Bryan K. *psychiatrist, educator*
Torras, Joseph Hill *pulp and paper company executive*
Underwood, Paul Benjamin *gynecologist, oncologist, educator*
Vakser, Ilya *biophysicist, educator*
Waller, John Louis *anesthesiologist, educator*
Wingo, Marshall Scott *urologist*
Wooten-Blanks, Leslie *biologist*
Wyatt, Justin K. *chemistry professor*
Wyrick, Charles Lloyd, Jr. *editor, writer*

Clemson
An, Yanming *philosopher, literature and language professor*
Aziz, Nadim Mahmoud *engineering educator*
Bailey, Beatrice Naff *language educator, researcher*
Bainbridge, Robert Warin *architect, consultant*
Barfield, Ray Elliott *literature and language professor*
Barker, James F. *academic administrator*
Bartley, Abel Alphonso *history professor*
Benjamin, Daniel Kelly *economics professor*
Bennett, Archie Wayne *academic administrator*
Brawley, Joel Vincent *mathematician, educator*
Burton, O'Neil B. III *academic administrator*
Chisman, James Allan *industrial engineering educator, consultant*
Clausen, Hugh Joseph *retired army officer*
Cox, Headley Morris, Jr. *lawyer, educator*
Cranston, Philip Edward *foreign language professional*
DesMarteau, Darryl Dwayne *chemistry professor*
Dunn, Charles Wythe *political science educator*
Frugoli, Julia Alice *research scientist*
Gartner, William B. *entrepreneur, educator*
Greenstein, Joel Sandor *industrial engineering educator*
Haller, William John *social sciences educator*
Hewitt, Robert Reid *landscape architect*
Jacobs, David P. *science educator*
Jalili, Nader *mechanical engineer, educator*
Kelly, John William, Jr. *academic administrator*
Kimbler, Delbert Lee, Jr. *retired industrial engineering educator*
King, Bruce Michael *psychology professor, department chairman*
Kurz, Mary E. *engineering educator*
Layne, Desmond R. *horticulturist, educator*
Luo, Jian *engineering educator, researcher*
Milhous, Elizabeth *social studies educator*
Owino, Tom Obuya *science educator, researcher*
Pang, Wei Chiang *civil engineer, educator*
Petzel, Florence Eloise *textiles educator*
Purnell, Oliver Gordon, Jr. *men's college basketball coach*
Pursley, Michael Bader *engineering educator, communications systems researcher, consultant*
Rajapakse, Nihal *horticulturist, educator*
Ravichandran, Nadarajah *civil engineer, researcher*
Sauer, Raymond D., Jr. *economics professor*
Scott, Mark C. *biologist, educator*
Shappell, Scott Allen *engineering educator, consultant*
Swinney, Dabo *college football coach*
Tritt, Terry *physicist*
Underwood, Richard Allan *English language educator*
Walker, Ian David *engineering educator*
Wheeler, Alfred George, Jr. *retired entomologist, biology professor, researcher*
Xuan, Xiangchun *engineering educator*
Yang, Tina *finance educator*
Zumbrunnen, David Arnold *engineering educator*

Clinton
Buckland, Karen Wisser *music educator*
Cornelson, George Henry, IV, *retired textile company executive*
Dutrow, Anita Marceca *education educator*
Meeker, Paige H. *science educator*
Rico, Christopher *artist*
Roth, Dale Davis *music educator, religious organization administrator*
Skinner, James Lister III *retired language educator*
Spiegel, John Franklin *theater educator*

Clio
McLeod, Marilynn Hayes *retired educational administrator, farmer*

Columbia
Almond, Carl Herman *surgeon, physician, educator*
Amidon, Roger Lyman *public health service officer, educator*
Ammal, Salai Cheettu *chemist*
Anderson, William H. *architect*
Barbieri, Katherine *political science professor*
Barnum, Mary Ann Mook *information management manager*
Barnum, William Douglas *retired communications executive*
Bates, Carol Henry *musicologist, music educator*
Bauer, R. Andre *lieutenant governor*
Beasley, David Muldrow *former governor, consultant*
Beatty, Donald W. *state supreme court justice*
Benner, Cristina Hill *literature and language educator*
Beyer, Christine E. *academic standards and assessment consultant*
Blanton, Hoover Clarence *lawyer*
Blue Sky, *artist, muralist*
Boggs, Jack Aaron *retired banker, municipal government official*
Bostick, Robert Maner *epidemiologist, family physician*
Boyce, Corrie Mosby *music educator*
Breedin, Berryman Brent *journalist, consultant, historian, public relations executive*
Briggs, Ward Wright *classics educator*
Brockelsby, Jeffrey Lind *investment executive*
Brosius, Karen *museum director*
Carr, Edward R. *environmentalist, educator*

Chaudhry, M. Hanif engineering educator, consultant, dean
Chellis, Converse A., II, state treasurer
Cofield, Virginia Riley elementary school educator, piano teacher
Conrad, Paul Ernest transportation consultant
Courson, John Edward state legislator, insurance company executive
Cunningham, Joseph Edward elementary school educator
Currie, Cameron McGowan federal judge
Datta, Timir physicist, solid state and materials consultant
Dawson, Katon political organization administrator
Day, Richard Earl lawyer, educator
Dilworth, Stephen James mathematics educator
Dobrasko, Rebekah cultural organization administrator, historian
Donald, Alexander Grant psychiatrist, educator
Drozda, Jeffery Allen insurance company executive, former state legislator
Duffy, John Joseph retired academic administrator, historian, educator
Duggan, Carol Cook research and development company executive
Duggan, Kevin information technology professional
Edgar, Walter Bellingrath historian, educator
Edge, Ronald Dovaston physics professor
Ellis, F. Earl, Jr. lawyer
Ellis, Yolanda Y. music educator, small business owner
Ezell, Elizabeth Anne music educator
Fazzino, Paul mechanical engineer
Finkel, Gerald Michael lawyer
Flanagan, Clyde Harvey, Jr. psychiatrist, psychoanalyst, educator
Foster, Robert Watson, Sr. law educator
Fowler, Carol Khare political organization administrator
Franklin, Benjamin, V, English language educator
Gaffney, Thomas Edward physician
Gibbons, Joseph Harrison engineering educator, farmer
Glad, Betty political scientist, educator
Grimball, Caroline Gordon retail sales professional
Hallman, Cecilia Ann real estate consultant
Hamilton, Clyde Henry federal judge
Hammond, Mark state official
Handel, Richard Craig lawyer
Harvey, Jonathan Matthew lawyer
Hearn, Kaye Gorenflo state judge
Hollis, Charles Eugene, Jr. finance company executive
Hooker, Steven P. sports medicine physician, educator
Hubbard, William C. lawyer
Hudson, Carolyn Brauer application developer, educator
Humphries, John O'Neal cardiologist, educator, dean
Hunter, C. Earl state agency administrator, environmental services administrator
Jabbari, Esmaiel polymer scientist, researcher
Jacobs, Louie A. state banking agency administrator
Janicki, Joseph S. physiologist, educator
Jeon, Donghyup research scientist
Kegley, Charles William, Jr. political science professor
Kendler, Bernhard retired editor
Kiker, Billy Frazier economics professor
Kittredge, John Williamson state supreme court justice
Koley, Goutam science educator
Krishnan, Balakrishnan engineering educator
Land, John Calhoun III lawyer, South Carolina State Senator
Larkin, William John religious studies educator
Leatherman, Hugh Kenneth, Sr. state legislator, engineering executive
Li, Xiang (Robert Li) tourism educator, director
Limehouse, Harry Bancroft, Jr. real estate developer, transportation consultant
Lindley, Lisa L. medical educator
Lloyd, Reginald Ivan state agency administrator, former prosecutor
Logan, Sandra Jean retired economics and business professor
Long, Eugene Thomas III philosophy educator, academic administrator
Martin, Robert William econometrician
Matthews, Steve Allen lawyer
McCaslin, Elizabeth Ann athletic trainer
McCray, Nikki Kesangame women's college basketball coach, former professional basketball player
McGhee, Carla Renee women's college basketball coach, retired professional basketball player
McGuire, Franklin Riley pulmonologist, educator
McKeown, Robert E. epidemiologist, educator
McLendon, Brian Andrew lab administrator, educator
McLeod, Walton James III state legislator, lawyer
McMaster, Henry Dargan state attorney general
Meyer-Brosdahl, Deborah J.C. educator, researcher
Monahan, Thomas Paul accountant
Mood, Francis P., Jr. lawyer, utilities executive
Morgan, Robert Marion educational research educator
Morris, Charlotte Ann media specialist, school librarian
Moskowitz, Jay health science association administrator, educator, dean
Nachtigal, Maurice pathology professor
Nexsen, Julian Jacobs lawyer
Nottingham, James M. surgeon, educator
Outin, Mary Louise business, multi-cultural history and geneology educator
Padgett, William Jowayne mathematics professor, researcher
Page, Randall state official
Palms, John Michael academic administrator, physicist
Papathanasiou, Thanasis D. chemical engineer, educator
Pastides, Harris academic administrator
Piper, Crystal Nicole medical researcher
Pleicones, Costa M. state supreme court justice
Popov, Branko Nestor engineering educator, educator
Powell, Donald Ashmore clinical research psychologist
Pratt, Walter F., Jr. dean, law educator
Preedom, Barry Mason physicist, researcher
Rawlinson, Helen Ann librarian
Rebollo, Anthony Ernest lawyer
Rex, Jim state official, school system administrator
Samuel, May Linda environmental scientist
Sanford, Mark (Marshall Clement Sanford Jr.) Governor of South Carolina, former United States Representative from South Carolina
Seigler, Ruth Queen college nursing administrator, educator, consultant
Sellers, Bakari T. state legislator
Sepulveda, Sonja Marian Atkinson choral director, accompanist
Shedd, Dennis W. federal judge
Sheppe, Joseph Andrew surgeon
Sherrer, John M. III cultural organization administrator
Shuler, Ellie Givan, Jr. retired military officer, museum administrator
Smith, Theresa Joanne research scientist, educator
Sorensen, Andrew Aaron retired academic administrator
Sproat, Ruth C. retired director, consultant
Spurrier, Steve (Steven Orr Spurrier) college football coach
Staley, Dawn Michelle women's college basketball coach, retired professional basketball player
Still, Charles Neal retired neurologist, medical educator, consultant
Strom, J. Preston, Jr. lawyer
Synnott, Marcia Graham history professor
Tate, Harold Simmons, Jr. lawyer
Teegen, Hildy dean, business educator
Thiruvanamalai, Valarmathi Mani pathologist, educator
Thomas, Latta Roosevelt religious educator, clergy
Timmerman, William B. utilities executive, accountant
Toal, Jean Hoefer state supreme court chief justice
Tripathi, Ramesh Chandra ophthalmologist, researcher, educator
Turnage, Scott E. history professor
Vogt, Thomas physics professor, director
Waldron, Robert Leroy, II, radiologist, educator
Waller, John Henry, Jr. state supreme court justice
Warren, Charles David library consultant
Weeks, J. David state representative, lawyer
Welch, Audrey B. retired music educator
Wideman, Ida Devlin science educator
Wilder, Ronald Parker economics professor
Wilkins, Walt (William Walter Wilkins III) prosecutor
Witherspoon, Walter Pennington, Jr. orthodontist
Wright, Harry Hercules psychiatrist
Xu, Zhi-Hui research scientist

Conway
Bachman, Maria K. English professor
Díaz, Barbara Beck educator
Gilman, Craig marine science professor
McMillan, Michael Reid retired orthopedic surgeon
Melcher, Martha Elena language educator
Monroe, Richard W. university professor
Sinclair, Frances Teresa music educator, musician
Stewart, Patricia Diane psychologist

Daniel Island
Gillespie, John David political science educator

Darlington
Gough, Herbert Frederick, Jr. minister
Ladson, Brenda Lee librarian

Denmark
Goodman, Jonathan M., II, engineering educator

Donalds
Carlock, John Bruce, Jr. retired language educator

Easley
Dyer, Jane Ballard pilot
Howe, Linda Arlene nursing educator, writer
Spearman, David Hagood retired veterinarian

Edisto Island
Van Metre, Margaret Cheryl performing company executive, dancer, educator

Florence
Baroody, Albert Joseph, Jr. pastoral counselor
Best, David Keith theater educator, department chairman
DeMichele, Domenic John neurologist, neuroradiologist
Foster, Jackie Green voice educator
Goradia, Hrishikesh J. engineering educator, researcher
Gourley, Alfred Glen, Jr. theater educator
Imbeau, Stephen Alan allergist
Singletary, Eloise business educator
Warters, T. Alissa political science professor, director

Fort Jackson
Brinsfield, John Wesley military officer, educator

Fort Mill
Dickey, Martin music educator

Gaffney
Berry, Scott D. physics professor, director
Griffin, Penni Oncken social worker, educator
Ivey, Elizabeth Reeves retired school system administrator
Spencer, Albert Franklin physical education educator
Witt, Betsy criminologist, educator

Georgetown
Ahearn, Arthur Mason orthopedist, surgeon, consultant
Bazemore, Trudy McConnell librarian

Graniteville
Learnard, James Michael conversational English professor, volunteer intellectual project, developmental English professor, retired collections and bad debt manager

Greenville
Alford, Robert Wilfrid, Jr. middle school educator
Baker, Harriet Kugley elementary school educator
Ballou, Kathryn Jeanne performing arts educator
Baur, Michael L. information technology executive
Belanger, Laura Hewlette environmental scientist, consultant
Blackwell, Christopher William literature educator
Bonner, Jack Wilbur III psychiatrist, educator, administrator
Brownlee, Noel Anderson pathologist, consultant
Crabtree, John Henry, Jr. retired English educator
Cureton, Claudette Hazel Chapman retired biology professor
DeMint, Jim (James Warren DeMint) United States Senator from South Carolina, former congressman
Dorman, D. Douglas human resources specialist, hospital administrator
Dreskin, Jeanet Steckler painter, medical artist, educator
Fallavollita, Paul financial analyst
Ferguson, Donald Littlefield retired lawyer
Gustafson, Dwight Leonard university dean
Higgins, Elizabeth Tate mathematics professor, director
Horton, James Wright retired lawyer
Hultstrand, Charles John architect
Hutson, Melvin Robert lawyer
Johnson, Jane Elizabeth medical technician
Jones, Bob III academic administrator
Jones, Robert Thaddues retired principal
Massey, Raymond David lawyer
Mauldin, John Inglis public defender
McCuen, Maureen E. history educator
Mears, Laine engineering educator
Mebane, William deBerniere newspaper publisher
Melton, Gary Bentley psychologist, educator
Morgan, Ruby Norris musician, educator
Oxner, George Dewey, Jr. lawyer
Payne, George Frederick academic administrator
Phillips, Joseph Brantley, Jr. lawyer
Riley, Richard Wilson lawyer, former United States Secretary of Education
Riordan, Michael C. hospital administrator
Rowe, Karen D. literature and language professor
Sanders, Harvey Gibert, Jr. lawyer
Schoolfield, Brenda Thompson history professor
Shi, David E. academic administrator, historian
Simmons, Charles Bedford, Jr. judge
Smith, Philip Daniel academic administrator, education educator
Stratton, Sally G. (Sara) retired school system administrator
Talley, Michael Frank lawyer
Traxler, William Byrd, Jr. federal judge
Walters, Johnnie McKeiver lawyer
Wei, Yanzhang microbiologist, educator
Westrope, Martha Randolph psychologist, consultant
White, Daniel Bowman lawyer
Wyche, Cyril Thomas lawyer
Wyche, Madison Baker III lawyer
Zou, Tong electrical engineer

Greenwood
Boxx, Rita McCord retired banker
Coon, Michael Dennard theater educator
Cushing, Sara Elizabeth language educator, writer
Jackson, Larry Artope retired college president
Moore, James E. former state supreme court justice
Phillips, Robert Kenney retired english literature and language professor
Schwartz, Charles E. medical geneticist, medical association administrator
Towles, Elizabeth W. engineering educator
Witherspoon, Kevin B. history professor

Greer
Evans, Philip G. media consultant, former sports association executive
Hu, Yiping metallurgical engineer
McAbee, Thomas Allen psychologist
McKenzie, Kathleen Julianna artist
Sundstrom, Harold Walter public relations executive

Hardeeville
Kadar, Karin Patricia librarian

Hartsville
Cuppett, Cathleen G. literature and language professor
DeLoach, Harris E.(Eugene), Jr. manufacturing executive, lawyer
Doubles, Malcolm Carroll college administrator
Menius, Espie Flynn, Jr. electrical engineer
Rubinstein, Joseph Harris education educator

Hilton Head
Drakeman, Donald Lee venture capitalist
Gallagher, Terrence Vincent editor
Harty, James D. former manufacturing company executive

Hilton Head Island
Adams, William Hensley ecologist, educator
Becker, Karl Martin retired lawyer
Brock, Karena Diane dancer, educator
Brown, Arthur Edmon, Jr. retired army officer
Burns, C(harles) Patrick hematologist, oncologist
Conn, Margaret Elbow human resources specialist
Cunningham, William Henry retired food products executive
Davis, Mary Martha (Marty Davis) small business owner, consultant
Engelman, Karl physician
Esposito, John Vincent lawyer
Field, James Bernard internist, educator
Gruchacz, Robert S. real estate company officer
Hagoort, Thomas Henry retired lawyer
Huckins, Harold Aaron chemical engineer
Jarvis, William Robert epidemiologist, educator
Kearney-Nunnery, Rose nursing administrator, educator, consultant
Lefer, Allan Mark physiologist
Levy, Maurice retired medical educator, researcher
Lewis, Gene Evans retired medical equipment company executive
McKeldin, William Evans management consultant
Ostergard, Paul Michael foundation executive
Patton, Joseph Donald, Jr. management consultant
Reed, Frances Boogher writer, actress
Roehrig, C(harles) Burns internist, consultant
Rose, William Shepard, Jr. lawyer
Rulis, Raymond Joseph manufacturing executive, consultant
Russell, Allen Stevenson retired metal products executive
Selvy, Barbara dance instructor
Shaheen, Jack George communications educator
Simons, Lawrence Brook lawyer
Wesselmann, Glenn Allen retired health facility administrator
Windman, Arnold Lewis retired mechanical engineer
Wright, Marshall manufacturing executive, diplomat
Yates-Williams, Linda Snow real estate broker

Hopkins
Moore, Willard S. oceanographer, educator

Indian Land
Pettus, Mildred Louise retired history professor, writer

Inman
D'Ambrosio, Jody (Gigi) Lynn art educator
Fogarty, Charles Michael pulmonologist, researcher

Irmo
Branham, Jennie Jones artist
Branham, Mack Carison, Jr. retired religious organization administrator, minister
Murphy, Jennifer H. (Buffy Murphy) elementary school educator

Isle Of Palms
Elliott, Larry Paul radiologist, educator
Lehr, Judy Brown educational consultant

Jackson
Smith, Mark Eugene nuclear engineering service company executive

Johns Island
Jackson, Mary craftswoman
Tarr, Robert Joseph, Jr. publishing and retail executive

Kiawah Island
Andria, Louis Matthew orthodontist
Warren, Russell Glen educational consultant

Lancaster
Bundy, Charles Alan retired foundation executive

Latta
Berry, Christy school librarian

Laurens
Griffin, Mary Frances retired media consultant

Lexington
MacNeill, Daniel Scott library director
Smith, John Powell entomologist, educator
Wilkins, Robert Pearce writer, lawyer

Marion
Harrelson, Nancy construction and real estate development company executive

Mauldin
Smith, Lisa Coleman autism and neurological disabilities special educator

Mc Cormick
Clayton, Verna Lewis state legislator
Soni, Jayshri science educator, director
Zeller, Michael James psychologist, educator

Mount Pleasant
Bilas, Richard A. economist
Bloder, Katharine Jean elementary school educator
Esnaola, Nestor F. surgeon, director
Gilbert, James Eastham academic administrator
Glenn, Edward Vernon Ferrell lawyer, consultant
Macdonald, Robert Rigg, Jr. retired museum director
Maize, John Christopher dermatologist, educator
Mosier, Arvin Ray chemist, researcher
Royall, Mary-Julia C. church organist, historian
Weininger, Markus radiologist

Myrtle Beach
Brogan, Richard Dennis retired civil engineer
Cazier, James Stanley social sciences educator, department chairman
Cohen, Stuart Colin science educator
Favaro, Mary Kaye Asperheim pediatrician, writer
Gravely, Mary Jeane volunteer
Harwell, David Walker retired judge
Lowes, Sandra Elaine chiropractor, educator
McCaffrey, Edmund F. abbot emeritus
Schwartz, Steve Wendelin physician
Sugishita, Jonea Gene marketing executive, copywriter

Nesmith
Pressley, Deloris N. retired literacy educator

New Zion
Gibbons, Robert Butler, Jr. *retired military officer*

Newberry
Horn, Charles *biology professor, department chairman*
McDowell, Betsy M. *critical care nurse, educator*
Partridge, William Franklin, Jr. *lawyer*

North Augusta
Champion, Susan Michele *music educator*

North Charleston
Hartnett, Richard James *literature and language professor, artist*
Heyward, Willie Bruce *lawyer, advocate*
Perry, Evelyn Reis *communications company executive*

North Myrtle Beach
Byrne, James Frederick *banker*

Orangeburg
Abdel-Kader, Wagih G. *physics professor*
Barnwell, Charles Brison, Jr. *lawyer*
Battle-Bryant, Rebecca *educational association administrator*
Brandes, Brian Todd *chemical engineer*
Byers, Keith Thomas *librarian*
Chen, Jianguo *biology professor*
Dalton, Cheryl Renee *entrepreneur*
Dees Grevious, Annette *speech educator, actress*
Foerster, Lisa Renee *voice educator*
Hill, Howard Darnell *consultant*
Hong, Jae-Dong *industrial engineering educator*
Hooker, Ward L. *economics professor*
Igwe, Kodilinye *art educator*
Kantor, Camelia Maria *geography instructor, researcher*
Konate, Dior *history professor*
Mahroof, Rizana M. *biology professor*
Manson, Bonita Yvonne *nutritionist, educator*
Martin, Frank C., II, *art educator*
Pearson, Melissa Berry *literature and language educator*
Silvestry, Ruben *philologist, educator*
Sims, Edward Howell *editor, writer*
Smoak, Randolph Duncan, Jr. *surgeon*
Wallace, Nathaniel Owen *English language educator*

Pauline
Burnett, E. C. III *former state supreme court justice*

Pawleys Island
Bodie, Joseph Russell *environmental services administrator*
Grubb, William Francis Xavier *consumer products company executive, marketing professional*
Justice, Franklin Pierce, Jr. *oil industry executive*
Kay, Thomas Oliver *agricultural consultant*
Matelic, Candace Tangorra *museum director, educator, organizational consultant*
Proefrock, Carl Kenneth *academic medical administrator*
Salmon, Robin Robertson *museum curator, editor*

Pendleton
Beyerlein, Anne MoYung *science educator*
Gilmour, Phillip Curtis *science educator*
Klaine, Stephen James *environmental toxicology educator*
Marshall, Gerald Lee *mathematician, educator*

Pickens
Hardin, Janet Becker *gifted and talented educator, music educator*
Wyche, Sam David *county official, former professional football coach*

Ridgeland
Cameron, Thomas William Lane *investment company executive*

Rock Hill
Bristow, Robert O'Neil *writer, educator*
Ford, Mary (Polly) Wylie *retired physical education educator*
Franklin, A. David *retired college dean, music educator, journalist*
Hale, Connie *music educator*
Manetta, Ameda Avrill *social sciences educator*
Sebhatu, Mesgun *physics professor*
Yilma, Almaz *biology professor*

Roebuck
Smith, Alan Wade *music educator*

Saint Helena Island
Googins, Sonya Forbes *state legislator, retired banker*
Tarr-Whelan, Linda *political organization worker, consultant*

Seneca
Kenelly, John Willis, Jr. *mathematician, educator*
Strong-Tidman, Virginia Adele *marketing professional*

Simpsonville
Kanzler, George *journalist, music critic*
Munley, William Edward *health services administrator*
Pratt, Harry Davis *retired entomologist*

Spartanburg
Augthun, Carol Elise *artist, educator*
Bullard, John Moore *religious studies educator, church musician*
Cann, Katherine Davis *history professor*
Chmiel, Mark E. *marketing professional, food service company executive*
Colloms, Vergene Jenkins *music educator, composer, producer*
Corden, Paul H. *retired college program director, food service executive*
Dille, Brice *ophthalmologist*
Harris, Carmen *history professor*
Johnson, Sarah J. *music educator*
Jones, William Osborne, II, *physician assistant, nephrologist*
Kay, Charles D. *philosophy educator*
Krick-Aigner, Kirsten Andrea *language educator*
Krout-Watson, Tracy *psychologist*
Lancaster, Amy *dean*
Leonard, Walter Raymond *retired biology professor*
Marchioli, Nelson Jerome *restaurant chain executive*
McGehee, Larry Thomas *retired academic administrator*
Milliken, Roger *textile and chemical company executive*
Moeller, John *biology professor*
Pae, Holly *special education educator*
Pollack, Elisa Erali *language educator*
Racine, Philip Noel *retired history educator*
Reback, Charles S. *economics professor*
Richard, Orr Kenneth *oncologist, educator*
Sellars, Christi von Lehe *music educator*
Smithart-Oglesby, Debra Lynn *restaurant chain executive*
Stephens, Bobby Gene *college administrator, consultant*
Wilde, Edwin Frederick *retired mathematics professor*
Wingo, Winston Alfonso *art educator*

Sullivans Island
Selby, John Bayne, Sr. *retired radiologist, medical educator*

Summerville
Burke, Rhonda Williams *counselor*
Deavers, James Frederick *optometrist, clinical nutritionist*
Reisman, Rosemary Moody Canfield *writer, humanities educator*

Sumter
Amirzadeh, Jafar *physics professor*
Barrow, Tawana Walker *psychiatrist, consultant*
Boyle, Ladson Hunter, Jr. *actor, educator*
Brown, Barbara Ann *county extension agent*
Fulcher, James P. *language educator*
Leavell, Elizabeth Boykin *retired pediatrician*

Sunset
Brodbeck, William Jan *marketing professional*

Taylors
Porter, Jean McRae *counselor*
Smith, Morton Howison *religious organization administrator, educator*

Tigerville
Gonzalez, Jorge Ivan *language educator*
NeSmith, Richard A. *education educator, consultant*
Shin, Hiewon *literature and language professor*

Travelers Rest
Bailey, Helen McShane *historian, consultant*

Trenton
Mims, Julian L. III *history professor, archivist*

Ulmer
Mathias, Lynda Rowell *retired secondary school educator*

Union
Whitener, William Jackson *retired military officer, dean*

Walterboro
Cone, George Wallis *lawyer*
Garrett, Darlynn Middleton *media specialist*
Refinetti, Roberto *biopsychologist*
Workman, William Douglas III *town manager; retired mayor, gas industry executive*

Wedgefield
McLaurin, Hugh McFaddin III *military officer, museum program director*

Wellford
Seay, Stephanie *elementary school educator*

West Columbia
Battista, Bradley Matthew *geophysicist*
Byars, Merlene Hutto *accountant, artist, writer*
Harmon, Horace Elmer, Jr. *retired museum director, cultural history consultant*
Klutzow, Friedrich Wilhelm *neuropathologist*
Phillips, Karen Diane *surgeon*
Wheeler, Hoyt Noland *management educator, arbitrator*

White Rock
Aull, James Stroud *retired bishop*

Whitmire
Kibler, James Everett, Jr. *English language educator, writer*

Williamston
Alewine, James William *financial executive*

Winnsboro
Meyer, Jack Allen *historian, consultant*

Woodruff
Childers, Bob Eugene *educational association executive*

Yemassee
Olendorf, William Carr, Jr. *small business owner*

York
Blackwell, Paul Eugene, Sr. *military officer*

SOUTH DAKOTA

Aberdeen
Anderson, Esther Elizabeth *retired pediatrician, educator*
Dohn, Ken W. *business educator*
Hedges, Mark Stephen *clinical psychologist*
Mendez, Celestino Galo *mathematics professor, dean*

Britton
Farrar, Frank Leroy *lawyer, former governor*

Brookings
Bailey, Harold Stevens, Jr. *retired educational administrator*
Beer, Betty Louise *lawyer*
Brooks, April Ahlers *history professor*
Chicoine, David Lyle *academic administrator*
Clay, Sharon A. *science educator*
Dalaly, Basil *nutritionist, educator*
Eischen, Michelle Robin *art educator*
Funchion, Michael F. *historian, educator*
Gienapp, David Ray *judge*
Johnston, Aaron *women's college basketball coach*
Kaushik, Radhey Shyam *microbiologist, educator, immunologist*
McFarland, Douglas C. *muscle biologist, educator*
McGee, Megan E. *coach, consultant*
Mix, Vickie Lynn *school librarian, educator*
Moldenhauer, William Calvin *soil scientist*
Perumal, Omathanu Pillai *research scientist, medical researcher, educator*
Rahman, Shafiqur *neuropharmacologist, scientist, professor, editor*
Rogers, Lawrence E. *education educator*
Schingoethe, David John *dairy cattle nutritionist*
Schumacher, Tom E. *soil scientist, educator*
Vanderpan, Norma *retired elementary school educator*

Bruce
Haertel, Lois Steben *education educator*

Canton
Perkinson, Robert Ronald *psychologist, consultant*

Eagle Butte
Eisenbraun, Monica T. *language educator*
Houston, Pamela Jo *humanities educator*
Webb, Yvonne M. *secondary school educator*

Freeman
Ries, Edward Richard *petroleum geologist, consultant*

Ipswich
Beck, Vaughn Peter *lawyer*

Jefferson
Gitter, Richard *thoracic surgeon*

Kadoka
Stout, Maye Alma *retired secondary school educator*

Lennox
Brendtro, Larry Kay *psychologist*

Lower Brule
Gerlach, Amy Louise *physical education educator*

Madison
John, Laflin H. *literature and language professor*

Mc Laughlin
Lehman, Carol Sue *school librarian*

Mobridge
Hall, Jo(sephine) Marian *editor*

Mud Butte
Ingalls, Marie Cecelie *former state legislator, retail executive*

Parker
Zimmer, John Herman *lawyer*

Pierre
Daugaard, Dennis M. *lieutenant governor*
Gerdes, David Alan *lawyer*
Gilbertson, David *state supreme court chief justice*
Gray, Bob *state legislator, political organization administrator*
Hollingsworth, Doneen B. *state agency administrator*
Konenkamp, John K. *state supreme court justice*
Larsen, Wallace Lawrence *retired transportation engineer, county official*
Larson, Vernon LeRoy *state treasurer*
Long, Larry *state attorney general*
Lucas, Larry James *state legislator*
Meierhenry, Judith Knittel *state supreme court justice*
Nelson, Chris A. *Secretary of State, South Dakota*
Novotny, Roger *state banking agency administrator*
Oster, Tom (Thomas J. Oster) *state official, school system administrator*
Repsys, Andrew J. *aquatic biologist, limnologist, water quality specialist, environmental biologist*
Riter, Robert C., Jr. *lawyer*
Rounds, Mike (Marion Michael Rounds) *Governor of South Dakota*
Severson, Glen Arthur *state supreme court justice*
Siebersma, Daniel *state librarian*
Thompson, Charles Murray *lawyer*
Weyer, Dianne Sue *health facility administrator*
Zinter, Steven L. *state supreme court justice*

Rapid City
Brookes, Leslie Joan *retired maternal/surgical nurse*
Buchanan, Carolee Horstman *special education educator, consultant*
Clark, Lynda Kay *artist*
Comcally, Tillian *historian, educator*
Corwin, Bert Clark *optometrist*
Cupich, Blase J. *bishop*
Foye, Thomas Harold *lawyer*
Hamilton, Douglas Warren *real estate executive*
Lien, Chris *construction executive*
Muci Küchler, Karim Heinz *mechanical engineering educator*
Patnaik, Anil Kumar *engineering educator, researcher*
Ramakrishnan, Venkataswamy *civil engineer, educator*
Roggenthen, William *geologist, educator*
Scofield, Gordon Lloyd *mechanical engineer, educator*
Smith, Paul Letton, Jr. *geophysicist*
Viken, Linda Lea Margaret *lawyer*
Voyles, C. Robert *electronics executive*
White, Ronald Joseph *biomedical researcher, physiologist, educator*
Wishard, Della Mae *former newspaper editor*
Wynia, Steven *industrial technical educator*
Yoon, Myungkeun *engineering educator*

Rosebud
Garriott, Wizipan *educational association administrator*

Rosholt
Swier, Carol Ann *English educator*

Saint Lawrence
Lockner, Vera Joanne *farmer, rancher, state legislator*

Sioux Falls
Aldern, Robert Judson *architectural, liturgical and landscape artist*
Ashworth, Julie *elementary school educator*
Bartling, Kimberly Kay *communications educator, theater educator*
Casas-Melley, Adela Teresa *pediatrician, surgeon*
Chapman, Cheryl K. *political organization administrator*
Christensen, David Allen *retired manufacturing executive*
Deering, Thomas Edwin *educator*
Dowling, Barbara R. *elementary school educator*
Gerdes, Anthony Martin *research scientist, health science association administrator*
Hagemeier, Deborah Anne *library director*
Hildebrand, Steve C. *consulting firm executive, political strategist*
Himler, Thomas Charles *psychologist*
Huseboe, Arthur Robert *American literature educator*
Jackley, Martin (Marty) J. *prosecutor*
Jaqua, Richard Allen *pathologist*
Jernberg, Beth L. *education educator*
Lunde, Lloyd William *vocational school educator*
Marshall, Mark F. *lawyer*
Munson, David Roy *Mayor, Sioux Falls, South Dakota*
Murdock, Rebecca Therese *management consultant, director*
Narendranath, Neelakantam V. *microbiologist, researcher*
Piersol, Lawrence L. *federal judge*
Rogers, David Hughes *banking and financial service professor, dean, real estate company executive*
Sanford, T(homas) Denny *bank executive*
Senay, Gabriel Bogale *research scientist, educator*
Sommer, Carol R. *elementary school educator*
Staggers, Kermit LeMoyne, II, *history and political science professor, state legislator, municipal official*
Swain, Paul Joseph *bishop*
Talley, Robert Cochran *academic administrator, cardiologist*
Tapken, Michelle G. *prosecutor*
Thompson, Ronelle Kay Hildebrandt *library director*
Viste, Arlen Ellard *chemistry professor*
Vorhes, Anna Kirstine *music educator*
Wegner, Karl Heinrich *retired pathologist, educator, farmer*
Welk, Thomas John *lawyer*
Wollman, Roger Leland *federal judge*

Spearfish
Colmenero-Chilberg, Laura Elizabeth *sociology professor*
Ellis, Mary Louise Helgeson *retired healthcare technology company executive*
King, Vincent Allan *literature and language professor*
Meyers, Kent *literature and language professor, writer*
Nsiah, Christian *economics professor, consultant*

Sturgis
Larson, Marlan T. *agricultural studies educator*

Vermillion
Balakier, James J. *literature and language professor*
Bucklin, Steven Jay *history professor*
Burton, Maureen B. *medical educator*
Clem, Alan Leland *retired political scientist, educator*
DiMond, Patricia Rae *literature and language professor*
Georgescu, Catalin *mathematician, educator*
Hilderbrand, Robert Clinton *history professor*
Hoover, Herbert Theodore *historian, educator*
Keifer, Joyce *science association director*
Kim, Young Ae *graphics designer, educator*
Knutson, Wayne Shafer *retired theater and English educator*
Melmer, Rick *dean, former state official, school system administrator*

Schlarman, Julie Jo *history professor, consultant*
Sevening, Diane Kay *alcohol/drug abuse studies educator, researcher*

Wall
Pederson, Gordon Roy *retired state legislator, military officer*

Wessington Springs
Mohling, Charlotte *middle school educator*

Yankton
Foster, James Caldwell *dean, historian*
Jorgensen, Katherine Lange *nursing educator*
Lofthus, Richard *history professor*

TENNESSEE

Allardt
Copeland, Patricia Ruth *elementary school educator*

Antioch
Mattice, Debora J. *special education educator, consultant*
Worthington, Melvin Leroy *minister, writer*

Arnold AFB
Davis, John William *government science and engineering executive*

Athens
Higdon, Linda Hampton *congressional staff*
Trent, Henry Gibson, Jr. *insurance company executive, educator*

Bartlett
Cheatham, Wanda M. *music educator*
Hatch, Margaret Oenone *secondary school educator*
Huffman, Delton Cleon, Jr. *pharmacy association executive*

Bolivar
Boyle, Candyace *psychologist*

Brentwood
Blackstock, James Fielding *lawyer*
Carpenter, William F. III *hospital management company executive, lawyer*
Clevenger, William Thomas *electrical engineer*
Davis, Deborah Lynn *music educator*
Fisher, Jeff (Jeffrey Michael Fisher) *professional football coach*
Heiser, Arnold Melvin *astronomer*
Lodowski, Charles Alan *retired trade association executive, lobbyist*
Pulikollu, Rajasekhar Venkata *materials engineer, researcher*
Taylor, Nicole Renée (Niki Taylor) *model, shop owner*
Wells, Dennis J. *dentist*
Winans, Cece *gospel vocalist*
Wright, James F. *agricultural products executive*
Xu, Luoyu Roy *engineering educator*

Bristol
Johnson, Opal Burton *retired elementary school educator*
Markison, Brian A. *pharmaceutical executive*
Overstreet, Catherine Ann *sales executive*
Teng, Wenyuan William *dean*
Werner, Dawn Heterick *elementary school educator*

Brownsville
Banks, Webb Follin *mayor*
Kalin, Robert *retired mathematics professor*

Byrdstown
Willis, Keith Alan *energy scientist, engineer*

Chattanooga
Allen, Sarah Frances *music educator, director*
Anderson, Larry Woodward *chemist, educator*
Bahner, Thomas Maxfield *lawyer*
Barioli, Francesco *mathematics professor*
Bishop, Liston, II, *insurance company executive*
Brooks, Ellyn Hersh *retired special education educator*
Carnes, Neil Patrick *mathematics educator*
Chopra, Prem Prem *engineering educator*
Cofer, Joseph Broaddus *surgeon*
Cothran, Dee Lisa *psychology professor*
Derthick, Alan Wendell *architect, firm executive*
Eason, Marcia Jean (Marcy Eason) *lawyer*
Easter, Anthony James *protective services official, educator*
Ebiefung, Aniekan Asukwo *mathematics professor, researcher*
Ellis, Fredrick Vernon *metallurgical engineer, consultant*
Fossel, Jon S. *retired investment company executive*
Franks, Herschel Pickens *judge*
Gartman, Max Dillon *language educator*
Greving, Robert C. *insurance company executive*
Harrison (Ingle), Bettye (Bettye Ingle) *real estate company executive*
Henderson, Joel Bridges *literature and language professor*
Kret, Robert A. *museum director*
Littlefield, Ron *Mayor, Chattanooga, Tennessee*
Long, Kathy Lynne *history professor*
Marshall, Willis Henry *psychiatrist*
Martin, Chester Y. *sculptor, painter*
Mattice, Harry Sandlin, Jr. *federal judge, former prosecutor*
McKenney, Richard P. *insurance company executive*
McNeill-Murray, Joan Reagin *volunteer, consultant*
Mills, Olan, II, *photography company executive*
Posey, Garry Lee *theater educator*
Quinn, Patrick *transportation executive*
Rabin, Alan A. *economics professor*
Resnick, Irven Michael *philosophy educator*
Santos, Benjamin Guzman *physician, anesthesiologist*
Segler, Christopher Paige *surgeon, researcher*
Stephens, Gregory D. *religious studies educator*
Stifler, William L., Jr. *literature and language professor*
Symes, Steven James Kenneth *chemistry professor*
Watjen, Thomas Ros *insurance company executive*
Wessels, Izak Frederick *ophthalmologist*
Wilson, Richard Lee *political science professor*

Christiana
Coppage, Laura Smith *music educator*

Clarksville
Amstutz, Julie Denise *elementary school educator*
Blanck, Harvey F. *retired chemistry professor*
Gold, Moniqueka E. *education educator*
Hunley, Eugene Allen *Physics Instructor*
Lowe, Kandia S. *radio director*
Smith, Gregory Dale *lawyer, judge*
Stoddard, Peter Hawkins *education educator, consultant*
Wilson, Patti L. *psychologist, educator*
Winters, David Douglas *lawyer*

Cleveland
Dale, Karen McCall *music educator*
Evans, Johnny L. *science educator*
Harper, James Edward, Jr. *academic administrator*
Hoffman, Daniel Lee *history professor, researcher*
Hunt, Andrew L. *library director*
Kraus, Ruby Jean *art educator*
McClung, Patricia Beatrice *special education educator*
Rhodes, Arthur Delano *benefits administrator*
Silverman, Patricia R. *communications educator*
Wilkins, James D. *language educator*

Coalfield
Justice, Jennifer Amanda *special education educator*

College Grove
Battle, William Robert (Bob Battle) *retired publishing executive*

Collegedale
Clark, Ann Rorabaw *English professor, consultant, writer*
Craven, Randall L. *graphics designer, educator, product designer*
Leatherman, Donn Walter *religious studies educator*
McKee, Ellsworth R. *food products executive*

Collierville
Springfield, James Francis *retired lawyer, banker*
Tesreau, Cynthia Lynn *elementary school educator*

Columbia
Cantrell, Sharron Caulk *principal*
Curry, Beatrice Chesrown *retired English educator*
Fleming, Emma Kae Brock *radiography educator*
Gardner, Hoyt Devane, Jr. *history professor*
Gidcomb, Barry Doyle *history professor*
Horner, Linda T. *mathematician, department chairman*

Cookeville
Abdallah, Mohammed *engineering educator*
Campana, Phillip Joseph *German language educator*
Chowdhuri, Pritindra *retired electrical engineer, educator*
Dainty, Helen Thompson *engineering educator*
Elkeelany, Omar *engineering educator, researcher*
Engelhardt, Robert Thomas *physicist, educator*
Kumar, Krishna *retired physics educator*
Mills, Hugh Harrison III *geologist, educator*
Panchagnula, Mahesh *engineering educator*
Qiu, Robert Caiming *engineering educator, consultant*
Rios, Marjorie Evans *language educator*
Sissom, Leighton Esten *engineering educator, dean, consultant*
Smolenski, Lisabeth Ann *physician*
Volpe, Angelo Anthony *retired academic administrator, chemist, educator*

Cordova
Bayakly, Nabil Abdulghani *biology professor*
Jacobs, M. Louise *secondary school educator*
Pugh, Dorothy Gunther *performing company executive*

Covington
Wright, Bonnie Shankle *assistant principal, choir director*

Crab Orchard
McBee, Christy Dawn *art educator*

Crossville
Bell, Charles Eugene, Jr. *retired industrial engineer*
Buechel, Eric *art gallery owner, visual artist*
Frazier, June Marie *retired public relations executive*
Hovmand, Svend *chemical engineer*
Marlow, James Allen *lawyer*

Cunningham
Mince, Carol Kirkham *history educator*

Dandridge
Bowers, Timothy J. *automotive executive*
Coley, Jan Brumback *biology educator*

Dayton
Boling, Paul C. *philosopher, educator*
Fitsimmons, Gary N. *library director, writer*
Ketchersid, William Lester *history professor*

Dickson
Larkins, Bessie Sullivan *education educator*

Dyersburg
Flatt, James Lynn *biology professor*
Northcutt, William Marion *English literature educator*
Strong, David A., Jr. *history professor*

Fall Branch
Douthat, Cheryl O. *music educator, director*

Fayetteville
Dickey, John Harwell *lawyer*
Matlock, Jack Foust, Jr. *diplomat*

Franklin
Carolin, Brian *automotive executive*
Fink, Robert Michael *pharmacist*
Kohan, Betsy Burns *lawyer*
Lankford, Monty J. *medical products executive*
Miller, Dennis Edward *health medical executive*
Petrie, William Marshall *psychiatrist*
Rosen, William Warren *lawyer*
Santini, Danilo John *energy economist, urban systems engineer*
Seifert, Rachel A. *lawyer*
Smith, Wayne Thomas *healthcare company executive*
Thornsberry, Clyde *microbiologist*
White, David R. *healthcare company executive*

Gallatin
Bradley, Nolen Eugene, Jr. *retired personnel executive, educator*
Douglas, Joseph C. *history professor*
Durham, Walter Thomas *historian, researcher*
Ellis, Joseph Newlin *retired wholesale distribution executive*
Loerakker, Jo Ann Katherine *retired chiropractor*
Schipper, Jan D. *language educator*

Gates
Nance, Helen Strayhorn *pre-school administrator, educator*

Gatlinburg
Catalfo, Alfred, Jr., (Alfio Catalfo) *lawyer*

Germantown
Beaty, James Harold *pediatric orthopaedic surgeon*
Ling, Frank W. *obstetrician, gynecologist*

Goodlettsville
Dreiling, Richard W. (Rick Dreiling) *retail executive*
Harper, Jewel Benton *pharmacist*
Lanigan, Susan S. *lawyer*
Tehle, David M. *retail executive*
van der Laan, Mikell F. *landscape artist*

Grand Junction
Godwin, Anna Marie *primary school educator*

Gray
Combs, Stephen Paul *pediatrician, health facility administrator*

Greenbrier
Newell, Paul Haynes, Jr. *engineering educator*

Greeneville
Dobson, Hugh Fredrick *supervisor*
Smith, Myron John, Jr. *librarian, author*

Harriman
Glenn, Betty Jean *finance educator*

Harrison
Rokicki, Phillip S. *career planning administrator, educator*

Harrogate
McGuire, Sandra Lynn *nursing educator*

Henderson
Gardner, Elmer Claude *academic administrator*

Hendersonville
Burt, Alvin Miller III *anatomist, cell biologist, writer, educator*
Davis, Jon C. Chris *minister*
McCaleb, Joe Wallace *lawyer*
Skaggs, Ricky *country musician*

Hickory Valley
Weaver, Peggy (Marguerite McKinnie Weaver) *plantation owner*

Huntingdon
King, Tracy Lynn *science educator*

Jackson
Agee, Bob R. *academic administrator, minister, educator*
Anderson, Stanley Thomas *federal judge*
Blanca, Acosta *literature and language professor, translator*
Boswell, G(eorge) Harvey *federal judge*
Cole, John Frankland *electrical engineer, educator*
Dodson, Frank *academic administrator*
Dubis, Kevin Mark *religious studies educator*
Hayes, Robert Mac *agronomy educator*
Holt, Michael Kenneth *management and finance educator, consultant, city councilman*
Hoyle, Shetina Yevette *librarian*
Hudacek, Vivian Susan *literature and language professor*
Jones, Dalan Dee *nursing educator*
Lindley, W. Lindley *history professor*
Nord, Keith Douglas *surgeon, director*
Swaim, Mark Wendell *physician, molecular biologist, hepatologist, essayist, gastroenterologist, photographer*
Todd, James Dale *federal judge*
Van Neste, Ray *religious studies educator, director*

Jefferson City
Austin, David Brian *philosopher, educator*
Baumgardner, James Lewis *history professor*
Bivens, Patricia Lynn *musician, director*
Bull, Connie Cruze *music educator*
Cordry, Sean Michael *physics professor*
Knight, Tori Hopper *academic administrator, educator*
Moffat, Charles Gordon *history professor, department chairman*

Jellico
Hausman, Keith Lynn *health facility administrator, physical therapist*
Walden, James William *accountant, educator*

Johnson City
Adebonojo, Festus O. *medical educator*
Ahmad, Zulfiqar *biochemist, educator*
Anthony, Margaret Alice *photographer, educator*
Clements, Andrea Deason *psychology educator*
Cupp, Horace Ballard *surgeon, educator*
Dotterweich, Douglas Pierce *economics professor, researcher*
Drinkard-Hawkshawe, Dorothy Lee *historian, educator, writer*
Fox, James J. III *psychology professor, researcher*
Freeman, Michael Byron *protective services official, consultant*
Gerhardt, E. Alvin, Jr. *retired museum director*
Giorgadze, Tamar Alfred *pathologist, physician*
Grover, Kathleen Higginson *literature and language educator*
Hamdy, Ronald Charles *geriatrician*
Henry, Robin Michelle *pharmacist, director*
Kao, Race Li-Chan *medical educator*
McIntosh, Cecilia Ann *biochemist, educator*
McKinney, Michael Merritt *law educator*
Mwinyelle, Jerome Banaya *language educator*
Olsen, Martin E. *obstetrician, educator*
Pandian, Shantha G. *psychiatrist*
Perry, Murvin Henry *communications educator*
Rahmani, Ramin Khosravi *mechanical engineer, researcher*
Scher, Rita Ann *librarian*
Snyder-Sowers, Mary Anne Sarah *performing company executive, choreographer, educator*
Stanton, Paul E., Jr. *academic administrator*
Storie, Melanie *history professor*
Taylor, Grant David *urologist*
Tollefson, Terrence Alfred *retired educator and consultant*
Turner, Krista Denise *director*
Waage, Frederick Oswin *English educator*

Kingsport
Bailey, William Henry *real estate appraiser*
Coover, Harry Wesley *manufacturing executive*
Espeland, Curtis E. *chemicals executive*
Ferguson, J. Brian *chemicals executive*
Groseclose, Clara Rita *retired secondary school educator*
Head, William Iverson, Sr. *retired chemical company executive*
Lee, Theresa K. *lawyer, chemicals executive*
Rigsby, Mary Sue *retired elementary school and adult education educator*
Rogers, James P. *chemicals executive*
Russell, Rob *academic administrator*
Smith, JoAnn Carroll *library and information scientist*
Tant, Martin Ray *chemical and biomedical engineer*
Weaver, Max Allen *chemist, consultant, inventor*

Kingston
Shacter, John *technology management and education consultant*

Knoxville
Abidi, Besma Roui *information scientist, educator*
Adabra, Kodjo *language educator*
Airee, Anita *pharmacist*
Alexeff, Igor *retired electrical engineering educator*
Allington, Richard Lloyd *literacy studies educator*
Ash, Stephen Vaughan *history professor, writer*
Barnes, Samuel Coleman *Senior Technical Talent Advisor*
Bass, William Marvin III *anthropology educator*
Beavers, James Earl *engineer, director, consultant*
Bell, Linda R. *writer, photographer*
Bingham, Carrol Reid *physicist*
Blaze, Doug A. *dean, law educator*
Boling, Edward Joseph *retired academic administrator*
Bose, Bimal Kumar *electrical engineering educator*
Brown, Donald Vaughn *retired engineer*
Burdette, Edwin Gordon *engineering educator, consultant*
Burman, Thomas Earl *history professor*
Butler, David *museum director*
Byrd, Debbie Curtis *medical educator*
Campbell, Michael L. *theatre company executive*
Cecil, William Thomas *health products executive, director*
Chapman, Jefferson *museum director*
Cheek, Jimmy Geary *academic administrator, agricultural studies educator*
Chen, Chung Hqo *research scientist*
Coleman, Shannon DeShae *lawyer, educator*
Cone, James Christopher *lawyer*
Cox, Anna Lee *retired administrative assistant*
Creasia, Joan Catherine *dean, nursing educator*
Cremins, William Carroll *lawyer*
Cummings, Peter Thomas *chemical engineering educator*
Davis, Wayne T. *dean*
Dedrick, James Russell *prosecutor*
DeGennaro, Ramon P. *finance educator, researcher*
Dewey, Barbara I. *librarian, dean*
Doak, Samuel Clements *lawyer*
Dunn, Gregory W. *theatre company executive*
Durairaj, Baskaran *chemistry professor*
Easterly, Joan Elizabeth *language educator*
Eckenrod, Edward Lee *advocate*
Farmer, Susan Baker *taxonomic botanist*
Felder-Hoehne, Felicia Harris *librarian, researcher*
Fender, Allison Jean *physical therapist, personal trainer*

Filston, Howard Church *pediatric surgeon*
Froula, James DeWayne *honor society administrator*
Fuller, Paul *sociology educator*
Gale, Richard Milton *retired philosopher*
Gaude, Emily Camp *elementary school educator*
Gentry, Robert Vance *physicist, researcher, writer*
Giordano, Lawrence Francis *lawyer*
Griffitts, Bobby R. *legislative staff member*
Haren, Elizabeth Gaye *counselor*
Harris, Diana Koffman *sociologist, educator*
Haslam, Bill *Mayor, Knoxville, Tennessee*
Hatcher, Robert Dean, Jr. *geologist, educator, research scientist*
Howard, Herbert Hoover *broadcasting and communications educator*
Hyman, Roger David *lawyer*
Infante, Isa Maria *political scientist, educator*
Irick, David Kim *engineering educator, consultant*
Jarvis, Howard E. *lawyer*
Jones, Carl Joseph *entomologist, educator*
Jones, Sherman J. *non profit organization executive, financial consultant, educator*
Jordan, Robert Leon *judge*
Kiffin, Lane *college football coach*
Kilgore, Tom D. *electric power industry executive*
King, John K. *retired lawyer*
Kliefoth, A. Bernhard III *neurosurgeon*
Koch, Erec R. *literature and language professor*
Koester, Rudolf *educator*
Kress, Tyler A. *biomedical engineer*
Landry, Mary Catherine *dance instructor, choreographer*
Lawson, Fred Raulston *banker*
Lee, Jan Louise *nursing educator*
Lee, Sharon Gail *state supreme court justice, lawyer*
Lowe, Kenneth W. *multimedia executive*
Mankel, Francis Xavier *retired principal, priest*
Markert, Cynthia Allin *artist*
McGuire, John Albert *dentist*
Mc Hargue, Carl Jack *lab administrator*
Miles, Amy E. *theatre company executive*
Mise, Jesse Sherden *structural engineer, consultant*
Moore, Marvelene C. *music educator*
Moore, Richard Wayne *electric power industry executive, former prosecutor*
Murrian, Robert Phillip *retired federal judge, educator*
Nazarewicz, Witold *nuclear scientist, educator*
Ownby, David H. *theatre company executive*
Paddison, Stephen John *engineering educator*
Prados, John William *retired engineering educator*
Pruitt, Jonathan Neal *research scientist*
Qiu, Wulin *chemist, materials scientist, materials engineer*
Reddick, Lovett Evan *biochemist*
Reynolds, Marjorie Lavers *nutritionist, educator*
Richards, Stephen Harold *engineering educator*
Ritchie, Albert *lawyer*
Roth, John Reece *electrical engineer, educator, researcher, inventor*
Rubenstein, Jay *history professor, writer*
Rukeyser, William Simon *journalist*
Russell, Rodney E. *school system administrator*
Sansom, William B. *consumer products executive*
Schlarbaum, Scott E. *forester, educator*
Schuler, Theodore Anthony *retired civil engineer*
Schweitzer, George Keene *chemistry professor*
Scott, Bob (Robert Scott) *retired chemical engineer, educator*
Shelby, Paulus P., Jr. *biology educator*
Simberloff, Daniel *biologist, educator*
Simek, Jan F. *academic administrator, anthropologist, educator*
Sorrells, Frank Douglas *retired mechanical engineer*
Stika, Richard F. *bishop*
Summitt, Pat (Patricia Sue Summit) *women's college basketball coach*
Thomas, Joyce Carol *author, educator*
Trotter, Donald Wesley *history professor*
Trout, Monroe Eugene *health facility administrator*
Vogel, Howard H. *lawyer*
Wade, Gary R. *state supreme court justice*
Wheeler, John Watson *lawyer*
White, Wesley Matthew *urologist*
Whiteside, Joan Robinson *administrative assistant, music educator*
Williams, Jan R. *dean, business educator*
Worthington, Robert Fletcher, Jr. *lawyer*
Wunderlich, Bernhard *retired physical chemistry professor*
Xiang, Shu *civil engineer, researcher*
Ye, Xiaofei *education educator*

Kodak
Sandberg, Ryne Dee *baseball coach, retired professional baseball player*

Lawrenceburg
Hayes, Sylvia Richmond *music educator*

Lebanon
Bryan, Danny Lee *biology professor*
Cochran, Sandra Brophy *restaurant chain company executive*
Eaton, Harvill Carlton *academic administrator*
Woodhouse, Michael A. *restaurant holdings company executive*

Lenoir City
Den Uyl, Helen *elementary school educator*
Edwards, C. Karen *consultant company executive*
Sproul, Harvey Leonard *lawyer*

Loudon
Horst, Teresa Dale *music educator*
Jones, Robert Gean *religion educator*
Randall, Marilyn Mae *writer*

Lynnville
Hollis, Bobby Allen, Jr. *music educator*

Madison
Campbell, Chester Douglas *writer*

Madisonville
Allen, Robert Howard *language educator*

Manchester
Dale, David L. *retired education educator*
Westberry, Anita Parrish *education educator*

Martin
Anderson, Pamela Susan *sports official, educator*
Baxter, Christopher M. *political science professor*
Bradshaw, Charles Callis *literature and language professor*
Brown, Laura L. *physical education educator*
Cook, Douglas J. *theater educator, department chairman*
Jarmon, Laura C. *retired literature and language professor*
Parker, Henry Herbin *humanities educator*
Parrish, Alissa Renee *nursing educator*
Phongkusolchit, Kiattisak *finance educator, researcher*
Schommer, John Joseph *mathematics professor*
Williams-Boyd, Deborah Kay *finance educator*

Maryville
Bradford, Tutt Sloan *retired publisher*
Howard, Cecil Byron *retired pediatrician*
McLemore, Carolyn Faye *elementary school educator*
Oakes, Lester Cornelius *retired electrical engineer, consultant*
Tabor, Curtis Harold, Jr. *retired librarian, minister*
Weeks, Robert Andrew *materials science researcher, educator*

Mason
Wilder, John Shelton *state legislator, former lieutenant governor*

Mc Ewen
Williams, John Lee *lawyer*

Mc Minnville
Grandey, Timothy Hal *social studies educator, farmer*

Memphis
Abston, Dunbar, Jr. *management consultant*
Adams-Graves, Patricia E. *medical educator*
Adsit, Russell Allan *landscape architect*
Allen, David Mark *psychiatrist, educator, director*
Bacopulos, Dionysia Stacey *mathematics professor*
Bargagliotti, Lillian Antoinette *nursing educator*
Barone, Tony, Sr. *professional sports team executive*
Bartow, Gene *professional sports team executive, retired men's college basketball coach*
Beranova-Giorgianni, Sarka *biomedical researcher, educator*
Bhattacharya, Sujoy *scientist, researcher*
Bibby, Henry (Charles Henry Bibby) *professional basketball coach*
Bobango, John Allen *lawyer*
Bollheimer, (Cecilia) Denise *marketing professional, finance company executive*
Boucher, Bradley Albert *pharmacist, educator*
Bowles, Grover Cleveland, Jr. *pharmacist, educator*
Brandon, Raymond Wilson *financial planner, securities principal*
Broffitt, Joyce Cassandra *judge*
Buckner, Thomas Randolph *lawyer*
Butts, Herbert Clell *retired dentist, educator*
Carr, Oscar Clark III *lawyer*
Carter, Robert B. *delivery service executive*
Cash, Kriner *school system administrator*
Castle, Darrell *lawyer*
Cetingok, Muammer *social sciences educator*
Chesney, Russell Wallace *pediatrician, educator*
Clarke, Dave F. *neurologist, educator*
Clippard, Richard F. *prosecutor*
Cohen, Harris L. *diagnostic radiologist, consultant*
Cook, August Joseph *lawyer, accountant*
Cox, Clair Edward, II, *urologist, medical educator*
Crain, Frances Utterback *retired dietitian*
Cupples, Douglas Wayne *education educator*
Currey, Thomas Arthur *ophthalmologist*
Desiderio, Dominic Morse, Jr. *chemistry and neurochemistry professor*
Dierkes, Judith Ann *artist, educator*
Donald, Bernice B. *judge*
Dreyfus, Susan Kahn *middle school educator*
Dunathan, Harmon Craig *college dean*
Eason, James David *surgeon*
Egidi, Maria Francesca *transplant physician*
English, Kelly *chef*
Evans, William Edward *hospital administrator, pharmacist, researcher*
Fain, John Nicholas *biochemistry educator*
Felix, Cheryl A. *air transportation executive*
Fitzgerald, Malinda E.C. *biology professor*
Ford, Harold Eugene *lobbyist, educator, former United States Representative from Tennessee*
Ford, Sylverna V. *dean university libraries*
Franceschetti, Donald Ralph *physicist, educator*
Freeman, Bob A. *retired microbiology educator, retired dean*
Freire, Amado X. *pulmonary physician, clinical researcher*
Fuller, Wayne Louis *logistics manager, retired air force officer*
Gay, Rudy Carlton, Jr. *professional basketball player*
Gerald, Barry *retired radiology educator, neuroscientist*
Geter, Jennifer L. *psychologist*
Gibbons, Julia Smith *federal judge*
Giles, William (Bill) T. *retail executive*
Gilman, Ronald Lee *federal judge*
Gilpatrick, Russell O. *dean, dental educator*
Glenn, T. Michael *delivery service executive*
Goldsmith, Harry Louis *lawyer*
Gourley, Dick R. *dean, pharmacy educator*
Graf, Alan B., Jr. *delivery service executive*
Graves, William H. *minister*
Green, Al *soul and gospel singer*
Green, Daniel Michael *pediatric oncologist*
Griffin, Clement M. *information technology executive*
Hackett, Richard Cecil *museum director, former mayor*
Hall, Arnita Rena *special education educator*
Haltom, William H. *lawyer*
Hawkins, O. Mason *investment company executive*
Hayes, Michael J. *retail executive*
Heda, Ghanshyam Das *molecular biologist, researcher*
Heimberg, Murray *pharmacologist, biochemist, physician*
Heiter, Matthew Stephen *lawyer*
Helton, Kathleen Jacobson *neuroradiologist*
Hermes, Clinton Daniel *lawyer*
Herrod, Henry Grady III *pediatrics professor, allergist, immunologist*
Hoffer, Fredric Alan *pediatric radiologist*
Holder, Janice Marie *state supreme court justice*
Hollins, Lionel *professional basketball coach*
Howe, Martha Morgan *microbiologist, educator*
Hughes, Walter Thompson *pediatrician, educator*
Hunt, James Calvin *physician, academic administrator*
Hymowitz, Steven *lawyer*
Jablonski, Monica Mary *science educator*
Jackson, Thomas Francis III *lawyer*
Jalenak, Peggy Eichenbaum *volunteer*
Jefferson, Daisy M. *social studies educator, english educator*
Johnson, Harry A. III *lawyer, finance company executive*
Johnson, Johnny *research psychologist, consultant*
Johnson, Joseph Erle *mathematician*
Johnson, Karen C. *epidemiologist, researcher*
Jordan, D. Bryan *bank executive*
Kaput, Jim L. *lawyer*
Karcioglu, Zeynel A. *ophthalmologist, educator*
Kelly, Aleda Mae *retired secondary education educator*
Kitabchi, Abbas Eqbal *medical educator*
Kitchin, Cameron (L. Cameron Kitchin) *museum director*
Korones, Sheldon Bernarr *pediatrician, educator*
Kozma, Robert *mathematics professor, director*
Krieger, Robert Lee, Jr. *human resource/management consultant, educator, writer, travel/meeting planner, political analyst, internet marketing consultant*
Kustoff, David F. *lawyer, former prosecutor*
Kutteh, William H. *medical educator, director*
Ledbetter, Paul Mark *lawyer, writer*
Leffler, Charles William *physiology and pediatrics educator*
Lewis, James Bryant, Jr. *physician*
Li, Ying Sing *chemistry professor*
Lyons, Al(pha) L. *museum director, retired manufacturing executive*
Majumdar, Sabita *biology professor*
Maksi, Gregory Earl *engineering educator*
Mallett, Veronica T. *medical educator, director*
Mansbach, Charles *gastroenterologist, researcher*
Marchetta, Jeffrey G. *mechanical engineer, educator*
Masterson, Kenneth Rhodes *lawyer*
McClinton, Joanie *elementary and secondary school educator*
Mc Creary, James Franklin *lawyer, mediator*
McDaniel, A. Stephen *lawyer*
McPherson, Larry Eugene *photographer, educator*
Morgan, Colby Shannon, Jr. *lawyer*
Morreim, E. Haavi *medical ethics educator*
Nemec, Christopher E. *music educator*
Nesin, Jeffrey David *academic administrator*
Newman, Charles Forrest *lawyer*
Nicholls, Tim S. *paper company executive*
Noel, Randall Deane *lawyer*
Norris, Charles Head *lawyer, manufacturing executive*
Osarogiagbon, Ray Uyiosa *oncologist, educator*
Ouzts, David Perry *church music director, organist*
Owen-Leinert, Susan Huff *voice educator, vocalist*
Pastner, Josh *men's college basketball coach*
Patay, Zoltán *radiologist, educator*
Patil, Shivaputra A. *research scientist*
Pfeffer, Lawrence Marc *cell biologist*
Philipp, Karla Ann *musician, educator, conductor*
Pileggi, Dominic J. *electronics executive*
Pope, Thaddeus Mason *law educator*
Pourciau, Lester John, Jr. *retired librarian*
Presley, Lisa Marie *singer*
Pruitt, Rosalyn Jolena *science educator*
Qi, Gang *mechanical engineer, educator*
Raines, Shirley Carol *academic administrator*
Ramsdell, Heather L. *speech pathology/audiology services professional, researcher*
Randolph, Zach *professional basketball player*
Ranta, Richard Robert *university dean*
Ratzlaff, David Edward *minister*
Razzouk, Bassem Ibrahim *hematologist, oncologist*
Reid, Karen Denise *aerospace transportation executive, writer*
Rhodes, William C. III *automotive executive*
Richards, Christine P. *delivery service executive, lawyer*
Robinson, Kenneth S. *pastor, former state agency administrator, physician*
Rubin, Rose Mohr *economics professor*
Russell, Thomas Arthur *humanities educator, religious studies educator, researcher*
Schelp, Richard Herbert *retired mathematics professor*
Schuler, Walter E. *lawyer*
Schwartzberg, Lee S. *internist, oncologist, hematologist*
Scroggs, Larry Kenneth *lawyer, state legislator*
Shan, Zuyao *medical researcher*
Shiue, Yeu-Sheng Paul *mechanical engineer, educator*
Shochat, Stephen Jay *pediatrician, surgeon*
Slagle, William F. *dental educator, dean*
Smallwood, Arwin Doremus *history professor*
Smith, Frederick Wallace *delivery service executive*
Smith, Karen Ann *nutritionist*
Smith, Maura Abeln *chief legal officer, paper company executive*
Spahr, Ronald W. *finance educator, department chairman*
Steib, James Terry *bishop*
Steinhauer, Gillian *lawyer*
Stoudamire, Damon Lamon *professional basketball coach, retired professional basketball player*
Suda, Katie Joy *pharmacist, educator*
Sunderman, Mark A. *finance educator*
Tabachnick, Stephen Ely *English literature educator*
Tate, Stonewall Shepherd *lawyer*
Tibbs, Martha Jane Pullen *civic worker, retired social worker*
Tonkin, Ina Lynn Dyer *physician, cardiovascular radiologist, educator*
Trammell, Bradley Ellis *lawyer*
Troutt, William Earl *academic administrator*
Tucker, Laurie A. *marketing executive*
Umholtz, Clyde Allan *financial analyst*
Van Middlesworth, Lester *physiology, biophysics and medicine educator, internist*
Vaughn, Cary Edward *minister, director*
Wallace, Chris *professional sports team executive*
Wallis, Carlton Lamar *librarian*
Webster, Robert G. *virologist, educator*
Wilcox, Harry Hammond *retired anatomist*
Williams, David Russell *retired music educator*
Williams, Edward F(oster) III *retired environmental engineer*
Winchester, Richard Lee, Jr. *lawyer*
Yasuda, Robert *painter*
Zeman, Herbert David *biomedical engineer*
Zhao, Wei *medical researcher*

Millington
Gray, Barbara L. *assistant principal, tax specialist*
Thomas-Harris, Yvonne Anita *writer, poet*

Morristown
Bolton, Kimberly D. *biology professor*
Comer, Evan Philip *manufacturing executive*
Culvern, Julian Brewer *chemist, naturalist, educator, writer, photographer*
Johnson, Evelyn Bryan *airport terminal executive*
Knowles, David L. *history professor*
McLain, Chippy A. *language educator*
Rouse, Viki Dasher *literature and language professor*

Mount Juliet
Chester, Thomas Wayne *state agency administrator*
Donovan, Gerard *management consulting company executive*
Holloway, Susan Master *elementary school educator*

Murfreesboro
Baily, Carol Ann *language educator*
Beckwith, Ruthie-Marie *financial consultant, director*
Breault, Kevin D. *social studies educator, researcher*
Bynum, Thomas L. *history professor*
Coleman, Jack Andrew, Jr. *otolaryngologist*
Corlew, Robert Ewing *history professor, academic administrator*
DeBoer, Angela Ruth *music educator*
Doyle, Delores Marie *retired principal*
Flanagan, Van Kent *journalist*
Ford, William F. *banker*
Heffington, Jack Grisham *lawyer, banker, insurance company executive, horse breeder*
Henderson, Ronald H. *science educator*
Linton, Michael Roy *music educator*
Scott, Rupert Neil *professor and capitalize university librarian*

Nashville
Abou-Khalil, Bassel William *neurologist, epileptologist*
Abram, Monroe J. *athletic trainer, educator*
Adams, Kenneth Stanley, Jr., (Bud Adams) *energy and professional sports team executive*
Adams, Ryan (David Ryan Adams) *musician*
Alexander, Lamar (Andrew Lamar Alexander) *United States Senator from Tennessee, former United States Secretary of Education*
Allison, Fred, Jr. *internist, retired medical educator*
Alvin, Glenda Marie *assistant director*
Archibald, Chestina Mitchell *minister*
Arnott, Jason *professional hockey player*
Arteaga, Carlos Luis *medical researcher, director*
Aschner, Judy Lynn *pediatrician, educator*
Atack, Jeremy *economics professor, history professor*
Autry, Philip Earl *music educator, musician*
Balcomb, Melanie S. *women's college basketball coach*
Baldwin, Harold Scott *pediatrician, educator*
Balser, Jeffrey R. *dean, medical educator*
Barfield, Henry Lee, II, *lawyer*
Barnett, Bruce Edwin *lawyer*
Bass, James Orin, Sr. *lawyer*
Bates, George William *obstetrician, gynecologist, educator*
Bauer, Avalyn *psychologist*
Beauchamp, Robert Daniel *surgeon, educator*
Benson, Edwin Welburn, Jr. *retired trade association executive*
Berlin, Jordan D. *gastrointestinal oncologist, healthcare educator*
Bernard, Louis Joseph *surgeon, educator*
Bigham, Wanda Durrett *religious organization administrator*
Bignall, Orville Newton *physicist, educator*
Bird, Caroline *author*
Boothby, Mark R. *immunologist*
Bostick, Charles Dent *retired lawyer*
Bottorff, Dennis C. *banker*
Bracken, Richard M. *healthcare company executive*
Bradford, James C., Jr. *brokerage house executive*
Bradford, James Warren, Jr. *dean, finance educator*
Bredesen, Philip Norman *Governor of Tennessee*
Brill, Aaron Bertrand *nuclear medicine educator*
Brock, John William III *surgeon, urologist, educator*
Brooks, Kix (Leon Eric Brooks) *musician*
Brophy, Jeremiah Joseph *retired finance company executive, military officer*
Brown, Joe Blackburn *judge*
Brown, Tommie Florence F. *state legislator, social work educator*
Burch, John Christopher, Jr. *investment banker*

Burnett, Lonnie Sheldon obstetrics and gynecology educator
Byrd, Andrew Wayne investment company executive
Byrne, John G. surgeon
Cannon, Sharon M. health facility administrator
Capdevila, Jorge H. medical educator, biochemistry educator
Carlton, Thomas I., Jr. lawyer, educator
Carroll, Frank Edward, Jr. radiologist, researcher
Catania, Kenneth C. neuroscientist, educator
Chang, Sam S. urologist, surgeon, educator
Chesney, Kenny country singer, songwriter
Choby, David Raymond bishop
Chytil, Frank biochemist
Clark, Cornelia A. state supreme court justice
Clemens, Peter J., IV, corporate financial executive
Cobb, Stephen A. lawyer
Cole, David A. psychology professor, department chairman
Collins, Kerry professional football player
Compton, John Joseph philosophy educator
Conner, Lewis Homer, Jr. lawyer
Cooil, Bruce Kimo mathematical statistician, statistics educator
Cook, E. Gary manufacturing executive
Cooper, Robert Elbert, Jr. state attorney general
Cooper, Susan R. state agency administrator
Coukos, Eleni Dianne education educator
Covington, Robert Newman retired law educator
Cowart, Richard G. lawyer
Craiglow, Hilary A. librarian
Crisp, Terry Arthur commentator, former professional hockey coach and player
Crowe, James Earl, Jr. pediatrician, educator
Crumpler, Algernon Darius (Alge Crumpler) professional football player
Cyrus, Cynthia J. dean, music educator
Daane, James Dewey banker
Dalton, James Edgar, Jr. health facility administrator
Daughtrey, Martha Craig federal judge
Davis, Stephen N. endocrinologist
Davis, Terry L. historical association executive
Dayan, Colin (A.K.A. Joan Dayan) professor of comparative literature, legal history and religion, writer
Dean, Karl Mayor, Nashville
Delbeke, Dominique nuclear medicine physician, educator
Demarcus, Jay (Stanley Demarcus) country musician, songwriter
Dickerson, Dennis Clark, Sr. historian, educator
Dillehay, Tom D. anthropologist, educator
Dmochowski, Roger urologist, educator
Dobbs, George Albert funeral director, embalmer
Dunn, Ronnie Gene musician
Duvenhage, Susan B. museum administrator
Echols, Robert L. federal judge
Edwards, Kathryn Margaret physician, researcher, educator
Ejiofor, Anthony Okechukwu microbiologist, educator
Ely, James Wallace, Jr. law educator
Epps, Anna Cherrie immunologist, educator, dean interim president
Estrin, Kari (Karen Ruth Estrin) music producer, agent, consultant
Fanning, Ellen biology professor, research scientist
Feng, Hua-Jun medical educator, researcher
Fields, James Perry dermatologist, dermatopathologist, allergist, pharmacologist, pharmacist
Finnegan, Cortland Temujin professional football player
Fisher, Jack medical educator, plastic surgeon
Fleischer, Arthur C. medical educator, radiologist
Followill, Caleb (Anthony Caleb Followill) musician
Followill, Jared (Michael Jared Followill) musician
Followill, Matthew (Cameron Matthew Followill) musician
Followill, Nathan (Ivan Nathan Followill) musician
Fonseca, Ricardo B. nuclear medicine physician
Ford, Donna education educator
Ford, Gerald J. (Jerry) finance company executive
Forrester, Chip political organization administrator
Fort, Tomlinson chemist, chemical engineering educator
Freeman, David Scott professional sports team executive, venture capitalist, lawyer
Frensley, Susanne H. history educator
Frist, Bill (William Harrison Frist) investment company executive, Former United States Senator from Tennessee, thoracic surgeon
Frist, Thomas Fearn, Jr. hospital management company executive
Frost, Richard W. manufacturing executive
Frost, Rick manufacturing executive
Galloway, Kenneth Franklin engineering educator
Gao, Benlian biochemist
Gauthier, Isabel cognitive neuroscientist
Giles, Joe W. music educator
Gingrass, Mary Katherine plastic surgeon
Girgus, Sam B. English literature educator
Gonzales, Greg state banking agency administrator
Gore, Steven Lowell accountant
Gore, Tipper (Mary Elizabeth Gore) wife of the former Vice President of the United States
Greelish, James P. cardiologist, surgeon, educator
Green, Lisa Cannon editor
Greer, John P. medical educator
Griffith, James Leigh lawyer
Grimes, R. Dale lawyer
Guha, Sujata education educator
Guthrie, Chris dean, law educator
Gwin, Dorothy Jean Bird retired psychology professor, dean
Hahn, George Thomas materials engineering educator, researcher
Hamilton, Joseph Hants, Jr. physicist, researcher
Hampton, Ralph Clayton, Jr. pastoral studies educator, clergyman
Hanselman, Richard Wilson entrepreneur
Hanusa, Timothy P. chemistry professor, director
Hargett, Tre state official
Hargrove, Erwin Charles, Jr. political science professor
Harris, Emmylou singer
Harris, J(acob) George health products executive
Harrison, Clifford Joy, Jr. banker
Hart, Richard Banner lawyer
Hartley, Michael J. travel company executive
Hassel, Rudolph Christopher language educator
Havens, Murray Clark political scientist, educator
Hays, Stephen Robert pediatrician, anesthesiologist
Haywood, Dave singer, musician
Head, David R. pathologist, educator
Hearn, Matthew Galen literature and language professor
Hedera, Peter neuroscientist, educator
Helderman, J. Harold transplant physician, immunologist, educator
Henderson, Milton Arnold professional society administrator
Hercules, David Michael chemistry professor, consultant
Hetherington, Marc J. political science professor
Hickson, Gerald Bennett pediatrician
Hildreth, James E.K. pharmacology and molecular science educator, dean
Hill, Faith musician
Hillenmeyer, Henry Reiling, Jr. restaurant company executive
Hinshaw, Carroll Elton economics professor
Hogan, Mark A. school system administrator
Holt, Trevor Joyce media specialist, educator
Hong, Charles C. cardiologist, medical educator
Hong, Liang engineering educator
Howell, John Floyd insurance company executive
Hwang, Jae-Kwang physicist, researcher
Inagami, Tadashi biochemistry professor
Jackson, Alan musician, lyricist
Jackson, Gretchen Purcell surgeon, educator
Janusek, John Wayne anthropologist, educator
Jarman, Mark Foster language educator
Jarquin Valdivia, Adrian Alberto internist, neurologist, researcher
Jennings, Henry Smith III cardiologist
Jensen, Gary Franklin sociology educator
Jiang, Xiaomo engineering researcher
Johnson, Bobby college football coach
Johnson, David Horton oncologist
Johnson, Hollis Eugene III foundation executive
Johnson, R. Milton healthcare executive
Joo, Myungsoo immunologist, researcher
Jordan, Benjamin T. engineering educator
Kaiser, Allen Bernard health facility administrator
Karim, Mohammad Rezaul chemistry professor
Kearse, Jevon professional football player
Kelley, Charles singer, musician
King, David A. lawyer
Klass, Judith Alexandra social studies educator, writer
Koch, William C., Jr. state supreme court justice
Krauss, Alison country musician
Kwami, Paul T. musical director and educator
Lachs, John philosopher, educator
Lagrange, Andre Hollis neurologist, educator
Lambert, Miranda vocalist
Land, Richard Dale minister, religious organization administrator
Lazar, Irving psychologist
Ledyard, Robins Heard lawyer
Lee, Donald Han surgeon, orthopedist
Lee, Douglas A. musicologist
Leuer, Mary Margaret elementary and secondary education educator
LeVan, Martin Douglas chemical engineering professor
Levox, Gary (Gary Wayne Vernon Jr.) country/rock singer
Li, Tong economics professor, researcher
Lillard, David H., Jr. state treasurer
Linton, MacRae Fort internist, educator
Livers, Thomas Henry not-for-profit fundraiser, consultant
Lukehart, Charles Martin chemistry professor
Lynch, John Brown plastic surgeon, educator
Lyon, Philip Kirkland lawyer
Madu, Leonard Ekwugha lawyer, human rights advocate, columnist
Marney, Samuel Rowe, Jr. retired allergist, immunologist, educator
Maron, David Joel cardiologist, educator
Martin, Charles Neil, Jr. health care management company executive
Martin, James Larence dentist, educator
Martin, Peter Robert psychiatrist, pharmacologist
Martin, William H. medical educator, director
Martinez Bland, Veronica Kay elementary school educator
Masys, Daniel Richard medical educator, department chairman
Mathew, Revi Puthenpurackal pediatrician, educator
Mathis, Dolores special education educator
Maurer, Christopher Herman foreign language educator
Mawae, Kevin James professional football player
May, Joseph Leserman (Jack May) retired lawyer
Mayer, John musician
McAnally, Mac musician, songwriter
McBride, Martina singer
McCammon, Holly sociologist, educator
McCarty, Richard Charles psychology professor, dean
McCowan, Otis Blakely mathematics professor
McIntyre, Edward Patrick, Jr. not-for-profit executive
McKenzie, Vashti Murphy bishop
McNutt, Mona Belle retired clinical social worker
Melvin, Willie Valentenia surgeon, educator
Melzer, Peter neuroanatomist, educator, research scientist
Merritt, Gilbert Stroud federal judge
Meyer, Ellen L. academic administrator
Midler, Bette singer, entertainer, actress
Miller, Richard L. architectural executive
Montgomery, Dillard Brewster musician, educator
Morales-Paliza, Manuel Angel electronic engineering educator
Morris, John Albert medical educator
Morton, Linda June academic administrator
Morton-Young, Tommie psychology professor, writer
Nagathihalli, Nagaraj biochemist, researcher
Neilson, Eric Grant physician, educator, health facility administrator
Nelson, Edward Gage brokerage house and bank executive, consultant
Oates, John Alexander III medical educator
O'Leary, Hazel Rollins academic administrator, former United States Secretary of Energy, lawyer
Osheroff, Neil biochemist, educator
Page, Frank S. head of religious order
Pagnani, Michael Joseph orthopaedic surgeon
Paisley, Brad musician
Pantelides, Sokrates Theodore research scientist
Parker, John Howard educator
Paul, William S. city health department administrator
Pearson, Sela poet, speaker
Perlin, Jonathan Brian health services company executive, former federal agency administrator
Pham, Wellington radiologist, educator
Pickard, Robert Evins history professor
Pickler, Kellie Dawn country singer
Pincus, Theodore microbiologist, rheumatologist, educator
Pinson, Charles Wright surgeon, educator, academic administrator
Plummer, Michael David mathematics professor
Poile, David Robert professional sports team executive
Policinski, Eugene Francis non-profit organization executive, syndicated columnist, editor, radio and television personality, producer
Polk, David Brent pediatrician, educator
Prince, Lawrence science educator
Rababaah, Haroun R. engineering educator, researcher
Radcliff, Joyce B. librarian
Ramsey, Ronald L. Lieutenant Governor of Tennessee
Rawlings, Jennifer Sue primary school educator
Ray, Wayne Allen epidemiologist, educator
Reed, Colin V. hotel company executive
Reed, Michael Eugene mathematics professor
Register, Jesse school system administrator
Reinfeldt, Mike (Michael Ray Reinfeldt) professional sports team executive, former professional football player
Reynolds, Doris Elizabeth management consultant, poet
Richmond, Marisa Jeanne columnist
Riggins-Ezzell, Lois museum administrator
Riley, Wayne Joseph academic administrator, medical educator
Rivera, Maximiano Marquez academic administrator, educator, researcher, writer
Roberts, John Robert cardiothoracic surgeon, consultant
Robertson, David physician, pharmacologist, educator
Robinson, Nathaniel David, Jr. physician, consultant
Robinson, William H. engineering educator
Rojas, Mario Augusto pediatrician, director
Rollins-Smith, Louise Ann immunologist, educator
Rooney, Joe Don country musician
Rose, Michael David hotel company executive
Ross, Joseph Comer pulmonologist, educator, academic administrator
Rubin, Edward law educator, former dean
Saff, Edward Barry mathematics professor, dean
Saltsman, John B., Jr., (Chip Saltsman) political organization administrator
Sargent, Mildred Crow retired history educator, writer
Sartor, David P. composer
Schaffner, William medical educator
Schnelle, Karl Benjamin, Jr. chemical engineering professor, consultant, researcher
Schneller, Pamela music educator
Schoggen, Phil H(oward) psychologist, educator
Schreiber, Kurt Gilbert lawyer
Schroeder, Joni Lynn secondary school educator
Scott, Hillary singer, musician
Seigenthaler, John Michael public relations executive, former newscaster
Seligson, Mitchell A. political science educator
Sevin, Dieter Hermann literature and language professor
Shack, Robert Bruce (Bruce Shack) plastic surgeon, department chairman
Shaw, Carole editor, publisher
Sheik, Duncan singer, songwriter
Shell, Owen Gladstone, Jr. retired bank executive
Shelton, Amy Elizabeth health facility administrator
Shockley, Ann Allen librarian, writer
Sidek, Naim information scientist
Sims, Wilson lawyer
Smith, Bradley E. anesthesiologist
Smith, Donnie Kay state agency administrator, retired military officer
Smith, Robin political organization administrator
Speece, Richard Eugene civil engineer, educator
Stahlman, Mildred Thornton pediatrician, pathologist, educator, researcher
Stallings, Kevin men's college basketball coach
Stassun, Keivan Guadalupe astronomer, educator
Steiger, James Hubert psychology professor
Stewart, David Marshall librarian
Stiles, Renee A. hospital administrator, educator
Stooksbury, William Claude minister
Stork, Travis Lane emergency physician
Stricklin, Cynthia J. middle school educator
Sugg, Jeanne D. library director
Sullivan, Steve professional hockey player
Summers, Paul G. lawyer, former state attorney general
Surowiec, Andrew Julius biophysicist, researcher
Swan, Patricia Brintnall academic administrator, researcher
Swensson, Earl Simcox architect
Swift, Taylor country singer
TeSelle, Eugene Arthur, Jr. religion educator
Thomas, Hazel Beatrice state official
Thomas, Robert Paige lawyer
Tolk, Norman Henry physics educator
Tong, Frank science educator
Trauger, Aleta Arthur judge
Trochtenberg, David Scott medical educator, director
Trotz, Barry professional hockey coach
Tuke, Robert Dudley lawyer, educator
Turk, Thomas Liebig arts consultant
Twain, Shania (Eilleen Regina Edwards) musician
Ullestad, Merwin Allan tax specialist, director
Urban, Keith country singer, songwriter
Uzzell-Baggett, Karon Lynette career officer
Valentine, Alan Darrell performing company executive, conductor
van der Harst, John Jay environmentalist
Van Mol, Louis John, Jr. public relations executive
Vermund, Sten Halvor epidemiologist, educator
Viscusi, W(illiam) Gregory Kip law and economics educator
Voegeli, Victor Jacque historian, educator, dean
Wahid, Abu N. M. economics professor
Walters, Arthur Scott neurologist, educator, clinical research scientist
Wang, Taylor Gunjin science administrator, educator, astronaut
Waterman, Robert A. lawyer
Watts, Carolyn Sue nurse
Webb, Timothy K. state official, school system administrator
Weber, Shea professional hockey player
Weingartner, H(ans) Martin finance educator
Westfield, Fred Meinhard economics professor
Whitlock, James Alan pediatrics educator
Williams, Anthony Ervin music educator
Williams, Carolyn Ruth Armstrong university official
Williams, Marsha Rhea computer scientist, educator, researcher, consultant
Wilson, Carolyn Taylor librarian
Wire, William Shidaker, II, retired apparel and footwear manufacturing company executive
Wisdom, Emma Nell Jackson writer, educator
Wiseman, Thomas Anderton, Jr. federal judge
Wyatt, Joe Billy academic administrator
Yarbrough, Edward Meacham prosecutor, lawyer
Yoakam, Dwight country western musician
Young, Vince Paul, Jr. professional football player
Yuspeh, Alan Ralph lawyer, health company executive
Zald, David H. cognitive neuroscientist
Zavalin, Andrey I. optics scientist, educator
Zeppos, Nicholas S. academic administrator
Zibart, Michael Alan wholesale book company executive

Newport
Ball, Travis, Jr. editor, retired school administrator
Gregg, Kimberly K. elementary school and adult education educator

Nunnelly
Crnkovich, Ruth Anne art appraiser, museum director

Oak Ridge
Biewer, Theodore Mathias physicist
Borie, Bernard Simon, Jr. retired physicist, educator
Colston, Freddie Charles political science professor
Cui, Xiaohui research scientist
Daniel, Claus materials scientist, researcher
Deiterding, Ralf research and development company executive
Galindo-Uribarri, Alfredo research scientist, educator
Haire, Marvin Jonathan nuclear scientist
Harvey, John Arthur nuclear physicist
Holloway, Jacqueline county commissioner
Jones, Virginia McClurkin retired social worker
Kim, Dongkyun computer scientist
Krause, Manfred Otto physicist
Kronenberg, Andreas nuclear chemist, radiochemist, nuclear technology consultant
Manges, Wayne William electrical engineer, researcher
McFarlane, Joanna chemist, researcher
Melnichenko, Yuri B. physicist
Mirzadeh, Saed nuclear scientist, researcher
Mook, Herbert Arthur research scientist
Nephew, Edmund A. physicist, retired mayor
Olama, Mohammed research scientist
Perry, Kelly Ann research scientist
Plasil, Franz physicist
Pouchard, Line Catherine research scientist, educator
Poutsma, Marvin L. retired chemical research administrator
Raridon, Richard Jay retired computer scientist
Read, Kenneth Francis, Jr. physics professor, researcher
Sorokine, Alexandre geographer, researcher
Spray, Paul Ellsworth retired surgeon
Stracener, Daniel W. physicist
Vishnivetskaya, Tatiana Aleksandrovna microbiologist, researcher
Yin, Tongming science educator
Zinkle, Steven John engineer, researcher

Ooltewah
Birch, Lorna May geriatrician

Parsons
Economos, Cora Matheny librarian

Pigeon Forge
Parton, Dolly singer, composer, actress

Pleasant Hill
Heald, Mark Aiken physicist, educator
Hull, Charles William retired special education educator

Pulaski
Dunavant, Richard Hannah prosecutor

Puryear
Hedges, Patrick Armand security firm executive

Ripley
Hartman, Joan Evans *educational consultant*

Rockford
Nesbit, Sandi Michelle *corporate financial executive*

Rockwood
Miller, Donald Eugene *anthropology educator*

Sevierville
Austin, Birgit Kuban *language educator*
Hicks, Deborah *music educator*
Koff, Shirley Irene *writer*
Waters, John B. *lawyer*

Sewanee
Croom, Frederick Hailey *academic administrator, mathematician, educator*
Cunningham, Joel Luther *academic administrator*
Gessell, John Maurice *minister, educator*
Patterson, William Brown *retired dean, history professor*
Perry, Charles Richard *history professor*
Poe, George Wilkinson *literature, culture and language professor*
Ridyard, Susan J. *history professor*
Varner, Marleen Allen *retired academic administrator*
Williamson, Samuel Ruthven, Jr. *historian, educator*
Winton, Calhoun *literature educator*
Yeatman, Harry Clay *biologist, educator*

Seymour
Dunlap, Sue Weaver *education educator*
Steele, Ernest Clyde *retired insurance company executive*

Shelbyville
Nelson, Clara Singleton *human resources consultant*

Shiloh
Allen, Stacy Dale *historian, parks director*

Signal Mountain
Cooper, Robert Elbert *state supreme court justice*
Hall, Thor *religion educator*
Howe, Lyman Harold III *chemist, researcher*

Smyrna
Essary, Pat A. *principal*

Soddy Daisy
Leitner, Paul Revere *lawyer*
Randall, Kay Temple *accountant, retired real estate agent*

Somerville
Macdonald, Sally Polk Bowers *retired addictions therapist*

Spring Hill
Lister, Thomas Mosie *composer, lyricist, publishing company executive, minister*

Springfield
Nutting, Paul John *city manager*
Wilks, Larry Dean *lawyer*

Talbott
Gresham, Chip *physician, researcher*

Trenton
Smith, Jeffrey A. *lawyer*

Tullahoma
Cheatham, Clarence Donald *political science educator*
Hill, Susan Sloan *safety engineer*
Johnson, Jacqueline Anne *physics professor*

Union City
Crist, Marilyn I. *social worker*

Washburn
Romeo, Joanne Josefa Marino *mathematics educator, department chairman*

Waverly
Hunter, William Michael *electrical engineer, civil engineer technician*

Waynesboro
Morris, Randy G. *small business owner*

Whites Creek
Coleman, John Daniel *political strategist*

Williamsport
Dysinger, Paul William *preventive medicine physician, educator*

TEXAS

Abilene
Alcorta, Joe H. *literature and language professor*
Armstrong, Randy Lee *communications educator*
Bentley, Clarence Edward *savings and loan association executive*
Berryhill, Carisse Mickey *University Librarian*
Betts, Joe Delton *retired religious studies educator*
Boyll, David Lloyd *retired broadcast executive*
Cardot, Joseph James *program director*
Datta, Amlan *economics and business educator*
Lloyd, Terry Lee *retired elementary school educator*
McCaleb, Gary Day *university official*
Morgan, Clyde Nathaniel *dermatologist*
Morrison, Shirley Marie *retired nursing educator*
Pender, Martha Helen *retired dramatic soprano*
Perry, Troy D. *retired minister, religious organization administrator*
Potter, Paul Eugene *communications educator, consultant*
Sartain, James Edward *lawyer*
Scherr, Bernard *music educator*
Specht, Alice Wilson *university libraries dean*
Stone, Meredith Jean *academic administrator*
Weller, David Allen *information technology executive, poet*
Wheeler, Floyd Larry *education educator*
Woodfin, Carol Gale *history professor*
Wortey, Elizabeth Norman *librarian, associate director*
Wright, Clell E. *music educator*

Addison
Beck, Charles Wesley, II, *lawyer*
Goldmann, James Allen *healthcare consultant*
Peiser, Robert Alan *turnaround executive*
Wellborn, W. Christopher *construction executive*

Aledo
Barton, David *religious studies educator, writer, historian, researcher*

Alice
Tetlie, Harold *soldier, priest*

Allen
Hu, Rose Qingyang *communications engineer, educator*
Johri, Vinod B. *retired astrophysics professor, writer, researcher*

Alpine
Antrim, Nancy Mae *linguistics professor, consultant*
Kittlitz, Rudolf Gottlieb, Jr. *chemical engineer, researcher*
Morgan, Raymond Victor, Jr. *mathematics professor*
Rohr, David Malcolm *geologist, educator*
Tucker Chambers, Johnnie L. *elementary school educator, rancher*

Alvin
Guess, Ann H. *literature and language professor, director*

Amarillo
Burnette, Susan Lynn *lawyer*
Carter, Edythe L. (Edie Carter) *mathematics educator*
Crowley, Cara J. *director*
Eimon, Pan Dodd *artist, writer*
Gladstein, John G. *language educator*
Klein, Jerry Lee, Sr. *minister, philosophy educator*
Laur, William Edward *retired dermatologist*
Madden, Wales Hendrix, Jr. *retired lawyer*
Marupudi, Sambasiva Rao *surgeon, educator*
Matthiesen, Leroy Theodore *bishop emeritus*
McCartt, Debra *Mayor, Amarillo, Texas*
McDonough, Raenell *musician, educator*
Mojtabai, Ann Grace *author, educator*
Parker, Gerald M. *osteopath, researcher*
Reed, Katherine (Kathy) E. *nursing educator*
Robertson, Pauline Durrett *publishing executive*
Saadeh, Constantine Khalil *internist, educator, health facility administrator*
Siddiqui, Afzal A. *medical educator*
Von Eschen, Robert Leroy *electrical engineer, consultant*
Wilson, Golder North *medical educator*
Yanta, John Walter *bishop emeritus*
Zurek, Patrick James *bishop*

Angleton
Fu, Cary T. *electronics executive*

Argyle
Pettit, John Douglas, Jr. *management educator*

Arlington
Ahmed, M. Basheer *psychiatrist, educator*
Akpom, Uchenna Nwabufo *finance educator, consultant*
Alfaro, Ashley Barden *speech educator*
Alfonzo, Edgardo Antonio *professional baseball player*
Armstrong, Daniel Wayne *chemist, educator*
Bagcal, Orlando Raza *engineering educator*
Basham, Randall E. *social worker, educator*
Benson, Kris (Kristin James Benson) *professional baseball player*
Brainerd, Charles J(on) *psychologist, mathematics professor*
Brown, Sandra *writer*
Burkart, Burke *geology educator, researcher*
Butte, Norine *marketing executive*
Chen, Wei *physics professor*
Cluck, Robert *Mayor, Arlington, Texas*
Copeland, Anita Bob *director, retired elementary school educator, senior consultant*
Cuntz, Manfred *astrophysicist, researcher, educator, writer*
Damuth, John Erwin *marine geologist*
Dragan, Irinel Chiril *mathematics educator*
English, Marlene Cabral *management consultant*
Ferrier, Richard Brooks *architect, educator*
Foss, Frank Wells *science educator*
Fouse, David Jesse *sr. web application developer*
Goodman, Toby Ray *lawyer*
Haji-Sheikh, Abdol Hossein *mechanical engineer, educator*
Han, Chien-Pai *statistics educator*
Harcrow, Edward Earl *lawyer*
Howell, Holly Lyn *athletic trainer*
Jones, Andruw Rudolf *professional baseball player*
Khan, Samee Ullah *computer scientist*
Kim, Choong-Un *science educator*
Kinsler, Ian Michael *professional baseball player*
Lingerfelt, B. Eugene, Jr. *minister*
Liu, Hanli *biomedical engineer, educator*
Mandal, Subhrangsu S. *chemistry professor, researcher*
McCuistion, Robert Wiley *hospital administrator, management consultant, lawyer*
Mc Keen, Chester M., Jr. *retired manufacturing executive*
McKizzie, Robert R. *economics professor*
Minnerly, Robert Ward *retired headmaster*
Munoz, Celia Alvarez *artist*
Nussbaum, Charles Oliver *philosopher, educator*
Oehler, Judith Jane Moody *retired counselor*
O'Quinn, Josie Lu *nursing educator*
Peterson, Lynn Meister *engineering educator*
Petroskey, Dale Alan *professional sports team executive, former museum director*
Pomerantz, Martin *chemistry educator, researcher*
Puppala, Anand Jagadeesh *engineering educator*
Ramsey, Charles Eugene *sociologist, educator*
Ray, Asok Kumar *physicist, researcher*
Reaser, Donald Frederick *retired geology educator*
Ren-Cang, Li *mathematician, educator*
Robinette, Gary Omer *landscape architect, educator*
Rodriguez, Ivan Torres *professional baseball player*
Rollins, Albert Williamson *civil engineer, consultant*
Roner, Michael Robert *virologist, educator*
Ryan, Nolan *professional baseball team executive, former professional baseball player*
Sawyer, Dolores *motel chain executive*
Shiakolas, Panos S. *mechanical engineer, educator*
Siegfried, Cary Ann *library director*
Smith, Charles Isaac *geology educator*
Sqenz, Sylvia *counseling administrator*
Stevens, Gladstone Taylor, Jr. *retired industrial engineer, retired educator*
Strom, E. (dwin) Thomas *chemistry professor, researcher*
Swanson, Peggy Eubanks *finance educator*
Thomas, Lois C. *musician, educator, religious organization administrator, composer*
Timmons, Richard Brendan *chemist, educator*
Tingley, Floyd Warren *retired internist*
Trevino, Roberto Rosalez *historian, educator*
Weekley, Frederick Clay, Jr. *lawyer*
Willoughby, Sarah-Margaret C. *retired chemist, educator, chemical engineer, consultant*
Wimberly, Clarence Ray *retired engineering educator*
Young, Michael Brian *professional baseball player*

Athens
Estep, William Merl *history educator*
Leeper, Marianne *history professor*
Price, Vernon L. *biological studies educator*
Wright, Marylyn Riley *music educator*

Aubrey
Pizzamiglio, Albert Theodore (Al Pierson) *conductor*

Austin
Aadnesen, Christopher *rail transportation executive, consultant*
Abbott, Greg *state attorney general, former state supreme court justice*
Abraham, Jacob A. *computer engineering educator, consultant*
Adams, Mary Louise *nursing educator, researcher*
Aldrich, Richard W. *biomedical researcher, neurobiology professor*
Allen, Barbara Rothschild *retired psychology professor*
Alofsin, Anthony *architect, art historian, writer, educator, artist*
Anand, Vaijayanthimala K. *software engineer*
Anderson, Urton Liggett *accounting educator*
Andrade, Hope (Esperanza Andrade) *Secretary of State, Texas*
Annis, Joseph P. *anesthesiologist, educator*
Antokoletz, Elliott Maxim *music educator*
Arens, Katherine Marie *language educator*
Armstrong, Lance *professional cyclist*
Ashworth, Kenneth Hayden *public information administrator*
Babuska, Ivo Milan *mathematics professor*
Bajaj, Chandrajit *science educator*
Baker, Lee Edward *biomedical engineering educator*
Baker, Mark Bruce *lawyer, educator*
Barbara, Paul Frank *chemistry professor*
Bard, Allen Joseph *chemist, educator*
Barnes, Rick (Richard Dale Barnes) *men's college basketball coach*
Barnes, Thomas Joseph *writer*
Barr, Ronald E. *educational association administrator*
Barrera, Elvira Puig *retired counselor, academic administrator*
Bartlett, Dan (Daniel Joseph Bartlett) *consulting firm executive, former federal official*
Bash, Frank Ness *astronomer, educator*
Baumgartner, Robert *investment company executive, consultant*
Beazley, Hamilton *writer, educator*
Benavides, Fortunato Pedro (Pete Benavides) *federal judge*
Bengtson, Roger Dean *physicist, department chairman*
Benkiser, Tina Johns *political organization administrator*
Beyer, Richard Michael *manufacturing executive*
Biegalski, Steven Robert *nuclear engineer*
Biesele, John Julius *biologist, educator*
Billings, Harold Wayne *retired library director, editor, writer*
Blunck, Tedde *lawyer, engineering company executive*
Bobbitt, Philip Chase *law educator, writer*
Bode, Joyce Scruggs *lawyer*
Boggs, James Ernest *chemistry professor*
Bolm, Deborah Dell *elementary school educator, consultant*
Borcherding, John David *civil engineer, educator*
Bordin, Cristina Stadolny *academic administrator*
Bose, Henry Robert, Jr. *molecular biologist, educator*
Bost, Jane Morgan *psychologist*
Botsford, David L. *lawyer*
Bowen, Sabine W. *geologist*
Breen, John Edward *civil engineer, educator*
Brewer, Thomas Bowman *retired university president*
Brister, Scott Andrew *state supreme court justice*
Brockett, Oscar Gross *retired theater educator*
Bronaugh, Edwin Lee *retired electrical engineer*
Brown, Mack *college football coach*
Brown, Norman Donald *history professor*
Bryant, William Thomas *theater educator*
Buchanan, Bruce, II, *political science professor*
Buell, Samuel W. *law educator, lawyer*
Burd, Gene Arnold *journalist, educator*
Burnham, Walter Dean *political science professor*
Caffarelli, Luis Angel *mathematician, educator*
Cankar, Paul Anthony *physical therapist, director*
Cannon, James Washington, Jr. *lawyer*
Carleton, Don Edward *academic administrator, writer*
Carstarphen, Meria Joel *school system administrator*
Chae, Chan Byoung *research scientist*
Choi, Jinwoo *engineer, researcher*
Cigarroa, Francisco Gonzalez *academic administrator, pediatric surgeon*
Clark, Charles T(aliferro) *retired statistician*
Clements, Jerry K. *lawyer*
Coleman, Gregory S. *lawyer*
Combs, Susan *state official*
Cooper, Charles G. *state banking agency administrator*
Cooper, William Wager *economics, accounting and finance professor, dean*
Corsi, Richard *environmental engineer, educator*
Crismon, Miles Lynn *clinical psychopharmacologist, dean, educator*
Cunningham, William Hughes *retired academic administrator, marketing professional, educator*
Davis, Robert Larry *lawyer*
Davis-Floyd, Robbie Elizabeth *anthropologist, educator*
Dealey, Amanda Mayhew *former foundation administrator*
Demkov, Alexander A. *physics professor*
Demond, Walter Eugene *lawyer*
Derrickson, William Borden *manufacturing executive*
Dessau, Nigel *computer company executive*
Dewhurst, David *Lieutenant Governor of Texas*
DeWitt-Morette, Cécile *physicist*
Dickie, Martha S. *lawyer*
Divine, Robert Alexander *history professor*
Doluisio, James Thomas *dean, pharmacy educator*
Dougal, Arwin Adelbert *electrical engineer, educator*
Dougherty, Molly Ireland *organization executive*
Dowd, Matthew John *communications executive, political consultant*
Doyle, Marcus H. *computer technology educator*
Drake, Stephen Douglas *psychologist, health facility administrator*
Drummond Borg, Lesley Margaret *geneticist*
Dubose, Kathryn Michaud *secondary school educator*
Dumas, Sara Lee *psychologist*
Duncombe, Raynor Lockwood *astronomer*
Dusansky, Richard *economist, educator*
Dyer, Cromwell Adair, Jr. *lawyer, legal association administrator*
Eakin, Richard T. *research scientist, consultant*
Elequin, Cleto, Jr. *retired physician*
Ellis, Martha McCracken *academic administrator, psychology professor*
Eluru, Naveen *research scientist*
Erskine, James Lorenzo *physics professor*
Fair, James Rutherford, Jr. *engineering educator, consultant*
Farrell, Edmund James *retired English language educator, writer*
Fearing, William Kelly *artist, educator*
Feazell, Vic *lawyer*
Fisher, William Lawrence *geologist, educator, dean*
Fleeger, David Clark *colon and rectal surgeon*
Fleming, Francine Faye *legal nurse consultant*
Flowers, Betty Sue *library director, educator*
Folk, Robert Louis *geologist, educator*
Fonken, Gerhard Joseph *retired chemistry professor, academic administrator*
Fowler, David Wayne *architectural engineering educator*
Franklin, Cynthia Southern *psychology professor, researcher*
Freeman, Robert Schofield *musicologist, pianist, educator*
Friedman, Alan Warren *humanities educator*
Friedman, Kinky (Richard S. Friedman) *writer, musician*
Fryxell, Greta Albrecht *marine botany educator, oceanographer*
Galbraith, James Kenneth *economics professor*
Galinsky, Gotthard Karl *classicist, educator*
Gallerano, Andrew John *lawyer*
Gallo, A.C. *food products executive*
Galloway, Gale Lee *oil and gas executive, rancher*
Garwood, William Lockhart *federal judge*
Garza, Antonio Oscar, Jr., (Tony Garza) *consulting firm executive, former ambassador*
Gau, George W. *finance educator, former dean*
Gavenda, J(ohn) David *physicist*
Gentle, Kenneth William *physicist*
George, Walter Eugene, Jr. *architect*
Georgiou, George *chemical engineer, educator*
Gilligan, Thomas W. *dean, finance educator*
Gimson, William H., III, (Bill Gimson) *health facility administrator*
Glade, William Patton, Jr. *economics professor*
Goestenkors, Gail Ann *women's college basketball coach*
Golemon, Ronald Kinnan *lawyer*
Gonzalez-Gerth, Miguel *literature and language educator, writer*
Goodenough, John Bannister *engineering educator, physicist, researcher*
Graglia, Lino Anthony *lawyer, educator*
Graham, Lawrence Sherman *political science educator, management consultant*
Graham, Seldon Bain, Jr. *lawyer, engineer*
Granof, Michael H. *finance educator, department chairman*
Graydon, Frank Drake *retired accounting educator, administrator*
Green, Paul Warren *state supreme court justice*

Green, Shirley Moore retired communications executive, public information officer
Greenhill, Joe Robert retired judge, lawyer
Gregory, Becky (Rebecca Ann Gregory) lawyer, former prosecutor
Greig, Brian Strother lawyer
Griffy, Thomas Alan physics professor
Groat, Charles George geologist, former federal agency administrator
Groten, Barnet energy executive
Gurasich, Stephen William, Jr. advertising executive
Haas, Joseph Marshall retired petroleum consultant
Hancock, Gerre Edward musician, educator
Harms, Robert Thomas linguist, educator
Harris, Ben M. education educator
Harris, Richard Lee engineering executive, retired military officer
Harrison, Richard Wayne lawyer
Heath, Fred Milton library director, educator
Hecht, Nathan Lincoln state supreme court justice
Helman, Stephen Jody lawyer
Henderson, Terry Lee electrical engineer, researcher
Hetzler, Susan Elizabeth Savage educational administrator
Higginbotham, Patrick Errol federal judge
Himmelblau, David Mautner chemical engineer
Hinich, Melvin J. economics professor
Hitchcock, Joanna publisher
Hixson, Elmer L. retired engineering educator
Holtzman, Wayne Harold psychologist, educator
Holz, Robert Kenneth retired geography educator
Hopkins, Antony Gerald history professor
Hopkins, Bill Everitt lawyer
Hopkins, William Everitt lawyer
Houston, Ron professional society administrator
Howell, Jefferson Davis, Jr. aerospace transportation executive, educator, retired military officer
Howell, John Reid mechanical engineering educator, director
Hughes, Karen Parfitt public relations executive, former federal agency administrator
Hughes, Thomas Joseph Robert mechanical engineering educator, consultant
Hull, David George aerospace engineering educator, researcher
Hull, Robert Joe lawyer
Hutchison, William Ray geologist
Ikard, Frank Neville, Jr. lawyer
Ingram, Jack musician
Injo, Ok biologist
Inman, Bobby Ray dean, educator, retired military officer
Irgang, Carole A. marketing executive
Ivy, John L. medical educator, researcher
Jacobson, Antone Gardner retired zoology educator
Jaimes, Becky S. Spanish language professor
Jansen, Donald Orville lawyer
Jefferson, Wallace B. state supreme court chief justice
Jentz, Gaylord Adair law educator
Johnson, Philip Wayne state supreme court justice
Jones, William Richard database administrator
Jordan, Bryce retired university president
Justice, William Wayne federal judge
Kallman, James William management consultant, educator
Kane, Robert Hilary philosophy educator
Kemp, Sue art educator
Kendrick, David Andrew economist, educator
Keys, Jerry Malcom lawyer, educator
Kimberlin, Sam Owen, Jr. financial consultant
Kirk, Terrence lawyer
Kirkpatrick, Mark A. biology professor
Knapp, Mark Lane communications educator, consultant
Knowles, Harry Jay Internet personality, blogger, film critic
Koen, Billy Vaughn mechanical engineering educator
Kolar, Mary Jane trade and professional association executive
Lakey, David L. state agency administrator
Lam, Simon Shin-Sing computer science educator
Lang, Roberta Lynn food products company executive, lawyer
Langlois, Peter Hayes epidemiologist
Lansford, James Lowell technologist
Larkam, Beverley McCosham clinical social worker, marriage and family therapist
Larson, Kermit Dean finance educator
Leiter, Brian R. law and philosophy professor, writer
Leslie, Steven W. pharmacologist, educator, former dean
Liljestrand, Howard Michael environmental engineering educator
Lim, Sang Hyun chemistry professor
Livingston, William Samuel retired academic administrator, political scientist, educator
Lochridge, Lloyd Pampell, Jr. lawyer
Lochridge, Patton G. lawyer
Lockett, Landon Johnson retired linguist
Loehlin, John Clinton psychologist, educator
Long, Bert Louis, Jr. artist
Loo, Lynn (Yueh-Lin) chemical engineer
Louis, William Roger historian
Lowry, Alaire Howard psychologist
Lukenbill, Willis Bernard adult education educator
Lynn, Laurence Edwin, Jr. academic administrator, educator
Mabry, Tom J. retired biological chemistry professor
Mackey, John P. food products executive
Mark, Hans Michael physicist, former federal agency administrator
Martin, Norman Marshall computer science educator
Mathias, Reuben Victor (Vic Mathias) organization executive, real estate investor
Matthews, Dan dentist
Mayes, Wendell Wise, Jr. former broadcasting company executive
McCarthy, John Edward bishop emeritus
McDaniel, Myra Atwell lawyer, former state official
McFadden, Dennis psychologist, educator
McGuffee, James W. engineering educator
McKeown-Moak, Mary Park educational consultant
Mc Ketta, John J., Jr. chemical engineering professor
McKetta, John J. III lawyer
McKinnon, Mark David consulting firm executive
Medina, David state supreme court justice
Meredith, Thomas J. investment company executive
Mickenberg, Julia Lynn American studies professor
Middleton, Christopher Germanic languages and literature educator
Mikels, Jo science educator
Miller, Richard Owen history professor
Mills, Stephen performing company executive
Moag, Rodney Frank language educator, country and bluegrass singer, musician, record producer
Mookherjee, Reetabrata computer scientist
Moore, J. Strother computer scientist, educator
Morton, R. Steven lawyer
Moss, Bill Ralph lawyer
Moss, Logan Vansen lawyer
Mountain, Janet M. foundation administrator, former computer company executive
Muchlinski, Magdalena Natalia anthropologist, educator
Mueller, Peggy Jean dance educator, choreographer, rancher
Mukai, Ai physiatrist
Mullenix, Linda Susan law educator
Neavel, Celia Beth medical association administrator
Neeld, Elizabeth Harper writer, educational business company owner
Neely, Stephanie librarian
Nevola, Roger lawyer
Nichols, Steven Parks mechanical engineer, educator, academic administrator, lawyer
Noriega, Rick (Richard Joel Noriega) state legislator
Novak, Gordon S., Jr. computer scientist, educator
Oden, John Tinsley engineering educator, mathematician, consultant
Olsen, Richard Galen biomedical engineer, consultant
O'Neill, Harriet state supreme court justice
Oshinsky, David M. history professor, writer
Otto, Byron Leonard retired lawyer, state agency administrator
Owen, Priscilla Richman federal judge, former state supreme court justice
Painter, Theophilus Shickel, Jr. internist, allergist
Pangle, Thomas Lee political scientist
Patzek, Tadeusz W. petroleum engineer, educator
Payne, John Ross archivist, educator, library and information scientist
Payne, Tyson Elliott, Jr. retired insurance executive
Peacock, Penne Korth ambassador
Pena, Richard lawyer
Peppas, Nicholas Athanassiou chemical and biomedical engineering educator, consultant
Perlak, Kimberley Shelley music educator
Perry, Rick (James Richard Perry) Governor of Texas
Pestorius, Eileen McGee art educator
Petrosky, Tomio Yamakoshi research scientist
Pintar, Elizabeth anthropologist, educator
Pluta, Joseph Edward economics professor
Pope, Andrew Jackson, Jr., (Jack Pope) retired judge
Powers, William Charles, Jr. academic administrator, law educator
Ramirez Garza, Elizabeth Ann biology professor, researcher
Rankin, Mary Ann dean, biology professor
Ray, Cread L., Jr. retired judge
Reible, Danny David environmental chemical engineer, educator
Rich, John Martin humanities educator, researcher
Richardson, James Michael lawyer
Roach, James Robert retired political science professor
Roan, Forrest Calvin, Jr. lawyer
Robbins, Mary concert pianist
Rodnick, Amie Bowman lawyer
Rodriguez, Daniel B. law educator
Rodriguez, Robert filmmaker
Roueche, John Edward, II, education educator, director
Roy, Loriene library and information scientist, association executive
Rylander, Henry Grady, Jr. mechanical engineering educator
Sager, Lawrence Gene dean, law educator
Sanchez, Eduardo J. academic administrator, former state agency administrator, physician
Sanchez, Isaac Cornelius chemical engineer, educator
Sandberg, Irwin Walter retired electrical and computer engineering educator
Sasse, Benjamin Eric public policy educator, former federal agency administrator
Schechter, Robert Samuel chemical engineer, educator
Schloss, Hadassah auditor
Schmandt, Jurgen A. public affairs educator
Schmitt, Karl Michael retired political scientist
Schneider, James M. bank executive, former computer company executive
Schuring, Elizabeth lawyer
Schwartz, Aaron Robert lawyer, former state legislator
Science, Carroll Thomas chemical engineer, educator
Scott, Robert state official, school system administrator
Serafine, Mary Louise psychologist, lawyer, educator
Sessions, Alice biology professor, department chairman
Shapiro, David L. lawyer
Shapiro, Liza J. anthropologist, educator
Shilling, Roy Bryant, Jr. academic administrator
Shine, Kenneth Irwin academic administrator, cardiologist, educator
Sialm, Clemens finance educator
Slivinske, Alec Joseph, Jr. economics professor
Smith, Jeffrey Chipps art educator
Smith, John Brewster library administrator
Smith, Patricia H. library association director
Smith, Todd Malcolm political consultant
Sparrow, Bartholomew Huntington political scientist, educator
Spelman, William social studies educator
Spence, Roy Milam, Jr. advertising executive
Springer, David William dean, social sciences educator
Stephen, John Erle lawyer, consultant
Stewart, Kent Kallam analytical biochemistry educator
Stice, James Edward chemical engineer, educator
Stoff, Michael B. history professor
Stokoe, Kenneth H., II, civil engineer, educator
Strauser, Robert Wayne lawyer
Sullivan, Jerry Stephen electronics executive
Sutton, Beverly Jewell psychiatrist
Sutton, Harry Eldon geneticist, educator
Sutton, John F., Jr. lawyer, dean, educator
Swartzlander, Earl Eugene, Jr. engineering educator, former electronics company executive
Sweeney, Mark dentist
Tate, John Torrence mathematics professor, researcher
Temple, Larry Eugene lawyer
Theriot, Edward C. museum director
Thompson, Sanna J. medical educator
Thornton, Joseph Scott research and development company executive, materials scientist
Tottenham, Terry Oliver lawyer
Trabulsi, Judy advertising and marketing executive
Trafton, Laurence Munro astronomer, researcher
Trudel, Tina M. psychologist, educator
Tuohy, Patricia Anne library director, consultant
Udagawa, Takeshi physicist, researcher
Ulman, Doug foundation administrator
Umberson, Debra sociologist, educator
Vacchio, Rene language educator
van Otteren, Juliet photographer
Voges, Linda Kay mathematics professor, communications engineer, educational coordinator
Volk, William R. lawyer
Wahl, William Bryan marketing professional, real estate company officer
Wainwright, Dale V. state supreme court justice
Walter, Virginia Lee psychologist, educator
Walton, Charles Michael civil engineering educator
Warren, Karen Cohen librarian
Wassenich, Red librarian
Weddington, Sarah Ragle lawyer, educator
Weinberg, Louise law educator, writer
Weintraub, Russell Jay lawyer, educator
Welch, Ashley James engineering educator
Wentworth, Earl Jeffrey state legislator, lawyer
Westbrook, Jay Lawrence law educator
Whitbread, Thomas Bacon language educator, writer
Whitney, Bret Meyers travel company executive
Wiese, William D. lawyer
Willett, Don R. state supreme court justice
Williams, Anna Lassiter psychologist, researcher
Williams, Mary Pearl judge
Williams, Roberton Capell III economics professor
Williamson, Barry Scott conductor, performing arts educator
Willson, C. Grant chemical engineering and chemistry professor
Wilson, Clark R. geophysicist, educator
Wilson, Margaret Scarbrough retail executive
Wink, Amy L. literature and language professor
Winters, Sam lawyer
Wood, Donald F. lawyer
Wurzbach, Linda educational consultant
Wynn, Will Mayor, Austin, Texas
Xie, Chi transportation engineer, researcher
York, Candace A. marketing professional, writer
Young, Phyllis Casselman music educator
Zheng, Shuang-Cai physics educator, researcher

Baird
Rodenberger, Charles Alvard aerospace engineer, consultant

Bandera
Bartley, Dee Gray information technology executive

Bastrop
Clemons, Barbara Gail history educator

Baytown
Britt, Johjn Carrigan history professor, academic administrator
Cao, Chunshe (James) chemical engineer
Gilbert, Tatyana S. engineering educator
Soileau, Veronica Demoruelle counselor, educator
Thomas, Charles Edward engineering educator
Williams, Drew Davis surgeon

Beaumont
Andes, Joan Keenen tax specialist
Baden, Sheri Louise primary school educator
Bahrim, Cristian physicist, educator, researcher
Baker, Mary Alice communications educator, consultant
Black, Robert Allen lawyer
Brooks, Jack Bascom former congressman
Corbett, Robert Wayne biology professor
Cover, Ellen Catherine biology professor, researcher
Guillory, Curtis John bishop
Hopper, Jack Rudd chemical engineering professor
Jao, Mien civil engineering educator
Kemble, Joe David mathematics professor
Koehn, Enno engineering educator, researcher
Lanoue, Stephanie Anne biology professor
Liu, Jiangjiang science educator
Lord, Evelyn Marlin mayor
Lozano, Jose nephrologist
Luviano, Damien M. ophthalmologist
Lyons, Wilburn Franklin college instructor, department chairman
Marquez, Alberto industrial engineering educator, researcher
Miller, Thomas Eugene lawyer, writer
Needham, Keith Alan language educator
Oxford, Hubert III lawyer
Peirce, Dwight A(lexander), Jr. music educator
Qian, Qin engineering educator
Roth, Lane communications educator
Scofield, Louis M., Jr. lawyer
Smith-Sterling, Carolyn Leola technology educator
Sooudi, Matthew M. retired surgeon
Tcheslavski, Gleb engineering educator
Tinsley, Judith Anne sonographer, program director

Bedford
Blackburn, Wyatt Douglas insurance executive
Dawes, Robert Leo mathematician, consultant
Riggs, Audrey psychologist
Vaught, Karin Hampton music educator

Beeville
Freeman, Patsy L. director
Littlejohn, John Joseph chemical engineer
Past, Kay Cude language educator

Bellaire
Cunningham, Robert Ashley mechanical engineer
Frazar, Kathy cosmetic dentist
Haywood, Theodore Joseph physician, educator
Jacobus, Charles Joseph lawyer, writer
Lundy, Victor Alfred architect, educator
Mayo, Clyde Calvin psychologist, educator

Belton
Crawford, Stephen J. music educator
Erlund, Cecilia Wharton psychology professor, small business owner
Peterson, Brady literature and language professor
Shelburne, D. Audell adult education educator
Shoemaker, Robert Morin retired military officer, commissioner
Wyrick, Stephen Von religion educator, minister

Bertram
Albert, Susan Wittig writer

Big Spring
Fryrear, Donald William agricultural engineer, researcher
Warner, William Dee nursing consultant

Blanco
Holleman, Curt Paul librarian

Boerne
Goode, Bobby Claude retired secondary school educator
Price, John Randolph writer
Richmond, James Ellis retired restaurant company executive
Wittmer, James Frederick preventive medicine physician, educator

Booker
Doerrie, Bobette retired secondary school educator

Breckenridge
Jones, Karen Annette civic volunteer

Brenham
Anglin, Karen Locher mathematics professor
Coston, Carrie Allen history professor
Dalman, Michael science educator
Drane, Clifford Conway economics professor
Lubbock, Mildred Marcelle (Midge Lubbock) former small business owner
Moorman, Richard Hal, IV, lawyer
Neill, Lisa literature and language professor
Richarz, Charisse Elaine language educator

Brooks City-Base
Balldin, Ulf Ingemar medical researcher
Miller, Carolyn Lyons microbiologist, military officer
Villarreal, Roberto Escamilla retired political science researcher, educator, administrator

Brownsville
Ahumada, Patricio M., Jr. Mayor, Brownsville, Texas
Emilio, Garrido Sanabria Rafael science educator, researcher
Ermolinsky, Boris Sergeevich chemist, educator
Garcia, Juliet Villarreal academic administrator
Harris, William literature and language professor
Holkup, Linda Patricia music educator
Langerbein, Helmut history professor, department chairman
McNabb Goodwin, Carol music educator
Nair, Saraswathy molecular biologist, educator
Oudshoorn, Michael John computer science educator
Pena, Raymundo Joseph bishop
Price, Richard H. physics professor
Sinha, Aum C. language educator
Stephenson, Mimosa Summers literature and language professor
Weisfeld, Sheldon lawyer
Yi, Taeil mathematician, educator
Zhou, Yong engineering educator

Brownwood
Bell, William Woodward lawyer
Bryant, Pamela L. chemistry professor
Campbell, Vicki F. counseling educator
DeHay, Jerry Marvin business educator, small business owner
Humfeld, Nancy Jo communications educator, director
Smith, Robert Leonard pastor, religious studies educator
Weeks, Patsy Ann Landry librarian, educator

Bryan
Bigham, Robert Eric engineer
Bryant, Keith Lynn, Jr. history professor
Fields, Sheila Crain elementary school educator
Loguinov, Dmitri computer scientist, educator

McIntyre, John Armin *physics professor*
Milford, Murray Hudson *retired soil science educator*
Piper, Lloyd Llewellyn, II, *engineer, government and service industry executive*
Samson, Charles Harold, Jr., (Car) *retired engineering educator, consultant*
Steelman, Frank (Frank Sitley) *lawyer*
Van Riper, Paul Pritchard *retired political science professor*

Bulverde
Lamoureux, Gloria Kathleen *nurse, consultant, retired military officer*

Burton
Knauss, Robert Lynn *corporate financial executive*

Bushland
Baumhardt, R. Louis *agronomist*
Howell, Terry Allen *agricultural engineer*
Payne, William Albert, Jr. *agronomist, educator*

Calvert
Alemán, Marthanne Payne *environmental scientist, consultant*

Canyon
Casso, Rebecca Lynn *music educator*
Frederickson, Mary Christine *conservator*
Long, Russell Charles *retired academic administrator*
Roper, Beryl Cain *writer, retired library director, publishing executive*
Tao, Shiquan *chemistry professor*
Thoman, Roy Edward *political scientist, educator*
Trela, Richard Joseph *conservator, educator*
Truitt, Edward Ray *performing arts educator, director*
Vanderpool, Guy Clifton *museum director*

Canyon Lake
Bowden, Virginia Massey *librarian*

Carrollton
Barland, Sarah Elizabeth *secondary school educator*
Illes, George Maximilian *retired food products executive*
Jacobson, Carrie *librarian*
Owen, Cynthia Carol *sales executive*
Riggs, Arthur Jordy *retired lawyer*
Withrow, Lucille Monnot *nursing home administrator*

Castroville
Wurn, Kathleen Marie *English educator*

Cedar Hill
Hickman, Traphene Parramore *retired library director, consultant, storyteller*
Jackson, Robert Roscoe *education educator*
Potter, Joe W. *dentist*
Stowers, Carlton Eugene *writer*
Wilson, Peggy Mayfield *retired chemist*

Cedar Park
Golden, John Thomas *language educator, consultant*
Lam, Pauline Poha *library director*
Love, Ben Howard *retired organization executive*

Channelview
Dunn, Donald Glenn *electrical engineer, consultant*

Chireno
Mayhar, Ardath Frances (Frank Cannon, John Killdeer, Frances Hurst) *writer*

Clarendon
Wiginton, Larry Micheal *chemistry professor*

Cleburne
MacLean, John Ronald *lawyer*

Coldspring
Dietterich, Thomas Glen *computer scientist, educator*

Coleman
Smith, Eva Joyce *retired counselor, social worker*

College Station
Abu Al-Rub, Rashid Kamel *engineering educator*
Adams, Ralph James Quincy *historian, educator*
Adkisson, Perry Lee *university system chancellor*
Akin, Bilal *electrical engineer*
Annamalai, Kalyan *engineering educator*
Arnowitt, Richard Lewis *retired physics professor*
Arosh, Joe A. *agricultural studies educator*
Atkins, Stephen Eugene *academic librarian, historian*
Bass, George Fletcher *retired archaeology educator*
Beaver, Bonnie Veryle *veterinarian, educator*
Bennett, G(eorge) Kemble *engineering educator*
Benzerga, A. Amine *engineering educator*
Bessler, David A *economist*
Blair, Gary *women's college basketball coach*
Bluemel, Janet *chemistry professor*
Borlaug, Norman Ernest *agricultural scientist*
Bowen, Ray Morris *academic administrator, engineering educator*
Buchanan, Walter Woolwine *electrical engineer, educator, academic administrator*
Byrne, C. William, Jr. *athletics program director*
Calvin, James Arthur *statistician, educator*
Cannon, Garland *linguist, educator*
Carlton, Paul Kendall, Jr. *physician*
Chilcoat, Richard Allen *military officer, university president*
Christiansen, James Edward *agricultural educator*
Cocanougher, Arthur Benton *academic administrator*
Colenda, Christopher Columbus III *psychiatrist, dean*
Cook, C. Colleen *librarian, dean*
Cook, Violetta Burke *university administrator*
Datta-Gupta, Akhil *engineering educator, consultant*
Daugherity, Walter C. *engineering educator*
Davis, Eddie Joe *foundation administrator*
Dessler, Alexander Jack *astrophysicist, educator*
Dethloff, Henry Clay *historian, educator*
Dickey, Nancy Wilson *chancellor, physician*
Dominguez, Elvis *research scientist*
Drees, Bastiaan Meijer *entomologist*
Duce, Robert Arthur *atmospheric chemist, oceanographer, educator*
Eaton, Gordon Pryor *geologist, consultant*
Edwards, George Charles III *political science professor, writer*
Ehsani, Mehrdad (Mark) *electrical engineering educator, consultant*
Erlandson, David Alan *education administration educator*
Finch, Warren Luenberg, Jr. *library and museum director, archivist*
Fletcher, Leroy Stevenson *mechanical engineer, educator*
Furubotn, Eirik Grundtvig *economics professor*
Galdo, Juan Carlos *literature and language professor*
Gali, Hariprasad *research scientist*
Gan, Jianbang *agricultural studies educator, economist*
Gegg, Brandon Christopher *engineering educator*
Ghanem, Hassan A. *education educator, researcher*
Gladysz, John Andrew *chemistry professor*
Godfrey, Cullen Michael *lawyer, academic administrator*
Goodman, David Wayne *research chemist, educator*
Greenberg, Les Paul *entomologist, researcher*
Guerrero, Tito III *university administrator*
Gunn, Clare Alward *travel consultant, writer, retired educator*
Hall, Kenneth Richard *chemical engineering professor, consultant*
Hann, Roy William, Jr. *civil engineer, educator*
Hardy, John Christopher *physicist, researcher, educator*
Harner, James Lowell *language educator*
Hawes, Catherine *medical educator, director*
Hise, Richard Todd *marketing professional, educator, consultant*
Hoagwood, Terence Allan *English educator*
Holcombe, Troy Leon *marine geologist*
Hueste, Mary Beth Deisz *engineering educator*
Hwang, Wonmuk *engineering educator*
Kersting, Erasmus Kristoffer *economist*
Kier, Ann B. *pathology educator*
Klemm, William Robert *scientist, educator*
Laane, Jaan *chemistry professor*
Li, Ming-Han *engineer, educator*
Loving, Jerome MacNeill *biographer*
Lowery, Lee Leon, Jr. *civil engineer*
Lu, Mi *computer engineer, educator*
Lytton, Robert Leonard *civil engineer, educator*
Mahajan, Arvind *finance educator*
Makogon, Yuri F. *engineering educator*
Martin, Carol Jacquelyn *artist, educator*
Mathewson, Christopher Colville *engineer, geologist, educator*
Matthews, Pamela R. *literature and language professor, dean*
McCrady, James David *veterinarian, educator*
McIntyre, Peter Mastin *physicist, researcher*
Meier, Kenneth John *political scientist*
Miller, Rhonda Kay *food scientist, educator*
Misemer, Sarah M. *theater educator*
Monroe, Haskell Moorman, Jr. *chancellor emeritus, retired history professor, dean*
Moroney, John Rodgers *economist, educator*
Murano, Elsa A. *agricultural studies educator, former academic administrator*
Nachman, Ronald James *chemist, researcher*
Nash, William Rhodes *retired psychology professor*
Ndubisi, Forster O. *landscape architect, educator*
Nite, Sandra Bonorden *mathematics educator*
Ntaimo, Lewis *engineering educator, researcher*
O'Connor, Rod *chemist, consultant, inventor*
Ory, Marcia Gail *social science researcher*
Page, Robert Henry *retired engineering educator, researcher*
Painter, John Hoyt *engineer*
Park, Yong Hun Sam *engineering company executive*
Pate, Andrew Lidden, Jr. *religious organization administrator*
Patton, Alton DeWitt *electrical engineering consultant*
Penson, John B., Jr. *economics professor, consultant*
Phillips, Charles David *gerontologist, health services researcher, public health professional*
Piscitelli, Felicia Ann *librarian, musician, musicologist*
Pokrovsky, Valery Leonidovich *physicist, researcher*
Qin, Qing-Ming *agriculturist*
Radovic, Miladin *engineering educator, researcher*
Rasmussen, Bryan Philip *engineering educator*
Richardson, Herbert Heath *retired mechanical engineer, educator, dean, academic administrator*
Rimer, Mendell de Jesus *healthcare educator*
Riskowski, Gerald Lee *engineering educator*
Roschke, Paul Norbert *engineering educator*
Rumpho-Kennedy, Mary Ellen *plant biochemistry educator*
Sadoski, Mark Christian *education educator*
Samollow, Paul B. *medical educator, researcher*
Saric, William Samuel *aerospace engineering educator*
Savari, Serap Ayse *engineering educator, researcher*
Sheather, Simon James *management educator*
Shepley, Mardelle McCuskey *architect, educator*
Sherman, Mike (Michael Francis Sherman) *college football coach, former professional football coach*
Sohrabji, Farida *neuroscientist, educator*
Solymosy, Edmond Sigmond Albert *marketing professional, retired military officer*
Stevenson, Douglass Edward *entomologist, toxicologist*
Stranges, Anthony Nicholas *science history educator*
Strawser, Jerry R. *dean*
Stroustrup, Bjarne *computer science and engineering professor*
Sun, Yuefeng *research scientist, educator*
Suntzeff, Nicholas Boris *research astronomer*
Sweet, Merrill Henry, II, *retired biology professor*
Tai-Seale, Ming *science educator, consultant*
Vitter, Jeffrey Scott *academic administrator, computer science educator, researcher*
Wang, Di *historian*
Wenger, Scott Andrew *orthopedist, surgeon*
Wichern, Dean William *business educator*
Wild, James Robert *biochemistry and genetics professor*
Woodcock, David Geoffrey *architect, educator*
Wu, Guoyao *animal scientist, nutritionist, educator*
Yapici, Murat Kaya *research scientist*
Zhao, Shengjie *electrical engineer, computer engineer*
Zheng, Qi *statistician, biomathematician*
Zollinger, Dan *engineering educator*

Colleyville
Allen, Julie Ann Snell *music educator*
Giesler, Karen Hofmann *middle school educator*
Hennessey, Audrey Kathleen *computer researcher, educator*
Sawyers, Norma Ann *elementary school educator, real estate agent, property manager*
Tigue, Virginia Beth (Ginny) *volunteer*

Commerce
Bertulani, Carlos A. *science educator*
Jacobs, Kathryn Elisabeth *educator*
Justice, Madeline Carol *education educator*
Linck, Charles Edward, Jr. *English language educator*
McBroom, James Randy *sociologist, educator*
Moseley, Ann *retired literature and language professor*
Ni, Bukuo *chemistry professor*
Scott, Joyce Alaine *academic administrator*
Vornberg, James Alvin *education educator*
Wicke, Jason *biochemist, educator*

Conroe
Johnson, Raymond K. *information technology manager*
Kramm, Deborah Ann *retired information technology executive*
Steed, Theresa Jean *manufacturing executive*
Waites, Houston Chase *theater educator*

Coppell
Aikman, Troy Kenneth *sportscaster, retired professional football player*
Khan, Amir Manzoor *orthopedist*
McCally, Charles Richard *construction company executive, consultant, mathematician, educator*
Smothermon, Peggi Sterling *middle school educator*

Copper Canyon
Nickon, Alex *chemist, educator*

Corinth
England, Barbara Jane *history professor*

Corpus Christi
Abdelsamad, Moustafa Hassan *dean*
Al-Akash, Samhar I. *pediatrician, nephrologist*
Blankenship, Billy Jim *surgeon*
Branscomb, Harvie, Jr. *lawyer*
Cain-Calloway, Jonizo *literature and language professor*
Carmody, Edmond *bishop*
Cassidy, Jack *academic administrator, educator*
Chodosh, Robert Ivan *retired elementary school educator, coach*
Cohn, Edward A. *economist, educator*
Crowley, Patrick M. *economics professor, consultant*
Crowson, Sue *literature and language professor*
Finley, George Alvin III *wholesale and oil industry executive*
Flores, Manuel C., Jr. *editor*
Flory, Neil *music educator, composer*
French, Dorris Towers Bryan *volunteer*
Garrett, Henry *Mayor, Corpus Christi, Texas*
Gracida, Rene Henry *bishop emeritus*
Head, Hayden Wilson, Jr. *federal judge*
Ihenetu, Kenneth Ugochukwu *agricultural studies educator*
Klein, Melvyn Norman *lawyer, investment executive*
Krnavek, Jennifier Diane *school librarian*
Leon, Rolando Luis *lawyer*
Lim, Alexander Rufasta *neurologist, clinical investigator and neurophysiologist, educator, writer*
McCollough, Cherie A. *science educator*
Oden, Derek *history professor*
Paulson, Bernard Arthur *oil industry executive, consultant*
Perkins, Cynthia O. *art educator*
Pohan, Cathy Ann *education educator, consultant*
Potter, Allan L. *lawyer*
Rabinowitz, Yaron Gil *psychologist, educator, military officer*
Robeau, Sally Garwood *secondary school educator*
Samocha, Tzachi Matzliach *research and development company executive, director*
Schmitt, Patricia Ann *health and physical education educator*
Scott, Gloria Randle *former college president*
Sisley, Nina Mae *physician, public health service officer*
Stukenberg, Michael Wesley *lawyer*
Sturman, Susan *music educator*
Susser, Sam L. *oil industry and consumer products company executive*
Valdez, Kristina Louise *secondary school educator*
Wooster, Robert *history professor*
Zamora, Antonio *music director, educator*

Corsicana
Harper, Richard Patrick *oral and maxillofacial surgeon*

Crane
Hugendubler, Richard Thomas *secondary school educator*

Crockett
LaClair, Patricia Marie *physical education director, paramedic*

Crosby
King, Vernon Dale *art educator*

Cypress
Hlozek, Carole Diane Quast *finance company executive*
Huss, Betty Jo *education educator*

Dale
LittleDog, Pat *writer*

Dallas
Abdo, Virginia Richie *retired secondary school educator*
Acker, Rodney *lawyer*
Ackerman, Deborah *lawyer*
Adams, Carl David *lawyer*
Adams, John Lewis *transportation executive*
Adams, Richard Lloyd *lawyer*
Adams, William Peter, Jr. *plastic surgeon, educator*
Aggarwal, Nalini K. *ophthalmologist, educator*
Ajlouni, Raed Fakhry *dentist, educator*
Alexander, Gail Susan *psychiatrist*
Allen, Jerry R. *Councilman*
Ammari, Habib *computer science educator, researcher*
Anderson, Barbara McComas *lawyer*
Anderson, E. Karl *lawyer*
Angelilli, Lawrence *construction executive*
Anwar, Azam *cardiologist*
Arpey, Gerard J. *air transportation executive*
Ashfaq, Raheela *pathologist, educator*
Ashley, George Edward *retired lawyer*
Atkins, Tennell *Councilman*
Attanasio, John Baptist *dean, law educator*
Augur, Marilyn Hussman *distribution executive*
Babb, Ralph W., Jr. *bank executive*
Baek, Hyeonman *research scientist*
Bailon, Gilbert *newspaper executive*
Baker, Katherine June *elementary school educator, minister, artist*
Baker, Tom *utilities executive*
Barnes, Madge Lou *physician*
Bartlett, Richard Chalkley *writer, conservationist*
Barton, Fritz Engel, Jr. *plastic surgeon, educator*
Baxter, Richard Henry Geoffrey *research scientist*
Bayne, James Elwood *investor*
Beer, James A. *information technology executive, former air transportation executive*
Bergstresser, Paul Richard *dermatologist, educator*
Bernstein, Ira Harvey *psychology professor*
Besio, Charles Arthur, Jr. *marketing educator*
Best, Robert Wayne *gas transmission company executive, lawyer*
Betts, Dianne Connally *economist, educator*
Beuttenmuller, Rudolf William *lawyer*
Bickel, John W., II, *lawyer*
Bidic, Sean Michael *plastic surgeon, orthopedist*
Birkeland, Bryan Collier *lawyer*
Black, Robert W. *executive*
Blackman, Rolando Antonio *professional sports team executive, retired professional basketball player*
Blessen, Karen Alyce *freelance/self-employed journalist, artist*
Blessing, Edward Warfield *petroleum company executive*
Bliss, Robert Harms *lawyer*
Blodgett, Lynn R. *information technology company executive*
Blue, John Ronald (J. Ronald Blue) *evangelical mission executive*
Bonte, Frederick James *radiologist, educator, physician*
Boone, Michael Mauldin *lawyer*
Bosch, Joseph A. *construction executive*
Boswell, George Marion, Jr. *orthopedist, health facility administrator*
Boyd, Dan Stewart *lawyer*
Bradford, William Edward *manufacturing executive*
Bradley, John Andrew *health facility administrator*
Brandt, Carole *theater educator, department chairman*
Branson, Frank Leslie III *lawyer*
Brice, Wanda R. *museum administrator*
Brin, Royal Henry, Jr. *lawyer*
Brinker, Nancy Goodman *foundation administrator, former ambassador*
Bromberg, Alan Robert *lawyer, educator*
Brooks, Carla Jo *financial services manager*
Brooks, Douglas H. *food service executive*
Brooks, James Elwood *geologist, educator*
Brown, Benjamin A. *investment advisor*
Brown, Karon Whitesell *education educator*
Brown, Michael Stuart *geneticist, educator, science administrator*
Brown, Nancy A. *health science association administrator*
Brown, Stephen F. *health facility administrator*
Browne, Richard Harold *statistician, consultant*
Bryant, L. Gerald *management consultant*
Buchanan, George R. *oncologist, hematologist, educator*
Buchholz, Donald Alden *stock brokerage company executive*
Bumpas, Stuart Maryman *lawyer*
Burke, William Temple, Jr. *lawyer*
Burlin, Tom *information technology executive*
Burns, Sandra *lawyer, educator*
Bush, Jack Eugene *retail executive*
Buthman, Mark A. *health products executive*
Butovich, Igor A. *biochemist, educator*
Buttigieg, Joseph J. *bank executive*
Byas, Teresa Ann Uranga *customer service administrator, interior designer, consultant*
Byrd, Steve (Henry Stephenson Byrd) *plastic surgeon, educator*
Caetano, Raul *psychiatrist, educator*

Callahan, Jack F., Jr. *food products executive*
Campbell, David *lawyer, utilities executive*
Campbell, Raymond III *publication director*
Cantrell, Scott *newspaper music critic*
Cantrill, Thomas H. *lawyer*
Caraway, Dwaine R. *Councilman*
Carlisle, Rick (Richard Preston Carlisle) *professional basketball coach, retired professional basketball player*
Carpenter, Gordon Russell *retired lawyer, banker*
Carroll, William Francis, Jr. *chemist*
Carrozza, Vincent A. *investment company executive*
Carson, Virginia Hill *oil and gas executive*
Case, Thomas Louis *lawyer*
Cavanagh, Harrison Dwight *ophthalmologist, educator*
Chavez, John Richard *historian, educator*
Chawner, Lucia Martha *language educator*
Cherry, William Speakman *real estate consultant and broker*
Chinnakotla, Srinath *surgeon, director*
Cho, Ho Soon Michelle L. *adult education educator*
Choi, Changho *physicist, educator*
Cirilo, Amelia Medina *educational consultant*
Clancy, Denyse Finn *lawyer*
Clifton, Matthew P. *petroleum refining company executive*
Cline, Bobby James *insurance company executive*
Cochran, George Calloway III *retired bank executive, lawyer*
Cockerham, Sidney Joe *professional society administrator*
Cocklin, Kim Roland *gas industry executive, lawyer*
Coggins, Paul Edward, Jr. *lawyer*
Cole, James S. *dean, dental educator*
Comini, Alessandra *art historian, educator*
Connolly, John E. *immunologist, educator*
Cook, Gary Raymond *academic administrator, minister*
Cowart, T(homas) David *lawyer*
Cowles, Jim E. *lawyer*
Cowling, Terianne *medical researcher*
Cox, Rody P(owell) *internist, educator*
Crain, John Walter *historian, educator*
Creamer, Barry Kenneth *humanities educator*
Crichton, Thomas, IV, *lawyer*
Crockett, Dodee Frost *brokerage house executive*
Crossland, Mary Helen *language educator*
Crotty, Robert Bell *religious organization administrator*
Crusemann, F(rederick) Ross *advertising agency official*
Cuban, Mark *professional sports team owner, Internet company executive*
Curran, Charles Edward *theology studies educator, priest*
Daves, Don Michael *minister*
Davis, Barry E. *energy executive*
Davis, Carolyn R. *Councilwoman*
Davis, Daisy Sidney *history professor*
Davis, Joe A. *lawyer*
Dawson, Edward Joseph *merger and acquisition executive*
Dealey, Lynn Townsend *artist*
Deason, Darwin *information technology executive*
Dee, Ronda *poet, photographer, small business owner, journalist*
Deisenhofer, Johann *biochemistry professor, researcher*
Delagi, Greg *electronics executive*
Devous, Michael David, Sr. *radiologist, educator*
Dhillon, Uttam *lawyer, former federal agency administrator*
Dillon, David Anthony *editor, educator*
Doke, Marshall J., Jr. *lawyer*
Donnell, Carolyn Faye *music educator*
Doran, Mark Richard *real estate financial executive*
Dozier, David Charles, Jr. *advertising and public relations executive*
Drapkin, Dennis B. *lawyer*
Durham, Michael Jonathan *investment professional*
Durovich, Christopher J. *hospital administrator*
Dutton, Diana Cheryl *lawyer*
Dyess, Bobby Dale *lawyer*
Dykeman, Alice Marie *public relations executive*
Early, Ann Marie *retired women's studies educator*
Easter, Glenda H. *communications educator*
Eberhart, Robert Clyde *biomedical engineering educator, researcher*
Einspruch, Burton Cyril *psychiatrist*
Ellis, Alfred Wright (Al Ellis) *lawyer*
Ellis, James A., Jr. *lawyer*
England, Julie Spicer *computer company executive*
Engles, Gregg L. *food products executive*
Estep, Robert Lloyd *lawyer*
Ethridge, Joseph Alfred *manufacturing executive*
Etter, Delores M. *engineering educator, former political appointee*
Eugene, Phillip Frenkel *hematologist*
Everbach, Otto George *lawyer*
Ewalt, David Harris *pediatrician, urologist*
Fagin, Stephen Andrew *historian*
Fairbairn, Ursula Farrell *human resources executive*
Falk, Robert Hardy *lawyer*
Falk, Thomas J. *health products executive*
Fankhauser, Mark A. *lawyer*
Fanning, Barry Hedges *lawyer*
Farrell, Kevin Joseph *bishop*
Feld, Alan David *lawyer*
Fenner, Suzan Ellen *lawyer*
Fenves, Andrew Zoltan *nephrologist*
Fetter, Trevor *healthcare industry executive*
Fielder, Charles Robert *retired oil industry executive*
Figari, Ernest Emil, Jr. *lawyer, educator*
Fijolek, Richard M. *lawyer*
Fillmore, Robert M. *lawyer*
Fish, A. Joe *federal judge*
Fisher, Richard Welton *bank executive*
Flatt, Adrian Ede *surgeon*
Fletcher, (Martha) Ann Messersmith *counseling administrator, educator*
Focht, Michael Harrison *health care industry executive*
Fordtran, John Satterfield *physician*
Forshey, Michael S. *lawyer*
Foutch, Michael James *actor, dancer, lighting designer, producer*
France, Newell Edwin *retired health facility administrator*
Franklin, Kirk *singer*
Free Hosford, Mary Moore *biological and medical anthropologist*
Freling, Richard Alan *lawyer*
Frenkel, Eugene Phillip *physician*
Freytag, Sharon Nelson *lawyer*
Friedberg, Errol Clive *pathology educator, researcher*
Frisbie, Curtis Lynn, Jr. *lawyer*
Fyfe, Alistair Ian *cardiologist, scientist, educator*
Galvin, Charles O'Neill *retired law educator*
García, Elba *city councilwoman, dentist*
Gardner, Stephen Henry *lawyer*
Garner, Bryan Andrew *law educator, writer, consultant*
Garner, Harold Ray *experimental research physicist, biochemist*
Gavish, Bezalel *computer science operations research, information systems educator*
George, Arthur L. *electronics executive*
German, Dwight Charles *neuroscientist, educator*
Ghormley, Jason Grant *sales executive*
Gibbs, James Alanson *geologist*
Gilchrist, Henry *lawyer*
Gillett, Grover *author*
Gilman, Alfred Goodman *dean, pharmacologist, educator*
Gleason, Sean *marketing executive*
Glendenning, Don Mark *lawyer*
Glines, Carroll Vane, Jr. *magazine editor*
Godwin, Donald Everett *lawyer*
Goldstein, Joseph Leonard *molecular biologist, educator*
González-Boles, Cristina M. *medical educator*
Gooden, Drew *professional basketball player*
Goodenberger, Daniel Marvin *medical educator*
Goodstein, Barnett Maurice *lawyer*
Goodwin, Stephen Arthur *lawyer*
Gores, Christopher Merrel *lawyer*
Grahmann, Charles Victor *bishop emeritus*
Grammer, John Colquitte *cardiologist*
Grant, Joseph Moorman *finance company executive*
Green, Hubert Gordon *university professor, pediatrician*
Gregory, Louis P. *lawyer, gas industry executive*
Gross, Gary Neil *allergist, physician*
Gruchalla, Rebecca Sue *medical researcher, educator*
Guerin, Dean Patrick *metal products executive*
Guleserian, Kristine Jane *surgeon, thoracic surgeon, educator*
Gunter, Jack Pershing *plastic surgeon, otolaryngologist*
Guthrie, M. Philip *corporate financial executive*
Gwinn, Robert Allen *technologist, director*
Gyemant, Robert Ernest *diversified financial services company executive*
Haley, Barbara Jean *oncologist, hematologist*
Hall, Neva L. *retail executive*
Hames, Michael J. *electronics executive*
Hamilton, David Lee *retired sports association administrator, environmental company executive*
Hammond, Herbert J. *lawyer, arbitrator, mediator*
Hamra, Sameer T. *plastic surgeon, educator*
Hardy, R. Doug *epidemiologist, educator*
Harran, Patrick G. *biochemistry professor*
Harrison, Frank *former university president*
Hartnett, Will Ford *state legislator, lawyer*
Hartt, Grover III *lawyer*
Hay, Jess Thomas *retired finance company executive*
Haynes, Catharina D. *federal judge, lawyer*
Heacock, David *electronics executive*
Hegi, Frederick B., Jr. *consumer products company executive*
Helfand, Marcy Caren *lawyer*
Henkel, Kathryn Gundy *lawyer*
Hennessy, Daniel Kraft *lawyer*
Henry, Vic Houston *lawyer*
Heslin, Peter A. *management consultant, researcher, educator*
Hester, Linda Hunt *retired dean, counselor, retired sociology, physical education and health professor*
Hicks, Marion Lawrence, Jr., (Larry Hicks) *lawyer*
Hill, Vonciel Jones *Councilwoman*
Hinnant, Jerry Herbert *surgeon*
Hinojosa, Michael *school system administrator*
Hinshaw, Chester John *lawyer*
Hirsch, Laurence Eliot *construction executive*
Hirschman, Karen L. *lawyer*
Hitt, David Hamilton, Sr. *retired health facility administrator*
Hobar, P. Craig *plastic surgeon, educator*
Hoffman, Marguerite Steed *former art gallery director*
Hoglund, Forrest Eugene *retired petroleum company executive*
Holman, James *allergist*
Holmes, Bert Otis E., Jr. *retired editor*
Horchow, S. Roger *marketing consultant*
Howard, Josh *professional basketball player*
Hubach, Joseph F. *lawyer, electronics executive*
Hudel, Chestella Alvis *athletics educator*
Huffman, Gregory Scott Combest *lawyer*
Hughes, Vester Thomas, Jr. *lawyer*
Humble, Monty Garfield *lawyer*
Hunt, Angela *city councilwoman*
Hunt, Ray Lee *petroleum company executive*
Hurd, Eric Ray *rheumatologist, internist, educator*
Hurwitz, Jodie Linda *cardiologist*
Hutchison, Ray Ray (E. Ray) *lawyer*
Irwin, Ivan, Jr. *lawyer*
Isaacson, Brandon *medical educator*
Jackson, Jewel *retired state agency administrator*
Jakes, T(homas) D(exter) *bishop, author*
Janis, Jeffery E. *plastic surgeon, educator*
Jayson, Melinda Gayle *lawyer*
Jester, Guy Earlscourt *engineering consultant*
Jeyarajah, Dhiresh Rohan *surgeon*
Jobe, Larry Alton *finance company executive*
Johnson, Madeleine Brinton *lawyer, air transportation executive*
Johnson, Mary Elizabeth *musician, educator*
Johnson, Robert Lee, Jr. *physician, educator, researcher*
Jones, June Sheldon III *college football coach*
Jordan, William Davis *lawyer*
Joyner, Oscar A. *communications executive*
Joyner, Tom *radio personality*
Jung, Peter Michael *lawyer*
Kadane, Sheffield A. *city councilman, investment company executive, real estate agent*
Kaiser, Fran Elizabeth *endocrinologist, gerontologist*
Kangas, Edward A. *healthcare company executive*
Katz, Karen W. *retail executive*
Keglevic, Paul *corporate financial executive*
Keithley, Bradford Gene *lawyer*
Kelly, Gary Clayton *air transportation executive*
Kemp, Mark D. *construction executive*
Kemper, Robert Van *anthropologist, minister, educator*
Kemps, Steven J. *lawyer, food products executive*
Kenkel, Jeffrey Miller *plastic surgeon, educator*
Kennedy, Marc J. *lawyer*
Kent, David Charles *lawyer*
Kernie, Steven Gerard *pediatrician, educator*
Kesterson, Ray Brent *dean, retired military officer*
Keyes, James Willard (Jim Keyes) *film rental company executive*
Kidd, Jason *professional basketball player*
Klein, Scott W. *publishing executive*
Kneese, Kyle Calvin *lawyer*
Kobdish, George Charles *lawyer*
Koeppel, Peter Stafford *advertising executive*
Kogan, Inna *psychiatrist, educator*
Kohl, Kathleen Allison Barnhart Hughes *lawyer*
Koop, Linda *city councilwoman*
Kriscunas, Suzanne B. (Suzy Kriscunas) *private equity firm executive*
Kruse, Ann Gray *computer programmer*
Kuhn, Willis Evan, II, *lawyer, mediator*
Kulkarni, Mak *electrical engineer*
Kyser, Kevin *information technology executive*
Lacy, John Ford *retired lawyer*
Lake, Charlene Farrell *telecommunications industry executive*
Lan, Donald Paul, Jr. *lawyer*
Landry, Jane Lorenz *architect*
Lane, John Rodger *art association administrator, retired museum director*
Lawson, Gary B. *lawyer*
Leedom, John Nesbett *manufacturing executive, state legislator*
Lemaster, Arthur James *educator*
Lenkovsky, Fima *anesthesiologist*
Leppert, Thomas C. *Mayor, Dallas, former construction executive*
Lerman, Mark Jeffrey *nephrologist, medical administrator*
Levenson, Stanley Richard *public relations and advertising executive*
Levin, Hervey Phillip *lawyer*
Lewis, Jerry M. *psychiatrist, educator*
Lichliter, Warren Eugene *surgeon, educator*
Lilyhorn, Gregory Dean *security firm executive*
Lindley, Hamilton P. *lawyer*
Linquist, Roger D. *telecommunications industry executive*
Lister, George *pediatrician*
Lites, Jim (James R. Lites) *sports association executive, former professional sports team executive*
Liu, George Tye *surgeon, educator*
Lockridge, Deborah Ann *minister, educator, small business owner*
Longford, Nicola *museum director*
Lovett, Melendy *electronics executive*
Lowe, Gregg A. *electronics executive*
Lowe, John Stanley *law educator*
Lowery, David J. *lawyer*
Lowry, Sharon Kathleen *history professor*
Luce, Thomas Warren III *educational association administrator, former federal agency administrator*
Lund, Steven *school system administrator*
Lynch, William Wright, Jr. *investment company executive, engineer*
Maddrey, Willis Crocker *medical educator, internist, academic administrator, consultant, researcher*
Makel, Larry A. *lawyer*
Malouf, Mark E. *structural engineer, consultant*
Mankoff, Ronald Morton *retired lawyer*
Manteuffel, Robert Lee *lawyer*
March, Kevin P. *electronics executive*
Marion, Shawn *professional basketball player*
Maris, Stephen S. *lawyer, educator*
Marlow, Patricia Bair Bond *realtor*
Marshall, John Harris, Jr. *geologist, oil industry executive*
Martin, Boe Willis *lawyer*
Mason, Thomas P. *lawyer*
Massman, Richard Allan *lawyer*
May, Kenneth Austin *former consumer products company executive*
McAtee, David Ray *lawyer*
McCallum, Scott *not-for-profit developer, former governor*
Mc Clelland, Robert Nelson *surgeon, educator*
McCrea, Marshall S. III *energy executive*
McCurley, Mary Johanna *lawyer*
McDowell, John Henry, Jr. *lawyer*
Mc Elhaney, John Hess *lawyer*
McElvain, David Plowman *retired manufacturing, finance company executive*
McInnis, Carolyn Crawford *real estate broker*
McKelvey, Gregory A. *food products executive*
McKnight, Joseph Webb *lawyer, educator, historian*
McNeil, Barry *lawyer*
McPherson, Gail *publishing and real estate executive*
McWilliams, Mike C. *lawyer*
Medrano, Pauline *city councilwoman, ESL educator*
Meisenheimer, Fred E. *gas industry company executive*
Melin, Stacy M. *literature and language educator*
Menges, John Kenneth, Jr. *lawyer*
Menter, M(artin) Alan *dermatologist*
Menzer, John Bruce *retail executive*
Meyer, Ferdinand Charles, Jr. *lawyer*
Meyerson, Morton Herbert *investor, real estate company executive*
Micciche, Daniel John *lawyer*
Mielke, Thomas J. *lawyer, health products executive*
Miers, Harriet Ellan *lawyer, former federal official*
Migdol, Marvin Jacob *public relations and marketing executive, consultant*
Mighell, Kenneth John *lawyer*
Miller, David Bruce *investment company executive*
Miller, Jo Carolyn Dendy *family and marriage counselor, educator*
Miller, Norman Richard *lawyer*
Miller, R. Terry *lawyer*
Mitchell, Jere Holloway *physiologist, researcher, medical educator*
Mitchell, Teddy Lee *physician*
Moddelmog, Hala *medical association administrator*
Mohieldin, Ahmed Nader *electrical engineer*
Mong, Robert William, Jr. *editor, publishing executive*
Montgomery, Will S. *lawyer*
Moore, Cheryl (Milkes) Jerome *lawyer*
Moore, Christopher Robertson Kinley *energy industry consultant*
Moore, Edward Warren *lawyer*
Moore, Hugh Leslie *retired pediatrician*
Moore, Stanley Ray *lawyer*
Moore, Thomas Joseph *finance company executive*
Morgan, Gregory Paul *financial investment advisor*
Moroney, James M. III *publishing executive*
Morris, Henry Madison III *minister, writer, speech professional, consultant*
Mortensen, Pamela S. *retail executive*
Mow, Robert Henry, Jr. *lawyer*
Mueller, Mark Christopher *lawyer*
Mulford, Clay (Ross Clayton Mulford) *think-tank executive, lawyer*
Murphy, John Joseph *manufacturing executive*
Muse, John R. *investment company executive*
Myers, Larry Leonard *otolaryngologist, educator*
Nabors, Marion Carroll *retired English educator*
Natinsky, Ron *city councilman, entrepreneur*
Naylor, Rebekah Ann *surgeon, educator*
Naziruddin, Bashoo *lab administrator, director*
Neeley, Beverly Evon *sociologist, consultant*
Nelson, Donnie *professional sports team executive*
Neumann, David A. *city councilman, small business owner*
Newman, Steven L. *health care executive*
Newton, Pauline T. *humanities educator*
Nichols, Henry Louis *retired lawyer*
Niemi, Albert William, Jr. *economics professor*
Nikopoulos, Beth *educational association administrator*
Noguchi, Hirofumi *surgeon*
Nolan, John Michael *lawyer*
Nowitzki, Dirk Werner *professional basketball player*
O'Connor, Reed Charles *federal judge*
Odom, Floyd Clark *surgeon*
O'Donnell, Peter, Jr. *foundation administrator*
O'Neil, Michelle May *lawyer*
Orwig, Matthew Dane *lawyer, former prosecutor*
O'Shaughnessy, Joyce Ann *oncologist, director*
Oualline, Viola Jackson *psychologist, consultant*
Overman, Ann Cathlene *school librarian, educator*
Pace, Carolina Jolliff *communications executive, investor*
Palmer, Anthony J. *health products executive*
Palmer, Christine (Clelia Rose Venditti) *opera singer, musician*
Palmer, Larry Garland *music educator, writer, musician*
Panos, Tas *information technology executive, lawyer*
Parada, Luis Fernando *science educator*
Parker, Stephen G. *linguist, consultant*
Parkey, Robert Wayne *radiology and nuclear medicine educator, research radiologist*
Parks, J. Michael *data processing executive*
Patricia, Mathes-Burnett G. *education educator*
Patterson, Joseph Redwine *retired lawyer*
Pauley, Shirley Stewart *religious organization executive*
Pearce, Ronald *retired cosmetic company executive*
Pearson, Robert Lawrence *executive recruiter*
Pell, Jonathan Laurence *performing company executive*
Pelletier, Sho-mei *musician, educator*
Pennington, Karen Harder *lawyer*
Perkins, Nancy Jane *industrial designer*
Peterson, Edward Adrian *lawyer*
Peterson, Eric H. *lawyer*
Pew, John Glenn, Jr. *lawyer*
Phelan, Robin Eric *lawyer*
Phelps, Steven *editor*
Philips, Brian D. *delivery service executive*
Phillips, Betty Lou (Elizabeth Louise Phillips) *writer, interior designer*
Phillips, Joseph Theodore, Jr. *neurologist, educator*
Pickens, T. Boone (Thomas Boone Pickens Jr.) *hedge fund manager, former oil industry executive*
Pingree, Bruce Douglas *lawyer*
Pinson, William Meredith, Jr. *pastor, writer, administrator, professor*
Pitman-Gelles, Bonnie Louise *museum administrator, educator*
Pleasant, James Scott *lawyer*
Porter, Biggs C. *corporate financial executive*
Portman, Glenn Arthur *lawyer*
Powell, Michael Vance *lawyer*
Powley, Susan Elizabeth *lawyer*
Price, Robert Eben *judge*
Purnell, Maurice Eugene, Jr. *lawyer*
Quinoy, Melisa *marketing and advertising executive*
Rabun, Daniel W. *oil and gas industry executive*
Rachofsky, Howard *retired investor, art collector, patron*
Raggio, Louise Ballerstedt *lawyer*
Raggio, Thomas Louis *lawyer*
Rasansky, Mitchell *city councilman*
Rather, Dan (Daniel Irvin Rather, Jr.) *news correspondent, former network news anchor*
Ray, Hillol Kumar *environmental engineer, poet*
Reid, Langhorne III *merchant banker*

Reinert, James A. *entomology educator*
Reynolds, Jackie Susan *biology professor*
Ricks, Ron *air transportation executive*
Riddle, Michael Lee *lawyer*
Ring, W(illiam) Steves *thoracic and cardiovascular surgeon*
Ringle, Brett Adelbert *lawyer, oil and gas industry executive, trustee*
Ritchey, Kathy J. *history professor*
Ritchie, Kevin *electronics executive*
Roach, John D. *building products company executive*
Roberts, Harry Morris, Jr. *lawyer*
Robertson, Beverly Carruth *retired steel company executive*
Rodgers, John Hunter *lawyer*
Rohrich, Rod(ney) James *plastic surgeon, educator*
Romersberger, Sara Jane *performing arts educator*
Roper, Richard B. III *lawyer, former prosecutor*
Rosenberg, Roger Newman *neurologist, educator, department chair*
Ross, Roman *retail executive*
Rosson, Glenn Richard *building products and furniture company executive*
Roth, James Frank *chemicals executive, chemist*
Ruff, Gary Kay *lawyer*
Sabat, Hemant Kumar *communications and information technology industry leader*
Sagalowsky, Arthur I. *urologist, educator*
Saint-Cyr, Michel *plastic surgeon*
Salazar, Steve *Councilman*
Salinas, Martin *energy executive*
Sargon, Simon A. *composer, professor of composition*
Schaeffler, Georg *lawyer, manufacturing executive*
Schecter, Arnold Joel *public health physician, researcher*
Schochet, Barry P. *health care executive*
Schreiber, Howard E. *lawyer*
Schreiber, Sally Ann *lawyer*
Selinger, Jerry Robin *lawyer*
Sell, Clay (Jeffrey Clay Sell) *energy company executive, former federal agency administrator*
Senkayi, Abu Lwanga *environmental scientist*
Sermyagin, Konstantin *petroleum engineer*
Shambaugh, Irvin Calvin, Jr. *aptitude test firm executive, consultant*
Shepherd, Jon Glen *lawyer*
Shepherd, Nick P. *film rental company executive*
Shimer, Daniel Lewis *finance company executive*
Silverstein, Russell L. *physician*
Simmons, Harold C. *investment and sugar company executive*
Simmons, Terry L. *lawyer*
Sims, Dale Benjamin *engineering educator*
Sizer, Phillip Spelman *retired oil and gas industry executive*
Skinner, James E. *retail executive*
Skinner, Jon *rehabilitation hospital administrator*
Slavine, Nikolai V. *science educator*
Smith, Frank Tupper *lawyer*
Smith, Sue Frances *newspaper editor*
Smith-Becker, Nancy Woolverton *public relations executive, art appraiser*
Smits, Jasper *humanities educator*
Son, Tae W. *physics professor*
Sostek, Bruce Steven *lawyer*
Spears, Ronald E. *telecommunications industry executive*
Spiegel, Lawrence Howard *advertising executive*
Stacy, Dennis William *architect*
Stalcup, Joe Alan *retired lawyer, dean*
Stankunas, Edward Joseph *banker*
Stastny, Peter *medical educator*
Steinberg, Lawrence Edward *lawyer*
Stephenson, Jane Connell *artist, educator*
Stephenson, Linda S. *school librarian*
Stewart, Robert S. *construction executive*
Stewart, William C. *medical researcher, director*
Stinnett, Mark Allan *lawyer*
Stockard, James Alfred *lawyer*
Stoffel, Paul T. *investment company executive*
Stone, Marvin Jules *hematologist, oncologist, educator*
Stordahl, Ann M. *retail executive*
Sucato, Daniel J. *orthopaedic surgeon*
Sundararajan, Vijay *systems engineer*
Suter, Robert Eduard *emergency physician, educator*
Szygenda, Stephen A. *electrical and computer engineering educator, researcher*
Tansky, Burton M. *department store executive*
Taulbee, Thomas Lester *psychotherapist, educator*
Tebbetts, John Beryl *plastic surgeon*
Templeton, Richard K. *electronics executive*
Templin, Donald C. *lawyer*
Terry, Jason Eugene *professional basketball player*
Thomas, Paul Lindsley *composer, musician, director*
Thomas, Philip Jordan *science educator*
Thomas, Sarah Elaine *music educator*
Thomas, Tim *professional basketball player*
Thompson, Heath *media consultant*
Thompson, Keith F. MacKechnie *geochemist, consultant*
Thompson, Zachary *city health department administrator*
Thomson, Basil Henry, Jr. *lawyer*
Thomson, Roger F. *lawyer*
Tomko, Edwin Joseph *lawyer*
Tran, Quoc-Hung *psychiatrist*
Trotter, James *physician*
True, Roy Joe *lawyer*
Tubb, James Clarence *lawyer*
Tucker, J. Walter, Jr. *manufacturing executive*
Turley, Linda *lawyer*
Turner, R. Gerald (Robert Gerald Turner) *academic administrator*
Umphrey, Donald Wayne *adult education educator, academic administrator, writer*
Unterberg, Craig Scott *lawyer*
Ussery, Terdema L., II, *professional sports team executive*
Valerin, Marcus Paul *school system administrator, director*
Vanderveld, John, Jr. *diversified financial services company executive*
Van de Ven, Michael G. *air transporation company executive*
Van Scoter, John C. *electronics executive*
van Zweden, Jaap *conductor, music director*
Veach, Robert Raymond, Jr. *lawyer*
Vest, Christina Weaver *private equity firm executive*
Vitetta, Ellen S. *microbiologist, immunologist, educator*
Voyles, Robb Lawrence *lawyer*
Waddell, Douglas Howard *family physician*
Waheed, Khurram *electrical and electronics engineer, educator*
Walkowiak, Vincent Steven *lawyer*
Wallace, Anderson, Jr. *lawyer, educator*
Wallace, Charles Alan *plastic surgeon*
Wallace, Timothy R. *manufacturing executive*
Walsh, Dawna Hamm *art educator*
Wansbrough, Ann *legal assistant*
Warman, Lynnette R. *lawyer*
Warren, Kelcy L. *energy executive*
Wassenich, Linda Pilcher *retired health policy analyst, social worker*
Watkins, Craig *prosecutor*
Watson, Claude Armstead *counselor*
Weakley, Clare George, Jr. *insurance company executive, theologian, entrepreneur*
Weber, David J. *history educator*
Weidman, David N. *chemicals executive*
Wells, Melanie Kay *marriage and family therapist, director*
West, Teresa L. (Terri West) *electronics executive*
Wheatley, Seagal V. *lawyer, legal association administrator*
Whitaker, Darla *electronics executive*
White, James Richard *lawyer*
Wildenthal, C(laud) Kern *physician, educator*
Wiles, Charles Preston *minister*
Will, Clark Bradford *lawyer*
Williams, Michael Edward, Sr. *dean*
Willingham, Clark Suttles *lawyer*
Wilson, Claude Raymond, Jr. *lawyer*
Wilson, Jean Donald *endocrinologist, educator*
Witte, Robert Jay *lawyer*
Wolford, Larry M. *surgeon*
Wolin, Robert Everett *lawyer*
Wood, Georgianna Adeline *primary school and language educator*
Woram, Brian J. *lawyer, construction executive*
Wortley, Micahel D. *lawyer*
Wright, Alan *lawyer*
Wright, Laura H. *corporate financial executive, air transportation executive*
Wu, John Guoqiang *literature and language professor*
Wyly, Charles Joseph, Jr. *entrepreneur*
Xie, Yang *medical educator*
Yancy, Clyde Warren, Jr. *cardiologist, educator*
Yang, Emeline *lawyer*
Yang, Li *electronics engineer*
Yaradanakul, Alp *biomedical researcher*
Young, Barney Thornton *lawyer*
Young, John F. *energy executive*
Yu, Gang *medical educator, researcher*
Zahn, Donald Jack *lawyer*
Zeitlin, Laurie *printing company and information technology executive*

Del Rio
Fernandez, Yolanda *literature and language educator*
Prather, Gerald Luther *management consultant, retired judge, military officer*

Denison
Bredberg, Kathleen Hope *nursing administrator, director*
Cameron, Frances Marilyn *elementary school educator*

Denton
Acevedo, Miguel F. *science and engineering educator*
Alatzas, George *delivery service company executive*
Alexander, Jim R. *social sciences educator*
Anand, Aman *research scientist*
Babcock, Mary Lynn *choreographer, educator*
Baker, Pamela Elaine *finance educator, consultant*
Bataille, Gretchen *academic administrator*
Belfiglio, Valentine John *political science professor*
Bertine, Dorothy Wilmuth *retired accountant, artist, art educator, genealogist, writer*
Cassella, Dean Marcel *language educator*
Choppali, Uma *physics professor*
Cobb, Steven Lee *economics professor*
Dadres, Susan Layne *economics professor*
Evangelopoulos, Nicholas E. *finance educator*
Eve, Susan Brown *science educator, dean*
Ferrell Chavez, Dawn Elizabeth *assistant principal*
Fuchs, Jannon Lou *neuroscientist, educator*
Gabriel, Eberhard John *lawyer, bank executive*
Garcia, Oscar Nicolas *computer science educator*
Gough, Clarence Ray *retired designer, educator*
Gough, Georgia Belle *art educator*
Greenlaw, Marilyn Jean *retired adult education educator*
Greer, Russell Alan *literature and language professor*
Groom, JoAn Charlene *music educator, director*
Gunter, Pete A.Y. *philosophy educator*
Hartsock, Ralph M. *music librarian*
Hayes, Marjorie *theater educator, director, actor*
Hays, Edith H. *mathematics educator*
Homick, Michael Wayne *program manager, educator*
Hossain, Muhammad Muazzem *educator*
Hurley, Alfred Francis *historian, academic administrator emeritus, retired air force officer*
Kesterson, David Bert *language educator, academic administrator*
Krokhin, Arkadii *physics professor*
Lawhon, John III *lawyer, retired county official*
McCaslin, Richard Bryan *history educator*
McCoy, Amy L. *special education educator*
McDonald-West, Sandi MacLean *director, consultant*
McMath, Elizabeth Moore *graphic artist*
Morton, Sophie *literature and language professor*
Munshi, Sadaf *linguistics professor, researcher*
Needleman, Alan *mechanical engineering educator*
Newell, Charldean *public administration educator*
Nievar, Angela M. *social sciences educator*
Novak, Rynell Stiff *retired academic administrator*
O'Rourke-Kaplan, Marian *dean*
Paul, Pamela Mia *concert pianist*
Pollack, Eunice G. *history professor*
Poole, Eva Duraine *librarian*
Preston, Michael James *social studies educator*
Renka, Robert Joseph *computer science educator, consultant*
Rozzi, Ricardo *philosopher, ecologist*
Saleh, Farida Yousry *chemistry professor*
Salimath, Manjula S. *management educator*
Scharf, Thomas W. *engineering educator*
Seaton, Lynn *music educator*
Seward, Rudy Ray *sociology educator*
Slater, Neil *music educator, composer*
Smith, Howard Wellington *education educator, retired dean*
Snapp, Elizabeth *librarian, educator*
Snapp, Harry Franklin *historian, educator*
Staples, Donald Edward *radio, film and television educator*
Surprise, Juanee *chiropractor, nutrition consultant*
Swigger, Keith *library and information scientist, educator*
Thompson, Frances McBroom *mathematics professor, writer*
Toulouse, Robert Bartell *retired college administrator*
Turner, Keith Whisnant *gerontologist, educator*
Turner, Philip Michael *academic administrator, writer*
Ver Duin, D'Arlene K. *sociologist, researcher*
Wodnicki, Adam Juliusz *pianist, educator*
Yang, Philip Q. *sociologist*
Yi, Zhixian *science educator*
Yuan, Xiaohui *engineering educator*
Zrnic, Reiko Lukic *physics educator*

Desoto
Campos, David *social sciences educator*
Ennis, Rodney Craig *pilot*

Dickinson
Fotsch, George Bernard III *chemical addiction counselor*
Neves, Kerry Lane *lawyer*
Sawyer, Cheryl Lynne *educational association administrator, consultant*

Driftwood
Miller, Charles E. (Chuck Miller) *judge*

Dripping Springs
Smith, Ellis Carlton *history educator, consultant*
Thompson, Larry Flack *nanotechnology and semiconductor process company executive*

Duncanville
Fewel, John Gerrard *government agency administrator, director*
Gawedzinski, Robert William *literature and language educator, department chairman*
Timpa, Vicki Ann *government health program administrator*

Edinburg
Abraham, John P. *computer engineer, educator*
Ahn, Seokyoung *science educator*
Anderson-Mejias, Pamela L. *applied linguistics professor*
Ayala, Kara J. *speech educator, researcher*
Chipara, Mircea *physicist*
Freeman, Robert Arthur *engineering educator*
Glover-Graf, Noreen M. *social sciences educator*
Kupczynski, Lori Pendley *instructional designer*
Leal, Hector *lab administrator*
Manuella, Frank *retired art and design educator*
Poletaeva, Elena *mathematician, researcher*
Wilson, Bruce Keith *consultant in men's health issues*
Yagdjian, Karen *mathematics professor*

Egypt
Krenek, Mary Louise *political scientist, researcher*
Wynn, John Thomas *retired academic administrator, farming executive, economic consultant, oil and gas producer*

El Lago
Chase, Jeanette Knapp *music educator*

El Paso
Adams, Bruce Douglas *physician, researcher*
Ansari, Fariba *physics professor*
Balcazar, Hector G. *dean*
Barfield, Lowry *lawyer*
Biswas, Amitava *engineering educator*
Boyd, Dana Kristin *elementary school educator*
Brey-Casiano, Carol A. *library director*
Briones, David *judge*
Colgin Abeln, Melissa Gail *music educator*
Combs, Don Carlos *counselor educator*
Cook, John *Mayor, El Paso, Texas*
Cross, Clinton Ferguson *lawyer*
Cuartas, Beatriz H. *humanities educator*
Czacki, Stanislas T. *manufacturing executive, consultant, retired automotive executive*
Dalke, Gary R. *oil industry executive*
Edmonds, Velma McInnis *nursing educator*
Feuille, Richard Harlan *lawyer, director*
Foged, Leslie Owen *mathematician, educator*
Foster, Paul L. *oil industry executive*
Garcia, Lorenzo *school system administrator*
Gardner, Kerry Ann *librarian*
Gibson, Sidney Kay *retired lawyer*
Gladstein, Mimi Reisel *theater and literature educator*
Goodman, Gertrude Amelia *civic worker*
Grieves, Robert Belanger *engineering and language educator*
Gutierrez, Richard *political science professor*
Hanbali, Fadi *neurosurgeon, educator*
Himelstein, Philip Nathan *psychology professor*
Jarvis, Richard S. *academic administrator*
Jordan, Shannon Collen *medical/surgical nurse*
Juarez, Antonio *psychotherapist, counselor, consultant, educator*
Kuczkowski, Krzysztof Marek *anesthesiologist, department chairman*
Lawrence, Milbourn *literature and language educator*
Leung, Ming-Ying *mathematics professor*
Lujan, Rosa Emma *bilingual specialist, trainer, consultant, assistant principal*
Marshall, Richard Treeger *lawyer*
Martinez-Lopez, Jorge Ignacio *internist, educator, cardiologist, consultant*
Mearns, Kenneth Crawford *retired communications educator*
Mitchell, Paula Rae *nursing educator, dean*
Moya, Eva M. *health services executive*
Mulla, Zuber *epidemiologist*
Mullins, Patrick *communications educator*
Natalicio, Diana Siedhoff *academic administrator*
Newman, Carla Ruth *science educator*
Nieto, Angelica Baylon *principal, educator*
Peralta-Videa, Jose R. *environmental scientist, researcher*
Roberts, Ernst Edward *marketing consultant*
Rodriguez-Torres, Jose German *retired veterinarian*
Salinas, Carlos Dominic *literature and language professor, consultant*
Sipiora, Leonard Paul *retired museum director, art appraiser*
Solórzano, Rosalía *sociologist, educator*
Sozer, Sadri Ozan *plastic surgeon*
Stevens, Jeff A. *oil industry executive*
Taber, David O. *urological surgeon*
Tabuenca-Moyer, Rosamaria *language educator*
Trussell, Robert Prescott *special education educator*
Waissman, Naomi Assadian *biology professor*
Webb, Robert Gravem *retired biology professor*
Zopfi, Emma G. *elementary school educator*

Elgin
Jordan, Charlene Hanson *writer*
Shelby, Nina Claire *special education educator*

Enchanted Oaks
Melton, Kathy A. *medical transcription educator*

Ennis
Swanson, Wallace Martin *lawyer*

Euless
Paran, Mark Lloyd *retired lawyer*
Pascal, Tracey Michele *software engineer, director*

Fair Oaks
Regan, William Joseph, Jr. *energy company executive*

Fairview
Hansen, Elizabeth (Beth) Stevens *human resources consultant*

Farmers Branch
Blachly, Jack Lee *lawyer*
Reyes, Czarina Suzanne *mathematics educator*
Walsdorf, Marisa *finance educator*

Flint
Young, Earle Michael III *history professor*

Flower Mound
Crosmer, Janie Lynn *insurance company executive*
Kolodny, Stanley Charles *oral surgeon, retired military officer*
Marrs, Carol Faye *performing arts educator, writer*
Ross, Lesa Moore *quality assurance professional*
Stokes, Linda Baer *elementary school educator*

Forney
Weatherford, Shirley Diane *special education educator*

Fort Sam Houston
Blueitt, Odis R. *financial analyst, military officer*
Coppola, Martin Nicholas *military officer, educator*
Givens, Melissa Lousie *emergency physician*
Hewitson, William Craig *physician, career officer*
Kulild, James Clinton *dentist, army officer*
Ryan, Kathy L. *physiologist, researcher*
Todd, Reeder Allen *pharmacist*
Wojcik, Barbara Elzbieta *statistician, researcher*

Fort Worth
Adams, Lavonne Marilyn Beck *critical care nurse, educator*
Alvarez, Jill Lynn *mechanical engineer, management consultant*
Appel, Bernard Sidney *marketing professional, consultant, retired electronics executive*
Araujo, Ilka Vasconcelos *musicologist, pianist*
Ard, Harold Jacob *library administrator*
Astrup, Jens Leo *retired civil engineer*
Auping, Michael G. *curator*
Bailey, Susan Rudd *physician*
Bass, Robert Muse *financier*
Bass, Sid Richardson *investment company executive*
Berce, Daniel Eugene *financial services company executive, accountant*
Berenson, William Keith *lawyer*
Boller, Paul Franklin, Jr. *retired American history educator, writer*
Bonderman, David *investment company executive, lawyer*
Boschini, Victor John, Jr. *academic administrator*
Brister, Gloria Nugent *small business owner, elementary school educator*
Brown, C. Harold *lawyer*
Brown, Richard Lee *lawyer*
Caldwell, Billy Ray *geologist*
Chalk, John Allen, Sr. *lawyer*
Choudhary, Adil Mushtaq *gastroenterologist*

Clark, Emory Eugene diversified financial services company executive
Cox, James Sidney physician
Cunningham, Atlee Marion, Jr. aeronautical engineer
Cunningham, Shirley Rose artist
Day, Julian C. retail executive
Dean, Beale lawyer
Dees, Sandra Kay Martin psychologist, research scientist
Dent, Edward Dwain lawyer
de Tonnancour, Paul Roger Godefroy library administrator
Dubin, Bruce medical educator, dean
Dunn, Connie lab administrator, educator
Durham, Jo Ann Fanning artist
Dwyer, Stacey H. construction executive
Elliott, Frank Wallace lawyer, educator
Everton, Jeanne Simpson theater educator
Ford, Jeanette White archivist, educator
Frizzell, Roger C. air transportation industry executive
Frost, Edmund Bowen lawyer
Garner, Jason W. biology professor
Garton, Daniel P. air transportation executive, marketing professional
Gattis, David Robert environmental scientist, state agency administrator
Gilbert, James Cayce minister
Gilderhus, Mark Theodore historian, educator
Haber, Marian Wynne journalism educator, writer
Hall, Randy Jarvis lawyer
Harbour, Ted Ira lawyer, construction executive
Hart, John Clifton lawyer
Harth-Bedoya, Miguel conductor
Hey, Wayne Albert urologic surgeon, medical association executive
Hodgkins, W. Grant supply chain improvements manager, project management professional, consultant
Hong, Xin optometrist
Horton, Donald R. construction executive
Horton, Thomas W. air transportation and former telecommunications company executive
Hoskins, Paul Matthew religious studies educator
Hull, Shelli Bigham chemistry professor
Hund, Thomas N. rail transportation executive
Hutton, Keith A. energy executive
Hyde, Clarence Brodie, II, oil industry executive
Ice, Carl R. rail transportation executive
Isik, Tela Mae obstetrical/gynecological nurse practitioner
Jackson, Donald Wilson political science professor, lawyer
Johnson, Abbie Mae language educator
Johnson, Melody school system administrator
Jones, Harlan Pierre medical educator
Jurgensen, Warren Peter retired psychiatrist, educator
Kelly, Raymond Boone III lawyer
Kemp, Thomas N. economics professor
Kennedy, Gary F. air transportation executive, lawyer
King, Steve Mason judge, lawyer
Kowalski, Debra Atkisson physician
Lanigan, John P., Jr. rail transportation executive
Lee, Eric McCauley museum director, art historian
Lee, Jason K. theology studies educator
Lewis, Frank Leroy electrical engineer, educator, researcher
Lewis, Leroy Frank engineering educator
Lichtman, David Michael orthopedist, health facility administrator, educator, retired military officer
Lycan, Anthony C. biology professor
Maldonado, Francisco Javier electrical research engineer
Matsumoto, Shinichi surgeon, researcher
Matveeva, Evgenia chemist
Mayyas, Mohammad A. mechanical engineer, researcher
McBryde, John Henry federal judge
McConnell, Michael Arthur lawyer
McDonald, Frank G. lawyer, energy executive
Means, Terry Robert federal judge
Minton, Jerry Davis retired banker, lawyer
Moncrief, Michael Joseph Mayor, Fort Worth, former state legislator
Motley, Travis surgeon
Mullendore, Walter Edward retired economist
Munn, Cecil Edwin lawyer
Nicholas, Nicholas Constantine retired military officer
Nichols, James Richard civil engineer, consultant
Nober, Roger rail transportation executive, lawyer
Ogle, Sarah Jean retired educational consultant, educator
Pai, Kalpana economics professor
Patterson, Gary college football coach
Patteson, Charles Lynn musician, retired music educator
Pettit, George Hunter lab administrator, researcher
Poole, David P. lawyer, utilities executive
Quarles, Carroll Adair, Jr. physicist, researcher
Quinn, Francis Xavier arbitrator, mediator, writer, law educator
Reade, Kathleen Margaret legal consultant, author, educator
Record, Phillip Julius journalist
Reding, Robert W. air transportation executive
Reinecke, Manfred G. chemistry professor
Reuter, Frank Theodore historian, educator
Rich, Harold W. history professor
Roberts, Leonard H. retail executive
Robin, Clara Nell (Claire Robin) English language educator
Robinson, Gleniece Armstrong library director
Rogers, Dale Craig finance company executive
Rose, Matthew K. rail transportation executive
Saenz, Michael college president
Scott, Janice Wilkie museum director
Scott, P. Mark musician, educator
Searcy, Marshall Mayes, Jr. lawyer
Sharma, Rajendra chemist, educator
Sikes, Mary Taggart librarian
Simmons, Jean Byers academic administrator, director
Simpson, Bob R. energy executive
Simpson, Dennis Dwayne psychologist, educator
Smith, Tracey real estate broker
Stevenson, Ben performing company executive
Thomas, Frank Nelson family therapist
Tillman, Massie Monroe mediator, arbitrator, art gallery owner, retired judge
Tobey, Martin Alan cardiologist
Tomnitz, Donald J. construction executive
Tucker, William Edward academic administrator, minister
Tyler, Ronnie Curtis museum director, art historian
Vann, Kevin William bishop
Wall, G. Michael medical chemist
Wallace, R. H., Jr. lawyer
Watson, Robert Francis lawyer
Weaber, Terry Lee information scientist
Wheat, Bill W. construction executive
Whitehead, Elizabeth Phillips lawyer
Wicker, Dorothy Baldwin physicist
Wicker, James Eugene retired psychologist
Williams, John B. lobbyist, consultant
Wilson-Webb, Nancy Lou educational association administrator
Witt, Jim executive editor
Wortel, Gary G. publishing executive
Yacante, Maria Lucy music educator, researcher

Fredericksburg
Malec, William Frank utilities company executive
Manhart, Marcia Y(ockey) retired art museum director
Miller, Charles Wallace historian, retired environmental geologist, educator

Freeport
Overton, Tim chemical engineer
Weaver, John D. (Bert Weaver) chemist, researcher
Zhou, Zhe research scientist

Frisco
Bell, Haney Hardy III lawyer
Cogen, Jeffrey David professional sports team executive
Crawford, Marc professional hockey coach
Forêt, Randy Blaise public relations executive, insurance company executive
Hawk, Phillip Michael service corporation executive
Hicks, Thomas O. professional sports team executive, real estate developer
Holmes, William Larry mechanical designer
Hull, Brett A. professional sports team executive, retired professional hockey player
Jackson, Les professional sports team executive
Malik, Imtiaz telecommunications industry executive, educator
Modano, Mike professional hockey player
Morrow, Brenden professional hockey player
Nieuwendyk, Joe professional sports team executive, retired professional hockey player
Richards, Brad professional hockey player
Robidas, Stephane professional hockey player
Taylor, Dave professional sports team executive, retired professional hockey player
Turco, Marty professional hockey player

Fulton
Lamb, Richard cultural organization administrator

Gainesville
McCormack, Lowell Ray oil industry and corporate financial executive, consultant

Galena Park
Fierro, Robert, Jr. librarian

Galveston
AL-Hendy, Ayman gynecologist, obstetrician
Anderson, Garland D. dean, obstetrician, gynecologist, educator
Ashizawa, Tetsuo neurologist, educator
Bloomfield, Maxwell Herron III retired history and law professor
Budelmann, Bernd Ulrich zoologist, educator
Bytautiene, Egle medical educator
Dawson, Earl Bliss medical educator
Duarte, Alexander medical educator
Esenaliev, Rinat Orozbekovich science educator, lab administrator
Estes, Ernest L. geologist, educator
Foster, William Edwin (Bill Foster) retired men's college basketball coach
Freeman, Daniel Herbert, Jr. biostatistician
Gonzalez, Emilio Bustamante rheumatologist, educator
Goodwin, Jean McClung psychiatrist
Gugala, Zbigniew medical educator
Gwak, Young Seob biomedical researcher
Hankins, Gary D.V. medical educator
Harirah, Hassan M. medical educator
Hawkins, Hal K(enneth) pathologist
Hirschfeld, Robert M.A. psychiatrist
Ingole, Sudeep Prabhakar engineering educator, researcher
Ismail, Nahed microbiologist, immunologist
James, Thomas Naum cardiologist, educator
Kanuth, Michelle Susan science educator
Klein, Gordon Leslie pediatrician, educator
Kumar, Santosh medical educator, research scientist
Lee, James Ching biochemistry researcher, educator
Loftin, Richard Bowen academic administrator
Malloy, Michael Howard pediatrician
McKendall, Robert Roland neurologist, virologist, educator
McLeod, E. Douglas real estate developer, lawyer
Mohanty, Aaron neurosurgeon, educator
Moody, Robert Lee insurance company executive
Munsell, Debra S. physician assistant, educator
Murphy, Frederick Augustus virologist, researcher
Nash, Kathleen nursing educator
Nguyen-Oghalai, Tracy Uyentrang medical educator, researcher
Oberhauser, Andres F. medical educator, researcher
Protas, Elizabeth J. physical therapist, academic administrator
Pyles, Richard B. medical educator
Rivaux, Lois Elaine music educator
Rosanio, Salvatore cardiologist, educator
Rose, Robert M. consultant interdisciplinary research netwoks
Sahu, Gautam K. medical educator
Salch, Steven Charles lawyer, mediator, arbitrator
Sandstead, Harold Hilton physician, researcher, educator, director
Savidge, Tor medical educator
Shelton, Kenneth R., Jr. real estate company executive, artist
Simmons, Anthony virology educator, physician, researcher
Smith, David English pathologist, educator
Srinivasan, Ganesan molecular biologist, educator
Stobo, John David academic administrator, physician
Theiler, Regan obstetrician, gynecologist, educator
Thompson, Edward Ivins Bradbridge biological chemistry and genetics educator, endocrinologist
Torres, Alfredo Gabriel biology professor, researcher
Townsend, Courtney M. surgeon
Willett, Donald historian
Willis, William Darrell, Jr. neuroscientist, educator
Zhu, Bao Ting pharmacologist, toxicologist, researcher

Garland
Burns, George Franklin archivist, retired English language educator
Driver, Joe Luther state legislator, insurance agent, consultant
Irby, Holt lawyer
Jones, Ronald E. mayor, Garland, Texas, assoc. pastor
Kemp, Pamela Jean marriage and family therapist
LeDoux, Ellen G. music educator
Lowell, Peggy Armstrong elementary school educator, writer
McGill, Maurice Leon corporate financial executive
McGrath, James Thomas real estate investment company executive
Taylor, Kelley M. music educator
Tucker, Kimberly Joan music educator, director

Georgetown
Browning, Grayson Douglas philosophy educator
Bryce, William Delf lawyer
Busfield, Roger Melvil, Jr. retired trade association executive, educator
Deviney, Marvin Lee, Jr. science administrator, director
Ferrari, Lois music educator, director
Gerding, Thomas Graham medical products executive
Lopreato, Joseph evolutionary sociologist, writer
Lovin, Keith Harold retired academic administrator, philosopher, educator
Manning, Robert Thomas internist, educator
Maxfield, Louise Fonda Gribble executive secretary
Moore, Pat Howard engineering and construction executive, educator
Nelsen, Hart Michael sociologist, educator
Parker, Lynda Michele psychiatrist
Pierce, Benjamin Allen biologist, educator
Proctor, Claude Oliver Russian language educator
Purdy, Jesse E. psychology professor
Sellers, Fred Evans accounting educator
Shelby, Roselle Price writer, retired special education educator
Smitheram, Margaret Etheridge health facility administrator, director
Tegtmeier, Ronald Eugene physician, surgeon
Tisdell, Ronald H. toxicologist, consultant

Giddings
Dismukes, Carol Jaehne county official

Glen Rose
Lane, Willa Joan Manes retired psychologist

Glenn Heights
Francis, Tamara physics educator, professional athletics manager
Rowe, Nancie E. director, minister

Gonzales
Ince, Laurel T. music educator

Graham
Richie, Boyd Lynn lawyer, political organization administrator

Granbury
Adams, Christopher Steve, Jr. retired electronics executive, military officer
Almy, Earle Vaughn, Jr., (Buddy) real estate executive
Curl, Samuel Everett retired dean, agriculturist, consultant

Grand Prairie
England, Charles Mayor, Grand Prairie, Texas
Solomon, Arthur Charles pharmacist

Grapevine
Blizzard, Linda Kay software engineer, consultant
Carlson, David W. computer software company executive
DeMatteo, Daniel A. computer game company executive
Fontaine, R. Richard computer game company executive
Franks, Jon Michael lawyer, mediator
Ghaffar, Faryal pediatrician, infectious disease specialist, educator
Hao, Yaowu education educator
Morgan, Steven R. computer game company executive
Raines, J. Paul computer company executive
Smith, Catherine R. computer software company executive
Stack, George Joseph philosopher, writer

Guthrie
Marion, Anne Windfohr rancher, museum administrator

Harker Heights
Bahr, Hubert Arthur retired computer engineer
Rose, Doris Ann secondary school educator

Harlingen
Cohn, Aaron I. anesthesiologist, educator
Llerandi Phipps, Carmen Guillermina nutritionist and dietitian
Lytle, Michael Allen forensic criminologist, consultant
Matz, James Richard municipal official
Pope, William L. lawyer, judge
Rendon, Jose Ruben library director
Salcedo-Dovi, Hector Eduardo anatomist, educator, surgeon

Heath
Kolodey, Fred James lawyer

Heathridge
Vaughan, Joseph Lee, Jr. entrepreneur, realtor, educational consultant

Helotes
Rojo, Ruth M. nutritionist, consultant, director

Hereford
Fangman, Karen Walker school nurse practitioner
Gilbert, Connie Fay secondary school educator
Yavornik, Barbara Ann pre-school educator

Hewitt
Ariyasinghe, Wickramasinghe M. physics professor
Walbesser, Henry Herman computer science educator

Hillsboro
Hyles, Vernon Ross literature and language professor

Hitchcock
Shaffer, Richard Paul financial planner, real estate company executive, military officer

Hockley
Williams, James Lee finance company executive

Horseshoe Bay
Anderson, Kenneth Ward investor, consultant
Jorden, James Roy oil industry executive, consultant
Simpson, H. Richard (Dick Simpson) retail merchandiser

Houston
Aardsma, David A. waste management executive
Abdalla, Eddie K. surgeon, educator
Aboul-Enein, Faisal H. family practice nurse practitioner, educator
Acaba, Joseph M. astronaut
Achenbaum, W(ilbert) Andrew historian, gerontologist
Adams, Wanda city councilwoman
Adelman, Rick (Richard Leonard Adelman) professional basketball coach
Adrogué, Sofia lawyer
Afify, Ahmed Aly engineer
Ahearne, Michael finance educator
Ajamie, Thomas Robert lawyer
Akers, William Walter chemical engineering educator
Alam, Mahboob internist
Alauddin, Mian M. chemist, educator
Alavi, Mehdi geologist
Aldape, Ken pathologist, researcher
Alexander, Leslie Lee professional sports team owner
Alexanian, Raymond hematologist
Alfini, James Joseph dean, lawyer, educator
Alford, Bobby Ray otolaryngologist, academic administrator, educator
Allender, John Roland lawyer
Allred, D. Craig pathologist, educator
Alt, Eckhard U. physician, educator
Amdur, Arthur R. lawyer
Anani, Tarig lawyer, software company executive
Anderson, Claire W. gifted and talented educator
Anderson, D(arryl) Kent bank executive
Anderson, Paul Milton energy executive
Anderson, Richard Carl geophysical exploration company executive
Anderson-Lehman, Ron air transportation executive
Antalffy, Leslie Peter mechanical engineer
Antignano, Angelo, IV, geologist
Antonelli, Dominic A. astronaut
Appel, Stanley Hersh neurologist, educator
Arafat, Raouf Raafat public health service officer
Archambault, Lee Joseph astronaut
Archibald, Lawrence E. (Larry Archibald) oil industry executive
Ariza, Trevor Anthony professional basketball player
Arjomand, Bijan medical educator
Armstrong, Greg L. oil industry executive
Arnold, Daniel Calmes retired finance company executive, lawyer
Arnold, John Douglas hedge fund manager
Aron, Doug oil industry executive
Ashby, Jeffrey S. astronaut
Asmus, David F. lawyer
Asselin, Heather E. lawyer
Atlas, Nancy Friedman judge
Atlas, Scott J. lawyer
Ayadi, Mary Olufemi health economist, educator
Ayus, Juan Carlos nephrologist
Bachmann, Richard H. lawyer, energy executive
Baggétt, Antrece Lynette historian, educator
Bahl, Saroj Mehta nutritionist, educator
Bailey, Harold Randolph surgeon, educator
Bair, Royden Stanley retired architect
Baker, C. Mark lawyer

Baker, James Addison, III, (Jim Baker) *lawyer, former United States Secretary of State*
Baker, Robert W. *lawyer*
Baker, Stephen Denio *physics professor*
Baldwin, Bonnie *physician*
Ball, George L. *investment banker*
Ball, Valdesha LeChante' *physician*
Ballanfant, Richard Burton *lawyer*
Ballas, Mark, Jr. *dancer*
Ballo, Matthew T. *radiation oncologist, educator*
Bally, Albert W. *retired geologist, educator*
Bargfrede, James Allen *lawyer*
Barham, Stephen R. *oil industry executive*
Barnea, Dan *information technology executive*
Barnett, Edward William *lawyer*
Barracano, Henry Ralph *retired oil company executive, management consultant*
Barratt, Michael Reed *astronaut*
Barrett, Bernard Morris, Jr. *plastic and reconstructive surgeon*
Barry, Brent Robert *professional basketball player*
Barshes, Neal Ryan *surgeon*
Bartling, Phyllis McGinness *oil company executive*
Bartsch, Joel A. *museum administrator, curator*
Bast, Robert Clinton, Jr. *medical researcher, educator*
Batchelder, Gene (Eugene Lewis Batchelder) *oil industry executive*
Batsakis, John George *pathology educator*
Battier, Shane *professional basketball player*
Battin, R. Ray (Rosabell Harriet Ray) *audiologist, neuropsychologist*
Bay, Annell R. *oil industry executive, geologist*
Beauchamp, Robert E. *information technology executive*
Bechtol, J. Currie *lawyer, oil industry executive*
Beckingham, Kathleen Mary *education educator, researcher*
Bedoya González, Cardenio *literature and language educator*
Beirne, Martin Douglas *lawyer*
Belk, Joan Pardue *language and literature educator*
Bellatti, Lawrence Lee *lawyer*
Bennett, Olga Salowich *civic worker, graphic arts researcher, consultant*
Bensaoula, Abdelhak *engineering educator, consultant*
Berg, David Howard *lawyer*
Berg, Geoffrey A. *lawyer*
Berg, Stacey Lynn *pediatric oncologist*
Bergsrud, Mark *air transportation executive*
Bering, Edgar Andrew III *physicist, educator*
Berkman, Lance *professional baseball player*
Betts, Nicole Lavette *elementary school educator, consultant*
Beyoncé, (Beyoncé Giselle Knowles) *singer*
Bhargava, Alok *economics professor, consultant*
Bidani, Akhil *biomedical researcher, educator*
Biery, Evelyn Hudson *lawyer*
Bigwood, David P. *librarian, writer*
Bilger, Bruce R. *lawyer*
Black, Donna Lord *school psychology specialist*
Blackburn, Sadie Gwin Allen *conservation executive*
Blackshear, A. T., Jr. *lawyer*
Bland, John Lloyd *lawyer*
Bluestein, Edwin A., Jr. *lawyer*
Bodey, Gerald Paul *retired medical educator*
Boe, Eric A. *pilot, astronaut*
Bogard, Donald Dale *planetary geochemist*
Bomba, John Gilbert *civil engineer, consultant*
Bonds, Michael P. *air transportation executive*
Bookout, John Frank, Jr. *oil industry executive*
Boren, William Meredith *manufacturing executive*
Bott, Simon Gregory *chemistry educator, researcher*
Bou Aram, Boura'a Abdul Karim *pediatrician, researcher*
Boule, Michelle L. *librarian, writer*
Boulware, Margaret A. *lawyer*
Boutros, Sean *plastic surgeon*
Bovay, Harry Elmo, Jr. *retired engineering company executive*
Bowen, Stephen G. *astronaut*
Bowles, James L. *oil industry executive*
Braden, John Alan *accountant*
Braiteh, Fadi *physician*
Bramanti, Frank J. *insurance company executive*
Brand, Stephen R. *oil industry executive*
Brandenstein, Daniel Charles *astronaut, retired military officer*
Brann, Richard R. *lawyer*
Braun, Michael C. *nephrologist, educator*
Brener, Daniel Michael *psychiatrist*
Brenner, Malcolm K. *pediatric and medical educator*
Brewer, Eileen D. (L. Eileen Doyle Brewer) *nephrologist, educator*
Brinkley, Douglas G. *historian, writer, educator*
Brinson, Gay Creswell, Jr. *retired lawyer*
Brito, Dagobert Llanos *economics professor*
Brotzen, Franz Richard *materials scientist, educator*
Brown, Dennison Robert *mathematician, educator*
Brown, Glenda Ann Walters *ballet director*
Brown, Peter *city councilman, architectural firm executive*
Brown, Powel H. *oncologist, educator*
Brown, Thaddeus B. *professional sports team executive*
Bryan, Nathan Scott *medical educator*
Bryan Green, Meva *hospital administrator, educator*
Bryant, John Bradbury *economics professor, consultant*
Buckingham, Edwin John III *lawyer*
Buckley, Vincent H. *lawyer*
Bue, Carl Olaf, Jr. *retired federal judge*
Bui, Khoi Tien *college counselor*
Buja, L. Maximilian *pathologist, academic administrator, educator*
Bullock, William L., Jr. *oil industry executive*
Bungo, Michael William *cardiologist, educator, administrator*
Burch, Voris Reagan *mediator, arbitrator, retired lawyer*
Burgert, David Lee *lawyer*
Burke, Kevin Charles Antony *geologist*
Burke, Michael Donald *oil and gas company executive*
Burnett, Susan Walk *personnel service company owner*
Burrus, (Charles) Sidney *electrical engineering educator*
Burzynski, Stanislaw Rajmund *internist*
Bush, George Herbert Walker *41st President of the United States*
Buster, John Edmond *obstetrician, researcher*
Butler, William Thomas *academic administrator, physician, educator*
Bux, William John *lawyer*
Buzdar, Aman U. *internal medicine educator*
Byerly, Diane Leslie *aerospace engineer, researcher*
Byreddy, Chakradhar R. *research and development company executive*
Caddell, Lynn M. *waste management executive*
Caddy, Michael Douglas *lawyer*
Caldwell, Barry H. *waste management executive*
Caldwell, Garnett Ernest *lawyer*
Caldwell, Richard H. *lawyer*
Caldwell, Rodney Kent *lawyer*
Caldwell, Tracy Ellen *surface chemist, researcher*
Caligur, Matthew W. *lawyer*
Callender, Norma Anne *counselor, public relations executive*
Campbell, Bert Louis *lawyer, arbitrator, mediator*
Campbell, Clifford Russell *research scientist*
Campbell, Eileen M. *oil industry executive*
Cantor, Scott Brian *medical educator*
Caram, Dorothy Farrington *educational consultant*
Carameros, George Demitrius, Jr. *natural gas company executive*
Carman, Carol A. *psychologist, educator*
Carr, Edward A. *lawyer*
Carrig, John A. *oil industry executive*
Carroll, Chuck (Charles A. Carroll) *manufacturing executive*
Carroll, James Vincent III *lawyer*
Carroll, Michael M. *dean, mechanical engineering educator*
Carroll, Milton *oil industry executive*
Carson, Daniel Douglas *biochemist, reproductive biologist*
Carter, John Francis, II, *lawyer*
Carter, John Loyd *lawyer*
Casscells, Samuel Ward III *cardiologist, educator, former federal agency administrator*
Cassimere, Brant *electrical engineer*
Caswell, Bryan *chef*
Catlin, Francis Irving *physician*
Caudill, William Howard *lawyer*
Cavaney, Red (Byron M. Cavaney Jr.) *oil industry executive, lobbyist*
Caviness, Alison Chantal *pediatrician, educator*
Cazalot, Clarence P., Jr. *oil industry executive*
Cazenave, Anita Washington *secondary school educator*
Cenatiempo, Michael J. *lawyer*
Chaiyarat, Walailuk *medical researcher*
Chalmers, David B. *petroleum executive*
Chamitoff, Gregory Errol *astronaut, aerospace engineer*
Chance, Jane *English literature educator*
Chandler, Richard E., Jr. *lawyer*
Chao, Albert *chemicals executive*
Chapman, Cynthia B. *lawyer*
Chavez, J. Anthony *lawyer*
Cheatham, John Bane, Jr. *retired mechanical engineering educator*
Chemaly, Roy F. *physician*
Chen, Eric *ophthalmologist*
Cheung, Min Rex *medical educator*
Chevray, Pierre M. *medical educator*
Chiang, W.C.W (Willie Chiang) *oil industry executive*
Chiao, Leroy *astronaut*
Chiou-Tan, Faye *physician, educator*
Chowdhury, Shafkat Ahmed *aerospace engineer*
Chu, Paul Ching-Wu *physicist, academic administrator, educator*
Chung, Paul W. *lawyer, energy executive*
Clark, Janet F. *oil industry executive*
Clarke, Robert Logan *lawyer*
Clayton, Benjamin J. *oil industry executive*
Cloninger, Dale Owen *retired finance educator, professor emeritus*
Clore, Lawrence Hubert *lawyer*
Clutterbuck, Anne *city councilwoman*
Cocanour, Christine Susan *surgery educator, researcher*
Coghlan, Kelly Jack *lawyer*
Cohen, Jeff *editor, publishing executive*
Cohn, William Ettlinger *cardiologist, thoracic surgeon, product designer*
Colbert, Kevin LeRoy *lawyer*
Coley, Randolph C. *lawyer*
Collings, Chris D. *lawyer*
Colson, John R. *electric power industry executive*
Compton, James E. *air transportation executive*
Condit, Linda Faulkner *retired economist*
Constantine, Kevin *professional hockey coach*
Conway, C.W. *oil industry executive*
Cook, Eugene Augustus *lawyer*
Cooper, Cecil Celester *professional baseball manager, retired professional baseball player*
Cooper, Valerie Gail *minister*
Corken, Heather Marie *lawyer*
Cornelison, Albert Otto, Jr., (Bert Cornelison) *lawyer, oil industry executive*
Cornelius, Sigmund L. (Sig Cornelius) *oil industry executive*
Corriere, Joseph N., Jr. *urologist, educator*
Cortes, Jorge *oncologist*
Couch, Jesse Wadsworth *retired insurance company executive*
Couch, Robert Barnard *physician, scientist, microbiologist, educator*
Cox, James Talley *lawyer*
Crain, Alan Rau, Jr. *lawyer, oil industry executive*
Crayton, Arnell *secondary school educator*
Creel, Michael Allen *energy executive*
Crinion, Gregory Paul *lawyer*
Crum, John A. *energy executive*
Cruz, José, Sr. *professional baseball coach, retired professional baseball player*
Cruz, Miguel Angel *biochemist, educator*
Cruz, R. Ted (R. Edward Cruz) *lawyer*
Cunningham, Ralph Sanford *energy executive*
Cunningham, Tom Alan *lawyer*
Cupp, Aneta Joan *music educator*
Cupp, B. Garland *information technology executive*
Curl, Robert Floyd, Jr. *chemistry professor*
Currie, John Thornton (Jack Currie) *retired investment banker*
Curry, George Evans *social sciences educator*
Cuthbertson, Gilbert Morris *political science professor*
D'Agostino, James Samuel, Jr. *corporate financial executive*
Daiger, Stephen P. *ophthalmologist, educator*
Dameris, Thad Thano *lawyer*
Dang, Kimberly Allen *energy executive*
Daugherty, John A., Jr. *realtor*
Davidson, Chandler *sociologist, educator*
Davidson, Charles D. *energy executive*
Davis, Debra Ann *secondary school educator*
Davis, (Alice) Marlece *secondary school educator, director*
Day, Jonathan S. *lawyer*
Deaton, Chad C. *oil and gas industry executive*
De Bremaecker, Jean-Claude *geophysics educator*
DeForest, Joanie *engineering educator*
DeGuerin, Dick *lawyer*
Delaney, William J. III *food products executive*
Del Valle, Teresa Jones *lawyer*
DeMent, James Alderson, Jr. *lawyer*
Demory-Luce, Debby Kay *dietitian, consultant*
DeMoss, Harold Raymond, Jr. *federal judge*
Demouy, Alyson M. *social studies educator*
DeNicola, T. Kevin *construction executive*
DeVault, John Lee *oil industry executive, geophysicist*
De Wree, Eugene Ernest *manufacturing executive*
Di, Francine *music educator, writer*
Dice, Bruce Burton *gas industry executive*
Dikeocha, Ndu *biology professor*
Dillard, Michael E. *lawyer*
Dillard, Stephen C. *lawyer*
DiNardo, Daniel Nicholas Cardinal *cardinal, archbishop*
Dinkins, Carol Eggert *federal official, lawyer*
Dinney, Colin P. *surgeon, urologist*
Djerejian, Edward Peter *academic administrator, retired ambassador*
Dobson, Rick *energy executive*
Dodd, Gerald Dewey, Jr. *radiologist, educator*
Doi, Takao *astronaut*
Dorman, Margaret K. *corporate financial executive*
Douglas, James Matthew *law educator, dean*
Downing, Margaret Mary *newspaper editor*
Doyle, Joseph Francis III *art educator*
Drew, Katherine Fischer *history professor*
Dreyer, Alec Gilbert *electric power industry executive*
Dronamraju, Krishna Rao *geneticist*
Drury, Leonard Leroy *retired oil company executive*
DuBois, Raymond N. *medical educator, researcher*
Dula, Arthur McKee III *lawyer, aerospace transportation executive*
DuMond, James Wilson, Jr. *biology professor, researcher*
Duncan, Charles William, Jr. *investor, former United States Secretary of Energy*
Duncan, Dan L. *energy executive*
Duncan, Robert D. *real estate company executive*
DuPont, Herbert Lancashire *medical educator, researcher*
Durand, Jean-Bernard *cardiologist, researcher*
Duston, Karen Lansford *biology professor*
Ebel, Gregory L. *energy executive*
Ehrmann, Susanna *language educator, photographer, writer*
Eichenwald, Eric *pediatrician, director*
Eichler, Rodney J. *energy executive*
Eiland, Gary Wayne *lawyer*
Eissa, Mona Ah *pediatrician, researcher, educator*
Ellis, Eric *dentist*
Elrod, Jennifer Walker *federal judge*
El-Zein, Randa *medical educator*
Engebretson, Joan C. *nursing educator*
Engelhardt, Hugo Tristram, Jr. *physician, educator*
Engerrand, Kenneth G. *lawyer, educator*
Erdin, Serkan *physicist*
Erikson, Sheldon R. *oil industry executive*
Ertan, Atilla *medical educator, physician, researcher, health facility administrator*
Erwin, Mark A. *air transportation executive*
Espree, Mildred Michelle *language educator, writer*
Esrey, William Todd *telecommunications company executive*
Estes, Mary K. *virologist, researcher*
Eubank, J. Thomas *lawyer*
Evans, Harry Launius *pathology educator*
Ewer, Michael S. *medical educator*
Eyharts, Leopold *astronaut*
Fadul, Nada Abdellatif *medical researcher*
Fakhri, Samer *otolaryngologist, educator*
Farenthold, Frances Tarlton *lawyer*
Farley, Andrew D. *lawyer, construction executive*
Farley, Martin Birtell *geologist*
Farner, Wendy Mineau *lawyer*
Farnsworth, T. Brooke *lawyer*
Farrell, John Marshall *architect*
Farris, G. Steven *energy executive*
Farrow, Anthony Raymond *management consultant*
Faulkner, Larry Ray *foundation administrator, retired academic administrator*
Feigon, Judith Tova *ophthalmologist, surgeon, educator*
Ferguson, Christopher J. *astronaut*
Fernandes, Edward F. *lawyer*
Fernández, Ariel *mathematics educator*
Ferrendelli, James Anthony *neurologist, educator*
Fiese, Richard Kelly *music educator*
Filiberto, Justin *geologist*
Filipp Beseda, Carolyn Francine *music educator, insurance agent*
Fine, David Jeffrey *hospital administrator, educator*
Fiorenza, Joseph Anthony *archbishop emeritus*
Fischer, Craig Peter *surgeon*
Fishman, Marvin Allen *pediatric neurologist, educator*
Flaitz, Catherine M. *former dean, dental educator*
Flato, William Roeder, Jr. *software development company executive*
Flesher, Robert G. *oil industry executive*
Florian-Lacy, Dorothy *psychologist, educator*
Focht, John Arnold, Jr. *engineer*
Foger, Frances Murchison *minister*
Ford, Thomas W., Jr. *lawyer*
Foreman, Michael J. *astronaut*
Fornage, Bruno Denis *radiologist, educator*
Foshee, Douglas L. *gas industry executive*
Fossum, Michael E. *astronaut*
Foster, Charles Crawford *lawyer, educator*
Fowler, W. Randall *energy executive*
Francis, James Stephen, Jr. *psychologist, educator*
Frank, Karen Denise *aerospace engineer*
Fredin, Todd W. *oil industry executive*
Freireich, Emil J *hematologist, educator*
Freud, Anthony Peter *opera company director*
Frey, Henry Wallace *research scientist*
Frick, Stephen N. *astronaut*
Frost, John Elliott *minerals company executive*
Fullenweider, Donn Charles *lawyer*
Fulwiler, Robert Neal *oil industry executive*
Gabbard, Glen Owens *psychiatrist, psychotherapist*
Gaelens, Albert Robert *retired director, educational administrator, priest*
Gagnon, Stewart Walter *lawyer*
Gaille, Shelby Scott *oil industry executive*
Galgana, Gerald Aguirre *geophysicist*
Galvin, Kerry A. *lawyer, chemicals executive*
Garan, Ronald J., Jr. *astronaut*
García, Ricardo Thomas *language educator*
Garner, Madelyn C. *librarian*
Gashawbeza, Ewenet *geophysicist*
George, Deveral D. *editor, journalist, advertising consultant*
Gerachis, George Matthew *lawyer*
Gershenson, David Marc *oncology educator, university administrator*
Gertzbein, Stanley David *orthopedic surgeon*
Giacchetti, Claudine A. *language educator*
Giadrossi, Nicoletta *manufacturing company executive*
Giardino, Angelo Peter *pediatrician, director*
Gibbs, James R. *oil industry executive*
Gibson, Everett Kay, Jr. *space scientist, geochemist*
Gibson, Rex Hilton *lawyer*
Gigli, Irma *dermatologist, academic administrator, educator*
Gilbert, Jill Barson *management consultant*
Gilbert, Mark R. *neuro-oncologist, educator*
Ginsberg, Lawrence David *psychiatrist, researcher*
Girotto, Ronald G. *hospital administrator*
Gladden, Dean Robert *arts administrator, educator, consultant*
Glick, William H. *dean, management educator*
Glowinski, Roland *mathematics professor*
Goff, Gregory J. *oil industry executive*
Goldman, Stanford Milton *medical educator*
Goldsmith, Billy Joe *real estate broker, rancher*
Goldstein, Stuart Leonard *pediatrician, educator*
Gonçalves, C. Lourenço *metal products executive*
Gong, Yun *cytologist, educator*
Gonzalez, Antonio *academic administrator, educator, title company executive*
Gonzalez, Raed *lawyer*
Gonzalez-Angulo, Ana Maria *medical educator*
Goodman, Barry Michael *lawyer*
Goodman, Herbert Irwin *petroleum company executive*
Gorenstein, David G. *chemistry and biochemistry professor*
Gorie, Dominic L. Pudwill *retired military officer, astronaut*
Goss, John Alan *surgeon, educator*
Gould, Andrew *oil industry executive*
Gould, Lance K. *medical scientist, professor*
Goux, Jean-Joseph Claude *humanities educator, writer*
Graf, Hans *conductor, music director*
Graves, Daniel Edward *medical association administrator, researcher*
Graving, Richard John *law educator*
Grawunder, Teresa A. *musician, educator*
Gray, Robert F., Jr. *lawyer*
Green, Ahman Rashad *professional football player*
Greenberg, Stephen Baruch *dean, medical educator*
Grigore, Alina M. *anesthesiologist*
Gritz, Ellen R. *behavioral scientist, educator*
Grizzle, J. David *air transportation executive*
Grossett, Deborah Lou *psychologist, consultant*
Grossman, Herbert Barton *urologist, researcher*
Grossman, Rex *professional football player*
Grossman, Robert George *neurosurgeon, department chairman*
Grunsfeld, John M. *astronaut, astronomer*
Gunn, Albert Edward, Jr. *internist, health facility administrator, lawyer, educator*
Gunn, Joan Marie *health facility administrator*
Gunter, Joseph Clifford III *lawyer*
Gupta, Monesha *pediatrician, educator*
Gutheinz, Joseph Richard, Jr. *criminal justice educator, consultant, lawyer*
Gutheinz, Stephanie Anne *legal assistant, musician*
Haensly, Patricia Anastacia *psychology professor*
Hall, Charles Washington *lawyer*
Hall, Robert Joseph *internist, educator*
Ham, Kenneth T. *astronaut, military officer*
Hamel, Douglas E. *lawyer*
Hamid, Basem *neurologist, consultant*
Hamilton, Carlos Robert, Jr. *endocrinologist, academic administrator, consultant*
Hamilton, Steven M. *plastic surgeon*
Han, Choongyong *petroleum engineer, researcher*
Handy, Beverly C. *medical educator*
Hankins, Christopher Lovell *plastic surgeon*
Hanks, George Carol, Jr. *state judge*
Hanna, Ehab Y. *otolaryngologist, educator*
Hanneman, Sandra K. Goodnough *nursing educator, researcher*
Hanrahan, Lawrence Martin *healthcare consultant*
Hardin, Rusty (Russell Hardin Jr.) *lawyer*
Harper, A(lfred) J(ohn), II, *lawyer*
Harrell, Charles E. *lawyer*
Harrington, Bruce Michael *lawyer, investor*

Harris, Venita Van Caspel *retired financial planner*
Harrison, Betty Carolyn Cook *retired education educator, administrator*
Harvin, David Tarleton *lawyer*
Hasen, Michael *engineering company executive, civil engineer*
Hassler, Robert J. *oil industry executive*
Hattaway, Karen Ann *literature and language professor*
Hawes, Clay Erik *lawyer*
Hawkins, Barbara Reed *mental health nurse*
Hayes, Elvin Ernest *retired basketball player*
Hayes-Jordan, Andrea Anita *surgeon, educator*
Haymond, Morey William *pediatrician, endocrinologist*
Haynes, Richard (Racehorse Haynes) *lawyer*
Haynie, Thomas Powell III *physician*
He, Renjie *medical researcher*
Heard, Larry *real estate company executive*
Heeg, Peggy A. *lawyer, former gas industry executive*
Heil, Anne Campochiaro *secondary school educator*
Heim, Michael A. *energy executive*
Heinrich, Randall Wayne *lawyer*
Heird, William Carroll *pediatrician, educator*
Helland, George Archibald, Jr. *manufacturing executive, federal official*
Hellerstein, Lewis Jan *hematologist, oncologist, consultant*
Heminger, Gary R. *oil industry executive*
Hempfling, Linda Lee *nurse*
Henington, David Mead *retired library director*
Henley, Ernest Justus *retired chemical engineering professor*
Henry, Margaret Elisabeth *dean, educator*
Hescht, Billy Wade *theater educator*
Heuser, Mark Charles *military officer, educator*
Hewitt, Lester L. *lawyer*
Hilfman, David L. *air transportation executive*
Hinchman, Steven B. *oil industry executive*
Hinde, Dan *judge*
Hinton, Paula Weems *lawyer*
Hissong, Douglas Wayne *chemical engineer*
Hittner, David *federal judge*
Hlavinka, Paul Thomas *lawyer*
Hobby, William Pettus *retired broadcast executive*
Hocker, Wesley Hardy *lawyer*
Hollyfield, John Scoggins *lawyer*
Holm, Pam *city councilwoman*
Holmes, Ann Hitchcock *journalist*
Holmes, Harry Dadisman *health care administrator*
Holsinger, Floyd Christopher *surgeon*
Holstead, John Burnham *retired lawyer*
Hook, Harold Swanson *former management consulting executive*
Horton, Thomas Edward, Jr. *mechanical engineering educator*
Horvitz, Paul Michael *finance educator*
Hoshide, Akihiko *astronaut*
Hough, Derek *dancer, actor*
Howard, Jerry *oil industry executive*
Howell, Kimberly *geologist, educator*
Hoyt, Mont Powell *lawyer*
Hsu, Sylvia *dermatologist, educator*
Hsu, Thomas Tseng-Chuang *civil engineer, educator*
Huang, Shawn Shaoping *engineer*
Hudson, Franklin *lawyer, real estate developer*
Hudspeth, Chalmers Mac *lawyer, educator*
Huff, Danny W. *paper products executive*
Hulet, Randall Gardner *physics professor*
Hunsaker, Barry, Jr. *lawyer*
Hunter, Jack E. *Senior District Judge*
Hurwitz, Richard Louis *medical sciences educator*
Hussain, Moinuddin Syed *geologist, engineer, consultant*
Hutchens, Jerome Enos *psychiatrist*
Hutchinson, William Kenneth *economics professor*
Hwang, Rosa F. *oncologist, educator*
Hwu, Patrick *oncologist*
Ifft, Lewis George III *company administrator*
Irwin, John Robert *oil and gas industry executive*
Ivey, Jack Todd *lawyer*
Jabbour, Elias *hematologist, oncologist, educator*
Jackson, George William *research scientist, consultant*
Jacobs, Mark M. *energy executive*
Jaeckle, Kurt Alfred *neuro-oncologist, neurologist, educator*
Jaffe, Amy Myers *energy executive, educator*
Jamail, Joseph Dahr, Jr. *lawyer*
James, Dean *librarian, writer*
Jamrich, Milan *science educator*
Jankovic, Joseph *neurologist, educator*
Jeevarajan, Antony S. *science administrator*
Jeevarajan, Judith A. *chemist*
Jefferies, John Lynn *cardiologist, educator*
Jenkins, Sheila Alnita *psychologist*
Jenkins nee McKellar, Peggy Ann *psychologist, educator*
Jennings, Michael C. *oil industry executive*
Jeske, Charles Matthew *lawyer*
Jhin, Michael Kontien *healthcare executive*
Jines, Michael L. *lawyer, energy executive*
Jneid, Hani *interventional cardiologist, researcher*
Johnson, Andre Lamont *professional football player*
Johnson, Gregory Harold *career officer, astronaut, experimental test and fighter pilot*
Johnson, Jarvis *city councilman*
Johnson, Sandra Ann *counselor, educator*
Johnson, Wayne D. *gas industry executive*
Jolibois, Marcus *professional sports team executive*
Jones, Dan *medical educator*
Jones, Dan Brigman *ophthalmologist, educator*
Jones, Darren C. *oil industry executive*
Jones, Edith Irby *internist*
Jones, Florence M. *music educator*
Jones, Frank Griffith *lawyer*
Jones, Jolanda F. *city councilwoman, lawyer*
Jordan, Carmen Angelle *bank executive*
Jordan, Charles Milton *lawyer*
Jordan, W. Carl *lawyer*
Josehart, Carl *rehabilitation hospital administrator*
Joyce, Rene R. *energy executive*
Jurtshuk, Peter, Jr. *microbiologist, educator*
Kagle, Joseph Louis, Jr. *artist, administrator, historian*
Kahan, Barry Donald *surgeon, educator*
Kaiser, Larry Robert *thoracic surgeon*
Kajander, John *hospital administrator*
Kakadiaris, Ioannis *computer science educator*
Kaplan, Alan Leslie *gynecology educator, oncologist, department chairman*
Karff, Samuel Egal *rabbi*
Katrana, David John *retired plastic and reconstructive surgeon, director*
Katz, Barry Jay *geologist, researcher*
Kaufman, Raymond Henry *physician, educator*
Kavraki, Lydia *computer scientist, educator*
Kay, Joel Phillip *lawyer*
Kean, Steven J. *energy executive*
Keller-McNulty, Sallie *statistician, educator, dean*
Kellner, Larry (Lawrence Wesley Kellner) *air transportation executive*
Kelly, Hugh Rice *lawyer, retired energy executive*
Kelly, Janet Langford *oil industry executive, lawyer*
Kelly, Mark E. *astronaut*
Ketchand, Robert Lee *lawyer*
Keyfitz, Barbara Lee *mathematics educator*
Keyomarsi, Khandan *medical educator*
Khan, M.J. *city councilman, real estate developer*
Khan-Mayberry, Noreen *toxicologist*
Khator, Renu *academic administrator, political science professor*
Kim, Daniel H. *neurosurgeon*
Kimbrough, Robert S. *astronaut*
Kinder, Richard Dan *natural gas pipeline, oil and gas company executive*
King, Carolyn Dineen *federal judge*
King, Katrina *bank executive*
Kinnear, Peter D. *energy executive*
Kinsey, James Lloyd *chemist, educator*
Klausmeyer, David Michael *scientific instruments manufacturing company executive*
Kliewer, Keith A. *oil industry executive*
Klish, William John *pediatrician, educator*
Kneese, Carolyn Calvin *retired education educator*
Knesek, Michael John *energy executive*
Knickel, Carin S. *oil industry executive*
Knobloch, Charles Saron *lawyer, geophysicist, computer scientist, inventor*
Knudsen, J.R. (Jim Knudsen) *oil industry executive*
Kobayashi, Riki *retired chemical engineer, educator*
Koenig, Rodney Curtis *lawyer, rancher*
Kohli, Rajiv *science administrator*
Kone, Bruce C. *medical educator, nephrologist, scientist, former dean*
Koo, Jaseok Peter *science educator*
Koo, Weoncheol *ocean engineer*
Kopra, Timothy L. *astronaut*
Kosten, Thomas Richard *psychiatrist, educator*
Kotarba, Joseph Anthony *sociologist, educator*
Koul, Dimpy *cell biologist, educator, researcher*
Kouri, Donald Jack *chemist, educator*
Kraft, Irvin Alan *retired psychiatrist*
Krajewski, Michael *conductor*
Kramer, Phillip D. *oil industry executive*
Kratochvil, L(ouis) Glen *lawyer*
Kraus, Gary Edward *neurosurgeon*
Krause, William Austin *retired engineering executive*
Krebs, Arno William, Jr. *lawyer*
Krieger, Paul Edward *lawyer*
Krishen, Kumar *research technologist*
Krohn, Tracy W. *oil industry executive, gas industry executive*
Kubiak, Gary *professional football coach*
Kundra, Vikas *radiologist, educator*
Kuntz, Hal Goggan *petroleum exploration company executive, rancher*
Kuznetz, Lawrence H. *research scientist*
Laderman, Gerald *air transportation executive*
LaFuze, William L. *lawyer*
Lai, Dejian *statistics educator*
Lake, Kathleen Cooper *lawyer*
Lally, Kevin P. *Pediatric Surgeon, Department Chairman*
Lamb, Sydney MacDonald *linguistics educator*
Lamont, Gene *professional baseball coach and former team manager*
Lance, Ryan M. *oil industry executive*
Lane, Neal Francis *physics professor, retired federal agency administrator*
Lang, Frederick F. *medical educator*
Langston, Claire *pathologist, educator*
Lanier, W. Mark *lawyer*
Lannie, Paul Anthony *lawyer, energy executive*
Larkin, Lee Roy *retired lawyer*
Larkin, William Vincent, Jr. *corporate financial executive*
Lassetter, Scott D. *lawyer*
Lawrence, Toni *city councilwoman, small business owner*
Lawrie, Gerald Murray *cardiovascular and thoracic surgeon, educator*
Lawson, Rhea Brown *library director*
Le, Weidong *neurologist, educator, neuroscientist*
Lee, Donghyung *psychologist*
Lee, Rebecca E *psychologist, educator*
Leebron, David Wayne *academic administrator, law educator*
Leeds, Norman E. *medical educator, radiologist*
Leguillon, Rolande Lucienne *French educator*
Lehrer, Kenneth Eugene *economic consulting company executive*
Lemmer, William C. *lawyer*
Lesar, David J. *oil industry executive*
Letsou, George Vasilios *cardiothoracic surgeon*
Levit, Max *wholesale distribution and food service executive*
Levy, Eugene Howard *planetary sciences and astrophysics educator, researcher*
Lewandowski, Jerome L. *physicist*
Lewis, Dorothy E. *medical educator*
Lewis, Edward Sheldon *chemistry professor*
Lewis, Kevin Paul *lawyer*
Lewis, Russell E. *pharmacist, educator*
Lewis, Valerae Olive *surgeon, educator*
Li, Gang *managing consultant*
Lienhard, John Henry, IV, *mechanical engineer, educator*
Lindsey, John H. *former insurance agency executive*
Lindsey, John William *neurologist, educator*
Linnehan, Richard M. *astronaut, veterinarian*
Lippman, Scott Michael *oncologist, educator*
Listengart, Joseph *lawyer, energy executive*
Liu, Jing *pathologist, educator*
Liu, Jinsong *pathologist*
Lofgren, Gary Ernest *Planetary Scientist*
Long, Delwin J., II, *professor*
Looper, Marcia Lynn *elementary school educator, consultant*
Looser, William Gregory *lawyer*
Lopez, David Tiburcio *lawyer, arbitrator, mediator, educator*
Lopez, Jose Aron *hematologist*
Lopez-Alegria, Michael Eladio *astronaut*
Loretta, Mark (David) *professional baseball player*
Lott, Marley *lawyer*
Love, Scott Anthony *lawyer*
Love, Stanley Glen *scientist, astronaut*
Lovell, Sue *city councilwoman*
Lowe, John E. *oil industry executive, accountant*
Lowman, Sara Allison *library director*
Lucid, Shannon W. *biochemist, astronaut*
Luigs, Charles Russell *retired gas and oil drilling industry executive*
Lynch, John F. *lawyer*
Lyons, A. Roy *oil industry executive*
Lyons, Lillian Carmina *periodontist, educator*
Lypka, Michael Alexander *surgeon, dentist*
Mackwell, Stephen Joseph *geophysicist, educator*
Magnus, Sandra H. *astronaut*
Mallia, Marianne *medical writer*
Mallory, George B. *pulmonologist, educator*
Mancias, Peedro *pediatrician*
Mann, Douglas Lowell *cardiologist*
Manzano-Ruiz, Juan José *mechanical engineer, researcher*
Mao, Li *molecular biologist, educator*
Marangell, Lauren Beth *psychiatrist, researcher*
Marcotte, Michael Steven *municipal official*
Margulis, Vitaly *urologist*
Mariotto, Marco Jerome *dean, psychology educator, researcher*
Markos, Louis A. *language educator*
Marriott, Susan *research scientist*
Marshburn, Thomas H. *astronaut, emergency physician*
Marston, Edgar Jean III *lawyer*
Martin, J. Clark *lawyer*
Martin, James Kirby *historian, educator*
Martin, Paul Edward *lawyer*
Martinez, David Roger *chemist, researcher*
Marzio, Peter Cort *museum director*
Mason, Dwayne L. *lawyer*
Massad, Stephen Albert *lawyer*
Massin, Edward Krauss *physician*
Massoud, Yehia *science educator*
Masters, Claude Bivin *lawyer*
Matthews, Kathleen Shive *biochemistry educator*
Mattox, Sharon M. *lawyer*
Mays, Randall T. *communications company executive*
McClanahan, David M. *energy executive*
McCleary, Beryl Nowlin *volunteer, travel company executive*
McCollam, Marion Andrus *consulting firm executive, educator*
McCollum, Mark A. *oil industry executive*
McCreary, Frank E. III *retired lawyer*
McDaniel, Jarrel Dave *lawyer*
McDavid, George Eugene (Gene) *retired newspaper executive*
McFall, Donald Beury *lawyer*
McFarlin, Brian Keith *medical educator, researcher*
Mc Ginty, John Milton *architect, consultant*
McGrady, Tracy *professional basketball player*
McGuire, Michael K. *periodontist*
McInnis, Richard Kavin *lawyer*
McKay, Lamar *oil industry executive*
McKechnie, John Charles *gastroenterologist, educator*
McKee, Rae Ellen (Rae Ellen McKee-Doucette) *special education educator*
McKenzie, Laurie Jane *medical association administrator*
McLeod, Chanse L. *lawyer*
McLeod, Harry O'Neal, Jr. *retired petroleum engineer, consultant*
McMahon, Catherine Driscoll *lawyer*
McMahon, Richard A. *finance educator*
McParland, Jeffrey J. *energy executive*
McPhail, JoAnn Winstead *writer*
McPhee, Jancy Crane *aerospace scientist*
McPherson, Alice Ruth *ophthalmologist, educator*
McPherson, David D. *cardiologist, educator*
McQuaid, Janet *lawyer*
Medlock, Kenneth Barry *economics professor, consultant*
Meehan, William A. *air transportation executive*
Melroy, Pamela Ann *astronaut*
Melton, Stephen Reid *lawyer*
Melvin, Leland D. *astronaut*
Mendelson, Robert Allen *polymer scientist, rheologist*
Menscher, Barnet Gary *steel company executive*
Mentz, Henry A. III *plastic surgeon*
Merel, Gail *lawyer*
Messier, Luc J. *oil industry executive*
Meyer, Ernst A. *oil industry executive, consultant*
Meyers, Kevin Omar *oil industry executive*
Miele, Angelo *engineering educator, researcher, consultant, author*
Milam, John Daniel *pathologist, educator*
Miles, Brian John *urologist*
Miller, Barry Rixmann *lawyer*
Miller, Charles Rickie *systems analyst, engineering executive*
Miller, Gary Evan *psychiatrist, mental health services professional*
Miller, Gray Hampton *federal judge, lawyer*
Miller, Harry Freeman *university administrator*
Miller, Janel Howell *psychologist*
Miller, Merrill Anthony, Jr. *energy executive*
Miller, Robert Harold *otolaryngologist, educator*
Miller, Sabrina Wares *librarian*
Miller, Steven L. *oil industry executive*
Miller, W. Thaddeus *energy executive*
Milliron, Nathan Joseph *lawyer*
Milosavljevic, Aleksandar *medical geneticist, educator*
Ming, Yao *professional basketball player*
Minter, David Lee *English literature educator*
Mintz-Hittner, Helen Ann *physician, researcher*
Mo, Yi-Lung *structural engineer, educator*
Moehlman, Michael Scott *lawyer*
Mohammadpour Velni, Javad *research scientist*
Moise, Kenneth Joseph, Jr. *medical educator*
Moncure, John Lewis *lawyer*
Montgomery, Cleothus *minister*
Montgomery, Denise Karen *nurse*
Moore, Edgar Allan *music educator*
Moore, Jack B. *oil industry executive*
Moore, Robert H. *pediatrician, educator*
Moore, Tim *lawyer*
Moorhead, Gerald Lee *architect*
Moran, Cesar A. *pathologist, educator*
Moran, Mark J. *air transportation executive*
Morey, Daryl R. *professional sports team executive*
Morris, Malcolm Stewart *title company executive, lawyer*
Morris, Owen Glenn *engineering corporation executive*
Morris, Stewart, Jr. *title insurance company executive*
Mosbacher, Robert Adam, Sr. *oil and gas industry executive, political organization executive, former United States Secretary of Commerce*
Mozzato, Luciano *manufacturing company executive*
Mulva, James Joseph *oil industry executive*
Munisteri, Joseph George *construction executive*
Munk, Zev Moshe *physician, researcher*
Murad, Ferid *physician*
Murphy, Ewell Edward, Jr. *lawyer*
Murphy, William Alexander, Jr. *diagnostic radiologist, educator*
Musher, Daniel Michael *medical educator, researcher, epidemiologist, director*
Myers, A. Maurice *waste management executive*
Myers, James Clark *advertising and public relations executive*
Naeem, Rizwan C. *geneticist, educator, lab administrator, director*
Nations, Howard Lynn *lawyer*
Nebgen, Denise R. *physician, researcher*
Nelson, David Loren *geneticist, educator*
Nelson, Flavia *neurologist, professor, researcher, consultant*
Nelson, Joelle Grace Kenney *lawyer*
Nesbitt, DeEtte DuPree *small business owner, investor*
Neuhaus, Philip Ross *investment banker*
Neul, Jeffrey Lorenz *medical educator, researcher*
Neumann, Henry W., Jr. *energy executive*
Ng, Chaan S. *radiologist, educator*
Nichols, Michael Cooper *food products executive, lawyer*
Niebruegge, Michael E. *lawyer*
Nielsen, Niels Christian, Jr. *retired religious studies educator*
Nimmer, Raymond T. *dean, law educator*
Noland, Mary Richerson *management consultant*
Nolen, Roy Lemuel *retired lawyer*
Noriega, Melissa *city councilwoman, educator*
Norris, Chuck (Carlos Ray) *actor*
Nosé, Yukihiko *surgeon, educator*
Novak, Jason P. *secondary school educator*
Nuwal, Tara C. *economics professor*
Nyberg, Karen L. *astronaut*
Oakes, Pamela R. *retired elementary school educator*
O'Brien, Eva Fromm *lawyer*
O'Connor, Ralph Sturges *investment company executive*
O'Donnell, Lawrence III *waste management executive*
Odum, Marvin E. *oil industry executive*
Oldham, Darius Dudley *lawyer*
Oldham, John Michael *physician, psychiatrist, educator*
O'Malley, Bert William *cell biologist, educator, physician*
Onn, Amir *medical educator, researcher*
O'Quinn, John M. *lawyer*
Ordemann, William *energy executive*
Orengo-Nania, Silvia *ophthalmologist*
Ornstein, David *urologist*
Osborne, C. Kent *oncologist, educator*
Osborne, Charles Kent *oncologist, researcher*
Oshman, Gene Jay *lawyer*
Osteen, Joel *minister*
Osterberg, Edward Charles, Jr. *lawyer*
Oswalt, Roy Edwards *professional baseball player*
O'Toole, Austin Martin *lawyer, mediator, arbitrator*
Pan, Hui-Lin *medical educator*
Paniagua, David *physician*
Papa, Mark Gary *oil and gas industry executive*
Papanicolaou, Andrew C. *neuroscientist, educator*
Parazynski, Scott E. *astronaut*
Parnas-Simpson, Marianna *chorus director, singer*
Partridge, Scott Francis *lawyer*
Passonno Stott, Nicole *astronaut*
Pate, Stephen Patrick *lawyer*
Patten, Robert Lowry *language educator*
Patterson, William J. *investment company executive*
Paul, Alida Ruth *retired elementary school educator*
Paul, Gordon Lee *behavioral scientist, psychologist*
Peabody, Arlene L. Howland Bayar *retired enterostomal therapy nurse*
Pefanis, Harry N. *oil industry executive*
Peng, Liang-Chuan *mechanical engineer*
Perich, Thomas J. *lawyer*
Perkins, Joe Bob *energy executive*
Perkyns, Jane Elizabeth *music educator, composer*
Perrier, Nancy *endocrinologist, educator*
Persse, David *emergency physician, director*
Pete, Eric E. *writer, claims representative*
Petropoulos, Dimitrios *oncologist, hematologist, educator*
Petrovich, Alisa Vladimira *historian, educator*
Pettit, Donald R. *astronaut, flight engineer, researcher*
Phillips, John L. *astronaut*
Phung, Nguyen Dinh *medical educator*

Pickering, James Henry III *academic administrator, educator*
Pierce, Frank Powell *lawyer, judge*
Plaeger, Frederick Joseph, II, *lawyer*
Plank, Roger B. *energy executive*
Poindexter, Alan *astronaut*
Ponomarev, Artem Lvovich *physicist, senior research scientist*
Porter, Thomas William III *lawyer*
Potluri, Venkateswara Rao *medical facility administrator*
Poulos, Michael James *insurance company executive*
Pourgol-Mohammad, Mohammad *manufacturing executive*
Powell, Alan *engineering educator, research scientist*
Prats, Michael *petroleum engineer, educator*
Probert, Tim *oil industry executive*
Pryor, William Daniel Lee *humanities educator*
Pulliam, Larry G. *food products executive*
Putra, Erwinsyah *petroleum engineer*
Qiao, Fengxiang *transportation engineer, educator*
Qisheng, Pan *transportation executive, educator*
Queller, David C. *ecology and biology professor*
Quiros-Tejeira, Ruben Eloy *pediatrician, educator, researcher*
Qureshi, Waqar A. *medical educator*
Raad, Issam I. *medical educator, researcher*
Radoff, Leonard Irving *retired librarian, consultant*
Ragauss, Peter A. *oil industry executive*
Raijman, Isaac *gastroenterologist, educator*
Ralls, W. Matthew *gas and oil industry drilling executive*
Ramsey, Michael W. *lawyer*
Ranieri, Lewis S. *investment company executive*
Rao, Nageswara Maddali *space and planetary scientist*
Rapini, Ronald Peter *dermatology educator*
Rappaport, Norman Harvey *plastic surgeon*
Rasekh, Abdi *cardiologist*
Raspino, Louis A. *energy executive*
Rauf, Zamir *energy executive*
Rauniar, Rupak *management educator*
Ray, Hugh Massey, Jr. *lawyer*
Ray, Hugh Massey III *lawyer*
Read, Michael Oscar *editor, consultant*
Ream, James B. (Jim Ream) *air transportation executive*
Reasoner, Harry Max *lawyer*
Reasor, Clayton (Craig Clayton Reasor, C.C. Reasor) *oil industry executive*
Reavley, Thomas Morrow *federal judge*
Reddy, J. Patrick *former energy executive*
Reed, Kathlyn Louise *occupational therapist, educator*
Reid, Katherine Louise *artist, educator, writer*
Reiff, Patricia Hofer *space physicist, educator*
Reinbolt, Paul C. *oil industry executive*
Remes, Robin Eva *secondary school educator, cartographer*
Reso, Anthony *geologist, educator, earth resources economist*
Rettig, Dwight W. *lawyer*
Rhoads, Jon Marc *pediatric gastroenterologist, educator*
Rhodes, Raymond Earl *professional football coach*
Ribble, John Charles *medical educator*
Richards, Leonard Martin *investment executive, consultant*
Rickel, John C. *automotive executive*
Ridge, Robert A. *oil industry executive*
Riedel, Alan Ellis *manufacturing executive, lawyer*
Rigby, Weldon *realtor*
Rigdon, Kevin Leigh *theater educator, lighting designer, set designer*
Riggenbach, Jeff *journalist, broadcaster*
Riley, William John *neurologist*
Ripley, Charlene A. *lawyer*
Risin, Semyon Aaron *pathologist, educator*
Rivenes, Shannon Marie *pediatric cardiologist*
Rivera, Victor M. *medical educator, director*
Rizzotto, Vincent Michael *bishop emeritus*
Roach, Robert Michael, Jr., (Randy Roach) *lawyer*
Robb, Geoffrey Lawrence *plastic surgeon*
Robbins, Susan Paula *social work educator*
Roberts, Charles Murray *retired publishing executive, writer*
Roberts, David E., Jr. *oil industry executive*
Rock, Douglas Lawrence *manufacturing executive*
Rodríguez, Félix M. *oil industry executive*
Rodriguez, James G. *city councilman*
Roff, J(ohn) Hugh, Jr. *energy executive*
Rolnik, Claire Yvette *literature and language professor*
Romans, Jay *waste management executive*
Rommel, A. Ross, Jr. *lawyer*
Rong, Shu *geophysicist, researcher*
Roos, Sybil Friedenthal *retired elementary school educator*
Rose, Beatrice Schroeder *harpist, educator*
Ross, Patti Jayne *obstetrics and gynecology educator*
Ross, R. Dale *medical products executive*
Rowe, Zane Conrad *air transportation executive*
Rowland, Kelly (Kelendria Trene Rowland) *singer*
Rowland, Robert Alexander III *lawyer*
Rozzell, Scott Ellis *lawyer, energy executive*
Rudley, John M. *academic administrator*
Runco, Mario, Jr. *astronaut, meteorologist, researcher*
Russell, John Francis *retired librarian*
Rustay, Jennifer Beth *lawyer*
Ryan, Jason Michael *lawyer*
Ryan, Stephen M. *lawyer*
Ryan, Thomas L. *funeral company executive*
Ryan, Vince *lawyer*
Sabek, Omaima M. *biology professor, director*
Safdar, Amar *medical educator, researcher*
Saizan, Paula Theresa *business consultant*
Salem, Philip Adeeb *medical educator*
Sales, James Bohus *lawyer*
Sallee, Wanda Jean *music educator*
Sanders, Joseph *law educator*
Sanderson, Mary Louise *medical association administrator*
Sandman, Bradford Aaron *coach, educator*
Sangi-Haghpeykar, Haleh *educator*
Sarofim, Fayez Shalaby *finance company executive*
Saunders, Charles Albert *lawyer*
Sawaya, Raymond *neurosurgeon*
Sazama, Kathleen *pathologist, lawyer*
Schachtel-Green, Barbara Harriet Levin *retired epidemiologist*
Scharold, Mary Louise *psychoanalyst, psychiatrist, educator*
Schaub, Matt (Matthew Rutledge Schaub) *professional football player*
Schechter, Arthur Louis *lawyer*
Scheyer, Eric Todd *dentist, periodontist, surgeon, educator*
Schick, Robert Michael *lawyer*
Schlegel, Hans *astronaut*
Schnoebelen, Anne Mary *musicologist, educator*
Schultze, Deborah *healthcare educator*
Schwartz, Charles Walter *lawyer*
Schwartzel, Charles Boone *lawyer*
Schwarz, Glenda M. *oil industry executive*
Schwind, William F., Jr. *lawyer, oil industry executive*
Scola, Luis *professional basketball player*
Seale, Robert Arthur *lawyer*
Secrest, George McCall, Jr., (Mac) *lawyer*
Selber, Jesse Creed *plastic surgeon, researcher*
Sellin, Joseph Henry *gastroenterologist*
Serrato, Darlene B. *finance educator*
Shaddock, Carroll Sidney *lawyer*
Shaffer, Anita Mohrland *counselor, educator*
Shakir, Huzefa *research scientist*
Shannon, Holden E. *air transportation executive*
Shannon, Margaret Barrett *lawyer*
Shaper, C. Park *energy executive*
Shearer, Linda *museum director*
Shearer, William Thomas *pediatrician, educator*
Sheets, Jeff W. *oil industry executive*
Shen, Ying H. *medical educator*
Sher, George Allen *philosophy educator*
Sherman, Steven I. *endocrinologist, educator*
Sherman, Vadim *surgeon, director*
Shiao, Shyang-Yun Pamela K. *nursing educator, researcher*
Shouse, August Edward *lawyer*
Shulman, Robert Jay *pediatrician, nutritionist, gastroenterologist, educator*
Si, Qimiao *physics professor*
Sickles, Robin C. *economics and statistics professor, consultant*
Sikma, Jack Wayne *professional basketball coach, retired professional basketball player*
Silva, Eugene Joseph *lawyer*
Simon-Campbell, E'Loria *nursing educator*
Simpson, Robert G. *waste management executive*
Simpson, Robert Louis *music educator*
Sing, William Bender *lawyer*
Skelly, Michael *energy executive*
Sledge, Charles M. *oil industry executive*
Sloan, Robert Bryan, Jr. *academic administrator*
Smirnakis, Stelios Manolis *medical educator*
Smisek, Jeffery A. *air transportation executive*
Smith, Alison Leigh *lawyer*
Smith, Arthur Kittredge, Jr. *academic administrator, political scientist, educator*
Smith, Dan F. *chemicals executive*
Smith, E. Ashley *lawyer, insurance company executive*
Smith, Jerry Edwin *federal judge*
Smith, Joellen *dean, literature and language educator*
Smith, Rick *professional sports team executive*
Smith, Roland Blair, Jr. *university administrator*
Smith, Stephen F. *food service executive*
Smythe, Cheves McCord *internist, geriatrician, educator, dean*
Sneed, Thomas K. *oil industry executive*
Snider, Stephen A. *oil industry company executive*
Snipes, Shedra Amy *research scientist*
Solomon, Marsha Harris *draftsman, artist*
Sondock, Ruby Kless *retired judge*
Sonfield, Robert Leon, Jr. *lawyer*
Sood, Anil K. *oncologist, researcher*
Sostman, Dirk *physician, clinical researcher, medical educator*
Spalding, Andrew Freeman *lawyer*
Sparks, Marvin Roosevelt, Jr. *music educator*
Speer, Michael Emery *neonatologist, educator*
Spikes, Patricia White *medical technologist*
Spitler, Kenneth F. *food products executive*
Spudich, John Lee *biochemist, molecular biologist, chemistry professor*
Staff, Joel V. *energy executive*
Stal, Samuel *plastic surgeon, educator*
Stallman, Kurt *composer, educator*
Stasney, C. Richard *otolaryngologist, director*
Steele, James Harlan *retired veterinarian*
Stefanyshyn-Piper, Heidemarie M. *astronaut*
Steiner, David P. *waste management executive*
Stephens, Sidney Dee *human resources specialist, retired chemical manufacturing company executive*
Stewart, David James *oncologist, educator*
Stewart, J.W. *energy executive, lawyer*
Stewart, Pamela L. *lawyer*
Still, Charles Henry, Sr. *lawyer*
Stockholder, Jessica *sculptor*
Stoops, James King *biochemistry researcher*
Stradley, William Jackson *lawyer*
Strassmann, Joan Elizabeth *evolutionary biologist*
Streng, William Paul *lawyer, educator*
Stryker, Steven Charles *lawyer*
Stubbs, William W. *interior designer*
Sturckow, Frederick W. (Rick) *astronaut*
Suarez-Almazor, Maria E. *rheumatologist, educator*
Subramanian, Shyam *sleep physician director*
Sugimoto, Mitsushige *medical association administrator, researcher*
Suki, Dima *epidemiologist*
Sullenbarger, Daniel James *oil industry executive, lawyer*
Sullivan, John F. III *lawyer*
Sullivan, Mike *city councilman, small business owner*
Sun, Yang *computer engineer*
Sunosky, James T. *lawyer*
Supak, Cathy Poerner *athletic trainer, educator*
Susman, Stephen Daily *lawyer*
Sutton, Jeffrey Paul *physician, scientist, administrator*
Sutton, Neal S. *lawyer*
Swan, Michael K. *lawyer*
Swanson, Al *oil industry executive*
Swanson, Steven R. *astronaut*
Swartz, Michael D. *statistical geneticist*
Sweeney, Jack *publishing executive*
Swick, Todd J. *medical association administrator*
Swift, David L. *manufacturing executive*
Swisher, Stephen G. *thoracic surgeon*
Sydow, Michael David, Sr. *executive lawyer*
Szalkowski, Charles C. *lawyer*
Talbert, Arthur Thomas *music educator*
Tani, Daniel M. *astronaut*
Tartt, Blake *lawyer*
Taylor, Cindy B. *oil industry executive*
Tee, Rebekah C. *art educator*
Tejada, Miguel Odalis *professional baseball player*
Thirsk, Robert Brent *astronaut*
Thomas, Byron Andrew *lawyer*
Thompson, Jon L. *retired oil industry executive*
Thompson, Tina Marie *professional basketball player*
Thorpe, Carlon Justine *engineering and operations executive*
Threet, John T. *principal*
Ting, Chin-Sen *physics professor*
Totten, Patricia A. *lawyer*
Toy, Eugene C. *gynecologist*
Traber, Peter George *medical educator, former academic administrator*
Tran, Qui-Phiet *English educator*
Trauber, Stephen M. (Steve Tauber) *investment banker*
Trice, David A. *oil industry executive*
Trichel, Mary Lydia *middle school educator*
Tucker, Susan *biomathematics and computational biology professor*
Tweardy, David John *physician, educator*
Untermeyer, Charles Graves (Chase Untermeyer) *real estate company executive*
Upton, Cindy McDonough *economics professor*
Urthaler, Yetzirah Yksya *Subsea Engineer*
Usher, Thomas James *metal products executive*
Utt, William P. (Bill Utt) *construction executive*
Uzman, James Akif *biology professor*
Vallbona, Carlos *physician*
Vallbona, Rima-Gretel Rothe *retired foreign language educator, writer*
Vallejo, Frances M. *oil industry executive*
Vallejo, Jesus G. *medical educator*
Valverde, José (Rafael) *professional baseball player*
Van Dyke, Gene *oil industry executive*
Van Fleet, George Allan *lawyer*
Varma, Datla G.K. *radiologist, researcher*
Varner, David Eugene *lawyer*
Vásquez, José Stephen *bishop*
Vaughan, Eugene H. *investment company executive*
Vierling, John Moore *physician*
Villinski, Jennifer C. *geochemist*
Vogel, Jennifer L. *lawyer, air transportation executive*
von der Mehden, Fred R. *political science professor*
Wagener, Christine Elizabeth *psychotherapist, educator*
Wagner, Charlene Brook *retired secondary school educator*
Wagner, Leslie *lawyer*
Wagner, Paul Anthony, Jr. *education educator*
Wakata, Koichi *astronaut*
Walheim, Rex J. *astronaut, military officer*
Walker, John E. (Ned Walker) *air transportation executive*
Walker, William Easton *surgeon, educator, lawyer*
Wall, Kenneth E., Jr. *lawyer*
Wallace, Mark Allen *hospital administrator*
Walls, Martha Ann Williams (Mrs. B. Carmage Walls) *publishing executive*
Walton, Dan Gibson *lawyer*
Waymire, Jack Calvin *medical educator*
Webb, Jack M. *lawyer*
Webb, Marty Fox *principal*
Weber, Fredric Alan *lawyer*
Weiner, Sanford Alan *lawyer*
Weinstein, Roy *physics professor*
Weisman, R(obert) Bruce *physical chemist, educator, entrepreneur*
Welch, Stanton *performing company executive*
Wells, Benjamin Gladney *lawyer*
Wells, Damon *investment company executive*
Welsh, H. Ronald *lawyer*
Werlein, Ewing, Jr. *federal judge*
Westby, Timothy Scott *lawyer, researcher*
Wheelock, Douglas H. *astronaut, military officer*
White, Bill (William Howard White) *Mayor, Houston*
Whiting, Hugh Richard *lawyer*
Whiting, S. Carol *music educator*
Whitlock, Gary L. *energy executive*
Whittenburg, Justin M. *lawyer*
Wiglesworth, Michael Bland *advertising executive*
Wike, D. Elaine *small business owner*
Wilde, William Key *lawyer*
Wilkin, Alana Zimmer *elementary school educator*
Wilkinson, Bruce W. *construction executive*
Willerson, James Thornton *cardiologist, researcher, medical educator*
Williams, Clay C. *energy executive*
Williams, Edward Earl, Jr. *entrepreneur, educator*
Williams, Lowell Craig *lawyer, employee relations executive*
Williams, Mario *professional football player*
Williamson, Bruce A. *gas industry executive*
Williamson, Peter David *lawyer*
Wilson, Carl Weldon, Jr. *construction company executive, civil engineer*
Wilson, David Vandiver, II, *lawyer*
Wilson, Edward Converse, Jr. *oil and natural gas production company executive*
Wilson, Floyd C. *oil industry executive*
Wilson, Jamia Weletha *science educator*
Wilson, Thomas Leon *physicist, researcher*
Wiseman, Melissa S. *economics professor*
Witmer, John Richard *librarian*
Wittenbraker, Rick L. *lawyer, waste management executive*
Womack, Guy Lee *lawyer, military officer*
Wong, Kwong-Kwok *medical educator*
Wood, Michael W. *lawyer*
Woodhouse, John Frederick *retired wholesale distribution executive*
Woodward, Wendy Ann *radiation oncologist*
Worthington, William Albert III *lawyer*
Wray, Thomas Jefferson *lawyer*
Wright, Clark Phillips *computer systems specialist*
Wright, Madeleine Elaine Pate *humanities educator*
Wuori, Stephen J. *energy executive*
Yampey-Jorg, Gloria Leonor *language educator*
Yang, Chao Yuh *biochemistry professor, medical educator*
Yatsenko, Yuri Petrovich *business professor, mathematician*
Yearwood, John *manufacturing executive*
Yeates, Marie R. *lawyer*
Yeh, Edward Tu-Hsing *cardiologist, educator, medical researcher*
Yeoman, Lynn Chalmers *medical educator*
Yetter, R. Paul *lawyer*
Young, John David *information systems analyst, consultant*
Youngdahl, Jay Thomas *lawyer*
Yu, Aiting Tobey *engineering executive*
Yu, Peirong *plastic surgeon, educator*
Zacharias, Nikolaos Marios *obstetrician, gynecologist, perinatologist*
Zamka, George D. *astronaut*
Zarrin-Khameh, Neda *pathologist*
Zeigler, Ann dePender *lawyer*
Ziemba, Lawrence M. *oil industry executive*
Zoghbi, William Antoine *cardiologist, educator*

Humble
Brown, Samuel Joseph, Jr. *engineer, scientist*
Douglass, Thelma Jean *educational administrator*
Hadlow, Vivian Jean *retired elementary school educator*
Trowbridge, John Parks *physician*

Hunt
Gambrell, James Bruton III *lawyer, educator*

Huntsville
Conwell, Halford Roger *physician*
Gutermuth, Mary Elizabeth *retired foreign language educator*
Huntsman, Silvia A. *literature and language professor*
Joo, Hee-Jong *criminology educator*
Lea, Stanley E. *artist, educator*
Payne, David Emer *university administrator*
Russell, George Haw *video production company executive*
Smith, Jonathan Charles *dancer, educator*
Vaughn, Michael S. *law educator*
Ward, Richard Hurley *education educator, writer*

Hurst
Bishara, Amin Tawadros *management and consulting firm executive*
Bowman, Karmien C. *sculptor, ceramist, educator*
Davidsson, John Paul *librarian*
Eamma, Kari Ann *biology professor*
Fox, Patrecia *literature and language educator*
Fuentes, Rosa *education educator*
Gallagher, Eddye Skillern *language educator, director*
Jacaruso, Diana *biology educator*
Kaluya, Michael David *finance educator*
Lindsey, Jerri Kay *biologist, educator*
Mabry, Philip T. *political scientist, consultant*
Wisdom, Rita Parker *literature and language professor*

Hutto
Hamilton, Elizabeth Ann *elementary school educator*

Industry
Huitt, Jimmie L. *rancher, oil and gas industry executive, real estate developer*

Ingleside
Vaden, William R. *oil industry executive, councilman*

Iola
Nelson, John Harrison *mathematics educator*

Iowa Park
Wright, Sabra Dell *music educator*

Irving
Albers, Mark W. *oil industry executive*
Barnard, Ray F. *engineering and construction management company executive*
Beach, Charles Addison *lawyer*
Bodily, Brett Hogan *literature and language professor*
Boeckmann, Alan L. *engineering and construction management company executive*
Caldwell, James D. *hotel executive*
Campo, Dave *professional football coach*
Cavanaugh, Lucille J. *oil industry executive*
Cejka, A. Tim *oil industry executive*
Cherri, Mona Y. *computer scientist, consultant, educator*
Cohen, Kenneth P. *oil industry executive, lawyer*
Deitemeyer, Michael J. *hotel executive*
Dingle, Philip *retired oil industry executive*
Dolan, Michael J. *oil industry executive*
Duffin, Neil W. *oil industry executive*
Dupree, Robert Scott *literature and language professor, library director*
Eaker, Charles William *chemistry professor*
Elmore, Phyllis Pearson *literature and language professor*

Flowers, Garry W. *engineering and construction management company executive*
Gears, Herbert A. *Mayor, Irving, Texas*
Gilbert, H. Steven *engineering and construction management company executive*
Glass, Sherman J., Jr. *oil industry executive*
Goldberg, Neal *retail executive*
Hawkins, William David *marketing executive*
Hernandez, Carlos Manuel *lawyer*
Hoops, Thomas *engineering educator*
Hubble, Henry H. *oil industry executive*
Humphreys, Donald D. *oil industry executive*
Jones, Jerry (Jerral Wayne Jones) *professional sports team executive*
Kelly, Alan J. *oil industry executive*
Kitna, Jon K. *professional football player*
Kling, Lewis M. *multi-industry executive*
Kruger, Richard M. *oil industry executive*
Lambert-Saul, Beth *real estate company executive*
Larson, William B. *metal products executive*
LaSala, Stephen R. *lawyer, oil industry executive*
Luxbacher, Roberta *oil industry executive*
Mace, Steven Douglas *academic administrator, educator*
Martin, Thomas Lyle, Jr. *academic administrator*
Matthews, Charles W., Jr. *oil industry executive, lawyer*
McClean, Murray R. *metal products executive*
Mulva, Patrick T. *oil industry executive*
Natour, Nahille I. *obstetrician, gynecologist*
Phillips, Wade *professional football coach*
Pisarczyk, Richard V. *oil industry executive*
Plaskett, Thomas George *transportation executive, director*
Potter, Robert Joseph *technical and business executive*
Pryor, Stephen D. *oil industry executive*
Rees, Frank William, Jr. *architect*
Romo, Tony (Antonio Ramiro Romo) *professional football player*
Sheffield, Scott D. *oil industry executive*
Sommerfeldt, John Robert *historian, educator*
Steele, C. William *scouting organization administrator*
Stuewer, Sherri K. *oil industry executive*
Sudbury, David Marshall *lawyer*
Swales, Larry D. *oil industry executive*
Swiger, Andrew P. *oil industry executive*
Tillerson, Rex W. *oil company executive*
Vega, Vanessa Leigh *English educator*
Walters, Thomas R. *gas and power company executive*
Ware, DeMarcus *professional football player*
Wicks, William Withington *retired public relations executive*
Wilkerson, Patricia Helen *retired director*
Williams, Roy Eugene, Jr. *professional football player*
Witten, Jason (Christopher Jason Witten) *professional football player*

Jacksonville
Blaylock, James Carl *clergyman, librarian*
Heflin, David Duane *literature and language professor*
Queen, Kay Wallace *education educator*
Thrall, Gordon Fish *publishing executive*

Joaquin
Gill, Madeline Kay *counselor*

Junction
Evans, Jo Burt *communications executive, rancher*

Justin
Delashmit, Walter Howard, Jr. *engineering executive, researcher, consultant, application developer*

Katy
Gray, Robert Steele *publishing executive, editor, writer*
Guest, Floyd Emory, Jr. *lawyer*
Puig, Carlos J. *plastic surgeon*
Smith, Theodore Glenn *technology educator, researcher*

Kaufman
Tygrett, Howard Volney, Jr. *judge, lawyer*

Keene
Doroftei, Mugur Gideon *music educator, conductor, composer, musician*
England, Michael *education educator*
Miller, Rebecca Lynn *software engineer*
Taroy-Valdez, Lolita B. *nursing educator*

Keller
Patterson, Ronald R(oy) *management consultant*

Kemp
Shugart, Jill *retired school administrator*

Kerrville
Frudakis, Evangelos William *sculptor*
Shaw, Alan Bosworth *geologist, retired paleontologist*

Kilgore
Buchanan, Paul Clarence *geologist, researcher*
Rorschach, Richard Gordon *lawyer*

Killeen
Jenkins, Sharon Leigh *special education educator*
Lapierre, Coady *psychology professor, consultant*
Peronto, Janice Lynn *principal*

Kingsville
Cox, Paul H. *physics professor*
Cruz Garza, Laura *psychology professor, researcher*
Hageman, Paul M. *music educator*
John, Kuruvilla *engineering educator*
Lee, Sangyong *engineering educator*
Li, Shuhui *engineer, educator*
Martinez, Alvaro Ignacio *science educator*
Melendy, Brenda *history professor, department chairman*
Moehring, Gregory *chemistry professor, department chairman*
Nekovei, Reza *engineering educator, researcher*
Nutan, Mohammad Tawhidul Haque *pharmacy educator, researcher*
Schueneman, Bruce R. *librarian*
Sethi, Rajat *cardiologist, educator*
Sun, Dazhi *engineering educator*
Tallant, Steven Hall *academic administrator, social worker*
Vela Córdova, Roberto J. *literature and language professor*

Kingwood
De Soignie, Roland C. *biology professor*
Heineman, Angela Gail *history professor*
Hullar, Leonard Earl *history professor*
Morgan, Betsy Elizabeth Robison *biology professor*
Swift, Constance Redmond *special education educator*

Kosse
Nicholas, Nickie Lee *retired industrial hygienist*

Kyle
Saunders, Patricia Gene Knight *freelance writer, editor*

La Grange
Morovich, George L. *rancher, contractor*

La Porte
Edwards, Kristina Nell *elementary school educator*
Kelling, David Henry *educational administrator, accountant*

La Ward
Lin, Ming T. *plant pathologist*

Lackland AFB
Fadare, Oluwole *pathologist, researcher, director*
Sabanegh, Edmund Sami, Jr. *urologist*
Westermann, Edward Burton *military officer, analyst, educator*

Lago Vista
Thompson, Dayle Ann *small business owner, consultant*

Lake Jackson
Alcorn, JoAnne Miller *librarian*
Gresham, Karen Renee *singer*
Hill, Diane Louise *educator*
Pryor, Wayne David *social sciences educator*
Tarrant, Sasha Ranae Adams *history professor*

Lakeway
Carlson, Lewis Herbert *history professor*
Conine, Ernest *columnist*

Lancaster
Lumbley, Sheryl Richardson *biology professor*
Rolling, Lincoln Curtis *history professor*

Laredo
Black, Clifford Merwyn *academic administrator, sociologist, educator*
Cepeda, Carmen Griselda *nurse*
Chavez, Mary Rose *counselor, educator*
Coats, Charles F. *physics and mathematics educator*
Gonzalez, Eugene Robert *investment banker*
Goonatilake, Rohitha *mathematician, educator*
Heimes, Charmaine Marie *elementary school educator, poet, writer*
Huang, Yu Mei *music educator*
Janamanchi, Balaji *operations management educator*
Kazen, George Philip *federal judge*
Liu, Shinhua *finance educator, researcher*
Maxstadt, John M. *librarian*
Mohamed Ben-Ruwin, Mohamed A. *political science professor*
Ni, Qingwen *engineering educator*
Nixon, Dennis E. *financial company executive*
Rivas, Andres Eloy *economics professor*
Sagafi-nejad, Tagi *business educator*
Salinas, Raul G. *Mayor, Laredo, Texas*
Seitel, Alan Lewis *speech pathology educator*
Soto, Gilberto D. *music educator*
Tamayo, James Anthony *bishop*

League City
Kanuth, James Gordan *chemical engineer*
Pandya, Utpal *microbiologist*

Leander
Fraley, Linda Williams Darnell *music educator*

Levelland
Carden, Ronald M. *history professor, department chairman*
Ham, Donna Olene *music educator*
Harbin, Paul B. *science educator*
Tackett, Billy John *electronics engineer, educator*

Lewisville
Dooley, Cristin Bevin *psychologist*
Hooten, John F *economics educator*
Lowe, Alan Conner *policy director*
Simpson, Carol Mann *librarian, editor, educator, attorney*
Whitney, Sharry Jan *science educator*

Little Elm
Milian, Ayda R. *secondary school educator*

Littlefield
Muller, Janice Elaine *secondary school educator*

Livingston
Hayes, Gordon Glenn *retired civil engineer*
Stovall, Jerry Coleman *insurance company executive*

Llano
Wallis, Olney Gray *lawyer*
Wilson, Dena Suzette *elementary school educator*

Lockhart
Scudday, Roy George *lawyer*

Longview
Castro, Juan Ramon *finance educator*
Cuba, Mattie Deneice *middle school educator*
Geer, Caroline L. *librarian*
Mann, True Sandlin *psychologist, consultant*
McMullen, Melody Mae *music educator*
Udy, Rae *columnist, writer*
Welge, Jack Herman, Jr. *lawyer*

Lubbock
Arwine, Alan Troy *political educator*
Ashcraft, Alyce Smithson *nursing educator*
Bagdure, Satish Ramesh *epidemiologist*
Bailey, Guy H. *academic administrator*
Baker, Robert J. *museum director, science educator, researcher*
Banda, Devender R. *education educator*
Bartsch, Richard Allen *chemist, educator*
Basu, Sukanta *science educator*
Beck, George Preston *anesthesiologist, educator*
Beyer, Gerry Wayne *lawyer, educator*
Buesseler, John Aure *ophthalmologist, management consultant*
Clausen, Jane *library director*
Conover, William Jay *statistics educator*
Dennison, Daniel Thomas *environmental compliance and lab administrator*
Duncan, Robert Lloyd *state legislator, lawyer*
Everse, Johannes *biochemist, researcher*
Frezza, Eldo E. *surgeon, educator*
Fullerton, Caren D. *finance educator*
Gill, Gurdev S. *orthopaedic surgeon*
Gonzales, Alberto R. *political science professor, former United States Attorney General*
Grammas, Paula *science educator, director*
Halldorsson, Ari *cardiologist*
Haragan, Donald Robert *academic administrator, geologist, educator*
Hartwell, William Gersham III *retired music educator*
Hentges, David John *microbiology educator*
Holaday, Allan Scott *biology educator*
Huffman, Walter B. *retired army officer, dean, law educator*
Hurley, Kristie DeLynn *primary school educator*
Jugenheimer, Donald Wayne *advertising executive, communications educator, academic administrator*
Kanu, Adaobi *pediatrician, educator*
Ketner, Kenneth Laine *philosopher, educator*
Kiesling, Ernst Willie *civil engineering educator*
Kristiansen, Magne *electrical engineer, educator*
Kumar, Ashwani *cardiologist*
Lakhani, Gopal *computer scientist, educator*
Laski, Melvin Edward *nephrologist, educator*
Leach, Mike (Michael C. Leach) *college football coach*
Lodhi, M. A.K. *physicist, educator*
Martin, Clyde F. *engineering educator*
Martin, Tom *mayor, Lubbock, Texas*
May, Donald Robert Lee *ophthalmologist, educator, academic administrator, farmer*
Mayer, Michael Frederick *chemistry professor*
McGinley, Mark Alan *biology professor*
Miller, Paul Allen *literature educator*
Mitchell, Ronald K. *finance educator*
Mitra, Sunanda Datta *engineering educator*
Moseley, Patricia Ann *lawyer*
Oberhelman, Harley Dean *retired educator*
Oliver, Marina Goodfield *University Librarian*
Phelan, Marilyn Elizabeth *law educator*
Poduslo, Shirley Ellen *neuroscientist*
Purdom, Thomas James *lawyer*
Raoufi, Azadeh *music educator*
Rodriguez, Placido *bishop*
Roy, Juliana W. *music educator*
Rudd, Loretta Cooper *education educator, researcher*
Sabatini, Sandra *physician*
Shabaneh AlTamimi, Hamed A. *medical educator, consultant*
Skoog, Gerald Duane *science educator*
Sobolewski, Michael Vladyslav *computer scientist*
Song, Lianfa *educator*
Spurgeon, Sara Louise *literature and language professor*
Straus, David Conrad *microbiologist, educator*
Tallent-Runnels, Mary K. *psychology professor, researcher*
Valle-Garcia, Esteban *social worker*
Vieth, Ronja *literature and language professor*
Wachtel, Mitchell Steven *pathologist*
Wendt, Charles William *soil scientist, educator*
White, Alice Virginia *academic administrator*
Wilson, Sarah Elizabeth *music educator*
Woodward, Jason E. *plant pathologist, educator*
Yoder-Wise, Patricia Snyder *nursing educator*

Lufkin
McFarland, Edward T. *lawyer*
Rankin, Daniel F., Jr. *humanities educator*

Madisonville
Rowley, Patti Mitchell *psychology educator*

Magnolia
Girard, Louis Joseph *retired ophthalmologist, educator*
Tarver, Betty Gail *music educator*

Mansfield
Parnell, Charles L. *speechwriter*

Marshall
Adams, Venesia Yevette *library director*
Alonzo, Jose Alfredo *language educator*
Boaz, Virginia Lile *music educator*
Falke, Cassandra Marie *literature and language professor*
Magrill, Rose Mary *library director*
Peterson, Cynthia Lynn *library director, educator*
Ravenell, Alma Rena *school librarian*
Sudhivoraseth, Niphon *pediatrician, immunologist, allergist*

Mc Kinney
Bahm, Matt Anthony *museum administrator, consultant*
Berry, Brian Joe Lobley *geographer, urban planner, political economist, educator*
Collins, Larry D. *history professor*
Daley, Tom *not-for-profit foundation executive*
Frank, Steven Neil *chemist*
Gill, David bRIAN *electrical engineer, educator*
McAndrew, Mark S. *insurance company executive*
Wright, Thomas Parker *artist*

Mcallen
Arredondo, Jenna Dolores *speech pathology/audiology services professional*
Casso, Ramiro Raul *physician, academic administrator*
Countryman, Karen Sue *nurse, educator*
Gonzalez, Rolando Noel *secondary school and theology studies educator, photographer*
Guerra, Luis S. *biology professor*
Hinojosa, Ricardo H. *federal judge*
Huber, Melba Stewart *dance studio owner, educator*
Lopez, Nereida *literature and language professor*
McGee, William Howard John *retired library director*
Ramirez, Leo Armando, Sr. *mathematics educator*
Snearley, Ed *biology professor*
Spyker, Leola Edith *missionary*
von Kuster, Lee Norman *retired mathematics professor*

Meadowlakes
Nussbaum, Paul Stowell *retired urologist*

Mesquite
Budd, Rose Antoinette *language educator*
Byrd, Kathryn Susan *psychologist, educator*
Cloud, Kevin *computer game company executive*
Dennis-Monzingo, Vivian Ann *mathematics professor*
Fawcett, Leah *school librarian*
Forrest, Mary L. *communications educator*
Fox-Balli, Christina Maria *language educator, translator*
Hollenshead, Todd *computer game company executive*
Holman, Morris H. *retired social sciences educator*
Huston, Elizabeth *literature professor*
Justice, Mahlon G. (Jay Justice) *physics professor*
Keylon, Dorothy Marie *mathematics professor*
Kotrany, Anne M. *school librarian*
Lo, Timothy P. *mathematics professor*
Sharp, Robert Gene *history professor*
Washington, Larissa Lenore *educator*
Wenrich, John William *college president*
Willits, Tim *computer game company executive*

Midland
Berner, Leo De Witte, Jr. *retired oceanographer*
Bridges, Judy Cantrell *gifted and talented education educator*
Dawkins, Diantha Dee *librarian*
Estes, Andrew Harper *lawyer*
Fredrickson, Mark Allan *health facility administrator, physiatrist*
Groce, James Freelan *financial adviser*
Grover, Rosalind Redfern *oil and gas company executive*
Hinton, Diana Davids *history professor, consultant*
MacDonald, Leland Lloyd *lawyer*
Meyers, Alan Hoge *lawyer*
Robertson, Melanie Anne *oil industry executive*
Syed, Elizabeth Chance *health facility administrator, critical care nurse*
Taylor, Nicholas C. *lawyer, state agency administrator, energy executive*

Mineola
Stevenson, David Wayne *municipal official*

Mineral Wells
Mei, Anhua *mechanical engineer, researcher*
Warfield, Gerald Alexander *composer, writer*

Mission
Eyre, Pamela Catherine *retired career officer*
Gomez, Roberto *engineering executive*
Guajardo, Graciela *librarian*
Herbalife, Allen Henneman Ralph *science educator*

Missouri City
de Kanter, Ellen Ann *retired English and foreign language educator*
Hodges, Jot Holiver, Jr. *retired lawyer, corporate financial executive*
Jenkins, Helen Bishop *academic administrator*
Rathnau, Heather Hearn *music educator, writer*
Starnes, Katie Gerard *retired community health nurse*
Weber, Katie *retired special education educator*

Monahans
Jones, Evelyn Rojean *theater educator, director*

Montgomery
Hargett, Kent *Education Foundation Administrator*

Mount Pleasant
McCauley, Dan Paul *dentist*
Posey, Pamela Gayle *special education educator*
Vaughn, William Preston *retired historian, educator*

Mountain Home
Schlechte, John Warren *research scientist*

Murchison
Taweel, Janice M. *artist, educator*

Nacogdoches
Carter, Evelyn *retired elementary school educator*
Doyle-Anderson, Ann *language educator*
Fante-Konwinski, Rhiannon Marie *psychology professor, consultant*
Howard, David L. *conductor, baritone*
Kennedy, Kyle Duane *theater educator, director, actor*
Kroll, Charles Elliot *literature language and cinema studies professor*
Markworth, Norman *astronomer, educator*
Moore, John Thomas *chemistry professor, writer*
Onchoke, Kefa K. *science educator*
Oswald, Tina Atkinson *librarian*
Scott, Debra Laurette *trombone professor*
Stroup, Michael D. *economics professor, dean*
Vaughan, Elizabeth Jean *education educator*
Wagner, Stephen C. *biology professor*

Navasota
Day, Kathryn Ann *history educator*

New Braunfels
Barragän, Celia Silguero *elementary school educator*
Benfield, Marion Wilson, Jr. *law educator*
Dugger, Roy Wesley *academic administrator, retired military officer*
Krueger, Robert Charles *former ambassador, congressman, senator*
Oestreich, Charles Henry *retired university president*
Pharis, Ruth McCalister *retired bank executive*
Rush, W.M. (Rusty) *trucking executive*

New Caney
Hayes, Ann Carson *computer company executive*

Normangee
Cox, Jack Ronald, Jr. *business educator*
Rector, M. Eugene *community pharmacist*
Stork, Vera Lee *retired elementary school educator*

North Richland Hills
Hildebrand, Phillip J. *insurance company executive*
Reed, Glenn W. *lawyer*

Odessa
Hadjicostandi, Joanna A. *social sciences educator*
Keast, Michelle *music educator*
Kipple, Mary Elizabeth *nursing educator*
Kunkel, Martha F. *director*
Kupper, Julie Ann *retired elementary school educator*
Lemons, Richard Mikel *agricultural studies educator*
León, Ana E. *humanities educator*
McMinn, J. B. *retired philosophy educator, composer*
Post, Diane *biology professor*
Richardson, Todd H. *literature and language professor*
Sofge, Steve Wayne *biology professor*
Stoudt, Emily Laws *geologist, educator*

Odonnell
Saleh, John *lawyer*
Stephens, Stephanic Mica *executive secretary, educator*

Orange
Coratti, John Edward *judicial clerk*

Paige
Trevino, Jerry Rosalez *retired secondary school principal*

Palestine
Camp, Ronald Edward *accounting and economics educator*
Nunnally, Charles Lynn *biology and agriculture professor*
Packard, Russell Calvert *deacon*
Williams, Franklin Cadmus, Jr. *bibliographer*

Palmer
Gabor, Leciana *middle school educator*

Pampa
Willingham, Jeanne Maggart *performing company executive, educator*

Panhandle
Sherrod, Lloyd Bruce *retired nutritionist*

Paris
Tyler, Cathie Ann *artist, educator*

Pasadena
Aquino, Dolores Catherine *chemistry professor*
Blue, Monte Lynn *college president*
Cartwright, Ann *chemistry professor, department chairman*
Gilley, Mickey Leroy *musician*
Gilmore, Jared Raphael *science educator*
Gross, Cynthia Sue *petrochemicals manufacturing executive*
Kenagy, Cheri Lynn *nurse*
LeMaster, David James *literature and language professor*
Moon, John Henry, Sr. *banker*
Mullins, Jack Allen *cardiologist, educator*
Ruiz, Miriam *secondary school educator*
Schumacher, Barbara J *biology professor*
Scott, William Floyd *accountant*
Shapiro, Edward Muray *dermatologist*
Shelton, Hal Terry *history professor*
Thornburg, John N. *literature and language professor*

Pearland
Buckelew, Stephen MIchael *basketball coach*
Hammond, Raymond William *pharmacotherapy specialist*
Horton, Terzah Marie *pediatrician*
Würsig, Bernd Gerhard *marine biology educator*

Penitas
Sandra, G. Koenig *school librarian*

Pflugerville
Schwitters, Kathleen Chantell *school psychologist specialist*
Upadhya, Girish *thermal mechanical engineer*

Pittsburg
Cogdill, Richard A. *food products executive*
Jackson, Donald *food products executive*
Pilgrim, Lonnie (Bo Pilgrim) *food products executive*

Placedo
Rivera, Josie *elementary school educator*

Plainview
Belshaw, Gary D. *music educator, composer*
Dayton, Leah Jane *secondary school educator*
Mosteller, Sandra Marie *music educator*
Pitts, Sharon Ann Gammage *nursing director*
Ray, Thomas M. *history professor*

Plano
Altabef, Peter Anthony *lawyer*
Bain, Travis Whitsett, II, *manufacturing and retail executive*
Becker, Doreen Doris *medical/surgical nurse*
Bober, Joanne L. *lawyer, retail executive*
Boylson, Michael J. *retail executive, marketing professional*
Brown, Peggy Ann *language educator, writer*
Cavanaugh, Robert B. *department store executive*
Cotter-Smith, Cathleen Marie *artist, educator*
Coulter, Matthew Ware *history professor, writer*
Cullen, David O'Donald *history professor*
Day, Kevin Thomas *retired business executive, investment banker, foundation administrator*
Dhillon, Janet L. *lawyer, retail executive*
Dillon, Donald Ward *management consultant*
Dougherty, F(rancis) Kelly *application developer*
Evans, Pat *Mayor, Plano, Texas*
Findley, John Sidney *dentist*
Gajraj, Noor *anesthesiologist, educator*
Gallardo, Henrietta Castellanos *writer*
Galloway, Marianne Thérèse *performing company executive*
Gideon, Sharon Lee *secondary school educator*
Gordon, Storrow Moss *lawyer, information technology executive*
Guyer, Richard *surgeon*
Haggard, Geraldine Langford *primary school educator, writer, consultant*
Helgeson, Jean Anne (Sorrels) *biology professor, consultant*
Heller, Jeffrey M. *data processing executive*
Hooper, Sandra *systems engineer*
Hu, Mei Melvin *interventional physiatrist*
Jordan, Michael Hugh *information technology executive*
Karr, Rosemary M. *mathematics professor*
Keathly, David Mark *electrical and computer engineer*
Liukin, Nastia *Olympic gymnast*
Mahadeva, Manoranjan *financial executive, accountant*
Markey, James Kevin *lawyer*
Miller, Waenard Livingston *cardiologist*
Mondul, Donald David *patent lawyer*
Musser, Cherri M. *information technology executive*
Naor, Daniel *food products executive*
Oden, William Bryant *bishop, educator*
O'Loughlin-Brooks, Jennifer L. *psychology professor*
Perot, Ross (H. Ross Perot, Henry Ross Perot) *real estate company, investment company, data processing executive*
Perot, Ross, Jr., (Henry Ross Perot Jr.) *real estate developer, professional sports team executive*
Rhodes, Sherry L. *educator*
Rittenmeyer, Ronald Allen *information technology executive*
Ryu, Manho *application developer*
Scott, Terry Lee *communications executive*
Shelton, James D. (Denny Shelton) *hospital investment company executive*
Shepherd, Karen Schiller *biology educator*
Shubert, Joseph Francis *librarian*
Speese, Mark E. *rental company executive*
Tong, John *ophthalmic plastic surgeon, pediatric ophthalmologist, educator*
Trebilcock, James R. *marketing executive*
Ullman, Myron Edward, III, (Mike Ullman) *retail executive*
Vargo, Ronald Paul *information technology executive*
Vickery, Karen S. *education educator, director*
Worsfold, Victor Leonard *retired social sciences educator*
Wyman, Richard Thomas *information technology manager, researcher*

Port Aransas
Schake, Lowell Martin *zoology educator, writer*
Turner, Elizabeth Adams Noble (Betty Turner) *real estate company executive, author*

Port Arthur
Goza, Jim *chemistry educator*
Munoz, Andrea Lee *human resources specialist*

Portland
Soliz, Eusebio *military officer*

Post
Neff, Marie Taylor *museum director, artist*

Pottsboro
Hanning, Gary William *utilities and water transportation executive, consultant*
Thomas, Ann Van Wynen *retired law educator*

Prairie View
Block, Harriette Howard-Lee *biology professor*
Ciftja, Orion *physicist, researcher*
Cofie, Penrose *engineering educator, researcher*
Cudnik, Brian *astronomer, educator*
Cuero, Raul G. *microbiologist, researcher, educator*
Goodwin, Ronald E. *history professor*
Gyamerah, Michael *engineering educator*
Howell, Kenneth Wayne *history professor*
Hritonenko, Natali *mathematics professor, researcher*
Kirschten, Robert *educator, author, videographer*
Michev, Dimitar Perov *mathematics professor*
Prestage, Jewel Limar *political scientist, educational consultant*
wWheaton, Elizabeth M. *finance company executive, educator*

Quinlan
Smith, Patsy Juanita *retired financial executive*

Rancho Viejo
Garza, Roberto Jesus *retired education educator*

Randolph AFB
Donovan, Edgardo *medical services corps officer*
Ellis, Edward R. *career officer*
Looney, William R. III *career military officer*

Red Oak
Jones, Genia Kay *critical care nurse, consultant*
Shaw, Sue Ann *medical transcriptionist*

Richardson
Atzori, Marco *neuroscientist, educator*
Baughman, Ray Henry *materials scientist*
Bluedorn, Todd M. *manufacturing executive*
Burke, Thomas William *benefits compensation analyst*
Byrd, Ellen Stoesser *school nurse practitioner*
Cantrell, Cyrus Duncan III *physics professor, engineering educator, director*
Conkel, Robert Dale *lawyer, consultant*
Daniel, David Edwin *academic administrator, civil engineer*
Dasgupta, Sajib *research scientist*
Dean, Denis Joseph *science educator*
Dholakia-Lehenbauer, Kruti Ravindra *associate dean*
Dogan, Kutsal *science educator*
Enthoven, Adolf Jan Henri *accounting educator*
Faria, Joao Ricardo *economist, educator*
Goodspeed, Linda A. *manufacturing executive*
Gray, Donald Melvin *molecular and cell biology educator*
Griffith, Daniel Alva *geography educator*
Henderson, Rashaunda *engineering educator*
Kaplan-Thornton, Karen Ellen *speech pathology/audiology services professional, educator*
Lingo, Kathy Price *theater director, communications educator*
Madden, Marie Frances *marketing professional*
Martin, Richard Kelley *lawyer*
McMechan, George *science educator*
Moltz, John Henry III *biology professor*
Pirkul, Hasan *dean, management educator*
Radhakrishnan, Suresh *finance educator*
Redman, Timothy Paul *language educator, writer*
Richards, Frederick Francis, Jr. *manufacturing executive, consultant*
Roemer, Nils H. *history professor*
Rutford, Robert Hoxie *geologist, educator*
Salk, Jane Ellen *educator*
Sall, Larry David *library director*
Salter, Elizabeth Mary *academic administrator*
Sandler, Todd Michael *economist, political scientist, educator*
Schjerven, Robert E. *retired manufacturing executive*
Snow, Linda E. *librarian*
Stern, Robert James *geologist, educator*
Strieter, Frederick John *engineering executive*
Tang, Chinpei *mechanical engineer, researcher*
Vijverberg, Wim Petrus Maria *economics educator*
Wiorkowski, John James *mathematics professor*
Yang, Duck Joo *research scientist, educator*

Richland Hills
Houston, Lowell E. *special education educator*

Richmond
Cox, Dorothy M. *language educator*
Elliott, Brady Gifford *judge*
O'Shea, Joyce Burnett *English educator*

Rockport
Berkebile, Charles Alan *geology educator, hydrogeology researcher*
Johnson, Marilyn *retired obstetrician, gynecologist*
Minor, Joseph Edward *civil engineer, educator*
Moroles, Jesús Bautista *sculptor*
Owen, Molly Jackson *music educator*

Rockwall
Fisher, Gene Jordan *retired chemical company executive*
Kotas, Robert Vincent *pediatrician, educator*

Rosenberg
Haygood, Eithel Marinella *artist, educator*
Slack, Molly Johanna *theater educator*

Rosharon
Lopez, Placida Ramos *elementary school educator*
Marya, Manuel Paul Claude *metallurgical and materials engineer, manager*

Round Rock
Bell, Paul D. *computer company executive*
Brennan, Deborah Dikeman *assistant principal*
Clarke, Jeffrey W. *computer company executive*
Cryer, Chad Lindsey *biology professor*
Dell, Michael Saul *computer company executive*
Garriques, Ronald G. *computer company executive*
Gladden, Brian T. *computer company executive*
Halter, Jon Charles *retired magazine editor, writer*
Nelson, Erin Mulligan *computer company executive, marketing professional*
Puri, Rajendra Kumar *business and tax specialist, consultant*
Ricklefs, Dale Lynne *library director*
Schuckenbrock, Steve (Stephen Francis Schuckenbrock) *computer company executive, former information technology executive*
Tu, Lawrence P. *lawyer, computer company executive*

Rowlett
Openshaw, Linda Leek *social worker, educator*
Sprague, Charles Warren *geologist*

Royse City
Borden, William Vickers *education educator, writer*

Sachse
Eichelberger, Charles Bell *retired career officer*

Salado
Parks, Lloyd Lee *oil industry executive*

San Angelo
Blount, Grady Price *dean, director*
Butler, Michael Ward *economics professor*
Chatfield, Mary Van Abshoven *independent researcher*
Cody, Karen *linguistics professor*
Dewar, David P. *humanities educator*
Ellery, Jon Christopher *literature and language professor*
Fischer, Duncan Kinnear *neurosurgeon*
Johnson, Harvey Douglas *mathematics educator*
McCoy, J. Kelly *biology professor*
Mobley, Nancy Elizabeth *artist, educator*
Pfeifer, Michael David *bishop*
Schonberg, Jeff Brett *literature and language professor, researcher*
Walther, Barbara Ann Lane *judge, former lawyer*
Worley, James Glenn *theater educator*
Zheng, Guoqiang *history professor*

San Antonio
Abramson, Hyman Norman *engineering and science research executive*
Acosta, Carlos L. *history professor, researcher*
Agaian, Sos Suien *electrical engineer, researcher*
Aguirre, Javier Ramos *historian, educator*
Alejos, Melba Casanova *music educator*
Anderson, Anita L. *psychology professor*
Armstrong, William Tucker III *lawyer*
Arthur, Gary L., Jr. *energy executive*
Atchley, Curtis Leon *mechanical engineer*
Aust, Joe Bradley *surgeon, educator*
Austin, Lola Houston *psychologist*
Avant, Patricia Kay *nursing educator*
Aycock, James J. *lawyer*
Ayon, Arturo A. *electrical engineer, educator*
Bachrach, Steven Maurice *chemistry educator*
Baker, Floyd Wilmer *surgeon, retired military officer*
Barilleaux, Rene Paul *curator*
Barton, James Cary *lawyer*
Becker, Quinn Henderson *orthopedic surgeon, military officer*
Beechinor, Diane Blanche *education educator*
Bellanger, Renee A. *pharmacist, educator*
Bellows, Thomas John *political scientist, educator*
Bennett, Sister Elsa Mary *retired secondary school educator*
Bennett, Steven Alan *lawyer, insurance company executive*
Bodenchuk, Michael J. *biologist, director*
Boozer, Lyndon K. *lobbyist*
Borron, Stephen W. *medical educator*
Bowers, Kim *lawyer, energy executive*
Brancaleon, Lorenzo *biophysicist, researcher*
Breit, William *economist, educator, writer*
Brewster, Olive Nesbitt *retired librarian*
Brooks, Franklin Ramon *psychologist, military officer*
Browning, Jay D. *energy executive, lawyer*
Budalur, Thyagarajan Subbanarayan *chemistry professor*
Buford, R.C. *professional sports team executive*
Buitron, Richard Arthur *literature and language professor*
Burch, James Leo *science research institute executive*
Burke, Betty Jane *retired real estate manager*
Bussineau King, Deborah Elaine *music educator*
Butler, Edward Franklyn *administrative law judge, educator*
Butt, Charles Clarence *food service executive*
Callaway, James W. (Jim) *telecommunications industry executive*
Callihan, Dorothy Jeanne *psychologist, educator*
Cantú, Oscar *bishop*
Cesur, Durmus *GIS expert*
Chen, Jiguo *microbiologist, researcher*
Cherukuri, Ravindranath Chowdary *research scientist*
Cibrian, Diane G. *Councilman*
Cicconi, James William *lawyer, telecommunications industry executive*
Ciskowski, Michael S. *energy executive*
Cisneros, Henry Gabriel *construction executive, former United States Secretary of Housing & Urban Development*
Cisneros, Mary Alice P. *Councilwoman*
Clamp, John G. *Councilman*
Clark, Leif Michael *federal judge*
Coker, Larry E. *college football coach*
Condos, Barbara Seale *real estate broker, developer, investor*
Condrill, Jo Ellaresa *small business owner, writer, consultant*
Conklyn, Elizabeth D. *insurance company executive*
Corrigan, Helen González *retired cytologist*
Cortez, Philip A. *Councilman*

Coughlin, Catherine M. *telecommunications industry executive*
Coughlin, Katherine M. *telecommunications industry executive*
Crabtree, Ben C. *neuromuscular therapy clinic director*
Crichton, Flora Cameron *volunteer, foundation administrator*
Crownover, Mike *energy executive*
Czerw, Russell J. *career military officer, dentist*
Daniels, Bruce C *history professor, author*
Darling, John Rothburn *business educator*
de la Vega, Ralph *telecommunications industry executive*
Diaz-Dennis, Patricia *lawyer, communications executive*
Donovan, John *telecommunications industry executive*
Dorff, Barbara L. *elementary and secondary school educator*
Downing, Jane Katherine *psychiatric nurse, lawyer*
Drutt, Matthew J. W. *museum director*
Duesterhoeft, Diane M. *librarian*
Dumitru, Daniel *physiatrist*
Duncan, A. Baker *investment banker*
Duncan, Tim (Timothy Theodore Duncan) *professional basketball player*
Dunne, Matthew *music educator*
Durbin, Richard Louis, Sr. *health facility administrator, consultant*
Duron, Robert J. *school system administrator*
Dyas, Anna Marie *gifted and talented educator*
Edwards, S. Eugene *energy executive*
Emamian, Vahid *engineering educator*
Espey, Lawrence Lee *biology professor*
Fabrique, Martha Helene *music educator*
Faules, Barbara Ruth *retired elementary school educator*
Fehrenbach, T.R. (Theodore Reed Fehrenbach) *writer*
Feldman, Marc D. *cardiologist, biomedical engineer, physiologist*
Finley, Michael Howard *professional basketball player*
Finnerty, William J. *oil industry executive*
Fisher, Dierdre Denise *mental health nurse, administrator, educator*
Fisher, Eric A. *energy executive, lawyer*
Flagg, C.A. (Chuck Flagg) *oil industry executive*
Flanagan, Thomas Joseph *bishop emeritus*
Flores, Patrick Fernandez *archbishop emeritus*
Focht-Hansen, Jane *literature and language professor*
Forgione, Dana Anthony *accounting educator*
Foster, Nancy Haston *columnist, writer*
Frazier, Eric David *information technology manager, consultant*
Fruth, Roman Martin *piano technician, musician*
Fuhrmann, Charles J., II, *financial consultant, educator*
Furgeson, William Royal *federal judge*
Galvan, Lourdes *Councilwoman*
Garcia, Henry Frank *supply and project management consultant*
Gardner, Kirsten Elizabeth *history professor*
Garrison, David H. *insurance company executive*
Garza, Emilio Miller *federal judge*
Ghosh, Amitava *mining engineer*
Gilbert, Steve *energy executive, lawyer*
Ginobili, Manu *professional basketball player*
Golden, Stephen L. *lawyer*
Goldstein, Gerald H. *lawyer*
Gomez, José Horacio *archbishop*
Gonzalez, Hector Hugo *nursing educator*
Gorder, Joseph W. *energy executive*
Gower, Patricia E. *history professor*
Gray, Shawn Scott *social services administrator*
Grimshaw, James Albert, Jr. *retired language educator*
Gruber, John Balsbaugh *physics professor*
Gwathmey, Joe Neil, Jr. *retired broadcast executive*
Han, Hai-Chao *engineering educator*
Hardberger, Phillip Duane *Mayor, San Antonio, judge, lawyer, journalist*
Hare, Henry Phillip, Jr. *psychiatrist*
Harris, Richard John *social sciences educator*
Harrison, Stephen A. *gastroenterologist*
Haywood, J. William *oil industry executive*
Henao, Andres Felipe *internist*
Henderson, Connie Chorlton *retired city planner, artist, writer*
Henderson, Dwight Franklin *dean, educator*
Hermann, Robert Charles, Jr. *neurologist, educator*
Herrera, Delicia *councilwoman*
Holt, Peter M. *professional sports team owner, agricultural products executive*
Hood, Sandra Dale *librarian*
Hornberger, Ronald *lawyer*
Horton, Granville Eugene *occupational medicine physician, retired air force officer*
Huang, Yufei *engineering educator*
Hudspeth, Almetra Kavanaugh *retired elementary school educator*
Hughes, Dan *professional basketball coach*
Irving, George Washington III *veterinarian, researcher, small business executive*
Jacobson, Helen Gugenheim (Mrs. David Jacobson) *civic worker*
Jaffe, David Bendix *neuroscientist, educator*
Jarmon, Sharon Irene *secondary school educator*
Jary, Mary Canales *business owner*
Jefferson, Richard *professional basketball player*
Jimenez, Daniel Angel *computer scientist, educator*
Jones, James Richard *business administration educator*
Kasinath, Balakuntalam S. *medical researcher*
Katz, Martin M. *psychologist, educator*
Kaylor, Maria *special education educator*
Keck, Judith Marie Burke *business owner, retired career officer*
Kellman, Steven G. *literature educator, author*
Killinger, Clayton *energy executive*
Klaerner, Curtis Maurice *gas industry executive*
Kline, John William *retired military officer, management consultant*
Kline, Kimberly Nicole *communications educator*
Klugman, Craig M. *humanities educator*
Labenz-Hough, Marlene *administrator*
Lanehart, Sonja Lanehart *language educator*
Lárraga, Maribel *language educator*
Larson, Lyle Thomas *commissioner*
Lefeber, Edward James, Jr. *internist, educator*
Leon, Robert Leonard *psychiatrist, educator*
Levin, Andrew W. *lawyer, communications executive*
Lewis, Everett D. *oil industry executive*
Lim, Seong Bae *business educator*
Lin, Ai-Ling *medical physicist, researcher in neuroscience and neuroimaging*
Lindner, Richard G. (Rick Lindner) *telecommunications industry executive*
Lonchar, Patricia Paulette *English educator*
Lyle, Robert Edward *chemist*
Manchester, Lucien Caleb *biology professor*
Marbut, Robert Gordon *communications, electronic security and broadcast executive, investor*
Marcogliese, Richard J. *energy executive*
Matus, Kristi Ann *insurance company executive*
Maxwell, Diana Kathleen *primary school educator*
May, S. Beth *music educator, composer*
Mays, L(ester) Lowry *broadcast executive*
Mays, Mark Pitman *communication company executive*
Mc Allister, Gerald Nicholas *retired bishop, minister*
McComas, David John *science administrator, space physicist*
McCoy, Joseph G. *oil industry executive*
McCracken, Richard Joseph *English educator, college administrator*
McDyess, Antonio Keithflen *professional basketball player*
McFee, Arthur Storer *physician*
McGill, Henry Coleman, Jr. *pathologist, educator, researcher*
McGuire, William Dennis *healthcare consultant*
McIntosh, Dennis Keith *veterinarian, consultant*
McKone, Timothy P. *lobbyist, telecommunications industry executive*
McNeil, Sheila D. *Councilwoman*
Michaels, Willard A. Bill (Bill Michaels) *retired broadcasting executive*
Miller, Forrest E. *telecommunications industry executive*
Monroe, Joseph M. *oil industry executive*
Moore-Sickmann, Susan *psychologist*
Moreau, Claude P. *oil industry executive*
Mortensen, Eric Michael *medical researcher*
Moynihan, John Bignell *retired lawyer*
Mulrow, Cynthia Diane *internist, editor*
Mustain, Megan Rust *philosopher, educator*
Myers, Ellen Howell *historian, educator*
Nath, Lopita *history professor*
Nelson, James Harold *health sciences administrator*
Newhauser, Richard Gordan *Medieval philology educator*
Newton, Virginia *archivist, historian, librarian*
Odom, Marjorie Mildred Morgan *retired librarian*
Ognibene, Andre John *internist, educator, retired military officer*
Oppenheim, Martha Kunkel *pianist, educator*
O'Rourke, Robert A. *cardiologist, educator*
Padmanabhan, Swaminathan *hematologist, oncologist, researcher*
Parekh, Dipen *medical educator*
Parker, Tony (William Anthony Parker II) *professional basketball player*
Parrish, Charles S. *lawyer, oil industry executive*
Passty, Jeanette Nyda Mendelssohn *literature and language professor, writer, editor*
Patterson, Jan Evans *epidemiologist, educator*
Pawel, Nancy Emma Ray *oil industry executive, educator, artist*
Perry, George *dean, neuroscientist, educator*
Perry, John *communications educator, researcher*
Perry, Robert Michael *lawyer, consultant, rancher*
Pestana, Carlos *surgeon, retired dean, educator*
Pitluk, Ellen Eidelbach *lawyer, mediator*
Popovich, Gregg *professional basketball coach*
Porter, Daniel J. *oil industry executive*
Prestigiacomo, Roberto *theater educator, art director*
Pruitt, Basil Arthur, Jr. *surgeon, retired military officer*
Pych, Rick *professional sports team executive*
Ramirez, Amelie G. *health facility administrator, director*
Ramos, Jennifer V. *Councilwoman*
Ramsinghani, Sushma *medical educator*
Ratliff, Dan A. *marriage and family therapist, educator*
Ratliff, Theo *professional basketball player*
Reams, Bernard Dinsmore, Jr. *law educator*
Redfield, Carol Ann Luckhardt *computer scientist, educator*
Reneau, Marvin Bryan *military officer, business professor*
Reser, Don Clayton *lawyer*
Restrepo, Ruben Dario *physician, educator*
Reuter, Stewart Ralston *retired radiologist*
Rezaie, Bahman *engineering educator, researcher*
Ribble, Ronald George *psychologist, educator, writer, behavioral consultant*
Rice, Chris *telecommunications industry executive*
Rivard, Robert *editor, publishing executive*
Roberson, Dawnlee *engineering educator*
Robertson, Samuel Luther, Jr. *psychotherapist, educator*
Robles, Josue, Jr. *insurance company executive*
Rodriguez, Justin *Councilman*
Rolin, Daniel Wayne, Jr. *military officer*
Rollin, Michael Fredrick *history professor*
Rouse, John Wilson, Jr. *technology consultant*
Rowe, Louis E. *Councilman*
Roy, Anuradha *statistician, educator, researcher*
Rubin, David Stuart *curator, art critic*
Rush, W. Marvin *trucking executive*
Salvucci, Linda *history professor*
Schembri, Chris *communications company executive, media specialist*
Schenker, Steven *internist, educator*
Schlueter, David Arnold *law educator*
Schmutz, John Francis *lawyer*
Schwethelm, Otto C. *oil industry executive*
Sculley, Patrick David *retired army officer, director*
Sebastian, Thomas *language educator*
Shanfield, Stephen B. *psychiatrist, educator*
Shanklin, Kenneth Dale *plastic surgeon*
Shapiro, Mark S. *neuroscientist, educator*
Shireman, Paula K. *medical educator*
Silantien, John Joseph *music educator*
Sinkfield, Carolin Ladell *agricultural studies educator*
Skelley, Dean Sutherland *clinical laboratory administrator*
Smith, Bruce Alfred *oil industry executive*
Smith, Reginald Brian Furness *retired anesthesiologist, educator*
Spears, Sally *lawyer*
Spencer, Roger Wayne *economics professor*
sStankey, John T. *telecommunications industry executive*
Stankey, John T. *telecommunications industry executive*
Steen, John Thomas, Jr. *lawyer*
Stephenson, Randall L. *telecommunications industry executive*
Stephenson, Thomas A. *publishing executive*
Strong, Wendi Ellen *insurance company executive*
Synek, Miroslav *physicist, chemist, world affairs consultant*
Terracina, Roy David *entrepreneur*
Titzman, Donna M. *energy executive*
Trichopoulos, Nikolaos *ophthalmologist*
Urbach, Adam Robert *chemistry professor*
Vadlamudi, Ratna K. *healthcare educator*
Vinson, Audrey Lawson *retired literature and language professor*
Wahl, Rosemarie *biologist, educator*
Walker, William Oliver, Jr. *retired humanities educator, dean*
Walmsley, Judith Abrams *chemistry professor*
Walsh, Nicolas Eugene *rehabilitation services professional, educator*
Wang, Lindsay L. *research and assessment director, principal*
Wang, Yufeng *science educator*
Ward, Michael T. *classicist, educator*
Watts, D. Wayne *telecommunications industry executive, lawyer*
Weinberg, Florence May *retired modern language and literature educator*
Weinstein, Martin *aerospace transportation and manufacturing executive, materials scientist*
Welch, Billy E. *retired government agency administrator, management consultant*
Westfall, Lynn D. *oil industry executive*
Widhelm, Jennifer Cochran *theater educator*
Wilkins, Rayford, Jr. *telecommunications industry executive*
Williams, Docia Schultz *small business owner*
Williams, Thomas Eugene *pediatric hematologist and oncologist, pharmaceutical executive*
Williams Adams, Annette Lynn *emergency physician*
Williams-Perry, Brenda Lee *pre-school educator*
Wolf, Steven E. *surgeon, educator*
Wood, Thomas Willard *retired health industry executive, retired military officer*
Wright, Gregory A. *oil industry executive*
Yang, Zhanbo *mathematics professor, researcher*
Young, James Julius *academic administrator, retired military officer*
Zesch, Hal *energy executive*
Zilveti, Carlos Benjamin *preventive medicine physician, pediatrician*

San Diego
Pena, Modesta Celedonia *retired principal*

San Marcos
Allsup, Roxane Cuellar *curriculum and instruction educator*
Blanda, Michael Thomas *chemist, researcher*
Charlton, Debra Lynn *theater educator*
Feakes, Debra Arliene *chemistry professor*
Garner, Lydia M. *history professor*
Imel, Elizabeth Carmen *retired physical education educator*
Mejía, Jaime Armin *language educator*
Nauert, Rick *healthcare educator, consultant*
Price, Larry R. *statistician, educator*
Rudzinski, Walter E. *chemistry professor, department chairman*
Shields, Patricia Mary *political science professor*
Skerpan-Wheeler, Elizabeth Penley *English language educator*
Stephan, Karl David *electrical engineering educator*
Stern, Harold Philip Elliott *electrical engineer, director*
Stovall, Frances Middagh *journalist, preservationist*
Suh, Taewon *marketing and business educator*
Tate, Jitendra S. *engineering educator*
Yazedjian, Ani *humanities educator*
Yun, Hyun Jung *political science professor*

Schertz
Vande Hey, James Michael *retired air force officer*

Seabrook
Fischer, Craig Leland *physician*
Patten, Bernard Michael *neurologist, writer, educator*

Seguin
Robinson, Ronald Alan *manufacturing executive*

Selma
Kent, Jeff (Jeffrey Franklin Kent) *business owner, retired professional baseball player*

Sheppard AFB
Cook, Sharla J. *career officer*

Sherman
Avard, Stephen Lewis *retired finance educator*
Melancon, Glenn *history professor*
Simmons, Kevin Mark *finance educator*
Williams, Ruby Jo *retired principal*

Smithville
Scofield, Virginia Lee *research scientist*

Snyder
Barnes, Maggie Lue Shifflett (Mrs. Lawrence Barnes) *nurse*
Gray, Donna Lea *small business owner*
Martini, Jason *academic administrator*

Southlake
Arafat-Johnson, Danyah *secondary school educator, director*
Bogdan, Michael Andrew *plastic surgeon*
Cruze, Jennifer Lea *secondary school educator*
Peluso, Michelle *Internet and travel company executive*
Smith, JoBeth *elementary school educator*
Sorge, Karen Lee *printing company executive, consultant*

Spearman
Jarvis, Billy Britt *lawyer*

Spring
Bartlow, Gene Steven *professional society executive, retired military officer*
Ciancimino, Joseph Andrew *data processing executive*
Corbett, Luke R. *former energy company executive*
Cox, Geoffrey F. *pharmaceutical executive*
Farley, Andrew Newell *lawyer, consultant*
Howard, Richard Carl *minister*
Hunt, T(homas) W(ebb) *retired religion educator*
Kehoe, John Kimball *finance educator, consultant*
Neill, Rebecca Anne *middle school educator*
Rex, Lonnie Royce *religious organization administrator*

Spring Branch
Barban, Arnold Melvin *advertising executive, educator, writer*
Geistfeld, James Gordon *veterinarian*

Spur
Warren, Jennifer Elizabeth *family nurse practitioner*

Stafford
Corley, Larry Steven *chemist*
Le, Duy-Loan *electrical engineer*

Stephenville
Bane, Alma Lynn *data research administrator*
Christopher, Joe Randell *retired language educator*
Collier, Boyd Dean *finance educator, management consultant*
McElroy, Linda Sue *retired elementary school educator*
Osei, Edward *economist, researcher*
Quazi, Moumin Manzoor *literature educator, consultant*
Schmelzer, Janet L. *history professor, researcher*

Sugar Land
Downs, Hartley H. III *chemist*
Finch, Robert David *mechanical engineer, educator, consultant*
Fox, Lori A. *psychologist*
Goodwin, Anthony Robert Holmes *chemist, editor*
Gross, Edmund Samuel *lawyer, oil industry executive*
Harribance, Sean Lalsingh *parapsychologist*
Heitzenrater, James F. *hospital administrator*
Hitchcock, Bion Earl *lawyer*
Hosley, Marguerite Cyril *civic worker*
Huston, Daniel Cliff *geophysicist*
Kakkanatt, George Mathew *psychotherapist, consultant*
Kulkarni, Sachin Rameshchandra *application developer*
Lipinski, John J. (Jack) *oil industry executive*
Morgan, Edward A. *oil industry executive*
Rider, Roger Alan *lawyer*
Riemann, Stanley A. *oil industry executive*
Schulze, Keith E. *dermatologist, surgeon*
Wagner, Donald Bert *health facility administrator*

Temple
Asea, Alexzander *research scientist*
Bennett, Daniel D *preventive medicine physician*
Breslin, Jerome W. *physiologist, cell biologist*
Butler, David Ford *dermatologist*
Clawson, James F., Jr. *judge, arbitrator, mediator*
Dehmer, Gregory Joseph *cardiologist*
Frankel, Arthur E. *oncologist, educator*
Furst, Cari Michelle *nursing educator*
Gaglani, Manjusha *medical educator*
Holleman, Vernon Daughty *internist, educator*
Mahabir, Raman Chaos *plastic surgeon, educator*
Meshack, Geneva Tucker *retired elementary school educator*
Northrup, Jason *marriage and family therapist*
Pickle, Jerry Richard *lawyer*
Rohack, John James *cardiologist*
Rosa, Robert H., Jr. *ophthalmologist, medical educator, researcher*
Sawyer, William Dale *internist, educator, dean, foundation administrator*
Smythe, William Roy *surgeon*
Tharakan, Binu *neuroscientist, researcher*

Texarkana
Bertrand, Betty Harleen *nurse*
Calhoun, John C., Jr. *academic administrator*
Peck, Leonard Warren, Jr. *lawyer*

Texas City
Hodges, Richard Dean *instrument and electrical technician*
Navy, Ernest Jude *educator, writer*
Orr, Tracy Clifford *anatomy, physiology professor*
Plasek, Susan G. *academic administrator*
Robertson, Paul Francis *mathematician, educator, technologist, entrepreneur*

The Colony
Culver, Jennifer Lynn *secondary school educator*
Mitchell, Melvin Clifford *music educator*

The Woodlands
Barker, Sam L. *pharmaceutical executive*
Benedetto, Anthony R. *religious mediator*
Bethea, Louise Huffman *allergist*
Broussard, Bruce D. *medical products executive*
Cagle, Melinda Reeves *editor*
Desjardins, Raoul *medical association administrator, financial consultant*
Ghosh, Supriyo *performing company executive*
Glenn, Gerald Marvin *marketing, engineering and construction executive*
Griffith, James William *systems engineer, consultant*
Gwin, Robert G. *oil industry executive*
Hackett, James T. *oil industry executive*
Hagerman, John David *lawyer, investment advisor*
Jones, Lincoln III *military officer*
Machle, Edward Johnstone *religious studies educator, philosopher*
Morrison, Scott David *management consultant, small business owner*
Reeves, Robert K. *lawyer, oil industry executive*
Sands, Arthur T. *biopharmaceutical executive, medical geneticist*
Schott, Sally Maria *music publisher, arts education consultant*
Shannon, Thomas O. *plastic surgeon*
Stolle, Russell Robert *chemicals executive*
Walker, R. A. *oil industry executive*
Wilcox, Raymond I. *oil industry executive*

Tomball
Fox, Clifton Robert *social studies educator*
Tynes, Alanna Marie *biology professor*

Trinidad
Conant, Allah B., Jr. *lawyer*

Tyler
Albertson, Christopher Adam *librarian*
Alworth, Charles Wesley *lawyer, engineer*
Brock, Dee Sala *television executive, writer, consultant, educator*
Corrada del Rio, Alvaro *bishop*
Davidson, Jack Leroy *academic administrator*
Doty, Duane Harold *business educator*
Dubre, Vandy *librarian*
Edwards, D. M. *retail, wholesale distribution and real estate company executive*
Ellis, Donald Lee *lawyer*
Fan, Wei *operations research specialist*
Gainer, Lindsey Adams *finance educator, consultant*
Gould, Tracy *medical educator*
Guthrie, Judith K. *federal judge*
Holland, Barbara *artist, educator*
Johnson, Thomas Allen *protective services official, educator*
Layton, Robert E., Jr. *retired aeronautical engineer*
Mastern, Dean Scott *personal growth and development consultant*
Patterson, Donald Ross *lawyer, educator*
Peters, Robert K. *dean, newscaster, journalist*
Prater, Emma Lou *retired academic administrator*
Pyle, Jeanne *library director*
Ross, Catherine Elizabeth *literature and language professor*
Sathyamoorthy, Muthukrishnan *engineering educator, associate provost*
Scott, Mary Sue *education educator*
Wrenn, Christopher Jay *physician*

Uvalde
Burchfield, Mitchel *education educator*
Graham, Robert Albert *physicist, researcher*
Kosub, Karla Ann *biology professor*
Ramsey, Frank Allen *veterinarian, retired army officer*

Valley Mills
Odell, Patrick Lowry *retired mathematics professor*

Valley View
Wallace, Donald John III *rancher*

Vernon
Ansley, Robert James *agricultural studies educator*
Coufal, Cindy *literature and language educator*
Malinowski, Dariusz Piotr *horticulturist, educator*
McCoy, Michael *economics professor*
Wofford, Garry *music educator*

Victoria
Fellhauer, David Eugene *bishop*
Harrington, Rick *psychology professor*
Kutach, Patricia Ann *counseling administrator*
McLain, Donald *engineering educator*

Waco
Ballenger, Erma Maxine *social studies educator, director*
Bassett, Randy L. *chemicals executive, director*
Beaujean, Alexander A. *psychology professor*
Belew, John Seymour *academic administrator, chemist*
Briles, Art *college football coach*
Brooks, Roger Leon *retired academic administrator*
Cleaver, Gerald Bryan *physicist, researcher*
Cobbs, Linda Ray *academic librarian*
Cunningham, Harold R. *academic administrator, accountant*
Dooley, Bill *language educator*
Drew, Scott *men's college basketball coach*
Farison, James Blair *electrical and biomedical engineer, educator*
Garland, David Ellsworth *academic administrator, theology studies educator*
Goforth, Thomas Tucker *retired geophysicist*
Grinols, Earl Leroy III *economist, educator*
Hein, Jay Forest *religious studies educator, former federal official*
Henderson, Johnny *mathematician, educator*
Karney, James A. *library director*
Kimsey-Davis, Beatrice Anna *civic worker, educator*
Leidner, Dorothy E. *science educator*
Lindsey, Jonathan Asmel *retired academic administrator, academic librarian*
Mackenzie, Charles Alfred *lawyer*
Mc Swain, Angus Stewart, Jr. *retired law educator*
Mulkey, Kim *women's college basketball coach*
Richie, Rodney Charles *critical care and pulmonary medicine physician*
Roldan-Figueroa, Rady *philosopher, educator*
Rolf, Howard Leroy *mathematician, educator*
Rose, John Thomas *finance educator*
Sheng, Qin *mathematics professor*
Shim, Jaeho *physical education educator*
Smith, Cullen *lawyer*
SoRelle, James *history professor*
Sorrels, Carolyn Jean *assistant to CIO*
Spencer, Vicki Carol *elementary school educator*
Stratton, Margaret Anne *minister*
Talbert, Charles Harold *theologian, educator*
Toben, Bradley J.B. *dean, law educator*

Waller
Evans, Nancy Peltier *behavioral specialist, educator*

Warda
Kunze, George William *retired soil scientist*

Waskom
Sullivan, Penny McIver *theater and speech educator*

Waxahachie
Collins, William Duane *religious studies educator*
Lewis, Diane Dunn *literature and language professor, department chairman*
Logue, Jeff *psychology professor, director*

Weatherford
Eppright, Carol A. *education educator*
King, Douglas Michael *lawyer, accountant*

Webster
Kobayashi, Herbert Shin *electrical engineer*

Weslaco
Fogarty, Elizabeth Jordan *retired librarian, researcher*
Wyatt, Debra Sue *speech educator*
Yang, Chenghai *agricultural engineer, researcher*

Wharton
Dees, Kevin W. *biology professor, consultant*
George, Lila Gene Plowe Kennedy *music educator*
Jeffery, Jennifer *biology professor*
Maxfield, Rose Mary *retired government official*
Rehak, Patricia *career planning administrator*

Whitewright
Burg, John Parker *construction panel executive*

Wichita Falls
Ballard, Mark Alan *secondary school educator*
Briley, Stephen Morris *lawyer*
Cook, Marcella Kay *retired theater educator*
Fowler, Robert Martin, Jr. *oil industry executive, consultant*
Hallford, Randal L. *chemistry professor*
Hancock, Carole Patricia *academic administrator*
Jordan-Aldaco, Judith Ann *music educator*
Leishner, Jane Carlson *retired director*
McClintock, Stuart *language educator*
Parker, Eva Annette *retired librarian*
Scherler, Kathy Louise *music educator, researcher*
Thornton, Brian *communication educator, researcher*
Walker, Randall Wayne *lawyer*
Waun, Roger *small business owner, minister*

Willis
Rappaport, Martin Paul *internist, nephrologist, educator*
Snider, Robert Larry *management consultant*

Wimberley
Brinsmade, Lyon Louis *retired lawyer*
Ellis, John *retired school system administrator, writer*
Skaggs, Wayne Gerard *retired diversified financial services company executive*

Woodway
Kunert, Holly Leigh *medical educator*
Packard, Joyce Hornaday *retired counselor*

Wylie
Carson, Charles Michael *composer, musician*
Cheng, Pauline Shyh-yi *mathematics educator*

Yoakum
Watson, David H. *physician*
Williams, Walter Waylon *lawyer, agricultural products supplier*

Zavalla
Devlin, Cynthia M. *air transportation executive, consultant*

UTAH

American Fork
Reinhold, Allen Kurt *graphic design educator*
Zhou, Bing-Nan *chemistry professor*

Bountiful
Andersen, Julie B. *elementary school educator*
Beesley, Kenneth Horace *educator*
Burningham, Kim Richard *educational association administrator, former state legislator*
Clay, Orson C. *insurance company executive, director*
Mangum, Garth Leroy *retired economist*

Brigham City
Halterman, Karen Annie *psychologist*

Brookside
McMahon, James Patrick *ecologist, consultant*

Castle Valley
Zavada, Barbara Johanna *artist, educator*

Cedar City
Blodgett, Terry Marvin *language educator*
Cotts, Laura Alford *physics professor, consultant*
Heuett, Brian L. *communications educator, small business owner*
Hill, Deborah Meyer *education educator*
Mayron, Lewis Walter *clinical ecology consultant*
Modesitt, Carol Ann *vocalist, music educator, opera director*
Modesitt, Leland Exton, Jr., (L.E. Modesitt Jr.) *writer, poet, consultant*
Ping, Larry Lee *history professor*
White, Lynn H. *psychology professor, researcher*
Wilks, Jill Ann *academic administrator, director*

Cedar Hills
Ashton, Dawne Belinda *retired secondary school educator*

Centerfield
Parkin, Fern Agnes Marvel *medical/surgical nurse, educator*

Centerville
Schwartz, Heidi K. *science educator*

Corinne
Ahmad, Rashid Ahmad *mechanical engineer*

Dugway
Davis, Vernon Thomas *military officer, researcher*

Genola
Newcomb, Helene E. *retired research scientist*

Holladay
McKell, Cyrus M. *retired dean, range plant physiologist, consultant*
O'Halloran, Thomas Alphonsus, Jr. *retired physicist, researcher*

Hyde Park
Bowen, Morgan *religious studies educator*

Kearns
Ohno, Apolo Anton *Olympic athlete*

Logan
Albee-Scott, Steven Robert *biologist, educator*
Baktur, Reyhan *engineering educator*
Baldwin, Debra *history educator*
Bowles, David Stanley *engineering educator, consultant*
Cao, Yongcan *research scientist*
Clement, Richard Wolcott *librarian, educator*
Daines, N. George *lawyer*
Fauth, Elizabeth Braungart *human development and family studies professor*
Gudmundson, Jon Karl *musician, director*
Hargreaves, George Henry *civil and agricultural engineer, researcher*
Hruby, George Geoffrey *writer, educator*
Keller, Jack *agricultural engineering educator, consultant*
Kohler, Brynja Raquel *mathematics professor*
Leidolf, Andreas *ecologist*
McNeal, Lyle Glen *science educator, rancher, consultant*
Moon, Todd Kay *engineering educator*
Rasmuson, Brent J. *photographer, small business owner*
Rasmussen, Harry Paul *horticulture and landscape educator*
Stucker, Brent *science educator*
Symanzik, Juergen *statistician, educator*
Tanner, David Arden *biologist, researcher*
Wagner, Dale R. *science educator*
West, Stephen Allan *lawyer*
Zhu, Lie *physics professor*

Manti
Funk, William Henry *retired environmental engineering educator*
Petersen, Benton Lauritz *paralegal*

Mapleton
Hillyard, Ira William *retired pharmacologist, educator*

Midvale
Smith, Mary Ellen *educational program facilitator*
Teerlink, J(oseph) Leland *real estate developer*

Midway
Zenger, John Hancock *training company executive*

Moab
Tallman, Eve *library director*

Montezuma Creek
Schaefer, Kim *music educator*

North Ogden
Heap, Joan S. *elementary school educator*

Oakley
Silverstone, Leon Martin *neuroscientist, cardiologist, educator, research scientist*

Ogden
Adams, J. Phillip *oil industry executive*
Berghout, Henry Laine *chemistry professor*
Buckner, Elmer La Mar *retired insurance company executive*
Carroll, Bradley W. *physics professor, department chairman*
Davidson, Thomas Ferguson *retired chemical engineer*
Elliott, Harold Marshall *geography educator*
Harrington, Mary Evelina Paulson (Polly) *writer, educator*
MacKay, Kathryn Leilani *social sciences educator*
Milner, Robert Seaton *toolmaker, manufacturing engineer, graphics designer, educator*
Pappas, Leah Aglaia *foundation administrator, political organization worker, secondary school educator*

Orem
Hall, Blaine Hill *retired librarian*
Hunt, H(arold) Keith *retired business management educator, marketing consultant*
Jackman, Roderick Victor *distance learning educator*
Ling, Jun Michael *mathematics professor*
McDonald, Richard Blaise *literature and language professor*
Moore, Hal G. *retired mathematician, educator*
Riley, Dyanne Schrock *music professor*
Sawyer, Thomas Edgar *management consultant*
Schofield, Anthony Wayne *lawyer*
Segelman, Alvin Burton *pharmaceutical executive, educator, research scientist*
Snow, Marlon O. *trucking executive, state agency administrator*
Takke, Karyn Coppock *social worker, educator*

Park City
Becker, William Watters *theater producer*
Cooley, Vernon Jackman *orthopedic surgeon*
Edwards, Howard Lee *retired oil and gas industry executive, lawyer*
Milner, Harold William *hotel executive*
Randt, Clark Thorp, Jr. *former ambassador, lawyer*
Vance, Dianne Sanchez *mathematician, educator*
White, Shaun Roger *Olympic athlete, professional snowboarder, professional skateboarder*

Price
Cha, Pamela Kandaris *communications educator*

Providence
Vest, Hyrum Grant, Jr. *retired horticultural sciences educator*

Provo
Allred, Ruel Acord *education educator*
Anderson, Neil J. *literature and language professor*
Ashworth, Brent Ferrin *lawyer*
Bahr, Howard Miner *sociologist, educator*
Bartlett, Leonard Lee *retired communications educator, advertising executive*
Baum, Kerry Robert *retired military officer, director*
Benzley, Steven E. *engineering educator*
Blake, George Rowland *soil and environmental scientist, educator, researcher*
Bott, Jay Cordell *oncologist, hematologist*
Boyter, Scott M. *academic administrator*
Brown, Ralph Browning *sociologist, educator*
Bullough, Robert Vernon, Jr. *teacher education*
Cheney, Brigham Vernon *physical chemist, consultant*
Christensen, Theodore Edward *educational consultant, educator*
Christianson, Frank Quinn *literature and language professor*
Cooper, Glen M. *history professor*
Cornia, Gary C. *dean, management educator*
Creer, Thomas Laselle *psychologist, educator, writer*
Crookston, R. Kent *agronomy educator*
Cutchins, Dennis R. *literature and language professor*
Fielding, Eric *set designer, educator*
Fox, Frank Wayne *retired history professor*
Geo-Jaja, Macleans A. *economics professor, education educator*
Hauglid, Brian Michael *ancient language educator*
Henderson, Douglas James *physicist, chemist, educator, researcher*
Hill, Ned Cromar *finance educator, consultant, former dean*
Hill, Richard Lee *lawyer*
Holt-Lunstad, Julianne *psychology professor, researcher*
Hoskisson, Paul *religious studies educator, director*
Hughes, (Robert) John *journalist, educator*
Hwang, Chun *cardiologist*
Izatt, Reed M. *chemistry researcher*
Jackson, James F. *nuclear engineer, educator*
Jensen, Clayne R. *retired academic administrator*
Jensen, Michael Allen *engineering educator*
Jensen, Richard Dennis *librarian*
Jensen, Robert J. *business strategy educator*
Johnson, Mark Joseph *art historian, educator*
Lockhart, Barbara Day *physical education educator*
Mendenhall, Bronco *college football coach*
Moss, Shawnda L. *theater educator*
Pedersen, Darhl Max *psychology professor*
Peer, Larry Howard *literature educator*
Pope, C. Arden III *economics professor*
Porter, Blaine Robert Milton *sociology professor, psychology professor*
Powley, Edward Harrison III *music educator*
Prater, Mary Anne *special education educator, researcher*
Rasband, James R. *dean, law educator*
Redford, Robert (Charles Robert Redford) *actor, film director*
Robins, Morris Joseph *chemistry professor, researcher*
Rose, Dave *men's college basketball coach*
Samuelson, Cecil O., Jr. *academic administrator*
Stone, Bernell Kenneth *finance educator*
Sudweeks, Sterling N. *medical educator*
Tanner, Stephen Lowell *retired literature educator*
Thomas, David Albert *law educator, director*
Towne, Justin *biology professor, researcher*
Turley, Robert Steven *physicist, researcher*
Valentine, John Lester *state legislator, lawyer*
Weber, Darrell Jack *plant biochemistry educator*

Willes, Mark Hinckley *media specialist*
Worthen, Kevin *academic administrator, law educator*
York, Neil Longley *history professor*
Youd, T. Leslie *retired civil engineer*

Richmond
Funk, Cyril Reed, Jr. *agronomist, educator*

Saint George
Atkin, Jerry C. *air transportation executive*
Bondanella, Peter *literature and language professor, writer*
Briggs, Robert Keith *musician*
Day, John Denton *small business owner, american quarter horse breeder*
Hodges, Sharon Green *editor, consultant, writer*
Kohl, John Preston *retired finance educator, consultant*
Terry, Gary A. *lawyer, director, former trade association executive*
Walker, Olene S. *former governor*

Salt Lake City
Adams, Joseph Keith *lawyer*
Agarwal, Neeraj *medical educator, researcher*
Allen, Ronald Carl *commissioner, artist, consultant, former state senator, computer company executive*
Anderson, Jeffrey Lance *cardiologist, educator*
Anderson, Ross Carl *Mayor, Salt Lake City, Utah, lawyer, human rights advocate*
Anderson, Stephen Hale *federal judge*
Antommarria, Armand Herbert Matheny *pediatrician, educator*
Barney, Kline Porter, Jr. *engineering company executive, consultant*
Barusch, Lawrence Roos *lawyer*
Bass, Brenda L. *biochemist, educator*
Baucom, Sidney George *lawyer*
Bauer, A(ugust) Robert, Jr. *surgeon*
Bausset Page, Ana *language educator*
Beall, Burtch W., Jr. *architect*
Beauchamp, Christine Marie *apparel executive*
Becker, Ralph Elihu, Jr. *Mayor, Salt Lake City, Utah*
Bell, Gregory S. *Lieutenant Governor of Utah, former state legislator*
Bendinger, Gary Frederick *lawyer*
Benjamin, Lorna Smith *psychologist*
Benson, Dee Vance *federal judge*
Berman, Daniel Lewis *lawyer*
Bhayani, Kiran Lilachand *environmental engineer, programs manager*
Bird, David R. *lawyer*
Bjorkman, David Jess *dean, gastroenterologist, educator*
Black, Wilford Rex, Jr. *state legislator*
Blackburn, Michael Dale *lawyer, educator*
Bliss, Anna Campbell *artist, architect, color consultant*
Bloom, Sherman *retired pathology educator, photographer*
Bodson, Marc *engineering educator*
Boozer, Carlos Austin, Jr. *professional basketball player*
Bouley, Sara Elizabeth *lawyer*
Boylen, Jim *men's college basketball coach*
Brady, Rodney Howard *diversified financial services and broadcast company executive, retired academic administrator, federal official*
Brandon, Kathleen Virginia *retired social studies educator*
Brems, David Paul *architect*
Brown, Carolyn Smith *communications educator, consultant*
Bruggers, Carol S. *pediatrician, educator*
Burke, John Patrick *internist, educator*
Callister, Louis Henry, Jr. *lawyer*
Capecchi, Mario Renato *genetics educator*
Carey, John Clayton *pediatrician, educator, medical geneticist*
Carnahan, Orville Darrell *state legislator, academic administrator*
Carroll, Dana *academic researcher, administrator, educator*
Cassell, Paul George *law educator, former federal judge*
Chillingworth, Lori *bank executive*
Chodosh, Hiram *dean, law educator*
Christensen, Bruce LeRoy *former academic administrator, commercial broadcasting executive*
Christensen, Harold Graham *lawyer*
Christensen, Ray Richards *lawyer*
Christopher, James Walker *architect, educator*
Clark, Deanna Dee *volunteer*
Cornaby, Kay Sterling *lawyer, retired state senator*
Curtis, D. Jay *lawyer*
Cutting, Patricia Grace *publishing executive, educator*
Davis, Gene *state legislator*
Davis, Loyd Evan *defense industry marketing professional*
Dee, David L. *museum director*
Derezotes, David S. *social services administrator, educator*
DeVries, Kenneth Lawrence *mechanical engineer, educator*
Dew, Bill *construction executive*
Dick, Bertram Gale, Jr. *physics professor*
Dole, Janice Gail Arnold *literacy educator*
Drew, Clifford James *psychologist, educator*
Durham, Christine Meaders *state supreme court chief justice*
Durrant, Matthew B. *state supreme court justice*
Elkins, Glen Ray *retired diversified management services company executive*
Ellis, Richard K. *state treasurer*
Esplin, J. Kimo *chemicals executive*
Eyring, Henry Bennion *head of religious order*
Facelli, Julio Cesar *physics researcher, university administrator*
Fehr, John William *newspaper editor*
Firmage, Edwin Brown *lawyer, educator*
Foster, Carol Marvel *pediatric endocrinologist*
Frank, Thomas *construction executive, management and design executive*
Fujinami, Robert Shin *pathologist, researcher*
Futrell, Nancy Nielson *neurologist*
Gandhi, Om Parkash *electrical engineer*
Gao, Zan *physical education educator*
Ghosh, Sambhunath (Sam) *environmental engineer, educator*
Gleich, Gerald Joseph *immunologist, researcher, educator*
Gortatowski, Melvin Jerome *retired chemist*
Graham, Bradley William *design educator*
Grant, Raymond Thomas *arts administrator*
Gray, Douglas D. *child and adolescent psychiatrist*
Greene, John Thomas *judge*
Greenwood, David A. *lawyer*
Gregersen, R(oald) George *newspaper publishing executive*
Grosser, Bernard Irving *psychiatrist, educator*
Guiora, Amos Neuser *law educator*
Hankins, Anthony P. *chemicals executive*
Hardman, Michael L. *dean*
Harris, Frank Ephraim *physics professor*
Haslam, Dennis V. *lawyer, former professional sports team executive*
Hatch, George Clinton *television executive*
Hawker, Charles Davis *biochemist, director*
Herbert, Gary Richard *Governor of Utah*
Ho, Chun-Hsing *civil engineer*
Holding, R(obert) Earl *oil industry executive*
Holland, Wayne, Jr. *political organization administrator*
Huelskamp, Willamarie Ann *artist*
Hull, Grafton Hazard, Jr. *social work educator*
Hulme, Paul G. *chemicals executive*
Huntsman, Jon Meade, Sr. *chemicals company executive*
Huntsman, Peter R. *chemicals executive*
Janát-Amsbury, Margit Maria *gynecologist, educator*
Janatova, Jarmila *biomedical investigator, educator*
Jarvis, Joseph Boyer *retired university administrator*
Jenkins, Bruce Sterling *federal judge*
Jensen, Dallin W. *lawyer*
Jepperson, Thomas C. *lawyer*
Johnson, Xan Stuart *performing arts educator*
Julander, Paula Foil *retired foundation administrator*
Keenan, Thomas J. *chemicals executive*
Kern, Michael J. *chemicals executive*
Kirilenko, Andrei *professional basketball player*
Kirkham, John Spencer *lawyer, director*
Kishore, Bellamkonda Krishna *biomedical researcher, educator*
Kolb, Helga Ellen *retired medical educator*
Krensky, Beth Ellen *artist, educator*
Krizaj, David *neuroscientist, ophthalmologist*
Leary, G. Edward *state banking agency administrator*
Lee, Blaine Nelson *consultant, life coach, writer, author*
Lee, Hosin *civil engineer, educator*
Livne, Nava Levia *psychologist, researcher*
Louie, Janis *chemistry professor*
Madsen, Brigham Dwaine *history professor*
Mango, Susan E. *biologist, educator*
Matlak, Michael Edward *pediatric general surgeon*
Mattis, Daniel Charles *physicist, researcher*
Mauger, John W. *dean, pharmacy educator*
McCleary, Lloyd E(verald) *education educator*
McConnell, Michael W. *federal judge, law educator*
McDermott, Kathleen E. *lawyer, corporate executive*
McKay, Monroe Gunn *federal judge*
Mecham, Glenn Jefferson *lawyer, mayor*
Melton, Arthur Richard *public health administrator*
Mendenhall, Robert W. *education technology executive*
Meyers, Rebecka Louise *pediatric general surgeon*
Middleton, Anthony Wayne, Jr. *urologist, educator*
Miller, Jan Dean *metallurgy educator*
Miller, William Charles *architect, educator*
Mishchenko, Eugene *physics professor*
Monson, Thomas Spencer *religious organization administrator, retired publishing executive*
Mooney, Jerome Henri *lawyer*
Moore, James R. *lawyer*
Morris, Donna Jones *library director*
Moser, Royce, Jr. *preventive medicine physician, educator*
Murphy, Michael R. *federal judge*
Nehring, Ronald E. *state supreme court justice*
Nelson, Roger Hugh *corporate financial executive, educator, consultant*
Nelson, Russell Marion *surgeon, educator*
Newman, Lance B. *literature and language professor*
Ninow, Kevin J. *chemicals executive*
Notarianni, Philip Frank *historian, program coordinator*
Nydegger, Rick D. *lawyer*
O'Connor, Kevin *professional sports team executive*
Okur, Mehmet *professional basketball player*
Olivera, Baldomero M. *biology professor*
Olsen, Steven Lloyd *museum administrator, educator*
Opitz, John Marius *clinical geneticist, pediatrician*
Pace, Nathan Leon *anesthesiologist, educator*
Page, Frank J. *music educator*
Palmer, David Keith *otolaryngologist*
Parkinson, William Woodall *theater educator*
Parrish, Jill Niederhauser *state supreme court justice*
Patel, Amit N. *surgeon, researcher*
Paulsen, Vivian *editor*
Peterson, Joel C. *investment company executive*
Picard, M(eredith) Dane *geologist*
Prospero, Moises *social studies educator, director*
Rattie, Keith O. *gas industry executive*
Reddy, Chakravarthy B. *pulmonologist, educator*
Ridd, Brian V. *chemicals executive*
Rodgers, George Marion *hematologist*
Romney-Manookin, Elaine Clive *retired music educator, composer*
Salisbury, Frank Boyer *botanist, educator, writer*
Salomonson, Vincent Victor *meteorologist, educator*
Saltz, Renato *plastic surgeon*
Sam, David *federal judge*
Sandquist, Gary Marlin *engineering educator, researcher, consultant, writer, military officer*
Scruggs, Samuel D. *lawyer, chemicals executive*
Shepherd, Karen *former congresswoman*
Shimp, Charles Patterson *psychologist, educator*
Shipko, Janet M. *human resources specialist*
Shipman, Jean Pugh *medical librarian*
Shiptsova, Rimma *economics professor*
Shumway, Larry K. *state official, school system administrator*
Shurtleff, Mark L. *state attorney general*
Sigal, Jill Lea *nuclear energy industry executive, former federal agency administrator*
Sillars, Malcolm O. *communications educator*
Simmons, Harris H. *bank executive*
Sklute, Adam *performing company executive, dancer*
Sloan, Jerry (Gerald Eugene Sloan) *professional basketball coach*
Smith, Cynthia M. *bank executive*
Smith, Robert B. *geophysicist, educator*
Sohn, Hong Yong *chemical and metallurgical engineer, educator*
Sorensen, John B. *surgeon*
Sorenson, Stephen Jay *lawyer*
Spangrude, Gerald John *hematologist, researcher*
Speer, William Dale *lab administrator, biology professor*
Stang, Peter John *organic chemist*
Stanutz, Donald J. *chemicals executive*
Stringfellow, Gerald B. *engineering educator*
Sundwall, David N. *state agency administrator, public health service officer*
Switzer, Kathleen Henderson *administrative law judge, clinical nurse specialist*
Tani, Lloyd Yasuo *pediatrician, educator*
Thompson, Neil Daniel *retired lawyer*
Tolman, Brett L. *prosecutor*
Tomsic, Peggy A. *lawyer*
Urie, Alan T. *bank executive*
Waddoups, Clark *federal judge*
Walker, Carlene Martin *state legislator*
Walker Neve, Diana *singer, voice educator*
Wallace, Matthew Walker *retired entrepreneur*
Wallis, M. Chad *medical educator*
Warner, Paul Michael *federal judge, former prosecutor*
Watt, Ronald G. *archivist*
West, Jason Brossard *education educator, consultant*
Wester, John Charles *bishop*
Whittingham, Kyle *college football coach*
Wilkins, Michael Jon *state supreme court justice*
Williams, Deron Michael *professional basketball player*
Williams, George Abiah *physics educator*
Wingate, Martha Anne *writer, publishing executive*
Wingate, Thomas Russell *writer*
Wolf, Harold Herbert *pharmacy educator*
Wolfinger, Nicholas H. *educator*
Wozniak, Steve (Stephen Gary Wozniak) *computer scientist, philanthropist*
Wright, Larry Jan *epidemiologist*
Yan, Xie *systems engineer*
Young, Michael Kent *academic administrator, law educator*
Zimmerman, Michael David *lawyer*

Sandy
Crittenden, Gary Lewis *private equity firm executive*
Durham, Lynn Ellen *school psychologist*
Gentry, Jeffery Scott *history professor*
Miller, Greg *professional sports team executive*
Phillips, Ted Ray *advertising executive*
Rigby, Randy *professional sports team executive*
Smith, Willard Grant *psychologist*
Snell, Marilyn Nelson *psychologist, researcher*
Sokolov, Yuri *engineer*

South Jordan
Larson, Bryan Alan *lawyer*

Springville
Francis, Rell Gardner *artist, photographer, writer*

Stansbury Park
Moyer, Linda Lee *artist, educator, author*

Vernal
Judd, Dennis L. *lawyer*

Washington
De Vany, Arthur Stacy *economics professor*

West Jordan
Gutman, Lucy Toni *social worker, educator*
James, Linda Coates *elementary school educator*

West Valley City
Woodward, Sandra S. *literature and language educator*

Woods Cross
Blackley, Cheryl Ann *musician, freelance/self-employed educator*
Hendriksen, Neil Evan *music educator*

VERMONT

Arlington
Cole, Ann Harriet *psychologist, consultant*
Pond, Thomas Alexander *physics professor, academic administrator*

Barnard
Larson, John Hyde *retired utilities executive*

Barre
Gilbert, Michael D. *secondary school educator*
Heath, Karen *secondary school educator*
Koch, Thomas F. *state legislator*

Bennington
Franklin, Jamie *curator, consultant*
Williams, Robert Joseph *retired museum director, educator*

Brandon
Farnsworth, Frank Albert *retired economics professor*

Brattleboro
Abrams, Jackie *artist, educator*
Agallianos, Dennis Dionysios *psychiatrist*
Ames, Adelbert III *neuroscientist, educator*
Reid, David G. *lawyer*
Smiley, Carol Anne *health facility administrator, sculptor*

Brownsville
Olderman, Gerald *retired medical device company executive*

Burlington
Angell, Kenneth Anthony *bishop emeritus*
Berger, Ritchie Eric *lawyer*
Carew, Lyndon B., Jr. *nutritionist, educator*
Carleton, Ian P. *lawyer, former political organization administrator*
Cate, Richard H. *academic administrator, former state official*
Coffin, Tristram J. *prosecutor*
Cooper, Sheldon Mark *immunologist, rheumatologist, educator, researcher*
Cutler, Stephen Joel *sociologist, educator*
Daniels, Robert Vincent *history professor, former state senator*
Davis, Christopher Lee *lawyer*
Davis, Wendy Sue *state agency administrator, public health service officer*
Dinitz, Jeffrey H. *mathematics professor*
Dinse, John Merrell *lawyer*
Drizo, Aleksandra *researcher, educator*
Escaja, Tina *social studies educator*
First, Lewis Richard *pediatrician*
Fogel, Daniel Mark *academic administrator, literature educator, writer*
Frank, Joseph Elihu *lawyer*
Gabriel, Diane Augusta *artist, educator*
Gennari, F(rank) John *medical educator*
Gogo, Prospero Barquero *cardiologist, director*
Grunberg, Steven Marc *medical educator*
Heinrich, Bernd *biologist, educator*
Hennessey, John William, Jr. *academic administrator, educator*
Hoar, Samuel, Jr. *lawyer*
Hutton, Patrick H. *retired history professor*
Kaelber, Lutz *sociologist, educator*
Kahn, Robbie Pfeufer *humanities educator*
Kascus, Marie Annette *librarian*
Kilpatrick, Charles William *biology professor*
Kuehne, Martin Eric *chemist, educator*
Kunin, Madeleine May *former Governor of Vermont*
Lidofsky, Steven David *medical educator*
Lucey, Jerold Francis *pediatrician*
Marshall, Jeffrey Scott *mechanical engineer, educator*
Matano, Salvatore Ronald *bishop*
Mintz, Keith Peter *research scientist*
Montroll, Andrew H. *lawyer, councilman*
Morin, Frederick C. *dean, pediatrician, educator*
Naylor, Magdalena Raczkowska *psychiatrist, educator*
Neiweem, David *music educator*
Nyborg, Wesley Lemars *physics professor*
Pinder, George Francis *engineering educator, research scientist*
Riddick, Daniel Howison *obstetrician, gynecologist, priest*
Rodgers, Robert Howard *ancient language educator*
Rohan, Kelly J. *psychology professor, researcher*
Sessions, William K. III *federal judge*
Shaw, Naomi *sales consultant, insurance agent, management consultant*
Shelton, Lawrence G. *social sciences educator*
Smith, David Young *physics professor*
Stout, Neil Ralph *retired history educator*
Tampas, John P. *radiologist*
Thomson, Ross David *economics professor*
Vincent, Jennifer A. *economics professor, consultant*
Wu, Junru *physics educator*

Castleton
Roper, Scott Christopher *geographer, researcher*

Charlotte
Melby, Edward Carlos, Jr. *veterinarian*
Naylor, Thomas Herbert *economist, educator, consultant*
Robinson, Sally Winston *artist*

Chester
Coleman, John Royston *writer*

Colchester
Blacketor, Paul Garber *minister*
Kujawa, Richard Stephen *social sciences educator*
Slaybaugh, Douglas Paul *history educator*
Sobel, Burton Elias *cardiologist, educator*
Umanzor-Yashimura, Marta A. *literature educator*

Danby
Peel, Harris *retired small business owner*

Dorset
Bamford, Joseph Charles, Jr. *gynecologist, obstetrician, educator, medical missionary, author*
Hittle, Richard Howard *oil and gas industry executive, consultant*
Marron, Pamela Anne *artist*

East Calais
Low, Anthony *language educator*

Essex Junction
Hook, Terence Blackwell *electrical engineer*
Tedd, Monique Micheline *artist*

Grand Isle
Dufrene, Brian M. *engineering executive*

Jacksonville
Dell, Ralph Bishop *retired pediatrician, researcher*
Hein, Karen Kramer *pediatrician, epidemiologist*

Johnson
Whitehill, Angela Elizabeth *artistic director*
Williams, Peggy Ryan *retired academic administrator*

Lincoln
Kompass, Edward John *consulting editor*

Londonderry
Powers, Ross *Olympic athlete*

Lyndon Center
Dame, William Page III *bank executive, educational administrator*
Downs, John Henry *lawyer*

Lyndonville
Atkins, Nolan Thomas *meteorologist, educator*
Hertz, Barry P. *education educator*
Werdenschlag, Lori B. *psychologist, educator*

Manchester
Carey, James Henry *banker*
Eichel, Charles Richard *lawyer*
Kouwenhoven, Gerrit Wolphertsen *retired museum director*

Manchester Center
Carr, Gerald Paul *retired astronaut, engineer, marketing professional, military officer*

Marlboro
Stevenson, Laura Caroline *writer, educator*

Middlebury
Albers, Jan Maria *historian, museum director*
Bumbeck, David *artist, retired educator*
Ferm, Robert Livingston *religion educator*
Forman, Michele *secondary school educator*
Geier, Philip Otto III *foundation executive, consultant, director, academic administrator*
Grindon, Leger *performing arts educator, writer*
Horlacher, David Edmund *economics professor, researcher*
Jacobs, Travis Beal *historian, educator*
Katz, Michael Ray *Slavic languages educator*
Lamberti, Marjorie *retired social studies educator*
Liebowitz, Ronald D. *academic administrator*
McKenna, William Michael *academic administrator*
McWilliams, John Probasco, Jr. *English literature educator*
Moss, Kevin *literature and language professor*
O'Brien, George Dennis *retired academic administrator*
Raum, Hans L. *librarian*
Robison, Olin Clyde *political science educator, former college president*
Vail, Van Horn *German language educator*
Winkler, Paul Frank, Jr. *astrophysicist, educator*

Montgomery Center
Sauvagnat, Henry Gabriel *entrepreneur, sales executive*

Montpelier
Barbieri, Christopher George *professional society administrator*
Bevans, Judy *political organization administrator*
Burgess, Brian Louis *state supreme court justice*
Diamond, M. Jerome *lawyer, retired state attorney general*
Dooley, John Augustine III *state supreme court justice*
Douglas, Jim (James Holley Douglas) *Governor of Vermont*
Dubie, Brian E. *Lieutenant Governor of Vermont*
Facos, James Francis *language educator*
Gibson, Ernest Willard III *retired state supreme court justice*
Guild, Alden *retired lawyer*
Johnson, Denise Reinka *state supreme court justice*
Keenan, Kathleen *state legislator, nurse*
MacLeay, Thomas H. *insurance company executive*
Markowitz, Deborah Lynn *Secretary of State, Vermont*
McShane, Sybil Brigham *retired library director, librarian*
Nuovo, Betty A. *state legislator, lawyer*
Paquin, Edward H., Jr. *state legislator, not-for-profit developer*
Reiber, Paul L. *state supreme court chief justice*
Roper, Robert *political organization administrator*
Saxman, Anna Esther *lawyer*
Skoglund, Marilyn *state supreme court justice*
Sorrell, William H. *state attorney general*
Spaulding, Jeb (George B. Spaulding) *state treasurer*
Thabault, Paulette J. *state banking agency administrator*
Thwaites, Christian William *investment company executive*
Vilaseca, Armando *state official, school system administrator*

Morrisville
Lechevalier, Hubert Arthur *microbiology educator*
Lechevalier, Mary Pfeil *retired microbiologist, educator*

Newbury
Doig, Jameson Wallace *political science professor*
McGarrell, James *artist, educator*

Newport
Pepyne, Edward Walter *lawyer, psychologist, educator*

North Pomfret
Crowl, John Allen *retired publishing company executive*

Northfield
Benabess, Najiba *economics professor, researcher*
Petrusa, Joshua H. *librarian*
Wick, William Shinn *clergyman, chaplain, pastor*

Norwich
Katz, Arnold Martin *medical educator*
Paine, Walter Cabot *journalist, consultant*
Parker, H. Worth *medical association administrator*
Snapper, Ernst *mathematics professor*
Stamelman, Richard Howard *French and humanities educator*

Pawlet
Buechner, Carl Frederick *minister, author*

Peacham
Barnes, Harry G., Jr. *advocate, consultant*
Engle, James Bruce *ambassador*

Perkinsville
Harris, Christopher *editor, writer, illustrator, graphics designer*

Plainfield
Jervis, Jane Lise *academic administrator, historian*

Poultney
Orr, Andrew S. *landscape artist*

Proctorsville
Harper, Jennifer *elementary school educator*

Putney
Gill, Jane Roberts *retired psychotherapist, clinical social worker*
Keil, John Mullan *advertising executive, artist*

Quechee
DeRouchey, Beverly Jean *investment company executive*
Vitty, Roderic Bemis *retired financial planner, publishing executive*
Wood, R. Stewart, Jr. *retired bishop*

Randolph
Ryerson, Marjorie Gilmour *journalist, poet, photographer, educator*

Richmond
Fary, Sandra Suzanne *science educator*

Rochester
Eddy, John Joseph *diplomat*

Rutland
Carroll, LaShun La Rue *dentist*
Crowley, Arthur Edward, Jr. *lawyer*
Ferraro, Betty Ann *retired state senator*
Haley, John Charles *retired bank executive*

Saint Albans
LeClair, John Clark *professional hockey player*

Saint Johnsbury
Gallagher, James C. *lawyer*
Marshall, John Henry *lawyer*

Shelburne
Anderson, Richard Louis *electrical engineer*
Canfield, Andrew Trotter *lawyer, writer*
Errecart, Joyce *lawyer, former state legislator*
Gilpin, Robert George, Jr. *political science professor*
Mead, Philip Bartlett *retired obstetrician, healthcare administrator, educator*
White, William North *retired chemistry professor*

South Burlington
Emery, Marla R. *geographer, researcher*
Foss, Jean Mitchell *school system administrator*
Gerson, William Thomas *pediatrician*
Hauptman, Robert *retired humanities educator*
Outwater, John Ogden *mechanical engineering educator*
Pizzagalli, James *construction and real estate company executive*
Schaberg, Paul G. *plant physiologist*
Shinozaki, Tamotsu *retired physician, anesthesiologist*

South Londonderry
Spiers, Ronald Ian *diplomat*

South Royalton
Doria, Anthony Notarnicola *college dean, educator*
Goodenough, Oliver Ramsdell *lawyer, educator*
Powers, Thomas Moore *writer*
Wroth, L(awrence) Kinvin *law educator*

Springfield
Guité, J. C. Michel *telephone company owner*
Putnam, Paul Adin *federal agency administrator*

Stowe
Whiteman, Joseph David *retired lawyer, manufacturing company executive*

Strafford
Manheim, Michael *English literature educator*
Williams, William Magavern *headmaster*

Swanton
Suitor, Dorcas P. *elementary school educator*

Thetford
Hoagland, Mahlon *biochemist, educator*

Underhill
Danforth, Elliot, Jr. *medical educator*

Vergennes
Grant, Edwin Randolph *retail and manufacturing executive*
Kamman, Alan Bertram *retired communications consulting company executive*

Waitsfield
Esty, David Cameron *marketing and communications executive*

Warren
Raphael, Albert Ash, Jr. *retired lawyer*
Sullivan, Kathleen *elementary school educator*

Waterbury
Donovan, Timothy *academic administrator*
Hilton, Linda D. *academic administrator*

West Burke
Van Vliet, Claire *artist*

West Glover
Weaver, John Borland *musician, department chairman, composer*

Weston
Stettler, Stephen F. *performing company executive*

White River Junction
Berman, Stephen Alan *neurologist*
Kainen, Michael Roland *lawyer, state representative*
Wallace, Amy Elizabeth *psychiatrist*

Williston
Laskarzewski, Debra Sue *language educator*

Wilmington
Little, Thomas M. *public relations executive*
Reeve, Franklin D. *writer, retired literature professor*

Windsor
Gilbert-Smith, Alma *museum director*

Wolcott
Fisher, Neal Floyd *religious organization administrator*

Woodstock
Billings, Franklin Swift, Jr. *federal judge*
Goulazian, Peter Robert *retired broadcasting executive*
Hoyt, Coleman Williams *postal consultant*
Matlins, Stuart M. *management consultant, publisher*
Zonay, Thomas A. *lawyer*

VIRGINIA

Abingdon
Jones, James Parker *federal judge*
Jones, Mary Trent *endowment fund trustee*
Quillen, Michael J. *energy executive*
Ramos-Cano, Hazel Balatero *caterer, chef, innkeeper, restaurateur, entrepreneur*

Afton
Anderson, Donald Norton, Jr. *retired electrical engineer*
McCoy, Sue *retired surgeon, biochemist, bioethicist*
Rhett, Haskell Emery Smith *educational association administrator*

Alberta
Walker, Stephen D. *history professor*

Alexandria
Adams, Ranald Trevor, Jr. *retired air force officer*
Allen, Ernie (Ernest Eugene Allen) *non-profit organization executive, lawyer*
Anderson, Maynard Carlyle *security firm executive*
Anderson, Steven C. *pharmacy association executive*
Armstrong, Cathal *chef*
Arundel, John Howard *journalist, publisher*
Bailey, Tracey L. *educational association administrator*
Balch, Charles M. *surgeon, educator*
Baroody, Michael Elias *trade association executive*
Barry, Lance Leonard *judge*
Bartels, Teresa Hall *non-profit organization administrator*
Bartlett, Elizabeth Susan *audio-visual specialist*
Beales, Char *marketing executive*
Berger, Patricia Wilson *retired librarian*
Beringer, Ivy *education educator*
Birely, William Cramer *investment banker*
Bombardt, John Nicholas *research scientist*
Bostetter, Martin V. B., Jr. *federal judge*
Bowman, Richard Carl *defense consultant, retired air force officer*
Braun, Michael A. *securities firm executive, retired federal agency administrator*
Brown, Frederic Joseph *military officer*
Bryant, Anne Lincoln *educational association administrator*
Buechner, Jack W(illiam) *lawyer, consultant, Former United States Representative, Missouri, educational association administrator*
Burch, John Thomas, Jr. *lawyer*
Bynum, Gayela A. *public information officer*
Cahill, Mary Beth *political strategist*
Carvalho, Julie Ann *psychologist*
Carville, James, Jr., (Chester James Carville) *political scientist, commentator*
Castellanos, Alex *media consultant*
Charlip, Ralph Blair *military officer, health facility administrator*
Chen, Fen *mathematician, educator, researcher*
Collins, Cardiss *retired congresswoman*
Connaughton, Sean Thomas *lobbyist, former federal agency administrator*
Connell, Mary Ellen *diplomat*
Cook, Charles William *aerospace engineer, educator, consultant*
Coons, Barbara Lynn *public relations executive, librarian*
Corrothers, Helen Gladys *criminal justice official*
Costagliola, Francesco *retired government official*
Cressey, Pamela J. *archaeologist, museum director*
Cross, Eason, Jr. *architect*
Crum, Richard *air transportation executive*
Crundwell, Duncan James *electronics executive*
Davis, Richard H. (Rick Davis) *lobbyist*
Devantier, Paul W. *religious organization administrator, broadcast executive*
Drennan, Joseph Peter *lawyer*
Duncan, Richard Ray *history professor*
Ebi, Kristie L. *consultant*
Ellis, Thomas Selby III *federal judge*
Ellmore, Mark *real estate consultant*
Falcon, Armando J., Jr. *consulting firm executive*
Fedorochko, William, Jr. *retired military officer, analyst*
Fisher, Donald Wayne *medical association administrator*
Fitton, Harvey Nelson, Jr. *former government official*
Fleming, Douglas Riley *journalist, publishing executive, consultant*
Flynn, Arlene A. *pharmacy association administrator*
Fosdick (Beebe), Cora Prifold *management consultant*
Foster, Robert Francis *communications executive*
Frommer, Lawrence Julian *retired travel company executive*
Fryzel, Michael E. *federal agency administrator, lawyer*
Gage, Alex P. *marketing consultant*
Gallagher, Anne Porter *communications executive*
Georges, Peter John *lawyer*
Gernand, Bradley Elton *archivist, librarian*
Goolrick, Robert Mason *legal consultant*
Gould, Phillip *engineer*
Greenstein, Ruth Louise *think-tank executive, lawyer*
Gurke, Sharon McCue *career officer*
Gurney, Robert M. *architectural firm executive*
Gwadosky, Dan A. *former state official, federal agency administrator*
Hammad, Alam E. *international business consultant, author educator*
Hark, William Henry *retired federal agency administrator, aerospace physician*
Harris, Dale William *systems engineer*
Harris, David Ford *management consultant, retired federal official*
Harrison, Marion Edwyn *lawyer*
Hausner, Laurence *health science association administrator*
Havens, Harry Stewart *retired federal official, management consultant*
Haygood, Alma Jean *elementary school educator*
Helman, Gerald Bernard *diplomat*
Hilton, Claude Meredith *federal judge*
Hirsch, Robert Louis *energy analyst, consultant*
Hobbs, Michael Edwin *retired broadcast executive*
Hood, Rodney Eugene *federal agency administrator*
Hudgins, David Drake *lawyer*
Hughes, Grace-Flores *federal agency administrator*
Hyland, Gigi (Christiane Hyland) *federal agency administrator*
Jacobson, Lawrence Albert *professional society administrator, lawyer*
Jenkins, John Smith *retired dean, lawyer*
Johnson, Edgar McCarthy *psychologist*
Jonas, Wayne B. *physician, researcher*
Kaplowitz, Lisa Glauser *physician, educator*
Kappos, David J. *federal agency administrator*
Karpiscak, John III *engineer, army officer*
Kelly, Nancy Frieda Wolicki *lawyer*
Knechtmann, James Allen *archivist, researcher*
Kolesnikov, Evgeni *surgeon, scientist, consultant*
Kollander, Mel *social scientist, statistician, economist*
Kopp, Eugene Paul *lawyer*
Kotlarchuk, Ihor O.E. *lawyer*
Krall, Jonathan Francis *physicist, researcher*
Kratovil, Jane Lindley *think tank associate, not-for-profit developer*
Kroesen, Frederick James *retired army officer, consultant*
Krueger, Gerald Peter *psychologist*
Kruse, Dennis K. *professional society administrator, retired military officer*
Lachance, Janice Rachel *professional association and federal agency administrator, lawyer*
Lang, William George, IV, *public policy administrator*
Laurent, Lawrence Bell *communications executive, retired journalist*
Leahy, Pat (P. Patrick Leahy) *geologist, former federal official*
Leestma, Robert *retired federal agency and educational association administrator*
Lenz, Edward Arnold *trade association administrator, lawyer*
Leonhart, Michele Marie *federal agency administrator*
Lichter, Allen S. *oncologist, medical association administrator*
Lightner, Candy (Candace Lynne Lightner) *non-profit management consultant, advocate*
Lipnick, Anne Ruth *advocate*
Lipnick, Robert Louis *chemist, toxicologist*
Loren, Donald Patrick *federal official, retired military officer*
Lundeberg, Philip Karl Boraas *curator, historian*
Mack, Carl B. *engineering executive*
Mackay, James Cobham *museum director*
MacLaren, William George, Jr. *engineering executive*
Malott, John Raymond *writer, consultant, not-for-profit executive*
Manson, Connie Jeane *librarian*
Markham, Ian Stephen *theology studies educator, dean*
Masterson, Kleber Sanlin, Jr. *physicist*
Matalin, Mary Joe *political consultant, editor*
McAndrews, Lawrence A. *medical association administrator*
McConville, Judy Allen *social studies educator*
McDowell, Charles Eager *lawyer, retired military officer*

McGuire, Edward David, Jr. *lawyer*
McKinnon, Russell F. *professional society administrator*
McMillan, Charles William *consulting company executive*
McNicol, David Leon *retired federal official, researcher*
Montague, Robert Latane III *lawyer*
Mossinghoff, Gerald Joseph *lawyer, educator*
Muir, Warren Roger *chemist, educator*
Nelson, David Leonard *business executive*
Neustadt, Arthur I. *lawyer*
Nodeen, Janey Price *information technology executive*
O'Grady, Liam *federal judge*
Pastin, Mark Joseph *health science association administrator, educator*
Paturis, E(mmanuel) Michael *lawyer*
Pearson, Lynda Ann *music educator*
Piecuch, Diane Marie *music educator*
Poehlein, Gary Wayne *retired chemical engineering professor*
Powell, Colin Luther *former United States Secretary of State, former chairman of the Joint Chiefs of Staff*
Puscheck, Elizabeth Ella *physician*
Pyle, Howard *lawyer, consultant*
Quirk, Frank Joseph *management consulting company executive*
Rabun, John Brewton, Jr. *criminal justice agency administrator*
Rayman, Russell Barry *physician*
Rector, John Michael *pharmaceutical association executive, lawyer*
Ritts, Leslie Sue *lawyer*
Romney, Carl F. *seismologist*
Saunders, Steven R. *international public policy specialist*
Scheibel, Kenneth Maynard *journalist*
Shern, David L. *mental health services professional, former dean*
Shirley, Craig P. *public relations executive, writer*
Smith, Elaine Diana *foreign service officer*
Smith, Jeffrey Greenwood *retired military officer*
Spencer, George Henry *lawyer*
Stanton, John Jeffrey *editor, director, journalist, government agency administrator, educator*
Stevens, Ron A. *lawyer, advocate, surveyor*
Stone, Ann Elizabeth *marketing agency executive, entrepreneur, volunteer, consultant*
Straub, Peter Thornton *lawyer*
Todd, Matthew *school librarian*
Toulmin, Priestley *retired geologist*
Trenga, Anthony John *federal judge*
Tucker, Alvin Leroy *retired government official*
Tucker, Howard McKeldin *investment banker, consultant*
Turner, Grace-Marie *non-profit organization executive*
Verburg, Edwin Arnold *management consultant*
Von Drehle, Ramon Arnold *lawyer*
Vosbeck, Elizabeth Just *retired geneticist*
Vosbeck, William Frederick, Jr. *architect*
Walker, Edward Keith, Jr. *retired management consultant, military officer*
Wasserstein, Ronald L. *statistics organization director*
Weinrich, Brian Erwin *mathematician, computer scientist*
Weisberg, Leonard R. *retired engineering executive, researcher*
Wilcox, David Eric *electrical engineering, educator, consultant, business owner*
Williams, John Edward *lawyer*
Wilson, Charles H. (Charles Harrison Wilson) *retired air force officer, financial planner, human resource development professional*
Winkenwerder, William, Jr. *consulting firm executive, former federal agency administrator*
Wolff, Robert D. *professional society administrator*
Yamamoto, Alan H. *lawyer*
Yoder, Edwin Milton, Jr. *columnist, educator, editor, writer*
Zissios, Patricia Ann *principal*

Altavista

McNiel, Robyn E. *psychologist*

Amissville

Hartke, Anita *real estate broker*
Hunter, Beverly Claire *research scientist, educator*

Annandale

Caporale, Jill Fredrica *biology professor*
Christianson, Geryld B. *government agency administrator, consultant*
Freeman, Baba Foster *editor*
Gorsen, Robert Marc *neurosurgeon*
Greinke, Everett Donald *management consultant*
Jollie, Susan Barbara *lawyer*
Khim, Jay Wook *information technology executive*
Kim, Stephen S. *surgeon, educator*
Lim, Hyunsik *lawyer*
Matuszko, Anthony Joseph *research chemist, administrator, educator*
Ochs, Walter J. *civil engineer, consultant*
Passut, Christine Diana *special education educator*
Peck, Nan J. *academic administrator*
Rogers, Stephen Hitchcock *retired ambassador*
Shamburek, Roland Howard *physician*
Vander Maten, Mary Ann *biology professor, dean*
Walters, Karen M. *mathematics professor*

Appomattox

Beatson, LeGrande Guerry *environmental health specialist*

Arlington

Adams, Jimmie Vick *communications systems company executive, retired military officer*
Adcock, Samuel Denton *lobbyist, former legislative director*
Aggrey, Orison Rudolph *former ambassador, consultant, academic administrator*
Allard, Dean Conrad *historian, retired historical center director*
Anthony, Robert Armstrong *lawyer, educator*
Armitage, Richard Lee *consulting firm executive, former federal agency administrator*
Arnold, Gary Howard *film critic*
Baginski, Maureen A. *former federal agency administrator*
Becker, Fred Reinhardt, Jr. *association executive, lawyer, retired military officer*
Beehler, Bruce McPherson *research zoologist, ornithologist, conservationist*
Bement, Arden Lee, Jr. *engineering educator, government agency administrator*
Berger, Dan (Brian Daniel Berger) *lobbyist*
Bigeleisen, Jacob *chemist, educator*
Blakey, Marion Clifton *aerospace association executive, former federal agency administrator*
Blum, Steven (H. Steven Blum) *career military officer*
Bolster, Archie Milburn *retired foreign service officer*
Bond, Phillip J. *technology association executive, former advertising executive*
Boorstein, Laurence *economist, educator*
Boudreau, Bruce *professional hockey coach*
Bowen, Stuart W., Jr. *federal official*
Brady, Jim (James M. Brady) *editor*
Brenner, Edgar H. *legal association administrator*
Brighton, John A. *mechanical engineer, academic administrator*
Bromley, Marilyn Modlin *librarian*
Buchanan, Louise *political organization worker, consultant*
Cadby, Carol *theater educator, director*
Calland, Albert M. III *information technology executive, former federal official, retired military officer*
Chatfield, William Austin *federal official*
Cheney, David Warren *science and technology policy analyst, executive*
Choksi, Mary Claire *investment company executive*
Chubb, Talbot Albert *physicist, consultant*
Clapman, Leah Meredith *public television editor*
Clark, Chris *professional hockey player*
Clarke, Richard Alan *management consultant, former federal official*
Claussen, Eileen Barbara *environmental services administrator, former federal agency administrator*
Clayton, James Edwin *journalist*
Coe, Doug *religious organization administrator*
Cofoni, Paul Michael *information technology executive*
Cohen, Sheldon Irwin *lawyer*
Cole, Steven Jay *trade association administrator*
Covington, James Edwin *government agency administrator, psychologist*
Cox, Henry *engineer, researcher*
Crouch, Richard Edelin *lawyer*
Culligan, Thomas M. *electronics executive*
David, Ruth A. *public service research institute executive*
Debney, George C. *mathematical physicist*
DeFeo, Charles Joesph *Internet company executive*
DeFilippi, George *retired air force officer*
Delaney, Raighne C. *lawyer*
Demetrion, James Thomas *retired museum director, consultant*
Dobbins, Jim (James Francis Dobbins Jr.) *think-tank executive, former federal agency administrator*
Dodgen, Larry J. *career military officer*
Dooley, Cal (Calvin Millard Dooley) *trade association administrator, former US Representative from California*
Dorman, Janet Lee Vosper *elementary school educator*
Drayton, Bill (William Drayton) *social entrepreneur, lawyer, management consultant*
Dunlap, William *artist, critic, educator*
Dunn, Michael M. *military association executive, retired military officer*
Earl, Sister Patricia Helene *director, educator*
Elsberg, John William *publishing executive, writer*
Erb, Karl Albert *physicist, government official*
Erwin, Frank William *human resources consultant*
Fay, Kevin J. *public relations executive*
Feinstein, Lee A. *political organization worker*
Ferraz, Francisco Marconi *neurological surgeon*
Fischer, Iván *conductor*
Flinn, Charles Gallagher *lawyer, priest*
Franklin, Jude Eric *electronics executive*
Frederick, William George DeMott *defense company executive, consultant*
Fuchs, Roland John *geography educator, academic administrator*
Fulton, Michael (C. Michael Fulton) *lobbyist*
Futrell, John William *environmental agency executive, lawyer*
Gabelnick, Henry Lewis *medical research administrator*
Gainer, Ronald Lee *lawyer*
Galloway, William Jefferson *retired foreign service officer*
Garcia, Eugene Ernest *federal agency administrator*
Gergely, Tomas Esteban *astronomer*
Giordano, James Joseph *neuroscientist, neuroethicist, pain specialist*
Glass, Andrew James *newspaper editor*
Gluski, Andrés R. *electric power industry executive*
Gracey, James Steele *retired coast guard officer, management consultant, director*
Graves, Bill (William Preston Graves) *transportation association executive, former Governor of Kansas*
Graves, Ernest, Jr. *retired army officer, consultant, engineer*
Green, Richard Alan *retired lawyer*
Gunderson, Steven Craig *association executive, former congressman*
Gunn, Joseph Ridgeway III *consulting economist*
Hackenson, Elizabeth *electric power industry executive*
Hall, Carl William *agricultural and mechanical engineer*
Hamilton, Anthony *singer*
Hanrahan, Paul Thaddeus *electric power industry executive*
Hansen, Kenneth D. *lawyer, ophthalmologist*
Hariadi, John Wesley *otolaryngologist, surgeon*
Harker, Victoria D. *electric power industry executive*
Harrison, Emmett Bruce, Jr. *corporate communications counselor*
Harrison, Virginia M. *federal agency administrator*
Heinemeier, Dan C. *science association director*
Hellmuth, George William *architect*
Helm, Bob (Robert Wilbur Helm) *lobbyist, former federal official*
Helm, Roger Charles *environmental services administrator*
Herbst, Robert LeRoy *organization executive*
Hickman, Elizabeth Podesta *retired counselor*
Hill, Christopher Thomas *professor*
Hokborg, Sven-Olof *military officer*
Houston, Paul David *educational association administrator*
Huff, Jimmy *finance company executive, director*
Hullin, Tod Robert *aerospace transportation executive*
Hunter, J(ohn) Robert *insurance consumer advocate*
Ifill, Gwen *moderator, political reporter*
Jacoby, Lowell Edwin (Jake Jacoby) *information technology executive, retired military officer*
Jarris, Paul *medical association administrator, former state agency administrator, physician*
Jehn, Christopher *economist*
Johnson, Charles Owen *retired lawyer*
Jones, Lawrence Andrew *research scientist, retired military officer*
Junker, Bobby Ray *research and development company executive, physicist*
Kang, Mikyung *application developer, researcher*
Kelly, John James *lawyer*
Kerger, Paula Arnold *broadcast executive*
Kerns, Wilmer Lee *researcher*
Kicklighter, Claude Milton (Mick Kicklighter) *academic administrator, former federal agency administrator*
Kneuer, John M.R. *information technology executive, former federal agency administrator*
Korman, James William *lawyer*
Kosarin, Jonathan Henry *lawyer, teacher, consultant*
Koury, Agnes Lillian *real estate property manager*
Krys, Sheldon Jack *retired diplomat*
Lala, Jaynarayan Hotchand *computer engineer*
Langley, Harold David *historian, retired educator*
Lee, Kangjin David *engineer*
Lehrer, Jim (James Charles Lehrer) *reporter, journalist*
Leland, Marc Ernest *trust company executive, consultant, lawyer*
Lenhardt, Alfonso Emanuel *federal official, retired career officer, foundation administrator*
Leslie, Gregg P. *lawyer*
Liddy, G. Gordon (George Gordon Liddy, Gordon Liddy) *radio personality, writer, former federal official*
Little, Caroline H. *publishing executive*
Lobstein, Marion Blois *biology professor*
Lohr, Michael F. *lawyer*
London, J. Phillip (Jack London) *information technology executive*
Loverde, Paul Stephen *bishop*
Luchok, Joseph Alan *communications executive, consultant*
Lundeen, William Bruce *radiologist*
MacDougall, William Lowell *magazine editor*
MacNeil, Robert Breckenridge Ware *retired journalist, writer*
Magrath, Michael P. *marketing executive, director*
Markessini, Joan *research scientist, psychologist*
Martin, Harry C. *lawyer*
Martin, Linda Gaye *demographer, economist*
Matthews, Allan Freeman *geologist*
McCaffrey, Barry Richard *consulting firm executive, retired military officer*
McDermott, Francis Owen *retired lawyer*
McDonald, Bernard Robert *retired federal agency administrator*
Mc Donald, Gail Faber *musician, educator*
Mc Donald, John Warlick *diplomat*
McKenzie, Walter L., Jr. *information technology executive, consultant*
McKinley, Craig R. *career military officer*
McPhee, George *professional sports team executive*
McTigue, Maurice P. *director*
Mellor, Chip (William H. Mellor) *lawyer*
Miles, Shirley *school system administrator*
Miller, Brian A. *lawyer, electric power industry executive*
Moore, Guy Will *retired public information officer, historian, writer*
Moris, Francisco *senior analyst*
Muller-Parker, Gisèle Thèrése *marine biologist, educator*
Muñoz, George *investment company executive, former federal agency administrator*
Musgrave, Marilyn Neoma *former United States Representative from Colorado*
Nash, Anthony J. *military analyst*
Nash, Bob J. *political organization worker*
Neikirk, William Robert *retired journalist*
Newburger, Beth Weinstein *communications executive*
Ng, Kam Wing *mechanical engineer, researcher*
Nirschl, Robert Phillip *orthopedic surgeon*
Ochmanek, David Alan *defense analyst*
Ochoa-Brillembourg, Hilda Margarita *investment banker*
O'Day, Paul Thomas *trade association executive*
O'Keefe, Sean Charles *manufacturing executive, former academic administrator*
Olsen, Kathie Lynn *science foundation director*
Ordway, Frederick Ira III *science educator, consultant, researcher, writer*
O'Sullivan, Lynda Troutman *lawyer*
Page, Harry Robert *business administration educator*
Palmer, Larry Leon *foundation administrator, former ambassador*
Parker, Jeffrey Scott *law educator*
Pendleton, Mary Catherine *retired foreign service officer*
Polsby, Daniel D. *dean, law educator*
Potvin, William Tracey *management consultant*
Pyatt, Everett Arno *federal official*
Rabbitt, Linda D. *construction executive*
Rahman, Muhammad Abdur *mechanical engineer*
Rajan, Ramkishen S. *economist, educator*
Rao, Neomi *law educator*
Ray, Gilbert T. *lawyer*
Regnery, Alfred Scattergood *publishing executive*
Ren, Chiang H. *aerospace engineer*
RisCassi, Robert W. *communications systems company executive, retired military officer*
Robb, Chuck (Charles Spittal Robb) *law educator, former United States Senator from Virginia*
Rockefeller, Sharon Percy *broadcast executive*
Rogers, Alan Victor *former career officer*
Rogers, James Frederick *banker, management consultant*
Rossides, Gale D. *federal agency administrator*
Rousselot, Peter Frese *lawyer, consultant*
Russell, William Trower III *small business owner*
Salmon, William Cooper *mechanical engineer, company executive*
Salter, Mark *speechwriter*
Sanz, Luis E. *gynecologist, educator*
Scarborough, Robert Henry, Jr. *entrepreneur*
Schaeffer, Eric D. *theater director, performing company executive*
Schmidt, Paul Wickham *lawyer*
Semin, Alexander *professional hockey player*
Sharp, Barry J. *school system administrator*
Shlesinger, Michael F *physicist, educator*
Siegel, Laurie F. *accountant, painter*
Simonson, David C. *retired newspaper association executive*
Smith, Louis John *historian*
Solis Doyle, Patti *political campaign worker*
Stevens, Donald King *retired aeronautical engineer, consultant*
Stickler, Richard E. *federal agency administrator*
Stombler, Robin *health science association administrator*
Stone, Stuart Lee Morrison *librarian, language educator*
Stoner, John Richard *federal agency administrator*
Stoto, Michael A. *statistician, epidemiologist*
Sullivan, Gordon R. *military association executive, retired military officer*
Sundquist, James Lloyd *retired political scientist*
Sundquist, M. Alexandra (Alix Sundquist) *diplomat, consultant*
Swetnam, Michael S. *think-tank executive*
Tang, William C. *electrical engineer*
Tannenwald, Peter *lawyer*
Tarpgaard, Peter Thorvald *naval architect*
Theodore, Jose *professional hockey player*
Tichenor, Charles Beckham III *operations research analyst*
Timperlake, Edward Thomas *writer*
Tolchin, Susan Jane *political science professor, writer*
Vitz, Paul Clayton *psychologist, educator*
Vuono, Carl E. *communications systems company executive, retired military officer*
Wagner, Caroline S. *research and development company executive*
Wagner, Robin Judy *interior designer, consultant*
Wahlquist, Andrew Folkman *government affairs executive*
Walcher, Greg E. *small business owner*
Walker, Woodrow Wilson *retired lawyer, real estate investor, farmer*
Walther, Larry Woodrow *federal agency administrator*
Warshawsky, Mark Joel *public finance and labor economist, former federal policy official*
Watkins, Birge Swift *real estate investment executive*
Watkins, Deborah Karen *epidemiology investigator, educator*
Wheat, Alan Dupree *former Congressman, political consultant*
Whitcomb, James Hall *geophysicist, foundation administrator*
White, Dale Timothy (Tim White) *television journalist, producer*
Whittier, Barbara J (Bobbie) *retired biology and chemistry educator*
Wilcox, Shirley Jean Langdon *genealogist*
Wilderotter, James Arthur *lawyer*
Williams, Maggie (Margaret Ann Williams) *political campaign manager, former federal official*
Wilson, Wendy Marie *elementary school educator, consultant*
Xuan, Jianhua Jason *engineering educator*
Zorthian, Barry *communications executive*
Zywicki, Todd Joseph *law educator*

Ashburn

Bawa, Raj *biotechnology educator, nanotechnologist*
Boyne, Walter James *writer, retired museum director*
Cerrato, Vinny *professional sports team executive*
Flaherty, Michael Paul *lawyer, investment banker*
Gold, George Myron *lawyer, editor, writer, consultant*
Green, James *medical educator*
Hall, DeAngelo *professional football player*
Harting, Harry Lloyd, Jr. *retired government agency administrator, military officer*
Haynesworth, Albert III *professional football player*
Moss, Santana Terrell *professional football player*
Newell, Rachel Pierce *music educator*
Nickle, Dennis Edwin *electronics engineer, consultant, deacon*
Pavsek, Daniel Allan *banker, educator*
Portis, Clinton *professional football player*
Rao, Jagadeesh Sridhara *research scientist*
Riddiford, Lynn Moorhead *biologist, educator*
Rubin, Gerald Mayer *biochemistry researcher, educator*
Sanfelici, Arthur H(ugo) *editor, writer*
Shannon, Thomas Alfred *retired educational association administrator emeritus*
Snyder, Daniel *professional sports team executive*
Zorn, Jim (James Arthur Zorn) *professional football coach, retired professional football player*

Ashland
Inge, Milton Thomas *American literature and culture educator, author*

Axton
Bestler, J. Michael *columnist, retired surgeon*

Baskerville
Boyd, John Wesley, Jr. *trade association administrator, farmer*

Bassett
Spilman, Robert Henkel *furniture company executive*

Bedford
Day, Mark Ronald *history educator, reenactor*
Rasoul, Sam *entrepreneur*

Bentonville
Halm, Nancye Studd *retired academic administrator*

Big Stone Gap
Moore, Rosa-lee *information technology executive*
Powers, Roy Daryl, Jr. *engineering educator*

Blacksburg
Agah, Masoud *electrical engineer, educator*
Akers, Robert Michael *physiologist, educator*
Aref, Hassan *fluid mechanics engineer, educator*
Arnold, Jesse Charles *retired statistician*
Asryan, Levon V. *physicist, electronics engineer, materials scientist*
Bailey, Annette F. *librarian*
Baisden, Andrew Carson *electrical engineer, researcher*
Ball, Sheryl *economics professor*
Batra, Romesh Chander *engineering educator, researcher*
Beamer, Frank *college football coach*
Benson, Richard Carter *mechanical engineer, educator, dean*
Bliznakov, Milka Tcherneva *architect, educator*
Brewer, Karen Jenks *chemistry educator*
Brown, Gary Sandy *electrical engineering educator*
Burkhart, Harold Eugene *forester, educator*
Campbell, Joan Virginia Loweke *secondary school and language educator*
Cao, Yang *research scientist, educator*
Cimini, Daniela *cell biologist, educator*
Cowles, Joe Richard *biology professor*
Dautartas, Mino (Minodaugas) Fernand *physical chemist*
De Datta, Surajit Kumar *soil scientist, agronomist, educator*
Dietrich, Andrea M. *environmentalist, educator*
Disney, Ralph L(ynde) *retired industrial engineering educator*
Doswald, Herman Kenneth *language educator, retired academic administrator*
Du, Yu *research scientist*
Edwards, Marc A. *civil engineer, educator*
Ekkad, Srinath V. *engineering educator, researcher*
Farmer, Ted Anthony *history professor*
Giovanni, Nikki (Yolanda Cornelia Giovanni) *poet, educator*
Gray, Festus Gail *electrical engineer, educator, researcher*
Graybeal, Jack Daniel *chemist, educator*
Greenberg, Seth *men's college basketball coach*
Grover, Norman LaMotte *theologian, philosopher*
Hong, Dennis Wonsuh *engineering educator, researcher*
Hovakimyan, Naira *mathematician, educator*
Jannuzi, F. Tomasson *economics professor*
Kelly, James Michael *plant and soil scientist*
Mahmoodi, Seyed Nima *engineering educator*
Mitchell, James Kenneth *civil engineer, educator*
Mo, Luke Wei *physicist, researcher*
Moore, Laurence John *business educator*
Nowak, Jerzy *educational association administrator, horticulture professor, director*
Pasupathy, Raghu *engineering educator*
Patterson, Douglas MacLennan *finance educator*
Phadke, Arun G. *engineering educator*
Pickrell, Gary R. *engineering educator, director*
Poole, Scott *architect, educator*
Price, Dennis Lee *industrial engineer, educator*
Randall, Clifford Wendell *civil engineer, educator*
Rodriguez-Camilloni, Humberto Leonardo *architect, historian, educator*
Saacke, Richard George *retired biology professor*
Schetz, Joseph Alfred *aerospace engineer, educator*
Schmittmann, Beate *physics professor*
Serrano, Elena Lidia *nutritionist, educator*
Squires, Arthur Morton *chemical engineer, educator*
Steger, Charles William *academic administrator*
Stremler, Mark Andrew *engineering educator, researcher*
Thorp, James Shelby *electrical engineering educator*
Torgersen, Paul Ernest *academic administrator, educator*
Uysal, Muzaffer Shamil *management educator*
Varadarajan, Srinidhi *computer scientist*
Walker, Richard David *retired civil engineer*
Wang, Shuo *engineering researcher*
Weaver, Pamela Ann *education educator*
Witonsky, Sharon *veterinarian, educator*
Yan, Jiao *marine biologist, educator*
Yuan, Lijuan *engineering educator*

Blue Ridge
Elmore, Walter A. *electrical engineer, consultant*

Bluemont
Kobetz, Richard William *criminologist, consultant*

Boston
Fisher, John Morris *association official, business executive, educator*

Bridgewater
Elick, Catherine Lilly *literature and language professor*
Porter, Lisa *sociologist, educator*
Siders, David L. *oil industry executive, educator*

Bristol
Tolbert, John Lee *literature and language educator*

Bristow
Schrock, Simon *wholesale executive*

Broadway
Helbert, Sharon Bunch *retired special education educator*

Buchanan
Cole, Evelyn Marie *day care administrator*

Burke
Bishop, Alfred Chilton, Jr. *lawyer*
Hipfel, Steven J. *lawyer*
Jeremiah, David Elmer *retired military officer*
Shen, Weixing *meteorologist*
Woodruff, C(harles) Roy *retired professional association executive, consultant*

Callao
Freeman, Anne Hobson *language educator, writer*

Capeville
Spady, Joanne Smith *secondary school educator*

Catlett
Broderick, Anthony James *air transportation executive*

Centreville
De Gennaro, Eida Mendoza *interpreter, real estate agent*
Fells, Robert Marshall *lawyer, business executive*

Chantilly
Austin, Wanda Murry *systems engineer*
Becker, James Richard *lawyer*
Carlson, Robert Charles *financial planner, writer*
Fimian, Keith *property inspection company executive*
Large, Scott F. *federal agency administrator*
Pocalyko, Michael Nicholas *investment banker, venture capitalist*

Charlottesville
Abbot, William Wright *history professor*
Abraham, Henry Julian *retired political science professor*
Aldrich, Clarence Knight *physician, educator*
Andrews, Minerva Wilson *retired lawyer*
Andrews, William Lester Self Self *chemistry educator*
Aylor, James Hiram *engineering educator*
Balogun, Rasheed Abiodun *physician and medical educator*
Battestin, Martin Carey *retired literature and language professor*
Bednar, Michael John *architecture educator*
Belanger, Terry *historian, educator*
Beller, George A. *cardiologist, educator*
Bennett, Tony (Anthony G. Bennett) *men's college basketball coach*
Berger, Toby *electrical engineer, educator*
Bonnie, Richard Jeffrey *lawyer, educator, consultant*
Bouchard, Larry Drennen *religious studies educator*
Brown, Holmes *public relations executive*
Bruner, Robert Frank *dean, business educator*
Bull, George Albert *retired banker*
Cannaday, Billy K., Jr. *dean, former state official, school system administrator*
Cannon, Jonathan Z. *law educator*
Cantrell, Robert Wendell *otolaryngologist, head and neck surgeon, educator*
Carey, Robert Munson *physician, educator*
Carter, Bruce Thomas *ophthalmologist*
Carter, William Walton *physicist, researcher*
Casey, John Dudley *writer, language educator*
Casteen, John Thomas III *academic administrator*
Chandler, Lawrence Bradford, Jr. *lawyer*
Chapel, Robert Clyde *theater director, educator*
Cherry, Kenneth Jerome, Jr. *surgeon*
Chevalier, Robert Louis *nephrologist, educator, medical researcher*
Chevalier, Roger Alan *astronomy educator, consultant*
Clore, Gerald L. *psychology professor*
Colker, Marvin Leonard *classics educator*
Colley, John Leonard, Jr. *management consultant, educator, writer*
Cornell, Dewey Gene *psychologist*
Cotton, William Donaldson, Jr. *astronomer*
Crabtree, Loren William *history professor, former academic administrator*
Crackel, Theodore Joseph *historian*
Crutchfield, William Gayle, Jr. *retail executive*
Daugherty, Leo *literature and language educator*
Davidson, Hugh MacCullough *French language and literature educator*
Davis, Edward Wilson *business administration educator*
De Colle, Simone *finance educator, researcher*
DeKosky, Steven Trent *dean, neurologist*
DeLoache, Judy Sprague *psychology professor*
DeMong, Richard Francis *finance and investments educator*
Dorning, John Joseph *nuclear engineering, applied physics and applied mathematics educator*
Dotson, Donald L. *lawyer*
Dove, Rita Frances *poet, language educator*
Drake, David Bartleson *medical educator*
Elzinga, Kenneth Gerald *economics professor*
Epstein, Robert Marvin *anesthesiologist, educator*
Fink, Lester Harold *retired engineering company executive, educator*
Finley, Robert Van Eaton *minister*
Fitchett, Taylor *law librarian*
Fitzgerald, Mark *engineering educator*
Flickinger, Charles John *anatomist, educator*
Forbes, John Douglas *architectural and economic historian*
Forrest, Patricia Anne *publishing executive, editor*
Fox, Charles Dunsmore, IV, *lawyer*
Fredrick, Laurence William *astronomer, educator*
Gaden, Elmer Lewis *retired engineering educator*
Galazka, Sim Stevens *medical educator, department chairman*
Gallagher, Thomas Francis *physicist*
Garber, Nicholas Jack *civil engineer, educator*
Garrett, Reginald Hooker *biology professor, researcher*
Garson, Arthur, Jr. *academic administrator, medical educator*
Gaskin, Felicia *biochemist, educator*
Gasman, Lydia Casto *art historian, educator*
Goetz, Charles John *law and economics educator*
Good, Richard Standish *geologist*
Goodrich, George Herbert *retired judge*
Graebner, Norman Arthur *historian, educator*
Grimes, Russell Newell *inorganic chemist, educator*
Guise, Theresa A. *endocrinologist, educator*
Gunter, Bradley Hunt *capital management executive*
Gwaltney, Jack Merrit, Jr. *physician, educator, scientist*
Haimes, Yacov Yosseph *systems and civil engineering educator, consultant*
Haines, Gerald Kenneth *retired historian*
Hammarskjold, Marie-Louise Anna *microbiologist, educator*
Handler, Jerome Sidney *anthropology educator*
Hanft, Ruth S. Samuels *economist, consultant*
Harding, Harry *dean, political scientist, educator, consultant*
Hartz, Jill *museum director*
Henderson, Stanley Dale *lawyer, educator, arbitrator*
Henry, Laurin Luther *public affairs educator*
Hirsch, Eric Donald, Jr. *language educator*
Hochberg, Bayard Zabdial *retired lawyer*
Hoel, Lester A. *civil engineering educator, department chairman*
Horgan, Cornelius Oliver *applied mathematics and mechanics professor, engineering educator*
Hostler, Sharon Lee *pediatrician, educator*
Howard, Arthur Ellsworth Dick *law educator*
Hudson, John Lester *chemical engineering professor*
Humphreys, Paul William *philosophy educator, consultant*
Hunt, William B. *pulmonologist*
Hurd, Nicole Farmer *director*
Jeffries, John Calvin, Jr. *law educator, former dean*
Johnston, Karen Chodack *neurologist, educator*
Jolly, Bruce Dwight *manufacturing executive*
Jordan, Daniel Porter, Jr. *foundation administrator, historian, educator*
Kaiserlian, Penelope Jane *publishing executive*
Kattwinkel, John *pediatrician, educator*
Kauffman, James Milton *special education educator, writer*
Keats, Theodore Eliot *radiologist, educator*
Keen, Rachel *psychology professor*
Kennedy, Cornelius Bryant *retired lawyer*
Kensington, Andrew Justus *litigation specialist*
Kesser, Bradley W. *otolaryngologist, educator*
Kiewra, Gustave Paul *psychologist, educator*
Krzysztofowicz, Sir Roman *systems engineering and statistical science educator, consultant*
Lane, Ann Judith *history and women's studies educator, director*
Lane, Mark *lawyer, educator, writer*
Lanham, Betty Bailey *anthropologist, educator*
Levenson, Jacob Clavner *language educator*
Li, Zuoping *biomedical engineer, researcher*
Lichtenstein, Nelson *history educator*
Little, Wm. A. (William Alfred Little) *language educator, researcher, musicologist*
Lo, Kwok-Yung *astronomer, educator, researcher, administrator*
Lobo, Peter Issac *physician*
Long, Charles Farrell *insurance company executive*
Loo, Beverly Jane *publisher, educator*
Mahoney, Paul G. *dean, law educator*
Marshall, John Crook *internal medicine educator, researcher*
Maslen, Eric Harvey *engineering educator, researcher*
Matherne, G. Paul *medical educator*
Matsumoto, Alan H. *radiologist, educator*
McCall, Anthony Leo *medical educator, researcher*
McCrimmon, Barbara Smith *writer, librarian*
McDonough, William Andrews *architect, former dean*
McGahren, Eugene Dewey III *surgeon*
McGann, Jerome John *language educator*
Meador, Daniel John *law educator*
Megill, Allan *historian*
Mellon, DeForest, Jr. *biology professor, researcher*
Menaker, Michael *biology professor*
Menefee, Samuel Pyeatt *lawyer, academic*
Mick, David Glen *finance educator*
Middleditch, Leigh Benjamin, Jr. *lawyer, educator*
Mikalson, Jon Dennis *classics educator*
Mintz, Paul David *pathologist*
Modesitt, Susan Carnall *oncologist, director*
Molhoek, Kerrington Ramsey *research scientist*
Moore, John Norton *lawyer, educator, diplomat*
Morgan, Raymond F. *plastic surgeon*
Nelson, Caleb Edward *law educator*
Nelson, Krysia Carmel *lawyer*
Nohrnberg, James Carson *language educator*
Nolan, Stanton Peelle *surgeon, educator*
O'Brien, David Michael *law educator*
O'Connell, Jeffrey *law educator*
Oldfield, Edward Hudson *neurosurgeon, researcher*
Olsen, Edgar Oliver *economics professor*
Onega, Esther E. *librarian*
O'Neil, Robert Marchant *law educator*
Owen, John Atkinson, Jr. *internist, educator*
Palanisamy, Prakash *research assistant*
Park, Byungkyu (Brian Park) *engineering educator*
Parshall, Brian J. *mathematician, educator*
Pate, Robert Hewitt, Jr. *retired counselor educator*
Pearson, William Raymond *biochemist, educator*
Peterson, Merrill Daniel *historian, educator*
Pinto, Jerald E. *financial analyst, director*
Platts-Mills, Thomas Alexander Evelyn *immunologist, educator, researcher*
Pope, Randolph D. *literature and language professor*
Proffitt, Dennis R. *psychology professor, department chairman*
Ragosta, Michael *cardiologist*
Rappaport, Yvonne Kindinger *educator*
Rehm, Patrice Koch *radiologist, educator*
Reppucci, Nicholas Dickon *psychologist, educator*
Rheuban, Karen Schulder *pediatric cardiologist, educator*
Rhoads, Steven Eric *political science professor*
Rini, Joel *language educator, linguist*
Rodgers, Bradley Moreland *pediatric, thoracic surgeon*
Rogol, Alan David *pediatric endocrinologist*
Root, James Benjamin *landscape architect*
Roseberry, Edwin Southall *retired state agency administrator*
Rowlingson, John Clyde *anesthesiologist, physician, educator*
Rubin, David Lee *humanities educator, critic, editor*
Russell, Mark A. *dermatologist*
Ryan, Debbie (Deborah A. Ryan) *women's college basketball coach*
Sabat, Michal *structural chemist*
Sabato, Larry Joseph *political science professor, director*
Sackett, Charles Ackley *physicist, educator*
Sahr, Morris Gallup *financial planner*
Saller, Devereux Nathaniel *medical educator, director*
Sarazin, Craig Leigh *astronomer*
Saulsbury, Frank T. *pediatric immunologist and rheumatologist*
Schauer, Frederick Franklin *law educator*
Scheld, William Michael *internist, educator*
Schuker, Stephen Alan *historian, educator*
Scott, Charlotte H. *business educator*
Sedgwick, Alexander *retired historian, educator*
Selfe, Terry Kit *medical researcher*
Shaw, Donald Leslie *Spanish language educator*
Shenkir, William Gary *business educator*
Shi, Weibin *medical educator*
Sibert, Polly Lou *conductor, educator*
Sihler, William Wooding *finance educator*
Skrutskie, Michael F. *science educator*
Slaughter, Edward Ratliff, Jr. *lawyer*
Smith, Clyde Ray *dean*
Spearing, Anthony Colin *English literature educator*
Stocker, Arthur Frederick *classics educator*
Strayer, Scott Merle *medical educator*
Stroud, Robert Edward *lawyer*
Sundberg, Richard Jay *chemistry professor*
Sutphen, James L. *pediatrician*
Sykes, Gresham M'Cready *sociologist, educator, artist*
Tai, Robert H. *science educator, researcher*
Thomas, Lawrence Eldon *mathematics professor*
Thomas, Mark Francis *history professor, economics professor, researcher*
Thornhill, Arthur H., Jr. *retired publishing executive*
Townsend, Miles Averill *aerospace and mechanical engineering educator*
Trindle, Carl *chemistry educator*
Truwit, Jonathon Dean *dean*
Turner, Robert Foster *law educator, writer*
Tuttle, Jeremy Ballou *neuroscientist*
Untaroiu, Costin Daniel *engineering educator, researcher*
Vanden Bout, Paul Adrian *astronomer, physicist, educator*
Wadlington, Walter James *law educator*
Wagner, Roy *anthropology educator, researcher*
Walker, William F. *medical educator*
Walt, Steven David *law educator*
Weary, Peyton Edwin *retired medical educator*
Weber, Hans Jürgen *physics professor*
Weinberger, Adrienne *artist, art appraiser*
Wenger, Larry Bruce *law librarian, educator*
Whitaker, John King *retired economics professor*
White, George Edward *lawyer, educator*
Whitehead, John Wayne *lawyer, educator, writer*
Wiggins, Barbara Sue *pharmacist, educator*
Wilkinson, J(ames) Harvie III *federal judge*
Wilson, Timothy D. *psychology professor*
Wittenborg, Karin *university librarian*
Wolcott, John Winthrop III *retired manufacturing executive*
Wood, Houston G. *engineering educator, researcher*
Worrell, Anne Everette Rowell *newspaper publisher*
Wright, Charles Penzel, Jr. *writer, educator*
Wulf, William Allan *engineering educator*
Yates, John Thomas, Jr. *chemistry professor, research scientist*
Zinberg, Cecile *retired history professor*
Zunz, Olivier Jean *history professor*

Chase City
Reams, Linda Pigg *elementary school educator*

Chesapeake
Barnes, Stacy Ray *finance educator, researcher*
Carter, Gene Thomas *interior designer*
Gorry, James A. III *lawyer*
Hill, Deborah Nixon *elementary school educator, minister*
Hudgins, Paul Granville *health facility administrator*
Jackson, Cynthia Ann *medical association administrator, health consultant*
Krasnoff, Alan P. *mayor, Chesapeake, Virginia*
Kringel, Deanna Lynn *music educator*
Locke, L. Muriel *mathematician, educator*
Mincheff, Donna Currie *special education educator*
Myrick, Bismarck *diplomat, history professor*
Notti, Donna Betts *special education educator*
Owens, Susan Elizabeth *realtor*
Potter, Cynthia M. *art educator, artist*
Sasser, Robert *retail executive*
Stillman, Margaret (Peggy Stillman) *library director*
Webb, Julia Jones *elementary school educator, minister*

Chester
Benn, Candace Marilea *elementary school educator*
Brooks, Marty Frances *language educator*

Gray, Charles Robert *lawyer*
Gray, Frederick Thomas, Jr., (Rick Gray) *journalist, actor, educator*
Law, Thomas Melvin *academic administrator*
Tiller, Charlene Teitelbaum *communications educator*

Chesterfield
Congdon, John Rhodes *transportation executive*
Davis, Bonnie Christell *judge*
Garnett, Douglas Acree *financial analyst, researcher*
Love, Dana Francis Ignatius *telecommunications industry executive*
Yohe, Robin M. *high school administration and music educator*

Chincoteague Island
Chagnon, Lucille Tessier *literacy acceleration consultant*

Christiansburg
Blanchard, Dorothy Hardt *academic administrator, volunteer*

Clarksville
Worth, Lynn Harris *writer*

Clifton
Brooks, Matthew Wayne *agrichemical regulatory chemist, consultant*
Hennesy, Gerald Craft *artist*
Hoffman, Karla Leigh *mathematician, educator*

Clifton Forge
Miller, Catherine H. *nursing administrator, property manager*

Cobbs Creek
Crum, John Kistler *management consultant*

Covington
Rohr, Dwight Mason *news director, radio marketing consultant*

Crozet
Detmer, Don Eugene *health informatics, management and policy researcher*
Reswick, James Bigelow *former government official, biomedical engineer*

Culpeper
Goddard, Frances Byrd *clinical social worker*

Dahlgren
Rayms-Keller, Alfredo *molecular biologist*

Daleville
Kinzie, Brenda Asburry *counselor*

Danville
Abreu, Luis Alberto *lawyer*
Lea, Robert Lee III *social sciences educator*
Martin, Marshall Wayne *finance educator*
Regan, Michael Patrick *lawyer*
Roberson, Janet *registrar*
Talbott, Frank III *lawyer*

Deltaville
Koedel, John Gilbert, Jr. *retired metal products executive*

Dinwiddie
McCray, Doris Raines *minister*

Dublin
Billaud, Louise Ann *musician, educator*
Douthat, Rebecca Arlene *retired secondary school educator*
Linzey, Juanita Bird *biology professor*

Dulles
Armstrong, Tim *Internet company executive*
Beecroft, Robert Stephen *United States Ambassador to Jordan*
Desmond, Ned *editor, writer*
Eastham, Alan Walter, Jr. *United States Ambassador to the Republic of Congo, lawyer*
Eikenberry, Karl Winfrid *United States Ambassador to Afghanistan*
Mussomeli, Joseph Adamo *ambassador*
North, Oliver Laurence (Ollie North) *syndicated columnist, retired military officer*
Parker, Ira H. *Internet company executive, lawyer*
Perry, June Carter *United States Ambassador to Sierra Leone*
Ricciardone, Francis Joseph, Jr. *Deputy Ambassador to Islamic Republic of Afghanistan Kabul*
Wayne, Earl Anthony *ambassador*

Dutton
Washburn, John Rosser *entrepreneur*

Earlysville
Brownell, Blaine Allison *educational association and academic administrator, history professor*

Eastville
Williams, Ida Jones *consumer and home economics educator, writer*

Edinburg
Trindal, Wesley Steele *mechanical engineer*

Emory
Denham, Robert Dayton *language educator*
Jones, Jerry Lee *computer educator*
Kellogg, Frederic Richard *religious studies educator*
Walker, Marilyn Suarez *educator*

Fairfax
Agnarsson, Geir *mathematics educator*
Agouris, Peggy *engineer, educator*
Aharonov, Yakir *physicist, researcher*
Anderson, LaKesha Nichole *communications educator*
Arnold, William McCauley *lawyer*
Baird, Charles Bruce *lawyer, consultant*
Baker, Daniel Richard *computer company executive*
Balakerskaia, Anna *music educator*
Barth, Michael Carl *economist*
Batten, Brian *research scientist*
Bennett, James Thomas *economics professor*
Best, Amy L. *education educator*
Bobzien, David P. *lawyer*
Boone, James Virgil *retired engineering executive, researcher*
Brown, Lorraine A. *literature educator*
Buchanan, James McGill *economist, educator*
Campana, Michael Phillip *secondary school foreign language educator*
Carty, Rita Mary *dean, emerita*
Chen, Chun-Hung *engineering educator*
Clay, Edwin S. III *library director*
Codding, Frederick Hayden *lawyer*
Cook, Gerald *electrical engineering educator*
Cowen, Tyler *economics professor*
Cramer, H. R. (Hal Cramer) *oil industry executive*
Cullison, Alexander C. (Doc Cullison) *mediator, arbitrator*
Dennis, Rutledge M. *sociologist, educator*
Downey, Richard Lawrence *lawyer*
Dutch, Nicole M. *researcher*
Emelianenko, Maria *mathematics professor*
Fagan, John Ernest *lawyer*
Farina, John Edward *religious studies educator*
Folk, Thomas Robert *lawyer*
Fox, Donna M. *dean, biology professor*
Ganesan, Rajesh *industrial engineer, researcher*
Geller, Harold Arthur *earth and space sciences executive, educator, author*
Gerber, Naomi Lynn Hurwirtz *physiatrist, educator*
Gertler, Janos John *electrical engineer, educator*
Gillette, Brian Kenneth *academic administrator*
Given, Barbara (Knight) *elementary school educator, secondary school educator*
Golden, James Leslie *information technology executive, retired military officer*
Haack, Barry N. *geographer, educator*
Haines, David W. *social sciences educator*
Hollans, Irby Noah, Jr. *retired trade association administrator*
Horton, Lois Elaine *history professor*
Houck, Mark Hedrich *engineering educator*
Hudson, William L. *conductor*
Hurt, Charlene Schmidt *library director*
Hutcheon, Wallace Schoonmaker *retired historian*
Jones, George Fleming *international consultant*
Kash, Don Eldon *political science professor*
Katz, Mark Norman *international relations educator, consultant, author*
Khan, Shahamat Ullah *environmental scientist, educator*
King, James Cecil *retired language and literature educator, medievalist*
Klopfenstein, Rex Carter *retired electrical engineer*
Kravitz, David Albert *finance educator*
Kurtz, Howard Vincent *theater educator*
LaPierre, Wayne R., Jr. *lobbyist*
Lapple, Judith A. *music educator, director*
Larranaga, Jim *men's college basketball coach*
Lawrence, James Franklin *mathematician, researcher*
Lindsey, Lawrence Benjamin (Larry Lindsey) *economist, former federal official*
Lomax, Michael Lucius *non-profit association administrator*
Longin, Thomas Charles *retired academic administrator*
Manheim, Frank Tibor *oceanographer*
Mann, Laura Ann *soprano*
Mann, Wendy *librarian*
McAllister, William Howard III *newspaper reporter, columnist, public affairs consultant*
McAndrews, James Patrick *retired lawyer*
McGavin, John David *lawyer*
McKnight, Patrick E. *medical educator, consultant*
Miller, Emilie F. *former state senator, consultant*
Miller, Patricia A. *music educator, opera and concert artist*
Morowitz, Harold Joseph *biophysicist, educator*
Nye, John Vincent Canizares *economics professor*
Palmer, James Daniel *information technology educator*
Parasuraman, Raja *psychology professor*
Pfiffner, James Price *political science professor*
Pruitt, Dean Garner *psychologist, educator*
Pugh, Arthur James (Jay Pugh) *retired retail executive*
Ramos-Pellicia, Michelle Frances *linguist, educator*
Rieger, Michael Ira *lawyer*
Roberts, Cecil Edward, Jr. *labor union administrator*
Robinson, Kayne B. *lobbyist, former political organization officer*
Rojahn, Johannes *psychology professor*
Rosenkranz, Robert Bernard *military officer*
Rust, John Howson, Jr. *lawyer, state legislator*
Sage, Andrew Patrick *systems engineering and management educator*
Sanderson, Douglas Jay *lawyer*
Saverot, Pierre-Michel *nuclear waste management company executive*
Schulman, Joseph Daniel *physician, health facility administrator, medical geneticist, educator*
Siddons, Joy Garbee *music educator*
Sikdar, Siddhartha *engineering educator*
Silcox, Gordon Bruce *executive coach*
Simpson, Carter B. *lawyer*
Smith, Richard Norton *historian, former library director*
Solomon, Ellen Joan *business owner, consultant*
Steele, Howard Loucks *economic development consultant, author*
Sturtevant, Brereton *retired lawyer, federal official*
Sun, Donglian *meteorologist*
Tadros, Nader K. *political organization worker, director*
Trefil, James Stanley *physicist, researcher*
Villarreal, Carlos Castañeda *engineering executive*
Wagner, Richard E. *economist, educator*
Wegman, Edward Joseph *statistician, educator, researcher*
Witek, James Eugene *retired public relations executive*
Wrbican, Sue *art educator*
Yang, Chaowei Phil *research scientist, educator*

Fairfax Station
Barringer, Joan Marie *counselor, educator, artist, writer*
Duff, William Grierson *electrical engineer, educator*
Randell, Cortes W. *news service executive*
Szczublewski, Wendy Sue *small business owner, musician, freelance/self-employed writer*

Falls Church
Abou-Ellail, Mohsen Mohamed *engineering educator, researcher*
Akkara, Joseph Augustine *chemist, educator, researcher*
Aukofer, Frank Alexander *journalist*
Barakat, Amin J. *pediatrician, pediatric nephrologist*
Barkley, Paul Haley, Jr. *architect*
Benton, Janine Schollnick *lawyer*
Benton, Nicholas Frederick *publisher*
Bingman, Charles Franklin *government executive, educator*
Boehm, Kenneth *legal association administrator*
Bokhari, Mazhar Ali *bank executive*
Borman, Karen Renee *surgeon*
Brady, Rupert Joseph *retired lawyer*
Bruck, Bill *business owner*
Calhoun, John Alfred *social services administrator*
Calkins, Susannah Eby *retired economist*
Chabraja, Nicholas D. *equipment manufacturing executive, lawyer*
Cherkasky, Michael Griffin *security firm executive, former insurance company executive*
Clegg, Roger Burton *lawyer*
Crawford, Kristina S. *psychologist*
Cromley, Allan Wray *retired journalist*
Deckelman, William L., Jr. *lawyer*
DeMuro, Gerard J *information technology executive*
Dewey-Balzhiser, Anne Elizabeth Marie *lawyer*
Diamond, Robert Michael *lawyer*
Evans, Peter Yoshio *ophthalmologist, educator*
Gallopoulos, Gregory Stratis *lawyer*
Green, James Wyche *sociologist, anthropologist, psychotherapist, consultant*
Hall, Charles M. *manufacturing executive*
Han, Syung D. *international trade consultant, financier*
Hart, C(harles) W(illard), Jr. *zoologist, curator*
Hays, Sharon Lynn *consulting company executive, former federal official*
Heebner, David K. *manufacturing executive, retired military officer*
Hibbs, Ernest G. *computer scientist, engineering executive*
Hjort, Howard Warren *economist, consultant*
Honigberg, Carol Crossman *lawyer*
Jo, Kenneth Yoon *electronics engineer*
Johnson, Jay L. *manufacturing executive, retired military officer*
Jones, Russel Cameron *civil engineer, educator*
Kaplow, Herbert Elias *journalist*
Kurtzke, John Francis, Sr. *neurologist, epidemiologist*
Lefrak, Edward Arthur *cardiovascular and thoracic surgeon*
Lorenzo, Michael *engineer, real estate broker, government official*
Luchini, Joseph S. *lawyer*
Mancuso, Michael John *corporate financial executive*
McCue, David J. *information systems specialist, entrepreneur*
Melnick, John Latane *lawyer*
Meserve, Richard Andrew *lawyer, administrator*
Mugavero, Thomas Collier *lawyer*
Mukherjee, Dipankar *surgeon*
Nguyen-Dinh, Thanh *internist, geriatrician, acupuncturist*
Orben, Robert *scriptwriter, writer*
Rahmandad, Hazhir *engineering educator*
Redd, L. Hugh *manufacturing executive*
Rooney, Kevin Davitt *federal agency administrator*
Savner, David A. *lawyer*
Schoomaker, Eric B. *career military officer*
Schoonover, Stanley R. *music educator, consultant*
Shah, Syed-Waqar *science educator*
Sveinsson, Linda Rodgers *engineering company executive*
Tether, Anthony John *aerospace executive*
Underwood, Paula Kay *military officer*
Wah, Robert M. *reproductive endocrinologist, obstetrician, gynecologist*
Ward, George Frank, Jr. *international programs executive, ambassador*
Ward, Joe Henry, Jr. *retired lawyer*
Weiss, Armand Berl *economist, association management executive*
Whitehead, Kenneth Dean *writer, translator, retired federal agency administrator, editor*
Wood, John Martin *lawyer*

Farmville
Dorrill, William Franklin *political scientist, educator*
Etheridge, Elizabeth Williams *history professor*
Garcia, Joseph Edward *earth science and geography educator*
Howe, Patricia Anne *librarian*
Lehr, David Leonard *economics professor*
Panzarello, Melissa *costume designer, educator*
Smith, Shawn *language educator*
Terry, Wayne Gilbert *healthcare educator, hospital administrator*
Witschey, Walter Robert Thurmond *anthropologist, educator, former museum director*

Fincastle
Huffman, Jerry Wayne *retired secondary school educator*

Flint Hill
Dietel, William Moore *former foundation executive*

Fort Belvoir
Anderson, Frank J., Jr. *retired career officer*
Crenshaw, Horace, Jr. *military officer*
DuBrow, Alexander Alan *information technology executive, consultant*
Dunwoody, Ann E. *career military officer*
Fyfe, Laura Jane *language educator*
Gould, Jay William III *science and technology systems engineer, management development educator, lecturer, author, international consultant*
Harms, John Kevin *lawyer*
O'Kane, Barbara Lynn *research psychologist*
Ratches, James Arthur *chief scientist*
Tegnelia, James A. *federal agency administrator*
Thompson, Alan S. *federal agency administrator, military officer*

Fort Lee
Leppo, Lisa Marie *forensic anthropologist*
Sakowitz, Philip E. *federal agency administrator*

Fredericksburg
Arnn, Nancy Shank *secondary school educator*
Braxton, Herman Harrison, Jr. *lawyer*
Bressler, Barry Lee *physicist, systems analyst*
Crippen, Timothy Alan *sociology educator*
Dorman, John Frederick *genealogist*
Edmunds, Jeffrey Garth *librarian*
Gill, Milvi Kosenkranius *artist, photographer*
Glessner, Thomas Allen *lawyer*
Hajek, Otomar *mathematician, educator*
Hample, Judy G. *academic administrator*
Harrod, Audrey Hunter *retired executive secretary*
Hasenfus, Harold Joseph *retired mechanical engineer, naval technical director*
Hoyt, John Arthur *cultural organization administrator, minister*
Jones, Harry Edward *diplomat, writer*
Liewehr, Frederick Russell *endodontist, educator*
Medding, Walter Sherman *retired environmental engineer*
Noel, Nancy W. *literature and language professor*
Raspen, Janice Ann *librarian, educator*
Rotter, Marcel Paul *literature and language professor*
Ryan, Kathy Ann *special education educator*
Sanford, Douglas Walker *archaeologist, educator*
Schmutzhart, Berthold Josef *sculptor, educator*
Sisk, Fred Dean *retired cartographer*
Stylianopoulos, Areti Leonidas *music educator*
Van Neste, Karen Lane *librarian, editor*

Front Royal
Andes, Larry Dale *minister*
Bonzagni, Vincent Francis *lawyer*
Douglas, J(ocelyn) Fielding *toxicologist, consultant*
Stevens, Loretta Marie *special education educator*

Gainesville
Cochran, Radeen M. *librarian*
French, Dorothy Marie *music educator*
Lee, Won Jay *radiologist*
Levell, Edward, Jr. *retired airport director, aviation consultant*
Lukowsky, Gerhard Hans *internist*
Tuck, Russell R., Jr. *college president emeritus*

Galax
Dunson, William Albert *biology professor, ecological consultant*
Kapp, John Paul *lawyer, physician, educator*

Garrisonville
Emely, Charles Harry *trade association executive, consultant*

Glen Allen
Anderson, James Frederick *clergyman*
Gulling, Mark V. *consumer products company executive*
Hossain, Deloar *pathologist, director*
Kirshner, Alan I. *insurance company executive*
Levit, Jay J(oseph) *lawyer*
Luke, John Anderson, Jr. *paper, packaging and chemical company executive*
Newby, Michael R. *lawyer*
Rajkowski, E. Mark *corporate financial executive*
Weaver, Mollie Little *lawyer*

Gloucester
Hicks, C. Flippo *lawyer*
James, Kay Coles *think-tank executive, former federal agency administrator*

Gloucester Point
Bush, Elizabeth Olney *marine lab technician*
Sandridge, Donald Otis *music educator*

Gordonsville
Wells, Mary Elizabeth Thompson *deacon, chaplain, spiritual director, iconographer*

Great Falls
Andrews, Betty Bauserman *retired secondary school educator, real estate manager*
Bachner, John Philip *business consultant*
Cass, Ronald Andrew *lawyer, former dean*
Cowhill, William Joseph *retired naval officer, consultant*
DiBona, Charles Joseph *retired trade association administrator*
Garrett, Wilbur Bill (Bill) *magazine editor*
Lillard, Mark Hill III *engineering consultant, retired military officer*
Minikes, Stephan Michael *ambassador, lawyer, banker*
Neidich, George *lawyer*
Railton, W(illiam) Scott *retired commissioner*
Turner, Stansfield *former CIA director, retired military officer*

Grundy
McGlothlin, Michael Gordon *lawyer*

Gum Spring
Dilworth, Robert Lexow *career military officer, educator*

Hampden Sydney
Bortz, Walter M. III *academic administrator*
Boykin, William G. (Jerry Boykin) *retired military officer*
Porterfield, William Wendell *chemist, educator*

Hampton
Abner, Harold Loyd *military officer, consultant*
Ali, Halima N. *mathematics professor, researcher*
Bai, Yingxin *optical engineer*
Barnes, Paula Cassandra *literature and language professor*
Barrow, Irene Marie *speech pathology educator*
Boonthum, Chutima *computer scientist, educator*
Brown, Ei Ei *science educator*
Cantrell, John Harris *physicist*
Carrington, Marian Denise *academic administrator, counselor, motivational speaker*
Courtney, Vernon S. *museum director, Museum Association Administrator*
Dildy, David Scott *lawyer*
Dillard, Royzell L. *music educator, director*
Enriquez, Manuel Hipolito *physician*
Gibson, Barbara S. *librarian*
Goode, Constance Loper *elementary school principal*
Goodson, Dorothy Moore *English educator, counselor*
Grierson, Kevin William *lawyer*
Halabuk, Michael Patrick *language educator*
Harris, Carl G. *music educator*
Holmes, Leonard George *psychologist*
Jahncke, Michael Lee *science educator, director*
Johnson, Leona Melissa *psychology professor, researcher*
Jones, Opel Tamian, I, *mathematics professor, director*
Khawaja, Mabel Masuda *English composition and literature educator*
Lohourou-Digbeu, Jacques *language educator, consultant*
Lowery, Alicia Carmen *language educator*
McAdaragh, Raymon Michael *aerospace engineer, researcher*
Miskolczi, Ferenc Mark *research scientist*
Nare, Otsebele E. *engineering educator, researcher*
Nazaryan, Hovakim *mathematician, researcher, atmospheric scientist*
Nazaryan, Vahagn *physicist, medical researcher*
Noor, Ahmed Khairy *engineering educator, researcher*
Redwanski, John *medical educator*
Refaat, Tamer F. *electrical engineer, researcher*
Roe, Lesa B. *federal agency administrator*
Smith, Stephen Mark *lawyer*
Sobieski, Jaroslaw *aerospace engineer*
Sypolt, Shirley Rae *elementary school educator*
Tripathi, Ram Kishore *physicist, researcher*
Verma, Arun K. *mathematician, educator*
Walsh, Joanne Claire *school librarian, educator*
Watson, Willie R. *research scientist*
Wechsler, Toni *healthcare educator, writer*

Hardyville
White, Gordon Eliot *historian, writer*

Harrisonburg
Adams, Tom *foreign language services executive*
Baker, George Harold III *physicist, educator*
Barnes, Susan K. *education educator, information technology executive*
Brickner, Aimee R. *communications educator*
Carrier, Ronald Edwin *academic administrator, director*
Choi, In Dal *music educator*
Congdon, Lee Walter *retired history professor*
Dalton, Claudette Ellis Harloe *anesthesiologist, educator, dean*
Duncan, Cheryl J. (Cheri Duncan) *systems administrator, librarian*
Geary, Robert Francis, Jr. *English educator*
Gill, Gerald Lawson *librarian*
Grayson, Joann Hess *psychology professor*
Hastedt, Glenn Peter *political science professor*
Henriques, Gregg Ros *psychology professor*
Johnson, Kia Noelle *speech pathology/audiology services professional, educator*
Marler, Jeffrey Allen *neuroscientist*
Palmer, Forrest Charles *librarian, educator*
Pappas, Eric Charles *director*
Shanahan, Maureen Gabrielle *academic administrator*
Taalman, Laura Anne *mathematics professor*
Theodore, Crystal *retired artist, educator*
Tkac, John Anthony *language educator*
White, Christopher Todd *language educator, anthropologist*
Whitmeyer, Steven J. *geologist, educator*

Hartfield
Johnson, Carl Randolph *chemist, educator*

Haymarket
Doolittle, Warren T. *retired federal official*
Frank, Jacob *lawyer*
Katz, Alan Charles *toxicologist*
Seely, James Michael *retired military officer, defense consultant, small business owner*

Heathsville
McKerns, Charles Joseph *lawyer*
Winkel, Raymond Norman *aerospace scientist, consultant, retired military officer*

Henrico
DiLorenzo, Francis X. *bishop*
Kevorkian, Richard *artist*

Herndon
Akin, Jeffrey *human capital consulting executive*
Allen, George Felix, Jr. *former United States Senator from Virginia, former Governor of Virginia*
Davis, Nathaniel (Nate) A. *broadcast executive*
Draper, William David *subject matter expert*
Gill, Jean Kennedy *chemistry professor*
Hall, John Reginald, II, *electronics company executive, retired army officer*
Hazel, William A., Jr. *orthopedist*
Jones, Reba (Becki) Pestun *elementary school and music educator*
Khazen, Ellida Moiseyevna *mathematician*
Nolan, Leslie Marian *artist*
O'Connor, Christopher John *information technology manager, consultant*
Price, James Michael *oceanographer*
Ryder, Robert T. *geologist, researcher*
Simanski, Claire Dvorak *art educator*
Wang, Zhengang *civil engineer, researcher*
Ward, Jeri *automotive company executive, marketing professional*
Young, Janet Cheryl *electrical engineer*

Hillsville
McGrady, Jonathan L. *lawyer*

Independence
Craig, James Hicklin *fine arts consultant*
Webb, Adam Paul *librarian*

Ivy
Nachmanovitch, Stephen *violinist, composer, author and educator*
Ubben, Donald Thomas *lawyer*
Wilcox, Harvey John *lawyer*

Jeffersonton
Hileman, Bette *journalist*

Kents Store
Brown, Nan Marie *retired minister*

Keswick
Frazier, Henry Bowen III *retired federal agency administrator*
Pochick, Francis Edward *financial consultant*
Rafajko, Robert Richard *science administrator*

Keysville
Lloyd, Judy M. *literature and language professor*

King George
Newhall, David III *retired federal official*

Lake Ridge
Ingrassia, Anthony Frank (Tony) *human resource specialist*
Stottlemyer, David Lee *federal official*

Lancaster
Kingsbury, Ellen Ann Dagon *anesthesiologist, general practitioner*

Langley AFB
Corley, John D. W. *career military officer*

Lansdowne
Colson, Charles Wendell (Chuck Colson) *lay minister, writer*
Miller, Dorothy Anne Smith *retired cytogenetics educator*

Leesburg
Brown, James Robert *retired air force officer*
Budiansky, Stephen Philip *writer*
De Barbieri, Mary Ann *not-for-profit management consultant*
Kutner, Lawrence Alan *executive director*
Levin, Mark Reed *radio personality, legal foundation administrator*
Lobanov-Rostovsky, Oleg *management consultant*
Macfarlane, David Gordon *defense systems design and development executive*
Mahood, Ken *music educator*
Strasser, Gabor *management consultant*

Lexington
Anderson, Michael Alan *economics educator*
Bang, James T. *economics professor*
Benefiel, Rebecca Ruth *ancient language educator*
Dellinger, Mary Ann *language educator*
DeVogt, John Frederick *management science and business ethics educator, consultant*
Elmes, David Gordon *psychologist, educator*
Gaines, James Edwin, Jr. *retired librarian*
Gutermuth, Karen *economics professor*
Hickman, Cleveland Pendleton, Jr. *biology professor*
Hyre, Matthew *engineering educator*
Jarrard, Leonard Everett *psychologist, educator*
John, Lewis George *retired political science educator*
Kiracofe, Clifford Attick, Jr. *political science professor*
Leach, Maurice Derby, Jr. *librarian, educator*
Mann, Sally M. *photographer*
Parker, Phyllis R. *secondary school educator*
Peay, J.H. Binford III *career military officer*
Phillips, Charles Franklin, Jr. *retired economist*
Rader, Angela Nichole *music educator*
Ruscio, Kenneth Patrick *academic administrator, political science professor*
Schwab, Frederic Lyon *geologist, educator*
Smolla, Rodney Alan *dean, law educator*
Spencer, Edgar Winston *geology educator*
Stephens, Laurence David, Jr. *linguist, investor, oil industry executive*
Stuart, Dabney *poet, language educator*
Wiant, Sarah Kirsten *law librarian, educator, director*
Williams, H. Thomas (Tom Williams) *academic administrator, physicist, educator*
Winfrey, John Crawford *economist, educator*

Locust Grove
Gulya, Aina Julianna *otolaryngologist*

Lorton
Celentano, Suzanne *movement educator*
Jackson, Gary Lee *security consultant*
Mastromarco, Dan Ralph *lawyer, consultant*
Shoemaker, Helen E. Martin Achor *civic worker*

Louisa
Small, William Edwin, Jr. *association and recreation executive*

Lovettsville
Flannery, John Philip *lawyer*
Foard, Douglas W. *historian*

Luray
Burzynski, Norman Stephen *editor*

Lynchburg
Akubue-Brice, Dorothy A. *history professor, researcher*
Bowman, Kathleen Gill *academic administrator*
Burnette, Ralph Edwin, Jr. *judge*
Bushong, Peggy *psychology professor*
Duff, Ernest Arthur *political scientist, educator*
Elson, James Martin *retired landmark director*
Gerdes, Darin L. *finance educator*
Gilmore, Philip Nathanael *finance educator, accountant*
Harvey, Aubrey Eaton III *retired industrial engineer*
Healy, Joseph Francis, Jr. *lawyer, retired air transportation executive*
Henderson, Horace Edward *World War II historian, peace advocate*
Hudson, Walter Tiree *artist*
Johnson, Robert Bruce *historic preservationist, director, small business owner*
LaHaye, Timothy F. *pastor, writer*
Lewis, Edward *engineering educator*
Lofaso, Cynthia R. *psychology professor*
Noronha, Silvester John *engineer, researcher*
Offield, Martin F. *biology professor*
Partie, David John *language educator*
Pursley, Frank James *retired personal development specialist*
Snead, George Murrell, Jr. *military officer, research scientist, consultant*
Solyom, Antal Endre *retired psychiatrist*
Stephens, Bart Nelson *former foreign service officer*
Sullivan, Gregory Paul *secondary school educator*
Webb, Evelyn Dunbar *middle school educator*
White, Kenneth Spencer, Sr. *lawyer*

Manakin Sabot
Bright, Craig Bartley *lawyer*

Manassas
Archer, Chalmers, Jr. *retired education educator*
Banville, Dominique *physical education educator*
Bruno, Irene Evelyn *mathematician, educator*
Cooper, James Nelson *medical educator*
Crum, Charles Noel *state magistrate*
Haddad, Nadim Fawzi *engineer, researcher*
Hayes, Linda Marie *middle school educator*
Isbister, Jenefir Diane Wilkinson *microbiologist, researcher, educator, consultant*
Kettlewell, Gail Biery *academic administrator, research professor*
Livingston, Jo Ellen Brooks *music educator*
Locigno, Paul Robert *public relations executive*
Storing, Paul Edward *retired foreign service officer*

Manassas Park
Knouse, Stacie *art educator*

Manquin
Osgood, Nancy Jean *medical educator, writer*

Markham
Ojeda Eiseley, Jaime de *former Spanish ambassador, educator*

Martinsville
Gette, Timothy J. *museum director*

Mason Neck
Mc Curdy, Patrick Pierre *editor*

Mc Dowell
Harkleroad, Jo-Ann Decker *special education educator*

Mc Lean
Allen, David *systems engineer*
Appler, Thomas L. *lawyer*
Aucutt, Ronald David *lawyer*
Auerbach, Anita L. *clinical psychologist*
Bailar, Gregor S. *finance company executive*
Barbiero, Victor Kelvin *health products executive, educator*
Black, Ginger Elizabeth *elementary school educator*
Blisk, Brenda Pack *financial consultant*
Bostrom, Robert Everett *lawyer, mortgage company executive*
Boyd, Ralph F., Jr. *mortgage company executive, former federal agency administrator*
Brown, Thomas Cartmel, Jr. *lawyer*
Brownlee, John Leslie *lawyer, former prosecutor*
Cahill, Harry Amory *diplomat, educator*
Cannon, Mark Wilcox *retired government official*
Card, Andy (Andrew Hill Card Jr.) *former White House chief of staff, former United States Secretary of Transportation*
Carnicero, Jorge Emilio *aeronautical engineer, transportation executive*
Chang, Michael *professional tennis player*
Church, Randolph Warner, Jr. *lawyer*
Cook, Patricia L. *mortgage company executive*
Degeorges, Paul Andre *ecologist, educator*
DeGiovanni-Donnelly, Rosalie Frances *biologist, educator*
Dempsey, James Raymon *manufacturing executive*
Dempsey, Joan Avalyn *consulting firm executive, former federal agency administrator*
Doyle, Frederick Joseph *retired government research scientist*
Dubow, Craig A. *publishing executive*
Duvall, Richard Osgood *lawyer*
Ellison, Earl Otto *computer scientist*
Estren, Mark James *communications executive, television producer, writer, editor*
Faga, Martin C. *engineer*
Fairbank, Richard D. *diversified financial services company executive*
Ferrante, Frank Edward *telecommunications systems engineer*
Filerman, Gary Lewis *healthcare educator*
Finneran, John G., Jr. *lawyer, diversified financial services company executive*
Fitzgerald, Peter Gosselin *bank executive, former United States Senator from Illinois*
Fleischer, Walter Hersch *lawyer*
Ford, Nelson M. *consulting firm executive*
Forman, Lee Lavinthal *museum administrator*
Gallagher, Brian *editor*
Gammon, James Alan *lawyer*
George, Paul G. *mortgage company executive*
Glassman, M. Melissa *lawyer*
Goktepe, Janet Rose *retired financial analyst*
Graham, Thomas, Jr. *lawyer*
Grasso, Alfred *engineering company executive, systems engineer*
Haldeman, Ed (Charles Edgar Haldeman Jr.) *mortgage company executive, former investment company executive*
Harbach, Ed (Frank Edwin Harbach) *management and technology consulting executive*
Hashemi, Nastaran *research assistant professor*
Hewitt, Lleyton Glynn *professional tennis player*
Hillen, John Francis *think-tank executive, former federal agency administrator*
Hillkirk, John M. *newspaper editor*
Horan, Richard T., Jr. *lawyer*
Hunke, David Lawrence *publishing executive*
Ingersoll, William Boley *lawyer, real estate developer*
Jackson, William Paul, Jr. *lawyer*
Jayne, Edward Randolph, II, *executive search consultant*
Johnson, Omotunde Evan George *economist*
Kane, Michael G. *publishing executive*
Kautt, Glenn Gregory *financial planner, consultant*
Knebel, John Albert *lawyer, former United States Secretary of Agriculture*
Koskinen, John Andrew *former mortgage company executive*
Layman, Lawrence *naval officer*
Layson, William McIntyre *retired research consulting company executive*
Leiter, Michael E. *federal official*
LeSourd, Nancy Susan Oliver *lawyer, writer*
Mahan, Clarence *federal agency administrator, writer*
Main, David C. *lawyer*
Malley, Raymond Charles *retired foreign service official, industrial executive*
Manikas, Kyle G. *prosecutor*
Marino, Michael Frank III *lawyer*
Mars, Forrest E., Jr. *candy company executive*
Mars, John Franklyn *candy company executive*
Martore, Gracia C. *publishing company executive*
Mathews, Linda McVeigh *newspaper editor*
Mayman, Todd A. *publishing executive, lawyer*
McClure, Roger John *lawyer*
McCorkindale, Douglas Hamilton *publishing executive*
McInerney, James Eugene, Jr. *trade association executive*
Meltzer, Steven Lee *lawyer*
Michaels, Paul S. *food products executive*
Miller, David L. *lawyer*
Miller, Donald Eugene *lawyer*
Molineaux, Charles Borromeo *lawyer, arbitrator, columnist, poet*
Morris, James Malachy *lawyer*
Mortensen, Robert Henry *landscape and golf course architect*
Murphy, Mary *retired librarian*
Nobil, James Howard, Jr. *real estate investor, developer, broker, consultant*
Nothaft, Frank Emile *economist*
Orkand, Donald Saul *management consultant*
Parshall, Gerald *journalist*
Perlin, Gary Laurence *diversified financial services company executive*
Perlman, Mike *mortgage company executive*
Pike, Lynn A. *bank executive*
Price, Ilene Rosenberg *lawyer*
Quinlan, J(oseph) Michael *lawyer*
Rath, Manik K. *lawyer*
Rose, Susan Porter *management and governmental affairs consultant*
Rosenbaum, David Mark *engineering executive, consultant, educator*
Russell, Theodore Emery *diplomat*
Safer, John *sculptor*
Salem, Rhonda Ziadeh *language and special education educator*
Saylor, Michael J. *computer software company executive*
Schneider, Peter Raymond *retired political scientist*
Schubert, Richard Francis *social services administrator, consultant*
Shapiro, Nelson Hirsh *lawyer*
Shortal, Terence Michael *retired systems company executive*
Shrader, Ralph William *consulting firm executive*
Sirilla, George M. *lawyer*
Stoddart, Veronica Gould *travel editor*
Strom, Leland A. *federal agency administrator*
Stump, John Sutton *retired lawyer*
Talbot, Lee Merriam *ecologist, educator, administrator*
Talbot, Martha Hayne *conservationist, biologist*
Tansill, Frederick Joseph *lawyer*
Taylor, George Peach, Jr. *aerospace transportation executive, retired military officer*
Theon, John Speridon *meteorologist, researcher*

Thernstrom, Abigail *federal agency administrator, writer*
Trout, Maurice Elmore *diplomat*
Van Lare, Wendell John *lawyer, director*
Wallace, Barbara Brooks *writer*
Wallace, Robert Bruce *retired surgeon*
Walsh, John Breffni *aerospace consultant*
Watson, Jerry Carroll *advertising executive*
Wilchins, Howard Martin *lawyer*
Witherell, Bruce M. *mortgage company executive*
Wright, William Evan *physician, consultant*
Yarborough, William Glenn, Jr. *military officer, forester, international business executive*
Zakheim, Dov Solomon *economist, former federal agency administrator*

Mclean
McBride, Timothy J. *lobbyist*
Rose, Mitch *lobbyist*

Meadowview
Kingsolver, Barbara Ellen *writer*

Mechanicsville
Avery, Eugene Leo *special education educator, retired automotive executive*
Beatty, Pamela Sanders *theater educator*
Bierman, James L. *health products executive*
den Hartog, Grace Robinson *lawyer, health products executive*
Gerrish, Brian Albert *theologian, educator, retired minister*
Hinkle, Barton Leslie *retired electronics company executive*
Minor, George Gilmer III *drug and hospital supply company executive*
Silver, Timothy Milton *physician, educator*
Smith, Craig R. *health products executive*
Wells, Mary Julia *psychologist*

Melfa
Grewe, Kim E. *literature and language professor*
Weitzel, Paul *finance educator*

Merrifield
Bumgarner, Robert L. *pathologist, retired military officer*

Middleburg
Boardman, Harold Frederick, Jr. *lawyer, corporate executive*
Langley, Rolland Ament, Jr. *engineering and management consultant*
McNichols, Gerald Robert *consulting company executive*
Paige, Wayne Leo *visual arts educator, artist*
Parkinson, James Thomas III *investment consultant*
Sodolski, John *retired professional society administrator*
Tourney, Michele Marie *archivist, historian*
vom Baur, Daphne de Blois *artist*
Yovanovich, Robyn Dobson *theater educator, department chairman*

Middletown
Brumbaugh, James *economics professor*

Midlothian
Cauthen, Charles Edward, Jr. *retired retail executive, management consultant*
Chapman, Gilbert Whipple, Jr. *publishing executive*
Friedel, Robert Oliver *physician*
Lamont-Gordon, Melissa Lynne *orchestra director, music educator*
Parrott, Neva *language educator*
Seay, William Claude, Jr. *history professor, geography educator*
Wadsworth, Robert David *advertising executive*

Mineral
Donald, James Robert *federal agency administrator, writer, economist*
Mayo, Louis Allen *policy management counseling company executive*
Speer, Jack Atkeson *publisher*
Stauffer, Ronald Eugene *lawyer, physicist*

Monterey
Tabatznik, Bernard *retired cardiologist*

Montross
Fountain, Robert Roy, Jr. *retired engineering company executive, farmer, military officer*

Mount Vernon
Belden, David Leigh *professional society executive, engineering educator*
Hartwell, Stephen *investment company executive*
Spiegel, H. Jay *lawyer*

Natural Bridge Station
Randolph-Broughman, Mary Etta *music educator*

Newington
Robertson, Jean Elizabeth *sociology educator*

Newport News
Buoncristiani, A. Martin *retired physics professor*
Cardman, Lawrence Santo *physics professor, researcher*
Cleeton, David Lawrence *economist, educational administrator*
Costa, Gerousis *physics professor*
Drummond, Neil Hiden *retired secondary school educator*
Forbes, Sarah Elizabeth *gynecologist, real estate company officer*
Fox, Margaret Louise *retired secondary school educator*
Frank, Joe S. *Mayor, Newport News, Virginia, lawyer*
Goldberg, Stanley Irwin *real estate company executive*
Hightower, John Brantley *retired museum administrator*
Hubbard, Harvey Hart *aeroacoustician, noise control engineer, consultant*
Hurst, Lon *theater educator, director, choreographer*
Hurst, Rebecca McNabb *language educator*
Kamp, Arthur Joseph, Jr. *lawyer*
Rossettini, Timothy James *music educator, director*
Sheaks, Barclay *artist*
Shwayder, James Mark *obstetrician-gynecologist*
Thro, William Eugene *lawyer, professor, university administrator*
Vachris, Michelle Albert *economist, educator*
Waller, George Darryl *music educator*
Williams, Cynthia Ann *small business owner, pediatrics nurse, writer, model, mentor*

Norfolk
Addis, Kay Tucker *newspaper editor*
Albert, Alan Dale *lawyer*
Baird, Edward Rouzie, Jr. *retired lawyer*
Ball, John David *clinical psychologist*
Barry, Richard Francis III *media executive*
Batten, Frank *newspaper publisher, cable broadcaster*
Bawab, Sebastian Y. *mechanical engineer, educator*
Baysal, Oktay *dean, educator*
Bishop, Bruce Taylor *lawyer*
Blount, Robert Haddock *management consultant, retired military officer*
Bonney, Hal James, Jr. *federal judge*
Bredehoft, John Michael *lawyer*
Brown, Mary Wilkes *secondary school educator*
Byrne, William Andrew *historian, educator*
Ciara, Barbara *news anchor*
Cobb, Brenda *gerontological medical social worker, counselor*
Cranford, Page Deronde *lawyer*
Crenshaw, Francis Nelson *retired lawyer*
Davidson, James Randall *educational consultant*
Davis, Mark S. *federal judge*
Davis, Russell Haden *counseling administrator, consultant*
Davis, Terry Hunter, Jr. *lawyer*
Dimino, Joseph C. *lawyer*
Donohue, David Patrick *retired engineering executive, military officer*
Drescher, John Webb *lawyer*
Faulconer, Robert Jamieson *pathologist, educator*
Filer, Larry *economics professor*
Finney, Fannie *minister, educator*
Fisher, Randall G. *pediatrician, educator*
Fraim, Paul D. *Mayor, Norfolk, Virginia*
Geddis, Demetris L. *engineering educator, researcher*
Goode, David Ronald *retired transportation company executive*
Gopinath, Mahesh *finance educator*
Habib, Imtiaz H. *language educator*
Han, Joseph Khristian *medical association administrator*
Heller, Dana A. *literature and language professor, director*
Hennessey, William John *museum director*
Hixon, James A. *lawyer, rail transportation executive*
Hubbard, Harold *political science professor*
Isekeije, Solomon Rowland *artist, educator*
Islam, Mohammed Nazrul *engineering educator, researcher*
Jamison, Joi Nichole *media specialist, performing company executive, educator*
Johnson, David Allan *internist, gastroenterologist, educator*
Karim, Mohammad Ataul *electrical engineering educator, researcher*
Kinzer, Amanda *performing arts educator*
Koch, James Verch *academic administrator, economist*
Kunz, Donald Lee *aeronautical engineer*
Lo, Bruce Mingyung *emergency physician*
Luttrell, William Ernest *naval officer, industrial hygienist, toxicologist, educator*
Maly, Kurt John *computer science educator*
Manion, Mark D. *rail transportation executive*
Martin, Howard W., Jr. *lawyer*
Mattis, James N. *career military officer*
McKee, Timothy Carlton *taxation educator*
McKinney, Sueanne E. *education educator*
Miller, Christine Marie *sales, marketing and public relations executive*
Miller, Khadijah Olivia *education educator*
Mohieldin, Taj Osman *engineering educator*
Moorman, Charles W. *transportation executive*
Naik, Dayanand N. *statistician, educator*
Neumann, Serina Ann Louise *psychologist, researcher*
Newkirk, Ingrid *animal rights organization administrator*
Nicholson, Myreen Moore *artist, researcher*
Oelberg, David George *neonatologist educator, researcher*
Okeke, Constance O. *ophthalmologist, educator*
Okpodu, Camellia Moses *biology professor, researcher*
Padgett, John David *lawyer*
Pariser, David Michael *dermatologist, educator*
Parker, Richard Wilson *lawyer, retired rail transportation executive*
Pasch, James Roy *consultant, military employee*
Pearson, John Yeardley, Jr. *lawyer*
Phillips, Richard *cargo ship captain*
Platsoucas, Chris Dimitrios *immunologist*
Popescu, Otilia *engineering educator*
Poston, Anita Owings *lawyer*
Qian, Sun *finance educator*
Ryan, John Morgan *lawyer*
Shannon, John Sanford *lawyer, retired rail transportation executive*
Sizemore, William Howard, Jr. *journalist*
Squires, James A. *rail transportation executive*
Steele, James Eugene *retired school system administrator*
Strasnick, Barry *otolaryngologist, health facility administrator, educator*
Taylor-Fishwick, David *immunologist, educator*
Teal, Gilbert Earle, II, *lawyer, coast guard officer*
Tolk, Andreas *computer scientist, researcher*
Train, Harry Depue, II, *retired naval officer*
Van Buren, William Ralph III *lawyer*
Weinberg, Jerrold G. *lawyer*
Werner, Eric James *pediatrician, director*
Wilson, Harold Stacy *history professor, writer*
Wiltse, James Clark *civil engineer*
Wolcott, Hugh Dixon *obstetrics and gynecology educator*
Wright, Sally Copeland *musician, educator*
Zalensky, Andrei O. *biology professor, researcher*

North
Fang, Joong *philosopher, mathematician, educator*

North Garden
Moses, Hamilton III *neurologist, hospital administrator, consultant, author*

Oak Hill
Le, Cuoc Van *mathematics educator, electrical engineer*

Oakton
Entzminger, John Nelson, Jr. *federal agency administrator, electrical engineer*
Farwell, Albert Edmond *retired government official, consultant*
Felsburg, David F. *engineering executive, educator*
Frost, S. David *retired naval officer*
Levin, Warren Mayer *family practice physician*

Occoquan
Nemecek, Albert Duncan, Jr. *retail executive, investment banker, management consultant*

Orange
Gore, Rebecca Estes *science educator*
Thompson, Louis Milton, Jr. *public investor relations consultant*

Paeonian Springs
Sloyan, Patrick Joseph *journalist*

Penhook
Hahn, John William *retired insurance company executive*
Rhodes, Rebecca Lane *school librarian*

Petersburg
Buck, Judith Brooks *principal, educator*
Dance, Gloria Fenderson *dance studio executive, ballet administrator*
Everitt, Alice Lubin *labor arbitrator*
Floyd-Savage, Karen Sue *music educator*
Garrott, Carl Lee *foreign language educator*
Gatrone, Ralph C. *chemistry professor*
Johnson, Cherlyn Ann *education educator*
Kabia, Mohamed Saidu *literature and language professor*
Lakew, Dejenie Alemayehu *mathematician*
Miles, Ruby Williams *secondary school educator*
Moore, Eddie N., Jr. *college president*
Newby, Earl Fernando *education educator*
Perdue, Diana S. *mathematician, educator*
Philipsen, Dirk Peter *history professor, consultant*
Proenza-Coles, Christina *history professor*
Rissel, Hildegard *language educator*
Slaughter, Gymama *engineering educator*
Stronach, Carey Elliott *physicist, researcher*
Townsel, A. Sylviane *language educator*

Poquoson
Holloway, Paul Fayette *retired aerospace transportation executive*
Tai, Elizabeth Shi-Jue Lee *library director*

Port Royal
Clarke-Hall, Deborah Renay *elementary school educator*

Portsmouth
DeMaio, Marlene *orthopedist, surgeon*
Jackson, Cheryl K. *English educator*
Mapp, Alf Johnson, Jr. *writer, historian, educator*
Monroe, Evelyn Jones *retired librarian*
Ojeda, Ana Maria *therapist, clinical caseworker*
Paquette, William Arthur *historian, educator*
Rampersaud Lundy, Sheryll *special education educator*
Reish, Joseph E. *psychology professor*
Weiss, Ronald Dean *biology professor*
Wolf, Jeffrey Stephen *physician*
Yarbrough, Terry Pinckney *physician*

Potomac Falls
Day, Charles Williamson *consultant*
Minton, Joseph Paul *retired safety organization executive*

Powhatan
Eberle, Charles Edward *paper and consumer products executive*

Prince George
Brown, Del M. Mauhrine *lawyer, educator*

Prospect
Shield, Julie Marie Karst *artist, educator*

Pulaski
McCarthy, Thomas James, Jr. *lawyer*

Purcellville
Grob, George Frederick *independent program evaluator*
McCurdy, Howard Earl *educator*
Sweeny, Peter Michael *lawyer, director*

Radford
Barris, Roann *art historian, educator*
Bay, Richard Joseph *art educator*
Carter, Fletcher Fairwick *university administrator, education educator retired*
Dunaway, Marsha Landrum *special education educator*
Hayes, David Lavern *librarian*
Hiltonsmith, Robert Warren *psychology professor*
James, Clarity *mezzo soprano*
Kovarik, William *communications educator, journalist, editor*
Orlov, Alexei G. *economics professor, researcher*
Radford, James H. *retired military officer, political science professor*
Turk, James Clinton, Jr. *lawyer*
Zeakes, Beverly Jean *physical education educator, department chairman*
Zeakes, Samuel John *biology professor*
Zweifel, Paul Frederick *retired physics professor*

Rapidan
Grimm, Ben Emmet *library director, consultant*

Reston
Ancell, Robert Manning *leadership organization executive*
Autor, Robert S. *finance company executive*
Biely, Debra Marie *retired military officer*
Blum, Edward Howard *investment banker*
Bradley, Murray L(ee) *librarian*
Bredehoft, Elaine Charlson *lawyer*
Brennan, Norma Jean *retired professional society administrator*
Brown, Dudley Earl, Jr. *retired health science association and federal agency administrator, retired military officer*
Brust, Robert H. *telecommunications industry executive*
Burgujian, Richard V. *lawyer*
Choe, Tae Eun *research scientist*
Christian, Eliot Jordan *information technology manager, consultant*
Clark, Jonathan C. *finance company executive*
Conway, William E., Jr. *telecommunications industry executive, venture capitalist*
Cowan, Keith O. *telecommunications industry executive*
Dears, Donn Dougherty *electric power industry executive*
Dziak, Jack *telecommunications industry executive*
East, Mary Ann Hildegarde *vocalist*
Epstein, Gary Marvin *lawyer*
Focazio, Michael Joseph *hydrologist, educator*
Foley, Christopher P. *lawyer*
Foosaner, Robert Stephen *telecommunications industry executive, lawyer*
Gates, James David *retired professional society administrator*
Grant, Carl Nothhaft III *business executive*
Gude, Atish *telecommunications industry executive*
Harrison, William Henry *retired medical educator*
Heleen, Mark L. *lawyer, finance company executive*
Hesse, Daniel Ryan *telecommunications industry executive*
Holdheim, William Wolfgang *retired comparative literature educator*
Hope, Samuel Howard *accreditation organization executive*
Hughes, Lauren *medical association administrator*
Jacyna, Garry Michael *research scientist*
Kahn, Robert E. *electrical engineer*
Kohlberg, Ira *physicist, mathematician*
Kramish, Arnold *physicist, historian, writer*
Kreyling, Edward George, Jr. *retired railroad executive*
LeFave, Richard T.C. *telecommunications industry executive*
Lord, Albert L. *finance company executive*
Madry-Taylor, Jacquelyn Yvonne *educational association administrator*
Maher, David Willard *Internet company executive*
Mogge, Harriet Morgan *educational association executive*
Myerson, Jay Barry *lawyer*
Naeser, Nancy Dearien *geologist, researcher*
Natale, Patrick J. *professional society administrator*
Palumbo, James Fredrick *finance company executive*
Payne, Roger Lee *geographer*
Pendergraft, David *lean six sigma consultant*
Plave, Lee Jonathan *lawyer*
Polemitou, Olga Andrea *accountant*
Powell, Anne Elizabeth *editor-in-chief*
Radhakrishnan, Rajesh *architect*
Rau, Lee Arthur *lawyer*
Redden, Shelton Dennis *telecommunications industry executive*
Reicin, Eric David *lawyer*
Remondi, John F. (Jack Remondi) *finance company executive*
Rosendhal, Jeffrey David *federal agency administrator, educator, astronomer, consultant*
Sarreals, Sonia *data processing executive, consultant*
Saville, Paul C. *construction executive*
Schar, Dwight C. *construction executive*
Scharff, Joseph Laurent *lawyer*
Scheeler, James Arthur *architect*
Scott, Betsy Sue *lawyer*
Shank, Fred Ross *food scientist*
Sharara, Fady Ihsan *reproductive endocrinologist, infertility specialist*
Smith, Ralph Lee *writer, musician*
Terracciano, Anthony Patrick *finance company executive*
Tucker, Robert David *geologist*
van Oss, Hendrik G. *geologist*
West, Barry J. *telecommunications industry executive*
Witt, Ruth Hutt *management consultant*
Young, Loretta Ann *auditor*

Rice
Hildebrandt, Susan A. *language educator*

Richlands
Sullivan, Sheila C. *critical care nurse, educator*

Richmond
Agee, G(eorge) Steven *federal judge, former state supreme court justice*

Allen, Jeffrey Rodgers *lawyer*
Amann, Patricia Burgess *special education educator*
Anderson, Bette (Bonnie) Ferguson *music educator*
Atkinson, Richard Lee, Jr. *internal medicine educator*
Austin, John D. *corporate financial executive*
Avrutin, Vitaliy *electrical engineer, researcher*
Ayers, Edward L. *academic administrator, history professor*
Bacon, Diane Briggs *music educator, consultant*
Ballentine, Ron *pharmacist, educator*
Balster, Robert Louis *Alcohol/Drug Abuse Educator Researcher*
Bartle, Samuel Thomas *pediatrician*
Bates, Hampton Robert, Jr. *pathologist*
Beran, David R. *food products executive*
Betts, James Edward *lawyer*
Black, Robert Perry *bank executive*
Blair, Robert E. *medical educator, researcher*
Blake, Peter A. *state agency administrator*
Blankenship, Don L. *energy executive*
Blumberg, Michael Zangwill *allergist*
Bolling, Bill (William T. Bolling) *Lieutenant Governor of Virginia*
Bonchev, Danail Georgiev *chemist, educator*
Booker, Lewis Thomas *lawyer*
Boudinot, F. Douglas *medical educator*
Boudinot, Frank Douglas *dean*
Bovender, Jack Oliver, Jr. *hospital management company executive*
Bray, Patricia Shannon *music educator, musician, small business owner*
Brewer, W. Keith *tobacco company executive*
Broadbent, Peter Edwin, Jr. *lawyer*
Brockenbrough, Henry Watkins *retired lawyer*
Brooks, Robert Franklin, Sr. *lawyer*
Brown, Marilyn Branch *retired educational administrator*
Browning, Keith D. *automotive executive*
Bryan, John Stewart III *newspaper publisher*
Bryson, William Hamilton *law educator*
Buckley, Kevin Joseph *lawyer*
Buford, Robert Pegram *lawyer*
Bunzl, Rudolph Hans *retired manufacturing executive*
Burrus, Robert Lewis, Jr. *lawyer*
Burton, Melvin Cosby, Jr. *economics professor, financial consultant*
Carlock, Margo *museum association administrator*
Carpenter, Everett E. *research scientist, educator*
Carrico, Harry Lee *retired judge*
Casini, Jane Sloan *wholesale distribution executive*
Catlett, Richard H., Jr. *retired lawyer*
Chandler, Theodore Lindy, Jr. *title insurance company executive, lawyer*
Charlesworth, Arthur Thomas *mathematics professor*
Chewning, Thomas N. *energy executive*
Christian, David A. *energy executive*
Coalter, Milton J., Jr. *library director, educator*
Cogbill, John Valentine III *lawyer*
Compton, Olin Randall *consulting electrical engineer, researcher*
Conti, Richard C. *museum director*
Cooper, William Edwin *professor, former academic administrator*
Corey, Linda Ann *medical educator, researcher*
Cornis-Pope, Marcel Horatiu *literature educator, literary critic, program director*
Cranwell, C. Richard *political organization administrator, lawyer*
Cutchins, Clifford Armstrong, IV, *lawyer*
Cuttino, Laurie Wright *medical educator*
Dan, Michael T. *security firm executive*
Daniel, Wilbon Harrison *retired history professor*
Davidson, C. Simon *lawyer, columnist*
Dehn, James Keith *investment company executive*
Dhillon, Gurpreet *economics professor*
Dias, Fiona P. *retail executive*
Dohnal, Dennis William *judge*
Dostart, Thomas J. *lawyer*
Doswell, Mary Cummings *energy executive*
Douglass, John G. *dean*
Drain, Cecil B. *dean, nursing educator, retired military officer*
Dray, Mark Stanley *lawyer*
Dunn, Linda Baugh *middle school educator*
Dunn, Philip J. *retail executive*
Eakin, Frank Edwin, Jr. *religious studies educator*
Effel, Laura *lawyer*
Ellis, Andrew Jackson, Jr. *lawyer*
Epstein, David Stanley *educator, consultant*
Face, E. Joseph, Jr. *state banking agency administrator*
Farrell, Nicholas Patrick *chemistry professor, researcher*
Farrell, Thomas Francis, II, *energy executive*
Fauls, Thomas E. (Ted) *lawyer*
Fenn, John Bennett *chemist, educator*
Folliard, Thomas J. *automotive executive*
Fraizer, Michael D. *insurance company executive*
Framme, Lawrence Henry III *political organization administrator, lawyer*
Freed, David Clark *artist*
Freeman, Edward Carl, Jr. *music minister*
Freeman, George C. III *tobacco company executive, lawyer*
Freeman, George Clemon, Jr. *lawyer*
Fuller-Seeley, Kathryn Helgesen *historian, educator*
Gad-el-Hak, Mohamed *aerospace and mechanical engineering educator, researcher*
Gandy, Gerald Larmon *rehabilitation counseling educator, psychologist, writer*
Ganeriwala, Manju S. *state treasurer*
Gary, Richard David *lawyer*
Gerner, John *financial consultant*
Giacobbe, George Antonino *special education educator, violinist*
Givens, Terryl L. *literature educator*
Glass, Carmen Cecilia *language educator*
Glasser, Wolfgang Gerhard *science researcher, educator*
Gluck, Michelle H. *lawyer*
Goodpasture, Philip Henry *lawyer*
Goodwyn, S. Bernard *state supreme court justice*
Goolsby, Allen Cunningham III *lawyer*
Gottwald, Floyd Dewey, Jr. *chemicals executive, director*
Green, Kristina F. *academic administrator, optician*
Gregory, Roger Lee *federal judge*
Grey, Robert J., Jr. *lawyer*
Griffith, Howard Morgan *state legislator, lawyer*
Gulbis, Natalie Anne *professional golfer, television personality*
Guney-Altay, Ozge *research scientist*
Hackney, Virginia Howitz *lawyer*
Hall, James H(errick), Jr. *philosophy educator, writer*
Hall, Stephen Charles *lawyer*
Hamel, Dana Bertrand *academic administrator*
Hanley, Katherine Keith *Secretary of the Commonwealth, Virginia*
Hardy, Richard Earl *rehabilitation counseling educator*
Harlow, John T. *electronics company executive*
Harris, Ruth Hortense Coles *retired finance educator*
Hassell, Leroy Rountree, Sr. *state supreme court chief justice*
Hayes, Curtis W. *radiologist, director*
Heaton, Stuart Alan *lawyer*
Hedgebeth, Reginald D. *lawyer, retail executive*
Heinicke, Craig Warren *economics professor*
Helwig, Arthur Woods *retired chemical company executive*
Henderson, Harriet *librarian, director*
Hettrick, George Harrison *lawyer*
Hetzer, G. Scott *energy executive*
Holm, George L. *food products executive*
Hughes, Mike *advertising executive*
Hunt, Ronald J. *dean, dental educator*
Hylton, Raymond Pierre *history professor, researcher*
Inlow, D. Ronald *academic administrator, consumerism lecturer, food service consultant*
Izyumskaya, Natalia *researcher*
Jacobs, Harry Milburn, Jr. *advertising executive*
Jenkins, William Schley III *theatrical designer*
Joel, William Lee, II, *interior and lighting designer*
Johnson, Craig A. *tobacco company executive*
Johnson, Patricia Lee *mathematics educator*
Jones, Dwight Clinton *Mayor, Richmond, Virginia*
Jones, Jeanne Pitts *pre-school administrator*
Jun, Jungwook *transportation engineer, researcher*
Kaine, Timothy Michael *Governor of Virginia*
Keane, Denise F. *lawyer, food products executive*
Kearfott, Joseph Conrad *lawyer*
Keenan, Barbara Milano *state supreme court justice*
Kelleher, Patrick B. *insurance company executive*
Kendler, Kenneth S. *medical educator*
Kennedy, Patricia Berry *retired music educator*
Kilgore, Jerry Walter *lawyer, former state attorney general*
King, Robert Leroy *business administration educator*
Kinser, Cynthia D. *state supreme court justice*
Knight, Wendy Diana *risk management officer*
Koonce, Paul D. *energy executive*
Koontz, Lawrence L., Jr. *state supreme court justice*
Kornstein, Susan G. *medical educator*
Kozlowski, Ronald Stephan *retired librarian*
Kukreja, Rakesh C. *medical educator*
Lacker, Jeffrey Malcolm *bank executive, economist*
Lacy, Elizabeth Bermingham *state supreme court justice*
Laskin, Daniel M. *oral and maxillofacial surgeon, educator*
Lawrence, Walter, Jr. *surgeon, educator*
LeBlanc, Daniel G. *state official*
Lee, Ivey Owen *multimedia designer*
Leggett, Gloria Jean *minister*
Lemons, Donald W. *state supreme court justice*
Levit, Héloïse B. (Ginger Levit) *art historian, journalist, art dealer, consultant*
Lutz, Jacob A., III, (Jake Lutz) *lawyer*
Margolin, Eric Mitchell *lawyer*
Marshall Traino, Heather M. *researcher*
Mattauch, Robert Joseph *retired electrical engineering educator, retired dean*
McCall, Shedrick Dwight *psychologist*
McClard, Jack Edward *lawyer*
McCrimmon, Miles *educator*
McCullough, James P., Jr. *psychology professor*
McDermid, Margaret E. (Lyn McDermid) *information technology executive, engineer*
McDonnell, Bob (Robert Francis) *former state attorney general, state legislator*
McFarlane, Walter Alexander *lawyer, educator*
McGee, Henry Alexander, Jr. *academic administrator*
McGettrick, Mark F. *energy executive*
Meath, James V. *lawyer*
Melcher, Elizabeth *musician*
Merrell, Ronald Clifton *surgeon, educator*
Miah, Abdul Jalil *library director*
Millette, LeRoy F., Jr. *state supreme court justice*
Mims, William Cleveland *state attorney general, lawyer*
Mollen, Edward Leigh *pediatrician, allergist, clinical immunologist*
Moore, Andrew Taylor, Jr. *banker*
Moore, David C. *tobacco company executive*
Moore, Thurston Roach *lawyer*
Morris, James Carl *architect*
Moss, Princess Renai *elementary school educator*
Munro, George E. *history professor*
Nadal, Anita *language educator*
Natarajan, Ramesh *medical educator*
Neal, Gail Fallon *physical therapist, educator*
Nelson, John Robert, Jr. *manufacturing executive*
Nestler, John Edwin *endocrinology educator*
Nixon, J.V. *cardiologist, educator*
Nyerges, Alexander Lee *museum director*
Ornato, Joseph P. *emergency physician, educator*
Owen, Duncan Shaw, Jr. *internist, retired educator*
Pagan, John Ruston *law educator*
Parrish, Steven C. *tobacco company executive*
Pearsall, John Wesley *lawyer*
Peart, Sandra Joan *dean*
Peebles, Robert M. *tobacco company executive*
Phillips, Thomas Edworth, Jr. *financial advisor, investment management consultant*
Pidaparti, Ramana M. *engineering educator*
Pinckney, Charles Cotesworth *lawyer*
Pithawalla, Yezdi Bahadur *chemist*
Pollard, Overton Price *retired lawyer*
Poma, John M. *mining company executive, lawyer*
Pope, Robert Dean *lawyer*
Powell, Lewis Franklin III *lawyer*
Pulley, (J.) Waverly. (III) *lawyer*
Pusey, William Anderson *lawyer*
Rader, Karen A. *director*
Rainey, Gordon Fryer, Jr. *lawyer*
Rawls, S. Waite III *museum director, investment company executive*
Redmond, David Dudley *lawyer*
Remley, Karen *state agency administrator, public health service officer*
Reshchikov, Michael A. *physics professor, researcher*
Rettig, James R. *university librarian, library association executive*
Rhoads, Mark B. *lawyer*
Richardson, David Walthall *cardiologist, educator, consultant*
Rigsby, Linda Flory *lawyer, director*
Rilling, John Robert *history professor*
Robertson, Gregory B. *lawyer*
Roday, Leon E. *lawyer, finance company executive*
Rogers, Steven A. *energy executive*
Rohr, Mark C. *chemicals executive*
Rolfe, Robert Martin *lawyer*
Salley, John Jones *retired academic administrator, oral pathologist*
Salomon, Dalal Maria *financial consultant*
Sanderlin, James L. *energy executive, lawyer*
Sawyer, Richard DeWight, Jr. *psychologist*
Schutz, Pamela S. *insurance company executive*
Schwarzschild, Jane L. *lawyer*
Sedaghat, Hassan *mathematician, educator*
Shall, Mary Snyder *physical therapist, educator*
Sharer, John Daniel *lawyer*
Shiembob, Mark S. *lawyer*
Sirica, Alphonse Eugene *pathology educator*
Slater, Thomas Glascock, Jr. *lawyer*
Slaughter, Alexander Hoke *lawyer*
Smith, R. Gordon *lawyer*
Spahn, Gary Joseph *lawyer*
Starke, Harold Eugene, Jr. *lawyer*
Sterling, Anne D. *not-for-profit developer*
Sterling, Keir Brooks *historian, educator*
Stone, Jacquelyn Elois *lawyer*
Stover, Jill S. *school librarian, writer*
Strauss, Jerome Frank III *medical researcher, educator*
Strickland, William Jesse *lawyer*
Stutts, James F. *lawyer, energy executive*
Sullivan, Walter Francis *bishop emeritus*
Sun, Qiang *scientist, educator*
Svikis, Dace Susan *medical educator*
Takabe, Kazuaki *surgeon, research scientist*
Talley, Charles Richmond *retired bank executive*
Taylor, Ashley L., Jr. *lawyer*
Terner, James *chemistry educator*
Thompson, Paul Michael *lawyer*
Tice, Douglas Oscar, Jr. *federal judge*
Torres Filho, Ivo *medical educator*
Trani, Eugene Paul *university president, educator*
Treadway, Sandra Gioia *library director*
Troy, Anthony Francis *lawyer*
Tuck, Grayson Edwin *real estate agent, gas industry executive*
Twigg, Judyth L. *political science professor*
Vetrovec, George Wayne *cardiologist, medical researcher, educator*
Waddell, William Robert *lawyer*
Walsh, William Arthur, Jr. *lawyer*
Wang, Qian *physicist, educator*
Warthen, Harry Justice III *lawyer*
Watkins, Hays Thomas *retired railroad executive*
Watts, Stephen Hurt, II, *lawyer*
Weistroffer, Heinz Roland *information systems professional, educator*
Whittemore, Anne Marie *lawyer*
Wilder, Doug (Lawrence Douglas Wilder) *Mayor, Richmond, Virginia, former governor*
Willard, Howard A. III *food products executive*
Williams, Amy McDaniel *lawyer*
Williams, Richard Leroy *federal judge*
Winslett, Stoner *artistic director*
Witt, Walter Francis, Jr. *lawyer*
Woodley, John Paul, Jr. *consulting firm executive, former civilian military employee*
Wright, Patricia I. *state official, school system administrator*
Wright, Wiley Reed, Jr. *lawyer, retired judge, mediator*
Yanchick, Victor A. *dean, educator*
Yelich, Nolan T. *library director*

Ridgeway

Martin, Leland Morris (Pappy) *historian, educator*

Roanoke

Al-Zubaidi, Amer Aziz *physicist, researcher*
Anderson, Phillip Verne *lawyer*
Bates, Harold Martin *lawyer*
Brouillard, Jack (John Charles Brouillard) *automotive parts company executive*
Burchfield, Donna Faye *dancer, educator*
Canavan, Jane Allison *psychologist*
Dagenhart, Betty Jane Mahaffey *nursing educator, administrator*
DeVries, James D. *insurance company executive*
Doan, Ruth Alden *history professor*
Dudley, Julia Campbell *prosecutor*
Estabrooks, Paul *science educator*
Fishwick, John Palmer *retired lawyer, railroad executive*
Freeland, Kevin Paul *automotive executive*
Gray, Nancy Ann Oliver *academic administrator*
Hess, Darla Bakersmith *cardiologist, educator*
Hutcheson, Jack Robert *hematologist, medical oncologist*
Jackson, Darren Richard *automotive parts company executive*
Johnson, Cynda Ann *physician, educator*
Kurtz, Jenifer *literature and language professor*
Landis, John William *retired engineering executive, consultant, government advisor*
Marshall, Heman Alexander III *lawyer*
Norona, Mike *automotive parts company executive*
Pace, G. Michael, Jr. *lawyer*
Powell, Sarah E. *lawyer, automotive executive*
Sebolt, Stephanie Ann *literature and language professor*
Steele, (Margaret) Anita Martin *law librarian, educator*
Stevens, Christopher Williams *lawyer*
Thomson, Paul Rice, Jr. *lawyer*
Turk, James Clinton *federal judge*
Wade, Jim L. (Jimmie L. Wade) *automotive executive*

Rockbridge Baths

Glidden, Robert Burr *academic administrator, music educator, consultant*

Rose Hill

Lane, Mary Winston *retired secondary school educator*

Roseland

Stemmler, Edward Joseph *physician, retired health facility administrator, dean*

Round Hill

Hillis, Catherine H. *artist*
Hillis, John David *broadcast executive, television producer, newswriter*
Schleede, Glenn Roy *marketing professional, consultant*
Tice, Raphael Dean *military officer*

Rural Retreat

Dutton, Sandra F. *music educator*
Evans, Susan W. *mathematics educator*

Saint Paul

Gregory, Ann Young *editor*

Salem

Bachelder, Elizabeth Young *musician, educator*
Bañuelos-Montes, Jose F. *language educator*
Brand, Edward Cabell *retail executive*
Brown, Gerald LaVonne *psychiatrist*
Fleenor, Matthew Clay *physics professor*
Gathercole, Patricia May *modern foreign languages educator*
Talbot, Lynn K. *language educator*
Young, James Marion *lawyer*

Sandy Point

Douglas, Daisy Howard *retired elementary school educator, writer, consultant*

Seaford

Badeaux, Earl Anthony *special education educator*
Jenkins, Margaret Bunting *human resources executive*

Smithfield

Cole, Michael H. *food products executive, lawyer*
Luter, Joseph Williamson III *meat packing and processing company executive*
Manly, Robert W., IV, *food products executive*
Pope, C. Larry *food products executive*
Zadeh, Mansour T. *food products executive*

South Hill

Huot, Rachel Irene *biomedical educator, research scientist, physician*

South Riding

Murray, Michael Patrick *lawyer*

Spotsylvania

Goforth, Deborah S. *school librarian, educator*
Hardy, Dorcas Ruth *business and government relations executive*
Hill, Jimmie Dale *retired federal agency administrator*
Manthei, Richard Dale *retired lawyer, health products executive*
Singleton, Tanya *nursing educator*

Springfield

Arifi, Fatana Baktash *artist, educator*
Benson, William Edward (Barnes) *geologist*
Bilodeau, John Edward *dental educator, consultant*
Brown, Margaret Catherine *artist*
Bruen, John Dermot *management consultant*
Campbell, Francis James *retired chemist*
Dake, Marcia Allene *retired nursing educator, dean*
de Haan, Henry John *research psychologist*
D'Elosua, Jennifer Dawn *music educator*
Englert, Roy Theodore *lawyer*
Ferrante, Jon Visconti *leadership and technology transfer executive, consultant*
Furst, Eric Jonathan *physician, surgeon*
Geiger, Richard Bernard *civil engineer, federal agency administrator*
Ginn, Richard Van Ness *retired military officer, healthcare executive*
Greer, Mark Francis *information technology executive*
Hart, Herbert Michael *military officer*
Heise, Dorothy Hilbert *retired librarian, government agency administrator*
Herbst, Ellen *federal agency administrator*
Kalkwarf, Leonard V. *minister*
Kieffer, Jarold Alan *publishing executive, writer*
Kurth, Ronald James *retired academic administrator, military officer*
Lambert, Vickie Ann *retired dean, nursing consultant*
Larson, Reed Eugene *foundation administrator*
Meikle, Philip G. *engineer, retired government agency executive*
Morsy, Mohamed Nageeb *electrical engineering educator, researcher*

Murri, Luella Davis *personnel and language professional*
Myers, Elissa Matulis *publishing executive, professional society administrator*
Shoemake, Angela Nichole *nursing educator*
Sonnemann, Harry *electrical engineer, consultant*
Starrs, James Edward *retired law and forensics educator, consultant*
Tian, Li *investment company executive, educator*
Wagner, Andrew James *retired meteorologist, elder, educator*
Williams, Cecilia Lee Pursel *optometrist*

Stafford
Dillard, Teresa Mary *school counselor*
Mezo, Richard Eugene *literature and language professor, writer*

Stanardsville
Anns, Arlene Eiserman *publishing company executive*
Anns, Philip Harold *brokerage house and pharmaceutical executive*
Keel, Alton Gold, Jr. *ambassador*

Staunton
Arnold, Albert James *retired foreign language educator, consultant*
Balsley, Philip Elwood *entertainer*
Cochran, George Moffett *retired judge*
Deeble, Paul D. *biology professor*
Garkov, Vladimir Nikolaev *chemistry professor*
Warren, Lisa Solod *writer*

Stephenson
Johnson, Eva Maria *retired translator*

Sterling
Austin, Lynne Hunzicker *secondary school educator*
Cooper, Cinder S. *literature and language professor*
Fiacco, Anthony Vincent *educator, researcher*
Friedheim, Jerry Warden *museum consultant*
Green, Darrell *retired professional football player*
Lacey, Aaron Michael *actor, director, film producer, scriptwriter*
Martin, Roger John *computer scientist*
Shepley, Magi D. *special education educator*
Souw, Bernard Eng-Kie *physicist, researcher, engineer, consultant*
Thompson, David Walker *astronautics company executive*

Suffolk
Bollinger, Michael *artistic director*
Brown, Alvenice Hortense Bryan *educator*
Burd, Joyce Ann *librarian*
Hall, Wayne Michael *management consultant*
Hines, Angus Irving, Jr. *petroleum marketing executive*
Holloway, Christopher Matthew *brokerage house executive*
Walker, Dale Maxwell *city official*

Sumerduck
McCamy, Sharon Grove *English educator*

Susan
Ambach, Dwight Russell *retired foreign service officer*

Sweet Briar
Muhlenfeld, Elisabeth Showalter *academic administrator, literature educator, writer*
Piepho, Lee (Edward Lee Piepho) *humanities educator*
Shea, Brent Mack *social sciences educator*

Tabb
Budd, Richard Wade *academic administrator, dean, priest*

Tappahannock
McGuire, Lillian (Elizabeth) Hill *historian, researcher, retired education educator, writer*

Tazewell
Weeks, Ross Leonard, Jr. *museum executive*

The Plains
Gibbons, John Howard (Jack, Jack Gibbons) *federal official, physicist*

Triangle
Thomas, Lindsey Kay, Jr. *research ecology biologist, educator, consultant*

Upperville
Powell Gebhard, Joy Lee (Bok Sin Lee) *small business owner*
Smart, Edith Merrill *civic worker*

Verona
Grizzel, Patsy (Pat) Pauline *human services administrator*
MacTavish, Susanne Hanna *retired library and information scientist*

Vienna
Anderson, Eric C. *aerospace transportation executive*
Beyer, Barbara Lynn *transportation executive, consultant*
Bhide, Manohar Gopal *nuclear scientist, educator*
Carr, Thomas A. *real estate company executive*
Chandler, Hubert Thomas *former army officer*
Cook, Jane Hampton *author, speaker, historian, commentator*
DeWitt, Charles Barbour *federal official*
Drumheller, Linda Blocher *language educator*
Edwards, Phillip Milton *retired import/export company executive*
Gardenier, John Stark *statistician, philosopher, researcher, writer*
Gardenier, Turkan Kumbaraci *statistician, researcher*
Gary, Stuart Hunter *lawyer*
Isaac, William Michael *brokerage house executive, retired federal official*
Jones, Terrence Dale *foundation executive, consultant*
Keiser, Bernhard Edward *engineering executive, communications engineer, consultant*
Mackesey, Daniel R. *lawyer*
Marx, Gary Dean *educational consultant, futurist, think-tank executive*
McElveen, Joseph James, Jr. *journalist, writer, newscaster, educator*
Monroe, Robert Rawson *national security consultant*
Olshaker, Mark Bruce *scriptwriter, filmmaker*
Olson, Walter Justus, Jr. *management consultant*
Patrick, Susan D. *educational association administrator, former federal agency administrator*
Peters, Geoffrey Wright *lawyer, fundraising executive*
Rogers, Raymond Jesse *retired federal railroad associate administrator*
Schwartz, Richard Harvey *pediatrician*
Stearns, Frank Warren *lawyer*
Titus, Bruce Earl *lawyer*
Whitaker, Thomas Patrick *lawyer*
Yamaguch, Yuriko Fujita *artist*

Virginia Beach
Agolini, Patricia *media specialist*
Alexander, William Powell *business advisor*
Antol, Joseph J. *artist*
Apperson, Jack Alfonso *retired army officer, management executive*
Baldwin, Stanley Forrest *lawyer, insurance company executive*
Barber, Vivian Kay *elementary school educator*
Carlson, James G. *healthcare services executive*
Carraway, James H. *plastic surgeon*
Carrington, Andrew Temple *education educator, consultant*
Chalk, Barbara Ann *surgical nurse*
Cheng, George Chiwo *computer scientist*
Choe, Kyle Seung *facial plastic surgeon*
de Guzman, Marsha Rhoda *special education educator*
Dixon, John Spencer *performing arts association administrator*
Felts, Margaret Jean *secondary school educator*
Fink, Eloise Bradley *art director*
Foster, Jeanne O'Cain *poet, fine arts educator*
Foster, Lori Ann Miller *psychologist*
Fraser, Ruth Hodges *city clerk*
Friedman, Andrew Mitchell *director housing and neighborhood preservation*
Grimsley, Joseph Wayne *history professor*
Hatt, Clifford Van *school system administrator, psychologist*
Hodapp, Heidi Francine *middle school educator*
Hopkins, Curtis L. *military officer, educator*
Hunter, Elizabeth M. *communications educator, director*
Ishmael, Laura Jeanne *music educator, pharmacologist*
Johnson, Janice Sims *library director*
Jones, Robert Clair *middle school educator*
Jones, Robert Griffith *law educator, mayor*
Jordan, Julia Mae *psychologist*
Lee, Marta *school librarian*
Lewis, Donald Sykes, Jr. *artist*
Lutsyshyn, Oksana *concert pianist, organist*
Melsheimer, Mel P(owell) *venture capitalist*
Melvin, Carole Ramey *educational consultant*
Morgan, Raymond Franklin *education educator*
Morrison, Jeffry H. *social sciences educator*
Oster, Gary Wayne *innovation and entrepreneurship educator*
Pickett, Owen Bradford *lawyer, former congressman*
Prescott, David L. C., Jr. *music educator*
Price, Alan Thomas *business and estate planner*
Quicke, Andrew Charles *cinema-television educator, consultant, writer*
Reece-Porter, Sharon Ann *international human rights educator*
Rephan, Jack *lawyer*
Robertson, Pat (Marion Gordon Robertson) *religious broadcasting executive, university president and chancellor*
Schreiber, Mark Traudt *psychiatrist*
Sears, Patricia Marie *elementary school educator, consultant*
Sekulow, Jay Alan *lawyer*
Selig, William George *academic administrator*
Sessoms, William D., Jr. *Mayor, Virginia Beach, Virginia, bank executive*
Shapiro, Richard N. *lawyer*
Shuttleworth, Thomas B., II, *lawyer*
Smith, Bruce *real estate company executive, retired professional football player*
Smith, Thelma Cheryl *principal, minister*
Spitzli, Donald Hawkes, Jr. *lawyer*
Spivak, Maurice Sidney *civil engineer, consultant*
Stansberry, James Wesley *air force officer*
Swail, Watson Scott *educational association administrator*
Talag, Trinidad Santos *retired educator*
Thomas, Jimi Elizabeth *elementary school educator*
Von Mosch, Wanda Gail *principal*
Wales, Lorene M. *film producer, educator*
Whitfield, Erica Sharon *director, career planning administrator*
Wick, Robert Thomas *retired supermarket executive*
Woodward, Lawrence H. *lawyer*
Ziegler, Rochelle Elizabeth *special education educator*

Ware Neck
McVey, Henry Hanna III *retired lawyer*
Tabb, Waller Crockett *retired allergist, immunologist*

Warrenton
Bobbitt, David Carroll *history professor*
Day, Bill S., Jr. *entrepreneur*
Howard, Blair Duncan *lawyer*
Keys, Robert Green *literature and language educator*
Killinger, John Eric *editor-in-chief, director*
Malmgren, Harald Bernard *economist*
Pribram, Karl Harry *neuroscience and psychology educator, brain researcher*

Washington
Arbelbide, C(indy) L(ea) *librarian, historian, author*
O'Connell, Patrick *chef*

Wattsville
Enright, William Maurice *retired literature and language educator*

Waynesboro
Alexander, William Woodward, Jr. *military officer*

Weems
Martin, William Raymond *retired financial manager*

Weyers Cave
Martinkosky, Jessica *art educator*

Wicomico Church
Kenna, Gail Ann *secondary and higher education educator*

Williamsburg
Al-Shalchi, Olla Najah *language educator*
Axtell, James Lewis *history professor*
Brooks, Philip Coolidge, Jr. *archivist, curator, historian*
Calver, Richard Allen *retired dean*
Campbell, Colin Goetze *foundation president*
Chappell, Miles Linwood, Jr. *art historian, educator*
Christison, Muriel Branham *retired museum director, art history educator*
Church, Dale Walker *lawyer*
Clark, Morton Hutchinson *lawyer*
Clavero, Cesar *research scientist*
Coakley, Richard Walker *retired chemical engineer*
Coleman, Henry Edwin *artist, educator*
Connell, Alastair McCrae *physician*
Connolly, Martha Taugher *voice educator*
Crapol, Edward P. *history professor*
Delos, John Bernard *physicist*
Denyes, James Richard *industrial engineer*
Douglas, Davison McDowell *dean, law educator*
Emerson, Philip G. *historic site director*
Esler, Anthony James *historian, novelist, educator*
Farrar, John Thruston *health facility administrator*
Fauvel, Maryse *language educator*
Finn, A. Michael *corporate communications specialist*
Fletcher, Mary Eason *voice educator*
Freeman, Rowland Godfrey III *retired manufacturing executive, military officer, consultant*
Gavaler, Joan Susan *dance educator*
Gentry, James William *retired state agency administrator*
Goldman, Alan H. *philosophy educator*
Gordon, Baron Jack *stockbroker*
Gottfried, Mark Ellis *accountant, consultant*
Graham, David Browning *lawyer*
Guastaferro, Angelo *space science administrator, consultant*
Heller, James Stephen *law librarian, educator*
Herrmann, Benjamin Edward *former insurance executive*
Hoffman, Ronald *historian, educator*
Holstein, William Kurt *business administration educator*
Hornsby, Bruce Randall *composer, musician*
Jacoby, William Jerome, Jr. *internist, retired military officer*
Kerns, Virginia B. *anthropologist, writer*
Kottas, John Frederick *business administration educator*
Landen, Robert Geran *retired historian, academic administrator*
Lange, Carl James *retired psychology professor*
Lynn, Larry (Verne Lauriston Lynn) *engineering executive*
Maloney, Milford Charles *retired internal medicine educator*
Marcus, Paul *law educator*
Margolin, Robert Jeremy *lawyer*
Martin, Fusi Fonkijom *film director, educator*
McCarthy, Connie Kearns *university librarian*
McGiffert, Michael *retired historian*
McLennan, Barbara Nancy *tax specialist*
Montgomery, Joseph William *financial consultant*
Nettels, Elsa *English language educator*
O'Connell, William Edward, Jr. *retired finance educator*
O'Connor, Sandra Day *retired United States supreme court justice*
Paige, Hilliard Wegner *corporate executive, consultant*
Pearson, Roy Laing *business administration educator*
Prokhorova, Elena V. *language educator*
Pulley, Larry (Lawrence B. Pulley) *dean, economics professor*
Rahman, Zia-Ur *research scientist*
Ramer, Deborah Lynne *special education educator*
Reiss, Mitchell B. *academic administrator, law educator, former ambassador*
Reveley, Walter Taylor III *academic administrator, former dean, law educator*
Ringlesbach, Dorothy Louise *retired nurse, writer*
Roberson, Robert S. *investment company executive*
Robinson, Jay (Thurston) *artist*
Rodman, Leiba *mathematician*
Sass, Arthur Harold *educational training administrator*
Schwartz, Miles Joseph *retired cardiologist*
Sherman, Richard Beatty *historian, educator*
Smith, Roger Winston *retired political theory educator*
Smith, William Henry Preston *freelance/self-employed writer, editor, former telecommunications industry executive*
Spitzer, Cary Redford *avionics consultant, electrical engineer*
Stanley, Shirley Davis *artist*
Starnes, Sofia Molina *writer, editor*
Starnes, William Herbert, Jr. *chemist, educator*
Starry, Donn Albert *retired aerospace corporate executive, retired military officer*
Sullivan, Timothy Jackson *museum administrator, retired academic administrator, educator*
Tanglao Aguas, Francis *performing arts association administrator, educator*
Towle, Leland Hill *retired federal agency administrator*
Vold, Robert Lawrence *science educator*
Voorhess, Mary Louise *pediatric endocrinologist*
Wallach, Alan *art historian, educator*
Wilkerson, Lawrence B. *former federal official, retired military officer*

Winchester
Aiosa, Charlotte Nelson *music educator*
Bechamps, Gerald Joseph *surgeon*
Bloom, Mary Ann *music educator*
Bonometti, Robert John *technology management and strategy executive*
Byrd, Harry Flood, Jr. *publishing executive, Former United States Senator, Virginia*
Conteh, Nabie Y. *information systems and computer technology educator*
Engelage, James Roland *commercial property manager*
Gouldey, Bruce K. *finance educator*
Helentjaris, Diane *physician*
Holland, James Tulley *retired plastics company executive*
Johnson, Carl Harold *trauma psychologist, director*
Kolt, Robert Paul *musicologist, conductor*
Larson, Robert Peter *music educator, director*
Lederer, Doris *musician*
Ludwig, George Harry *retired physicist, electrical engineer*
Rahman, Ateequr *pharmacist, educator*
Roberts, Charles Stewart *surgeon*
Romano, Charlene Baughan *music educator*
Schweitzer, Petra *literature and language professor*
Sproul, Joan Heeney *retired elementary school educator*
Tillmann, Richard *literature and language educator*

Wise
Kellogg, Melinda Jane *physics professor*
Ponce - Ortiz, Esteban *literature and language professor*
Smiddy, Joseph Charles *retired academic administrator*
Volk, David Paul *music educator*
Wolny, Witold Paul *social studies educator, consultant*

Woodberry Forest
Campbell, Dennis Marion *academic administrator, theologian, educator*

Woodbridge
Binder, L. James *retired magazine editor, journalist*
Figueroa, Carmen R. *language educator, assistant dean*
Flori, Anna Marie DiBlasi *health facility administrator, nurse, anesthesiologist*
Garon, Richard Joseph, Jr. *political organization worker*
Gilmore, Marjorie Havens *retired civic worker, lawyer*
Hood, Ronald Chalmers III *historian, writer*
Kellermann, Charles William *information scientist, educator*
Lanza, William Paul *academic administrator*
Messerschmidt, William Harclerode *retired non-commissioned officer, musician*
Peck, Dianne Kawecki *architect*
Rebhan, Gail *art educator*
Rethmel, Carol Ann *voice educator, director*
Sandler, Betty Moore *lawyer*
Tin, Jan *economist*
Zhao, Tong *management consultant*

Woodstock
Walton, Morgan Lauck III *lawyer*

Wytheville
Linzey, Donald Wayne *biologist, educator, researcher*

Yorktown
Faron, Kathleen Adams *elementary school educator, department chairman*
Henney, Frederic Allison *retired English language educator*
Pinelli, Thomas Edward *information scientist*
Wood, James Edward, Jr. *religion educator, author*

WASHINGTON

Anacortes
Businger, Joost Alois *atmospheric scientist, educator*
Cavanaugh, Michael Everett *lawyer, arbitrator, mediator*
Higgins, Robert (Walter) *career naval officer, physician*
Hoffmann, Manfred Walter *consulting company executive*
Kozloff, Eugene Nicholas *zoologist, educator, author*
Mc Cracken, Philip Trafton *sculptor*
Pratt, David Terry *engineering consultant*
Stoebe, Thomas Gaines *materials science educator*
Tornow, L. William *musician*

Arlington
Gerwick, Madeline Carol *marketing and timing professional*

Auburn
Ma, Zhenkui *remote sensing applications scientist, consultant*

Bainbridge Island
Berg, Walter Louis *retired history professor*
Brians, Paul Edward *retired literature and language professor*
Burns, Shirley MacDonald *artist, educator*
Carlson, Robert Michael *artist*
Cassella, William Nathan, Jr. *retired not-for-profit organization executive*
Harrison, Cynthia L. *librarian*

Battle Ground
Caltagirone, Paul John *psychologist*
Ezelle, Robert Eugene *diplomat*

Belfair
Hager, Robert Worth *retired aerospace executive*

Bellevue
Andersen, James A. *retired state supreme court justice*
Anderson, David Coryell *lawyer, automotive executive*
Brockenbrough, Edwin Chamberlayne *surgeon*
Cardillo, James G. *automotive executive*
Cheevarunothai, Patikhom *transportation engineer*
Connors, John G. *venture capitalist, former computer software company executive*
Cremin, Robert W. *manufacturing executive*
de Sá e Silva, Elizabeth Anne *secondary school educator*
Dolgen, Jonathan L. *former motion picture company executive, investor*
Ellison, Herbert Jay *retired historian, educator*
Fiske, Neil S. *retail executive*
Gangl, Kenneth R. *automotive executive*
Graham, John Robert, Jr. *financial executive*
Hackett, Carol Ann Hedden *physician*
Hackett, John Peter *dermatologist*
Hall, Eleanor Williams *public relations executive*
Jakkula, Vikramaditya Reddy *computer scientist, researcher*
Johnson, Lynn Barbara *artist, civic worker*
Khan, Arif *psychiatrist, educator*
Khosrowshahi, Dara *travel company executive*
Lepore, Dawn Gould *Internet pharmaceutical company executive*
Lisaius, Frederic Albert *artist*
Lynch, Juneann M. *medical/surgical nurse, nursing educator*
McReynolds, Neil Lawrence *management consultant*
Myhrvold, Nathan P. *technology executive*
Olson, Robert William *writer, retired counselor*
Page, Roy Christopher *periodontist, scientist, educator*
Parks, Donald Lee *mechanical engineer, human factors engineer*
Pigott, Mark C. *automotive executive*
Plimpton, Thomas E. *automotive executive*
Post, Denny Marie *telecommunications industry executive, marketing professional*
Rand, Richard Pierce *plastic surgeon*
Reams, Patricia Lynn *retired elementary school educator*
Reynolds, Stephen Philip *utility company executive*
Rice, Kay Diane *elementary school educator, consultant*
Santel, Patrick Francis X. *lawyer*
Schroder, Sigrid Caroline *lawyer, consultant*
Scott, J. Lennox *real estate company executive*
Sebris, Robert, Jr. *lawyer*
Shifrin, Donald Lee *pediatrician*
Sims, Dave *sportscaster*
Stewart, Anne Matsumoto *language educator*
Swailes, Heidi Robin *counselor*
Sweeney, David Brian *lawyer*
Tembreull, Michael A. *automotive executive*
Thompson, Winston Mark Obed *entomologist, consultant, writer*
Tian, Hongqi *application developer, researcher*
Warren, James Ronald *retired museum director, journalist*
Wells-Henderson, Ronald John *investment counselor*
Whatmore, George Bernard *research scientist, writer, internist, neurophysiologist*
Wilkens, Lenny (Leonard Randolph Wilkens Jr.) *sportscaster, former professional sports team executive, retired professional basketball player*
Williamson, Charles R. *retired energy company executive*

Bellingham
Acevedo-Gutierrez, Alejandro *biology professor*
Anderson, David Bowen *lawyer*
Arthurs, Eugene Gerard *professional society administrator*
Boudreaux, Andrew *physics professor*
Bourm, Roger Michael *real estate broker, investor, property manager*
Burdge, Rabel James *sociology educator*
Clark-Langager, Sarah Ann *curator, academic administrator*
Cox, David Jackson *biochemistry professor*
Dooley, Kathleen Ann *elementary school educator*
Gogröf-Voorhees, Andrea Elizabeth *foreign language educator*
Howe, Warren Billings *physician*
Jansen, Robert Bruce *consulting civil engineer*
Johnston, Robert M. *retired literature and language professor*
Larner, Daniel M. *theater educator, playwright, writer*
Matthews, Robin Adele *environmental scientist, educator*
Meals, Pamela F. *publishing executive*
Packer, Mark Barry *lawyer, financial consultant, foundation official*
Ross, June Rosa Pitt *biologist, educator*
Stevenson, Joan Catharine *anthropologist, educator*
Thompson, Roger Roy *history professor*
Vajda, Edward J. *literature and language professor*
Whyte, Nancy Marie *performing arts educator*
Wolters, Curt Cornelis Frederik *economic consultant, retired foreign service officer*

Benton City
Omel, June M. *elementary school educator*

Bothell
Constantino, Karen Marie *elementary school educator*
Gude, Veera Gnaneswar *civil engineer, researcher*
Hauser, Robert G. *cardiologist, medical products executive*
Oflazoglu, Ezogelin *oncologist, science administrator*
Soltani, Azita *director of research*
Watts, Linda Susan *humanities educator*

Brinnon
Strom, Are *biologist*

Brush Prairie
Edlich, Richard French *biomedical engineer, educator*

Burien
Burgess, Charles Orville *history professor*
Risse, Guenter Bernhard *physician, historian, educator*

Burton
Dyer, Carolyn Price *artist, writer*

Camano Island
Clowes, Garth Anthony *electronics executive, consultant*
Hartley, Celia Love *author, consultant, retired nursing educator, administrator*

Camas
Howe, Robert Wilson *education educator*
Kotsovos, Jerry Frank *retired secondary school educator*

Carnation
Beshur, Jacqueline E. *retired animal trainer, farmer, writer*
Burner, Darcy *application developer*

Centralia
Buzzard, Steven Ray *lawyer*
Gimbel, Hervey Willis *public health physician, medical administrator*
Kirk, Henry Port *academic administrator*
Spiegelberg, Marc Steven *secondary school educator*

Cheney
Smith, Grant William *language educator, volunteer*
Steiner, Henry-York *English language and literature educator*
Wainwright, Paul Edward Blech *construction company executive*

Clarkston
Migaki, James M. *education educator*
Torgerson, Linda Belle *music educator*

Clinton
Holtby, Kenneth Fraser *retired manufacturing executive*
Powers, David Richard *educational administrator*
Westergaard, George Henry *secondary school educator*

Clyde Hill
Condon, Robert Edward *surgeon, educator, consultant*

Colville
Culton, Sarah Alexander *psychologist, educator*
Gray, Edmund Wesley *physician*
Monroe, John B. *history professor*

Cosmopolis
Luark, Lillian *retired city clerk*

Coupeville
Goodman, William Lee *retired naval officer, aerospace engineer and commercial pilot*
Lotzenhiser, George William *musician, educator, academic administrator, composer*
Mayhew, Eric George *medical researcher, educator, consultant*
Menzel, Paul Theodore *philosopher, educator*
Piercy, Gordon Clayton *bank executive, educator*
Thom, Richard David *retired electronics executive*

Deer Park
Forman, Robert Edgar *retired sociology professor*

Des Moines
Akaka, Sheryl Hung Lan Lokelani *music educator*
Tuell, Jack Marvin *retired bishop*
wBarclay, Gerry *biology professor*

Dupont
Pettit, Ghery St. John *electronics engineer*

East Wenatchee
Fluegge, Matthew W. *dentist*

Eastsound
de Boor, Carl-Wilhelm R. *mathematician*
Hoagland, Karl King, Jr. *lawyer*

Edmonds
Bell, Nancy Lee Hoyt *real estate investor, middle school educator, volunteer*
Daum, David Ernest *machinery manufacturing company executive*
Monroe, James Walter *retired corporate financial executive*
Schmit, Lucien André, Jr. *retired structural engineer*

Ellensburg
Hoover, Amy Lynn *pilot, educator*
McIntyre, Jerilyn Sue *academic administrator*
Miller, Maxine Lynch *retired home economist, interior designer, educator*
Rosell, Sharon Lynn *physics and chemistry professor*
Takei, Hideki *business educator*

Everett
Byrne, Patrick J. *information technology executive*
Mestel, Mark David *lawyer*
Nelson, Carol Kobuke *bank executive*
Oliver, William Donald *orthodontist*
Olsen-Estie, Jeanne Lindell *golf course owner*
Ostergaard, Joni Hammersla *lawyer*
Valentine, Mark Conrad *dermatologist*

Fairchild Air Force Base
Files, Douglas Scott *flight surgeon, military officer*

Federal Way
Bedient, Patricia M. *paper company executive*
Blywise, Barbara *mental health services professional*
Fulton, Daniel S. *paper company executive*
Gideon, Thomas F. *paper company executive*
Hooper, John A. *human resources specialist*
McDade, Sandy D. *lawyer, paper company executive*
Rossi, Ruth Harris *special education educator*

Fort Lewis
Jacoby, Charles H., Jr. *career military officer*

Friday Harbor
Agosta, William Carleton *chemist, educator*
Geyman, John Payne *physician, educator*
MacGinitie, Walter Harold *psychologist, educator*

Gig Harbor
Bernard, Lowell Francis *retired academic administrator, educator*
McClung, J(ames) David *corporate executive, lawyer, academic administrator*
Meacham, Charles Harding *federal agency administrator*
Stover, Miles Ronald *management consultant*
Thompson, Ronald Edward *lawyer*

Goldendale
Skillern, Michael Phillip *museum administrator*

Grandview
Verhoeven, Linda Stransky *librarian, educator*

Granite Falls
Peterson, Andrea *elementary school educator*

Hansville
Lenski, Ann Blalock *evaluation researcher, editor, writer*

Hoquiam
Kessler, Keith Leon *lawyer*

Hunts Point
Ebsworth, Barney A. *retired travel company executive*

Indianola
Gutsche, Carl David *chemistry professor*

Issaquah
Barchet, Stephen *obstetrician, gynecologist, retired military officer*
Benoliel, Joel *lawyer*
Brotman, Jeffrey H. *wholesale distribution executive*
Cain, Coleen W. *writer, educator*
Curre, Cora Lee *medical laboratory manager*
DiCerchio, Richard D. *wholesale distribution executive*
Evans, Ersel Arthur *engineering executive, consultant*
Galanti, Richard A. *wholesale business executive*
Matthews, John *human resources specialist, wholesale distribution executive*
Oles, Stuart Gregory *lawyer*
Ptacek, William H. *library director*
Reid, John Mitchell (Jack Reid) *biomedical engineer, researcher, consultant*
Sinegal, James D. (Jim Sinegal) *wholesale distribution executive*
von Speyer, Jacques *financier*

Kenmore
Gilleland, John Rogers *technology company executive*
Guy, Arthur William *electrical engineering educator, researcher*
Jennerich, Edward John *academic administrator, dean*
Montague, Deborah Marie *elementary school and music educator, consultant*
Sobolewski, John Stephen *computer scientist, director, consultant*
Sokol, Jennifer Marie *musician, writer*
Springer, Floyd Ladean *architect*

Kennewick
Brewton, Wesley Hopkins (Wes Brewton) *retired chef, retired real estate manager*
Camp, Kimberly N. *museum administrator, artist*
Cochran, James Alan *emeritus mathematics professor, department chairman, dean*
Fearing, George B. *lawyer*
Merkel, Patricia Mae *retired school system administrator*
Scott, Pamela J. *educational consultant*

Kent
Booth, Pieter *research and development company executive, consultant*
Dumitrescu, Cristina M. *intensive care nurse*
Goo, Abraham Meu Sen *retired manufacturing executive*
Hebeler, Henry Koester *retired electronics executive, aerospace engineer*

Keyport
Treacy, Gerald Bernard, Jr. *lawyer*

Kirkland
Barto, Deborah Ann *physician*
Chapple, John H. *investment company executive*
Dunn, Jeffrey Edward *neurologist*
Kowalski, Waldemar *theology studies educator*
McDonald, Joseph Lee *insurance broker*
Mitchell, Joseph Patrick *architect*
Nelson, Matt *psychology professor*
Ryles, Gerald Fay *investor, finance company executive*
Scranton, Pierce Edward *orthopedist, department chairman*
Szablya, Helen Mary *writer, language educator*

La Conner
Garcia, John *psychologist, educator*
Knopf, Kenyon Alfred *economist, educator*

La Push
Krueger, Katherine Kamp *lawyer*

Lacey
Caplan, Frank *retired management consultant, educator*
Fett, James D. *epidemiologist, director*
Siera, Steven G. *career planning administrator, educator*

Lake Forest Park
Adams, Hazard Simeon *retired language educator, writer*

Lakewood
Gilchrist, Debra L. *college librarian*
McEwen, Doris Ann *education educator*

Langley
Cammermeyer, Margarethe *retired medical/surgical nurse*
Le Roy, Robert Powell *retired minister, educator, writer*

Liberty Lake
Mielke, Clarence Harold, Jr. *hematologist*

Lilliwaup
McGrady, Corinne Young *design company executive*

Longview
Foster, Virginia *retired botany educator*
Uthmann, Richard W. *retired music educator*

Lopez Island
Brownstein, Barbara Lavin *geneticist, educator, director*

Lummi Island
Hanson, Polly (Pauline) Mae Early *librarian*

Lynnwood
Jenes, Theodore George, Jr. *retired military officer*
Olsen, Kenneth Harold *geophysicist, astrophysicist, historian*
Sandahl, Bonnie Beardsley *nursing administrator*
Schein, Rodney M. *electronics engineer, educator*
Schneider, Robert Kerry *electric utility engineer*

Manchester
Fearon, Lee Charles *chemist*

Maple Valley
Brown, Thomas Andrew *retired aircraft and weaponry manufacturing executive*

Marysville
Bart, Rick *retired protective services official*

Medina
Dagnon, James Bernard *human resources executive*
Schlotterbeck, Walter Albert *manufacturing executive, lawyer*

Mercer Island
Anderson, Peter MacArthur *retired lawyer*
Dunner, David Louis *medical educator*
Dykstra, David Charles *management executive, consultant, accountant, author, educator*
Elgee, Neil Johnson *retired internist, endocrinologist, educator*
Gould, Alvin R. *manufacturing executive*
Hilst, Glenn Rudolph *environmental sciences administrator, researcher*
Reed, May J. *medical educator*

Mill Creek
Aagard, Todd Allen *electronics company executive*
O'Keefe, Kathleen Mary *state official*

Mount Vernon
Church, Pamela Sue *academic administrator, educator*
Heinze, Susanna Lynn Christie *biology professor*
Klein, Henry *architect*
Langworthy, William Clayton *retired college official*

Mountlake Terrace
Baxter, Richard Alan *plastic surgeon, educator*
Schweyen, Stephen Gregory *engineering company executive*

Mukilteo
Bohn, Dennis Allen *engineering executive*
Brown, Bruce Baden *accountant*
Edmondson, Frank Kelley, Jr. *lawyer, legal administrator*

White, Lowell Elmond, Jr. *retired medical educator*

Newcastle
Erxleben, William Charles *lawyer, data processing executive*

Nine Mile Falls
Grubbs, Paul Alan *educator pilot*

Nordland
Kramnicz, Rosanne *freelance writer*

North Bend
Brumbaugh, Harley Aaron *retired music educator, conductor*

Oak Harbor
Daugherty, Kenneth Earl *research company executive, educator*
Lightbourne, Alesa M. *writer, educator, mediator*
Miller, Robert Scott *clinical social worker, project manager*
Shaw, Kathleen M. Troutner *retired librarian*

Olympia
Alexander, Gerry L. *state supreme court chief justice*
Bates, Charles Walter *attorney*
Calabria, Lalita *research scientist, educator*
Chambers, Thomas Jefferson *state supreme court justice*
Cheng, Yuk Wing *biometrician*
Coontz, Stephanie Jean *history professor, writer*
Dorn, Randy (Randolph I. Dorn) *state official, school system administrator*
Esbeck, Edward S. *retired educator*
Fairhurst, Mary E. *state supreme court justice*
Fisher, Nancy Louise *pediatrician, geneticist, retired nurse*
Gregoire, Christine O'Grady *Governor of Washington, former state attorney general*
Haseltine, James Lewis *artist, consultant*
Hayes, Maxine Delores *public health service officer, physician, pediatrician*
Hutchins, Diane Elizabeth Rider *librarian*
Isaki, Lucy Power Slyngstad *lawyer*
Jackson, Thelma Harrison *educational consultant, researcher*
Jarvis, Scott *state banking agency administrator*
Johnson, Charles William *state supreme court justice*
Johnson, James Martin *state supreme court justice, lawyer*
Kreidler, Myron (Mike) *State Insurance Commissioner of Washington, Fomer United States Representative, Washington, optometrist*
Long, Jeanine Hundley *state legislator*
Louis, Glen *music educator*
Macduff, Ilone Margaret *music educator*
Madsen, Barbara A. *state supreme court justice*
Markham, J. David *secondary school educator, writer, historical consultant*
McIntire, James L. *state treasurer*
McKenna, Rob *state attorney general, former councilman*
Miller, Allen Terry, Jr. *lawyer*
Oberbillig, Molly Castleman *utilities executive*
Owen, Bradley Scott *Lieutenant Governor of Washington*
Owens, Susan *state supreme court justice*
Randlett, Mary Willis *photographer*
Reed, Sam *Secretary of State, Washington*
Roe, Charles Barnett *lawyer*
Sanders, Richard Browning *state supreme court justice*
Selecky, Mary C. *state agency administrator*
Sesonske, Alexander *nuclear and chemical engineer*
Smith, Charles Z. *retired state supreme court justice*
Stephens, Debra L. *state supreme court justice*
Walker, Francis Joseph *lawyer*
Walsh, Jan *library director*

Omak
Pearce, Donald W. *music educator*

Orcas
Greever, John *retired mathematics professor*

Parkland
Johnson, LuAn K. *disaster management consultant*

Pasco
Cruz, Antonio *language educator*
Meadows, Deborah Renee *dean, educator*
Wyatt, Paige A. *mechanical engineer, educator*

Port Angeles
Andrew, Louise Briggs *emergency physician, medical legal consultant*
Brewer, John Charles *journalist*
Kessler, Lynn Elizabeth *state legislator*
Taylor, S. Brooke *lawyer*

Port Ludlow
Krugman, Stanley Lee *international management consultant*

Port Orchard
Thoman, Mark Edward *pediatrician*

Port Townsend
Merwin, William Stanley *poet*
Wheeler, Lorna Raven *literature and language educator*

Poulsbo
Romaine, Grant Hirsch *retired protective services official*

Prosser
Capener, Regner Alvin *minister, electronics engineer, writer*
Cooper, Lynn Dale *retired minister, retired navy chaplain*
Davenport, Joan R. *agriculturist, educator*
Harbertson, James Foster *research scientist*
Proebsting, Edward Louis, Jr. *retired horticulturist*

Pullman
Arthur, Linda Louise *sociologist, educator*
Balla, Vamsi Krishna *research scientist*
Banas, Emil Mike *physicist, researcher*
Bennett, Dick *college basketball coach*
Bone, Ken *men's college basketball coach*
Bose, Susmita *engineering educator*
Campbell, R. Keith *pharmacist, educator*
Condon, William Francis, Jr. *literacy educator*
Ding, Jow-Lian *engineering educator*
Dobney, Fredrick John *academic administrator*
Dodgen, Harold Warren *chemistry and physics professor*
Espinola-Arredondo, Ana *researcher*
Floyd, Elson Sylvester *academic administrator*
Haarsager, Dennis Lee *broadcast executive*
Hassold, Terry Jon *geneticist, educator*
Hinman, George Wheeler *physics professor*
Hust, Stacey Jolene *communications educator, researcher*
Hyde, Virginia Crosswhite *literature and language educator*
Jiang, Zhihua *geneticist, educator*
Kallaher, Michael Joseph *mathematics professor*
Keller, C. Kent *science educator*
Kim, Hyun Jeong *tourism educator*
Klavano, Paul Arthur *veterinary pharmacologist, anesthesiologist, educator*
Krueger, James Martin *physiology educator*
Lawrence, Holder *engineering educator*
Lewis, Norman G. *academic administrator, researcher, consultant*
McNamara, John Patrick *nutritionist, educator*
McSweeney, Frances Kaye *psychology professor*
Meier, Kathryn Elaine *pharmacologist, educator, academic administrator*
Monroe, Kelvin Jonathan *musician, educator*
Moss, Jeffrey P. *language educator*
O'Fallon, Andrew Steven *software engineer, educator*
Pavel, D. Michael *art educator*
Paznokas, Lynda Sylvia *elementary school educator*
Pearce, Gregory *botanist*
Rawlins, V. Lane *economics professor, retired academic administrator*
Rosa, Eugene Anthony *sociologist, environmental scientist, educator, artist*
Shen, Shihui *research assistant*
Stetler, Larry D. *geologist*
Tashman, Laith *civil engineer, educator*
Warner, Dennis Allan *psychology professor*
Washida, Haruhiko *botanist*
Yan, Jia *economics professor*
Zbib, Hussein Mustapha *engineering educator*
Zhong, Weihong (Katie Zhong) *engineering educator*

Redmond
Abu-Hadba, Walid *computer software company executive*
Allard, J. *computer software company executive*
Andersen, Klaus Holse *computer software company executive*
Anderson, Brad *computer software company executive*
Anderson, Nancy J. *computer software company executive, lawyer*
Arbogast, Brian *computer company executive*
Ayala, Orlando *computer software company executive*
Bach, Robert J. (Robbie Bach) *computer software company executive*
Ballmer, Steven Anthony *computer software company executive*
Belfiore, Joe *computer software company executive*
Bevington, Sue *computer software company executive*
Blakeley-Perez, Jose Alfredo *software architect*
Bottenberg, Joyce Harvey *writer, social services administrator*
Brod, Frank H. *computer software company executive, accountant*
Brooks, Brad *computer software company executive*
Brummel, Lisa E. *computer software company executive*
Burt, Thomas William *computer software company executive, lawyer*
Capossela, Chris *computer software company executive*
Charney, Scott *computer software company executive, lawyer*
Chayes, Jennifer Tour *mathematical physicist, educator*
Chrapaty, Debra J. *computer software company executive*
Christie, Doug (Douglas Dale Christie) *entrepreneur, former professional basketball player*
Crozier, Alain *computer software company executive*
Cutler, David Neil, Sr. *software engineer*
Davis, T. Ronald *marketing professional*
DelBene, Kurt *computer software company executive*
Delman, Michael *computer software company executive*
DeVaan, Jon S. *computer software company executive*
Domeniconi, Robin *computer company executive, former publishing executive*
Dunaway, Cammie *marketing executive*
Eisler, Craig *computer software company executive*
Elop, Stephen A. *computer software company executive*
Fathi, Ben *computer software company executive*
Ferguson, Donald *computer company executive*
Flake, Gary William *computer software company executive*
Flowers, Melvin *computer software company executive*
Gates, Bill (William Henry Gates III) *computer software company executive*
George, Grant *computer software company executive*
Gibbons, Tom *computer software company executive*
Golden, L. Michael *computer software company executive*
Gounares, Alexander *computer software company executive*
Guggenheimer, Steve *computer software company executive*
Gupta, Anoop *computer software company executive*
Guthrie, Scott *computer software company executive*
Gutiérrez, Horacio E. *computer software company executive*
Hardin, Bryan David *occupational safety and health specialist*
Hey, Tony *computer software company executive*
Higuchi, Yasuyuki *computer software company executive*
Ho, Roz *computer software company executive*
Hogan, Kathleen *computer software company executive*
Holland, Todd *computer software company executive*
Homldahl, Todd *computer software company executive*
Huston, Darren *computer software company executive*
Jeffress, Rusty *computer company executive*
Jha, Rajesh K. *computer software company executive*
Jones, Chris *computer software company executive*
Jorgensen, Erik *computer software company executive*
Kaplan, Rich *computer software company executive*
Kelly, Bob *computer software company executive*
Kennedy, William *computer software company executive*
Khaki, Jawad *computer software company executive*
Kim, Shane *computer software company executive*
Kimishima, Tatsumi *computer game company executive*
Klein, Peter *computer software company executive*
Koch, Mitchell L. *computer software company executive*
Kummert, Ted *computer software company executive*
Laing, Bill *computer software company executive*
Larson-Green, Julie *computer software company executive*
Leblond, Antoine *computer software company executive*
Lees, Andrew *computer software company executive*
Leung, Simon *computer software company executive*
Lichtman, Moshe *computer software company executive*
Liddell, Christopher P. *computer software company executive*
Liffick, Steve *computer software company executive*
Lomet, David Bruce *computer scientist*
Lu, Qi *computer software company executive*
MacDonald, Brian *computer software company executive*
Markezich, Ron *computer software company executive*
Mathews, Mich *computer company executive*
Mattrick, Donald A. *computer software company executive*
Matz, Joseph S. *computer software company executive*
Mehdi, Yusuf *computer software company executive*
Meshii, Masahiro *materials science educator*
Michener, John Russell *electrical engineer*
Mital, Amit *computer software company executive*
Mitchell, William H. *computer software company executive*
Mount, Mindy (Melinda J. Mount) *computer software company executive*
Muglia, Bob (Robert L. Muglia) *computer software company executive*
Mulinder, Austen *computer software company executive*
Mundie, Craig James *computer software company executive*
Myerson, Terry *computer software company executive*
Nackman, Lee *computer software company executive*
Nadella, Satya *computer software company executive*
Nan, Fei *application developer*
Nash, Mike *computer software company executive*
Nelson, Kimberly Terese *computer software company executive, former federal agency administrator*
Neupert, Peter *computer software company executive*
Niehaus, Michael *application developer, consultant*
Numoto, Takeshi *computer software company executive*
Ozzie, Ray (Raymond E. Ozzie) *computer software company executive*
Pall, Gurdeep Singh *computer software company executive*
Panke, Helmut *retired automotive executive*
Paolucci, Umberto *computer software company executive*
Park, Michael S. *computer software company executive*
Parthasarathy, Sanjay *computer software company executive*
Passman, Pamela S. *computer software company executive*
Phelps, Marshall C., Jr. *computer software company executive*
Pitasky, Scott *computer software company executive*
Porter, David *computer software company executive*
Rashid, Richard F. *computer software company executive*
Reed, Daniel A. *computer software company executive*
Reller, Tami *computer software company executive*
Ritchie, J. *computer software company executive*
Rodriguez, Enrique *computer software company executive*
Rosini, Eduardo B. *computer software company executive*
Roskill, Jon *computer software company executive*
Rudder, Eric D. *computer company executive, information technology executive*
Schiro, Steve *computer software company executive*
Schneider, Roy Lester *former Governor of Virgin Islands*
Scott, Tony *computer software company executive*
Shaw, Frank X. *computer software company executive*
Sheldon, Jeanne *computer software company executive*
Shum, Harry *computer software company executive*
Sinofsky, Steven J. *computer software company executive*
Smith, Bradford Lee *computer software company executive, lawyer*
Smith, Burton Jordan *computer designer*
Snapp, Mary E. *computer software company executive, lawyer*
Sobey, Edwin J. C. *museum director, oceanographer, consultant*
Somasegar, Sivarama Kichenane *computer software company executive*
Sowder, Robert Robertson *architect*
Srivastava, Amitabh *computer software company executive*
Taneja, Rajat *computer software company executive*
Tatarinov, Kirill *computer software industry expert*
Teper, Jeffrey Allen *computer software company executive*
Thompson, David M. *computer software company executive*
Thompson, Rick *computer software company executive*
Tobey, Brian *computer software company executive*
Treadwell, David *computer software company executive*
Turner, Kevin (B. Kevin Turner) *computer software company executive*
Ul-Mustafa, Raza *application developer, researcher*
Valencia Lavao, Jesus M. *electrical engineer, consultant*
van der Kooi, Rik *computer software company executive*
Vaskevitch, David *computer software company executive*
Veghte, Bill *computer software company executive*
Vigil, Henry P. *computer software company executive*
Wahbe, Robert *computer software company executive*
Watson, Allison L. *computer software company executive*
Westlake, Blair *computer software company executive*
Willard, H(arrison) Robert *electrical engineer*
Witts, Simon *computer software company executive*
Yan, Jingyu *computer graphics designer*
Youngjohns, Robert H. *computer software company executive*
Zecher, Linda *computer software company executive*
Zhang, Ya-Qin *computer software company executive*
Zinn, George *computer software company executive*

Renton
Bengelink, Ronald Lee *aerodynamics engineer*
Holmgren, Mike (Michael George Holmgren) *professional football coach*
Houshmandzadeh, T.J. (Touraj Houshmandzadeh) *professional football player*
James, Edgerrin Tyree *professional football player*
Longbrake, William Arthur *bank executive*
Mora, Jim (James Lawrence Mora) *professional football coach*
Ruskell, Tim *professional sports team executive*
Thomas, Brian Chester *retired state legislator, engineer*

Republic
Chambers, Milton Warren *retired architect*

Richland
Arntzen, Evan *geologist*
Bair, William J. *retired radiobiologist*
Bevelacqua, Joseph John *physicist, researcher*
Chikalla, Thomas David *retired science facility administrator*
Cox, Gary Robert *engineer*
Darby, Nancy *secondary school educator*
Devarakonda, Maruthi N. *research scientist, educator*
Doctor, Steven Richard *engineer*
Elderkin, Charles Edwin *retired meteorologist*
Felmy, Andrew Robert *research scientist*
Fryxell, Glen Edward *chemist, educator, materials scientist*
Glennen, Robert Eugene, Jr. *retired academic administrator*
Harutyunyan, Satenik *mechanical engineer*
Hoppe, Eric W. *chemistry professor, researcher*
Kathren, Ronald *health physicist*
Kim, Jin Yong *research scientist*
Lo Presti, Charles Arthur *research scientist*
Lu, Ning *electrical engineer, researcher*
Lyubinetsky, Igor *research scientist*
Miller, James Vince *university president*
Moore, Emmett Burris, Jr. *physical chemist, educator*
Murphy, Mark Kenneth *physicist, researcher*
Roop, Joseph McLeod *economist*
Sanfilippo, Antonio *chief scientist*
Shin, Yongsoon *research scientist*
Singhal, Subhash C. *engineer*
Westergard, Billie *project engineer*
Xantheas, Sotiris Stavros *chemist, researcher*

Sammamish
Yocam, Eric Wayne *engineer*

Seatac
Wells, Roger Stanley *software engineer*

Seattle
Agler, Brian *professional basketball coach*
Albaugh, James F. *aerospace transportation executive*

Alberg, Tom Austin *investment company executive, lawyer*
Albrecht, Richard Raymond *retired manufacturing executive, lawyer*
Alexie, Sherman Joseph, Jr. *writer*
Allan, Susan *academic administrator, former public health service officer*
Allen, Paul Gardner *professional sports team executive, computer company executive*
Alokolaro, Ann O. *secondary school educator*
Alstead, Troy *food service executive*
Anderson, Robert T. *lawyer, educator, former federal agency administrator*
Anderson, Roger Harris *retired physics professor*
Andrew, Lucius Archibald David III *bank executive*
Andrews, J. David *lawyer*
Anna, Kagley Nicole *biologist*
Ansell, Julian S. *urologist, educator*
Anzai, Yoshimi *radiologist, director*
Appelbaum, Frederick Ray *oncologist*
Aprikyan, Andranik Andrew Goorgen *molecular biologist, biomedical researcher*
Archibald, Sandra Orr *dean, political science professor, economist*
Atwater, Brian F. *geologist, educator*
Ayer, William S. *air transportation executive*
Backous, Douglas D. *otolaryngologist, director*
Baillie, Thomas A. *dean, former pharmaceutical executive*
Bain, William James, Jr. *architect*
Baker, David *biochemist*
Baker, K. Scott *pediatrician, educator*
Baker, Roland Jerald *finance educator*
Baker-Johnson, Marcia J. *dental hygienist*
Banks, James Albert *research director, educator*
Barton, Richard N. *computer company executive*
Baum, William Alvin *astronomer, educator*
Beale, Jane Guthrie *music publisher, music educator, pianist*
Bedard, Erik Joseph *professional baseball player*
Beighle, Douglas Paul *aerospace transportation executive*
Beltre, Adrian *professional baseball player*
Beren, Steve *Internet marketing professional*
Berman, Robert G. *dentist*
Bernard, Eddie Nolan *oceanographer*
Berni, Rosemarian Rauch *rehabilitation and oncology nurse*
Bevan, Michael J. *immunologist, educator, researcher*
Beyers, William Bjorn *geography educator*
Bezos, Jeffrey Preston *mail order services company executive*
Bichsel, Hans *physicist, consultant, researcher*
Bird, Sue (Suzanne Brigit Bird) *professional basketball player*
Birmingham, Richard Joseph *lawyer*
Bishop, Michael Joshua *medical educator*
Bishop, Virginia Wakeman *retired librarian, humanities educator*
Blair, M. Wayne *lawyer*
Blanco, Hilda J. *urban planner, educator*
Blethen, Frank A. *newspaper publisher*
Blom, Daniel Charles *lawyer, investor, retired insurance company executive*
Blumenfeld, Charles Raban *lawyer*
Boal, Peter Cadbury *performing company executive*
Boardman, David *editor*
Bodansky, David *physicist, researcher*
Boeder, Thomas L. *lawyer*
Boersma, P. Dee *conservation biologist, educator*
Boggs, Paula Elaine *lawyer, beverage service company executive*
BonJour, Laurence Alan *philosopher, educator*
Borgatta, Edgar F. *sociologist, educator*
Bosworth, Thomas Lawrence *architect, retired educator*
Boucek, Robert Joseph, Jr. *pediatrician, educator*
Bowden, Douglas McHose *neuropsychiatric scientist, neuroinformaticist*
Bowen, Jewell Ray *chemical engineering professor*
Boylan, Merle Nelson *librarian, educator*
Brammer, Lawrence Martin *psychologist, educator*
Brentnall, Teresa A. *gastroenterologist, educator*
Breslow, Norman Edward *biostatistics educator, researcher*
Bridge, Herbert Marvin *retail executive*
Bridge, Jonathan Joseph *lawyer, retail executive*
Bringman, Joseph Edward *lawyer*
Brock, Isaac *musician*
Brodsky, Anatol M. *research scientist*
Brown, Robert Alan *geophysicist, educator*
Brownlee, Donald Eugene, II, *astronomer, educator*
Brunett, Alexander Joseph *archbishop*
Buck, Linda B. *medical educator*
Buckner, Philip Franklin *newspaper publisher*
Burke, Wylie *medical geneticist*
Cahn, John Werner *metallurgist, educator*
Callan, Josi Irene *museum director*
Campbell, Robert Hedgcock *investment banker, lawyer*
Carithers, Robert L. *medical educator*
Carlson, Dale Arvid *retired dean*
Carson, Scott E. *aerospace transportation executive*
Cauce, Ana Mari *dean, psychology professor*
Chalodhorn, Rawichote *computer scientist*
Char, Patricia Helen *lawyer*
Chicoine, Nicole Mooney *lawyer*
Chirot, Daniel *sociology and international studies educator*
Christian, Gary D. *chemistry professor*
Claflin, Arthur Cary *lawyer*
Clark, Annette *dean*
Clausen, Mark A. *lawyer*
Cochran, Wendell Albert *science editor*
Coldewey, John Christopher *English literature educator*
Collier, Ann *epidemiologist, researcher*
Collier, Tom Ward *musician, educator*
Corey, Lawrence *medical educator*
Coughenour, John Clare *federal judge*
Cowan, Darrel *geologist, educator*
Cox, Frederick Moreland *retired dean, social worker*
Creager, Joe Scott *geology and oceanography educator*
Crenshaw, Edward Lee, Sr. *aviation electronics technician*
Cross, Bruce Michael *lawyer*
Culver, John *food service executive*
Cunningham, Janis Ann *lawyer*
Dale, David C. *physician, educator*
Davidson, Ernest Roy *chemist, educator*
Davis, Earl James *chemical engineering professor emeritus*
Davis, James *physician, educator*
Davis, John MacDougall *lawyer*
Davydow, Dimitry *psychiatrist, educator*
Dawson, Geraldine *psychologist, educator*
Dawson, Patricia Lucille *surgeon*
Day, Robert Winsor *preventive medicine physician, researcher*
De Alessi, Ross Alan *lighting designer*
Dear, Ronald Bruce *retired social work educator*
Delavar, Michael *pilot*
Denke, Conrad William *motion picture producer*
Denny, Brewster Castberg *retired university dean*
Denson, Nikkole E. *beverage company executive, film producer*
Desouza, Kevin Clyde *application developer, educator*
Devinatz, Ethan Sander *mathematics professor*
Dial, Ellen Conedera *lawyer*
Diddams, Margaret Ann DuPlissis *psychology professor, consultant*
Dimmick, Carolyn Reaber *federal judge*
Dong, Nelson G. *lawyer*
Doran, Charles Francis, Jr. *mathematician, professor*
Dunbar, Bonnie J. *engineer, astronaut, museum administrator*
Durran, Dale Richard *geophysicist, educator*
Eddy, Allison *nephrologist, educator*
Efimov, Vitaly *physicist, researcher, educator*
Elgin, Ron Alan *advertising executive*
Elizondo Almaguer, Eusebio L. *bishop*
Eller, Marlin *security firm executive*
Elyn, Mark *retired vocalist*
Emery, Helen Margaret *pediatric rheumatologist*
Emmert, Mark Allen *academic administrator, educator*
Enders, Eva *marine biologist, researcher*
Esser, Luke *political organization administrator*
Estes, Kenneth William *history professor, military officer*
Evans, Bernard William *geologist, educator*
Evans, Daniel Jackson *former senator, management consultant*
Fancher, Michael Reilly *editor, publishing executive*
Feigl, Eric Otto *physiology educator*
Feldman, Kenneth W. *pediatrician*
Feldman, Roger Lawrence *artist, educator*
Felsenstein, Joseph *science educator*
Ferrante, Antonino *aeronautical engineer, researcher*
Fidel, Raya *information science educator*
Fiedler, Fred Edward *retired organizational psychology educator, consultant*
Fine, Arthur I. *philosopher, educator*
Finlayson, Bruce Alan *retired chemical engineering professor*
Fischer, Edmond Henri *biochemistry educator*
Fischer, Thomas Covell *law educator, consultant, writer*
Fisher, Jeffrey L. *lawyer*
Fleming, David W. *city health department director*
Fletcher, Betty Binns *federal judge*
Fluke, Lyla Schram (Mrs. John M. (Lyla) Fluke Sr.) *publisher*
Foster, Barry Alan *cultural organization researcher, educator*
Foster, Susan Eileen *lawyer*
Franza, B. Robert, Jr. *science association director, educator*
Franza, Bernard Robert *science association director*
Fredriksen Goldsen, Karen I. *social welfare administrator, educator*
Friedman, Alexander Stephen *foundation administrator, investment banker*
Friedman, Andy *realtor*
Fuller, Mark *chef*
Gaffney, Joseph M. *lawyer*
Galloway, Patricia Denese *civil engineer*
Gardiner, John Jacob Zucker *writer, educator, philosopher*
Gardiner, T(homas) Michael *artist*
Garfield, Leonard *museum director*
Gass, Michelle Petkers *beverage service company executive, marketing executive*
Gassner, Holger Guenther *surgeon, consultant*
Gates, Melinda French *foundation administrator*
Gates, R. Jordan *delivery service executive*
Gaulke, Linda Strande *civil engineer, researcher*
Gentry, Roger Lee *research wildlife biologist*
Gerrard, Keith *lawyer*
Giblett, Eloise Rosalie *retired hematologist*
Gilbert, Paul H. *engineering executive, consultant*
Gittinger, D. Wayne *lawyer*
Glomset, John Asbjorn *medical educator*
Golden, Matthew *epidemiologist*
Goldin, Adam *medical educator*
Golub, Mike *sports and entertainment company executive*
Goodkin, Robert *neurosurgeon, educator*
Goodlad, John Inkster *education educator, writer*
Goodloe-Johnson, Maria L. *school system administrator*
Gores, Thomas C. *lawyer*
Gorton, Slade (Thomas Slade Gorton III) *lawyer, lobbyist, former senator*
Gould, Ronald Murray *federal judge*
Gouldthorpe, Kenneth Alfred Percival *state official, editor*
Grace, Ryan Thomas *lawyer*
Gradel, James D. *lawyer*
Graham, Stephen Michael *lawyer*
Gralow, Julie Ruth *physician*
Graney, Pat *choreographer*
Gray, Marvin Lee, Jr. *lawyer*
Green, Philip P. *mathematician, educator, computer scientist*
Green, William L. *lawyer*
Greenberg, E. Peter *microbiologist*
Greenwald, Anthony Galt *psychology educator*
Griffey, Ken, Jr., (George Kenneth Griffey Jr.) *professional baseball player*
Gross, Edward *retired sociologist*
Groudine, Mark Terry *oncologist*
Gunn, John T. *oceanographer, researcher*
Guntheroth, Warren Gaden *pediatrician, educator*
Gwinn, Mary Ann *editor*
Halver, John Emil *nutritional biochemist*
Haman, Raymond William *retired lawyer*
Hansen, Thomas Nanastad *hospital administrator, pediatrician*
Hansten, Philip Douglas *pharmacist, educator*
Harlan, John Marshall *medicine educator*
Harmon, Daniel Patrick *classics educator*
Hartwell, Leland Harrison (Lee Hartwell) *geneticist, educator*
Hasselbeck, Matt *professional football player*
Hauschka, Stephen Denison *developmental biologist, educator*
Hazelton, Penny Ann *law librarian, educator*
Hazzard, William Russell *geriatrician, educator*
Healey, Ada M. *real estate developer*
Heath, George Ross *oceanographer*
Heath, Richard Raymond *retired investment company executive*
Heer, Nicholas Lawson *language educator*
Heinsen, Kaare *computer game company executive, application developer*
Hellström, Ingegerd *medical researcher*
Hellström, Karl Erik *science educator, researcher*
Henderson, Maureen McGrath *medical educator*
Henley, Ernest Mark *physics professor, retired dean*
Hernandez, Felix Abraham *professional baseball player*
Hicks, Gregory Alan *dean, law educator*
Higgins, Robert *finance educator*
Hildreth, Susan *library director*
Hill, Chrystie R. *library and information scientist*
Hille, Bertil *physiology educator*
Hills, Regina J. *web manager*
Hilpert, Edward Theodore, Jr. *retired lawyer*
Hirschman, Charles, Jr. *sociologist, educator*
Hirschmann, Franz Gottfried *aerospace executive*
Hoffman, Allan Sachs *chemical engineer, educator*
Hollender, Lars Gösta *dental educator*
Holley, Rick R. *lumber company executive*
Holzworth, Robert Haviland, II, *geophysics and physics educator*
Hopkins, Kathleen Joan *lawyer*
Hornbein, Thomas Frederic *anesthesiologist*
Houston, Janeanne Currier *vocalist, educator*
Hunthausen, Raymond Gerhardt *archbishop emeritus*
Huston, John Charles *law educator*
Irving, Ron *mathematics professor*
Ishimaru, Akira *electrical engineering educator*
Isik, Frank *plastic surgeon*
Iyer, Nalini *literature and language professor*
Jackson, Lauren *professional basketball player*
Jacobs, Deborah L. *foundation administrator, former library director*
Jacobson, Phillip Lee *architect, educator*
Jaffe, Robert Stanley *lawyer*
Jassy, Andrew R. *retail sales company executive*
Jenkins, Speight, Jr. *opera company director*
Jessen, Joel Anne *not-for-profit executive, art educator*
Jiambalvo, James *dean*
Johjima, Kenji *professional baseball player*
Johnson, Bruce Edward Humble *lawyer*
Johnson, Darryl Norman *former ambassador*
Johnston, Norman John *retired architecture educator*
Jones, Grant Richard *landscape architect*
Jones, Julius Andre Maurice *professional football player*
Jones, Richard A. *federal judge*
Jorgensen, Jens Erik *mechanical engineer, educator*
Jump, Christina M. *research scientist*
Kahn, Steven Emanuel *medical educator*
Kalet, Ira Joseph *medical computer scientist*
Kane, Alan Henry *lawyer*
Kaplan, Robert David *lawyer*
Kapur, Kailash Chander *industrial engineering educator*
Kareiva, Peter Michael *zoology educator, research ecologist*
Karl, Mike O. *medical researcher*
Kates, Carolyn Louise *physical therapist*
Keegan, John E. *lawyer*
Kenny, George Edward *pathobiology educator*
Keyt, David *philosophy and classics educator*
Kharasch, Evan David *physician*
Kilpatrick, John Aaron *construction and development company executive*
Kim, Yongmin *electrical and biomedical engineer, educator*
Kimball, Harry Raymond *medical association administrator, educator*
King, Ivan Robert *astronomy educator*
King, Mary-Claire *geneticist, educator*
Kirk, Judd *real estate development executive*
Klebanoff, Seymour Joseph *medical educator*
Kliot, MIchel *neurosurgeon*
Knight, W. H., Jr., (Joe Knight) *law educator, former dean*
Kobayashi, Albert Satoshi *mechanical engineering educator*
Koehler, Reginald Stafford III *lawyer*
Kolb, Keith Robert *architect, educator*
Koppel, Michael G. *retail executive*
Korg, Jacob *English literature educator*
Koster, John Frederick *insurance executive*
Kraft, George Howard *physician, educator*
Krebs, Edwin Gerhard *biochemistry educator*
Krochalis, Richard F. *federal agency administrator*
Krohn, Kenneth Albert *radiologist, educator*
Kruse, Shari *real estate agent*
Kunkel, Georgie Bright *freelance writer, retired counselor*
Kwiram, Alvin L. *retired chemistry professor, academic administrator*
Lacitis, Erik *journalist*
Laing, Sharon S. *research scientist*
Landefeld, Stewart M. *lawyer*
Larson, Anne M. *internist*
Larson, Eric B. *medical educator, director, internist*
Lazowska, Edward Delano *computer science educator*
Leale, Olivia Mason *small business owner, import marketing executive*
Leavens, Ileana Beatriz *art educator*
Lee, John Marshall *mathematics professor*
Lehman, Constance Dobbins *radiologist, researcher*
Lemly, Thomas Adger *lawyer*
Lidstrom, Mary E. *chemical engineering and microbiology professor*
Lincoln, Howard *manufacturing company and sports team executive*
Linnell, Albert Paul *physics and astronomy educator*
Liu, Chen-Ching *electrical engineering educator*
Loeb, Lawrence A. *medical educator, director*
Loftus, Thomas Daniel *lawyer*
Lubatti, Henry Joseph *physicist, researcher*
Lundin, Norman Kent *artist, educator*
Lynass, Lori *researcher*
MacDonald, Don *psychology educator*
MacLachlan, Douglas Lee *marketing educator*
Madis, Eric Stephen *musician*
Maier, Ronald Vitt *surgeon, educator*
Manning, J. Richard *lawyer*
Marchese, Lisa Marie *lawyer, educator*
Martin, Thomas Reed *medical educator, medical association administrator*
Marty, Raymond *nuclear physician*
Mason, Marilyn Gell *retired library administrator, writer, consultant*
Mason, Robert McSpadden *information scientist, educator, dean*
Matchett, William H(enry) *English literature educator*
Matsen, Frederick Albert III *orthopedic educator*
Matsuoka, Yoky *medical educator*
Mayo, Robert N. *computer science researcher*
McAndrews, Brian Patrick *venture capitalist, former computer software company executive*
McCaw, John Elroy, Jr. *investment company executive, professional sports team executive*
McClure, R. Dale *physician*
McCracken, Peter H. *librarian*
McCune, Philip Spear *lawyer*
Mc Feron, Dean Earl *mechanical engineer, educator*
McKay, John *law educator, former prosecutor*
McKay, Michael Dennis *lawyer*
McKenrick, Laurence Lee *environmentalist*
McLaughlin, John F. *pediatrician, educator*
McPhaden, Michael James *oceanographer, educator*
Meehan, John J. *pediatrician, educator*
Meier, R. Paul *lawyer*
Merkle, Alan Ray *lawyer*
Mesher, Barry Neal *lawyer*
Michael, Ernest Arthur *mathematics professor*
Mills, Richard Pence *ophthalmologist*
Milton, Catherine Higgs *entrepreneur*
Mizumori, Sheri J.Y. *psychology professor, department chairman*
Montgomery, David R. *geologist, educator, writer*
Montoya, Gonzalo *chemical engineer, educator*
Moore, Daniel Charles *retired anesthesiologist*
Mostaghel, Elahe A. *medical educator*
Motulsky, Arno Gunther *internist, geneticist, educator*
Moudon, Anne Vernez *urban design educator*
Mull, Robert W. *filmmaker, curator*
Munch, David *retired chemistry professor*
Murray, Christopher J.L. *medical educator*
Mussehl, Robert Clarence *lawyer*
Muy-Rivera, Martin *biochemist, researcher*
Neal, Joseph M. *anesthesiologist, educator*
Neligan, Peter C. *plastic surgeon, educator*
Nelson, Allen F. *proxy solicitation company executive*
Nelson, Arleen Bruce *social worker*
Nelson, James Alonzo *radiologist, educator*
Neppe, Vernon Michael *neuropsychiatrist, behavioral neurologist, psychopharmacologist, writer, phenomenologist, conciousness researcher, forensic specialist, philosopher*
Neuhouser, Marian L. *nutritionist, researcher*
Nghiem, Paul T. *dermatologist, educator*
Nickels, Greg *Mayor, Seattle*
Niemi, Janice *retired lawyer, state legislator, judge*
Ning, Xue-Han (Hsueh-Han Ning) *physiologist, researcher*
Nordstrom, Blake W. *retail executive*
O'Brien, Kevin D. *medical educator*
O'Donnell, Matthew *electrical engineering, computer science educator, dean*
Oehler, Richard William *lawyer*
Olsen, Harold Fremont *lawyer*
Olson, David John *political science professor*
Olson, Maynard V. *science educator, researcher*
Olstad, Roger Gale *science educator*
Oman, Henry *retired electrical engineer, engineering executive*
Ostrow, Jay Donald *gastroenterology educator, researcher*
Otto, Catherine Mary *cardiologist, educator*
Page, Richard Leighton *cardiologist, medical educator, researcher*
Paget, Joel Hathaway *lawyer*
Pagon, Roberta Anderson *pediatrician, educator*
Palmer, Douglas S., Jr. *lawyer*
Parikh, Jay R. *radiologist*
Parks, Michael James *editor*
Pedersen, Jamie D. *state legislator, lawyer*
Pelz, Dwight *political organization administrator*
Perkins, James D. *surgeon*
Perrin, Edward Burton *biomedical researcher, public health educator*
Petrie, Gregory Steven *lawyer*
Phillips, Vicki L. *foundation administrator, former school system administrator*
Pilat, Michael Joseph *engineering educator*
Piven, Peter Anthony *architect, management consultant*
Plotnick, Robert David *economic consultant, educator*
Popovic, Zoran *environmental engineer, educator*
Porter, Stephen Cummings *geologist, educator*
Prentke, Richard Ottesen *lawyer*
Pressly, Thomas James *history professor*

Price, John R. lawyer, educator
Pritchard, Llewelyn George lawyer
Punyon, Ellen principal
Quinn, LeBris Smith cell biologist
Rabak, David William retired family practice physician, educator, consultant
Rabinovich, Regina pediatrician, epidemiologist, director
Rabinovitch, Benton Seymour chemist, educator emeritus
Raese, David Senna aerospace and mass properties engineer, consultant
Raikes, Jeffrey Scott foundation administrator, former computer software company executive
Ramsey, Paul Glenn dean, internist
Ramsey, Scott D. researcher, educator
Rand, Jim Francis science educator
Ravenholt, Reimert Thorolf epidemiologist, researcher
Ray, Charles Kendall retired dean
Redman, Eric lawyer
Reeves, Joan Hutchins painter
Reh, Thomas Andrew biologist, educator
Rehr, John J. physicist, researcher
Reidmiller, David R. atmospheric chemist
Reinhardt, William Parker chemical physicist, educator
Ritter, Daniel Benjamin lawyer
Rivara, Frederick Peter pediatrician, educator
Robb, John Wesley religion educator
Robbins, Stephen J. M. lawyer
Robinson, Jeffery P. lawyer
Romar, Lorenzo men's college basketball coach
Rose, Peter J. delivery service executive
Rosellini, Albert D. former governor
Rosen, Jacob engineering educator
Rosen, Jon Howard lawyer
Rotella, Stephen J. former bank executive
Roth, Mark research scientist
Rubenstein, Jeffrey Elliot prosthodontist, professor
Ruckelshaus, William Doyle investment company executive, former federal agency administrator
Ruggerone, Gregory T. research scientist
Rule, Ann writer
Rummage, Stephen Michael lawyer
Russell, Francia retired ballet director, educator
Salmon, Marla E. dean, nursing educator
Samiljan, Katriana lawyer
Saneto, Russell Patrick pediatric neurologist, epileptologist, neurobiologist
Sarason, Irwin G. psychology professor
Sari, Robert B. lawyer, retail executive
Sasenick, Joseph Anthony health care company executive
Sathyanarayana, Sheela pediatrician, educator
Schaie, K(laus) Warner human development and psychology educator
Schiffrin, Milton Julius physiologist
Schimmelbusch, Werner Helmut psychiatrist
Schoenfeld, Walter Edwin manufacturing executive
Schultz, Howard D. beverage service company executive
Schwab, Evan Lynn lawyer
Schwartz, Irwin H. lawyer
Schwarz, Gerard conductor, musician, music director
Scott, Cheryl M. foundation administrator, healthcare educator
Scranton, George Alfred theater educator
Segal, Jack mathematics professor
Seidl, R(obert) Bryce museum director, former manufacturing company executive, city official
Senczuk, Anna Maria cell biologist, researcher
Shadle, Steven Curtis librarian
Shahn, Judith voice educator
Shankaran, Nishanth application developer
Sher, Bartlett theater director
Sidbury, Robert pediatrician
Silver, Michael education educator
Simon, Gregory E. psychiatrist, researcher
Simonyi, Charles software engineer
Sin, Mo-Kyung nurse
Skerrett, Shawn Joseph physician
Smith, Scott A. lawyer
Smith-DiJulio, Kathleen psychosocial clinical nurse specialist
Sobel, Michael vascular surgeon, researcher
Song, Kit M. orthopedist, educator
Spafford, Michael Charles artist
Squires, William Randolph III lawyer
Stapleton, F. Bruder pediatric nephrologist, academic administrator
Starr, Isidore law educator
Staryk, Steven Sam violinist, concertmaster, educator
Stearns, Susan Tracey lighting design company executive, lawyer
Stein, Julie K. museum director, educator
Stenchever, Morton Albert obstetrician, gynecologist
Stern, Edward Abraham physics professor
Stoebuck, William Brees law educator
Stoelinga, Mark Theodore meteorologist, educator
Stolov, Walter Charles medicine physiatrist, educator
Stowell, Kent retired ballet director
Stricherz, Vincent C. journalist
Stringer, William Jeremy university official
Stross, Cynthia lawyer
Sullivan, Jeffrey C. prosecutor
Suzuki, Edward M. chemist
Suzuki, Ichiro professional baseball player
Szkutak, Tom corporate financial executive
Tallman, Richard C. federal judge, lawyer
Tang, Qiuhong research scientist
Tarleton, Earl Russell, Jr. lawyer
Tatupu, Lofa professional football player
Taylor-Brochet, Andrea language educator
Thirlby, Richard Coller surgeon
Thomas, Carol Guggenheim history professor, writer
Thomas, Edward Donnall internist, hematologist, retired medical educator
Thomas, Herbert Cushing, Jr. physician, educator
Thomas, Irv writer, journalist
Thomas, John Val architect
Thompson, Elizabeth Alison mathematics professor
Thouless, David James retired physicist, educator
Tift, Mary Louise artist
Tolich, Nikolai physicist, educator
Tomas, Alejandro photographer
Tonelli, Mark R. cardiologist, educator
Townes, David Andrew medical educator
Treiger, Irwin Louis lawyer
Trier, William Cronin retired medical educator, plastic surgeon
True, Lawrence pathologist, educator
True, William L. (Bill True) retired real estate company executive
Tschernisch, Sergei P. academic administrator
Tune, James Fulcher lawyer
Turnovsky, Stephen John economics professor
Tuthill, Oliver W., Jr. psychologist, consultant, independent film producer, director
Tyson, Joseph Jude bishop
Urban, Nicole D. biostatistician
van den Berghe, Pierre Louis sociologist
Vater, Youri L. medical educator
Vedder, Nicholas Blair plastic surgeon, educator
Wagner, Edward Harris epidemiologist, educator
Wagoner, David Everett lawyer, arbitrator
Wakamatsu, Don (Wilbur Donald Wakamatsu) professional baseball coach
Ward, Ronald R. lawyer
Wasserheit, Judith N. social services administrator
Waterston, Robert Hugh medical educator, researcher, medical geneticist, department chairman
Weaver, Lois Jean physician, educator
Webster Stratton, Carolyn Hinde psychology professor
Wechsler, Mary Heyrman lawyer
Wei, Pax S.P. research scientist
Weinberg, John Lee federal judge
Wellner, Jon August statistician, educator
Wenk, Edward, Jr. civil engineer, educator, writer, policy analyst
Wessells, Hunter urologist, researcher
Wetteland, John Karl professional baseball coach, retired professional baseball player
Whisner, Mary librarian
Wilets, Lawrence physicist, educator
Williams, J. Vernon retired lawyer
Willingham, Tyrone college football coach
Wilson, L. Michelle (Michelle Wilson) lawyer, information technology executive
Wilson, Lizabeth Anne (Betsy Wilson) dean, library director
Wilson, Richard Randolph lawyer
Wise, Phyllis M. physiologist, educator
Woods, James Sterrett toxicologist
Woods, Nancy Fugate nursing educator
Woodward, Janet Claire school librarian, educator
Wright, Bagley venture capitalist, entrepreneur, art collector
Wurster, Charles Frederick environmental scientist, educator
Yang, Yang statistician, medical researcher
Yashruti, Salah Hadi retired surgeon
Yee, Cassian K. oncologist, researcher
Yee, Shirley Jo-Ann history professor
Yue, Agnes Kau-Wah otolaryngologist
Zieniewicz, Stephen hospital administrator
Zilly, Thomas Samuel federal judge
Zimmerman, Gary A(lan) chemistry educator, academic administrator, profl. genealogists
Zumeta, William Mark public policy educator

Selah
Ring, Lucile Wiley lawyer

Sequim
Huntley, James Robert government official, international affairs scholar
Karr, James Richard ecologist, educator, research director
Kretschmer, Keith Hughes investor

Shelton
Barnard, Susan literature and language educator
McNabb, David E. educator, author
Milander, Henry Martin educational consultant

Shoreline
Bailey, Sandra secondary school educator, department chairman
Dolacky, Susan K. music educator
Hanson, Kermit Osmond business administration educator, retired dean
Merendino, K. Alvin surgeon, educator

Silverdale
Shaw, Annita Louise art educator

Snohomish
Ellis, Stephen Charles lawyer
Hill, Valerie Charlotte nurse
Tuengel, Lisa Marie elementary school educator

Spanaway
Campbell, Thomas J. state legislator, chiropractor
Parker, Lynda Christine Rylander secondary school educator

Spokane
Baker, Danial Edwin pharmacist, educator
Bender, Betty Wion librarian
Beqiri, Mirjeta S. operations management educator
Bulan, Liana dentist
Bynagle, Hans Edward library director, philosophy educator
Cameron, Alex Brian accountant, educator
Carriker, Robert Charles history professor
Chamberlain, Barbara Kaye communications executive
Cohen, Arnold Norman gastroenterologist
Connolly, Kenneth Thomas lawyer
Covey, Michael J. forest products and real estate executive
Cowles, William Stacey newspaper publisher
Crosby, Glenn Arthur chemistry professor
Danke, Virginia educational administrator, travel consultant
Edwards, James Robert minister, educator
Eliassen, Jon Eric retired corporate financial and utilities executive
Ely, Gary G. utilities company executive
Eymann, Richard Charles lawyer
Few, Mark men's college basketball coach
Friends, Todd Hart finance educator
Grant, William Joseph retired judge
Halvorson, Marjory opera director
Horton, Susan Pittman bank executive
Houseman, Gerald L. political science professor, writer
Kafentzis, John Charles journalist, educator
Koegen, Roy Jerome lawyer
Kostelec, William A. photographer, educator
Kovacevich, Robert Eugene lawyer
Krizan, Kelly Joe physician, leather craftsman
Kunkel, Richard Lester public radio executive
Lamon, Laurie JoAnne literature and language professor
Lee, Hi Young physician, acupuncturist
Lee, Richard Francis James evangelical clergyman, media consultant, lawyer
Martin, Earl F. dean, law educator
May, Richard B. psychology professor
Mays, Roy Mark, Jr., (Mark Mays) psychologist, educator
McCulloh, Thayne Martin university administrator, consultant
McDevitt, James A. prosecutor, lawyer
McWilliams, Edwin Joseph banker
Migliazzo, Arlin C. history professor
Murray, James Michael librarian, lawyer
Nawash, Jalal Mohammad physics professor
Novak, Terry Lee dean, educator
Ogden, C(hester) Robert insurance company executive
Polley, Harvey Lee retired missionary, math and science educator
Powell, Darren D. medical educator
Quackenbush, Justin Lowe federal judge
Robinson, Herbert Henry III psychotherapist, educator
Saha, Sandeep Ajoy medical educator, researcher
Siegel, Louis Pendleton retired forest products executive
Sines, Randy D. retail executive
Skylstad, William Stephen bishop
Stackelberg, John Roderick history professor
Stanley, Heidi B. bank executive
Steele, Karen Dorn journalist
Teets, Walter Ralph accounting educator
Ueberroth, Peter Victor sports association executive
Verner, Mary Mayor, Spokane, Washington
Wirt, Michael James library director

Spokane Valley
Linn, Diana Patricia retired elementary school educator

Stanwood
Birkestol, Annabelle Mollie Elsie retired elementary school educator

Sumas
Hemry, Larry Harold former federal agency official, writer, inventor

Sumner
Gosselin, Cheryl Block media specialist, librarian

Tacoma
Baarsma, Bill Mayor, Tacoma
Bartlett, Norma Thyra retired administrative assistant
Bryan, Robert J. federal judge
Butchart, Ronald Eugene social foundations educator, researcher, administrator
Cloud, Douglas R. lawyer
Fischer, Mary E. special education educator
Flemming, Stanley Lalit Kumar physician, mayor, state legislator
Frantz, Dale Nelson automobile import processing company executive
George, Nicholas lawyer, entrepreneur
Gerganov, Bogomil E. physics professor
Gordon, Joseph Harold lawyer
Hitz, Ralph geologist, educator
Holt, William E. lawyer, managing partner
Houston, Phillip Thomas social worker
Krueger, James A. lawyer
La Fond, John Quinn retired law educator
Magden, Ronald Earnest education educator
Martin, Mark Owen biology professor
McGraw, Leigh Kyle family practice nurse practitioner, researcher
Mowery, Gerald Eugene publishing executive, writer
Nelson, Eric Dolaine literature educator, consultant
Nicandri, David L. museum director
Rickman, Connie Garza retired principal
Rimbach, Evangeline Lois retired music educator
Rousslang, Kenneth W. retired chemistry professor
Settle, Benjamin Hale federal judge
Stebich, Stephanie A. museum director
Stuart, Jeffrey L. mathematics professor, consultant
Tang, Kwong-Tin physics professor, researcher
Ward, Keith Charles music educator
Wiegman, Eugene William minister, academic administrator
Wimberger, Peter Hans museum director, educator

Toppenish
Ross, Kathleen Anne academic administrator

Tukwila
Fitzpatrick, Thomas Mark lawyer
Talmadge, Philip Albert retired judge, state senator

Tumwater
Mallory, Tim librarian

University Place
Bourgaize, Robert G. economist
Panerio, Robert Major, Sr. music educator, composer
Seiber, Richard Allan retired chaplain United States Air Force

Vancouver
Archer, Stephen Hunt economist, educator
Bridgewater, Rachel library and information scientist
Dettman, Donald Reese loss control inspector
Diggs, Marylynne literature and language professor
Donovan, Thomas John retired humanities educator
Engelker, Lynsey L. athletic trainer, professional athletics manager
Karmy-Jones, Riyad Caradog surgeon, educator
Karpinski, John Stanley lawyer
Kim, Dave Dae-Wook engineering educator
Lenfant, Claude Jean-Marie physician, director
Middlewood, Martin Eugene writer, consultant
Ogden, Daniel Miller, Jr. public official, educator
Ogden, Valeria Munson management consultant, state representative
Pollard, Royce Mayor, Vancouver, Washington
Probst, Tahira M. psychology professor
Robertson, Joel Thomas railroad executive
Shamrell, Richard T. physics professor
Sutherland, Roxane Y. communications educator
Tang, Liang optics scientist
Vossler, Deborah J. mathematics and science educator

Vashon
Cushman, Karen Lipski writer

Veradale
Keating, Eugene Kneeland animal scientist, educator

Walla Walla
Bridges, George S. academic administrator, sociology educator
Carlsen, James Caldwell retired systematic musicologist
McIlvaine, Patricia Morrow physician
Perry, Louis Barnes retired insurance company executive
Purcell, Cynthia D. bank executive
Rasmussen, Lisa Anne art educator, department chairman, gallery director
Reese, John M. lawyer
Simon, Nancy Lynn performing arts educator, director
Wade, Leroy Grover, Jr. chemistry educator

Washougal
Harness, William Edward tenor

Wenatchee
Beausoleil, Richard A. animal scientist
Daling, LaiLee T. librarian
Elfving, Don C. horticulturist, educator
Hall-Thur, Celia Marie history professor
Howard, Nancy D. literature and language professor
Primm, Richard Kirby physician
Reilly, Joan nursing educator

West Richland
Ellis, Patricia primary school educator

White Salmon
Chapin, F. Stuart, Jr. science educator, director

Woodinville
Couser, William Griffith nephrologist, academic administrator, educator
Radtke, Derek Paul lawyer
Sanders, Richard Kinard actor

Woodland
Hansen, Walter Eugene insurance executive

Yakima
Beehler, Tobi Lorraine elementary school educator, education educator
Lopez, George E. mathematics professor
Phillips, Kathleen Gay small business owner
Sevilla, Carlos Arthur bishop
Suko, Lonny Ray judge

WEST VIRGINIA

Athens
Marsh, Joseph Franklin, Jr. retired academic administrator
O'Haynes, Delilah Ferne literature and language professor
Turnbull, Robert B. librarian

Beckley
Fragile, Stacey Lynn lawyer
Hitt, Frank dean, consultant
Rhode, Marye Frances paralegal

Berkeley Springs
Morris, Sarah literature and language educator

Bethany
Fletcher, Adam C. mathematics professor
Smith, G(odfrey) T(aylor) college president

Bluefield
Chryssikos, Alexandra Gianelos secondary school educator
Cochran, Dana Stoker literature and language professor
Foster, Lewis C. physics professor
Gearheart, Gary sales executive
Kantor, Isaac Norris lawyer

Bridgeport
McClure, Charles Richard retired superintendent

Buckhannon
Waggoner, Eric *literature and language professor*

Chapmanville
Wilson, Terilyn Barrett *elementary school educator*

Charles Town
McDonald, Angus Wheeler *farmer*
Na, Tsung Shun (Terry Na) *Chinese studies educator, writer*

Charleston
Alkhateeb, Fadi Mohammad Ali *pharmacist, educator*
Barth, Elizabeth Anne *former aide*
Benjamin, Brent D. *state supreme court chief justice, lawyer*
Bennett, Robert Menzies *retired gas pipeline company executive*
Betts, Rebecca A. *lawyer*
Boland, James Pius *surgeon, educator*
Brewer, Lewis Gordon *judge, educator*
Brown, James Knight *lawyer*
Casey, Nick (G. Nicholas Casey Jr.) *lawyer, political organization administrator*
Chapman, John Andrew *retired chamber of commerce executive*
Chilton, Elizabeth Easley Early *newspaper executive*
Cline, Sara McLaughlin *state banking agency administrator*
Curtis, Chris *state agency administrator*
Davis, Robin Jean *state supreme court justice*
Dissen, James Hardiman *lawyer*
Douglass, Gus Ruben *Commissioner of Agriculture, West Virginia*
Gillespie, William Harry *forestry executive, geology educator*
Haught, James Albert, Jr. *journalist, editor*
Hechler, Ken *retired state official, congressman, writer, political science professor*
Hodges, Adam *museum director*
Ketchum, Menis E., II, *state supreme court justice*
King, Robert Bruce *federal judge*
Linger, Rebecca Susan *chemistry professor*
Love, Charles Marion III *lawyer*
McCabe, Brooks Fleming, Jr. *state legislator*
Mc Graw, Darrell Vivian, Jr. *state attorney general*
McHugh, Thomas Edward *state supreme court justice, lawyer*
McKinney, Doug *political organization administrator, urologist*
Mellert, Lucie Anne *writer, photographer*
Michael, M. Blane *federal judge*
Miller, Charles T. *prosecutor*
Neely, Richard *lawyer*
O'Connor, Otis Leslie *retired lawyer, director*
Paine, Steven L. *state official, school system administrator*
Pasinetti, Nina Denton *dance educator, artistic director, choreographer*
Perdue, John D. *state treasurer*
Prichard, John David *minister*
Richardson, Sally Keadle *academic administrator*
Robinson, E. Glenn *lawyer*
Rowe, Larry Linwell *lawyer, former state senator*
Scott, Olof Henderson, Jr. *priest*
Smith, Stuart Lewis *community volunteer*
Tennant, Natalie E. *state official*
Tomblin, Earl Ray *state legislator, Lieutenant Governor of West Virginia*
Udall, John Nicholas, Jr. *medical educator, researcher*
Walker, Martha Yeager *state agency administrator, former state senator*
Workman, Margaret Lee *state supreme court justice, lawyer*
Zak, Robert Joseph *lawyer*

Clarksburg
Leuliette, Connie Jane *secondary school educator*
Payne, Johnny F. *minister*

Daniels
Buratynski, Theresa Joan *physician*

Dunbar
Russell, James Alvin, Jr. *college administrator*

Elkins
Cruz, Lora N. *mental health nurse, educator*
Maxwell, Robert Earl *federal judge*

Fairmont
Aloi, Michael John *lawyer*
Frasure, Carl Maynard *political science professor*
Freeman, Philip M. *architect, educator*
Hardway, Wendell Gary *retired academic administrator*
McKeen, Angela Anne *science educator*
Swiger, Elizabeth Davis *chemist, educator*

Frankford
Mazzio-Moore, Joan L. *retired radiology educator, physician*

Fraziers Bottom
Talbott, Charles W., Jr. *agricultural studies educator*

Gandeeville
Hameed, Omar *pathologist*

Glenville
Tubesing, Richard Lee *library director*

Greenville
Warner, Kenneth Wilson, Jr. *editor, publishing executive*

Harpers Ferry
Bailey, Nancy Joyce *elementary school educator*
Boucher, Wayne Irving *policy analyst*
Kodak, Don *museum director*

Hedgesville
Boland, Gerald Lee *health facility administrator*

Huntington
Babiuc-Hamilton, Maria Cristina *physics professor*
Bledsoe, Kathleen Elizabeth *academic librarian, educator*
Chrol, E. Del *classicist, educator*
Cocke, William Marvin, Jr. *plastic surgeon, educator*
Confer, Jennifer *pharmacist, educator*
Delidow, Beverly *medical educator*
Dennison, Corley Francis III *dean*
Foster, Earl James *orthopedist*
Hayes, Robert Bruce *former college president, educator*
Jenkins, Evan H. *state legislator*
Jude, David C. *medical educator*
Kawada, Ikuyo *language educator*
Mufson, Maurice Albert *infectious diseases physician, educator*
Nguyen, Que Huong *physics professor*
Petrany, Stephen Michael *medical educator, director*
Pratt, Mary Louise *librarian, writer*
Reese, Clara Cook *educator*
Wenzel, Loren Alvin *accounting professor*
Wietholter, Jon Patrick *pharmacist, educator*
Woodward, David Reid *retired history professor*

Hurricane
Hage, Lillian C. *religious organization administrator, director, dean*

Institute
Bird, John D. *finance educator, consultant*

Kearneysville
Biggs, Alan Richard *plant pathologist, educator*
Brown, Eric Wayne *geneticist*

Keyser
Falkowski, Theresa Gae *chemistry educator*
Smoot, Stephen Annese *columnist, educator*

Kingwood
Moyers, Sylvia Dean *retired medical librarian*

Lewisburg
Ford, Richard Edmond *lawyer*

Marlinton
Sharp, Jane Price *retired editor*

Martinsburg
Ayers, Anne Louise *small business owner, consultant, counselor*
Foley, Diana Kay Teets *mental health nurse, educator*
Hill, Philip Bonner *lawyer*
Radosh, Ronald *history professor*

Matewan
Call, Bridget Kay *literature and language educator*

Montgomery
Carlson, George Theodore *physics professor*
Munasinghe, Ranjith Arachchige *mathematics professor, engineer*

Morgantown
Albrink, Margaret Joralemon *medical educator*
Allamong, Betty Davis *retired academic administrator, biology professor*
Bang, Ki Moon *epidemiologist, professor*
Blaydes, Sophia Boyatzies *English language educator*
Bucklew, Neil S. *former academic administrator, educator*
Carver, Jeffrey Scott *science educator*
Cheng, Yueming *engineering educator*
Cho, Eung Ha *engineering educator*
Choudhry, Muhammad Akram *engineering educator*
Cochrane, Robert Lowe *biologist*
Collins, James William *health science association administrator, epidemiologist, mechanical engineer*
Constantinescu, Adi *physicist, educator*
Eck, Ronald Warren *civil engineer, educator*
Ernest, John Richard *literature and language professor*
Etherton, John Richard *safety engineer*
Fisher, John Welton, II, *lawyer, educator, academic administrator*
Fleming, William Wright, Jr. *retired pharmacology professor*
Fusco, Andrew G. *lawyer*
Garrison, Michael S. *lawyer, educator, former academic administrator*
Glover, Douglas Dennis *obstetrics, gynecology and pharmacology educator*
Griffith, Charles T. *accountant, consultant*
Haff, Guy Gregory *exercise science educator, researcher*
Halabe, Udaya Bhatta *civil engineering educator, researcher*
Hardesty, David Carter, Jr. *president emeritus and professor of law, former academic administrator*
Kemp, Emory Leland *civil engineering educator*
Khan, Tapan Kumar *adult education educator*
Kim, Hong Nack *political science professor*
Kurian, Sobha *medical educator*
Lambert, H. Wayne *medical educator, researcher*
McCluskey, Stephen C. *retired history professor*
Morris, Greg *director, former federal agency administrator*
Morris, William Otis, Jr. *lawyer, educator*
Nugent, George Robert *neurosurgeon*
Peng, Syd S. *mining engineer, educator*
Prabhu, Vikram Clifford *physician*
Pyles, Rodney Allen *archivist, county official*
Rao, Katikineni Murali Krishna *medical researcher*
Rentch, James Spencer *forester, educator*
Ringer, Darrell Wayne (Dan) *lawyer*
Schaeffer, Peter (Peter Viktor Schaeffer) *urban and regional planning educator*
Scudiere, Debra Hodges *lawyer*
Sears, Robert Stephen *finance educator, former dean*
Siriwardane, Hema J. *science educator*
Spenik, James L. *research scientist*
Stewart, Bill *college football coach*
Stout, Nancy Ann *health science association administrator, director*
Tauger, Mark Bernard *historian*
Vatsa, Mayank *computer scientist, researcher*
Vehse, Charles Theodore *humanities educator*
Wenger, Sharon Louise *cytogeneticist, researcher, educator*
Wiedebusch, Mary Kathryne *dance educator*
Wilson, Mary Alice *musician, educator*
Witt, Tom *economics researcher, educator*
Zhang, Yadong *medical researcher*

Oak Hill
Hamilton, Pat R. *retired lawyer, state representative*

Parkersburg
Francis, Lynne Ann *music educator*
Gaston, Patricia Sullivan *educator*
Heiss, Harry Glen *archivist*
McClung, Phil Oran *psychology professor*
McKenzie, Lawrence J. *composition educator*
Notturno, Mark Amadeus *philosopher*
Wilson, Roberta Bush *retired psychotherapist, accountant*
Zeck, Van *federal agency administrator*

Pennsboro
Poling, Kermit William *minister*

Philippi
Shearer, Richard Eugene *educational consultant*

Pullman
Fearn, Noelle E. *criminologist, educator*

Ranson
Rudacille, Sharon Victoria *medical technician*

Ravenswood
Barber, Donald Gene, Jr. *supply chain professional*

Ronceverte
Hooper, Anne Dodge *pathologist, educator*

Saint Albans
Smith, Robert Carlisle *retired department administrator, retired welding educator*

Salem
Bullion, Keith Alan *coach, director*
Raad, Virginia *pianist, educator*

Shepherdstown
Abbrecht, Peter Herman *medical educator*
Elliott, Jean Ann *retired library director*
Snyder, Joseph John *editor, lecturer, consultant, historian, writer*
Strasser, William Carl, Jr. *retired college president, educator*
Wilson, Miriam Janet Williams *publishing executive*

Shinnston
Spears, Jae *state legislator*

South Charleston
Fishkin, Anne Sonya *retired special education educator*

Spencer
Parker, Theresa Ann Boggs *records manager, retired special education educator, retired music educator*

Stonewood
Guido, Ben L. *principal*

Summit Point
Taylor, Harold Allen, Jr. *industrial minerals consultant*

Teays
Lamb, Carl Vernon *writer, retired engineer*

Weirton
Fahey, William Thomas, II, *lawyer*

West Columbia
Fowler, Sandra Lynn *poet*

West Liberty
Domyan, Steve Richard *audiologist, educator*
Fliess, Robert F. *mathematics professor*
Hattman, John William *literature and language professor*
Lasch, Meta M. *communications and art educator*
Thomas, David Joseph *literature and language professor*

Wheeling
Akhavan-Heidari, Mehdi *cardiothoracic surgeon*
Bailey, John Preston *federal judge, lawyer*
Bransfield, Michael Joseph *bishop*
Danford, Thomas R. *biology professor*
Hill, Barry Morton *lawyer*
Johnston, Thomas E. *judge*
Michaels, James Edward *bishop emeritus*
Peace, Bernie Kinzel *art educator, artist*
Phillis, Marilyn Hughey *artist*
Potter, Sharon Lynn *prosecutor*
Schmitt, Bernard William *bishop emeritus*
Stamp, Frederick Pfarr, Jr. *federal judge*
Thurston, Bonnie Bowman *religious studies educator, minister, poet*
Whelton, Beverly Jean *philosopher, educator*

White Sulphur Springs
Henry, Cynthia Ann *retired gerontology nurse, educator*

WISCONSIN

Algoma
Golomski, William Arthur Joseph *consulting company executive*

Appleton
Albrecht, Roberta J. *writer*
Beck, Jill *academic administrator, dancer, educator*
Boldt, Oscar Charles *construction executive, director*
Boren, Clark Henry, Jr. *general and vascular surgeon*
Chaney, William Albert *retired history professor*
Cook, David Marsden *physics professor*
De Stasio, Elizabeth Ann *biology educator*
Froehlich, Harold Vernon *judge, retired congressman*
Goldgar, Bertrand Alvin *literary historian*
Grayson, David S. *paper company executive*
Luther, Thomas William *retired dermatologist*
Malaney, Stephanie J. *reading specialist*
Oppmann, Andrew James *newspaper editor*
Petinga, Charles Michael *transportation executive*
Rence, Bradford G. *biology professor*
Stellmacher, Jon Michael *corporate financial executive*
Wieckert, Steven Kelly *real estate developer, former state legislator*

Ashland
Brouder, Mark Joseph *fishery field station supervisor, manager*
Gorman, Owen Thomas *biologist*
Joyal, Richard Dale *economics professor*
Saxild, Christine Ann *science educator*
Smith, Jane Schneberger *retired city administrator*

Balsam Lake
Anjulis, Stanley Joseph *retired church administrator*

Baraboo
Lang, Gregory P. *music educator*
Umhoefer, Aural M. *retired dean, educational consultant*

Barneveld
Kolb, Victoria L. *retired mathematics educator*

Barron
Kienbaum, Janice Mae *reading specialist*

Beaver Dam
Butterbrodt, John Ervin *real estate company officer*

Beloit
Boros-Kazai, Andras *political science professor*
Buchanan, Gregory McClellan *psychology professor*
Davis, Harry Rex *political science professor*
Green, Harold Daniel *dentist*
Gustafson, Jerry William *entrepreneur educator, economics professor*
Knueppel, Henry W. *manufacturing executive*

Black River Falls
Lister, Thomas Edward *lawyer*

Bloomer
Prenzlow, Elmer John-Charles, Jr. *minister*

Boscobel
Young, Gary William *minister, educator, retired military officer*

Brookfield
Carter, Charlene Ann *psychologist*
Carter, Rodney William *lawyer*
Dillon, Donald F. *data processing executive*
Jones, Richard K. *information technology executive*
Pottebaum, Sharon Mitchell *farm manager, retired health educator*
Rooney, Carol Bruns *dietitian*
Schmitz, John J. *writer, educator*
Sprague, Charles W. *lawyer, finance company executive*
Vierthaler, Bonnie Louise *artist, educator*
Winsten, Saul Nathan *lawyer*
Yabuki, Jeffrey W. *data processing company executive, former accounting company executive*

Cascade
Baumann, Carol Edler *retired political scientist*

Chetek
Fossum, Robert Merle *mathematician, educator*

Chippewa Falls
Sutherland, Marion Ida *music educator*

Clintonville
Primmer, Lillian Juanda *science educator*

Colgate
Earl, Marcia Hunt *music educator, director*

Cottage Grove
Baird, Robert Dahlen *retired theology studies educator*
Lund, Daryl Bert *retired food science educator*

Cumberland
Nyseth, Elizabeth Ann *retired secondary school educator*

Darien
Miller, Malcolm Henry *manufacturing sales executive, real estate developer*

De Forest
Morjan, Wilmar *entomologist, researcher*

De Pere
Aerts, Rita Jane *retired elementary school educator*

Baeten, Jane Ellen *educator, school counselor*
Crowley, Karlyn *educator*
Harris, John T., IV, *religious organization administrator*
Humphrey, Nicolas Scott *literature and language professor*
Risden, Edward L. *literature and language professor*

Delafield
Haugner, Carolyn M. *elementary school educator*

Delavan
Barnett, Maryann Fau *special education educator*

Dodgeville
Angel, Timothy Luke *lawyer*

Dousman
Zettl, Gary T. *engineering educator*

Eau Claire
Berg-Peck, Catherine *literature and language professor*
Bogstad, Janice Marie *Literature & Language Professor Women Studies, Academic Librarian*
Brill, Donald Maxim *researcher, educator*
Diggle-Dehne, Theresa A. *science educator*
Field, Barbara Kay *elementary school educator*
Frank, John LeRoy *commissioner, lawyer, educator*
King, Frederick W. *chemistry professor, researcher*
Kirkhorn, Lee-Ellen Charlotte *community health nurse, educator*
Menard, John R., Jr. *home improvement retail executive*
Mirr, Joseph R. *lawyer*
Stanton, Sandra Sunquist *consultant, educator*
Stark, Paul *small business owner*
Stoddard, Glenn McDonald *lawyer*
Tiefel, Virginia May *librarian*
Weil, D(onald) Wallace *business administration educator*

Edgerton
Peck, David Blackman *electrical engineer*

Egg Harbor
Schultz, Richard Otto *ophthalmologist, educator*

Elkhart Lake
Harper, Carrie Lynn *school counselor*

Elkhorn
Dunn, Walter Scott, Jr. *writer, museum director, consultant*
Eberhardt, Daniel Hugo *lawyer*
Janners, Erik Nikolas *music educator, conductor*
Reinke, Doris Marie *retired elementary school educator*
Sostarich, Mark Edward *lawyer*

Ferryville
Tedeschi, John Alfred *historian, librarian, educator*

Fish Creek
Abegg, Martin Gerald *retired academic administrator*

Fitchburg
Bhargava, Ashok *retired economics professor*
Buchholz, Ronald Lewis *retired architect*
Gurkow, Helen J. *retired physician*
Haslanger, Philip Charles *minister*
Kaus, Michael *research and development company executive*

Fond Du Lac
Denow, Thomas D. *research scientist, educator*
Henken, Willard John *retired university dean*
Schimpf, David Michael *theology studies educator, department chairman*
Treffert, Darold Allen *psychiatrist, writer, hospital administrator*

Fort Atkinson
Jones, Alan Porter, Jr. *food manufacturing executive*
Schumacher, Mabel G. *director, consultant*

Fox Point
Froemming, Barbara G. *retired home economics educator*

Franklin
Graef, Luther William *civil engineer*
Stenzel, Mary Francis *social worker*
Tittl, Matthew Paul *medical technician, educator*

Franksville
Palecek, Michael R. *information technology manager*

Genesee Depot
Kaldhusdal, Terry Lee *elementary school educator*

Germantown
Rudebeck, Carol A. *special education educator*

Glendale
Sterner, Frank Maurice *manufacturing executive*
Wright, Mary Ann *automotive components company executive*

Grafton
Maynard, John Ralph *lawyer*
Stock, E. Lee *ophthalmologist, consultant*

Green Bay
Alesch, Daniel James *social sciences educator, researcher*
Banks, Robert J. *bishop emeritus*
Capers, Dom (Dominic Capers) *professional football coach*
Conley, William Cleland *statistician, educator*
Daley, Arthur James *retired magazine publisher*
Driver, Donald Jerome *professional football player*
Edgar, Terence S. *pediatric neurologist*
Gard, John *state legislator*
Grosso, Cheryl Ann *art educator*
Harris, Al (Alshinard Harris) *professional football player*
Kurenok, Vladimir *mathematics professor*
LaRue, Lillian Jayne *electrical engineer, educator*
Malloy, Kaoime Elin *costume designer, educator*
McCarthy, Mike *professional football coach*
Morneau, Robert Fealey *bishop*
Murphy, Mark Hodge *professional football team executive, retired professional football player*
Ricken, David Laurin *bishop*
Telzrow, Michael E. *museum director, historian*
Thompson, Ted Clarence *professional sports team executive, retired professional football player*
Weyers, Larry Lee *energy executive*
Wolf, Barth Joel *lawyer, energy executive*
Woodson, Charles C. *professional football player*

Greendale
Patterson, Amanda Margaret *music educator*
Vinent-Cantoral, Aida R. *mediator*

Hales Corners
Case, Karen Ann *lawyer*
McNally, Vincent Joseph *historian, educator*

Hartford
Aubuchon, Richard E. *engineering executive*

Hartland
Stamsta, Jean F. *artist*

Hollandale
Colescott, Warrington Wickham *artist, printmaker, educator*

Holmen
Meyer, Karl William *retired university president*

Hortonville
Habeck, Carolyn R. *library director*

Hudson
Dahle, Carol Jo *secondary school choral director*
Witthuhn, Burton Orrin *retired university official*

Iola
Krause, Chester Lee *publishing executive*
Mishler, Clifford Leslie *publisher*

Janesville
Buechler, Dale *engineering educator*
Detert-Moriarty, Judith Anne *graphic designer, educator, volunteer*
Fingerson, Kyle R. *history professor*
Fitzgerald, James Francis *broadcast executive*
Kubina, June M. *instrumental music educator, music educator*

Jefferson
Smith, Dena Michele *physical education educator*

Johnson Creek
Braunschweig, Cynthia S. *art educator*

Kenosha
Boe, Barbara Louise *retired dean*
Cyr, Arthur I. *political science and economics professor*
Earns, Lane Robert *academic administrator, historian, educator*
Garcia, Alvaro *music educator*
Hegrenes, Scott Grayson *biology professor*
Iaquinta, Leonard Phillip *academic administrator, writer, consultant, not-for-profit fundraiser*
Joyce, Daniel James *curator*
Kulke, Erik C. *language educator*
Kummings, Donald Dale *language educator*
Mast, Joy Nystrom *biogeographer educator*
Morales, Maria Isabel *language educator*
Pinchuk, Nicholas Thomas *manufacturing executive*
Potente, Eugene, Jr. *interior designer*
Rattigan, Denise *special education educator*
Renaud, Christine *classicist, educator*
Robinson-Gustin, Brenda Sue *retired art educator, painter*
Sleeter, Christine Elaine *education educator*
Stern, Walter Wolf III *lawyer*
Udry, Stephen Potter *history professor*

Kohler
Kohler, Herbert Vollrath, Jr. *diversified manufacturing company executive*
O'Keefe, Tamra Lynn *psychologist, school system administrator, director*

La Crosse
Ancius, Michael J. *corporate financial executive*
Byom, Carolyn E. *lab administrator*
Chilton, Galadriel *academic librarian*
Clark, Malcolm Gene, Sr. *artist, consultant, historian*
Davy, Michael Francis *civil engineer, consultant*
DePaolo, Anthony *literature and language educator*
Doberstein, Scott T. *athletic trainer educator*
Gorman, Kathleen Jean *performing arts educator, choreographer*
Gow, Joe *academic administrator*
Graham, Lise N. *finance educator*
Haro, Roger John *biology professor*
Kooiman, Barbara Marlene *historian*
Lenards, Nishele Dyan *medical educator*
Listecki, Jerome Edward *bishop*
Luckner, Brian William *choir director, organist, composer*
Morehouse, Richard Edward *psychology professor*
Periyasamy, Kasilingam *engineering educator*
Rademacher, Dana Ellis *urologist*
Rude, Brian David *utilities executive*
Simpson, Steven Vincent *social sciences educator*
Sleik, Thomas Scott *lawyer*
Smuksta, Michael J. *history professor*
Vogt, Kimberly Ann *sociologist, educator*
Webster, Stephen Burtis *dermatologist, educator*

Lake Geneva
Braden, Berwyn Bartow *lawyer*
Dobray, Alan Michael *theoretical physicist, research scientist*

Lancaster
Croft, Candace Ann *psychology professor, academic administrator, small business owner*
Halferty, James Burkhardt *lawyer*

Land O Lakes
Sharpee, Rhoda Anderson *social worker*

Lomira
Kittelson, Roger *marketing professional*

Luxemburg
Riley, Dan *entertainer*

Madison
Abrahamson, Shirley Schlanger *state supreme court chief justice*
Adler, Julius *biochemist, educator, biologist*
Albers, Sheryl Kay *state legislator*
Albert, Daniel Myron *ophthalmologist, educator*
Aldag, Ramon John *management and organization educator*
Allen, David Bruce *endocrinologist, educator*
Anderson, David R. *insurance company executive*
Anderson, Louis Wilmer, Jr. *physicist, researcher*
Andreano, Ralph Louis *economist, educator*
Antonioni, David *professor, director*
Arndt, George Arthur *anesthesiologist, consultant*
Askey, Richard Allen *mathematician, educator*
Atalla, Rajai H. *science administrator, educator*
Auerbach, Emily K. *language educator, director*
Barger, Amy J. *astronomer, educator*
Barger, Vernon Duane *physicist, educator*
Barnhill, Charles Joseph, Jr. *lawyer*
Barrett, Bruce *medical educator, researcher*
Bartley, Linda L. *musician, music educator*
Basting, Thomas J., Sr. *lawyer*
Beachley, Norman Henry *mechanical engineer, educator*
Beck, Anatole *mathematician, educator*
Begum, Ayesha *astronomer, researcher*
Bennett, Kenneth Alan *retired biological anthropologist*
Berg, William James *language educator, writer, translator*
Berghahn, Klaus Leo *German and Jewish studies educator*
Beyer-Mears, Annette *physiologist*
Bird, Robert Byron *chemical engineering educator, author*
Bogue, Allan George *historian, educator*
Botez, Dan *physicist*
Bradley, Ann Walsh *state supreme court justice*
Brennan, Robert Walter *association executive*
Brewster, Francis Anthony *lawyer*
Bringmann, Kathrin *mathematician, educator*
Brock, Thomas Dale *retired microbiology professor*
Brock, William Allen III *economist, educator*
Bruch, Ludwig W. *physicist, researcher*
Bullock, William Henry *bishop emeritus*
Bunge, Charles Albert *library science educator*
Burgess, Richard Ray *oncologist, biotechnologist, educator*
Burns, Dixie L. *astronomer, educator*
Burris, Robert Harza *biochemist, educator*
Busby, Edward Oliver *retired dean*
Cao, Guoping *research scientist*
Carnell, Kent I. *lawyer*
Cassinelli, Joseph Patrick *astronomy educator*
Chandler, Richard Gates *lawyer*
Chapman, Loren J. *psychology professor*
Chinn, Menzie David *economics educator*
Christensen, Nikolas Ivan *geophysicist, educator*
Churchwell, Edward Bruce *astronomer, educator*
Cieslewicz, David J. *Mayor, Madison, Wisconsin*
Ciplijauskaite, Birute *humanities educator*
Clay, Clarence Samuel *acoustical oceanographer*
Cleland, W(illiam) Wallace *biochemistry educator*
Connors, Kenneth Antonio *retired pharmacy educator*
Cooper, Peggy (Mary Margaret) *artist, educator*
Coppersmith, Susan Nan *physicist*
Crim, Forrest Fleming, Jr. *chemist, educator*
Crone, Wendy Catherine *engineering educator*
Cronon, William *history professor*
Crooks, Neil Patrick *state supreme court justice*
Crow, James Franklin *retired genetics educator*
Curtis, Charles G., Jr. *lawyer*
Curtis, Paul David *lawyer*
Dale, Thomas Ernest Abell *art educator*
Darling, Alberta Helen *state legislator*
Davis, Kenneth Boone, Jr. *dean, law educator*
DeMain, John *opera company director*
Dempsey, Robert J. *neurosurgeon*
Derzon, Gordon M. *hospital administrator*
Devine, Patricia G. *psychology professor, department chairman*
DeWerd, Larry Albert *medical physicist, educator*
DeWitt, David J. *computer scientist*
Diawara, Yacouba *physicist, researcher*
Dietmeyer, Donald Leo *retired electrical engineering educator*
Dimick, Barbara L. *library director*
Dorn, Dennis L. *theater educator*
Dott, Robert Henry, Jr. *geologist, educator*
Doyle, Jim (James Edward) *Governor of Wisconsin, former state attorney general*
Draper, Norman Richard *statistician, educator*
Drechsel, Robert Edward *journalism educator*
Dubrow, Heather *literature educator*
Earl, Anthony Scully *former governor, lawyer*
Eichelman, Burr Simmons, Jr. *psychiatrist, researcher, educator*
Emmert, Gilbert Arthur *retired engineering educator*
Evan, Amato Tomas *climate scientist*
Evenson, Merle Armin *chemist, educator*
Evers, Tony (Anthony Evers) *state official, school system administrator*
Evert, Ray Franklin *botany educator*
Fahien, Leonard August *physician, educator*
Farrar, Thomas C. *chemist, educator*
Farrell, Philip M. *pediatrician, medical educator, former dean*
Faulkner, Julia Ellen *opera singer*
Ferris, Michael C. *mathematics professor*
Field, Henry Augustus, Jr. *lawyer*
Fleischman, Stephen *museum director*
Foldy, Seth Leonard *state agency administrator, public health officer, physician, educator*
Fonck, Raymond John *physicist, educator*
Fox, Michael Vass *theology studies educator*
Frazier, Kenneth L. *university librarian*
Frykenberg, Robert Eric *historian, educator*
Gableman, Michael J. *state supreme court justice*
Galanter, Marc Selig *law educator*
Garver, Fanny P. *art gallery owner*
Garver, Thomas Haskell *curator, consultant, writer*
Gilbert, Pupa *physics professor, director*
Goldberger, Arthur Stanley *economics professor*
Goll, James Gerard *chemistry professor*
Gooding, Diane Carol *psychology educator, researcher*
Graf, Truman Frederick *agricultural economist, educator*
Greaser, Marion Lewis *science educator*
Greenfield, Norman Samuel *psychologist, educator*
Greenler, Robert George *physics professor, researcher*
Greller, Jason Anthony *lawyer*
Gruber, John Edward *editor, historian, photographer*
Guenther, Erik Richard *lawyer*
Haimson, Bezalel Cecil *engineering educator*
Hamerow, Theodore Stephen *historian, educator*
Hamers, Robert J. *chemistry educator, researcher*
Hammel, Kenneth Edward *biochemist, educator*
Han, Tao *physics professor*
Hannouchi, Said *language educator*
Hansen, Sherri M. *psychiatrist*
Hansen, W. Lee *economics professor*
Hanson, David James *lawyer*
Harvey, William D. *utilities executive, lawyer*
Hawkinson, Lorraine A. *librarian*
Heatley, Gregg Alan *ophthalmologist*
Heinrich, Carolyn J. *political science professor, director*
Hester, Donald Denison *economics professor*
Hetsko, Cyril Michael *internist*
Hill, Charles Graham, Jr. *chemical engineering educator*
Hokin, Lowell Edward *biochemist, educator*
Hood, Leroy Edward *molecular biologist, educator*
Hopen, Herbert John *horticulture educator*
Horning, Kathleen T. *library director*
Howell, Roberta F. *lawyer*
Hoyt, James Lawrence *journalism educator, writer*
Hu, Kejin *molecular and stem cell biologist*
Huang, Ming-Huang *engineer, materials scientist*
Iltis, Hugh Hellmut *botanist, educator, environmental advocate*
Jacobs, Harvey M. *urban planner, educator*
Jacobsen, Kendra *health facility administrator*
Jahn, Molly M. *dean, biologist, educator*
Jalil, Qamar *social studies educator*
Javid, Manucher J. *retired neurosurgeon, educator*
Jeanne, Robert Lawrence *entomologist, educator*
Jefferson, James Walter *psychiatrist, educator*
Ji, Li Li *biomedical researcher*
Johnson, Clark Montgomery *geologist, educator*
Johnson, Jean Elaine *nursing educator*
Johnson, Maryl Rae *cardiologist*
Johnson, Richard Arnold *statistics educator, consultant*
Joranson, David Eric *research scientist*
Julian, Thomas Michael *gynecologic surgeon, educator*
Kaesberg, Paul Joseph *virology researcher*
Kang, Iksoon *research scientist*
Katen-Bahensky, Donna *health facility administrator*
Keating Heinemann, Lorrie T. *state banking agency administrator*
Kendall, Nancy *education educator, consultant*
Khazins, David Mikhailovich *retired research scientist*
Kleinhenz, Christopher *foreign language educator, researcher, director*
Knechtle, Stuart Johnston *medical educator, transplant immunologist*
Knetter, Michael Mark *dean*
Knowles, Richard Alan John *language educator*
Koski, Ann Louise *museum director*
Kresse, Kerry L. *library director*
K-Turkel, Judith Leah Rosenthal (Judi K-Turkel) *writer, editor, publisher*
Kudsk, Kenneth Allan *surgeon*
Kurtz, Thomas Gordon *mathematics professor*
Kutler, Stanley Ira *historian, lawyer, educator*
Laessig, Ronald Harold *preventive medicine and pathology educator, state official*
La Follette, Douglas J. *Secretary of State, Wisconsin*
Lagally, Max Gunter *physics professor*
Lan, Que *science educator*
Landry, Gregory L. *pediatrician, educator*
Langer, Richard J. *lawyer*
Lardy, Henry A(rnold) *biochemistry professor*
Latta, Richard Allen *lawyer*
Lautenschlager, Peggy A. *former state attorney general*
Lawler, James Edward *physics professor*
Lawton, Barbara *Lieutenant Governor of Wisconsin*
Leavitt, Judith Walzer *history of medicine educator*
Lewandowski, Gina *engineering educator*
Lewandowski, Richard J. *lawyer*
Li, Fumin *research scientist*
Li, Kai *chemist, research scientist*
Li, Lingjun *chemistry professor*
Lightfoot, Edwin Niblock, Jr. *retired chemical engineering educator*
Lin, Chun Chia *research physicist, educator*
Lincoln Michel, Karen *journalist*
Linstroth, Tod Brian *lawyer*
Linton, William A., Jr. *medical products executive*

Long, Willis Franklin *electrical engineering educator, researcher*
Lorimer, Craig Gordon *ecologist, educator*
Lovell, Edward George *mechanical engineering educator*
Ma, Zhenqiang *engineering educator*
MacDougall, Priscilla Ruth *lawyer*
Madureira, Luis Manuel *literature and language professor*
Maher, Louis James, Jr. *geologist, educator*
Mahoney, Jane E. *medical educator, director*
Maki, Dennis G. *epidemiology educator*
Malkus, David Starr *mathematician*
Marlett, Judith Ann *nutritional sciences educator, researcher*
Marshall, Kathryn Sue *lawyer*
Martin, Biddy (Carolyn Arthur Martin) *academic administrator*
Martin, Robert David *judge, educator*
Martin-Berg, Laurey *literature and language professor*
Mash, Donald J. *college president*
Mau, Bob *statistician, evolutionary biologist*
Maynard, James Harold *chemistry professor*
McNelly, John Taylor *retired journalist, educator*
Meisner, Lorraine Faxon *geneticist*
Meisner, Maurice J. *history professor*
Melli, Marygold Shire *law educator*
Mertz, Janet Elaine *molecular biology researcher, educator, consultant*
Misran, Jennifer *language educator*
Morlino, Robert Charles *bishop*
Morton, Stephen Dana *chemist, consultant*
Mostaghimi, Ladan *psychiatrist*
Mowris, Gerald William *lawyer*
Moyer-Horner, Lucas *conservationist, educator*
Mueller, Willard Fritz *economics professor*
Mukerjee, Pasupati *chemistry professor*
Nagel, Alexander *mathematics professor*
Newcomb, Eldon Henry *retired botany educator*
Nordby, Eugene Jorgen *orthopedic surgeon*
Novotny, Donald Wayne *electrical engineer, educator*
O'Brien, Andrea Maxworthy *education teacher*
Odden, Allan Robert *education educator*
Olson, Norman Fredrick *not-for-profit developer, retired food science educator*
Ozeki, Akichika *statistician*
Panczenko, Russell *museum director*
Parter, Seymour Victor *computer science and mathematics educator*
Peercy, Paul Stuart *engineering educator*
Pella, Milton Orville *science educator*
Pfotenhauer, John M. *engineering educator, researcher*
Pillaert, E(dna) Elizabeth *museum director*
Pitot, Henry Clement III *pathologist, educator*
Post, Jeffrey H. *insurance company executive*
Powell, Barry Bruce *classicist, educator*
Prange, Roy Leonard, Jr. *lawyer*
Prosser, David Thomas, Jr. *state supreme court justice, former state legislator*
Ramayya, Edwin Bosco *engineer, researcher*
Ranallo, Frank N. *medical researcher*
Ranney, Joseph Austin *lawyer*
Rao, Velcheru Narayana *south asian professor*
Record, M. Thomas, Jr. *biochemist, educator*
Reps, Thomas William *science educator, small business owner*
Reynolds, Ernest West *retired internist, educator*
Rice, Joy Katharine *psychologist, education educator*
Riley, Jocelyn Carol *writer, television producer*
Ring, Gerald J. *real estate developer, insurance company executive*
Roberts, Jeanette C. *dean, pharmacy educator*
Roberts, Leigh Milton *psychiatrist*
Robinson, Stephen Michael *mathematician, educator*
Rodwell, John Dennis *biochemist*
Roggensack, Patience Drake *state supreme court justice*
Roseberry, James Alan *retired science educator*
Ryan, Bo (William F. Ryan Jr.) *men's college basketball coach*
Sakidja, Ridwan *research scientist*
Salzwedel, Jack C. *insurance company executive*
Sass, Dawn Marie *state treasurer*
Sauer, Jeff *university hockey coach*
Schejbal, David *dean*
Scherer, Victor Richard *physicist, computer scientist, musician, consultant*
Schultz, Daniel R. *insurance company executive*
Schweber, Simone *education educator*
Schwendinger, Laura Elise *composer, humanities educator*
Shabaz, John C. *judge*
Shafer, Byron Edwin *political science professor*
Shain, Irving *retired chemicals executive, academic administrator*
Sheffield, Lewis Glosson *physiologist*
Shi, Yu *engineer, researcher*
Sibert, Edwin L. *chemistry professor*
Sinnott, Stephen P. *former prosecutor*
Skilton, John Singleton *lawyer*
Skinner, James Lauriston *chemist, educator*
Sondel, Paul Mark *pediatric oncologist, educator*
Sonnedecker, Glenn Allen *pharmaceutical historian, educator*
Spencer, C. Stanley *insurance company executive*
Spencer, Cheryl L. *literature and language educator*
Spencer, Christopher S. *lawyer, insurance company executive*
Stein, James Howard *medical educator, researcher*
Susman, Millard *geneticist, educator*
Swan, Barbara J. *lawyer, utilities executive*
Taber, Christopher Robert *finance educator*
Temkin, Harvey L. *lawyer*
Theron, Peter *mathematics professor*
Thomas, J. Mark *sociologist, educator, minister*
Thompson, Barbara Storck *state official*
Thomson, James Alexander *molecular biologist, educator*
Timmins, Robert *biologist*
Tishler, William Henry *landscape architect, educator*
Turng, Lih-Sheng *education educator*
Tvedt, Ryan Robert *theater educator*
Van Hollen, J(ohn) B(yron) *state attorney general, former prosecutor*
Vaughan, Michael Richard *lawyer*
Vaughan, Worth Edward *retired chemistry professor*
Vowles, Richard Beckman *literature educator*
Wald, Arnold *gastroenterologist*
Waldo, Robert Leland *retired insurance company executive*
Webster, John Goodwin *biomedical engineering educator, researcher*
Weinbrot, Howard David *language educator*
Wenger, Ronald David *surgeon*
Westman, Jack Conrad *child psychiatrist, educator*
Whiffen, James Douglass *surgeon, educator*
Whitlon, Donna Sue *neuroscientist, researcher*
Whitney, Lori Ann *legislative staff member*
Wiesenfarth, Joseph John *retired literature educator*
Wiley, John D. *academic administrator, educator*
Wineke, Joseph Steven *political organization administrator, former state legislator*
Wirz, George Otto *bishop emeritus*
Wolfe, Barbara L. *economics professor, researcher*
Wuethrich, Marcel *research scientist*
Young, Merwin Crawford *political science professor*
Zell, Josephine May *retired language educator*
Ziegler, Annette Kingsland *state supreme court justice*
Zimmerman, Howard Elliot *chemist, educator*
Zinder, Newton Donald *investment advisor, consultant*
Zweifel, David Alan *newspaper editor*

Manitowoc
Bandt, Tracy Tadych *psychologist*
Jones, Maurice D. *lawyer*
Muraski, Sister Rosalyn *special education educator*
Nelson, Robert Louis *education educator, consultant*
Tellock, Glen E. *manufacturing executive*
Trader, Joseph Edgar *orthopedic surgeon*

Marinette
Ceccarelli, Michael Paul *technologist*
Malmstadt, Mary Jane *music educator*
Rice, Karolyn Kaye *elementary school educator*

Markesan
Chamberlain, Robert Glenn *retired tool manufacturing executive*

Marshfield
Balz, Jean Arlynn *physician assistant*
Islam, Tasbirul *physician*
Kuehner, Marvin Ernest *surgeon*
Okon, Tomasz R. *palliative medicine physician, educator*

Mc Naughton
Bradshaw, Glenn Raymond *art educator*

Menasha
Gonya, Teresa Joanne *biology professor*
Zimmerman, Lynda Diane *music educator*

Menomonee Falls
Brennan, Donald A. *retail executive*
Eskenasi, Peggy *retail executive*
Gardner, Julie *retail executive*
Hinnrichs-Dahms, Holly Beth *elementary school educator*
Janzen, Norine Madelyn Quinlan *clinical laboratory scientist*
Jeffries, Telvin *retail executive*
Lanier, Bob *promotional products company executive, retired professional basketball player*
Mansell, Kevin B. *retail executive*
McDonald, Wesley S. *retail executive*
Montgomery, Larry (R. Lawrence Montgomery) *retail executive*
Nelson, Mary Ellen Genevieve *retired adult education educator*
Schepp, Richard D. *lawyer, retail executive*
Worthington, John M. *retail executive*

Menomonie
Asthana, Rajiv *engineering educator, researcher*
Eggert, James Edward *economics professor, writer*
Raut, Usha *physics professor*
Schuler, Robert Jordan *language educator, writer*

Mequon
Besch, Michael D. *academic administrator*
Bloom, James Edward *sales and marketing director, commodity trading and financial executive*
Elias, Paul S. *retired marketing executive*
Ellis, William Grenville *academic administrator, management consultant*
Kopfmann, Beverly Jean *small business owner*
Krueger, Doreen *language educator*
Menuge, Angus Jl *philosopher, educator*
Richman, Stephen Erik *retired lawyer, consultant*
Sisney, Ned *education educator*
Stephens, Carolyn King *retired literature and language professor*
Sullivan, Patricia W. (Terry Sullivan) *real estate trainer*
Terry, Leon Cass *neurologist, educator*
Wallace, Harry Leland *lawyer*

Merrill
Goessl, Celine *head of religious order*

Merton
Rheineck, Wendy Lynn *science educator*

Middleton
Berman, Ronald Charles *lawyer, accountant*
Dorner, Peter Paul *retired economist, educator*
Lee, Leslie Warren *marketing executive, educator*
Olive, David L. *endocrinologist, educator*
Sweet, Harvey *set and lighting designer*

Milton
Enlow, Donald Hugh *retired anatomist, dean*

Milwaukee
Aaron, Gordon K. *lawyer*
Ali, Omar *medical educator*
Allen, Will *urban farmer*
Alred, Gerald James *writing and language professor*
Aman, Mohammed Mohammed *dean, library and information science professor*
Amster, Ellen Jean *history professor*
Andrekopoulos, William G. *school system administrator*
Arbit, Bruce *direct marketing executive, consultant*
Babler, Wayne E., Jr. *lawyer*
Bader, Alfred Robert *chemist*
Ball, Elizabeth Fikenscher *gynecologist*
Ballman, Patricia Kling *lawyer*
Bannen, John Thomas *lawyer*
Bardenwerper, Fred Louis *lawyer*
Barnett, Robert L. *retired communications executive*
Barrett, Thomas M. (Tom Barrett) *Mayor, Milwaukee, former United States Representative from Wisconsin*
Barth, Karl Luther *retired seminary president*
Baumann, Roxanne Lee *industrial products international executive*
Beals, Vaughn Le Roy, Jr. *retired motorcycle manufacturing executive*
Beard, Daniel Andrew *medical educator*
Behrendt, David Frogner *retired journalist*
Beilke, Mark A. *medical educator*
Belfer, Beverly Rochelle Eigen *music educator, writer*
Benoit, Edward A. III *researcher*
Bergmann, Thomas E. *corporate financial executive*
Biller, Joel Wilson *lawyer, retired diplomat*
Biskupic, Steven M. *lawyer, former prosecutor*
Bleustein, Jeffrey L. *motorcycle company executive*
Bogut, Andrew *professional basketball player*
Bohn, Michael J. *psychiatrist, director*
Boie, Charles A. *museum administrator*
Bowen, Michael Anthony *lawyer, writer*
Bowles, Jacqueline Moore *marketing executive*
Boyd, Colin *manufacturing executive*
Boylan, Jim *professional basketball coach*
Braun, Ryan Joseph *professional baseball player*
Brenner, Elizabeth (Betsy Brenner) *publishing executive*
Brodwin, Paul Eric *medical educator*
Buntin, John D. *biology professor*
Burch, Thaddeus Joseph, Jr. *physics professor, priest*
Burke, William Ulick (Chip) *lawyer*
Busch, John Arthur *lawyer, business executive*
Buss, Daniel Frank *environmental scientist*
Callahan, William Patrick *bishop*
Cannon, David Joseph *lawyer*
Carter, Michael G. *insurance company executive*
Casey, John Alexander *lawyer*
Casper, Richard Henry *lawyer*
Chan, Carlyle Hung-lun *psychiatrist, educator*
Cheatham, Wallace McClain *music educator*
Chen, Qinghua *engineering educator*
Christiansen, Keith Allan *lawyer*
Chrzanowska-Wodnicka, Magdalena B. *research scientist*
Colbert, Virgis W. *food products executive*
Connelly, Mark *writer, educator*
Connolly, Gerald Edward *lawyer*
Cronin, Vincent Sean *geologist*
Culver, Curt S. *diversified financial services company executive*
Cutler, Richard W. *lawyer*
Cutler, Verne Clifton *engineering educator, consultant*
Daily, Frank J(erome) *lawyer*
Daniels, John W., Jr. *lawyer*
Davis, Susan F. *manufacturing executive*
Delfs, Andreas *conductor, musical director*
Diaz, Luis Alberto *dermatologist, educator*
Dyszelski, Aaron M. *theater educator, director*
Earing, Michael G. *cardiologist, director*
Ellis, Dwight Holmes III *lawyer*
Emanuel, John F. *lawyer*
Erickson, Randall J. *lawyer*
Eshetu, Gwendelbert Lewis *retired social worker*
Evans, Terence Thomas *federal judge*
Factor, Kim A.S. *mathematics professor, educational consultant*
Farrell, Patrick *artist*
Farris, Trueman Earl, Jr. *retired newspaper editor*
Feinsilver, Donald Lee *psychiatry professor*
Fielder, Prince Semien *professional baseball player*
Finley, Daniel Mark *museum administrator, former county official*
Flamboe, Jennifer M. *language educator, interpreter*
Florsheim, Richard Steven *lawyer*
Flynn, Mary *professor*
Forner, Sean A. *historian, educator*
Fraser, Alexander Paul *lawyer*
Frauen, Kurt Herman *lawyer*
Frautschi, Timothy Clark *lawyer*
Friebert, Robert Howard *lawyer*
Friedman, James Dennis *lawyer*
Furlong, Mark Francis *diversified financial services company executive, bank executive*
Gaggioli, Richard Arnold *mechanical engineering educator*
Gagne, Eric (Serge) *professional baseball player*
Gaines, Irving David *lawyer*
Galanis, John William *lawyer*
Gallagher, Richard Sidney *lawyer*
Gallop, Jane (Jane Anne Gallop) *women's studies educator, writer*
Garland, George Arthur *engineering educator, consultant*
Gauthier, Janice Lorraine *lawyer*
Gefke, Henry Jerome *lawyer*
Gemignani, Joseph Adolph *lawyer*
Gennarelli, Thomas A. *neurosurgeon, consultant*
Geske, Janine Patricia *law educator*
Gettel, James Joseph *lawyer, consultant*
Ghiardi, James Domenic *lawyer, educator*
Giacinti, Louis Anthony *science educator, writer*
Goodkind, Conrad George *lawyer*
Graham, Richard Harris, Jr. *theater educator*
Green, Edward Anthony *museum director*
Griffith, Owen Wendell *biochemistry professor*
Gudausky, Todd *cardiologist, educator*
Guerin, D. Michael *lawyer*
Guse, Christopher J. *art educator*
Haberman, F. William *lawyer*
Habush, Robert Lee *lawyer*
Hagerman, Douglas M. *consumer products company executive, lawyer*
Hamlin, Christine M. *archaeologist, educator*
Hammond, John R. *professional sports team executive*
Hansen, John Herbert *university administrator, accountant*
Hassler, John Michael *engineering educator*
Haworth, Daniel Thomas *emeritus chemistry professor*
Heinen, James Albin *electrical engineering educator*
Henrickson, Kelly John *pediatrician, medical educator*
Hernandez, Lyndon Joseph DeVera *medical educator*
Hoffman, Nathaniel A. *lawyer*
Hoffman, Trevor William *professional baseball player*
Holz, Harry George *lawyer*
Horsman, Lenore Lynde (Eleanora Lynde) *singer, voice educator*
Hubka, Thomas C. *architecture educator*
Hunt, Kenneth Charles *lawyer*
Huntington, David Mack Goode *foundation administrator*
Hur, Su-Ryong *physician, anesthesiologist*
Jackson, Tamara Nicole *lawyer*
Jang, Jaejin *engineering educator, consultant*
Joerres, Jeffrey A. *employment services executive*
Johnson, Sheri *medical educator, former state agency administrator*
Jones, Paul W. *manufacturing executive*
Jordan, Ruth Ann *retired physician*
Josyula, Kanth V. *research and development company executive*
Kaiser, Martin *editor-in-chief*
Karkheck, John Peter *physics professor, researcher*
Karp, David Barry *lawyer*
Kearney, Joseph D. *dean, law educator*
Keegan, Daniel T. *museum director*
Kendall, Jason Daniel *professional baseball player*
Kennedy, John Patrick *lawyer, corporate financial executive*
Kerr, Dorothy Marie Burmeister *marketing executive, consultant*
Keshvala, Seelpa H *educational opportunity fund director*
Kessler, Joan F. *judge, lawyer*
Kircher, John Joseph *law educator*
Klappa, Gale E. *energy executive*
Kochar, Mahendr Singh *physician, health facility administrator, research scientist, educator, writer, consultant*
Kohls, Heather Lynne Hipke *economics professor, consultant*
Kopps-Wagner, Jennifer *lawyer, insurance company executive*
Korn, Jeffrey Bernard *engineering educator*
Koss, John Charles *consumer electronics products manufacturing company executive*
Kringel, Jerome Howard *lawyer*
Kroft, Steven Howard *hematopathologist, medical educator*
Krueger, Raymond Robert *lawyer*
Kubale, Bernard Stephen *lawyer*
Kuchan, Anthony Mark *psychologist, educator*
Kuester, Dennis J. *diversified financial services company and bank executive*
Kushner, Beth *lawyer*
Kwiatt, James T. *physician*
Lacy, William H. *retired mortgage company executive*
LaDosa, John *medical researcher*
Layde, Joseph Bernard *psychiatrist, educator*
Lea, Filomena *English language educator, writer*
Lehninger, Paul David *theology studies educator*
Levit, William Harold, Jr. *lawyer*
Lione, Gail Ann *lawyer, automotive executive*
Little, Robert David *library science professor*
Liu, Qingmin *software engineer, materials engineer*
Llaurado, Thadd J. *lawyer*
Lu, Bin *electrical engineer, inventor, researcher*
Lucey, Patrick Joseph *former Governor of Wisconsin*
Lueders, Wayne Richard *lawyer*
Macha, Ken (Kenneth Edward Macha) *professional baseball manager*
Mandernack, Scott Bryan *librarian*
Manista, Raymond J. *lawyer, insurance company executive*
Manning, Kenneth Paul *specialty chemical company executive*
Marquis, William Oscar *lawyer*
Massey, Patrick Baber *internist, health facility administrator*
Masterson, Joseph Daniel *lawyer*
McCaw, Robert John *language educator*
McDonald, R. Bruce *manufacturing executive*
McGaffey, Jere D. *retired lawyer*
McGilligan, Patrick Michael *writer, editor*
Mehail, James Joseph *aerospace engineer, educator*
Melin, Robert Arthur *lawyer*
Melvin, Doug *professional baseball team manager*
Meus, Jonathan A. *engineering educator*
Moberg, David Oscar *sociology educator*
Mossbrucker, Joerg *engineering educator*
Mulcahy, Robert William *lawyer*
Munroe, Stephen H. *biology professor*
Munson, Ethan Vincent *engineering educator*
Murphy, Judith Chisholm *trust company executive*
Namdari, Bahram *surgeon*
Nasiri, Adel *retired engineering educator*
Nattinger, Ann B. *internist, researcher, medical educator*
Neuner, Joan Marie *medical educator*
Nosbusch, Keith D. *multi-industry high-technology company executive*
Okarma, Jerome D. *lawyer, manufacturing executive*
Olds, Glenn Richard *medical educator, department chairman*
Pagel, Paul Stanley *cardiac anesthesiologist*
Paulson, Belden Henry *political scientist, educator*

Peltz, Cissie Jean *art gallery director, cartoonist*
Peoples, Robert William *biomedical researcher*
Perlman, Richard Wilfred *economist, educator*
Phillips, Thomas John *lawyer*
Pindyck, Bruce Eben *lawyer, corporate financial executive*
Pink, Michael *performing company executive*
Poliner, Gary A. *insurance company executive*
Prantil, Vincent Carl *science educator*
Priebus, Reince *lawyer, political organization administrator*
Quereshi, Mohammed Younus *retired psychology professor*
Quirk, James *museum director*
Randolph, Willie (Willie Larry Randolph Jr.) *professional baseball coach, retired professional baseball player*
Redd, Michael *professional basketball player*
Rilling, William S. *radiologist*
Roell, Stephen A. *manufacturing executive*
Rosenberg, Lucille Glicklich *retired child psychiatrist*
Sampson, Kelvin Dale *professional basketball coach, former college basketball coach*
Samson, Richard Max *theater director, investment company executive*
Santo Tomas, Linus Hipolito *pulmonologist*
Schaefer, Jame *religious studies educator*
Schneider, John David *theatre director, playwright, actor, jazz singer*
Schnoll, Howard Manuel *financial consultant, investment company executive*
Schnur, Robert Arnold *lawyer, educator*
Schoenfeld, Howard Allen *management consultant, lawyer*
Schott, Sarah E. *lawyer*
Schroeder, John H. *university chancellor*
Seery, Carol Hubbard *communication sciences educator*
Sennett, Nancy J. *lawyer*
Shapiro, James Edward *judge*
Shapiro, Robyn Sue *lawyer, educator*
Shear, Alan James *theologian*
Shetty, Kaup Rajmohan *endocrinologist, educator*
Shiely, John Stephen *manufacturing executive, lawyer*
Shriner, Thomas L., Jr. *lawyer*
Siegel, Robert Harold *English literature educator, writer*
Simmons-Welburn, Janice *dean, library director*
Sims, Deloris *bank executive*
Skiles, Scott Allen *professional basketball coach*
Sklba, Richard John *bishop*
Soergel, Konrad Hermann *physician*
Spore, Keith Kent *newspaper executive*
Stadtmueller, Joseph Peter *federal judge*
Steinmiller, John F. *professional sports team executive*
Stemper, Brian D. *biomedical engineer, educator*
Stockdale, Christopher *physics professor*
Stoffel, Virginia Carroll *occupational therapist, educator*
Stoiber, Karen Callan *psychologist, educator*
Strayer, Jacqueline F. *manufacturing executive*
Sturm, William Charles *lawyer*
Surridge, Stephen Zehring *lawyer, writer*
Suster, Saul *medical educator, director*
Sutherlin, Michael W. *paper company executive*
Sveum, Dale Curtis *professional baseball coach*
Swanson, Roy Arthur *classicist, educator*
Sykes, Diane S. *federal judge, former state supreme court justice*
Szwarc, Wlodzimierz *operations research professor*
Talano, Julie M. *medical educator*
Theoharis, Athan George *history professor*
Thrall, Arthur Alvin *artist, educator*
Trattner, Walter Irwin *humanities educator, educator*
Tully, Catherine T. *lawyer*
Tysoe, Wilfred Tjalke *chemistry professor*
Ullman, Pierre Lioni *retired Spanish literature and language educator*
Vairavan, Kasivisvanathan *electrical engineering and computer science educator*
Vanderheyden, Jennifer Sue *language educator*
Vang, Chia Youyee *history professor*
Wandell, Keith E. *motorcycle company executive*
Wang, Marjorie *medical educator*
Warren, Richard M. *experimental psychologist, educator*
Weakland, Rembert George *archbishop emeritus*
Weening, Richard William, Jr. *venture capitalist, media communications executive, entrepreneur*
Wentz, Blake E. *engineering educator*
Whelan, Harry T. *neurologist, educator*
Widera, Georg Ernst Otto *mechanical engineering educator, consultant*
Wild, Robert Anthony *academic administrator*
Wiley, Edwin Packard *retired lawyer*
Williams, Allen W., Jr. *lawyer*
Williams, Brent (Buzz Williams) *men's college basketball coach*
Winters, Jill Mary *nursing educator, director*
Wrate, Glenn Thomas *engineering educator*
Yancey, Kim Bruce *dermatology researcher*
Zhang, Jin *information educator*
Zhu, Shankuan *epidemiologist, educator*
Zore, Edward John *financial services executive*

Monona
Jensen, Jill Susan *music educator*

Mount Horeb
Becker, David *artist, retired educator*

Mukwonago
Breeden, David Marion *Parish minister, English language educator, writer*

Nashotah
Hollister, Winston Ned *pathologist*
Vincent, Norman L. *retired insurance company executive*

Neenah
Orm, Sally S. *music educator, piano vocal coach*
Smaby, Mary Ellen *elementary school educator*
Theisen, Henry J. *manufacturing executive*

New Berlin
Belich, Kay S. *music educator*
Gebhard, LaVerne Elizabeth *retired accounting educator*
Kumar, Gagan *physician, educator*
Marsh, Clare Teitgen *retired school psychologist*
Vissers, Michelle *psychologist*
Weiner, Louis Max *retired mathematics educator*
Winkler, Dolores Eugenia *retired health facility administrator*

New Holstein
Amundson, Richard Arlen, Jr. *principal*

New Richmond
Zuberbier, Jo Ann *elementary school educator*

Oak Creek
Stroik, Marilyn L. *elementary school educator*

Oconomowoc
Bleke, Diane K. *music educator, director*
Conrader, Constance Ruth *artist, writer*
Kneiser, Richard John *accountant*
Peebles, Allene Kay *retired manufactured housing company executive*
Sieckert, Kristine Ellen *school psychologist, consultant*
Stout, William E. *science educator*

Ogema
Giese, Robert James *minister*

Onalaska
Waite, Lawrence Wesley *osteopathic physician, educator*

Orfordville
Griffin, Julie Marie *literature educator*

Oshkosh
Barwig, Regis Norbert James *priest*
Blankfield, Bryan J. *lawyer, automotive executive, accountant*
Bohn, Robert G. *transportation company executive*
Cheng, Theresa *neurosurgeon*
Cooper, Janelle Lunette *neurologist, educator*
Curtis, George Warren *lawyer*
Gruberg, Martin *political science professor*
McLaughlin, Jeffrey R. *orthopedist, director*
Olejniczak, Bernard Charles *education educator*
Perkins, Troy *filmmaker*
Ristow, Thelma Frances *retired elementary school educator*
Sagehorn, David M. *transportation company executive*
Szews, Charles *transportation executive*
Turnmeyer, Denise L. *pediatrics nurse, educator*

Pewaukee
Holtzman, Steven *engineering educator*
Johnson, Patricia Lynn *nursing educator*
Ostruszka, Kathleen Zelek *economics professor*
Schlei, Thomas K *social sciences educator*

Platteville
Cornils, Margaret A. *music educator*
Gregg, Matthew Douglas *music educator, director*
Kuhle, Christina Marie *women's college basketball coach*
Tigerman, Kathleen *humanities educator*

Pleasant Prairie
Morrone, Frank *electronics executive*

Plover
Drew, Richard Allen *retired electrical engineer*

Plymouth
Albrinck, Meg *literature and language professor*
Gentine, Lee Michael *marketing professional*

Racine
Baker, Joyce Mildred *medical/surgical nurse, volunteer*
Baumgardt, George Francis *bank executive, musician, director*
Burke, Thomas A. *manufacturing executive*
Coates, Glenn Richard *lawyer*
Johnson, H(erbert) Fisk *manufacturing executive*
Johnson-Leipold, Helen P. *outdoor recreation company executive*
Klein, Gabriella Sonja *retired communications executive*
Konz, Gerald Keith *retired manufacturing executive*
Nielsen, Mark Francis *lawyer*
Pepich, Bruce Walter *museum director, curator*
Sahakian, Lillian Zarouhi *artist, designer*
Schneider, David Alan *information technology manager*
Stewart, Richard Donald *internist, educator, writer*
Wambold, Richard Lawrence *manufacturing executive*
Wright, Betty Ren *children's book writer*

Reedsburg
Mockler, Jolee Marie *art educator*

Rhinelander
Burmaster, Elizabeth *academic administrator, former state official*

Rice Lake
Hoeft, Mary Elizabeth *communications educator*

Richland Center
Gollata, James Anthony *library director, educator*
Heinen, John Timothy *environmental engineer*
Zorea, Aharon W. *history professor*

Ripon
Amsden, Robert Lee *theater educator*
Jeffries, Paul Franklin *philosophy professor*
Reed, Timothy Peter *language educator*

River Falls
Biluk, Evelyn J. *education educator*
Ghenciu, Ioana *mathematics professor*
Hammarback, Bernt J. *dental association administrator*
Hoffman, Cheryl *media specialist*
Krey, DeAn Marie *retired education educator*
Montgomery, Karen E. *retired library and information scientist*
Pavlov, Vladimir Grigorievich *language educator*
Schneider-Rebozo, Lissa Price *literature and language professor*
Thibodeau, Gary A. *academic administrator*

Seymour
Kempen, Peter M. *secondary school educator*

Shawano
Mutter, John J., Jr. *writer, researcher*

Sheboygan
Abler, Ronald Francis *geography educator*
Fritz, Kristine Rae *retired secondary school educator*
Weinhold, David *library director*
Yurk, Todd Michael *retired health products executive*

Shell Lake
Aderman, Oscar Darrell *retired music educator*

Soldiers Grove
Ewing, Brian Kim *retired engineering executive, writer*

South Milwaukee
Kitzke, Eugene David *research and development company executive*

Sparta
Tripp, Tyler J. *lawyer*

Spooner
Frey, Paul Howard *chemical engineer, engineering consultants company executive*

Stevens Point
Biasca, Karyn *science educator*
Francis, Edgar Walter, IV, *history professor*
Long, Charles Alan *retired biology professor, museum director*
Mertz, Paul Eric *retired history professor, writer*
Rosenfield, Robert Norman *biology professor*
Schuh, Dale R. *insurance company executive*
Smith, David Lyle *artist, educator*
Stevens, Dwight Marlyn *educational administrator*

Sturgeon Bay
Maher, Virginia Jones *art historian, educator*

Sturtevant
Johnson, S. Curtis *chemicals executive*
Lonergan, Edward F. *manufacturing executive*
Marschke, Sean M. *chief of police, emergency management director*

Sun Prairie
Amstadt, James R. *cosmetic dentist*
Eustice, Francis Joseph *lawyer*

Superior
Christensen, Peter Forsyth *bishop*
Fliss, Raphael Michael *bishop emeritus*
Glazman, Charles M. *education educator*
Haugland, John Clarence *emeritus university vice chancellor*
Morden, Annette Sonja Knudson *retired education educator*
Nordgren, Debra *librarian, educator*
Robek, Mary Frances *business education educator*
Scott, David Edmund *music educator, conductor, consultant*
Stewart, Richard Dow *science educator*

Sussex
Stromberg, Gregory *printing ink company executive*

Thiensville
Roselle, William Charles *librarian*

Three Lakes
Holtz, Barbara Belle *retired pre-school educator*

Tomah
Neurohr, Shirley Ann *retired special education educator*

Union Grove
Dawson, Rose Dorothy *retired elementary school educator*

Verona
Buelow, Frederick Henry *agricultural engineering educator*

Washburn
Stewart, John Miller *psychologist, educator*

Washington Island
Raup, David Malcolm *paleontology educator*
Schweikert, Norman Carl *retired musician*

Waterford
Hanson, Jody Elizabeth *special education educator*
Karraker, Louis Rendleman *retired corporate executive*

Watertown
Midcalf, Randall *language educator, director*
Schott, Katharine Sue *nursing educator*

Waukesha
Cauley, James Robert *lawyer*
Debrecht, Dennis Michael *economics professor, researcher*
Gustafson, Mardel Emma *secondary school educator, writer*
Kelly, Lori Duin *literature and language professor*
Schwartz, Robert Terry *industrial designer, director*
Smith, Alexandra Helena *microbiologist, director*
Stringham, Phyllis Joan *retired music educator*

Waunakee
Conaway, Jane Ellen *retired elementary school educator*

Waupaca
Feldt, Mary *elementary school educator*
Hansen, Louise Hill *music educator, retired application developer*

Waupun
Wendt, Thomas *finance company executive*

Wausau
Builer, Dorothy Marion *business owner*
Drengler, William Allan John *lawyer*
Loftus, Stephen Edward *elementary art educator*
Orr, San Watterson, Jr. *lawyer*
Prey, Yvonne Mary *real estate broker*
Sexauer, Cornelia F. *history professor*
Veninga, James Frank *humanities educator, editor, writer*
Wadzinski, Mary Beth *administrative assistant*

Wautoma
Tennessen, Kenneth J. *retired entomologist*

Wauwatosa
Heath, Robert F. *lawyer*
Kalogjera, Ikar Jaksa *psychiatrist, educator*
Savage, Thomas Ryan *lawyer*
Stubbe, Ray William *minister, writer*

West Bend
Schaefer, Gordon Emory *food products executive*

Weyauwega
Maasch, Lloyd Palmer *physician*

Whitefish Bay
Hawkins, Brett William *retired political science professor*
Hendee, William Richard *medical physics educator, academic administrator, radiologist*

Whitewater
Adams, Rick Alan *biologist, educator*
Baica, Malvina Florica *mathematics professor, researcher*
Bren, Barbara R. *librarian*
Busse, Eileen Elaine *special education educator*
Chapman, Stephanie Lynn *education educator*
Choi, Sang D. *researcher, educator*
Connor, James Richard *retired academic administrator*
Drucker, Thomas Lyndon *mathematics professor*
Grubel, Barbara Lynn *dancer, educator*
Han, Baocheng *chemistry professor, department chairman*
Heyning, Katharina E. *academic administrator, educator*
Kumpaty, Hephzibah J. *chemistry professor*
Laurent, Jerome King *retired economics professor*
Nam, Ki-Bong *mathematics professor*
Oravec, Jo Ann Rose *computing and public policy educator*
Weber, Curt Michael *law educator*

Williams Bay
Hobbs, Lewis Mankin *astronomer*

Windsor
McDonald, David Michael *church administrator*

Wisconsin Rapids
Engelhardt, LeRoy A. *retired paper company executive*
Olson-Hellerud, Linda Kathryn *elementary school educator*

WYOMING

Afton
Nethercott, Mark A. *physics educator*

Big Horn
Canterbury, Jacqueline Lee *biology professor*
Schultz, Harry Pershing *chemistry researcher, retired educator*

Casper
Anderson, Kevin Stuart *archivist, librarian*
Bennion, Scott Desmond *physician*
Blesi, Jonathan W. *engineering educator*
Cotherman, Audrey Mathews *educational administrator, management consultant*
Durham, Harry Blaine III *lawyer*
Eskew, Sandra Caye *elementary school educator*
Fagan, Tucker *legislative staff member, former state agency administrator*
Foster, Vicki Anne *secondary school educator*
Hartsock, Jane Marie *nurse, educator*
He, Jianjun *music educator, composer*
Hinchey, Bruce Alan *environmental engineering company executive, state legislator, state legislator*
Keim, Michael Ray *dentist*
Lowe, Robert Stanley *lawyer*
Nganga, Lydiah Wangui *education educator*
Petersen, Leslie *political organization administrator*
Prypchan, Lida D. *psychiatrist*
Ptasynski, Harry *geologist, oil industry executive*
Rickabaugh, René Lane *principal*

Scaling, Sam T. *obstetrician, gynecologist*
Schellberg, Thomas *economics professor*
Stroock, Thomas Frank *oil and gas company executive*
Wildman, Peter Roberts *mathematics professor*
Wold, John Schiller *geologist, former congressman*

Cheyenne
Breen, Nathan David (Nate Breen) *historian, educator*
Brimmer, Clarence Addison *federal judge*
Brorby, Wade *federal judge*
Burke, E. James *state supreme court justice, lawyer*
Carlson, Kathleen Bussart *law librarian*
Cornish, Nancy Lee *music educator*
Crank, Patrick J. *lawyer, former state attorney general*
Freudenthal, Dave (David D. Freudenthal) *Governor of Wyoming*
Freudenthal, Steven Franklin *lawyer, political organization worker*
Gamst, Frederick Charles *social anthropologist*
Golden, T. Michael *state supreme court justice*
Hart, Joseph Hubert *bishop emeritus*
Hill, William U. *state supreme court justice, former state attorney general*
Johnson, Wayne Harold *state legislator*
Kite, Marilyn S. *state supreme court justice, lawyer*
Knight, Robert Edward *bank executive, educator*
Kunz, April Brimmer *state legislator, lawyer*
Lain, Sheryl A. *literacy coach*
Maxfield, Max R. *Secretary of State, Wyoming*
Meyer, Joseph B. *state treasurer*
Moore, Mary French (Muffy) *potter, advocate*
Myers, Rolland Graham *investment counselor*
Noe, Guy *retired social services administrator*
O'Brien, Terrence Leo *federal judge*
Panopoulos, Nick Antonios *retired speech and drama educator*
Parrish, Denise Kay *regulatory accountant*
Rankin, Kelly Harrison *prosecutor*
Salzburg, Bruce A. *state attorney general*
Sansonetti, Thomas L. *lawyer, former federal agency administrator*
Sherard, Brent D. *state agency administrator, physician*
Speight, John Blain (Jack Speight) *lawyer*
Thomson, Thyra Godfrey *former state official*
Vogel, Jeffrey C. *state banking agency administrator*
Voigt, Barton R. *state supreme court chief justice*
Weigner, Brent James *secondary school educator*
White, Daniel Eugene *lawyer*
Woodhouse, Gay Vanderpoel *former state attorney general, lawyer*

Cody
Donoghue, Ann Marie *museum administrator, consultant*
Garry, James B. *historian, naturalist, storyteller, writer*
Jackson, Harry Andrew *artist*
Simpson, Alan Kooi *lawyer, former senator*

Evanston
Harris, Mark W. *former mayor, lawyer*

Fairview
Luginbuehl, Marsha Lee *psychologist*

Gillette
Bailey, Daniel B. *lawyer, entrepreneur*
Degnan, Paula *professional development specialist*

Jackson
Cox, Paul Alan *ethnobotanist, educator*
Herrick, Gregory Evans *computer company executive*
Hirschfield, Alan James *entrepreneur*
Law, Clarene Alta *small business owner, state legislator*
Massy, William Francis *education educator, consultant*
Schuster, Robert Parks *lawyer*
Spence, Gerry (Gerald Leonard Spence) *lawyer, writer*
Trauner, Gary *entrepreneur*
Vaughan, Diana *political organization administrator*

Jackson Hole
McNutt, James Charles *museum director*

Kelly
Knowles, William Standish *retired chemist*

Lander
Field, Francis Edward *electrical engineer, educator*
Raynolds, David Robert *buffalo breeder, writer*
Robeson, Terry Lazuk *elementary school educator, priest*

Laramie
Allen, John Logan *retired geographer*
Bogard, Theresa Lynn *music educator*
Boresi, Arthur Peter *writer, educator*
Brown, Michael R. *communications educator*
Chai, Winberg *political science professor, foundation administrator*
Crocker, Thomas Dunstan *economics professor*
Darnall, Roberta Morrow *educational association administrator*
Dickman, Francois Moussiegt *former foreign service officer, educator*
Farrell, Mary M(aggie) *dean of libraries*
Ford, Stephen P. *biology professor*
Gill, George Wilhelm *retired anthropologist*
Godby, Robert William *economics professor, department chairman*
Hansen, Matilda *former state legislator*
Hind, Emily *language educator*
Kinney, Lisa Frances *lawyer*
Kirkwood, Carol *literature and language educator*
Langlois, Walter Gordon *writer, retired literature and language professor*
Lauer, Warren A. *lawyer*
Lewis, Randolph Vance *molecular biologist, researcher*
Lockwood, Jeffrey Alan *entomologist*
Maxfield, Peter Charles *state legislator, lawyer, educator*
Mercer, Jennifer Lynn *research scientist*
Meyer, Edmond Gerald *retired chemistry professor, energy scientist, academic administrator*
Mingle, John Orville *engineer, educator, lawyer, consultant*
Nye, Eric W. *English language and literature educator*
Rechard, Paul Albert *retired civil engineering company executive, consultant*
Reif, (Frank) David *artist, educator*
Schatz, Mona Claire Struhsaker *social worker, educator, consultant, researcher*
Shaffer, Sherrill Lynn *economist*
Spiegelberg, Emma Jo *business education educator, academic administrator*
Stefanovic, Margareta *science educator*
Towler, Brian Francis *petroleum engineer, educator*
Tschirhart, John Thomas *economist, educator*
Williams, Roger Lawrence *historian, educator*

Powell
Brophy, Dennis Richard *psychology and philosophy professor, academic administrator, minister*
Myers, Rex Charles *historian, educator, retired dean*
Patrick, H. Hunter *retired judge, lawyer*

Riverton
Bebout, Eli Daniel *state legislator*
Girard, NettaBell *lawyer*

Rock Springs
Conover, Dustin *educational association administrator*
Thompson, Josie *nurse*

Sheridan
Korsch, Tobin Anne *dental hygienist, educator*
Marshall, Anne Bradley *lawyer*

Teton Village
McCollister, Christopher Michael *forester*

Torrington
Nesbitt, John Dunville *literature and language professor, writer*
Smith, Walter Lloyd *Middle School Educator*

Wheatland
Hunkins, Raymond Breedlove *lawyer, rancher*

Wilson
Chrystie, Thomas Ludlow *investor*
Davis, Shelby Moore Cullom *investment company executive, consultant*
Gordon, Stephen Maurice *manufacturing company executive, rancher*
Hall, Zach Winter *former scientist and research administrator*

Worland
Woods, Lawrence Milton *airline company executive*

Yellowstone National Park
Lewis, Suzanne *parks director*

TERRITORIES OF THE UNITED STATES

AMERICAN SAMOA

Pago Pago
Jyothibhavan, Joserose S. *chemistry educator*
Kruse, F. Michael *Chief Justice, American Samoa High Court*
Langkilde, Fagafaga Daniel *communications executive, political organization administrator*
Laumoli, Tuiasina Salamo *state agency administrator, public health service officer*
Poumele, Claire Tuia *state official, school system administrator*
Richmond, Lyle L. *Associate Justice, American Samoa High Court*
Ripley, Afa, Jr., (Fepulea'i A. Ripley Jr.) *attorney general*
Schuster, Su'a Carl *political organization administrator, bishop*
Sunia, Ipulasi Aitofele Toese F. *Lieutenant Governor of American Samoa*
Tulafono, Togiola T.A. *Governor of American Samoa*
Weitzel, John Quinn *bishop*

FEDERATED STATES OF MICRONESIA

Pohnpei
Akapito Skilling, Vita *state agency administrator*
Falcam, Leo A. *former Micronesian government official*

GUAM

Agana
Flores, Philip Joseph *bank executive, former political organization administrator*

Agana Heights
Leon-Guerrero, Jillette Torre *nonprofit organization executive, consultant, writer*
Torres, Susie Apuron *special education educator*

Barrigada
Ilagan, Artemio B. *territorial banking agency administrator*
McDonald Terlaje, Patricia *counselor*

Hagatna
Bretania-Shafer, Nerissa *school system administrator*
Camacho, Felix Perez *Governor of Guam*
Carbullido, F. Philip *Associate Justice, Guam Supreme Court*
Charfauros, Tony (Anthony Charfauros) *political organization administrator*
Cruz, Michael W. *Lieutenant Governor of Guam, surgeon*
Flores, Christina Rosalie *art educator*
Limtiaco, Alicia Garrido *state attorney general, former prosecutor*
Maraman, Katherine Ann *associate justice, Guam Supreme Court*
Mullins, Christopher M. *physical education educator*
Rapadas, Leonardo M. *prosecutor*
Torres, Robert J., Jr. *Chief Justice, Guam Supreme Court*
Unpingco, John Walter Sablan *federal judge*

Mangilao
Dames, Vivian Loyola *social sciences educator*
Roberto, J. Peter *state agency administrator*
Strauch, Edward Hugo *writer, retired literature and language professor*
Wang, Chih *retired librarian, educator*
Yang, Jian *food scientist, educator*

Tamuning
Cahinhinan, Nelia Agbada *retired public health nurse, health facility administrator*

NORTHERN MARIANA ISLANDS

Saipan
Baka, Gregory *acting attorney general*
Camacho, Charlotte DLG *principal, elementary school educator*
Castro, Alexandro Cruz *commonwealth supreme court justice*
Dela Cruz, Acelia Castro *elementary school educator*
Demapan, Miguel S. *commonwealth supreme court justice*
Fitial, Benígno Repeki *Governor of Northern Mariana Islands*
Inos, Eloy Songao *Lieutenant Governor of the Northern Mariana Islands*
Lamkin, Celia Belocora *physician*
Manglona, John A. *commonwealth supreme court justice*
Sablan, Rita Aldan *state official, school system administrator*
Villagomez, Joseph K. *state agency administrator, public health service officer*

PUERTO RICO

Arecibo
Friedman, Jonathan S. *environmental scientist*

Bayamon
Berio, Blanca *editor, writer, language educator*
Cabrera-Otero, Sylvia *physician*
Carro, Eric F. *neurosurgeon*
Morales-Zeno, Ana J. *literature and language professor*

Cayey
Montes-Pizarro, Errol L. *mathematician, researcher*

Dorado
Glickman, Marlene *non-profit organization administrator*
Spector, Michael Joseph *agribusiness executive*

Fajardo
Fernós, Manuel J. *academic administrator*

Guaynabo
Guisasola Gamez, Elina *psychologist*

Gurabo
Kuruganty, Sastry Pratap *electrical engineering educator*

Hatillo
Santos, Isabel Rodriguez *marketing educator*

Hato Rey
Ferrer, Miguel Antonio *brokerage house executive*

Humacao
Pinto, Nicholas Joaquim *physics professor*

Manati
Martinez, Heriberto *human resources and management professional*

Mayaguez
Collins, Dennis Glenn *mathematics professor*
Goyal, Vijay K. *engineering educator, researcher*
Jury, Mark Robert *metrologist, educator*
Lopez, Gustavo E. *chemistry professor*
Montalvo-Rodriguez, Rafael R. *microbiologist, educator*
Pastrana, Belinda *science educator, researcher*
Perales-Perez, Oscar J. *engineering educator*
Ruiz-Vargas, Yolanda *finance educator*
Sahai, Hardeo *medical statistics educator*
Suarez, Luis Edgardo *civil engineering educator*

Mercedita
Perez-Nieves, Roberto *plastic surgeon, educator*

Ponce
Garcia, Joxel *dean, former federal agency administrator*
Quintana-Alsina, Myriam *chemistry professor*
Rivera-Amill, Vanessa *medical educator*
Toro Vargas, Cirilo *library director, educator*

Rio Piedras
Hilerio, Cibel M. *psychologist, researcher*

San Juan
Acosta, Raymond Luis *federal judge*
Almodovar, Edna *pharmacist, educator*
Aponte Martinez, Luis Cardinal *cardinal, archbishop emeritus*
Bonilla-Felix, Melvin A. *pediatrician, educator*
Carreras, Francisco José *retired academic and foundation administrator*
Casiano, Kimberly *publishing executive*
Chardán, Carlos R. *school system administrator*
Cordero, Jose Fernando *pediatrician, dean*
Corrada del Rio, Baltasar *lawyer, retired former state supreme court justice*
Daddy Yankee, (Raymond Ayala) *musician*
Dunbar, Donald Churchill *neuroscientist, anthropologist*
Engman, Martin Feeney *mathematics professor*
Espino, Ana M. *parasitology and immunology educator, researcher*
Ferre, Antonio Luis *newspaper publisher*
Fiol Matta, Liana *territorial supreme court justice*
Folch-Serrano, Karen D. *psychologist, consultant*
Fortuño, Luis Guillermo *Governor of Puerto Rico*
Frontera, Walter R. *dean, physiatrist, educator*
Gioda, Adriana *chemistry professor*
González Nieves, Roberto Octavio *archbishop*
Hernández Denton, Federico *territorial supreme court justice*
Joshipura, Kaumudi Jinraj *epidemiologist*
Katar, Sri Lakshmi *science educator*
Kolthoff Caraballo, Erick V. *territorial supreme court justice*
Kumar, Ashok *research scientist, educator*
Lasa-Ferrer, Armando *lawyer*
Martinez Torres, Rafael L. *territorial supreme court justice*
Matheu, Federico Manuel *university chancellor*
McClintock, Kenneth D. (Kenneth D. McClintock-Hernandez) *Puerto Rican secretary of state, former state legislator*
Méndez, Carlos (Don Carlos Méndez Martínez) *political organization administrator, mayor*
Montes, Ingrid *chemistry professor*
Montilla, Victor Javier *broadcast executive*
Negron-Garcia, Antonio S. *law educator, former commonwealth of Puerto Rico supreme court justice*
Ortiz, Alexis *physical therapist, educator*
Pabon Charneco, Mildred G. *territorial supreme court justice*
Padilla, Alfredo *territorial banking agency administrator*
Pasnicu, Cornel *mathematician, educator*
Pérez-Cardona, José Manuel *cardiologist*
Prats Palerm, Robert L. *political organization administrator*
Rivera-Dueño, Jamie *state agency administrator, public health service officer*
Rivera Pérez, Efraín E. *territorial supreme court justice*
Rodriguez, Annabelle *territorial supreme court justice, former attorney general*
Rodriguez-Diaz, Juan E. *lawyer*
Rodriguez-Velez, Rosa Emilia *prosecutor*
Rosso de Irizarry, Carmen (Tutty Rosso de Irizarry) *finance executive*
Saavedra-Arias, José Javier *physics professor*
Sagardía, Antonio (Antonio Miguel Sagardía De Jesus) *attorney general*
Santini, Jorge A. *Mayor, San Juan, Puerto Rico*
Santos Pico, Jose V. *neurosurgeon*
Torres, Daniel Fernandez *bishop*
Valcárcel, Marta Iris *pediatric educator*
Vélez-Cardona, Waldemiro *education educator, consultant*
Wexler, David B. *law educator*

Santa Isabel
Lugo-Paoli, Luz Minerva *counselor, educator*

Santurce
Residante, El (René Pérez) *singer, composer*
Visitante, El (Eduardo Cabra) *singer, musician*

Trujillo Alto
Crespo de Sanabia, María Milagros *retired education educator*

Viejo San Juan
Casellas, Salvador E. *judge*

VIRGIN ISLANDS

Charlotte Amalie
Barnard, Geoffrey W. *judge*
Feuerzeig, Henry Louis *lawyer*
Francis, Georgia *music educator*
Garfield, Winifred L. *nursing administrator*
Thomas, Elliott Griffin *bishop emeritus*

Christiansted
Bland, James Theodore, Jr. *lawyer*
Centeno, Robert Francis *plastic surgeon*
Christian, Cora L.E *health facility administrator, physician*
Finch, Raymond Lawrence *judge*
Francis, Gregory R. *Lieutenant Governor of US Virgin Islands*
Schoenbohm, Herbert L. *political organization administrator, radio personality*

Frederiksted
Birbahadur, Dindial *secondary school educator*

Kingshill
Bryson, Valrica *music educator*

St Croix
Cannon, George W., Jr. *United States Magistrate Judge, VI District Court*
Lee, Sidney Phillip *chemical engineer, state senator*

St John
Walker, Ronald R. *editor, educator, writer*

St Thomas
Benjamin, Cecil *political organization administrator*
Berry, Lorraine Ledee *state senator*
Bevard, Herbert Armstrong *bishop*
Cabret, Maria *territorial supreme court justice*
Carty, Amos W. *lawyer*
de Jongh, John Percy, Jr. *Governor of the United States Virgin Islands, real estate company executive*
Donastorg, Adlah, Jr., (Foncie Donastorg) *territorial legislator*
Frazer, Vincent F. *attorney general*
Gomez, Curtis V. *Chief Judge, United States District Court of VI*
Hodge, Rhys S. *territorial supreme court chief justice*
Holcombe, Justin K. *lawyer*
King, Lillia Elise *histologist, educator*
Larsen, Lauren *school system administrator*
Michael, Noreen *academic administrator*
Prior, Cornelius Bernard, Jr. *utilities executive, financial consultant*
Seipel, Peter *physical education educator, athletic director*
Sheen-Aaron, Julia *state agency administrator, public health service officer*
Swan, Ive Arlington *territorial supreme court justice*
Terry, Lavern *school system administrator*
Turnbull, Charles Wesley *former governor*

MILITARY ADDRESSES OF THE UNITED STATES

EUROPE

APO
Anderson, Curtis Thorwald, II, *military officer*
Bowker, Rayanne Sones *elementary school educator*
Carner, George *foreign service executive, economic strategist*
Dempsey, Martin E. *career military officer*
Leibrecht, Murl Edwin *preventive medicine physician, consultant, retired military officer*
Marshall, Brian Laurence *federal official*
Salerno, Patricia J. *elementary school educator*
Simpson, Sandra Kay *logistics specialist*

PACIFIC
Stanton, William Anthony *diplomat*

CANADA

ALBERTA

Calgary
Bird, J. Richard *energy executive*
Bouwmeester, Jay *professional hockey player*
Campbell, Finley Alexander *geologist, consultant*
Daniel, Patrick D. *energy executive*
Glockner, Peter G. *civil and mechanical engineering educator*
Grand-Maitre, Jean *performing company executive*
Hotchkiss, Harley N. *professional hockey team owner, oil industry executive*
Iginla, Jarome *professional hockey player*
Jokinen, Olli *professional hockey player*
Jones, Geoffrey Melvill *physiology research educator*
King, Ken *professional sports team executive*
Kiprusoff, Miikka *professional hockey player*
Lam, Galen Ka-Ron *electrical engineer*
Maier, Gerald James *gas industry executive*
Major, John Charles *judge*
Malik, Om Parkash *electrical engineering educator, researcher*
McEwen, Alexander Campbell *legal association administrator, consultant, cadastral studies educator, former Canadian government official, land use planner*
Milone, Eugene Frank *astronomer, educator*
Palileo, Hazel Valencia *videographer*
Phaneuf, Dion *professional hockey player*
Playfair, Jim *professional hockey coach*
Raeburn, Andrew Harvey *performing arts consultant*
Robottom, David T. *lawyer, energy executive*
Smith, Eldon *cardiologist, physiologist, educator*
Southern, Nancy C. *utilities executive*
Stebbins, Robert Alan *sociology educator*
Sutter, Brent Colin *professional hockey coach, retired professional hockey player*
Sutter, Darryl John *professional sports team executive, former professional hockey coach*

Canmore
Janes, Robert Roy *museum director, archaeologist, editor, consultant*

Devon
Ng, Siauw-Hoi *research scientist*

Edmonton
Babiuk, Lorne Alan *virologist, immunologist, researcher*
Beaulieu, Norman C. *engineering educator, writer*
Fleming, Wayne *professional hockey coach*
Gilbert, Tom *professional hockey player*
Gough, Denis Ian *geophysics educator*
Gyenes, Gábor *physician, educator*
Halloran, Philip Francis *nephrologist, immunologist*
Hemsky, Ales *professional hockey player*
Katz, Daryl A. *pharmaceutical executive, entrepreneur, professional sports team executive*
Kay, Cyril Max *biochemist, educator*
Keown, Lauriston Livingston, Jr. *consulting psychologist*
Khabibulin, Nikolai *professional hockey player*
Lock, Gerald Seymour Hunter *retired mechanical engineering educator*
Lowe, Kevin Hugh *professional sports team executive, professional hockey player*
Mardon, Austin *geographer, writer, researcher*
Moreau, Ethan *professional hockey player*
Oberg, Lyle *physician, academic administrator*
Offenberger, Allan Anthony *retired electrical engineering educator*
Penner, Dustin *professional hockey player*
Quinn, Pat (John Brian Patrick Quinn) *professional hockey coach*
Renney, Tom *professional hockey coach*
Rutter, Nathaniel Westlund *geologist, educator*
Souray, Sheldon *professional hockey player*
Stelck, Charles Richard *geology educator*
Stevenson, William Alexander *retired justice of Supreme Court of Canada*
Tambellini, Steve *professional sports team executive, former professional hockey player*

Lethbridge
Los, Cornelis Albertus *economist, finance educator, risk analyst*

Red Deer
Donald, Jack C. *oil industry executive*

BRITISH COLUMBIA

Anmore
Ribary, Urs *neuroscientist, educator*

Burnaby
Brantingham, Paul Jeffrey *criminologist, educator*
Brinkman, Fiona Susan *bioinformaticist, educator, molecular biologist*
Kimura, Doreen *psychology professor, researcher*
Kitchen, John Martin *historian, educator*
Tung, Rosalie L. *business educator, consultant*
Wainwright, David Stanley *patent agent*

Cobble Hill
Cox, Albert Reginald *retired dean, retired cardiologist*

Cowichan Station
Grauer, Sherrard *artist*

Delta
Russell, Richard Doncaster *geophysics educator, academic administrator*

Fernie
McFarlin-Kosiec, Barbara Ann *elementary school educator, secondary school educator, literature and language professor, small business owner*

Heriot Bay
Bringhurst, Robert *poet*

Kelowna
Basdeo, Sahadeo *government official, educator, politician*
Krysko, Dave *Internet company executive*
Merrifield, Lane *Internet company executive*
Milani, Abbas Sadeghzadeh *professor*
Priebe, Lance *Internet company executive, application developer*

Lake Country
Muggeridge, Derek Brian *engineering executive, consultant*

Langley
Ferris, Ronald Curry *retired bishop*
Thomas, Howard Paul *civil engineer, consultant*

Mayne Island
Cavoukian, Raffi (Raffi) *folksinger, children's entertainer*

North Saanich
Saddlemyer, Ann (Eleanor Saddlemyer) *humanities educator, critic, theater historian*

Parksville
Weir, Bryce Keith Alexander *neurosurgeon, neurologist, educator*

Richmond
Durrant, Geoffrey Hugh *retired language educator*

Salt Spring Island
Raginsky, Nina *artist*

Sidney
Bigelow, Margaret Elizabeth Barr (M.E. Barr) *retired botany educator*
Kendrick, William Bryce *biologist, consultant, editor, writer*
van den Bergh, Sidney *astronomer*

Surrey
Igali, Baraladei Daniel *Olympic athlete, coach, motivational speaker*

Vancouver
Affleck, Ian Keith *physics educator*
Aquilini, Francesco *investment company executive, professional sports team executive*
Austin, Jacob (Jack Austin) *retired Canadian government official*
Baird, Patricia Ann *physician, educator*
Blair, Robert *animal science administrator, educator, researcher*
Bonifacho, Bratsa *artist*
Clark, Colin Whitcomb *mathematics professor*
Cohen, Leonard (Norman Cohen) *poet, writer, musician*
Conway, John S. *history professor*
Cynader, Max Sigmund *neuroscience professor, researcher*
Demitra, Pavol *professional hockey player*
Donaldson, Edward Mossop *research scientist, marine biologist, consultant*
Evans, John deCourcey *real estate company officer*
Feldman, Joel Shalom *mathematician*
Finnegan, Cyril Vincent *retired dean, zoology educator*
Friedman, Sydney M. *anatomist, educator, medical researcher*
Gillis, Mike (Michael David Gillis) *professional sports team executive, retired professional hockey player*
Granirer, Edmond Ernest *mathematician, educator*
Hardwick, David Francis *pathologist*
Hardy, Walter Newbold *physics professor, researcher*
Holsti, Kalevi Jacque *political scientist, department chairman*
Jones, David Robert *retired zoology educator*
Jones, Norah (Geethali Norah Jones Shankar) *singer*
Kane, Nolan C. *editor, researcher*
Keevil, Norman B. *mining executive*
Kesselman, Jonathan Rhys *economics professor, public policy researcher*
Laponce, Jean A. *political scientist, educator*
Lavigne, Avril *singer*
Lindsey, Casimir Charles *zoologist, educator*
Littrell, Mark *media specialist*
Luongo, Roberto *professional hockey player*
Lyons, Terrence Allan *mining executive*
Marchak, Maureen Patricia *retired anthropology and sociology educator, academic administrator*
Mattessich, Richard Victor (Alvarus) *business administration researcher*
McGeer, Edith Graef *retired neurological science educator*
Mc Lean, Donald Millis *microbiologist, educator, pathologist, pediatrician*
McNeill, John Hugh *pharmaceutical sciences educator*
McWhinney, Edward Watson *Canadian government legislator*
Mitchell, Joni (Roberta Joan Anderson) *singer, songwriter, artist*
Mizgala, Henry F. *physician, consultant, retired medical educator*
Nemetz, Peter Newman *economist, researcher, policy analysis educator*
Newmeyer, Frederick Jaret *linguist, educator*
Olsen, Inger Anna *retired psychologist*
Overmyer, Daniel Lee *humanities educator*
Pacheco-Ransanz, Arsenio *language educator, historian, educator*
Packer, James Innell *theology studies educator, writer*
Phillips, Anthony George *neurobiology researcher*
Piternick, Anne Brearley *librarian, educator*
Rothstein, Samuel *librarian, educator*
Salcudean, Martha Eva *mechanical engineer, educator*
Schaller, Jane Green *pediatrician*
Schneider, Mathieu *professional hockey player*
Sedin, Daniel *professional hockey player*
Sedin, Henrik *professional hockey player*
Shaw, Michael *biologist, educator*
Shearer, Ronald Alexander *economics professor*
Sinclair, Alastair James *geology educator*
Sion, Maurice *mathematics professor*
Suedfeld, Peter *psychologist, educator*
Sundin, Mats Johan *professional hockey player*
Tees, Richard Chisholm *psychology professor emeritus*
Tolle, Eckhart *writer*
Unger, Richard Watson *history professor*
Vigneault, Alain *professional hockey coach*
Walker, Michael Angus *economist, director*
Wieman, Carl E. *physics professor*
Yaffe, Barbara Marlene *journalist*
Zimmerman, Chris *professional sports team executive*

Victoria
Antoniou, Andreas *electrical engineering educator*
Barrie, Len *real estate developer, professional sports team executive*
Batten, Alan Henry *astronomer*
Best, Melvyn Edward *geophysicist*
Copes, Parzival *economist, researcher*
Finlay, James Campbell *retired museum director*
Hutchings, John Barrie *astronomer, researcher*
Israel, Werner *physicist, educator*
Manning, Eric *computer scientist, educator, dean, researcher*
Meadow, Charles *information scientist, writer*
Morton, Donald Charles *astronomer*
Nuttall, Richard Norris *management consultant, physician*
Richards, Vincent Philip Haslewood *librarian*
Singleton-Wood, Allan James *communications executive*
Wiles, David McKeen *chemist*

West Kelowna
Wedepohl, Leonhard Martin *electrical engineering educator*

West Vancouver
Wynne-Edwards, Hugh Robert *geologist, educator, entrepreneur*

White Rock
Phillips, John Edward *zoologist, educator*

Winfield
Horton, William Russell *retired utilities executive*

MANITOBA

Winnipeg
Cohen, Harley *engineering educator*
Eyre, Ivan *artist*
Filmon, Gary Albert *Canadian provincial premier, civil engineer*
Haworth, James Chilton *pediatrics educator*
Lewis, André Leon *performing company executive*
MacKenzie, George Allan *company director*
Mufti, Aftab A. *civil engineering educator*
Persaud, Trivedi Vidhya Nandan *anatomy educator, researcher, consultant*
Rozumnyj, Jaroslav *literature educator*
Schnoor, Jeffrey Arnold *lawyer*
Smith, Ian Cormack Palmer *biophysicist*
Turner, Robert Comrie *composer*

NEW BRUNSWICK

Fredericton
Grotterod, Knut *retired paper company executive*
Kenyon, Gary Michael *gerontologist, educator*
Strange, Henry Hazen *judge*

Saint Andrews
Anderson, John Murray *operations research specialist, consultant, retired academic administrator*

Saint John
Condon, Thomas Joseph *university historian*

NEWFOUNDLAND AND LABRADOR

Saint John's
Crosbie, John Carnell *retired Canadian government official, university administrator, lawyer*
Gibbons, Rex Vincent *geologist*
Rochester, Michael Grant *geophysics educator*

Torbay
Dabinett, Diana Frances *artist*

NOVA SCOTIA

Antigonish
Sweet, William *educator, author, administrator*

Bayfield
Blair, Rosemary Miles *retired art educator, environmentalist*

Canning
Ogilvie, Kelvin Kenneth *academic administrator, chemist, educator*

Chester Basin
Parr-Johnston, Elizabeth *economist, consultant*

Dartmouth
Horrocks, Norman *librarian, educator, editor*

Glasgow
Williams, Edna Aleta Theadora Johnston *journalist*

Halifax
Dexter, Robert Paul *lawyer*
Fillmore, Peter Arthur *mathematician, educator*
Glube, Constance Rachelle *retired judge*
Gray, James *English literature educator*
Hall, Brian Keith *biology professor, writer*
Jaeger, Leslie Gordon *academic administrator*
Kulyk, Karen Gay *artist*
Langley, George Ross *medical educator*
Laursen, Finn *political science professor*
Mann, Kenneth Henry *marine ecologist*
Matta, Chérif Farid *chemistry professor*
Murray, Thomas John (Jock Murray) *physician, neurologist, educator*
Stairs, Denis Winfield *political science professor, department chairman*

Mahone Bay
Collins, John Alfred *retired obstetrician, gynecologist, educator*

North Sydney
Nickerson, Jerry Edgar Alan *business executive*

Stellarton
Sobey, David Frank *food company executive*

Tatamagouche
Roach, Margot Ruth *retired biophysicist, educator*

Wallace
Boyle, Willard Sterling *physicist, researcher*

ONTARIO

Aurora
Lanthier, Ronald Ross *retired manufacturing executive*

Bracebridge
Evans, John David Daniel *judge*

Brampton
Paikeday, Thomas M. *lexicographer, linguistic consultant*

Brantford
Hanna, William Brooks *publishing executive, literary agent*

Brockville
Spalding, James Stuart *retired telecommunications industry executive*

Burlington
Harris, Philip John *retired engineering educator*

Cambridge
MacBain, William Halley *minister, theology studies educator, academic administrator*
White, Joseph Charles *manufacturing and retailing company executive*

Chatham
McKeough, William Darcy *retired supply company executive*

Deep River
Milton, John Charles Douglas *nuclear physicist, researcher*

Don Mills
French, William Harold *retired newspaper editor*

Dorchester
Fanning, William James *professional sports team executive, commentator*

Etobicoke
Scholefield, Peter Gordon *health facility administrator*

Freelton
Sonnenberg, Hardy *data processing executive, researcher, electrical engineer*

Guelph
Bewley, John Derek *botany researcher, educator*
Dickinson, William Trevor *hydrologist, educator*
Land, Reginald Brian *library administrator*

Hamilton
Bandler, John William *electrical engineering educator, consultant*
Blajchman, Morris Aaron *science educator, physician*
Datars, William Ross *physicist, researcher*
Etches-Johnson, Amanda *library and information scientist*
Garland, William James *nuclear engineer, educator*
George, Peter James *economist, educator*
Hirsh, Jack *medical researcher*
Schwarcz, Henry Philip *geologist, educator*
Spenser, Ian Daniel *chemistry professor*
Williams, David R. (Dafydd Rhys Williams) *research scientist, medical educator, retired astronaut*
Wong, Kon Max *electrical engineer educator*

Kanata
Alfredsson, Daniel *professional hockey player*
Heatley, Dany *professional hockey player*
Leeder, Cyril *professional sports team executive*
Melnyk, Eugene N. *professional sports team executive, retired pharmaceutical executive*
Murray, Bryan Clarence *professional sports team executive, former professional hockey coach*
Spezza, Jason *professional hockey player*

Kingston
Gerson, Donald Franklin *pharmaceutical executive*
Kaliski, Stephan Felix *economics professor*
Leggett, William C. *biology professor, academic administrator*
Lewis, William John *aerospace engineer*
Low, James A. *physician*
MacKinnon, James Gordon *economist, educator*
Meisel, John *political scientist*
Nielsen, Morten Ørregaard *economics professor*
Spencer, John Hedley *biochemistry educator*
Stewart, Alec Thompson *physicist, educator*
Szarek, Walter Anthony *chemist, educator*
Tchegus, Robert Paul *lawyer*
Wall, Wendy Lynn *history professor, writer*
Wyatt, Gerard Robert *biology professor, researcher*

Kitchener
Coles, Graham *conductor, composer*
Eldred, Gerald Marcus *performing company executive*
Winger, Roger Elson *retired church administrator*

London
Bancroft, George Michael *chemical physicist, educator*
Bauer, Michael Anthony *computer scientist, educator*
Borwein, David *mathematics professor*
Dreimanis, Aleksis *emeritus geology educator*
Fyfe, William Sefton *geochemist, educator*
Gerber, Douglas Earl *classics educator*
Inculet, Ion I. *electrical engineer, educator, science association director, consultant*
Kang, Chil-Yong *virologist, immunology educator*
Laidler, David Ernest William *economics professor*
Lala, Peeyush Kanti *research scientist, educator*
Marotta, Joseph Thomas *medical educator*
Osbaldeston, Gordon Francis *finance educator, retired federal agency administrator*
Perinpanayagam, Hiran *dental educator*
Poole, Nancy Geddes *art gallery curator, writer*
Théberge, Jean *biophysicist*
William, David *theater director, actor*
Wonnacott, Ronald Johnston *retired economics professor*

Manotick
Hobson, George Donald *retired geophysicist*
Osmond, Dennis Gordon *anatomist, researcher, medical educator*

Markham
Gulden, Simon *lawyer, management consultant, consultant*
Tsubouchi, David H. *Canadian provincial official*

Mississauga
Dempsey, William G. *pharmaceutical executive*
Gupta, Rajesh *engineer, consultant*

Nepean
Chudobiak, Walter James *electronics executive*
Kallmann, Helmut Max *musicologist, retired librarian*

Niagara-on-the-Lake
Augustine, Jerome Samuel *merchant banker*
Olley, Robert Edward *economist, educator*

Nobleton
Embleton, Tony Frederick Wallace *retired Canadian government official*

North York
Adelman, Howard *philosophy educator*
Blundell, William Richard Charles *retired electric company executive*
Buzacott, John Alan *engineering educator*
Davey, Kenneth George *biologist, educator, academic administrator*
Gasparrini-Etheridge, Claudia *publishing executive, research scientist, writer*
Regan, David *neuroscientist*
Thomas, Clara McCandless *retired literature educator*
Tse, Philip Kui *airport engineering maintenance consultant*

Oshawa
Elias, Arturo S. *automotive executive*
Zhang, Dan *engineering educator, researcher*

Ottawa
Alper, Howard *chemistry professor*
Altman, Samuel Pinover *mechanical engineer, research consultant*
Armstrong, Henry Conner *former Canadian government official, consultant*
Bacon, Lise *Canadian senator*
Baum, Bernard Rene *research scientist*
Beare-Rogers, Joyce Louise *retired research and development executive*
Binnie, William Ian Corneil *judge*
Bozozuk, Michael *civil engineer*
Brooks, David Barry *resource economist*
Buchanan, John MacLennan *Canadian provincial official*
Campbell, Don *information technology executive*
Carty, Arthur John *science policy advisor, research administrator*
Clouston, Cory *professional hockey coach*
Coleman, John Morley *transportation engineering executive*
Comrie, Mike (Michael William Comrie) *professional hockey player*
Copps, Sheila *former Canadian government official, political journalist, commentator*
Courtois, Bernard Andre *communications executive*
Cruickshank, John Douglas *broadcast executive*
d'Aquino, Thomas *lawyer, educator, entrepreneur, global strategist*
Davey, Clark William *newspaper publisher*
de Bold, Adolfo J. *pathologist, educator, physiologist, researcher*
de Chastelain, A(lfred) John G(ardyne) D(rummond) *Canadian army officer, diplomat*
Dlab, Vlastimil *mathematics professor, researcher*
Dray, William Herbert *philosophy educator*
Dryden, Ken *legislator, former sports team executive, retired professional hockey player*
Fairbairn, Joyce *Canadian government official*
Fellegi, Ivan Peter *statistician*
Georganas, Nicolas D. *electrical engineering educator, academic administrator*
Gillingham, Bryan Reginald *music educator*
Halliday, Ian *astronomer*
Harington, Charles Richard *vertebrate paleontologist*
Hervieux-Payette, Céline *Canadian senator*
Holahan, Matthew Richard *science educator*
Holmes, John Leonard *chemistry professor*
Hurteau, Gilles David *retired obstetrician, gynecologist, educator, dean*
Ingold, Keith Usherwood *chemist, educator*
Jordan, Joseph Louis *education educator, government official*
Kates, Morris *biochemist, educator*
Kovalev, Alexei *professional hockey player*
Labarge, Margaret Wade *medieval history professor, historian, writer*
Lapointe, Martin *professional hockey player*
Lavoie, Lionel A. *physician, health science association administrator*
Leiss, William Carl *political science professor*
MacFarlane, John Alexander *retired federal agency administrator*
MacKenzie, Lewis Wharton *military officer*
Macklem, Michael Kirkpatrick *publisher*
Malone, David Michael *diplomat, educator*
Mantsch, Henry Horst *chemistry professor*
Margeson, Theodore Earl *judge*
McAvity, John Gillis *museum director, association executive, museologist*
McLachlin, Beverley *Canadian supreme court chief justice*
McLure, John Douglas *management consultant, former Canadian government official*
O'Connor, Gordon James *Canadian government official*
Penner, Keith *former Canadian government official*
Perry, Malcolm Blythe *biologist, researcher*
Philogene, Bernard J. R. *academic administrator, science educator*
Rock, Allan Michael *academic administrator, lawyer, former Canadian government official*
Runte, Roseann O'Reilly *academic administrator*
Scott, Marianne Florence *retired librarian, educator*
Shiari, Behrouz *mechanical engineer, researcher*
Silverman, Ozzie *consulting strategist*
Silvestri, Claudio *information technology executive*
Squire, Anne Marguerite *retired humanities educator*
Staines, David McKenzie *language educator*
Stanford, Joseph Stephen *diplomat, lawyer, educator*
St-Onge, Denis Alderic *geologist, research scientist, educator*
Storey, Kenneth Bruce *biology professor*
Strayer, Barry Lee *retired judge*
Sylvestre, Jean Guy *former national librarian*
Tassé, Roger *lawyer, former Canadian government official*
Urie, John James *retired lawyer, former Canadian federal judge*
Vassilyadi, Michael *pediatric neurosurgeon*
Veizer, Ján *geology educator*
Whitehead, J. Rennie *science administrator, consultant*
Yalden, Maxwell Freeman *Canadian diplomat*
Yeomans, Donald Ralph *Canadian government official, consultant*
Zambonini, Ron (Renato Zambonini) *information technology executive*

Peterborough
Dumas, Michael Godfrey Joseph *artist*

Rexdale
Kraemer, Philipp *retired manufacturing company executive, inventor*

Richmond Hill
Fong, Maryanne T.P. *telecommunications industry executive, researcher*
Liew, Choong Chin *research scientist, educator*
Zulfi, Tasleem Elahi (Tasleem Elahi Qureshi) *broadcast executive, television personality*

Saint Catharines
Miller, Jack (John Peter Miller) *journalist*
Stevenson, Garth *social sciences educator*

Scarborough
Cetín, Anton *artist*
White, Calvin John *zoo executive, zoological association executive, financial manager*

Stittsville
MacLeod, Robert Angus *retired microbiology educator, researcher*

Thorold
O'Mara, John Aloysius *bishop emeritus*

Thunder Bay
Bo, Myint Win *principal, educator*

Toronto
Amon, Cristina Hortensia *mechanical engineering educator, researcher*
Angel, Aubie *endocrinologist, academic administrator*
Are, Ayokunnu *financial advisor, investment banker*
Armstrong, Robin Louis *physics professor, physicist*
Arthurs, Harry William *lawyer, educator, academic administrator*
Astman, Barbara Ann *artist, educator*
Bandeen, Robert Angus *management consultant*
Bargnani, Andrea *professional basketball player*
Beckwith, John *musician, composer, educator*
Blake, Jason *professional hockey player*
Blewett, David Lambert *English literature educator*
Bohme, Diethard Kurt *chemistry professor*
Boland, Janet Lang *judge*
Bosh, Chris *professional basketball player*
Brook, Adrian Gibbs *chemistry professor*
Bryant, Josephine Harriet *library executive*
Budrevics, Alexander *landscape architect*
Burke, Brian *professional sports team executive*
Carrothers, Gerald Arthur Patrick *environmental and city planning educator*
Cefis, Alberta M. *bank executive*
Chandra, Ranjit Kumar *research scientist, educator, physician*
Chester, Robert Simon George *lawyer*
Clark, Wendel *retired professional hockey player*
Colangelo, Bryan *professional sports team executive*
Colgrass, Michael Charles *composer*
Connell, Philip Francis *food industry executive*
Cook, Stephen Arthur *mathematics and computer science educator*
Cooke, Michael *editor-in-chief, publishing executive*
Cowan, Benson *travel company executive, lawyer*
Curlook, Walter *management consultant*
Dale, Robert Gordon *investment company executive*
Davison, Edward Joseph *electrical engineering educator*
Dick, John E. *medical geneticist, educator*
Dimma, William Andrew *real estate executive*
Dobson, Wendy Kathleen *economics professor*
Dunlop, David John *geophysics educator, researcher*
Eagles, Stuart Ernest *real estate company officer*
Egoyan, Atom *film director*
Elder, Richard Bruce *artist, writer*
English, Alexander *professional basketball coach, retired professional basketball player*
Evans, John Robert *academic administrator, cardiologist*
Eyton, John Trevor *business executive*
Farquharson, Gordon MacKay *lawyer, director*
Fatt, William Robert *hotel executive*
Fierheller, George Alfred *retired communications executive*
Finlay, Terence Edward *retired archbishop*
Fletcher, Cliff (George Clifford Fletcher) *professional sports team executive*
Fox, Wayne C. *stock exchange and corporate financial executive*
Fraser, William Neil *retired government agency administrator*
Friedlander, John Benjamin *mathematician, educator*
Fullerton, R. Donald *banker*
Furtado, Nelly Kim *vocalist*
Garbajosa (Chaparro), Jorge *professional basketball player*
Gaston, Clarence Edwin (Cito Gaston) *professional baseball team manager*
Gerber, Martin *professional hockey player*
Gilmour, Doug *professional hockey coach, retired professional hockey player*
Godsoe, Peter Cowperthwaite *retired banker*
Goh, Chan Hon *ballerina*
Goodwin, Pamela J. *oncologist, educator*
Goring, David Arthur Ingham *chemist, educator*
Gotlieb, Allan E. *former ambassador*
Gotlieb, Calvin Carl *computer scientist, educator*
Granatstein, Jack Lawrence *historian*
Grimes, Shenae Sonya *actress*
Gruia, Ronald Floriano *systems analyst*
Halladay, Roy (Harry Leroy Halladay III) *professional baseball player*
Healy, Glenn *sports association administrator, commentator, retired professional hockey player*
Helleiner, Gerald Karl *economics professor*
Hofmann, Theo *biochemist, educator*
Holyday, Douglas Charles *city councillor*
Hore, John Edward *retired commodity futures educator*
Iavaroni, Marc (Marcus John Iavaroni) *professional basketball coach, retired professional basketball player*
Janischewskyj, Wasyl *electrical engineering educator*
Jaworska, Tamara *artist*
Johnston, Colleen M. *bank executive*
Joseph, Curtis Shayne *professional hockey player*
Kaberle, Tomas *professional hockey player*
Kain, Karen Alexandria *performing company executive, ballet dancer*
Kaufman, Nathan *retired pathologist, educator*
Kerr, David Wylie *managing partner, director*
Kloet, Thomas A. *stock exchange executive*
Knowlton, Thomas A. *retired dean, food products executive*
Kolzig, Olaf *professional hockey player*
Komisarek, Mike *professional hockey player*
Kramer, Burton *graphics designer, artist, educator*
Kumar, Subodh *investment banker*
Kushner, Eva *academic administrator, educator, author*
Leech, Jim (James William Leech) *investment company executive*
Lewis, Robert *journalist, media executive*
Lindsay, Roger Alexander (Baron of Craighall) *investment executive*
Litherland, Albert Edward *physics professor*
Liversage, Richard Albert *cell biologist, educator*
MacDonald, Brian Scott *management consultant*
Macdonald, Donald Stovel *public policy advisor*
Macdonald, Hugh Ian *economics professor, public policy professor, academic administrator*
MacDougall, Hartland Molson *retired bank executive*
MacLaren, Roy *retired Canadian government official*
MacLennan, David Herman *research scientist, educator*
Maidment, Karen E. *bank executive*
Mann, George Stanley *diversified financial services company executive, real estate company officer*
Martin, Robert William *retired utilities executive*
Masui, Yoshio *zoology educator*
Mc Culloch, Ernest Armstrong *internist, educator*
McMurtry, R. Roy *federal judge*
Mercier, Eileen Ann *pension fund chairman*
Milbury, Mike (Michael James Milbury) *sports analyst, former professional sports team executive*
Millgate, Michael (Henry) *retired literature educator*
Moore, Carole Irene *librarian*
Moore, Christopher Hugh *writer*
Morey, Carl Reginald *musicologist*
Moritz, A.F. (Albert Frank) *poet, educator*
Morneau, William *pension and benefits company executive*
Munk, Peter *mining executive*
Naylor, C. David *academic administrator*
Nesbitt, Richard *bank executive, former stock exchange executive*
Nesterovic, Rasho *professional basketball player*
Nguyen, San Duy *psychiatrist, educator*
Novak, David *theology studies educator, rabbi*
Ogilvie, Richard Ian *clinical pharmacologist*
Oundjian, Peter *conductor, music director*
Pawson, Anthony J. *molecular biologist*
Peacock, Molly *poet, educator, writer*
Peddie, Richard A. *professional sports team executive*
Pickren, Wade Edward *historian*
Piggott, Michael Rantell *chemical engineer, educator*
Polanyi, John Charles *chemist, educator*
Polley, Sarah *actress*
Pollock, Bruce Godfrey *psychiatrist, educator*
Poon, Alan Ming Wang *sports association executive, director*
Poprawa, Andrew *diversified financial services company executive, accountant*
Pratt, Robert Cranford *political scientist, educator*
Price, Timothy R. *accountant*
Pritchard, Huw Owen *chemist, educator*
Ronald, Thomas Iain *retired financial services executive*
Rooney, Paul George *mathematics professor*
Rose, Jeffrey Raymond *retired economist, public servant, trade unionist*
Rowe, David John *physics professor*
Ryan, William Francis *priest*
Salama, C. Andre Tewfik *electrical engineering educator*
Scardamalia, Marlene *education educator, researcher*
Schwartz, Gerald Wilfred *business executive*
Semak, Michael William *photographer, educator*
Sessle, Barry John *adult education educator, researcher*

Shepherd, Gordon Greeley *space physics educator, researcher*
Siminovitch, Louis *geneticist, educator, scientist*
Slemon, Gordon Richard *electrical engineering educator*
Smith, Mike (Michael A. Smith) *former professional sports team executive*
Smith, Peter William Ebblewhite *electrical engineer, educator, research scientist, physicist*
Sole, Michael Joseph *cardiologist*
Steffer, Robert Wesley *clergyman*
Stymiest, Barbara *bank executive*
Tanenbaum, Joey *real estate developer*
Tanenbaum, Larry (Lawrence Tanenbaum) *construction executive, professional sports team executive*
Taylor, Allan Richard *retired banker*
Taylor, Kathleen P. *hotel executive*
Thomson, David Kenneth Roy *publishing executive*
Tobe, Stephen Solomon *zoology educator*
Triano, Jay *professional basketball coach*
Turkoglu, Hedo (Hidayet) *professional basketball player*
Turnbull, John Cameron *retired pharmacist, consultant*
van Ginkel, Blanche Lemco *architect, educator*
Venetsanopoulos, Anastasios Nicolaos *electrical engineer, educator*
Wilson, Lynton Ronald *telecommunications industry executive, academic administrator*
Wilson, Ronald Lawrence *professional hockey coach, former professional hockey player*
Wleugel, John Peter *manufacturing executive*
Wonham, Walter Murray *electrical engineer, educator*

Unionville
Pazak, John Stephen *bishop*

Waterloo
Aczél, János Dezsö *mathematician*
Anis, Mohab *engineering educator*
Balsillie, Jim *information technology executive*
Berczi, Andrew Stephen *academic administrator, educator*
Fallding, Harold Joseph *sociology educator*
Lazaridis, Mike *information technology executive, entrepreneur*
Paldus, Josef *mathematics professor*
Penlidis, Alexander *chemical engineering professor*
Saini, Simarjeet Singh *electronics engineer*
Sedra, Adel Shafeek *engineering educator, academic administrator*
Urquhart, Tony *artist, educator*
Van Seters, John *retired biblical literature educator*
Vlach, Jiri *electrical engineering educator, researcher*
Warner, Barry Gregory *ecologist, educator*

West Toronto
Iacobucci, Frank *lawyer, judge, former academic administrator*

Willowdale
Kerner, Fred *book publisher, writer*

Windsor
Bertman, Stephen Samuel *languages, literatures and civilizations educator, writer*
Ferguson, John Duncan *medical research educator*
Hackam, Reuben *electrical engineering educator*
La Rocque, Eugene Philippe *retired bishop*
Thibert, Roger Joseph *clinical chemist, educator*
Zhang, Guoqing *engineering educator*
Doolittle-Romas, Monique *health science association administrator*
Mohler, Brian Jeffery *diplomat*

PRINCE EDWARD ISLAND

Belfast
Weber, Jean Macphail *retired museum director*

Charlottetown
Sanborn, George Freeman, Jr. *genealogist*

QUEBEC

Beaconsfield
Harder, Rolf Peter *graphic designer, painter*

Ile Perrot
Lalonde, Marc *lawyer, former Canadian government official*

Kirkland
Baroudy, Bahige Mourad *biochemist, researcher*

Laval
Bourget, Edwin Robert *marine ecologist, educator*
Talbot, Pierre Joseph *microbiologist, researcher*

Leclercville
Morin, Pierre Jean *retired management consultant, social services administrator*

Montpellier
Poirier, Louis Joseph *neurology educator*

Montreal
Barrette, Jean *physicist, researcher*
Beauregard, Luc *public relations executive*
Bisignani, Giovanni *air transportation association executive*
Bisson, Claude *retired Chief Justice of Quebec*
Brecher, Michael *political science professor*
Bruemmer, Fred *writer, photographer*
Burgess, John Herbert *cardiologist, educator*
Cammalleri, Mike *professional hockey player*
Carroll, Robert Lynn *biology professor, paleontologist, curator, museum director*
Cedraschi, Tullio *retired investment company executive*
Chang, Thomas Ming Swi *research scientist, biotechnologist, educator*
Charney, Melvin *artist, architect, educator*
Cruess, Richard Leigh *orthopedic surgeon, dean*
Cyr, J. V. Raymond *telecommunications industry executive*
Demers, Jacques *legislator, sports analyst, former professional hockey coach*
Desmarais, Paul *diversified management and holding company executive*
Eisenberg, Adi *chemist*
Franco, Eduardo L.F. *epidemiologist, educator*
Freedman, Samuel Orkin *retired university official*
Freeman, Carolyn Ruth *oncologist*
Gabbour, Iskandar *city and regional planning educator*
Gainey, Bob (Robert Michael Gainey) *professional sports team executive, retired professional hockey player*
Genest, Jacques *nephrologist, clinical scientist, science administrator*
Gillespie, Thomas Stuart *lawyer*
Gillett, George Nield, Jr. *professional sports team executive, communications executive*
Gionta, Brian *professional hockey player*
Gold, Phil *immunologist, educator, researcher*
Goldbloom, Victor Charles *pediatrician*
Goltzman, David *endocrinologist, educator, researcher*
Gomez, Scott *professional hockey player*
Gratton, Robert *diversified financial services company executive*
Haccoun, David *electrical engineering educator*
Ikawa-Smith, Fumiko *anthropologist, educator*
Johnston, Donald James *lawyer, educator*
Jones, Barbara Ellen *neurologist, educator*
Jones, Hank *jazz musician*
Kamal, Musa Rasim *chemical engineer, consultant*
Kinsley, William Benton *literature educator*
Kramer, Michael Stuart *pediatric epidemiologist*
Ladanyi, Branko *civil engineer, educator*
Lamarre, Bernard *engineering executive*
Large, John Andrew *library and information service professor*
Laurin, Pierre *finance company executive*
Leroy, Claude *physics professor, researcher*
Lessard, Michel M. *finance company executive*
Li, Chao-Jun *chemistry professor, researcher*
Limperopoulos, Catherine *occupational therapist, researcher*
Lock, Edouard *performing company executive*
Lowy, Frederick Hans *academic administrator, psychiatrist*
Mac Lean, Lloyd Douglas *surgeon*
Markov, Andrei *professional hockey player*
Martin, Jacques *professional hockey coach, former professional sports team executive*
Matziorinis, Kenneth N. *economist*
Melzack, Ronald *psychology professor*
Milic-Emili, Joseph *physiologist, educator*
Milner, Brenda Atkinson Langford *neuropsychologist*
Molson, Andrew T. *management consultant*
Molson, Geoffrey Eric *brewery company executive*
Mulder, David S. *cardiovascular surgeon*
Mulroney, Brian (Martin Brian Mulroney) *former Prime Minister of Canada*
Mysak, Lawrence Alexander *oceanographer, climatologist and mathematics educator*
Nagano, Kent George *conductor, music director*
Nattel, Stanley *cardiologist, research scientist*
Normandeau, Andre Gabriel *criminologist, educator*
Normore, Calvin *philosophy professor*
Ohayon, Maurice M. *research center administrator, psychiatrist*
Paidoussis, Michael Pandeli *mechanical engineering educator*
Pankov, Gradimir Krunislav *performing company executive*
Pasternac, André *cardiologist, educator*
Paterson, David J. *paper company executive*
Perlin, Arthur Saul *chemistry professor*
Pierre, Samuel J. *engineering educator*
Podgorsak, Ervin B. *medical physicist, educator, administrator*
Popovici, Adrian *law educator, emeritus professor*
Pound, Richard William Duncan *lawyer, accountant, former academic administrator*
Price, Carey *professional hockey player*
Ramachandran, Venkatanarayana Deekshit *electrical engineering educator*
Rivest, Jean-François *conductor*
Robb, James Alexander *retired lawyer*
Rochette, Louis *water transportation executive*
Rolland, Lucien Gilbert *paper company executive, director*
Scriver, Charles Robert *medical researcher, human geneticist, retired medical educator*
Selvadurai, Antony Patrick Sinnappa *civil engineer, mathematician, educator, consultant*
Snell, Linda S. *internist, educator*
Sourkes, Theodore Lionel *biochemistry professor*
Speirs, Derek James *diversified financial services company executive*
Steinberg, Arnold (H. Arnold Steinberg) *academic administrator, former diversified financial services company executive*
Suen, Ching Yee *computer scientist, educator, researcher*
Szabo, Denis *criminologist, educator*
Taras, Paul *physicist, researcher*
Torrey, David Leonard *investment banker*
Turcotte, Jean-Claude Cardinal *cardinal, archbishop*
Vaillancourt, Jean-Guy *sociology educator, researcher*
Wainberg, Mark Arnold *medical educator, director*
Waller, Harold Myron *political science professor*
Webster, Norman Eric *journalist, foundation administrator*
Whitehead, Michael Anthony *chemistry professor*
Williams, John D. *paper company executive*

Mount Royal
Elie, Jean André *investment banker*

North Hatley
Jones, Douglas Gordon *retired literature educator*

Outremont
Dufour, Jean-Marie *economist, statistician, educator*
Gulkin, Harry *arts administrator, film producer*

Pointe-Claire
Bachynski, Morrel Paul *physicist*
Kaminsky, Ben *chemist*

Quebec City
Belanger, Gerard *economics professor*
Dinan, Robert Michael *lawyer*
LeMay, Jacques *lawyer*
Morin, Louis *lawyer*
Potvin, Pierre *physiologist, educator*
Prothro, Jerry Robert *lawyer*
Roy, Patrick *professional sports team executive, coach, retired professional hockey player*
Stavert, Alexander Bruce *archbishop*
Verge, Pierre *legal educator*

Rimouski
Blanchet, Bertrand *archbishop*

Rosemere
Hopper, Carol *trade association administrator*

Saint Hubert
Payette, Julie *astronaut, electrical engineer, computer engineer*

Saint Jean Sur Richelieu
Trudel, Marc J. *botanist, educator*

Saint-Faustin-Lac-Carre
Des Marais, Pierre, II, *communications holding company executive*

Saint-Laurent
Dion, Stéphane *Canadian legislator*

Sainte Croix
Grenier, Fernand *geographer, consultant*

Sainte-Foy
Normand, Robert *retired lawyer*
Tremblay, Marc Adélard *anthropologist, educator*

Sherbrooke
Tremblay, André-Marie *physicist*

Varennes
Bartnikas, Raymond *electrical engineer, educator*

Westmount
Coolidge, Robert Tytus *deacon, historian, educator*

SASKATCHEWAN

Regina
Bayda, Edward Dmytro *retired chief justice*
MacKay, Harold Hugh *lawyer*
Semenov, Andrei Yurievich *research scientist*

Saskatoon
Billinton, Roy *engineering educator*
Blakeney, Allan Emrys *Canadian government official, lawyer, educator*
Bornstein, Eli *artist, sculptor*
Huang, Pan Ming *soil science educator*
Ish, Daniel Russell *law educator, academic administrator*
Kennedy, Marjorie Ellen *librarian*
Kerrich, Robert *geologist, educator*

Burnaby
Alava Saltos, Juan Jose *research scientist*

Cape Ray
Harnack, Robert P. *retired professor*

Laval
Déziel, Eric *microbiologist, educator*

Montreal
Jablonski, Zygmunt *lawyer*
Vachon, Jacques P. *lawyer, paper company executive*

North Hatley
Salt, Alfred Lewis *priest*

Sainte Anne de Bellevue
Grant, William Frederick *geneticist, biosystematist, educator*

Sherbrooke
Deslongchamps, Pierre *chemistry professor*

Whistler
Rae, Barbara Joyce *staging company*

AFGHANISTAN

Kabul
Karokhel, Danish *broadcast executive*

ALBANIA

Durres
Kukeli, Agim *economics professor*

ALGERIA

Algiers
Bouteflika, Abdelaziz *President of Algeria*

El-Biar
Ford, Robert Stephen *United States Ambassador to Algeria*

ANGOLA

Luanda
Lavrador, Sebastiao Bastos *bank executive*

ANTIGUA AND BARBUDA

St John's
Carlisle, James B. *former head of state*

ARGENTINA

Buenos Aires
Bergel, Meny *physician, researcher*
Frasch, Alberto Carlos C. *molecular genetics educator*
Montes, Leopoldo Feliciano *dermatologist, educator*
Parisier, Carlos *lawyer, economist*
Petracchi, Enrique Santiago *judge*

Córdoba
Cabrera, Angel Leopoldo *professional golfer*

ARMENIA

Yerevan
Sargsyan, Davit *library director*

ARUBA

Oranjestad
Oduber, Nelson Orlando *Prime Minister of Aruba*

AUSTRALIA

Adelaide
Sharma, Sanjeev *engineer, researcher*

Altona
Daniel-Dreyfus, Susan B. Russe *information technology executive*

Armadale
Neil, Sandra Eilleen Silverberg *psychologist*

Balmain
Jakuba, Rachel Wisniewski *environmental scientist*

Barton
Evans, Gareth *Australian government and international official*

Camberwell
Edwards, F(rederick) Gary *architectural firm executive, health facility planner*
Peterson, Douglas Brian (Pete Peterson) *former ambassador, former United States Representative from Florida*

Canberra
Cosgrove, P. J. *military officer*
Craig, David Parker *retired chemistry professor*
Fletcher, Neville Horner *physicist*
Taylor, Stuart Ross *geochemist, writer*

Caulfield
Le Grand, Homer *emeritus professor*

Clayton
Tonge, Bruce John *psychiatrist*

Clermont
Mepham, Derek John Amoore *business investor*

Crawley
Street, Robert *retired academic administrator, physicist*
Sweeney, Jillian C. *marketing professor*

Darwin
Rao, Akkinepalli Badri Narayan *physician, educator*

Double Bay
Guerin, Didier *magazine executive*

Footscray Victoria
Wheeler, Tony (Anthony Ian Wheeler) *travel publishing executive*

Hillaries
Jones, John Brian *agriculturist*

Lindfield
Morgan, Vincent Thomas *research scientist, consultant*

Malanda
Cooper, William Thomas *natural history artist*

Melbourne
Collis, Gavin E. *chemist*

Denton, Derek Ashworth *medical researcher, foundation administrator*
Fahour, Ahmed *investment company executive*
MacKinnon, Dolly *historian, music educator*
Prescott, John Barry *resource industry executive*
Rosenfeld, Jeffrey Victor *neurosurgeon*
Wolfram, David Anthony *information technology executive*

Milsons Point
Foster, Milo George *manufacturing executive*

Nedlands
Oxnard, Charles Ernest *anatomist, anthropologist, biologist, educator*

New Farm
Ward, Megan Mae *yoga therapist*

New South Wales
Mozer, Attila Janos *materials scientist, researcher*

North Ryde
Ryan, Louise *statistician, educator*
Selley, Michael L. *pharmaceutical company executive*

North Sydney
Crowe, Russell *actor*
Dienst, Daniel W. *metal products executive*
Scott, Brian Walter *management consultant*

Parkville
Boger, David Vernon *chemical engineer, educator*

Perth
Verbitsky, Vladimir *conductor*

Rankin Park
Chapman, Barry Lloyd *retired cardiologist, educator, army officer*

Redfern
Campion, Jane *film director, screenwriter*

South Yarra
Stephen, Ninian Martin *judge*

Southport
Mayne, Alfred R. *research scientist*

Springfield
Spalvins, Janis Gunars *steamship company executive*

Surry Hills
Marchetta, Melina *writer*

Sydenham
Marasigan, Rodel Castillo *systems analyst*

Sydney
Bishop, Rosalinda Matubis *information manager*
Brennan, Hon. Sir Gerard *judge*
Cardona, Beatriz *research scientist*
Clancy, Edward Bede Cardinal *cardinal, archbishop emeritus*
Geiger, Mark Watson *history educator*
Hora, Heinrich *physicist*
Huckstep, Ronald Lawrie *traumatic and orthopaedic surgery educator, consultant*
Shine, John *molecular geneticist, researcher, biochemist*

Townsville
Dobbs, Kirstin Anne *marine life administrator*
Ho, Yik Hong *colon and rectal surgeon*

Victoria
Bana, Eric *actor*
Johnston, Colin Ivor *medical educator, researcher*

AUSTRIA

Graz
Gee, Erin *composer*

Grossgmain
Mueller, Christa *radiologist*

Linz
Davies, Dennis Russell *conductor, music director, pianist*
Strasser, Rudolf *law educator*

Reutte
Knippscheer, Sven *mechanical engineer, materials scientist*

Salzburg
González, Ricardo *surgeon, educator*

Steinerkirchen
Handel, Norbert Erasmus Freiherr van *marketing professional*

Vienna
Cetto, Ana Maria *physicist, researcher*
Dahinden, Justus *architect*
Magariños, Carlos Alfredo *international association administrator*
Schulte, Gregory L. *United States Ambassador to United Nations, Vienna*

Wien
Cotrubas, Ileana *opera singer, retired lyric soprano*
Hornykiewicz, Oleh *retired biochemical pharmacologist*
Wirth, Gerald *conductor, composer*
Finley, Julie Hamm *United States Ambassador to Organization for Security and Cooperation in Europe*

AZERBAIJAN

Baku
Garayev, Abulfas Mursal *government official*

THE BAHAMAS

Nassau
Beck, Jan Scott *lawyer*

BAHRAIN

Manama
Al-Salman, Jameela M.R. *public health service officer, consultant*

Riffa
Al-Khalifa, Sheikh Hamad bin Isa *King of Bahrain*

BANGLADESH

Dhaka
Alam, Nazmul *medical researcher*
Brooks, W. Abdullah *pediatrician, researcher*
Marino, Joseph *archbishop, diplomat*

Kushtia
Latifur Rahaman, Rasul Boaksh *legal association administrator*

BELARUS

Grodno
Hrakhouskaya, Tatsiana Cheslavovna *biochemist, researcher*

Minsk
Aleinikov, Gennady *bank executive*
Dailyudenko, Victor *physicist, researcher*
Prokopovich, Petr *federal official*
Swiatek, Kazimierz Cardinal *cardinal, archbishop emeritus*

BELGIUM

Antwerp
Saal, Ilka *literature and language professor*
Snyders, Dirk Johan *electrophysiologist and biophysicist educator*

Beersel
Alfons Remi Emiel, Viscount Verplaetse *bank administrator*

Brussels
Albert II, King (Albert Félix Humbert Théodore Chrétien Eugène Marie) *Monarch of Belgium*
Barnum, John Wallace *lawyer*
Boon, Thierry *biomedical researcher*
Buysse, Paul Henri Maria *manufacturing executive*
Ciarka, Agnieszka *cardiologist*
Daalder, Ivo H. *United States Permanent Representative to NATO*
de Duve, Christian René *chemist, educator*
Flory, Peter Cyril Wyche *international organization official, former federal agency administrator*
Freizer, Louis A. *radio producer*
Godfraind, Theophile Joseph *pharmacologist, educator*
Gray, C(layland) Boyden *federal official, former United States Ambassador to European Union, lawyer*
Houziaux, Léo Narcisse Omer *astronomer, educator*
Lengele, Benoît G. *surgeon, educator*
Maisin, Jean René Simon *medical researcher, educator*
Muccioli, Giulio G. *science educator*
Ruding, Herman Onno *banker, former cabinet minister*
Rzewski, Frederic *composer*
Vinje, Thomas C. *lawyer*

Genappe
Williams, Jody *political organization administrator*

Habay-la-Neuve
Nothomb, Charles Ferdinand *Belgian government official, minister*

Liège
Mosora-Stan, Florentina Ioana *physics professor*

Namur
Kelly, Sister Marie *school system administrator*

Sambreville
Boskovic, Bojan O. *physicist, engineer*

BELIZE

Belmopan
Young, Sir Colville *Belizean government official*

BENIN

Cotonou
Blume, Michael August *archbishop*

BERMUDA

Hamilton
McCormick, Hugh Thomas *lawyer*
Pitman, Gary Robert *oil industry executive*
Wiegley, Roger Douglas *lawyer*

Pembroke
Alexander, Barbara Toll *financial consultant*

BHUTAN

Lungtenphu
Dorji, Lam (Goongloen Gongma Lam Dorji) *military officer*

BOSNIA-HERZEGOVINA

Sarajevo
John, C. Dayton *literature and language professor*

BRAZIL

Belém
Lainson, Ralph *parasitologist, researcher*

Brasília
Falcão, José Freire Cardinal *cardinal, archbishop emeritus*

FlorianÓpolis
Lopes, Elizeu Pereira *communications educator, researcher*

Florianópolis
Lopes, Eliezer Pereira *communications educator*

Fortaleza
Teixeira, Eduardo V. *mathematics professor*

Paranagua
Novak, Alfredo Ernest *bishop emeritus*

Pelotas
Valente, Ana Luisa Schifino *animal scientist, educator*

Ribeirao Preto
Roque, Eliana Mendes S. Teixeira *social worker, educator*

Rio de Janeiro
de Araújo, Aloisio Pessoa *mathematics professor*
Sales, Eugenio Cardinal de Araujo *cardinal, archbishop emeritus*

Salvador
Agnelo, Geraldo Majella Cardinal *archbishop*

Sorocaba
Martins, Nelson *physics professor*

São Paulo
Antunes, Celina *real estate company executive*
Arns, Paulo Evaristo Cardinal *cardinal, archbishop emeritus*
Dini, Gal Moreira *plastic surgeon, researcher, university teacher*
Lopes, Maria-Cecilia *pediatrician*
Riecken, Claudia *researcher, director*

Varginha
Pereira, Renato Claudio Costa *air transportation executive*

BRITISH VIRGIN ISLANDS

Tortola
Chalwell-Brewley, Lavon Patricia *biology educator*

BRUNEI

Bandar Seri Begawan
Todd, William E. *United States Ambassador to Brunei Darussalam*

BULGARIA

Rousse
Loukantchevsky, Milen *telecommunications industry executive*

Sofia
Georgiev, Svetlin Georgiev *mathematics professor, researcher*
Harsev, Emil Manolov *bank executive*
Valev, Ventzeslav Vassilev *computer scientist, educator, researcher*

CAMBODIA

Phnom Penh
Chhang, Youk *Cambodian government official*

CAMEROON

Yaoundé
Biya, Paul *President of the Republic of Cameroon*

CAYMAN ISLANDS

Georgetown
James, Winston Clive *agriculturist, environmental services administrator, department chairman*

CHANNEL ISLANDS

Saint Helier
Bailhache, Sir Philip Martin *judge*

CHILE

Santiago
Jimenez, Juan Pablo *economist, educator*
Wilkey, Malcolm Richard *retired ambassador, judge*

Talca
Casaretto, Jose A. *plant biologist*

CHINA

Beijing
Bai, Chunli *professional society administrator, educator*
Christianson, Jon L. *lawyer*
Christianson, Wei Sun *diversified financial services company executive*
Deng, John (Zhonghan Deng) *electrical engineer, researcher*
Dingman, Michael David *manufacturing executive, investor*
Gu, Bing-Lin *academic administrator, physics professor*
Jiabao, Wen *Chinese government official*
Li, Fang-hua *physicist*
Li, Xiaodong *architect, educator*
Li, Xing Zhong *physics educator*
Liu, Limin *academic administrator, educator*
Liu, Yi-Xun *reproductive biologist, academician, researcher*
Ma (Xuezheng), Mary *retired computer company executive*
Sheng, Zhi (Chih) Yong *surgeon, educator*
Thornton, John Lawson *economics professor, former diversified financial services company executive*
Tu, Chuanyi *space physics educator, researcher*
Xu, Xiangyuan *academic administrator, educator*
Yan, Gao *power company executive*
Yang, Chen Ning Franklin *physicist, educator*
Yang, Guangrong *physicist, researcher, educator*
Yu, Qingjuan *astrophysicist, educator*
Yuan, Longping *agronomist*
Zhang, Chuhan *civil engineer, educator*
Zhou, Bang Rong *physicist, researcher*

Dalian
Zhao, Zhongkui *researcher*

Dongguan
McIlvain, Peter James *literature and language professor*

Guangzhou
Ren-Heidenreich, Lifen *engineering executive*
Wang, Jing *lawyer*

Hangzhou
Xiuzi, Ye *engineering educator*

Hi-Tech Zone Xian
Leighton, Lawrence Ward *investment banker*

Hong Kong
Che, Chi-Ming *chemist, educator*
Halperin, David Richard *lawyer*
Ka-Shing, Li *international entrepreneur*
Kwong, Peter Kong-Kit *retired archbishop*
Lau, Lawrence Juen-Yee *academic administrator, economics professor, consultant*
Nelson, Steven Craig *lawyer*
Pacter, Paul Allan *accounting standards researcher*
Yu, Benita Ka Po *lawyer*

Macau
Veiga Jardim, Oswaldo *conductor, composer, researcher*

Nanjing
Han, Lixin *information scientist, educator*
Wang, Xin *geologist, researcher*
Xie, Kai Ji *aeronautical engineering educator*
Yu, Jurong *chemist*

Pudong
Wan, Zehong *research and development company executive*

Shanghai
Cheng, Mei Wei *automotive executive*
Cohn, David Stephen *lawyer*
Hu, Song *oceanographer, educator*
Lin, Maria C.H. *lawyer*
Lu, Bao-Liang *computer scientist, educator*
Prosser, Michael Hubert *communications educator*
Zhu, Xinyuan *chemistry professor*

Shantou
Leyden, Michael Joseph, II, (Lei Jie Ming) *business finance educator, entrepreneur, writer*

Shenzhen
Yandle, Stephen Thomas *dean*
Yu, Gang *science educator*

Wuhan
Li, Chaoying *biomedical researcher, researcher*

Xi'an
Yao, Xi *ceramics engineer, educator*
Zhao, Wenming *retired biochemistry and molecular biology educator*

COLOMBIA

Bogota
Bookwalter, William Keith *principal*
Delgado, Alberto *engineering educator, researcher*
Reina, Carrillo José Gabriel *physician, surgery educator*

COSTA RICA

San José
Arias Sanchez, Oscar *President of Costa Rica*
Hoffman, Irwin *orchestra conductor*
Perez Esquivel, Adolfo *human rights activist*
Scharf, Eric *lawyer, educator*

COTE D'IVOIRE

Abidjan
Gbagbo, Laurent *President of Cote d'Ivoire*

CROATIA

Rijeka
Bosnar, Alan *medical university administrator, physician*

Split
Buble, Nikola *musicologist, conductor*

Zagreb
Drazancic, Ante *obstetrician, gynecologist, educator*
Kniewald, Jasna *toxicologist, educator, scientist*

CUBA

Havana
Gonzalez, Gisela *immunologist, researcher*

CYPRUS

Nicosia
Christodoulou, Christodoulos *business consultant*
Evangelou, Alecos Costa *former Cyprian government official*
Hadjipapas, Andreas *publishing executive*
Karageorghis, Vassos *archaeologist*
Vrontis, Demetris *dean, marketing professor*

CZECH REPUBLIC

Brno
Gröger, Roman *research scientist*
Hřib, Jiří Emil *plant physiologist*
Klapka, Jindřich Ludvík *mathematician, physicist, educator, researcher*

Frenstat
Kusin, Vladimir Victor *retired communications executive*

Nymburk
Cusumano, James Anthony *filmmaker, vocalist, retired pharmaceutical, hotel, and recording industry executive*

Olomouc
Merta De Velehrad, Jan *safety engineer, psychologist*

Prague
Čejka, Jiří *retired chemist, researcher*
Dienstbier, Jiří *diplomat, writer, political scientist, journalist*
Dostál, Jan *hotel, tourist and gaming industry executive*
Kalkus, Stanley *librarian, administrator, consultant*
Kočárnik, Ivan *insurance company executive*
Kotrla, Miroslav *physicist*
Kozma, Peter *physicist*
Kučera, Vladimír *control engineering educator*
Neuzil, Petr *cardiologist, researcher*
Potmesil, Petr *pharmacologist*
Říman, Josef *biology professor*
Sebek, Michael *research scientist, entrepreneur, educator*
Tuma, Stanislav Josef *radiologist*

Zlin
Kolomaznik, Karel *engineering educator*

DEMOCRATIC REPUBLIC OF CONGO

Kinshasa
Garvelink, William John *United States Ambassador to the Democratic Republic of Congo*

DENMARK

Aalborg
Caspersen, Sven Lars *academic administrator, statistician*

Aarhus
Gjedde, Albert Hellmut *neurology educator, neurobiology researcher*

Bagsvaerd
Erhardtsen, Elisabeth *pharmaceutical executive*

Copenhagen
Bohr, Aage Niels *physicist, researcher*
Hoffmeyer, Erik *former bank executive*
Kinch, Kjartan Münster *physicist*
Moller, Maersk Mc-Kinney *shipowner*
Mottelson, Ben Roy *physicist*
Nielsen, Erland Kolding *library director*
Parrott, Jeffrey Keith *linguist, researcher*
Petersen, Niels Helveg *Danish government official*
Pethick, Christopher John *physicist*
Rifbjerg, Klaus Thorvald *writer*

Farum
Larsen, Poul Steen *retired information science educator*

Frederiksberg
Buch, Jan *retired medical research administrator, director*

Lyngburg
Federspiel, Ulrik *diplomat*

Nordborg
Clausen, Jørgen Mads *engineering executive*

Risskov
Smith, Donald Frederick *psychologist, pharmacologist*

Roskilde
Skov, Leif *performing arts association administrator, entrepreneur*

DOMINICAN REPUBLIC

Santo Domingo
Fernandez Reyna, Leonel *President of The Dominican Republic*

ECUADOR

Quito
Del Pino, Eugenia M. *biology professor*

EGYPT

Alexandria
Eldakar, Youssef I. *software engineer*
Noweir, Madbuli Hamed *chemical engineer, educator*
Zahran, Mohsen Moharram *architect, educator*

Cairo
Anderson, Lisa *academic administrator, political science professor, researcher*
Hamza, Ahmed Mohamed *pediatrician, researcher*
Marei, Mamdouh Mohey Eddine *Egyptian government official*
Sullivan, Earl Le Roy *political science professor, former academic administrator*

Giza
El-Mougy, Nehal Samy *plant pathologist, researcher*
Zaki, Kamal El-Din Mahmoud *veterinarian, educator*

Manyal
Kandil, Doaa Adel *tour guidance*

Rossitta line
Hafez, Shireen Abdelgawad *veterinarian, educator, anatomist*

ENGLAND

Ampthill
Horlock, John Harold *academic administrator, engineer*

Ashford
Prickett, Stephen *retired literature and language professor*

Askett Bucks
Irons, Jeremy *actor*

Beaconsfield
Lindley, David *mechanical engineer*

Beaworthy
Richards, Sir Rex Edward *research scientist, academic administrator*

Beckenham
Lader, Malcolm Harold *pharmaceutical consultant*

Bedfordshire
Patel, Nildeep Mukundray *mechanical engineer, researcher*

Berkshire
Everitt-Newton, Katherine Evelyn *international management consultant, business coach*

Beverley
Edles, Gary Joel *lawyer, educator*

Birmingham
Swadener, John Gregory *mechanical engineering lecturer*

Bournemouth
Darvill, Timothy Charles *archaeology educator*

Bradford
Morrison, Kenneth Duncan *retired retail grocery executive*
Sherwin, James Terry *lawyer*

Brentford
Bondy, Rupert *pharmaceutical executive, lawyer*

Bristol
Haggett, Peter *geographer, educator*

Cambridge
Baker, Alan *mathematician*
Baulcombe, David C. *plant scientist*
Buckingham, Amyand David *chemistry professor*
Chadwick, Owen *academic administrator, historian, educator*
Cottrell, Alan *materials scientist*
Edwards, Sir Samuel Frederick *physicist, researcher*
Garrow, David Jeffries *historian, author*
Gurdon, Sir John Bertrand *cell biologist*
Hawking, Stephen William *astrophysicist, mathematician, educator*
Hawthorne, Sir William Rede *aerospace and mechanical engineer, educator*
Heisler, Lora Katherine *neuroscientist*
Hinde, Robert Aubrey *biologist, psychologist, educator*
Hoare, Sir Charles Antony Richard *computer scientist, researcher*
Hogwood, Christopher Jarvis Haley *music educator*
Kermode, (John) Frank *literary critic, educator*
Klug, Aaron *molecular biologist*
Lynden-Bell, Donald *astronomer*
Milner, Robin *computer scientist*
Moffatt, Henry Keith *science educator*
Rees, Martin John *astronomy educator*
Renfrew, Andrew Colin (Lord Renfrew of Kaimsthorn) *archaeologist, educator, director*
Steiner, George (Francis Steiner) *author, educator*
Walker, John Ernest *molecular biologist, researcher*
Wilkes, Sir Maurice V. *computer science emeritus professor, computer scientist*

Cardiff
Tumlinson, Alexandre Rex *biomedical engineer, researcher*

Charlbury
Belkin, Boris David *violinist*

Cheltenham
Winwood, Stephen Lawrence *musician, composer*

Cheshunt
Leahy, Sir Terry *food products executive, marketing professional*

Coventry
Feelisch, Martin *research scientist, consultant*
Thomas, Howard *business educator*
Varghese, George *systems engineer*

Dartford
Goodman, Len *former dancer, television personality*

East Sussex
Katin, Peter Roy *pianist*

Edgware
Walji, Jabir Mohamed *strategist, futurist and systematic innovation consultant*

Essex
Collins, Joan Henrietta *actress*

Exeter
Wyatt, Adrian Frederick *physicist, researcher*

Gloucester
Angus, Sir Michael Richardson *chemical company executive*

Hampshire
Morris, Paul *psychologist, educator*

Henley-on-Thames
Bullock, Peter Bradley *company director, consultant*

Hertfordshire
Bishop, Malcolm Graham Hamilton *medical essayist, dental surgeon*

Hull
Pettman, Barrie Owen *entrepreneur*

Kent Cranbrook
Hattersley-Smith, Geoffrey Francis *retired government research scientist*

Leavesden
Watson, Emma *actress*

Leeds
De Frutos, Javier *performing company executive, choreographer, dancer*
Ichino, Yoko *ballerina*
Nixon, David *dancer*
Phillips, Oliver *tropical forest ecologist, researcher*
Slechta, Jiri *theoretical physicist*

Leicester
Crowther, David *education educator*
Jeffreys, Sir Alec John *geneticist, educator*

Leicestershire
Levendorskii, Serge Zakhar *mathematics educator*

London
Abu-Deeb, Kamal Mikha'il *humanities educator*
Adele, (Adele Laurie Blue Adkins) *singer*
Aguoru, Kingsley Chibuzor, Sr. *computer engineer, systems analyst, consultant*
Ahrendts, Angela J. *apparel executive*
Alexeev, Dmitri Konstantinovich *pianist*
Amaechi, John *motivational speaker, retired professional basketball player*
Anderson, Kevin C. *actor*
Armstrong-Jones, Antony Earl (Antony Charles Robert Armstrong-Jones, 1st Earl of Snowdon) *photographer, writer*
Arulpragasam, Mathangi (M.I.A.) *singer, artist*
Ashkenazy, Vladimir Davidovich *concert pianist, conductor*
Bailey, Christopher *apparel designer*
Baird, Dugald Euan *automotive executive*
Batla, Raymond John, Jr. *lawyer*
Beck, Jeff (Geoffrey Arnold Beck) *guitarist*
Beckham, Victoria Caroline *singer, apparel designer*
Bell, Joshua *musician*
Bertolucci, Bernardo *film director*
Binney, Robert Harry *bank executive*
Blethyn, Brenda Anne *actress*
Blood, David *investment company executive*
Blunt, Emily *actress*
Bono, (Paul David Hewson) *singer, songwriter*
Bremer, J. Marco *Internet company executive, director*
Brennan, David R. *pharmaceutical executive*
Broers, Lord Alec Nigel *engineering educator*
Butler, Peter E. *plastic surgeon*
Carey, George Leonard (Lord Carey of Clifton) *former archbishop of Canterbury*
Carroll, Cynthia B. *mining executive*
Chadwick, Derek James *foundation administrator*
Chammah, Walid A. *diversified financial services company executive*
Chevalier, Tracy Rose *writer*
Christie, Julie *actress*
Cleese, John Marwood *writer, comedian*
Codron, Michael Victor *theater producer*
Collins, Paul John *banker*
Colson, Christian *film producer*
Cope, Wendy *poet*
Cowell, Simon *television personality, music producer*
Cowles, James C. *bank executive*
Darling, Peter *choreographer*
Daughtry, Christopher Adam *singer*
Davis, Brian Keith *biophysicist, researcher*
Davis, Sir Colin Rex *conductor*
Day-Lewis, Daniel (Michael Blake) *actor*
Deighton, Len *author*
Dempsey, Clint (Clinton Drew Dempsey) *professional soccer player*
Dench, Judi (Judith Olivia Dench) *actress*
de Savorgnani, Adriane Aldrich *healthcare administrator, nurse*
Diederichs, Klaus *diversified financial services company executive*
Duffy, Simon P. *telecommunications industry executive*
Duffy, (Aimée Ann Duffy) *singer*
Duncan, Lindsay *actress*
Elizabeth II, (Elizabeth Alexandra Mary) *By the Grace of God of the United Kingdom of Great Britain and Northern Ireland and of Her Other Realms and Territories Queen, Head of the Commonwealth, Defender of the Faith*
Evans, Christopher *biotechnologist*
Evans, Richard C.S. *bank executive*
Fabricant, Arthur E. *lawyer, corporate financial executive*
Fine, Anne *writer*
Finney, Albert *actor, theater director*
Fisher, Rick *lighting designer*
Flor, Claus Peter *conductor*
Fo, Dario *playwright*
Foster, Norman Robert (Lord Baron Norman Robert Foster of Thames Bank) *architect*
Fraser, Jane *bank executive*
Frayn, Michael *playwright*
Frears, Stephen *film director*
Fuller, Simon *music company executive, television producer*
Galloway, Janice *writer, editor*
Gelenbe, Sami Erol *computer scientist, engineering educator*
Gervais, Ricky *actor, scriptwriter*
Glazer, Barry David *lawyer*
Glocer, Thomas Henry *publishing executive*
Goosen, Retief *professional golfer*
Gordon, Anthony Grant *psychologist, audiologist, independent scientist*
Gottesman, A(rthur) Edward *lawyer*
Greener, Sir Anthony *computer company executive, director*
Gwynne, Haydn *actress*
Gyllenhammar, Pehr Gustaf *finance company executive, writer, retired automotive executive*
Habgood, Anthony John *corporate executive*
Haitink, Bernard J. H. *conductor*

Hakim, Nadey Subhy *surgeon*
Hall, Lee *playwright, screenwriter*
Hall, Sir Peter Geoffrey *urban and regional planning educator*
Hallissey, Michael *retired management consultant*
Hannah, John *actor*
Harris, Thomas *writer*
Harwood, Ronald *screenwriter, playwright*
Hatley, Tim *set designer, costume designer*
Hegarty, John F., Jr. *advertising executive*
Hicks, Taylor Reuben *singer*
Hinduja, Srichand Parmanand *association executive, hospital administrator*
Hodge, Douglas *actor*
Hunter Blair, Pauline Clarke *author*
Hurt, John Vincent *actor*
Ioannou, Constantinos Elia *accountant*
Irvine, Ian Alexander Noble *media company executive, director*
Ischinger, Wolfgang *ambassador, diplomat*
Ivory, James Francis *film director*
Jacobson, Dan *writer*
James, P(hyllis) D(orothy) (Baroness James of Holland Park of Southwold in County of Suffolk) *author*
Janossy, George *immunologist, educator*
Jeet, Surjit Singh (Surjit Singh) *historian, research scholar*
John, Sir Elton Hercules (Reginald Kenneth Dwight) *musician*
Jourdren, Marc Henri *investment banking company executive*
Kallakis, Ambassador Achilleas Michalis S. (His Excellency Ambassador Achilleas M. Kallakis of the Republic of *transportation executive, real estate company executive*
Kandel, Christopher Nelson *lawyer*
Kapranos, Alexander (Franz Ferdinand) *singer, musician*
Kingsley, Sir Ben *actor*
Kinsella, Sophie (Madeleine Sophie Wickham) *writer*
Knightley, Keira *actress*
Knopfler, Mark *rock guitarist, singer, composer*
Koch, Martin *composer*
Kuper, Adam Jonathan *anthropologist, educator*
Kwei-Armah, Kwame (Ian Roberts) *playwright, actor, singer*
Leaf, Robert Stephen *public relations executive*
LeBaron, Richard B. *ambassador*
Leigh, Mike *film director*
Lessing, Doris (Doris May Tayler) *writer*
Lewis, Leona Louise *singer*
Lindahl, Göran *manufacturing and engineering executive*
Lipworth, Sir (Maurice) Sydney *solicitor, finance company executive*
Litton, Andrew *conductor, music director*
Lloyd Webber, Lord Andrew (Baron of Sydmonton) *composer*
Lowenthal, David *historian, geographer*
Lynch, Gary G. *diversified financial services company executive, lawyer*
MacClean, Walter Lee *dentist*
Maciejowsky, Boris *economist, researcher*
Mackerras, Sir Charles (Alan Maclaurin) *conductor*
Maini, Sir Ravinder Nath *rheumatologist, educator*
Mantegazza, Sergio *finance company executive*
Markoski, Joseph Peter *lawyer*
Martin, Sir George Henry *recording industry executive*
Massenet, Natalie *internet entrepreneur*
Masur, Kurt *conductor, music director*
May, Robert McCredie (Lord May of Oxford) *biology educator*
McAvoy, James Andrew *actor*
McGrath, Patrick *writer*
McGregor, Ewan Gordon *actor*
McKellen, Sir Ian *actor*
McPhee, Katharine Hope *singer*
McShane, Ian *actor*
Mellon, Tamara *apparel executive*
Meyer, Sir Christopher J.R. *former ambassador*
Micklethwait, John *editor-in-chief*
Minnick, Mary E. *investment company executive, former beverage company executive*
Minton, Yvonne Fay *mezzo-soprano*
Montgomery, John Warwick (Baron of Kiltartan and Lord of Morris, Comte de St. Germain de Montgommery) *law educator, theologian*
Moody, Ron *actor, writer*
Mooney, James F. *telecommunications industry executive*
Morris, Desmond (John) *zoologist, writer, artist*
Moss, Kate *model*
Mosselmans, Carel Maurits *investment banker*
Muir-Taylor, Douglas James *ophthalmologist*
Murphy-O'Connor, Cormac Cardinal *cardinal, archbishop*
Nagra, Parminder *actress*
Newell, Mike *film director*
Nighy, Bill Francis *actor*
Okonedo, Sophie *actress*
Oliver, Jamie *chef, television personality*
Oppenheimer, Deanna Watson *bank executive*
Ormsby, Eric Linn *writer, educator*
Page, Jimmy (James Patrick Page) *musician*
Patel, Dev *actor*
Paton Walsh, Jill *writer*
Pattinson, Robert (Robert Thomas-Pattinson) *actor*
Pavlova, Anna *finance educator*
Penny, Nicholas Beaver *museum director*
Pessl, Marisha *writer, artist*
Piot, Peter (Baran) *global health professor*
Plant, Robert Anthony *singer*
Plapinger, William A. *lawyer*
Plowright, Joan Ann *actress*
Portes, Richard David *economics professor*
Powles, Trevor James *physician, oncologist*
Pryce, Jonathan *actor*
Quillen, Cecil Dyer III *lawyer*
Quint, David Paul *investment banking executive*
Radcliffe, Daniel (Daniel Jacob Radcliffe) *actor*
Ralston, Anthony *computer scientist, mathematician, educator*
Rees, David William Alan *engineering educator, researcher, writer*
Reza, Yasmina *author, playwright*
Richardson, Miranda *actress*
Rickman, Alan *actor*
Romano, Fernanda (Fefa Romano) *advertising executive*
Rossi, Paul *publishing executive*
Rowling, J.K. (Joanne Kathleen Rowling) *writer*
Rutter, Michael Llewellyn *child psychology educator*
Sarkis, Ziad Joseph *private equity executive*
Scardino, Dame Marjorie Morris *publishing executive*
Shankar, Ravi *composer, musician*
Sheen, Michael *actor*
Sher, Sir Antony *actor, author, artist*
Sherwood, Michael S. *diversified financial services company executive*
Sillitoe, Alan *writer*
Slootweg, Caroline *marketing executive*
Smith, Dame Maggie (Margaret Natalie Smith Cross) *actress*
Smith, Zadie (Sadie Smith) *writer*
Sorrell, Martin Stuart *advertising and marketing executive*
Spacey, Kevin *actor*
Stelle, Kellogg Sheffield *physicist*
Stevens, Robert Bocking *lawyer*
Stoppard, Tom (Tomas Straussler) *playwright*
Sukawaty, Andrew J. *telecommunications industry executive*
Swarovski, Nadja *apparel designer*
Swinton, Tilda (Katherine Matilda Swinton) *actress*
Townshend, Pete (Peter Dennis Blandford Townshend) *musician, composer*
Uchida, Mitsuko *pianist*
Venzago, Mario *conductor, former music director*
Wainwright, Geoffrey John *archaeologist*
Wallace, Bonnie Ann *biochemist, biophysicist, educator*
Walsh, Paul S. *beverage executive*
Warner, Scott Dennis *investment banker*
Weisz, Rachel *actress*
White, Walter Hiawatha, Jr. *lawyer*
Winner, Michael Robert *film director, producer, writer*
Winters, William Thomas (Bill Winters) *diversified financial services company executive*
Wyn-Jones, Alun (William Wyn-Jones) *software developer, mathematician*
Zennström, Niklas *Internet company executive, entrepreneur*
Zonana, Victor *lawyer, educator*

Lymington
Martin, Giles *recording industry executive*

Macclesfield
Lovell, Sir (Alfred Charles) Bernard *astronomer, educator*

Malton
Habgood, John Stapylton *archbishop*

Marlow
Le Blanc, Bart *banker*

Middlesex
Bonfield, Sir Peter Leahy *international business executive*

Milton Keynes
Gourley, Brenda *educational institution administrator*

Newcastle
De Jong, Nanette *musicologist, educator*

Newton Abbot
Baker, James Barnes *architect*

Norfolk
Roberts, Sir Denys (Tudor Emil) *judge*

North Wales
Hands, Terence David (Terry) *theater and opera director*

Oxford
Bell Burnell, S(usan) Jocelyn *astrophysicist, physics professor*
Bodmer, Sir Walter Fred *cancer research administrator*
Dewey, John Frederick *geologist, educator*
Down, William John Denbigh *bishop*
Hanson, Sir John Gilbert *academic administrator*
Hirsch, Sir Peter Bernhard *metallurgist*
Johnson, Louise Napier *molecular biophysicist, educator*
Krebs, John Richard *zoologist, science administrator*
Morpurgo Davies, Anna Elbina *philologist, educator*
Nasmyth, Kim *science association director*
North, Peter Machin *academic administrator, barrister*
Peto, Sir Richard *medical researcher*
Raz, Joseph *philosophy and law educator*
Shaw, Dennis Frederick *former library director, chartered physicist, consultant*
Thomas, Keith Vivian *historian, former college president*
Vaisey, David George *librarian, archivist*
Varese, Federico *sociology professor*

Plymouth
Totterdell, Michael Standforth *education educator, researcher*

Redhill
Donaldson, David *pathologist*

Richmond
Armfield, Diana Maxwell *artist, educator*

Roecliffe
Hilsum, Cyril *physicist*

Saint Ives
Biggs, Peter Martin *veterinary scientist, virologist*

Salford
Madan, Vishal *dermatologist*

Southampton
Brebbia, Carlos Alberto *engineering educator, consultant*
Morton, Newton Ennis *human geneticist*

Stevenage
Follett, Kenneth Martin *author*

Stroud
Robinson, John Beckwith *development management consultant*

Sturminster Newton
Seaford, John Nicholas *clergyman, retired dean*

Sunderland
Puttnam, Lord David Terence *film producer*

Surrey
Holm, Sir Ian *actor*
Immelman, Trevor *professional golfer*
Karlsson, Robert *professional golfer*
Naldrett, Anthony James *geology educator*
Weston, Sir John (Sir Philip John Weston) *retired diplomat*

Sutton Bonington
Campbell, Keith H. S. *cell biologist, embryologist, educator*

Temple
Bingham, Thomas Henry (Lord Bingham of Cornhill) *judge*

Uxbridge
Dere, Willard Honglen *medical products executive*

Whitchurch
Adams, Richard George *writer*

Wigan
Talapatra, Indrajit *endocrinologist*

Wiltshire
Dyson, Sir James *manufacturing executive, inventor*
Stern, Claudio Daniel *medical educator, embryological researcher*

ESTONIA

Tallinn
Köörna, Arno *economist, educator*
Lippmaa, Endel *science educator, researcher*

Tartu
Eeber, Ludmilla *acquisition librarian*
Voznesensky, Nikolay Boris *mechanical engineering educator*

ETHIOPIA

Addis Ababa
Simon, John Andrew *United States Ambassador to the African Union*
Wolde Giorgis, Girma *President of Ethiopia*

FIJI

Suva
Rabuka, Sitiveni Ligamamada *Fijian government official, army officer*

FINLAND

Espoo
Watson, Gregory Harriss *consulting company executive*

Helsinki
Ilus, Erkki Hannu *marine biologist, researcher*
Langbacka, Ralf Runar *theater director, educator*
Liewendahl, Bo Kristian *retired pathologist, nuclear medicine physician*
Ollila, Jorma Jaakko *telecommunications industry executive*

Jyväskylä
Lartillot, Olivier *computer scientist, educator, researcher*

Raisio
Haavisto, Heikki Johannes *retired Finnish government official*

Tampere
Salonen, Pekka Olavi *electrical engineer*

Turku
Granö, Olavi Johannes *geography educator*

FRANCE

Amiens
Barpanda, Prabeer *researcher*

Aubagne
Chermann, Jean Claude *virologist, researcher*

Bages
Kitzinger, Uwe *college president*

Bayon
Cochran, John M. III *lawyer*

Besancon
Boillat, Guy Maurice Georges *mathematical physicist*

Blagnac
Joye, Jacky *flight test engineer*

Chatenay-Malabry
Evesque, Pierre Henri *physics researcher*

Chevilly Larue
Chenay, Christian Jean-Marie *biomedical engineer*

Clichy
Attal, Laurent *cosmetics executive*

Compiegne
Dubuisson, Bernard Louis *science educator, administrator*

Creteil
Renoux, André *retired physicist researcher*

Dissay
Marchessou, Helene Daisy *English and American literature educator*

Ecully
Comte-Bellot, Genevieve Marie *engineering educator*

Fontainebleau
Hawawini, Gabriel Alfred *finance educator, former dean*

Fontenay-aux-Roses
Dauguet, Julien Charles *computational biomedicine researcher, educator*

Fontenay-sous-Bois
Doucas, Vassilis *biologist, researcher*

Gif-sur-Yvette
Cesarsky, Catherine *astrophysicist*
Duplessy, Jean Claude *research scientist*
Le Bihan, Denis *radiologist*
Rho, Mannque *theoretical physicist, researcher*

Guyancourt
Criqui, Bernard Claude *materials processes engineer, researcher*

Hénin Beaumont
Fournier, Eric *internist, pulmonologist*

Illkirch-Graffenstaden
Simpson, Michael Kevin *academic administrator, political science professor*

Issy Les Moulineaux
Pouzilhac, Alain Duplessis de *advertising executive*

La Fossette
Barnes, Wallace Ray *retired lawyer*

La Tour d Aigues
Xingjian, Gao *writer*

Lacoste
Strauss, Gwen B. *writer, editor*

Le Chillou
Gourvest, Alain *retired finance educator*

Le Vesinet
Fourt, Bernard-Francois P. *retired engineer*
Hillion, Pierre Théodore Marie *mathematical physicist*

Levallois-Perret
Filipacchi, Daniel *publishing executive*

Limoges
Menier, Robert Joseph *physiologist*

Lyon
Gardner, David *electronics executive*

Lys-Lez-Lannoy
Ledoux, Jean-Marie *veterinarian*

Malaucene Vaucluse
Langenkamp, Mary Alice (M.A. Langenkamp) *artist, educator*

Marseille
Boutterin, Emmanuel *public relations executive*

Morlaix
Baillet, Gilles Pierre *orthodontist*

Mulhouse
Donnet, Jean Baptiste *physical chemist, educator, consultant*

Neuilly-sur-Seine
de Homem-Christo, Guy-Manuel *musician*

Nozay
Betgé-Brezetz, Stéphane *computer scientist, researcher*

Orleans
Price, David Cecil Long *physicist, researcher*

Orsay
Friedel, Jacques *retired physics professor*

Palaiseau
Basdevant, Jean-Louis Henri *physicist, researcher*

Paris
Alaïa, Azzedine *fashion designer*
Allais, Maurice Felix *economist*
Arnault, Bernard Jean Etienne *consumer products company executive*
Askey, Thelma J. *international organization official, former federal agency administrator*
Baum, Axel Helmuth *lawyer*
Beffa, Jean-Louis Guy Henri *manufacturing executive*
Bensimon, Aaron *biotechnology company executive*
Blokh, Alexandre (Jean Blot) *writer*
Cagle, William Rae *retired librarian*
Cardin, Pierre *fashion designer*
Cariddi, Alan Francis *lawyer*
Carlier, Bertrand *nuclear engineer*
Cherkaoui, Mohamed *sociologist*
Chiquet, Maureen *consumer products company executive*
Choay, Patrick Henri *pharmaceutical executive*
Cohen-Tannoudji, Claude Nessim *physics professor*
Cotillard, Marion *actress*
Courtois, Jean-Philippe *computer software company executive*
Crawford, John Fort *lawyer*
Dassault, Serge *media and software company and air transportation executive, French senator*
de Havilland, Olivia Mary *actress*
de Menil, Georges *economist, educator*
Deneuve, Catherine (Catherine Dorleac) *actress*
De-Thé, Guy Blaudin *research scientist, educator*
Egan, Christopher F. *United States Ambassador to the Organization for Economic Cooperation & Development*
Elbaz, Alber *apparel designer*
Fitoussi, Jean-Paul Samuel *economics professor*
Gaultier, Jean-Paul *fashion designer*
Jacob, François *biologist, educator*
Jeantelot, Charles Marcel Jean *retired French diplomat*
Jolas, Betsy *composer, educator*
Jones, Richard Henry *international organization official, retired ambassador*
Kouchner, Bernard *French government official, humanitarian*
Kourilsky, François Michel *research scientist*
Kouymjian, Dickran *art historian, educator*
Lacroix, Christian Marie Marc *fashion designer*
Lagarde, Christine *French government official, lawyer*
Lagardere, Arnaud *media company executive*
Lagerfeld, Karl Otto *fashion designer*
Lahrs, Claus-Dietrich *apparel executive*
Lehalle, Charles-Albert *mathematician*
Le Roy Ladurie, Emmanuel Bernard *historian, educator*
Louvard, Daniel François *cell biologist, researcher*
Marcus, Claude *advertising executive*
Mercadal, Lucile *nephrologist*
Montagnier, Luc Antoine *virologist*
Myerson, Jacob Myer *retired diplomat*
Nehmé, Paul J. *beverage company executive*
Oliver, Louise V. *United States Ambassador to UNESCO*
Payri, Joel *pharmaceutical marketing executive*
Pecker, Jean-Claude *astronomer, educator, author*
Peugeot, Patrick *insurance executive*
Piano, Renzo *architect*
Piza, Arthur Luiz *painter*
Poloujadoff, Michel Eugene *electrical engineering educator*
Raharinaivo, André Léon *research scientist, educator*
Raimondi, Ruggero *opera singer*
Rappeneau, Jean-Paul *film director, scriptwriter*
Redburn, Tom *editor*
Renouf, Edda *artist*
Ricol, Rene Jean *accountant*
Rocard, Michel Louis Léon *French politician*
Ross, Charles *artist*
Roussely, Francois *electric power industry executive*
Salans, Carl Fredric *lawyer*
Schiray, Michel *economist, research scientist, consultant*
Schmemann, Serge *journalist*
Serre, Jean-Pierre *mathematician, scholar*
Sulkowski, Hubertus Victor *lawyer*
Terry, Sara *photographer, reporter*
Todorov, Tzvetan *scientific researcher*
Tribouillard, Daniel Jean Louis *fashion executive*
Tufano, Paul J. *telecommunications industry executive*
Vandame, Jean-Marie Richard *financial professional services firm executive*
Weymuller, Bruno *oil and gas industry executive*
Yuechiming, Roger Yue Yuen Shing *mathematics professor*

Poitiers
Giraud, René Ernest *academic administrator, economist, educator*

Port-Fréjus
Crapon de Caprona, Count Noël François Marie *retired senior United Nations official*

Rocquencourt
Jacquet, Philippe Pierre *research scientist, educator*

Roissy
Spinetta, Jean-Cyril *airline executive*

Roques
White, Norval Crawford *architect*

Saint Ceols
Saisselin, Remy Gilbert *fine arts educator*

Saint Cloud
Atassi, Ghanem *retired oncologist*
Perrier, Piérre Claude *aeronautical engineer, researcher*

Saint Etienne
Vergnaud, Jean-Maurice *science educator, researcher*

Saint Maur des Fosses
Heggy, Essam *planetary scientist*

Saint-Cyr-sous
Aubry, Cecile (Anne-José Bénard) *writer*

Strasbourg
Elkomoss, Sabry Gobran *retired physicist*
Ungerer, Jean Thomas (Tomi Ungerer) *writer, artist*
van Regenmortel, Marc Hubert Victor *virologist, educator, director*

Suresnes
Monnet, Jacques Charles Louis *automotive executive*

Toulouse
Sarramon, Jean-Pierre Fernand Louis *urologist, educator*

Tours
Barthelemy, Jean-Paul Francois *orthopedic surgeon*

Valbonne
Junker, Ulrich Martin *computer scientist, researcher*

Vandoeuvre-les-Nancy
Blazy, Pierre François *science educator, consulting metallurgist*

Villefranche-sur-Mer
Legendre, Louis *oceanographer, educator, research scientist*

Villeurbanne
Legendre, Serge *paleontologist, researcher*

GEORGIA

Covington
Zha, Shitong *research scientist*

Tbilisi
Gamkrelidze, Thomas Valerian *linguist, educator*

GERMANY

APO
Adams, Julian Timothy *psychologist*

Aachen
Pischinger, Franz Felix *engineer, researcher, educator*

Alstadt
Richter, Gerhard *artist*

Bad Homburg
Klatten, Susanne Quandt *pharmaceutical executive*

Bad Nauheim
Engel, Felix Benedikt Salomon *cell biologist, researcher*

Berlin
Barenboim, Daniel *conductor, pianist, music director*
Eichler, Hans Joachim *physics professor*
Ertl, Gerhard *retired institute director*
Holzmann, Ruth Dorothee *dermatologist*
Inbal, Eliahu *conductor*
Jahnke, Kristoph *internist, hematologist, oncologist, researcher*
Jochmann, Frank *mathematician*
Jung, Dieter *multimedia artist*
Kocka, Juergen *history professor*
Loboda-Cackovic, Jasna *physicist, artist, sculptor, painter, research scientist*
Piper, Adrian Margaret Smith *philosopher, artist, educator*
Schlink, Bernhard *law educator, writer*
Spur, Günter *engineering educator*
Stabreit, Immo Friedrich Helmut *diplomat*
Tsatsaronis, George *mechanical engineering educator, researcher*

Bielefeld
Brock, Norbert *retired pharmacologist*
Roeckner, Michael G. *mathematics professor*

Bonn
Albach, Horst *economist*
Korte, Bernhard Hermann *mathematician, researcher*
Rampacher, Hermann Hans *writer, consultant*

Braunschweig
Leseberg, Dieter Wolfgang Michael *mathematician*

Bremen
Bathrick, David *foreign language educator, academic administrator*
Fahle, Manfred *ophthalmology researcher*
Wells, Raymond O'Neil, Jr. *mathematics professor, researcher*

Cologne
Meisner, Joachim Cardinal *cardinal, archbishop*
Thiede, Walther *research scientist, consultant, writer*
Tomaszewski, Christian *artist*

Damsatadt
McChrystal, Stanley A. *career military officer*
McKiernan, David D. *retired military officer*
Rodriguez, David M. *career military officer*

Drolshagen
Arend, Peter *retired biologist, physician, allergist, lab administrator*

Duedenbuettel
Pfennigstorf, Werner *lawyer*

Duisburg
Kumm, Dietmar Alfred *orthopedist, consultant, surgeon*

Düsseldorf
Bove, Carol *sculptor*
Schulz, Ekkehard D. *metal products executive*

Essen
Soltesz, Stefan *conductor*

Frankfurt
Bader, W(illiam) Reece *lawyer*
Greiner, Walter Albin Erhard *physicist*
Herold, Karl Guenter *lawyer, consultant*
Leckey, Mark *artist*
Maucher, Helmut Oswald *food products executive*
Simitis, Spiros *legal educator*

Freiberg
Van Calker, Dietrich O. *psychiatrist, educator*
Zabecki, David Tadeusz *engineer, educator, military historian, military officer*

Fulda
Beckman, James Wallace Bim *management consultant, educator*

Furth im Wald
Rau, Magda *ophthalmologist*

Garching bei Muenchen
Van Hemmen, J. Leo *physics professor, researcher*

Göttingen
Oellerich, Michael *clinical chemistry professor, chemical pathologist*
Roesky, Herbert Walter *chemistry professor*
Starck, Christian Walter *law educator*
Toennies, Jan Peter *research chemical physicist*

Halle
Parthier, Benno *biologist*
Schmoll, Hans Joachim *hematology and oncology educator*

Hamburg
Ayvazyan, Valeri *computer scientist, researcher, physicist, consultant*
Lüst, Reimar *foundation president*
Neumeier, John *choreographer, ballet company director*
Pawlik, Kurt F. *psychologist, social science educator*
Schaper, Herbert Walter August *retired chemist, researcher*

Hanau
Rink, Thomas *nuclear medicine physician*

Hannover
Allen, Bruce *physicist*

Heidelberg
Lyko, Frank *molecular biologist*

Herzogenaurach
Schaeffler, Maria-Elisabeth *manufacturing executive, small business owner*

Hessen
Teichler, Ulrich Christian *higher education educator, researcher*

Holzkirchen
George, Jeff *pharmaceutical executive*

Jülich
Grünberg, Peter Andreas *materials scientist*

Koln
Lee, Catherine *sculptor, painter*

Kunzelsau
Würth, Reinhold *manufacturing executive*

Leipzig
Pääbo, Svante *molecular biologist, biochemist*

Ludwigshafen
Strube, Juergen F. *chemical company executive*

Lübeck
Fligge, Jörg *librarian, library director*

Mainz
Binder, Kurt *physics professor*

Mannheim
Isaak, Robert Allen *international management and political economy educator, writer*

Mayen
Gartz, Rolf F. *foundation administrator*

Meerbusch
Schulze, Juergen Helmut *engineering executive*

Munich
Araiza, Francisco (José Francisco Araiza Andrade) *opera singer*
Heinzl, Joachim Lothar *engineering educator*
Heywang-Koebrunner, Sylvia H. *radiologist, educator*
Langenscheidt, Florian *publisher*
Schmidt, Stefan *mechanical engineer, economist*
Schwarz, Markus J. *psychoneuroimmunologist, neurochemist*

Münster
Spevack, Marvin *language educator*

Neu Isenburg
Hoare-Temple, Piers Howard *building maintenance executive*

Nuremberg
Doerries, Reinhard René *historian, educator*

Obernzell-Erlau
Kunze, Reiner Alexander *writer, poet*

Oststeinbek
Willamowski, Michael *academic librarian*

Ottilienstr
Clarke, Ingrid Gadway *retired academic ombudsman, consultant*

Potsdam
Flick, Friedrich Christian *art collector*

Regensburg
Eisenmann-Klein, Marita *plastic surgeon*
Stetter, Karl Otto *microbiologist, educator*

Rostock
Vaupel, James W. *demographer*

Rüsselheim
Demant, Hans Henrich *automotive executive*

Saarbruecken
Zhukovsky, Mikhail Andreyevich *biophysicist*

Schleusingen-Gethles
Frank, Dieter *retired chemicals executive*

Seeheim-Jugenheim
Halama, Niels *physician, researcher*

St Augustin
Feldkämper, Ludger Bernhard *religious organization administrator*

Starnberg
Huber, Franz *retired research director*

Stutensee
Barbian, Otto Alfred *physicist*

Stuttgart
Anderson, Reid Bryce *performing company executive*
Cardona, Manuel *physics professor*
Geh, Hans-Peter *retired library director, consultant*
Ward, William E. (Kip Ward) *career military officer*
Warnecke, Hans-Jürgen *retired engineering educator*
Yates, Mary Carlin *diplomat*
Zakim, David *biochemist*
Zetsche, Dieter *automotive executive*

Taunusstein
Ruppert (Metzger), Thomas Erich *cell and molecular biologist, quality assurance and regulatory professional*

Tübingen
Küng, Hans *theologian, educator*
Nüsslein-Volhard, Christiane *medical researcher*

Vaihingen
Stavridis, Jim (James George Stavridis) *career military officer*

Witten
Gaengler, Peter Wolfgang *dentist, researcher*

Worms
Elkins, Tabitha M. *music educator, composer, jazz singer, pianist, writer*

Wuppertal
Schubert, Guenther Erich *pathologist*

Wyk-Wrixum
Friese, Brigitte *federal agency administrator*

Würzburg
Keil, Gundolf *medical historian*
Manara, Jochen Walter *physicist, researcher*

GHANA

Accra
Jones, Monty P. *science administrator*

Kumasi
Jafar, Muhammad Mamun *non governmental organization executive*

GREECE

Athens
Angelopoulos-Daskalaki, Gianna *lawyer, ambassador, former International Olympic Committee Executive*

Boudoulas, Harisios *cardiologist, researcher, medical educator*
Brilakis, Harry Stylianos (Harilaos Stylianos Brilakis) *ophthalmologist*
Brissimis, Sophocles Nicholas *economist*
Floratos, Emmanuel *physicist, educator*
Kalamotousakis, George John *economist, merchant banker, educator*
Kerameus, Konstantinos D. *law educator, legal consultant*
Lapatsanis, Petros Dimitris *pediatrician*
Larounis, George Philip *manufacturing executive, director*
Meletiadis, Joseph *microbiologist, educator*
Miliotis, Demitrios *physics professor*
Papadakis, Panagiotis Agamemnon *corporate financial executive*
Papoulias, Karolos *President of the Republic of Greece*
Tsalamata, Vicky Dimitrios *artist, educator, painter, printmaker*
Tzannetakis, Tzannis *Greek government official*
Zevgolis, Ioannis *geotechnical engineer, researcher*

Chania
Karystinos, George N. *engineering educator*
Lagoudakis, Michail G. *engineering educator*

Larissa
Zacharoulis, Dimitris *surgeon, researcher*

Marousi
Joannou, Dakis *businessman*

Piraeus
Papachristou, Costas John *physicist, researcher*

Ptolemaida
Tsachouridis, Vassilios A. *electrical and control engineer, researcher*

Thessaloniki
Baloyannis, Stavros Joannis *neurologist, educator, researcher*
Rodopoulos, Panteleimon Evaggelos *clergyman*

GRENADA

Saint Georges
Forde, Martin S. *science educator*

GUANA ISLAND

Barrigada
Perez, Annie Rivera *elementary school educator*

GUATEMALA

Antigua
Rodgers, Frank *librarian*

Guatemala City
Mayora, Eduardo A. *lawyer, educator, author*
Mishaan, Emilio *transplant surgeon, educator*

HONDURAS

Comayaga
Scarpone Caporale, Gerald D. Joseph *bishop emeritus*

HONG KONG

Central
Arculli, Ronald Joseph *Hong Kong government official*
Evans, J. Michael *diversified financial services company executive*
Roach, Stephen S. *diversified financial services company executive*
Roppel, Mark *lawyer*
Wen, Carson *lawyer, legislator*

Happy Valley
Onne, Madeleine *performing company executive, dancer*

Ho Man Tin
Leong, John Chi-Yan *academic administrator, orthopaedic surgeon, educator*

Hong Kong
Leung, Ka-Cheong *engineering educator*
Tsui, Lap-Chee *academic administrator, molecular genetics educator*
Wong, Joseph Wing Ping *Hong Kong government official*
Wong, Richard Yue-Chim *academic administrator, economics professor*

Hong Kong Island
Zen Ze-kiun, Joseph Cardinal *cardinal, bishop*

Kowloon
de Waart, Edo *conductor, music director*
Liu, Hugh *engineering company executive, electronics engineer*
Ma, Bianca Kin-san *broadcast executive*
Woo, Chia-Wei *physicist, educator*

Kwun Tong
Tunkey, James Peter *security firm executive*

North Point
Apcar, Leonard M. *editor*
Chung, Chi Yung *college administrator*
Lee, Shau Kee *real estate developer*

Pokfulam
Gould, Gaye *linguist, educator*

Shatin
Ding, Quan Long *research and development company executive*
Lee, Wendy Wan-Ki *music professor*
Mirrlees, Sir James Alexander *economics professor*

Wanchai
Fung, Daniel R. (Daniel Wah-kin Fung) *lawyer, broadcasting agency administrator*
Suen, Stephen *investment company executive*
Wong, Albert Wing Kuen *finance educator*
Chai, Nelson J. *bank executive, former stock exchange executive*
Thomas, Owen D. *diversified financial services company executive*

HUNGARY

Budapest
Horn, Gyula *former Prime Minister of Hungary*
Karpati, Attila *engineering educator, consultant, research scientist*
Meszaros, Milan *astrophysicist*
Michelberger, Pal *mechanical engineer, educator*
Pal, Lenard *physicist*
Pungor, Ernö *chemist, educator*
Shattuck, John *foundation administrator, former ambassador*
Szigeti, János *physicist*
Teplán, István, Sr. *biochemist, researcher*

Debrecen
Csikai, Gyula *physicist, researcher*

Sopron
Sitkei, György *engineer, educator*

Szeged
Keszthelyi, Lajos *science educator*

ICELAND

Mos
Hannibalsson, Jon Baldvin *Icelandic ambassador, politician*

Reykjavik
Gunnarsson, Birgir Isleifur *bank executive, legislator*
Oddsson, David *former Prime Minister of Iceland, bank executive*
Wallevik, Jon Elvar *engineer, researcher*

INDIA

Ajmer
Menezes, Ignatius *bishop*

Alleppey
Chenaparampil, Peter Michael *bishop*

Assam
Menamparampil, Thomas S.D.B. *archbishop*

Bangalore
Kulkarni, Rahul Ravindra *research scientist*
Rajuk, Venugopal Kuppanna *computer engineer, educator*
Rao, Ramachandra U. *aerospace scientist*

Bombay
Pimenta, Simon Ignatius Cardinal *cardinal, archbishop emeritus*

Burdwan
Bandyopadhyay, Ranjan *sociology educator*

Chandigarh
Chhabra, Tarlok Singh *advertising executive*

Chennai
Punnoose, A. John *hospital administrator*

Haryana
Katariya, Kushagra *cardiothoracic surgeon, educator, healthcare developer, stratigist*

Hyderabad
Gummaraju, Srinivas Chakravarthy *oncologist, hematologist*
Raychowdhury, Subhendu *research scientist*

Kanpur
Joglekar, Satish Dinkar *physicist, educator*

Karnal
Dhanker, Sultan Singh *agriculturist, researcher*

Kerala
Vithayathil, Varkey Cardinal *cardinal, archbishop*

Kolkata
Kothari, Hemraj *mechanical engineer, management consultant*
Moideen, Rafeeq *dermatologist, consultant*
Patra, Amlan Kumar *animal scientist, educator*

Kurnool
Teegala, Brahmananda Reddy *electrical engineer, educator*

Manipal
Pai, Satish Upendra *publishing executive*

Mumbai
Sen, Pranab *computer scientist, researcher*

New Delhi
Bagla, Pallava *journalist, photographer*
Dikshit, Sheila *state official*
Kaushal, Radhey Shyam *theoretical physicist, researcher*
Kumar, Virender *weed scientist*
Machan, Polly Joseph *hotel manager*
Mitra, Asoke Nath *retired physicist, educator*
Pandey, Girdhar Kumar *molecular biologist*
Plianbangchang, Samlee *world organization administrator*
Podewils, Ulrich *academic administrator*
Singh, Kushal Pal (K.P.) *real estate developer*
Srivastava, Radhey Shyam *research scientist*
Tripathy, Baishnab C. *science educator*

Noida
Jain, Prem Chand *mechanical engineer*
Mitra, Raja *electronics engineer*

Pune
Abhyankar, Aditya *dean, director*

Secunderabad
Velamakanni, Gopala Krishna *geophysicist, seismologist, researcher*

Trivandrum
Valiathan, Marthanda Varma Sankaran *cardiac surgeon*

INDONESIA

Jakarta
Darmaatmadja, Julius Riyadi Cardinal *cardinal, archbishop*
Hsi, Edward Yang *lawyer, venture capitalist, industrialist*
Mulhadiono, Yoga Pratomo *petroleum geologist, consultant*
Tilaar, Henry A.R. *social sciences educator*

Manado
Sarundajang, Sinyo Harry *government official*

IRAN

Shiraz
Ahmadizadeh, Mehdi *engineering educator, consultant*

IRELAND

Cork
Lyons, Nona Mary *adult education educator*

Derry
Hume, John *retired politician of Northern Ireland*

Donegal
Friel, Brian (Bernard Patrick Friel) *author*

Dublin
Ahern, Dermot *Irish government official*
Cotter, John *finance educator*
Downes, Paul Edward *psychology lecturer, research consultant*
Farrell, Colin James *actor*
Fottrell, Patrick *biochemistry professor, former university president*
McDaid, Jim *government official*
Murray, John Loyola *judge*
Sheridan, Jim *film director, screenwriter*

Galway
Hynes, Garry *theater director*

Mullingar
Donleavy, James Patrick *writer, artist*

ISRAEL

Arad
Hollander, Samuel *economist, educator*

Be'er Sheva
Brosilow, Coleman Bernard *chemical engineering educator*
Frenkel, David Arie *law professor*
Glick, Shimon Michael *medical educator*
Oz, Amos (Amos Klausner) *writer, educator*

Givat Brener
Tritter, Richard Paul *strategic consultant*

Haifa
Ciechanover, Aaron Judah *biochemist, educator*

Jerusalem
Cole, Peter *poet, translator*
Hazboun, Viveca *psychiatrist*
Hrushovski, Ehud *mathematics professor*
Lehman, Meir (Manny Lehman) *computer scientist, software engineer, consultant*
Menses, Jan *artist, draftsman, muralist*
Merrick, Joav *pediatrician, government agency administrator, researcher*
Page, Ernest *retired medical educator*
Peres, Shimon *President of Israel*

Maale Efraim
Gur, Itzhak *physician, researcher*

Netanya
Tsitverblit, Naftali Anatol *physicist, fluid mechanics engineer, researcher*

Ra'anana
Hayon, Elie M. *chemist, educator*

Rehovot
Arnon, Ruth *immunologist, educator, researcher*
Katchalski-Katzir, Ephraim *biophysicist, educator*
Sachs, Leo *geneticist, educator*
Sela, Michael *immunologist, chemist*

Savyon
Bushinsky, Jay (Joseph Mason) *journalist, news correspondent*

Tel Aviv
Dekel-Tabak, Eddie *economics educator*
Naharin, Ohad *choreographer, performing company executive*

ITALY

Bergamo
Donizetti, Mario *painter, essayist*

Bologna
Biffi, Giacomo Cardinal *cardinal, archbishop emeritus*
Caffarra, Carlo Cardinal *cardinal, archbishop*
Giacomelli, Giorgio Maria *emeritus physics professor*
Venturi, Margherita *chemistry professor, researcher*

Capranica VT
Liberati, Emilio *psychology doctor, sociologist, consultant*

Ciserano di Zingonia
Vieri, Christian *professional soccer player*

Citta del Vaticao
Harvey, James Michael *archbishop*

Civitanova Marche
Rogante, Massimo *nuclear scientist, researcher*

Como
Casati, Giulio *theoretical physics professor*

Cremia
Malipiero, Victoria Schneider *opera singer*

Firenze
Santiago, Claudi *manufacturing executive*

Florence
Blondel, Jean Fernand *political science educator*
Cecil, Charles Harkless *artist, educator*
Giannini, Frida *apparel designer*
Nicolodi, Maria *neuropharmacologist, medical researcher*
Olschki, Alessandro *book publishing executive*

Genoa
Canestri, Giovanni Cardinal *cardinal, archbishop emeritus*
Morchio, Renzo Giulio *retired biophysicist, researcher, educator*

Mestre
Maguire, Janet *composer*

Milan
Berlusconi, Marina *publishing executive*
Bisiachi, Irene Maria Giulia *press office consultant*
Calasso, Roberto *writer, publisher*
Cavalli, Roberto *fashion designer*
Del Vecchio, Leonardo *manufacturing executive*
Dolce, Domenico *fashion designer*
Gabbana, Stefano *fashion designer*
Goldwurm, Gian Franco *psychiatrist, psychologist, psychotherapist*
Honegger, Federico *artist*
Prada, Miuccia Bianca *fashion designer*
Ronaldinho, (Ronaldo de Assis Moreira) *professional soccer player*
Tonon, Giovanni *medical researcher*
Versace, Donatella *fashion designer*
Zambelli, Angelo *lawyer*
Zara, Claudio *finance educator, management consultant*

Monza
Lanzetta, Marco *hand surgeon, microsurgeon*

Naples
Giordano, Michele Cardinal *cardinal, archbishop*

Padua
Beatrice, Pier Franco *humanities educator*
Grossi, Francis Xavier, Jr. *lawyer, educator*
Piccoli, Giuliano *paleontologist, educator*
Shea, William Rene *historian, history and philosophy professor*

Palermo
Fiumara, Ettore *neurosurgeon*

Pavia
Rubbia, Carlo *physicist*

Pisa
Mannelli, Italo Marcello *physics professor*
Most, Glenn Warren *classics professor*

Povo
Palpanas, Themis *engineering educator, consultant*

Ravenna
Conti, Matteo Coker *biochemist, researcher*

Rieti
Truini Palomba, Maria Giuseppina *supreme court lawyer, judge*

Rimini
Mazza, Domenico *orthodontist*

Rome
Angelini, Fiorenzo Cardinal *cardinal, archbishop emeritus*
Antonelli, Ennio Cardinal *cardinal, archbishop*
Baum, William Wakefield Cardinal *cardinal, archbishop emeritus*
Benedict XVI, His Holiness Pope (Joseph Alois Ratzinger) *Pope of the Roman Catholic Church, Bishop of Rome*
Berlusconi, Silvio *Prime Minister of Italy, professional sports team executive*
Bile, Franco *judge*
Brachetti Peretti, Aldo Maria *gas industry executive*
Burke, Raymond Leo *archbishop*
Celant, Attilio *economic geographer, educator*
Cordero Lanza di Montezemolo, Andrea Cardinal *cardinal, archbishop*
Di Noia, Joseph Augustine *archbishop, theologian*
Etchegaray, Roger Marie Élie Cardinal *cardinal, archbishop*
Flood, Gregory Charles *human resources management specialist retired*
Foley, John Patrick Cardinal *cardinal, archbishop*
Gros-Pietro, Gian Maria *economics professor*
Guarguaglini, Pier Francesco *aerospace transportation executive*
Herranz Casado, Julián Cardinal *cardinal, archbishop*
Kasper, Walter Cardinal *cardinal, archbishop*
Khamzayev, Almaz N. *ambassador*
Levada, William Joseph Cardinal *cardinal, archbishop emeritus*
Levi-Montalcini, Rita *neurobiologist, researcher*
Maraviglia, Bruno *physicist, researcher*
McGurn, William Barrett III *lawyer*
Poli, Roberto *oil industry executive*
Poupard, Paul Cardinal *cardinal, archbishop*
Salvini, Giorgio *physicist, researcher*
Sanchez, Jose Tomas Cardinal *cardinal, archbishop*
Scognamiglio Pasini, Carlo *economics and finance professor, former senator, defense minister*
Shiner, Josette Sheeran (Josette Sheeran) *international organization official, former federal agency administrator*
Sisulu, Sheila Violet Makate *international organization official, diplomat*
Stigliano, Jose Maria *information technology executive, computer scientist*
Szoka, Edmund Casimir Cardinal *cardinal, archbishop*
Vasquez, Gaddi H. *United States Ambassador to the United Nations, Rome*
Vento, Sergio *former ambassador*
Westley, John Richard *economist*
Zeffirelli, Franco *theater and film director*

Siena
Tiezzi, Enzo *physical chemistry educator*

Trieste
Rao, Chintamani Nagesa Ramachandra *science educator, Indian government official, academic administrator*

Turin
Bouchard, Giorgio *minister, religious organization administrator*
Challet, Damien Cyrille *physicist, researcher*
Elia, Michele *mathematics professor*
Rizzi, Gianfranco *artist*
Rossi, Guido A(ntonio) *mathematics professor, researcher*

Vatican City
Deskur, Andrzej Maria Cardinal *cardinal, archbishop*
Dias, Ivan Cardinal *archbishop, cardinal*
Martinez Somalo, Eduardo Cardinal *cardinal, archbishop*
Martino, Renato Raffaele Cardinal *cardinal, archbishop, diplomat*
Mejia, Jorge Maria Cardinal *cardinal, archbishop*
Noe, Virgilio Cardinal *cardinal, archbishop*
Schleck, Charles Asa *archbishop emeritus*
Stafford, James Francis Cardinal *cardinal, archbishop*

Venice
Pasinetti, Pier Maria *author*
Tagliapietra, Lino *glass artist*

Verona
Pozzo, Riccardo *philosophy educator*

JAPAN

Agatsuma
Kozai, Yoshihide *astronomer*

Aichi
Hachisuka, Keisuke *mechanical engineer, researcher*
Kato, Nobuo *bacteriology educator*
Okazaki, Masaharu *chemist*
Toyoda, Shuhei *automotive executive*

Aizu-Wakamatsu
Watanabe, Shigeru *mathematician, researcher*

Ashikaga
Ando, Yasutaka *materials scientist, researcher*

Bunkyo
Kasagi, Nobuhide *mechanical engineering educator*
Mori, Kenji *chemistry professor*
Shirayanagi, Peter Seiichi Cardinal Seiichi *cardinal, archbishop*

Chiba
Arai, Toshihiko *retired microbiology and immunology educator*
Hattori, Naozo *science educator*
Matsuda, Masafumi *research scientist, educator*
Suzuki, Makoto *thoracic surgeon*
Valentine, Bobby (Robert John Valentine) *professional baseball manager*

Chigasaki
Hirota, Sadao *engineering educator, researcher*

Fukui
Taniguchi, Keiji *engineering educator*

Fukuoka
Ishibashi, Akira *mechanical engineer, educator*
Kajiyama, Tisato *academic administrator, materials physics and chemistry educator*

Futtsu
Fujisaki, Keisuke *electrical researcher*

Gifu
Hatada, Kazuyuki *mathematician, educator*

Gunma
Hironaka, Heisuke *mathematics professor, academic administrator*

Gyoda
Shibasaki, Yoshio *chemistry professor, researcher*

Hamamatsu
Kaneko, Masao *radiology educator, researcher, specialist*
Suzuki, Osamu *automotive executive*

Hirakata
Shigemitsu, Toshiro *ophthalmologist, researcher*

Hiratsuka
Ayano, Katsutoshi *management educator*

Hirosaki
Fukui, Atsushi *gynecologist, immunologist, physician*
Sakai, Takehiro *surgeon*
Sato, Hiroyuki *materials engineer, researcher*

Hokkaido
Iida, Yoichi *chemist, molecular biologist*

Hyogo
Goto, Yukio *academic administrator*
Sugiyama, Takeharu *physical chemist*

Ibaraki
Chung, Inho *special education educator*
Taniguchi, Shoichi *library and information scientist, educator*
Urabe, Tohsuke *mathematics professor, researcher*

Kagawa
Fujita, Masayuki *biologist, educator*

Kagoshima
Arima, Eitoku *surgeon*

Kanagawa
Itako, Kazutaka *engineering educator, researcher*
Okada, Ellie *business educator*

Kashihara
Tsujimoto, Tatsuhiro *gastroenterologist, researcher*

Kashiwa
Oguchi, Takashi *geoscientist, educator*

Kashiwara
Hori, Keiko *English literature educator*

Kasugai
Watanabe, Makoto *engineering educator*

Kawagoe
Maki, Atsushi *economics professor*

Kawasaki
Yoshida, Kenichi *veterinarian, biology educator*

Kinokawa
Yamawaki, Nobuyuki *engineering educator, biomedical engineer, researcher*

Kitakyushu
Noda, Nao-Aki *mechanical engineering educator, researcher*

Kobe
Inoue, Shun *sociologist*
Kingetsu, Toshiki *retired materials physicist, researcher*
Mizukoshi, Koshi *metal products executive*
Tanaka, Ichiro *fluid mechanics scientist, educator*

Kochi
Hojo, Masashi *chemistry professor*

Koriyama
Goto, Noboru *neuroanatomist, neuropathologist*

Kureshiki
Oiwa, Hiroshi *surgeon*

Kushimoto
Akura, Junsuke *ophthalmologist, researcher*

Kyoto
Iwayama, Tajiro *university president, educator*
Tsuji, Toshizo *hospital administrator, educator*

Machida
Miyazaki, Koichi *economics professor*

Mie
Isshiki, Masayuki *sociologist, educator, dean*
Kitashirakawa, Michihisa *head of religious order*

Mitaka
Kazama, Toshio *retired humanities educator*

Miyagi
Adachi, Saburo *electrical engineering educator, researcher*
Tan, Masaki *surgeon, director*

Nagasaki
Tsurumoto, Toshiyuki *orthopaedic surgeon, researcher*

Nagoya
Kajitani, Motohisa *sociology educator*
Kasuya, Hideki *medical researcher, surgeon*
Kawaguchi, Fumio *electric power industry executive*
Nakanishi, Kiyoshi *retired automotive executive*
Sakai, Toshihiko *engineer*
Sendo, Takeshi *mechanical engineering educator, researcher, writer*

Niigata
Suzuki, Noriyasu *physician, psychologist, journalist*
Takizawa, Hideaki *gastroenterologist*

Oita
Higashino, Makoto *environmental scientist*

Okayama
Kamiya, Hidehiko *statistics and economics professor*
Morooka, Hiroshi *neurosurgeon*
Nii, Shiro *director, virologist, educator*

Okinawa
Nishihara, Minoru *surgeon*

Osaka
Akase, Masako *humanities educator*
Honnami, Shoichi *retired law educator, researcher*
Kamitani, Takayuki *engineering educator*
Morita, Katsura *chemical company executive*
Nagae, Yoshio *English educator*
Ohnami, Masateru *mechanical engineering educator*
Otsuka, Ryo *medical educator*
Shindo, Katsuhisa *surgeon*
Tanaka, Junji *educational administrator*
Usami, Masahisa *physician, director*
Yamada, Kohei *retired art educator*

Otawara
Tatsuro, Baba *health products executive, medical educator*

Saitama
Furuya, Kenichi *reproductive endocrinologist, gynecologic surgeon*
Ito, Masao *neuroscience researcher*
Muto, Takasuke *sociologist, educator*

Sanyo-Onoda
Kobayashi, Shunsuke *science educator*

Sendai
Hozawa, Atsushi *medical educator*

Shiga
Matsuda, Wakoto *neurosurgeon, researcher*

Shinjuku
Ikari, Katsunori *geneticist, rheumatologist, orthopedic surgeon*
Morikawa, Shunichi *medical educator*
Tatsuta, Kuniaki *organic chemistry educator*

Shizuoka
Anma, So *engineer, consultant*

Suita
Iida, Norihiko *physiatrist, educator*

Takarazuka
Takahashi, Yoriko *psychology professor*

Takasaki
Matsushiro, Nobuhito *engineering executive, researcher*

Tamano
Kunio, Saito *electronics engineer*

Tochigi
Ara, Katsutoshi *environmental engineer, researcher*
Honma, Koichi *pathologist, researcher*
Hyodo, Haruo *radiologist, educator*

Tokorozawa
Nakamura, Hiroshi *urology educator*

Tokyo
Abe, Nobuyasu *ambassador*
Aihara, Hironori *electronics executive*
Akihito, Emperor *Emperor of Japan*
Akiyama, Shinichiro *oncologist, hematologist, researcher*
Anderson, Ronald J. *insurance company executive*
Aoyama, Hiroyuki *structural engineering educator*
Clyde, Robert W. *insurance company executive*
de la Fuente Ramirez, Juan Ramon *psychiatrist, former academic administrator*
Esaki, Leo (Esaki Leona, Esaki Reiona) *physicist, foundation executive, university president*
Eto, Hajime *retired information scientist, educator*
Farrar, Stanley F. *lawyer*
Fujino, Kazuo *marine geneticist*
Fukushima, Kiyohiko *economist*
Fukuyama, Yukio *child neurologist, pediatrics educator*
Hagiwara, Toshitaka *manufacturing executive*
Harada, Norio *software engineer, researcher, educator*
Hirai, Makiko *physician*
Hori, Yukio *engineering educator, scientific association administrator, researcher*
Ichikawa, Yoshio *wood trade company executive*
Iida, Shuichi *physicist, educator*
Inoguchi, Takashi *political scientist, educator*
Ishii, Akira *parasitologist, allergist, malariologist*
Jameson, Samuel Walter *newspaperman, foreign correspondent*
Jyoji, Yoshizawa *medical educator*
Kamimura, Hiroshi *theoretical physicist*
Kaneko, Isao *air transportation executive*
Karatsu, Osamu *research and development company executive*
Kasahara, Yasushi *chemist*
Kato, Shuichi *information scientist, educator*
Kawahara, Hiroyuki *molecular cell biologist professor*
Kawakami, Masaya *medical educator*
Kitajima, Yoshitoshi *printing company executive*
Kitani, Osamu *agriculture educator*
Kiyohara, Takehiko *publishing executive*
Kobayashi, Noritake *business educator*
Koshiba, Masatoshi *physicist, educator*
Krisher, Bernard *foreign correspondent*
Kumagai, Takashi *physician, researcher*
Kunii, Tosiyasu Laurence *information science educator*
Kurokawa, Kaneyuki *science administrator*
Kuroyanagi, Noriyoshi *engineering educator*
Kusakari, Takao *transportation executive*
Mitarai, Fujio *electronics company executive*
Mizuno, Atsushi *economist*
Nagao, Makoto *academic administrator, engineering educator*
Nagata, Minoru *retired electronics engineer*
Nakajima, Hiroshi *education educator*
Nishiyama, Chiaki *economist, educator*
Nomakuchi, Tamotsu *electronics executive*
Ogata, Shijuro *retired central banker*
Ohashi, Yoji *air transportation executive*
Ohga, Norio *retired electronics executive*
Omura, Satoshi *research scientist, administrator*
Ozawa, Seiji *conductor, music director*
Petersen, Barry Rex *news correspondent*
Rice, Edward A., Jr. *military officer*
Saito, Makoto *economics professor*
Sakurada, Yutaka *retired chemist*
Sasaki, Akihiko *cardiologist*
Sasaki, Mikio *trading company executive*
Shibata, Tadashi *engineering educator*
Shirai, Shun *law educator, lawyer*
Suzuki, Akira *physics professor*
Suzuki, Tadao *retired corporate financial executive*
Suzuki, Yoichiro *retired asset management company executive*
Tachi, Susumu *robotics educator*
Takenaka, Toichi *pharmaceutical executive*
Takizawa, Yukio *medical ecologist*
Togo, Hisatake *research institute administrator*
Tokoro, Mario *computer scientist*
Toyoshima, Chikashi *structural biologist, educator*
Watanabe, Satoshi Patten *economist, researcher*
Watanabe, Takahiro *medical educator*
Yaku, Takeo T. *computer scientist, educator*

Toride shi
Okabe, Katsumi *retired special education educator*

Toyota
Toyoda, Eiji *automotive executive*
Toyoda, Tatsuro *automobile company executive*

Tsukuba
Akiyama, Kayo *neuroscientist, researcher*
Imaizumi, Yoko (Ima-Izumi) *literature and film educator*
Murayama, Yuji *geographer, science professor*
Shimizu, Kazuhiko *education educator*
Shiotani, Seiji *diagnostic radiologist*
Sutoo, Den'etsu *neuroscientist, researcher*
Tanaka, Hiroshi L. *atmospheric scientist*
Yamamoto, Hiro-Aki *toxicology and pharmacology educator*

Utsunomiya
Yorikawa, Hiroharu *physicist, researcher*

Yatomi
Sakai, Yu *pathologist*

Yokkaichi
Tanaka, Ichirou *science educator*

Yokohama
Ito, Noboru *electric power industry executive*
Kato, Masaharu *materials scientist, educator*
Kida, Shinichiro *oceanographer*

Yonago
Maeda, Kazuo *obstetrician, gynecologist, educator*

JORDAN

Amman
Batayneh, Malek Khaled *finance company executive, consultant*
Habboushe, Mudhafer Petros *orthopedist, educator*
Masri, Taher Nashat *Jordanian government official*
Saadeh, Sherif Nabil *gastroenterologist, hepatologist, researcher*

KAZAKHSTAN

Almaty
Mansurov, Zulkhair Aimukhametovich *chemist*

KENYA

Nairobi
Kionga-Kamau, Stephen Githii *engineering executive, educator*
Maathai, Wangari *environmentalist, consultant*
Tibaijuka, Anna Kajumulo *international organization official, advocate, economics professor*

KUWAIT

Kuwait
Rahman, Abdur *neuroscientist, educator*

Safat
Alazmi, Waleed *medical educator*
Al-Turki, Abdul Aziz Abdallah *oil industry association executive*
Jallad, Karim N. *chemistry professor*

KYRGYZSTAN

Bishkek
Koichuev, Turar Koichuevich *economist, science association executive*

Bul Erkinduk
Sultanov, Marat *bank executive*

LATVIA

Riga
Kabashkin, Igor *telecommunications industry executive*
Lācis, Aris *health facility administrator, cardiac surgeon*
Ulmanis, Guntis *former President of Latvia*

LEBANON

Beirut
Hamdan, Abdul-latif H. *otolaryngologist, educator*
Khatib, Rustom Atfat *gynecologist, endocrinologist, researcher, consultant*
Shehadi, Sameer Ibrahim *plastic surgeon*
Waterbury, John *political science professor, writer, former academic administrator*

Beyrouth
Kolvenbach, Peter Hans *priest, head of religious order*

Byblos
Sheikh-Taha, Marwan *medical educator, researcher*

LITHUANIA

Vilnius
Brazauskas, Algirdas Mykolas *Prime Minister Republic of Lithuania*

LUXEMBOURG

Buschdorf
Kamanda, Kama Sywor *poet, writer*

Luxembourg
Kokott, Julia Beate *advocate general*

Niederkorn
Meder, Cornel *retired archivist, director*

Senningerberg
Fulci, Francesco Paolo *former diplomat*

MALAWI

Lilongwe
Malewezi, Justin *Malawian government official*

MALAYSIA

Cyberjaya
Muthaiyah, Saravanan *dean*

Johor
Wong, Kuan Yew *engineering educator, researcher*

Kuala Lumpur
Abdel-Rahim, Muddathir *political scientist, educator*

Putrajaya
Omar, Salem *physician, gastroenterologist, researcher*

Selangor
Azer, Samy Aziz *gastroenterologist, educator*
Manaf, Mohammed Zaini *management consulting company executive*

Shah Alam
Zainal-Abidin, Siti-Zaleha *computer scientist, educator*

MALDIVES

Malé
Deen, Mohamed Waheed *small business owner*

MALTA

Valletta
Fenech, Joseph *former Maltese government official, lawyer*

MAURITIUS

Port Louis
Glover, Sir Victor Joseph Patrick *former chief justice*
Ramgoolam, Navinchandra *Prime Minister of the Republic of Mauritius*

MEXICO

Alvaro Obregon
Sepúlveda Amor, Jaime *public health service officer*

Baja California
Montero Alpírez, Gisela *chemical engineer, researcher*

Ciudad Juarez
Tabuenca-Cordoba, Maria-Socorro *education educator, researcher*

Districto Federal Mexico
Quiroz Robles, Fernando *bank executive*

Garza Garcia
Zambrano, Lorenzo H. *manufacturing executive*

Guadalajara
Durand, Jorge *anthropologist*
Romano Gomez, Miguel *bishop*

Jiutepec
Patino-Gomez, Carlos *hydrologist*

Mexico City
Aramburúzabála De Garza, Maria Asunción *food products executive*
Azuela Güitrón, Mariano *judge*
Bruton, John Macaulay *trade association executive, consultant*
Cardenas Solorzano, Cuauhtemoc *Mexican government official*
Carreto-Chavez, Gerardo *lawyer*
De La Riva, Myriam Ann *artist*
Flores-Moreno, Roberto *research scientist*
Frenk, Julio Jose *minister of health for Mexico, health systems researcher, consultant*
Goeser, Louise K. *retired automotive executive*
Knaul, Felicia Marie *economist, health policy researcher*
Legorreta, Ricardo *architectural firm executive*
Medina-Mora, Manuel *bank executive*
Mendelejis, Leonardo Nierman *artist*
Ramirez-Mireles, Fernando *electronics engineer, consultant*
Suarez-Iñiguez, Enrique *education educator*
Téllez Kuenzler, Luis *former government official, investment banker*
Vargas Legaspi, Juan *manufacturing executive*
Zorilla Fullaondo, Enrique *bank executive*

Queretaro
Lesser-Carrillo, Luis Ernesto *civil engineer, educator*

Tepic
Watty Urquidi, Ricardo *bishop*

Tijuana
Chayet, Arturo S. *ophthalmologist, surgeon, consultant*

Tlaquepaque
Cueva-Zepeda, Alfredo *mechanical engineer, educator*

MOLDOVA

Floresti
Palii, Larisa P. *language educator*

Kishinev
Pyshkin, Sergei L. *physics professor, researcher*

MONACO

Charlotte
Vicari, Andrew *artist*

Monte Carlo
Lovett, Laurence Dow *retired real estate and steamship executive*

MONGOLIA

Ulaanbaatar
Gantsog, Tserensodnom *academic administrator, educator*
Mandel, Leslie Ann *investment advisor, writer*
Nymadawa, Pagbajabyn *physician, public health administrator*

MONTENEGRO

Podgorica
Vujanović, Filip *President of Republic of Montenegro*

MOROCCO

Rabat
Rafi, Mostafa *ophthalmologist*

Sale
Hamzaoui, Ahmed *literature and language professor*

MOZAMBIQUE

Maputo
dos Santos, Alexandre José Maria Cardinal *cardinal, archbishop emeritus*

NAMIBIA

Windoek
Nujoma, Sam Daniel *President of Namibia*

NEPAL

Kathmandu
Rana, Pashupati S.J.B. *legislator*

NETHERLANDS

Amsterdam
Andriessen, Louis *composer*
Dahan, Rene *retired oil industry executive*
Drenth, Pieter Johan Diederik *psychology professor, consultant*
Groenink, Rijkman Willem Johan *bank executive*
Martinez, Arthur C. *bank executive, retired retail executive*
Momin, Alhaj Babul Ahmed *investigation bureau director, poet, writer*
Sawyer, Errol *photographer*

Breukelen
Uhlaner, Lorraine Marie *finance educator*

De Bilt
Van Ginkel, Johannes Auguste *geographer, educator*

Delft
Buice, Eric Steve *mechanical engineer, researcher*
Haak, Alex Johan Henri *architect, educator*

Eindhoven
Huiskes, Hendrik W.J. (Rik Huiskes) *biological engineer*

Groningen
Holz, Hans Heinz *philosophy educator*

Haren
Alonso, David *ecologist*

Maastricht
Van Praag, Herman Meir *psychiatrist, educator, researcher*

Rijswijk
Pickard, Ann *oil industry executive*

Rotterdam
Gallogly, James Lawrence (Jim Gallogly) *chemical company executive, retired oil industry executive*
van Wachem, Lodewijk Christiaan *petroleum company executive*

The Hague
Allison, Richard Clark *judge*
Beatrix, Her Majesty Queen (Beatrix Wilhelmina Armgard van Oranje-Nassau) *Queen of The Netherlands*
Boed, Roman A. *legal administrator*
Buergenthal, Thomas *international judge*
Higgins, Dame Rosalyn *judge*
Jiuyong, Shi *judge*
Kaul, Hans-Peter *international judge*
Koroma, Abdul G. *judge*
Kourula, Erkki *international judge*
Owada, Hisashi *judge*
Parra-Aranguren, Gonzalo *judge*
Ranjeva, Raymond *judge*
Tomka, Peter *diplomat, arbitrator, judge, lawyer*
Vincent, Jim *performing company executive*

Utrecht
't Hooft, Gerardus (Gerard) *physicist, researcher*
Tielman, Rob A.P. *social sciences educator*

Vlaardingen
Smith, Arlan Robert *plastic and reconstructive surgeon*

Zaandam
Vuursteen, Karel *beverage industry executive*

NETHERLANDS ANTILLES

Willemstad
Saleh, Jaime *former Netherlands Antilles government official*

NEW ZEALAND

Auckland
Sims, Francis Harding *retired medical researcher*
Su, Bin *architecture educator*

Waikanae
Williams, Thomas Stafford Cardinal *cardinal, archbishop*

Wellington
Balvo, Charles Daniel *archbishop*
Clement, Jemaine *actor, musician*
Jackson, Peter *film director*
Keith, Sir Kenneth James *law commissioner, educator, judge*
Paquin, Anna Helene *actress*

NICARAGUA

Bluefields Zelaya Norte
Zywiec Sidor, David Albin *bishop*
Schmitz Simon, Pablo Ervin *bishop*

NIGERIA

Enugu
Ozumba, Benjamin Chukwuma *obstetrician, gynecologist, educator*

Lekki Peninsula
Ogunlade, Abimbola Adegoke *systems engineer*

NORTHERN IRELAND

Belfast
McCanny, John Vincent *engineering educator, executive*

NORWAY

Hosle
Drevvatne, Dag *lawyer, investor*

Lillestrøm
Gjessing, Dag Trygveson *physicist*

Oslo
Fenstad, Jens Erik *mathematics professor*
Gjønnes, Jon Kjell *physics professor*
Harald V, King *King of Norway*
Haug, Charlotte J. *editor, educator*
Karlsen, Paul Johan *psychologist, researcher, writer*
Lodgaard, Sverre *nuclear disarmament researcher*
Loenning, Per *bishop*
Pettersen, Suzann *professional golfer*
Vibe, Kjeld *ambassador*
Winnem, Bjørn Magne *anesthesiologist*

Tananger
Warwick, Paul C. *oil industry executive*

Trondheim
Lavrov, Alexandre Vadimovich *research scientist*
Popescu, Mihaela *elementary school educator, researcher*

PAKISTAN

Islamabad
Qureshi, Iqbal Hussain *nuclear chemist*

Karachi
Khan, Nadeem Kamal Mustafa *health facility administrator, accountant*

Lahore
Armacost, Peter Hayden *academic administrator*
Asif, Muhammad *physicist, researcher*
Geoffrey, Iqbal (Mohammed Jawaid Iqbal Jafree) *artist, educator, lawyer, department chair, consultant*

Kotlyakov, Vladimir Mikhailovich *geographer, researcher*
Krikalev, Sergei Konstantinovich *flight engineer, cosmonaut, researcher*
Novikov, Sergei Petrovich *mathematician*
Paulson, Andrew *publishing executive, Internet company executive*
Perminov, Anatoly *aerospace agency executive*
Romanovski, Mikhail Rem *mathematician*
Tsapenko, Nikolai Evgenievich *mathematician, educator*
Ushakov, Yury Viktorovich *Russian government official, former ambassador*
Vladimirov, Vasiliy Sergeyevich *mathematician*
Zaretskaya, Elena *social sciences educator, dean*
Zolotov, Yury Alexandrovich *chemist*

Nizhniy Novgorod
Bityurin, Nikita *physicist, researcher*

Novosibirsk
Skrinsky, Alexander Nikolaevich *physicist, researcher*
Vasilyev, Vladislav Yurievich *chemist, researcher, engineer*

Rostov-on-Don
Pogorelov, Vadim Alekseevich *engineer*

Saint Petersburg
Birshtein, Tatiana Maximovna *physicist, educator, researcher*

Yurga
Apasov, Alexander Mikhailovich *physicist, educator*

RWANDA

Moscow
Grigoriev, Sergei Aleksandrovich *political scientist, researcher*

SAINT KITTS AND NEVIS

Basseterre
Mohammed, Hamish *epidemiologist, educator*

SAINT LUCIA

Castries
Louisy, Pearlette *governor general of Saint Lucia*

SAINT VINCENT AND THE GRENADINES

Bequia
Mitchell, Sir James Fitzallen *former Prime Minister of Saint Vincent and The Grenadines, agronomist, hotelier*

SAUDI ARABIA

Al Madinah
Molla, Ahmed Abdin *surgeon*

Jeddah
Ainsleigh, Susan Anita *special education educator, consultant*

Riyadh
Alharbi, Abeer Ali *physics professor*
Al-Shaikh, Abdallah Muhammad Ibrahim Al *Saudi Arabian government official*
Alshareef, Fehied Fahad *government agency leader*
Wagoner, Michael D. *ophthalmologist*

SCOTLAND

Aberchirder
Talbot, Nyna Lucille *psychologist, writer*

Dundee
Hillman, John Richard *agricultural and biotechnological studies educator, researcher, consultant*

Edinburgh
Atiyah, Sir Michael Francis *mathematician*
Finney, David John *biometrician*
Mackay, James Peter Hymers (Lord Mackay of Clashfern) *retired university official*
Macneil, Ian Roderick *lawyer, educator*
Tsirikos, Athanasios Ioannis *orthopedist, spinal surgeon, educator*

Fife
Roff, William Robert *historian, educator, writer*

Glasgow
Iolana, Patricia Elvira *foundation administrator, consultant*
Moosa, Ahmed Shafeeq Ibrahim (Sappé) *journalist*
Tiffany, John *theater director*

Shetland
Kynastone, Vivien Rebecca *export company executive*

St Andrews
Lee, Thomas Alexander *accountant, educator*

Stirling
Lenman, Bruce Philip *historian, educator*
Masocha, Walter *finance educator*

SENEGAL

Dakar
Bernicat, Marcia Stephens Bloom *United States Ambassador to Republics of Senegal and Guinea-Bissau*
Wade, Abdoulaye *President of Senegal*

SERBIA

Belgrade
Milutinovic, Milan A. *former President of the Republic of Serbia*
Mitrasinovic, Petar M. *chemistry professor, engineer, research scientist*

Pancevo
Trivic, Dusan Nikola *retired research scientist*

SEYCHELLES

Victoria
Michel, Alix James *President of Seychelles*

SIERRA LEONE

Freetown
Rapp, Stephen John *international prosecutor*
Swaray, Steven Mustapha *banker, economist*

SINGAPORE

Singapore
Aung, Naing Naing *technologist, researcher*
Bompard, Julien *chef*
Guaning, Su *academic administrator*
Henretta, Deborah A. *consumer products company executive*
Hong, Song-Iee *social studies educator*
Hunter, Howard Owen *academic administrator, law educator*
Kong, Adams Wai Kin *electrical engineer, researcher*
Lau, John Hon Shing *electronics scientist*
Lim, Tai Wei *communications educator, researcher*
Low, Cze Hong *ophthalmologist*
McNamara, Michael *electronics executive*
Swain, Judith Lea *cardiologist, educator*
Yoo, Byounghyun *research scientist*

SLOVAKIA

Voderady
Neisser, Hentike *editor, writer*

SLOVENIA

Ljubljana
Bernik, France *literature educator*
Nabergoj, Andrej *entrepreneur*

SOUTH AFRICA

Bloemfontein
Stulting, Andries Andriessen *ophthalmologist*

Cape Town
Cleary, Sean Michael *risk management executive, founding chair, director*

Johannesburg
Pesic, Ratnik Josip *application developer, management consultant, mathematician, educator*

Mmabatho Northwest
Mangope, Lucas Manyane *tribal chief, politician*

North West
Lumadi, Mutendwahothe Walter *educational association administrator*

Port Alfred
Stocks, Rundell Kingsley *management, construction, education and general consultant*

Pretoria
Daniel, George Francis *archbishop*
Green, James Patrick *archbishop*

Rondebosch
Ellis, George Francis Rayner *mathematics professor*
van der Merwe, Nikolaas Johannes *archaeologist*

Witbank
Jansen van Rensburg, Dirkie Johanna *physician, medical researcher*

SPAIN

Adeje
Grindley, Bruce Alan *real estate agency executive*

Alicante
Castejon-Costa, Juan Luis *psychologist, educator*

Badajoz
Gómez Galán, José *historian, philosopher, writer, theologian, educator*

Barcelona
Badell, Mariana *research scientist, consultant*
Carles Gordo, Ricardo Maria Cardinal *cardinal, archbishop emeritus*
Huidobro, Fernando López *economist, biologist*
Rissech, Carme *research scientist*
Vilardell, Francisco *gastroenterologist, educator*

Barcelonass
Laricchia-Robbio, Leopoldo *molecular biologist, educator*

Betlem
Cecchini, Leo *entrepreneur*

Cordoba
Vaamonde-Martin, Diana Maria *biologist, embryologist, researcher, educator*

La Gomera
Wells, Melissa Foelsch *retired ambassador*

Madrid
Abellan, José Luis *humanities educator*
Botín, Ana Patricia *bank executive*
Feltenstein, Harry David, Jr. *chemicals executive*
Frühbeck de Burgos, Rafael *conductor*
Garcia-Palencia, Rafael *lawyer*
Herrero Rodriguez de Miñon, Miguel *lawyer, legislator, consultant*
Juan Carlos, His Majesty , I, (Juan Carlos de Borbón y Borbón) *King of Spain*
Mayor Zaragoza, Federico *biochemistry educator*
Mortier, Gerard *opera company director*
Pérez-Díaz, Víctor Miguel *sociology educator*
Santiago, Francisco José Hernando *judge*

Santiago de Compostela
Touriñán López, José Manuel *education educator*

Segovia
Wojcieszak, Magdalena Elzbieta *communications educator, researcher*

Seville
Sanchez, Leonedes Monarrize Worthington (His Royal Highness Duke de Leonedes of Spain Sicily Greece) *fashion designer*

Toledo
Ruiz, Luis M. *physical education educator*

Valencia
Docavo Alberti, Ignacio *zoology educator*
Maazel, Lorin Varencove *conductor, composer, violinist*

Villareal
Altidore, Jozy (Josmer Volmy Altidore) *professional soccer player*

Zaragoza
Hernandez Altemir, Francisco *surgeon*
Yadav, Prashant *economics educator*

SRI LANKA

Colombo
Wirasinha, Hemamali Anushka *computer scientist, researcher*

SUDAN

Malakal
Wieu, Andrew W. Riang *government agency administrator*

SURINAME

Paramaribo
Goedschalk, Henk Otmar *banker, educator*

SWEDEN

Goteborg
Martinovski, Bilyana *language educator, researcher*

Gothenburg
Svensson, Robert Charles Wilhelm *physicist, researcher*

Helsingborg
Kamprad, Ingvar *former consumer products company executive*

Jönköping
Picard, Robert Georges *writer, educator*

Kiruna
Hultqvist, Bengt Karl Gustaf *physicist, educator*

Kista
Fodor, Gabor Andras *electrical engineer, researcher*

Lerum
Borei, Sven Hans Emil *translator, writer, educator*

Linköping
Spaeth, Mary Shepard *marketing communications executive*

Ornskoldsvik
Forsberg, Peter *professional hockey player*

Solna
Ljøstad, Torstein Torberg *retired airline company executive*

Stockholm
Ax:son Johnson, Antonia Margaret *industrial, marketing and trading company executive*
Cavalli-Björkman, Görel *professor*
Farahbakhshazad, Neda *research scientist*
Gradin, Anita *former ambassador and European Commission member*
Gustafsson, Jan-Åke *molecular endocrinologist, medical nutritionist*
Hallberg, Rolf Oskar *biogeochemist*
Hedelius, Tom Christer *banker*
Holm, Christer A. *lawyer*
Johnson, Antonia Ax:son *food products executive*
Käll, Lukas *biotechnologist*
Lidman, Tomas Erik *national archivist*
Olsson, Curt Gunnar *banker*
Sohlman, Michael *foundation administrator*
van den Bosch, Margareta *apparel company executive*
Wachtmeister, Count Wilhelm H.F. *retired diplomat*
Wallenberg, Peter *banker, investor*
Wastberg, Olle M. *nation branding organization administrator*

Uppsala
Champion, Margrét Gunnarsdóttir *literature and language educator*
Laurent, Torvard Claude *biochemist, educator*
Scheicher, Ralph Hendrik *research scientist*

Västerås
Xiong, Ning *computer scientist*

Örebro
Persliden, Jan R. G. *physicist*

SWITZERLAND

Aargau
Bodis, Stephan B. *radiologist, oncologist, educator*

Alpnach
Bocker, Hans Jurgen *finance educator, editor-in-chief, consultant*

Basel
Arber, Werner *microbiologist*
Eriksen, Erik Fink *endocrinologist, internist, researcher*
Gehring, Walter Jakob *biology professor, geneticist*
Nidecker, Andreas Cornelis *radiologist, educator*

Bern
Carlson, Dale Bick *writer*
Shaha, Maya *nursing educator*

Berne
Blocher, Christoph *Swiss government official*

Bottmingen
Burger, Max Marcel *biochemist*

Bulle
Haeusler, Jean-Marc C. *global medical director*

Busingen
Friede, Reinhard L. *neuropathologist, educator*

Chambésy
Helland, Douglas Rolf *retired intergovernmental organization computer executive*

Chateau d'Oex
Berman, Joshua Mordecai *lawyer, manufacturing executive*

Geneva
Annan, Kofi Atta *international organization administrator, former secretary general of the United Nations*
Brown, Kent Newville *ambassador*
Duboule, Denis *biology researcher, educator*
Gueudet, Edouard Philippe *banker*
Niskala, Markku *international organization administrator*
Schwab, Klaus Martin *foundation administrator*
Sommaruga, Cornelio *foundation administrator, diplomat*
Steinberger, Jack *physicist, researcher*
Tichenor, Warren W. *United States Ambassador to the United Nations, Geneva*

Geneve
Dubrule, Paul Jean-Marie *hotel and restaurant company executive, vintager*

Hergiswil
Bröder, Ernst-Günther *financial executive, economist*

Hinterkappelen
Reuter, Harald *pharmacologist*

Hinwil
Sala, Marzio Giuseppe *research and development company executive*

Hunenberg
Buehler, Kevin J. *pharmaceutical executive*

Langenthal
Maleck, Wolfgang Helmut *anesthesiologist*

Lausanne
Camilleri, Louis Carey *tobacco company executive*
Carrard, Francois Denis *international organization administrator, lawyer*
Chakravarthy, Balaji Srinivasan *strategic management educator, consultant*
Nikolaou, Lambis W. *International Olympic Committee board member*
Rozza, Gianluigi *mathematician, aerospace engineer*
Wall, Charles R. *tobacco company executive, lawyer*

Meggen
Galway, Sir James *flutist*

Muttenz
L'Eplattenier, Francois *venture capitalist*

Rolle
Aaronson, Robert Jay *air transportation executive*

Schaffhausen
Poses, Frederic M. *manufacturing executive, former engineering company executive*

Vandoeuvres
Ortiz, George *artist*

Verbier
Gyll, John Sören *marketing executive*

Versoix
Mahler, Halfdan Theodor *physician, health organization executive*

Vevey
Frick, David P. *lawyer*

Waldenburg
Hamm, Palma *art historian, writer, researcher, art expert, educator, art collector*

Windisch
Anderegg, Roland *mechanical engineer, researcher*

Yverdon-les-Bains
Egolf, Peter William *physicist*

Zurich
Calatrava, Santiago *architect, structural engineer, artist*
Dewar, Brent (Walter William Brent Dewar) *automotive executive*
Dougan, Brady W. *diversified financial services company executive*
Dunitz, Jack David *retired chemistry educator, researcher*
Eschenmoser, Albert *chemist*
Hammesfahr, Robert Winter *lawyer*
Hogan, Joseph M. *engineering company executive*
Kohli, Ulrich A. *lawyer*
Morari, Manfred *chemical engineer, educator*
Müller, Karl Alexander (K. Alex Mueller) *physicist, researcher*
Schiro, James Joseph *insurance company executive*
Seebach, Dieter *chemistry professor*
Stevens, Eric R. *automotive executive*
Wassmer, Rudolf Andreas *entrepreneurial engineer*
Wüthrich, Kurt *molecular biologist, biophysicist, educator*

TAIWAN

Chiayi
Ku, Maurice S. B. *agricultural studies educator*

Chupei
Chou, Richard Chi-Chang *mechanical engineer*

Hsinchu
Wang, David *finance educator*

Jhongli
Tseng, Dyi-Hwa *environmental engineer, educator, dean*

Kaohsiung
Lambert, Marianne T. *retired elementary school educator*
Shan Kuo-hsi, Paul Cardinal *cardinal, bishop emeritus*
Wang, Gwo Jaw *orthopedic surgery educator*

Keelung
An, John F. *engineering educator*
Chin-Feng, Lin *science educator*
Wu, Jenq-Lang *engineering educator*

Nankang
Shiue, Yunn-Shin Jessie *materials scientist, researcher*

Pingtung
Fan, Tai-Sheng Allen *social scientist, educator*
Ou, Shan-Hwei *academic administrator, engineering educator*

Taichung
Chang, Pao-Long *management sciences educator, academic administrator*
Chuo, Liang-Jen *psychiatrist, researcher*
Wang, Matthew Nai-Hwei *surgeon, educator*

Taichung Hsien
Peng-Chi, Peng *metallurgical engineer*

Tainan
Huang, Ting-Chia *chemical engineering professor, researcher*

Taipei
Chao, Hsia Fu *gastroenterologist, administrator*
Chen, Chien-Jen *epidemiologist, Minister of Health, Minister of Science*
Chen, Peng-Jen (Ting-Cheng) *political educator, writer*
Chien, Fredrick Fu *Taiwan government official, foundation administrator*
Chu, Tzong-Shinn *physician scientist, medical educator*
Huang, Song-Yuan *health educator*
Jan, Ming-Yie *biomedical engineer, consultant*
Lee, Hsuan-Shu *biotechnologist*
Lee, Lin-Shan *electrical engineering educator, research and development company executive*
Lee, Teng-Hui *Former President of Taiwan*
Lien Chan, *Chinese government official*
Lin, Chia-Hsiang *electrical and electronics technologist*
Ling, Chung-Mei *pharmaceutical executive*
Pan, Joshua Jih *architect*
Sicart, Pierre-Alexandre Serge Henry *writer, scholar*
Sun, Andy *dentist*
Tsai, Ming-Hung *internist, researcher*
Tsung, Christine Chai-yi *financial executive, treasurer*
Tzyy-Jiann, Wang *science educator*
Wang, Pei-Ling *geochemist*
Wu, Cheng-Hung *engineering educator, researcher*

Yilan County
Yu, Yuan Hsiang *chemist, electronics engineer, educator*

TAJIKISTAN

Dushanbe
Alimardonov, Murotali *bank executive*
Oqilov, Oqil Ghaybulloyevich *Prime Minister of Tajikistan*

THAILAND

Bangkok
Bovornkitti, Somchai *internist*
Intuwongse, Chai-Sit *orthopedist, consultant*
John, Eric G. *United States Ambassador to Thailand*
Kitbunchu, Michael Michai Cardinal *cardinal, archbishop emeritus*
McMillion, Margaret Kim *foreign service officer*
Meensook, Charoen *physician, consultant*
Narayan, Amarendra *telecommunications executive*
Pinkaew, Prachya *film producer and director*
Russell, Paul George *lawyer*
Suwat, Liptapanlop *Thailand government official*
Warrasak, Sukhuma *ophthalmologist*

Phasicharoen
Mongkhonvanit, Pornchai *academic administrator*

Phucket
Pianko, Theodore A. *lawyer*

Pranakorn
Tepvorachai, Gorn *financial analyst*

TRINIDAD AND TOBAGO

Diego Martin
Walcott, Derek Alton *poet, playwright*

Port of Spain
Gilbert, Edward Joseph *archbishop*
Gullickson, Thomas Edward *archbishop*

Saint Augustine
Shaw, Timothy Milton *political science professor*

San Fernando
Mahabir, Errol Edward *company executive*

TUNISIA

Carthage
Sehili, Mahmoud *artist*

Tunis
Ben Ali, Zine El-Abidine *President of Tunisia*

TURKEY

Ankara
Elbasi, Ersin *computer scientist, researcher*
Gül, Abdullah *President of Turkey*
Kirecci, Akif *economics professor*

Edirne
Aricak, Osman Tolga *education educator*

Istanbul
Utku, Senol *civil engineer, computer science educator, mathematics professor*
Yamak, Sibel *social sciences educator, researcher*

Sariyer
Alkan, Emre *mathematics professor*

Van
Tapan, Mucip *engineering educator, consultant*

UKRAINE

Dnipropetrovsk
Bolshakov, Vladimir Ivanovich *metallurgist, educator*

Kiev
Antonov, Alexander Alexandrovich *engineering executive, researcher*
Reznykov, Illya Igorevich *mathematician, application developer*

UNITED ARAB EMIRATES

Abu Dhabi
Cleaves, Peter Shurtleff *foundation administrator*

Al Ain
AbuQamar, Synan F. *biology professor, researcher*

Al-Ain Abu-Dhabi
Ijaz, Muhammad Khalid Khalid *virologist, immunologist*

Dubai
Chohan, Gulshan-Naseem *office manager*
Hegazy, Abdelatif M. *real estate company executive*
Jarade, Elias Fares *ophthalmologist*
Rabbat, Guy *electronics executive, consultant*
Subair, Saad Osman Abdalla *science educator*

Sharjah
Abed, Farid H. *science educator*
al-Qasimi, Sheikh Sultan bin Muhammad (Sheikh Sultan bin Muhammad Al-Qasimi) *Emir of Sharjah*

UZBEKISTAN

Tashkent
Azimov, Rustam Sadikovich *bank executive*
Shakirov, Zair Saatovich *biologist, researcher*

VATICAN CITY

Poggi, Luigi Cardinal *cardinal, archbishop emeritus, archivist*

VENEZUELA

Caracas
Chang-Mota, Roberto *electrical engineer*
Cisneros, Gustavo Alfredo *retail executive*

VIETNAM

Binh An Ward
Israel, Barry John *lawyer*

Hanoi
Nam, Ha Hai *computer science educator, researcher*
Tran, Huong Mai *editor-in-chief*
Vu, Nhat Tan *composer*

WALES

Aberystwyth
Lairikyengbam, Shyam Kishore Singh *cardiologist*
Walters, Kenneth *applied mathematics educator*

Cardiff
Jiles, David Collingwood *physicist, materials science educator*

Jeffreyston
Woodman, Grey Musgrave *psychiatrist*

WEST INDIES

Schoelcher Martinica
Saffache, Pascal Marie *dean, educator*

ZAMBIA

Mongu
Duffy, Paul Francis *bishop*

Nangoma
Hansen, Florence Marie Congiolosi (Mrs. James S. Hansen) *social worker*

ADDRESS UNPUBLISHED

Aamodt, Roger Louis *retired federal agency administrator*
Abanilla, Patricia Karen Amarillas *psychiatrist*
Abate, Carol Elizabeth *humanities educator, writer*
Abbas Borhan, Richat *research and development company executive*
Abbe, Elfriede Martha *sculptor, graphics designer*
Abbett, Robert Kennedy *artist, writer*
Abbott, Charles Favour *lawyer*
Abbott, Edward Leroy *finance executive*
Abdel-Hadi, Ali Ismail *engineer, educator*
Abdelkarim, Ahmad *dentist, educator*
Abdellah, Faye Glenn *retired public health service officer*
Abdelrahman, Talaat Ahmad Mohammad *financial executive*
Abdollahian, Mark *medical educator*
Abdul-Aziz, Rana *language educator*
Abel, Barbara Ellen *photographer*
Abeles, Kim Victoria *artist*
Abelin, Theodor *retired medical educator, epidemiologist*
Abell, Anna Ellen *primary school educator*
Abell, Dawn Gabbitas *elementary and secondary school educator, administrator*
Abella, Isaac David *physicist, researcher*
Abernathy, Jennifer P. *music educator*
Abetti, Pier Antonio *electrical engineer, management consultant, educator*
Abey, Kathy Michele *district representative, retired congressional caseworker*
Abiose, Ademola *cardiologist, educator*
Ablard, Charles David *administrative judge*
Able, Kenneth Paul *biology professor*
Aboussie, Marilyn *retired judge*
Abraham, F. Murray (Fahrid Murray Abraham) *actor, educator*
Abraham, Francine Dinneen *sales executive, banker*
Abram, Ruth Jacobeth *museum founder*
Abrams, Arthur Jay *retired physician*
Abrams, Dan *media strategy firm executive, former broadcast executive*
Abrams, Fredrick Ralph *physician, clinical ethicist*
Abramson, Leslie Hope *lawyer*
Abrevaya, Jason *economics professor*
Abu-Khalaf, Murad *electrical engineer, computer scientist, educator*
Abulhab, Saad Dean *librarian, Information Technology Director & Type Designer*
Abu-Lughod, Janet Lippman *sociologist, educator*
Abuzeineh, Alisa Amanda *research scientist*
Acar, Cenk *engineering company executive*
Accorsi, Ernie (Ernest William Accorsi Jr.) *retired professional sports team executive*
Acerra, Michele (Mike Acerra) *engineering and construction company executive*
Acevedo-Vilá, Aníbal *former Governor of Puerto Rico*
Acheampong, Joseph Kofi *pharmacist, researcher*
Achord, James Lee *retired gastroenterologist*
Achorn, Robert Comey *retired newspaper publisher*
Acker, Raymond Abijah *retired minister and army chaplain*
Acker, Robert Flint *retired microbiologist*
Ackerman, Melvin *investment company executive*
Ackerman, Raymond Basil *advertising executive*
Ackermann, Barbara Bogel *counselor*
Ackermann, Bradley Lynn *research scientist*
Acosta, Alex (Rene Alexander Acosta) *former prosecutor, former federal agency administrator*
Acosta, Catherine *psychologist, special education educator*
Acta, Manny (Manuel Elias Acta) *former professional baseball manager*
Adair, Irmalee Traylor *social worker*
Adair, Stefan Rene *plastic surgeon*
Adam, John, Jr. *insurance company executive emeritus*
Adam, Justine E. *psychologist*
Adamchuk, Viacheslav Ivanovych *educator*
AdamLichtman, Adam David *medical educator, director*
Adams, Arlin Marvin *lawyer, retired judge, arbitrator, mediator*
Adams, Daniel Fenton *law educator*
Adams, David Orin *aeronautical engineer*
Adams, David Parrish *historian, epidemiologist, educator*
Adams, Edwin Melville *retired diplomat, actor, writer*
Adams, Forrest H. *retired pediatrician*
Adams, James Frederick *psychologist, academic administrator, educator*
Adams, James Thomas *surgeon*
Adams, John Carter, Jr. *retired insurance executive*
Adams, Leocadia Donat *secondary school educator, writer*
Adams, Lorraine *reporter*
Adams, Margaret Bernice *retired museum official*
Adams, Phyllis Yewell *foreign language educator*
Adams, Robert McCormick *anthropologist, educator*
Adams, Thomas Lynch, Jr. *lawyer*
Adams, Timothy D. *former federal agency administrator*
Adams, Weston *former diplomat, military officer, lawyer*
Adamson, Lynda G. *literature educator, writer*
Adcock, Robert H., Jr., (Bunny Adcock) *former state banking agency administrator*
Addae-mensah, Kweku *biomedical researcher*
Addington, David S. *former federal official, lawyer*
Addo, Charles Kwame *science educator*
Adegbile, Isaiah Olanipekun *history professor, poet*
Adelman, Kenneth Lee *journalist, former ambassador*
Adelstein, Robert S. *medical researcher*
Ader, Pauletta *technologist*
Adesogan, Adegbola *nutritionist, educator*
Adesola, Oluseye *language educator*
Adeyemi, Oluwadamilola Adebola *infectious diseases physician*
Adeyemi, Sele *social studies educator*
Adler, Brent H. *radiologist*
Adler, Jack Saul *retired accountant*
Adler, Raphael *retired humanities educator, speech pathology/audiology services professional*
Adler, Richard Melvin *architect, planner*
Adrogue, Horacio Esteban *nephrologist, educator*
Adsumilli, Chowdary B. *research scientist*
Aduen, Javier Francisco *physician, researcher*
Adzamli, Kofi *radiologist scientist & patent agent*
Aehlert, Barbara June *health facility administrator*
Afon, Yinka *environmental engineer, consultant*
Afraz, Arash Seyed-Reza *research scientist*
Agan, Cami D. *literature and language professor*
Agapito, Luis Alberto *research scientist*
Agar, Beatrice Arlene *nutritionist, educator*

Agarwal, Pranab *engineering company executive*
Agarwala, Ranjeet *science educator*
Agashe, Janhavi *research scientist*
Aggarwal, Sanjeev *manufacturing executive, director*
Agrawal, Amit *medical educator, researcher*
Aguilera, Christina *singer*
Aguilera, Richard Warren (Rick Aguilera) *retired professional baseball player*
Aguinsky, Richard Daniel *electrical engineer, engineering executive*
Aguirregabiria, Victor *science educator*
Agut, Calin M. *mathematics professor*
Ahearne, John Francis *science foundation director, researcher*
Ahmadzadeh, Hossein *chemistry professor*
Ahmed, Ali *epidemiologist, researcher*
Ahmed, Walid Khairy Mohamed *electrical engineer*
Aho, Melissa Kay *librarian, educator, writer*
Ahrari, Ehsan M. *political science professor, dean*
Ahrens, Franklin Alfred *veterinary pharmacology educator*
Ahrens, Kent *museum director, art historian*
Ahuja, Sanjiv *telecommunications industry executive*
Aigen, Betsy P. *psychotherapist*
Aiken, Clay (Clayton Holmes Aiken) *singer*
Aiken, Michael Thomas *former academic administrator*
Aikman, Albert Edward *lawyer*
Ain, Diantha *poet, artist, educator*
Aipperspach, Ryan *computer engineer*
Aires, Julie H. *biology professor*
Airoldi, Edoardo Maria *statistician, researcher, computer scientist, consultant*
Aisen, Ari *economist, researcher*
Aiyer, Meenakshy K. *medical educator*
Akanbi, Linda Barbara *education educator*
Akasheh, Osama Z. *geophysicist*
Akasofu, Syun-Ichi *geophysicist, educator*
Akay, Hasan U. *engineering educator*
Akbani, Rehan *research scientist*
Akers, Sharron Loella *language educator*
Akhavan, Farhad *electrical engineer*
Akinci, Necip Onder *structural engineer*
Akindemowo, Olujoke Eniola *law educator, researcher*
Akintimoye, Akindele D. *lawyer, consultant*
Akiyama, Carol Lynn *motion picture industry executive*
Akkor, Gundogdu *retired architectural firm and engineering executive, foundation administrator*
Aksamija, Zlatan *engineer, researcher*
Alam, Nadia M. *language educator, researcher*
Alasio, Teresa Marie *pathologist, educator*
Alasti, Hadi *electrical engineer, researcher*
Albanese, Jay Samuel *criminologist, educator*
Albanese, Thomas *entrepreneur*
Albano, Pasquale Charles *management educator, management consultant*
Alban-Salazar, Miguel F. *language educator*
Albers, Charles Edgar *retired investment company executive*
Albert, Gerald *retired clinical psychologist*
Alberti-Thomson, Marie J. (Marie Joyce Salisbury) *musician, educator*
Albrecht, Chris *talent agency executive, former broadcast executive*
Albrecht, Rebekah S. *mathematician, educator*
Albright, Joseph William *management consultant*
Albritton, William Harold III *federal judge*
Alcantara, Adriana *science educator*
Alden, Ingemar Bengt *pharmaceuticals executive*
Alderfer, Clayton Paul *professor, organizational consultant, writer*
Alderson, Vanessa *administrative assistant*
Aldredge, Theoni Vachliotis *costume designer*
Aldrich, Patricia Anne Richardson *retired magazine editor*
Aldrich, Seth F. *psychologist*
Aldridge, Adrienne Yingling *accountant, writer*
Aldridge, Donald O'Neal *military officer*
Aldrin, Buzz *retired astronaut*
Aleinikov, Andrei Grigoryevich *linguist, educator*
Alemu, Fitsum Achamyeleh *lawyer, researcher*
Alessi, David Alan *research scientist*
Alessio, Adam *medical educator, researcher*
Alexander, George Jonathon *lawyer, educator, dean*
Alexander, Hope *actor, educator, theater director*
Alexander, Icie Mae *communications executive*
Alexander, Jason (Jay Scott Greenspan) *actor*
Alexander, Jessica Aronow *anesthesiologist*
Alexander, Jonathan *cardiologist, consultant*
Alexander, Judd Harris *retired paper company executive*
Alexander, Nancy A. *information technology manager, director*
Alexander, Shaun *professional football player*
Alexandra, Allison Melissa *artist, writer, educator*
Alfano, Robert R. *science and engineering educator*
Alfonso-Bica, Kristy Lynn *elementary school educator*
Alford, Renee Marie *speech pathology/audiology services professional, educator*
Alfred, Stephen Jay *retired lawyer*
Alfriend, Kyle Terry *aerospace engineer*
Alholm, Björn-Olof Georg *diplomat*
Ali, Asem *Computer Vision Researcher*
Ali, Hamad Abdulkareem *academic administrator*
Ali, Kamal Mahmood *computer scientist*
Ali, Mohammed Zamshed *information technology executive, researcher*
Ali, Muhammad (Cassius Marcellus Clay) *retired professional boxer*
Alia, Valerie *humanities educator, writer*
Aliber, Robert Z. *economist, educator*
Alinder, Mary Street *writer, educator*
Allan, Sarah Katherine *Oriental studies educator*
Allard, Michael Alan *music educator, conductor*
Allard, Wayne (Allan Wayne Allard) *retired US Senator from Colorado, veterinarian*
Allbritton, Cliff *personal and organizational consultant*
Allday, Martin Lewis, Jr. *retired lawyer*
Alleeta, Julie *retired lawyer*
Allemang, Arnold A. *chemicals executive*
Allen, Bennie Carnel *employee relations specialist*
Allen, Betty Noldon *education educator, consultant*
Allen, Bruce Templeton *retired economics professor*
Allen, Charles E. *consulting firm executive, former federal agency administrator*
Allen, Charlotte *secondary school educator*
Allen, Donald Vail *investment company executive, pianist*
Allen, Elma Leitch *special education educator*
Allen, Frances Elizabeth *computer scientist*
Allen, Janet Lee *special education educator*
Allen, Laurie Ann *elementary school educator*
Allen, Louis Alexander *management consultant*
Allen, Marilyn Myers Pool *theater director, video specialist*
Allen, Merrill James *marine biologist*
Allen, Pamela Smith *retired psychologist, writer*
Allen, Patricia J. *retired library director*
Allen, Ralph Carnell *retired assistant principal*
Allen, Roberta *writer, photographer, conceptual artist*
Allen, Toni K. *lawyer*
Allen, William Hayes *lawyer, educator*
Allen, Woody (Allen Stewart Konigsberg) *film director, actor*
Allender, Julie Ann *psychologist*
Allison, Andrew Marvin *church administrator*
Allison Haslach, Linda *music educator*
Allred, Stephen (Coral Stephen Allred) *former federal agency administrator*
Allred, Susan G. *school system administrator*
Allston, Charita Capers *music educator*
Alm, John Richard *beverage company executive*
Almas, Tabish *medical researcher*
Almeida, Richard Joseph *finance company administrator*
Almodovar, Pedro *filmmaker, film director, film producer*
Almore-Randle, Allie Louise *special education educator, academic administrator*
Almour, Vicki Lynn *elementary school educator*
Aloff, Mindy *writer*
Alou, Felipe Rojas *former professional baseball team manager*
Alper, Andrew Michael *former investment banker*
Alper, Merlin Lionel *corporate financial executive*
Alpern, Andrew *lawyer, architect, historian*
Alpert, Ann Sharon *retired insurance claims examiner*
Alpher, Victor Seth *clinical psychologist, consultant*
Alramahi, Bashar *oil industry researcher*
Alroy, John *research scientist*
Alshahrani, Saad Ali *economist*
Altekruse, Joan Morrissey *retired preventive medicine physician*
Altenburger, Karl Marion *allergist*
Alter, Edward T. *former state treasurer*
Althoff, Robert R. *psychiatrist, educator*
Althouse, Gary Carl *veterinary physiologist*
Altman, Irwin *psychologist, educator*
Altman, Lawrence Gene *biologist, educator*
Altman, Louis *lawyer, author, educator*
Al-Tonsi, Abbas Ahmed *language educator, consultant*
Altschaeffl, Adolph George *retired civil engineering educator*
Altshuler, Kenneth Z. *psychiatrist, educator*
Alvarado, Shannon *professional athletics coach*
Alvare, Charles Daguerre *financial advisor, educator*
Alvarez, Veronica Iris *language educator*
Alvarez-Galloso, Roberto C. *mental health professional*
Alvi, Mohammed Haroon *process engineer*
Amacher, Arthur Loren *neurosurgeon*
Amann, Charles Albert *mechanical engineer, researcher*
Amar, Akhil Reed *law educator*
Amara, Lucine *vocalist*
Amatangelo, Nicholas S. *retired financial printing company and document management executive, educator*
Amato Chiaramonte Bordonaro, Baron Carlo Camillo *ambassador, consultant*
Amatulli, Rosa *literature educator*
Ambach, Gordon Mac Kay *educational association executive*
Ambrose, John Anthony *cardiologist, educator*
Ambrozic, Aloysius Matthew Cardinal (His Eminence Aloysius Cardinal Ambrozic) *cardinal, archbishop emeritus*
Amerasekera, Ekanayake Ajith *electronics engineer, director*
Ames, Donald Paul *retired air research director*
Ames, Marc L. *retired lawyer*
Ames, Sandra Cutler *secondary school educator*
Amestoy, Jeffrey Lee *former state supreme court chief justice, educator*
Amgott, Madeline *television producer, consultant*
Amidon, Edwin H., Jr. *lawyer*
Amiel, Howard *ophthalmologist, corneal surgeon*
Amis, Edward Stephen, Jr. *radiologist, retired military officer*
Ammanamanchi, Sudhakar *cancer biologist, educator*
Amonte, Tony (Anthony Lewis Amonte) *retired professional hockey player*
Amoroso, Richard Louis *psychologist, educator*
Amundson, John Kay *electrical engineer*
Amylon, Michael David *physician, educator*
An, Chungming *telecommunications industry executive*
An, Songon *research scientist*
Anagnostou, Dimitris E. *engineering educator, researcher*
Anastasopoulos, Panagiotis Ch. *transportation engineer, economist*
Anaya, Henry Daniel *research scientist, consultant*
Anbar, Michael *biophysics professor*
Anchin, Jack C. *psychologist, educator*
Ancker-Johnson, Betsy *physicist, engineer, retired automotive executive*
Ancoli-Israel, Sonia *psychologist, researcher*
Ancona, George Efrain *photographer, author*
Ancona, Kier Alexis *zoologist*
Anderer, Joseph Henry *textile company executive*
Andersen, Dan Edward *physicist, entrepreneur*
Andersen, David Charles *lawyer*
Andersen, Kurt Byars *writer*
Andersen, Linda *retired literature and language educator*
Andersen, Roy Stuart *physicist*
Anderson, Alan Stewart *lawyer*
Anderson, Allamay Eudoris *retired health educator, home economist*
Anderson, Bernard E. *economist*
Anderson, Elaine Janet *science educator*
Anderson, Geraldine Louise *medical researcher*
Anderson, Gillian Leigh *actress*
Anderson, Gregory Thomas *secondary school educator, researcher, historian*
Anderson, Herschel Vincent *retired librarian*
Anderson, Hugh George *bishop*
Anderson, Iris Anita *retired secondary school educator*
Anderson, James George *sociologist, educator, communications educator*
Anderson, Joan R. *secondary school educator*
Anderson, John Firth *retired religious organization administrator, retired librarian*
Anderson, John Gaston *electrical engineer, consultant*
Anderson, Jon Stephen *newswriter*
Anderson, Joseph Norman *retired food products executive, academic administrator*
Anderson, Lance Eric *management consultant*
Anderson, Laurie *experimental performance artist, musician*
Anderson, Linda Jean *critical care nurse, psychiatric nurse practitioner*
Anderson, Lisa D. *graphics designer, educator*
Anderson, Maria Watkins *financial analyst*
Anderson, Mark Robert *data processing executive, biochemist*
Anderson, Mary Ann Grasso *business executive*
Anderson, N. Christian III *former newspaper publisher*
Anderson, Ned, Sr. *Apache tribal official*
Anderson, Nona Louise *literature and language professor*
Anderson, Pam (Pamela Denise Anderson) *actress*
Anderson, Paul Irving *management executive*
Anderson, Paulette Elizabeth *real estate developer, entrepreneur, retired elementary school educator*
Anderson, Porter Warren, Jr. *retired pediatrics educator*
Anderson, Rachael Keller (Rachael Keller) *retired library director*
Anderson, Russell *research and development company executive*
Anderson, Russell A. *former state supreme court justice*
Anderson, Tom *former Internet company executive*
Anderson, Wayne Carl *global public affairs officer, retired corporate executive*
Anderson-Spivy, Alexandra *arts correspondent, editor, critic, writer, historian*
Andersson, Bo I. *automotive executive*
Andersson, Craig Remington *retired chemical company executive*
Andersson, Helen Demitrous *artist*
Andjaba, Martin *ambassador*
Ando, Yushi *chemicals executive*
Andrade, Joel T. *forensic specialist*
Andrawis, Alfred Samuel *engineering educator*
Andre, Anthony D. *management consultant*
Andrea, Mario Iacobucci *retired engineer, scientist, gemologist, appraiser*
Andreasson, Kim J. *writer, consultant*
Andreessen, Marc Lowell *venture capitalist, software company executive*
Andreeva, Valentina A. *medical researcher*
Andreoli, Thomas Eugene *physician*
Andretti, Mario *retired race car driver*
Andreu, Helene C. *dancer, educator*
Andrews, C.E. (Charles Elliot Andrews Jr.) *former finance company executive*
Andrews, David Ralph *lawyer*
Andrews, David Wallace *medical educator*
Andrews, Dame Julie (Julia Elizabeth Wells) *actress, singer*
Andrews, Marion E. *artist, calligrapher*
Andrews, Pat R. *political science professor*
Andrews, Richard Otis *former art gallery director, curator*
Andrews, William Cooke *physician*
Andreychuk, David *former professional hockey player*
Andriole, Vincent Thomas *medical educator, researcher*
Andrisani, John Anthony *editor, writer*
Andruk, Marjorie Dean *artist, educator*
Angell, Richard Bradshaw *philosophy educator*
Angle, Thomas E. *history professor*
Angle, Tracy Joyce *theater educator*
Anglim, Paul *biochemist*
Anis, Munazza *radiologist, educator*
Anisimov, Victor *chemist, researcher*
Annen, Margaret T. *language educator*
Annesi, Adele Mary *editor, writer*
Annus, John Augustus *artist*
Ansari, Rashid *engineering educator*
Ansbro, John Joseph *philosopher, educator*
Anschutz, Philip F. *communications and professional sports team executive*
Ansley, Shepard Bryan *lawyer*
Anstee, Jaime Lee Kelly *medical researcher*
Antebi, Guy *language educator*
Anthony, Joan Caton *administrative judge*
Anthony, Tisi Paul *recreational facility executive*
Anthony, Wilma Tylinda *retired customer service administrator*
Anthony-Perez, Bobbie Cotton Murphy *retired psychology professor*
Antich, Peter *radiologist, educator*
Aon, Frank Joseph Garcia *lab administrator, materials scientist*
Aouizerat, Bradley Eric *nursing educator*
Apfelbach, George Leonard, Jr. *urologist*
Aponte, Frances *psychologist, educator*
Appell, Louise Sophia *retired consulting company executive*
Appenzeller, Otto *neurologist, researcher*
Applebaum, Edward Leon *otolaryngologist, educator*
Applegate, Edward C. *writer, advertising educator*
Appleton, Kevin *academic administrator*
Apps, Jerold Willard *writer*
Apsel, Alyssa *electrical and computer engineer*
Apted, Michael David *film director*
Apuron, Anthony Sablan *archbishop*
Arakawa, Fumiyasu *archaeologist, researcher*
Aranguri, Cesar *internist, cardiologist, educator*
Archer, Lillian Patricia *academic administrator, dean*
Archey, William T. *retired trade association administrator*
Archibald, Nolan D. *household and industrial products company executive*
Archuleta, David James *singer*
Arciniega, Armando *mathematics professor*
Arciszewski, Tomasz Tadeusz *engineering educator*
Arcos, Cresencio S. *ambassador*
Arcus, Sam George *social worker, educator, author and writer*
Arden, Bruce Wesley *retired computer scientist, engineering educator*
Arditi, Aries Robert *research scientist*
Arditti, Paul *sound designer*
Areen, Judith Carol *law educator*
Arenal, Julie (Mrs. Barry Primus) *choreographer*
Arenberg, Julius Theodore, Jr. *retired accounting company executive*
Argiris, Athanassios *oncologist, researcher*
Arif, Ronald *electronics engineer*
Arif, Sally A. *pharmacist, educator*
Arking, Lucille Musser *nurse, epidemiologist, consultant*
Arking, Robert *geneticist, gerontologist, educator*
Arkless, David *employment services executive*
Arlen, Michael J. *writer*
Arlidge, John Walter *retired utilities executive*
Armacost, Mary-Linda Sorber Merriam *educational consultant*
Armaingaud, Franck *engineer*
Armbruster, Paula *social worker, director, child mental health educator*
Armen, Margaret Meis *lawyer*
Armey, Dick (Richard Keith Armey) *former United States Representative from Texas*
Armistead, Katherine Kelly (Mrs. Thomas B. Armistead III) *interior designer, travel consultant, civic worker*
Armour, Robert Alexander *literature and language professor, researcher*
Armstrong, Donald *biochemistry, pathophysiology educator*
Armstrong, Douglas Dean *journalist*
Armstrong, F(redric) Michael *retired insurance company executive, consultant*
Armstrong, (Arthur) James *minister, educator, consultant, writer*
Armstrong, James Francis III *retired language educator, writer*
Armstrong, L. C. *artist*
Armstrong, Marsha Susan *elementary school educator*
Armstrong, Thomas Newton III *art and garden specialist*
Arndt, Dianne Joy *artist, photographer*
Arndt, Laura Denise Lyons Bodeen *mathematics educator, composer of miracles*
Arnett, Edward McCollin *chemistry educator, researcher*
Arnold, Alanna S. Welling *lawyer*
Arnold, Charlotte S. *criminal justice agency executive, activist*
Arnold, George Lawrence *retired advertising company executive*
Arnold, Henri *cartoonist*
Arnold, James Oliver *aerospace executive, researcher*
Arnold, Janet Nina *health facility administrator, consultant*
Arnold, Jerome Gilbert *lawyer*
Arnold, Marygwen Suella *language educator, medical/surgical nurse*
Arnott, Howard Joseph *biology professor, dean*
Arquette, Patricia *actress*
Arrabal, Fernando *writer*
Arriaga, Moises Alberto *biomedical researcher, educator*
Arrigo, Jan Elizabeth *photographer, writer, artist*
Arrington, Michael (Jack Michael Arrington) *web publishing company executive, blogger, lawyer*
Arrott, Patricia Graham *artist, educator*
Arsht, Leslye Alene *retired federal agency administrator*
Arsie, Alessandro *mathematician, researcher*
Artemova, Alina *music educator*
Arthur (II), Hugh Thomas *lawyer*
Arthur, John Morrison *retired utilities executive*
Artis, LaToya CheRee *medical researcher*
Arunajatesan, Srinivasan *research scientist*
Asadorian, Diana C. *electrical engineer, educator*
Asamizu, Hirokuni *electronics engineer*
Asato, Evan Masami *artist, architect, designer*
Ascencao, Erlete Malveira *psychologist, educator*
Aschauer, Charles Joseph, Jr. *retired health products executive*
Aschheim, Eve Michele *artist, educator*
Ash, Jennifer Gertrude *writer, editor*
Ash, Roy Lawrence *former federal official*
Ashanti, Baron James *poet, educator*
Ashby, Franklin Charles, Jr. *corporate financial executive, educator*
Ashe, Bernard Flemming *arbitrator, lawyer, educator*
Ashe, Victor Henderson *former United States Ambassador to Poland, former mayor*
Ashford, Rob *choreographer, dancer*
Ashmore, Pamela Jean *music educator*
Ashton, Betsy Finley *artist, writer*
Ashton, Harris John *lawyer*
Ashworth, Bessie *benefits compensation analyst, writer*
Asiabanpour, Bahram *engineering educator*
Asirvatham, Sulochana Ruth *philologist, educator*
Askay, Richard R. *philosopher, educator*

Askew, Rilla *author*
Askins, Nancy Ellen Paulsen *training services executive*
Aslakson, Kenneth Randolph *law educator*
Asman, Bub (Henry B. Asman) *sound editor*
Asmussen, Angie *communications educator*
Astolfi, Jeri-Mae G. *music educator*
Astorino, Todd Anthony *exercise psychologist educator*
Astwood, Sir James Rufus *court administrator*
Atchison, Joseph Edward *pulp and paper industry consultant*
Atchison, Richard Calvin *retired trade association director*
Atherton, Barbara Klein *elementary school educator*
Atkin, J Myron *science educator*
Atkins, Erica *singer*
Atkins, Paul Stewart *former commissioner*
Atkins, Tina (Trecina Evette Atkins) *singer*
Atkins, Victor Kennicott, Jr. *private investor*
Atkins, William Paul *lawyer*
Atkinson, Holly Gail *physician, journalist, educator, human rights activist, writer*
Atlas, David *meteorologist, research scientist*
Atlee, John Light *retired physician, consultant*
Attebery, Louie Wayne *language educator*
Atwater, Phyllis Y. *municipal official*
Atwood, Donna Elaine *retired financial manager*
Atwood, Genevieve *geologist*
Au, Algie *biology professor*
Au, Howard *manufacturing executive*
Aubut, Marcel *lawyer, sports association official*
Auerbach, David I. *health policy analyst*
Auerbach, Ernest Sigmund *lawyer, insurance company executive, writer*
Auerbach, Norma Lent *educational administrator*
Aufhauser, David D. *lawyer, former federal agency administrator*
Augenstein, Ralf Gerald *physician*
August, Gilbert Paul *pediatrician, educator*
Augustine, Norman Ralph *not-for-profit and business executive, educator, retired federal agency administrator*
Augustine, Samuel Charles *medical educator, consultant*
Aulbach, George Louis *retired real estate company executive*
Aumann, Robert John *economics professor*
Aurin, Robert James *entrepreneur*
Aurongzeb, Deeder *research scientist*
Austin, Jacqueline Jean *exceptional student services educator*
Austin, John DeLong *retired judge*
Austin, John H.M. *retired radiologist*
Austin, Marion Russell *education educator, consultant*
Austin, Philip Edward *university professor, president emeritus*
Aust-Keefer, Mary Beth *library administrator*
Autrey, Wesley James *construction worker*
Auyang, Edward D. *surgeon*
Avary, Roger Roberts (Frank Brauner) *film director, producer, writer*
Aved, Barry *retail executive, consultant*
Avery, Carolyn Elizabeth *artist*
Avery, John Gates *retired engineering executive*
Avery, Mary Ellen *pediatrician, educator*
Avery, Stephen Neal *playwright, writer*
Avila, Charlie A. (Carlos A. Avila) *physics researcher, inventor*
Avila, Marvin Arthur *assistant principal student services*
Aviles, Alice Alers *psychologist*
Avinor, Eleanor Zeitlen *marriage and family therapist*
Avnet, Jonathan Michael *motion picture company executive, film director*
Avrett, Roz (Rosalind Case) *writer*
Awazu, Yukika *corporate executive, researcher, consultant, writer*
Awokuse, Titus O. *economics professor*
Axford, Roy Arthur *nuclear engineering educator*
Axilrod, Stephen Harvey *global economic consultant, economist*
Ayanso, Anteneh Wondimu *information systems educator*
Aykroyd, Daniel Edward *actor, writer*
Ayon, Xochitl *school librarian*
Ayotte, Kelly A. *former state attorney general*
Aziz, Noreen *oncologist, senior program director*
Baab-Hohman, Roberta (Robin) *artist, writer, stage manager*
Babar, Sardar Ijlal *pulmonologist*
Babauta, Darlyn Salas *customer service associate*
Babb, Roberta Joan *educational administrator*
Babb, Tracie *communications educator*
Babbitt, Samuel Fisher *retired university official*
Baca, Jim *mayor*
Baca, Joseph Francis *retired judge*
Baca, Vera Jennie Schulte *art educator*
Baccini, Laurance Ellis *lawyer*
Bach, Jan Morris *composer, educator*
Bach, Mary Irene *music educator*
Bacharach, Melvin Lewis *venture capitalist*
Backlar, Patricia *education educator*
Bäckman, Cristina M. *molecular biologist, biomedical researcher*
Backman, Gerald Stephen *retired lawyer*
Backus, Marcia Ellen *lawyer*
Bacolod, Marigee *economist, educator*
Bacon, Leslie Edward *operations analysis manager*
Bacon, Phillip *geographer, author, consultant*
Baddour, Anne Bridge *pilot*
Bader, William Banks *historian, former corporate executive, foundation executive*
Bae, Frank S.H. *retired law librarian*
Bae, Soo Hyun *research scientist*
Baer, Harold, Jr. *federal judge*
Baertschi, Steven W. *Pharmaceutical Researcher*
Bagert, Donald Joseph *computer scientist, educator*
Baggett, Donnis Gene *newspaper editor*
Bagley, Ronald Laird *military officer, educator*
Bagley, William Thompson *lawyer*
Bagnall, Joseph Albert *history professor*
Bagshaw, Malcolm A. *radiation oncologist, educator*
Bahbah, Bishara Assad *investment company executive, consultant*
Bahl, Tracy L. *healthcare executive*
Bahukutumbi, Radha *research scientist, educator*
Bai, He *research scientist*
Baier, Edward John *retired public health service officer, industrial hygiene engineer, consultant*
Bailar, Barbara Ann *retired statistician*
Bailes, Katherine *lawyer, educator*
Bailey, Burck *lawyer*
Bailey, Charles-James Nice *retired linguistics educator*
Bailey, Janet Dee *publishing executive*
Bailey, Margaret Elizabeth *nurse, retired military officer*
Bailey, Robert C. *opera company executive*
Bain, Douglas G. *retired aerospace transportation executive, lawyer*
Bain, Kevin T. *pharmacist, educator*
Bain, William Donald, Jr. *lawyer, chemicals executive*
Bainbridge, Dona Bardelli *marketing professional*
Bains, Harrison MacKellar, Jr. *retired corporate financial executive*
Bainton, Donald J. *diversified manufacturing company executive*
Baird, Alice Knar *retired language educator*
Bakeman, Carol Ann *travel writer, singer*
Baker, Augustus L., Jr. *retired surgeon*
Baker, Bonnie *nursing educator*
Baker, Carolyn Simmons *library director, consultant, researcher*
Baker, D. James *oceanographer, administrator, science and management consultant*
Baker, Deborah *physiology, geology, astronomy, meteorology, oceanography educator*
Baker, Edward Kevin *retail executive*
Baker, Eva Lee *education educator, researcher*
Baker, Gary Anthony *police officer and supervisor*
Baker, Henry S., Jr. *retired bank executive*
Baker, Ian Archbald *explorer, educator, writer, photographer*
Bákér, J. A., II, *executive management advisor and consultant, monetary architect, financial engineer emeritus*
Baker, Jimmy H. *former state finance administrator*
Baker, John David *health facility administrator, not-for-profit fundraiser, real estate agent*
Baker, Kathleen *music educator*
Baker, Paul Scott *ophthalmologist*
Baker, Ronald James *language educator, academic administrator*
Baker, Stewart Abercrombie *former federal agency administrator, lawyer*
Baker, Vincent Lamont *former professional basketball player*
Baker, William Franklin *retired broadcast executive*
Baker, William Thompson, Jr. *lawyer*
Baker, Zachary Moshe *librarian*
Bakht, Baidar *civil engineer, researcher, educator*
Bakken, Gordon Morris *law educator*
Bakkensen, John Reser *lawyer*
Baktir, Selcuk *electrical and computer engineer, researcher*
Bala, Sriram *clinical research professional*
Balázsi, Gábor *biophysicist, researcher*
Baldassano, Corinne Leslie *radio executive*
Baldrige, Letitia *writer, management consultant*
Baldwin, Allen Adail *retired lawyer, writer*
Baldwin, George Curriden *physicist, researcher*
Baldwin, Irene S. *hotel executive, real estate developer*
Baldwin, John Charles *surgeon, researcher*
Baldwin, William Russell *optometrist, foundation administrator*
Baliga, Ragavendra Ramakrishna *cardiologist, researcher*
Balish, Ruth Reitz *retired community health nurse*
Balisle, Jenny E. *artist*
Ball, Carroll Raybourne *anatomist, researcher, medical educator*
Ball, Cathi Rosanne *art educator*
Ball, Howard Guy *association administrator, educator*
Ball, James Herington *retired lawyer*
Ball, John Robert *healthcare executive*
Ball, Robert Edwin *engineering educator*
Ballantine, Betty *editor*
Ballhaus, William Louis *engineering executive*
Balstad, Roberta *social scientist*
Baltazzi, Evan Serge *retired engineering research consulting company executive*
Balter, Frances Sunstein *civic worker*
Baltzell, Kimberly *research scientist*
Bamberger, Gerald Francis *plastics marketing consultant*
Bamberger, Phylis Skloot *lawyer, educator, retired judge*
Banbury, Demby Bowman *director*
Bandar, Prince bin Sultan bin Abd al-Aziz Al Saud *former ambassador*
Bandy, Jack D. *lawyer*
Bandyopadhyay, Aparajita *research scientist*
Bangalore Prakash, Somashekar *Senior design Engineer*
Bankhurst, Arthur Dale *medical educator, researcher*
Banks, Charles Augustus III *distribution executive*
Banks, Deirdre Margaret *retired church organization administrator*
Bannister, Robert Corwin, Jr. *historian, educator*
Bansak, Stephen A., Jr. *investment banker, financial consultant*
Banta, James Elmer *epidemiologist, educator, dean*
Bantry, Bryan *entrepreneur*
Baptiste, La Verne Johnson *retired secondary school educator*
Baquet, Charles R. III *former federal agency administrator, international studies educator*
Barad, Jill Elikann *former family products company executive*
Baranchuk, Nina *finance educator*
Baranowski, Marcin *biology professor*
Baranski, Christine *actress*
Barasch, Marc Ian *writer*
Barber, James Alden *navy officer, educator*
Barbo, Dorothy Marie *obstetrician, gynecologist, educator*
Barbosa, Patricia R. *radar engineer*
Barca, George Gino *international winery executive, financial investor, consultant*
Barcenas-Mooradian, Martha *academic administrator, literature and language professor*
Bar-Cohen, Avram *mechanical engineering educator*
Bardaglio, Peter Winthrop *humanities and sustainability educator, former academic administrator*
Barefoot, Aldos Cortez, Jr. *retired forester, educator*
Bareither, Christopher *research scientist*
Barger, William James *management consultant, educator*
Barham, Charles Dewey, Jr. *electric power industry executive, lawyer*
Barham, Patte *publisher, author, columnist*
Barish, Matthew Adam *radiologist*
Barkan-Clarke, Jacqueline Mia *author, jewelry designer*
Barker, Virginia Lee *nursing educator*
Barkley, Terrell Wayne *archivist, curator, school librarian*
Barkmeier, Wayne W. *dentist, researcher, educator*
Barlowe, Dorothea *art educator, illustrator*
Barnard, Donald Roy *medical and veterinary entomologist*
Barner, Mark E. *minister, consultant*
Barnes, Frances Johnson *educational consultant*
Barnes, Robert F *agronomist*
Barnes, Robert Vincent *retired elementary and secondary school art educator*
Barnes, Sheila Kaye *Executive Director*
Barnes, Wesley Edward *energy and environmental executive*
Barnett, Amy DuBois *editor-in-chief*
Barnett, Benjamin Lewis, Jr. *retired physician, educator*
Barnett, Joyce Lyndel *freelance/self-employed writer*
Barnett, Patricia Ann *development professional*
Barney, Austin Dunham, II, *real estate developer*
Barnhardt, Zeb Elonzo, Jr. *lawyer*
Barnhurst, Christine Louise *broadcast executive*
Barnickol, Karl R. *lawyer*
Barnum, William Milo *architect*
Baron, Jeffrey *retired pharmacologist*
Baron, Seymour *engineering and research executive*
Baron, Stanley N. *retired electrical engineer*
Barr, Adam *biology educator*
Barr, James III *telecommunications company executive*
Barr, James Norman *retired federal judge*
Barr, John Baldwin *chemist, research scientist*
Barr, John Gladden *music educator*
Barr, Michael Charles *research director, lawyer*
Barranger, Milly Slater *theater educator author*
Barrett, Austin John *hematologist, researcher*
Barrett, Beverly Frances *public relations specialist*
Barrett, Janet Tidd *academic administrator*
Barrett, Lida Kittrell *mathematics professor*
Barrett, Richard David *university director, consultant, retired bank executive*
Barricks, Michael Eli *retinal surgeon*
Barrie, Erin Evelyn *school psychologist*
Barr-Marinetti, Shannon Evette *management consultant*
Barrow, Charles Herbert *investment banker*
Barrow, Thomas Davies *retired oil and mining company executive, consultant*
Barrow, Thomas Francis *artist, educator*
Barrows, Frank Clemence *journalist*
Barry, John M. *historian, writer*
Bartel, Arthur Gabriel *retired principal, alderman, culinary arts instructor*
Bartell, Angela Gina Baldi *retired judge*
Barth, David Keck *retired wholesale distribution executive, consultant*
Barth, Frances *artist*
Bartlett, Arthur Eugene *real estate company executive*
Bartlett, Bruce Reeves *writer*
Bartlett, David *media consultant*
Bartlett, Dede Thompson *association executive*
Bartlett, Denise Margaret *science educator*
Bartlett, Eugene Fred *retired surgeon*
Bartlett, Heather *cardiologist, educator*
Bartlett, Shirley Anne *accountant*
Barton, Gregory Mark *Olympic athlete*
Bartrem, Duane Harvey *retired military officer, residential designer, consultant*
Bartz, David John *lawyer*
Barua, Susamma *associate dean*
Barzilay, Joshua Israel *endocrinologist, educator*
Barzun, Jacques *writer, historian, lecturer*
Bascom, John Upton *retired surgeon*
Basescu, Neil *physics professor*
Basha-Soliman, Iman Ismail *literature and language educator*
Baskins, Ann O'Neil *lawyer, former computer company executive*
Baskovitz, Diana *retired elementary school educator*
Basnett, Margaret G. *reading and language arts educator, consultant*
Basova, Yulia *chemical engineer, researcher*
Bass, Aaron *school system administrator*
Bass, Charles Foster *former United States Representative from New Hampshire*
Bass, Lynda D. *retired medical/surgical nurse, nursing educator*
Bass, Steven Craig *computer science educator*
Bassett, Elizabeth Ewing (Libby Bassett) *writer, editor, consultant*
Bassett, Leslie Raymond *composer, educator*
Bassford, Lynn Foster *physicist, engineer manager*
Bassingthwaighte, Sarah Louise *music educator*
Basu, Nikhil Kumar *research scientist*
Basu, Sandip *research scientist*
Batakian, Manuel *bishop*
Batchelder, Alice M. *federal judge*
Batchelder, William Howard *psychology educator*
Batchu, Ravi Venkata *software engineer, researcher*
Batdorf, Linda *administrator*
Bateman, Charles Gregory *music educator*
Bateman, David Alfred *lawyer*
Bateman, Mitchell Ray *psychologist*
Bateman, Robert McLellan *artist*
Bates, Barbara J. Neuner *retired municipal official*
Bates, Gerald Earl *retired bishop*
Bates, Gwen Lee *health facility administrator, consultant*
Bates, Kim *history professor*
Bateson, Mary Catherine *retired anthropology educator, writer, lecturer*
Bathala, Neeti *science educator*
Batman, Keith *healthcare educator*
Battaglia, Francine *mechanical engineering educator, researcher*
Batteen, Mary Louise *oceanographer*
Battocchi, Ronald Silvio *lawyer*
Batts, Warren Leighton *retired manufacturing executive*
Bauer, Barbara Ann *marketing consultant*
Bauer, Henry Hermann *chemistry and science educator*
Bauer, Natalie Renee *medical educator*
Bauer, Patricia E. *journalist*
Bauer, Richard Carlton *nuclear engineer*
Baugh, Charles Milton *biochemistry educator, dean*
Baugh-Bennett, Grace L. *musician, educator*
Bauhan, Hobart Baker *retired mining engineer, farmer*
Baum, Eleanor *electrical engineering educator*
Baum, Jules Leonard *ophthalmologist, educator*
Bauman, Frederick Carl *lawyer, mining executive*
Bauman, Winfield Scott *finance educator*
Baumgarten, Jon A. *lawyer*
Baumgartner, Andrew C. *retired elementary school educator*
Baumgartner, John H. *gas industry executive*
Baumhart, Raymond Charles *religious organization administrator*
Bavuso, Craig *psychologist*
Baxter, John Darling *internist, endocrinologist, educator, health facility administrator*
Baxter, Nevins Dennis *bank consultant*
Baxter, Sheila R. *career military officer*
Bayles, Carmon Salter *special education educator*
Baylor, Elgin Gay *former professional sports team executive, retired professional basketball player*
Baym (Stillinger), Nina *literature educator, researcher, writer, editor*
Baymiller, Lynda Doern *social worker*
Baynes, Thomas Edward, Jr. *retired judge, lawyer, mediator, educator*
Bayoumi, Hassan *engineer*
Bayoumi, Moustafa *social studies educator*
Beach, Michael Lindsay *statistician*
Beadle, Elizabeth Ahrens *retired elementary school educator*
Beagrie, George Simpson *dentist, educator, retired dean*
Beal, Merrill David *conservationist, museum director*
Beals, L(oren) Alan *association executive*
Bear, Geraldine M. *nursing assistant, poet*
Beard, Ann Southard *diplomat, oil industry executive*
Beard, James K. *retired aeronautical engineer*
Beasley, Barbara Starin *sales executive, marketing professional*
Beasley, James George *civil engineer*
Beattie, Michael Stephen *neuroscientist, educator*
Beatts, Anne Patricia *writer*
Beatty, Frances *civic worker*
Beatty, Virginia Lewis *librarian, archivist, environmental education & urban horticulture consultant*
Beatty, Warren *actor, film director, film producer*
Beauchamp, Valdivia Vânia Siqueira *translator*
Beaudet-Francès, Patricia Suzanne *senior photography editor*
Beauprez, Bob (Robert L. Beauprez) *former congressman*
Beaven, Michael Anthony *biomedical researcher*
Beaver, Barbara Leann *elementary school educator, writer*
Beavers, Roy Lackey *retired utilities executive, volunteer, writer*
Beck, Albert *manufacturing executive*
Beck, Barbara J. *employment services executive*
Beck, Jane *dance educator, choreographer*
Beck, Susan Rebecca *voice educator, consultant*
Becker, Gail Roselyn *museum director*
Becker, Lawrence Carlyle *philosopher, educator, writer*
Becker, Nancy May *nursing educator*
Beckerman, Nancy Lisa *psychotherapist, educator*
Beckett, Victoria Ling *physician*
Beckjord, Eric Stephen *nuclear engineer, researcher*
Beckson, Mace *psychiatrist*
Bedford, Hilary Evans *history educator*
Bedigian, Dorothea *botanist*
Bednoff, Stuart Leon *obstetrician, gynecologist, educator*
Beecher, Graciela Fernandez *language educator, writer*
Beeler, Charles Alan *retired music educator*
Beer, Christian Walter *economics educator*
Beers, Charlotte Lenore *retired advertising executive, former federal agency administrator*
Beezer, Robert Renaut *federal judge*
Beggs, William H. *microbiologist, researcher*
Begovich, Michael *criminal defense attorney, law educator*
Beguin, Bernard Auguste *retired broadcast executive, columnist*
Behr, Marion Ray *artist*
Behrendt, John Charles *geophysicist, researcher, writer*
Beiswenger, Jane Miller *retired science educator*
Bekavac, Nancy Yavor *retired academic administrator, lawyer*
Bekkali, Younes *pharmaceutical executive, director*
Beldock, Donald Travis *investor*
Beldock, Myron *lawyer*
Beldon, Sanford T. *publisher*
Belfer, Inna *research scientist, medical educator*
Belfour, Ed *former professional hockey player*
Belgrave, Faye *social sciences educator*
Belieu, Erin *literature educator*
Belinger, Harry Robert *retired business executive*

Belk, Leotis S. *language educator*
Bell, Angela Marie *accountant*
Bell, Jack *federal agency administrator*
Bell, Janet S. *interior designer, developer, event producer*
Bell, Jeff *former computer software marketing executive*
Bell, Jerry Alan *science education consultant*
Bell, Larry Stuart *artist*
Bell, Robert Morrall *retired lawyer*
Bell, Sharon Kaye *small business owner*
Bell, Susan Jane *nurse*
Bellak, Sharon Lee *middle school educator*
Bellamy, James Carl *retired insurance company executive*
Belleville, Philip Frederick *lawyer*
Bellmon, Henry Louis *former Governor of Oklahoma*
Bello, Maria Elana *actress*
Bell-Rose, Stephanie *foundation administrator*
Belluomini, Frank Stephen *accountant*
Belmonte-Alcantara, Thelma *education educator*
Belnap, Nuel Dinsmore, Jr. *philosophy educator*
Belnick, Mark Alan *lawyer, educator*
Beltran, Felix *graphic designer*
Beluso, Karen Mae *performing company executive, music educator*
Ben-Amots, Ofer *composer, educator*
Bencardino, Jenny Teresa *musculoskeletal radiologist*
Bencini, Sara Haltiwanger *concert pianist*
Benedetti, Michael M. *science educator*
Benedict, Stewart H. *writer, playwright*
Benfield, Ann Kolb *retired lawyer*
Benfield, John Richard *surgeon, educator*
Benjamin, Arlin James *physicist*
Benjamin, Croxton G. *history professor*
Benjamin, Latanya T. *dermatologist*
Benkert, Joseph A. *former federal agency administrator*
Bennet, Douglas Joseph, Jr. *former academic administrator*
Bennett, Alan M. *retired insurance company executive*
Bennett, Amanda *former editor*
Bennett, Barbara Virginia *fashion consultant, concert pianist*
Bennett, Bryce Hugh, Jr. *lawyer*
Bennett, Charles Leonard *astrophysicist, educator*
Bennett, Clay *cartoonist*
Bennett, Curtis Dwight *mathematician*
Bennett, Edward Virdell, Jr. *surgeon*
Bennett, Lerone, Jr. *retired magazine editor, author*
Bennett, Peter Dunne *retired marketing educator*
Bennett, Robert LeRoy *computer software development company executive*
Bennett, Robert Thomas *lawyer, former political organization administrator, accountant*
Bennett, Stephen M. *former computer software company executive*
Bennett, Tony (Anthony Dominick Benedetto) *entertainer*
Bennett, Velma Jean *elementary school educator*
Benney, Douglas Mabley *direct marketing executive, consultant*
Benning, James *film director*
Benoit, Danielle Sw *medical researcher*
Benoit, Philip Grosvenor *communications executive, educator, writer*
Benson, Allen B. *chemist, educator, consultant*
Benson, Craig Robert *former governor*
Benson, Donald Charles *mathematician, educator*
Benson, Donald Erick *finance company executive*
Bensussen, Melia *theater director, professor*
Bentley, Charles Raymond *geophysics educator*
Bentley, Charmaine Clark O'Fallon *secondary school educator*
Bentley, Donald Lyon *statistics professor, minister*
Bentley, Kenneth Chessar *oral and maxillofacial surgeon, educator*
Benton, Malu *language educator*
Benyshek, Denita Maree *psychotherapist, educator, artist*
Benzahra, Sidi Cherkawi *physics professor*
Beracha, Barry Harris *retired food products executive*
Beranek, Kim Marie *music educator*
Berard, Barbara *performing arts educator*
Berard, Bryan *professional hockey player*
Berardi, John M. *nutritionist, educator*
Bercovitch, Sacvan *English language professional, educator*
Bercu, Barry Bernard *pediatric endocrinologist*
Berding, Kenneth *biblical studies and biblical greek eduactor*
Beredjiklian, Pedro Kirkor *physician*
Berenbaum, Michael Gary *theology educator*
Berg, Darla Gaye *writer*
Berg, Helen MacDuffee *retired university program director, statistician*
Berg, Sanford Vern *economics professor, director*
Bergan, Edmund Paul, Jr. *lawyer*
Bergau, Frank Conrad *real estate, commercial and investment properties executive*
Bergen, Candice *actress, writer, photojournalist*
Berger, Barbara *special education educator, consultant*
Berger, Frank Stanley *management consultant*
Berger, Michael *physician, educator*
Berger, Robert Bertram *lawyer*
Berger, Sanford Jason *retired lawyer, securities dealer, real estate broker*
Berger, Steven R. *retired lawyer, state official*
Berger, Stuart *medical educator*
Bergeron, Patricia Ann *education educator, consultant*
Bergin, Allen Eric *clinical psychologist, educator*
Bergland, Robert Selmer *former United States Secretary of Agriculture*
Berglund, Robin G. *psychiatrist, management consultant*
Bergman, Andrew *scriptwriter, film director*
Bergman, Hermas John (Jack Bergman) *retired college administrator*
Bergstein, Daniel Gerard *lawyer*
Berhe, Asmeret Asefaw *science educator*
Beringer, William Ernst *mediator, arbitrator, lawyer, retired manufacturing executive*
Berka, Marianne Guthrie *health and physical education educator*
Berka, Randy M. *molecular biologist, director*
Berkery, Rosemary Theresa *lawyer, former diversified financial services company executive*
Berkley, Peter Lee *lawyer*
Berkley, Stephen M. *entrepreneur, investor*
Berkoff, Charles Edward *pharmaceutical and biotech consultant*
Berkowitz, Henry *artist*
Berlin, Kenneth Darrell *chemistry professor, consultant, researcher*
Berlin, Robert Harry *historian, educator*
Berlind, Roger Stuart *stage and film producer*
Berlinger, Warren *actor*
Berman, Jeff *former Internet company executive*
Berman, Louise Marguerite *education educator, writer*
Berman, Michael P. *photographer*
Berman, Miriam Naomi *librarian*
Berman, Richard Angel *health facility administrator*
Berman, Sandra Rita *retired personnel director*
Berman, William H. *retired publishing company executive*
Bern, Dorrit J. *former apparel executive*
Bernard, Cathy S. *management corporation executive*
Bernard, Jennifer *music educator*
Bernath, John (Jack) Charles, Jr. *electronics and reliability engineer*
Bernhardt, Arthur Dieter *urban planner, consultant*
Bernsen, Harold John *political scientist, educator, retired military officer*
Bernstein, Carl *writer, journalist*
Bernstein, Edward Charles *rabbi*
Bernstein, I. Melvin *dean, materials scientist*
Bernstein, Mary *sociologist, educator*
Bernstein, Merton Clay *law educator, arbitrator*
Bernstein-Siegel, Debra Lynn *marketing administrator, dance educator*
Bernthal, Harold George *health products executive, director*
Berra, Kathy *rehabilitation nurse, researcher*
Berra, P. Bruce *computer science educator*
Berresford, Susan Vail *retired foundation administrator*
Berrien, James Stuart *environmental news and information web site executive, former magazine publisher*
Berry, Gail W. *psychiatrist, educator*
Berry, Iris Elizabeth *academic administrator*
Berry, Jacob Obadiah *not-for-profit developer, rancher*
Berry, Robert Vaughan *retired electrical manufacturing company executive*
Berry, Sharon *medical/surgical nurse, legal nurse consultant*
Berry, William Willis *retired utilities executive*
Bers, Abraham *electrical engineering and physics educator*
Bers, Donald Martin *physiology educator*
Bersell, Sean Devlin *trade association executive*
Bershad, Neil Jeremy *electrical engineering educator*
Bertolet, Jennifer L. *historian*
Bertram, Phyllis Ann *retired lawyer, communications executive*
Bertrand, Frederic Howard *retired insurance company executive*
Bertrand, Luc *former stock exchange executive*
Besch, Lorraine W. *special education educator*
Beschloss, Michael *historian, writer, lecturer, commentator*
Beshai, John *cardiologist, educator*
Besing, Ray Gilbert *lawyer, educator*
Besley, Athlone Christine *education educator, researcher*
Bess, Michael Demaree *history professor*
Best, Laurence Edward *lawyer*
Bestwick, Warren William *retired construction company executive*
Besur, Siddesh V. *medical educator*
Betancourt-Bryant, Sonia *music educator*
Bethke, Louise Virginia *music educator, writer*
Betti, John Anso *federal official, retired automotive executive*
Beumer, Richard Eugene *retired engineering executive*
Beuning, Penny J. *chemistry professor*
Beuthien, Gayle Dawn *special education educator, swim coach*
Bevan, Tim *film producer*
Bevelhymer, Darlene Pearl *lawyer, retired secondary school educator*
Be Vier, William A. *retired religious studies educator*
Bevilacqua, Anthony Joseph Cardinal *cardinal, archbishop emeritus*
Bevington, Edmund Milton *electrical machinery manufacturing company executive*
Bewley, Peter David *corporate director, investor*
Bey, Gwendolyn *legal association administrator*
Beyer, Dana D. *music educator*
Beyer, Lisa *journalist*
Beyer, Norma H. *nursing educator*
Bhada, Rohinton Khurshed *chemical engineering educator*
Bhadra, Jayanta *computer scientist, electrical engineer*
Bhanja, Sanjukta *engineering educator*
Bhanot, Sanjay *pharmaceutical executive, researcher*
Bhatia, Rajan *engineer, physicist, researcher*
Bhatia, Sneha P. *writer*
Bhatt, Jagdish Jeyshanker *retired science educator, author*
Bhattacharya, Tilak *mathematics professor*
Bhattacherjee, Anol *finance educator*
Bi, Jian *senior statistician, consultant*
Biasin, Giovanni *language educator*
Bick, Katherine Livingstone *neuroscientist, educator, researcher*
Bickford, Margaret Wyatt *minister*
Bidwell, James Truman, Jr. *lawyer*
Bidwell, Roger Grafton Shelford *biologist, educator*
Biederman, Edwin Williams, Jr. *retired geologist*
Biegel, David Eli *social worker, educator*
Bielory, Leonard *allergist, immunologist, medical school administrator*
Bielucke, Edward Anthony III *transportation executive, writer*
Bierig, Jack R. *lawyer, educator*
Bierring, Ole *ambassador*
Bierstedt, Peter Richard *entertainment industry consultant, lawyer*
Bies, Susan Schmidt *former federal official*
Biester, Edward George, Jr. *judge, former congressman*
Bigby, JudyAnn *medical educator*
Bigelow, Robert P. *lawyer, arbitrator, mediator, journalist*
Bigelow, Vivian Lou *elementary school educator, secondary school educator*
Biggs, Edmund Logan *retired college administrator*
Bighta, Anna *educator*
Biglaiser, Glen *science educator*
Bijur, Peter I. *retired petroleum company executive*
Bikales, Norbert M. *chemist, science administrator*
Biklen, Stephen Clinton *retired diversified financial services company executive*
Bikoff, J. Darius *beverage company executive*
Bilbray, James Hubert *Former United States Representative from Nevada, lawyer, consultant*
Bilirakis, Michael *former congressman, lawyer, corporate financial executive*
Billingham, Clare *elementary school educator*
Bimstein, Phillip Kent *composer*
Bina, Robert W *psychologist*
Bingham, Marian *artist, printmaker*
Binkley, David Martin *electrical engineer, educator, musician*
Binkley, Howell *lighting designer*
Binkley, Timothy *computer graphics designer, educator*
Binnie, Nancy Catherine *retired nurse, educator*
Binoche, Juliette *actress*
Binzen, Peter Husted *journalist*
Biondi, Frank J., Jr. *entertainment company executive*
Birch, Adolpho A., Jr. *retired state supreme court justice*
Birch, Ian *former editor-in-chief*
Birch, Michael *Internet company executive, application developer*
Bircher, Andrea Ursula *retired psychiatric mental health clinical nurse specialist*
Bircher, Daniel Trevor *musician*
Bird, Kai *journalist, historian*
Bird, Mary Lynne Miller *professional society administrator*
Birder, Lori A. *medical educator*
Birdsall, William Forest *retired librarian*
Bird-Soto, Nancy I. *language educator*
Birk, John Richard *management consultant*
Birkenmaier, Anke *educator*
Birky, John Edward *banker, financial consultant*
Birnbaum, Milton *laser physicist, educator, researcher*
Bishop, Anne Hughes *retired nursing educator*
Bishop, Budd Harris *retired museum director*
Bishop, C. Diane *state agency administrator, educator*
Bishop, Charles Edwin *academic administrator, economist, educator*
Bishop, Charles Joseph *retired manufacturing executive*
Bishop, Claire DeArment *small business owner, retired librarian*
Bishop, Douglas Krumbhaar *biologist, educator*
Bishop, Gordon Bruce *journalist*
Bishop, Kim Irene *pharmaceutical consultant, cognitive psychopharmacologist*
Bishop, William Peter *management consultant, rancher, musician*
Bishop-Haynes, Aisha Suzette *materials scientist*
Bissell, James Dougal III *motion picture production designer*
Biswas, Pinaki *statistician*
Bittner, David Michael *engineering educator and professional engineer*
Bitzas, Penelope *music educator*
Bivens, Carolyn Vesper *former sports association administrator*
Biziou, Peter *cinematographer*
Blacher, Joan Helen *psychotherapist, educator*
Black, Charles Ray, Jr., (Charlie Black) *lobbyist*
Black, David *writer, educator*
Black, Dustin Lance *scriptwriter, television and film producer*
Black, Hillel Moses *publisher*
Black, Sir James Whyte *retired academic administrator, pharmacologist*
Black, Kathleen Marie *literature and language professor*
Black, Kris Susan Lynn *marketing company executive, speaker, author, poet*
Black, Lewis *comedian, actor*
Black, Susan Harrell *federal judge*
Black, William Rea *lawyer*
Blackbourn, David Gordon *history professor*
Blackburn, John W. *retired psychologist*
Blackburn, Larry H. *builder*
Blackford, Robert Newton *lawyer, director*
Blackman, Jeffrey William *lawyer*
Blackmun, Barbara Winston *art historian, educator, academic administrator*
Blackstone, Dara *music educator, conductor*
Blackwell, James E. *retired science educator*
Blackwell, Lois Moore *fashion designer, educator, visual artist*
Blackwell, Vickie Jan *small business owner*
Blagden, Susan Lowndes *retired small business owner*
Blagojevich, Rod R. (Milorad Blagojevich) *former Governor of Illinois, former United States Representatives from Illinois*
Blaine, David (David Blaine White) *magician*
Blaine, Davis Robert *valuation consultant, investment banker*
Blair, Anita K. *former civilian military employee*
Blair, David Clark *information scientist, educator*
Blaise, J. Harry *engineering educator*
Blaise, Oliver N., Jr. *educational consultant, retired school system administrator*
Blake, Gerald Rutherford *retired banker*
Blake, Kimberly Bosworth *pharmacist*
Blake, King Charles *humanities educator, writer*
Blake Ramos, Debra Barbara *writer*
Blalock, Carol Douglass *psychologist, educator*
Blalock, Louise *librarian, public administrator, executive coach*
Blanchard, Richard Frederick *construction executive*
Blanchard, Townsend Eugene *retired service companies executive*
Blanco, Kathleen Babineaux *former governor*
Blank, Rebecca Margaret *federal agency administrator, economist*
Blankfein, Robert Jerome *retired neurologist*
Blatz, Linda Jeanne *sales executive*
Blauer, Derwin Ann Taylor *educator*
Blaylock, Russell Lane *biology professor, retired neurosurgeon*
Bleck, Phyllis Claire *surgeon*
Bleicher, Samuel Abram *law professor, consultant*
Blencke, Carl Joseph *finance educator*
Bleszinski, Cliff (Clifford Michael) *game designer*
Bletzer, Keith Valery *secondary school educator*
Blickwede, Donald Johnson *retired metal products executive*
Blige, Mary Jane *singer*
Blinn, William Frederick *television writer and producer*
Bliss, Donald Tiffany, Jr. *retired ambassador*
Blissett, William Frank *English literature educator*
Blix, Hans Martin *retired international organization official*
Blizard, Marjorie Claire *small business owner*
Blizzard, James Michael *engineering educator*
Bloch, Anthony Michael *mathematician, educator*
Bloch, Erich *retired electrical engineer, science foundation director*
Bloch, Julia Chang *foundation president*
Bloch, Richard M. *psychology professor, director*
Bloch, Stuart Marshall *lawyer, banker*
Block, Emil Nathaniel, Jr. *retired air force officer*
Block, Gene David *academic administrator, biologist, educator*
Block, Lawrence *writer*
Bloemen, Harmanna *economics professor*
Blomquist, Alan Charles *film producer*
Blondin, C. J. *trade association administrator, lawyer*
Bloodworth, Gladys Leon *elementary school educator*
Bloodworth, Glen Alexander *nuclear medicine physician*
Bloomer, Harold Franklin, Jr. *retired lawyer*
Bloomfield, Lincoln Palmer *political scientist*
Bloomquist, Kenneth Gene *music educator, director*
Bloomquist, Rodney Gordon *geologist*
Blos, Joan Winsor *writer, critic, educator*
Blossom, Beverly *choreographer, educator*
Blount, Benroe Wayne *physician, department chairman*
Blount, Vyren William *finance educator*
Blow, George *lawyer*
Blue, China *artist*
Blum, Barbara Davis *investor*
Blum, Bradley Dickerson *restaurant chain executive*
Blum, Gerald Henry *retired retail executive*
Blum, Samuel *retired research scientist*
Blumberg, Mark Stuart *health service researcher, scientist, director*
Blume, Sheila Bierman *retired psychiatrist*
Blumencranz, Peter William *surgeon*
Blumenfeld, Thomas Jefferson *orthopedist*
Blumenthal, Susan Jane *physician, psychiatrist, educator*
Blumenthal, W. Michael (Werner Michael Blumenthal) *retired manufacturing company executive, former United States Secretary of the Treasury*
Bluth, B. J. (Elizabeth Jean Catherine Bluth) *sociologist, aerospace technologist*
Blyth, Myrna Greenstein *publishing executive*
Boal, Dean *retired arts center administrator, educator*
Boal, Ellis *lawyer*
Boardman, Elizabeth Drake *computer security professional*
Boardman, Paul Craig *science educator*
Bobrow, Davis Bernard *public policy educator*
Bobzien, Susanne *philosopher, educator*
Bocchetta, Maurizio *molecular biologist, educator*
Bockius, Ruth Bear *nursing educator*
Bodensteiner, Lisa M. *former utilities executive, lawyer*
Bodey, Richard Allen *minister, educator*
Bodman, Helene Dunn *musicologist, arts administrator*
Bodman, Samuel Wright III *former United States Secretary of Energy*
Bodsworth, Fred *writer, ecologist*
Bodycomb, Jeffrey Taylor *engineering company executive*
Boe, David Stephen *musician, educator, dean*
Boehle, William Randall *music educator emeritus*
Boff, Kenneth Richard *engineering research psychologist*
Boggs, Charles Harmon, Jr. *retired surgeon*
Bogren, Carol Ferrer *secondary school educator*
Bohanon, Kathleen Sue *neonatologist*
Bohrman, Catherine Leuchs *sculptor*
Bohstedt, John *retired history professor*
Boise, Audrey Lorraine *retired special education educator*
Boitano, Brian *Olympic athlete*
Bokat, Stephen Arthur *lawyer, former business association executive*
Bokhari, Naila Qureshi *mathematician, educational consultant*
Bolas, Gerald Douglas *museum director, art historian, educator*
Bolden, Marion A. *former school system administrator*
Bolen, David Benjamin *former ambassador*

Bolger, David P. *former insurance company executive*
Bolie, Victor Wayne *molecular biologist, researcher*
Bolinder, Scott W. *former publishing company executive*
Bollapragada, Ramesh *information scientist, educator*
Bollenbacher, Herbert Kenneth *steel company official*
Bolley, Sue Rebecca *mathematics educator*
Bollinger, Sharon Moore *psychotherapist*
Bollon, Steven A. *financial analyst, educator*
Bolnick, Howard Jeffrey *consultant, investor*
Bolsterli, Margaret Jones *English professor, farmer*
Bolten, Joshua Brewster *former White House chief of staff*
Bolton, Caroline Joy *retired quality assurance professional*
Bolton, Claude M., Jr. *former civilian military employee, retired military officer*
Boly, Lillian Byronell *retired language educator*
Bomes, Stephen D. *lawyer*
Bonardi De Bretignon, Claude-David *ambassador*
Bonates, Tiberius Oliveira *management consultant*
Bonati, Ralph L. *biology educator*
Bonazzi, Elaine Claire *mezzo soprano*
Bond, Julian *civil rights association executive*
Bond, Rose *artist, educator*
Bondi, Harry Gene *lawyer*
Bondi, Joseph Charles, Jr. *education educator, consultant*
Bonds, Alfred B. III *engineering educator, consultant*
Bonds, Barry Lamar *professional baseball player*
Bondy, Alison A. *music educator*
Bonekemper, Edward Henry III *history professor*
Bonesio, Woodrow Michael *lawyer*
Bonilla, Fernando J. *former Puerto Rican government official*
Bonilla-Ríos, Daniel Cecilio *ancient language educator*
Bon Jovi, Jon (John Francis Bongiovi Jr.) *musician, singer, songwriter, actor, professional sports team executive*
Bonnard, Raymond *theater director*
Bonnell, Bruno *information technology executive*
Bonner, David Calhoun *chemical company executive*
Bonner, John Tyler *biology professor*
Bonnett, James W. *retired engineer*
Bonnie, Shelby W. *Internet company executive*
Bon Tempo, Michael III *middle school educator*
Bontha, Srikanth *milling system engineer*
Boo, Katherine *newswriter*
Bookbinder, Russ *professional sports team executive*
Booker, Nana Laurel *art gallery owner, honorary consul*
Booker-Reed, Shundria NeKesha *educational consultant*
Boone, Donna Clausen *physical therapist, statistician, researcher*
Boone, Earle Marion *marketing executive, investor*
Booth, Catherine Kate Mary *art educator*
Booth, Debra *theater educator*
Boothby, Richard Alfred *gynecologist, educator*
Boothe, Leon Estel *academic administrator emeritus, consultant*
Boral, Sougato *chemist, researcher*
Boras, Scott D. *professional sports agent*
Borda, Richard Joseph *retired insurance company executive*
Bordelon, Suzanne Mackie *writing and rhetoric educator*
Borden, David M. *former state supreme court justice*
Borden, Ernest Carleton *oncologist, educator*
Borgman, Matthew *pediatrician*
Borgnine, Ernest *actor*
Boriboonsomsin, Kanok *transportation engineer*
Boris, Neil Walden *psychiatrist, consultant*
Borisy, Gary G. *science administrator, researcher, molecular biology professor*
Bork, Robert Heron *law educator, retired federal judge*
Borkowski, Francis Thomas *music educator*
Borkowski, John Joseph *lawyer*
Borowitz, Albert Ira *lawyer, writer*
Borum, Rodney Lee *corporate financial executive*
Borwein, Jonathan Michael *mathematics professor*
Borysewicz, Mary Louise *editor*
Bos, Gary D. *orthopedist*
Boschmann, Erwin *chemistry professor*
Bosco, Philip Michael *actor*
Bose, Sudip *statistician, educator*
Bosl, Phillip L. *retired lawyer*
Bosmajian, Haig Aram *speech communication educator*
Boss, Kevin Korey *military officer*
Bossidy, Larry (Lawrence Arthur) *pharmaceutical company and former industrial manufacturing executive*
Bosson, Richard Campbell *state supreme court justice*
Boswell, Vivian Nicholson *protective services official*
Botelho, Bruce Manuel *mayor, retired state attorney general*
Boterbloem, Kees *humanities educator*
Botkin, James W. *leadership and executive coach*
Botkin, Monty Lane *computer company executive*
Botsford, Mary Henrich *retired ophthalmologist*
Bottolfson, Wahnita Joan *parochial school educator*
Boucher, Richard A. *former federal agency administrator*
Boudoulas, Olga *dermatologist*
Boudreau, Daniel J. *retired state supreme court justice*
Boudreau, Thomas M. *lawyer, health products executive*
Boudreaux, John *marketing and public relations executive*
Bougas, James Andrew *physician, surgeon, educator*
Boulais, Robert Charles *mathematics educator*
Boulanger, Carol Seabrook *lawyer*
Boulez, Pierre *composer, conductor*
Bounds, Sarah Etheline *historian*
Bourdain, Anthony *chef, writer*
Bourguignon, Erika Eichhorn *anthropologist, educator*
Bourguignon, Lilly Y. *medical educator, researcher*
Bourke, Anthony Thomas Conal *retired medical researcher, microbiologist*
Bourque, Boyd D. *secondary school educator*
Bouvier, Linda Fritts *publishing executive*
Bouvier, Monica Renee *traffic director*
Bova, Benjamin William *writer, editor*
Bow, Stephen Tyler, Jr. *business executive*
Bowden, William P., Jr. *retired lawyer, finance company executive*
Bowen, Barton Richard *economics professor*
Bowen, Bonnie T. *literature and language professor*
Bowen, Jean *retired librarian, consultant*
Bowen, Lowell Reed *retired lawyer*
Bowen, Otis Ray *former United States Secretary of Health and Human Services, former Governor of Indiana*
Bowen, Richard Lee *retired academic administrator, political scientist, educator*
Bowen, Tim *former recording industry executive*
Bower, Janet Esther *writer, educator*
Bower, Jean Ramsay *lawyer, writer*
Bowers, Christi C. *mediator, lawyer, writer*
Bowers, Richard Philip *manufacturing executive*
Bowes, Frederick III *publishing executive, consultant*
Bowick, Susan D. *retired computer company executive*
Bowles, Barbara Landers *retired investment company executive*
Bowling, Woodrow Wilson *telecommunications industry executive, insurance company executive*
Bowman, Bruce Alan *civil engineer*
Bowman, Craig Thomas *mechanical engineer, educator*
Bowman, Leah *retired fashion designer, educator consultant*
Bowman, Ned David *medical administrator*
Bowman, Roger Manwaring *real estate company officer*
Bowne, Shirlee Pearson *real estate consultant*
Bowser, Osen Felton *literature and language professor*
Box, Thadis Wayne *university dean emeritus, educator*
Boyarchenko, Svetlana Ivanovna *economics professor, mathematician*
Boyatt, Thomas David *retired ambassador*
Boyce, Joseph Nelson *retired journalist, consultant, educator*
Boyce, Martha Jo *artist, educator*
Boyce, Ralph L., Jr., (Skip Boyce) *former ambassador*
Boyd, Alan Stephenson *retired United States Secretary of Transportation*
Boyd, David James *retired social sciences educator*
Boyd, Mary Frances *retired school nurse, pastor*
Boyd, Richard Lyn *secondary school educator*
Boyd, Sue Marston *retired music educator*
Boyda, Nancy E. *former United States Representative from Kansas*
Boyer, Albert Bruce *optometrist, educator*
Boyer, Dale Kenneth *English educator*
Boyer, Herbert Wayne *retired biochemist, biotechnology company executive*
Boyer, Robert Allan *finance company executive*
Boykin, Robert Heath *retired banker*
Boyle, B. B. *mathematics educator*
Boyle, Lara Flynn *actress*
Boyle, Michael Dermot *medical educator*
Boyle, Tatiana Gennadievna *research scientist*
Boyles, Robert Strickland, Jr. *financial consultant*
Boyles-Jernigan, Carol Ann Patterson *career planning administrator*
Boynes, Sean G. *dental anesthesiologist, researcher*
Boyte, Harry Chatten *social worker, director*
Boyter, Judy B *music educator*
Bozack, Amanda R. *education educator*
Braasch, John William *retired surgeon, consultant*
Bracey, Earnest *political science professor*
Brack, O. M., Jr. *language educator*
Bradbeer, Clive *biochemistry educator*
Bradbury, Bill (William Chapman Bradbury III) *former state official*
Braddock, Richard S. *Internet company executive*
Bradford, Louise Mathilde *social work administrator*
Bradford, Mary Rosen *lawyer*
Bradlee, Marcia Joy Beck *adult education educator*
Bradley, Amelia Jane *lawyer*
Bradley, Jennette B. *former state official, lieutenant governor*
Bradley, Josephine B. *social worker, educator*
Bradley, Melvin LeRoy *communications executive*
Brady, Donna Elizabeth *sales, marketing and performing company executive*
Brady, Edmund Matthew, Jr. *lawyer*
Brady, Edward Thomas, Jr. *lawyer, writer*
Brady, Jean Stein *retired librarian*
Brady, Mary Rolfes *music educator*
Brady, Nicholas Frederick *investment company executive, former United States Secretary of the Treasury*
Brady, Rebecca *medical educator*
Brady, Roger A. *career military officer*
Brady, Sharon *actor, theater educator*
Brady, Terrence Joseph *mediator, arbitrator, retired judge*
Brady-Borland, Karen *retired reporter, columnist*
Braen, Bernard Benjamin *retired psychology professor*
Brafford, William Charles *lawyer*
Braganza, Jennifer *engineering educator*
Bragg, Michael Ellis *lawyer, insurance company executive*
Braggs, Patricia *account manager*
Brahmbhatt, Chaitali J. *academic administrator, educator*
Braithwaite, Dawn O. *communication educator*
Bram, Leon Leonard *publishing company executive*
Bramhall, Debra A. *information technology manager, consultant*
Bramson, Leon *retired social scientist, educator*
Branagan, James Joseph *lawyer*
Brancato, Leo John *manufacturing executive*
Brand, Rachel Lee *former federal agency administrator, lawyer*
Brand, Vance Devoe *astronaut, director*
Brandeis, Barry *retired apparel executive*
Brandom, Barbara Wendeborn *anesthesiologist, consultant*
Brandon, Kathryn Elizabeth Beck *pediatrician*
Brandon, Liane *filmmaker, educator, photographer*
Brandt, Robert Frederic III *retired editor, journalist*
Brandt-Soetermans, Valerie *dancer, educator*
Brant, Nataliya Borisovna *language educator*
Brant, Sandra J. *magazine publisher*
Brantz, George Murray *retired lawyer*
Brar, Gurdarshan Singh *soil scientist, researcher*
Brasher, George Walter *physician, consultant*
Braswell, Jackie Boyd *state agency administrator*
Bratko, Dusan *chemistry professor, researcher*
Braude, Robert Michael *retired medical librarian*
Brauer, Rhonda Lyn *proxy solicitor, lawyer, corporate governance consultant*
Braun, Jerome Irwin *lawyer*
Braun, Mary Lucile Dekle (Lucy Braun) *psychotherapist, counseling administrator, educator*
Braun, Stanley *orthodontist, educator*
Braunstein, Diane Karen *non-profit association executive, government administrator, government relations professional*
Bravo, Rose Marie *former apparel company executive, food products executive*
Brawley, Otis Webb *oncologist, educator*
Brawner, Gerald Andre, Jr. *paralegal*
Brayer, Edith Marie *marriage and family therapist, consultant*
Brazelton, Garth Adam *economist*
Brazinski, Frank William *composer, educator*
Brdlik, Carola Emilie *retired accountant*
Breathed, Berkeley *cartoonist*
Brechtel, Unda Jurka *retired library director*
Brecker, Randal Edward *musician, arranger*
Bredfeldt, John Creighton *economics educator, writer, retired military officer*
Breece, Robert William, Jr. *lawyer, investment company executive*
Breen, Judith Snyder *mathematics professor*
Brees, Michael Paul *controller*
Brega, Kerry Elizabeth *physician, researcher*
Brehl, James William *lawyer*
Brelis, Matthew Dean Burns *journalist*
Bremer, Paul (Lewis Paul Bremer III, Jerry Bremer) *former diplomat*
Bremer, Ronald Allan *genealogist, editor*
Brenes, Jeremy *homeopath, researcher*
Brennan, Donna Lesley *public relations company executive*
Brennan, James Joseph *lawyer, bank executive*
Brennan, Lawrence Edward *retired electronics engineer*
Brennan, Mark Joseph *physiatrist*
Brenneman, Serena C. *finance educator*
Brennen, Reid Alyn *research scientist*
Brennen, Stephen Alfred *management consultant*
Brenner, Dean Elliott *medical oncology and pharmacology educator*
Brent, Robert Leonard *medical educator*
Brent, Thomas Peter *retired molecular pharmacologist*
Brentegani, Teresa E. *language educator*
Bretthauer, Erich Walter *chemist, educator*
Breuer, William Bentley *author*
Breunig, Joshua Joshn *biologist, researcher*
Brewer, Angela Sue *middle school educator*
Brewer, Barbara Bagdasarian *nursing administrator*
Brewer, Roy Edward *lawyer*
Brewer, Timothy Francis III *retired cardiologist*
Brewerton, Francis J. *business educator*
Brewster, Abenaa Marcia *oncologist, educator*
Brewster, Daryl G. *former food services company executive*
Brewster, Elizabeth Winifred *literature educator, poet, writer*
Brewster, Jamie Susan *theater educator*
Brewster, Mary Moorhead *retired educational association administrator*
Brickell, Charles Hennessey, Jr. *marine engineer, retired military officer*
Bricker, Harvey Miller *retired anthropology educator*
Bricker, Victoria Reifler *anthropologist, educator*
Bridge, Bobbe Jean *former state supreme court justice*
Bridger, Baldwin, Jr. *electrical engineer*
Bridges, Jeff *actor*
Briese, Michael W. *writer, priest, inventor*
Brigden, John *lawyer*
Briggle, Gary Lee *actor, director*
Briggs, Bonnie Sue *school librarian, minister*
Briggs, Martijna Aarts *language educator*
Briggs, Niwana Page *editor, writer*
Briggs, William Benajah *retired aerospace engineer*
Brill, Kenneth C. *federal official, former ambassador*
Brill, Maria *psychologist*
Brillie, M. Scott *savings and loan association executive*
Brim, Orville Gilbert, Jr. *former foundation administrator, writer*
Brin, Foster Blake *psychiatrist*
Brinberg, Herbert Raphael *publishing executive*
Brisbane, Arthur Seward *newspaper publisher*
Briskin, Jacqueline Elizabeth *author*
Brister, Trudy Ann *counseling administrator*
Bristow, Walter James, Jr. *retired judge*
Britt, Joseph John *religious studies educator*
Britt, Ronald Leroy *retired manufacturing company executive*
Brizio-Molteni, Loredana *surgeon, educator*
Broady, Christel H. *language educator*
Brobston, Stanley Heard *music educator, writer*
Brock, Eric John *urban planner, historian, consultant*
Brock, Geoffrey *literature and creative writing professor*
Brock, Greg J. *professor*
Brock, John Morgan (Juno), Jr. *composer, performer, producer*
Brock, William Emerson, III, (Bill Brock) *former United States Secretary of Labor*
Broderick, James Allen *painter, educator*
Brodeur, Catherine Reckart *artist*
Brodhead, David Crawmer *lawyer*
Brodsky, Beverly Anne *writer, consultant, editor*
Brodsky, Marc Herbert *physicist, research and publishing executive*
Brodsky, Sheldon *economics professor, consultant*
Brody, Alan Samuel *radiologist, researcher*
Brody, Arthur *industrial executive*
Brody, Saul Nathaniel *retired English literature educator*
Brodzik, Lester Leonard *artist, retired occupational therapist*
Brogliatti, Barbara Spencer *retired television and motion picture executive, consultant*
Brokaw, Tom (Thomas John Brokaw) *news correspondent, former network news anchor*
Brokke, Catherine Juliet *retired mission executive*
Bromund, Alice A. *retired elementary school educator*
Bronfman, Edgar Miles, Sr. *retired liquor company executive*
Bronkar, Eunice Dunalee *artist, educator*
Brook, Douglas Alan *former civilian military employee*
Brook, Scott Jonathan Bradley *mayor, lawyer*
Brooke, Edward William III *lawyer, former United States Senator from Massachusetts*
Brooke, Francis John III *retired academic administrator*
Brooke, Ralph Ian *dental educator*
Brooks, Alfred R. *bank executive*
Brooks, Andrée Aelion *journalist, educator, writer*
Brooks, Babert Vincent *publisher*
Brooks, Deborah June *art educator*
Brooks, Garth (Troyal Garth Brooks) *musician, singer*
Brooks, Kenneth N. *forestry educator*
Brooks, Lorraine Elizabeth *retired music educator*
Brooks, Michael Paul *retired urban planning educator*
Brooks, Timothy H. *broadcast executive*
Brooks-Turner, Myra *music educator*
Broome, Claire Veronica *epidemiologist, researcher*
Broome, Oscar Whitfield, Jr. *finance educator*
Brosnan, Pierce *actor*
Brothers, John Alfred *retired oil company and chemicals executive*
Brotman, David Joel *architectural firm executive, consultant*
Brotman, Stuart Neil *management consultant, law educator, communications executive*
Brott, Walter Howard *retired cardiac surgeon, educator, military officer*
Broude, Ronald *music publisher*
Broughton, Hazel Callen *rehabilitation counselor, consultant*
Browder, Felix Earl *mathematician, educator*
Brown, Alberta Mae *nurse*
Brown, Alice Elste *artist*
Brown, Alton C. *television personality, chef*
Brown, B. Andrew *lawyer*
Brown, Barbara *librarian, educator*
Brown, Barbara June *hospital and nursing administrator*
Brown, Beth A. *language educator*
Brown, Bruce Maitland *philanthropy consultant*
Brown, Carol Ann *librarian, director*
Brown, Charles Dodgson *lawyer*
Brown, Charles Samuel *singer, composer, retired educator*
Brown, Dale Susan *retired federal agency administrator, website manager, keynote speaker*
Brown, David Nelson *lawyer*
Brown, David Richard *school system administrator, minister*
Brown, Donald Douglas *transportation executive, consultant, retired military officer*
Brown, Edward J III *bank executive*
Brown, Elizabeth Eleanor *retired librarian*
Brown, Emery N. *neuroscientist, educator, statistician, anesthesiologist*
Brown, Eric M. *research scientist*
Brown, Frank R. *judge*
Brown, Geraldine *nurse, freelance writer*
Brown, Hank *former academic administrator, former senator*
Brown, Herbert Graham *entrepreneur*
Brown, Herbert Russell *lawyer, writer*
Brown, J. E. (J.E. Buster Brown) *lawyer, consultant*
Brown, James Nelson, Jr. *retired accountant*
Brown, Jeannette Elizabeth *retired science educator*
Brown, Jerry Milford *health products executive*
Brown, John Robert *lawyer, community volunteer, librarian*
Brown, June Gibbs *retired government official*
Brown, Kimberly D. *performing arts educator, choreographer, director*
Brown, Laima Adomaitis *art therapist, artist, writer*
Brown, Lee Patrick *retired mayor, former federal official*
Brown, Lora Alice *entertainment company executive, educator*
Brown, Marcia Joan *author, artist, photographer*
Brown, Marvin Thomas *philosopher, educator*
Brown, Melvin F. *finance company executive*
Brown, Michael John *retired judge*
Brown, Michael Robert *literature and language educator*
Brown, Robert Laidlaw *state supreme court justice*
Brown, Ronald Delano *endocrinologist*
Brown, Stephen Ira *mathematics and philosophy of education professor emeritus*
Brown, Stephen S. *telecommunications industry executive*
Brown, Steven Harry *engineering executive*
Brown, Viseeta *health science association administrator*
Brown, William Ferdinand *artist, writer*
Brown-Barton, Grace Olive *music educator*
Browne, Frederick Douglas *physiologist, educator*
Browne, Jackson *singer, songwriter*

Browne, John (Lord Browne of Madingley) *financial company executive, former oil industry executive*
Browne, John Charles *physicist, researcher, lab administrator*
Browne, Ray *insurance agent, former United States Shadow Representative, DC*
Brownell, Blanche Parisi *retired secondary school educator*
Browning, Peter Crane *manufacturing executive*
Brown Klinger, Stephen *financial analyst*
Brown Leatherberry, Thomas Henry *performing company executive, clergyman*
Brownlee, Les (Romie Leslie Brownlee) *former civilian military employee*
Brownlee, Paula Pimlott *higher education consultant*
Brownlee, Robert Calvin *pediatrician, educator*
Brownrigg, Walter Grant *cartoonist*
Brown Spitzmueller, Janiece Marie *lawyer*
Broyles, Jeffrey Lynn *school psychologist*
Bru, Abelardo E. *retired food products executive*
Brubaker, Crawford Francis, Jr. *federal agency administrator, aerospace scientist, consultant*
Bruce, Gregory Ellis *theater educator, director*
Bruckert, Vincent *literature and language professor, playwright*
Bruess, Charles Edward *lawyer*
Brugger, David John *media consultant*
Brumback, Charles Tiedtke *retired newspaper executive*
Brumbaugh, Steven Gerard *biology professor*
Brunelle, Daniel J. *retired chemist*
Brungraber, Robert J. *civil engineer, educator*
Brunner, Kathleen Marie *humanities educator*
Bruzoni, Matias *physician*
Bryan, Billie Marie (Mrs. James A. Mackey) *retired biologist*
Bryan, J(ames) P(erry), Jr. *energy executive*
Bryan, Karen Smith *lawyer*
Bryan, Lawrence Dow *retired college president, consultant*
Bryan, Vernanne *author, historian*
Bryant, Bertha Estelle *retired medical/surgical nurse*
Bryant, La Kesha Joy *physical education educator*
Bryant, Paul Thompson *language educator*
Bryant, Thomas Lee *retired magazine editor*
Bryant, Warren F. *former retail executive*
Bryner, Alexander O. *former state supreme court justice*
Bryson, Nancy Southard *lawyer, former federal agency administrator*
Bubak, Vit *research scientist*
Bubrick, Melvin Phillip *surgeon*
Buchanan, J(ohn) Robert *physician, educator*
Buchanan, Pat (Patrick Joseph Buchanan) *journalist, author, political commentator*
Buchanan, William H., Jr. *retired lawyer, venture capitalist*
Buchbinder, Darrell Bruce *lawyer*
Bucheister, Patricia Louise (Patt Parrish) *writer, artist*
Buchman, Craig *otolaryngologist*
Buck, David R. *history professor*
Buck, Jane Louise *retired psychology professor*
Buck, Louise Bryden *psychiatrist*
Buck, Martina *medical researcher*
Buckels, Marvin Wayne *savings and loan association executive*
Buckingham, Albert William *retired college administrator, physical education educator*
Buckingham, David Cowan *judge*
Buckley, Eleanor Jane *retired elementary school educator*
Buckley, Frederick Jean *retired lawyer*
Buckley, John Joseph, Jr. *healthcare executive*
Buckman, Raymond William, Jr. *engineering educator*
Buckner, Sally Beaver *literature and language professor, writer*
Bucknum, Michael John *chemist, crystallographer, educator*
Bucksbaum, Melva *foundation administrator*
Bucy, J. Fred, Jr. *retired electronics company executive*
Buda, Thaddeus J., Jr. *retired lawyer*
Budd, Ann F. *geologist, educator*
Budgeon, Mark K. *mechanical engineer, consultant*
Budimirovic, Dejan B. *academic child psychiatrist*
Budington, William Stone *retired librarian*
Budwig, Ralph Sanders *engineering educator, researcher*
Budynas, Richard Gordon *engineering educator, writer*
Buell, Lawrence Ingalls *language educator*
Buhl, Cynthia Maureen *advocate, educator*
Buhler, Jill Lorie *editor, writer*
Bui, Yen Kim *pediatrician, researcher*
Buist, Kathy *artist*
Buist, Neil Robertson MacKenzie *pediatric educator, medical association administrator*
Buker, Robert Hutchinson, Sr. *army officer, thoracic surgeon*
Bulkley, Gregory Bartlett *cattle rancher, retired academic surgeon and research scientist*
Bull, Bergen Ira *retired equipment manufacturing company executive*
Bull, Inez Stewart *musician, educator, curator*
Bullard, Ervin Trowbridge *tropical horticulturist*
Bullard, Judith Eve *psychologist, systems engineer*
Bullard, Lofton Alexander *mathematics professor*
Bullas, Leonard Raymond *retired microbiology professor*
Bullerdick, Kim H. *lawyer, petroleum executive*
Bullock, Mary Brown *political science professor, former academic administrator*
Bullock, Molly *retired elementary school educator*
Bullock, Sandra (Sandra Annette Bullock) *actress*
Bumbry-Bronson, Venetta *music educator*
Bump, Elizabeth Bertha *music educator*
Bunch, Jennings Bryan, Jr. *retired electrical engineer*
Bundy, Annalee Marshall *retired library director*
Bunkowske, Eugene Walter *religious studies educator*
Bunn, Ronald Freeze *retired lawyer, academic administrator, political scientist*
Bunyan, Ellen Lackey Spotz *retired chemist*
Burack, Michael Leonard *lawyer*
Burch, Michael Ray *computer company executive*
Burchard, John Kenneth *retired chemical engineer*
Burchman, Leonard *federal official, journalist*
Burch-Martinez, Berkeley Alison *primary school educator*
Burden, Ordway Partridge *investment banker*
Burgdoerfer, Jerry J. *marketing and distribution executive*
Burge, John Wesley, Jr. *management consultant*
Burger, Glenn Douglas *literature and language professor*
Burgher Schweppe, Pauline Menefee *retired marriage and family therapist*
Burgstaler, Edwin Allen *medical technologist*
Buritz, Robert Samson *retired electrical engineer*
Burk, Raymond Franklin, Jr. *internist, educator, researcher*
Burk, Robert S. *retired lawyer*
Burke, Brooke *actress, model*
Burke, William Thomas *lawyer, educator*
Burkes, Lionel Seaton *science educator, writer, researcher*
Burket, John McVey *retired dermatologist*
Burkett, Lawrence V. *retired insurance company executive, lawyer*
Burkey, Lee Melville, Sr. *lawyer*
Burkhart, Catherine Ray *retired secondary school educator*
Burki, Fred Albert *labor union official*
Burkle, Ronald W. *entrepreneur, retired food service executive*
Burleigh, Judith Cushing *education educator*
Burleigh, William Robert *retired media executive*
Burman, Darryl Michael *lawyer*
Burman, Leonard Emanuel *tax specialist, director*
Burnbaum, Michael William *lawyer*
Burnett, Iris Jacobson *corporate communications specialist*
Burnette, Brandon R. *librarian*
Burnham, Christopher Bancroft *former international organization official, former federal agency administrator*
Burnham, J. V. *retired sales executive*
Burns, Cora Lea *music educator, director*
Burns, Edward J., Jr. *actor, film director*
Burns, Ellen Jean *distance education administrator*
Burns, Max *former congressman*
Burns, Michael J. *former automotive parts company executive*
Burrow, Gerard Noel *internist, educator*
Burrow, Harold *retired gas industry executive*
Burrows, Donald Albert *artist, painter, photographer*
Burrows, Edwin Gladding *retired broadcaster, writer, poet*
Burson, Betsy Lee *librarian*
Bursten, Stuart Lowell *physician, biochemist*
Burstyn, Ellen (Edna Rae Gillooly) *actress*
Burt, Richard *lawyer*
Burtley, Calvin *art director*
Burton, Bruce Arthur *education educator*
Burton, Lawrence DeVere *agriculturist, educator*
Burton, Richard Jay *lawyer*
Burwick, David A. *marketing executive*
Busby, Daniel Gary *music educator, theater educator*
Busch, Annie *retired library director*
Busch, August Anheuser III *retired brewery company executive*
Busch, August Anheuser, IV, *former brewery company executive*
Busch, Joyce Ida *small business owner*
Buschke, Herman *neurologist*
Bush, Barbara Pierce *former First Lady of the United States, volunteer*
Bush, Brett Charles *oceanographer*
Bush, Eileen Shanin *voice educator*
Bush, Ellen D. *music educator*
Bush, Frederick Morris *former federal agency administrator*
Bush, George Walker *43rd President of the United States*
Bush, Jeb (John Ellis Bush) *former governor*
Bush, Laura Welch *former First Lady of the United States*
Bush, Norman *research and development company executive*
Bush, Sarah Lillian *retired historian*
Bush, William Merritt *retired lawyer*
Bush, William Read *computer scientist*
Bush, Yvonne *writer, counselor*
Busquet, Anne M. *Internet company executive*
Bussabarger, Mary Louise *mental health services professional*
Busse, Leonard Wayne *banker, financial consultant*
Butchko, Harriett Hays *physician*
Butenis, Patricia Agatha *former ambassador*
Butler, Denise Elizabeth *primary school educator*
Butler, Donald Philip *electrical engineer, educator*
Butler, Donna Marcia *retired mathematics educator*
Butler, James Newton *retired chemist, educator*
Butler, John Musgrave *financial consultant*
Butler, Louis Bennett, Jr. *former state supreme court justice*
Butler, Orton Carmichael *retired climatologist, educator*
Butler, Robert Thomas *retired advertising executive*
Butler, Serena Jane Johnson *computer networking educator, small business owner*
Butler, William Joseph *lawyer, educator*
Butman, John Anthony *radiologist*
Butte, Amy S. *former brokerage house executive*
Butterfield, Bruce Scott *executive, editor, author, educator, consultant*
Buttner, Edgar Arnold *medical educator*
Buttrey, Donald Wayne *lawyer*
Büyükanit, Yasar *career military officer*
Buzard, James Albert *biomedical start-up consultant*
Buzard, Kurt Andre *ophthalmologist*
Byerly, Steven Lee *educational consultant*
Bynes, Amanda *actress*
Bynes, Frank Howard, Jr. *physician*
Byrd, Isaac Burlin *retired biologist*
Byrd, Marc Robert *floral designer*
Byrne, Edmund Francis *philosophy educator*
Byrne, Gabriel *actor*
Byrne, John Edward (JEB Byrne) *retired federal official*
Byrne, Lawrence John *literature and language professor*
Byrne-Dempsey, Cecelia (Cecelia Dempsey) *journalist*
Byrnes, Hope Huska *singer, volunteer*
Caan, James *actor, director*
Cabcabin, Diana M. *middle school educator, consultant*
Cabot, Hugh III *painter, sculptor*
Cacciatore, Ronald Keith *lawyer*
Cacciavillan, Agostino Cardinal *cardinal, archbishop*
Cacioppo, John Terrance *psychologist, educator, researcher*
Cadambe, Viveck R. *research scientist*
Cade, Gregory Brian *fireman, former federal agency administrator*
Cadore, Tayesha Anne *elementary school educator*
Cadwallader, Gwen Natalie *elementary school educator, music educator*
Cage, Jack Hays *executive search consultant*
Cai, Chaozhong *chemist*
Cai, Mei *materials engineer, researcher*
Cai, Ming Zhi *chemist, researcher, film producer*
Cai, Ying *engineer, researcher*
Cai, Yuanfang *engineering educator*
Caicedo, Patricia *singer, musicologist, physician*
Cain, William Howard *secondary school educator*
Calabrese, Karen Ann *artist, educator*
Calame, Byron Edward *journalist*
Calarco, Vincent Anthony *specialty chemicals company executive*
Calavia, Jose Emilio *physics professor*
Calcagni, Gianluca *physicist*
Calcanis, Jason McCabe *Internet company executive*
Calder, Iain Wilson *publishing executive*
Caldera, Louis Edward *law educator, former federal official*
Calderón, Sila Maria *former Governor of Puerto Rico*
Calderwood, Stuart Keith *medical educator, consultant*
Caldwell, Elwood Fleming *food scientist, educator*
Caldwell, Heather Kingsley *biology professor*
Caldwell, William Mackay, IV, *cloning and stem cell research company executive*
Caletti, Deb L. *writer*
Califano, Filomena *chemistry professor*
Callaham, Jeffery *artist*
Callahan, Vincent Francis, Jr. *state legislator, retired publishing executive*
Callahan, Vivian *broadcast executive*
Callander, Bruce Douglas *journalist, freelance writer*
Callard, David Jacobus *investment company executive*
Callaway, Matthew Stephen *application developer*
Calleo, David Patrick *history professor, political economy international relations*
Calley, John *former motion picture company executive, film producer*
Callier, Maria Cecile *journalist, senior technical writer, radio producer*
Callow, William Grant *retired judge*
Calman, Craig David *actor, writer*
Calvert, Berta Alicia *language educator*
Calvert, Jack George *atmospheric chemist, educator*
Calvert, William Preston *radiologist*
Calvin, Robert Joseph *professor, author, management consultant*
Calvo, Esteban *sociologist, researcher*
Cambone, Stephen Anthony *former federal agency administrator*
Cameron, Kirk MacGregor Drummond *statistician*
Cameron, Lucille Wilson *retired dean*
Cameron-Mickens, Vertrelle Diane *singer, conductor, voice educator*
Campanelli, Joseph P. *former bank executive*
Campasino, Ellen Marie *elementary school educator*
Campbell, Andrew William *immunotoxicology physician*
Campbell, Arthur Andrews *retired federal agency administrator*
Campbell, Byron Chesser *newspaper publishing executive*
Campbell, Charles Edward *scientist, opthalmic consultant*
Campbell, Daniel Glen *dean*
Campbell, Edwin Denton *educational association administrator, consultant, accountant*
Campbell, Henry Cummings *librarian*
Campbell, James P. *manufacturing executive*
Campbell, Janet Coral *architect*
Campbell, John *engineering educator*
Campbell, John *former ambassador*
Campbell, Joyce S. *language educator, department chairman*
Campbell, Judith E. *retired insurance company executive*
Campbell, Judy *medical/surgical nurse, educator*
Campbell, Levin Hicks *federal judge*
Campbell, Louis Adams *secondary school educator*
Campbell, Mary Stinecipher *retired chemist*
Campbell, Melissa Lynnsimmons *music educator*
Campbell, Reginna Gladys *medical/surgical nurse*
Campion, Thomas Francis *lawyer*
Canaday, Steven *literature and language professor*
Canady, John W. *medical educator*
Candler, Steven *education educator*
Candlish, Malcolm *manufacturing executive*
Cannavale, Bobby (Roberto Cannavale) *actor*
Cannizzaro, Linda Ann *geneticist, researcher*
Cannon, Christopher Black *former United States Representative from Utah, lawyer*
Cannon, Steven M. *chemist*
Canny, Priscilla Forney *senior vice president*
Cansev, Mehmet *physician, researcher*
Canter, Maria P. *gynecologist*
Cantero-Exojo, Monica *language educator*
Cantor, Alan Bruce *management consultant, application developer*
Cantu, Jose Francisco *retired postal worker*
Cantus, H. Hollister *marketing and government relations consultant*
Canty, John M., Jr. *medical educator, researcher*
Cao, Xinde *chemist*
Caparro, James *entertainment industry executive*
Capasso, Federico *physicist*
Capiro, Natalie *research scientist*
Capka, J. Richard (Joseph Richard Capka) *former federal agency administrator, retired military officer*
Caplan, Allan *biology professor*
Caplovitz, Coleman David *retired physician*
Caplow, Theodore *sociologist*
Capra, Frances M. *retired telecommunications industry executive*
Carbonneau, Guy *former professional hockey coach, retired professional hockey player*
Carbunar, Bogdan *engineer, researcher*
Cardell, Silvana *choreographer, educator*
Carder, Paul Charles *retired advertising executive*
Cardno, Donald Barry *retired personnel director*
Cardona, Julio Jose *assistant dean, educational researcher*
Cardoso, Anthony Antonio *artist, educator*
Cardoza, David *aerospace scientist*
Cardwell, Nancy Lee *editor, writer*
Careau, James Thomas *music educator*
Caren, Robert Poston *aerospace scientist*
Carey, Drew *actor*
Carey, Jana Howard *lawyer*
Carfora, John Michael *economics professor, research and academic administrator, author*
Carini, Gabriella *research scientist*
Cariola, Robert Joseph *artist*
Carl, Schanbacher F. *dermatologist, director*
Carlesimo, P.J. (Peter J. Carlesimo) *former professional basketball coach*
Carley, Kurt *actor*
Carlin, John William *educator, Former Governor, Kansas*
Carlin, Marian P. *secondary school educator*
Carliner, Geoffrey Owen *economist, director*
Carling, Tobias John Eric *surgeon, research scientist*
Carlock, Barbara E. *librarian*
Carlock, Sandra Lynn *musician, educator*
Carlsen, Mary Baird *clinical psychologist*
Carlson, Janet Frances *psychologist, educator*
Carlson, Kimberly R. *veterinarian*
Carlson, Lynn Redding *astrophysicist*
Carlson, Natalie Traylor *publisher*
Carlson, Richard Warner *journalist, broadcast executive, federal agency administrator, diplomat*
Carlson, Robert Codner *industrial engineering educator*
Carlson, Roger David *psychologist, educator, minister*
Carlson, Theodore Joshua *lawyer, retired utilities executive*
Carlstrom, Charlotte Mahr *education educator*
Carlucci, Frank Charles III *former United States Secretary of Defense*
Carlyle, Bobbie Kristine *sculptor*
Carlyon, David James *writer, actor, theater director*
Carmack, Mona *library administrator*
Carnahan, Brice *chemical engineer, educator*
Carnes, Tara Lea Barker *music educator*
Carnesale, Albert *engineering educator, former academic administrator*
Carney, Amy Beth *history instructor*
Carney, John C., Jr. *former Lieutenant Governor of Delaware*
Carney, Timothy Michael *ambassador*
Carnicom, Gene E. *health services administrator*
Carol, Clericuzio Louise *geneticist, researcher*
Caroleo, Linn E. *mathematics professor, writer, freelance/self-employed photographer*
Carone, Nicolas *artist*
Carpenter, Denise A. *social worker*
Carpenter, Derr Alvin *retired landscape architect*
Carpenter, Lynn *language educator*
Carpenter, Marlene *retired philosopher, educator*
Carpenter, Pearl Elizabeth *artist*
Carpenter, Robert J. *epidemiologist*
Carpenter, Rosalie T. *education educator, consultant*
Carpenter, Scott (Malcolm Scott Carpenter) *retired astronaut, oceanographer*
Carpenter-Mason, Beverly Nadine *quality assurance professional*
Carpentieri, Sarah C. *neuropsychologist, researcher, clinical psychologist*
Carr, Bessie *retired elementary school educator*
Carr, E. Barbara *librarian*
Carr, Lloyd H. *retired college football coach*
Carr, Mindy Lea *healthcare educator*
Carr, Patricia Ann *community health nurse*
Carr, Winifred Walker *artist, historian*
Carraher, Mary Lou Carter *art educator*
Carrara, Benjamin J., II, *psychologist*
Carrasquilla, Kurt Frank *finance educator*
Carrion, Richard L. *bank executive*
Carroll, John Millar *computer science and psychology educator*
Carroll, Joseph J(ohn) *lawyer*
Carroll, Karen Colleen *pathologist, infectious diseases specialist*
Carroll, M(argaret) Lizbeth Carr *art educator, graphics designer, photographer*
Carron, Ronald Joseph *retired electric power industry executive*
Carsley, John E. *metallurgical engineer, researcher*
Carson, Brad Rogers *former congressman*
Carson, Denise Wilkinson *retired gifted and talented educator*
Carson, Regina E. *healthcare administrator, geriatric specialist*
Carstairs, Sharon *legislator*
Carstens, David Henry *military officer*
Carswell, Jane Triplett *retired family physician*
Carter, Betsy L. *editor, writer*
Carter, Cynthia (Cindy) Lynn *writer*
Carter, Henry Moore, Jr. *retired foundation executive*

Carter, Hodding, III, (William) *foundation executive, retired journalist, commentator, educator*
Carter, James E. *mining company executive*
Carter, Jeanne Wilmot *lawyer, publishing executive*
Carter, Jeffrey Richard *music educator*
Carter, John Swain *retired museum director*
Carter, La Rae Dunn *music educator*
Carter, Mel Keith *chemist*
Carter, Melva Jean *retired medical technician*
Carter, Nanette Carolyn *artist*
Carter, Steve *former state attorney general*
Carter, Thomas Allen *retired engineering executive*
Carter, Thomas Smith, Jr. *retired rail transportation executive*
Carter, Tonya M. *science educator*
Carter, Tracy Gail *elementary school educator*
Carter, Yvonne Breaux *retired librarian*
Carthey, Joseph Howard *economics professor*
Carton, Lonnie Caming *educational psychologist*
Cartwright, Brian Grant *lawyer*
Cartwright, Elizabeth *science educator*
Cartwright, Talula Elizabeth *leadership consultant, educator*
Carty, Donald J. *former computer company executive, former air transportation executive*
Caruso, Joan Robertson *special education educator*
Carver, Kendall Lynn *insurance company executive*
Carver, Stephen D. *publishing executive, former broadcast executive*
Casanova, Aldo John *sculptor*
Casazza, John Andrew *electrical engineer, energy executive*
Case, Edward Espenett *former United States Representative from Hawaii, lawyer*
Case, Elizabeth Joy *psychology and educational assessment director*
Case, Reginald *artist*
Casei, Nedda *mezzo soprano*
Casella, Peter F(iore) *patent and licensing executive*
Casella, Russell Carl *physicist*
Casey, Dwane L. *former professional basketball coach*
Casey, Harry Wayne *performer, songwriter, record producer*
Cash, Joseph Carl *history educator, government educator*
Cash, Mary Frances *minister, retired civilian military employee*
Cash, W. Larry *health products executive*
Cason, James Caldwell *retired ambassador*
Cason, Nica Virginia *retired nursing educator*
Caspers, Jean S. *librarian*
Cassagnol, Manouchkathe *pharmacist, educator*
Cassel, Robert Uriah *chemist*
Cassell, Eric Jonathan *physician*
Cassell, Kay Ann *librarian*
Casserly, Charley *former professional football team executive*
Cassiani Ingoni, Riccardo *medical researcher*
Cassidy, Carl Eugene *physician*
Cassidy, James Mark *construction company executive*
Cassidy, John Harold *lawyer*
Cassidy, Shelley *psychologist*
Casson, Joseph Edward *lawyer*
Cassou, Steven Peter *economics professor*
Castagna, Vanessa J. *retired retail executive*
Castaldi, David Lawrence *health products executive*
Castel, Amanda Derryck *pediatrician*
Castel, Jean Gabriel *lawyer, educator, international arbitrator*
Castellarin, John Stephen *literature and language professor*
Castellino, Ronald Augustus Dietrich *radiologist, educator*
Castelloes, Frederico Lemos *language educator*
Castelluzzo, Julie Anne *school librarian*
Castile, Rand (Jesse Randolph III) *retired museum director*
Castle, Howard Blaine *retired religious organization administrator*
Castle, James Cameron *information technology executive*
Castle-Hughes, Keisha *actress*
Caston, J(esse) Douglas *retired medical educator*
Castor, Jon Stuart *technology executive*
Castro, Maria Graciela *medical educator, geneticist, researcher*
Castro, Raul Hector *lawyer, Former Governor, Arizona, ambassador*
Castro, Teresa Jacira *small business owner*
Caswell, Dorothy Ann Cottrell *performing arts association administrator*
Catalano, Louis William, Jr. *neurologist*
Catalano, Patrick M. *medical educator, researcher*
Catelan, Paolo *environmental services administrator*
Cates, Dennis Lynn *minister*
Cathell, Dale Roberts *former Judge, Maryland Court of Appeals*
Catherine, Anne Scine *theology educator*
Cathey, Wade Thomas *electrical engineering educator*
Cathou, Renata Egone *chemist, consultant*
Catling, Douglas George *product development company executive*
Caucia, Louisa B. *retired elementary school educator*
Cavaco, Sofia C.F.M. *engineering educator*
Cavalli-Sforza, Luigi Luca *geneticist, educator*
Cavanagh, Richard Edward *corporate chairman, director*
Caviani, Laura Susan *music educator*
Caviezel, James Patrick *actor*
Cavin, Susan Elizabeth *sociologist, writer*
Cawley, Joseph Douglas *retired reading professor*
Cayne, James E. (Jimmy Cayne) *former diversified financial services company executive*
Cazalas, Mary Rebecca Williams *lawyer, nurse*
Cazayoux, Don (Donald J. Cazayoux Jr.) *former United States Representative from Louisiana*
Cecil, David Rolf *mathematician, educator*
Cecil, Elizabeth Jean *writer*
Cedar, Paul Arnold *church executive, minister*
Cedeno, Amy A. *regulatory affairs, quality assurance professional*
Celebi, M. Emre *engineering educator*
Celentano, Francis Michael *artist, educator*
Cellarius, Richard Andrew *biology professor*
Censullo, Michael *radiologist*
Centafont, Lucy Ann Alexander *occupational therapist, consultant*
Cermak, James Frank *theater educator*
Cerny, Louis Thomas *civil and transportation engineer, consultant*
Cerutti, Steven Matthew *ancient language educator*
Cerveny, David John *lawyer*
Cesarman, Ethel *physician scientist*
Cha, Byung Ho *research scientist*
Cha, Soyoung Stephen *mechanical engineer, educator*
Chaban, Victor *medical educator, consultant*
Chabot, Steven Joseph *former United States Representative from Ohio, lawyer*
Chacko, George Kuttickal *management science educator, consultant*
Chacko, Samuel *association official*
Chae, Moo Sung *electrical engineer*
Chafel, Judith Ann *education educator*
Chagarov, Evgueni A. *physicist*
Chahinian, A(ram) Philippe *oncologist*
Chaifetz, David Harvey *lawyer*
Chaiyasate, Kongkrit *surgeon*
Chakrabarti, Anjan K. *preventive medicine physician*
Chakraborti, Rajat Kanti *engineer, consultant*
Chakraborty, Arpan *research scientist*
Chakravarty, Swapnajit *electrical engineer, researcher*
Chalcraft, Elena Marie *actress, singer*
Chalif, Ronnie *medical association co-founder, artist*
Chalikian, Alice Beatrice *chiropractor*
Challagulla, Venkata Udaya Bhaskar *computer engineer*
Challis, Richard Bracebridge *art dealer, educator*
Chamberlain, William Edwin, Jr. *management consultant*
Chamberlin, Michael Meade *lawyer*
Chambers, Bettye Thomas *language educator*
Chambers, Elenora Strasel *artist*
Chambers, Heather Lynn *reading specialist*
Chambers, Setsuko *gynecologic oncologist*
Chan, Jeanette K. *lawyer*
Chan, Tsz Ping *research scientist*
Chance, F. Earlayne *artist, genealogist*
Chandler, Alice *retired academic administrator, educational consultant*
Chandler, James John *surgeon, educator*
Chandler, Robert Leslie *public relations executive*
Chandra, Satish *psychologist*
Chaney, Laura D. *humanities educator*
Chang, Byoung-Yong *chemist*
Chang, Clarence Dayton *retired chemist*
Chang, David Z. *oncologist*
Chang, Edward H. *consulting and marketing company executive*
Chang, Hernan Robert *infectious disease consultant*
Chang, Herng-Hua *research scientist*
Chang, John B. *surgeon*
Chang, Kevin Jeffrey *radiologist, educator*
Chang, Ren Fang *retired physicist, researcher*
Chang, Victor Tsu-Shih *oncologist, researcher, educator*
Chang, Winston Wen-tsuen *economist, educator*
Chang, Ying Chih *engineering educator, researcher*
Chang, Yun Kyung *researcher*
Changchun, Liu *research scientist*
Chanos, George J. *former state attorney general*
Chao, James Min-Tzu *architect*
Chao, Ronald Philip *plastic surgeon*
Chao, Ruth *psychologist, educator*
Chaplin, Tara M. *medical researcher*
Chapman, Daniel P. *epidemiologist*
Chapman, Richard LeRoy *public affairs researcher*
Chapman, Robert Foster *federal judge*
Chapman, William *baritone*
Chappell, Annette M. *educational consultant, minister*
Chappell, Fred Davis *language educator, poet*
Charles, Luenda E. *public health service officer, researcher*
Charles, Marilyn Kay *secondary school educator*
Charles, Robert Bruce *lawyer, former federal agency administrator*
Charles, Walter *actor*
Charleton, Margaret Ann *child care administrator, consultant*
Charwat, Andrew Franciszek *engineering educator*
Chase, Helen Louise *bank executive*
Chase, J. Vincent *property manager*
Chase, James Richard *retired college president*
Chase, Lee P. *religious studies educator, consultant*
Chase, Peter Paul *retired science educator*
Chase, Robin M. *entrepreneur*
Chase, Sandra Lee *clinical pharmacist, consultant*
Chaseman, Joel *communications consultant*
Chasnoff, Ira Jay *pediatrician*
Chassin, Jameson Lewis *retired surgeon*
Chassman, Leonard Fredric *retired labor union administrator*
Chastain, Kenneth Duane *retired foreign language educator, writer*
Chatterjee, Anindya *economist, researcher*
Chattman, Raymond Christopher *association executive*
Chaturvedi, Anil Dass *telecommunications executive, researcher*
Chaudhuri, Jyoti Prakash *geneticist*
Chauhan, Parth Randhir *paleontologist*
Chauvette, Claude R. *retired executive secretary*
Chavan, Prithviraj Vasantrao *environmental engineer*
Chave, Carol *arbitrator, retired lawyer*
Chávez, Denise Elia *performance writer, actress*
Chawla, Soni Chander *medical educator, consultant*
Chaykin, Robert Leroy *manufacturing and marketing executive*
Cheah, Boon-Siang *electrical engineer*
Chealander, Steven Russell *former federal agency administrator*
Cheatham, Carl Wade *minister, educator*
Cheatham, Robert William *retired lawyer*
Checchi, Alfred A. *air transportation executive, financial consultant*
Cheddie, Denver Faron *engineering educator, researcher*
Cheeks, Maurice Edward *former professional basketball coach, retired professional basketball player*
Cheetham, Jonathan *surgeon, researcher*
Chelios, Chris (Christos K. Chelios) *professional hockey player*
Chelle, Robert Frederick *electric power industry executive, educator*
Chem, Widhya *ambassador*
Chen, Chun-Da *finance educator*
Chen, Del-Min Amy *lawyer*
Chen, Di *electronics executive, optical engineer, consultant*
Chen, James Kenneth *chemical biology professor*
Chen, Jiangping *science educator*
Chen, Jiwei *computer engineer*
Chen, Kuen Hai *physician*
Chen, Nong *electronics engineer, researcher*
Chen, Philip Minkang *strategic consultant*
Chen, Shiping *information scientist*
Chen, Shoei-Sheng *retired mechanical engineer*
Chen, Wei *chemist, researcher, materials scientist, polymer engineer*
Chen, Wei *mechanical engineer*
Chen, Weifeng *science educator*
Chen, Xiaotian *librarian, educator*
Chen, Yijian *research scientist*
Chen, Yue *research and development company executive, director*
Chen, Zu-yan *language educator*
Cheney, Dick (Richard Bruce Cheney) *former Vice President of the United States, United States Secretary of Defense*
Cheng, Boyle C. *medical educator*
Cheng, Hefa *civil engineer, educator*
Cheng, Jing-Ru C. *computer scientist, researcher*
Cheng, Wan-Lee *mechanical engineer, educator*
Cheng, Yiling J. *epidemiologist*
Cheng, Yue *molecular geneticist, pathologist*
Cher, (Cherilyn Sarkisian) *singer, actress*
Chercover, Murray *television executive*
Cherepanov, Genady Petrovich *mathematician, mechanical engineer*
Cher-Killigm, Beatrice M. *history professor, art educator*
Chernavsky, George Y. *composer, producer, song writer*
Chernichaw, Mark *broadcast executive, corporate communications executive, television director, television producer, media consultant, educator*
Chernin, Peter F. *former multimedia company executive*
Chernoff, Amoz Immanuel *hematologist, consultant*
Chernow, Ron *writer, journalist*
Cherry, Caroline Lockett *educational association administrator*
Cherry, Robert Steven III *municipal official*
Chesnut, Nondis Lorine (Angel Love) *education educator, writer, learning specialist, scriptwriter*
Chesson, Michael Bedout *history professor, writer*
Chevalier, Denise Ann *teacher, professor*
Chevalier, Paul Edward *retired retail executive, lawyer*
Chhaochharia, Vidhi *economics professor*
Chiang, I-Ting *engineer*
Chiang, Michael Fred *physician*
Chiara, Margaret Mary *former prosecutor, lawyer*
Chibani, Omar *physicist*
Chibucos, Pamela E. *education educator*
Chicoine, Eldred *school system administrator*
Chicone, Carmen *mathematics professor*
Chidley, Matthew *optical engineer*
Chiechi, Carolyn Phyllis *federal judge*
Chien, Nguyen Tam *ambassador*
Chihorek, John Paul *electronics company executive*
Chiklis, Michael *actor*
Child, Margaret Smillie *retired consultant, former government official*
Childers, Joshua Brandon *psychologist, educator*
Chiles, Stephen Michael *retired lawyer*
Chilingarian, George Varos (Chilingar) *petroleum, environmental educator*
Chilvers, Derek *insurance company executive*
Chiorini, Matt *theater educator, director*
Chirico-Elkins, Ursula *retired librarian*
Chirinko, Robert S. *economics professor*
Chisman, Amy Elynn *lighting designer, educator*
Chitnis, Ashay *research scientist*
Chiu, Bella Chao *astrophysicist, writer*
Chizhikov, Viktor Viktorovich *research scientist*
Chloros, George *surgeon*
Chmielinski, Edward Alexander *retired electronics company executive*
Cho, Alfred Yi *electrical engineer*
Cho, Hyeonjoong *computer engineer, researcher*
Cho, Jaedong *engineering company executive, researcher*
Chodorow, Nancy Julia *psychoanalyst, educator*
Choi, David Kyu *electronics engineer*
Choi, Eunmi *research scientist*
Choi, Im Ja Park *non-profit executive*
Choi, Samuel *medical researcher*
Choi, Sheena *education educator*
Choi, Stephen Sukjun *physicist*
Choi, Wooyoung *mathematics professor*
Choi, Yoonsu *research scientist*
Choi, Young Eui *English language professor*
Cholewka, Patricia Anne *nursing educator*
Chollet, Philippe Jean Marie *oncologist, educator*
Chong, Andy Chinyu *research scientist*
Choo, Christie *pharmacist, educator*
Chopin, Christopher Allen *lawyer*
Chou, Chung-Kwang *bio-engineer*
Chouery, Farid Alexandre *electrical and structural engineer, consultant*
Choukas-Bradley, Melanie *writer, photographer, naturalist*
Chow, Judy *library and information scientist, educator*
Chow, Rita Kathleen *nursing consultant*
Chow, Timothy Yi-Chung *mathematician, systems engineer*
Chow, Winston *engineering executive, researcher*
Chowdhury, Mashrur *engineering educator*
Chretien, Jane Henkel *internist*
Chrétien, Raymond A.J. *retired ambassador*
Chrisanthopoulos, Peter *advertising executive*
Christensen, C. Lewis *real estate developer*
Christensen, Lindsey *research scientist*
Christenson, Gregg Andrew *bank executive*
Christian, Carole Ann *psychologist, academic administrator*
Christian, James Wayne *economist*
Christiansen, Richard Dean *retired newspaper editor*
Christiansen, Richard Louis *orthodontist, educator, dean*
Christie, Christopher James *former prosecutor, lawyer*
Christie, Laurence Glenn, Jr. *surgeon, educator*
Christie, Thomas Philip *former federal agency administrator*
Christoffersen, Ralph Earl *chemist, researcher, director*
Christopher, Alexander George *transportation company executive*
Christopher, Russell Lewis *baritone*
Christopherson, Myrvin Frederick *college president*
Christou, Carol Thomas *physicist, educator*
Christy, Nicholas Pierson *physician*
Chu, Benjamin Thomas Peng-Nien *chemistry professor*
Chu, Ellin Resnick *librarian, consultant*
Chu, Jack J. (Zhu) *electrical engineer*
Chu, Katherine K. *music educator*
Chu, Ting-Heng *educator*
Chuah, Mooi Choo *electrical engineer*
Chubb, Stephen Darrow *health products executive*
Chun, Asaph Y. *research scientist*
Chun, Jacqueline Clibbett *artist, educator*
Chung, Benjamin Inbeh *urologist*
Chung, Doo-ri *apparel designer*
Chung, Kevin C. *medical educator*
Church, Eugene Lent *physicist, consultant*
Churchill, Myla *art educator, writer*
Churchill, Robert Wilson *state legislator, lawyer*
Churchill, Stephen Perry *graphic designer*
Churchill, Ward LeRoy *social sciences educator, advocate*
Churgin, Amy *former publishing executive*
Chusid, Martin *retired musicologist, educator*
Cianciosa, Carolyn Lucy *radiologic technologist, educator*
Cibes, William Joseph, Jr. *retired academic administrator*
Cicero, Carmen Louis *artist, educator*
Cicolani, Angelo George *research and development company executive, operating engineer*
Ciesielka, Debbie *nurse, educator*
Ciesla, Fred John *astrophysicist, meteoriticist, researcher*
Cikovsky, Nicolai, Jr. *retired curator, art historian, educator*
Cintron-Laguna, Pilar Teresa *language educator*
Citro, Yolande *real estate agent*
Cittone, Henry Aron *hotel and restaurant management educator*
Ciullo, Rosemary *psychologist*
Civetta, Peter Joseph *literature and language professor, researcher*
Claiborne, Kenya Wynette *secondary school educator*
Claiborne, William *journalist*
Clamon, Christopher *state attorney general*
Clancy, Mathew P. *chemical engineer, application developer*
Clancy, Thomas L., Jr. *novelist, producer*
Clarizio, Lynda M. *former information technology advertising executive, lawyer*
Clark, Alicia Garcia *political party official*
Clark, Caleb Morgan *political scientist, educator*
Clark, Candy *actress*
Clark, Celia Rue *lawyer*
Clark, Donald Otis *lawyer*
Clark, Edgar Sanderford *insurance broker, expert witness, consultant*
Clark, Eve Vivienne *linguist, educator*
Clark, Hilary J. *mathematics professor*
Clark, Jack Ivor *civil engineer, researcher*
Clark, James Covington *journalist, historian*
Clark, Karen Heath *lawyer*
Clark, LeRoy D. *law educator*
Clark, Mary Higgins *writer, communications executive*
Clark, Matt *writer*
Clark, Merrell Edward, Jr. *retired lawyer*
Clark, Michell C. *former federal agency administrator*
Clark, Peter Bruce *retired publishing executive*
Clark, Philip Raymond *nuclear utility executive, engineer*
Clark, Ramsey (William Ramsey Clark) *lawyer, former United States Attorney General*
Clark, Sandra Helen Becker *geologist*
Clark, Thomas Carlyle *retired banker*
Clark, Wesley M. *manufacturing executive*
Clark, William Arthur V. *geographer*
Clarke, Amy J. *metallurgist*
Clarke, Ciana Bernadine Bennett *education educator, researcher*
Clarke, Cordelia Kay Knight Mazuy *management consultant, artist*
Clarke, Gregory *sound designer*
Clarke, Henry Lee *foreign service officer, ambassador*
Clarke, Hughette Naomi *elementary school educator*
Clarke, Janet Morrison *marketing executive*
Clarke, Kester D. *metallurgist*
Clarke, Logan, Jr. *management consultant*
Clark Johnson, Kimberly *singer, educator*
Clark-Johnson, Susan *retired publishing executive*
Clark-Shanks, K. Audrey *biology professor*
Clarkson, Allen Cornelius *academic administrator*
Clarkson, Charles Eugene *medical technician*
Clarkson, Kelly Brianne *singer*
Clasen, Milton G. *university librarian*
Claus, Alison S. *mathematics education professor*
Claus, Carol Jean *small business owner*
Clausen, Jeanne Lorraine *musician*
Clauson, Kathleen Jo *writer, library operations associate*

Claver, Robert Earl *television producer, director*
Clawson, John Addison *investment company and retired chemicals executive*
Clay, John Peter *investment company executive*
Clayton, David A(lvin) *biology professor*
Clayton, Glenn N. *literature and language professor*
Clayton, Raymond Edward *municipal official*
Clayton, Richard Reese *retired diversified financial services company executive*
Claytor, Richard Anderson *retired federal agency administrator*
Cleary, Manon Catherine *artist, retired educator*
Cleave, Mary L. *environmental engineer, former astronaut*
Clees, Kelly Marie *school psychologist*
Cleeton, Lorraine *special education educator*
Cleghorn, John Edward *retired bank executive*
Clemen, Robert T. *decision analysis educator*
Clemendor, Anthony Arnold *obstetrician, educator, gynecologist, educator*
Clemens, Alvin Honey *insurance company executive*
Clemens, Roger (William Roger Clemens) *former professional baseball player*
Clement, Yvonne Madeline *librarian*
Clements, Thomas Frank *writer*
Clemmensen, Larry P. *investment company executive*
Clerides, Glafcos John *former President of Cyprus, lawyer*
Cleveland, David Michael *geologist*
Clifford, Brother Peter *academic administrator, religious studies educator*
Clifton, Douglas C. *retired newspaper editor*
Clifton, Russell B. *retired mortgage company executive, consultant*
Clinard, Marshall Barron *sociologist, educator*
Cline, Carolyn Joan *plastic and reconstructive surgeon*
Clinton, Thomas William *physicist, researcher*
Clogan, Paul Maurice *English language and literature educator*
Cloonan, Yona Keich *epidemiologist*
Clooney, George *actor*
Close, Glenn *actress*
Closen, Michael Lee *retired law educator*
Clote, Peter George *computer scientist, mathematician, educator*
Cloud, Stanley Wills *journalist, writer, editor, reporter*
Clough, Patricia G. *literature and language professor*
Clough, Ray William, Jr. *civil engineering educator*
Clow, Richmond L. *professor*
Clubb, Bruce Edwin *retired lawyer*
Clymer, Adam *journalist, writer*
Coakley, Erin Louise *internist*
Coan, Patricia A. *retired judge*
Cobabe, Alvin Fred *retired surgeon, small business owner*
Cobb, John Boswell, Jr. *clergyman, educator*
Cobb, John Candler *medical educator*
Cobb, Kay Beevers *retired state supreme court justice, state senator*
Cobb, Virginia Horton *artist, educator*
Coberly, Elaine K. *psychologist*
Cobitz, Walthea V. *dean, educator*
Coburn, D(onald) L(ee) *playwright*
Coccia, Michel Andre *retired lawyer*
Cochran, John P. *economics professor*
Cochran, Kathy Holcombe *music educator, conductor*
Cochran, Robert Carter *surgical educator*
Cochrane, Walter E. *retired academic administrator, music supervisor, clarinet soloist*
Cockrel, Kenneth Vern, Jr. *former mayor*
Cockrum, William Monroe III *investment banker, educator*
Cody, Christopher B. *secondary school educator*
Cody, Judith *composer, writer*
Coffee, Joseph Denis, Jr. *retired college chancellor*
Coffey, John Louis *federal judge*
Coffey, Sharon Marie *music educator*
Coffey, Timothy *physicist*
Coffin, Bertha Louise *retired telecommunications industry executive*
Coffin, Bruce *literature and language educator*
Coffman, Diana *biology professor*
Cofield, Cheryl Yvonne *elementary and secondary school educator*
Cohen, Alvin P. *language educator*
Cohen, Aryell *music educator*
Cohen, Burton Jack *otolaryngologist, educator*
Cohen, Christopher B. *lawyer*
Cohen, Claire Gorham *investment company executive*
Cohen, Gloria Ernestine *elementary school educator*
Cohen, Jay M. *consulting firm executive, former federal agency administrator, retired military officer*
Cohen, Joel J. *lawyer, investment banker*
Cohen, Larry *computer software company executive*
Cohen, Malcolm Martin *psychologist, researcher*
Cohen, Margaret Ann *artist, consultant*
Cohen, Mark Herbert *broadcast executive*
Cohen, Michael Paul *statistician*
Cohen, Neal Stuart *air transportation executive*
Cohen, Rachel Rutstein *financial planner*
Cohen, Roberta Jane *think-tank associate*
Cohen, Stanley *retired biochemistry educator*
Cohen, William Nathan *radiologist*
Cohn, Gary Dennis *journalist, educator*
Cohn, Marianne Winter Miller *civic activist*
Coker, Ayodeji *research scientist*
Coker, Donald William *banking, management and economic consultant*
Colaianni, Joseph Vincent *judge*
Colaianni, Louis Edward *voice educator*
Colantuono, Thomas Paul *former prosecutor, state legislator*
Colberg, Talis James *mayor, former state attorney general*
Colbern, Steven Garrett *chemist, researcher*
Colbert, Stephen (Stephen Tyrone Colbert) *comedian, actor*
Colburn, Kenneth Hersey *retired financial executive*
Cole, Nikki Jo *music educator*
Cole, Stephen Mark *investment banker*
Coleman, Claire Kohn *public relations executive*
Coleman, Dabney W. *actor*
Coleman, Gary William *retired elementary school educator*
Coleman, Jean Black *nurse, physician assistant*
Coleman, Marsha Lee *mathematics educator*
Coleman, Mary Sue *academic administrator*
Coleman, Norman, Jr. *former United States Senator from Minnesota, mayor*
Coleman, Robert Lee *retired lawyer*
Coleman, Robert Winston *lawyer*
Coleman, Ted *health educator, consulting executive*
Coletta, Nancy Joy *vision scientist, educator*
Colfax, Toyoko Suzuki *language educator*
Colip, Olga Shearin *retired home economist, volunteer*
Colker, Edward *artist, educator*
Collette, Frances Madelyn *retired tax specialist, lawyer, consultant, advocate*
Collier, Herman Edward, Jr. *retired college president*
Collier, William Gayle *psychology professor, researcher*
Collins, Brian David *archivist*
Collins, Eileen Marie *astronaut*
Collins, Frank, Jr. *dentist, educator*
Collins, J. Michael *retired public broadcasting executive*
Collins, James Duffield *marine engineer, editor*
Collins, Kathleen Anne *artistic director*
Collins, Lois M. Rylander *artist*
Collins, Martha *English language educator, writer*
Collins, Richard Stratton (Dick Collins) *retired public relations executive*
Collins, Ronald Leslie Leopold *neurosurgeon*
Collins, Sherri Smith *music educator*
Collins, Terry *health educator*
Collins, Walter Lloyd George *editor*
Collins-McNeil, Janice *nursing professor, researcher*
Collmer, Robert George *retired language educator*
Colman, Jenny Meyer *psychiatrist*
Colodny, Edwin Irving *lawyer, retired air transportation executive*
Colombo, Rose Marie *freelance/self-employed newswriter, television personality*
Colonnier, Marc Leopold *retired anatomist*
Colón Robles, Marilé *research scientist*
Colosimo, Mary Lynn Sukurs *psychology professor*
Colton, John P. *nuclear scientist, engineering executive*
Colton, Sterling Don *retired lawyer, hotel executive*
Columbus, Chris J. *film director, screenwriter*
Colwell, Bryan York *private investor, philanthropist*
Colwell, Howard Otis *advertising executive*
Combs, Holly Marie *actress*
Combs, Roy James, Jr. *systems analyst, researcher*
Combs, Sean (Diddy) *record company executive, producer, actor*
Comisky, Ian Michael *lawyer*
Common, (Lonnie Rashid Lynn, Common Sense) *rap artist*
Compton, Diane Groat *professional counselor, researcher*
Compton, Norma Haynes *retired dean, artist*
Compton, Robert H. *lawyer*
Compton, W. Dale *physicist, researcher, engineer*
Conaway, Edward C. *corporate communications specialist*
Conaway, Mary Ann *education educator, academic administrator*
Condon, Tom (Thomas Joseph Condon) *sports agent, retired professional football player*
Condra, Allen Lee *retired lawyer, state official*
Condry, Robert Stewart *retired hospital administrator*
Conger, Harry Milton *mining company executive*
Conley, Ruth Irene *poet*
Connanghey, Mc. William Eugene *chemical engineer*
Connell, Carol Matheson *corporate communications specialist, consultant*
Connell, Shirley Hudgins *public relations professional*
Connell, William D. *lawyer*
Connelly, Sharon Rudolph *nuclear energy industry executive*
Conner, Chuck (Charles F. Conner) *former federal agency administrator*
Conner, Lindsay Andrew *lawyer*
Connery, Sir Sean (Thomas Sean Connery) *actor*
Connolly, Thomas Joseph *engineering educator*
Connolly, Violette M. *small business owner*
Connor, Daniel F. *child and adolescent psychiatrist, researcher*
Connor, Geoffrey Scott *former state official, lawyer*
Connor, Joseph E. *former international organization official*
Connor, Laurence Davis *retired lawyer*
Conomy, John Paul *neurologist, educator, lawyer*
Conover, Lloyd Hillyard *retired research scientist*
Conover-Carson, Anne *writer*
Conrad, Harold Theodore *psychiatrist*
Conran, James Michael *consumer advocate, public policy consultant*
Conrath, Barney Jay *astrophysicist*
Conrey, Thomas Joseph *psychologist*
Conroy, Tamara Boks *artist, retired special education educator*
Conroy, Thomas Francis *insurance company consultant*
Consey, Kevin Edward *museum administrator*
Constantine, Larry L. *software designer, design and consulting company executive*
Constantine, Madonna G. *psychology professor, researcher*
Constantine, Michael *actor*
Conte, Julie Villa *nurse, administrator*
Conti, Indalicio Palomar *finance educator*
Conway, David Antony *marketing professional*
Conway, John Thomas *federal agency administrator, lawyer, engineer*
Conway, Richard Ashley *environmental engineer*
Conway-Langguth, Rebecca Joan *dance school owner and instructor*
Coohill, Thomas Patrick *biophysicist, photobiologist*
Cook, Charles Wilkerson, Jr. *retired bank executive, municipal official*
Cook, David Roland *singer, musician*
Cook, Edward Joseph *college president*
Cook, Hardy Merrill III *retired literature and language professor*
Cook, Linda Z. *former oil industry executive*
Cook, Lisa Connelly *historian, educator*
Cook, Martha E. *retired language educator*
Cook, Sister Mary Mercedes *school system administrator, director*
Cook, Myrtle *special education and elementary school educator*
Cook, Quentin LaMar *church leader, healthcare executive, lawyer*
Cook, Renay *elementary school educator*
Cook, Richard Kelsey *aerospace transportation executive*
Cook, Sharki Jo *humanities educator*
Cook, Sharon Lee Delancey *retired elementary school educator, musician*
Cook, William Alfred *medical products executive*
Cooke, Robert William *retired science journalist, author and photographer*
Cooledge, Richard Calvin *retired lawyer*
Cooley, Denton Arthur *surgeon, educator*
Coonts, Stephen Paul *writer*
Coop, Frederick Robert *retired city manager*
Cooper, Austin Morris *chemist, engineer, researcher, consultant*
Cooper, Charles Gordon *retired insurance company executive*
Cooper, Charles Howard *retired photojournalist, publishing executive*
Cooper, Elva June *artist*
Cooper, Eugene Bruce *speech pathology/audiology services professional, educator*
Cooper, Hal *television director*
Cooper, Hal Dean *lawyer*
Cooper, Jacqueline M. *career planning administrator, director*
Cooper, Jacquelyn Barber *librarian*
Cooper, James Michael *education educator*
Cooper, Josephine Smith *trade association and public affairs executive*
Cooper, Judith Kase *retired theater educator, playwright*
Cooper, Kathleen Bell *dean, retired federal agency administrator*
Cooper, Ken Errol *retired management educator*
Cooper, Norton J. (Sky) *liquor, wine and food company executive*
Cooper, Paula K. *psychologist*
Cooper, Rebecca *art dealer*
Cooper, William S. *retired state supreme court justice*
Cooperman, Jack Morris *nutrition educator*
Cope, Jeannette Naylor *minister*
Cope, John R(obert) *retired lawyer*
Cope, Kenneth Wayne *retail executive*
Cope, Melba Darlene *volunteer, photographer*
Copeland, Angie Denise *communications educator*
Copeland, Henry Jefferson, Jr. *former college president*
Copeland, Robert Glenn *lawyer*
Coplin, Mark David *lawyer*
Copperfield, David (David Kotkin) *illusionist, director, producer*
Coppersmith, Clifford Patrick *academic administrator, educator*
Coppie, Comer Swift *retired state official*
Coppola, Sofia Carmina *film director, film producer, scriptwriter*
Coppotelli, Blake Albert *lawyer*
Corbet, Kathleen A. *investment company executive, former financial information company executive*
Corbett, Brooke Myers *science educator*
Corbett, Donna M. *historian*
Corbett, Lenora Meade *mathematician, community college educator*
Corbin, Veronica L. *secondary school educator, information scientist, consultant*
Corcoran, James B. *bank executive*
Corderman, Douglas George *retired non-profit organization executive*
Cordero-Román, Arnaldo *humanities educator*
Cordes, Brett McCormack *otolaryngologist*
Cordes, Kathleen Ann *retired physical education educator, director*
Cordova, Ruben Charles *art historian, curator, photographer*
Cordray, Richard A. *state attorney general*
Cordray-Van de Castle, Karen *retired elementary school educator*
Corey, Kenneth Edward *urban planning and geography educator, researcher*
Corey, Orlin Russell *publishing executive*
Corkins, Bob *school system administrator*
Cormie, Donald Mercer *investment company executive*
Cormier, Jon *computer engineer*
Cormier, Joseph Bowman *private investigator, consultant*
Cornejo-Patterson, Deanna Hortensia *language educator*
Cornelius, Nathalie *language educator*
Cornell, Robert Arthur *retired federal official*
Cornish, Jay (Thelbert Bernard Cornish Jr.) *research and development company executive, former internet company executive*
Cornish, Jeannette *lawyer*
Cornish, Katrina *research scientist*
Cornish, Randall *educator, graphic artist*
Correa, Jaime *architectural firm executive*
Correa-de-Araujo, Rosaly Lia *medical researcher, educator*
Correll, Alston Dayton, Jr., (Pete) *forest products company executive*
Corrigan, Brian Jay *literature educator, writer*
Corry, Aline Lahusen *art educator*
Cortese, Richard Anthony *computer company executive*
Cortes Zavala, Luis Alberto *systems engineer, security researcher, consultant*
Cosby, Bill *actor, television producer*
Cosimano, Thomas Francis *finance educator*
Cosman, Francene Jen *former government official*
Costa, Fabricio *research scientist*
Costa, Mary *soprano*
Costa-Gavras, (Constantin Gavras) *film director, writer*
Costantini, Mary Ann C. *writer, adult education educator*
Costantini, William Joseph *educator*
Costanza, Michael C. *retired statistics professor*
Costello, Elvis (Declan Patrick McManus) *musician, songwriter, singer*
Costes, George T. *retired state judge*
Cottam, Gene Larry *retired biochemistry educator*
Cottam, Keith M. *librarian, educator, administrator*
Cotten, Annie Laura *psychologist, educator*
Cotter, Robert F. *hotel executive*
Cotter, William Reckling *foundation administrator*
Cotting, James Charles *manufacturing executive, director*
Cottone, Anthony Matthew *investment advisor*
Cottrell, David Milton *sound recording engineer, producer, singer, songwriter*
Cottrell, Mary-Patricia Tross *bank executive*
Couch, Daniel Michael *healthcare executive*
Coughlin, Jack *printmaker, sculptor, art educator*
Cougill, Roscoe McDaniel *retired military officer*
Couillard, Elizabeth L. *secondary school educator, department chairman*
Coulter, Jack Benson, Jr. *financial planner*
Coulter, Stephanie Michelle Benedict *photographer, sales consultant*
Counter, James Nicholas III *trade association executive, lawyer*
Courington, Leigh Ann *history professor*
Court, Iain Maxwell *lighting designer*
Courtenay, William James *historian, educator*
Courtés, Joseph Jean-Marie *humanities educator, writer*
Courtnay, Wiliam Gerard *osteopathic physician*
Courtney, Edward *retired classics educator*
Courtney, Hischke J. *dancer, educator*
Couvillion, David Irvin *retired federal judge*
Covalt, Robert Byron *chemicals executive*
Covassin, Tracey *athletic training educator*
Covintree, George E. *retired anesthesiologist*
Cowan, Andrew Glenn *television writer, producer, performer*
Cowher, Bill (William Laird Cowher) *sportscaster, former professional football coach*
Cowles, Charles *art dealer*
Cowles, Lois Anne Fort *social worker, educator, poet*
Cowperthwait, Lindley Murray, Jr. *lawyer*
Cox, Beulah Elizabeth *violinist, music educator*
Cox, Chapman Beecher *retired lawyer, charitable organization and aerospace executive*
Cox, Christopher (Charles Christopher Cox) *former United States Representative from California*
Cox, John Francis *retired cosmetic company executive*
Cox, Marshall *lawyer*
Cox, Robert Hames *chemist, consultant*
Cox, Tiffany L. *researcher*
Cox, William Andrew *cardiovascular thoracic surgeon*
Coyle, Marie Bridget *retired microbiologist, lab administrator*
Coyle, Martin Adolphus, Jr. *lawyer*
Coyle, Mary Bridget *humanities educator*
Coyne, Brian J(oseph) *pharmaceutical researcher*
Cozma, Raluca *journalist, educator*
Crabbs, Roger Alan *publishing executive, director, small business owner, military officer, educator*
Craft, Edmund Coleman *retired manufacturing executive*
Craft, Suzanne *neuroscientist, educator*
Crafton-Masterson, Adrienne *retired real estate company executive*
Crahan, Elizabeth Schmidt *librarian*
Craig, Carol Mills *marriage, family and child counselor*
Craig, Larry Edwin *consulting company executive, former United States Senator from Idaho*
Craik, Mary Bernice *artist, art gallery owner*
Crain, Mary Ann *retired elementary school educator*
Craioveanu, Mihai Dorin *musician*
Cramer, John McNaight *lawyer*
Cramer, Mark Clifton *lawyer*
Cramer, Robert Vern *retired college administrator, consultant*
Crane, Frederick Loring *biochemistry educator*
Crane, Roger Ryan, Jr. *lawyer*
Cranney, Marilyn Kanrek *retired lawyer*
Crary, Michael A. *medical educator*
Crary, Miner Dunham, Jr. *lawyer*
Cravats, Monroe *science educator*
Craven, Wes *film director*
Cravens, Thomas D. *literature and language professor*
Crawford, Bruce Edgar *advertising executive*
Crawford, Carol Tallman *law educator*
Crawford, Constance *performance artist, educator*
Crawford, Edward E. *retired psychologist*
Crawford, James Leroy *minister, retired theology studies educator*
Crawford, Kenneth Charles *retired academic administrator*
Crawford, Mallory *counselor*
Crawford, Muriel Laura *lawyer, educator, writer*
Crawford, Peggy (Margaret Elizabeth Frank Crawford) *photographer*
Crawford, Sheila Jane *librarian, reading specialist retired*
Crawford, William Walsh *retired consumer products company executive*
Crawford Walden, Sandra D. *media specialist*
Crawley, Cheryl K. *school system administrator*
Crea, Vivien S. *retired military officer*
Creech, John Lewis *botanist, consultant*
Crennel, Romeo *former professional football coach*
Cretara, Domenic Anthony *artist, educator*
Crewdson, John Mark *journalist, writer*
Crews, Mara Lynne *writer*
Crinklaw, Katherine Mary *artist*
Crino, Marjanne Helen *anesthesiologist*
Crisci, Mathew G. *financial consultant and author*

Crisci, Pat Devita retired psychology educator
Criscuolo, Esperanza retail executive
Crist, Paul Grant retired lawyer
Criswell, Kimberly Ann executive coach, communications consultant, performance artist
Croan, Robert James music critic
Crocker, Ryan Clark former ambassador
Crocker, Saone Baron lawyer
Crocker, Suzanne painter
Cromwell, Florence Stevens occupational therapist
Cron, Kenneth D. former interactive software and gaming executive
Cronce, Paul Calvin retired dermatologist
Cronenberg, David film director
Cronin, Stephen Burke science educator
Cronson, Robert Granville retired lawyer
Croskell, Madelon Byrd music educator, classical vocalist
Crosley, Jannell Mary special education educator
Cross, Kathryn Patricia education educator
Crossley, Nancy Ruth retired federal agency administrator
Crossley, Pamela Kyle history professor, writer
Crouch, Peter E. engineering educator
Crouch, Sarah Harris music educator, writer
Crovitz, Louis Gordon (Gordon Crovitz) former publishing executive, journalist
Crow, Rita Jane secondary school educator
Crow, Sheryl singer, songwriter, musician
Crowder, Heather Elizabeth mental health services professional, consultant
Crowder, Mary Ellen artist, educator, photographer, real estate broker
Crowe, James Joseph lawyer
Crowell, Craven H., Jr. retired federal agency administrator
Crowell, Dring Needham biology educator
Crowell, Kenneth Leland biology educator
Crowl, Steven Craig aerospace engineer
Crozer, Norman P. special education educator, director
Crozier, William Marshall, Jr. bank holding company executive
Cruciani, Ricardo Alberto physician
Crumbley, Esther Helen Kendrick retired real estate agent, retired secondary school educator, councilwoman
Crume, Richard V. engineering educator
Crumley, Martha Ann charity fundraising executive
Crumpton, Henry A. (Hank Crumpton) former federal agency administrator
Crusan, Ronald L. retired museum director
Cruz, Theresa Lavaina mental health services professional, educator
Cruz, Zoe diversified financial services company executive
Cruz-Romo, Gilda soprano
Crvenkovski, Branko former president of Macedonia
Cryer, Rodger Earl educational administrator
Csikszentmihalyi, Mark language educator
Cubin, Barbara Lynn former United States Representative from Wyoming
Cuddihy, Robert Vincent, Jr. finance and marketing executive
Cueto, Rochelle E. retired elementary school educator
Cuetter, Albert Cayetano neurologist
Cuffe, Stafford Sigesmund business, technology, manufacturing and management consultant
Cui, Hongliang engineering company executive, researcher
Cui, Minghao application developer, researcher
Cui, Ying research scientist
Culkin, Macaulay actor
Culleeney, Maureen Ann information technology executive, educator
Cullen, Fergus P. small business owner, former political organization administrator
Cullen, James G. telecommunications industry executive
Culligan, Sean Louis theater educator
Cullingford, Elizabeth literature and language professor, department chairman
Culp, Courtney Ann history professor
Culp, Michael Bronston investor, writer, publisher
Culp, Mildred Louise corporate financial executive
Culwell, Charles Louis retired manufacturing executive
Cumba, Mark T. lawyer
Cumming, Robert Hugh artist, photographer
Cummings, Blake landsman
Cummings, David William artist, retired educator
Cummins, John Stephen bishop emeritus
Cummins, Nancyellen Heckeroth electronics engineer
Cummins, Wilma Jeanne actress, comedienne
Cunniff, Suzanne surgical technician
Cunningham, Alice Jeanne chemistry educator, author, consultant
Cunningham, Alice Welt law and mathematics educator
Cunningham, Kathy artist, art educator
Cunningham, Kimberly Ellen medical transcriptionist
Cunningham, Michael Gerald composer, writer, music educator emeritus
Cunningham, Ronnie Walter venture capitalist
Cunningham, Terence Thomas III hospital administrator
Cunningham, Valerie S. historic preservationist, researcher
Cupp, Lucy Paschall retired elementary school educator, minister
Cupp, Robert Erhard golf course architect, land use planner
Curie, Charles G. former federal agency administrator
Curler, (Mary) Bernice writer, educator
Curott, David Richard retired physics professor
Curran, Tom biology professor, researcher
Currence, Carol J. retired education educator
Currie, Robert Bruce psychology professor
Currie, Steven Ray artist
Curry, Carlton E. broadcast and waterworks executive, councilman
Curry, Catharine Terrill marketing and sales corporate executive
Curry, John Michael investment banker
Curry, Nancy S. radiologist, educator
Curry Scott, Shirley Goodman retired director
Curson, Theodore musician
Curtin-Wilding, Leigh media consultant, writer
Curtis, Drew Internet company executive
Curtis, George Clifton psychiatrist, educator, researcher
Curtis, James L. psychiatrist
Curtis, Jamie Lee actress
Curtis, John Joseph lawyer, writer
Curtis, Joyce Mae retired physical education educator
Curtis, Mary E. (Mary Horowitz) publishing executive
Curtis, Thomas Pelham, II, artist, educator, small business owner
Curto, Paul Allen retired research scientist
Curvin, Peggy freelance/self-employed photographer
Cusanovich, Michael Anthony biochemist
Cussler, Clive Eric author
Cutler, Deborah literature and language professor
Cutsinger, Roger Lynn engineering company executive
Cyr, Conrad Keefe federal judge
Czarnecki, Gerald Milton investment banker, venture capitalist
Dabbagh, Mahmoud language educator, linguist, researcher
Dable, Carol M. primary school educator
D'Abruzzo, Stephanie actress
Dackow, Orest Taras insurance company executive
da Cruz, Eduardo M. cardiologist, educator
Dacus, Judy McLellan biology professor
Daffron, MaryEllen retired librarian
Daglis, Lisa Genine deputy attorney general
Dagne, Getachew A. biostatistician
D'Agustino, Steven communication and technology educator
D'Agusto, Karen Rose lawyer
Dahan, Andre telecommunications industry executive
Daher, Edouard cardiologist
Dahl, John film director
Dahlburg, John-Thor Theodore news correspondent
Dahlgren, Carl Herman Per performing company executive, educator
Dahling, Gerald Vernon retired lawyer, director
Dahouk, Abbas military officer
Dahse, Kenneth William photographer, writer, educator
Dai, Qi science educator
Dai, Shengyang research scientist
Daie, Jaleh investment company executive
Dailey, Dell Lee former federal agency administrator, retired military officer
Dailey, Dianne K. lawyer
Dailey, Jim former mayor
Daily, Deirdre Lynn systems analyst
Dale, Shana Leigh former federal agency administrator
Dale, T.D. architectural firm executive
D'Alesandro, Philip Anthony parasitologist, immunologist, retired medical educator
Dalessandri, Kathie Marie surgeon, educator
D'Alessandro, Dominic retired financial executive
D'Alessio, Valaida Corrine artist, consultant
Daley, Jennifer internist, educator
Daley, Sandra retired artist, filmmaker, photographer
Dallek, Robert historian, writer
'Dally, James William mechanical engineering educator, consultant
Daly, Benjamin marine biologist, researcher
Daly, Miriam Shamer retired family physician
Dalzell, Rick information technology executive
Dam, Q. Binh engineering educator, researcher
Damas, Marie Chantale physicist, academic administrator
Damavandi, Nader electrical engineer
Dame, Richard Franklin marine biology educator
Damon, Matt (Matthew Paige Damon) actor
Damon, Shirley Stockton art gallery owner
Damsgaard, Patricia Rae artist, educator
Danaher, John Anthony III prosecutor
Danaher, Mallory Millett (Mallory Jones) actress, photographer, film and theater producer
D'Andrade, Hugh A(lfred) retired pharmaceutical company executive, lawyer
Danehy, Robert Joseph aquatic biologist
Danforth, Arthur Edwards finance executive
D'Angelo, Joseph F. secondary school educator, principal
D'Angelo, Lawrence M. humanities educator
Dangoor, David Ezra Ramsi consumer goods company executive
Dangremond, David W. art history educator
Dani, (Shirley Leyrer) sculptor, painter
Daniel, Coldwell III economist, educator, entrepreneur
Daniel, Elinor Perkins (Perky Daniel) clergywoman
Daniel, Ronald George theater, film and opera director
Daniels, Diana M. lawyer
Daniels, James Maurice retired physicist
Daniels, Lydia M. health care administrator
Daniels, William Burton retired physicist, educator
Danielsen, Albert Leroy economics professor, energy and utilities consultant
Danilov, Alexey V. hematologist
Dann, Marc E. former state attorney general, former state senator
Danne, Richard Franklin graphic designer
Danowitz, Mary Ann education educator
Danse, Ilene Homnick Raisfeld physician, educator, toxicologist, sculptor
Danso-Boafo, Kwaku education educator
Danticat, Edwidge writer, educator
Danzig, Richard Jeffrey former federal agency administrator
Da Pena, Eileen psychologist
Daquila, Richard mathematics professor
Darabont, Frank screenwriter, director
Darby, Joseph M. reservist
Darden, Derrick Carolyle retired military
Darling, Jeremy astrophysicist, educator
Darmofal, David political scientist, educator
Darnell, Riley Carlisle lawyer, former state official
Darrow, William Richard retired pharmaceutical company executive, consultant
Darvarova, Elmira musician, concertmaster
Darzynkiewicz, Zbigniew D. research scientist
Das, Koel research scientist
Das, Samik research assistant
Daschle, Linda Hall lobbyist
Daschle, Tom (Thomas Andrew Daschle) former United States Senator from South Dakota
Dashiell, Georgette Elaine actor, director
Daskalova, Sasha molecular biologist
Dasso, Jerome Joseph real estate educator
Dastin, Samuel J. aerospace engineer, consultant
Date, Elaine Satomi physiatrist, educator
Datta, Utpal science educator, researcher
Dattilo, Thomas A. retired manufacturing executive
Dattolo, Alphonse A. language educator
Daube, Jonathan Mahram retired academic administrator
Daugherity, Brian James historian, educator, historian, writer
Davenport, Deborah Ann elementary school educator
Davenport, Lawrence Franklin academic administrator
DaVerne, Steven Richard advertising director, artist, illustrator
David, Clive events executive
David, Larry television scriptwriter and producer, actor
Davids, Robert Norman retired petroleum exploration geologist
Davidson, John Kenneth, Sr. sociologist, educator, researcher, writer, consultant
Davidson, Mayer B. endocrinologist, educator, researcher
Davidson, Rick employment services executive
Davies, Don education educator
Davies, Raymond Douglas musician, songwriter
Davis, Brian Lee mathematics professor
Davis, C. VanLeer III lawyer
Davis, Christine Maria education educator
Davis, Clarence Clinton, Jr. lawyer
Davis, David Lee former United States Representative from Tennessee
Davis, Dempsie Augustus military officer, educator, financial planner
Davis, Donald Alan news correspondent, author
Davis, Donald Robert nutritionist, researcher, consultant
Davis, Earon Scott environmental policy writer, teacher, massage therapist, legal consultant
Davis, Elizabeth Eileen education educator
Davis, Evelyn Cleveland educational association administrator, consultant
Davis, Frederic Emery corporate executive
Davis, Geena (Virginia Elizabeth Davis) actress
Davis, Harley Cleo retired military officer
Davis, Helen R. elementary and middle school educator
Davis, John Ripoll manufacturing executive
Davis, John Warren retired real estate broker, consultant
Davis, John William toxicologist
Davis, Joseph Lloyd academic administrator, consultant
Davis, Kate K. literature and language professor
Davis, Katherine Sarah physical therapist
Davis, Lanita Irene secondary school educator
Davis, Linda Lennon McConnell critical care nurse
Davis, Mamie (Denise Davis) writer
Davis, Mary Helen psychiatrist, educator
Davis, Mellar Pilgrim oncologist
Davis, Michelle Denise writer
Davis, Morris D. retired military officer, lawyer
Davis, Osceola A. opera singer
Davis, Patricia Margaret Alice psychology and religion educator
Davis, Robert W. computer company executive
Davis, Roger Edwin lawyer, retired retail executive
Davis, Ruth Margaret information technology executive
Davis, Ryan Justin director, researcher
Davis, Samuel hospital administrator, educator, consultant
Davis, Wanda Rose lawyer
Davis, William Allison, II, retired lawyer
Davis, William Edwin retired science educator
Davoudi, Ali research scientist
Dawdy, Doris Ostrander writer
Dawson, David Lynn theater educator
Dawson, Geraldine medical educator, social worker
Dawson, Suzanne Stockus lawyer
Day, Donald Lee retired engineering educator
Day, Kahlil Amyn mediator, lawyer
Day, Richard Allen retired chemistry professor
Day, Richard M. computer educator
Dayton, Mark Brandt former senator
Dea, Peter Allen gas industry executive, geologist
Deabes, Wael Abdelrahman electrical engineer, educator
Deaciuc, Ion Victor molecular biologist, researcher
Deacon, David Emmerson advertising executive
Deakins, Roger Alexander photographer, cinematographer
Dean, Carole Lee film company executive
Dean, Edwin Becton entrepreneur
Dean, John Wesley III investment banker, former federal official
Dean, Leslie Alan (Cap Dean) international economic, social and political development consultant, interagency and defense analyst
Dean, Patrecea Louise lawyer, educator, small business owner
De Angelis, Rosemary Eleanor actress
De Antoni, Edward Paul retired lab administrator
Deats, Suzanne writer, editor, artist
DeBakey, Lois science administrator, educator
DeBakey, Selma communications educator, writer, editor
Debbie, Gipson S. pediatrician, educator
deBear, Richard Stephen library planning consultant
De Blasi, Tony (Anthony Armando De Blasi) artist
de Blasis, James Michael performing company executive, theater producer
DeBock, Ronald Gene real estate company executive
DeBow, Faith pianist, music educator
DeBow, Thomas Joseph, Jr. advertising executive
DeBrincat, Susan Jeanne nutritionist
de Casal, Carole Anita education educator
deCastro, Cristina L. secondary school educator
Dechant, Virgil C. retired fraternal organization administrator
Dechar, Peter Henry artist
Decker, Josephine I. health clinic official
Decker, Mark Jonathan radiologist
Decker, Murray Steven social studies educator
Decker, Susan Lynne former Internet company executive
Decker, Walter Johns toxicologist
Decker, Wyatt W. emergency physician, educator
De Concini, Dennis lawyer, lobbyist, retired senator, consultant
De Cou-Landberg, Michelle V. retired language educator
Dede, Ercan M. mechanical engineer, researcher
DeDio, Robert otolaryngologist
Dedman, Bill journalist
Dee, Brian Michael pharmacist
Deeds, Virginia Williams volunteer
Deems, Sherran Ellen (Sherry) artist, educator, editor
De Felitta, Frank Paul film producer, writer
Defever, Susanna Ethel retired language educator
DeGabrielle, Donald J., Jr. former prosecutor
Degann, Sona Irene obstetrician, gynecologist, educator
Degener, Carol M. lawyer
Degn, Douglas J. retired retail executive
Degos, Laurent hematology professor, public health administrator
DeGroff, Dale food service executive
DeHart, Paul Robert political science professor
Dehm, Scott M. medical educator, researcher
Dehmelt, Hans Georg retired physicist
DeHoff, Valerie S. music educator
Deily, Linnet Frazier former ambassador
Deiro, Judith Anne chemical dependency educator
de Jager, Cornelis retired astronomer
DeJarnatt, Kitty M. retired special education educator
de Jong, Robert L. chemical engineer
Dejud, Carlos psychologist
de Keczer, Steve A. research scientist
Dela Cruz, Jose Santos retired commonwealth supreme court justice
Delaney, Marnie Patricia retail executive
DeLapp, Tina Davis retired nursing educator
de la Rocha, Zack singer, musician
de La Sabliere, Jean-Marc former international organization official
de la Torre, Jack Carlos clinical neuroscientist
de la Torre, Otto J. language educator, minister
DeLaTorre, Phillip Eugene law educator
De Laurentiis, Giada chef
de Lavallade, Carmen dancer, choreographer
DeLay, Tom (Thomas Dale DeLay) former United States Representative from Texas
De La Zerda, David Joseph internist
Del Corso, Robert Engel retired history professor
Delehant, Joseph Henry lawyer
de Leon, Lidia Maria magazine editor
DeLeon, Richard Edward retired political science professor
Delgadillo, Maria Lorena language educator, translator
Delgado, Roger Rodriguez surgeon, educator
Delgado-Norris, Evelyne Mattie language educator
Delk, Charlotte Turley elementary school educator
Dell, Charlene Elizabeth music educator
Dell, Christopher William United States Ambassador to the Republic of Kosovo
DellaPina, Mario John academic administrator
DellaVecchia, Michael Anthony ophthalmologist, pathologist educator, scientist
Dellwo, Robert Dennis lawyer
DeLong, Joseph Ireland theology studies educator
De Long, Katharine retired secondary school educator
del Toro, Guillermo film director
De Lutis, Donald Conse investment advisor, consultant
Dely, Steven retired aerospace company executive
DeMane, Michael F. former medical products executive
Demant, Margaret H. retired interior designer
de Margitay, Gedeon acquisitions and management consultant
DeMary, Jo Lynne retired school system administrator, elementary school educator
Demas, Tula Ann retired counseling administrator
de Masi, Kenneth Forrest secondary school educator
de Matteo, Drea actress
DeMille, Dale Esther LPN director
DeMille, Nelson Richard writer
Deming, Rust M. ambassador, educator
Deming, Thomas Edward publishing executive
Demme, Jonathan director, producer, writer
DeMorrow, Sharon molecular biologist, educator
Dempsey, Edward Joseph lawyer
Demskis, Erinn Elisabeth language educator
Denecker, Christine language educator
Denevan, William Maxfield geographer, historical ecologist, educator
Deneve, Jeremiah Lee surgeon
Deng, Hai engineering educator, researcher
Deng, Qian finance company executive
Deng, Shaoping lab administrator, director
Deng, Weiling chemical engineer
Denis, Anne Cara musician, educator
Denison, Dwight Val finance educator
Denn, Cyril Joseph retired financial advisor
Denneen, John Paul lawyer
Dennis, Steven J. performing arts educator, actor
Dennis-Bay, Laura language educator

Denniston, George Clinton *medical activist, medical association administrator*
Denny, Terry Anne *elementary school educator*
Denoya, Laila Edna *bilingual educational consultant*
Dent, Frederick Baily *retired textiles executive, former United States Secretary of Commerce*
Dent, Julie *executive director*
Denton, Ray Douglas *insurance company executive*
Denver, Eileen Ann *retired editor*
Deo, Chaitanya Suresh *materials scientist, researcher*
de Oliveira Maciel, Marco Antonio *former Brazilian Vice President*
De Palma, Catherine S. *insurance adjuster, paralegal*
DePalma, Ralph George *surgeon, educator, medical administrator*
De Palma-Iozzi, Frances M. *music educator, conductor*
DePaoli, Lou *former professional sports team executive*
de Puget, Albert Borg Olivier *magistrate judge*
Depuglio, Joseph *physics educator*
Derber, Dana M. *graphic and web designer*
Derbes, Daniel William *retired manufacturing executive*
Derbyshire, William Wadleigh *language educator, translator*
Der-Houssikian, Haig *retired linguist, educator*
Der Kaloustian, Vazken Movses *pediatrics and medical genetics educator*
Dermanis, Paul Raymond *architect*
Dern, Laura *actress*
Deromedi, Roger K. *food products executive*
De Rosa, Eve *psychology professor*
Derr, Kenneth Tindall *retired oil industry executive*
Der Torossian, Papken *engineering executive*
Derwinski, Edward Joseph *former United States Secretary of Veterans Affairs*
DeSando, John Anthony *film critic, retired humanities educator*
Desbarats, Peter Hullett *journalist, educator, academic administrator*
Desbiens, Norman A. *medical educator, researcher*
de Schoutheete de Tervarent, Philippe *ambassador*
de Silva, Santhusht S. *educator*
DeSilvey, Dennis Lee *cardiologist, educator, academic administrator*
Desio, Delores Jean *writer, artist, retired elementary school educator*
Desjardins, Eric *retired professional hockey player*
Desloge, Christopher Davis, Sr. *real estate company, merchant banking and consulting executive*
Desnoyers, Megan Floyd *retired archivist, educator*
De Sofi, Oliver Julius *data processing executive*
de Soto, Simon *mechanical engineer*
DeSousa, Maria Ab *immunologist, educator*
Despommier, Dickson Donald *microbiology educator, parasitologist*
Despot, Shirley Ann *artist*
DeStafeno, John J. *ophthalmologist*
Destrempes, Sandra Lee *elementary school educator*
Deutsch, Herbert Arnold *music educator*
Deutsch, James I. *curator*
DeVaney, Carol Susan *management consultant*
Devaney, Earl E. *federal official*
Deverts, Denise Janicki *health psychology researcher*
DeVivo, Ange *retired small business owner*
Devlin, Michael Coles *bass-baritone*
DeVore, Daun Aline *lawyer*
DeVries, Robert Allen *foundation administrator*
deVries-White, Donna Lynn *education educator, consultant*
DeVylder, Edgar Paul, Jr. *lawyer*
Dewar, James McEwen *marketing, aerospace and defense executive, developing nations consultant*
Dewey, Arthur Eugene *former federal agency administrator*
Dewey, Nancy *mathematics educator*
deWilde, David Michael *management consultant, lawyer, finance company executive, retired recruiter*
DeWine, Mike (Richard Michael DeWine) *former senator, lawyer*
DeWitt, Eula *retired accountant*
Dewji, Nazneen N. *medical educator, small business owner*
DeWolfe, Christopher T. *former Internet company executive*
DeWoskin, Robert S. *toxicologist*
Dey, Madan Mohan *economics professor*
DeYoung, Marilyn Brant-Chandler *retired urban planner, farmer*
Dezube, Bruce Jeffrey *internist, oncologist, hematologist*
Dhanda, Abhishek *engineering company executive*
Dhoble, Abhijeet *internist*
Diakunchak, Ihor S. *retired mechanical engineer*
Diamond, Stuart *lawyer, educator, business executive*
Diamond, Susan Zee *management consultant*
Diao, Xiumin *medical researcher*
Diaz, Laura O. *secondary school educator*
Diaz-Castillo, Carlos *research scientist*
DiBenedetto, Gary *composer, educator*
DiCaprio, Leonardo *actor*
Di Cecco, James *real estate company executive*
Dichter, Barry Joel *lawyer*
Dick, James Cordell *concert pianist*
Dickens, Joyce Rebecca *retired addictions therapist, educator*
Dickens, Justin Kirk *nuclear physicist*
Dickeson, Robert Celmer *retired foundation administrator, management consultant*
Dickinson, Donald Charles *library science professor*
Dickinson, Gail Krepps *library science educator*
Dickman, James Bruce *photojournalist*
Dicksheet, Sharadkumar *plastic surgeon*
Dickson, James Francis III *surgeon*
Dickstein, Michael Ethan *mediator, arbitrator, lawyer*
Dickstein, Morris *language educator, writer*
DiCristino, Dia *health facility administrator*
DiDomenico, Mauro, Jr. *communications executive*
Diederichs, Janet Wood *public relations executive*
Diefenbacher, Eric H. *science educator*
Diefenderfer, Dan *filmmaker*
Diefendorf, Jeffry M. *history professor*
Diehl, Deborah Hilda *lawyer*
Diehl, Louis F. *hematologist*
Diehl, Stephen Anthony *human resources consultant*
Diem, Richard A. *social studies educator, educational consultant*
Diemer, Emma Lou *composer, educator*
Dierickx, Constance Ricket *psychologist, management consultant*
Dierolf, Volkmar *physics professor*
Dietel, James Edwin *lawyer, consultant*
Dietrich, Klaus *physicist, retired professor*
Diez de Velasco, Manuel *barrister, educator*
Diffrient, Niels *industrial designer*
Diggavi, Suhas *research scientist*
Di Giacomo, Fran *artist*
Di Giovanni, Anthony *retired coal mining company executive*
di Giovanni, Julian *economist*
DiGregorio, Amanda Elizabeth *medical products executive*
DiLiberto, Frank E. *physical therapist*
Dill, Ellen Renée *educator, minister, writer*
Dill, Laddie John *artist*
Dillon, Robert Sherwood *retired diplomat*
Dimaira, Ann B. *medical/surgical nurse*
Dimancescu, Mihai D. *neurosurgeon, researcher, educator*
DiMartino, Margaret Mary *elementary school educator*
Di Martino, Rita *utility company executive, government representative*
Di Massa, Ernani Vincenzo, Jr. *communications executive, television producer, writer*
Dinallo, Eric Robert *former state official*
Dincauze, Dena Ferran *retired archaeologist, educator*
Dincecco, Jennie Elizabeth Williams Swanson *healthcare administrator, mentor, educator, volunteer*
Dincer, Umit Deniz *pharmacologist, researcher*
Dinerstein, Staci *broadcast executive, educator*
Ding, Jinwen *biomedical researcher*
Dingman, Stanley Lawrence *retired science educator*
Dinwiddie, Granger *psychology professor*
Dinwiddie, William James *environmental operator*
DioGuardi, Richard James *psychologist, researcher*
Di Palma, Sunday Lynn *retired humanities educator*
DiPasqua, Aimee Dora *physician*
DiPentima, Renato Anthony *information technology executive*
DiPiazza, Michael Charles *insurance company executive*
DiPietro, Ralph John *lawyer*
Dipko, Thomas Earl *retired minister, religious organization administrator*
DiRienzo, Casey *economics professor*
Dirks, Roger L. *mathematics educator*
Dirsmith, Jessica *psychologist*
Dirvin, Gerald Vincent *retired consumer products company executive*
DiSalvatore, William P. *lawyer*
Dishy, Bob *actor*
Dispenza, Mary Catherine *director, educator, photographer*
Ditta, Joseph Michael *literature and language professor*
Dittenhafer, Brian Douglas *banker, economist*
Dittenhafer, Daniel Webster, II, *computer scientist*
Ditter, J. William, Jr. *federal judge*
Ditton, Patricia Granville *psychologist, educator*
Dix, Carol *writer*
Dixit, Avinash Kamalakar *economics professor*
Dixon, Albert Truman *mathematician, educator*
Dixon, Ben Harold *musician, educator*
Dixon, Gordon Henry *biochemist, educator*
Dixon, Jane Frazier *elementary school educator, consultant*
Dixon, William Robert *musician, educator*
Dixon-Nielsen, Judy E(arlene) *mortgage banker specialty in government lending, marketing professional, consultant*
Djalilian, Hamid Reza *medical educator, neurologist*
Djang, David S.W. *physician*
Djordjevic, Dimitrije *historian, educator*
Dnes, Antony William *economist*
Doak, Wesley Allen *school librarian, educator*
Doan, Lurita Alexis *former federal agency administrator*
Dobbs, Lou (Louis Earl Dobbs) *commentator, former broadcast executive*
Dobelle, Evan Samuel *academic administrator*
Doberenz, Alexander R. *retired nutrition educator, chemist*
Dobler, Donald William *retired procurement and materials executive, dean*
Dobrzynski, Judith Helen *journalist, commentator*
Dobson, Donald Alfred *retired electrical engineer*
Dockery, J. Lee *retired medical school administrator*
Dockstader, Deborah Ruth *minister*
Dodd, Emmeline Irwin *retired biology educator*
Dodds, Amy Noelle Shawler *music educator*
Dodgen, Daniel W. *health policy advisor, psychologist*
Dodson, Carolyn McCroskey *biology professor, consultant*
Dodson, Daryl Theodore *ballet administrator, consultant*
Dodson, Samuel Robinette III *retired investment banker*
Doering, Kelly Bell Scribner *marketing executive*
Doerper, John Erwin *journal editor, publishing executive*
Dofflemyer, Leonard *retired history professor*
Dogan, Gokhan *research scientist*
Dogançay, Burhan C. *artist, photographer, sculptor*
Doherty, Peter Charles *immunologist*
Dohmen, Mary Holgate *retired primary school educator*
Dohn, Julianne *child protective services specialist*
Dohrmann, Russell William *retired manufacturing executive*
Dolan, Andrew Kevin *retired lawyer*
Dolan, Edward Francis *writer*
Dolan, Michael J. *former multimedia company and advertising executive*
Dolan, Peter Brown *lawyer*
Dole, Arthur Alexander *former psychology professor, department chairman*
Dole, Elizabeth Hanford *former United States Senator from North Carolina*
Doligosa, Annie Lumampao *elementary school educator, researcher*
Dolim, Henry Philip, Jr. *retired engineering educator*
Dolins, Steven Barnett *engineering educator*
Dollens, Ronald W. *pharmaceutical executive*
Dollinger, Marc Lindsey *historian*
Dolph, Wilbert Emery *lawyer*
Doman, Elvira *retired science administrator*
Dombalis, Constantine Nicholas *minister, writer*
Domenici, (Pete) Vichi *retired United States Senator from New Mexico*
Domenick, Julie D. *lobbyist*
Domiano, Joseph Charles *lawyer*
Dominguez, Alvio *mathematics professor*
Dominguez, Cari M. *former federal official*
Dominguez, Michael L. *federal agency administrator, former civilian military employee*
Domjan, Laszlo Karoly *journalist*
Donald, Aida DiPace *retired publishing executive*
Donald, James Lloyd (Jim Donald) *former beverage service company executive*
Donaldson, Eva G. *chemist, writer*
Donaldson, William Henry *investment banker, former federal agency administrator*
Donberger, Karen Shepard *special education and elementary school educator*
Doncarlos, Lydia *medical educator*
Dong, Beibei *finance educator*
Dong, Ren Guang *mechanical engineer*
Dong, Wei *research scientist*
Donley, Russell Lee III *small business owner, former state legislator*
Donlon, William James *retired lawyer*
Donna, Stewart *researcher*
Donnally, Patricia Broderick *writer*
Donnell, Harold Eugene, Jr. *retired professional society administrator*
Donner, Jörn Johan *film director, writer, state legislator*
Donoff, R. Bruce *dean, oral surgeon, dental educator*
Donoghue, John Francis *archbishop emeritus*
Donohoe, Jerome Francis *lawyer*
Donohue, Marc David *chemical engineering professor*
Donovan, Brian *journalist, author*
Donovan, Dennis Dale *priest*
Donovan, Helen W. *editor*
Doody, William E. *secondary school educator*
Doolittle, Deborah Hope *language educator, writer*
Doolittle, John Taylor *former United States Representative from California*
Dorel, Theresa Garfield *humanities educator, department chairman*
Doria, Cataldo *transplant surgeon*
Dorkin, Frederic Eugene *lawyer*
Dorman, David Christopher *toxicologist, researcher*
Dornbush, K. Terry *former ambassador, consulting company executive, educator*
Dorsey, Dolores Florence *retired corporate treasurer, finance company executive*
Dorvil, Judith Marie *psychologist*
Doss, Delia L. *mathematics educator*
Doss, Jessica Yarina *incentive program manager*
Dossin, Ernest Joseph III *credit manager*
Doten, David R. *social worker*
Doty, Scott William *science educator*
Doud, Guy R. *motivational speaker, former secondary education educator*
Doueihi, Stephen Hector Youssef *bishop emeritus*
Dougherty, John Chrysostom III *retired lawyer*
Douglas, Dewey L. *theater educator, lighting designer*
Douglas, James *retired professional boxer*
Douglas, Karin Nadja *engineer*
Douglas, P C *producer, director, reporter, editor*
Douglass, Jane Dempsey *retired theology educator*
Douglass, Robert Royal *bank executive, lawyer*
Dow, David Sontag *retired ophthalmologist*
Dow, Ronald F. *librarian, dean*
Dow, William Hatfield *healthcare educator*
Dowd, Morgan Daniel *retired political science professor, dean*
Dowdy, Charles Wayne *former United States Representative from Mississippi*
Dowdy, Robert Alan *retired lawyer, director*
Dowling, Edward Thomas *economics professor*
Dowling, Michael Paul *think-tank executive*
Dowling, Vincent John *retired lawyer*
Downes, Rackstraw *artist*
Downey, John Alexander *physician, educator*
Downing, Hudson Urquhart *retired securities trader, bank executive*
Downs, Dorothy Rieder *art historian, consultant, writer*
Downs, Jon Franklin *drama educator, director, writer*
Doyle, Gillian *actress*
Doyle, Irene Elizabeth *retired electronic sales executive, retired nurse*
Doyle, L. F. Boker *retired trust company executive*
Doyle, Tom *sculptor*
Dozier, Glenn Joseph *diversified financial services company executive*
Dozier, James Lee *former army officer*
Dozier, Therese Knecht *department of education advisor, former education association administrator*
Drabkin, Murray *lawyer*
Dracos, Theodore Michael *journalist, television producer*
Dragon, William, Jr. *footwear and apparel company executive*
Dragoumis, Paul *electric utility company executive*
Drahos, Sandra P. *retired chemist*
Drake, Dallas *retired professional hockey player*
Drake, Donald Charles *journalist, playwright*
Drake, Evelyn Downie *retired secondary school educator*
Drake, George Albert *retired academic administrator, historian, educator*
Drake, Martin Harvey *counseling administrator, educator*
Drake, Miriam Anna *retired librarian, educator, writer, consultant*
Drake, Rodman Leland *investment company executive, consultant*
Drake, Thelma Day *former United States Representative from Virginia*
Drance, Stephen Michael *ophthalmologist, educator*
Draney, Clark Lloyd *literature and language educator*
Draper, Edgar *psychiatrist*
Draper, E(rnest) Linn, Jr. *retired electric utility executive*
Draughon, Scott *lawyer, social worker, educator*
Drazan, Joseph Gerald *retired librarian*
Drechsel, Edward Russell, Jr. *retired utilities executive*
Drechsler, Beatrice Krain *lawyer*
Drennan, Catherine Luschinsky *chemistry professor*
Drennen, William Miller, Jr. *cultural organization administrator, film producer, writer*
Drescher, Judith Altman *library director*
Dreskin, Stephen Charles *immunologist, allergist*
Dressler, David Charles *retired construction materials executive*
Drew, Fraser Bragg Robert *language educator*
Drews, Jürgen *pharmaceutical researcher*
Drey, Philip *religious studies educator*
Dreyer, Nancy Ann *epidemiologist, researcher*
Driscoll, Kimberlee Marie *lawyer*
D'Rivera, Paquito *clarinetist, saxophonist, conductor, composer*
Drosdick, John Girard *retired oil industry executive*
Drozd, Leszek Stanislaw *educational video producer, music composer for films, CEO story tellers producer*
Drozdeck, Steven Richard *management consultant*
Drucker, Carol R. *medical educator*
Drue, Kerry Erica *former attorney general*
Druffel, Ann Bernice *researcher, writer, public speaker*
Drum, Alice *academic administrator, educator*
Drummond, Carol Cramer *voice educator, lyricist, writer, artist*
Druskin, Robert A. *retired diversified financial services company executive*
Druskoff, Barbara Therese *retired elementary school educator*
Druz, Regina Shmukler *cardiologist, researcher*
Dryden, Stephen David *artist, product designer*
Dryman, Amy *epidemiologist*
Du, Jianxin *research scientist*
Duan, Xiaochun *electrical engineer*
Dubik, James M. *career military officer*
Dubin, David Meyer *lawyer, educator*
Dubin, Howard Victor *dermatologist*
Dubin, Stephen Victor *lawyer*
Du Boff, Michael H(arold) *lawyer*
Dubs, Gloria L. *artist, realtor*
Dubuc, Carroll Edward *lawyer*
Dubuque, Theodore Julien, Jr. *retired surgeon*
Duchesne, Juan Carlos *surgeon, director*
Duchovny, David *actor*
Duckstein, Susan L. *reading teacher, life skills teacher*
Duclos, Laura M. *research and development company executive, director*
Duddy, Patrick Dennis *former ambassador*
Duderstadt, James Johnson *academic administrator, engineering educator*
Dudman, Richard Beebe *journalist*
Duelfer, Charles Alfred *aerospace transportation executive, weapons inspector, director*
Duenes, Annette S. *science educator, consultant*
Duerksen, George Louis *music therapist, educator*
Duff, Gill *advertising executive*
Duff, Patricia *civic activist*
Duffield, David A. *application developer, former computer software company executive*
Duffy, Bill *former professional sports team executive*
Dufour, Jack Edward *retired small business owner, special education educator, athletic director, coach*
Dugan, Patrick Raymond *microbiologist, educator, dean*
Duggirala, Rajesh *electrical engineer, researcher*
Duhl, Olga Anna *literature educator, researcher*
Duhme, Carol McCarthy *civic worker*
Duke, Patty (Anna Marie Duke) *actress*
Duke, Robin Chandler Tippett *retired public relations executive, former ambassador*
Dulberg, Loretta *psychologist*
Duley, Margot Iris *historian, educator*
Dull, William Martin *retired engineering executive*
Dulski, Jennifer *Internet company executive*
Dumanoski, Dianne *journalist, writer*
Dumas, Sandra Lee *medical technician, microbiologist*
Dumett, Miguel *mathematician*
Dummett, Sir Michael Anthony Eardley *philosopher, educator*
Dumont, Allan Eliot *retired physician, educator*
Dumont, Mary *chef*
Dunaway, Faye (Dorothy Dunaway) *actress*
Dunaway, Frank Rosser III *emergency physician*
Dunbar, Diana (Diane) L. *educator, videographer, dancer, artist, writer*
Duncan, Allyson K. *federal judge*
Duncan, David Ewing *editor, writer*
Duncan, Mike (Robert Michael Duncan) *former political organization administrator*
Duncan, Robert Bannerman *finance educator, former dean*
Duncombe, Tcherina Swilley *biology professor*
Dunford, James Christopher *military officer*
Dunham, Archie Wallace *retired oil industry executive*

Dunham, Benjamin Starr *editor, art association administrator*
Dunlop, Matthew William *engineering educator*
Dunn, Adrian John *neuroscientist*
Dunn, Arnold Samuel *biochemistry educator*
Dunn, Bruce Sidney *materials scientist, educator*
Dunn, David *educational association administrator, former federal agency administrator*
Dunn, Helen Elizabeth *retired secondary school educator*
Dunn, Jack Newton *urologist*
Dunn, John Francis *lawyer, state representative*
Dunn, Kimberly Dawn *chemist, research scientist*
Dunn, Linda Kay *retired physician*
Dunn, M(orris) Douglas *lawyer*
Dunn, Patricia C. *retired social work educator*
Dunn, Richard Joseph *retired investment advisor*
Dunn, Robert Giddings *writer, educator, publisher*
Dunn, Robert Lawrence *lawyer*
Dunnam, James Robert *state legislator, lawyer*
Dunne, Diane C. *marketing professional*
Duplessis, Audrey Joseph *school system administrator*
Dupureur, Cynthia *chemistry professor*
Duquette, Jim *professional sports team executive*
Duran, Victor Manuel *literature and language professor*
Durantini, Marta Rosa *psychology professor, researcher*
Durbha, Surya *science educator*
Durell, Jack *psychiatrist*
Durell, Viviane G. *psychologist, small business owner*
Durkee, Dianna *medical/surgical nurse*
Durnin, John H. *education educator*
Duro, Debora *gastroenterologist*
Durr, Robert Joseph *construction executive, mechanical engineer*
Durrani, Sajjad Haidar *retired aerospace and communications engineer*
Dusan, Sorin *director of research*
Dusevich, Vladimir M. *electronics executive, researcher*
Duteil, Hervé Pierre *bank executive, musician*
Dutile, Fernand Neville *law educator*
Dutta, Achyut Kumar *electrical and electronics engineer*
Dutta, Anirban *biomedical engineer*
Dutta, Kaushik *biologist*
Duval, Olivia Blackmon *music educator*
Dwan, Dennis Edwin *broadcast executive, photographer*
Dwight, Harvey Alpheus *retired small business owner*
Dworzan, Helene Liberman *writer, poet, playwright*
Dwyer, Gerald Paul, Jr. *economist, bank executive*
Dyar, Kathryn Wilkin *pediatrician*
Dybul, Mark Richard *immunologist, former ambassador*
Dyck, Walter Peter *gastroenterologist, educator, academic administrator*
Dye, Michele Yvette *librarian*
Dye, Sharon Elizabeth Herndon *speech pathologist*
Dyer, Wayne Walter *psychologist, writer, radio and television personality*
Dykewicz, Mark Steven *physician*
Dylan, Jakob *musician, singer*
Dy-Liacco, Gabriel S. *psychotherapist, social sciences educator*
Dymally, Mervyn Malcolm *retired state legislator*
Dysart, Benjamin Clay III *conservationist, engineer, consultant*
Dyson, Allan Judge *retired librarian*
Dyson, Tim *public relations executive*
Dzhandzhulyan, Lev *business analyst, consultant*
Dziewanowska, Zofia Elizabeth *pharmaceutical executive*
Eagle, Kim Allen *cardiologist*
Eaglet, Robert Danton *electrical engineer, aerospace scientist, consultant, retired military officer*
Eaker, Sherry Ellen *editor*
Earhart, Gammon M. *physical therapist, researcher*
Earle, Timothy Keese *anthropology educator*
Earle, Victor Montagne III *lawyer*
Early, Bert Hylton *retired lawyer, consultant*
Earp, Naomi Churchill *former federal official*
Easley, Michael Francis *former Governor of North Carolina*
Easley, Robert J. *retail executive*
Easterson, Sam *artist*
Eastin, Keith E. *former civilian military employee*
Eastland, Grant *physicist*
Eastman, Francesca Marlene *volunteer, art historian*
Easton, Charles Clement, Jr. *corporate financial executive*
Easton, John H. *engineering educator, consultant*
Easton, Michelle *foundation executive*
Easton, Roger L. *former operations research specialist, consultant*
Eaton, Dorel *elementary school educator*
Eaton, Shirley M. *medical/surgical nurse*
Ebbs, George Heberling, Jr. *university executive*
Ebell, Mark Herbert *physician, researcher*
Eberhart, Steven Wesley *psychologist*
Eberstein, Arthur *former biomedical engineering educator, researcher*
Ebert, Robert Peter *German language professor*
Ebie, William D. *retired museum director*
Ebraheim, Nabil Anwar *orthopedist, surgeon*
Eccleston, Charles H. *environmental and nuclear consultant*
Echols, Mary Evelyn *motivational speaker and business consultant, writer*
Eck, Robert Edwin *retired physicist*
Eckel, Christine Marie *medical educator*
Eckelmann, Frank Donald *retired geology educator, dean*
Eckstein, Jerome *philosopher, retired educator*
Economou, Greg *professional sports team executive*
Ecton, Donna R. *business executive*
Eddy, Don *artist*
Edelman, David A. *surgeon*
Edelman, Eric Steven *former federal agency administrator, former ambassador*
Edelsberg, Sally Comins *retired physical therapist, educator*
Edelson, Mary Beth *artist, educator*
Edelson, Zelda Sarah Toll *retired editor, artist*
Eden, Benjamin *economics professor*
Edmar, Désirée Anna Elisabeth *retired museum director*
Edmo, Jean Umiokalani *artist, poet*
Edmonds, Anne Carey *librarian*
Edmonds, Crystal D. *language educator, department chairman, distance learning coordinator*
Edmonds, Elizabeth A. *lawyer*
Edoh, Kossi *mathematics professor*
Edson, Evelyn *history professor, writer*
Eduardo, Lau C. *molecular biologist, researcher*
Edward, Sir David Alexander Ogilvy *retired judge*
Edwards, Ardis Lavonne Quam *retired elementary education educator*
Edwards, Bruce George *retired ophthalmologist, military officer*
Edwards, Charles *neuroscientist, educator*
Edwards, David *engineering educator*
Edwards, Geoffrey Hartley *newspaper publisher*
Edwards, Kathleen *real estate broker, former educator*
Edwards, Larry David *internist, educator, dean*
Edwards, Lynn A. *retired school system administrator*
Edwards, Patrick Ross *retail executive, lawyer, management consultant*
Edwards, Randall *former state treasurer*
Edwards, Richard Alan *retired lawyer*
Edwards, Robert Hazard *retired college president*
Edzwald, James K. *engineering educator*
Efird, Jimmy Thomas *statistician*
Egan, Edward Michael Cardinal *archbishop emeritus, cardinal*
Egan, Wesley William *former ambassador*
Egas, Eric *artist*
Egger-Halbeis, Christoph B. (Chris Egger-Halbeis) *medical educator, director*
Eglee, Charles Hamilton *scriptwriter, film and television producer*
Eglinton, Daniel Thomas *orthopedist*
Egloff, Fred Robert *manufacturers representative, writer, historian*
Ehigie, Benjamin Odion *radiographer, technologist*
Ehlers, Kathryn Hawes (Mrs. James D. Gabler) *physician*
Ehling, Stefan *food scientist*
Ehrenreich, Barbara *writer*
Ehrlich, Annette *psychologist, educator*
Ehtesham, Moneeb *neurologist, educator*
Eich, Jennifer L. *literature educator*
Eichler, Duane Curtis *biochemist, educator*
Eick-Gamm, Kimberly Marie *social worker*
Eickhoff, Harold Walter *college president, humanities educator*
Eimers, Jeri Anne *retired counselor*
Einhorn, Martin B. *physicist, educator*
Eire, Carlos *historian, educator, writer*
Eischen, Donald F. *psychologist, educator, writer*
Eisenberg, Carola *psychiatrist, educator*
Eisenberg, Patricia Lee *medical/surgical nurse*
Eisenhower, John Sheldon Doud *former ambassador, writer*
Eisenstat, Theodore Ellis *colon and rectal surgeon, educator*
Eisenstein, Edward Milton *psychologist, physiologist, radiologist, educator*
Eisler, Colin Tobias *art historian, curator*
Eisner, Sigmund *retired English language educator*
Eisold, John Francis *physician*
Ekeus, Rolf Carl *diplomat*
Ekpenyong, Boniface Esong *physics professor*
Elam, Fred Eldon *retired military officer*
Elam, Leslie Albert *retired museum director*
Elam, Matthew *industrial engineer, educator*
El-Attar, Heba Ahmed Nabil *language educator*
el-Azhary, Rokea Adel *dermatologist, educator*
Elbert, Sarah *retired history professor*
Elder, Mary Louise *retired librarian*
Elderfield, John *art historian, museum curator*
Elebiyo, Vivian Bukola *writer*
Elfenbein, Gerald Jay *physician, scientist, educator*
Elgart, Edward Guerry *civilian military employee*
Elgawady, Mohamed *structural engineer, researcher, educator*
Eliasson, Jan Kenneth *former Swedish government official, former President of United Nations General Assembly and Minister for Foreign Affairs*
Elicker, Gordon Leonard *retired lawyer*
Eliot, Theodore Lyman, Jr. *former ambassador, consultant*
Elisha, Larisa *musician, performer, educator*
Elix, Douglas Thorne *retired information technology executive*
Elkins, Kathryn Marie *alcohol/drug abuse services professional, recreational therapist*
Ellenberger, Jack Stuart *law librarian*
Ellender, Timothy James *emergency physician, educator*
Eller, Christina Hull *librarian*
Ellerbrock-Bendele, Lynette *psychologist*
Ellett, Alan Sidney *real estate developer*
Ellig, Bruce Robert *retired personnel director*
Elliot, Jared *financial management consultant*
Elliott, David LeRoy *mathematics and engineering educator*
Elliott, J. Raymond *medical products executive*
Elliott, Kenneth Yates *theater educator*
Elliott, Stuart Jay *editor, journalist*
Ellis, Anne Elizabeth *fundraiser*
Ellis, Cynthia Sue *music educator*
Ellis, James D. *retired telecommunications industry executive, retired lawyer*
Ellis, Joseph John Michael III *writer, history professor*
Ellis, Laurel Glynn *retired entrepreneur*
Ellis, Lawrence Dobson *internist, educator*
Ellis, Robert Harry *retired broadcast executive, academic administrator*
Ellis, Roger Barry *communications educator*
Ellis, Sophia (Lugene) Holley *retired secondary school educator*
Ellis, Steven George *public relations and corporate communications executive*
Ellison, Lois Taylor *internist, educator, medical association administrator*
Ellner, Paul Daniel *retired microbiologist*
Ellwanger, Steven Joseph *statistician*
Elman, Noel *entrepreneur, electrical engineer*
Elmore, Kimberly Pruett *literature and language professor*
El-Moursy, Magdy *electronics engineer*
Elrick, Donald *retired literature educator*
Elrod, Deborah Lee *special education educator*
Else, Carolyn Joan *retired library director*
El-Serag, Hashem Beshir *gastroenterologist, educator*
Elsey, George McKee *retired foundation administrator*
Elson, Edward Elliott *diplomat*
Elstun, Esther Nies *foreign language educator*
Eltahawy, Hazem A. *neurosurgeon, educator*
Eltayeb, Emil *pharmacist, researcher*
Elverum, Gerard William *retired electronics and aerospace transportation executive*
Elwood-Akers, Virginia Edythe *librarian, retired archivist*
Ely, Duncan Cairnes *not-for-profit executive*
Elysee, Yves Jean *literature and language educator*
Elzay, Richard Paul *retired dean, dental educator, department chairman*
Emanuel, Ari (Ariel Zev Emanuel) *talent agency executive*
Embry, Stephen Creston *lawyer*
Emek, Sharon Helene *risk management consultant*
Emerling, Carol G. *corporate governance consultant*
Emerson, Alex Louise *literature and language professor*
Emerson, Anne Devereux *retired museum administrator*
Emerson, Claudia *poet, language professor*
Emerson, Daniel Everett *retired communications company executive*
Emery, Alan Roy *scientist, museum administrator, business executive*
Emmett, Rita *professional speaker*
Emmons, Robert Duncan *diplomat*
Emry, Betsy *librarian*
Endicott, William F. *journalist*
Endres, Kelly J. *psychologist*
Eng, Adrienne Rose *corporate financial executive*
Eng, Clare Sher Ling *music educator*
Engdahl, Todd Philip *editor*
Engel, Albert Joseph *retired federal judge*
Engel, Bernard Theodore *psychologist, educator*
Engelhardt, Jeffery Allen *pathologist*
Engelhardt, John Hugo *lawyer, bank executive*
Engelman, Rosalyn Ackerman *artist*
Engels, Beatrice Ann *artist, poet, retired real estate company executive*
Engels, Lawrence Arthur *retired metal products executive*
Engelson, Leslie *librarian*
England, Gordon Richard *former federal agency administrator*
Englert, Brian Carl *environmental scientist*
English, Bertis Deon *history professor*
English, Floyd Leroy *telecommunications industry executive*
English, Patricia Dorzell *women's health nurse practitioner*
English, Philip Sheridan *former United States Representative from Pennsylvania*
English, Stephen Raymond *lawyer*
Engvold, Oddbjørn *astrophysics educator*
Enhorning, Goran *obstetrician, gynecologist*
Ennis, Edgar William, Jr. *lawyer*
Enoch, Craig Trively *retired judge*
Enraght-Moony, Thomas *former internet company executive*
Enroth-Cugell, Christina Alma Elisabeth *neurophysiologist, educator*
Ensminger, Luther Glenn *retired chemist*
Ephron, Nora *writer*
Epp, Dianne Naomi *secondary school educator*
Epp, Eldon Jay *religion educator*
Epp, Menno Henry *clergyman*
Epperly, Kermit Lowell *dean, accountant*
Eppolito, Mary *assistant principal, educator*
Epps, Charles Harry, Jr. *retired orthopaedic surgery educator, dean*
Epstein, Adam *theater producer*
Epstein, Judith Ann *judge*
Erb, James Bryan *conductor, musicologist, educator*
Erb, Thomas Owen *education educator*
Erbe, Yvonne Mary *music educator, marketing specialist, guidance counselor*
Erdas, Andrea *physics professor*
Erdil, Deger Cenk *computer scientist*
Ergen, Mustafa *engineer*
Erichsen, Peter Christian *lawyer*
erick, William Joseph *hydrologist*
Erickson, Alan Eric *librarian*
Erickson, Carol Jean *literature and language professor*
Erickson, Donna Joy *writer, editor, publisher*
Erickson, Edward Leonard *biotechnologist, consultant*
Erickson, Mitchell Drake *chemist, environmental scientist*
Ericson, David Frank *political scientist, educator*
Erives, Albert J. *biology professor*
Erkonen, William Edward *radiologist, medical educator*
Erlicht, Lewis Howard *broadcasting company executive*
Ernst, Daniel Pearson *lawyer*
Ernst, Suzanne *retired academic administrator, educator*
Erpek, Tugba *electrical engineer*
Ertel, Karen *epidemiologist, researcher*
Ertosun, Mehmet Günhan *electrical engineer*
Ertugrul, Mine *finance educator*
Ervin, Kathleen Gwen *journalist*
Erwin, Barbara F. *school system administrator*
Erwin, Elmer Louis *vintager, consultant*
Erwin, Linda McIntosh *retired librarian*
Eskay, Michael K. *special education educator*
Eskew, Henry Lawrence, Jr. *economist, consultant*
Esmer, Burcu *finance educator*
Espinosa, Wellington Rafael *educator*
Esposito, Bonnie Lou *marketing professional*
Esquivel, Agerico Liwag *retired research physicist*
Estelle, (Estelle Fanta Swaray) *singer*
Estes, Carl Lewis, II, *lawyer*
Estes, Elaine Rose Graham *retired librarian*
Estes, Jack Charles *entrepreneur, oil industry executive, research scientist*
Estes, Mary Caroline Bailey *special education educator*
Estrada, Arnoldo Delfino *research scientist, consultant*
Estrin, Herbert Alvin *financial consultant, film company executive*
Estrin, Richard William *real estate and business broker, retired editor*
Esty, John Cushing, Jr. *writer, educator, not-for-profit counsel*
Etchegoyen Lynch, Martin *lawyer, consultant*
Etheridge, Diana Carol *Internet business executive*
Etra, Lionel *lawyer*
Etters, Ronald Milton *retired lawyer, former government official*
Ettinger, Harry Joseph *retired industrial hygiene engineer, consultant*
Ettinger, Joseph Alan *lawyer*
Ettinger, Lawrence Jay *pediatric hematologist, oncologist, educator*
Euster, Joanne Reed *retired librarian*
Eustis, Albert Anthony *lawyer, diversified financial services company executive*
Eustis, Steven M. *electrical engineer*
Evans, Barton, Jr. *retired analytical instrument company executive*
Evans, Bonita Dianne *education educator*
Evans, Bruce Dwight *lawyer*
Evans, Charlotte Mortimer *communications consultant, writer*
Evans, Geraldine Ann *former academic administrator*
Evans, Jack R. (J. Glenn) *writer, poet*
Evans, James Handel *academic administrator, architect*
Evans, James Hurlburt *retired transportation and natural resources executive*
Evans, John Derby *telecommunications industry executive*
Evans, Joy *foundation administrator*
Evans, Lane Allen *Former United States Representative, Ill*
Evans, Margaret Utz *secondary school educator*
Evans, Michael Duane *coach*
Evans, Pamela R. *sales and marketing executive*
Evans, Richard Austin *education educator, consultant*
Evans, Rosemary Hall *civic worker*
Evans, Tyler Jonah *mathematics professor*
Evans, William Lee *biologist, educator*
Evelyn, Rev Phyllis *spiritual care administrator*
Everdell, William *retired lawyer*
Everett, Terry (Robert Terry Everett) *retired United States Representative from Alabama*
Everett, Tom *actor*
Everhart, Gloria Elaine *music educator*
Evert, Chris (Christine Marie Evert) *retired professional tennis player*
Eviatar, Lydia *pediatrician, neurologist*
Evmenenko, Guennadi Alexandrovich *physicist*
Ewald, Robert Frederick *insurance executive, consultant*
Ewald, Roberta Grant *artist, writer*
Ewen, H. I. *physicist*
Ewing, Elisabeth Anne Rooney *priest*
Ewing, James E. *priest*
Ewing, Mary Eileen *radiologic technologist*
Ewing, Raymond Charles *retired ambassador*
Ewing, Scott Edwin *physician, psychiatrist, educator*
Exner, Frank Kepler *information scientist, indexer*
Eyde, Lorraine Dittrich *psychologist, researcher*
Eyler, John H., Jr. *retail toy and game company executive*
Eyman, Earl Duane *electrical science educator, consultant*
Eyraud, Henri Louis Charles *chemical engineer*
Eyzaguirre, Eduardo Javier *medical educator, researcher*
Ezer, Mitchel J. *lawyer*
Ezzat, Hazem A(hmed) *research executive, consultant*
Faber, Michael Warren *lawyer*
Fabiano, Nicola *physicist, researcher*
Fabre, Niza Elsie *African studies and hispanic literature educator*
Fabricatore, Carol Diane *artist, educator*
Fabunan, Ruben G. *physician, research scientist, inventor*
Fabus, Renee Laura *communications educator*
Fagan, Drew Stephen *language educator*
Fagg, George Gardner *retired federal judge*
Faggin, Federico *electronics executive*
Fagin, David Kyle *mining executive*
Fahrenkrog, Eugene Henry, Jr. *lawyer*
Fahringer, Catherine Hewson *retired savings and loan association executive*
Fairfield, Paula Kathleen *sound recording engineer*
Faison, Edmund "Ted" Winston, Jr. *software architect*
Faison, Edward Kerr *ecologist*
Faivre, Bertrand *film producer*
Fajardo-Acosta, Sergio *astronomer*
Fakahany, Ahmass L. *retired investment company executive*
Falcon, Yvonne *management consultant*
Falcone, Frank S. *former academic administrator*
Fales, Haliburton, II, *lawyer*
Falvey, Mark A. *entrepreneur*
Fan, Xingzhe *engineering educator*
Fan, Zhenchuan *medicine studies educator*
Fan, Zihong J. *epidemiologist*
Fang, Haw-ren *research scientist*
Fanton, Jonathan Foster *retired foundation administrator*
Fanwick, Ernest *lawyer*

Farah, Ibrahim O. *microbiologist, biomedical researcher*
Farah, Martha J. *neuroscientist, educator*
Fararo, Thomas John *sociologist, educator*
Farber, Roselee Cora *counselor*
Farewell, Susan *journalist, writer*
Fargo, Heather *Former Mayor, Sacramento, California*
Faria, Me'Shell Anita *special education educator*
Faricy, John Hartnett, Jr. *lawyer*
Faris, James Vannoy *cardiologist, educator, health facility administrator*
Fariss, Bruce Lindsay *endocrinologist, consultant*
Farkas, Daniel Frederick *food science and technology educator*
Farley, John Edward *retired sociologist, educator, researcher*
Farmakides, John Basil *lawyer*
Farmer, Cornelia Griffin *lawyer, consultant, county hearings official*
Farmer, Crofton Bernard *atmospheric physicist*
Farmer, Roger Edward Alfred *economics professor*
Farney, Charlotte Eugenia *musician, educator*
Farquhar, Robin Hugh *educational consultant, former university president*
Farquhar, William G. *chief analyst, researcher*
Farr, Barry Miller *physician, epidemiologist*
Farr, Ivanne Estelle *small business owner, artist, consultant*
Farrar, Elaine Willardson *artist*
Farrar, John Edson, II, *finance company executive, consultant, investment advisor*
Farrell, Brian J. *computer game company executive*
Farrell, Suzanne (Roberta Sue Ficker) *ballerina*
Farrell, W. James *retired metal products manufacturing company executive*
Farrelly, Peter John *screenwriter*
Farren, J. Michael *former federal official, lawyer*
Farrington, Bertha Louise *retired nursing administrator*
Farrington, Carole Chaney *literature and language professor*
Farris, Jerome *federal judge*
Farris, Ronald M. *retired intelligence officer*
Fasick, Adele Mongan *library and information scientist, educator*
Fasman, Marjorie Lesser *artist, writer*
Fassler, Kerin Irene *retired systems accountant*
Fast, Heinz Gerhard *music educator, conductor*
Fatemi, Faramarz Saifpour *history and political science professor, consultant*
Fathallah, Hassana *research scientist*
Faulkner, Frances Mayhew *retired federal agency administrator*
Fausett, Laurene Van Camp *mathematics professor*
Faw, Richard Earl *nuclear engineering educator*
Fawcett, John Thomas *archivist*
Fay, Conner Martindale *retired marketing executive*
Fay, Donald P. *lawyer*
Fay, Miriam Soler *school counselor, educator*
Fay, Peter Thorp *federal judge*
Fay, Sarah *former advertising executive*
Fay, William Frederick *film producer*
Fayngold, Moses *physics professor, researcher*
Fazio, Evelyn M. *publisher, agent*
Feal, Gisele Catherine *foreign language educator*
Fearon, Charlene O'Brien *special education educator*
Feaster, Jay (Harry Jay Feaster) *former professional sports team executive*
Federing, Eric K. *legislative staff member, public information officer, business executive*
Feeney, Maryann McHugh *not-for profit professional*
Feeney, Matthew Edward *linguist, educator*
Feeney, Tom (Thomas Charles Feeney III) *former United States Representative from Florida, lawyer*
Feeser, Larry James *retired civil engineering educator, researcher*
Fehler, Timothy *history professor*
Feigenbaum, David Louis *lawyer*
Feigin, Barbara Sommer *marketing consultant*
Feiler, Jo Alison *artist*
Fein, Seymour Howard *pharmaceutical executive*
Feinstein, Amy *literature and language professor*
Feinstein, Robert P. *dermatologist*
Feist, Patrick J. *principal, consultant*
Feisthammel, Audrey Marie *museum director, educator*
Feld, Carole Leslie *marketing executive*
Feldhamer, Thelma Leah *retired architect*
Feldkamp, John Calvin *retired lawyer, educator*
Feldman, Eva Lucille *neurology educator*
Feldman, H. Larry *lawyer*
Feldman, Marc David *psychiatrist*
Feldman, Roger David *lawyer*
Feldman, Shana Madigan *legal assistant*
Feldstein, Joshua *educational administrator*
Felgar, Raymond Eugene *pathologist, educator*
Felicetti, Daniel A. *academic administrator*
Fell, Elizabeth P. *education educator*
Fell, Samuel Kennedy (Ken) *retired infosystems executive*
Feller, Robert William Andrew *public relations executive, retired professional baseball player*
Fellner, Eric *film producer*
Felos, Kimberly *humanities educator*
Felstiner, Mary Lowenthal *retired history professor*
Felton, Helen Martin *retired adult education educator, writer*
Fenech, Daniel Thomas *cartoonist*
Fenech, Joseph Charles *lawyer*
Feng, Chengde *mathematician, educator*
Feng, Lei *medical researcher*
Feng, Qianmei *engineering educator*
Feng, Rui *statistician, educator*
Fenimore, George Wiley *management consultant*
Fenton, Thomas Trail *journalist*
Fenwick, James Henry *editor, writer, columnist*
Ferencz, Charlotte *retired pediatrician, epidemiologist*
Ferencz, Nicholas *pharmacist, educator*
Ferguson, Bradford Lee *lawyer*
Ferguson, Charles Austin *retired newspaper editor*
Ferguson, Gary Lee *public relations and security management executive*
Ferguson, Jeannette E. *research technician*
Ferguson, Michael A. (Mike) *former United States Representative from New Jersey*
Ferguson McGinnis, Kathryn Joan (Kathy Ferguson McGinnis) *flight attendant*
Fergusson, Frances Daly *former academic administrator*
Fernald, Harold Allen *publishing executive*
Fernandes, Marlos Ramalho *physician, researcher*
Fernandez, Fernando Lawrence *aeronautical engineer, research and development company executive*
Ferraro, Cristiana S. *language educator, interior designer*
Ferreira, Francisco Hollanda Guimaraes *economist, researcher*
Ferreira, Jo Ann Jeanette Chanoux *management consultant, delivery service executive*
Ferri-Grant, Carson (Carson Grant) *actor, director, artist, writer, digital film video editor*
Ferris, Roger Patrick *architect*
Ferry, Joan Evans *school counselor*
Ferry, Martha Morton *non-profit executive*
Ferstenfeld, Julian Erwin *internist, educator*
Fetscherin, Marc Philippe *business educator*
Fetter Filho, Antonio Fernando Härter *research scientist*
Fetters, Norman Craig, II, *retired banker*
Fey, John Theodore *retired insurance company executive*
Fey, Willard *global environmental researcher, educator*
Fiddick, Paul William *public official, broadcast executive*
Fiedler, Carl E *retired forestry professor*
Fields, Douglas Philip, Sr. *real estate and investment company executive*
Fields, Ruth Peedin *artist*
Fields, Tina Rae *artist, ecopsychologist*
Fields, Velma Archie *retired medical/surgical nurse*
Fields, Victor Lee *music educator*
Fields-Harris, Deborah Carol *mathematician, educator*
Fiennes, Ralph (Ralph Nathaniel Twisleton-Wykeham Fiennes) *actor*
Fierman, Ella Yensen *retired psychotherapist*
Fiero-Maza, Lorraine Doris *music educator*
Fietsam, Robert, Jr. *physician*
Figueredo, Danilo H. *librarian, writer*
Figueroa, Yolanda *cardiologist*
Fike, Edward Lake *newspaper editor*
Filchock, Ethel *education educator*
Filer, Emily Symington Harkins *retired foundation administrator, writer, associate chaplain*
Filerman, Michael Herman *television producer*
Filley, Christopher Mark *neurologist, researcher*
Fillmore, John Dillon *artist*
Finale, Frank L. *retired elementary school educator, writer*
Finch, Janet Buswell *musician*
Finckenauer, James O. *criminal justice educator, researcher*
Fine, Andrea Joiner *writer*
Fine, Lawrence B. *lawyer*
Finger, Harold Ben *nuclear engineer*
Fingerson, Leroy Malvin *engineering executive, mechanical engineer*
Fink, Alma *retired elementary school educator*
Fink, Daniel Julien *management consultant*
Fink, Raymond *medical educator*
Finkel, Jaclyn Dawn *history educator*
Finkelstein, Daniel *ophthalmologist*
Finkelstein, Richard *set designer, educator*
Finlay, Robert Derek *food products executive*
Finlayson, John Sylvester *retired biochemist*
Finley, Emma Rosemary *retired science educator*
Finley, Harry *artist, museum director*
Finley, Phillip E. *architecture educator*
Finley, Sarah Maude Merritt *retired social worker*
Finnegan, Sara Anne (Sara F. Lycett) *publisher*
Finnessy, John P. *mortgage company executive, director*
Finnigan, Robert Emmet *retired small business owner*
Finocchiaro, Alfonso G. *bank executive*
Finzel, Barry Craig *research scientist*
Fiorito, Edward Gerald *lawyer*
Firebaugh, Francille Maloch *academic administrator*
Fischbach, Charles Peter *rail transportation executive, consultant, lawyer, arbitrator, mediator, government official*
Fischbach, Cheryl L. *nursing educator*
Fischer, Carl Robert *retired health facility administrator*
Fischer, Charlotte Froese *research scientist, educator*
Fischer, David J. *retired mayor*
Fischer, Joseph L. *pharmaceutical executive*
Fischer, Maxim *electronics engineer*
Fischer, Michael Ludwig *environmental executive*
Fischer, Russell Leonard *public relations executive*
Fischer, William Samuel *composer, lecturer*
Fish, Howard Math *aerospace transportation executive*
Fish, Janet Isobel *artist*
Fishburn, Janet Forsythe *dean*
Fisher, Andrew, IV, *retired journalist*
Fisher, Bruce Albert *anatomy and physiology educator*
Fisher, Carrie Frances *actress, writer*
Fisher, Charles Harold *retired chemistry educator, researcher*
Fisher, Dale Dunbar *animal scientist, dairy nutritionist*
Fisher, Frances *actress*
Fisher, Nancy *writer, producer, director*
Fisher, Robert Charles Haru *publishing executive, editor*
Fishman, Harriet J. *artist, educator, writer*
Fishman, Joshua Aaron *sociolinguist, educator*
Fiske-Rusciano, Roberta Louise *anthropologist*
Fiskin, Arthur Max, Jr. *retired biologist, educator*
Fiszer-Szafarz, Berta (Berta Safars) *research scientist*
Fitch, Brooke *biology professor*
Fitch, Frank Wesley *pathologist, immunologist, educator*
Fitch, Fred Emmett *communications educator*
Fitch, Robert McLellan *research and development company executive, consultant*
Fitts, Catherine Austin *investment advisor*
Fitz-Enz, David G. *retired military officer, television producer, novelist*
Fitzgerald, James J. III *former state supreme court justice*
Fitzgerald, Joan V. *artist*
FitzGerald, John Edward III *lawyer*
Fitzmaurice, Laurence Dorset *social services administrator*
Fitzpatrick, Christopher *musician, educator*
Fitzpatrick, Lorraine *retired accountant*
Fitzpatrick, Nancy Hecht *editor*
Fitzroy, Nancy deLoye *engineering executive, mechanical engineer*
FitzSimons, Dennis Joseph *former broadcast and publishing executive*
Fix, John Neilson *banker*
Flanagan, James Loton *electrical engineer, educator, researcher*
Flanagan, Nancy A. *nursing educator, researcher*
Flanders, Donald Hargis *manufacturing executive*
Flanders, Robert G., Jr. *lawyer, educator, association administrator*
Flato, Gwyndolynn Sue *fine art educator*
Flavin, Sonja *artist*
Fleck, Bela *country musician*
Fleetwood, Clifford Gene ("The Father of Philosophical Art") *lawyer, publishing and recording industry executive, author*
Fleisher, Frederic Elliott *communications executive*
Fleishman, Philip Robert *internist*
Fleming, Carolyn Elizabeth *religious organization administrator, interior designer*
Fleming, Gavin John *lawyer*
Fleming, Gina Marie *music educator*
Fleming, Julie A. *attorney, legal consultant*
Fleming, Rhonda *actress, singer, philanthropist*
Fleming, Thomas A. *retired educator*
Fleming, Thomas James *writer*
Flemming, David Paul *biologist*
Fletcher, Denise Koen *strategic and financial consultant*
Fletcher, Donald Rodgers *writer, religious studies educator*
Fletcher, Donna Angella *secondary school educator*
Fletcher, Ernie (Ernest Lee Fletcher) *Former Governor of Kentucky*
Fletcher, James Erving *academic administrator, educator*
Fletcher, Ronald Darling *microbiologist educator*
Fleury, Paul Aimé *physicist*
Flick, John Edmond *retired lawyer*
Flinn, Paul Anthony *materials scientist*
Flint, John E. *retired historian*
Flitcraft, Richard Kirby, II, *former chemical company executive*
Flock, Kelly *computer game company executive*
Flory, Curt Alan *research physicist*
Flory, Margaret Martha *retired religious organization administrator*
Flournoy, John Craig *journalism educator*
Flowers-Schoen, Marylu Utley *art educator*
Floyd, Brian A. *electrical engineer, researcher*
Floyd, Kristy A. *elementary school educator*
Floyd, Otis Henry *retired military officer, adult education educator*
Floyd, Tim *former men's college basketball coach, former professional basketball coach*
Floyd, William R. *former health facility administrator*
Flynn, George William *retired music educator*
Flynn, Paul Bartholomew *retired foundation executive*
Flynt, Larry Claxton, Jr. *publisher*
Fofana, Amadou Tidiane *literature and language professor*
Fogel, Evan Lloyd *gastroenterologist*
Fogel, Joshua *psychologist, researcher*
Fogelman, Ann Florence *nutrition consultant, educator, researcher*
Fogg, Richard Lloyd *food products executive*
Fogleman, Guy Carroll *physicist, mathematician, educator*
Fogu, Claudio *literature and language professor*
Foley, David Edward *bishop emeritus*
Foley, Gary J. *chemical engineer, computer scientist, federal agency administrator, researcher*
Foley, Kevin Thomas *neurosurgeon, educator*
Foley, Mark Adam *former congressman*
Folsom, Amanda L. *mathematician, educator*
Folz, Carol Ann *benefits compensation analyst*
Fonda, Peter *actor, director, producer*
Fondiller, Shirley Hope Alperin *nursing educator, journalist, historian*
Fons, Eric Wallace *physics professor*
Fonseca, Christine Nel *psychologist, consultant*
Fontaine, Joan *actress*
Fontana, Dominic Joseph (D.J. Fontana) *musician*
Fontes, Manuel Lopes *medical educator, researcher*
Fontes, Patricia J. *psychologist*
Fontijn, Claire *musician, educator*
Foote, Beverly Alice *language educator*
Foote, Evelyn Patricia *retired military officer*
Foote, William Chapin *manufacturing executive*
Forbes, Mary Allison *psychology educator*
Forbes, Michael Patrick *former congressman*
Ford, Alma Regina *retired union official, educator*
Ford, Barbara Jean *librarian, educator*
Ford, Charles A. *former ambassador*
Ford, Ford Barney *retired federal official*
Ford, Harrison *actor*
Ford, Kenneth William *physicist*
Ford, Loretta C. *retired dean, educator, consultant, nurse*
Ford, Tom *apparel designer and executive*
Fordyce, James Stuart *retired non-profit organization executive*
Foreman, George Edward *retired boxer, commentator, minister*
Foreman, Spencer (Spike Foreman) *retired hospital administrator, pulmonologist*
Foresman, George W. *consulting company executive, former federal agency administrator*
Forest, Eva Brown *retired nursing home supervisor, composer*
Forgeard, Noël *retired aerospace and defence company executive*
Forget, Mark Alan *educational consultant, educator*
Forlines, Clifton *research scientist*
Forman, Edgar Ross *mechanical engineer*
Forman, Miloš *film director*
Fornari, Victor M. *psychiatrist*
Fornoni, Alessia *medical educator*
Forrester, Jay Wright *management consultant, educator*
Forry, John Ingram *lawyer*
Forsleff, Louise Stewart *psychologist, educator*
Forslund, Catherine *history professor*
Forster, Geoffrey Peter *company director*
Forster, Merlin Henry *foreign languages educator, writer, researcher*
Forster, Robert Arthur III *retired research scientist*
Forsyth, Ben Ralph *retired academic administrator, medical educator*
Fort, Randall Martin *corporate executive*
Fortenbaugh, Samuel Byrod III *lawyer*
Fossella, Vito John, Jr. *former United States Representative from New York*
Foster, Charles Henry Wheelwright *former foundation officer, consultant, author*
Foster, David Lee *lawyer*
Foster, Deborah Megivern *counselor, consultant*
Foster, Judith Christine *lawyer, writer*
Foster, Martha Tyahla *pre-school administrator*
Foster, Virginia Ramos *language educator*
Foulkes, William David *psychologist, educator*
Fountain, Joanna Fraser *library consultant, business owner*
Fountain, Karen Schueler *retired physician*
Fournier, Dudley John *surgeon*
Fournier, Maureen Mary *physical education educator*
Fournier, R. E. Keith *retired biologist*
Fowke, Benjamin G.S. III *energy executive*
Fowler, Alan Bicksler *retired physicist*
Fowler, Flora Daun *retired lawyer*
Fox, Betty *financial services executive*
Fox, Daniel Michael *author, advisor*
Fox, David Jeffery *literature and language educator*
Fox, Deborah Lee *elementary school educator*
Fox, Edward Alan *retired finance company executive*
Fox, Eleanor Mae Cohen *lawyer, educator, writer*
Fox, Joan Phyllis *environmental engineer, company executive*
Fox, Karen C. *medical educator, health science association administrator*
Fox, Michael Wilson *veterinarian, animal scientist*
Fox, Robin *social studies educator*
Fox-Clarkson, Anne C. *fundraising company executive*
Foxman, Abe (Abraham Henry Foxman) *advocacy organization administrator*
Foxworthy, Jeff *comedian, writer, actor*
Foy, Betty Lou Jones *educational administrator*
Foy, Charles Daley *retired soil scientist*
Foys, Roger Joseph *bishop*
Fradkin, David Milton *physicist, researcher*
Fraenkel, Liana *rheumatologist, researcher*
Fralix Gold, Carolyn M. *medical/surgical nurse, educator, consultant*
Frame, Robert M. *lighting designer, theater director*
Francis, Jerome Leslie *lawyer*
Francis, Karen *painter, television producer, writer*
Francis, Mildred Elaine *retired statistician, epidemiologist*
Francis, Steve D'Shawn *professional basketball player*
Francis, Warren William *retired surgeon, educator*
Francke, Linda Bird *journalist*
Franco, Sharone Elizabeth *psychiatrist*
Frank, Edgar Gerald *retired finance company executive*
Frank, Glenda *performing arts educator, writer*
Frank, Karen Susanna *lawyer*
Frank, Larry James *library director*
Frank, Linda Maria *science educator*
Frank, Michael Victor *risk assessment engineer*
Frank, Philippe G. *medical educator*
Frank, Ronald Edward *marketing educator*
Frank, Stephen Edward *retired electric power industry executive*
Frankel, James Burton *retired lawyer*
Frankenstein, John *international management educator, consultant*
Franklin, Aretha Louise *singer*
Franklin, Edward Ward *international investment consultant, lawyer, actor*
Franklin, Renty B. *medical educator*
Franklin, William Price *information technology manager*
Franks, Allen P. *retired research institute executive, educator*
Frankson-Kendrick, Sarah Jane *publisher*
Frankston, Robert M. *computer software executive, developer*
Frantz, Ray William, Jr. *retired librarian*
Franz, Frank Andrew *academic administrator, physicist, educator*
Franz, John E. *bio-organic chemist, researcher*
Franz, Judy R. *physics professor*
Frase, Katharine *information technology executive*
Fraser, Donald MacKay *retired mayor, Former United States Representative, Minnesota*
Fratto, Tony (Salvatore Antonio Fratto) *former federal official*
Frauenhoffer, Rose Marie *visual artist*
Frazier, Eloise M. *minister*
Fredeman, Betty Coley (Betty Coley) *retired librarian, editor*
Frederick, Peter J. *medical researcher*
Frederick-Mairs, T(hyra) Julie *administrative health services official*
Frederickson, Christine Magnuson *reporter, researcher, editor, writer*

Free, Sheela Sitaram poet, educator
Freed, Richard (Donald) music critic
Freedland, Kenneth E. psychologist, educator
Freedman, Aaron David retired medicine and biochemistry educator, dean
Freedman, Brett Arthur orthopedist, surgeon
Freedman, Gerald Stanley radiologist, educator, healthcare administrator
Freedman, Russell Bruce author
Freeland, Richard Middleton former academic administrator, historian
Freeland, Stephen John biology professor
Freeman, Charles E. state supreme court justice
Freeman, Herbert retired computer engineering educator
Freeman, Margaret Helen language educator
Freeman, Michael Elliot science educator
Freeman, Morgan actor
Freeman, Phillip psychiatrist
Freeman, Richard Francis banker
Freeman, Rosalind Alter retired library and information scientist
Freeman, Theodore Monroe physician
Frehm, Lynne artist, painter
Freilicher, Jane artist
Freitas, Beatrice B(otty) musician, educator
Frelinghuysen, Peter Hood Ballantine, Jr. Former United States Representative, New Jersey
French, Candace Lee elementary school and music educator
French, Daniel J. former prosecutor
French, John Robert Putnam III biologist
French, Julia McAllister (Judy) environmental consultant
French, Laurence Armand social sciences educator
French, Mary B. editor, photographer, poet, retired literature educator
French, Roderick Stuart university chancellor
French, Shelley language educator
Frenkel, Alexander L. applied mathematics professor
Freston, Tom (Thomas E. Freston) former broadcast executive
Frey, Glenn songwriter, vocalist, guitarist
Freyermuth, Virginia Karen art educator
Fri, Robert Wheeler retired museum director
Frick, David Rhoads lawyer, retired insurance company executive
Frick, Ivan Eugene retired academic administrator, educational consultant
Fricker, Brenda actress
Fricker, Janet S. library director
Friday, Elbert Walter, Jr. federal agency administrator, meteorologist
Fried, Charles law educator
Friedensohn, Henry retired physician
Friedlander, Charles Douglas (Chuck Friedlander) aerospace scientist, consultant
Friedman, Howard W. retired real estate company executive
Friedman, James Winstein economist, educator
Friedman, Jane M. former publishing executive
Friedman, Joan M. retired accountant, educator
Friedman, Mildred architecture educator, design educator, curator
Friedman, Paul Richard lawyer
Friedman, Richard Everett curator, art appraiser
Friedman, Richard Joel orthopaedic surgeon
Friedman, Samuel Robert HIV/AIDS epidemiologist
Friedman, Tully Michael finance company executive
Friedmann, Mark engineering company executive
Friedrich, Jon M. chemistry professor
Frieling, Gerald Harvey, Jr. specialty steel company executive
Friend, William Benedict bishop emeritus
Frisby, Herbert Russell lawyer
Frisch, Sidney, Jr. lawyer, real estate and insurance broker
Frisco, Louis Joseph retired electronics executive, electrical engineer
Fritz, Ethel Mae Hendrickson writer
Fritz, Rene Eugene manufacturing executive
Froberg, Brent Malcolm classics educator
Frohman-Bentchkowsky, Dov electrical engineer, retired computer company executive
Froman, Michael Braverman insurance company executive
Fromm, Joseph retired editor, foreign correspondent, foreign affairs consultant
Frost, Barbara Sherry lawyer
Frost, Ellen Louise political economist
Frost, Michelle librarian
Frost, Sterling Newell arbitrator, mediator, management consultant
Frot-Coutaz, Cecile television producer
Frowner, Byron retired electrical engineer, researcher
Frudakis, Zenos Antonios sculptor, artist
Frue, William Calhoun lawyer
Frush, Donald Paul radiologist
Frye, Christine Marie school system and counseling administrator
Fryer, Thomas Waitt, Jr. editor, writer
Frymer, Murry writer, film and theater critic, columnist
Fu, Cindy Yan psychologist
Fu, Engang research scientist
Fuchs, Alan chemistry professor
Fudge, Ann Marie former advertising executive
Fuentes, Carlos writer, retired ambassador
Fuentez, Tania Michele journalist
Fuerch, Richard Edmund engineering educator
Fuerstner, Fiona Margaret Anne ballet company executive, educator
Fugett, Roberta Lynn special education educator
Fuhr, Patti Sue Wimbs optometrist, director
Fukasawa, Natsuki music educator
Fukuda, Atsuo physicist, materials science researcher, educator
Fukuta, Naoki computer scientist, researcher
Fulbright, Harriet Mayor educational association administrator
Fulcher, Samuel F.A. medical educator
Fuld, Richard Severin, Jr., (Dick Fuld) former investment company executive
Fuller, Anne Elizabeth Havens English language and literature educator, consultant
Fuller, Bonnie publishing executive
Fuller, Bryan television producer, scriptwriter
Fuller, Dale L. software security company executive
Fuller, Jack William writer, retired publishing executive
Fuller, Maxine Compton retired secondary school educator
Fuller, Nancy MacMurray mathematics professor
Fuller, Samuel Ashby retired lawyer, mining executive
Fuller, Sandra Vivian oil and gas industry executive
Fulmer, Vincent Anthony retired college president
Fulton, John agricultural engineer, educator
Fumagalli, Barbara Merrill artist, printmaker
Funakoshi, Yuji meteorologist
Funk, Edith Kay retired minister, psychotherapist, social worker
Funseth, Robert Lloyd Eric Martin international consultant, retired diplomat
Furash, Edward Elliott investment company executive, banker, educator, writer, theater producer
Furlan, Connie SaLoutos actress, educator
Furlotti, Alexander Amato real estate and investment company executive
Furnas, David William plastic surgeon, educator
Furst, E. Kenneth accountant
Gabor-Hotchkiss, Magda research scientist, librarian
Gabrisch, Heike engineering educator
Gach, Jay Anthony composer
Gaddis, Paul Otto university dean
Gaddy, Sidney Warren government agency administrator
Gadiesh, Orit management consulting executive
Gadomski, Robert Eugene gas industry executive
Gaffin, David Morris meteorologist, researcher
Gaffney, Thomas retired banker
Gage, L. Patrick (Leonard Patrick Gage) biotechnology & pharmaceutical industry consultant
Gagnon, Paul Michael former prosecutor
Gahagan, Kevin Thomas engineering company executive
Gai, Neville research scientist
Gaillard, George Siday III architect
Gainer, Robert theater educator, department chairman
Gaines, Boyd actor
Gaines, Brenda J. retired financial services company executive
Gainey, Lilah Leigh librarian
Gainor, Thomas Edward bank executive
Galagan, Carol Anne special education educator
Galante, Jane Hohfeld musician, historian
Galbraith, William Bruce internist, educator
Galda, Dwight William finance company executive
Gale, Holly Ruth music educator
Gale, Lacey Andrews research scientist
Gale, Michael Johnathan entrepreneur
Gale, Stanley William psychiatrist
Galindo, Karla Rae retired secondary school educator
Gall, Robert Stephen philosophy educator
Gallagher, Gerard James maritime legal practitioner, educator, researcher
Gallagher, Michael Robert retired consumer products company executive
Gallagher, Peter actor
Gallardo, Sandra Silvana television producer, actress
Galli, John Ronald physicist, educator
Gallini, Richard psychologist, consultant
Gallucci-Breithaupt, Adrianne psychologist, social worker
Galvin, Matthew Reppert psychiatry educator
Galvis, Camilo Andres real estate company executive, researcher
Gamache, Claudette Theresa artist, nurse
Gamble, Desirata artist, poet
Gambrell, Luck Flanders business executive
Gamer, Carlton Edwin composer, music educator
Gammon, Samuel Rhea III retired association executive, former ambassador
Gan, Chenny Quan musician, artist, educator
Gan, Juis interior designer
Gan, Quan medical researcher
Gandal, Keith literature and language professor
Gandolf, Raymond L. media correspondent
Gandolfini, James actor
Ganguly, Arijit software engineer
Ganis, Sidney film company executive, former motion picture association executive
Ganley, James Powell retired ophthalmologist
Gannon, Sister Ann Ida retired philosophy educator
Ganske, Ingrid medical researcher
Ganske, J. Greg former congressman, plastic surgeon
Gantt, Jean Wallace economics professor
Gantz, Carroll Melvin industrial design consultant, consumer product designer
Ganzi, Victor Frederick former publishing executive
Gao, Zhiming research scientist
Garcia, Erika elementary school educator
Garcia, Jorge actor
Garcia, Julia Theresa secondary school educator
Garcia, Luis Fernando photographer
Garcia-Granados, Sergio Eduardo portfolio manager, writer, historian
García-Paine, José María education educator
Garcia Tormo, Xavier physicist
García-Valdecasas Y Fernández, Rafael judge
Garcia y Carrillo, Martha Xochitl pharmacist
Gardenhire, Douglas Shawn health facility administrator
Gardin, Hershel academic administrator, dean, management consultant
Gardiner, Hobart Clive petroleum company executive
Gardiner, Lester Raymond, Jr. retired lawyer
Gardner, Bernard surgeon, educator
Gardner, Donna L. psychologist, educator
Gardner, Elizabeth Ann Hunt artist, poet, genealogist
Gardner, James Carson (Jim Gardner) former lieutenant governor, congressman
Gardner, John Howland III neurologist
Gardner, Meredith Lee communication consultant
Gardner, Sandi B. retired biology professor
Gardner, Wilford Robert physicist, researcher
Gardom, Garde Basil former lieutenant governor of British Columbia
Gareau, Jean L. application technology executive
Garelnabi, Mahdi Omer Hamid research scientist
Garetto, Lawrence P. dean
Garfield-Woodbridge, Nancy writer
Garfinkle, Elaine Myra writer
Garland, Elsie M. adolescent and family violence counselor
Garland, Robert Lee secondary school educator, writer
Garlin, Jeff actor
Garman, David Kline former federal agency administrator
Garner, Algean, II, healthcare company administrator, consultant
Garner, Carlene Ann not-for-profit fundraiser, consultant
Garner, Jay Montgomery retired military officer
Garner, Jennifer Anne actress
Garnier, Jean-Pierre retired pharmaceutical executive
Garnjost, Kurt lawyer
Garofalo, Janeane actress, comedienne
Garrett, Marshall Lee anesthesiologist, educator
Garrett, Nataki theater director
Garrido, Terhilda health science association administrator, consultant
Garrison, Linda Susan fundraising consultant, writer
Garrison, Robert Frederick astronomer, educator
Garrison, Steve R. political science professor
Garruto, Ralph Michael biomedical anthropologist, biologist, educator
Gartenberg, Seymour Lee retired recording industry executive
Gartner, Lawrence Mitchell pediatrician, medical educator
Garton, Robert Dean state legislator
Garvey, Jane F. diversified financial services company executive, former public relations firm executive
Garwin, Richard Lawrence physicist
Gary, Marc lawyer, financial services industry executive, former telecommunications industry executive
Garza, Cutberto nutrition educator
Garza, Ed former mayor
Gashi, Qendrim research scientist, mathematics professor
Gasich, Welko Elton retired aerospace defense executive, management consultant
Gasper, Jo Ann social services administrator, consultant
Gasper, Ruth Eileen real estate executive
Gasque, Thomas James retired English educator
Gassaway, William Brooks retired manufacturing executive, writer
Gasser, Michael J. consumer products company executive
Gatch, Milton McCormick, Jr. library director, clergyman, educator
Gates, Jay Rodney retired museum director
Gates, Mimi Gardner retired museum director
Gates, Stephen Frye lawyer, retired oil industry executive
Gates, Susan Inez magazine publisher
Gatewood, George David science educator
Gatewood, Tela Lynne lawyer
Gatewood, Willard Badgett, Jr. retired historian, writer
Gaudio, Maxine Diane biofeedback therapist, stress management consultant
Gaulke, Mary Florence retired library administrator
Gaustad, Edwin Scott historian, educator
Gavin, Donald Glenn lawyer, educator
Gavril, Jean (Jean Van Leeuwen) writer
Gay, William Ingalls veterinarian, retired health science association administrator
Gaye, Zachariah Zarzar education educator
Gaylin, Willard physician, educator
Gaylord, Kimberly Buck engineering educator
Gayoom, Maumoon Abdul former president of Maldives
Gear, Emily museum director, curator
Geary, Stephen R. engineer, educator, engineering executive
Gebelein, Richard Stephen judge, former state attorney general
Gechtoff, Sonia artist
Geddy, Vernon Meredith, Jr. lawyer
Gee, Glendon W. retired soil scientist
Geertz, Hildred Storey anthropology educator
Geffen, David Lawrence film company executive
Geha, Alexander Salim cardiothoracic surgeon, educator
Gehani, Ray R. finance educator
Geiger, Melissa S. art history professor
Geisler, Thomas Milton, Jr. lawyer, educator
Geistfeld, Ronald Elwood retired dental educator
Geithner, Paul Herman, Jr. retired banker
Gelber, Robert Cary retired law librarian
Gelboin, Harry Victor biochemistry educator, researcher
Geldard, Richard Gordon publisher, writer, retired philosophy educator
Gelfand, Israil Moiseevich (Izrail) mathematician, biologist
Geller, Scott A. management consultant
Gelman, Deborah healthcare educator
Gelmi, Alessandra Valentina Maria Romana Valeria author, educator
Gelston, Philip A. lawyer
Geltzer, Robert Lawrence lawyer, arbitrator, mediator, retired retail executive
Gemeinhardt, Judith M. (Judi Gamin) writer, poet
Gemignani, Michael Caesar clergyman, retired mathematics professor
Genaro, Donald Michael industrial designer
Genesoni, Jacqueline mathematics educator
Gengler, Richelle Ruth musician, educator
Genieser, Nancy Branom radiologist
Genkins, Gabriel physician
Gens, Ralph Samuel electrical engineering consultant
Gentilcore, Eileen Marie Belsito principal
Gentry, Donald William engineering executive, mining engineer
Georg, Manfred research scientist
George, Faye poet
George, Gay lawyer
George, Gerald William editor, writer, administrator
George, Joey Russell lawyer
George, Joyce Jackson lawyer, writer, retired judge
George, Kiranraj assistant professor, electrical engineer, researcher
George, Rohini medical physicist
Gephardt, Donald Louis retired music professor
Geraci, Matthew James pharmacist
Gerald, Michael Charles pharmacy educator, dean
Gerard, Roy Dupuy retired oil company executive
Gerberding, Julie Louise former federal agency administrator
Geren, Gerald S. lawyer
Geren, Pete (Preston M. Geren III) former United States Representative from Texas
Gerlach, Jeanne Elaine English language educator
Germain, Pichop Nkengoum economics professor
Gerritsen, Mary Ellen vascular and cell biologist
Gerson, Donald Jerome computer scientist, consultant, photographer, small business owner
Gerson, Elliot Francis foundation administrator
Gerstner, Louis Vincent, Jr. retired private equity firm executive
Geschke, Charles M. computer company executive
Gessaman, Margaret Palmer mathematician, educator, retired dean
Getty, Amorette Rose Klug research scientist
Gewitz, Michael Harold pediatric cardiologist
G. Giorges, Aklilu Tilahun mechanical engineer, researcher
Ghaffari, Avideh Behrouz interior designer
Ghanem, Eman biochemist
Gharabawi Garibaldi, George Milad psychiatrist, neuroscientist
Ghattas, Jacqueline Samy elementary school educator
Ghazvinian, John H. historian, writer
Ghebrhiwet, Freweiny Wendy real estate broker, consultant
Gherman, Paul M. retired university librarian
Ghibesi, Jason Joseph political science professor
Ghosal, Anima research scientist
Ghosh, Ramya economist
Giaccio, Anthony lawyer
Giacobbe, Alice C. special education educator
Gianturco, Delio Emanuele management consultant, educator, author
Gibbons, Sam Melville former United States Representative, Florida, government agency administrator
Gibbs, David Richard musician, journalist, photographer, writer
Gibbs, Dawn Ann media specialist, educator
Gibbs, Frederick Winfield lawyer, communications executive
Gibbs, Johnie Elizabeth information technology manager, educator, consultant
Giberson, Joan Alyne retired school nurse
Gibert, Stephen P. political scientist
Giblin, Patrick David retired bank executive
Gibney, Alex producer, director, writer
Gibson, Donald Bernard literature educator, educator
Gibson, Mel actor, film director and producer
Gibson, Michael Troy political science professor
Gibson, Milton Eugene cardiologist
Gibson, Pamela Hemenway elementary school educator
Gibson, Wesley Cullen writer
Gibson, William Willard, Jr. law educator
Giele, Janet Zollinger sociologist, educator
Gifford, Marjorie Fitting mathematician, educator, consultant
Gift, James Joseph aquatic toxicologist
Gilbert, Allan Arthur retired manufacturing executive
Gilbert, Charles D. neurobiologist
Gilbert, Elayne Rhoda writer
Gilbert, Frederick E. development planner, Africanist, consultant
Gilbert, Harriette Gurley retired music educator
Gilbert, Melissa former actors guild executive, actress
Gilbert, Sandee R. art educator
Gilburne, Miles R. venture capitalist
Gilchrest, Thornton Charles retired association executive
Gilchrest, Wayne Thomas former United States Representative from Maryland, secondary school educator
Gilchrist, Gerald Seymour pediatric hematologist, oncologist, educator
Gilchrist, William Aaron architect
Giles, James Francis financial executive
Giles, Melva Theresa nursing educator
Giles, Patricia Cecelia Parker retired art educator, graphic designer
Gill, Henry Herr photojournalist
Gill, Thomas James III pathologist, educator
Gillan, Rebecca Jane music educator, composer
Gillespie, Gerald Ernest Paul comparative literature educator, writer
Gillett, James Warren retired ecotoxicology educator
Gillett, Mary Caperton military historian
Gillette, Nancy E. entomologist, researcher
Gilliam, Terry Vance film director, actor, writer, illustrator
Gillis, John Lamb, Jr. lawyer
Gillispie, Billy Clyde former men's college basketball coach
Gilmore, Dawn S. music educator
Gilroy, Frank Daniel playwright
Gim, Dong-Woo display designer
Gimenes, Sonia Regina Rosendo family therapist, psychologist
Gimple, W. Thomas sales executive

Gimzewski, James K. *chemistry professor*
Gines, Ernest *finance educator*
Gingerich, David Earl *aerospace engineer, educator*
Gingold, Dennis Marc *lawyer*
Gingras, Michele *music educator*
Ginossar, Tamar *medical researcher, educator*
Ginsberg, Ernest *lawyer, banker*
Ginsberg-Fellner, Fredda *retired pediatric endocrinologist, researcher*
Gioconda, Thomas F. *program manager, retired military officer*
Gioia, Dana (Michael Dana Gioia) *poet, critic, former cultural organization administrator*
Gipson, Melinda *publishing executive*
Girgis, Michael M. *physician*
Girman, Dee-Marie *retired artist, singer*
Gitelson, Susan Aurelia *corporate executive, philanthropist*
Gitner, Gerald L. *air transportation executive, investment banker*
Gittinger, Laurie Ellen *music educator*
Giuliani, Judith *not-for-profit executive*
Giulianti, Mara Selena *former mayor*
Giusti, Joseph Paul *retired academic administrator, consultant*
Giza, David Alan *lawyer*
Gladden, Vivianne Cervantes *healthcare consultant, writer*
Gladysheva, Inna *biochemist, researcher*
Glancy, Walter John *retired lawyer*
Glasberg, Laurence Brian *investment company executive*
Glascoff, Susan Titus *public advocate, former secondary school educator, school board member, securities trader*
Glaser, Diana Andreeva *engineer*
Glaser, Robert Joy *retired internist, foundation administrator*
Glashow, Sheldon Lee *physicist, researcher*
Glass, Dorothea Daniels *physiatrist, educator*
Glass, Kenneth Edward *management consultant*
Glass, Margie Lee Loudd *secondary school educator*
Glasser, Ira Saul *former civil liberties organization administrator*
Glassheim, Jeffrey Wayne *allergist, immunologist, pediatrician*
Glassick, Charles Etzweiler *foundation administrator*
Glassman, Cynthia Aaron *former federal agency administrator*
Glassman, James Kenneth *former federal agency administrator*
Glasson, Lloyd *sculptor, educator*
Glavine, Tom (Thomas Michael Glavine) *professional baseball player*
Glazer, Jack Henry *retired lawyer*
Gleaves, Leon Rogers *marketing and sales executive*
Gleichman, John Alan *protective services expert*
Gleim, Kathy Marie *music educator, performer, composer*
Glendon, Mary Ann *US Ambassador to the Holy See, law educator*
Glenn, Constance White *art museum director, educator, consultant*
Glenn, Violetta Colleen *retired secondary school educator*
Glesk, Ivan *physicist, educator, researcher*
Glick, J. Leslie *management consultant*
Glick, Jane Mills *retired biomedical researcher*
Glick, Ruth Burtnick *literature educator, writer*
Glickman, Daniel Robert *motion picture association executive, former United States Secretary of Agriculture*
Glindeman, Henry Peter, Jr. *real estate developer*
Glismann, Clementine *retired elementary school educator*
Glohr, Eric A. *academic administrator*
Glover, Sherry Register *nursing educator*
Gloyd, Lawrence Eugene *retired diversified manufacturing company executive*
Glück, Louise Elisabeth *poet, educator*
Glysch, Randall Lee *research scientist*
Gnanadesikan, Ramanathan *retired statistics educator, researcher*
Goble, Patrick *composer, educator*
Goble, Paul *writer, illustrator, artist*
Godbille, Lara *museum director*
Godbold, John Cooper *federal judge*
Goddard, Janet Sniffin *artist*
Goddess, Lynn Barbara *real estate investor*
Godhardt, Karen *information technology executive*
Godin, Seth Warren *entrepreneur, blog website writer, marketing professional*
Godlas, Alan *religious studies educator*
Goduti, Philip Anthony, Jr. *history professor*
Godwin, Hilary A. *chemistry professor, research scientist*
Godwin, Ralph Lee, Jr. *real estate executive*
Goel, Tushar *application developer, researcher*
Goeltz, Richard Karl *finance company executive*
Goelz, Susan *biochemist, director*
Goericke, Fabian Thomas *research scientist*
Goerke, Glenn Allen *university administrator*
Goetsch, Peggy *biology professor*
Goetz, Jozef *engineering educator*
Goff, Renee Rosenstock *gifted and talented educator*
Gofferje, Hadwig *retired language educator*
Goffman, Thomas Edward *radiation oncologist*
Goffredi, Shana Kaye *marine biologist, educator*
Goforth, Jill Hastings *principal*
Gogbashian, Andrew *surgeon, researcher*
Goines, Leonard *music educator, consultant*
Gokulakrishnan, Ponnuthurai *chemical engineer*
Gold, Judith Hammerling *psychiatrist*
Gold, Leonard Singer *librarian, translator, curator*
Goldberg, Burton David *pathologist, researcher, educator*
Goldberg, C. Jeffrey *mathematics educator, accountant*
Goldberg, David Alan *investment banker, lawyer*
Goldberg, Edwin *rehabilitation specialist, interfaith clergyman*
Goldberg, Lee Winicki *furniture company executive*
Goldberg, Lois D. *health facility administrator, disability analyst*
Goldberg, Mark Arthur *neurologist*
Goldberg, Martin *internist, educator*
Goldberg, Michael Ellis *neurologist, neuroscientist*
Goldberg, Nancy G. *business owner, community volunteer*
Goldberg, Samuel *retired mathematician, foundation administrator*
Goldberg, Victor Joel *retired data processing company executive*
Goldberg, Whoopi (Caryn Elaine Johnson) *actress, comedienne*
Goldberger, Arthur Earl, Jr. *information technology executive*
Goldberger, George Stefan *finance company executive*
Goldberger, Paul Jesse *dean, architecture critic, writer*
Golden, David Edward *physicist*
Golden, Gerald Samuel *retired national medical board executive*
Golden, Joseph Aaron *lawyer*
Golden, Judith Greene *artist, educator*
Golden, Robert Neal *psychiatrist, researcher, dean, medical educator*
Goldenberg, Kim *retired academic administrator, internist, consultant*
Goldfarb, Eric Daniel *information technology executive*
Goldfarb, Muriel Bernice *marketing and advertising consultant*
Goldman, Bert Arthur *retired psychology professor*
Goldman, Bruce Dale *biology educator*
Goldman, Jeri Joan *psychologist*
Goldman, Judith *writer, editor, curator, consultant, publisher*
Goldman, William *writer, scriptwriter*
Goldmann, Morton Aaron *cardiologist, educator*
Goldner, Sheldon Herbert *retired import/export company executive*
Goldsborough, Robert Gerald *publishing executive, author*
Goldsmith, Jay Paul *pediatrician, educator*
Goldsmith, Jeff Charles *management consultant*
Goldsmith, Michael Allen *oncologist, educator*
Goldstein, Alfred George *consumer products company executive*
Goldstein, Avram *pharmacology educator*
Goldstein, Bernard *metal recycling, transportation and casino executive*
Goldstein, Burton Benjamin, Jr. *university professor*
Goldstein, Burton Jack *psychiatrist*
Goldstein, Carl *art educator*
Goldstein, Dora Benedict *pharmacologist, educator*
Goldstein, Irving Solomon *chemistry professor, consultant*
Goldstein, Julius Lester *biomedical engineer, consultant*
Goldstein, Leonard Barry *dentist*
Goldstein, Norman Ray *international trading company executive, consultant*
Gole, Anand *engineering educator, researcher*
Golemon, Patricia Lynn *marketing professional, educator, writer*
Golson, Randal L. *social sciences educator, department chairman*
Golub, Evan *computer science educator*
Golub, Sharon Bramson *retired psychologist, educator*
Gomes, Kevin *application developer*
Gomez, Larry *former prosecutor*
Gomez-Mejia, Luis R. *educator*
Gonnering, Russell Stephen *ophthalmic plastic surgeon*
Gonwa, Thomas Arthur *nephrologist, educator*
Gonzales, Ernesto Luis B. *bank executive*
Gonzalez, Caleb *ophthalmologist, educator*
Gonzalez, Juan G. *engineering company executive*
Gonzalez, Karen Eileen *middle school educator*
Gonzalez, Rose Marie Juarez *retired education educator*
Gonzalez-Flecha, Beatriz *biology professor*
Good, Brenton Earl *art educator, artist*
Good, Laurance Frederic *retired hospital administrator*
Good, Linda Lou *elementary school educator*
Good, Walter Raymond *investment company executive*
Goodall, Jane *zoologist*
Goode, Stephen Hogue *publishing executive*
Goode, Virgil Hamlin, Jr. *former United States Representative from Virginia*
Goodenow, Robert W. *lawyer, former sports association administrator*
Gooden-Young, Phyllis Karron *dance instructor*
Goodfellow, Robin Irene *surgeon*
Gooding, Charles Arthur *radiologist, physician, educator*
Goodland, Robert J. A. *environmental scientist*
Goodlett, David Eugene *history professor*
Goodman, Charles David *physicist, researcher*
Goodman, Cynthia Diane *public health physician*
Goodman, Elizabeth Ann *retired lawyer*
Goodnough, Robert Arthur *artist*
Goodrich, James A. *veterinarian, researcher*
Goodrich, Kenneth Paul *retired dean*
Goodsell, Charles True *public administration educator, researcher*
Goodyear, John L. *artist, educator*
Goold, Douglas *think-tank executive*
Gora, Susannah Porter Martin *journalist, poet*
Gorbaty, Martin Leo *chemist, researcher*
Gordis, David Moses *academic administrator, rabbi*
Gordon, James S. *retired lawyer, director*
Gordon, Leonard H(erman) D(avid) *history educator*
Gordon, Lonny Joseph *artist, educator, dean*
Gordon, Marjorie *lyric-coloratura soprano, opera producer, educator*
Gordon, Sharon Ann *mathematics and pre-school educator*
Gordon, William Edwin *physicist, electrical engineer, academic administrator, educator*
Gorelick, Ellen Catherine *museum executive director, chief curator, artist, educator, civic volunteer, retired*
Gorelik, Gennady *research scientist, writer*
Gorence, Patricia Josetta *judge*
Goreniuc, Mircea C. Paul *sculptor*
Gorfe, Alemayehu A. *medical educator*
Gorman, Marcie Sothern *retired personal care industry executive*
Gorodeski, George *medical educator*
Gorodeski, George I. *medical educator*
Gorske, Robert H. *lawyer*
Gorsline, Stephen Paul *security specialist*
Goss, Jerome Eldon *craftsman, retired cardiologist*
Goss, Joel Francis *writer*
Goss, Porter Johnston *former CIA director, retired United States Representative from Florida*
Gottlieb, Alan Merril *advertising, fundraising and broadcasting executive, writer*
Gottlieb, Gary L. *hospital administrator, psychiatrist*
Gottlieb, H. David *podiatrist*
Gottlieb, Klaus T. *gastroenterologist, educator*
Gottlieb, Michah *religious studies educator*
Gotto, Jamie L. *medical educator*
Gottschalk, Charles M. *international energy consultant*
Gould, Elliott *actor*
Gould, Martha Bernice *retired librarian*
Goulet, Charles Ryan *retired insurance company executive*
Goulet, Lorrie *sculptor*
Gourley, Sara J. *lawyer*
Gourvitz, Elliot Howard *lawyer*
Gouse, S. William, Jr. *mechanical engineering executive, researcher*
Gouw, Julia Suryapranata *bank executive*
Govindjee, *biophysics, biochemistry, and biology professor*
Gowan, Donald Elmer *religion educator*
Gowans, Sir James Learmonth *retired science administrator, immunologist*
Grabowski, Tom *art educator*
Grace, Cynthia *lawyer, educator*
Grace, Marcia Bell *advertising executive*
Grachek, Marianna Kern *healthcare administrator*
Grady, Joan Butterworth *principal*
Grady, Lee Timothy *pharmaceutical chemist*
Grady, Sandra C. *minister, counselor*
Grady, Wayne Joseph *retired government official*
Graebner, James Herbert *transportation executive*
Graff, George Leonard *lawyer*
Graham, Clarence E., Jr., (Jay Graham) *humanities educator, literature and language educator*
Graham, David F. *lawyer*
Graham, David G. *preventive medicine physician, psychiatrist*
Graham, Ginger L. *pharmaceutical executive*
Graham, Howard Lee, Sr. *finance company executive*
Graham, James Herbert *retired dermatologist*
Graham, Jewel Freeman *social worker, lawyer, educator*
Graham, Joy Francine *pediatric clinical nurse specialist*
Graham, Lanier *art historian, curator*
Graham, Laurie *editor, writer*
Graham, Olive Jane *retired medical/surgical nurse*
Graham, Stuart Edward *construction company executive*
Graham, Terrence Lee *plant pathologist, educator*
Graham, Wallace Karl *chemicals executive*
Graham-Moore, Brian Edward *retired educator, consultant*
Graisse, Jean-Jacques *former international organization official*
Gralla, Lawrence *publishing company executive*
Gralla, Milton *retired publisher*
Granato, Catherine (Cammi Granato) *former olympic athlete, sports association executive*
Grandy, Walter Thomas, Jr. *physicist, researcher*
Granger, Loretha *special education educator*
Grann, Phyllis E. *editor, former publisher executive*
Granott, Nira *psychologist, researcher*
Grant, Alexander Marshall *retired ballet director*
Grant, Carmen Hill *psychologist, psychotherapist*
Grant, Frances Elizabeth *retired educator*
Grant, Gerald A. *neurosurgeon*
Grant, Isabella Horton *retired judge*
Grant, Kathleen J. *history professor*
Grant, Ken A. *history professor*
Grant, Lee (Lyova Haskell Rosenthal) *actress, television and film director*
Grant, Mark Antonio *organization administrator*
Grant, Merrill Theodore *television producer*
Grant, Richard Earl *retired medical and legal consultant*
Grantham, Joyce Carol *small business owner, music educator*
Grantham, Walter J. *mechanical engineer, educator*
Granville, Richard Scott *information technology executive*
Grassell, Duane V. *secondary school educator*
Gratz, Loren William *school administrator*
Gravel, Mike (Maurice Robert Gravel) *former United States Senator from Alaska*
Graveline, Jeremy James *finance educator*
Graves, Lorraine Elizabeth *dancer, educator, coach*
Graves, Wallace Billingsley *retired university executive*
Gray, Francine du Plessix *writer*
Gray, Gordon L. *communications educator*
Gray, Jan Charles *lawyer, business owner*
Gray, Karla Marie *retired state supreme court chief justice*
Gray, Mary Jane *retired obstetrician, gynecologist*
Gray, Paul *retired engineering educator*
Gray, Phebe Xu *language educator*
Gray, Richard Alexander, Jr. *retired chemical company executive*
Gray, Richard Arden *retired transportation executive*
Graziano, Michael Steven Anthony *medical educator*
Grdina, David John *radiation biologist, educator*
Greaser, Constance Udean *communications executive, researcher*
Grebstein, Sheldon Norman *academic administrator*
Grechka, Vladimir *geophysicist*
Greco, Christopher Jon *musician, composer, educator*
Greco, Richard, Jr. *former civilian military employee*
Green, Carol H. *consultant, retired lawyer, journalist, educator*
Green, Carole L. *lawyer*
Green, David *hematologist*
Green, Howard *actor*
Green, Keith DeWayne *humanities educator*
Green, Louis Harry *retired surgeon*
Green, Morris *retired pediatrician, educator*
Green, Nancy Loughridge *publishing executive*
Green, Patricia Pataky *school system administrator, consultant, superintendents of schools*
Green, Paul John *critic*
Greenberg, Alan Courtney (Ace Greenberg) *retired diversified financial services company executive*
Greenberg, Albert *art director*
Greenberg, Carolyn Phyllis *retired anesthesiologist*
Greenberg, Ira Arthur *psychologist*
Greenberg, Irving *rabbi*
Greenberg, Jack M. *former food products executive*
Greenberg, Marvin *retired music educator*
Greenberg, Maurice Raymond (Hank Greenberg) *insurance company executive*
Greenberg, Ronald David *lawyer, educator*
Greenblatt, Hellen Chaya *immunologist, microbiologist*
Greenburg, Dan *author*
Greene, Alvin *management consultant*
Greene, Diane B. *information technology executive*
Greene, Donald Richard *dermatologist, educator*
Greene, Geoffrey Lloyd *physicist*
Greene, Jo *school system administrator*
Greene, John Joseph *lawyer*
Greene, Jule Blounte *lawyer*
Greene, Katrina Tomar *anthropologist, educator*
Greene, Lynne Jeannette *wellness consultant, artist*
Greenebaum, Leonard Charles *retired lawyer*
Greenfield, James Robert *lawyer*
Greenfield, Lee *state legislator*
Greenfield, Val Shea *ophthalmologist*
Greenhouse, Linda Joyce *journalist, educator*
Greenman, Jane Friedlieb *lawyer, human resources executive*
Greenspan, Robert Edward *physician*
Greenstein, Merle Edward *import/export company executive*
Greenwald, John Edward *publishing executive, journalist*
Greenway, Joan M. *dean*
Greenwood, Frank *information scientist, educator*
Greenwood, Gordon Edward *retired education educator*
Greenwood, Janet Kae Daly *psychologist, academic administrator, marketing professional*
Greenwood, William Warren *journalist*
Greer, K. Gordon *banker*
Greer, Robert Bruce III *orthopedist, educator*
Greetham, Elizabeth M. *former health products executive*
Gregg, Dawn G. *engineering educator*
Gregor, Dorothy Deborah *retired librarian*
Gregory, Bettina Louise *journalist*
Gregory, Daniel Hayes *gastroenterologist*
Gregory, Frederick Drew *retired federal agency administrator*
Greiner, Nicole K. Hudak *physical education educator*
Greiner, William Donald *artist*
Grella, Luca *physicist*
Grenier, Laura Margiotta *medical/surgical nurse*
Gresham, Glen Edward *physician*
Greve-Carroll, Marie-Jean *artist, retired educator*
Grévisse, Fernand *judge*
Grew, Raymond Edward *mechanical engineer*
Grewe, Maria *literature and language educator*
Grey, Joel *actor*
Grey, Robert Dean *biology professor, former academic administrator*
Gribbin, Robert E. III *diplomat*
Gribble, Mary Louise *freelance/self-employed poet, writer*
Gribbon, Deborah *museum director*
Griese, Brian *professional football player*
Griffin, Campbell Arthur, Jr. *retired lawyer*
Griffin, Carleton Hadlock *accountant, educator*
Griffin, James Anthony *bishop emeritus, academic administrator*
Griffin, Michael Douglas *aerospace scientist, former federal agency administrator*
Griffin, Richard J. *federal agency administrator*
Griffin, Tim (John Timothy Griffin) *former prosecutor*
Griffith, B(ezaleel) Herold *retired plastic surgeon, educator*
Griffith, Clark Dexter *corporate financial executive*
Griffith, Douglas *research scientist*
Griffith, Heather Marie *psychologist*
Griffith, Rosita Denise *elementary school educator*
Griffiths, Jonathan Barrick *music producer, arranger, consultant*
Griffiths, Phillip A. *mathematician, retired academic administrator*
Grigg, William Humphrey *utilities executive*
Grigorian, Siran *language educator*
Grijalva, Carlos Gabriel *medical educator*
Grim, Charles W. *former federal agency administrator*
Grimaldi, Nicholas Lawrence *fundraising executive*
Grimm, Dean Lain *psychologist*
Grimmer, Johannes Fredrik *otolaryngologist, educator*
Grinell, Sheila *museum director, consultant*
Grinenko, Elena *dancer*
Griner, Brenda *choreographer, director*
Grisham, Therese Elizabeth *humanities educator*
Griskey, Pauline Becker *education educator, researcher*
Griswold, Frank Tracy III *retired bishop*
Gromen, Richard John *historian, educator*
Grooms, Henry Randall *retired civil engineer*
Grosbard, Ulu *film director*
Groskopf, Aubrey Bud *broadcast executive, lawyer*

Grosland, Emery Layton *retired banker*
Gross, Deborah Anne *literature and language professor*
Gross, Lawrence Alan *lawyer*
Gross, Leon Jay *psychometrician*
Gross, Mark *lawyer, food products executive*
Gross, Richard Benjamin *lawyer, film producer*
Grossman, Barbara *artist, educator*
Grossman, Carolyn Sylvia Cort *retired elementary school educator*
Grossman, Edward Jerome *music educator, composer*
Grossman, Ginger Scheflin *advocate*
Grossman, Robert Allen *retired transportation executive*
Grosso, Sue Jane Rivas *radiologist*
Grothendieck, Alexandre *retired mathematician*
Grove, Myrna Jean *retired elementary school educator*
Grove, Richard Charles *retired power tool company executive*
Grove, Terrie *school librarian*
Groves, Bernice Ann *retired elementary and secondary school coordinator, educator*
Groves, Ray John *accountant*
Grow, Daniel R. *gynecologist*
Growick, Philip *advertising executive*
Gruber, Ira Dempsey *historian, educator*
Gruberg, Cy *educational administrator*
Gruen, Margaret *actress*
Gruen, Shirley Schanen *artist*
Gruetzmacher, Nancy Lynn *retired middle school educator*
Grühn, Daniel *psychologist, educator*
Grumbach, Doris *novelist, editor, critic, educator, bookseller*
Grunder, Fred Irwin *retired industrial hygienist, consultant*
Grunder, Hermann A. *science administrator, director, research scientist*
Grunt, Jerome Alvin *retired pediatric endocrinologist*
Grushow, Sandy *broadcast executive*
Grutman, Jewel Humphrey *lawyer, writer*
Gruver, William Rolfe (Bill Gruver) *finance educator, retired investment banker*
Gu, Yu *engineering educator*
Guan, Yabo *research scientist*
Gubbins, Keith Edmund *chemical engineering educator*
Gubser, Peter Anton *political scientist, writer, educator*
Guda, Kishore *research scientist*
Gudlavalleti, Seshu Kumar *research scientist*
Guerra, Alma Del Rosario *retired music educator*
Guerrera, Lisa E. *financial planner*
Guffey, Trisha Rae *assistant principal*
Gugel, Craig Thomas *research and planning executive*
Gugler, Mary Dugan *composer, music educator*
Guhin, Michael Alan *ambassador*
Gui, James Edmund *architect*
Guild, Clark Joseph, Jr. *lawyer*
Guild, Jeffrey K. *mathematics professor*
Guillet, David Wilber *anthropologist, educator*
Guinn, Janet Martin *psychologist, consultant*
Guinn, Kenny C. (Kenneth Carroll Guinn) *former governor*
Gulbrandsen, Patricia Hughes *physician*
Gulcher, Robert Harry *aerospace transportation executive*
Gulick, Sidney (Denny) L. III *mathematics professor, writer*
Gulledge, Sandra Smith *publicist*
Gullo, Stephen Pernice *psychologist, corporate executive*
Gulmahamad, Hanif *entomologist, consultant*
Gumaste, Ashwin *engineering educator*
Gumbel, Bryant Charles *broadcaster*
Gumpert, Carolyn L. *secondary school educator*
Gumpper, Karella Ann *federal government official*
Gunasekera, Hitihamy Mudiyanselage *economics professor*
Gundersheimer, Werner Leonard *library director*
Gunderson, Judith Keefer *golf association executive*
Gunderson, Ted Lee *security consultant*
Gundlach, Heinz Ludwig *doctor juris*
Gunsul, Katherine (Kate) Elma *retired secondary school educator*
Guo, Fulai *astrophysicist*
Guo, Jiantao *biotechnologist*
Guo, Mingruo *food scientist, educator*
Guo, Yang *research scientist*
Guo, Yong *statistician*
Guo, Zhichang *environmental scientist*
Guoqiang, Shu *research scientist*
Gupta, Abhay *plastic and reconstructive surgeon, medical educator*
Gupta, Amit *physician, consultant*
Gupta, Ram *software company executive*
Gurfein, Jared L. *wine and spirits executive, lawyer*
Gurgulino de Souza, Heitor *government organization consultant*
Gurian, Mal *telecommunications executive*
Gurram, Prudhvi Krishna *research scientist*
Gurstel, Norman Keith *lawyer*
Gurudas, Ullas *retired research scientist*
Gurudu, Suryakanth R. *gastroenterologist, educator*
Gurumurthi, Sudhanva *science educator*
Gurwitch, Arnold Andrew *communications executive*
Gussow, Sue Ferguson *artist, educator, writer*
Gustafson, Richard Alrick *retired university president*
Gustafsson, Lars Erik Einar *writer, educator*
Guth, Amber Azniv *surgeon, educator*
Gutheinz, James O'Leary *military officer, law clerk*
Gutheinz, Jean *public relations executive*
Guthrie, Janet *professional race car driver*
Gutknecht, Gil (Gilbert William Gutknecht Jr) *former congressman, former state legislator*
Gutman, David Andrew *psychiatrist*
Gutman, Richard Edward *lawyer*
Gutmann, Ronald J. *consultant, expert witness, retired electrical engineering educator*
Guttenberg, Steve *actor*
Guy, Mary (Penny) Whytlaw *secondary school educator and librarian*
Guyer, Rick *psychometrician*
Guyker, William Charles, Jr. *electrical engineer, researcher*
Guzman, Carole L. *small business owner*
Gyllenhaal, Jake *actor*
Ha, Chong Wan *information technology executive*
Haaland, Gordon Arthur *retired academic administrator*
Haas, Edward Lee *management consultant*
Haas, Frederick Carl *retired paper company and chemicals executive*
Haas, Howard Green *retired bedding manufacturing company executive*
Haas, Suzanne Alberta *elementary and secondary school educator*
Haas-Belluz, Sigrid Charlotte *literature and language professor, director*
Habecker, Eugene Brubaker *academic administrator*
Haber, Geoffrey John *rabbi*
Haber, Ralph Norman *psychology consultant, researcher, educator*
Habermann, Helen *botanist, educator*
Habibi, Reza *radiologist, researcher*
Habicht, Frank Henry *retired manufacturing executive*
Haborak, George Edward *retired academic administrator, educator*
Hackel-Sims, Stella Bloomberg *lawyer, former government official*
Hackett, John Byron *retired advertising executive, lawyer*
Hackett, Robert John *lawyer*
Hackett, Wesley Phelps, Jr. *lawyer*
Hackney, James Acra III *industrial engineer, consultant, retired manufacturing executive*
Hadaway, Christopher Kirk *sociologist, research administrator*
Hadda, Janet Ruth *language educator, lay psychoanalyst*
Haddady, Shirin *physician*
Haddock, Raymond Earl *retired career officer*
Haddy, Theresa Brey *pediatrician, hematologist, oncologist, educator*
Haden, Clovis Roland *retired academic administrator, engineering educator*
Hadley, Stephen John *former National Security Advisor*
Hadley, Susan *health educator*
Hadley, William Melvin *retired dean*
Haenlein, Nathan *art educator*
Hagan, Joseph Henry *educational consultant*
Hagel, Chuck (Charles Timothy Hagel) *retired United States Senator from Nebraska*
Hagel, John III *management consultant*
Hagel, Raymond Charles *publishing company executive, educator*
Hagelstein, Robert Philip *publisher*
Hageman, Richard Philip, Jr. *educational administrator*
Hagenlocker, Edward E. *retired automobile company executive*
Hager, John Henry *former political organization administrator, former federal agency administrator*
Haggerty, Robert Johns *pediatrician, educator*
Hagood, William Edward *history educator*
Hahn, Frank Horace *economics professor*
Hahn, Virginia Lynn *reservations agent*
Hahn, Walter Humphrey *artist, educator, consultant*
Haibach, Pamela S. *science educator*
Haig, Alexander Meigs, Jr. *former United States Secretary of State, retired military officer*
Haile, L. John, Jr. *journalist, publishing executive*
Hain, Pamela Chase *historian, writer*
Haines, David Harry *consulting executive*
Haines, Richard Foster *retired psychologist*
Haining, Jeane *psychologist*
Hainsworth, Melody May *library and information scientist, researcher*
Hairfield-Marrs, Judy L. *retired school educator*
Hairston, William *author, poet, former actor*
Haisch, Bernard Michael *astronomer, researcher*
Hajek, Robert J., Sr. *lawyer, real estate broker*
Hajj, Elie Youssef *civil engineer, consultant*
Hakala, Karen Louise *retired real estate specialist*
Hake, Ralph F. *former appliance manufacturing executive*
Hakkila, Eero Arnold *retired nuclear safeguards technology chemist*
Hakobyan, Yeranuhi *research scientist*
Halaska, Terrell Lynn *consulting firm executive, former federal agency administrator*
Halberstam, Heini *mathematics professor*
Haldeman, Joe William *writer*
Halder, Indrani *research scientist*
Hale, Margaret Smith *insurance company executive, educator*
Hale, Nancy Annette Bills *elementary school educator*
Hales, Charles Albert *physician, educator*
Haley, George Brock, Jr. *retired lawyer*
Halfen, David *retired publishing executive*
Hall, Charles Worth Leo *college administrator*
Hall, Christopher George Longden *academic administrator*
Hall, Courtney D. *medical educator, researcher*
Hall, Dale (Henry Dale Hall) *former federal agency administrator*
Hall, Delma L. *academic administrator*
Hall, Donald *poet*
Hall, Ella Taylor *clinical school psychologist*
Hall, Gregory *composer, engineer*
Hall, Hansel Crimiel *communications executive*
Hall, Howard Pickering *engineering and mathematics educator*
Hall, James Evan *lawyer*
Hall, James Stanley *jazz guitarist, composer*
Hall, James William *university chancellor*
Hall, Jay *social psychologist*
Hall, John Hopkins *retired lawyer*
Hall, John N. *news service executive*
Hall, Lawrence *secondary school educator*
Hall, Monty *television producer, actor*
Hall, Paul J. *lawyer*
Hall, Susan Laurel *artist, educator, writer*
Hall, Teresa Ruth *publishing executive*
Hall, Tony P. *retired congressman, former ambassador*
Halle, Bruce T. *automotive products company executive*
Halleck, Charles White *lawyer, photographer, former judge*
Halleck, Donna P. *piano educator*
Halliburton, Lloyd *retired Romance philology educator*
Halliday, William Ross *retired physician, speleologist, writer*
Halperin, Jerome Arthur *retired pharmaceutical executive*
Halpern, Alvin Michael *retired physicist, educator, consultant*
Halpern, James Bladen *lawyer*
Halpern, Joel Martin *anthropologist, photographer*
Halpin, Daniel William *engineering educator, consultant, writer*
Halverstadt, Robert Dale *mechanical engineer, metal products executive*
Ham, Sommy L. *publisher, writer*
Hamadeh, Shirine *history professor, researcher*
Hambidge, Douglas Walter *archbishop*
Hamblen, Lapsley Walker, Jr. *retired judge*
Hamdan, Lubna K. *science educator, researcher*
Hamecs, Francella Cheslock *elementary and secondary school educator*
Hamed, Martha Ellen *retired federal government official, small business owner*
Hamel, Louis Reginald *retired systems analyst*
Hamel, Robert Arthur *military officer*
Hamel, Rodolphe *retired lawyer, pharmaceutical executive*
Hamelin, Marcel *historian, educator*
Hamil, Burnette Wolf *science educator*
Hamill, (William) Pete *newspaper columnist, author, editor*
Hamilton, Dagmar Strandberg *lawyer, retired educator*
Hamilton, David Eugene *minister, educator*
Hamilton, James William *psychiatrist, writer, artist*
Hamilton, Jean *financial services executive, e-commerce and software executive*
Hamilton, John A. *engineering educator*
Hamilton, Laird John *professional surfer*
Hamilton, Marc C. *psychologist*
Hamilton, Mark Wade *literature educator*
Hamilton, Michael Seymour *political scientist, educator*
Hamilton, Robert Woodruff *retired legal association administrator, educator*
Hamilton, Virginia Van der Veer *historian, educator*
Hamit, Francis Granger *novelist, playwright*
Hamlin, Harriett E. *educational consultant*
Hamlin, Sonya B. *communications specialist*
Hammel, Ernest Martin *medical educator, academic administrator*
Hammer, Robert Eugene *psychologist*
Hammer, Wade Burke *retired oral and maxillofacial surgeon, educator*
Hammerschmidt, John Paul *former United States Representative, Arkansas, lumber company executive*
Hammond, Ann P. *retired elementary, high school and college educator, poet*
Hammond, Glenn Barry, Sr. *judge, electrical engineer*
Hammond, Graeme Lord *surgeon, educator*
Hammond, Mary Sayer *art educator*
Hammond, Paul Young *political science professor*
Hammond, Robie Lee *health science association administrator*
Hammoud, Riad *research scientist*
Hampton, Christopher James *writer, translator*
Hampton, Lori Beth *psychologist*
Hampton, Pastella T. *educational consultant*
Han, Eunice Myunghee *priest, educator*
Han, Jibin *engineer, researcher*
Han, Joseph *systems engineer, director*
Han, Nong *artist, sculptor, painter*
Han, Renzhi *research scientist*
Han, Sang M. *engineering educator*
Hanawalt, Christina Ann *art educator*
Hanaway, Catherine Lucille *lawyer, former prosecutor*
Hancock, Artemus Ward, Sr. *music educator*
Hancock, Charles R. *education educator*
Hancock, John C. *pharmacologist*
Hancock, Patricia Ann *artist*
Hand, Ivan Leslie *pediatrician, researcher*
Hand, Peter James *neurobiologist, educator*
Hand, Roger *physician, educator*
Handler, Carole Enid *lawyer, city planner*
Handler, Harold Robert *lawyer*
Handler, Lowell Stuart *photographer, educator*
Handy, Edward Otis, Jr. *retired diversified financial services company executive*
Handy, Rollo Leroy *philosopher, researcher*
Hanes, Carol Louise *language educator*
Haney, Marlene Carol *music educator*
Hanfelt, Peggy Jean *speech educator*
Hanford, George Hyde *retired educational association administrator*
Hanks, Brian *science educator*
Hanley, Joan *media specialist*
Hanlon, Glen A. *professional hockey coach, retired professional hockey player*
Hanmer, Stephen Read, Jr. *retired federal official*
Hanna, Duke Ellsworth *retired neurological surgeon*
Hanna, Noreen Anelda *adult education educator, consultant*
Hannaford, Peter Dor *public relations executive, writer*
Hannah, John Peter *former federal official*
Hannaman, Alberta Anna *artist*
Hannau, Lucia *literature and language professor*
Hanneman, Rodney Elton *metallurgical engineer*
Hannon-Odom, Roxanne Denise *literature and language professor, department chairman*
Hanotiau, Bernard Raoul *lawyer*
Hansell, John Royer *retired pathologist*
Hansen, B. J. (Bobby J. Hansen) *management consultant, real estate investor and developer*
Hansen, Cory Cooper *literature educator*
Hansen, Nancy C. Urdahl *retired special education educator, small business owner*
Hansen, Richard Emory *psychologist*
Hanson, Arnold Philip *retired lawyer*
Hantzis, Peter C. *psychologist, educator*
Hanushek, Eric Alan *economics professor*
Hapner, Mary Lou *securities trader, writer*
Haque, Anwarul *engineering educator*
Harari, Haim *physicist, researcher*
Harbaugh, Janice M. *counselor, consultant*
Hardage, Page Taylor *retired elementary school educator*
Hardaway, Robert Morris III *retired surgeon*
Hardaway, Timothy Duane *retired professional basketball player*
Hardcastle, Marcia E. (Marcia E. Temme) *retired journalist*
Harder, Robert Clarence *state official*
Hardie, Michael Howard *mathematician, educator*
Hardie Boys, Sir Michael *former New Zealand governor general*
Hardin, Bobby Ott *engineering educator*
Hardin, Hal D. *lawyer, judge, former US attorney*
Hardin, James Neal *language educator, publisher*
Hardin, Mary L. *interior designer*
Harding, Philip Andreae *retired communications and marketing researcher*
Hardock, Linda *music educator*
Hardwicke, Catherine Helen *film director, set designer*
Hardy, Ashton Richard *retired lawyer*
Hardy, Chester Alfred *engineer*
Hardy, Clarence Earl, Jr. *government, nonprofit and corporate sector executive*
Hardy, Ernest Edward *academic official, consultant*
Hardy, Nat W. *literature and language professor*
Hardy, Ralph W. F. *biochemist*
Hardy, Richard Allen, Jr. *psychologist, educator*
Hare, Norma Q. *retired school system administrator*
Harff, Charles Henry *retired lawyer, manufacturing executive*
Harford, Robert R. *dermatologist*
Hargrove, William Richard *education educator, lawyer*
Haring, Ellen Stone *philosophy educator*
Harkins, Thomas Edward *literature educator*
Harlech, Pamela *journalist*
Harlin, Marilyn Miler *marine botany educator, researcher, consultant*
Harman, Jennifer (Jennifer Harman-Traniello) *professional poker player*
Harman, Maryann Whittemore *artist, educator*
Harmatuk, Frances A. *retired psychiatrist, anesthesiologist*
Harmel, Merel Hilber *anesthesiologist, educator*
Harmer, Mark A. *research scientist*
Harmon, Lynn Astrid *announcer, writer*
Harmon-Jones, Eddie *psychology professor*
Harms, Nancy Ann *nursing educator*
Harnedy, Joan Catherine Holland *retired systems analyst*
Harner, Michael James *anthropologist, educator*
Harold, Constance Cammille *theater educator, artist*
Harper, Conrad Kenneth *lawyer*
Harper, Cynthia Channing *medical researcher, educator*
Harper, Henry H. *retired military officer*
Harper, James Weldon III *finance consultant*
Harper, Marsha Wilson *retired religious organization administrator*
Harrell, Charles Lydon, Jr. *retired lawyer*
Harrell, Eric *theater professor*
Harrell, Margaret Ann *writer, photographer, editor*
Harrell, Richard Godwin *alcohol/drug abuse services professional*
Harrigan, Rosanne Carol *medical educator*
Harrington, Gerard III *marketing and communications executive, business consultant*
Harrington, Jean Patrice *academic administrator*
Harrington, John Tolan *internist, nephrologist, educator, retired dean*
Harrington, Robert Dudley, Jr. *retired printing company executive*
Harrington, Roger Fuller *electrical engineering educator, retired*
(Reyes) Harrington, Sandra J. *translator, educator*
Harris, Alice *linguist, educator*
Harris, Allen K. *lawyer*
Harris, Cynthia Viola *principal*
Harris, Cyril Manton *physicist, acoustical engineer, architect, educator*
Harris, Dale Hutter *retired judge*
Harris, Delmarie Jones *retired elementary school educator*
Harris, Dolores M. *retired academic administrator, adult education educator*
Harris, Elaine K. *medical consultant*
Harris, Erica Renee *researcher*
Harris, Frederick John *foreign language and literature educator*
Harris, Fredric Joel *engineering educator, consultant*
Harris, Harriet *actress*
Harris, Jeremy *former mayor*
Harris, Joe Frank *former governor*
Harris, Marcelite Jordan *retired career officer*
Harris, Merle Wiener *retired academic administrator*
Harris, Nicholas George *publisher*
Harris, Randall Edward *preventive medicine physician*
Harris, Robert A. *retired music educator*
Harris, Robert Norman *advertising executive, educator*
Harris, Stephanie L. *Government Agency Secretary*
Harris-Barber, Daisy *elementary school educator*
Harrison, Alonzo *construction executive*
Harrison, Blake Andrew *social sciences educator*
Harrison, Gordon Ray *engineering executive, consultant, research scientist*
Harrison, John Raymond *foundation administrator, retired publishing executive*
Harrison, Michael *former opera company director*
Harrison, Robin Fonclara *music educator*
Harrop, Daniel Smith III *psychiatrist*

Hart, Cecil William Joseph *otolaryngologist, surgeon*
Hart, Cherie Ann *music educator*
Hart, James Warren *retired athletic administrator, professional football player*
Hart, Karen E. *psychologist, consultant*
Hart, Robert Lee *retired English educator*
Hartfield, Elizabeth Ann (Libby Hartfield) *museum director*
Hartger, Barbara J. *marketing professional*
Hartling, Linda M. *human services administrator, researcher*
Hartman, David G. *retired actuary*
Hartman, Earl Kenneth *writer*
Hartman, Michelle Sharon *elementary school educator*
Hartman, Rosemary Jane *retired special education educator*
Hartmann, George Herman *retired manufacturing executive*
Hartnett, David *physics professor, researcher*
Hartsburg, Craig William *former professional hockey coach, retired professional hockey player*
Hartsock, Linda Sue *retired management consultant*
Hartzell, Irene Janofsky *psychologist, mediator*
Hartzell, Pam L. *media specialist*
Harvey, Francis J. *former civilian military employee*
Harvey, James Cardwell *political science and history professor, consultant*
Harvey, Marc S(an) *lawyer, historian, educator*
Harvey, Thomas Edward *former federal agency administrator*
Harville, Martha Louise *special education educator*
Harwell, Denise *researcher*
Harwell, William Earnest (Ernie Harwell) *retired commentator*
Harwell, Xenia Srebrianski *language educator, researcher*
Harwit, Martin Otto *astrophysicist, writer, educator, museum director*
Haryono, Ignatius Wibisono *writer*
Hasan, Mahbub *research scientist*
Hasek, Dominik *retired professional hockey player*
Hashemi, Shohreh S. *science educator, researcher*
Hashimoto, Sozo *information technology executive*
Haskett, Dianne Louise *retired mayor, lawyer, consultant*
Haskins, Steve *retired veterinarian*
Haslett, Jared Wooddell *physicist, educator*
Hassan, Ibne *lawyer, diplomat, political philosopher, international strategist*
Hassanein, Nevine Gamal *elementary school educator*
Hasse, John Edward *music curator*
Hasselmo, Nils *retired academic administrator, linguist*
Hastings, L(ois) Jane *architect, educator*
Hatami, Mehrangiz *obstetrician, gynecologist, researcher*
Hatchwell, Eli *research scientist*
Hatfield, Julie Stockwell *journalist*
Hatfield, Stacey *elementary school educator*
Hathorne, Gayle Gene *musician, family historian*
Hatley, Ellen Delores *elementary school educator*
Hatton, Caroline Kim *sports anti-doping scientist*
Hauck, Jeffrey Peter Artorius Martel *lawyer, protective services official, consultant*
Hauptmann, Randal Mark *biotechnologist*
Hausdorfer, Gary Lee *management consultant*
Hauser, Joyce Roberta *marketing professional*
Hauver, Constance Longshore *lawyer*
Haver-Allen, Ann *communications director*
Hawes, Sue *lawyer*
Hawke, Ethan Green *actor*
Hawkes, Mary Newgeon *retired minister, educator*
Hawkins, Brian Lee *former educational association administrator*
Hawkins, Charles Travis *retired physics professor*
Hawkins, Kellye Danielle *language educator*
Hawkins, Mary Ellen Higgins *state legislator, public relations executive*
Hawthorne, Bruce N. *lawyer, former telecommunications industry executive*
Hawthorne, Margaret Rush *historian, director*
Hawthorne, Roy John *retired music educator*
Hayanga, Awori Jeremiah *surgeon*
Haydel, Shelley E. *microbiologist, researcher*
Hayden, Michael Vincent *consulting firm executive, former CIA Director, retired military officer*
Hayden, Paul Allan *speech pathology educator, consultant, researcher*
Hayek, Carolyn Jean *financial consultant, retired judge*
Hayes, Byron Jackson, Jr. *retired lawyer*
Hayes, Charles Franklin III *retired museum director*
Hayes, Cynthia Ann (C.A. Hayes) *writer*
Hayes, David Ryan *mathematics professor*
Hayes, David Vincent *sculptor*
Hayes, Janet Gray *retired management consultant, mayor*
Hayes, John Patrick *retired manufacturing company executive*
Hayes, Patricia Thornton *music educator, retired director*
Hayes, Paula Freda *federal agency administrator*
Hayes, Robert Francis *psychologist, educator*
Hayes, Robin (Robert Cannon Hayes) *former United States Representative from North Carolina*
Hayhurst, James Frederick Palmer *career and business consultant, inspirational speaker, author*
Hayman, Russell *lawyer*
Haynes, Alora Dawn *performing arts educator*
Haynes, David Donald *electrical engineer*
Haynes, Kevin *pharmacist, researcher*
Hays, Robert William *retired communications educator, writer*
Haywood, H(erbert) Carl(ton) *psychologist, educator*
Hayworth, J.D. (John David Jr.) *former congressman*
Hazard, Robert Culver, Jr. *retired hotel executive*
Hazel, Mary Belle *university administrator*
Hazelip, Linda Ann *musician, small business owner, executive assistant*
H'Doubler, Francis Todd, Jr. *surgeon*
He, Biyu Jade *neuroscientist*
He, Jin *electronics engineer, researcher*
He, Yi *marketing educator*
He, Zhiguo *research scientist*
Headings, Michael D. *elementary school educator, reading specialist*
Healey, Kerry Murphy *former lieutenant governor*
Healy, Daniel Thomas *secondary school educator*
Healy, Steven Michael *accountant, city official*
Heaphy, Janis Besler *retired publishing executive*
Hearl, Peter R. *former food service executive*
Hearn, Fil *retired architectural history professor*
Hearn, Joyce Camp *retired state legislator, educator, consultant*
Heath, John Robert *music educator*
Heath, Joseph Nounnan *retired literature and language educator, writer*
Heath, Kevin Kevin *literature and language professor*
Heath, Richard Eddy *lawyer*
Heatherley, James Lawrence *psychotherapist, educator*
Heaton, Haidee *theater educator*
Heaton, Jean Mossman *retired early childhood educator*
Heaton, Larry Cadwalder *estate planner, security firm executive*
Hebert, William N. *lawyer*
Heche, Anne (Anne Celeste Heche) *actress*
Heck, James Baker *retired education educator*
Heck, Jennifer Leigh *neonatal clinical nurse specialist, educator*
Heckadon, Robert Gordon *plastic surgeon*
Hecker, Michael Hanns Louis *retired electrical engineer, speech scientist*
Hecker, Scott Jonathan *pharmaceutical research director*
Heckler, Margaret Mary *former ambassador, former United States Secretary of Health & Human Services*
Hector-Skinner, Vicki L. *artist*
Hedahl, Gorden Orlin *theater educator, retired dean*
Hedberg, Paul Clifford *broadcast executive*
Hedreen, Richard C. *real estate developer*
Hedrick, Amy *health facility administrator, educator*
Hedstrom, Mitchell Warren *banker*
Heed, Peter W. *former state attorney general*
Heerman, Barbara L. *retired secondary school educator*
Heeschen, David Sutphin *astronomer, educator*
Hefferan, Colien Joan *economist*
Heffernan, James Anthony Walsh *language and literature educator*
Heffron, Howard A. *lawyer*
Hefner, Christie Ann *former publishing executive*
Hegarty, George John *university president, literature and language professor*
Hegde, Vinod R. *medical association administrator, researcher*
Heggers, John Paul *retired surgery, immunology and microbiology educator*
Heginbotham, Jan Sturza *sculptor*
Heidelberg, Paul *writer*
Heider, Jon Vinton *retired lawyer*
Heidt-Dunwell, Debra Sue *vocational school educator*
Heileman, John Phillip *endocrinologist*
Heiligenstein, Christian Enric *lawyer*
Heilmeier, George Harry *electrical engineer, researcher*
Heimbinder, Isaac *lawyer*
Heimbold, Charles Andreas, Jr. *former ambassador*
Heimbold, Margaret Byrne *realtor, publisher, poet, consultant*
Heineman, Andrew David *retired lawyer*
Heineman, Ben Walter *corporation executive*
Heiner, Douglas Cragun *pediatrician, educator, immunologist, allergist*
Heiney, John Weitzel *former utilities executive*
Heinicke, Ralph Martin *science administrator, consultant*
Heininger, S(amuel) Allen *retired chemical company executive*
Heintz, Michael Alfred *biology professor*
Heirman, Donald Nestor *training engineering company executive, research scientist, consultant, educator, director*
Heise, John Irvin, Jr. *lawyer*
Heiss, Mary Wynne *artist*
Heitman, Kristin *medical educator*
Heitzman, Deborah Ann *cell biologist*
Helber, Robert William *oceanographer*
Helfand, Arthur Erwin *podiatrist*
Helfand, Eugene *chemist*
Helfgott, Roy B. *economist, educator*
Helgenberger, Marg *actress*
Helgeson, John Paul *plant pathology and botany educator*
Heller, Adam *chemist, researcher*
Heller, Arthur *advertising executive*
Heller, Robert *financial executive, economist*
Hellerstein, David Joel *psychiatrist, researcher, writer*
Hellmers, Norman Donald *retired historic site director*
Helm, DeWitt Frederick, Jr. *professional society administrator, consultant*
Helprin, Mark *author*
Helton, Sandra Lynn *telecommunications industry executive*
Hemann, Raymond Glenn *research company executive*
Hemby, James Benjamin, Jr. *college president*
Hemingway, Richard William *law educator*
Hemmingsen, Barbara Bruff *retired microbiologist*
Hendershott, Anna Lorraine *educational director*
Henderson, John Drews *architect*
Henderson, Melford J. *epidemiologist, molecular biologist, chemist*
Henderson, Thomas Henry, Jr. *lawyer, former legal association executive*
Henderson, Wiley Joseph *biology educator*
Hendrick, Joseph Riddick, III, (Rick Hendrick) *race team owner*
Hendricks, David Wesley *engineering executive*
Hendricks, James Powell *artist*
Hendrickson, William George *business executive*
Hendrix, Mary Elizabeth *assistant professor in education, language educator, researcher*
Hendrix, Stephen C. *financial executive, consultant*
Hendry, Jean Sharon *psychopharmacologist*
Hendry, Robert Ryon *lawyer*
Henes, Donna *ceremonial artist, writer*
Heng, Iem H. *application developer, educator*
Henikoff, Leo M., Jr. *academic administrator, medical educator*
Henkel, Cynthia Leigh *elementary school educator*
Henley, Richard James *health facility administrator*
Hennessey, Keith B. *former federal official*
Hennessey, Patrick Daniel *musician, educator, musicologist*
Hennessey, William Joseph *physician*
Hennessy, Dean McDonald *lawyer, municipal official, director*
Henney, Christopher Scot *immunologist*
Henning, George Thomas, Jr. *retired steel company executive*
Henninger, Nancy *retired voice educator, singer*
Henrnadez, Gladys A. *education educator*
Henry, Barbara Ann *retired publishing executive*
Henry, Dale *artist*
Henry, Rene Arthur *writer*
Henry, Robert John *lawyer*
Hensley, Ralph Henry III *federal management analyst*
Henson, Anna Resnick *music educator*
Henson, Robert Frank *retired lawyer*
Heppe, Karol Virginia *lawyer, educator*
Hepper, Carol *artist, educator*
Heptinstall, Robert Hodgson *physician*
Herbert, Adam William, Jr. *former academic administrator, educator*
Herbert, Gavin Shearer *health care products company executive*
Herbert, James Charles *writer, researcher*
Herbold, Patricia Louise *retired ambassador*
Herbst, Jurgen *historian, educator*
Heredia, Juanita *language educator*
Herenton, Willie W. *retired mayor*
Hergenhan, Joyce *communications executive*
Hergo, Jane Antoinette *music educator, composer*
Herguth, Robert John *retired columnist*
Hering, Doris Minnie *dance critic*
Herley, Daveen Dorothy *artist, educator*
Herlihy-Chevalier, Barbara Doyle *retired mental health nurse*
Herman, David Jay *orthodontist*
Herman, Ellen Rombs *retired literature and language educator, painter*
Herman, William Arthur *engineering and physics laboratory director*
Hermann, Donald Harold James *law educator*
Hermann, Robert Bell *physical chemist, consultant*
Hermannsson, Steingrimur *former Prime Minister of Iceland*
Hermodson, Amy E. *communications educator*
Hernandez, Michelle A. *lawyer*
Hernandez, Ramon Robert *retired minister, librarian, educator*
Hernández, Sandra R. *foundation administrator*
Hernandez-Garduno, David *electrical engineer*
Hernández-Ortiz, José A. *retired lawyer, literature and language educator*
Herndon, James Marvin *nuclear scientist, consultant*
Hernick, Linda VanAller *paleontologist, researcher*
Hero, Aphrodite S. *retired real estate developer, retired personnel director*
Herod, Charles Carteret *Afro-American studies educator*
Herold, Rochelle Snyder *early childhood educator*
Herrell, Roger Wayne *lawyer*
Herrera, Enrique *language educator*
Herrera, Silvia Patricia *special education educator*
Herriford, Robert Levi, Sr. *retired military officer*
Herring, Jerone Carson *retired lawyer, bank executive*
Herring, Joan Sanders *secondary school educator*
Herringer, Frank Casper *retired diversified financial services company executive*
Herrmann, Mary Anne *elementary school educator*
Herrnkind, Hilda Marie *writer, military volunteer*
Herron, Edwin Hunter, Jr. *energy consultant*
Herron, Orley R. *college president*
Hersey, David Kenneth *theatrical lighting designer*
Hershatter, Richard Lawrence *lawyer, writer*
Herson, Arlene *television producer, journalist, television personality, radio commentator*
Herstand, Theodore *retired theatre artist, educator*
Hertog, Roger *retired investment company executive*
Hertrich, Rainer *aerospace and defense company executive*
Hervey, Nina Fern *retired church administrator, minister*
Herz, Irene Laurel *web site design company executive, librarian*
Herzberg, Thomas *artist, educator, illustrator*
Herzberger, Eugene E. *retired neurosurgeon*
Herzfeld, Siegfried *manufacturing executive, consultant*
Herzog, Peter Emilius *retired legal educator*
Heslop, Michael George *economics professor*
Hess, Wendi Elizabeth *secondary school educator*
Hester, James McNaughton *retired foundation administrator, artist*
Hester, Nancy Elizabeth *county government official*
Hesterberg, Earl J. *automotive executive*
Hetland, James Lyman, Jr. *banker, lawyer, educator*
Heuer, Martin Frederick *retired human resources specialist*
Hey, Robert Pierpont *retired editor*
Heyer, Steven J. *former hotel and beverage company executive*
Heyman, Ira Michael *federal agency administrator, law educator, museum executive*
Heymann, C(lemens) David *author*
Heyward, Andrew John *former broadcast executive*
Hiatt, Arnold *apparel and retail executive*
Hickey, Barry James *archbishop*
Hickey, Joseph Michael *investment banker*
Hickey, Kevin Francis *software company executive*
Hickman, Lucille *physical therapist*
Hicks, Allen Morley *retired hospital administrator*
Hicks, Greta Patterson *accountant, lecturer, writer*
Hicks, Lewis Edward *history professor, political science professor, department chairman*
Hicks, Ritchie B. *physical education educator*
Hicks, Wayland R. *rental company executive*
Hidden-Dodson, Nancy *retired psychologist, consultant, educator*
Hietala, Valerie Grace *alpaca rancher, realtor, environmentalist, educator*
Higbee, Donna Good *writer, researcher*
Higdon, Pamela Leis *writer*
Higginbotham, Edith Arleane *radiologist, researcher*
Higginbotham, John Taylor *lawyer*
Higginbottom, Heather A. *federal official*
Higginbottom, Samuel Logan *retired air transportation executive*
Higgins, Dorothy Marie *dean, educator*
Higgins, Kathryn O'Leary (Kitty Higgins) *former federal agency administrator, former consulting firm executive*
Hight, B. Boyd *retired lawyer*
Hightower, Jack English *retired judge, former congressman*
Hilbrands, Peggy G. *psychologist*
Hildebrandt, Friedhelm *medical educator, researcher*
Hildreth, Patricia Yvonne *retired finance company executive*
Hildrum, Kirsten *research scientist*
Hilgraves, Rebekkah *opera singer voice instructor poet marketing consultant*
Hill, David Warren *lawyer*
Hill, Jerry Dean *elementary school educator*
Hill, John Edward *lawyer*
Hill, Kent Richmond *foundation administrator, former federal agency administrator*
Hill, Lowell Dean *agricultural marketing educator*
Hill, Michael Anthony *mathematics professor*
Hill, Patricia Francine *information technology executive, educator*
Hill, Richard Allan (Rick Hill) *former congressman*
Hill, Virgil Lusk, Jr. *academic administrator, military officer*
Hill, Willie L., Jr. *music educator*
Hillenburg, Stephen *writer, television producer, animator*
Hiller, David Dean *former publishing executive*
Hilliard, Sam Bowers *geography educator*
Hillis, William Daniel *biology professor*
Hillman, Gracia M. *former management consultant, federal agency administrator*
Hillman, Jennifer Anne *international official*
Hillman, Leon *electrical engineer*
Hillman, Richard Stanley *retired political science professor*
Hilton, Jean Bull *musician*
Hilton, Nicky (Nicholai Olivia Hilton) *apparel designer*
Hilton, Paris *actress*
Himes, Diane A. *buyer, fundraiser, actress, lobbyist*
Himes, John Harter *medical researcher, educator*
Himmelfarb, Gertrude *writer, educator*
Hinchey, Tim *former professional sports team executive*
Hincks, Marcia Lockwood *retired insurance company executive*
Hind, Harry William *pharmaceutical company executive*
Hindman, Leslie Susan *auction company executive*
Hinds, Sallie Ann *retired township official*
Hines, Andrew Hampton, Jr. *utilities executive*
Hines, Colleen M. *clinical nurse specialist*
Hines, Mary Jane *retired elementary school teacher*
Hines, Walter James *former stock exchange executive*
Hinkley, Everett David, Jr. *physicist*
Hinshaw, Edward Banks *retired broadcast executive*
Hinterbuchner, Catherine N. *physician, medical educator*
Hinton, Velecia Ann *academic administrator*
Hintz, Gerald R. *engineer, educator*
Hirai, Kazuo (Kaz) *electronics executive*
Hirokawa, Shoji *retired chemistry professor*
Hirose, Teruo Terry *surgeon educator, essayist, medical writer*
Hirsch, George Aaron *publishing executive*
Hirsch, Horst Eberhard *metal products executive, consultant*
Hirsch, Lawrence Leonard *physician, retired educator*
Hirshfield, Stuart *lawyer*
Hirsh-Pasek, Kathryn Ann *psychology educator*
Hirshtal, Edith *retired concert pianist, educator, chamber musician*
Hitchcock, Frederick E., Jr., (Fritz) *automotive company executive*
Hitchcock, Walter Anson *retired educational consultant*
Hitz, Frederick Porter *public and international affairs educator*
Hladik, Florian *research scientist*
Ho, Chih-Ming *physicist, researcher*
Hobbins, William T. *retired military officer*
Hobbs, Franklin Dean III *lawyer*
Hobson, Jade *journalist, consultant*
Hochhalter, Gordon Ray *advertising communications executive*
Hochschild, Adam *writer, journalist*
Hochschild, Carroll Shepherd *computer company and medical equipment executive, educator*
Hock, Roger R. *psychology professor*
Hockeimer, Henry Eric *engineering executive*
Hockin, Robert *business educator, consultant*
Hodel, Donald Paul *former United States Secretary of the Interior*
Hodge, Ian Moir *physical chemist*
Hodge, Jacqueline Celeste *freelance/self-employed radiologist*
Hodge, Verne Antonio *judge*
Hodgen, Maurice Denzil *retired history professor, writer*
Hodges, Adele E. *career military officer*
Hodges, Ann *actress, singer, dancer*
Hodges, Ann *retired television editor, columnist*
Hodges, David Parmer *architect*
Hodges, Shirley Marie *secondary school educator*
Hodgson, Suzanne Andree *secondary school educator*

Hodsoll, Francis Samuel Monaise *government official*
Hodzic, Edin *engineer, educator*
Hoefler, Torsten *research scientist*
Hoeg, Donald Francis *chemist, consultant, research and development company executive*
Hoel, Anne Kelly *finance educator, consultant*
Hoerder, Dirk *history educator*
Hofbauer, Eric M. *musician, educator*
Hofer, Stephen Robert *lawyer*
Hoff, Benjamin Lloyd *writer, scriptwriter*
Hoff, Charles Worthington III *retired banker*
Hoffheimer, Michael Harry *law educator*
Hoffman, Daniel (Gerard Hoffman) *literature educator, poet*
Hoffman, Darnay Robert *management consultant*
Hoffman, Franklin Thomas *artist, printmaker, retired army officer*
Hoffman, James Simon *engineering educator*
Hoffman, Jerry Irwin *retired dental educator*
Hoffman, John Fletcher *retired lawyer*
Hoffman, Kevin Michael *psychologist, researcher*
Hoffman, Lucas Raphael *medical educator*
Hoffman, Marian Ruth *singer, voice educator*
Hoffman, S. David *lawyer, engineer, military officer, educator, artist*
Hoffman, Sharon Lynn *adult education educator*
Hoffman, William *writer*
Hoffman, William Moses *theater educator*
Hoffmann, Christoph Ludwig *lawyer*
Hoffmann, Frances Porter *librarian*
Hofmann, Paul Bernard *healthcare consultant*
Hofmeister, John D. *retired oil industry executive*
Hofseth, Lorne John *medical researcher, educator*
Hogan, Neville John *mechanical engineering educator, consultant*
Hogan, Robert Henry *trust company executive*
Hogle, Ann Meilstrup *painter, art educator*
Hohlt, Richard Frederick *lobbyist*
Hokana, Gregory Howard *retired engineering executive*
Hoke, Sheila Wilder *retired librarian*
Hokenson, Jan Walsh *literature and language professor*
Holbrook, Karen Ann *retired academic administrator, biologist*
Holbrooke, Richard Charles Albert *diplomat*
Holcomb, Gene Ann *federal loan officer*
Holdaway, Ronald M. *retired federal judge*
Holden, Donald *artist, writer*
Holden, William Willard *insurance executive*
Holder, Maxine E. *writer*
Holdridge, Barbara *recording and book consultant, editor*
Holford, Theodore Richard *biostatistician, educator*
Holiday, Edith Elizabeth *former presidential adviser, cabinet secretary*
Holifield-Kennedy, Linda R. *physician*
Holik, Bobby (Robert Holik) *retired professional hockey player*
Holl, Roger Elmo *lawyer, educator*
Holland, Beth *actress*
Holland, Branti Latessa *science educator*
Holland, David Thurston *former editor*
Holland, Randy James *state supreme court justice*
Holle, Reginald Henry *retired bishop*
Holleb, Doris B. *urban planner, economist*
Hollerbach, Paula Elizabeth *demographer, researcher*
Holley, Linda Ann *secondary school educator*
Holli, Melvin George *retired history professor*
Holliday, Darrell Thaggard, Jr. *engineering educator*
Hollings, Fritz (Ernest Frederick) *former senator*
Hollis, Deborah D. *systems analyst, application developer*
Hollister, Jeffrey William *ecologist*
Holloran, Thomas Edward *business educator*
Holloway, Ernest Leon *retired university president*
Hollowell, John W. *retired urologist*
Holly, Lauren (Lauren Michael Holly) *actress*
Holm, Celeste *actress*
Holman, Bill *composer*
Holman, Dixon Wade *retired judge*
Holmes, Dallas Scott *judge, educator*
Holmes, David Richard, Jr. *cardiologist*
Holmes, Henry Allen *diplomat, educator*
Holmes, Larry *epidemiologist, educator*
Holmes, Myke *actor, educator*
Holmes, Paul Luther *political scientist, educational consultant*
Holmes, Richard Brooks *mathematical physicist*
Holmes, Willa B. *writer, former educator*
Holmstrom, Lynda Lytle *sociologist, educator*
Holochwost, Steven John *psychology professor, researcher*
Holowchak, Mark *philosopher, educator*
Holstein, Adora De Los Santos *economics professor*
Holt, George, Jr. *information technology executive*
Holt, Marjorie Sewell *lawyer, Former United States Representative, Maryland*
Holte, Debra Leah *investment company executive, financial analyst*
Holtkamp, Susan Charlotte *elementary school educator*
Holton, Grace Holland *accountant*
Holtzman, Robert Neil Nehemiah *neurosurgeon, neurologist*
Holtzschue, Karl Bressem *lawyer, author, educator*
Holz, Carl Wayne *retired theologian*
Holzer, Harry Joseph *economist, educator*
Homayoon, Kaveh *urologist*
Homer, Melodie Antonette *clinical nursing instructor*
Honaker, Jimmie Joe *lawyer, educator*
Honeystein, Karl *lawyer, media specialist*
Honig, Alice Sterling *psychologist*
Honour, Lynda Charmaine *research scientist, psychotherapist, educator*
Honsa, Thomas Patrick *secondary school educator, history professor*
Hood, William Boyd, Jr. *cardiologist, educator*
Hoog, Thomas W. *public relations executive*
Hook, Jerry B. *pharmaceutical consultant*
Hooks, Benjamin Lawson *civil rights advocate, retired civil rights association executive*
Hooley, Darlene Kay Olson *former United States Representative from Oregon*
Hooper, Emmanuel *engineer, consultant*
Hooper, Henry Olcott *retired academic administrator, physicist*
Hooper, Josh *advertising executive, speaker, writer, director*
Hooper, Robert Alexander *television producer, educator*
Hooper, William Douglas *retired diversified financial services company executive, photographer, digital imaging artist*
Hootman, Harry Edward *English professor, retired nuclear engineer*
Hoover, John Elwood *former military officer, consultant, writer, educator*
Hopkins, Sir Anthony (Philip) *actor*
Hopkins, Daniel Nelson *materials engineer*
Hopkins, Lisa Ann *multimedia designer, educator*
Hopkins, Robert Charles *chemistry and biophysics educator*
Hopkins, William Hayes *lawyer, writer*
Hopp, Phillip Edward *gifted and talented educator*
Hoppe, Melli *choreographer, educator*
Hopping, Richard Lee *retired academic administrator*
Horlick, Gary Norman *lawyer, educator*
Horlick, Ruth *photographer*
Horn, Andrew Warren *lawyer*
Horn, Lee Shawn *sports analyst*
Horn, Wade Frederick *psychologist, former federal agency administrator*
Hornby, Kenneth Peter *self-employed*
Hornby, Sara Ann *metallurgical engineer, marketing professional*
Horne, Marjorie *production stage manager, event consultant*
Horner, Judith Anne *music educator*
Horner, Matina Souretis *retired academic administrator, corporate financial executive*
Horning, Barbara Hortense Scheer *retired elementary school educator*
Hornyak, Roy Robert *music educator, minister*
Horsley, Tip Alonzo *mathematics educator, military officer*
Horsman, David A. Elliott *writer, finance company executive, educator*
Horswill, C. Weir *retired obstetrician-gynecologist, photographer*
Horton, Linda Rae *lawyer*
Horton, Robert Carlton *geologist*
Horvat, Vashti *principal*
Horvath, Annette *home care administrator*
Horvath, Debora D. *bank executive*
Horward, Donald David *retired history professor*
Horwitz, Donald Paul *lawyer*
Hosansky, Anne *writer*
Hoskinson, Katherine Thayer *school psychologist*
Hosman, Sharon Lee *retired music educator*
Hostert, Sharon Ann *elementary school educator, assistant principal*
Hostettler, John Nathan *former congressman*
Hostovich, Teena Maria *insurance brokerage executive*
Hot, Aliya *optometrist, educator*
Hotchkiss, Andrew *biologist*
Hoty, JoAnn *biology professor*
Hou, Jianhui *chemist*
Hou, Songming *science educator*
Hou, Tingjun *research scientist*
Hough, Jason Wayne *communication educator*
Hough, Sigmund *neuropsychologist*
Hough, Thomas Henry Michael *retired lawyer, educator*
Houghtaling, Pamela Ann *communications consultant, writer*
Houghton, James Richardson *retired manufacturing executive*
Houghton, Katharine *actress*
Houk, Irene Miller *dentist*
Hourihan, Meg *entrepreneur, blog site host*
House, Karen Elliott *former publishing executive, editor, journalist*
Houseman, Ann Elizabeth Lord *educational administrator*
Houshiar, Bobbie Kay *retired language arts educator*
Houston, Alma Faye *retired psychiatrist*
Houston, Stanley Dunsmore *retired public relations executive*
Houtz, Duane Talbott *hospital administrator*
Howard, Darryl E. *religious studies educator*
Howard, David *ballet master, school administrator*
Howard, Dean Denton *electrical engineer, researcher, consultant*
Howard, Donald Searcy *banker*
Howard, James E. *physicist, researcher*
Howard, James Webb *brokerage house executive, engineer, lawyer*
Howard, John W.S. *mental health services professional, alcohol/drug abuse services professional, theology studies educator*
Howard, Joseph Harvey *retired librarian*
Howard, Karrelldo J. *protective services official*
Howard, Marilyn *retired school system administrator*
Howard, Robert Elliott *former federal official, consultant, educator*
Howard, Robert Franklin *observatory administrator, astronomer*
Howard, Sheryl Andrea *lawyer*
Howard, Terry Thomas *obstetrician, gynecologist*
Howard-Peebles, Patricia N. *clinical cytogeneticist*
Howards, Stuart S. *pediatric urologist*
Howe, Gordon *retired professional hockey player, sports association executive*
Howe, John Prentice III *health facility administrator, physician*
Howell, Della *hematologist, oncologist*
Howell, Donald Lee *lawyer*
Howell, Embry Martin *researcher*
Howell, Joel DuBose *internist, educator*
Hower, Frank Beard, Jr. *retired banker*
Howes, Sophia DuBose *writer*
Howrey, Eugene Philip *retired economics and statistics professor*
Hoy, Gilbert R. *retired physics educator*
Hoye, Robert Earl *systems science educator*
Hoyt, Mary Finch *writer, media consultant, retired federal official*
Hratchian, Hrant Patrick *research scientist*
Hricak, Hedvig *radiologist*
Hsieh, Din-Yu *applied mathematics professor*
Hsieh, I-Wei *research scientist*
Hsieh, Tsui-Hsia *artist, educator*
Hsu, Apo (Ching Hsin) *conductor*
Hsu, Emilie Tien-Jung *lawyer*
Hsu, Hugo Y. *ophthalmologist, educator*
Hu, Gusheng *mechanical engineer*
Hu, Hongde *mathematics professor*
Hu, Hua-ling Wang *writer, historian*
Hu, Jie *engineering educator*
Hu, Shouping *education educator*
Hu, Weigang *software engineer*
Hu, Xiaolin *professor*
Hu, Yongyou *chemical engineer, researcher*
Huajiang, Huang *research scientist*
Huang, Dongzhou *civil engineer, educator, consultant, research scientist*
Huang, Jidong *engineering educator*
Huang, Lan *statistician*
Huang, Rick Y. *application developer*
Huang, Verna D. *music educator*
Huang, Xiao *engineer*
Huang, Yun *application developer, research scientist*
Hubalek, Shirley Kay *music educator, art educator*
Hubbard, Elizabeth *actress*
Hubbard, Gregory Scott *physicist*
Hubbe, Henry Ernest *financial forecaster, trading manager*
Huber, Colleen Adlene *artist*
Huber, David L. *retired prosecutor*
Huber, Wesley David *accountant, lawyer, financial planner, educator*
Hubley, Reginald Allen *publishing executive*
Hubnik, Sandi J. *literature and language professor*
Hubona, Geoffrey Stuart *information systems educator, computer scientist*
Huckabee, Mike (Michael Dale Huckabee) *former Governor of Arkansas*
Hudachek-Buswell, Mary R. *mathematics professor*
Hudak, Thomas F(rancis) *finance company executive*
Huddle, Franklin Pierce, Jr. *diplomat*
Huddleston, Mark *religious studies educator*
Huddleston, Vicki Jean *former ambassador*
Hudkins, John W. *lawyer*
Hudlicka, Eva *research scientist*
Hudnut, Robert Kilborne *clergyman, writer*
Hudnut, William Herbert III *political scientist*
Hudson, Donald J. *retired stock exchange executive*
Hudson, Franklin Donald *manufacturing executive, consultant*
Hudson, Sharon Marie *communications executive*
Hudson, Stanton Harold, Jr. *public relations, development executive, academic administrator, educator*
Huegel, Donna Marie *historian, author*
Hueppi, Rolf *financial services executive*
Huey, Constance Anne Berner *mental health counselor*
Huffington, Anita *sculptor*
Huffman, Brenda S. *information technology executive*
Huffman, Carol Cicolani *retired educational association administrator*
Huffman, Carol Koster *retired middle school educator*
Huffman, Durward Roy *academic administrator, electrical engineer*
Huffman, James Thomas William *oil industry executive*
Huffman, John William *chemist, educator*
Hughes, Ann Hightower *retired economist*
Hughes, Francis P. *medical association administrator*
Hughes, Harry Roe *lawyer, former Governor of Maryland*
Hughes, Mary Alice *adult education educator, consultant*
Hughes, Nicholas Melvin *mining company executive*
Hughes, Pam *retired secondary school educator*
Hughes, Sue Margaret *retired librarian*
Hughes, Thomas C., Jr. *lawyer*
Hughes-Hallett, Karen P. *language educator*
Huja, Sarandeep *orthodontist, educator*
Hulet, Ervin Kenneth *retired nuclear chemist*
Hull, Bobby (Robert Marvin Hull) *retired professional hockey player*
Hull, Brian P. *former investment company executive*
Hull, Clifford, Sr. *retired chemical operator, retired military non commissioned officer, military officer*
Hull, Geordan *finance educator, director*
Hull, Jane Dee *former governor, state legislator*
Hull, McAllister Hobart, Jr. *retired university administrator*
Hull, Richard Thompson *retired philosophy educator, not-for-profit executive*
Huls, Glenna L. *retired sociology educator, photographer*
Hulse, Russell Alan *physicist*
Hulshof, Kenny Charles *former United States Representative from Missouri*
Hultstrand, Donald Maynard *bishop*
Humetewa, Diane J. *former prosecutor*
Humke, Ramon Lyle *utilities executive*
Hummel, Marian *retired art educator, photographer*
Humphrey, Phyllis A. *writer*
Humphreys, Robert Russell *lawyer, arbitrator, consultant*
Humphries, Jefferson *literature and language educator*
Humphries, M. Clayton, Jr. *lawyer*
Hundley, Carol Marie Beckquist *music educator*
Hundt, Reed Eric *management consultant, former federal agency administrator*
Hung, James Chen *engineering educator, consultant*
Hunger, J(ohn) David *business educator*
Huning, Devon Gray *actress, audiologist, dancer, photographer*
Hunnicutt, Victoria Anne Wilson *educational consultant*
Hunsucker, Robert Dudley *physicist, electrical engineer, educator, researcher*
Hunt, Aaron Andrew *music educator*
Hunt, Andrea Wheaton *nurse*
Hunt, Arthur William *communications educator*
Hunt, Helen (Helen Elizabeth Hunt) *actress*
Hunt, Lorraine T. *former lieutenant governor*
Hunt, Oliver Raymond, Jr. *thoracic and cardiovascular surgeon*
Hunt, Sarah Mincey *elementary school educator*
Hunt, William W. *former investment company executive*
Hunter, Duncan Lee *retired United States Representative from California*
Hunter, Frances Ellen Croft *music educator*
Hunter, Jack Duval *retired lawyer*
Hunter, James Edward *chemist, consultant*
Hunter, Jeffrey Glen *finance educator, director*
Hunter, Juanita Walters *minister*
Hunter, Malcolm Llewellyn, Jr. *biology professor*
Hunter-Bowington, Dorothy Diana *educator, consultant*
Huntington, Lawrence Smith *investment banker*
Huntoon, Marc Alan *anesthesiologist, educator*
Huo, Bonnie Kwan *artist*
Huo, Jinshan *materials scientist*
Huppert, George *historian*
Huras, William David *retired bishop*
Hurd, Richard Nelson *pharmaceutical executive*
Hurley, Francis T. *archbishop emeritus*
Hurmuzlu, Yildirim *mechanical engineering educator*
Hurn, D. Kent *retired academic administrator, finance educator*
Huron, Roderick Eugene *minister, writer*
Hurt, William Holman *investment management company executive*
Husarik, Stephen *music educator*
Hushen, John Wallace *manufacturing executive*
Huston, Margo *journalist*
Hut, A. Stephen *lawyer*
Hutcheon, Duncan Elliot *physician educator*
Hutchins, Robert Ayer *architectural consultant*
Hutchinson, Barbara Jane *retired library director, history educator*
Hutchinson, Edna M. *home care nurse*
Hutchinson, Michael Philip *education educator*
Hutson, Henry Critchfield *retired academic administrator*
Huttenback, Robert Arthur *academic administrator, educator*
Hutter, Adolph Matthew, Jr. *cardiologist, educator*
Hutton, Lori *music educator*
Hutton, Timothy *actor*
Huvos, Andrew *internist, cardiologist, educator*
Huynh, My Hang Vo *energetic materials chemist*
Hwang, Cordelia Jong *retired chemist*
Hwang, David Henry *playwright, screenwriter*
Hwang, Jason Kao *composer, violinist, music educator*
Hwang, Jungseek *physics professor, researcher*
Hwang, Myun Joong *research scientist*
Hwynn, Julie Huynh *internal medicine physician*
Hyatt, Kathryn Lees *music educator*
Hybl, William Joseph *lawyer, foundation administrator*
Hyde, Alan Litchfield *retired lawyer*
Hyde, Lawrence Henry, Jr. *manufacturing executive*
Hyde, Tristram Tupper *aeronautical engineer*
Hyland, Geoffrey Fyfe *retired energy executive*
Hynes, Brian *lawyer, lobbyist*
Hynes, Thomas John *academic administrator*
Iamele, Richard Thomas *retired law librarian*
Ibach, Robert Daniel, Jr. *retired library director*
Ibanez, Manuel Luis *academic administrator, biologist, educator*
Ibbs, Charles William *civil engineer, consultant*
Ickert, Rachel Artho *civil engineer*
Idaszak, Jerome Joseph *economic journalist*
Idilbi, Ahmad *physicist, researcher*
Idzik, Daniel Ronald *retired lawyer*
Ienner, Donald S. *former recording industry executive*
Iglehart, Sheralee Hill *elementary school educator, writer*
Iglesias, Maria Estrella *language educator, writer*
Ignatius, Roger *educator, consultant*
Ignatonis, Sandra Carole Autry *retired special education educator*
Ihrig, Colin J. *application developer*
Ijames, Lisa Diane *educator*
Iklé, Richard Adolph *lawyer*
Ilag, Liza Luna *endocrinologist, educator*
Iler, Robert *actor*
Iles, Warthell Browne *retired nursing educator, consultant*
Illanes, Katarina *nephrologist*
Illukpitiya, Prabodh *agriculture economist*
Immel, Barbara Kay Kephart *management consultant*
Immergut, Karin J. *prosecutor*
Impellizzeri, Anne Elmendorf *insurance company executive, non-profit executive*
Imperato, Pascal James *physician, healthcare administrator, writer, historian*
Imperato, Robert L. *religious studies educator*
Imperiale, Michael *medical educator*
Impoco, Jim *editor*
Iñárritu, Alejandro González *film director, producer*
Ingberman, Sima Blumenfeld *real estate company officer*
Ingelfinger, Julie R. *physician, researcher*
Ingersoll, Paul Mills *banker*
Ingham, John Norman *retired history professor*
Ingle, James Newell *oncologist, consultant*
Ingram, Barbara Averett *minister*
Ingram, George Conley *judge*
Ingram, James Carlton *economist, educator*
Ingram, Jerrilyn Jenkins *academic administrator*
Inlow, Rush Osborne *chemist*
Inman, Lydia Lucille *retired university dean*
Innis, Daniel Eugene *dean, consultant*
Inos, Rita Hocog *retired school system administrator*
Inoue, Michael Shigeru *industrial and electrical engineer*

Insalaco-De Nigris, Anna Maria Theresa *middle school educator*
Ioffe, Grigory *geography educator, researcher*
Ipsen, Grant Ruel *state legislator, insurance and investments professional*
Iqbal, Shahed *epidemiologist*
Ireland, Betty *former state official*
Iriart, Celia Beatriz *public health specialist, consultant, researcher, sociologist*
Irving, George Steven *actor*
Irving, Janell NaKia *fundraising consultant*
Irving, Jeffrey Alan *management consultant, educator, lawyer*
Irving, John Winslow (John Wallace Blunt Jr.) *writer*
Irwin, Linda Belmore *public relations/marketing consultant*
Irwin, Nina *neuroscientist, educator*
Irwin, Paul Garfield *minister, social services executive*
Irwin, Peter John *orthopaedic surgeon*
Isaac, Carol A. *physical therapist, researcher*
Isaac, Teresa Ann *former mayor, lawyer*
Isaacs, Jessica B. *literature and language educator, department chairman*
Isaacs, Jonathan William *oil industry executive*
Isaacs, Susan *writer, scriptwriter*
Isbell, Marcia Annette *management consultant*
Isenberg, Jane Frances *writer, retired language educator*
Iserson, Kenneth Victor *bioethicist, writer, medical educator*
Ishaque, Mashhood *application developer, researcher*
Islam, Saleem *pediatric surgeon, researcher*
Ismach, Arnold Harvey *retired journalism educator*
Ismail, Ari *computer scientist*
Ismail, John Y. H. *dentist, prosthodontist*
Ison, John Montgomery *language educator, writer*
Israel, Leo *accountant*
Istook, Ernest James, Jr., (Jim) *former congressman, lawyer*
Ivanchenko, Lauren Margaret Dowd *pharmaceutical executive*
Ivers, Donald Louis *retired federal judge*
Ivers, Louise H. *retired art history professor*
Iverson, Thomas Edwin *retired academic administrator, mathematician, educator*
Ivester, M(elvin) Douglas *investment company executive, retired beverage company executive*
Ivey, Denise Hassell *publishing executive*
Ivey, Elizabeth Spencer *retired physicist, educator*
Ivey, Mary Bradford *counselor, vice president*
Ivie, Evan Leon *computer science educator*
Iwunze, Maurice O. *education educator, researcher*
Ix, Robert Edward *food products executive*
Iyer, Sundar *systems engineer*
Iyigun, Cem *science educator*
Izadi, Behnaz *language educator*
Izadjoo, Mina Jassemzadeh *microbiologist*
Izaguirre, George *retired microbiologist*
Izawa, Chizuko *psychologist, researcher*
Jaber, Suzanne Joy *psychologist*
Jabs, Aura Lee *minister, educator*
Jachimiak, Terry Dana, II, *theater educator*
Jackoboice, Sandra Kay *artist*
Jackson, Alphonso Roy *former United States Secretary of Housing and Urban Development*
Jackson, Barbara Ann Garvey *music educator*
Jackson, Barry Steven *former federal official*
Jackson, Charles Ian *writer, consultant*
Jackson, Deborah Cheryl *mathematician*
Jackson, Felicity Anne *performing arts organization administrator*
Jackson, Guida Myrl *writer, editor, literature educator*
Jackson, Janet *singer, dancer*
Jackson, John Wyant *biotechnology company executive*
Jackson, Kenneth Arthur *physicist, researcher*
Jackson, Miles Merrill *retired university dean*
Jackson, Nagle *stage director, playwright*
Jackson, Phillip Ellis *marketing executive, writer*
Jackson, Robert William *retired utilities executive*
Jackson, Thomas Humphrey *former academic administrator*
Jackson, William Elmer, Jr. *retired packaging company administrator*
Jackson-Vanier, Linda M. *retired art educator, counselor*
Jackson Wright, Adrienne A. *educational consultant*
Jacobi, Bonnie Schaffhauser *music teacher, pianist*
Jacobi, Derek George *actor*
Jacobowitz, Ellen Sue *curator, museum administrator*
Jacobs, Arthur Dietrich *health services executive, educator, researcher*
Jacobs, Bradley S. *former rental company executive*
Jacobs, Deborah Ann *English language educator*
Jacobs, Gretchen Huntley *physician, psychiatrist*
Jacobs, John Patrick *lawyer*
Jacobs, Laurence Stanton *physician, educator*
Jacobs, Marianne *anthropologist, medical/surgical nurse, educator*
Jacobs, Nancy Carolyn Baker *writer*
Jacobs, Richard Alberto *mechanical engineer*
Jacobsen, Diane DeMell *foreign policy specialist*
Jacobson, Dale *physicist, electronics executive*
Jacobson, James Bassett *retired insurance and financial services company executive*
Jacobson, Joan Leiman *writer*
Jacobson, Louis Alan *journalist*
Jacobson, Norman L. *retired agricultural educator, researcher*
Jacoby, Beverly Schreiber *art consultant*
Jacoby, Erika *social worker*
Jacoud, Adriana *art director*
Jae-Il, Kim *research scientist*
Jaffe, Norman *oncologist, educator*
Jagasia, Kaushalya Ghanshyam *secondary school educator*
Jagerman, Adrienne *retired elementary school educator, nurse*
Jahns, Angela Marie *mathematics professor*
Jain, Geetika Pathania *communications educator*
Jain, Sudhanshu *emergency physician, educator*
Jakubauskas, Edward Benedict *college president*
Jakubowski, Marek Krzysztof *research scientist*
Jalba, Mihai Sergiu *epidemiologist, pulmonologist, physician, researcher*
Jalonen, Nancy Lee *professor, arts administrator, educational television producer*
Jambor, Robert Vernon *lawyer*
James, Allix Bledsoe *retired university president*
James, Bruce Richard *publishing executive*
James, Charles Franklin, Jr. *retired engineering educator*
James, Estelle *economist, educator*
James, Kevin *actor*
James, Louis Meredith *personnel executive*
James, Randall S. *former state banking agency administrator*
James, Ronald J. *former civilian military employee, lawyer*
James, William Hall *former state official, educator*
Jameson, Patricia Marian *government agency administrator*
Jamiel, John *theater educator*
Jamison, Daniel Oliver *lawyer*
Jamison, Erica Leigh *psychology educator*
Jamison, John Callison *business educator, investment banker*
Jamison, Philip *artist*
Jamison, Richard *college athletics administrator*
Jampole, Emma Joy *music educator, composer*
Jan, Yuh Nung *biochemistry and physiology educator*
Janczewski, Colleen *social worker*
Janelli, Roger L. *literature and language professor*
Janeway, Richard *retired academic administrator*
Jang, Won-Suk *civil engineer, researcher*
Jang, Young-Il *research and development scientist*
Jangid, Kamlesh *microbiologist*
Janicak, Philip Gregory *psychiatrist, educator*
Janke, Norma E. *legal nursing consultant*
Jankowski, John Edward, Jr. *government administrator*
Janney, Kay Print *retired performing arts educator, theater director*
Jannyavula Venkata, Sumanth *electrical engineer*
Jansen, Angela Bing *artist, educator*
Jansen, Daniel Ervin *former professional speedskater, marketing professional, former olympic athlete*
Jansen, Koen *medical association administrator*
Januszewicz Ekstrom, von Lubitz Dag Konrad *scientist consultant*
Japuntich, Daniel Allan *chemical engineer, researcher*
Jarmusch, Jim *film director, actor*
Jarrett, David G. *emergency physician*
Jarrett, Jeffrey D. *energy companies association executive, former federal agency administrator*
Jaska, Susan Park *retired radar systems engineer*
Jason, Hilliard *physician, educator*
Jasper, Norman Hans *engineer*
Jasti, Srichand *statistician*
Jauhar, Sandeep *physician, director*
Javed, Faizan *application developer*
Javernick, Amy Sue *special education educator*
Javits, Eric Moses *ambassador, lawyer*
Javits, Joshua Moses *lawyer*
Javitt, Daniel C. *psychiatrist, researcher*
Javitt, Gail Hannah *lawyer, educator*
Javitt, Jonathan C. *ophthalmologist*
Jaworski, Justin W. *research scientist*
Jay, Corrigan R. *economics professor*
Jay, Norma Joyce *artist*
Jayaraman, Balaji *research scientist*
Jaynes, Mike *literature and language professor*
Je, Sang-Soo *engineer, researcher*
Jean, Claudette R. *retired elementary school educator*
Jeck, Richard Kahr *research meteorologist*
Jefferson, Monica Louise *nueropsychologist*
Jeffery, Michael *retired government agency administrator*
Jeffords, James Merrill *former United States Senator from Vermont*
Jeffries, Clark D. *mathematician, educator*
Jegga, Anil G. *medical educator*
Jemal, Ahmedin *epidemiologist*
Jen, Joseph Jwu-Shan *academic administrator, former federal agency administrator*
Jen, Philip Hung Sun *science educator, researcher*
Jenai, Marilyn *psychotherapist*
Jenkins, Anthony Jerome *former prosecutor*
Jenkins, Brenda Gwenetta *pre-school administrator, special education educator*
Jenkins, Charles H., Jr. *retail company executive*
Jenkins, Darrell Lee *librarian*
Jenkins, Debra *psychology professor*
Jenkins, Lekelia Danielle *ecologist, researcher*
Jenkins, Richard Dale *actor, theater director*
Jenkins, Stephen Philip *biology professor*
Jennings, Joseph Ashby *banker*
Jennings, Thomas Parks *lawyer*
Jennings, Toni (Antoinette Lee Jennings) *former lieutenant governor, former state senator*
Jennings, Sister Vivien *retired literature and language professor*
Jennison, Brian (Lester) *retired environmental specialist*
Jensen, Arthur Seigfried *retired physicist*
Jensen, Eva Marie *medical/surgical nurse*
Jensen, Nancy Daggett *music educator*
Jepson, Robert Scott, Jr. *bank executive*
Jerdee, Sylvia Ann *retired minister*
Jesse, H. William, Jr. *investment banker*
Jessen, Shirley Agnes *artist*
Jetley, Karun *software company executive, consultant*
Jett, Stephen Clinton *geography and textiles educator, researcher*
Ji, Zhenyu *cell biologist*
Jiang, Bai-Chuan *optical educator*
Jiang, Tianyi *computer company executive*
Jiang, Wei *application developer*
Jiao, Guansheng *medical researcher*
Jiler, Linda Cerise *retired fire and aviation program support specialist, fire emergency dispatcher, consultant, researcher, writer*
Jiménez, Tomás Roberto *sociologist, educator*
Jin, Di *research scientist*
Jin, Guohua *computer scientist, educator*
Jindal, Rohit *medical researcher*
Jing, Xiangpeng *information technology manager*
Joanou, Phillip *advertising executive, artist*
Joel, Billy (William Martin Joel) *musician*
Joel, Katie Lee (Katherine Lee) *television personality*
Joelson, Mark René *lawyer*
Joghi Thatha Gowder, Sivakumar *research scientist*
Johansen, Terri *psychologist*
Johanson, David Richard *lawyer*
Johansson, Alicia Barbara *musician*
Johns, Tammy *employment services executive*
Johns, Warren LeRoi *retired lawyer*
Johnsen, Barbara Parrish *retired writer, educator*
Johnson, Albert Wesley *retired political science professor, public official*
Johnson, Arthur William, Jr. *retired research scientist*
Johnson, Benjamin F., VI, *economist, consultant*
Johnson, Brad *former state official*
Johnson, Bruce E. *former lieutenant governor, state legislator*
Johnson, Camille *media executive*
Johnson, Carl Thor *former federal agency administrator*
Johnson, Charles Felzen *retired medical educator*
Johnson, Charles Lavon, Jr. *clinical neuropsychologist, consultant*
Johnson, Charles Minor *retired physicist*
Johnson, Clay III *former federal official*
Johnson, Craig N. *management consultant*
Johnson, Dale Arthur *church history professor*
Johnson, David *retired lobbyist*
Johnson, David L. *federal agency administrator, retired military officer*
Johnson, David Wilfred, Jr. *ceramics engineer, researcher*
Johnson, Deborah Lorraine *not-for-profit executive, consultant*
Johnson, Denis Hale *writer, poet*
Johnson, Donald Clay *retired librarian, curator*
Johnson, Eugene Laurence *lawyer*
Johnson, Frank Edward *surgeon educator*
Johnson, Freda S. *financial analyst, consultant*
Johnson, Gary Earl *former governor*
Johnson, Hazel Winifred *nurse, retired army officer*
Johnson, Herbert Frederick *sales executive, retired academic administrator, librarian*
Johnson, Irving Stanley *pharmaceutical executive, biomedical research consultant*
Johnson, James Terence *lawyer, writer, minister, educator*
Johnson, Janet Hovey *English language educator*
Johnson, Jay David *writer, consultant*
Johnson, Jeanne Jordan *music educator, department chairman*
Johnson, Jennifer Rose *lawyer*
Johnson, John *broadcast journalist, artist*
Johnson, John Prescott *retired philosophy educator*
Johnson, Joyce *retired military officer*
Johnson, Lael Frederic *lawyer*
Johnson, Laymon, Jr. *management analyst*
Johnson, Lennart Ingemar *materials engineering consultant*
Johnson, Leonard Morris *retired pediatric surgeon*
Johnson, Lois Brooks *retired elementary guidance counselor*
Johnson, Martin Clifton, Sr. *retired physician*
Johnson, Maryann Elaine *educational administrator*
Johnson, Maurice Verner, Jr. *agricultural research and development executive*
Johnson, Michael Warren *international relations specialist*
Johnson, Nichole Sharese *school nurse practitioner, basketball coach*
Johnson, Noel Lars *biomedical engineer*
Johnson, Patricia B. *retired surgical and mental health nurse*
Johnson, Reverdy *lawyer*
Johnson, Richard Tenney *lawyer*
Johnson, Sally A. *nurse, educator*
Johnson, Sandra Kay *music educator*
Johnson, Scott William *former lawyer, manufacturing executive*
Johnson, Stephen L. *former federal agency administrator*
Johnson, Stewart Willard *civil engineer*
Johnson, Suzanne Nora *retired diversified financial services company executive, lawyer*
Johnson, Sylvia Sue *university administrator, educator*
Johnson, William Potter *publishing executive, director*
Johnson, William Ray *insurance company executive*
Johnson, Yvonne Thomas *elementary school educator*
Johnson-Ferrell, June Alexis *counselor, social worker*
Johnson-McKee, Marian *biology professor*
Johnston, Carolyn S. *elementary school educator, reading specialist*
Johnston, Gregory L. *retail executive*
Johnston, John Devereaux, Jr. *retired law educator*
Johnston, Laurance Scott *foundation director, healthcare educator*
Johnston, Lawrence R. (Larry Johnston) *retired food products executive*
Johnston, Phillip Michael *retired museum director, curator*
Johnston, Zenda Jo *special education educator*
Johnstone, D. Bruce *education educator, academic administrator*
Johnstone, Douglas Inge *retired state supreme court justice, lawyer*
Johnstone, Iain Murray *statistician, educator, consultant*
Johnstone, John William, Jr. *retired chemical company executive*
Joliat, Jay Frederick *venture capitalist, marketing consultant*
Jolly, Charles Nelson *lawyer, pharmaceutical executive*
Jonason, Louisa *musician, educator*
Jonckheere, Edmond Alphonse *electrical engineer, consultant*
Jones, Abbott C. *investment company executive*
Jones, Anita Katherine *computer scientist, educator*
Jones, Bettye Wright *education and reading educator*
Jones, Carleton Shaw *information technology executive, lawyer*
Jones, Cecil Paul *retired surgeon*
Jones, Charles Hill, Jr. *banker*
Jones, Christine Massey *retired furniture company executive*
Jones, Claire Burtchaell *artist, educator, writer*
Jones, Cleopatra Celeste *retired gerontologist, sociologist, educator*
Jones, Constance Coralie *retired music educator*
Jones, David Charles *former Chairman of the Joint Chiefs of Staff*
Jones, Douglas Wiley *lawyer*
Jones, Edith Hollan *federal judge*
Jones, Edward Paul *writer, editor*
Jones, Elaine R. *former legal association administrator, civil rights advocate*
Jones, Frank Joseph *retired securities exchange executive*
Jones, George L. *retail executive*
Jones, Gerre Lyle *marketing and public relations consultant*
Jones, Jack Bristol *education educator*
Jones, Joe Kenley *journalist*
Jones, John *materials engineer*
Jones, John Harris *retired lawyer*
Jones, Joshua *military officer*
Jones, Keith Alden *lawyer*
Jones, Kellie *medical educator*
Jones, Lawrence Neale *retired dean, minister*
Jones, Leander Corbin *history professor, media specialist*
Jones, Lisa Maria Draper *counselor*
Jones, Lupe Sirena *insurance agent*
Jones, Norma Dell *association executive*
Jones, Peter d'Alroy *historian, writer, retired educator*
Jones, Phyllis Gene *judge*
Jones, Richard Hunn *biostatistician, researcher, educator*
Jones, Robert Henry *automotive distribution executive*
Jones, Ruth A. *retired secondary school educator*
Jones, Shirley *actress, singer*
Jones, Suejette Albritton *basic skills educator*
Jones, Thomas Claburn *poet, educator*
Jones, Thomas Owen *computer company executive*
Jones, Wayne Allen *psychotherapist, publisher*
Jones, William Adrian *musician, educator, program developer*
Jones, William Rex *law educator*
Jones-Eddy, Julie Margaret *retired librarian*
Jones-Webb, Rhonda Jean *epidemiologist, educator*
Jong, Ing-Chang *engineering educator*
Jonsen, Eric Richard *lawyer*
Jordan, Deovina Nasis *nursing administrator, educator*
Jordan, Howard Emerson *retired engineering executive, consultant*
Jordan, James Lowell *writer, educator*
Jordan, Jerry Dale *lawyer, gas industry executive*
Jordan, Lisa Anne *dancer, educator*
Jordan, Marvin Evans, Jr. *record company executive, vocalist, actor, composer*
Jordan, Michelle Denise *judge*
Jordan, Nikisa S. *environmental scientist*
Jordan, Richard Charles *pathologist, educator*
Jordan, Robert Reed *retired geologist, educator*
Jordan, Robert Smith *political science professor, civilian military employee*
Joselyn, Jo Ann *space scientist*
Joseph, Elizabeth *literature and language professor*
Joseph, J. Jonathan *interior designer*
Joseph, Michael Thomas *broadcast consultant*
Joseph, Ramon Rafael *internist, educator*
Joseph, Robert G. *former federal agency administrator*
Josephs, Kelly Baker *literature and language educator*
Josephson, Kenneth Bradley *artist, retired educator*
Joshi, Bharat *engineering educator*
Jourdan, Toni Christina *small business owner, actress, writer*
Jow, Shin-Yao *mathematics professor*
Judell, Harold Benn *lawyer*
Jugulum, Rajesh *engineer, researcher*
Juliá, Mercedes *literature and language professor*
Juliber, Lois D. *retired consumer products company executive*
Jumper, John Phillip *retired military officer*
Jun, Jangeun *computer engineer*
Jun, Soojin *medical educator, researcher*
Jung, Kwan Yee *artist*
Jung, Rodney C. *internist, academic administrator*
Jung, Woo *special education educator, researcher*
Jungeberg, Thomas Donald *lawyer*
Junger, Sebastian *writer*
Juran, Sylvia Louise *retired editor*
Jurgelski, Annette Elizabeth *retired academic administrator*
Jurgensen, Barbara *writer*
Juricic, Davor *engineering educator*
Jurkovic, Sinisa *electrical engineer, researcher*
Jurkowitz, Daniel S. *lawyer, prosecutor, judge*
Juskowiak, Terry Eugene *career military officer, information technology executive*
Juviler, Peter Henry *political scientist, educator*
Kaakaji, Wayel *neurosurgeon, educator*
Kaback, David Brian *molecular biologist*
Kaback, Michael *medical educator*
Kabel, Robert Lynn *emeritus chemical engineering professor*
Kachuck, Beatrice *retired education educator, women's studies educator*
Kacines, Juliette Rosette *dialectical behavior therapist*
Kaczmarek, Zdzislaw *environmental engineer, scientist, educator*
Kadambi, Narasimha Prasad *nuclear engineer*
Kaddoum, Roland *anesthesiologist, researcher*

Kadel, Lee A. *information security analyst*
Kadota, Takashi Theodore *mathematician, electrical engineer*
Kaehele, Bettie Louise *accountant*
Kahana, Eva Frost *sociology educator*
Kahn, Herta Hess (Mrs. Howard Kahn) *retired investment company executive*
Kahn, James Steven *retired museum director*
Kahn, Steven Michael *astrophysicist, educator*
Kahn, Susan *artist*
Kahn, Victoria Elaine Hopkins *special education educator*
Kaiser, Robert A. *telecommunications industry executive*
Kaiser, Suzanne Billo *investment banker, writer*
Kaisershot, A. Kevin *composer*
Kalaany, Nada Y. *biomedical researcher*
Kalafatoglu, Tugba *marketing and public relations professional, business and political communications consultant*
Kalaitzidou, Kyriaki *engineering educator*
Kalbacken, Joan Muriel *foreign language educator, author*
Kalbfleisch, John McDowell *retired cardiologist*
Kalemli-Ozcan, Sebnem *economics professor*
Kalin, Ronald V. *electrical engineer*
Kaling, Mindy *actress, scriptwriter, television producer*
Kaliski, Lucy Anne *science educator, consultant*
Kalkstein, Laurence Saul *geography educator*
Kallay, Michael Frank, II, *medical products executive*
Kallenberg, John Kenneth *retired librarian*
Kallgren, Edward Eugene *lawyer*
Kalo, Michele Christine *music educator*
Kamalasadan, Sukumar *electrical and computer engineering educator, researcher*
Kamarajan, Chella *medical researcher*
Kambach, Bel *travel & tourism educator*
Kambutu, John *adult education educator*
Kamel, Haidy Nasr *pharmacist*
Kamerick, Eileen Ann *financial executive, lawyer*
Kamerin, Kim K. *music educator*
Kamin, Blair Douglass *architecture critic*
Kaminski, Janusz Zygmunt *cinematographer*
Kaminski, Patricia Joyce *lab administrator*
Kaminsky, Alice Richkin *retired literature educator*
Kamrin, Michael Arnold *toxicology educator*
Kan, Marni L. *psychologist*
Kanarfogel, Ephraim *religious studies professor*
Kander, John Harold *composer*
Kandula, Praveen *medical educator*
Kane, Cynthia A. *retired special education educator*
Kane, Frank Lester *physician*
Kane, Karen Marie *public affairs consultant*
Kane, Michael Barry *social science research executive*
Kang, Chang Yong *electrical engineer, researcher*
Kang, Kyongha *materials scientist*
Kang, Steven S. *surgeon*
Kang, Un Jung *neurologist, educator*
Kannan, Govind *engineer, researcher*
Kanter, Jolie Lynn *psychologist*
Kantor, Mark Alan *lawyer, arbitrator*
Kanuk, Leslie Lazar *management consultant, educator*
Kao, Tzu-Jen *research scientist*
Kaplan, Aaron Val *cardiologist, educator*
Kaplan, Gabriela Diana *radiologist*
Kaplan, Harriet Smith *psychiatrist, educator*
Kaplan, Helene Lois *lawyer*
Kaplan, Justin *medical educator*
Kaplan, Leonard Eugene *accountant*
Kaplan, Richard Alan *government official*
Kaplan, Richard James *film producer and director, educator, consultant, scriptwriter*
Kaplan, Robert B. *linguistics educator, consultant, researcher*
Kaplan, Susan *retired lawyer*
Kaplowitz, Neil *gastroenterologist, educator*
Kapnick, Richard Bradshaw *lawyer*
Kapur, Amit *former Internet company executive*
Karacaovali, Baybars *economics professor*
Karalekas, Anne *media executive*
Karalis, John Peter *computer company executive, lawyer*
Karanovich, Milenko *educator, researcher*
Karasik, Miriyam Beth *artist, musician, writer*
Karayanis, Plato Steven *opera company executive*
Karben, Shelley Valerie *elementary and special education educator*
Karchov, Michael *electronics executive*
Karetzky, Stephen *library director, educator, writer, researcher*
Karhade, Omkar *research scientist*
Karim, Jawed *Internet company executive, application developer*
Karim, Muhammad Bazlul *political scientist, educator*
Karle, Isabella L. *chemist*
Karle, Jerome *physicist, researcher*
Karol, Michael Alan *editor*
Karoui, Abdennaceur *physics professor*
Karp, Donald Mathew *lawyer, banker*
Karp, Rosanne *oncology and women's health nurse*
Karraker, Angela Rene *special education educator*
Karre, Kathleen Mary *lawyer*
Karson, Samuel *psychologist, educator*
Kartha, Kutty Krishnan *retired plant pathologist*
Karuna, Christo *finance educator*
Kaser, David *retired librarian, educator, consultant*
Kashcheyeva, Olga *mathematics professor, researcher*
Kashyap, Purna Chandra *gastroenterologist*
Kasi, Vijay *management consultant*
Kaskowitz, Edwin *social services executive*
Kaslick, Ralph Sidney *dentist, educator*
Kaslow, Florence Whiteman *psychologist, educator, family business consultant*
Kass, Mary Elizabeth *pathologist, hospital administrator*
Kastenbaum, Robert Jay *life course educator, researcher*
Kastenmeier, Robert William *former Congressman*
Kaster, Laura A. *lawyer*
Kastor, Frank Sullivan *language educator*
Kataoka, Teruyuki *engineer, researcher*
Katazkos, Victoria Elena *nurse*
Katers, Nicholas *history professor*
Katona, Peter Geza *biomedical engineer, educator*
Katsiyannis, Antonis *school administrator*
Katz, Colleen *publisher*
Katz, Jeffrey A. *television and radio personality, newspaper columnist, public speaker*
Katz, Lawrence Sheldon *lawyer*
Katz, Natasha *lighting designer*
Katz, Sanford Noah *lawyer, educator*
Katz, William Loren *author*
Katz, William Michael *writer*
Katzenbach, Nicholas deBelleville *former United States Attorney General*
Kauffman, B. Suzanne *historian, genealogist*
Kaufman, David Joseph *lawyer*
Kaufman, Lawrence Charles *professional chess player*
Kaufman, Stephen Lawrence *radiologist, educator*
Kaul, Sanjeev A. *urologist, consultant*
Kaulaity, Marlinda *literature and language educator*
Kaur, Judith Salmon *oncologist*
Kaushal, Shalesh *ophthalmologist, biochemist*
Kaushik, Prashant *rheumatologist, educator*
Kavakci, Merve *social sciences educator*
Kavalek, Lubomir *chess expert*
Kavanaugh, Frank James *film producer, educator*
Kavesh, Eden *fraud investigator, financial consultant*
Kavli, Fred *retired manufacturing and engineering executive, physicist*
Kay, Irene Pramisloff *school system administrator*
Kay, Joshua B. *attorney, educator*
Kaylan, Howard Lawrence *musical entertainer, screenwriter, composer*
Kaymak, Baris *environmental engineer*
Kaz, Nathaniel *sculptor*
Kaza, Aditya K. *physician*
Kazakov, Aleksey V. *architectural designer, artist*
Kazan, Alexandra Khan *photographer, web designer*
Keala, Betty Ann Lyman *computer scientist*
Keala, Francis Ahloy *security executive*
Kean, Joanne Aylsworth *retired secondary school educator*
Kearney, John D. *history professor*
Kearns, James Joseph *artist*
Kearns, Merle Grace *state agency administrator*
Kearns-Simmons, Shannon Marie *theater educator, director*
Keatinge, Robert Reed *lawyer*
Keaton, Michael *actor, comedian*
Keaton, William Thomas *academic administrator, pastor*
Kebrle, John Michael *aerospace engineer*
Keech, Elowyn Ann *interior designer*
Keegan, John Charles *former mayor, retired military officer, former state legislator*
Keele, Zudora Brown *school librarian*
Keeler, James Leonard *food products executive*
Keeler, William Henry Cardinal *cardinal, archbishop emeritus*
Keeling, J(ohn) Michael *lawyer, trade association executive*
Keenan, Anthony Lee *trucking executive*
Keenan, Mike (Micheal Edward Keenan) *former professional hockey coach, professional sports team executive*
Keene-Burgess, Ruth Frances *military official*
Keeney, Virginia T. *retired child psychiatrist*
Keenum, Mark Everett *former federal agency administrator*
Keeny, Spurgeon Milton, Jr. *professional society administrator*
Keffer, Charles Joseph *retired physics professor, academic administrator*
Kehew, George Mansir *artist*
Kehler, Dorothea Faith *retired English educator*
Kehlmann, Robert *artist, critic*
Kehoe, L. Paul *state judge*
Kehoe, Nita L. *art educator, gallery director*
Kehrer, Tracy Carl *chemical engineer*
Keil, M. David *retired international association executive*
Keill, Stuart Langdon *psychiatrist*
Keim, Betty Lou *actress, literary consultant*
Keith, Kelly Ann *language educator*
Keith, Robert William *banker*
Keith, Toby (Toby Keith Covel) *country singer, songwriter, producer*
Keith, William Douglas *lawyer*
Kekatpure, Rohan D. *research scientist*
Kelder, Dorothy Mae *science educator*
Kelehear, Carole Marchbanks Spann *legal assistant*
Kellar, William Henry *retired academic administrator, historian, educator*
Kelleher, Herbert David *retired air transportation executive, lawyer*
Kelleher, Kathleen *marketing professional*
Keller, Gail *psychologist, consultant*
Keller, Nadya Clark *retired biochemistry educator, researcher*
Keller, Paul *retired advertising executive researcher*
Keller, Ric (Richard A. Keller) *lawyer, former United States Representative from Florida*
Keller, Sarah Natasha *communications educator*
Kelley, Edward Allen *publisher*
Kelley, James Francis *lawyer*
Kelling, Angela S. *psychology professor*
Kellogg, Kathy *psychologist*
Kellogg, Peter R. *securities dealer*
Kelly, Anthony Odrian *textiles executive*
Kelly, Beverly Ann *elementary school educator*
Kelly, Charles Arthur *lawyer*
Kelly, Craig James *retired bank executive*
Kelly, Lucie Stirm Young *retired nursing educator*
Kelly, Michele Patrice *neuroscientist, researcher*
Kelly, Paul V. *lawyer, former sports association administrator*
Kelly, Sue W. (Susan Weisenbarger Kelly) *consulting firm executive, former congresswoman*
Kelly, Timothy Johnston *secondary school educator*
Kelsch, Phyllis Arlene *assistant principal*
Kelso, Charlotte Elizabeth *elementary school educator, health and physical education specialist*
Kemp, Aaron Shane *neuropsychiatry, researcher*
Kempe, Janet *elementary school educator*
Kemper, John Dustin *mechanical engineering educator*
Kempf, Donald G., Jr. *retired lawyer*
Kempisty, Michael *artist, writer*
Kempner, Jonathan L. *lobbyist*
Kempner, Maximilian Walter *dean, lawyer*
Kempthorne, Dirk Arthur *former United States Secretary of the Interior*
Kemraj, Bharati S. *reporter, television producer*
Kendall, Dorothy Irene *secondary school educator*
Kendig, William Lamar *retired federal official, financial manager*
Kendrick, Beverly Ann *medical/surgical nurse, small business owner*
Kendrick, Budd Leroy *psychologist*
Kendrick, Peter Murray *communications executive, investor*
Kennan, Dan *counselor*
Kennard, Lydia H. *former airport terminal executive*
Kennedy, Cynthia Carolyn Marshall *language educator*
Kennedy, Jonny D. *language educator*
Kennedy, Karen Syence *advertising agency executive*
Kennedy, Leo Raymond *engineering executive*
Kennedy, Mark Raymond *former congressman*
Kennedy, Maydra Jane Penisson (J.P. Kennedy) *poet*
Kennedy, Megan Catherine *music educator*
Kennedy, Sheryl J. *elementary school educator*
Kennedy, Thomas J. *lawyer*
Kennett, Lee Boone, Jr. *historian, educator*
Kenney, Estelle Koval *artist, educator*
Kenney-Baden, Linda *lawyer*
Kenny, Charles Francis *lawyer, educator*
Kenny, Robert Wade *sociology, ethics and rhetoric educator*
Kenny, Shirley Strum *retired academic administrator*
Kenrich, John Lewis *retired lawyer*
Kent, Gary Warner *film director, writer*
Kent, Matthew *law clerk*
Kenworthy, William Eugene *judge*
Keohane, Nannerl Overholser *political scientist, academic administrator*
Kercheval, John William III *finance professor, aerospace and defense executive, vulture capitalist, former investment banker*
Kerins, Francis Joseph *college president*
Kern, Charles William *retired academic administrator, chemist, educator*
Kern, Eugene Barton *plastic surgeon, director*
Kern, Irving John *retired food company executive*
Kern, Martin *social studies educator*
Kern, Ronald Paul *dean, consultant*
Kernan, Barbara Desind *government agency administrator*
Kerr, Donald MacLean, Jr. *federal official, physicist*
Kerr, Frederick Hohmann *retired health facility and academic administrator*
Kerr, Gregory Peter *biology professor*
Kerr Walker, Joi Mechelle *literacy educator, consultant*
Kertzer, David Israel *academic administrator, anthropology educator, writer*
Keshavanarayana, Suresh *engineering educator, researcher*
Kessler, Edwin *meteorology educator, consultant*
Kessler, Gale Suzanne *psychologist, educator*
Kester, Helen Mary *minister*
Ketchie, Diane *singer, music educator*
Ketchum, Peradine Elizabeth *elementary school educator*
Kettelkamp, Donald Benjamin *retired orthopedist*
Keum, JongMin *research scientist*
Kevles, Bettyann Holtzmann *writer, historian, educator*
Key, Shawnda R. *elementary school educator*
Keyes, Alan Lee *political activist, radio talk show host, former diplomat*
Keyes, James Henry *retired manufacturing executive*
Keyes, Joan Ross Rafter *education educator, writer*
Keynton, Robert S. *engineering educator*
Keys, John W. III *former federal agency administrator*
Keys, Martha Elizabeth *former congresswoman*
Keywood, Kay Hill *mathematics educator, small business owner*
Kezlarian, Nancy Kay *marriage and family therapist*
Khachemoune, Amor *physician*
Khaligh, Alireza *engineering educator*
Khalil, DiaaEldin *integrated circuit research & development engineer*
Khalil, Imane *mechanical engineer, educator*
Khalilzad, Zalmay Mamozy *former Permanent United States Representative to the United Nations*
Khan, Abu M. *physics professor*
Khan, Ahmed Mohiuddin *insurance company executive*
Khan, Ahsan Yaqoob *psychiatrist, educator*
Khan, Fareesa Ghousia *gynecologist*
Khan, Mohamed K. *oncologist, educator*
Khan, Sohel *principal engineer*
Khatena, Joe *psychology professor*
Khatib, Kathy *school administrator, educator*
Khersonsky, Yuri *retired research and development company executive*
Khodier, Majid Mahmoud *engineering educator, researcher*
Khokhar, M. Inam *language educator*
Khoroshev, Mark I. *electrical engineer, consultant*
Khosla, Ved Mitter *oral and maxillofacial surgeon, educator*
Khuong, Loc Huu *finance educator*
Khuri, Marcus A. *mathematics professor*
Khvost-Vostrikova, Natalia S. *art educator, consultant*
Kidd, Michael Hayden *translator, educator*
Kieffer, Tara L. *virologist*
Kiel, Jeff E. *former publishing executive*
Kiely, Dan Ray *fund manager, real estate company executive, consultant*
Kienitz, LaDonna Trapp *lawyer, librarian, municipal official*
Kiesler, Charles Adolphus *psychologist, academic administrator*
Kihega, Harold G. *biology professor*
Kikareas, Panagiotis *foundation administrator, retired military officer*
Kilbourn, William Douglas, Jr. *law educator*
Kilby, Heidi Lynn *psychologist, educator*
Kildee, Jennifer *translator, editor*
Kilgore, Rebecca S. *secondary school educator*
Kilgus, Edward Chip *singer, actor, writer, poet*
Killeen, Michael John *lawyer*
Killian, William Paul *manufacturing executive*
Killinger, Kerry Kent *retired bank executive*
Kilmann, Ralph Herman *business educator*
Kilpatrick, James Jackson, Jr. *retired columnist, retired writer*
Kim, Caroline Choi *dermatologist, director*
Kim, Chwail *research scientist*
Kim, Deok-Ho *biomedical researcher*
Kim, Do Nyeon *research scientist*
Kim, Doh-Khul *economics professor*
Kim, Dow *investment company executive*
Kim, Ellen Ye *music educator*
Kim, Heather *director*
Kim, Hee-Young *otolaryngologist*
Kim, Minju *educator*
Kim, Ryoung-han *research scientist*
Kim, Sang Wu *engineering educator*
Kim, Sarang *medical educator*
Kim, Soonhyang *literature and language professor*
Kimball, Alexa Boer *dermatologist*
Kimbrell, Deborah Ann *geneticist, educator*
Kimes, Alane S. *medical researcher*
Kim-Farley, Robert James *epidemiologist, educator*
Kim Jong Il, *Democratic People's Republic of Korea Supreme Leader*
Kimmel, Mark *author, venture capital company executive*
Kimmitt, Mark (Mark Traecey Patrick Kimmitt) *former federal agency administrator, retired military officer*
Kimura, Suguru Roy *pharmaceutical executive, researcher*
Kincannon, Charles Louis (Louis Kincannon) *retired federal agency administrator*
Kind, Joshua B. *retired art history professor*
Kindberg, Shirley Jane *pediatrician*
Kinder, Suzanne Fonay Wemple *retired historian, educator*
King, Alfred Meehan *financial executive*
King, Algin Braddy *retired marketing educator*
King, Amy Cathryne Patterson *retired mathematics educator, researcher*
King, Cynthia Bregman *writer*
King, David A. *aerospace engineer*
King, Hueston Clark *retired otolaryngologist, educator*
King, Jack A. *lawyer*
King, James Calvin *mathematics educator*
King, Jane Cudlip Coblentz *volunteer educator*
King, John *composer, musician*
King, Joy Riemer *art educator, linguist*
King, Larry L. *playwright, actor*
King, Michael Howard *lawyer*
King, Paul J. *orthopedist*
King, Philip Gordon *public relations counselor*
King, Quintin L. *trade association administrator, lobbyist*
King, Rebecca J. *lawyer, consultant*
King, Robert Lucien *retired lawyer*
King, Robert Thomas *editor, writer*
King, Ronald Lee *retired accountant, government agency administrator*
King, Rosalyn Mercita *social sciences educator, psychologist, researcher*
King, Sheldon Selig *health facility administrator, educator*
King, Sheryl Jayne *retired secondary school educator, counselor*
King, Susan Marie *retired special education educator*
King, William Collins *retired oil industry executive*
Kingdon, Henry Shannon *retired internist, biochemist, science administrator*
Kingdon, Robert McCune *historian, educator*
Kingsbery, Walton Waits, Jr. *retired accounting firm executive*
Kingston, Maxine Hong *writer, educator*
Kinnear, Greg *actor, film producer*
Kinnison, Willard Wayne *physics professor*
Kinrys, Gustavo *psychiatrist, director*
Kinsey, Angela *actress*
Kinslow, Margie Ann *volunteer*
Kinzie, Jeannie Jones *radiation oncologist, nuclear medicine physician*
Kipniss, Robert *artist*
Kipniss MacDonald, Betty Ann *artist, educator*
Kipper, Barbara Levy *wholesale distribution executive*
Kircher, Kimberly Lauren *behavior analyst, educational consultant*
Kirchmeier, Emmalou Handford *minister, writer*
Kirk, Carmen Zetler *data processing executive and science fiction writer*
Kirk, Donald Evan *electrical engineering educator, dean*
Kirk, John Robert, Jr. *retired lawyer, consultant*
Kirkland, Glenda Anderson *music educator*
Kirkland, Rebecca Trent *endocrinologist*
Kirkland, Virgil Wayne *retired electrical engineer*
Kirkpatrick, Charles Harvey *immunologist, researcher*
Kirkpatrick, Kent *political science professor*
Kirkpatrick, Ronald Crecelius *aerospace engineer, researcher*
Kirsch, Nancy Rosenthal *physical therapist, educator*
Kirsch, Nathan C. *retired pharmaceutical executive, consultant*
Kirsch, Roslyn Ruth *artist, painter, printmaker, educator*
Kirsteuer, Ernst Karl Eberhart *biologist, curator*
Kirtman, Bernard *chemistry professor*
Kirwan, R. DeWitt (Kyle) *lawyer*
Kiryluk, Krzysztof *nephrologist, researcher*

Kiser, Colin Lee *military officer, government contractor*
Kiser, Jackson L. *federal judge*
Kiser, Nagiko Sato *retired librarian*
Kish, Kathleen V. *academic administrator*
Kisor, Henry Du Bois *retired editor, columnist, critic, writer*
Kiss, Ronald K. *naval architect*
Kissinger, Henry Alfred *international consulting company executive, former United States Secretary of State*
Kister, James Milton *retired mathematician, educator*
Kistiakowsky, Vera *physical researcher, educator*
Kist-Tahmasian, Candace Lynee *psychologist*
Kitchen, Paul Howard *hockey historian*
Kitchka, Jennifer Lyn *psychologist*
Kitridou, Rodanthi C. *medical educator*
Kitt, Tom *composer, musician*
Kivikoski, Asko Ilmari *retired obstetrician, gynecologist*
Kizilisik, Aydin Tarik *surgeon, researcher*
Kjersten, Erin R. *social services administrator*
Klaehne, Eberhard O.W. *pharmaceutical executive, chemist*
Klafter, Cary Ira *lawyer*
Klamon, Lawrence Paine *lawyer*
Klampe, Craig Allen *composer*
Klarich, David John *lobbyist, lawyer*
Klaus, Charles *retired lawyer*
Klausner, Richard Daniel *cell biologist, researcher*
Klaviter, Helen Lothrop *magazine editor, retired*
Klearman, Kimberly J. *lighting designer*
Kleiman, Alan Boyd *artist*
Klein, Bernard Joseph *management specialist*
Klein, Charlotte Conrad *public relations executive*
Klein, Chuck *retired private investigator, writer*
Klein, Edward *writer*
Klein, James Edgar *actor*
Klein, Linda Ann *lawyer*
Klein, Lynn Ellen *artist*
Klein, Marc *retired neuroscientist*
Klein, Martin *ocean engineering consultant*
Klein, Mary Ann *special education educator*
Klein, Michael Stuart *former diversified financial services company executive*
Klein, Susan Elaine *librarian*
Kleinlein, Kathy Lynn *training and development executive*
Kleinsorge, William Peter *metallurgical engineer*
Klemens, Thomas Lloyd *editor*
Klemm, John Donald, Jr. *finance company executive, director*
Klesse, William R. (Bill Klesse) *energy executive*
Klett, Gordon A. *retired savings and loan association executive*
Klett, James Dean *physicist, consultant, small business owner*
Kliebhan, Sister M(ary) Camille *academic administrator*
Klimo, Paul *neurosurgeon*
Klinck, Cynthia Anne *retired library director*
Kline, Frank Menefee *psychiatrist*
Kline, John P. *psychologist, researcher*
Kline, Leona Ruth *nurse, volunteer*
Kline, Norman Douglas *retired judge*
Klinghoffer, Judith Apter *historian, consultant*
Klippert, Richard Hobdell, Jr. *engineering executive*
Klotman, Robert Howard *retired music educator*
Klott, David Lee *lawyer*
Kloves, Steven *film director, scriptwriter*
Klute, Allan Aloys *retired physicist, retired economist*
Knapp, Lonnie Troy *elementary school educator*
Knapp, Thomas Joseph *lawyer*
Knappen, Mary *mathematics educator*
Knaub, Clete *engineering educator*
Knefel, Ann Margaret *researcher*
Knickrehm, Glenn Allen *management executive*
Knies, Robert Carl, Jr. *critical care nurse*
Knight, Billy (William R. Knight) *former professional sports team executive*
Knight, Eric A. *aerospace executive, entrepreneur, inventor*
Knight, Francine *administrative assistant, economics professor*
Knight, Gary *lawyer, writer, educator*
Knight, Herbert Borwell *manufacturing executive*
Knight, James Arthur *agricultural studies educator*
Knight, Margaret L. *librarian, educator*
Knight, Patricia Marie *biomedical engineer, consultant*
Knighten, Latrenda *elementary school educator, consultant*
Knobloch, Ferdinand J. *psychiatrist, educator*
Knockemus, Mark *engineering educator, director*
Knollenberg, Joseph Castl (Joe Knollenberg) *former United States Representative from Michigan*
Knott, Wiley Eugene *retired electronics engineer*
Knowles, Julie Nall *secondary school educator*
Knowles, Richard Norris *chemist*
Knowles, Tony (Anthony Carroll Knowles) *former governor*
Knox, James Russell, Jr. *biophysical chemistry educator*
Knoxville, Johnny (Philip John Clapp) *actor*
Knupps, Terri Crouse *music educator*
Knutsen, Gregg Evan *transportation executive*
Ko, Jonghan *agronomist*
Kobashigawa, Suzan *educator*
Kobayashi, Koichi S. *immunologist, educator*
Kobza, Donna Ann *special education educator, consultant*
Kocel, Katherine Merle *psychology professor, researcher*
Koch, Margaret Rau *writer, artist, historian*
Koch, Molly Brown *parent educator*
Koch, Patricia W. *media specialist*
Koch, Virginia Greenleaf (Virginia M. Greenleaf) *painter*
Kocherginsky, Nikolai M. *chemistry educator*
Koelmel, Lorna Lee *data processing executive*
Koenig, Allen Edward *higher education consultant*
Koenig, Maureen Catherine *science educator*
Koenig, Thomas Howard *social studies educator*
Koenigstein, David *librarian, educator*
Koepke, Allen Henry *music educator, composer*
Koerber, Dolores Jean *music educator*
Koffler, Aviele Melissa *psychologist*
Kogan, Esther *education educator, director*
Kogan, Richard J. *former pharmaceutical company executive*
Koglin, Terry Lee *mechanical engineer, consultant*
Kohan, Dennis Lynn *finance educator*
Kohn, Jean Gatewood *retired health facility administrator, pediatrician*
Kohn, Liberty Lee *language educator*
Kohrman, Arthur Fisher *pediatrics educator*
Kohrt, Carl Fredrick *former research and development institute executive*
Koka, Sai Sudha *research scientist*
Kolaitis, Marinna Mallis *language educator, writer*
Kolb, Gloria Ro *medical products executive*
Kolb, Harold Hutchinson, Jr. *language educator*
Kolb, James A. *science foundation director, writer*
Kolbe, Jim (James Thomas Kolbe) *former United States Representative, Arizona*
Kolenda, Joanne L. *elementary and secondary school educator, volunteer*
Koletsky, Alan Jared *oncologist, educator*
Kolevar, Kevin M. *investment company executive, former federal agency administrator*
Kollaer, Jim C. *real estate executive, architect*
Koller, Loren D. *veterinary medicine educator*
Kollias, Jim Harry *music educator*
Kolmanovsky, Ilya *aerospace and automotive engineer, researcher*
Kolodny, Stephen Arthur *lawyer*
Kolodziejski, Vinci J. *artist, educator*
Koltun, Frances Lang *editor, publisher, broadcaster*
Komar, Vitaly *artist*
Komechak, Marilyn Gilbert *retired psychologist, writer*
Komisar, David Daniel *retired academic administrator*
Komisarjevsky, Christopher P.A. *retired public relations executive*
Konchitsky, Alon *electronics engineer, communications executive*
Konduru, Srinivasa *economics professor*
Koneru, Vamsi Krishna *psychologist*
Kong, Soon-Cheol *research scientist*
Konner, Joan Weiner *academic administrator, writer, educator, television producer and retired executive*
Kono, Toshihiko *cellist*
Konola, Claudette June *consultant*
Konwinski, Lisa Michele *federal official, lawyer*
Koo, George Ping Shan *business consultant*
Koo, Shou-Eng *economics professor*
Koo, Simon G.M. *engineering educator*
Kooijmans, Pieter Hendrik *former judge*
Kooluris Dobbs, Linda Kia *artist, photographer*
Kopan, Raphael *molecular biologist, consultant, medical educator, researcher*
Kopelson, Arnold *film producer*
Koperski, Nanci Carol *legal nurse consultant, women's health nurse*
Kopielski, Camille Ann *counseling administrator, volunteer*
Koplan, Stephen *former federal official*
Kopp, Achim *language educator*
Kopytine, Mikhail L. *physicist*
Kordahi, Maurice *mechanical engineer, director*
Kordish, Heike Christiane *retired library director*
Koren, Edward Benjamin *cartoonist, educator*
Korenic, Lynette Marie *librarian*
Korinek, Karl *retired judge, law educator*
Kormondy, Edward John *retired academic administrator, science educator*
Korn, Jessica Susan *research scientist, educator, program manager*
Kornel, Ludwig *medical educator, physician, scientist*
Kornhaber, Donna Marie *theater educator*
Korobkov, Alexander *engineer*
Korologos, Ann McLaughlin *communications executive, former United States Secretary of Labor*
Korotkova, Olga *physics professor*
Kosik, Daniel W. *physics professor*
Kosner, Edward A(lan) *editor*
Kossina, Mary Helen *retired elementary school educator*
Kosslyn, Stephen M. *psychologist, educator*
Kostic, Dina *musician, educator*
Koszarski, Richard *film historian, curator*
Kotcher, Shirley J.W. *lawyer*
Koten, John F. *editor-in-chief*
Kothary, Nishita *radiologist, consultant*
Kotter, John Paul *organizational behavior educator, management consultant*
Kottkamp, Jeffrey Dean *Lieutenant Governor of Florida, lawyer*
Kotz, Nathan Kallison (Nick Kotz) *news correspondent, author*
Kounavis, Michael E. *research scientist*
Koutal, Reuben Kamiar *mechanical engineer*
Kovach, Andrew Louis *human resources specialist, consultant*
Kovach, Bill *educational foundation administrator*
Kovacs, Malcolm *sociologist, educator*
Kozak, Elizabeth *biology professor*
Koziara, Gene (Eugene Harry) *retired aerospace engineer, operations research analyst economist, systems analyst*
Koziol, Christopher Jude *architecture professor*
Kozlowski, Rob *performing arts educator*
Krabbe, Thomas Joseph *music educator*
Kraft, Yvette *art educator*
Kraimer, Rebecca *environmental scientist*
Krakower, Bernard Hyman *management consultant*
Kramer, Dale Vernon *retired language educator*
Kramer, Gerhard *electrical engineer, educator*
Kramer, Keith Allan *music educator, composer*
Kramer, Kenneth Bentley *retired federal judge, former congressman*
Kramer, Peter Robin *computer company executive, artist*
Kramer, Richard Jay *gastroenterologist, educator*
Kramp, Suzan Marie *systems programmer*
Krantz, Steven George *mathematics professor, writer*
Kratt, Peter George *lawyer*
Kraus, Jan P. *research scientist, educator*
Krause, Sonja *chemistry professor*
Kravetz, Katharine *education educator*
Kravitch, Phyllis A. *federal judge*
Kravitz, Ellen King *musicologist, educator*
Kravitz, Rubin *chemist*
Krawetz, Stephen Andrew *molecular medicine and genetics scientist, educator*
Kregg, Helen Christine *foundation administrator*
Kreider, Clement Horst, Jr. *neurosurgeon*
Kreitlow, Burton William *retired adult education educator*
Kreitzburg, Marilyn June *academic librarian*
Kreizinger, Loreen I. *lawyer*
Kremer, Honor Frances (Noreen Kremer) *real estate broker, small business owner*
Kremer, Michael *surgeon*
Krenicki, John, Jr. *manufacturing executive*
Kreps, Juanita Morris *retired economics professor, former United States Secretary of Commerce*
Kretschmer, Frank Frederick, Jr. *electrical engineer, researcher, consultant*
Kribel, Robert Edward *consultant, retired physicist, academic administrator*
Krieg, Kenneth Joseph *former federal agency administrator*
Kriegsman, Sali Ann *performing arts executive, consultant, writer*
Kriger, Yefim G. *engineering educator*
Krishna, Kiran *risk management consultant*
Krishnaswamy, Mukunda *information technology executive, entrepreneur*
Kriz, Otakar *retired electrical engineer, researcher*
Krohn, Christy Anne *special education educator*
Krohnke, Duane W. *retired lawyer*
Krominga, Lynn *cosmetics executive, lawyer, director*
Krongard, Howard J. *former federal agency administrator, lawyer*
Kronman, Andrea C. *medical educator*
Kroske, Mary Louise *family practice nurse practitioner*
Krueger, Arlin James *physicist*
Krueger, Chris A. *physical education educator*
Kruesi, Frank Eugene *lobbyist, former government executive*
Krug, Edward Charles *environmental scientist*
Krug, John Carleton (Tony Krug) *academic administrator, library director, consultant*
Kruger, Linda Lee *retired military officer*
Krugman, Stanley Liebert *retired science administrator, geneticist*
Krulik, Barbara S. *cultural management consultant, curator, writer*
Krulitz, Leo Morrion *retired business executive, director*
Krupa, Shiva *cell biologist*
Krupp, James Arthur Gustave *management consultant*
Krych, Margaret A. *retired religious organization administrator, educator*
Kryzhniy, Vladimir V. *mathematics professor, researcher*
Kubilus, Norbert John *information technology executive*
Kucera, Daniel William *archbishop emeritus*
Kudo, Toshifumi *surgeon, researcher*
Kudrow, Lisa (Marie Diane) *actress*
Kuehn, Lucille M. *retired humanities educator*
Kuenn, Marjorie Asp *retired music educator*
Kuhl, Randy (John R. Kuhl Jr.) *former United States Representative from New York, lawyer*
Kuhler, Deborah Gail *grief therapist, former state legislator*
Kuhlmann, Martin *electrical engineer*
Kuhlmann-Wilsdorf, Doris *materials scientist, inventor, retired educator*
Kuhn, Thomas Joseph, Sr. *assistant principal*
Kulander, Byron Rodney *geologist, educator*
Kulathumani, Vinod *engineering educator*
Kulkarni, Ambarish Jayant *mechanical engineer*
Kulstad, Guy Charles *public works official*
Kultermann, Udo *architectural and art historian, educator, writer*
Kumar, Kanagaraj Ganesh *biologist, educator*
Kumar, Rita *literature and language educator*
Kumar, Sathish Alampalyam Poru *computer scientist, engineering educator, information technology manager*
Kumar, Vivek *urologist, surgeon*
Kumazawa, Risa *science educator*
Kumble, Steven Jay *lawyer*
Kundel, Harold Louis *radiologist, educator*
Kung, Douglas C. *systems engineer*
Kung, Patrick Chung-Shu *biotechnologist*
Kunkle, William Joseph *judge, lawyer*
Kunkler, Arnold William *retired surgeon, educator*
Kunselman, JoAn Dorothy *librarian, educator, editor, writer*
Kunstadter, Geraldine Sapolsky *foundation executive*
Kunz, Alexandra Cavitt *physician, anthropologist, owner*
Kunze, Otto Robert *retired agricultural engineering educator*
Kuo, Chun-Fang Frank *counselor, educator*
Kuo, Hong-Hsiang (Harry Kuo) *automotive executive, researcher*
Kupchella, Charles Edward *retired academic administrator, writer, educator*
Kupelian, Louise Paulson *musician, educator*
Kuppermann, Nathan *emergency physician*
Kuramoto, André Seichi Ribeiro *electronics engineer*
Kuriansky, Judy *television and radio personality, reporter, clinical psychologist, writer, educator*
Kurnick, Nathaniel Bertrand *retired oncologist, hematologist*
Kuroda, Yasumasa *political science professor, researcher*
Kurtz, Harold Paul *foundation executive*
Kushlan, James Anthony *science administrator, educator, conservationist, writer*
Kushner, Harvey David *management consultant*
Kushner, Tony *playwright, scriptwriter*
Kusserow, Richard Phillip *federal agency administrator, corporate financial executive*
Kusterer, Thomas *program director*
Kustin, Kenneth *chemist*
Kutasov, Israel Mayer *petroleum engineering and geothermics researcher, consultant*
Kutrzeba, Joseph S. *theater producer, director*
Kutscher, Ronald Earl *retired federal agency administrator*
Kutyna, Donald Joseph *air force officer*
Kuusisto, Lucina Marcia de Mello *chemistry educator*
Kuwajima, Shirou *physician*
Kuwayama, S. Paul *physician, immunologist, allergist*
Kuznetsova, Lyubov P. *research scientist*
Kvint, Vladimir Lev *economist, strategist, mining engineer, finance educator*
Kwasinski, Andres *electronic engineer*
Kwiram, Bernard Rudolph Alvin *music educator, conductor*
Kwitek, Benjamin Joseph *entrepreneur, consultant*
Kwon, Do-Kyoung *electrical engineer*
Kwon, Jaimyoung (Jaimie Kwon) *science educator*
Kwon, Jeff Soonchuel *physician*
Kwon, Jin-Ah *research scientist*
Kwong, Eva *artist, educator*
Kyesmu, Pius Michael *biology professor, researcher*
Kyle, Gene Magerl *merchandise presentation artist*
Kyle, Jeffrey A. *medical educator*
Kyle, Richard House *federal judge*
La, Wayne H. *mathematics professor*
LaBeouf, Shia *actor*
La Blanc, Robert Edmund *information technology executive*
LaBonte, Melissa J. *biology professor*
Labor, Earle Gene *literature and language professor*
Labrecque, Richard Joseph *retired industrial executive*
Lachapelle, Cleo Edward *retired social worker, real estate broker*
Lackland, John *lawyer, nurseryman*
LaCrue, Alexis Nichole *parasitologist*
Ladd, Diane *actress, writer, film director, producer*
Ladd, Joseph Carroll *retired insurance company executive*
Ladewig Goodman, Jeanne Margaret *artist*
Lafever, Howard Nelson *botanist, educator, geneticist*
Laffer, Arthur Betz *economist*
La Gamma, Edmund Francis *pediatrician*
Lagunoff, David *pathologist, educator*
LaHood, Marvin John *retired language educator*
Lahoud, Émile Jamil *former president of Lebanon, retired military officer*
LaHue, Christine *history educator*
Lai, Feng-Qi *instructional designer, educator*
Lai, Yurong *medical researcher*
Lai, Zhian *optical engineer*
Laidlaw, Robert Richard *retired publishing executive*
Laimbeer, Bill *former professional basketball coach, retired professional basketball player*
Laing, Malcolm Brian *geologist, consultant*
Laird, Cheryl F. *mental health services professional, paralegal*
Laird, Gwendolyn Ann *history professor, bank executive*
Laird, Melvin Robert, Jr. *former United States Secretary of Defense*
Lake, I. Beverly, Jr. *retired state supreme court chief justice*
Laksanalamai, Pongpan *microbiologist*
Lakshmikanthan, Preetham *coponent design engineer*
Lal, Geeta *surgeon*
Lala, Dominick Joseph *manufacturing executive*
Lalgudi, Hariharan Ganesh *engineer, researcher*
Laliberte, Brian J. *lawyer*
LaMantia, Charles Robert *management consulting company executive*
Lamb, Charles Franklin *biology professor, neuroscientist*
Lamb, Tiffany Dean *biology professor*
Lambert, Daniel Michael *retired academic administrator*
Lambert, George H. *physician, director*
Lambert, John Walton *music educator*
Lambert, Joseph Earl *retired state supreme court chief justice*
Lambert, Kirsten Schnoor *public relations executive, writer*
Lambert, Richard Bowles, Jr. *freelance writer*
Lamborn, LeRoy Leslie *law educator*
Lamel, Linda Helen *lawyer, arbitrator, director, professional society and retired insurance company executive, college president*
Lamkin, Martha Dampf *lawyer, foundation executive*
Lamon, Harry Vincent, Jr. *lawyer*
Lamont, Alice *accountant, consultant*
Lamont, Lee *retired music company and communications executive*
LaMorte, Joyce E. *music educator*
LaMotta, Connie Frances *public relations agency owner*
Lampert, Eleanor Verna *retired human resources specialist*
Lampson, Butler Wright *computer scientist*
Lampson, Nick (Nicholas Valentino Lampson) *former United States Representative from Texas*
Lampton, Dunn O. *retired prosecutor*
Lamy, M. Rebecca (Mary Rebecca Lamy) *consultant, land developer, government official*
Lan, Zhiling *engineering educator*
Lanahan, Daniel Joseph *lawyer*
Lancaster, Carroll Townes, Jr. *health services executive*
Lancaster, John Howard *civil engineer, consultant*
Lancaster, Kirsten Kezar *psychologist*
Landau, Ellis *hotel executive*
Landau, Emily Fisher *art collector, foundation administrator*
Landau, Felix *lawyer*
Landau, Jon *music producer, manager*
Landau, Judith *psychiatrist*
Lande, Alexander *physicist, researcher*

Landeck, Carl corporate financial executive
Landes, George Miller biblical studies educator
Landes, Nicholas civil engineer, researcher
Landesman, Rocco (Fredric Rocco Landesman) theatre executive
Landgarten, Helen Barbara art psychotherapist, educator
Landis, Kenneth H. entrepreneur, private investor, venture capitalist
Landon, John William retired minister, social worker, educator
Landon, Susan N. humanitarian, arts and environmental advocate, poet
Landon, William J. retired intelligence officer
Lane, Nathan (Joseph Lane) actor
Lane, Richard Allan preventive medicine physician, educator
Lane, Ted A. music educator, musician
Lane, William W. electronics executive
Lang, William Charles retail executive
Langbo, Arnold Gordon retired food products company executive
Langdale, Mark former ambassador, former hotel executive
Lange, William Michael retired lawyer
Langenkamp, Sandra Carroll retired human services administrator
Langer, Dennis Henry pharmaceutical company executive
Langer, Glenn Arthur cellular physiologist, educator
Langer, Ralph Ernest journalist, retired editor
Langfeldt, Andrew engineer
Langford, Roland Everett safety engineer, writer
Langridge, Robert biophysicist, educator, computational biologist
Langston, James Leland electronics engineer
Langton, Cleve Swanson author, advertising executive
Langton (Tomasiewicz), Dawn Theresa literature and language educator
Lann, Martha Marie psychology professor, consultant
Lanni, Terry (Joseph Terrence Lanni) retired hotel corporation executive
Lanphear, AErin Marie school system administrator
Lansing, Elizabeth Ellen science educator
Lansing, Sherry Lee foundation administrator, former film company executive
Lanterman, Jennifer L. researcher, educator
Lantz, Joanne Baldwin retired academic administrator
Lantzer, Jason Scott historian, educator
Lanzerotti, Mary Yvonne physicist, editor
Laowattana, Somchai neurologist, educator
Lape, Robert Cable broadcast journalist
Lapin, Sharon Vaughn interior designer
Lapiz-Bluhm, Maria Danet Sanchez neuroscientist, medical/surgical nurse
Laporte, Leo Frederic geologist, educator, paleontologist
Lappe, Frances Moore author, lecturer
Laqueur, Walter history professor, writer
Larkin, Joan poet, literature and language educator
Larkin, Michael John editor, journalist
LaRobardier, Genevieve Krause lawyer
La Rocca, Isabella artist, educator
Laroche, Helena Hillman medical researcher
LaRocque, Marilyn Ross Onderdonk writer, editor, public relations executive, consultant
Larsdotter, Anna-Lisa retired translator, artist
Larson, Charles Fred management consultant
Larson, Janice Talley application developer
Larson, Joan Isbell musician, educator
Larson, Richard Smith pathologist, researcher
Larson, Vicki Lord academic administrator, communication disorders educator
Lash, Barbara Platten art historian, educator
Lasher, Lara Elaine epidemiologist, researcher
Lashley, Felissa Rose dean, nursing educator, researcher
Lasker, Joseph L. artist, illustrator
Laskey, Richard Anthony biomedical device executive
Lasky, Richard Donald psychoanalyst, educator
La Spata, Michelle Gayle school psychologist
Lass, Diane marriage and family therapist
Lasser, Lawrence J. former investment company executive
Lassman, Adrienne community volunteer
Latchford, Wayne Harry physics professor
Latimer, James Harold musician, conductor, composer, music educator
Latta, George Haworth III neonatal/perinatal nurse practitioner
Lattanzio, Stephen Paul astronomy educator
Lattimore, Louise Joan elementary school educator
Lau, David L-C. cardiologist
Lau, Joann M. biology professor
Lau, Stephanie economics professor
Laudone, Anita Helene lawyer
Lauer, Jeanette Carol dean, history educator, writer
Laughlin, Louis Gene economic analyst, consultant
Laurence, Michael Marshall retired editor
Laurent, Pierre-Henri retired history professor
Lauria, Rita Marie attorney, media and communications researcher, consultant
Laursen, Krista aerospace scientist, director
Laursen, Lin L. retired women's college basketball coach
Lautenbacher, Conrad Charles, Jr. former federal agency administrator, retired naval officer
Lauter, Judith Larue neuroscientist
Lavassani, Fereshteh science educator
Lavelle, John Paul urologist
LaVerdiere, Claudette Marie nun, head of religious order
Laverty, Lyle (Robert Lyle Laverty) former federal agency administrator
Lavezzi, John Charles retired art history educator, archaeologist
Lavidge, Robert James marketing research executive
Lavine, Alan columnist, writer
Laviolette, Peter former professional hockey coach
Law, Bernard Francis Cardinal cardinal, retired archbishop
Law, Kevin meteorologist, educator
Law, Phillip Garth scientist, Antarctic explorer, educationaist
Law, Shek Hang medical educator
Lawer, Betsy banker, small business owner, vintner, director
Lawhon, Tommie Collins Montgomery humanities educator
Lawless, Michael Rhodes pediatrics educator
Lawless, Thomas William lawyer
Lawrence, Christine physician
Lawrence, Janice Fletcher psychologist
Lawrence, Margery H. (Margery Hulings Lawrence) marketing consultant
Lawrence, Sally Clark retired academic administrator
Lawrenson, Peter John electrical engineer, entrepreneur, educator
Lawson, Carolina-Donadio language educator, translator
Lawson, John Joseph vocational educator, consultant
Lawton, Kelly Marie Lee secondary school educator, performing arts director
Lax, Philip land developer, space planner, retired
Laybourne, Geraldine B. (Geraldine Bond) retired broadcast executive
Layfield, Lester James pathologist, educator
Layke, John C. plastic surgeon, researcher
Layne, James Nathaniel retired vertebrate biologist
Layton, John Robert writer
Layton, Robert Glenn radiologist
Layton, William George consultant, retired human resources and import/export company executive
Lazar, Charna L. education educator, retired CIA officer, security consultant
Lazar, Zoe L. psychologist
Lazarus, Adrienne B. retail executive
Lazell, James Draper biologist
Lazo, Mariana epidemiologist, researcher
Lazovsky, Lorna Deane minister
Le, Hung Qui application developer
Lea, Lorenzo Bates lawyer
Leach, Jim (James Albert Smith Leach) political science professor, former United States Representative from Iowa
Leach, Robin producer, writer, television host
Leach, Ronald J. computer science educator
Leachman, Cloris actress
Leahy, Jeannette (Jeannette Oliver Leahy Tinen Kaehler) actress
Leahy, T. Liam business development and technology investor
Lear, M. Kathleen artist, music educator, small business owner
Leary, Thomas Barrett lawyer, former federal agency administrator
Leath, Kenneth Thomas plant pathologist, educator, agriculturist, consultant
Leath, Mary Elizabeth medical/surgical nurse
Leather, Victoria Potts college librarian
Leavitt, Michael Okerlund former United States Secretary of Health and Human Services
Leavy, Herbert Theodore publisher
Leazenby, Tresa case conference chairperson
LeBar, Mark computer products company executive
LeBlanc, Hugh Linus political science professor, consultant
LeBlanc, Leonard Joseph retired electronics company executive
LeBlond, Paul Henri oceanographer, educator
Lebon, Rachel L. musician, educator
Lebowitz, Charlotte Meyersohn social worker
LeBrecht, Thelma Jane Mossman retired reporter
Lecat, Robert J. retired aeronautical engineer
Leclerc, Monique Marie Yvonne meteorologist, educator
Ledbetter, Hassel research scientist, educator
Lederer, Peter David lawyer
Lederer, William Jonathan medical association administrator, educator
Lederman, Leon Max physicist, researcher
Ledogar, Stephen J. retired diplomat
Ledwig, Donald Eugene election official, association executive, retired broadcast executive, military officer
Lee, Alvin A. literary educator, scholar, author
Lee, Christopher Frank Carandini actor, writer, singer
Lee, David B.N. internist, educator, nephrologist, consultant
Lee, Gwendolin Kuei retired ballet educator
Lee, Harper (Nelle Harper Lee) writer
Lee, Harrison Hon librarian, consultant
Lee, Heung-Man otolaryngologist, educator
Lee, Ho Jin economist
Lee, Jae-Seung physicist, researcher
Lee, Jeong Keun oral, maxillofacial surgeon, director
Lee, Jeong-Kyu education educator, researcher, academic administrator
Lee, Jong Nam materials engineer
Lee, Jongdoo researcher
Lee, Karen An-hwei english professor, poet
Lee, Katrina LaShawn health insurance business consultant
Lee, Marvina Sue science educator
Lee, Mordecai political scientist, educator
Lee, Nelda S. art appraiser, art dealer, film producer
Lee, Pali Jae retired librarian, writer
Lee, Richard Kenneth software company executive
Lee, Richard William physicist, researcher
Lee, Sihyung electronics engineer
Lee, Steve Chi Kong bank executive
Lee, Tabia (T. Lee) social studies educator
Lee, Thomas Tehwen neurosurgeon
Lee, Tony analyst developer
Lee, William Franklin III composer, musician
Leeds, Douglas Brecker advertising executive, theater producer
Leeds, Nancy Brecker sculptor, lyricist
Leeson, David Brent electrical engineer, educator, former electronics company executive
Leet, Richard Hale oil industry executive
Leetch, Brian Joseph retired professional hockey player
LeFante, Carolyn J. medical association administrator
Leff, Ilene J(afnel) management consultant, social sector organization and companies corporate executive, federal official
Leff, Joseph Norman yarn manufacturing company executive
Lefferts, George television producer
Legault, Pierre retail executive, pharmaceutical executive
Leggett, Roberta Jean (Bobbi Leggett) retired social services administrator
Legters, W. Matthew medical educator
Lehman, Jeffrey Sean academic administrator
Lehmann, Noreen Veronica insurance company executive
Lehner, Paul Edward systems engineer, researcher
Lehner-Quam, Alison Lynn library administrator
Lehrman, Irving rabbi
Lehtola, Lori A. history professor
Lehtonen, Hannu Jalmari fluid mechanics engineer
Leiber, Gerson August artist
Leiber, Judith Maria designer, manufacturer
Leibler, Kenneth Robert finance company executive
Leibowitz, Jack Richard physicist, educator
Leibowitz, Marvin lawyer
Leibowitz, Rosalind psychologist, educator
Leidel, Katherine journalist, newscaster
Leidy, Charlotte military officer
Leijonhufvud, Axel Stig Bengt economics professor
Leimkuhler, Gerard Joseph diversified financial services company executive
Leinweber, David Walter history professor
Leipzig, Arthur photographer, retired educator
Leistner, Mary Edna retired secondary school educator
Leitao, Dave men's college basketball coach
Lelyveld, Joseph Salem former newspaper editor, news correspondent, writer
LeMaistre, Charles Aubrey internist, epidemiologist, educator
Lembark, Connie Wertheimer art consultant
Lemke, Carol Ann music educator, pianist Vocalist Teacher of Piano & Voice, CPA
Lemke, Greg Erwin biology professor
Lemlich, Robert retired chemical engineer, educator
Lemos, Arthur retired music educator
Lempert, Philip advertising executive, writer, news correspondent
Lempert, Richard Owen lawyer, educator
Lenden-Holt, Jessica Marie speech pathology/audiology services professional
Lenert, Petar S. medical researcher
Lenhart, Cynthia Rae conservation organization executive
Lennon, Joseph Luke retired academic administrator, priest
Lennox, William James, Jr. retired military officer
Lent, Michael Stephen artist, curator
Lentini, Francine retired physical education educator
Lenz, Carl Otto international organization official
Leon, Nellie health educator
Leonard, Sister Anne C. school system administrator
Leonard, Bill (John William Leonard) former federal agency administrator
Leonard, Hasse A. psychologist, educator
Leonhardt, Thomas Wilburn librarian, library director
Leonowich, Paul mechanical engineer, science educator
Leos, Kathleen former federal agency administrator
Lepage, Robert actor, playwright
Le Pensec, Louis French government official
Lepke-Sims, Barbara Weiger music educator
Lepore, Natasha medical researcher
Le Quéré, Jean François Marie scientific instrumentation researcher
Lerner, Herbert J. tax consultant
Lescroart, John Thomas writer, composer, singer
Leslie, Maureen Heelan university director
Leslie, Teresa Elizabeth anthropologist, educator
Lesnewski, Ruth physician, director
Lesnik, Julie anthropologist, educator
Less, Anthony Albert retired naval officer
Lesser, Ruth language educator
Lessie, Douglas Louis physics educator
Lester, Alicia Louise financial analyst
Lester, Julius B. author
Lester, Mark Charles neurosurgeon
Lester, Robin Dale historian, educator, writer, former headmaster
Lettow, Lucille Jane retired school librarian, education educator
Lev, Elise L. nursing educator
Leveille, Gilbert Antonio food products executive
Level, Leon Jules investor, director
Leventhal, Nathan performing company executive, lawyer, municipal official
Levesque, George research scientist
Levey, Robert Frank columnist, not-for-profit fundraiser
Levi, Josef Alan artist
Levick, Richard Scott communications executive, lawyer, consultant, educator
Levin, A. Leo retired law educator, government official
Levin, Alan Scott pathologist, allergist, immunologist, lawyer
Levin, Morton D(avid) artist, printmaker, educator
Levin, Pavel science educator, researcher
Levin, Richard I. dean, cardiologist, researcher
Levin, Steven Jonathan physician
Levine, Alan J. entertainment company executive
Levine, Michael E. law educator, researcher
Levine, Susan Beth history professor
Levine, Thomas Jeffrey Pello lawyer
Levins, John Raymond investment advisor, educator, management consultant
Levins, Richard biologist, educator
Levinsky, Frieda Libby language educator
Levinsohn, Gary producer
Levinson, Herbert Sherman civil and transportation engineer
Levinson, Riki art director
Levinson, Stephen Eliot electrical engineer, educator
Levitas, Miriam C. Strickman documentary filmmaker
Levitt, Seymour Herbert radiologist, educator
Levitte, Jean-David former ambassador
Levy, Arthur James public relations executive, writer
Levy, David retired lawyer, insurance company executive, consultant
Levy, I. Richard lawyer
Levy, Leah Garrigan federal official
Levy, Leslie Ann application developer
Levy, Louis Edward retired accounting firm executive
Levy, Marv (Marvin Daniel) former professional football team executive, retired professional football coach
Levy, Norman B. psychiatrist, educator
Levy, Robert Edward retired management consultant
Levy, Stephen H. philosopher, logician computer scientist, author
Lew, Roger Alan manufacturing executive
Lewie, Reva Goodwin artist, educator
Lewin, Leif I. finance executive
Lewins, Steven financial analyst, investment company executive, legislative staff member, retired military officer
Lewis, Albert James, Jr. energy executive, director
Lewis, Andrew Lindsay, Jr., (Drew Lewis) former United States Secretary of Transportation
Lewis, Anthony columnist, educator
Lewis, Charles Leonard psychologist
Lewis, David Charles historian, educator
Lewis, David L. security firm executive, consultant
Lewis, Dennis Carroll writer, spiritual teacher
Lewis, Douglas retired art historian
Lewis, Emanuel Raymond historian, psychologist, retired librarian
Lewis, Floyd Wallace former electric utility executive
Lewis, Frederick A. library director
Lewis, Homer Dick retired nuclear engineer
Lewis, Hunter investment advisor, writer
Lewis, James Kevin music educator
Lewis, Justin Harley religious studies educator
Lewis, Kay interior designer, consultant
Lewis, Martha Andreé elementary school educator
Lewis, Martin Edward transportation executive, oil trader, foreign government concessionary
Lewis, Martin R. paper company executive, consultant
Lewis, Mary-Frances civic volunteer
Lewis, Ned Lehmon secondary school educator
Lewis, Perry Joshua investment banker
Lewis, Rita Hoffman plastic products manufacturing company executive
Lewis, Robert Enzer editor, educator
Lewis, Ron (Ronald E. Lewis) former United States Representative from Kentucky
Lewis, Samuel Winfield retired federal agency administrator, diplomat
Lewitt, Miles Martin computer engineering company executive
Lewy, Helen Crosby artist, writer, translator, painter
Leybourn, Carol musician, educator
Li, Charlene market trend analyst, media strategist
Li, Eugene S. physics professor
Li, Jichun mathematics professor, director
Li, Lide mathematician, financial engineer
Li, Lihong electrical engineer, educator
Li, Linghong physics professor
Li, Min Research Scientist in Analytical Organic Chemistry
Li, Qian research scientist
Li, Ting-Kai retired federal agency administrator, biologist
Li, Tingye electrical engineer
Li, Xiaojie senior research associate
Li, Xin computer scientist, researcher
Li, Xiong geophysicist
Li, Yawen research scientist
Li, Youzhi research scientist
Lian, Jie biomedical engineer
Liang, Jian application developer
Liang, Kathleen economics professor
Liang, Qing research scientist
Liang, Qingqing electronics engineer
Liao, Yuyun computer engineer
Libassi, Frank Peter lawyer
Libby, Billy W. (Bill Libby) religious studies educator
Liberati, Maria Theresa lifestyle company executive, writer, chef
Liberman, Gail Jeanne editor
Lichtenstein, Harvey performing arts association administrator
Lichtenstein, Lawrence Mark immunologist, allergist, educator
Lichtman, Emily Ann radiologist
Licke, Wallace John lawyer
Liddy, Edward M. retired insurance company executive
Lidsky, Ella retired law librarian
Lieberfarb, Warren N. digital media pioneer
Lieberman, Louis (Karl Lieberman) artist
Liebman, Ronald Stanley lawyer
Liebowitz, Daniel S.F. retired medical educator
Liegl, Dorothy M. retired library director
Liftin, John Matthew lawyer
Lifton, Robert Jay psychiatrist, author
Liggett, Thomas Jackson retired seminary president
Light, Marion Jessel retired elementary school educator
Ligon, Demond L., Sr. sales executive
Ligon, Duke R. lawyer
Ligon, Nikimya psychologist
Liguori, Robert lawyer, insurance company executive
Li-lan, artist
Liles, Virginia Rembert (Virginia Pitts Rembert) retired art educator
Lilien, Robert Jarrett (Jarrett Lilien) former diversified financial services company executive

Liljegren, Frank Sigfrid *art association administrator, artist, educator*
Lillehoff, Piper *psychiatrist*
Lilley, John Mark *academic administrator*
Lilley, William III *business executive*
Lilly, Edward Guerrant, Jr. *retired utilities executive*
Lilly, Thomas Gerald *retired lawyer*
Lilly-Hersley, Jane Anne Feeley *nursing researcher*
Lim, Hee Chuan *physics professor, researcher*
Limbacher, Randy L. *oil industry executive*
Limerick, Dianne A. *mathematics educator, athletic trainer*
Limouze, Henry S. *literature and language professor, department chairman*
Lin, Chengxian *research scientist*
Lin, David C. *biomedical researcher*
Lin, Henry *research scientist*
Lin, Hsiu Ling *literature and language professor*
Lin, Jenny Mei Hwa *paralegal, painter*
Lin, Maya *architect, sculptor*
Lin, Paul P. *mechanical engineer, educator*
Lin, Qiuyun *education educator*
Lin, Ray-Qing *physicist, researcher*
Lin, Xi *medical educator*
Lincicome, David Richard *biomedical scientist, animal scientist*
Lincoln, Grace *elementary school educator*
Lincoln, Walter Butler, Jr. *marine engineer, educator*
Lind, Niels Christian *civil engineering educator*
Lind, Owen Thomas *biology professor*
Linda, Gerald *advertising and marketing executive*
Lindberg, Francis Laurence, Jr. *management consultant*
Linde, Maxine Helen *lawyer, corporate financial executive, investor*
Linde, Ronald Keith *investor*
Lindell, Dennis Michael *medical educator*
Lindeman, Carolynn Anderson *music educator*
Lindenberger, Herbert Samuel *writer, literature educator*
Lindenmayer, Elisabeth *international organization administrator*
Lindgren, William Dale *librarian*
Lindros, Eric *retired professional hockey player*
Lindsay, Diane Miller *music educator*
Lindsey, Joyce Rebecca *secondary school educator*
Lindsey, Roberta Lewise *music researcher, historian, educator*
Lindstrom, Rosetta Arline *retired medical technician*
Lineen, Edward M. *lawyer, information technology executive*
Liner, Ernest *biologist*
Linett, David *retired lawyer*
Ling, Elizabeth M. *research engineer*
Lingle, Marilyn Felkel *journalist, columnist, writer*
Lingren, Wesley Earl *chemistry educator*
Linhares, Judith Yvonne *painter, educator*
Link, Phoebe Forrest *educator, author, social worker, poet*
Link, Phyllida Korman *artist, educator*
Link, Steven Otto *environmental scientist, statistician*
Linn, Richard *federal judge*
Lintner, Roberta Pompilio *art educator, artist*
Linton, Michael Alan *Internet company executive*
Linz, Anthony James *osteopathic physician, consultant, educator*
Lioi, Sara Elizabeth *judge*
Lipkind, Lynne *publishing executive, educator*
Lipkowitz, George S. *surgeon, director*
Lippard, Lucy Rowland *writer, educator, critic, curator*
Lippincott, James Andrew *retired biochemistry and biological sciences educator*
Lippincott, Philip Edward *retired paper company executive*
Lippitt, Mary B. *finance company executive*
Lipschutz, Michael Elazar *chemistry professor, consultant, researcher*
Lipset, Robert *engineering educator, consultant*
Lipsey, Joseph, Jr. *retired wholesale distribution executive*
Lipsey, Richard George *economist, educator*
Lipsky, Burton G. *lawyer*
Lipson, Abigail *psychologist*
Lipson, Allen S. *former entertainment company executive, lawyer*
Lipson, Daniel N. *political science professor*
Lipton, Ann Lynn *Educator*
Lipton, Glenn E. *orthopaedic surgeon*
Lipton, Robert Steven *lawyer*
Lisio, Donald John *historian, educator*
Lithgow, John Arthur *actor*
Litman, Harry Peter *lawyer, educator*
Litou, Hendry *Internet company executive, researcher*
Litscher, Eveline *biology professor*
Little, Arthur Dehon *investor*
Little, Charlotte Louise *poet, writer*
Little, (William) Grady *former professional baseball coach, team manager*
Little, James W. *retired dental educator*
Littleton, Harvey Kline *artist*
Littleton, Heavenly Denise *video editor, producer, filmmaker*
Littman, Earl *advertising and public relations executive*
Litvack, Sanford Martin *lawyer*
Liu, Hongjie *biotechnologist, educator*
Liu, Huimin *physicist, educator*
Liu, Katherine Chang *artist, art educator*
Liu, Song *computer engineer*
Liu, Songtao *medical researcher*
Liu, Te Hua *retired neuroradiologist*
Liu, Weiping *metallurgist*
Liu, Young King *biomedical engineering educator*
Livdahl, Todd Philip *biology professor*
Liverman, Betty Jean *elementary school educator*
Livingston, Gwendell Sheawanna *education educator*
Livingstone, Susan Morrisey *management consultant, former federal agency administrator*
Llora, Xavier *computer scientist, educator*
Lloyd, Michael Jeffrey *recording producer*
Lloyd, Robert Blackwell, Jr. *retired lawyer*
Lo, Shui-yin *physicist*
Loacker, Lynn J. *lawyer*
Lober, Irene Moss *educational consultant*
Lobo, Arthur Peter *electrical engineer*
Lobo, Lucía *language educator*
Lobue, Ange *psychiatrist, author*
Lochner, Philip Raymond *retired communications executive, former commissioner*
Lock, Evgeniya Hristova *research scientist*
Locke, Edwin Allen III *retired psychologist, educator*
Locklear, Heather *actress*
Locklin, Muriel Lucie *artist*
Lockwood, Robert W. *management consultant*
Lockwood, Theodore Davidge *retired academic administrator*
Loeser, Eric *chemist*
Loewald, Elizabeth Longshore *retired psychiatrist*
Loftin, Craig Michael *history professor*
Lofton, James David *former professional football player, professional football coach*
Lofton, Kevin Eugene *medical facility administrator*
Loftus, Elizabeth F. *psychology professor*
Logan, Joseph E. *research scientist*
Logan, Kent *retired securities industry executive*
Logan, Latania K. *physician scientist*
Logan, Robert Alexander *literature and language professor*
Loge, Krista Fields *psychologist*
Logsdon, Vicki Dianne *librarian, director*
Logue, James Nicholas *epidemiologist*
Logue, Jean Evelyn *music educator*
Loh, Wai Kiew *oil industry executive*
Lohan, Lindsay Dee *actress*
Lohman, Gordon Russell *retired manufacturing executive*
Lohmann, George Young, Jr. *neurosurgeon, health facility administrator, artist*
Lohmuller, Martin Nicholas *bishop emeritus*
Loiello, John Peter *diplomat, international consultant*
Loken, Barbara *marketing educator, social psychologist*
Lolo, Eduardo Calixto *writer, journalist, educator*
Lombardi, Mary Luciana *musician, historian*
Lonchyna-Lisowsky, Maria *music educator*
Long, Clarence Dickinson III *lawyer*
Long, Harry (On-Yuen Eng) *chemist, science and technology executive, consultant*
Long, Lillian F. *music educator*
Long, Mary E. *medical researcher*
Long, Peter Avard Chipman *retired military officer*
Long, Robert Emmet *author*
Long, Roger Leonard *artist*
Longaberger, Tami *home decor accessories company executive*
Longobardo, Anna Kazanjian *engineering executive*
Longobardo, Guy Alfred *lawyer*
Longstreet, John Charles *retired computer scientist*
Longsworth, Robert Morrow *language educator*
Lonsdale, Howard Charles *physician*
Looney, Gerald Lee *medical educator, administrator*
Loos, Roberta Alexis *advocate, artist, educator*
Looser, Donald William *academic administrator*
Loper, James Leaders *broadcasting executive*
Lopes, Jacqueline Cunha *language educator*
Lopez, Barry Holstun *writer*
Lopez, Harold Lee *special education educator*
Lopez, Patricia Nell *minister, educator*
Loppnow, Milo Alvin *clergyman, former church official*
Lord, Jerome Edmund *education administrator, writer*
Lorelli, Elvira Mae *artist, art educator*
Lorelli, Michael Kevin *consumer products company executive*
Loren, Allan Z. *former financial services company executive*
Lorenz, Marie *architect, sculptor*
Loring, Gloria Jean *vocalist, actress, writer*
Loring, John Robbins *artist, writer*
Los, Marinus *retired agrochemical researcher*
Lo Schiavo, Francesca *set designer*
Losi, Maxim John *medical communications executive*
Lotas, Judith Patton *advertising executive*
Lotsch, Alexander *scientist*
Lotspiech, Jeffrey *computer scientist, consultant*
Lotz, George Michael *retired computer company executive, graphics designer, photographer*
Louargand, Marc Andrew *real estate executive, financial consultant*
Louie, Steven Gwon Sheng *physics professor, researcher*
Loumiet, Carlos Ernesto *lawyer*
Love, Courtney *singer, actress*
Love, Robert Lyman *retired educator, consultant*
Love, Shirley *mezzo-soprano*
Loveland, Eugene Franklin *retired gas industry executive*
Lovell, James Arthur, Jr. *retired astronaut*
Lovell, Malcolm Read, Jr. *public information officer, educator, retired trade association administrator, federal official*
Lovelle, William *language educator*
Lovett, Clara Maria *retired academic administrator, historian*
Lovett, Elizabeth Michelle *music educator*
Lovisone, Sylvia Ruth *lawyer*
Lovvorn, Audrey Marie *mental health therapist*
Low, Harry William *judge*
Low, Morton David *retired neuroscientist, healthcare educator, consultant*
Low, Philip Stewart *chemistry professor, biochemistry company executive*
Low, Ron Albert *former professional hockey coach*
Lowe, John C. *medical researcher, director*
Lowenberg, Georgina Grace *retired elementary school educator*
Lowenthal, Constance *art historian, consultant*
Lowrance, Larry *special education educator, psychologist*
Loy, Frank Ernest *retired federal official diplomat*
Lozančić, Niko *former President of Federation of Bosnia and Herzegovina*
Lu, Chung-Cheng Jason *engineering educator*
Lu, Jin *engineer, researcher*
Lu, Ning H. *research scientist*
Lu, Zhao *engineering professor*
Lubaroff, David Martin *immunologist, educator*
Lubell, Ellen *writer*
Lubezki, Emmanuel *cinematographer*
Lubic, Ruth Watson *health facility administrator, nurse midwife*
Lubich, Frederick Alfred *language educator*
Lubich, Mark Walter *artist*
Lubick, Donald Cyril *lawyer*
Lubick, Sonny *former college football coach*
Lubin, Steven *concert pianist, musicologist*
Lubner, Mary F. *retired elementary school educator*
Lubotsky, Darren Howard *economics professor, researcher*
Lucas, Jane Meekins *writer, educator*
Lucas, Michele Angelyn *learning consultant, special education educator*
Lucas, Paul David Mark *lawyer*
Lucas, Phillip Charles *religious studies educator*
Lucas, Teri Kathleen *secondary school educator*
Lucas, William Ray *aerospace scientist, consultant*
Luce, Edward Andrew *plastic surgeon*
Lucht, Orren Jesse *retired mechanical engineer*
Lucier, P. Jeffrey *publishing executive*
Lucker, Jay *library consultant*
Luckey, Doris Waring *civic volunteer*
Luddy, Paula Scott *nursing educator*
Luder, Owen (Harold Luder) *architect, construction executive, consultant, mediator*
Ludwig, Allan Ira *photographer, educator, artist, writer*
Ludwig, Christa *retired mezzo soprano*
Luedeman, Gerald Warren *radiologist*
Luening, Robert Adami *retired agricultural studies educator*
Luetkehoelter, Gottlieb Werner (Lee Luetkehoelter) *retired bishop, clergyman*
Luftman, Jerry *dean, educator*
Lufty, JoyBeth *minister*
Lugenbeel, Edward Elmer *publisher*
Luh, William *engineer, researcher*
Luhrs, Claudia C. *materials scientist, educator*
Luk, Debra K. *psychologist*
Lukacs, Michael Edward *electro-optics researcher*
Luke, David Lincoln III *retired paper company executive*
Luke, Karen *chemist, researcher*
Luke, Robert George *nephrologist, medical educator*
Luker, Rebecca *actress, soprano*
Lumbard, Devon Andrew *structural engineer, educator*
Lumelsky, Vladimir Jacob *engineering educator*
Lund, James Louis *lawyer*
Lundberg, George David, II, *medical editor-in-chief, pathologist*
Lundgren, Colleen Bowling *elementary school educator, consultant*
Lundquist, Daniel Merritt *educational consultant, former dean*
Luo, Lei *materials engineer, researcher*
Luo, Xuanwen *electrical engineer*
Lupash, Lawrence Ovidiu *computer analyst, researcher*
Lupu, Radu *pianist*
Lurie, Alvin David *lawyer*
Luskin, Frederic Michael *psychologist, educator*
Lussier, Alexandre *research scientist*
Luther, Nicole *language educator*
Luthi, Randall B. *former federal agency administrator*
Luthy, Richard Godfrey *environmental engineering educator*
Luti, Bill (William Joseph Luti) *federal official, retired military officer*
Luttner, Edward F. *consulting company executive*
Lutz, Matthew Charles *oil industry executive, geologist*
Lutz, Tamara Jean *nursing consultant*
Lyall, Katharine Culbert *former academic administrator, economist, educator*
Lyford, Ronald Lee *music educator*
Lyles, Mark Bradley *advanced technology company executive, military officer*
Lynch, Catherine Gores *social services administrator*
Lynch, Charles Andrew *chemicals executive*
Lynch, Dennis James *retired plastic surgeon*
Lynch, Gerald Weldon *former academic administrator, psychologist*
Lynch, Jessica *military officer*
Lynch, John Thomas *retired science administrator, physicist*
Lynch, Robert Emmett *mathematics professor*
Lynch, Thomas Wimp *lawyer*
Lynch, Timothy Jeremiah-Mahoney *lawyer, educator, theologian, realtor, writer*
Lynd, Phyllis *artist, educator*
Lynds, Gayle Hallenbeck *writer*
Lyne, Dorothy-Arden *secondary school educator*
Lynn, Naomi B. *academic administrator*
Lynne, Michael *film company executive*
Lynton, Sandra M. *psychologist*
Lyon, Bruce Arnold *lawyer, educator*
Lyon, Gholson *psychiatrist*
Lyon, Martha Sue *research engineer, retired military officer*
Lyons, Champ, Jr. *state supreme court justice*
Lyons, John David *literature and language professor*
Lyons, John W(inship) *retired civilian military employee, chemist, consultant*
Lyons, Richard Kent *dean, finance educator*
Lyons, Susanne D. *information technology executive*
Lyons-Hunt, Jennifer K. *history professor*
Lysne, Allen Bruce *laboratory director*
Ma, Wenjing *application developer*
Maatman, Gerald Leonard *insurance company executive*
Mabey, Ralph R. *lawyer*
Mac Alister, Robert James *executive recruiter*
MacAlister, Rodney J. *former president African Development Foundation*
MacAulay, Lawrence A. *former Canadian government official, member of Parliament*
MacAvoy, Thomas Coleman *manufacturing executive, educator*
MacCarthy, Talbot Leland *civic volunteer*
MacCormack, Jean F. *academic administrator*
MacCracken, Michael Calvin *atmospheric scientist*
MacDevitt, Brian *lighting designer*
MacDonald, Alan Hugh *academic administrator*
MacDonald, Donald Paul *lawyer*
MacDonald, Elizabeth Hutton *artist, educator*
MacDonald, J. Randall *information technology executive, human resources specialist*
Macdonald, Lenna Ruth *executive lawyer, business advisor*
Mace, Michael Jay *architect*
Macedo de la Concha, Rafael *former Mexican government official*
Machina, Mark Joseph *economist*
MacHovec, Frank J. *psychologist*
Maciewski, Bryan Jon *finance educator, consultant*
Mackay, Leo Sidney, Jr. *healthcare company executive, former federal agency administrator*
MacKenzie, Donald Murray *health facility administrator*
Mackenzie, Kendra *art educator*
Mackey, Jeffrey Allen *priest*
Mackin, Randal Thomas *literature and language professor*
MacKinnon, John Alexander *lawyer*
Maclay, Sarah *poet, educator*
MacLean, Doug *former professional hockey coach, former sports team executive*
MacLellan, Steve *bank executive*
MacLennan, Beryce Winifred *psychologist*
MacLeod, Gordon C. *surgeon*
Macnab, Alistair Murdoch *retired writer*
MacNeill, James William *environmental energy and management consultant*
Maco, Paul Stephen *securities and exchange administrator*
MacTavish, Craig *former professional hockey coach, retired professional hockey player*
MacWilliams, Kenneth Edward *investment banker*
Madapusi, Arun *educator, consultant*
Madden, John *retired sportscaster, retired professional football coach*
Madden, John Philip *motion picture director, actor*
Madden, Richard Blaine *forest products executive*
Maddin, Robert *metallurgist, educator*
Maddux, Greg (Gregory Alan Maddux) *retired professional baseball player*
Madeira, Francis King Carey *conductor, educator*
Madhavaram, Sreedhar *marketing educator*
Madix, Robert James *chemical engineer, educator*
Madrid, Cirilo L. *health facility administrator*
Madsen, Michael *actor*
Madsen, Virginia *actress*
Maeda, Kenji *medical researcher*
Maeda, Koichi *pathologist*
Maehl, William Harvey *retired historian*
Magana, Melanie G *psychologist, consultant*
Magee, Alan *artist*
Magee, Elaine *dietician, consultant*
Magee, John Francis *research and development company executive*
Maghelal, Praveen Kumar *engineering educator*
Magid, Laurie *prosecutor*
Magliocchetti, Paul *lobbyist*
Magnan, Morris Allen *nursing researcher, educator*
Magnano, Salvatore Paul *retired finance company executive, treasurer*
Magne, Michel Jaques *dental educator, ceramist*
Magnes, Harry Alan *physician*
Magno, Gil D. *music educator, personal development consultant*
Magoni, Despo *artist*
Magor, Louis Roland *conductor*
Magpili, Luna *systems engineer, consultant*
Magrill, Joe Richard, Jr. *religious organization administrator, minister*
Magro, Cynthia Maria *pathologist*
Maguire, Martie (Martha Elenor Erwin Maguire) *musician*
Magurno, Richard Peter *lawyer*
Mah, Silvia Armitano *director, educator*
Mahaffey, Marcia Hixson *retired educational administrator*
Mahajan, Anita *oncologist, educator*
Mahaney, Jack *engineering educator*
Maharidge, Dale Dimitro *journalist, educator, writer*
Maher, Cormac Oliver *neurosurgeon, pediatrician, researcher*
Maheras, Thomas G. *former diversified financial services company executive*
Mahesh, Virendra Bhushan *endocrinologist*
Mahle, Christoph Erhard *electrical engineer*
Mahler, Ronald Paxton Sheets *engineer, mathematician*
Mahmood, Arshad *former academic administrator*
Mahmood, Nafeesa F. *physician, consultant*
Mahmoodian, Roza *research scientist*
Mahmud, Enad *civil engineer, researcher*
Mahmud, Shireen Dianne *photographer*
Mahoney, George LeFevre *lawyer*
Mahoney, John *actor*
Mahoney, John L. *English literature educator*
Mahoney, Michael Robert Taylor *art historian, educator*
Mahoney, Robert William *electronic and security systems manufacturing executive*
Mahoney, Tim (Timothy Edward Mahoney) *former United States Representative from Florida*
Mahood, R. Wayne *education educator*
Mai, Chao Chen *engineer*
Maier, Robert Henry *retired real estate executive*
Maier, Theodore Joseph *literature and language educator*
Main, Robert Gail *communications educator, training services executive, television and film producer, retired military officer*
Main, Terena Ann *music educator, corporate financial executive*
Mainella, Fran (Frances P. Mainella) *educator, former federal agency administrator*
Maines, Natalie Louise *musician*
Mair, Bruce Logan *interior designer, architectural firm executive*

Maisto, John F. *former ambassador*
Majeed, D. Hadayai S. *publishing executive, writer*
Major, Patrick Webb III *principal*
Mak, Linda L. *dermatologist*
Makdisi, Tony *medical educator*
Makki, S. Kami *education educator*
Makriyannis, Alexandros *medicinal chemist, educator*
Maksem, John Adelbert *pathologist*
Mala, Theodore Anthony *physician, consultant*
Malach, Monte *physician*
Malafronte, Judith Adelia *music educator*
Maldonado, Antonio *lawyer*
Maldonado, Gustavo Omar *engineering educator, researcher*
Malek, Marlene Anne *foundation administrator*
Malewski, Jennifer Jean *clergy member*
Malhotra, Madhu Bala *psychiatrist*
Mali, Paul *publisher, retired management educator*
Malick, Terrence (David Whitney II) *film director*
Malin, Robert Abernethy *retired investment company executive*
Maling, George Croswell, Jr. *physicist*
Malins, Donald Clive *biochemist, researcher*
Malishenko, Timothy Peter *retired aerospace company executive*
Malkan, Stacy *communications executive, director*
Malks, Betty F. *social worker*
Mallchok, Jeanne *retired special education educator*
Mallison, Howard Danford *retired corporate communications specialist*
Mallory, Arthur Lee *dean, retired state official*
Mallory, Kristin L. *community college administrator*
Malloy, John Richard *lawyer, chemicals executive*
Malloy, Michael Terrence *journalist, reporter*
Malluche, Hartmut Horst *nephrologist, medical educator*
Malone, Claudine Berkeley *management consultant*
Malone, Dorothy *actress*
Maloney, James Henry *community development executive, former congressman*
Malphurs, Roger Edward *biomedical marketing executive*
Mancera Aguayo, Miguel *retired banker*
Manchester, Kenneth Edward *electronics executive, consultant*
Mancuso, John Henry *retired lawyer, bank executive*
Mandal, Prabir Kumar *biologist, educator*
Mandel, Jeffrey S. *psychologist*
Mandelbrot, Benoit B. *mathematician, research scientist, educator*
Mandell, Gerald A. *nuclear medicine physician*
Mandell, Gerald Lee *internist, educator*
Mandle, Roger *museum administrator, former academic administrator*
Mandyam, Giridhar Dhati *electronics engineer*
Maneker, Roberta S(ue) *frelance writer*
Mangalpally, Kiran Kumar Ramchander *medical researcher*
Mangano, Salvatore Nicholas *retired surgeon*
Mangla, Sundeep *radiologist, research scientist*
Manglona, Ramona V. *judge, former attorney general*
Mangold, John Frederic *manufacturing executive, retired military officer*
Mangravite, Ronald *filmmaker, writer*
Manion, Bonnie J. *volunteer, poet, composer*
Manivannan, Dakshnamoorthy *computer scientist, educator*
Manjunath, Prashanth *anesthesiologist, researcher*
Mankin, Robert Stephen *diversified financial services company executive*
Manley, Joan A(dele) Daniels *retired publishing executive*
Manley, Judith L. *director*
Manlove, Benson *retired gas industry executive, secondary school educator*
Mann, Eric Louis *retired military officer, mathematics professor, researcher*
Mann, Joan Ellona *artist, editor*
Mann, Mary Anneeta *author*
Manner, Jennifer Fouse *social worker*
Mannes, Elena Sabin *film and television producer, television director*
Manning, David Geoffrey *former ambassador*
Manning, John Warren III *retired surgeon, medical educator*
Manning, Sylvia *academic administrator, language educator*
Manning, William Dudley, Jr. *retired specialty chemical company executive*
Mannino, J(oseph) Robert *medical educator*
Manos, Christopher Lawrence *lawyer, mediator*
Manrique, Jaime *writer, educator*
Mansergh, Gordon Dwight *health maintenance and prevention researcher*
Mansfield, Gordon Hall *former federal agency administrator*
Mansfield, Jerry W. *literature and language professor*
Mansfield, Stephen Lee *writer, educator*
Manso, Leira A. *Latin American literature educator, poet, translator*
Mansour, Mohamad Y. *structural engineer, researcher*
Mansur, Louis K. *materials scientist, nuclear engineer*
Mantei, Lorraine E. *school system administrator*
Mantena, Ravi *business educator*
Mantz, Arlan W. *physics professor*
Manuel, Ralph Nixon *retired private school executive*
Manville, Greta Craig *writer*
Manyam, Bala Venkatesha *medical researcher, neurology educator*
Manyame, Comfort *systems administrator*
Mao, Weidong *science educator*
Mao, Yuan *research scientist, educator*
Maples, Philip G. *retired museum director*
Maplesden, Carol Harper *marriage and family therapist, music educator*
Mapp, Catherine *performing arts educator, department chairman*
Mapp, Edward Charles *speech educator*
Maraldo, Ushana *multimedia designer, artist, photographer, writer*
Marans, J. Eugene *lawyer*
Marburger, John Harmen III *former federal official*
Marc, David Tischler *cardiologist, director*
Marcdante, Karen Jean *medical educator*
Marcello, Patrick Ryan *dentist*
March, Michael F. *propulsion systems analyst, consultant*
Marchant, Barbara *performing arts educator, acting coach*
Marchenko, Tamara G. *music educator*
Marciano, Sonia *finance educator*
Marcu, Aaron R. *lawyer*
Marcum, James Walton *library director, educator*
Marcus, Bernard *foundation administrator, retired retail executive*
Marcus, Greil Gerstley *critic*
Marcuse, Aida E. *writer, translator, educator*
Marcuse, Dietrich *retired physicist*
Marcy, Kevin Michael *film producer, lawyer*
Mardi, Shalva Josef *research scientist*
Margolis, Bernard Allen *library administrator*
Margolis, Daniel Herbert *lawyer*
Margolis, Jay M. *former apparel company executive*
Margoshes, Miriam Kagan *information specialist*
Margules, Cecelia *composer, poet*
Margulies, Julianna *actress*
Margulis, Alexander Rafailo *physician, educator*
Mariano, Ana Virginia *retired pathologist*
Mari Aparici, Carina *nuclear medicine physician*
Mariash, Cary Norman *medical educator, researcher*
Marin, Cheech (Richard Anthony Marin) *actor, writer, director*
Marine, Michael W. *former ambassador*
Marineau, Eric Christian *research scientist*
Marinetti, Guido V. *biochemistry professor*
Marinis, Thomas Paul, Jr. *lawyer*
Marino, Deirdre J. *science educator*
Marion, John Louis *former fine arts auctioneer and appraiser*
Marion, Marjorie Anne *literature and language professor, educational consultant*
Mark, Hon Fong Louie *cytogeneticist*
Mark, Michael Laurence *retired music educator*
Mark, Reuben *retired consumer products company executive*
Markel, Anna *pharmacist, educator*
Marker, Marc Linthacum *lawyer, investor, entrepreneur*
Markham, Charles Henry *neurologist*
Markhotok, Anna *physics professor*
Marklin, George *physicist*
Markopolos, Harry M. *financial investigator, former investment company executive*
Markovich, Alexandria *assistant principal*
Markovich, Patricia H. *economist*
Marks, Bruce *performing company executive, choreographer*
Marks, John *engineer, consultant*
Marks, Kathryn Allan *dancer, educator*
Marks, Roberta Barbara *artist, educator*
Marlowe, Willie *artist, fine arts educator*
Marmer, Nancy *editor*
Marolda, Anthony Joseph *management consulting company executive*
Maron, Marc *comedian, actor, writer*
Marone, Anthony F., Jr. *quality assurance professional*
Marquand, Jean MacMurtry *educational association administrator*
Marra, Vincent J., Jr. *economics professor*
Marrin, Charles Ainsworth Staveley *cardiovascular and thoracic surgeon, educator*
Marro, Anthony James *retired newspaper editor*
Marron, Donald Baird, Jr. *economist*
Marsh, Don Ermal *supermarket executive*
Marsh, Jack, Jr., (John Otho Marsh) *lawyer, former United States Representative from Virginia*
Marsh, Joan Knight *educational film company executive, video company executive, publishing executive*
Marsh, Karyn B. *lawyer*
Marshak, Robert Reuben *retired dean, medical educator, veterinarian*
Marshall, Charles Noble *rail transportation executive*
Marshall, Frank W. *film producer, director*
Marshall, Freddie Ray *former United States Secretary of Labor*
Marshall, John Paul *broadcast engineer*
Marshall, Kathleen *choreographer, theater director*
Marshall, Robert Charles *computer company executive*
Marshall, Robert Norman *hotel executive*
Marshall, Terrylynne *art educator, painter, sculptor*
Marshall, Thomas Carlisle *retired applied physics professor*
Marshall, Wayne Keith *anesthesiology educator*
Marte-Bautista, Helen I. *retired performing arts educator*
Martens, Leslie Vernon *retired dentistry educator, consultant*
Martin, Albert Charles *manufacturing executive, lawyer*
Martin, Alice Howze *former prosecutor*
Martin, Andrea Louise *actress, comedienne, writer*
Martin, Daniel C. *surgeon, gynecologist, educator*
Martin, Edwin Wilson *mayor*
Martin, Elliot Edwards *theatrical producer*
Martin, Jacqueline Briggs *writer*
Martin, James Kay *policy and management consultant*
Martin, Jeanine Kay *retired elementary school educator*
Martin, John Carl *astronomer, educator*
Martin, John F. *academic administrator*
Martin, John William, Jr. *retired lawyer, automotive executive*
Martin, Joseph Vinson *neuroscientist, educator*
Martin, Judson Phillips *retired education educator*
Martin, Kathryn A. *endocrinologist*
Martin, Kevin Jeffrey *former federal official*
Martin, Laura *secondary school educator*
Martin, Lynn Morley *former United States Secretary of Labor*
Martin, Marcia D. *science educator*
Martin, Paul *former Prime Minister of Canada*
Martin, Thomas MacDonald *lawyer*
Martin, Tony *retired humanities educator*
Martin, William Collier *hospital administrator*
Martineau, Robert John *retired law educator*
Martinez, Mel (Melquiades Rafael Martinez) *former United States Senator from Florida, former United States Secretary of Housing and Urban Development*
Martinez, Ronald L. *literature and language professor*
Martinez Diez, Fernando *engineer*
Martinez-Munoz, Gloria Angelica *biochemist, researcher*
Martini, John *engineering educator, department chairman*
Martin-Lowry, Beverly Anne *writer, columnist*
Martino, Joseph Paul *research scientist, researcher*
Martino, Silvana *osteopath, medical oncologist*
Martorana, Barbara Joan *retired secondary school educator*
Marty, Martin Emil *theology studies educator*
Martyl, (Mrs. Alexander Langsdorf Jr.) *artist*
Martyn, Evi *musician, educator*
Martz, Mike J. *former professional football coach*
Maruyama, Magoroh *business educator, researcher, consultant*
Marvin-Basta, Laura Lynn *art educator*
Marx, Gary T. *sociologist, writer*
Marx, Michael William *language educator, writer*
Mase, Raymond James *musician, educator*
Masekela, Barbara Joyce Mosima *former ambassador*
Mashberg, Arthur *medical educator*
Mashnik, Stepan G. *physicist*
Masi, Julia A. *elementary school educator*
Masiello, Rocco Joseph *air transportation executive, consultant*
Masih, Tara Lynn *book editor, writer*
Maskaev, Oleg *professional boxer*
Masket, Edward Seymour *television executive*
Mason, Connie Jeanne *writer*
Mason, Frank Henry III *automotive and rental company executive*
Mason, John Latimer *engineering executive*
Mason, Linda *physical education educator, coach*
Mason, Lois E. (J. Day Mason) *painter, poet, actress, educator*
Mason, Thomas Albert *retired lawyer*
Mason, Thomasine Grayson *judge*
Masoner, Jason R. *hydrologist*
Massey, Keith Andrew *language educator*
Massey, Robert Unruh *internist, educator, dean*
Massey, Stephen Charles *rare book dealer, consultant*
Massey, Thomas Benjamin *retired university president*
Massoudi, Bahram Barry *management consultant*
Masten, Jacqueline Gwendolyn *small business owner*
Masters, Ann Browning *educator, poet*
Masters, George Windsor, Jr. *electrical engineer, educator*
Masterson, Peter *actor, film producer*
Mastro, Christopher P. *secondary school educator*
Mata, Linda Sue Proctor *writer, consultant*
Matarasso, Seth L. *dermatologic surgeon*
Matasar, Ann B. *retired dean, finance educator*
Matenopoulos, Debbie *television personality*
Matera, Frances Lorine *retired elementary school educator*
Materia, Kathleen Patricia Ayling *nurse*
Mates, Lawrence A., II, *medical company executive, consultant*
Mates, Robert Edward *mechanical engineering educator*
Mates, Susan Onthank *physician, educator, musician, writer*
Matheny, Adam Pence, Jr. *child psychologist, educator, consultant, researcher*
Mathes, Rachel Clarke *voice educator, singer*
Mathews, E. Anne Jones *retired library educator, academic administrator*
Mathews, Jack Wayne *journalist, film critic*
Mathews, Mary Kathryn *retired government official*
Mathieu, Michele Suzanne *grant writer, computer scientist, consultant*
Mathis, John Prentiss *lawyer*
Mathis, Luster Doyle *academic administrator, political scientist, educator*
Matiya, Jim *psychology professor*
Matlock, John Hudson *retired science administrator, materials engineer*
Matoax, Louise *mathematics educator curriculum development, consultant*
Matschullat, Robert W. *former consumer products company executive*
Matsuda, Fujio *retired academic administrator*
Matsuda, Masatake *former rail transportation executive*
Mattano, Rebecca L. *environmentalist, educator*
Matterson, Joan McDevitt *physical therapist*
Matthew, Lyn *sales executive, consultant, marketing professional*
Matthews, Barbara Caridad *lawyer*
Matthews, Elizabeth Woodfin *law librarian*
Matthews, Norman Stuart *retail executive*
Matthews, Rondra J. *publishing executive*
Matthews, Waide Kareem *librarian*
Matthiessen, Peter *author*
Mattice, Howard LeRoy *education educator*
Mattingly, Mack Francis *former ambassador, Former United States Senator, Georgia, entrepreneur*
Mattoon, Scott Alexander *private school educator*
Mattox, Johnny Lynn *biologist, educator*
Mattson, Harold Frazyer, Jr. *mathematics professor*
Matusiak, Frederick *military analyst, educator*
Mauch, Robert Carl *energy and financial services executive*
Maul, Kevin Jay *financial consultant, economist*
Maunder, Addison Bruce *agronomic research company executive*
Mauner, Claudia Anne *design educator*
Maupin, Michael Dennis *quality assurance professional*
Mauskopf, Seymour Harold *history professor*
Maxwell, Barbara Ruth *not-for-profit developer*
Maxwell, George Patrick *plastic surgeon*
Maxwell, Jerome Eugene *corporate executive*
Maxwell, W(ilbur) Richard *retired management consultant*
May, Gary Stephen *electrical engineer*
May, Ingrid Barbara *elementary school educator*
May, Janet Sue *playwright, lyricist*
May, Kenneth Nathaniel *retired food industry consultant*
May, Phyllis Jean *financial executive*
Mayer, Alisande Fountain *media specialist*
Mayer, Allan *public relations executive, consultant*
Mayer, Anthony John *investment company executive*
Mayer, James Joseph *retired corporate lawyer*
Mayer, John William (Bill Mayer) *lawyer*
Mayer, Sister Patricia E. *retired elementary school educator*
Mayer, Susan Martin *art educator*
Mayfield, Robert Charles *academic administrator, geographer, educator*
Mayfield, Sandra J. *literature and language professor*
Mayfield-Clarke, Ann Bernadette *speech, language pathologist*
Maynard, Natalie Ryshna *pianist, educator*
Mayo, Dana Walker *chemistry professor*
Mayro, Karl R. *realtor*
Mayweather, Floyd, Jr. *retired professional boxer*
Mazak, Arlene Patricia *marriage and family therapist*
Mazankowski, Donald Frank *Canadian government official*
Mazzilli, Lee *sportscaster, former professional baseball manager*
Mazzola, Marjorie Ellen *humanities educator*
Mbulaiteye, Sam *medical researcher*
McAfee, Noelle Claire *philosopher, educator*
McAlexander, Melissa *chemistry professor, researcher*
McAmis, Edwin Earl *retired lawyer*
McAndrews, Lawrence John *history professor*
McAniff, Nora P. *former publishing executive*
McAnuff, Des *artistic director*
McAnulty, William E., Jr. *former state supreme court justice*
McAuliffe, Terry (Terence Richard McAuliffe) *former political organization administrator*
McBride, Anita Bevacqua *former federal official*
McBride, Mildred Maylea *retired elementary school educator*
McBurney, Margot B. *retired librarian*
McCabe, Linda Jean *elementary school educator*
McCall, Brian David *history educator, political science educator*
McCallum, Robert Davis, Jr. *former ambassador*
McCambridge, John James *retired civil engineer*
McCandless, Carolyn Keller *retired human resources executive*
McCann, Elizabeth Ireland *theater, television and film producer*
McCann, Peter Paul *biology researcher, educator*
McCann, Renetta *former advertising executive*
McCann, Robert James *former diversified financial services company executive*
McCants, William David *lawyer, writer*
McCarey, Wilma Ruth *retired lawyer*
McCarrick, Theodore Cardinal *cardinal, archbishop emeritus*
McCarthy, April C. *elementary school educator*
McCarthy, Daniel William *management consultant*
McCarthy, Harold Charles *retired insurance company executive*
McCarthy, J. Thomas *lawyer, educator*
McCarthy, Jeanne *literature and language professor*
McCarthy, Karen P. *former congresswoman, state legislator*
McCarthy, Michael *military officer*
McCarthy, Paul Fenton *aerospace transportation executive, retired military officer*
McCarthy, Vincent Paul *lawyer*
Mc Carthy, Walter John, Jr. *retired utilities executive*
McCartney, David L. *ophthalmologist, department chairman*
McCartney, Sir Paul (James Paul McCartney) *musician*
McCarty, Shirley Carolyn *retired aerospace executive*
McCarty, Wendy Lynette *education educator*
McCash, June Hall *writer, retired language educator*
McCaskey, Raymond F. *retired health insurance company executive*
McCausland, Peter *technology company executive*
McCausland, Thomas James, Jr. *retired brokerage house executive*
McCaw, Susan Rasinski *former ambassador*
McClain, Lena Alexandria *protective services official*
McClanahan, Rue (Eddi-Rue McClanahan) *actress*
McClane, Robert Sanford *entrepreneur, bank executive*
McClatchy, Kevin S. *professional sports team executive*
McClellan, Roger Orville *toxicologist*
McClelland, Shearwood III *physician*
Mc Clendon, William Hutchinson III *retired lawyer*
McClennen, Miriam J. *former state official*
McClintock, Anne *literature and language professor*
McClinton, Donald George *retired diversified holding company executive*
McCloskey, J(ohn) Michael *retired environmental policy organization manager*
McCloud, Anece Faison *retired academic administrator*
McCloy, Shirley *adapted physical education specialist*
McConaughey, Matthew *actor*
McConnell, Edward Bosworth *legal association administrator, lawyer*
McConnell, Mike (John Michael McConnell) *former Director of National Intelligence, retired military officer*
McCord, Arline Fujii *retired university administrator, educator*

McCorkle, Robert Ellsworth *agribusiness educator*
McCormack, David Richard *lawyer*
Mc Cormack, Francis Xavier *lawyer, former oil company executive*
McCormack, Mike *former congressman*
McCormack, Sean Ian *former federal agency administrator*
McCormick, David Arthur *venture capitalist*
McCormick, Donald Bruce *retired biochemist, educator*
McCormick, John Owen *retired comparative literature educator*
McCormick, Joseph B. *healthcare educator*
McCormick, Robert Junior *former federal agency administrator*
McCosham, Joyce L. *retired secondary school educator*
McCoy, Gordon R. *minister*
McCoy, Mary Nell *music educator*
Mc Coy, Tidal Windham *former government official*
McCrary, Victor R., Jr. *engineering company executive*
McCready, Sam *theater educator and director, actor*
McCuistion, Peg Orem *retired health facility administrator*
McCullough, Laurence Bernard *medical educator, consultant*
McCurdy, Larry Wayne *automotive parts company executive*
McCurdy, Michael Charles *illustrator, author*
McCurley, Robert Lee, Jr. *lawyer, educator*
McCutcheon, Debra *school librarian*
McDade, James Russell *management consultant*
McDermott, Agnes Charlene Senape *philosophy educator*
Mc Dermott, John Francis *psychiatrist, physician*
McDiarmid, Lucy *literature educator, writer*
McDonald, April D. *writer*
McDonald, Bradley G. *lawyer*
Mc Donald, Shirley Peterson *social worker*
McDonald, William Henry *venture capitalist*
McDonnell, Joseph B. *lawyer*
McDonough, Richard Michael *philosophy educator*
McDonough, William J. *diversified financial services company executive*
McDougall, Donald Blake *retired provincial official, librarian*
McDougall, Roderick Gregory *lawyer*
McDowell, Elizabeth Mary *retired pathology educator*
McDowell, Laura Oneita *secondary school educator*
McDowell, Malcolm *actor*
McDowell, Wilbur Benedict *retired chemist consultant*
McEliece, Michelle *biology professor*
McElwreath, Sally Chin *corporate communications executive*
McEnroe, John Patrick, Jr. *retired professional tennis player*
McEwen, Megan *research scientist*
Mc Fadden, George Linus *retired army officer*
Mc Fadden, Joseph Michael *historian, educator*
McFadden, Lee Vernon *religious organization administrator*
McFadden, Peter William *retired mechanical engineering educator*
McFarlane, Donovan Anthony *finance educator, consultant*
McFarlane, Seth Woodbury *television producer, animator*
McFarling, Usha Lee *journalist*
McFate, Patricia Ann *foundation executive, science educator*
McFeatters, Ann Carey *journalist*
McGann, Lisa B. Napoli *language educator*
McGarry, Marcia *retired community service coordinator*
McGarvey, Daniel John *ecologist, educator*
McGee, Harold Johnston *former academic administrator*
McGee, Humphrey Glenn *retired architect*
McGee, Jane Marie *retired elementary school educator*
McGee, Liam E. *former bank executive*
McGee, Patrick Edgar *postal service clerk*
McGee, Robert Merrill *oil industry executive*
McGee, Stacie *social worker, educator*
McGhee, Laura L. *molecular biologist, researcher*
McGill, Dan Mays *insurance business educator*
McGill, Lisa M. *semiconductor engineer*
McGill, Robert M. *lawyer*
McGinnies, Elliott Morse *psychologist, educator*
McGinnis, Charles Irving *civil engineer*
McGlashan, Thomas Hamel *psychiatrist, educator*
McGlothlen, John M. *librarian*
McGough, Duane Theodore *economist, consultant, retired federal official*
McGovern, George Stanley *former United States Senator from South Dakota*
McGowan, Susan *gifted and talented educator*
McGrath, J. Paul *lawyer*
McGrath, Mary Helena *plastic surgeon, educator*
McGregor, John M. *medical educator*
McGregor, Theodore Anthony *chemical company executive*
McGuffey, Carroll Wade, Jr. *lawyer*
McGuigan, Michael DeTurck *research scientist*
McGuinn, Martin Gregory *retired bank executive, lawyer*
McGuinness, Kevin Michael *psychologist, director*
McGuire, James Kavanaugh *retired education educator*
McGuire, John W., Sr. *advertising executive, marketing professional, writer*
McGuire, Michael John *environmental engineer*
McGuire, Vail H. *literature and language professor*
McGuirk, Ronald Charles *retired bank executive, economic advisor*
McGuirk, Terrence *former broadcasting company executive*
McGurk, Christopher Jamie *film company executive*
McHenry, Barnabas *lawyer*
McHenry, Bart *academic administrator*
McIlroy, Alan F. *manufacturing executive*
McInerney, Elaine F. *medical educator*
McIntier, Russell J. *retired writer*
McIntosh, Terrie Tuckett *lawyer*
McIntyre, Virgie M. *retired elementary school educator*
McKale, Michael *religious studies educator, director*
McKay, Kenneth Gardiner *retired physicist, electronics company executive*
McKay, Margo Marquita *lawyer, former federal agency administrator*
McKay, Michael Kevin *nurse, priest, chaplain*
McKay, Patricia A. *corporate financial executive*
McKay, Paul Patrick *healthcare educator*
McKay, Renee *artist*
McKean, Robert Jackson, Jr. *retired lawyer*
McKee, Betty Davis *English language educator*
McKee, Roger Curtis *retired federal judge*
McKeever-Thompson, Claire L. *nurse, educator, consultant, human services manager*
McKenna, Erin Nicole *history professor*
McKenna, Stephen James *retired lawyer, corporate executive*
McKenna, Terence Patrick *retired insurance company executive*
McKennon, Keith Robert *chemical company executive*
McKenzie, Bret *musician, actor*
McKeown, Mary Elizabeth *retired academic administrator*
McKeown, William P. *retired lawyer*
Mc Keown, William Taylor *magazine editor, author*
McKinley, Ellen Bacon *priest*
McKinnell, Hank (Henry A. McKinnell Jr.) *retired pharmaceutical executive*
McKinney, Bart *orthopedist, researcher*
McKinney, Brett *medical educator*
McKinney, Joseph Crescent *bishop emeritus*
McKinzie, Barbara Anne *educational association administrator*
McKlenshaw, Irvin Lee *retired small business owner, advocate*
McKneely, Joey *choreographer*
McKnight, Lee Holland *literature and language professor*
McKowen, Dorothy Keeton *educator, librarian*
McLauchlin, Vera Ann *history professor*
McLaughlin, Frank E. *nursing educator*
McLaughlin, John Edward *former federal agency administrator*
McLaughlin, Joseph *lawyer*
McLaughlin, Leighton Bates, II, *retired journalist, reporter, educator*
McLaughlin, William Irving *space technical manager, writer*
McLaurin, Lambert Paschal *retired medical educator*
McLawhon, Ronald William *pathology educator, biochemist*
McLean, Walter Franklin *government agency administrator, business consultant, legislator, minister*
McLellon, Richard Steven *aerospace engineer, consultant*
Mclendon, Roger Edwin *neuropathologist, educator*
McLeskey, Charles Hamilton *anesthesiologist, educator, pharmaceutical executive*
McLure, Victoria *literature and language professor*
McMahan-Woneis, Celestine *integrative medical educator, health psychologist, educator, educational therapist, health psychology educator*
McMahon, Harry Thomas *investment company executive*
McMahon, James E. *lawyer, former prosecutor*
McManus, Alesia *librarian*
McManus, Jason Donald *retired editor-in-chief*
McManus, John Coyne *educator, writer*
McManus, Patrick Francis *editor, educator, writer*
McManus, Richard Philip *lawyer, agricultural products executive*
McManus, William Paul *police chief*
McMaster, Belle Miller *religious organization administrator*
McMaster, Brian John *artistic director*
McMaster, Juliet Sylvia *English language educator*
McMenamin, Sarah Kelly *biologist, educator*
McMillan, Robert Ralph *lawyer*
McMillin, Stephen Scott *former federal official*
McMurtry, R. Cody *physical education educator*
McNair, John William, Jr. *civil engineer*
McNally, Mark Thomas *history professor*
McNally, Regina C. *marketing educator*
McNamara, Brenda Norma *retired secondary school educator*
McNamara, Kristin Tara *literature and language educator, small business owner*
McNamara, Thomas Edmund (Ted) *federal official, former ambassador*
McNamee, Lawrence Ross, Jr. *manufacturing executive*
McNeal, Monica Malone *medical educator, director*
McNealey, Billie *psychologist*
McNeil, Edward Warren *real estate company executive*
McNeill, Dan K. *retired military officer*
McNeill, Robert Patrick *investment advisor*
McNitt, Willard Charles *food products executive*
McNulty, Kathleen Anne *social worker, consultant, psychologist*
McNulty, Michael Robert *former United States Representative from New York*
McPeters, Sharon Jenise *artist, writer*
McPhearson, Geraldine June *retired medical/surgical nurse*
McPhee, John Angus *writer*
McPheeters, Edwin Keith *architect, educator*
McPherson, Donald Scott *labor and employment arbitrator/mediator*
McPherson, James Alan *writer, educator*
McPherson, Naemi Tanaka *language educator*
Mc Quade, Lawrence Carroll *lawyer, investment company executive*
McQueen, Regenia *writer*
McQuerry, Patricia Ann *painter, retired secondary school educator*
McShefferty, John *retired research executive personal care, industry executive consultant*
Mc Sheffrey, Gerald Rainey *architect, educator, city planner, author*
McSorley, Rita Elizabeth *adult education educator*
McSwain, Byrdie Engle *laboratory scientist, immunohematologist*
McSwain, Robert G. *former federal agency administrator*
McSweeny, William Francis *petroleum company executive, author*
McTaggart, Timothy Robert *state agency administrator, lawyer*
McTague, John Paul *materials scientist, educator, chemist, researcher*
McWethy, Patricia Joan *educational association administrator*
McWhirter, Jamila LeAnn *choral conductor*
McWhorter, Diane *writer*
McWilliams, Karen Joan *writer*
McWilliams, Michael *writer, publisher*
McWilliams, Teressa Wylie *choreographer*
Meacham, David Adam *biologist*
Meacham, Susan *dietician, educator*
Meadors, Constance Yvonne *engineering educator, researcher*
Meadows, Gwendolyn Joann *retired behavioral disorders educator*
Meads, Donald Edward *management services company executive*
Meara, Anne *actress, playwright, writer*
Mears, Walter Robert *retired journalist*
Mecca, Kimberly Ann *psychologist*
Mecklenburg, Gary Alan *retired hospital administrator*
Medavoy, Mike (Morris Mike Medavoy) *film company executive, producer*
Medders, Emily Anna *speech pathology/audiology services professional*
Medina, Mariemma *lawyer, educator*
Medina, Sandra *social worker, educator*
Meding, Stephen Mercer *research scientist*
Mednick, Robert *accountant*
Meehan, Patrick Leo *former prosecutor*
Meek, Forrest Burns *retired trading company executive*
Meerschaert, Joseph Richard *retired physician*
Meffert, Roland Matthew *retired periodontist*
Megna, Steve Allan *retired secondary school educator*
Mehne, Paul Randolph *consultant, retired medical educator*
Meigher, S. Christopher III *communications and media executive, publisher*
Meigs, Montgomery Cunningham, Jr. *retired military officer, educator*
Meiksin, Zvi H. *electrical engineering educator*
Meilan, Celia *food products executive*
Meilman, Edward *physician*
Meinwald, Jerrold *retired chemistry professor*
Meisel, David Dering *retired astronomer*
Mejia, Sister Cristel *language educator*
Mejico, Luis J. *neurologist, educator*
Melanson, Dorothy *political organization administrator*
Melczek, Dale Joseph *bishop*
Melder, Keith E. *retired curator*
Meldman, Robert Edward *lawyer*
Meldrum, Deirdre Ruth *electrical engineer, educator*
Mele, Joanne Theresa *dentist*
Melillo, Joseph Vincent *theater producer*
Mellerick-Dressler, Dervla M. *medical association administrator*
Mellinkoff, Sherman Mussoff *medical educator*
Mellins, Claude Ann *psychologist*
Mellins, Harry Zachary *radiologist, educator*
Mellott, John C. *retired publishing executive*
Melody, Michael Edward *publishing company executive*
Meloy, Judith Marie *retired humanities educator*
Melton, William Everett *retired music educator*
Meltzer, Jay H. *lawyer, consultant*
Melvin, Billy Alfred *clergyman*
Melvin, Peter Joseph *astrophysicist, educator*
Menaker, Daniel *former publishing executve, television producer*
Menaker, Ronald Herbert *retired bank executive*
Mench, John William *retail executive, electrical engineer*
Mencher, Joan Phyllis *anthropology educator*
Mende, Robert Graham *retired engineering association executive*
Mendels, Joseph *psychiatrist, educator*
Mendelson, Joan Rintel *lawyer*
Mendoza, George *poet, author*
Menefee, Linnea-Norma *antique dealer*
Menicucci, Audrey *artist*
Menlove, Frances Lee *psychologist*
Menn, Julius Joel *retired research scientist, consultant*
Menna, Sári *artist, educator*
Menon, Jai M. *information technology manager*
Menzel, Jiří *film and theater director, actor*
Mercay, Jessie Jardine *academic administrator, educator*
Mercer, Dorothy May *real estate company executive*
Mercer, Edwin Wayne *lawyer*
Mercer, Richard James *lawyer*
Merchant, Rahul *former mortgage company executive*
Mercurio, Renard Michael *real estate company executive*
Meredith, Andrea L. *medical educator*
Meredith, Lisa Ann Marie *literacy coach, consultant*
Meredith, Thomas Brian *healthcare consultant*
Meredith, Wendi Sue *music educator*
Merino, Adriana Graciela *language educator*
Meriwether, Heath J. *newspaper consultant, retired publisher, educator*
Merkin, Albert Charles *pediatrician, allergist*
Merriam, Robert W. *engineering executive, educator*
Merrill, Jean Fairbanks *writer*
Merrill, Joseph Melton *medical educator*
Merritt, Bruce Gordon *lawyer*
Merritt, Libbie *safety engineer*
Merritt, Nancy-Jo *lawyer*
Merritt, Susan Mary *computer science educator, dean*
Merriweather, Freda E. *education educator*
Mersfelder, Tracey *pharmacist, educator*
Merson, Susan Ilene *actor, writer, producer*
Merwade, Venkatesh M. *hydrologist*
Meschan, Lynn *psychology professor*
Meshejian, Wayne Kit *retired physics professor*
Meshel, Harry *former state senator, political party official*
Meshkaty, Shahra *academic administrator*
Meskill, Victor P. *academic administrator, educator*
Mesney, Kathryn *theater educator*
Messa, Charles Angelo III *plastic surgeon*
Messer, Donald Edward *author, theology educator, administrator*
Messerle, Judith Rose *retired medical librarian, public relations executive*
Messier, Pierre *lawyer, manufacturing executive*
Messmer, Donald Joseph *business management educator, marketing consultant*
Messner, Robert Thomas *lawyer, bank executive*
Mestel, Sherry Y. *social worker, school psychologist, art therapist*
Mestres, Ricardo A. III *film company executive*
Metallo, Claudine *language educator*
Metcalf, Karen *retired foundation executive*
Metcalf, Laurie (Lauren Ophelia Metcalfe) *actress*
Metcalf, William Edwards *museum curator, educator*
Metcalfe, Robert Davis III *lawyer*
Metz, T(heodore) John *librarian, educator*
Meurer, William Joseph *emergency physician, educator*
Mewshaw, Richard Eric *chemist*
Meyer, Charlotte Lois *medical geriatric social worker, consultant*
Meyer, Dorothy Jean *nursing consultant, director*
Meyer, Henry Lewis III *bank executive*
Meyer, Max Earl *lawyer*
Meyer, Philip Edward *journalism educator*
Meyer, Piotr Jan *electronics engineer*
Meyer, Pucci *editor*
Meyer, Richard W. *retired university librarian*
Meyer, Robert R. *retired science educator*
Meyer, Theo E. *cardiologist*
Meyerhoff, James Lester *medical researcher*
Meyerink, Victoria Paige *film producer, actress*
Meyers, Robert Allen *chemist, publisher*
Meyers, Tedson Jay *lawyer*
Meyerson, Ivan D. *lawyer, former corporate financial executive*
Michael, George T. *real estate manager, developer*
Michael, Jerrold Mark *public health service officer, educator, retired dean*
Michael, Mark Alber *cardiologist, researcher*
Michael, Simon R. *physician scientist, educator*
Michaud, Georges Joseph *physics professor*
Michel, George Frederick *psychology professor, researcher*
Michel, Mary Ann Kedzuf *retired nursing educator*
Michelle, Millay Kathleen *sculptor*
Mick, Diane Joan *nurse*
Mickes, Laura *psychology professor*
Mick III, Leonard Silas *language educator*
Middaugh, Robert Burton *artist*
Middelhoek, André J. *retired international organization administrator, auditor*
Middleman, Raoul Fink *artist*
Midelfort, Hans Christian Erik *retired history professor*
Miekka, Jeanette Ann *retired science educator*
Miele, Joel Arthur, Sr. *civil engineer*
Migaj, David *language educator*
Miguda, Edith Atieno *history professor*
Migue, Jean Luc *economics professor*
Miguel, Luis *musician*
Mihaly, Laszlo *physics professor*
Mihram, George Arthur *mathematician*
Mikaelian, Tsoline *aerospace engineer*
Mikeska, Noel Rhea *entrepreneur, health advocate*
Mikhelashvili, Tim *pharmaceutical executive*
Mikhelson, Sergei *mathematician, educator*
Mikiewicz, Anna Daniella *marketing and international business export manager*
Mikitka, Gerald Peter *brokerage house executive, consultant*
Mikulics, Michael P. *literature and language educator*
Milan, Stojanovic P. *medical educator, director*
Milch, Peter Stephen *retired finance educator*
Miles, Frank Charles *retired newspaper executive*
Miles, Laveda Ann *advertising executive*
Miley, Bryan S. *language educator, real estate broker*
Millane, Lynn *retired municipal official*
Millar, John Donald *physician, occupational & environmental health services consultant, musician*
Millard, Charles Warren III *retired museum director, writer*
Millea, Thomas Francis *photographer*
Miller, Alan J. *retired financial company executive*
Miller, Allen Richard *retired mathematician*
Miller, Anthony Bernard *physician, researcher*
Miller, Arjay *retired university dean*
Miller, Beverly A(nn) *reference librarian, professor*
Miller, Brenda *Johrei practitioner*
Miller, Carole Ann Lyons *writer, editor, publisher, marketing executive*
Miller, Dale Eugene *philosopher, educator*
Miller, Donald LeSessne *publishing executive*
Miller, Edmund Kenneth *retired electrical engineer, educator*
Miller, Elizabeth Gamble *literature and language professor, translator*
Miller, Ellen S. *marketing executive*
Miller, Gay Davis *lawyer*
Miller, G(erson) H(arry) *science administrator, mathematician, computer scientist, chemist*
Miller, Harold Edward *retired manufacturing conglomerate executive, consultant*
Miller, Harriet Sanders *former art center director*
Miller, Jack David R. *radiologist, physician, educator*
Miller, Jacqueline Winslow *library director*
Miller, Jerry Huber *retired university chancellor*
Miller, John Lester *electro-optical physicist*
Miller, Jonathan S. *former state treasurer*
Miller, Laura M. *former mayor, journalist*

Miller, Lisa Ann *lawyer*
Miller, Marilyn Lea *library and information scientist, educator*
Miller, Mark David *orthopedist, surgeon, educator*
Miller, Matthew Jason *science educator, director*
Miller, Norman Charles, Jr. *editor, reporter*
Miller, Patrick William *research scientist, educator*
Miller, R. Charles *lawyer*
Miller, Richard Glen *financial planning executive*
Miller, Richard Steven *lawyer*
Miller, Roberta Doris *elementary school educator*
Miller, Ross Hays *retired neurosurgeon*
Miller, Shannon *Olympic athlete*
Milligan, Cynthia Hardin *dean, lawyer*
Milligan, Victor *consulting engineer*
Millikan, Diane Linda *insurance company executive*
Millimet, Erwin *lawyer*
Millon, Henry Armand *art educator*
Mills, Corinne C. *music educator*
Mills, Dale Douglas *journalist*
Mills, David L. *retired electrical engineer, computer scientist, educator*
Mills, Elizabeth Shown *historical writer, genealogist*
Mills, Eugene Sumner *academic administrator*
Mills, Helene Audrey *retired education educator*
Mills, Kevin Lee *computer scientist, researcher*
Mills, Richard Paul *former state official, school system administrator*
Mills, Steven A. *information technology executive*
Mills-Koonce, William Roger *psychologist, director*
Milner, Irvin Myron *retired lawyer*
Milnor, Hazel *nurse*
Milunas, J. Robert *health care organization executive*
Milway, Phyllis Louise *human services manager*
Min, Janice Byung *former editor-in-chief*
Min, Misun *mathematician*
Minagawa, Teiichi *molecular biologist*
Minahan, Daniel Francis *lawyer, retired manufacturing executive*
Mindlin, Paula Rosalie *retired reading educator*
Minehan, Cathy Elizabeth *retired bank executive*
Minner, Ruth Ann *former Governor of Delaware*
Minners, Howard Alyn *federal agency administrator, researcher, preventive medicine physician*
Minnich, Donna *social sciences educator*
Minshall, Greg *computer programmer*
Mintz, M. J. *lawyer*
Mintz, Morton Abner *writer, reporter*
Miquelon, Miriam F. *former prosecutor, lawyer*
Mir, Montserrat *education educator*
Miracle, Doris Jean *retired medical/surgical nurse*
Miranda-Levi, Jason *film producer, writer*
Mirfakhraie, Koorosh *systems engineer, educator*
Miriam, Frazure Amanda *research scientist*
Mirren, Helen (Ilynea Lydia Mironoff) *actress*
Mirza, Zakir Hussain *aerospace company consultant*
Mirzaei, Ahmad *electrical engineer*
Mishin, Evgeny Vilenovich *physicist*
Miskimen, Theresa Marie *psychiatrist, educator*
Miskus, Michael Anthony *electrical engineer*
Mislow, Kurt Martin *chemist, educator*
Misrack, Tana Marie *counselor, minister, writer*
Mistry, Percy Shiavak *investment banker*
Mitchell, Brian Stokes *actor*
Mitchell, Carol Ann *nursing educator*
Mitchell, David Benjamin *lawyer, arbitrator, mediator*
Mitchell, John Charles *marketing professional*
Mitchell, Sam *former professional basketball coach*
Mitchell, Steve Harold *psychologist*
Mitchell, William D. (Bill Mitchell) *lawyer*
Mitchell, William Marvin *pathology educator*
Mitchem, Cheryl E. *accounting educator*
Mitman, Meghan Fehlig *transportation engineer*
Mitra, Abhijit *chemistry professor*
Mitra, Pritha *economist*
Mitra, Rupak *molecular biologist*
Mitroff, Ian I. *finance educator*
Mitteldorfer, Shirley Justis *education educator, consultant*
Mittendorf, Kimberly Ann *retired secondary school educator, real estate consultant*
Mittleider, Rebecca Ann *elementary school educator*
Mitzner, Kenneth Martin *electrical engineer, consultant*
Mixon, Victoria *writer*
Miyake, Yasuji *computer science educator*
Mize, Ronald L. *social studies educator*
Miziorko, Henry M. *research scientist, educator*
Mladick, Richard Anthony *plastic surgeon*
Mlakar, Roy A. *former professional sports team executive*
Moazed, Khosrow L. *retired engineering educator*
Mobley, William Hodges *management consultant, educator, writer, researcher*
Moch, Peggy L. *mathematics professor*
Modisher, Melvin Wayne *obstetrician, gynecologist, educator*
Modny, Cynthia Jean *dermatologist*
Moe, Lonn Andre *state revenue official*
Moeller, Joseph John, Jr. *university official*
Moenssens, Sandra Birkelbach *licensed marriage and family therapist, licensed mental health counselor*
Moffat, MaryBeth *consulting company executive*
Moffatt, Joyce Anne *performing company executive*
Moffatt, Katy (Katherine Louella Moffatt) *musician, lyricist, vocalist*
Moffett, David McKenzie *former mortgage company executive, retired bank executive*
Mogae, Festus Gontebanye *former president of Botswana*
Mogel, Leonard Henry *writer*
Moghimzadeh, Mahmood *economics professor*
Mogilnicki, Eric J. *legislative staff member*
Mohaideen, A. Hassan *surgeon, consultant, health products executive*
Mohajer Iravani, Baharak *engineer*
Mohamadi, Masoud *retired surgeon*
Mohammad, Asif Iqbal *algorithms engineer, researcher*
Mohan, Jyoti *history professor*
Mohan, Tungesh Nath *television and film producer, film educator*
Mohanty, Saraju P. *computer scientist, educator*
Mohler, Ronald Rutt *electrical engineering educator*
Mohr, Jay *comedian, actor*
Mohseni Languri, Ehsan *mechanical engineer, researcher*
Mok, Samuel Tinsing *management consultant, former federal agency administrator*
Mokhatab, Saeid *gas industry technical consultant*
Molholm, Kurt Nelson *retired federal agency administrator*
Molinaro, Joseph Daniel *dentist, director*
Moline, Jennifer M. *corporate financial executive*
Moll, David Carter *civil engineer*
Moll, Lloyd Henry *retired bank executive*
Moll, Maryann Elizabeth *education educator*
Mollenauer, Linn Frederick *retired physicist, writer*
Moloney, Stephen Michael *lawyer*
Moloney, William J. *former state official, school system administrator*
Molz, Redmond Kathleen *public affairs educator*
Monaco, Chris *historian, writer, documentary filmmaker*
Moncrieff, Mitchell William *atmosphere physicist researcher*
Mondlin, Marvin *publisher, appraiser, consultant*
Mone, Peter John *lawyer*
Mongo, Karen Mathis *speech educator*
Monjan, Andrew Arthur *retired neuroscientist*
Monroe, Carl Dean III *lawyer*
Monroe, Frederick Fales *geologist, oceanographer*
Monroe, Stephanie Johnson *lobbyist, former federal agency administrator*
Monroe, William Lewis *human resources executive*
Monsen, Elaine Ranker *nutritionist, educator, editor*
Monson, Nancy Peckel *writer, editor, book collaborator, spokesperson*
Montague, Brian John *consulting company executive*
Monteith, Larry King *chancellor emeritus*
Montelongo, Michael D. *marketing executive, former civilian military employee*
Montero, Sylvia *former pharmaceutical executive*
Montford, John Thomas *communications executive, lawyer, former state legislator*
Montgomery, Betty Dee *former state attorney general, state legislator*
Montgomery, Cliff Wilson *journalist, writer, researcher*
Montgomery, Hubert Theron, Jr. *physician, health care administrator*
Montgomery, John Richard *pediatrician, educator*
Montgomery, Lani Lynn *art educator*
Montgomery, Roy Delbert *retired gas industry executive*
Montoya, Regina T. *lawyer*
Montrone, Paul Michael *former scientific instruments company executive*
Moody, Myriam Sylvie *mathematics professor*
Moon, Barbara G. *lawyer*
Moon, Craig A. *retired publishing executive*
Moon, Il-Ju *meteorologist*
Moon, Jane Anderson *systems engineer, consultant*
Moon, Loretta Marie *recreational therapist*
Mooney, Michael Joseph *university professor*
Mooney, Robert Thurston *healthcare educator*
Mooney, Ted (Edward Comstock Mooney) *editor, art critic, writer*
Moore, Alan *writer*
Moore, Andrew Given Tobias, II, *investment banker, law educator*
Moore, Betty Jo *retired legal assistant*
Moore, Billy Don *scriptwriter, film producer*
Moore, Cornell Leverette *financial services executive, lawyer*
Moore, Demi (Demi Guynes, Demetria Gene Guynes) *actress*
Moore, Derrick Lanier *military officer*
Moore, Donald Walter *retired academic administrator*
Moore, Donnica Lauren *physician, medical writer*
Moore, Fay Linda *systems engineer*
Moore, Jean E. *social worker, academic administrator, educator, radio personality*
Moore, John Eddy *former lieutenant governor*
Moore, John Ronald *manufacturing executive*
Moore, Malcolm Frederick *manufacturing executive*
Moore, Marla W. *school librarian*
Moore, Michael *filmmaker, writer*
Moore, Mike (Michael C.) *lawyer, former state attorney general*
Moore, Nancy M. *secondary school educator*
Moore, Pamela Gay *retired music educator*
Moore, Richard Hancock *lawyer, former state treasurer*
Moore, Robert Henry *writer, editor, communications consultant*
Moore, Robert William *professional organization executive*
Moore, Ronald Lee *physicist*
Moore, Stanley Wayne *retired political science professor*
Moore, Thomas Andrew *biotechnology executive*
Moore, Thomas David *academic administrator*
Moore, Thomas Holmes *retired school administrator*
Moore, Thomas Paul *retired broadcast executive*
Moore, William Henry *radiologist*
Moore, William Vegh *sports medicine physician*
Moorer, Emily Hall *literature and language educator*
Moore-Wleklinski, Patricia Marie *secondary school educator*
Moorhead, Lucy Galpin *writer*
Moossy, John *neurologist, consultant, pathologist*
Moradi, Ahmad F. *software company executive*
Moran, Charles A. *security firm executive, educator*
Moran, Kevin J. *publishing operations director*
Moran, Thomas Harry *retired academic administrator*
Morcott, Southwood Jelks (Woody Morcott) *retired automotive parts company executive*
Morden, John Reid *security-international relations consultant*
Morden, Robert Dean *biology professor*
Mordohai, Philippos *engineering educator*
Morduch, Jonathan *economist, educator*
Moreau, Nancy A. *physics professor*
Morelan, Paula Kay *choreographer*
Moreland, Richard Paul *musician, educator*
Morella, Constance Albanese *former United States Representative from Maryland*
Morelli, James Kevin *biochemist*
Morello, Joseph Albert *musician, educator*
Morello, Tom *musician*
Moreno, Albert F. *lawyer, former apparel executive*
Moreno, Carlos Sanchez *aerospace engineer*
Moreno, Rita (Rosita Dolores Alverio) *actress*
Moretti, August Joseph *pharmaceutical executive, lawyer*
Morgan, Anne Marie G. *broadcast journalist, educator*
Morgan, Betsy L. *former publishing executive*
Morgan, Christopher Donald *mechanical engineer, consultant*
Morgan, Edmund Sears *retired history professor*
Morgan, Jeff *literature and language professor*
Morgan, Joyce Elizabeth *retired elementary school educator*
Morgan, M. Jane *computer systems consultant*
Morgan, Marlene *education educator, consultant*
Morgan, Oliver WC *epidemiologist*
Morgan, Ruth Prouse *academic administrator, educator*
Morgan, Sandra *science educator*
Morgan, Timi Sue *lawyer*
Morgan, William J. *independent director, leadership development consultant and retired accounting company executive*
Morgenstein, William *shoe company executive*
Morgenstern, Kenneth E. *plastic surgeon*
Morgenthaler, Alisa *lawyer*
Moriarty, Donald William, Jr. *bank executive*
Morin, Lynn P. *music educator, director, secondary school educator*
Morissette, Alanis Nadine *singer*
Morita, Linå *pianist, educator*
Moritz, Chad Henry *research scientist*
Moriyama, Karen Ito *retired educational association administrator*
Morley, Jeffrey Joshua *dentist, educator*
Morley, Lloyd Albert *electrical engineering educator*
Morof, Jeffrey W. *lawyer*
Morphew, Dorothy Richards-Bassett *artist, real estate broker*
Morrell, Ayako M. *language educator*
Morrell, Robert Hanly *television producer, director*
Morris, Brenda Denise *music educator, director*
Morris, Errol *filmmaker*
Morris, G. Ronald *automotive executive*
Morris, John *composer, conductor, arranger*
Morris, John Woodland, II, *retired engineering consultant, military officer*
Morris, Lissa Camille *music educator*
Morris, Robert Gemmill *retired foreign service officer*
Morris, Tammy Kay *bank executive*
Morris, William Clinton, Jr. *petroleum engineer*
Morrisett, Lloyd N. *retired foundation executive*
Morrison, Donald William *lawyer*
Morrison, Martin *writer*
Morrison, Paul J. *former state attorney general, prosecutor*
Morrison, Robert Scheck *former manufacturing executive, former food products executive*
Morrison, Shelley *actress*
Morrison, Toni (Chloe Ardelia Wofford) *writer, educator, editor*
Morrison, Winifred Elaine Haas *social sciences educator*
Morrissette, Jerusha M. *music educator*
Morrissey, Charles Thomas *historian, educator*
Morrow, Rob *actor*
Morse, Carmel Lei *professor*
Morse, Gayle Skawennio *psychologist, consultant*
Morse, Judith *music educator, conductor*
Morse, Robert Harry *lawyer*
Morse-McNeely, Patricia *poet, writer, retired secondary school educator*
Mortensen, Viggo *actor, writer*
Mortimer, Richard Walter *mechanical engineer, educator*
Morton, Donald John *librarian*
Morton, James Carnes, Jr. *retired automotive executive*
Mosbacher, Robert Adam, Jr. *former investment company executive*
Moseley, April Lowe *artist*
Moseley, Julia W. *music educator, preservationist*
Mosemann, Lloyd Kenneth, II, *retired research and development company executive*
Moser, Barry *artist*
Moser, Jeffery Richard *not profit developer, director, grant writer*
Mosier, Virginia Lou *school system administrator*
Mosier, William Arthur *psychiatrist, psychotherapist, director, medical educator, researcher*
Mosiman, Rita Esther *music educator, performing artist*
Moskow, Michael Harold *retired bank executive*
Moss, Madison Scott *retired editor*
Moss, Marc *medical educator*
Moss, Thomas Henry *science foundation director, physicist*
Mossavar-Rahmani, Sharmin *diversified financial services company executive*
Moss Greenberg, Jill *special education administrator, civil rights activist*
Mosteller, Darla Brooks *singer, educator*
Motaghiannezam, Reza Mohammad *engineering educator*
Motamed, Thomas Firouz *insurance company executive*
Motheral, Brenda R. *health products executive*
Motroni, Hector John *retired printing company executive*
Mott, Rodney B. *metal products executive*
Motto, Jerome Arthur *psychiatrist, educator*
Mottola, Tommy (Thomas Daniel Mottola) *recording industry executive*
Mouillet, Alain Charles *retired engineering educator, researcher*
Moulds, Eric Shannon *professional football player*
Mouledous, Pierrette Marie *music educator*
Mounasamy, Varatharaj *orthopedist, educator*
Movahedzadeh, Farahnaz *medical researcher, educator*
Mow, Van C. *engineering educator, researcher*
Mower, Morton Maimon *cardiologist*
Moya, Patrick Robert *lawyer*
Moyano, Marcela *communications educator*
Moyer, R. Charles *finance company executive, educator, retired dean*
Moynahan, John Daniel, Jr. *retired insurance executive*
Moyse, Hermann III *banker*
Mozilo, Angelo R. *retired mortgage company executive*
Mracky, Ronald Sydney *marketing executive, tourism consultant, media specialist*
Mramor, Marti *engineer, linguist*
Mudavanhu, Blessing *research scientist*
Mudigonda, Ashwin *electrical engineer, researcher*
Mudry, Michael *pension and benefit consultant*
Mueller, Ada Rose *elementary school educator*
Mueller, Berndt *physics professor*
Mueller, Gary Alfred *software engineer*
Mueller, Robert Louis *manufacturing executive*
Mueller-Heubach, Eberhard *medical educator*
Mugambi, Helen Nabasuta *literature educator*
Muhammad, Claudette Marie *religious organization administrator*
Muhn, Judy Ann *psychologist, genealogist, trainer*
Muir, J. Dapray *lawyer*
Mujica-Parodi, Mauro E. *architect*
Mulawka, Diane I. *mathematics educator*
Mulcahy, Gabriel M. *pathologist*
Mulcahy, Robert Edward *management consultant*
Mullen, Terri Ann *retired special education educator*
Mullen, William Joseph III *retired career army officer*
Muller, Henry James *journalist, magazine editor*
Muller, Henry Nicholas III *retired foundation administrator*
Muller, Peter *lawyer, film company and retail executive*
Mullins, Charles Brown *physician, academic administrator*
Mullis, Kary Banks *biochemist*
Muluzi, Elson Bakili *former President of Malawi*
Mulvee, Robert Edward *bishop emeritus*
Mulvey, Victoria A. *counselor*
Mulvihill, Maureen Esther *writer, professor*
Mumma, Albert Girard, Jr. *architect*
Munitz, Barry A. *former foundation administrator*
Munoz, Mario Alejandro *civil engineer, retired consultant*
Muñoz Dones De Carrascal, Eloisa (Eloise Munoz Dones) *hospital administrator, pediatrician, educator*
Muñoz-Solá, Haydeé Socorro *retired library administrator*
Munro, Barbara Hazard *retired nursing educator, dean, researcher*
Munro, Donald William, Jr. *non-profit organization executive*
Munsell, Elsie Louise *retired lawyer*
Munsey, Virdell Everard, Jr. *retired utilities executive*
Munson, Ronald Alfred *retired chemist*
Munt, Janet Staples *state senator*
Munver, Ravi *urologist*
Munzner, Robert Frederick *biomedical engineer*
Murarka, Shyam Prasad *science and engineering educator, administrator*
Murat, Yusef J. *plastic surgeon*
Murchison, David Claudius *lawyer*
Murdock, John Gustaf *physics professor*
Murdock, Larry Paul *religious studies educator, director*
Murdock, Steven H. *former federal agency administrator*
Murff, Elizabeth Jane Tipton *mathematician, statistician, educator*
Murin, Joseph J. *former mortgage company executive*
Murphey, Sheila Ann *infectious diseases physician, educator, researcher*
Murphy, Evelyn Frances *economist*
Murphy, Francis *language educator*
Murphy, Gerald *retired federal official*
Murphy, Kimberly Ann *biology professor*
Murphy, Lesley Ryann *geneticist*
Murphy, Marilyn Jane *library director*
Murphy, Marion Colucci *writer, poet*
Murphy, Mary Leigh *artist*
Murphy, Michael Joseph *former state treasurer*
Murphy, Randall Kent *writer, educator, consultant*
Murphy, Remington Morris *clerk*
Murphy, Stacia *former health service association executive*
Murray, Carla Mary *sound effects artist*
Murray, David George *architect*
Murray, Julia Kaoru (Mrs. Joseph E. Murray) *occupational therapist*
Murray, Robert Gray *sculptor*
Murray, Timothy Patrick *Lieutenant Governor of Massachusetts, former mayor*
Murray Shaw, Juleen *actress*
Murry, J. Warren *surgeon, educator*
Musa, Samuel Albert *university executive*
Musante, Tony (Anthony Peter Musante Jr.) *actor*
Musick, Katherine M. *research scientist*
Musihin, Konstantin K. *electrical engineer*
Muson, Howard Henry *writer, consultant*
Musselman, Larry L. *retired chemical engineer*
Mustard, Lewis Williams *management consultant, educator*
Muszynska, Agnieszka (Agnes) *mechanical engineering researcher, consultant*
Mutale, Christian Thales *research scientist*
Muthukrishnan, Swarna *research scientist*
Myer, Donald Beekman *architect*
Myerowitz, P(aul) David *cardiac surgeon, educator, writer*
Myers, Allen Richard *rheumatologist*

Myers, Angela Michelle *music educator, department chairman*
Myers, Caitlin Knowles *economics professor*
Myers, Dee Dee (Margaret Jane Myers) *television personality, former White House press secretary*
Myers, Donald Alan *transportation executive*
Myers, Dorothy Roatz *artist*
Myers, Franklin *oil industry executive*
Myers, Jeffrey Daniel *concert pianist, music educator*
Myers, Jesse Jerome *lawyer*
Myers, Mark D. *geologist, former federal official*
Myers, Michele Tolela *former academic administrator*
Myers, Phillip Fenton *corporate financial, technology executive*
Myers, Robert David *judge*
Myers, Sophia M. *writer, researcher, artist, cartographer, translator*
Myren, Richard Albert *criminologist, consultant*
Myrth, Judy G. *retired editor*
Mysore, Shashidhar C. *computer scientist*
Nabors, Robert Lee, Sr. *military officer*
Nachman, Gerald Weil *columnist, critic, writer*
Nadeau, Robert M. *geophysicist*
Nadel, Elliott *investment company executive*
Nadolski, Dora J. *social sciences educator, researcher*
Naes, Jennifer Le *medical technologist*
Nagaraj, Vengalattore Thattai *aerospace engineer*
Nagashima, Masayuki *chemical and mechanical engineer, researcher*
Nagel, Thomas *philosopher, lawyer, educator*
Nagle, Eugenia Susan Karabacz *retired sociologist, psychologist*
Nagler, Stewart Gordon *retired insurance company executive*
Nagy, Elizabeth Garver *artist*
Nahman, Norris Stanley *electrical engineer*
Naidoo, Robin *biologist, researcher*
Naidorf, Louis Murray *architect*
Naik, Rupali K. *researcher*
Najjar, Samer S. *internist, educator*
Nam, Seung Yeob *network technician, researcher*
Nampet, Wajira *psychology professor*
Nance, Mary Joe *retired secondary school educator*
Nance, Tony Max-Perry *designer, illustrator*
Nanda, Ved Prakash *law educator, director, academic administrator*
Nandikolla, Vidya K. *engineering educator, researcher*
Nanos, George Peter, Jr. *former science administrator, military officer, physicist*
Naoumova, Irina Yevgenievna *business educator, consultant*
Napier, Cameron Mayson Freeman *historic preservationist*
Narbon, Lilian *writer*
Narita, Hiro *cinematographer*
Narron, Jerry Austin *former professional baseball manager*
Narumanchi, Sreekant Venkat Jagannath *energy executive*
Nasgaard, Roald *museum curator*
Nash, Linda Kay *music educator*
Nash, Melvin Samuel *lawyer*
Nashat, Guity *historian, education educator, researcher*
Naslund, Markus *retired professional hockey player*
Nason, Dolores Irene *computer company executive, social services administrator, minister*
Nass, Thomas P. *religious studies educator*
Natani, Kirmach *forensic psychologist*
Natarajan, Sriraam *research scientist*
Natcher, Stephen Darlington *retired lawyer, electronics executive*
Nathan, Gerald Dale *retired psychologist, researcher, writer*
Nation, David Arthur *retired computer scientist, sculptor*
Naumer, Carola *art historian, educator*
Naumer, Janet Noll *retired dean*
Naval, Neeraj *medical educator*
Navas, William Antonio, Jr. *former civilian military employee, retired military officer*
Navasky, Victor Saul *journalism professor, director, publisher emeritus*
Navetta, Christopher J. *metal products executive*
Naviaux, LaRee DeVee *retired psychologist, academic administrator, director*
Nawab, Syed Hamid *engineering educator*
Nawalkha, Sanjay K. *finance educator*
Naylor, Rhonda *mathematics instructor*
Ndibongo-Traub, Lulama *economist, educator*
Neal, Darwina Lee *retired federal agency administrator*
Neal, Teresa Schreibeis *secondary school educator*
Neame, Ronald *director, producer*
Nearine, Robert James *educational psychologist*
Neary, Patricia Elinor *ballet director*
Neblett, Carol *soprano*
Nederlander, James Laurence *theater producer*
Neece, Olivia Helene Ernst *investment company executive, consultant*
Needles, Belverd Earl, Jr. *accountant, educator*
Neel, Judy Murphy *management consultant*
Neff, Donald Lloyd *news correspondent, writer*
Negron-Soto, Lizzie *psychologist*
Negroponte, John Dimitri *former federal agency administrator, former Director of National Intelligence*
Neher, Andrew W. *psychologist, educator*
Nehrt, Lee Charles *management educator*
Neill, Debra R. *history professor*
Neilson, Benjamin Reath *lawyer*
Nekritz, Edward Steven *lawyer*
Nelligan, William David III *professional association executive*
Nelms, Michelle *pre-school educator*
Nelson, Alice Carlstedt *retired nursing educator*
Nelson, Allyson Lyn *lawyer*
Nelson, Carl Roger *retired lawyer*
Nelson, Christopher Grant *dermatologist*
Nelson, Craig T. *actor*
Nelson, David Aldrich *retired federal judge*
Nelson, Dean B. *media company executive*
Nelson, Delores Privette *nurse*
Nelson, Glen David *health products executive, physician*
Nelson, John Woolard *neurology educator, physician*
Nelson, Kay LeRoi *chemist, educator*
Nelson, Kristin Schad *otolaryngology, facial plastic surgeon*
Nelson, Nancy Eleanor *retired pediatrician, educator*
Nelson, Norman Daniel *government official*
Nelson, Ron *composer, educator, conductor*
Nelson, Thomas Adams *electrical engineer, consultant*
Nelson, Walter Gerald *retired insurance company executive*
Nemec, Josef *retired organic chemist, researcher*
Nemfakos, Charles Panagiotis *defense industry executive, strategic consultant*
Nemiroff, Maxine Celia *small business owner, art historian*
Nemirow, Arnold Myles *paper company executive*
Neophytou, Neophytos *research scientist*
Nesanovich, Stella Ann *literature educator, poet*
Nesbitt, Mitzi Evalee *voice educator, director*
Neslund, Scott *former marketing and communications company executive*
Ness, Bernice Hagie *retired music educator*
Ness, Norman Frederick *retired astrophysicist, educator, administrator*
Netherland, Louis Victor *military officer, educator*
Netto, Amba Cecile *military officer*
Neufeld, Mace *film company executive*
Neufeld, Ronald David *environmental engineer, educator*
Neumann, David *theater educator*
Neumann, Forrest Karl *retired health facility administrator*
Nevill, William Albert *chemistry professor*
Neville, Elizabeth Egan *artist, educator*
Neville, Phoebe *choreographer, dancer, educator*
Nevin, Phillip *retired professional baseball player*
Nevins, Sheila *television producer*
Nevins, Tracy Anne *elementary school educator*
New, Rosetta Holbrook *retired secondary school educator, retired department chairman, retired nutrition consultant*
Newbern, William David *retired state supreme court justice*
Newborn, Jud *anthropologist, writer, curator, educator, historian*
Newbrun, Ernest *oral biology and periodontology educator*
Newell, Shirley Ann Cecil *retired art dealer, artist*
Newell, Stephen *finance educator, department chairman*
Newkirk, John Burt *retired metallurgical research administrator*
Newman, Bruce Murray *retired antiques gallery owner*
Newman, Carol L. *lawyer*
Newman, Edwin Harold *news commentator*
Newman, Eileen *not-for-profit organization executive*
Newman, Joan Meskiel *lawyer*
Newman, Philip Robert *psychologist*
Newman, Phyllis *actress*
Newman, R. Donald *retired paper company executive*
Newman, Rachel *editor*
Newman, Richard *history professor*
Newman, Stacey Clarfield *artist, curator*
Newman, Theodore Roosevelt, Jr. *Senior Judge, DC Court of Appeals*
Newmark, Leonard Daniel *linguistics educator*
Newsome, James Eugene *former mercantile exchange executive*
Newsome, Lisa Testa *anesthesiologist, educator*
Newton, Francis Chandler, Jr. *lawyer*
Newton, Roger Gerhard *educator, physicist*
Ng, Choon Hoe *process engineer*
Ng, Tse Nga *research scientist*
Nguyen, Charles Cuong *engineering educator, researcher, dean*
Nguyen, Clifford Ham-Thiem *telecommunications engineer*
Nguyen, Dong *computer scientist, researcher, software engineer, educator*
Nguyen, Khanh Gia *medical educator*
Nguyen, Quang *chemical engineer*
Nguyen, Tila (Tila Tequila) *entertainer, model, singer*
Nicholas, Lawrence Bruce *company executive*
Nicholas, Lynn Holman *historian, researcher, writer*
Nicholl, Matthew James *music educator, director*
Nicholls, Richard Aurelius *retired obstetrician, gynecologist*
Nicholls, Robert Lee *civil engineer, educator*
Nichols, Argie Nell *science educator*
Nichols, Dennis Witt *rector*
Nichols, Donald Arthur *economist, educator*
Nichols, Gregory Dawson *playwright, educator*
Nichols, Harvey *biology professor*
Nichols, Iris Jean *retired illustrator*
Nichols, Mike *stage and film director*
Nichols, Robert Leighton *civil engineer*
Nicholson, Cie (Cynthia Nicholson) *marketing professional*
Nicholson, Henry Hale, Jr. *retired surgeon*
Nicholson, Leland Ross *retired utilities executive, energy consultant*
Nicoara, Andreea Carina *mathematics professor*
Nicolas, Kenneth Lee *import/export company executive*
Nicolás, Sherwood-Droz *electrical engineer, researcher, computer engineer, researcher*
Nicoll, Edward J. *information technology company executive*
Niculescu, Peter S. *former mortgage company executive*
Niehoff, Karl Richard Besuden *finance company executive*
Nielsen, Jakob *computer interface engineer*
Niemeyer, Sandra Kay *retired secondary school educator*
Niemiec, Edward Walter *retired professional association executive*
Nieto, Juan Manuel *emergency medicine physician*
Nigro, Kenneth Michael *musician, educator*
Niguidula, Kathleen Ann *musician, educator*
Nigwekar, Sagar U. *dentist, researcher*
Nikaido, Hiroshi *microbiologist*
Niloff, Paul Hyman *surgeon, educator*
Nilsson, Edward Olof *architect*
Nirenberg, Marshall Warren *biochemist*
Nishimura, Joseph Yo *retired retail executive, accountant*
Nissen, Varina *employment services executive*
Nistala, Ravi *nephrologist*
Nitzarim, Yoel David *language educator*
Niu, Feng *research and development company executive*
Nix, Patricia *artist*
Nixon, Marni *singer*
Nkansah, Franklin Daniel *electrical engineer, educator*
Nkoy, Flory Lumu *medical educator*
Nobert, Frances *music educator*
Noble, Helen Bonner *artist*
Nobles, Laurence Hewit *retired geology educator*
Nochman, Lois Wood Kivi (Mrs. Marvin Nochman) *retired literature educator*
Noddings, Nel *education educator, writer*
Noe, Elnora (Ellie) *retired chemicals executive*
Nolan, Jeanada H. *retired state agency administrator, social worker, educator*
Noland, Carrie Jaurès *educator*
Noland, Kenneth Clifton *artist*
Nolen, William Giles *lawyer, accountant*
Nolff, Susan D. *web site designer, small business owner*
Noll, Jeanne C. *retired music educator*
Nolles, Niki *literature and language professor*
Nolte, Nick *actor*
Nonna, John Michael *lawyer*
Noonan, Jacqueline Anne *pediatrician, educator*
Noonan, Patrick Sutton *author management educator*
Noor, Ronny *language educator, writer*
Nora, James Jackson *physician, writer, educator*
Norbeck, Jane S. *retired nursing educator*
Norberg, Arthur Lawrence, Jr. *historian, physicist, educator*
Norden, Ernest Elwood *retired foreign language educator*
Norgren, William Andrew *retired religious denomination administrator*
Norkin, Cynthia Clair *retired physical therapist*
Norman, Bobby Don *artist, writer, research scientist*
Norman, Christina *broadcast executive*
Norman, Donald Arthur *psychologist, educator*
Norman, Gregory John *professional golfer*
Norman, Thena Monts Durham *microbiologist, researcher, health facility administrator*
Norrid, Henry Gail *osteopathic physician and surgeon, researcher, educator, healthcare facility administrator*
Norris, Darell Forest *retired insurance company executive*
North, Gary L. *career military officer*
Northcutt, Eleen Marie *secondary school educator*
Norton, Jane Ellen Bergman (Jane Bergman) *former lieutenant governor*
Norton, Peter K. *retired computer utilities programmer, writer*
Noski, Charles H. *former telecommunications executive*
Noto, Lucio A. *investment company executive, retired oil industry executive*
Nottingham, Edward Willis, Jr. *former federal judge*
Nottingham, William Jesse *retired religious organization administrator, minister*
Nova, Craig *writer*
Novack, Alvin John *physician*
Novak, Barbara *art history educator*
Novak, James Edmund *nephrologist*
Novello, Antonia Coello *pediatric nephrologist, former state health commissioner, former United States Surgeon General*
Novick, Julius Lerner *theater critic, educator*
Nowel, Andrew F. *academic administrator*
Nowell, Linda Gail *not-for-profit executive*
Nuchtern, Jed G. *surgeon, educator*
Nugent, Helen Jean McClelland *history professor*
Nugent, Walter Terry King *historian*
Nuland, Victoria J. *former United States permanent representative to NATO*
Nunis, Doyce Blackman, Jr. *historian, educator*
Nunn, Charles Burgess *retired religious organization administrator*
Nurenberg, David *retired oil company executive*
Nurick, Carl J. *author, consultant, poet*
Nurnberg, Charles Gordon *publishing executive*
Nutzell, Natalie *financial analyst*
Nuzzo, Anthony Gerald *bank executive*
Nyberg, Donald Arvid *oil industry executive*
Nyberg, Stanley Eric *research scientist*
Nye, Bernard Carl *educational administrator*
Nye, Dorothy Mae *freelance journalist, educator*
Nye, Linda Purcell *secondary school educator*
Nygren, Malcolm Ernest *minister*
Nyirjesy, Istvan *retired obstetrician, gynecologist*
Oakes, Ellen Ruth *psychotherapist, health facility administrator*
Oakley, Andrew Arthur *journalist, educator*
Oaks, Sunny *child and family advocate, consultant, author, lyricist*
O'Baire-Kark, Marika *nurse, educator, writer*
Ober, Doris Ann *writer, editor, consultant*
Ober, Richard Francis, Jr. *lawyer, director, banker*
Obermann, Richard Michael *governmental technology and policy analyst*
Obermayer, Herman Joseph *newspaper publisher*
Oberndorf, Meyera E. *Former Mayor, Virginia Beach, Virginia*
Oberste, Steve *microbiologist*
Obiozor, George Achulike *former ambassador*
Oblinger, James L. *former academic administrator*
Obot, Isidore Silas *public health scholar*
O'Brien, Denise Diane *medical/surgical nurse, perianesthesia nurse*
O'Brien, J. Willard *lawyer, educator*
O'Brien, John Wilfrid *economist, educator, retired university president*
O'Brien, Morgan Edward *communications executive, lawyer*
O'Brien, Raymond Francis *transportation executive*
O'Brien, Robert John, Jr. *public relations executive, former government official, air force officer*
O'Brien, Timothy Andrew *journalist, writer, lawyer, educator*
O'Byrne, Michael *retired management consultant*
Ochoa, Armando Xavier *bishop*
Ochs, Michael *editor, librarian, music educator*
Ockey, Ronald J. *lawyer*
O'Connell, William Raymond, Jr. *educational consultant, retired academic administrator*
O'Connor, Doris Julia *not-for-profit fundraiser, consultant*
O'Connor, Edward Vincent, Jr. *lawyer*
O'Connor, James John *retired utility company executive*
O'Connor, John Joseph *information technology manager*
O'Connor, Marilyn Jane *paralegal*
O'Connor, Paul Daniel *lawyer*
O'Connor, R. D. *retired healthcare executive*
Oden, Jean P(hifer) *special education educator*
Odenigbo, Innocent Chukwunwike *linguist, writer, consultant*
Odermatt, Robert Allen *architect*
Odhiambo, David Nandi *literature and language educator*
Odom, G. David (Dave Odom) *retired men's college basketball coach*
O'Donnell, Chris *actor*
O'Donnell, F. Scott *former state agency administrator*
O'Donnell, Kathleen C. *artist*
O'Donnell, Kevin *retired metal products executive*
O'Donnell, Rosie *television personality, actress, comedienne*
O'Driscoll, Seamas Stiofan *literature and language professor*
Odya, Gregory Matthew *musician, educator*
Oehler, Michael Glenn *humanities educator, social sciences educator, researcher, administrator*
Oerter, Cynthia Lynn *medical technologist*
Oesterlin, Lovye Gwendolyn *retired chemist, educator, retired educational consultant*
O'Garden, Irene *writer, actress*
Ogata, Katsuhiko *engineering educator*
Ogawa, Ayako *language educator, writer*
Oglesby, Elaine Sue *elementary school educator*
Ogletree, Glenda L. *education educator*
Ogliaruso, Michael Anthony *retired chemist, educator, actor*
Oh, Mark Edward *minister*
Oh, Sandra *actress*
O'Hare, Denis *actor*
O'Hare, James Raymond *energy executive*
O'Hare, Joseph Aloysius *priest, editor-in-chief, former academic administrator*
Ohsfeldt, Robert L. *health economist, educator*
Ojwang, J.G.O. *research scientist*
Ok, Efe A. *economics professor*
O'Keefe, Gary Raymond *actor*
O'Keefe, James William, Jr. *investment manager and banker*
Okoshi-Mukai, Sumiye *artist*
Okoye-Johnson, Ogo *education educator*
Oktem, Ozgur *medical doctor, researcher*
Oladunni, Olutayo O. *consultant*
Oldenburg, Claes Thure *artist*
Olds, Jacqueline *psychiatrist, educator*
Olearchyk, Andrew *cardiothoracic surgeon, educator*
Olenchak, Frank Richard *retired music educator, musician*
Oles, Douglas Stuart *lawyer*
Olgin, Gregory B. *pharmacy technician, educator*
Olinger, Chauncey Greene, Jr. *investment company executive, editorial consultant*
Olins, Robert Abbot *communications research executive*
Olive, David Michael *journalist, editor*
Oliveira, Katrina R.K. *educator*
Oliver, Jerry Alton *former police chief*
Oliver, Kimberly *primary school educator*
Oliver, Nuria Maria *computer science researcher*
Oliveros, Pauline *composer, performer*
Olivier, Leonard James *bishop emeritus*
Olkinetzky, Sam *artist, educator, retired museum director*
Olmsted, Jennifer *interior design consultant*
O'Loughlin, Katie Eileen Bridget *poet*
Olsen, Glen A. *church musician, educator*
Olshan, Judd David *human ecologist*
Olson, Dale C. *public relations executive*
Olson, Keith Waldemar *historian, educator*
Olson, Lute (Robert Luther Olson) *retired men's college basketball coach*
Olson, Mark Walter *former non-profit corporation administrator*
Olson, Paula Sue *director, educational consultant*
Olson, Peter W. *former publishing executive*
Olson, Robert Edward *coal mining executive*
Ölveczky, Peter Csaba *science educator*
Olyphant, Timothy *actor*
O'Malley, Susan *former professional sports team executive*
Omholt, Bruce Donald *product designer, mechanical engineer, consultant*
Omidi, C. Julian *plastic surgeon*
Omtvedt, Irvin Thomas *academic administrator, educator*
O'Neal, Kathleen Len *communications executive, writer, management speaker, financial consultant*
O'Neal-Seralathan, Crescentia *advocate*
O'Neill, Beverly Lewis *former mayor, college president*
O'Neill, Harry William *retired research market and opinion company executive*
O'Neill, Mary Jane *not-for-profit administrator, consultant*
O'Neill, Megan O. *biology professor*
Ong, Han Chuan *biology professor*

Perkowski, Jan Louis *language, literature and folklore educator*
Perl, Harold *neonatologist, pediatrician*
Perlingieri, Ilya Sandra *art historian, writer*
Perlman, Barry Arnold *astronomy educator*
Perlmutter, Barbara S. *retired public relations executive*
Perlov, Dadie *management and executive search consultant*
Pero, Colin Daniel *facial plastic surgeon researcher*
Perotti, Rose Norma *lawyer*
Perrot, Paul Norman *museum director*
Perrotta, Antonio *trust company executive*
Perry, Anne Marie Litchfield *educator*
Perry, George Wilson *oil and gas company executive*
Perry, James Benn *former hotel and gaming company executive*
Perry, Nancy Bland *accountant*
Perry, Tyler A. *playwright, actor, theater director and producer*
Perry, William Brian *colorectal surgeon*
Persad, Chadee *information technology manager*
Perschbacher, Peter Wesley *environmental science educator, research scientist*
Persico, Joseph Edward *historian*
Persky, Marla Susan *lawyer*
Persoff, Nehemiah *actor, artist*
Persson, Erland Karl *retired electrical engineer, researcher, executive*
Pervouchine, Dmitri *science educator*
Pescatore-Shirey, Hope Jean *middle school reading educator*
Pesch, Ellen P. *lawyer*
Pesci, Joe (Joseph Frank Pesci) *actor*
Pesola, Gene Raymond *physician*
Peszke, Michael Alfred *psychiatrist, writer*
Peters, Douglas Alan *appeals nurse supervisor*
Peters, Jennifer R. *music educator*
Peters, Mary Elizabeth *former United States Secretary of Transportation*
Peters, Rosemary Alison *literature and language professor*
Peters, Sue Ellen *retired elementary school educator*
Peters, Todd *psychiatrist*
Petersen, Dorothy Virginia *investment company executive*
Petersen, Jean Snyder *retired educational association administrator*
Petersen, John D. *former academic administrator*
Petersen, Martin Eugene *curator*
Petersen, William (William Louis Petersen) *actor*
Peterson, Alfred Edward *retired family physician*
Peterson, Ann Sullivan *physician, consultant*
Peterson, Anne Elizabeth Wallace *music educator, composer*
Peterson, Barbara Ann Bennett *history professor, television personality*
Peterson, Betty W. *language educator, writer*
Peterson, Bruce D. *lawyer, energy executive*
Peterson, Bruce Ernest *social studies educator*
Peterson, Carl Eric *metal products executive, banker*
Peterson, David Lynn *research scientist*
Peterson, Dawn Michelle *entrepreneur, writer*
Peterson, Erik Charles *prosecutor*
Peterson, Hikaru Hanawa *agricultural studies educator*
Peterson, John E. *former United States Representative from Pennsylvania*
Peterson, Keith Stanley *literature and language professor*
Peterson, Martha *artist*
Peterson, Robert Austin *retired manufacturing executive*
Peterson, Rosetta Hicks *retired music educator*
Peterson, Steven W. *neonatal nurse*
Petranovich, Danilo *political science professor*
Petrascheck, Michael *biologist, researcher*
Petrelli, Heather Mw *academic administrator, director*
Petrequin, Harry Joseph, Jr. *foreign service officer*
Petri, Peter Alexander *economist, educator, director*
Petriashvili, Marina *physician*
Petrillo, Leonard Philip *lawyer, retired investment company executive*
Petrovic, Bojan D *diagnostic radiologist*
Petru, Suzanne Mitton *retired health care finance executive*
Petrunger, Dennis Keith *school system administrator, educator*
Pettener, Emanuele *literature and language professor*
Pettigrew, L. Eudora *retired academic administrator*
Pettis-Roberson, Shirley McCumber *former US Representative, California*
Pettit, Marilyn Hilley *historian, educator, archivist, consultant*
Pettitt, Jay S. *architect, consultant*
Petty, George Oliver *retired lawyer*
Petzal, David Elias *retired editor, writer*
Petzold, Carol Stoker *state legislator*
Pevear, Roberta Charlotte *state legislator*
Pewitt, James Dudley *retired academic administrator*
Peyton, John *Mayor, Jacksonville, Florida*
Pezeshk, Violet *psychologist, educator*
Pflum, Barbara Ann *retired allergist*
Pfund, Randy (Randall C. Pfund) *former professional sports team executive*
Pfuntner, Walter Alan, Jr. *marketing executive, educator*
Pham, Lee *literature and language professor, consultant*
Phansalkar, Shobha *health facility administrator, researcher*
Phelan, Stephanie Ellen *artist, graphics designer*
Phelps, Bonnie Noreen *retired secondary school educator*
Phelps, Charles Elliott *economics professor, director*
Phelps, Mark D. *music educator*
Phelps, Michael Edward *biophysics professor*
Philips, Laura Alma *former pharmaceutical executive*
Phillips, Caroline L. *lab administrator*
Phillips, Dorothy K. *lawyer*
Phillips, Elaine Anderson *religious studies educator*
Phillips, James Dickson, Jr. *retired federal judge*
Phillips, James Harold *retired lawyer*
Phillips, John P(aul) *retired neurosurgeon*
Phillips, Julia Mae *physicist*
Phillips, Julien L. *theater educator*
Phillips, Katharine Anne *psychiatrist*
Phillips, Laughlin *retired museum director, editor*
Phillips, Leo Harold, Jr. *lawyer*
Phillips, Melannie *medical educator*
Phillips, Peggie L. *medical educator*
Phillips, Richard A. *retired literature and language educator*
Phillips, Stefanie Pannell *school system administrator*
Phillips, Stone (Stone Stockton Phillips) *newscaster*
Phillips, Winifred Patricia *composer*
Phipps, Robert Lee *information technology manager*
Phitayakorn, Roy *surgeon*
Piagentini, Susan *music educator*
Pianka, Eric Rodger *population biologist, educator*
Piazza, Mike (Michael Joseph Piazza) *retired professional baseball player*
Pick, Donald Lowell *urologist*
Pickering, Chip (Charles Willis Pickering Jr.) *former United States Representative from Mississippi*
Pickering, Howard William *metallurgy engineer, educator*
Pickering, Thomas Reeve *retired aerospace transportation executive*
Pickering, Willa Earline *electrical engineer, educator*
Pickett, Eugenia Valdivia *retired social worker*
Pickett, Terry Hill *language professional educator*
Pickle, Linda Williams *biostatistician*
Pickrel, Paul *language educator*
Picower, Warren Michael *editor*
Picton, Earla Wise *retired music educator, director*
Piecuch, Jim *history professor, writer*
Piedimonte, Giovanni *pediatrician*
Pieper, Darold D. *lawyer*
Pierangeli, Silvia Susana *medical educator, consultant*
Pierce, Barbara A. *elementary school educator*
Pierce, Charles Eliot, Jr. *retired library director, educator*
Pierce, David Hyde *actor*
Pierce, Donald Shelton *retired orthopedic surgeon, educator*
Pierce, Hilda (Hilda Herta Harmel) *painter*
Pierce, Lawrence Warren *retired federal judge*
Pierce, Michael Norman *internist*
Pierce, Patricia Ann *retired university administrator*
Pierce, Susan Resneck *academic administrator, literature educator, consultant*
Pierce, Tamora *writer*
Pierro, Richard Salvatore *electrical engineer*
Pierskalla, William Peter *dean, finance and engineering educator*
Pietrocarlo, Nick *artist, consultant, information technology director*
Piga, Stephen Mulry *retired lawyer*
Pike, Diane Kennedy *writer, educator*
Pilisuk, Marc *psychology educator*
Pilla, Venkata *systems analyst*
Pimiento, Jose Mario *physician*
Pine, Charles Joseph *clinical psychologist*
Pineda, Albert Anthony *obstetrician, gynecologist, educator*
Pinero, Maria Anabel *language educator*
Pineyro, Michele *psychologist*
Ping-Robbins, Nancy Regan *musician, writer, artist*
Pinter, Gabriel George *retired physiology educator*
Pinto, Rosalind *retired secondary school educator, volunteer*
Piprek, Joachim *solid state physicist*
Pirchner, Herman, Jr. *foreign policy specialist*
Pirkle, Earl Charnell *retired geologist*
Pirodsky, Donald Max *psychiatrist, educator*
Pirro, Alfred Anthony, Jr. *emergency physician*
Pirro, Jeanine Ferris *television personality, former prosecutor*
Pisano, Linda Maureen *costume designer, educator*
Pitcher, Griffith Fontaine *lawyer*
Pitcock, James Allison *retired pathologist*
Pitici, Felicia *biophysicist*
Pitman, LaVern Frank *librarian*
Pitofsky, Robert *federal agency administrator, law educator*
Pitt, George *lawyer, investment banker*
Pittman, Roy Clinton, Jr. *neurosurgeon, theologian, lawyer, philosopher*
Pitts, Roger L. *psychologist*
Placeres, Martha *music educator*
Placke, James Anthony *retired diplomat*
Plaks, Albert I. *electrical engineer, educator*
Plant, Jackson Vaughn *minister*
Plant, Jeff *architecture educator*
Platis, Chris Steven *adult education educator*
Platis, James George *secondary school educator*
Platt, Robert L. *retired industrial hygienist, consultant*
Plauche, Nancy Caroline *retired counselor*
Pletcher, Eldon *retired cartoonist*
Plews-Ogan, Margaret L. *pediatrician, department chairman*
Pliskin, Berenice Rita Chaplan *artist*
Plombon, John Joseph *electronics engineer*
Plotkin, Horacio *pediatric endocrinologist, orthopedic surgeon, educator*
Plotkin, Stanley Alan *virologist*
Plotnick, Harvey Barry *publishing executive*
Plumb, Marjorie Jane *social worker, consultant*
Plummer, Anita Ellescas *artist*
Pniakowski, Andrew Frank *structural engineer*
Pocock, J. Michael *communications executive*
Podichetty, Vinod Kumar *medical researcher*
Podkul, Theodore B., Jr. *healthcare executive*
Poehling, Katherine *pediatrician*
Poehner, Raymond Glenn *retired bank executive*
Pogue, Linda Sue *science educator*
Poindexter, Mark Carey *university administrator communications educator, critic*
Pointurier, Yvan *computer scientist*
Poirier, Therese Irene *pharmacist, pharmacy educator*
Pokala, Naveen *urologist*
Pokras, Sheila Frances *retired judge*
Poleway, Christopher J. *former publishing executive*
Polfliet, Sarah Jean *physician*
Poliakoff, Gary A. *lawyer, educator*
Policastro, Felice *research scientist*
Pollack, Gerald Alexander *economist, educator, federal agency administrator*
Pollack, Gerald Leslie *physicist, researcher, educator*
Pollack, Jonathan Duker *political science professor*
Pollack, Marsha *secondary school educator*
Pollard, Kate *photographer, art educator*
Pollock, Karen Anne *computer analyst*
Polomsky, Michael Douglas *psychology professor*
Polsby, Allen Isaac *retired lawyer*
Polsgrove, Carol Claxon *writer, retired communications educator*
Polster, James *writer, film producer*
Pombo, Richard William *former congressman, rancher, farmer*
Pomeroy, Heather Aline *sales and marketing executive*
Pomfret, Bonnie *music educator*
Ponitz, David H. *former academic administrator*
Ponturo, Anthony T. (Tony Ponturo) *former brewery company executive*
Poon, Peter Tin-Yau *engineer, physicist*
Poor, Janet Meakin III *landscape designer*
Poos, Jacques Francois *former foreign minister, member of European Parliament*
Pope, Ingrid Bloomquist *sculptor, poet, painter*
Pope, John *retired law educator*
Pope, John Charles *former airline company executive*
Pope, Katherine Collins *former broadcast executive*
Pope, Kenneth Sayle *psychologist*
Popova, Marina *engineering educator*
Popp, Bernard Ferdinand *bishop emeritus*
Popp, Lilian Mustaki *writer, educator*
Poppe, Laurie Catherine *matrimonial lawyer, social worker, real estate executive*
Poppel, Harvey Lee *management consultant, investment banker*
Poppers, Paul Jules *anesthesiologist, educator*
Porras, Vicki *language educator*
Portal, Gilbert Marcel Adrien *oil industry executive*
Porte-Lewis, Ami Lynn *special education educator, school psychologist*
Porter, Dan A. *biology professor, director*
Porter, Dixie Lee *retired insurance company executive, consultant*
Porter, James Morris *retired judge*
Porter, John Ridgely III *lawyer*
Porter, John Wilson *educational association administrator, director*
Porter, Michael Pell *lawyer*
Porter, Philip Thomas *retired electrical engineer*
Porter, Terry *former professional basketball coach, retired professional basketball player*
Porter, W. Thomas *retired bank executive*
Portland, Rene (Maureen Portland) *retired women's college basketball coach*
Portnoy, Sara S. *lawyer*
Portocarrero, Melvy R. *language educator*
Portway, Patrick Stephen *telecommunications consulting company executive, educator*
Poser, Ernest George *psychologist, educator*
Posner, Kenneth *lighting designer*
Posner, Sylvie Pérez *lawyer*
Pospisil, JoAnn *historian, archivist*
Poss, Jeffery Scott *architect, educator*
Post, Avery Denison *retired church official*
Post, Gaines, Jr. *retired history professor, dean, academic administrator*
Post, Richard Bennett *retired human resources executive*
Potash, Charles *lawyer*
Potash, Stephen Jon *public relations executive*
Poteete, Anthony R. *molecular biologist, educator*
Potrepka, Daniel M. *electronics engineer*
Potsic, Amie Sharon *photographer, artist, educator*
Pottekat, Anita *cell biologist*
Potter, Everett *travel writer*
Potter, James Earl *retired international hotel management company executive*
Potts, Christopher Gerard *language educator*
Potts, Gerald Neal *manufacturing executive*
Potts, Rebecca *literature and language professor*
Potts, Timothy F. *former museum director*
Potvin, Alfred Raoul *retired engineering executive*
Poulos, Clara Jean *retired nutritionist*
Pound, Frank R., Jr. *lawyer*
Pounds, Kevin D. *social studies educator*
Poundstone, William Nicholas, Jr. *writer*
Pourbeik, Pouyan *power engineering consultant and researcher*
Pourchot, Georgeta Valentina *political science educator*
Povich, Lynn *journalist, Internet executive, editor*
Powell, Alma Johnson *writer, advocate, foundation administrator*
Powell, Ardal *music company executive, editor*
Powell, Bradford Scott *research scientist, educator*
Powell, Donald E. *former federal official*
Powell, J. Braxton *retired state treasurer*
Powell, John *composer*
Powell, John Livingston *retired obstetrician and gynecologist*
Powell, Matthew *oncologist, educator*
Powell, Thomas Edward III *biological supply company executive, physician*
Powell-Hunt, Sue Rose *art educator*
Power, Katherine *Internet company executive*
Powers, Elizabeth Whitmel *lawyer*
Powers, Joan *artist, photographer, educator*
Powers, Scott *medical association administrator*
Poza, Ernesto *management consultant, educator*
Pozzatti, Rudy Otto *artist*
Prabhakar, Swaroop *medical educator*
Prabhu, Krish Anant *former telecommunications industry executive, educator*
Prado, Edward Charles *federal judge*
Prado, William Manuel *psychologist, educator*
Prance, Sir Ghillean Tolmie *botanical gardens administrator, botanist*
Prange, Hilmar Walter *neurology educator*
Prasad, Ashok *science educator*
Prasad, Navin *ophthalmologist*
Prasad, Vibha *computer engineer*
Prather, Kimberly Ann *chemistry professor*
Prather, Lenore Loving *former state supreme court chief justice*
Pratt, David M. *education educator*
Pratt, Robert Windsor *lawyer*
Prawoto, Yunan *materials scientist*
Prchal, Josef Tomas *hematologist, researcher*
Preciado, Pamela *artist*
Preddy, Raymond Randall *retired newspaper publisher, educator*
Preer, Joan C. *retired assistant principal, science educator*
Preiser, Wolfgang Friedrich Ernst *retired architect, educator, consultant, researcher*
Prem, F. Herbert, Jr. *retired lawyer*
Prema, Nitya *marriage and family therapist, artist*
Premack, David *psychologist*
Prentice, Howard Malcolm *research scientist, educator*
Prescott, Barbara Lodwich *educational association administrator*
Prescott, Richard Chambers *writer*
Presniakov, Alexander *artist, sculptor, inventor, writer*
Pressler, Larry *former senator, lawyer*
Pressman, Jacob *retired rabbi*
Prestine, Joan Singleton *writer, editor, educator*
Preston, Seymour Stotler III *chemicals executive*
Preston, Steven C. *former United States Secretary of Housing and Urban Development*
Preudhomme, Marcia Denrique *marketing executive, writer*
Prewitt, Lena Voncille Burrell *management educator*
Prewoznik, Jerome Frank *retired lawyer*
Price, Alfred Lee *lawyer, mining executive*
Price, Betty Jeanne *chimes musician*
Price, Daniel Martin *federal official, lawyer*
Price, Jack F. *cardiologist*
Price, Robert Ira *coast guard officer*
Price, Steven *venture capitalist, communications executive, lawyer*
Price, Tom *journalist*
Price, William James, IV, *investment banker*
Pridmore, Roy Davis *retired federal official*
Priest, Jessie Shaw *media specialist*
Prilipko, Olga *medical researcher*
Prince, Anna Lou *composer, music publisher, construction executive*
Prince, Faith *actress, singer*
Prince, Martin Raymond *radiologist*
Prins, Robert Jack *retired academic administrator*
Prising, Jonas *employment services executive*
Pristoop, Simon Morris *retired physicist, systems engineer, consultant*
Pritchard, Claudius Hornby, Jr. *retired university president*
Privett, Ronna *literature and language professor*
Procter, Robert J. *economics professor, consultant*
Proctor, Kenneth Gordon *physiology educator*
Proctor, Richard James *geologist, consultant*
Proenza, Bill (Xavier William Proenza) *meteorologist, former federal agency administrator*
Prokasy, William Frederick *academic administrator*
Promod Kumar, Ramachandran Pillai *neurosurgeon, educator*
Propst, Christopher M. *literature and language professor*
Propst, Michael Truman *pathologist*
Proulx, (Edna) Annie *writer*
Provensen, Alice *artist, writer*
Pruden, Wesley (James Pruden) *retired editor*
Pruis, John J. *manufacturing executive*
Pruitt, Robert E. *geneticist, educator*
Pry, George Lawrence *art institute administrator*
Pryce, Deborah Denine *former United States Representative from Ohio*
Pryer, Mary Jane *retired lawyer*
Pryor, Carol Graham *retired obstetrician, gynecologist*
Pryor, Harold S. *retired college president*
Pryor, Richard Walter *telecommunications executive, retired air force officer*
Puck, Wolfgang *chef*
Puddy, William Curtiss *retired military officer, not-for-profit developer*
Puig, Steve *ancient language educator*
Pulhamus, Marlene Louise *retired elementary school educator*
Pulitzer, Emily Rauh (Mrs. Joseph Pulitzer Jr.) *art historian, consultant*
Pullen, Penny Lynne *non-profit organization administrator, state legislator*
Pullman, Jennifer King *artist, educator*
Pulwers, Jack Edward *public affairs specialist, news executive, writer, historian, journalism educator, lecturer, broadcaster*
Purcell, Christine M. *music educator, music company executive*
Purcell, Steven Richard *international management consultant, engineer, economist*
Pure, Pamela J. *former health products executive*
Puris, Martin Ford *media company executive*
Purtle, John Ingram *lawyer, former state supreme court justice*
Purves, William Kirkwood *biologist, educator*
Purvis, Gail *elementary school educator*
Puryear, Martin *artist, educator*
Pust, Ronald E. *physician, educator*
Puthoff, Harold E. *physics researcher*
Putzy, Karry Ann *secondary school educator*
Puzzo, Joseph Anthony, Jr. *middle school educator*
Pyatt, Kedar Davis, Jr. *research and development company executive*
Pylant, Bethany S. *engineering educator*
Pyle, Robert Milner, Jr. *financial consultant*
Pylipow, Stanley Ross *retired manufacturing company executive*
Pyrgiotis, Yannis N. *former sports association administrator*
Pytell, Robert Henry *retired lawyer, judge*
Pytlewski, Laura Jean *chemistry professor*

Pytlinski, Jerzy Teodor physicist, educator, research scientist
Pytte, Agnar physicist, retired academic administrator
Qi, Li research scientist
Qi, Xiaoning electrical engineer, electronics engineer, research scientist
Qi, Zhenyu research scientist
Qian, Zifen artist, editor-in-chief
Qiang, Mei biomedical researcher, educator
Qin, Xiaofa medical educator, research scientist
Qiu, Shenfeng medical researcher
Qiu, Xiangjun mining engineer
Qu, Dongxia physicist, researcher
Qu, Liangti research scientist
Qu, Wei research scientist
Quade, Vicki editor, writer, theater producer
Qualls, Robert L. manufacturing and bank executive, educator, retired state official
Qualls, Roxanne mayor
Quant, Harold Edward retired financial services company executive, rancher
Quarles, James Linwood III lawyer
Quattrone, Frank P. investment company executive
Quay, Thomas Emery lawyer
Quaye, Sylvia Sissuh lawyer
Queen, James E. automotive executive
Quencer, Robert Moore neuroradiologist, researcher
Quenon, Robert Hagerty retired mining consultant and holding company executive
Query, Lois A. elementary school educator
Quezada Toruño, Rodolfo Cardinal cardinal, archbishop
Quiala, Maribel psychotherapist, consultant
Quick, Renee mathematics professor, department chairman
Quigley, Martin Schofield writer, educator
Quillen, Cecil Dyer, Jr. engineer, lawyer, consultant
Quillen, William Tatem retired judge, lawyer, educator
Quillian, Warren Wilson, II, pediatrician, educator
Quinly, Scott Anderson secondary school educator
Quinn, Charles Nicholas journalist
Quinn, Eugene Frederick diplomat, minister
Quinn, Kevin Anthony investment banker
Quintana-Allenson, Ana M. government agency executive
Quintero, Elias Matthew biomedical researcher
Quitoriano, Nathaniel J. research scientist
Quock, Raymond Mark pharmacologist, health sciences educator, biomedical researcher
Qutub, Musa Yacub hydrogeologist, educator, consultant
Rabb, Bruce lawyer
Rabeja, Irina Rodica Olga electronics engineer, computer scientist, writer
Rabinowitz, David Lincoln research scientist
Race, George Justice pathology educator
Rachor, Jeffrey C. former automotive supplies company executive
Rada, Mihai Catalin application developer
Rada, Ruth Byers retired dean
Radde-Gallwitz, Andrew theology studies educator
Rader, Dotson Carlyle writer, journalist
Radev, Ivan electronics engineer, educator
Radford, R. S. lawyer, law educator
Radulović, Novak Aleksandar economist, composer
Radzik, Albin F. federal analyst, military consultant
Raffegeau, Jean Michel audit and consulting company executive
Ragent, Boris physicist
Ragins, Herzl retired surgeon
Ragland, Kathryn Marie dancer, educator
Rago, Dorothy Ashton retired elementary school educator
Rahmati, Ahmad electrical engineer, researcher
Rahming, Etta Lorraine social worker, psychotherapist, school psychologist, consultant
Rai, Alexander K. international affairs executive
Raichle, Marcus Edward radiology and neurology educator
Railsback, Sherrie Lee management consultant, educator
Raimi, Samuel M. film director
Rainer, Rex Kelly civil engineer, educator
Raines, Franklin Delano former mortgage company executive
Raines, Jeff biomedical scientist, medical research director
Rainey, Jean Osgood public relations executive
Rajan, Raghuram economist, educator
Rajendra, Kunwar retired engineering educator, consultant
Raju, Minnie M. application analyst, critical care nurse
Raker, Irma S. retired Judge, Maryland Court of Appeals
Rakes, Ganas Kaye retired finance and banking educator
Rakkolainen, Ismo research scientist
Rako, Susan psychiatrist, writer, producer, filmmaker
Raleigh, Cecil Baring geophysicist
Raley, Beverly Spickelmier retired systems administrator, writer
Rall, Wilfrid neuroscientist, sculptor
Rallo, James Gilbert retired management company executive
Ralston, Martha Jane retired medical/surgical nurse
Ram, Chitta Venkata physician
Raman, Baranidharan research scientist
Ramasamy, Shaker Gnanasekaran science educator
Ramer, James LeRoy civil engineer
Ramey, Eudora Malois minister
Ramirez, Mary Catherine retired secondary school educator
Ramirez, Tina performing company executive
Ramirez-Rivera, Jose physician
Ramirez Rubio, Deborah school librarian
Ramis, Harold Allen film director, screenwriter, actor
Rammohan, Kottil Walappil neurologist, educator
Ramos, Jorge Rafael computer scientist, researcher
Ramos, Marta language educator
Rampersad, Sally Elizabeth anesthesiologist
Ramsay, J. Russell psychologist
Ramsey, Lloyd Brinkley retired savings and loan executive, retired army officer
Ramstad, James Marvin (Jim Ramstad) former United States Representative from Minnesota, lawyer
Rand, Calvin Gordon art educator, consultant
Rand, Joella Mae retired nursing educator, counselor
Randall, Peter retired plastic surgeon
Randall, Richard Rainier geographer
Randazzo, Beverly Paulina retired assistant principal
Randazzo, Marisa R. psychologist
Randinelli, Tracey Anne magazine editor
Randolph, Virgella retired federal official
Rangappa, Sunil cardiologist
Rangaswamy, Padma historian, director, author, interculturist
Ranjan, Srikant mechanical engineer
Rankin, Scott David artist, educator
Rannala, Bruce biology professor
Ranney, George A., Jr. lawyer
Ranney, Helen Margaret retired internist, hematologist, educator
Ranney, Richard Raymond periodontist educator, researcher, dean
Ransom, Roger L. retired history professor
Ransom, Tasha Elana perspective production field producer
Rao, Anil Vithala science educator
Rao, Korcherlakota Ramchandar mechanical engineer, consultant
Rao, Rama Krishna R. pharmaceutical company executive
Rapaport, Michael actor
Raphael, Carol health care administrator
Raphael, Molly (Mary E. Raphael) retired library director
Rapolu, Praveen physician
Rapoport, Ronald Jon journalist
Rappaport, Irving S. entrepreneur, lawyer IP consultant
Rapsomanikis, Themistoklis Theodore independent electrical engineering researcher
Raschke, Jeanne M. psychologist
Rascon, Alfred V. former federal agency administrator
Rash, Wayne, Jr. journalist
Rasi, Humberto Mario editor, educator
Raskin, Michael A. retail executive, director
Rasor, Dina Lynn journalist, private investigator
Rastogi, Anjali health care executive
Rasu, Rafia S. pharmacy and nursing educator researcher
Ratha, Nalini K. computer scientist, researcher
Ratner, Buddy Dennis biomedical engineer, educator
Ratner, Michael D. lawyer
Ratterree, John Eric academic administrator
Ratti, Ricardo Allen lawyer
Rattner, Steven Lawrence former private equity firm executive
Raucher, Gary M. psychotherapist, educator
Raucher, Herman screenwriter, novelist
Raval, Ma Florena Tenazas retired pathologist
Ravdin, Peter Marcus internist, educator, oncologist
Raven, Francis Harvey mechanical engineer, educator
Raven, Patricia Elaine (Penny Raven) real estate broker, developer, columnist
Ravi, Sujith environmental scientist
Ravindran, Cholapurath Nishal physician
Ravinsky, Anthony music educator
Rawleigh, Sara Lynette elementary school educator
Rawls, Frank Macklin lawyer
Rawnsley, Howard Melody pathologist, educator
Rawool-Sullivan, Mohini research scientist
Rawson, Richard J. telecommunications industry executive, lawyer
Ray, Clyde Hosea retired educator, writer
Ray, Dipan B. director
Ray, Jane Zimrude retired machine shop executive
Ray, Marilyn Anne nursing educator, researcher
Ray, Marjorie retired financial planner
Ray, Paul Richard, Jr. executive recruiter, consultant
Ray, Priyadip research scientist
Ray, Susan Elaine principal
Raymond, David Walker lawyer
Raymond, Ural Wayne retired retail executive
Rayner, William Alexander retired newspaper editor, author
Rayward, Warden Boyd librarian, educator
Rea, Anne E. lawyer
Read, Richard Eaton newspaper reporter
Read, Virginia Hall retired biochemistry professor
Reagan, Nancy Davis (Anne Francis Robbins) former First Lady of the United States, volunteer
Reath, George, Jr. lawyer, mediator, arbitrator
Rebay, Luciano language educator, literary critic
Rebhun, Joseph allergist, immunologist, medical educator
Rebollo López, Francisco retired Associate Justice, PR Supreme Court
Recht, Ray set designer
Reciniello, Richard physicist
Reck, Elizabeth Torre social worker, educator
Rector, Donna Lynn writer, photographer, poet, artist
Redd, J. Diane not-for-profit fundraiser
Redd, Scott (John Scott Redd) former federal official, retired military officer
Redden, Taylor Tilghman musician
Reddy, Chakradhar M. gastroenterologist, educator
Reddy, Ravinder medical educator, director
Redfield, Pamela A. state legislator
Redlo, Mitchell economics professor, consultant
Redmont, Bernard Sidney dean, communications educator
Redwine, John Newland state legislator, physician
Reece, Belynda M. minister, military officer, consultant
Reece, David Bryson information systems administrator
Reece, Julia Ruth systems analyst, entrepreneur
Reece, Karyn Lynn business owner, consultant
Reed, Adam Victor psychologist, engineer, information scientist
Reed, Angelica Denise sculptor, writer, illustrator
Reed, Anne F. Thomson management consultant
Reed, Austin F. lawyer
Reed, David Patrick information scientist
Reed, John Shepard retired diversified financial services company executive
Reed, Kit writer
Reed, Leon Samuel secondary school educator, photographer
Reed, Mark Lafayette III retired humanities educator
Reed, Mary Carolyn Camblin retired music educator, county official
Reed, Susan J. elementary school educator
Reeder, Robert Harry retired lawyer
Reeder, Stacy Lynn geologist
Rees, Raymond F. military officer
Reese, Hayne Waring psychologist, educator
Reese, Pokey former professional baseball player
Reeves, Hallie Lawson retired music educator, chaplain
Reeves, Keanu actor
Refaat, Marwan lebanon cardiology fellow
Regal, Randall Nathaniel policy analyst
Regan, Judith Terrance former publishing executive
Regan, Peter Francis III physician, medical educator
Regan, Susan Wright dance educator, small business owner, choreographer
Regatte, Ravinder R. medical educator
Regelbrugge, Roger Rafael steel company executive
Regenstreif, Herbert lawyer
Regula, Ralph Straus former United States Representative from Ohio, lawyer
Rehak, James Richard orthodontist
Rehth, Ann counselor
Reich, John M. former federal agency administrator
Reich, Laurence lawyer
Reichard, Ulrich H. anthropologist, educator
Reiche, Frank Perley lawyer, former federal commissioner
Reichenbach, Linda Louise mathematician, language educator
Reichs, Kathy (Kathleen Joan Toelle Reichs) forensic anthropologist, educator, writer
Reid, Dolores B. retired social services administrator, consultant
Reid, Geraldine Wold (Geraldine Reid Skjervold) retired artist
Reid, Helen Veronica provost
Reid, Irvin D. former academic administrator
Reid, Ivonne Figueroa language educator
Reid, Robert Alfred physician
Reid, Robert Lelon engineering educator, dean
Reidy, Thomas Michael financial executive
Reifenheiser, Thomas V. banker
Reigel, Marissa M. research and development company executive
Reilly, Dinah physical therapist
Reilly, John C. actor
Reilly, William Kane private equity firm executive, preservationist, former federal agency administrator
Reiman, Donald Henry language educator
Rein, Catherine Amelia retired insurance company executive, lawyer
Rein, Linda S. broadcast executive
Reinhard, Joao Pedro chemicals company executive
Reinhardt, Stephen Roy federal judge
Reinhardt, Steven K. computer scientist
Reinike, Irma retired civilian military employee, writer, artist, poet, lyricist
Reinke, Ralph Louis retired academic administrator
Reinleitner, Katherine Mindlin psychologist, foundation administrator
Reinoehl, Richard Louis artist, scholar, martial artist
Reinsmoen, Nancy Louise medical educator, director
Reinus, William R. radiology educator
Reis, Ricardo economics professor
Reisenauer, Eric Michael humanities educator
Reisman, Judith Ann Gelernter media communications executive, educator
Reiss, Jerome retired lawyer
Reiss, John Charles bishop emeritus
Reiss, Robert Francis physician
Reiter, Brandt artist
Reiter, Glenn Mitchell lawyer
Rejman, Diane Louise business analyst
Relyea, Harold Clarence political scientist, writer
Remkus, Connie Elaine nutritional consultant
Remley, Audrey Wright retired academic administrator, psychologist
Remlinger, Rolf music educator, composer
Rempt, Rodney P. retired academic administrator, career military officer
Ren, Shunlin medical educator
Ren, Xing Jian physician
Ren, Zhaohui engineer
Renard, Paul Steven music educator
Renaud, Bernadette Marie Elise author
Renda, Patrick Blake investment company executive
Renda-Tanali, Irmak program director, consultant
Rendich, Ana painter, collage artist
Rendl-Marcus, Mildred artist, economist
Renfro, Patricia Elise library director, academic administrator
Renner, Swen zoologist
Renouf, Anne corporate financial executive, consultant
Ren-Patterson, Renee Feng neuropathologist, neuroscientist
Rent, Clyda Stokes academic administrator
Renzi, Rick (Richard George Renzi) former United States Representative from Arizona
Repinski, Sara library director
Resch, Rita Marie retired music educator
Reschly, Daniel J. education educator, psychologist
Resnick, Alice Robie retired state supreme court justice
Resnick, Elaine Bette psychotherapist, licensed clinical social worker
Resnick, Myron Jay retired insurance company executive, lawyer
Ress, Regina story telling and language professor, actor
Restrepo, Humberto gynecologist, obstetrician, educator
Reuber, Grant Louis banking insurance company executive
Reucroft, Philip J. retired materials science professor
Reuszer, Diane Curtis humanities educator
Reveal, Ernest Ira III retired lawyer
Reverdin, Bernard J. lawyer
Rew, Lawrence Boyd lawyer
Rewcastle, Neill Barry neuropathologist
Rexroat, Larry P environmental scientist
Reyes, M. Jude food products distribution executive
Reynik, Robert John retired materials scientist, science educator
Reynolds, John Hughes, IV, retired research and development executive
Reynolds, Karen Ann retired elementary school educator
Reynolds, Lloyd George economist, educator
Reynolds, Patricia Ellen artist
Reynolds, Robert artist, educator
Reynolds, William Bradford lawyer
Reynolds-Hufner, Jo S. (Jo S. Scholze) retired, educational administrator
Reznikov, Vladimir Lvovich (Vadim Lesnikov) historian, playwright
Rhoads, James Berton archivist, consultant, federal official, educator
Rhodes, Alice Graham retired lawyer, not-for-profit community development consultant
Rhodes, Daisy Chun writer, researcher, historian
Rhodes, Deborah Jean Johnson former prosecutor
Rhodes, Eric Foster employee relations consultant, writer
Rhodes, Lawrence artistic director
Rhodes, Linda Jane psychiatrist
Rhodes, Peter Edward label company executive
Rhodes, Sandra Lavern retired elementary school educator
Riabov, Vladimir Victor aerospace, mechanical, computer engineer, consultant
Riasanovsky, Nicholas Valentine retired historian, educator
Ribley-Borck, Joan Grace medical/surgical rehabilitation nurse
Ricciardi, Lawrence Robert lawyer
Riccio, Cira art educator
Rice, Alan R. geophysicist
Rice, Anne writer
Rice, Claretha Mayes medical/surgical nurse, educator
Rice, Ferill Jeane writer
Rice, Gary Russell retired special education educator
Rice, Jerry Lee retired professional football player
Rice, Joseph Albert retired bank executive
Rice, Mary Kathleen literature and language professor
Rice, Patricia Oppenheim Levin retired special education educator, consultant
Rice, Stuart Alan chemist, educator
Rich, Andrea Louise former museum administrator
Rich, Jeffrey A. former information technology company executive
Rich, Karen nursing educator
Rich, Michael Joseph lawyer
Rich, Robert Stephen lawyer
Richard, A. Kerber medical educator
Richard, Candace L. music educator
Richard, N. Landers psychology professor
Richard, Robert Carter psychological consultant
Richards, David Gleyre German language educator
Richards, Earl Frederick electrical engineer, educator
Richards, Patricia Jones artist, poet, musician, composer
Richardson, Charles Clifton biochemist, educator
Richardson, Edward R. former academic administrator
Richardson, John Carroll lawyer, financial consultant
Richardson, Laurel Walum sociology educator
Richardson, Margaret Milner lawyer
Richardson, Robert cinematographer
Richardson, Robert Dale, Jr. language educator
Richardson, Stephen Giles biotechnologist, research and development company executive, writer
Richardson, William Chase retired university and foundation executive
Richardson, Willie Forrest, Jr. physician, consultant
Richards-Vital, Claudia small business owner, recreational facility executive
Riche, Dennis M. retired history professor
Richey, James D., Jr. literature and language professor
Richman, Alan magazine editor, educator
Richman, Paul semiconductor industry executive, educator
Richman, Peter electronics executive
Richmond, Angela music educator
Richmond, Rocsan television executive producer, investigative reporter, small business owner
Richter, W.D. screenwriter, director, producer
Rick, Roseleen P. lawyer
Rickard, Margaret Lynn library director, consultant
Rickel, Annette Urso psychology and psychiatry researcher, educator
Rickert, Jonathan Bradley retired foreign service officer
Ricketson, Mary E. former dean, lawyer
Ricks, Joycia Camilla retired lawyer
Ricks, Mark G. former lieutenant governor, state senator
Ricks, Thomas Miller retired historian, faculty researcher, academic administrator, independent scholar
Riddell, Malcolm investment banker
Ridgway, Rozanne LeJeanne corporate director, retired ambassador
Ridings, Dorothy Sattes former association executive
Ridolfi, Patrick Murphy music educator, tenor
Riedesel, Clark Alan retired education educator

Riehecky, Janet Ellen writer
Ries, Marcie Berman former ambassador
Rieselman, Deborah Sue editor
Riffenburgh, Gerrye H. artist, educator
Riffenburgh, Robert Harry biostatistician, researcher
Rifkin, Ned former museum director
Rifkin, Stephen nephrologist
Rigg, Charles Andrew pediatrician
Riggins, Tracy neurologist, educator
Riggio, Kerry Kerstin elementary school worker, researcher
Riggs, Michael David editor, writer
Riggs, Penny Kaye molecular geneticist
Righini, Marilou Mausteller editor, consultant
Righter, Walter Cameron retired bishop
Riley, Monica microbiologist, educator
Riley, Nancy Mae retired secondary school educator
Riley, Rebecca Michelle music educator
Riley, Sally Jean retired science educator
Rimel, Ira Wesley writer, US Navy supply officer, real estate specialist, real estate appraiser, real estate broker
Rinaldi, Emilia finance educator
Rincon, Fred neurologist, researcher
Rinebold, Alice June environmental scientist
Ring, Nancy Gail artist, educator, writer
Ring, Renee Etheline lawyer
Ringel, Judy G. writer
Rinker, Charles F., II, surgeon
Rino, Barbara Elizabeth musician, educator
Riofrio, José Antonio electronics engineer
Ripley, Alice H. actress
Rippert, Eric Theodore oral and maxillofacial surgeon, healthcare consultant, author, writer
Rips, Lance Jeffrey psychology professor
Rischbieter, Michael O. biology professor
Risdon, Michael Paul manufacturing executive
Risebrough, Doug former professional sports team executive
Risi, Louis James, Jr. manufacturing executive
Risin, Diana biomedical researcher
Rising, Catharine Clarke author
Risinger, Petra Everest school librarian
Riskas, Mike retired physical education educator, coach, actor
Rissman, Burton Richard lawyer
Ritchey, Samuel Donley, Jr. retired retail executive
Ritman, Barbara Ellen counselor
Ritter, Ann Marie pediatric neurosurgeon
Ritvo, Roger Alan research management professor, health management-policy educator
Rivadeneira, David Edward colon and rectal surgeon, researcher
Rivero, Andria psychology educator
Rivers, Beverly D. former district secretary
Rivkind, Perry Abbot federal railroad agency administrator
Rivlin, Rachel lawyer
Rizowy, Carlos Guillermo lawyer, educator, political analyst
Rizza, Frank Alfonso retired surgeon, educator
Rizzo, Jeffrey F. corporate and non-profit financial executive
Roach, Margaret former publishing executive
Roa-Prada, Sebastian engineering educator
Roark, Barbara Ann librarian
Roark, Ian R. school system administrator
Robb, Sarah Rainey biology professor
Robbins, Christiane Patricia media director, artist, designer, educator
Robbins, Richard James endocrinologist, researcher
Robe, Thurlow Richard retired engineering educator, dean
Roberson, James O. foundation executive
Roberts, David Glen prospector, investor, ceo
Roberts, Doris actress
Roberts, Edwin Albert, Jr. editor, journalist
Roberts, Gary retired professional hockey player
Roberts, Jonathan dancer
Roberts, Karlene Ann education educator
Roberts, Lawrence Gilman telecommunications industry executive
Roberts, Lillian retired principal
Roberts, Margaret Harold editor, publisher
Roberts, Marilyn Gottlieb artist, educator
Roberts, Melville Parker neurosurgeon
Roberts, Patricia Lee education educator
Roberts, Samuel Smith television news executive
Roberts, Suzanne Catherine artist
Roberts, Thomas George retired physicist
Roberts, William B. lawyer
Roberts, William H. lawyer
Robertson, A. Haeworth actuary, foundation executive, benefits consultant
Robertson, Charles James museum director emeritus
Robertson, Cliff (Clifford Parker Robertson III) actor, writer, director
Robertson, David Stuart art educator
Robertson, Jack Clark accounting educator
Robertson, John Archibald Law nuclear scientist
Robertson, Julian Hart, Jr. hedge fund manager
Robertson, LaVerne minister
Robertson, Michael Internet company executive
Robertson, Paul John music educator
Robertson, Robert Graham Hamish physicist
Robertson, Sara Stewart investor, entrepreneur
Robins, Linda Carol language educator
Robinson, Bob Leo retired international investment service executive
Robinson, David Brooks retired naval officer
Robinson, David Zav not-for-profit consultant
Robinson, Davis Rowland lawyer, international arbitrator
Robinson, Devette Lorraine music educator
Robinson, Frank former professional baseball manager, retired professional baseball player
Robinson, Gail Patricia retired mental health counselor
Robinson, Geoffrey Laurence lawyer
Robinson, Howard Arthur, Jr. minister
Robinson, Hugh Granville consulting management company executive
Robinson, James Arthur political scientist
Robinson, Linda Gosden communications executive
Robinson, Marguerite Stern anthropologist, educator, consultant
Robinson, Mary Elizabeth Goff retired historian, researcher
Robinson, Mary Jo pathologist
Robinson, Molly Jahnige statistician, educator
Robinson, Paula LeKatz artist
Robinson, Rebecca Lynne medical researcher
Robinson, Ronald Gene military officer, political science professor
Robinson, Sara Curtis arts administrator
Robinson, Stephanie Nicole education educator
Robinson, Thomas Christopher health science educator
Robinson, William Andrew retired health service executive, physician
Robison, Emily Burns musician
Robison, Paula Judith flutist
Robison, Sara Anne middle school educator, band director
Robitaille, Carolyn Ann music educator
Rocca, Christina B. ambassador, former federal agency administrator
Roche, James Richard pediatric dentist, university dean
Roche, Pauline Jennifer artist
Roche de Coppens, Peter George sociologist, educator
Rochelle, Lugenia academic administrator
Rockaway, Eytan film producer, director
Rockburne, Dorothea Grace artist
Rockwell, John Sargent critic, writer, former arts administrator
Rodbell, Clyde Armand retired distribution executive
Rode, Daniel L. engineering educator
Rodecker, Stephen Bailey science specialist, secondary school educator
Rodgers, Bruce Alan government agency administrator, psychologist
Rodgers, Lawrence Rodney internist, educator
Rodin, Eugene aerospace scientist, researcher, engineering educator
Rodin, Howard Alan periodontist
Roditti, Esther C(laire) lawyer, writer
Rodman, Sue A. wholesale company executive, artist, writer
Rodnunsky, Sidney lawyer, educator
Rodriguez, Jai television personality
Rodriguez, Louis Joseph academic administrator, economist, educator
Rodriguez, Rick former executive editor
Rodriguez, Timothy Allen language educator
Rodriguez-Cintron, William pulmonologist
Roe, Mary Ann retired postmaster
Roe, Thomas Coombe former utility company executive
Roebuck, Judith Lynn retired secondary school educator
Roeder, Gloria Jean civil rights specialist, retired private investigator
Roeg, Nicolas Jack film director
Roehm, Julie Ann marketing executive
Roeller, Herbert Alfred biology professor
Roenick, Jeremy retired professional hockey player
Roesner, Peter Lowell manufacturing executive
Rogalski, Lois Ann speech and language pathologist
Rogeness, Mary Speer retired state legislator
Rogers, Barbara J. musician
Rogers, Betsy elementary school educator
Rogers, David playwright, actor
Rogers, E. Kennedy dentist
Rogers, Elizabeth London retired geriatrics services professional
Rogers, Frederic Halsey economist
Rogers, Hugh Daniel electrical engineer, educator
Rogers, Jack David plant pathologist, educator
Rogers, Justin Towner, Jr. retired utility company executive
Rogers, Margaret Ellen Jonsson civic worker
Rogers, Ruth Frances retired microbiologist
Rogers, Wanda Faye vocalist
Rohatgi, Pradeep Kumar engineering educator
Rohde, James Vincent medical devices company executive
Rohr, Davis Charles aerospace consultant, retired military officer
Rohrbach, Heidi A. lawyer
Rohrer, Heinrich physicist
Roitman, Judith mathematician, educator, poet
Rojas, Victor Hugo Macedo retired vocational education educator
Rojas-Primus, Constanza language educator
Roll, Todd M. library director
Rolland, Jannick P. medical educator
Rolle, Andrew historian, writer
Roller, Pamela Jo elementary school educator
Rollins, Diann Elizabeth retired occupational health nurse, primary school educator, activist and advocator
Rollins, Edward J., Jr. political commentator
Rollins, Faye Lorraine medical transcriptionist
Rollins, Ken (Quinton C. Rollins) museum director
Rollins, Lisa Kay medical educator, director
Rollins, Tree (Wayne Monte Rollins) former professional basketball coach, retired professional basketball player
Roman, Alfred Victor science education educator
Roman, James Warren performing arts educator
Roman, Kenneth business consultant, corporate communications executive
Roman, Nancy Grace astronomer, consultant
Romano, Joseph Anthony healthcare education and marketing consultant
Romanos, Jack (John Romanos Jr.) retired publishing executive
Romanow, Josh lawyer
Romanowski, Thomas Andrew physicist, educator
Romanucci-Ross, Lola anthropologist, educator
Romero Aguero, Julio Enrique electrical engineer, educator
Romero-González, Mauricio psychiatrist, educator, consultant
Romes, Rekina psychologist
Rook, Judith Rawie television producer, writer
Rook, Vicki Lynn safety specialist
Rooke, David Lee retired chemical company executive
Rooney, Andrew Aitken writer, journalist
Rooney, Francis (Laurence Francis Rooney III) construction executive, former ambassador
Roorda, John Francis, Jr. manufacturing executive, consultant
Roosa, Stephen Allen energy engineer
Roost, Alisa theater educator
Rooth, Signe Alice editor, consultant
Rosales, Monica D. social studies educator
Rosario, Bedda L. statistician
Roscoe, Kevin Jay radiologist, physician
Rose, Ernst dentist
Rose, James Turner aerospace engineer, consultant
Rose, (Robert) Kevin Internet company executive, blogger
Rose, Michael Dean retired lawyer, educator
Rose, Patricia artist, educator
Rose, Paul Edward systems administrator, educator
Rose, Robert Edgar retired state supreme court justice
Rose, Robert John bishop emeritus
Rose, Tessie E. special education educator, consultant
Roseman, Jack computer services company executive
Rosen, Arthur Marvin advertising executive
Rosen, Judah Ben computer scientist
Rosen, Michael Howard real estate executive
Rosen, Paul Peter pathologist
Rosenberg, Alison P. retired public policy officer
Rosenberg, David Alan military historian, strategic analyst
Rosenberg, Eli Ira physicist, educator
Rosenberg, Raymond David special education educator, consultant
Rosenberg, Rudy chemical company executive
Rosenberg, Sheli Zysman retired finance company executive
Rosenblatt, Roger writer
Rosenblum, Estelle H. retired dean, nursing educator
Rosenfield, James Harold, Sr. communications executive
Rosenkilde, Carl Edward retired physicist
Rosenn, Harold lawyer
Rosenow, Mitchell Paul sound recording engineer, studio owner, musician, music producer
Rosensaft, Lester Jay management consultant, lawyer
Rosenthal, Howard Gary psychotherapist, educator, author
Rosenthal, James D. retired federal official, retired ambassador
Rosenthal, Joel chemist, researcher
Rosenthal, Lee electrical engineer, educator
Rosenthal, Michael Ross retired academic administrator, consultant
Rosenthal, Nan curator, educator, author
Rosenthal, Susan Barbara retired librarian
Rosett, Daniel J. film company executive
Rosha, Uzi lawyer
Rosicki, Maria Trzetrzewinska-Trett clinical psychologist
Rosky, Burton Seymour lawyer
Ross, Amanda Joanne biology professor
Ross, Bobby (Robert Joseph Ross) retired college football coach
Ross, Carol retired women's college basketball coach
Ross, Charlotte Pack social services administrator
Ross, Darrin composer
Ross, Dennis B. diplomat, writer
Ross, Dennis E. retired automotive executive, lawyer
Ross, Donald Keith retired insurance company executive
Ross, Gerald Fred electrical engineering executive, researcher
Ross, Gerald Harvey family practice and environmental medicine physician
Ross, Leonard Lester retired academic administrator
Ross, Michael Aaron lawyer
Ross, Molly Owings small business owner, sculptor
Ross, Tracey actress
Rossin, Lawrence George ambassador
Ross-Nazzal, James history professor
Rosso, Kevin Michael geochemist, director
Roster, Michael lawyer
Roth, Harvey Paul retired publishing executive
Roth, Jeffrey geophysicist
Roth, Karl Sebastian retired pediatrician
Roth, Michael lawyer
Roth, Philip Milton writer
Rothenberg, Albert psychiatrist, educator
Rothenberg, Elliot Calvin lawyer, writer
Rothman, Howard Joel lawyer
Rothman, Kenneth Jay epidemiologist
Rothschild, Jennifer Ann artist, educator
Rothschild, Rick entertainment company executive
Rothstein, Gerald Alan investment consultant
Rothwell, Robert Alan investing and consulting company executive, writer
Rotman, Joseph Jonah mathematician, educator
Rotman, Marvin radiation oncologist, radiologist, educator
Rottenberg, Hagai medical educator
Rotunda, Adam Michael dermatologist
Roukema, Lorae Teresa education educator, consultant
Rouman, James Christ anesthesiologist
Rouman, John Christ classics educator
Roumbos, Maria K. elementary school educator
Rouphael, Nadine G. physician
Rouse, Roscoe, Jr. retired librarian, educator
Rouse, Terrie Suzitte museum director
Rousseau, Eugene Ellsworth musician, educator, consultant
Roussel, Lee Dennison economist
Rove, Karl Christian political analyst, former federal official
Rowe, Devona Powell retired counseling administrator, director, social worker, secondary school educator
Rowe, G. Steven former state attorney general
Rowe, Thomas Dudley, Jr. law educator
Rowell, Barbara Caballero retired academic administrator
Rowell, Lester John, Jr. retired insurance company executive
Rowe-Maas, Betty Lu real estate analyst
Rowley, Maxine Lewis education educator, retired academic administrator
Roy, Biswadev environmental scientist
Roy, Matthew G. secondary school educator, social studies educator
Roy, Michelle E. musician, information technology consultant
Roy, Sanjoy health outcomes researcher
Roy, Thomas Fredrick history professor
Roy, Valeria Acosta language educator
Royal, Darrell K. university official, retired football coach
Royce, Paul Chadwick healthcare administrator
Roy Chowdhury, Ayan engineer
Rozenberg, Valeria chemist, researcher
Ruan, Jiening language and literacy professor, director, writer
Rubbert, Paul Edward retired engineering executive
Rubello, David Jerome artist
Rubenstein, Atoosa Behnegar former editor-in-chief
Rubenstein, David Aaron military officer, healthcare administrator
Rubenstein, Judith Louise psychologist
Rubin, Alan physician
Rubin, Bruce Kalman medical professor, researcher
Rubin, Ellen education/access consultant
Rubin, Gretchen Craft author
Rubin, Jay retired literature and language professor
Rubin, Louis Decimus, Jr. retired language educator, writer, publishing executive
Rubin, Phyllis Getz health association executive
Rubin, Richard Allan lawyer
Rubin, Rick (Frederick Jay Rubin) recording industry executive
Rubin, Robert Edward former diversified financial services company executive, former United States Secretary of the Treasury
Rubin, Robert Joseph internist, nephrologist, consultant
Rubin, Sandra Mendelsohn artist
Rubin, Zick lawyer, writer, psychology professor
Rubinoff, Ira biologist, researcher, conservationist
Rubinstein, Eva (Anna) photographer
Rubner, Michael international relations educator, university administrator
Ruby, Norman F. research scientist
Ruccolo, Margaret Rose Roebke music educator, violinist
Rudd, Ann Talton psychologist, artist
Rudd, D(ale) F(rederick) chemical engineering professor
Ruddy, Kathy Aakre paralegal
Ruder, Tia L. music educator
Rudi, Langston Cilibrasi software engineer
Rudin, Anne retired mayor, nursing educator
Rudner, Sara dancer
Rudolph, Andrew Henry retired dermatologist, educator
Rudolph, James Robert psychologist
Rudy, Raymond Bruce, Jr. retired food company executive
Rudy, Ruth Corman former state legislator
Rueger, George Edward bishop emeritus
Rufanova, Victoriya medical researcher
Ruffin, Herbert George, II, history professor
Ruggiero, Matthew John bassoonist
Ruggles, Rudy Lamont, Jr. international security advisor
Rukeyser, Robert James manufacturing executive
Ruland, Mildred Ardelia retired retail executive and buyer
Rumfolo, Marilu financial analyst
Rumpakis, E. John realtor emeritus
Rumpf, Ann psychologist
Rundquist, Elizabeth Ann art therapist
Runge, Marschall Stevens cardiologist, educator
Runge, Val Murray medical educator
Ruof, Richard Alan minister, poet, writer
Rupert, Hoover minister, writer
Rus, Teodor computer scientist, educator
Rusaw, Sally Ellen librarian
Rush, Julia Ann Halloran (Mrs. Richard Henry Rush) artist, writer
Rush, Loretta G. biology professor
Rush, Richard Henry finance company executive, educator, writer
Rush, Sophia A. law educator
Rushforth, Ann Fay artist, educator
Rushing, John Alan business educator
Russ, Edmond Vincent, Jr. marketing professional
Russ, Joanna author
Russack, John A. federal official
Russell, Beatrice Nibigira performing arts educator
Russell, Bill (William Felton Russell) former professional basketball team executive, retired professional basketball player
Russell, Carol Ann city council member, retired company executive
Russell, Florence L. elementary school educator
Russell, Kurt actor
Russell, Liane Brauch retired geneticist
Russell, Louise retired education educator
Russell, Mason Webster economist, consultant
Russell, Walter Dallas, Jr. diversified financial services company executive
Russo, Jose pathologist
Russo, Patricia F. former telecommunications company executive
Russo, Richard writer
Russo, Roy Lawrence retired electronics engineer
Russo, Vincent Joseph surgeon
Rutherford, John Sherman, III, (Johnny Rutherford) retired professional race car driver
Rutherford, Lisa school psychologist
Rutsala, Vern A. poet, writer, language educator
Rutsky, Lester retired textiles executive, writer

Ruttenberg, Ruth A. *economist*
Ruud, Clayton Olaf *engineering educator*
Ruviella-Knorr, Jeanne L. *music educator, consultant*
Ryan, Arthur Frederick *retired diversified financial services company executive*
Ryan, Christine Brett *music educator*
Ryan, Daniel John *university administrator*
Ryan, Deborah Lorraine *music educator*
Ryan, George William *manufacturing executive*
Ryan, Ione Jean Alohilani Rathburn *retired education educator, counselor*
Ryan, James *insurance company executive*
Ryan, John Joseph *physician*
Ryan, John Michael *landscape architect*
Ryan, John William *educational association administrator*
Ryan, Kay Pedersen *poet*
Ryan, Kelli Lorraine *ballerina, educator*
Ryan, Leo Vincent *business educator*
Ryan, Marleigh Grayer *language educator*
Ryan, Melbagene T. *retired food service and nutrition director*
Rybczyk, Joseph Anthony *physicist, researcher, writer, inventor*
Ryckman, Eric Michael *research scientist, educator*
Rydén, Bengt Gunnar *retired stock exchange executive*
Rydholm, Ralph Williams *advertising executive*
Rylance, Mark (Mark Waters) *actor, performing company executive*
Rymar, Julian W. *manufacturing executive, director*
Rynearson, Arthur John *lawyer*
Ryskamp, Charles Andrew *museum director, educator*
Saalfeld, Fred Erich *science educator, researcher*
Saavedra, Abelardo *former school system administrator*
Sabatini, Nelson John *healthcare executive*
Sabb, Annmarie Louise *retired chemist*
Sabbath, Joseph Waters *academic administrator*
Sabbatini, Marcello *journalist, motor sports weekly director*
Sabeti, Mike A. *endodontist, periodontist, educator*
Sabharwal, Sunil *emergency physician*
Sablik, Martin John *research physicist*
Sabo, Martin Olav *former congressman*
Sabodash, Vladlena *economics professor, researcher*
Sacco, Louis John *software design architect*
Sackett, Susan Deanna *writer*
Sacks, Temi J. *public relations executive*
Sacripanti, Peter John *lawyer*
Sade, Donald Stone *anthropology educator*
Sadek, Sanaa Mounir *literature and language professor*
Sadjadi, Firooz Ahmadi *electrical engineer, consultant, researcher, lecturer*
Sadler, Irene Constance *retired language educator*
Sadler, Judith K. *retired special education educator, school system administrator*
Sadock, Geoffrey Johnston *English professor*
Sadoh, Godwin Simeon *music educator*
Sadow, Harvey S. *healthcare company executive*
Saeed, Shehzad *pediatrician, educator*
Saeks, Richard Ephraim *engineering executive*
Safai, Nick M. *chemical engineer, director*
Safer, Alan *statistician, educator*
Safren, Cheryl *artist, educator*
Sagan, M. J. *architectural firm executive*
Sager, Donald Jack *librarian, consultant, retired publishing executive*
Saha, Abhijit *astronomer*
Saha, Santosh Chandra *history educator*
Sahai, Tuhin *research scientist*
Sahid, Joseph Robert *lawyer*
Sahin Sariisik, Asli *engineer*
Sahoo, Bishwabhusan *chemist*
Sahota, Puneet *medical researcher*
Sahrakorpi, Seppo *senior research engineer*
Saigo, Roy Hirofumi *academic administrator, botanist*
Saile, David George *architecture educator, researcher*
Saini, Viney *research scientist*
Saint, Eva Marie *actress*
St. Amant, Kirk *communications educator*
St. Clair, Donald David *lawyer*
St. Clair, Thomas McBryar *mining and manufacturing company executive*
St. Germain, Fernand Joseph *Former United States Representative, Rhode Island*
Saint-Girard, Christian *theater director, actor, educator, choreographer, theater producer*
Saint-Jacques, Bernard *linguistics educator*
St. John, Kristoff *actor*
Saint-Pierre, Guy *engineering executive*
Saito, Robert Shunichi *writer, poet*
Sak, Gilbert *music educator*
Sakic, Joe (Joseph Steven Sakic) *retired professional hockey player*
Saks, Judith-Ann *artist*
Saks, Stephen Howard *accountant, health organization executive*
Salahuddin, Parveen *information scientist, researcher*
Salama, Aman *language educator*
Salama, Mohammad *literature and language professor*
Salamone, Joseph Charles *polymer chemistry professor*
Salamone-Kochowicz, Jean Gloria *retired bank executive*
Salapatek, John (John Franklin) *literature and language educator, writer*
Salathe, John, Jr. *retired manufacturing executive*
Salava, Jennifer Anne *psychologist*
Salazar, Omar Mauricio *radiation oncologist, educator*
Salcedo, Claudia S. *language educator, lab administrator*
Saldivar, Enrique *bioengineer, researcher*
Saleh, Brian Behrooz *aerospace transportation executive*
Saleh, Paul N. *former telecommunications executive*
Sali, Bill (William Thomas Sali) *former United States Representative from Idaho*
Saligman, Harvey *retired consumer products and services company executive*
Salins, Peter D. *political science professor, academic administrator*
Salisbury, Alan Blanchard *information technology officer*
Salisbury, John *chemist, researcher*
Saliterman, Richard Arlen *lawyer*
Salkind, Michael Jay *science administrator, metallurgical engineer*
Sallis, James *writer*
Salman, Abduljabbar A. *agronomist*
Salman, Robert Ronald *lawyer*
Salminen, Seppo Ossian *plant biochemist*
Saltz, Leonard Bruce *oncologist*
Saltzman, Brian *physician, surgeon, educator*
Saltzman, Philip *television producer, writer*
Salyer, Kenneth E. *surgeon*
Salzman, Arthur George *retired architect*
Samaranch, Juan Antonio (Marqués de Samaranch) *former international sports organization executive*
Samardjiev, Ivan Jordanov *medical researcher*
Sambora, Richie (Richard Stephen Sambora) *musician, singer, songwriter*
Samec, Diane Patricia *retired elementary school educator*
Sami, Sedat *civil engineering, educator*
Samkoff, Lawrence Mark *neurologist, educator*
Sammons, Morgan Taylor *psychologist*
Samolyk, Keith Andrew *cardiovascular perfusionist, director*
Sampram, Ellis Senanu Kojo *physician*
Sampson, Donna Rene *mathematics educator*
Sampson, Robert Neil *professional society administrator, consultant*
Samuels, Janet Lee *lawyer*
Samuels, John Stockwell III *mining company executive, financier*
San Agustin, Joe Taitano *political organization worker, educator*
Sanborn, Kathy *musician, recording artist and author*
Sanchez, Alita Cassandra *physical education educator, personal trainer*
Sanchez, Ricardo S. *retired military officer*
Sanchez-Kennedy, Maria *museum director*
Sanchez-Ramos, Roberto J. *former attorney general*
Sander, Elliot Gene (Lee Sander) *former transportation executive*
Sanders, Barry *retired professional football player*
Sanders, Franklin D. *retired insurance company executive*
Sanders, Heywood T. *finance educator*
Sanders, Joe Maxwell, Jr. *pediatrician*
Sanders, Marion Yvonne *retired geriatrics nurse*
Sanders, Marlene *news correspondent, journalism educator*
Sanders, Patricia Smith *language educator, consultant*
Sanders, Walter Jeremiah, III, (Jerry Sanders) *retired computer company executive*
Sanderson, James Richard *retired naval officer, financial consultant*
Sanderson, Jihong W. *finance educator, consultant*
Sandford, Virginia Adele *retired motivational speaker, writer*
San Diego, Armando G. *retired military officer, pathologist, consultant*
Sandoval, Rik (Charles Sandoval) *broadcast executive*
Sands, Rick (Richard Sands) *former film company executive*
Sandwell, Kristin Ann *special education educator*
Sanger, Frederick *retired molecular biologist*
Sanger, Stephen W. *retired consumer products company executive*
Sang-Sik, Yeo *civil engineer, consultant*
Sangster, Paul Edward *retired radiologist*
Saniga, Erwin Martin *educator, painter*
Sanjian, Ara *history professor*
San Miguel, Manuel *painter, historian, composer, poet*
Sanquist, Nancy Johnson *real estate technology consultant, educator*
Santana, Suzette M. *language educator*
Santangelo, Gaspare Charles *education educator, retired principal*
Santhanaraman, Gopalakrishnan *computer scientist*
Santina, Dalia *nutritionist, writer, skin care specialist*
Santisi, Terri M. (Theresa M. Santisi) *multimedia company executive*
Santman, Leon Duane *lawyer, former federal government executive*
Santomero, Anthony M. *financial consultant, former bank executive, public policymaker*
Santos, Santos V. *literature and language professor, researcher*
Santry, Barbara Lea *venture capitalist*
Sapienza, Madeline *historian, researcher*
Sapoff, Meyer *retired electronics executive*
Sapp, John Raymond *lawyer*
Sapsowitz, Sidney H. *entertainment and media company executive*
Saravolatz, Louis Donald *epidemiologist, medical educator*
Sarbanes, Paul Spyros *former United States Senator from Maryland*
Sargent, Thomas Andrew *retired political science professor*
Sargent, William Winston *retired anesthesiologist*
Sarkar, Joy *engineer, educator*
Sarris, Andrew George *film critic*
Sarry, Christine *ballerina*
Sarsgaard, Peter *actor*
Sas, Robert Joseph, Jr. *geologist, researcher*
Sass, Cynthia N. *lawyer*
Sass, Mary Martha *freelance writer, artist*
Sasser, James Ralph *former United States Senator from Tennessee*
Sasso, John *advertising and public strategies executive*
Satpathy, Ruby *cardiologist, researcher*
Satterfield, David Michael *federal official*
Sattler, Bruce Weimer *lawyer*
Sattler, Rolf *retired plant morphologist, educator*
Satz, Louis K. *publishing executive*
Saucier, Gene Duane *state legislator, import/export company executive*
Saucier, Guylaine *corporate financial executive*
Saumell, Eileen Mary *psychologist*
Saunders, Lonna Jeanne *lawyer, broadcast journalist, talk host, writer*
Saunders, Terry Rose *lawyer*
Savage, Kim I. *academic administrator*
Savard, Denis Joseph *former professional hockey coach*
Savenor, Betty Carmell *painter, printmaker*
Savitripriya, Swami *Hindu religious leader, author*
Savitt, Susan Schenkel *lawyer, mediator*
Savitz, Maxine Lazarus *retired aerospace transportation executive*
Savoy, Suzanne Marie *nursing educator*
Sawai, Dahleen Emi *language educator*
Sawczuk, Ihor S. *urologist*
Sawyer-Morse, Mary Kaye *nutritionist, educator*
Sawyers, Elizabeth Joan *retired librarian, director*
Sax, Joseph Lawrence *lawyer, educator*
Saxena, Parul *special education educator, psychologist*
Saxon, Burton Roy *humanities educator*
Saxon, Wolfgang Erik Georg *journalist, writer*
Saxton, Jim (Hugh James Saxton) *former United States Representative from New Jersey*
Saygili, Gokhan *civil engineer, researcher*
Sayles, Leonard Robert *management educator, consultant*
Sayre, Donna *elementary school educator*
Sayre, John Marshall *retired lawyer, former government official*
Scala, James *health facility administrator, consultant, writer*
Scales, Pat R. *retired library association executive, director*
Scanlan, Thomas Joseph *former academic administrator*
Scannell, Herb *broadcast executive*
Scarchuk, Lynn Nettleton *retired music educator*
Scarlett, Elizabeth Ann *foreign language educator*
Scarlett, Lynn (Patricia Lynn Scarlett) *former federal agency administrator*
Scerno, Joseph Benedict *management consultant executive, arbitrator*
Schaap, James Ike *finance educator*
Schachter, James Robert *editor*
Schadow, Karen E. *public speaking trainer, educator*
Schaefer, Mary K. *school system administrator*
Schaelicke, Lambert *computer engineer*
Schafer, Ed (Edward Thomas Schafer) *former United States Secretary of Agriculture, former Governor of North Dakota*
Schaffner, Adam David *plastic surgeon*
Schaller, Jean *geneticist*
Schanfield, Fannie Schwartz *community volunteer*
Schaper, Leonard W. *retired engineering educator*
Scharf, Michael Paul *law educator*
Scharf, William *artist*
Scharlemann, Robert Paul *theology studies educator, minister*
Scharschmidt, Bruce Frederick *physician*
Schatz, Gottfried *biochemistry educator*
Schauf, Victoria *pediatrician, educator*
Schaupp, Joan Pomprowitz *trucking executive, writer*
Scheel, Nels Earl *corporate financial executive, accountant*
Scheff, Thomas Joel *sociologist, educator*
Scheffler, Linda Weingarten *psychologist, educator*
Schegloff, Emanuel Abraham *social studies educator*
Scheidel, Walter *historian*
Schein, Edgar Henry *management educator*
Schein, Virginia Ellen *psychologist*
Scheinman, Nancy Jane *psychologist*
Schell, Allan Carter *retired electrical engineer*
Schell, Melvin Frank, Jr. *real estate agent*
Schellenberger, Robert Earl *retired management educator, department chairman*
Schellman, John A. *chemistry professor*
Schenck, Jack Lee *retired electric utility executive*
Schenker, Marc Benet *preventive medicine physician, medical educator, department chairman*
Schenkkan, Robert Frederic *playwright, screenwriter*
Scherer, James R. *research scientist*
Scherer, Ronald Callaway *voice scientist, educator*
Scherger, Joseph Edward *family physician, educator*
Schexnayder, Charlotte Tillar *state legislator*
Schexnider, Virginia Reeves *school psychologist*
Scheyer, Daniel *lawyer*
Schiff, Jeffrey Allen *environmental sculptor, educator*
Schiff, Martin *physician, surgeon*
Schiff, Molly Jeanette *artist, researcher*
Schiffman, Howard Scott *law and environmental educator*
Schifrin, Lalo *composer*
Schiller, Lawrence Julian *film producer, writer*
Schilling, Emily Gaenzle *research scientist*
Schindler, Jo Ann *retired library director*
Schlaepfer, Isabel Rubio *research scientist*
Schlafly, Hubert Joseph, Jr. *communications executive*
Schlagel, Richard H. *retired philosophy educator*
Schlageter, Robert William *museum administrator*
Schlesinger, Deborah Lee *retired librarian*
Schlesinger, James Rodney *economist, former United States Secretary of Defense*
Schlesinger, Lisa *playwright, educator*
Schless, Phyllis Ross *investment banker*
Schlicher, Ronald Lewis *former ambassador*
Schlossman, John Isaac *architect*
Schloter, Philipp *information technology executive*
Schmaeman, Cynthia *biology professor*
Schmalz, Carl Nelson, Jr. *artist, educator, art historian, printmaker*
Schmandt-Besserat, Denise *archaeologist, educator*
Schmider, Mary Ellen Heian *American studies educator, academic administrator*
Schmidt, David Kelso *engineering educator*
Schmidt, Harvey Martin *economist, educator, financial analyst, consultant*
Schmidt, Hildred Doris *music educator*
Schmidt, Karl A. *lawyer*
Schmidt, Mike (Michael Jack Schmidt) *retired professional baseball player*
Schmidt, Parbury P., Jr. *chemist*
Schmidt, Torrance *horticulturist*
Schmidtke, Suzanne de Fine *retired social worker*
Schmitt, William Gerard *writer, editor, magazine manager*
Schmitz, Barbara *art preservationist*
Schmitz, Dennis Mathew *retired language educator*
Schmults, Edward Charles *lawyer*
Schnackenberg, Gjertrud Cecelia *poet*
Schnackenberg, Roy Lee *artist*
Schnapp, Diana Corley *communications educator*
Schneck, Stuart Austin *retired neurologist, educator*
Schneewind, Sarah Katherine *history professor*
Schneider, Allen Morris *psychology professor*
Schneider, Amanda E. *literature and language professor*
Schneider, Calvin *physician*
Schneider, Carl Edward *law educator*
Schneider, Carl Stanley *retired physics professor, researcher*
Schneider, Catherine Chemin *occupational therapist, consultant, writer*
Schneider, Duane Bernard *English literature educator*
Schneider, Edgar Rolf Gottfried *retired mathematician, application developer, writer*
Schneider, Gisela *art educator*
Schneider, Jan *retired obstetrics and gynecology educator*
Schneider, Janet M. *museum administrator, painter, curator*
Schneider, Phillip Harry Leonard (Phil Schneider) *healthcare organization executive*
Schneider, Rob *actor*
Schneider, Valerie Lois *retired speech educator*
Schneider, William George *chemist, research consultant*
Schneller, Marina Velentgas *lawyer*
Schnitzer, Howard Joel *physics professor, researcher*
Schock, Robert Norman *geophysicist*
Schoen, Robert *demographer*
Schoen, Robert Taylor *rheumatologist*
Schoenberger, James Edwin *retired federal agency administrator*
Schofield, Robert E. (Robert Edwin Schofield) *historian, educator, academic administrator*
Scholes, Edison Earl *military officer*
Scholz, Thomas *plastic surgeon, researcher*
Schonberg, Alan Robert *personnel director*
Schonhorn, Harold *chemist, researcher*
Schoof, Rosalind *toxicologist*
Schoomaker, Peter Jan *retired military officer*
Schoonmaker Powell, Thelma *film editor*
Schoonover, Philip J. *former retail executive*
Schorr, Daniel Louis *broadcast journalist, author, lecturer*
Schott, Donald Karl *lawyer*
Schott, John Robert *international consultant, educator*
Schottenheimer, Marty (Martin Edward Scottenheimer) *former professional football coach*
Schowalter, William Raymond *college dean, educator*
Schrader, Dennis R. *former federal agency administrator*
Schrag, Philip Gordon *law educator*
Schrage, Rose *retired academic administrator*
Schram, Ronald Byard *lawyer*
Schramm, Bernard Charles, Jr. *retired advertising agency executive*
Schrand, Richard Henry, Sr. *broadcast executive, advertising bureau owner, educator*
Schreckinger, Sy Edward *advertising executive, consultant*
Schreiber, Alan Hickman *lawyer*
Schreiber, Horst *information technology manager*
Schreiber, Kai Markus *neuroscientist*
Schreiber, Paul Solomon *lawyer*
Schreider, Larry Stephen *director, educator*
Schrenko, Linda C. *former school system administrator*
Schroeder, Brian S. *philosopher, educator, theologian*
Schroeder, LaVerne *medical/surgical nurse*
Schubert, Barbara Schuele *retired performing arts association administrator*
Schubert, Helen Celia *public relations executive*
Schuchard, Robert L. *lawyer*
Schuelke, John Paul *religious organization administrator*
Schuessler, John T. (Jack Schuessler) *retired food service executive*
Schuldt, Barbara Jean *school librarian*
Schulhofer-Wohl, Samuel *economics professor*
Schulman, Alan *lawyer*
Schulman, Harold *obstetrician, gynecologist*
Schulman, Sidney *neurologist, educator*
Schultz, Albert Barry *engineering educator*
Schultz, Caitlin G. *psychologist, educator*
Schultz, Daniel G. *former federal agency administrator*
Schultz, Dennis Bernard *lawyer*
Schultz, Harley *consulting company executive*
Schultz, Stanley George *physiologist, educator, dean*
Schulz, William Frederick *human rights scholar and advocate*
Schulzke, Margot Seymour *artist, author, educator*
Schunicht, Shannon Anthony *retired military officer, political scientist*
Schupp, Russ *computer professor, web site designer*
Schur, Lucille S. *artist*
Schurenberg, Eric P. *magazine editor*
Schuster, Carol Joyce *special education educator, consultant*
Schuster, Elaine *retired civil rights professional*
Schutz, Donald Frank *geochemist, environmental corporate executive*
Schutz, Richard Phillip *special education educator*
Schwab, Eileen Caulfield *lawyer, educator*

Schwab, Howard Joel *retired judge*
Schwab, Judith *artist, sculptor, curator, educator*
Schwartz, Bernard Julian *lawyer*
Schwartz, Brian Michael *philosopher, think-tank executive*
Schwartz, Carol Levitt *government official*
Schwartz, Daniel Bennett *artist*
Schwartz, Eleanor Brantley *academic administrator*
Schwartz, Eliezer *psychologist, educator*
Schwartz, George R. *physician, researcher*
Schwartz, Judy Ellen *thoracic surgeon*
Schwartz, Leon *foreign language educator*
Schwartz, Lillian Feldman *artist, filmmaker, critic, nurse, writer*
Schwartz, Michael *professor, researcher*
Schwartz, Michael Robinson *management consultant*
Schwartz, Sheila Ruth *education and English educator*
Schwartz, Shirley E. *retired chemist, researcher*
Schwartz, Sima M. *music educator*
Schwartz, Stephen Lawrence *composer, lyricist*
Schwartzman, Jason Francesco *actor, musician*
Schwary, Ronald Louis *motion picture producer*
Schwarz, Jan *literature and language professor*
Schwarz, Joe (John J.H. Schwarz) *former congressman, physician*
Schwarz, M. Roy *retired physician, administrator*
Schwarz, Udo Dietmar *physicist, researcher*
Schwarzer, William W. *federal judge*
Schwebel, Renata Manasse *sculptor*
Schweiker, Richard Schultz *former trade association administrator, former United States Secretary of Health & Human Services*
Schwendinger, Julia Rosalind Siegel *sociology researcher*
Schwerdtner, Frederick Howard *lawyer, retired police commander, real estate broker*
Schwimmer, David *actor*
Sciuva, Margaret W. *counselor*
Scobey, Margaret *former ambassador*
Scollard, Patrick John *hospital executive*
Scoppetta, Nicholas *fire commissioner*
Scorsese, Martin *film director, film producer*
Scotland, S. J. (Susan Rose Scotland) *artist, educator*
Scott, Benjamin *retired electrical engineer*
Scott, Carol *science educator*
Scott, Catherine Dorothy *library and information scientist, consultant*
Scott, Charles David *chemical engineer, consultant*
Scott, David Clinton *research scientist*
Scott, G. Judson, Jr. *lawyer, federal judge*
Scott, Joyce *writer*
Scott, Karen Elizabeth *advocate*
Scott, Karen N. *language educator*
Scott, Lesli *psychologist*
Scott, Michael Dennis *lawyer*
Scott, Renay Marie *academic administrator, educator*
Scott, T. Gordon *chemistry and math educator, writer*
Scott-Battle, Gladys Natalie *retired social worker*
Scott-Burton, Jennifer Marie *special education educator*
Scully, Marlan Orvil *physics professor*
Scully, Robert William (Bob Scully) *retired diversified financial services company executive*
Sczudlo, Walter Joseph *lawyer*
Seabolt, Robert D. *lawyer*
Seaden, George *civil engineer*
Seader, Junior DeVere (Bob Seader) *retired chemical engineering professor*
Seale, James Millard *retired religious organization administrator, minister*
Seals, Margaret Louise Crumrine *retired journalist*
Seamans, William *writer, retired reporter, commentator*
Searle, Rodney Newell *state legislator, farmer, insurance agent*
Sears, Mary Helen *lawyer*
Sears, Sandra Jones *medical/surgical nurse, consultant*
Seary, Jennifer *language educator*
Sease, Gene Elwood *communications executive*
Seawell, Thomas Robert *artist, retired educator*
Seay, Charlotte J. *artist*
Sebastian, Peter *political scientist, consultant, retired diplomat*
Secchiutti, Ronald *electrical engineering designer*
Sechrist, Chalmers Franklin, Jr. *electrical engineering educator*
Seck, Ousmane *economics professor*
Secretan, Jimmy *application developer, researcher*
Sedelmaier, John Josef *filmmaker*
Sedghizadeh, Parish Paymon *dentist, oral and maxillofacial pathologist, educator*
Sedighi, Artin *application developer, researcher*
Seeborg, Michael C. *economics professor*
Seelam, Seetharami *research scientist*
Seeley, Cathy Lynn *director, secondary school educator, consultant*
Seelig, Gerard Leo *management consultant*
Seemann, Rosalie Mary *international business and foreign policy association executive*
Segal, Erich *author, educator*
Segal, Vladimir M. *retired metallurgist, researcher*
Segars, Kelly Scott, Sr. *physician, banker*
Segger, Martin Joseph *museum director, educator, art historian*
Segreto, Linda Mary Janeczek *special education educator, librarian*
Segrove, David Anthony *information technology manager*
Sehring, Adolf *artist, sculptor*
Seible, Frieder *structural engineer, educator*
Seidel, Selvyn *lawyer, educator*
Seidenman, Neil Arnold *interpreter*
Seidman, Stephen Benjamin *dean, computer science educator*
Seigenthaler, John Lawrence *retired newspaper executive*
Seinfeld, Jerry *comedian, actor, television producer, scriptwriter*
Seiple, John W., Jr. *corporate financial executive*
Selders, Jean E. *retired psychology professor*
Seldner, Betty Jane *environmental engineer, aerospace transportation executive, consultant*
Seleznev, Vadim Eugenjevich *mathematician, researcher*
Seli, Emre Utku *reproductive endocrinology and infertility specialist, physician researcher*
Seligman, Nicole Kay *broadcast executive, lawyer*
Seligson, Carl Harold *corporate financial executive*
Selke-Kern, Barbara Ellen *university official, writer*
Selkowitz, Arthur *retired advertising executive*
Sell, LeeLou *retired elementary school educator*
Seller, Robert Herman *cardiologist, physician*
Sells, Boake Anthony *private investor*
Seltser, Raymond *epidemiologist, educator, preventive medicine physician*
Seltzer, Vicki Lynn *obstetrician, gynecologist*
Selvaraju, Raghuram *medical researcher*
Semancik, Stephen *physicist*
Semel, Terry S. *retired Internet company executive*
Seminara, Lynda Anne *editor*
Semler, William Ludwig *retired obstetrician, retired gynecologist*
Semyonov, Oleg G. *research scientist*
Sen, Alper *engineering educator*
Sen, Dipankar *technology manager, principal*
Sena, Charalena *dental office executive*
Sendaula, Henry Musoke *engineering educator*
Sendlinger, Shawn Crowley *chemistry professor, department chairman*
Seney, Erin E. *biologist, marine biologist*
Sengupta, Abhijit *molecular and optical physicist*
Sennema, David Carl *arts consultant*
Sens, Alexander *classicist, educator*
Sentell-Perez, Jo *psychologist*
Sentenne, Justine *corporate ombudsman consultant*
Seow, Steven C. *research scientist*
Sepehr, Ali *physician*
Serag, Engy *claims consultant*
Serenbetz, Robert *manufacturing executive, financial planner*
Serkes, Jeffrey D. *former energy executive*
Serling, Joel Martin *educational psychologist*
Sernoffsky, Michael A. *elementary school educator*
Serrie, Hendrick *retired anthropology and international business educator*
Servodidio, Pat Anthony *broadcast executive*
Serwatka, Walter Dennis *publishing executive*
Sessions, Roy Brumby *otolaryngologist, educator*
Sessums, T. Terrell *lawyer*
Setser, Carole Sue *food scientist, educator*
Settles, Jeanne Dobson *retired librarian*
Sever, John Louis *medical researcher, educator*
Severo, Richard *writer*
Severson, Katie LeAnn *music educator*
Sevier, Michael Christopher *engineer*
Sevilla, Emerita Nepomuceno *writer*
Sewell, Daniel D. *psychiatrist, educator*
Seymour, Daniel Keith *human services administrator*
Seymour, Joseph John *air transportation executive*
Seyon, Patrick L. N. *social sciences educator, educational consultant*
Seyoum, Berhane *medical educator*
Sfekas, Stephen James *lawyer, educator*
Sha, William T. *senior nuclear scientist, consultant*
Shabani, Javad *research scientist*
Shabot, Myron Michael *hospital administrator*
Shackelford, Scott Addison *air force officer, retired, civilian research chemist*
Shader, Richard Irwin *psychiatrist, pharmacologist, educator*
Shaevitz, Joshua William *physics professor*
Shaffer, Bernard William *mechanical and aerospace engineering educator*
Shaffer, Kitt *radiologist, educator*
Shaffer, Richard James *lawyer, retired manufacturing executive*
Shaffert, Kurt *retired lawyer, chemical engineer*
Shagam, Janet Yagoda *educator, microbiologist*
Shagan, Bernard Pellman *endocrinologist, educator*
Shah, Bipin Chandra *banker*
Shaheen, Gerald L. *retired manufacturing executive*
Shahied, Ishak I. *science educator*
Shaker, William Haygood *marketing professional, public policy reformer*
Shakespeare, Valerie Monroe *curator, director, art gallery owner*
Shakoor, Abdul *geologist, educator*
Shaktini, Namascar *language educator*
Shalikashvili, John Malchase *former Chairman of the Joint Chiefs of Staff*
Shambaugh, Stephen Ward *lawyer*
Shan, Xi *research scientist*
Shan, Ying *computer scientist*
Shanahan, Mike (Michael Edward Shanahan) *former professional football coach*
Shanbhag, Sachin *science educator, researcher*
Shane, Jeffrey *physics professor*
Shane, Jeffrey Neil *lawyer*
Shane, John Marder *endocrinologist*
Shank, Maurice Edwin *aerospace engineer, consultant*
Shannon, Marilyn McCusker *biologist, educator*
Shannon, Mary Lou *adult health nursing educator*
Shannon, Peter Michael, Jr. *lawyer*
Shaoman, Yin *research scientist*
Shapiro, Harvey *poet*
Shapiro, Judith R. *former academic administrator, anthropology educator*
Shapiro, Leo J. *social researcher*
Shapiro, Marc Robert *retail executive*
Shapiro, Perry *economics educator*
Shapiro-Mathes, Angela *former broadcast executive*
Shapoury, Alireza *research scientist*
Sharifi, Neda A. *scientist*
Sharkey, Vincent Joseph *finance company executive*
Sharma, Brahama D. *chemistry professor*
Sharma, Divesh Shankar *finance educator*
Sharma, Sushil K. *medical educator*
Sharma, Vivek *finance educator*
Sharman, Robert D. *meteorologist, researcher*
Sharman, William *professional basketball team executive*
Sharp, Anne Catherine *artist, educator*
Sharp, Dan Steven *epidemiologist*
Sharp, William *retired advertising executive*
Sharpe, William Forsyth *economics professor*
Shartle, Stanley Musgrave *engineering executive, consultant, surveyor*
Shasteen, Donald Eugene *retired government official, small business consultant*
Shatin, Judith *composer, educator*
Shaughnessey, Gail *educator*
Shaughnessy, Allen F. *pharmacist, educator*
Shaw, Diane *artist, educator*
Shaw, Eleanor Jane *newspaper editor*
Shaw, Harold *retired performing arts association administrator*
Shaw, Helen Lester Anderson *nutrition educator, researcher, retired dean*
Shaw, Jack Allen *communications company executive*
Shaw, John Frederick *retired naval officer*
Shaw, Judy Browder *engineer*
Shaw, Kenneth Alan *former university president*
Shaw, Leonard Glazer *retired electrical engineering educator, consultant*
Shaw, Nancy Rivard *museum curator, art historian, consultant*
Shaw, Richard Thomas *humanitarian, retired federal agent, retired military officer*
Shaw, Ronald Ahrend *physician, educator*
Shaw, Theodore Michael *former legal association administrator*
Shaye, Robert Kenneth *film company executive*
Shays, Christopher H. *former United States Representative from Connecticut*
Shea, Christopher *chemicals executive, director*
Sheaffer, Richard Allen *electrical engineer*
Sheaffer, Suzanne Frances *geriatrics nurse*
Shealy, Harry E., Jr. *biology professor, consultant*
Shearing, Miriam *retired state supreme court chief justice*
Shedaker, Kathleen Edith *publishing executive*
Shedd, Arthur B. *retired school system administrator*
Shedd, Donald Pomroy *surgeon*
Sheeder, Robert Elwood *lawyer*
Sheehan, Robert James, II, *retired management and market research consultant*
Sheen, Charlie (Carlos Irwin Estevez) *actor*
Sheen, Martin (Ramon Estevez) *actor*
Sheesley, Mary Frank *art educator*
Sheffey, Ruthe T. *language educator*
Shehab, Tariq *engineering educator, researcher*
Sheild, Carolyn Jean *science educator*
Sheindlin, Judith (Judge Judy) *television personality, judge*
Sheldon, Stephen *pediatric sleep medicine educator, researcher*
Sheldon, Terry Edwin *lawyer, investment advisor*
Shelley, Charles Arthur, Jr. *retired academic administrator*
Shellman-Lucas, Elizabeth C. *special education educator, researcher*
Shelor, Belva Jean *psychologist*
Shelton, Hugh (Henry Hugh Shelton) *former Chairman of the Joint Chiefs of Staff*
Shelton, James Douglas *banker*
Shelton, Kathryn H. *retired librarian*
Shelton, Stephani *broadcast journalist, consultant*
Shemesh, Lorraine R. *painter*
Shen, Zheng-Xuan *researcher*
Sheng, Jinhua *research scientist*
Shenoy, Sachindev Shantaram *astronomer*
Shepard, Christy J. *special education educator*
Shepard, Richard Blount *surgeon, educator*
Shepard, Sam (Samuel Shepard Rogers) *playwright, actor*
Shepherd, Bobby E. *federal judge*
Shepherd, Cybill Lynne *actress, singer*
Shepp, Bryan Eugene *psychologist, educator*
Sheppard, April Spring *school librarian*
Sheppard, Jennifer Modlin *genealogist, retired government employee*
Sher, Leo *psychiatrist*
Sherbell-Na, Rhoda *artist, sculptor*
Shere, Dennis *lawyer, writer, retired publishing executive*
Sheridan, Edward Patrick *college dean*
Sheridan, Judson Dean *academic executive*
Sheridan, Patrick Michael *retired finance company executive*
Sheridan, Sonia Landy *artist, retired educator*
Sherin, Edwin *theater, film and television director, actor*
Sherman, Howard D. *financial consultant*
Sherman, Jeffrey Barry *retired retail executive*
Sherman, Jimmie Lee *mathematician, educator*
Sherman, John Foord *biomedical consultant*
Sherman, Richard Morton *composer, lyricist*
Sherrard, William Robert *retired operations management educator*
Sherrer, Charles David *dean, clergyman*
Sherris, David Allan *surgeon, researcher, educator*
Sherrod, Danny Troy *writer, educator*
Sherry, George Leon *political science professor*
Sherwood, Gloria N. *graphics designer, genealogist, small business owner*
Shestack, Alan *retired museum administrator*
Shevchuk, Nikolai Alexandrovich *biologist*
Shi, Dexiu *laser and optics scientist*
Shi, Tianchen *research scientist*
Shields, Andrea Lyn *psychologist, coach, educator*
Shields, Brooke Christa Camille *actress, model*
Shields, Cynthia Rose *college administrator*
Shields, Joan Marie *microbiologist, parasitologist*
Shields, Stephanie *psychology professor*
Shier, Gloria Bulan *mathematics professor*
Shier, Susan Lynne *music educator*
Shiffrin, Nancy *writer, educator*
Shihab, Fuad Said *medical educator, researcher*
Shihabi, Zak K. *lab administrator, director*
Shikuma, Eugene Yujin *travel company executive*
Shilling, Lilless McPherson *healthcare educator*
Shillingburg, Constance Joanne *historian, retired history professor*
Shils, Maurice Edward *physician, educator, research scientist*
Shim, Sang Eun *engineering educator*
Shimoda, Jerry Yasutaka *retired national historic park manager*
Shin, Jae Cheol *research scientist*
Shin, Jaewon *research scientist*
Shin, Shung Jae *management educators*
Shindle, William Richard *retired musicologist, educator*
Shindler, Steven M. *telecommunications industry executive*
Shinn, George Latimer *investment banker, consultant, finance educator*
Shinn, James Joseph (Jim Shinn) *former federal agency administrator*
Shiotsu, Masahiro *engineering educator*
Shipman, Barbara Lowther *librarian*
Shirer, Robert LLoyd *clergyman*
Shirilau, Mark Steven *utilities executive*
Shirley, Jon Anthony *former computer software company executive*
Shirley-Quirk, John *singer, educator*
Shisler, Arden L. *insurance and transportation company executive*
Shlimovich, Pavel *internist*
Shockley, Edward Julian *retired air transportation executive*
Shoemaker, Lawrence R. *pediatrician, educator*
Shoji, Kakuko *language educator*
Shore, Eleanor Gossard *retired medical school dean*
Shorris, Anthony Ernest *former state agency administrator*
Shorter, Walter Wyatt *paper company executive*
Shotwell, Malcolm Green *minister*
Shoul, Melvin I. *retired surgeon*
Shoup, Andrew James, Jr. *retired oil industry executive*
Shoupe, Donna *obstetrician-gynecologist, educator*
Shreve, Susan Richards *writer, educator*
Shrivastava, Amitesh *materials engineer*
Shriver, Robert Sargent, Jr., (Sargent Shriver) *lawyer*
Shrotriya, Vishal *research scientist*
Shubb, William Barnet *judge*
Shuchart, Eugene Joseph *retired accountant*
Shuhy, David E. *theater educator, set designer*
Shuler, Caroletta Alexis *criminal justice educator*
Shulman, Bernard H. *psychiatrist, educator*
Shulman, Mildred *artist*
Shulman, Yechiel *engineering educator*
Shultis, Robert Lynn *finance educator, consultant, retired professional society administrator*
Shuman, Samuel Irving *lawyer, educator*
Shuman, Stanley S. *investment banker*
Shumate, David John *literature and language professor*
Shuster, Frederick *retired internist, gastroenterologist*
Shuster, Robert G. *electronics executive, consultant*
Sia, Ka Cheung *application developer*
Sibo, Elsa Lynette *secondary school educator*
Sidereas, Panagiotis *physicist*
Sieben, J(ohn) Kenneth *retired humanities educator, writer, editor*
Sieburth, Richard *literature educator, interpreter*
Siegal, Allan Marshall *journalist, consultant*
Siegal, Rita Goran *engineering company executive*
Siegel, George Henry *management consultant*
Siegel, Herbert Bernard *management consultant*
Siegel, Ira T. *retired publishing executive*
Siegel, Jack Morton *retired pharmaceutical executive*
Siegel, Stanley *financial executive*
Siegfried, Jan Brooks *music educator, director*
Siemer, Deanne Clemence *lawyer*
Sieverts, Jorgen Francois *engineering executive*
Siffert, Robert Spencer *orthopedic surgeon*
Sifton, David Whittier *retired magazine editor*
Sigety, Charles Edward *lawyer, financial planner*
Sigle, John Walter *science educator*
Sigler, Jamie-Lynn *actress*
Sigler, John Charles *former firearms association executive*
Sigman, Stanley T. *retired telecommunications industry executive*
Sigmon, J. Lewis, Jr. *medical educator*
Sigmond, Carol Ann *lawyer*
Sikes, Cynthia Lee *actress, singer*
Sil, Samik *geophysicist*
Silberling, Louise Stillman *sociologist, writer, editor*
Silberman, Laurence Hirsch *federal judge*
Sills, Scott E. *nanotechnologist*
Silva, Omega Logan *physician*
Silva, Robert Owen *retired protective service official*
Silva-Guzman, Angelica *literature and language educator*
Silver, Audrey Wilma *nurse, educator, writer*
Silver, Lynn Leslie *research scientist, consultant*
Silver, Malcolm David *pathologist, educator*
Silverberg, Kristen Lee *former ambassador*
Silverman, Ira Norton *news producer*
Silverman, Jerry Mark *political science professor, consultant*
Silverman, Kenneth Eugene *language educator, writer*
Silverman, Stanley Wayne *chemical company executive*
Silverstein, Barbara Ann *producer, musician*
Silvey, Anita Lynne *editor*
Simecka, Betty Jean *marketing executive*
Simendinger, Theodore John *writer, publishing executive*
Simeral, William Goodrich *retired chemical company executive*
Simin, Grigory *science educator*
Simmonds, Robert Maurer *operations research analyst*
Simmons, Lynda Merrill Mills *retired principal*
Simmons, Richmond Hogle *retired obstetrician, gynecologist*
Simmons, Russell *recording industry executive*
Simmons (Neumann), Sylvia *advertising executive, writer*
Simms, Maria Kay *small business owner, writer, artist, publisher*
Simon, Adam F. *political science professor*
Simon, Bernece Kern *retired social worker*
Simon, Donald John *financial planner, theta healer, small business owner*
Simon, J. Stephen *retired oil industry executive*

Simon, Norma Plavnick *psychologist*
Simon, Peter E. *publishing executive*
Simon, Robert G. *lawyer*
Simon, Ronald Isaac *financial executive*
Simon, Sandra Ruth Waldman *retired state agency administrator*
Simon, William Leonard *scriptwriter, television and film producer, writer*
Simonelli, Lorenzo *manufacturing executive*
Simons, Anneke Prins *artist, educator*
Simons, Lynn Osborn *educator*
Simonson, Lee Stuart *broadcast executive*
Simpson, Andrea Lynn *communications executive*
Simpson, Frederick James *retired science administrator*
Simpson, Hugh L. *news correspondent, newswriter*
Simpson, Jack Benjamin *medical technologist, business executive*
Simpson, Joanne Malkus *meteorologist*
Simpson, Michael Marcial *science and technology specialist, consultant*
Simpson, Murray *electrical engineer, consultant*
Simpson, Robert Homer *meteorologist, consultant*
Sims, Dale *former state treasurer*
Sims, John R. *lawyer*
Sims, Kent Otway *economist*
Sims, Lowery Stokes *museum curator, administrator, writer, educator*
Sims, Pamela Jan (Cerussi) *writer, minister*
Simson, Jo Anne *retired anatomy and cell biology educator*
Sinagra, Jack G. *former state senator*
Sinai, Allen Leo *economist, educator*
Sinclair, Carole *publishing executive, editor*
Sinclair, Patricia White *language educator*
Sinclair, Virgil Lee, Jr. *judge, writer*
Sincoff, Michael Z. *human resources and marketing executive, educator*
Sindler, Brian Paul *artist*
Singer, Dale *reporter, editor*
Singer, David Michael *marketing and public relations executive*
Singer, Donna Lea *writer, editor, educator*
Singer, Jack Wolfe *medical educator*
Singer, Markus Morton *retired trade association administrator*
Singh, Chitranjan K. *electronics engineer*
Singh, Jatinder Pal *research scientist, consultant*
Singh, Kunwar Pal *manufacturing executive, researcher*
Singh, Madhu *social sciences educator*
Singleton, David Michael *chemist, researcher*
Singleton, Jonetta Williams *poet, retired special education educator*
Sinha, Rakesh Kumar *computer scientist, researcher*
Sinkford, Jeanne Craig *dental association administrator, retired dentist, dean, educator*
Sinno, R. Ralph *civil engineer, educator*
Sinor, Howard Earl, Jr. *lawyer*
Sipowicz, Sharie *pharmaceutical executive, researcher*
Sirna, Gail Carolyn *artist, educator, writer*
Sischy, Ingrid Barbara *editor, art critic*
Sisk, Eileen Victoria *writer, journalist*
Sisk, Jane Elizabeth *economist, educator*
Sissman, Liron *artist, painter*
Sites, Kevin *news correspondent, journalist, web blogger*
Sitomer, Richard Allen (Ricky Sitomer) *air transportation executive*
Sittig, James Christopher *art dealer, painter, sculptor, landscape artist, poet*
Siu, Wang-Ngai *solicitor*
Siv, Sichan Aun *former ambassador*
Sivacolundhu, Ramesh Kumar *veterinarian*
Sivak-Callcott, Jennifer A. *ophthalmologist*
Sjostrand, Fritiof Stig *biologist, educator*
Skaff, Joseph John *state agency administrator, retired military officer*
Skaggs, Stacy L. *elementary school educator*
Skalsky, Askold *retired literature and language professor*
Skarecky, Douglas William *lab administrator*
Skeen, David Ray *systems engineer, consultant, engineering executive, educator*
Skelland, Anthony Harold Peter *chemical engineering professor*
Skenderian, Jessica Josephine *psychologist*
Skiff, Frederick Norman *physics educator, researcher*
Skigen, Patricia Sue *lawyer*
Skinner, Cathy JoAnn *school system administrator*
Skinner, Frederick William *retired history professor*
Skinner, Patricia Morag *state legislator*
Skol, Armand George *lawyer*
Skolnik, Barnet David *retired lawyer*
Skov, Arlie Mason *petroleum engineer, consultant*
Skowronski, Vincent Paul *musician, recording industry executive*
Skramstad, Harold Kenneth, Jr. *museum consultant*
Skromme, Lawrence H. *consulting agricultural engineer*
Slachta, Gregory Andrew *urologist*
Slater, Christian *actor*
Slattery, Edward James *bishop*
Slaugh, Lynn H. *retired chemist*
Slaughter, Freeman Cluff *retired dentist*
Slavens, Thomas Paul *library science educator*
Slavit, David Hal *otolaryngologist*
Slavitt, David Walton *retired lawyer*
Slayman, Carolyn Walch *geneticist, educator*
Slesnick, Timothy *cardiologist, educator*
Slichter, Charles Pence *physicist, researcher*
Sliesoraitis, Sarunas *pharmacist, educator*
Sliger, Herbert Jacquemin, Jr. *lawyer*
Sliger, Rebecca North *mechanical engineer*
Slim, Michel S. *surgeon, educator, health facility administrator*
Slinger, Michael Jeffery *law librarian, director*
Sljivic-Simsic, Biljana B. *retired Slavic and Baltic languages educator*
Sloan, Anne Elizabeth *food scientist, writer*
Sloan, Carolyn *music educator, composer, lyricist*
Sloan, Hugh Walter, Jr. *automotive executive*
Sloan, Michael Allan *neurologist*
Sloane, Neil James Alexander *mathematician, researcher*
Slockett, Deena *medical educator*
Slocum, Kay Brainerd *history professor, musician*
Slonaker, Norman Dale *lawyer*
Slosberg, Mike *advertising executive*
Slotkin, Todd *diversified financial services company executive*
Slover, William Lewis *lawyer*
Sloyan, Gerard Stephen *theology studies educator, priest*
Slutz, Pamela Jo Howell *former ambassador*
Small, Lawrence M. *former museum executive*
Small, Sarah Mae *volunteer*
Smally, Donald Jay *consulting engineering executive*
Smarr, Larry Lee *science administrator, astrophysicist, educator*
Smart, James Anthony *music educator*
Smelser, June *librarian*
Smelser, Neil Joseph *sociologist*
Smetana, Pavel Amos *religious organization administrator*
Smiley, Jane Graves *author, educator*
Smith, A. Robert *editor, author*
Smith, Anne Day *writer*
Smith, Anne Marie Schoefer *application developer*
Smith, Barbara Barnard *music educator*
Smith, Barbara Jeanne *retired librarian*
Smith, Betty *writer, not-for-profit developer*
Smith, Carl Brent *retired chemist*
Smith, Carole Dianne *retired lawyer, editor, writer, product developer*
Smith, Catherine H. *bank executive*
Smith, Catherine Marie *science educator*
Smith, Charles Haddon *geologist, consultant, retired federal agency administrator*
Smith, Charlotte Reed *retired music educator*
Smith, Cora Adele *retired writer*
Smith, Darvin Scott *internist*
Smith, David Horton *social science researcher-theorist, writer, consultant, nonprofit organization founder, internet business founder*
Smith, David Julian *educational consultant*
Smith, Elise Fiber *international non-profit development agency administrator*
Smith, Ellen Louise *retired language educator*
Smith, Elmer *telecommunications industry executive*
Smith, Erin Ann *science educator*
Smith, Floyd Leslie *insurance company executive*
Smith, Frederick Coe *retired manufacturing executive*
Smith, George Drury *publishing executive*
Smith, George Patrick, II, *lawyer, educator*
Smith, Harold Charles *pension fund administrator*
Smith, J. Kellum, Jr. *foundation administrator, lawyer*
Smith, Jack David *lawyer*
Smith, James A. *lawyer*
Smith, Janice Yoder *biology professor*
Smith, Jason *retired professional hockey player*
Smith, John Francis, Jr., (Jack Smith) *retired automotive executive*
Smith, John Mortimer Fourette *bishop*
Smith, John W(esley), Jr. *data processing executive, consultant*
Smith, Julious Perry, Jr. *lawyer*
Smith, Kathryn Lee *artist, educator*
Smith, Kathryn Nally *history educator*
Smith, Kerry Clark *lawyer*
Smith, Leonard R. *information technology executive, educator*
Smith, Leonore Rae *artist*
Smith, Linda Gene (Gene Smith) *former legislative staff member*
Smith, Liz (Mary Elizabeth Smith) *columnist, newscaster*
Smith, Lois Arlene *actress, writer*
Smith, Margaret Taylor *volunteer*
Smith, Marie F. *lobbyist, former association executive*
Smith, Martha Virginia Barnes *retired elementary school educator*
Smith, Martin Bernhard *retired journalist*
Smith, Martin Henry *retired pediatrician*
Smith, Mary Louise *former real estate broker*
Smith, Monica *chiropractor, researcher*
Smith, Nick H. *former congressman, archivist, farmer*
Smith, Orin Robert *chemical company executive*
Smith, Ozzie (Osborne Earl Smith) *retired professional baseball player*
Smith, Patricia Ann (Pat Smith) *elementary school educator*
Smith, Patricia Lynne *artist*
Smith, Paul Vergon, Jr. *retired gas industry executive*
Smith, Phillip Walton *retired surgeon*
Smith, Phyllis *actress*
Smith, Raymond Leigh *plastic surgeon*
Smith, Richard Alan *publishing and specialty retailing executive*
Smith, Rita Rex *mechanical engineer*
Smith, Robert Hugh *retired engineering construction company executive*
Smith, Robert Powell *former ambassador, retired foundation administrator*
Smith, Rod *retired professional football player*
Smith, Ronald Lynn *health system executive*
Smith, Russell B. *surgeon*
Smith, Samuel Howard *academic administrator, plant pathologist*
Smith, Scott Clybourn *retired publishing executive*
Smith, Stuart Lyon *psychiatrist, corporate financial executive*
Smith, Thomas F. *immunologist*
Smith, Vme Edom (Verna Mae Smith) *social sciences educator, freelance photographer, writer*
Smith, Wendy L. *foundation executive*
Smither, Howard Elbert *musicologist, educator*
Smith II, Leon M. *chemist*
Smits, Kathleen Curran *artist, educator*
Smock, Raymond William *historian*
Smolinski, Bryan *professional hockey player*
Smollett, Jurnee Diana *actress*
Smoot, Julianna *political fundraiser*
Smukal, Michael William *musician, educator, composer*
Smyntek, John Eugene, Jr. *editor*
Smyth, Ellen Gray Menees *systems support specialist*
Snader, Jack Ross *retired publishing company executive*
Sneeringer, Stephen Geddes *lawyer*
Snell, Patricia Poldervaart *retired librarian, consultant*
Snelling, Barbara W. *retired state legislator*
Snider, L. Britt *federal official*
Snook, Paul *real estate company executive*
Snowden, Lawrence Fontaine *retired air transportation executive, retired military officer*
Snyder, Joan *painter*
Snyder, John Leighton *lawyer*
Snyder, Marvin *neuropsychologist*
Snyder, Nathan *entrepreneur, investor*
Snyder, William Burton *insurance company executive*
Sobin, Leslie Howard *pathologist, educator*
Sobkowicz, Hanna Maria *retired neurologist*
Socol, Sheldon Eleazer *university official*
Socolow, Robert Harry *engineering educator, physicist*
Soderberg, Nancy *former ambassador*
Soe, Kyaw K. *medical educator*
Soeteber, Ellen *journalist, editor*
Sohn, Livia *music educator*
Sohn, Sung Won *former bank executive*
Soileau, Monica Marie *economist*
Sojka, Gary Allan *biologist, educator, academic administrator*
Sokol, Ronald Jay *pediatric gastroenterologist, researcher*
Solá, Victoria M. *announcer, writer*
Solano, Julio Rafael *priest, educator*
Solberg, Amy Kathleen *director*
Solberg, Ronald Louis *investment adviser, portfolio manager*
Solkoff, Jerome Ira *lawyer, educator*
Sollender, Joel David *accountant, consultant, financial executive*
Solls, Mark A. *lawyer*
Solmssen, Peter *retired academic administrator*
Solomon, Abraham Lev *mathematics professor*
Solomon, Susan *atmospheric chemist*
Soltero-Harrington, Luis Rubén *retired surgeon, educator*
Somasundaran, Ponisseril *surface and colloid engineering educator*
Somers, Louis Robert *retired food company executive*
Somerville, Christopher Roland *biochemist, educator*
Somes, Joan Marie *emergency nurse practitioner*
Sommerfeld, Jude Thomas *chemical engineer, educator*
Sondheim, Stephen Joshua *composer, librettist, lyricist*
Sonego, Ian G. *retired assistant attorney general*
Song, Byung Youn *electronics executive, consultant*
Song, Qi *electrical engineer*
Sonnenschein, Hugo Freund *academic administrator, writer, economist, educator*
Sontag, James Mitchell *oncologist, researcher*
Soran, Z. Ozlem *medical educator*
Sorel, Edward *artist*
Sorensen, Carl Edward *manufacturing executive*
Sorensen, Jack *computer game company executive*
Sorenstam, Annika *retired professional golfer*
Sorkin, Aaron *scriptwriter, television producer, playwright*
Sorstokke, Ellen Kathleen *marketing executive, educator*
Sosa, Ernest *philosopher, educator*
Sosa, Julie A. *medical educator*
Sotos, John George *cardiologist, writer*
Sottile, Joseph James *elementary school educator, poet*
Souganidis, Panagiotis Emmanuel *mathematician, educator*
Souler, Benjamin Kerwin *retired research chemist, pharmacist, consultant*
Soules, Aline *librarian, writer*
Sourial, Alfy Saif *surgeon*
Sourirajan, Karthik *research scientist*
Souter, David Hackett *retired United States supreme court justice*
South, Frank Edwin *physiologist, educator*
South, Michael Shane *oncologist*
Southerland, S. Duane *manufacturing executive*
Sowande, Beverly Folasade *lawyer, educator*
Spackman, Thomas James *radiologist*
Spadafora, David Charles *historian, educator*
Spainhour, J. Patrick (James Patrick Spainhour) *outsourcing company executive, former apparel executive*
Spanfeller, James John, Jr. *former publishing executive*
Spangenberg, Norman Earl *retired hydrologist educator*
Spangler, Beulah Stark (Bes Spangler) *retired literature and language professor*
Sparks, John Edward *lawyer*
Sparks, Jordin Brianna *singer*
Sparks, Robert Ronold, Jr. *lawyer*
Sparrow, Alison Kidder *painter, sculptor*
Spaulding, Anne C. *epidemiologist, educator*
Spector, Rose *former state supreme court justice*
Speelman, Patrick J. *history professor*
Speer, Richard John *security consultant*
Speers, Roland Root, II, *lawyer*
Speicher, Carl Eugene *pathologist*
Spellman, Mitchell Wright *surgeon, academic administrator, educator*
Spelman, Nancy Latting *developmental psychologist*
Spence, Andrew *artist, painter*
Spence, James Robert, Jr. *broadcast executive, educator, mediator*
Spence, Joseph Thomas *biochemist*
Spence, Nancy Elizabeth *workshop developer, psychology educator, literature educator, writer*
Spencer, Bennion L. *college instructor*
Spencer, John Daniel *former mayor*
Spencer, Tricia Jane *writer*
Sperelakis, Nicholas, Sr. *retired physiology and biophysics educator, researcher*
Spero, Nancy *artist*
Spidlik, Tomas Cardinal *cardinal, priest, theologian*
Spiegel, Jayson Leslie *lawyer, educator, professional society administrator*
Spiegel, Melvin *retired biology professor*
Spiess, Eliot Bruce *biologist, educator*
Spillane, Nancy Marie *primary school educator*
Spillman, Marjorie Rose *theater producer, dancer*
Spinrad, Robert Joseph *computer scientist*
Spiro, Herbert John *political scientist, ambassador*
Spitzberg, Irving Joseph, Jr. *lawyer*
Spitzer, Eliot Laurence *political science professor, former Governor of New York*
Spitzer, John J. *retired economics professor*
Spivak, Joan Carol *communications executive*
Splane, Richard Beverley *social work educator*
Spodek, Bernard *early childhood educator*
Spomer, Penny Sue *elementary school educator*
Spong, Donald A. *physicist*
Spottswood, Lydia Carol *nurse, health facility administrator*
Spraggins, Johnnie David *sociology and cultural studies educator*
Sprague, Esther Sparks *art history educator*
Sprecher, Baron William Gunther *pianist, composer, conductor, diplomat*
Sprince, Leila Joy *retired librarian*
Spring, Anita *anthropologist, educator*
Spring, Bonnie Joan *preventive medicine professor*
Springer, Debra Ann *psychologist*
Springer, Marlene *retired academic administrator*
Springer, Paul David *lawyer, film company executive*
Springer, Robert Dale *retired air force officer, consultant, lecturer*
Springer-Scott, Gladys Lorraine *educator, consultant*
Sprinthall, Norman Arthur *psychology educator*
Sproul, Sarah Lee *conductor, musician, educator*
Spruill, Louise Elam *retired mathematics educator*
Spurlock, Morgan *television producer, film producer*
Squibb, John R. *history professor*
Squibb, Samuel Dexter *chemistry professor*
Squier, Jack Leslie *sculptor, retired art educator*
Squires, Kathleen Elaine *internal medicine educator*
Squires, Nina Grace *artist*
Sreenivas, Mytheli *history professor*
Sridharan, Arvind *engineer*
Srinivasagupta, Deepak *chemical engineer, researcher*
Srinivasan, Asha *music educator, composer*
Srinivasan, Rangaswamy *chemical physicist*
Srinivasan, Vedanth *engineer*
Srinivasan, Venkataraman *marketing and management educator*
Srivastava, Vinod K. *research scientist, educator*
Stabler, Scott Lawrence *historian, educator*
Stackhouse, Max Lynn *religious studies educator*
Stadelman, William Ralph *chemicals executive*
Stadler, Selise McNeill *laboratory and x-ray technician, medical assistant*
Stafford, William Henry, Jr. *federal judge*
Staggers, Mary E. *minister*
Staivisky, Jeanne Louise *counselor, alcohol/drug abuse services professional*
Staley, Airica *biologist*
Staley, Thomas Fabian *literature and language professor, museum director*
Stalker, Jacqueline D'Aoust *academic administrator, educator*
Stallone, Sylvester Gardenzio *actor, film director, scriptwriter, producer*
Stallworth, Monica Lavaughn *geriatrician*
Stalnaker, Judith Ann *education educator*
Staloff, Arnold Fred *financial services executive*
Stamm, Brad *economics professor*
Stamoolis, James John *academic administrator, educator*
Stancell, Arnold Francis *chemical engineering educator, retired oil industry executive*
Stanek, Alan Edward *retired music educator, performing arts association administrator*
Stanfill, Dennis Carothers *corporate financial executive*
Stankovich, Alla (Tsykalo) *research scientist*
Stanley, Kenneth *statistician, educator*
Stanley, Margaret King *performing arts administrator*
Stanley, Paul *physics professor*
Stanley, Robert Anthony *artist, educator*
Stanley, Scott, Jr. *editor*
Stanley, Steven Mitchell *paleontologist, educator*
Stansell, Leland Edwin, Jr. *lawyer, mediator, educator*
Stansell, Ronald Bruce *retired investment banker*
Stanton, Louis Lee *federal judge*
Stapleton, Beverly Cooper *aerospace executive*
Stapleton, Craig Roberts *former ambassador*
Stapp, Joshua Paul *computer engineer*
Stark, Diana *public relations executive*
Stark, Joan Scism *education educator*
Stark, Nellie May *forester, ecologist, educator*
Starkweather, Frederick Thomas *retired data processing executive*
Starr, Kimberly Ann *assistant principal, school system administrator*
Starr, Steven Dawson *photographer*
Stasek, Lorraine Anne *elementary school educator*
Stashower, Daniel Meyer *writer*
Stauderman, Albert Philip, Jr. *media production consultant*
Stave, Anna M. *education educator*
Stavropoulos, William S. *retired chemical company executive*
Steadman, David Wilton *retired museum director, deacon*
Stearns, Marilyn Tarpy *music educator*
Stearns, Stewart Warren *charitable association executive*
Stebel, Michael David *marketing professional, consultant*
Steele, Charles, Jr. *retired civil rights association executive, former state legislator*
Steele, Judith McConnell *writer*
Steele, Mildred Romedahl *educator*

Steele, Valerie Fahnestock *museum director, writer, educator*
Steelman, Sara Gerling *retired art association administrator*
Steenland, Douglas M. *former air transportation executive*
Steffen, Jason H. *astrophysicist*
Steffy, Marion Nancy *state agency administrator*
Stegenga, James Jay *senior compliance examiner*
Steier, Michael Edward *cardiac surgeon*
Stein, Adam Matthew *military officer*
Stein, Daniel *hotel and resort operations executive*
Stein, Robert Alan *electronics executive*
Stein, Sandra Therese *pharmacist*
Steinbach, Lynne Susan *radiologist, educator*
Steinback, Thomas R. *business management educator*
Steinberg, Andrew B. *former federal agency administrator, lawyer*
Steinberg, Craig Russell *mediator*
Steinberg, Russell Max *behavioral pediatrician, educator*
Steiner, Elizabeth *philosopher, psychologist, educator*
Steiner, Heinz *science professor, researcher*
Steiner, Robert L. *economist*
Steinhardt, Alicia Ann *biology professor, director*
Steinhauer, Josefa Melissa *biologist*
Steinhoff, Raymond O(akley) *consulting geologist*
Stellar, Arthur Wayne *school system administrator*
Stemerman, David H. *radiologist*
Stendahl, Brita Kristina *humanities and social studies educator*
Stengel, James R. *retired consumer products company executive*
Stengel, Ronald Francis *management consultant*
Štěpánek, Petr *computer science educator*
Stephens, Donald R(ichards) *investor*
Stephens, Edward Carl *communications educator, writer*
Stephens, Norris Lynn *school librarian*
Stephens, Robert Oren *retired English language educator*
Stephenson, Herman Howard *retired banker*
Stephenson, Toni Edwards *publishing, internet domain communications and investment company executive*
Stephens-Rich, Barbara E. *minister, educator*
Steptoe, Mary Lou *lawyer*
Steptoe, Sonja *legal firm administrator*
Stern, Arthur Paul *electronics executive*
Stern, Joseph A. *lawyer, former publishing executive*
Stern, Julian Nathaniel *lawyer, pharmaceutical executive*
Stern, Kenneth P. *former broadcast executive, information technology executive*
Stern, Robin Lauri *medical physicist*
Stern, S(eesa) Beatrice *executive secretary, medical/surgical nurse*
Sterne, Hedda *artist*
Sternheimer, Karen *sociologist, writer*
Sterrett, James Kelley, II, *lawyer*
Sterrett, Samuel Black *lawyer, former judge*
Stetson, Robert Francis *retired metallurgist*
Stetz, Melba Del Carmen *psychologist*
Stevens, Art *public relations executive*
Stevens, Berton Louis, Jr. *data processing executive*
Stevens, Kenneth Allen *retired defense department worker*
Stevens, Lori Ann LaBeau *public librarian, administrator*
Stevens, May *artist*
Stevens, Rebecca Ann *sociologist, educator*
Stevens, Robert J. *aerospace transportation executive*
Stevens, Shane *novelist*
Stevens, Sheila Maureen *retired teachers union administrator*
Stevens, Ted (Theodore Fulton Stevens) *former United States Senator from Alaska*
Stevens, Warren *actor*
Stevenson, Deborah L. *government official, educator*
Stevenson, Earl *communications executive, entrepreneur*
Stevenson, Joyce R.L. *retired psychologist*
Stevenson, Marshall Field, Jr. *history professor*
Stevenson, Michael Keith *elementary school educator*
Stever, Horton Guyford *aerospace scientist, engineer, educator, consultant*
Stewart, Albert Elisha *safety engineer, engineering executive*
Stewart, Annette *retired judge*
Stewart, Charles Leslie *lawyer*
Stewart, Dorothy K. *librarian*
Stewart, Gordon Curran *retired insurance institute executive*
Stewart, Gwendolyn M. *elementary school educator*
Stewart, John Wray Black *college dean*
Stewart, Lucille Marie *retired special education coordinator, educator*
Stewart, Michael Glenn *otolaryngologist, educator*
Stewart, Murray Baker *retired lawyer*
Stewart, Rod *retired literature and language professor*
Stewart, S. Evelyn *child psychiatrist, researcher*
Stewart, Thomas Clifford *investment company executive*
Stewart, Timothy Glen *organist*
Stickney, Jessica *former state legislator*
Stickney, John Moore *lawyer*
Stiebing, William Henry, Jr. *retired history professor*
Stief, Louis John *chemist*
Stiff, Robert Martin *newspaper editor*
Stiffler, Jack Justin *electrical engineer*
Stiggall, Corin J. *musician*
Stiles, Beverly Lynn *sociologist, educator*
Stiles, Thomas Beveridge, II, *retired investment company executive*
Still, Homer Ibson *information technology executive*
Stiller, Ben *actor, television producer*
Stiller, Shale David *lawyer, educator*
Stillman, Elinor Hadley *retired lawyer*
Stimpert, Michael Alan *retired agricultural products company executive*
Stimpson, Jim P. *medical educator*
Stinsmuehlen-Amend, Susan *artist*
Stiritz, Marette McCauley *English language educator, consultant*
Stittich, Eleanor Maryann *retired nursing educator*
Stivers, Tenille Marie *psychology educator*
Stock, Carl William *geology educator*
Stock, Wendy *physician, educator*
Stockbauer, Roger Lewis *retired physicist, researcher*
Stockdale, Nancy L. *historian, educator*
Stocker, Christine Marie *language educator*
Stoeckel, Luke Edward *psychologist, researcher*
Stohlman, Connie Suzanne *neonatal intensive care unit nurse, obstetrical gynecological nurse*
Stoiber, Carlton Ray *nuclear law consultant, freelance/self-employed cartoonist*
Stoiber, Susanne A. *health science association administrator*
Stojkovic, Dusan *lawyer*
Stokes, Harvey J. *musician, educator, composer*
Stolarik, M. Mark *history professor*
Stolier, Alan J. *surgeon*
Stollerman, Gene Howard *internist, educator*
Stolley, Paul David *medical educator, researcher*
Stomfay-Stitz, Aline Maria *education educator*
Stone, Alan John *manufacturing and real estate company executive*
Stone, Brian *engineering educator*
Stone, Donald Raymond *lawyer*
Stone, Edmund Crispen III *banker*
Stone, Edward Herman *lawyer*
Stone, James Howard *management consultant*
Stone, Jin *language educator*
Stone, Jonathan Francis *biology professor*
Stone, Joss (Joscelyn Eve Stoker) *singer*
Stone, Oliver *film director, producer, scriptwriter*
Stone, Richie Eugene *engineering educator*
Stone, Sharon *actress*
Stone, Susan Ridgaway *marketing educator*
Stone, Sylvia *voice educator, singer*
Storer, Thomas W. *medical educator*
Storm, J. Reni *nurse, consultant*
Story, Joyce Ann *retired language educator*
Story, Timothy Kevin (Tim Story) *film director*
Stott, Terri Jeuan *residential services director*
Stotter, Harry Shelton *banker, lawyer*
Stoytcheva, Lilia Stefanova *concert pianist, educator*
Stoytcheva, Petia *economics professor*
Strain, James Ellsworth *pediatrician, educator, retired medical association administrator*
Strait, George *musician*
Strait, Viola Edwina Washington *librarian*
Straling, Phillip Francis *bishop emeritus*
Strand, Mark *poet*
Strand, Theresa *educational consultant*
Strange, Donald Ernest *healthcare company executive*
Strangman, Thomas *aerospace engineer*
Strantz, Nancy Jean *law educator, consultant*
Strathairn, David *actor*
Stratton, Mariann *retired military nursing executive*
Stratton, Robert *retired electronics executive*
Stratton, Walter Love *lawyer*
Stratton-Gonzalez, Sandra *dance educator, administrator*
Straub, Peter Francis *novelist*
Strauch, Berish *plastic surgeon, hand and cosmetic surgeon*
Strauss, Peter *actor*
Strawn, Evelyn Rae *artist*
Street, John Charles *linguistics educator*
Street, John Franklin *former mayor*
Strem, Ryan David *educator*
Strickholm, Jean *musician, company executive, retired elementary school educator*
Strider, Marjorie Virginia *artist, educator*
Stridiron, Iver Allison *former attorney general*
Strieder, William Christian *chemical engineering educator, consultant*
Striker, Cecil Leopold *archaeologist, educator*
Stringer, John *retired materials scientist*
Stritch, Elaine *singer, actress*
Strobel, Pamela B. *former energy executive*
Strodel, Robert Carl *lawyer*
Stroik, Adrienne Lisbeth *dance educator*
Strom, Victoria *small business owner*
Strong, Annsley Chapman *interior designer, volunteer*
Strong, John David *insurance company executive*
Strong, John Scott *finance educator*
Strong, Virginia Wilkerson *freelance writer, former special education educator*
Strong-Cuevas, Elizabeth *sculptor*
Strongin, Jonathan David *physician*
Strother, Patrick Joseph *public relations executive*
Strothman, James Edward *editor-in-chief*
Stroud, Rhoda M. *elementary school educator*
Stroud, Robert Michael *biophysicist, educator, biotechnologist*
Stroup, Kala Mays *former education commissioner, educational alliance administrator*
Strouse, Jean *writer, cultural organization administrator*
Strouth, Baron Howard Steven *geologist, mining engineer*
Strubel, Richard Perry *Internet company executive*
Strukoff, Rudolf Stephen *retired music educator*
Strum, Jay Gerson *retired lawyer*
Strunz, Kai *research scientist, educator*
Stryker, Richard Ripley, Jr. *museum director*
Stryker, Robin *social sciences educator*
Stryker, Sheldon *sociologist, educator*
Stuart, Alice Melissa *lawyer*
Stuart, Gerard William, Jr. *investment company executive, alderman, city official*
Stuart, Joseph Martin *museum administrator*
Stuart, Nancy Rubin (Nancy Zimman Stetson) *journalist, author, television producer*
Stuart, Sherry Blanchard *artist*
Stubbs, Gerald *biochemist, educator*
Stubbs, Kendon Lee *retired librarian*
Stubbs, Lu *sculptor, educator*
Studebaker, Forrest E. *history educator*
Stuebner, James Cloyd *real estate developer, contractor*
Stuhr, Elaine Ruth *former state legislator*
Stults, Walter Black *management consultant, trade association administrator*
Stultz, Cilla Holmes *psychologist*
Stumpe, Warren Robert *county official, retired engineering executive*
Sturgell, Robert Allan (Bobby Sturgell) *former federal agency administrator*
Sturges, John Siebrand *management consultant*
Sturner, Lynda *performing company executive*
Stycos, Maria Nowakowska *retired adult education educator*
Subedi, Bidya Raj *school system administrator, statistician, consultant*
Subramanian, Vijay *mechanical engineer*
Sudan, Ravindra Nath *electrical engineer, physicist, educator*
Sudarsky, Jerry M. *industrialist*
Sugiyama, Masano *chemical engineer, researcher*
Sui, Lei *technical leader*
Sukoff Rizzo, Stacey J. *research scientist*
Šulc, Vladimír *mechanical engineer*
Sullam, JoAnne D. *environmental artist*
Sullenberger, Chesley Burnett, III, (Sully Sullenberger) *pilot, airline safety consulting company executive*
Sullivan, Amanda *science educator*
Sullivan, Charles *dean, educator, author*
Sullivan, Colleen Anne *anesthesiologist, educator*
Sullivan, Daniel Joseph *theater critic*
Sullivan, Eugene John Joseph *manufacturing executive, director*
Sullivan, Eugene Raymond *federal judge*
Sullivan, George Edward *writer*
Sullivan, Gregory Patrick *principal engineer*
Sullivan, Harry Truman *research scientist*
Sullivan, James Leo *organization executive*
Sullivan, Jane *theater educator, director*
Sullivan, John Dominic *theater producer, writer*
Sullivan, John Louis, Jr. *retired search company executive*
Sullivan, Kathryn D. *geologist, former astronaut, science association executive*
Sullivan, Mary Ann *artist*
Sullivan, Mary Rose *retired English language educator*
Sullivan, Owen *employment services executive*
Sullivan, Roy Michael *aerospace engineer, researcher*
Sullivan Stemberg, Maureen *interior designer*
Sultanik, Evan Andrew *computer scientist*
Sumlin, Margaret Brown (Margie Sumlin) *retired special education educator*
Summerfield, John Robert *textile curator*
Summers, Carol *artist*
Summers, Cathleen *film producer*
Summers, David Stewart *neurologist, consultant*
Summers, Lorraine Dey Schaeffer *retired librarian*
Sun, Changquan Calvin *medical researcher, educator*
Sun, Hongwei *mechanical engineer*
Sun, Hui *industrial engineer, operations research analyst*
Sun, Jiaming *social sciences educator*
Sun, Jie *R & D engineer*
Sun, Lipeng *chemist*
Sun, Wei *pharmaceutical executive, researcher*
Sun, Yongsheng Victor *educator*
Sun, Zuo *aerospace engineer, researcher*
Sundaram, Narayan *electrical engineer*
Sundaram, Senthil K. *pediatrician, educator*
Sunde, Douglas *plastic surgeon*
Sunderman, Duane Neuman *chemist, research and development company executive*
Suneja, Manish *physician*
Sung, Kyongje *medical researcher*
Sung, Kyu-Taik *social worker, gerontologist, educator, researcher*
Sununu, John Edward *former United States Senator from New Hampshire*
Supino, Phyllis Gail *medical researcher, educator*
Suppa-Friedman, Janice DeStefano *secondary school educator, consultant*
Suppes, Patrick *statistician, philosopher, psychologist, educator*
Suput, Ray Radoslav *librarian*
Suraci, Patrick Joseph *clinical psychologist*
Suranovic, Steven M. *science educator*
Surawicz, Borys *physician, educator*
Surbone, Antonella *medical oncologist, bioethics researcher*
Surles, Richard Hurlbut, Jr. *retired law librarian*
Susman, Morton Lee *lawyer*
Sussberg, Milton Joel *marketing professional*
Sussman, Barry *writer, demographer, editor*
Sussman, Gerald *social sciences educator*
Sussman, Janet I. *social sciences educator*
Sussman, Laureen Glicklin *retired elementary school educator*
Suter, Scott Hamilton *literature and language educator*
Sutherland, Donald *actor*
Sutin, Norman *senior chemist emeritus, researcher*
Sutnick, Alton Ivan *internist, dean, educator, researcher, consultant*
Sutter, Jane Elizabeth *conservationist, science educator*
Sutter, Laurence Brener *lawyer*
Suttie, John Weston *biochemist*
Suttle, Helen Jayson *retired elementary school educator*
Sutton, George Paul *rocket propulsion engineer, writer, educator*
Sutton, Joe *playwright, educator*
Sutton, Johnny Keane *lobbyist, former prosecutor*
Sutton, Julia *musicologist, dance historian*
Sutton, Lee *biology professor*
Sutton, Peter Campbell *museum director*
Sutton-Creech, Donna Lynn *gifted and talented educator*
Sutton-Straus, Joan M. *journalist*
Suzuki, Hidetaro *violinist*
Suzuki, Yukiko *language educator*
Svarovsky, Sergei A. *engineering educator*
Svoboda, Janice June *nurse*
Swad, Stephen Mark *former mortgage company executive*
Swailes, William E. *counseling administrator*
Swain, Donald Christie *retired academic administrator, historian, educator*
Swalm, Thomas Sterling *aviations systems and weapons consultant, retired military officer*
Swan, Mara E. *employment services executive*
Swann, Charena Rai *psychotherapist, social worker*
Swanson, Victoria Clare Heldman *lawyer*
Swanstrom, Thomas Evan *economist*
Swartz, Jon David *psychologist, educator*
Swayne, Kenneth E. *engineering educator*
Sweeney, Deidre Ann *lawyer*
Sweeney, James *application developer*
Sweeney, John E. *former United States Representative from New York*
Sweet, Chad Creighton *consulting firm executive, former federal official*
Swenson, Sara *librarian, educator*
Swerdlow, Martin Abraham *retired pathologist, educator*
Swett, Richard Nelson (Dick) *former ambassador, former congressman*
Swift, Michael Ronald *internist, educator*
Swimm-McMahon, Katherine Lynn *educator*
Swinburn, Charles *retired rail transportation executive*
Swistek, Ronald James *special education educator*
Switzer, Janet *psychologist administrator*
Switzer, Maurice Harold *journalist*
Swoap, David Bruce *government and state agency administrator, consultant, art director*
Swope, Donald Downey *retired banker*
Sykora, Petr *professional hockey player*
Symons, Edward Leonard, Jr. *lawyer, educator, investment advisor*
Sypolt, Diane Gilbert *retired judge*
Syron, Richard Francis *former mortgage company executive, economist*
Syverud, Kent Douglas *dean, law educator*
Szabo, Barna Aladar *engineering educator*
Szabo, Istvan *film director*
Szakal, Andras Kalman *immunologist, anatomist, educator*
Sze, Sarah *sculptor*
Szelenyi, Ivan *adult education educator*
Szetela, Cheryl Wahl *educator*
Szydlowski, Ralph *retired metal products engineer*
Szymanski, Edna Mora *academic administrator*
Taar, Mireille *language educator, interpreter*
Tackett, Stephen Douglas *retired education services specialist*
Tadros, Fawzi M. *educator*
Tadros, Mohsen Shokry *agriculturist*
Taft, Sheldon Ashley *retired lawyer*
Tagiuri, Consuelo Keller *child psychiatrist, educator*
Taher, Cecilia *music educator*
Taheri, Saied *engineering educator*
Tai, Tsze Cheng *aerodynamicist, researcher*
Taifi, Mohamed *language educator, researcher*
Takhar, Pawan S. *food and biological engineer*
Talaga, Stephen C. *pianist, composer, music educator*
Talamo, Jonathan Haskell *ophthalmologist, educator*
Talbot, Mary Lee *minister*
Talent, James Matthes *former United States Senator from Missouri*
Taliaferro, Philip III *lawyer*
Tallett, Elizabeth Edith *biopharmaceutical company executive*
Talley, Robert Morrell *aerospace company executive*
Talley, Truman Macdonald *retired publisher, editor*
Tallman, Ann Marie *lawyer*
Talmadge, Mary Christine *nursing educator administrator*
Talmage, David Wilson *retired microbiologist, educator, dean*
Talor, Zvi *nephrologist*
Tam, Sunny Wing Yee *physicist*
Tamaro, George John *retired consulting engineer*
Tambour, Sophie *research scientist*
Tambs, Lewis Arthur *diplomat, historian, educator*
Tammeus, William David *journalist, columnist*
Tamura, Shigemi *electric power industry executive*
Tan, Dongfeng *pathologist, educator*
Tan, Songxin *science educator*
Tanachaiwiwat, Sapon *information technology manager*
Tanaka, J(eannie) E. *lawyer*
Tancredo, Tom (Thomas Gerard Tancredo) *retired United States Representative from Colorado*
Tandler, Bernard *cell biology educator*
Tandon, Rajiv *psychiatrist, educator*
Tandy, Carla M. *dancer, educator*
Tandy, Karen Pomerantz *communications executive, former federal agency administrator*
Tane, Susan Jaffe *retired manufacturing company executive*
Tanenbaum, Jay Harvey *lawyer*
Tang, Irving Che-hong *mathematician, educator*
Tang, Shensheng *research scientist*
Tang, Wei *software engineer*
Tang, Xiaoli *medical educator*
Tang, Yue *financial analyst*
Tangherlini, Frank Robert *physics educator*
Tannenberg, Dieter E.A. *retired manufacturing executive*
Tanner, Laurel Nan *education educator*
Tanner, W(alter) Rhett *lawyer*
Tanyuk, Kathryn Mary *medical/surgical nurse, educator*
Tao, Jiang *engineering educator*
Tao, Jianning *research scientist*
Taplin, Mary-Ellen *medical educator*
Taragin, Davira Spiro *curator*
Tarantino, Cheryl *literature and language professor*
Tarasiewicz, Tamara *painter*
Tarazaga, Pablo Alberto *research scientist*
Tarbutton, Lloyd T. *hotel executive, consultant*
Tarleton, Jesse S. *retired business educator*
Tarr, Curtis W. *management consultant, educator*
Tarr, Kenneth J. *retired investment company executive*
Tarrance, Vernon Lance, Jr. *research and development company executive*

Tarrant, Christine Gloria *music educator*
Tarro, Giulio *virologist*
Tartakovsky, Daniel M. *applied mathematician*
Tartir, Samir *science educator*
Tasse, Marie Jeanne *retired art educator*
Tassler, Nina *broadcast executive*
Tasto, James P. *orthopedist, educator*
Tata, Giovanni *publishing executive*
Tate, Deborah Taylor *former commissioner*
Tate, Kristopher *Internet company executive*
Tatlock, Anne M. *retired trust company executive*
Tatum, Arthur III *lexicographer, educator, pianist*
Taubin, Alexander *computer scientist, educator*
Taubman, A. Alfred *real estate developer*
Tauc, Jan *retired physics professor*
Taviss, Patricia Ann *management consultant, library association executive*
Tay, Savas *physicist, researcher*
Tayler, Irene *retired English literature educator*
Taylor, Alice P. *medical researcher*
Taylor, Anthony Baldwin *civil engineer*
Taylor, Barbara Ann Olin *writer, educational consultant*
Taylor, Charles Hart *former United States Representative from North Carolina*
Taylor, Charolette Olivia *primary school educator*
Taylor, Cora Hodge *social worker*
Taylor, Edna Jane *retired employment program counselor*
Taylor, Henry Splawn *retired literature educator, poet*
Taylor, Holly Ann *music educator*
Taylor, James C. *language educator*
Taylor, Jeffrey Lee *political science educator, writer*
Taylor, Job III *lawyer*
Taylor, Joel Sanford *retired government agency administrator, retired lawyer*
Taylor, John Calvin *dentist*
Taylor, John Jackson (Jay) *writer, retired diplomat*
Taylor, Joshua Aaron *computer scientist*
Taylor, June Ruth *retired minister*
Taylor, LaVonne Troy *editor*
Taylor, Leslie Ronald *psychologist*
Taylor, Marisa *literature and language professor*
Taylor, Mary Lee *retired academic administrator*
Taylor, Nathalee Britton *retired nutritionist, freelance/self-employed writer*
Taylor, Nellie Ruby *artist, author, dramatist, director, producer, host, poet, singer, filmmaker*
Taylor, Paulette Ann *special education educator, consultant*
Taylor, Peyton Troy, Jr. *oncologist, educator*
Taylor, Robert Morgan *electronics executive*
Taylor, Ronald Lewis *sociology educator*
Taylor, Sarah Ann *oncologist, educator*
Taylor, Volney *retired information company executive*
Taylor, William Colton *physician, educator*
Taylor-Clark, Kalahn Alexandra *medical researcher*
Taylor-Dunn, Corliss Leslie *marriage and family therapist*
Taype, Carmen Amelia *physician*
Teaford, Jon Christian *retired history professor*
Tecco, Romuald Gilbert Louis Joseph *violinist, concertmaster*
Tedford, Charles Franklin *biophysicist*
Teeters, Nancy Hays *economist*
Teets, Peter B. *former civilian military employee*
Tehovnik, Edward Joseph *neuroscientist*
Teitelbaum, Michael Edward *electrical engineer*
Tejnil, Edita *engineering company executive*
Teleman, Silviu *mathematician, educator*
Telford, Sam Rountree, Jr. *zoologist*
Teman, Elly *medical researcher*
Temerlin, Liener *advertising executive*
Templeman, Lydia *retired assistant principal*
Temsch, Richard *research and development company executive, consultant*
Tenhagen, Allison Mae *psychologist*
TenHoeve, Thomas *academic administrator*
Tenorio, Pedro Agulto *former Resident Representative from Northern Mariana Islands*
Teodorescu, Victoria Jean *surgeon*
Teplow, Theodore Herzl *retired valve company executive*
Tepper, Lloyd Barton *occupational and preventive medicine physician, educator*
Terada, Alice Masae *retired elementary school educator*
Teresi, Jeanne A. *medical researcher, director*
Termini, Roseann Bridget *law educator*
Terrell, G. Irvin *lawyer*
Terrell, Hellenna L. *education educator*
Terrell, Hope Price *assistant principal*
Terris, Susan *physician, cardiologist, researcher*
Terry, Carole Cosgrove *retired small business owner, historian, researcher*
Terry, Clifford Lewis *journalist*
Terry, Edwin Wellington *college librarian*
Terry, Frances Jefferson *retired psychiatric nurse practitioner*
Terry, John David *telecommunications industry executive, educator*
Terry, Mickey Thomas *music educator, director*
Tersine, Brenda L. *funeral director*
Tesler, Lawrence Gordon *technology company executive*
Teulé, Florence *research scientist*
Teutsch, Clifford L. *editor-in-chief*
Tew, E. James, Jr. *management services company executive*
Tewari, Shubha *physics professor*
Textor, Robert Bayard *cultural anthropology educator, writer, consultant*
Thacker, Patricia Ann *nursing educator*
Thackeray, Jonathan E. *lawyer*
Thackston, Edward Lee *civil engineering educator*
Thai, My T. *engineering educator*
Thain, John Alexander *former diversified financial services company executive*
Thaler, Richard Winston, Jr. *investment banker*
Thaller, Michelle Lynn *astronomer*
Tharoor, Shashi *former international organization official, writer*
Tharp, Stephen John *organist, pianist, artist*
Tharpe, Frazier Eugene *journalist*
Thaxton, Jessie J. *elementary school educator*
Thayer, Jane Hillis *psychologist*
Theophilou, Theophilos Sotiri *mechanical engineer*
Thernstrom, Stephan *historian, educator*
Theroux, Paul Edward *author*
Therrell, Bradford Leon, Jr. *medical researcher*
Therrien, Michel *former professional hockey coach*
Theus, Reggie Wayne *former professional basketball coach, retired professional basketball player*
Thiel, Philip *retired design educator*
Thiele, Gloria Day *librarian, small business owner*
Thiele, Howard Nellis, Jr. *lawyer*
Thiessen, Delbert Duane *psychologist*
Thiessen, Marc A. *journalist, former federal official*
Thigpen, Richard Elton, Jr. *retired lawyer*
Thistlethwaite, David Richard *architect*
Thodesen, Carl Christian *civil engineer*
Thomas, Beverly Irene *special education educator, counseling administrator, educational diagnostician*
Thomas, David Lindsey *lawyer, member of former state board education former state senator*
Thomas, Donald Lee *construction technology educator*
Thomas, Forsthuber G. *immunologist, educator*
Thomas, Franklin Augustine *lawyer, consultant*
Thomas, Harry K., Jr. *former federal agency administrator*
Thomas, Joe Carroll *retired human resources director*
Thomas, John Howard *astrophysicist, mechanical engineer, educator*
Thomas, Kenneth Glyndwr *mining executive*
Thomas, Lynnell L. *language educator*
Thomas, Patricia Anne *retired law librarian*
Thomas, Ralph Charles III *attorney*
Thomas, Regena L. *former state official*
Thomas, Sara Alice Folger *school librarian, curator*
Thomas, Sean Michael *journalist, writer*
Thomas, Suzanne *educational consultant*
Thomas, Teresa Ann *retired microbiologist, educator*
Thomas, Timothy Wayne *mathematics educator, athletic director*
Thomas, Tom *retired plastics company executive*
Thomason, Christia R. *librarian*
Thomason, James Brant *history professor*
Thompson, Alan Eric *economics professor*
Thompson, Craig Snover *corporate communications executive*
Thompson, Dean M., II, *knowledge management and learning executive*
Thompson, Deborah G. *secondary school educator*
Thompson, Dennis Peters *plastic surgeon*
Thompson, Edleeca Payne *humanities educator*
Thompson, Ewa M. *foreign language educator*
Thompson, Herbert Alden *microbiologist, public health scientist*
Thompson, Holley Marker *lawyer, marketing professional, consultant*
Thompson, Jack Edward *mining company executive*
Thompson, James Alexander, Jr. *lawyer*
Thompson, Jerry E. *oil industry executive*
Thompson, Jill Lynette Long *former congressman*
Thompson, Kenneth *software engineer*
Thompson, Laura *theater producer*
Thompson, Martin Christian *retired news executive*
Thompson, Nels F. *biology professor*
Thompson, Philip Douglas *federal agency administrator, educator*
Thompson, Ralph Gordon *retired federal judge*
Thompson, Ralph Newell *former chemical corporation executive*
Thompson, Richard Leon *pharmaceutical executive, lawyer*
Thompson, Susan A. *communications educator*
Thompson, Wenoka Shenaile *television producer, writer*
Thompson, William Ancker *intramural-recreational sports director, educator*
Thoms, Norman Wells *retired cardiovascular and thoracic surgeon*
Thomson, Alexander Bennett, Jr. *financial planner, tax and management consultant*
Thomson, Keith Stewart *biologist, author*
Thomson, Todd Stuart *investment company executive*
Thomson, Virginia Winbourn *humanities educator, writer*
Thoreen, Mary Louise *elementary school educator, consultant*
Thorn, Terence Hastings *energy executive, consultant, writer*
Thorne, James Dana *astronautical engineer, researcher*
Thorne, William Albert *retired lawyer*
Thornhill, Harlen Webster *retired aircraft engineer*
Thornton, Felicia D. *food service company executive*
Thornton, James F. *plastic surgeon, former military officer*
Thornton, Peter A. *engineering educator, consultant*
Thornton, Richard C. *history professor*
Thornton, Rita Louise *environmental scientist, lawyer*
Thornton, Thomas Noel *former publishing executive*
Thornton, Yvonne Shirley *obstetrician, writer, musician*
Thorp, Benjamin A. III *retired paper company executive*
Thorsen, Marie Kristin *radiologist, educator*
Thorson, Connie Capers *library educator*
Thrasher, Rose Marie *critical care and community health nurse*
Thulean, Donald Myron *symphony conductor*
Thurman, Cynthia Denise *former human services administrator, writer*
Thurman, Uma *actress*
Thurmond, George Murat *judge*
Thurmond, J. Strom, Jr. *lawyer, former prosecutor*
Thursby, Jacqueline Schuster *literature and language professor, director*
Thurston, Jacqueline Beverly *retired artist, writer, educator*
Tian, Feng *biologist, researcher*
Tiburcio, Nelson Jose *criminologist, consultant*
Tideman, T. Nicolaus *economics educator*
Tiedge, Henri *medical educator, researcher*
Tiefenbrun, Jonathan *surgeon*
Tielke, James Clemens *retired retail and manufacturing executive*
Tiffany, James Robert, Jr. *physical education educator, physical fitness company executive*
Tijardovic, Ivica *research scientist*
Tikalsky, Paul J. *civil engineering educator, structural engineer*
Tilford, Terry Trent *translator*
Tillinghast, John Avery *utilities executive*
Tillman, Celestine *chemistry professor*
Tilson, Whitney R. *investment company executive*
Timmermann, Allan Gilling *management and economics professor*
Timmins, George Emerson *physics professor*
Timmons, Sharon L. *retired elementary school educator*
Tincher, Laura Marie *literature and language educator, photographer*
Tingler, Marlene Johannsen *music educator, insurance agent*
Tingstrum, Nancy Ash *dietitian*
Tingus, Steven James *physiologist, researcher*
Tippett, Dave *former professional hockey coach*
Tipping, William Malcolm *social services administrator*
Tisch, Wilma Stein *foundation administrator*
Tise, Larry Edward *historian, cultural organization administrator*
Tishman, Lynn P. *psychologist, psychoanalyst*
Titcomb, Caldwell *music and theatre historian*
Tkach, Dianne *educator*
To, Kenneth Kin Wah *medical educator, researcher*
Toay, Thelma M. *columnist, poet*
Tobacman, Joanne Kramer *medical educator, researcher*
Tobias, Veronica Ann (Roni Tobias) *psychologist*
Tobiassen, Barbara Sue *systems analyst, consultant, volunteer*
Tobin, James Edward *communications educator, writer*
Tobin, James Robert (Jim Tobin) *retired biomedical device manufacturing company executive*
Tobin, Paul Edward, Jr. *museum director, retired admiral*
Tocco, Elaine Kay *technical expert*
Todd, William Mills III *literature educator*
Todd, Zane Grey *retired utilities executive*
Todhunter, John Anthony *toxicologist, consultant*
Todorova, Valentina K. *biochemist, educator*
Toedt, D(ell) C(harles) III *lawyer*
Tognoli, Era M. *opera company director*
Tokofsky, Jerry Herbert *film producer*
Tolbert, Cornelia Emma *music educator*
Tolia, Vasundhara K. *pediatric gastroenterologist, educator*
Tolins, Roger Alan *lawyer*
Toll, John Sampson *retired academic administrator, physics professor*
Tolle, Brenda Kay *secondary school educator, computer scientist, consultant*
Tollenaere, Lawrence Robert *retired industrial products company executive*
Tolmacheva, Marina Aleksandrovna *academic administrator*
Tolman, Philip D. *lawyer, corporate financial executive*
Tombros, Peter George *pharmaceutical executive*
Tomlin-Houston, Lisa *executive, career coach workforce strategist*
Tomlinson, Carol Ann *education educator, writer*
Tomlinson, Susan Elizabeth *language educator*
Tompkins, Ellen Beth *retired elementary school educator*
Tondel, Lawrence C. *lawyer*
Tonioli, Bruno *choreographer, dancer*
Tonjes, Marian Jeannette Benton *education educator*
Tontiruttananon, Channarong *electrical engineer, researcher*
Toomey, Patrick Joseph *former United States Representative from Pennsylvania*
Toomey, Richard Andrew, Jr. *lawyer*
Top, Franklin Henry, Jr. *physician, researcher*
Topaloglu, Zeynep *economics professor*
Toplin, Robert Brent *history professor, television producer*
Topper, Elisa Freiden *former librarian, consultant*
Torbica, Zeljko Marko *construction executive, educator*
Torda, Elinor A. *language educator*
Torgerson, Larry Keith *lawyer*
Torgerson, William T. *lawyer, retired electric power industry executive*
Torkildsen, Peter Gerard *former United States Representative from Massachusetts*
Torrance, Sam *professional golfer*
Torre, Gary Jerome *retired lawyer*
Torres, Arelis *elementary school educator*
Torres, Rudy Arnold *artist*
Torrez, Michelle Marie *artist, educator*
Torrie, Jane Marie *chiropractor, secondary school educator*
Torson, Dianna May *retired small business owner*
Toshach, Clarice Oversby *real estate developer, retired computer company executive*
Tosun, Duygu *research scientist*
Toth, Myra Bernstein *artist, educator*
Toupin, Harold Ovid *retired chemical company executive*
Tourtellotte, Wallace William *neurologist, educator*
Tovesson, Fredrik *nuclear scientist*
Tower, Mollie Gregory *writer, educator, consultant*
Towfighi, Amytis *neurologist*
Towle, Alexis Charles (Lex Towle) *education advocate, director*
Towler, Evelyn Wheeler *retired elementary school educator*
Towler, Katherine *writer*
Town, Terrence Christopher *research scientist*
Townsend, Fran (Frances Fragos Townsend) *former federal official*
Townsend, Frances (Fran Townsend) *healthcare educator, writer*
Townsend, Kathleen Kennedy *former lieutenant governor*
Townsend, Tiffany G. *psychology professor*
T-Pain, (Faheem Najm) *rap artist*
Trachtenberg, Matthew J. *arts administrator, financial services executive, philanthropist*
Tract, Marc Mitchell *lawyer*
Traeger, Charles Henry III *educator and innovator*
Trammel, Denise *science educator*
Tramonte, Michael Robert *retired education educator*
Tramonto, Rick *chef*
Tran, Nam Van *secondary school educator*
Tran, Tammie *language educator*
Tranquada, Robert Ernest *retired internist, educator*
Transou, Lynda Lou *advertising art administrator*
Trask, Thomas Edward *religious organization administrator*
Trattner, Laura V. *retired middle school educator*
Travis, Vance Kenneth *petroleum business executive*
Traynham, Earle Campbell *retired economics professor, dean*
Trebon, Thomas *academic administrator*
Trebunskaya, Anna *dancer*
Trechsel, Stefan *law educator*
Tregub, Alexander (Alex Tregub) *electronics engineer*
Treible, Kirk *retired academic and foundation administrator*
Treichel, Dixie Ann *writer, composer*
Trelease, Allen William *historian, educator*
Trelles, Ana *art educator*
Trenholm, Laurie E. *horticulturist, educator*
Trent, Robert Harold *retired business educator*
Tresnowski, Bernard Richard *retired health insurance company executive*
Trevathan, Edwin *neurologist, educator*
Trevathan, James E. *waste management executive*
Trezza, Alphonse Fiore *librarian, educator*
Tribus, Myron *management consultant, educator*
Triipan, Maive *library director*
Trimble, Phillip Richard *law educator*
Trimble, Sandra Ellingson *lawyer*
Trimble, William Cattell, Jr. *retired lawyer*
Trinchet, Jorge *language educator*
Trindade, Arvind Julius *internist, researcher*
Tringale, Anthony Rosario *insurance executive*
Tripeny, Patrick *architect, educator*
Tripp, Amanda *psychologist*
Tripplehorn, Jeanne *actress*
Tritsch, George Leopold *retired biochemist, educator*
Tritten, James John *retired federal agency administrator*
Trongale, Nicholas Albert *entrepreneur, researcher, educator*
Troop, Paul Melvin *public relations executive, journalist*
Trop, Sandra *former museum director*
Tropez-Sims, Susanne *pediatrician, educator*
Trost, Glenn W. *lawyer*
Trotter, Suzanne Michelle *psychologist*
Trout, Linda Copple *former state supreme court justice*
Troy, Daniel E. *pharmaceutical executive, lawyer*
Troyer, Alice Kay *library and computer skills educator*
Trubeck, William Lewis *former diversified financial services company executive*
Truesdale, John Cushman *federal agency administrator, lawyer*
Trumbull, William Ernest *retired surgeon, educator*
Trusdell, Mary Louise Cantrell *retired academic administrator*
Trussell, Jacqueline *theology studies educator*
Trutor, Genevieve Williamson *museum director*
Tryon, Elizabeth Anne *educational association administrator*
Trythall, Harry Gilbert *music educator, composer*
Trzcinski, Eileen *social studies educator, director*
Tsai, Chi Chun *engineering educator*
Tsai, Wen-Ying *sculptor, painter, engineer*
Tsay, Ching Sow *retired anesthesiologist*
Tschetter, Ronald Allen *former federal agency administrator*
Tschoepe, Gary Joseph *retired political science professor*
Tse, Charles Yung Chang *pharmaceutical executive, lawyer*
Tse, Florence *director*
Tse, Stephen *artist, educator*
Tsigelny, Igor *research scientist*
Tsiligaridis, John *education educator, researcher*
Tsoukalas, Lefteri H. *engineering educator, department chairman*
Tsuang, John *psychiatrist*
Tsui, Sze-Kai Jack *mathematics educator*
Tu, Yufeng *business educator*
Tubb, Gary Alan *humanities educator*
Tubis, Arnold *physics professor*
Tucci, Oscar Maximillian *restauranteur, radio host, writer, philanthropist*
Tuchman, Avraham (Avi) *physicist, researcher*
Tuck, Amy *former lieutenant governor*
Tucker, H. Richard *oil industry executive*
Tucker, Laurey Dan *lawyer*
Tucker, Thomas Deane *humanities educator*
Tuft, Mary Ann *executive search firm executive*
Tuitele, Lui *retired school system administrator*
Turaga, Deepak Srinivas *electrical and computer engineer, researcher*
Turczyn, Christine Lilian *writer, educator*
Turek, Sonia Fay *journalist*
Turigliatto-Fahrney, Terri A. *educational association administrator, educator*
Turk, Eleanor Louise *history professor*
Turk, Richard Errington *retired psychiatrist*
Turnage, Fred Douglas *retired lawyer*
Turnau, Vivian Williamson *retired literature and language educator*
Turnbull, Vernona Harmsen *retired education educator, counseling administrator*
Turndorf, Herman *anesthesiologist, educator*
Turner, Bonese Collins *artist, educator*
Turner, Elvin L. *retired school system administrator*

Turner, Harry Spencer preventive medicine physician, educator
Turner, Henry Brown finance company executive, director
Turner, Jean L. astronomer, educator
Turner, John Freeland former federal agency administrator, state legislator
Turner, John Sidney, Jr. retired otolaryngologist, educator
Turner, Natalie A. retired consultant
Turner, Terry Campbell lawyer
Turnley, David Carl photojournalist
Turock, Betty Jane retired library and information science professor
Turok, Paul Harris composer, commentator, music critic
Turteltaub, Jon film director
Turturro, Aida actress
Tussing, Lewis Benton, III, (Tony) secondary education educator, coach
Tutt, Karl Fleming literature and language professor
Tuttle, Robert Holmes former ambassador
Tuul, Johannes physics professor, researcher
Twardy, Stanley Albert, Jr. lawyer
Twenhafel, Nancy Ann pathologist, director
Twichell, Chase poet
Twiddy, Elizabeth writer, educator
Twigg-Smith, Thurston newspaper publisher
Twitchell, Theodore Grant music educator, composer
Twomey, Kevin retail executive
Tyler, Anne (Mrs. Taghi M. Modarressi) writer
Tyler, Carl Walter, Jr. retired epidemiologist, health science association administrator
Tyler, John Duke psychologist, educator
Tyler, Peggy Lynne Bailey retired lawyer
Tyler, Steven (Stephen Victor Tallarico) singer
Tyree, Rebecca Young music educator
Tyrl, Paul mathematics professor, researcher
Tyrrell, Gerald Gettys banker
Tyson, Lucille R. health facility administrator, geriatrics nurse
Tytler, Linda Jean emergency manager, state legislator
Tyzack, Margaret actress
Tzeng, Jung-Ying statistician, researcher
Uberall, Herbert Michael Stefan physicist, professor emeritus
Uchrin, Christopher George environmental engineer and scientist
Ucko, Barbara Clark writer
Uddin, Mohammed Rafique biology professor
Udupi, Yathiraj Bhat software engineer
Uehling, Barbara Staner academic administrator
Uffelman, Malcolm Rucj electronics executive
Ufford, Charles Wilbur, Jr. lawyer
Ufimtsev, Pyotr Yakovlevich physicist, electrical engineer, educator
Ugalde, Arantza language educator
Uggams, Leslie entertainer
Ugorowski, Philip Brien nuclear scientist, researcher
Uhler, Walter Charles government official, writer
Ulate, Isai engineering educator
Ulevich, Neal Hirsh photojournalist
Ulfelder, Jay political scientist, director
Ulick, Susan E. investment company executive
Ullberg, Kent Jean sculptor
Ullestad, Charles Lee humanities educator
Ullman, Edwin Fisher biotechnologist, consultant
Ullman, Nelly Szabo statistician, educator
Ulloa, Leonor Alvarez de language educator
Ulsh, Gordon A. battery manufacturing company executive
Umpenhour, Ken Eugene protective services official
Underhill, Jacob Berry III retired insurance company executive
Unger, Barbara poet, writer, retired literature and language professor
Unger, Gere Nathan emergency physician, lawyer
Unger, Paul Walter retired soil scientist
Unger, Roger Harold physician, research scientist
Unruh, Gary Lee retired music educator
Unsworth, Richard Preston minister, educator, director
Unterberger, Betty Miller retired history professor
Unwin, Stephen Forman advertising executive, educator
Upatnieks, Juris retired optical engineer
Upbin, Shari theater producer, director
Upchurch, Leslie Purcell music educator
Upenieks, Valda V. nursing educator
Upshaw, Harry Stephan psychologist, educator
Upton, Becky J. secondary school educator
Urbano, Arthur Peter historian, theologian
Uribe, Fernando, Jr. law educator
Urkowitz, Michael banker
Urofsky, Melvin Irving historian, educator, director
Uscinski, Ronald Henry medical educator
Usery, Willie J., Jr. former United States Secretary of Labor
Ushakov, Sergey V. research scientist
Usher, Timothy Dwight physics professor
Ushijima, Jean M. retired city official
Utgoff, Kathleen Platt former federal agency administrator
Uyeda, Steven biology professor
Uys, Jurgen Peter Brinker securities analyst
Uysal, Ismail research scientist
Uzgoren, Eray science educator
Vacchelli, Robert Francis judge
Vacco, Dennis C. lawyer, former state attorney general
Vaidyanathan, Vijay V. engineering educator
Vail, Nancy L. Scott retired elementary school educator, artist
Vailakis, Ivonne G. literature educator
Vakili, Bahman Fakhimi urologist
Valcic, Branka finance educator
Valdez, Patricia language educator
Valdivia, Annarella psychologist
Valencia, Margarita Spanish language educator
Valentine, Charles Francis retired educational administrator
Valentine, Gene C. securities dealer
Valentine, Phyllis Louise counseling administrator
Valentine, Ralph Schuyler chemical engineer, director
Valentine, William Newton retired physician, educator
Valentino, (Valentino Garavani) retired fashion designer
Valeri, Tony Canadian government official, small business owner
Valero, René Arnold retired bishop
Vallabhan, Girish C. urologist
Valles, Judith president, former mayor, retired academic administrator
Vallier, Nanette psychologist
Valtier, Sandra toxicologist
Van Arsdale, Sharon A. nurse
Vanbiesbrouck, John Robert hockey analyst, retired professional hockey player
VanButsel, Michael R. real estate broker, construction executive
Vancastle, Robin bank executive
van Daalen, Albert A. religious minister, CEO
Van de Bogart, Debra Scherwerts medical/surgical nurse, researcher
Vandeputte, Dixie Dianne retired psychologist, educator
Van der Horst, Brian Christopher communications consultant, author, educator
Vanderlinde, Roger social sciences educator
van der Marck, Jan art historian
Vanderwagen, W. Craig (William Craig Vanderwagen) physician, former federal agency administrator
Van Dine, Alan Charles advertising agency executive, writer
Van Dine, Harold Forster, Jr. architect, artist
Vandiver, Sara Elizabeth Sharp Rankin retired postmaster
Van Dyk, Frederick Theodore political scientist, writer
Van Dyke, Debbie K. special education services professional
Vanek, Francis Michael engineering educator, researcher
Van Etten, Peter Walbridge foundation executive
Van Exel, Nickey Maxwell retired professional basketball player
van Gestel, Allan mediator, arbitrator
Van Goor, Anthony Jay retired military officer, medical executive
Van Gorder, John Frederic lawyer
Van Ha, Thuong G. radiologist, educator
Van Handel, Michael J. employment services executive
Van Heertum, Ronald Lanny physician
Van Hoey, Nicole pharmacist, writer
Van Horn, Hugh M. physicist, astronomer, educator
vanHorn, Kate Raudenbush retired school psychologist
Van Horn, Keith retired professional basketball player
Van Houten, G. David, Jr. beverage company executive
Van Houten, Ronald psychology professor
Vanier, Jacques physicist
Van Inwegen, Patrick F. political science professor
VanItallie, Theodore Bertus physician
VanMeter, Vandelia L. retired library director
Vann, David James author, professor
Vann, Esther Martinez science educator
van Nagell, John Rensselaer oncologist, gynecologist
Van Ness, Ross Howard education educator
Van Orden, Phyllis Jeanne librarian, educator
Van Patten, James Jeffers education educator
Van Praagh, James spiritual medium
van Tienhoven, Ari education educator, educator
Van Valkenburgh, Holly Viola librarian, consultant
Van Vleet, William Benjamin lawyer, retired insurance company executive
Vanzura, Liz (Elizabeth K. Vanzura) automotive executive
Varakin, Donald Alexander psychology professor
Varda, Agnes scriptwriter, film director
Vargo, Louise landscape artist, music educator
Varjavand, Reza finance educator
Varner, Joyce Ehrhardt retired librarian
Varner, Joyce McCullers geriatric nurse practitioner, educator
Vasconcelos, Marco psychologist
Vasholz, Lothar Alfred retired insurance company executive
Vasko, Peter Theodore Frederick priest
Vasquez, Margarita M. pediatrician, educator
Vasquez, Sabrina Claudine choreographer, educator
Vasseur, Alexis Frederic mathematics professor
Vasu, Subith research scientist
Vasudev, Brahm Sarup nephrologist
Vaughan, Samuel Snell editor, writer, publishing executive
Vaughn, John Rolland retired auditor
Vaughn-Daniels, Kymberly Louise healthcare educator, consultant
Vaux, Henry James, Jr. economics professor
Vavala, Domenic Anthony medical research scientist, educator, retired military officer
Vayalakkara, Jyothi neuropsychologist, director, educator
Vayanian, Solara Zakeli artist, educator, researcher
Vayghan, Jamshid Abdollahi architectural engineer
Vazacopoulos, Alkis application developer, educator
Vaze, Shilpa Arun software, firmware, modeling engineer
Vedder, Eddie singer
Veeramalai, Mallika research scientist
Vega, Edwin Salvador media specialist, educator
Velazquez, Omaida Caridad vascular surgeon, researcher
Velev, Miroslav N. electrical and computer engineer, educator, entrepreneur, inventor
Velikanova, Olga historian, educator
Velisek, Libor medical educator
Vella, Ruth Ann real estate executive
Vellanki, Gangadhar B. information scientist, consultant
Vellenga, Kathleen Osborne state legislator
Veloso, Francisco science educator
Velzy, Charles O. mechanical engineer
Vendé, Sandra lab administrator
Vendituoli, Elizabeth Ann special education educator
Venema, Jeremy literature and language professor
Venkatesh, Murali engineering educator
Venters, Harley Eugene lawyer
Ventura, Jesse (James Janos, "The Body") former Governor of Minnesota, retired professional wrestler
Vér, István László acoustical engineer, consultant
Verlich, Jean Elaine writer, public relations executive, consultant
Verma, Surjit Kumar retired school system administrator
Vermeil, Dick (Richard Albert Vermeil) retired professional football coach
Vermylen, Paul Anthony, Jr. oil industry executive
Vernazza, Trish Brown (Trish Eileen Brown) visual artist, art therapist, sculptor, psychotherapist
Vernon, Alex literature and language professor
Vernon, Carl Atlee, Jr. retired wholesale food distributor executive
Vernon, Dean Matthew psychology educator
Vernon, Lawrence Gordon librarian
Vernon, Margaret Katherine psychologist
Veronis, George geophysics educator
Versch, Esther Marie artist
Veselinovič, Draško stock exchange executive
Vespa, Ned Angelo photographer
Vessey, John William, Jr. former Chairman of the Joint Chiefs of Staff
Vest, Gayle Southworth obstetrician, gynecologist
Vicencio, Alfin Gemil pediatrician
Vichiola, Christopher Michael writer, educator
Vick, Dwight Harold educator
Victor, John C. epidemiologist
Vidal, Gore (Eugene Luther Vidal Jr.) writer
Viegas, Jennifer journalist, writer
Viest, Ivan Miroslav structural engineer, consultant
Vieth, Christopher W. former publishing executive
Vike-Freiberga, Vaira former President of Latvia
Villa-Komaroff, Lydia molecular biologist, educator, health product executive, academic administrator
Villalobos, Ligiah former international programming manager, film producer, scriptwriter
Villarosa, Shari former ambassador
Villarrubia, Glenda Boone reading specialist and coordinator, educator, consultant
Villella, Edward Joseph dancer, choreographer, performing arts association administrator
Villforth, John Carl engineer, health physicist
Villoch, Kelly Carney art director
Vincent, Francis Thomas, Jr., (Fay Vincent) former baseball commissioner
Vincent, Hal Wellman retired military officer, investor
Vincent, James Louis biotechnology company executive
Vincent, Sam (James Samuel Vincent) former professional basketball coach, former professional basketball player
Vine, Kimberly Ann public relations executive
Vines, John R. career military officer
Vinkey, Rachel Burdick psychiatrist
Viorst, Judith Stahl writer
Viorst, Milton writer
Virkhaus, Taavo conductor
Visocki, Nancy Gayle information services consultant
Vita, Steven poet
Vitale, Ruth Ann former film company executive
Vitt, David Aaron health products executive
Vittetoe, Marie Clare retired clinical laboratory science educator
Vladeck, Bruce Charney healthcare consultant, former academic administrator
Vlazny, John George archbishop
Vliet, Marni health policy and health program consultant
Voegtlin-Anderson, Mary Margaret music educator, small business owner
Voell, Richard Allen retired private investor
Vogel, H. Victoria psychotherapist, educator, writer, stress disorder and addiction recovery counselor
Vohra, Amit mechanical engineer
Vohs, James Arthur health plan administrator
Voight, Jon actor
Vojnovic, Igor Zoran geographer, urban planner, educator
Voketaitis, Arnold Matthew bass-baritone, educator
Volk, Austin N. retired insurance company executive
Volk, Patricia Gay novelist, essayist
Volkay, Chris John investment company executive
Volker, Kurt Douglas former United States permanent representative to NATO
Volkhardt, John Malcolm retired food products executive
Voloshin, Beverly R. literature and language professor
Volpe, Doris artist
Volpe, Eileen Rae retired special education educator
von Bothmer, Bernard Nicholas history professor
von Eschenbach, Andrew C. oncologist, former federal agency administrator
von Furstenberg, Betsy actress, writer
von Furstenberg, Diane fashion designer, writer, entrepreneur
von Hake, Margaret Joan librarian
von Hoffman, Nicholas writer, retired reporter
Von Mayrhauser, Jennifer costume designer
von Moltke, Gebhardt retired diplomat
von Wachter, Till Marco economics professor
Vook, Frederick Ludwig physicist, consultant
Voorhees, James Dayton, Jr. lawyer
Voorhees, Kent Jay chemist
Voorhis, Brenda Heath Jacobsen retired psychiatrist
Vorce-Tish, Helene R. writer
Vosevich, Kathi Ann writer, editor
Vosk, Ted W. lawyer
Voss, Omer Gerald farm equipment executive
Voss, Regis Dale agronomist, educator
Votaw, John Frederick, Sr. educational association administrator, educator
Voyles, Kyle research scientist
Voytek, Mary Sullivan sculptor
Vozzella, Thomas R. musician, conductor, composer, organist
Vreeland, Russell Glenn senior tax manager, accountant, consultant
Vroom, Victor Harold management consultant, educator
Vu, Joseph Duong financial educator
Vulgamore, Allison Beth performing arts association administrator
Vuong, Joseph Trung humanities educator
Vuong, Lynette Dyer literature and language professor
Vuoto, Anthony (Tony) F. bank executive
Vyas, Deepti pharmacist
Vyhmeister, Nancy Jean retired religious studies educator
Vyn, Eleanor Mears physical therapist
Waaland, Irving T. retired aerospace engineer
Wachtman, Jeanette Marie art educator, artist, writer
Wacker, Kelly Lynn audiologist, educator
Wadden, Thomas Antony psychologist, educator
Waddill, Cynthia Kay orthopaedic nurse practitioner
Wade, Heather A. archivist, educator
Wade, June Booth secondary school educator
Wadkins, Theresa A. psychology professor, researcher
Wadley, M. Richard consumer products executive
Waggoner, Cheri psychologist
Wagman, Robert John journalist, writer
Wagner, Anthony E. academic administrator, former state official
Wagner, Antonin economics professor
Wagner, Arthur Ward, Jr. lawyer
Wagner, Bruce Herman school librarian, educator
Wagner, Ellyn Santi retired mathematics educator
Wagner, Harvey M. finance educator, consultant
Wagner, Helen Adeene elementary school educator
Wagner, Karel retired nuclear engineer, educator
Wagner, Michael medical researcher, educator
Wagner, Paula film company executive
Wagner, Ron entrepreneur
Wagoner, Geraldine Vander Pol music educator
Wagoner, Rick (George Richard Wagoner Jr.) former automotive executive
Wahl, Floyd Michael geologist
Wahome, Joseph Muriuki zoologist, educator
Wahweah, Linda McNeil insurance agent, writer
Waidmann, Brian K. former federal agency administrator
Waitkus, Jay writer
Wakefield, Sarah Rebecca literature and language professor
Walberg, Tim (Timothy Lee Walberg) former United States Representative from Michigan, former state legislator
Walden, Joseph Lawrence career officer
Waldkoetter, Raymond Oliver psychologist, consultant
Waldmeir, Peter Nielsen retired journalist
Waldon, Alton Ronald, Jr. judge
Wales, Jimmy Donal (Jimbo Wales) Internet company executive
Walk, Barbra Denise customer service administrator, tutor
Walker, Annette retired counseling administrator
Walker, Antoine Devon professional basketball player
Walker, Bernice Baker artist
Walker, Beverly Ann minister, health facility administrator
Walker, Carolyn Mae retired secondary school educator
Walker, Clarence Eugene psychology professor
Walker, David H. medical educator
Walker, Donald Burke retired music educator, archivist, composer
Walker, Fred Elmer broadcast executive
Walker, George Herbert III former ambassador, retired investment banking company executive
Walker, Gloria Lee training services executive
Walker, Gordon Davies government official, writer, lecturer, consultant
Walker, James Edward humanities educator
Walker, Joae Brooks retired psychiatrist
Walker, Karen Louise music educator
Walker, Linda Lee lawyer
Walker, Mark A. lawyer
Walker, Mary Alexander writer
Walker, Pamela mathematics educator
Walker, Philip Chamberlain, II, retired health facility administrator
Walker, Philip Doolittle retired literature and language professor, composer
Walker, Rachel Brady retired literature and language professor
Walker, Richard Henry lawyer
Walker, Ronald Edward psychologist, educator
Walker, Roslyn Adele retired museum director
Walker, Ruth Charlotta language educator, real estate broker
Walker, Steven Charles literature and language professor
Wall, M. Danny retired finance company executive
Wall, Sonja Eloise nursing administrator
Wallace, Dee actress
Wallace, F. Blake retired aerospace transportation executive, retired mechanical engineer
Wallace, Jane House retired geologist
Wallace, Joyce Irene Malakoff internist
Wallace, Linda Kay mathematics professor
Wallace, Michele writer, educator
Wallace, Mike (Myron Leon Wallace) newscaster, television personality
Wallace, Nicolle (Nicolle Devenish) former federal official
Wallace, Robert Bruce neuroscience educator
Wallace, Teresa Lynn art educator
Wallach, Patricia councilman, retired mayor
Waller, Eunice McLean retired educator
Waller, Steven R. engineer

Waller-Niewold, Marilyn J. *podiatric surgeon*
Wallerstein, Betty Cooper *clinical social worker, family therapist*
Wallerstein, Robert Solomon *retired psychiatrist*
Walling, Donovan Robert *editor, writer*
Wallis, Diana Lynn *artistic director*
Wallot, Jean-Pierre *archivist, historian*
Walmer, Edwin Fitch *retired lawyer*
Walsh, Diana Chapman *former academic administrator, sociologist, educator*
Walsh, Dolores Ann Gonczo (Lorry Walsh) *special education educator*
Walsh, John E., Jr. *business educator, consultant*
Walsh, Joseph Fidler (Joe Walsh) *recording artist, record producer*
Walsh, Joseph Thomas *retired state supreme court justice*
Walsh, M. Emmet *actor*
Walsh, Michael P. *mechanical engineer*
Walsh, Michael Thomas *historian, musician*
Walsh, Nan *artist, painter, sculptor, consultant*
Walsh, Patrick M. *career military officer*
Walsh, William Albert *management consultant, retired military officer*
Walsh, William Desmond *investor*
Walsh Mitchell, Diana *school psychologist, consultant*
Walstedt, Russell Erwin *physicist*
Walter, Carmel Monica *security consultant, writer*
Walter, Patricia L. *psychotherapist, consultant*
Walters, Farah M. *health services company administrator, former hospital administrator*
Walters, Glen Robert *retired banker*
Walters, Jerry B. *retired art educator*
Walters, Robert Ancil *physicist, mathematician*
Walters, Sylvia Solochek *art educator*
Waltner, Beverly Ruland *artist*
Walton, Alice Louise *bank executive*
Walton, Anthony John (Tony Walton) *set and costume designer, illustrator, writer*
Walton, Christy R. *philanthropist*
Waltrip, Michael Curtis *professional race car driver*
Waltz, Kathleen M. *former publishing executive*
Walz, Edward George *protective services official*
Wan, Hung-da *mechanical engineer, educator*
Wan, Rong-Yu *metallurgist*
Wander, Joseph Day *chemist*
Wang, Chen-ku *retired library director*
Wang, Gongyao *materials scientist*
Wang, Haibin *systems administrator, consultant*
Wang, Haiqin *computer scientist*
Wang, Jin *engineering educator*
Wang, Lawrence K. *engineering educator*
Wang, Mian *education educator*
Wang, Mo *psychology professor*
Wang, Nancy *pathologist, educator*
Wang, Richard G. *literature educator*
Wang, Wanlin *research scientist*
Wang, Ye-Yi *computer scientist*
Wang, Ying *chemist, researcher*
Wang, Youru *philosopher, educator*
Wang, Yu *science educator*
Wang, Yung-Ho Ophelia *geographer, educator*
Wang, Zhiyong *optical engineer, researcher*
Wanger, Eugene Gilkison *retired lawyer*
Wangsness, Genna Stead *retired hotel executive, innkeeper*
Wannier, Mario Marc-Antoine *research scientist, multi-media specialist, director*
Wantland, William Charles *retired bishop, lawyer*
Warberg, Willetta *concert pianist, music educator*
Warcken, Nancy B. *elementary school educator*
Ward, Anne Starr Minton *musician, educator*
Ward, Chester Lawrence *physician, consultant*
Ward, George Truman *architect*
Ward, Jacqueline Ann Beas *nurse, healthcare administrator, legal nurse consultant*
Ward, Jeannette Poole *retired psychologist, educator*
Ward, Mal Yvonne *special education educator*
Ward, Wanda Louise Dobbs *educational administrator*
Warder, Richard Currey, Jr. *dean, mechanical aerospace engineering educator*
Ware, D. Clifton *vocalist, educator*
Ware, Gwendolyn C. *retired counseling administrator*
Ware, Marilyn *former ambassador, former utilities company executive*
Warey, Alok *diesel engineer*
Warfel, M(artha) Kay *speech pathology/audiology services professional*
Warian, Christine Barbara *elementary school educator*
Warma, Mahamadi Jacob *mathematics professor*
Warman, Linda K. *retired secondary school educator*
Warnasooriya, Nilanthi *research scientist*
Warne, William Robert *economist*
Warner, Don Lee *dean emeritus*
Warner, Douglas Alexander, III, (Sandy Warner) *retired diversified financial services company executive*
Warner, John Hilliard, Jr. *technical services company executive*
Warner, Malcolm-Jamal *actor, director, producer*
Warner, Susan *federal agency administrator*
Warner, William Hamer *mathematician*
Warren, Alice Louise *artist*
Warren, Daniel Churchman *health facility administrator*
Warren, Dwight William III *physiology educator*
Warren, Marie Antoinette *elementary school educator*
Warrior, Della C. *academic administrator, art educator*
Warwick, Margaret Ann *retired health science facility administrator, consultant*
Warwick, Shelly *library director, researcher*
Washburn, Donald Arthur *retired business executive, investor*
Washington, Denzel *actor*
Watabe, Norimitsu *marine biologist, educator*
Watanabe, Kyoichi A(loysius) *pharmacology educator, chemist*
Waterhouse, Keith *urologist, educator, retired surgeon*
Waters, William Carter III *retired internist, educator*
Watford, Dolores *elementary school educator*
Watkins, Ann Esther *mathematics professor*
Watkins, Dean Allen *electronics executive, educator*
Watkins, George Daniels *physics professor*
Watkins, James David *former United States Secretary of Energy, retired military officer*
Watkins, Jeffrey Clifton *neuroscientist*
Watkins, Julia M. *educational association administrator*
Watrous, Robert Thomas *academic director*
Watson, Donald Charles, Jr. *cardiothoracic surgeon, educator*
Watson, George Henry, Jr. *broadcaster, journalist*
Watson, Jack Crozier *retired state supreme court justice*
Watson, Jack H., Jr. *lawyer, former White House chief of staff*
Watson, James Dewey *retired molecular biologist*
Watson, Patty Jo *anthropology educator*
Watson, Robert Joe *retired health facility administrator, retired career officer*
Watt, James Gaius *lawyer, former United States Secretary of the Interior*
Watt, Stephanie Denise *musician, educator, department chairman*
Watt, William Stewart *retired physical chemist*
Watta, David Anthony *product manager*
Watters, Ann Oliva *psychologist, educator*
Watters, Linda A. *former state banking agency administrator*
Watts, Anthony Lee *bank executive*
Watts, John Ransford *academic administrator*
Watts, Mary Ann *retired elementary school educator*
Watts, Wendy Hazel *wine consultant*
Waud, Roger Neil *economist, educator*
Waugh, Theodore Rogers *orthopedic surgeon*
Wavle, James Edward, Jr. *pharmaceutical company executive, lawyer*
Wax, Alan S. *language educator*
Wax, Martin Bruce *ophthalmologist*
Waxman, Allen Perry *former pharmaceutical executive, lawyer*
Waxman, Ronald *computer engineer*
Way, Barbara Haight *retired dermatologist*
Way, Jacob Edson III *museum director*
Wayne, Kyra Petrovskaya *writer*
Weathersby, George Byron *management company executive*
Weaver, Anne Genevieve Hera *writer*
Weaver, Franklin Thomas *retired newspaper executive*
Weaver, James Howard *former Congressman*
Weaver, John B. *library director*
Weaver, William Charles *manufacturing executive*
Weaver, William Schildecker *retired electric power industry executive*
Webb, Katharine *counselor*
Webb, Martha Jeanne *writer, educator, film producer*
Webb Girard, Amy *research scientist*
Webel, Charles Peter *human science and psychology educator*
Weber, Darren Lee *neuroscientist, researcher*
Weber, Donald B. *advertising executive, marketing professional*
Weber, Gloria Richie *retired minister, state legislator*
Weber, Idelle *artist, educator*
Weber, John Walter *insurance company executive*
Weber, Larry Francis *retired electrical engineer*
Weber, Randal Scott *head and neck surgeon, educator*
Weber, Susan A. *lawyer*
Weber, Yvonne Roebuck *research administrator, educator*
Webster, Christopher White *foreign service officer*
Webster, Harold Frank *physicist*
Webster, Henry de Forest *neuroscientist*
Webster, John Crosby Brown *minister, educator*
Webster, Owen Wright *chemist*
Webster, Robert Kenly *lawyer*
Weckler, Nora *retired psychology educator, psychotherapist*
Wedgeworth, Ann *actress*
Weekes, Kevin *professional hockey player*
Weeks, Brigitte *publishing executive*
Weeks, Clifford Myers *musician, academic administrator*
Weeks, William Rawle, Jr. *oil industry executive*
Weems, Kerry N. *former federal agency administrator*
Weerasinghe, Kumudini Mangala (Kelly Weise) *science educator*
Weers, Vesta L. *secondary school educator, department chairman*
Wefald, Jon *former academic administrator*
Wegner, Harold Claus *lawyer, educator, consultant*
Wehn, Karen Swaney *education educator, consultant*
Wehner, André *psychologist, educator*
Wei, Maria L. *dermatologist, educator*
Weickert, Wanda Opal *child welfare and attendance counselor, psychotherapist, educator*
Weiherer, Patricia Dee *retired librarian*
Weil, Lynne Amy *communications executive, writer*
Weil, Peter Henry *retired lawyer*
Weil, Randolph Allen *executive*
Weil, Richard III *surgeon, medical educator*
Weil, Rolf Alfred *economist, retired university president*
Weil, Thomas P. *retired health services consultant*
Weiland, Barbara J. *neuroscientist*
Weiland, Scott Richard *singer*
Weiler, John M. *physician, educator, executive*
Weinbach, Lawrence Allen *computer services company executive, private equity managing director*
Weinberg, Gerhard Ludwig *history professor, writer*
Weinberg, Richard M. *internist, pulmonary and critical care physician, consultant*
Weinberg, Steven *physics professor*
Weinberg, Teri Ellen *former broadcast executive*
Weinberger, Steven *lawyer, educator*
Weiner, Ferne *psychologist*
Weiner, Louis Marc *oncologist*
Weiner, Matthew *television producer, scriptwriter*
Weiner, Max *psychology professor*
Weiner, Richard *public relations executive*
Weiner, Ruth Fleischmann *science educator*
Weingand, Darlene Erna *librarian, educator*
Weingarten, Joseph Leonard *aerospace engineer*
Weingarten, Michael S. *surgeon, educator*
Weingust, Don *theater educator*
Weinkauf, Mary Louise Stanley *retired clergywoman, educator*
Weinshenker, Naomi Joyce *clinical psychiatrist, educator, researcher*
Weinstein, Michael P. *marine scientist, administrator*
Weinstein, Milton Charles *decision scientist, educator*
Weinstein, Philip Merrill *lawyer*
Weintraub, Sam *retired reading educator*
Weir, Anne *writer*
Weir, Jeffrey Michael *history professor, consultant*
Weir, Sara Hart *science and health policy consultant*
Weis, Frederick M. *former academic administrator*
Weis, Margaret Edith *writer, editor*
Weisberg, Barbara *writer, editor*
Weisberg, Robert Irving *former ambassador*
Weisburger, Elizabeth Kreiser *retired chemist*
Weisman, Leonard E. *medical educator*
Weismantel, Gregory Nelson *management consultant, computer company executive*
Weiss, Alvin Harvey *chemical engineer, educator, research scientist, consultant*
Weiss, Avery H. *ophthalmologist, educator*
Weiss, Glenn P. *television director*
Weiss, Joan Oppenheimer *social worker, educator*
Weiss, Joanne Marion *writer*
Weiss, Kenneth Andrew *lawyer, educator*
Weiss, Lyn Denise *physician*
Weiss, Nancy Passman *artist*
Weiss, Stephen J. *lawyer*
Weissenburger, David Allen *psychologist, educator, consultant*
Weissman, Jack (George Anderson) *retired editor*
Weiswasser, Stephen *electronics executive*
Weisz, Deborah *trombonist, music educator, composer*
Weisz, Paul B(urg) *physicist, researcher, chemical engineer*
Weitz, Lesley Anne *aerospace engineer, researcher*
Weitz, Melissa *environmentalist*
Weizmann, Howard Charles *consulting firm executive, former federal agency administrator*
Welburn, Edward T. *automotive executive*
Welch, C. David (Charles David Welch) *former federal agency administrator*
Welch, Martin E. III *investor, former rental company executive*
Welch, Richard L. *priest, lawyer*
Weldon, David Joseph, Jr. *former United States Representative from Florida*
Weldon, Jeffrey Alan *lawyer*
Weller, Gerald C. (Jerry Weller) *former United States Representative from Illinois*
Welles, Ferne Bingham Malcolm *retired archivist*
Wellisz, Stanislaw *economics professor*
Wellner, Marcel Nahum *research scientist, educator*
Wells, Christine Louise *physical education educator*
Wells, Robert Hartley *chemist, consultant*
Wells, Stephen Michael *engineering educator*
Welmaker, Gregory S. *medical researcher*
Welsh, Christabel Jane *neuroimmunologist*
Welsh, Dorothy Dell *columnist, writer*
Welsh, John Beresford, Jr. *retired lawyer*
Welsome, Eileen *journalist, writer*
Welter, William Michael *marketing and advertising executive*
Weltman, Joel Kenneth *immunologist*
Welzel, Tania M. *physician*
Wendel, Charles Allen *retired lawyer*
Wendlinger, Robert Matthew *communications and memory consultant*
Wendt, E. Allan *international affairs consultant*
Weng, Daniella *pharmacist, researcher*
Wenger, James L. *education educator*
Wenglowski, Joyce *painter*
Wenk, Robert E. *pathologist*
Wentz, Jeffrey Lee *information systems executive*
Wentz, William Henry, Jr. *aerospace engineer, educator*
Werkman, Rosemarie Anne *former public relations professional, volunteer*
Werman, Thomas Ehrlich *record producer*
Werner, Robert Joseph *dean, music educator*
Werner, Stuart Lloyd *computer services company executive*
Werner-Jacobsen, Emmy Elisabeth *developmental psychologist*
Werthan, Jeffrey Michael *lawyer*
Wertlieb, Donald Lawrence *psychologist, educator*
Wertsman, Vladimir Filip *librarian, writer, library and information scientist, translator*
Wertz, Gail Williams *microbiologist, educator*
Wesley, John E. *photographer, educator*
Wessel, Morris Arthur *retired pediatrician*
Wesselink, David Duwayne *finance company executive*
Wessling, Robert Bruce *retired lawyer*
West, Catherine G. *former retail executive*
West, Janet Elaine Olson *elementary school educator*
West, Jerry Alan *former professional sports team executive, retired professional basketball player*
West, Mildred Marie *art educator*
West, Rexford Leon *retired bank executive*
West, W. Richard, Jr. *retired museum director*
Westbie, Barbara Jane *retired graphics designer*
Westerhoff, John Henry III *priest, theologian, educator*
Westerhout, Gart *retired astronomer*
Westerman, Donna Day *artist*
Westernoff, Trent H. *surgeon*
Westhead, Paul *former professional basketball coach*
Weston, Francine Evans *secondary school educator*
Westring, Christian Gustav *geneticist, consultant*
Wetherbe, Herbert John *pharmacist*
Wetherell, Albert A. *secondary school educator*
Wetherill, Eikins *lawyer, stock exchange executive*
Wettels, Nicholas Benjamin *biomedical engineer*
Wexler, Sandra M. *artist, medical illustrator*
Weyman, Steven Aloysius *retired military officer*
Whale, Arthur Richard *retired lawyer*
Whalen, Charles William, Jr. *writer, retail executive, Former United States Representative, Ohio*
Whalen, Norma Jean *retired special education educator*
Whaley, Ross Samuel *environmentalist, educator*
Wharton, Margaret Mary *nun, educator*
Whatley, Jillian Katri *physiologist, educator*
Wheatland, Richard, II, *fiduciary services executive, museum executive*
Wheaton, Douglas B. *city manager, lawyer*
Wheeler, Albin Gray *retired military officer, educator*
Wheeler, Barbara J. *management consultant*
Wheeler, Burton M. *language educator, dean*
Wheeler, Cass (M. Cass. Wheeler) *healthcare consultant, former health science association administrator*
Wheeler, David Laurie *university dean*
Wheeler, George Charles, Jr. *materials and process engineer*
Wheeler, John Oliver *retired geologist*
Wheeler, R(ichard) Kenneth *lawyer, educator*
Wheeler, Stephen Frederick *legal administrator*
Wheeler, William Joe *retired research scientist*
Whelan, James Robert *investor, mining company executive*
Whelan, Stephen Thomas, Jr. *lawyer*
Whelchel, Sandra Jane *writer*
Whipple, Judith Roy *retired editor*
Whisler, James Steven *retired mining executive, lawyer, rancher*
Whitaker, Stephen Taylor *geologist, oil exploration consultant*
Whitaker, Thomas Kenneth *former university chancellor*
Whitaker, Thomas O'Hara *theater educator, director*
Whitburn, Merrill Duane *English literature educator*
White, Allen Bradley *meteorologist*
White, Beverly Jane *retired cytogeneticist*
White, Charles Sidney John *retired humanities educator*
White, Florence May *retired special education educator*
White, Gerald Andrew *retired chemical company executive*
White, James Edmund *architect, educator*
White, Jill Carolyn *lawyer*
White, John Wesley, Jr. *retired academic administrator*
White, Judith Miriam *biology professor*
White, Katherine Russell *lawyer*
White, Kendred Alan *lawyer*
White, Kerr Lachlan *retired physician, foundation administrator*
White, Lonnie Joe *retired history educator*
White, Luther G. *finance educator*
White, Michael Lee *executive producer, writer*
White, Pamela Jo *elementary school educator*
White, Ralph Paul *automotive executive, consultant*
White, Rebecca E. *advocate*
White, Ronald Leon *retired business executive*
White, Stanley Archibald *electrical engineer, researcher*
White, Tayloe McDonald *artist*
White, Tony L. *former health and medical products executive*
White, Yonsenia S. *artist, educator*
Whitehead, John Cunningham *former bank executive*
Whitehead, Tanya Dianne Grubbs *psychologist, educator, researcher*
Whiteley, Benjamin Robert *retired insurance company executive*
White-Means, Shelley *healthcare educator*
Whitener, Ronnie Dale *physics professor*
Whitesell, John Edwin *retired motion picture company executive*
Whitesell, Patrick *talent agency executive*
Whitman, Gregory Theodore *neurologist*
Whitman, Martin J. *portfolio manager*
Whitman, Meg (Margaret Cushing Whitman) *former Internet company executive*
Whitney, Edward Bonner *retired investment banker*
Whitney, Jane *foreign service officer*
Whitsell, John Crawford, II, *general surgeon*
Whittell, Polly (Mary K.) *editor, journalist*
Wiatt, Jim (James Anthony Wiatt) *talent agency executive*
Wicks, David O., Jr. *communications executive*
Widman, Rudolph Paul *college administrator*
Widner, Ralph Randolph *retired public administrator*
Widner, Roberta Ann *accountant, artist*
Wieand, Lou Ann *psychology educator, psychotherapist*
Wiebenson, Dora Louise *architectural historian, editor, writer*
Wiehl, Lis W. *legal analyst, educator*
Wieland, Gilbert Darryl *medical researcher, anthropologist, gerontologist*
Wiernik, Peter Harris *oncologist, educator*
Wiese, Richard *explorer, field scientist, journalist*
Wieselthier, Jeffrey E. *electronics engineer, researcher*
Wiesen, Donald Guy *retired diversified manufacturing company executive*
Wiessler, David Albert *news correspondent*
Wiest, Dianne *actress*
Wiggins, Charles Henry, Jr. *lawyer*
Wightman, Sharon Leilani *retired librarian*
Wigler, Andrew Jeffrey *lawyer*
Wikina, Suanu Bliss *human resources specialist*
Wiklund, Tommy Gert *astrophysicist*
Wilchek, Meir *biochemist, educator*
Wilcox, Mark Dean *lawyer*
Wilde, Daniel Underwood *computer engineering educator*
Wilder, Gene (Jerry Silberman) *actor, film director, writer*
Wilder, Janet Mary *performing company executive*
Wildhack, William August, Jr. *lawyer*
Wilding, Diane *computer scientist, consultant*

Wilds, Daniel O. *health products executive*
Wiles, Edwin McKinley *education educator, librarian*
Wiley, Carl Ross *timber company executive*
Wiley, Richard Arthur *lawyer*
Wilhelmi, Cynthia Joy *business and information technology manager, information scientist executive consultant*
Wilhelmsen, Harold John *accountant*
Wilhjelm, Christian *conductor, artist*
Wilk, Ronald *physician*
Wilkening, Laurel Lynn *academic administrator, aerospace scientist*
Wilkerson, Matt *biology professor*
Wilkie, Robert Leon, Jr. *former federal agency administrator*
Wilkin, Richard Edwin *clergyman, religious organization administrator*
Wilkins, Barratt (George Wilkins) *librarian*
Wilkins, Fred Clayton *physician, educator, engineer*
Wilkinson, Ann E. *theater educator, actress*
Wilkinson, Doris *medical sociology educator*
Wilkinson, Harry Edward *management educator, consultant*
Wilkinson, Richard H. *archaeologist, educator*
Wilkinson, Stanley Ralph *retired agronomist*
Wilkomirski, Josef *conductor, writer, composer, educator, journalist*
Will, Christina *school librarian*
Will, Fritz G. *physical chemist, consultant*
Will, Katherine Haley *former academic administrator*
Will, Roland Tracy, II, *writer, editor, journalist, publisher, television producer*
Willard, Richard Kennon *lawyer, former pharmaceutical company executive*
Willauer, Whiting Russell *retired manufacturing executive, systems engineer*
Willbanks, T. Shawn *educational association administrator*
Willenbecher, John *artist*
Willey, Frieda Anders *adult education educator*
Williams, Albert Nathaniel *writer, educator*
Williams, Alfred B. *retired management educator*
Williams, Barbara Kitty *nursing educator*
Williams, Billy Dee *actor*
Williams, Charles Wesley *retired engineering executive, consultant, researcher*
Williams, Darcel Patrice *writer, editor*
Williams, Edward Joseph *banker*
Williams, Elizabeth *human services administrator*
Williams, Ervin Eugene *religious organization administrator*
Williams, Freda Videll *speech pathology/audiology services professional*
Williams, George Christopher *biologist, ecology and evolution educator*
Williams, Howard Walter *aerospace engineer, engineering executive*
Williams, Ian George *writer*
Williams, James Buchanan *retired surgeon*
Williams, James Kendrick *bishop emeritus*
Williams, Jatika *social worker, educator*
Williams, Jean-Pierre *research scientist*
Williams, JoBeth *actress*
Williams, John Leicester *mechanical engineer, educator*
Williams, Kim Allan *cardiologist, educator*
Williams, Linda Frances *public nutrition administrator*
Williams, Lisa A. *music educator*
Williams, Louis Clair, Jr. *public relations executive*
Williams, Michael Maurice Rudolph *nuclear engineering consultant*
Williams, Michael Richard *protective services official*
Williams, Michael Shadden *art director*
Williams, Neville *solar power company executive*
Williams, Nicole Leann *human resources specialist, director*
Williams, Patricia Badia *retired counselor, academic administrator, mathematics educator*
Williams, Paul Stratton *executive recruiter*
Williams, Phyllis Cutforth *retired realtor*
Williams, Rachel D. *literature and language professor*
Williams, Robert Leon *retired psychiatrist, neurologist, educator*
Williams, Ronald Dean *minister, religious organization administrator*
Williams, Ronald Oscar *mathematician*
Williams, Scott Matthew *science educator*
Williams, Shannon Renee *mental health services professional*
Williams, Terrie Michelle *public relations executive*
Williams, Thelma B. *retired principal*
Williams, Thomas W. *electrical engineer*
Williams, Wesley Samuel, Jr. *lawyer*
Williamson, Douglas Franklin, Jr. *lawyer*
Williamson, Thomas Arnold *publishing executive*
Willingham, Mary Maxine *fashion retailer*
Willis, Bruce *actor*
Willis, Paul Allen *retired librarian, dean*
Willis, Ruth *freelance/self-employed theater director, actress*
Willis, Selene Lowe *electrical engineer, application developer, consultant, information technology manager*
Willis, Solomon Lee *mathematics educator*
Willison, Bruce Gray *dean*
Willocks, Kristin *psychology educator*
Wills, J. Robert *retired academic administrator, theater educator, writer*
Wills, John Elliot, Jr. *retired historian, writer*
Wills, William Ridley, II, *retired insurance company executive, historian*
Wilmut, Ian *biologist*
Wilson, Annette Sigrid *retired elementary school educator*
Wilson, Bruce Duxbury *lawyer*
Wilson, Chester Goodwin *electrical engineer, educator*
Wilson, Colin Henry *writer*
Wilson, Gretchen *vocalist*
Wilson, Heather Ann *former United States Representative from New Mexico*
Wilson, James Lawrence *retired chemical company executive*
Wilson, James Miller, IV, *cardiovascular surgeon, educator*
Wilson, Jane *artist*
Wilson, John Pasley *retired law educator*
Wilson, Joseph Charles, IV, *former ambassador*
Wilson, Karen Lee *museum staff member, researcher*
Wilson, Kenneth Geddes *physics research administrator*
Wilson, Lanford *playwright*
Wilson, Lois M. *minister*
Wilson, Lynn Deyo *radiation oncologist*
Wilson, Mark Stephen *research scientist*
Wilson, Mary Elizabeth *epidemiologist, physician, educator*
Wilson, Melinda J. *psychologist*
Wilson, Melvin Edmond *retired civil engineer*
Wilson, Myron Robert, Jr. *retired psychiatrist*
Wilson, Patricia Potter *library and information science educator*
Wilson, Paul Lowell *mortgage company executive, lawyer*
Wilson, Rainn D. (Rainn Dietrich Wilson) *actor*
Wilson, Rhys Thaddeus *lawyer*
Wilson, Robin Scott *retired academic administrator, writer*
Wilson, Ronald A. *judge*
Wilson, Ross *former ambassador*
Wilson, Scott Thomas *psychologist, researcher*
Wilson, Stanley Charles *artist, educator, curator, art gallery director, consultant*
Wilson, Thomas Buck *lawyer*
Wilson, Walter Clinton *retired oil and gas industry executive*
Wilson, Wayne Jerome *psychology professor*
Wiltschko, Wolfgang *zoology educator*
Wimbs, Cassandra M. *musician, educator, writer*
Wimmer, Kathryn *retired elementary school educator*
Wimpffen, Otto Rudolph *mathematics professor*
Wimpress, Gordon Duncan, Jr. *management consultant, foundation administrator*
Winand, René Fernand Paul *retired metallurgy educator*
Wincheski, Russell A. *research scientist*
Winder, Robert Owen *mathematician, computer engineer, geophysicist*
Windhauser, John William *retired journalism educator, consultant*
Windsor, Harriet Smith *former state official*
Windsor, Patricia (Katonah Summertree, Perrin Winters, Anna Seeling) *author, educator, lecturer*
Wine-Banks, Jill Susan *lawyer*
Winer, Karen K. *endocrinologist*
Wingert, Hannelore Christiane *author, realtor, chemicals executive*
Winkler, Agnieszka M. *marketing executive*
Winkler, Donny W. *physics professor*
Winkler, Heather Starr *music educator*
Winn, Carolyn Pautke *librarian, consultant*
Winn, Joseph Lampher *retired electronics executive*
Winneker, Richard Craig *pharmacologist, researcher*
Winnowski, Thaddeus Richard (Ted Winnowski) *investment banker, consultant*
Winokur, Marissa Jaret *actress*
Winold, Helga Ulsamer *retired music educator*
Winrow, Brian Paul *law educator*
Winslet, Kate *actress*
Winslow, David Allen *chaplain, retired military officer*
Winslow, John Franklin *lawyer*
Winstead, Melody *science educator*
Winter, Judy Elaine *author, speaker*
Winter, Roger Jay *artist*
Winter, Roger Paul *former federal agency administrator*
Winter, Terence *writer, television producer*
Winter-Neighbors, Gwen Carol *special education and art educator, consultant*
Wintersheimer, Donald Carl *retired state supreme court justice*
Winterstein, James Fredrick *academic administrator*
Wira, Charles Ryan *physician, educator*
Wirebaugh, Amy *physical therapist, educator*
Wirth, Russell D. L., Jr. *investment and merchant banker*
Wirtschafter, David *talent agency executive*
Wise, Patricia *opera singer, educator*
Wise, Ronnie W. *retired library director*
Wisehart, Mary Ruth *retired religious organization administrator*
Wisely, Donna *secondary school educator, athletic trainer*
Wiseman, Alan M(itchell) *lawyer*
Wiseman, Douglas Carl *education educator, department chairman, dean*
Wiseman, Patryce Avsharian *ecologist*
Wish, LeslieBeth Berger *psychotherapist, writer, management consultant*
Wishengrad, Marcia H. *lawyer*
Wishnick, Marcia Margolis *pediatrician, geneticist, educator*
Wisniewski, P. Michelle *retired obstetrician, gynecologist*
Wiswall, Dorothy Roller *language educator*
Witcher, Michael H. *homeland and national security expert*
Witcover, Jules Joseph *columnist, writer*
Witt, Hugh Ernest *manufacturing executive, consultant*
Witt, Melvin Sylvan *periodical editor, publisher*
Wittbrodt, Edwin Stanley *financial planner, consultant, retired military officer*
Witte, Ann Dryden *economics educator*
Witte, Owen Neil *microbiologist, molecular biologist, educator*
Wittich, John Jacob *retired academic administrator, finance company executive*
Wittig, Don *judge*
Wittig, Raymond Shaffer *lawyer, intellectual property technology manager*
Wittig, Sigmar *academic administrator, researcher, retired aerospace transportation executive*
Wixen, Joan Saunders *journalist*
Wizda, Christine Anne *history professor*
Wodlinger, Mark Louis *broadcast executive*
Wofsy, Steven Charles *astrophysicist, researcher*
Wojahn, R. Lorraine *retired state senator*
Wojcik, Cass *decorative supply company executive, retired municipal official*
Wolanskyj, Alexandra *hematologist*
Woldman, Sherman *pediatrician*
Woldt, Harold Frederick, Jr. *newspaper publishing executive*
Wolf, Dale B. *former health care company executive*
Wolf, Dale Edward *former Governor of Delaware*
Wolf, Gary Wickert *retired lawyer*
Wolfberg, Melvin Donald *optometrist, educational association administrator, consultant*
Wolfe, Gregory Baker *international relations educator*
Wolfe, Margaret Ripley *historian, educator, consultant*
Wolfen, Werner F. *lawyer*
Wolfensohn, James David *former President of the World Bank, diplomat*
Wolfersteig, Jean Lois *retired medical association administrator*
Wolff, Eleanor Blunk *actress*
Wolff, Manfred Ernst *chemist, pharmaceutical executive*
Wolfram, Dietmar *Information Scientist Educator*
Wolfson, Michael George *retired lawyer*
Wolfson, Sarah Elizabeth *singer, educator, physical education educator*
Wolkoff, Neal Lawrence *stock exchange executive*
Woll, Harry J. *electrical engineer*
Wollert, Gerald Dale *retired food products executive, securities trader*
Wolman, William *economist, journalist, broadcaster*
Woloch, Isser *history educator*
Wolpert Richard, Chava *artist*
Wolynez, Allen Lawrence *psychology professor*
Womack, Bobby (Robert Dwayne Womack) *musician, songwriter*
Wonders, William Clare *geography educator*
Wong, Ah-San *planetary scientist, musician, writer*
Wong, Albert J. *medical educator*
Wong, Edward Vincent *investment company executive*
Wong-Diaz, Francisco Raimundo *lawyer, educator*
Woo, Derek *electrical and computer engineer*
Woo, Honguk *research scientist*
Woo, Kenneth Roger *urologist*
Wood, Corinne Gieseke *former lieutenant governor*
Wood, Frank Maxwell *former prosecutor, lawyer*
Wood, Janis Louise *retired assistant principal*
Wood, Joseph S. *academic administrator*
Wood, Maurice *medical educator*
Wood, Robert Charles *lawyer, real estate developer*
Wood, Terry Lee *mathematics educator*
Wood, Vivian Poates *mezzo soprano, educator, author*
Wood, Willis Bowne, Jr. *retired utilities executive*
Woodard, Joseph Lamar *law librarian, emeritus professor*
Wooden, John Robert *retired college basketball coach*
Woodland, N. Joseph *retired optical engineer, retired mechanical engineer*
Woodring, Carl *English language educator*
Woodruff, Judy Carline *broadcast journalist*
Woodruff, Mary Brennan *elementary school educator*
Woodruff, Virginia *broadcast journalist, writer*
Woodrum, Patricia Ann *librarian*
Woods, Dan *information technology manager, consultant*
Woods, Eleanor C. *music educator*
Woods, Jason C. *medical educator*
Woods, Sandra Kay *real estate executive*
Woodside, Lisa Nicole *retired humanities educator*
Woodsworth, Anne *retired academic administrator, librarian*
Woodward, Clinton Benjamin, Jr. *civil engineer, educator*
Woodward, James Franklin *science educator*
Woodward, Ralph Lee, Jr. *retired historian, educator*
Wooldridge, William Charles *lawyer*
Woolf, William Blauvelt *retired association executive*
Woolsey, Robert Paul *church musician*
Woolston-Catlin, Marian *retired psychiatrist*
Wooten, Cecil Aaron *retired religious organization administrator*
Wooton, David L. *chemist, consultant*
Wopat, Tom *actor, singer*
Worboys, Roger Dick *retired communications executive*
Worden, Skip *writer*
Worenklein, Jacob Joshua *lawyer*
Workman, John Mitchell *chemist*
Workman, John P., Jr. *marketing professor*
Worner, Theresa Marie *internist, educator*
Worrell, Richard Vernon *orthopedic surgeon, dean*
Worrell, Stewart Phillip *lawyer, diversified financial services company executive*
Worth, John Eugene *anthropologist, educator*
Worthington, Bruce R. *lawyer, energy executive*
Worthington, Tracy *retired operations research analyst*
Woteki, Catherine Ellen *nutritionist*
Wott, John Arthur *retired arboretum and botanical garden executive, horticulture educator*
Wozniak, A. Rachel *educator*
Wren, Casey Leigh *broadcast technician, department chairman*
Wren, Stephen Corey *mathematician, inventor*
Wright, David John *telecommunications systems specialist, educator*
Wright, David L. *food and beverage company executive*
Wright, Dell *residential care and treatment facility executive*
Wright, Douglas Tyndall *former university administrator*
Wright, Ethel *secondary school educator*
Wright, Frederick Lewis, II, *lawyer*
Wright, Gladys Stone *music educator, writer, composer*
Wright, James Ralph *retired lawyer*
Wright, Jeanne Elizabeth Jason *retired advertising executive*
Wright, Joan L. *artist*
Wright, John W. *social studies educator*
Wright, Josephine Rosa Beatrice *musicologist, educator*
Wright, Judith Rae *retired accountant*
Wright, Lori Dunkle *musician, educator*
Wright, Robert Payton *lawyer*
Wright, Theodore Robert Fairbank *biologist, educator*
Wright, Tony *advertising executive*
Wrobel, Bruce J. *energy and utilities company executive*
Wroble, Arthur Gerard *judge*
Wrong, Dennis Hume *retired sociologist, educator*
Wroth, James Melvin *retired military officer*
Wruble, Bernhardt Karp *lawyer*
Wruble, Brian Frederick *investor*
Wu, Fengtao *language educator*
Wu, Hong *economics professor*
Wu, Huiquan *chemical engineer*
Wu, Jian Young *science educator*
Wu, Man-Li C. *research scientist*
Wu, Naijun *senior fellow*
Wu, Wei *research scientist*
Wu, Xianren *telecommunications industry executive, researcher*
Wu, Xin *electrical engineer, researcher, educator*
Wu, Xingru *petroleum engineer*
Wu, Yider *research scientist*
Wu, Yongjun *application developer*
Wu, Yu-Chien *medical researcher*
Wyatt, Marcia Jean *fine arts and speech educator, administrative assistant*
Wyckoff, E. Lisk, Jr. *lawyer*
Wykoff, Gary Lee *writer*
Wylie, James Malcolm *adult education educator*
Wyman, Milton *ophthalmologist*
Wynar, Bohdan Stephen *retired librarian, writer, editor*
Wyner, Yehudi *composer, pianist, conductor, educator*
Wyngaarden, James Barnes *retired physician*
Wynne, Patricia M *finance company executive*
Wyrtki, Klaus *oceanography educator*
Xi, Yutao *medical researcher*
Xia, Guohua *scientist, psychiatrist, psychologist*
Xia, Yuan-Qing *research scientist*
Xiao, Jing *science educator, researcher*
Xie, Haiyong *computer scientist*
Xie, Lexing *computer scientist*
Xing, Jun *academic administrator, educator*
Xingguo, Xiong *engineering educator*
Xu, Cailin *research scientist*
Xu, Dong *physicist, researcher*
Xu, Dongmei *molecular biologist, director*
Xu, Guangyao *research scientist*
Xu, Jinghai J. (Jim Xu) *toxicologist, researcher*
Xu, Jingye *research scientist*
Xu, J.M. (Jimmy Xu) *physicist, educator, engineer*
Xu, Juncheng *engineer, researcher*
Xu, Zhijie *research scientist*
Xue, Yuan *engineering educator*
Yadavalli, Gopala Krishna *medical educator*
Yadavalli, Kameshwar *electronics engineer*
Yadrick, Robert Martin *operations analyst*
Yalam, Arnold Robert *allergist, immunologist, consultant*
Yalamanchili, Praveen Raj *nephrologist*
Yale (Yeleyenide-Yale), Melpomene Fotine *researcher, anthropologist, archaeologist, art historian, conservator*
Yamamoto, Joe *retired psychiatrist, educator*
Yamamoto, Nobuto *immunologist, director*
Yamanouchi-Rynn, Midori *retired social sciences educator*
Yan, Wei *research scientist*
Yan, Xin *preventive medicine physician, educator*
Yanez, Antonio, Jr. *lawyer*
Yang, Bin *pathologist, molecular biologist*
Yang, Bing-Shiang *engineering educator*
Yang, Bo *electrical engineer*
Yang, Guo-Yuan *neuroscientist*
Yang, Jerry *former Internet company executive*
Yang, Jidong *transportation engineer*
Yang, Li *geography and tourism educator*
Yang, Shujun *electrical engineer*
Yang, Weibin *physician*
Yankey, Kofi *economics professor*
Yannella, Donald *literature and language professor*
Yantz, Patricia E. *art educator*
Yao, Frances *music educator, small business owner*
Yao, Yi *electrical engineer, researcher*
Yarbrough, Robert Allen *literature and language professor*
Yarchoan, Robert *clinical immunologist, researcher*
Yard, Michael *anatomy and physiology educator, retired military officer*
Yardibi, Tarik *research scientist*
Yarrow, Peter *folksinger*
Yastine, Barbara A. *former diversified financial services company executive*
Yates, David John C. *chemist, researcher*
Yavarkovsky, Jerome Harold *university librarian emeritus*
Yawney, Trent *former professional hockey coach, retired professional hockey player*
Ybarra, Kimberly Elizabeth *music and elementary school educator*
Ye, Weilan *scientist*
Yeager, Chuck (Charles Elwood Yeager) *retired air force officer, test pilot*
Yeager, Kurt Eric *research and development company executive*
Yeager, Phillip Charles *transportation company executive*
Yearwood, Trisha *country music singer, songwriter*
Yehia, Baligh R. *physician*
Yemelyanov, Alexander M. *mathematician, educator*
Yenko, Jayne M. *education educator*
Yeosock, John John *military officer*
Yepes, Enrique *language educator*

Professional Index

AGRICULTURE

UNITED STATES

ALABAMA

Auburn University
Mosjidis, Jorge *agricultural studies educator, researcher*
Reddy, Munagala *agricultural studies educator*

Town Creek
Ford, Stephen Allyn *farmer, educator*

Tuskegee Institute
Hill, Walter A. *agricultural sciences educator, researcher*

ARKANSAS

Beebe
Sites, Jerry *agricultural studies educator*

Fayetteville
Kellogg, David Wayne *agricultural studies educator, researcher*

CALIFORNIA

Berkeley
Ligon, Ethan Andrew *agricultural studies educator*

Davis
Alston, Julian Mark *agricultural studies educator*

Fresno
Epperson, Robert Dale *farmer*

Livingston
Foster, Ron *agricultural products supplier and executive*

Napa
Chiarella, Peter Ralph *vintner*

Orange
Williams, Patricia Sue *agricultural studies educator*

Pacific Palisades
Jennings, Marcella Grady *rancher, investor*

Rancho Mirage
Pais, Claudette Rachel *former horse breeder, political consultant*

San Francisco
Hills, Austin Edward *vineyard executive*

San Jose
D'Arrigo, Stephen, Jr. *agricultural company executive*

COLORADO

Denver
Decker, Peter Randolph *rancher, retired state official*

Montrose
Kontny, Vincent L. *rancher, retired engineering executive*

Springfield
Wessler, Melvin Dean *farmer, rancher*

FLORIDA

Fort Pierce
McMullian, Anke Hilde *agricultural studies educator*

Gainesville
Nair, Ramachandran P.K. *agroforestry educator, researcher*
Schmitz, Andrew *agricultural studies educator*
Seale, James Lawrence, Jr. *agricultural studies educator, trade association administrator, researcher*
Spreen, Thomas H. *agricultural studies educator*

Ocala
Ray, Ruth Alice Yancey *retired rancher, real estate developer*

HAWAII

Honolulu
Ching, Chauncey Tai Kin *agricultural studies educator, economist*

ILLINOIS

Centralia
Sickmeyer, Kent A. *agricultural studies educator*

Deerfield
Wilson, Stephen Ray *fertilizer manufacturing company executive*

Freeport
Setterstrom, James Robert *agricultural studies educator*

Urbana
Hoeft, Robert Gene *agricultural studies educator*
Spitze, Robert George Frederick *agricultural studies educator*

INDIANA

Fort Wayne
Marine, Clyde Lockwood *agricultural products supplier, consultant*

Indianapolis
Hegel, Carolyn Marie *farm owner and organization executive*

West Lafayette
Lechtenberg, Victor L. *agricultural studies educator*

IOWA

Akron
Hultgren, Dennis Eugene *farmer, management consultant*

Ames
Topel, David Glen *agricultural studies educator*

KANSAS

Claflin
Burmeister, Paul Frederick *farmer*

Concordia
Damman, Patrick Kelly *agricultural studies educator*

Manhattan
McKee, Richard Miles *retired agricultural studies educator*

LOUISIANA

Baton Rouge
Subudhi, Prasanta Kumar *agricultural studies educator*

Rayne
Sha, Xueyan *agricultural studies educator*

MINNESOTA

Goodridge
Hanson, Norma Lee *farmer*

MISSISSIPPI

Ackerman
James, Lee J. *agriculture educator*

Alcorn State
Cuadra, Evelin J. *agricultural studies educator*

Moorhead
Corley, Barry James *agricultural studies educator, farmer*

MISSOURI

Huntsville
Newbrough, Warren Wade *farmer*

MONTANA

Helena
McDonald, Dennis *rancher, political organization administrator*

Missoula
Chung, Woodam *agricultural studies educator*

NEVADA

Yerington
Scatena, Lorraine Borba *retired rancher, women's rights advocate, researcher*

NEW YORK

Cobleskill
Hunsinger, Todd W. *agricultural studies educator, researcher*

Ithaca
Hoffmann, Michael Peter *agricultural studies educator*

OHIO

Columbus
Ockerman, Herbert W. *agricultural and international studies educator*

Pickerington
Basinger, Ned Naden *farmer, educator*

Wooster
Steward, Larry G. *agricultural studies educator, consultant*

SOUTH DAKOTA

Saint Lawrence
Lockner, Vera Joanne *farmer, rancher, state legislator*

Sturgis
Larson, Marlan T. *agricultural studies educator*

TENNESSEE

Hickory Valley
Weaver, Peggy (Marguerite McKinnie Weaver) *plantation owner*

TEXAS

Athens
Price, Vernon L. *biological studies educator*

College Station
Arosh, Joe A. *agricultural studies educator*
Christiansen, James Edward *agricultural educator*
Gan, Jianbang *agricultural studies educator, economist*
Murano, Elsa A. *agricultural studies educator, former academic administrator*

Corpus Christi
Ihenetu, Kenneth Ugochukwu *agricultural studies educator*

Guthrie
Marion, Anne Windfohr *rancher, museum administrator*

Industry
Huitt, Jimmie L. *rancher, oil and gas industry executive, real estate developer*

La Grange
Morovich, George L. *rancher, contractor*

Odessa
Lemons, Richard Mikel *agricultural studies educator*

San Antonio
Sinkfield, Carolin Ladell *agricultural studies educator*

Valley View
Wallace, Donald John III *rancher*

Vernon
Ansley, Robert James *agricultural studies educator*

WEST VIRGINIA

Charles Town
McDonald, Angus Wheeler *farmer*

Fraziers Bottom
Talbott, Charles W., Jr. *agricultural studies educator*

WISCONSIN

Milwaukee
Allen, Will *urban farmer*

WYOMING

Lander
Raynolds, David Robert *buffalo breeder, writer*

SCOTLAND

Dundee
Hillman, John Richard *agricultural and biotechnological studies educator, researcher, consultant*

TAIWAN

Chiayi
Ku, Maurice S. B. *agricultural studies educator*

ADDRESS UNPUBLISHED

Brooks, Kenneth N. *forestry educator*
Bulkley, Gregory Bartlett *cattle rancher, retired academic surgeon and research scientist*
Erwin, Elmer Louis *vintager, consultant*
Fan, Zhenchuan *medicine studies educator*
Jacobson, Norman L. *retired agricultural educator, researcher*
Johnson, Maurice Verner, Jr. *agricultural research and development executive*
Knight, James Arthur *agricultural studies educator*
Luening, Robert Adami *retired agricultural studies educator*
McCorkle, Robert Ellsworth *agribusiness educator*
Peterson, Hikaru Hanawa *agricultural studies educator*
Stimpert, Michael Alan *retired agricultural products company executive*
Voss, Omer Gerald *farm equipment executive*

ARCHITECTURE & DESIGN

UNITED STATES

ALABAMA

Auburn
Heck, Ross *design educator, consultant*
Millman, Richard George *architect, educator*

Birmingham
Simon, Cliff *design educator*

Madison
Vo, Hieu N. *architect*

ALASKA

Anchorage
Maynard, Kenneth Douglas *architect*

ARIZONA

Gold Canyon
Johnson, Charles Foreman *architectural firm executive*

Payson
Hershberger, Robert Glen *architect, educator*

Phoenix
Hawkins, Jasper Stillwell, Jr. *architect*
Jones, Eddie *architect*
Schiffner, Charles Robert *architect*

Scottsdale
Brown, Shirley Margaret Kern (Peggy Brown) *interior designer*
Lloyd-Lee, Beverly *interior designer*

Tucson
Cook, William Howard *architect*
Nelson, Edward Humphrey *architect*
Seehausen, Richard Ferdinand *architect*
Wallach, Leslie Rothaus *architect*

ARKANSAS

Little Rock
Chilcote, Lugean Lester *retired architect, researcher*
Levy, Eugene Pfeifer *architectural firm executive, architect*
Truemper, John James, Jr. *retired architect*

CALIFORNIA

Bakersfield
McAlister, Michael H. *architect*

Belvedere
Hugenberg, Patricia Ellen Petrie *product designer*

Berkeley
Brocchini, Ronald Gene *architect*
Cardwell, Kenneth Harvey *architect, educator*
Stoller, Claude *architect*

Corona Del Mar
Yeo, Ron *architect*

El Cerrito
Burger, Edmund Ganes *architect*

Escondido
Devine, Walter Bernard *naval architect, marine engineer*

Fresno
Patnaude, William Eugene *architect*
Pings, Anthony Claude *architect*

Gardena
Shelby, Carroll Hall *automotive designer*

Greenbrae
Tyng, Anne Griswold *architect*

Highland
MacQueen, Cherie K. *interior designer, artist, retired newscaster, retired sportscaster*

Huntington Beach
Foose, Chip *automotive designer, television personality*

Irvine
Kraemer, Kenneth Leo *architect, urban planner, educator*

Laguna Woods
Badgley, John Roy *architect*

Los Angeles
Corrigan, Timothy *interior designer, former advertising executive*
Denari, Neil M. *architectural firm executive, educator*
Dworsky, Daniel Leonard *architect, educator*
Fickett, Edward Hale *architect, educator, arbitrator*
Gehry, Frank Owen *architect*
Man, Lawrence Kong *architect, art dealer, entrepreneur*
Moe, Stanley Allen *architect, consultant*

Manhattan Beach
Blanton, John Arthur *architect, writer*

Mill Valley
D'Amico, Michael *architect, urban planner*

Mojave
Rutan, Burt (Elbert Leander Rutan) *aircraft designer, aircraft company executive*

Mountain View
Kobza, Dennis Jerome *architect*

Newport Beach
Bissell, George Arthur *architect*
Blankenship, Edward G. *architect*
Butera, Barclay *interior designer*

Oak Hills
Whiting, Gary Brian *design educator*

Oxnard
O'Connell, Hugh Mellen, Jr. *retired architect*

Redlands
Bricker, Lauren Weiss *architectural historian*

Rowland Heights
Chou, George Kechung *architect, civil engineer, small business owner, urban planner*

Sacramento
Lionakis, George *architect*
Wasserman, Barry L(ee) *architect*

San Francisco
Bull, Henrik Helkand *architect*
Field, John Louis *architect*
Jennings, Jim *architect*
Kriken, John Lund *architect*
Lucas S.J., Thomas Martin *art and architecture professor*
Minar, Paul G. *interior designer, consultant*
Moris, Lamberto Giuliano *architect*
Pfeffer, Patrick *architect*

San Jose
Tanaka, Richard Koichi, Jr. *architect, planner*

San Luis Obispo
Pohl, Jens Gerhard *architecture educator, director*

San Rafael
Manny, Carter Hugh, Jr. *architect, retired foundation administrator*

Santa Barbara
Burgee, John Henry *architect*
Kruger, Kenneth Charles *architect*

Santa Monica
Campbell, Douglas Allen *landscape architect, consultant*
Mayne, Thom *architect*
Smith, Michael S. *interior designer, furniture designer*

South Pasadena
Girvigian, Raymond *architect*

Stanford
Eustis, Robert Henry *design company executive, mechanical engineer*

Tarzana
Smith, Mark Lee *architect*

Topanga
Curedale, Robert A. *industrial designer*

Turlock
Shirvani, Sir Hamid *architect, educator, philosopher, writer, university president*

Walnut Creek
Hassid, Sami *architect, educator*

Windsor
Matkin, Judith Conway *product designer*

COLORADO

Broomfield
Williams, John James, Jr. *architect*

Denver
Anderson, John David *architect*
Brownson, Jacques Calmon *architect*
Fuller, Robert Kenneth *architect, urban designer*

Fort Collins
Grandin, Temple *industrial designer, science educator*

Highlands Ranch
Vosbeck, Robert Randall *architect*

Pueblo
Greenlaw, Roger Lee *interior designer*

CONNECTICUT

Centerbrook
Grover, William Herbert *architect*

Cheshire
Rowland, Ralph Thomas *retired architect*

Fairfield
Guise, David Earl *architect, educator*

Greenwich
Matthaei, Gay Humphrey *interior designer*

New Canaan
Dean, Robert Bruce *architect*
Papp, Laszlo George *retired architect*
Risom, Jens *furniture designer, consultant, manufacturing executive*

New Haven
Bloomer, Kent Cress *architecture educator*
Newick, Craig David *architect*
Pelli, Cesar *architect*
Roth, Harold *architect*

Niantic
Butler, Jonathan Putnam *architect*

Northford
Gregan, Edmund Robert *landscape architect*

South Kent
Baker, John Milnes *architect*

Trumbull
Watson, Donald Ralph *architect, dean, writer, artist*

DISTRICT OF COLUMBIA

Washington
Ayers, Stephen Thomas *architect*
Bagnoli, David Christopher *architect*
Burton, Douglas *interior designer*
Cox, Warren Jacob *architect*
Jacobsen, Hugh Newell *architect*
Kulski, Julian Eugeniusz *architect, writer*
Lewis, Anne McCutcheon *architect*
Lewis, Roger Kutnow *architect, educator, author*
Miller, Ewing Harry *retired architect*
Murray, Christopher Charles III *architect*
Oehme, Wolfgang Walter *landscape architect*
Price, Travis L. III *architectural firm executive, educator*
Ramberg, Walter Dodd *architect*
Schlesinger, B. Frank *architect, educator*
Siegel, Lloyd Harvey *architect, real estate developer, consultant*
Williams, Terrance Reynolds *architecture educator*
Woofter, Vivien Perrine *interior designer, consultant*
Yerkes, David Norton *architect*

FLORIDA

Avon Park
Markel, Tanna Michelle *design educator*

Boca Raton
Harris, S. Buddy *architect, interior designer*

Daytona Beach
Amick, William Walker *golf course architect*

Deerfield Beach
Ruga, Wayne *architect*

Delray Beach
Rippeteau, Darrel Downing *retired architect*

Fort Lauderdale
Galvis, J. Alberto *architect, educator*

Fort Myers
Sappenfield, Charles Madison *architect, educator*
Trudnak, Stephen Joseph *landscape architect*

Gulf Breeze
French, Jere Stuart *landscape architect*

Jacksonville
Morgan, William Newton *architect, educator*

Key West
Klimowich, Edward John *architecture educator*

Miami
Feito, Jose *architect*
Hampton, Mark Garrison *architect*

Miramar
Stewart Simpson, Donnamay Angela *interior designer*

Naples
Bradley, Charles MacArthur *retired architect*
Lewis, Gordon Gilmer *golf course architect*
Lickhalter, Merlin *architect*
Liebenson, Gloria Krasnow *retired interior design executive, freelance writer*

Palatka
O'Leary, Robert William *design educator, lighting designer*

Pensacola
Epperson, David Ross *architect, planner, photographer*
Torgersen, Torwald Harold *architect, consultant*
Woolf, Kenneth Howard *architect*

Pompano Beach
Gorman, Robert Saul *architect*

Saint Augustine
Wilkes, Delano Angus *architect*

Saint Petersburg
Ginn, Ronn *architect, environmental planner, general contractor*
Wedding, Charles Randolph *architect*

Sebastian
Lagin, Neil *landscape designer, consultant*

Stuart
Ankrom, Charles Franklin *landscape architect, consultant*

Tallahassee
Wiedegreen, Eric Albert *interior designer, educator*

Tampa
Howey, John Richard *architect, writer*
Jennewein, James Joseph *architect*
Lashley, Keith Livingstone *architect, educator*

Vero Beach
Ahrens, William Henry *architect*

West Palm Beach
Marshall-Beasley, Elizabeth *landscape architect*
Ross, Edward Joseph *architect*

Winter Haven
Burns, Arthur Lee *architect*

GEORGIA

Atlanta
Bainbridge, Frederick Freeman III *architect*
Cooper, Jerome Maurice *architect*
Diedrich, Richard Joseph *architect*
Hatch, Helen Davis *architect*
Khandelwal, Madhur *architectural firm executive*
Lewcock, Ronald Bentley *architect, educator*
Peponis, John *architect, educator*
Pulgram, William Leopold *architect, space designer*
Sizemore, Michael Maynard *architectural firm executive*

Augusta
Woodhurst, Robert Stanford, Jr. *architect*

Columbus
Manuel, Kimberly Ann *design educator*
Simpson, Minnie Peach *interior designer*

Decatur
Mc Intosh, James Eugene, Jr. *interior designer*

Kennesaw
Chen, Ming *design educator*

Kingsland
Huygens, Remmert William *architect*

Macon
Dunwody, Eugene Cox *architect*

Marietta
Shpuza, Ermal *architecture educator*

Moultrie
McCall, John Clark, Jr. *interior designer*

Norcross
Greene, Don Howard *product designer*

HAWAII

Honolulu
Ashraf, Kazi K. *architecture educator*
Steinmann, John Colburn *architect*
Vidal, Alejandro Legaspi (Andy Vidal) *architect*
Yeh, Raymond Wei-Hwa *architect, educator*

Kaneohe
Fisette, Scott Michael *landscape and golf course architect*

Waipahu
Chang, Walter Tuck, Sr. *draftsman, real estate agent, religious studies educator*

IDAHO

Moscow
Mead, Phillip Gunn *architect, educator*

ILLINOIS

Barrington
Amatangelo, Kathleen Driscoll *interior designer, educator*

Bloomington
Switzer, Jon Rex *architect*

Champaign
Baker, Jack Sherman *retired architect*
Boubekri, Mohamed *architecture educator*
Kim, Michael Kyong-il *professor, architect*
Riley, Robert Bartlett *landscape architect*

Chicago
Balasi, Mark Geoffrey *architect*
Compagnon, Odile Anne *architecture educator*
Gold, Allan Harold *architect, structural engineer, educator*
Hackl, Donald John *architect*
Herbst, Walter Brown *industrial designer*
Holabird, John Augur, Jr. *retired architect*
Kerbis, Gertrude Lempp *architect*
Kriegshauser, John *architecture educator*
Mack, Alan Wayne *interior designer*
Matthei, Edward Hodge *architect*
McCullagh, Grant Gibson *retired architect*
McCurry, Margaret Irene *architect, furniture and interior designer, educator*
Phillips, Frederick Falley *architect*
Robertson, Donna Virginia *architect, educator, dean*
Schroeder, Douglas Fredrick *architect*
Smith, Adrian Devaun *architect*
Tigerman, Stanley *architect, educator*
Valerio, Joseph Mastro *architectural firm executive, educator*
Weber, Hanno *architect*
Whitney, Patrick Foster *design educator*

Evanston
Grunsfeld, Ernest Alton III *architect*
Kuzmanic, Ana *design educator*
Macsai, John *retired architect*
Piper, Robert Johnston *retired architect, urban planner*

Highland Park
Tobin, Calvin Jay *retired architect*

Hinsdale
Unikel, Eva Taylor *interior designer*

Lake Zurich
Krolopp, Rudolph William *retired industrial designer, consultant*

Lisle
Al-Banna, Ayham *architect*

Northbrook
Dubin, Arthur Detmers *retired architect*

Oak Park
Heitzman, Frank Edward *architect*

Palatine
Dittburner, Carl Michael *architect, educator*

Schaumburg
Otis, James, Jr. *architect*

Skokie
Siegal, Burton Lee *product designer, consultant, inventor*

Wheaton
Martin, Marcia Gray *retired architecture educator, artist, designer*

Winnetka
Weber, John Bertram *architect*

INDIANA

Carmel
Eden, Barbara Janiece *commercial and residential interior designer*
McLaughlin, Harry Roll *architect*

Indianapolis
Florestano, Dana Joseph *architect*

Mishawaka
Troyer, LeRoy Seth *architect*

Notre Dame
Stamper, John W. *architecture educator, academic administrator*

South Bend
Horsbrugh, Patrick *architect, educator, environologist*

IOWA

Ames
Lewis, Calvin Fred *architect, educator*
Palermo, Gregory Sebastian *architect*

Clear Lake
Broshar, Robert Clare *retired architect*

Iowa City
Neumann, Roy Covert *architect*

KANSAS

Lawrence
Grabow, Stephen Harris *architecture educator*

Manhattan
Foerster, Bernd *architecture educator*

KENTUCKY

Lexington
Aynsley, Richard Michael *architect, researcher*
Romanowitz, Byron Foster *architect, engineer*

LOUISIANA

Lafayette
Malinowski, Jerome Joseph *design educator*

Metairie
Mirzai, Pirooz (Victor Mirzai) *architect, educator, consultant*

New Orleans
Bookhardt, Fred Barringer, Jr. *architect*
Filson, Ronald Coulter *architect, educator, dean*
Klingman, John Philip *architect, educator*
Waggonner, Joseph David III *architect*

Ruston
Carwile, Guy Winstead *architect, educator*

MAINE

Edgecomb
Carlson, Suzanne Olive *architect*

New Harbor
Fradley, Frederick Macdonell *retired architect*

Southwest Harbor
Forbes, Peter *architect*

MARYLAND

Annapolis
Miller, Richards Thorn *naval architect, engineer*

Baltimore
Adams, Harold Lynn *retired architect*
Brodie, Menasha Jacob (Jay) *architect, city planner, government executive*

Bowie
Stone, Edward Harris, II, *landscape architect*

Chevy Chase
Auerbach, Seymour *architect*
Oudens, Gerald Francis *architect, architectural firm executive*

Olney
Delmar, Eugene Anthony *architect*

Potomac
Yerman, Anne Veronica *interior designer*

Rockville
Morgan, William Bruce *naval architect*

MASSACHUSETTS

Amherst
Cornish, Geoffrey St. John *golf course architect*

Bedford
Payne, Harry Morse, Jr. *architect*
Shepley, Hugh *architect*

Boston
Finegold, Maurice Nathan *architect*
Goody, Joan Edelman *architect*
Pisani, Anthony Michael *architect*
Stull, Donald LeRoy *architect*
Tappé, Albert Anthony *architect*

Cambridge
Anderson, Stanford Owen *architect, architectural historian, educator*
Campbell, Robert *architect, writer*
Koolhaas, Remment *architect, educator*
Kruger, Kenneth *architect*
Necipoglu, Gülru *art history and architecture professor*
Porter, William Lyman *architect, educator*
Woo, Kyu Sung *architect*

Edgartown
Rosenfeld, Walter David, Jr. *architect, writer*

Marblehead
Green, Richard John *architect*

Newton
Ardalan, Nader *architect*

Springfield
Engebretson, Douglas Kenneth *architect, interior designer*

Waltham
Notkin, Leonard Sheldon *architect*

Wellesley
Birkerts, Gunnar *architect*

Woods Hole
Newman, John Nicholas *naval architect educator*

MICHIGAN

Ann Arbor
Beckley, Robert Mark *architect, educator*

Detroit
Francis, Edward D. *architect*
Orikri, Timothy UfuomaEfe *landscape artist*

Flushing
Demankowski, Lisa Renee *architect, educator*

Kalamazoo
Carver, Norman Francis, Jr. *architect, photographer*

South Haven
LaRocque, Linda Lou *interior designer, educator, playwright*

Ypsilanti
Ilozor, Benedict Dozie *architect, researcher, facility manager, planner*

MINNESOTA

Duluth
Salmela, David Daniel *architect*
Whiteman, Richard Frank *architect*

Minneapolis
Clemence, Roger Davidson *landscape architect, educator*
Jacob, Bernard Michel *architect*
Martin, Roger Bond *landscape architect*
Roe, Sharon Louise *architect, educator*

Northfield
Sovik, Edward Anders *architect, consultant*

Winona
Mayer, Kit *scenic designer, director*

MISSISSIPPI

Columbus
Rood, Cynthia Hooper *landscape architect, consultant*

Mississippi State
Martin, Edward Curtis, Jr. *landscape architect, educator*

Starkville
Ford, Robert MacDonald III *architect, educator*

MISSOURI

Branson
Ownby, Jerry Steve *landscape architect, educator*

Columbia
Yoon, So-Yeon *design educator*

Kansas City
Seligson, Theodore H. *architect, interior designer, urban planner*

Saint Louis
Bextermiller, Theresa Marie *architect, computer engineer*
Marti, Paul Edgar, Jr. *architect, educator*
Michaelides, Constantine Evangelos *architect, educator*

MONTANA

Bozeman
DeHaas, John Neff, Jr. *retired architecture educator*

NEBRASKA

Lincoln
Stange, James Henry *architect*
Unthank, Michael George *architectural firm executive*

NEVADA

Las Vegas
Feiner, Edward A. *architect*
Serfas, Richard Thomas *architecture educator, urban planner, municipal official*

Reno
Schweigert, Lynette Aileen *interior designer, consultant*

NEW HAMPSHIRE

Exeter
Richardson, Artemas P(artridge) *retired landscape architect*

Hanover
Brooks, H. Allen *architectural educator, author*

NEW JERSEY

Bound Brook
Shive, Richard Byron *architect*

Cape May Point
Jordan, Joe J. *architect*

East Orange
Fielo, Muriel Bryant *interior designer*

Englewood
Schmidt, Ronald Hans *architect*

Middletown
Chiu, Angela Lan *architect, researcher*

Newark
Goldman, Glenn *architect, educator*

Paterson
Kagan, Vladimir *furniture and interior designer*

Princeton
Diller, Elizabeth E. *architect, educator, artist*
Ford, Jeremiah III *architect*
Graves, Michael *architect, educator*
Hillier, J(ames) Robert *architect*
Holt, Philetus Havens III *architect*
Lerner, Ralph *architect, university dean*

Trenton
Jones, Sophia LaShawn *architect*

Upper Saddle River
Cappitella, Mauro John *architect*

NEW MEXICO

Albuquerque
Foster, Judi *interior designer, artist*
Pirkl, James Joseph *industrial designer, educator, writer*

Corrales
Hooker, Van Dorn *architect, educator, artist*

Santa Fe
Franzen, Ulrich J. *architect*
Leon, Bruno *architect, educator*

NEW YORK

Astoria
Araki, Henry Angel *industrial designer*

Buffalo
Coles, Robert Traynham *architect*

Cranberry Lake
Glavin, James Edward *landscape architect*

Cross River
Thorn, Susan Howe *interior designer*

Dobbs Ferry
Guggenheimer, Tobias Immanuel Simon *architect*

East Hampton
Delson, Sidney Leon *architect*

Hastings On Hudson
Weinstein, Edward Michael *architect, consultant*

Jamaica
Gati, William Eugene *architect, industrial designer, educator*

Locust Valley
Bentel, Frederick Richard *architect, educator*

Mount Vernon
McBride, Susan Alyse *interior designer, consultant*

New Rochelle
Menzies, Henry Hardinge *architect*

New York
Bailey, Preston *Event Designer*
Baird, Campbell Atkinson III *design educator*
Balmori, Diana *landscape designer*
Bartlett, Elizabeth Easton *interior designer*
Bell, Robin *interior designer*
Bland, Frederick Aves *architect*
Borrelli, John Francis *architect*
Buatta, Mario *interior designer*
Buttrick, Harold *architect*
Childs, David M. *architectural firm executive*
Cobb, Henry Nichols *architect*
Cook, Richard A. (Rick Cook) *architect*
Cushing, Charles R. *architectural firm executive*
David, Theoharis Lambros *architect, educator*
Dennis, Diane Joy Milam *retired architect*
De Vido, Alfredo Eduardo *architect*
Edelman, Judith H. *architect*
Eisenman, Peter David *architect, educator*
Fox, Robert Frederick, Jr. *architect*
Halsband, Frances *architect*
Hinz, Theodore Vincent *architect*
Kliment, Robert Michael *architect*
Krebs, Carl F. *architectural firm executive*
Lefferts, Gillet, Jr. *architect*
Libeskind, Daniel *architect*
Liebman, Theodore *architect*
Maria Antonella, Pelizzari *art history educator*
Marino, Peter *architect*
Masey, Jack *exhibition designer*
Meier, Richard Alan *architect*
Minskoff, Edward J. *architectural firm executive*
Pennoyer, Peter Morgan *architect*
Quennell, Nicholas *landscape architect, educator*
Ripka, Judith *jewelry designer*
Robertson, Jaquelin Taylor *architect, educator*
Rockwell, David *architectural firm executive*
Shah, Shamir *architect*
Slomanson, Lloyd Howard *architect, musician, photographer*
Smotrich, David Isadore *architect*
Solomonoff, Galia *architect*
Stern, Robert Arthur Morton *architect, educator, writer*
Taylor, Marilyn Jordan *architectural firm executive*
Tozer, Elizabeth Farran *interior and floral designer*
Varney, Carleton Bates, Jr. *interior designer, columnist, educator*
Voorsanger, Bartholomew *architect*
Vossoughian, Nader *architecture educator, curator*
Weine, Seth Joseph *architectural and graphic designer, writer*
Williams, Tod Culpan *architect, educator*
Willis, Beverly Ann *architect*
Wilson, Robin *interior designer*

Nyack
Degenshein, Jan *architect, planner*

Richfield Springs
Walters, Marjorie Anne *interior designer, consultant*

Rochester
Remington, Royce Roger *design educator*

Rye
Rolland, Peter George *landscape architect*

Syracuse
Smardon, Richard Clay *landscape architect, environmental studies professor*

Troy
Haviland, David Sands *retired architectural educator, researcher, administrator*
Kilgallon, Susan Margaret *architect, educator*

Wappingers Falls
Johnson, Jeh Vincent *architect*

Westhampton Beach
Flood, Angela *interior designer, artist*

NORTH CAROLINA

Asheville
King, Joseph Bertram *architect*
Latta, Diana Lennox *retired interior designer*

Boone
Oelberg, Robert Nathan *landscape architect*

Carrboro
Dixon, Frederick Dail *architect*

Chapel Hill
Godschalk, David Robinson *architect, urban development planner, educator*

Charlotte
Ferebee, Stephen Scott, Jr. *retired architect*
Gantt, Harvey B. *architect, former mayor*
Huberman, Jeffrey Allen *architect*
Montague, Edgar Burwell, III, (Monty Montague) *industrial designer*

Kinston
Baker-Gardner, Jewelle *interior designer, business consultant*

Raleigh
Clarke, Lewis James *landscape architect*
Flournoy, William Louis, Jr. *retired landscape architect*
Khachatoorian, Haig Nmn *industrial designer, educator*

Malecha, Marvin John *architect, academic administrator*

Research Triangle Park
Atkins, John L. III *architect*

OHIO

Celina
Fanning, Ronald Heath *architect, engineer*

Cincinnati
Chatterjee, Jayanta *architecture and planning educator*
Glendening, Everett Austin *architect*
Goetzman, Bruce Edgar *architecture educator*
Luckner, Herman Richard III *interior designer*
Nielsen, George Lee *architect*
Scheer, Brenda Case *architect, educator*

Cleveland
Bowen, Richard Lee *architect*
Gibans, James David *architect, consultant*
Madison, Robert Prince *architect*
Melsop, James William *architect*
Sande, Theodore Anton *architect, educator, foundation executive*
Zung, Thomas Tse-Kwai *architect*

Columbus
Osgood, Robert T., Jr. *architect, strategic planner*
Weinhold, Virginia Beamer *interior designer*

Mason
Cuff, Virginia Evelyn *architectural firm executive, consultant*

North Royalton
Holliday, Walter William *architectural firm executive*

Oxford
Sanabria, Sergio Luis *architecture educator*

Toledo
Martin, Robert Edward *architect*

OKLAHOMA

Norman
Henderson, Arnold Glenn *architect, educator*

Oklahoma City
Halpin, Anna Marie *retired architect*

Stillwater
Hebert, Paulette R. *design educator*
Jones, Nigel R. *architect, educator*

OREGON

Ashland
Mularz, Theodore Leonard *architect*

Beaverton
Hatfield, Tinker L. *architect, apparel and product designer*

Depoe Bay
Eaton, Leonard Kimball *retired architecture educator*

Eugene
Cheng, Nancy Yen-wen *architecture educator*

Hillsboro
Dubrulle, Françoise M. *architect, painter, interior designer*

Lorane
Plésums, Guntis *architect, retired educator*

Medford
Straus, David A. *architectural firm executive*

Portland
Hacker, Thomas Owen *architect*
Vanderslice, Ellen *architect, composer*

Welches
Merrill, William Dean *retired architect, medical facility planning consultant*

PENNSYLVANIA

Bethlehem
Spillman, Robert Arnold *architect*

Camp Hill
Brandow, Theo *architect*

Greencastle
Scott, Leighton Reeves *interior designer, artist, writer*

Harrisburg
Knackstedt, Mary V. *interior designer*

Narberth
Grenald, Raymond *architectural lighting designer*

New Cumberland
Peters, Ralph Edgar *architectural firm and engineering executive*

Philadelphia
Braham, William Walter III *architecture educator*
Breiner, David M. *architecture educator*
Brown, Denise Scott *architect, urban planner*
Eiswerth, Barry Neil *architect, educator*
Farley, Richard John *architect, engineer*
Hayes, John Freeman *architect*
Lawson, John Quinn *architect*
Magaziner, Henry Jonas *architect, writer*
Maxman, Susan Abel *architect*
Mertins, Detlef *architect, educator*
Rybczynski, Witold Marian *architect, educator, writer*
Saylor, Peter M. *architect*
Venturi, Robert *architect*
Whinnery, Peter B. *design educator*

Pittsburgh
Damianos, Sylvester *architect, sculptor*
Lam, Khee Poh *architecture educator, consultant*

Pottstown
Trahan, Kelly *design educator*

State College
Haas, John C. *architect*

Williamsport
Hintz, Harry W., Jr. *residential construction educator, contractor*
Wozniak, Robert Andrew *architectural technology professor*

Willow Grove
Suer, Marvin David *architectural consultant*

RHODE ISLAND

Newport
Cutler, Laurence Stephan *architect, museum administrator, writer, advertising executive, educator*
Hence, Jane Knight *architectural designer*

Providence
St. Florian, Friedrich Gartler *architect, educator*

SOUTH CAROLINA

Clemson
Bainbridge, Robert Warin *architect, consultant*
Hewitt, Robert Reid *landscape architect*

Columbia
Anderson, William H. *architect*

Greenville
Hultstrand, Charles John *architect*

TENNESSEE

Chattanooga
Derthick, Alan Wendell *architect, firm executive*

Goodlettsville
van der Laan, Mikell F. *landscape artist*

Memphis
Adsit, Russell Allan *landscape architect*

Nashville
Miller, Richard L. *architectural executive*
Swensson, Earl Simcox *architect*

TEXAS

Arlington
Ferrier, Richard Brooks *architect, educator*
Robinette, Gary Omer *landscape architect, educator*

Austin
Alofsin, Anthony *architect, art historian, writer, educator, artist*
George, Walter Eugene, Jr. *architect*

Bellaire
Lundy, Victor Alfred *architect, educator*

College Station
Ndubisi, Forster O. *landscape architect, educator*
Shepley, Mardelle McCuskey *architect, educator*
Woodcock, David Geoffrey *architect, educator*

Dallas
Landry, Jane Lorenz *architect*
Perkins, Nancy Jane *industrial designer*
Stacy, Dennis William *architect*

Denton
Gough, Clarence Ray *retired designer, educator*

Edinburg
Kupczynski, Lori Pendley *instructional designer*

Houston
Bair, Royden Stanley *retired architect*
Farrell, John Marshall *architect*
Mc Ginty, John Milton *architect, consultant*
Moorhead, Gerald Lee *architect*
Solomon, Marsha Harris *draftsman, artist*
Stubbs, William W. *interior designer*

Irving
Rees, Frank William, Jr. *architect*

UTAH

Salt Lake City
Beall, Burtch W., Jr. *architect*
Brems, David Paul *architect*
Christopher, James Walker *architect, educator*
Graham, Bradley William *design educator*
Miller, William Charles *architect, educator*

VERMONT

Poultney
Orr, Andrew S. *landscape artist*

VIRGINIA

Alexandria
Cross, Eason, Jr. *architect*
Gurney, Robert M. *architectural firm executive*
Vosbeck, William Frederick, Jr. *architect*

Arlington
Hellmuth, George William *architect*
Tarpgaard, Peter Thorvald *naval architect*
Wagner, Robin Judy *interior designer, consultant*

Blacksburg
Bliznakov, Milka Tcherneva *architect, educator*
Poole, Scott *architect, educator*
Rodriguez-Camilloni, Humberto Leonardo *architect, historian, educator*

Charlottesville
Bednar, Michael John *architecture educator*
McDonough, William Andrews *architect, former dean*
Root, James Benjamin *landscape architect*

Chesapeake
Carter, Gene Thomas *interior designer*

Falls Church
Barkley, Paul Haley, Jr. *architect*

Mc Lean
Mortensen, Robert Henry *landscape and golf course architect*

Reston
Radhakrishnan, Rajesh *architect*
Scheeler, James Arthur *architect*

Richmond
Joel, William Lee, II, *interior and lighting designer*
Morris, James Carl *architect*

Woodbridge
Peck, Dianne Kawecki *architect*

WASHINGTON

Kenmore
Springer, Floyd Ladean *architect*

Kirkland
Mitchell, Joseph Patrick *architect*

Mount Vernon
Klein, Henry *architect*

Redmond
Sowder, Robert Robertson *architect*

Republic
Chambers, Milton Warren *retired architect*

Seattle
Bain, William James, Jr. *architect*
Bosworth, Thomas Lawrence *architect, retired educator*
Jacobson, Phillip Lee *architect, educator*
Johnston, Norman John *retired architecture educator*
Jones, Grant Richard *landscape architect*
Kolb, Keith Robert *architect, educator*
Moudon, Anne Vernez *urban design educator*
Piven, Peter Anthony *architect, management consultant*
Thomas, John Val *architect*

WEST VIRGINIA

Fairmont
Freeman, Philip M. *architect, educator*

Summit Point
Taylor, Harold Allen, Jr. *industrial minerals consultant*

WISCONSIN

Fitchburg
Buchholz, Ronald Lewis *retired architect*

Kenosha
Potente, Eugene, Jr. *interior designer*

Madison
Tishler, William Henry *landscape architect, educator*

Milwaukee
Hubka, Thomas C. *architecture educator*

Waukesha
Schwartz, Robert Terry *industrial designer, director*

CANADA

ONTARIO

Toronto
Budrevics, Alexander *landscape architect*
van Ginkel, Blanche Lemco *architect, educator*

MEXICO

Mexico City
Legorreta, Ricardo *architectural firm executive*

AUSTRALIA

Camberwell
Edwards, F(rederick) Gary *architectural firm executive, health facility planner*

AUSTRIA

Vienna
Dahinden, Justus *architect*

CHINA

Beijing
Li, Xiaodong *architect, educator*

EGYPT

Alexandria
Zahran, Mohsen Moharram *architect, educator*

ENGLAND

London
Foster, Norman Robert (Lord Baron Norman Robert Foster of Thames Bank) *architect*

Newton Abbot
Baker, James Barnes *architect*

FRANCE

Paris
Piano, Renzo *architect*

Roques
White, Norval Crawford *architect*

NETHERLANDS

Delft
Haak, Alex Johan Henri *architect, educator*

NEW ZEALAND

Auckland
Su, Bin *architecture educator*

PERU

Lima
Canepa, Giacomo Giovannini *architect*

REPUBLIC OF KOREA

Seoul
Choi, Young-Hwan *architecture educator*
Kim, Won *architect*

SWITZERLAND

Zurich
Calatrava, Santiago *architect, structural engineer, artist*

TAIWAN

Taipei
Pan, Joshua Jih *architect*

ADDRESS UNPUBLISHED

Adler, Richard Melvin *architect, planner*
Akkor, Gundogdu *retired architectural firm and engineering executive, foundation administrator*
Armistead, Katherine Kelly (Mrs. Thomas B. Armistead III) *interior designer, travel consultant, civic worker*
Armstrong, Thomas Newton III *art and garden specialist*

Barnum, William Milo *architect*
Bell, Janet S. *interior designer, developer, event producer*
Brotman, David Joel *architectural firm executive, consultant*
Campbell, Janet Coral *architect*
Carpenter, Derr Alvin *retired landscape architect*
Chao, James Min-Tzu *architect*
Correa, Jaime *architectural firm executive*
Cupp, Robert Erhard *golf course architect, land use planner*
Dale, T.D. *architectural firm executive*
Demant, Margaret H. *retired interior designer*
Dermanis, Paul Raymond *architect*
Diffrient, Niels *industrial designer*
Feldhamer, Thelma Leah *retired architect*
Ferris, Roger Patrick *architect*
Finley, Phillip E. *architecture educator*
Friedman, Mildred *architecture educator, design educator, curator*
Gaillard, George Siday III *architect*
Gan, Juis *interior designer*
Gantz, Carroll Melvin *industrial design consultant, consumer product designer*
Genaro, Donald Michael *industrial designer*
Ghaffari, Avideh Behrouz *interior designer*
Gilchrist, William Aaron *architect*
Gui, James Edmund *architect*
Hardin, Mary L. *interior designer*
Hastings, L(ois) Jane *architect, educator*
Henderson, John Drews *architect*
Hodges, David Parmer *architect*
Hutchins, Robert Ayer *architectural consultant*
Joseph, J. Jonathan *interior designer*
Kazakov, Aleksey V. *architectural designer, artist*
Keech, Elowyn Ann *interior designer*
Kiss, Ronald K. *naval architect*
Koziol, Christopher Jude *architecture professor*
Lai, Feng-Qi *instructional designer, educator*
Lapin, Sharon Vaughn *interior designer*
Lewis, Kay *interior designer, consultant*
Lin, Maya *architect, sculptor*
Lorenz, Marie *architect, sculptor*
Luder, Owen (Harold Luder) *architect, construction executive, consultant, mediator*
Mace, Michael Jay *architect*
Mair, Bruce Logan *interior designer, architectural firm executive*
Mauner, Claudia Anne *design educator*
McGee, Humphrey Glenn *retired architect*
McPheeters, Edwin Keith *architect, educator*
Mc Sheffrey, Gerald Rainey *architect, educator, city planner, author*
Mujica-Parodi, Mauro E. *architect*
Mumma, Albert Girard, Jr. *architect*
Murray, David George *architect*
Myer, Donald Beekman *architect*
Naidorf, Louis Murray *architect*
Nilsson, Edward Olof *architect*
Odermatt, Robert Allen *architect*
Olmsted, Jennifer *interior design consultant*
Omholt, Bruce Donald *product designer, mechanical engineer, consultant*
Paulsen, Serenus Glen *retired architect, educator*
Pei, I.M. (Ieoh Ming Pei) *architect*
Pettitt, Jay S. *architect, consultant*
Plant, Jeff *architecture educator*
Poor, Janet Meakin III *landscape designer*
Poss, Jeffery Scott *architect, educator*
Preiser, Wolfgang Friedrich Ernst *retired architect, educator, consultant, researcher*
Ryan, John Michael *landscape architect*
Sagan, M. J. *architectural firm executive*
Saile, David George *architecture educator, researcher*
Salzman, Arthur George *retired architect*
Schlossman, John Isaac *architect*
Strong, Annsley Chapman *interior designer, volunteer*
Sullivan Stemberg, Maureen *interior designer*
Takhar, Pawan S. *food and biological engineer*
Thiel, Philip *retired design educator*
Thistlethwaite, David Richard *architect*
Tripeny, Patrick *architect, educator*
Van Dine, Harold Forster, Jr. *architect, artist*
Vargo, Louise *landscape artist, music educator*
Ward, George Truman *architect*
White, James Edmund *architect, educator*
Ytterberg, Michael Roger *architect, educator*

ARTS: LITERARY *See also* COMMUNICATIONS MEDIA

UNITED STATES

ALASKA

Anchorage
Strohmeyer, John *writer, retired editor*
Thomas, Lowell, Jr. *writer, retired military officer, state senator*

ARIZONA

Mesa
St. Cyr, Margaret Ann (Peggy St. Cyr) *writer*

Phoenix
Duyck, Kathleen Marie *poet, musician, retired social worker*
Ellison, Cyril Lee *literary agent, retired publishing executive*
Holaday, Barbara (Bobbie) Hayne *writer*

Scottsdale
La Vista, Frank William *writer, educator*
Taylor, James C. *writer*

Sun City West
Bowkett, Gerald Edson *editorial consultant, writer*

Tempe
Parent, Annette Richards *freelance writer, artist*
Raby, William Louis *writer, consultant*

Tucson
Butcher, Russell Devereux *writer, photographer*
Deming, Alison Hawthorne *writer, poet, academic administrator*
Nord, Myrtle Selma *writer, researcher*
Stitt, Mari Leipper *poet*
Williams, Joy *writer*

ARKANSAS

Cabot
Tackett, Viti Lee *writer*

Hot Springs
Selix, Karen Elizabeth *writer, artist, vocalist*

Little Rock
Nunn, Patarica Dian *poet*

Springdale
Strong, B. Jean *writer, publisher*

CALIFORNIA

Aromas
Fleischman, Paul *children's author*

Atascadero
Locke, Virginia Otis *writer*

Berkeley
Brooke, Tal (Robert Taliaferro) *writer*
Callenbach, Ernest *retired writer, editor*
Chetin, Helen Campbell *writer*
Hass, Robert Louis *poet, literature educator*
Kluger, Richard *writer, editor*
Knox, Helene Margrethe *poet, editor*
Pollan, Michael *author, journalist, professor*

Beverly Hills
Alberghetti, Adriana *literary agent*
Apatow, Judd *scriptwriter, television and film producer*
Ball, Alan *screenwriter*
Chase, David (David DeCaesare) *scriptwriter, television director and producer*
Cody, Diablo (Brooke Busey-Hunt) *scriptwriter*
Gaghan, Stephen *scriptwriter, film director*
Greenberg, Richard *playwright*
Groening, Matthew (Abram) *writer, cartoonist*
Kaufman, Charlie *scriptwriter*
Mendelsohn, Daniel *writer, humanities professor*
Pezzullo, Ralph Michael *writer, playwright*
Roth, Eric *screenwriter*
Schulian, John (Nielsen Schulian) *screenwriter, author*
Shanley, John Patrick *playwright, screenwriter*
Slade, Bernard *playwright*
Wellins, Cori *literary agent*

California City
Flakes, Susan *playwright, screenwriter, non-fiction writer, hotel reviewer, theater director*

Camarillo
Truman, Ruth Dixon *administrator, writer, lecturer, consultant*

Cambria
Gray, Thomas Stephen *writer*

Carpinteria
Rau, Margaret E. *writer*

Castro Valley
Wycoff, Charles Coleman *writer, retired anesthesiologist*

Century City
Ward, David Schad *scriptwriter, film director*

Chico
Cummings, Anne Alexandra *retired writer*
Livingston, Myran Jay *author, film writer, director and producer*

Chula Vista
Nelson, Carl Alfred *author, international business educator, Former Captain USN*

Citrus Heights
Daves, Sandra Lynn *poet, lyricist*

Claremont
Wachtel, Albert *writer, educator*

Clovis
Engle, Margarita *writer, poet*
Shields, Allan Edwin *writer, educator, photographer*

Colton
Allen, Blair Hamilton *writer, poet, artist, editor, photographer*

Corona
Everett Nollkamper, Pamela Irene *writer, educator*

Cromberg
Kolb, Ken Lloyd *writer*

Dana Point
Walker, Doris Isaak *writer, historian, educator*

Davis
Bunch, Richard Alan *writer, educator, poet, philosopher*
Major, Clarence Lee *writer, painter, poet, educator*
Rooks, George Malcolm *writer, educator, small business owner*

Del Mar
Morton, Frederic *author*

Dove Canyon
Bird, Brian Rex *writer, producer television/film*

Fresno
Garrison-Finderup, Ivadelle Dalton *writer, educator*
Lanter, Lanore *writer, educator*

Glendale
Landau, Annette Henkin *writer, librarian*

Grass Valley
Cheney, Margaret *writer, retired editor*
Washington, Allyn Jarvis *writer*

Healdsburg
Castellini, Mary Mercer *author*
Myers, Robert Eugene *writer, educator*

Hollywood
Melchior, Ib Jorgen *scriptwriter, author, film director*

La Jolla
Antin, David *poet, critic*
Havis, Allan Stuart *playwright, theatre educator*

Los Altos
Hickman, Martha Whitmore *writer*

Los Angeles
Axelrod, Jeremiah Borenstein *writer, educator*
Baumbach, Noah *screenwriter*
Chaiken, Stacie Rae *writer, performer, theater director, educator*
Corwin, Norman *scriptwriter, film producer, film director*
Gilroy, Tony *scriptwriter, film director*
Kaplan, Nadia *writer*
Koepp, David *screenwriter*
Manelli, Donald Dean *scriptwriter, film and television producer*
Patrick, Robert *playwright*
Shagan, Steve *scriptwriter, film producer*

Mendocino
Feehan, Christine *writer*

Menlo Park
Heller, Esther A. *writer, educator*

Mill Valley
Coulter, Catherine (Jean Catherine Coulter Pogany) *writer*

Newport Beach
Koontz, Dean Ray *writer*
Wentworth, Diana von Welanetz *author*

North Hollywood
Campos, Luis *puzzle writer*

Northridge
Boberg, Dorothy Kurth *author*

Norwalk
Kouns, Alan Terry *writer, consultant*

Oakland
Foley, Jack (John Wayne Harold Foley) *poet, writer, editor-in-chief*
Haiman, Franklyn Saul *writer, communications educator*
Schacht, Henry Mevis *writer, consultant*

Ontario
Kloepfer, Marguerite Fonnesbeck *writer*

Palm Springs
Nelson, K. Bonita *literary agent*
Wouk, Herman *writer*

Pasadena
Brogden-Stirbl, Shona Marie *writer, researcher*

Penngrove
Haslam, Gerald William *writer, educator*

Petaluma
Pronzini, Bill John (William Pronzini) *writer*
Spiegelman, Art *writer, cartoonist*

Playa Del Rey
McNeill, Daniel Richard *writer*

Pomona
Mezey, Robert *poet*

Rancho Santa Fe
Byrd, Betty Rantze *writer*

Rancho Santa Margarita
Shusterman, Neal Douglas *writer, scriptwriter*

Riverside
Minot, Stephen *writer*

Ross
Godwin, Sara *writer*

San Diego
Skwara, Erich Wolfgang *writer, poet, critic, literature educator*

San Francisco
Alyesh, Jason R. *writer*
Cohn, Kathleen Mandry *writer*
Eggers, Dave *fiction writer, magazine editor*
Gold, Herbert *author*
Rivlin, Gary *writer, reporter*
Rusher, William Allen *writer, commentator, columnist*
Sachs, Marilyn Stickle *writer, editor, educator*
Saunders, Sally Love *poet, educator*

San Jose
Fitzgerald, Timothy Kevin *writer, political organizer*
Loventhal, Milton *writer, playwright, lyricist*

San Luis Rey
Williams, Elizabeth Yahn *poet, writer, educator, lawyer*

San Marino
Sherwood, Midge *writer*

San Rafael
Hart, John *writer*
Turner, William Weyand *writer*

Santa Barbara
Behrens, June Adelle *writer*
Ramsay, William Charles *writer, composer*

Santa Clara
Kalinovsky, Tatiana *writer*
Simmons, Janet Bryant *writer, publishing executive*

Santa Monica
Scott, Jill *poet, musician*

Stanford
Djerassi, Carl *writer, retired chemistry professor*
Steele, Shelby *writer, educator*
Wolff, Tobias (Tobias Jonathan Ansell Wolff) *writer, English professor*

Studio City
Parish, James Robert *writer, cinema historian*

Van Nuys
Becker, Frawley *writer, dialogue director, location manager*

Venice
Eliot, Alexander *writer*

Vista
Wright, Kirby Michael *writer, editor*

Woodland Hills
Jason, Sonya *writer*

COLORADO

Bayfield
Korns, Leota Elsie *writer, mountain land developer, insurance broker*

Boulder
Coel, Margaret Speas *writer*
Kaye, Evelyn Patricia (Evelyn Patricia Sarson) *author, publisher, travel expert*

Denver
Buckstein, Caryl Sue *writer*
Carlson, Robert Ernest *freelance writer, architect, lecturer*
Corriere, Jules *playwright, theater director*
Kundert, Judy A. *writer and publisher*
MacGregor, George Lescher, Jr. *freelance/self-employed writer*
Nemiro, Beverly Mirium Anderson *author, educator*

Lakewood
Peters, Julie Anne *writer*

Trinidad
Tamez, Lorraine Diane *writer, nurse*

Wheat Ridge
Morriss, Frank *writer, educator*

CONNECTICUT

Bolton
Reyna, Magdalena Bessy *writer*

East Hampton
Tucceri, Clive Knowles *writer, science educator, consultant*

Easton
Maloney, John Joseph *writer*

Greenwich
Ewald, William Bragg, Jr. *writer, consultant*
Hoberman, Mary Ann *author*
Wallach, Magdalena Falkenberg (Carla Wallach) *writer*

Madison
Pauley, Barbara Anne *author, educator*

New Canaan
Fredericks, Jeanne Maria Judson *literary agent*

New Haven
Alexander, Elizabeth *poet, English language educator*
Hayden, Dolores *author, educator*
Phillips, Caryl *writer*
Sommer, Miriam Goldstein (Mimi G. Sommer) *writer, photographer*

Sharon
Lisle, Laurie *author*

Storrs Mansfield
Rimland, Lisa Phillip *writer, composer, lyricist*

Waterford
Commire, Anne *playwright, writer, editor*
Morgan, John Richard *writer, publishing executive*

West Hartford
Calip, Roger *writer, educator*

Weston
Diforio, Robert George *literary agent*
Kilty, Jerome Timothy *playwright, theater director, actor*

Westport
Hotchner, Aaron Edward *author*
Ogintz, Eileen *travel writer*

DELAWARE

Wilmington
Gilmore, Clare Mae *writer*

DISTRICT OF COLUMBIA

Washington
Alperovitz, Gar *author, educator*
Alwood, Edward McQueen *author, journalist, professor*
Arndt, Richard Tallmadge *writer, consultant, cultural administrator*
Atlas, Liane Wiener *writer*
Birnbaum, Norman *writer, humanities educator*
Burnham, David Bright *writer, educator*
Burns, David Mitchell *writer, musician, retired diplomat*
Coulter, Ann Hart *writer, political columnist, lawyer*
Cox, Ana Marie *writer, former political blogger*
Davies, J. Clarence (Terry Davies) *author, consultant*
Dunbar, Leslie Wallace *writer, consultant*
Freeman, Charles W., Jr., (Chas Freeman) *writer, former ambassador*
Furgurson, Ernest Baker, Jr., (Pat Furgurson) *writer*
Gallo, Anthony Ernest *playwright, theatrical artistic director, economist*
Gingrich, Newt (Newton Leroy Gingrich) *writer, former United States Representative from Georgia*
Hiebert, Ray Eldon *writer, educator*
Leamer, Laurence Allen *writer*
Mallon, Thomas *writer*
May, Stephen *writer, federal official, historian*
McGurn, William Joseph *speechwriter, editor*
Merrell, Jesse Howard *writer*
Nash, James Lee *poet, security official*
O'Rourke, P.J. (Patrick Jake O'Rourke) *writer, political satirist, journalist*
Shaw, Russell Burnham *writer, journalist*
Violante, Patricia *translator, language expert, writer, interpreter*
Whittemore, Edward Reed, II, *poet, retired educator*

FLORIDA

Belleair Beach
Fuentes, Martha Ayers *playwright*

Boca Raton
Keyes, Daniel *author*

Bradenton
Blanchard, Leonard Albert *writer, consultant, educator*

Cape Coral
Hopkins, Lee Bennett *writer, educator*

Coral Gables
Clay, Cynthia Joyce *writer, editor-in-chief*

Eustis
Chorosinski, Eugene Conrad *writer, poet, author*

Fort Lauderdale
Schneider, Ursula Wilfriede *author*

Gainesville
Carlson, David Edward *jounalism educator, journalist, consultant*

Hallandale Beach
Geller, Bunny Zelda *poet, writer, publisher, sculptor, artist*

Hobe Sound
Houser, Constance W. (Connie Houser) *writer, artist*

Key Biscayne
Cardozo, Arlene Rossen *writer*

Key West
Mathews, Harry Burchell *poet, writer, educator*

Longboat Key
Hazan, Marcella Maddalena *writer, educator, consultant*

Miami
Alperin, Stanley I. *writer, editor, consultant*
Goodman-Milone, Constance B. (Connie Goodman-Milone) *writer*
Meltzer, Brad *writer*

Naples
Capelle-Frank, Jacqueline Aimee *writer*
Mills, Dorothy Jane (Dorothy Z. Seymour, Dorothy Seymour Mills) *writer, editor, consultant*

Neptune Beach
Chambers, Ruth Coe *writer*

Orlando
Comfort, Iris Tracy *writer*

Palm Beach
Kay, Marcia Chellis *writer*

Panama City
Schafer, John Stephen *poet*

Placida
McClister, Michael *writer*

Port Orange
Mc Collister, John Charles *writer, minister, educator*

Saint Petersburg
Carlson, Jeannie Ann *writer*
Mikals-Adachi, Eileen B. *translator, educator*

Sarasota
Jones, Sally Daviess Pickrell *writer*
North, Marjorie Mary *writer*
Stevens, Elisabeth Goss (Mrs. Robert Schleussner Jr.) *writer, graphic artist*
Weeks, Albert Loren *writer, educator, journalist*

Tallahassee
Fielding, Raymond Edwin *writer, communications educator*
Johnson, Margaret Anderson *writer, publishing and agricultural products executive*

Venice
Harlow, Joan Beverley Hiatt (Joan Hiatt Harlow) *writer*

West Palm Beach
Bergmann, Arthur M. *writer, retired journalist, retired county official*
Passy, Charles *writer*

Winter Park
Rooks, Linda *writer*

GEORGIA

Atlanta
Rushdie, Sir Salman (Ahmed Salman Rushdie) *writer, educator*

Barnesville
Freeman, Angelia Brown *poet*

Carrollton
Williams, Mary Eleanor Nicole *retired writer*

Pine Mountain
Bishop, Michael *writer*

Saint Marys
Berry, Stephen L. (Steve Berry) *writer, lawyer*

Savannah
Coffey, Thomas Francis, Jr. *retired writer*
Thomas, Dwight Rembert *writer*

HAWAII

Ewa Beach
Croddy, Eric *translator*

Honolulu
Halloran, Richard Colby *writer, reporter, communications executive, editor*
Tjarks, Mark Damon *playwright, literature and language professor*

IDAHO

Hailey
Dolas, Evelyn Ann *poet, musician*

ILLINOIS

Barrington
Verschoor, Curtis Carl *author, consultant*

Belleville
Pounds, Regina Dorothea *writer*

Champaign
Ruggles, D. Fairchild *writer*
Watson, Jessica Lewis *writer*

Chicago
Bryan, Ashley F. *children's book author, illustrator*
Camper, John Jacob *writer, academic administrator*
Crane, R.H. *poet*
Hallinan, Joseph Thomas *writer*
Madsen, Dorothy Louise (Meg) *writer*
McKinney, Megan *writer*
Melnick, Jane Fisher *writer, educator, photographer*
Plotnik, Arthur *writer, columnist*
Turow, Scott F. *writer, lawyer*

Evanston
Gibbons, Reginald *poet, literature and language professor*
Gibbons, William Reginald, Jr. *poet, writer, translator, editor*
Kertész, Imre *writer*

Highland Park
Greenblatt, Miriam *writer, editor, educator*

Northfield
Mamet, David Alan *playwright, scriptwriter*

Oak Lawn
Laird, Jean Elouise Rydeski (Mrs. Jack E. Laird) *author, adult education educator*

Oakland
Eriksen, Barbara Ann *writer, researcher*

Ottawa
Ballowe, James *writer, educator*

Palatine
Pohl, Frederik *freelance/self-employed writer*

Peoria Heights
Grebner, Bernice Prill *author, astrological counselor*

Rockford
Kampfe, Doris Elaine *storyteller, folk artist, poet*

Roscoe
Sears, Donna Mae *writer, illustrator*

South Barrington
Kissane, Sharon Florence *writer, consultant, educator*

Stoy
Rhoten, Kenneth Dale *writer*

University Park
Alozie, Emmanuel C. *writer, educator*

Urbana
Lieberman, Laurence *poet, educator*

Wilmette
Miripol, Jerilyn Elise *poet, writer, writing therapist*

INDIANA

Chesterton
Petrakis, Harry Mark *author*

Elkhart
Eddy, Darlene Mathis *poet, educator*

Frankfort
Borland, Kathryn Kilby *writer*

Muncie
Thornbro, William Graden *writer*

IOWA

Cedar Falls
Skaine, Rosemarie Keller *writer, publisher, consultant*

Council Bluffs
Moeller, James Charles *writer, educator*

Des Moines
Hunter, Linda Mason *author*

Iowa City
Bell, Marvin Hartley *poet, language educator*
Johnson, Nicholas *writer, lawyer, educator*
Merrill, Christopher Lyall *writer*

Sioux City
Hassenger, James Michael *writer, retired small business owner*

Windsor Heights
Beadel, Stephen Jay *author*

KANSAS

Leawood
Garwood, Julie *writer*

Olathe
Kamberg, Mary-Lane *writer, journalist*

Overland Park
Gray, Thomas Alva, Jr. *writer, retired protective services official*

Pittsburg
Beer, Pamela Jill Porr *writer, retired vocational school educator*

KENTUCKY

Georgetown
Arnson Svarlien, Diane *translator, educator*

Lexington
Johnson, Jane Penelope *freelance/self-employed writer*

LOUISIANA

Baton Rouge
Madden, David *author*
Mueller, Lisel *writer, poet*

New Orleans
Pizer, Donald *author, educator*

Shreveport
Kendrick, Rhonda Lynn *poet, small business owner*

MAINE

Allagash
Hafford, Faye O'Leary *writer*

Bangor
King, Stephen Edwin *writer, scriptwriter*

Brunswick
Peacher, Georgiana Melicent *poet, educator*

Gardiner
Dunbar, Robert Everett *writer, educator*

Milbridge
Enslin, Theodore Vernon *poet*

Portland
Manuel, Peter Jay *poet, singer/songwriter, dramatist, language professor, librettist*

Scarborough
Doermann, Humphrey *writer, consultant*

Waterville
Easton, Thomas Atwood *writer, educator*

MARYLAND

Annapolis
Miller, John Grider *writer*

Baltimore
Epstein, Daniel Mark *poet, dramatist, biographer*
Fisher, Alan Hall *guidebook writer*
Grossman, Allen Richard *poet, educator*
Schultheis, Patricia Ann *writer, editor*

Bethesda
Josephson, Julian *writer*
Kingsley, Mary Lee *writer, researcher, consultant, retired marketing executive*
Schaeffer, Charles Perry *writer, editor*

Chevy Chase
Bacon, Donald Conrad *writer, editor*

Fort Washington
Cameron, Rita Giovannetti *writer, publishing executive*

Frederick
Randall, Frances *technical writer*

Gaithersburg
Naylor, Phyllis Reynolds *writer*

Owings Mills
Cymet, Tyler Childs *medical writer, researcher*

Rockville
Kruger, Mollee Coppel *writer*
Madle, Robert Albert *writer*

Saint Marys City
Clifton, Lucille Thelma *author*

Salisbury
Booker, Betty Mae *poet*

Silver Spring
Whitten, Leslie Hunter, Jr. *writer, poet, reporter*

West Bethesda
Vogelgesang, Sandra Louise *writer, consultant, former ambassador*

MASSACHUSETTS

Amherst
Black, Holly *writer*

Boston
Angelou, Maya (Marguerite Annie Johnson) *writer, actress*
Kaptchuk, Ted J. *writer, acupuncturist*
Khan, Lurey *writer*
Lahiri, Jhumpa (Nilanjana Sudeshna) *writer*
Lowry, Lois (Lois Hammersberg) *writer*
Sheff, David *writer, editor*
Strothman, Wendy Jo *literary agent*
Terrill, Ross Gladwin *writer, educator*
Wiesel, Elie *writer, educator*

Brighton
Valianti, Deborah L. *playwright*

Byfield
Kozol, Jonathan *writer*

Cambridge
Díaz, Junot *writer, educator*
DiCamillo, Kate *writer*
Heaney, Seamus Justin *poet, educator*
Hiaasen, Carl *writer, reporter*
Hughes, Libby *writer*
Kaplan, Justin *author*
Yergin, Daniel Howard *writer, consultant*

Chestnut Hill
Valette, Jean Paul *writer*

Cohasset
Whipple, Jacqueline Conant *writer, media specialist*

Cummington
Wilbur, Richard Purdy *writer, educator*

Hatfield
Yolen, Jane *writer*

Lexington
Kennedy, X.J. (Joseph Kennedy) *writer*

North Chelmsford
Erkkila-Ricker, Barbara Howell *writer, photographer*

Northampton
Kherdian, David *writer*
Newman, Lesléa *writer*

Provincetown
Oliver, Mary *poet*

Roslindale
Spada, James *writer, photographer, publishing executive*

Southborough
Mylotte, John Arnold *writer, educator*

Taunton
Ricciardi, Cynthia Booth *writer, researcher, educator*

Wellesley
Jacobs, Ruth Harriet *poet, playwright, sociologist, gerontologist*

Wellfleet
Piercy, Marge *poet, writer*

West Roxbury
Ellenbogen, George *poet, educator*

Williamstown
Burns, Joan Simpson *writer, editor*

Worthington
Bagg, Robert Ely *poet, educator, translator*

MICHIGAN

Ann Arbor
Gregerson, Linda Karen *poet, language educator, critic*
Lach, Alma Elizabeth *food and cooking writer, consultant*

Belleville
Schaefer, James Theodore *writer, editor, educator*

Charlotte
Coirolo, Christina *writer, author representative*

Detroit
Madgett, Naomi Long *poet, editor, publisher, educator*

East Lansing
Perrin, Robert *writer, consultant*
Wakoski, Diane *poet, educator*

Grand Rapids
Rumney, Helene Vosburgh *retired poet, peace activist*

Holland
Nieuwsma, Milton John *writer, journalist*

Hudson
Kauffman, Janet *writer*

Idlewild
Wooley, Geraldine Hamilton *poet, writer*

Kalamazoo
Light, Christopher Upjohn *freelance/self-employed writer, photographer*

Mount Pleasant
Smallwood, Carol *writer*

Okemos
Klunzinger, Thomas Edward *writer, actor, film director*

Republic
Wixtrom, Donald Joseph *translator*

Sodus
Handy, Virginia Mae *writer*

MINNESOTA

Minneapolis
Baldwin, Trista *playwright*
Erdrich, Louise *writer, poet*
Hampl, Patricia *writer, educator*
Korotkin, Fred *writer, philatelist*
Miller, Alan M. *writer, educator, television host*
Pate, Alexs Delaney *writer, educator*
Tatlock, Ann *writer*

Moorhead
Zinober, Richard Neil *playwright, educator*

Saint Paul
Keillor, Garrison (Gary Edward Keillor) *writer, radio personality*
Swanson, Susan Marie *children's book author, educator*

MISSISSIPPI

Jackson
Redmon, Cynthia Ann *poet, songwriter*

MISSOURI

Columbia
McDaniel, Sue Powell *writer*

Kansas City
Kirch, Donald Allen *writer, composer*
Kofler, Silvia Maria *writer, educator*

Maryville
Tennihill, Sally Kay *writer, music educator*

Saint Charles
Hickenlooper, George Loening, Sr. *playwright, educator*

Saint Louis
Burgin, Richard Weston *writer, educator, editor*
Gass, William H. *writer, educator*
Lubbock, James Edward *retired writer, photographer, media consultant*
Lutz, John Thomas *author*
Miller, Judith Braffman *writer*
Phillips, Carl *poet, educator*
Schlafly, Phyllis Stewart *writer*
Swinson, Sara Hope *writer, artist*

MONTANA

Bigfork
Wetzel, Betty Preat *writer*

Bonner
Smith, Annick *writer*

NEBRASKA

Lincoln
Magorian, James *poet, writer*

NEVADA

Cold Springs
Turner VanLydegraf, Claudia Beth *writer, researcher*

Las Vegas
Gardner, Grace Joely *writer, psychologist, consultant*

Reno
Scrimgeour, Gary James *writer, educator*

NEW HAMPSHIRE

Durham
Ford, Daniel (Daniel Francis Ford) *writer*

Etna
Picoult, Jodi Lynn *writer*

New London
Gepfert, Alan Harry *copywriter, finance educator, sculptor, management consultant*

Wentworth
Bixby, Roland Maurice *writer, adult education educator*

NEW JERSEY

Bergenfield
Davidson, Marilyn Copeland *writer, musician, educator*

Cape May Court House
Cohen, Daniel Edward *writer*
Cohen, Susan Lois *writer*

Elizabeth
Lucco, James Perry *writer*

Englewood
Albee, Gloria *playwright*

Jackson
Heck, Roberta M. *poet, writer*

Lebanon
Barto, Susan Carol *writer*

Long Branch
Lagowski, Barbara Jean *writer, editor*
Stewart, Georgiana Liccione *writer*

Maplewood
Lally, Michael David *writer, actor*

Martinsville
Baxter, Nancy *medical writer*

Medford
Henderson, Rita Elizabeth *literary agent, journalist*

Montclair
Delgado, Ramon Louis *theater educator, author, director, playwright, lyricist*

New Brunswick
Jenkins, Alyce Mitchem *writer, educator*

Newark
Rittenhouse, Michele Raper *playwright, theater educator*

Princeton
Cheiten, Marvin Harold *playwright, manufacturing executive*
Muldoon, Paul B. *poet, educator*
Rampersad, Arnold *writer, literature educator*

Princeton Junction
Norback, Craig Thomas *writer*

Teaneck
Wallmann, Jeffrey Miner *author*

Titusville
Christopher, Klim *writer*

Toms River
Tamm, Jayanti *writer*

Trenton
Obed, Leonora Rita Villegas *writer, educator*

Whiting
Willis, Ben *writer, artist*

NEW MEXICO

Albuquerque
Anaya, Rudolfo *writer, educator*
Gahala, Estella Marie *writer, consultant*
Harden, Neva Ninette *writer, consultant*
Priem, Richard Gregory *writer, executive*

Las Vegas
Howard, Leland William *writer*

Los Alamos
Eads, Damian R. *open source software author*

Santa Fe
Cooper, Sandra Lenore *writer, artist*
Momaday, Navarre Scott *writer, poet*
Mora, Pat *writer, speech professional*

NEW YORK

Albany
Kennedy, William Joseph *novelist, educator*

Annandale On Hudson
Achebe, Chinua *writer, humanities educator*
Sourian, Peter *writer, educator*

Ardsley
Silman, Roberta Karpel *fiction writer, critic*

Ardsley On Hudson
Lapine, Missy Chase *writer, chef*

Bedford Hills
Lustbader, Eric Van *writer*

Brightwaters
North, E(dward) Lee *retired writer, former aerospace company professional*

Bronx
Kornfeld, Robert Jonathan *playwright, photographer*
Shapiro, David Joel *poet, art critic, educator*

Bronxville
Rosenthal, Lucy Gabrielle *writer, editor, educator*

Brooklyn
Bradshaw, Thomas *playwright, educator*
Chambers, William Edmond *writer*
Donaldson, Stephen Reeder *author*
Gioseffi, Daniela *poet, writer, playwright, critic*
Leary, Gordon *playwright, lyricist*
Pearlman, Ellen Lois *writer, filmmaker, critic, curator*
Reynolds, Nancy Remick *writer, researcher, editor*
Rogers, Michael Alan *writer*

Buffalo
Macomber, Debbie *writer*

Cairo
Ludwig, Laura Lonshein *poet*

Catskill
Philp, Richard Nilson *writer, editor, journalist, historian*

Chappaqua
George, Jean Craighead *author, illustrator*

Copake
Johnson, Paul Edward *poet, writer*

Croton Falls
Jakes, John *author*

Dobbs Ferry
Pesetsky, Bette *writer, educator*

Flushing
Goldsmith, Howard *writer, consultant*
Zinnes, Harriet Fich *poet, fiction writer, retired English educator, literary and art critic*

Forest Hills
Henley, Arthur *writer, editor*

Geneseo
Kelly, David Michael *poet, creative writing educator*

Germantown
Linney, Romulus *author, educator*

Great Neck
Hurwitz, Johanna (Johanna Frank) *writer*

Greenfield Center
Bruchac, Joseph *writer, storyteller*

Hamilton
Berlind, Bruce Peter *poet, educator*

Henrietta
Byfield, Bert A. *conservative humanitarian novelist*

Interlaken
Bleiler, Everett Franklin *writer, publishing company executive*

Katonah
McCauley, Gerard Francis *literary agent*

New Rochelle
Branch, William Blackwell *playwright, producer, professor*
Saperstein, David *writer, film director, television personality*
Sommer, Jay *writer, literature and language educator*

New York
Adichie, Chimamanda Ngozi (Amanda N.) *writer*
Albee, Edward Franklin *playwright, writer*
Alessandrini, Gerard *playwright, theater director*
Ashdown, Marie Matranga *writer, educator, cultural organization administrator*
Ashton, Dore *writer, educator*
Atwood, Margaret Eleanor *writer*
Auster, Paul *writer*
Baldacci, David *writer*
Balogh, Mary *writer*
Barnett, LaShonda Katrice *writer, educator*
Bauer, Marion Dane *writer*
Beattie, Ann *writer, educator*
Begley, Louis *writer, lawyer*
Beim, Norman *playwright, actor, theater director, writer*
Bell, Hilari *writer, former librarian*
Bell, Theodore Augustus, III, (Ted Bell) *writer, former advertising executive*
Benioff, David *writer*
Bentley, Eric *writer, playwright, educator*
Berendt, John Lawrence *writer, editor*
Berg, A(ndrew) Scott *writer*
Berger, Thomas Louis *author*
Berman, Claire Gallant *freelance/self-employed writer*
Birstein, Ann *writer, educator*
Block, Francesca Lia *writer*
Blum, Howard Robert *writer*
Blume, Judy *author*
Bogen, Nancy *writer, English educator*
Box, C.J. *writer*
Bradbury, Ray Douglas *writer*
Bradford, Barbara Taylor *writer, journalist*
Branch, Taylor *writer*
Braudy, Susan Orr *writer*
Briggs, Patricia *writer*
Broad, William J. *science writer*
Brooks, Geraldine *writer, reporter, news correspondent*
Brown, Dan *writer*
Brown, Rita Mae *writer*
Bujold, Lois McMaster *writer*
Burroughs, Augusten (Christopher Robison) *writer*
Callo, Joseph Francis *writer*
Canin, Ethan *writer*
Carey, Peter Philip *writer, educator*
Castro, Jan Garden *writer, art educator, consultant*
Charbonnet, Gabrielle *writer*
Cherryh, C. J. *writer*
Child, Lee (Jim Grant) *writer*
Choi, Susan *writer*
Christensen, Kate *writer*
Cisneros, Sandra *poet, short story writer, essayist*
Cleary, Beverly Atlee (Mrs. Clarence T. Cleary) *writer*
Coben, Harlan *writer*
Collins, Jackie (Jacqueline Jill Collins) *writer*
Connelly, Michael *writer*
Conniff, Richard *writer*
Conroy, Pat (Donald Patrick Conroy) *writer*
Cornwell, Patricia Daniels *writer*
Crouch, Stanley *writer, musician*
Curry, Jane Louise *writer*
Curtis, Christopher Paul *writer*
Czajkowski, Jim (James Rollins, James Clemens) *writer*
Dailey, Janet *writer*
Danto, Arthur Coleman *writer, philosopher, critic*
Deaver, Jeffery (William Jefferies) *writer, former lawyer*
Decter, Midge *writer*
Desai, Kiran *writer*
Deveraux, Jude *writer*
Diamonstein-Spielvogel, Barbaralee *writer*
Didion, Joan *writer*
Dobell, Byron Maxwell *magazine consultant*
Doctorow, E.L. (Edgar Lawrence Doctorow) *writer, English educator*
Doty, Mark *poet*
Dowling, Danielle *writer*
Dubus, Andre III *writer*
Duffy, James Henry *writer, retired lawyer*
Earling, Debra Magpie *writer, educator*

Eckert, Allan Wesley *writer*
Eichenwald, Kurt *writer*
Ellroy, James *writer*
Evanovich, Janet *writer*
Ferrigno, Robert *writer*
Fleischman, Albert Sidney (Sid Fleischman) *writer*
Flory, Marjorie Anne *writer, editor*
Fowler, Karen Joy *writer*
Fox, Paula *writer*
Frank, Elizabeth *writer, educator*
Frazier, Charles Robinson *writer*
French, Patrick *writer*
Friedman, B(ernard) H(arper) *writer*
Gaiman, Neil Richard *novelist, comics writer, screenwriter*
Gelb, Leslie Howard *writer, lecturer, consultant*
George, (Susan) Elizabeth *writer*
Ghosh, Amitav *writer, educator*
Giblin, James Cross *writer, publishing executive*
Giffin, Emily Fisk *writer*
Gilbert, Elizabeth *writer*
Gladwell, Malcolm *writer*
Goddard, Donald Letcher *writer, editor*
Goldman, Peter Louis *writer*
Golomb, Susan L. *literary agent*
Goodman, George Jerome Waldo (Adam Smith) *writer, television journalist, consultant*
Gordon, Mary Catherine *writer*
Goulden, Joseph Chesley *author*
Grafton, Sue Taylor *writer*
Grau, Shirley Ann (Mrs. James Kern Feibleman) *writer*
Green, Jane (Jane Green Warburg) *writer*
Greenwald, Sheila Ellen *writer, illustrator*
Gregory, Philippa *writer*
Grisham, John (John Ray Grisham) *writer*
Grogan, John *writer, journalist*
Hackbarth, Steven Lyle *writer, educator, audio-visual specialist*
Hague, William Edward *writer*
Hamilton, Laurell Kaye *writer*
Harris, Charlaine *writer*
Harrison, Jordan *playwright*
Harrison, Kim *writer*
Haynes, Todd *film writer, producer, director*
Hesse, Karen (Karen Sue Hesse) *writer, educator*
Hjortsberg, William Reinhold *writer*
Hosseini, Khaled *writer*
Hotz, Robert Lee *writer, editor*
Howard, Richard (Joseph) *poet, literary translator*
Hughes, Jeff *playwright, lyricist*
Iglauer, Edith *writer, reporter*
Iles, Greg *writer*
Jannuzzi, Luigi *playwright, educator*
Jhabvala, Ruth Prawer *writer*
Johansen, Iris *writer*
Jones, Diana Wynne *writer*
Jong, Erica Mann *writer*
Kauffmann, Stanley Jules *author*
Kaufman, Bel *author, educator*
Keene, Donald *writer, translator, language educator*
Kehret, Peg *writer*
Kellerman, Faye Marilyn *writer*
Kellerman, Jonathan Seth *writer, pediatric psychologist, educator*
Kennedy, Adrienne Lita *playwright*
Kenyon, Sherrilyn *writer*
Kinney, Jeff *writer*
Klein, T(heodore) E(ibon) D(onald) *writer*
Kleinzahler, August *poet*
Koch, Stephen Bayard *writer, language educator*
Kostelanetz, Richard *writer, media artist*
Kotlowitz, Robert *writer, editor*
Krantz, Judith Tarcher *novelist*
Kumin, Maxine Winokur *poet, writer*
LaBute, Neil *scriptwriter, director, playwright*
Lamb, Wally *writer*
Lamm, Donald Stephen *literary agent*
Lapine, James Elliot *playwright, director*
Laurents, Arthur *playwright, theater director*
Lawson, Nigella *cookbook writer, celebrity chef*
Lee, Kate *literary agent*
Lehane, Dennis *writer*
Levine, Gail Carson *writer*
Levoy, Myron *author*
Lewis, Michael *writer, journalist*
Lindsey, (Helen) Johanna *writer*
Lorch, Maristella De Panizza *writer, educator*
Luce, William *playwright, librettist, screenwriter*
Lurie, Alison *writer*
Macer-Story, Eugenia Ann *writer*
Maguire, Gregory *writer*
Mason, Bobbie Ann *writer*
Mazzucelli, Colette Grace Celia *author, educator*
McCarthy, Cormac (Charles Joseph McCarthy) *writer*
McCullough, David *writer*
McDermott, Alice *writer*
McInerney, Jay *writer*
McMillan, Terry L. *writer, educator*
McMurtry, Larry Jeff *writer*
McNally, Terrence *playwright*
McQuown, Judith Hershkowitz *writer, consultant, financial planner*
Meehan, Thomas *writer*
Meltzer, Milton *author*
Menza, Claudia Marcella *literary agent*
Meyer, Stephenie *writer*
Milch, David *screenwriter, producer*
Monk Kidd, Sue *writer*
Mooney, Richard Emerson *writer*
Moore, Christopher *writer*
Mosley, Walter Ellis *writer*
Mullaney, Craig Michael *writer*
Munro, Alice Ann *writer*
Navarra, Tova *writer, artist*
Neier, Aryeh *author, human rights organization administrator*
Nicol, Dominik *writer, photographer*
Nixon, Agnes Eckhardt *television writer, producer*
North, Charles Laurence *poet, educator*
Nottage, Lynn *playwright*
Oates, Joyce Carol *writer, educator*
O'Doherty, Brian *writer*
O'Donnell, Mark Patrick *writer, drama educator*
Offit, Sidney *writer, educator*
O'Neill, Joseph *writer*
Palahniuk, Chuck (Charles Michael Palahniuk) *writer, journalist*
Pall, Ellen Jane *writer*
Park, Barbara Lynne *writer*
Parker, Pippin *playwright, theater director*
Parker, Robert Brown *writer*
Paterson, Katherine Womeldorf *writer*
Patterson, James Brendan, Jr. *writer*
Pérez-Rivera, Francisco (Frank Rivera) *writer*
Perry, Thomas Edmund *novelist, television screenwriter, producer*
Piccirilli, Thomas Edward *writer*
Pool, Mary Jane *writer, editor*
Powell, Julie *writer*
Price, Richard *writer*
Pynchon, Thomas Ruggles, Jr. *writer*
Reich, Christopher *writer*
Rendell, Ruth Barbara (Barbara Vine) *writer*
Revkin, Andrew C. *writer, reporter*
Rhodes, Richard Lee *writer*
Rice, Luanne *writer*
Rich, Adrienne *poet*
Roberts, Nora (Eleanor Marie Robertson) *writer*
Robinson, Marilynne *writer*
Robinson, Roxana Barry *writer, art historian*
Rothenberg, Jerome *writer, literature educator*
Rumaker, Michael *writer, language educator*
Sachar, Louis *writer*
Salinger, J.D. (Jerome David Salinger) *author*
Salter, James *writer*
Salter, Mary Jo *poet*
Sandford, John (John Roswell Camp) *writer, journalist*
Sargent, Pamela *writer*
Schisgal, Murray *playwright*
Schultz, Philip *poet*
Scieszka, Jon *children's author*
Sedaris, David Raymond *writer, comedian*
Segal, Lore *writer*
Shawn, Wallace *playwright, actor*
Sheehan, Susan *writer*
Shmailo, Larissa *poet, director*
Shreve, Anita *writer*
Shulevitz, Uri *writer, illustrator*
Silbersack, John Walter *literary agent*
Silva, Daniel Joseph *writer*
Sittenfeld, Curtis *writer*
Smith, Ian K. *writer, columnist, physician*
Smith, Warren Allen *writer, director, columnist*
Sparks, Nicholas *writer*
Steel, Danielle (Danielle Fernande Dominique Schuelein-Steel) *author*
Stephenson, Neal Town *writer*
Stine, R. L. (Robert Lawrence Stine) *children's book author*
Strout, Elizabeth *writer, educator*
Sypher, Francis J. *writer, editor, educator*
Talese, Gay *writer, former journalist*
Tan, Amy Ruth *writer*
Taylor, Mildred D. *author*
Thor, Brad *writer*
Tomkins, Calvin *writer*
Toobin, Jeffrey Ross *writer, legal analyst*
Trillin, Calvin *writer, journalist*
Urban, Amanda (Binky Urban) *literary agent*
Walker, Alice Malsenior *writer*
Ward, Geoffrey Champion *writer, editor*
Washburn, Anne *playwright*
Wasserman, Steve *literary agent*
Weiner, Jennifer Agnes *writer*
Weiss, Allen S. *writer, educator, playwright*
Wender, Phyllis Bellows *literary agent*
Weschler, Lawrence Michael *writer, journalist*
West, Paul Noden *writer, playwright*
Wolf, Naomi *writer*
Wolfe, Tom (Thomas Kennerly Wolfe Jr.) *writer, journalist*
Wolff, Virginia Euwer *writer*
Woods, Stuart *writer*
Wren, Gayden *playwright, theater director*
wVollmann, William Tanner *writer*
Yaffe, James *writer*

Nyack
Hendin, David Bruce *literary agent, writer, numismatist, educator*

Painted Post
Kirk, Connie Ann *writer*

Pawling
Lester, Helen Doughty *writer*

Poughkeepsie
Willard, Nancy Margaret *writer, educator*

Purchase
Rachlin, Harvey Brant *writer*

Rhinebeck
Sloane, Beverly LeBov *writer, instructor, consultant*

Riverhead
Banfelder, Robert Joseph *award-winning novelist, lecturer and outdoors writer*

Rochester
Rothberg, Abraham *writer*

Roslyn Heights
Faber, Adele *author, educator*

Rye
Hurwitz, Sol *writer, consultant*
Ketchum, William Clarence *author, educator*

Scarsdale
Topping, Seymour *writer*

Shady
Malkine-Falvey, Fern Sylvie *writer, journalist, painter*

Staten Island
Foster, Paul *playwright*
Porter, Darwin Fred *writer*

Syracuse
Luft, Eric v.d. *writer, educator, publisher*
Staples, Heidi L *poet, writer*

Wainscott
Herzog, Arthur III *author*

Warwick
Linnéa, Sharon *writer, playwright*

West Nyack
Pringle, Laurence Patrick *writer*

Woodstock
Godwin, Gail Kathleen *writer*

NORTH CAROLINA

Chapel Hill
Spencer, Elizabeth *writer*

Charlotte
Ethridge, Mark Foster III *writer, publishing executive, consultant*
Finley, Glenna *writer*

Cullowhee
Rash, Ron *writer, educator*

Denver
Gleasner, Diana Cottle *author*

Durham
Vick, Marsha Cook *writer, humanities educator*

Fayetteville
Dandy, Roscoe Greer *author, psychotherapist, educator, retired public health service officer*

Greensboro
Watson, Robert Winthrop *poet*

Greenville
Gilham, Hanna Kaltenbrunner *writer*

Raleigh
Tucker, Helen Welch *writer*

Spindale
Tucker, Tom *science and invention writer, literature and language professor*

Winston Salem
Ehle, John Marsden, Jr. *writer*
Hanes, Frank Borden *writer, former business executive, farmer*

OHIO

Cedarville
Moore, Julie L. *writer, director, poet*

Cincinnati
Birmingham, Stephen *writer*
Craft Davis, Audrey Ellen *writer, educator*

Cleveland
Finn, Robert *writer, educator*
Kovel, Terry Horvitz *writer, antiques authority*

Cleveland Heights
Sandburg, Helga *author*

Dayton
Boice, Martha Hibbert *writer, publishing executive*
Finkelstein, Leo, Jr. *writer, communications executive, director, educator*

Euclid
Adrine-Robinson, Kenyette *writer, educator, poet, artist, photographer, percussionist*

Gambier
MacLeod, Wendy *playwright, performing arts educator*

Glendale
Strom, Kristina Chase *writer, consultant*

Kent
Wakabayashi, Judy *translator, educator*

Middletown
McClain, Michael H. *writer*

Napoleon
Meekison, MaryFran *writer*

Perrysburg
Weaver, Richard L., II, *writer, educator, lecturer*

Willoughby
Guy, Eleanor Bryenton *retired writer*

Worthington
Vladem, Steven Allen *writer, film producer, motivational speaker*

OKLAHOMA

Mustang
Wood, Jean Carol *poet, lyricist*

OREGON

Culver
Siebert, Diane Dolores *author, poet*

Eugene
Wilhelm, Kate (Katy Gertrude) *author*

Portland
Hoffman, Alice *writer*
Larson, Wanda Z. *writer, poet*
McGregor, Michael N. *writer, educator*
Neavoll, George Franklin *writer*
Tuska, Jon *writer, publishing executive*

PENNSYLVANIA

Boyers
Shiloh, Allen *writer*

Kennett Square
Martin, George (Whitney) *writer*

King Of Prussia
Schumann, Paula M. L. *writer*

Lancaster
Shenk, Lois Elaine Landis *writer*
Taylor, Ann *writer, educator*

Milford
Le Guin, Ursula Kroeber *writer*

Oxford
Bowden, Mark Robert *writer*

Philadelphia
Bernstein, Charles *poet, writer, educator*
Fuller, Charles H, Jr. *playwright*
Givens, Janet Eaton *writer*
Kinsella, Thomas *poet*
Owens, Rochelle *poet, playwright*
Paglia, Camille *writer, humanities educator*
Wallace, Emily Mitchell *writer, editor, educator*

Pittsburgh
Favorini, Attilio Anthony *playwright, educator*

Pottstown
Hylton, Thomas James *author*

State College
Gillan, Garth Jackson *writer, retired philosopher, deacon, psychoanalytic psychotherapist*

Wayne
Faust, Christa *writer*

RHODE ISLAND

Charlestown
Huetteman, Susan Bice *writer*

Providence
López-Morillas, Frances (Mapes) *translator*
Steinbach, Meredith Lynn *writer, educator*
Wright, Carolyn D. *poet, literature and language professor*

SOUTH CAROLINA

Aiken
Smith, Gregory White *writer*

Anderson
Kline, George Louis *writer, translator, retired philosophy and literature educator*

Hilton Head Island
Reed, Frances Boogher *writer, actress*

Lexington
Wilkins, Robert Pearce *writer, lawyer*

Rock Hill
Bristow, Robert O'Neil *writer, educator*

Summerville
Reisman, Rosemary Moody Canfield *writer, humanities educator*

TENNESSEE

Knoxville
Bell, Linda R. *writer, photographer*
Thomas, Joyce Carol *author, educator*

Loudon
Randall, Marilyn Mae *writer*

Madison
Campbell, Chester Douglas *writer*

Millington
Thomas-Harris, Yvonne Anita *writer, poet*

Nashville
Bird, Caroline *author*
Pearson, Sela *poet, speaker*
Wisdom, Emma Nell Jackson *writer, educator*

Sevierville
Koff, Shirley Irene *writer*

TEXAS

Amarillo
Mojtabai, Ann Grace *author, educator*

Arlington
Brown, Sandra *writer*

Austin
Barnes, Thomas Joseph *writer*
Beazley, Hamilton *writer, educator*
Friedman, Kinky (Richard S. Friedman) *writer, musician*
Neeld, Elizabeth Harper *writer, educational business company owner*

Boerne
Price, John Randolph *writer*

Canyon
Roper, Beryl Cain *writer, retired library director, publishing executive*

Cedar Hill
Stowers, Carlton Eugene *writer*

Chireno
Mayhar, Ardath Frances (Frank Cannon, John Killdeer, Frances Hurst) *writer*

Dale
LittleDog, Pat *writer*

Dallas
Bartlett, Richard Chalkley *writer, conservationist*
Dee, Ronda *poet, photographer, small business owner, journalist*
Gillett, Grover *author*
Phillips, Betty Lou (Elizabeth Louise Phillips) *writer, interior designer*

Elgin
Jordan, Charlene Hanson *writer*

Georgetown
Shelby, Roselle Price *writer, retired special education educator*

Houston
Mallia, Marianne *medical writer*
McPhail, JoAnn Winstead *writer*
Pete, Eric E. *writer, claims representative*

Mansfield
Parnell, Charles L. *speechwriter*

Plano
Gallardo, Henrietta Castellanos *writer*

San Antonio
Fehrenbach, T.R. (Theodore Reed Fehrenbach) *writer*

UTAH

Cedar City
Modesitt, Leland Exton, Jr., (L.E. Modesitt Jr.) *writer, poet, consultant*

Logan
Hruby, George Geoffrey *writer, educator*

Salt Lake City
Lee, Blaine Nelson *consultant, life coach, writer, author*
Wingate, Martha Anne *writer, publishing executive*
Wingate, Thomas Russell *writer*

VERMONT

Chester
Coleman, John Royston *writer*

Marlboro
Stevenson, Laura Caroline *writer, educator*

South Royalton
Powers, Thomas Moore *writer*

Wilmington
Reeve, Franklin D. *writer, retired literature professor*

VIRGINIA

Alexandria
Malott, John Raymond *writer, consultant, not-for-profit executive*

Arlington
Timperlake, Edward Thomas *writer*

Ashburn
Boyne, Walter James *writer, retired museum director*

Blacksburg
Giovanni, Nikki (Yolanda Cornelia Giovanni) *poet, educator*

Charlottesville
Casey, John Dudley *writer, language educator*
Dove, Rita Frances *poet, language educator*
McCrimmon, Barbara Smith *writer, librarian*
Wright, Charles Penzel, Jr. *writer, educator*

Clarksville
Worth, Lynn Harris *writer*

Falls Church
Orben, Robert *scriptwriter, writer*
Whitehead, Kenneth Dean *writer, translator, retired federal agency administrator, editor*

Leesburg
Budiansky, Stephen Philip *writer*

Lexington
Stuart, Dabney *poet, language educator*

Mc Lean
Wallace, Barbara Brooks *writer*

Meadowview
Kingsolver, Barbara Ellen *writer*

Portsmouth
Mapp, Alf Johnson, Jr. *writer, historian, educator*

Reston
Smith, Ralph Lee *writer, musician*

Staunton
Warren, Lisa Solod *writer*

Stephenson
Johnson, Eva Maria *retired translator*

Vienna
Olshaker, Mark Bruce *scriptwriter, filmmaker*

Virginia Beach
Foster, Jeanne O'Cain *poet, fine arts educator*

Williamsburg
Smith, William Henry Preston *freelance/self-employed writer, editor, former telecommunications industry executive*
Starnes, Sofia Molina *writer, editor*

WASHINGTON

Bellevue
Olson, Robert William *writer, retired counselor*

Issaquah
Cain, Coleen W. *writer, educator*

Kirkland
Szablya, Helen Mary *writer, language educator*

Nordland
Kramnicz, Rosanne *freelance writer*

Oak Harbor
Lightbourne, Alesa M. *writer, educator, mediator*

Port Townsend
Merwin, William Stanley *poet*

Redmond
Bottenberg, Joyce Harvey *writer, social services administrator*

Seattle
Alexie, Sherman Joseph, Jr. *writer*
Gardiner, John Jacob Zucker *writer, educator, philosopher*
Kunkel, Georgie Bright *freelance writer, retired counselor*
Rule, Ann *writer*
Thomas, Irv *writer, journalist*

Vashon
Cushman, Karen Lipski *writer*

WEST VIRGINIA

Charleston
Mellert, Lucie Anne *writer, photographer*

Teays
Lamb, Carl Vernon *writer, retired engineer*

West Columbia
Fowler, Sandra Lynn *poet*

WISCONSIN

Appleton
Albrecht, Roberta J. *writer*

Brookfield
Schmitz, John J. *writer, educator*

Elkhorn
Dunn, Walter Scott, Jr. *writer, museum director, consultant*

Madison
K-Turkel, Judith Leah Rosenthal (Judi K-Turkel) *writer, editor, publisher*
Riley, Jocelyn Carol *writer, television producer*

Milwaukee
Connelly, Mark *writer, educator*
McGilligan, Patrick Michael *writer, editor*

Racine
Wright, Betty Ren *children's book writer*

Shawano
Mutter, John J., Jr. *writer, researcher*

WYOMING

Laramie
Boresi, Arthur Peter *writer, educator*
Langlois, Walter Gordon *writer, retired literature and language professor*

TERRITORIES OF THE UNITED STATES

GUAM

Mangilao
Strauch, Edward Hugo *writer, retired literature and language professor*

CANADA

BRITISH COLUMBIA

Heriot Bay
Bringhurst, Robert *poet*

Vancouver
Cohen, Leonard (Norman Cohen) *poet, writer, musician*
Tolle, Eckhart *writer*

ONTARIO

Toronto
Moore, Christopher Hugh *writer*
Moritz, A.F. (Albert Frank) *poet, educator*
Peacock, Molly *poet, educator, writer*

QUEBEC

Montreal
Bruemmer, Fred *writer, photographer*

AUSTRALIA

Surry Hills
Marchetta, Melina *writer*

DENMARK

Copenhagen
Rifbjerg, Klaus Thorvald *writer*

ENGLAND

Cambridge
Steiner, George (Francis Steiner) *author, educator*

London
Chevalier, Tracy Rose *writer*
Cleese, John Marwood *writer, comedian*
Cope, Wendy *poet*
Deighton, Len *author*
Fine, Anne *writer*
Fo, Dario *playwright*
Frayn, Michael *playwright*
Galloway, Janice *writer, editor*
Hall, Lee *playwright, screenwriter*
Harris, Thomas *writer*
Harwood, Ronald *screenwriter, playwright*
Hunter Blair, Pauline Clarke *author*
Jacobson, Dan *writer*
James, P(hyllis) D(orothy) (Baroness James of Holland Park of Southwold in County of Suffolk) *author*
Kinsella, Sophie (Madeleine Sophie Wickham) *writer*
Kwei-Armah, Kwame (Ian Roberts) *playwright, actor, singer*
Lessing, Doris (Doris May Tayler) *writer*
McGrath, Patrick *writer*
Ormsby, Eric Linn *writer, educator*
Paton Walsh, Jill *writer*
Pessl, Marisha *writer, artist*
Reza, Yasmina *author, playwright*
Rowling, J.K. (Joanne Kathleen Rowling) *writer*
Sillitoe, Alan *writer*
Smith, Zadie (Sadie Smith) *writer*
Stoppard, Tom (Tomas Straussler) *playwright*

Stevenage
Follett, Kenneth Martin *author*

Whitchurch
Adams, Richard George *writer*

FRANCE

La Tour d Aigues
Xingjian, Gao *writer*

Lacoste
Strauss, Gwen B. *writer, editor*

Paris
Blokh, Alexandre (Jean Blot) *writer*

Saint-Cyr-sous
Aubry, Cecile (Anne-José Bénard) *writer*

Strasbourg
Ungerer, Jean Thomas (Tomi Ungerer) *writer, artist*

GERMANY

Bonn
Rampacher, Hermann Hans *writer, consultant*

Obernzell-Erlau
Kunze, Reiner Alexander *writer, poet*

IRELAND

Donegal
Friel, Brian (Bernard Patrick Friel) *author*

Mullingar
Donleavy, James Patrick *writer, artist*

ISRAEL

Be'er Sheva
Oz, Amos (Amos Klausner) *writer, educator*

Jerusalem
Cole, Peter *poet, translator*

ITALY

Milan
Calasso, Roberto *writer, publisher*

Venice
Pasinetti, Pier Maria *author*

LUXEMBOURG

Buschdorf
Kamanda, Kama Sywor *poet, writer*

POLAND

Cracow
Szymborska, Wislawa (Wislawa Symborska) *poet*

SWEDEN

Jönköping
Picard, Robert Georges *writer, educator*

SWITZERLAND

Bern
Carlson, Dale Bick *writer*

TRINIDAD AND TOBAGO

Diego Martin
Walcott, Derek Alton *poet, playwright*

ADDRESS UNPUBLISHED

Ain, Diantha *poet, artist, educator*
Alinder, Mary Street *writer, educator*
Allen, Roberta *writer, photographer, conceptual artist*
Aloff, Mindy *writer*
Andersen, Kurt Byars *writer*
Andreasson, Kim J. *writer, consultant*
Applegate, Edward C. *writer, advertising educator*
Apps, Jerold Willard *writer*
Arlen, Michael J. *writer*
Arrabal, Fernando *writer*
Ash, Jennifer Gertrude *writer, editor*
Ashanti, Baron James *poet, educator*
Askew, Rilla *author*
Avery, Stephen Neal *playwright, writer*
Bakeman, Carol Ann *travel writer, singer*
Baldrige, Letitia *writer, management consultant*
Barnett, Joyce Lyndel *freelance/self-employed writer*
Bartlett, Bruce Reeves *writer*
Barzun, Jacques *writer, historian, lecturer*
Bassett, Elizabeth Ewing (Libby Bassett) *writer, editor, consultant*
Beatts, Anne Patricia *writer*
Beauchamp, Valdivia Vânia Siqueira *translator*
Benedict, Stewart H. *writer, playwright*
Berg, Darla Gaye *writer*
Bergman, Andrew *scriptwriter, film director*
Bernstein, Carl *writer, journalist*
Bhatia, Sneha P. *writer*
Black, David *writer, educator*
Black, Dustin Lance *scriptwriter, television and film producer*
Blake Ramos, Debra Barbara *writer*
Block, Lawrence *writer*
Blos, Joan Winsor *writer, critic, educator*
Bodsworth, Fred *writer, ecologist*
Bova, Benjamin William *writer, editor*
Bower, Janet Esther *writer, educator*

Breuer, William Bentley *author*
Briese, Michael W. *writer, priest, inventor*
Briskin, Jacqueline Elizabeth *author*
Brodsky, Beverly Anne *writer, consultant, editor*
Brown, Marcia Joan *author, artist, photographer*
Bryan, Vernanne *author, historian*
Bucheister, Patricia Louise (Patt Parrish) *writer, artist*
Bush, Yvonne *writer, counselor*
Caletti, Deb L. *writer*
Carlyon, David James *writer, actor, theater director*
Carter, Cynthia (Cindy) Lynn *writer*
Cecil, Elizabeth Jean *writer*
Chernow, Ron *writer, journalist*
Choukas-Bradley, Melanie *writer, photographer, naturalist*
Clancy, Thomas L., Jr. *novelist, producer*
Clark, Mary Higgins *writer, communications executive*
Clark, Matt *writer*
Clements, Thomas Frank *writer*
Coburn, D(onald) L(ee) *playwright*
Conley, Ruth Irene *poet*
Conover-Carson, Anne *writer*
Coonts, Stephen Paul *writer*
Costantini, Mary Ann C. *writer, adult education educator*
Cowan, Andrew Glenn *television writer, producer, performer*
Crews, Mara Lynne *writer*
Curler, (Mary) Bernice *writer, educator*
Cussler, Clive Eric *author*
Danticat, Edwidge *writer, educator*
Darabont, Frank *screenwriter, director*
David, Larry *television scriptwriter and producer, actor*
Davis, Earon Scott *environmental policy writer, teacher, massage therapist, legal consultant*
Davis, Mamie (Denise Davis) *writer*
Davis, Michelle Denise *writer*
Dawdy, Doris Ostrander *writer*
Deats, Suzanne *writer, editor, artist*
DeMille, Nelson Richard *writer*
Desio, Delores Jean *writer, artist, retired elementary school educator*
Dix, Carol *writer*
Dolan, Edward Francis *writer*
Donnally, Patricia Broderick *writer*
Druffel, Ann Bernice *researcher, writer, public speaker*
Dunn, Robert Giddings *writer, educator, publisher*
Dworzan, Helene Liberman *writer, poet, playwright*
Eglee, Charles Hamilton *scriptwriter, film and television producer*
Ehrenreich, Barbara *writer*
Elebiyo, Vivian Bukola *writer*
Ellis, Joseph John Michael III *writer, history professor*
Emerson, Claudia *poet, language professor*
Ephron, Nora *writer*
Erickson, Donna Joy *writer, editor, publisher*
Esty, John Cushing, Jr. *writer, educator, not-for-profit counsel*
Evans, Jack R. (J. Glenn) *writer, poet*
Farrelly, Peter John *screenwriter*
Fine, Andrea Joiner *writer*
Fisher, Nancy *writer, producer, director*
Fleming, Thomas James *writer*
Fletcher, Donald Rodgers *writer, religious studies educator*
Fox, Daniel Michael *author, advisor*
Free, Sheela Sitaram *poet, educator*
Freedman, Russell Bruce *author*
Fritz, Ethel Mae Hendrickson *writer*
Frymer, Murry *writer, film and theater critic, columnist*
Fuentes, Carlos *writer, retired ambassador*
Fuller, Jack William *writer, retired publishing executive*
Garfield-Woodbridge, Nancy *writer*
Garfinkle, Elaine Myra *writer*
Gavril, Jean (Jean Van Leeuwen) *writer*
Gelmi, Alessandra Valentina Maria Romana Valeria *author, educator*
Gemeinhardt, Judith M. (Judi Gamin) *writer, poet*
George, Faye *poet*
Gibson, Wesley Cullen *writer*
Gilbert, Elayne Rhoda *writer*
Gilroy, Frank Daniel *playwright*
Gioia, Dana (Michael Dana Gioia) *poet, critic, former cultural organization administrator*
Glück, Louise Elisabeth *poet, educator*
Goble, Paul *writer, illustrator, artist*
Goldman, Judith *writer, editor, curator, consultant, publisher*
Goldman, William *writer, scriptwriter*
Goss, Joel Francis *writer*
Gray, Francine du Plessix *writer*
Greenburg, Dan *author*
Gribble, Mary Louise *freelance/self-employed poet, writer*
Grumbach, Doris *novelist, editor, critic, educator, bookseller*
Gustafsson, Lars Erik Einar *writer, educator*
Hairston, William *author, poet, former actor*
Haldeman, Joe William *writer*
Hall, Donald *poet*
Hamit, Francis Granger *novelist, playwright*
Hampton, Christopher James *writer, translator*
Harrell, Margaret Ann *writer, photographer, editor*
Hartman, Earl Kenneth *writer*
Hayes, Cynthia Ann (C.A. Hayes) *writer*
Heidelberg, Paul *writer*
Helprin, Mark *author*
Henry, Rene Arthur *writer*
Herbert, James Charles *writer, researcher*
Herrnkind, Hilda Marie *writer, military volunteer*
Heymann, C(lemens) David *author*
Higbee, Donna Good *writer, researcher*
Higdon, Pamela Leis *writer*
Hillenburg, Stephen *writer, television producer, animator*
Himmelfarb, Gertrude *writer, educator*
Hochschild, Adam *writer, journalist*
Hoff, Benjamin Lloyd *writer, scriptwriter*
Hoffman, William *writer*
Holder, Maxine E. *writer*
Holmes, Willa B. *writer, former educator*
Horsman, David A. Elliott *writer, finance company executive, educator*
Hosansky, Anne *writer*
Howes, Sophia DuBose *writer*
Hoyt, Mary Finch *writer, media consultant, retired federal official*
Hu, Hua-ling Wang *writer, historian*
Humphrey, Phyllis A. *writer*
Hwang, David Henry *playwright, screenwriter*
Irving, John Winslow (John Wallace Blunt Jr.) *writer*
Isaacs, Susan *writer, scriptwriter*
Isenberg, Jane Frances *writer, retired language educator*
Jackson, Charles Ian *writer, consultant*
Jackson, Guida Myrl *writer, editor, literature educator*
Jacobs, Nancy Carolyn Baker *writer*
Jacobson, Joan Leiman *writer*
Johnsen, Barbara Parrish *retired writer, educator*
Johnson, Denis Hale *writer, poet*
Jones, Edward Paul *writer, editor*
Jones, Thomas Claburn *poet, educator*
Jordan, James Lowell *writer, educator*
Junger, Sebastian *writer*
Jurgensen, Barbara *writer*
Katz, William Loren *author*
Katz, William Michael *writer*
Kennedy, Maydra Jane Penisson (J.P. Kennedy) *poet*
Kevles, Bettyann Holtzmann *writer, historian, educator*
Kidd, Michael Hayden *translator, educator*
Kildee, Jennifer *translator, editor*
Kimmel, Mark *author, venture capital company executive*
King, Cynthia Bregman *writer*
King, Larry L. *playwright, actor*
Kingston, Maxine Hong *writer, educator*
Klein, Edward *writer*
Koch, Margaret Rau *writer, artist, historian*
Kushner, Tony *playwright, scriptwriter*
Lambert, Richard Bowles, Jr. *freelance writer*
Lappe, Frances Moore *author, lecturer*
Larkin, Joan *poet, literature and language educator*
LaRocque, Marilyn Ross Onderdonk *writer, editor, public relations executive, consultant*
Larsdotter, Anna-Lisa *retired translator, artist*
Layton, John Robert *writer*
Lee, Harper (Nelle Harper Lee) *writer*
Lescroart, John Thomas *writer, composer, singer*
Lester, Julius B. *author*
Lewis, Dennis Carroll *writer, spiritual teacher*
Lindenberger, Herbert Samuel *writer, literature educator*
Lippard, Lucy Rowland *writer, educator, critic, curator*
Little, Charlotte Louise *poet, writer*
Long, Robert Emmet *author*
Lopez, Barry Holstun *writer*
Lubell, Ellen *writer*
Lucas, Jane Meekins *writer, educator*
Lynds, Gayle Hallenbeck *writer*
Maclay, Sarah *poet, educator*
Macnab, Alistair Murdoch *retired writer*
Mann, Mary Anneeta *author*
Manrique, Jaime *writer, educator*
Mansfield, Stephen Lee *writer, educator*
Manville, Greta Craig *writer*
Marcuse, Aida E. *writer, translator, educator*
Martin, Jacqueline Briggs *writer*
Martin-Lowry, Beverly Anne *writer, columnist*
Mason, Connie Jeanne *writer*
Mata, Linda Sue Proctor *writer, consultant*
Mathieu, Michele Suzanne *grant writer, computer scientist, consultant*
Matthiessen, Peter *author*
May, Janet Sue *playwright, lyricist*
McCash, June Hall *writer, retired language educator*
McDonald, April D. *writer*
McIntier, Russell J. *retired writer*
McPhee, John Angus *writer*
McPherson, James Alan *writer, educator*
McQueen, Regenia *writer*
McWhorter, Diane *writer*
McWilliams, Karen Joan *writer*
McWilliams, Michael *writer, publisher*
Mendoza, George *poet, author*
Merrill, Jean Fairbanks *writer*
Messer, Donald Edward *author, theology educator, administrator*
Miller, Carole Ann Lyons *writer, editor, publisher, marketing executive*
Mills, Elizabeth Shown *historical writer, genealogist*
Mintz, Morton Abner *writer, reporter*
Mixon, Victoria *writer*
Mogel, Leonard Henry *writer*
Monson, Nancy Peckel *writer, editor, book collaborator, spokesperson*
Moore, Alan *writer*
Moore, Billy Don *scriptwriter, film producer*
Moore, Robert Henry *writer, editor, communications consultant*
Moorhead, Lucy Galpin *writer*
Morrison, Martin *writer*
Morrison, Toni (Chloe Ardelia Wofford) *writer, educator, editor*
Morse-McNeely, Patricia *poet, writer, retired secondary school educator*
Mulvihill, Maureen Esther *writer, professor*
Murphy, Marion Colucci *writer, poet*
Murphy, Randall Kent *writer, educator, consultant*
Muson, Howard Henry *writer, consultant*
Myers, Sophia M. *writer, researcher, artist, cartographer, translator*
Narbon, Lilian *writer*
Nichols, Gregory Dawson *playwright, educator*
Nova, Craig *writer*
Nurick, Carl J. *author, consultant, poet*
Ober, Doris Ann *writer, editor, consultant*
O'Garden, Irene *writer, aetress*
O'Loughlin, Katie Eileen Bridget *poet*
Oransky, Ivan *writer, editor*
Orkin, Jenna *writer*
Ostriker, Alicia Suskin *poet*
Ozick, Cynthia *writer*
Paci, Ruth A. *freelance/self-employed writer*
Paine, Alan *poet*
Pakula, Hannah *writer*
Panchyk, Richard Robert *writer*
Paolucci, Anne Attura *playwright, poet, literature educator, educational consultant*
Patterson, Richard North *writer, lawyer*
Peck, Richard Wayne *writer*
Pendergrast, Mark H. *writer*
Pennino, Anthony Paul *playwright, educator*
Perry, Tyler A. *playwright, actor, theater director and producer*
Pierce, Tamora *writer*
Pike, Diane Kennedy *writer, educator*
Polsgrove, Carol Claxon *writer, retired communications educator*
Polster, James *writer, film producer*
Popp, Lilian Mustaki *writer, educator*
Potter, Everett *travel writer*
Poundstone, William Nicholas, Jr. *writer*
Powell, Alma Johnson *writer, advocate, foundation administrator*
Prescott, Richard Chambers *writer*
Prestine, Joan Singleton *writer, editor, educator*
Proulx, (Edna) Annie *writer*
Quigley, Martin Schofield *writer, educator*
Rader, Dotson Carlyle *writer, journalist*
Raucher, Herman *screenwriter, novelist*
Rector, Donna Lynn *writer, photographer, poet, artist*
Reed, Kit *writer*
Renaud, Bernadette Marie Elise *author*
Rhodes, Daisy Chun *writer, researcher, historian*
Rice, Anne *writer*
Rice, Ferill Jeane *writer*
Richter, W.D. *screenwriter, director, producer*
Riehecky, Janet Ellen *writer*
Rimel, Ira Wesley *writer, US Navy supply officer, real estate specialist, real estate appraiser, real estate broker*
Ringel, Judy G. *writer*
Rising, Catharine Clarke *author*
Rogers, David *playwright, actor*
Rooney, Andrew Aitken *writer, journalist*
Rosenblatt, Roger *writer*
Roth, Philip Milton *writer*
Rubin, Gretchen Craft *author*
Russ, Joanna *author*
Russo, Richard *writer*
Rutsala, Vern A. *poet, writer, language educator*
Ryan, Kay Pedersen *poet*
Sackett, Susan Deanna *writer*
Saito, Robert Shunichi *writer, poet*
Sallis, James *writer*
Schenkkan, Robert Frederic *playwright, screenwriter*
Schlesinger, Lisa *playwright, educator*
Schnackenberg, Gjertrud Cecelia *poet*
Scott, Joyce *writer*
Seamans, William *writer, retired reporter, commentator*
Segal, Erich *author, educator*
Severo, Richard *writer*
Sevilla, Emerita Nepomuceno *writer*
Shapiro, Harvey *poet*
Shepard, Sam (Samuel Shepard Rogers) *playwright, actor*
Sherrod, Danny Troy *writer, educator*
Shiffrin, Nancy *writer, educator*
Shreve, Susan Richards *writer, educator*
Simendinger, Theodore John *writer, publishing executive*
Simon, William Leonard *scriptwriter, television and film producer, writer*
Sims, Pamela Jan (Cerussi) *writer, minister*
Singer, Donna Lea *writer, editor, educator*
Singleton, Jonetta Williams *poet, retired special education educator*
Sisk, Eileen Victoria *writer, journalist*
Smiley, Jane Graves *author, educator*
Smith, Anne Day *writer*
Smith, Betty *writer, not-for-profit developer*
Smith, Cora Adele *retired writer*
Sorkin, Aaron *scriptwriter, television producer, playwright*
Spencer, Tricia Jane *writer*
Stashower, Daniel Meyer *writer*
Steele, Judith McConnell *writer*
Stevens, Shane *novelist*
Strand, Mark *poet*
Straub, Peter Francis *novelist*
Strong, Virginia Wilkerson *freelance writer, former special education educator*
Strouse, Jean *writer, cultural organization administrator*
Sullivan, George Edward *writer*
Sussman, Barry *writer, demographer, editor*
Sutton, Joe *playwright, educator*
Tatum, Arthur III *lexicographer, educator, pianist*
Taylor, Barbara Ann Olin *writer, educational consultant*
Taylor, John Jackson (Jay) *writer, retired diplomat*
Theroux, Paul Edward *author*
Tilford, Terry Trent *translator*
Tower, Mollie Gregory *writer, educator, consultant*
Towler, Katherine *writer*
Treichel, Dixie Ann *writer, composer*
Turczyn, Christine Lilian *writer, educator*
Twichell, Chase *poet*
Twiddy, Elizabeth *writer, educator*
Tyler, Anne (Mrs. Taghi M. Modarressi) *writer*
Ucko, Barbara Clark *writer*
Unger, Barbara *poet, writer, retired literature and language professor*
Varda, Agnes *scriptwriter, film director*
Verlich, Jean Elaine *writer, public relations executive, consultant*
Vichiola, Christopher Michael *writer, educator*
Vidal, Gore (Eugene Luther Vidal Jr.) *writer*
Viorst, Judith Stahl *writer*
Viorst, Milton *writer*
Vita, Steven *poet*
Volk, Patricia Gay *novelist, essayist*
von Hoffman, Nicholas *writer, retired reporter*
Vorce-Tish, Helene R. *writer*
Vosevich, Kathi Ann *writer, editor*
Waitkus, Jay *writer*
Walker, Mary Alexander *writer*
Wallace, Michele *writer, educator*
Wayne, Kyra Petrovskaya *writer*
Weaver, Anne Genevieve Hera *writer*
Webb, Martha Jeanne *writer, educator, film producer*
Weir, Anne *writer*
Weis, Margaret Edith *writer, editor*
Weisberg, Barbara *writer, editor*
Weiss, Joanne Marion *writer*
Whalen, Charles William, Jr. *writer, retail executive, Former United States Representative, Ohio*
Whelchel, Sandra Jane *writer*
Will, Roland Tracy, II, *writer, editor, journalist, publisher, television producer*
Williams, Albert Nathaniel *writer, educator*
Williams, Darcel Patrice *writer, editor*
Williams, Ian George *writer*
Wilson, Colin Henry *writer*
Wilson, Lanford *playwright*
Windsor, Patricia (Katonah Summertree, Perrin Winters, Anna Seeling) *author, educator, lecturer*
Winter, Terence *writer, television producer*
Worden, Skip *writer*
Wykoff, Gary Lee *writer*
Yingling, Phyllis Stuckey *writer*
Zaillian, Steven *screenwriter, director*
Zeilig, Nancy Meeks *writer, editor*
Zulauf, Sander (Sander William Zulauf) *poet, educator, editor*

ARTS: PERFORMING

UNITED STATES

ALABAMA

Birmingham
Hubbard, Ron *performing arts educator*
Laeger, Therese Roach *performing arts educator*
Lawhon, Sharon Leding *music educator, director*
Sanchez, Fabian *dancer*
Sen, Bisakha Pia *performing arts educator*
Shelton, Bessie Hunter *music educator, director*

Chickasaw
Erwin, Sandra Kay *music educator*

Florence
Ruebhausen, David K. *theater educator*

Huntsville
Gill, Glenda Eloise *theater educator*
Kruja, Mira *music educator*

Madison
Lee, Soojeong *music educator, soprano*

Montevallo
Killian, Tammy Lee *theater educator, director*

Montgomery
Washington, Kara Elizabeth *music educator*

Rogersville
Oldham, Dewey Lindon (Spooner Oldham) *musician, songwriter*

Talladega
Lanier, Anita Suzanne *musician, educator*

Thorsby
Pounders, Stephen C. *music educator*

ALASKA

Anchorage
David, Edgecombe P. *theater educator*
Gazaway, Barbara Ann *music and art educator*
Strid-Chadwick, Karen S. *musician, educator*

Palmer
Burton, Jamin L. *music educator*

Valdez
Moore, Dawson *performing company executive, playwright*

ARIZONA

Flagstaff
Scott, Louise H. *music educator*

Florence
Mosby, Nora Jane *music educator*

Fountain Hills
Tyl, Noel Jan *retired vocalist, astrologer, writer*

Glendale
Cotton, Sally Jean *retired music educator*

Holbrook
Solomonson, Michael *performing arts, department chairman*

Marana
Evarts, Caren Goodin *music educator, recording artist, performer, pianist*

Mesa
Dutson, Lyn *theater educator*

Weiskopf, Wanda *mezzo soprano, writer, poet*
Wonder, Stevie (Steveland Hardaway Judkins, Stevland Morris) *musician*
Zimmer, Hans Florian *composer*

Campbell
Browne, Sylvia (Sylvia Shoemaker) *spiritual medium, writer*

Canoga Park
Taesch, Richard Edmund *music educator*

Castro Valley
West, Doyle Thomas *retired music educator*

Claremont
Bennett, William John (Bill Bennett) *radio personality, former United States Secretary of Education*
Huang, Hao H. *music educator, department chairman*
Lerner, Jesse *filmmaker*
Nelson, Mark D. *music educator, arts education administrator*
Schroerlucke, Leslie Jean *music educator*

Clovis
Kawashima, Hope Nozomi *musician*
van der Paardt, Tamara Ann *music educator*

Colfax
Deaderick, John F. *actor, educator*

Concord
Accatino, Steven C. *instrumental music educator, orchestra conductor*
Blair, Virginia Devoto *music educator*

Corona
Chambers-Belida, Candace R. *radio personality, writer, television producer, educator*
Holt, Chifra *dancer, educator, choreographer*

Corona Del Mar
Karson, Burton Lewis *musician, educator*

Costa Mesa
Berkompas, Susan K. *theater director*

Culver City
Brooks, James L. *film producer, director*
Brooks, Mel *film producer and director, actor, scriptwriter*
Chaffin, Ceán *producer*
Duncan, Michael Clarke *actor*
Fincher, David *film director and producer*
Kaufman, Richard Stuart *conductor*
Lee, Ang *film director*
Mark, Laurence Maurice *film producer*
Marshall, Garry K. (Garry Kent Marsciarelli) *film producer, director, writer*
Phoenix, Joaquin Raphael *actor*
Taylor, Regina *actress*
Wick, Douglas *producer*

Dana Point
Kramer, Kathryn Leslie *film director, educator*

Davis
Cole, Kimberly Ree *music educator, musician*
Iacovelli, John Chesley *performing arts educator*
Ortiz, Pablo *composer*

Diamond Bar
Chih, Luke *music educator, conductor*
Snoop Dogg, (Calvin Broadus) *vocalist, actor*

Emeryville
Bird, Brad (Phillip Bradley Bird) *film director, writer, animator*

Encino
Ingels, Marty *agent, broadcast executive*
Shire, David Lee *composer*
Westmore, Michael George *make-up artist, writer*
Willard, Fred *actor*

Fairfield
Ornellas, Maile Louise *filmmaker, educator*

Fort Bragg
Gjerde, Rosalie Carolyn *music educator, conductor*

Fountain Valley
de Jong-Pombo, Teresa Maria *concert pianist, educator*
Treadway-Dillmon, Linda Lee *actress, stuntwoman, dancer, dispatcher, athletic trainer*

Fremont
Blank, Thomas *theater educator*
Hsu, Gloria *piano educator*
LaRose, Katherine Stencel *music educator*
Yamamoto, Masako *music educator, director*

Fresno
Riggs, Krista Dyonis *music educator, librarian*

Fullerton
Frost, Jacqueline Beth *cinematographer, educator*
Ketter, Charles David *theater educator, director*
Zeballos, Abel *theater educator, make-up artist, consultant*

Glendale
Filosa, Gary Fairmont Randolph, II, *film and television producer*
Jacobson, Nina R. *film producer, former company executive*
Prager, Dennis *radio talk show host*
Sotelo, Eduardo (El Piolín) *radio personality*

Hayward
Fajilan, Ann *theater educator*

Hollywood
Berryman, Guy *musician*
Buckland, Jon *musician*
Burke, Cheryl *dancer*
Champion, Will *musician*
DioGuardi, Kara *songwriter, producer*
Greenwood, Colin Charles *musician*
Greenwood, Jonathan Richard Guy (Jonny Greenwood) *musician*
Lynne, Shelby (Shelby Lynn Moorer) *country singer*
Martin, Chris *singer*
Miles, Joanna *actress, playwright, director*
O'Brien, Edward John *musician, vocalist*
Selway, Phillip James *musician*
Will.i.am, (William James Adams Jr.) *rap artist*
Yorke, Thom (Thomas Edward Yorke) *singer*

Huntington Beach
Carter, Henrietta McKee *music educator, department chair*

Irvine
Ruyter, Nancy Lee Chalfa *dance educator*
Wilderson, Frank B. III *performing arts educator, writer*
Yamamoto, Lisa Maria *music educator*

Kentfield
Halprin, Anna Schuman (Mrs. Lawrence Halprin) *dancer*

La Crescenta
Baldwin, Alec (Alexander Rae Baldwin III) *actor*

La Jolla
Rubinstein, Kim *theater educator*

La Mesa
Canzoneri, Lois H. *retired church musician*

La Mirada
Mumford, Lawrence R. *composer, educator*

La Palma
Levy, Elaine Ann *music educator*

Laguna Woods
McClure, Hal H. *film producer*

Lake View Terrace
Troyer, Verne *actor*

Lancaster
Kim, Gloria Seunghee *music educator, singer, director*

Lompoc
Belisle-Foreman, Karen *music educator*

Long Beach
deAlbuquerque, Joan Marie *conductor, music educator*
Engelhardt, James F. *theater educator*
Engle, Robert Irwin *music educator, translator*

Los Angeles
Affleck, Ben *actor*
Aniston, Jennifer *actress*
Annaud, Jean-Jacques *film director, producer, scriptwriter*
Arnett, Will *actor*
Ashforth, Alden *musician, educator*
Bacharach, Burt *composer, conductor*
Baker, Dylan *actor*
Balaski, Belinda L. *actress, educator, writer, artist, photographer*
Banks, Elizabeth *actress*
Banks, Tyra (Tyra Lynne Banks) *television personality, retired model*
Bardem, Javier *actor*
Barker, Bob (Robert William Barker) *television personality*
Bassett, Angela Evelyn *actress*
Bates, Kathy *actress*
Begley, Ed, Jr. *actor*
Bell, Drake (Jared Drake Bell) *actor, singer*
Bell, Kristen *actress*
Bell, Lee Phillip *television personality, producer*
Bell, William J., Jr. *television producer*
Benedict, Diane *theater educator, director*
Bening, Annette *actress*
Bennington, Chester Charles *singer*
Berry, Halle Maria *actress*
Biggs, Jason *actor*
Bilson, Rachel *actress*
Blair, Selma (Selma Blair Beitner) *actress*
Bloom, Claire *actress*
Bourdon, Robert Gregory *musician*
Braxton, Toni *singer, actress*
Brenneman, Amy *actress*
Brody, Adrien *actor*
Brolin, James (James Brunderlin) *actor*
Buffett, Jimmy (James William Buffett) *vocalist, songwriter, writer*
Burnett, Charles *film director, screenwriter, producer*
Burnett, T-Bone (Henry John Burnett) *music producer, musician*
Burrows, James *television and motion picture director, producer*
Burton, Brian Joseph (Danger Mouse) *sound recording engineer, musician*
Burton, Tim (Timothy William Burton) *film director, film producer*
Caine, Sir Michael (Maurice Joseph Micklewhite, Jr.) *actor*
Carnicke, Sharon Marie *theater director, educator, theater specialist*
Carolla, Adam *actor, radio personality, film producer, scriptwriter*
Carrey, Jim *actor*
Carter, Chris *producer, director*
Cates, Gilbert *television and film producer, theater director*
Cee-Lo, (Thomas DeCarlo Callaway) *singer*
Champlin, Charles Davenport *television personality, critic, writer*
Cheadle, Donald Frank *actor*
Clark, Dick *performer, producer*
Clayburgh, Jill *actress*
Cooper, Chris *actor*
Copeland, Stewart *composer, musician*
Corman, Roger William *film director*
Craig, Daniel *actor*
Crawford, Chace *actor*
Crockett, Donald Harold *composer, music educator*
Cruise, Tom (Thomas Cruise Mapother IV) *actor*
Cruz, Penélope *actress*
Cyrus, Billy Ray *country music performer, actor*
D'Accone, Frank Anthony *music educator*
Daldry, Stephen *theater director, film director*
Daly, Timothy *actor*
Dano, Paul Franklin *actor*
Davis, LaVan *actor*
Dawson, Rosario *actress, singer*
Dee, Ruby (Ruby Dee Davis) *actress, writer, film director*
Delson, Brad Phillip *musician*
Del Toro, Benicio (Benicio Monserrate Rafael del Toro Sánchez) *actor*
Dennehy, Brian *actor*
Dillon, Kevin *actor*
Dinklage, Peter *actor*
Domingo, Plácido (José Plácido Domingo Embil) *tenor, conductor, opera company director*
Donaldson, Roger *film director, film producer*
Downey, Robert, Jr. *actor, singer*
Dr. Dre, (Andre Ramelle Young) *rap musician, record producer*
Driver, Minnie *actress*
Duritz, Adam *musician*
Eckhart, Aaron *actor*
Efron, Zac *actor, singer*
Electra, Carmen (Tara Leigh Patrick) *actress*
Elrod, Lu *music professor emerita, actress*
Elswit, Robert *cinematographer*
Etheridge, Melissa Lou *singer, lyricist*
Farrell, David Michael *musician*
Farrell, Joseph *film producer and company executive, financial analyst*
Ferrera, America Georgine *actress*
Field, Sally Margaret *actress*
Fischer, Jenna (Regina Marie Fischer) *actress*
Fisher, Isla Lang *actress*
Fleming, Andrew Macdonald *film director*
Fletcher, Louise *actress*
Fonda, Jane *actress*
Forte, Will (Orville Willis Forte IV) *actor, scriptwriter*
Fossum, Louis Eric *theater educator, writer*
Foster, Sutton *actress*
Gere, Richard *actor*
Gondry, Michel *film director*
Gordon-Levitt, Joseph Leonard *actor*
Gosling, Ryan (Ryan Thomas Gosling) *actor*
Graham, Heather *actress*
Grammer, Kelsey *actor*
Greenberg, Barry Michael *talent executive*
Gugino, Carla *actress*
Gyllenhaal, Maggie *actress*
Hackman, Gene (Eugene Alden Hackman) *actor*
Hahn, Joseph *disc jockey, video director*
Hanks, Tom *actor, film producer, director*
Hardison, Kadeem *actor*
Harper, Hill (Frank Harper) *actor*
Harrelson, Woody *actor*
Hart, Melissa Joan *actress*
Hartke, Stephen Paul *composer, educator*
Harvey, PJ (Polly Jean Harvey) *singer*
Hayek, Salma *actress*
Heigl, Katherine Marie *actress*
Henkel, Kathy *composer*
Henley, Don *singer, drummer, songwriter*
Henson, Taraji Penda *actress*
Hirsch, Judd *actor*
Hoffman, Philip Seymour *actor*
Holbrook, Hal (Harold Rowe Holbrook Jr.) *actor*
Horovitz, Adam Keefe (Adrock, King Ad-Rock) *musician*
Hounsou, Djimon Gaston *actor*
Hudson, Kate *actress*
Hurd, Gale Anne *film producer*
Hurt, William *actor*
Ice-T, (Tracy Marrow) *rap artist, actor*
Inaba, Carrie Ann *choreographer, dancer*
Ireland, Kathy *actress, apparel designer*
Jackman, Hugh *actor*
Jackson, Joshua Carter *actor*
Jackson, Samuel L. *actor*
Johansson, Scarlett *actress*
Johnson, Kym *dancer*
Jones, January *actress*
Jones, Sir Tom (Thomas Jones Woodward) *singer*
Kahane, Jeffrey Alan *conductor, pianist, music director*
Keith, David *symphony orchestra conductor*
Kelley, David E. *producer, writer*
Kendell, Ken *music educator*
Kennedy, George *actor*
Keyes, Cheryl L. *musician, educator*
Kidman, Nicole *actress*
Klauss, Kenneth Karl *composer, music educator*
Kollatz-Florido, Rebecca Lynn *music educator*
Koules, Oren D. *film producer, professional sports team executive*
Krause, Peter *actor*
Kutcher, Ashton (Christopher Ashton Kutcher) *actor*
Kyles, Cedric Antonio (Cedric the Entertainer) *comedian, actor*
Lange, Jessica Phyllis *actress*
Larry the Cable Guy, (Daniel Lawrence Whitney) *comedian, radio personality*
Larter, Ali (Alison Elizabeth Larter) *actress*
Lauridsen, Morten Johannes *composer, music educator*
LeBeau, Mary Delle *dancer, educator, writer*
Lennox, Annie *rock musician*
Leoni, Téa (Elizabeth Tea Pantaleoni) *actress*
Letterman, David *talk show host, producer, comedian, writer*
Liman, Doug *film director, film producer*
Linkletter, Arthur Gordon *radio and television broadcaster*
London, Andrew Barry *film editor*
Long, Justin Jake *actor*
Lopez, George *actor, comedian*
Lopez, Jennifer *actress, singer, dancer*
Lovato, Demi (Demetria Devonne Lovato) *actress*
MacLachlan, Kyle *actor*
Macy, William H. *actor*
Malkovich, John *actor*
Manheim, Camryn *television and film actress*
Marsden, James Paul *actor*
Masterson, Mary Stuart *actress*
Matthews, Dave *singer, musician*
McBride, Danny R. *actor*
McQueen, Justice Ellis (L. Q. Jones) *actor, television director*
Medak, Peter *film director*
Milano, Alyssa *actress*
Milchan, Arnon *film producer*
Muldaur, Diana Charlton *actress*
Murphy, Eddie *actor, comedian*
Murphy, (Frances) Elaine *musician, harpist, flutist*
Murray, Chad Michael *actor*
Neuwirth, Bebe (Beatrice Neuwirth) *dancer, actress*
Newhart, Bob (George Robert Newhart) *entertainer*
Nicholson, Jack *actor*
Nielsen, Leslie *actor*
O'Connell, Taaffe Cannon *actress, publishing executive*
O'Hurley, John *actor*
Olsen, Ashley Fuller *actress, apparel designer*
Olsen, Mary-Kate *actress, apparel designer*
O'Neal, Tatum *actress*
Osment, Haley Joel *actor*
Owen, Clive *actor*
Palmer, Keke (Lauren Keyana Palmer) *actress*
Paltrow, Gwyneth *actress*
Penn, Sean *actor*
Perry, Katy (Katheryn Elizabeth Hudson) *singer*
Perry, Matthew *actor*
Pervan, Nenad Neno *theater educator*
Phillips, Todd *film director, film producer*
Pinto, Freida *actress*
Pittman, Amanda Nelson *music educator*
Piven, Jeremy *actor*
Poitier, Sidney *actor, film director*
Pompeo, Ellen *actress*
Portman, Natalie *actress*
Pressly, Jaime Elizabeth *actress*
Pullman, Bill *actor*
Ratzenberger, John Deszo *actor, writer, film director*
Rickles, Donald Jay *comedian, actor*
Riggen, Patricia *film director, film producer*
Roberts, Emma Rose *actress*
Roberts, Julia Fiona *actress*
Rock, Chris *actor, comedian*
Rogen, Seth *actor*
Rosenberg, Alan *actors guild executive*
Ross, Marion *actress*
Roth, Tim *actor*
Rourke, Mickey (Philip Andre Rourke Jr.) *actor*
Rowell, Victoria *actress*
Rubin, Stanley Creamer *television producer, film producer*
Ruskin, Joseph Richard *actor, director*
Ryan, Meg (Margaret Mary Emily Ann Hyra) *actress, film producer*
Santaolalla, Gustavo *musician, composer, record producer*
Schallert, William Joseph *actor*
Schiff, Richard *actor*
Schlesinger, Adam *musician*
Schott, Robert W. (Bob Schott) *film producer, actor, film director*
Scott-Thomas, Kristin *actress*
Seal, (Seal Henry Olusegun Olumide Adelo Samuel) *musician*
Selleck, Tom *actor*
Serkis, Andy *actor*
Shaiman, Marc *composer, arranger, orchestrator*
Shinoda, Michael Kenji *musician, artist*
Shyamalan, M. Night (Manoj Nelliyattu Shyamalan) *film director*
Simpson-Wentz, Ashlee Nicole *singer*
Sinbad, (David Adkins) *actor, comedian*
Sisko, Diane *film producer*
Smart, Amy *actress*
Smiley, Tavis *television talk show host, writer*
Snow, Brittany *actress*
Snyder, Zack *film director*
Sobieski, Leelee (Liliane Rudabet Gloria Eslveta Sobieski) *actress*
Sorvino, Mira *actress*
Springsteen, Bruce (Bruce Frederick Joseph Springsteen) *musician, singer*
Stahl, Nick *actor*
Stamp, Terence Henry *actor*
Statham, Jason *actor*
Stevenson, Robert Murrell *music educator*
Streep, Meryl (Mary Louise Streep) *actress*
Streisand, Barbra Joan *singer, actress, film director*
Swofford, Beth *agent*
Thicke, Alan *actor*
Thomas, Rob (Robert Kelly Thomas) *singer, songwriter*
Thomson, William Ennis *music theorist, author*
Tomlin, Lily *actress*
Turturro, John *actor*
Ullman, Tracey *actress, singer*
Underwood, Carrie Marie *singer*
Valli, Frankie (Francis Castelluccio) *singer*
Veasey, Pamela Renea *television producer*
Walden, Olga Ascher *music educator*
Walken, Christopher *actor*
Walsh, Kate *actress*
Waterston, Sam *actor*
Watts, Naomi *actress*
Whitaker, Forest *actor*
Williams, Michelle *actress*
Williams-Paisley, Kimberly *actress*
Wilson, Chandra Danette *actress*
Wilson, Patrick Joseph *actor*

Winters, Barbara Jo *musician*
Witherspoon, Reese (Laura Jean Reese Witherspoon) *actress*
Wood, Evan Rachel *actress*
Woodley, Shailene Diann *actress*
Wright, Mary Ellen *theater educator*
Wyle, Noah *actor*
York, Michael (Michael York-Johnson) *actor*
Zellweger, Renée *actress*
Zemeckis, Robert L. *film director*

Los Osos
Kreitzer, Jacalyn Bower *vocalist, educator*

Malibu
Almond, Paul *film director and producer, scriptwriter, novelist*
Bush, Kristian *musician*
Harris, Ed (Edward Allen Harris) *actor*
Kirkland, Geoffrey Alan *motion picture production designer*
Nettles, Jennifer *singer*

Mendocino
Eckert, Rinde *composer, librettist*

Mill Valley
Adessa, Lori *music educator*
Padula, Fred David *filmmaker*
Schiff, Jan Pedersen *conductor, voice educator*

Modesto
Jones, Mary Cunningham *music educator*

Moorpark
Kessner, Dolly Eugenio *music educator, concert pianist*

Mountain View
Isaacs, Nicholas Stephen *music educator, director*

Newport Beach
Landau, Martin *actor*
Steinberg, Leigh William *sports agent*

North Hollywood
English, Diane *television producer, writer, communications executive*
Fanning, Dakota *actress*
Holmes, Michael *performing arts company executive, educator*
McMartin, John *actor*
Smothers, Tom *actor, singer*
Toplitt, Gloria H. *music educator, actress, vocalist*
Toussieng, Yolanda *make-up artist*

Northridge
Bostrom, Sandra Janine *music educator*
Cartwright, Nancy *actress, television producer*
Luedders, Jerry Duane *music educator, academic administrator*

Norwalk
DeMichele, Anna Tina *music educator*

Oakland
DeFazio, Lynette Stevens *dancer, choreographer, violinist, actress, educator*
Duran, Claudio E. *composer, writer*
Terry, Keith *performing company executive, dancer, body musician*
Zschau, Marilyn *singer*

Orange
Tamiko, Washington Suzette *theater educator*

Oroville
Manera, Rose Ellen *music educator, elementary school educator*

Pacific Palisades
Goodman, John *actor*
Ritter, Jason *actor*

Pacifica
Latham, Benjamin Erwin *music educator*

Palo Alto
Cashion, Susan *retired performing arts educator*
Lo, Yee On *composer*

Pasadena
Childs, Billy *composer*
Halsted, Margo *music educator, carillonneur*
Hicklin, Ronald Lee *music production company executive*
Horak, Jan-Christopher *filmmaker, educator, curator*
Jones, Jennifer *actress*
Menefee, John William III *cinematographer, film producer*
Pinsky, Drew (David Drew Pinsky) *television personality, psychotherapist*
Robinson, Roger *actor, director*

Petaluma
Bailey, Preston Edward *music educator*

Port Hueneme
Schneider, Arthur Paul *retired videotape and film editor, author*

Porterville
Kusserow, James *music educator*

Ramona
Pordon, William Philip *music educator*

Redondo Beach
Richards, Denise *actress*

Rialto
Robertson, Carey Jane *musician, educator*

Riverside
Lee, Raejin *music educator, soprano*

Rocklin
Stanley, Elizabeth Kathryn *music educator*

Sacramento
Braden, Charles Goetzman III *theater educator*
Mazzaferro, James Joseph *music educator*
McCann-Lawson, Kim *theater educator, director*
Nice, Carter *conductor*
Piper, Jami Kathleen *music educator, composer, musician*
Rainwater, Eric *composer, music educator*

San Diego
Bates-Romeo, Delores Alvenia *music educator, consultant*
Befort, Carlene Mae *music educator*
Campbell, Ian David *opera company director*
Crump-Pace, Jacqueline Anita *music educator*
Flettner, Marianne *opera administrator*
Korneitchouk, Igor *music educator, composer*
Liang, Lei *composer*
Noel, Craig *performing arts company executive, producer*
O'Brien, Jack George *artistic director*
Overton, Marcus Lee *performing arts association administrator, actor, writer*
Pagan, Keith Areatus *music educator, academic administrator*
Pfiffner, Patrick Meehan *musician, educator*
Stein, Franklin Joseph *music educator*
Treger, Marjorie Mae *theater director, educator*

San Francisco
Alesi, Tommy *musician*
Breaux, Jimmy *musician*
Brevig, Eric *special effects expert, executive*
Burtt, Ben *sound designer, director, editor*
Caniparoli, Val William *choreographer, dancer*
Coppola, Francis Ford *film director, film producer, scriptwriter*
Doucet, David *musician*
Doucet, Michael *musician, songwriter*
Emunah, Renee *drama therapist, professor*
Gibbard, Ben *singer, musician*
Gockley, David (Richard David Gockley) *opera company director*
Goode, Joe *performing company executive*
Guggenheim, Davis *film and TV director, producer*
Hastings, Edward Walton *theater director*
Hirst, Karen L. *actor, singer, theater educator*
King, Alonzo *artistic director, choreographer*
Kitundu, Walter *sound artist, instrument designer, composer*
Knoll, John *visual effects supervisor*
Kochetkova, Maria *dancer*
Leap, Emily *dancer, acrobat*
McGegan, Nicholas *conductor*
McGuire, Kathleen Alison *conductor*
Muren, Dennis E. *special effects expert*
Runnicles, Donald *conductor*
Shorenstein Hays, Carole *theater producer*
Tomasson, Helgi *performing company executive, dancer, choreographer*
Walla, Chris *musician, music producer*
Ware, Billy *musician*

San Jose
Dalis, Irene *mezzo soprano, performing arts association administrator*
Hughes, Daniel David *performing company executive*
Masters, Gary *dancer, choreographer*
Nahat, Dennis F. *performing company executive, choreographer*
Near, Timothy *theater director*

San Luis Obispo
Suhr, Moon Ja Minn *dance educator*

San Marcos
Houk, Benjamin Noah *performing company executive, choreographer*

San Rafael
Brubeck, David Warren *musician*
Lucas, George Walton, Jr. *film director, producer, scriptwriter*
Santana, Carlos *musician*

Santa Ana
Donchey, Sheryl Diane *theater educator*

Santa Barbara
Brodhead, James E(aston) *actor, writer*
Feigin, Joel *composer, educator*
Horne, Marilyn Berneice *mezzo-soprano*
Howorth, David *producer, director*
Laris, Katherine Elizabeth *theater director, educator*
Pilafian, Christopher *choreographer*
Pyron, Nona Faye *music educator, director*

Santa Clarita
Feldman Nebenzahl, Bernardo *composer, educator*
Mays, Kenneth Robert *music educator*

Santa Cruz
Carson, Benjamin Leeds *composer, educator*
Leikin, Anatole *music educator*
Weiner, Claire Zundell (CZ Cameron) *theatrical director*

Santa Maria
Moret, Jeanine *film educator*

Santa Monica
Akerman, Malin Maria *actress*
Angel, Steven *musician*
Bratt, Benjamin *actor*
Bruckheimer, Jerry Leon *producer*
Cameron, James *film director, screenwriter, producer*
Cole, Gary Michael *actor*
Curran, Leigh *actress, playwright*
DeLonge, Thomas Matthew, Jr. *musician*
Eminem, (Marshall Mathers III) *rap artist*
Falco, Edie *actress*
Ferrell, Conchata Galen *actress, performing arts educator*
Handler, Chelsea Jane *comedian, television personality*
Hannigan, Alyson *actress*
Kennedy, David *musician*
Kennedy, Kathleen *film producer*
Lady Gaga, (Stefani Joanne Angelina Germanotta) *singer*
Louis-Dreyfus, Julia *actress*
McGinley, John C. *actor*
McNall, Bruce *film producer, former professional sports team executive*
Meester, Leighton (Leighton Marissa Claire Meester) *actress*
Peña, Michael Anthony *actor*
Seyfried, Amanda Louise *actress*
Shannon, Molly Helen *actress*
Sonnenfeld, Stefan *film editor*
Spacek, Sissy (Mary Elizabeth Spacek) *actress*
Summer, Donna (La Donna Adrian Gaines) *singer, songwriter, actress*
Tamblyn, Amber Rose *actress*
Taylor, James Vernon *musician*
The Edge, (David Howell Evans) *musician*
Valentine, Dean *film producer*
Watson, Doc (Arthel Lane Watson) *vocalist, guitarist, banjoist, recording artist*
Wexler, Haskell *film producer*
Willard, Atom (Adam Willard) *musician*

Sebastopol
Griggs, Lewis Brown *executive producer, speaker, trainer*

Sherman Oaks
Beck, Glenn *radio personality, commentator*
Clark, Susan (Nora Goulding) *actress*
Douglas, Michael Kirk *actor, film director, film producer*
Elfman, Danny *composer*
Fogerty, John Cameron *musician, composer*
Howard, Alison Koi *singer, music licensing consultant, lyricist*
Jordan, Bonnie *television producer*
Taylor, Elizabeth (Dame Elizabeth Rosemond Taylor) *actress*

Stanford
Cohen, Albert *musician, educator*

Stevenson Ranch
Krainin, Julian Arthur *film director, producer, cinematographer, writer*

Stockton
Acoba, Valerie Lee *performing arts educator*
Wilcox, Helena Marguerita (Helena Rita Wilcox) *music educator*

Studio City
Barrett, Dorothy *performing company executive*
Boyett, Joan Reynolds *performing company executive*
Esposito, Jennifer *actress*
Hudson, Jennifer *singer, actress*
Kenney, H. Wesley, Jr., (Harry Wesley Kenney Jr.) *television producer and director*
King, Carole (Carole Klein) *lyricist, singer*
Smart, Jean *actress*

Sun City
Schmoll, Edith Margaret *music educator*

Sunnyvale
Lanaro, Clara Marrama *music educator, writer*

Sylmar
Foster, Dudley Edwards, Jr. *musician, educator*

Tarzana
Jones, Dean Carroll *actor*
Richman, Peter Mark *actor, painter, writer, film producer*

Templeton
Girolo, Nella Sue *retired voice educator*

Thousand Oaks
Kroeger, Chad *musician*
Kroeger, Mike *musician*
Loren, Sophia *actress*
Peake, Ryan *musician*
Rooney, Mickey (Joe Yule Jr.) *actor*

Toluca Lake
Costner, Kevin *actor*
Nunez, Oscar *actor*

Torrance
Nachef, Joanna Medawar *performing company executive*
Scarlata, Ronald Alan *theater educator, director*

Tujunga
Corea, Chick (Armando Corea) *pianist, composer*
Loehwing, Lord Rudi Charles *film producer, director, publicist, radio broadcasting executive, journalist*

Twentynine Palms
Panter, Nicole Olivieri *film educator, writer, film critic*

Universal City
Chavira, Ricardo Antonio *actor*
Cross, Marcia *actress*
Huffman, Felicity (Flicka Huffman) *actress*
Longoria, Eva (Eva Longoria Christopher, Eva Longoria Parker) *actress*
Merkerson, S. Epatha *actress*
O'Brien, Conan *talk show host, writer, performer*
Quinto, Zachary John *actor*
Reitman, Ivan *film director, producer*
Sheridan, Nicollette *actress*
Silberling, Bradley Mitchell *film director*
Spielberg, Steven Allan *film director, producer*
Wolf, Dick (Richard A. Wolf) *television producer*

Valencia
Smith, Ishmael Wadada Leo (Wadada Leo Smith) *musician, composer*

Valley Village
Barkin, Elaine Radoff *composer*
Diller, Phyllis (Phyllis Ada Driver Diller) *actress, writer*

Visalia
Porterfield-Pyatt, Chaumonde R. *music educator, advocate*

Walnut Creek
Grandi, Lois A. *theater director, choreographer, actor*

Weed
Schaefer, M. Elaine *music educator, conductor*

West Hills
Geeting, Joyce Ann *musician, educator*

West Hollywood
Cage, Nicolas (Nicolas Coppola) *actor*
Cole, Natalie Maria *singer*
Cyrus, Miley (Destiny Hope Cyrus, Hannah Montana) *actress, singer*
de Rossi, Portia *actress*
Duvall, Robert (Robert Selden Duvall) *actor*
Foster, Jodie (Alicia Christian Foster) *actress, film director, producer*
Franklyn, Audrey Pozen *talent promoter, television personality*
Goodwin, Ginnifer *actress*
Harden, Marcia Gay *actress*
Harper, Robert *actor*
Holloway, Josh *actor*
Jackson, Randy *music producer, television personality, musician*
Jbara, Gregory *actor*
McDormand, Frances *actress*
Pine, Chris Whitelaw *actor*
Presley, Priscilla (Pricilla Ann Wagner, Priscilla Beaulieu Presley) *actress*
Routh, Brandon *actor*
Ryan, Amy *actress*
Sackett, Barnard (Barney) *actor, film producer, director, scriptwriter*
Schreiber, Liev (Isaac Liev Schreiber) *actor*
Stein, Ben (Benjamin Jeremy Stein) *television personality, writer, lawyer, economist*
Stipe, Michael *musician, film producer*
Tarantino, Quentin Jerome *film director, scriptwriter*
Thornton, Billy Bob *actor, film producer*
Tomei, Marisa *actress*
Trachtenberg, Michelle *actress*
Washington, Kerry *actor*
Wright Penn, Robin *actress*
Zombie, Rob (Robert Cummings) *musician, filmmaker*

Woodland Hills
O'Connor, Brian D.A. *music educator, French horn musician*

COLORADO

Aspen
Berkeley, Edward *opera company director, music educator*

Aurora
Hughes, Christopher Adam *conductor, educator*

Boulder
Fink, Robert Russell *music educator and theorist, retired dean*
Hayes, Deborah *musicology educator, college administrator*
Mooney, William Piatt *actor*
Sable, Barbara Kinsey *retired music educator*

Castle Rock
Cooper, Kathryn Dupuy *musician, educator*
Wolfer, Dale *retired music educator*

Colorado Springs
Ansorge, Iona Marie *musician, educator, real estate agent*
Chandler Mills, Leah *theater educator*
Glenn, Shannon Lea *music educator*
Scott, Carla Anne *musician, educator*
Scott, Stephen *composer, musician, educator*

Denver
Boggs, Gil *principal ballet dancer*
Bondelevitch, David Joseph *film music editor*
Fredmann, Martin *ballet company artistic director, educator, choreographer*

Durango
Lee, Nathan K. *theater educator, director*

Englewood
Rowe, Mike (Michael Gregory Rowe) *television personality*

Estes Park
Varilek, Julie *music educator*

Grand Junction
Waggoner, Heather E. *theater educator*

Greeley
Malde, Melissa *singer, educator*
Murray, Robert Patrick *musician, educator*

Lakewood
Brownson, Sue McPherson *music educator*

Littleton
Asbjörnson, Kevin Donald *musician, small business owner*
Day, Susan Marie *music educator, composer*
Keats, Donald Howard *composer, educator*

Longmont
Coleman, Bud *choreographer, educator*

Loveland
Balsiger, David Wayne *television director, writer, television producer, television director, researcher*

Northglenn
Kappler, Karen L. *musician, educator*

U S A F Academy
Galema, Joseph M. *music director*

Westminster
Kopperud, Marilyn Sue *music educator*
White, John David *composer, author*

Wheat Ridge
Hockenberry, E'Rena *music educator*

CONNECTICUT

Bloomfield
Mamlok, Walter Joseph *music educator, musician*

Bridgeport
Richard, Ellen *theater executive*

Canaan
Thorne, Francis *composer*

Canton
Richardson, Dana Roland *technology consultant*

Chaplin
Wood, Wendy Deborah *filmmaker*

Colchester
Bartkowski, Kathleen Susan *musician*

Danbury
Jennings, Alfred Higson, Jr. *music educator, actor, singer*
Nelson, Willie Hugh *musician, lyricist*

Fairfield
LoMonaco, Martha Schmoyer *theater educator, director*

Farmington
Treggor, Josef Philip *music educator, composer, researcher*

Hartford
Mardinly, Susan J. *musician, music educator*

Meriden
Curran, Louis Jerome, Jr. *choral master*

New Haven
Fassler, Margot Elsbeth *music educator, religious studies educator*
Feldman, Grace A. *music educator*
Gerow, Aaron *performing arts educator*
Tirro, Frank Pascale *music educator, composer, writer*

Newington
Anderson, Kathryn Parks *music educator*
Cohen, Fern K. *music educator*

Oakville
Carroll, Constance Marie *pianist, music educator*

Old Saybrook
Geer, Lois Margaret *music educator*

Ridgefield
Taylor, Edwin R. *music director*

South Windsor
Murtha, Roger Gerry *music educator*

Stamford
Karp, Steve *agent*
Macurdy, John Edward *bass*
Novikova, Tatyana *music educator*

Storrs Mansfield
Rose, Dale A.J. *performing arts educator*

Torrington
Rolfe, Ellen Mary *retired music educator*

West Hartford
Braus, Ira L. *music educator, researcher*

Weston
Fredrik, Burry *theater producer, director*

Westport
Solum, John Henry *flutist, educator, author, advocate for arts*

Willimantic
Brodie, Ellen Faith *theater educator, director*

DELAWARE

Bear
Hudson, Kelly Marie *music educator*

Greenville
Parets, Paul L. *music educator*

New Castle
Shafer, Yvonne *theater educator, writer*

Wilmington
Lockhart-Videtto, Elizabeth Mary *music educator, director*

DISTRICT OF COLUMBIA

Washington
Ames, Frank Anthony *musician, film producer*
Buckley, Mary A. *dancer*
Crawford-Mason, Clare Wootten *television producer, journalist*
Day, Doris (Doris von Kappelhoff) *singer, actress*
Fischer, Elizabeth (Betsy) *television producer*
Fricke, Heinz *conductor*
Hamlisch, Marvin Frederick *composer, conductor, musician, entertainer*
Hay, Austin (George A. Hay) *actor, artist, pianist, writer*
Kahn, Michael *stage director*
Kaiser, Michael M. *performing arts center executive*
Kamalidiin, Saïs Telmeth *music educator*
Kendall, Peter Landis *television news executive*
Lelyveld, Gail Annick *actress*
McCann, John Michael *performing arts company professional*
Smith, Robin L. *television personality, psychologist, writer*
Stone, Florence Smith *film presenter, festival producer, consultant*
Tetreault, Paul R. *theater director, museum administrator*
Walsh, John *television show host, missing children and victims' rights advocate*
Webre, Septime *performing company executive, choreographer*
Weidenfeld, Sheila Rabb *television producer, writer*
Weinstein, Mark Jay *opera general director*
Williams, Armstrong *radio and television show host, political commentator*

FLORIDA

Boca Raton
Barry, Barbara Rosamond *music educator, writer*
Burganger, Judith *concert pianist*
Zaitz, Cynthia Louise *creativity, music, theatre and dance educator*

Clermont
Sides, I. Ruth S. *retired music educator*

Coral Gables
de Graaf, Melissa Jenny *music educator*
Sandoval, Arturo *jazz musician*

Davie
Walkinshaw, Nicole M. *performing arts educator*

Daytona Beach
Niemann, Judith A. *vocalist, educator*
Picott, Jerry Lee, Jr. *music educator*
Poitier, Constance Rena *music specialist, educator*

Deerfield Beach
Schwarz, Susan Bowers Young *piano teacher*

Doral
Heuer, Robert Maynard, II, *opera company executive*

Fort Lauderdale
LeRoy, Miss Joy *model, apparel designer*
Randi, James (Randall James Hamilton Zwinge) *magician, educator*
Spangler, David Sheridan *composer, director, creative arts educator, writer*
Webster, Ernest Wesley *musician, educator*

Gainesville
DesForges, Deborah Waln *music educator*
Forrester, Sheila Mary *music educator, composer*
Jaeger, Ina Claire *music educator, violinist*
Lowe, John Thomas, Jr. *church and concert musician*
Paul, Ouida Fay *music educator*
Selmore, Dametria Suzanne *actor*

Gulfport
Carroll, Charles Michael *music educator*

Hallandale
Vaserstein, Ludmila *music educator*

Hialeah
Lester, Timothy M. *music educator, vocalist*

Jacksonville
Fernandez, Ileana Barbara *musician, educator*
Homsley, Denise Louise *music educator*
Jordan, Deborah Ann *theater educator, director*
Page, Willis *conductor*
Stanley, Helen Camille *composer, musician*
Stewart, Sandra Kay *music educator*

Kissimmee
Schonauer, Lisa Lynn *music educator*

Lakeland
Bawek, Paul D. *theater educator, director, actor*
Jacobson, Barbara Dinger *music educator*

Largo
Inserra, Lisa *radio producer, educator*

Lecanto
Wheatley, Deborah A. *music educator*

Maitland
Nelson, Stephen D. *music educator*

Miami
Allen, Charles Norman *television, film and video producer*
Bergmann, Elizabeth Helene *dance educator, arts administrator*
De Sena, Ferdinando *composer, educator*
Floyd, Suzanne Elvira Izzo *music educator*
Galatas, Ruth Ann *musician, publishing executive, educator*
Harmon, Monica Renee *music educator*
Ibberson, Amy Kristen *musician, director*
Juanes, (Juan Esteban Aristizábal Vásquez) *musician*
Kahn, Jack Merrill *television producer*
Kerstetter, Kathleen Marie *music educator*
Madurga, Gonzalo F. *performing company executive, actor, singer, director*
Moody, Jacqueline Elaine *music educator*
Pilafian, Audrey Kalenian *music educator*
Saralegui, Cristina Maria *Spanish language television personality, journalist*
Walkley, Mary L. *voice and music educator*

Miami Beach
Rosenhaus, Drew *professional sports agent*

Milton
Leddy, Amanda Collier *music educator*

Monticello
Burkart, Arnold Emil *music educator*

Naples
Kirby, Charles William, Jr. *dancer, choreographer*
White, Roy Bernard *performing arts association administrator*

North Palm Beach
Hayman, Richard Warren Joseph *conductor*

Ocala
Hudson, Ann Elizabeth *music educator*

Orlando
Atwell, George Michael *composer, conductor, musician*
Beckner, Cynthia Byrd *music and elementary school educator*
Harris, Lani M. *theater educator*
Jordan, Grace Carol *music educator*
Rosene, Paul Earl *music educator*
Schultz, Victoria L. *harpist, entertainer, music educator*
Wittenburg, Michael Shane *concert pianist, music educator*

Ormond Beach
Granville, Paulina *independent music scholar, educator*
Hodkinson, Sydney Phillip *composer, educator, musician, conductor*

Palatka
Bratcher, Freddick *dancer, educator*

Palm Bay
Marshall, Kenneth Robert *music educator*

Palm Harbor
Katzen-Guthrie, Joy *performance artist, engineering executive*

Panama City Beach
Birdwell, Michelle Marie *music educator*

Pembroke Pines
Hudson, Brenda Louise *opera singer, piano and vocal coach, genealogist*

Pensacola
Lauderdale, Lynne Allison *music educator*
Rubardt, Peter Craig *conductor, educator*

Plant City
Neel, Sandra King *conductor*

Port Richey
Fry, Ronald Sylvan *music educator, director*

Port Saint Lucie
Rothschild, Mary Ann *music educator*

Punta Gorda
Cushman, Jaclyn Ellen *musician, director*

Ruskin
Dickson, Tim *music educator, marina general manager*

Saint Petersburg
Honein, Berthe *music educator*

Sarasota
Allen, Charles Franklin *music educator*
Carstens, Charlene B. *composer, music educator*
Faron, Sally Rogers *performing arts association administrator, consultant*
McCollum, John Morris *tenor*
McMaster, Gloria (Gloria Bugni Juhn) *mezzo-soprano, educator*
Sparrow, Carol Sweeney *music educator*
Stewart, Donald George *musician, composer, music industry executive*
Vasilaki, Linda Boozer *music educator*

Silver Springs
Tillis, Mel *entertainer, songwriter*

Tallahassee
Corzine, Jennifer Jean *music educator*
Houlihan, Gerri Paige *choreographer, educator*
Madsen, Clifford Kimball *music educator, therapist*
Rogers, Nancy Marie *music educator*
Zwilich, Ellen Taaffe *composer*

Tampa
Fung, Chi-Keung Victor *music educator, researcher*
Leopold, Blake *music educator*
Moore, Janet L.S. *music educator, dean*
Owen, Chuck *composer, music educator*
Plays, Dana *film director, educator*

Treasure Island
Dunn, Craig Andrew *entertainer, conductor, writer, composer, educator*

Valparaiso
Merritt, Phyllis June *music educator, director*

Venice
Tausan, Carol A. *music educator*

West Palm Beach
Castiglione, Anita *pianist, music educator*
Hale, Marie Stoner *performing company executive*
Robinson, Raymond Edwin *conductor, music educator, writer*

Weston
Berry, Becky *music educator*

Windermere
Rudzik, Lynne A. *musician, educator*

Winter Park
Cavenaugh, Jennifer Jones *theater educator, department chairman*
Wallace, Curtis Wilbern, Jr. *music director, organist*
Wrancher, Elizabeth Ann *retired music educator, opera singer*

GEORGIA

Alpharetta
Michele, Chrisette (Chrisette Michele Payne) *singer*

Athens
Buck, Peter *musician, guitarist*
Mills, Mike *musician*

Atlanta
Flannery, James William *performing arts educator, theater director and producer, singer*
Fletcher, Kathy Jordan *music educator*
Harris, Clifford Joseph, Jr., (T.I., Tip Harris) *rap artist*
Kingsbury, Michael Bryant *organist, retired elementary and secondary school educator*
Klughart, Toni Anne *musician, singer, educator*
McFall, John *performing company executive*
Raymond, Usher, IV, (Usher) *singer, actor*
Reese, Audrey Maria *music educator*
Spano, Robert *conductor, music director*
Taylor, Leslie M. *theater educator*
Wallace, Peter Marsden *radio personality and producer, commentator, writer*
Willis, Sharon J. *music educator, director*
Woodard, Diane E. *music educator*

Augusta
Meyers, Nicholaus *music educator*

Austell
Pope, Jacqueline Privette *music educator*

Bainbridge
Kuhn-Hancock, Lori Ann *performing arts educator, director*

Buford
Smith, Rebecca L. *musician*

Canton
Frady, Rita R. *music educator, information technology manager*
Jones-Kelner, Barbara Teryl *music educator*

Columbus
Golden, Joseph David *music educator*
Hiatt, Florence Ellen *musician*
Norah, Patricia Ann *retired music educator*

Decatur
Hamilton, Frank Strawn *musician, composer, educator*

Duluth
Moss, Shad Gregory (Bow Wow, Lil' Bow Wow) *rap artist*

East Point
Bridgewater, Herbert Jeremiah, Jr. *radio personality*

Fort Gaines
Chaffin, LaVerne *music educator*

Fort Valley
Williams, Barbara B. *retired music educator*

Gainesville
Jones, David Leland *music educator*
Pinson, Vicki Faye *music educator, director*

Hartwell
Rushing, Tonnie Austin Page *musician, educator*

Hephzibah
Smith, Charles Joe, Sr. *music educator*

Lagrange
Barber Knoll, Kim *performing arts educator, department chairman*

Lawrenceville
Folds, Frank Elliott *music educator*

Leesburg
Hilley, Mary Kay *music educator*

Loganville
McGonigle, Terry L. *theater educator, consultant*

Mableton
Reeves, Denise Moseley *dancer, educator*

Marietta
Roach, Carole Hyde *music educator*
Sigler, Paulette Terry *music educator*

Mcdonough
Wilson, Russell Edward *music educator*

Milledgeville
Caldwell, Ann B. *music educator*
Ragan, Charlotte Ann *music educator*
Tolbert, Patti McClure *music educator*

Oakwood
Phillips, Ernie Howard *music educator*

Peachtree City
Day, Annette J. *music educator*

Richmond Hill
Dasher, Donna Shearouse *music educator*

Rome
Davis, Susan Lynn *musician, educator*

Roswell
Ludacris, (Chris Bridges) *musician, actor*
Siepi, Cesare *opera singer*

Savannah
Deen, Paula H. *television personality, restaurant owner, chef*
Schultz, Lucinda D. *music educator*

Statesboro
Kwan, Yin Ling Eva *music educator*

Stone Mountain
Fairweather, Daniel Edward *music educator*

Sylvania
Harper, Michael Christopher *music educator*

Tallapoosa
Abney, Martha McEachern *music educator*

Thomaston
Thomas, Joan E. *music educator*

Tifton
Haywood, Mary Gwendolyn *music educator*

Waleska
Naylor, Susan Embry *music educator*

Whitesburg
Noell, Beverly Ann *music educator*

Woodstock
Soh-Harbin, Julie *music educator*

Young Harris
Richardson, Vernal Edward *retired music educator*
Wolfersteig, Eloise Smith *retired music educator*
Wolfersteig, Robert Frederick *retired musician*

HAWAII

Hilo
Besio, Kathryn Jean *performing arts educator*

Honolulu
Baker, Tammy Hailiopua *theater educator*
Cazimero, Robert *musician*
Lu, Caixia *television director, language educator*

Kaneohe
Lewis, Mary Jane *film producer, director, scriptwriter*
Young-Pohlman, Colette Lisa *music educator*

Waianae
Bourke-Faustina, Marlene Frances *music educator*

IDAHO

Boise
Aitken, Paul Arthur *composer, conductor*
Holt, Isabel Rae *radio program producer*

Moscow
Bathurst, Pamela *music educator*

Post Falls
Hasalone, Annette Leona *radio personality, research and development company executive*

Rexburg
Barrus, Charles LaMar, Jr. *music educator*

Sandpoint
Daarstad, Erik *cinematographer*

Twin Falls
Cowger, Shari Ann *music educator*

ILLINOIS

Algonquin
Dooley, Meeghan Elizabeth *music educator*

Aurora
Pappas, Margene *retired music educator*

Barrington
Carter, Jeanie *performing company executive*

Belleville
Jones, Donald Leigh *retired music educator*

Bloomington
Brown, Jared *theater director, educator, writer*
Lindberg, Sandra D. *theater educator, director, actor*
Vayo, David Joseph *composer, music educator*

Bourbonnais
Dalton, Martha Gomer *music educator*

Carbondale
Davenport, Susan Gail *music educator, director*

Carol Stream
Janssen, Carron Joyce *music educator*

Carterville
Seagle, Mike *theater educator*

Cary
Irey, Robin Elizabeth *performing company executive, performing arts educator*

Champaign
Fredrickson, L(awrence) Thomas *composer*
McKay, JoAnn *retired musician, composer*

Charleston
Faires, Joel Brooks *music educator*
Weidner, Robert Wright *retired musician, musicologist, educator*

Chicago
Bauer, Karen *music educator*
Bird, Andrew *musician*
Bridges, Cynthia Elaine *music educator*
Card, Deborah R. *orchestra administrator*
Choi, Kyong Mee *composer, musician, educator*
Cohan, Ryan *composer, pianist*
Dabrowski, Edward John *television technical director*
Daniel, T. *mime performer, theater director, choreographer*
Dunagan, Deanna *actress*
Farina, Dennis *actor*
Glass, Ira *radio producer, radio personality*
Guy, Buddy *blues guitarist*
Inojosa, Franklin *music educator*
Jaskot-Inclan, Maria *theater director, educator*
Kalver, Gail Ellen *dance company executive, musician*
Lavey, Martha *performing company executive*
Lazar, Ludmila *concert pianist, music educator*
Letts, Tracy *actor, playwright*
Mason, William *opera company director*
Matesky, Elisabeth Anne *international solo violinist, educator, composer, arranger*
May, Aviva Rabinowitz *music educator, musician, linguist*
Muti, Riccardo *conductor, music director*
Noel, Carol Adele *music educator, opera singer*
Padberg, Helen Swan *violinist*
Patterson, Carly *singer, former Olympic gymnast*
Pollak, Lisa *radio producer*
Reed, Rondi *actress, theater director*
Robertson, Anne Walters *music educator, music historian*
Savage, Terry *television personality, journalist, stockbroker*
Schmitt, Natalie Crohn *theater educator*
Schmitz, Jeffrey Michael *performing arts educator*
Tallchief, Maria *former ballerina*
Wang, Albert James *violinist, educator*
Wasson, Jeffrey *music educator*
Wheater, Ashley C. *former dancer, performing company executive*
Winfrey, Oprah *television talk show host, actress, television producer*

Chicago Heights
Reed, Scott C. *musician, educator, writer*

Country Club Hills
McClelland, Helen *music educator*

Dekalb
Chitwood, Judith *performing arts educator*
Cosenza, Glenda Lee *music educator*
Gately, Kathryn *theater educator*
Gelman, Alexander *theater director, educator*
Goldenberg, William Bruce *musician, educator*

Downers Grove
Hornish, Ronald Frederick *music educator*

East Peoria
Wadsworth Walker, Cherilee *music educator*

Edwardsville
Anop, Lenora-Marya *violinist, music educator*
Claudson, William Dolan *music educator*
Schultz, Norbert J. *retired music educator*
Stranc, Cathleen L. *music educator*

Elmhurst
Weiger, Alan W. *theater director, educator*

Evanston
Cantor, Daniel Adam *theater educator*
Eberley, Helen-Kay *opera singer, recording industry executive, poet*
Hall, Bruce A. *music educator*
Hemke, Frederick L. *music educator*
Kan-Walsh, Karen Chih Pah *music educator*
Kujala, Walfrid Eugene *musician, educator*
Peters, Gordon Benes *retired musician*
Shapiro, Anna D. *theater director*
Zimmerman, Mary Alice *performing arts educator, director, playwright*

Galesburg
Polay, Bruce *musician, conductor, educator*

Glen Ellyn
Evans, Margarita Sawatzky *retired voice educator, academic administrator*

Godfrey
Parton-Stanard, Susan *music educator, voice educator, musician*

Grayslake
Turska, Joanna *music educator*

Greenville
Stampfli, Leonard Thomas *music educator, department chairman*

Herscher
Cessna, Katrina J. *music educator, composer*

Highland Park
Hobson, Stephen Gilbert *conductor, music educator*

Lemont
Marx, Kenneth R. *music educator*

Lincolnshire
Criglar, Melinda L. *retired dancer, educator*

Lisle
Flock, Maryann *musician, director*

Loves Park
Dixon, John James *retired music educator*

Macomb
Walker, Tammie Leigh *music educator*

Mascoutah
Setterlund, Tina A.M. *music educator*

Mattoon
Bagger, Edward Duke James *retired performing arts educator*
Black, Todd Ronald *music educator*

Moline
Kasinger, Thomas Paul *music educator*

Mundelein
Berg, Nancy Jeanne *music educator*

Naperville
Jack, Zachary Michael *performing arts educator*
Lanham-Murray, Nickole Cynthia *theater educator*
VerHoven, Victoria *voice educator*

Normal
Koch, John Michael *music educator, singer*
Vetere, Michael J. III *theater educator*

Northfield
Broos, Carol Linville *music educator*

Olive Branch
Shumaker, Jarod Kyle *music educator*

Oswego
Schneider, Glen Walter *music educator, director*

Paris
Hiddle, Susan K. *musician, educator*

Park Forest
Billig, Etel Jewel *theater director, actress*

Peoria
Arnold, Rebecca Leigh *theater educator*
Wright, Gina A. *voice educator*

River Forest
Goetz-Sota, Germaine Helen *theatre and speech educator, department chairman*

Rockford
Cole, Richie Thomas *musician, composer, educator*
Robinson, Donald Peter *musician, retired electrical engineer*

South Holland
Anderson, Paul Martin *musician, educator*

Springfield
Cobb-Myers, Janet Lea *music educator*

Urbana
Lee, Esther Kim *theater educator*
Vaughn, Linda F. *musician, educator*
Yeung, Ann *music educator*

Vernon Hills
Kim, Sachiko O. *music educator*

Villa Park
Antonelli, Joseph K. *musician, educator*
Ellingsen, Barbara Joyce *music educator*

Waterloo
Hoffmann, Mary Jukich *voice educator*

Waukegan
Houle, Jeanne Larson *retired music educator*

West Chicago
Noonan, Josette Marie *music educator*

Wheaton
Lim, Cheryl Cheon-Ae *music educator*

Wilmette
Wentz, Pete (Peter Lewis Kingston Wentz III) *musician*

Winnetka
Ladd, David Scott *music educator*

INDIANA

Anderson
Chappell, Rebecca A. *music educator*

Auburn
Johnson, George Axil III *television producer*

Bloomington
Brown, Keith *musician, educator*
Effron, David Louis *conductor, performing company executive*
Gouker, Jane Ann *music educator*
Kallaur, Barbara *music educator*
Kiesgen, Paul *music educator*
McCraw, Michael *music educator*
McDonald, Susann Hackett *music educator*
Mellencamp, John (John Cougar) *singer, lyricist*
Phillips, Harvey G. *musician, performing arts educator*
Spera, Dominic Gregorio *music educator, writer*
Ward-Steinman, David *composer, music educator, pianist*

Carmel
Priestley, Jason (Jason Bradford Priestley) *actor*

Columbus
Bowden, David *conductor*

Crawfordsville
Fisher, A. James *theater educator, director, actor*

Elkhart
Carnall, Timothy W. *music educator*

Evansville
Dallinger, Carol J. *music educator*
Fiedler, Anne Hastings *music educator*
Reed, R. Douglas *music educator*

Greencastle
Phang, May *music educator*

Hammond
Hansen, Jack Winsor *musician, educator*

Hanover
Batchvarova, Madlen Todorova *music educator, conductor*
Fearnow, Mark Allen *theater educator, writer*
Nickels, Ruth Elizabeth *band director*

Hebron
Walker, Joyce L. *music educator*

Indianapolis
Burgomaster, Frederick *music director*
Everly, Jack *conductor*
Murphy, Meissa Bleu *music educator, behaviorist*
Schmid, John A. *musician, voice educator*
Tudor, Tamara *theater educator*

Marion
Miller, Peter Karl *music educator*

Michigan City
Wiegand, Elizabeth Grieger *musician, educator*

Mishawaka
Kendall, Michael Jay *musician, educator*

Muncie
Mackey, Elizabeth Jocelyn *music educator*
Richter, Elizabeth Margot *music educator*
Vayman, Anna *music educator*

New Albany
Pieper, Michael Joseph *television producer, actor, talk show host*

Notre Dame
Juan, Anton Manauis *director/playwright, senior professor*

Oakland City
Spitler, Carolyn Elizabeth *music educator*

Plainfield
Clark, Debra Elizabeth *music educator*

Rensselaer
Thiel, Robb G. *musician, director*

South Bend
Bell, Wishart Bryan *music educator, conductor*
Muniz, Jorge *composer, music educator*
Skarbek, Denise Marie *music educator*

Terre Haute
Papadopoulos, Peter Joseph *theater educator, playwright*

Upland
Bade, Christopher *musician, educator*

West Lafayette
Holtvedt, Kristine June *performing arts educator, director*

IOWA

Alden
Oliver, Kerryn Hinrichs *music and religious studies educator*

Bettendorf
Greenhoe, David Stanley *performance artist, music educator*
Myatt, William Howard *theater educator, director, actor*
Schulz, Sally Ann *pastoral musician, conductor, educator*

Cedar Falls
Buckholz, Christopher *music educator*
Chesnutt, Rod Martin *music educator*
Fanelli, Michael Paul *musician, educator, writer*

Cedar Rapids
Nassif, Shakeeb Joseph *performing arts educator*

Cherokee
Gordon, Roma Dianne *music educator*

Coralville
Thomas, Carole Lesniak *retired music educator*

Council Bluffs
Kurt, Johnny Thomas *music educator*

Davenport
Dcamp, Charles Barton *music educator*
Eitrheim, Kristofer James *theater educator*

Decorah
Monson, Larry Lee *music educator*
Noble, Weston Henry *music educator*

Dubuque
Dunker, Amy *music educator*

Estherville
Ayres, Carol J. *music educator, director*

Forest City
Fiebig, Jeremy Ray *theater educator*
Taylor, Kristín Jónína *musician, educator*

Fort Dodge
Naeve, Denise R. *music educator*

Grinnell
Rommereim, John Christian *music educator*

Iowa City
Gompper, David *composer, music educator*
Joselson, Rachel *voice educator*
Kottick, Edward Leon *musician, educator*
Mather, Roger Frederick *retired music educator, writer*
Preucil, Doris Bogen *music educator*

Mount Pleasant
Crane, Frederick Baron *retired music educator*

Orange City
Josselyn-Cranson, Heather Rene *music educator*

Pella
Sodd, Mary Jo *theatre educator*

Sioux City
Dye, Lana L. *music educator*

Storm Lake
Keeler, Paula A. *music educator, director*
Safley, Holli Ewoldt *music educator*

Washington
Buchholz, Lee William (Leroy William Buchholz) *retired music educator*

Waverly
O'Konski, Marjorie Katherine *music educator*

KANSAS

Blue Rapids
Hood, Carol A. *music educator*

Emporia
Aman, M. Robert *music educator*

Haysville
Brown, Linda Carolyn *music educator*

Hutchinson
Wendelburg, Norma Ruth *composer, educator, pianist*

Iola
Piazza, Tony *theater educator*

Kansas City
Minter, Karen Celeste *music educator*

Lawrence
Bial, Henry *theater educator*
Mattila, Edward Charles *music educator*
Tsubaki, Andrew Takahisa *theater director, educator*

Lenexa
Warenskjold, Dorothy *singer, educator*

Liberal
Workman, Darin D. *music educator*

Lindsborg
LeGault, Gregory Lee *theater educator, playwright*

Manhattan
Ollington, David McKenna *performing arts educator*

Mcpherson
Hopkins, Kyle Darin *music educator, director*

Olathe
Colson, Judy C. *music educator*

Overland Park
Davis, Maureen *performing arts educator*

Paola
Buntin, Sandra Lynn *music educator*

Parsons
Walker, Robert R. *music educator*

Topeka
Prece, Paul M. *theater educator, department chairman*

Wichita
Hittle, Lisa Lynn *musician, educator*
McArthur, Tillian (Tilly McMac) *freelance/self-employed music educator, small business owner*

KENTUCKY

Calvert City
Madison, Vicki DiAnne *retired music educator*

Cawood
Shepherd, William Michael *music educator, musician*

Frankfort
Fletcher, Winona Lee *theater educator*

Georgetown
Hall, Sara Y. *retired music educator*

Lexington
Lugo, Noemi G. *voice educator*
Maloney, Doreen M. *performing arts educator*
Partain, Gregory L. *composer, educator*

Louisville
Hardin, Carmen Marie *music educator*
Lin, Stephen Houng Tze *music educator*

Morehead
Blair, Suanne Hower *music educator*

Murray
Hill, Todd Edwin *band director*

Richmond
James, Rob *performing arts association administrator, consultant*
Smith, Carla Anne *music educator*

Somerset
Sexton, Scotty Eugene *music educator, gifted and talented educator*

LOUISIANA

Baton Rouge
Buchmann, Molly O'Banion *choreographer, educator*
Lusted, Dona Sanders *music educator, consultant, organist*
Mathews, Sharon Walker *performing company executive, secondary school educator*
McCoy, Wesley Lawrence *musician, educator, conductor*
Smith, Richard James *retired music educator*
Tandberg, Gerilyn Gay *theater educator, retired costume designer*
Yarbrough, Martha Cornelia *music educator*

Bossier City
Johnson, Russell W. *video editor*

Franklin
Rouly, Ellie Arceneaux *dancer, educator*

Hammond
Hemberger, Glen James *university band director, music educator*

Lake Charles
Batchelor, Karen Sue *music educator*
Belew, Barbara Jeanne *music educator*
Lines, Carol Fuqua *voice educator*
Pace, (Audrey) Joy *theater educator*

Metairie
Grotkowski, Edward Michael *music educator, director*

Monroe
Trapp, A. C. *retired music educator*

Morgan City
Grant-Dupuy, Jennifer W. *music educator*

Natchitoches
Allen, Burt M. *music educator, director*
Derby-McDermott, Dennette S. *flutist, educator*

New Orleans
Blanchard, Terence *musician, composer*
Gendusa, Charles Patrick *performing arts educator*
St. Julien, Thais Mary *soprano, musician*

Ruston
Thompson, Laura Ann Mobley *music educator*

Sulphur
Fuller, Betty Stamps *music educator*

Thibodaux
Hebert, Frances Cynthia *music educator*
Soares, Luciana *music educator*

Zachary
Rogillio, Kathy June *musician, director, small business owner, educator*

MAINE

Castine
Davis, Peter Frank *filmmaker, writer*

Gorham
Kilroy, Wil *theater educator*

Orono
Hardy, Sandra E. *theater educator, director*

Sidney
Gooldrup, Marjorie Shepard *music educator*

South Freeport
Schwartz, Elliott Shelling *composer, writer, retired music educator*

Sullivan
Davis-Wexler, Ginia *singer, director*

MARYLAND

Annapolis
Seep, Dorothy M. *music educator*

Arnold
Fitzgerald, Lynda P. *dancer, director*
Macaulay, Janice Michel *music educator, composer*

Baltimore
Alsop, Marin *conductor, violinist, music director*
Dawkins, Stuart Earl *theater producer*
Diaz-Starr, Lucía López *performing arts educator, singer*
Grabill, Vin *performing arts educator, department chairman*
Huggins, Amy Branum *music educator*
Hulbert, Jarl O. *music educator*
Mydlack, Daniel James *filmmaker, educator*
Otal, Monica D. *music educator*
Sutherland, Donald Sinclair *musician, educator*
Temirkanov, Yuri Khatuevich *conductor, music director*
Teter, Eston Joe *musician, educator*

Bowie
Hillsman, Joan Rucker *music educator*
Lewis, Patricia Ann *music educator*
Parr-Corretjer, Polly *singer, music educator*

Chestertown
Clarke, Garry Evans *composer, academic administrator, musician*

College Park
Montgomery, William Layton *musician, educator*
O'Hara, Michael M. *theater educator*

Columbia
Carter, Karen Zepp *music educator, elementary school educator*
Kearns, Ronald Edwin *music educator, performance artist*

Crofton
Mahaffey, Redge Allan *movie producer, director, writer, actor, scientist, business executive*
Smith, Rebecca Anstine *harpist, educator*

Ellicott City
Benjamin, Thomas Edward *music educator, composer, conductor*

Emmitsburg
Tortora, Anne Halloran *music educator, director*

Fort Washington
Harrison, Ronnette *music educator, director*

Frostburg
Bauman, Jon Ward *retired music educator*
Horner, Ronald George *musician, educator*

Hagerstown
Hull, Michele Lynn *music educator*

Indian Head
Bailey, Louella C. *music educator*

Kensington
Forrest, Sidney *clarinetist, music educator*

La Plata
Herdman-Fisher, Carolyn A. *music educator*

Owings
O'Neill, Patricia Tydings *performing arts educator, language educator*

Potomac
Tressel, George Walter *television producer, science educator, consultant*

Princess Anne
Nagoski, Marcelle *music educator*

Salisbury
Cockey, Linda Essick *music educator*
Folger, William Michael *music educator*

Silver Spring
Snyder, Donald Ivandale *musician, educator*

Towson
Ahearn, Elizabeth Lowe *performing arts educator, dance department chair*
Forrest, Juliet *dancer, choreographer, educator*
Jothen, Michael Jon *music educator*
Levin, Marguerite Baker *music educator*
Luchese, Diane *music educator*
McFalls, James C. *trombonist and music educator*

Wye Mills
Peterson, Richard Stewart *theater director*

MASSACHUSETTS

Amherst
Donohue, Therese Brady *artistic director, choreographer, costume and set designer*
Rexroth, Laura Jayne *conductor*
Sawyer, Eric Warren *composer, music educator*
Spratlan, Lewis *composer, educator*

Boston
Barker, Edwin Bogue *musician*
Chambers, Richard Wadsworth *theater educator*
Firth, Everett Joseph *timpanist*
Fox, Donal *composer, jazz musician, pianist*
Harvey, Mark Sumner *composer, educator, retired minister, musician*
Hoffman, Stanley Marc *composer, editor*
Hoyt, Herbert Austin Aikins *television producer*
Hughson, Barry C. *performing arts association administrator*
Jaguaribe, Maira Clodes *music educator*
Jochum, Veronica *pianist*
Lockhart, Keith Alan *conductor, music director*
Loizou, Maria Jane *singer, librarian*
Marsh, Milton R.W. *composer*
Moriarty, John *opera administrator, artistic director*
Nickole, Leonidas A. *performing arts educator, director*
Nissinen, Mikko Pekka *dancer, performing arts company executive, artistic director*
Wheeler, W(illiam) Scott *composer, conductor, music educator*
Williams, John Towner *composer, conductor*
Young, Laura *choreographer, educator*

Braintree
Hallenbeck, Rachel Kirsten *music educator, director*

Cambridge
Cassino, Peter Frank *music educator, musician*
Connick, Harry, Jr. *musician, actor, vocalist, composer, lyricist*
de Varon, Lorna Cooke *choral conductor*
Hatfield, Juliana *vocalist*
Kirchner, Leon *composer, pianist, conductor*
Kraus, Rozann B. *performing company executive*
Orchard, Robert John *theater producer, educator*
Parker, Lisa Frederick *music educator, Dalcroze specialist*
Sims, Ezra *composer*
Ward, John Milton *music educator*
Wood, Pamela Sharon *music educator, soprano*

Chelsea
Sutter, Diane *television executive*

Dedham
Magner, Jerome Allen *performing company executive*

Eastham
Tipton, Noel Martin, Jr. *musician, writer, composer*

Falmouth
Brock, Nancy Jeanne *music educator, writer*

Franklin
Ferguson, Dennis Edward *musician, educator*

Great Barrington
Curtin, Phyllis *music educator, dean, vocalist*

Holyoke
Damon, Steven William *music educator*
Dower-Gold, Catherine Anne *music history educator*

Hopkinton
Moran, Wendy Jacqueline *musician, educator*

Hyannis
Campbell, Roy Niel *music educator*

Lee
Thomas, Augusta Read *composer*

Longmeadow
Dovolani, Tony (Driton Dovolani) *dancer*

Marblehead
Kennedy, Elizabeth Mae *musician*

Mashpee
Jamison, John L. *musician, educator*

Mattapan
Walker, Dianne *dancer, performing company executive*

Medford
Barwell, Nina *music educator*

Needham
Di Domenica, Robert Anthony *musician, composer*

Newton
Wahlberg, Mark *actor*

Newton Center
Schuller, Gunther Alexander *composer*

North Adams
McConnell, Matthew Stephen *composer, educator*

North Attleboro
Flynn, Kate Elizabeth *music educator, director*

Northampton
Naegele, Philipp Otto *musician, educator*

Orleans
Patterson, Elizabeth C. *choir director*

Pittsfield
Guzzo, Jessica Ann *music educator*
Shanahan, Ellen C. *music educator*

Plymouth
Gregory, Dick *comedian, volunteer*

Salem
McLyman, Meghan *dance professor*
Staples, Mavis *singer*

Shirley
Hoffmann, Micheal Joseph *theater director*

Somerville
Curwood, Steve *television producer, host*
Fitzpatrick, Terry *public radio reporter, producer*

Vineyard Haven
Breuer, Joann Green *theater director*

Waltham
Boykan, Martin *composer, music educator*
Chang, Yu-Hui *composer*
Krstansky, Adrianne Marie *actress, performing arts educator*

Wellesley
Olsen, David Teng *performing arts educator*

Wellesley Hills
Tang, Jenny CC *music educator*

West Barnstable
Rapoza, Elizabeth *theater educator, playwright, director*

Westfield
Aldrich-Jones, Jean Elizabeth *music educator*

Weston
Tenney, Sarah G. *music educator*

Williamstown
Shainman, Irwin *musician, educator*

Woburn
Guo, Ling *musician, consultant*

Worcester
Delorey, John Francis *music educator*
Hatfield, Renee S.J. *music educator*
Lamothe, Donat Romeo *music educator*
McDaniels, Darryl (D.M.C.) *rap artist*

Worthington
Schrade, Rolande Maxwell Young *composer, pianist, educator*

MICHIGAN

Adrian
Dodson, John Thomas *orchestra conductor*

Albion
Balke, Maureen A. *voice educator*

Ann Arbor
Allen, Geri A. *composer, pianist*
Bolcom, William Elden *composer, educator, musician*
Paxton, Tom *songwriter, entertainer, author*
Peng Chen, Hsiu-Hui *music educator*
Scavarda, Donald Robert *composer, artist*
Verrett, Shirley *soprano*

Battle Creek
Matthews, Wyhomme S. *retired music educator, academic administrator*

Berrien Springs
Ritzenthaler, Beatriz Augusta *musician, educator*

Bloomfield Hills
Swift, Jonathan *television personality, educator*

Commerce Township
Thibideau, Carolyn C. *musician, educator*

Detroit
Calarco, N. Joseph *theater educator*
Collins, Christopher Brian *musician*
DiChiera, David *opera company director*
Engelhardt, Regina *cosmetologist, artist, small business owner*
Slatkin, Leonard Edward *music director, conductor*
Vander Weg, John D. *music educator*

East Lansing
Kirk, Edgar Lee *retired musician, educator*

Farmington Hills
Purdy, Jan Rae *music educator*

Frankfort
Storrer, William Allin *theater educator, consultant*

Grand Rapids
Horn, Joyce Elaine *retired music educator*
Metzler, James Robert *musician*

Hillsdale
Brandon, James M. *theater educator*

Holland
Kearns, Bobbi Lynn *music educator*

Jackson
Livesay, Jacqueline Ryder *music educator, choir director*
Nugent, Ted (Theodore Anthony Nugent) *musician, radio personality*

Kalamazoo
Baas, Jane Thornbury *dancer, educator*
Berkow, Jay *theater director*
Griffin, Monica Leigh *voice educator*
Ratner, Carl Joseph *opera stage director, baritone*

Lake Orion
Berger, Laura Ann *dance studio owner*

Lansing
Otten, Roberta Ann *theater and dance educator, choreographer*

Livonia
Nelson, Troy Alan *music educator, church musician, assistant principal*

Mount Pleasant
Martin, Sue Ann *theater educator*
Mascolo-David, Alexandra *music educator*

Northport
Scripps, Douglas Jerry *musician, educator, conductor*

Romeo
Tsukamoto, Daniel *piano instructor, church organist*

Saginaw
Coughlin, Jeannine Marie *music educator*

Sebewaing
Corrion, Samantha Jae *music educator*

South Haven
Tyrrell, Cole Brooks *music educator*

Traverse City
Faulmann, Roger Ray *retired music educator*

Troy
Zoubareff, Kathy Olga *actress, model*

Warren
Cutter, Jeffrey S. *music educator*

Waterford
Pronovost, Amy Lynne *dancer, educator*

Wayland
Stephenson-Bennett, Michelle Annette *music educator*

MINNESOTA

Apple Valley
Becker, Bruce Warren *music educator*

Arden Hills
Lahann, Jon Clifford *retired music educator*

Bloomington
Smith, Henry Charles III *symphony orchestra conductor*

Cambridge
Van Alstine, Sharri Kay *music educator*

Chanhassen
Prince, (Prince Rogers Nelson) *musician, actor*

Coon Rapids
McCarthy, Thomas Gregory *theater educator*
Vogel, Scott Charles *music educator*
Wilson, Sylvia Alyce *musician, educator*

Duluth
Morath, Max Edward *entertainer, composer, writer*

Eden Prairie
De Bono, Luella Elizabeth *music educator*

Falcon Heights
Jackson, Donna Cardamone *retired music educator*

Golden Valley
Spake, Mary Barbara *music educator*

Minneapolis
Bizri, Hisham M. *filmmaker, educator*
Boyce, Karin R. *music educator*
Brown, Carlyle *performing company executive, playwright*
Fetler, Paul *retired composer*
Malmin, Cindy Lou *music educator*
Martenson, Edward Allen *theater manager*
Nash, Elizabeth Hamilton *music and theater educator, vocalist, writer*
Vänskä, Osmo *conductor, music director*

Morris
Seggelke, Martin Heinrich *conductor, music professor*

Saint Cloud
Wentworth, Brenda Kathryn *theater educator*

Saint Joseph
Dillard, Leigh Williams *theater educator*

Saint Paul
Mennicke, David *music educator, director*
Murray, Bill *actor, writer*
Thompson, Steven Bruce *music educator, director*
Waters, Harry T., Jr. *theater educator, actor*
You, Yali *music educator*

Saint Peter
Maatman, Micah Joel *theater educator*

Thief River Falls
Anderson, Steven Keith *musical entertainer, writer*

Wayzata
Skrowaczewski, Stanislaw *conductor, composer*

Woodbury
Bunch, William Franklin *retired music educator*

Worthington
Benton, Galen Lee *retired music educator*

MISSISSIPPI

Clinton
Durham, Carol Elise *musician, educator*
Wilder, Brenda *music specialist*

Columbus
Kantack, Catherine Margaret *retired music educator, international and bank broker*
Segrest, Linda Hudson *music educator*

Ellisville
Strickland, Carrie D *music educator*

Gautier
Feris, Alessandra Schmidt *music educator*

Grenada
Thomas, Ouida Power *music educator*

Hattiesburg
Stockstill, David H. *musician, research historian, lecturer*

Jackson
Frost, Joseph D. *theater educator*
Sachs, Stephen Warren *music educator, director*
Smith, Carnice *music educator, director*

Meridian
Nabors, Steven Thomas *theater educator*

Southaven
Butler, Elizabeth Rosanne *music educator, director*

Sumrall
Downey, James Cecil *retired music and humanities educator*

University
Dor, George W. K *music educator*

MISSOURI

Ballwin
Cowell, Kimberly *music educator*

Blue Springs
Washburn, Gladys Haase *retired church musician, educator, director*

Bolivar
Hooper, William Loyd *music educator, university administrator*

Bowling Green
Bruce, Judith Esther *retired music educator, elementary school educator*
Carty, Elaine Smith *music educator*

Butler
Turner, Vicky Jo *music educator*

Chesterfield
Baker, Sandra Kay *music educator*

Columbia
Burgoyne, Suzanne *theater educator, writer*
Vale, Patrice J. *musician, consultant*

Creve Coeur
Randle, Bernadette *musician, composer, graphics designer*

Doniphan
McCann, Lawrence Alton *music educator*

Fulton
McClain, Cindy Dunstan *music educator*

Jefferson City
Govang, Don C. *performing arts association administrator*

Joplin
Wostal, Holly Ann *music educator*

Kansas City
Lindsay, Twyla Lynn *music educator*
Londré, Felicia Mae Hardison *theater educator*
Mobberley, James *music educator, composer*
Myers, Betty J. *retired music specialist*
Rudy, Paul *composer*
Setser, Patricia A. *music educator*
Sherburn, Rebecca Sue *voice educator*
Whitener, William Garnett *dancer, choreographer*

Liberty
Coleman, Ian David *music educator*
Harriman, Richard Lee *performing arts administrator, educator*

Marshall
Sayer, Ronald J. *composer, educator*

Maryville
Kling, Carl Andrew *music educator*

Platte City
Jones, Jay Robert *music educator*

Rogersville
Hover, Tryphena Machael *music educator*

Saint Charles
Grooms, Pamela Gayle *music educator*

Saint James
Stevens, Helen Jean *music educator*

Saint Louis
James, James Edward *music educator*
Pileggi, Annamaria *theater director, educator*
Robertson, David *conductor, music director*
Schvey, Henry I. *performing arts educator*
Schweizer, Gregory Paul *music educator*
Scoggins, Rob *choreographer, director*
Stallings, Charles Kendall *music educator, composer*
Stewart, John Harger *music educator*
Stookesberry, Denise *musician, educator*
Sutherland, Mary (Marcus) *pianist, composer, conductor*
Swearingen, Laura Colleen *music educator, director*
Turner-Richard, Lana R. *musician, director, composer*
Woolf, Steven Michael *artistic director*

Saint Peters
Poettker, Mary Therese *music educator*
Ranner, Shanna *music educator*

Springfield
Blake, Loretta L. *music educator*
Cassity, Michael David *music therapy educator*
Harris, Jane Marie *music educator*
Heyboer, Jill L. *musician, educator*
Jenkins, Bonnie Lee *music educator*
Spicer, Holt Vandercook *retired theater educator*
Wilkins, Sharon Kay Ramsey *music educator, director*

Trenton
Gentry, Shirley *music educator, writer*

Wildwood
Hapner, Barry Nathan *performing arts educator*

MONTANA

Bozeman
Biegel, Debra Jeanne *music educator*
Vick, Jeffrey Harrison *musician, educator*

Butte
Clark, Gloria A. *music educator*

Eureka
Kessler-Hodgson, Lee Gwendolyn *actress, marketing company executive*

Great Falls
Hugg, Harold J. *music educator, director*

Missoula
Brown, Firman Hewitt, Jr. *drama educator, theater director*

NEBRASKA

Chadron
Mays, Roger William *theater educator*
Winkle, William Allan *music educator*

Fremont
Elsberry, James *retired music educator, director*
Regier, Bryan L. *music educator*

Hastings
White, George William *theater educator*

Kearney
Schnoor, Neal Henry *music educator*

Lincoln
Collier, Nathan Morris *musician, educator*
Dixon, Wheeler Winston *film and video studies educator, writer*
Koch Johns, Patricia A. *theater educator*
Parkhurst, Jack Lee *theater educator*

Lyons
Rose, Dwight Dean *music educator*

Mc Cook
Watts, Susan Helene *theater educator*

Omaha
Johnson, James David *concert pianist, organist, educator*
Storm, Christopher *music educator*
Williams, Steven L. *theater educator, director*

NEVADA

Boulder City
Schultheis, Adam John *music educator, consultant*

Elko
Lovell, Walter Benjamin *music educator, radio personality*

Indian Springs
Dvorak, DeLyle Dennis *music and early childhood educator, consultant*

Las Vegas
Baley, Virko *composer, conductor, pianist*
Bernstein, Maureen Ann *theater educator, director*
Canfield, James *artistic director*
Collins, Clarence *musician*
Gourdine, Jerome Anthony (Anthony Gourdine, Little Anthony) *musician*
Hall, Zuladawn *music educator*
Kalb, Benjamin Stuart *television producer, director*
Lewis, Jerry (Joseph Levitch) *comedian*
Muhlenbruck-Fleischer, Deborah Lynn *music educator*

North Las Vegas
Janzen, Donna Lee (Bricker) *music educator, singer*
Roth, Kelly *choreographer, educator*
Talley, Brenda S. *performing arts center director, theatrical light designer*

Reno
Aldrich, Gary O. *singer, educator*
Daniels, Ronald Dale *conductor*
Kurkul, Wen Wang *musician, educator, administrator*

Sandy Valley
Viscuglia, Jenny Lou *music educator*

NEW HAMPSHIRE

Dover
Spires, Diane Hayes *music educator*

Hanover
Ehrlich, David Gordon *film director, educator*

Orford
Karol, John J., Jr. *producer, filmmaker*

Walpole
Burns, Ken *documentary filmmaker*

NEW JERSEY

Allendale
Ruth, Rodney *musician, music consultant, contractor, educator*

Cherry Hill
Pfeuffer, Robert John *musician*

Chester
Albert-Vespignani, Kathleen M.G. *performing arts educator*

Cinnaminson
Edwin, Robert *voice educator*

Cream Ridge
Jacobs, Jim *actor, composer, librettist, playwright*

Delanco
Lane, Carrie Belle (Hairston) *retired music educator*

East Brunswick
Braun, Anna M. *music educator*

Edison
Chen-Maxham, Li-Chan *soprano*

Elizabeth
de la Viña-Sierra, Diana Maria *music educator*

Flemington
Nowak, Jerry (Gerald C. Nowak) *music educator, Musician Writer Conductor*

Fort Lee
Thomopoulos, Michael *music educator*

Glassboro
Zuponcic, Veda Helen *music educator, art director*

Hackensack
Pero, Victoria *performing arts educator*

Hawthorne
Clavijo, Pío *music educator, director*

Hillside
Wilson, Bertina Iolia *retired music educator*

Jersey City
Howard, Terrence Dashon *actor*
Minnelli, Liza *singer, actress*
Queen Latifah, (Dana Elaine Owens) *actress, musician*
Warren, Maredia Delois *music educator*

Lakewood
Appello, Patrick Paul *guitarist, lutenist, educator*
Malamut, Myra Lewinter *music educator, director*

Leonia
Deutsch, Nina *pianist, vocalist*
Dondysh, Victoria *pianist*

Lincroft
Benham, Helen *music educator*

Linden
Dunn, John Mark *music educator, director*

Manalapan
Lin, Chiu-Tze *conductor, musician*

Mays Landing
Gross, Michelle Bayard *dancer, educator*
McNeal, Jane Erskine *musician, educator*

Medford
Sheffer, James Thomas *music educator*

Montclair
Craig, Mary Ann *music educator*
Walker, George Theophilus, Jr. *composer, music educator, pianist*

Mount Laurel
Jones, Marian C. *music educator*

New Brunswick
Lustig, Graham *performing company executive*
Saltz, Amy *theater educator, director*
Schuld, Susan Marie *performing arts educator*
Whitener, Scott *music educator, researcher*

Newark
Barron, Kenny *musician*
Järvi, Neeme *conductor, music director*
Mácal, Zdenìk *conductor, music director*
Santiago, Diana *music educator*

Newton
Boulware, Bobbie L. *music educator*

Oceanport
Ruggeri, Dianne Ellen *music educator, band director*

Old Bridge
Nanton, Lisa Seeman *music educator*

Paramus
Bonnaffons, Ken J. *theater director, Professor ESL*
Saltzman, Jared *performing arts educator, lighting designer*

Paterson
Richardson, Cynthia Teresa *music educator*

Plainfield
Mazur, Thomas A. *music educator*

Pomona
Mallett, Mark Edmund *theater educator*

Princeton
Orphanides, Nora Charlotte *ballet educator*
White, Barbara Ann *composer*

Red Bank
Smith, Kevin *film director, writer, actor*

Richwood
Robinette, Joseph Allen *playwright*

Ridgefield
Chmerkovskiy, Maksim *dancer*
Tracey, Matthew Sean *musician, educator*

Riverdale
Bullough, John Frank *musician, educator*

Rockaway
Steier, Audrey Keller *music educator*

Scotch Plains
Kraemer, Ira B. *symphony conductor*

Sicklerville
Simpson, Eugene Thamon *music educator, singer*

Somerset
DeMonic, Betty Lee *music educator*

South Orange
Nowik, John David *musician, educator*

Sparta
Jacobs-Quam, Vivien Marie *retired music educator*

Teaneck
Reid, Rufus Lamar *jazz bassist, composer*

Tenafly
Tall, Susan Porter *music educator*

Trenton
Demitry, Elpis Hope *retired music educator*

Warren
Maull, George Marriner *conductor, educator*

West Long Branch
Anderson, Sheri *theater educator*

West Orange
Atkins, Richard Bart *film and television producer*

NEW MEXICO

Albuquerque
Liotta, William A. *theater educator*
Mock, Joan Bodet *music educator*
Schacht, Catherine Ann *musician, mezzo soprano*
Severs, William Floyd *actor*
Wild, Richard *music educator, musician*

Artesia
Jensen, Eric Reinhard *music educator*

Edgewood
Hamilton, Jerald *musician*

Farmington
Carson, Theresa Ann *theater director*

Hobbs
Starling, Virginia R. *music educator, consultant*

Los Lunas
Jolly, Jeffrey Russell *musician, educator*

Portales
Carr, Tracy A. *musician, educator*
Dal Porto, Mark Daniel *music educator*
Paschke, Donald Vernon *music educator*

Santa Fe
Gaddes, Richard *former opera company director*
Jonas, Chris *composer*
Knight, Kenneth Hugh *conductor*
MacKay, Charles *opera company director*
Newhall, Mary Anne *dancer, educator*
Sturges, Molly *performing company executive, composer*
Zlatoff-Mirsky, Everett Igor *violinist*

NEW YORK

Albany
Evoskevich, Paul Joseph *music educator*
Merrill, Andrea O. *music educator*

Astoria
Ethier, Scott *composer*
Francesa, Mike (Michael Patrick Francesa) *radio personality*

Attica
Rogers, Donald L. *music educator, department chairman, animal breeder*

Bayside
Bonous-Smit, Barbara *music educator, pianist, librarian*
Mullany, Kevin Fergus *music educator, director*
Zinn, William *musician, composer*

Bedford
Chase, Chevy (Cornelius Crane Chase) *comedian, actor, writer*
Palminteri, Chazz *actor*

Binghamton
Choi, Janey *violinist, artist*
Scholtz, Andrew *music educator*
Valencia, Melanie Laine *music educator, performer*
Wildoner, Nancy Schamu *music educator, fine arts department chairman*

Bohemia
Grandmaster Flash, (Joseph Saddler) *disc jockey*

Briarcliff Manor
Wheeler, Margaret Jane *actress, soprano, voice educator*

Brockport
McGhee, Diane Baumann *dance instructor, consultant*
Sarrazin, Natalie Rose *music educator, researcher*

Bronx
Ask-Nanko, Lorraine Charlotte *music educator*
Lagares, Portia Octavia *music educator*
Mittler, Diana (Diana Mittler-Battipaglia) *music educator, pianist*
Rolón, Rosalba *performing company executive*
Rubensky, Mitchell *band director*

Bronxville
Biscardi, Chester *composer, educator*

Brookhaven
Desiderio, Joseph Gerard *music educator*

Brooklyn
Bateman, Jason *actor*
Bielawa, Lisa *composer*
Brown, Ronald K. *performing company executive, choreographer*
Bullard, Thomas *theater educator, director*
Gordon, Michael *composer*
Hopkins, Karen Brooks *performing arts executive*
Kanza, Dominic *musician*
Lang, David *composer*
Latif-Zade, Alisher *composer*
Lee, Spike (Shelton Jackson Lee) *film director and producer*
Morris, Mark William *choreographer*
Niesen, James Louis *theater director*
O'Farrill, Arturo *composer*
Rucker, Bronwyn *actress, writer, social worker*
Skrobela, Katherine Creelman *music producer, data processing executive*
Snyder, Allegra Fuller *dancer, film director, educator*
Thompson, Iola Pointer *choreographer, educator*
Vidal, Maureen Eris *theater educator, actress*
Yokoshi, Yasuko *choreographer*

Brookville
Hynes, Maureen Deirdre *cellist, conductor, teacher*

Buffalo
Beckley, Carol *theater educator, set designer*
Boyar, Benjamin *music educator*
Lombardo Appleby, Linda Rose *music educator*

Camillus
Alvaro, Anthony Joseph *music educator*

Canandaigua
McGuire, David Robert *music educator, composer*

Cheektowaga
Kipler, James Michael *musician, educator*

Cicero
Pink, (Alecia Beth Moore) *singer*

Clifton Park
Nair, Laura *retired music educator*

Cornwall On Hudson
Cameron, Elsa Gerow *music educator*

Derby
Cuomo, Rivers *singer, songwriter*

Dix Hills
Mymit, Chuck W. *music educator, musician*

East Amherst
Ennis, Carol Robbins *retired music educator*

Elmira
Kelly, John J. *performing arts educator, director*

Floral Park
Daloia, Rachel Rosemary *music educator*

Flushing
Cesarano, Michael Ferdinand *theater educator, actor*
Einhorn, Susan *theater educator, director*
Hart, Antonio Maurice *musician, educator*

Forest Hills
Polakoff, Abe *baritone*

Garden City
Einenkel, Robert Herbert *theater educator, actor, director*
Wetherill, Linda Marie *musician, educator, performing arts association administrator*

Germantown
Farberman, Harold *conductor, composer*

Grand Island
Remson, Debra S. *music educator*

Greenvale
Senft, Mason George *musician*
Sugar, Joseph Robert *musician, conductor, educator*

Hamburg
Wolfe, Peter J. *retired performing arts educator*

Hempstead
Coleman, Benjamin Joseph *music educator*
Heuermann-Nowik, Patricia Calhoun *theater director*
Schechtman, Saul *conductor*

Hicksville
Kasimakis, Debra Ann *performing company executive*

Houghton
Congdon, Judy Ann *music educator*

Howard Beach
Leiter, Samuel L. *theater educator*

Huntington
Masear, Claude *music educator, musician*

Ithaca
Fonder, Mark Leslie *music educator*
Haywood, Jennifer Sarah *music educator*
Herskowitz, Richard Julian *arts manager*
Husa, Karel *composer, conductor, educator*
Merrill, Andrea Tai *musician, educator*
Onishi, Deidre *theater educator, director*
Rifkin, Deborah *music educator*
Shepherd, Sean *composer*

Jackson Heights
Stevenson, Amanda (Sandy Stevens) *librettist, composer, songwriter*

Jericho
Sapan, Joshua Ward *cable television executive*

Jewett
Khanzadian, Vahan *tenor*

Katonah
Brownlee, Delphine *actress, musician*

Kinderhook
Glynn, Carlin (Carlin Masterson) *actress*

Kings Park
LaFantano, Elizabeth *music educator*

Liverpool
Federico, Josephine A.M. *music educator*
Landers, Mary Dean J. *music educator*

Long Eddy
Hoiby, Lee *composer, concert pianist*

Long Island City
Westwick, Ed *actor*

Loudonville
Karimi-Hakak, Mahmood *film director, educator*

Manhasset
Brand, Oscar *folk singer, writer, educator*

Massapequa
Turk, Elizabeth Ann *music educator*

Melville
Sobol, Elise Schwarcz *music educator*

Millerton
Hastings, Donald Francis *actor, writer*

Monroe
Furman-Markowitz, Joanna Florence *dance educator*

Mount Kisco
Starobin, Michael *composer, orchestrator*

Narrowsburg
Krause, Gloria Rose *music educator*

New Hartford
Weiss, Holly Anne *music educator, singer*

New Hyde Park
Esiason, Boomer (Norman Julius Esiason) *radio personality, sportscaster, retired professional football player*

New Rochelle
Swire, Edith Wypler *music educator, violist, violinist*

New York
Abrams, Muhal Richard *pianist, composer*
Adams, John Coolidge *composer, conductor*
Adams, Yolanda Yvette *singer*
Ahrens, Lynn *lyricist*
Akon, (Aliaune Thiam) *singer*
Alda, Alan *actor, film director, scriptwriter*
Alexander, Jane (Jane Quigley) *actress, theater educator, writer*
Alvarez, David (David Alvarez-Gonzalez) *actor, dancer*
Anania, Vincent Jay *film director, educator*
Andersen, Mark *musician*
Arkin, Alan Wolf *actor*
Armitage, Karole *dancer, choreographer*
Arroyo, Martina *soprano*
Asakawa, Takako *dancer, choreographer, educator, director*
Ashanti, (Ashanti Shequoiya Douglas) *vocalist*
Asner, Ed *actor*
Austin, Patti *singer*
Ax, Emanuel *pianist*
Azenberg, Emanuel *theatrical producer*
Baker, Leslie David *actor*
Barbour, Catherine Jean *actress, set designer, director, american mime*
Bart, Roger *actor*
Bates, Mason *composer, disc jockey*
Baumgartner, Brian *actor*
Bedingfield, Natasha *singer*
Bednar, Rudy *television producer, director*
Beeson, Jack Hamilton *composer, educator, writer*
Behar, Joy *television personality*
Belzer, Richard *actor, comedian*
Benanti, Laura *actress*
Besterman, Douglas *composer, orchestrator*
Birkenhead, Thomas Bruce *theater producer, educator*
Björk, (Björk Guðmundsdóttir) *singer, composer*
Bledel, Alexis (Kimberly Alexis Bledel) *actress*
Bogart, Anne Dean *theater director, educator*
Bond, Victoria Ellen *conductor, composer*
Borras, Yolanda *music program administrator, educator, consultant*
Bozeman, Beverley (Beverly B. Fuller) *dancer, singer, actress, choreographer, director*
Bracco, Lorraine *actress*
Brendel, Alfred *concert pianist*
Brokaw, Mark *theater director*
Brothers, Joyce Diane *television personality, psychologist*
Brown, Chris (Christopher Maurice Brown) *singer*
Brown, David *film producer, writer*
Brown, Trisha *dancer*
Bundchen, Gisele *model*
Burnett, Mark *television producer*
Burstein, Danny *actor*
Burstein, Nanette *film and television director, producer*
Burwell, Carter *composer*
Butler, Kerry *actress*
Byer, Diana *performing company executive*
Byrd, Debra Ann *actor, theater producer, performing company executive*
Byrne, David *musician, composer, artist, director*
Byrne, Rhonda *television producer, writer*
Campbell, Naomi *model*
Cantrell, Lana *actress, lawyer, singer*
Capalbo, Carmen *theater director, producer*
Carell, Steve *comedian, actor*
Carey, Mariah *singer*
Carlson, Ann Marie *choreographer, performance artist*
Carlson, Marvin Albert *theater educator*
Cavenaugh, Matt *actor*
Cazeaux, Isabelle Anne Marie *retired music educator*
Chang, Marian S. *filmmaker, composer*
Chenoweth, Kristin *actress*
Church, Thomas Haden *actor*
Clapp, Stephen Henry *violinist*
Conway, Kevin *actor, performing company executive*
Corddry, Rob *comedian, actor*
Corsaro, Frank Andrew *theater director*
Cory, Eleanor Thayer *composer, educator*
Curtin, Jane Therese *actress, writer*
Curtis, Paul James *mime, director*
Daltrey, Roger (Roger Harry Daltrey) *singer*
d'Amboise, Jacques Joseph *former dancer, choreographer, educator, director*
Danitz, Marilynn Patricia *choreographer, video specialist*
David, Michael *theater producer*
Davidovsky, Mario *retired composer*
Davis, Christopher James *television producer*
Davis, Viola *actress*
Del Forno, Anton *classical guitarist, recording artist, composer, educator*
De Niro, Robert *actor, film producer and director, restaurant owner*
DePreist, James Anderson *conductor*
DeWoody, Beth Rudin *film producer*
Deyn, Agyness (Laura Hollins) *model*
Dillon, Matt *actor*
Doyle, John *artistic director, designer*
Drake, Laura *theater director, performer*
Dratch, Rachel *comedienne, actress*
Du Boff, Jill Bonnie Candise *sound effects artist, educator*
Duchin, Peter Oelrichs *musician*
Duff, Hilary Ann *singer, actress*
Dukakis, Olympia *actress*
Dylan, Bob (Robert Allen Zimmerman) *singer, musician*
Edward, John (John Edward McGee Jr.) *spiritual medium, writer*
Elliott, Missy (Melissa Arnette Elliot) *musician*
Eschenbach, Christoph *conductor, musician, music director*
Fairchild, Megan *dancer*
Farley, Carole *soprano*
Feld, Eliot *dancer, choreographer, performing company executive*
Fenley, Molissa *choreographer, performing company executive*
Fifty Cent, (Curtis James Jackson) *rap artist*
Fiorato, Hugo *conductor*
Flannery, Kate *actress*
Fleming, Renée L. *opera singer*
Fogler, Dan *actor*
Fontana, Thomas Michael *television producer, scriptwriter*
Ford, Eileen Otte (Mrs. Gerard W. Ford) *modeling agency executive*
Foreman, Richard *theater director, playwright*
Fox, Matthew *actor*
Fox, Michael J. (Michael Andrew Fox) *actor*
Frank, Gabriela Lena *composer*
Frith, Michael Kingsbury *artistic director, illustrator, writer, production company executive, actor*
Frost, David *music producer*
Gelb, Peter *performing company executive*
Giamatti, Paul *actor*
Giannini, Giancarlo *actor, director, screenwriter*
Gifford, Kathie Lee *television personality, vocalist*
Gilbert, Alan T. *conductor, music director*
Gillinson, Sir Clive Daniel *music executive, former musician*
Giraldi, Robert Nicholas *film director*
Glass, Philip *composer, musician*
Goldsmith, Merwin *actor, theater director*
Goldsmith-Thomas, Elaine *film producer*
Goodman, Roger Mark *television director*
Gordon, Mark *actor, theater director, educator*
Greenfield, Lucille Jean *music educator, composer*
Greif, Michael *theatre director*
Griffel, L. Michael *music educator, researcher*
Griffey, Anthony *tenor*
Haggerty, Luane Ruth Davis *theater director, actress, educator*
Halmi, Robert, Sr. *film, television producer*
Hamilton Jackson, Marilyn J. *dancer, choreographer, educator*
Hamingson, Andrew Dean *theater director*
Hammett, Kirk Lee *musician*
Hanning, Barbara Russano *music educator*
Harari, Saar *choreographer, dancer*
Hardin, Melora *actress*
Hargitay, Mariska Magdolina *actress*
Harmon, Jane *theater producer*
Harrell, Ray Evans *performing company executive, conductor, educator*
Harris, Julie (Ann) *actress*
Harry, Deborah Ann *singer*
Harter, Theo C. *music educator, composer*
Hasselbeck, Elisabeth *television personality*
Hays, Kathryn *actress*
Hebert, Bliss Edmund *opera director*
Helm, Lenora Zenzalai *musician, educator*
Helms, Ed *comedian, actor*
Hensley, Shuler *actor, vocalist*
Herman, Jerry *composer, lyricist*
Herrera, Paloma *dancer*
Herzog, Werner (Werner Stipetic) *film director*
Hetfield, James *singer*
Hirokami, Junichi *conductor, former music director*
Hirschorn, Michael W. *television producer, entertainment company executive*
Ho, Betty Juenyü Yülin *retired musician, physiologist, educator*
Houston, Whitney *singer*
Hughes, Doug *theater director*
Hyman, Earle *actor, educator*
Imus, Don (John Donald Imus Jr.) *radio personality*
Irvin, Michael Jerome *television personality, retired professional football player*
Jackson, Anne (Anne Jackson Wallach) *actress*
Jacobs, Paul A. *music educator*
Jagger, Sir Mick (Michael Philip Jagger) *singer, musician*
James, Brian d'Arcy *actor*
Jamison, Judith *performing company executive, dancer*
Jean, Wyclef *musician, recording industry executive*
Josefowicz, Leila Bronia *violinist*
Judd, Karlan *composer*
Jung, Doris *soprano*
Kamlot, Robert *performing arts executive*
Kanakaredes, Melina *actress*
Kandel, Karen *actress*
Karchin, Louis Samuel *composer, educator*
Kassel, Virginia Weltmer *television producer, writer*
Kaufman, Moisés *theater director, playwright*
Kent, Linda Gail *dancer*
Keys, Alicia (Alicia Augello Cook) *singer*
Kid Rock, (Robert James Ritchie) *singer*
Kilik, Jon *film producer*
Kilmer, Val *actor*
Kind, Richard J. *actor*
King, B.B. (Riley B. King) *singer, guitarist*
Kistler, Darci Anna *ballet dancer*
Kline, Kevin Delaney *actor*
Korf, Anthony *composer, artistic director*
Kowalik, Trent Matthias *actor, dancer*
Kozak, Harley Jane *actress, writer*
Krasinski, John *actor*
Kubiak, Teresa Wojtaszek *soprano*
Kulish, Kiril Jacob *actor, dancer*
Kurman, Juta *music educator*
Kya-Hill, Robert *actor, educator*
Lacamoire, Alex *composer*
Lacombe, Jacques *conductor*
Lane, Stewart F. *theater owner, producer*
Lauer, Matt *television personality*
Leary, Denis *actor, comedian*
LeCompte, Elizabeth *theater director*
Legrand, Michel Jean *composer*
Lemon, Ralph *choreographer*
Lents, Stacie *performing arts educator*
Leppard, Raymond John *conductor, musician*
Leritz, Lawrence R. *choreographer, singer, dancer*
Levine, James Lawrence *conductor, music director, pianist*
Levy, Reynold *performing arts center administrator, retired telecommunications industry executive*
Lil Wayne, (Dwayne Michael Carter Jr.) *rap artist*
Lima, Adriana Francesca *model*
Limbaugh, Rush Hudson III *radio talk show host*
Lipkin, Seymour *musician, conductor, educator*
Lipton, James *television personality*
Lively, Blake Christina *actress*
Loney, Glenn Meredith *theater educator*
Lumet, Sidney *film director*
LuPone, Patti *actress*
Lyman, Peggy *artistic director, dancer, choreographer, educator*
Ma, Yo-Yo *cellist*
MacFarlane, Seth Woodbury *television producer, scriptwriter*
MacNeil, Ian *theatrical set & costume designer*
Maddow, Rachel Anne *radio and TV personality, political activist*
Malkin, Barry *film editor, consultant*
Mansouri, Lotfollah (Lotfi Mansouri) *retired performing company executive*
Marceau, Yvonne *ballroom dancer, educator*
Margolis, Mark Neal *actor*
Marsalis, Wynton *musician*
Martin, Demetri (Demitri Martin) *comedian, scriptwriter*
Martin, Ricky (Enrique Martin Morales IV) *vocalist, actor, producer, composer*
Martins, Peter *performing company executive, choreographer*
Mason, Marshall W. *theater director, educator, author*
Maysles, Albert H. *filmmaker*
Mazzo, Kay *ballet dancer, educator*
Mazzola, John William *retired performing company executive, consultant*
McCall, Anthony *filmmaker, conceptual artist*
McCarthy, Andrew *actor*
McDonald, Audra Ann *actress, vocalist*
McGraw, Nancy McCall *singer, theater producer*
McKenzie, Kevin Patrick *performing company executive*
McTeer, Janet *actress*
Mehta, Zarin *performing company executive*
Menzel, Idina *actress, singer*
Michaels, Lorne *television producer*
Michelson, Sarah *choreographer*
Miller, Dennis *comedian*
Miller, Stephanie Katherine *radio personality, comedian*
Miller-Sydney, Audrey Yvonne *music educator*
Miranda, Lin-Manuel *actor, composer, lyricist*
Mitchell, Arthur *dancer, choreographer, performing company executive, educator*
Monaghan, Dominic *actor*
Monaghan, Michelle *actress*
Monk, Meredith Jane *artistic director, composer, choreographer, filmmaker*
Moore, Jason *theater director*
Morrison, Matthew *actor*
Morse, David *actor*
Muller, Jennifer *choreographer, dancer*
Murphy, Donna *actress*
Murphy, Rosemary *actress*
Muskal, Tamar *composer*
Neal, Patricia *actress*
Nederlander, James Morton *theater executive*
Newman, Randy *singer, songwriter, musician*
Ne-Yo, (Shaffer C. Smith) *singer*
Nicholaw, Casey *theater director, choreographer*
Nickson, Robert Frazier *film producer, educator*
Noth, Chris *actor*
Novak, B.J. Manaly (Benjamin Joseph Novak) *actor, television producer, scriptwriter*
Nugent, Nelle *theater, film and television producer*
Oberst, Conor Mullen *singer, musician*
O'Hara, Kelli *singer, actress*
Olivo, Karen *actress*
O'Neal, Hank *entertainment producer, small business owner*
Oppenheim, Tom *performing company executive*
Overlie, Mary G. *choreographer, theater educator*
Page, Ellen *actress*
Panettiere, Hayden *actress*
Pardee, Margaret Ross *violinist, violist, educator*
Parker, Alice *composer*
Parsons, Estelle *actress, director, theater producer*
Paulus, Diane *performing company executive, theater director*
Payton-Wright, Pamela *actress*
Pepe, Neil *performing company executive*
Perlman, Itzhak *violinist*
Perry, Douglas *opera singer*
Peters, Bernadette (Bernadette Lazzara) *actress*
Philbin, Regis (Francis Xavier) *television personality*
Pisoni, Lorenzo *actor*
Poler-Buzali, Gabriela *performing arts association administrator*
Poor, Peter Varnum *television producer and director*
Port, Whitney Eve *television personality, apparel designer*
Posin, Kathryn Olive *choreographer*
Power, Will *writer, composer, rap artist*
Powers, Scott *television producer, actor*
Price, (Mary Violet) Leontyne *retired concert and opera singer, soprano*
Rainer, Yvonne *choreographer, filmmaker*
Randolph, David *conductor*
Ratmansky, Alexei *performing company executive, dancer, choreographer*
Reeves, Jennifer Todd *filmmaker*
Refaeli, Bar *model*
Reich, Steve *composer*
Reig, June Wilson *writer director and producer*
Reinking, Ann H. *dancer, actress*
Reuben, Gloria *actress, singer*
Rhoden, Dwight *performing company executive, choreographer, dancer*
Rhodes, Randi *radio personality*
Rhodes, Samuel *violist, educator*
Rice, Barbara Lynn *stage manager*
Richards, Keith *musician*
Richards, Michael *actor, comedian*
Richardson, Desmond *dancer*
Rihanna, (Robyn Rihanna Fenty) *singer, actress*
Ripa, Kelly Maria *television personality, actress*
Rivera, Geraldo *television personality, journalist*
Robbins, Tim (Timothy Francis Robbins) *actor, film director*
Rodewald, Heidi *musician, composer*
Rogoff, Tamar *choreographer*
Rollins, Sonny (Theodore Rollins) *composer, musician*
Ross, Diana *singer, actress, entertainer, fashion designer*
Ross, Jerrold *music educator*
Roth, Daryl *theater producer*
Rothfeld, Michael B. *theatrical producer, investor*
Rothschild, Amalie Randolph *filmmaker, producer, director, photographer*
Rouse, Christopher Chapman III *composer, educator*
Rudel, Julius *conductor*
Rudin, Scott *film and theatre producer*
Rutenberg, Michael Elliot *theater educator*
Salonen, Esa-Pekka *conductor, music director*
Sams, Jeremy *theater director, composer*
Sarandon, Susan *actress*
Savran, David *theater educator*
Schechner, Richard *theater director, educator*
Scheeder, Louis *theater producer, director, educator*
Schmit, Timothy Bruce *musician*
Schorer, Suki *ballet teacher*
Schrade, Robert Warren *classical pianist, educator*
Schreiber, Pablo *actor*
Seary, Lawrence Anthony *cinematographer, television producer*
Seder, Sam (Samuel Lincoln Seder) *radio personality, comedian, writer*
Seeger, Pete *folk singer, songwriter*
Seidelman, Susan *film director*
Seidler, Alan *composer, musician, music company executive*
Seldes, Marian *actress*
Seller, Jeffrey *theatre producer*
Serebrier, José *musician, composer, conductor*
Shankel, Lynne *conductor, composer*
Shattuck, Scott Harlan *performing company executive*
Shelley, Carole *actress*
Shen, Wei *performing company executive, choreographer*
Sherman, Arthur *theater educator, writer, actor, composer, sculptor*
Shick, Vicky *dancer, choreographer*
Shuman, Earl Stanley *songwriter, music publisher*
Silver, Joan Micklin *film director, screenwriter*
Silverman, Allison *television producer, scriptwriter*
Silvers, Sally *choreographer, performing company executive*
Simmons, Joseph (Run Simmons, Rev Run) *musician*
Simpson, Jessica Ann *singer, actress*
Sitomer, Sheila Marie *television producer and director*
Smith, Malcolm Sommerville *bass vocalist*
Smith, Philip J. *performing arts organization administrator*
Snyder, Arlen Dean *actor*

Solís, Marco Antonio *singer, composer*
Solomons, Gus, Jr., (Gustave Martinez) *choreographer, dancer, writer*
Soyer, David *cellist, music educator*
Spears, Britney *singer*
Stang, Rolf Kristian *vocalist, educator, actor, advertising executive, writer*
Steel, George Robert *opera company director*
Stein, Jared J. *theater director, educator*
Stepleton, James *composer*
Stern, Howard Allan *radio personality, television show host*
Stew, (Mark Stewart) *musician*
Stewart, Ellen D. *theater producer*
Stewart, Jon (Jonathan Stewart Leibowitz) *television personality, comedian*
Stiefel, Ethan *dancer, performing company executive, dean*
Sting, (Gordon Matthew Sumner) *musician, songwriter, actor*
Stoltzman, Richard Leslie *clarinetist*
Storch, Arthur *theater director*
Stroman, Susan *choreographer, theater director*
Stucky, Steven (Edward) *composer, conductor*
Studdard, (Christopher) Ruben *singer*
Szot, Paulo *baritone, singer, actor*
Talmi, Yoav *conductor, composer*
Taylor, Paul B. *choreographer*
Taymor, Julie *theater, film and opera director, designer*
Thompson, Donald Raymond *film producer, playwright*
Thompson, Fred Dalton *actor, former United States Senator from Tennessee*
Thompson, Jewel Taylor *music educator*
Threadgill, Henry *musician*
Tilson Thomas, Michael *conductor, music director*
Timberlake, Justin Randall *singer*
Trujillo, Robert *musician*
Tyner, McCoy (Alfred McCoy Sulaimon Saud Tyner) *jazz pianist, composer*
Ulrich, Lars *musician*
Upshaw, Dawn *soprano*
Vaccariello, Patrick *conductor*
Vachon, Christine *film producer*
Van Amstel, Louis *dancer*
Vieira, Meredith *television personality*
Wainwright, Rufus *musician, singer*
Walker, Charles Dodsley *conductor, organist*
Walker, Thomas Scott *actor*
Wallace, Stewart F. *composer*
Wallach, Eli *actor*
Wankel, Robert Edmond *performing arts organization administrator*
Ward, Anthony *theatrical scenic and costume designer*
Waters, Sylvia *performing company executive, dancer*
Wek, Alek *model*
West, Kanye *rap artist*
Wheeldon, Christopher *performing company executive, choreographer*
White, George Cooke *theater director, foundation administrator*
White, Jack (John Anthony Gillis) *musician*
White, Nicholas John *musician, director, composer*
Whittingham, Kenneth *television director*
Wile, Joan *composer, lyricist, singer, author*
Williams, Montel *television talk show host*
Williams, Vanessa L. (Vanessa Lynn Williams) *recording artist, actress*
Wilson, Cassandra *singer*
Wilson, Reggie *artistic director, choreographer, dancer*
Wittstein, Edwin Frank *theater director, set designer*
Wolfe, George C. *theater director, producer, playwright*
Wong, Elizabeth Hung *organist, choirmaster*
Woodward, Joanne Gignilliat *actress*
Woodward, Kirk *theater director*
Woodward, Patricia *theater director, educator*
Wu, Man *musician*
Yamaguchi, Masaya *musician, educator*
Zenón, Miguel *musician*
Zorn, John *composer, musician*
Zosike, Joanie Fritz *theater director, actress, writer*
Zukerman, Pinchas *concert violinist, violist, conductor*

Newburgh
Teutul, Paul John, Sr. *television personality, mechanic*

Newcomb
Chatzky, Herbert *music educator*

Nyack
Flansburgh, John Conant *musician*
Linnell, John Sidney *musician*

Oakdale
Bertsch-Wells, Jane A. *theater educator*

Oakland Gardens
McGill, Georgia *theater educator, director*

Oneonta
Gruenhagen, Lisa M. *music educator*

Oswego
Shore, Amy Elizabeth *performing arts educator, director*

Pawling
Jones, James Earl *actor*

Peekskill
Black, Carolyn Rebecca *music educator*

Pocantico Hills
Humphrey, Jordan *theater producer*

Port Washington
van Schenkhof, Carol Dougherty (Carol Dovan) *soprano, educator*

Poughkeepsie
Pisani, Michael Vincent *music educator*
Wilson, Richard Edward *composer, music educator, pianist*

Purchase
Joyce-Walter, Mary Ann *music educator, composer*
Magaziner, Elliot Albert *musician, conductor, educator*
Munro, Doug *musician, director*

Red Hook
Gudenzi-Ruess, Ida Carmen V. *music educator, artist*

Rochester
Argetsinger, Gerald Scott *drama educator*
Gauldin, Robert L. *music educator, composer*
Hess, Benton Edward *music educator*
Laires, Fernando *concert piano educator*

Rocky Point
Knapp, Craig Brian *musician, educator*

Rosendale
Trompetter, Amy Clemens *theater director*

Saint Regis Falls
O'Bryan, Margaret Sundberg *music educator*

Saratoga Springs
Porter, David Hugh *musician, classicist, academic administrator, music educator*

Schenectady
Steckler, Charles N. *theater educator*
Szokody, Aniko *pianist, educator*

Sea Cliff
Popova, Nina *retired dancer, choreographer, director*

Shelter Island Heights
Wolosoff, Bruce Germont *composer*

Shrub Oak
Vaccaro, Annette Andréa *music educator*

Skaneateles
Veverka, Karen Elizabeth *music educator*

Slingerlands
Jacobs, Karen Louise *musician, medical technician, educator*

Sparkill
Dahl, Arlene *actress, writer, designer, cosmetics executive*

Staten Island
Fusco, Jo Ellen *music educator*
Trogan, Roland Bernard *composer, educator*

Syracuse
Caravan, Ronald L. *music educator, composer*
Dekaney, Elisa Macedo *music educator, researcher*
Elms, Ben *actor, theater director*
Orentlicher, John *video research educator, artist*
Waggoner, Andrew *composer*
Wolff, Catherine Elizabeth *opera company executive*

Troy
Snyder, Patricia Di Benedetto *theater director, producer*

Uniondale
Sanchez, Laura Ann *music educator*

Valhalla
Fachnie, H(ugh) Douglas *film manufacturing company official*

Valley Cottage
Bridgman, Art *choreographer, dancer*
Packer, Myrna *choreographer, dancer*

Vestal
O'Connell, Patricia Ellen *musician, educator*

Wading River
Volonts, Marguerite Louise *music educator, singer*

Walden
Murphy, Pamela Ann *musician, educator, actress*

Wallkill
Strauser, Susan Parkyn *performing arts educator, singer, professional soloist*

Wantagh
Berk, Adele L. *composer, music educator*

Washingtonville
Marcialis, Angelo Vincent *musician, educator*

West Point
Williams, Craig Stewart *organist, choirmaster, music educator, director*

White Plains
Chase, Jenny Wei-Lang Kao *singer, music educator*

Woodstock
De Johnette, Jack *musician*

Yonkers
Baumel, Herbert *violinist, conductor*

NORTH CAROLINA

Black Mountain
Belue, Janie A. *music educator*

Boiling Springs
Lahaie, Scot *theater educator*

Boone
Lacy, Hollie Hutchison *musician, educator*
Mendel, Traci *composer, educator*
Mills, Susan Wilson *music educator*

Buies Creek
Hight, H. K. *theater technical director*

Chapel Hill
Kindem, Gorham Anders *filmmaker, educator*
Moeser, James Charles *music educator, former academic administrator*
Neff, Severine *music educator*

Charlotte
Bonnefoux, Jean-Pierre *choreographer, dancer*
Harris, Corey *blues musician*
Linda, Sickler Suda *music educator*
Thompson, Jocelyn Pharr *organist, director, educator*

Concord
Howard, Vivian Amick *music educator*

Cullowhee
Armfield, Terri Elaine *music educator, musician*
Beam, Richard Squires *theater educator*

Davidson
Sprague, Raymond *music educator*

Durham
Davis, Chuck *dance company executive, dancer*
Daw, Amy W. *music educator*
Eger, Joseph *conductor*
Krakowski, Jane *actress*
Nakarai, Charles Frederick Toyozo *music educator*

Elon
Buckmaster, Matthew Tobe *musician, educator*
Gang, Richard Philip *theater educator*
Rubeck, Fredrick John *performing arts educator*

Fayetteville
Barnicle, Mary Anne *music educator, piano accompanist*
Turner, Gwendolyn Marie *band director, musician*
Widdows, Marianne Shuta *orchestra director*

Franklinton
Elmore, Cenieth Catherine *music educator*

Gastonia
Fayssoux, Patricia Ann Paysour *music educator*

Greensboro
Deere, James Dickson *singer, pianist, music educator and writer*
Hammond, David Alan *stage director, educator*
Heil, John Eric *theater educator*
Locke, John R. *music educator, director*
Middleton, Herman David, Sr. *retired theater educator*
Moffett, Mondre *musician, educator*

Greenville
Darby, F. Leonard *theater educator*
Dashiell, Carroll Vaughn, Jr. *musician, educator*
Moore, Charles Willard *music educator*
Tahaney, Michael Hamilton *theatre professor, actor and director*

Indian Trail
Brewer, James Timothy *music educator, director*

Lexington
Mabe, Walter Lee *music educator*

Louisburg
Miller, Brian Daniel *music educator, organist*

Lowell
Myers, Jeanette Moore *music educator, director*

Mars Hill
Newton, Paul George *musician, retired librarian*

Monroe
Casstevens, Charles Franklin, Jr. *music educator, minister*

New Bern
Tolmich, Andrea J. *music educator, department chairman*

Raleigh
Poe, Terry Lynn *music educator*
Sorrell, Rozlyn *singer, actress, theater director, educator*
Thompson Cornwall, Lonieta Aurora *music educator, consultant*
Torres, Talani *performing arts educator*
Vogel, Phyllis Jean *music educator*
Youngman, Lola Jeanne *music educator*

Rich Square
Baugham, Samuel McCoy *actor, painter*

Roseboro
Cobb, Katherine Simon *theater educator*

Salisbury
Hagy, David Lee *conductor*
Higbee, Dale (Strohe) *musician, retired psychologist*

Swannanoa
Whittington, Lorin Dale *retired music educator*

Todd
Cole, Susan Stockbridge *retired theater educator*

Wake Forest
Johnson, Ben Sigel *music educator*

Warrenton
Weddington, Elizabeth Gardner (Liz Gardner) *actress*

Wilmington
Nice, Scott Dean *voice educator*

Winston Salem
Placilla, Christina Dawn *music educator*
Stewart, Gwendolyn Johns *music educator*

NORTH DAKOTA

Bismarck
Knoll, Gloria Jean *music educator*

Bottineau
Roemmich, Dalonnes Kay *music educator*

Devils Lake
Rygg, Glenn *retired music educator*

Fargo
Horvik, Lori Ann *theater educator, consultant*
Schultz, Ed (Edward Andrew Schultz) *radio personality*

Grand Forks
Rheude, Elizabeth Anne *music educator*
Towne, Gary Spaulding *music educator*

OHIO

Alliance
Boehm, Patricia *music educator*

Ashtabula
Carrel, Marianne Eileen *music educator*

Athens
Sayrs, Elizabeth *music educator*
Scott, Madeleine *performing arts educator*
Winters, Robert Louis *theater educator, consultant*

Berea
Winget, Jack B. *theater educator, director, actor*

Bowling Green
Leclair, Jacqueline Fairchild *musician, educator*

Canfield
Scurich, Kelly Lemos *music director*

Chagrin Falls
Shakley, Elaine M. *organist, department chairman*

Cincinnati
Galloway, Lillian Carroll *modeling agency executive, consultant*
Järvi, Paavo *conductor, music director*
Morgan, Victoria *performing company executive, choreographer*
Smarelli, David John *music educator, musician*
Smith, Timothy W. *musician, educator*
Weinstein, Anna *music educator*
Winfrey, Marcellene S. *music educator, church musician*

Cleveland
Adams, H. Leslie *composer*
Burton, Gary *musician*
Cutler, Timothy Spence *music educator, composer*
Hoffman, Barbara G. *filmmaker, educator*
Hruby, Frank Michael *musician, educator, critic*
Lawrence, Estelene Yvonne *musician, transportation executive*
Morris, Thomas William *symphony orchestra administrator*
Updegraff, David *music educator*
Warner, Carolyn G. *musician, music educator*
Weir, Dame Gillian Constance *musician*
Welser-Möst, Franz *conductor, music director*

Columbus
Allen, Lois Arlene Height *musician*
Barlow-Ware, Jacqueline Sue *music educator*
Charles, Gerard *performing company executive, choreographer*
Cordell, Philip Granvile *music educator, musician*
Hildreth, James David *musician, educator*
Rosenstock, Susan Lynn *orchestra administrator*

Dayton
Novak, Jason *music educator*

Delaware
Gardner, Bonnie Milne *theater educator, playwright*

Dublin
Calucci, Tony *performing arts educator*

Elyria
Sanders, Phyllis May *musician*

Findlay
Hanson, David Alan *music educator*

Fremont
Ziebold, Barbara M. *music educator*

Grove City
Williams, Linda Dianne *retired music educator*

Hilliard
McNutt, Suzanne Michaelene *music educator*
Pyles, Selma Broadway *music educator*

Holland
Conlin, Thomas *conductor*

Kent
Karpanty, Kimberly A. *choreographer, educator*
Reiss, Richard Arnold *theater director, actor*

Kettering
Meckstroth, Wilma Jean *piano and organ educator, accompanist*

Lima
Ignatieva, Maria *theater educator*

Lorain
Murrell, Jill Pongracz *music educator, director*

Medina
Skidmore, Tyler Lee *music educator*

New Concord
Schumann, Laura Elaine *conductor*

North Olmsted
Janson, Patrick *vocalist, educator, actor*

Oak Harbor
Sievert, Vicki Lee *retired music educator*

Oberlin
Rutstein, Sedmara Zakarian *concert pianist, educator*

Oxford
Chung, Hsinglin Tracy *theater educator*

Parma
Musat, Katherine Gadus *retired music educator*
Pitcher, Megan Louise *dancer, director*

Saint Marys
Dickerson, Janice Eileen *music educator*

Solon
Bane, Glenice Gail *music educator*

Springfield
Todd, Carol *music educator*

Strongsville
Webb, Tara Yvette *music educator*

Toledo
Alby, Irene *theater educator, director*
Ashton, Dyrk Michael *performing arts educator*
Chambers, Virginia Anne *music educator*
Girgis-Hanna, Mary Fahim *music educator*
Koskoski, Jarrod Francis *music educator*

Wapakoneta
Lusk Barlage, Mary Margaret *music educator*

Willoughby
Baker, Charles Stephen *music educator*
Linsenmeier, Carol Vincent *music educator*

Wilmington
Alexander, J. Wynn *theater educator, director*

Zanesville
McLaughlin, James Lee *musician, director*
Strahm, Mary Ellen *music educator*

OKLAHOMA

Chickasha
Hanson, Dan Lewis *music educator, entertainer, composer*

Claremore
Blakely, David *theater educator, playwright*

Durant
Adair, Aaron Lucas *theater educator*
Cunningham, James Grady *theater educator*

Edmond
Bristow, Donald Gene *theater educator*

Inola
Paul, Gary Wayne *music educator*

Lawton
Detweiler, Stanley Bruce *music educator*
Gagliardi, Charlotte Marie *music educator, secondary school educator*
Underwood, Kirsten Fedje *musician, educator*

Mounds
Halsey, James Albert *entertainer, theater producer*

Newalla
Hixson, Janice Vee *music educator, composer*

Norman
Ambrosini, Armand Anthony *music educator*
Buchwald, Michael Carl *theater educator*
Dorrough, Vicki Lee *theater educator*
Tussing, Marilee Appleby *music educator*

Oklahoma City
Green, Vickie *music educator*
Hilger, Robyn *music educator*
Jackson, Wanda Lavonne *country western musician*
Kelly, Vicky Leloie *music educator*
Mellott, Greg L. *film producer, writer, director*
Payne, Gareld Gene *vocal music educator, medical transcriptionist*
Price Boday, Mary Kathryn *choreographer, small business owner, educator*

Stillwater
Adams, Brant *music educator, director*
Doolen, J. Kevin *theater educator*

Tulsa
Angelini, Marcello *performing company executive*
Collins, Laura Jane *music educator, singer*
LaBelle, Patti (Patricia Louise Holte) *singer, entertainer*
Owens, Jana Jae *entertainer*
Sowell, Laven *retired music educator*
Weinstock Rad, Katheryn Louise *music educator*

Valliant
House, Janie Burdette *music educator*

OREGON

Ashland
Kristina, Foltz *musician, educator*
Rauch, Bill *performing company executive, theater director*
Severin, Ezra B. *musician*

Central Point
Savage, Michael (Michael Alan Weiner) *radio personality, commentator*

Corvallis
Headrick, Charlotte Jane *theater educator*

Eugene
Bailey, Exine Margaret Anderson *soprano, educator*
Bergquist, Peter *retired music educator*
Farrington, Marianne Patricia *choreographer, educator*

Forest Grove
Burch-Pesses, Thomas Michael *music educator*

La Grande
Bush, Ken *theater educator*
Espinosa, Leandro *composer, conductor, educator*

Monmouth
Lee, Gordon *composer, educator*

Portland
Berentsen, Kurtis George *music educator, conductor*
Cheifetz, Hamilton *music educator*
Friesen, David Douglas *musician, educator, composer*
Harris, Charles David *music educator*
Hays, Daniel J. *theater educator*
Hunt, Barry L. *performing arts educator, director*
Kalmar, Carlos *conductor, music director*
Kohne, Heidi Ann *church musician*
Stowell, Christopher R. *performing company executive, choreographer, retired dancer*

Salem
Wu, Hekun Andre *music educator, director*

PENNSYLVANIA

Abington
Anderson, Valerie B. *actress, writer*

Akron
Leithmann, David Edward *music educator*

Allentown
Beltzner, Gail Ann *music educator*
Dearborn, Karen *performing arts educator, director*
Hemerly, Dorothea M. *music educator, director*
Jacobs, Michelle Munno *performing arts educator*
Liebhaber, Barbara *music educator*

Altoona
Cutsforth-Huber, Bonnie Bridget *music educator, singer*

Annville
Mecham, Mark Leonidas *music educator, department chairman*

Bala Cynwyd
Hancock, Herbert Jeffrey (Herbie Hancock) *composer, pianist, publisher*

Beaver Falls
Copeland, Robert Marshall *music educator, department chairman*

Bethel Park
Florig, Patricia Stickle *music educator*

Bethlehem
Allen, Beatrice *music educator, pianist*
Binford, Hilde Marga *music educator*
Diggs, David B. *musician*

Birdsboro
Dieffenbach, Lisa M. *music educator*

Blue Bell
Edwards, Joselle Elizabeth *performing arts educator*

Boyertown
Lydic, Nadine K. *music educator*

Bryn Mawr
Goutman, Lois Clair *retired drama educator*

Carlisle
Bowers, Teresa Marie *music educator*

Center Valley
Lewis, Anne M. *actress, educator*
Razze, Dennis *theater educator, director*

Cheyney
Bagley, Edythe Scott *theater educator*

Delta
Withrow, James A. *music educator*

Derry
Baltzer, Cynthia Louise *music educator*

Doylestown
Solly, Richard Peter *music educator*

Dresher
Levicoff, Valerie Ann *music educator*

Drexel Hill
Benglian, Barbara Mason *music educator*
Martino, Michael Charles *entertainer, musician, actor*

Edgemont
Davis, Scott Charles *music educator, political activist*

Ephrata
Reed, Galen K. *music educator*

Erie
Hay, Christine Marie *dancer, educator*

Everett
Whetstone, Joni Lee *music educator*

Fallsington
Foote, Kathryn Ann *music educator*

Fort Washington
Hallman, Patricia L. *retired musician*

Fredericksburg
Daubert, Harlan Aaron *music educator, director*

Gettysburg
Sasnett, Kathleen Beth *theater educator, director*

Glenmoore
Fix, Irene M. *pianist*

Glenside
Kleckner, Chris J. *theater educator*
Willig, Barbara Adele *music educator*

Grantham
Cornacchio, Rachel Ann *music educator*
Gulde, Katharine Haynes *musician, educator*

Greencastle
Wertime, Timothy Ray *music educator*

Grove City
Moser, Mary Ann *music educator, director*

Haverford
Wernick, Richard Frank *composer, conductor, educator*

Hershey
Sheaffer, Cristal S. *music educator*

Indiana
Hood, Michael James *theater educator, arts administrator*
McCreary, Patrick *theater educator, director*

King Of Prussia
Helmetag, Diana *music educator*

Kingston
Weisberger, Barbara *artistic director, advisor, educator*

Lancaster
Buchanan, Lovell *entertainer*
Markley, Jill L. *music educator*

Lansdale
Didden, Lynn Williams *music educator*

Lansdowne
Geist, Lorraine Pinnelli *music educator, director*

Lewisburg
Muller, Riana Ricci *musician, educator*

Loysburg
Stuckey, Ellen Mae *music educator*

Mansfield
Monkelien, Sheryl L. *music educator*

Milford Square
Sewell, Gloriana *music educator*

Moon Township
Elliott, Lisa J. *choreographer, educator*

Mount Pleasant
Collins, Frederick George *music educator, secondary school educator*

New Wilmington
Lind, Robin Anna-Karin *music educator*
Pitman, Grover Allen *music educator*

Newtown
Sheridan, John J. *musician, educator*

Philadelphia
Ben-amos, Dan *Folklore Educator*
Blavat, Jerry (Gerald Joseph Blavat) *radio and television personality, actor*
Colson, Rosemary *music educator*
Crumb, George Henry *composer, educator*
Daugherty, F(rancis) Mark *music educator, conductor, theater director*
Decherney, Peter *media educator*
Driver, Robert Baylor, Jr. *opera company director*
Garonzik, Sara Ellen *stage producer*
Hoke-Scedrov, Bonnie Carol *music educator, soprano*
Hong, Riyehee *musician, litrugist, educator, researcher*
Julian, Melanie Blair *voice educator*
Kaiser, Roy *performing company executive*
Miller, Buffy *dancer*
Pasternak, Jill Margot *radio producer, host, musician, educator*
Prischmann Gryniewicz, Deborah Anne *vocalist, educator*
Sawallisch, Wolfgang *conductor*
Sheldon, Deborah Ann *music educator, consultant*
Smith, Lloyd *musician*
Tuttle, Karen Ann *violist, educator*
Weesner, Anna *composer, music educator*

Pipersville
Block, Caryn S. *composer*

Pittsburgh
Bardyguine, Patricia Wilde *dancer, performing company executive*
Gray, Matthew Ian *performing arts educator, communications educator, consultant*
Harth, Sidney *musician, educator*
Hollingsworth, Samuel Hawkins, Jr. *bassist*
Honeck, Manfred *conductor, music director*
Jukes, D. E. *actor, theater director, educator*
Kline, Gary R. *music educator*
Li, Hanna Wu *music educator*
Orr, Terrence S. *dancer, ballet master, artistic director*
Thuma, Holly Diane *performing arts educator*
Zahler, Clara Tatar *music educator*

Pottstown
Holladay, Victor Mason *music educator*

Pottsville
Thomas, Mark P. *conductor, educator*

Reading
Constantine, Andrew *conductor, music director*

Saegertown
Ralph, NancyJo *retired music educator*

Selinsgrove
Tober, Nina *music educator, department chairman*

Slippery Rock
Gray, Colleen Gail *music educator*
Nolen Holland, Nola *choreographer*
Payne, Ursula Octavia *choreographer, educator*

Southampton
Lenox, Gina Marie *music educator*

Strasburg
Goss, Stephen D. *musician, educator*

Swarthmore
Devin, Lee (Philip) *consultant, dramaturg, author*
Mee, Erin B. *theater educator*

Swiftwater
Brooks, Joyce Maria *music educator*

Vandergrift
Aikins, Candace Sue *music educator, consultant*

Villanova
Petropoulos, Kostas *music educator*

Waynesburg
Powers, Edward Lewis *theater educator*

West Chester
Albert, Kristen Ann *music educator*
Briselli, Carol *music educator*
Dobrzelewski, Jean-Christophe *music educator*
McFarland, Ann Louise *music educator*
Rovine, Harvey *theater educator*

Woodlyn
Turso, Aimee Lynn *music educator*

Yardley
Tice, Jennifer S. *music educator*

York
McGhee, James Hamill *theatre director, teacher, poet*
Yeater, Kathleen Wecker *musician, educator*

RHODE ISLAND

Chepachet
Jubinska, Patricia Ann *ballet instructor, choreographer*

Cranston
Burge, David Russell *concert pianist, composer, educator*
Livingston, Carolyn Harris *music educator*
Torelli, Anthony-Alexander *musician, conductor, educator*

Lincoln
Marsden, Herci Ivana *classical ballet artistic director*

Newport
Englander, Roger *television producer, director*
Malkovich, Mark Paul III *musician, performing company executive*
Raum, Mary Beth *performing arts educator*
Roos, Casper *actor*

Pawtucket
Orson, Barbara Tuschner *actress*

Providence
Barnhill, James Orris *theater educator*
Faraone, Philip *organist, director, consumer products company executive*
Rosenbaum, Randall *arts association administrator*
Wilmeth, Don Burton *theatre arts educator and historian, administrator, writer, editor, actor, director*

Scituate
Neves, David *musician, educator*

Warwick
Amante y Zapata, Joseph John *music professor*
Kaiser, Audrey Kathleen *music educator*
Kelley, James Edward *actor, writer*

SOUTH CAROLINA

Aiken
Losey, Mary Haejung *music educator*

Anderson
Williford, Sandra Simmons *music educator*

Charleston
Cantwell, Don *artistic director*
Gunn, Morey Walker, Jr. *director music organist*

Clinton
Buckland, Karen Wisser *music educator*
Roth, Dale Davis *music educator, religious organization administrator*
Spiegel, John Franklin *theater educator*

Columbia
Boyce, Corrie Mosby *music educator*
Ellis, Yolanda Y. *music educator, small business owner*
Ezell, Elizabeth Anne *music educator*
Sepulveda, Sonja Marian Atkinson *choral director, accompanist*
Welch, Audrey B. *retired music educator*

Conway
Sinclair, Frances Teresa *music educator, musician*

Edisto Island
Van Metre, Margaret Cheryl *performing company executive, dancer, educator*

Florence
Best, David Keith *theater educator, department chairman*
Foster, Jackie Green *voice educator*
Gourley, Alfred Glen, Jr. *theater educator*

Fort Mill
Dickey, Martin *music educator*

Greenville
Ballou, Kathryn Jeanne *performing arts educator*
Morgan, Ruby Norris *musician, educator*

Greenwood
Coon, Michael Dennard *theater educator*

Hilton Head Island
Brock, Karena Diane *dancer, educator*
Selvy, Barbara *dance instructor*

Mount Pleasant
Royall, Mary-Julia C. *church organist, historian*

North Augusta
Champion, Susan Michele *music educator*

Orangeburg
Foerster, Lisa Renee *voice educator*

Rock Hill
Hale, Connie *music educator*

Roebuck
Smith, Alan Wade *music educator*

Spartanburg
Colloms, Vergene Jenkins *music educator, composer, producer*
Johnson, Sarah J. *music educator*
Sellars, Christi von Lehe *music educator*

Sumter
Boyle, Ladson Hunter, Jr. *actor, educator*

SOUTH DAKOTA

Sioux Falls
Vorhes, Anna Kirstine *music educator*

TENNESSEE

Bartlett
Cheatham, Wanda M. *music educator*

Brentwood
Davis, Deborah Lynn *music educator*
Taylor, Nicole Renée (Niki Taylor) *model, shop owner*
Winans, Cece *gospel vocalist*

Chattanooga
Allen, Sarah Frances *music educator, director*
Posey, Garry Lee *theater educator*

Christiana
Coppage, Laura Smith *music educator*

Clarksville
Lowe, Kandia S. *radio director*

Cleveland
Dale, Karen McCall *music educator*

Cordova
Pugh, Dorothy Gunther *performing company executive*

Fall Branch
Douthat, Cheryl O. *music educator, director*

Hendersonville
Skaggs, Ricky *country musician*

Jefferson City
Bivens, Patricia Lynn *musician, director*
Bull, Connie Cruze *music educator*

Johnson City
Snyder-Sowers, Mary Anne Sarah *performing company executive, choreographer, educator*

Knoxville
Landry, Mary Catherine *dance instructor, choreographer*
Moore, Marvelene C. *music educator*

Lawrenceburg
Hayes, Sylvia Richmond *music educator*

Loudon
Horst, Teresa Dale *music educator*

Lynnville
Hollis, Bobby Allen, Jr. *music educator*

Martin
Cook, Douglas J. *theater educator, department chairman*

Memphis
Green, Al *soul and gospel singer*
Nemec, Christopher E. *music educator*
Ouzts, David Perry *church music director, organist*
Owen-Leinert, Susan Huff *voice educator, vocalist*
Philipp, Karla Ann *musician, educator, conductor*
Presley, Lisa Marie *singer*
Williams, David Russell *retired music educator*

Murfreesboro
DeBoer, Angela Ruth *music educator*
Linton, Michael Roy *music educator*

Nashville
Adams, Ryan (David Ryan Adams) *musician*
Autry, Philip Earl *music educator, musician*
Brooks, Kix (Leon Eric Brooks) *musician*
Chesney, Kenny *country singer, songwriter*
Demarcus, Jay (Stanley Demarcus) *country musician, songwriter*
Dunn, Ronnie Gene *musician*
Estrin, Kari (Karen Ruth Estrin) *music producer, agent, consultant*
Followill, Caleb (Anthony Caleb Followill) *musician*
Followill, Jared (Michael Jared Followill) *musician*
Followill, Matthew (Cameron Matthew Followill) *musician*
Followill, Nathan (Ivan Nathan Followill) *musician*
Giles, Joe W. *music educator*
Harris, Emmylou *singer*
Haywood, Dave *singer, musician*
Hill, Faith *musician*
Jackson, Alan *musician, lyricist*
Kelley, Charles *singer, musician*
Krauss, Alison *country musician*
Kwami, Paul T. *musical director and educator*
Lambert, Miranda *vocalist*
Levox, Gary (Gary Wayne Vernon Jr.) *country/rock singer*
Mayer, John *musician*
McAnally, Mac *musician, songwriter*
McBride, Martina *singer*
Midler, Bette *singer, entertainer, actress*
Montgomery, Dillard Brewster *musician, educator*
Paisley, Brad *musician*
Pickler, Kellie Dawn *country singer*
Rooney, Joe Don *country musician*
Sartor, David P. *composer*
Schneller, Pamela *music educator*
Scott, Hillary *singer, musician*
Sheik, Duncan *singer, songwriter*
Swift, Taylor *country singer*
Twain, Shania (Eilleen Regina Edwards) *musician*
Urban, Keith *country singer, songwriter*
Valentine, Alan Darrell *performing company executive, conductor*
Williams, Anthony Ervin *music educator*
Yoakam, Dwight *country western musician*

Pigeon Forge
Parton, Dolly *singer, composer, actress*

Sevierville
Hicks, Deborah *music educator*

Spring Hill
Lister, Thomas Mosie *composer, lyricist, publishing company executive, minister*

TEXAS

Abilene
Pender, Martha Helen *retired dramatic soprano*
Scherr, Bernard *music educator*
Wright, Clell E. *music educator*

Amarillo
McDonough, Raenell *musician, educator*

Arlington
Thomas, Lois C. *musician, educator, religious organization administrator, composer*

Athens
Wright, Marylyn Riley *music educator*

Aubrey
Pizzamiglio, Albert Theodore (Al Pierson) *conductor*

Austin
Antokoletz, Elliott Maxim *music educator*
Brockett, Oscar Gross *retired theater educator*
Bryant, William Thomas *theater educator*
Hancock, Gerre Edward *musician, educator*
Ingram, Jack *musician*
Mills, Stephen *performing company executive*
Mueller, Peggy Jean *dance educator, choreographer, rancher*
Perlak, Kimberley Shelley *music educator*
Robbins, Mary *concert pianist*
Rodriguez, Robert *filmmaker*
Williamson, Barry Scott *conductor, performing arts educator*
Young, Phyllis Casselman *music educator*

Beaumont
Peirce, Dwight A(lexander), Jr. *music educator*

Bedford
Vaught, Karin Hampton *music educator*

Belton
Crawford, Stephen J. *music educator*

Brownsville
Holkup, Linda Patricia *music educator*
McNabb Goodwin, Carol *music educator*

Canyon
Casso, Rebecca Lynn *music educator*
Truitt, Edward Ray *performing arts educator, director*

College Station
Misemer, Sarah M. *theater educator*

Colleyville
Allen, Julie Ann Snell *music educator*

Conroe
Waites, Houston Chase *theater educator*

Corpus Christi
Flory, Neil *music educator, composer*
Sturman, Susan *music educator*
Zamora, Antonio *music director, educator*

Dallas
Brandt, Carole *theater educator, department chairman*
Donnell, Carolyn Faye *music educator*
Foutch, Michael James *actor, dancer, lighting designer, producer*
Franklin, Kirk *singer*
Johnson, Mary Elizabeth *musician, educator*
Joyner, Tom *radio personality*
Palmer, Christine (Clelia Rose Venditti) *opera singer, musician*
Palmer, Larry Garland *music educator, writer, musician*
Pell, Jonathan Laurence *performing company executive*
Pelletier, Sho-mei *musician, educator*
Romersberger, Sara Jane *performing arts educator*
Sargon, Simon A. *composer, professor of composition*
Thomas, Paul Lindsley *composer, musician, director*
Thomas, Sarah Elaine *music educator*
van Zweden, Jaap *conductor, music director*

Denton
Babcock, Mary Lynn *choreographer, educator*
Groom, JoAn Charlene *music educator, director*
Hayes, Marjorie *theater educator, director, actor*
Paul, Pamela Mia *concert pianist*
Seaton, Lynn *music educator*
Slater, Neil *music educator, composer*
Wodnicki, Adam Juliusz *pianist, educator*

El Lago
Chase, Jeanette Knapp *music educator*

El Paso
Colgin Abeln, Melissa Gail *music educator*
Gladstein, Mimi Reisel *theater and literature educator*

Flower Mound
Marrs, Carol Faye *performing arts educator, writer*

Fort Worth
Everton, Jeanne Simpson *theater educator*
Harth-Bedoya, Miguel *conductor*
Patteson, Charles Lynn *musician, retired music educator*
Scott, P. Mark *musician, educator*
Stevenson, Ben *performing company executive*
Yacante, Maria Lucy *music educator, researcher*

Galveston
Rivaux, Lois Elaine *music educator*

Garland
LeDoux, Ellen G. *music educator*
Taylor, Kelley M. *music educator*
Tucker, Kimberly Joan *music educator, director*

Georgetown
Ferrari, Lois *music educator, director*

Gonzales
Ince, Laurel T. *music educator*

Houston
Ballas, Mark, Jr. *dancer*
Beyoncé, (Beyoncé Giselle Knowles) *singer*
Brown, Glenda Ann Walters *ballet director*
Cupp, Aneta Joan *music educator*
Di, Francine *music educator, writer*
Fiese, Richard Kelly *music educator*
Filipp Beseda, Carolyn Francine *music educator, insurance agent*
Freud, Anthony Peter *opera company director*
Gladden, Dean Robert *arts administrator, educator, consultant*
Graf, Hans *conductor, music director*
Grawunder, Teresa A. *musician, educator*
Hescht, Billy Wade *theater educator*
Hough, Derek *dancer, actor*
Jones, Florence M. *music educator*
Krajewski, Michael *conductor*
Moore, Edgar Allan *music educator*
Norris, Chuck (Carlos Ray) *actor*
Perkyns, Jane Elizabeth *music educator, composer*
Rigdon, Kevin Leigh *theater educator, lighting designer, set designer*
Rose, Beatrice Schroeder *harpist, educator*
Rowland, Kelly (Kelendria Trene Rowland) *singer*
Sallee, Wanda Jean *music educator*
Simpson, Robert Louis *music educator*
Sparks, Marvin Roosevelt, Jr. *music educator*
Stallman, Kurt *composer, educator*
Talbert, Arthur Thomas *music educator*
Welch, Stanton *performing company executive*
Whiting, S. Carol *music educator*

Huntsville
Russell, George Haw *video production company executive*
Smith, Jonathan Charles *dancer, educator*

Iowa Park
Wright, Sabra Dell *music educator*

Keene
Doroftei, Mugur Gideon *music educator, conductor, composer, musician*

Kingsville
Hageman, Paul M. *music educator*

Lake Jackson
Gresham, Karen Renee *singer*

Laredo
Huang, Yu Mei *music educator*
Soto, Gilberto D. *music educator*

Leander
Fraley, Linda Williams Darnell *music educator*

Levelland
Ham, Donna Olene *music educator*

Longview
McMullen, Melody Mae *music educator*

Lubbock
Hartwell, William Gersham III *retired music educator*
Raoufi, Azadeh *music educator*
Roy, Juliana W. *music educator*
Wilson, Sarah Elizabeth *music educator*

Magnolia
Tarver, Betty Gail *music educator*

Marshall
Boaz, Virginia Lile *music educator*

Mcallen
Huber, Melba Stewart *dance studio owner, educator*

Mineral Wells
Warfield, Gerald Alexander *composer, writer*

Missouri City
Rathnau, Heather Hearn *music educator, writer*

Monahans
Jones, Evelyn Rojean *theater educator, director*

Nacogdoches
Howard, David L. *conductor, baritone*
Kennedy, Kyle Duane *theater educator, director, actor*
Scott, Debra Laurette *trombone professor*

Odessa
Keast, Michelle *music educator*

Pampa
Willingham, Jeanne Maggart *performing company executive, educator*

Pasadena
Gilley, Mickey Leroy *musician*

Plainview
Belshaw, Gary D. *music educator, composer*
Mosteller, Sandra Marie *music educator*

Plano
Galloway, Marianne Thérèse *performing company executive*

Richardson
Lingo, Kathy Price *theater director, communications educator*

Rockport
Owen, Molly Jackson *music educator*

Rosenberg
Slack, Molly Johanna *theater educator*

San Angelo
Worley, James Glenn *theater educator*

San Antonio
Alejos, Melba Casanova *music educator*
Bussineau King, Deborah Elaine *music educator*
Dunne, Matthew *music educator*
Fabrique, Martha Helene *music educator*
Fruth, Roman Martin *piano technician, musician*
May, S. Beth *music educator, composer*
Oppenheim, Martha Kunkel *pianist, educator*
Prestigiacomo, Roberto *theater educator, art director*
Silantien, John Joseph *music educator*
Widhelm, Jennifer Cochran *theater educator*

San Marcos
Charlton, Debra Lynn *theater educator*

The Colony
Mitchell, Melvin Clifford *music educator*

The Woodlands
Ghosh, Supriyo *performing company executive*

Vernon
Wofford, Garry *music educator*

Waskom
Sullivan, Penny McIver *theater and speech educator*

Wharton
George, Lila Gene Plowe Kennedy *music educator*

Wichita Falls
Cook, Marcella Kay *retired theater educator*
Jordan-Aldaco, Judith Ann *music educator*
Scherler, Kathy Louise *music educator, researcher*

Wylie
Carson, Charles Michael *composer, musician*

UTAH

Cedar City
Modesitt, Carol Ann *vocalist, music educator, opera director*

Logan
Gudmundson, Jon Karl *musician, director*

Montezuma Creek
Schaefer, Kim *music educator*

Orem
Riley, Dyanne Schrock *music professor*

Park City
Becker, William Watters *theater producer*

Provo
Moss, Shawnda L. *theater educator*
Powley, Edward Harrison III *music educator*
Redford, Robert (Charles Robert Redford) *actor, film director*

Saint George
Briggs, Robert Keith *musician*

Salt Lake City
Grant, Raymond Thomas *arts administrator*
Johnson, Xan Stuart *performing arts educator*
Page, Frank J. *music educator*
Parkinson, William Woodall *theater educator*
Romney-Manookin, Elaine Clive *retired music educator, composer*
Sklute, Adam *performing company executive, dancer*
Walker Neve, Diana *singer, voice educator*

Woods Cross
Blackley, Cheryl Ann *musician, freelance/self-employed educator*
Hendriksen, Neil Evan *music educator*

VERMONT

Burlington
Neiweem, David *music educator*

Johnson
Whitehill, Angela Elizabeth *artistic director*

Middlebury
Grindon, Leger *performing arts educator, writer*

West Glover
Weaver, John Borland *musician, department chairman, composer*

Weston
Stettler, Stephen F. *performing company executive*

VIRGINIA

Alexandria
Pearson, Lynda Ann *music educator*
Piecuch, Diane Marie *music educator*

Arlington
Cadby, Carol *theater educator, director*
Clapman, Leah Meredith *public television editor*
Fischer, Iván *conductor*
Hamilton, Anthony *singer*
Liddy, G. Gordon (George Gordon Liddy, Gordon Liddy) *radio personality, writer, former federal official*
Mc Donald, Gail Faber *musician, educator*
Schaeffer, Eric D. *theater director, performing company executive*

Ashburn
Newell, Rachel Pierce *music educator*

Charlottesville
Chapel, Robert Clyde *theater director, educator*
Sibert, Polly Lou *conductor, educator*

Chesapeake
Kringel, Deanna Lynn *music educator*

Chesterfield
Yohe, Robin M. *high school administration and music educator*

Dublin
Billaud, Louise Ann *musician, educator*

Fairfax
Balakerskaia, Anna *music educator*
Hudson, William L. *conductor*
Kurtz, Howard Vincent *theater educator*
Lapple, Judith A. *music educator, director*
Mann, Laura Ann *soprano*
Miller, Patricia A. *music educator, opera and concert artist*
Siddons, Joy Garbee *music educator*

Falls Church
Schoonover, Stanley R. *music educator, consultant*

Fredericksburg
Stylianopoulos, Areti Leonidas *music educator*

Gainesville
French, Dorothy Marie *music educator*

Gloucester Point
Sandridge, Donald Otis *music educator*

Hampton
Dillard, Royzell L. *music educator, director*
Harris, Carl G. *music educator*

Harrisonburg
Choi, In Dal *music educator*

Ivy
Nachmanovitch, Stephen *violinist, composer, author and educator*

Leesburg
Kutner, Lawrence Alan *executive director*
Levin, Mark Reed *radio personality, legal foundation administrator*
Mahood, Ken *music educator*

Lexington
Rader, Angela Nichole *music educator*

Lorton
Celentano, Suzanne *movement educator*

Manassas
Livingston, Jo Ellen Brooks *music educator*

Mechanicsville
Beatty, Pamela Sanders *theater educator*

Middleburg
Yovanovich, Robyn Dobson *theater educator, department chairman*

Natural Bridge Station
Randolph-Broughman, Mary Etta *music educator*

Newport News
Hurst, Lon *theater educator, director, choreographer*
Rossettini, Timothy James *music educator, director*
Waller, George Darryl *music educator*

Norfolk
Kinzer, Amanda *performing arts educator*
Wright, Sally Copeland *musician, educator*

Petersburg
Dance, Gloria Fenderson *dance studio executive, ballet administrator*
Floyd-Savage, Karen Sue *music educator*

Radford
James, Clarity *mezzo soprano*

Reston
East, Mary Ann Hildegarde *vocalist*

Richmond
Anderson, Bette (Bonnie) Ferguson *music educator*
Bacon, Diane Briggs *music educator, consultant*
Bray, Patricia Shannon *music educator, musician, small business owner*
Freeman, Edward Carl, Jr. *music minister*
Kennedy, Patricia Berry *retired music educator*
Melcher, Elizabeth *musician*
Winslett, Stoner *artistic director*

Roanoke
Burchfield, Donna Faye *dancer, educator*

Rural Retreat
Dutton, Sandra F. *music educator*

Salem
Bachelder, Elizabeth Young *musician, educator*

Springfield
D'Elosua, Jennifer Dawn *music educator*

Staunton
Balsley, Philip Elwood *entertainer*

Sterling
Lacey, Aaron Michael *actor, director, film producer, scriptwriter*

Suffolk
Bollinger, Michael *artistic director*

Virginia Beach
Dixon, John Spencer *performing arts association administrator*
Ishmael, Laura Jeanne *music educator, pharmacologist*
Lutsyshyn, Oksana *concert pianist, organist*
Prescott, David L. C., Jr. *music educator*
Wales, Lorene M. *film producer, educator*

Williamsburg
Connolly, Martha Taugher *voice educator*
Fletcher, Mary Eason *voice educator*
Gavaler, Joan Susan *dance educator*
Hornsby, Bruce Randall *composer, musician*
Martin, Fusi Fonkijom *film director, educator*
Tanglao Aguas, Francis *performing arts association administrator, educator*

Winchester
Aiosa, Charlotte Nelson *music educator*
Bloom, Mary Ann *music educator*
Kolt, Robert Paul *musicologist, conductor*
Larson, Robert Peter *music educator, director*
Lederer, Doris *musician*
Romano, Charlene Baughan *music educator*

Wise
Volk, David Paul *music educator*

Woodbridge
Rethmel, Carol Ann *voice educator, director*

WASHINGTON

Anacortes
Tornow, L. William *musician*

Bellingham
Larner, Daniel M. *theater educator, playwright, writer*
Whyte, Nancy Marie *performing arts educator*

Clarkston
Torgerson, Linda Belle *music educator*

Coupeville
Lotzenhiser, George William *musician, educator, academic administrator, composer*

Des Moines
Akaka, Sheryl Hung Lan Lokelani *music educator*

Kenmore
Sokol, Jennifer Marie *musician, writer*

Longview
Uthmann, Richard W. *retired music educator*

North Bend
Brumbaugh, Harley Aaron *retired music educator, conductor*

Olympia
Louis, Glen *music educator*
Macduff, Ilone Margaret *music educator*

Omak
Pearce, Donald W. *music educator*

Pullman
Monroe, Kelvin Jonathan *musician, educator*

Seattle
Beale, Jane Guthrie *music publisher, music educator, pianist*
Boal, Peter Cadbury *performing company executive*
Brock, Isaac *musician*
Collier, Tom Ward *musician, educator*
Denke, Conrad William *motion picture producer*
Elyn, Mark *retired vocalist*
Graney, Pat *choreographer*
Houston, Janeanne Currier *vocalist, educator*
Jenkins, Speight, Jr. *opera company director*
Madis, Eric Stephen *musician*
Mull, Robert W. *filmmaker, curator*
Russell, Francia *retired ballet director, educator*
Schwarz, Gerard *conductor, musician, music director*
Scranton, George Alfred *theater educator*
Shahn, Judith *voice educator*
Sher, Bartlett *theater director*
Staryk, Steven Sam *violinist, concertmaster, educator*
Stowell, Kent *retired ballet director*

Shoreline
Dolacky, Susan K. *music educator*

Spokane
Halvorson, Marjory *opera director*

Tacoma
Rimbach, Evangeline Lois *retired music educator*
Ward, Keith Charles *music educator*

University Place
Panerio, Robert Major, Sr. *music educator, composer*

Walla Walla
Simon, Nancy Lynn *performing arts educator, director*

Washougal
Harness, William Edward *tenor*

Woodinville
Sanders, Richard Kinard *actor*

WEST VIRGINIA

Charleston
Pasinetti, Nina Denton *dance educator, artistic director, choreographer*

Morgantown
Wiedebusch, Mary Kathryne *dance educator*
Wilson, Mary Alice *musician, educator*

Salem
Raad, Virginia *pianist, educator*

WISCONSIN

Baraboo
Lang, Gregory P. *music educator*

Chippewa Falls
Sutherland, Marion Ida *music educator*

Colgate
Earl, Marcia Hunt *music educator, director*

Elkhorn
Janners, Erik Nikolas *music educator, conductor*

Greendale
Patterson, Amanda Margaret *music educator*

Kenosha
Garcia, Alvaro *music educator*

La Crosse
Gorman, Kathleen Jean *performing arts educator, choreographer*
Luckner, Brian William *choir director, organist, composer*

Luxemburg
Riley, Dan *entertainer*

Madison
Bartley, Linda L. *musician, music educator*
DeMain, John *opera company director*
Dorn, Dennis L. *theater educator*
Faulkner, Julia Ellen *opera singer*
Schwendinger, Laura Elise *composer, humanities educator*
Tvedt, Ryan Robert *theater educator*

Marinette
Malmstadt, Mary Jane *music educator*

Menasha
Zimmerman, Lynda Diane *music educator*

Milwaukee
Belfer, Beverly Rochelle Eigen *music educator, writer*
Cheatham, Wallace McClain *music educator*
Delfs, Andreas *conductor, musical director*
Dyszelski, Aaron M. *theater educator, director*
Graham, Richard Harris, Jr. *theater educator*
Horsman, Lenore Lynde (Eleanora Lynde) *singer, voice educator*
Pink, Michael *performing company executive*
Samson, Richard Max *theater director, investment company executive*
Schneider, John David *theatre director, playwright, actor, jazz singer*

Monona
Jensen, Jill Susan *music educator*

Neenah
Orm, Sally S. *music educator, piano vocal coach*

New Berlin
Belich, Kay S. *music educator*

Oconomowoc
Bleke, Diane K. *music educator, director*

Oshkosh
Perkins, Troy *filmmaker*

Platteville
Cornils, Margaret A. *music educator*
Gregg, Matthew Douglas *music educator, director*

Ripon
Amsden, Robert Lee *theater educator*

Shell Lake
Aderman, Oscar Darrell *retired music educator*

Superior
Scott, David Edmund *music educator, conductor, consultant*

Washington Island
Schweikert, Norman Carl *retired musician*

Waukesha
Stringham, Phyllis Joan *retired music educator*

Waupaca
Hansen, Louise Hill *music educator, retired application developer*

Whitewater
Grubel, Barbara Lynn *dancer, educator*

WYOMING

Casper
He, Jianjun *music educator, composer*

Cheyenne
Cornish, Nancy Lee *music educator*
Panopoulos, Nick Antonios *retired speech and drama educator*

Laramie
Bogard, Theresa Lynn *music educator*

TERRITORIES OF THE UNITED STATES

PUERTO RICO

San Juan
Daddy Yankee, (Raymond Ayala) *musician*

Santurce
Residante, El (René Pérez) *singer, composer*
Visitante, El (Eduardo Cabra) *singer, musician*

VIRGIN ISLANDS

Charlotte Amalie
Francis, Georgia *music educator*

Kingshill
Bryson, Valrica *music educator*

CANADA

ALBERTA

Calgary
Grand-Maitre, Jean *performing company executive*
Palileo, Hazel Valencia *videographer*
Raeburn, Andrew Harvey *performing arts consultant*

BRITISH COLUMBIA

Mayne Island
Cavoukian, Raffi (Raffi) *folksinger, children's entertainer*

Vancouver
Jones, Norah (Geethali Norah Jones Shankar) *singer*
Lavigne, Avril *singer*
Mitchell, Joni (Roberta Joan Anderson) *singer, songwriter, artist*

MANITOBA

Winnipeg
Lewis, André Leon *performing company executive*
Turner, Robert Comrie *composer*

ONTARIO

Kitchener
Coles, Graham *conductor, composer*
Eldred, Gerald Marcus *performing company executive*

London
William, David *theater director, actor*

Ottawa
Gillingham, Bryan Reginald *music educator*

Toronto
Beckwith, John *musician, composer, educator*
Colgrass, Michael Charles *composer*
Egoyan, Atom *film director*
Furtado, Nelly Kim *vocalist*
Goh, Chan Hon *ballerina*
Grimes, Shenae Sonya *actress*
Kain, Karen Alexandria *performing company executive, ballet dancer*
Oundjian, Peter *conductor, music director*
Polley, Sarah *actress*

QUEBEC

Montreal
Jones, Hank *jazz musician*
Lock, Edouard *performing company executive*
Nagano, Kent George *conductor, music director*
Pankov, Gradimir Krunislav *performing company executive*
Rivest, Jean-François *conductor*

AUSTRALIA

North Sydney
Crowe, Russell *actor*

Perth
Verbitsky, Vladimir *conductor*

Redfern
Campion, Jane *film director, screenwriter*

Victoria
Bana, Eric *actor*

AUSTRIA

Graz
Gee, Erin *composer*

Linz
Davies, Dennis Russell *conductor, music director, pianist*

Wien
Cotrubas, Ileana *opera singer, retired lyric soprano*
Wirth, Gerald *conductor, composer*

BELGIUM

Brussels
Freizer, Louis A. *radio producer*
Rzewski, Frederic *composer*

CHINA

Macau
Veiga Jardim, Oswaldo *conductor, composer, researcher*

COSTA RICA

San José
Hoffman, Irwin *orchestra conductor*

CZECH REPUBLIC

Nymburk
Cusumano, James Anthony *filmmaker, vocalist, retired pharmaceutical, hotel, and recording industry executive*

DENMARK

Roskilde
Skov, Leif *performing arts association administrator, entrepreneur*

ENGLAND

Askett Bucks
Irons, Jeremy *actor*

Cambridge
Hogwood, Christopher Jarvis Haley *music educator*

Charlbury
Belkin, Boris David *violinist*

Cheltenham
Winwood, Stephen Lawrence *musician, composer*

Dartford
Goodman, Len *former dancer, television personality*

East Sussex
Katin, Peter Roy *pianist*

Essex
Collins, Joan Henrietta *actress*

Leavesden
Watson, Emma *actress*

Leeds
De Frutos, Javier *performing company executive, choreographer, dancer*
Ichino, Yoko *ballerina*
Nixon, David *dancer*

London
Adele, (Adele Laurie Blue Adkins) *singer*
Alexeev, Dmitri Konstantinovich *pianist*
Anderson, Kevin C. *actor*
Arulpragasam, Mathangi (M.I.A.) *singer, artist*
Ashkenazy, Vladimir Davidovich *concert pianist, conductor*
Beck, Jeff (Geoffrey Arnold Beck) *guitarist*
Beckham, Victoria Caroline *singer, apparel designer*
Bell, Joshua *musician*
Bertolucci, Bernardo *film director*
Blethyn, Brenda Anne *actress*
Blunt, Emily *actress*
Bono, (Paul David Hewson) *singer, songwriter*
Christie, Julie *actress*
Codron, Michael Victor *theater producer*
Colson, Christian *film producer*
Cowell, Simon *television personality, music producer*
Darling, Peter *choreographer*
Daughtry, Christopher Adam *singer*
Davis, Sir Colin Rex *conductor*
Day-Lewis, Daniel (Michael Blake) *actor*
Dench, Judi (Judith Olivia Dench) *actress*
Duffy, (Aimée Ann Duffy) *singer*
Duncan, Lindsay *actress*
Finney, Albert *actor, theater director*
Flor, Claus Peter *conductor*
Frears, Stephen *film director*
Gervais, Ricky *actor, scriptwriter*
Gwynne, Haydn *actress*
Haitink, Bernard J. H. *conductor*
Hannah, John *actor*
Hicks, Taylor Reuben *singer*
Hodge, Douglas *actor*
Hurt, John Vincent *actor*
Ivory, James Francis *film director*
John, Sir Elton Hercules (Reginald Kenneth Dwight) *musician*
Kapranos, Alexander (Franz Ferdinand) *singer, musician*
Kingsley, Sir Ben *actor*
Knightley, Keira *actress*
Knopfler, Mark *rock guitarist, singer, composer*
Koch, Martin *composer*
Leigh, Mike *film director*
Lewis, Leona Louise *singer*
Litton, Andrew *conductor, music director*
Lloyd Webber, Lord Andrew (Baron of Sydmonton) *composer*
Mackerras, Sir Charles (Alan Maclaurin) *conductor*
Masur, Kurt *conductor, music director*
McAvoy, James Andrew *actor*
McGregor, Ewan Gordon *actor*
McKellen, Sir Ian *actor*
McPhee, Katharine Hope *singer*
McShane, Ian *actor*
Minton, Yvonne Fay *mezzo-soprano*
Moody, Ron *actor, writer*
Moss, Kate *model*
Nagra, Parminder *actress*
Newell, Mike *film director*
Nighy, Bill Francis *actor*
Okonedo, Sophie *actress*
Page, Jimmy (James Patrick Page) *musician*
Patel, Dev *actor*
Pattinson, Robert (Robert Thomas-Pattinson) *actor*
Plant, Robert Anthony *singer*
Plowright, Joan Ann *actress*
Pryce, Jonathan *actor*
Radcliffe, Daniel (Daniel Jacob Radcliffe) *actor*
Richardson, Miranda *actress*
Rickman, Alan *actor*
Shankar, Ravi *composer, musician*
Sheen, Michael *actor*
Sher, Sir Antony *actor, author, artist*
Smith, Dame Maggie (Margaret Natalie Smith Cross) *actress*
Spacey, Kevin *actor*
Swinton, Tilda (Katherine Matilda Swinton) *actress*
Townshend, Pete (Peter Dennis Blandford Townshend) *musician, composer*
Uchida, Mitsuko *pianist*
Venzago, Mario *conductor, former music director*
Weisz, Rachel *actress*
Winner, Michael Robert *film director, producer, writer*

North Wales
Hands, Terence David (Terry) *theater and opera director*

Sunderland
Puttnam, Lord David Terence *film producer*

Surrey
Holm, Sir Ian *actor*

FINLAND

Helsinki
Langbacka, Ralf Runar *theater director, educator*

FRANCE

Neuilly-sur-Seine
de Homem-Christo, Guy-Manuel *musician*

Paris
Cotillard, Marion *actress*
de Havilland, Olivia Mary *actress*
Deneuve, Catherine (Catherine Dorleac) *actress*
Jolas, Betsy *composer, educator*
Raimondi, Ruggero *opera singer*
Rappeneau, Jean-Paul *film director, scriptwriter*

GERMANY

Berlin
Barenboim, Daniel *conductor, pianist, music director*
Inbal, Eliahu *conductor*

Essen
Soltesz, Stefan *conductor*

Hamburg
Neumeier, John *choreographer, ballet company director*

Munich
Araiza, Francisco (José Francisco Araiza Andrade) *opera singer*

Stuttgart
Anderson, Reid Bryce *performing company executive*

Worms
Elkins, Tabitha M. *music educator, composer, jazz singer, pianist, writer*

HONG KONG

Happy Valley
Onne, Madeleine *performing company executive, dancer*

Kowloon
de Waart, Edo *conductor, music director*

Shatin
Lee, Wendy Wan-Ki *music professor*

IRELAND

Dublin
Farrell, Colin James *actor*
Sheridan, Jim *film director, screenwriter*

Galway
Hynes, Garry *theater director*

ISRAEL

Tel Aviv
Naharin, Ohad *choreographer, performing company executive*

ITALY

Cremia
Malipiero, Victoria Schneider *opera singer*

Mestre
Maguire, Janet *composer*

Rome
Zeffirelli, Franco *theater and film director*

JAPAN

Tokyo
Ozawa, Seiji *conductor, music director*

NETHERLANDS

Amsterdam
Andriessen, Louis *composer*

The Hague
Vincent, Jim *performing company executive*

NEW ZEALAND

Wellington
Clement, Jemaine *actor, musician*
Jackson, Peter *film director*
Paquin, Anna Helene *actress*

POLAND

Cracow
Penderecki, Krzysztof *composer, conductor*

Warsaw
Dawidow, Boguslaw *music director*
Zanussi, Krzysztof *film director, producer, scriptwriter*

SCOTLAND

Glasgow
Tiffany, John *theater director*

SPAIN

Madrid
Frühbeck de Burgos, Rafael *conductor*
Mortier, Gerard *opera company director*

Valencia
Maazel, Lorin Varencove *conductor, composer, violinist*

SWITZERLAND

Meggen
Galway, Sir James *flutist*

TAIWAN

Taipei
Sicart, Pierre-Alexandre Serge Henry *writer, scholar*

THAILAND

Bangkok
Pinkaew, Prachya *film producer and director*

VIETNAM

Hanoi
Vu, Nhat Tan *composer*

ADDRESS UNPUBLISHED

Abernathy, Jennifer P. *music educator*
Abraham, F. Murray (Fahrid Murray Abraham) *actor, educator*
Aguilera, Christina *singer*
Aiken, Clay (Clayton Holmes Aiken) *singer*
Alberti-Thomson, Marie J. (Marie Joyce Salisbury) *musician, educator*
Albrecht, Chris *talent agency executive, former broadcast executive*
Alexander, Hope *actor, educator, theater director*
Alexander, Jason (Jay Scott Greenspan) *actor*
Allard, Michael Alan *music educator, conductor*
Allen, Marilyn Myers Pool *theater director, video specialist*
Allen, Woody (Allen Stewart Konigsberg) *film director, actor*
Allison Haslach, Linda *music educator*
Allston, Charita Capers *music educator*
Almodovar, Pedro *filmmaker, film director, film producer*
Amara, Lucine *vocalist*
Amgott, Madeline *television producer, consultant*
Anderson, Gillian Leigh *actress*
Anderson, Pam (Pamela Denise Anderson) *actress*
Andreu, Helene C. *dancer, educator*
Andrews, Dame Julie (Julia Elizabeth Wells) *actress, singer*
Angle, Tracy Joyce *theater educator*
Apted, Michael David *film director*
Archuleta, David James *singer*
Arditti, Paul *sound designer*
Arenal, Julie (Mrs. Barry Primus) *choreographer*
Arquette, Patricia *actress*
Artemova, Alina *music educator*
Ashford, Rob *choreographer, dancer*
Ashmore, Pamela Jean *music educator*
Asman, Bub (Henry B. Asman) *sound editor*
Astolfi, Jeri-Mae G. *music educator*
Atkins, Erica *singer*
Atkins, Tina (Trecina Evette Atkins) *singer*
Avary, Roger Roberts (Frank Brauner) *film director, producer, writer*
Aykroyd, Daniel Edward *actor, writer*
Bach, Jan Morris *composer, educator*
Bach, Mary Irene *music educator*
Bailey, Robert C. *opera company executive*
Baker, Kathleen *music educator*
Baranski, Christine *actress*
Barr, John Gladden *music educator*
Barranger, Milly Slater *theater educator author*
Bassett, Leslie Raymond *composer, educator*
Bassingthwaighte, Sarah Louise *music educator*
Bateman, Charles Gregory *music educator*
Baugh-Bennett, Grace L. *musician, educator*
Beatty, Warren *actor, film director, film producer*
Beck, Jane *dance educator, choreographer*
Beck, Susan Rebecca *voice educator, consultant*
Beeler, Charles Alan *retired music educator*
Bello, Maria Elana *actress*
Beluso, Karen Mae *performing company executive, music educator*
Ben-Amots, Ofer *composer, educator*
Bencini, Sara Haltiwanger *concert pianist*
Bennett, Tony (Anthony Dominick Benedetto) *entertainer*
Benning, James *film director*
Bensussen, Melia *theater director, professor*
Beranek, Kim Marie *music educator*
Berard, Barbara *performing arts educator*
Bergen, Candice *actress, writer, photojournalist*
Berlind, Roger Stuart *stage and film producer*
Berlinger, Warren *actor*
Bernard, Jennifer *music educator*
Betancourt-Bryant, Sonia *music educator*
Bethke, Louise Virginia *music educator, writer*
Bevan, Tim *film producer*
Beyer, Dana D. *music educator*
Bimstein, Phillip Kent *composer*
Binoche, Juliette *actress*
Bircher, Daniel Trevor *musician*
Bissell, James Dougal III *motion picture production designer*
Bitzas, Penelope *music educator*
Biziou, Peter *cinematographer*
Black, Lewis *comedian, actor*
Blackstone, Dara *music educator, conductor*
Blaine, David (David Blaine White) *magician*
Blige, Mary Jane *singer*
Blinn, William Frederick *television writer and producer*
Blomquist, Alan Charles *film producer*
Bloomquist, Kenneth Gene *music educator, director*
Blossom, Beverly *choreographer, educator*
Boe, David Stephen *musician, educator, dean*
Boehle, William Randall *music educator emeritus*
Bonazzi, Elaine Claire *mezzo soprano*
Bondy, Alison A. *music educator*
Bon Jovi, Jon (John Francis Bongiovi Jr.) *musician, singer, songwriter, actor, professional sports team executive*
Bonnard, Raymond *theater director*
Booth, Debra *theater educator*
Boras, Scott D. *professional sports agent*
Borgnine, Ernest *actor*
Borkowski, Francis Thomas *music educator*
Bosco, Philip Michael *actor*
Boulez, Pierre *composer, conductor*
Bouvier, Monica Renee *traffic director*
Boyd, Sue Marston *retired music educator*
Boyle, Lara Flynn *actress*
Boyter, Judy B *music educator*
Brady, Mary Rolfes *music educator*
Brady, Sharon *actor, theater educator*
Brandon, Liane *filmmaker, educator, photographer*
Brandt-Soetermans, Valerie *dancer, educator*
Brazinski, Frank William *composer, educator*
Brecker, Randal Edward *musician, arranger*
Brewster, Jamie Susan *theater educator*
Bridges, Jeff *actor*
Briggle, Gary Lee *actor, director*
Brobston, Stanley Heard *music educator, writer*
Brock, John Morgan (Juno), Jr. *composer, performer, producer*
Brooks, Garth (Troyal Garth Brooks) *musician, singer*
Brooks, Lorraine Elizabeth *retired music educator*
Brooks-Turner, Myra *music educator*
Brosnan, Pierce *actor*
Brown, Alton C. *television personality, chef*
Brown, Charles Samuel *singer, composer, retired educator*
Brown, Kimberly D. *performing arts educator, choreographer, director*
Brown, Lora Alice *entertainment company executive, educator*
Brown-Barton, Grace Olive *music educator*
Browne, Jackson *singer, songwriter*
Brown Leatherberry, Thomas Henry *performing company executive, clergyman*
Bruce, Gregory Ellis *theater educator, director*
Bull, Inez Stewart *musician, educator, curator*
Bullock, Sandra (Sandra Annette Bullock) *actress*
Bumbry-Bronson, Venetta *music educator*
Bump, Elizabeth Bertha *music educator*
Burke, Brooke *actress, model*
Burns, Cora Lea *music educator, director*
Burns, Edward J., Jr. *actor, film director*
Burstyn, Ellen (Edna Rae Gillooly) *actress*
Busby, Daniel Gary *music educator, theater educator*
Bush, Eileen Shanin *voice educator*
Bush, Ellen D. *music educator*
Bynes, Amanda *actress*
Byrne, Gabriel *actor*
Byrnes, Hope Huska *singer, volunteer*
Caan, James *actor, director*
Caicedo, Patricia *singer, musicologist, physician*
Calman, Craig David *actor, writer*
Cameron-Mickens, Vertrelle Diane *singer, conductor, voice educator*
Campbell, Melissa Lynnsimmons *music educator*
Cannavale, Bobby (Roberto Cannavale) *actor*
Caparro, James *entertainment industry executive*
Cardell, Silvana *choreographer, educator*
Careau, James Thomas *music educator*
Carey, Drew *actor*
Carley, Kurt *actor*
Carlock, Sandra Lynn *musician, educator*
Carnes, Tara Lea Barker *music educator*
Carter, Jeffrey Richard *music educator*
Carter, La Rae Dunn *music educator*
Casei, Nedda *mezzo soprano*
Casey, Harry Wayne *performer, songwriter, record producer*
Castle-Hughes, Keisha *actress*
Caswell, Dorothy Ann Cottrell *performing arts association administrator*
Caviani, Laura Susan *music educator*
Caviezel, James Patrick *actor*
Cermak, James Frank *theater educator*
Chalcraft, Elena Marie *actress, singer*
Chapman, William *baritone*
Charles, Walter *actor*
Chávez, Denise Elia *performance writer, actress*
Cher, (Cherilyn Sarkisian) *singer, actress*
Chernavsky, George Y. *composer, producer, song writer*
Chiklis, Michael *actor*
Chiorini, Matt *theater educator, director*
Christopher, Russell Lewis *baritone*
Chu, Katherine K. *music educator*
Chusid, Martin *retired musicologist, educator*
Clark, Candy *actress*
Clarke, Gregory *sound designer*
Clark Johnson, Kimberly *singer, educator*
Clarkson, Kelly Brianne *singer*
Clausen, Jeanne Lorraine *musician*
Claver, Robert Earl *television producer, director*
Clooney, George *actor*
Close, Glenn *actress*
Cochran, Kathy Holcombe *music educator, conductor*
Cody, Judith *composer, writer*
Coffey, Sharon Marie *music educator*
Cohen, Aryell *music educator*
Colaianni, Louis Edward *voice educator*
Colbert, Stephen (Stephen Tyrone Colbert) *comedian, actor*
Cole, Nikki Jo *music educator*
Coleman, Dabney W. *actor*
Collins, Kathleen Anne *artistic director*
Collins, Sherri Smith *music educator*
Columbus, Chris J. *film director, screenwriter*
Combs, Holly Marie *actress*
Common, (Lonnie Rashid Lynn, Common Sense) *rap artist*
Condon, Tom (Thomas Joseph Condon) *sports agent, retired professional football player*
Connery, Sir Sean (Thomas Sean Connery) *actor*
Constantine, Michael *actor*
Conway-Langguth, Rebecca Joan *dance school owner and instructor*
Cook, David Roland *singer, musician*
Cooper, Hal *television director*
Cooper, Judith Kase *retired theater educator, playwright*
Copperfield, David (David Kotkin) *illusionist, director, producer*
Coppola, Sofia Carmina *film director, film producer, scriptwriter*
Cosby, Bill *actor, television producer*
Costa, Mary *soprano*
Costa-Gavras, (Constantin Gavras) *film director, writer*
Costello, Elvis (Declan Patrick McManus) *musician, songwriter, singer*
Cottrell, David Milton *sound recording engineer, producer, singer, songwriter*
Courtney, Hischke J. *dancer, educator*
Cox, Beulah Elizabeth *violinist, music educator*
Craioveanu, Mihai Dorin *musician*
Craven, Wes *film director*
Crawford, Constance *performance artist, educator*
Cronenberg, David *film director*
Croskell, Madelon Byrd *music educator, classical vocalist*
Crouch, Sarah Harris *music educator, writer*
Crow, Sheryl *singer, songwriter, musician*
Cruz-Romo, Gilda *soprano*
Culkin, Macaulay *actor*
Culligan, Sean Louis *theater educator*
Cummins, Wilma Jeanne *actress, comedienne*
Cunningham, Michael Gerald *composer, writer, music educator emeritus*
Curson, Theodore *musician*
Curtis, Jamie Lee *actress*
D'Abruzzo, Stephanie *actress*
Dahl, John *film director*
Dahlgren, Carl Herman Per *performing company executive, educator*
Damon, Matt (Matthew Paige Damon) *actor*
Danaher, Mallory Millett (Mallory Jones) *actress, photographer, film and theater producer*
Daniel, Ronald George *theater, film and opera director*
Darvarova, Elmira *musician, concertmaster*
Dashiell, Georgette Elaine *actor, director*
Davies, Raymond Douglas *musician, songwriter*
Davis, Geena (Virginia Elizabeth Davis) *actress*
Davis, Osceola A. *opera singer*
Dawson, David Lynn *theater educator*
De Angelis, Rosemary Eleanor *actress*
de Blasis, James Michael *performing company executive, theater producer*
DeBow, Faith *pianist, music educator*
De Felitta, Frank Paul *film producer, writer*
DeHoff, Valerie S. *music educator*
de la Rocha, Zack *singer, musician*
de Lavallade, Carmen *dancer, choreographer*
Dell, Charlene Elizabeth *music educator*
del Toro, Guillermo *film director*
de Matteo, Drea *actress*
Demme, Jonathan *director, producer, writer*
Denis, Anne Cara *musician, educator*
Dennis, Steven J. *performing arts educator, actor*
De Palma-Iozzi, Frances M. *music educator, conductor*
Dern, Laura *actress*
Deutsch, Herbert Arnold *music educator*
Devlin, Michael Coles *bass-baritone*
DiBenedetto, Gary *composer, educator*
DiCaprio, Leonardo *actor*
Dick, James Cordell *concert pianist*
Diefenderfer, Dan *filmmaker*
Diemer, Emma Lou *composer, educator*
Dishy, Bob *actor*
Dixon, Ben Harold *musician, educator*
Dixon, William Robert *musician, educator*
Dodds, Amy Noelle Shawler *music educator*
Dodson, Daryl Theodore *ballet administrator, consultant*
Donner, Jörn Johan *film director, writer, state legislator*
Douglas, Dewey L. *theater educator, lighting designer*
Douglas, P C *producer, director, reporter, editor*
Downs, Jon Franklin *drama educator, director, writer*
Doyle, Gillian *actress*
D'Rivera, Paquito *clarinetist, saxophonist, conductor, composer*
Drozd, Leszek Stanislaw *educational video producer, music composer for films, CEO story tellers producer*
Drummond, Carol Cramer *voice educator, lyricist, writer, artist*
Duchovny, David *actor*
Duke, Patty (Anna Marie Duke) *actress*
Dunaway, Faye (Dorothy Dunaway) *actress*
Duval, Olivia Blackmon *music educator*
Dylan, Jakob *musician, singer*
Elisha, Larisa *musician, performer, educator*
Elliott, Kenneth Yates *theater educator*
Ellis, Cynthia Sue *music educator*
Emanuel, Ari (Ariel Zev Emanuel) *talent agency executive*
Eng, Clare Sher Ling *music educator*
Epstein, Adam *theater producer*
Erb, James Bryan *conductor, musicologist, educator*
Erbe, Yvonne Mary *music educator, marketing specialist, guidance counselor*
Estelle, (Estelle Fanta Swaray) *singer*
Everett, Tom *actor*
Everhart, Gloria Elaine *music educator*
Fairfield, Paula Kathleen *sound recording engineer*
Faivre, Bertrand *film producer*
Farney, Charlotte Eugenia *musician, educator*
Farrell, Suzanne (Roberta Sue Ficker) *ballerina*
Fast, Heinz Gerhard *music educator, conductor*
Fay, William Frederick *film producer*
Fellner, Eric *film producer*
Ferri-Grant, Carson (Carson Grant) *actor, director, artist, writer, digital film video editor*
Fields, Victor Lee *music educator*
Fiennes, Ralph (Ralph Nathaniel Twisleton-Wykeham Fiennes) *actor*
Fiero-Maza, Lorraine Doris *music educator*
Filerman, Michael Herman *television producer*
Finch, Janet Buswell *musician*
Fischer, William Samuel *composer, lecturer*
Fisher, Carrie Frances *actress, writer*
Fisher, Frances *actress*
Fitzpatrick, Christopher *musician, educator*
Fleck, Bela *country musician*
Fleming, Gina Marie *music educator*
Fleming, Rhonda *actress, singer, philanthropist*
Flynn, George William *retired music educator*
Fonda, Peter *actor, director, producer*
Fontaine, Joan *actress*
Fontana, Dominic Joseph (D.J. Fontana) *musician*
Fontijn, Claire *musician, educator*
Ford, Harrison *actor*
Forman, Miloš *film director*
Foxworthy, Jeff *comedian, writer, actor*
Frank, Glenda *performing arts educator, writer*
Franklin, Aretha Louise *singer*
Freeman, Morgan *actor*
Freitas, Beatrice B(otty) *musician, educator*
Frey, Glenn *songwriter, vocalist, guitarist*
Fricker, Brenda *actress*
Frot-Coutaz, Cecile *television producer*
Fuerstner, Fiona Margaret Anne *ballet company executive, educator*
Fukasawa, Natsuki *music educator*
Fuller, Bryan *television producer, scriptwriter*
Furlan, Connie SaLoutos *actress, educator*
Gach, Jay Anthony *composer*
Gainer, Robert *theater educator, department chairman*
Gaines, Boyd *actor*
Galante, Jane Hohfeld *musician, historian*
Gale, Holly Ruth *music educator*
Gallagher, Peter *actor*
Gallardo, Sandra Silvana *television producer, actress*
Gamer, Carlton Edwin *composer, music educator*
Gan, Chenny Quan *musician, artist, educator*
Gandolfini, James *actor*
Garcia, Jorge *actor*
Garlin, Jeff *actor*
Garner, Jennifer Anne *actress*
Garofalo, Janeane *actress, comedienne*
Garrett, Nataki *theater director*
Gengler, Richelle Ruth *musician, educator*
Gephardt, Donald Louis *retired music professor*
Gibbs, David Richard *musician, journalist, photographer, writer*
Gibney, Alex *producer, director, writer*
Gibson, Mel *actor, film director and producer*
Gilbert, Harriette Gurley *retired music educator*
Gillan, Rebecca Jane *music educator, composer*
Gilliam, Terry Vance *film director, actor, writer, illustrator*
Gilmore, Dawn S. *music educator*
Gingras, Michele *music educator*
Gittinger, Laurie Ellen *music educator*
Gleim, Kathy Marie *music educator, performer, composer*
Goble, Patrick *composer, educator*
Goines, Leonard *music educator, consultant*
Goldberg, Whoopi (Caryn Elaine Johnson) *actress, comedienne*
Gooden-Young, Phyllis Karron *dance instructor*
Gordon, Marjorie *lyric-coloratura soprano, opera producer, educator*
Gould, Elliott *actor*
Grant, Alexander Marshall *retired ballet director*
Grant, Lee (Lyova Haskell Rosenthal) *actress, television and film director*
Grant, Merrill Theodore *television producer*
Graves, Lorraine Elizabeth *dancer, educator, coach*
Greco, Christopher Jon *musician, composer, educator*
Green, Howard *actor*
Greenberg, Marvin *retired music educator*
Grey, Joel *actor*
Griffiths, Jonathan Barrick *music producer, arranger, consultant*
Grinenko, Elena *dancer*
Griner, Brenda *choreographer, director*
Grosbard, Ulu *film director*
Grossman, Edward Jerome *music educator, composer*
Gruen, Margaret *actress*
Guerra, Alma Del Rosario *retired music educator*
Gugler, Mary Dugan *composer, music educator*
Guttenberg, Steve *actor*
Gyllenhaal, Jake *actor*
Hall, Gregory *composer, engineer*
Hall, James Stanley *jazz guitarist, composer*
Hall, Monty *television producer, actor*
Halleck, Donna P. *piano educator*
Hancock, Artemus Ward, Sr. *music educator*
Haney, Marlene Carol *music educator*
Harding, Philip Andreae *retired communications and marketing researcher*
Hardock, Linda *music educator*
Hardwicke, Catherine Helen *film director, set designer*
Harold, Constance Cammille *theater educator, artist*
Harrell, Eric *theater professor*
Harris, Harriet *actress*
Harris, Robert A. *retired music educator*
Harrison, Michael *former opera company director*
Harrison, Robin Fonclara *music educator*
Hart, Cherie Ann *music educator*
Hathorne, Gayle Gene *musician, family historian*
Hawke, Ethan Green *actor*
Hawthorne, Roy John *retired music educator*
Hayes, Patricia Thornton *music educator, retired director*
Haynes, Alora Dawn *performing arts educator*
Hazelip, Linda Ann *musician, small business owner, executive assistant*
Heath, John Robert *music educator*
Heaton, Haidee *theater educator*
Heche, Anne (Anne Celeste Heche) *actress*
Hedahl, Gorden Orlin *theater educator, retired dean*
Helgenberger, Marg *actress*
Hennessey, Patrick Daniel *musician, educator, musicologist*
Henninger, Nancy *retired voice educator, singer*
Henson, Anna Resnick *music educator*

Hergo, Jane Antoinette *music educator, composer*
Herson, Arlene *television producer, journalist, television personality, radio commentator*
Herstand, Theodore *retired theatre artist, educator*
Hilgraves, Rebekkah *opera singer voice instructor poet marketing consultant*
Hill, Willie L., Jr. *music educator*
Hilton, Jean Bull *musician*
Hilton, Paris *actress*
Hirshtal, Edith *retired concert pianist, educator, chamber musician*
Hodges, Ann *actress, singer, dancer*
Hodges, Ann *retired television editor, columnist*
Hofbauer, Eric M. *musician, educator*
Hoffman, Marian Ruth *singer, voice educator*
Hoffman, William Moses *theater educator*
Holland, Beth *actress*
Holly, Lauren (Lauren Michael Holly) *actress*
Holm, Celeste *actress*
Holman, Bill *composer*
Holmes, Myke *actor, educator*
Hooper, Robert Alexander *television producer, educator*
Hopkins, Sir Anthony (Philip) *actor*
Hoppe, Melli *choreographer, educator*
Horne, Marjorie *production stage manager, event consultant*
Horner, Judith Anne *music educator*
Hornyak, Roy Robert *music educator, minister*
Hosman, Sharon Lee *retired music educator*
Houghton, Katharine *actress*
Howard, David *ballet master, school administrator*
Hsu, Apo (Ching Hsin) *conductor*
Huang, Verna D. *music educator*
Hubalek, Shirley Kay *music educator, art educator*
Hubbard, Elizabeth *actress*
Hundley, Carol Marie Beckquist *music educator*
Huning, Devon Gray *actress, audiologist, dancer, photographer*
Hunt, Aaron Andrew *music educator*
Hunt, Helen (Helen Elizabeth Hunt) *actress*
Hunter, Frances Ellen Croft *music educator*
Husarik, Stephen *music educator*
Hutton, Lori *music educator*
Hutton, Timothy *actor*
Hwang, Jason Kao *composer, violinist, music educator*
Hyatt, Kathryn Lees *music educator*
Iler, Robert *actor*
Iñárritu, Alejandro González *film director, producer*
Irving, George Steven *actor*
Jachimiak, Terry Dana, II, *theater educator*
Jackson, Barbara Ann Garvey *music educator*
Jackson, Felicity Anne *performing arts organization administrator*
Jackson, Janet *singer, dancer*
Jackson, Nagle *stage director, playwright*
Jacobi, Bonnie Schaffhauser *music teacher, pianist*
Jacobi, Derek George *actor*
James, Kevin *actor*
Jamiel, John *theater educator*
Jampole, Emma Joy *music educator, composer*
Janney, Kay Print *retired performing arts educator, theater director*
Jarmusch, Jim *film director, actor*
Jenkins, Richard Dale *actor, theater director*
Jensen, Nancy Daggett *music educator*
Joel, Billy (William Martin Joel) *musician*
Joel, Katie Lee (Katherine Lee) *television personality*
Johansson, Alicia Barbara *musician*
Johnson, Jeanne Jordan *music educator, department chairman*
Johnson, Sandra Kay *music educator*
Jonason, Louisa *musician, educator*
Jones, Constance Coralie *retired music educator*
Jones, Shirley *actress, singer*
Jones, William Adrian *musician, educator, program developer*
Jordan, Lisa Anne *dancer, educator*
Kaisershot, A. Kevin *composer*
Kaling, Mindy *actress, scriptwriter, television producer*
Kalo, Michele Christine *music educator*
Kamerin, Kim K. *music educator*
Kaminski, Janusz Zygmunt *cinematographer*
Kander, John Harold *composer*
Kaplan, Richard James *film producer and director, educator, consultant, scriptwriter*
Karayanis, Plato Steven *opera company executive*
Katz, Jeffrey A. *television and radio personality, newspaper columnist, public speaker*
Kavanaugh, Frank James *film producer, educator*
Kaylan, Howard Lawrence *musical entertainer, screenwriter, composer*
Kearns-Simmons, Shannon Marie *theater educator, director*
Keaton, Michael *actor, comedian*
Keim, Betty Lou *actress, literary consultant*
Keith, Toby (Toby Keith Covel) *country singer, songwriter, producer*
Kennedy, Megan Catherine *music educator*
Kent, Gary Warner *film director, writer*
Ketchie, Diane *singer, music educator*
Kilgus, Edward Chip *singer, actor, writer, poet*
Kim, Ellen Ye *music educator*
King, John *composer, musician*
Kinnear, Greg *actor, film producer*
Kinsey, Angela *actress*
Kirkland, Glenda Anderson *music educator*
Kitt, Tom *composer, musician*
Klampe, Craig Allen *composer*
Klein, James Edgar *actor*
Klotman, Robert Howard *retired music educator*
Kloves, Steven *film director, scriptwriter*
Knoxville, Johnny (Philip John Clapp) *actor*
Knupps, Terri Crouse *music educator*
Koepke, Allen Henry *music educator, composer*
Koerber, Dolores Jean *music educator*
Kollias, Jim Harry *music educator*
Kono, Toshihiko *cellist*
Kopelson, Arnold *film producer*
Kornhaber, Donna Marie *theater educator*
Kostic, Dina *musician, educator*
Kozlowski, Rob *performing arts educator*
Krabbe, Thomas Joseph *music educator*
Kramer, Keith Allan *music educator, composer*
Kriegsman, Sali Ann *performing arts executive, consultant, writer*
Kudrow, Lisa (Marie Diane) *actress*
Kuenn, Marjorie Asp *retired music educator*
Kupelian, Louise Paulson *musician, educator*
Kuriansky, Judy *television and radio personality, reporter, clinical psychologist, writer, educator*
Kutrzeba, Joseph S. *theater producer, director*
Kwiram, Bernard Rudolph Alvin *music educator, conductor*
LaBeouf, Shia *actor*
Ladd, Diane *actress, writer, film director, producer*
Lambert, John Walton *music educator*
LaMorte, Joyce E. *music educator*
Landesman, Rocco (Fredric Rocco Landesman) *theatre executive*
Lane, Nathan (Joseph Lane) *actor*
Lane, Ted A. *music educator, musician*
Larson, Joan Isbell *musician, educator*
Latimer, James Harold *musician, conductor, composer, music educator*
Leach, Robin *producer, writer, television host*
Leachman, Cloris *actress*
Leahy, Jeannette (Jeannette Oliver Leahy Tinen Kaehler) *actress*
Lebon, Rachel L. *musician, educator*
Lee, Christopher Frank Carandini *actor, writer, singer*
Lee, Gwendolin Kuei *retired ballet educator*
Lee, William Franklin III *composer, musician*
Lefferts, George *television producer*
Lemke, Carol Ann *music educator, pianist Vocalist Teacher of Piano & Voice, CPA*
Lemos, Arthur *retired music educator*
Lepage, Robert *actor, playwright*
Lepke-Sims, Barbara Weiger *music educator*
Leventhal, Nathan *performing company executive, lawyer, municipal official*
Levine, Alan J. *entertainment company executive*
Levinsohn, Gary *producer*
Levitas, Miriam C. Strickman *documentary filmmaker*
Lewis, James Kevin *music educator*
Leybourn, Carol *musician, educator*
Lichtenstein, Harvey *performing arts association administrator*
Lindeman, Carolynn Anderson *music educator*
Lindsay, Diane Miller *music educator*
Lindsey, Roberta Lewise *music researcher, historian, educator*
Lithgow, John Arthur *actor*
Littleton, Heavenly Denise *video editor, producer, filmmaker*
Locklear, Heather *actress*
Logue, Jean Evelyn *music educator*
Lohan, Lindsay Dee *actress*
Lombardi, Mary Luciana *musician, historian*
Lonchyna-Lisowsky, Maria *music educator*
Long, Lillian F. *music educator*
Loring, Gloria Jean *vocalist, actress, writer*
Love, Courtney *singer, actress*
Love, Shirley *mezzo-soprano*
Lovett, Elizabeth Michelle *music educator*
Lubezki, Emmanuel *cinematographer*
Lubin, Steven *concert pianist, musicologist*
Ludwig, Christa *retired mezzo soprano*
Luker, Rebecca *actress, soprano*
Lupu, Radu *pianist*
Lyford, Ronald Lee *music educator*
Madden, John Philip *motion picture director, actor*
Madeira, Francis King Carey *conductor, educator*
Madsen, Michael *actor*
Madsen, Virginia *actress*
Magno, Gil D. *music educator, personal development consultant*
Magor, Louis Roland *conductor*
Maguire, Martie (Martha Elenor Erwin Maguire) *musician*
Mahoney, John *actor*
Main, Terena Ann *music educator, corporate financial executive*
Maines, Natalie Louise *musician*
Malafronte, Judith Adelia *music educator*
Malick, Terrence (David Whitney II) *film director*
Malone, Dorothy *actress*
Mangravite, Ronald *filmmaker, writer*
Mannes, Elena Sabin *film and television producer, television director*
Mapp, Catherine *performing arts educator, department chairman*
Marchant, Barbara *performing arts educator, acting coach*
Marchenko, Tamara G. *music educator*
Marcy, Kevin Michael *film producer, lawyer*
Margules, Cecelia *composer, poet*
Margulies, Julianna *actress*
Marin, Cheech (Richard Anthony Marin) *actor, writer, director*
Mark, Michael Laurence *retired music educator*
Marks, Bruce *performing company executive, choreographer*
Marks, Kathryn Allan *dancer, educator*
Maron, Marc *comedian, actor, writer*
Marshall, Frank W. *film producer, director*
Marshall, Kathleen *choreographer, theater director*
Marte-Bautista, Helen I. *retired performing arts educator*
Martin, Andrea Louise *actress, comedienne, writer*
Martin, Elliot Edwards *theatrical producer*
Martyn, Evi *musician, educator*
Mase, Raymond James *musician, educator*
Masterson, Peter *actor, film producer*
Matenopoulos, Debbie *television personality*
Mathes, Rachel Clarke *voice educator, singer*
Maynard, Natalie Ryshna *pianist, educator*
McAnuff, Des *artistic director*
McCann, Elizabeth Ireland *theater, television and film producer*
McCartney, Sir Paul (James Paul McCartney) *musician*
McClanahan, Rue (Eddi-Rue McClanahan) *actress*
McConaughey, Matthew *actor*
McCoy, Mary Nell *music educator*
McCready, Sam *theater educator and director, actor*
McDowell, Malcolm *actor*
McFarlane, Seth Woodbury *television producer, animator*
McKenzie, Bret *musician, actor*
McKneely, Joey *choreographer*
McMaster, Brian John *artistic director*
McWhirter, Jamila LeAnn *choral conductor*
McWilliams, Teressa Wylie *choreographer*
Meara, Anne *actress, playwright, writer*
Melillo, Joseph Vincent *theater producer*
Melton, William Everett *retired music educator*
Menzel, Jiří *film and theater director, actor*
Meredith, Wendi Sue *music educator*
Merson, Susan Ilene *actor, writer, producer*
Mesney, Kathryn *theater educator*
Metcalf, Laurie (Lauren Ophelia Metcalfe) *actress*
Meyerink, Victoria Paige *film producer, actress*
Miguel, Luis *musician*
Mills, Corinne C. *music educator*
Miranda-Levi, Jason *film producer, writer*
Mirren, Helen (Ilynea Lydia Mironoff) *actress*
Mitchell, Brian Stokes *actor*
Moffatt, Joyce Anne *performing company executive*
Moffatt, Katy (Katherine Louella Moffatt) *musician, lyricist, vocalist*
Mohan, Tungesh Nath *television and film producer, film educator*
Mohr, Jay *comedian, actor*
Moore, Demi (Demi Guynes, Demetria Gene Guynes) *actress*
Moore, Michael *filmmaker, writer*
Moore, Pamela Gay *retired music educator*
Morelan, Paula Kay *choreographer*
Moreland, Richard Paul *musician, educator*
Morello, Joseph Albert *musician, educator*
Morello, Tom *musician*
Moreno, Rita (Rosita Dolores Alverio) *actress*
Morin, Lynn P. *music educator, director, secondary school educator*
Morissette, Alanis Nadine *singer*
Morita, Lina *pianist, educator*
Morrell, Robert Hanly *television producer, director*
Morris, Brenda Denise *music educator, director*
Morris, Errol *filmmaker*
Morris, John *composer, conductor, arranger*
Morris, Lissa Camille *music educator*
Morrison, Shelley *actress*
Morrissette, Jerusha M. *music educator*
Morrow, Rob *actor*
Morse, Carmel Lei *professor*
Morse, Judith *music educator, conductor*
Mortensen, Viggo *actor, writer*
Moseley, Julia W. *music educator, preservationist*
Mosiman, Rita Esther *music educator, performing artist*
Mosteller, Darla Brooks *singer, educator*
Mouledous, Pierrette Marie *music educator*
Murray, Carla Mary *sound effects artist*
Murray Shaw, Juleen *actress*
Musante, Tony (Anthony Peter Musante Jr.) *actor*
Myers, Angela Michelle *music educator, department chairman*
Myers, Dee Dee (Margaret Jane Myers) *television personality, former White House press secretary*
Myers, Jeffrey Daniel *concert pianist, music educator*
Narita, Hiro *cinematographer*
Nash, Linda Kay *music educator*
Neame, Ronald *director, producer*
Neary, Patricia Elinor *ballet director*
Neblett, Carol *soprano*
Nederlander, James Laurence *theater producer*
Nelson, Craig T. *actor*
Nelson, Ron *composer, educator, conductor*
Nesbitt, Mitzi Evalee *voice educator, director*
Ness, Bernice Hagie *retired music educator*
Neumann, David *theater educator*
Neville, Phoebe *choreographer, dancer, educator*
Nevins, Sheila *television producer*
Newman, Phyllis *actress*
Nguyen, Tila (Tila Tequila) *entertainer, model, singer*
Nicholl, Matthew James *music educator, director*
Nichols, Mike *stage and film director*
Nigro, Kenneth Michael *musician, educator*
Niguidula, Kathleen Ann *musician, educator*
Nixon, Marni *singer*
Nobert, Frances *music educator*
Noll, Jeanne C. *retired music educator*
Nolte, Nick *actor*
O'Donnell, Chris *actor*
O'Donnell, Rosie *television personality, actress, comedienne*
Odya, Gregory Matthew *musician, educator*
Oh, Sandra *actress*
O'Hare, Denis *actor*
O'Keefe, Gary Raymond *actor*
Olenchak, Frank Richard *retired music educator, musician*
Oliveros, Pauline *composer, performer*
Olsen, Glen A. *church musician, educator*
Olyphant, Timothy *actor*
Ordway, Mark Franklin *cinematographer*
Osbourne, Ozzy (John Osbourne) *singer*
O'Shea, Anna Belle Marie *music educator, liturgy administrator*
Osmond, Marie *singer*
Ossello, Kristie *music educator*
Ostrow, Stuart *theatrical producer, educator, author*
Otto, Devin Theophil *music educator*
Page, Anthony *theater director, film director*
Paige, Paul *retired music educator*
Panovski, Naum *theater director*
Paolino, Ray *theater director*
Parkinson, Rebecca *music educator*
Pasquier, Joël *music educator*
Peabody, Dossy *performing arts educator, actor*
Peck, Leslie *dancer, educator*
Pederson, Linda L. *music educator*
Persoff, Nehemiah *actor, artist*
Pesci, Joe (Joseph Frank Pesci) *actor*
Peters, Jennifer R. *music educator*
Petersen, William (William Louis Petersen) *actor*
Peterson, Anne Elizabeth Wallace *music educator, composer*
Peterson, Rosetta Hicks *retired music educator*
Phelps, Mark D. *music educator*
Phillips, Julien L. *theater educator*
Phillips, Winifred Patricia *composer*
Piagentini, Susan *music educator*
Picton, Earla Wise *retired music educator, director*
Pierce, David Hyde *actor*
Ping-Robbins, Nancy Regan *musician, writer, artist*
Pirro, Jeanine Ferris *television personality, former prosecutor*
Placeres, Martha *music educator*
Pomfret, Bonnie *music educator*
Powell, John *composer*
Price, Betty Jeanne *chimes musician*
Prince, Anna Lou *composer, music publisher, construction executive*
Prince, Faith *actress, singer*
Purcell, Christine M. *music educator, music company executive*
Ragland, Kathryn Marie *dancer, educator*
Raimi, Samuel M. *film director*
Rako, Susan *psychiatrist, writer, producer, filmmaker*
Ramirez, Tina *performing company executive*
Ramis, Harold Allen *film director, screenwriter, actor*
Ransom, Tasha Elana *perspective production field producer*
Rapaport, Michael *actor*
Ravinsky, Anthony *music educator*
Redden, Taylor Tilghman *musician*
Reed, Mary Carolyn Camblin *retired music educator, county official*
Reeves, Hallie Lawson *retired music educator, chaplain*
Reeves, Keanu *actor*
Regan, Susan Wright *dance educator, small business owner, choreographer*
Reilly, John C. *actor*
Remlinger, Rolf *music educator, composer*
Renard, Paul Steven *music educator*
Resch, Rita Marie *retired music educator*
Rhodes, Lawrence *artistic director*
Richard, Candace L. *music educator*
Richardson, Robert *cinematographer*
Richmond, Angela *music educator*
Richmond, Rocsan *television executive producer, investigative reporter, small business owner*
Ridolfi, Patrick Murphy *music educator, tenor*
Riley, Rebecca Michelle *music educator*
Rino, Barbara Elizabeth *musician, educator*
Ripley, Alice H. *actress*
Roberts, Doris *actress*
Roberts, Jonathan *dancer*
Robertson, Cliff (Clifford Parker Robertson III) *actor, writer, director*
Robertson, Paul John *music educator*
Robinson, Devette Lorraine *music educator*
Robison, Emily Burns *musician*
Robison, Paula Judith *flutist*
Robitaille, Carolyn Ann *music educator*
Rockaway, Eytan *film producer, director*
Rodriguez, Jai *television personality*
Roeg, Nicolas Jack *film director*
Rogers, Barbara J. *musician*
Rogers, Wanda Faye *vocalist*
Roman, James Warren *performing arts educator*
Rook, Judith Rawie *television producer, writer*
Roost, Alisa *theater educator*
Rosenow, Mitchell Paul *sound recording engineer, studio owner, musician, music producer*
Ross, Darrin *composer*
Ross, Tracey *actress*
Rothschild, Rick *entertainment company executive*
Rousseau, Eugene Ellsworth *musician, educator, consultant*
Roy, Michelle E. *musician, information technology consultant*
Ruccolo, Margaret Rose Roebke *music educator, violinist*
Ruder, Tia L. *music educator*
Rudner, Sara *dancer*
Ruggiero, Matthew John *bassoonist*
Russell, Beatrice Nibigira *performing arts educator*
Russell, Kurt *actor*
Ruviella-Knorr, Jeanne L. *music educator, consultant*
Ryan, Christine Brett *music educator*
Ryan, Deborah Lorraine *music educator*
Ryan, Kelli Lorraine *ballerina, educator*
Rylance, Mark (Mark Waters) *actor, performing company executive*
Sadoh, Godwin Simeon *music educator*
Saint, Eva Marie *actress*
Saint-Girard, Christian *theater director, actor, educator, choreographer, theater producer*
St. John, Kristoff *actor*
Sak, Gilbert *music educator*
Saltzman, Philip *television producer, writer*
Sambora, Richie (Richard Stephen Sambora) *musician, singer, songwriter*
Sanborn, Kathy *musician, recording artist and author*
Sarry, Christine *ballerina*
Sarsgaard, Peter *actor*
Scarchuk, Lynn Nettleton *retired music educator*
Schifrin, Lalo *composer*
Schiller, Lawrence Julian *film producer, writer*
Schmidt, Hildred Doris *music educator*
Schneider, Rob *actor*
Schoonmaker Powell, Thelma *film editor*
Schubert, Barbara Schuele *retired performing arts association administrator*
Schwartz, Sima M. *music educator*
Schwartz, Stephen Lawrence *composer, lyricist*
Schwartzman, Jason Francesco *actor, musician*
Schwary, Ronald Louis *motion picture producer*
Schwimmer, David *actor*
Scorsese, Martin *film director, film producer*
Sedelmaier, John Josef *filmmaker*
Seinfeld, Jerry *comedian, actor, television producer, scriptwriter*
Severson, Katie LeAnn *music educator*
Shatin, Judith *composer, educator*
Shaw, Harold *retired performing arts association administrator*
Sheen, Charlie (Carlos Irwin Estevez) *actor*
Sheen, Martin (Ramon Estevez) *actor*

Sheindlin, Judith (Judge Judy) *television personality, judge*
Shepherd, Cybill Lynne *actress, singer*
Sherin, Edwin *theater, film and television director, actor*
Sherman, Richard Morton *composer, lyricist*
Shields, Brooke Christa Camille *actress, model*
Shier, Susan Lynne *music educator*
Shirley-Quirk, John *singer, educator*
Shuhy, David E. *theater educator, set designer*
Siegfried, Jan Brooks *music educator, director*
Sigler, Jamie-Lynn *actress*
Sikes, Cynthia Lee *actress, singer*
Silverman, Ira Norton *news producer*
Silverstein, Barbara Ann *producer, musician*
Skowronski, Vincent Paul *musician, recording industry executive*
Slater, Christian *actor*
Sloan, Carolyn *music educator, composer, lyricist*
Smart, James Anthony *music educator*
Smith, Barbara Barnard *music educator*
Smith, Charlotte Reed *retired music educator*
Smith, Lois Arlene *actress, writer*
Smith, Phyllis *actress*
Smollett, Jurnee Diana *actress*
Smukal, Michael William *musician, educator, composer*
Sohn, Livia *music educator*
Sondheim, Stephen Joshua *composer, librettist, lyricist*
Sparks, Jordin Brianna *singer*
Spillman, Marjorie Rose *theater producer, dancer*
Sprecher, Baron William Gunther *pianist, composer, conductor, diplomat*
Sproul, Sarah Lee *conductor, musician, educator*
Spurlock, Morgan *television producer, film producer*
Srinivasan, Asha *music educator, composer*
Stallone, Sylvester Gardenzio *actor, film director, scriptwriter, producer*
Stanek, Alan Edward *retired music educator, performing arts association administrator*
Stanley, Margaret King *performing arts administrator*
Stearns, Marilyn Tarpy *music educator*
Stevens, Warren *actor*
Stewart, Timothy Glen *organist*
Stiggall, Corin J. *musician*
Stiller, Ben *actor, television producer*
Stokes, Harvey J. *musician, educator, composer*
Stone, Joss (Joscelyn Eve Stoker) *singer*
Stone, Oliver *film director, producer, scriptwriter*
Stone, Sharon *actress*
Stone, Sylvia *voice educator, singer*
Story, Timothy Kevin (Tim Story) *film director*
Stoytcheva, Lilia Stefanova *concert pianist, educator*
Strait, George *musician*
Strathairn, David *actor*
Stratton-Gonzalez, Sandra *dance educator, administrator*
Strauss, Peter *actor*
Strickholm, Jean *musician, company executive, retired elementary school educator*
Stritch, Elaine *singer, actress*
Stroik, Adrienne Lisbeth *dance educator*
Strukoff, Rudolf Stephen *retired music educator*
Sturner, Lynda *performing company executive*
Sullivan, Jane *theater educator, director*
Sullivan, John Dominic *theater producer, writer*
Summers, Cathleen *film producer*
Sutherland, Donald *actor*
Suzuki, Hidetaro *violinist*
Szabo, Istvan *film director*
Taher, Cecilia *music educator*
Talaga, Stephen C. *pianist, composer, music educator*
Tandy, Carla M. *dancer, educator*
Tarrant, Christine Gloria *music educator*
Taylor, Holly Ann *music educator*
Tecco, Romuald Gilbert Louis Joseph *violinist, concertmaster*
Terry, Mickey Thomas *music educator, director*
Tharp, Stephen John *organist, pianist, artist*
Thompson, Laura *theater producer*
Thompson, Wenoka Shenaile *television producer, writer*
Thulean, Donald Myron *symphony conductor*
Thurman, Uma *actress*
Tingler, Marlene Johannsen *music educator, insurance agent*
Tognoli, Era M. *opera company director*
Tokofsky, Jerry Herbert *film producer*
Tolbert, Cornelia Emma *music educator*
Tonioli, Bruno *choreographer, dancer*
T-Pain, (Faheem Najm) *rap artist*
Trebunskaya, Anna *dancer*
Tripplehorn, Jeanne *actress*
Trythall, Harry Gilbert *music educator, composer*
Turok, Paul Harris *composer, commentator, music critic*
Turteltaub, Jon *film director*
Turturro, Aida *actress*
Twitchell, Theodore Grant *music educator, composer*
Tyler, Steven (Stephen Victor Tallarico) *singer*
Tyree, Rebecca Young *music educator*
Tyzack, Margaret *actress*
Uggams, Leslie *entertainer*
Unruh, Gary Lee *retired music educator*
Upbin, Shari *theater producer, director*
Upchurch, Leslie Purcell *music educator*
Van Praagh, James *spiritual medium*
Vasquez, Sabrina Claudine *choreographer, educator*
Vedder, Eddie *singer*
Villella, Edward Joseph *dancer, choreographer, performing arts association administrator*
Virkhaus, Taavo *conductor*
Voegtlin-Anderson, Mary Margaret *music educator, small business owner*
Voight, Jon *actor*
Voketaitis, Arnold Matthew *bass-baritone, educator*
von Furstenberg, Betsy *actress, writer*
Vozzella, Thomas R. *musician, conductor, composer, organist*
Vulgamore, Allison Beth *performing arts association administrator*
Wagoner, Geraldine Vander Pol *music educator*
Walker, Donald Burke *retired music educator, archivist, composer*
Walker, Karen Louise *music educator*
Wallace, Dee *actress*
Wallis, Diana Lynn *artistic director*
Walsh, Joseph Fidler (Joe Walsh) *recording artist, record producer*
Walsh, M. Emmet *actor*
Warberg, Willetta *concert pianist, music educator*
Ward, Anne Starr Minton *musician, educator*
Ware, D. Clifton *vocalist, educator*
Warner, Malcolm-Jamal *actor, director, producer*
Washington, Denzel *actor*
Watt, Stephanie Denise *musician, educator, department chairman*
Wedgeworth, Ann *actress*
Weeks, Clifford Myers *musician, academic administrator*
Weiland, Scott Richard *singer*
Weiner, Matthew *television producer, scriptwriter*
Weingust, Don *theater educator*
Weiss, Glenn P. *television director*
Weisz, Deborah *trombonist, music educator, composer*
Whitaker, Thomas O'Hara *theater educator, director*
White, Michael Lee *executive producer, writer*
Whitesell, Patrick *talent agency executive*
Wiatt, Jim (James Anthony Wiatt) *talent agency executive*
Wiest, Dianne *actress*
Wilder, Gene (Jerry Silberman) *actor, film director, writer*
Wilder, Janet Mary *performing company executive*
Wilhjelm, Christian *conductor, artist*
Wilkinson, Ann E. *theater educator, actress*
Wiłkomirski, Josef *conductor, writer, composer, educator, journalist*
Williams, Billy Dee *actor*
Williams, JoBeth *actress*
Williams, Lisa A. *music educator*
Willis, Bruce *actor*
Willis, Ruth *freelance/self-employed theater director, actress*
Wilson, Gretchen *vocalist*
Wilson, Rainn D. (Rainn Dietrich Wilson) *actor*
Wimbs, Cassandra M. *musician, educator, writer*
Winkler, Heather Starr *music educator*
Winokur, Marissa Jaret *actress*
Winold, Helga Ulsamer *retired music educator*
Winslet, Kate *actress*
Wirtschafter, David *talent agency executive*
Wise, Patricia *opera singer, educator*
Wolff, Eleanor Blunk *actress*
Wolfson, Sarah Elizabeth *singer, educator, physical education educator*
Womack, Bobby (Robert Dwayne Womack) *musician, songwriter*
Wood, Vivian Poates *mezzo soprano, educator, author*
Woods, Eleanor C. *music educator*
Woolsey, Robert Paul *church musician*
Wopat, Tom *actor, singer*
Wright, Gladys Stone *music educator, writer, composer*
Wright, Lori Dunkle *musician, educator*
Wyner, Yehudi *composer, pianist, conductor, educator*
Yao, Frances *music educator, small business owner*
Yarrow, Peter *folksinger*
Ybarra, Kimberly Elizabeth *music and elementary school educator*
Yearwood, Trisha *country music singer, songwriter*
Yorkey, Brian *lyricist*
Younker, Kathleen Teuber *pianist, music educator*
Yui, Lisa *music educator*
Yuriko, (Yuriko Kikuchi) *dancer, choreographer*
Zahler, Adam Troy *stage director, theatre professor*
Zandstra, Greta Marie *theater educator, actor*
Zawadzki-Janusz, Stacy Lynn *performing arts director, owner, educator*
Zentz, Laurie Funderburk *music educator*
Zeta-Jones, Catherine *actress*
Zhao, Zhen *music educator*
Zheng, Yin Ping *performing arts educator*
Ziemba, Karen *actress*
Zien, Chip *actor*
Zimmerman, Phyllis Elaine *music educator, composer, director*
Zwick, Edward M. *director, producer, scriptwriter*

ARTS: VISUAL

UNITED STATES

ALABAMA

Auburn
Hatfield, Donald Gene *retired art educator*

Birmingham
Rankin, Don *art educator, educator*

Fairfield
McCaslin, LaTanya *art educator*

Florence
Knight, Karen Anne McGee *artist, educator, educational research administrator*

Hartselle
Coon, Elizabeth M. *artist*

Huntsville
Benzle, Curtis Munhall *artist, educator*

Jacksonville
Skinner, Jauneth *graphic artist, educator*

Montevallo
Stephens, Scott *art educator*

Tuscaloosa
Hopkins, Martha Ann *artist*

ALASKA

Fairbanks
Matusevich, Yelena *artist, educator*
Nakoneczny, Michael Martin *artist*

ARIZONA

Chandler
Winterer-Schulz, Barbara Jean *graphics designer, writer*

Chinle
Coor, Caren Barbara *art educator*

Chino Valley
Casey, Bonnie Mae *artist, educator*

Green Valley
de Soto, Ernest Frank *artist, writer*

Mesa
Doyle, Matthew Brian *computer graphics designer*

Oracle
Rush, Andrew Wilson *artist*

Patagonia
La Noue, Terence David *artist, educator*

Payson
Salomon, Marilyn *artist*

Peoria
Bailey, Claudia Jean *artist, retired librarian*
Willard, Garcia Lou *artist*

Phoenix
Tyus, Gordon *graphics designer, educator*

Scottsdale
Afsary, Cyrus *artist*
Magenta, Muriel *artist*
Schrader, Carol Ann *artist, painter*

Sedona
Coleman, M.L. (Michael Lee) *artist*

Sun Lakes
Hall, Barbara Louise *interior designer, artist*

Tucson
Conant, Howard Somers *artist, educator*
Crooks, Roselyn June *artist, writer*
Dredge, Jill Ann *artist*

ARKANSAS

Fayetteville
Wilson, Charles Banks *artist*

Palestine
Taylor, Barbara Mae Helm *artist, educator*

Rose Bud
Spradley, Pamela Claire *art educator*

Salem
Harber-Hurtt, Lisa Lynn *art educator*

Siloam Springs
Martin, Bobby C. *graphics designer, educator*

CALIFORNIA

Agoura Hills
Hancock, Lani Jane *artist*

Arcata
Land-Weber, Ellen *photography professor*

Auburn
Blaney, Suzanne Avery *artist, writer*
Rothwell, Elaine B. *artist*

Bakersfield
Reep, Edward Arnold *artist*

Berkeley
Cantor, Rusty Sumner *artist*
Genn, Nancy *artist*
Hartman, Robert Leroy *artist, educator*
Miyasaki, George Joji *artist*
Simpson, David William *artist, educator*

Beverly Hills
Ferretti, Dante *display designer*
Greenberg, Jill *photographer*

Bolinas
Harris, Paul *sculptor*

Camarillo
Bowman, Bruce *art educator*
Mihalopoulos, Catherine Elizabeth *art educator*

Cambria
Harden, Marvin *artist, educator*

Carmel
Hobbs, C. Fredric *artist, filmmaker, writer*
Jacobs, Ralph, Jr. *artist*

Carmichael
Ryan, Gretchen Margarete Frieda *art educator*

Carpinteria
Hansen, Robert William *artist, educator*

Carson
Hirsch, Gilah Yelin *artist, writer*

Chatsworth
Strieby, B. Lorraine *artist*

Chico
Hornaday, Richard H. *artist, retired educator*

Claremont
Benjamin, Karl Stanley *artist, educator*
Rankaitis, Susan *artist*

Concord
Broadbent, Amalia Sayo Castillo *graphic arts designer*

Corona
Lincoln, Tami Marie *art educator*

Coronado
Hubbard, Donald *marine artist, writer*

Costa Mesa
Muller, Jerome Kenneth *photographer, art director, editor*

Cottonwood
Stewart, John Norman *scenic artist*

Culver City
Arceneaux, Edgar *artist*
Gordon, Florence Irene *graphics designer, illustrator*
Grant, Joan Julien *artist*
Ochoa, Ruben *artist*
Simmons, Kimora Lee (Kimora Lee Perkins) *apparel designer, television personality, model*

Daly City
Kennedy, Gwendolyn Debra *artist, scriptwriter, playwright*

Dana Point
Blacketer, James Richard *artist*

Danville
Monheit, Molly Jane *artist*

Davis
Morgan, Maggie *costume designer, design educator*

Desert Hot Springs
Laws, Maurice Wesley *set decorator, museum exhibit designer*

Emeryville
Doctor, Pete *animator, film director, scriptwriter*
Peterson, Bob III *animator, film director, scriptwriter*
Stanton, Andrew *animator, film director, film producer, scriptwriter*

Fair Oaks
Potter, George Kenneth *artist*

Fallbrook
Ragland, Jack Whitney *artist*

Fountain Valley
Worden, Mark K. *multimedia designer, educator*

Garberville
Nyokka, Suzette *artist, natural health educator*

Gilroy
Wu, Wayne Wen-Yau *artist*

Glendale
Cobey, Virginia Branum *artist, actress, art collector*

Glendora
Starobin, Nancy *photographer*

Greenbrae
Blatt, Morton Bernard *medical illustrator*
Teller, Pauline Ivancovich *artist*

Hayward
Jordahl, Kathleen Patricia (Kate Jordahl) *photographer, educator*
Wong, Wanda Yuk-Wa *graphics designer, educator*

Hollister
Miller, Alisa Dorothy Norton *artist*

Indio
Zorick, Nancy Lee *artist, actress*

Irvine
Carson, Juli Christine *art educator*
Leung, Simon *artist*

Kingsburg
Olson, Maxine Louise *artist, lecturer*

La Jolla
Imana, Jorge Garron *artist*

La Puente
Vetter, Lawrence Anthony *art educator, consultant*

Laguna Beach
Darrow, Paul Gardner *painter, printmaker, cartoonist, illustrator*

Lagunitas
Holman, Arthur Stearns *artist*

Lincoln
Johnson, Ursula Anne *artist*

Long Beach
Barron, (Mary Lou) Slater *artist, retired educator*

Los Altos
Alexander, Kathryn Jean Macaulay (Kay) *retired art curriculum writer, consultant*

Los Angeles
Apt, Charles *artist*
Avenaim, Jerry *commercial photographer*
Brendel, Bettina *abstract artist*
Caroompas, Carole Jean *artist, educator*
Curran, Darryl Joseph *photographer, educator*
Fairey, Shepard *printmaker*
Farnham, Katherine A. *recording artist*
Hamilton, Patricia Rose *art dealer*
Hockney, David *artist*
Layton, Harry Christopher *art director*
LeMay, Harry Adrian *artist, educator*
Lhuillier, (Diane) Monique *apparel designer*
McCarthy, Paul *artist*
Negro, Mary Joan *art educator*
Park, Lee (Lee Parklee) *artist*
Ray, Charles *sculptor*
Salicki, Roman *commercial photographer*
Sanditz, Lisa *painter*
Sargent, Margaret Holland *portrait artist, actress, writer*
Stickler, Stephen H. *photographer*
Todd, Michael Cullen *sculptor, painter*
Wayne, June Claire *artist*

Los Gatos
Carson, Sol Kent *artist, educator*
Mintz, Marilyn D. *artist, writer*

Los Osos
Kreitzer, David Martin *artist*

Mckinleyville
Berry, Glenn *artist, educator*

Morgan Hill
Freimark, Robert (Bob Freimark) *artist*

Newport Beach
Belic Weiss, Zoran *artist, design educator, director*
Spitz, Barbara Salomon *artist*

North Hollywood
Vasilyeva, Anna *artist, writer*

Northridge
Bassler, Robert Covey *artist, educator*

Novato
McNamara, John Stephen *artist, educator*

Oakdale
Saletta, Mary Elizabeth (Betty Saletta) *sculptor*

Oakland
Beasley, Bruce Miller *sculptor*
Horning, Robert Eugene *artist, educator*
Melchert, James Frederick *artist, educator*
Sutter, Elouise C. *retired art educator*

Orange
Banning, Donna Rose *art educator*
Stephen, Berens *artist, educator*

Pacific Grove
Elinson, Henry David *artist, language educator*
Tanguy-Tracey, Sheila Anne *artist, poet*

Pacific Palisades
Chesney, Lee Roy, Jr. *artist*
Kaufer, Shirley Helen *artist, painter*

Pacifica
Petersen, Roland *artist, printmaker*

Palm Springs
Carnase, Thomas Paul *graphics designer, consultant*

Palo Alto
Lobdell, Frank *artist*

Panorama City
Janis, Elinor Raiden *artist, educator*

Pasadena
Gill, Gene *artist*
Pashgian, M. Helen *artist*

Pebble Beach
Mortensen, Gordon Louis *artist, printmaker*

Penn Valley
Sands, Sharon Louise *graphics designer, artist*

Petaluma
Skalagard, Hans Martin *artist*

Pomona
Hargis, Barbara Picasso *artist*

Quartz Hill
McAllister, Bruce Richard *art educator*

Ramona
Newman, Malane L. *computer graphics designer, cartoonist, illustrator, computer graphics designer, educator*

Rancho Palos Verdes
Mac Innes, David Harold *artist, small business owner*
MacInnes, Margaret E. *retired art educator*

Redding
Matenaer, Tegwin A. *artist, retired educator, consultant*

Redlands
Goto, Toshiko *retired art educator*

Richmond
Wessel, Henry *photographer*

Ridgecrest
Miears-Cutsinger, Mary Ellen *artist, gallery owner*

Riverside
Bell, Helen Lavin *artist*

Rosemead
Jin, Jing Yi *photographer, film director*

Roseville
Smith, Kaye Train *artist*

Sacramento
Karsiere, Sarma *art educator*
Piskoti, Carol Lee *art educator*

Salinas
Puckett, Richard Edward *artist, former recreation executive*

San Bernardino
Baluyut, Pearlie Rose Salaveria *art educator*

San Diego
Edmonds, Jason Lemuel *art educator, writer*
Gardella, Duane MacIntyre *set designer, educator*
Moore, Linda A. *art dealer, curator*
Nelson, Kadir *illustrator, artist*
Nyiri, Joseph Anton *sculptor, art educator*

San Francisco
Babcock, Jo *artist, educator*
Baker, Joy Doreen *art educator, artist*
Beall, Dennis Ray *artist, educator*
Chin, Sue Soone Marian (Suchin Chin) *artist, photojournalist*
Dickinson, Eleanor Creekmore *artist, educator*
Goldstine, Stephen Joseph *art educator*
Martin, Fred *artist, academic administrator*
McClintock, Jessica *fashion designer*
Monteith, Matthew *photographer*
Stermer, Dugald Robert *designer, writer, illustrator, consultant*
Tantum, James Kent *artist, publisher*
Ternar, Mine Y. *artist, educator*

San Jose
Estabrook, Reed *artist, educator*

San Juan Bautista
Nutzle, Futzie (Bruce John Kleinsmith) *artist, writer, animator*

San Juan Capistrano
Ealy, Cynthia Pike *artist, real estate agent*

San Mateo
Huxley, Mary Atsuko *artist*

San Rafael
Thelen, Phyllis B. *artist*
Tosti, Annette Brewer *artist*

Santa Barbara
Eguchi, Yasu *artist*
Holly, Dianne Jean *costume designer, educator*

Santa Clara
Hofstetter, Jane Robinson *artist, educator*

Santa Monica
Craig, Stuart N. *film production designer*
Masucci, Michael James *artist*
Weber, Bruce *photographer, filmmaker*

Santa Rosa
Fruiht, Dolores Giustina *artist, educator, poet*
Rider Stevenson, Jane *artist, educator*

Sonoma
Fellows, Alice Combs *artist*

South Pasadena
Askin, Walter Miller *artist, educator*

Stanford
Ramsaur, Michael F. *lighting designer*

Studio City
Hight, Jeremy James *artist, writer*
Lasarow, Marilyn Doris *artist, educator*
Leonard, Herman *photographer*

Thousand Oaks
Miller, Elizabeth Joan *artist, guidance counselor*

Valencia
Kersels, Martin *conceptual artist*

Van Nuys
Graham, Roger John *photography and journalism professor*

Venice
Alf, Martha Joanne *artist*
Eversley, Frederick John *sculptor, engineer*

Ventura
Koch, Gerd Hermann *artist, educator*

Walnut Creek
Reimann, Arline Lynn *artist*

West Hills
Abdo, Lynda Lee *art director*

Westlake Village
Richardson, Leatrice Joy *artist*

Wilton
Abraham, Bondi Corinne *artist*

COLORADO

Aspen
Soldner, Paul Edmund *artist, ceramist, educator*

Boulder
Bolomey, Roger Henry *sculptor*
Charteris, Frances I.A. *art educator, artist*

Colorado Springs
Cockrille, Stephen *art director, business owner*
Stansbry, Michael David *set designer, educator*

Delta
Lowell, Lauretta Jane *craftsman, poet*

Denver
Argent, Lawrence *artist, educator*
Graham, Pamela Smith *artist, educator*
Shwayder, Elizabeth Yanish *sculptor*
Witold, Kaczanowski *painter, sculptor*

Dolores
Rice, Wayne *artist, educator, small business owner*

Durango
Balas-Whitfield, Susan *artist*

Fort Collins
Jacobs, Peter Alan *artist, educator*
Yust, David E. *artist, educator*

Lake George
Norman, John Barstow, Jr. *graphics designer, educator*

Laporte
Riba, Shirley *artist*

Montrose
Radovich, Donald *painter, illustrator, retired art educator*

Pueblo
Furman, Jane Christine *art educator*

Salida
Hubicki, Frederick R. *artist*

Sterling
Jacquelyn, Rae Mathis *graphics designer, educator*

CONNECTICUT

Brooklyn
McIlvane, Edward James *stained glass artist, educator*

Fairfield
Walker, Jonathan J. *art educator*

Falls Village
Cronin, Robert Lawrence *painter*

Gaylordsville
Dunn, Virginia *artist*

Greenwich
Perless, Robert L. *sculptor*

Guilford
Pease, David Gordon *artist, educator*

Hartford
Hammer, Alfred Emil *artist, educator*

Lyme
LaForge, Mary Green *artist, educator*

Meriden
Tamburine, Jean Helen *sculptor, painter, illustrator*

Milford
Fagan, Alanna *artist, printmaker*

Naugatuck
Mannweiler, Mary-Elizabeth *painter*

New Canaan
Kovatch, Jak Gene *artist*

New Haven
Bailey, William Harrison *artist, educator*
Humphrey, David Aiken *painter, printmaker, educator*
Johnson, Lester Fredrick *artist*
Reynolds, Jock *artist, curator, art gallery director*
Yeargan, Michael *scenic designer*

Newtown
Cottingham, Robert *artist*

Norwalk
Perry, Charles Owen *sculptor*

Ridgefield
Benton, Suzanne *sculptor, mask ritualist, printmaker, painter*

Sharon
Johns, Jasper *artist*

Southbury
Rorick, William Calvin *portrait artist, retired librarian*

Stamford
Babson, Jane Frances *artist, writer*
Cassidy, Denis Andrew *artist, architect*

Stonington
Elliott, Inger McCabe *apparel designer, textiles executive, consultant*

Voluntown
Caddell, Foster *artist*

Wallingford
Lauttenbach, Carol *artist*

West Cornwall
Estern, Neil Carl *sculptor*
Simont, Marc *artist*

West Hartford
Keller, Dorothy Bosch *art educator*

Weston
Bleifeld, Stanley *sculptor*

Westport
Chernow, Ann Levy *artist, educator*
Fisher, Leonard Everett *artist, educator, writer*
Reilly, Nancy (Anne Caulfield Reilly) *painter*
Siff, Marlene Ida *artist, designer*

DELAWARE

Dagsboro
Hanna, Anne Marie *artist*

Greenville
Reynolds Cooch, Nancy D. *sculptor*

Lewes
Costigan, Constance Frances *artist, educator*

New Castle
Almquist, Don *illustrator, artist*

Newark
Breslin, Nancy Ann *photographer, educator*
Breslin, Wynn Boin *artist*
Brown, Hilton *artist, educator*
Homer, William Innes *art history educator, expert, writer*
Korber, Louise Ann *artist*
Rowe, Charles Alfred *artist, graphics designer, educator*

Wilmington
Bounds-Seemans, Pamella J. *artist*
Messina, Charles *artist*

DISTRICT OF COLUMBIA

Washington
Blair, James Pease *freelance photographer*
Brown, Pamela Wedd *artist*
Colton Skolnick, Judith A. *artist*
DiPerna, Frank Paul *photographer, educator*
Gumpert, Gunther *artist*
Hogan, Felicity *artist*
Jecklin, Lois Underwood *art corporation executive, consultant*
Kapikian, Catherine Andrews *artist*
Kimes, Don Mark *artist, educator*
Klein, Charlotte Feuerstein *art consultant*
Krebs, Rockne *artist*
Rode, Meredith Eagon *artist, educator*
Tacha, Athena *sculptor, artist, educator*
Wasko-Flood, Sandra Jean *artist, educator*
Wright, Frank *artist, educator*

FLORIDA

Atlantic Beach
Gartland, Alice Johnson *artist*

Bonita Springs
Elliott, Donna Louise *artist*

Bradenton
Gedeon, Peter Ferenc *photographer, director*

Clearwater
Slade, Roy *artist, college president, museum director*

Cocoa Beach
Webb, Garfield *art educator*

Davie
Myers, Debbie *graphics designer, educator*

Delray Beach
St. George, Elaine *art educator*

Elfers
Milana-Panopoulos, Maria *artist, model*

Fort Myers
Schwartz, Carl Edward *artist, printmaker*
Vavrina, Charles Laurel *art director*

Fort Pierce
Jefferson, Zanobia Bracy *artist, educator*
Swenson, Ada Perez *artist*

Gainesville
Favini, Paul Furey *costume designer, educator*

Hobe Sound
Mark, Marsha Yvonne Ismailoff *artistic director*

Hollywood
Moore, Victoria *artist*

Indialantic
Pavlakos, Ellen Tsatiri *sculptor*

Jacksonville
Pelton, Margaret Marie Miller *retired art educator, academic administrator, artist*
Sheridan, Alice Virginia *photographer, educator*

Jensen Beach
Skrupky, Elaine Charlotte *art educator*

Key Biscayne
de la Cruz, Rosa *art collector*

Key West
McIntosh, Jon Charles *illustrator, graphics designer, painter*

Kissimmee
McCann, Jean Friedrichs *artist, educator*

Lake Mary
Bachmann, Bill *photographer*

Lakeland
Rogers, James Gordon, Jr. *art educator*
Stark, Bruce Gunsten *artist*

Land O Lakes
O'Connell, Carmela Digristina *appraisal executive, consultant*

Largo
Seidel, Richard L. *artist*

Miami
Bannard, Walter Darby *artist, critic*
Damian, Carol Esposito *art educator, director*
Farrell, Patrick *photographer, photojournalist*
Kislak, Jean Hart *art director*
Morgan, Andrew Wesley *artist, educator*
Pfeiffer, Mary Louise *artist, educator*
Steinbaum, Bernice *art dealer*

Mount Dora
Kirton, Jennifer Myers *artist*

Naples
Eldridge, David Carlton *art and antique appraiser*
Vickrey, Robert Remsen *artist*
York, Tina *painter*

Nokomis
Novak, Joyce Keen *artist, secondary school educator*

North Palm Beach
Kaplan, Muriel Sheerr *sculptor*

Ocala
Hornick, Susan Florence Stegmuller *artist, secondary education educator, fine arts educator, curriculum specialist, retired*

Orange Park
Hunt, J(ulian) Courtenay *artist*

Osprey
Gross, Marilyn Agnes *artist, audiologist, small business owner*

Palm Beach Gardens
Samuels, Fern Jacqueline *artist, educator*

Palm Harbor
Kanelous, Kanelos John *graphics designer*

Pensacola
Breed, Glenn Avery *costume designer, educator*
Larson, Barbara Jean *art history professor*
Maki, Hope Marie (Countess Hope Marie Maki) *artist, educator*

Punta Gorda
Pollard, Herschel Newton *artist, psychologist*

Rotonda West
Durham, Olga Kalapaca *retired art educator, volunteer*

Saint Augustine
Troemel, Jean Wagner-Willhite *artist*

Sanford
Vienneau, Laurence Edward, Jr. *art educator*

Sarasota
Lengyel, Alfonz *art history, archeology and museology educator*
Wendlandt, Dorothea Schnepf *artist, writer*

Tallahassee
Cooper, Martha H. *costume designer, educator*

Tampa
O'Brien, Mary Ellen Christina *artist, educator*
Sopher, Vicki Elaine *appraiser*

Temple Terrace
Kashdin, Gladys Shafran *painter, educator, volunteer*

Vero Beach
Ferrell, Catherine K. *sculptor, painter*
Jonason, Pauline Marie *retired art educator*

West Palm Beach
Baker, Dina Gustin *artist*

Weston
Firgau, Conchita *artist*

Winter Haven
Schepis, Anthony Joseph *artist, educator*

GEORGIA

Alpharetta
Bolton, Robin Jean *artist, painter*

Athens
Dunham, Richard E. III *lighting and set designer, consultant, educator*
Herbert, James Arthur *retired art educator, artist, filmmaker*
Kaufman, Glen Frank *art educator*
Oliveri, Michael Steven *art educator*
Olsen, Richard James *artist, educator*
Paul, William Dewitt, Jr. *retired art educator, collector, artist*
Rittenberry, Harold W., Jr. *sculptor*
Smith (Cavanagh), Susan Carlton *artist, illustrator, sculptor*

Atlanta
Grumet, Priscilla Hecht *fashion specialist, consultant, writer*
Hung, Chin-Cheng *artist, educator*
McLean, James Albert *artist, educator*
Wilmer, Mary Charles *artist*

Augusta
Schultz, Nancy Jansson *artist*

Brunswick
LeMieux, Jeffery Alan *art educator*

Canton
Alexander, Constance Joy (Connie Alexander) *stone sculptor*

Columbus
Graver, Steven F. *costume designer, educator*

Greensboro
Copelan, Ann Hanson *artist, psychologist*

Hiawassee
Davis, Nighta J. *photographer, artist*

Macon
Weaver, Jacquelyn Kunkel Ivey *artist, educator*

Marietta
Lahtinen, Silja Liisa *artist*

Mount Berry
Mew, Thomas Joseph, III, (Tommy) *artist, educator*

Savannah
Aja-Herrera, Marie *fashion designer, educator*

Villa Rica
McKibbin, William Alex *artist*

HAWAII

Honolulu
Betts, Barbara Stoke *artist, educator*

Kihei
Galesi, Deborah Lee *artist*

Lihue
Lai, Waihang *art educator*

Makawao
Huff, Harriet *artist, educator*

IDAHO

Aberdeen
Krehbiel, Jennifer Nell *art educator*

Boise
Grambo, Isaac *art educator*

Coeur D' Alene
Clabby, Michael *computer graphics designer, educator*

Gooding
Larson, Lynn Wood *artist, musician*

Harrison
Carlson, George Arthur *artist*

Meridian
Looney, Daniel Stephen *artist*

Pocatello
Frazier, Timothy Howard *art educator*
Stucki, Margaret Elizabeth *painter, writer*

ILLINOIS

Carbondale
Gertsman, Elina *art educator*

Champaign
Kotoske, Roger Allen *artist, educator*

Chicago
Ajayi, Murphy M. *sculptor, educator*
Alcantara, Anita Luisa *community arts administrator*
Aubin, Barbara Jean *artist*
Burroughs, Margaret Taylor Goss *artist*
Castillo, Mario Enrique *artist, educator*
Coffey, Susanna Jean *artist, educator*
Crane, Barbara Bachmann *photographer, educator*
Edelstein, Teri J. *art educator, director, consultant*
Himmelfarb, John David *artist*
Hunt, Richard *sculptor*
Kearney, John Walter *sculptor, painter*
King, Andre Richardson *architectural graphic designer*
Martin, Ionis Bracy *artist, educator*
McElheny, Josiah G. *sculptor*
McGrail, Jeane Kathryn *artist*
Morris, Rebecca *painter*
Niffenegger, Audrey Anne *artist, writer*
Pallasch, Magdalena Helena (Mrs. Bernhard Michael Pallasch) *artist*
Postiglione, Corey M. *artist, critic, educator*
Steinberg, Rubin *retired art educator, artist*

Cissna Park
McCullough, Edward L. *artist, educator*

Des Plaines
Banach, Art John *retired graphic artist*
Henrikson, Arthur Allen *political cartoonist, educator*

Dixon
Huber, Marianne Jeanne *art dealer and appraiser*

Edwardsville
Malone, Robert Roy *artist, educator*

Evanston
Conger, William Frame *artist, educator*
Griffith, Jeanne Ballard *retired medical illustrator*
Rosenthal, Todd *set designer*

Glen Ellyn
Marszalek, Elizabeth A. *computer graphics designer, educator*
Venezia, Anthony D. *multimedia designer*

Glencoe
Siske, Regina *artist*

Glenview
Hough, Winston *artist*

Highland Park
Slavick, Ann Lillian *retired art educator*

Lombard
Ahlstrom, Ronald Gustin *artist*

Matteson
Chatman, Gloria Lynn *art educator*

Mount Prospect
Eliason, Birdell *painter, educator*

Naperville
Finzer, Carolyn Lauing *artist*

Oak Brook
Klinger, Gail Greaves *art educator, illustrator*

Oak Lawn
Jachna, Joseph David *photographer, educator*

Oak Park
Senese, Suzanne Marie *art and music educator, performance artist*

Park Forest
Cribbs, Maureen Ann *artist, educator*

River Grove
McNamara, Dennis K. *art educator*

Saint Charles
Malinowski, MaryEllen *photographer, artist*

Serena
Freese, Carolyn Lee *art educator*

Table Grove
Thomson, Helen Louise *artist*

Waukegan
Miller, Helen Elizabeth *art and adult education educator, artist*

Winnetka
Plowden, David *photographer*

INDIANA

Bloomington
O'Hearn, Robert Raymond *stage designer*

Evansville
Baker, Gloria Marie *artist*
Roth, Carolyn Louise *art educator*

Indianapolis
Rutledge, Joanne *retired artist consultant*
Schaad, Dee Edwin *art educator*

Muncie
Shawger, David C. *set designer, educator*
Turcotte, Elizabeth Anne *art educator*

New Albany
Stallard, Donna *art educator*

Notre Dame
Coleman, Robert Randolf *art educator*

Seymour
Lewis, Judith Susanna *artist*

Shelbyville
Campbell, Wayne Edward *artist*

South Bend
Larkin, Eugene David *artist, educator*

Terre Haute
Chen, Ray Gow Hwei *artist, educator, department chair*

West Lafayette
Ichiyama, Dennis Yoshihide *art educator, educational association administrator*
Lord, Victoria Lynn *artist*

Winamac
Ligocki, Gordon Michael *artist, educator*

IOWA

Burlington
Koehler-Trickler, Sally Jo *illustrator*

Cedar Falls
Blakesley, Kimberly Kay *art educator, consultant*

Davenport
Townsend, Julie Rae *artist, educator*

Des Moines
Reece, Maynard Fred *artist, writer*

Iowa City
Myers, Virginia Anne *art educator*

Toledo
Lyon, Norma Duffield *sculptor, agriculturist*

KANSAS

Chase
Stull, Evalyn Marie *artist*

Dodge City
Sewell, Carol Ann *artist*

Lenexa
Amundson, Beverly Carden *retired artist*

KENTUCKY

Danville
Holman, Deborah Young *art educator*

Fort Wright
Sullivan, Connie Castleberry *artist*

Franklin
Law, Jerriann Marcella *artist, poet, writer*

Grayson
McDaniel, Charles J. *art educator*

Lexington
Sandoval, Arturo Alonzo *artist, educator*

Murray
Guy, Sallie T. *artist*

Wickliffe
Frueh, Deborah K.A. (Debi) *artist, poet*

Winchester
Snowden, Ruth O'Dell Gillespie *artist*

LOUISIANA

Baton Rouge
Rutledge, Katherine Burck *artist*

Houma
Babin, Regina-Champagne *artist, educator, musician, consultant*

Lafayette
Barry, Mildred Castille *artist*
Groh, William C. *artist*
Guidry, Amy Michelle *artist*

Metairie
Crosby, Deborah Berry *artist*

New Orleans
Bryan, Amy *art educator, director*
Liljeberg, Genevieve Brocato *artist*

Poretto, Jodi *art dealer*

Shreveport
Hughes, Mary Sorrows *artist*
Morelock, Jasmine Crawford *artist*

MAINE

Alna
Beerits, Janet Penrose Robinson *sculptor*

Farmington
Barigar, Elizabeth Gayle *painter, art educator*

Georgetown
Ipcar, Dahlov *artist, writer, illustrator*

Lewiston
Feintuch, Robert *painter*

New Harbor
Lyford, Cabot *sculptor*

Ogunquit
West, Norman Ellsworth *artist*

Rockland
Anne, Lois *artist, educator*

Vinalhaven
Indiana, Robert (Clark) *artist*

Wilton
O'Donnell, Patricia Eileen *art educator*

Wiscasset
Leslie, Seaver *artist*

York
Haley, Priscilla Jane *printmaker*
Hallam, Beverly (Beverly Linney) *artist*

MARYLAND

Annapolis
Fry, Virginia Milne *artist, poet*
Markman, Ronald *artist, educator*

Arnold
Hepner, Donna Terese *art educator*

Baltimore
Tenser, Beth Hillary *graphics designer, art director*
Tucker, James L., Jr. *artist, educator*

Bethesda
Benson, Elizabeth Polk *art specialist*
Dignac, Geny (Eugenia M. Bermudez) *sculptor*
Elliott, George Armstrong III *artist, journalist*
Fleming, Patricia Stubbs (Patsy Fleming) *artist*
Grais, Alexandra *art appraiser, director*
Koenig, Elizabeth Barbara *sculptor*
Nasseripour, Mohammad Michel *artist, architect*
Sarnoff, Lili-Charlotte (Lolo Sarnoff) *artist*

Boyds
Bu, Rulei *artist, educator*

Chestertown
Amos, James Lysle *photographer*

Chevy Chase
Asher, Lila Oliver *artist*
Kranking, Margaret Graham *artist, retired educator*

College Park
Richardson, W. C. *painter*

Columbia
Blackwell-Taffel, Camellia Ann *art educator, consultant*

Denton
Doster, Rose Eleanor Wilhelm *artist*

Derwood
Mylonakis, Stamatios Gregory *artist, research scientist, retired lawyer*

Galena
Hunsperger, Elizabeth Jane *art and design consultant, educator*

Lothian
Messenger, Barbara Beall *artist*

Mount Airy
Foley, Cornelia MacIntyre *retired artist*

Silver Spring
Aranya, Gwendalin Qi *painter, priest, educator, yoga instructor, reiki master*
Davis, Marica Nanci Ella Riggin *retired artist*
Peiperl, Adam *sculptor, photographer*

Stevenson
Stanley, Gregory V. *art educator*

Towson
Ruppert, John Hutchins *sculptor*

Trappe
Burns-Bowie, Maureen Elizabeth *sculptor*

MASSACHUSETTS

Amherst
Anderson, Ronald Trent *artist, educator*
Hayashi, Robert Terry *educator*
Liebling, Jerome *photographer, educator*
Reed-Penttinen, Daphne Stevenson *artist*
Yarde, Richard Foster *art educator*

Boston
Ablow, Joseph *artist, educator*
Bokhari, Afshan *art educator, curator*
Eder, Esther Garcia *artist*
Fink, Aaron *artist*
Francis, Keith M. *graphics designer, artist*
Goldstein, Nathan *artist, writer*
Hershey, Nona *artist, printmaker, educator*
Huckaby, Sedrick Ervin *painter*
McFarland Lord, Jenna *set designer, educator*
Nixon, Nicholas *photographer*
Parker, Olivia *photographer*
Picker, Sebastián *artist*
Scollans, Carol G. J. *art educator*
Wiesner, David *illustrator, children's writer*

Bridgewater
Cochran, Michael G. *artist, educator*
Dondero, Mary E. *artist, educator*

Brookline
Barron, Ros *artist*
Swirnoff, Lois *artist, educator*

Cambridge
Bakanowsky, Louis Joseph *artist, architect, educator*
Chandler, Fay Martin *artist*
Feininger, Theodore Lux *artist*
Jonas, Joan (Joan Amerman Edwards) *artist*
Slosburg-Ackerman, Jill Rose *artist, educator*

Chelsea
Gaetani, Kristina L. *art educator*

Concord
Ihara, Michio *sculptor*
MacNeill, Frederick Douglas *artist*

East Orleans
Burkert, Robert Randall *artist*

Fall River
Wilner, Marion Leonard *art educator*

Framingham
Starobin, Leslie Ann *art educator*

Gloucester
Steele-Goetemann, Judith Ann *artist, gallery owner, educator*

Haydenville
Rupp, Sheron Adeline *photographer, educator*

Lancaster
Richards, Glenora *artist*

Lowell
Minkkinen, Arno Rafael *photographer, educator*

Natick
Geller, Esther (Bailey Geller) *artist*

Newtonville
Polonsky, Arthur *artist, educator*

North Dartmouth
Fisher, Elaine *art educator, photographer*

Norwell
Brett, Jan Churchill *illustrator, author*

Provincetown
Collins, Larry Richard *artist, educator, art gallery director*
Hutchinson, Peter Arthur *artist*

Reading
Frey, Joanne Alice Tupper *art educator*
Nordstrand, Nathalie Elizabeth Johnson *artist*

Rockport
Martin, Roger Hemenway *artist, educator*
Nicholas, Thomas Andrew *artist*

Sagamore Beach
Corn, Wanda Marie *retired fine arts educator*

Shrewsbury
Kranich, Margaret Mansley *artist*

South Hadley
Hall, Lee *artist, educator, writer*

Sudbury
Aronson, David *artist, retired educator*

Truro
Lazeren, Elizabeth *artist*
Preston, Malcolm *artist, art critic*

Wakefield
Fioravanti, Jeff *artist*

Waltham
Bohlen, Nina *artist*
Fleming, Andrea L. *art educator, director*

Wayland
Dergalis, George *artist, educator*

Wellfleet
Henry, Robert S. *art educator*

West Brookfield
Higgins, Brian Alton *artist*

West Tisbury
Howes, Ann M. *watercolor artist, cultural organization administrator, educator*

Williamstown
Blair, Phyllis E. *artist*
Scullin, Dorothy Dodworth *artist, writer*

Winchester
Ferrara, Lee *graphics designer, artist, educator*
Neuman, Robert Sterling *artist, educator*

Winthrop
Kearney, Eva M. *art educator*

MICHIGAN

Ann Arbor
Biro, Matthew *art educator, consultant*
Eisenberg, Marvin Julius *retired art history educator*
Kopinski, Keith Lowell *art director, educator*

Bloomfield Hills
Burnett, Patricia Hill *artist, educator*

Dearborn
Al-Tawil, Hashim M. *art educator, researcher*
Cape, James Odies E. *fashion designer*

Detroit
Abt, Jeffrey *art educator, art historian, artist, writer*
Day, Burnis C. *artist, educator*
Johnson, Lester Larue, Jr. *artist, educator*

Flint
Baird, Darryl Glenn *photographer, educator*
Smith, Catherine Jean *artist, educator*

Hillsdale
Frudakis, Anthony Parker *sculptor, educator*

Holly
Stolpin, William Roger *printmaker*

Howell
Watkins, Curtis WinthroP *artist*

Kalamazoo
Desmett, Don *art educator*

Marquette
Leuthold, Steven Michael *art educator*

Mount Pleasant
Traines, Rose Wunderbaum *sculptor, educator*

Novi
Barr, David John *retired art educator*

Petoskey
Switzer, Carolyn Joan *artist, educator*

Port Huron
Rowark, Maureen *fine arts photographer*

MINNESOTA

Duluth
Chee, Cheng-Khee *artist, educator*

Harmony
Webster, Jeffrey Leon *graphic designer*

Minneapolis
Katsiaficas, Diane *artist, educator*
Newman, Mari Alice *artist, architect, art designer*
Ramalho-Ahrndt, Maria Gabriela *art educator*
Rose, Thomas Albert *artist, educator*
Slettehaugh, Thomas Chester *retired art educator*

Minnetonka
Sussman, Bonnie Kaufman *art dealer, interior designer, consultant*

Saint Cloud
Specht-Jarvis, Roland Hubert *fine arts and humanities educator, dean*

Saint Paul
Hand, Mary Jane *artist, poet, educator*
Lasansky, Leonardo *artist, educator*
Olson, Bettye Johnson *artist, retired educator*

MISSISSIPPI

Carriere
Stanton, Sylvia Doucet *artist, gallery owner*

Clinton
Gore, Samuel Marshall *art educator, sculptor*
Hataway, Michael Willis *graphics designer, educator*

Columbus
Summer, Emily Eugenia *artist, educator*

Meridian
Marshall, John Steven *artist, educator, museum administrator*

Moorhead
Stone-Street, Nancy Harrington *painter, printmaker, educator*

Natchez
Golden, Rolland Harve *artist*

Wesson
Ross, Thomas Albert *art educator*

MISSOURI

Bowling Green
Farris, Donald Herach *art educator*

Chillicothe
Crouch, Frances Nadine *art educator*

Cleveland
Harper, Bill J. *floral designer, consultant, educator*

Columbia
Stack, Frank Huntington *painter, retired art educator*

Florissant
Bommarito, Florence Ann *graphics designer, educator*

Hollister
Canfield, Cindy Sue *art educator*

Kansas City
Gowin, Elijah *photographer*
Lee, Margaret Norma *artist*
Mast, Kande White *artist*
Mendenhall, Kathleen F. *art educator*
Schaffer, Sandra Sue *artist, educator*

Pierce City
Cummings, Richard William *art educator*

Platte City
Kalin, D(orothy) Jean *artist, educator*

Saint Louis
Buggs, Dwayne Andre *fine arts coordinator, music educator*
Colangelo, Carmon *artist, printmaker, educator*
Fondaw, Ronald Edward *artist, educator*
Hansman, Robert G. *artist, educator*
Knoblauch-O'Neal, Christine Ann *artist*
Metcalfe, Elizabeth Brokaw *art educator*
Rosen, Adrienne *artist, educator*
Savoie, Sean Michael *lighting designer, educator*
Zonia, Dhimitri *artist*

Springfield
Armstrong, Bill Howard *artist, educator*

Sturgeon
Dawkins, Amy *artist*

NEBRASKA

Lincoln
Hoff, Michael C. *art educator*

North Platte
Haneline, Richard Dik *art educator*

NEVADA

Las Vegas
Garn, Susan Lynn *art educator*
Goldblatt, Hal Michael *photographer*
Martinez, Adriana *photographer*

Reno
Davidson, Jane P. *art educator*
Goin, Peter Jackson *art educator*
Hilts, Ruth *artist*

NEW HAMPSHIRE

Amherst
Johnson, Daryl Diane *painter*

Concord
Resnick, Kenneth *photography director*

Francestown
Milton, Peter Winslow *artist*

Hanover
Boghosian, Varujan Yegan *sculptor, educator*
Riley, Enrico *painter*

Newport
Gayvoronsky, Ludmila *artist, educator*

Silver Lake
Wilkins, David George *fine arts educator*

Wolfeboro
Bonin, Suzanne Jean *artist*

NEW JERSEY

Atlantic Highlands
Tice, George A(ndrew) *photographer*

Avon By The Sea
Mataranglo, Robert Patrick *artist, educator*

Belmar
Swett, Stephen Frederick, Jr. *artist, educator*

Bernardsville
Spofford, Sally (Hyslop) *artist*

Bridgewater
Patton, Diana Lee Wilkoc *artist, educator, illustrator*

Califon
Rosen, Carol Mendes *artist*

Camden
Tan, LiQin *artist, educator*

Egg Harbor Township
Robbins, Hulda Dornblatt *artist, printmaker*
Schreiber, Eileen Sher *artist*

Englewood
Koons, Irvin Louis *graphics designer, consultant, marketing professional*

Hackensack
Parisi, Cheryl Lynn *art educator*

Hackettstown
Lamour, Kenol *artist, educator*

Jersey City
D'Alessandro, Kathryn Carol *art educator*
Gurevich, Grigory *visual artist, educator, mime*
Yoshimoto, Midori *art educator, director*

Keasbey
Hari, Kenneth Stephen *painter, sculptor, writer*

Lakewood
Pilgram, Suzanne *artist, educator*

Laurel Springs
Roma, Aida Clara *artist*

Leonia
Thiesfeldt, Sheila M. *artist, educator, small business owner*

Lodi
Kelly, Mary Ann Therese *visual artist, educator*

Maplewood
Woods, Krystyna Janina *artist, pharmacist*

Medford
Mayer, Joyce Harris *artist*

Metuchen
Arbeiter, Joan *artist, educator*

Millburn
Pace, Stephen Shell *artist, educator*

Morristown
Prystauk, Elissa *artist*

New Brunswick
Kenfield, John Fawcett III *art educator*

Newton
Hollander, Roslyn *artist, educator*

Paramus
Jacobs, Helen Nichols *artist*

Penns Grove
Reilley, James Clark *artist, cartoonist, retired small business owner*

Piscataway
Rosalsky, Barbara Ellen *artist, community health nurse*

Pompton Plains
Kettlewood, Bea Card *artist, retired educator*

Princeton
Bunnell, Peter Curtis *retired art educator, curator*
George, Thomas *artist*
Grabar, Oleg *retired art educator*
Kahn, Eiko Taniguchi *artist*
McVicker, Charles Taggart *artist, educator*
Seawright, James L., Jr. *sculptor, educator*

Ridgewood
Cutrona, Louis John, Jr. *computer system designer, neuroscientist*

Salem
Kates, Joan M. *art educator*

Somerset
Staub, Carol Anne *artist*

Stockton
Mahon, Robert *photographer*
Schoenherr, John (Carl) *artist, illustrator*

Summit
Baker, Alden *artist*

Teaneck
Indick, Janet *sculptor*

Trenton
Leipzig, Melvin *art educator*

Verona
Ayaso, Manuel *artist*

Wayne
Garcia, Ofelia *art educator, administrator*

Williamstown
Murashima, Kumiko *artist, educator*

NEW MEXICO

Albuquerque
Barry, Steve *sculptor, educator*
Duke, Wanda K. *artist*
Hovel, Esther Harrison *art educator*
Nelson, Mary Carroll *artist, writer*
Qualley, Charles Albert *art educator*
Ré, Paul Bartlett *artist, writer, peace worker*
Sisson, Laurence P. *artist*
Truby, Betsy Kirby *artist, illustrator, photographer*
Williams, Juanita Rosalie *artist*
Witkin, Joel-Peter *photographer, poet*

Arroyo Seco
McHenry, Jonathan Keith *artist*

Bloomfield
Espinosa, Nancy Sweet *artist, anthropologist, curator*

Corrales
Eaton, Pauline *artist, educator*

Gallup
Cattaneo, Jacquelyn Annette Kammerer *artist, educator*

Las Cruces
Huber, Wayne Carl *administrator, educator and artist*
Lopez, Carol Sue *artist*

Las Vegas
Lbdell, David *art educator*
Lobdell, David *art educator*

Penasco
Marx, Nicki Diane *sculptor, painter, jeweler*

Portales
YSikes, Juanita Lou *art educator*

Roswell
Peterson, Dorothy Hawkins *artist, educator*

Santa Fe
Evans, Dick *artist*
Gorski, Daniel Alexander *art educator, artist*
Harroun, Dorothy Sumner *artist*
Perroni, Carol *artist*
Sloan, Jeanette Pasin *artist*

NEW YORK

Albany
Carson, JoAnne *artist, educator*
Goldstein, Kenneth Scott *set designer*

Alfred
Higby, Wayne (Donald) *artist, educator*
Scheer, Joseph H. *artist, education educator*

Amenia
Hale, Nathan Cabot *sculptor, artist, poet*

Ancram
Blechman, R. O. *artist, filmmaker*

Ancramdale
Weinstein, Joyce *artist*

Annandale On Hudson
LÊ, An-My *photographer, educator*
Pfaff, Judy *artist*
Sandström, Sigrid *painter*

Bellerose
Stecher, Pauline *painter, educator*

Brentwood
DeSario, James M. *art educator, photographer, writer*

Bronx
Adams, Alice *sculptor*
Bacarella, Flavia *artist, educator*
Behnken, William Joseph *artist, educator*
Kassoy, Hortense (Honey Kassoy) *artist, sculptor, painter*
Kitt, Olga *artist*
Korman, Barbara *sculptor*
Serrano, Helen *art educator*
Spinka, William J. *art educator*

Brooklyn
Dinnerstein, Harvey *artist*
Fischer, R.M. *sculptor*
Gianlorenzi, Nona Elena *art dealer, painter*
Gisolfi, Diana (Pechukas) *art history educator*
Grado, Angelo John *artist*
Haber, Ira Joel *artist, educator*
Hoyt, Ellen *artist, educator*
Kemp, James William *graphic artist*
Lazansky, Edward *artist, art educator*
Litto, Judith Cheryl *art educator*
Mallory, Michael *art educator*
Miller, Greg *photographer*
Nii, Yuko *artist*
Padovano, Anthony John *fine arts educator, artist*
Piene, Chloe *artist, filmmaker*
Pitynski, Andrzej Piotr *sculptor*
Rauschenbusch, Stephanie *artist, educator, poet*
Schaefer, Marilyn Louise *artist, writer, educator*
Shaw, Kendall (George) *artist, educator*
von Rydingsvard, Ursula Karoliszyn *sculptor*
Zakanitch, Robert Rahway *artist*
Zinnes, Alice Fich *artist, educator*
Zollar, Jawole Willa Jo *artist, choreographer*

Buffalo
Houseknecht, Stephen *artist, educator*
Martin, Margaret M. *artist, educator, Author*
Parks, Michael E. *art educator, department chairman*
Price, Justine D. *art educator*
Schweitzer, Shannon Troy *lighting designer, design educator*
Townsend, Carol Agnes *artist, educator*

Buskirk
Johanson, Patricia Maureen *artist, architect, park designer*

Campbell Hall
Greenly, Colin *artist*

Canaan
Walker, William Bond *painter, retired librarian*

Cazenovia
Wyckoff, Sylvia Spencer *art educator, artist*

Cochecton
Berlind, Robert Elliot *artist, educator*

Corning
Buechner, Thomas Scharman *artist, museum director, retired glass manufacturing company executive*

Croton On Hudson
Wandel, Sharon Lee *sculptor*

East Amherst
Garver, Walter Raymond *artist*

East Hampton
Jaudon, Valerie *artist*
Praetorius, William Albert, Sr. *artist, retired real estate company officer, retired advertising executive*
Scott, Rosa Mae *artist, educator*

East Setauket
Badalamenti, Fred Leopoldo *artist, educator*

Elmira
Miran, Patricia Marie *art educator*

Fayetteville
Hadyk-Wepf, Sonia Margaret *artist, real estate manager*

Flushing
Carlson, Cynthia Joanne *artist, educator*
Chang, Jason *artist, educator*
Feng, Ying *painter, educator*
Gonzalez, Tony *artist, educator*
Shen, Ronger *artist, educator*
Yeo, Kim Eng *artist*

Fly Creek
Dusenbery, Walter Condit *sculptor*

Forest Hills
Morgan, Jacqui *illustrator, painter, art educator, writer*

Franklin Square
Indiviglia, Salvatore Joseph *artist, retired military officer*

Garden City
Russell, Stella Pandell *artist, author, educator*

Glen Head
Newmark, Marilyn *sculptor*

Glenford
Rieder, Naomi *artist*

Great Neck
Seidler, Doris *artist*

Great River
Edwards, Christine E. *artist*

Hopewell Junction
Sellingsloh, Hulda Knipling *retired artist*

Hudson Falls
Leary, Daniel *artist*

Ithaca
Ashdown, Susan P. *art educator*
Grippi, Salvatore William *artist*
Mikus, Eleanore Ann *artist*
Poleskie, Stephen Francis *retired art educator, artist, writer, publisher*
Schuler, Mary Callaghan *artist, educational association administrator*

Jackson Heights
Dacey, Paul *artist*
Imayeva, Olga Borisovna *artist*

Jamaica
Cade, Walter III *artist, actor, musician, vocalist*

Jefferson
Sullivan, Jim *artist*

Jeffersonville
Craft, Douglas Durwood *artist*
Harms, Elizabeth Louise *artist*

Johnson City
McMillen, Marieta Louise *art educator*

Katonah
Giobbi, Edward Giacchino *artist*

Lawrence
Henriquez, Allen *artist*

Long Island City
Madden, Steven *footwear designer*

Lynbrook
Cangemi, Lisa Lynne *art director, graphics designer*

Manhasset
Stevens, Thelma Kaplan *artist, educator*

New Hampton
Sinnard, Elaine Janice *painter, sculptor*

New Rochelle
Metz, Roxie Anne *art educator*

New York
Abish, Cecile *artist*
Adrian, Barbara (Mrs. Franklin C. Tramutola) *artist*
Alpert, William Harold (Bill) *artist, painter*
Anastasi, William Joseph *artist*
Anthony, William Graham *artist*
Armani, Giorgio *fashion designer*
Arms, Anneli (Anna Elizabeth) *artist, educator*
Backstedt, Roseanne Joan *artist*
Badgley, Mark *fashion designer*
Baldessari, John Anthony *artist*
Banerjee, (Bimal) *artist, educator*
Banker, Amy Beth Cohen *artist, writer, educator, curator, actress, poet*
Banks, Jeffrey *fashion designer*
Barnet, Will *artist, educator*
Barnet, Will *painter*
Barney, Matthew *sculptor, filmmaker*
Barr-Sharrar, Beryl *artist, art historian*
Bendet, Stacey *apparel designer*
Ben-Haim, Zigi *artist*
Bensimon, Gilles *photographer*
Biddle, Flora Miller *art patron, museum administrator*
Birch, Willie *artist*
Blair, Dike *sculptor, painter*
Bloom, Martha Louise *artist, educator*
Bochner, Mel *artist*
Bonino, Fernanda *art dealer*
Bontecou, Lee *artist, sculptor*
Bourgeois, Louise *sculptor*
Boutis, Tom *artist, painter, printmaker*
Bradshaw, Dove *artist*
Brett, Nancy Heléne *artist*
Brody-Lederman, Stephanie *artist*
Bruder, Harold Jacob *artist, educator*
Bunts, Frank Emory *artist*
Burch, Tory *apparel designer*
Burrows, Stephen *apparel designer*
Cajori, Charles Florian *artist, educator*
Campbell, Ronald Neil *retired graphics designer*
Campo, Carlos *apparel designer*
Cappellazzo, Amy *art appraiser, writer*
Cardile, Paul Julius *fine arts dealer*
Castoro, Rosemarie *sculptor*
Celmins, Vija *painter*
Chapman, Georgina *apparel designer, actress*
Chermayeff, Ivan *graphics designer*
Chin, Mel *sculptor*
Chinn, Yuen Yuey *art educator, painter*
Christensen, Irene *artist*
Close, Chuck (Charles Thomas Close) *artist*
Coe, Sue *artist, journalist*
Coffin, Anne Gagnebin *arts administrator, editor*
Cohen, Cora *artist*
Colette, S. *artist*
Costa, Francisco *fashion designer*
Cota, Christian *apparel designer*
Crown, Roberta Lila *artist, educator*
Cunningham, Francis *artist*
Dana, F(rank) Mitchell *theatrical lighting designer*
de la Renta, Oscar *fashion designer*
Demarchelier, Patrick *photographer*
DeMonte, Claudia Ann *artist, educator*
Denes, Agnes C. *environmental artist*
Dennis, Donna Frances *sculptor, art educator*
Dennison, Lisa *auction house executive*
Di Meo, Dominick *artist, sculptor, painter*
Dion, Mark *installation sculptor, photographer*
Dobbs, John Barnes *artist, educator*
Donneson, Seena Sand *artist*
Donovan, Tara *sculptor*
Drum, Sydney Maria *artist*
Duff, John Ewing *sculptor*
Dunkelman, Loretta *artist*
Dyyon, Mario (LeRoy Frazier) *artist*
Ecko, Marc (Marc Milecofsky) *apparel designer*
Eins, Stefan *artist, curator, science researcher, writer*
Elgort, Arthur *photographer*
Enders, Elizabeth McGuire *artist*
Erwitt, Elliott Romano *photographer, cinematographer*
Fasnacht, Heide Ann *artist, educator*
Feigen, Richard L. *art dealer, collector, writer*
Feltus, Alan Evan *artist*
Fernández, Teresita *sculptor*
Fetherston, Erin *apparel designer*
Field, Patricia *apparel designer, stylist*
Fischer, Carl *photographer, graphic designer, actor*
Floret, Evelyn *sculptor*
Florin, Sharon *artist*
Foulkes, Llyn *artist, educator*
Frankenthaler, Helen *artist*
Fyfe, Joe *painter*
Gagosian, Larry Gilbert *art dealer*
Gallo, David *scenic designer*
Geissbuhler, Stephan *graphics designer*
Gibson, Ralph H. (Ralph Holmes Gibson) *photographer*
Ginzel, Andrew H. *artist*
Glaser, Milton *graphics designer, illustrator*
Greenwold, Mark *painter*
Griefen, John Adams *artist, educator*
Grigely, Joseph Constantine, Jr. *artist, language educator*
Gutman, Robert William *retired art educator*

Haacke, Hans Christoph Carl *artist, educator*
Haas, Richard John *artist*
Haessle, Jean-Marie Georges *artist*
Halaby, Samia Asaad *painter, educator, writer*
Hammons, David *sculptor*
Hamoy, Carol *artist*
Handforth, Mark *sculptor*
Hardy, John *artist*
Henselmann, Caspar Gustav Fidelis *sculptor*
Herman, Stan *fashion designer*
Herrera, Carolina *fashion designer*
Highstein, Jene Abel *sculptor*
Hilfiger, Tommy (Thomas Jacob Hilfiger) *apparel designer*
Holstad, Christian *artist*
Holzman, Eric *painter*
Hort, Michael *art collector*
Hort, Susan *art collector*
Hostvedt, Anna *painter*
Howard, Mildred *sculptor*
Hull, Cathy *artist, illustrator*
Hyde, James *artist*
Iacono, John *photographer*
Incandela, Gerald Jean-Marie *artist*
Ireland, Patrick *artist*
Iturbide, Graciela *photographer*
Jacobs, Marc *fashion designer*
Jacquette, Yvonne Helene *artist*
Jenkins, Paul *artist*
Johnson, Betsey Lee *fashion designer*
Kahn, Wolf *artist*
Kaish, Luise Clayborn *sculptor, painter, educator*
Kaish, Morton *artist, educator*
Kamali, Norma *fashion designer*
Kan, Diana Artemis Mann Shu *painter, art educator, writer*
Karan, Donna (Donna Faske) *fashion designer*
Kelley, Mike *artist*
Keno, Leslie B. *antiques dealer, appraiser*
Kentridge, William *visual artist*
King, Marcia Gygli *artist*
Kinstler, Everett Raymond *artist*
Klausen, Ray *theatre set and television production designer, sculptor*
Klein, Calvin Richard *fashion designer*
Klein, Cynthia *art appraiser*
Klein, Steven *photographer*
Klein, William *photographer, filmmaker*
Knowles, Alison *artist*
Koons, Jeff *artist*
Koppelman, Chaim *artist, educator*
Koppelman, Dorothy Myers *artist, consultant*
Korins, David *set designer*
Kors, Michael (Karl Anderson Jr.) *fashion designer*
Kotlowitz, Dan *lighting designer*
Kramarsky, Werner H. *art collector*
Krementz, Jill *photographer, author*
Krivonos, Sergey *pianist, educator*
Kroell, Devi *accessories designer*
Kurahara, Ted Naomi *artist, educator*
Lam, Derek *apparel designer*
Lanyon, Ellen *artist, educator*
Lash, Stephen Sycle *auction company executive*
Lasker, Jonathan Lewis *artist*
Lauren, Ralph *fashion designer*
Leech, Katharine (Kitty Leech) *costume designer, educator*
Leibovitz, Annie *photographer*
Lekberg, Barbara *sculptor*
Lerner, Sandra *artist*
Levine, Sherrie *conceptual artist*
Levy, Builder *photographer*
Lins, Pam *sculptor*
Lipsky, Pat *artist*
Loengard, John Borg *photographer, editor*
Long, Charles *sculptor*
Lou, Liza *artist*
Lovell, Whitfield *artist*
Malandrino, Catherine *apparel designer*
Mann, Frank Bert *artist, educator*
Mark, Mary Ellen *photographer*
Marton, Tutzi *artist*
Maxmen, Mimi (Mary Elizabeth Maxmen) *costume and scenic designer*
Mayer, Rosemary *artist*
McCartney, Stella *apparel designer*
McCredie, James Robert *fine arts educator*
McElhinney, James Lancel *artist, educator*
Mc Gowin, William Edward *artist*
McKinley-Haas, Mary *artist*
McLane, Derek *set designer*
McMullan, Patrick *photographer*
Mehretu, Julie *artist*
Meisel, Steven *advertising photographer*
Meyers, Dale (Mrs. Mario Cooper) *artist*
Miano, Louis Stephen *arts advisor*
Miller, Nicole Jacqueline *fashion designer*
Miller, Richard Kidwell *artist, actor, educator*
Mir, Aleksandra *artist*
Mischka, James *fashion designer*
Miyake, Issey *fashion designer*
Mizrahi, Isaac *fashion designer*
Mortimer, Tinsley Randolph *apparel designer*
Mutu, Wangechi *collage artist, painter*
Natori, Josie Cruz (Josefina Almeda Cruz Natori) *apparel designer*
Nauman, Bruce *artist*
Neiman, LeRoy *artist*
Niccolini, Dianora *photographer*
Ohlson, Douglas Dean *artist, educator*
Okuhara, Tetsu *artist, photographer*
Oldenburg, Richard Erik *auction company executive*
Oldham, Todd *fashion designer*
Ono, Yoko *conceptual artist, singer, recording artist*
Pask, Scott *set designer*
Passlof, Pat *artist, educator*
Peckolick, Alan *painter, graphies designer, photographer*
Perlis, Donald M. *artist*
Picasso, Paloma *fashion designer*
Pilati, Stefano *apparel designer*
Poons, Larry *artist*
Porter, Liliana Alicia *artist, photographer, painter, printmaker, filmmaker*
Posen, Zac *apparel designer*
Quiles, Esther *art educator*
Quinson, Bruno Andre *painter, retired publishing executive*
Raftery, Andrew Stein *printmaker*
Rathbone, Peter B. *art appraiser*
Reddy, Krishna Narayana *artist, educator*
Reese, Tracy *fashion designer*
Reininghaus, Ruth *retired artist*
Resika, Paul *artist*
Ringgold, Faith *artist*
Rodriguez, Narciso *fashion designer*
Roi, Alice (Roy Blumenthal) *apparel designer*
Rosenberg, Alex Jacob *art appraiser and dealer, educator*
Rowley, Cynthia *apparel designer*
Roy, Rachel *fashion designer*
Rubinfien, Leo H. *photographer, writer*
Ruscha, Edward *artist*
Russotto, Paul *artist, educator*
Sanchez, Angel *apparel designer*
Sandler, Lucy Freeman *art history educator*
Saul, Peter A. *artist, educator*
Schapiro, Miriam *artist*
Schenk, Thomas *photographer*
Schnabel, Julian *artist, film director*
Schneider, JoAnne *artist*
Scofidio, Ricardo *artist, architect, educator*
Selznick, Brian *illustrator, writer*
Serra, Richard *sculptor*
Shatter, Susan Louise *artist, museum administrator, educator*
Sherrod, Philip Lawrence *artist, composer, painter, poet*
Sigal-Ibsen, Rose *artist*
Sleigh, Sylvia *artist, educator*
Sloat, Richard Joel *artist*
Slone, Sandi *artist*
Smith, Kiki *artist*
Smith, Robert Michael *sculptor, educator*
Smith, Shirley *artist*
Sonneman, Eve *artist*
Sorrenti, Mario *photographer*
Spade, Kate (Katherine Noel Spade) *apparel designer*
Spence, Sique (Mary Stewart Spence) *art dealer*
Spikol, Eileen *artist*
Stainrook, Harry Richard *photographer, retired bank executive*
Stuart, Jill *apparel designer*
Sui, Anna *fashion designer*
Swain, Robert *artist*
Tahari, Elie *fashion designer*
Taylor, David J. *photographer*
Terruso, Luigi Leonardo *artist, educator*
Tipton, Jennifer *lighting designer*
Toledo, Isabel *apparel designer*
Tooker, George *painter, printmaker*
Torreano, John Francis *painter, sculptor*
Trujillo, Marc *painter*
Tsao, Vivian J. *artist, educator*
Tscherny, George *graphics designer*
Turner, Bracha *painter*
Tuttle, Richard *artist*
Twardus, Susan M. *artist, art gallery owner, display designer*
Unithan, Dolly *visual artist*
Upright, Diane Warner *art dealer*
Wagner, Robin Samuel Anton *stage and set designer*
Wahlgren, Francis J. *art appraiser*
Wald, Sylvia *artist*
Walker, Kara *artist*
Wall, Jeff *photographer*
Wang, Alexander *apparel designer*
Wang, Vera *fashion designer*
Warren, Richard *fashion photographer*
Weiner, Lawrence Charles *artist*
Weiss, Marilyn Ackerman *artist*
Welker, Jennifer Carol Marie *artist*
Wexler, Peter John *artist, sculptor, photographer, theatre designer, producer, director*
Widing, Eric P. *auction specialist*
Winkfield, Trevor *painter*
Woo, Alex *jewelry designer*
Wright, Faith-dorian *artist*
Wunderman, Jan Darcourt *artist*
Wurmfeld, Sanford *artist, educator*
Zarish, Janet Ann *art educator, director, actress*
Zimmerman, Elyn *artist*
Zimmerman, Kathleen Marie *artist*

North White Plains
Erla, Karen *artist, painter, collagist, printmaker*

Northport
Hohenberger, Patricia Julie *fine arts and antique appraiser, consultant*

Nyack
Chien, Jennie *sculptor*

Oneonta
Freckelton, Sondra *artist*

Ossining
Sadan, Mark *photographer, film producer, artist*

Oswego
Fox, Michael David *retired art educator*
Macey, Kitty *costume designer, educator*

Oyster Bay
Prey, Barbara Ernst *artist*

Piermont
Berkon, Martin *artist*

Pittsford
Dunsky, Annie *artist*

Port Chester
Sayles, Eva *artist*

Port Jervis
Healy, Julia Schmitt *artist, educator*

Queens Village
Megherian, Yefkin *sculptor*

Rhinebeck
Ewald, Wendy Taylor *photographer, writer, educator*

Rochester
Sheppard, Luvon *art educator*
Singer, Alan Daniel *artist*
Wolsky, Jack *retired art educator*

Rockville Centre
Derbentli, Betty Ann *art educator, curator*

Roslyn
Finke, Leonda Froehlich *sculptor, educator*

Sagaponack
Isham, Sheila *artist*

Saratoga Springs
Stake, Peter *artist, educator*

Shelter Island Heights
Culbertson, Janet Lynn *artist*
Gage, Beau *artist*

Snyder
Breverman, Harvey *artist*

Somers
Bensen, Annette Wolf *graphic art company consultant*

South Salem
Carpentieri, Carol Ellen *artist, educator*

Southampton
Swift, Mary Lou *art dealer, financial consultant*
Tuma, Mym *sculptor, painter, educator*

Stony Brook
Pekarsky, Melvin Hirsch *artist*

Sugar Loaf
Endico, Mary Antoinette *artist*

Syracuse
Cohen-Cruz, Jan *art educator, director*
Forbes, Peter Edwin *sculptor*
Heath, Patti *art educator, musician*
Thomas, Sidney *fine arts educator, researcher*

Vestal
Adour, Colleen McNulty *artist, educator*

Wainscott
Russo, Alexander Peter *artist, educator*

Wallkill
Koch, Edwin Ernest *artist, interior designer*

Warwick
Fletcher, Robert Alexander *artist, writer*

White Plains
Machover, Carl *computer graphics designer, engineer, consultant*

Williamsville
Fortunato, Pat Deakin *fine artist*

Woodmere
Winick, Bernyce Alpert *artist, photographer*

Woodstock
Banks, Rela *sculptor*

Yonkers
Speirs, Greg *sports artist*
Viola, Mary Jo *art history educator*

NORTH CAROLINA

Asheville
Tynes, Robert Dick *artist, educator*

Boone
Neff, Alice Elaine *costume designer*
Yaukey, Margaret Ann *art educator*

Burnsville
Doyle, John Lawrence *artist*

Canton
Hand, Clelia *artist, art educator*

Dallas
Easter, Willie, Jr. *artist, writer*

Franklin
Kinard, Cynthia Cochran *artist writer poet*

Gastonia
Patterson, Elaine Wilcox *art educator*

Greenville
Wallin, Leland Dean *artist, educator*

Hendersonville
Tatreau, (Dolores) Maxine *artist*

Leasburg
Treacy, Sandra Joanne Pratt *retired art educator, illustrator*

Lexington
Frontz, Leslie Kay *art educator*

Lillington
Jewell, Eileen Kathryn *art educator*

Mount Olive
Hooks, Cheryl *art educator*

Pittsboro
Kachergis, Joyce W. *book designer*

Raleigh
Robinson, Charlotte Hill *artist*

Rocky Mount
Evans, Emma *retired art educator*

Salisbury
Dougherty, Erin Brooke *costume designer, educator*

Statesville
Flake, Mark Wayde *artist*

Williamston
Denny, Brenda S. *art educator*

Winston Salem
Faccinto, Victor Paul *artist, gallery administrator*

Zebulon
Ruffing, Anne Elizabeth *artist*

OHIO

Ashtabula
Morisue, Glenn T. *graphics designer*

Aurora
Lawton, Florian Kenneth *artist, educator*

Bowling Green
Hershberger, Andrew E. *art educator*
Ocvirk, Otto George *artist*

Cincinnati
Attee, Joyce Valerie Jungclas *artist*
Bollen, Sharon Kesterson *artist, educator*
Brod, Stanford *graphics designer, educator*
Daniels, Astar *artist*
Wygant, Foster Laurance *art educator*

Cleveland
Bergengren, Charles Lang *art educator*
Deming, David Lawson *art educator*
Fallon, Pat *artist, educator*
Kiernan, Maureen *art educator*

Columbus
Hamilton, Ann Katherine *sculptor*
Marsh, Fredrik *photographer*
Nelson, Ardine *photographer*
Russell, Nas'Naga R. *illustrator*
Wagner, Robert Walter *photographer, communications educator, film producer, consultant*

Dayton
Wikstrom, Loretta Wermerskirchen *artist*

Elyria
Robinson-Odom, June Frances Margaret A. *art educator*

Fairfield
Allen, Lois Faye *art educator*
Cimini, Eric Michael *lighting designer, director*

Hilliard
Cupp, David Foster *photographer, journalist*

Hudson
Carducci, Judith Weeks Barker *artist, retired social worker*

Kirtland
Armstrong, Mary Ogden *artist, graphics designer*

Marion
Beery, Arthur *artist*

Oxford
Ewing, Susan R. *artist, educator*

Perrysburg
Autry, Carolyn *artist, educator*
Catalano, Dominic *art educator, illustrator*

Seven Hills
Stanczak, Julian *artist, educator*

Springfield
Humphries, Jimmy *set designer, educator*

Sylvania
Collins, Penny *graphics designer, illustrator*

Willoughby
Krider, Margaret Young *art educator*

OKLAHOMA

Broken Arrow
Huff, Melinda Louise *art educator*
Jones, Jp *graphics designer*

Guthrie
Womack, Destiny Mary Louise *artist*

Lawton
Liontas-Warren, Katherine *art educator*
Mays, Quincey *art educator*

Norman
Wood, Betty Jean *conceptual artist, educator*

Oklahoma City
Alaupovic, Alexandra Vrbanic *artist, educator*
Boston, Billie *costume designer, history educator*
Hoge, Margaret R. *art educator*

Seminole
Kirk, Kelly D. *art educator, department chairman*

Tulsa
Valero, Maria Teresa *photographer, art educator*

OREGON

Ashland
Hay, Richard Laurence *theater set designer*

Bandon
Handley, Louise Patricia *artist*
Lindquist, Louis William *artist, researcher, writer*

Cannon Beach
Greaver, Harry *artist*

Eugene
Frederick, Elizabeth Eleanor Tatum *watercolor artist, retired educator*

Medford
Schubert, Ruth Carol Hickok *artist, educator*

Newberg
Keith, Pauline Mary *artist, illustrator, writer*

Newport
Gilhooly, David James III *artist*

Portland
Boutwell, Anne Dielschneider *artist, painter*
Ebert, Leslie *artist*
Farner, Darla A. *artist*
Street, Terry M. *artist, educator*
Walker, Morgan Wailes *art educator*

Roseburg
Gugel, Merilynn Sue *artist*

Stayton
Gay, Larry Kenneth *artist, automotive executive, consultant*

PENNSYLVANIA

Allentown
Battle, Turner Charles III *art educator, educational association administrator*
Kocsis, James Paul *artist*
Osterweil, Ara Cybele *art educator*

Ardmore
Levy, Rochelle Feldman *artist*
Zito, Allison Ann *textile weaver, member*

Audubon
Williams, Lawrence Soper, Jr. *photographer*

Camp Hill
McGeary, Barbara Joyce *artist, educator*

Cochranville
Sazegar, Morteza *artist*

Doylestown
Katsiff, Bruce *artist*

Easton
Bellissimo, Mary E. *art educator*

Elkins Park
Erlebacher, Martha Mayer *artist, educator*

Erie
Staniunas Hopper, Jodi Ann *graphics designer, educator*

Glenside
Medel, Rebecca Rosalie *artist*

Haverford
Williams, William Earle *artist, educator, curator*

Jim Thorpe
Meneeley, Edward Sterling *artist*

Lancaster
Poser, Joan Rapps *artist, writer*

Marshalls Creek
Svoboda, Joanne Dzitko *artist, educator*

New Hope
Freyer, Victoria C. *fashion and interior design executive*

Pennsburg
Hovanec, Julia Lynne *art educator*

Philadelphia
d'Agostino, Peter *art educator*
Goschke, Linda Fry *artist*
Granger, Randy William *art educator, consultant*
Lewis, E(arl) B(radley) *artist, illustrator*
Miyamori, Keiko *artist*
Newman, Libby *painter, printmaker, curator*
Paone, Peter *artist*
Spandorfer, Merle Sue *artist, educator, writer*
Willet, E. Crosby (Everett Crosby Willet) *artist*

Pittsburgh
Bates, Beverly Jo-Anne *artist, educator*
Herrington, Howard Ray *artist*

Reading
Garrison, Matthew Moore *artist, educator*
Horacek, Constance Heller *graphic designer, educator*

Rochester
Douglas, Elizabeth Asche *artist, musician, educator, writer*

Scranton
Hinkle Maria, Lisa *photographer, educator*

Selinsgrove
Livingston, Valerie A. *art educator, consultant*

Solebury
Anthonisen, George Rioch *sculptor, artist*

Tower City
Adams, Susan L. *art educator*

Upper Black Eddy
Wechsler, Gil *lighting designer*

West Chester
da Costa, Virginia Marie *art educator*

West Grove
Allman, Margo Hutz *sculptor, painter*

RHODE ISLAND

Charlestown
Rohm, Robert Hermann *sculptor, educator*

Jamestown
Worden, Katharine Cole *sculptor*

Narragansett
Bentley-Scheck, Grace Mary *artist*

Providence
Feldman, Walter Sidney *artist, educator*
Golden, Hal *artist, consultant*
Heyman, Lawrence Murray *printmaker, painter*
Howes, Lorraine de Wet *fashion designer, educator*

Wakefield
Leete, William White *retired artist*

Warwick
Brown, Ann Eckert *artist, educator*

SOUTH CAROLINA

Clinton
Rico, Christopher *artist*

Columbia
Blue Sky, *artist, muralist*

Greenville
Dreskin, Jeanet Steckler *painter, medical artist, educator*

Greer
McKenzie, Kathleen Julianna *artist*

Inman
D'Ambrosio, Jody (Gigi) Lynn *art educator*

Irmo
Branham, Jennie Jones *artist*

Johns Island
Jackson, Mary *craftswoman*

Orangeburg
Igwe, Kodilinye *art educator*
Martin, Frank C., II, *art educator*

Spartanburg
Augthun, Carol Elise *artist, educator*
Wingo, Winston Alfonso *art educator*

SOUTH DAKOTA

Brookings
Eischen, Michelle Robin *art educator*

Rapid City
Clark, Lynda Kay *artist*

Sioux Falls
Aldern, Robert Judson *architectural, liturgical and landscape artist*

Vermillion
Kim, Young Ae *graphics designer, educator*

TENNESSEE

Chattanooga
Martin, Chester Y. *sculptor, painter*
Mills, Olan, II, *photography company executive*

Cleveland
Kraus, Ruby Jean *art educator*

Collegedale
Craven, Randall L. *graphics designer, educator, product designer*

Crab Orchard
McBee, Christy Dawn *art educator*

Johnson City
Anthony, Margaret Alice *photographer, educator*

Knoxville
Markert, Cynthia Allin *artist*

Memphis
Dierkes, Judith Ann *artist, educator*
McPherson, Larry Eugene *photographer, educator*
Yasuda, Robert *painter*

Nunnelly
Crnkovich, Ruth Anne *art appraiser, museum director*

TEXAS

Amarillo
Eimon, Pan Dodd *artist, writer*

Arlington
Munoz, Celia Alvarez *artist*

Austin
Fearing, William Kelly *artist, educator*
Kemp, Sue *art educator*
Long, Bert Louis, Jr. *artist*
Pestorius, Eileen McGee *art educator*
Smith, Jeffrey Chipps *art educator*
van Otteren, Juliet *photographer*

College Station
Martin, Carol Jacquelyn *artist, educator*

Corpus Christi
Perkins, Cynthia O. *art educator*

Crosby
King, Vernon Dale *art educator*

Dallas
Dealey, Lynn Townsend *artist*
Stephenson, Jane Connell *artist, educator*
Walsh, Dawna Hamm *art educator*

Denton
Gough, Georgia Belle *art educator*
McMath, Elizabeth Moore *graphic artist*

Edinburg
Manuella, Frank *retired art and design educator*

Fort Worth
Cunningham, Shirley Rose *artist*
Durham, Jo Ann Fanning *artist*

Houston
Doyle, Joseph Francis III *art educator*
Kagle, Joseph Louis, Jr. *artist, administrator, historian*
Reid, Katherine Louise *artist, educator, writer*
Stockholder, Jessica *sculptor*
Tee, Rebekah C. *art educator*

Huntsville
Lea, Stanley E. *artist, educator*

Hurst
Bowman, Karmien C. *sculptor, ceramist, educator*

Kerrville
Frudakis, Evangelos William *sculptor*

Mc Kinney
Wright, Thomas Parker *artist*

Murchison
Taweel, Janice M. *artist, educator*

Paris
Tyler, Cathie Ann *artist, educator*

Plano
Cotter-Smith, Cathleen Marie *artist, educator*

Rockport
Moroles, Jesús Bautista *sculptor*

Rosenberg
Haygood, Eithel Marinella *artist, educator*

San Angelo
Mobley, Nancy Elizabeth *artist, educator*

Tyler
Holland, Barbara *artist, educator*

UTAH

American Fork
Reinhold, Allen Kurt *graphic design educator*

Castle Valley
Zavada, Barbara Johanna *artist, educator*

Logan
Rasmuson, Brent J. *photographer, small business owner*

Provo
Fielding, Eric *set designer, educator*

Salt Lake City
Bliss, Anna Campbell *artist, architect, color consultant*
Huelskamp, Willamarie Ann *artist*
Krensky, Beth Ellen *artist, educator*

Springville
Francis, Rell Gardner *artist, photographer, writer*

Stansbury Park
Moyer, Linda Lee *artist, educator, author*

VERMONT

Brattleboro
Abrams, Jackie *artist, educator*

Burlington
Gabriel, Diane Augusta *artist, educator*

Charlotte
Robinson, Sally Winston *artist*

Dorset
Marron, Pamela Anne *artist*

Essex Junction
Tedd, Monique Micheline *artist*

Middlebury
Bumbeck, David *artist, retired educator*

Newbury
McGarrell, James *artist, educator*

West Burke
Van Vliet, Claire *artist*

VIRGINIA

Arlington
Dunlap, William *artist, critic, educator*

Charlottesville
Weinberger, Adrienne *artist, art appraiser*

Chesapeake
Potter, Cynthia M. *art educator, artist*

Clifton
Hennesy, Gerald Craft *artist*

Fairfax
Wrbican, Sue *art educator*

Farmville
Panzarello, Melissa *costume designer, educator*

Fredericksburg
Gill, Milvi Kosenkranius *artist, photographer*
Schmutzhart, Berthold Josef *sculptor, educator*

Harrisonburg
Theodore, Crystal *retired artist, educator*

Henrico
Kevorkian, Richard *artist*

Herndon
Nolan, Leslie Marian *artist*
Simanski, Claire Dvorak *art educator*

Independence
Craig, James Hicklin *fine arts consultant*

Lexington
Mann, Sally M. *photographer*

Lynchburg
Hudson, Walter Tiree *artist*

Manassas Park
Knouse, Stacie *art educator*

Mc Lean
Safer, John *sculptor*

Middleburg
vom Baur, Daphne de Blois *artist*

Newport News
Sheaks, Barclay *artist*

Norfolk
Isekeije, Solomon Rowland *artist, educator*
Nicholson, Myreen Moore *artist, researcher*

Prospect
Shield, Julie Marie Karst *artist, educator*

Radford
Bay, Richard Joseph *art educator*

Richmond
Freed, David Clark *artist*
Jenkins, William Schley III *theatrical designer*
Lee, Ivey Owen *multimedia designer*
McCrimmon, Miles *educator*

Round Hill
Hillis, Catherine H. *artist*

Springfield
Arifi, Fatana Baktash *artist, educator*
Brown, Margaret Catherine *artist*

Vienna
Yamaguch, Yuriko Fujita *artist*

Virginia Beach
Antol, Joseph J. *artist*
Fink, Eloise Bradley *art director*
Lewis, Donald Sykes, Jr. *artist*

Weyers Cave
Martinkosky, Jessica *art educator*

Williamsburg
Coleman, Henry Edwin *artist, educator*
Robinson, Jay (Thurston) *artist*
Stanley, Shirley Davis *artist*

Woodbridge
Rebhan, Gail *art educator*

WASHINGTON

Anacortes
Mc Cracken, Philip Trafton *sculptor*

Bainbridge Island
Burns, Shirley MacDonald *artist, educator*
Carlson, Robert Michael *artist*

Bellevue
Johnson, Lynn Barbara *artist, civic worker*
Lisaius, Frederic Albert *artist*

Burton
Dyer, Carolyn Price *artist, writer*

Lilliwaup
McGrady, Corinne Young *design company executive*

Olympia
Haseltine, James Lewis *artist, consultant*
Randlett, Mary Willis *photographer*

Pullman
Pavel, D. Michael *art educator*

Redmond
Yan, Jingyu *computer graphics designer*

Seattle
De Alessi, Ross Alan *lighting designer*
Feldman, Roger Lawrence *artist, educator*
Gardiner, T(homas) Michael *artist*
Leavens, Ileana Beatriz *art educator*
Lundin, Norman Kent *artist, educator*
Reeves, Joan Hutchins *painter*
Spafford, Michael Charles *artist*
Stearns, Susan Tracey *lighting design company executive, lawyer*
Tift, Mary Louise *artist*
Tomas, Alejandro *photographer*

Silverdale
Shaw, Annita Louise *art educator*

Spokane
Kostelec, William A. *photographer, educator*

Walla Walla
Rasmussen, Lisa Anne *art educator, department chairman, gallery director*

WEST VIRGINIA

Wheeling
Peace, Bernie Kinzel *art educator, artist*
Phillis, Marilyn Hughey *artist*

WISCONSIN

Brookfield
Vierthaler, Bonnie Louise *artist, educator*

Green Bay
Grosso, Cheryl Ann *art educator*
Malloy, Kaoime Elin *costume designer, educator*

Hartland
Stamsta, Jean F. *artist*

Hollandale
Colescott, Warrington Wickham *artist, printmaker, educator*

Janesville
Detert-Moriarty, Judith Anne *graphic designer, educator, volunteer*

Johnson Creek
Braunschweig, Cynthia S. *art educator*

Kenosha
Robinson-Gustin, Brenda Sue *retired art educator, painter*

La Crosse
Clark, Malcolm Gene, Sr. *artist, consultant, historian*

Madison
Cooper, Peggy (Mary Margaret) *artist, educator*
Dale, Thomas Ernest Abell *art educator*

Mc Naughton
Bradshaw, Glenn Raymond *art educator*

Middleton
Sweet, Harvey *set and lighting designer*

Milwaukee
Farrell, Patrick *artist*
Guse, Christopher J. *art educator*
Thrall, Arthur Alvin *artist, educator*

Mount Horeb
Becker, David *artist, retired educator*

Oconomowoc
Conrader, Constance Ruth *artist, writer*

Racine
Sahakian, Lillian Zarouhi *artist, designer*

Reedsburg
Mockler, Jolee Marie *art educator*

Stevens Point
Smith, David Lyle *artist, educator*

Wausau
Loftus, Stephen Edward *elementary art educator*

WYOMING

Cheyenne
Moore, Mary French (Muffy) *potter, advocate*

Cody
Jackson, Harry Andrew *artist*

Laramie
Reif, (Frank) David *artist, educator*

TERRITORIES OF THE UNITED STATES

GUAM

Hagatna
Flores, Christina Rosalie *art educator*

CANADA

BRITISH COLUMBIA

Cowichan Station
Grauer, Sherrard *artist*

Salt Spring Island
Raginsky, Nina *artist*

Vancouver
Bonifacho, Bratsa *artist*

MANITOBA

Winnipeg
Eyre, Ivan *artist*

NEWFOUNDLAND AND LABRADOR

Torbay
Dabinett, Diana Frances *artist*

NOVA SCOTIA

Bayfield
Blair, Rosemary Miles *retired art educator, environmentalist*

Halifax
Kulyk, Karen Gay *artist*

ONTARIO

Peterborough
Dumas, Michael Godfrey Joseph *artist*

Scarborough
Cetín, Anton *artist*

Toronto
Astman, Barbara Ann *artist, educator*
Elder, Richard Bruce *artist, writer*
Jaworska, Tamara *artist*
Kramer, Burton *graphics designer, artist, educator*
Semak, Michael William *photographer, educator*

Waterloo
Urquhart, Tony *artist, educator*

QUEBEC

Beaconsfield
Harder, Rolf Peter *graphic designer, painter*

Montreal
Charney, Melvin *artist, architect, educator*

SASKATCHEWAN

Saskatoon
Bornstein, Eli *artist, sculptor*

MEXICO

Mexico City
De La Riva, Myriam Ann *artist*
Mendelejis, Leonardo Nierman *artist*

AUSTRALIA

Malanda
Cooper, William Thomas *natural history artist*

ENGLAND

London
Armstrong-Jones, Antony Earl (Antony Charles Robert Armstrong-Jones, 1st Earl of Snowdon) *photographer, writer*
Bailey, Christopher *apparel designer*
Fisher, Rick *lighting designer*
Hatley, Tim *set designer, costume designer*
Swarovski, Nadja *apparel designer*

Richmond
Armfield, Diana Maxwell *artist, educator*

FRANCE

Malaucene Vaucluse
Langenkamp, Mary Alice (M.A. Langenkamp) *artist, educator*

Paris
Alaïa, Azzedine *fashion designer*
Cardin, Pierre *fashion designer*
Elbaz, Alber *apparel designer*
Gaultier, Jean-Paul *fashion designer*
Lacroix, Christian Marie Marc *fashion designer*
Lagerfeld, Karl Otto *fashion designer*
Piza, Arthur Luiz *painter*
Renouf, Edda *artist*
Ross, Charles *artist*
Terry, Sara *photographer, reporter*

Saint Ceols
Saisselin, Remy Gilbert *fine arts educator*

GERMANY

Alstadt
Richter, Gerhard *artist*

Berlin
Jung, Dieter *multimedia artist*

Cologne
Tomaszewski, Christian *artist*

Düsseldorf
Bove, Carol *sculptor*

Frankfurt
Leckey, Mark *artist*

Koln
Lee, Catherine *sculptor, painter*

Potsdam
Flick, Friedrich Christian *art collector*

GREECE

Athens
Tsalamata, Vicky Dimitrios *artist, educator, painter, printmaker*

ISRAEL

Jerusalem
Menses, Jan *artist, draftsman, muralist*

ITALY

Bergamo
Donizetti, Mario *painter, essayist*

Florence
Cecil, Charles Harkless *artist, educator*
Giannini, Frida *apparel designer*

Milan
Cavalli, Roberto *fashion designer*
Dolce, Domenico *fashion designer*
Gabbana, Stefano *fashion designer*
Honegger, Federico *artist*
Prada, Miuccia Bianca *fashion designer*
Versace, Donatella *fashion designer*

Turin
Rizzi, Gianfranco *artist*

Venice
Tagliapietra, Lino *glass artist*

JAPAN

Osaka
Yamada, Kohei *retired art educator*

MONACO

Charlotte
Vicari, Andrew *artist*

NETHERLANDS

Amsterdam
Sawyer, Errol *photographer*

PAKISTAN

Lahore
Geoffrey, Iqbal (Mohammed Jawaid Iqbal Jafree) *artist, educator, lawyer, department chair, consultant*

SPAIN

Seville
Sanchez, Leonedes Monarrize Worthington (His Royal Highness Duke de Leonedes of Spain Sicily Greece) *fashion designer*

SWITZERLAND

Vandoeuvres
Ortiz, George *artist*

TUNISIA

Carthage
Sehili, Mahmoud *artist*

ADDRESS UNPUBLISHED

Abbe, Elfriede Martha *sculptor, graphics designer*
Abbett, Robert Kennedy *artist, writer*
Abel, Barbara Ellen *photographer*
Abeles, Kim Victoria *artist*
Aldredge, Theoni Vachliotis *costume designer*
Alexandra, Allison Melissa *artist, writer, educator*
Ancona, George Efrain *photographer, author*
Anderson, Laurie *experimental performance artist, musician*
Anderson, Lisa D. *graphics designer, educator*
Andersson, Helen Demitrous *artist*
Andrews, Marion E. *artist, calligrapher*
Andruk, Marjorie Dean *artist, educator*
Annus, John Augustus *artist*
Armstrong, L. C. *artist*
Arndt, Dianne Joy *artist, photographer*
Arrigo, Jan Elizabeth *photographer, writer, artist*
Arrott, Patricia Graham *artist, educator*
Asato, Evan Masami *artist, architect, designer*
Aschheim, Eve Michele *artist, educator*
Avery, Carolyn Elizabeth *artist*
Baab-Hohman, Roberta (Robin) *artist, writer, stage manager*
Baca, Vera Jennie Schulte *art educator*
Balisle, Jenny E. *artist*
Ball, Cathi Rosanne *art educator*
Bangalore Prakash, Somashekar *Senior design Engineer*
Barkan-Clarke, Jacqueline Mia *author, jewelry designer*
Barlowe, Dorothea *art educator, illustrator*
Barnes, Robert Vincent *retired elementary and secondary school art educator*
Barrow, Thomas Francis *artist, educator*
Barth, Frances *artist*
Bateman, Robert McLellan *artist*
Behr, Marion Ray *artist*
Bell, Larry Stuart *artist*
Beltran, Felix *graphic designer*
Bennett, Barbara Virginia *fashion consultant, concert pianist*
Berkowitz, Henry *artist*
Berman, Michael P. *photographer*
Bingham, Marian *artist, printmaker*
Binkley, Howell *lighting designer*
Binkley, Timothy *computer graphics designer, educator*
Blackwell, Lois Moore *fashion designer, educator, visual artist*
Blue, China *artist*
Bohrman, Catherine Leuchs *sculptor*
Bond, Rose *artist, educator*
Booth, Catherine Kate Mary *art educator*
Bowman, Leah *retired fashion designer, educator consultant*
Boyce, Martha Jo *artist, educator*
Broderick, James Allen *painter, educator*
Brodeur, Catherine Reckart *artist*
Brodzik, Lester Leonard *artist, retired occupational therapist*
Bronkar, Eunice Dunalee *artist, educator*
Brooks, Deborah June *art educator*
Brown, Alice Elste *artist*
Brown, William Ferdinand *artist, writer*
Buist, Kathy *artist*
Burrows, Donald Albert *artist, painter, photographer*
Burtley, Calvin *art director*
Byrd, Marc Robert *floral designer*
Cabot, Hugh III *painter, sculptor*
Calabrese, Karen Ann *artist, educator*
Callaham, Jeffery *artist*
Cardoso, Anthony Antonio *artist, educator*
Cariola, Robert Joseph *artist*
Carlyle, Bobbie Kristine *sculptor*
Carone, Nicolas *artist*
Carpenter, Pearl Elizabeth *artist*
Carr, Winifred Walker *artist, historian*
Carraher, Mary Lou Carter *art educator*
Carroll, M(argaret) Lizbeth Carr *art educator, graphics designer, photographer*
Carter, Nanette Carolyn *artist*
Casanova, Aldo John *sculptor*
Case, Reginald *artist*

Celentano, Francis Michael *artist, educator*
Challis, Richard Bracebridge *art dealer, educator*
Chambers, Elenora Strasel *artist*
Chance, F. Earlayne *artist, genealogist*
Chisman, Amy Elynn *lighting designer, educator*
Chun, Jacqueline Clibbett *artist, educator*
Chung, Doo-ri *apparel designer*
Churchill, Myla *art educator, writer*
Churchill, Stephen Perry *graphic designer*
Cicero, Carmen Louis *artist, educator*
Cleary, Manon Catherine *artist, retired educator*
Cobb, Virginia Horton *artist, educator*
Cohen, Margaret Ann *artist, consultant*
Colker, Edward *artist, educator*
Collins, Lois M. Rylander *artist*
Conroy, Tamara Boks *artist, retired special education educator*
Cooper, Elva June *artist*
Cooper, Rebecca *art dealer*
Cornish, Randall *educator, graphic artist*
Corry, Aline Lahusen *art educator*
Coughlin, Jack *printmaker, sculptor, art educator*
Coulter, Stephanie Michelle Benedict *photographer, sales consultant*
Court, Iain Maxwell *lighting designer*
Cowles, Charles *art dealer*
Craik, Mary Bernice *artist, art gallery owner*
Crawford, Peggy (Margaret Elizabeth Frank Crawford) *photographer*
Cretara, Domenic Anthony *artist, educator*
Crinklaw, Katherine Mary *artist*
Crocker, Suzanne *painter*
Crowder, Mary Ellen *artist, educator, photographer, real estate broker*
Cumming, Robert Hugh *artist, photographer*
Cummings, David William *artist, retired educator*
Cunningham, Kathy *artist, art educator*
Currie, Steven Ray *artist*
Curtis, Thomas Pelham, II, *artist, educator, small business owner*
Curvin, Peggy *freelance/self-employed photographer*
Dahse, Kenneth William *photographer, writer, educator*
D'Alessio, Valaida Corrine *artist, consultant*
Daley, Sandra *retired artist, filmmaker, photographer*
Damsgaard, Patricia Rae *artist, educator*
Dangremond, David W. *art history educator*
Dani, (Shirley Leyrer) *sculptor, painter*
Danne, Richard Franklin *graphic designer*
Deakins, Roger Alexander *photographer, cinematographer*
De Blasi, Tony (Anthony Armando De Blasi) *artist*
Dechar, Peter Henry *artist*
Deems, Sherran Ellen (Sherry) *artist, educator, editor*
Derber, Dana M. *graphic and web designer*
Despot, Shirley Ann *artist*
Di Giacomo, Fran *artist*
Dill, Laddie John *artist*
Dogançay, Burhan C. *artist, photographer, sculptor*
Downes, Rackstraw *artist*
Doyle, Tom *sculptor*
Dryden, Stephen David *artist, product designer*
Dubs, Gloria L. *artist, realtor*
Easterson, Sam *artist*
Eddy, Don *artist*
Edelson, Mary Beth *artist, educator*
Edmo, Jean Umiokalani *artist, poet*
Egas, Eric *artist*
Engelman, Rosalyn Ackerman *artist*
Engels, Beatrice Ann *artist, poet, retired real estate company executive*
Ewald, Roberta Grant *artist, writer*
Fabricatore, Carol Diane *artist, educator*
Farrar, Elaine Willardson *artist*
Fasman, Marjorie Lesser *artist, writer*
Feiler, Jo Alison *artist*
Fields, Ruth Peedin *artist*
Fields, Tina Rae *artist, ecopsychologist*
Fillmore, John Dillon *artist*
Finkelstein, Richard *set designer, educator*
Finley, Harry *artist, museum director*
Fish, Janet Isobel *artist*
Fishman, Harriet J. *artist, educator, writer*
Fitzgerald, Joan V. *artist*
Flato, Gwyndolynn Sue *fine art educator*
Flavin, Sonja *artist*
Flowers-Schoen, Marylu Utley *art educator*
Ford, Tom *apparel designer and executive*
Frame, Robert M. *lighting designer, theater director*
Francis, Karen *painter, television producer, writer*
Frauenhoffer, Rose Marie *visual artist*
Frehm, Lynne *artist, painter*
Freilicher, Jane *artist*
Freyermuth, Virginia Karen *art educator*
Frudakis, Zenos Antonios *sculptor, artist*
Fumagalli, Barbara Merrill *artist, printmaker*
Gamache, Claudette Theresa *artist, nurse*
Gamble, Desirata *artist, poet*
Garcia, Luis Fernando *photographer*
Gardner, Elizabeth Ann Hunt *artist, poet, genealogist*
Gechtoff, Sonia *artist*
Gilbert, Sandee R. *art educator*
Giles, Patricia Cecelia Parker *retired art educator, graphic designer*
Gim, Dong-Woo *display designer*
Girman, Dee-Marie *retired artist, singer*
Glasson, Lloyd *sculptor, educator*
Goddard, Janet Sniffin *artist*
Golden, Judith Greene *artist, educator*
Goldstein, Carl *art educator*
Good, Brenton Earl *art educator, artist*
Goodnough, Robert Arthur *artist*
Goodyear, John L. *artist, educator*
Gordon, Lonny Joseph *artist, educator, dean*
Goreniuc, Mircea C. Paul *sculptor*
Goss, Jerome Eldon *craftsman, retired cardiologist*
Goulet, Lorrie *sculptor*
Grabowski, Tom *art educator*
Greenberg, Albert *art director*
Greiner, William Donald *artist*
Greve-Carroll, Marie-Jean *artist, retired educator*
Grossman, Barbara *artist, educator*
Gruen, Shirley Schanen *artist*
Gussow, Sue Ferguson *artist, educator, writer*
Haenlein, Nathan *art educator*
Hahn, Walter Humphrey *artist, educator, consultant*
Hall, Susan Laurel *artist, educator, writer*
Hammond, Mary Sayer *art educator*
Han, Nong *artist, sculptor, painter*
Hanawalt, Christina Ann *art educator*
Hancock, Patricia Ann *artist*
Handler, Lowell Stuart *photographer, educator*
Hannaman, Alberta Anna *artist*
Harman, Maryann Whittemore *artist, educator*
Hayes, David Vincent *sculptor*
Hector-Skinner, Vicki L. *artist*
Heginbotham, Jan Sturza *sculptor*
Heiss, Mary Wynne *artist*
Hendricks, James Powell *artist*
Henes, Donna *ceremonial artist, writer*
Henry, Dale *artist*
Hepper, Carol *artist, educator*
Herley, Daveen Dorothy *artist, educator*
Hersey, David Kenneth *theatrical lighting designer*
Herzberg, Thomas *artist, educator, illustrator*
Hilton, Nicky (Nicholai Olivia Hilton) *apparel designer*
Hindman, Leslie Susan *auction company executive*
Hoffman, Franklin Thomas *artist, printmaker, retired army officer*
Hogle, Ann Meilstrup *painter, art educator*
Holden, Donald *artist, writer*
Hopkins, Lisa Ann *multimedia designer, educator*
Horlick, Ruth *photographer*
Hsieh, Tsui-Hsia *artist, educator*
Huber, Colleen Adlene *artist*
Huffington, Anita *sculptor*
Hummel, Marian *retired art educator, photographer*
Huo, Bonnie Kwan *artist*
Jackoboice, Sandra Kay *artist*
Jackson-Vanier, Linda M. *retired art educator, counselor*
Jacoby, Beverly Schreiber *art consultant*
Jacoud, Adriana *art director*
Jamison, Philip *artist*
Jansen, Angela Bing *artist, educator*
Jay, Norma Joyce *artist*
Jessen, Shirley Agnes *artist*
Jones, Claire Burtchaell *artist, educator, writer*
Josephson, Kenneth Bradley *artist, retired educator*
Jung, Kwan Yee *artist*
Kahn, Susan *artist*
Karasik, Miriyam Beth *artist, musician, writer*
Katz, Natasha *lighting designer*
Kaz, Nathaniel *sculptor*
Kazan, Alexandra Khan *photographer, web designer*
Kearns, James Joseph *artist*
Kehew, George Mansir *artist*
Kehlmann, Robert *artist, critic*
Kehoe, Nita L. *art educator, gallery director*
Kempisty, Michael *artist, writer*
Kenney, Estelle Koval *artist, educator*
Khvost-Vostrikova, Natalia S. *art educator, consultant*
Kind, Joshua B. *retired art history professor*
King, Joy Riemer *art educator, linguist*
Kipniss, Robert *artist*
Kipniss MacDonald, Betty Ann *artist, educator*
Kirsch, Roslyn Ruth *artist, painter, printmaker, educator*
Klearman, Kimberly J. *lighting designer*
Kleiman, Alan Boyd *artist*
Klein, Lynn Ellen *artist*
Koch, Virginia Greenleaf (Virginia M. Greenleaf) *painter*
Kolodziejski, Vinci J. *artist, educator*
Komar, Vitaly *artist*
Kooluris Dobbs, Linda Kia *artist, photographer*
Kraft, Yvette *art educator*
Krulik, Barbara S. *cultural management consultant, curator, writer*
Kwong, Eva *artist, educator*
Kyle, Gene Magerl *merchandise presentation artist*
Ladewig Goodman, Jeanne Margaret *artist*
Lakshmikanthan, Preetham *coponent design engineer*
Landau, Emily Fisher *art collector, foundation administrator*
La Rocca, Isabella *artist, educator*
Lasker, Joseph L. *artist, illustrator*
Lavezzi, John Charles *retired art history educator, archaeologist*
Lear, M. Kathleen *artist, music educator, small business owner*
Lee, Nelda S. *art appraiser, art dealer, film producer*
Leeds, Nancy Brecker *sculptor, lyricist*
Leiber, Gerson August *artist*
Leiber, Judith Maria *designer, manufacturer*
Leipzig, Arthur *photographer, retired educator*
Lembark, Connie Wertheimer *art consultant*
Lent, Michael Stephen *artist, curator*
Levi, Josef Alan *artist*
Levin, Morton D(avid) *artist, printmaker, educator*
Levinson, Riki *art director*
Lewie, Reva Goodwin *artist, educator*
Lewy, Helen Crosby *artist, writer, translator, painter*
Lieberman, Louis (Karl Lieberman) *artist*
Li-lan, *artist*
Liles, Virginia Rembert (Virginia Pitts Rembert) *retired art educator*
Linhares, Judith Yvonne *painter, educator*
Link, Phyllida Korman *artist, educator*
Lintner, Roberta Pompilio *art educator, artist*
Littleton, Harvey Kline *artist*
Liu, Katherine Chang *artist, art educator*
Locklin, Muriel Lucie *artist*
Long, Roger Leonard *artist*
Lorelli, Elvira Mae *artist, art educator*
Loring, John Robbins *artist, writer*
Lo Schiavo, Francesca *set designer*
Lubich, Mark Walter *artist*
Ludwig, Allan Ira *photographer, educator, artist, writer*
Lynd, Phyllis *artist, educator*
MacDevitt, Brian *lighting designer*
MacDonald, Elizabeth Hutton *artist, educator*
Mackenzie, Kendra *art educator*
Magee, Alan *artist*
Magoni, Despo *artist*
Mahmud, Shireen Dianne *photographer*
Mann, Joan Ellona *artist, editor*
Maraldo, Ushana *multimedia designer, artist, photographer, writer*
Marion, John Louis *former fine arts auctioneer and appraiser*
Marks, Roberta Barbara *artist, educator*
Marlowe, Willie *artist, fine arts educator*
Marshall, Terrylynne *art educator, painter, sculptor*
Martyl, (Mrs. Alexander Langsdorf Jr.) *artist*
Marvin-Basta, Laura Lynn *art educator*
Mason, Lois E. (J. Day Mason) *painter, poet, actress, educator*
Mayer, Susan Martin *art educator*
McCurdy, Michael Charles *illustrator, author*
McKay, Renee *artist*
McPeters, Sharon Jenise *artist, writer*
McQuerry, Patricia Ann *painter, retired secondary school educator*
Menefee, Linnea-Norma *antique dealer*
Menicucci, Audrey *artist*
Menna, Sári *artist, educator*
Michelle, Millay Kathleen *sculptor*
Middaugh, Robert Burton *artist*
Middleman, Raoul Fink *artist*
Millea, Thomas Francis *photographer*
Millon, Henry Armand *art educator*
Montgomery, Lani Lynn *art educator*
Morphew, Dorothy Richards-Bassett *artist, real estate broker*
Moseley, April Lowe *artist*
Moser, Barry *artist*
Murphy, Mary Leigh *artist*
Murray, Robert Gray *sculptor*
Myers, Dorothy Roatz *artist*
Nagy, Elizabeth Garver *artist*
Nance, Tony Max-Perry *designer, illustrator*
Neville, Elizabeth Egan *artist, educator*
Newell, Shirley Ann Cecil *retired art dealer, artist*
Newman, Stacey Clarfield *artist, curator*
Nichols, Iris Jean *retired illustrator*
Nix, Patricia *artist*
Noble, Helen Bonner *artist*
Noland, Kenneth Clifton *artist*
Norman, Bobby Don *artist, writer, research scientist*
Novak, Barbara *art history educator*
O'Donnell, Kathleen C. *artist*
Okoshi-Mukai, Sumiye *artist*
Oldenburg, Claes Thure *artist*
Olkinetzky, Sam *artist, educator, retired museum director*
Ortman, George Earl *artist*
Otani, Yuriko L. (Charko) *retired artist*
Paravano, Dino *artist*
Parent, Elizabeth Schiro *costume designer, educator*
Parsons, Ivy *art educator, sculptor, digital and multi media artist*
Paskell, Linda Ruth *art educator, photojournalist*
Paul, Arthur *artist, illustrator, graphics designer*
Paulsen, Brian Oliver *art educator, artist*
Payne, Barbara Ann *artist, educator*
Peckham, Ellen *artist, poet*
Perez, Suzanne *art educator, consultant*
Peterson, Martha *artist*
Phelan, Stephanie Ellen *artist, graphics designer*
Pierce, Hilda (Hilda Herta Harmel) *painter*
Pietrocarlo, Nick *artist, consultant, information technology director*
Pisano, Linda Maureen *costume designer, educator*
Pliskin, Berenice Rita Chaplan *artist*
Plummer, Anita Ellescas *artist*
Pollard, Kate *photographer, art educator*
Pope, Ingrid Bloomquist *sculptor, poet, painter*
Posner, Kenneth *lighting designer*
Potsic, Amie Sharon *photographer, artist, educator*
Powell-Hunt, Sue Rose *art educator*
Powers, Joan *artist, photographer, educator*
Pozzatti, Rudy Otto *artist*
Preciado, Pamela *artist*
Presniakov, Alexander *artist, sculptor, inventor, writer*
Provensen, Alice *artist, writer*
Pullman, Jennifer King *artist, educator*
Puryear, Martin *artist, educator*
Qian, Zifen *artist, editor-in-chief*
Rand, Calvin Gordon *art educator, consultant*
Rankin, Scott David *artist, educator*
Recht, Ray *set designer*
Reed, Angelica Denise *sculptor, writer, illustrator*
Reid, Geraldine Wold (Geraldine Reid Skjervold) *retired artist*
Reinoehl, Richard Louis *artist, scholar, martial artist*
Reiter, Brandt *artist*
Rendich, Ana *painter, collage artist*
Rendl-Marcus, Mildred *artist, economist*
Reynolds, Patricia Ellen *artist*
Reynolds, Robert *artist, educator*
Riccio, Cira *art educator*
Richards, Patricia Jones *artist, poet, musician, composer*
Riffenburgh, Gerrye H. *artist, educator*
Ring, Nancy Gail *artist, educator, writer*
Robbins, Christiane Patricia *media director, artist, designer, educator*
Roberts, Marilyn Gottlieb *artist, educator*
Roberts, Suzanne Catherine *artist*
Robertson, David Stuart *art educator*
Robinson, Paula LeKatz *artist*
Robinson, Sara Curtis *arts administrator*
Roche, Pauline Jennifer *artist*
Rockburne, Dorothea Grace *artist*
Rose, Patricia *artist, educator*
Rothschild, Jennifer Ann *artist, educator*
Rubello, David Jerome *artist*
Rubin, Sandra Mendelsohn *artist*
Rubinstein, Eva (Anna) *photographer*
Rush, Julia Ann Halloran (Mrs. Richard Henry Rush) *artist, writer*
Rushforth, Ann Fay *artist, educator*
Safren, Cheryl *artist, educator*
Saks, Judith-Ann *artist*
San Miguel, Manuel *painter, historian, composer, poet*
Sass, Mary Martha *freelance writer, artist*
Savenor, Betty Carmell *painter, printmaker*
Scharf, William *artist*
Schiff, Jeffrey Allen *environmental sculptor, educator*
Schiff, Molly Jeanette *artist, researcher*
Schmalz, Carl Nelson, Jr. *artist, educator, art historian, printmaker*
Schmitz, Barbara *art preservationist*
Schnackenberg, Roy Lee *artist*
Schneider, Gisela *art educator*
Schulzke, Margot Seymour *artist, author, educator*
Schur, Lucille S. *artist*
Schwab, Judith *artist, sculptor, curator, educator*
Schwartz, Daniel Bennett *artist*
Schwartz, Lillian Feldman *artist, filmmaker, critic, nurse, writer*
Schwebel, Renata Manasse *sculptor*
Scotland, S. J. (Susan Rose Scotland) *artist, educator*
Seawell, Thomas Robert *artist, retired educator*
Seay, Charlotte J. *artist*
Sehring, Adolf *artist, sculptor*
Sennema, David Carl *arts consultant*
Sharp, Anne Catherine *artist, educator*
Shaw, Diane *artist, educator*
Sheesley, Mary Frank *art educator*
Shemesh, Lorraine R. *painter*
Sherbell-Na, Rhoda *artist, sculptor*
Sheridan, Sonia Landy *artist, retired educator*
Sherwood, Gloria N. *graphics designer, genealogist, small business owner*
Shulman, Mildred *artist*
Simons, Anneke Prins *artist, educator*
Sindler, Brian Paul *artist*
Sirna, Gail Carolyn *artist, educator, writer*
Sissman, Liron *artist, painter*
Sittig, James Christopher *art dealer, painter, sculptor, landscape artist, poet*
Smith, Kathryn Lee *artist, educator*
Smith, Leonore Rae *artist*
Smith, Patricia Lynne *artist*
Smits, Kathleen Curran *artist, educator*
Snyder, Joan *painter*
Sorel, Edward *artist*
Sparrow, Alison Kidder *painter, sculptor*
Spence, Andrew *artist, painter*
Spero, Nancy *artist*
Squier, Jack Leslie *sculptor, retired art educator*
Squires, Nina Grace *artist*
Stanley, Robert Anthony *artist, educator*
Starr, Steven Dawson *photographer*
Sterne, Hedda *artist*
Stevens, May *artist*
Stinsmuehlen-Amend, Susan *artist*
Strawn, Evelyn Rae *artist*
Strider, Marjorie Virginia *artist, educator*
Strong-Cuevas, Elizabeth *sculptor*
Stuart, Sherry Blanchard *artist*
Stubbs, Lu *sculptor, educator*
Sullam, JoAnne D. *environmental artist*
Sullivan, Mary Ann *artist*
Summers, Carol *artist*
Sze, Sarah *sculptor*
Tarasiewicz, Tamara *painter*
Tasse, Marie Jeanne *retired art educator*
Taylor, Nellie Ruby *artist, author, dramatist, director, producer, host, poet, singer, filmmaker*
Thurston, Jacqueline Beverly *retired artist, writer, educator*
Torres, Rudy Arnold *artist*
Torrez, Michelle Marie *artist, educator*
Toth, Myra Bernstein *artist, educator*
Trelles, Ana *art educator*
Tsai, Wen-Ying *sculptor, painter, engineer*
Tse, Stephen *artist, educator*
Turner, Bonese Collins *artist, educator*
Ullberg, Kent Jean *sculptor*
Valentino, (Valentino Garavani) *retired fashion designer*
Vann, David James *author, professor*
Vayanian, Solara Zakeli *artist, educator, researcher*
Vernazza, Trish Brown (Trish Eileen Brown) *visual artist, art therapist, sculptor, psychotherapist*
Versch, Esther Marie *artist*
Vespa, Ned Angelo *photographer*
Villoch, Kelly Carney *art director*
Volpe, Doris *artist*
von Furstenberg, Diane *fashion designer, writer, entrepreneur*
Von Mayrhauser, Jennifer *costume designer*
Voytek, Mary Sullivan *sculptor*
Wachtman, Jeanette Marie *art educator, artist, writer*
Walker, Bernice Baker *artist*
Wallace, Teresa Lynn *art educator*
Walsh, Nan *artist, painter, sculptor, consultant*
Walters, Jerry B. *retired art educator*
Walters, Sylvia Solochek *art educator*
Waltner, Beverly Ruland *artist*
Walton, Anthony John (Tony Walton) *set and costume designer, illustrator, writer*
Warren, Alice Louise *artist*
Weber, Idelle *artist, educator*
Weiss, Nancy Passman *artist*
Wenglowski, Joyce *painter*
Wesley, John E. *photographer, educator*
West, Mildred Marie *art educator*
Westbie, Barbara Jane *retired graphics designer*
Westerman, Donna Day *artist*
Wexler, Sandra M. *artist, medical illustrator*
White, Tayloe McDonald *artist*
White, Yonsenia S. *artist, educator*
Willenbecher, John *artist*
Williams, Michael Shadden *art director*
Wilson, Jane *artist*
Wilson, Stanley Charles *artist, educator, curator, art gallery director, consultant*
Winter, Roger Jay *artist*
Wolpert Richard, Chava *artist*
Wright, Joan L. *artist*
Wyatt, Marcia Jean *fine arts and speech educator, administrative assistant*
Yantz, Patricia E. *art educator*
Youens, Rachel P. *painter*
Zapf, Hermann *book and type designer*

Zekman, Terri Margaret *graphic designer*
Zeleny, Ann Douglas *sculptor*
Zelinsky, Paul O. *illustrator, artist, writer*
Zhao, Hongbin *artist*
Zoe, Rachel (Rachel Zoe Rosenzweig) *fashion stylist*

ASSOCIATIONS AND ORGANIZATIONS *See also* specific fields

UNITED STATES

ALABAMA

Auburn
Turnham, Joe (Joseph R. Turnham) *political organization administrator*

Birmingham
Carter, Frances Tunnell (Fran Carter) *fraternal organization administrator*
Diasio, Ilse Wolfartsberger *volunteer*
Gross, Iris Lee *not-for-profit association executive*

Mobile
Spechalske, Frank Herman *retired educational administrator*

Montevallo
Seagle, Mary Jane *educational association administrator*

Selma
Calhoun-Bates, Carolyn E. *social services administrator*

Tuscaloosa
Jemison, Sandra J. *educational association administrator, educator*

ALASKA

Anchorage
Higgins, Patti Carolyn *political organization administrator*
Ruedrich, Randy *political organization administrator*

Juneau
Smith, Charles Anthony *foundation administrator, director*

ARIZONA

Cottonwood
Groseta, Andy (Peter Andrew Groseta) *lobbyist*

Phoenix
King, Robert L. *foundation and former academic administrator*
McCain, Cindy (Cindy Lou Hensley McCain) *philanthropist, wholesale distribution executive*
Pullen, Randy *political organization administrator*
Yzaguirre, Raul Humberto *civil rights leader*

Prescott
Garvey, Daniel Edward *foundation administrator, educator*

Scottsdale
Ferree, John Newton, Jr. *fundraising specialist, consultant*
Morrison, James William, Jr. *lobbyist, government agency administrator, consultant*
Wojcik, Martin Henry *not-for-profit executive*

Tubac
Chilcote, Samuel Day, Jr. *trade association administrator*

Tucson
Davenport, Sandra *cultural organization administrator, eldercare specialist*
Grand, Marcia *civic worker*
Harcleroad, Fred Farley *higher education administrator, consultant*
Mikesell, Elizabeth Bremond *foundation administrator*
Mullen, Rod *nonprofit organization executive*
Orr, Ethan *non-profit organization executive*
Riggs, Lew *foundation executive*
Schimberg, Barbara *organizational development consultant*
Thorpe, Jason M. *non-profit organization director*
Tirrell, John Albert *organization executive, consultant*
Walker, Ronald Hugh *foundation administrator*

ARKANSAS

Bentonville
McKenna, Margaret Anne *foundation administrator, former academic administrator*

Fayetteville
Malone, David Roy *public fund consultant retired educational association administrator, director*

Little Rock
Turner, Todd *political organization administrator, lawyer*
Webb, Doyle L. *political organization administrator, former state legislator*

Searcy
Yecke, Cheri Pierson *educational researcher, administrator, policymaker, writer*

CALIFORNIA

Auburn
Miller, Susan L. *social services administrator*

Bakersfield
Huerta, Dolores Clara (Dolores Fernández) *labor union administrator*

Berkeley
Buell, Evangeline Canonizado *advocate*
Green, David *nonprofit organization administrator*
McLaughlin, Sylvia Cranmer *volunteer, environmentalist*
Myers, Miles Alvin *educational association administrator, researcher*
Odermatt, Diana B. *development consultant*

Beverly Hills
Ahmanson, Howard F., Jr. *philanthropist*
Schaff, Manya *foundation administrator*
Sherak, Thomas Mitchell (Tom Sherak) *motion picture association executive*
Siciliano, Rocco Carmine *cultural institute executive*

Burbank
Rawlinson, Joseph Eli *foundation administrator, lawyer*

Canoga Park
Lederer, Marion Irvine *cultural administrator*

Carmel
Bohannon-Kaplan, Margaret Anne *non-profit organization executive, lawyer*

Claremont
Kennedy, Brian T. *think-tank executive*
Stokes, Anne Dorothy *retired educational association administrator*

Covina
Nguyen, Loc H. *social services administrator*

Culver City
Netzel, Paul Arthur *fundraising management executive, consultant*

Danville
Cross, Christopher T. *educational association administrator, consultant*

Davis
Maurer, Frank W., Jr. *land trust administrator*

Emeryville
Penhoet, Edward E. *retired foundation administrator, former biochemicals company executive, former dean*

Encino
Irmas, Audrey Menein *not-for-profit developer*

Fresno
Shmavonian, Gerald S. *political organization administrator*

Fullerton
Sadrudin, Moe *humanitarian organization executive*

Hercules
Tyson, Kathleen Hayhurst *educational association administrator*

Imperial Beach
Gerlach, Murney *foundation administrator, historian, educator*

Irvine
Ahmanson, Roberta Green *philanthropist*
Fulton, Kenneth Ray *professional association administrator*

Keene
Rodriguez, Arturo Salvador *labor union official*

Kentfield
Blum, Joan Kurley *retired fundraising consultant, copy editor and graphics designer*

La Jolla
Davidow, Jeffrey *think-tank executive, former ambassador*

Lafayette
Edwards, Aura C. *political organization worker, volunteer*

Long Beach
Fischler, Sandy Lynn *charitable and informational organization executive*

Los Altos
Larson, Carol S. *foundation administrator, lawyer*

Los Angeles
Barrios, Jarrett Tomas *civils rights organization executive, former state legislator*
Broad, Eli *foundation administrator, art collector*
Daly, Robert Anthony *international relief organization, former professional sports team and film company executive*
Durnil, John Michael *civil rights organization executive*
Glasgow, Istiharoh *art administrator*
Gomez, Diana L. *professional society administrator, engineer*
Lizarraga, David C. *non-profit community development corporation administrator*
Marrow, Deborah *foundation administrator*
Marshall, Mary Jones *civic worker*
Powell, James Lawrence *educational association administrator, museum director, geologist*
Prewitt, Jean *not-for-profit organization executive*
Wood, James Nowell *foundation administrator, retired museum director*

Los Gatos
Allan, Lionel M. *director for-profit and non-profit companies, Legal and Business Advisor*

Marina Del Rey
Stebbins, Gregory Kellogg *foundation executive*

Menlo Park
Altman, Drew E. *foundation executive*
Brest, Paul A. *foundation administrator, law educator*
Collins, Nancy Whisnant *foundation administrator*
Smith, Marshall Savidge *foundation executive*

Mill Valley
Schreyer, Chara *foundation administrator, art collector*

Modesto
Whiteside, Carol Gordon *foundation executive*

Mountain View
Bills, Robert Howard *political party executive*

Newport Beach
Wallis, Mary Camilla *civic leader*

Oakland
Alexander, Stewart A. *political organization worker*
Hargrave, Charles R. *nonprofit organization supervisor*
Macmeeken, John Peebles *foundation executive, educator*
Widener, Mary Lee *non-profit financial executive*

Oxnard
Tolmach, Jane Louise *community activist, municipal official*

Pacific Palisades
Caster, Jacqueline Jacobs *not-for-profit executive*
Hubbs, Donald Harvey *foundation executive*
Snowhook, Ann Laferty *social services administrator*

Palm Springs
Ellsworth, Frank L. *not-for-profit executive*
Wlaschin, Ken *cultural organization administrator, writer*

Palmdale
Phillips, Ruthanne *special education administrator*

Palo Alto
Bush, Barbara Pierce *not-for-profit executive, volunteer, former first daughter*
McCormick, Steven J. *foundation administrator*
Nichols, William Ford, Jr. *foundation, health science association administrator, educator*
Skoll, Jeffrey S. *philanthropist, former Internet company executive*

Pasadena
Ellner, Carolyn Lipton *non-profit organization executive, dean, consultant*
Staehle, Robert L. *foundation executive*

Penn Valley
McDonald, Douglas Robert *retired non profit agency executive*

Redwood City
Spangler, Nita Reifschneider *volunteer*

Riverside
Peterson, Arthur Laverne *foundation administrator*

Ross
Giovinco, Joseph *non profit agency administrator, writer*

Sacramento
Nehring, Ron *political organization administrator*
Torres, Art *former political organization administrator, former state legislator*

San Diego
Afzali, Abdi *alumni association administrator, infosystems specialist*
Ballinger, Charles Edwin *educational association administrator*
Lane, Gloria Julian *foundation administrator*
McBrayer, Sandra L. *educational director, homeless outreach educator*
Spira, Patricia Goodsitt *retired association executive*
Wallace, Candy *culinary association administrator*

San Francisco
Bereuter, Douglas Kent *foundation administrator, former congressman*
Bitterman, Mary Gayle Foley *foundation executive*
Burton, John L. *political organization administrator, retired state legislator*
Canales, James Earl, Jr. *foundation president*
Dachs, Lauren Bechtel *non-profit organization executive*
Egan, Patricia Jane *foundation administrator, retired director*
Fisher, Martin J. *not-for-profit executive*
Fisher, Robert Morton *foundation and academic administrator*
Foster, Kenneth J. *art association administrator*
Guttentag, Lucas *advocate, lawyer*
Johnson, Chalmers *educational association administrator, retired political science professor*
LaRiva, Gloria *labor union administrator, advocate*
Lehane, Christopher S. *political consultant*
Mattern, Douglas James *think-tank executive*
Mitchell, Theodore Reed *educational association administrator, former academic administrator*
Tripp, Alan H. *educational association administrator, consultant*

San Jose
Hutton, Carole Leigh *not-for-profit executive, former newspaper editor*

San Juan Capistrano
Barreto, Hector V., Jr. *not-for-profit organization executive, former federal agency administrator*

San Luis Obispo
Jamieson, James Bradshaw *foundation administrator*

Santa Barbara
McCoy, Lois Clark *retired social services administrator, county official, editor*
Obern, Vivian Marie Hapeman *volunteer*

Santa Clarita
Boyer, Carl III *not-for-profit developer, retired mayor, municipal official*

Santa Monica
Davis, Paul Kensil *strategic planner*
Milken, Michael R. *think-tank executive, philanthropist*
Rich, Michael David *think-tank executive, lawyer*
Thomson, James Alan *think-tank executive*

Stanford
Bryk, Anthony S. *educational association administrator*
Lyman, Richard Wall *foundation and academic administrator, historian*
Raisian, John *think-tank executive, economist*
Seelig, Tina L. *entrepreneurship program director, educator*
Shulman, Lee S. *former educational association administrator*

Stinson Beach
Metz, Mary Seawell *retired foundation and academic administrator*

Sylmar
Froelich, Beverly Lorraine *foundation administrator*

Turlock
Lee, Virginia Fern *community volunteer*

Woodland Hills
Ross, Robert K. *foundation administrator, physician*

Woodside
Blum, Richard Hosmer Adams *foundation administrator, educator, writer*

Yorba Linda
Stavropoulos, Rose Mary Grant *community activist, volunteer*

COLORADO

Boulder
Hayes, Richard Johnson *association executive, retired lawyer*
Hess, John Warren *professional society administrator*
Sanders, Lucinda (Lucy Sanders) *information technology organization executive*

Centennial
Bryan, A(lonzo) J(ay) *retired service club official*
Lessey, Samuel Kenric, Jr. *foundation administrator*

Colorado Springs
Killian, George Ernest *retired educational association administrator*
Miller, Zoya Dickins *civic worker, consultant*

Denver
Chu, Roderick Gong-Wah *educational association administrator*
Hogan, Curtis Jule *labor union administrator, industrial relations specialist, consultant*
McConnell, John *environmental activist, founder of Earth Day*
Schrenk, Gary Dale *foundation executive*
Waak, Patricia Ann *political organization administrator*
Wimett, Lynn Cathy *educational association administrator, director*

Englewood
Keesling, Ruth Morris *foundation administrator*

Fort Collins
Chappell, Barbara Kelly *retired child welfare consultant*
Eddy, Gladys Louise *retired educational administrator*

Greeley
Bond, Richard Randolph *retired foundation administrator*

Greenwood Village
Neiser, Brent Allen *foundation executive, public affairs and personal finance speaker, consultant*

Wadhams, Richard Ivory (Dick Wadhams) *policitcal organization administrator*

Lakewood
Isely, Henry Philip *association and business executive, integrative engineer, writer, educator*

Littleton
Keogh, Heidi Helen Dake *advocate*

Longmont
Rayback, Cynthia Ann *educational association administrator*

Loveland
Rodman, Alpine C. *arts and crafts company executive, photographer*

Superior
Olatunji, Thabiti Shawki (Reverend Thabiti) *executive director, motivational speaker, advisor, educator*

CONNECTICUT

Avon
Griggs, Julie Hinds *foundation administrator*

Brookfield
Oderwald, Susan *professional society administrator*

Chaplin
Chatel, Regina G. *educational association administrator*

Fairfield
Dorn, Nancy Patricia *lobbyist, former federal official*

Greenwich
Kovner, Kathleen Jane *civic worker, portrait artist*

Groton
Kennedy, Evelyn Siefert *foundation and textiles executive*

Guilford
Stevens, Lydia Hastings *community volunteer*

Hamden
Schwartz, Douglas *public opinion poll director*

Hartford
DiNardo, Nancy *political organization administrator*
Eshoo, Barbara Anne Rudolph *non-profit administrator*
Healy, Christopher *political organization administrator*

New Britain
Stathos, Lifteria K. *retired educational association administrator*

New Haven
Anderson, Carl Albert *fraternal organization administrator, lawyer, dean*
Leo, Martha E. *advocate, counselor*

Newtown
Forger, Robert Durkin *retired professional association administrator*

Riverside
Coulson, Robert *retired professional society administrator, arbitrator, writer*

Trumbull
Norcel, Jacqueline Joyce Casale *educational association administrator*

Waterbury
Harper, Barbara Clara *educational program administrator, counselor*

West Hartford
Einfeldt, Teri Lynn *cultural organization administrator*

Westport
MacCormack, Charles Frederick *international relief organization executive*

Willimantic
Jennings, Julianne *cultural organization administrator*
Peterson, Elizabeth Holly *art association administrator*

Wilton
Kaskell, Peter Howard *professional society administrator, lawyer*

DELAWARE

Lewes
Spence, Sandra *retired trade association administrator*
Warden, Richard Dana *government labor union official*

Wilmington
Baxter, Beverley Veloris *economic association administrator, educator*
Daniello, John D. *political organization administrator*
Emmert, Richard Eugene *retired industrial and professional association executive*
Ross, Thomas Stuart *political organization administrator*

DISTRICT OF COLUMBIA

Washington
Abbott, Jim (James Anthony Abbott) *advocate, retired professional baseball player*
Able, Edward H. *association executive*
Abrams, David B. *nonprofit organization director, former federal agency administrator*
Ackil, Josh *lobbyist*
Aguillen, Dean *lobbyist*
Allen, Jeanne *educational association administrator*
Allen, Tom (Thomas Hodge Allen) *trade association administrator, former United States Representative from Maine*
Andres, Gary *lobbyist*
Arlook, Ira Arthur *advocate, communications executive*
Arnold, William Edwin *health advocate, consultant*
Ashcroft, John David *lobbyist, law educator, former United States Attorney General*
Atkinson, Robert David *think tank administrator, economic policy analyst*
Ayres, David T. *lobbyist*
Babby, Ellen Reisman *educational association executive*
Bailey, Pamela Giles *trade association administrator*
Baker, Richard Hugh *lobbyist, former congressman*
Balcombe, Jonathan Peter *animal advocate*
Ball, William Lockhart III *lobbyist, former civilian military employee*
Barno, David W. *think-tank executive, retired military officer*
Bartlett, Doyle *lobbyist*
Baskerville, Lezli *educational association administrator*
Beddow, Thomas F. *lobbyist*
Bender, David Ray *retired library association executive*
Bentsen, Kenneth E., Jr. *lobbyist, former United States Representative from Texas*
Berman, Michael S. *lobbyist, lawyer*
Berman, Wayne L. *lobbyist*
Bernardi, Roy A. (Romolo Albert Bernardi) *lobbyist, former federal agency administrator*
Bernthal, Frederick Michael *research association executive*
Betancourt Lopez, Antonio L. *association executive*
Blackwill, Robert Dean *lobbyist, former federal agency administrator*
Blunt, Matt (Matthew Roy Blunt) *lobbyist, former Governor of Missouri*
Boaz, David Douglas *foundation executive*
Bockorny, David A. *lobbyist*
Boggs, George Robert *educational association administrator*
Boggs, Thomas Hale, Jr. *lobbyist, lawyer*
Bonds, Anita *political organization administrator*
Bonosaro, Carol Alessandra *professional society and retired federal agency administrator*
Booker, Salih *human rights organization executive*
Borg, Joseph Philip *securities association administrator, lawyer*
Boston, Daniel T. *lobbyist*
Brain, Charles M. (Chuck Brain) *lobbyist*
Broad, Molly Corbett (Margaret Corbett Broad) *educational association administrator*
Brobeck, Stephen James *consumer advocate*
Brooks, Arthur C. *think-tank executive*
Brosnan, Carol Raphael Sarah *retired art association administrator*
Buis, Tom (Thomas Paul Buis) *alternative energy advocate, former labor union administrator*
Burger, Anna B. *labor union administrator*
Burrus, William Henry *labor union administrator*
Calingaert, Michael *non-profit organization executive*
Carmen, David M. *lobbyist*
Cassidy, Gerald *lobbyist, lawyer*
Castagnetti, David A. *lobbyist, political strategist*
Chadwick, Kirsten Ardleigh *lobbyist*
Chamberlin, Wendy J. *think-tank executive, former ambassador*
Champlin, Steven M. *lobbyist*
Chan, Wing-Chi *cultural consultant and organization administrator, musicologist*
Chavez-Thompson, Linda *political organization administrator, retired labor union administrator*
Chocola, Chris (Joseph Christopher Chocola) *political organization executive, former United States Representative from Indiana*
Cicerone, Ralph John *foundation administrator, research scientist*
Cino, Maria *political organization administrator, former federal agency administrator*
Cipolla, Vin *foundation administrator, entrepreneur*
Cizik, Rev. Richard L. *lobbyist, minister*
Coffey, Matthew B. *senior advisor to industry*
Cohen, Howard *lobbyist*
Cohen, Larry *labor union administrator*
Cohen, Michael *educational association administrator*
Cole, Lorraine *women's association executive*
Cole, Ray *lobbyist*
Corts, Paul Richard *educational association and former federal agency administrator*
Courson, John A. *lobbyist*
Cramer, Bud (Robert Edward Cramer Jr.) *lobbyist, former United States Representative from Alabama*
Crane, Edward Harrison III *think-tank executive, financial analyst*
Crawford, George C. *lobbyist*
Crawford, Lester Mills, Jr. *scientic consultant, former federal agency administrator*
Crawford, Stephen *think tank manager*
Curris, Constantine William *educational association administrator*
Datri, James Edmund *advertising association executive, lawyer*
Davidson, Jo Ann *political organization administrator, state legislator*
Davis, Lance Alan *foundation administrator, research and development executive, metallurgical engineer*
Day, Mary Louise *volunteer*
Deal, Timothy *association executive, former diplomat*
DeFrancis, Suzanne Cox *international relief organization executive, former federal agency administrator*
DeMuth, Christopher Clay *think-tank executive*
DeWaal, Caroline Smith *education and advocacy organization executive, lawyer*
Diaz, Eduardo *cultural organization administrator*
Dillon, Jennifer O'Malley *political organization administrator*
Dole, Bob (Robert Joseph Dole) *lobbyist, lawyer, retired United States Senator from Kansas*
Donahue, Thomas Reilly *trade union official*
Donatelli, Frank J. *lobbyist, lawyer*
Donohue, Tom J. (Thomas Joseph Donohue) *business association administrator*
Dorn, Jennifer Lynn *professional association executive, former federal agency administrator*
Dorsey, David Byard *non-profit executive*
Downey, Thomas Joseph *lobbyist, former congressman*
Duberstein, Kenneth Marc *lobbyist, former White House chief of staff, management consultant*
Echaveste, Maria *lobbyist, former federal official*
Edelman, Marian Wright *not-for-profit developer, lawyer*
Edwards, Mickey (Marvin Henry Edwards) *think-tank executive, former congressman*
Eisenberg, Pablo Samuel *non-profit organization executive*
Elcano, Mary S. *international non-profit organization executive, lawyer*
Elliott, Thomas Michael *retired association executive, educator, consultant*
Elmendorf, Steven A. *lobbyist*
Emely, Mary Ann *association executive*
Ericsson, Sally Claire *not-for-profit consultant*
Evans, Donald Louis *think-tank executive, former United States Secretary of Commerce*
Everett, Ralph Bernard *think-tank executive*
Farrow, Frank *think-tank executive*
Fazio, Vic (Victor Herbert Fazio Jr.) *lobbyist, lawyer, former congressman*
Ferguson, William, Jr., (Bill Ferguson) *lobbyist*
Feulner, Edwin John, Jr. *think-tank executive*
Finkle, Jeffrey Alan *professional association executive*
Fiorina, Carly (Cara Carleton Sneed Fiorina) *think-tank executive, former computer company executive*
Forkan, Patricia Ann *foundation executive*
Francois, Francis Bernard *retired professional society administrator, lawyer, transportation consultant*
Friedman, Alan Jacob *educational association administrator, former museum director*
Gage, John *labor union administrator*
Gainsborough, Jenni *advocate*
Geduldig, Sam *lobbyist*
George, Warren S. *labor union administrator*
Gerard, Jack N. *trade association administrator*
Germond, Alice Travis *political organization administrator*
Giblin, Vincent J. *labor union administrator*
Gifford, Rufus (John Rufus Gifford) *political organization administrator*
Gillespie, Ed (Edward Walter Gillespie) *lobbyist, former political organization administrator*
Giordano, Nick (Nicholas P. Giordano) *lobbyist*
Goelzer, Daniel Lee *non-profit corporation administrator*
Gold, Martin B. *lobbyist, lawyer*
Gold, Richard M. *lobbyist, lawyer*
Golodner, Jack *labor association official, consultant*
Gradison, Bill (Willis David Gradison Jr.) *non-profit corporation administrator, former United States Representative from Ohio*
Graham, John H., IV, *association executive*
Green, Madeleine F. *educational association administrator*
Griffenhagen, George Bernard *trade association executive*
Griffith, Lanny *lobbyist, lawyer*
Hallman, Linda D. *foundation administrator*
Hamilton, Lee Herbert *think-tank executive, former United States Representative from Indiana*
Hamre, John J. *think-tank executive, former federal agency administrator*
Hansen, Christopher W. *trade association administrator*
Hansen, Joseph T. *labor union administrator*
Harbert, Karen Alderman *think-tank executive, former federal agency administrator*
Harlow, Larry (Bryce Larimore Harlow) *lobbyist, former federal official*
Harris, Leslie *think-tank executive, lawyer*
Harris, Steven Brown *non-profit corporation administrator, lawyer*
Hart, Jack Steven *lobbyist, lawyer, accountant*
Hartley, Gregg L. *lobbyist*
Height, Dorothy I. *former foundation administrator*
Heinz Kerry, Teresa (Maria Teresa Thierstein Simoes-Ferreira) *foundation administrator*
Henke, Tracy Ann *lobbyist, former federal agency administrator*
Hickok, Gene (Eugene Welch Hickok) *lobbyist, former federal agency administrator*
Hill, Edwin D. *labor union administrator*
Hirschmann, Susan B. *lobbyist*
Hodge, Linda M. *former educational association administrator*
Hoffa, James Phillip *labor union administrator*
House, W(illiam) Michael *lobbyist, lawyer*
Howard, Muriel A. *educational association administrator, former academic administrator*
Huang, Margaret *human rights advocate*
Huband, Frank Louis *educational association executive director, electrical engineer, lawyer*
Hughes, Thomas Lowe *foundation executive*
Hunt, Wayne Robert, Sr. *non-profit organization executive*
Iezzi, Carmen K. *trade association administrator, director*
Ignagni, Karen Marie *lobbyist*
Indyk, Martin Sean *think-tank executive, former ambassador*
Insulza, José Miguel *international organization official, former Chilean government official*
Irion, Mark S. *lobbyist, management consultant*
Isaacson, Walter Seff *think-tank executive, writer*
Isakowitz, Mark W. *lobbyist*
Jacobs, Madeleine *professional society administrator, writer*
Jacobson, Michael Faraday *consumer advocate, writer*
Jankowsky, Joel *lobbyist, lawyer*
Jennings, Chris *lobbyist*
Johnson, Joel *lobbyist*
Johnson, Ralph Raymond *lobbyist, retired ambassador*
Jones, Diane Auer *educational association administrator, former federal agency administrator*
Josten, R. Bruce *lobbyist*
Kahn, Charles N., III, (Chip Kahn) *lobbyist*
Kamber, Victor Samuel *political consultant*
Kanner, Marty (Martin B. Kanner) *lobbyist*
Karpinski, Gene Brien *political organization executive*
Katzen, Sally *lobbyist, lawyer, educator*
Kaufman, Ronald C. *lobbyist*
Keelen, Matt *lobbyist*
Keenan, Nancy *pro-choice association executive*
Kelley, Colleen M. *labor union administrator*
Kennedy, Ethel Skakel *philanthropist*
Kies, Kenneth J. *lobbyist, lawyer*
Kilgore, Peter George *trade association executive, lawyer*
Knapp, Richard Maitland *association executive*
Kohr, Howard A. *lobbyist*
Kolb, Charles Chester *foundation administrator*
Kolb, Charles Edward Mealey *think-tank executive, lawyer, former federal offical*
Kreig, Andrew Thomas *trade association executive*
Krenik, Edward D. *lobbyist*
Krumholtz, Jack *lobbyist*
Lane, William C. *lobbyist*
Lawson, Peter H. *lobbyist, automotive executive*
Lee, Gwendolyn B. *educational association administrator*
Lee, Nicole C. *human rights advocate*
Leff, Deborah *foundation administrator*
Lendsey, Jacquelyn L. *foundation administrator*
Leonard, Robert J. *lobbyist*
Levine, Felice J. *educational association administrator*
Limbaugh, Mark A. *lobbyist, former federal agency administrator*
Liu, Michael Minoru Fawn *lobbyist, former federal agency administrator*
Livingston, Bob (Robert Linlithgow Livingston Jr.) *lobbyist, former United States Representative from Louisiana*
London, Herbert Ira *think-tank executive, humanities educator*
Lott, Trent *lobbyist, former United States Senator from Mississippi*
Lowery, Clay *lobbyist, former federal agency administrator*
Lowery, William David (Bill Lowery) *lobbyist, former congressman*
Lujan, Manuel, Jr. *think-tank executive, former United States Secretary of the Interior, retired congressman*
Mack, David L. *think-tank executive, former federal agency administrator*
Maddaloni, Martin J. *retired labor union administrator*
Malcolm, Ellen Reighley *political advocacy association administrator*
Maloney, Drew *lobbyist*
Margo, Adair *art association administrator, art gallery owner*
Marincola, Elizabeth Mark *nonprofit executive*
Marques, Christine Schon *political organization administrator*
Marshall, William III *think-tank executive*
Marvel, Kevin Boyd *professional society administrator, astronomer*
Masters, Edward Eugene *association executive, former foreign service officer*
Mathews, Jessica Tuchman *think-tank executive, former federal official, columnist*
Mattoon, Daniel J. *lobbyist*
Maxwell, Mary Beth *labor advocate*
McBee, Steve *lobbyist*
McCarron, Douglas J. *labor union administrator*
McCormick, Walter Bernard, Jr. *trade association administrator*
McCrery, Jim (James Otis McCrery) *lobbyist, former United States Representative from Louisiana*
McCurdy, David Keith *trade association administrator, former congressman*
McElveen-Hunter, Bonnie *international relief organization executive*
McEntee, Gerald W. *labor union administrator*
McGinnis, Patricia Gwaltney *non-profit organization executive*
McGrath, Raymond J. *lobbyist, former congressman*
McGuire, Jack (John F. McGuire) *international relief organization executive*
Mc Kay, Emily Gantz *civil rights and nonprofit professional*
McKay, Kenneth K. *political organization administrator*
McPherson, Peter (M. Peter McPherson) *educational association administrator, former publishing executive*
McSlarrow, Kyle E. *lobbyist, former federal agency administrator*
McSweeny, Dorothy Pierce *art association administrator*
Mehlman, Bruce P. *lobbyist, lawyer, formal federal agency administrator*
Mercado, Moses C. *lobbyist*
Merrigan, John A. *lobbyist, lawyer*
Meyerson, Adam *foundation administrator*
Michel, Bob (Robert Henry Michel) *lobbyist, former United States Representative from Illinois*

Milligan, Robert S. *business association administrator*
Mishel, Lawrence *think-tank executive, economist, researcher*
Molinari, Susan *lobbyist, former congresswoman*
Monroe, Loren *lobbyist*
Moore, Barbara C. *fraternal organization administrator*
Moore, Dale *lobbyist, former federal agency administrator*
Moore, Gregory T. *civil rights association executive*
Moore, Jacquelyn Cornelia *retired labor union administrator, editor*
Mueller, Sharon Lee (Sherry Mueller) *educational organization executive*
Murguia, Janet *non-profit organization administrator*
Murphy, Gerard Norris *trade association executive*
Nader, Ralph *advocate, lawyer, writer*
Natividad, Irene *women's rights advocate*
Niemeier, Charles D. *non-profit corporation administrator, accountant*
Nunn, Sam (Samuel Augustus Nunn Jr.) *think-tank executive, former United States Senator from Georgia, lawyer*
Oblinger, Diana G. *educational association administrator*
O'Brien, Lawrence Francis, III, (Larry O'Brien) *lobbyist, lawyer*
O'Neill, Terry Anne *feminist organization executive, lawyer*
Ortiz, Manuel *lobbyist*
O'Sullivan, Terence M. *labor union administrator*
Overby, Charles L. *foundation administrator*
Pacelle, Wayne *animal rights organization administrator*
Padilla, Christopher Alan *lobbyist, former federal agency administrator*
Paulson, Kenneth Alan *foundation administrator, former editor-in-chief*
Paxon, Bill (L. William Paxon) *lobbyist, former congressman*
Pearson, Roger *organization executive*
Pelavin, Sol Herbert *research company executive*
Petito, Margaret L. *foundation president*
Pfotenhauer, Kurt Paul *trade association administrator*
Pitts, Jim (James L. Pitts) *lobbyist*
Plattner, Marc Florea *foundation administrator, editor*
Platts, Howard Gregory *cultural organization administrator, non for profit trustee*
Podesta, Heather Miller *lobbyist, lawyer*
Podesta, John David *think-tank executive, law educator, former White House chief of staff*
Podesta, Tony (Anthony T. Podesta) *lobbyist*
Porter, John Edward *lobbyist, lawyer, former congressman*
Porter, Jon Christopher, Sr. *lobbyist, former United States Representative from Nevada*
Portnoy, Elliott Ivan *lobbyist, lawyer*
Prager, Susan Westerberg *educational association administrator, law educator, former academic administrator*
Prioleau, Florence W. *lobbyist, lawyer*
Puryear, Eugene *advocate, writer*
Quinn, Jack (John M. Quinn) *lobbyist, lawyer*
Raben, Robert *lobbyist, lawyer*
Rademaker, Stephen Geoffrey *lobbyist, former federal agency administrator*
Radin, Alex *former association executive, consultant*
Raffaelli, John D. *lobbyist, lawyer*
Rand, A. Barry (Addison Barry Rand) *retirement association executive*
Reger, Lawrence Lee *trade association administrator*
Reinsch, William Alan *association executive, educator*
Reischauer, Robert D. *think-tank executive*
Rice, Louise Allen *fraternal organization administrator, reading educator*
Richardson, Ann Bishop *foundation executive, lawyer*
Riehle, B. Hudson *trade association executive*
Robinson, Sharon Porter *educational association administrator*
Rogan, Elizabeth A. *professional society administrator*
Rogers, Edward Maurice, Jr. *lobbyist, lawyer*
Rolando, Fredric V. *labor union administrator*
Romer, Roy R. *educational association administrator, former Governor of Colorado*
Rosenberg, Simon *think-tank executive*
Rother, John *association executive, lawyer*
Rotherham, Andrew J. *educational association administrator*
Rothkopf, Arthur J. *business association executive*
Ruskin, Robert Sterling *educational association administrator*
Russell, William Joseph *educational association administrator*
Rutherford, Boyd Kevin *political organization administrator, former federal agency administrator*
Ryan, James (Jimmy) *lobbyist, diversified financial services company executive*
Salyer, Stephen Lee *educational program administrator*
Saunders, Harold Henry *foundation administrator*
Scanlon, Terrence Maurice *think-tank executive*
Scheunemann, Randy (Randall J. Scheunemann) *lobbyist*
Schneider, Carol Geary *educational association administrator*
Schofield, Regina Brown *foundation administrator, former federal agency administrator*
Schulman, Melissa A. *lobbyist, former legislative staff member*
Schwartz, Victor Elliot *lobbyist, lawyer, educator*
Selig, William Paul *advocate*
Shackelford, Lottie Holt *political organization administrator*
Sharp, Philip Riley *think-tank executive, former congressman*
Shaw, Rhod *lobbyist*
Shust, Diane Marie *educational association administrator, lawyer, educator*
Sikorski, Gerry *lobbyist, lawyer, former congressman*
Sippel, Serra *advocate*
Slater, Rodney Earl *lobbyist, lawyer, former United States Secretary of Transportation*
Smith, Edward M. *labor union administrator*
Smith, Gordon Harold *lobbyist, former United States Senator from Oregon*
Smith, Jessie P. Dowling *retired social services administrator*
Smith, William S., Jr. *education association administrator*
Solomon, Richard Harvey *think-tank executive*
Splete, Allen Peterjohn *educational association administrator, educator*
Staats, Elmer Boyd *foundation executive, former government official*
Stanton, Matt *lobbyist, beverage company executive*
Steele, Michael S. *political organization administrator, former lieutenant governor*
Stenholm, Charles Walter *lobbyist, former congressman*
Stern, Andrew L. (Andy Stern) *labor union administrator*
Stetson, Jane Watson *political organization administrator*
Stich, Roberta Lynn *not-for-profit fundraiser, social worker*
Stockman, Jennifer Blei *political organization administrator*
Stonesifer, Patty (Patricia Q. Stonesifer) *former foundation administrator*
Stottlemyer, Todd A. *business association executive*
Stuart, Sandi *lobbyist*
Sullivan, Michael J. *lobbyist, former prosecutor*
Sullivan, Michael J. *labor union administrator*
Sundquist, Don *lobbyist, former governor*
Sweeney, John Joseph *labor union administrator*
Swonger, Chris *lobbyist, beverage company executive*
Talbott, Strobe *think-tank executive*
Tanielian, Matt *lobbyist*
Tarplin, Linda E. *lobbyist*
Tarplin, Richard J. *lobbyist, former federal agency administrator*
Tate, Daniel Clyde, Jr. *lobbyist, former legislative aide*
Taylor, Nancy Elizabeth *lobbyist, lawyer*
Tedeschi, George *labor union administrator*
Tharpe, Don I. *foundation administrator*
Theodore, Eustace D. *educational association administrator, consultant*
Tijerino, Jose A. *foundation administrator*
Tobias, Robert Max *labor leader, lawyer*
Tonkin, Leo Sampson *educational association administrator*
Trumka, Richard Louis *labor union administrator*
Utley, Jon Basil *think-tank executive, journalist*
Van Scoyoc, Stu (H. Stewart Van Scoyoc) *lobbyist, lawyer*
Vine, Howard A. *lobbyist, lawyer*
Vogel, Alex N. *lobbyist, lawyer*
Vogel, Jon *political organization executive*
Walker, Robert Smith *lobbyist, former United States Representative from Pennsylvania*
Walsh, James Thomas (Jim Walsh) *lobbyist, former United States Representative from New York*
Walters, John P. *think-tank executive, former federal official*
Warren, David Liles *educational association administrator*
Wartell, Sarah Rosen *think-tank executive*
Washburn, Eric *lobbyist*
Watts, J. C. (Julius Caesar Watts Jr.) *lobbyist, former United States Representative from Oklahoma*
Weaver, Reg(inald) *educational association administrator*
Weber, Vin (John Vincent Weber) *lobbyist, former United States Representative from Minnesota*
Weingarten, Randi *labor union administrator, lawyer*
Weinstein, Kenneth R. *think-tank executive*
Wertheimer, Fredric Michael *public policy advocate*
White, Robert Edward *think-tank executive*
Wilhelm, John W. *labor union administrator*
Wilhoit, Gene *educational association administrator*
Williams, Anthony Allan (Tony Williams) *lobbyist, former mayor*
Williams, Eddie Nathan *retired think-tank executive*
Williams, James A. *labor union administrator*
Williams, Jimmy (James F. M. Williams) *lobbyist*
Wilson, Charles Nesbitt *lobbyist, former United States Representative from Texas*
Wise, Bob (Robert Ellsworth Wise Jr.) *educational association administrator, former governor, congressman*
Wortley, George Cornelius *lobbyist, former United States Representative from New York*
Wynn, Albert Russell *lobbyist, former United States Representative from Maryland*
Yingling, Edward L. *banking association executive*
Young, William H. *labor union administrator*
Zeidman, Fred S. *civic leader, corporate financial executive*

FLORIDA

Boca Raton
Goldstein, Jerome Charles *retired professional society administrator, otolaryngologist, surgeon*
Jessup, Jan Amis *arts volunteer, writer*
Leary, William James *educational association administrator, educator*

Bonita Springs
Liebman, Phyllis Janice *volunteer, educator*

Coral Springs
Autry, Herman Allen, Sr. *lobbyist, writer, music executive*
Burg, Ralph *art association executive*

Delray Beach
Stewart, Patricia Carry *foundation administrator*

Estero
Brown, William Robert *trade association administrator, consultant*

Fort Lauderdale
Crawford, Claire Cressman *volunteer, educator*
Hills, John Merrill *educational association administrator, consultant, public relations executive, researcher*

Gainesville
Gets, Lispbeth Ella *retired educational administrator*

Harbour Heights
Nash, Ruth S. *foundation administrator*

Holmes Beach
Dunne, Nancy Anne *retired social services administrator*

Key Biscayne
Klarreich, Sue Friedman *education administrator, consultant*

Lady Lake
Langevin, Thomas Harvey *retired educational association administrator, consultant*

Lauderdale By The Sea
Wynne, Brian James *retired professional society administrator*

Longboat Key
Dorsey, Eugene Carroll *former foundation and communications executive*

Miami
Cooper, Johnnie Edward, Jr. *advocate*
Culmer, Leome Frances *volunteer*
Fontanals-Cisneros, Ella *art association administrator, information systems specialist*
Garcia, Joe *not-for-profit fundraiser*
Ibarguen, Alberto *foundation administrator, former publishing executive*
Sanchez, Manuel *retired social services administrator, writer*
Tice, Dianne Lisa *social services administrator*

Naples
Caldwell Portenier, Patty Jean Grosskopf *advocate, educator*
Rowe, Herbert Joseph *retired trade association executive*

Okeechobee
Bishop, Sid Glenwood *union official*

Orange Park
Miller, Martin Eugene *management labor negotiator, lobbyist*

Palm Beach
Elson, Suzanne Goodman *social services administrator*
Floeckher, Louise Byrne Weldon *volunteer*
Hope, Margaret Lauten *retired civic worker*
Levine, Audrey Pearlstein *foundation administrator*

Palm Beach Gardens
Falk, Bernard Henry *trade association executive*

Palm Coast
Boyer, Kaye Kittle *association management executive*

Ponte Vedra Beach
Watson, John Lawrence III *former trade association executive*

Port Orange
Collyer, Robert B. *retired trade association administrator*

Sanibel
Ball, Armand Baer *former association executive, consultant*

Sarasota
Culkin, Charles Walker, Jr. *retired trade association administrator*

Tallahassee
Greer, Jim *political organization administrator*
Hammer, Marion Price *association executive*
Stipanovich, John McKager (Mac Stipanovich) *lobbyist, lawyer*
Thurman, Karen L. *political organization administrator, former congresswoman, lobbyist*
Turnbull, Marjorie Reitz *educational consultant, state legislator*

Tampa
Islam, Arif *educational association administrator, researcher*
Schumacher, Margaret Lynn *not-for-profit fundraiser, director*

Vero Beach
Holloman, Marilyn Leona Davis *lobbyist, non profit administrator*
McNamara, Francis Joseph, Jr. *retired foundation executive, lawyer*

GEORGIA

Athens
Algeo, John Thomas *association executive, retired educator*

Atlanta
Anthony, Barbara Cox *foundation administrator*
Bankoff, Joseph R. *art center administrator*
Copenhaver, John Barns *not-for-profit executive, lawyer*
Dotson, Albert *not-for-profit fundraiser*
Everhart, Sue *political organization administrator*
Kidd, Jane V. *political organization administrator, former state legislator*
Miller, Joseph (Buzz) *lobbyist, nuclear energy industry executive*
Spillett, Roxanne *social services administrator*
Tillman, Mary Norman *urban affairs consultant*
Wylly, Barbara Bentley *volunteer*

Decatur
Wheelan, Belle S. *educational association administrator*

Dublin
Clark, Gail Brooks *educational association administrator*

Fayetteville
De Revere, David Wilsen *retired professional society administrator*

Macon
Harvey, James Mathews, Jr. *public relations administrator*

Marietta
Kelly, William Watkins *retired educational association executive*

Peachtree City
Nix, Kemie Richards *educational association administrator, editor*

Saint Simons Island
Bell, Ronald Mack *university foundation administrator, consultant*

Savannah
Thomson, Audrey Shire *volunteer*

Tyrone
Bernard, Sallie *non-profit organization executive*

HAWAII

Honolulu
Hack, Randolph C. *advocate, counselor, educator*
Lee, Willes K. *political organization administrator*
Morrison, Charles Edward *think-tank executive*
Ramler, Siegfried *foundation administrator, researcher*
Robinson, Robert Blacque *foundation administrator*
Schatz, Brian E. *political organization administrator, environmentalist, former state legislator*
White, Emmet, Jr. *retirement community administrator*

IDAHO

Boise
Semanko, Norman M. *political organization administrator*

ILLINOIS

Chicago
Brown, Elizabeth McCarthy *social services administrator*
Browne, Bliss Williams *social welfare administrator*
Byther-Smith, Ida W. *social services administrator*
Cassens Weiss, Debra Sue *professional association administrator, publishing executive*
Craine, Thomas Knowlton *not-for-profit developer*
Dolan, Thomas Christopher *professional society administrator*
Fetridge, Bonnie-Jean Clark *civic volunteer*
Gallucci, Robert Louis *foundation administrator*
Heineman, Natalie *civic worker*
Jackson, Rev. Jesse Louis *civil rights activist, clergyman*
Johnson, Gary Thomas *cultural organization and museum administrator*
Jones, Sharon Elaine *cultural organization administrator, lawyer*
Keenan, Barbara Byrd *professional society administrator*
Kelly, Jerry Bob *social services administrator*
Lenihan, Dermot Patrick *public health administrator*
Lowenkron, Barry Frederick *foundation administrator, former federal agency administrator*
Lurie, Ann LaSalle *foundation administrator*
MacDougal, Gary Edward *corporate board member, foundation trustee*
Minow, Josephine Baskin *civic volunteer*
Olsen, Rex Norman *trade association executive*
Parker, Bonita M. *civil rights organization executive*
Shanahan, Betty *professional society administrator*
Simmons, Adele Smith *foundation executive, former educator*
Thomas, Barbara L. *not-for-profit executive*
Vogelzang, Jeanne Marie *professional society administrator, lawyer*

Crystal Lake
Plinske, Kathleen A. *educational association administrator associate vice president*

Des Plaines
Fortman, Fred J. *professional society administrator*
Sampson, David Allan *insurance association executive, former federal agency administrator*

Evanston
Arrington, Michael Browne *foundation administrator*
Gordon, Julie Peyton *foundation administrator*
Lewis, Charles A. *foundation administrator*
Rielly, John Edward *educational association administrator*
Thrash, Patricia Ann *retired educational association administrator*

Galena
Sipiera, Paul P., Jr. *foundation administrator, retired geology and astronomy professor*

Grayslake
Bronner, Gwethalyn JeTaun *art association administrator, director*

Hazel Crest
Freed, Melvyn Norris *retired educational association administrator, writer*

Jacksonville
Mathews, Jack Sherman *foundation administrator, retired insurance company executive*

Kildeer
Muffoletto, Mary Lu *retired educational association administrator, editor*

La Grange Park
Bradley, Harry A. *professional society administrator*

Lake Barrington
Worrell, Sharyn Dianne Kelley *volunteer, retired flight attendant*

Lake Forest
Morell, William Nelson, Jr. *retired foreign trade association executive, government agency administrator*

Mchenry
Chamberlain, Charles James *railroad labor union executive*

Morton Grove
McKenna, Andrew, Jr. *political organization administrator, printing company executive*

O Fallon
Brown, Jessie Marquita *elementary information specialist*

Oak Brook
John, Richard C. *enterprise development organization executive*

Ottawa
Thornton, Edmund B. *philanthropist*

Park Ridge
Pannke-Smith, Peggy *president*

River Grove
Jeans, Mary Millicent *educational association administrator*

Rock Island
Rafferty, Genevieve Kennedy *social service agency administrator*

Rockford
King-Sturdivant, Constance Maria *social services administrator*

Rosemont
Good, William Allen *professional society executive*

Schaumburg
Tompson, Marian Leonard *professional society administrator*

Springfield
Everingham, Karen E. *museum association administrator*
Khaund, Munindra *educational association administrator*

Sycamore
Stone, Van Courtright *not-for-profit developer*

Wilmette
Brink, Marion Francis *trade association administrator*

INDIANA

Bloomington
Brinkman, Paul Del(bert) *retired foundation administrator, journalist, educator*
Mobley, Tony Allen *foundation administrator, former dean, recreation educator*

Indianapolis
Barcus, Robert Gene *retired educational association administrator*
Braun, Robert Clare *retired association and advertising executive*
Chism, Lauren P. *educational association administrator*
Clark, J. Murray (Murray Clark) *political organization administrator, lawyer*
Everson, Mark Whitty *commissioner*
Finley, Katherine Mandusic *professional society administrator*
Morris, James Thomas *former international organization official*
Parker, Dan J. *political organization administrator*
Robbins, N. Clay *foundation administrator*
Smith, Curt *think tank executive, journalist*
Vereen, Robert Charles *retired trade association administrator*

Lafayette
Scaletta, Helen Marguerite *volunteer*

Newburgh
Saum, Elizabeth Pape *community volunteer*

South Bend
Hunt, Mary Reilly *organization executive*

Terre Haute
Goode, Gregory Justin *lobbyist*

Wabash
Ford, Richard Edwin *volunteer*

West Lafayette
Baumgardt, Billy Ray *professional society administrator, agriculturist*
Murray, Keith *educational association administrator*

IOWA

Ames
Benson, Neala Lawrence *volunteer*

Des Moines
Kiernan, Michael *political organization administrator*
Strawn, Matthew N. *political organization administrator*

Holstein
Soseman, Eleanor Douglass *volunteer*

Iowa City
Croft, Laurie Jane *social services administrator*
Ferguson, Richard L. *educational association administrator*

North Liberty
Brenneman, Tami K. *not-for-profit fundraiser*

KANSAS

Mcpherson
Barber, Carla *museum association administrator*

Shawnee Mission
Gates, Lawrence C. *political organization worker, lawyer*

Topeka
Adkins, Amanda *political organization administrator*
Frahm, Sheila *association executive, academic administrator, former government official*

Wichita
Gable, Wayne E. *lobbyist*

Winfield
Gray, Ina Turner *fraternal organization administrator*

KENTUCKY

Burlington
Kahmann, Sarah Stuber Blanken *retired foundation administrator*

Corbin
Barton-Collings, Nelda Ann *retired political organization worker, bank executive, entrepreneur*

Florence
Gorman, Gayla Marlene Osborne *consumer affairs executive*

Frankfort
Robertson, Steve *political organization administrator*
Williams, Ellen C. *lobbyist, political organization worker*

Lexington
Lewis, Robert Kay, Jr. *fundraising executive*
Sexton, Robert Fenimore *educational organization executive*
Simon, Lisa *travel association executive*

Louisville
Early, Jack Jones *foundation executive*
Yahyaoui, Nasr E. *educational association administrator*

LOUISIANA

Baton Rouge
Breaux, John Berlinger *lobbyist, former senator*
Villere, Roger F., Jr. *political organization administrator*

Mandeville
Landry, Joseph L., Jr. *retired affirmative action specialist*

New Orleans
Sullivan, Daniel Edmond *fundraising executive*

MAINE

Augusta
Gervais, Paul Nelson *foundation administrator, psychotherapist, writer, public relations executive*
Knutson, John *political organization administrator*

Bangor
Coffman, Michael S. *international organization official, ecologist*

Brunswick
Sprague, Edward Auchincloss *retired professional society administrator, economist*

Falmouth
Toomey, Jeanne Elizabeth *animal activist*

Farmington
Webster, Charles M. *political organization administrator*

Georgetown
Chapin, Maryan Fox *civic worker*

York
Smart, Mary-Leigh Call *civic worker*

MARYLAND

Annapolis
Hite, William P. *labor union administrator*
Turnbull, Susan W. *political organization administrator*

Baldwin
Derwart, Gregory M. *non-profit executive*

Baltimore
Brock, Roslyn McCallister *civil rights association executive*
Fuentealba, Victor William *professional society administrator*
Hayes, Dennis Courtland *civil rights association executive, lawyer*
Jealous, Benjamin Todd *civil rights association executive, foundation administrator*
Lazar, John Edward *social services administrator, not-for-profit developer*
Nelson, Douglas W. *foundation administrator*
Saini, Uma Arya *educational association administrator*

Bethesda
Beall, Robert Joseph *foundation executive*
Cassimatis, Emmanuel G. *educational association administrator, psychiatrist, educator*
Cleary, Timothy Finbar *professional society administrator*
Dahlberg, Gregory Robert *lobbyist*
Day, Robert Dwain, Jr. *foundation administrator, lawyer*
Grau, John Michael *trade association executive*
Nelson, Ethelyn Barnett *civic worker*
Reed, Berenice Anne *cultural organization administrator, artist, educator*
Salisbury, Franklin C., Jr. *foundation administrator*
Saunders, Charles Baskerville, Jr. *retired association executive*
Shlaes, John B. *foundation administrator*
Stone, Jeremy Judah *professional society administrator*

Bowie
Littlefield, Roy Everett III *association executive, law educator*

California
Powell, Melchior Daniel *educational administrator, lawyer*

Chevy Chase
Hunt, Frederick Talley Drum, Jr. *association executive*

College Park
Chodos, Alan *professional society administrator*
Hakim, Toufic Maurice *educational association administrator*
Murdoch, Amelia Clara *educational association administrator*

Columbia
Purcell, James Nelson, Jr. *international organization administrator*
Scornaienchi, Joan Webb *educational association administrator, consultant*

Frederick
Gordon, Rita Simon *civic leader, former nurse, educator*

Germantown
Kinniburgh, Alan James *not-for-profit administrator, molecular biologist*

Greenbelt
Matthews, Darryl R., Sr. *not-for-profit fundraiser*

Lanham
Miller, Alwin Vermar *educational association administrator, consultant*

Largo
Ryan, Carol J. *educational administrator*

Mitchellville
Hammer, Jane Amelia Ross *advocate*

Potomac
Keefe, Arthur Thomas III *non-profit fund raising executive*
Rosenberg, Sarah Zacher *retired cultural organization administrator*

Rockville
Kline, Raymond Adam *professional organization executive*
Marcuccio, Phyllis Rose *retired educational association administrator, editor*

Silver Spring
Maddy, Jim *museum association administrator*
Smedley, Lawrence Thomas *retired organization executive*
Stover, Carl Frederick *foundation executive*

Stevenson
DiSalvo, Diane *art administrator, director, curator*

Stevensville
Engel, Bradford Charles *educational association administrator, secondary school educator*

Sykesville
Crist, Gertrude H. *civic worker*
Williams, Alice Noel Tuckerman *retired foundation administrator*

Upper Marlboro
Buffenbarger, R. (Robert) Thomas *labor union administrator*

Waldorf
Raiman, Rosemary A. *advocate*

MASSACHUSETTS

Amherst
MacKnight, Carol Bernier *educational association administrator*

Boston
Cabot, Louis Wellington *foundation trustee*
DiCamillo, Curt Jonathan Gough *non-profit executive*
Gilbert McDonald, Patricia Kelly *director, educational publishing*
Glass, Renée *educational health foundation executive*
Kennedy, Caroline Bouvier (Caroline Bouvier Kennedy Schlossberg) *foundation executive, writer, lawyer*
McGovern, Gail J. *international organization executive, former investment company executive*
Meisner, Mary Jo *foundation administrator, former newspaper editor*
Seitter, Keith L. *professional society administrator, meteorologist*
Simons, D. Brenton *not-for-profit executive*
Walsh, John Edward *political organization administrator, insurance company owner*

Brookfield
Couture, Ronald David *art association administrator, web site designer, consultant*

Cambridge
Berlowitz, Leslie *cultural organization administrator*
Lee, Barbara *political activist, foundation administrator*
White, Shelby *art association administrator*

Chatham
Cogan, Mary Hart *community activist, philanthropist*
Daly, Charles Ulick *foundation executive*

Dorchester
Smith, Survilla Marie *social services administrator, artist, poet*

Framingham
Harrington, Joseph Francis *educational company executive, history educator*

Hull
Anderson, Timothy Christopher *educational association administrator*

Ipswich
Wilson, Doris H. *volunteer*

Lexington
Garing, Ione Davis *civic worker*

Malden
Guild, Richard Samuel *trade association management company executive*
Von Stein, Nicholas *political organization worker*

Milford
Nassour, Jennifer A. *political organization administrator*

Milton
Corcoran, Robert Joseph *fundraising executive*

New Bedford
Bullard, John Kilburn *educational association administrator*

Pittsfield
Wenner, Gene Charles *arts management executive*

Plymouth
Baker, Peggy MacLachlan *cultural organization administrator, museum director*

Quincy
Holway, David J. *labor union administrator*

Revere
Anthony, Sylvia *social welfare organization executive*

Southborough
Warren, John Coolidge *educational administrator*

Wayland
Humphrey, Diana Young *fundraiser*

Westford
Geary, Marie Josephine *art association administrator*

Westwood
Phillips, Marion Grumman *civic volunteer, writer*

MICHIGAN

Ann Arbor
Diana, Joseph A. *retired foundation executive*
Kennedy, David Boyd *foundation executive, lawyer*

Battle Creek
Overton-Adkins, Betty Jean *foundation administrator*
Speirn, Sterling K. *foundation administrator*

Clinton Township
Holland, Ruby Mae *social welfare administrator*

Dearborn
Ojakli, Ziad S. *lobbyist, automotive executive*
Tomlinson, Mark C. *professional society administrator*

Detroit
Baytarian, P. Jeffrey *not-for-profit fundraiser*
Gettelfinger, Ronald A. *labor union administrator*
Noland, Mariam Charl *foundation executive*

Flint
White, William Samuel *foundation executive*

Gaylord
Smith, Frank Earl *retired trade association administrator*

Grand Rapids
Jones, Ora McConner *retired foundation administrator*
Sieger, Diana R. *foundation administrator*

Hesperia
Yob, Chuck (Charles Walter Yob) *political organization administrator*

Kalamazoo
Petersen, Anne C. (Cheryl Petersen) *foundation administrator, educator*

Lansing
Brewer, Mark Courtland *political organization administrator*
Weiser, Ronald *political organization administrator, former ambassador*
Wise, Sharon *political organization administrator*

Saint Joseph
Moore, Melissa *professional society administrator*

Troy
Marshall, John Elbert III *foundation executive*
Rapson, Richard (Rip Rapson) *foundation administrator*

MINNESOTA

Lake Lillian
Marquardt, Steve Robert *advocate*

Little Falls
Stobb, Mary Jean *retired association administrator*

Minneapolis
Binger, Erika L. *foundation administrator*
Horsch, Kathleen Joanne *social services administrator, educator, consultant*
Johnson, John Warren *retired professional society administrator*
Leuchovius, Deborah *advocate, special education services professional, consultant*

North Mankato
Solo, Joyce Rubenstein *volunteer*

Saint Cloud
Prout, Robert Stephen *higher education consultant, law enforcement consultant*

Saint Paul
Anderson, Gordon Louis *foundation administrator*
Carey, Ron *political organization administrator*
Pratt, Jon *not-for-profit executive*
Sisson, Bernice Belair *advocate*
Skillingstad, Constance Yvonne *social services administrator, educator*

MISSISSIPPI

Jackson
Carmichael, Sally W. *volunteer*
Risley, Rod Alan *educational association administrator*
Seivers, Lana C. *educational association administrator, former state official*
White, Brad *political organization administrator*

MISSOURI

Ballwin
Pallozola, Christine *not-for-profit executive*

Bridgeton
Kenison, Raymond Robert *fraternal organization administrator*

Chesterfield
Diamandis, Peter H. *foundation administrator, entrepreneur*

Columbia
Brushwood, Mack Lewis *labor union administrator*

Jefferson City
Smith, Lloyd Franklin *political organization administrator*

Kansas City
Bugher, Robert Dean *professional society administrator*
Lenaghan, Michael John *association executive*
Rasmus, John Charles *retired trade association administrator, lawyer, consultant*

Saint Louis
Bascom, C. Perry *retired foundation administrator, lawyer*
Fletcher, Bill, Jr. *political organization executive, activist*
Hunter, Earle Leslie III *retired professional association executive*
Kimmey, James Richard, Jr. *foundation administrator*
Pope, Robert E(ugene) *fraternal organization administrator*

Springfield
O'Block, Robert *association, publishing executive*

MONTANA

Billings
Sample, Joseph Scanlon *foundation executive*

Bozeman
Mortenson, Greg *not-for-profit fundraiser, writer*

Butte
Alvarado, Arlene *educational association administrator*

Cut Bank
Johnson, Liane *political organization administrator*

NEBRASKA

Harrison
Coffee, Virginia Claire *civic worker, former mayor*

Lincoln
Hardin, Martha Love Wood *civic leader*
Rosenow, John Edward *foundation executive*

Omaha
Strawhecker, Paul Joseph *fundraising consultant*

NEVADA

Carson City
Ayres, Janice Ruth *social services administrator*

Henderson
Freyd, William Pattinson *not-for-profit fundraiser, director*

Las Vegas
Lieberman, Sam *political organization administrator*
Lowden, Sue *political organization administrator*
Mackey, Barbara *museum association administrator, director*
Manley, Edward Harry, Jr. *food safety and management trainer, professional association administrator, food products executive, retired military officer*
Martin, Myron Gregory *foundation administrator*
Nicholson, R. Stephen *former cultural organization administrator*
Tate, Eleanor Ann *educational association administrator*

Reno
De Sa Kono, Denise Ann Rene *cultural organization administrator*
LoSasso, Vicki Rae *political organization worker, artist*

NEW HAMPSHIRE

Concord
Buckley, Raymond Carl, II, *political organization administrator, former state legislator*

Dunbarton
Kimball, Philip C. *professional society administrator*

Hampton Falls
Sununu, John Henry *political organization administrator, former White House chief of staff, former governor of New Hampshire*

Peterborough
Eppes, William David *arts and humanities advocate*

Portsmouth
Hardy, Victoria Elizabeth *non profit administrator*

NEW JERSEY

Atlantic City
Jamieson, John Edward, Jr. *social services administrator, minister*

Bernardsville
Cooperman, Saul *retired educational administrator*

Caldwell
Ryan, Joanne Winona *art administrator, artist, consultant, educator*

Edison
Blanco, Virgil Harold *college professor, administrator*

Flemington
Saylor-Castelgrant, Elizabeth Ann *educational association administrator*

Highland Park
Kolodzei, Natalia A. *art association administrator, curator*

Jackson
Klostreich, Eva Tricules *educational association administrator*

Montclair
Campbell, Stewart Fred *foundation administrator, consultant*

New Brunswick
Bunch, Charlotte *advocate*

New Vernon
Dugan, John Leslie, Jr. *foundation executive*

Newark
Cicerchi, Eleanor Ann Tomb *not-for-profit fundraiser*
Kennedy, Alyson *advocate, garment worker*

Oradell
Mcglynn, Mary Aspinwall *artist, juror instructor*

Paramus
Noguere, Suzanne *trade association administrator, poet*

Pennington
Calvo, Roque John *professional society administrator*

Plainfield
Limpert, John H., Jr. *fund raising executive*

Princeton
Balch, Stephen Howard *professional society administrator*
Jeffers, Beverly Maynard *volunteer*
Landgraf, Kurt M. *educational association administrator*
Yao, Nan *educational association administrator*

Sewell
Hallenbeck, Ralph Henry *retired educational administrator*

Shiloh
Garrison, John Raymond *organization executive*

Trenton
Wilson, Tom *political organization administrator*

West Orange
Rinsky, Judith Sue Lynn *foundation administrator, consultant, educator*

NEW MEXICO

Albuquerque
Cole, Terri Lynn *organization administrator*
Silas, Pamala M. *professional society administrator*

Raton
Schmeits, Ronald L. *advocacy organization executive, bank executive*

NEW YORK

Albany
Lynch, Patricia *lobbyist*
Treadwell, Alexander F. *foundation executive, former state official*

Amherst
Clark, Donald Malin *professional association executive*

Arcade
Ezzo, David Albert *not-for-profit executive, anthropologist, educator*

Bayside
Madden, Joseph Daniel *trade association executive*

Briarcliff Manor
Read, John Conyers *non-profit company executive*

Brooklyn
Al-Islam, Amir *social services administrator, educator*
French, Stephanie Taylor *grantmaking and philanthropy expert*
Russell, Wayne Delano *activist, educator, poet*
Wilson, Robert Warne *philanthropist*

Buffalo
Clarkson, Elisabeth Ann Hudnut *volunteer*
Vela, Diana *educational association administrator*

Chappaqua
de Janosi, Peter Engel *research manager*

Commack
Price, Amelia Ruth *not-for-profit foundation president, artist, small business owner*

Dobbs Ferry
Sutton, Francis Xavier *social services administrator, consultant*

East Hampton
Hope, Judith H. *former political organization administrator*

Flushing
Fichtel, Rudolph Robert *retired association executive*

Glenmont
Bellizzi, John J. *law enforcement association administrator, pharmacist, educator*

Hastings On Hudson
Tarlov, Alvin Richard *foundation administrator, physician, educator*

Hudson
Miner, Jacqueline *political consultant*

Ithaca
Hemmings, Madeleine Blanchet *retired, not-for-profit administrator, grant writer, public policy director, media consultant*

Jamestown
Thompson, Birgit Dolores *civic worker, writer*

Katonah
Bergson, Henry Paul *professional society administrator, consultant*

Larchmont
Hinerfeld, Ruth G. *civic organization executive*

Manhasset
Foerst, John George, Jr. *retired fundraising executive*

Montauk
Butler, Thomas William *retired health and social services administrator*

New Rochelle
Black, Page Morton *civic worker, vocalist, musician*

New York
Anderson, Richard Theodore *trade association administrator, urban planner*
Ashley, Dwayne *not-for-profit fundraiser*
Baird, Zoë *foundation administrator*
Ban, Ki-Moon (Ban Ki-Moon) *Secretary General of the United Nations, former South Korean government official*
Belknap, Norton *foundation administrator*
Berger, Elizabeth H. *lobbyist*
Bergman, Charles Cabe *foundation executive*
Berkley, Seth Franklin *epidemiologist, international health specialist*
Bial, Deborah *educational association administrator*
Bias, Val *foundation administrator*
Bischoff, Theresa Ann *not-for-profit association executive*
Bowen, William Gordon *foundation administrator, economist*
Bowers, John M. *labor union administrator*
Brooks, Deborah W. *foundation administrator*
Calero, Róger *advocate, editor, writer*
Canada, Geoffrey *social welfare administrator, writer*
Caperton, Gaston (William Gaston Caperton III) *educational association administrator, former Governor of West Virginia*
Caputo, Lucio *trade company executive*
Carter, Virgil R. *professional society administrator*
Cheng-Hopkins, Judy *international organization administrator*
Christopher, Maurine Brooks *foundation administrator, writer, editor*
Cohen, Jonathan Elliot *international human rights advocate*
Conarroe, Joel Osborne *foundation administrator, editor, educator*
Connor, W(alter) Robert *foundation administrator, classicist, educator*
Covello, Vincent Thomas *environmental science and medicine educator, foundation administrator*
Cunningham, Jennifer *lobbyist, consultant*
Dajani, Virginia *art association administrator*
D'Amato, Alfonse Marcello *lobbyist, former United States Senator from New York*
Davis, Florence Ann *foundation administrator, lawyer*
Dennis, Everette Eugene, Jr. *foundation executive, educator, writer*
Desai, Vishakha N. *professional society administrator*
d'Escoto Brockmann, Miguel *President of United Nations General Assembly, priest*
Diggins, Peter Sheehan *arts administrator*
Duarte, Sergio de Queiroz *international organization official*
Ellis, Ross *non-profit organization executive*
Engelhardt, Sara Lawrence *retired organization executive*
Ewing, John Harwood *professional math organization executive*
Fehr, Donald M. *labor union administrator*
Fernandez, Charissa L. *educational association administrator*

Finan, Chris *foundation administrator, historian*
Gerner, Joan *executive vice president*
Goldberg, Beverly *foundation administrator, consultant*
Gomory, Ralph Edward *foundation administrator, mathematician*
Goodwin, Michael *labor union administrator*
Gore Schiff, Karenna *nonprofit organization administrator, lawyer, writer*
Grayer, Jonathan *education company executive*
Gregorian, Vartan *foundation administrator*
Grignon, Perianne *trade association administrator, marketing professional*
Guehenno, Jean Marie *international organization official*
Haass, Richard Nathan *think-tank executive*
Hanley, William Herbert *professional society administrator*
Harris, David Alan *not-for-profit organization executive*
Hatter, Richard Wayne *foundation administrator, artist*
Hemphill, Clara Jacobs *advocate*
Hesselbein, Frances Richards *speaker, writer, editor*
Hill, Janine *foreign policy think-tank*
Hoffman, Linda R. *social services administrator*
Holtan, Tor *foundation administrator*
Hong, Chung-Wha *advocacy organization director*
Hoye, J.D. *foundation administrator*
Hughes, Denis M. *labor union administrator*
Hughes, Richard P., Jr. *labor union administrator*
Innis, Niger *advocate, civil rights organization administrator*
Isenberg, Steven Lawrence *literary association administrator, retired publishing executive*
Jacobsen, Theodore H. (Ted H. Jacobsen) *labor union administrator, secondary school educator*
Jones, David R. *not-for-profit executive*
Kaggen, Lois Sheila *non-profit organization executive, advocate*
Kasirer, Suri *lobbyist*
Katzowitz Shenfield, Lauren *philanthropy consultant*
Knoll, Monica *not-for-profit organization administrator, marketing professional*
Kopp, Wendy *educational association administrator*
Labunski, Stephen Bronislaw *professional society administrator*
LaFayette, Reggie (Reginald A. LaFayette) *political organization administrator*
Larberg, John Frederick *retired social welfare executive, wine consultant, educator*
Lauder, Jo Carole *art association administrator*
Lawson-Johnston, Peter Orman *foundation executive*
Lee, Thomas F. *art association administrator*
Leet, Mildred Robbins *social welfare administrator, consultant*
Leffler, Marvin *foundation administrator, writer*
Lewis, Alan James *foundation administrator, pharmacologist*
Linder, Bertram Norman *foundation administrator, horse breeder, actor*
Loar, Peggy Ann *foundation administrator, museum administrator*
London, Nora *foundation administrator*
Loughlin, Thomas G. *professional society administrator*
Mahoney, Margaret Ellerbe *foundation executive*
Mathisen, Harold Clifford *foundation administrator*
Maynard, Virginia Madden *foundation administrator*
McCrary, Eugenia Lester (Mrs. Dennis Daughtry McCrary) *civic worker, writer*
McPherson, Mary Patterson *charitable foundation executive*
Migiro, Asha-Rose *international organization official*
Migro, Asha-Rose *international organization official*
Miller, Harvey S. Shipley *foundation trustee, philanthropist*
Mirrer, Louise *professional society administrator, former language educator*
Mone, Lawrence J. *think-tank executive*
Montalvo, Elba *social services administrator*
Moran, Martin Joseph *fundraising company executive*
Morial, Marc Haydel *civil rights association executive, former mayor*
Moskowitz, Eva S. *educational association administrator*
Mumford, Robin Bruce *foundation administrator, director, lighting designer*
O'Neill, June F. *political organization administrator, county official*
Otunnu, Olara A. *childrens organization official*
O'Brien, Patricia *international organization official*
Pascoe, B. Lynn *international organization official, former ambassador*
Polin, Jane L. *foundation official*
Randel, Don Michael *foundation administrator, former academic administrator, musicologist*
Rapoport, Miles S. *advocate, former state official*
Rodin, Judith Seitz *foundation administrator, former academic administrator*
Rose, Joanna Semel *volunteer*
Rosenthal, Jacob (Jack Rosenthal) *foundation executive*
Ross, Carne *international relations specialist, former diplomat*
Roth, Kenneth *human rights advocate*
Rothman, Esther Pomeranz *social services administrator, psychologist*
Rover, Edward Frank *foundation administrator, lawyer*
Rupp, George Erik *international relief organization executive*
Ryan, T. Timothy (Thomas Timothy Ryan Jr.) *securities industry association executive*
St. Martin, Charlotte *trade association administrator*
Schnur, Jonathan *educational association administrator*
Sidamon-Eristoff, Anne Phipps *not-for-profit developer*
Slutsky, Lorie A(nn) *foundation executive*
Smith, Barry Hamilton *foundation administrator, physician*
Smith, Rick *foundation administrator*
Spero, Joan Edelman *foundation administrator*
Spindler, James Andrew *not-for-profit executive*
Steedman, Doria Lynne Silberberg *foundation administrator*
Sussman, Leonard Richard *foundation executive*
Tanner, Jonathan D. *educational association administrator*
Tenenbaum, Ann G. *art association administrator*
Toussaint, Roger *labor union administrator*
Traverse, Lyn D. *not-for-profit fundraiser, communications executive*
Tudryn, Joyce Marie *professional society administrator*
Ubiñas, Luis Antonio *foundation president*
Veneman, Ann Margaret *international organization official, former United States Secretary of Agriculture*
Vergne, Philippe *art foundation administrator*
Walker, David Michael *foundation administrator*
Wanner, Eric *foundation executive*
Wright, Suzanne Werner *foundation administrator, volunteer*
Wylde, Kathryn S. *business organization executive*
Yale (Yeleyenide-Yale), Serina *philanthropist, apparel designer*
Yamazaki, Jun *international organization official*

Niagara Falls
Hawkins De Golier, Danielle *political activist*

Pleasant Valley
Becofsky, Arthur Luke *arts administrator, writer*

Rhinebeck
Lesser, Elizabeth *not-for-profit organization administrator, writer*

Rochester
Anderson, Kristin T. *educational association administrator, director*
Ebenhack, Ben Wright *not-for-profit company executive*
Klinke, Louise Hoyt *volunteer*
Lebman, Robert Richard *social services administrator*
Pacala, Leon *retired professional society administrator*

Saratoga Springs
Carovano, John Martin *retired not-for-profit developer*

Scarsdale
Paulin, Amy Ruth *civic activist, consultant, state legislator*
Port, Lilly Bruck Lieb *retired advocate, columnist, commentator*
Stamas, Stephen *not-for-profit administrator*

Schenectady
Hull, Roger Harold *foundation and former academic administrator*

Spring Valley
Neal, Leora Louise Haskett *social services administrator*

Stony Brook
Brandwein, Ruth Ann *social welfare educator, social services administrator, writer*

Stony Creek
La Grasse, Carol Winter *property rights advocate, retired civil engineer*

Syracuse
Colvin, Ruth Johnson *literacy organization founder*
Irwin, Peter C. *not-for-profit fundraiser*

Tarrytown
Brownstein, Alan P. *health foundation executive, consultant*
Teicher, Oren Jonathan *trade association executive*

Westbury
Mondello, Joseph N. *political organization administrator*

White Plains
Howse, Jennifer Louise *foundation administrator*
Slaughter, John Brooks *professional society administrator*

NORTH CAROLINA

Cary
Bryant, Mynora Joyce *not-for-profit fundraiser*
Martin, William Royall, Jr. *retired professional society administrator*

Chapel Hill
Krasno, Richard Michael *foundation executive, educator*

Charlotte
Locke, Elizabeth Hughes *retired foundation administrator*
McClure, Howard Jean, Jr. *advocate*
Spiro, Robert Harry, Jr. *foundation and business executive, educator*

Clinton
Griffin, Betty Lou *not-for-profit developer, educator*

Greensboro
Revell, Henry, Jr. *social services administrator, retired education educator*
Ryan, John R. *educational association administrator, former academic administrator, career military officer*

Raleigh
Allen, Barbara Kirkman *politcal organization administrator*
Daves, Linda *political organization administrator*
Lee, Howard N. *educational association administrator*
Young, David *political organization administrator*

Statesville
Johnston, Betty Parker *retired social service worker*

Wilson
McCain, Betty Landon Ray *political party and state official*

NORTH DAKOTA

Bismarck
Emineth, Gary *political organization administrator*
Karls, Ken *foundation executive, former political organization administrator*
Sand, Duane *think-tank associate*
Strauss, David *political organization administrator, former legislative staff member*

Grand Forks
Jones, Arthur Frederick *art university administrator, educator*

Williston
Yockim, James Craig *foundation administrator*

OHIO

Akron
Brake, Yvonne Marie *not-for-profit development director*
Collier, Alice Elizabeth Becker *retired social administrator, educational administrator*

Berlin Center
Haynali, Carolyn Ann *social services administrator*

Canton
McFarren, Leland Cullen *educational association administrator, educator*

Chagrin Falls
Vail, Iris Jennings *civic worker*

Cincinnati
Motch, Marjorie McCullough *service organization executive*

Cleveland
Albano, Albert P. *Museum Association Administrator*
Calkins, Hugh *foundation executive*
Distelhorst, Garis Fred *trade association executive*
Futhey, Mike (Malcolm B. Futhey) *labor union administrator*
Lord, James Gregory *organizational, community and philanthropic counsel*
Parry, Michael *not-for-profit fundraiser, singer, actor*
Penman, Robbie Mae *volunteer, political organization worker*
Pike, Kermit Jerome *cultural organization administrator*
Smith, Jerome *not-for-profit developer, film producer, writer*

Columbus
DeWine, Kevin *political organization administrator, former state legislator*
Laidlaw, William K. *not-for-profit developer*
Newman, Diana S. *foundation administrator, consultant, writer*
Selby, Diane Ray Miller *retired fraternal organization administrator*
Trent, Elton Roger *educational assessment administrator, writer*

Coshocton
Freund, Carol Louise *freelance staff development consultant*

Dayton
Clark, Jim *labor union administrator*
Daley, Robert Emmett *retired foundation executive*
Mathews, David (Forrest David Mathews) *foundation executive, former United States Secretary of Health Education and Welfare*

Fairfield
Gruenwald, James Howard *association executive, consultant*

Greenville
Thieme, Jean Louise *retired art association administrator*

Hudson
Frank, John V. *foundation administrator*

Kettering
Kent, Lawrence *retired association executive, education and mental health director*

Lewis Center
Heinlen, Daniel Lee *alumni organization administrator, consultant*

North Canton
Fernandez, Kathleen M. *cultural organization administrator*

Oxford
Miller, Robert James *education association administrator*

Richfield
Lewis, Sylvia Davidson *foundation executive*

Silver Lake
Cantor, Arnold *labor relations official*

Youngstown
Redfern, Chris *political organization administrator, former state legislator*

OKLAHOMA

Oklahoma City
Holmes, Ivan *political organization administrator*
Johnson, Glen D., Jr. *educational association administrator*
Jones, Gary *political organization administrator*
Kerr, Lou C. *foundation administrator*
Weddington, Stacey Lee *not-for-profit developer*

Tulsa
Ekdahl, Richard William *educational association executive*

OREGON

Ashland
Kreisman, Arthur *higher education consultant, retired humanities educator*

Corvallis
Wilkins, Caroline Hanke *advocate, political organization worker*

Portland
Collins, Maribeth Wilson *retired foundation administrator*
Hudson, Jerry E. *foundation administrator*
Smith, Meredith Wood *political organization administrator*
Tiernan, Bob (Robert Tiernan) *political organization administrator, former state legislator*

Summerville
Hopkins, Gerald Frank *trade association administrator*

PENNSYLVANIA

Elkins Park
Pak, Hyung Woong *community advocate*

Gladwyne
Cooney, Patricia Ruth *civic worker*

Glenside
Block, Isaac Edward *professional society administrator*

Harrisburg
Gleason, Robert A., Jr. *political organization administrator*
Rooney, Terence Joseph (T.J.) *political organization administrator, former state legislator*

Haverford
Meyers, Mary Ann *foundation administrator, consultant, writer*

Havertown
Wing, Kennard Thompson *educational organization official*

Lewisburg
Neuman, Nancy Adams Mosshammer *civic leader*

Monroeville
Skolnick, Marilyn *civic worker*

Newtown
Bernstine, Daniel O'Neal *educational association administrator, law educator*

Philadelphia
Capanna, Robert *educational association administrator, composer*
Mallery, David *education leader, teacher seminars, consultant*
Muhammad, Mike *advocate*
Murray, Dwayne M. *fraternity organization administrator, lawyer*
Reed, Sally Gardner *cultural organization administrator*
Rimel, Rebecca Webster *foundation administrator*

Pittsburgh
Boyce, Doreen Elizabeth *foundation administrator, educator*
Brean, Richard Joseph *labor union administrator, lawyer*
Gerard, Leo W. *labor union administrator*
Vagt, Robert F. *foundation administrator, former academic administrator*

Rydal
Fernberger, Marilyn Friedman *not-for-profit developer, consultant, volunteer*

State College
Book, Edward Raymond *retired trade association administrator*
Phillips, Janet Colleen *retired educational association administrator, editor*

Villanova
Friend, Theodore Wood III *foundation executive, historian, writer*

Warrendale
Rumbaugh, Max Elden, Jr. *professional society administrator*
Schutt, David L. *engineering association executive*

Wayne
Etris, Samuel Franklin *trade association research consultant*

York
Dzubak, Cora M. *educational association administrator*
Foster, Timothy Edward *educational association administrator*

RHODE ISLAND

Kingston
Molloy, David Scott, Jr. *labor relations educator*

Providence
Lynch, William Joseph *political organization administrator, lawyer*
Scott, Jonathan P. *think-tank executive*

SOUTH CAROLINA

Anderson
Bailey, Jake Schultz *volunteer, retired electrical engineer*

Columbia
Dawson, Katon *political organization administrator*
Dobrasko, Rebekah *cultural organization administrator, historian*
Fowler, Carol Khare *political organization administrator*
Sherrer, John M. III *cultural organization administrator*

Hilton Head Island
Ostergard, Paul Michael *foundation executive*

Lancaster
Bundy, Charles Alan *retired foundation executive*

Myrtle Beach
Gravely, Mary Jeane *volunteer*

Orangeburg
Battle-Bryant, Rebecca *educational association administrator*

Saint Helena Island
Tarr-Whelan, Linda *political organization worker, consultant*

Woodruff
Childers, Bob Eugene *educational association executive*

SOUTH DAKOTA

Rosebud
Garriott, Wizipan *educational association administrator*

Sioux Falls
Chapman, Cheryl K. *political organization administrator*

TENNESSEE

Brentwood
Lodowski, Charles Alan *retired trade association executive, lobbyist*

Chattanooga
McNeill-Murray, Joan Reagin *volunteer, consultant*

Knoxville
Eckenrod, Edward Lee *advocate*
Froula, James DeWayne *honor society administrator*

Memphis
Ford, Harold Eugene *lobbyist, educator, former United States Representative from Tennessee*
Jalenak, Peggy Eichenbaum *volunteer*
Tibbs, Martha Jane Pullen *civic worker, retired social worker*

Nashville
Benson, Edwin Welburn, Jr. *retired trade association executive*
Davis, Terry L. *historical association executive*
Forrester, Chip *political organization administrator*
Henderson, Milton Arnold *professional society administrator*
Johnson, Hollis Eugene III *foundation executive*
Livers, Thomas Henry *not-for-profit fundraiser, consultant*
McIntyre, Edward Patrick, Jr. *not-for-profit executive*
Saltsman, John B., Jr., (Chip Saltsman) *political organization administrator*
Smith, Robin *political organization administrator*

Whites Creek
Coleman, John Daniel *political strategist*

TEXAS

Austin
Barr, Ronald E. *educational association administrator*
Benkiser, Tina Johns *political organization administrator*
Dealey, Amanda Mayhew *former foundation administrator*
Dougherty, Molly Ireland *organization executive*
Houston, Ron *professional society administrator*
Kolar, Mary Jane *trade and professional association executive*
Mountain, Janet M. *foundation administrator, former computer company executive*
Ulman, Doug *foundation administrator*

Breckenridge
Jones, Karen Annette *civic volunteer*

Cedar Park
Love, Ben Howard *retired organization executive*

College Station
Davis, Eddie Joe *foundation administrator*

Colleyville
Tigue, Virginia Beth (Ginny) *volunteer*

Corpus Christi
French, Dorris Towers Bryan *volunteer*

Dallas
Brinker, Nancy Goodman *foundation administrator, former ambassador*
Cockerham, Sidney Joe *professional society administrator*
Lane, John Rodger *art association administrator, retired museum director*
Luce, Thomas Warren III *educational association administrator, former federal agency administrator*
McCallum, Scott *not-for-profit developer, former governor*
Mulford, Clay (Ross Clayton Mulford) *think-tank executive, lawyer*
Nikopoulos, Beth *educational association administrator*
O'Donnell, Peter, Jr. *foundation administrator*

Dickinson
Sawyer, Cheryl Lynne *educational association administrator, consultant*

El Paso
Goodman, Gertrude Amelia *civic worker*

Fort Worth
Williams, John B. *lobbyist, consultant*
Wilson-Webb, Nancy Lou *educational association administrator*

Fulton
Lamb, Richard *cultural organization administrator*

Georgetown
Busfield, Roger Melvil, Jr. *retired trade association executive, educator*

Houston
Bennett, Olga Salowich *civic worker, graphic arts researcher, consultant*
Faulkner, Larry Ray *foundation administrator, retired academic administrator*
Ifft, Lewis George III *company administrator*
McCleary, Beryl Nowlin *volunteer, travel company executive*

Irving
Steele, C. William *scouting organization administrator*

Mc Kinney
Daley, Tom *not-for-profit foundation executive*

Mcallen
Spyker, Leola Edith *missionary*

San Antonio
Boozer, Lyndon K. *lobbyist*
Crichton, Flora Cameron *volunteer, foundation administrator*
Gray, Shawn Scott *social services administrator*
Jacobson, Helen Gugenheim (Mrs. David Jacobson) *civic worker*
McKone, Timothy P. *lobbyist, telecommunications industry executive*

Spring
Bartlow, Gene Steven *professional society executive, retired military officer*

Sugar Land
Hosley, Marguerite Cyril *civic worker*

Waco
Kimsey-Davis, Beatrice Anna *civic worker, educator*

UTAH

Bountiful
Burningham, Kim Richard *educational association administrator, former state legislator*

Ogden
Pappas, Leah Aglaia *foundation administrator, political organization worker, secondary school educator*

Salt Lake City
Clark, Deanna Dee *volunteer*
Derezotes, David S. *social services administrator, educator*
Holland, Wayne, Jr. *political organization administrator*
Julander, Paula Foil *retired foundation administrator*

VERMONT

Middlebury
Geier, Philip Otto III *foundation executive, consultant, director, academic administrator*

Montpelier
Barbieri, Christopher George *professional society administrator*
Bevans, Judy *political organization administrator*
Roper, Robert *political organization administrator*

Peacham
Barnes, Harry G., Jr. *advocate, consultant*

VIRGINIA

Afton
Rhett, Haskell Emery Smith *educational association administrator*

Alexandria
Allen, Ernie (Ernest Eugene Allen) *non-profit organization executive, lawyer*
Anderson, Steven C. *pharmacy association executive*
Bailey, Tracey L. *educational association administrator*
Baroody, Michael Elias *trade association executive*
Bartels, Teresa Hall *non-profit organization administrator*
Bryant, Anne Lincoln *educational association administrator*
Connaughton, Sean Thomas *lobbyist, former federal agency administrator*
Davis, Richard H. (Rick Davis) *lobbyist*
Greenstein, Ruth Louise *think-tank executive, lawyer*
Jacobson, Lawrence Albert *professional society administrator, lawyer*
Kratovil, Jane Lindley *think tank associate, not-for-profit developer*
Kruse, Dennis K. *professional society administrator, retired military officer*
Lachance, Janice Rachel *professional association and federal agency administrator, lawyer*
Lenz, Edward Arnold *trade association administrator, lawyer*
Lipnick, Anne Ruth *advocate*
McKinnon, Russell F. *professional society administrator*
Rabun, John Brewton, Jr. *criminal justice agency administrator*
Rector, John Michael *pharmaceutical association executive, lawyer*
Turner, Grace-Marie *non-profit organization executive*
Wolff, Robert D. *professional society administrator*

Arlington
Adcock, Samuel Denton *lobbyist, former legislative director*
Becker, Fred Reinhardt, Jr. *association executive, lawyer, retired military officer*
Berger, Dan (Brian Daniel Berger) *lobbyist*
Blakey, Marion Clifton *aerospace association executive, former federal agency administrator*
Bond, Phillip J. *technology association executive, former advertising executive*
Buchanan, Louise *political organization worker, consultant*
Cole, Steven Jay *trade association administrator*
David, Ruth A. *public service research institute executive*
Dobbins, Jim (James Francis Dobbins Jr.) *think-tank executive, former federal agency administrator*
Dooley, Cal (Calvin Millard Dooley) *trade association administrator, former US Representative from California*
Dunn, Michael M. *military association executive, retired military officer*
Feinstein, Lee A. *political organization worker*
Fulton, Michael (C. Michael Fulton) *lobbyist*
Futrell, John William *environmental agency executive, lawyer*
Gunderson, Steven Craig *association executive, former congressman*
Helm, Bob (Robert Wilbur Helm) *lobbyist, former federal official*
Herbst, Robert LeRoy *organization executive*
Houston, Paul David *educational association administrator*
Hunter, J(ohn) Robert *insurance consumer advocate*
Nash, Bob J. *political organization worker*
O'Day, Paul Thomas *trade association executive*
Palmer, Larry Leon *foundation administrator, former ambassador*
Solis Doyle, Patti *political campaign worker*
Sullivan, Gordon R. *military association executive, retired military officer*
Swetnam, Michael S. *think-tank executive*
Williams, Maggie (Margaret Ann Williams) *political campaign manager, former federal official*

Ashburn
Shannon, Thomas Alfred *retired educational association administrator emeritus*

Baskerville
Boyd, John Wesley, Jr. *trade association administrator, farmer*

Blacksburg
Nowak, Jerzy *educational association administrator, horticulture professor, director*

Boston
Fisher, John Morris *association official, business executive, educator*

Burke
Woodruff, C(harles) Roy *retired professional association executive, consultant*

Charlottesville
Jordan, Daniel Porter, Jr. *foundation administrator, historian, educator*

Chincoteague Island
Chagnon, Lucille Tessier *literacy acceleration consultant*

Earlysville
Brownell, Blaine Allison *educational association and academic administrator, history professor*

Fairfax
Cullison, Alexander C. (Doc Cullison) *mediator, arbitrator*
Hollans, Irby Noah, Jr. *retired trade association administrator*
LaPierre, Wayne R., Jr. *lobbyist*
Lomax, Michael Lucius *non-profit association administrator*
Roberts, Cecil Edward, Jr. *labor union administrator*
Robinson, Kayne B. *lobbyist, former political organization officer*
Tadros, Nader K. *political organization worker, director*

Falls Church
Calhoun, John Alfred *social services administrator*
Han, Syung D. *international trade consultant, financier*

Flint Hill
Dietel, William Moore *former foundation executive*

Fredericksburg
Hoyt, John Arthur *cultural organization administrator, minister*

Garrisonville
Emely, Charles Harry *trade association executive, consultant*

Gloucester
James, Kay Coles *think-tank executive, former federal agency administrator*

Great Falls
DiBona, Charles Joseph *retired trade association administrator*

Leesburg
De Barbieri, Mary Ann *not-for-profit management consultant*

Lorton
Shoemaker, Helen E. Martin Achor *civic worker*

Louisa
Small, William Edwin, Jr. *association and recreation executive*

Lynchburg
Johnson, Robert Bruce *historic preservationist, director, small business owner*

Mc Lean
Hillen, John Francis *think-tank executive, former federal agency administrator*
McInerney, James Eugene, Jr. *trade association executive*
Schubert, Richard Francis *social services administrator, consultant*

Mclean
McBride, Timothy J. *lobbyist*
Rose, Mitch *lobbyist*

Middleburg
Sodolski, John *retired professional society administrator*

Mount Vernon
Belden, David Leigh *professional society executive, engineering educator*

Norfolk
Newkirk, Ingrid *animal rights organization administrator*

Potomac Falls
Minton, Joseph Paul *retired safety organization executive*

Reston
Ancell, Robert Manning *leadership organization executive*
Brennan, Norma Jean *retired professional society administrator*
Gates, James David *retired professional society administrator*
Hope, Samuel Howard *accreditation organization executive*
Madry-Taylor, Jacquelyn Yvonne *educational association administrator*
Mogge, Harriet Morgan *educational association executive*
Natale, Patrick J. *professional society administrator*

Richmond
Carlock, Margo *museum association administrator*
Cranwell, C. Richard *political organization administrator, lawyer*
Framme, Lawrence Henry III *political organization administrator, lawyer*
Sterling, Anne D. *not-for-profit developer*

Springfield
Larson, Reed Eugene *foundation administrator*

Upperville
Smart, Edith Merrill *civic worker*

Vienna
Jones, Terrence Dale *foundation executive, consultant*

Patrick, Susan D. *educational association administrator, former federal agency administrator*

Virginia Beach
Swail, Watson Scott *educational association administrator*

Williamsburg
Campbell, Colin Goetze *foundation president*
Sass, Arthur Harold *educational training administrator*

Woodbridge
Garon, Richard Joseph, Jr. *political organization worker*
Gilmore, Marjorie Havens *retired civic worker, lawyer*

WASHINGTON

Bainbridge Island
Cassella, William Nathan, Jr. *retired not-for-profit organization executive*

Bellingham
Arthurs, Eugene Gerard *professional society administrator*

Seattle
Esser, Luke *political organization administrator*
Foster, Barry Alan *cultural organization researcher, educator*
Fredriksen Goldsen, Karen I. *social welfare administrator, educator*
Friedman, Alexander Stephen *foundation administrator, investment banker*
Gates, Melinda French *foundation administrator*
Jacobs, Deborah L. *foundation administrator, former library director*
Jessen, Joel Anne *not-for-profit executive, art educator*
Pelz, Dwight *political organization administrator*
Phillips, Vicki L. *foundation administrator, former school system administrator*
Raikes, Jeffrey Scott *foundation administrator, former computer software company executive*
Scott, Cheryl M. *foundation administrator, healthcare educator*
Wasserheit, Judith N. *social services administrator*

WEST VIRGINIA

Charleston
Chapman, John Andrew *retired chamber of commerce executive*
McKinney, Doug *political organization administrator, urologist*
Smith, Stuart Lewis *community volunteer*

WISCONSIN

Madison
Brennan, Robert Walter *association executive*
Olson, Norman Fredrick *not-for-profit developer, retired food science educator*
Wineke, Joseph Steven *political organization administrator, former state legislator*

Milwaukee
Huntington, David Mack Goode *foundation administrator*

WYOMING

Casper
Cotherman, Audrey Mathews *educational administrator, management consultant*
Petersen, Leslie *political organization administrator*

Cheyenne
Noe, Guy *retired social services administrator*

Jackson
Vaughan, Diana *political organization administrator*

Laramie
Darnall, Roberta Morrow *educational association administrator*

Rock Springs
Conover, Dustin *educational association administrator*

TERRITORIES OF THE UNITED STATES

AMERICAN SAMOA

Pago Pago
Schuster, Su'a Carl *political organization administrator, bishop*

GUAM

Agana Heights
Leon-Guerrero, Jillette Torre *nonprofit organization executive, consultant, writer*

Hagatna
Charfauros, Tony (Anthony Charfauros) *political organization administrator*

PUERTO RICO

Dorado
Glickman, Marlene *non-profit organization administrator*

San Juan
Méndez, Carlos (Don Carlos Méndez Martínez) *political organization administrator, mayor*
Prats Palerm, Robert L. *political organization administrator*

VIRGIN ISLANDS

Christiansted
Schoenbohm, Herbert L. *political organization administrator, radio personality*

St Thomas
Benjamin, Cecil *political organization administrator*

CANADA

QUEBEC

Montreal
Bisignani, Giovanni *air transportation association executive*

Outremont
Gulkin, Harry *arts administrator, film producer*

MEXICO

Mexico City
Bruton, John Macaulay *trade association executive, consultant*

AUSTRIA

Vienna
Magariños, Carlos Alfredo *international association administrator*

BELGIUM

Brussels
Flory, Peter Cyril Wyche *international organization official, former federal agency administrator*

Genappe
Williams, Jody *political organization administrator*

CHINA

Beijing
Bai, Chunli *professional society administrator, educator*

COSTA RICA

San José
Perez Esquivel, Adolfo *human rights activist*

ENGLAND

London
Chadwick, Derek James *foundation administrator*
Hinduja, Srichand Parmanand *association executive, hospital administrator*
Piot, Peter (Baran) *global health professor*

Milton Keynes
Gourley, Brenda *educational institution administrator*

FRANCE

Paris
Askey, Thelma J. *international organization official, former federal agency administrator*

GERMANY

Berlin
Ertl, Gerhard *retired institute director*

Hamburg
Lüst, Reimar *foundation president*

Mayen
Gartz, Rolf F. *foundation administrator*

HUNGARY

Budapest
Shattuck, John *foundation administrator, former ambassador*

INDIA

New Delhi
Plianbangchang, Samlee *world organization administrator*

ITALY

Rome
Shiner, Josette Sheeran (Josette Sheeran) *international organization official, former federal agency administrator*
Sisulu, Sheila Violet Makate *international organization official, diplomat*

JAPAN

Osaka
Tanaka, Junji *educational administrator*

KENYA

Nairobi
Tibaijuka, Anna Kajumulo *international organization official, advocate, economics professor*

LUXEMBOURG

Luxembourg
Kokott, Julia Beate *advocate general*

SCOTLAND

Glasgow
Iolana, Patricia Elvira *foundation administrator, consultant*

SOUTH AFRICA

North West
Lumadi, Mutendwahothe Walter *educational association administrator*

SWEDEN

Stockholm
Sohlman, Michael *foundation administrator*
Wastberg, Olle M. *nation branding organization administrator*

SWITZERLAND

Geneva
Annan, Kofi Atta *international organization administrator, former secretary general of the United Nations*
Niskala, Markku *international organization administrator*
Schwab, Klaus Martin *foundation administrator*
Sommaruga, Cornelio *foundation administrator, diplomat*

Lausanne
Carrard, Francois Denis *international organization administrator, lawyer*

UNITED ARAB EMIRATES

Abu Dhabi
Cleaves, Peter Shurtleff *foundation administrator*

ADDRESS UNPUBLISHED

Ambach, Gordon Mac Kay *educational association executive*
Anderson, Ned, Sr. *Apache tribal official*
Archey, William T. *retired trade association administrator*
Atchison, Richard Calvin *retired trade association director*
Augustine, Norman Ralph *not-for-profit and business executive, educator, retired federal agency administrator*
Babb, Roberta Joan *educational administrator*
Ball, Howard Guy *association administrator, educator*
Balter, Frances Sunstein *civic worker*
Bartlett, Dede Thompson *association executive*
Beals, L(oren) Alan *association executive*
Beatty, Frances *civic worker*
Bell, Jerry Alan *science education consultant*
Bell-Rose, Stephanie *foundation administrator*
Berresford, Susan Vail *retired foundation administrator*
Berry, Jacob Obadiah *not-for-profit developer, rancher*
Bird, Mary Lynne Miller *professional society administrator*
Black, Charles Ray, Jr., (Charlie Black) *lobbyist*
Blix, Hans Martin *retired international organization official*
Bloch, Julia Chang *foundation president*
Blondin, C. J. *trade association administrator, lawyer*
Boal, Dean *retired arts center administrator, educator*
Bond, Julian *civil rights association executive*
Bradford, Louise Mathilde *social work administrator*
Bradley, Josephine B. *social worker, educator*
Braunstein, Diane Karen *non-profit association executive, government administrator, government relations professional*
Brewster, Mary Moorhead *retired educational association administrator*
Brim, Orville Gilbert, Jr. *former foundation administrator, writer*
Brown, Bruce Maitland *philanthropy consultant*
Bucksbaum, Melva *foundation administrator*
Buhl, Cynthia Maureen *advocate, educator*
Burki, Fred Albert *labor union official*
Burnham, Christopher Bancroft *former international organization official, former federal agency administrator*
Campbell, Edwin Denton *educational association administrator, consultant, accountant*
Carnicom, Gene E. *health services administrator*
Carter, Henry Moore, Jr. *retired foundation executive*
Carter, Hodding, III, (William) *foundation executive, retired journalist, commentator, educator*
Chacko, Samuel *association official*
Chassman, Leonard Fredric *retired labor union administrator*
Chattman, Raymond Christopher *association executive*
Cherry, Caroline Lockett *educational association administrator*
Choi, Im Ja Park *non-profit executive*
Clark, Alicia Garcia *political party official*
Cohen, Roberta Jane *think-tank associate*
Cohn, Marianne Winter Miller *civic activist*
Colwell, Bryan York *private investor, philanthropist*
Connor, Joseph E. *former international organization official*
Conran, James Michael *consumer advocate, public policy consultant*
Cooper, Josephine Smith *trade association and public affairs executive*
Cope, Melba Darlene *volunteer, photographer*
Corderman, Douglas George *retired non-profit organization executive*
Cotter, William Reckling *foundation administrator*
Counter, James Nicholas III *trade association executive, lawyer*
Crumley, Martha Ann *charity fundraising executive*
Daschle, Linda Hall *lobbyist*
Davis, Evelyn Cleveland *educational association administrator, consultant*
Dechant, Virgil C. *retired fraternal organization administrator*
Deeds, Virginia Williams *volunteer*
de La Sabliere, Jean-Marc *former international organization official*
DeVries, Robert Allen *foundation administrator*
Dickeson, Robert Celmer *retired foundation administrator, management consultant*
Domenick, Julie D. *lobbyist*
Donnell, Harold Eugene, Jr. *retired professional society administrator*
Dowling, Michael Paul *think-tank executive*
Drennen, William Miller, Jr. *cultural organization administrator, film producer, writer*
Duff, Patricia *civic activist*
Duhme, Carol McCarthy *civic worker*
Duncan, Mike (Robert Michael Duncan) *former political organization administrator*
Dunn, David *educational association administrator, former federal agency administrator*
Eastman, Francesca Marlene *volunteer, art historian*
Easton, Michelle *foundation executive*
Ellis, Anne Elizabeth *fundraiser*
Elsey, George McKee *retired foundation administrator*
Ely, Duncan Cairnes *not-for-profit executive*
Evans, Joy *foundation administrator*
Evans, Rosemary Hall *civic worker*
Fanton, Jonathan Foster *retired foundation administrator*
Feeney, Maryann McHugh *not-for profit professional*
Ferry, Martha Morton *non-profit executive*
Filer, Emily Symington Harkins *retired foundation administrator, writer, associate chaplain*
Fitzmaurice, Laurence Dorset *social services administrator*
Flynn, Paul Bartholomew *retired foundation executive*
Ford, Alma Regina *retired union official, educator*
Fordyce, James Stuart *retired non-profit organization executive*
Foster, Charles Henry Wheelwright *former foundation officer, consultant, author*
Fox-Clarkson, Anne C. *fundraising company executive*
Foxman, Abe (Abraham Henry Foxman) *advocacy organization administrator*
Fulbright, Harriet Mayor *educational association administrator*
Gammon, Samuel Rhea III *retired association executive, former ambassador*
Garner, Carlene Ann *not-for-profit fundraiser, consultant*
Garrison, Linda Susan *fundraising consultant, writer*
Gasper, Jo Ann *social services administrator, consultant*
Gerson, Elliot Francis *foundation administrator*
Gilbert, Melissa *former actors guild executive, actress*
Gilchrest, Thornton Charles *retired association executive*
Giuliani, Judith *not-for-profit executive*
Glascoff, Susan Titus *public advocate, former secondary school educator, school board member, securities trader*
Glassick, Charles Etzweiler *foundation administrator*
Goold, Douglas *think-tank executive*

Graisse, Jean-Jacques *former international organization official*
Grant, Mark Antonio *organization administrator*
Grimaldi, Nicholas Lawrence *fundraising executive*
Grossman, Ginger Scheflin *advocate*
Gunderson, Judith Keefer *golf association executive*
Hager, John Henry *former political organization administrator, former federal agency administrator*
Hanford, George Hyde *retired educational association administrator*
Hardy, Clarence Earl, Jr. *government, nonprofit and corporate sector executive*
Harrison, John Raymond *foundation administrator, retired publishing executive*
Hawkins, Brian Lee *former educational association administrator*
Helm, DeWitt Frederick, Jr. *professional society administrator, consultant*
Hernández, Sandra R. *foundation administrator*
Hester, James McNaughton *retired foundation administrator, artist*
Hill, Kent Richmond *foundation administrator, former federal agency administrator*
Himes, Diane A. *buyer, fundraiser, actress, lobbyist*
Hohlt, Richard Frederick *lobbyist*
Hooks, Benjamin Lawson *civil rights advocate, retired civil rights association executive*
Huffman, Carol Cicolani *retired educational association administrator*
Irving, Janell NaKia *fundraising consultant*
Jankowski, John Edward, Jr. *government administrator*
Jarrett, Jeffrey D. *energy companies association executive, former federal agency administrator*
Johnson, David *retired lobbyist*
Johnson, Deborah Lorraine *not-for-profit executive, consultant*
Johnston, Laurance Scott *foundation director, healthcare educator*
Kaskowitz, Edwin *social services executive*
Keeny, Spurgeon Milton, Jr. *professional society administrator*
Keil, M. David *retired international association executive*
Kempner, Jonathan L. *lobbyist*
Keyes, Alan Lee *political activist, radio talk show host, former diplomat*
Khatib, Kathy *school administrator, educator*
Kikareas, Panagiotis *foundation administrator, retired military officer*
King, Jane Cudlip Coblentz *volunteer educator*
King, Quintin L. *trade association administrator, lobbyist*
Kinslow, Margie Ann *volunteer*
Kjersten, Erin R. *social services administrator*
Klarich, David John *lobbyist, lawyer*
Kovach, Bill *educational foundation administrator*
Kregg, Helen Christine *foundation administrator*
Kruesi, Frank Eugene *lobbyist, former government executive*
Kunstadter, Geraldine Sapolsky *foundation executive*
Kurtz, Harold Paul *foundation executive*
Landon, Susan N. *humanitarian, arts and environmental advocate, poet*
Lansing, Sherry Lee *foundation administrator, former film company executive*
Lassman, Adrienne *community volunteer*
Ledwig, Donald Eugene *election official, association executive, retired broadcast executive, military officer*
Leggett, Roberta Jean (Bobbi Leggett) *retired social services administrator*
Lenhart, Cynthia Rae *conservation organization executive*
Lenz, Carl Otto *international organization official*
Lewis, Mary-Frances *civic volunteer*
Liljegren, Frank Sigfrid *art association administrator, artist, educator*
Lindenmayer, Elisabeth *international organization administrator*
Loos, Roberta Alexis *advocate, artist, educator*
Luckey, Doris Waring *civic volunteer*
Lynch, Catherine Gores *social services administrator*
MacAlister, Rodney J. *former president African Development Foundation*
MacCarthy, Talbot Leland *civic volunteer*
Magliocchetti, Paul *lobbyist*
Malek, Marlene Anne *foundation administrator*
Manion, Bonnie J. *volunteer, poet, composer*
Marcus, Bernard *foundation administrator, retired retail executive*
Marquand, Jean MacMurtry *educational association administrator*
Maxwell, Barbara Ruth *not-for-profit developer*
McAuliffe, Terry (Terence Richard McAuliffe) *former political organization administrator*
McFate, Patricia Ann *foundation executive, science educator*
McGarry, Marcia *retired community service coordinator*
McKinzie, Barbara Anne *educational association administrator*
McWethy, Patricia Joan *educational association administrator*
Melanson, Dorothy *political organization administrator*
Mende, Robert Graham *retired engineering association executive*
Metcalf, Karen *retired foundation executive*
Miller, Harriet Sanders *former art center director*
Monroe, Stephanie Johnson *lobbyist, former federal agency administrator*
Moore, Robert William *professional organization executive*
Moriyama, Karen Ito *retired educational association administrator*
Morrisett, Lloyd N. *retired foundation executive*
Moser, Jeffery Richard *not profit developer, director, grant writer*
Muller, Henry Nicholas III *retired foundation administrator*
Munitz, Barry A. *former foundation administrator*
Munro, Donald William, Jr. *non-profit organization executive*
Nelligan, William David III *professional association executive*
Newman, Eileen *not-for-profit organization executive*
Niemiec, Edward Walter *retired professional association executive*
Nowell, Linda Gail *not-for-profit executive*
Oaks, Sunny *child and family advocate, consultant, author, lyricist*
O'Connor, Doris Julia *not-for-profit fundraiser, consultant*
Olson, Mark Walter *former non-profit corporation administrator*
O'Neal-Seralathan, Crescentia *advocate*
O'Neill, Mary Jane *not-for-profit administrator, consultant*
Park, Won Kuk *foundation administrator*
Petersen, Jean Snyder *retired educational association administrator*
Porter, John Wilson *educational association administrator, director*
Prance, Sir Ghillean Tolmie *botanical gardens administrator, botanist*
Prescott, Barbara Lodwich *educational association administrator*
Pullen, Penny Lynne *non-profit organization administrator, state legislator*
Redd, J. Diane *not-for-profit fundraiser*
Richardson, William Chase *retired university and foundation executive*
Ridings, Dorothy Sattes *former association executive*
Roberson, James O. *foundation executive*
Robinson, David Zav *not-for-profit consultant*
Roeder, Gloria Jean *civil rights specialist, retired private investigator*
Rogers, Margaret Ellen Jonsson *civic worker*
Ross, Charlotte Pack *social services administrator*
Ryan, John William *educational association administrator*
Samaranch, Juan Antonio (Marqués de Samaranch) *former international sports organization executive*
Sampson, Robert Neil *professional society administrator, consultant*
San Agustin, Joe Taitano *political organization worker, educator*
Schanfield, Fannie Schwartz *community volunteer*
Schulz, William Frederick *human rights scholar and advocate*
Schuster, Elaine *retired civil rights professional*
Schweiker, Richard Schultz *former trade association administrator, former United States Secretary of Health & Human Services*
Scott, Karen Elizabeth *advocate*
Seemann, Rosalie Mary *international business and foreign policy association executive*
Sigler, John Charles *former firearms association executive*
Singer, Markus Morton *retired trade association administrator*
Small, Sarah Mae *volunteer*
Smith, Elise Fiber *international non-profit development agency administrator*
Smith, J. Kellum, Jr. *foundation administrator, lawyer*
Smith, Margaret Taylor *volunteer*
Smith, Marie F. *lobbyist, former association executive*
Smith, Wendy L. *foundation executive*
Stearns, Stewart Warren *charitable association executive*
Steele, Charles, Jr. *retired civil rights association executive, former state legislator*
Steelman, Sara Gerling *retired art association administrator*
Stevens, Sheila Maureen *retired teachers union administrator*
Sullivan, James Leo *organization executive*
Sutton, Johnny Keane *lobbyist, former prosecutor*
Tharoor, Shashi *former international organization official, writer*
Tipping, William Malcolm *social services administrator*
Tisch, Wilma Stein *foundation administrator*
Towle, Alexis Charles (Lex Towle) *education advocate, director*
Transou, Lynda Lou *advertising art administrator*
Tryon, Elizabeth Anne *educational association administrator*
Turigliatto-Fahrney, Terri A. *educational association administrator, educator*
Van Etten, Peter Walbridge *foundation executive*
Vliet, Marni *health policy and health program consultant*
Votaw, John Frederick, Sr. *educational association administrator, educator*
Walton, Christy R. *philanthropist*
Watkins, Julia M. *educational association administrator*
Watta, David Anthony *product manager*
White, Rebecca E. *advocate*
Willbanks, T. Shawn *educational association administrator*
Woolf, William Blauvelt *retired association executive*
Zaid, Shakir Tor Ishaq *not-for-profit developer, minister*
Zharikov, Alexander Nikolaevich *trade union federation executive*
Zimmerman, Gary J. *retired utilities association executive*
Zimny, Max *labor union administrator, lawyer, arbitrator*

ATHLETICS

UNITED STATES

ALABAMA

Auburn
Chizik, Gene *college football coach*
Fortner, Nell *women's college basketball coach*
Housel, David *emeritus athletic director*
Lebo, Jeff *men's college basketball coach*

Birmingham
Slive, Michael Lawrence *sports association executive, lawyer*

Montgomery
Hester, Hortense *retired physical education educator*

Tuscaloosa
Grant, Anthony *men's college basketball coach*
Saban, Nick (Nicholas Lou Saban) *college football coach, former professional football coach*

ALASKA

Eagle River
Cotten, Samuel Richard *fisheries consultant, fisherman, former state legislator, consultant*

ARIZONA

Glendale
Doan, Shane *professional hockey player*
Gretzky, Wayne Douglas *professional hockey coach, retired professional hockey player*
Jovanovski, Ed *professional hockey player*
Maloney, Don *professional sports team executive, retired professional hockey player*
Moss, Douglas G. *professional sports team executive*
Porter, Kevin *professional hockey player*

Phoenix
Barbosa, Leandro Mateus *professional basketball player*
Boldin, Anquan *professional football player*
Byrnes, Eric James *professional baseball player, radio, television personality*
Cartwright, James William (Bill Cartwright) *professional basketball coach, retired professional basketball player*
Eckstein, David Mark *professional baseball player*
Fitzgerald, Larry Darnell, Jr. *professional football player*
Gaines, Corey *professional basketball coach*
Gentry, Alvin *professional basketball coach*
Gibson, Kirk Harold *professional baseball coach, retired professional baseball player*
Graves, Rod *professional sports team executive*
Haren, Dan (Daniel John Haren) *professional baseball player*
Hill, Grant *professional basketball player*
Hinch, A.J. (Andrew Jay Hinch) *professional baseball coach*
Kerr, Steve (Stephen Douglas Kerr) *professional sports team executive, retired professional basketball player*
Leinart, Matthew Stephen *professional football player*
Lemieux, Claude *retired professional hockey player*
Majerle, Daniel Lewis *professional basketball coach, retired professional basketball player*
Nash, Steve *professional basketball player*
Pitman, Jim *professional sports team executive*
Pondexter, Cappie *professional basketball player*
Richardson, Jason Anthony *professional basketball player*
Sarver, Robert G. *professional sports team owner*
Schilling, Curt (Curtis Montague Schilling) *retired professional baseball player*
Stoudemire, Amare Carsares *professional basketball player*
Taurasi, Diana Lurena *professional basketball player*
Webb, Brandon (Tyler Webb) *professional baseball player*
Welts, Rick *professional sports team executive*
Wilson, Adrian (Adrian Lemar Wilson) *professional football player*

Scottsdale
Mediate, Rocco *professional golfer*

Tempe
Erickson, Dennis *college football coach, former professional football coach*
Grimm, Russ *professional football coach, retired professional football player*
Sendek, Herb *men's college basketball coach*
Turner Thorne, Charli *women's college basketball coach*
Warner, Kurt (Kurtis Eugene Warner) *professional football player*
Whisenhunt, Ken *professional football coach*

Tucson
Kearney, Joseph Laurence *retired athletic conference administrator*
Miller, Sean *men's college basketball coach*
Stoops, Mike *college football coach*

ARKANSAS

Fayetteville
Broyles, Frank (John Franklin Broyles) *athletic director, retired college football coach*
Petrino, Bobby *college football coach*

Hot Springs
Pelton, Elois Bleidt *retired physical education educator*

State University
Brady, John E. *men's college basketball coach*

CALIFORNIA

Alameda
Asomugha, Nnamdi *professional football player*
Cable, Thomas Lee (Tom Cable) *professional football coach*
Davis, Al (Allen Davis) *professional football team executive*
Garcia, Jeff (Jeffrey Jason Garcia) *professional football player*
Lechler, Shane (Edward Shane Lechler) *professional football player*
McFadden, Darren *professional football player*
Russell, JaMarcus *professional football player*

Aliso Viejo
Cohen, Sasha (Alexandra Pauline Cohen) *ice skater*

Anaheim
Abreu, Bobby (Bob Kelly Abreu) *professional baseball player*
Carlyle, Randy *professional hockey coach, retired professional hockey player*
Figgins, Chone (Desmond DeChone Figgins) *professional baseball player*
Fuentes, Brian Christopher *professional baseball player*
Getzlaf, Ryan *professional hockey player*
Giguere, Jean-Sebastien *professional hockey player*
Guerrero, Vladimir Alvino *professional baseball player*
Hedican, Bret *professional hockey player*
Hunter, Torii Kedar *professional baseball player*
Kazmir, Scott (Edward) *professional baseball player*
Koivu, Saku *professional hockey player*
Moreno, Arturo (Arte Moreno) *professional sports team executive, former advertising executive*
Murray, Bob (Robert Frederick Murray) *professional sports team executive, former professional hockey player*
Niedermayer, Scott *professional hockey player*
Nonis, David *professional sports team executive*
Reagins, Tony *professional baseball team executive*
Schulman, Michael *professional sports team executive, lawyer*
Selanne, Teemu *professional hockey player*

Berkeley
Boyle, Joanne *women's college basketball coach*
Montgomery, Mike *men's college basketball coach*

Beverly Hills
Johnson, Magic (Earvin Johnson Jr.) *professional sports team and development company executive, retired professional basketball player*

Camarillo
Bryan, Bob Charles *professional tennis player*
Bryan, Mike Carl *professional tennis player*

Carson
Arena, Bruce *professional soccer coach*
Beckham, David (Robert Joseph) *professional soccer player*

El Segundo
Abdul-Jabbar, Kareem (Lew Alcindor, Lewis Ferdinand Alcindor) *professional basketball coach, retired professional basketball player*
Bryant, Kobe *professional basketball player*
Buss, Jerry (Gerald Hatten Buss) *professional sports team owner*
Bynum, Andrew *professional basketball player*
Fisher, Derek Lamar *professional basketball player*
Gasol, Pau *professional basketball player*
Kupchak, Mitchell *professional sports team executive, retired professional basketball player*
Milton-Jones, DeLisha *professional basketball player*
Odom, Lamar Joseph *professional basketball player*

La Jolla
Bavasi, Peter Joseph *sports management executive*

La Verne
Mosley, Shane *boxer*

Long Beach
Monson, Dan *men's college basketball coach*

Los Angeles
Artest, Ron (Ronald William Artest Jr.) *professional basketball player*

Bowa, Larry (Lawrence Robert Bowa) *professional baseball coach, retired professional baseball player*
Brown, Dustin *professional hockey player*
Caldwell, Nikki *women's college basketball coach*
Camby, Marcus D. *professional basketball player*
Carroll, Pete *college football coach*
Colletti, Ned Louis, Jr. *professional sports team executive*
Cooper, Michael Jerome *professional basketball coach, former professional basketball player*
Davis, Baron *professional basketball player*
De La Hoya, Oscar *retired boxer*
Dunleavy, Mike (Michael Joseph Dunleavy Jr.) *professional basketball coach*
Frolov, Alexander *professional hockey player*
Griffin, Blake Austin *professional basketball player*
Guerrero, Daniel G. *sports association administrator*
Hextall, Ron *professional sports team executive, former professional hockey player*
Hopkins, Bernard *professional boxer*
Howland, Ben *men's college basketball coach*
Hudson, Orlando Thill *professional baseball player*
Jackson, Philip Douglas *professional basketball coach*
Kopitar, Anze *professional hockey player*
Kuroda, Hiroki *professional baseball player*
Lasorda, Tommy (Thomas Charles Lasorda) *retired professional baseball team manager*
Leslie, Lisa DeShaun *professional basketball player*
Lombardi, Dean *professional sports team executive*
Martin, Russell (Nathan Coltrane Jeanson), Jr. *professional baseball player*
McCourt, Jamie *professional sports team executive*
Murray, Terry (Terence Rodney Murray) *professional hockey coach*
Mussina, Michael Cole (Mike Mussina) *retired professional baseball player*
Neuheisel, Rick (Richard Gerald Neuheisel, Jr.) *college football coach*
Ng, Kim (Kimberly J. Ng) *professional sports team executive*
O'Neill, Kevin *men's college basketball coach*
Parker, Candace Nicole *professional basketball player*
Pierre, Juan *professional baseball player*
Ramirez, Manny (Manuel Aristides Ramirez) *professional baseball player*
Robitaille, Luc *professional sports team executive, retired professional hockey player*
Roeser, Andy *professional sports team executive*
Scuderi, Rob *professional hockey player*
Shaw, Brian K. *professional basketball coach, retired professional basketball player*
Thome, Jim *professional baseball player*
Thornton, Al *professional basketball player*
Torre, Joe (Joseph Paul Torre) *professional baseball team manager*
Vizcaino, Jose Luis Pimental *professional baseball coach, retired professional baseball player*

Monterey Park
Stankevitz, Diane Lynn *athletic trainer*

Moraga
Bennett, Randy *men's college basketball coach*

Oakland
Cheaney, Calbert Nathaniel *professional sports team executive, retired professional basketball player*
Cohan, Christopher J. *professional sports team owner*
Ellis, Monta *professional basketball player*
Garciaparra, Nomar (Anthony Nomar Garciaparra) *professional baseball player*
Geren, Bob (Robert Peter Geren) *professional baseball manager*
Harris, Larry *professional basketball coach*
Jackson, Stephen *professional basketball player*
Maggette, Corey Antoine *professional basketball player*
Mullin, Christopher Paul *professional sports team executive, retired professional basketball player*
Nelson, Donald Arvid (Nellie Nelson) *professional basketball coach*
Richmond, Mitchell James *professional sports team executive, retired professional basketball player*
Rowell, Robert *professional sports team executive*
Yamaguchi, Kristi Tsuya *ice skater*

Playa Del Rey
Lewis, Carl (Frederick Carlton Lewis) *retired Olympic track and field athlete*

Sacramento
Abdur-Rahim, Shareef (Julius Shareef Abdul-Rahim) *professional basketball coach, retired professional basketball player*
Carril, Pete (Peter J. Carril) *professional basketball consultant*
Lawson, Kara *professional basketball player*
Maloof, Gavin Patrick *professional sports team executive*
Maloof, Joseph *professional sports team owner*
Nocioni, Andres Marcelo *professional basketball player*
Petrie, Geoffrey Michael *professional sports team executive, retired professional basketball player*
Reynolds, Jerry Owen *professional sports team executive*
Thomas, John *professional sports team executive*
Westphal, Paul *professional basketball coach*
Whisenant, John *professional basketball coach*

San Diego
Black, Bud (Harry Ralston Black) *professional baseball manager*
Edmonds, Jim (James Patrick Edmonds) *professional baseball player*
Gates, Antonio *professional football player*
Giles, Brian Stephen *professional baseball player*
Gonzalez, Adrian *professional baseball player*
Merriman, Shawne DeAndre *professional football player*
Moorad, Jeff *professional sports team executive*
Prior, Mark William *professional baseball player*
Rivers, Philip *professional football player*
Seau, Junior (Tiana Baul Seau Jr.) *professional football player*
Smith, A.J. *professional sports team executive*
Sproles, Darren Lee *professional football player*
Tomlinson, LaDainian *professional football player*
Turner, Norv (Norval Eugene Turner) *professional football coach*
Winfield, Dave (David Mark Winfield) *professional sports team executive, sportscaster, retired professional baseball player*

San Francisco
Affeldt, Jeremy David *professional baseball player*
Johnson, Randy (Randall David Johnson) *professional baseball player*
Kelly, Roberto Conrado (Bobby Kelly) *professional baseball coach, retired professional baseball player*
Lincecum, Timothy LeRoy *professional baseball player*
Lomong, Lopez (Lopepe Lomong) *Olympic track and field athlete*
Magowan, Peter Alden *professional sports team and retail executive*
Neukom, William H. *professional sports team executive, lawyer*
Penny, Brad (Bradley Wayne Penny) *professional baseball player*
Policy, Carmen A. *professional sports team executive*
Renteria, Edgar Enrique *professional baseball player*
Righetti, David Allen (Dave Righetti) *professional baseball coach, retired professional baseball player*
Sanchez, Freddy (Frederick Phillip Sanchez) *professional baseball player*

San Jose
Blake, Rob *professional hockey player*
Boyle, Dan *professional hockey player*
Cheechoo, Jonathan *professional hockey player*
Jamison, Gregory John *professional sports team executive*
Marleau, Patrick *professional hockey player*
McLellan, Todd *professional hockey coach*
Nabokov, Evgeni *professional hockey player*
Thornton, Joe *professional hockey player*
Wilson, Douglas Frederick *professional sports team executive, retired professional hockey player*

Santa Clara
Bruce, Isaac Isidore *professional football player*
Dolich, Andrew Bruce *professional sports team executive*
McCloughan, Scot G. *professional sports team executive*
Singletary, Mike *professional football coach, retired professional football player*
Smith, Alex (Alexander Doug Smith) *professional football player*
Spikes, Takeo *professional football player*
Willis, Patrick L. *professional football player*

Solvang
Roberts, Monty *horse trainer, writer*

Stanford
Grousbeck, Harold Irving *professional sports team owner, management educator*
Harbaugh, Jim (James Joseph Harbaugh) *college football coach, retired professional football player*
VanDerveer, Tara *women's college basketball coach*

Stockton
Murphy, Jeremiah T. *professional sports team, construction executive*

Torrance
Zartman, Charleen Therese *physical education educator*

Vista
Hawk, Tony *professional skateboarder*

West Hollywood
Pacquiao, Manny (Emmanuel Dapidran Pacquiao) *boxer*

COLORADO

Colorado Springs
Beard, Amanda *Olympic swimmer*
Cheek, Joey *Olympic athlete*
Clay, Bryan Ezra *Olympic track and field athlete*
Colangelo, Jerry John *professional sports team executive*
Coughlin, Natalie *Olympic swimmer*
Kwan, Michelle Wing *professional figure skater*
May-Treanor, Misty *Olympic athlete*
Peirsol, Aaron *Olympic swimmer*
Phelps, Michael *Olympic swimmer*
Schultz, Richard Dale *national athletic organization executive*
Torres, Dara *Olympic athlete*
Walsh, Kerri Lee *Olympic athlete*
Wariner, Jeremy *Olympic track and field athlete*

Denver
Anthony, Carmelo *professional basketball player*
Billups, Chauncey *professional basketball player*
Chapman, Rex *professional sports team executive, retired professional basketball player*
Dantley, Adrian *professional basketball coach, retired professional basketball player*
Foote, Adam *professional hockey player*
Giambi, Jason Gilbert *professional baseball player*
Hejduk, Milan *professional hockey player*
Karl, George *professional basketball coach*
Knight, Greg *professional sports team executive*
Lacroix, Pierre *professional sports team executive*
Martin, Kenyon *professional basketball player*
Nenê, (Maybyner Rodney Hilario) *professional basketball player*
Sacco, Joe *professional hockey coach, retired professional hockey player*
Sherman, Greg *professional sports team executive*
Smyth, Ryan *professional hockey player*
Street, Huston Lowell *professional baseball player*
Tierney, Bill *university athletic coach*
Tracy, Jim (James Edwin Tracy) *professional baseball manager*
Tulowitzki, Troy Trevor *professional baseball player*
Warkentien, Mark *professional sports team executive*

Englewood
Bailey, Champ *professional football player*
Dawkins, Brian Patrick *professional football player*
Jordan, LaMont *professional football player*
McDaniels, Josh *professional football coach*
Nolan, Mike *professional football coach*
Orton, Kyle *professional football player*
Xanders, Brian *professional sports team executive*

Greenwood Village
Elway, John Albert *professional sports team executive, retired professional football player*

CONNECTICUT

Litchfield
Kennedy, Susan Orpha *physical education educator, consultant, sports official*

New Haven
Williams, Tom *college football coach*

South Windsor
Baretta, Marsha Motyl *elementary school physical education educator*

Stamford
Goldsmith, Donna *sports entertainment company executive*

Storrs
Edsall, Randy Douglas *college football coach*

Storrs Mansfield
Auriemma, Geno *women's college basketball coach*
Calhoun, Jim *men's college basketball coach*

Uncasville
Thibault, Mike *professional basketball coach*

DISTRICT OF COLUMBIA

Washington
Arenas, Gilbert *professional basketball player*
Backstrom, Nicklas (Lars Nicklas Backstrom) *professional hockey player*
Biche, Peter *professional sports team executive*
Butler, Caron (James Caron Butler) *professional basketball player*
Cassell, Samuel James *professional basketball coach, retired professional basketball player*
Dunn, Adam Troy *professional baseball player*
Fishman, Ira *sports association executive, lawyer*
Foye, Randy *professional basketball player*
Green, Mike *professional hockey player*
Grunfeld, Ernie *professional sports team executive, retired professional basketball player*
Jamison, Antawn Cortez *professional basketball player*
Jones, Jeffrey Allen (Jeff Jones) *men's college basketball coach*
Kenlaw, Jessie *professional basketball coach*
Moreno, Jaime *professional soccer player*
Morrison, Brendan *professional hockey player*
Ovechkin, Alexander *professional hockey player*
Patrick, Dick (Richard M. Patrick) *professional sports team executive*
Plank, Julie *professional basketball coach*
Pollin, Abe *professional sports team owner, construction executive*
Riggleman, Jim (James David Riggleman) *professional baseball coach*
Saunders, Flip (Philip D. Saunders) *professional basketball coach*
Smith, DeMaurice Fitzgerald *sports association executive, lawyer*
Strasburg, Stephen *professional baseball player*
Tapscott, Ed *professional sports team executive*
Thompson, John III *men's college basketball coach*
Wittman, Randy Scott *professional basketball coach*
Zierden, Don *professional basketball coach*
Zimmerman, Ryan Wallace *professional baseball player*

FLORIDA

Boca Raton
Jarvis, Mike *men's college basketball coach*
Roddick, Andy Stephen *professional tennis player*

Bradenton
Haas, Tommy (Thomas Mario Haas) *professional tennis player*

Coral Springs
Becker, Benjamin *professional tennis player*

Davie
Henning, Dan *former professional football coach*
Ireland, Jeff *professional sports team executive*
Long, Jake *professional football player*
Parcells, Bill (Duane Charles Parcells) *professional sports team executive, retired professional football coach*
Pennington, Chad (James Chadwick Pennington) *professional football player*
Porter, Joseph Eugene (Joey Porter) *professional football player*
Sparano, Tony *professional football coach*
Taylor, Jason Paul *professional football player*

Daytona Beach
Castrale, Nicole *professional golfer*
Creamer, Paula *professional golfer*
Evans, Marsha Johnson *ladies professional golf association commissioner, retired military officer*
France, Brian Z. *sports association executive*
Inkster, Juli *professional golfer*
Jang, Jeong *professional golfer*
Kerr, Cristie *professional golfer*
Kim, Mi Hyun *professional golfer*
Lincicome, Brittany *professional golfer*
Miyazato, Ai *professional golfer*
Ochoa, Lorena *professional golfer*
Pak, Se Ri *professional golfer*
Prammanasudh, Stacy *professional golfer*
Pressel, Morgan *professional golfer*
Steinhauer, Sherri *professional golfer*
Tseng, Yani *professional golfer*
Webb, Karrie *professional golfer*
Whitworth, Kathrynne Ann *professional golfer*
Wie, Michelle Sung *professional golfer*

Deerfield Beach
King, Don *boxing promoter*

Fort Lauderdale
Mahan, Mary Hoyle *retired physical educator*

Gainesville
Butler, Amanda *women's college basketball coach*
Donovan, Billy (William John) *men's college basketball coach*
Meyer, Urban *college football coach*
Tebow, Tim (Timothy Richard Tebow) *student athlete*

Hollywood
Gonzalez, Fredi *professional baseball manager*

Jacksonville
Del Rio, Jack *professional football coach, former professional football player*
Holt, Torry *professional football player*
Jones-Drew, Maurice Christopher *professional football player*
Shula, Mike (Michael John Shula) *professional football coach, former college football coach*
Sifford, Charlie (Charles Luther Sifford) *professional golfer*
Smith, Gene *professional sports team executive*

Jupiter
Vanatta, Bob *athletic administrator*

Miami
Banks, Marcus (Arthur Lamarcus III) *professional basketball player*
Beasley, Michael Paul *professional basketball player*
Haith, Frank James, Jr. *men's college basketball coach*
Loria, Jeffrey H. *sports team executive*
O'Neal, Jermaine *professional basketball player*
Ramirez, Hanley *professional baseball player*
Riley, Patrick James *professional sports team executive*
Rothstein, Ronald *professional basketball coach*
Samson, David P. *professional baseball team executive*
Shannon, Randy Lannard *college football coach*
Slice, Kimbo (Kevin Ferguson) *mixed martial arts fighter*
Spoelstra, Erik *professional basketball coach*
Thomas, Isiah Lord III *men's college basketball coach, retired professional basketball player*
Underwood, Joseph Warren *athletic trainer, educator, actor*
Wade, Dwyane (Dwyane Tyrone Wade Jr.) *professional basketball player*
Woolworth, Eric S. *professional sports team executive*

Naples
Frazer, John Howard *tennis association and retired manufacturing executive*

North Palm Beach
Nicklaus, Jack William *professional golfer, sports apparel executive*

Ocala
Rollerson, Corey L. *professional basketball coach*

Orlando
Carter, Vince *professional basketball player*
DeVos, Richard Marvin, Sr. *professional sports team owner, former network marketing company executive*
Ewing, Patrick Aloysius *professional basketball coach, retired professional basketball player*
Fritz, Jim *professional sports team executive*
Howard, Dwight David, II, *professional basketball player*
Lewis, Rashard Quovon *professional basketball player*
Martins, Alex *professional sports team executive*
Nelson, Jameer *professional basketball player*
Redick, J.J. (Jonathan Clay Redick) *professional basketball player*
Smith, Otis Fitzgerald *professional sports team executive, retired professional basketball player*
Vander Weide, Bob *professional sports team executive*
Van Gundy, Stan *professional basketball coach*

Williams, Jason Chandler *professional basketball player*
Williams, Pat *professional sports team executive*

Palm Beach Gardens
Couples, Frederick Steven *professional golfer*
Furyk, Jim (James Michael Furyk) *professional golfer*
Leonard, Justin (Justin Charles Garret Leonard) *professional golfer*
Mickelson, Phil (Philip Alfred Mickelson Jr.) *professional golfer*
Verplank, Scott Rachal *professional golfer*
Wadkins, Lanny Lanston *professional golfer*
Woods, Tiger (Eldrick Woods) *professional golfer*

Palm Harbor
Jordan, Patricia Colgan *physical education educator*

Ponte Vedra
Hart, Dudley *professional golfer*
O'Hair, Sean *professional golfer*
Perry, Kenny (James Kenneth Perry) *professional golfer*
Weekley, Boo (Thomas Brent Weekley) *professional golfer*

Ponte Vedra Beach
Agassi, Andre Kirk *retired professional tennis player*
Austin, Woody *professional golfer*
Blake, James Riley *professional tennis player*
Campbell, Chad *professional golfer*
Cink, Stewart *professional golfer*
Cook, John (Nueman) *professional golfer*
Coria, Guillermo *professional tennis player*
Curtis, Ben Clifford *professional golfer*
Els, Ernie (Theodore Ernest Els) *professional golfer*
Finchem, Tim *Professional Golfers' Association of America Tour commissioner*
Garcia, Sergio *professional golfer*
Gaudio, Gaston *professional tennis player*
Ginepri, Robby (Robert Louis Ginepri) *professional tennis player*
Grosjean, Sebastien Rene *professional tennis player*
Johnson, Zach (Zachary Harris Johnson) *professional golfer*
Kim, Anthony *professional golfer*
Mahan, Hunter *professional golfer*
Montgomerie, Colin Stuart *professional golfer*
Moya, Carlos *professional tennis player*
Nalbandian, David *professional tennis player*
Romero, Andrés *professional golfer*
Scott, Adam *professional golfer*
Singh, Vijay *professional golfer*
Stricker, Steve *professional golfer*
Villegas, Camilo *professional golfer*
Yang, Yong-Eun *professional golfer*
Young, Mark Vernon *sports association executive, lawyer*

Saint Petersburg
Allaster, Stacey *sports association executive*
Burrell, Pat (Patrick Brian Burrell) *professional baseball player*
Crawford, Carl Demonte *professional baseball player*
Dementieva, Elena *professional tennis player*
Garza, Matthew Scott (Matt Garza) *professional baseball player*
Huber, Liezel *professional tennis player*
Kuznetsova, Svetlana *professional tennis player*
Longoria, Evan Michael *professional baseball player*
Maddon, Joe (Joseph John Maddon) *professional baseball manager*
Myskina, Anastasia *professional tennis player*
Pena, Carlos Felipe *professional baseball player*
Raymond, Lisa *professional tennis player*
Sharapova, Maria *professional tennis player*
Upton, B.J. (Melvin Emanuel Upton) *professional baseball player*
Zimmer, Donald William *former professional baseball coach, professional baseball manager, retired professional baseball player*

Sunrise
Cohen, Alan Phillip *professional sports team executive, former pharmaceutical executive*
DeBoer, Peter *professional hockey coach*
Sexton, Randy J. *professional sports team executive*
Stillman, Cory *professional hockey player*
Yormark, Michael *professional sports team executive*

Tallahassee
Bowden, Bobby (Robert Cleckler Bowden) *college football coach*
Hamilton, Leonard *men's college basketball coach*
Hogan, Dexter L. *football coach*
Semrau, Sue *women's college basketball coach*
Yerg, Beverly Johnson *retired physical education educator, researcher*

Tampa
Alstott, Michael Joseph (Mike Alstott) *retired professional football player*
Barber, Ronde (Jamael Oronde Barber) *professional football player*
Campbell, Ron *professional sports team executive*
Dominik, Mark *professional sports team executive*
Lawton, Brian R. *professional sports team executive*
Lecavalier, Vincent *professional hockey player*
Leftwich, Byron Antron *professional football player*
Morris, Raheem *professional football coach*
St. Louis, Martin *professional hockey player*
Stamkos, Steven *professional hockey player*
Tanguay, Alex *professional hockey player*
Tocchet, Rick *professional hockey coach, retired professional hockey player*
Winslow, Kellen Boswell, II, *professional football player*

Vero Beach
Fish, Mardy *professional tennis player*

Viera
Nessel, Edward Harry *swimming coach*

West Palm Beach
Floyd, Raymond Loran *professional golfer*

Weston
Williams, Ricky (Errick Lynne Williams) *professional football player*

Winter Springs
Hall, Gene Christian (Chris Hall) *coach, educator*

GEORGIA

Athens
Fox, Mark *men's college basketball coach*
Richt, Mark *college football coach*

Atlanta
Aaron, Hank (Henry L. Aaron) *professional baseball team executive*
Anderson, Garret *professional baseball player*
Anderson, John *professional hockey coach, retired professional hockey player*
Belkin, Steven *professional sports team executive*
Bibby, Mike *professional basketball player*
Cox, Bobby (Robert Joe Cox) *professional baseball manager*
Crawford, Aaron Jamal (Jamal Crawford) *professional basketball player*
Dimitroff, Thomas G., Jr. *professional sports team executive*
Dudley, Rick (Richard C. Dudley) *professional sports team executive, retired professional hockey player*
Enstrom, Tobias *professional hockey player*
Erving, Julius (Winfield), (II) *business executive, retired professional basketball player*
Gearon, John Michael, Jr., (Michael Gearon) *professional sports team owner, communications executive*
Hill, Tyrone *professional basketball coach, retired professional basketball player*
Horford Reynoso, Alfred Joel (Al Horford) *professional basketball player*
Johnson, Joe Marcus *professional basketball player*
Johnson, Paul *college football coach*
Jones, Chipper (Larry Wayne Jones Jr.) *professional baseball player*
Kovalchuk, Ilya *professional hockey player*
Kubina, Pavel *professional hockey player*
Lowe, Derek (Derek Christopher Lowe) *professional baseball player*
McCann, Brian Michael *professional baseball player*
McLouth, Nathan Richard (Nate McLouth) *professional baseball player*
Meadors, Marynell *professional basketball coach*
Mutombo, Dikembe (Dikembe Mutombo Mpolondo Mukamba Jean Jacque Wamutombo) *retired professional basketball player*
Price, Mark (William Mark Price) *professional basketball coach, retired professional basketball player*
Riccio, Felix *professional sports team owner*
Rucchin, Steve *professional hockey player*
Schuerholz, John Boland, Jr. *professional baseball executive*
Smith, Joe (Joseph Leynard Smith) *professional basketball player*
Sund, Rick (Richard W. Sund) *professional sports team executive*
Vazquez, Javier Carlos *professional baseball player*
Waddell, Don *professional sports team executive*
Wilkins, Dominique (Jacques Dominique Wilkins) *professional sports team executive, retired professional basketball player*
Williams, Bob *professional sports team executive*
Woodson, Mike *professional basketball coach*
Wren, Frank *professional baseball team executive*
Zhitnik, Alexei *professional hockey player*

Fairburn
Holyfield, Evander *professional boxer*

Flowery Branch
Abraham, John *professional football player*
Blank, Arthur M. *professional sports team and retired lumber company executive*
Elam, Jason *professional football player*
Gonzalez, Tony (Anthony David Gonzalez) *professional football player*
McKay, Richard James *professional sports team executive*
Ryan, Matt (Matthew Thomas Ryan) *professional football player*
Smith, Mike *professional football coach*
Turner, Michael *professional football player*

Morrow
Totty, Totty Okoro *soccer coach*

HAWAII

Honolulu
McMackin, Greg *college football coach*

IDAHO

Boise
Petersen, Chris *college football coach*

ILLINOIS

Carbondale
Lowery, Christopher M. *men's college basketball coach*

Champaign
Weber, Bruce *men's college basketball coach*
Zook, Ron *college football coach*

Chicago
Baines, Harold Douglass *retired professional baseball player, baseball bench coach*
Bickerstaff, Bernie (Bernard Tyrone Bickerstaff Sr.) *professional basketball coach*
Bondra, Peter *professional hockey player*
Bowman, Scotty (William Scott Bowman) *professional sports team executive, retired professional hockey coach*
Bowman, Stan *professional sports team executive*
Bradley, Milton Obelle *professional baseball player*
Buehrle, Mark Alan *professional baseball player*
Campbell, Brian Wesley *professional hockey player*
Colon, Bartolo *professional baseball player*
Del Negro, Vincent Joseph (Vinny Del Negro) *professional basketball coach*
Dempster, Ryan (Scott) *professional baseball player*
Deng, Luol *professional basketball player*
Dupree, Candice *professional basketball player*
Dye, Jermaine *professional baseball player*
Forman, Gar *professional sports team executive*
Foudy, Julie Maurine *retired professional soccer player, Olympic athlete*
Fowles, Sylvia Shaqueria *professional basketball player*
Fukudome, Kosuke *professional baseball player*
Gervais, Mark G. *physical education educator*
Guillen, Ozzie (Oswaldo Jose Barrios Guillen) *professional baseball manager*
Hamm, Mia (Mariel Margaret Hamm) *retired professional soccer player*
Hemond, Roland A. *professional baseball team executive*
Hossa, Marian *professional hockey player*
Hucles, Angela Khalia *professional soccer player*
Kane, Patrick *professional hockey player*
Key, Steven *professional basketball coach*
Kotsay, Mark Steven *professional baseball player*
Lilly, Ted (Theodore Roosevelt Lilly) *professional baseball player*
Madden, John *professional hockey player*
McDonough, John F. *professional sports team executive*
Miller, Brad (Bradley Allen Miller) *professional basketball player*
O'Reilly, Heather Ann *Olympic athlete*
Paxson, John *professional sports team executive, retired professional basketball player*
Peavy, Jake (Jacob Edward Peavy) *professional baseball player*
Piniella, Lou (Louis Victor Piniella) *professional baseball team manager*
Pizer, Howard Charles *sports and entertainment executive*
Quenneville, Joel *professional hockey coach*
Reinsdorf, Jerry Michael *professional sports team owner, real estate company executive, accountant, lawyer*
Reyna, Claudio *retired professional soccer player*
Rios, Alexis Israel *professional baseball player*
Rose, Derrick Martell *professional basketball player*
Schanwald, Steve *professional sports team executive*
Soriano, Alfonso Guilleard *professional baseball player*
Soto, Geovany *professional baseball player*
Tallon, Dale *professional sports team executive*
Toews, Jonathan *professional hockey player*
Westbrook, Brian Collins *professional football player*
Wirtz, Rocky (W. Rockwell Wirtz) *professional sports team executive, beverage company executive*
Zambrano, Carlos Alberto *professional baseball player*

Evanston
Fitzgerald, Pat *college football coach*

Glenview
King, Billie Jean Moffitt *retired professional tennis player*

Lake Forest
Angelo, Jerry *professional sports team executive*
Cutler, Jay *professional football player*
Forte, Matt *professional football player*
Hester, Devin *professional football player*
Marinelli, Rod *professional football coach*
Pace, Orlando Lamar *professional football player*
Smith, Lovie *professional football coach*
Urlacher, Brian Keith *professional football player*

Park Ridge
Delany, Jim (James Edward Delany) *sports association administrator, lawyer*

Schaumburg
Colberg, Linda *physical education educator*

Springfield
Hicks, David Eric *retired sports association executive*

Sterling
Moran, Joan Jensen *physical education and healthcare educator*

INDIANA

Bloomington
Crean, Tom (Thomas Aaron Crean) *men's college basketball coach*

Indianapolis
Bird, Larry Joe *professional sports team executive, retired professional basketball player*
Caldwell, Jim *professional football coach*
Catchings, Tamika Devonne *professional basketball player*
Cato, Mo M. *professional soccer coach, educator*
Dunn, Lin *professional basketball coach*
Faulk, Marshall Williams *retired professional football player*
Ford, Terrence Jerod (T.J. Ford) *professional basketball player*
Granger, Danny, Jr. *professional basketball player*
Hansbrough, Tyler *professional basketball player*
Irsay, James Steven *professional football team owner*
Lagat, Bernard *Olympic track and field athlete*
Manning, Peyton Williams *professional football player*
Morway, David S. *professional sports team executive*
O'Brien, Jim *professional basketball coach*
Patrick, Danica Sue *race car driver*
Polian, Bill *professional football team executive*
Sanders, Bob (Demond Sanders) *professional football player*
Shaheen, Greg A. *sports association executive*
Stevens, Brad K. *men's college basketball coach*
Vinatieri, Adam Matthew *professional football player*
Wheldon, Dan (Daniel Clive Wheldon) *race car driver*
Williams, Bernard *Olympic athlete*

Muncie
Hoke, Brady *college football coach*

New Castle
Cole, Adelaide Meador *retired physical education educator*

Notre Dame
Brey, Mike *men's college basketball coach*
McGraw, Muffet *women's college basketball coach*
Swarbrick, John Brian, Jr. *athletics director, lawyer*
Weis, Charlie *college football coach*

Rochester
Neff, Kathy S. *swimming and water safety educator*

West Lafayette
Painter, Matt *men's college basketball coach*

IOWA

Ames
Fennelly, William (Bill Fennelly) *women's college basketball coach*

Cedar Falls
Jacobson, Ben *men's college basketball coach*

Davenport
Foster, James Franklin *professional sports management executive*

Des Moines
Phelps, Mark *men's college basketball coach*

Iowa City
Ferentz, Kirk *college football coach*
Lickliter, Todd *men's college basketball coach*

West Des Moines
Johnson, Shawn Machel *Olympic gymnast*

KANSAS

Emmett
Byers, Walter *athletic association executive*

Lawrence
Mangino, Mark Thomas *college football coach*
Manning, Danny (Daniel Ricardo Manning) *men's college basketball coach, retired professional basketball player*
Self, Bill *men's college basketball coach*

Manhattan
Patterson, Deb *women's college basketball coach*

Mcpherson
Coppock, Doris Ellen *retired music and physical education educator*

Topeka
Craw, Nicholas Wesson *motor sports association executive*

KENTUCKY

Bowling Green
Navalta, James W. *physical education educator*

Lexington
Calipari, John Vincent *men's college basketball coach*

Louisville
Evans, Robert L. *sports venue executive*
Kragthorpe, Steve *college football coach*
Pitino, Rick *men's college basketball coach*
Walz, Jeff (Jeffrey J. Walz) *women's college basketball coach*

Williamsburg
Blackmore-Haus, Margaret Ann *athletic trainer, educator*

LOUISIANA

Baton Rouge
Chancellor, Van *women's college basketball coach*
Johnson, Trent *men's college basketball coach*

Li, Li *physical education educator*
Miles, Les (Leslie Edwin Miles) *college football coach*
Reeve, Thomas Gilmour *physical education educator*
Starkey, Bob (Robert G. Starkey) *women's college basketball coach*

Grambling
Duckett, Rick *men's college basketball coach*

Metairie
Brees, Drew (Drew Christopher Brees) *professional football player*
Bush, Reggie *professional football player*
Colston, Marques *professional football player*
Harrington, Joey (John Joseph Harrington) *professional football player*
Loomis, Mickey *professional sports team executive*
Payton, Sean (Patrick Sean Payton) *professional football coach*
Shockey, Jeremy Charles *professional football player*
Vilma, Jonathan Polynice *professional football player*

New Orleans
Bower, Jeff *professional sports team executive*
Daniels, Antonio Robert *professional basketball player*
Okafor, Emeka (Chukwuemeka Noubuisi Okafor) *professional basketball player*
Paul, Chris *professional basketball player*
Reed, Willis *professional sports team executive*
Scott, Byron *professional basketball coach, retired professional basketball player*
Shinn, George *professional sports team owner*
Stojakovic, Peja *professional basketball player*
Weber, Hugh *professional sports team executive*
West, David Moorer *professional basketball player*

MAINE

Portland
Blair, Bonnie Kathleen *former professional speedskater, Olympic athlete*

MARYLAND

Baltimore
Angelos, Peter G. *professional sports team executive, lawyer*
Flacco, Joe (Joseph Vincent Flacco) *professional football player*
Huff, Aubrey Lewis *professional baseball player*
Jones, Adam La Marque *professional baseball player*
Lewis, Ray Anthony *professional football player*
MacPhail, Andrew B. *professional sports team executive*
Markakis, Nick (Nicholas William Markakis) *professional baseball player*
McClain, Le'Ron De'Mar *professional football player*
McGahee, Willis Andrew *professional football player*
Ngata, Haloti (Etuini Haloti Ngata) *professional football player*
Reed, Ed (Edward Earl Reed Jr.) *professional football player*
Rice, Ray *professional football player*
Ripken, Cal (Calvin Edwin Ripken Jr.) *retired professional baseball player, sportscaster*
Smith, L.J. *professional football player*
Suggs, Terrell (Terrell Raynonn Suggs) *professional football player*

Bethesda
Johnson, Robert Louis *professional sports team owner, former broadcast executive*

Bowie
Baker, Marshina *physical education educator*

College Park
Frese, Brenda S. *women's college basketball coach*
Friedgen, Ralph Harry *college football coach*
Yow, Deborah A. *athletic director*

Frederick
Butler, Jay *women's college basketball coach*

Owings Mills
Cameron, Cam (Malcolm G. Cameron III) *professional football coach*
Harbaugh, John *professional football coach*
Newsome, Ozzie *professional sports team executive*
Smith, Troy *professional football player*

Rockville
Foreman, Todd Matthew *professional sports team owner, communications executive*
Levenson, Bruce *professional sports team owner, communications executive*
Peskowitz, Ed *professional sports team owner, communications executive*

MASSACHUSETTS

Boston
Ainge, Danny Ray *professional sports team executive, retired professional basketball player*
Allen, Ray (Walter Ray Allen) *professional basketball player*
Allen, Tony *professional basketball player*
Amaker, Tommy *men's college basketball coach*
Bay, Jason Raymond *professional baseball player*
Beckett, Joshua Patrick *professional baseball player*
Blendon, Robert Jay *health policy educator*
Bourque, Ray *retired professional hockey player*
Chara, Zdeno *professional hockey player*
Chiarelli, Peter *professional sports team executive*
Drew, J.D. (Jonathan David Drew) *professional baseball player*
Epstein, Theo N. *professional sports team executive*
Fernandez, Manny (Emmanuel Fernandez-Lemaire) *professional hockey player*
Francona, Terry Jon *professional baseball manager, former professional baseball player*
Garnett, Kevin Maurice *professional basketball player*
Gay, Tyson *track and field athlete*
Gotham, Richard Ernest *professional sports team executive*
Henry, John William, II, *professional sports team executive*
Jacobs, Charlie (Charles M. Jacobs) *professional sports team executive*
Julien, Claude *professional hockey coach*
Kessel, Phil *professional hockey player*
Lester, Jonathan Tyler *professional baseball player*
Lowell, Mike (Michael Averett Lowell) *professional baseball player*
Lucchino, Lawrence *sports team executive, lawyer*
Martinez, Victor Jesus *professional baseball player*
Matsuzaka, Daisuke *professional baseball player*
Neely, Cam (Cameron Michael) *professional sports team executive, retired professional hockey player*
Ortiz, David (David Americo Ortiz Arias) *professional baseball player*
Papelbon, Jon(athan) (Robert) *professional baseball player*
Parker, Jack *men's college hockey coach*
Pedroia, Dustin Luis *professional baseball player*
Pierce, Paul Anthony *professional basketball player*
Ramirez, Ramon Santo *professional baseball player*
Recchi, Mark *professional hockey player*
Rivers, Doc (Glenn Anton Rivers) *professional basketball coach*
Rondo, Rajon Pierre *professional basketball player*
Savard, Marc *professional hockey player*
Thomas, Tim *professional hockey player*
Varitek, Jason *professional baseball player*
Wagner, Billy (William Edward Wagner) *professional baseball player*
Wakefield, Timothy Stephen (Tim Wakefield) *professional baseball player*
Wallace, Rasheed *professional basketball player*
Youkilis, Kevin *professional baseball player*

Braintree
Malloy, Ellen Ann *athletic trainer*

Charlestown
Orr, Bobby (Robert Gordon Orr) *retired professional hockey player, sports agent*

Chestnut Hill
Spaziani, Frank *college football coach*
York, Jerry *men's college hockey coach*

Foxboro
Belichick, Bill (William Stephen Belichick) *professional football coach*
Brady, Tom (Thomas Edward Patrick Brady Jr.) *professional football player*
Caserio, Nick *professional sports team executive*
Dillon, Corey *professional football player*
Gostkowski, Stephen Carroll *professional football player*
Johnson, Thomas (Pepper Johnson) *professional football coach, retired professional football player*
Kraft, Robert K. *professional sports team executive*
Mayo, Jerod *professional football player*
Moss, Randy Gene *professional football player*
Reese, Floyd *professional sports team executive*
Taylor, Fred *professional football player*

Lexington
Grousbeck, Wycliffe *professional sports team owner, venture capitalist*

Lowell
MacLean, John *professional hockey coach, former professional hockey player*

Lynnfield
Kerrigan, Nancy *professional figure skater, retired Olympic athlete*

North Andover
Kravette, Ronald Irwin *professional athletics coach, educator*

MICHIGAN

Allen Park
Culpepper, Daunte *professional football player*
Cunningham, Gunther *professional football coach*
Hanson, Jason Douglas *professional football player*
Johnson, Calvin *professional football player*
Linehan, Scott Thomas *professional football coach*
Mayhew, Martin R. *professional sports team executive, retired professional football player*
Schwartz, Jim *professional football coach*
Stafford, Matt (John Matthew Stafford) *professional football player*

Ann Arbor
Rodriguez, Rich *college football coach*

Auburn Hills
Brown, Kwame *professional basketball player*
Davidson, Karen W. *professional sports team executive*
Dumars, Joe III *professional sports team executive, retired professional basketball player*
Ford, Cheryl *professional basketball player*
Gordon, Ben *professional basketball player*
Hamilton, Richard Clay *professional basketball player*
Hill, Brian A. *professional basketball coach*
Kuester, John *professional basketball coach*
Mahorn, Rick (Derrick Allen Mahorn) *professional basketball coach, retired professional basketball player*
Nolan, Deanna Nicole *professional basketball player*
Ostfield, Alan *professional sports team executive*
Perry, Scott *professional sports team executive*
Prince, Tayshaun Durell *professional basketball player*
Smith, Katie (Katherine May Smith) *professional basketball player*
Wallace, Ben *professional basketball player*
Wilson, Thomas S. *professional sports team executive*

Cheboygan
Ostrowski, Stacey *athletic trainer, educator*

Davison
West, Stacy Kathlena *athletic trainer*

Dearborn
Larionov, Igor (Igor Nikolayevich Larionov) *retired professional hockey player*

Detroit
Babcock, Mike *professional hockey coach*
Bertuzzi, Todd *professional hockey player*
Cabrera, Miguel (Jose Miguel Cabrera) *professional baseball player*
Datsyuk, Pavel *professional hockey player*
Devellano, Jim (James Charles Devellano) *professional sports team executive*
Draper, Kris *professional hockey player*
Filppula, Valtteri *professional hockey player*
Franzen, Johan *professional hockey player*
Granderson, Curtis, Jr. *professional baseball player*
Holland, Ken *professional sports team executive*
Holmstrom, Tomas *professional hockey player*
Ilitch, Marian *professional hockey team and food service executive*
Ilitch, Michael *professional hockey team and food products executive*
Leyland, Jim (James Richard Leyland) *professional baseball manager*
Lidstrom, Nicklas *professional hockey player*
Maltby, Kirk *professional hockey player*
McCarty, Darren *professional hockey player*
Nabozny, Heather *professional sports team groundskeeper*
Ordonez, Magglio Jose *professional baseball player*
Osgood, Chris *professional hockey player*
Polanco, Placido Enrique *professional baseball player*
Rafalski, Brian *professional hockey player*
Rogers, Kenny (Kenneth Scott Rogers) *professional baseball player*
Samuelsson, Mikael *professional hockey player*
Stuart, Brad *professional hockey player*
Van Slyke, Andrew James *professional baseball coach, retired professional baseball player*
Verlander, Justin Brooks *professional baseball player*
Washburn, Jarrod *professional baseball player*
Willis, Dontrelle (Wayne) *professional baseball player*
Yzerman, Steve (Stephen Gregory Yzerman) *professional sports team executive, retired professional hockey player*
Zetterberg, Henrik *professional hockey player*

East Lansing
Dantonio, Mark *college football coach*
Izzo, Thomas (Tom Izzo) *men's college basketball coach*
Merchant, Suzy *women's college basketball coach*

Livonia
Gilbert, Daniel *professional sports team owner, mortgage company executive*

MINNESOTA

Eden Prairie
Allen, Jared Scot *professional football player*
Brzezinski, Rob *professional sports team executive*
Childress, Brad *professional football coach*
Favre, Brett Lorenzo *professional football player*
Hutchinson, Steve *professional football player*
Spielman, Rick *professional sports team executive*
Williams, Kevin *professional football player*

Lakeland
Housley, Phil F. *coach, retired professional hockey player*

Minneapolis
Cabrera, Orlando Luis *professional baseball player*
DeForge, Anna *professional basketball player*
Gillom, Jennifer *professional basketball coach, retired professional basketball player*
Gomes, Ryan *professional basketball player*
Grudzielanek, Mark James *professional baseball player*
Jefferson, Al *professional basketball player*
Kahn, David *professional sports team executive*
Mauer, Joe *professional baseball player*
Monroe, Craig (Keystone) *professional baseball player*
Moor, Rob *professional sports team executive*
Morneau, Justin Ernest George *professional baseball player*
Nathan, Joseph Michael (Joe Nathan) *professional baseball player*
Peterson, Adrian Lewis *professional football player*
Rambis, Kurt (Darrell Kurt Rambis) *professional basketball coach, retired professional basketball player*
Ryan, Terry *professional sports team executive*
Smith, Bill *professional sports team executive*
Smith, Tubby *men's college basketball coach*
Stack, Jim *professional sports team executive*
Wiggins, Candice Dana *professional basketball player*
Wright, Chris *professional sports team executive*
Young, Delmon Damarcus *professional baseball player*

Saint Paul
Backstrom, Niklas *professional hockey player*
Fletcher, Chuck (George C. Fletcher) *professional sports team executive*
Havlat, Martin *professional hockey player*
Leipold, Craig L. *professional sports team executive*
Lynn, Tom *professional sports team executive*
Nolan, Owen *professional hockey player*
Richards, Todd *professional hockey coach*

MISSISSIPPI

Jackson
Bynum, CeDric Darnell *professional baseball coach, elementary school educator*
Fowler, Paul David *coach*
McAllister, Deuce (Dulymus Jenod McAllister) *professional football player*

Mississippi State
Stansbury, Rick *men's college basketball coach*

University
Nutt, Houston Dale, Jr. *college football coach*

MISSOURI

Archie
Schulte, Troy Anthony *coach, director*

Columbia
Anderson, Mike *men's college basketball coach*
Pinkel, Gary *college football coach*

Earth City
Bulger, Marc *professional football player*

Kansas City
Carney, John Michael *professional football player*
Cassel, Matt *professional football player*
Glass, David D. *professional sports team executive, retired retail executive*
Greinke, Donald Zachary (Zach Greinke) *professional baseball player*
Haley, Todd *professional football coach*
Hillman, Trey (Thomas Brad Hillman) *professional baseball manager*
Johnson, Larry (Larry Alphonso Johnson Jr.) *professional football player*
Pioli, Scott *professional sports team executive*
Thomas, Zach Michael (Zachary Michael Thomas) *professional football player*

Maryland Heights
Hahn, Mark A. *coach, educator*

Oregon
Lynn, Brenda *physical education educator*

Palmyra
Wosman, Brian D. *physical education educator, director*

Saint Louis
Armstrong, Doug *professional sports team executive*
Brewer, Eric *professional hockey player*
Checketts, Dave (David Wayne Checketts) *professional sports team executive*
Davidson, John *professional sports team executive, former hockey analyst*
Glaus, Troy Edward *professional baseball player*
Greene, Khalil Thabit *professional baseball player*
Holliday, Matt *professional baseball player*
Jackson, Steven Rashad *professional football player*
Kariya, Paul *professional hockey player*
La Russa, Tony, Jr., (Anthony La Russa Jr.) *professional baseball manager*
Long, Christopher Howard *professional football player*
MacInnis, Al *professional sports team executive, retired professional hockey player*
Molina, Yadier B. *professional baseball player*
Murray, Andy *professional hockey coach*
Pleau, Larry (Lawrence Winslow Pleau) *professional sports team executive*
Pujols, Albert (Jose Alberto Pujols) *professional baseball player*
Saunders, Alan Keith *professional football coach*
Smoltz, John Andrew *professional baseball player*
Softli, Tony *professional sports team executive*
Spagnuolo, Steve *professional football coach*
Tkachuk, Keith *professional hockey player*
Wolfard, Jason *basketball coach, educator*

Springfield
Garrett, Dale Lee *football coach, educator*

NEBRASKA

Brady
Novacek, Jay McKinley *retired professional football player*

Lincoln
Mulvaney, Mary Jean *retired physical education educator*
Osborne, Tom (Thomas William Osborne) *college athletic director, former United State Representative from Nebraska*
Pelini, Bo *college football coach*

Stromsburg
Waltman, Bob Ray *coach, educator*

NEVADA

Las Vegas
Fertitta, Frank J. III *sports association and casino executive*
Fertitta, Lorenzo J. *sports association and casino executive*
Primeau, Keith *professional sports team executive, retired professional hockey player*
Schneiter, George Malan *professional golfer, real estate developer*

NEW HAMPSHIRE

Goshen
Wright, Lilyan Boyd *physical education educator*

Keene
Bleam, Nancy Kay *physical education educator*

Newmarket
Jernigan, David Bruce *men's college basketball coach*

Sugar Hill
Miller, Bode (Samuel Bode Miller) *professional skier*

NEW JERSEY

Camden
Mazzoli, Linda Fabrizio *personal trainer, consultant, marketing professional*

East Rutherford
Carr, David *professional football player*
Coughlin, Tom (Thomas Richard Coughlin) *professional football coach*
Frank, Lawrence *professional basketball coach*
Gilbride, Kevin *professional football coach*
Harris, Devin Lamar *professional basketball player*
Jacobs, Brandon *professional football player*
Lamping, Mark C. *professional sports team executive*
Manning, Eli (Elisha Nelson Manning) *professional football player*
Mara, John Kevin *professional sports team executive*
Pierce, Antonio *professional football player*
Reese, Jerry *professional sports team executive*
Snee, Christopher *professional football player*
Thorn, Rodney King *professional sports team executive, retired professional basketball player*
Tuck, Justin Lee *professional football player*
Umenyiora, Osi *professional football player*
Vanderweighe, Kiki (Ernest Maurice Vanderweighe III) *professional sports team executive, retired professional basketball player*
Vandeweghe, Ernest Maurice, III, (Kiki Vandeweghe) *professional sports team executive, retired professional basketball player*
Yi, Jianlian *professional basketball player*
Yormark, Brett D. *professional sports team executive*

Fairfield
Fassel, Jim (James E. Fassel) *professional football coach*

Far Hills
Glover, Lucas Hendley *professional golfer*

Little Falls
Berra, Yogi (Lawrence Peter Berra) *former professional baseball player, coach, manager*

Montclair
Chemidlin, Michele Lynn *athletic trainer, consultant*

New Brunswick
Dougherty, Neil Joseph *physical education educator, consultant*

Newark
Brodeur, Martin *professional hockey player*
Elias, Patrik *professional hockey player*
Lamoriello, Lou (Louis Anthony Lamoriello) *professional sports team executive*
Langenbrunner, Jamie *professional hockey player*
Laperriere, Jacques (Joseph Hughes Laperriere) *professional hockey coach, retired professional hockey player*
Lemaire, Jacques *professional hockey coach*
Parise, Zach *professional hockey player*
Raines, Tim (Timothy Raines) *baseball coach, retired professional baseball player*
Robinson, Larry Clark *professional hockey coach, retired professional hockey player*
Rolston, Brian *professional hockey player*
Shanahan, Brendan Frederick *professional hockey player*
Stevens, Scott *retired professional hockey player*
Vanderbeek, Jeffrey *professional sports team executive*

Piscataway
Schiano, Greg *college football coach*
Stringer, C. Vivian (Charlene Vivian Sringer) *women's college basketball coach*

Secaucus
Austin, Ski *sports association executive*
Criqui, Robert J. *sports association executive*
Denenberg, David Scott *sports association executive, lawyer*
Hellmuth, Stephen M. *sports association executive*
Koenig, William S. *sports association executive*

Totowa
Peter, Samuel (Okon) *professional boxer*

NEW MEXICO

Abiquiu
Howlett, Phyllis Lou *retired athletics administrator*

Albuquerque
Alford, Steve (Steven Todd Alford) *men's college basketball coach*

NEW YORK

Brentwood
Burgess, John Thomas *physical education educator, consultant*

Bronx
Afterman, Jean *professional sports team executive*
Burnett, A.J. (Allen James Burnett) *professional baseball player*
Cano, Robinson Jose *professional baseball player*
Chamberlain, Joba *professional baseball player*
Damon, Johnny *professional baseball player*
Girardi, Joe (Joseph Elliot Girardi) *professional baseball manager, retired professional baseball player*
Hinske, Eric Scott *professional baseball player*
Jackson, Reggie (Reginald Martinez Jackson, Mr. October) *retired professional baseball player*
Jeter, Derek Sanderson *professional baseball player*
Levine, Randy Lewis *professional baseball team executive, lawyer*
Lienert, Christoph *physical education educator*
Matsui, Hideki *professional baseball player*
Peña, Tony (Antonio Francisco Peña) *professional baseball coach, retired professional baseball player*
Pettitte, Andy (Andrew Eugene Pettitte) *professional baseball player*
Posada, Jorge Rafael *professional baseball player*
Rivera, Mariano *professional baseball player*
Rodriguez, Alex (Alexander Emmanuel Rodriguez) *professional baseball player*
Sabathia, C.C. (Carsten Charles Sabathia) *professional baseball player*
Steinbrenner, George Michael III *professional baseball team and shipbuilding company executive*
Steinbrenner, Hal (Harold Zeig Steinbrenner) *professional baseball team executive*
Swisher, Nick (Nicolas Thompson Swisher) *professional baseball player*
Tarver, Antonio Deon *professional boxer*
Teixeira, Mark Charles *professional baseball player*

Brooklyn
Leung, Raymond W. *physical education educator*
Ratner, Bruce C. *professional sports team owner, real estate developer*

Buffalo
Gill, Turner *college football coach*
Miller, Ryan *professional hockey player*
Numminen, Teppo *professional hockey player*
Quinn, Larry (Lawrence Quinn) *professional sports team executive*
Regier, Darcy John *professional sports team executive*
Ruff, Lindy *professional hockey coach*
Vanek, Thomas *professional hockey player*
Vanini, J. Tim *environmental educator, coach, consultant*

Canastota
Perkins, Eddie *retired professional boxer*

Cobleskill
Westervelt, Gayle Gaetano *physical education educator*

Cooperstown
Henderson, Rickey Henley *retired professional baseball player, former professional baseball coach*
Mays, Willie Howard, Jr., (Say Hey Kid) *retired professional baseball player*

Flushing
Beltran, Carlos *professional baseball player*
Delgado, Carlos Juan *professional baseball player*
Hernandez, Livan (Eisler Livan Carrera Hernandez) *professional baseball player*
Manuel, Jerry *professional baseball team manager*
Minaya, Omar *professional sports team executive*
Perez, Oliver *professional baseball player*
Putz, J.J. (Joseph Jason Putz) *professional baseball player*
Reyes, Jose Bernabe *professional baseball player*
Rodriguez, Francisco Jose *professional baseball player*
Santana, Johan (Johan Alexander Santana Araque) *professional baseball player*
Sheffield, Gary Antonian *professional baseball player*
Wilpon, Fred *professional sports team executive*
Wright, David Allen *professional baseball player*

Hempstead
Callahan, Bill (William E. Callahan) *professional football coach*
Faneca, Alan Joseph, Jr. *professional football player*
Ryan, Rex *professional football coach*
Sanchez, Mark *professional football player*
Tannenbaum, Mike (Michael B. Tannenbaum) *professional sports team executive*
Washington, Leon *professional football player*

Irvington
Jackson, Billy Ray *physical education educator*

Ithaca
Donahue, Steve *men's college basketball coach*

Jamaica
Desormeaux, Kent J. *jockey*
Roberts, Norm *men's college basketball coach*

Lake Placid
Rossi, Ronald Aldo *sports association administrator, Olympic athlete*

Loudonville
McCaffery, Fran *men's college basketball coach*

Mamaroneck
McEnroe, Patrick *former professional tennis player, sports commentator*

New York
Angel, Steven M. *sports association executive*
Avery, Sean *professional hockey player*
Bantom, Michael Allen *sports association executive*
Barnett, Michael *professional sports team executive*
Behrens, Kathleen *sports association executive*
Bettman, Gary Bruce *National Hockey League commissioner*
Blazejowski, Carol Ann *professional sports team executive, retired professional basketball player*
Brosnan, Timothy J. *sports association executive*
Brown, Reneé M. *sports association executive*
Buchanan, Richard W. (Richard W. Buchanan) *sports association executive, lawyer*
Canseco, Jose *retired professional baseball player*
Capriati, Jennifer Maria *professional tennis player*
Carelli, Thomas A. *sports association executive*
Collins, Emilio *sports association executive*
Collins, John *sports association executive*
Cottrell, Ted (Theodore John Cottrell) *professional football coach*
D'Antoni, Mike (Michael Andrew D'Antoni) *professional basketball coach*
Dellapina, John *sports association executive, writer*
Deutsch, Ayala *sports association executive, lawyer, educator*
Donovan, Anne *professional basketball coach*
Drury, Chris *professional hockey player*
Dubinsky, Brandon *professional hockey player*
Duhon, Chris *professional basketball player*
DuPuy, Bob (Robert A. DuPuy) *major league baseball executive*
Gaborik, Marian *professional hockey player*
Gilroy, Matt *professional hockey player*
Gliedman, Michael Seth *sports association executive*
Goodell, Roger Stokoe *National Football League commissioner*
Granger, Christopher *sports association executive*
Graves, Adam *professional sports team executive, retired professional hockey player*
Green, Dennis E. *professional football coach*
Gregory, Jim (James Michael) *sports association executive, former professional sports team executive*
Grubman, Eric P. *sports association executive*
Hanson, Paula *sports association executive*
Harrington, Al (Albert Harrington) *professional basketball player*
Haslett, Jim (James Donald Haslett) *professional football coach*
Higgins, Christopher *professional hockey player*
Houston, Allan Wade *professional sports team executive, retired professional basketball player*
Jackson, Stu *sports association executive, former men's college basketball coach*
Jennings, Brian *sports association executive*
Johnson, Ronald Lee *sports association executive, retired military officer*
LaRocca, Salvatore *sports association executive*
Lee, David *professional basketball player*
Litvin, Joel M. *sports association executive, lawyer*
Louganis, Greg E(fthimios) *retired Olympic athlete, actor*
Lundqvist, Henrik *professional hockey player*
Mariner, Jonathan D. *major league baseball executive*
Martin, Michael Townsend *sports association executive, marketing professional, consultant*
McHale, John Joseph, Jr. *major league baseball executive, former professional sports team executive*
McIntyre, Brian P. *sports association executive*
Meiseles, Daniel *sports association executive*
Messier, Mark Douglas *professional sports team executive, retired professional hockey player*
Milicic, Darko *professional basketball player*
Orender, Donna *sports association executive*
Redden, Wade *professional hockey player*
Reed, Dan *sports association executive*
Richard, Stephen O. *sports association executive*
Robinson, Nate (Nathaniel Robinson) *professional basketball player*
Ruta, Thomas V. *professional sports team and accounting executive*
Sampras, Pete *retired professional tennis player*
Sather, Glen Cameron *professional sports team executive, former professional hockey coach and player*
Schoenfeld, Jim *professional sports team executive, professional hockey coach*
Selig, Bud (Alan Huber Selig) *Major League Baseball commissioner*
Silver, Adam *sports association executive*
Stern, David Joel *National Basketball Association commissioner*
Tatum, Mark A. *sports association executive*
Tolbert, Bernard *sports association executive*
Tortorella, John *professional hockey coach*
Ueberroth, Heidi J. *sports association executive*
Walsh, Donnie (Joseph Donald Walsh Jr.) *professional sports team executive*
Zahnd, Richard H. *sports association executive, lawyer*

Orchard Park
Brandon, Russ *professional sports team executive*
Jauron, Dick (Richard M. Jauron) *professional football coach*
Lynch, Marshawn Terrell *professional football player*
Owens, Terrell Eldorad *professional football player*
Schobel, Aaron Ross *professional football player*
Wilson, Ralph Cookerly, Jr. *professional football team executive*

Port Jefferson
Tovornik, Mary Rose *physical education educator*

Rochester
Nolan, Ted (Theodore John Nolan) *professional sports team executive, former professional hockey coach*
Shannon, Danielle *coach*

Syracuse
Boeheim, Jim *college basketball coach*

Uniondale
Biron, Martin *professional hockey player*
Dey, Chris *professional sports team executive, entrepreneur*
DiPietro, Rick *professional hockey player*
Gordon, Scott *professional hockey coach*
Snow, Garth *professional sports team executive, former professional hockey player*
Streit, Mark *professional hockey player*
Trottier, Bryan John *professional sports team executive, former professional hockey player and coach*
Wang, Charles B. *professional sports team executive, former computer company executive*
Weight, Doug *professional hockey player*

White Plains
Davenport, Lindsay *professional tennis player*
Williams, Serena *professional tennis player, apparel designer*
Williams, Venus *professional tennis player*

NORTH CAROLINA

Chapel Hill
Davis, Butch (Paul Hilton Davis) *college football coach*
Hatchell, Sylvia R. *women's college basketball coach*
Smith, Dean Edwards *retired men's college basketball coach*
Williams, Roy *men's college basketball coach*

Charlotte
Bell, Raja *professional basketball player*
Brown, Larry (Lawrence Harvey Brown) *professional basketball coach*
Chandler, Tyson Cleotis *professional basketball player*
Delhomme, Jake Christopher *professional football player*
Diaw, Boris (Boris Diaw-Riffiod) *professional basketball player*
Earnhardt, Dale, Jr. *race car driver*
Fox, John *professional football coach*
Gordon, Jeff *race car driver*
Gross, Jordan Alan *professional football player*
Guelli, Pete *professional sports team executive*
Higgins, Rod (Roderick Dwayne Higgins) *professional sports team executive, retired professional basketball player*
Hurney, Marty *professional sports team executive*
Johnson, Jimmie (James Kenneth Johnson) *race car driver*
Jordan, Michael Jeffrey *professional sports team executive, retired professional basketball player*
Mohammed, Nazr *professional basketball player*
Muhammad, Muhsin, II, *professional football player*
Peppers, Julius (Frazier) *professional football player*
Smith, Stevonne Latrall (Steve Smith) *professional football player*
Whitfield, Fred, Jr. *professional sports team executive*
Williams, DeAngelo *professional football player*

Concord
Biffle, Greg *race car driver*
Edwards, Carl *race car driver*
Franchitti, Dario *race car driver*
Kahne, Kasey (Kenneth) *race car driver*
Kenseth, Matt Roy *race car driver*
Montoya, Juan Pablo *professional race car driver*
Smith, (Ollen) Bruton *sports association executive*

Durham
Case, Richard W. *sports association executive*
Cutcliffe, David *college football coach*
Johnson, Davey (David Allen Johnson) *professional baseball coach*
Krzyzewski, Mike (Michael William Krzyzewski) *college basketball coach*
McCallie, Joanne P. *women's college basketball coach*
White, Kevin M. *athletic director*

Huntersville
Busch, Kyle *race car driver*
Gibbs, Joe Jackson *professional sports team executive, former professional football coach*
Logano, Joey *race car driver*

Kannapolis
Mayfield, Jeremy (Allen) *race car driver*
Newman, Ryan Joseph *race car driver*
Stewart, Tony (Anthony Wayne Stewart) *professional race car driver*

Mooresville
Busch, Kurt Thomas *professional race car driver*
Castroneves, Hélio *race car driver*
Dixon, Scott (Ronald) *race car driver*
Petty, Richard *retired race car driver*

Raleigh
Barrasso, Tom *professional hockey coach, retired professional hockey player*

Brind'Amour, Rod *professional hockey player*
Cole, Erik *professional hockey player*
Francis, Ron *professional sports team executive, retired professional hockey player*
Lowe, Sidney *men's college basketball coach*
Maurice, Paul *professional hockey coach*
Rutherford, Jim *professional sports team executive*
Staal, Eric *professional hockey player*
Ward, Aaron *professional hockey player*
Wesley, Glen *retired professional hockey player*

Welcome
Bowyer, Clint *professional race car driver*
Burton, Jeff Brian *race car driver*

Winston Salem
Gaudio, Dino Joseph *men's college basketball coach*
Grobe, Jim *college football coach*

NORTH DAKOTA

Fargo
Phillips, Saul *men's college basketball coach*

OHIO

Aurora
Eakin, Thomas Capper *sports promotion executive*

Berea
Kokinis, George *professional sports team executive*
Lewis, Jamal *professional football player*
Mangini, Eric *professional football coach*
Quinn, Brady (Brady Tyler Quinn) *professional football player*

Cambridge
Zalenski, Amy Ralynn *athletic trainer, small business owner*

Canton
Tippett, Andre *retired professional football player*
Zimmerman, Gary Wayne *professional football player*

Cincinnati
Baker, Dusty (Johnnie B. Baker Jr.) *professional baseball team manager, retired professional baseball player*
Benson, Cedric *professional football player*
Bruce, Jay A. *professional baseball player*
Coles, Laveranues *professional football player*
Cordero, Francisco Javier *professional baseball player*
Cronin, Mick *men's college basketball coach*
Jocketty, Walt (Walter J. Jocketty) *professional baseball team manager, professional sports team executive*
Kelly, Brian *college football coach*
Lewis, Marvin *professional football coach*
Mack, Chris *men's college basketball coach*
McGuff, Kevin *women's college basketball coach*
Ochocinco, Chad (Chad Javon Johnson) *professional football player*
Palmer, Carson *professional football player*
Phillips, Brandon Emil *professional baseball player*
Rolen, Scott Bruce *professional baseball player*
Tobin, Duke *professional sports team executive*
Volquez, Edinson *professional baseball player*

Cleveland
Brown, Mike *professional basketball coach*
Federer, Roger *professional tennis player*
Ferry, Danny *professional sports team executive, retired professional basketball player*
Hafner, Travis Lee *professional baseball player*
Henman, Tim *retired professional tennis player*
Ilgauskas, Zydrunas *professional basketball player*
James, LeBron Raymone *professional basketball player*
Komoroski, Len *professional sports team executive*
Kosar, Bernie Joseph, Jr. *professional sports team executive, retired professional football player*
Lopez, Nancy *retired professional golfer*
O'Neal, Shaquille Rashaun *professional basketball player*
Seles, Monica *retired professional tennis player*
Varejao, Anderson Franca *professional basketball player*
Wedge, Eric (Michael Wedge) *professional baseball team manager*
Williams, Maurice (Mo Williams) *professional basketball player*
Wood, Kerry (Lee) *professional baseball player*

Columbus
Bartels, Robert Louis *retired physical education educator, coach*
Commodore, Mike *professional hockey player*
Foster, Jim (James S. Foster) *women's college basketball coach*
Hitchcock, Ken *professional hockey coach*
Howson, Scott *professional sports team executive*
Mason, Steve *professional hockey player*
Matta, Thad Michael *men's college basketball coach*
Modin, Fredrik *professional hockey player*
Nash, Rick *professional hockey player*
Peca, Michael *professional hockey player*
Priest, Michael b *professional sports team executive*
Schmid, Sigi *professional soccer coach*
Smith, Gene *athletic director*
Tressel, Jim (James Patrick Tressel) *college football coach*

Dayton
Gregory, Brian *men's college basketball coach*
O'Keefe, Linda Lee *physical education educator*

Wooster
Lovato, Monica *boxer*

Youngstown
Pavlik, Kelly (Robert) *boxer*

OKLAHOMA

Norman
Bradford, Sam *student athlete*
Capel, Jeff III *men's college basketball coach*
Coale, Sherri *women's college basketball coach*
Stoops, Bob *college football coach*

Oklahoma City
Adelson, Kenneth I. *professional sports team executive*
Barth, Danny *professional sports team executive*
Bennett, Clayton Ike *professional sports team owner*
Binning, Bette Finese (Mrs. Gene Hedgcock Binning) *athletic association official*
Brooks, Scott William *professional basketball coach*
Durant, Kevin Wayne *professional basketball player*
Fernandez, Lisa *softball player*
Green, Jeff *professional basketball player*
Krstic, Nenad *professional basketball player*
Presti, Sam *professional sports team executive*
Sanchez, Cindi Asbury *physical education educator*
Thomas, Etan *professional basketball player, poet*

Stillwater
Gundy, Mike *college football coach*

OREGON

Corvallis
Riley, Michael *college football coach*
Riley, Mike *college football coach*

Eugene
Bellotti, Mike *college football coach*

Portland
Fernandez, Rudy *professional basketball player*
Glanville, Jerry *college football coach, former professional football coach*
Hickcox, Leslie Kay *health education educator consultant*
Levi, Alexis *professional sports team executive, owner, agent*
McMillan, Nathaniel (Nate McMillan) *professional basketball coach*
Miller, Andre Lloyd *professional basketball player*
Miller, Larry G. *professional sports team executive*
Oden, Greg *professional basketball player*
Pritchard, Kevin *professional sports team executive*
Roy, Brandon Dawayne *professional basketball player*

PENNSYLVANIA

Aldan
Stegmuller, Agnes Leonore *physical education educator*

Allison Park
Toerge, Lynn *athletic trainer*

Easton
Holmes, Larry *retired professional boxer*

Erie
Ftorek, Robbie Brian (Robert Brian Ftorek) *professional hockey coach, retired professional hockey player*

Philadelphia
Akers, David *professional football player*
Allen, Keith *professional sports team executive*
Ayers, Randy *professional basketball coach*
Boucher, Brian *professional hockey player*
Brand, Elton Tyron *professional basketball player*
Briere, Daniel *professional hockey player*
Cardoza, Tonya *women's college basketball coach*
Carle, Matt *professional hockey player*
Carter, Jeff *professional hockey player*
Clarke, Robert Earle (Bobby Clarke) *professional sports team executive, commentator*
Dalembert, Samuel Davis *professional basketball player*
DiLeo, Tony *professional sports team executive*
Dunphy, Fran *men's college basketball coach*
Emery, Ray *professional hockey player*
Gagné, Simon *professional hockey player*
Hamels, Cole (Colbert Michael Hamels) *professional baseball player*
Hatcher, Darien *retired professional hockey player*
Heckert, Tom *professional sports team executive*
Holmgren, Paul *professional sports team executive, retired professional hockey player*
Howard, Ryan James *professional baseball player*
Ibanez, Raul Javier *professional baseball player*
Iguodala, Andre Tyler *professional basketball player*
Jordan, Eddie Montgomery *professional basketball coach*
Lee, Cliff (Clifton Phifer Lee) *professional baseball player*
Leyva, Nick (Nicholas Tomas Leyva) *professional baseball coach*
Lidge, Brad (Bradley Thomas Lidge) *professional baseball player*
Luukko, Peter A. *professional sports team executive*
Lynam, Jim *professional basketball coach*
Martelli, Phil *men's college basketball coach*
Martinez, Pedro Jaime *professional baseball player*
McLaren, Kyle *professional hockey player*
McNabb, Donovan *professional football player*
Mornhinweg, Marty *professional football coach*
Moyer, Jamie *professional baseball player*
Paddock, John (Alvin John Paddock) *professional sports team executive, former professional hockey coach*
Park, Chan Ho *professional baseball player*
Price, Lara *professional sports team executive*
Pronger, Chris *professional hockey player*
Reid, Andy (Andrew Walter Reid) *professional football coach*
Richards, Mike *professional hockey player*
Rollins, Jimmy (James Calvin Rollins) *professional baseball player*
Samuel, Asante T. *professional football player*
Snider, Edward Malcolm *professional sports team executive*
Stefanski, Edward A. *professional sports team executive*
Stevens, John *professional hockey coach, retired professional hockey player*
Utley, Chase *professional baseball player*
Vick, Michael (Michael Dwayne Vick) *professional football player*
Victorino, Shane Patrick *professional baseball player*

Pittsburgh
Adams, Craig *professional hockey player*
Berenato, Agnus McGlade *women's college basketball coach*
Bylsma, Dan *professional hockey coach, former professional hockey player*
Colbert, Kevin *professional sports team executive*
Crosby, Sidney *professional hockey player*
Dixon, Jamie P., II, *men's college basketball coach*
Farrior, James *professional football player*
Fedotenko, Ruslan *professional hockey player*
Fleury, Marc-Andre *professional hockey player*
Gonchar, Sergei *professional hockey player*
Granato, Tony *professional hockey coach, retired professional hockey player*
Guerin, Bill *professional hockey player*
Harrison, James, Jr. *professional football player*
Holmes, Santonio, Jr. *professional football player*
Huntington, Neal A. *professional sports team executive*
Kennedy, Tyler *professional hockey player*
Kunitz, Chris *professional hockey player*
LeBeau, Dick (Charles Richard LeBeau) *professional football coach*
Lemieux, Mario *professional sports team executive, retired professional hockey player*
Malkin, Evgeni *professional hockey player*
Morehouse, David *professional sports team executive*
Polamalu, Troy (Trou Aumua Polamalu) *professional football player*
Roethlisberger, Ben *professional football player*
Russell, John William *professional baseball team manager, retired professional baseball player*
Satan, Miroslav *professional hockey player*
Shero, Ray (Rejean Shero) *professional sports team executive*
Staal, Jordan *professional hockey player*
Talbot, Maxime *professional hockey player*
Tomlin, Mike *professional football coach*
Wannstedt, David Raymond *college football coach, former professional football coach*
Ward, Hines, Jr. *professional football player*

Reading
Hornish, Sam, Jr., (Samuel Jon Hornish Jr.) *race car driver*

University Park
DeChellis, Ed *men's college basketball coach*
Paterno, Joe (Joseph Vincent Paterno) *college football coach*
Vairo, Giampietro Luciano *professional athletic trainer*

Villanova
Wright, Jay *men's college basketball coach*

Youngstown
Palmer, Arnold Daniel *professional golfer*

RHODE ISLAND

Providence
Marinatto, John *sports association executive*
Tranghese, Michael A. *sports association executive*

SOUTH CAROLINA

Clemson
Purnell, Oliver Gordon, Jr. *men's college basketball coach*
Swinney, Dabo *college football coach*

Columbia
McCaslin, Elizabeth Ann *athletic trainer*
McCray, Nikki Kesangame *women's college basketball coach, former professional basketball player*
McGhee, Carla Renee *women's college basketball coach, retired professional basketball player*
Spurrier, Steve (Steven Orr Spurrier) *college football coach*
Staley, Dawn Michelle *women's college basketball coach, retired professional basketball player*

Gaffney
Spencer, Albert Franklin *physical education educator*

Rock Hill
Ford, Mary (Polly) Wylie *retired physical education educator*

SOUTH DAKOTA

Brookings
Johnston, Aaron *women's college basketball coach*
McGee, Megan E. *coach, consultant*

Lower Brule
Gerlach, Amy Louise *physical education educator*

TENNESSEE

Brentwood
Fisher, Jeff (Jeffrey Michael Fisher) *professional football coach*

Knoxville
Kiffin, Lane *college football coach*
Summitt, Pat (Patricia Sue Summit) *women's college basketball coach*

Kodak
Sandberg, Ryne Dee *baseball coach, retired professional baseball player*

Martin
Anderson, Pamela Susan *sports official, educator*
Brown, Laura L. *physical education educator*

Memphis
Barone, Tony, Sr. *professional sports team executive*
Bartow, Gene *professional sports team executive, retired men's college basketball coach*
Bibby, Henry (Charles Henry Bibby) *professional basketball coach*
Gay, Rudy Carlton, Jr. *professional basketball player*
Hollins, Lionel *professional basketball coach*
Pastner, Josh *men's college basketball coach*
Randolph, Zach *professional basketball player*
Stoudamire, Damon Lamon *professional basketball coach, retired professional basketball player*
Wallace, Chris *professional sports team executive*

Nashville
Abram, Monroe J. *athletic trainer, educator*
Arnott, Jason *professional hockey player*
Balcomb, Melanie S. *women's college basketball coach*
Collins, Kerry *professional football player*
Crumpler, Algernon Darius (Alge Crumpler) *professional football player*
Finnegan, Cortland Temujin *professional football player*
Freeman, David Scott *professional sports team executive, venture capitalist, lawyer*
Johnson, Bobby *college football coach*
Kearse, Jevon *professional football player*
Mawae, Kevin James *professional football player*
Poile, David Robert *professional sports team executive*
Reinfeldt, Mike (Michael Ray Reinfeldt) *professional sports team executive, former professional football player*
Stallings, Kevin *men's college basketball coach*
Sullivan, Steve *professional hockey player*
Trotz, Barry *professional hockey coach*
Weber, Shea *professional hockey player*
Young, Vince Paul, Jr. *professional football player*

TEXAS

Arlington
Alfonzo, Edgardo Antonio *professional baseball player*
Benson, Kris (Kristin James Benson) *professional baseball player*
Howell, Holly Lyn *athletic trainer*
Jones, Andruw Rudolf *professional baseball player*
Kinsler, Ian Michael *professional baseball player*
Petroskey, Dale Alan *professional sports team executive, former museum director*
Rodriguez, Ivan Torres *professional baseball player*
Ryan, Nolan *professional baseball team executive, former professional baseball player*
Young, Michael Brian *professional baseball player*

Austin
Armstrong, Lance *professional cyclist*
Barnes, Rick (Richard Dale Barnes) *men's college basketball coach*
Brown, Mack *college football coach*
Goestenkors, Gail Ann *women's college basketball coach*

College Station
Blair, Gary *women's college basketball coach*
Sherman, Mike (Michael Francis Sherman) *college football coach, former professional football coach*

Corpus Christi
Schmitt, Patricia Ann *health and physical education educator*

Dallas
Blackman, Rolando Antonio *professional sports team executive, retired professional basketball player*
Carlisle, Rick (Richard Preston Carlisle) *professional basketball coach, retired professional basketball player*
Cuban, Mark *professional sports team owner, Internet company executive*
Gooden, Drew *professional basketball player*
Hamilton, David Lee *retired sports association administrator, environmental company executive*
Howard, Josh *professional basketball player*
Hudel, Chestella Alvis *athletics educator*
Jones, June Sheldon III *college football coach*
Kidd, Jason *professional basketball player*
Lites, Jim (James R. Lites) *sports association executive, former professional sports team executive*
Marion, Shawn *professional basketball player*
Nelson, Donnie *professional sports team executive*
Nowitzki, Dirk Werner *professional basketball player*
Terry, Jason Eugene *professional basketball player*
Thomas, Tim *professional basketball player*

Ussery, Terdema L., II, *professional sports team executive*

Fort Worth
Patterson, Gary *college football coach*

Frisco
Cogen, Jeffrey David *professional sports team executive*
Crawford, Marc *professional hockey coach*
Hicks, Thomas O. *professional sports team executive, real estate developer*
Hull, Brett A. *professional sports team executive, retired professional hockey player*
Jackson, Les *professional sports team executive*
Modano, Mike *professional hockey player*
Morrow, Brenden *professional hockey player*
Nieuwendyk, Joe *professional sports team executive, retired professional hockey player*
Richards, Brad *professional hockey player*
Robidas, Stephane *professional hockey player*
Taylor, Dave *professional sports team executive, retired professional hockey player*
Turco, Marty *professional hockey player*

Galveston
Foster, William Edwin (Bill Foster) *retired men's college basketball coach*

Houston
Adelman, Rick (Richard Leonard Adelman) *professional basketball coach*
Alexander, Leslie Lee *professional sports team owner*
Ariza, Trevor Anthony *professional basketball player*
Barry, Brent Robert *professional basketball player*
Battier, Shane *professional basketball player*
Berkman, Lance *professional baseball player*
Brown, Thaddeus B. *professional sports team executive*
Constantine, Kevin *professional hockey coach*
Cooper, Cecil Celester *professional baseball manager, retired professional baseball player*
Cruz, José, Sr. *professional baseball coach, retired professional baseball player*
Green, Ahman Rashad *professional football player*
Grossman, Rex *professional football player*
Hayes, Elvin Ernest *retired basketball player*
Johnson, Andre Lamont *professional football player*
Jolibois, Marcus *professional sports team executive*
Kubiak, Gary *professional football coach*
Lamont, Gene *professional baseball coach and former team manager*
Loretta, Mark (David) *professional baseball player*
McGrady, Tracy *professional basketball player*
Ming, Yao *professional basketball player*
Morey, Daryl R. *professional sports team executive*
Oswalt, Roy Edwards *professional baseball player*
Rhodes, Raymond Earl *professional football coach*
Sandman, Bradford Aaron *coach, educator*
Schaub, Matt (Matthew Rutledge Schaub) *professional football player*
Scola, Luis *professional basketball player*
Sikma, Jack Wayne *professional basketball coach, retired professional basketball player*
Smith, Rick *professional sports team executive*
Supak, Cathy Poerner *athletic trainer, educator*
Tejada, Miguel Odalis *professional baseball player*
Thompson, Tina Marie *professional basketball player*
Valverde, José (Rafael) *professional baseball player*
Williams, Mario *professional football player*

Irving
Campo, Dave *professional football coach*
Jones, Jerry (Jerral Wayne Jones) *professional sports team executive*
Kitna, Jon K. *professional football player*
Phillips, Wade *professional football coach*
Romo, Tony (Antonio Ramiro Romo) *professional football player*
Ware, DeMarcus *professional football player*
Williams, Roy Eugene, Jr. *professional football player*
Witten, Jason (Christopher Jason Witten) *professional football player*

Lubbock
Leach, Mike (Michael C. Leach) *college football coach*

Pearland
Buckelew, Stephen MIchael *basketball coach*

Plano
Liukin, Nastia *Olympic gymnast*

San Antonio
Buford, R.C. *professional sports team executive*
Coker, Larry E. *college football coach*
Duncan, Tim (Timothy Theodore Duncan) *professional basketball player*
Finley, Michael Howard *professional basketball player*
Ginobili, Manu *professional basketball player*
Holt, Peter M. *professional sports team owner, agricultural products executive*
Hughes, Dan *professional basketball coach*
Jefferson, Richard *professional basketball player*
McDyess, Antonio Keithflen *professional basketball player*
Parker, Tony (William Anthony Parker II) *professional basketball player*
Popovich, Gregg *professional basketball coach*
Pych, Rick *professional sports team executive*
Ratliff, Theo *professional basketball player*

San Marcos
Imel, Elizabeth Carmen *retired physical education educator*

Waco
Briles, Art *college football coach*
Drew, Scott *men's college basketball coach*
Mulkey, Kim *women's college basketball coach*
Shim, Jaeho *physical education educator*

UTAH

Kearns
Ohno, Apolo Anton *Olympic athlete*

Park City
White, Shaun Roger *Olympic athlete, professional snowboarder, professional skateboarder*

Provo
Lockhart, Barbara Day *physical education educator*
Mendenhall, Bronco *college football coach*
Rose, Dave *men's college basketball coach*

Salt Lake City
Boozer, Carlos Austin, Jr. *professional basketball player*
Boylen, Jim *men's college basketball coach*
Gao, Zan *physical education educator*
Kirilenko, Andrei *professional basketball player*
O'Connor, Kevin *professional sports team executive*
Okur, Mehmet *professional basketball player*
Sloan, Jerry (Gerald Eugene Sloan) *professional basketball coach*
Whittingham, Kyle *college football coach*
Williams, Deron Michael *professional basketball player*

Sandy
Miller, Greg *professional sports team executive*
Rigby, Randy *professional sports team executive*

VERMONT

Londonderry
Powers, Ross *Olympic athlete*

Saint Albans
LeClair, John Clark *professional hockey player*

VIRGINIA

Arlington
Boudreau, Bruce *professional hockey coach*
Clark, Chris *professional hockey player*
McPhee, George *professional sports team executive*
Semin, Alexander *professional hockey player*
Theodore, Jose *professional hockey player*

Ashburn
Cerrato, Vinny *professional sports team executive*
Hall, DeAngelo *professional football player*
Haynesworth, Albert III *professional football player*
Moss, Santana Terrell *professional football player*
Portis, Clinton *professional football player*
Snyder, Daniel *professional sports team executive*
Zorn, Jim (James Arthur Zorn) *professional football coach, retired professional football player*

Blacksburg
Beamer, Frank *college football coach*
Greenberg, Seth *men's college basketball coach*

Charlottesville
Bennett, Tony (Anthony G. Bennett) *men's college basketball coach*
Ryan, Debbie (Deborah A. Ryan) *women's college basketball coach*

Fairfax
Larranaga, Jim *men's college basketball coach*

Manassas
Banville, Dominique *physical education educator*

Mc Lean
Chang, Michael *professional tennis player*
Hewitt, Lleyton Glynn *professional tennis player*

Radford
Zeakes, Beverly Jean *physical education educator, department chairman*

Richmond
Gulbis, Natalie Anne *professional golfer, television personality*

Sterling
Green, Darrell *retired professional football player*

WASHINGTON

Carnation
Beshur, Jacqueline E. *retired animal trainer, farmer, writer*

Pullman
Bennett, Dick *college basketball coach*
Bone, Ken *men's college basketball coach*

Renton
Holmgren, Mike (Michael George Holmgren) *professional football coach*
Houshmandzadeh, T.J. (Touraj Houshmandzadeh) *professional football player*
James, Edgerrin Tyree *professional football player*
Mora, Jim (James Lawrence Mora) *professional football coach*
Ruskell, Tim *professional sports team executive*

Seattle
Agler, Brian *professional basketball coach*
Allen, Paul Gardner *professional sports team executive, computer company executive*
Bedard, Erik Joseph *professional baseball player*
Beltre, Adrian *professional baseball player*
Bird, Sue (Suzanne Brigit Bird) *professional basketball player*
Golub, Mike *sports and entertainment company executive*
Griffey, Ken, Jr., (George Kenneth Griffey Jr.) *professional baseball player*
Hasselbeck, Matt *professional football player*
Hernandez, Felix Abraham *professional baseball player*
Jackson, Lauren *professional basketball player*
Johjima, Kenji *professional baseball player*
Jones, Julius Andre Maurice *professional football player*
Romar, Lorenzo *men's college basketball coach*
Suzuki, Ichiro *professional baseball player*
Tatupu, Lofa *professional football player*
Wakamatsu, Don (Wilbur Donald Wakamatsu) *professional baseball coach*
Wetteland, John Karl *professional baseball coach, retired professional baseball player*
Willingham, Tyrone *college football coach*

Spokane
Few, Mark *men's college basketball coach*
Ueberroth, Peter Victor *sports association executive*

Vancouver
Engelker, Lynsey L. *athletic trainer, professional athletics manager*

WEST VIRGINIA

Morgantown
Stewart, Bill *college football coach*

Salem
Bullion, Keith Alan *coach, director*

WISCONSIN

Green Bay
Capers, Dom (Dominic Capers) *professional football coach*
Driver, Donald Jerome *professional football player*
Harris, Al (Alshinard Harris) *professional football player*
McCarthy, Mike *professional football coach*
Murphy, Mark Hodge *professional football team executive, retired professional football player*
Thompson, Ted Clarence *professional sports team executive, retired professional football player*
Woodson, Charles C. *professional football player*

Jefferson
Smith, Dena Michele *physical education educator*

La Crosse
Doberstein, Scott T. *athletic trainer educator*

Madison
Ryan, Bo (William F. Ryan Jr.) *men's college basketball coach*
Sauer, Jeff *university hockey coach*

Milwaukee
Bogut, Andrew *professional basketball player*
Boylan, Jim *professional basketball coach*
Braun, Ryan Joseph *professional baseball player*
Fielder, Prince Semien *professional baseball player*
Gagne, Eric (Serge) *professional baseball player*
Hammond, John R. *professional sports team executive*
Hoffman, Trevor William *professional baseball player*
Kendall, Jason Daniel *professional baseball player*
Macha, Ken (Kenneth Edward Macha) *professional baseball manager*
Melvin, Doug *professional baseball team manager*
Randolph, Willie (Willie Larry Randolph Jr.) *professional baseball coach, retired professional baseball player*
Redd, Michael *professional basketball player*
Sampson, Kelvin Dale *professional basketball coach, former college basketball coach*
Skiles, Scott Allen *professional basketball coach*
Steinmiller, John F. *professional sports team executive*
Sveum, Dale Curtis *professional baseball coach*
Williams, Brent (Buzz Williams) *men's college basketball coach*

Platteville
Kuhle, Christina Marie *women's college basketball coach*

TERRITORIES OF THE UNITED STATES

GUAM

Hagatna
Mullins, Christopher M. *physical education educator*

CANADA

ALBERTA

Calgary
Bouwmeester, Jay *professional hockey player*
Hotchkiss, Harley N. *professional hockey team owner, oil industry executive*
Iginla, Jarome *professional hockey player*
Jokinen, Olli *professional hockey player*
King, Ken *professional sports team executive*
Kiprusoff, Miikka *professional hockey player*
Phaneuf, Dion *professional hockey player*
Playfair, Jim *professional hockey coach*
Sutter, Brent Colin *professional hockey coach, retired professional hockey player*
Sutter, Darryl John *professional sports team executive, former professional hockey coach*

Edmonton
Fleming, Wayne *professional hockey coach*
Gilbert, Tom *professional hockey player*
Hemsky, Ales *professional hockey player*
Khabibulin, Nikolai *professional hockey player*
Lowe, Kevin Hugh *professional sports team executive, professional hockey player*
Moreau, Ethan *professional hockey player*
Penner, Dustin *professional hockey player*
Quinn, Pat (John Brian Patrick Quinn) *professional hockey coach*
Renney, Tom *professional hockey coach*
Souray, Sheldon *professional hockey player*
Tambellini, Steve *professional sports team executive, former professional hockey player*

BRITISH COLUMBIA

Surrey
Igali, Baraladei Daniel *Olympic athlete, coach, motivational speaker*

Vancouver
Demitra, Pavol *professional hockey player*
Gillis, Mike (Michael David Gillis) *professional sports team executive, retired professional hockey player*
Luongo, Roberto *professional hockey player*
Schneider, Mathieu *professional hockey player*
Sedin, Daniel *professional hockey player*
Sedin, Henrik *professional hockey player*
Sundin, Mats Johan *professional hockey player*
Vigneault, Alain *professional hockey coach*
Zimmerman, Chris *professional sports team executive*

ONTARIO

Dorchester
Fanning, William James *professional sports team executive, commentator*

Kanata
Alfredsson, Daniel *professional hockey player*
Heatley, Dany *professional hockey player*
Leeder, Cyril *professional sports team executive*
Melnyk, Eugene N. *professional sports team executive, retired pharmaceutical executive*
Murray, Bryan Clarence *professional sports team executive, former professional hockey coach*
Spezza, Jason *professional hockey player*

Ottawa
Clouston, Cory *professional hockey coach*
Comrie, Mike (Michael William Comrie) *professional hockey player*
Kovalev, Alexei *professional hockey player*
Lapointe, Martin *professional hockey player*

Toronto
Bargnani, Andrea *professional basketball player*
Blake, Jason *professional hockey player*
Bosh, Chris *professional basketball player*
Burke, Brian *professional sports team executive*
Clark, Wendel *retired professional hockey player*
Colangelo, Bryan *professional sports team executive*
English, Alexander *professional basketball coach, retired professional basketball player*
Fletcher, Cliff (George Clifford Fletcher) *professional sports team executive*
Garbajosa (Chaparro), Jorge *professional basketball player*
Gaston, Clarence Edwin (Cito Gaston) *professional baseball team manager*
Gerber, Martin *professional hockey player*
Gilmour, Doug *professional hockey coach, retired professional hockey player*
Halladay, Roy (Harry Leroy Halladay III) *professional baseball player*
Healy, Glenn *sports association administrator, commentator, retired professional hockey player*
Iavaroni, Marc (Marcus John Iavaroni) *professional basketball coach, retired professional basketball player*
Joseph, Curtis Shayne *professional hockey player*
Kaberle, Tomas *professional hockey player*
Kolzig, Olaf *professional hockey player*
Komisarek, Mike *professional hockey player*
Nesterovic, Rasho *professional basketball player*
Peddie, Richard A. *professional sports team executive*
Poon, Alan Ming Wang *sports association executive, director*
Smith, Mike (Michael A. Smith) *former professional sports team executive*
Triano, Jay *professional basketball coach*
Turkoglu, Hedo (Hidayet) *professional basketball player*
Wilson, Ronald Lawrence *professional hockey coach, former professional hockey player*

QUEBEC

Montreal
Cammalleri, Mike *professional hockey player*
Gainey, Bob (Robert Michael Gainey) *professional sports team executive, retired professional hockey player*
Gillett, George Nield, Jr. *professional sports team executive, communications executive*
Gionta, Brian *professional hockey player*
Gomez, Scott *professional hockey player*

Markov, Andrei *professional hockey player*
Martin, Jacques *professional hockey coach, former professional sports team executive*
Price, Carey *professional hockey player*

Quebec City
Roy, Patrick *professional sports team executive, coach, retired professional hockey player*

ARGENTINA

Córdoba
Cabrera, Angel Leopoldo *professional golfer*

ENGLAND

London
Dempsey, Clint (Clinton Drew Dempsey) *professional soccer player*
Goosen, Retief *professional golfer*

Surrey
Immelman, Trevor *professional golfer*
Karlsson, Robert *professional golfer*

ITALY

Ciserano di Zingonia
Vieri, Christian *professional soccer player*

Milan
Ronaldinho, (Ronaldo de Assis Moreira) *professional soccer player*

JAPAN

Chiba
Valentine, Bobby (Robert John Valentine) *professional baseball manager*

NORWAY

Oslo
Pettersen, Suzann *professional golfer*

SPAIN

Toledo
Ruiz, Luis M. *physical education educator*

Villareal
Altidore, Jozy (Josmer Volmy Altidore) *professional soccer player*

SWEDEN

Ornskoldsvik
Forsberg, Peter *professional hockey player*

SWITZERLAND

Lausanne
Nikolaou, Lambis W. *International Olympic Committee board member*

ADDRESS UNPUBLISHED

Accorsi, Ernie (Ernest William Accorsi Jr.) *retired professional sports team executive*
Acta, Manny (Manuel Elias Acta) *former professional baseball manager*
Aguilera, Richard Warren (Rick Aguilera) *retired professional baseball player*
Alexander, Shaun *professional football player*
Ali, Muhammad (Cassius Marcellus Clay) *retired professional boxer*
Alou, Felipe Rojas *former professional baseball team manager*
Alvarado, Shannon *professional athletics coach*
Amonte, Tony (Anthony Lewis Amonte) *retired professional hockey player*
Andretti, Mario *retired race car driver*
Andreychuk, David *former professional hockey player*
Baker, Vincent Lamont *former professional basketball player*
Barton, Gregory Mark *Olympic athlete*
Baylor, Elgin Gay *former professional sports team executive, retired professional basketball player*
Belfour, Ed *former professional hockey player*
Berard, Bryan *professional hockey player*
Berka, Marianne Guthrie *health and physical education educator*
Bivens, Carolyn Vesper *former sports association administrator*
Boitano, Brian *Olympic athlete*
Bonds, Barry Lamar *professional baseball player*
Bookbinder, Russ *professional sports team executive*
Bryant, La Kesha Joy *physical education educator*
Buckingham, Albert William *retired college administrator, physical education educator*
Carbonneau, Guy *former professional hockey coach, retired professional hockey player*
Carlesimo, P.J. (Peter J. Carlesimo) *former professional basketball coach*
Carr, Lloyd H. *retired college football coach*
Casey, Dwane L. *former professional basketball coach*
Casserly, Charley *former professional football team executive*
Cheeks, Maurice Edward *former professional basketball coach, retired professional basketball player*
Chelios, Chris (Christos K. Chelios) *professional hockey player*
Clemens, Roger (William Roger Clemens) *former professional baseball player*
Cordes, Kathleen Ann *retired physical education educator, director*
Covassin, Tracey *athletic training educator*
Crennel, Romeo *former professional football coach*
Curtis, Joyce Mae *retired physical education educator*
DePaoli, Lou *former professional sports team executive*
Desjardins, Eric *retired professional hockey player*
Douglas, James *retired professional boxer*
Drake, Dallas *retired professional hockey player*
Duffy, Bill *former professional sports team executive*
Duquette, Jim *professional sports team executive*
Economou, Greg *professional sports team executive*
Evans, Michael Duane *coach*
Evert, Chris (Christine Marie Evert) *retired professional tennis player*
Feaster, Jay (Harry Jay Feaster) *former professional sports team executive*
Floyd, Tim *former men's college basketball coach, former professional basketball coach*
Foreman, George Edward *retired boxer, commentator, minister*
Fournier, Maureen Mary *physical education educator*
Francis, Steve D'Shawn *professional basketball player*
Gillispie, Billy Clyde *former men's college basketball coach*
Glavine, Tom (Thomas Michael Glavine) *professional baseball player*
Granato, Catherine (Cammi Granato) *former olympic athlete, sports association executive*
Greiner, Nicole K. Hudak *physical education educator*
Griese, Brian *professional football player*
Guthrie, Janet *professional race car driver*
Hamilton, Laird John *professional surfer*
Hanlon, Glen A. *professional hockey coach, retired professional hockey player*
Hardaway, Timothy Duane *retired professional basketball player*
Harman, Jennifer (Jennifer Harman-Traniello) *professional poker player*
Hart, James Warren *retired athletic administrator, professional football player*
Hartsburg, Craig William *former professional hockey coach, retired professional hockey player*
Hasek, Dominik *retired professional hockey player*
Hendrick, Joseph Riddick, III, (Rick Hendrick) *race team owner*
Hicks, Ritchie B. *physical education educator*
Hinchey, Tim *former professional sports team executive*
Holik, Bobby (Robert Holik) *retired professional hockey player*
Howe, Gordon *retired professional hockey player, sports association executive*
Hull, Bobby (Robert Marvin Hull) *retired professional hockey player*
Jamison, Richard *college athletics administrator*
Jansen, Daniel Ervin *former professional speedskater, marketing professional, former olympic athlete*
Kaufman, Lawrence Charles *professional chess player*
Kavalek, Lubomir *chess expert*
Keenan, Mike (Micheal Edward Keenan) *former professional hockey coach, professional sports team executive*
Kitchen, Paul Howard *hockey historian*
Knight, Billy (William R. Knight) *former professional sports team executive*
Krueger, Chris A. *physical education educator*
Laimbeer, Bill *former professional basketball coach, retired professional basketball player*
Laursen, Lin L. *retired women's college basketball coach*
Laviolette, Peter *former professional hockey coach*
Leetch, Brian Joseph *retired professional hockey player*
Leitao, Dave *men's college basketball coach*
Lentini, Francine *retired physical education educator*
Levy, Marv (Marvin Daniel) *former professional football team executive, retired professional football coach*
Lindros, Eric *retired professional hockey player*
Little, (William) Grady *former professional baseball coach, team manager*
Lofton, James David *former professional football player, professional football coach*
Low, Ron Albert *former professional hockey coach*
Lubick, Sonny *former college football coach*
MacLean, Doug *former professional hockey coach, former sports team executive*
MacTavish, Craig *former professional hockey coach, retired professional hockey player*
Maddux, Greg (Gregory Alan Maddux) *retired professional baseball player*
Martz, Mike J. *former professional football coach*
Maskaev, Oleg *professional boxer*
Mason, Linda *physical education educator, coach*
Mayweather, Floyd, Jr. *retired professional boxer*
McClatchy, Kevin S. *professional sports team executive*
McEnroe, John Patrick, Jr. *retired professional tennis player*
McMurtry, R. Cody *physical education educator*
Miller, Shannon *Olympic athlete*
Mitchell, Sam *former professional basketball coach*
Mlakar, Roy A. *former professional sports team executive*
Moulds, Eric Shannon *professional football player*
Narron, Jerry Austin *former professional baseball manager*
Naslund, Markus *retired professional hockey player*
Nevin, Phillip *retired professional baseball player*
Norman, Gregory John *professional golfer*
Odom, G. David (Dave Odom) *retired men's college basketball coach*
Olson, Lute (Robert Luther Olson) *retired men's college basketball coach*
O'Malley, Susan *former professional sports team executive*
Palmeiro, Rafael Corrales *former professional baseball player*
Parins, Robert James *professional football team executive, judge*
Patterson, Steve *former professional sports team executive*
Pfund, Randy (Randall C. Pfund) *former professional sports team executive*
Piazza, Mike (Michael Joseph Piazza) *retired professional baseball player*
Porter, Terry *former professional basketball coach, retired professional basketball player*
Portland, Rene (Maureen Portland) *retired women's college basketball coach*
Pyrgiotis, Yannis N. *former sports association administrator*
Reese, Pokey *former professional baseball player*
Rice, Jerry Lee *retired professional football player*
Risebrough, Doug *former professional sports team executive*
Riskas, Mike *retired physical education educator, coach, actor*
Roberts, Gary *retired professional hockey player*
Robinson, Frank *former professional baseball manager, retired professional baseball player*
Roenick, Jeremy *retired professional hockey player*
Rollins, Tree (Wayne Monte Rollins) *former professional basketball coach, retired professional basketball player*
Ross, Bobby (Robert Joseph Ross) *retired college football coach*
Ross, Carol *retired women's college basketball coach*
Russell, Bill (William Felton Russell) *former professional basketball team executive, retired professional basketball player*
Rutherford, John Sherman, III, (Johnny Rutherford) *retired professional race car driver*
Sakic, Joe (Joseph Steven Sakic) *retired professional hockey player*
Sanders, Barry *retired professional football player*
Savard, Denis Joseph *former professional hockey coach*
Schmidt, Mike (Michael Jack Schmidt) *retired professional baseball player*
Schottenheimer, Marty (Martin Edward Scottenheimer) *former professional football coach*
Shanahan, Mike (Michael Edward Shanahan) *former professional football coach*
Sharman, William *professional basketball team executive*
Smith, Jason *retired professional hockey player*
Smith, Ozzie (Osborne Earl Smith) *retired professional baseball player*
Smith, Rod *retired professional football player*
Smolinski, Bryan *professional hockey player*
Sorenstam, Annika *retired professional golfer*
Sykora, Petr *professional hockey player*
Therrien, Michel *former professional hockey coach*
Theus, Reggie Wayne *former professional basketball coach, retired professional basketball player*
Tiffany, James Robert, Jr. *physical education educator, physical fitness company executive*
Tippett, Dave *former professional hockey coach*
Torrance, Sam *professional golfer*
Van Exel, Nickey Maxwell *retired professional basketball player*
Van Horn, Keith *retired professional basketball player*
Vermeil, Dick (Richard Albert Vermeil) *retired professional football coach*
Vincent, Francis Thomas, Jr., (Fay Vincent) *former baseball commissioner*
Vincent, Sam (James Samuel Vincent) *former professional basketball coach, former professional basketball player*
Walker, Antoine Devon *professional basketball player*
Waltrip, Michael Curtis *professional race car driver*
Weekes, Kevin *professional hockey player*
Wells, Christine Louise *physical education educator*
West, Jerry Alan *former professional sports team executive, retired professional basketball player*
Westhead, Paul *former professional basketball coach*
Wooden, John Robert *retired college basketball coach*
Yawney, Trent *former professional hockey coach, retired professional hockey player*

BUSINESS *See* FINANCE: INDUSTRY

COMMUNICATIONS *See* COMMUNICATIONS MEDIA; INDUSTRY: SERVICE

UNITED STATES

NEW YORK

New York
Turner, Kelli *diversified media and merchandising company executive*

COMMUNICATIONS MEDIA *See also* ARTS: LITERARY

UNITED STATES

ALABAMA

Auburn University
Carvalho, John *communications educator*

Birmingham
Clemmensen, Jon L. *communications educator*
Culpepper, Mary Kay *editor*
Griffin, Eleanor *publishing executive, editor*
Hanson, Victor Henry, II, *newspaper publisher*
Kennedy, Joe David, Jr., (Joey Kennedy) *editor*
Powell, Larry *communications educator*
Scarritt, Thomas Varnon *newspaper editor*
Seitz, Karl Raymond *editor*
Stephens, James T. (J.T. Stepehens) *publishing executive*

Dothan
Williams, Claudia Baxter *retired media specialist, school librarian*

Hueytown
Nelson, Susan Rhodes *media specialist, educator*

Jacksonville
Harbor, Kingsley Okoro *communications and journalism educator, researcher*

Montgomery
Bristol, Caterina *music company executive*

Trussville
Jacobson, James Edmund *retired newspaper editor*

Tuscaloosa
Reinhart, Kellee Connely *journalist*

ARIZONA

Carefree
Mangouni, Norman *publishing executive*

Gilbert
Kenney, Thomas Frederick *retired broadcast executive*

Marana
Steckler, Larry *publishing executive, writer*

Phoenix
Breland, Sandy Ann *broadcast executive, director*
Edens, Gary Denton *broadcast executive*
Leach, John F. *editor, director, journalist, educator*
Lovely, Randy *editor-in-chief*
Moyer, Alan Dean *retired newspaper editor*
Stahl, Richard G. C. *journalist, editor*
Wu, Xu *communications educator*
Zidich, John M. *publishing executive*

Prescott
Beatty, Jametha Ann *communications educator*

Scottsdale
Joseph, Gregory Nelson *media critic, writer, actor, advocate*

Sedona
Sasmor, James Cecil *publishing representative, educator*

Tucson
Allvin, Paul G. *communications educator*
Martin, June Johnson Caldwell *journalist*

ARKANSAS

Fayetteville
Fosu, Ignatius *communications educator*

Fort Smith
Norin, Lori Ann *communication educator*

Little Rock
Greenberg, Paul *editor*
Hussman, Walter E., Jr. *publishing executive*
Parkhurst, Ted A. *publishing executive*
Portis, Charles McColl *reporter, writer*
Smith, Griffin *executive editor*

CALIFORNIA

Agoura Hills
Chagall, David *journalist, writer*

Alhambra
Duke, Donald Norman *publishing executive*

Alta Loma
Straka, Laszlo Richard *retired publishing consultant*

Arcadia
Belnap, David F. *journalist*

Atascadero
Rios, Evelyn Deerwester *columnist, musician, artist, writer*

Belvedere Tiburon
Rosenthal, Robert Jon *newspaper editor, journalist*

Berkeley
Bagdikian, Ben Haig *journalist, educator*
Browne, G.M. Walter Shawn *journalist, publisher*
Helson, Henry Berge *publisher, retired educator*
Hertelendy, Paul *critic, writer, poet*
Lesser, Wendy *editor, writer, consultant*
Susskind, Teresa Gabriel *publishing executive*

Beverly Hills
Billick, Brian Harold *sportscaster, former professional football coach*
Corwin, Stanley Joel *book publisher*
Friedman, Robert Lee *film company executive*
Gabler, Elizabeth Brand *film company executive*
Grazer, Brian *film company executive*
Hill, David *broadcast executive*
Hudlin, Reginald Alan *broadcast executive, film director, writer*
Jaffe, Stephen Singer *media specialist*
Lond, Harley Weldon *editor, publishing executive*
Minnillo, Vanessa Joy *news correspondent*
Rapino, Michael *music company executive*
Schneider, Charles Ivan *newspaper executive*
Sherwood, (Karen) Kehela *broadcast executive*
Siragusa, Tony (Anthony Siragusa) *sportscaster, retired professional football player*
Stern, Leonard Bernard *television and motion picture production company executive*
Strauss, Ricky *film company executive, producer*
Switzer, Barry *sportscaster, retired professional football coach*
Wiczyk, Modi *media company executive*
Wolper, David Lloyd *motion picture and television executive*

Brea
Hewitt, Hugh *editor, writer, radio talk show host*

Burbank
Aviv, Oren R. *film company executive*
Berwick, Frances *broadcast executive*
Bird, Andy *film company executive*
Cohen, Polly *film company executive*
Cook, Richard W. (Dick Cook) *film company executive*
Fleishman, Susan Nahley *entertainment company executive*
Horn, Alan F. *film company executive*
Iger, Bob (Robert Allen Iger) *entertainment company executive*
Kroll, Sue (Susan A. Kroll) *film company executive*
Kwan-Rubinek, Veronika *broadcast executive*
Marinelli, Janice *broadcast executive*
McLoughlin, Hilary Estey *broadcast executive*
McPherson, Stephen *broadcast executive*
Meyer, Barry Michael *motion picture executive*
Michel, Donald Charles *editor*
Ostroff, Dawn T. *broadcast executive*
Robinov, Jeff (Jeffrey Stephen Robinov) *film company executive*
Roth, Peter *broadcast executive*
Shuler, Dennis W. *entertainment company executive*
Staggs, Thomas O. *entertainment company executive*
Sweeney, Anne M. *cable television company executive*
Tarrant, Alison *broadcast executive, marketing professional*
Zucker, Jeffrey A. *broadcast executive*

Burlingame
Anders, George Charles *journalist, writer*
Corcoran, Elizabeth Anne *journalist*

Carlsbad
Howard, Robert Staples *newspaper publisher*

Carmel
Koeppel, Gary Merle *publishing executive, art gallery owner, writer*
Mollman, John Peter *publishing executive*

Chula Vista
Blankfort, Lowell Arnold *newspaper publisher*

Culver City
Jacobs, Betty Jane Lazaroff *communications educator*
Pascal, Amy Beth *film company executive*
Vollack, Lia *broadcast executive*

Daly City
Batlin, Robert Alfred *retired newspaper editor*

Del Mar
Marcus, Larry David *broadcast executive*

Dublin
Woodson, Roderick Kevin *sportscaster, football coach, retired professional football player*

El Cajon
Russell, Anne M. *editor-in-chief*

El Segundo
Churchill, Bruce B. *broadcast executive*
Doyle, Patrick T. *broadcast executive*
Guyardo, Paul *broadcast company executive*
Hunter, Larry Dean *broadcast executive, lawyer*
Palkovic, Michael W. *broadcast executive*
Pontual, Romulo *broadcast executive*

Emeryville
Bangs, Richard Johnston *publishing executive, explorer*
Catmull, Edwin Earl *film company executive, computer graphics engineer*
Lasseter, John Alan *film company executive, computer animator*

Fresno
Wilson, James Ross *communications educator, broadcast executive*

Fullerton
Lewandoski, Robert Henry *editor, publisher*
Puente, Henry *communications educator*

Glendale
Daly, Ann Michelle *broadcast executive*
GLobe, Anne *film company executive*
Katzenberg, Jeffrey *film company executive*
MacDonald, Laurie *film company executive*
Parkes, Walter F. *film company executive*
Snider, Stacey *film company executive*

Greenbrae
Freedman, Albert Z. *publishing executive*

Happy Camp
Brown, Barbara Black *publishing company executive*

Hollywood
Salzman, David Elliot *entertainment industry executive*

Huntington Beach
De Massa, Jessie G. *media specialist*
Garofalo, David P. *publishing executive, former mayor*

Inglewood
Sludikoff, Stanley Robert *publisher, writer*

Irvine
Bartkus, Richard Anthony *magazine publisher*
Horne, Terry *publishing executive*
Lesonsky, Rieva *editor-in-chief*
Osborne, Burl *retired publishing executive*
Power, Francis William *newspaper publisher*
Siegel, Barry *journalist, writer, literature educator*

La Canada
Paniccia, Patricia Lynn *journalist, writer, lawyer, educator*

La Jolla
Copley, David C. *publishing executive*
Freedman, Jonathan Borwick *journalist, writer, educator*
Harris, T. George *editor*
Morgan, Neil *editor, journalist, writer*
Pfeiffer, Phyllis Kramer *publishing executive*
Ramirez, Michael P. *editorial cartoonist*

La Verne
Pollock, Donald *communications educator, filmmaker*

Long Beach
Yousef, Fathi Salaama *communications educator, management consultant*

Los Angeles
Archerd, Army (Armand A. Archerd) *columnist, retired commentator*
Arthur, John M. *editor*
Bangalter, Thomas *recording industry executive, musician*
Berry, Stephen Joseph *reporter*
Blue, Violet (Ada Mae Johnson) *blogger*
Boyle, Barbara Dorman *film company executive*
Bryson, Louise Henry *retired broadcast executive*
Cannon, Reuben *casting company executive, film producer*
Chavez, Michael Robinson *photojournalist*
Clarke, Peter *communications and health educator*
Cole, Carolyn *photojournalist*
Cole, K.C. *journalist, writer*
Cowan, Louis Geoffrey *communications educator, writer*
Delugach, Albert Lawrence *journalist*
de Passe, Suzanne *record company executive*
Dwyre, William Patrick *journalist*
Edwards, Marion *broadcast executive*
Field, Ted (Frederick) *film company and former recording industry executive*
Firstenberg, Jean Picker *retired film institute executive*
Gardner, Joseph Lawrence *editor, writer*
Gazzale, Bob *film institute executive*
Gianopulos, Jim *film company executive*
Goren, Edward Gerald (Ed Goren) *broadcast executive*
Green, Trent Jason *sportscaster, retired professional football player*
Guider, Elizabeth Grier *editor*
Hamm, Catherine *travel editor*
Hartenstein, Eddy W. *publishing executive, former electronics executive*
Hefner, Hugh Marston *editor-in-chief*
Hilton, Perez (Mario Armando Lavandeira Jr.) *celebrity gossip blogger*
Hobbs, Pamela *communications educator, retired lawyer*
Hollihan, Thomas Andrew *communications educator*
Jacobson, Sidney *editor*
Jarrin, Jaime Leonardo *sportscaster, broadcast executive*
Jones, Quincy *producer, composer, arranger, conductor, trumpeter*
Klunder, Jack D. *publishing executive*
Lazarus, David *journalist*
Lee, Stan (Stanley Martin Lieber) *cartoon publisher, writer*
Levin, Harvey Robert *reporter, television producer, lawyer*
Levine, Pamela *film company executive*
Levinsohn, Peter *film company executive*
Lewis, Claudia *film company executive*
Liebling, Debbie (Deborah Liebling) *film company executive*
Litewka, Albert Bernard *entertainment executive*
Lozano, Monica Cecilia *publishing executive*
Maharaj, Davan R. *editor*
Malkin, Michelle *columnist, political commentator*
Martin, Roland S. *journalist, former editor*
McLaren, Mary *film company executive*
McSavaney, Raymond S. *photojournalist*
Meyer, Nick *film company executive*
Parent, Mary Campbell *film company executive*
Parks, Michael Christopher *journalist, educator*
Piller, Charles Leon *journalist*
Ramos, Jorge *newscaster*
Rice, Peter *broadcast executive*
Rich, Alan *music critic, writer*
Rothman, Tom (Thomas Edgar Rothman) *film company executive*
Rush, Herman E. *television executive*
Saltzman, Joseph *journalist, educator, television producer*
Sarnoff, Thomas Warren *television executive*
Shuster, Alvin *journalist, reporter*
Silverman, Ben *broadcast executive, television producer*
Singh, Bedi Ajay *film company executive*
Sloan, Harry Evans *film company executive*
Stanton, Russ W. *editor-in-chief*
Stephens, Loren M. *publishing executive, writer, film producer*
Taati, Poopak *media director*
Tellem, Arn *media company executive, agent*
Tellem, Nancy Reiss *broadcast executive*
Tiles, Neal *broadcast executive*
Trembly, Cristy *television executive*
Utley, Nancy *film company executive*
Uva, Joe *broadcast executive*
Van Buren, Abigail (Jeanne Phillips) *columnist, educator*
Walden, Dana *broadcast executive*
Watts, Emma *film company executive*
Weiss, Kenneth R. *newswriter*
Williams, Kenneth Scott *entertainment and advertising company executive*
Wilson, Ed *broadcast executive*
Yari, Bob *film company executive, producer*

Los Gatos
Hastings, Reed (Wilmot Reed Hastings Jr.) *film rental company executive, former education association administrator*

Malibu
McCall, Elizabeth Kaye *columnist, consultant, writer*

Manhattan Beach
Maisel, David *entertainment company executive*

Marina Del Rey
Lindheim, Richard David *broadcast executive, director*

Mill Valley
Leslie, Jacques Robert, Jr. *journalist*

Monterey
Goldstein, Kenneth F. *entertainment and publishing company executive*

Monterey Park
Stapleton, Jean *journalism educator*

Mount Shasta
Stienstra, Stephani Ann *editor, writer*

Murrieta
Yates, Ronald Eugene *newspaper editor, educator, author, journalist*

National City
Beauchamp, Miles Philip *editor, columnist, consultant*

Northridge
Dart, John Seward *journalist, editor*

Oakland
Dailey, Garrett Clark *publisher, lawyer*
McKinney, Judson Thad *broadcast executive*
Schrag, Peter *editor, writer*
Westergren, Timothy Brooks *music company executive*
Wood, Larry (Mary Laird) *journalist, writer, public relations executive, educator, environmental consultant*

Pacific Grove
Davis, Robert Edward *retired communications educator*
Sproule, James Michael *communications educator, writer*

Pacific Palisades
Kirkgaard, Valerie Anne *marketing company partner, media group executive, radio host, producer, writer, consultant*

Palm Desert
Ayling, Henry Faithful *editor, consultant, journalist, poet*

Palm Springs
Gerard, James Wilson *publishing consultant*

Palo Alto
Diamond, Diana Louise *editor, journalist*
Gubins, Samuel *publishing executive*
Wojcicki, Esther Denise *journalist, educator*

Pasadena
Matthews, Mildred Shapley *retired editor*

Paso Robles
Brown, Benjamin Andrew *retired journalist*

Placentia
Klapthor, James *broadcast media executive*

Rancho Mirage
Sheldon, Deena Lynn *television camera operator, film producer*

Riverside
James, Etta (Jamesetta Hawkins) *recording artist*
Sokolsky, Robert Lawrence *journalist*
Tinianow, Dan Eric *communications educator*

Rolling Hills Estates
Conrad, Paul Francis *cartoonist*

Sacramento
Dell, Cheryl Elbright *publishing executive*
Henson, Glenda Maria *newswriter*
Pruitt, Gary B. *publishing company executive*
Shriver, Maria Owings *former news correspondent*
Sill, Melanie *editor-in-chief*
Walsh, Denny Jay *reporter*
Williams, Arthur Cozad *retired broadcasting executive*

San Diego
Breen, Stephen P. *editorial cartoonist*
Olshevsky, George *editor*
Rowe, Peter A. *columnist*
Steen, Paul Joseph *retired broadcasting executive*
Winner, Karin E. *editor*

San Francisco
Adkins, Mark *publishing executive*
Anderson, Chris W. *editor-in-chief*
Bauerlein, Monika *magazine editor*
Bronstein, Phil *publishing executive*
Bushee, Ward III *editor*
Davidson, Keay *newswriter*
Duscha, Julius Carl *journalist*
Fox, Mitchell B. *publishing executive*
Fox, Steve *editor-in-chief*
Garchik, Leah Lieberman *journalist*
German, William *newspaper editor*
Graysmith, Robert *political cartoonist, author*
Greenwald, Glenn *columnist, lawyer*
Hafner, Katie *reporter*
Hale, Cecil *communications and business educator*
Jeffery, Clara *magazine editor*
Markoff, John *reporter*
McCracken, Harry *journalist*
McGinnis, Christopher *travel correspondent, editor*
Perlman, David *journalist*
Richtel, Matt (Theron Heir) *reporter, cartoonist*
Rosenheim, Daniel Edward *journalist, television news director*
Russell, Sabin *newswriter*
Sansweet, Stephen Jay *journalist, writer, marketing executive*
Smith, Patrick (Patrick Santosuosso) *columnist, pilot*
Vega, Frank J. *publishing executive*
Wolaner, Robin Peggy *Internet and magazine publisher*

San Jose
Butler, David J. *newspaper editor*
Carey, Peter Kevin *reporter*
Hanasaki, Philip Toshifusa *communications educator*
Trousdale, Stephen Richard *newspaper editor*
Tully, Mac *publishing executive*

San Rafael
Morgan, Michael Brewster *publishing executive*

Santa Ana
Brusic, Ken *editor-in-chief*
Katz, Tonnie *newspaper editor*

Santa Barbara
Ackerman, Marshall *publishing executive*
Brilliant, Ashleigh Ellwood *cartoonist, writer*
Brown, J'Amy Maroney *journalist, media consultant, investor*
Jackson, Beverley Joy Jacobson *columnist, educator*
Peck, Abraham *editor, media consultant, educator*

Santa Clarita
Sturges, Sherry Lynn *recording industry executive*

Santa Monica
Berman, Gail *former film company executive, media company executive*
Greenberg, Sarah *film company executive*
Huffington, Arianna *columnist, writer, editor*
Iovine, Jimmy *recording industry executive*
Levin, Gerald M. (Jerry Levin) *former media and entertainment company executive*
Mancuso, Frank G. *entertainment and communications company executive*
Palmatier, Malcolm Arthur *editor, consultant*
Rifkin, Arnold *film company executive*
Shearmur, Alli *film company executive*
Timbaland, (Timothy Z. Mosley) *recording industry executive, rap artist*

Santa Rosa
Callum, Myles *magazine editor, writer*
Person, Evert Bertil *retired newspaper and radio executive*

Sausalito
Brand, Stewart *editor, writer, multimedia designer*

Seaside
May, James Harvey *communications educator*

Sebastopol
O'Reilly, Tim *computer book publishing company executive, open sourcer advocate*

Sherman Oaks
Drudge, Matt (Matthew Nathan Drudge) *journalist, celebrity blogger*
Platus, Libby *journalist, art educator, sculptor, artist*

Signal Hill
Adler, Jeffrey D. *political consultant, crisis management expert*

Sonoma
Beckmann, Jon Michael *publishing company executive*

Stanford
Andreopoulos, Spyros George *writer*
Joffe, Josef *editor, columnist*
Suppes, Christine Johnson *publishing executive*

Stockton
Whittington, Robert Bruce *retired publishing company executive*

Summerland
Cannon, Louis Simeon *journalist, writer*

Tehachapi
Mitchell, Betty Jo *publishing executive, writer*

Toluca Lake
Ragan, Ann Talmadge *media and production consultant, actor*

Universal City
Baker, Bridget *broadcast executive*
Bromstad, Angela *broadcast executive*
Graboff, Marc J. *broadcast executive*
Langley, Donna *film company executive*
Linde, David *film company executive*
Madison, Paula *broadcast executive*
Menendez, Belinda *broadcast executive*
Meyer, Ron *film company executive*
Rocco, Nikki *film company executive*
Zigler, Vivi *broadcast executive, marketing professional*

Valley Springs
Anema-Garten, Durlynn C. *communications educator, counseling administrator, writer*

Victorville
Augustine-Carreira, Jacqueline *communications educator*

Vista
Linhart, Letty Lemon *editor*

West Hollywood
Fein, Irving *television and motion picture executive*
Grey, Brad *film company executive*
Huntsberry, Frederick D. *film company executive*
Powell, Amy Ruth *film company executive*

Wilton
Harrison, George Harry, III, (Hank Harrison) *publishing executive, author*

Woodland Hills
Latona, Valerie Ann *editor-in-chief*
McCluggage, Kerry *film and television executive*
Windrum, Ken *communications educator*

Yreka
Smith, Vin *editor, small business owner, writer*

COLORADO

Aspen
Hayes, Mary Eshbaugh *editor, writer*

Centennial
Udevitz, Norman *publishing executive*

Cherry Hills Village
Stapleton, Katharine Hall (Katie Stapleton) *commentator, writer*

Denver
Cohen, Andrew *news analyst, lawyer*
Dance, Francis Esburn Xavier *communication educator*
Drake, Sylvie (Jurras) *theater critic*
Kern, Jerome H. *consulting firm executive*
Moore, Gregory L. *editor*
Price, Kathleen McCormick *editor, writer*
Rothman, Paul A. *publishing executive*
Saltz, Howard Joel *newspaper editor*
Sheeler, Jim *journalist, educator*
Singleton, William Dean *publishing executive*

Durango
Van Mols, Brian *publishing executive*

Evergreen
Dobbs, Gregory Allan *journalist*

Fort Collins
May, Stephen James *communications educator, writer*

Georgetown
Stern, Mort(imer) P(hillip) *communications educator, editor, reporter, consultant*

Golden
Baron, Robert Charles *publishing executive*
Zimmer, Larry William, Jr. *sports announcer*

Greeley
Crandall, James L. *communications educator*

Greenwood Village
Abbott, William J. *broadcast executive*

Gunnison
Gelwicks, James M. *retired communications educator*

Highlands Ranch
Harris, Douglas Clay *retired newspaper executive*

Pueblo
Rawlings, Robert Hoag *newspaper publisher*

CONNECTICUT

Bethel
Shepard, Jean Heck *retired publishing consultant*

Bristol
Berman, Chris *sportscaster*
Bodenheimer, George *broadcast executive*
Brown, Hubie (Hubert Jude Brown) *sportscaster, retired professional basketball coach*
Edwards, Herman Lee *sportscaster, former professional football coach*
Gammons, Peter *columnist, commentator*
Gruden, Jon David *sportscaster, former professional football coach*
Jackson, Mark *sportscaster, retired professional basketball player*
Knight, Bobby (Robert Montgomery Knight) *sportscaster, retired men's college basketball coach*
Lieberman-Cline, Nancy *sportscaster, former professional basketball coach and player*
Lobo, Rebecca *sportscaster, retired professional basketball player*
Mashburn, Jamal *sportscaster, retired professional basketball player*
Melrose, Barry James *studio analyst, former professional hockey coach and player*
Rose, Jalen *sportscaster, retired professional basketball player*
Smith, Emmitt (Emmitt James Smith III) *sportscaster, retired professional football player*
Theismann, Joe (Joseph Robert Theismann) *sportscaster, retired professional football player*
Van Gundy, Jeff *sportscaster, former professional basketball coach*
Vina, Fernando *sportscaster, retired professional baseball player*
Vitale, Dick *sportscaster, commentator*
Wallace, Rusty *sportscaster, retired race car driver*
Walsh, John A. *broadcast executive, editor*
Walton, William Theodore, III, (Bill Walton) *sportscaster, former professional basketball player*

Chester
Frost-Knappman, (Linda) Elizabeth *publishing executive, editor, writer*

Danbury
Reynolds, Jean Edwards *publishing executive*

Darien
Becker, Ralph Edward *broadcast executive, consultant*
Brooke, Avery Rogers *publisher*
Workman, Sharon Joy *journalist*

Easton
Enos, Randall *cartoonist, illustrator*
Lorenz, Lee Sharp *cartoonist*

Fairfield
Kaff, Albert Ernest *reporter, writer*
Kudlow, Lawrence Alan (Larry Kudlow) *financial news correspondent, economist*

Greens Farms
Deford, Frank *sportswriter, commentator, writer*

Greenwich
Brant, Peter M. *publishing executive, real estate developer*

Hartford
Graziano, Richard J. *publishing executive*
Hazell, Naedine *editor*
Noel, Don Obert, Jr. *retired editor, columnist*
Pach, Peter Barnard *columnist, editor*

Ivoryton
Bendig, William Charles *editor, artist*

Lakeville
Estabrook, Robert Harley *journalist*

Lyme
Purcell, Bradford Moore *publishing company executive*

Madison
Egbert, Emerson Charles *retired publisher*

Milford
Henderson, Albert Kossack *publishing and food products executive, consultant*

Moodus
Cumming, Robert Emil *editor, writer*

New Canaan
Allen, Joseph Henry *retired publishing company executive*

New Haven
Balay, Robert Elmore *editor, librarian*
Fuchs, Elinor *theater critic, playwright, educator*
McClatchy, J. D. *editor, writer, educator*

Norwalk
DeCesare, Donald E. *broadcast executive*
Johnston, Catherine Viscardi *former magazine publisher*

Old Greenwich
Dixon, John Morris *magazine editor*

Old Saybrook
Gilmore, Clarence Percy *editor-in-chief, writer*

Sharon
Gordon, Nicholas *broadcast and performing arts executive*

Shelton
Kantrowitz, Jonathan Daniel *publishing executive, educator, lawyer*

Simsbury
Osborne, Louise *publishing executive*

Stamford
Duncan, Thomas Webb *media executive*
Lane, Hana Umlauf *editor*
McCarrick, Edward R. *publishing executive*

Terryville
Block, Fran *library media specialist*

Washington
Brimelow, Peter *journalist*

Waterbury
Pape, William James, II, *newspaper publisher*

Westport
Kramer, Sidney B. *publishing executive, literary agent, lawyer*
McCormack, Donald Paul *newspaper consultant*
Wussler, Robert Joseph *broadcast executive, media consultant*

Wilton
Seitz, Nicholas Joseph *editor, journalist*

Wolcott
Cordone, Kathleen Ann *media specialist*

DELAWARE

Dover
Smyth, Joel Douglas *newspaper executive*

New Castle
Cansler, Leslie Ervin *retired newspaper editor*
O'Donnell, Christine T. *political commentator, marketing consultant*

Newark
DeVivo, Sal J. *newspaper executive*
Jackson, Marvin Dennis *retired journalism educator, writer*

DISTRICT OF COLUMBIA

Washington
Adams, Robert Edward *journalist*
Alper, Jill *political consultant*
Alterman, Eric Ross *journalist, writer, English professor*
Arana, Marie *editor, writer*
Arnovitz, Benton Mayer *editor*
Asker, James Robert *magazine editor*
Barber, Ben Bernard Andrew *journalist*
Barnes, Frederic Wood, Jr. *journalist, political analyst*
Barone, Michael D. *political correspondent, writer, editor*
Baskin, Roberta *television correspondent*
Beinart, Peter Alexander *editor, journalist*
Bellows, Keith Adams *editor-in-chief, writer*
Blitzer, Wolf *journalist, news correspondent*
Bradlee, Ben (Benjamin Crowninshield Bradlee) *publishing executive, retired editor-in-chief*
Bradley, David G. *publishing executive*
Brauchli, Marcus Walker *editor*
Braverman, Jordan *columnist*
Brock, Gregory E. *editor*
Broder, David Salzer *journalist, writer*
Brown, Campbell (Alma Dale Campbell Brown) *newscaster*
Brown, John Patrick *publishing executive, financial consultant*
Bruzelius, Nils Johan Axel *journalist*
Cafferty, Jack *news anchor*
Centanni, Steve *national news correspondent*
Chandrasekaran, Rajiv *editor, writer*
Clemente, Rosa Alicia *journalist, advocate*
Clift, Eleanor *journalist, writer*
Cosgrove, John Patrick *editor*
Cowan, Edward *journalist, editor*
Crenshaw, Albert Burford *retired journalist*
Cutler, Bernard Joseph *editor-in-chief, writer*
De Borchgrave, Arnaud *editor, writer, lecturer*
Deeb, Mary-Jane *editor, educator, librarian*
DeFrank, Thomas Michael *journalist*
Devine, Tad (Thomas A. Devine) *media consultant*
Dillin, John Woodward, Jr. *retired editor, reporter*
Dillon, Veronica *publishing executive, lawyer*
Donohoe, Cathryn Murray *journalist*
Dorn, James Andrew *editor*
Douthat, Ross Gregory *editor, columnist, writer*
Dowd, Maureen *columnist*
Downie, Leonard, Jr. *publishing executive, retired editor, professor*
Drew, Elizabeth *commentator, journalist, writer*
Edwards, Bob (Robert Alan Edwards) *radio news anchor*
Elfin, Mel *magazine editor*
Elsasser, Glen Robert *journalist*
Entman, Robert Mathew *communications educator, consultant*
Faherty, Robert Louis *publishing executive*
Fahey, John M., Jr. *magazine and book publishing executive*
Favreau, Jonathan *speechwriter*
Feld, Karen Irma *journalist, commentator, speech professional*
Fineman, Howard David *columnist, writer, news correspondent*
Foer, Franklin *editor*
Franzen, Byron T. (John Franzen) *media specialist*
Friedman, Thomas Loren *foreign correspondent, writer*
Frum, David *columnist*
Gerson, Michael John *journalist*
Givhan, Robin Deneen *journalist*
Goldberg, Jonah Jacob *political columnist*
Graham, Donald Edward *publishing company executive*
Greene, David *reporter*
Gregory, David Michael *journalist, news correspondent*
Griffin, Paul L. *publishing executive, fraternal organization administrator*
Grosvenor, Gilbert Melville *journalist, educator, publishing executive*
Grubisich, Tom *web editor*
Grunwald, Mandy *media consultant*
Gurdon, Hugo *editor-in-chief*
Guzy, Carol *photojournalist*
Gwaltney, Corbin *publishing executive, editor*
Hiatt, Fred *editor, journalist*
Hills, Stephen P. *publishing executive*
Hinden, Stanley Jay *newspaper editor*
Hines, Barbara Bealor *communications educator, director*
Hitchens, Christopher Eric *columnist, writer*
Hume, Brit (Alexander Britton Hume) *journalist*
Jenkins, Loren B. *broadcast executive, publisher, writer*
Johns, Christopher George *editor-in-chief, photojournalist*
Johnson, Richard Kent *publishing executive*
Jones, Boisfeuillet, Jr., (Bo Jones) *publishing executive*
Jones, Hal S. *publishing executive*
Joo, Douglas D.M. *video production and aviation executive*
Joyce, Anne Raine *editor*
Kagan, Robert William *foreign policy commentator, historian*
Kelly, Brian J. *editor*
Kennedy, Katherine *freelance/self-employed media consultant*
King, Colbert Isaiah *columnist*
King, Larry (Lawrence Harvey Zeiger) *broadcaster, radio personality*
Kiplinger, Knight Austin *journalist, publishing executive*
Kirk, Donald *journalist*
Klose, Kevin *broadcast executive*
Knight, Athelia Wilhelmenia *journalist*
Kondracke, Morton Matt *journalist, commentator*
Krauthammer, Charles *columnist, editor*
Kristol, William (Bill Kristol) *political analyst, editor*
Kuttner, Robert Louis *editor, writer, columnist*
Lamb, Brian Patrick *broadcast executive*
Lambro, Donald Joseph *columnist*
Lardner, George, Jr. *journalist, writer*
Lawson, Jennifer *broadcast executive*
Lee, Debra Louise *cable television company executive*
Leeds, Charles Alan *publishing executive*
Lehrman, Margaret McBride *broadcast executive, television producer*
Leubsdorf, Carl Philipp *publishing executive*
Lewis, Charles Joseph *journalist*
Lewis, Robert David Gilmore *retired editor*
Lichtblau, Eric *journalist*
Locker, Raymond Duncan *editor*
Logan, Lara *news correspondent*
Lubar, Jeffrey Stuart *journalist, trade association executive*
Malley, Claudia *publishing executive*
Margolis, Doris May Rosenberg *editor, writer*
Marshall, Joshua Micah *publisher, blog writer, columnist, editor, political journalist*
McBee, Susanna B. *freelance journalist*
McLaughlin, John J. *broadcast executive, television producer, journalist, political commentator*
McMahon, Francine *publishing executive*
Melendy, David Russell *newscaster, reporter*
Mitchell, Andrea *journalist, television news anchor*
Murray, Alan Stewart *publishing executive*
Naím, Moisés *editor-in-chief*
Narisetti, Raju *editor*
Ohanian, Bernard Jay *writer, editor*
Ottaway, David Blackburne *journalist*
Parsons, Gary M. *broadcast executive*
Peirce, Neal R. *journalist*
Peretz, Martin *publishing executive, educator*
Pincus, Walter Haskell *news editor*
Pratt, Dana Joseph *publishing consultant*
Priest, Dana *journalist*
Putzel, Michael *journalist, editor*
Rankin, Robert Arthur *journalist*
Ravenal, Earl Cedric *international relations educator, writer*
Ricks, Thomas Edwin *journalist, writer*
Ridgeway, James Fowler *journalist*
Risen, James E. *journalist*
Roberts, Cokie (Corinne Boggs Roberts) *newscaster*
Roberts, John *news anchor*
Robinson, Eugene H. *journalist, newspaper columnist*
Rosen, Gerald Robert *editor*
Safire, William *journalist, foundation administrator*
Samuelson, Robert Jacob *journalist*
Sanger, David E. *news correspondent*
Satter, David Arnold *author, journalist*

Schieffer, Bob *newscaster*
Schiller, Vivian L. *broadcast executive, former Internet company executive*
Schmidt, Susan *journalist*
Schram, Martin Jay *journalist*
Scoblic, J. Peter *magazine editor*
Selingo, Jeffrey J. *editor, reporter*
Semas, Philip Wayne *editor*
Shales, Thomas William *television and film critic, writer, journalist*
Shanks, Hershel *editor, writer*
Shannon, Donald Hawkins *retired editor*
Shapiro, Walter Elliot *columnist*
Sheehan, Neil *reporter, writer*
Shenon, Philip *journalist*
Siegel, Robert Charles *broadcast journalist*
Simons, Carol Lenore *magazine editor*
Smith, John B. *publishing executive*
Smith, R. Jeffrey *national investigative correspondent*
Smith, Stephen Grant *journalist*
Spayd, Elizabeth Terry (Liz Spayd) *editor*
Sperling, Godfrey, Jr. *retired journalist*
Stephanopoulos, George Robert *political reporter*
Stern, Carl Leonard *retired news correspondent, federal official, educator*
Stern, Marcus A. *journalist*
Stolberg, Sheryl Gay *journalist*
Taubman, Philip M. *editor*
Terzian, Philip Henry *journalist*
Thomasson, Dan King *newspaper executive, columnist*
Tiede, Tom Robert *journalist*
Tobias, Andrew Previn *columnist, educator*
Toedtman, James Smith *journalist, editor*
Tolchin, Martin *journalist, writer*
Trafford, Abigail *columnist, editor, writer, public speaker*
Walsh, George William *publishing company executive, editor, author*
Weiss, Rick *reporter*
Westfall, Sandra Sobieraj *journalist*
Weymouth, Katharine Bouchage *publishing executive*
Whitaker, Mark Theis *broadcast executive, editor*
Whitworth, William A. *magazine editor*
Will, George Frederick *editor, journalist, commentator*
Williams, Earl Patrick, Jr. *retired editor, freelance writer*
Williams, Juan *news correspondent*
Willman, David *investigative journalist*
Winfrey, Carey Wells *journalist, editor*
Winter, Thomas Swanson *publishing executive*
Wood, James *magazine editor, literary critic*
Woodward, Bob (Robert Upshur Woodward) *editor, writer*
Yen, Hope S. *journalist, lawyer*
Zelman, Susan Tave *broadcast executive, former state official, school system administrator*

FLORIDA

Boca Raton
Handel, Morton Emanuel *film company executive, management consultant*
Jackson, Stephanie A. *communications educator, consultant*
McQueen, Scott Robert *broadcast executive*

Boynton Beach
Jacobs, Wendy *editor, realtor*
Klein, Bernard *publishing executive*

Bradenton
White, Dale Andrew *journalist*

Cocoa Beach
Quinn, John Collins *publishing executive, editor*

Cooper City
Kelly, Brian J. *media specialist*

Dade City
Barnes, Andrew Earl *former newspaper executive*

Delray Beach
Salsberg, Arthur Philip *publishing executive*

Dover
Pearson, Walter Donald *editor, columnist*

Fort Lauderdale
Bolanos, Michael Templeton *media production executive*
Greenberg, Howard *publishing executive*
Markus, Robert Michael *retired journalist*
Maucker, Earl Robert *editor, publishing executive*
Williamson, William Paul, Jr. *journalist*

Fort Myers
Barbour, William Rinehart, Jr. *retired book publisher*

Gainesville
Barber, Charles Edward *publishing executive, journalist*
Kelly, Kathleen S(ue) *communications educator*

Heathrow
Argirion, Michael *editor*

Hialeah
Arrarás, Maria Celeste *newscaster, journalist*
Browne, Donald Victor *broadcast executive*

Hollywood
Barnes, Gregory *media specialist, educator*

Inverness
Barrow, Sally Settle *retired media specialist, librarian*
Crouse, John Oliver, II, *journalist, publisher*

Jacksonville
Davis, Fred *journalist, educator*
Hartmann, Frederick William *newspaper editor*
Lehmbeck, John Pierce *journalist, writer*
Parmelee, John H. *communications educator*
Vincent, Norman Fuller *broadcast executive*

Key Biscayne
Pope, John Edwin *editor, columnist*

Lake Helen
Finn, Stephen Martin *media producer, venture capitalist*

Lake Mary
Strang, Stephen Edward *editor*

Lake Worth
Asher, Kathleen May *communications educator*
Willis, Clayton *broadcaster, government official, educator, arts consultant*

Lakeland
MacDonald, Susan Priest *media specialist, writer*

Lutz
Kolb, Richard Maurice *sports writer, sportscaster*

Miami
Barry, Dave *columnist, writer*
Birsh, Arthur Thomas *publishing executive*
Black, Creed Carter *newspaper executive*
Cenziper, Debbie *journalist*
Cotayo, Charles *journalist, critic, film producer*
Gyllenhaal, Anders *editor*
Harrison, Stanley L. *editor, educator, writer*
Landsberg, David A. *publishing executive*
Lawrence, David, Jr. *journalist, early childhood advocate*
Lew, Salvador *radio station executive*
Perkel, Robert Simon *photojournalist, educator*
Russell, James Webster, Jr. *retired editor, columnist*
Savage, James Francis *retired editor*
Wax, William Edward *photojournalist*

Mount Dora
Trundle, W(infield) Scott *publishing executive newspaper, lawyer*

Naples
Blevins, Charles Russell *publishing executive*
Clapp, Roger Howland *retired publishing executive*
Clarke, John Patrick *retired newspaper publisher*
Cobb, Brian Eric *broadcast executive*
Jones, Philip Howard *broadcast journalist*
Moore, Oliver Semon III *publishing executive, consultant*
Penniman, Nicholas Griffith, IV, *retired newspaper publisher*
Silvestri, Vito Nicholas *communications educator*

Niceville
Warren, J. Richard *editor, retired humanities educator*

Orlando
Adubato, Richard Adam (Richie Adubato) *sportscaster, former professional basketball coach*
Dunn, William Bruna III *journalist*
Hall, Charlotte Hauch *editor*
Maupin, Elizabeth Thatcher *theater critic*
Pierce, Jerry Earl *publishing executive*
Ramos, Elmo, Jr. *music company executive*

Palm Bay
Pattyn, Sue *publishing executive*

Palm Coast
Afflick, Gilbert Leslie *editor, journalist*
Franco, Annemarie Woletz *editor*

Palm Harbor
Barker, Larry Lee *communications educator*
Jones, Winona Nigels *retired media specialist*

Panama City
Lucas, Truett LaVan *retired communications technician*

Parkland
Froehlich, Fritz Edgar *communications educator, telecommunications scientist*

Pensacola
App, Cynthia *communications educator*
Bowden, Jesse Earle *editor, writer, cartoonist*

Port Richey
VanMeer, Mary Ann *publishing executive, writer, webmaster*

Saint Augustine
Nolan, Joseph Thomas *journalism educator, communications consultant*

Saint Petersburg
Belich, John Patrick, Sr. *journalist, private investigator*
Corty, Andrew P. *publishing executive*
DeGregory, Lane *journalist, features writer*
Haiman, Robert James *editor, journalist, educator, media consultant, expert witness, critic*
Jenkins, Robert Norman *reporter, editor*
Kubiet, Leo Lawrence *media consultant*
Naughton, James Martin *journalist*
Patterson, Eugene Corbett *retired editor, publishing executive*
Petty, Marty *publishing executive*
Pittman, Robert Turner *retired newspaper editor*
Pizana, Orlando Akhiem *communications educator*
Tash, Paul Clifford *editor, publishing executive*

Sanford
Scott, Mellouise Jacqueline *retired media specialist*

Sarasota
Hughes, Allen *music critic*
Marino, Eugene Louis *publishing executive, director*
Proffitt, Waldo, Jr. *newspaper editor*

Tallahassee
Clifford, Dorothy Ring *journalist*
Dadisman, Joseph Carrol *retired newspaper executive*
Grable, Bettye Ann *communications educator*
Morgan, Lucy Ware *senior correspondent, journalist*
Sanchez, Robert Francis *journalist*

Tamarac
Thaung, U *journalist*

Tampa
Bowman, Janet *media specialist*
Coats, Janet S. (Janet Weaver) *editor*
Friedlander, Edward Jay *journalist, educator*
Luddington, Betty Walles *retired media specialist*
Palmer, Denise E. *publishing executive*
Schueler, John R. *newspaper executive*
Tully, Darrow *newspaper publisher*

Tarpon Springs
Leisner, Anthony Baker *publishing company executive*

Venice
Cool, Kim Patmore *editor, publishing and retail executive*

West Palm Beach
Hunter, Michael *publishing executive*
Johnson, Martin Allen *publishing executive, artist*
Kessler, Ronald Borek *journalist, writer*
Rukeyser, M.S., Jr. *television consultant, writer*

Weston
Marino, Dan (Daniel Constantino Marino Jr.) *sportscaster, retired professional football player*

Winter Park
Federle, Michael *publishing executive*

GEORGIA

Albany
Moises, Alfonso Arturo *communications educator*

Athens
Fink, Conrad Charles *journalist, communications executive, consultant*
Soloski, John *journalism and communications educator*

Atlanta
Albert, Marv *sportscaster, program director*
Alleyne, Mark Dacosta *communications educator, journalist*
Amanpour, Christiane *news correspondent*
Barkley, Charles Wade *sportscaster, retired professional basketball player*
Bisher, James Furman *journalist, writer*
Blackmon, Douglas A. *newspaper reporter, writer*
Collins, Doug (Paul Douglas Collins) *sportscaster, former professional basketball coach*
Connelly, Terrence John, Sr. *broadcast executive*
Dupri, Jermaine *recording industry executive, music producer*
Fratello, Mike (Michael Robert Fratello) *sportscaster, former professional basketball coach*
Freeman, Brenda *broadcast executive*
Gwynn, Anthony Keith (Tony Gwynn) *sportscaster, retired professional baseball player*
Kennedy, James Cox *publishing and media executive*
Kent, Philip I. *broadcast executive*
Kernis, Jay *broadcast executive*
Klein, Jonathan *broadcast executive*
Kloer, Philip Baldwin *journalist*
Luckovich, Michael Edward *cartoonist*
Malveaux, Suzanne *news correspondent*
Mullin, Bernard James *media consultant*
Neil, Robert F. *broadcast executive*
O'Brien, Soledad *news anchor*
Polk, James Ray *journalist*
Sams, Louise S. *broadcast executive, lawyer*
Sander, John L. *broadcast executive*
Sloan, Mary Jean *retired media specialist*
Taylor, Susan L. *former magazine editor, philanthropist*
Toner, Michael F. *journalist*
Turner, Ted (Robert Edward Turner III) *retired broadcast company executive, philanthropist*
Wallace, Julia Diane *editor*
Walton, Jim *broadcast executive*

Columbus
Wells, Kelly L. *media specialist*

Decatur
Knight, Walker Leigh *publishing executive, minister*
Shaw, Jeanne Osborne *editor, poet*

Fayetteville
Turnipseed, Barnwell Rhett III *journalist, broadcaster, public relations consultant*

Gainesville
Coakley, Deirdre *columnist, writer*

Kennesaw
Williamsen, Dannye Sue *personal development educator, publisher, ordained minister*

Mableton
Rowe, Bonnie Gordon *music company executive*

Macon
Savage, Randall Ernest *journalist*

Marietta
Opre, Thomas Edward *retired editor, film company executive*

Maysville
Leach, Claudia Rylee *media specialist, educator*

Oxford
Sitton, Claude Fox *newspaper editor*

Powder Springs
Creighton, Peggy Milam *media specialist, writer*

Sandy Springs
Eckert, Michael Joseph *television and technology executive*

Savannah
Smith, David Lee *retired editor*

Statesboro
Adhikari, Dharma Nanda *journalist, writer, educator*

Woodstock
Olton, Patricia McKinley *media specialist*

HAWAII

Honolulu
Simonds, John Edward *retired newspaper editor*
Sparks, Robert William *retired publishing executive*

Kahului
Yamamoto, Irwin Toraki *editor, publishing executive*

IDAHO

Boise
Boren, Robert Reed *communications educator*
Gowler, Vicki Sue *editor-in-chief*
McLuskie, Ed *communications educator*

ILLINOIS

Arlington Heights
Lampinen, John A. *newspaper editor*

Bloomington
Merwin, Davis Underwood *newspaper executive*

Buffalo Grove
Kuennen, Thomas Gerard *journalist*

Burr Ridge
Wyatt, Robert Odell *journalism educator*

Carol Stream
Bemis, Mary Ferguson *magazine editor*
Franzen, Janice Marguerite Gosnell *magazine editor*

Champaign
Kroner, Fred L. *journalist*
Meyer, August Christopher, Jr. *broadcast executive, lawyer*
Watts, Robert Allan *publisher, lawyer*

Charleston
Coutant, Mary McElwee *retired editor*

Chicago
Anderson, Karl Stephen *retired journalist*
Barron, John *editor*
Bates, Zeline Kelly *media specialist, director*
Belden-Adams, Kris K. *journalist, educator*
Bigelow, Chandler III *publishing executive*
Curwen, Randall William *retired journalist, editor*
Cusac, Anne-Marie *journalist, educator*
Dee, Ivan Richard *book publisher*
Dold, Robert Bruce *journalist*
Ebert, Roger Joseph *film critic*
Feder, Robert *columnist*
Fetridge, Clark Worthington *publishing executive*
Francuch, Paul Charles *broadcast journalist*
Giangreco, Mark *sportscaster, director*
Hayes, M. M.M. *publishing executive*
Hayner, Donald *editor-in-chief*
Hirt, Jane *editor*
Hlavacek, Roy George *publishing executive*
Hollandsworth, Todd Mathew *sportscaster, retired professional baseball player*
Huebner, Jeff *art journalist, freelance writer*
Hunter, Tony *publishing executive*
Idol, Anna Catherine *magazine editor*
Judge, Bernard Martin *retired editor, publishing executive*
Kamyszew, Christopher D. *film executive, educator, curator*
Kern, Gerould W. *publishing executive, editor*
Klatt, Wayne Roy *editor, writer*
Krashesky, Alan *newscaster*
Krueger, Bonnie Lee *editor, writer*
Loesch, Katharine Taylor *communications educator, theater educator*
Longworth, Richard Cole *journalist, writer*
Lowe, Mira *editor*
Madigan, John William *publishing executive*
Mansueto, Joseph Daniel *publishing executive*
McNally, Andrew, IV, *publishing executive, director*
Michaels, Randy (Benjamin Homel) *multimedia company executive*
Migala, Lucyna J. *journalist, broadcast executive, artistic director*
Nash, Jessie Madeleine *journalist, science writer*
Nault, William Henry *publishing executive*
Patrick, Dan *sportscaster*
Plouffe, David *political strategist*

Primm, Earl Russell III *publishing executive*
Reardon, John E. *broadcast executive*
Rice, Linda Johnson *publishing executive*
Rice, William Edward *journalist*
Ross, Michael Neil *publishing executive*
Ross, Sharon Marie *communications educator*
Roy, Kevin *newscaster*
Rynkiewicz, Stephen Michael *journalist*
Salopek, Paul F. *reporter, foreign correspondent*
Scheppach, Tracey L. *communications media company executive*
Shebel, Heather A. *editor*
Smith, Sam *columnist, writer*
Stone, Steven Michael *sports announcer, former baseball player*
Thompson, George Fletcher *editor, publishing executive*
von Rhein, John Richard *music critic, journalist, writer*
Wier, Patricia Ann *publishing executive, consultant*
Wille, Lois Jean *retired editor*

Dekalb
Gunkel, David J. *communications educator*

Elmhurst
Pruter, Margaret Franson *editor*

Evanston
Borcover, Alfred Seymour *journalist*
Galvin, Kathleen Malone *communications educator*
Ghiglione, Loren Frank *journalism professor*
Jacobs, Norman Joseph *publishing executive*
Jones, Robert Russell *retired magazine editor*
Kuenster, John Joseph *editor*
McCarron, John Francis *editor*
Otwell, Ralph Maurice *retired newspaper editor*
Youngman, Owen Ralph *newspaper executive, educator*

Highland Park
Pattis, S. William *publishing executive*
Rutenberg-Rosenberg, Sharon Leslie *retired journalist*

Huntley
Balk, Alfred William *journalist*

Kenilworth
Cook, Stanton R. *media company executive*

Lake Forest
Schulze, Franz, Jr. *critic, educator*

Libertyville
True, Raymond Stephen *editor, writer*

Macomb
Siddiqi, Mohammad A. *journalist, educator*

Mount Vernon
LeMay, Nicholas K. *broadcast executive*
Withers, W. Russell, Jr. *broadcast executive*

Naperville
Larson, Roy *journalist, retired publishing executive*

Northbrook
Pesmen, Sandra (Mrs. Harold William Pesmen) *journalist, educator*

Oak Brook
Biedron, Theodore John *publishing and advertising executive*

Oak Park
Bedrossian, Ursula Kay Kennedy *editor*

Oregon
Haynes, Gary Allen *photojournalist, editor*

Palatine
Neeley, Henrietta Nance *music school administrator*

Rockford
Jacobi, Fredrick Thomas *newspaper publisher*

Urbana
Andersen, Kenneth Eldon *speech communication educator, consultant*
Christians, Clifford Glenn *communications educator*
Dash, Leon DeCosta, Jr. *journalist*

Wilmette
Boyle, Antonia Barnes *writer, editor*

Winnetka
Quaal, Ward Louis *broadcast executive*

INDIANA

Anderson
Clanin, Douglas Edward *editor, researcher*

Bloomington
Franklin, Timothy A. *communications educator*
Jacobi, Peter Paul *journalism educator, writer*
Lee, Don Yoon *publishing executive, academic administrator, writer*
Schurz, Scott Clark *newspaper executive*

Bristow
James, Marion Ray *retired publishing executive, editor*

East Chicago
Platis, Mary Lou *media specialist*

Fort Wayne
Klugman, Stephan Craig *newspaper editor*

Franklin
Nuwer, Henry Joseph (Hank Nuwer) *journalist, educator*

Greensburg
Mills, Linda Lou *media specialist*

Huntington
Spenner, Richard Lee *media specialist*

Indianapolis
Dorrel, Ruth *editor*
Garmel, Marion Bess Simon *retired arts journalist*
McKeand, Patrick Joseph *newspaper publisher, educator*
Russell, Frank Eli *retired newspaper publishing executive*
Ryerson, Dennis R. *editor*
Wright, David Burton *retired newspaper publishing company executive*

Lafayette
Renzetti, Phyllis Jean *retired technical editor, paleontologist*

Michigan City
Varro, Barbara Joan *retired editor*

Munster
Potempa, Philip Matthew *journalist, columnist, communications educator*

Plymouth
Merle, Patrick F. *communications educator*

South Bend
Storin, Matthew Victor *retired editor*

Terre Haute
Vincent, Richard C. *communications educator, researcher*

West Lafayette
Dutta, Mohan *communications educator*

IOWA

Ames
Alumbaugh, JoAnn McCalla *magazine editor*

Cedar Falls
Siddens, Paul Jackson III *communication educator*
Skaine, James C. *retired communications educator*

Cedar Rapids
Keller, Eliot Aaron *broadcast executive*
Thompson-Stanton, Mary Jean *communications educator*

Des Moines
Butler, Gayle *editor-in-chief*
Gartner, Michael Gay *editor, baseball and television executive*
Hollingsworth, Laura L. *publishing executive*
Kerr, William T. *publishing and broadcast executive*
Lacy, Stephen M. *publishing and broadcasting executive*
Washburn, Carolyn K. *editor-in-chief*
Witke, David Rodney *retired newspaper editor, consultant*

Iowa City
Becker, Samuel Leo *retired communications educator*
Gronbeck, Bruce Elliot *communications educator*
Singer, Jane Bess *communications educator*
Yao, Qingjiang *communications educator, researcher*

Mason City
Collison, Jim *publishing executive*

West Des Moines
Myers, Mary Kathleen *publishing executive*

KANSAS

Arkansas City
Ewing, Dejon L. *communications educator*

Chanute
Weilert, Mary E. *communications educator*

Hutchinson
Baumer, Beverly Belle *journalist*
Buzbee, Richard Edgar *retired newspaper editor*

Lawrence
Dickinson, William Boyd, Jr. *media consultant*
Hale, Richard Lee *magazine editor*
Simons, Dolph Collins, Jr. *publishing executive, editor*

Manhattan
An, Soontae *communications educator*
Gould, Thomas HP *communications educator*
Seaton, Edward Lee *editor, publishing executive*

Mission Hills
Rose, Stephen F. *columnist*

Olathe
Dodd, James B. *Internet executive*
Peterson, Cynthia L. *communications educator*

Overland Park
Christian, Shirley Ann *journalist, author*
Wornall, Ilah Ruth (Ruthie Wornall) *publishing executive, educator*

Shawnee Mission
Martin, Donna Lee *retired publishing company executive*

Wichita
Hatteberg, Larry Merle *photojournalist*

KENTUCKY

Benton
Denial, Roy *editor, author*

Crestview Hills
Bryant, Gregory A. *instructional technologist and designer, educator*

Fedscreek
Bottom, Jean Bertrand *media specialist*

Fort Mitchell
Silvers, Gerald Thomas *retired publishing executive*

Greenville
Walters, Sue Fox *broadcast executive, accountant*

Lexington
Carroll, John Sawyer *educator, former newspaper editor*
Cross, Alvin Miller (Al Cross) *journalist*
Kelly, Timothy Michael *newspaper publisher*
Kissling, Fred Ralph, Jr. *publishing and insurance agency executive*

Louisville
Garson, Arnold Hugh *publishing executive*
Ivory, Bennie L. *executive editor*
Towles, Donald Blackburn *retired publishing executive*

Paducah
Stice, Dwayne Lee *broadcasting company executive, professional organist*

Pewee Valley
Gill, George Norman *newspaper publishing company executive*

LOUISIANA

Baton Rouge
Camp, John Bliss *journalist, television producer*
Miller, Andrea Lynn *communications educator*

Boutte
Patricia, Pitre Agnes *media specialist*

Grambling
Laleh Parvaran, Parvin *communications educator*

La Place
Fiffie Proctor, JoAnn *media and technology specialist*

New Orleans
Crumley, David Oliver *publishing executive, writer*
Moreno, Helena *newscaster*
Phelps, Ashton, Jr. *newspaper publisher*
Pope, John Marvin *journalist*
Roesler, Robert Harry *media consultant*

Shreveport
Lazarus, Allan Matthew *retired newspaper editor*

MAINE

Belfast
Griffith, Patricia King *journalist*

Cape Elizabeth
Rich, John Hubbard, Jr. *retired news correspondent*

Castine
Bernstein, Lester *editorial consultant*

Chebeague Island
Traina, Salvatore Albert *publishing executive*

East Boothbay
Gibson, Barry Joseph *editor*

Penobscot
dePaolo, Ronald Francis *editor-in-chief, writer*

MARYLAND

Baltimore
Cook, J. Montgomery (Monty Cook) *editor*
Hirsh, Allan Thurman, Jr. *retired publishing executive*
Muccie, Mary Rose *publishing executive*
Ryan, Timothy E. *publishing executive*
Sanders, Julius Ray *music company executive*
Scott, Frederick Isadore, Jr. *editor, management consultant*
Stone, Precious *communications educator*

Bethesda
Chronister, Gregory Michael *newspaper editor*
Cornish, Edward Seymour *magazine editor*
Edwards, Virginia B. *editor, publishing executive*
Frank, Richard Sanford *retired magazine editor*
Herman, Edith Carol *journalist*
Holmberg, Ted *journalist, consultant*
Johnson, Thomas Dale *consultant and publishing executive*
Kempster, Norman Roy *journalist*
Larrabee, Donald Richard *publishing executive*
Nelson, John Howard (Jack Howard Nelson) *journalist*
Pickerell, James Howard *photojournalist*
Wagner, Cynthia Gail *editor, writer*

Cheverly
Miller, Mark Karl *journalist, editor*

Chevy Chase
Adler, James Barron *publishing executive*
Bruno, Harold Robinson, Jr. *retired journalist, writer*
Cowen, Eugene Sherman *broadcast executive*
Gottschall, Edward Maurice *editor, writer*
Kilborn, Peter Thurston *journalist, author*
Kriegsman, Alan M. *arts critic*
Shipler, David Karr *journalist, writer*
Shogan, Robert *news correspondent*
Smith, Hedrick Laurence *journalist, television producer*
Toth, Robert Charles *retired journalist*

College Park
Beasley, Maurine Hoffman *journalism educator, historian*
Fink, Edward Laurence *communications educator*
Gomery, Douglas *communications educator, writer*
Johnson, Haynes Bonner *journalist, writer, commentator*

Easton
Potter, Blair Burns *editor*

Garrett Park
Kornberg, Warren Stanley *journalist*

Havre De Grace
Wetter, Virginia Forwood Pate *broadcast executive*

Lanham
Freese, Rich *publishing executive*
Hughes, Catherine L. (Cathy Hughes) *broadcast executive, radio personality*

Lutherville Timonium
Cedrone, Louis Robert, Jr. *retired critic*

Monkton
Parker, Robert M., Jr., (Bob Parker) *wine critic, writer*

Potomac
Christian, John Kenton *publishing executive, marketing professional, consultant*
Fox, Arthur Joseph, Jr. *editor*
Karnow, Stanley *journalist, writer*
Penczner, Marius *media company executive*
Sundick, Sherry Small *journalist, writer, poet*

Rockville
Kohlmeier, Louis Martin, Jr. *newspaper reporter*
Miller, Claire Ellen *editor, educator, writer*

Saint Michaels
Trippi, Joe *media consultant*

Salisbury
Kleiman, Gary Howard *broadcast, advertising and cellular communications consultant*

Severna Park
Pumphrey, Janet Kay *editor, publishing executive*

Sherwood Forest
Richards, Carol Ann Rubright *lecturer, retired editor, journalist*

Silver Spring
Bennett, Carol(ine) Elise *retired reporter, actress*
Dolan, Liz *multimedia company executive, marketing professional*
Hendricks, John S. *broadcast executive*
Kaplan, Marjorie *broadcast executive*
Rodgers, Johnathan *broadcast executive*
Vernon, Weston, III, (Wes Vernon) *broadcaster, writer, actor*
Zaslav, David M. *broadcast executive*

Spencerville
Whitaker, Joel *publishing executive, public official*

Street
Spangler, Ronald Leroy *retired television and aircraft executive, automobile consultant*

Sunderland
Franklin, Jon Daniel *writer, journalist, educator*

Taneytown
Wisner, Gail Ann *media specialist*

University Park
Beckenstein, Myron *journalist*

MASSACHUSETTS

Boston
Ainsley, P. Steven (Steve Ainsley) *publishing executive*
Baron, Martin *editor*
Cohen, Rachelle Sharon *journalist*
Daniloff, Nicholas *journalist, educator*
Feeney, Mark *journalist*
Golden, Daniel *journalist*
Hostetter, Amos Barr, Jr. *cable television executive*
James, Bill *baseball writer, statistician*
Lawrence, Merloyd Ludington *editor*
Leland, Timothy *retired newspaper executive*
Mason, Charles Ellis III *magazine editor*
Morris, Gerald Douglas *newspaper editor*
Purcell, Patrick Joseph *publishing executive*
Redo, Philip Lappano *broadcast executive*

Rice, Jim (James Edward Rice) *sportscaster, professional baseball coach, retired professional baseball player*
Solomon, Caleb P. *editor*
Twombly, Stephen Doane *magazine publisher*
Tyson, Peter *editor-in-chief*
Williams, Brown F *media specialist*
Xue, Yong *columnist, educator*

Braintree
Smyth, Peter Hayes *radio executive*

Brookline
Bourne, Katherine Day *journalist, educator*

Cambridge
Aronson, Michael Andrew *editor*
Giles, Robert Hartmann *journalist, educator*
Goodman, Ellen Holtz *journalist*
Lenger, John Richard *journalism educator*
Nordell, Hans Roderick *journalist, retired editor*
Urbanowski, Frank *publishing company executive*
Wilcox, Maud *editor*

Chestnut Hill
Olufowote, James *communications educator*

Concord
Heinle, Beverly Diane *publishing executive*

Framingham
Levy, Joseph Louis *publishing company executive*

Hingham
Menzies, Ian Stuart *newspaper editor*

Hudson
Osoff, Jeffrey Arlin *media company executive*

Leeds
Deane, James Garner *editor, conservationist*

Needham
Greenway, Hugh Davids Scott *journalist*

Needham Heights
Forman, Leonard P. *former publishing executive*
Salhany, Lucille S. (Lucy Salhany) *broadcast executive*

North Adams
Thurston, Donald Allen *broadcast executive*

North Chelmsford
Kotelly, George Vincent *editor, writer, electrical engineer*

Pittsfield
Rich, Philip Dewey *publishing executive*

Plymouth
Flood, H. Gay (Hulda Gay Flood) *editor, consultant*

Quincy
Lippincott, Joseph P. *photojournalist, educator*
Zoulas, Soterios C. *communications educator, consultant*

Rockport
Bissell, Phil (Charles P. Bissell) *cartoonist*

Somerville
Hume, Ellen Hunsberger *media analyst, educator, journalist*

South Hadley
Elleman, Barbara *editor*

Springfield
Starr, David *editor, publisher*

Waltham
Goodheart, Eugene *literary critic*

Wayland
Huff, William Braid *retired publishing company executive*

Wellfleet
Limpitlaw, John Donald *publishing executive, clergyman*

West Falmouth
King, Richard Hood *retired newspaper executive*

West Tisbury
Méras, Phyllis Leslie *journalist*

Westport
Gormley, Robert John *retired publishing executive*

Winthrop
Flockhart, Barbara Townsley *retired publishing executive*

MICHIGAN

Adrian
Bleam, Sheri Reeves *communication educator, consultant*

Ann Arbor
Alterman, Eddie *editor-in-chief, writer*
Beaver, Frank Eugene *critic, historian*
Driscoll, John C., Jr. *publishing executive*
Eisendrath, Charles Rice *journalism educator, farmer, consultant*
Gloeckner, Phoebe Louise *cartoonist, author, illustrator*
Hessler, David William *information and multimedia systems educator*
Schmitz, Philip Charles *editor, researcher*

Baroda
Reckline, Sigmund Joseph *publishing executive, editor*

Bay City
Hiner, John Patrick *newspaper editor*

Birmingham
McCuen, John Joachim *columnist, educator, US military counterinsurgery and hybrid war consultant*

Canton
Reed, Gary Brian *publishing executive*

Dearborn
Hogan, Brian Joseph *editor*
Kiska, Timothy Olin *communications educator, radio producer*

Detroit
Andrews, Caesar *editor*
Anger, Paul *newspaper editor*
Parry, Dale D. *publisher, editor*
Wolman, Jonathan Paley *newspaper editor, journalist*

East Lansing
Freedman, Eric *journalist, educator, writer*
Greenberg, Bradley Sander *communications educator*

Grand Rapids
Bytwerk, Randall Lee *communication educator*

Grosse Pointe
Bryfonski, Dedria Anne *publishing executive*
Ruffner, Frederick G., Jr. *book publisher*

Grosse Pointe Park
Elsila, David August *editor*

Grosse Pointe Woods
McWhirter, Glenna Suzanne (Nickie) *retired columnist*

Herron
Elkie, Kimberly K. *medical editor*

Kalamazoo
Jamison, Frank Raymond *independent video producer, retired communications educator*

Kentwood
Kelley, DeVere Orin *media specialist*

Manistee
Trussell, Charles Tait *columnist*

Mount Pleasant
Norris, Darcy Janelle *sign language teacher*
Petrick, Michael Joseph *journalism educator*

Rochester
Baker, Susan Gail *communication educator*

Saginaw
Chaffee, Paul Charles *newspaper editor, publisher*

Southfield
Clifford, Carolyn *news correspondent, reporter*
Margolis, Sherry *newscaster*
Osborne, Marie-Angela *journalist*
Timmons, Robbie *news anchor*

Waterford
James, William Ramsay *broadcast executive*

Wixom
Alpert, Daniel *broadcast executive*

Ypsilanti
Evans, Gary Lee *communications educator, consultant*

MINNESOTA

Edina
Bisping, Bruce Henry *photojournalist*

Minneapolis
Barnes, Nancy *editor-in-chief*
Cope, Lewis *journalist*
Cowles, John, Jr. *publishing executive, women's sports promoter, civic activist*
Flanagan, Barbara *journalist*
Harte, Christopher M. *publishing executive, investment manager*
Laing, Karel Ann *publishing executive*
Lerner, Harry Jonas *publishing executive*
Murphy, Joseph Edward, Jr. *broadcast executive*
Opperman, Dwight Darwin *retired publishing company executive*
Reichgott Junge, Ember Darlene *broadcast commentator, retired state senator, lawyer, writer, radio personality*
Ridder, Par *former publishing executive*
Scallen, Thomas Kaine *broadcast executive*
Trouten, Douglas James *journalist*
White, Robert James *retired columnist*

Rochester
Shampo, Marc Anthony *retired editor*

Saint Bonifacius
Grainger, Johnny Loujack *communications educator, consultant*

Saint Cloud
Bruestle, Gregory J. *media specialist*

Saint Paul
Amidon, Paul Charles *publishing executive*
Fladung, Thom *editor-in-chief*
Gilmore, Guy L. *publishing executive*
Hubbard, Stanley Stub *broadcast executive*
Kling, William Hugh *broadcast executive*
Lofquist, Vicki L. *journalist*
Maxa, Rudolph Joseph, Jr. *journalist*

West Saint Paul
Cento, William Francis *retired newspaper editor*

Winona
Hokanson, A. Drake *communications educator*

MISSISSIPPI

Hattiesburg
Xue, Fei *communications educator*

Jackson
Mitchell, Jerry *reporter*

Natchez
Kirk, Susanne Smith *editor*

MISSOURI

Birch Tree
Holden, Janet L. *media specialist*

Bolivar
Miller, Brett *communications educator, consultant*

Cape Girardeau
Jeter Yanow, Cindie *communications educator*

Carthage
McAfee, Diana Mae *media specialist, music educator*

Columbia
Davis, Charles Nelson *journalism educator*
Loory, Stuart Hugh *journalist*
Sanders, Keith Page *journalism educator*
Taft, William Howard *retired journalism educator*
Wanta, Wayne *communications educator*

Kansas City
Busby, Marjean (Marjorie Jean Busby) *retired journalist*
Gray, Helen Theresa Gott *editor*
Gusewelle, Charles Wesley *journalist, writer*
Zieman, Mark *editor, publishing executive*

Parkville
Noe, J. Mark *communications educator*

Saint Louis
Engelhardt, Thomas Alexander *editorial cartoonist*
Gauen, Patrick Emil *news correspondent*
Holt, Glen Edward *editor*
Mowbray, Kevin D. *publishing executive*
Pollack, Joe *retired columnist, critic, writer*
Randolph, Jennings, Jr., (Jay Randolph) *sportscaster*
Rice, Patricia Jane *journalist*
Robbins, Arnie *editor*

Smithville
Johnson, Darryl Thomas *communications educator*

Springfield
Glazier, Robert Carl *publishing executive*

Troy
Krumlinde, Georganna *media specialist*

MONTANA

Bigfork
Harvey, Nancy Melissa *media specialist, art educator*

Billings
Larsen, Kimbert E. *journalist*

NEBRASKA

Lincoln
Dyer, William Earl, Jr. *retired newspaper editor*

Omaha
Derrick, Deborah Ball *editor, writer*
Gottschalk, John E. *newspaper publishing executive*
Ress, Patricia Colleen *editor, writer*

NEVADA

Henderson
Kelley, Michael John *newspaper editor*
Wills, Robert Hamilton *retired publishing executive*

Las Vegas
Berghel, Hal L. *columnist, inventor, consultant, lecturer, educator*
Huston, Joyce A. *entertainment and publishing company executive*

Reno
Hengstler, Gary Ardell *publisher, editor, lawyer*

NEW HAMPSHIRE

Concord
Brown, Tom Christian *newspaper publishing executive*

Dover
Wentworth, William Edgar *retired journalist*

Dublin
Hale, Judson Drake, Sr. *publishing executive, editor, writer*

Exeter
Wicklein, John Frederick *journalist, educator*

Keene
Salcetti, Marianne *newswriter, educator*

Lyme
Dwight, Donald Rathbun *publishing executive, corporate communications specialist*

Manchester
Jago, Barbara Jeanne *communications educator*

Nashua
Horn, Jennifer *former columnist, talk show host*

Portsmouth
Hopkins, Jeannette Ethel *book publisher, editor*

NEW JERSEY

Belleville
Salvini, Emil Robert *publishing executive, writer, historian*

Cape May
Fox, Matthew Ignatius *publishing executive*

Chatham
Meagher, James Proctor *editor*

Cherry Hill
Rudman, Solomon Kal *magazine publisher*

Cranbury
Yoseloff, Julien David *publishing company executive*

Deal
Becker, Richard Stanley *music publisher*

East Brunswick
Meningall, Evelyn L. *retired educational media specialist*

East Rutherford
Kluge, John Werner *broadcast and advertising executive*

Englewood Cliffs
Bartiromo, Maria Sara *financial news correspondent*
Burnett, Erin Isabelle *financial news correspondent*
Faber, David *broadcast business news network correspondent*
Hoffman, Mark *broadcast executive*
Quick, Becky (Rebecca Quick) *financial news correspondent*
Saible, Stephanie Irene *editor-in-chief*

Fords
Blond, Stuart Richard *magazine editor*

Fort Lee
Knopf, Claire *editor, writer*
Orman, Suze (Susan Lynne Orman) *news correspondent, writer*
Stuart, Carole *publishing executive*

Franklinville
Moyer, Mary A. *media specialist*

Gillette
Nathanson, Linda Sue *publishing executive, writer*

Glen Ridge
Addison, Herbert John *consulting editor, writer*

Hackensack
Ahearn, James *columnist*

Haddonfield
Baltake, Joe *film critic*

Haworth
Biesel, Diane Jane *editor, publishing executive*

Highland Park
Fogiel, Max *publishing executive*

Hoboken
Tardiff, Jill Alexandria *publishing executive, photographer*
Ubell, Robert Neil *editor, educator, publishing executive, consultant*

Jackson
Wagner, Edward Kurt *publishing company executive*

Lakewood
Forbes, Gordon Maxwell *sportswriter, retired commentator*

Lawrenceville
Oram, Fern Amy *content director*

Little Falls
Aregood, Richard Lloyd *editor*

Little Ferry
Dauber, Sheila *media specialist, school librarian*

Maplewood
Gilbert, Rose Bennett *journalist*

Matawan
Liggett, Twila C. *broadcast executive, educator*

Monmouth Junction
Prestbo, John Andrew *editor, writer, journalist*

Montclair
Delbourgo, Joëlle Lily *publishing executive*
Glasser, Stephen Andrew *publishing executive, lawyer*
Gollob, Herman Cohen *retired publishing executive*

Montvale
Politi, Beth Kukkonen *publishing services company executive*

Morristown
Koyce, Terence G. *communications educator*

New Brunswick
Friedrich, Gustav William *communications educator*
Horowitz, Irving Louis *publisher, educator*

Newark
Arwady, George E. *publishing executive*
Daniel, Carter Anderson *business communications educator, author*
Dauth, Frances Kutcher *journalist, editor*
Emrick, Mike (Doc Emrick) *sportscaster*
Newhouse, Mark William *publishing executive*
Steinbaum, Robert S. *publishing executive, lawyer*
Willse, James Patrick *editor*

Nutley
To, Stephen Edward *editor, writer*

Oakland
Keough, Daniel Emmet *retired magazine editor*

Oldwick
Snyder, Arthur *publishing executive*

Piscataway
Israel, Paul Bryan *editor, director*

Plainfield
Allen (Sup), Stuart *film and television company executive*

Princeton
Christopherson, Elizabeth Good *foundation executive*
Levine, Richard James *publishing executive*
Lippincott, Walter Heulings, Jr. *retired publishing executive*
O'Donnell, Laurence Gerard *retired managing editor*
Weiss, Renée Karol *editor, musician*

Ridgewood
Ostling, Richard Neil *journalist*

Saddle River
Noyes, Robert Edwin *publisher, writer*

Secaucus
Crowley, Monica *political commentator*
Larkin, Barry Louis *sportscaster, retired professional baseball player*
Payton, Gary Dwayne *sportscaster, retired professional basketball player*
Ratigan, Dylan *journalist, financial news correspondent*
Webber, Chris (Mayce Edward Christopher Webber III) *sportscaster, retired professional basketball player*
Weissmann, Arnie *editor-in-chief, travel writer*

Short Hills
Austin, Danforth Whitley *media executive*
Schaefer, Eleanor Montville *retired publishing executive*
Winter, Ruth Grosman (Mrs. Arthur Winter) *journalist*

Skillman
Eiger, Richard William *retired publisher*

South Amboy
Ghezzi, Lawrence Victor *media specialist, educator*

South Orange
Gainsburg, Roy Ellis *publishing executive, researcher*

Southampton
Callaway, Ben Anderson *retired journalist*

Sparta
Spence, Robert Leroy *publishing executive*

Weehawken
Hobson, Burton Harold *publishing executive*

West Caldwell
Soderlind, Sterling Eugene *publishing executive, consultant*

Woodland Park
Margulies, James Howard *editorial cartoonist*

NEW MEXICO

Albuquerque
Hadas, Elizabeth Chamberlayne *editor*
Lang, Thompson Hughes *publishing executive*
Maddy, Coleen *editor*
Werder, Olaf H. *communications educator, researcher*

Los Alamos
Mendius, Patricia Dodd Winter *retired editor, educator, writer*

Raton
Carroll, William *publishing company executive*

Rio Rancho
Baehr, Karl Joseph *broadcasting executive*

Santa Fe
Andrews, John Frank *editor, author, educator*
Burns, Scott *columnist*
Dirks, Lee Edward *newspaper executive*
Groseclose, Everett Harrison *retired editor*
Lichtenberg, Maggie Klee *publishing executive*
Stolley, Richard Brockway *journalist*

Silver City
Fryxell, David Allen *publishing executive*

NEW YORK

Albany
Morga Bellizzi, Celeste *editor*
Rosenfeld, Harry Morris *editor*
Smith, Rex William *journalist*

Ancramdale
Ditto, David Thomas *inventor, artist*

Ardsley On Hudson
Seaman, Alfred Barrett *journalist, writer*

Bedford
Bowman, James Kinsey *publishing executive, rare book dealer*

Bellport
Townsend, Terry *publishing executive*

Bethpage
Dolan, Charles Francis (Chuck Dolan) *media and entertainment company executive*
Ratner, Hank J. *broadcast executive*

Bronx
Abdul, Raoul *music critic*
Ahmose, Nefertari A. *journalism educator*
Andersen, Robin *media specialist, educator*

Bronxville
Lee, Clement William Khan *media consultant*
Lombardo, Philip Joseph *broadcasting company executive*

Brooklyn
Fox, Cynthia F. *journalist, writer*
Greaves-Venzen, Gail-Ann G. *communications educator*
Klein, Laura Colin *publishing executive*
Ortner, Everett Howard *magazine editor, writer*
Rosado, Rossana *publishing executive, editor-in-chief*
Sanford, David Boyer *journalist, editor*
Wiener, Hesh (Harold Frederic Wiener) *publishing executive, consultant*

Buffalo
Lipsey, Stanford *newspaper publisher*
Sullivan, Margaret M. *editor-in-chief*
Trotter, Herman (Eager), Jr. *retired music critic*
Urban, Henry Zeller *publishing executive*

Campbell Hall
Ottaway, James Haller, Jr. *newspaper publisher*

Cobleskill
Sanchez, Joanna Marie *communications educator*

Delmar
FitzAlan-Howard, Bennett-Thomas Henry Robert *news analyst, consultant, political scientist, theologian*

Dobbs Ferry
Anbinder, Paul *publishing executive, consultant*
Simon, Lothar *publishing executive*

East Hampton
Jaroff, Leon Morton *retired magazine editor*
Threlkeld, Richard Davis *retired broadcast journalist*

Elba
Kauffman, William Joseph *editor, writer*

Elmsford
Miranda, Robert Nicholas *publishing executive, director*

Flushing
Torrence-Thompson, Juanita Lee *editor, public relations executive*

Forest Hills
Brooks, Martin *electronic media executive*
Reis, Don *publishing executive*

Garrison
Kaebnick, Gregory E. *editor, researcher*

Glens Falls
Mahoney, Mark *newspaper editor*

Great Neck
Bender, Bruce F. *book publishing executive*
Kahn, David *editor, author*
Panes, Jack Samuel *publishing executive*

Hamilton
Edmonston, William Edward, Jr. *retired publishing executive, writer, psychology professor*

Hastings On Hudson
Landau, Peter Edward *editor*
Reich, Herb *editor*

Hempstead
Masheck, Joseph Daniel *art critic, educator*

Huntington
Connor, Joseph Robert *editor*

Ithaca
Hardy, Jane Elizabeth *communications educator*
Schwartz, Donald Franklin *communication scientist*

Katonah
Fry, John *magazine editor*

Lancaster
Stoffel, Shelley L. *library media specialist*

Levittown
Massie, Clifford Michael *music company executive*

Locust Valley
Fairman, Joel Martin *retired broadcast executive*

Manhasset
Burke, Alexander James, Jr. *publishing executive*
Evans, Bob (Robert Evans) *publishing executive*
Preston, Rob *editor-in-chief*
Weitzner, Steve *publishing executive*

Manlius
Harriff, Suzanna Elizabeth Bahner *media consultant*

Melville
Handelsman, Walt *cartoonist*
Hildebrand, John Frederick *columnist, educator*
Knight, Timothy P. *publishing executive*
Mancini, John *editor, publishing executive*
Rossetti, George A. *editor, director*

Middletown
Bedell, Barbara Lee *journalist*

Millbrook
Hall, Penelope Coker *editor, writer*

New Hyde Park
Lehrer, Stanley *magazine publisher, editorial director, museum exhibitor*

New Rochelle
Ong, Bruce Nelson *communication skills consultant*

New York
Abelson, Alan *columnist*
Abelson, Reed V. *reporter*
Adams, Cindy *journalist*
Adams, Scott *cartoonist*
Adler, Edward I. *media and entertainment company executive*
Adler, Jerry *journalist, writer*
Adler, Margot Susanna *journalist, radio producer, correspondent, writer*
Adler, Stephen J. *editor-in-chief*
Ailes, Roger Eugene *broadcast executive*
Akselrad, Hal (Harold Eaton) *broadcast executive, lawyer*
Allan, Col *editor-in-chief*
Allyn, Susan M. *publishing executive, marketing professional*
Alter, Jonathan Hammerman *journalist*
Ambrosio, Anthony G. *broadcast executive*
Ames, Roger *recording industry executive*
Amster, Linda Evelyn *newspaper executive, consultant*
Ancier, Garth Richard *broadcast executive*
Anderson, David Poole *sportswriter*
Anderson, Jon *publishing executive, children's book author*
Andre, Michael (Kenneth Andre) *editor-in-chief*
A.O., Leon Hertz *publishing executive*
Arnold, Martin *editor, journalist*
Ascheim, Tom (Thomas Eliot Ascheim) *publishing executive*
Astley, Amy Taran *editor-in-chief*
Atlas, James Robert *editor, writer*
Auster, David L. *theatre executive*
Azzoli, Val *music company executive*
Baer, Amy Bosley *film company executive*
Bahr, Lauren S. *publishing executive*
Bailey, Glenda *editor-in-chief*
Bair, Thomas J. *publishing executive*
Baker, Deborah *editor, writer*
Baker, Elizabeth Calhoun *magazine editor*
Balis, Janet *diversified media and merchandising company executive*
Ball, John Paul *publishing company executive*
Barber, Tiki (Atiim Kiambu Barber) *sportscaster, retired professional football player*
Bardos, Karoly *television and film educator, writer, director*
Barolini, Teodolinda *literary and cultural critic*
Barron, James Turman *journalist*
Barry, Dan *columnist*
Barstow, David *journalist, investigative reporter*
Bartels, Steve *music company executive*
Bearak, Barry Leon *journalist*
Beckman, Richard David *publishing and advertising executive*
Behar, Richard *investigative journalist*
Belson, Ken *reporter*
Bender, Judith *journalist, editor*
Bennack, Frank Anthony, Jr. *publishing company executive*
Berenson, Alex *reporter, writer*
Berry, John Nichols III *publishing executive, editor*
Bettis, Jerome Abram *sports commentator, retired professional football player*
Betts, Katherine Hadley (Kate Betts) *editor*
Birnbaum, Debra Gail *magazine editor*
Black, Carole *broadcast executive*
Black, Cathie P. (Cathleen Prunty Black) *publishing executive*
Blair, William Granger *retired reporter*
Blangiardi, Barbara *broadcast company executive, marketing professional*
Blank, Matthew C. *broadcast company executive*
Blumenthal, Sidney Stone *political columnist*
Bodley, Harley Ryan, Jr. *sportswriter, editor, announcer*
Boffey, Philip M. *journalist*
Bookspan, Martin *broadcaster, writer*
Borland, Virginia Ann *journalist, fiber company executive*
Bossert, Rex Thomas *editor-in-chief*
Bowers, Brent *editor*
Bowles, Hamish *editor*
Bratten, Millie Martini *editor-in-chief*
Brener, Richard *film company executive*
Britt, Glenn Alan *media company executive*
Brody, Jane Ellen *journalist, researcher*
Bronfman, Edgar Miles, Jr. *recording industry executive*
Brooks, David B. *editor, columnist*
Brown, Darrell James *publishing executive*
Brown, Helen Gurley *editor-in-chief*
Brown, Tina (Christina Hambley Brown) *journalist, television personality*
Browne, Arthur *newspaper editor*
Brun, Henry *publishing executive*
Bruni, Frank *restaurant critic*
Bryan, Stephen *music company executive*
Buchholz, Todd *journalist, social sciences educator, consultant*
Buck, Joe (Joseph Francis Buck) *sportscaster*
Buckley, Christopher Taylor *editor, author*
Bumiller, Elisabeth *journalist, writer*
Burgheim, Richard *magazine editor*
Burns, John F. *reporter*
Burstein, Lawrence C. *publishing executive*
Bushnell, Candace *columnist, writer*
Byrne, Gerard Anthony (Gerry) *publishing executive, consultant*
Cagle, Jess *editor*
Caine, Paul Jason *publishing executive*
Calpeter, Lynn Ann *broadcast executive*
Campos, Fernando *entertainment editor*
Carey, Chase (Charles G. Carey) *broadcast executive*
Carey, David *publishing executive*
Carlson, Tucker (Tucker Swanson McNear Carlson) *political analyst, writer, television host*
Carlucci, Paul V. *publishing executive*
Carr, Gladys Justin *publishing executive, editor, writer*
Carr, James T. *publishing executive*
Carter, Graydon (Edward Graydon Carter) *editor-in-chief*
Carter, John Mack *publishing company executive*
Casella, Jim *publishing executive*
Casey, Susan *editor*
Cavuto, Neil Patrick *financial news correspondent*
Centrello, Gina *publishing executive*
Chang, Laura *editor, journalist*
Chesnutt, Jane *editor-in-chief*
Chestnut, Colette *broadcast executive*
Chubb, Sarah Caldecot *publishing executive*
Cisneros, Bettina Lynn *multimedia company executive, marketing professional*
Clark, Joan Hardy *retired journalist*
Clayton, Joseph Paul *broadcast executive*
Coddington, Grace *publishing executive*
Coen, Jessica *blog writer, editor*
Cohen, Adam *reporter, lawyer*
Cohen, Lyor C. *recording industry executive*
Cohen, Richard Martin *journalist*
Coles, Joanna *magazine editor-in-chief*
Collins, Gail *journalist*
Collins, Richard Lawrence *editor*
Collinsworth, Cris *sportscaster, retired professional football player*
Colmes, Alan Samuel *political commentator, radio personality*
Cona, Louis *publishing executive*
Connolly, John Joseph *publishing executive*
Cooney, Joan Ganz *broadcast executive, director*
Cooper, Anderson Hays *news correspondent, cable news anchor*
Cooper, Michael *reporter*
Corcoran, David *newspaper editor*
Corporon, John Robert *broadcast executive*
Costas, Bob (Robert Quinlan Costas) *sportscaster*
Cotter, Holland *art critic, writer*
Couric, Katie (Katherine Anne Couric) *newscaster, journalist*
Cowdell, Phil *media communications agency executive*
Cramer, Douglas Schoolfield *broadcasting executive*
Crist, Judith *film and drama critic*
Croce, Arlene *critic*
Cross, Theodore Lamont *publisher, author*
Crowdus, Gary Alan *film company executive*
Cuozzo, Steven David *newspaper editor*
Curley, Thomas *newspaper executive*
Curren, Lois Clark *music company executive, television producer*
Curry, Ann *correspondent, anchor*
Daintith, Stephen *publishing executive*
D'Angelo, Joseph Francis *publishing executive*
Daniels, Susanne *broadcast executive*
Danziger, Lucy *editor*
Darling, Ronald Maurice (Ron Darling) *sportscaster, retired professional baseball player*
Dash, Damon *recording industry executive, consumer products company executive*
Dauman, Philippe P. *multimedia company executive*
Davidson, Bruce *photojournalist*
Davidson, Louise T. *editor*
Davis, Clive Jay *recording industry executive*
De Angelis, Judy *anchorwoman*
DeLorenzo, Matt *editor-in-chief*

de Menil, Joy Alexandra *editor*
Denton, Nick *publishing executive*
Derow, Peter Alfred *publishing executive*
DeVoe, David F., Sr. *publishing executive*
Doerfler, Ronald John *publishing executive*
Dohle, Markus *publishing executive*
Donnelly, John *publishing executive*
Dooley, Thomas E. *multimedia company executive*
Dormann, Henry O. *magazine publisher*
Dreifus, Claudia *journalist, educator*
Dugger, Celia Williams *journalist*
Dukmejian, Michael V. *publishing executive*
Dungy, Tony *sportscaster, retired professional football coach*
Dunn, Martin *editor-in-chief*
Easton, Nina Jane *journalist*
Ebersol, Dick (Duncan Dickie Ebersol) *television broadcasting executive*
Edmiston, Mark Morton *publishing company executive*
Edsall, Thomas Byrne *reporter*
Edwards, Duncan *publishing executive*
Eichhorn, Guenther *publishing executive*
Eleta, Graciela (Graciela Eleta de Cacho) *broadcast company executive, marketing professional*
Ellis, Lisa *music company executive*
Ellis, Rosemary *editor-in-chief*
Elsen, Jon *editor*
Emmerich, Toby *film company executive*
Engstrom, Erik *publishing executive*
Essig, Jack *magazine publishing executive*
Esterow, Milton *publishing executive*
Evans, Greg *cartoonist*
Fabrikant, Geraldine *journalist*
Fager, Jeffrey *broadcast executive*
Farber, Michael *sportswriter*
Fargis, Paul McKenna *publishing executive, consultant*
Favorule, Denise *publishing executive*
Faxon, Roger *music company executive*
Fears, Linda *editor-in-chief*
Feder, Barnaby *reporter*
Feldman, Ruth *publishing executive*
Feniger, Jerome Roland, Jr. *broadcast executive*
Feretic, Eileen Susan *editor*
Fertig, Howard *publishing executive*
Feyer, Thomas *editor*
Filkins, Dexter Price *journalist*
Finel-Honigman, Irene Elizabeth *communications educator*
Finkelstein, James A. *media executive*
Finn, Edwin Anthony, Jr. *publishing executive*
Finn, Peter Michael *broadcast executive*
Fiori, Pamela *publishing executive, writer*
Firth, Nicholas *recording industry executive*
Florio, Thomas A. *publishing executive*
Folio, James M. *publishing executive*
Forbes, Steve (Malcolm Stevenson Forbes Jr.) *publishing executive*
Forbes, Timothy Carter *publishing executive*
Ford, Mark Patrick *publishing executive*
Forden, Diane Claire *magazine editor*
Fox, Keith *publishing executive*
Foxman, Ariel *editor*
France, Kim *editor-in-chief*
Frankel, Max *retired journalist*
Franks, Lucinda Laura *journalist*
Franks, Martin Davis *broadcast executive*
Freudenheim, Milton B. *journalist*
Friedman, Arthur *editor, educator*
Gallo, William Victor *cartoonist*
Garafola, Lynn *dance critic, educator*
Garcia, Nina *publishing executive*
Gardino, Vincent Anthony *broadcast executive*
Gaspin, Jeffrey M. *broadcast executive*
Gehringer, Richard George *publishing executive*
Geiser, Elizabeth Able *publishing company executive*
Gellman, Barton David *correspondent*
Gersh, Lisa *broadcast executive, lawyer*
Ghost, Amanda (Amanda Louisa Gosein) *music company executive, songwriter*
Gibson, Charles DeWolf *newscaster*
Gigot, Paul Anthony *editor*
Gissler, Sigvard Gunnar, Jr. *journalist, educator, retired editor*
Glowczewska, Klara Maria *editor-in-chief, translator*
Golden, Michael *publishing executive*
Gollan, Douglas D. *travel magazine editor-in-chief*
Goodman, Michael B(arry) *communications educator*
Gotti, Victoria *columnist, writer, actress*
Grace, Nancy Ann *news correspondent, former prosecutor*
Graham, Alma Eleanor *editor, writer, educational consultant*
Graham, Fred Patterson *news correspondent, journalist*
Granger, David *editor*
Graves, Earl G., Jr., (Butch Graves) *publishing executive*
Graves, Earl Gilbert *publishing executive*
Green, Dan *publishing executive*
Green, George Joseph *publishing executive*
Greenberg, Peter S. *travel editor, news correspondent, writer*
Greenblatt, Robert *broadcast company executive, producer*
Greenburg, Ross *broadcast executive, television producer*
Greene, Joshua *publishing executive, editor*
Greene, Richard H. *journalist, writer, policy analyst*
Greenwald, Julie *recording industry executive*
Greenwald, Martin *publishing company executive*
Grenquist, Peter Carl *publishing executive, consultant*
Grossman, Lev *journalist, writer*
Grune, Steven Bryan *publishing executive*
Guiher, James Morford, Jr. *publisher, writer*
Guzmán, Pilar *editor-in-chief*
Hackett, George *editor*
Hackett, Larry *editor*
Haegele, Patricia *publishing executive*
Haire, Jack *magazine publisher*
Hammer, Bonnie *broadcast executive*
Handler, Howard N. *music company executive, marketing professional*
Hansell, Saul Henry *reporter*
Harrow, Nancy (Mrs. Jan Krukowski) *editor, composer, singer*
Hart, Clare *information company executive*
Hauck, Marguerite Hall *broadcast executive*
Hauser, Gustave M. *media executive*
Headlam, Bruce *editor*
Heartney, Eleanor *art critic*
Heekin-Canedy, Scott H. *publishing executive*
Herbert, Bob *journalist*
Hersh, Seymour Myron *journalist, writer*
Hicks, Tyler Gregory *publishing company executive, writer*
Hinton, Leslie Frank *publishing executive*
Hippeau, Eric *publishing executive*
Hodge, Roger D. *editor*
Hoge, Warren M. *editor*
Holt, Sidney Clark *journalist*
Horyn, Cathy B. *editor*
Houghtlin, Robert G. *publishing executive*
Hoyt, Clark Freeland *editor, journalist*
Huey, John Wesley, Jr. *editor*
Hughes, Lisa Henriques *publishing executive*
Hurley, Cheryl Joyce *book publishing executive*
Hutchins, Traver *publishing executive*
Ianniello, Joseph R. *broadcast executive*
Ingrassia, Lawrence *editor*
Irish, George Butler *media company executive*
Jackson, Keith MacKenzie *retired sports commentator*
Jacobs, Lawrence A. *media company executive, lawyer*
Jamison, Jayne *publishing executive*
Jay-Z, (Shawn Corey Carter) *music company executive, rap artist*
Johnson, Brooke Bailey *broadcast executive*
Johnson, Gus *sportscaster*
Johnson, Richard C. *editor*
Jones, Laurie Lynn *magazine editor*
Jones, Richard M. *broadcast executive*
Jones Reynolds, Star (Starlet Marie Jones) *television host, lawyer, former prosecutor*
Jordan, Tina *publishing association executive*
Kagan, Julia Lee *magazine editor*
Kahan, Phyllis Irene *editor, writer, educator*
Kalajian-Lagani, Donna *publishing executive*
Kaminer, Ariel *editor*
Kandel, Myron *newscaster, columnist*
Kane, Susan *editor*
Kann, Peter Robert *retired publishing executive, journalist*
Kaplan, Janice *editor*
Kaplan, Rick (Richard N. Kaplan) *broadcast executive*
Karlgaard, Rich *publishing executive*
Karpel, Craig S. *journalist, editor*
Kaufman, Victor A. *broadcast and retired film company executive*
Kaye, Joyce Rutter *publishing executive*
Kelleher, Kevin *music company executive*
Keller, Bill G. *executive editor*
Kelley, Jacki *media communications agency executive, marketing professional*
Kellogg, Clark *sportscaster*
Kenney, Brian *editor-in-chief*
Kerr Redniss, Andrea *media agency executive, marketing and communications professional*
Kessler, Eric *broadcast executive*
King, Gayle *editor, radio and television personality*
Kissel, Howard William *drama critic*
Klein, Jason Evan *publishing executive*
Klein, Joe *journalist, columnist, writer*
Kliger, Jack *publishing executive*
Kluger, Jeffrey *reporter, author*
Knobler, Peter Stephen *magazine editor, writer*
Kolata, Gina *journalist, writer*
Kolatch, Myron *magazine editor*
Koster, Elaine *publishing executive*
Koteff, Ellen *editor*
Kozinn, Allan *music critic, reporter*
Kramer, Marc Z. *publishing executive*
Kremins, Carolyn *magazine publishing executive*
Kristof, Nicholas Donabet *journalist, columnist*
Kushner, Jared Corey *publishing executive, real estate developer*
Lafavore, Michael J. *editor-in-chief*
Lagani, Daniel *publishing executive*
Lamadrid, Carlos *publishing executive*
Lamont, Lansing *journalist, writer, public affairs and trust executive*
Landau, Sidney Ivan *lexicographer*
Landman, Jonathan *editor*
Lapham, Lewis Henry *editor, television personality, writer*
Larsen, Jonathan Zerbe *journalist*
Lawrence, Nina *publishing executive*
Leahey, Lynn *editor-in-chief*
Leahy, Michael Joseph *retired newspaper editor*
Leaver, Marcus E. *publishing executive*
Lee, Frances Helen *editor*
Lee, Jennifer *journalist*
Lee, Sally A. *editor-in-chief, publishing executive*
Lees, Alfred William *former magazine editor, writer, retired*
Leiter, Al (Alois Terry Leiter) *sportscaster, retired professional baseball player*
Leive, Cindi (Cynthia M. Leive) *editor-in-chief*
Lemarchand, Alain *publishing executive*
Leo, Jacqueline M. *on-line publishing executive, former editor-in-chief*
Lerer, Kenneth B. *publishing executive, investor*
Levinson, Warren Mitchell *broadcast journalist*
Levitz, Paul Elliot *publishing executive*
Levy, Clifford J. *investigative journalist*
Liles, Kevin *music company executive*
Lohr, Steve *reporter*
Longley, Marjorie Watters *newspaper executive*
Loomis, Carol J. *journalist*
Lurie, Ranan Raymond *political cartoonist, artist, journalist*
Lyons, Nick *retired publishing executive*
MacArthur, John Roderick C. G. (Rick MacArthur) *magazine publisher, journalist*
MacGowan, Sandra Firelli *publishing executive, consultant*
Mapes, Glynn Dempsey *newspaper editor*
Marino, Robin L. *multi-media company executive*
Marriott, Michel *reporter*
Marshall, Tom *publishing executive*
Martin, Judith Sylvia *journalist*
Marzorati, Gerald *editor*
Mastrangelo, Matt *publishing executive*
Mathis, Catherine J. *publishing executive*
Matters, Craig *editor*
Matthews, Christopher John *political commentator, writer*
Matz, Alison Adler *publishing executive*
Maurer, Gilbert Charles *media specialist*
Mayer, Jane *journalist*
Mayer, Margery Weil *publishing executive*
Mazzola, Anthony Thomas *editor, graphics designer, consultant, curator*
McCartney, Scott *travel editor, columnist*
McCarty, V. K. *publishing executive, chaplain, librarian, editor*
McCormack, Thomas Joseph *retired publishing executive, playwright*
McDonell, Terry *publishing executive, writer, editor*
McEwen, Laura Ellen *publishing executive*
McFadden, Robert Dennis *reporter*
McFeely, William Drake *publishing company executive*
McGrath, Judy (Judith Ann McGrath) *broadcast executive*
McGraw, Harold Whittlesey, Jr. *publishing executive*
McGuire, Pierre *sports analyst, former professional hockey coach*
McManus, Sean Joseph *broadcast executive*
Meacham, Jon E. *editor*
Medina, Kate (Kathryn Bach Medina) *associate publisher*
Meigs, James B. *editor-in-chief*
Melloan, George Richard *editor*
Mencher, Melvin *journalist, educator*
Menicheschi, Edward John *publishing executive*
Meyer, Karl Ernest *retired journalist*
Michaels, Al (Alan Richard Michaels) *sportscaster*
Millard, Wenda Harris *multi-media company executive*
Miller, Michael Jeffrey *editor, analyst*
Miller, Sarah Gray *editor-in-chief*
Millstein, Lincoln *media company executive*
Minick, Michael *publishing executive*
Mirenburg, Barry Leonard *publishing executive, educator*
Mitchell, Alison N. *newspaper reporter, editor*
Mitchell, Chris *publishing executive*
Mohler, Mary Gail *magazine editor*
Moonves, Leslie *broadcast executive*
Moore, Alma C. *publishing executive, consultant*
Moore, Ann S. *publishing executive*
Morgan, Mary E. *publishing executive*
Morris, Dick *columnist, political consultant*
Morris, Doug (Douglas Peter Morris) *recording industry executive*
Morrison, Stacy Lynne *editor*
Moskin, John Robert *editor, writer*
Moss, Adam *editor-in-chief*
Moyers, Bill *journalist, writer, former White House press secretary*
Murdoch, Rupert (Keith Rupert Murdoch) *multi media company executive*
Murphy, Helen *recording industry executive*
Murphy, Suzanne *publishing executive*
Murray, Brian *publishing executive*
Myers, Michelle *publishing executive*
Myers, Roberta A. (Robbie Myers) *editor-in-chief*
Nachtwey, James Alan *photojournalist*
Naegle, Sue E. (Suzanne) *broadcast executive*
Nalder, Eric Christopher *investigative reporter*
Nantz, Jim (James William Nantz) *sportscaster*
Nelson, Anne *media consultant, educator, writer*
Nelson, Bill *broadcast executive*
Nelson, Jim *editor-in-chief*
Nelson, Kathy *broadcast executive*
Nelson, Martha Jane *editor*
Newman, Diane *publishing executive*
Nocera, Joseph *columnist*
Noonan, Peggy (Margaret Ellen Noonan) *columnist, writer*
Novitz, Charles Richard *broadcast executive, reporter*
Novogrod, Nancy Gerstein *editor*
Obogeanu, Madalina Maria *reporter*
O'Connor, Anahad S. *journalist*
O'Donnell, Norah *news correspondent*
Okura-Marszycki, Mindy Emi *editor*
Olbermann, Keith Theodore *news analyst, sportscaster*
O'Neill, Paul Andrew *sportscaster, retired professional baseball player*
O'Reilly, Bill (William O'Reilly Jr.) *commentator, writer*
Oreskes, Michael H. *editor, journalist*
Ortenberg, Tom *film company executive*
Osgood, Charles *news broadcaster, journalist*
Palsho, Dorothea Coccoli *information services executive*
Pareene, Alex E. *blog editor*
Penn, Stanley William *journalist*
Perlmutter, Isaac *entertainment company executive*
Perram Frank, Heather *editor-in-chief*
Pfeiffer, Jane Cahill *former broadcasting company executive, consultant*
Pines, Burton Yale *media executive*
Pinkwater, Julie *publishing executive*
Plepler, Richard L. *broadcast executive*
Pollock, Ellen Joan *editor*
Pope, Liston, Jr. *writer, journalist*
Porterfield, Christopher *magazine editor, writer*
Pressman, Gabe Stanley *reporter*
Price, Frank *motion picture and television company executive*
Promaulayko, Michele *editor-in-chief*
Putnam, Keri *film company executive*
Quindlen, Anna *journalist, writer*
Quinn, Jane Bryant *journalist, writer*
Race, Tim *editor*
Raines, Howell Hiram *columnist, former newspaper editor*
Ratner, Ellen Faith *news analyst and correspondent, writer*
Raven, Abbe *broadcast executive*
Redstone, Sumner Murray *broadcast executive, lawyer*
Reichl, Ruth Molly *editor-in-chief*
Reid, Antonio (L.A. Reid) *music company executive*
Reid, Robert Harden III *news correspondent, journalist*
Reidy, Carolyn Kroll *publishing executive*
Remnick, David Jay *journalist, editor-in-chief*
Rennie, John *editor-in-chief*
Rescigno, Richard Joseph *editor*
Reynolds, Harold Craig *sportscaster, retired professional baseball player*
Rhoads, Geraldine Emeline *editor, consultant*
Rhone, Sylvia Marie Miller *recording industry executive*
Rich, Frank *journalist, writer*
Rieff, David Sontag *editor, critic*
Rizzuto, Katherine *publishing executive*
Roberts, Robin *newscaster*
Robinson, Janet L. *publishing executive*
Robinson, Richard *publishing executive*
Rogin, Gilbert Leslie *editor, author*
Roker, Al *newscaster*
Ronson, Mark Daniel *recording industry executive, disc jockey*
Rose, Charlie (Charles Peete Rose Jr.) *television journalist*
Rosenthal, Andrew Mark *newspaper editor*
Rosenthal, Jane L. *film company executive*
Rosenthal, Shirley Lord *cosmetics magazine executive, novelist*
Ross, Alex *music critic*
Ross, Brian Elliott *chief investigative correspondent*
Rosset, Barnet Lee, Jr. *publishing executive*
Rothberg, Gerald *editor, publishing executive*
Ryan, Regina Claire (Mrs. Paul Deutschman) *editor, literary agent*
Salembier, Valerie Birnbaum *publishing executive*
Salvatore, Diane J. *publishing executive*
Samuels, Dorothy J. *journalist, writer*
Sanders, Gina Susan *publishing executive*
Sandler, Irving Harry *art critic, art historian*
Santelli, Rick *news correspondent, former financial executive*
Sareyan, Andy *publishing executive*
Sarnelle, Joseph R. *publishing executive*
Sarnoff, Ann M. *publishing executive, former sports association executive*
Sarnoff, Richard *digital publishing executive*
Sasman, Irene Deak Handberg *publishing executive*
Savage, Charles *reporter, news correspondent*
Sawyer, Diane *newscaster, journalist*
Scarborough, Chuck (Charles Bishop Scarborough III) *newscaster*
Scarborough, Joe (Charles Joseph Scarborough) *newscaster, former United States Representative from Florida*
Schamus, James Allan *film producer and company executive, screenwriter*
Schenck, Will *publishing executive*
Schiesel, Seth *reporter*
Schlosser, Herbert S. *broadcasting company executive*
Schmertz, Mildred Floyd *editor-in-chief, writer*
Schmidt, William E. *editor*
Schmidt-Holtz, Rolf *music company executive*
Schneider, Martin Aaron *photojournalist, ecologist, engineer, writer, artist, television director, filmmaker, public advocate, medical researcher, educator*
Schuman, Patricia Glass *publishing company executive, educator*
Schutte, Drew *publishing executive*
Schwartz, Gil (Stanley Bing) *broadcast executive, writer*
Sciutto, Jim *news correspondent*
Seelig, Jill *publishing executive*
Seife, Charles *communications educator*
Semple, Robert Baylor, Jr. *editor, journalist*
Serwer, Andy (Andrew E. Serwer) *editor, journalist*
Seymour, Lesley Jane *editor-in-chief*
Shah, Vivek R. *publishing executive*
Shain, Harold I. *publishing executive*
Shapiro, Gary Evan *newspaper journalist*
Shapiro, Neal *broadcast executive, television producer*
Shea, Martin M. *broadcast executive*
Shepard, Stephen Benjamin *journalist, educator, retired editor*
Shier, Shelley M. *production company executive*
Shnayerson, Robert Beahan *editor, consultant*
Shoket, Ann E. *editor-in-chief*
Shortz, Will *puzzle editor*
Sibley, Jessica *publishing executive*
Siegel, Marvin *newspaper editor*
Siegel, Randy *publishing executive*
Sifton, Sam *editor*
Siklos, Richard *reporter*
Silverman, Al *editor*
Silvers, Robert B. *editor*
Simmons, Sue *newscaster*
Singer, Joy Daniels *journalist, consultant*
Singer, Niki *media consultant*
Singleton, Donald Edward *retired journalist*
Singleton, Ken *sportscaster, retired professional baseball player*
Sleed, Joel *columnist*
Sloan, Allan Herbert *journalist*
Smith, Carol A. *publishing executive*
Smith, Joseph Phelan *film company executive*
Smith, Patrick John *editor, writer*
Smith, Richard Mills (Rick) *former publishing executive*
Smith, Shepard (David Shepard Smith Jr.) *newscaster*
Smyth, Rich *publishing executive*
Soocher, Stan *editor, lawyer*
Sparkman, Robin Hamilton *editor*
Squires, John *publishing executive*
Stahl, Lesley Rene *news correspondent*
Steiger, Paul Ernest *editor-in-chief, journalist*

Stengel, Richard *editor*
Stern, Mitchell *broadcast executive*
Stern, Robert D. *publishing executive*
Stern, Roslyne Paige *magazine publisher*
Strahan, Michael Anthony *sportscaster, retired professional football player*
Straka, Angeline C. *broadcast executive*
Strauss, Carolyn L. *former broadcast executive*
Studin, Jan *publishing executive*
Sturtevant, Peter Mann, Jr. *television news executive*
Sugihara, Kenzi *publishing executive*
Sullivan, Andrew Michael *online journalist, editor, news blogger*
Sulzberger, Arthur Ochs, Jr. *newspaper publisher*
Suskind, Ronald Steven *journalist, writer*
Sussman, Gerald *publishing company executive*
Sweed, Phyllis *publishing executive*
Talley, André Leon *editor-at-large*
Tanenhaus, Sam *editor*
Tang, Terry *editor, lawyer*
Tapper, Jake *television journalist, news correspondent*
Tarde, Jerry (Gerard Tarde) *editor-in-chief*
Taylor, Terry R. *editor, educator*
Teague, Lettie *editor*
Tetzeli, Rick *magazine editor*
Thomas, Brooks *publishing executive, director*
Thomas, Helen Amelia (Mrs. Douglas B. Cornell) *editor-in-chief, former White House correspondent*
Thomson, Robert James *editor*
Thurm, David Aaron *publishing executive*
Tillman, Vickie A. *publishing executive, former financial information company executive*
Tober, Barbara D. (Mrs. Donald Gibbs Tober) *editor*
Todd, Chuck (Charles David Todd) *news correspondent*
Tofel, Richard Jeffrey *non-profit publishing executive*
Toff, Nancy Ellen *book editor*
Tomashoff, Craig L. *magazine editor*
Tomlinson, James Francis *retired news agency executive*
Tonchi, Stefano *editor*
Tong, Kaity *anchor*
Townsend, Alair Ane *publishing executive*
Townsend, Chuck (Charles H. Townsend) *publishing executive*
Treaster, Joseph B(land) *journalist*
Tuchman, Phyllis *critic*
Turitzin, John N. *entertainment company executive, lawyer*
Turner, Alice Kennedy *editor*
Tuschman, Bob *broadcast executive*
Uchitelle, Louis *journalist*
Ulanoff, Lance *editor-in-chief*
Umansky, Diane *editor*
Unger, David C. *journalist*
Vanden Heuvel, Katrina *publishing executive, editor*
Van Susteren, Greta Conway *newscaster, lawyer*
Vargas, Elizabeth *newscaster*
Vien, Patrick *music company executive*
Wackermann, William J. *publishing executive*
Wade, Nicholas Michael Landon *journalist*
Wald, Richard Charles *media consultant, educator*
Waldman, Steven *editor*
Walk, Charlie *music company executive*
Walker, Mort *cartoonist*
Wallace, Thomas C. *editor, publishing executive*
Walters, Barbara Jill *broadcast journalist*
Waricha, Joan *publishing executive*
Weiner, Timothy Emlyn *reporter, writer*
Weinstein, Bob (Robert Weinstein) *film company executive*
Weinstein, Harvey *film company executive*
Weisberg, Jacob *web magazine editor*
Weisenberg, Shari *broadcast executive, marketing professional*
Weisman, Eric *music company executive*
Weiss, Barry *recording industry executive*
Wells, David Lee *sportscaster, retired professional baseball player*
Wells, Linda Ann *editor-in-chief*
Wen, George Walter Sun *publishing executive, editor*
Wenner, Jann Simon *editor, publisher*
Westin, David Lawrence *broadcast executive, lawyer*
White, Denise *multimedia company executive*
White, Kate *editor-in-chief*
Whiteman, Douglas E. *publishing executive*
Whitney, Craig Richard *journalist*
Wiesenthal, Robert S. *Entertainment Company Executive*
Wilford, John Noble, Jr. *science news correspondent*
Wilkins, Amy P. *publishing executive*
Williams, Brian *network news anchor*
Williams-Rude, Beatrice *editor*
Willis, John Alvin *retired editor*
Winkler, Matthew Adam *editor-in-chief, reporter*
Winship, Frederick Moery *journalist*
Wintour, Anna *editor-in-chief*
Witmer, Carey *publishing executive*
Wolf, Brana *editor-at-large*
Wong, Andrea J. *broadcast executive*
Woodruff, Bob (Robert Warren Woodruff) *newscaster*
Young, Genevieve Leman *publishing executive, editor*
Zagat, Nina *publishing executive*
Zagat, Tim *publishing executive*
Zakaria, Fareed Rafiq *editor, journalist*
Zalaznick, Lauren Jane *broadcast executive*
Zarghami, Cyma *broadcast executive*
Zaslow, Jeffrey Lloyd *journalist, columnist*
Zimbalist, Michael *publishing executive*
Zinczenko, David *editor-in-chief*
Zuckerman, Mortimer Benjamin *publishing executive, real estate developer*

Oakdale
Bouquet, Theresa F. *journalist, educator*

Old Westbury
O'Brien, Adrienne Gratia *communications educator*

Ontario
Blackman, Lani Modica *copy editor*

Pleasantville
Alston, Alyce C. *publishing executive, former diamond company executive*
Balaban, Anne *publishing executive*
Berner, Mary G. *publishing executive*
Dillon, Eva A. *publishing executive*
Grimes, Suzanne *publishing executive*
McCarty, Todd C. *publishing executive, former retail executive*
Northrop, Peggy *editor-in-chief*

Port Washington
Candido, Arthur Aldo *publishing and distribution company executive*
Jay, Frank Peter *retired writer, lexicographer, educator*

Poughkeepsie
Kim, David Sang Chul *publishing executive, evangelist, retired academic administrator*
Stridsberg, Albert Borden (Paul Borden) *advertising consultant, editor, educator*

Purchase
Martin-Ruiz, Beatriz *music company executive*
Schmitz, Robert Allen *executive, investor*

Remsenburg
Billman, Irwin Edward *publishing executive*

Rochester
Fallesen, Gary David *journalist, lay worker, not-for-profit developer*
Kaidy, Mitchell *retired journalist, legislative staff member*
Lank, Edith Handleman *journalist, educator*
Lester, Howard Elliot *film company executive*
Palvino, Jack Anthony *retired broadcasting executive*

Rye
Nelson, Vita Joy *editor, publisher*

Sag Harbor
Brody, Jacqueline *editor*
Epstein, Jason *publishing company executive*

Saratoga Springs
Moran, Paul James *journalist, columnist*

Scarsdale
Erbsen, Claude Ernest *retired journalist*
Goodman, Jordan Elliot *journalist*
O'Neill, Michael James *editor, author*
Topping, Audrey Ronning *photojournalist*

Skaneateles
O'Connell, Sharon Kay *media specialist*

Sleepy Hollow
Flynn-Connors, Elizabeth Kathryn *reporter, editor*
Melvin, Russell Johnston (Jay Melvin) *magazine publishing consultant*
Neill, Richard Robert *retired publishing executive*

Somers
Cohn, Howard *retired magazine editor*

South Setauket
Poli, Kenneth Joseph *editor, writer, photographer*

Staten Island
Newhouse, Donald E. *newspaper publishing executive*
Newhouse, Samuel Irving, Jr., (Si Newhouse Jr.) *publishing executive*
Prince, Danforth *publishing executive, journalist*

Troy
Friedman, Sue Tyler *technical publications executive*

Vestal
Weil, Joseph David *editor, writer*

Wainscott
Henderson, William Charles *editor*

Warwick
Simon, Dolores Daly *copy editor*

White Plains
Leish, Kenneth William *retired publishing company executive*

Williamsville
Levite, Laurence A. *publishing executive*

Willsboro
Reuther, David Louis *retired children's book publisher, writer*

Woodhaven
Lipscomb, Thomas Heber III *media company executive*

Yonkers
Hough, Barbara *library media specialist, educator*
Kleman, Kimberly C. *editor-in-chief*
McKean, Kevin S. *publishing executive, writer*
Westphal, Carol Jean *media specialist*

Yorktown Heights
Wade, James O'Shea *editor, writer*

NORTH CAROLINA

Asheville
Merrill, Jonathan Alden *retired newsletter editor*

Brevard
Phillips, Euan Hywel *publishing executive*

Cary
Swanson, David C. *publishing executive*

Chapel Hill
Bailey, Herbert Smith, Jr. *retired publisher*
Bowers, Thomas Arnold *journalism educator, dean*
Cole, Richard Ray *communications educator, former dean*
Lauder, Valarie Anne *editor, educator*
Ravenel, Shannon *book publishing professional*

Charlotte
Armstrong, James David *editor, educator, minister*
Bauroth, Nancy Ann *journalist, former marketing executive*
Caulkins, Ann *publishing executive*
Clark-Claytor, Elizabeth B. *media specialist*
Gotta, Joseph D. *music company executive*
Haines, Kenneth H. *sports television broadcasting and marketing executive*
Hayes, Corlis Angela *communications educator, actor, director*
Kistenberg, Cindy J. *communications educator, theater educator*
Thames, Rick *publishing executive, editor-in-chief*

Conover
Jarrett, Dale (Arnold) *commentator, retired professional race car driver*

Durham
Cayne, Bernard Stanley *editor*
Fiske, Edward B. *editor, journalist*
Rossiter, Alexander, Jr. *publishing executive, author*

Elon
Copeland, David *communications educator*

Fayetteville
Flagg, Garrett Cortez *communications educator*

Greensboro
Blackwell, William Ernest *broadcast executive*
Jellicorse, John Lee *communications and theatre educator*

Greenville
Fraley, Todd *communications educator*

Harrisburg
Economaki, Chris Constantine (Christopher Economaki) *publishing executive*

Hickory
Drendel, Frank Matthew *cable company executive*

Jefferson
Franklin, Robert McFarland *book publisher*

Pembroke
Curtis, Anthony R. *communications educator*

Raleigh
Farr, A. Celeste *communications educator*
Kauffman, Terry *broadcast and communications educator, artist*
McKinney, Donald Lee *magazine editor*
Pittman, James Morris (Jack Pittman) *cartoonist, illustrator, character designer, consultant*
Reeves, Ralph Bernard III *publishing executive*

Sanford
Harrington, Anthony Ross *radio announcer, educator*

Southport
Pepper, Jeffrey Mackenzie *publishing executive*

Warrenton
Harrison-Jervay, Evelyn Yvonne *publishing executive*

Wilmington
Jones, David Meredith *retired communications educator*

Winston Salem
King, Wayne Edgar *journalist, educator*
Price, Henry Escoe *broadcast executive*
Zagoria, Sam D(avid) *reporter, educator, federal agency administrator*

Wrightsville Beach
Mc Ilwain, William Franklin *newspaper editor, writer*

OHIO

Alliance
Bergmann, Mark Allan *broadcast executive, educator*

Amherst
Gerstenberger, Valerie *media specialist*

Athens
McKerrow, Raymie E. *communications educator*
Scott, Charles Lewis *retired photojournalist*
Snow, Andrew P *communications educator, researcher*
Stempel, Guido Hermann III *journalism educator*

Avon Lake
Pascarella, Perry James *editor, writer*

Bexley
Finley, Charles Edwin *communications educator*

Bowling Green
Gabel, Rodney M. *communications disorders educator*
Park, Sung-Yeon *communications educator*

Cincinnati
Boehne, Richard A. *newspaper company executive*
Buchanan, Margaret E. *publishing executive*
Callinan, Tom *editor-in-chief*
Irwin, Miriam Dianne Owen *publishing executive, writer*
King, Margaret Ann *communications educator*
Knue, Paul Frederick *newspaper editor*
Krome, Frederic *editor*
McMullin, Ruth Roney *retired publishing executive*
Mechem, Charles Stanley, Jr. *retired broadcast executive*
Pepper, John Ennis, Jr. *entertainment company executive, former consumer products company*
Trent, Judith Swanlund *communication educator*

Cleveland
Bellamy, Gail Anne Ghetia *magazine editor, author, speaker*
Brandt, John Reynold *editor, journalist*
Conrad, Robert David *broadcast executive, educator*
Egger, Terrance C.Z. *publishing executive*
Giannetti, Louis Daniel *film critic, educator*
Goldberg, Susan *editor*
Jensen, Kathryn Patricia (Kit Jensen) *broadcast executive*
Lee, Jae-won *communications educator, political campaign consultant*
Soltis, Katherine *editor*

Columbus
Cox, Mitchel Neal *editor*
Curtin, Michael Francis *publishing executive, writer*
Dimmick, John W. *communications educator*
Fiorile, Michael J. *publishing executive*
Gribble, Charles Edward *editor, language educator*
Grossberg, Michael Lee *theater critic, writer*
Hopkins, Christiana *communications educator*
Kefauver, Weldon Addison *publishing executive*
Marrison, Benjamin J. *editor-in-chief*
McCoy, Bernard Rogers *television anchor*
Sherrill, Thomas Boykin III *retired newspaper publishing executive*
Wolfe, John F. *publishing executive*

Dayton
Gaines, Elliot *communications educator*
Matheny, Ruth Ann *editor*

Hudson
Clark, Robert Phillips *editor, consultant*

Kent
Kim, Junghyun Frannie *communications educator*

Mason
Smith, C. LeMoyne *retired publishing executive*

Oxford
Sanders, Gerald Hollie *communications educator*

Pepper Pike
O'Neill, Katherine Templeton *journalist, former nursing educator, museum administrator*
Vail, Thomas Van Husen *retired publishing executive*

Rocky River
Condon, George Edward *journalist*

Sidney
Stevens, Robert Jay *magazine editor*

Toledo
Royhab, Ronald *journalist, editor*

Trotwood
Oluyitan, Emmanuel Funso *communications educator*

Vandalia
Scinto, Michael Jospeph *broadcast executive*

Waverly
Cornish, Carol A. *media specialist*

Wooster
August, Robert Olin *retired journalist*
Schreiber, Clare Adel *journalist*

Yellow Springs
Cawood, Albert McLaurin (Hap Cawood) *retired newspaper editor*

OKLAHOMA

Altus
Shelby, Karla Jane *music company executive, director*

Bethany
Feisal, Marcia Moon *communications educator*
Murrow, Wayne Lee *retired communications educator, dean*

Lawton
Heflin, James L. *communications educator*

Norman
Dunbar, Norah Ellen *communications educator*
Miller, Claude Harold *communications educator*
Weber, Jerome Charles *human relations educator, retired academic administrator*

Oklahoma City
Gourley, James Leland *editor, publishing executive*
Kelley, Ed *editor-in-chief*

Thompson, David *publishing executive*
Triplett, E. Eugene *editor*

Stillwater
Senat, Joey *communications educator*

Tecumseh
Moser, Glenda Faye *media specialist*

Terlton
Bender, John Henry, Jr., (Jack Bender) *editor, cartoonist*

Tulsa
Haring, Robert Westing *newspaper editor*
Nyikos, Stacy Ann *publishing executive*

Wewoka
Trimble, Vance Henry *retired newspaper editor*

OREGON

Ashland
Risser, James Vaulx, Jr. *journalist, educator*

Central Point
Ingraham, Laura Anne *political commentator, radio talk show host*

Christmas Valley
Johnson, Mary Alice *magazine editor*

Coos Bay
Gee, Nina Foran *retired journalist, elementary school educator, writer*

Corvallis
Hall, Don Alan *editor, writer*

Eugene
Baker, Alton Fletcher III *editor, publishing executive*

Milton Freewater
Gipson, Stephen Richard *journalist, construction executive*

Portland
Bates, Doug *editor*
Bhatia, Peter K. *editor, journalist*
Bunza, Linda Hathaway *editor, writer, composer, director*
Johnston, Virginia Evelyn *retired editor*
Ritchie, David *communications educator, researcher*
Rowe, Sandra Mims *editor*
Stickel, Frederick A. *publishing executive*

Salem
Mainwaring, William Lewis *publishing company executive, author*

PENNSYLVANIA

Bensalem
Kang, Benjamin Toyeong *journalist, minister*

Bloomsburg
Bertelsen, Dale Alan *communications educator*
Brasch, Walter Milton *journalist, educator*
Defenbaugh, Nicole Lynn *communications studies professor*

Carlisle
Fish, Chester Boardman, Jr. *retired editor*

Clearfield
Krebs, Margaret Eloise *publishing executive*

Delta
Quesenbery, Erika Lynn *media specialist, curator*

Elizabethtown
Lobdell, Jared Charles *editor, educator*
Wennberg, Hans-Erik *communications educator*

Emmaus
Dorn, Jonathan Andrew *editor-in-chief*
Murcko, Mary *publishing executive*
Rodale, Ardath Harter *publishing executive*
Rodale, Maria *publishing executive*

Erie
Welch, William James *journalist, educator*

Greensburg
Freidheim, Cyrus F., Jr. *former publishing and food products executive*

Harleysville
Smagalski, Carolyn M. *publishing executive, webmaster, director*

Harrisburg
Gover, Raymond Lewis *retired newspaper executive*

Havertown
Hendrickson, Paul Joseph *journalist, writer, educator*

Hollidaysburg
McPhee, Norma Howatt *publishing executive, author*

Honesdale
Brown, Kent Louis, Jr. *magazine editor*

Kennett Square
Landstrom, Elsie Hayes *retired editor*

Lancaster
Shaw, Charles Raymond *journalist*

Mechanicsburg
Juditz, Lillian Mickley *retired communications educator*

Philadelphia
Biddle, Daniel R. *editor, reporter*
Burke, Stephen B. *broadcast executive*
Carey, Arthur Bernard, Jr. *editor, columnist*
Days, Michael *editor*
Gamble, Kenneth *recording industry executive, music producer*
Gordon, Anne Kathleen *editor*
Halpern, Eric Franklin *university publishing director*
Harper, Christopher *journalist, educator*
Huff, Leon A. *music producer, composer*
Jackson, Harold *journalist*
Klein, Julia Meredith *freelance journalist, editor*
Leiter, Robert Allen *journalist, editor, writer*
Lent, John Anthony *journalist, educator*
Marimow, William K. (Bill Marimow) *editor*
Parry, Lance Aaron *publishing executive*
Pedersen, Darlene Delcourt *publishing executive, writer, psychotherapist*
Porter, Jill *journalist*
Rorer, John Whiteley *publisher, consultant*
Tierney, Brian Patrick *publishing executive, former advertising and public relations executive*
Vazirani, Kavita *broadcast company executive*

Pittsburgh
Block, John Robinson *newspaper publisher, editor-in-chief*
Hopey, Stephen Donald *journalist, educator*
Scaife, Richard Mellon *publishing executive, philanthropist*
Shribman, David Marks *editor*

Reading
Fitzpatrick, Caroline *communications educator, director*

Scranton
Lynett, William Ruddy *publishing and broadcast executive*

Southampton
Nathan, Dusty *journalist, shop owner*

Warrington
Ward, Hiley Henry *journalist, educator*

Washington Crossing
Roche, Gail Connor *editor*

Wayne
Fabbri, Anne R. *critic, curator*

West Chester
Mahoney, William Francis *editor, writer*

West Conshohocken
Lenfest, Harold FitzGerald *former cable television executive, lawyer*

Wyncote
Booker, Alvin Eugene *publishing executive, consultant*

RHODE ISLAND

Bristol
Moffa, John L. *media specialist, director*

Kingston
Smith, Jason Kemmitt *communications educator*

Newport
Cowley, Robert William *editor, writer, editorial consultant*

Portsmouth
Needham, Richard Lee *magazine editor*

Providence
Farmer, Susan Lawson *retired broadcast executive, former secretary of state*
Rosenberg, Alan Gene *editor*

SOUTH CAROLINA

Bennettsville
Kinney, William Light, Jr. *editor, publishing executive*

Cayce
McElveen, William Lindsay *broadcast executive, educator*

Charleston
Bass, Jack *journalism educator*
Schreadley, Richard Lee *newswriter, retired editor*
Wyrick, Charles Lloyd, Jr. *editor, writer*

Columbia
Breedin, Berryman Brent *journalist, consultant, historian, public relations executive*
Kendler, Bernhard *retired editor*
Morris, Charlotte Ann *media specialist, school librarian*

Greenville
Mebane, William deBerniere *newspaper publisher*

Greer
Evans, Philip G. *media consultant, former sports association executive*

Hilton Head
Gallagher, Terrence Vincent *editor*

Hilton Head Island
Shaheen, Jack George *communications educator*

Johns Island
Tarr, Robert Joseph, Jr. *publishing and retail executive*

Laurens
Griffin, Mary Frances *retired media consultant*

Orangeburg
Sims, Edward Howell *editor, writer*

Simpsonville
Kanzler, George *journalist, music critic*

Walterboro
Garrett, Darlynn Middleton *media specialist*

SOUTH DAKOTA

Mobridge
Hall, Jo(sephine) Marian *editor*

Rapid City
Wishard, Della Mae *former newspaper editor*

Sioux Falls
Bartling, Kimberly Kay *communications educator, theater educator*

TENNESSEE

Cleveland
Silverman, Patricia R. *communications educator*

College Grove
Battle, William Robert (Bob Battle) *retired publishing executive*

Johnson City
Perry, Murvin Henry *communications educator*

Knoxville
Howard, Herbert Hoover *broadcasting and communications educator*
Lowe, Kenneth W. *multimedia executive*
Rukeyser, William Simon *journalist*

Maryville
Bradford, Tutt Sloan *retired publisher*

Murfreesboro
Flanagan, Van Kent *journalist*

Nashville
Crisp, Terry Arthur *commentator, former professional hockey coach and player*
Green, Lisa Cannon *editor*
Holt, Trevor Joyce *media specialist, educator*
Policinski, Eugene Francis *non-profit organization executive, syndicated columnist, editor, radio and television personality, producer*
Richmond, Marisa Jeanne *columnist*
Shaw, Carole *editor, publisher*
Turk, Thomas Liebig *arts consultant*

Newport
Ball, Travis, Jr. *editor, retired school administrator*

TEXAS

Abilene
Armstrong, Randy Lee *communications educator*
Boyll, David Lloyd *retired broadcast executive*
Potter, Paul Eugene *communications educator, consultant*

Amarillo
Robertson, Pauline Durrett *publishing executive*

Austin
Burd, Gene Arnold *journalist, educator*
Knapp, Mark Lane *communications educator, consultant*
Mayes, Wendell Wise, Jr. *former broadcasting company executive*

Beaumont
Baker, Mary Alice *communications educator, consultant*
Roth, Lane *communications educator*

Brownwood
Humfeld, Nancy Jo *communications educator, director*

Coppell
Aikman, Troy Kenneth *sportscaster, retired professional football player*

Corpus Christi
Flores, Manuel C., Jr. *editor*

Dallas
Bailon, Gilbert *newspaper executive*
Blessen, Karen Alyce *freelance/self-employed journalist, artist*
Cantrell, Scott *newspaper music critic*
Dillon, David Anthony *editor, educator*
Easter, Glenda H. *communications educator*
Glines, Carroll Vane, Jr. *magazine editor*
Holmes, Bert Otis E., Jr. *retired editor*
Keyes, James Willard (Jim Keyes) *film rental company executive*
Klein, Scott W. *publishing executive*
Mong, Robert William, Jr. *editor, publishing executive*
Moroney, James M. III *publishing executive*
Phelps, Steven *editor*
Rather, Dan (Daniel Irvin Rather, Jr.) *news correspondent, former network news anchor*
Shepherd, Nick P. *film rental company executive*
Smith, Sue Frances *newspaper editor*
Thompson, Heath *media consultant*

Denton
Staples, Donald Edward *radio, film and television educator*

El Paso
Mearns, Kenneth Crawford *retired communications educator*
Mullins, Patrick *communications educator*

Fort Worth
Haber, Marian Wynne *journalism educator, writer*
Record, Phillip Julius *journalist*
Witt, Jim *executive editor*
Wortel, Gary G. *publishing executive*

Houston
Cohen, Jeff *editor, publishing executive*
Downing, Margaret Mary *newspaper editor*
George, Deveral D. *editor, journalist, advertising consultant*
Hobby, William Pettus *retired broadcast executive*
Holmes, Ann Hitchcock *journalist*
McDavid, George Eugene (Gene) *retired newspaper executive*
Read, Michael Oscar *editor, consultant*
Riggenbach, Jeff *journalist, broadcaster*
Roberts, Charles Murray *retired publishing executive, writer*
Sweeney, Jack *publishing executive*
Wagner, Charlene Brook *retired secondary school educator*
Walls, Martha Ann Williams (Mrs. B. Carmage Walls) *publishing executive*

Jacksonville
Thrall, Gordon Fish *publishing executive*

Katy
Gray, Robert Steele *publishing executive, editor, writer*

Kyle
Saunders, Patricia Gene Knight *freelance writer, editor*

Lakeway
Conine, Ernest *columnist*

Longview
Udy, Rae *columnist, writer*

Mesquite
Forrest, Mary L. *communications educator*

Round Rock
Halter, Jon Charles *retired magazine editor, writer*

San Antonio
Foster, Nancy Haston *columnist, writer*
Gwathmey, Joe Neil, Jr. *retired broadcast executive*
Kline, Kimberly Nicole *communications educator*
Marbut, Robert Gordon *communications, electronic security and broadcast executive, investor*
Mays, L(ester) Lowry *broadcast executive*
Michaels, Willard A. Bill (Bill Michaels) *retired broadcasting executive*
Perry, John *communications educator, researcher*
Rivard, Robert *editor, publishing executive*
Stephenson, Thomas A. *publishing executive*

San Marcos
Stovall, Frances Middagh *journalist, preservationist*

The Woodlands
Cagle, Melinda Reeves *editor*
Schott, Sally Maria *music publisher, arts education consultant*

Tyler
Brock, Dee Sala *television executive, writer, consultant, educator*

Wichita Falls
Thornton, Brian *communication educator, researcher*

UTAH

Cedar City
Heuett, Brian L. *communications educator, small business owner*

Price
Cha, Pamela Kandaris *communications educator*

Provo
Bartlett, Leonard Lee *retired communications educator, advertising executive*
Hughes, (Robert) John *journalist, educator*
Willes, Mark Hinckley *media specialist*

Saint George
Hodges, Sharon Green *editor, consultant, writer*

Salt Lake City
Brown, Carolyn Smith *communications educator, consultant*
Cutting, Patricia Grace *publishing executive, educator*
Fehr, John William *newspaper editor*

Gregersen, R(oald) George *newspaper publishing executive*
Hatch, George Clinton *television executive*
Paulsen, Vivian *editor*
Sillars, Malcolm O. *communications educator*

VERMONT

Lincoln
Kompass, Edward John *consulting editor*

North Pomfret
Crowl, John Allen *retired publishing company executive*

Norwich
Paine, Walter Cabot *journalist, consultant*

Perkinsville
Harris, Christopher *editor, writer, illustrator, graphics designer*

Randolph
Ryerson, Marjorie Gilmour *journalist, poet, photographer, educator*

Woodstock
Goulazian, Peter Robert *retired broadcasting executive*

VIRGINIA

Alexandria
Arundel, John Howard *journalist, publisher*
Castellanos, Alex *media consultant*
Fleming, Douglas Riley *journalist, publishing executive, consultant*
Hobbs, Michael Edwin *retired broadcast executive*
Scheibel, Kenneth Maynard *journalist*
Stanton, John Jeffrey *editor, director, journalist, government agency administrator, educator*
Yoder, Edwin Milton, Jr. *columnist, educator, editor, writer*

Annandale
Freeman, Baba Foster *editor*

Arlington
Arnold, Gary Howard *film critic*
Brady, Jim (James M. Brady) *editor*
Clayton, James Edwin *journalist*
Elsberg, John William *publishing executive, writer*
Glass, Andrew James *newspaper editor*
Ifill, Gwen *moderator, political reporter*
Kerger, Paula Arnold *broadcast executive*
Lehrer, Jim (James Charles Lehrer) *reporter, journalist*
Little, Caroline H. *publishing executive*
MacDougall, William Lowell *magazine editor*
MacNeil, Robert Breckenridge Ware *retired journalist, writer*
Neikirk, William Robert *retired journalist*
Regnery, Alfred Scattergood *publishing executive*
Rockefeller, Sharon Percy *broadcast executive*
Simonson, David C. *retired newspaper association executive*
White, Dale Timothy (Tim White) *television journalist, producer*

Ashburn
Sanfelici, Arthur H(ugo) *editor, writer*

Axton
Bestler, J. Michael *columnist, retired surgeon*

Charlottesville
Forrest, Patricia Anne *publishing executive, editor*
Kaiserlian, Penelope Jane *publishing executive*
Loo, Beverly Jane *publisher, educator*
Thornhill, Arthur H., Jr. *retired publishing executive*
Worrell, Anne Everette Rowell *newspaper publisher*

Chester
Gray, Frederick Thomas, Jr., (Rick Gray) *journalist, actor, educator*
Tiller, Charlene Teitelbaum *communications educator*

Covington
Rohr, Dwight Mason *news director, radio marketing consultant*

Dulles
Desmond, Ned *editor, writer*
North, Oliver Laurence (Ollie North) *syndicated columnist, retired military officer*

Fairfax
Anderson, LaKesha Nichole *communications educator*
McAllister, William Howard III *newspaper reporter, columnist, public affairs consultant*

Fairfax Station
Randell, Cortes W. *news service executive*

Falls Church
Aukofer, Frank Alexander *journalist*
Cromley, Allan Wray *retired journalist*
Kaplow, Herbert Elias *journalist*

Great Falls
Garrett, Wilbur Bill (Bill) *magazine editor*

Harrisonburg
Brickner, Aimee R. *communications educator*

Herndon
Davis, Nathaniel (Nate) A. *broadcast executive*

Jeffersonton
Hileman, Bette *journalist*

Luray
Burzynski, Norman Stephen *editor*

Mason Neck
Mc Curdy, Patrick Pierre *editor*

Mc Lean
Dubow, Craig A. *publishing executive*
Gallagher, Brian *editor*
Hillkirk, John M. *newspaper editor*
Hunke, David Lawrence *publishing executive*
Kane, Michael G. *publishing executive*
Martore, Gracia C. *publishing company executive*
Mathews, Linda McVeigh *newspaper editor*
Mayman, Todd A. *publishing executive, lawyer*
McCorkindale, Douglas Hamilton *publishing executive*
Parshall, Gerald *journalist*
Stoddart, Veronica Gould *travel editor*

Midlothian
Chapman, Gilbert Whipple, Jr. *publishing executive*

Norfolk
Addis, Kay Tucker *newspaper editor*
Barry, Richard Francis III *media executive*
Batten, Frank *newspaper publisher, cable broadcaster*
Ciara, Barbara *news anchor*
Jamison, Joi Nichole *media specialist, performing company executive, educator*
Sizemore, William Howard, Jr. *journalist*

Paeonian Springs
Sloyan, Patrick Joseph *journalist*

Potomac Falls
Day, Charles Williamson *consultant*

Radford
Kovarik, William *communications educator, journalist, editor*

Reston
Powell, Anne Elizabeth *editor-in-chief*

Richmond
Bryan, John Stewart III *newspaper publisher*

Round Hill
Hillis, John David *broadcast executive, television producer, newswriter*

Saint Paul
Gregory, Ann Young *editor*

Springfield
Kieffer, Jarold Alan *publishing executive, writer*
Myers, Elissa Matulis *publishing executive, professional society administrator*

Stanardsville
Anns, Arlene Eiserman *publishing company executive*

Vienna
McElveen, Joseph James, Jr. *journalist, writer, newscaster, educator*

Virginia Beach
Agolini, Patricia *media specialist*
Hunter, Elizabeth M. *communications educator, director*
Quicke, Andrew Charles *cinema-television educator, consultant, writer*
Robertson, Pat (Marion Gordon Robertson) *religious broadcasting executive, university president and chancellor*

Warrenton
Killinger, John Eric *editor-in-chief, director*

Winchester
Byrd, Harry Flood, Jr. *publishing executive, Former United States Senator, Virginia*

Woodbridge
Binder, L. James *retired magazine editor, journalist*

WASHINGTON

Bellevue
Dolgen, Jonathan L. *former motion picture company executive, investor*
Sims, Dave *sportscaster*
Wilkens, Lenny (Leonard Randolph Wilkens Jr.) *sportscaster, former professional sports team executive, retired professional basketball player*

Bellingham
Meals, Pamela F. *publishing executive*

Port Angeles
Brewer, John Charles *journalist*

Pullman
Haarsager, Dennis Lee *broadcast executive*
Hust, Stacey Jolene *communications educator, researcher*

Seattle
Blethen, Frank A. *newspaper publisher*
Boardman, David *editor*
Buckner, Philip Franklin *newspaper publisher*
Cochran, Wendell Albert *science editor*
Fancher, Michael Reilly *editor, publishing executive*
Gwinn, Mary Ann *editor*
Lacitis, Erik *journalist*
Parks, Michael James *editor*
Stricherz, Vincent C. *journalist*

Spokane
Cowles, William Stacey *newspaper publisher*
Kafentzis, John Charles *journalist, educator*
Kunkel, Richard Lester *public radio executive*
Steele, Karen Dorn *journalist*

Sumner
Gosselin, Cheryl Block *media specialist, librarian*

Tacoma
Mowery, Gerald Eugene *publishing executive, writer*

Vancouver
Middlewood, Martin Eugene *writer, consultant*
Sutherland, Roxane Y. *communications educator*

WEST VIRGINIA

Charleston
Chilton, Elizabeth Easley Early *newspaper executive*
Haught, James Albert, Jr. *journalist, editor*

Greenville
Warner, Kenneth Wilson, Jr. *editor, publishing executive*

Keyser
Smoot, Stephen Annese *columnist, educator*

Marlinton
Sharp, Jane Price *retired editor*

Parkersburg
McKenzie, Lawrence J. *composition educator*

Shepherdstown
Snyder, Joseph John *editor, lecturer, consultant, historian, writer*
Wilson, Miriam Janet Williams *publishing executive*

West Liberty
Lasch, Meta M. *communications and art educator*

WISCONSIN

Appleton
Malaney, Stephanie J. *reading specialist*
Oppmann, Andrew James *newspaper editor*

Green Bay
Daley, Arthur James *retired magazine publisher*

Iola
Krause, Chester Lee *publishing executive*

Janesville
Fitzgerald, James Francis *broadcast executive*

Madison
Drechsel, Robert Edward *journalism educator*
Gruber, John Edward *editor, historian, photographer*
Hoyt, James Lawrence *journalism educator, writer*
Lincoln Michel, Karen *journalist*
McNelly, John Taylor *retired journalist, educator*
Zweifel, David Alan *newspaper editor*

Milwaukee
Behrendt, David Frogner *retired journalist*
Brenner, Elizabeth (Betsy Brenner) *publishing executive*
Farris, Trueman Earl, Jr. *retired newspaper editor*
Kaiser, Martin *editor-in-chief*
Seery, Carol Hubbard *communication sciences educator*
Spore, Keith Kent *newspaper executive*

Rice Lake
Hoeft, Mary Elizabeth *communications educator*

River Falls
Hoffman, Cheryl *media specialist*

WYOMING

Laramie
Brown, Michael R. *communications educator*

TERRITORIES OF THE UNITED STATES

PUERTO RICO

Bayamon
Berio, Blanca *editor, writer, language educator*

San Juan
Casiano, Kimberly *publishing executive*
Ferre, Antonio Luis *newspaper publisher*
Montilla, Victor Javier *broadcast executive*

VIRGIN ISLANDS

St John
Walker, Ronald R. *editor, educator, writer*

CANADA

BRITISH COLUMBIA

Vancouver
Kane, Nolan C. *editor, researcher*
Littrell, Mark *media specialist*
Yaffe, Barbara Marlene *journalist*

NOVA SCOTIA

Glasgow
Williams, Edna Aleta Theadora Johnston *journalist*

ONTARIO

Brantford
Hanna, William Brooks *publishing executive, literary agent*

Don Mills
French, William Harold *retired newspaper editor*

North York
Gasparrini-Etheridge, Claudia *publishing executive, research scientist, writer*

Ottawa
Cruickshank, John Douglas *broadcast executive*
Davey, Clark William *newspaper publisher*

Richmond Hill
Zulfi, Tasleem Elahi (Tasleem Elahi Qureshi) *broadcast executive, television personality*

Saint Catharines
Miller, Jack (John Peter Miller) *journalist*

Toronto
Cooke, Michael *editor-in-chief, publishing executive*
Lewis, Robert *journalist, media executive*
Milbury, Mike (Michael James Milbury) *sports analyst, former professional sports team executive*
Thomson, David Kenneth Roy *publishing executive*

Willowdale
Kerner, Fred *book publisher, writer*

QUEBEC

Montreal
Webster, Norman Eric *journalist, foundation administrator*

AFGHANISTAN

Kabul
Karokhel, Danish *broadcast executive*

AUSTRALIA

Double Bay
Guerin, Didier *magazine executive*

BRAZIL

FlorianÓpolis
Lopes, Elizeu Pereira *communications educator, researcher*

Florianópolis
Lopes, Eliezer Pereira *communications educator*

CHINA

Shanghai
Prosser, Michael Hubert *communications educator*

CYPRUS

Nicosia
Hadjipapas, Andreas *publishing executive*

ENGLAND

Cambridge
Kermode, (John) Frank *literary critic, educator*

London
Fuller, Simon *music company executive, television producer*
Glocer, Thomas Henry *publishing executive*
Irvine, Ian Alexander Noble *media company executive, director*
Martin, Sir George Henry *recording industry executive*
Micklethwait, John *editor-in-chief*
Rossi, Paul *publishing executive*
Scardino, Dame Marjorie Morris *publishing executive*

Lymington
Martin, Giles *recording industry executive*

FRANCE

Levallois-Perret
Filipacchi, Daniel *publishing executive*

Paris
Dassault, Serge *media and software company and air transportation executive, French senator*
Lagardere, Arnaud *media company executive*
Redburn, Tom *editor*
Schmemann, Serge *journalist*

HONG KONG

Kowloon
Ma, Bianca Kin-san *broadcast executive*

North Point
Apcar, Leonard M. *editor*

INDIA

Manipal
Pai, Satish Upendra *publishing executive*

New Delhi
Bagla, Pallava *journalist, photographer*

ISRAEL

Savyon
Bushinsky, Jay (Joseph Mason) *journalist, news correspondent*

ITALY

Florence
Olschki, Alessandro *book publishing executive*

Milan
Berlusconi, Marina *publishing executive*

JAPAN

Tokyo
Jameson, Samuel Walter *newspaperman, foreign correspondent*
Kiyohara, Takehiko *publishing executive*
Krisher, Bernard *foreign correspondent*
Petersen, Barry Rex *news correspondent*

NORWAY

Oslo
Haug, Charlotte J. *editor, educator*

PERU

Lima
Yardley, Jonathan *journalist*

REPUBLIC OF KOREA

Gyeonggi
Yoon, Hyung-Doo *publisher, educator, writer*

Incheon
Kwak, Kyung Sup *communications educator*

Seoul
Han, Youngyearl *communications educator*
Park, Myungkark *president, publisher, physicist*

RUSSIA

Moscow
Paulson, Andrew *publishing executive, Internet company executive*

SCOTLAND

Glasgow
Moosa, Ahmed Shafeeq Ibrahim (Sappé) *journalist*

SINGAPORE

Singapore
Lim, Tai Wei *communications educator, researcher*

SLOVAKIA

Voderady
Neisser, Hentike *editor, writer*

SPAIN

Segovia
Wojcieszak, Magdalena Elzbieta *communications educator, researcher*

VIETNAM

Hanoi
Tran, Huong Mai *editor-in-chief*

ADDRESS UNPUBLISHED

Abrams, Dan *media strategy firm executive, former broadcast executive*
Achorn, Robert Comey *retired newspaper publisher*
Adams, Lorraine *reporter*
Adelman, Kenneth Lee *journalist, former ambassador*
Akiyama, Carol Lynn *motion picture industry executive*
Aldrich, Patricia Anne Richardson *retired magazine editor*
Anderson, Jon Stephen *newswriter*
Anderson, N. Christian III *former newspaper publisher*
Anderson-Spivy, Alexandra *arts correspondent, editor, critic, writer, historian*
Andrisani, John Anthony *editor, writer*
Annesi, Adele Mary *editor, writer*
Armstrong, Douglas Dean *journalist*
Arnold, Henri *cartoonist*
Arrington, Michael (Jack Michael Arrington) *web publishing company executive, blogger, lawyer*
Ashton, Betsy Finley *artist, writer*
Asmussen, Angie *communications educator*
Avnet, Jonathan Michael *motion picture company executive, film director*
Babb, Tracie *communications educator*
Baggett, Donnis Gene *newspaper editor*
Bailey, Janet Dee *publishing executive*
Baker, William Franklin *retired broadcast executive*
Baldassano, Corinne Leslie *radio executive*
Ballantine, Betty *editor*
Barham, Patte *publisher, author, columnist*
Barnett, Amy DuBois *editor-in-chief*
Barnhurst, Christine Louise *broadcast executive*
Barrows, Frank Clemence *journalist*
Bartlett, David *media consultant*
Bauer, Patricia E. *journalist*
Beaudet-Francès, Patricia Suzanne *senior photography editor*
Beguin, Bernard Auguste *retired broadcast executive, columnist*
Bennett, Amanda *former editor*
Bennett, Clay *cartoonist*
Bennett, Lerone, Jr. *retired magazine editor, author*
Berman, William H. *retired publishing company executive*
Beyer, Lisa *journalist*
Bierstedt, Peter Richard *entertainment industry consultant, lawyer*
Binzen, Peter Husted *journalist*
Birch, Ian *former editor-in-chief*
Bird, Kai *journalist, historian*
Bishop, Gordon Bruce *journalist*
Blyth, Myrna Greenstein *publishing executive*
Bolinder, Scott W. *former publishing company executive*
Boo, Katherine *newswriter*
Borysewicz, Mary Louise *editor*
Bouvier, Linda Fritts *publishing executive*
Bowen, Tim *former recording industry executive*
Bowes, Frederick III *publishing executive, consultant*
Boyce, Joseph Nelson *retired journalist, consultant, educator*
Brady-Borland, Karen *retired reporter, columnist*
Braithwaite, Dawn O. *communication educator*
Bram, Leon Leonard *publishing company executive*
Brandt, Robert Frederic III *retired editor, journalist*
Brant, Sandra J. *magazine publisher*
Breathed, Berkeley *cartoonist*
Brelis, Matthew Dean Burns *journalist*
Briggs, Niwana Page *editor, writer*
Brinberg, Herbert Raphael *publishing executive*
Brisbane, Arthur Seward *newspaper publisher*
Brogliatti, Barbara Spencer *retired television and motion picture executive, consultant*
Brokaw, Tom (Thomas John Brokaw) *news correspondent, former network news anchor*
Brooks, Andrée Aelion *journalist, educator, writer*
Brooks, Timothy H. *broadcast executive*
Broude, Ronald *music publisher*
Brownrigg, Walter Grant *cartoonist*
Brugger, David John *media consultant*
Brumback, Charles Tiedtke *retired newspaper executive*
Bryant, Thomas Lee *retired magazine editor*
Buchanan, Pat (Patrick Joseph Buchanan) *journalist, author, political commentator*
Buhler, Jill Lorie *editor, writer*
Burleigh, William Robert *retired media executive*
Burrows, Edwin Gladding *retired broadcaster, writer, poet*
Byrne-Dempsey, Cecelia (Cecelia Dempsey) *journalist*
Calame, Byron Edward *journalist*
Calder, Iain Wilson *publishing executive*
Callahan, Vivian *broadcast executive*
Callander, Bruce Douglas *journalist, freelance writer*
Calley, John *former motion picture company executive, film producer*
Callier, Maria Cecile *journalist, senior technical writer, radio producer*
Campbell, Byron Chesser *newspaper publishing executive*
Cardwell, Nancy Lee *editor, writer*
Carlson, Richard Warner *journalist, broadcast executive, federal agency administrator, diplomat*
Carter, Betsy L. *editor, writer*
Carver, Stephen D. *publishing executive, former broadcast executive*
Chercover, Murray *television executive*
Chernichaw, Mark *broadcast executive, corporate communications executive, television director, television producer, media consultant, educator*
Christiansen, Richard Dean *retired newspaper editor*
Churgin, Amy *former publishing executive*
Claiborne, William *journalist*
Clark, James Covington *journalist, historian*
Clark, Peter Bruce *retired publishing executive*
Clark-Johnson, Susan *retired publishing executive*
Clifton, Douglas C. *retired newspaper editor*
Cloud, Stanley Wills *journalist, writer, editor, reporter*
Clymer, Adam *journalist, writer*
Cohen, Mark Herbert *broadcast executive*
Cohn, Gary Dennis *journalist, educator*
Collins, J. Michael *retired public broadcasting executive*
Collins, Walter Lloyd George *editor*
Colombo, Rose Marie *freelance/self-employed newswriter, television personality*
Combs, Sean (Diddy) *record company executive, producer, actor*
Cooke, Robert William *retired science journalist, author and photographer*
Cooper, Charles Howard *retired photojournalist, publishing executive*
Copeland, Angie Denise *communications educator*
Corey, Orlin Russell *publishing executive*
Cowher, Bill (William Laird Cowher) *sportscaster, former professional football coach*
Cozma, Raluca *journalist, educator*
Crabbs, Roger Alan *publishing executive, director, small business owner, military officer, educator*
Crawford Walden, Sandra D. *media specialist*
Crewdson, John Mark *journalist, writer*
Croan, Robert James *music critic*
Crovitz, Louis Gordon (Gordon Crovitz) *former publishing executive, journalist*
Curry, Carlton E. *broadcast and waterworks executive, councilman*
Curtin-Wilding, Leigh *media consultant, writer*
Curtis, Mary E. (Mary Horowitz) *publishing executive*
D'Agustino, Steven *communication and technology educator*
Dahlburg, John-Thor Theodore *news correspondent*
Davis, Donald Alan *news correspondent, author*
Dean, Carole Lee *film company executive*
DeBakey, Selma *communications educator, writer, editor*
Dedman, Bill *journalist*
de Leon, Lidia Maria *magazine editor*
Deming, Thomas Edward *publishing executive*
Denver, Eileen Ann *retired editor*
DeSando, John Anthony *film critic, retired humanities educator*
Desbarats, Peter Hullett *journalist, educator, academic administrator*
Dickman, James Bruce *photojournalist*
Dinerstein, Staci *broadcast executive, educator*
Dobbs, Lou (Louis Earl Dobbs) *commentator, former broadcast executive*
Dobrzynski, Judith Helen *journalist, commentator*
Doerper, John Erwin *journal editor, publishing executive*
Dolan, Michael J. *former multimedia company and advertising executive*
Domjan, Laszlo Karoly *journalist*
Donald, Aida DiPace *retired publishing executive*
Donovan, Brian *journalist, author*
Donovan, Helen W. *editor*
Dracos, Theodore Michael *journalist, television producer*
Drake, Donald Charles *journalist, playwright*
Dudman, Richard Beebe *journalist*
Dumanoski, Dianne *journalist, writer*
Duncan, David Ewing *editor, writer*
Dunham, Benjamin Starr *editor, art association administrator*
Dwan, Dennis Edwin *broadcast executive, photographer*
Eaker, Sherry Ellen *editor*
Edelson, Zelda Sarah Toll *retired editor, artist*
Edwards, Geoffrey Hartley *newspaper publisher*
Elliott, Stuart Jay *editor, journalist*
Ellis, Robert Harry *retired broadcast executive, academic administrator*
Ellis, Roger Barry *communications educator*
Endicott, William F. *journalist*
Engdahl, Todd Philip *editor*
Erlicht, Lewis Howard *broadcasting company executive*
Ervin, Kathleen Gwen *journalist*
Fabus, Renee Laura *communications educator*
Farewell, Susan *journalist, writer*
Fenech, Daniel Thomas *cartoonist*
Fenton, Thomas Trail *journalist*
Fenwick, James Henry *editor, writer, columnist*
Ferguson, Charles Austin *retired newspaper editor*
Fernald, Harold Allen *publishing executive*
Fike, Edward Lake *newspaper editor*
Fisher, Andrew, IV, *retired journalist*
Fisher, Robert Charles Haru *publishing executive, editor*
Fitch, Fred Emmett *communications educator*
Fitzpatrick, Nancy Hecht *editor*
FitzSimons, Dennis Joseph *former broadcast and publishing executive*
Flournoy, John Craig *journalism educator*
Francke, Linda Bird *journalist*
Frederickson, Christine Magnuson *reporter, researcher, author, writer*
Freed, Richard (Donald) *music critic*
French, Mary B. *editor, photographer, poet, retired literature educator*
Freston, Tom (Thomas E. Freston) *former broadcast executive*
Friedman, Jane M. *former publishing executive*
Fromm, Joseph *retired editor, foreign correspondent, foreign affairs consultant*
Fryer, Thomas Waitt, Jr. *editor, writer*
Fuentez, Tania Michele *journalist*
Fuller, Bonnie *publishing executive*
Gandolf, Raymond L. *media correspondent*
Ganis, Sidney *film company executive, former motion picture association executive*
Ganzi, Victor Frederick *former publishing executive*
Gartenberg, Seymour Lee *retired recording industry executive*
Gates, Susan Inez *magazine publisher*
Geffen, David Lawrence *film company executive*
Geldard, Richard Gordon *publisher, writer, retired philosophy educator*
George, Gerald William *editor, writer, administrator*
Gibbs, Dawn Ann *media specialist, educator*
Gill, Henry Herr *photojournalist*
Gipson, Melinda *publishing executive*
Glickman, Daniel Robert *motion picture association executive, former United States Secretary of Agriculture*
Goldsborough, Robert Gerald *publishing executive, author*
Goode, Stephen Hogue *publishing executive*
Gora, Susannah Porter Martin *journalist, poet*
Graham, Laurie *editor, writer*
Gralla, Lawrence *publishing company executive*
Grann, Phyllis E. *editor, former publisher executive*
Gray, Gordon L. *communications educator*
Green, Nancy Loughridge *publishing executive*
Green, Paul John *critic*
Greenhouse, Linda Joyce *journalist, educator*
Greenwald, John Edward *publishing executive, journalist*
Greenwood, William Warren *journalist*
Gregory, Bettina Louise *journalist*
Groskopf, Aubrey Bud *broadcast executive, lawyer*
Grushow, Sandy *broadcast executive*
Gulledge, Sandra Smith *publicist*
Gumbel, Bryant Charles *broadcaster*
Hagel, Raymond Charles *publishing company executive, educator*
Haile, L. John, Jr. *journalist, publishing executive*
Halfen, David *retired publishing executive*
Hall, Teresa Ruth *publishing executive*
Ham, Sommy L. *publisher, writer*
Hamill, (William) Pete *newspaper columnist, author, editor*
Hanley, Joan *media specialist*
Hardcastle, Marcia E. (Marcia E. Temme) *retired journalist*
Harlech, Pamela *journalist*
Harmon, Lynn Astrid *announcer, writer*
Hartzell, Pam L. *media specialist*
Harwell, William Earnest (Ernie Harwell) *retired commentator*
Hatfield, Julie Stockwell *journalist*
Hays, Robert William *retired communications educator, writer*
Heaphy, Janis Besler *retired publishing executive*
Hedberg, Paul Clifford *broadcast executive*
Hefner, Christie Ann *former publishing executive*
Henry, Barbara Ann *retired publishing executive*
Herguth, Robert John *retired columnist*
Hering, Doris Minnie *dance critic*
Hermodson, Amy E. *communications educator*
Hey, Robert Pierpont *retired editor*
Heyward, Andrew John *former broadcast executive*
Hiller, David Dean *former publishing executive*
Hinshaw, Edward Banks *retired broadcast executive*
Hirsch, George Aaron *publishing executive*
Hobson, Jade *journalist, consultant*
Holdridge, Barbara *recording and book consultant, editor*
Holland, David Thurston *former editor*
Horn, Lee Shawn *sports analyst*
Hough, Jason Wayne *communication educator*
House, Karen Elliott *former publishing executive, editor, journalist*
Hubley, Reginald Allen *publishing executive*
Hunt, Arthur William *communications educator*
Huston, Margo *journalist*
Idaszak, Jerome Joseph *economic journalist*
Ienner, Donald S. *former recording industry executive*
Impoco, Jim *editor*
Ismach, Arnold Harvey *retired journalism educator*
Ivey, Denise Hassell *publishing executive*
Jacobson, Louis Alan *journalist*
Jain, Geetika Pathania *communications educator*
James, Bruce Richard *publishing executive*
Johnson, John *broadcast journalist, artist*
Johnson, William Potter *publishing executive, director*
Jones, Joe Kenley *journalist*
Jordan, Marvin Evans, Jr. *record company executive, vocalist, actor, composer*
Joseph, Michael Thomas *broadcast consultant*
Juran, Sylvia Louise *retired editor*
Kamin, Blair Douglass *architecture critic*
Karalekas, Anne *media executive*
Karol, Michael Alan *editor*
Keller, Sarah Natasha *communications educator*
Kemraj, Bharati S. *reporter, television producer*
Kiel, Jeff E. *former publishing executive*
Kilpatrick, James Jackson, Jr. *retired columnist, retired writer*
King, Robert Thomas *editor, writer*
Kisor, Henry Du Bois *retired editor, columnist, critic, writer*
Klaviter, Helen Lothrop *magazine editor, retired*
Klemens, Thomas Lloyd *editor*
Koch, Patricia W. *media specialist*
Koltun, Frances Lang *editor, publisher, broadcaster*
Koren, Edward Benjamin *cartoonist, educator*
Kosner, Edward A(lan) *editor*
Koten, John F. *editor-in-chief*
Kotz, Nathan Kallison (Nick Kotz) *news correspondent, author*
Krulitz, Leo Morrion *retired business executive, director*
Laidlaw, Robert Richard *retired publishing executive*
Lamont, Lee *retired music company and communications executive*
Landau, Jon *music producer, manager*
Langer, Ralph Ernest *journalist, retired editor*
Lape, Robert Cable *broadcast journalist*
Larkin, Michael John *editor, journalist*
Laurence, Michael Marshall *retired editor*
Lavine, Alan *columnist, writer*

Laybourne, Geraldine B. (Geraldine Bond) *retired broadcast executive*
LeBrecht, Thelma Jane Mossman *retired reporter*
Leidel, Katherine *journalist, newscaster*
Lelyveld, Joseph Salem *former newspaper editor, news correspondent, writer*
Levey, Robert Frank *columnist, not-for-profit fundraiser*
Lewis, Anthony *columnist, educator*
Lewis, Robert Enzer *editor, educator*
Liberman, Gail Jeanne *editor*
Lieberfarb, Warren N. *digital media pioneer*
Lingle, Marilyn Felkel *journalist, columnist, writer*
Lipkind, Lynne *publishing executive, educator*
Lipson, Allen S. *former entertainment company executive, lawyer*
Lloyd, Michael Jeffrey *recording producer*
Lolo, Eduardo Calixto *writer, journalist, educator*
Loper, James Leaders *broadcasting executive*
Lucier, P. Jeffrey *publishing executive*
Lundberg, George David, II, *medical editor-in-chief, pathologist*
Lynne, Michael *film company executive*
Madden, John *retired sportscaster, retired professional football coach*
Maharidge, Dale Dimitro *journalist, educator, writer*
Main, Robert Gail *communications educator, training services executive, television and film producer, retired military officer*
Majeed, D. Hadayai S. *publishing executive, writer*
Malloy, Michael Terrence *journalist, reporter*
Manley, Joan A(dele) Daniels *retired publishing executive*
Marcus, Greil Gerstley *critic*
Marmer, Nancy *editor*
Marro, Anthony James *retired newspaper editor*
Marsh, Joan Knight *educational film company executive, video company executive, publishing executive*
Masih, Tara Lynn *book editor, writer*
Masket, Edward Seymour *television executive*
Mathews, Jack Wayne *journalist, film critic*
Matthews, Rondra J. *publishing executive*
Mayer, Alisande Fountain *media specialist*
Mazzilli, Lee *sportscaster, former professional baseball manager*
McAniff, Nora P. *former publishing executive*
McFarling, Usha Lee *journalist*
McFeatters, Ann Carey *journalist*
McGuirk, Terrence *former broadcasting company executive*
McGurk, Christopher Jamie *film company executive*
Mc Keown, William Taylor *magazine editor, author*
McLaughlin, Leighton Bates, II, *retired journalist, reporter, educator*
McManus, Jason Donald *retired editor-in-chief*
McManus, Patrick Francis *editor, educator, writer*
Mears, Walter Robert *retired journalist*
Medavoy, Mike (Morris Mike Medavoy) *film company executive, producer*
Mellott, John C. *retired publishing executive*
Melody, Michael Edward *publishing company executive*
Menaker, Daniel *former publishing executve, television producer*
Meriwether, Heath J. *newspaper consultant, retired publisher, educator*
Mestres, Ricardo A. III *film company executive*
Meyer, Philip Edward *journalism educator*
Meyer, Pucci *editor*
Miles, Frank Charles *retired newspaper executive*
Miller, Donald LeSessne *publishing executive*
Miller, Norman Charles, Jr. *editor, reporter*
Mills, Dale Douglas *journalist*
Min, Janice Byung *former editor-in-chief*
Mondlin, Marvin *publisher, appraiser, consultant*
Montgomery, Cliff Wilson *journalist, writer, researcher*
Moon, Craig A. *retired publishing executive*
Mooney, Ted (Edward Comstock Mooney) *editor, art critic, writer*
Moore, Thomas Paul *retired broadcast executive*
Moran, Kevin J. *publishing operations director*
Morgan, Anne Marie G. *broadcast journalist, educator*
Morgan, Betsy L. *former publishing executive*
Moss, Madison Scott *retired editor*
Mottola, Tommy (Thomas Daniel Mottola) *recording industry executive*
Moyano, Marcela *communications educator*
Muller, Henry James *journalist, magazine editor*
Myrth, Judy G. *retired editor*
Nachman, Gerald Weil *columnist, critic, writer*
Neff, Donald Lloyd *news correspondent, writer*
Neufeld, Mace *film company executive*
Newman, Edwin Harold *news commentator*
Newman, Rachel *editor*
Norman, Christina *broadcast executive*
Novick, Julius Lerner *theater critic, educator*
Nurnberg, Charles Gordon *publishing executive*
Nye, Dorothy Mae *freelance journalist, educator*
Oakley, Andrew Arthur *journalist, educator*
Obermayer, Herman Joseph *newspaper publisher*
O'Brien, Timothy Andrew *journalist, writer, lawyer, educator*
Ochs, Michael *editor, librarian, music educator*
Olive, David Michael *journalist, editor*
Olson, Peter W. *former publishing executive*
Oppedahl, John Frederick *newspaper publisher, executive*
Ortner, Bonnie *media specialist, librarian*
O'Shea, James E. *former editor-in-chief*
Pace, Eric Dwight *retired journalist*
Packer, Billy *former sports announcer*
Pakenham, Rosalie Muller Wright *magazine and newspaper editor*
Parker, Mel *editor*
Parkyn, John William *editor, writer, columnist*
Parrish, David Walker, Jr. *retired legal publishing company executive*
Paul, Kenneth *newspaper editor*
Peacock, Mary Willa *magazine editor, consultant*
Perenchio, Andrew Jerrold *film and television executive*
Peres, Judith May *journalist*
Petzal, David Elias *retired editor, writer*
Phillips, Stone (Stone Stockton Phillips) *newscaster*
Picower, Warren Michael *editor*
Pletcher, Eldon *retired cartoonist*
Plotnick, Harvey Barry *publishing executive*
Poindexter, Mark Carey *university administrator communications educator, critic*
Poleway, Christopher J. *former publishing executive*
Pope, Katherine Collins *former broadcast executive*
Povich, Lynn *journalist, Internet executive, editor*
Powell, Ardal *music company executive, editor*
Preddy, Raymond Randall *retired newspaper publisher, educator*
Price, Tom *journalist*
Priest, Jessie Shaw *media specialist*
Pruden, Wesley (James Pruden) *retired editor*
Puris, Martin Ford *media company executive*
Quade, Vicki *editor, writer, theater producer*
Quinn, Charles Nicholas *journalist*
Randinelli, Tracey Anne *magazine editor*
Rapoport, Ronald Jon *journalist*
Rash, Wayne, Jr. *journalist*
Rasi, Humberto Mario *editor, educator*
Rasor, Dina Lynn *journalist, private investigator*
Rayner, William Alexander *retired newspaper editor, author*
Read, Richard Eaton *newspaper reporter*
Regan, Judith Terrance *former publishing executive*
Rein, Linda S. *broadcast executive*
Richman, Alan *magazine editor, educator*
Rieselman, Deborah Sue *editor*
Riggs, Michael David *editor, writer*
Righini, Marilou Mausteller *editor, consultant*
Roach, Margaret *former publishing executive*
Roberts, Edwin Albert, Jr. *editor, journalist*
Roberts, Margaret Harold *editor, publisher*
Roberts, Samuel Smith *television news executive*
Rockwell, John Sargent *critic, writer, former arts administrator*
Rodriguez, Rick *former executive editor*
Rollins, Edward J., Jr. *political commentator*
Romanos, Jack (John Romanos Jr.) *retired publishing executive*
Rooth, Signe Alice *editor, consultant*
Rosett, Daniel J. *film company executive*
Roth, Harvey Paul *retired publishing executive*
Rubenstein, Atoosa Behnegar *former editor-in-chief*
Rubin, Rick (Frederick Jay Rubin) *recording industry executive*
Sabbatini, Marcello *journalist, motor sports weekly director*
St. Amant, Kirk *communications educator*
Sanders, Marlene *news correspondent, journalism educator*
Sandoval, Rik (Charles Sandoval) *broadcast executive*
Sands, Rick (Richard Sands) *former film company executive*
Santisi, Terri M. (Theresa M. Santisi) *multimedia company executive*
Sapsowitz, Sidney H. *entertainment and media company executive*
Sarris, Andrew George *film critic*
Satz, Louis K. *publishing executive*
Saxon, Wolfgang Erik Georg *journalist, writer*
Scannell, Herb *broadcast executive*
Schachter, James Robert *editor*
Schmitt, William Gerard *writer, editor, magazine manager*
Schnapp, Diana Corley *communications educator*
Schorr, Daniel Louis *broadcast journalist, author, lecturer*
Schrand, Richard Henry, Sr. *broadcast executive, advertising bureau owner, educator*
Schurenberg, Eric P. *magazine editor*
Seals, Margaret Louise Crumrine *retired journalist*
Seigenthaler, John Lawrence *retired newspaper executive*
Seligman, Nicole Kay *broadcast executive, lawyer*
Seminara, Lynda Anne *editor*
Servodidio, Pat Anthony *broadcast executive*
Serwatka, Walter Dennis *publishing executive*
Shapiro-Mathes, Angela *former broadcast executive*
Shaw, Eleanor Jane *newspaper editor*
Shaye, Robert Kenneth *film company executive*
Shedaker, Kathleen Edith *publishing executive*
Shelton, Stephani *broadcast journalist, consultant*
Siegal, Allan Marshall *journalist, consultant*
Siegel, Ira T. *retired publishing executive*
Sifton, David Whittier *retired magazine editor*
Silvey, Anita Lynne *editor*
Simmons, Russell *recording industry executive*
Simon, Peter E. *publishing executive*
Simonson, Lee Stuart *broadcast executive*
Simpson, Hugh L. *news correspondent, newswriter*
Sinclair, Carole *publishing executive, editor*
Singer, Dale *reporter, editor*
Sischy, Ingrid Barbara *editor, art critic*
Sites, Kevin *news correspondent, journalist, web blogger*
Smith, A. Robert *editor, author*
Smith, George Drury *publishing executive*
Smith, Liz (Mary Elizabeth Smith) *columnist, newscaster*
Smith, Martin Bernhard *retired journalist*
Smith, Richard Alan *publishing and specialty retailing executive*
Smith, Scott Clybourn *retired publishing executive*
Smyntek, John Eugene, Jr. *editor*
Snader, Jack Ross *retired publishing company executive*
Soeteber, Ellen *journalist, editor*
Solá, Victoria M. *announcer, writer*
Spanfeller, James John, Jr. *former publishing executive*
Spence, James Robert, Jr. *broadcast executive, educator, mediator*
Stanley, Scott, Jr. *editor*
Stauderman, Albert Philip, Jr. *media production consultant*
Stephens, Edward Carl *communications educator, writer*
Stephenson, Toni Edwards *publishing, internet domain communications and investment company executive*
Stern, Kenneth P. *former broadcast executive, information technology executive*
Stiff, Robert Martin *newspaper editor*
Strothman, James Edward *editor-in-chief*
Stuart, Nancy Rubin (Nancy Zimman Stetson) *journalist, author, television producer*
Sullivan, Daniel Joseph *theater critic*
Sutton-Straus, Joan M. *journalist*
Switzer, Maurice Harold *journalist*
Tammeus, William David *journalist, columnist*
Tassler, Nina *broadcast executive*
Tata, Giovanni *publishing executive*
Taylor, LaVonne Troy *editor*
Terry, Clifford Lewis *journalist*
Teutsch, Clifford L. *editor-in-chief*
Tharpe, Frazier Eugene *journalist*
Thiessen, Marc A. *journalist, former federal official*
Thomas, Sean Michael *journalist, writer*
Thompson, Martin Christian *retired news executive*
Thompson, Susan A. *communications educator*
Thornton, Thomas Noel *former publishing executive*
Toay, Thelma M. *columnist, poet*
Tobin, James Edward *communications educator, writer*
Turek, Sonia Fay *journalist*
Turnley, David Carl *photojournalist*
Twigg-Smith, Thurston *newspaper publisher*
Ulevich, Neal Hirsh *photojournalist*
Vanbiesbrouck, John Robert *hockey analyst, retired professional hockey player*
Vaughan, Samuel Snell *editor, writer, publishing executive*
Vega, Edwin Salvador *media specialist, educator*
Viegas, Jennifer *journalist, writer*
Vieth, Christopher W. *former publishing executive*
Villalobos, Ligiah *former international programming manager, film producer, scriptwriter*
Vitale, Ruth Ann *former film company executive*
Wagman, Robert John *journalist, writer*
Wagner, Paula *film company executive*
Waldmeir, Peter Nielsen *retired journalist*
Walker, Fred Elmer *broadcast executive*
Wallace, Mike (Myron Leon Wallace) *newscaster, television personality*
Walling, Donovan Robert *editor, writer*
Waltz, Kathleen M. *former publishing executive*
Watson, George Henry, Jr. *broadcaster, journalist*
Weaver, Franklin Thomas *retired newspaper executive*
Weeks, Brigitte *publishing executive*
Weinberg, Teri Ellen *former broadcast executive*
Weissman, Jack (George Anderson) *retired editor*
Welsh, Dorothy Dell *columnist, writer*
Welsome, Eileen *journalist, writer*
Werman, Thomas Ehrlich *record producer*
Whipple, Judith Roy *retired editor*
Whitesell, John Edwin *retired motion picture company executive*
Whittell, Polly (Mary K.) *editor, journalist*
Wiessler, David Albert *news correspondent*
Williamson, Thomas Arnold *publishing executive*
Windhauser, John William *retired journalism educator, consultant*
Witcover, Jules Joseph *columnist, writer*
Witt, Melvin Sylvan *periodical editor, publisher*
Wixen, Joan Saunders *journalist*
Wodlinger, Mark Louis *broadcast executive*
Woldt, Harold Frederick, Jr. *newspaper publishing executive*
Woodruff, Judy Carline *broadcast journalist*
Woodruff, Virginia *broadcast journalist, writer*
Wren, Casey Leigh *broadcast technician, department chairman*
Young, Nerissa Ann *journalist*
Young, Patrick *editor, writer*
Zahn, Paula *newscaster*
Zappe, John Paul *city editor, newspaper executive, educator*
Zerman, Melvyn Bernard *retired publishing executive, writer*
Zimmerman, Debbie *communications educator*
Zimmerman, William Edwin *editor, writer*
Zulker, Charles Bates *broadcasting company executive*
Zweifel, Donald Edwin *editor, lobbyist, consultant*

EDUCATION *See also* specific fields for postsecondary education

UNITED STATES

ALABAMA

Alabaster
McChesney, Robert Michael, Sr. *retired academic administrator*

Athens
Glenn, Robert Kyle *academic administrator*
Smith, Patricia Crawford *elementary school educator*

Auburn
Galbraith, Ruth Legg *retired dean, home economist*
Groccia, James Edward *education educator*
Miller, Wilbur Randolph *academic administrator*
Zallen, Harold *academic administrator, chemist*

Auburn University
Evans, R. Lee *dean*
Gogue, Jay (G. Jay Gogue) *academic administrator*
Strom, Paris Scott *education educator*

Bay Minette
Hollinger, Faron Lavaughn *school system administrator*

Bessemer
Garlikov, Patricia Moodie *education educator*
Stringfellow, Mary Willingham *mathematics educator*

Birmingham
Berte, Neal Richard *academic administrator*
Deal, William Brown *medical school dean, physician, educator*
Donmoyer, Jay Frank *retired private school educator*
Mc Callum, Charles Alexander *academic administrator*
McKinley, Cameron Sharbel *elementary school educator*
Moorer, Douglass Charles *educator*
Morgan, Kathryn Diane *criminology educator*
Pollick, G. David *academic administrator, philosopher*
Rich, Robert Regier *academic administrator, immunologist, medical educator*
Solomon, Gloria Lee *educational consultant*
Westmoreland, Andrew *academic administrator*
Wilson, Tracey L. *biology educator*

Brilliant
Franks, Gracie G. *elementary school educator*

Citronelle
Surry, Melinda Owen *reading coach*

Clanton
Tidwell, Betty Davenport *special education educator*

Coosada
Reynolds, Linda Ann *elementary school educator*

Crossville
Blessing, Maxine Lindsey *secondary school educator*

Cullman
Ivey, Mona Kay *secondary school educator, association administrator, consultant*

Decatur
Julich, Nancy C. *secondary school educator*
Smith, Trina *academic administrator*

Dothan
Fleming, Jennie M *retired education educator*
Flowers, V. Anne *retired academic administrator*
Jones, Sandra Lee *retired dean*
Phillips, Kenneth Edward *history educator, writer*
Thomas, Shannon Lawson *academic administrator, educator*

Eclectic
Tracy, Patricia Ann Koop *secondary school educator*

Eufaula
Conniff, Alexandra Acosta *secondary school educator*

Florence
Cale, William Graham, Jr. *university administrator, environmental sciences educator, researcher*
Reynolds, Celia Robinson *academic librarian, educator*

Fultondale
Taylor, Patricia Nail *mathematics and science educator*

Gadsden
Reynolds, Sharon Jones *elementary school educator*

Hamilton
Barnes, Judith Ann *director, educator*

Hanceville
Holmes, Kristen Jones *academic administrator*

Helena
Coulter, Fern Goshen *retired secondary school educator*

Huntsville
Baird, James Kern *educator, consultant, academic administrator*
Hawley, Harold Patrick *educational consultant*
Lundquist, Charles Arthur *academic administrator*
Ratchford Merchant, Betty Jo *retired elementary school educator*
Turner, Mary Alice *curriculum specialist*

Jasper
Sparkman, Brandon Buster *educator, consultant, writer*

Leeds
Wilson, Maggie Isabelle Lovell *secondary school educator*

Livingston
Green, Asa Norman *academic administrator*

Madison
Brannan, Eulie Ross *educational consultant*
Jones, Christine Regina *secondary school educator*
Petty, Margaret *elementary school educator*

Marion
Cleveland, Willie Mae *elementary school educator*

Maylene
Copes, Marvin Lee *academic administrator*

Mobile
Copeland, Lewis *principal*
Crowell, Tangie Michelle *elementary school educator*
Franks, Ronald Dwyer *dean, psychiatrist, educator*

Giles, Rebecca McMahon *education educator*
Phan, Anh-Vu *adult education educator, researcher*
Smith, Anne Sisson *private school educator*

Montgomery
Gravatt, Lincoln Edmund *history educator*
Kennedy, Kamela Denise *director*
King, Andrea S. *secondary school educator*
Luce, Dena Lahue *university librarians*
May, Cecil Richard, Jr. *academic administrator*
Tennimon, Dannie Earl *academic administrator, educator*
Wortham, Joycelyn Foy *education specialist*

Moody
Brasher, Terrie Walker *secondary school educator*
Sublett, Sherry Lake *junior high school educator*

Northport
Burry-Stock, Judith Anne (Anne Burry) *education educator*

Slocomb
Vikcers, Tom M. *secondary school educator*

Troy
Davidson, Barry Sheldon *academic administrator, comparative and adult education educator*
Kline, John Alvin *distinguished professor of leadership*
Schubert, Donna Clark *public relations educator, professional society administrator*

Tuscaloosa
Fields, Ruth Kinniebrew *secondary and elementary educator, consultant*
McNealey, Ernest *college president*
Randall, Kenneth C. *dean, law educator*
Taaffe, James Griffith *retired academic administrator, educator*
Thomas, Joab Langston *retired academic administrator, biologist, educator*
Witt, Robert E. *academic administrator*
Wright, Darrell Dean *educator*

Tuskegee
Green, Elbert P. *retired academic administrator*
White, Mildred Virginia *secondary school educator, retired counseling administrator*

Tuskegee Institute
Sumbry, Jo Ann *academic administrator, educator*

ALASKA

Anchorage
Byrd, Milton Bruce *academic administrator*
Comeau, Carol Smith *school system administrator*
Sandberg, Arlene *elementary school educator*
Sellers, Sheila Renea *special education educator*
Ulmer, Frances Ann *academic administrator, retired state official*

Auke Bay
Waldrip, Karen Marie *career planning administrator*

Chiniak
Griffin, Elaine B. *educator*

Dillingham
Bouker, Ina B. *elementary school educator*

Eagle River
Sparks, Jack Norman *dean*

Fairbanks
Doran, Timothy Patrick *academic administrator*
Hamilton, Mark R. *academic administrator*
Jones, Stephen B. *academic administrator*

Valdez
Devens, John Searle *natural resources administrator*

Wrangell
Miller, Jennifer L. *elementary school educator, small business owner*

ARIZONA

Anthem
Hagerty, George James III *former academic administrator, educator, consultant*

Buckeye
Brown, Kyle Daniel *elementary school principal*

Chandler
Casteel, Camille *school system administrator*
Penley, Larry Edward *former academic administrator, finance educator*

Chinle
Hodson, William David *elementary school educator, consultant*

Coolidge
Schiller, Marjorie A. *special education professor*

Desert Hills
Evans, Carol Ann *reading specialist*

Florence
Brahms, Katheryn Ann *early childhood educator*

Fountain Hills
Wright, C. T. Enus *former academic administrator*

Glendale
Flanigan, Sean *education educator, coach*
Gutierrez, Michael Edward *elementary school educator, department chairman*
Heathcotte, Toby Fesler *retired educator, writer*
Smelser, Philip Sidney *history educator*

Green Valley
Smith, Raymond Lloyd *former university president, consultant*

Lakeside
Seely, Dennis M. *secondary school educator*

Mesa
Duvall, Debra *school system administrator*

Page
Hoodenpyle, Sandra Kay *elementary school educator*

Peoria
Jenkins, Carol Anne *educator*

Phoenix
Cook, Michael David *academic administrator, director*
Covey, Donald David *school system administrator*
Edwards, Vicki Ann *director, consultant*
Frehner, Patricia Ann *education educator, consultant*
Halford, Sharon Lee *academic administrator, educational consultant*
Hudson, Karen G. *special education educator*
Lee, Barbara S. *special education educator*
McConnell, Albert Lynn *dean of education*
Peralta, Everett Figueroa *college professor, department chairman*
Schrader, Susan Rae *elementary school educator*
Sperling, John Glen *educational services company executive*
White, Danny Levius *counselor, consultant, educator*

Pinetop
Gilbert-Tiegs, Marion Ann *gifted and talented educator, consultant*

Prescott
Newton, Ray C. *university official*
Sandum, Allan Ira *retired biology educator*
Slominski, Elena Gregoryevna *mathematics educator*

Rio Verde
Vanselow, Neal Arthur *retired academic administrator, internist*

San Luis
Kryger, Jerri Renee *elementary school educator*

Scottsdale
Bruhn, John Glyndon *retired university provost and dean*
Hill, Louis Allen, Jr. *retired dean, civil engineer, consultant*
Jenkins, Charles Franklin *educator*
Phillips, Wanda Charity *secondary school educator, writer*
Stone, Alan Jay *retired academic administrator*

Sun Lakes
Dean, Charles Thomas *industrial arts educator, academic administrator*
Thompson, Loring Moore *retired academic administrator, writer*

Surprise
Bradford, Mariah *elementary school educator, consultant*
Burns, Clare Marie *retired elementary school educator*
Hosmer, Eileen Gaylord *special education educator*
Rosenbaum, Mary Louise *elementary school educator*

Tempe
Crow, Michael M. *academic administrator*
Dustman, Patricia (Jo) Allen *elementary school educator, consultant*
Haggerson, Nelson Lionel, Jr. *education educator*
Milke, Linda Jean *elementary school educator*
Mittelstaedt, Robert E., Jr. *dean*
Rivers, Patrick A. *education educator, researcher*
Schiff Berman, Paul *dean, law educator*
Tabbara, Hadi *director, researcher*
Thor, Linda M. *college president*
Volek, Emil *educator*
Zucker, Stanley Howard *special education educator*

Thatcher
Bapat, Madhuri R. *physics educator*

Tsaile
Vecenti, Gene Ortizio Juanajillo Alitizar *educator*

Tucson
Aiello, Antonio J. *education educator*
Bootman, J. Lyle *dean, pharmacy educator*
Celania-Fagen, Elizabeth *school system administrator*
Crist, William Miles *academic administrator, pediatrician, educator*
Dadante, Elizabeth Frances *history educator, cognitive coach*
Garner, Girolama Thomasina *retired educational administrator, educator*
Heywood, Stanley John *educator*
Johnson, John Gray *retired university chancellor*
Kaltenbach, C(arl) Colin *dean, educator*
Likins, Peter William *retired academic administrator*
Massaro, Toni Marie *retired dean, law educator*
Moten, Darlene *elementary school educator*
Nikolich-Zugich, Janko *biomedical scientist, educator*
Peterson, John Kenneth *elementary school educator*
Ponoroff, Lawrence *dean, law educator, consultant*
Popson, Lucy (Maria D. Popson) *elementary school educator*
Portney, Paul Rogers *dean*
Reff, Steven M. *economics educator*
Shelton, Robert Neal *academic administrator, physics professor, researcher*
Stoffle, Carla Joy *university library dean*
Thomson, Donald Arthur *education educator*

ARKANSAS

Arkadelphia
Dunn, Charles DeWitt *academic administrator*
Elrod, Ben Moody *academic administrator*
Grant, Daniel Ross *retired academic administrator*
Johnson, Trina Lynn *special education educator*
Woodall, Peggy Keaton *special education educator*

Batesville
McNamee, Kathleen Metzger *academic administrator*

Bentonville
Tuthill, John G. *academic administrator*
Zumwalt, Kenneth Wayne *assistant principal*

Blytheville
Thomasson, Emily *mathematics educator*

Camden
Gunnels, Robert D. *academic administrator*
Owen, Larry Gene *academic administrator, educator, electronics engineer, consultant*

Conway
Courtway, Thomas C. *academic administrator, former state legislator*
Harlan, Mary Hope *education educator, department chairman*
Meadors, Allen Coats *academic administrator, educator*
Spatz, Kenneth Chris(topher), Jr. *statistics educator*

Earle
Swift, Peggy Lynette *elementary school educator*

Fayetteville
Gearhart, G. David *academic administrator, education educator*
Kohler, Peter Ogden *retired academic administrator, internist, educator*
Nance, Cynthia Eleanor (Cyndi Nance) *dean, law educator*
Schoppmeyer, Martin William *education educator*
Schoppmeyer, Martin William, Jr. *school system administrator*
Smith, Robert Victor *academic administrator, educator*

Heber Springs
Stroud, Peggy *secondary school educator*

Hot Springs
Farris, Jefferson Davis *university administrator*

Jonesboro
Smith, Eugene Wilson *retired academic administrator, education educator*

Little Rock
Banks, Alicia *elementary school educator*
Bass, Evelyn Elizabeth *elementary school educator*
Calloway, Billie Jean *retired educator*
Fribourgh, James Henry *retired university administrator*
Geffken, Carolyn D. *special education educator*
Pennington, Jodie A. *education outreach educator*
Sugg, Barney Alan *academic administrator*
Truex, Dorothy Adine *retired university administrator*

Magnolia
Clark, James R. *secondary school educator, director*

Montrose
Bates, Jimmy W. *secondary school educator, director, minister*

Perryville
McCallister, Carolyn G. *secondary school educator*

Pine Bluff
Scott, Vicki Sue *retired school system administrator*

Rogers
Goff, Deborah Oleta *elementary school educator*

Russellville
Morris, Lois Lawson *retired education educator*

Searcy
Wood, Michael B. *principal*

Sherwood
Cantu, Jennifer St. John *gifted and talented educator*

Springdale
Holman, L. Charlene *elementary school educator*
Minkel, Justin *elementary school educator*

Texarkana
Petty, Marsha *chemistry educator*

CALIFORNIA

Agoura Hills
Stagg, Enid *educational consultant*

Alameda
Robinson, Joanne Adele *retired secondary school educator, volunteer*

Alhambra
Suzuki, Bob H. *retired academic administrator*

Anaheim
Goodspeed, Kathryn Ann *pre-school educator*
Unan, George Vincent *adult education educator*

Antioch
Stamm, Barbara Marie Anderson *elementary school educator, interior designer*

Apple Valley
Jackson, Betty Eileen *music and elementary school educator*

Aptos
Bohn, Ralph Carl *educational consultant*
Coe, Virginia L. *literature and language educator*

Arcadia
Matsuura, Kenneth Ray *counseling administrator*

Arcata
McCrone, Alistair William *retired academic administrator*
Wang, Rui *dean, educator*

Azusa
Aguilar, Gladys Maria *counselor, educator*
Harrell, Shelley Renee *school librarian*
Pacino, Maria Antonieta *education educator, department chairman*
Parham, Thomas David *education educator*

Bakersfield
Zarra, Ernest Joseph III *secondary school educator, researcher*

Beaumont
Youngren, Delvana Hope *secondary school educator*

Berkeley
Birgeneau, Robert Joseph *academic administrator, physicist, researcher*
Gray, Paul Russell *academic administrator, electrical engineering educator*
Hasegawa, Yoko *educator*
Heathcock, Clayton Howell *chemistry educator, researcher*
Kunanbaeva, Alma B. *history educator*
Linn, Marcia Cyrog *education educator*
McKenzie, Jean Hazel *academic librarian*
McPhail-Geist, Karin Ruth *secondary school educator, musician*
Raphael, Steven P. *dean, political science professor*
Richards, Mark A. *dean, earth and planetary science professor*
Steigmann, David John *professor*

Beverly Hills
Grant, Michael Ernest *educational administrator, management educator*

Big Bear Lake
Mix, Jill Kaye *secondary school educator, artist*

Bloomington
Lawrence, William, Jr. *retired elementary school educator*

Blythe
Wells, James Wayne *retired secondary school educator*

Brawley
Kinder, Joseph Donald *retired principal*

Burbank
Ballew, Pat *elementary school educator*
Nielsen, Kenneth Ray *academic administrator*

Burlingame
Villavicencio, José Antonio *secondary school educator*

Calabasas
Hawkins, John N. *education educator, writer*

Camarillo
David, Marie M. *pre-school educator*
Moffett, Kenneth Lee *superintendent*
Rush, Richard R. *academic administrator*
Wakelee, Daniel William *academic administrator*

Capitola
Jackson, Kingsbury Temple *educational and financial consultant*

Carlsbad
Golden, Paula Englander *psychology social work and addiction educator, consultant*

Carmel
Freed, Sharon Lou *retired principal*

Carmichael
Friedman, Mary Kathleen *secondary school educator*

Carson
Paige, Dorothy Billiard *consultant-academic coach*

Chico
Zingg, Paul Joseph *academic administrator*

Chino Hills
Wood, Terri Lynn *secondary school educator*

Claremont
Alexander, John David, Jr. *college administrator*
Benjamin, Beverly Paschke *retired education educator*
Bettison-Varga, Lori *academic administrator, geologist, educator*
Gann, Pamela Brooks *academic administrator*
Kerchner, Charles Taylor *educator*
Klawe, Maria Margaret *academic administrator, engineering and computer science educator*
O'Kelly, Crystal Kathleen *secondary school educator, television producer*
Oxtoby, David William *academic administrator, chemistry professor*
Platt, Joseph Beaven *former college president*
Skandera Trombley, Laura Elise *academic administrator, literature educator*
Strauss, Jon Calvert *retired academic administrator*

Clayton
Bower, Fay Louise *academic administrator, nursing educator*

Clovis
Miner, Craig Alan *special education educator*

Costa Mesa
Triggs, Ray Ellis, Jr. *history educator*

Covina
Baker, Elenora Frances *retired elementary school educator*

Culver City
Thomas, Geraldine Hoge *elementary school educator*

Cupertino
Podolny, Joel M. *academic administrator, management educator, former dean*

Cypress
Mosqueda-Ponce, Therese *counselor, professor*

Danville
Harks, Helene Louise *elementary school educator*

Davis
Currall, Steven C. *dean, management educator*
Johnson, Kevin Raymond *dean, law educator*
Katehi, Linda P.B. *academic administrator, engineering educator*
Kraft, Rosemarie *dean, educator*
Pritchard, William Roy *former university systems administrator*
Springer, Sally Pearl *university administrator*
Tanno, John W. *university librarian*

Denair
Hale, Lois J. *retired mathematics educator*

Downey
Meysenburg, Mary Ann *principal*
Robles, Darline P. *school system administrator*

El Cajon
Thomas, Esther Merlene *elementary and adult education educator*
Tuttle, Sandia Lou DeWaide *literature and language educator*

El Cerrito
Herzberg, Dorothy Crews *retired secondary school educator*

El Dorado Hills
Tierney, Kevin Allen *elementary school educator*

Encino
Silva, Carole *elementary school educator*

Escondido
Carlson, Mary Lou *elementary school educator, sister*
Sanders, Adrian Lionel *retired educational consultant*
Walker, Patricia Ann *special education educator*

Fair Oaks
Hutton, Essex Clark, Sr. *adult education educator*

Fairfield
Forssell, Linda Lee *secondary school educator, illustrator*
Kirkorian, Donald George *retired academic administrator*
Mary, Diane Bradley *elementary school educator, secondary school educator*
Williams, Lena Rose *academic administrator*

Fillmore
Orozco, Marc Peter *secondary school educator*

Fremont
Brown, Michael Gene *vice principal*
Peebles, Lucretia Neal Drane *education educator*
Venturini, Judith Anne *education educator*

Fresno
Genini, Ronald Walter *retired history educator*
Girvin, Shirley Eppinette *retired elementary school educator, journalist*
Misakian, Jo Ellen Priest *school librarian*
Tudman, Cathi Graves *elementary school educator*

Fullerton
Donoghue, Mildred Ransdorf *education educator*
Fischer, Robert Blanchard *academic administrator, researcher*
Jensen, Robert Russell *dean, consultant*
Smith, Ephraim Philip *academic administrator*

Goleta
Everhart, Thomas Eugene *retired academic administrator, engineering educator*

Granada Hills
Silver, Vanessa Marie *educational therapist, consultant*

Hayward
Garcia, Melva Ybarra *counseling administrator, educator*
Kwon, Myoung-ja Lee *retired academic librarian*
Rees, Norma S. *academic administrator*

Healdsburg
Flores-Deras, Ever J. *counseling administrator*

Hemet
Monk, Sharon Anne *special education educator*

Hughson
Hailey, Kathleen Wilson *elementary school educator*

Huntington Beach
Houck, Aleda Jean *dean*
Ramphal, Julie Frances *retired secondary school educator*

Indio
Houghton, Robert Charles *secondary school educator*

Irvine
Bras, Rafael Luis *dean, engineering educator*
Chemerinsky, Erwin *dean, law educator*
Drake, Michael V. *academic administrator, ophthalmologist, educator*
Fleischer, Everly Borah *academic administrator, department chairman*
Jorion, Philippe *education educator*
Munoff, Gerald J. *university librarian*
Policano, Andrew J. *dean, finance educator*
Sexton, Jared *African American studies professor*

Kelseyville
Berry, John Joseph *educational administrator*

La Jolla
Atkinson, Richard Chatham *academic administrator, cognitive scientist*
Brenner, David Allen *academic administrator, medical educator*
Colbert, James, Jr. *academic administrator, educator, pharmacist*
Gabay, Janis T. *literature and language educator*
Kay, Steve A. *dean, molecular biologist, educator*
Miller, David R. *academic administrator*
Pound, Glenn Simpson *university dean*
Ries, Andrew *dean, educator*
Schottlaender, Brian E.C. *university librarian*
Sullivan, Robert S. *college dean*
Topol, Eric Jeffrey *academic administrator, cardiologist, educator, geneticist*

La Mirada
Burke, Peggy A. *education educator*
Weathers, Matthew *educator*

La Puente
Chico, Darlene Ehrich *elementary school educator*
Pleitez, Concepcion Maria *elementary school educator*
Ver Kuilen, Marion Jane *retired instructional aide*

La Quinta
Puente, Maria Luz *bilingual educator*

La Verne
Fleck, Raymond Anthony, Jr. *retired academic administrator*
Morgan, Stephen Charles *academic administrator*

Ladera Ranch
Skidmore, Michelle Marie *elementary school educator, principal*

Laguna Beach
Fry, Edward Bernard *retired education educator*

Lancaster
Dumas, Louise Isabelle *elementary school educator*
Jones, Betty Ann *retired elementary school educator*

Lawndale
Robinson, Mary Beth *educational administrator*

Lemoore
Krend, William John *secondary school educator*

Live Oak
Spilman, Janet Lynne *special education educator*

Lodi
Reinold, Christy Diane *school counselor, consultant*

Loma Linda
Carter, Ronald *academic administrator*

Long Beach
Alexander, F. King *academic administrator*
Amouzegar, Mahyar *dean, systems analyst*
Burnett, Ella M. Glenn *education educator*
Duran, Matias Martin *retired adult education educator*
Elston, Joan Wilma *adult education educator, real estate agent*
Fenton, Gayle B. *academic administrator*
Fleming, Jane Williams *retired elementary school educator, writer*
Jeynes, William Hettich *education educator, religious organization administrator, minister*
Lathrop, Irvin Tunis *retired dean*
Murray, John Patrick *education educator*
Springer, Wilma Marie *retired elementary school educator*

Los Angeles
Allums, Henriene *elementary school educator*
Ansley, Julia E. *retired elementary school educator, poet, writer*
Armstrong, Lloyd, Jr. *academic administrator, physics professor*
Bice, Scott Haas *dean, law educator*
Brown, Deborah Ellen *gifted and talented educator, writer*
Burcham, David W. *academic administrator, law educator*
Caywood, KayDee *special education educator*
Chapman Collins, Janice *school system administrator*
Cheeseboro, Margrit *retired economics educator*
Colacurcio, Michael J. *English professor*
Davis-Fernandes, Tina Denise *secondary school educator, coach*
Dewey, Donald Odell *dean, academic administrator*
Donner, Neal Arvid *educator*
Dunkel Schetter, Christine *psychology educator*
Dutta, Shantanu *dean*
Erdos, Joanna E. *school counselor, secondary school educator*
Ghez, Andrea Mia *astronomy and physics educator*
Gilliam, Franklin D., Jr. *dean, political science professor*
Gold, Victor J. *dean, academic administrator, law educator*
Gothold, Stuart Eugene *school system administrator, education educator*
Guarnieri, Roberta Jean *elementary school educator, consultant*
Gubera, Jon Christien *secondary school educator*
Haley, Roslyn Trezevant *educational program director*
Herscher, Uri David *academic administrator, history educator, rabbi*
Hill, Millicent E. *English educator*
Hoi, Samuel Chuen-Tsung *academic administrator*
Hubbard, John Randolph *retired academic administrator, diplomat*
Kleingartner, Archie *dean, educator, academic administrator*
Knott, Jack H. *dean, political science professor*
Legohn, Lisa Marie *vocational school educator*
Lyder, Courtney Harvey *dean, nursing educator*
Lynch, Beverly Pfeifer *education and information studies educator*
McGregor, Judith Ann *education educator*
McKinney, Virginia Elaine Zuccaro *educational administrator*
Mentzer, Roslyn *academic administrator*
Morisky, Donald E. *director, medical educator*
Moriuchi, K. Derek *secondary school educator*
Needleman, Jack *education educator, researcher*
Olian, Judy D. *dean, management educator*
Puliafito, Carmen Anthony *dean, ophthalmologist, healthcare executive*
Rasmussen, Robert Kenneth *dean, law educator*
Rivera, John Zarate *director*
Sample, Steven Browning *academic administrator*
Schill, Michael H. *dean, law educator*
Shideler, Ross Patrick *literature and language educator, writer, translator, poet*
Skotheim, Robert Allen *retired academic administrator, educator*
Strong, Gary Eugene *university librarian*
Tigue, William Bernard *adult education educator*
Tribble, Denise Hall *registrar*
Vanderveen, R. Pete (Randall L. Vanderveen) *dean, pharmacist, educator*
Veitch, Jonathan *academic administrator*
Vredevoe, Donna Lou *academic administrator, microbiologist, educator, biomedical researcher*
Wagner, William Gerard *dean, information scientist, consultant, physicist, investment manager*
Wakimoto, Roger Masao *meteorology educator, researcher*
Waterman, Christopher *dean*
Wexler, Robert *academic administrator*
Whalen, Lucille *retired academic administrator*

Los Gatos
Rachlin, Jeanne-Marie *mathematics educator*

Lynwood
Sitomer, Alan Lawrence *literature and language educator*

Malibu
Benton, Andrew Keith *academic administrator, lawyer*
Phillips, Ronald Frank *academic administrator*
Starr, Kenneth Winston *dean, law educator, lawyer*
Warder, Michael Young *academic administrator*

Menifee
Balow, Irving Henry *retired education educator*

Menlo Park
Chapin, June Roediger *education educator*

Merced
Tomlinson-Keasey, Carol Ann *academic administrator*

Milpitas
Allen, Irma M. *adult education educator*

Mission Viejo
Lake, Jane Burford *retired special education educator, hypnotherapist, small business owner*

Modesto
Brown, Candy Lee *elementary school educator*

Monterey
Cornish, Bonita Clark *retired secondary school educator*
Opperman, Rosanna Resendez *vice principal*

Moraga
Thier, Herbert David *director, retired academic administrator*

Moreno Valley
Bajor, Renee Allyson *special education educator*
Marshall, Debra Lynn *secondary school educator*
Phillips-Brown, Exa *educator*

Moss Landing
Williams, Phyllis Eleanor *retired educator*

Napa
Stauffer, Thomas Michael *university president*

National City
Caruana, Sean David *education educator*

North Hills
Deets, Richard M. *secondary school educator, consultant*

North Hollywood
Chang, Wung *academic administrator, investment advisor, educator*

Northridge
Afifi, Marianne H. *dean*
Mitchell, James Andrew *education educator*
Nama, Adilifu *educator*
O'Sullivan, Donal *educator*
Rowlands, Kathleen Dudden *education educator*

Novato
Lane, Michele Jeanne *special education educator*
Patterson, W. Morgan *college president*

Oakland
Brock, Theresa Jean (Terry) *retired elementary school educator*
Diaz, Sharon *education administrator*
Greer, Sandra Charlene *academic administrator, chemistry professor*
Griffin, Betty Jo *elementary school educator*
Yudof, Mark George *academic administrator, law educator*

Oceanside
Daniel, Susan Qualls *secondary school educator*

Ojai
Shagam, Marvin Hückel-Berri *private school educator*

Olivehurst
Green, Tim M. *mathematics educator*

Orange
Kraft, Arthur *dean*
Machan, Tibor Richard *college professor, newspaper columnist*
Post, Barbara J. *retired mathematics educator*

Orinda
Counelis, James Steve *education educator*

Pacific Grove
Ericson, Jon Meyer *academic administrator, language educator*

Pacific Palisades
Outcalt, David Lewis *academic administrator, mathematics professor, consultant, musician*

Palm Desert
Baxter, Betty Carpenter *life coach, consultant*

Palm Springs
O'Neill, Michael James *retired special education educator*

Palo Alto
Heneveld-Story, Christy Jean *educational researcher*
Pizzo, Philip A. *dean, pediatrician, educator*
Whitaker, Urban George, Jr. *educational consultant, former dean*

Palos Verdes Estates
Lazzaro, Anthony Derek *academic administrator*

Paradise
Barr, Donald Roy *statistics and operations research educator, statistician*

Pasadena
Arnold, Frances Hamilton *chemistry educator*
Chameau, Jean-Lou *academic administrator*
Douglas, Kimberly *university librarian*
Gilman, Richard Carleton *retired academic administrator*
Lingenfelter, Sherwood Galen *academic administrator, retired anthropologist*
Winbush, Olga Joyce *education educator, consultant*

Pebble Beach
Sullivan, James Francis *university administrator*

Petaluma
Thomas, Nancy Hinckley *special education educator*

Placerville
Maxfield, John Edward *retired university dean*

Playa Del Rey
Baker, Robert M.L., Jr. *academic administrator, research scientist*
Hite, Janet Sue *retired elementary school educator*

Pleasant Hill
Bastrenta, Brigitte Elisabeth *school administrator*
Nelson, Bette Sturr *secondary school educator*

Pleasanton
Roshong, Dee Ann Daniels *dean, educator, counselor*

Pomona
Ambrose, William Wright, Jr. *dean, educator, academic administrator*
Callaway, Linda Marie *special education educator*

Poway
Conant, Kim Untiedt *retired elementary school educator*

Rancho Cordova
Hendrickson, Elizabeth Ann *retired secondary school educator*

Rancho Palos Verdes
Petak, William John *systems management educator*

Rancho Santa Margarita
Hoppe, Dorothe Anna *chemistry educator*

Redding
Wertz, Carol R. *education educator*

Reseda
Banks, Carol T. *elementary school educator*

Rialto
Elliott, Susan Donise *secondary school educator*

Richmond
Sibitz, Michael William *school system administrator*

Riverside
Day, Renee Noelle *special education and secondary school educator*
Fontana, Sandra Ellen Frankel *special education educator*
Jackson, Ruth Moore *university librarian*
Khoury, Sarkis Joseph *professor, consultant*
Kroeger, Dennis Michael *school system administrator*
Rainey, Susan J. *school system administrator*
Russo, Marisa Natalina *educational consultant*
Suyenaga, Elsie Sakae *retired elementary school educator*
White, Timothy Peter *academic administrator*

Rocklin
Erickson, William Lawrence *academic administrator*
Haley, James Brian *dean*
Herzog, Nathan Braden *professor, consultant*

Rohnert Park
Babula, William *dean, writer*

Roseville
Gerth, Donald Rogers *retired university president, educator*
Yates, Coleen Denise *special education educator*

Sacramento
Amezcua, Esther Hernandez *elementary school educator*
Barankin, Joseph Paul *director, consultant*
Callahan, Edward J. *dean*
Clover, Haworth Alfred *elementary school educator, historian*
Hinks, Lyle Allen *special education educator*
Parker, Elizabeth Rindskopf *dean, law educator*
Pomeroy, Claire *dean, academic administrator, medical educator*
Scott, Jack Alan *academic administrator, former state senator*
Trzyna, Thaddeus Charles *academic institution administrator*
Warriner, Kristin Palmquist *retired public school educator*
Young, Heather M. *academic administrator, nursing educator*
Zaidi, Emily Louise *retired elementary school educator*

San Bernardino
Legutki, Gregg *project specialist*
Nam, Sang Seok *special education educator*
Terrell, Charles Shaul, Jr. *educational administrator*

San Bruno
Browne, Kathryn Williams *education educator*

San Diego
Brody, William Ralph *academic administrator, radiologist, educator*
Cole, Kevin *dean, law educator*
Golding, Brage *university president*
Grier, Terry B. *school system administrator*
Hardin, Sally Brosz *dean, nursing educator*
Idos, Margarita de Leon *elementary school educator*
Kasbeer, Stephen Frederick *retired university official, investor*
Lyons, Mary E. *academic administrator*
Maloney, Ellen Claire *elementary school educator*
Maurer, Lawrence Michael *retired acting school administrator, educator*
Porras, Jess *special education educator*
Rodenberg, Johanna Kristine *education educator, consultant*
Scorgie, Kathryn *education educator*
Uribe, Jennie Ann *elementary school educator*
Vega, Carolyn Jane *elementary educator, consultant, writer*
Weber, Stephen Lewis *academic administrator*

San Dimas
Mori, Allen Anthony *retired academic administrator*

San Francisco
Abbott, Richard Lee *physician*
Brand, Jeffrey S. *dean, law educator*
Bratton, Christopher Alan *academic administrator, videographer, art educator*
Cary, Stephen *educational consultant*
Clifford, Geraldine Joncich *retired education educator*
Corrigan, Robert Anthony *academic administrator*
Desmond-Hellmann, Susan *academic administrator, former medical products manufacturing executive*
Dracup, Kathleen Anne *dean, nursing educator*
Dugoni, Arthur A. *dean emeritus, orthodontics educator*
Garcia, Carlos *school system administrator*
Hawgood, Sam *dean, pediatrician, medical educator*
Heyda, Pamela *elementary school educator*
Johnson, Matilee Howard *retired headmistress*
Kozloff, Lloyd M. *dean, microbiologist, educator*
Lewis, Hilda Present *academic administrator, educator*
Martinez, Leo *dean, law educator*
Nye, Margaret Bien *middle school educator*
Privett, Stephen A. *academic administrator, priest*
Robertson, Merle Greene *art historian, academic administrator*
Sakamoto, Katsuyuki *retired academic administrator, psychologist, educator*
Stephens, Elisa *college president*
Warner, Rollin Miles, Jr. *economics educator, real estate broker*

San Gabriel
Tomich-Bolognesi, Vera *educator*

San Jose
Alire, Camila A. *dean emerita, librarian, educator*
Arvizu, Charlene Sutter *elementary school educator*
Boac, Thelma Blantucas *principal*
Haycock, Kenneth Roy *academic administrator, educator, consultant*
Iglesias, Don *school system administrator*
Okerlund, Arlene Naylor *academic administrator, writer*
Whitmore, Jon Scott *academic administrator, play director*

San Leandro
Dolgin, Stephen Mark *secondary school educator, retired social worker*

San Luis Obispo
Baker, Warren J(oseph) *university president*

San Pedro
Gaines, Jerry Lee *retired secondary school educator*
Ingerson, Nancy Nina Moore *special education educator*

San Rafael
Adcock, Muriel W. *special education educator*
Fink, Joseph Richard *academic administrator*
Thomas, Mary Ann McCrary *counselor, school system administrator*

Santa Ana
Lawson, Barbara Slade *elementary school educator, artist*
Schaefer, Ronald Dean *secondary school educator*

Santa Barbara
Allaway, William Harris *retired academic administrator*
Boyan, Norman J. *retired education educator*
Gallo, Marta Irene *retired literature and language educator*
Jullien, Dominique M. *literature and language educator*
Norris, Virginia Oakley *secondary school educator*
O'Dowd, Donald Davy *retired university president*
Sinsheimer, Robert Louis *retired academic administrator, educator*
Yang, Henry T.Y. *academic administrator, educator*

Santa Clara
Goodchild, Lester Francis *higher education educator*
Locatelli, Paul Leo *academic administrator*
Polden, Donald *dean, law educator*

Santa Clarita
Lavine, Steven David *academic administrator*
Perrault, Penni Marilyn *elementary school educator*

Santa Cruz
Blumenthal, George *academic administrator, astronomy and astrophysics professor*
Garcia-Luna-Aceves, J.J. *education educator*
Steel, Virginia (Ginny Steel) *university librarian*

Santa Monica
Kuzmanovic, Jane Violet *academic administrator*

Santa Rosa
Webb, Charles Richard *retired university president*

Saratoga
Barna, Lillian Carattini *school system administrator*

Seal Beach
Pipes, Doris Perry *secondary school educator, consultant*

Seaside
Anderson, David Louis *academic administrator, history professor*

Sherman Oaks
O'Neill, Sallie Boyd *educational consultant, sculptor, small business owner*

Signal Hill
Vandament, William Eugene *retired academic administrator*

Sonoma
Hobart, Billie *retired education educator*

South Lake Tahoe
Triano, Carolyn P. *special education educator*

South Pasadena
Fuller, Kathy J. *special education educator, consultant, researcher*

Spring Valley
Love, Michael *secondary school educator*

Stanford
Anderson, Theodore Wilbur *statistics educator*
Boaler, Jo *education educator*
Darling-Hammond, Linda *education professor*
Eisner, Elliot W. *education educator*
Evers, Williamson Moore (Bill Evers) *education policy analyst, former federal agency administrator*
Gosling, John Arthur *education educator*
Hennessy, John L. *academic administrator*
Joss, Robert L. *dean, business educator*
Kamil, Michael *education educator*
Kays, William Morrow *academic administrator, mechanical engineer*
Kramer, Larry *dean, lawyer, educator*
Laughlin, Robert B. *academic administrator, physics professor*
Riggs, Henry Earle *academic administrator, engineering educator*
Selfridge-Field, Eleanor *educator*
Spence, Andrew Michael *former dean, finance educator*
Stone, William Edward *academic administrator, consultant*
Strober, Myra Hoffenberg *education educator, consultant*
Whitney, Rodger Franklin *academic administrator*
Yuen, Richard Joseph *university dean*

Stockton
Blodgett, Elsie Grace *elementary school educator, small business owner, property manager*
Cobb, Judy Lynn *elementary school educator*
DeRicco, Lawrence Albert *retired college president*
DeRosa, Donald V. *academic administrator*
Gilbertson, Philip *academic administrator*
Ren, Jianhua *education educator*
Sorby, Donald Lloyd *retired dean*

Sun Valley
Cinnamon, William III *elementary and special education educator*
Mayhue, Richard Lee *dean, minister, writer*

Sunnyvale
Schwartz, Eleanore Anita *retired elementary school educator, small business owner*

Tarzana
Zeitlin, Herbert Zakary *college administrator, educational consultant, writer*

Tehachapi
Sprinkle, Martha Clare *elementary school educator*

Thousand Oaks
Lieberman, Judith L. *retired special education educator*

Tiburon
Stotter, Ruth *retired college program director*

Torrance
Kuc, Joseph A. *research scientist*

Turlock
Burns, James Wesley *academic administrator, researcher, consultant*

Twentynine Palms
Clemente, Patrocinio Ablola *secondary school educator*

Union City
Muñoz, Eduardo Rafael *elementary school educator*

Valencia
Blake, Laurence *dean, educator*

Vallejo
Foushee-Higgs, Rosa *elementary school educator, artist*
Wilson, Carrie Lee Stroud *principal*

Valley Ford
Mulkern-Kolosey, Sandy Kathleen *college counselor, educator, realtor*

Van Nuys
Crawford, Marvin Leonard, Sr. *retired school system administrator*

Venice
Beery-Polglase, Penelope (Pixie) *education educator*

Ventura
Stauffer, Jeffery Dean *education educator*

Victorville
Kildal, Lori Ann *dean*

Walnut Creek
Lilly, Luella Jean *retired academic administrator*
Merrill, Richard James *retired educational director*
Stupak, Ronald Joseph *dean, management educator, researcher, author, consultant*

Weimar
Kerschner, Lee R(onald) *academic administrator, political scientist, educator*

West Sacramento
Hakala, Nila Virginia *primary school educator*

Whittier
Cruz, Denis J. *elementary school educator*

Woodland Hills
Berry, Barbara Cochran *education educator, writer*
Phoenix, David D. *special education educator*

Yorba Linda
Esparza, Karen Ann *history educator*
Lunde, Dolores Benitez *retired secondary school educator*

Yuba City
Leverett, Dawn R. *disability education consultant*

Yucaipa
Gomez, Louis Salazar *college president*

COLORADO

Arvada
Bert, Carol Lois *retired educational assistant*
Krohnfeldt, Gretchen Ann *secondary school educator, genealogist*

Aspen
Heyman, Juliane Marion *retired history educator, language educator*

Aurora
Altiere, Ralph J. *dean, pharmacy educator*
Cowee, John Widmer *retired university chancellor*
Hamrick, Eliza Carney *secondary school educator, consultant*
Rivera, Susan Frances *elementary school educator*

Bayfield
Horton, Frank Elba *academic administrator, geographer, educator*

Beulah
Anderson, Ronald Delaine *education educator*

Boulder
Borko, Hilda *education educator*
DiStefano, Philip P. *academic administrator*
Gleeson, Todd Timothy *dean, biology professor*
Williams, James Franklin, II, *dean, librarian*

Broomfield
Parker, Bobby Douglas *radio broadcaster, photographer, educator*

Centennial
Greenberg, Elinor Miller *director, consultant*

Colorado Springs
Adams, Bernard Schroder *retired college president*
Blake, Esther Jean *retired elementary school educator*
Celeste, Richard F. *academic administrator, retired ambassador, Former Governor, Ohio*
Fielden, C. Franklin III *early childhood education consultant*
Lomas, Clara A. *educator, researcher*
Madsen, Karen F. *retired elementary school educator*
McDade, Roberta Clark *secondary school educator*
Robran, Conrad John *retired education educator*
Shockley-Zalabak, Pamela Sue *academic administrator*
Steinhoff, Lynnette Kay *special education educator*

Denver
Benson, Bruce Davey *academic administrator, oil and gas company executive*
Boasberg, Tom *school system administrator*
Burrows, Bertha Jean *retired academic administrator*
Byyny, Richard Lee *former academic administrator, physician, educator*
Carbone, Rocco William III *elementary school educator*
Coombe, Bob (Robert D.) *academic administrator*
Emmet, Thomas Addis, Jr. *college administrator, consultant*
Jarles, Ruth Sewell *education educator*
Larson, Ruth Elaine *elementary school educator*
McCall, Laura *education educator, writer*
Meeks, Patricia Lowe *literature and language educator, consultant*
Newman, Kimberly Eileen *adult education educator*
Rubin, Cathy Ann *secondary school educator*
Slotta, Oliveann Davis *mathematics educator, consultant*

Estes Park
Ryder, Susan R. *elementary school educator*

Evans
Geisendorfer, Nancy Kay *mathematics educator*

Falcon
Jackson, Kathlynn L. *special education educator, behavior specialist*
Meek, Lisa K. S. *intervention coordinator, psychotherapist*

Fort Collins
Baldwin, Lionel Vernon *retired university president*
Bloemen, Crystal Lynn *secondary school educator*
Cochenour, Donnice *academic librarian*
Frank, Anthony A. (Tony Frank) *academic administrator*
Harper, Judson Morse *retired university administrator, consultant, educator*
Maher, Thomas George *academic administrator, producer, media educator*

Treaster, Melba Mauck *retired educational consultant and educator*

Fruita
Harvey, Barbara Lou *special education educator*

Golden
Bickart, Theodore Albert *university president emeritus*
Chouinard, Karen Reiko *elementary school educator*
Gordon, Douglas H. *literature and language educator*
Scoggins, M. W. (Bill Scoggins) *academic administrator*

Greeley
Banerjee, Rashida *special education educator*
Rittner, Linda *educational consultant, director*

Lakewood
McBride, Guy Thornton, Jr. *college president emeritus*
Reed, Joan-Marie *special education educator*

Littleton
Mosier, Cheryl Angeline *secondary school educator, consultant*

Longmont
Moats, Louisa Cook *educational consultant, researcher*

Louisville
Bravo, Adele *elementary school educator*

Monument
Posey, Carolyn Ann *secondary school educator*

Parachute
Leonard, Betsy Ann *director, writer*

Pueblo
Becker, Charles A. *adult education educator*
Sisson, Ray L. *retired dean, author*
Turner, Dorothy Jean *school librarian*

Snowmass Village
DiBiaggio, John A. *university president*

Sterling
Walsh, Shari M. *literature and language educator*

Thornton
Johnson, Michael *principal*

Towner
Fees, Ruth Anna *secondary school educator*

Walden
Ary, Bonnita Ellen *registrar, federal official*

CONNECTICUT

Bloomfield
Foster, Benjamin, Jr. *educational administrator*
Nelson-Kauffman, Wendy *history educator*
Rendock, Mary Kay *elementary school educator*

Bridgeport
Hendricks, Edward David *educator, consultant, speaker, trainer*

Columbia
Stockmal, Henry F., Jr. *retired principal*

Coventry
Dimmock, Virginia Ellen *literature and language educator, consultant*

Danbury
Arbitelle, Ronald Alan *retired elementary school educator*
Hawkes, Carol Ann *academic administrator*
Pszota, Gabor *physics educator*

Darien
Lim, Ralph Wei Hsiong *academic administrator*

Deep River
Nidzgorski, Barbara Helen *gifted and talented educator, puppeteer*

East Hartford
Smith, Edmund Johnston *middle school educator*

Enfield
Doty, Victoria Skower *middle school educator*

Fairfield
Baron, Shari Ann *academic administrator*
Li, Cindy *academic librarian*
Maxwell, Carole Ann *director*
Miles, Leland Weber *retired academic administrator*

Falls Village
Purcell, Mary Louise Gerlinger *retired adult education educator*

Farmington
Melekote, Swathanthra Kumar *education educator*
Robinson, Peter J. *retired dean, periodontal educator, pathologist*

Greenwich
Mullen, Anthony J. *special education educator*
Sternberg, Betty J. *school system administrator*

Groton
English, James Fairfield, Jr. *former college president*
Galbraith, Marian *elementary school educator*

Hamden
Cooley, Francis Rexford *dean*
Oddi, Marie Caporale *educational administrator*

Hartford
Carter, David George, Sr. *academic administrator*
Coleman, George A. *school system administrator*
Frost, James Arthur *former university president*
Hay, Leroy E. *school system administrator*
Jones, James Fleming, Jr. *academic administrator, language educator*
Kedderis, Pamela Jean *academic administrator*
Lauter, Paul *literature and language educator*
Paul, Jeremy Ralph *dean, law educator*
Reynolds, Scott Walton *academic administrator*

Madison
Anderson, G. Ernest, Jr. *retired education educator*

Middletown
Roth, Michael S. *academic administrator, historian*

Monroe
Kranyik, Elizabeth Ann *secondary school educator*

Naugatuck
Sasso, Ruth Maryann *retired educator*

New Britain
Klonoski, Edward D. *academic administrator*
Mulcahy, Daniel G. *education educator*
Shen, Xiaoping *geography educator*

New Canaan
Despres, Louise Fay *secondary school educator*
McKeough, Susan Anne *elementary school educator*

New Haven
Alpern, Robert J. *dean, medical educator*
Birnbaum, Irwin Morton *educational consultant, lawyer*
Brenzel, Jeffrey *dean*
Daly, Radley Hutchinson *retired academic administrator*
Gray, Margaret *dean, nursing educator*
Greene, Liliane *literature and language educator, editor*
Hamilton, Andrew D. *academic administrator, chemistry professor*
Lamar, Howard Roberts *academic administrator, historian*
LaPalombara, Joseph *political science educator, industrial management educator*
Levin, Rick (Richard Charles Levin) *academic administrator, economist*
Mendelsohn, Robert *educator*
Oster, Sharon M. *dean, management educator*
Paveza, Gregory J. *dean*
Post, Robert Charles *dean, law educator*
Salovey, Peter *academic administrator, psychology professor*
Speth, James Gustave *dean, environmental studies educator, lawyer*

New London
Higdon, Leo Ignatius, Jr., (Lee Higdon) *academic administrator*

Norfolk
O'Malley, John Patrick *dean*

North Branford
Gasparine, Barbara Ellen *elementary school educator*

North Haven
Hudson, Richard L. *retired adult education educator, minister*
Moeller, Judith Stone *reading educator, consultant*

Northford
James, Virginia Stowell *retired elementary and secondary school educator*

Norwalk
Johnson, Robert James *psychology educator*

Orange
Zitnay, Jill M. *educational consultant, educator*

Pomfret Center
Sweatt, Ermelinda Espinola *retired mathematics educator*

Redding
Poulos, Christopher *literature and language educator*

Ridgefield
Brewster, Carroll Worcester *former academic administrator*

Southington
Bagwell, Carol Tessier *special education educator, consultant*

Stamford
Handler, Evelyn *former academic administrator*
Monson, Robert Joseph *education educator*

Storrs
Shah, Farhed *economics educator*

Storrs Mansfield
Adelson, Jill Lynn *assistant professor, educational research consultant*
Baxter, Donald Leon Murray *education educator*
Hogan, Michael J. *academic administrator*
Kerr, Kirklyn M. *academic administrator, veterinarian, pathologist*
MacDonald, John Thomas *school system administrator*
Nicholls, Peter J. *academic administrator*

Woods, David G. *dean*

Stratford
Giordano, Kathryn M. *psychology educator*

Taconic
Medvecky, Patricia *retired elementary school educator*

Waterbury
DeCesare, Joyce Shiel *retired guidance counselor*
Lang, Christine JoAnn *middle school educator*
Martone, Eric Anthony Domenic *history educator*

Waterford
Weidenbaum, Rhoda Sussman *history educator, researcher*

West Hartford
Chase, Carol Johnson *mathematics educator*
Harrison, Walter Lee *university president*
Jepsen, Jane Barry *secondary school educator*
Malone, Thomas Francis *academic administrator, meteorologist*
Markham, Claire Agnes (M. Clare Markham) *retired chemistry educator, consultant*
McAuliffe-Curnias, Susan Eileen *secondary school educator*
Reid, Pamela Trotman *college president, psychology professor*
Tonkin, Humphrey Richard *academic administrator, educator*

Westport
Davidson, JoAnn W. *retired elementary school educator*
Warner, Kerstin Julianna *gifted and talented educator*

Willimantic
Barbuto, Leah M. *early childhood and technology educator, consultant*

Woodbury
O'Brien, Bonnie Jeanne *counseling administrator*

DELAWARE

Bethany Beach
Jacobsen, Julia Mills *educational administrator*

Dover
Jones, Geraldine Ann Johnson *secondary school educator*
Wilson, Clealyn Bullock *elementary school educator*

Harrington
Bulischeck, Anita Marie *guidance counselor, special education educator*

Hockessin
Mitchell, Peter Kenneth *educational consultant*
Yasik, Christine Marie *literature and language educator*

Laurel
Lydic, Garrett Walton *elementary school educator*
Selby, Cora Norwood *retired elementary school educator*

Lewes
Donovan, James Francis *retired school system administrator*

New Castle
Doberstein, Audrey K. *college president*
Price, Leon R. *elementary school educator*
Sanderson, Devon Lee *elementary school educator*
Williamson, Sandra Kaye *education educator*

Newark
Bailey, Daniel Carl *higher education administrator*
Harker, Patrick Timothy *academic administrator, systems engineer, educator*
Kwansa, Francis A. *educator*

Wilmington
Alonso, Caridad *elementary school educator*
Baron, Stuart *academic administrator, art educator, artist*
Fullerton, Ann Elizabeth *retired biology educator*
Higgins, Roxanne Snelling *educational consultant*
Roselle, David Paul *retired academic administrator, mathematician, educator*
Wasson, Ellis Archer *history educator*

DISTRICT OF COLUMBIA

Washington
Aleinikoff, Thomas Alexander *dean, law educator*
Arnez, Nancy Levi *educational leadership educator*
Bangura, Abdul Karim *academic administrator, researcher, scientist*
Bowden, Aisha L. *elementary school educator*
Burgin, Walter Hotchkiss, Jr. *retired academic administrator*
Burke-Ables, Kim S. *biology educator*
Buser, Carolyn Elizabeth *adult education educator*
Cadogan, Rene Felipe *counseling administrator, educator*
Churchill, John Hugh *college academic administrator*
Clewell, Beatriz Chu *director, researcher*
Cook, Mary Ann *adult education educator*
Craig, John Charles *educational consultant*
Daly, George Garman *dean*
DeGioia, John J. *academic administrator*
Duffey, Joseph Daniel *academic administrator*
Elliott, Emerson John *education consultant, policy analyst*
Englund, Julie Irene *academic administrator*
Fisher, Miles Mark, IV, *education and religious studies educator, minister*
Fusco, Aurilla Marie *director*
Futrell, Mary Alice Hatwood *dean, education association administrator*
Gerety, Tom R. *former academic administrator, lawyer, educator, philosopher*
Gormley, William T. *dean, political science professor*
Greenhalgh, Paul *academic administrator*
Grossman, Claudio M. *dean, law educator*
Jones, Judith Miller *director*
Kamras, Jason *mathematics educator*
Keaney, Thomas Addis *academic administrator, management consultant, military officer*
Keeley, Robert Vossler *retired academic administrator, ambassador*
Kerwin, Cornelius Martin *academic administrator, educator*
Kim, Mikyong Minsun *education educator*
Kirk, Artemis G. *university librarian*
Kirkpatrick, Laird Clifford *dean, law educator*
Knapp, Steven *academic administrator*
Lawrence, Frederick M. *dean, law educator*
Lawson, Donna Yvette *special education educator*
Luttwak, Edward Nicolae *academic administrator, policy and business consultant, senior advisor*
Magrath, C. Peter *academic administrator, educational association executive*
Mantyla, Karen *distance learning consultant*
Miles, Veryl Victoria *dean, law educator*
Milman, Natalie Bordelon *education educator*
Mitchell, Stephen Ray *dean, rheumatologist*
Mohrman, Kathryn J. *academic administrator*
Muller, Steven *international studies educator, academic administrator*
Natarajan, Githa *elementary school educator*
Nelson, Charles J. *academic administrator, diplomat, consultant*
Nwagbaraocha, Joel Onukwugha *academic administrator, educator*
O'Connell, David M. *academic administrator, priest*
O'Hara, Sabine U. *academic administrator, dean, economist, educator*
Phillips, Susan Meredith *dean, economist, educator*
Ranck, Edna Runnels *academic administrator, researcher*
Reddel, Carl Walter *academic administrator*
Reece, Gwendolyn J. *academic administrator*
Rhee, Michelle A. *school system administrator, former educational association administrator*
Ribeau, Sidney A. *academic administrator*
Rope, William Frederick *educator*
Sclafani, Susan K. *educational consultant, former federal agency administrator*
Scott, James L. *dean, emergency physician, educator*
Sessoms, Allen Lee *academic administrator, physicist, educator, retired diplomat*
Smith, Abbie Oliver *college administrator, educator*
Spillane, Robert Richard *school system administrator*
Steigman, Andrew L. *academic dean*
Stevenson, Zollie Julius, Jr. *former school system and government agency administrator, consultant*
Strange, Sharon Louise *special education educator, musician*
Tate, Rosemary *special education educator*
Thomas-Razza, Constance *retired elementary school educator*
Thompson, Bernida Lamerle *principal, consultant, educator*
Vasquez, Vivian *education educator*
Ward, David *educational consultant, former educational association administrator, academic administrator*
Weiner, Stephen Francis *academic administrator, communications educator*
Weingold, Marjorie Nassau *retired special education educator*
Weiss, Charles, Jr. *educator*
Williams, Ella Marilyn *mathematics educator*
Wise, Lorraine E. *educational consultant*

FLORIDA

Apopka
Carlson, Donna Marie *elementary school educator*
Fiorenza, Veronica Eve *pre-school educator*

Arcadia
Cline, Adrian H. *academic administrator*

Belle Glade
Grear, Effie Carter *principal*

Belleview
Savage, Sherelyn Sue *secondary school educator*

Boca Raton
Arden, Eugene *retired university provost*
Braisted, Mary Jo *elementary school educator*
Brehm, Patricia Christman *principal*
Comment, Anna Mae *retired principal*
Friedland, Michael Lawrence *dean, medical educator*
Lichtstein, Daniel M. *dean, internist*
Pellen, Rita M. *associate dean*
Rebel, Amy Louise *elementary school educator*
Smith, Dawn Mercedes *assistant dean*
Tennies, Robert Hunter *headmaster*

Bonita Springs
Becker, Richard Charles *retired academic administrator*
Borchers, Janet Marise *elementary school educator, school counselor*
Johnson, Franklyn Arthur *academic administrator*

Boynton Beach
Hughes, Richard G. *principal, consultant*

Bradenton
Alex, Elizabeth Robins *retired adult education educator, retired preschool director*
Driscoll, Constance Fitzgerald *education educator, writer, consultant*
Wolf, John M. Jack *adult education seminar consultant*

Brooksville
Chamberlain, Daniel Robert *retired college president*

Cape Coral
Bradley, Jean Irene *elementary school educator*
Graham, Dorothy E. *elementary school educator*
Vilardi, Charles Ronald *principal*

Clearwater
Campbell, Martha Etheredge *dean, educator*
Lovik, Eric Gordon *academic administrator, director*

Coral Gables
Shalala, Donna Edna *academic administrator, former United States Secretary of Health and Human Services*
Tien, James M. *dean, engineering educator, consultant*
White, Patricia Denise *dean, law educator*

Davie
Roddy, Christopher *academic administrator, educator*

Daytona Beach
Green, Betty Nielsen *education educator, consultant*
Hartsell, Horace Ed *college president*

DeLand
Libby, Wendy B. *academic administrator*

Debary
Coble, Alicia Sharon *retired elementary and secondary school educator*

Deerfield Beach
Martin, Dianna Luise *retired school administrator*

Deland
Dascher, Paul Edward *dean, accounting educator*
Langston, Paul T. *dean, composer, music educator*
Sharpe, Virginia Deegan *educational consultant*
Wright, Jane Lanier *school librarian*

Delray Beach
Leeds, Susanne *special education educator, writer*
Smith, Robin Debra *primary school educator*
Sparrow, Kathleen Gail *retired secondary school educator*
Templeton, Chelneca (Chelly Templeton) *education educator*

Destin
O'Brien, Gregory Michael St. Lawrence *academic administrator*

Dover
Scholtes, Linda Marie *elementary school educator*

Dunedin
Tapley, Earl Mays *retired college dean*

Eagle Lake
Farr, Ausonia Ann *special education educator*

Fort Lauderdale
Carter-Miller, Jocelyn *educational services company executive, former retail executive*
Edmund, Norman Wilson *educational researcher*
Fischler, Abraham Saul *retired academic administrator, educator*
Hanbury, George Lafayette, II, *academic administrator*
Hilburn, Dawn *special education educator*
Pollinger, Teresita A. *multi-cultural resource educator*
Spungin, Charlotte Isabelle *retired secondary school educator, writer*
Uchin, Robert Allen *dean, endodontist*

Fort Myers
Colgate, Doris Eleanor *sailing school owner, administrator*
Goodell, Warren Franklin *retired academic administrator*
Robertson, Mary Amos *mathematics educator*
Tinker, Thomas Eaton *retired headmaster*
Wilder, Lynn K. *education educator*

Fort Pierce
Alvarez, Camila *literature and language educator*
Schwenger, Wilbur John *mathematics educator*

Fort Walton Beach
Hicks, Patricia J. *secondary school educator*
Moran, Kimberly Dianne *secondary school educator, artist*

Gainesville
Brown, Myra Suzanne *university librarian*
Bryan, Robert Armistead *academic administrator, educator*
Chambers, Robert Hunter III *academic administrator, consultant, historian, educator*
Dolan, Teresa A. *dean, educator, researcher*
Jerry, Robert Howard, II, *dean, law educator*
Kirkland, Nancy Childs *secondary school educator, consultant*
Kraft, John *dean, management educator*
Krohn, Marvin D. *dean, educator*
Lowenstein, Ralph Lynn *university dean emeritus*
Machen, James Bernard *academic administrator*
Maple, Marilyn Jean *educational media coordinator*
Marshall, Kevin A. *director*
Mills, Jon *dean emeritus, law educator*
Peters, Jorg *professor*
Phillips, Winfred Marshall *academic administrator, professor, mechanical engineer*
Resnick Carswell, Sarah Jacqueline *registrar*
Riffee, William H. *dean, pharmacy educator*
Saucerman, Alvera Adeline *elementary school educator*
York, E. Travis *retired academic administrator*

Graceville
Kinchen, Thomas Alexander *college president*

Hialeah
Gallego, Jose Miguel *special education educator*

Hollywood
Clark, Deborah A. *secondary school educator*
Lutchman, Eva *middle school educator*

Indialantic
Scrivener, Lois Doing *retired principal, educator*

Jacksonville
Cagle, Margaret Broughton *retired parochial school educator*
Davis, Craig Anderson *school system administrator, educator*
Delaney, John Adrian *academic administrator*
Hughes, Carolyn Wright *elementary school educator, director*
Jamrich, John Xavier *retired university administrator*
Jones, David Marshall *school librarian, director*
Khan, Marty Z. *academic administrator*
Kinne, Frances Bartlett *academic administrator*
Main, Edna Dewey (June Main) *education educator*
Olin, Marilyn *secondary school educator*
Osborn, Marvin Griffing, Jr. *educational consultant*
Otto, Elizabeth Hall *education educator*
Pratt-Dannals, Ed *school system administrator*
Rogers, Linda L. *middle school educator*

Jensen Beach
Dahn, Conney Colley *special education educator*

Kissimmee
Haynes, Ulric St. Clair, Jr. *retired dean*
Roberds, Richard Mack *professor emeritus*
Severance, Jeri-Lynne White *elementary school educator*

Lake Worth
Carlisle, Ervin Frederick *university provost, educator*
Ramos, Carlos F. *physics educator*
Rudayeva, Yelena *biology educator*

Lakeland
Moseley, Lisa Lent *counseling administrator*
Taylor, Cheryl Meagan *pre-school administrator*
Washington, Gloria Dunn *secondary school educator*

Leesburg
Greata, Joanne Dixon *educational consultant*

Longwood
Campbell, David A. *secondary school educator*

Loxahatchee
Russell-Tyson, Pearl Leonie *elementary school educator*

Melbourne
Catanese, Anthony James *academic administrator*
Weaver, Lynn Edward *academic administrator, consultant, editor*

Miami
Addy, Dawn Emerson *adult education labor educator*
Banya, Kingsley *dean*
Bush, Gregory Wallace *director*
Clarkson, John G. *academic administrator, ophthalmologist*
Felton, Sandra Haley *special education educator*
Greer, Pedro Jose, Jr., (Joe Greer) *dean*
Hildenbrand, Susan Elaine *education educator*
Ishmael, Annesa Fazeela *elementary school educator*
Kaplan, Betsy Hess *retired school board member*
Katz, Sandra *educational consultant, psychologist, educator*
Klonarides, Geraldine *education educator*
Mallery, Charles Henry *college associate dean, biology educator*
McCabe, Robert Howard *college president*
McLaughlin, Margaret Brown *adult education educator, writer*
O'Neill, William Walter *dean, cardiologist, educator*
Patrie, Cheryl Christine *elementary school educator*
Penick, John E. *educator*
Rodriguez, Josefa Nieves *special education and language educator*
Rosenberg, Mark B. *academic administrator*

Miami Beach
Foote, Gwendolyn Sue *educator, artist*

Miami Gardens
Conley, James W. *English and language arts educator*
Medina-Pascu, Isabel M. *academic administrator*
Robinson, Beatriz Gonzalez *academic administrator*

Miami Shores
Esposito, Luigi Gennaro *educator*

Miramar
Florio, Donamarie Rose *secondary school educator*

Montverde
Revis-Pyke, Robin Lynn *director*

Mount Dora
Shepp, Judith Rosser *retired elementary school educator*

Naples
Dobranski, Bernard *dean, law educator*
Mahalawich, Anne Mary *retired mathematics educator*
Wedel-Cowgill, Millie Redmond *secondary school, performing arts, communication and education educator*

New Port Richey
Brice, Jeanine Lynn *associate dean*
Johnson, Henry Eugene III *middle school educator*
Plant, John Maxime *educator*

New Smyrna Beach
Shaffer, Joye Coy *reading specialist*

North Lauderdale
Dunham, Laura *elementary school educator*

North Miami Beach
Sorosky, Jeri P. *academic administrator*

Ocala
Brown, Warren Donald *adult education educator, retired police officer*
Cecil, Joseph Terry *education educator*
Tait, Patricia Ann *secondary school educator*

Odessa
Lawson, Mary Carolyn *elementary and middle school educator*

Opa Locka
Sample, Althea Merritt *retired secondary education educator, conductor*

Orlando
Carter, Glenn Arnold *academic administrator, consultant*
Chacon, Delia C. *secondary school educator*
Connolly, Joseph Francis, II, *academic administrator, government consultant*
Dieker, Lisa A. *special education educator*
Graham, Eleanore Davis *elementary school educator*
Jacobs, Diane Margaret *academic administrator*
Karwowski, Waldemar *adult education educator*
Profitt, Donald Ralph *secondary school educator*
Wilson, Brenda Marie *secondary school educator*
Wood, Nancy J. *secondary school educator*

Ormond Beach
Martin, Charles John *professor*

Osprey
Weathermon, Sidney Earl *retired elementary school educator*

Oviedo
MacKenzie, Charles Sherrard *academic administrator*

Palm Bay
Colman, Charles Kingsbury *academic administrator, criminologist*
Krause, Mary Alice *elementary school educator*
Merrell, Keith P. *elementary school educator*

Palm Beach Gardens
Fagan, Richard *mathematics educator*
Más, Beverley Berlin *counseling advisor, career planning advisor*
Peck, Maryly VanLeer *retired academic administrator, chemical engineer*
Turner, V(eras) Dean *dean*

Palm City
Kronk, Bernadette Rago *elementary school educator, consultant*

Palm Coast
Raffo, Kristin L. *elementary school educator*

Palm Harbor
Hewitt, Sarah Nichole *educational consultant, researcher*
Perkins, Robert Edward *retired secondary school educator*

Panama City
Rockhill, Marsha *special education educator*

Pensacola
Franklin, Godfrey *adult education educator*
Surles, Carol D. *academic administrator*

Pompano Beach
Baslaw-Finger, Annette *education educator, consultant*
Bookbinder, Robert Max *retired school system administrator, educational consultant, writer*
Endahl, Ethelwyn Mae *elementary education educator, consultant*
Williams, Cloretta Mae *retired elementary school educator*

Port Charlotte
Hill, Richard Earl *academic administrator*
Norris, Dolores June *elementary school educator*

Port Orange
Johnson, Susan F. *elementary school educator*

Port Saint Lucie
Guglielmino, Lucy Margaret Madsen *education educator, researcher, consultant*
Guglielmino, Paul Joseph *educator*

Reddick
Romanski, Joyce Marie *secondary school educator, small business owner, instructor*

Rockledge
Anderson, Robert Aeiker *college administrator*

Saint Augustine
Sappington, Sharon Anne *retired school librarian*

Saint Leo
Hammond, Bruce Ray *academic administrator, consultant, communications educator*
Persky, David William *lawyer*

Saint Petersburg
Carfora, Joan C. *elementary school educator*
Chapin, Lloyd Walter *academic administrator*
Coraggio, James Thomas *educational researcher, measurement consultant*
Dinsdale, Carol Ellen *special education educator*
Dukes, Lyman Lee III *special education professor*
Notaro, Gerald Anthony *university librarian*
Robinson, Chester Hersey *retired dean*
Smith, Betty Robinson *retired elementary school educator*
Southworth, William Dixon *retired education educator*
Young, June Hurley *elementary school educator, writer*

Sarasota
Atwell, Robert Herron *academic administrator*
Christ-Janer, Arland Frederick *college president*
Church, Martha Eleanor *retired academic administrator*
Cleland, Sherrill *college president*
Michalson, Gordon E., Jr. *academic administrator*
Miller, Peggy Gordon Elliott *retired academic administrator*
St. John, Terri *secondary school educator*
Scanlon, Janice Lynn *retired gifted and talented educator*

Sebring
Parrett, Janelle Swilley *secondary school educator*
Schumacher, Cynthia Jo *retired elementary and secondary education educator*

South Daytona
Fernández, Lianne *elementary school educator, consultant*

Spring Hill
Mathia, Mary Loyola *parochial school educator, nun*
Wood, Shelton Eugene, Jr. *education educator, minister, consultant*

Sugarloaf
Greenberg, Linda Garrett *education educator, volunteer, singer*

Summerfield
Heflin, Jimmie Lee *elementary school educator*

Sun City Center
Chapman, Lenora Rosamond *day care provider, social service organization director*

Tallahassee
Bert, Clara Virginia *retired secondary school educator, administrator*
Bye, Raymond Erwin, Jr. *academic administrator*
Carter, Tina A. *educator*
Ervin, Charles Phifer, Jr. *education educator, retired military officer*
Jeong, Allan C. *education educator*
Lick, Dale Wesley *educational leadership educator, mathematician*
Mooney, Krista Michele *academic administrator*
Pla, Arthur James *school system administrator*
Waas, Harriet Issner *elementary school educator*
Weidner, Donald J. *dean, law educator*
Wetherell, Thomas Kent *academic administrator*

Tamarac
Galipault, Lorraine D. *adult education educator*

Tampa
Branch, Mary Fletcher Cox *secondary school educator*
Genshaft, Judy Lynn *academic administrator, psychologist, educator*
Jones, Franklin Ross *education educator*
Kruschwitz, Walter Hillis *retired physics educator*
Leto, Sharon Ann *secondary school educator, consultant*
Loiselle, Joan Brenda *elementary school educator, art educator*
Meisels, Gerhard George *academic administrator, chemist, educator*
Morrill, Donald *dean, director*
Pauly, Jennifer L. *director, graphics designer*
Sanchez, Mary Anne *retired secondary school educator*
Sbramaniam, Chitra P. *educational consultant*
Weizmann, Maria Pia *associate dean*

Tierra Verde
Gaffney, Thomas Francis *principal*

Titusville
O'Sullivan, Patricia Ann *principal, writer*

Valrico
McCrystal, Jennifer Cross *elementary school educator*

Venice
Felker, Ouida Jeanette Weissinger *special education educator*

Finlay, Susan Sparling *education educator*
Seiler, Charlotte Woody *retired education educator*

West Palm Beach
Hardin, Luther *academic administrator, former state legislator*
Kendall, Carla P. *school system administrator, mathematician*
Pingpank, Robert Charles *retired mathematics educator*

Wewahitchka
de Abreu, Sue *elementary school educator*

Winter Garden
Gillet, Pamela Kipping *special education educator*

Winter Haven
Bennett, Samuel *elementary school educator*
Cloud, Linda Beal *retired secondary school educator*

Winter Springs
McNeal, Mary Kay *secondary school educator*

Zephyrhills
Barron, Ilona Eleanor *elementary school educator, consultant*

GEORGIA

Albany
Bryant, Thedis W. *academic librarian*
Calhoun, Roy *school librarian*
Forsyth, Rosalyn Moye *middle school educator*
Johnson, Debra Pope *education educator*
King, Hanh *literature and language educator*
Willis, Jakie Arleta *elementary and secondary educator*

Alpharetta
Filliat, Elizabeth Hartley *retired secondary school educator*
Wind, Alan Michael *history educator*

Americus
Capitan, William Harry *university president emeritus*

Athens
Aaron, Ira Edward *retired educator*
Adams, Michael Fred *academic administrator, political scientist, educator*
Jackson, Lori Lee *elementary school educator*
Krasnostchekova, Elena Alexander *literature and language educator*
Lauth, Thomas P. *dean, political science professor*
Potter, William Gray, Jr. *university librarian*
Smagorinsky, Peter *education educator*
Sumichrast, Robert T. *dean, business educator*
White, Rebecca Hanner *dean, law educator*

Atlanta
Aaberg, Thomas Marshall, Sr. *academic administrator*
Addison, Abby Ayer *middle school educator*
Affonso, Dyanne D. *dean*
Alexander, Cecil Abraham *academic administrator, consultant, retired architect*
Becker, Mark Paul *academic administrator, statistician, educator*
Bellamy, Ivory *elementary school educator, consultant*
Benveniste, Lawrence M. *dean*
Brown, Carlton E. *academic administrator*
Cilella, Mary Winifred *director*
Davis, Erroll Brown, Jr. *academic administrator, former utilities executive*
Eaddy, Felton Eugene *literature and language educator*
Franklin, Robert Michael, Jr. *academic administrator, theology studies educator*
Gonzalez-Ruiz, Julio *literature and language educator*
Henry, Ronald James Whyte *academic administrator, physicist, educator*
Henry, Thomas Reid *education educator, researcher*
Hogan, John Donald *retired college dean, finance educator*
Kaminshine, Steven J. *dean, law educator*
Koplan, Jeffrey Powell *academic administrator, epidemiologist*
LaDuke, Bettie *academic administrator*
Lewis, Earl *academic administrator*
Luce, Richard *university librarian*
Mahaley-Johnson, Hosanna *school system administrator*
McCauley, Linda A. *dean, nursing educator*
Partlett, David F. *dean, law educator*
Peterson, George P. (Bud Peterson) *academic administrator*
Rojas, Carlos *literature and language educator*
Salbu, Steve *dean, business educator*
Sanfilippo, Fred Paul *academic administrator, medical educator, pathologist*
Schuster, Gary Benjamin *academic administrator, chemistry professor*
Tatum, Beverly Daniel *academic administrator, writer, psychology and education educator*
Wagner, James Warren *academic administrator, engineering educator*
Wilson, Michael W. *academic librarian, educator*
Young, Charles Edward *former academic administrator*

Augusta
Jackson, Rosa M. *retired elementary school educator*
Nzeh, Okoroafor Ogbajie *director*

Austell
Scott, Yvonnie Michelle *special education educator, diagnostician, paralegal*

Bainbridge
Miley, Jenna Yvonne *education educator, consultant*

Baxley
Williams, David Alfred *elementary school music specialist*
Williams, Sonia Kay *retired secondary school educator*

Blairsville
Stainback, Susan Bray *professor emeritus*

Calhoun
Orfield, Robert Allen *special education director*

Canton
Hamby, Ira Ben III *elementary school educator*

Carnesville
Royston, Pamela Jean *special education educator*

Carrollton
Larkin, Martha Jane *higher education educator*
Sethna, Beheruz Nariman *academic administrator, educator, management consultant*
Trotman Scott, Michelle Frazier *special education educator*

Cataula
Averill, Ellen Corbett *retired secondary education science educator, administrator*

Columbus
Duncan, Frances Murphy *retired special education educator*
Riggsby, Dutchie Sellers *education educator*

Conyers
Grider, Rhonda Patriece *elementary school educator, writer*

Covington
Norwood, Brandi Aisha *middle school educator*

Dallas
Gilbert, Martha W. *literature and language educator*
Jackson, Cynthia Williford *special education educator*

Dalton
Smith, Janet Susannah *literature and language educator, department chairman*

Dawsonville
Jorgensen, Alfred H. *retired information technology educator*

Decatur
Bryant, Erika Knight *mathematics educator*
Keaton, Mollie M. *elementary school educator*
Kiss, Elizabeth *academic administrator, philosophy educator*

Demorest
Rogers, Elizabeth (Betty) Carlisle *educator, consultant*

Douglasville
Smith, Stephanie Renae *middle school educator*
Walker, Pam *biology educator*

Dublin
Shuman-Riley, Brenda *literature and language educator*

Duluth
Cothrun, Thomas Keith *secondary school educator*
Guillory, Barbara Ann *elementary school educator*

Dunwoody
Askew Cain, Peggy *elementary school educator, consultant*

Eatonton
Digby, Pamela Annette *elementary school educator*

Evans
Owen, Shaun Sonia *elementary school educator, small business owner, consultant*

Fairburn
Martin, Terry Malone *assistant principal*
Milam, Lynne Morgan *special education educator*
Williams, Pedelaphe *education educator*

Flowery Branch
Coll, Edward Girard, Jr. *university president*

Fort Oglethorpe
Christensen, Brian Duaine *education educator*

Gainesville
Burd, John Stephen *retired academic administrator, music educator*
Mills, Hugh Milton, Jr. *retired college president*
Nichols, Dana *literature and language educator*

Hephzibah
Albarado, Rebecca Hill *elementary school educator*

Ila
Greene, Sheree' Jeane *elementary school educator, consultant*

Jeffersonville
Hawthorne, Sarah Beck *reading educator*

Jonesboro
Mahone, Antonio *elementary school educator*
Perez, Maritza E. *special education educator*
Vaughn, Rosalyn Mae *academic administrator*

Kennesaw
Siegel, Betty Lentz *president emeritus*

Lake Park
Tucker, Glenn Gorham *retired educational administrator*

Lawrenceville
Harris, Melba Iris *elementary and secondary school educator, state agency administrator*

Lilburn
Bendelius, Bonnie Sue *elementary school educator*

Macon
Davis, David Scott *academic administrator, chemistry professor*
Floyd, Daisy Hurst *dean, law educator*
Pilcher, Christie W. *retired special education educator*
Shomaker, Andrea Kay *secondary school educator*
Steeples, Douglas Wayne *retired university dean, consultant, researcher*

Marietta
Downs, Claudia Peery *special education educator*
Houston, Dorothy Middleton *elementary school educator*
Laframboise, Joan Carol *middle school educator*
Overstreet, Regina Nix *mathematics educator*

Mcdonough
Mauney, Brandi Savage *special education educator*

Milledgeville
Mizelle, Nancy Batson *education educator, consultant*

Roopville
Huckeba, Emily Causey *retired elementary school educator*

Saint Marys
Hall, Lois Bremer *secondary school educator, volunteer*

Savannah
Cannon, Major Tom *retired special education educator*
Chong, Bruce Simon *dean, broadcast executive*
Dirlam, David Kirk *education educator*
Leighton, Richard Frederick *retired dean*
Polite, Evelyn C. *retired elementary school educator, evangelist*
Postell, Cindy Deborah *secondary school educator*
Rowan, Richard G. *former academic administrator*
Wallace, Paula S. *academic administrator*

Smoke Rise
Dees, Julian Worth *retired academic/research administrator*

Snellville
Blankenship, Colleen Marie-Krick *secondary school educator, writer*

Springfield
Guggino, Nelson Maurice *secondary school educator*

Statesboro
Tootle, Kathleen Maloof *special education educator*

Stone Mountain
Brown, Rhonda Jean *special education educator*
Jones, Ellen *elementary school educator*

Summerville
Perry, Alan Eugene *literature and language educator, department chairman*

Suwanee
Smith, Kimberly M. *assistant principal, educational consultant*
Wilson, Duane Bubba Regan *secondary school educator*

Swainsboro
Sapp, Gena Johnson *secondary school educator*

Temple
O'Dell, Connie Vincent *special education educator*

Thomaston
Hardy, Christina Brown *dean*

Toccoa Falls
Gardner, Donna Rae (Donna Rae Diehl) *education educator*

Trion
Robinson, Wynnelle Ann *counseling administrator*

Tucker
Stewart, Connie Ward *retired academic administrator*

Valdosta
Bailey, Hugh Coleman *academic administrator*
Blanton, Vallye J. Jean *educator*
Gunter, Philip Lee *special education educator, dean*
Pollock, Michael E. *mathematics educator, football coach, director*

Warner Robins
Childs, Vivian L. *retired principal*

Young Harris
Cox, Cathy *academic administrator, former state official*

HAWAII

Ewa Beach
Butler, Debra Yvonne *special education educator, small business owner*

Hana
Stevens, Muriel Kauimaeole Lee *retired elementary school educator*

Hilo
Pezzuto, John Michael *dean, pharmacology educator*

Honolulu
Castle, Alfred *administrator, executive*
Cook, Bryan G. *education educator*
Englert, Peter *academic administrator, director*
Gee, Chuck Yim *dean*
Greenwood, M.R.C. *academic administrator, biologist, nutrition educator*
Ingersoll, Caroline Yee *director*
Keith, Kent Marsteller *academic administrator, motivational speaker, lawyer, writer*
Kim-Rupnow, Weol Soon *education educator*
LaBelle, Thomas Jeffrey *research executive, academic administrator*
Muranaka, Jami *biology educator*
Pickens, Alexander Legrand *retired education educator*
Plourde, William E. *secondary school educator*
Silva, Mary Barnes *retired elementary school educator*
Soifer, Aviam *dean, law educator*
Uejo, Colleen Misaye *elementary school educator*

Kailua
Tubbs, Mary S. *curriculum coordinator*

Kailua Kona
Diama, Benjamin *retired secondary school educator, composer, writer*

Kaneohe
Ashley, Elizabeth *dean, educator*
Ko, Seung Kyun *international relations educator, consultant*
Maeshiro, Mitzi (Mikilani) *literature and language educator*

Kilauea
Caspillo, Carol A. *retired secondary school educator*

Laie
Miller, Ronald Mellado *education educator*

IDAHO

Boise
Andrus, Cecil Dale *academic administrator, former United States Secretary of the Interior*
Hart, Richard LaVerne *retired college dean*
Lazare, Michael *principal*
Lojek, Helen Heusner *associate dean*
Maloof, Giles Wilson *academic administrator, educator, author*
Pound, Kathleen Last *elementary school educator*

Caldwell
Hendren, Robert Lee, Jr. *academic administrator*
Hoover, Robert Allan *university president*

Coeur D' Alene
Finney, Andrew W. *academic administrator*

Idaho Falls
Castle, Lyle William *dean*

Jerome
Rice, Melissa Ann *mathematics educator*

Moscow
Daley-Laursen, Steven B. *academic administrator, dean, environmental scientist, educator*

Ola
Farr, Reeta Rae *special education administrator*

Parma
Sharkey, (John) Mick *biology educator*

Pocatello
Lawson, Jonathan Nevin *academic administrator, educator*
Olson, Gary Andrew *academic administrator, English language professor*
Piel, John A. *education educator*
Robinson, Evelyn Etta *principal*

Rexburg
Weyland, Jack Arnold *physics educator, writer*

Rigby
Henry, Esther Kaye *secondary school educator*

Rogerson
Boss, Marylin Jeanette *elementary school educator*

Shelley
Fleming, Chris K. *literature and language educator*

Sun Valley
Cassell, William Comyn *retired college president*

Twin Falls
Gentry, James Robert *education educator*

ILLINOIS

Alexander
Eck, Gail Ann *elementary school educator*

Arlington Heights
Placek-Zimmerman, Ellyn Clare *school system administrator, educator, consultant*

Aurora
Daugherty, Patricia Ann *retired elementary school educator*
Ross, Kristen Ann *school system administrator*

Belleville
Grandberry-Edwards, Vera Lynn *elementary school educator*
Hilgenbrink, Robert J. *academic administrator*

Bloomington
Bolen, Charles Warren *university dean*

Bolingbrook
Mell, Patricia *dean*

Bourbonnais
Spruce, Sara Elizabeth *education educator*

Cahokia
Schwemmer, Gabrielle *academic administrator, coach*

Carbondale
Dixon, Billy Gene *academic administrator, educator*
Poshard, Glenn (Glendal W. Poshard) *academic administrator, former congressman*

Carol Stream
Armerding, Hudson Taylor *retired college president, consultant*

Champaign
Cutcher-Gershenfeld, Joel E. *dean, professor*
DeBrock, Larry *dean, economics professor*
Herman, Richard H. *academic administrator*
Ikenberry, Stanley Oliver *education educator, director, former university president*
McConkie, George Wilson *education educator*
Okazawa, Hiromi *school librarian*
Smith, Bruce P. *dean, law educator*
Summerfield, Gale *director, educator*
Tettegah, Sharon Yvonne *university professor*

Charleston
Rives, Stanley Gene *retired academic administrator*
Swartzbaugh, Dorothy Stoeppelwerth *middle school educator*
Thornburgh, Daniel Eston *retired university administrator, journalism educator*

Chebanse
McLaughlin, Barbara Lyn *elementary school educator*

Chicago
Adelman, Pamela Bernice Kozoll *education educator*
Allen, Armstead *educator*
Allen-Meares, Paula G. *academic administrator, social work educator*
Anderson, John Leonard *academic administrator, chemical engineering educator*
Ayers, Bill (William Charles Ayers) *education professor, writer*
Bauman, Jerry L. *dean, pharmacy researcher, educator*
Beestrum, Molly A. *school librarian, educator*
Benson, Moses, Jr. *retired education services specialist*
Bigg, Susan Jeanette *educational consultant*
Bindenagel, James Dale *university executive*
Binion, Celious *retired parochial school educator*
Birnbaum, Barry William *special education educator*
Bowman, Barbara Taylor *early childhood educator*
Brawner, Cynthia D. *elementary school educator*
Buniak, Raymond *educational professional*
Cafferty, Pastora San Juan *education educator*
Campbell Lee, Sally Ann *academic administrator, director*
Chanyungco, Delly Yangco *dean*
Chauhan, Vyjayanti *biology educator*
Chinniah, Nim *academic administrator*
Clark, Gerda Margarete *special education educator*
Davis, Addie L. *mathematics educator*
Dreher, Melanie Creagan *dean, nursing educator*
Froehle, Bryan Thomas *professor, director*
Garanzini, Michael J. *academic administrator, priest*
Gislason, Eric Arni *academic administrator, chemistry professor*
Hamada, Robert S(eiji) *dean, economist, entrepreneur, educator*
Harris, Shirley *elementary, secondary and adult education educator*
Hayes, Alice Bourke *academic administrator, biologist, researcher*
Holaday Royster, Lynn Christine *academic administrator, educator*
Huberman, Ron *school system administrator*
Inwang, Rosie L. *education educator*
Jameson, James Larry *dean, educator, internist, endocrinologist*
Johnson, Barbara Elaine Spears *retired education educator*
Jones, Tony *academic administrator*
Keiderling, Timothy Allen *chemistry educator, researcher*
Khan, M. Wasiullah *academic administrator*
Kim, Mi Ja *dean, academic administrator*
Konrad, Beth *professor, consultant*
Krent, Harold J. *dean, law educator*
Kuner, Charles *retired secondary school educator*
Landerholm, Elizabeth Jane *early childhood education educator*
Levandowski, Barbara Sue *education educator*
Levmore, Saul *dean, law educator*
Lipinski, Ann Marie *academic administrator, former publishing executive*
Lusk, Peggy June *retired counseling administrator*
Madara, James Lee *dean, pathologist, educator, epitheliologist, CEO*
Mason, Gregory Wesley, Jr. *secondary school educator*
Mayer, Susan E. *dean, political science professor*
Mayo, Cora Louise *educator*
McCrank, Lawrence J. *dean, university librarian*
McMath, Lula Wray *retired elementary school educator, realtor*
Meisels, Samuel J. *education educator*
Miceli, William Cyril, Sr. *director*
Mirza, Leona Lousin *elementary school educator, director*
Morgan, Anita L. *academic librarian*
Noesen, Darlene Dorothy *mathematics educator*
Reilly, Anne Huedepohl *university educator, researcher*
Reynolds, Ruth Carmen *school administrator, secondary school educator*
Roberson, Carolyn A. *counseling administrator*
Roberts, Jo Ann Wooden *school system administrator*
Sanders, J. Ted *academic administrator, former educational association administrator*
Schieser, Hans Alois *education educator*
Schonfeld, Dan *educator*
Schubert, William Henry *curriculum studies educator*
Shaver, Joan Louise Fowler *dean, women's health nurse*
Snyder, Edward Adams *dean, economics professor*
Standberry, Herman Lee *school system administrator, educational consultant, corporate executive*
Steinberg, Salme Elizabeth Harju *academic administrator, historian*
Stewart, Donald M. *college president*
Sulkin, Howard Allen *academic administrator*
Swanson, Don Richard *university dean*
Uretz, Robert Benjamin *biophysics educator, university dean*
Van Zandt, David E. *dean, law educator*
Wagner, Susan Laurene *elementary gifted education educator*
Walton, Surrey Max *educator*
Wasan, Darsh Tilakchand *academic administrator, chemical engineer, educator*
Wham, David Buffington *secondary school educator*
Whitaker, Eric E. *academic administrator, former state agency administrator*
White, C. Vanessa *director*
Wolfson, Warren D. *dean, law educator, former judge*
Wyndewicke, Kionne Annette (Annette Johnson Moorer) *retired secondary school educator*
Yellen, David N. *dean, lawyer*
Yu, Clement Tak *educator, researcher, consultant*
Zimmer, Robert Jeffrey *academic administrator, mathematician, educator*

Chicago Heights
Rohwedder, Christopher *elementary school educator*

Crystal Lake
Haas, Sheila Jean *secondary school educator*

Deerfield
Meyer, Mara Ellice *special education educator, consultant, academic administrator*
Wrobbel, Karen *education educator, consultant*

Dekalb
Monat, William Robert *university official*
Nissen, Christopher Karl *educator*
Peters, John G. *academic administrator, political scientist*
Thomas, Lynne M. *academic librarian, researcher, blogger*

Des Plaines
Lee, Margaret Burke *college president, language educator*
McClure, Matthew K. *secondary school educator*

Du Quoin
Ibendahl, Jean Ayres *retired elementary and secondary educator*

East Saint Louis
Wright, Katie Harper *educational administrator, journalist*

Edwardsville
Karanovich, Frances Ann Bridger *education educator, retired superintendent, consultant*

Elgin
Del Genio, Irina L. *dean*
Mao, Ruixuan (Rick Mao) *dean*

Elmhurst
Niziolek, Alice *academic administrator*

Eureka
Edge, Rhea Arlene *dean*
Fulop, Ann *psychology educator*
Hearne, George Archer *academic administrator*

Evanston
Boye, Roger Carl *academic administrator, journalism educator*
Christian, Richard Carlton *dean, former advertising agency executive*
Hedges, Larry V. *educator*
Jain, Dipak Chand *dean, marketing educator, consultant*
Kimbrough, Lorelei *retired elementary and secondary school educator*
Lewis, Dan Albert *education educator*
Power, Peggy Ann *elementary school educator*
Schapiro, Morton Owen *academic administrator*
Tybout, Alice Marie *educator*
Weber, Arnold Robert *academic administrator*

Evergreen Park
Wigsmoen, Susan Catania *elementary school educator*

Galesburg
Haywood, Bruce *retired academic administrator*
Leath, Cheryl Lynn *retired pre-school educator, poet, painter*
Miller, Michael D. *mathematics educator*
Schroth, Stephen Timothy *education educator, researcher*
Taylor, Roger Lee *academic administrator, lawyer*

Glen Carbon
Lazerson, Earl Edwin *retired academic administrator*

Glen Ellyn
Neurauter, Elizabeth Strain *secondary school educator*

Glenview
Corley, Jenny Lynd Wertheim *elementary school educator*

Gurnee
Bedore, Lenora T. *elementary school educator*

Harrisburg
McKinstry, Glenn Allen *secondary school educator*

Harwood Heights
Rudel, Barbara Elizabeth *elementary school educator*

Highland Park
Slavsky, David Bruce *academic administrator, educator*

Hillside
Savic, Jelena *mathematics educator*

Hoffman Estates
McCullough, Gary E. *education company executive*
Peterson, Susan Carl *secondary school educator, gifted and talented educator*

Jacksonville
Anderson, Michael R. *elementary school educator, writer*
Johns, Beverley Anne Holden *special education administrator*

Joliet
Manning-Smith, Kelly Ann *dean of students*
Reed, Brian Alan *school system administrator*
Thompson, Gregory Lynn *secondary school educator*
Tokatlioglu, Theresa Diaz Lopez *elementary school educator*

Justice
Casselle, Corene *pre-school educator*

Kankakee
Crady, Paula Gannon *secondary school educator*

La Grange
Sessions, Joan T. *administrator, educator*

Lemont
Doebert, Sandra L. *school system administrator*

Loves Park
Saporito-Hines, Lucille Ann *special education educator*

Lyons
Gordon, Mark Harry *education professor*

Macomb
Drea, John Thomas *academic administrator, consultant*
Hayes, Paul Robert *retired field and clinical experiences coordinator*
Lindner, Reinhard W *education educator*

Maple Park
Carter, Ethel Ilene *secondary school educator*

Maywood
Ludwig, Logan T. *dean, consultant*

Moline
Pearce, Jay Thomas *history educator*

Morton
Sutter, Elaine Joyce *elementary school educator*

Mossville
Clary, Wendy Anne *principal*

Mount Prospect
Ullman, Christopher Charles *school librarian, educator*

Naperville
Gilmore, Brenda René *literature and language educator, theater director*
Wilde, Harold Richard *college president*

New Lenox
Heffernan, Debra Jane *administrator*

Normal
Bowman, Clarence Alvin (Al Bowman) *academic administrator*

Northbrook
Ben-Arie, Ronit Peleg *elementary school educator*

Oak Brook
Hoffmann, Joan Carol *retired academic dean*

Oak Park
Adelman, William John *retired academic administrator, industrial relations specialist*
Venerable, Shirley Marie *retired gifted and talented educator*

Oakbrook Terrace
Taylor, Ronald Lee *academic administrator*

Orland Park
Burfeind, Betty Ruth *retired secondary school educator, coach*

Oswego
Johnson, Dawn Sundene *chemistry educator*

Palatine
Edstrom, James A. *academic librarian*

Palos Heights
Powell, Patricia Lynn *education and special education educator*

Palos Hills
Stratton, Pauline A. *retired elementary school educator, alderman*

Paris
Essinger, Susan Jane *special education educator*

Park Forest
Dalke, Carl D. *school system administrator, consultant*
Orr, Marcia *primary school educator, consultant, director*
Sullivan, Patricia Marie *elementary school educator*

Park Ridge
Lampert, Joan *school system administrator*

Peoria
Kelly, Grace Dentino *secondary school educator*

Prospect Heights
Jenkins, Marlys J. *special education educator*

Quincy
Auluck, Nitin *educator*
Straub, Sunny L. *retired elementary school educator*
Tomczak, Patricia Ann *dean, archivist*

Richton Park
Pierce, Mary E. *retired elementary school educator, public relations consultant*

River Forest
Coe, Donald Kirk *retired academic administrator*
Johnson, Arvid C. *dean*

Rock Island
Horstmann, James Douglas *retired academic administrator*

Rockford
Bienen, Henry Samuel *former academic administrator, political scientist, educator*
Homewood, Elizabeth Holmes Nash *elementary school educator*
Johnson, Elizabeth Ericson *retired educator*
Koch, Carol Sue *secondary school educator*
Steele, Carl Lavern *academic administrator*

Rockton
Bolger, Jacqueline E. *literature and language educator*

Round Lake Beach
Harold, Kathleen T. *elementary school educator*

Saint Charles
Didier, James William *academic administrator, consultant*
Larsen, David Allen *educational consultant*

Schaumburg
Firsel, Lynne Marie *education educator*
MacDonald, William Burke *secondary school educator, consultant*

South Holland
Burton, Art T. *history educator*
Larsen, Mary Ann Indovina *counselor, educator*

Spring Grove
Mason, Janice M. *principal, director*

Springfield
Chriswell, Linda D. *special education educator*
Kocis, Janet Kay *elementary school educator*
Laubersheimer, David E. *academic administrator*
Poorman, Robert Lewis *retired academic administrator*
Schroeder, Raymond Ernest *educational administrator*

Sycamore
Johnson, Yvonne Amalia *elementary school educator, consultant*

University Park
Casey, Diane Dates *dean*
Maimon, Elaine Plaskow *academic administrator*

Urbana
Ghosh, Avijit *academic administrator, business educator, former dean*

Henderson, Robert Arthur *educator*
Kaufman, Paula T. *university librarian*
Knobloch, Neil A. *education educator*
Maeda, Akio *educator*

Vernon Hills
Cho, Yong Hyo *education educator, consultant*

Westmont
Baule, Steven Michael *superintendent*

Wheaton
Cook, Edward David *institute executive director*
Douglas, Cynthia *paraprofessional*
Juhl, Nicole Marie *secondary school educator*
Litfin, Duane *academic administrator*

Wilmette
Olson, Patricia Hagey *retired elementary school educator*
Smutny, Joan Franklin *academic director, educator*

Winnetka
McKee, Judith Nelson *elementary school educator, educational consultant*

Woodridge
Jandes, Kenneth Michael *retired superintendent of schools*
Kolek, Mary Eileen *principal*

Zion
Akouris, Dianne *elementary school educator*

INDIANA

Anderson
Nicholson, Dorothy Nelis *retired pre-school educator*
Nicholson, Robert Arthur *college president*

Angola
Deller, Jean A. *academic administrator*

Avon
Alsop, Thomas Walter *secondary education educator*

Bloomington
Arnove, Robert Frederick *education educator*
Barnes, A. James *dean*
Bornholdt, Laura Anna *academic administrator*
Brescia, William Fred, Jr. *development officer*
Chaifetz, Marshal Lawrence *educational consultant, educator*
Graham, John David *dean, former federal agency administrator*
McRobbie, Michael Alexander *academic administrator, computer scientist, educator*
Mehlinger, Howard Dean *education educator*
Robel, Lauren *dean, law educator*
Robinson, Jennifer Meta *senior lecturer, consultant*
Ryan, John William *academic administrator*
Smith, Carl Bernard *education educator*
Smith, Daniel C. *dean, finance educator*
Webb, Charles Haizlip, Jr. *retired dean*

Carmel
Rand, Leon *academic administrator*

Columbia City
Gust, Korrine Marie *education educator*

Connersville
Newton, Cindy Lynn *middle school educator, media specialist*

Corydon
Miller, Judith Elaine *retired middle school educator, musician*

Crawfordsville
White, Patrick E. *academic administrator*

Evansville
Jennings, Stephen Grant *academic administrator*

Fishers
Shults, Anna *elementary school educator*

Fort Wayne
Bard, Gary G. *academic administrator, dean*
Maiko, Saneta Morara *educator and director*
Shuster, Kirk Steven *retired primary school educator*

Frankfort
Sayers Butler, Patricia Ann *secondary school educator*

Gary
Morgan, Dorothy Ann *literature and language educator*
Smith, Vernon G. *education educator, Indiana State Representative*

Goshen
Meyer, Albert James *educational researcher*

Granger
Marino, Joseph Paul, Sr. *dean, chemist, researcher*
Morgan, Ardys Nord *school improvement consultant*

Greencastle
Bottoms, Robert Garvin *academic administrator, director*
Casey, Brian William *academic administrator, history professor*
Farber, Robert Holton *retired dean*

Griffith
Luetschwager, Mary Susan *educational consultant*

Indianapolis
Bailey, Dustin A. *school system administrator, secondary school educator*
Bepko, Gerald Lewis *retired academic administrator, law educator*
Brenner, Mark Lee *academic administrator, physiologist, educator*
Broome, Marion E. *dean, nursing educator*
Clark, Charles M., Jr. *medical school administrator*
Dai, Yuan-Shun *education educator*
Dale, Robert Howard Ingleby *psychology educator*
Fife, Rose Spitz *educator*
Floyd, James M., Jr. *adult education educator*
Gooldy, Patricia Alice *retired elementary school educator*
LaGrotto, Louisa *middle school educator*
Malone, Jean Hambidge *educational consultant*
Najjar, Diana *elementary school educator*
Roberts, Gary Raymond *dean, law educator*
Slocum, Judith Ann *retired elementary school educator*
Stewart, Sandra Kay *dean*
Sullender, Joy Sharon *retired elementary school educator*
Sykes, Linda Diane *retired elementary school educator*
White, Eugene G. *school system administrator*
Williams, Luida K. *retired elementary school educator*

Kokomo
Sarratore, Steven T. *academic administrator*
Tucker, Katherine Louise *elementary school educator*

Kouts
Miller, Sarabeth *secondary school educator*

La Porte
Johnson, Bruce Ross *elementary school educator*

Lafayette
Jischke, Martin C. *retired academic administrator*
Troutner, Joanne Johnson *director, consultant, secondary school educator*

Lagrange
Schmidt, David Joseph *senior resource specialist, consultant*

Lizton
King, Richard Gene *superintendent*

Middlebury
Dickey, Lucy Jane *elementary school educator*

Muncie
Amman, E(lizabeth) Jean *academic administrator*
Lawhead, Victor Bernard *education educator*
Stewart, Rita Joan *academic administrator*
Yssel, Nina *special education educator*

New Albany
Rea, Patrick Shaw *secondary school educator*
Riehl, Jane Ellen *education educator*

New Castle
Dye, Mary Jane *elementary school educator*

North Manchester
Schilling, Heather Anne *education educator*
Switzer, Jo Young *college president*

Notre Dame
Burish, Thomas Gerard *academic administrator, psychology professor*
Crosson, Frederick James *retired dean, humanities educator*
Jenkins, John I. *academic administrator*
Malloy, Edward Aloysius *academic administrator*
Newton, Nell Jessup *dean, law educator*
O'Meara, Onorato Timothy *academic administrator, mathematician*
Scheidt, W. Robert *chemistry educator, researcher*
Woo, Carolyn Yauyan *dean*
Younger, Jennifer A. *university librarian*

Plymouth
Jurkiewicz, Margaret Joy Gommel *retired secondary school educator*

Princeton
Clem, Nancy Gayle *secondary school educator*

Russiaville
Berry, Patricia A. *middle school educator*

Scottsburg
Burns, Paul D. *assistant principal*

South Bend
Harriman, Gerald Eugene *retired business administrator, economics professor*
Karns, Elizabeth A. (Libby Karns) *retired daycare administrator*
Mooney, Elizabeth Kaatz *adult education educator*
Shepherd, Terry Lynn *special education educator*
Spitzer, Bruce Alan *education educator*

Spencerville
Clark, Donna M. *retired elementary school educator*

Terre Haute
Dando, William Arthur *academic administrator, geography and geology educator*
Hunt, Effie Neva *retired dean, literature educator*
Malooley, David Joseph *electronics and computer technology educator*

Valparaiso
Heckler, Mark Alan *academic administrator*
Mundinger, Donald Charles *retired college president*

Warsaw
Pfeiffer, Isobel Lorraine *education educator*

West Lafayette
Beering, Steven Claus *academic administrator, medical educator*
Carney, Thomas Quentin *academic administrator, educator, professional pilot*
Córdova, France Anne-Dominic *academic administrator, astrophysicist*
Cosier, Richard A. *dean, finance educator*
Cox, Beverly E. *educational researcher, educator*
Ford, Frederick Ross *retired university official*
Moyars-Johnson, Mary Annis *retired academic administrator*
Reckowsky, Michael J. *academic administrator*
Shertzer, Bruce Eldon *education educator*
Wendt, Oliver *special education educator*

Westfield
Bradbury, Betty Marie *retired history and music educator*

IOWA

Albia
Jones, Betsy Lea *literature and language educator*

Allison
Reese, Susan Marie *elementary school educator*

Ames
Bugeja, Michael Joseph *director, educator, writer*
Crabtree, Beverly June *retired dean*
Ebbers, Larry Harold *education educator*
Geoffroy, Gregory L. *academic administrator, educator*
Hoffman, Elizabeth *academic administrator, economics professor*
Jackson, George Arthur *dean, educator*
Kozak, John Joseph *provost, chemistry educator*
Manatt, Richard *retired education educator*

Ankeny
Keese, Jan *elementary school educator*

Anthon
Herrick, Cynthia Jean *literature and language educator*

Cedar Falls
Licari, Michael J. *dean, political science professor*

Cedar Rapids
Perkins, Marcus Matthew *special education educator*
Russell, Steve D. *elementary school educator*
Underwood, Richard Lee *educator*

Coralville
Van Arendonk, Susan Carole *special education educator*

Creston
Dillenburg, Carolyn Eva Lauer *retired secondary school educator*

Davenport
Herzig, Stella *reference librarian*
Hudson, Celeste Nutting *education educator, consultant, reading clinic administrator*
Sheehey, Patricia Ann *secondary school educator*

Des Moines
Burn, Barbara Louise *literature and language educator*
Gaines, Ruth Ann *secondary school educator*
Vestal, Allan W. *dean, law educator*

Dubuque
Lee, Becky Glasson *education educator*
Meier, Joyce *education educator*

Earlham
Latham, Howard Douglas *school system administrator*

Elk Horn
Conklin, Virginia Ruth *school librarian, educator*

Emmetsburg
Hoover, Thomas R. *secondary school educator*

Fort Madison
Sodey, Angela Ann *gifted and talented educator*

Grinnell
Bonath, Gail Jean *Librarian*
Osgood, Russell King *academic administrator*

Iowa City
Boyd, Willard Lee *academic administrator, educator, lawyer, museum director*
Brennan, Robert Lawrence *educational director, psychometrician*
Feldt, Leonard Samuel *academic administrator, educator*
Frantz, Rita *dean, nursing educator*
Harper, Dennis Carlin *education educator*
Hunter, William Curt *dean, finance educator*
Jepsen, David Andrew *retired counselor, educator*
Jones, Carolyn C. *dean, law educator*
Jones, Catherine Clarissa *retired secondary school educator*
Kopelson, Kevin *literature and language educator*
Letendre, Donald E. *dean*
Mason, Sally Kay Frost *academic administrator, biology professor*
Morphew, Christopher Clark *education educator*
Plapp, Bryce Vernon *biochemistry educator*
Robillard, Jean Eugene *academic administrator*
Rothman, Paul B. *dean, medical educator*
Rushton, Gerard *geography professor, researcher*
Schulz, Rudolph Walter *university dean emeritus*
Spriestersbach, Duane Caryl *academic administrator, speech pathology/audiology services professional, educator*
Stone, Gerald Lee *university administrator, educator, psychologist*

Maquoketa
Krum, Dee *secondary school educator*

Mount Vernon
Cotton, Gregory Mark *librarian*

New Providence
Reece, Marlene Williams *elementary school educator*

Newton
Ponder, Marian Ruth *mathematics educator*
Ward, Doree Maxine *secondary school educator*

Oelwein
Flaucher-Falck, Velma Ruth *retired special education educator*

Oskaloosa
Burrow, Nancy Kay *special education educator*
Burrow, Paul Irving *secondary school educator*

Sabula
McKone, Brenda Kay *elementary school educator, coach*

Sioux City
Clovis, Samuel Harvey, Jr. *academic administrator*
Hamilton, Ruth Milton Green *retired college administrator, consultant*
Warnstadt, Jacqueline Rae *elementary school educator*

Sloan
Ullrich, Roxie Ann *special education educator*

Storm Lake
Bochtler, Stanley Edwin *education educator*
Musel, Donna Sue *academic administrator*

Waterloo
Alfrey, Marian Antoinette *retired education educator*
Kober, Arletta Refshauge (Mrs. Kay L. Kober) *retired supervisor*

KANSAS

Caldwell
Struble, Thelma Pauline *elementary school educator*

Caney
Wilmoth, Marsha H. *elementary school educator*

Chanute
Harris, Tosca Dugan *academic administrator*

Clearwater
Taverner, Pamela Johnson *secondary school educator*

Emporia
Phelps, Connie Lea *special education gifted educator*

Fort Leavenworth
Stentiford, Barry Maxfield *education educator, military officer*

Great Bend
Rittenhouse, Nancy Carol *elementary school educator*

Halstead
Sigmund, Cynthia Marie *elementary school educator*

Hays
Budig, Jeanette *special education educator*
Mercer, Debbie K. *dean*

Hope
Hottman, Geneva Rae *elementary school educator*

Kansas City
Atkinson, Barbara F. *academic administrator, dean, medical educator*
Naima, Hasan A. *academic administrator, department chairman*
Warne, Alan M. *continuing education educator, consultant*

Larned
Dodez, Diane M. *retired principal*

Lawrence
Agrawal, Gail *dean, law educator*
Audus, Kenneth L. *dean, pharmaceutical researcher*
Clowes, Edith W. *literature and language educator, consultant*
Cravens, Thomas E. *physics educator, researcher*
Finneran, Lanell Rene *special education educator, drama therapist*
Frederickson, Horace George *retired academic administrator, humanities educator*
Gray-Little, Bernadette *academic administrator, psychology professor*
Riffel, Laura Ann *director, special education educator*

Lenexa
Hackett, Jill M. *academic administrator*

Liberal
Hicks, Linda Reona *elementary school educator*
Smothermon, Reba Maxine *elementary school educator*

Manhattan
Coffman, James Richard *academic administrator, veterinarian, educator*
Lynch, Judith Arlene *academic administrator, director*
Schulz, Kirk H. *academic administrator*

North Newton
Ediger, Marlow *retired education educator*

Olathe
Henning, Lillian Joyce *special education educator*
Stevens, Diana Lynn *elementary school educator*

Overland Park
Diviney, Nancy Lynn *elementary school educator*
Ghahramani, Katie K. *associate professor*
Halloran, Rachelle *pre-school educator*
Velicer, Janet Schafbuch *retired elementary school educator*
Willsie, Sandra Kay *internist, educator*

Oxford
Browning, Terri L. *secondary school educator*

Shawnee
Clifton, Thomas E. *academic administrator, minister*

Stilwell
Hodgell, Murlin Ray *dean*

Topeka
Dennis, Dale M. *school system administrator*
McFarland, William Joseph (Joe) *academic administrator*

Valley Center
Greenwood, Riley MacGregor *biology educator*

KENTUCKY

Ashland
Beasley, Paul Wayland *academic administrator*

Auburn
Buster-Kemplin, Katina Joy *educational consultant*

Benton
Robichaud, Carolyn Wommack *retired secondary school educator*

Berea
Boggs, Bennett Gibson *academic administrator*
Haddix, Susan Ann *secondary school educator*

Bowling Green
Dahl, Darwin B. *educator*
Haynes, Robert Vaughn *retired academic administrator, historian*
Watkins, Leslie M. *academic administrator*

Campbellsville
Conner, Jeanette Jones *retired elementary school educator*
Meece, Drewry *retired education educator, minister*

Covington
Berg, Lorine McComis *retired guidance counselor*

Danville
Breeze, William Hancock *academic administrator*
Roush, John A. *academic administrator*

Elizabethtown
Buckles, Adrian Dale *dean, educator*

Fort Thomas
Yelton, Dianne Burgess *secondary school educator*

Frankfort
Bennett, Charles H. *dean*
Lancaster, Susan Abramson *education educator, consultant*
Sisney, Sherleen Sue *secondary school educator*
Trammell, Jerry Powell *literature and language educator*

Franklin
Starks, Venessa G. *retired elementary school educator*

Glasgow
Fritsch, Jennifer Lynne *middle school educator, artist*

Grethel
Hughes, Cindi Baker *special education educator*

Guston
Yundt, Betty Brandenburg *elementary school educator*

Hardin
Morrow, Bruce William *academic administrator, management consultant*

Hopkinsville
Redmon-Holliday, Rose Marie *secondary school educator*

Lexington
Allison, Jonathan Mackinnon *university professor, researcher*
Brennen, David A. *dean, law educator*
Collins, Martha Layne *academic administrator, former governor*
Diedrichs, Carol Pitts *library dean*
Ferzacca, William *retired education educator*
Gallaher, Art, Jr. *university chancellor emeritus, anthropology educator*
Guskey, Thomas Robert *education educator*
Isenhour, Kathleen Chaney *special education educator*
Jackson, Judy Faye *academic administrator*
Todd, Lee Trover, Jr. *academic administrator, electrical engineer*
Turner, Sharon P. *dean, dentist, educator*

Louisville
Bratton, Ida Frank *retired secondary school educator*
Cantwell, Patricia A. *guidance counselor*
Carroll, Jean Gray *retired mathematics educator*
Chen, James Ming *dean, law educator*
Choi, Namok *education educator*
Clover, Richard D. *dean*
Daugherty, Kimberly *academic administrator, educator*
Goldstein, Irvin L. *elementary school educator*
Greaver, Joanne Hutchins *mathematics educator, writer*
Hasan, Hammam Adib *education educator*
Howard, Deanna Jean *elementary school educator*
Jenne, Sue Oak *elementary school educator*
Koppel, Sheree Powers *dean*
Martinez-Maldonado, Manuel *academic administrator, dean, medical and science educator*
Mohler, Richard Albert, Jr. *academic administrator, theologian*
Newell, Elizabeth Carolyn *retired secondary school educator*
Ruter, Ruth Evelyn *elementary school educator*
Sauk, John Joseph *dean, educator*
Wright, Jeffrey A. *biology, physics educator*

Madisonville
Parker, Faye C. *elementary school educator*

Morehead
Caric, Ric Northrup *educator*
Dean, Lloyd *retired high school counselor*
Klecker, Beverly McCauley *academic administrator*

Mount Sterling
Aileen-Donohew, Phyllis Augusta *educational consultant*

Murray
Dunn, Randy J. *academic administrator*
Matlock, Pamela Durbin *special education educator*

Nicholasville
Armstrong, Marcy Lynn *literature and language educator*
Midkiff, Dinah Lee *retired elementary and middle school educator*

Owensboro
Olssen, Jennifer Leigh *elementary school educator*

Paducah
Talbert, Debra Kaiser *elementary school educator, artist*

Paint Lick
Donaldson, Kathleen *special education educator*

Pikeville
Mutter, Jennie *secondary school educator, artist*
Smith, Harold Hasken *university administrator*
Venters, Teresa Anne *elementary school educator*

Princeton
Earnest, Melissa Webb *education educator*
Noffsinger, Nancy Leigh *retired special education educator*

Richmond
McQueen, Keven Darryl *literature and language educator*

Russellville
Jukes, Jonathan H. *school librarian*

Simpsonville
Burkhardt, Susanne M. *elementary school educator*

Somerset
Eastham, Donna Saunders *interdisciplinary early childhood educator*
Watson, Rollin J. *former academic administrator, educator, writer*

Vanceburg
Phillips, Susan Diane *secondary school educator*

LOUISIANA

Alexandria
Wesse, David Joseph *higher education administrator, consultant*

Baker
Baker, Yvonne Bell *elementary school educator*

Baton Rouge
Banks, Willie Ivory *educational administrator*
Bensman, Stephen J. *school librarian, researcher*
Caffey, Horace Rouse *academic administrator, agricultural company executive*
Cerise, Frederick P. *academic administrator, former state agency administrator*
Hamilton, John Maxwell *university dean, writer*
Harper, Sandra Stecher *academic administrator*
Jenkins, William L. *academic administrator*
Jolly, Jennifer L. *education educator*
Lombardi, John V. *academic administrator, historian*
Martin, Michael V. *academic administrator, economics professor*
Mc Cameron, Fritz Allen *retired university administrator*
Prestage, James Jordan *consultant*
Risinger, Beth N. *elementary school educator*
Slaughter, Ralph *academic administrator*
Spearman, Diane Negrotto *art/special education educator*
Vallas, Paul G. *school system administrator*
Weiss, Jack Meyar *academic administrator, law educator*

Benton
Lynn, Jeff Wilson *history educator, farmer*

Choudrant
Lofton, Brenda M. *secondary school educator*

Deridder
Smith, Mabel Hargis *retired secondary school educator, musician*

Franklin
Fairchild, Phyllis Elaine *school counselor*

Frierson
Cobb, Kathleen Littlejohn *retired school administrator*

Gonzales
Kidd, Ruth Price *retired secondary school educator*

Grambling
Favors, Steve Alexander *academic administrator*
Porter, Wilma Jean *retired educational consultant*

Hammond
Kirylo, James David *education educator, consultant*
Parker, Clea Edward *retired university president*

Houma
Ponvelle, Brittany Gomez *elementary school educator*

Lafayette
Authement, Ray Paul *college president*
Cain, Judith Sharp *mathematics educator, consultant*
Simon, Carmon Serena *biology educator*

Lake Charles
Fields-Gold, Anita *retired dean*
Lee, Brandi Gremillion *elementary school educator*

Mandeville
Arrowsmith, Marian Campbell *elementary school educator, supervisor, educator*

Many
Quarles, Mary Jo *school librarian, educator*

Marrero
Love, Gayle Magalene *school system administrator*

Metairie
Crosby, Marena Lienhard *retired academic administrator*
Sanderson, Christine Graves *literature and language educator*

Monroe
Profit, Loretha Spurs *retired elementary school educator*

Natchitoches
Wall, Jerry Leon *dean, management educator, university administrator*
Wolfe, George Cropper *retired private school educator, artist, writer*

New Orleans
Adriaan, St. Claire Marlin *elementary school principal*
Bardell, Derek D. *academic administrator*
Cody, Wilmer St. Clair *educational policy consultant*
Cowen, Scott S. *academic administrator*
DeNisi, Angelo *dean*
Gordon, Joseph Elwell *university official, educator*
Griffin, Stephen M. *dean, law educator*
Harris, Frances Flintroy *retired university administrator assistant, civic worker*
Legrand, Benjamin David *elementary school educator, consultant*
Lyons, Sue Ellen Landry Landry *private school educator, consultant*
McArthur, Janet Davis Penland *literature and language educator*
McCall, John Patrick *college president, educator*
Melson, Lisa *psychology educator*
Mogabgab, Rose-Warren Berryman *academic administrator, writer*
Paradise, Louis Vincent *education educator, dean*
Query, Lance D. *dean, university librarian*
Watson, James Raymond *education educator*

Newllano
Boren, Lynda Sue *gifted education educator*

Opelousas
Underwood, Lorainne Ballard *literature and language educator*

Prairieville
Biri, Toni Roppolo *elementary school educator*

Ruston
Freasier, Aileen W. *special education educator*
Nassar, Raja *statistics educator, researcher, consultant*

Saint Martinville
Fournet, Patricia Sibley *retired secondary school educator*

Shreveport
Glasgow, Dianne Britt *education educator, writer, consultant*
Smith, Karen L. *elementary school educator*
Testerman, Traci L. *educator*

Sicily Island
Dale, Sam E., Jr. *retired educational administrator*

Slidell
Dabdoub, Paul Oscar *academic administrator*
Fincher, Margaret Ann *retired secondary school educator*

Springhill
Thomas, Faye Evelyn J. *elementary and secondary school educator*

Thibodaux
Hulbert, Stephen Thompson *academic administrator*

West Monroe
Ford, Mary Ann *secondary school educator*

Zachary
Price, Carol Leah *mathematics educator*

MAINE

Augusta
Randall, Richard J. *academic administrator*

Bangor
MacTaggart, Terrence Joseph *education educator, researcher, former academic administrator*
Pattenaude, Richard Louis *academic administrator, educator*

Bar Harbor
Krevans, Julius Richard *academic administrator, internist*
Swazey, Judith Pound *academic administrator, science educator*

Brewer
Davis, William Edmund *retired education educator*

Brownfield
Kloskowski, Vincent John, Jr. *educational consultant, author, educator*

Brunswick
Mills, Barry *academic administrator, lawyer*

Cape Porpoise
Glasser, William Arnold *academic administrator*

Farmington
Kalikow, Theodora June *academic administrator*

Harrington
Ray, Brittany E. *literature and language educator*

Houlton
Michael, Hannigan Owen *biology educator*

Kennebunkport
Featherman, Sandra *retired academic administrator, political science professor*

Lewiston
Hansen, Elaine Tuttle *academic administrator*
Tardif, Donna Lynn *elementary school educator*

New Harbor
Woolf-Wade, Sarah Jane *retired elementary school educator, writer*

Newfield
Patten, Ronald James *university dean*

North Yarmouth
Fecteau, Rosemary Louise *educational administrator, consultant*

Old Orchard Beach
Day, Marlene E. *elementary school educator*

Orono
Butterfield, Stephen Alan *education educator*
Kennedy, Robert Alan *educational administrator*
Rice, Edward Perry *secondary school educator*
Wiersma, G. Bruce *dean, forester, educator*

Portland
Botman, Selma *academic administrator, political science professor*
Dill, William Rankin *college president*
Pitegoff, Peter Robert *dean, law educator*

Presque Isle
Gentile, Caroline D. *adult education educator*

Skowhegan
Ross, James Owen *education educator, researcher*

Spruce Head
Bird, John Adams *educational consultant*

Topsham
Wilson, Linda Smith *retired academic administrator*

Waterville
Adams, William D. *academic administrator*

Armstrong, Darlene L. *elementary school educator*

Yarmouth
Bischoff, David Canby *retired university administrator*
Hart, Loring Edward *academic administrator*

MARYLAND

Accokeek
Kutchi, Judith Ann *elementary school educator*

Adelphi
de Jong, Mark E. *academic librarian*
Kirwan, William English, II, *academic administrator, mathematics professor*

Annapolis
Bowen, Linnell R. *director*
Cheek, Graham Terry *chemistry educator, researcher*
Fowler, Jeffrey L. *academic administrator, career military officer*
Kushner, Jack *physician executive*
Nuesse, Celestine Joseph *retired university official*
Stern, Margaret Bassett *retired special education educator, author*

Baltimore
Allan, Janet D. *dean, nursing educator*
Arrindell, Nicholas J. *academic administrator, educator*
Baltzley, Patricia Creel *mathematics educator*
Boughman, Joann Ashley *dean*
Boyd, Amanda D. *elementary school educator*
Brewer, Nevada Nancy *elementary school educator*
Carver, Wendy Gage *elementary school educator*
Daniels, Ronald J. *academic administrator, law educator*
Elias, Sarah Davis *retired English language educator*
Ellis, Brother Patrick (H. J.) *academic administrator*
Falk, Adam *dean, physics professor*
Gallagher, Michela *academic administrator, psychology professor*
Gifford, Donald George *dean, law educator, consultant*
Ginsberg, Benjamin *political science educator*
Guler, Osman *education educator, researcher*
Gupta, Yash P. *dean*
Haddon, Phoebe Anniese *dean, law educator*
Hill, Martha N. *dean, community health nurse*
Jackson, Stanley Edward *retired special education educator*
Lazarus, Fred, IV, *academic administrator*
Leffell, Mary Sue *educator*
McDaniel, Mildred Gage *elementary school educator*
McPartland, James Michael *academic administrator*
Panuska, Joseph Allan *retired academic administrator*
Pittenger, Arthur O., Jr. *mathematics educator*
Reece, E. Albert *dean, obstetrician, gynecologist, perinatologist*
Rhodes, Sharyn S. *education educator, consultant*
Ross, Richard Starr *retired medical school dean, cardiologist, educator*
Sadak, Diane Marie *director, performing arts educator*
Valentine, April Sue *elementary school educator, department chairman*

Bel Air
Alegi, Marc Patrick *middle school educator*
Miller, Dorothy Eloise *education educator*

Beltsville
Bruckner, Daniel Raymond *history educator*

Berlin
Hammond, Michelle *middle school educator*

Bethesda
Corn, Milton *dean, physician, consultant*
Hemming, Val G. *retired dean, educator*
Hutchins, Michael *non-profit scientific society administrator, conservation biologist*
Solomon, Henry *university dean*

Brooklandville
Schlitz, Laura Amy *school librarian, writer*

Brooklyn
Young-Wilson, Brenda L. *special education educator*

Burtonsville
Hudson, Yvonne Morton *retired elementary school educator*

California
Shoemaker, Cynthia Cavenaugh Jones *academic dean*

Chevy Chase
Meltzer, Jack *retired dean*

College Park
Anandalingam, Gnanalingam *dean, management educator*
DeLoatch, Nicole T. *academic administrator*
Dieter, George Elwood, Jr. *academic administrator*
Egel, Andrew *education educator*
Fetter, Steve *dean, physicist, educator*
Finkelstein, Barbara *education educator*
Imig, David Gregg *professor practise, retired educational association administrator*
Ingold, Catherine White *academic administrator*
Kosco Cossard, Patricia Ann *school librarian*
Langenberg, Donald Newton *retired academic administrator, physicist*
Mote, Clayton Daniel, Jr. *academic administrator, mechanical engineer, educator*
Wiseman, Donna L. *dean, education educator*

Columbia
Davis, Janet Marie Gorden *secondary school educator*
Gross, Linda Maria *secondary school educator*
Jones-Wilson, Faustine Clarisse *retired education educator*
Whiting, Albert Nathaniel *former university chancellor*

Crownsville
Campbell, Walter Everett *adult education educator*

Cumberland
Frederick, Sharon L. *education educator*

District Heights
McDowell-Craig, Vanessa Dennise *supervisor, consultant*

Edgewater
Whaley, Beth Dowling *retired elementary school educator*

Ellicott City
Bruley, Duane Frederick *academic administrator, consultant, engineer*

Frostburg
Root, Edward Lakin *education educator, academic administrator*

Gaithersburg
Bremenstuhl, David P. *elementary school educator*

Glen Burnie
Horine, Nelson Charles, II, *educator, educational administrator*
Watts, Virginia Agnes *retired special education educator*

Greenbelt
Bernstein, Kenneth J. *secondary school educator*
McCarter, Sharondia Renee *elementary school educator*

Havre De Grace
Tabor, Pamela Dalton *elementary school educator, career planning administrator*

Hyattsville
Spencer, Catherine Ellen *academic administrator*

Joppa
Bates, Martha Copenhaver *elementary school educator*

Kennedyville
Schiff, Gary Stuart *academic administrator, educator, consultant*

Kensington
Ellwanger, Albert Thompson III *secondary school educator*

La Plata
Miklos, Athena Pauline *educator*

Lanham
Ingraham, Cynthia Louise Johnson *educational consultant*

Laurel
Dorsey, John Wesley, Jr. *retired academic administrator, economist*
Williams, Barbara Ivory *retired educational researcher*

Lusby
Ladd, Culver Sprogle *secondary school educator*

Marion Station
Handy, Mary Thomas *retired elementary school educator*

Millersville
Culver, Catherine Marie *secondary school educator*

Ocean Pines
Crawford, Norman Crane, Jr. *academic administrator, consultant*

Potomac
Bulger, Roger James *academic administrator*
Hey, Nancy Henson *retired educational administrator*
Ingram, Richard Thomas *retired academic administrator, writer, consultant*
Kuykendall, Crystal Arlene *educational consultant, lawyer*

Princess Anne
Thompson, Thelma Barnaby *university president, classical languages educator*

Rockville
Ayafor, Isaiah M. *education educator*
Stansfield, Charles W. *educational administrator*

Saint Marys City
O'Brien, Jane Margaret *academic administrator*

Saint Michaels
Feisel, Lyle Dean *retired dean, electrical engineer, educator*

Salisbury
Gorrow, Teena Ruark *education educator*

Silver Spring
Bauer, Norman James *retired education educator*
Clark, Mizzell Phillips (Mitzi) *school librarian*
Coles, Anna Louise Bailey *retired dean, nurse*
Makris, Margaret Lubbe *retired elementary school educator*
Scheuerman, William E. *academic administrator, political science professor*

Stevenson
Hyman, Mary Bloom *science education programs coordinator*
Manning, Kevin James *academic administrator*

Suitland
Wilder, Elmon *retired university administrator*

Swanton
Cummins, Delmer Duane *academic administrator, historian*

Takoma Park
Kranidis, Rita S. *educator*
Ogora, Jane *university librarian*

Towson
Caret, Robert Laurent *academic administrator*
Douglas, Paul H. *university professor*
Hairston, Joe A. *school system administrator*

Trappe
Bowie, Norman Ernest *university official, educator*

Union Bridge
Hannah, Judy Challenger *private education tutor*

Walkersville
Welty, Sarah Osborn *secondary school educator*

MASSACHUSETTS

Agawam
Goodwin, Beverly Ann *elementary school educator*
Schilling-Nordal, Geraldine Ann *retired secondary school educator*

Amherst
Blair, Rhonda Louise *educator, actor*
Holub, Robert Charles *academic administrator, language educator*
Marx, Anthony W. *academic administrator*
May, Ernest Dewey *academic administrator, musician*
Prince, Gregory Smith, Jr. *retired college president*

Auburn
Mitchell, Karen Lee *special education educator, consultant*

Ayer
Sizer, Theodore R. *education educator*

Babson Park
Schlesinger, Leonard Arthur *academic administrator*
Tadepalli, Raghu *dean*

Bedford
White, Alan Frederick *academic administrator*

Beverly
Eastman, W. Dean *secondary school educator*

Bolton
Wintle, Suzanne *elementary school educator*

Boston
Abby, Dean R. *academic administrator, director*
Aeschliman, Michael David *education educator, writer*
Alden, Vernon Roger *academic administrator*
Aoun, Joseph E. *academic administrator, linguistics educator, researcher*
Ash, Barbara Lee *education and human services professor*
Auger, Jessie L. *elementary school educator*
Blandford, Gaynor E. *academic administrator*
Brown, Robert Arthur *academic administrator, chemical engineering professor*
Chang, Shan Nan *education educator, academic administrator*
Dienstag, Jules Leonard *dean, hepatologist, researcher*
Eisner, Sister Janet Margaret *college president*
Federman, Daniel David *academic administrator, endocrinologist, educator*
Flier, Jeffrey S. *dean, endocrinologist*
Grant, Barbara Hurwitz *history educator*
Harris-Sharples, Susan Hoffman *education educator*
Hedlund, Ronald David *academic administrator, researcher, educator*
Hopey, Christopher Edward *academic administrator*
Johnson, Carol R. *school system administrator*
Lataif, Louis Edward *dean*
Lawrence, Paul Roger *retired professor*
Le Quesne, Philip William *chemistry educator, researcher*
Light, Jay O. *dean*
Lutchen, Kenneth R. *dean, biomedical engineer, educator*
Myers, Robert K. III *director, musician, composer*
Norris, Lonnie Harold *dean*
O'Rourke, Maureen A. *dean, law educator*
Penney, Sherry Hood *academic administrator, consultant*
Royo, Sebastian *dean, finance educator*
Sargent, David Jasper *academic administrator*
Silber, John Robert *retired academic administrator, law and philosophy educator*
Simmons, Sylvia Jeanne Quarles *academic administrator, educator*
Sloan, Katherine (Kay Sloan) *college president*
Spieler, Emily A. *dean, law educator*
Westling, Jon *university administrator*
Wilson, Jack Martin *academic administrator, science educator*
Woods, Ryan John *education director*
Zelen, Marvin *statistics educator*

Braintree
Watts, Kisha Mann *school system administrator, secondary school educator*

Bridgewater
St. Aubin, Kendra Jane *Librarian*

Brookline
Ruthchild, Rochelle Goldberg *education educator*

Cambridge
Abadi, Abraham Albert *education educator*
Chernoff, Herman *statistics educator*
Clay, Phillip L. *academic administrator*
Dye, Nancy Schrom *academic administrator, historian, educator*
Edley, Christopher Fairchild, Jr. *dean, law educator*
Ellwood, David Tabor *dean, public policy educator*
Faust, Drew Gilpin (Catharine) *academic administrator, historian*
Fischer, Kurt Walter *education educator*
Forst, Edward C. *academic administrator, former diversified financial services company executive*
Graham, Patricia Albjerg *education educator*
Gray, Paul Edward *academic administrator*
Grosz, Barbara Jean *dean, computer scientist, educator*
Hammonds, Evelynn Maxine *dean, history professor*
Hockfield, Susan *academic administrator, medical educator*
Howitt, Arnold Martin *academic administrator, educator*
Johnson, Howard Wesley *retired academic administrator, finance company executive*
Kelman, Steven Jay *education educator*
Khoury, Philip S. *academic administrator*
LaGuardia, Cheryl M. *school librarian, writer*
Meyer, Dorothy Virginia *retired education educator*
Minow, Martha Louise *dean, law educator*
Perelman, Leslie C. *academic administrator*
Purcell, Bill *academic administrator, former mayor*
Reif, L. Rafael *academic administrator, engineering educator*
Schmittlein, David C. *dean, marketing professor*
Shinagel, Michael *dean, English literature educator*
Smith, Michael D. *dean, electrical engineering and computer science professor*
Sollors, Werner *literature and language educator*
Thiemann, Ronald Frank *dean, religious studies educator*
Whitlock, Charles Preston *former university dean*
Wones, Suzanne L. *academic librarian*

Canton
Trupe, Mary-Ann *secondary school educator*

Carver
Baldo, Robert Voisine *elementary educator*

Chatham
Stout, Sharon Sparkes *elementary school educator, counselor*

Chestnut Hill
Altbach, Philip *director, educator*
Beaton, Albert Eugene *education educator*
Boynton, Andrew C. *dean*
Gaiser, Ted Joseph *academic administrator, minister*
Leahy, William Patrick *academic administrator, historian, educator*
Monan, James Donald *university chancellor*

Dartmouth
Souza, Kathleen Anne *middle school educator*

Dorchester
Allen, Desser Lewis *retired elementary school educator*

Douglas
Bachelder, Beverly Brandt *secondary school educator, assistant principal, director*

Easthampton
Davis-Harris, Jeannette Gardrine *educator, historian*

Everett
Blake, Margaret Mary *director*

Fiskdale
Costello, Christine Ann *fine arts director, church organist*

Framingham
Flanagan, Timothy James *academic administrator, criminal justice educator*
Lucci, Dorothy Ann *educational consultant, psychologist*

Franklin
Benjamin, Bernard Edward *school system administrator, director*

Harwich
Caretti, Ann M. *school system administrator*

Haydenville
Shallcross, Doris Jane *education educator*

Holden
O'Neil, William Francis *academic administrator*

Ipswich
Lombardo, Ann Marie *special education educator, writer, artist*

Lancaster
Dugan, Maureen *biology educator, consultant*

Lexington
Cazden, Courtney B(orden) *education educator*
Collins, Allan Meakin *education educator*
Wilson, Wendy Scott *history educator*

Longmeadow
Ezrin, Myer *retired director*
Katz, Barbara Stein *special education educator*
Leary, Carol Ann *academic administrator*

Lowell
Abdelal, Ahmed T. *academic administrator, biology professor*
Lewis, Diane *educator*
Meehan, Martin Thomas (Marty Meehan) *academic administrator, former congressman, lawyer*
Ting, John M. *dean, engineering educator*

Lynn
Ryder, Edward Francis *secondary school educator*

Marstons Mills
Martin, David Standish *education educator*

Medford
Bacow, Lawrence Seldon *academic administrator, environmental scientist, educator*
Sternberg, Robert Jeffrey *dean, psychology professor, researcher*

Needham
Karr, P. J. *education educator, writer*
Miller, Richard Keith *academic administrator, engineering educator*

New Bedford
Matsumoto, Carolee Setsuko *researcher, education developer and administrator*

Newburyport
Robinson, Joyce McPeake *academic administrator, consultant*

Newton
Matteson, Carol J. *academic administrator*

Newton Center
Carter, Nick *academic administrator, minister*
Garvey, John Hugh *dean, law educator*

Newtonville
Harris, Paul Lansley *education professor*

North Andover
Keohan, Robert Daniel *literature and language educator, columnist*

North Dartmouth
Fields, Keota *education educator*

North Easton
Lema, Karen Anne *special education educator*

Northampton
Christ, Carol Tecla *academic administrator*

Northborough
Cradler, Judith A. *science educator*

Norton
Crutcher, Ronald Andrew *academic administrator, music educator*

Pittsfield
Kersten, Christian George *university administrator*
Wood, Elizabeth Ann *special education educator*

Provincetown
Wolfman, Brunetta Reid *education educator*

Salem
Doran, Kathleen Brewer *dean, consultant*

Sheffield
Kaufman, Raun Kahlil *education center adminstrator, teacher*

Shrewsbury
Onorato, Nicholas Louis *retired program director, economist*

Somerville
Austill, Allen *dean emeritus*

South Dartmouth
Ward, Richard Joseph *university dean, educator, author*

South Hadley
Creighton, Joanne Vanish *academic administrator*
Kaltenbach, Jane Couffer *biology educator*
Mullins, John Madison *educational consultant*

Springfield
Caprio, Anthony S. *academic administrator*
Leslie, George J. *professor*

Sudbury
Campbell, Elaine Josephine *retired academic administrator, writer, critic*

Waltham
Reinharz, Jehuda *academic administrator, history educator*
Sullivan, Mary E. *retired secondary educator, former state legislator*
Wawrzaszek, Susan V. *university librarian*

Wellesley
Auerbach, Jerold S. *educator*
Bottomly, (H.) Kim *academic administrator, biology professor, researcher*

West Newton
Fox, John Bayley, Jr. *retired university dean*

West Roxbury
Roach, Maureen S. *primary school educator*

West Springfield
Moore, Kelly Ann *secondary school educator*

Westborough
Jackson, Frederick Herbert *educational administrator*

Westwood
Ragone, David Vincent *former university president*

Williamstown
Canova, Jane E. *international education administrator*
Swift, Jane Maria *educational consultant, former governor*
Wagner, William G. *academic administrator*

Winchester
Harris, Carole Ruth *education educator, researcher, consultant*
Irving, Gitte Nielsen *secondary school educator*

Woods Hole
Adams, Rex *dean*

Worcester
Bassett, John E. *academic administrator, language educator*
Berkey, Dennis Dale *academic administrator*
Brenneman, Betsey Jean *college librarian*
Collins, Michael F. *academic administrator, medical educator*
Flotte, Terence Robin *dean, researcher, medical educator*
Indic, Premananda *education educator, researcher*
Mardilovich, Ivan P. *education educator, researcher*
McFarland, Michael C. *academic administrator*
Stutz, Cathleen Kinsella *education educator*

Yarmouth Port
Hall, James Frederick *retired college president*

MICHIGAN

Allendale
Haas, Thomas Joseph *academic administrator, chemistry educator*

Alma
Henry, David L. *political science educator, researcher*

Ann Arbor
Annchild, Cynthia *educational consultant*
Ascione, Frank Joseph *dean, pharmacy educator*
Balkrishnan, Rajesh *education educator*
Caminker, Evan H. *dean, law educator*
Collins, Susan Margaret *dean, political science professor*
Courant, Paul Noah *university librarian, economist, educator*
Dolan, Robert J. *dean*
Fleming, Suzanne Marie *academic administrator, freelance/self-employed writer*
Kalbfleisch, John David *statistics educator*
Kelch, Robert Paul *former dean, pediatric endocrinologist*
Leabo, Dick A. *retired statistics educator*
Omenn, Gilbert Stanley *academic administrator, internist, scientist*
Paul, Ara Garo *university dean*
Polverini, Peter J. *dean, dental educator*
Potempa, Kathleen M. *dean, nursing educator*
Robbins, Jerry Hal *educational administration educator*
Rogers, Bryan Leigh *dean, artist, educator*
Scarnecchia, Suellyn *academic administrator, lawyer*
Schacht, Jochen Heinrich *biochemistry educator*
Ulaby, Fawwaz Tayssir *academic administrator, engineering educator*
Warner, Kenneth E(dgar) *dean, public health educator, consultant*
Webber, Bonny A. *educational consultant*
Woolliscroft, James O. *dean, medical educator*

Berrien Springs
Lesher, William Richard *retired academic administrator*
Murray-Nseula, Marlene *educator*

Beverly Hills
Pardington, Mary Elizabeth *elementary school educator*

Big Rapids
Ryan, Ray Darl, Jr. *academic administrator*
Westman, Craig Ellery *academic administrator*

Bloomfield Hills
Jurkiewicz, Mary Louise *elementary school educator*

Caro
Hile, Michele Vera *middle school educator*

Clawson
Smith, Paulette Weatherwax *secondary school educator*

Dearborn
Beyer, Roberta Bonnie *dean, education professor, writer, researcher*
Zhu, Qiang *education educator*

Dearborn Heights
Johns, Diana *secondary school educator*

Detroit
Barrett, Nancy Smith *academic administrator*
Brown, Gloria Diane *elementary school educator*
Gueyser, Teresa N. *school system administrator, lawyer*
Issa, Diane Christine *special education educator, consultant*
Kyff, Kimberly *elementary school educator*
Little, Laura Ann *elementary school educator, art educator*
Rogers, Richard Lee *academic administrator, educator*
Ronnick, Michele Valerie *education educator*
Schirmer, Barbara Rose *special education educator, academic administrator*
Smith, Gary Richard *technology educator*

East Lansing
Flegler, Stanley Lewis *academic administrator, educator*
Ladenson, Sharon *university librarian*
Rappley, Marsha D. *dean, physician, educator*
Rothert, Marilyn L. *dean, nursing educator*
Simon, Lou Anna Kimsey *academic administrator*
Snoddy, James Ernest *education educator*
Strampel, William Derkey *dean, medical educator*
Warrington, Willard Glade *retired university official*

Eastpointe
Backus, Joseph A. *mathematics educator*

Edwardsburg
Moellenberndt, Scott D. *principal*

Elk Rapids
Thompson, Richard Thomas *academic administrator*

Escanaba
Weydt, Eric Charles *private school educator*

Fair Haven
Lenhausen, Georgia Rowena *secondary school educator*

Flint
Marcinkoski, Annette Marie *retired elementary school educator*
Simmons, Robert Randolph *principal*

Grand Rapids
Balog, C. Edward *academic administrator*
Diekema, Anthony J. *college president, consultant*
Hruby, Norbert Joseph *former college president, educational consultant, playwright*
Lubbers, Arend Donselaar *retired academic administrator*
Maupin, Karin Louise *secondary school educator*
VanScoy, Holly Carole *social and educational researcher*

Holland
Nyenhuis, Jacob Eugene *academic administrator*
Van Wylen, Gordon John *former college president*

Holt
Wood, Mary Elizabeth *retired secondary school educator, church musician*

Houghton
Abdelkhalik, Ossama *computer science educator, researcher*
Hungwe, Kedmon Nyasha *education educator, researcher*

Jackson
Smith, Jeff M. *secondary school educator*

Kalamazoo
Burns, James W. *education educator*
Dahlinger, Martha Louise *elementary school educator*
Freedman, Lauren *education educator, consultant*
Katrovas, Richard *literature and language educator, director*
Showalter, Shirley H. *former academic administrator*
Sinclair, Michael David *mathematics and science educator*

Lake Orion
Leonard, Jacquelyn Ann *retired elementary school educator*

Lansing
Straus, Kathleen Nagler *academic administrator, educator*

Lawrence
Applewhaite, Carlisle S. *special education educator, consultant*

Livonia
Budd, Jennifer Kathleen *literature and language educator*
Kujawa, Sister Rose Marie *academic administrator*

Ludington
Puffer, Richard Judson *retired college chancellor*

Macomb
Farmakis, George Leonard *retired education educator*

Marquette
Cotter, June Ann *special education educator*
Manning, Robert Hendrick *retired audio-visual services director, retired communications educator*

Millington
Bickel, Elaine Carol *academic administrator*

Mount Pleasant
Nowak-Fabrykowski, Krystyna Teresa *early childhood education educator*

Muskegon
Ross, Annette Lee *educational consultant*

New Buffalo
Roemer, James Anthony *retired director*

Northville
Allen, Janet Louise *school system administrator*

Novi
Serenson, Lynn Ann *mathematics educator*

Okemos
Edwards, Caryn Louise *educational consultant, special education educator*

Pontiac
Love, Sharon Irene *elementary school educator*
Riley, Mary Jane Stewart *secondary school educator*

Portage
Schultheis, Ann Lucia *retired curriculum specialist*

Rochester
Kraemer, Elizabeth Wallis *academic librarian*
Packard, Sandra Podolin *education educator, consultant*

Roscommon
Giacobazzi, Frederic David *literature and language educator*

Saint Clair
Wittig, Carol Hill *special education educator*

Saint Clair Shores
Coleman, Fay *literature and language educator, director*

South Haven
Llorens, Merna Gee *elementary school educator, retired music educator*

South Lyon
Melkvik, Jennifer Kent *retired mathematics educator*

Southfield
Hentrel, Bobbie Kuykendall *elementary school principal*

Spring Lake
Bussard, Janice Wingeier *retired secondary school educator*

Traverse City
Zimmerman, Paul Albert *retired academic administrator, minister*

University Center
Bledsoe, David Martin *educator*

West Bloomfield
Simpson, Robert Lee *academic administrator, department chairman, biologist, educator*

Williamston
Schab, Daniel J. *mathematics educator*

Wyoming
Couch, Katrina Denise *elementary school educator*

Ypsilanti
Block, Judith Florence *university librarian, distance education specialist*
Lewis-White, Linda Beth *elementary school educator*
Thueme, William Harold *secondary school educator, counselor, travel coordinator*
Willis, Craig Dean *academic administrator*

MINNESOTA

Ada
Sillerud, Arlen Roger *retired secondary school educator*

Afton
Robb, Babette *retired elementary school educator*

Alexandria
Lillestol, Jane Brush *educational consultant*

Baxter
Tomonovich, Kristin L. *special education educator*

Bemidji
Gilbertson, Troy *criminology educator*
Rogers, Patricia Louise *education educator, consultant, dean*
Sonsteng, Kathleen A. *education educator*

Bloomington
Sandok, Scott *economics educator, healthcare educator*

Caledonia
Dibert, Wendy Katherine *parochial school educator*

Cloquet
Belanger, Sharon Amling *special education educator*

Duluth
Stauber-Johnson, Elizabeth Jane *retired elementary school educator*

Excelsior
Pfeifer, Polly Lee *elementary school educator*

Falcon Heights
Kreuter, Gretchen Von Loewe *academic administrator*

Grand Rapids
Welch, Wayne Willard *educator*

Hastings
McGovern, Jillaine *literature and language educator*

Hibbing
Carey, Jan *school librarian*

Lakeville
Kasella, Nancy E. *psychology educator*

Little Falls
Perfetti, Robert Nickolas *educational consultant*

Long Lake
Lowthian, Petrena *academic administrator*

Maple Grove
Kirpes, Anne Irene *elementary school educator*

Mendota Heights
Friedrichs, Terence Paul *special and gifted education teacher*

Minneapolis
Atwood, John Brian *dean, political science professor*
Bruininks, Robert H. *academic administrator, psychologist, educator*
Davis-Blake, Alison *dean, management educator*
DiGangi, Frank Edward *academic administrator*
Dragseth, Kenneth Allen *retired superintendent and educational consultant of schools*
Huntzicker, William Edward *journalism educator, writer*
Johnson, Walter Heinrick, Jr. *retired educator, university administrator*
Lindell, Edward Albert *academic and religious organization administrator*
Lougee, Wendy Pradt *university librarian, educator*
McNaron, Toni A.H. *literature and language educator, director*
Montgomery, Lynn Marie *educational consultant*
Narciso, Carmen Veronica *elementary school educator*
O'Keefe, Thomas Michael *academic administrator*
Roth, Margaret Agnes *child development educator*
Stephens, Lee-Ann Williams *elementary school educator*
Stouder, Robin Renee *academic administrator, realtor*
Sullivan, Alfred Dewitt *academic administrator*
Svendsbye, Lloyd August *retired academic administrator, theologian, educator*
Warring, Douglas Franklin *education educator, psychologist*
Wippman, David *dean, law educator*

Morris
Hauger, Susan Mary *secondary school educator*
Kim, Jong-Min *education educator*

New Hope
McDaniel, Randall Cornell *substitute teacher, retired professional football player*

Northfield
Anderson, David R. *academic administrator*
Oden, Robert A., Jr. *academic administrator*
Olson, Deanna *school librarian*

Osseo
Anya, Adamma Chukwudi *special education educator*

Plymouth
Vieth, William Chapman *secondary school educator*

Prior Lake
Anderson, C. Wilson, Jr. *learning specialist*

Richfield
Devlin, Barbara Jo *retired school district administrator*

Rochester
Stockwell, Linda M. *principal*

Saginaw
Stauber, Marilyn Jean *retired elementary and secondary school educator*

Saint Cloud
Burgeson, John C. *dean*
Motin, Susan Hubbs *school librarian*
Russell, Patrick L. *psychology educator*

Saint Joseph
Fabres, Jose Antonio *educator*

Saint Paul
Brushaber, George Karl *academic administrator, minister*
Caine, Clifford James *educational administrator, consultant*
Dybvig, Mary McIlvaine *educational consultant, psychologist*
Dykstra, Robert *retired education educator*
Elde, Robert P. *dean, neuroscientist, educator*
Maxfield, Lori Rochelle *education educator*
McCormick, James Harold *academic administrator*
Rodríguez, Liliana Cristina *mathematics educator*
Rosenberg, Brian C *academic administrator*
Runge, Carlisle Ford *trade and environmental policy educator*
Sonday, Arlene W. *educational consultant*

Sartell
Morgan, Mary Jo *school system administrator*

Stillwater
Erwin, Raymond Maurice *secondary school educator*

Waseca
Frederick, Edward Charles *university official*

Waterville
Pettis, Patricia Amanda *secondary school educator, farmer*

Winona
Beyer, Mary Edel *primary education educator*
Nasstrom, Roy Richard *educational consultant*

Winthrop
Leitheiser, Mark Steven *literature and language educator*

MISSISSIPPI

Alcorn State
Wyatt, Helen J. *special education educator*

Booneville
Russell, Belinda *education educator*

Brandon
Wand, Kimberly Joanne *assistant principal*

Clarksdale
Presley, Vivian Mathews *junior college administrator*

Clinton
Campbell, Edward Wesley *elementary school educator*

Columbus
Mahoney, Linda L. *education educator, consultant*
Traynham, Lurene Jones *retired secondary school educator*

Crystal Springs
Nixon, Brenda Joyce *elementary school educator, small business owner*

Ellisville
Ross, Lisa Sims *special education educator*

Flowood
Verneuille, Kim R. *dean, educator*

Gautier
Moak, Rex R. *psychology educator*

Goodman
Diffey, Steven Dwayne *academic administrator, director*

Grenada
Rummage, James Mark *history educator*

Gulfport
Egland, Katherine Tatum *educational consultant, director*
Opel, Pamela Lynn *elementary school educator*

Hattiesburg
Bedenbaugh, Angela Lea Owen *chemistry educator, researcher*
Diket, Mary Read M. *academic administrator, educator*
Gunther, William David *academic administrator, economics professor*
Lucas, Aubrey Keith *retired university president*
Mazher, Waseem *special education educator*
McNeese, Rose Marie *retired education educator*
Noonkester, James Ralph *retired college president*
Reinshagen, Yolanda P. *elementary school educator*
Roy, Stephanie *academic administrator, educator*

Jackson
Bounds, Hank M. *school system administrator*
Carlisle, Peggy Jane *elementary school educator*
Chambers-Camper, Fransenna Ethel *special education educator*
Easley, Ray R. *seminary official, clergyman*
Mayeaux, Anne Russell *education educator*
McLin-Bronson, Hattie Rogers *school system administrator*

Madison
Watts, Thomas Parrish *history educator, consultant*

Meridian
Thomas, Olin C. *secondary school educator*

Minter City
Mitchell, Patsy Malier *religious school founder, administrator*

Mississippi State
Foglesong, Robert H. *academic administrator, career military officer*
Hopper, Peggy F. *education educator*
Rabideau, Peter Wayne *dean, chemistry professor, educator*
Ruby, Roy Harris *academic administrator*

Monticello
Clyburn, Esmond Steve *secondary school educator*

Natchez
Foster, Evaline L. *education educator, researcher*

Ocean Springs
Jenkins, Lawanna *retired middle school educator*

Olive Branch
Leary, Frances Elizabeth Cooper *secondary school educator*

Oxford
Moorhead, Sylvester Andrew *retired education educator*
Walton, Gerald Wayne *retired university official, retired university official*

Picayune
Penton-Smith, Tammy L. *elementary school educator*

Raymond
Cook, Jeanne Wells *literature and language educator*
Flanders, Helen Juanita *school librarian, academic administrator*

Saltillo
Hopkins, Betty Belinda *elementary school educator*

Scooba
Monk, Suzanne Renee *academic administrator*

Starkville
Mabry, Donald Joseph *retired academic administrator, history professor*
Mosley, Mary Nell H. *retired elementary school educator*

Tupelo
Cleveland, Mary Heloise *elementary school educator*

University
Davis, Samuel Marion *dean, law educator, researcher*
Sam, Joseph *retired university dean*

Utica
Marshall, Sophia S.L. *director*

Vicksburg
Pace, Carol Rebecca *elementary school educator*

Waynesboro
Crager, Ginny Lee *gifted and talented educator*

MISSOURI

Advance
Thomas, Rich L. *secondary school educator*

Arnold
Kasey, Arthur R. III *secondary school educator*

Bakersfield
Barnes, Sandra Lynn *special education educator*

Belton
Daggett, Kathleen *retired special education educator*
Hoye, Linda Lee *special education educator*

Bethel
Coonrod, Delberta Hollaway (Debbie) *retired educator, consultant*

Boonville
Cline-Denney, Dorothy May Stammerjohn *education educator, consultant*

Bosworth
Ireland, Betty Jean *retired principal, music educator*

Cape Girardeau
Suhr, Karl Friedrich *school librarian*

Chesterfield
Chambers, Jerry Ray *school system administrator, consultant*

Columbia
Deaton, Brady J. *academic administrator*
Dessem, R. Lawrence *dean, law educator*
Forsee, Gary D. *academic administrator, former telecommunications industry executive*
Miller, Paul Ausborn *adult education educator*

Farmington
Kellogg, Margaret *elementary school educator*

Fayette
Inman, Marianne Elizabeth *academic administrator*

Florissant
Ackley, Robert Arthur *mathematics educator, retired military officer*
Conrad, Mary Trench *elementary school educator*
Kralemann, William Joseph *retired chemistry educator*
Sikora, Diana Marie *elementary school educator*

Forsyth
Klinefelter, Sarah Stephens *retired dean, broadcast executive*

Granby
Sparkman, Lyle Bruce *academic administrator, education educator*

Hannibal
Schafer, Bette Jane *education educator*

Hillsboro
Adkins, Gregory D. *higher education administrator*
Cummiskey, Raymond Vincent *academic administrator*

Holt
Merrill, Donna *special education educator*

Humansville
Richler, Zenia H. *naturopath educator, health facility administrator*

Independence
Franklin, J. Richard *principal*
Johnson, Sharon Elaine *elementary school educator*
Shover, Joan *retired secondary school educator*

Jackson
Patrick, John *secondary school educator*

Jefferson City
Brandt, William Edmund *retired school system administrator*
Scott, Gary Kuper *retired academic administrator*

Kansas City
Amerison, Janice Earline *special education educator*
Caulfield, Joan *director, educator*
Churchman, Michael Steele Bright *educational consultant, educator*
Collins, Kathleen *academic administrator, art educator*
Eubanks, Eugene Emerson *education educator, consultant*
Gould, Charlene J. *dean, educator*
Hamilton, Richard Alfred *retired academic administrator, marketing executive*
Jonas, Harry S. *medical education consultant*
McCollum, Clifford Glenn *college dean emeritus*
Sizemore, William Christian *retired academic administrator, county official*
Slaughter, Rochelle Denise *elementary school educator*
Snelling, Troy Wayne *history educator*
Suni, Ellen Y. *dean, law educator*
Swaffar, Glenda Jean *director*
Woods-Taylor, Cleora Lynesia *mathematics educator, consultant*

Laurie
Currier, Mike *elementary school educator, writer*

Liberty
Haistings, Jeanine Lee *education educator*
Tanner, Jimmie Eugene *retired dean*

Marshfield
Frame, Susan S. *special education educator*

Mexico
Holman, Mark D. *secondary school educator*

Moberly
Agee, Patricia Ann *school librarian, director*

Mooresville
Totten, Tina Rosene *special education educator*

Neosho
Allman, Ann Lowrance *counseling administrator*
Williams, Bethia *education educator*

Nevada
Besaw, Jeanne Marie *school librarian*

Park Hills
Young, Shawn *education educator*

Poplar Bluff
Nunnery, Pamela L. *literature and language educator*
Sievers, David *secondary school educator*

Raymore
Spainhower, James Ivan *retired college president*

Riverside
Curry, Debbie Ann *school librarian*

Rolla
Carney, John F. III *academic administrator*
Mitchell, Owen Robert *dean, electrical engineering educator*

Saint Ann
Lema, Pickett Pat *school system administrator*

Saint Charles
Leavitt, Lynda *professor*

Saint Joseph
Bogle, Deborah Confer *education educator*
Saravanabhavan, Sheila *education educator*

Saint Louis
Abdul-Hafidh, Jamal *educator*
Baker, Shirley Kistler *academic administrator, university librarian*
Biondi, Lawrence *academic administrator, priest*
Blankenship, Robert Eugene *biochemistry educator*
Blanton, Elizabeth Anne *secondary school educator*
Booth, Betty Jean *retired daycare administrator, poet*
Cain, James Nelson *arts school and concert administrator*
Chittooran, Mary M. *education educator*
Danforth, William Henry *retired academic administrator, physician*
Dreessen, Chuck R. *mathematics educator*
George, Thomas Frederick *academic administrator*

Hickman, Clark Joseph *education educator*
Huestis, Jeffrey Charles *academic administrator, dean*
Janis, Larry Williard *secondary school educator*
Jordan, Julia Crawford *secondary school educator*
Koff, Robert Hess *academic administrator, adult education educator*
Lackey, Kayle Diann *elementary school educator*
Lewis, Jeffrey E. *dean, law educator*
Mahan, David James *retired academic administrator*
McNamee, Sister Catherine *educator*
McReynolds, Patricia Randolph *retired education educator*
Monteleone, Patricia L. *dean*
Overall, Dianna *elementary school educator*
Rice, Rose Ann M. *secondary school educator*
Sansalone, Mary Jane *dean, structural engineer, educator*
Scheffing, Dianne Elizabeth *special education educator*
Shapiro, Larry J. *dean, educator, pediatrician*
Staines, Gail M. *academic administrator*
Sykes, Charles E. *dean*
Walker, Doretta Anita *director*
Weiss, Robert Francis *retired academic and religious organization administrator, consultant*
Wrighton, Mark Stephen *academic administrator, chemistry professor*

Saint Peters
Caples, Linda Griffin *retired secondary school educator*
Huckshold, Wayne William *elementary school educator*
Thornton, Girard B., Jr., (Jerry) *elementary school educator*

Springfield
Abidogun, Jamaine Marie *education educator, researcher*
Allcorn, Terry Alan *principal, educator*
Beisswenger, Drew (Donald Andrew Beisswenger) *music librarian*
Frizell, Michael *director*
Kavanaugh, Rosa Jean *dean*
Reed, Peggy Anne *education educator*
Salley, C. DeWitt, Jr. *education educator, director*
Sherman, Ruth Todd *counseling administrator, educator*
Smith, Gregory Arnold *dean*
Toste, Anthony Paim *chemistry educator, researcher*

Troy
Bockhorst, Barbara Alice *retired secondary school educator*
Mills, Marsha Lee *retired secondary school educator*

Wildwood
Truitt, William Harvey *private school educator*

Windyville
Condron, Daniel Ralph *academic administrator, metaphysics educator*

MONTANA

Billings
Kerr, Shauna Gay *secondary school educator*
Mahlke, Amy Gerilyn *pre-school teacher*

Boulder
Kelly, Mark *secondary school educator*

Bozeman
Buonamici, April Graham *elementary school and music educator*

Butte
Gilmore, W. Franklin (Frank) *academic administrator*

Dayton
Catalfomo, Philip *retired university dean*

Helena
Pettit, Lawrence Kay *university president*

Missoula
Barnett, Mary Louise *elementary school educator*
Brown, Perry Joe *dean*

Montana City
Shaver, James Porter *retired education educator, dean*

Wolf Point
Morin, JoyAnn Hauge *education educator*

NEBRASKA

Arlington
Moskus, Jerry Ray *retired academic administrator*

Bellevue
Hawkins, Mary Bess *academic administrator*
Kayne, Jon Barry *academic administrator, psychologist*
Muller, John Bartlett *academic administrator*

Hastings
Dux-Ideus, Sherrie Lee *school librarian, history educator*

Kearney
Forster, Bruce Alexander *dean*
Snider, Daren *educator*

Lincoln
Bradley, Richard Edwin *retired academic administrator*
Dunlap, Michael S. *student loan company executive*
Giles-Watson, Maura *educator*
Grew, Priscilla Croswell *academic administrator, geologist, educator, museum director*
Hansen-Daberkow, Michelle Len *elementary school art educator*
Kern, Jeanne Rustemeyer Wood *retired secondary school educator*
Mendola, Joseph Robert *philosophy professor, department chairman*
Perlman, Harvey Stuart *academic administrator*
Willborn, Steven L. *dean, law educator*

Omaha
Baker, Gail *director, ESL educator*
Brock, Barbara Louise *education educator*
Felton, Melanie K. *special education educator*
Fennell, Madaline *elementary school educator*
Foster, Betty Louise *secondary school educator*
Gollan, John Lachlan *dean, medical educator*
Haselwood, Eldon LaVerne *retired education educator*
Louis, Virgie Lee *retired secondary school educator*
Newton, John Milton *academic administrator, psychologist, educator*
Pamies, Rubens John *dean*
Ranks, Anne Elizabeth *retired elementary and secondary education educator*
Riepe, Charleine Williams *secondary school educator*

Scottsbluff
Alkire, Garry R. *dean*

Staplehurst
Harre, Alan Frederick *retired academic administrator*

Tekamah
Cooper, Velma J. *elementary school educator*

Waverly
Jensen, Daniel *history educator*

York
Eckman, Steven William *academic administrator*

NEVADA

Carson City
Brant, James William *educational consultant, mathematician*
Eftimoff, Anita Kendall *retired educational consultant*

Elko
Lesbo, Paula Mae *secondary education educator*

Hawthorne
Funk, Gary A. *secondary school educator*

Henderson
Holmes, BarbaraAnn Krajkoski *retired secondary school educator*
Kapel, David Edward *academic administrator, researcher, education educator*
Keene, Richard Brian *school system administrator, educational consultant*
Martin, Gale D. *adult education educator*
Teemant, Melanie J. *middle school educator*
Thanki, Sandip G. *educator*

Las Vegas
Ananias, José *retired school system administrator*
Andolina, Nancy Jean *retired middle school educator, dancer, English and language arts educator*
Arteaga, Deborah *educator*
Ashley, David B. *academic administrator, engineering educator*
Chung, Sue Fawn *educator, researcher*
Edualino, Emilio Quial *school educator*
Gaspar, Anna Louise *retired elementary school educator, consultant*
Gerdes, Denise M. *school librarian*
Guinan, Mary Elizabeth *academic administrator, public health service officer, physician, researcher*
Hall, Gene E. *education educator*
Johnston, Sally Jo *dean, department chairman*
Nathanson, Rebecca *education educator, law educator*
Pierce, Thresia Korte (Tish Pierce) *primary school educator*
Pravica, Michael Gojko *education educator*
Shuman, R. Baird *academic administrator, consultant, language educator, writer*
Sileo, Nancy M. *special education educator*
Silverman, Elaine Ann *mathematics educator*
Walker, Gwendolyn Kaye *guest teacher elementary education*
White, John Valery *dean*
Willis, Tricia Lee *special education educator*

North Las Vegas
Manley, Audrey Forbes *retired academic administrator, pediatrician, military officer*
Neff, William *educator*
Wyckoff, Theri Lynne *education educator*

Reno
Ceppos, Jerry (Jerome Merle Ceppos) *dean, former newspaper editor*
Dietrich, Dean Forbes *academic administrator*
Dillard, Robert Lee *academic administrator*
Glick, Milton Don *academic administrator, chemist*
McCarty-Puhl, J-Petrina *chemistry educator*
Perry, Jean Louise *academic administrator*
Rubalcava, Micaela *education educator*

Winnemucca
Smith, Jack N. *secondary school educator*

NEW HAMPSHIRE

Brentwood
Boozer-Blasco, Claudia Ruth *family and consumer resources educator*

Chester
Volpe, Christopher Thomas *history educator*

Concord
Denham, Robin Richardson *secondary school educator*
Kenney, Kimberly *elementary school educator*

Dover
Pelletier, Marsha Lynn *secondary school educator, poet*

Durham
Gao, Mingchu *education educator*
Huddleston, Mark Wayne *academic administrator, political scientist, educator*
Loy, James Brent *education educator*
MacKay, Edward R. *academic administrator*

Epping
Whitesell, Ann Therese *elementary school educator*

Exeter
Kelley, Carolyn *biotechnology educator*

Hanover
Danos, Paul *dean, accounting educator*
Green, Ronald Michael *bioethics educator*
Helble, Joseph John *dean, chemical engineer, educator*
Kim, Jim Yong *academic administrator, preventive medicine physician*

Keene
Herold, Irene M.H. *academic librarian*

Manchester
DeFelice, Jonathan Peter *academic administrator, priest*
Reno, Stephen Jerome *former academic administrator*

Milford
Queeney, Deborah Ann *special education educator*

Nashua
Arthur, Rose Ann Horman *dean*
Leech, John Warner *research scientist*

North Hampton
Southworth, Robert Alexander, Jr. *education researcher, educator*

Plaistow
Wilder, Dwight Safford *academic administrator*

Portsmouth
Krajeck, Amy Jo *literature and language educator*

Rindge
Birge, James *academic administrator*

West Lebanon
Halperin, George Bennett *education educator, retired military officer*

NEW JERSEY

Basking Ridge
Cleaves, Graham Robert *secondary school educator*

Bayville
Atkins, Yvette *special education educator*
Tozer, Jean Frame *gifted and talented educator*

Bernardsville
Venezia, William Thomas *school system administrator, counseling consultant*

Bridgewater
Hart, Karen Jean *special education educator*

Browns Mills
Di Nunzio, Dominick *educational administrator*

Burlington
Cobb, Vanessa Wyvette *elementary school educator*

Butler
Kerler, Dov-Ber Boris *academic administrator*

Caldwell
Savage, Joseph George *academic administrator*
Werner, Patrice (Patricia Ann Werner) *academic administrator*

Camden
Gordon, Walter Kelly *retired academic administrator, language educator*
Solomon, Rayman Louis *dean, law educator*

Colts Neck
Crowder-Pagano, Linda Louise *special education educator*

Cranbury
Kimmich, Christoph Martin *former academic administrator, educator*

East Orange
Wright, Jameelah R. *pre-school educator*

Edgewater
Teicher, Henry Earl *retired education educator*

Edison
Biunno, Theresa *physical education educator*

Egg Harbor City
Farris, Vera King *former college president*

Egg Harbor Township
Carney, Michelle Catherine *assistant principal*

Elizabeth
Ferrara, Joseph Anthony, Sr. *vice principal*

Ewing
Garrett, Leigh Ann *elementary school educator*

Flanders
Kuzma, Deborah J. *vice principal, music educator*

Fort Lee
Sugarman, Alan William *educational consultant*

Glassboro
D'Augustine, Robert *academic administrator, lawyer*
Holdcraft, Janet Rulon *school system administrator*

Glen Rock
Keenaghan, Patricia Anne *principal, educator*

Hackensack
Williamson, (Eulah) Elaine *elementary school educator*

Hackettstown
Iaione, Robin Jan *elementary school educator*

Haddon Heights
Weinberg, Ruthmarie Louise *special education educator, researcher*

Hamilton
Kilbourne, Claire Anne *retired gifted and talented education educator*
Turnbull-Bruehl, Jo'Ann Hazel *special education educator*

Hightstown
Elliott, Frank Nelson *retired college president*

Hillside
Dickerson, Martin Lee *principal*

Hoboken
Matthews, Charles *school disciplinarian*
Raveché, Harold Joseph *academic administrator*

Jersey City
Ross, John G. *educator*
Soo Hoo, Tsung (Bill) Yao *security studies educator, consultant*

Lakewood
Doak, Nancy Ann *mathematics educator*
Williams, Barbara Anne *retired academic administrator*

Lanoka Harbor
Lake, William Robert *educator*

Lawrenceville
Hnasko, Amy Marie *primary school educator*
Jordan, Mildred Rice Loretta *education educator*
Lackie, Robert Jonathan *university librarian, educator, consultant*
Rozanski, Mordechai *academic administrator*
Tharney, Leonard John *education educator, consultant*

Lincroft
Ruiz Madas, Yesenia *educational counselor*

Linwood
Sutman, Frank Xavier *retired academic administrator, chemist, writer, educator*

Little Falls
Luing, Larry Lee *educational administrator*

Madison
Bull, Vivian Ann *retired academic administrator, educator*

Mahwah
D'Antonio, Lawrence *mathematics educator*

Maplewood
Fiorito, Frank Anthony *secondary educator*

Marlton
Cheney, Eleanora Louise *retired secondary school educator*

Martinsville
Raby, John Cornelius *secondary school educator*

Mays Landing
Wilinski, Grant W. *dean*

Middletown
Shields, Patricia Lynn *educational broker, consultant*

Monmouth Beach
Ginty, Karen *elementary school educator*

Monroe Township
Sullivan-Szuts, Betty Anne *academic administrator, educator*
Treatman, Paul *retired school system administrator*

Montclair
Cooke, Nicole *school librarian*

Hadzic, Gorica *literature and language educator*
Kripalani, Lakshmi Assudomal *educator*

Morristown
Mertz, Francis James *university president*

Mullica Hill
Tosti, Susan Marie *educational consultant*

New Brunswick
Greenberg, Douglas Stuart *dean, history professor*
Greenberg, Michael Richard *urban studies and community health educator*
Haugerud, Angelique *professor of anthropology*
McCormick, Richard Levis *academic administrator*
Nelson, Jack Lee *education educator*
Stanley, Jason *education educator*
Stauffer, George B. *dean, musician, historian, consultant*
Strawderman, William E. *statistics educator*
Strickland, Dorothy *education educator*
Tanner, Daniel *education educator*
Turshen, Meredeth *educator*

New Monmouth
Santos, Sharon Lee *parochial school educator*

New Providence
Hirsch, Maxine K. *special education educator, councilman*

Newark
Altenkirch, Robert A. *academic administrator*
Bergen, Stanley Silvers, Jr. *retired academic administrator*
Farmer, John Joseph, Jr. *dean, lawyer, former state attorney general*
Givens, Theartis Tina Mansfield *primary school educator*
Graycar, Adam *dean, former Australian government official*
Hobbs, Patrick Esmond *dean, law educator*
Janey, Clifford Bernard *school system administrator*
Lieb, Janice Rose *primary school educator*
Owen, William Franklin, Jr. *academic administrator, former research and development company executive*
Petillo, John J. *former academic administrator, priest*
Sabio, Dorothy *elementary school educator*
Tedesco, Barbara L. *dean, educator*
Vincenti, Gene A. *director, consultant*

Norwood
Murburg, Thelma D. *retired elementary school educator*

Oakland
Butterfield, Charles Edward, Jr. *educational consultant*

Paramus
Chenoweth, Okey Everett *literature and language educator, writer, actor, director*
Jenkins, Elaine *middle school educator*
Russell, Carol Ann Lamken *special education educator*
Tamburro, Peter James, Jr. *secondary school educator*

Parsippany
Weisberg, Joseph Simpson *retired dean*

Paterson
Fields, Marvin Leon *secondary school educator*

Pennington
Townsend, Peggy (Stephanie G.) *headmaster*

Piscataway
Amaral, Andre Renato Sales *education educator, researcher*
Dill, Ellis Harold *university dean*
Klein, Michael Tully *dean, chemical engineer, consultant*

Plainfield
Ruiz, Pedro Javier *education educator*

Pomona
Herath, Ajantha *education educator*
Jones, Joseph E. *elementary school educator*

Pompton Plains
Pischl, Adolph John *school administrator*

Princeton
Dawes, Trevor A. *school librarian*
Duncan, Dianne Walker *elementary school educator*
Goddard, Peter *academic administrator, mathematical physicist*
Hollander, Toby Edward *education educator*
Paxson, Christina Hull *dean, economics and public affairs professor*
Pimley, Kim Jensen *financial training consultant*
Tilghman, Shirley Marie *academic administrator, biology professor*
Ueda, Atsuko *educator*

Randolph
Ghosh, Ajit Kumar *daycare administrator*

Ridgewood
Friedrich, Margret Cohen *guidance and student assistance counselor*

Roselle
Wilson, Arthur Theodore *education consultant*

Short Hills
Robbins-Wilf, Marcia *educational consultant*

Sicklerville
Miller, Audrey Thornton *retired vice principal*

South Orange
Holmes, Paul A. *academic administrator*
Talar, Anita Louise *university librarian*

Southampton
O'Connor, Sheryl Broderick *retired literature and language educator*

Succasunna
London, Fran *special education educator*

Sussex
Puzio, Bonnie Jean *special education educator*

Teaneck
Farrell, Mary Lupiani *education educator*
Lichtenstein, Robert *education executive*
Mabli, Peter H. *history educator*

Tinton Falls
Ostar, Allan William *educational consultant*

Trenton
Donohue, Patricia Carol *academic administrator*
Pruitt, George Albert *academic administrator*
Riccards, Michael Patrick *academic administrator*
Scheiring, Michael James *college official*
Smallwood, Robert Albian, Jr. *retired secondary education educator*

Union
Lederman, Susan Sturc *public administration professor*

Union City
Englese, Damon Joseph *director*

Upper Montclair
Gil, Eduardo *academic administrator*

Voorhees
Leontiades, Milton *retired dean*

Wall
Height, Kelly A. *literature and language educator*

Wallington
Jarotski, Diane *guidance director*

Warren
Hennings, Dorothy Grant *education educator*

Wayne
Benedict, Theresa Marie *retired mathematics educator*
Speert, Arnold *academic administrator, chemistry educator*

West Long Branch
Gaffney, Paul Golden, II, *academic administrator, retired military officer*

Westfield
Fitts, Leonard Donald *educational administrator*

Westwood
Cullen, Ruth Enck *reading specialist, elementary school educator*

Whippany
Vallee, Michelle Linda *pre-school educator*

Willingboro
Denslow, Deborah Pierson *primary school educator*

Woodbridge
Seidman, Barbara R. *mathematics educator*

NEW MEXICO

Alamogordo
Hobson, Suellen Ann Weber *retired elementary school educator*

Albuquerque
Caplan, Edwin Harvey *retired dean, finance educator*
de Gouvea, Raul *educator, consultant*
Draper, Dorothy E. *middle school mathematics educator*
Everitt, Elizabeth M. *school system administrator*
Frias, Shirlee N. *elementary school educator*
Garcia, F. Chris *academic administrator, political scientist, educator*
Graff, Pat Stuever *secondary school educator*
Harris, David W. *academic administrator*
Hopfinger, Anton Joseph *education educator, consultant*
Lambert, Jeffrey Scott *secondary school educator*
Lattman, Laurence Harold *retired academic administrator*
Pieper, John Albert *dean, educator*
Qi, Huaqing *special education educator*
Roth, Paul Barry *dean, educator, emergency medicine physician*
Schmidly, David J. *academic administrator, biology professor*
Wade, Gaylia Suzanne *secondary school educator*
Washburn, Kevin *dean, law educator*

Carlsbad
Christopherson, Ron *mathematics educator*
Pinching, Deborah Anne Odell *special education educator*

Cerrillos
Lutz, Nancy Cole *educational consultant*

Dulce
Tiong, Tamra A. *elementary school educator*

Farmington
Anderson, Evelyn Louise *elementary school educator*

Grants
Barnes, Ina Jean *retired elementary educator*

La Luz
Gonzales, Victor S. *principal*

Las Cruces
Cruzado, Waded *academic administrator*
Gale, Thomas Martin *university dean*
Heger, Herbert Krueger *education educator*
Nothom, Theodore John *professor*
Zakahi, Walter R. *dean, communications educator*

Las Vegas
Fries, James A. *academic administrator*

Lordsburg
Moralez, Joselyn Hope *special education educator*

Los Alamos
Benjamin, Susan Selton *elementary school educator*
Willerton, Beverly Kay *mathematics educator*

Moriarty
Cox, Darlene Beth *secondary school educator*

Placitas
Watson-Boone, Rebecca A. *dean, researcher, library and information scientist, educator*

Portales
Frost, Everett Lloyd *academic administrator, anthropologist*
Good, Kathie *special education educator, consultant, dean*
Howard, Carolyn F. *elementary school educator*

Reserve
Wiley, James Dee *retired history and biology educator, national park service ranger*

Santa Fe
Cerny, Charlene Ann *director*
Wilson-Segura, Channell Monique *secondary school educator*

Silver City
Snedeker, John Haggner *university president*
Tolar, Trinidad Uribe *education educator, director*

NEW YORK

Albany
Brademas, John *retired academic administrator, former congressman*
Lipetz, Ben-Ami *dean, information science educator*
O'Connor, John Joseph, Jr. *academic administrator*
Philip, George Michael *academic administrator, former pension fund administrator*
Plowman, Travis S. *education educator, consultant*
Robbins, Cornelius (Van Vorse) *educational administration educator*
Straussman, Jeffrey *dean, political science professor*
Verdile, Vincent Paul *dean, emergency physician*
Zimpher, Nancy Lusk *academic administrator*

Alfred
La Course, William Carl *glass science educator, researcher*

Amherst
Brazeau, Gayle Ann *associate dean*

Annandale On Hudson
Botstein, Leon *academic administrator, conductor, historian*

Attica
Morgan, Claire Marie *elementary school educator*

Auburn
Bartolotta, Kristen *literature and language educator*

Babylon
DaSilva, Lynn Judith *special education educator*
Herbst, Jane Elizabeth *school librarian*
Schnepp, Angela J. *secondary school educator*
Schwarz, Barbara Ruth Ballou *elementary school educator*

Baldwin
Aliano, Joy Caryl *retired elementary school educator*

Baldwinsville
Pretzat, Julie *academic administrator, conductor*

Beacon
Rousseau, Christina Jeannie *elementary school educator*

Bellport
Coonerty, Mary Elizabeth *special education educator*
Schultheis, Edwin Milford *dean, business educator*

Bemus Point
Rollinger, Mary Elizabeth *retired school counselor, clinical director*

Binghamton
Bobinski, George S., Jr. *associate dean*
DeFleur, Lois B. *academic administrator*
Kowalik, Thomas Frederic *director community programs*
Meador, John Milward, Jr. *dean, librarian*
Morello, Debra A. *dean*
Philips, George K. *parochial school educator*
Sileo, Richard Nicholas *physics educator*
Skinner, Timothy Joseph *educator*
Spanfelner, Deborah Calabro *college librarian*
Swain, Mary Ann Price *university official*

Brockport
Bowdler, Jane Maxon *mathematics educator*
Gemmett, Robert J. *dean, English language educator*

Bronx
Antwi, Ebenezer Yaw *education educator*
Berman, Stephen Leonard *mathematics and statistics educator*
Bowers, Francis Robert *educational consultant, literature educator*
Keating, Tedd Michael *adult education educator*
Laruccia, Stephen Dominic *academic administrator*
McShane, Joseph Michael *academic administrator, priest*
Mueser, John Alan *elementary school educator*
O'Donnell, Brennan Patrick *academic administrator, literature and language professor*
Payson, Martin Saul *mathematics educator*
Piderit, John J. *educational consultant and author, former university president*
Rhinehart, Alycia Celeste *principal*
Robinson, Gwendolyn Niema *elementary school educator*
Rothstein, Anne Louise *academic administrator, educator*
Sanchez-Silkman, Jennifer Christine *elementary school educator*
Schneider, Scott Michael *academic administrator*
Shanklin, Elizabeth E. *secondary school educator*
Spiegel, Allen Michael *dean, internist*
Wertheim, Mary Danielle *educational coordinator*
Yuan Gee, Ka Chuen Carol *school librarian*

Bronxville
Dodds, Jerrilynn D. *dean, art historian, lecturer, writer*
Lawrence, Karen R. *academic administrator, literature and language professor*

Brooklyn
Bugliarello, George *academic administrator, educator*
Chung, Ping-Tsai *education educator*
Dealy, Michael Thomas *psychology educator*
D'Elia, Nicholas *secondary school educator*
Foronda, Elena Isabel *secondary school educator*
Gamble, Cahtina Robyne *elementary school educator*
Hill, Elizabeth Anne *academic administrator, lawyer*
Ierardi, Eric Joseph *school system administrator*
Kinard-Wright, Judith Lauretta *elementary school educator, secondary school educator, special education educator*
Lambert, Jeffrey Warren *special education educator, director*
Macchiarola, Frank Joseph *academic administrator, educator*
Panwar, Shivendra Singh *education educator, researcher*
Rosario-Olmedo, Carmen Gloria *principal*
Schweikert, Mary Lou *elementary school educator*
Shivcharran, Jaigobin *secondary school educator, consultant*
Simons, Barbara *retired elementary school educator*
Taylor, Ian Logan *dean*
Wexler, Joan G. *dean, law educator*
Witherspoon, Maria Bernarda Pena *principal*
Wolfe, Ethyle Renee *academic administrator*

Brookville
Swaner, Lynn E. *education educator*

Buffalo
Anderson, Wayne Keith *dean, educator*
Beigel, Andrew Richard *education educator*
Brathwaite, Frank B. *education educator*
Leavitt-Noble, Kimberly A. *special education educator*
Lee, Jaekyung *education educator, researcher*
Meshlovitz, Mary E. *educational consultant, special education educator*
Mutua, Makau Wa *dean, law educator*
Putnam, Susan K. *psychology educator*
Russo, Kelly Anne *secondary school educator*
Simpson, John Barclay *academic administrator*
Triggle, David John *dean, pharmacist, consultant*
Tucker, Melvin Jay *education educator, researcher*
Zieziula, Charmayne C. *education educator*

Canastota
Mirante, Thomas Anthony *retired secondary education educator*

Canton
Fox, William Lloyd, Jr. *academic administrator, educator, minister*
Sullivan, Daniel F. *retired academic administrator, sociologist, educator*

Catskill
Ferrara, Lorraine Mary *literature and language educator*

Cedarhurst
Lagnado, Jennifer M. *assistant principal*

Central Islip
James, Sharon Ann *elementary school educator*

Chautauqua
Jackson, Juanita Wallace *educational consultant*

Cheektowaga
Wagle, A. Tina *education educator, researcher*

Churchville
Balch, Glenn McClain, Jr. *academic administrator, minister, writer*

Clifton Park
Valenti, Laurie M. *elementary school educator*

Clinton
Stewart, Joan Hinde *academic administrator*

Cobleskill
Puciato, Kathleen *education educator*
Zingale, Donald Paul *academic administrator, educator*

Commack
Cohen, Judith W. *retired academic administrator*

Corinth
Dingman, Carolyn *school librarian*

Corning
Dunbar, Deborah S. *instructor*
Wilson, Cecilia Ann *special education educator*

Cornwall On Hudson
Peirce, Karen Patricia *education educator*

Cortland
McMahon, Joseph M. *economics educator*

Dix Hills
Somerville, Daphine Holmes *retired elementary school educator*

Dobbs Ferry
Postman, Robert Derek *dean, mathematics professor, writer*

Dryden
Powell, Marsha *director, educator*

East Amherst
Kirdani, Esther May *retired school counselor*
Raven, Ronald Jacob *education educator, researcher, consultant*

East Aurora
Woodard, Carol Jane *educational consultant*

East Hampton
Bancheri, Louis P., Jr. *training specialist, retired educator*

East Meadow
Beyer, Norma Warren *secondary school educator*

East Setauket
Petrey, Sandy *educator*

Eastchester
Kravath, Alan Wolfe *retired education evaluator*

Elmira
Burke, Rita Hoffmann *retired educational administrator*
Reddick, Bryan DeWitt *academic administrator*
Smith, Martha C. *college librarian*

Endicott
Goodwin, Charles Hugh *technology education educator*

Fayetteville
Krathwohl, David Reading *retired education educator*

Floral Park
Curci, Paula *counseling educator, poet, radio personality*
Sottile, Kathleen M. *principal, music educator*

Flushing
Missick, Patricia Ann *secondary school educator*

Forest Hills
Buhks, Ephraim *college administrator, technology educator*
Weber-Levine, Phyllis *secondary school educator*

Freeport
Mitchell, Alice Joyce Jones *retired secondary school educator, dietician*

Fresh Meadows
Vigoda, Paul Evan *secondary school educator*

Fulton
Dowd, Kenneth Robert *elementary school educator*

Gainesville
Drumma, Eric Matthew *elementary school educator*

Garden City
Scott, Robert Allyn *academic administrator*
Shuart, James Martin *retired academic administrator*

Garnerville
Chapman, Margaret Elizabeth *elementary school educator*

Geneseo
Mooney, Michael C. *academic administrator, coach*

Glen Cove
Rothberg, Judith *elementary school educator, researcher*

Glenwood
Chambers, Denning Jessyca *middle school educator*

Great Neck
Marcus, Philip *associate dean*

Greenvale
Regazzi, John James III *dean, publishing executive*
Steinberg, David Joel *academic administrator, historian, educator*

Hamburg
Witt, Dennis Ruppert *mathematics educator*

Hamilton
Johnston, Michael (William) *political science educator, university administrator*
Pruitt, Nancy Louise *educator*
Roelofs, Lyle Dean *academic administrator, physics professor*

Hampton Bays
Bucicchia, Carolanne Stephanie *elementary school educator*
Wille, Rosanne Louise *educational consultant*

Hauppauge
Reid, Margaret Elizabeth *elementary and secondary school educator*

Hempstead
Berliner, Herman Albert *academic administrator, economist, educator, dean*
Demleitner, Nora Verena *dean, law educator*
Wu, Michelle M. *dean, law educator*

Hornell
Hunter, John Orr *retired college president*

Horseheads
Clark, Judy Ann *elementary school educator*
Krauss, Patricia Richardson *educator*

Huntington Station
Stevens, Susan Seltenreich Cirillo *special education educator*

Ilion
Vivacqua, Ritamarie Lillian *psychology educator*

Inwood
Cohan, Delorie Rose *elementary music educator*

Islip
Libert, Nancy Porta *retired elementary school educator*

Ithaca
Ben Daniel, David Jacob *entrepreneurship educator, consultant*
Halpern, Bruce Peter *academic administrator, researcher, educator*
Kenney, Anne *university librarian*
McConkey, James Rodney *literature and language educator, writer*
Norton, Mary Beth *history educator, writer*
Paau, Alan Shiukee *academic administrator, biotechnologist, educator*
Rhodes, Frank Harold Trevor *academic administrator, geologist*
Rochon, Thomas Richard *academic administrator*
Schwab, Stewart Jon *dean, law educator*
Seznec, Alain *dean, language educator*
Skorton, David Jan *academic administrator*
Thomas, Louis Joseph *dean, management educator*
Viele, Patricia Thompson *physics and astronomy librarian*
Weinstein, Leonard Harlan *institute program director, educator*
Wikoff, Karin *school librarian*

Jackson Heights
Ryan, Judith Ann *dean*

Jamaica
Boghosian, Stella Maris *education educator*
Bunshaft, Charles Edward *elementary school educator, consultant*
Edwards, Cynthia E. *principal*
Holmes, Aliya E. *educational technology educator*
Kaplan, Carolyn Sue *elementary school educator*
Pratt-Johnson, Yvonne Karen *education professor*
Sciame, Joseph *university administrator*
Simons, Michael A. *dean, law educator*

Kenmore
Gielow, Kathleen Louise *career planning administrator, special education educator, consultant*

Kings Point
Stern, Marilyn *technical services, academic librarian*

Lake Katrine
Konior, Jeannette Mary *retired elementary and secondary school educator*

Lake Placid
Pappalardo, Rosa Gloria *secondary school educator*
Reiss, Paul J. *academic administrator*

Levittown
Braverman, Lisa Rene *dean*

Little Falls
Lowery, Kathleen Ann *elementary school educator*

Loch Sheldrake
Arnold, Richard Walter *academic librarian, artist*

Long Island City
Lucca, Louis Anthony *academic administrator*

Loudonville
Doyle, Mathias Francis *academic administrator, political scientist, educator*
Toal, James Francis *academic administrator*

Mamaroneck
Martin, Roger Harry *retired college president*

Manhasset
Smith, Lawrence Gerard *dean, medical educator, health facility administrator*

Marcy
Rishel, Kenn Charles *school superintendent*

Massapequa
Faust, Naomi Flowe *education educator*

Memphis
Woolson, Gloria Jean *education educator*

Mendon
Munson, Harold Lewis *education educator*

Merrick
Garfinkel, Lawrence Saul *academic administrator, television producer, educator*
Glogau, Lillian Flatow Fleischer Zeigen *retired educational administrator*
Harrison, Marjorie Freeman *secondary education educator, librarian*

Middleburgh
Mau, Lisa Anne *special education educator*

Montgomery
Feldman, Arlene Karp *special education educator, director*

Mount Kisco
Buglione, Anna Maria *pre-school educator*

Mount Vernon
Addesso, Angela Joyce *school system administrator*

New Hartford
Boyle, William Leo, Jr. *educational consultant, retired academic administrator*

New Paltz
Poskanzer, Steven Gary *academic administrator, lawyer*

New Rochelle
Cohen, Saul Bernard *retired academic administrator, geographer*
Donahue, Richard James *secondary school educator*
Reddington, Mary Jane *retired secondary school educator*

New York
Adler, Norman Tenner *psychology educator, dean*
Alfano, Michael Charles *university administrator*
Altman, Stan *academic administrator, educator*
Arndt, Cynthia *educational administrator*
Benson, Thomas Luther *academic administrator*
Berne, Robert *academic administrator*
Best, Wanda *career planning consultant*
Bloom, Alfred Howard *academic administrator, educator*
Bollinger, Lee Carroll *academic administrator, law educator*
Boullosa, Carmen *educator, writer*
Boylan, Elizabeth Shippee *academic administrator, biologist, educator*
Brabeck, Mary Margaret *dean, psychology professor*
Brizendine, Ellanor N. (Bodie) *headmaster*
Brown, Joyce F. *academic administrator*
Burgess, Clara Skipwith *retired principal*
Burns, Red *academic administrator*
Campbell, Mary Schmidt *dean*
Cartelli, Mary Anne *literature and language educator*
Claster, Jill Nadell *academic administrator, history educator*
Consagra, Sophie Chandler *academic administrator*
Cooley, Thomas F. *dean, economics professor*
Cullinan, Bernice Ellinger *education educator*
Davidson, Anthony R. *education educator, consultant*
Davis, D. Lavelda *dean, academic administrator*
Diller, Matthew *dean, law educator*
Dobrinsky, Herbert Colman *university administrator*
Dorman, Peter Fitzgerald *academic administrator, anthropologist, educator*
Durkin, Dorothy Angela *university official*
Fried, Linda Phyllis *dean, medical educator*
Friedman, Stephen J. *dean*
Fu, Fang *literature and language educator*
Fuhrman, Susan H. *academic administrator, education educator, researcher*
Gatto, John Taylor *educational analyst, public speaker*
Germano, William Paul *dean, former publishing executive*
Geurts, Tom Geerd *real estate educator, consultant*
Ghnassia (Fortunato), Barbara *counseling administrator*
Gillespie, John Thomas *retired university administrator*
Goldman, Lee *dean, cardiologist, educator*
Goldstein, Matthew *academic administrator*
Gotto, Antonio Marion, Jr. *dean, internist, medical educator*
Gottschalk, Alfred *retired academic and museum administrator*
Grossman, Robert Ivin *dean, neuroradiologist, scientist, educator*
Grueskin, William Steven (Bill Grusekin) *dean, educator, former editor*
Haffner, Alden Norman *academic administrator*
Halperin, Jonathan L. *medical school administrator*
Hamilton, Dorothy Cann *academic administrator*
Hood, Donald Charles *academic administrator, psychologist, vision neuroscientist, educator*
Hubbard, Glenn (Robert Glenn Hubbard) *dean, former federal official*
Ilchman, Warren Frederick *academic and foundation administrator, educator*
Jansky, Jeannette Jefferson *learning disabilities specialist*
Jennings, Bruce *research institute director*
Joel, Richard Marc *academic administrator, law educator*
Jones, (L.) Serene *academic administrator, theology professor*
Katzman, John S. *educational organization executive*
Kean, Thomas Howard *retired academic administrator, former Governor of New Jersey*
Kerrey, Bob (Joseph Robert Kerrey) *academic administrator, former United States Senator from Nebraska*
Klein, Joel Irwin *school system administrator*
Korsten, Susan Snyder *mathematics educator*
Lamm, Norman *academic administrator, rabbi*
Lander, Bernard *academic administrator, sociologist, clergyman*
Lange, Phil C. *retired education educator*
Lemann, Nicholas Berthelot *dean, journalist*
Levine, Naomi Bronheim *academic administrator*
Linsky, Marty *education educator*
Lloyd, Jean *retired early childhood educator*
Love-Hassell, Esther Boyer *special education educator, consultant*
Malinowska-Sempruch, Kasia *director*
Mandel, Carol Ann *university librarian*
Marcuse, Adrian Gregory *academic administrator*
McCrie, Robert Delbert *prison reformer, editor, educator*
Moody-Adams, Michele Marcia *dean, philosophy professor*
Morreale, Joseph Constantino *academic administrator, educator, economist, consultant*
Neal, James G. *university librarian*
Nurse, Sir Paul M. *academic administrator*
Paige, Roderick Raynor *educational consultant, former United States Secretary of Education*
Parkin, Gerard Francis Ralph *chemistry educator, researcher*
Pawliczko, George Ihor *academic administrator*
Polisi, Joseph William *academic administrator*
Pouncey, Peter Richard *academic administrator, classics educator*
Powel, Jane C. *educational consultant*
Raab, Jennifer J. *academic administrator*
Rabb, Harriet Schaffer *academic administrator, lawyer*
Reidenberg, Joel R. *academic administrator, law educator*
Reutter, Eberhard Edmund, Jr. *education and law educator*
Revesz, Richard Luis *dean, law educator*
Rhodes, David *academic administrator*
Richards, Craig Edward *academic administrator, educator*
Richardson, Richard Colby, Jr. *leadership and policy studies educator, researcher*
Robert, Jackson L. *education professor, literature and language professor*
Rowland, Esther E(delman) *retired dean*
Rudenstine, Neil Leon *former academic administrator, educator*
Schall, Ellen *dean, political science professor*
Schizer, David Michael *dean, law educator*
Schoonmaker, Frances G. *education educator*
Selby, Cecily Cannan *dean, science educator*
Sexton, John Edward *academic administrator, law educator*
Snyder, Jon David *dean*
Spar, Debora Lynn *academic administrator*
Steele, Claude Mason *academic administrator, psychology professor*
Szalda, David Joseph *chemistry educator*
Travis, Jeremy *academic administrator*
Treanor, William Michael *dean, law educator*
Van Nort, Sydney C. *school librarian, archivist*
Wands, Bruce *academic administrator, musician, writer*
Waren, Stanley Arnold *academic administrator, performing company executive*
Yepes-Baraya, Mario *educational research and evaluation consultant*
Yetman, Leith Eleanor *academic administrator*
Young, Carol Ann *elementary school educator, graphics designer, writer*
Yu, Pauline Ruth *former dean, educational association administrator*

Newburgh
Joyce, Mary Ann *principal*

Niagara University
Cowden Esq, Peter Alexander *education educator, consultant*
Praetzel, Gary D. *dean*

North Babylon
Galligan, James *retired guidance counselor*

Northport
Allen, Marilyn Grace *school librarian*
Weaver, Eric James *educational administrator*

Oakdale
Miller, Rhoda *academic administrator*

Olean
Gates, Richard Wade *education educator*

Oneonta
Larkin, F. Daniel *academic administrator, educator*

Oswego
Davis, R. Deborah *education educator*
Hockey, Christopher Lawrence *academic administrator*

Ovid
Scoles, Marie Y. *elementary school educator*

Ozone Park
Bellamy, Renee Adele *secondary school educator*

Pittsford
Bernstein, Paul *retired academic dean*
Sproull, Robert Lamb *retired academic administrator, physicist, director*
Thompson, Brian John *academic administrator, optics scientist, educator*

Plattsburgh
Jablonski, John E. *academic administrator, engineering educator*

Port Chester
Benoit, Mary *school librarian*

Port Jefferson
MacKinnon, Ann Laurie *retired elementary school educator*

Port Jefferson Station
Drucker, Matthew Douglas *secondary school educator*

Port Jervis
Martinez, Andres Manuel, Jr. *mathematics educator*

Port Washington
Gordon-Tennant, Jennifer Jay *secondary school educator*

Potsdam
Collins, Anthony G. (Tony Collins) *academic administrator*
Ha, Andrew Kwangho *education educator*
Kim, Eugene *education educator*
Rudiger, Lance Wade *secondary school educator*

Poughkeepsie
Conklin, Donald David *academic administrator*
Coyne, Therese Anne *school librarian*
Hill, Catharine Bond (Cappy) *academic administrator, economics professor*
Opdycke, Leonard Emerson *retired literature and language educator, publishing executive, writer*

Purchase
Bodenrader, Andrew *academic administrator, educator*
Schwarz, Thomas J. *academic administrator, lawyer*
Vardin, Patricia Anne *education educator*
West, Kazuko Ito *mathematics educator, department chair*

Rexford
Schmitt, Roland Walter *retired academic administrator*

Rochester
Adams, Carol H. *dean*
Blanda-Holtzberg, Marianne Lourdes *education educator, consultant*
Campbell, Alma Jacqueline Porter *elementary school educator*
Cohen, Jules *former dean, internist, educator*
Dannefer, William Dale *educator, dean*
Destler, William W. *academic administrator*
Everett, Claudia Kellam *retired special education educator*
French, Lucia Ann *education educator, director*
Guzick, David S. *dean, educator*
Jacobs, Richard L. *secondary school educator, coach*
Joynt, Robert James *academic administrator, physician*
Kirschenbaum, Howard *education educator*
Krober, Alfred *school librarian, director*
Lake, Matthew *director*
Lucas, Diane Marie *school librarian*
Parker, Kathy P. *dean, nursing educator*
Penwarden, Ann P *assistant director*
Seligman, Joel *academic administrator*
Zupan, Mark A. *dean, economics professor*

Rockville Centre
Lynch, Peter K. *education educator*

Rotterdam Junction
Cox, Paulyn Mae *retired elementary school educator*

Saint James
Kelly, Michael Joseph *academic administrator, consultant*

Sanborn
Michalak, Janet Carol *childhood education educator, coordinator*
Nowak (Jarosz), Linda Therese *special education educator, consultant*

Saratoga Springs
Abrams, Kenneth Theodore *retired academic administrator*
Glotzbach, Philip A. *academic administrator, philosopher, educator*

Saugerties
Falzano, Colleen *special education educator*

Sayville
Vigliotta, Margaret D. *retired secondary school educator, art educator, artist*

Schenectady
Ainlay, Stephen Charles *academic administrator, educator*
Hartkern, Danielle Anne *elementary school educator*
Lorang, George Joseph *special education educator*
Pritchard, Mary D'Ercole *elementary school educator*

Seaford
Bongiovi, Stephen *literature and language educator*

Selden
Connors, William Francis, Jr. *academic administrator*

Seneca Falls
Norman, Mary Marshall *academic administrator, alcohol/drug abuse services professional, educator*

Sharon Springs
Pfau, Richard Anthony *retired university president*

Skaneateles
Behrend, Donald Fraser *academic administrator, educator*

Smithtown
Mead-Haskins, Debra *educational consultant, academic administrator, educator*

Somers
Concepcion, David *assistant principal*

Staten Island
Berci, Margaret Elizabeth *education educator*
Wilson, Van Ray *secondary school educator*

Stony Brook
Cochran, James Kirk *dean, oceanographer, educator, geochemist*
Edelman, Norman Herman *dean, medical educator, academic administrator*
Kaler, Eric William *academic administrator*
Rifkin, Barry R. *dean, dental educator, researcher*
Shamash, Yacov *dean, electrical engineering educator*
Stanley, Samuel Leonard, Jr. *academic administrator, medical educator*
Tewarson, Reginald Prabhakar *retired mathematics educator, consultant*

Syracuse
Arterian, Hannah R. *dean, law educator*
Broadnax, Walter Doyce *former academic administrator, educator*
Cantor, Nancy *academic administrator*
Freund, Deborah A. *academic administrator*
Murphy, Cornelius B., Jr., (Neil Murphy) *academic administrator*
Pearson, Gretchen Elaine *college librarian*
Scheinman, Steven Jay *dean, medical educator*
Thorin, Suzanne E. *dean, university librarian*
Wallerstein, Mitchel Bruce *dean, political science professor*

Troy
Baker, Kim Pearson *education educator*
Clemmons, Byard Quigg *guidance counselor, prosecutor*
Cramb, Alan W. *dean, engineering educator*
Jackson, Shirley Ann *academic administrator, physicist*
Kahl, William Frederick *retired academic administrator*
Mayo, Robert Raymond (Bob Mayo) *university librarian*
Nagy, George *education educator*
Zagorevski, Dmitri *academic administrator*

Utica
Cattat, Vincent Joesph *retired education educator*

Valhalla
Hankin, Joseph Nathan *college president*
Jenks, Eileen A. *academic administrator, real estate agent*
O'Connell, Ralph Anthony *dean, psychiatrist, educator*

Walden
Miranda, Hermes *school counselor*

Wantagh
Cahill, Kathleen J. *director*

Wappingers Falls
Robinson, Paul David *literature and language educator*
Stabile, Patrice Christine *mathematics educator*

Webster
Powers, Richard Gerard *history educator*

West Point
Hagenbeck, Franklin Lee *academic administrator, career military officer*

Westbury
Greenberger, Roni Susan *elementary school educator*
Ross-Lee, Barbara *dean, educator*

White Plains
High, Kemba M. *special education educator*
Ottinger, Richard Lawrence *dean emeritus, former congressman*
Szolnoki, John Frank *special education educator, administrator*
Waterhouse, Lynette *mathematics educator*

Whitesboro
Blake, Edward Stephens *secondary school educator*

Whitestone
Lodico, Cheryl Madeline *secondary school educator*

Yonkers
Ismail, Jeanne *elementary school educator*
Liggio, Jean Vincenza *adult education educator, artist*
Trentanelli, John Anthony *educational administrator*

Yorktown Heights
Schiller, Barbara *retired special education educator*

NORTH CAROLINA

Asheville
Brown, David G. *academic administrator*
Fedock, Barbara C. *primary school educator, consultant*
Fernandes, Jane K. *academic administrator, sign language professional*
Merrill, Deane Whitney, Jr. *education educator, consultant*
Polite, Lettie Wilson *retired middle school educator, librarian*
Ponder, Anne *academic administrator*

Burlington
Phillips, Ruth Ann *retired secondary school educator*

Cary
Summers, Suzanne Frances Hemenway *elementary school educator*

Chapel Hill
Andrews, Richard Nigel Lyon *academic administrator, educator*
Blouin, Robert A. *dean, pharmacy educator*
Bowles, Erskine Boyce *academic administrator, former White House chief of staff*
Campbell, Bobby Jack *academic administrator*
Carroll, Roy *retired academic administrator*
Cronenwett, Linda r. *dean, educator, hospital administrator*
Dean, James W., Jr. *dean, finance educator*
Ganley, Oswald Harold *retired director*
Gil, Karen M. *dean, psychology professor*
Griffiths, José-Marie *dean, library and information science educator*
Hunt, Douglass *retired university official*
Joyner, Leon Felix *university administrator, retired*
Levine, Madeline Geltman *literature and language educator, translator*
Magill, Samuel Hays *academic administrator, consultant*
Rimer, Barbara K. *dean, healthcare educator*
Roper, William Lee *dean, preventive medicine physician, administrator*
Sanders, John Lassiter *retired academic administrator*
Smith, Michael R. *dean, academic administrator*
Thorp, H. Holden *academic administrator, chemistry professor*
Vargha, Rebecca Brogden *librarian, library association executive*
Williams, John N. *dean, dental educator*

Charlotte
Boe, Christopher Scott *education educator*
Dubois, Philip Leon *academic administrator, political scientist, educator*
Eppley, Frances Fielden *secondary school educator, writer*
Fretwell, Elbert K., Jr. *retired university chancellor, consultant*
Gorman, Peter C. *school system administrator*
McAfee, Larry W. *chemistry educator*
Mercer, Evelyn Lois *retired counseling administrator*
Peterson, Evonne Stewart *elementary school educator*
Tyson, Cynthia Haldenby *academic administrator*
Woodward, James Hoyt *academic administrator, engineering educator*
Wright, Bonnie H. *middle school educator*

Cove City
Miller, Wendy A. *elementary school educator*

Cullowhee
Coulter, Myron Lee *retired academic administrator*
Reed, Alfred Douglas *retired academic administrator*

Davidson
Dixon, Stephanie Bell *elementary school educator*
Ross, Thomas Warren, Sr. *academic administrator, former judge*

Durham
Andrews, Nancy Catherine *dean, pediatrician, hematologist, educator*
Brodhead, Richard H. *academic administrator*
Dennis, Helen Oldham *elementary school educator*
Doyle, Gloria Thorpe *secondary school educator*
Feaver, Peter Douglas *political science educator, consultant, defense analyst*
Gilliss, Catherine Lynch *vice chancellor, dean, nursing educator*
Jakubs, Deborah *university librarian*
Kuniholm, Bruce Robellet *academic administrator, educator*
Levi, David F. *dean, former federal judge*
Moore, Joy Jittaun *dean*
Parker, William *education educator*
Sheppard, Blair H. *dean, finance company executive, educator*
Stanley, Carol Jones *academic administrator, educator*
Takahashi, Toku *education educator, researcher*

Elon
Tolley, Jerry Russell *academic administrator*

Fairview
Brown, Gregory Neil *academic administrator, forester, educator*

Fayetteville
Barringer-Brown, Charletta Hope *professor, educational consultant*
Farrior, Helen Hooks *retired assistant principal*
Roe, Kathryn Jane *elementary school educator*

Forest City
Watson, Tanya Parton *school system administrator, director*

Fort Bragg
Laney, Patricia Ann *elementary school educator*

Gastonia
Bostic, Jerry Jackson *principal*
Crissman, Katherine Kolb *counseling administrator*

Glendale Springs
Carter, Roy *secondary school educator, coach*

Greensboro
Barber, Elizabeth Anne *education educator*
Dugda, Mulugeta Tuji *education educator*
French, Lenny Sue *middle school educator*
Humburg, Patricia A. *supervisor*
Malveaux, Julianne Marie *academic administrator, economist, writer*
Michalak, Sarah C. *university librarian*
Oliver, Donna H. *academic administrator, former secondary school educator*
Rogers, William Raymond *retired academic administrator, psychologist, educator*
Schunk, Dale Hansen *dean*
Sullivan, Patricia A. *academic administrator*
Zopf, Evelyn LaNoel Montgomery *retired guidance counselor*

Greenville
Anderson, James Franciscous *criminal justice educator*
Bearden, James Hudson *university official*
Cunningham, Paul Raymond Goldwyn *dean, medical educator*
Howell, John McDade *retired academic administrator, political scientist, educator*
Leggett, Donald Yates *academic administrator*
Phillips, Phil E. *professor, academic administrator*
Smith Canter, Lora Lee *special education educator*

Hickory
Beasley, Diana F. *biology educator*
Pasour, Katherine Meador *dean, educator*
Sims, Janette Elizabeth Lowman *retired educational director*

High Point
Carter, Kathleen Sharp *educational consultant, shop owner*
Palmer, Pamela Murrill *educator*
Peoples-Marwah, Andrea Michelle *educational consultant, researcher*

Hudson
Council, Jimmy *director*

Huntersville
Tompkins, James Richard *retired special education educator*

Kinston
Petteway, Samuel Bruce *college president*

Lake Junaluska
Martinson, Jacob Christian, Jr. *academic administrator*
Stanton, Donald Sheldon *retired academic administrator*

Lexington
Carlton, Robbin Briley *elementary school educator*

Littleton
Skinner, Sue Dossett *retired vocational director*

Mars Hill
Payne, John Kenneth *acadmic administrator*

Mount Airy
Joyce-Norris, Elaine Rozelle *elementary school educator*

Mount Olive
Raper, William Burkette *retired college president*

Murfreesboro
White, Martin Christopher *academic administrator*

Murphy
Holcomb, Linda Laine *elementary school educator, director*

Nags Head
Heinrich, Katharine Ann *gifted and talented educator*

Nashville
Penick, Angela Lucas *elementary school educator*

Newland
Company, Kay Hudkins *biology educator, assistant principal*

Raleigh
Barnhardt, Robert Alexander *retired dean*
Brisson, E. Carson *registrar*
Bruck, Robert Ian *education educator*
Burris, Craven Allen *retired college administrator, professor*
Dolce, Carl John *education administration educator*
Foxe, Marye Anne *academic administrator*
Hartford, Maureen A. *academic administrator*
Hoch, Paul Frederick, Jr. *history educator*

Jarrett, Polly Hawkins *retired secondary school educator*
Martin-Vega, Louis A. *dean, engineering educator*
Nelson, Larry A. *statistics educator, consultant*
Niu, Steve *director*
Ogirri, Esther O. *Academic Librarian*
Parramore, Barbara Mitchell *education educator*
Rahmani, Carol Hipp *retired school system administrator, psychologist*
Robinson, Prezell Russell *academic administrator*
Showalter, David Scott *teaching professor*
Sosower, Mark Lawrence *educator*
Watson, Kimberly *director, educator*

Research Triangle Park
Burris, John Edward *academic administrator, biologist, educator*

Rocky Mount
Griffiths, Deborah Holmes *academic administrator*

Rougemont
Holeman, Betty Jean *counseling administrator*

Salisbury
Troxler, Willie Thomasene *retired elementary school educator*
Turner, Willard Craig *academic administrator*

Seven Lakes
Reilly, David Henry *retired university dean*

Shelby
Gash, Chavis Dennord *coordinator*
Putnam, James Dean *secondary school educator*

Southern Pines
Cardwell, Nina Fern *special education educator*

Statesville
Elliott, Carolyn Cole *secondary school educator, department chairman*

Supply
Wescott, Joseph Warren, II, *academic administrator, education educator*

Tarboro
Jordan, Michael J. *academic administrator*

Wake Forest
Kimrey, Karen Goss *secondary school educator*

Wilmington
Gray, Marilyn F. Grinwis *elementary school educator, music educator*

Windsor
Bazemore, Naomi Smith *elementary school educator*

Winston Salem
Applegate, William Brown *dean, researcher, medical educator*
Carlton, Capers Baity *secondary school educator, director*
Hatch, Nathan Orr *academic administrator*
Jester, Jane Harris *school librarian*
Morant, Blake *dean, law educator*
Reinemund, Steven S. *dean, educator, retired food products executive*
Roth, Marjory Joan Jarboe *special education educator*
Stroupe, Henry Smith *university dean*

Winton
Moore, Clemmie Archer *retired elementary school educator*

Woodland
Wilson, Lloyd Lee *registrar, educator*

Youngsville
Burwell, Edith Brodie *retired elementary school educator*

Zebulon
Privette, Janet Brown *elementary school educator*

NORTH DAKOTA

Bismarck
Hilzendeger, Cori Lynn *principal*

Ellendale
Schlieve, Hy C. J. *school administrator*

Fargo
Meester, Holly *elementary school educator, music educator, sales executive*
Reid, Michele M. *school librarian, dean*

Grand Forks
Aune, Adonica Schultz *education educator, consultant*
Chalmers, Lynne *special education educator*
Kelley, Robert Otis *academic administrator, anatomist*
Nordlie, Robert Conrad *biochemistry educator*
Page, Sally Jacquelyn *university official, management educator*
Swanson, Zona Luciel *retired elementary school educator*

Hatton
Strand, Fred P. *mathematics educator*

Minot
Allen, Warren George *college administrator*
Srock, Marlene *elementary school educator*

Wahpeton
Donahe, Peggy Yvonne *gifted and talented educator, librarian, English elementary teacher*

OHIO

Ada
Baker, Kendall L. *academic administrator*
Freed, Catherine Carol Moore *education educator*
Jao, Feng *education educator*

Akron
Barker, Harold Kenneth *former university dean*
Buzzelli, Charlotte Grace *special education educator*
Martin, Jack *educational services company executive, former federal agency administrator*
Revay, Linda Ann *principal, educator*
von Spiegel, Janice Krieger *mathematics educator*

Amelia
Kahles, Cheryl Mary *elementary school educator*

Ashland
Seifert, Nancy Faye Eshelman *retired special education educator, consultant*

Athens
Bruning, James Leon *academic administrator, educator*
Cooper-Chen, Anne *journalism educator, researcher*
Crowl, Samuel Renninger *retired dean, language educator*
Grant, Anita H. *academic librarian*
Hazler, Richard John *counselor educator*
McDavis, Roderick J. *academic administrator*
Muhammad, Najee Emerson *education educator*
Safran, Stephen Philip *educational program coordinator*

Aurora
Ross, Violet Bica *retired elementary school educator, psychologist*

Bay Village
Sprague, Vicki L. *educational consultant*

Berea
Durst, Richard Wayne *academic administrator*
Gesink, Indira Falk *educator*

Beverly
Sprague, Cathy L. *secondary school educator*

Bowling Green
Cartwright, Carol Ann *academic administrator*
Umbarger, Gardner Thompson III *special education educator, researcher*

Broadview Heights
Jergens, Maribeth Joie *school counselor*

Brunswick
Sandvick, Janet Rose *history educator*

Burton
Lynch, Deborah Ann *college administrator*

Cambridge
Barzda, Susan Marie *special education educator, music educator*

Canton
Peck, Douglas Caton *dean, educator*
Pelanda, Raymond Victor *retired director*
Trapani, John G., Jr. *philosophy professor*
Walker, James William *physics educator, freelance/self-employed writer*

Cedarville
Grigorenko, Margaret Crook *education educator, consultant*
Humphreys, Donald Stephen Ray *academic administrator*

Chagrin Falls
Brown, Jeanette Grasselli *retired director*

Chillicothe
Jayne, Cristina Marsh *retired elementary school educator*

Chippewa Lake
Javorek, Richard Alan *history educator, consultant*

Cincinnati
Alexander, Wilma Jean *business education educator, management consultant*
Ates, Delories *retired counseling administrator*
Auyang, Grace Chao *education educator, consultant*
Bilionis, Louis D. *dean, law educator*
Briggs, Henry Payson, Jr. *headmaster*
Bryant, Irene Melba *retired elementary school educator, artist*
Cunningham, Margaret Gast *faculty member*
Easley, Joanne L. *vocational evaluator*
Farrell, Pamela Christine *secondary school educator*
Greengus, Samuel *academic administrator, theology studies educator*
Hall, Madelon Carol Syverson *retired elementary school educator*
Harrison, Donald Carey *academic administrator, cardiologist, educator*
Kessinger, Thomas Anthony *education and social studies educator, researcher, consultant*
Meisner, Patricia Ann *assistant principal*
Moomaw, Sally Coup *education educator*
Plevyak, Linda Huether *education educator, researcher*
Spicer, Emily Taylor *school system administrator*
Spohn, Dorothy M. *retired elementary school educator*
Stern, David Mark *dean, medical educator*
Wagner, Thomas Edward *academic administrator, educator*
Winkler, Henry Ralph *retired academic administrator, historian*
Woods, Carol Smith *private school educator*

Circleville
Wentz, Mary H. *gifted and talented educator*
Wolford, Joanne M. *academic administrator, director*

Cleveland
Blazar, Kathleen Casteel *academic librarian, director*
Burns, Michael Kent *retired educator, chemical dependency counselor*
Callesen-Gyorgak, Jan Elaine *special education educator*
Cerone, David *academic administrator*
Eustis, Joanne D. *university librarian*
Flynn, Patricia M. *director, special education and gifted and talented educator*
Grossman, Mary Margaret *retired elementary school educator*
Locke, Carl Eugene *secondary school educator*
McCollum, Delores LaRheine *secondary school educator*
McCullough, Joseph *retired academic administrator*
McDonald, Mary Beth *academic administrator*
Nickerson, Gary Lee *educational consultant*
Pekarek, Thomas *substitute teacher*
Quigney, Theresa Ann *special education educator*
Schwartz, Michael *academic administrator, sociology educator*
Snyder, Barbara Rook *academic administrator*
Sposet, Barbara Ann *secondary school educator*
Tien, Norman C. *dean, engineering educator*
Weidenthal, Maurice David (Bud Weidenthal) *academic administrator, journalist*
Wertheim, Sally Harris *director, academic administrator, dean, education educator, consultant*
Wykle, May L. *dean, educator, researcher*

Cleveland Heights
Challenger, Vicki Lee *elementary school educator*

Columbia Station
Goll, Paulette Susan *education educator*

Columbus
Alutto, Joseph Anthony *academic administrator, former dean, management educator*
Bell, Karen A. *dean*
Blomquist, Laura Louise Gavrelis *academic librarian*
Brueggemeier, Robert W. *dean, medical educator*
Cole, Clarence Russell *college dean*
Gabbe, Steven Glenn *dean, obstetrician, gynecologist, educator*
Ganschinietz, Deepa *elementary school educator*
Gee, Elwood Gordon *academic administrator*
Griffith, Dennison W. *academic administrator, artist, educator*
Harris, Gene T. *school system administrator*
Janies, Daniel Andrew *biology educator*
Lee, Mei-Ling Ting *professor*
Michael, Alan C. *dean, law educator*
Miller, Wayne Clayton *academic administrator*
Moore, James L. III *counselor, educator*
Oxley, Margaret Carolyn Stewart *elementary school educator*
Poon, Christine A. *dean, business educator, retired pharmaceutical company executive*
Sedmak, Daniel D. *academic administrator*
Stephens, Thomas M(aron) *education educator*
White, Ora Dade *educational consultant, writer, activist, counselor, community volunteer*
Willke, Thomas Aloys *academic administrator, statistician, educator*

Dayton
Curran, Daniel J. *academic administrator, sociologist, educator*
DiSalvo, Debra Sue *gifted and talented educator*
Huang, Shan Chun *physics educator*
Keane-Sexton, Maureen Bridget *literature and language educator*
Lasley, Thomas J., II, *education educator*
Mrozek, Lawrence James *educator*
Sableski, Thomas Lee *secondary school educator*

Delaware
Kent, Conrad A. *education educator*
Lemke, Stacy J. *secondary school educator*
Thomas, John Edward *educational consultant*

Delta
Miller, Beverly White *former college president, educational consultant*

East Cleveland
England, Diana Whitten *elementary school educator*

Fairborn
Combs, Eric A. *social studies educator*
Goetz, Douglas Neil *contract management educator*

Fairfield
Masanek, Michele *secondary school educator, soccer coach*
Moreland, Vicki Ann *education educator*

Findlay
Freed, DeBow *academic administrator*

Gambier
Nugent, S. Georgia *academic administrator*

Georgetown
Fite, Tom W. *retired mathematics educator, farmer*

Granville
Knobel, Dale Thomas *academic administrator, historian, educator*

Hemlock
Johnson, George Warner *gifted and talented educator, consultant*

Hillsboro
Flum, Terry Eugene *biology educator*

Hudson
Goheen, Janet Moore *counseling administrator, sales executive*
Lambacher, Kathleen Hartwell *retired education educator*

Huron
Leser, Anne Elizabeth *education educator*

Ironton
Curry, Estella Roberta *education educator, school psychologist, consultant*
Thomas, Timothy Franklin *secondary school educator*

Johnstown
Fiedler, Karen E. *science curriculum coordinator*

Kent
Balan, Christine *special education educator*
Bedrosian, Wendy Kowalyk *pre-school educator*
Buttlar, Rudolph Otto *retired college dean*
Gaston, Paul Lee *academic administrator, language educator*
Henderson, James George *curriculum studies educator*
Kotun, Carol Ann *mathematics educator*

Lancaster
Lieber, Marla *secondary school educator*

Leetonia
Foreman, Gail Lynne *secondary school educator*

Lewis Center
Thomason, Sandra Lee *elementary school educator*

Lima
MacBenn, Joseph Vernon *director*

Loveland
Voluse, Charles Rodger III *retired education educator*

Mansfield
Gregory, Deirdre Dianne *secondary school educator*
Riedl, John Orth *retired university dean*

Marietta
Montgomery, Jerry Lynn *retired education educator*

Massillon
Eckhart, Marylouise Christine Santilli *pre-school educator*

Medina
Pilat, Janet Louise B. Oberholtzer *adult education educator*

Miamiville
Franz, (Iris) Vivian *dean, director*

Morrow
Suddendorf, Matthew L. *band director*

Mount Vernon
Shriver, William Russell *secondary school educator*

New Lexington
Harper, Toni Jane *secondary school educator*

Niles
Ruman, Renee *principal*

North Canton
Cooney, Sondra Miley *literature and language educator*

Oberlin
Brown, John Lott *former university president, retired educator*
Krislov, Marvin *academic administrator, lawyer, educator*
MacKay, Alfred F. *dean, philosophy educator*
McGuire, Charles Edward *musicology educator*

Orrville
Hennell, Robert William III *secondary school educator*

Orwell
Strong, Marcella Lee *music specialist, educator*

Oxford
Earhart, Eileen Magie *retired elementary school and child and family life educator*
Forren, John Patrick *academic administrator, educator*
Jaeger, Herbert *physics educator*
Marshall, Bryan William *educator*
McKinney, Mark *educator*
Sessions, Judith Ann *dean, university librarian*
Shriver, Phillip Raymond *academic administrator*

Painesville
Davis, Barbara Snell *education educator*

Parma
Petrus, Sally A. *elementary school educator*
Romanovich, Patricia M. *parochial school educator*

Tener, Carol Joan *retired secondary school educator, consultant*

Peninsula
Sigler, Theresa Jane *school system administrator*

Perrysburg
Filippova, Daria Vladimirovna *private school educator*

Piqua
Retman, Deborah W. *biology educator*

Port Clinton
Ewersen, Mary Virginia *retired school system administrator, poet*

Portsmouth
Johnson, Janice E. *education educator, writer*

Rio Grande
Hatfield, Barbara Scott *academic administrator*

Sagamore Hills
Miller, Susan Ann *retired school system administrator*

Scio
Prusha, Jeffrey A. *elementary school educator*

Shaker Heights
Brachna, Gabor (Samuel) *elementary school educator*

Solon
Williams, Jeffery Lynn *secondary school educator, consultant, writer*

Springfield
Kinnison, William Andrew *retired university president*
Stelzer, Patricia Jacobs *retired secondary school educator*

Stow
Castillo, Katherine Lynn *secondary school educator, business owner*

Streetsboro
Cielec, Greg J. *literature and language educator*

Strongsville
Yates, Patricia Lawrence *elementary school educator*

Sylvania
Masten, Barbara Jean *education educator, department chairman*
Sampson, Earldine Robison *education educator*

Toledo
Closius, Phillip J. *dean, law educator*
Gutteridge, Thomas G. *academic administrator, arbitrator, consultant*
Konwinski, Jacqueline Marie Koralewski *secondary school educator*
Pham, David Lan *secondary school educator, writer*
Ray, Douglas Ellsworth *dean, law educator*
Reichert, Christine Edwards *academic administrator*
Romanoff, Marjorie Reinwald *retired education educator*
Sherry, Mark Dominic *educator, researcher*

University Heights
Seaton, Shirley Smith *academic administrator, consultant*

University Hts
Ford, Theron N. *education educator*

Upper Arlington
Bordelon, Carolyn Thew *elementary school educator*

Vincent
Meek, Barbara Susan *retired elementary school educator*

Wadsworth
Wilhelm, Cathy S. *elementary school educator*

Walton Hills
Wareham, L. Marie *elementary school educator*

Wellston
Loxley, Kathryn *retired elementary school educator*

Westerville
Kerr, Thomas Jefferson, IV, *academic administrator*
Wilson, Edward Allyn *educational administrator*

Willoughby
Pennington, John Robert *biology educator, department chairman*

Youngstown
Yozwiak, Bernard James *retired mathematics educator, academic administrator*

Zanesville
Childers, Susan Lynn Bohn *special education educator, school system administrator, human resources and transition specialist, consultant*

OKLAHOMA

Ardmore
Molander, Deborah Jean *special education educator*

Bartlesville
Baker-Morris, Kay *special education educator*
Rockey, Peggy Ann *pre-school educator*

Bixby
McManus, Delana Ann *elementary school educator*
Walker, Jerald Carter *academic administrator, minister*

Bristow
Caudle, Letha Grace *secondary school educator*

Broken Arrow
Hong-Nam, Kyungsim Kay *education educator, consultant*
Vargas, Traci Junelle *special education educator*

Claremore
Heidlage, Patsy Jo *physical education educator*

Disney
Hamilton, Carl Hulet *retired academic administrator*

Duncan
Burum, Sharon *educator*

Durant
Turner, Michael Dan *academic administrator*

Edmond
Sibley, William Arthur *retired academic administrator, physics professor, consultant*

Inola
Mullen, Deborah W. *elementary school educator*

Langston
Haysbert, JoAnn Wright *academic administrator*
Showalter, Betsy S. *mathematics educator*

Lookeba
Davis, Michael D. *principal, coach*

Maramec
Blair, Marie Lenore *elementary school educator*

Mcloud
Goats, Debbie *elementary school educator*

Midwest City
Cheek, Norma Jean *retired elementary school educator*
Wier, Leanne May *life sciences educator*

Moore
Chiles, Mary Jane *secondary school educator*

Muskogee
Hasler-Reid, Linda *elementary school educator*

Norman
Biscoe, Belinda P. *academic administrator, psychologist*
Boren, David Lyle *academic administrator, former senator*
Jones, Charlotte *director*
Pappas, James Pete *university administrator*
Risser, Paul Gillan *academic administrator, botanist*
Sasaki, Yoshi Kazu *meteorology educator, researcher*
Van Horn, Richard Linley *academic administrator*
Winters, Martha P. *history and language educator*
Zapffe, Nina Byrom *retired elementary school educator*
Zhai, Yan *education educator, researcher*

Nowata
Acebo, Ronnie Vic *literature and language educator, coach*

Oklahoma City
Coats, Andrew Montgomery *dean, lawyer, former mayor*
Halligan, James Edmund *retired academic administrator, retired chemical engineer, state legislator*
Hardeman, Carole Hall *education educator*
Kriesel, Deanna *education educator*
Lavender, Maxine Knight *special education educator*
Paris, Lee Anne Hagewood *academic librarian*
Springer, Karl *school system administrator*
Weigel, Paul Henry *biochemistry educator, researcher, consultant*
Williamson, Marvel *dean, nursing administrator, sexologist, educator*
Woods, Pendleton *college director, author*

Oologah
Thomas, Rick W. *school system administrator*

Ponca City
Rice, Sue Ann *retired dean, psychologist*

Poteau
Long, Sheila Joan *academic administrator*

Shawnee
Sharp, Ron *secondary school educator*

Stillwater
Hargis, V. Burns (Burns Hargis) *academic administrator, lawyer*
Strathe, Marlene I. *academic administrator*

Tahlequah
Duncan, Janice Marie *education educator*
Haskins, V. Lyle *retired academic administrator*

Tulsa
Buthod, Mary Clare *school administrator*
Donaldson, Robert Herschel *university administrator, educator*
Lewis, Patricia Mohatt (Patty) *special education educator*
Nell, Gay *pre-school educator*
Siddons, Jeffrey G. *school librarian*
Thornton, Charlie Mae *secondary school educator*
Trennepohl, Gary Lee *academic administrator, finance educator*
Upham, Steadman *academic administrator, anthropologist, educator*

OREGON

Beaverton
Duncan, Richard Fredrick, Jr. *retired secondary school educator, consultant*

Cannon Beach
Wismer, Patricia Ann *retired secondary school educator*

Corvallis
Byrne, John Vincent *educational consultant*
Davis, John Rowland *academic administrator*
Verts, Lita Jeanne *academic administrator*

Eugene
Doty, Angela *career planning administrator*
Frohnmayer, David Braden *retired academic administrator*
Gall, Meredith (Mark) Damien *education professor emeritus, writer*
Lariviere, Richard Wilfred *academic administrator, educator*
Melnick, Robert *dean*
Moseley, John Travis *academic administrator, physicist, researcher*
Paris, Margaret L. *dean, law educator*
Pickett, Stephen Wesley *academic administrator, consultant*
Weatherhead, Andrew Kingsley *educator*

Fall Creek
Light, Betty Jensen Pritchett *retired dean*

Grants Pass
Murdock, Doris Dean *special education educator, program developer*

Gresham
Cooke, Jackie (Jacqueline Marie Cooke) *elementary school educator*
Waagen, Linda Louise *elementary school educator*

Joseph
Gilbert, David Erwin *academic administrator, physicist*

Lake Oswego
Wicklund, Lee Arthur *retired school system administrator*

Lowell
Boyle, John Howard *history educator*

Mcminnville
Walker, Charles Urmston *retired university president*

Medford
Dixon, Andrew Derart *retired academic administrator*
Franklin, Darlene Kay *elementary school educator*

Milton Freewater
Piefer, Thomas R. *history educator*

Monmouth
Dunn, Doris Marjory *retired secondary school educator, volunteer*

Newberg
Johnson, Thomas Floyd *former academic administrator, educator*

Oceanside
Wadlow, Joan Krueger *retired academic administrator, construction executive*

Portland
Bartlett, Thomas Alva *retired educational administrator*
Bleich, Michael Robert *dean, nursing educator*
Bragdon, Paul Errol *retired academic administrator, educator*
Diver, Colin S. *academic administrator, educator*
Engelberg, Elaine A. *retired secondary school educator*
Fan, Lee Siu *professional-technical training educator, entrepreneur, business executive, management consultant*
Hochstettler, Thomas John *academic administrator, historian*
Johnson, Virginia Macpherson *secondary school educator, consultant*
Leupp, Edythe Peterson *retired education educator*
Lopez, Stephanie Ann *elementary school educator, consultant*
Njoku, Scholastica Ibari *retired college librarian, writer*
Smith, Carole *school system administrator*
Wood, Cynthia Wilder *elementary school educator*

Roseburg
Ball, Char Lee Frances *retired special education educator*

The Dalles
Hayden, I. Jill *secondary school educator*

Yachats
Robeck, Mildred Coen *retired education educator, writer*

PENNSYLVANIA

Acme
Boggs, Brenda Lee *religious studies educator, librarian*

Adrian
Hogg, Yvonne Marie *principal*

Aliquippa
Staby, Dorothy Louise *elementary school educator*

Allentown
Pavelich, Judith *retired secondary school educator*

Ambridge
Powell, Pamela Baker *education educator, minister*

Aspinwall
Eckert, Jean Patricia *elementary school educator*

Aston
Kain, James P. *literature and language educator*

Atglen
Souders, Roberta Belshaw *literature and language educator*

Bala Cynwyd
Oswald, James Marlin *education educator, researcher*

Bath
Ditty, Mary Dawn *secondary school educator*

Beaver
Strock, Robert S. *retired education educator*

Bensalem
O'Toole, Michael Anthony *academic administrator*

Bentleyville
Blasko, Barbara Ann *secondary school educator*

Berwick
Pasukinis, Cheryl Renee *elementary school educator*

Bethel Park
Menees, Katherine Determan *retired parochial school educator*

Bethlehem
Agbeh, Anthony Odey *education educator, consultant*
Gast, Alice Petry *academic administrator, chemical engineering educator*
Treisner, George Henry, Jr. *vocational educator, electrical contractor, financial advisor and tax consultant*
Wu, S. David *dean, industrial and systems engineering educator*

Bloomsburg
Obiozor, Williams Emeka *special education educator*
Trapane, Ruth *educator, artist*

Bradford
Hopkins, Judy G. *literature and language educator*

Brownsville
Martin, Richard H. *principal*

Bryn Mawr
Baird, John Absalom, Jr. *retired academic administrator*
Frank, Edward David, II, *history educator*
Hirsh, Sharon Latchaw *academic administrator, art history educator*
McAuliffe, Jane Dammen *academic administrator, religious studies and Islamic studies educator*
Pietrzak, Rona *dean, director*
Vickers, Nancy J. *retired academic administrator*

Butler
Walsh, Joy Irene *literature and language educator*

Canonsburg
Mascetta, Joseph Anthony *principal*

Carlisle
Durden, William G. *academic administrator*
Efird, Cynthia Grissom *academic administrator, former ambassador*
McConnaughay, Philip J. *dean, law educator*

Center Valley
Gambet, Daniel G(eorge) *academic administrator, minister*

Chalfont
Ashley, Kathleen Labonis *elementary school educator*

Chester
Bruce, Robert James *retired academic administrator*
Harris, James Thomas III *college administrator, educator*

Cheyney
Mullaney, Beth Jo *school librarian*

Clarion
Goodman, Greg S. *education educator*

Collegeville
Strassburger, John Robert *academic administrator*

Connellsville
Humbert, Kimberly Ramsay *secondary school educator*
Shearer, Linda Rae *English educator*

Coplay
Stockman, Kathleen Helen *elementary school educator*

Dallas
Rogan, Joseph P. *special education educator*

Devon
Toth, Marian Davies *Teacher, Author Educational Administrator,*

Dover
Butterfield, Andrea Christine *school system administrator*

Downingtown
Romanosky, LuAnn *elementary school educator*

Doylestown
Thomas, Ellen Louise *school system administrator*

Dresher
Faust, Carrissima Washington *educational consultant*

East Stroudsburg
Kansfield, Norman J. *former seminary president*
Romano, Stephanie Anne *education educator, consultant*
Waters, Faith H. *retired education educator*

Easton
Hughes, Michael P. *principal*
Stull, Frank Walter *elementary school educator*
Teboh-Ewungkem, Miranda Ijang *education educator*
Weiss, Daniel H. *academic administrator, former dean*

Edinboro
Gendlin, Gerry *political science educator*

Elizabethtown
Dietz, William Dunfee, Jr. *elementary school educator*
Garber, Margaret Mary *elementary school educator*
Gordon, Laurie Anne *academic director*
Ritsch, Frederick Field *academic administrator, historian*
Sample, Frederick Palmer *former college president*

Elkins Park
Burnley, June Williams *secondary school educator*
Stinnett, Hester *art school administrator, educator*

Emlenton
Berg, Janice Carol *elementary school educator*

Erie
Burgoyne, Noel Jaeger *retired secondary school educator*
Daly, Mary *college administrator*
Evans, Karen L. *education educator, director*
Glaser, Earleen R. *school librarian, archivist*
Jones, Darci *school librarian, director*
Sucha, George R. *education educator*
Zelazny, Catherine *retired elementary school educator*

Everett
Barr, Tony *special education educator*

Fairview
Graziani, Linda Ann *secondary school educator*
Stern, Marilyn Jean *special education educator*

Flourtown
Cooke, Sara Mullin Graff *daycare provider, kindergarten educator, medical assistant*

Franklin
Sauer, Mary Julia *special education educator*

Fredericktown
Molinaro-Thompson, David Robert *secondary school educator*

Gettysburg
Riggs, Janet Morgan *academic administrator, psychology professor*

Gibsonia
Lichina, April Marie *elementary school educator*

Grantham
Patrick, Nancy J. *special education educator, researcher*

Greensburg
Neff, Mary Ellen Andre *retired elementary school educator*

Greenville
Reinhart, Connie S. *academic administrator, educator*

Harrisburg
Brown, John Walter *vocational education supervisor*
Cavanaugh, John C. *academic administrator, psychology professor*
Derk, Patricia Keach *retired secondary school educator*
Fulmer, Deborah Lee *education educator, oncological nurse*
Koones, Donald Gregory *associate dean, educator*

Hatfield
Jesberg, Robert Ottis, Jr. *educational consultant, science educator*

Haverford
Emerson, Stephen G. *academic administrator, oncologist, hematologist, educator*

Havertown
Crouse, Carol K. Mavromatis *elementary school educator*
Evarts, Mary H. *retired mathematics educator*
Wright, Cecilia Powers *gifted and talented educator*

Hershey
Jones, Marshall Bush *education educator, researcher*

Honesdale
Barbe, Walter Burke *education educator*

Huntingdon
Kepple, Thomas Ray, Jr. *college administrator*

Huntingdon Valley
Holland, Burt S. *statistics educator, consultant*

Indiana
Atwater, Tony *university president*
Hwang, Eun Jin *education educator*
Jalongo, Mary Renck *educator*

Irwin
Perich, Terry Miller *retired secondary school educator*

Jefferson Hills
Smith, Leslie Edgar *vocational school administrator*

Jenkintown
Hidalgo, Alfreda Edith *elementary school educator*
Oh, Soojin Susan *elementary school educator*

Jim Thorpe
Bickel, Jean Louise *school librarian*

Johnstown
Alcamo, Frank Paul *retired principal*
McGrath, John Michael *educator*

Knox
Rupert, Elizabeth Anastasia *retired dean*

Kutztown
Watson, Carol Elizabeth *education educator*

La Plume
Boehm, Edward Gordon, Jr. *college administrator, educator*
Jennings, Patricia A. *literature and language educator*

Lafayette Hill
Delacato, Janice Elaine *special education educator, consultant*

Lake Ariel
Petrosky, Michele Marie *school librarian*

Lancaster
Ebersole, Mark Chester *emeritus college president*
Fry, John Anderson *academic administrator*
Kneedler, (Alvin) Richard *academic administrator*

Langhorne
Schoenstadt, Barbara Laison *special education educator*

Latrobe
Porembka, Michael Richard *assistant principal, supervisor*
Quinlivan, Gary M. *dean, educator*
Towey, Jim (H. James Towey) *academic administrator, former federal official*

Lawrenceville
Kipferl, Christiana A. *special education educator*

Lehman
Williams, Thomas Alan *high school guidance counselor, small business owner*

Levittown
Edson, Megan *school librarian*

Lewisburg
Mitchell, Brian Christopher *academic administrator*
Smith, Marguerite Irene *gifted and talented educator*

Lincoln University
Nelson, Ivory Vance *academic administrator*
Van Dover, James Kenneth *education educator*

Lititz
Sandercox, Robert Allen *academic administrator, minister*

Lock Haven
Lima, Sally Murphy *education educator*

Lower Burrell
Croushore, James *counseling administrator*

Macungie
Rubin, Arthur Herman *retired academic administrator*

Malvern
Qiu, Robin G. *adult education educator*

Martinsburg
Neff, Robert Wilbur *academic administrator, educator, minister*

Mc Elhattan
Garner, Charles William *retired educational administration educator, consultant*

Mc Keesport
House, Audrey Ann *school librarian*

Mechanicsburg
Page, William J. *criminal justice educator*

Media
Bonnell, Allen Thomas *college president emeritus, consultant*
Bortner, Doyle McClean *retired college dean*
Bury, Lorraine *secondary school educator*

Millersville
Briola, Richard David *literature and language educator*

Montoursville
Huff, Carl Raymond *academic administrator*

Moon Township
Cellante, Donna L. *dean*

Mount Pleasant
Dangelo, Eugene Michael *elementary school educator*

Nanticoke
Bassham, Mia Wang *university librarian*

Nazareth
Ferraro, Margaret Louise (Peg) *secondary school educator*

Nelson
Kyofski, Bonelyn Lugg *retired education educator*

New Holland
Sheaffer, M. P. A. *educator*

New Hope
Coyle, Diane Bonanomi *special education educator*

New Milford
Cunningham, Mary Ann Michael *secondary school educator*

Newtown
Booraem, Hendrik, V, *education educator, historian*

Newtown Square
Bertolet, Caroline Lynne Georgeanne *special education educator, labor union administrator*
Swing, Elizabeth Sherman *education educator*

Norristown
DeMedio, Kathleen Marie *chemistry educator*

Oil City
Clemente, Nancy Ellen *school librarian*

Oxford
Cole, Charles Chester, Jr. *academic administrator*

Penn Run
Thibadeau, Eugene Francis *education educator, consultant*

Philadelphia
Ackerman, Arlene C. *school system administrator, education professor*
Brucker, Paul C. *academic administrator, physician*
Caplan, Arthur Leonard *university program director, educator*
Clair, Angelina Theresa *principal*
Cohen, David Walter *academic administrator, educator, periodontist*
Epps, JoAnne A. *dean, law educator*
Fernandez, Happy Craven (Gladys) *academic administrator*
Fitts, Michael Andrew *dean, law educator*
Goon, Arthur David *academic administrator, educator*
Graffman, Gary *academic administrator, pianist, educator*
Gutmann, Amy *academic administrator, political science and philosophy educator*
Hart, Ann Weaver *academic administrator*
Homan, Richard V. *dean*
Lewis, Edward Ted *academic administrator*
Liacouras, Peter James *academic administrator, lawyer, arbitrator, educator*
Meleis, Afaf Ibrahim *dean, nursing educator*
Modla, Virginia Bordonaro *education educator*
Onley, Sister Francesca *academic administrator*
Porat, M. Moshe *dean, management educator*
Porter, Andrew Calvin *dean, psychologist, educator*
Potero, Valerie Jane *elementary school educator*
Price, Vincent Edward *academic administrator, communications and political science professor*
Robertson, Thomas Sinclair *dean, marketing educator*
Romer, Daniel *university official, psychologist, educator*
Rubenstein, Arthur Harold *dean, internist, educator*
Rudczynski, Andrew B. *academic administrator, medical researcher*
Sibolski, Elizabeth Hawley *academic administrator*
Slaughter-Defoe, Diana Tresa *education educator, psychologist*
Smarkola, Claudia *education educator*
Tritton, Thomas Richard *former academic administrator, biologist, educator*
Veitz, Sister Mary Frances *director*
Verlin, Jonathan R. *secondary school educator*

Pittsburgh
Baldis, Sean R. *elementary school educator*
Cohon, Jared L. *academic administrator*
Crossely, Mary A. *dean, law educator*
Cubbage, Bobbie Danielle *pre-school educator*
Davis, Larry E. *academic administrator*
Dougherty, Charles John *academic administrator*
Dunbar-Jacob, Jacqueline *dean, nursing educator, researcher*
Dunn, Kenneth B. *dean, economics professor*
Kroboth, Patricia Dowley *dean, pharmacy educator*
Kupfer, David J. *psychiatry professor*
Larsen, Ronald L. *dean, information scientist, educator*
Lehoczky, John Paul *statistics educator*
Miller, Ronald Lynn *director*
Murray, John Edward, Jr. *academic administrator, law educator*
Nolting, Daniel Lincoln *school librarian*
Nordenberg, Mark Alan *academic administrator, law educator*
Packard, Rochelle Sybil *retired elementary school educator*
Rebich, Lois J. *elementary school educator*
Ross, Madelyn Ann *academic administrator, newspaper editor*
Smartschan, Glenn Fred *educational consultant*
Walls Perry, J(oyce) Lorraine *elementary school educator*
Weidman, John Carl, II, *education and sociology educator, consultant*

Pocono Summit
Yorke-Viney, Sally Anne *elementary school educator*

Quakertown
Babb, Lisa Marie *physical education educator*

Radnor
George, Marie Angelella *academic administrator*

Reading
Hamwi, Bonnie L. *education educator, consultant*
Pumariega, JoAnne Buttacavoli *mathematics educator*
Rodgers, Lana Loretta Lusch *retired elementary school educator*

Renfrew
Meredith, Joanne Cusick *retired special education educator*

Scottdale
Lee, John Lawrence, Jr. *educational administrator*

Scranton
Arter, Patricia Sullivan *special education educator*
Elvidge, Christina Marie *director*
Jaeger, Gale Albano *education educator*
Passon, Richard Henry *retired academic administrator, language educator*
Sethi, Arjinder P. S. *program director*
Stufft, Derry L. *education educator*

Secane
Hudiak, David Michael *academic administrator, lawyer*

Shippensburg
Bao, Julie Qiu *education professor*
Basler, Linda Gerber *retired elementary school educator*

Slippery Rock
Colbert-Lewis, Sean C.D., Sr. *educator, consultant*

South Park
Furman, L. Robert *principal, music educator*

Southampton
Gniewek, Debra Lyman *school librarian, consultant*

State College
Byrnes, Lisa T. *instructional designer*
Dupuis, Victor Lionel *retired curriculum and instruction educator*
Hoffa, Harlan Edward *retired university dean, art educator*
McKeel, Lillian Phillips *retired education educator*

Summerdale
Pickel, Diane Dunn *education educator*

Swarthmore
Chopp, Rebecca S. *academic administrator*
Guardiola, Maria Luisa *literature and language educator*

Telford
Boughter, Barbara B. *retired mathematics educator*

Townville
Rudy, Elaine Kim *elementary school educator*

Turbotville
Brewer, Elizabeth Ann *elementary school counselor*

University Park
Antle, Charles Edward *statistics educator*
Heid, Mary Kathleen *mathematics educator*
Herr, Edwin Leon *educator, academic administrator*
Spanier, Graham Basil *academic administrator*

Villanova
DelTosto Brogan, Doris *dean, law educator*
Heitzmann, Ray *education educator, athletic coach*
Lucky, Crystal J. *educational consultant*

Warminster
Ciao, Frederick J. *school system administrator, educator*
Weaver-Stroh, Joanne Mateer *education educator, consultant*

Washington
Haring-Smith, Tori *academic administrator*

Longo, James McMurtry *academic administrator*

Washington Crossing
Means, John Barkley *director, language educator*

Wayne
Ziglar, William Larry *academic administrator, historian, religious studies educator*

West Chester
Dowdell, Crystal *assistant principal*
Nicastro, Anthony Joseph *academic administrator, educator*

West Grove
Olson, Leroy Calvin *retired educational administration educator*

Wexford
Roy, Suzanne Scully *reading specialist*

Wilkes Barre
Horoszy, Albert John *mathematics educator*
Loomis, Richard Morgan *literature and language educator*
Murray-Galella, Suzanne *special education educator, consultant*

Willow Street
Henderson, Joseph Ralston *educator*

Yardley
Breitenfeld, Frederick, Jr. *retired educational consultant, broadcast executive*
Millner, Rachel Erin *psychology educator, occupational therapist*

RHODE ISLAND

Barrington
Moody, Marilyn Leavitt *retired special education educator*

Jamestown
Ullrich, Robert Albert *academic administrator*

Kingston
Carothers, Robert Lee *academic administrator*
Dunson, Stephanie *literature and language educator, consultant*
Shim, Minsuk Kim *education educator*

Lincoln
Marini, Kelly Jean *elementary school educator*

Middletown
Jackson, John Edward *adult education educator, retired military officer*

Newport
Antone, M. Therese *academic administrator, nun*
Gerety, Jane *academic administrator, nun*

North Kingstown
Morse, Barbara *mathematics educator*

Providence
Greer, David Steven *dean, educator, physician*
Grossi, Linda Marie *elementary school educator*
Hemmasi, Harriette Ann *university librarian*
Hobday, Debra J. *dean*
Kennedy, David William *academic administrator, law educator*
Maeda, John *academic administrator, graphics designer, artist, computer scientist*
Simmons, Ruth J. *academic administrator*

Warwick
Hayes, Catherine Davis *elementary school educator*
Izzi, John *mathematics educator, writer, actor*

Westerly
Crowley, Cynthia Warner Johnson *secondary school educator*

Woonsocket
Crowley, Rosa Quinonez *literature and language educator*

SOUTH CAROLINA

Adams Run
Stewart, Shirley S. *retired elementary school educator*

Anderson
Kaiser, Louise Martin *elementary school educator*
Millwood, Kenneth Andrew *university librarian*

Beaufort
Vido, Karen Phinney *education educator*

Bluffton
Markwood, Stephen Ernest *Educational Consultant*

Central
Sinnamon, Walter Bruce *college administrator, biology educator*

Charleston
Appleget, Terri Lynn *elementary school educator*
Benson, P. George *academic administrator, finance educator*
Cadwallader, Stephen Wayne *history and government educator*
Carnell, Claude Mitchell, Jr. *academic administrator*
DiPiro, Joseph Thomas *dean, pharmacy educator*
Egelson, Pauline C. *director*
Greenberg, Raymond Seth *academic and health facility administrator, educator*
Jenkins, Pearl G. *retired secondary school educator, realtor*
Rosa, John William *academic administrator, career military officer*
Simms, Lois Averetta *retired secondary school educator*
Strauch, Katina Parthemos *college librarian, publishing executive*

Clemson
Barker, James F. *academic administrator*
Bennett, Archie Wayne *academic administrator*
Burton, O'Neil B. III *academic administrator*
Kelly, John William, Jr. *academic administrator*

Clinton
Dutrow, Anita Marceca *education educator*

Clio
McLeod, Marilynn Hayes *retired educational administrator, farmer*

Columbia
Benner, Cristina Hill *literature and language educator*
Cofield, Virginia Riley *elementary school educator, piano teacher*
Cunningham, Joseph Edward *elementary school educator*
Duffy, John Joseph *retired academic administrator, historian, educator*
Li, Xiang (Robert Li) *tourism educator, director*
Meyer-Brosdahl, Deborah J.C. *educator, researcher*
Morgan, Robert Marion *educational research educator*
Outin, Mary Louise *business, multi-cultural history and geneology educator*
Palms, John Michael *academic administrator, physicist*
Pastides, Harris *academic administrator*
Pratt, Walter F., Jr. *dean, law educator*
Sorensen, Andrew Aaron *retired academic administrator*
Sproat, Ruth C. *retired director, consultant*
Teegen, Hildy *dean, business educator*

Conway
Díaz, Barbara Beck *educator*
Monroe, Richard W. *university professor*

Gaffney
Ivey, Elizabeth Reeves *retired school system administrator*

Graniteville
Learnard, James Michael *conversational English professor, volunteer intellectual project, developmental English professor, retired collections and bad debt manager*

Greenville
Alford, Robert Wilfrid, Jr. *middle school educator*
Baker, Harriet Kugley *elementary school educator*
Gustafson, Dwight Leonard *university dean*
Jones, Bob III *academic administrator*
Jones, Robert Thaddues *retired principal*
McCuen, Maureen E. *history educator*
Payne, George Frederick *academic administrator*
Shi, David E. *academic administrator, historian*
Smith, Philip Daniel *academic administrator, education educator*
Stratton, Sally G. (Sara) *retired school system administrator*

Greenwood
Jackson, Larry Artope *retired college president*

Hartsville
Doubles, Malcolm Carroll *college administrator*
Rubinstein, Joseph Harris *education educator*

Hilton Head Island
Levy, Maurice *retired medical educator, researcher*

Irmo
Murphy, Jennifer H. (Buffy Murphy) *elementary school educator*

Isle Of Palms
Lehr, Judy Brown *educational consultant*

Kiawah Island
Warren, Russell Glen *educational consultant*

Latta
Berry, Christy *school librarian*

Mauldin
Smith, Lisa Coleman *autism and neurological disabilities special educator*

Mount Pleasant
Bloder, Katharine Jean *elementary school educator*
Gilbert, James Eastham *academic administrator*

Orangeburg
Hill, Howard Darnell *consultant*
Pearson, Melissa Berry *literature and language educator*

Pawleys Island
Proefrock, Carl Kenneth *academic medical administrator*

Pickens
Hardin, Janet Becker *gifted and talented educator, music educator*

Rock Hill
Franklin, A. David *retired college dean, music educator, journalist*

Simpsonville
Munley, William Edward *health services administrator*

Spartanburg
Corden, Paul H. *retired college program director, food service executive*
Lancaster, Amy *dean*
McGehee, Larry Thomas *retired academic administrator*
Pae, Holly *special education educator*
Racine, Philip Noel *retired history educator*
Stephens, Bobby Gene *college administrator, consultant*

Taylors
Porter, Jean McRae *counselor*

Tigerville
NeSmith, Richard A. *education educator, consultant*

Ulmer
Mathias, Lynda Rowell *retired secondary school educator*

Wellford
Seay, Stephanie *elementary school educator*

SOUTH DAKOTA

Brookings
Bailey, Harold Stevens, Jr. *retired educational administrator*
Chicoine, David Lyle *academic administrator*
Mix, Vickie Lynn *school librarian, educator*
Rogers, Lawrence E. *education educator*
Vanderpan, Norma *retired elementary school educator*

Bruce
Haertel, Lois Steben *education educator*

Eagle Butte
Webb, Yvonne M. *secondary school educator*

Kadoka
Stout, Maye Alma *retired secondary school educator*

Mc Laughlin
Lehman, Carol Sue *school librarian*

Rapid City
Buchanan, Carolee Horstman *special education educator, consultant*

Sioux Falls
Ashworth, Julie *elementary school educator*
Deering, Thomas Edwin *educator*
Dowling, Barbara R. *elementary school educator*
Jernberg, Beth L. *education educator*
Lunde, Lloyd William *vocational school educator*
Sommer, Carol R. *elementary school educator*
Talley, Robert Cochran *academic administrator, cardiologist*

Vermillion
Melmer, Rick *dean, former state official, school system administrator*

Wessington Springs
Mohling, Charlotte *middle school educator*

Yankton
Foster, James Caldwell *dean, historian*

TENNESSEE

Allardt
Copeland, Patricia Ruth *elementary school educator*

Antioch
Mattice, Debora J. *special education educator, consultant*

Bartlett
Hatch, Margaret Oenone *secondary school educator*

Bristol
Johnson, Opal Burton *retired elementary school educator*
Teng, Wenyuan William *dean*
Werner, Dawn Heterick *elementary school educator*

Chattanooga
Brooks, Ellyn Hersh *retired special education educator*

Clarksville
Amstutz, Julie Denise *elementary school educator*
Gold, Moniqueka E. *education educator*
Stoddard, Peter Hawkins *education educator, consultant*

Cleveland
Harper, James Edward, Jr. *academic administrator*
McClung, Patricia Beatrice *special education educator*

Coalfield
Justice, Jennifer Amanda *special education educator*

Collegedale
Clark, Ann Rorabaw *English professor, consultant, writer*

Collierville
Tesreau, Cynthia Lynn *elementary school educator*

Columbia
Cantrell, Sharron Caulk *principal*

Cookeville
Volpe, Angelo Anthony *retired academic administrator, chemist, educator*

Cordova
Jacobs, M. Louise *secondary school educator*

Covington
Wright, Bonnie Shankle *assistant principal, choir director*

Cunningham
Mince, Carol Kirkham *history educator*

Dandridge
Coley, Jan Brumback *biology educator*

Dickson
Larkins, Bessie Sullivan *education educator*

Gates
Nance, Helen Strayhorn *pre-school administrator, educator*

Grand Junction
Godwin, Anna Marie *primary school educator*

Greeneville
Dobson, Hugh Fredrick *supervisor*

Harrison
Rokicki, Phillip S. *career planning administrator, educator*

Henderson
Gardner, Elmer Claude *academic administrator*

Jackson
Agee, Bob R. *academic administrator, minister, educator*
Dodson, Frank *academic administrator*

Jefferson City
Knight, Tori Hopper *academic administrator, educator*

Johnson City
Grover, Kathleen Higginson *literature and language educator*
Stanton, Paul E., Jr. *academic administrator*
Tollefson, Terrence Alfred *retired educator and consultant*
Turner, Krista Denise *director*

Kingsport
Groseclose, Clara Rita *retired secondary school educator*
Rigsby, Mary Sue *retired elementary school and adult education educator*
Russell, Rob *academic administrator*

Knoxville
Blaze, Doug A. *dean, law educator*
Boling, Edward Joseph *retired academic administrator*
Cheek, Jimmy Geary *academic administrator, agricultural studies educator*
Creasia, Joan Catherine *dean, nursing educator*
Davis, Wayne T. *dean*
Gaude, Emily Camp *elementary school educator*
Mankel, Francis Xavier *retired principal, priest*
Russell, Rodney E. *school system administrator*
Shelby, Paulus P., Jr. *biology educator*
Simek, Jan F. *academic administrator, anthropologist, educator*
Williams, Jan R. *dean, business educator*
Ye, Xiaofei *education educator*

Lebanon
Eaton, Harvill Carlton *academic administrator*

Lenoir City
Den Uyl, Helen *elementary school educator*

Manchester
Dale, David L. *retired education educator*
Westberry, Anita Parrish *education educator*

Maryville
McLemore, Carolyn Faye *elementary school educator*

Memphis
Cash, Kriner *school system administrator*
Cupples, Douglas Wayne *education educator*
Dreyfus, Susan Kahn *middle school educator*
Dunathan, Harmon Craig *college dean*
Ford, Sylverna V. *dean university libraries*
Gilpatrick, Russell O. *dean, dental educator*
Gourley, Dick R. *dean, pharmacy educator*
Hall, Arnita Rena *special education educator*
Kelly, Aleda Mae *retired secondary education educator*
McClinton, Joanie *elementary and secondary school educator*
Nesin, Jeffrey David *academic administrator*
Raines, Shirley Carol *academic administrator*
Ranta, Richard Robert *university dean*
Troutt, William Earl *academic administrator*

Millington
Gray, Barbara L. *assistant principal, tax specialist*

Mount Juliet
Holloway, Susan Master *elementary school educator*

Murfreesboro
Doyle, Delores Marie *retired principal*
Scott, Rupert Neil *professor and capitalize university librarian*

Nashville
Balser, Jeffrey R. *dean, medical educator*
Bradford, James Warren, Jr. *dean, finance educator*
Coukos, Eleni Dianne *education educator*
Cyrus, Cynthia J. *dean, music educator*
Ford, Donna *education educator*
Frensley, Susanne H. *history educator*
Guha, Sujata *education educator*
Guthrie, Chris *dean, law educator*
Hogan, Mark A. *school system administrator*
Leuer, Mary Margaret *elementary and secondary education educator*
Martinez Bland, Veronica Kay *elementary school educator*
Mathis, Dolores *special education educator*
Meyer, Ellen L. *academic administrator*
Morton, Linda June *academic administrator*
O'Leary, Hazel Rollins *academic administrator, former United States Secretary of Energy, lawyer*
Parker, John Howard *educator*
Rawlings, Jennifer Sue *primary school educator*
Register, Jesse *school system administrator*
Riley, Wayne Joseph *academic administrator, medical educator*
Rivera, Maximiano Marquez *academic administrator, educator, researcher, writer*
Sargent, Mildred Crow *retired history educator, writer*
Schroeder, Joni Lynn *secondary school educator*
Seligson, Mitchell A. *political science educator*
Stricklin, Cynthia J. *middle school educator*
Swan, Patricia Brintnall *academic administrator, researcher*
Williams, Carolyn Ruth Armstrong *university official*
Wyatt, Joe Billy *academic administrator*
Zeppos, Nicholas S. *academic administrator*

Newport
Gregg, Kimberly K. *elementary school and adult education educator*

Pleasant Hill
Hull, Charles William *retired special education educator*

Ripley
Hartman, Joan Evans *educational consultant*

Sewanee
Croom, Frederick Hailey *academic administrator, mathematician, educator*
Cunningham, Joel Luther *academic administrator*
Patterson, William Brown *retired dean, history professor*
Varner, Marleen Allen *retired academic administrator*

Seymour
Dunlap, Sue Weaver *education educator*

Smyrna
Essary, Pat A. *principal*

Washburn
Romeo, Joanne Josefa Marino *mathematics educator, department chairman*

TEXAS

Abilene
Berryhill, Carisse Mickey *University Librarian*
Cardot, Joseph James *program director*
Lloyd, Terry Lee *retired elementary school educator*
McCaleb, Gary Day *university official*
Specht, Alice Wilson *university libraries dean*
Stone, Meredith Jean *academic administrator*
Wheeler, Floyd Larry *education educator*
Wortey, Elizabeth Norman *librarian, associate director*

Alpine
Tucker Chambers, Johnnie L. *elementary school educator, rancher*

Amarillo
Carter, Edythe L. (Edie Carter) *mathematics educator*
Crowley, Cara J. *director*

Arlington
Copeland, Anita Bob *director, retired elementary school educator, senior consultant*
Han, Chien-Pai *statistics educator*
Minnerly, Robert Ward *retired headmaster*
Pomerantz, Martin *chemistry educator, researcher*
Sqenz, Sylvia *counseling administrator*

Austin
Bolm, Deborah Dell *elementary school educator, consultant*
Bordin, Cristina Stadolny *academic administrator*
Brewer, Thomas Bowman *retired university president*
Carleton, Don Edward *academic administrator, writer*
Carstarphen, Meria Joel *school system administrator*
Cigarroa, Francisco Gonzalez *academic administrator, pediatric surgeon*
Cunningham, William Hughes *retired academic administrator, marketing professional, educator*
Doluisio, James Thomas *dean, pharmacy educator*
Dubose, Kathryn Michaud *secondary school educator*
Ellis, Martha McCracken *academic administrator, psychology professor*
Gilligan, Thomas W. *dean, finance educator*
Gonzalez-Gerth, Miguel *literature and language educator, writer*
Graham, Lawrence Sherman *political science educator, management consultant*
Harris, Ben M. *education educator*
Hetzler, Susan Elizabeth Savage *educational administrator*
Inman, Bobby Ray *dean, educator, retired military officer*
Jordan, Bryce *retired university president*
Livingston, William Samuel *retired academic administrator, political scientist, educator*
Lukenbill, Willis Bernard *adult education educator*
Lynn, Laurence Edwin, Jr. *academic administrator, educator*
McKeown-Moak, Mary Park *educational consultant*
Powers, William Charles, Jr. *academic administrator, law educator*
Rankin, Mary Ann *dean, biology professor*
Roueche, John Edward, II, *education educator, director*
Sager, Lawrence Gene *dean, law educator*
Sanchez, Eduardo J. *academic administrator, former state agency administrator, physician*
Shilling, Roy Bryant, Jr. *academic administrator*
Shine, Kenneth Irwin *academic administrator, cardiologist, educator*
Springer, David William *dean, social sciences educator*
Wurzbach, Linda *educational consultant*

Bastrop
Clemons, Barbara Gail *history educator*

Beaumont
Baden, Sheri Louise *primary school educator*

Beeville
Freeman, Patsy L. *director*

Belton
Shelburne, D. Audell *adult education educator*

Boerne
Goode, Bobby Claude *retired secondary school educator*

Booker
Doerrie, Bobette *retired secondary school educator*

Brownsville
Garcia, Juliet Villarreal *academic administrator*

Brownwood
Campbell, Vicki F. *counseling educator*

Bryan
Fields, Sheila Crain *elementary school educator*

Canyon
Long, Russell Charles *retired academic administrator*

Carrollton
Barland, Sarah Elizabeth *secondary school educator*

Cedar Hill
Jackson, Robert Roscoe *education educator*

College Station
Adkisson, Perry Lee *university system chancellor*
Atkins, Stephen Eugene *academic librarian, historian*
Bowen, Ray Morris *academic administrator, engineering educator*
Byrne, C. William, Jr. *athletics program director*
Cocanougher, Arthur Benton *academic administrator*
Cook, Violetta Burke *university administrator*
Dickey, Nancy Wilson *chancellor, physician*
Erlandson, David Alan *education administration educator*
Ghanem, Hassan A. *education educator, researcher*
Guerrero, Tito III *university administrator*
Monroe, Haskell Moorman, Jr. *chancellor emeritus, retired history professor, dean*
Nite, Sandra Bonorden *mathematics educator*
Sadoski, Mark Christian *education educator*
Sheather, Simon James *management educator*
Strawser, Jerry R. *dean*
Vitter, Jeffrey Scott *academic administrator, computer science educator, researcher*

Colleyville
Giesler, Karen Hofmann *middle school educator*
Sawyers, Norma Ann *elementary school educator, real estate agent, property manager*

Commerce
Jacobs, Kathryn Elisabeth *educator*
Justice, Madeline Carol *education educator*
Scott, Joyce Alaine *academic administrator*
Vornberg, James Alvin *education educator*

Coppell
Smothermon, Peggi Sterling *middle school educator*

Corpus Christi
Abdelsamad, Moustafa Hassan *dean*
Cassidy, Jack *academic administrator, educator*
Chodosh, Robert Ivan *retired elementary school educator, coach*
Krnavek, Jennifier Diane *school librarian*
Pohan, Cathy Ann *education educator, consultant*
Robeau, Sally Garwood *secondary school educator*
Scott, Gloria Randle *former college president*
Valdez, Kristina Louise *secondary school educator*

Crane
Hugendubler, Richard Thomas *secondary school educator*

Crockett
LaClair, Patricia Marie *physical education director, paramedic*

Cypress
Huss, Betty Jo *education educator*

Dallas
Abdo, Virginia Richie *retired secondary school educator*
Attanasio, John Baptist *dean, law educator*
Baker, Katherine June *elementary school educator, minister, artist*
Brown, Karon Whitesell *education educator*
Cho, Ho Soon Michelle L. *adult education educator*
Cirilo, Amelia Medina *educational consultant*
Cole, James S. *dean, dental educator*
Cook, Gary Raymond *academic administrator, minister*
Early, Ann Marie *retired women's studies educator*
Fletcher, (Martha) Ann Messersmith *counseling administrator, educator*
Gilman, Alfred Goodman *dean, pharmacologist, educator*
Green, Hubert Gordon *university professor, pediatrician*
Harrison, Frank *former university president*
Hester, Linda Hunt *retired dean, counselor, retired sociology, physical education and health professor*
Hinojosa, Michael *school system administrator*
Kesterson, Ray Brent *dean, retired military officer*
Lund, Steven *school system administrator*
Melin, Stacy M. *literature and language educator*
Niemi, Albert William, Jr. *economics professor*
Overman, Ann Cathlene *school librarian, educator*
Patricia, Mathes-Burnett G. *education educator*
Shambaugh, Irvin Calvin, Jr. *aptitude test firm executive, consultant*
Stephenson, Linda S. *school librarian*
Turner, R. Gerald (Robert Gerald Turner) *academic administrator*
Umphrey, Donald Wayne *adult education educator, academic administrator, writer*
Valerin, Marcus Paul *school system administrator, director*
Williams, Michael Edward, Sr. *dean*
Wood, Georgianna Adeline *primary school and language educator*

Del Rio
Fernandez, Yolanda *literature and language educator*

Denison
Cameron, Frances Marilyn *elementary school educator*

Denton
Bataille, Gretchen *academic administrator*
Ferrell Chavez, Dawn Elizabeth *assistant principal*
Greenlaw, Marilyn Jean *retired adult education educator*
Hartsock, Ralph M. *music librarian*
McCaslin, Richard Bryan *history educator*
McCoy, Amy L. *special education educator*
McDonald-West, Sandi MacLean *director, consultant*
Novak, Rynell Stiff *retired academic administrator*
O'Rourke-Kaplan, Marian *dean*
Smith, Howard Wellington *education educator, retired dean*
Toulouse, Robert Bartell *retired college administrator*
Turner, Philip Michael *academic administrator, writer*
Zrnic, Reiko Lukic *physics educator*

Dripping Springs
Smith, Ellis Carlton *history educator, consultant*

Duncanville
Gawedzinski, Robert William *literature and language educator, department chairman*

Egypt
Wynn, John Thomas *retired academic administrator, farming executive, economic consultant, oil and gas producer*

El Paso
Balcazar, Hector G. *dean*
Boyd, Dana Kristin *elementary school educator*
Combs, Don Carlos *counselor educator*
Garcia, Lorenzo *school system administrator*
Jarvis, Richard S. *academic administrator*
Lawrence, Milbourn *literature and language educator*
Natalicio, Diana Siedhoff *academic administrator*
Nieto, Angelica Baylon *principal, educator*
Trussell, Robert Prescott *special education educator*
Zopfi, Emma G. *elementary school educator*

Elgin
Shelby, Nina Claire *special education educator*

Farmers Branch
Reyes, Czarina Suzanne *mathematics educator*

Flower Mound
Stokes, Linda Baer *elementary school educator*

Forney
Weatherford, Shirley Diane *special education educator*

Fort Worth
Boschini, Victor John, Jr. *academic administrator*
Johnson, Melody *school system administrator*
Ogle, Sarah Jean *retired educational consultant, educator*
Saenz, Michael *college president*
Simmons, Jean Byers *academic administrator, director*
Tucker, William Edward *academic administrator, minister*

Galveston
Anderson, Garland D. *dean, obstetrician, gynecologist, educator*
Loftin, Richard Bowen *academic administrator*
Stobo, John David *academic administrator, physician*

Garland
Lowell, Peggy Armstrong *elementary school educator, writer*

Georgetown
Lovin, Keith Harold *retired academic administrator, philosopher, educator*

Glenn Heights
Francis, Tamara *physics educator, professional athletics manager*
Rowe, Nancie E. *director, minister*

Granbury
Curl, Samuel Everett *retired dean, agriculturist, consultant*

Grapevine
Hao, Yaowu *education educator*

Harker Heights
Rose, Doris Ann *secondary school educator*

Hereford
Gilbert, Connie Fay *secondary school educator*
Yavornik, Barbara Ann *pre-school educator*

Houston
Alfini, James Joseph *dean, lawyer, educator*
Anderson, Claire W. *gifted and talented educator*
Beckingham, Kathleen Mary *education educator, researcher*
Bedoya González, Cardenio *literature and language educator*
Betts, Nicole Lavette *elementary school educator, consultant*
Bott, Simon Gregory *chemistry educator, researcher*
Bui, Khoi Tien *college counselor*
Butler, William Thomas *academic administrator, physician, educator*
Caram, Dorothy Farrington *educational consultant*
Carroll, Michael M. *dean, mechanical engineering educator*
Cazenave, Anita Washington *secondary school educator*
Crayton, Arnell *secondary school educator*
Davis, Debra Ann *secondary school educator*
Davis, (Alice) Marlece *secondary school educator, director*
Djerejian, Edward Peter *academic administrator, retired ambassador*
Flaitz, Catherine M. *former dean, dental educator*
Gaelens, Albert Robert *retired director, educational administrator, priest*
Glick, William H. *dean, management educator*
Gonzalez, Antonio *academic administrator, educator, title company executive*
Greenberg, Stephen Baruch *dean, medical educator*
Harrison, Betty Carolyn Cook *retired education educator, administrator*
Heil, Anne Campochiaro *secondary school educator*
Henry, Margaret Elisabeth *dean, educator*
Khator, Renu *academic administrator, political science professor*
Kneese, Carolyn Calvin *retired education educator*
Leebron, David Wayne *academic administrator, law educator*
Long, Delwin J., II, *professor*
Looper, Marcia Lynn *elementary school educator, consultant*
Mariotto, Marco Jerome *dean, psychology educator, researcher*
Matthews, Kathleen Shive *biochemistry educator*
McKee, Rae Ellen (Rae Ellen McKee-Doucette) *special education educator*
Miller, Harry Freeman *university administrator*
Nimmer, Raymond T. *dean, law educator*
Novak, Jason P. *secondary school educator*
Oakes, Pamela R. *retired elementary school educator*
Parnas-Simpson, Marianna *chorus director, singer*
Paul, Alida Ruth *retired elementary school educator*
Pickering, James Henry III *academic administrator, educator*
Remes, Robin Eva *secondary school educator, cartographer*
Roos, Sybil Friedenthal *retired elementary school educator*
Rudley, John M. *academic administrator*
Sangi-Haghpeykar, Haleh *educator*
Sloan, Robert Bryan, Jr. *academic administrator*
Smith, Arthur Kittredge, Jr. *academic administrator, political scientist, educator*
Smith, Joellen *dean, literature and language educator*
Smith, Roland Blair, Jr. *university administrator*
Threet, John T. *principal*
Trichel, Mary Lydia *middle school educator*
Wagner, Paul Anthony, Jr. *education educator*
Webb, Marty Fox *principal*
Wilkin, Alana Zimmer *elementary school educator*

Humble
Douglass, Thelma Jean *educational administrator*
Hadlow, Vivian Jean *retired elementary school educator*

Huntsville
Payne, David Emer *university administrator*
Ward, Richard Hurley *education educator, writer*

Hurst
Fox, Patrecia *literature and language educator*
Fuentes, Rosa *education educator*

Hutto
Hamilton, Elizabeth Ann *elementary school educator*

Iola
Nelson, John Harrison *mathematics educator*

Irving
Mace, Steven Douglas *academic administrator, educator*
Martin, Thomas Lyle, Jr. *academic administrator*
Wilkerson, Patricia Helen *retired director*

Jacksonville
Queen, Kay Wallace *education educator*

Keene
England, Michael *education educator*

Kemp
Shugart, Jill *retired school administrator*

Killeen
Jenkins, Sharon Leigh *special education educator*
Peronto, Janice Lynn *principal*

Kingsville
Tallant, Steven Hall *academic administrator, social worker*

Kingwood
Swift, Constance Redmond *special education educator*

La Porte
Edwards, Kristina Nell *elementary school educator*
Kelling, David Henry *educational administrator, accountant*

Lake Jackson
Hill, Diane Louise *educator*

Laredo
Black, Clifford Merwyn *academic administrator, sociologist, educator*
Heimes, Charmaine Marie *elementary school educator, poet, writer*

Lewisville
Hooten, John F *economics educator*

Little Elm
Milian, Ayda R. *secondary school educator*

Littlefield
Muller, Janice Elaine *secondary school educator*

Llano
Wilson, Dena Suzette *elementary school educator*

Longview
Cuba, Mattie Deneice *middle school educator*

Lubbock
Bailey, Guy H. *academic administrator*
Banda, Devender R. *education educator*
Conover, William Jay *statistics educator*
Haragan, Donald Robert *academic administrator, geologist, educator*
Hurley, Kristie DeLynn *primary school educator*
Oliver, Marina Goodfield *University Librarian*
Rudd, Loretta Cooper *education educator, researcher*
Song, Lianfa *educator*
White, Alice Virginia *academic administrator*

Madisonville
Rowley, Patti Mitchell *psychology educator*

Marshall
Ravenell, Alma Rena *school librarian*

Mcallen
Gonzalez, Rolando Noel *secondary school and theology studies educator, photographer*
Ramirez, Leo Armando, Sr. *mathematics educator*

Mesquite
Fawcett, Leah *school librarian*
Kotrany, Anne M. *school librarian*
Washington, Larissa Lenore *educator*
Wenrich, John William *college president*

Midland
Bridges, Judy Cantrell *gifted and talented education educator*

Missouri City
Jenkins, Helen Bishop *academic administrator*
Weber, Katie *retired special education educator*

Montgomery
Hargett, Kent *Education Foundation Administrator*

Mount Pleasant
Posey, Pamela Gayle *special education educator*

Nacogdoches
Carter, Evelyn *retired elementary school educator*
Vaughan, Elizabeth Jean *education educator*

Navasota
Day, Kathryn Ann *history educator*

New Braunfels
Barragán, Celia Silguero *elementary school educator*
Dugger, Roy Wesley *academic administrator, retired military officer*
Oestreich, Charles Henry *retired university president*

Normangee
Stork, Vera Lee *retired elementary school educator*

Odessa
Kunkel, Martha F. *director*
Kupper, Julie Ann *retired elementary school educator*

Paige
Trevino, Jerry Rosalez *retired secondary school principal*

Palmer
Gabor, Leciana *middle school educator*

Pasadena
Blue, Monte Lynn *college president*
Ruiz, Miriam *secondary school educator*

Penitas
Sandra, G. Koenig *school librarian*

Placedo
Rivera, Josie *elementary school educator*

Plainview
Dayton, Leah Jane *secondary school educator*

Plano
Gideon, Sharon Lee *secondary school educator*
Haggard, Geraldine Langford *primary school educator, writer, consultant*
Rhodes, Sherry L. *educator*
Shepherd, Karen Schiller *biology educator*
Vickery, Karen S. *education educator, director*

Port Arthur
Goza, Jim *chemistry educator*

Prairie View
Kirschten, Robert *educator, author, videographer*

Rancho Viejo
Garza, Roberto Jesus *retired education educator*

Richardson
Daniel, David Edwin *academic administrator, civil engineer*
Dholakia-Lehenbauer, Kruti Ravindra *associate dean*
Pirkul, Hasan *dean, management educator*
Salk, Jane Ellen *educator*
Salter, Elizabeth Mary *academic administrator*

Richland Hills
Houston, Lowell E. *special education educator*

Rosharon
Lopez, Placida Ramos *elementary school educator*

Round Rock
Brennan, Deborah Dikeman *assistant principal*

Royse City
Borden, William Vickers *education educator, writer*

San Angelo
Blount, Grady Price *dean, director*
Johnson, Harvey Douglas *mathematics educator*

San Antonio
Beechinor, Diane Blanche *education educator*
Bennett, Sister Elsa Mary *retired secondary school educator*
Dorff, Barbara L. *elementary and secondary school educator*
Duron, Robert J. *school system administrator*
Dyas, Anna Marie *gifted and talented educator*
Faules, Barbara Ruth *retired elementary school educator*
Henderson, Dwight Franklin *dean, educator*
Hudspeth, Almetra Kavanaugh *retired elementary school educator*
Jarmon, Sharon Irene *secondary school educator*
Kaylor, Maria *special education educator*
Maxwell, Diana Kathleen *primary school educator*
Perry, George *dean, neuroscientist, educator*
Williams-Perry, Brenda Lee *pre-school educator*
Young, James Julius *academic administrator, retired military officer*

San Diego
Pena, Modesta Celedonia *retired principal*

San Marcos
Allsup, Roxane Cuellar *curriculum and instruction educator*

Sherman
Williams, Ruby Jo *retired principal*

Snyder
Martini, Jason *academic administrator*

Southlake
Arafat-Johnson, Danyah *secondary school educator, director*
Cruze, Jennifer Lea *secondary school educator*
Smith, JoBeth *elementary school educator*

Spring
Neill, Rebecca Anne *middle school educator*

Stephenville
McElroy, Linda Sue *retired elementary school educator*

Temple
Meshack, Geneva Tucker *retired elementary school educator*

Texarkana
Calhoun, John C., Jr. *academic administrator*

Texas City
Navy, Ernest Jude *educator, writer*
Plasek, Susan G. *academic administrator*

The Colony
Culver, Jennifer Lynn *secondary school educator*

Tyler
Davidson, Jack Leroy *academic administrator*
Peters, Robert K. *dean, newscaster, journalist*
Prater, Emma Lou *retired academic administrator*
Scott, Mary Sue *education educator*

Uvalde
Burchfield, Mitchel *education educator*

Vernon
Coufal, Cindy *literature and language educator*

Victoria
Kutach, Patricia Ann *counseling administrator*

Waco
Belew, John Seymour *academic administrator, chemist*
Brooks, Roger Leon *retired academic administrator*
Cobbs, Linda Ray *academic librarian*
Cunningham, Harold R. *academic administrator, accountant*
Garland, David Ellsworth *academic administrator, theology studies educator*
Lindsey, Jonathan Asmel *retired academic administrator, academic librarian*
Spencer, Vicki Carol *elementary school educator*
Toben, Bradley J.B. *dean, law educator*

Weatherford
Eppright, Carol A. *education educator*

Wharton
Rehak, Patricia *career planning administrator*

Wichita Falls
Ballard, Mark Alan *secondary school educator*
Hancock, Carole Patricia *academic administrator*
Leishner, Jane Carlson *retired director*

Wimberley
Ellis, John *retired school system administrator, writer*

Wylie
Cheng, Pauline Shyh-yi *mathematics educator*

UTAH

Bountiful
Andersen, Julie B. *elementary school educator*
Beesley, Kenneth Horace *educator*

Cedar City
Hill, Deborah Meyer *education educator*
Wilks, Jill Ann *academic administrator, director*

Cedar Hills
Ashton, Dawne Belinda *retired secondary school educator*

Holladay
McKell, Cyrus M. *retired dean, range plant physiologist, consultant*

Logan
Baldwin, Debra *history educator*

Midvale
Smith, Mary Ellen *educational program facilitator*

North Ogden
Heap, Joan S. *elementary school educator*

Orem
Jackman, Roderick Victor *distance learning educator*

Provo
Allred, Ruel Acord *education educator*
Boyter, Scott M. *academic administrator*
Bullough, Robert Vernon, Jr. *teacher education*
Christensen, Theodore Edward *educational consultant, educator*
Cornia, Gary C. *dean, management educator*
Jensen, Clayne R. *retired academic administrator*
Prater, Mary Anne *special education educator, researcher*
Rasband, James R. *dean, law educator*
Samuelson, Cecil O., Jr. *academic administrator*
Worthen, Kevin *academic administrator, law educator*

Salt Lake City
Bjorkman, David Jess *dean, gastroenterologist, educator*
Carroll, Dana *academic researcher, administrator, educator*
Chodosh, Hiram *dean, law educator*
Christensen, Bruce LeRoy *former academic administrator, commercial broadcasting executive*
Hardman, Michael L. *dean*
Jarvis, Joseph Boyer *retired university administrator*
Mauger, John W. *dean, pharmacy educator*
McCleary, Lloyd E(verald) *education educator*
West, Jason Brossard *education educator, consultant*
Wolfinger, Nicholas H. *educator*
Young, Michael Kent *academic administrator, law educator*

West Jordan
James, Linda Coates *elementary school educator*

West Valley City
Woodward, Sandra S. *literature and language educator*

VERMONT

Barre
Gilbert, Michael D. *secondary school educator*
Heath, Karen *secondary school educator*

Burlington
Cate, Richard H. *academic administrator, former state official*
Fogel, Daniel Mark *academic administrator, literature educator, writer*
Hennessey, John William, Jr. *academic administrator, educator*
Morin, Frederick C. *dean, pediatrician, educator*

Colchester
Slaybaugh, Douglas Paul *history educator*

Johnson
Williams, Peggy Ryan *retired academic administrator*

Lyndonville
Hertz, Barry P. *education educator*

Middlebury
Forman, Michele *secondary school educator*
Liebowitz, Ronald D. *academic administrator*
McKenna, William Michael *academic administrator*
O'Brien, George Dennis *retired academic administrator*

Plainfield
Jervis, Jane Lise *academic administrator, historian*

Proctorsville
Harper, Jennifer *elementary school educator*

South Burlington
Foss, Jean Mitchell *school system administrator*

South Royalton
Doria, Anthony Notarnicola *college dean, educator*

Strafford
Williams, William Magavern *headmaster*

Swanton
Suitor, Dorcas P. *elementary school educator*

Warren
Sullivan, Kathleen *elementary school educator*

Waterbury
Donovan, Timothy *academic administrator*
Hilton, Linda D. *academic administrator*

VIRGINIA

Alexandria
Bartlett, Elizabeth Susan *audio-visual specialist*
Beringer, Ivy *education educator*
Haygood, Alma Jean *elementary school educator*
Jenkins, John Smith *retired dean, lawyer*
Todd, Matthew *school librarian*
Zissios, Patricia Ann *principal*

Annandale
Passut, Christine Diana *special education educator*
Peck, Nan J. *academic administrator*

Arlington
Dorman, Janet Lee Vosper *elementary school educator*
Earl, Sister Patricia Helene *director, educator*
Hill, Christopher Thomas *professor*
Kicklighter, Claude Milton (Mick Kicklighter) *academic administrator, former federal agency administrator*
McTigue, Maurice P. *director*
Miles, Shirley *school system administrator*
Polsby, Daniel D. *dean, law educator*
Sharp, Barry J. *school system administrator*
Whittier, Barbara J (Bobbie) *retired biology and chemistry educator*
Wilson, Wendy Marie *elementary school educator, consultant*

Bedford
Day, Mark Ronald *history educator, reenactor*

Bentonville
Halm, Nancye Studd *retired academic administrator*

Blacksburg
Campbell, Joan Virginia Loweke *secondary school and language educator*
Steger, Charles William *academic administrator*
Torgersen, Paul Ernest *academic administrator, educator*
Weaver, Pamela Ann *education educator*

Bristol
Tolbert, John Lee *literature and language educator*

Broadway
Helbert, Sharon Bunch *retired special education educator*

Buchanan
Cole, Evelyn Marie *day care administrator*

Capeville
Spady, Joanne Smith *secondary school educator*

Charlottesville
Bruner, Robert Frank *dean, business educator*
Cannaday, Billy K., Jr. *dean, former state official, school system administrator*
Casteen, John Thomas III *academic administrator*
DeKosky, Steven Trent *dean, neurologist*
Garson, Arthur, Jr. *academic administrator, medical educator*
Hurd, Nicole Farmer *director*
Kauffman, James Milton *special education educator, writer*
Mahoney, Paul G. *dean, law educator*
Rappaport, Yvonne Kindinger *educator*

Smith, Clyde Ray *dean*
Truwit, Jonathon Dean *dean*
Wittenborg, Karin *university librarian*

Chase City
Reams, Linda Pigg *elementary school educator*

Chesapeake
Hill, Deborah Nixon *elementary school educator, minister*
Mincheff, Donna Currie *special education educator*
Notti, Donna Betts *special education educator*
Webb, Julia Jones *elementary school educator, minister*

Chester
Benn, Candace Marilea *elementary school educator*
Law, Thomas Melvin *academic administrator*

Christiansburg
Blanchard, Dorothy Hardt *academic administrator, volunteer*

Danville
Roberson, Janet *registrar*

Dublin
Douthat, Rebecca Arlene *retired secondary school educator*

Emory
Walker, Marilyn Suarez *educator*

Fairfax
Best, Amy L. *education educator*
Campana, Michael Phillip *secondary school foreign language educator*
Carty, Rita Mary *dean, emerita*
Fox, Donna M. *dean, biology professor*
Gillette, Brian Kenneth *academic administrator*
Given, Barbara (Knight) *elementary school educator, secondary school educator*
Longin, Thomas Charles *retired academic administrator*
Silcox, Gordon Bruce *executive coach*

Fincastle
Huffman, Jerry Wayne *retired secondary school educator*

Fredericksburg
Arnn, Nancy Shank *secondary school educator*
Hample, Judy G. *academic administrator*
Ryan, Kathy Ann *special education educator*

Front Royal
Stevens, Loretta Marie *special education educator*

Gainesville
Tuck, Russell R., Jr. *college president emeritus*

Great Falls
Andrews, Betty Bauserman *retired secondary school educator, real estate manager*

Hampden Sydney
Bortz, Walter M. III *academic administrator*

Hampton
Carrington, Marian Denise *academic administrator, counselor, motivational speaker*
Goode, Constance Loper *elementary school principal*
Goodson, Dorothy Moore *English educator, counselor*
Sypolt, Shirley Rae *elementary school educator*
Walsh, Joanne Claire *school librarian, educator*

Harrisonburg
Barnes, Susan K. *education educator, information technology executive*
Carrier, Ronald Edwin *academic administrator, director*
Pappas, Eric Charles *director*
Shanahan, Maureen Gabrielle *academic administrator*

Herndon
Jones, Reba (Becki) Pestun *elementary school and music educator*

Lexington
Anderson, Michael Alan *economics educator*
John, Lewis George *retired political science educator*
Parker, Phyllis R. *secondary school educator*
Ruscio, Kenneth Patrick *academic administrator, political science professor*
Smolla, Rodney Alan *dean, law educator*
Williams, H. Thomas (Tom Williams) *academic administrator, physicist, educator*

Lynchburg
Bowman, Kathleen Gill *academic administrator*
Sullivan, Gregory Paul *secondary school educator*
Webb, Evelyn Dunbar *middle school educator*

Manassas
Archer, Chalmers, Jr. *retired education educator*
Hayes, Linda Marie *middle school educator*
Kettlewell, Gail Biery *academic administrator, research professor*

Mc Dowell
Harkleroad, Jo-Ann Decker *special education educator*

Mc Lean
Black, Ginger Elizabeth *elementary school educator*

Mechanicsville
Avery, Eugene Leo *special education educator, retired automotive executive*

Middleburg
Paige, Wayne Leo *visual arts educator, artist*

Midlothian
Lamont-Gordon, Melissa Lynne *orchestra director, music educator*

Newport News
Drummond, Neil Hiden *retired secondary school educator*
Fox, Margaret Louise *retired secondary school educator*

Norfolk
Baysal, Oktay *dean, educator*
Brown, Mary Wilkes *secondary school educator*
Davidson, James Randall *educational consultant*
Davis, Russell Haden *counseling administrator, consultant*
Koch, James Verch *academic administrator, economist*
McKinney, Sueanne E. *education educator*
Miller, Khadijah Olivia *education educator*
Steele, James Eugene *retired school system administrator*

Oak Hill
Le, Cuoc Van *mathematics educator, electrical engineer*

Penhook
Rhodes, Rebecca Lane *school librarian*

Petersburg
Buck, Judith Brooks *principal, educator*
Johnson, Cherlyn Ann *education educator*
Miles, Ruby Williams *secondary school educator*
Moore, Eddie N., Jr. *college president*
Newby, Earl Fernando *education educator*

Port Royal
Clarke-Hall, Deborah Renay *elementary school educator*

Portsmouth
Rampersaud Lundy, Sheryll *special education educator*

Purcellville
McCurdy, Howard Earl *educator*

Radford
Carter, Fletcher Fairwick *university administrator, education educator retired*
Dunaway, Marsha Landrum *special education educator*

Richmond
Amann, Patricia Burgess *special education educator*
Ayers, Edward L. *academic administrator, history professor*
Boudinot, Frank Douglas *dean*
Brown, Marilyn Branch *retired educational administrator*
Cooper, William Edwin *professor, former academic administrator*
Douglass, John G. *dean*
Drain, Cecil B. *dean, nursing educator, retired military officer*
Dunn, Linda Baugh *middle school educator*
Epstein, David Stanley *educator, consultant*
Giacobbe, George Antonino *special education educator, violinist*
Green, Kristina F. *academic administrator, optician*
Hamel, Dana Bertrand *academic administrator*
Hunt, Ronald J. *dean, dental educator*
Inlow, D. Ronald *academic administrator, consumerism lecturer, food service consultant*
Johnson, Patricia Lee *mathematics educator*
Jones, Jeanne Pitts *pre-school administrator*
McGee, Henry Alexander, Jr. *academic administrator*
Moss, Princess Renai *elementary school educator*
Peart, Sandra Joan *dean*
Rader, Karen A. *director*
Rettig, James R. *university librarian, library association executive*
Salley, John Jones *retired academic administrator, oral pathologist*
Stover, Jill S. *school librarian, writer*
Trani, Eugene Paul *university president, educator*
Yanchick, Victor A. *dean, educator*

Roanoke
Gray, Nancy Ann Oliver *academic administrator*

Rockbridge Baths
Glidden, Robert Burr *academic administrator, music educator, consultant*

Rose Hill
Lane, Mary Winston *retired secondary school educator*

Rural Retreat
Evans, Susan W. *mathematics educator*

Sandy Point
Douglas, Daisy Howard *retired elementary school educator, writer, consultant*

Seaford
Badeaux, Earl Anthony *special education educator*

Spotsylvania
Goforth, Deborah S. *school librarian, educator*

Springfield
Kurth, Ronald James *retired academic administrator, military officer*
Lambert, Vickie Ann *retired dean, nursing consultant*

Stafford
Dillard, Teresa Mary *school counselor*

Sterling
Austin, Lynne Hunzicker *secondary school educator*
Fiacco, Anthony Vincent *educator, researcher*
Shepley, Magi D. *special education educator*

Suffolk
Brown, Alvenice Hortense Bryan *educator*

Sweet Briar
Muhlenfeld, Elisabeth Showalter *academic administrator, literature educator, writer*

Tabb
Budd, Richard Wade *academic administrator, dean, priest*

Vienna
Marx, Gary Dean *educational consultant, futurist, think-tank executive*

Virginia Beach
Barber, Vivian Kay *elementary school educator*
Carrington, Andrew Temple *education educator, consultant*
de Guzman, Marsha Rhoda *special education educator*
Felts, Margaret Jean *secondary school educator*
Hatt, Clifford Van *school system administrator, psychologist*
Hodapp, Heidi Francine *middle school educator*
Jones, Robert Clair *middle school educator*
Lee, Marta *school librarian*
Melvin, Carole Ramey *educational consultant*
Morgan, Raymond Franklin *education educator*
Sears, Patricia Marie *elementary school educator, consultant*
Selig, William George *academic administrator*
Smith, Thelma Cheryl *principal, minister*
Talag, Trinidad Santos *retired educator*
Thomas, Jimi Elizabeth *elementary school educator*
Von Mosch, Wanda Gail *principal*
Whitfield, Erica Sharon *director, career planning administrator*
Ziegler, Rochelle Elizabeth *special education educator*

Warrenton
Keys, Robert Green *literature and language educator*

Wattsville
Enright, William Maurice *retired literature and language educator*

Wicomico Church
Kenna, Gail Ann *secondary and higher education educator*

Williamsburg
Calver, Richard Allen *retired dean*
Douglas, Davison McDowell *dean, law educator*
McCarthy, Connie Kearns *university librarian*
Pulley, Larry (Lawrence B. Pulley) *dean, economics professor*
Ramer, Deborah Lynne *special education educator*
Reiss, Mitchell B. *academic administrator, law educator, former ambassador*
Reveley, Walter Taylor III *academic administrator, former dean, law educator*

Winchester
Conteh, Nabie Y. *information systems and computer technology educator*
Sproul, Joan Heeney *retired elementary school educator*
Tillmann, Richard *literature and language educator*

Wise
Smiddy, Joseph Charles *retired academic administrator*

Woodberry Forest
Campbell, Dennis Marion *academic administrator, theologian, educator*

Woodbridge
Lanza, William Paul *academic administrator*

Yorktown
Faron, Kathleen Adams *elementary school educator, department chairman*

WASHINGTON

Anacortes
Stoebe, Thomas Gaines *materials science educator*

Bellevue
de Sá e Silva, Elizabeth Anne *secondary school educator*
Reams, Patricia Lynn *retired elementary school educator*
Rice, Kay Diane *elementary school educator, consultant*

Bellingham
Dooley, Kathleen Ann *elementary school educator*

Benton City
Omel, June M. *elementary school educator*

Bothell
Constantino, Karen Marie *elementary school educator*

Camas
Howe, Robert Wilson *education educator*
Kotsovos, Jerry Frank *retired secondary school educator*

Centralia
Kirk, Henry Port *academic administrator*
Spiegelberg, Marc Steven *secondary school educator*

Clarkston
Migaki, James M. *education educator*

Clinton
Powers, David Richard *educational administrator*
Westergaard, George Henry *secondary school educator*

Ellensburg
McIntyre, Jerilyn Sue *academic administrator*

Federal Way
Rossi, Ruth Harris *special education educator*

Gig Harbor
Bernard, Lowell Francis *retired academic administrator, educator*

Granite Falls
Peterson, Andrea *elementary school educator*

Kenmore
Jennerich, Edward John *academic administrator, dean*
Montague, Deborah Marie *elementary school and music educator, consultant*

Kennewick
Merkel, Patricia Mae *retired school system administrator*
Scott, Pamela J. *educational consultant*

Lacey
Siera, Steven G. *career planning administrator, educator*

Lakewood
Gilchrist, Debra L. *college librarian*
McEwen, Doris Ann *education educator*

Mount Vernon
Church, Pamela Sue *academic administrator, educator*
Langworthy, William Clayton *retired college official*

Olympia
Esbeck, Edward S. *retired educator*
Jackson, Thelma Harrison *educational consultant, researcher*
Markham, J. David *secondary school educator, writer, historical consultant*

Pasco
Meadows, Deborah Renee *dean, educator*

Port Townsend
Wheeler, Lorna Raven *literature and language educator*

Pullman
Dobney, Fredrick John *academic administrator*
Floyd, Elson Sylvester *academic administrator*
Hyde, Virginia Crosswhite *literature and language educator*
Lewis, Norman G. *academic administrator, researcher, consultant*
Paznokas, Lynda Sylvia *elementary school educator*

Richland
Darby, Nancy *secondary school educator*
Glennen, Robert Eugene, Jr. *retired academic administrator*
Miller, James Vince *university president*

Seattle
Allan, Susan *academic administrator, former public health service officer*
Alokolaro, Ann O. *secondary school educator*
Archibald, Sandra Orr *dean, political science professor, economist*
Baillie, Thomas A. *dean, former pharmaceutical executive*
Banks, James Albert *research director, educator*
Carlson, Dale Arvid *retired dean*
Cauce, Ana Mari *dean, psychology professor*
Clark, Annette *dean*
Cox, Frederick Moreland *retired dean, social worker*
Denny, Brewster Castberg *retired university dean*
Emmert, Mark Allen *academic administrator, educator*
Goodlad, John Inkster *education educator, writer*
Goodloe-Johnson, Maria L. *school system administrator*
Hicks, Gregory Alan *dean, law educator*
Jiambalvo, James *dean*
Punyon, Ellen *principal*
Ramsey, Paul Glenn *dean, internist*
Ray, Charles Kendall *retired dean*
Salmon, Marla E. *dean, nursing educator*
Silver, Michael *education educator*
Stringer, William Jeremy *university official*
Tschernisch, Sergei P. *academic administrator*
Wilson, Lizabeth Anne (Betsy Wilson) *dean, library director*
Woodward, Janet Claire *school librarian, educator*
Zimmerman, Gary A(lan) *chemistry educator, academic administrator, profl. genealogists*

Shelton
Barnard, Susan *literature and language educator*
Milander, Henry Martin *educational consultant*

Shoreline
Bailey, Sandra *secondary school educator, department chairman*

Snohomish
Tuengel, Lisa Marie *elementary school educator*

Spanaway
Parker, Lynda Christine Rylander *secondary school educator*

Spokane
Baker, Danial Edwin *pharmacist, educator*
Danke, Virginia *educational administrator, travel consultant*
Martin, Earl F. *dean, law educator*
McCulloh, Thayne Martin *university administrator, consultant*
Novak, Terry Lee *dean, educator*

Spokane Valley
Linn, Diana Patricia *retired elementary school educator*

Stanwood
Birkestol, Annabelle Mollie Elsie *retired elementary school educator*

Tacoma
Fischer, Mary E. *special education educator*
Magden, Ronald Earnest *education educator*
Rickman, Connie Garza *retired principal*

Toppenish
Ross, Kathleen Anne *academic administrator*

Vancouver
Vossler, Deborah J. *mathematics and science educator*

Walla Walla
Bridges, George S. *academic administrator, sociology educator*

West Richland
Ellis, Patricia *primary school educator*

Yakima
Beehler, Tobi Lorraine *elementary school educator, education educator*

WEST VIRGINIA

Athens
Marsh, Joseph Franklin, Jr. *retired academic administrator*

Beckley
Hitt, Frank *dean, consultant*

Berkeley Springs
Morris, Sarah *literature and language educator*

Bethany
Smith, G(odfrey) T(aylor) *college president*

Bluefield
Chryssikos, Alexandra Gianelos *secondary school educator*

Bridgeport
McClure, Charles Richard *retired superintendent*

Chapmanville
Wilson, Terilyn Barrett *elementary school educator*

Charleston
Richardson, Sally Keadle *academic administrator*

Clarksburg
Leuliette, Connie Jane *secondary school educator*

Dunbar
Russell, James Alvin, Jr. *college administrator*

Fairmont
Hardway, Wendell Gary *retired academic administrator*

Harpers Ferry
Bailey, Nancy Joyce *elementary school educator*

Huntington
Bledsoe, Kathleen Elizabeth *academic librarian, educator*
Dennison, Corley Francis III *dean*
Hayes, Robert Bruce *former college president, educator*
Reese, Clara Cook *educator*

Keyser
Falkowski, Theresa Gae *chemistry educator*

Matewan
Call, Bridget Kay *literature and language educator*

Morgantown
Allamong, Betty Davis *retired academic administrator, biology professor*
Bucklew, Neil S. *former academic administrator, educator*
Khan, Tapan Kumar *adult education educator*
Morris, Greg *director, former federal agency administrator*

Parkersburg
Francis, Lynne Ann *music educator*
Gaston, Patricia Sullivan *educator*

Philippi
Shearer, Richard Eugene *educational consultant*

Saint Albans
Smith, Robert Carlisle *retired department administrator, retired welding educator*

Shepherdstown
Strasser, William Carl, Jr. *retired college president, educator*

South Charleston
Fishkin, Anne Sonya *retired special education educator*

Spencer
Parker, Theresa Ann Boggs *records manager, retired special education educator, retired music educator*

Stonewood
Guido, Ben L. *principal*

WISCONSIN

Appleton
Beck, Jill *academic administrator, dancer, educator*

Baraboo
Umhoefer, Aural M. *retired dean, educational consultant*

Barneveld
Kolb, Victoria L. *retired mathematics educator*

Barron
Kienbaum, Janice Mae *reading specialist*

Cumberland
Nyseth, Elizabeth Ann *retired secondary school educator*

De Pere
Aerts, Rita Jane *retired elementary school educator*
Baeten, Jane Ellen *educator, school counselor*

Delafield
Haugner, Carolyn M. *elementary school educator*

Delavan
Barnett, Maryann Fau *special education educator*

Eau Claire
Field, Barbara Kay *elementary school educator*
Stanton, Sandra Sunquist *consultant, educator*

Elkhart Lake
Harper, Carrie Lynn *school counselor*

Elkhorn
Reinke, Doris Marie *retired elementary school educator*

Fish Creek
Abegg, Martin Gerald *retired academic administrator*

Fond Du Lac
Henken, Willard John *retired university dean*

Fort Atkinson
Schumacher, Mabel G. *director, consultant*

Fox Point
Froemming, Barbara G. *retired home economics educator*

Genesee Depot
Kaldhusdal, Terry Lee *elementary school educator*

Germantown
Rudebeck, Carol A. *special education educator*

Holmen
Meyer, Karl William *retired university president*

Hudson
Dahle, Carol Jo *secondary school choral director*
Witthuhn, Burton Orrin *retired university official*

Janesville
Kubina, June M. *instrumental music educator, music educator*

Kenosha
Boe, Barbara Louise *retired dean*
Earns, Lane Robert *academic administrator, historian, educator*
Iaquinta, Leonard Phillip *academic administrator, writer, consultant, not-for-profit fundraiser*
Rattigan, Denise *special education educator*
Sleeter, Christine Elaine *education educator*

La Crosse
Chilton, Galadriel *academic librarian*
DePaolo, Anthony *literature and language educator*
Gow, Joe *academic administrator*

Madison
Busby, Edward Oliver *retired dean*
Davis, Kenneth Boone, Jr. *dean, law educator*
Frazier, Kenneth L. *university librarian*
Hamers, Robert J. *chemistry educator, researcher*
Jahn, Molly M. *dean, biologist, educator*
Johnson, Richard Arnold *statistics educator, consultant*
Kendall, Nancy *education educator, consultant*
Knetter, Michael Mark *dean*
Martin, Biddy (Carolyn Arthur Martin) *academic administrator*
Mash, Donald J. *college president*
O'Brien, Andrea Maxworthy *education teacher*
Odden, Allan Robert *education educator*
Roberts, Jeanette C. *dean, pharmacy educator*
Schejbal, David *dean*
Schweber, Simone *education educator*
Spencer, Cheryl L. *literature and language educator*
Turng, Lih-Sheng *education educator*
Wiley, John D. *academic administrator, educator*

Manitowoc
Muraski, Sister Rosalyn *special education educator*
Nelson, Robert Louis *education educator, consultant*

Marinette
Rice, Karolyn Kaye *elementary school educator*

Menomonee Falls
Hinnrichs-Dahms, Holly Beth *elementary school educator*
Nelson, Mary Ellen Genevieve *retired adult education educator*

Mequon
Besch, Michael D. *academic administrator*
Ellis, William Grenville *academic administrator, management consultant*
Sisney, Ned *education educator*

Milwaukee
Aman, Mohammed Mohammed *dean, library and information science professor*
Andrekopoulos, William G. *school system administrator*
Barth, Karl Luther *retired seminary president*
Feinsilver, Donald Lee *psychiatry professor*
Flynn, Mary *professor*
Hansen, John Herbert *university administrator, accountant*
Kearney, Joseph D. *dean, law educator*
Keshvala, Seelpa H *educational opportunity fund director*
Schroeder, John H. *university chancellor*
Simmons-Welburn, Janice *dean, library director*
Wild, Robert Anthony *academic administrator*
Zhang, Jin *information educator*

Neenah
Smaby, Mary Ellen *elementary school educator*

New Holstein
Amundson, Richard Arlen, Jr. *principal*

New Richmond
Zuberbier, Jo Ann *elementary school educator*

Oak Creek
Stroik, Marilyn L. *elementary school educator*

Oshkosh
Olejniczak, Bernard Charles *education educator*
Ristow, Thelma Frances *retired elementary school educator*

Rhinelander
Burmaster, Elizabeth *academic administrator, former state official*

Ripon
Jeffries, Paul Franklin *philosophy professor*

River Falls
Biluk, Evelyn J. *education educator*
Krey, DeAn Marie *retired education educator*
Thibodeau, Gary A. *academic administrator*

Seymour
Kempen, Peter M. *secondary school educator*

Sheboygan
Fritz, Kristine Rae *retired secondary school educator*

Stevens Point
Stevens, Dwight Marlyn *educational administrator*

Superior
Glazman, Charles M. *education educator*
Haugland, John Clarence *emeritus university vice chancellor*
Morden, Annette Sonja Knudson *retired education educator*

Three Lakes
Holtz, Barbara Belle *retired pre-school educator*

Tomah
Neurohr, Shirley Ann *retired special education educator*

Union Grove
Dawson, Rose Dorothy *retired elementary school educator*

Waterford
Hanson, Jody Elizabeth *special education educator*

Waukesha
Gustafson, Mardel Emma *secondary school educator, writer*

Waunakee
Conaway, Jane Ellen *retired elementary school educator*

Waupaca
Feldt, Mary *elementary school educator*

Whitewater
Busse, Eileen Elaine *special education educator*
Chapman, Stephanie Lynn *education educator*
Connor, James Richard *retired academic administrator*
Heyning, Katharina E. *academic administrator, educator*

Wisconsin Rapids
Olson-Hellerud, Linda Kathryn *elementary school educator*

WYOMING

Afton
Nethercott, Mark A. *physics educator*

Casper
Eskew, Sandra Caye *elementary school educator*
Foster, Vicki Anne *secondary school educator*
Nganga, Lydiah Wangui *education educator*
Rickabaugh, René Lane *principal*

Cheyenne
Lain, Sheryl A. *literacy coach*
Weigner, Brent James *secondary school educator*

Gillette
Degnan, Paula *professional development specialist*

Jackson
Massy, William Francis *education educator, consultant*

Lander
Robeson, Terry Lazuk *elementary school educator, priest*

Laramie
Farrell, Mary M(aggie) *dean of libraries*
Kirkwood, Carol *literature and language educator*

Torrington
Smith, Walter Lloyd *Middle School Educator*

TERRITORIES OF THE UNITED STATES

AMERICAN SAMOA

Pago Pago
Jyothibhavan, Joserose S. *chemistry educator*

GUAM

Agana Heights
Torres, Susie Apuron *special education educator*

Barrigada
McDonald Terlaje, Patricia *counselor*

Hagatna
Bretania-Shafer, Nerissa *school system administrator*

Mangilao
Wang, Chih *retired librarian, educator*

NORTHERN MARIANA ISLANDS

Saipan
Camacho, Charlotte DLG *principal, elementary school educator*
Dela Cruz, Acelia Castro *elementary school educator*

PUERTO RICO

Fajardo
Fernós, Manuel J. *academic administrator*

Ponce
Garcia, Joxel *dean, former federal agency administrator*

San Juan
Carreras, Francisco José *retired academic and foundation administrator*
Chardán, Carlos R. *school system administrator*
Frontera, Walter R. *dean, physiatrist, educator*
Matheu, Federico Manuel *university chancellor*
Vélez-Cardona, Waldemiro *education educator, consultant*

Trujillo Alto
Crespo de Sanabia, María Milagros *retired education educator*

VIRGIN ISLANDS

Frederiksted
Birbahadur, Dindial *secondary school educator*

St Thomas
Larsen, Lauren *school system administrator*
Michael, Noreen *academic administrator*
Seipel, Peter *physical education educator, athletic director*
Terry, Lavern *school system administrator*

MILITARY ADDRESSES OF THE UNITED STATES

EUROPE

APO
Bowker, Rayanne Sones *elementary school educator*
Salerno, Patricia J. *elementary school educator*

CANADA

BRITISH COLUMBIA

Cobble Hill
Cox, Albert Reginald *retired dean, retired cardiologist*

Fernie
McFarlin-Kosiec, Barbara Ann *elementary school educator, secondary school educator, literature and language professor, small business owner*

Kelowna
Milani, Abbas Sadeghzadeh *professor*

Vancouver
Finnegan, Cyril Vincent *retired dean, zoology educator*

NOVA SCOTIA

Antigonish
Sweet, William *educator, author, administrator*

Canning
Ogilvie, Kelvin Kenneth *academic administrator, chemist, educator*

Halifax
Jaeger, Leslie Gordon *academic administrator*

ONTARIO

Kingston
Spencer, John Hedley *biochemistry educator*

Ottawa
Jordan, Joseph Louis *education educator, government official*
Philogene, Bernard J. R. *academic administrator, science educator*
Rock, Allan Michael *academic administrator, lawyer, former Canadian government official*
Runte, Roseann O'Reilly *academic administrator*

Thunder Bay
Bo, Myint Win *principal, educator*

Toronto
Evans, John Robert *academic administrator, cardiologist*
Knowlton, Thomas A. *retired dean, food products executive*
Kushner, Eva *academic administrator, educator, author*
Naylor, C. David *academic administrator*
Scardamalia, Marlene *education educator, researcher*
Sessle, Barry John *adult education educator, researcher*

Waterloo
Berczi, Andrew Stephen *academic administrator, educator*

QUEBEC

Montreal
Freedman, Samuel Orkin *retired university official*
Lowy, Frederick Hans *academic administrator, psychiatrist*
Steinberg, Arnold (H. Arnold Steinberg) *academic administrator, former diversified financial services company executive*

MEXICO

Ciudad Juarez
Tabuenca-Cordoba, Maria-Socorro *education educator, researcher*

Mexico City
Suarez-Iñiguez, Enrique *education educator*

ARGENTINA

Buenos Aires
Frasch, Alberto Carlos C. *molecular genetics educator*

AUSTRALIA

Caulfield
Le Grand, Homer *emeritus professor*

Crawley
Street, Robert *retired academic administrator, physicist*

Sydney
Geiger, Mark Watson *history educator*

BELGIUM

Namur
Kelly, Sister Marie *school system administrator*

BRITISH VIRGIN ISLANDS

Tortola
Chalwell-Brewley, Lavon Patricia *biology educator*

CHINA

Beijing
Gu, Bing-Lin *academic administrator, physics professor*
Liu, Limin *academic administrator, educator*
Xu, Xiangyuan *academic administrator, educator*

Hong Kong
Lau, Lawrence Juen-Yee *academic administrator, economics professor, consultant*

Shenzhen
Yandle, Stephen Thomas *dean*

COLOMBIA

Bogota
Bookwalter, William Keith *principal*

CYPRUS

Nicosia
Vrontis, Demetris *dean, marketing professor*

DENMARK

Aalborg
Caspersen, Sven Lars *academic administrator, statistician*

EGYPT

Cairo
Anderson, Lisa *academic administrator, political science professor, researcher*

Manyal
Kandil, Doaa Adel *tour guidance*

ENGLAND

Ampthill
Horlock, John Harold *academic administrator, engineer*

Cambridge
Chadwick, Owen *academic administrator, historian, educator*

Leicester
Crowther, David *education educator*

London
May, Robert McCredie (Lord May of Oxford) *biology educator*

Oxford
Hanson, Sir John Gilbert *academic administrator*
North, Peter Machin *academic administrator, barrister*
Varese, Federico *sociology professor*

Plymouth
Totterdell, Michael Standforth *education educator, researcher*

FRANCE

Bages
Kitzinger, Uwe *college president*

Illkirch-Graffenstaden
Simpson, Michael Kevin *academic administrator, political science professor*

Poitiers
Giraud, René Ernest *academic administrator, economist, educator*

GERMANY

Hessen
Teichler, Ulrich Christian *higher education educator, researcher*

Oststeinbek
Willamowski, Michael *academic librarian*

Ottilienstr
Clarke, Ingrid Gadway *retired academic ombudsman, consultant*

Starnberg
Huber, Franz *retired research director*

GUANA ISLAND

Barrigada
Perez, Annie Rivera *elementary school educator*

HONG KONG

Ho Man Tin
Leong, John Chi-Yan *academic administrator, orthopaedic surgeon, educator*

Hong Kong
Tsui, Lap-Chee *academic administrator, molecular genetics educator*
Wong, Richard Yue-Chim *academic administrator, economics professor*

North Point
Chung, Chi Yung *college administrator*

INDIA

New Delhi
Podewils, Ulrich *academic administrator*

Pune
Abhyankar, Aditya *dean, director*

IRELAND

Cork
Lyons, Nona Mary *adult education educator*

JAPAN

Fukuoka
Kajiyama, Tisato *academic administrator, materials physics and chemistry educator*

Hyogo
Goto, Yukio *academic administrator*

Ibaraki
Chung, Inho *special education educator*

Kyoto
Iwayama, Tajiro *university president, educator*

Okayama
Nii, Shiro *director, virologist, educator*

Tokyo
Nagao, Makoto *academic administrator, engineering educator*
Nakajima, Hiroshi *education educator*

Toride shi
Okabe, Katsumi *retired special education educator*

Tsukuba
Shimizu, Kazuhiko *education educator*
Yamamoto, Hiro-Aki *toxicology and pharmacology educator*

MALAYSIA

Cyberjaya
Muthaiyah, Saravanan *dean*

MONGOLIA

Ulaanbaatar
Gantsog, Tserensodnom *academic administrator, educator*

NORWAY

Trondheim
Popescu, Mihaela *elementary school educator, researcher*

PAKISTAN

Lahore
Armacost, Peter Hayden *academic administrator*

PHILIPPINES

Cebu City
Oro, Felisa Panal *education supervisor*

REPUBLIC OF KOREA

Cheongju
Sa, Tongmin *education educator*

Daegu
Han, Younglim *education educator*

Dongdaemun
Lee, Hyunjeong *vocational school educator*

Gwangju
Hwang, Yunhan *academic administrator*
Rowe, Sung Man *university executive, educator*

Pohang
Park, Chan-Mo *academic administrator, educator*

Seoul
Chung, Un-Chan *former academic administrator*
Lee, Ho-In *academic administrator, engineering educator*
Lee, Sungho H. *education educator, consultant, academic administrator*
Song, Mi-Yeon *education educator, physician*
Yoo, Jang Hee *academic administrator, economist*

SAUDI ARABIA

Jeddah
Ainsleigh, Susan Anita *special education educator, consultant*

SCOTLAND

Edinburgh
Mackay, James Peter Hymers (Lord Mackay of Clashfern) *retired university official*

SINGAPORE

Singapore
Guaning, Su *academic administrator*
Hunter, Howard Owen *academic administrator, law educator*

SPAIN

Madrid
Mayor Zaragoza, Federico *biochemistry educator*

Santiago de Compostela
Touriñán López, José Manuel *education educator*

SWEDEN

Uppsala
Champion, Margrét Gunnarsdóttir *literature and language educator*

TAIWAN

Kaohsiung
Lambert, Marianne T. *retired elementary school educator*

Pingtung
Ou, Shan-Hwei *academic administrator, engineering educator*

Taipei
Chen, Peng-Jen (Ting-Cheng) *political educator, writer*

THAILAND

Phasicharoen
Mongkhonvanit, Pornchai *academic administrator*

TURKEY

Edirne
Aricak, Osman Tolga *education educator*

WALES

Aberystwyth
Walters, Kenneth *applied mathematics educator*

WEST INDIES

Schoelcher Martinica
Saffache, Pascal Marie *dean, educator*

ADDRESS UNPUBLISHED

Abell, Anna Ellen *primary school educator*
Abell, Dawn Gabbitas *elementary and secondary school educator, administrator*
Adamchuk, Viacheslav Ivanovych *educator*
Adams, Leocadia Donat *secondary school educator, writer*
Aiken, Michael Thomas *former academic administrator*
Akanbi, Linda Barbara *education educator*
Alfonso-Bica, Kristy Lynn *elementary school educator*
Ali, Hamad Abdulkareem *academic administrator*
Allen, Betty Noldon *education educator, consultant*
Allen, Charlotte *secondary school educator*
Allen, Elma Leitch *special education educator*
Allen, Janet Lee *special education educator*
Allen, Laurie Ann *elementary school educator*
Allen, Ralph Carnell *retired assistant principal*
Allred, Susan G. *school system administrator*
Almore-Randle, Allie Louise *special education educator, academic administrator*
Almour, Vicki Lynn *elementary school educator*
Ames, Sandra Cutler *secondary school educator*

Glismann, Clementine *retired elementary school educator*
Glohr, Eric A. *academic administrator*
Goerke, Glenn Allen *university administrator*
Goff, Renee Rosenstock *gifted and talented educator*
Goforth, Jill Hastings *principal*
Goldberg, C. Jeffrey *mathematics educator, accountant*
Goldberger, Paul Jesse *dean, architecture critic, writer*
Goldenberg, Kim *retired academic administrator, internist, consultant*
Gomez-Mejia, Luis R. *educator*
Gonzalez, Karen Eileen *middle school educator*
Gonzalez, Rose Marie Juarez *retired education educator*
Good, Linda Lou *elementary school educator*
Goodrich, Kenneth Paul *retired dean*
Gordis, David Moses *academic administrator, rabbi*
Gordon, Sharon Ann *mathematics and pre-school educator*
Grady, Joan Butterworth *principal*
Graham-Moore, Brian Edward *retired educator, consultant*
Granger, Loretha *special education educator*
Grant, Frances Elizabeth *retired educator*
Grassell, Duane V. *secondary school educator*
Gratz, Loren William *school administrator*
Graves, Wallace Billingsley *retired university executive*
Grebstein, Sheldon Norman *academic administrator*
Green, Patricia Pataky *school system administrator, consultant, superintendents of schools*
Greene, Jo *school system administrator*
Greenway, Joan M. *dean*
Greenwood, Gordon Edward *retired education educator*
Grewe, Maria *literature and language educator*
Griffith, Rosita Denise *elementary school educator*
Griskey, Pauline Becker *education educator, researcher*
Grossman, Carolyn Sylvia Cort *retired elementary school educator*
Grove, Myrna Jean *retired elementary school educator*
Grove, Terrie *school librarian*
Groves, Bernice Ann *retired elementary and secondary school coordinator, educator*
Gruberg, Cy *educational administrator*
Gruetzmacher, Nancy Lynn *retired middle school educator*
Guffey, Trisha Rae *assistant principal*
Gumpert, Carolyn L. *secondary school educator*
Gunsul, Katherine (Kate) Elma *retired secondary school educator*
Gustafson, Richard Alrick *retired university president*
Guy, Mary (Penny) Whytlaw *secondary school educator and librarian*
Haaland, Gordon Arthur *retired academic administrator*
Haas, Suzanne Alberta *elementary and secondary school educator*
Habecker, Eugene Brubaker *academic administrator*
Haborak, George Edward *retired academic administrator, educator*
Haden, Clovis Roland *retired academic administrator, engineering educator*
Hadley, William Melvin *retired dean*
Hagan, Joseph Henry *educational consultant*
Hageman, Richard Philip, Jr. *educational administrator*
Hagood, William Edward *history educator*
Hairfield-Marrs, Judy L. *retired school educator*
Hale, Nancy Annette Bills *elementary school educator*
Hall, Charles Worth Leo *college administrator*
Hall, Christopher George Longden *academic administrator*
Hall, Delma L. *academic administrator*
Hall, James William *university chancellor*
Hall, Lawrence *secondary school educator*
Hamecs, Francella Cheslock *elementary and secondary school educator*
Hamlin, Harriett E. *educational consultant*
Hammond, Ann P. *retired elementary, high school and college educator, poet*
Hampton, Pastella T. *educational consultant*
Hancock, Charles R. *education educator*
Hanna, Noreen Anelda *adult education educator, consultant*
Hansen, Nancy C. Urdahl *retired special education educator, small business owner*
Hardage, Page Taylor *retired elementary school educator*
Hardy, Ernest Edward *academic official, consultant*
Hare, Norma Q. *retired school system administrator*
Hargrove, William Richard *education educator, lawyer*
Harrington, Jean Patrice *academic administrator*
Harris, Cynthia Viola *principal*
Harris, Delmarie Jones *retired elementary school educator*
Harris, Dolores M. *retired academic administrator, adult education educator*
Harris, Merle Wiener *retired academic administrator*
Harris-Barber, Daisy *elementary school educator*
Hartman, Michelle Sharon *elementary school educator*
Hartman, Rosemary Jane *retired special education educator*
Harville, Martha Louise *special education educator*
Hassanein, Nevine Gamal *elementary school educator*
Hasselmo, Nils *retired academic administrator, linguist*
Hatfield, Stacey *elementary school educator*
Hatley, Ellen Delores *elementary school educator*
Hayhurst, James Frederick Palmer *career and business consultant, inspirational speaker, author*
Hazel, Mary Belle *university administrator*
Headings, Michael D. *elementary school educator, reading specialist*
Healy, Daniel Thomas *secondary school educator*
Heath, Joseph Nounnan *retired literature and language educator, writer*
Heaton, Jean Mossman *retired early childhood educator*
Heck, James Baker *retired education educator*
Heerman, Barbara L. *retired secondary school educator*
Hegarty, George John *university president, literature and language professor*
Heidt-Dunwell, Debra Sue *vocational school educator*
Hemby, James Benjamin, Jr. *college president*
Hendershott, Anna Lorraine *educational director*
Henikoff, Leo M., Jr. *academic administrator, medical educator*
Henkel, Cynthia Leigh *elementary school educator*
Henrnadez, Gladys A. *education educator*
Herbert, Adam William, Jr. *former academic administrator, educator*
Herman, Ellen Rombs *retired literature and language educator, painter*
Herold, Rochelle Snyder *early childhood educator*
Herrera, Silvia Patricia *special education educator*
Herring, Joan Sanders *secondary school educator*
Herrmann, Mary Anne *elementary school educator*
Herron, Orley R. *college president*
Hess, Wendi Elizabeth *secondary school educator*
Higgins, Dorothy Marie *dean, educator*
Hill, Jerry Dean *elementary school educator*
Hill, Virgil Lusk, Jr. *academic administrator, military officer*
Hines, Mary Jane *retired elementary school teacher*
Hinton, Velecia Ann *academic administrator*
Hitchcock, Walter Anson *retired educational consultant*
Hodges, Shirley Marie *secondary school educator*
Hodgson, Suzanne Andree *secondary school educator*
Hoffman, Sharon Lynn *adult education educator*
Holbrook, Karen Ann *retired academic administrator, biologist*
Holley, Linda Ann *secondary school educator*
Holloway, Ernest Leon *retired university president*
Holtkamp, Susan Charlotte *elementary school educator*
Honsa, Thomas Patrick *secondary school educator, history professor*
Hooper, Henry Olcott *retired academic administrator, physicist*
Hopp, Phillip Edward *gifted and talented educator*
Hopping, Richard Lee *retired academic administrator*
Horner, Matina Souretis *retired academic administrator, corporate financial executive*
Horning, Barbara Hortense Scheer *retired elementary school educator*
Horsley, Tip Alonzo *mathematics educator, military officer*
Horvat, Vashti *principal*
Hostert, Sharon Ann *elementary school educator, assistant principal*
Houseman, Ann Elizabeth Lord *educational administrator*
Howard, Marilyn *retired school system administrator*
Hu, Shouping *education educator*
Hu, Xiaolin *professor*
Huffman, Carol Koster *retired middle school educator*
Huffman, Durward Roy *academic administrator, electrical engineer*
Hughes, Mary Alice *adult education educator, consultant*
Hughes, Pam *retired secondary school educator*
Hull, McAllister Hobart, Jr. *retired university administrator*
Humphries, Jefferson *literature and language educator*
Hunnicutt, Victoria Anne Wilson *educational consultant*
Hunt, Sarah Mincey *elementary school educator*
Hunter-Bowington, Dorothy Diana *educator, consultant*
Hurn, D. Kent *retired academic administrator, finance educator*
Hutchinson, Michael Philip *education educator*
Hutson, Henry Critchfield *retired academic administrator*
Huttenback, Robert Arthur *academic administrator, educator*
Hynes, Thomas John *academic administrator*
Ibanez, Manuel Luis *academic administrator, biologist, educator*
Iglehart, Sheralee Hill *elementary school educator, writer*
Ignatonis, Sandra Carole Autry *retired special education educator*
Ijames, Lisa Diane *educator*
Ingram, Jerrilyn Jenkins *academic administrator*
Inman, Lydia Lucille *retired university dean*
Innis, Daniel Eugene *dean, consultant*
Inos, Rita Hocog *retired school system administrator*
Insalaco-De Nigris, Anna Maria Theresa *middle school educator*
Isaacs, Jessica B. *literature and language educator, department chairman*
Iverson, Thomas Edwin *retired academic administrator, mathematician, educator*
Iwunze, Maurice O. *education educator, researcher*
Jackson, Miles Merrill *retired university dean*
Jackson, Thomas Humphrey *former academic administrator*
Jackson Wright, Adrienne A. *educational consultant*
Jacobs, Deborah Ann *English language educator*
Jagasia, Kaushalya Ghanshyam *secondary school educator*
Jagerman, Adrienne *retired elementary school educator, nurse*
Jakubauskas, Edward Benedict *college president*
Jalonen, Nancy Lee *professor, arts administrator, educational television producer*
James, Allix Bledsoe *retired university president*
Jamison, Erica Leigh *psychology educator*
Janeway, Richard *retired academic administrator*
Javernick, Amy Sue *special education educator*
Jean, Claudette R. *retired elementary school educator*
Jen, Joseph Jwu-Shan *academic administrator, former federal agency administrator*
Jenkins, Brenda Gwenetta *pre-school administrator, special education educator*
Johnson, Lois Brooks *retired elementary guidance counselor*
Johnson, Maryann Elaine *educational administrator*
Johnson, Sylvia Sue *university administrator, educator*
Johnson, Yvonne Thomas *elementary school educator*
Johnston, Carolyn S. *elementary school educator, reading specialist*
Johnston, Zenda Jo *special education educator*
Johnstone, D. Bruce *education educator, academic administrator*
Jones, Bettye Wright *education and reading educator*
Jones, Jack Bristol *education educator*
Jones, Lawrence Neale *retired dean, minister*
Jones, Norma Dell *association executive*
Jones, Ruth A. *retired secondary school educator*
Josephs, Kelly Baker *literature and language educator*
Jung, Woo *special education educator, researcher*
Jurgelski, Annette Elizabeth *retired academic administrator*
Kachuck, Beatrice *retired education educator, women's studies educator*
Kahn, Victoria Elaine Hopkins *special education educator*
Kambutu, John *adult education educator*
Kane, Cynthia A. *retired special education educator*
Karanovich, Milenko *educator, researcher*
Karben, Shelley Valerie *elementary and special education educator*
Karraker, Angela Rene *special education educator*
Katsiyannis, Antonis *school administrator*
Kaulaity, Marlinda *literature and language educator*
Kay, Irene Pramisloff *school system administrator*
Kean, Joanne Aylsworth *retired secondary school educator*
Keaton, William Thomas *academic administrator, pastor*
Keele, Zudora Brown *school librarian*
Kellar, William Henry *retired academic administrator, historian, educator*
Kelly, Beverly Ann *elementary school educator*
Kelly, Timothy Johnston *secondary school educator*
Kelsch, Phyllis Arlene *assistant principal*
Kelso, Charlotte Elizabeth *elementary school educator, health and physical education specialist*
Kempe, Janet *elementary school educator*
Kempner, Maximilian Walter *dean, lawyer*
Kendall, Dorothy Irene *secondary school educator*
Kennedy, Sheryl J. *elementary school educator*
Kenny, Shirley Strum *retired academic administrator*
Kerins, Francis Joseph *college president*
Kern, Charles William *retired academic administrator, chemist, educator*
Kern, Ronald Paul *dean, consultant*
Kerr Walker, Joi Mechelle *literacy educator, consultant*
Kertzer, David Israel *academic administrator, anthropology educator, writer*
Ketchum, Peradine Elizabeth *elementary school educator*
Key, Shawnda R. *elementary school educator*
Keyes, Joan Ross Rafter *education educator, writer*
Keywood, Kay Hill *mathematics educator, small business owner*
Kilgore, Rebecca S. *secondary school educator*
Kim, Heather *director*
Kim, Minju *educator*
King, James Calvin *mathematics educator*
King, Sheryl Jayne *retired secondary school educator, counselor*
King, Susan Marie *retired special education educator*
Kircher, Kimberly Lauren *behavior analyst, educational consultant*
Kish, Kathleen V. *academic administrator*
Klein, Mary Ann *special education educator*
Kliebhan, Sister M(ary) Camille *academic administrator*
Knapp, Lonnie Troy *elementary school educator*
Knappen, Mary *mathematics educator*
Knighten, Latrenda *elementary school educator, consultant*
Knowles, Julie Nall *secondary school educator*
Kobza, Donna Ann *special education educator, consultant*
Koch, Molly Brown *parent educator*
Koenig, Allen Edward *higher education consultant*
Kogan, Esther *education educator, director*
Kolenda, Joanne L. *elementary and secondary school educator, volunteer*
Komisar, David Daniel *retired academic administrator*
Konner, Joan Weiner *academic administrator, writer, educator, television producer and retired executive*
Kopielski, Camille Ann *counseling administrator, volunteer*
Kormondy, Edward John *retired academic administrator, science educator*
Kossina, Mary Helen *retired elementary school educator*
Kravetz, Katharine *education educator*
Kreitlow, Burton William *retired adult education educator*
Krohn, Christy Anne *special education educator*
Krug, John Carleton (Tony Krug) *academic administrator, library director, consultant*
Kuhn, Thomas Joseph, Sr. *assistant principal*
Kumar, Rita *literature and language educator*
Kupchella, Charles Edward *retired academic administrator, writer, educator*
Kuusisto, Lucina Marcia de Mello *chemistry educator*
LaHue, Christine *history educator*
Lambert, Daniel Michael *retired academic administrator*
Langton (Tomasiewicz), Dawn Theresa *literature and language educator*
Lantz, Joanne Baldwin *retired academic administrator*
Larson, Vicki Lord *academic administrator, communication disorders educator*
Lashley, Felissa Rose *dean, nursing educator, researcher*
Lattimore, Louise Joan *elementary school educator*
Lauer, Jeanette Carol *dean, history educator, writer*
Lawrence, Sally Clark *retired academic administrator*
Lawson, John Joseph *vocational educator, consultant*
Lawton, Kelly Marie Lee *secondary school educator, performing arts director*
Lazar, Charna L. *education educator, retired CIA officer, security consultant*
Leather, Victoria Potts *college librarian*
Leazenby, Tresa *case conference chairperson*
Lee, Jeong-Kyu *education educator, researcher, academic administrator*
Lehman, Jeffrey Sean *academic administrator*
Leistner, Mary Edna *retired secondary school educator*
Lennon, Joseph Luke *retired academic administrator, priest*
Leonard, Sister Anne C. *school system administrator*
Leslie, Maureen Heelan *university director*
Lester, Robin Dale *historian, educator, writer, former headmaster*
Lettow, Lucille Jane *retired school librarian, education educator*
Levin, Richard I. *dean, cardiologist, researcher*
Lewis, Martha Andreé *elementary school educator*
Lewis, Ned Lehmon *secondary school educator*
Li, Min *Research Scientist in Analytical Organic Chemistry*
Liggett, Thomas Jackson *retired seminary president*
Light, Marion Jessel *retired elementary school educator*
Lilley, John Mark *academic administrator*
Limerick, Dianne A. *mathematics educator, athletic trainer*
Lin, Qiuyun *education educator*
Lincoln, Grace *elementary school educator*
Lindsey, Joyce Rebecca *secondary school educator*
Link, Phoebe Forrest *educator, author, social worker, poet*
Lipton, Ann Lynn *Educator*
Liverman, Betty Jean *elementary school educator*
Livingston, Gwendell Sheawanna *education educator*
Lober, Irene Moss *educational consultant*
Lockwood, Theodore Davidge *retired academic administrator*
Looser, Donald William *academic administrator*
Lopez, Harold Lee *special education educator*
Lord, Jerome Edmund *education administrator, writer*
Love, Robert Lyman *retired educator, consultant*
Lovett, Clara Maria *retired academic administrator, historian*
Lowenberg, Georgina Grace *retired elementary school educator*
Lowrance, Larry *special education educator, psychologist*
Lubner, Mary F. *retired elementary school educator*
Lucas, Michele Angelyn *learning consultant, special education educator*
Lucas, Teri Kathleen *secondary school educator*
Luftman, Jerry *dean, educator*
Lundgren, Colleen Bowling *elementary school educator, consultant*
Lundquist, Daniel Merritt *educational consultant, former dean*
Lyall, Katharine Culbert *former academic administrator, economist, educator*
Lynch, Gerald Weldon *former academic administrator, psychologist*
Lyne, Dorothy-Arden *secondary school educator*
Lynn, Naomi B. *academic administrator*
Lyons, Richard Kent *dean, finance educator*
MacCormack, Jean F. *academic administrator*
Madapusi, Arun *educator, consultant*
Mah, Silvia Armitano *director, educator*
Mahaffey, Marcia Hixson *retired educational administrator*
Mahmood, Arshad *former academic administrator*
Mahood, R. Wayne *education educator*
Maier, Theodore Joseph *literature and language educator*
Major, Patrick Webb III *principal*
Makki, S. Kami *education educator*
Mallchok, Jeanne *retired special education educator*
Mallory, Arthur Lee *dean, retired state official*
Mallory, Kristin L. *community college administrator*
Manley, Judith L. *director*
Manning, Sylvia *academic administrator, language educator*
Mantei, Lorraine E. *school system administrator*
Manuel, Ralph Nixon *retired private school executive*
Markovich, Alexandria *assistant principal*
Marshak, Robert Reuben *retired dean, medical educator, veterinarian*
Martin, Jeanine Kay *retired elementary school educator*
Martin, John F. *academic administrator*
Martin, Judson Phillips *retired education educator*
Martin, Laura *secondary school educator*
Martorana, Barbara Joan *retired secondary school educator*
Masi, Julia A. *elementary school educator*
Massey, Thomas Benjamin *retired university president*
Masters, Ann Browning *educator, poet*
Mastro, Christopher P. *secondary school educator*
Matasar, Ann B. *retired dean, finance educator*
Matera, Frances Lorine *retired elementary school educator*
Mathis, Luster Doyle *academic administrator, political scientist, educator*
Matoax, Louise *mathematics educator curriculum development, consultant*

Matsuda, Fujio *retired academic administrator*
Mattice, Howard LeRoy *education educator*
Mattoon, Scott Alexander *private school educator*
May, Ingrid Barbara *elementary school educator*
Mayer, Sister Patricia E. *retired elementary school educator*
Mayfield, Robert Charles *academic administrator, geographer, educator*
McBride, Mildred Maylea *retired elementary school educator*
McCabe, Linda Jean *elementary school educator*
McCall, Brian David *history educator, political science educator*
McCarthy, April C. *elementary school educator*
McCarty, Wendy Lynette *education educator*
McCloud, Anece Faison *retired academic administrator*
McCloy, Shirley *adapted physical education specialist*
McCord, Arline Fujii *retired university administrator, educator*
McCosham, Joyce L. *retired secondary school educator*
McCutcheon, Debra *school librarian*
McDowell, Laura Oneita *secondary school educator*
McGee, Harold Johnston *former academic administrator*
McGee, Jane Marie *retired elementary school educator*
McGowan, Susan *gifted and talented educator*
McGuire, James Kavanaugh *retired education educator*
McHenry, Bart *academic administrator*
McIntyre, Virgie M. *retired elementary school educator*
McKeown, Mary Elizabeth *retired academic administrator*
McManus, John Coyne *educator, writer*
McNamara, Brenda Norma *retired secondary school educator*
McNamara, Kristin Tara *literature and language educator, small business owner*
McSorley, Rita Elizabeth *adult education educator*
Megna, Steve Allan *retired secondary school educator*
Mehne, Paul Randolph *consultant, retired medical educator*
Mercay, Jessie Jardine *academic administrator, educator*
Merriweather, Freda E. *education educator*
Meshkaty, Shahra *academic administrator*
Meskill, Victor P. *academic administrator, educator*
Meyer, Richard W. *retired university librarian*
Mikulics, Michael P. *literature and language educator*
Miller, Arjay *retired university dean*
Miller, Jerry Huber *retired university chancellor*
Miller, Roberta Doris *elementary school educator*
Milligan, Cynthia Hardin *dean, lawyer*
Mills, Eugene Sumner *academic administrator*
Mills, Helene Audrey *retired education educator*
Mir, Montserrat *education educator*
Mitteldorfer, Shirley Justis *education educator, consultant*
Mittendorf, Kimberly Ann *retired secondary school educator, real estate consultant*
Mittleider, Rebecca Ann *elementary school educator*
Moeller, Joseph John, Jr. *university official*
Moll, Maryann Elizabeth *education educator*
Monteith, Larry King *chancellor emeritus*
Mooney, Michael Joseph *university professor*
Moore, Donald Walter *retired academic administrator*
Moore, Marla W. *school librarian*
Moore, Nancy M. *secondary school educator*
Moore, Thomas David *academic administrator*
Moore, Thomas Holmes *retired school administrator*
Moorer, Emily Hall *literature and language educator*
Moore-Wleklinski, Patricia Marie *secondary school educator*
Moran, Thomas Harry *retired academic administrator*
Morgan, Joyce Elizabeth *retired elementary school educator*
Morgan, Marlene *education educator, consultant*
Morgan, Ruth Prouse *academic administrator, educator*
Mosier, Virginia Lou *school system administrator*
Moss Greenberg, Jill *special education administrator, civil rights activist*
Mueller, Ada Rose *elementary school educator*
Mulawka, Diane I. *mathematics educator*
Mullen, Terri Ann *retired special education educator*
Musa, Samuel Albert *university executive*
Myers, Michele Tolela *former academic administrator*
Nance, Mary Joe *retired secondary school educator*
Naumer, Janet Noll *retired dean*
Navasky, Victor Saul *journalism professor, director, publisher emeritus*
Neal, Teresa Schreibeis *secondary school educator*
Nelms, Michelle *pre-school educator*
Nevins, Tracy Anne *elementary school educator*
New, Rosetta Holbrock *retired secondary school educator, retired department chairman, retired nutrition consultant*
Nichols, Dennis Witt *rector*
Niemeyer, Sandra Kay *retired secondary school educator*
Noddings, Nel *education educator, writer*
Noland, Carrie Jaurès *educator*
Northcutt, Eleen Marie *secondary school educator*
Nowel, Andrew F. *academic administrator*
Nye, Bernard Carl *educational administrator*
Nye, Linda Purcell *secondary school educator*
Oblinger, James L. *former academic administrator*
O'Connell, William Raymond, Jr. *educational consultant, retired academic administrator*
Oden, Jean P(hifer) *special education educator*
Odhiambo, David Nandi *literature and language educator*
Oglesby, Elaine Sue *elementary school educator*
Ogletree, Glenda L. *education educator*
Okoye-Johnson, Ogo *education educator*
Oliveira, Katrina R.K. *educator*
Oliver, Kimberly *primary school educator*
Olson, Paula Sue *director, educational consultant*
Omtvedt, Irvin Thomas *academic administrator, educator*
Oprsal, Nancy Upshaw *retired elementary school educator*
Orr, Kenneth Bradley *academic administrator*
Ou, Chaohua *academic administrator*
Outt, Helen May *retired elementary school educator, psychologist*
Packard, Sophie S. *elementary school educator*
Paddio-Johnson, Eunice Alice *school system administrator*
Palatnick, Frank Sidney *educational consultant*
Palmer, Irene Sabelberg *retired dean, nursing educator, genealogist*
Paris-De Monte, Ileana M. *assistant principal*
Parisi, Leah Evans *dean, nursing educator, lawyer*
Parisi, Valerie Marie *dean, medical educator*
Parker, Donald Fred *dean, human resources specialist, educator*
Parker, Lynette *elementary school educator, secondary school educator*
Parmenter, Kelli Denise *middle school educator, small business owner*
Parsons, Alexandra Clare *literature and language educator*
Patrick, Pauline Margaret *secondary school educator*
Patterson, Oscar III *retired academic administrator*
Patton, Carl Vernon *retired academic administrator*
Paul, Carol Ann *retired academic administrator, biology educator*
Paxton, J. Willene *retired academic administrator*
Payne, Ladell *retired academic administrator*
Peitscher, Judith *elementary school educator*
Pencola, Annamaria Regina *elementary school educator*
Pendarvis, Edwina Dawn *retired gifted and talented educator*
Pennington, Aubrey El *director*
Peoples, John Arthur, Jr. *former university president, consultant*
Perger, Donna Spagnoli *retired secondary school mathematics educator*
Perkner, Stanislav *academic administrator, educator*
Perry, Anne Marie Litchfield *educator*
Pescatore-Shirey, Hope Jean *middle school reading educator*
Peters, Sue Ellen *retired elementary school educator*
Petersen, John D. *former academic administrator*
Petrelli, Heather Mw *academic administrator, director*
Petrunger, Dennis Keith *school system administrator, educator*
Pettigrew, L. Eudora *retired academic administrator*
Pewitt, James Dudley *retired academic administrator*
Phelps, Bonnie Noreen *retired secondary school educator*
Phillips, Richard A. *retired literature and language educator*
Phillips, Stefanie Pannell *school system administrator*
Pierce, Barbara A. *elementary school educator*
Pierce, Patricia Ann *retired university administrator*
Pierce, Susan Resneck *academic administrator, literature educator, consultant*
Pierskalla, William Peter *dean, finance and engineering educator*
Pinto, Rosalind *retired secondary school educator, volunteer*
Platis, Chris Steven *adult education educator*
Platis, James George *secondary school educator*
Pollack, Marsha *secondary school educator*
Ponitz, David H. *former academic administrator*
Porte-Lewis, Ami Lynn *special education educator, school psychologist*
Pourchot, Georgeta Valentina *political science educator*
Pratt, David M. *education educator*
Preer, Joan C. *retired assistant principal, science educator*
Prins, Robert Jack *retired academic administrator*
Pritchard, Claudius Hornby, Jr. *retired university president*
Prokasy, William Frederick *academic administrator*
Pry, George Lawrence *art institute administrator*
Pryor, Harold S. *retired college president*
Pulhamus, Marlene Louise *retired elementary school educator*
Purvis, Gail *elementary school educator*
Putzy, Karry Ann *secondary school educator*
Puzzo, Joseph Anthony, Jr. *middle school educator*
Query, Lois A. *elementary school educator*
Quinly, Scott Anderson *secondary school educator*
Rada, Ruth Byers *retired dean*
Rago, Dorothy Ashton *retired elementary school educator*
Ramirez, Mary Catherine *retired secondary school educator*
Ramirez Rubio, Deborah *school librarian*
Randazzo, Beverly Paulina *retired assistant principal*
Ratterree, John Eric *academic administrator*
Rawleigh, Sara Lynette *elementary school educator*
Ray, Clyde Hosea *retired educator, writer*
Ray, Dipan B. *director*
Ray, Susan Elaine *principal*
Redmont, Bernard Sidney *dean, communications educator*
Reed, Leon Samuel *secondary school educator, photographer*
Reed, Susan J. *elementary school educator*
Reid, Helen Veronica *provost*
Reid, Irvin D. *former academic administrator*
Reinke, Ralph Louis *retired academic administrator*
Remley, Audrey Wright *retired academic administrator, psychologist*
Rempt, Rodney P. *retired academic administrator, career military officer*
Renda-Tanali, Irmak *program director, consultant*
Rent, Clyda Stokes *academic administrator*
Reschly, Daniel J. *education educator, psychologist*
Reynolds, Karen Ann *retired elementary school educator*
Reynolds-Hufner, Jo S. (Jo S. Scholze) *retired, educational administrator*
Rhodes, Sandra Lavern *retired elementary school educator*
Rice, Gary Russell *retired special education educator*
Rice, Patricia Oppenheim Levin *retired special education educator, consultant*
Richardson, Edward R. *former academic administrator*
Ricketson, Mary E. *former dean, lawyer*
Riedesel, Clark Alan *retired education educator*
Riggio, Kerry Kerstin *elementary school worker, researcher*
Riley, Nancy Mae *retired secondary school educator*
Risinger, Petra Everest *school librarian*
Ritvo, Roger Alan *research management professor, health management-policy educator*
Rivero, Andria *psychology educator*
Roark, Ian R. *school system administrator*
Roberts, Karlene Ann *education educator*
Roberts, Lillian *retired principal*
Roberts, Patricia Lee *education educator*
Robinson, Stephanie Nicole *education educator*
Robison, Sara Anne *middle school educator, band director*
Rochelle, Lugenia *academic administrator*
Rodriguez, Louis Joseph *academic administrator, economist, educator*
Roebuck, Judith Lynn *retired secondary school educator*
Rogers, Betsy *elementary school educator*
Rojas, Victor Hugo Macedo *retired vocational education educator*
Roller, Pamela Jo *elementary school educator*
Roman, Alfred Victor *science education educator*
Rose, Tessie E. *special education educator, consultant*
Rosenberg, Raymond David *special education educator, consultant*
Rosenblum, Estelle H. *retired dean, nursing educator*
Rosenthal, Michael Ross *retired academic administrator, consultant*
Ross, Leonard Lester *retired academic administrator*
Roukema, Lorae Teresa *education educator, consultant*
Roumbos, Maria K. *elementary school educator*
Rowe, Devona Powell *retired counseling administrator, director, social worker, secondary school educator*
Rowell, Barbara Caballero *retired academic administrator*
Rowley, Maxine Lewis *education educator, retired academic administrator*
Roy, Matthew G. *secondary school educator, social studies educator*
Royal, Darrell K. *university official, retired football coach*
Rubin, Ellen *education/access consultant*
Russell, Florence L. *elementary school educator*
Russell, Louise *retired education educator*
Ryan, Daniel John *university administrator*
Ryan, Ione Jean Alohilani Rathburn *retired education educator, counselor*
Saavedra, Abelardo *former school system administrator*
Sabbath, Joseph Waters *academic administrator*
Sadler, Judith K. *retired special education educator, school system administrator*
Saigo, Roy Hirofumi *academic administrator, botanist*
Salapatek, John (John Franklin) *literature and language educator, writer*
Samec, Diane Patricia *retired elementary school educator*
Sampson, Donna Rene *mathematics educator*
Sanchez, Alita Cassandra *physical education educator, personal trainer*
Sandwell, Kristin Ann *special education educator*
Santangelo, Gaspare Charles *education educator, retired principal*
Savage, Kim I. *academic administrator*
Saxena, Parul *special education educator, psychologist*
Sayre, Donna *elementary school educator*
Scanlan, Thomas Joseph *former academic administrator*
Schaefer, Mary K. *school system administrator*
Schowalter, William Raymond *college dean, educator*
Schrage, Rose *retired academic administrator*
Schreider, Larry Stephen *director, educator*
Schrenko, Linda C. *former school system administrator*
Schuldt, Barbara Jean *school librarian*
Schuster, Carol Joyce *special education educator, consultant*
Schutz, Richard Phillip *special education educator*
Schwartz, Eleanor Brantley *academic administrator*
Schwartz, Michael *professor, researcher*
Schwartz, Sheila Ruth *education and English educator*
Scott, Renay Marie *academic administrator, educator*
Scott-Burton, Jennifer Marie *special education educator*
Seeley, Cathy Lynn *director, secondary school educator, consultant*
Segreto, Linda Mary Janeczek *special education educator, librarian*
Selke-Kern, Barbara Ellen *university official, writer*
Sell, LeeLou *retired elementary school educator*
Sernoffsky, Michael A. *elementary school educator*
Shapiro, Judith R. *former academic administrator, anthropology educator*
Shaughnessey, Gail *educator*
Shaw, Kenneth Alan *former university president*
Shedd, Arthur B. *retired school system administrator*
Shelley, Charles Arthur, Jr. *retired academic administrator*
Shellman-Lucas, Elizabeth C. *special education educator, researcher*
Shepard, Christy J. *special education educator*
Sheppard, April Spring *school librarian*
Sheridan, Edward Patrick *college dean*
Sheridan, Judson Dean *academic executive*
Sherrer, Charles David *dean, clergyman*
Shields, Cynthia Rose *college administrator*
Shore, Eleanor Gossard *retired medical school dean*
Sibo, Elsa Lynette *secondary school educator*
Silva-Guzman, Angelica *literature and language educator*
Simmonds, Robert Maurer *operations research analyst*
Simmons, Lynda Merrill Mills *retired principal*
Simons, Lynn Osborn *educator*
Skaggs, Stacy L. *elementary school educator*
Skinner, Cathy JoAnn *school system administrator*
Smith, David Julian *educational consultant*
Smith, Kathryn Nally *history educator*
Smith, Martha Virginia Barnes *retired elementary school educator*
Smith, Patricia Ann (Pat Smith) *elementary school educator*
Smith, Samuel Howard *academic administrator, plant pathologist*
Socol, Sheldon Eleazer *university official*
Solberg, Amy Kathleen *director*
Solmssen, Peter *retired academic administrator*
Sonnenschein, Hugo Freund *academic administrator, writer, economist, educator*
Sottile, Joseph James *elementary school educator, poet*
Spence, Nancy Elizabeth *workshop developer, psychology educator, literature educator, writer*
Spencer, Bennion L. *college instructor*
Spillane, Nancy Marie *primary school educator*
Spodek, Bernard *early childhood educator*
Spomer, Penny Sue *elementary school educator*
Springer, Marlene *retired academic administrator*
Springer-Scott, Gladys Lorraine *educator, consultant*
Spruill, Louise Elam *retired mathematics educator*
Stalker, Jacqueline D'Aoust *academic administrator, educator*
Stalnaker, Judith Ann *education educator*
Stamoolis, James John *academic administrator, educator*
Stark, Joan Scism *education educator*
Starr, Kimberly Ann *assistant principal, school system administrator*
Stasek, Lorraine Anne *elementary school educator*
Stave, Anna M. *education educator*
Steele, Mildred Romedahl *educator*
Stellar, Arthur Wayne *school system administrator*
Stephens, Norris Lynn *school librarian*
Stevens, Lori Ann LaBeau *public librarian, administrator*
Stevenson, Michael Keith *elementary school educator*
Stewart, Gwendolyn M. *elementary school educator*
Stewart, John Wray Black *college dean*
Stewart, Lucille Marie *retired special education coordinator, educator*
Stivers, Tenille Marie *psychology educator*
Stomfay-Stitz, Aline Maria *education educator*
Strand, Theresa *educational consultant*
Stroud, Rhoda M. *elementary school educator*
Studebaker, Forrest E. *history educator*
Stycos, Maria Nowakowska *retired adult education educator*
Subedi, Bidya Raj *school system administrator, statistician, consultant*
Sullivan, Charles *dean, educator, author*
Sumlin, Margaret Brown (Margie Sumlin) *retired special education educator*
Suppa-Friedman, Janice DeStefano *secondary school educator, consultant*
Sussman, Laureen Glicklin *retired elementary school educator*
Suter, Scott Hamilton *literature and language educator*
Suttle, Helen Jayson *retired elementary school educator*
Sutton-Creech, Donna Lynn *gifted and talented educator*
Swailes, William E. *counseling administrator*
Swain, Donald Christie *retired academic administrator, historian, educator*
Swimm-McMahon, Katherine Lynn *educator*
Swistek, Ronald James *special education educator*
Syverud, Kent Douglas *dean, law educator*
Szelenyi, Ivan *adult education educator*
Szetela, Cheryl Wahl *educator*
Szymanski, Edna Mora *academic administrator*
Tackett, Stephen Douglas *retired education services specialist*
Tanner, Laurel Nan *education educator*
Taylor, Charolette Olivia *primary school educator*
Taylor, Jeffrey Lee *political science educator, writer*
Taylor, Mary Lee *retired academic administrator*
Taylor, Paulette Ann *special education educator, consultant*
Templeman, Lydia *retired assistant principal*
TenHoeve, Thomas *academic administrator*
Terada, Alice Masae *retired elementary school educator*
Terrell, Hellenna L. *education educator*
Terrell, Hope Price *assistant principal*
Terry, Edwin Wellington *college librarian*
Thaxton, Jessie J. *elementary school educator*
Thomas, Beverly Irene *special education educator, counseling administrator, educational diagnostician*
Thomas, Sara Alice Folger *school librarian, curator*
Thomas, Suzanne *educational consultant*
Thomas, Timothy Wayne *mathematics educator, athletic director*
Thompson, Deborah G. *secondary school educator*
Thompson, William Ancker *intramural-recreational sports director, educator*
Thoreen, Mary Louise *elementary school educator, consultant*
Timmons, Sharon L. *retired elementary school educator*
Tincher, Laura Marie *literature and language educator, photographer*

Toll, John Sampson *retired academic administrator, physics professor*
Tolle, Brenda Kay *secondary school educator, computer scientist, consultant*
Tolmacheva, Marina Aleksandrovna *academic administrator*
Tomlinson, Carol Ann *education educator, writer*
Tompkins, Ellen Beth *retired elementary school educator*
Tonjes, Marian Jeannette Benton *education educator*
Torres, Arelis *elementary school educator*
Towler, Evelyn Wheeler *retired elementary school educator*
Tramonte, Michael Robert *retired education educator*
Tran, Nam Van *secondary school educator*
Trattner, Laura V. *retired middle school educator*
Trebon, Thomas *academic administrator*
Treible, Kirk *retired academic and foundation administrator*
Trusdell, Mary Louise Cantrell *retired academic administrator*
Tse, Florence *director*
Tsiligaridis, John *education educator, researcher*
Tuitele, Lui *retired school system administrator*
Turnau, Vivian Williamson *retired literature and language educator*
Turnbull, Vernona Harmsen *retired education educator, counseling administrator*
Turner, Elvin L. *retired school system administrator*
Tussing, Lewis Benton, III, (Tony) *secondary education educator, coach*
Uehling, Barbara Staner *academic administrator*
Upton, Becky J. *secondary school educator*
Vail, Nancy L. Scott *retired elementary school educator, artist*
Valentine, Charles Francis *retired educational administrator*
Valentine, Phyllis Louise *counseling administrator*
vanHorn, Kate Raudenbush *retired school psychologist*
Van Ness, Ross Howard *education educator*
Van Patten, James Jeffers *education educator*
van Tienhoven, Ari *education educator, educator*
Venditouli, Elizabeth Ann *special education educator*
Verma, Surjit Kumar *retired school system administrator*
Vernon, Dean Matthew *psychology educator*
Vick, Dwight Harold *educator*
Volpe, Eileen Rae *retired special education educator*
Wade, June Booth *secondary school educator*
Wagner, Anthony E. *academic administrator, former state official*
Wagner, Bruce Herman *school librarian, educator*
Wagner, Ellyn Santi *retired mathematics educator*
Wagner, Helen Adeene *elementary school educator*
Walker, Annette *retired counseling administrator*
Walker, Carolyn Mae *retired secondary school educator*
Walker, Pamela *mathematics educator*
Waller, Eunice McLean *retired educator*
Walsh, Diana Chapman *former academic administrator, sociologist, educator*
Walsh, Dolores Ann Gonczo (Lorry Walsh) *special education educator*
Wang, Mian *education educator*
Warcken, Nancy B. *elementary school educator*
Ward, Mal Yvonne *special education educator*
Ward, Wanda Louise Dobbs *educational administrator*
Warder, Richard Currey, Jr. *dean, mechanical aerospace engineering educator*
Ware, Gwendolyn C. *retired counseling administrator*
Warian, Christine Barbara *elementary school educator*
Warman, Linda K. *retired secondary school educator*
Warner, Don Lee *dean emeritus*
Warren, Marie Antoinette *elementary school educator*
Warrior, Della C. *academic administrator, art educator*
Watford, Dolores *elementary school educator*
Watrous, Robert Thomas *academic director*
Watts, John Ransford *academic administrator*
Watts, Mary Ann *retired elementary school educator*
Weber, Yvonne Roebuck *research administrator, educator*
Weers, Vesta L. *secondary school educator, department chairman*
Wefald, Jon *former academic administrator*
Wehn, Karen Swaney *education educator, consultant*
Weis, Frederick M. *former academic administrator*
Wenger, James L. *education educator*
Werner, Robert Joseph *dean, music educator*
West, Janet Elaine Olson *elementary school educator*
Weston, Francine Evans *secondary school educator*
Wetherell, Albert A. *secondary school educator*
Whalen, Norma Jean *retired special education educator*
Wheeler, David Laurie *university dean*
Whitaker, Thomas Kenneth *former university chancellor*
White, Florence May *retired special education educator*
White, John Wesley, Jr. *retired academic administrator*
White, Lonnie Joe *retired history educator*
White, Pamela Jo *elementary school educator*
Widman, Rudolph Paul *college administrator*
Wiles, Edwin McKinley *education educator, librarian*
Wilkening, Laurel Lynn *academic administrator, aerospace scientist*
Will, Christina *school librarian*
Will, Katherine Haley *former academic administrator*
Willey, Frieda Anders *adult education educator*
Williams, Thelma B. *retired principal*
Willis, Solomon Lee *mathematics educator*
Willison, Bruce Gray *dean*
Willocks, Kristin *psychology educator*
Wills, J. Robert *retired academic administrator, theater educator, writer*
Wilson, Annette Sigrid *retired elementary school educator*
Wilson, Robin Scott *retired academic administrator, writer*
Wimmer, Kathryn *retired elementary school educator*
Winter-Neighbors, Gwen Carol *special education and art educator, consultant*
Winterstein, James Fredrick *academic administrator*
Wisely, Donna *secondary school educator, athletic trainer*
Wiseman, Douglas Carl *education educator, department chairman, dean*
Wittich, John Jacob *retired academic administrator, finance company executive*
Wittig, Sigmar *academic administrator, researcher, retired aerospace transportation executive*
Wood, Janis Louise *retired assistant principal*
Wood, Joseph S. *academic administrator*
Woodruff, Mary Brennan *elementary school educator*
Woodsworth, Anne *retired academic administrator, librarian*
Wozniak, A. Rachel *educator*
Wright, Douglas Tyndall *former university administrator*
Wright, Ethel *secondary school educator*
Wylie, James Malcolm *adult education educator*
Xing, Jun *academic administrator, educator*
Yenko, Jayne M. *education educator*
Yohe, Harry Edward, Jr. *special education educator*
Young, Gail Diane *secondary school educator*
Young, Ruth Brooks *retired elementary school educator*
Young, Teresa Gail Hilger *retired adult education educator*
Youngs, Diane Campfield *learning disabilities specialist, educator*
Yuill, Thomas MacKay *academic administrator, microbiology educator*
Zahner Kraeft, Dorothy Simkin *retired elementary school educator, school librarian*
Zang, Kathleen Ann *pre-school educator*
Zatsiorsky, Vladimir Moiseevich (Michailovich) *biomechanics educator, researcher*
Zeilinger, Elna Rae *elementary school and gifted and talented educator*
Zhang, Lixuan *education educator*
Zito, Rae Nanette *retired elementary school educator*
Zold, Robert Kenneth *educational administrator*

ENGINEERING

UNITED STATES

ALABAMA

Auburn
Chin, Bryan A. *materials engineer, educator*
Cochran, John Euell, Jr. *aerospace engineer, lawyer, educator*
Crocker, Malcolm John *mechanical engineer, educator*
Cutchins, Malcolm Armstrong *aerospace engineer, educator, researcher*
Hanley, Thomas Richard *engineering educator*
Jaeger, Richard Charles *electrical engineer, educator, science association director*
Mao, Shiwen *engineering educator*
Sforzini, Richard Henry *aerospace engineer, educator*

Auburn University
Clement, Prabhakar T. *engineering educator, researcher*
Eden, Mario Richard *engineering educator*

Birmingham
Ayasoufi, Anahita *engineer, researcher*
Goldman, Jay *industrial engineer, educator, dean emeritus*
Goodrich, Thomas Michael *engineering and construction executive, lawyer*
Jo, Young Gyun *nuclear engineer*
Kuhn, Kenneth August *electrical engineer, educator*
Potter, John Leith *retired mechanical and aerospace engineer, educator, consultant*
Rajendra, Anand Laxmikantrao *electrical engineer*
Scripa, Rosalia *engineering educator, researcher*
Sisiopiku, Virginia P. *civil engineer*

Daphne
Jeffreys, Elystan Geoffrey *petroleum consultant*

Decatur
Smith, Troy Alvin *aerospace research engineer*

Hartselle
Johnson, Loyd *agricultural engineer, researcher*

Huntsville
Daussman, Grover Frederick *electrical engineer, consultant*
Ho, Fat Duen *engineering educator*
Howard, Richard T. *aerospace engineer*
Karbhari, Vistasp M. *engineering educator, researcher*
Pastrick, Harold Lee *aeronautical engineer*
Pittman, William Claude *electrical engineer*
Sackheim, Robert Lewis *aerospace engineer, educator*
Sun, Yuzhi *mechanical engineer, researcher*
Wang, Zhi Jian *aerospace engineer*
Wells, Buren Earl *computer engineer, educator*
Wieland, Paul Otto *environmental control systems engineer*
Zuo, Qiuhai Ken *engineering educator, researcher*

Loachapoka
Schafer, Robert Louis *agricultural engineer, researcher*

Madison
Morgan, John Derald *foundation director, electrical engineer, educator, writer, researcher*
Robertson, Glen A. *aerospace engineer*

Montgomery
Pan, Chai-Fu *engineering educator*

Mosul
Southern, Terry Keith *engineering executive*

Normal
Bhattacharjee, Sudip *engineering educator*

Opp
Bundrick, Tracy Lee *engineering educator*

Salem
Gibbons, Dona Alden Coe *electrical engineer, technical education coordinator*

Spanish Fort
van Aken, John Henry *retired marine engineer*

Thomasville
Moore, Chester *engineering educator*

Tuscaloosa
Bao, Ningzhong *chemical engineer*
Doughty, Julian Orus *mechanical engineer, educator*
Gibson, George Edward, Jr. *civil engineering educator, consultant, researcher*
Moynihan, Gary Peter *industrial engineering educator*
Ray, Paul Sukhamay *engineering educator, researcher*

Tuskegee
Jiang, Li *engineering educator*
Lester, Cynthia Yvette *engineering educator*

Tuskegee Institute
Triggs, Eldon Dale, II, *aerospace engineer, educator*

ALASKA

Anchorage
Bothum, Mark Sumner *engineering educator*
Dutta, Utpal *engineering educator*
Olofsson, John Arndt *engineering educator*
Smithers, Paul T (Smithers T) *civil engineer, educator*

Fairbanks
Lin, Chuen-Sen *mechanical engineer, educator*
Tilsworth, Timothy *retired environmental/civil engineering educator*

ARIZONA

Cave Creek
Collins, Jack Adam *mechanical engineer*

Chandler
Braunisch, Henning *electronics engineer, researcher*
Pietambaram, Srinivas V. *engineer*
Wang, Jinlin *chemical engineer*
Zhang, (Mike) Tao *electrical engineer, researcher*

Clarkdale
Silvern, Leonard Charles *retired engineering executive*

Fountain Hills
Erickson, Edward Grant *electrical engineer*

Gilbert
Ring, Jack *systems engineer, educator*

Glendale
Bai, Haowei *aerospace engineer and scientist*

Green Valley
Hanson, John M. *structural engineer, consultant*

Hereford
Hirth, John Price *metallurgical engineering educator*

Mesa
Baxter, Gene Kenneth *mechanical engineer, engineering company executive*
Biekert, Russell George *engineering educator, consultant*
Singhal, Avinash Chandra *engineering administrator, educator*

Paradise Valley
Russell, Paul Edgar *electrical engineering educator*
Weinberger, Arnold *retired electrical engineer*

Phoenix
Frank, Tim *engineering educator*
Freyermuth, Clifford L. *structural engineering consultant*
Lee, Wontae *environmental engineer, researcher*
Robertson, Samuel Harry III *transportation safety research engineer, educator*

Prescott
Bieniawski, Zdzislaw Tadeusz Richard *engineering educator, writer, consultant*
Chesson, Eugene *retired civil engineering educator, consultant, volunteer*
Kahne, Stephen James *systems engineering educator, engineering company executive, academic administrator*

Scottsdale
Ballinger, Charles William *sanitary engineer, consultant*
Gookin, Thomas Allen Jaudon *civil engineer*

Sun City
Davies, Percy (Pete) Charles *mechanical engineer*

Sun City West
Brown, Ruth Geisler *retired electronics engineer*

Tempe
Abedinpour, Siamak *electrical engineer*
Barnaby, Hugh James *engineering educator*
Berman, Neil Sheldon *retired chemical engineering professor*
Black, John Arthur, Jr. *electrical engineer, computer scientist, publisher*
Cao, Yu *engineering educator, researcher*
Chiriac, Victor Adrian *aerospace engineer, researcher*
Fafitis, Apostolos *engineering educator, researcher*
Ferry, David Keane *electrical engineering educator*
Fu, Yue *electrical engineer*
Jang, Jin-Wook *electronics engineer*
Karády, George György *electrical engineering educator, consultant*
Lacroix, Zoé *engineering educator, researcher*
Lee, Tae-Woo *aerospace engineer, researcher, educator*
Mahajan, Subhash *electronic materials educator*
Montgomery, Douglas Carter *industrial engineering educator*
Skromme, Brian J. *engineering educator*
Vasileska, Dragica *electrical engineer, educator*
Vittal, Vijay *electrical engineer, educator*
Zhou, Ding-Wei *mechanical engineer, researcher*

Tucson
Arnell, Walter James William *engineering educator, consultant*
Brubaker, Galen Wayne *engineering educator*
Cuello, Joel L. *biosystems engineer, professor*
Gaither, William Samuel *civil engineering executive, consultant*
Kerwin, William James *electrical engineering educator, consultant*
Kohloss, Frederick Henry *retired engineer*
Mense, Allan Tate *research and development engineering executive*
Ogilvie, T(homas) Francis *marine engineering educator*
Riley, Mark Richard *biochemical engineer, educator*
Slack, Donald Carl *agricultural engineer, educator*
Smerdon, Ernest Thomas *engineering educator*
Venkata, Subrahmanyam Saraswati *engineering educator, researcher*
Ziolkowski, Richard Walter *electrical engineer, educator*

ARKANSAS

Conway
Friedman, William H. *engineering educator*

Fayetteville
Bajwa, Sreekala G. *agricultural engineer, educator*
Gaddy, James Leoma *chemical engineer, educator*
Hajihashemi, Mohammad Reza *engineer*
Kim, Jin Woo *engineering educator*
Malshe, Ajay P. *engineering educator*
Rardin, Ronald L. *engineering educator*
White, John Austin, Jr. *engineering educator, retired academic administrator*
Yang, Jie *electrical engineer, researcher*
Yoon, Hargsoon *engineering educator*

Little Rock
Xi, Jinxiang *engineering educator, researcher*

North Little Rock
Herron, Ronald Leroy *aeronautical engineer, educator*

Searcy
Gastineau, Zane D. *engineering educator, department chairman*

CALIFORNIA

Alameda
Griffith, Saul *engineering innovations inventor*

Aliso Viejo
Kister, Henry Z. *chemical engineer*
Steuert, Douglas Michael *engineering and construction management company executive*

Alpine
Roberts, Dwight Loren *engineer, writer*

Altadena
Coles, Donald Earl *retired engineering educator*

Anaheim
McNulty, James Francis *engineering executive*

Arcadia
Burbano, Arturo A. *process engineer*
Trussell, R(obert) Rhodes *environmental engineer*

Arcata
Grafman, Lonny *engineering educator, editor*

Arroyo Grande
Hoffmann, Jon Arnold *retired aeronautical engineer*

Atherton
Hooper, Mark Scheller *electrical engineer, educator*
Lowry, Larry *engineering company executive*
Morel-Seytoux, Hubert Jean *civil engineer, educator*

Azusa
Alam, Maksudul M. *chemical engineer*

Belmont
Renwick, Stephen P. *engineer*

Berkeley
Bell, Alexis T. *chemical engineer, educator*
Berger, Stanley Allan *mechanical and biomechanical engineering educator*
Bogy, David B(eauregard) *mechanical engineering educator*
Cairns, Elton James *chemical engineering professor, consultant*
Chua, Leon O. *electrical engineering and computer science educator*
Dornfeld, David Alan *engineering educator*
Fuerstenau, Douglas Winston *mineral engineering educator*
Garrison, William Louis *civil engineering educator*
Grigoropoulos, Costas *mechanical engineering educator*
Hsu, Chieh Su *applied mechanics engineering educator, researcher*
Hu, Chenming *engineering educator*
Javey, Ali *engineering educator*
Kastenberg, William Edward *engineering professor, former academic administrator*
King, Cary Judson III *chemical engineer, educator, academic administrator*
Leitmann, George *mechanical engineer, educator*
Lewis, Edwin Reynolds *biomedical engineering educator, academic administrator*
Ma, Fai *mechanical engineering educator*
Majumdar, Arunava *mechanical engineer, educator*
Monismith, Carl Leroy *civil engineering educator*
Muller, Richard Stephen *electrical engineer, educator*
Onishi, Lisa *chemical engineer, researcher*
Ott, David Michael *engineering company executive*
Pagni, Patrick John *mechanical engineering science educator, safety engineer, researcher*
Pigford, Thomas Harrington *nuclear engineering educator*
Pister, Karl Stark *engineering educator*
Polak, Elijah *engineering educator, computer scientist*
Prausnitz, John Michael *chemical engineer, educator*
Sastry, Sosale Shankara *electrical engineer, computer scientist, dean, educator*
Smith, Otto J. M. *electrical engineering educator*
Tirrell, Matthew V. *engineering educator, department chairman*
White, Richard Manning *electrical engineering educator*
Wiegel, Robert Louis *consulting engineering executive*
Yeung, Ronald Wai-Chun *engineering educator, researcher*

Buellton
Porter, Bruce Jackman *computer engineer, application developer, portfolio manager, civil engineer*

Campbell
Levy, Salomon *mechanical engineer*
Ross, Hugh Courtney *electrical engineer*

Carlsbad
Ghiu, Silvana Melania Stefania *process and development engineer*
Kim, Kyehee *environmental engineer, consultant*
Wilson, Donald Grey *engineering management consultant*

Carmichael
Throner, Guy Charles, Jr. *aerospace engineering executive, scientist, inventor, consultant*

Carson
Buehlmann, Urs K. *engineering educator, researcher*
Siegel, Neil Gilbert *computer engineer, consultant*

Cerritos
Zhang, Lianfeng *chemical engineer*

Chatsworth
Gunn, Stanley Veerin *retired engineer*
Nalbandian, Ruben *engineering company executive*

Chico
Roth, Ronald Lee *engineering educator*

Claremont
Dym, Clive Lionel *engineering educator*
Molinder, John Irving *engineering educator, consultant*
Monson, James Edward *electrical engineer, educator*
Phillips, John Richard *engineering educator*
Pray, Ralph Emerson *metallurgical engineer*

Compton
Wang, Charles Ping *engineering executive*

Concord
Tkachuk, Andrei *engineering company executive*

Costa Mesa
Brady, John Patrick, Jr. *electronics educator, consultant*

Covina
Paulson, Raymond Arnold *science engineering executive*

Culver City
Pierstorff, Erik *biomedical engineer*

Cupertino
Haskell, Barry Geoffry *computer engineer, researcher*
Merdinger, Charles John *civil engineer, educator, military officer, academic administrator*
Tetsuro, Motoyama *electronics engineer*

Cypress
Guzman, Indira Rita *information science educator, researcher*

Daly City
Mobley, Clarence Fowler *retired civil engineer*

Davis
Chancellor, William Joseph *agricultural engineering educator*
Cheney, James Addison *civil engineering educator*
Gates, Bruce Clark *chemical engineer, educator*
Lavernia, Enrique Jose *materials science and engineering educator, dean*
Marino, Miguel Angel *engineering educator*
Tchobanoglous, George *civil engineering educator*
Wallender, Wesley William *engineering professor*
Wang, Shih-Ho *electrical engineer, educator*

Del Mar
Wilkinson, Eugene Parks *nuclear engineer, director*

Diamond Bar
Mirisola, Lisa Heinemann *program supervisor*

El Segundo
Hsia, Irene Yee *electrical engineer*
Kim, Sung Jin *computer engineer*
Lee, Anne Lim *electrical engineer*
Mende, Howard Shigeharu *mechanical engineer*
Nguyen, Tien Manh *technical executive*

Emeryville
Zwoyer, Eugene Milton *retired consulting engineering executive*

Encinitas
Deets, Dwain Aaron *retired aerospace technology executive*

Encino
Friedman, George Jerry *aerospace engineering executive*
Knuth, Eldon Luverne *engineering educator*

Escondido
Ghandhi, Sorab Khushro *electrical engineering educator*

Fairfield
Edson, William Alden *retired electrical engineer, researcher*

Folsom
Ettlich, William F. *electrical engineer*

Fremont
Chao, Kwang-Chu *chemical engineer, educator*
Chen, Wai-Kai *electrical engineering and computer science educator, consultant*
Engelbart, Douglas C. *engineering executive*
Le, Thuy Trong *nuclear engineer, educator*
Rangavajhula, Krishna *mechanical engineer, educator*
Wu, James Chen-Yuan *aerospace engineering educator*
Zhu, Sha *materials engineer*

Fresno
Hunter, Timothy *industrial technology educator*

Fullerton
Clymer, John *electrical engineer, educator*
Kwon, Young D. *engineering educator, researcher*
Tehrani, Fleur Taher *electrical engineer, educator, researcher*
Tiwari, Binod *civil engineer*

Huntington Beach
Leveton, Ian Sinclair *civil engineer*

Irvine
Alexopoulos, Nicolaos George *electrical engineer, educator, dean*
Chelapati, Chunduri Venkata *civil engineering educator*
Fahim, Amr *electrical engineer*
Guo, Yifan *electronics engineer, educator*
Kaneko, Tadashi S. *engineer, researcher*
Kwon, Young Jik *bioengineering researcher and educator*
Lampert, Seymour *retired mechanical engineering educator, consultant*
Meiselbach, James Vincent *mechanical engineer, educator*
Mirnajafizadeh, Seyed Ali *engineering educator, researcher*
Qu, Qi *communications engineer*
Ray Chaudhuri, Samit *civil engineer, researcher*
Samueli, Henry *electrical engineer, educator, professional sports team executive*
Sirignano, William Alfonso *aerospace and mechanical engineer, educator*
Sklansky, Jack *electrical and computer engineering educator, researcher*
Ting, Albert Chia *biomedical engineer, researcher*
Wickramasinghe, Hemantha Kumar *electrical engineer, physicist*
Wolken, Matthew J. *mechanical engineer, educator*
Won, Kwang Woong *chemical engineer*
Zhang, guohao (Gary) *electronics engineer*

La Canada Flintridge
Macmillan, Robert Smith *electronics engineer*

La Jolla
Chang, William Shen Chie *electrical engineering educator*
Chau, Pao C. *engineering educator*
Chien, Shu *physiology and bioengineering educator*
Cortes, Jorge *engineering educator*
de Callafon, Raymond *engineering educator*
Fung, Yuan-Cheng Bertram *bioengineering educator, writer*
Levy, Ralph *engineering executive, consultant*
Lieber, Richard Louis *biomedical engineering scientist, educator*
Liu, Bao *engineering educator*
Liu, Zhaowei *engineering educator*
Milstein, Laurence Bennett *electrical engineering educator, researcher*
Nahavandi, Amir Nezameddin *retired engineering firm executive*
Penner, Stanford Sol *engineering educator*
Schmid-Schoenbein, Geert Wilfried *biomedical engineer, educator*
Thompson, Steve Charles *engineer*
Zeidler, James Robert *electrical engineer, researcher*

Lafayette
Krueger, Robert Edward *mechanical engineer, manufacturing executive*

Laguna Hills
Hammond, R. Philip *chemical engineer*

Lake Forest
Schroeder, John A. *systems engineering consultant, educator*

Livermore
Hallquist, John O. *engineering company executive*
King, Ray John *electrical engineering educator, engineering company executive*

Lompoc
Means, James Andrew *retired engineer*

Long Beach
Dillon, Michael Earl *mechanical engineering executive, educator*
Hsu, John C. *system, aerospace mechanical engineer*
Killian, Thomas J. *engineering educator*
Kumar, Rajendra *electrical engineering educator*
Philpott, Lindsey *civil engineer, researcher, educator*
Sciortino, Antonella *engineering educator*
Sidhwa, Frank N. *engineering executive*
Tsang, Chit-Sang *engineering educator*

Los Altos
Aryanfar, Farshid *electrical and electronics engineer*
Mackey, Sean Charles *anesthesiologist, electrical engineering consultan*
Oh, Kyung Suk (Dan Oh) *electrical engineer*
Peterson, Victor Lowell *aerospace engineer, consultant*

Los Altos Hills
Sharpe, Roland Leonard *structural engineer, consultant*

Los Angeles
Barone, Sherry Joy *test engineer*
Bendiksen, Oddvar Olav *aerospace engineer, educator*
Buffington, Gary Lee Roy *safety engineer, construction executive*
Chang, Jane P. *chemical engineering educator*
Danziger, Bruce Edward *structural engineer*
Dhir, Vijay K. *engineering educator*
Dorman, Albert A. *engineering executive, consultant, architect*
Fathpour, Sasan *optical engineer, researcher*
Felton, Lewis Peter *engineering educator*
Hollander, Sidney *computer systems engineer*
Hovanessian, Shahen Alexander *electrical engineer, educator, consultant*
Itoh, Tatsuo *engineering educator*
Jacobson, Marcus J. *retired mechanical engineer*
Ken, Susanto Suwarno *engineer*
Kim, Jeongbin John *mechanical engineering educator*
Kuehl, Hans Henry *electrical engineering educator*
LeMoyne, Robert *biomedical engineer*
Maxworthy, Tony *mechanical and aerospace engineering educator*
Mendel, Jerry Marc *electrical engineering educator*
Muntz, Eric Phillip *aerospace and mechanical engineering educator, consultant*
Nathanson, Theodore Herzl *aeronautical engineer, architect*
Newman, Richard G. *engineering company executive*
Nobe, Ken *chemical engineering professor*
Okrent, David *engineering educator*
Ozcan, Aydogan *electrical engineer, educator*
Pakbaznia, Ehsan *electrical engineer*
Parente, Robert Bruce *electrical engineer, consultant*
Park, Daeyoung *engineer, researcher*
Perrine, Richard Leroy *environmental engineer, educator*
Ramo, Simon *retired engineering executive*
Reed, Irving Stoy *electrical engineer*
Rubinstein, Moshe Fajwel *engineering educator*
Sadraie, Hamid Reza *civil engineer, researcher*
Safonov, Michael George *electrical engineering educator, consultant*
Sahimi, Muhammad *engineering educator*
Scholtz, Robert Arno *electrical engineering educator*
Settles, F. Stan, Jr. *engineering educator, manufacturing executive*
Sewell, William George III *electronics engineer, writer*
Stenstrom, Michael Knudson *civil engineering educator*
Stephenson, Gary Van *aerospace engineer*
Strong, Pamela Kay *material and process engineer*
Swamikannu, Xavier *environmental engineer, state official*
Tsotsis, Theodore Thomas *engineering educator*
Udwadia, Firdaus Erach *engineering educator, consultant*
Urena-Alexiades, Jose Luis *electrical engineer*
Wagner, Christian Nikolaus Johann *materials engineering educator*
Welch, Lloyd Richard *electrical and communications engineer, educator, consultant*
Willner, Alan Eli *electrical engineer, educator*
Yen, Teh Fu *civil and environmental engineering educator*
Yortsos, Yannis C. *petroleum engineer, educator, dean*
Zou, Qiyue *systems engineer*

Los Gatos
Rosenheim, Donald Edwin *electrical engineer*
Sonkusale, Sahcin Ramrao *electrical engineer*
Waydo, Stephen *aeronautical engineer, researcher*

Malibu
Bedrosian, Edward *retired electrical engineer*
Dominguez, Sylvia Margarita *electrical engineer, researcher*

Menlo Park
Honey, Richard Churchill *retired electrical engineer*
Labiosa, William Bruce *civil engineer, researcher*
Levenson, Milton *chemical engineer, consultant*

Milpitas
Zheng, Min *engineer*

Moffett Field
Colombano, Silvano Pietro *aeronautical engineer, researcher*
Sharma, Surendra Prasad *technical manager, scientist*
Statler, Irving Carl *aerospace engineer*

Monrovia
Edwards, Kenneth Neil *chemical engineering executive*

Monterey
Butler, Jon Terry *computer engineering educator, researcher*
Fargues, Monique P. *electrical engineer, educator*
McNelley, Terry R. *engineering educator*
Vu, Bruce Thanh *aerospace engineer, educator*

Mountain View
Chu, Wai C. *engineer, researcher*
Hoagland, Albert Smiley *electrical engineer, researcher*
Jing, Tong *electrical engineer*
Johnson, Conor Deane *mechanical engineer*
Jonaris, George G. *electrical and computer engineer*
Perrella, Anthony Joseph *electronics engineer*

Murrieta
Geffe, Philip Reinhold *electrical engineer, consultant*

Newport Beach
Alvarado, John *computer game engineer*
Kraus, John Walter *former aerospace engineering company executive*
Lee, Kyehyung *systems engineer*
Parks, Fredrick Scott *systems engineer*

North Hollywood
de la Houssaye, Brette Angelo-Pepe *electrical engineer, researcher, educator*

North Tustin
Dean, William Evans *aerospace engineer, engineering company executive, consultant*

Northridge
Bradshaw, Richard Rotherwood *engineering executive*
Kabo, J. Michael *mechanical engineering educator*
Palerm, Cesar C. *electrical engineer, researcher*

Novato
McAllister, Todd *biomedical engineer*
Minogue, Robert Brophy *retired nuclear engineer*

Oakland
Ji, Jun *engineering company executive*
Lee, Low Kee *electronics engineer, consultant*
Penzien, Joseph *structural engineering educator*
Schell, Farrel Loy *transportation engineer*

Occidental
Rumsey, Victor Henry *electrical engineering educator emeritus*

Oceanside
Jennex, Murray Eugene *engineering educator, consultant*
Yurist, Svetlan Joseph *mechanical engineer*

Orange
Bauer, Bruce F. *retired aerospace engineer*

Pacific Palisades
Herman, Elvin E. *retired consulting electronic engineer*

Palo Alto
Brown, David Randolph *electrical engineer*
Chaturvedi, Nalin A. *aerospace engineer, researcher*
Hodge, Philip Gibson, Jr. *mechanical and aerospace engineering educator*
Jain, Vivek *electronics and communication engineer, researcher*
Kanumuri, Sandeep *communications engineer, researcher*

Kim, Wan Hee *engineering educator*
Moll, John Lewis *retired electronics engineer*
Quate, Calvin Forrest *engineering educator*
Schafer, Ronald William *electrical engineering educator*
Taylor, John Joseph *nuclear engineer, researcher*

Palos Verdes Estates
Abbott, A. Dwight *retired astronautical engineer*
Raue, Jorg Emil *electrical engineer*
Seide, Paul *civil engineering educator*
Yarbrough, Allyson Debra *electrical engineer*

Palos Verdes Peninsula
Mirels, Harold *aerospace engineer*

Pasadena
Bass, Deborah Simone *engineering company executive*
Breckinridge, James Bernard *optical scientist*
Bridges, William Bruce *electrical engineer, educator, researcher*
Dubovitsky, Serge *engineering educator, researcher*
Elachi, Charles *aerospace engineer*
Hornung, Hans Georg *aeronautical engineering educator, science administrator*
Jennings, Paul Christian *civil engineering educator, academic administrator*
List, Ericson John *environmental engineering science educator, consultant*
Losh, Samuel Johnston *engineering administrator*
Martin, Craig Lee *engineering company executive*
Murray, Richard M. *engineering educator*
Ortiz, Michael *engineering educator*
Parker, Jeffrey Scott *systems engineer, researcher*
Phillips, Robert *engineering educator, researcher*
Rutledge, David B. *electrical engineer, educator*
Sabersky, Rolf Heinrich *mechanical engineer*
Sarani, Siamak *aerospace engineer*
Seinfeld, John Hersh *chemical engineering professor*
Sengupta, Anita *aerospace engineer, researcher*
Shimada, Katsunori *retired electrical engineer*
Smith, Michael Robert *electro-optical engineer, physicist*
Wood, Lincoln Jackson *aerospace engineer*
Yariv, Amnon *electrical engineering educator, research scientist*

Playa Del Rey
Weir, Alexander, Jr. *chemical engineer, consultant*

Pleasanton
Novak, Randi Ruth *systems engineer, computer scientist*
Van Dreser, Merton Lawrence *ceramics engineer*

Pomona
Bhandari, Subodh *engineering educator*
Chalkiadakis, Fanourios *electrical engineer, educator*
Dobbs, Steven Kent *aerospace engineer, educator*
Li, Mingheng *engineering educator*
Lou, Yiming *chemical engineer*
Nise, Norman S. *engineering educator*
Teague, Lavette Cox, Jr. *systems educator, consultant*
Tomiyasu, Kiyo *retired consulting engineer*
Turner, Howard *engineering educator, consultant*

Rancho Cucamonga
Alvarez, Tirso Reyes, Jr. *engineer*
Stewart, Howard L. *engineering educator*

Redondo Beach
Brodsky, Robert Fox *aerospace engineer, educator, author*

Redwood City
Deng, Shiming *engineer*

Reseda
Mirzaei, Shahnam *engineering educator*

Richmond
Qiu, Zhijun *engineer, researcher*

Riverside
Balandin, Alexander A. *electrical engineer, educator*
Beni, Gerardo *electrical engineer, educator*
Khayer, Mohammad Abul *electrical engineer, researcher*

Running Springs
Liddle, Sidney George *retired mechanical engineer, researcher*

Sacramento
Crimmins, Philip Patrick *retired metallurgical engineer, lawyer*
Forsyth, Raymond Arthur *civil engineer, consultant*
Kerri, Kenneth Donald *civil engineering educator*
Lathi, Bhagawandas Pannalal *retired electrical engineering educator*
Luo, Zairen *transportation engineer*
McDonald, Kelly Kristin *engineering educator*
Merayyan, Saad M. *engineering educator*
Pang, Jing *engineering educator*
Zhang, Du *engineering educator*

San Diego
Anderson, Paul Maurice *electrical engineering educator, researcher, consultant*
Auld, Robert Henry, Jr. *biomedical engineer, educator, consultant, writer*
Beck, Niels Johannes *mechanical engineer*
Bhargava, Valmik *biomedical engineer, researcher*
Buyuksonmez, Fatih *environmental engineer, researcher*
Cao, Zhiheng *engineer*
Chen, Kun-Mu *electrical engineering educator*
Dahlberg, Kenneth C. *engineering executive*
De Angelis, Flavio *electrical engineer, researcher*
El-Khamy, Mostafa *electrical engineer, researcher*
Friedman, Arthur Daniel *electrical engineer, computer scientist, investment company executive, educator*
Fu, Peilin *engineering educator*
Gupta, Madhu Sudan *electrical engineering educator*
Hauck, James Pierre *scientist*
Hua, Guogang *engineer*
Jing, Zhigang *electrical engineer*
Kim, Namsoo *electrical engineer*
Larom, David Lee *engineering educator*
Larson, Arvid Gunnar *electrical engineer*
Lee, Ki Dong *communications engineer*
Nosseir, Nagy Sabet *engineering educator*
Paget, John Arthur *mechanical engineer*
Plotkin, Allen *aerospace engineer, educator*
Rowson, Sebastian *engineering executive*
Ruane, James Edward, Jr. *engineering executive*
Seo, Dongwon *communications engineer, design scientist*
Shah, Hemang J. *systems engineer*
Sharma, Satish Kumar *engineering educator*
Venkataraman, Satchi *engineering educator*
Zhou, Bo *systems engineer*

San Francisco
Abramson, Norman *retired engineering educator, electronics executive*
Bechtel, Riley Peart *engineering company executive*
Bechtel, Stephen Davison, Jr. *retired engineering company executive*
Dolby, Ray Milton *electrical engineer, company executive*
Frenkel, Val S. *environmental engineer*
Hotchkiss, Ralf David *engineer, educator*
Hui, Jonathan Wing Yan *engineer*
Khatri, Sikandar Khan *engineering educator*
Koffel, Martin M. *engineering company executive*
Lee, Samuel Sangwon *civil, environmental and agricultural engineer*
Mahmoodi, Hamid *engineer*
Merrick, Fred Harold *retired marine engineer*
Shushkewich, Kenneth Wayne *structural engineer*
Smith, Bernard Joseph Connolly *retired civil engineer*
Solo, Ashu M. G. *engineer, researcher*

San Gabriel
Shao, Zhenhua *electrical engineer, consultant*

San Jose
Contos, Paul Anthony *engineer, investment consultant*
Dennison, Ronald Walton *engineer*
Iben, Icko Eric Timothy *electrical engineer*
Jiang, Lijun *mechanical engineer*
Lee, Sung-Chang *mechanical engineer*
Morelos-Zaragoza, Robert Henry *communications engineer*
Rosenblum, Frank Michael *civil engineer, consultant, surveyor*
Rushdi, Ahmad A. *systems engineer*
Tretz, Christophe Robert *electrical engineer*
Yu, Weider D. *engineering educator*
Zhu, Lin *engineer*

San Luis Obispo
Anderson, Warren Ronald *electrical engineering educator*
Bing, Qu *engineering educator*
Self, Brian P *engineering educator*
Taufik, Taufik *electrical engineer, educator*

San Marcos
Purdy, Alan Harris *biomedical engineer*

San Mateo
Kim, Joseph Ho *engineering educator*

San Pedro
McCarty, Frederick Briggs *electrical engineer, consultant*
Simmons, William *retired aerospace engineer, research and development company executive*

San Rafael
Douglas, James *construction engineering educator*

San Ramon
Vatannia, Shahla *mechanical engineer*

Sand City
Coile, Russell Cleven *electrical engineer, consultant*

Santa Ana
Amoroso, Frank *retired communication system engineer, consultant*
Kelly, James Patrick, Jr. *retired engineering executive*

Santa Barbara
Bruch, John Clarence, Jr. *engineer, educator*
Kramer, Edward John *materials engineering educator*
Kroemer, Herbert *electrical engineering educator*
McMeeking, Robert Maxwell *mechanical engineer, educator*
Mitra, Sanjit Kumar *electrical and computer engineering educator*
Pei, Yi *electronics engineer, researcher*
Sensiper, Samuel *electrical engineer*
Theofanous, Theofanis G. *engineering educator, consultant*

Santa Clara
Chan, Shu-Park *electrical engineering educator*
Gope, Dipanjan *computer engineer*
Goyal, Shalabh *electronics engineer*
Kamal, Abu Hena M. *electrical engineer, researcher*
Lee, Hyung Jai *material scientist*
Nassif, Nabil *engineering executive, director*
Parden, Robert James *engineering educator, management consultant*
Pattanayak, Deva Narayan *engineering company executive*
Ranjan, Rahul *engineer, researcher*
Vu, Quat Thuong *electrical engineer*
Yang, Cary *engineering educator*

Santa Cruz
Kang, Sung-Mo (Steve Kang) *electrical engineering educator*
Kubby, Joel *electrical engineer, educator*
Wang, Xin *computer engineer, researcher*
Wiberg, Donald Martin *electrical engineering educator, consultant*

Santa Maria
Arnold, Stephen L. *systems engineer*

Santa Monica
Gritton, Eugene Charles *nuclear engineer, director*
Kayton, Myron *engineering company executive*
Sherman, Zachary *civil engineer, aerospace engineer, consultant*

Santa Rosa
Grundy, Richard David *engineer*
Marougi, Salam D. *engineering educator*

Seal Beach
Matz, Sean Cormick *electrical engineer*

Sonoma
Muchmore, Robert Boyer *engineering executive, consultant*

South Pasadena
Kopp, Eugene Howard *communications and electrical engineer, consultant*

South San Francisco
Hull, Cordell William *engineering, construction, and project management executive, investor*

Stanford
Aziz, Khalid *petroleum engineering educator*
Baer, Thomas M. *optical engineer*
Bejerano, Gill *engineering educator*
Boudart, Michel *chemical engineer, consultant, educator*
Cannon, Robert Hamilton, Jr. *aerospace engineering educator*
Cox, Donald Clyde *electrical engineering educator*
Davis, Jennifer *engineering educator, researcher*
Glynn, Peter Winston Gunnar *engineering educator*
Hesselink, Lambertus *electrical engineering and physics educator*
Horowitz, Mark A. *electrical engineering and computer science educator*
Huang, Kerwyn Casey *engineering educator*
Iglehart, Donald Lee *engineering educator*
Jeong, Min-Wook *electrical engineer*
Kailath, Thomas *electrical engineer, educator*
Khosla, Chaitan S. *chemical engineer*
Kino, Gordon Stanley *electrical engineering educator*
Kruger, Paul *nuclear civil engineering educator*
Liang, Chunlei *mechanical engineer, researcher*
Linehan, John H. *engineering educator, biomedical engineer*
Ludwig, Francis Leonidas *retired engineering educator*
Macovski, Albert *electrical engineer, educator*
McCarty, Perry Lee *civil and environmental engineering educator*
Meng, Teresa H. *electrical engineer, educator*
Ott, Wayne Robert *environmental engineer*
Parkinson, Bradford Wells *astronautical engineer, educator*
Paté-Cornell, Marie-Elisabeth Lucienne *engineering educator*
Perry, William James *engineering educator, former United States Secretary of Defense*
Plummer, James D. *electrical engineering educator, dean*
Saha, Mitul *engineer*
Shaqfeh, Eric Stefan G. *engineering educator*
Skogstad, Philipp Leo *engineering company executive, director*
Springer, George Stephen *mechanical engineering educator*
Steele, Charles Richard *biomedical and mechanical engineering educator*
Street, Robert Lynnwood *civil, mechanical and environmental engineer*
Sweeney, James Lee *engineering educator*
Tomlin, Claire J. *aeronautical engineer, educator*
Vincenti, Walter Guido *aeronautical engineer, emeritus educator*
White, Robert Lee *electrical engineer, educator*
Zhou, Ping *physical engineer*

Studio City
Delnik, Alexander *engineering executive, consultant*

Sunnyvale
Banerjee, Sourav *mechanical engineer, researcher*
Ensminger, Dale *retired mechanical and electrical engineer*
Goo, Jung-Suk *semiconductor company research engineer*
Guan, Xiang *electrical engineer*
Leong, Chia Ken *mechanical engineer*
Mehta, Swati *electrical engineer, researcher*
Oei, Lok S. *digital communications systems and DSP engineer, researcher*
Petersen, Kurt Edward *electrical engineer, researcher, entrepreneur*
Vig, John *electronics engineer, consultant*
Weinberg, William Henry *chemical engineer, physicist, educator*
Zhang, Chi *engineer*

Tarzana
Hansen, Robert Clinton *electrical engineer, consultant*
Lindley, Charles Alexander *aerospace engineer, consultant*

Torrance
Bae, Bonho *electrical engineer*
Grzesik, Jan Alexander *electronics engineer, mathematician*
Marston, Douglas Robert *engineering educator*

Ventura
Gaynor, Joseph *chemical engineer, management consultant*

Victorville
Sedeño, Eugene Raymond *electronics engineer, consultant*

Walnut
Kelkar, Vaibhav *chemical engineer*

Walnut Creek
Cassidy, John Joseph *hydraulic and hydrologic engineer*
Hanson, Robert Duane *engineering educator*

Watsonville
Brown, Alan Charlton *retired aeronautical engineer*

Westlake Village
Caligiuri, Joseph Frank *retired engineering executive*

Whittier
Ekenel, Mahmut *civil engineer, researcher*

Wilmington
Hands, Eric William *civil and electrical engineer researcher*

Windsor
Bradley, Matthew Joseph *engineering company executive*

Yorba Linda
Lynch, Frank Thomas *aeronautical engineer, consultant*
Porcello, Leonard Joseph *engineering research and development executive*

COLORADO

Bayfield
Collins, William Leroy *retired telecommunications engineer*

Bellvue
Candelora, Deborah Michael *engineer, sculptor*

Boulder
Amadei, Bernard Paul *civil engineer, not-for-profit developer, educator*
Banerjee, Arghya *aerospace engineer, researcher*
Barnes, Frank Stephenson *electrical engineer, educator*
Carlson, Lawrence Evan *mechanical engineering educator*
Corotis, Ross Barry *civil engineer, educator, academic administrator*
Datta, Subhendu K. *mechanical engineer, educator*
Hanna, William Johnson *electrical engineering educator*
Hauser, Ray Louis *engineer, researcher, entrepreneur*
Hill, David Allan *electrical engineer*
Jin, Xiaoying *software technical lead, electrical and computer engineer, researcher*
Joy, Edward Bennett *electrical engineer, educator, consultant*
Kim, Sudook A. *materials engineer, researcher*
Kim, Tae-Hyung *engineering educator*
Krarti, Moncef *engineer*
Maley, Samuel Wayne *electrical engineering educator*
Peters, Max Stone *chemical engineer, educator*
Podhajsky, Ronald J. *biomedical engineer, researcher*
Reitsema, Harold James *aerospace engineer*
Sani, Robert LeRoy *chemical engineering professor*
Smith, Ernest Ketcham *electrical engineer*
Snyder, Howard Arthur *aerospace engineering educator, consultant*
Sodal, Ingvar Edmund *retired electrical engineer, science administrator*
Song, Won Jay *electrical engineer, educator*
Timmerhaus, Klaus Dieter *chemical engineering professor*
Zable, Jack Louis *mechanical engineer, educator*

Broomfield
Andreiev, Yura (George) *electronics engineer*
Boulos, Paul Fares *civil and environmental engineer*
Bressler, Marcus Nathan *engineer, consultant*

Centennial
Goughnour, Roy Robert *civil engineer, educator, director*

Colorado Springs
Adnet, Jacques Jim Pierre *astronautical and electrical engineer, consultant*
Ferguson, Jackson Robert, Jr. *astronautical engineer*
Laubhan, Matt *engineering educator*
Morris, Steven Lynn *engineering consultant, retired military officer*
Watts, Oliver Edward *engineering company executive*

Columbine Valley
Gagin, Lawrence Vincent *ceramics engineer, consultant*

Denver
Annandale, George William *engineer*
Balle, James Christian *systems engineer*

Fay, Richard James *mechanical engineering executive, educator*
Frevert, Donald Kent *hydraulic engineer*
Glunz, Gregory *engineer*
McCandless, Bruce, II, *aerospace engineer, retired astronaut*
Papantoni Kazakos, Titsa *engineering educator*
Reshotko, Eli *aerospace engineer, educator*

Englewood
Olcer, Nuri Yelman *engineering researcher, educator*
Polland, Anthony Travis *engineering company executive, director*

Estes Park
Ojalvo, Morris *civil engineer, educator*
Webb, Richard C. *engineering company executive*

Fort Collins
Abt, Steven R. *civil engineer, educator*
Barbezat, Eugene LaVar *retired computer engineer, military officer*
Chong, Edwin K. P. *engineering educator*
Evans, Norman Allen *retired civil engineering educator*
Kaufman, Harold Richard *mechanical engineer, physics educator*
Matthies, Frederick John *civil and environmental engineer*
Richardson, Everett Vern *hydraulic engineer, educator, administrator, consultant*
Roesner, Larry August *civil engineer*
Rubin, Binyamin *aerospace engineer*
Santoni, Brandon Gerad *engineering educator, researcher*
Venayagamoorthy, Subhas Karan *civil engineer, educator*

Golden
Arora, Manohar Lal *engineering educator*
Ciobanu, Cristian V. *engineering educator*
Dickenson, Eric Reyvell Velázquez *engineering educator*
Hamm, Nathaniel Paul *engineering educator*
Mohagheghi, Ali *chemical engineer*
Nozik, Arthur Jack *research physical chemist*
Skokan, Catherine *engineering educator*
Sloan, Earle Dendy, Jr. *chemical engineering educator*
Suryanarayanan, Siddharth *electrical engineer, educator*
Van Kirk, Craig William *petroleum engineer, educator*

Grand Junction
Rybak, James Patrick *retired engineering educator*

Greenwood Village
Arvizu, Dan Eliab *mechanical engineer*
Haliw, Jerome Michael *civil engineer*

Highlands Ranch
Maucec, Marko *nuclear engineer, researcher*
Rogers, Benjamin Talbot *mechanical engineer, consultant*

Lakewood
Barrett, Michael Henry *civil engineer*
Lu, Paul Haihsing *mining engineer, geotechnical consultant*

Longmont
Nordgren, Ronald Paul *retired engineering educator, researcher*

Louisville
Syed, Yasser Fouad Khaderi *electrical engineer*

Loveland
Fleischer, Gerald Albert *industrial engineer, educator*

Superior
Middlebrooks, Eddie Joe *environmental engineer*

U S A F Academy
Cummings, Russell Mark *aerospace engineer, educator*

Westminster
Zhang, Li Larry *engineer, researcher, educator*

CONNECTICUT

Bloomfield
Cornell, Robert Witherspoon *retired mechanical engineer*
De Maria, Anthony John *electrical engineer*

Bridgeport
Syed, Rizvi Sajjad Haider *engineering educator, researcher*

Cheshire
Eppler, Richard Andrew *chemical engineer, educator, consultant*

East Hartford
Staroselsky, Alexander *mechanical engineer, materials scientist*

Fairfield
Bubencik, John William, II, *civil engineer, consultant, transportation engineer*

Farmington
Laurencin, Cato Thomas *biomedical engineer, orthopaedic surgeon, dean*

Greenwich
Van Houten, Leonard Erskine *consulting engineer*

Hartford
Bronzino, Joseph Daniel *electrical engineer*

Mansfield Center
DiBenedetto, Anthony Thomas *engineering educator*

Mystic
Thompson, Robert Allan *aerospace engineer*

New Britain
Czajkowski, Eva Anna *aerospace engineer, educator*
Naoumov, Viatcheslav I. *mechanical and aerospace engineer, educator*

New Haven
Duncan, James S. *engineering educator*
Narendra, Kumpati Subrahmanya *electrical engineer, educator*

New Milford
Jeyapalan, Jey K. *civil engineer*

North Branford
Mead, Lawrence Myers, Jr. *retired engineering executive*

Norwalk
Bays, John Theophanis *consulting engineer*

Pawcatuck
Gitzendanner, Robert *manufacturing engineer, director*

Ridgefield
McConnell, John Edward *retired electrical engineering company executive*

Stamford
Engel, Gerald L. *engineering educator*

Storrs Mansfield
Bzymek, Zbigniew Marian *engineering educator*
Chiu, Wilson K. S. *engineering educator*
Grasso, Domenic *civil engineering educator*
Kim, Jeong-Ho *engineering educator*
Pitkin, Edward Thaddeus *aerospace engineer, consultant*
Zofka, Adam *civil engineer, educator*

Stratford
Blair, Sylvia H. *project engineer*

West Haven
Collura, Michael Anthony *chemical engineer, educator*

West Redding
Sinha, Bikash Kumar *mechanical engineer, researcher*

DELAWARE

Bear
Yannul, Edward *chemical engineer, writer*

Hockessin
Igwe, Godwin Joseph *chemical engineer*

Lewes
Beaufait, Frederick W(illiam) *retired engineering educator*

Newark
Barteau, Mark Alan *chemical engineering and chemistry educator*
Beris, Antony Nicolas *chemical engineer, educator*
Boncelet, Charles George *engineering educator*
Buma, Takashi *electrical engineer, educator*
Byrne, John Michael *energy and environmental educator*
Chajes, Michael Joseph *civil engineer, educator*
Chen, Jingguang G. *chemical engineer, educator*
Dursun, Derya *environmental engineer, researcher*
Krishnan, Palaniappa *agricultural engineering educator*
Ma, Xu *engineer, researcher*
Russell, Thomas William Fraser *chemical engineer, educator*
Sandler, Stanley Irving *chemical engineering educator*
Szeri, Andras Z. *engineering educator*
Vinson, Jack Roger *mechanical engineer, educator*
Zhang, Yuhong *mechanical engineer, researcher*

Wilmington
Diemer, Russell Bertrum, Jr. *chemical engineer, educator*
Koch, Carl Mark *retired environmental engineering executive*

DISTRICT OF COLUMBIA

Washington
Arkilic, Galip Mehmet *mechanical engineer, educator*
Bainum, Peter Montgomery *aerospace engineer, consultant*
Blanchard, Bruce *civil engineer, consultant*
Cheng, Xiuzhen *engineering educator*
Day, Gordon W. *electrical engineer*
Deland, Michael Reeves *attorney-at-law, disability and environmental consultant*
Efimba, Robert *engineering educator, consultant*
Eisner, Howard *engineering executive, educator*
Fertel, Marvin S. *civil engineer*
Garris, Charles Alexander *mechanical engineer, educator*
Giallorenzi, Thomas Gaetano *optical engineer*
Hamdar, Samer Hani *civil engineer, educator*
Hartman, Patrick James *mechanical engineer, researcher*
Hershey, Robert Lewis *mechanical engineer, management consultant*
Kahn, Walter Kurt *engineering and applied science educator*
Kao, Timothy Wu *civil engineering educator*
Kappaz, Michael H. *engineering and energy executive*
Kinney, George Patrick *broadcast engineering executive*
Kyriakopoulos, Nicholas *engineering educator*
Marventano, David *engineering and construction management company executive*
Motevalli, Vahid *engineering educator*
Ososanya, Esther Titilayo *engineering educator*
Page, Robert Wesley *engineering and construction company executive, federal official*
Pardavi-Horvath, Martha Maria *engineering educator, researcher*
Pickholtz, Raymond Lee *electrical engineering educator, consultant*
Saidi, Reza *engineering educator*
Sherali, Zeadally *engineering educator*
Skinner, Robert Earle, Jr. *civil engineer, engineering executive*
Skolnik, Merrill I. *electrical engineer*
Townsend, Marjorie Rhodes *aerospace engineer, engineering executive*
Vest, Charles Marstiller *engineering educator, former academic administrator*
Vojcic, Branimir R. *engineering educator, consultant*
Wang, John Cheng Hwai *communications engineer, researcher*
Wang, Zhaoyang *engineering educator*
Whitesides, John Lindsey, Jr. *aerospace engineering educator, researcher*
Whitworth, Horace Algernon *mechanical engineer*

FLORIDA

Aventura
Wolfenson, Azi U. *electrical, mechanical and industrial engineer, consultant*

Boca Grande
Marini, Robert Charles *environmental engineering executive*

Boca Raton
Gallaher, Ryan M. *engineering company executive, director*
Lin, Yukweng M. *engineer, educator*
Mussenden, Georg Antonio *electronics engineer*
Wang, Xin *engineering educator*

Brandon
Stephens, Robert David *environmental engineering executive*

Coral Gables
Giancaspro, James *engineering educator, researcher*
Mantell, Murray I. *engineering educator*
Matta, Fabio *structural engineer, educator*
Wong, Kau-Fui Vincent *engineering educator, educator*

Davie
Upadhiaya, Umesh Chandra *engineer, consultant*

Daytona Beach
Helfrick, Albert Darlington *electronics engineering educator, consultant, department chairman*
Steinhauer, Heidi Marie *manufacturing engineer, educator*
Yang, Thomas *electrical engineer, educator*

Deland
Freeman, Ronald Eugene *environmental engineer*

Fort Lauderdale
Roush, Robert Warren *electrical engineer, director*

Fort Myers
Moeschl, Stanley Francis *electronics and electrical engineer, management consultant*

Fort Walton Beach
Lord, William *retired electrical engineer*

Gainesville
Anderson, Timothy J. *chemical engineering distinguished professor*
Balabanian, Norman *electrical engineering educator*
Batich, Christopher David *biomedical engineer, educator*
Blanch, Paul Bradford *biomedical engineer, researcher*
Cabrera, Victor Elias *environmental engineer, researcher*
Capehart, Barney Lee *industrial and systems engineer, educator*
Cristescu, Nicolaie Dan *engineering educator*
Delfino, Joseph John *environmental engineering sciences educator*
Fossum, Jerry George *electrical engineering educator*
Hahn, David Worthington *engineering educator*
Hollien, Harry Francis *communications engineer*
Isaacs, Gerald William *retired agricultural engineering educator, consultant*
Khargonekar, Pramod Prabhakar *engineering educator*
Kurzweg, Ulrich Hermann *engineering science educator*
Law, Mark Edward *electrical engineer, educator*
Lin, Jenshan *engineering educator*
O, Kenneth Kyongyop *engineering educator*
Sah, Chih-Tang *electrical and computer engineering educator*
Sherif, S. A. *engineering educator*
Slavickas, Rimas Anthony *electrical engineer, educator, researcher*
So, Franky *engineering educator*
Uhrig, Robert Eugene *nuclear engineer, educator*
Viessman, Warren, Jr. *professor emeritus*
Wachsman, Eric D. *engineering educator*
Wheeler, Bruce C. *engineering educator*

Indialantic
Preece, Betty P. *electrical engineer, educator*

Jacksonville
Elsafty, Adel *engineering educator*
McGovern, Jay *aeronautical engineer, consultant*
Mueller, Edward Albert *retired transportation engineer*
Vasana, Susan (Chun-Ye) *engineering educator*

Jupiter
Migliaro, Marco William *electrical engineer*
Wolff, Edward Alvin *electronics engineer*

Kennedy Space Center
Amador, José Jorge *computer engineer, researcher*

Keystone Heights
Ohanian, Mihran Jacob *nuclear engineer, educator, dean, researcher*

Lady Lake
Granger, Robert Alan *mechanical and aerospace engineering educator*

Lake Mary
DiPaolo, Peter Thomas *engineering executive, educator*
Koser, Gary Richard *civil engineer*

Lakeland
Garrott, Frances Carolyn *architectural engineer*

Melbourne
Choi, Youngsik *engineering educator*

Miami
Dede, Mehmet Ismet Can *robotics researcher, educator*
Khan, Ahmad Arshan *engineer, researcher*
Maidique, Modesto Alex *engineering educator, former academic administrator*
Makki, Shamila *project manager engineer, researcher*
Veziroglu, Turhan Nejat *mechanical engineering educator, researcher*

Naples
Portenier, Walter James *aerospace engineer*
Sowman, Harold Gene *ceramics engineer, researcher*
Suziedelis, Vytautas A. *retired engineering corporation executive*

Nokomis
Novak, Robert Louis *civil engineer, pavement management consultant*

Orlando
An, Linan *engineering educator*
Bevc, Frank Peter *electrical engineer*
Boreman, Glenn David *electrical engineer*
Dorleus, Joseph Alphonse Raoul *electronics engineer*
Gao, Xingbo *engineering educator*
Murali, Supraja *optical engineer, researcher*
Simaan, Marwan *electrical engineering educator*
Yeh, Gour-Tsyh *environmental engineer, educator*

Osprey
Boldt, Heinz *retired aerospace engineer*

Palm Beach
Callahan, Edward William *chemical engineer, retired manufacturing executive*

Palm Beach Gardens
Gillette, Frank C., Jr. *retired mechanical engineer*

Panama City
D'Arcy, Gerald Paul *engineering executive, consultant*

Port Charlotte
Kok, Hans Gebhard *consulting engineer*

Port Orange
Millar, Gordon Halstead *mechanical engineer, agricultural products executive*

Riviera Beach
Schmidt, Thomas Charles *biomedical engineer, researcher*

Saint Augustine
Lund, Frederick Henry *aerospace and electrical engineer*

Saint Cloud
Everett, Woodrow Wilson *electrical engineer, educator*

Saint Petersburg
Cardenas-Valencia, Andres Manuel *chemical engineer, researcher*
Collins, Carl Russell, Jr. *industrial engineer*

Sarasota
Derr, Frederick Mueller *civil engineer*
Deutsch, Sid *biomedical engineer, educator*
Long, Robert Radcliffe *fluid mechanics engineer, educator*
Metzger, Sidney *retired communications engineer*

Sunrise
Goldenberg, Felix *retired electrical engineer, researcher*

Tallahassee
Coloney, Wayne Herndon *civil engineer*
Dalban-Canassy, Matthieu *mechanical engineer*
De Forest, Sherwood Searle *agricultural engineer, products executive*
Gor'kov, Peter (Lev Petrovich) *biomedical engineer*
Hayek, Saleh *engineer, researcher*
Islam, Tanveerul Tanveer *engineering educator*
Meyer-Baese, Uwe *engineering educator*
Shih, Chiang *mechanical engineer, educator*
Standridge, Charles Robert *engineering educator, consultant*
Sutterfield, J. S. *engineering educator*
Wu, Tien-Shuenn *engineer, researcher, consultant*
Yu, Ming *engineering educator, researcher*

Tampa
Carnahan, Robert Paul *civil engineer, educator, researcher, consultant*
Dubey, Rajiv *engineering educator*
Huang, Jimin *civil engineer, consultant*
Hunter, Larry Lee *retired electrical engineer*
Kasturi, Rangachar *electrical engineer, educator*
Lu, Jian John *engineering educator*
Macferran, Ernest Leslie *mechanical engineer*
Okogbaa, Geoffrey Obitor *engineering educator*
Pendyala, Ram Mohan *civil engineering educator*
Ranganathan, Nagarajan *engineering educator*
Ross, Mark Allen *engineering educator, consultant*
Szonntagh, Eugene L. *chemical engineer, educator, chemist, historian, archaeometrist, organologist*

Tavares
Kaiser, Robert Lee *retired engineering executive*

The Villages
Dupies, Donald Albert *retired civil engineer*

Wellington
Cohen, Edward *civil engineer*

Winter Haven
Johnson, Gordon Selby *consulting electrical engineer*

Winter Park
Granberry, Edwin Phillips, Jr. *safety engineer, consultant*

GEORGIA

Albany
Marbury, Ritchey McGuire III *engineering executive, surveyor*

Alpharetta
Yeatman, Henry Clay *mechanical engineer*

Athens
McCutcheon, Steven Clifton *ecological and environmental engineer, hydrologist*
Nelson, Stuart Owen *agricultural engineer, researcher, educator*
Roberts, Ken *electrical engineer, director*

Atlanta
Abdel-Khalik, Said Ibrahim *nuclear and mechanical engineering educator*
Bao, Gang *biomedical engineer, educator*
Bellanca, Joseph Paul *engineering construction executive*
Berryman, Robert Mogabgab *systems engineer*
Cherkaoui, Mohammed *aerospace engineer, educator*
Cressler, John David *electrical engineering educator*
del Valle, Yamille Ellend *engineer, researcher*
Ellingwood, Bruce Russell *structural engineer, educator*
Erera, Alan *engineering educator*
Faber, Olaf Ulrich *structural engineer*
Forney, Larry J. *chemical engineer, educator*
Giddens, Don Peyton *engineering educator, researcher*
Guerra, Larry Cacao *engineer, researcher*
Harrison, George Brooks *engineer, researcher, retired military officer*
Hess, Dennis William *chemical engineering educator*
Hodges, Dewey Harper *aerospace engineer, educator*
Howard, Ayanna MacCalla *electrical and robotics engineer, educator*
Jackson, Robert Benton, IV, *environmental engineer*
Kenney, James Stevenson *engineering educator, consultant*
Kim, Yoon Jo *mechanical engineer, researcher*
Madisetti, Vijay Krishna *electrical engineer, educator*
McCann, Martin Bruce *civil engineer*
McDowell, David Lynn *mechanical engineering educator*
McIntire, Larry Vern *biomedical engineering educator*
Meindl, James Donald *electrical engineering educator, academic administrator*
Papapolymerou, John *engineering educator*
Petrovic, Bojan *nuclear engineer, educator*
Price, Edward Warren *retired aerospace engineer*
Rodgers, Michael Owen *civil engineer, educator*
Rouhani, Shahrokh *civil engineering environmental educator, consultant*
Rousseau, Ronald William *chemical engineering educator, researcher*
Salant, Richard Frank *mechanical engineer, educator*
Shinohara, Minoru *engineering educator*
Spain, Jim C. *environmental engineer, educator*
Stacey, Weston Monroe, Jr. *nuclear engineer, physicist, educator*
Thuesen, Gerald Jorgen *industrial engineer, educator*
Vachon, Reginald Irenee *mechanical engineer*
Vuola, Olli *engineering company executive*
Winer, Ward Otis *mechanical engineer, educator*
Yoganathan, Ajit Prithiviraj *biomedical engineer, educator*
Yuan, Jiahui *electronics engineer, researcher*

Austell
O'Rear, Clarence Michael *engineering company executive*

Avondale Estates
Bastin, Clinton *retired chemical engineer, nuclear scientist*

Big Canoe
Bendelius, Arthur George *engineering firm executive*

Dillard
Aldridge, Melvin Dayne *engineering educator*

Doraville
Wempner, Gerald Arthur *engineering professor*

Duluth
Colwell, Gene Thomas *engineering educator*

Gainesville
Jones, William Benjamin, Jr. *retired electrical engineering educator*

Jasper
Wiltse, James Cornelius *retired electrical engineer*

Macon
Hails, Robert Emmet *retired aerospace engineer, manufacturing executive, military officer*
Leonard, Michael Steven *industrial engineering educator*

Marietta
Asgill, Austin Blanshard *electrical engineer, educator*
Atkins, Robert Wayne *engineering educator, consultant*
Bernal, Barbara V. *engineering educator*
Kim, Sung Hee *engineering educator*
Miles, Thomas Caswell *mechanical engineer*
Patterson, Philip Edward *engineering educator*
Sampath, Ramanathan *chemical engineer, educator*
Sanner, George Elwood *electrical engineer*

Norcross
Nuyan, Seyhan *control engineer*

Savannah
Mustafa, Mohamad *engineering educator*
Tan, Yong *electronics engineer*

Sky Valley
Geer, Ronald Lamar *mechanical engineer, consultant, retired oil industry executive*

Statesboro
Piltner, Reinhard *engineering educator*
Vlcek, Brian L. *engineering educator*

Stone Mountain
Bacon, Louis Albert *retired consulting civil engineer*
Nerem, Robert Michael *engineering educator, consultant*

Tucker
Das, Jagdish Chander *engineer, consultant*

Warner Robins
DePriest, C(harles) David *engineering executive, retired military officer*

HAWAII

Hilo
Vesper, Karl Hampton *business and mechanical engineering educator*

Honolulu
Chen, Wai-Fah *civil engineering educator*
Cotlar, Morton *organizational scientist, educator*
Cox, Richard Horton *civil engineering executive*
Ghasemi Nejhad, Mehrdad N. *mechanical engineering educator*
Hamada, Harold Seichi *civil engineer, educator*
Kim, Albert Sechurl *civil engineer, educator*
Koide, Frank Takayuki *electrical engineering educator*
Liu, Clark C. K. *engineering educator, director*
Ma, Tianwei *engineering educator*
Prevedouros, Panos D. *engineering educator, consultant*
Saint Georges Chaumet, Eric *electronics engineer*
Shimotsu, Ryan *biomedical engineer*
Shiroma, Wayne A. *engineering educator*
Wang, Jaw-Kai *bioengineering educator*
White, Gary Richard *electrical engineer*
Yee, Alfred Alphonse *structural engineer, consultant*

Kamuela
Adkins, Sean Michael *electrical, computer science and optical engineer*

Kapaau
McFee, Richard *electrical engineer, physicist*

Mililani
Camery, John William *computer engineer*

IDAHO

Boise
Durcan, D. Mark *engineering executive*
Eggert, Rudolph J. *engineering educator*
Papic, Milorad *electrical engineer, researcher*
Zarges, Thomas H. *engineering executive*

Eagle
Chung, Caleb *inventor, toymaker, toy company executive*

Idaho Falls
Bruemmer, David Jonathan *robotics engineer*
Chang, Gray S. *nuclear engineer, consultant*
Oh, Chang *chemical engineer, consultant*
Riemke, Richard Allan *nuclear engineer*

Inkom
Ambrose, Tommy W. *chemical engineer, engineering executive*

Moscow
Abdel-Rahim, Ahmed *engineering educator*
Aston, D. Eric *engineering educator*
DeShazer, James Arthur *biological engineer, educator, research administrator*

Pocatello
Jacobsen, Richard T. *mechanical engineering educator*
Naidu, D. Subbaram *electrical engineer, educator*

ILLINOIS

Argonne
Aliberti, Gerardo *nuclear engineer*
Chang, Yoon Il *nuclear engineer*
Kumar, Romesh *chemical engineer*

Batavia
Darve, Christine *mechanical engineer*

Bloomington
Pannell, Thierry Edgard *engineer, information technology manager*

Carbondale
Farhang, Kambiz *engineering educator*
Koc, Rasit *ceramics engineer, educator*
Ma, Xingmao *environmental engineer, educator*
Mahajan, Ajay *engineering educator*

Champaign
Korst, Helmut Hans *mechanical engineer, educator*

Chicago
Anthony, Donald Barrett *engineering executive*
Babcock, Lyndon Ross, Jr. *environmental engineer, educator*
Carreira, Domingo Jose *structural engineer*
Chowdhury, Masud H. *computer engineer, educator*
Chudnovsky, Alexander *engineering educator, consultant*
Chung, Paul Myungha *mechanical engineer, educator*
Dix, Rollin C(umming) *mechanical engineering educator, consultant*
Fowler, Martin *software engineer, consultant*
Fukui, Yoshio *engineering educator*
Lee, Gyungho *engineering educator*
Lin, James Chih-I *biomedical and electrical engineer, educator*
Lin, Jie *engineering educator, researcher*
Linden, Henry Robert *chemical engineer, researcher*
Mahani, Mohammad Shadbakht *engineering educator*
Manafzadeh, Saeed *engineering educator, director*
McCaul, Joseph Patrick *chemical engineer*
Miller, Irving Franklin *chemical and biomedical engineer, academic administrator, educator*
Minkowycz, W. J. *mechanical engineering educator*
Minneste, Viktor, Jr. *retired engineering executive*
Muehleisen, Ralph T. *architectural engineer, educator*
Murata, Tadao *engineering and computer science educator*
Noll, Kenneth Eugene *air resources engineering educator*
Rikoski, Richard Anthony *electrical engineering executive*
Riley, Benjamin Robertson *engineering educator*
Russo, Gilberto *engineering educator*
Ryan, William Arthur *mechanical engineer*
Wong, Thomas Tang Yum *engineering educator*
Xu, Yang *engineering educator*

Clarendon Hills
Moritz, Donald Brooks *mechanical engineer, consultant*

Decatur
Koucky, John Richard *metallurgical engineer, manufacturing executive*

Des Plaines
Winfield, Michael D. *engineering company executive*

Downers Grove
Ahmadzadeh, Azita *chemical engineer*

Elmhurst
Parker, James John *engineer, marketing professional*

Evanston
Achenbach, Jan Drewes *engineering scientist*
Backman, Vadim *biomedical engineer, educator*
Belytschko, Ted *engineering educator*
Bobco, William David, Jr. *consulting engineering company executive*
Brazelton, William Thomas *chemical engineer, educator, dean*
Carr, Stephen Howard *materials engineer, educator*
Daskin, Mark Stephen *engineering educator*
Fessler, Raymond R. *metallurgical engineering consultant*
Frey, Donald Nelson *industrial engineer, educator, retired manufacturing executive*
Keer, Leon Morris *engineering educator*
Kliphardt, Raymond A. *engineering educator*
Krizek, Raymond John *engineering educator, consultant*
Messersmith, Phillip B. *biomedical engineer, educator*
Murphy, Gordon John *electrical engineer, educator*
Ottino, Julio Mario *engineering educator*
Packman, Aaron Ian *environmental engineer, educator*
Smith, Spencer Bailey *engineering and business educator*
Taflove, Allen *electrical engineer, educator, researcher, consultant*
Van Ness, James Edward *electrical engineering educator*
Warren, Todd *engineering educator, retired computer company executive*
Weertman, Julia Randall *materials engineering educator*

Glenview
Brady, Sharon *engineering executive*
Brunner, Robert E. *engineering executive*
Flaum, Russell M. *engineering executive*
Gerstner, Robert William *structural engineering educator, consultant*
Gresh, Philip M. *engineering executive*
Hansen, Thomas J. *engineering executive*
Hindman, Craig A. *engineering executive*
Kropp, Ronald D. *engineering executive*
Martel, Roland M. *engineering executive*
Panarese, William C. *civil engineer*
Parry, David C. *engineering executive*
Santi, E. Scott *engineering executive*
Sutherland, Allan C. *engineering executive*
Van Zelst, Theodore William *civil engineer, engineering company executive*
Zentmyer, Hugh J. *engineering executive*

Grayslake
Bates, Ben *ceramics engineer, educator*

Gurnee
Sommerlad, Robert Edward *environmental research engineer*

Hinsdale
Norton, John W., Jr. *chemical engineer, educator*

La Grange
Hoisington, Steven H. *industrial engineer*
Mehlenbacher, Dohn Harlow *civil engineer, consultant*

Lake Forest
Lambert, John Boyd *chemical engineer, consultant*

Libertyville
Jeyaraj, Arulsaravana *electronics engineer*
Thiruppukuzhi, Srikanth Vankeepuram *electronics engineer*

Lindenhurst
Theis, Peter Frank *engineering executive*

Lisle
Morrison, Delmar R. *chemical engineer*

Moline
Badmos, Adebayo Yekeen *engineering educator, researcher*
Taylor, Byron Keith *industrial engineer*

Mossville
Silver, Ronald G. *chemical engineer, researcher*
Son, Youngjin *mechanical engineer*

Naperville
Kreipke, Merrill Vincent *civil engineer, consultant*
Kucera, Jane *chemical engineer*
Vora, Manu Kishandas *chemical engineer, consultant*

New Lenox
Turner, Thomas J. *engineering company executive*

Norridge
Petrakis, Myron Titos *retired mechanical engineer*

Oak Park
Clark, John Peter III *engineer, consultant*

Palatine
Albanese, Jim *electrical engineer*

Park Forest
Williams, Jack Raymond *retired civil engineer*

Peoria
Alkhouli, Osama Mohammad *engineer*
Hindi, Riyadh *engineering educator, researcher*
Liu, Shuangbiao (Jordan) *mechanical engineer*
Lu, Yufeng *engineering educator*
Malinowski, Aleksander *engineering educator*
Opdenbosch, Patrick *mechanical engineer, researcher*

Plainfield
Chakrabarti, Subrata Kumar *offshore research engineer*

Rockford
Gieras, Jacek Franciszek *engineering educator, research scientist*
Roberts, James Brian *engineer*

Rolling Meadows
Yang, Shing Lung Steven *antenna engineer*

Romeoville
Streit, Michael K. *aeronautical engineer, educator*

Skokie
Corley, William Gene *engineering research executive*

South Barrington
Murarka, Narayan P. *electronics engineer, engineering executive*

Sugar Grove
Morrical, Art Andrew *communications engineer*

Summit Argo
Fleischman, Gregory Joseph *chemical engineer, researcher*

Urbana
Adesida, Ilesanmi *engineering educator, researcher, dean*
Andrawes, Bassem *engineering educator*
Barenberg, Ernest John *engineering educator, consultant*
Bergeron, Clifton George *engineer, educator*
Blahut, Richard Edward *electrical and computer engineering educator*
Brunet, Marie-Christine *engineering educator*
Chato, John Clark *mechanical and bioengineering educator*
Cheng, Keh-Yung *electrical engineering educator*
Coleman, Paul Dare *physics and electrical engineering educator*
Conry, Thomas Francis *mechanical engineering educator*
Daruka, Govind Prasad *engineering educator, researcher, small business owner, consultant*
Eden, James Gary *electrical engineer, physicist, educator, researcher*
Fang, Nicholas X. *engineering educator*
Fernandez, Rocio Luz *civil engineer, researcher*
Garcia, Marcelo Horacio *engineering educator, consultant*
Hall, William Joel *retired civil engineer, educator*
Hannon, Bruce Michael *engineering educator*
Hasegawa-Johnson, Mark Allan *electrical engineer, educator*
Hess, Karl *engineering and science educator*
Holonyak, Nick, Jr. *electrical engineering educator*
Huang, Thomas Shi-Tao *electrical engineering educator, researcher*
Jacobson, Sheldon Howard *engineering educator*
Jones, Benjamin Angus, Jr. *retired agricultural engineering educator, science administrator*
Kumar, Panganamala Ramana *electrical and computer engineering educator*
Leon, Arturo Segundo *civil engineer, researcher*
Loui, Michael Conrad *engineering educator*
Lu, Stephen Chih-Yang *engineering educator, researcher, consultant*
Luo, Nie *professor engineering physics*
Makela, Jonathan James *engineering educator*
Maxwell, William Hall Christie *civil and environmental engineer, educator*
May, Walter Grant *chemical engineer, educator*
Miley, George H. *nuclear and electrical engineering educator, plasma engineer, energy conversion scientist*
Murtha, Joseph Patrick *civil engineer, educator*
Olson, Scott M. *civil engineer, educator*
Rao, Nannapaneni Narayana *electrical engineer*
Sivapalan, Murugesu *engineer educator, consultant*
Snoeyink, Vernon L. *civil engineer, educator*
Stallmeyer, James Edward *engineering educator*
Swenson, George Warner, Jr. *engineering educator*
Wah, Benjamin Wan-Sang *electrical and computer engineering educator*

Wilmette
Wadden, Richard Albert *environmental engineer, educator, science administrator, consultant*

INDIANA

Angola
Lin, Ping-Wha *engineering educator, consultant*

Chesterfield
Fry, Meredith Warren *retired civil engineer*

Columbus
Izadian, Afshin *electrical engineer, researcher*

Fort Wayne
Mahmoud, Aly Ahmed *electrical engineering educator*
Njock Libii, Josué *mechanical engineer, educator*
Streeter, Robert Davenport *electrical engineer, consultant*

Hammond
Fathizadeh, Masoud *engineering educator*
Marrero, Benjamin *electrical engineer, educator*
Neff, Gregory Pall *mechanical engineer, educator*
Pierson, Edward Samuel *engineering educator, consultant*

Indianapolis
Hsu, Andrew To-ming *engineering educator*
Kalwara, Joseph John *engineer*
Poinsette, Donald Eugene *engineering executive, management consultant*
Rovnyak, Steven Michael *engineering educator*
Turner, Charles Hall *biomedical engineer, educator*

Lafayette
Etzel, James Edward *environmental engineering educator*
Gustafson, Winthrop Adolph *retired engineering educator*
Liley, Peter Edward *retired engineering educator*
Osborn, John Robert *retired engineering educator*
Pipes, Robert Byron *mechanical engineer, educator*

Muncie
Seymour, Richard Deming *technology educator*
Xu, Renmei *engineering educator*

Munster
Wang, Xiuling *engineering educator*

Notre Dame
Incropera, Frank Paul *mechanical engineering educator*
Kwon, Dae Kun *civil engineer, researcher*
Merz, James Logan *electrical and materials engineering educator, researcher*
Schmitz, Roger Anthony *chemical engineer, educator, academic administrator*
Smith, James Ormal *engineering educator*
Stadtherr, Mark A. *chemical engineer, educator*

Seymour
Paulson, James Marvin *retired engineering educator*

South Bend
Vrajitoru, Dana *engineering educator*

Terre Haute
Badar, M. Affan *engineering educator*

Valparaiso
Cohen, Raymond *retired mechanical engineer, educator*

West Lafayette
Albright, Lyle Frederick *chemical engineering educator*
Ariyur, Kartik Balasubramanian *control systems engineer, researcher*
Barany, James Walter *industrial engineering educator*
Corvalan, Carlos Maria *engineering educator*
Delleur, Jacques William *retired engineering educator*
Drnevich, Vincent Paul *engineering educator*
Givan, Robert *engineering educator*
Grace, Richard Edward *engineering educator*
Hambrusch, Susanne E. *computer engineering educator*
Jackson, Mark James *engineering educator*
Jamieson, Leah H. *engineering educator, dean*
Jenkins, Jere H. *nuclear engineer, director*
Jevremovic, Tatjana *nuclear engineer, researcher*
Labi, Samuel *civil engineering educator, researcher*
Ladisch, Michael R. *engineering educator*
Landgrebe, David Allen *electrical engineer*
Lee, Hanil *electrical engineer, researcher*
Lin, Pen-Min *electrical engineer, educator*
Liu, Chunghorng Richard *engineering educator*
Marshall, Francis Joseph *aerospace engineer*
Naik, Sameer Vijaykumar *mechanical engineer, educator*
Ohland, Matthew William *engineering educator, consultant*
Pierret, Robert F. *electrical engineering educator*
Prabhu, Nagabhushana *industrial engineer, educator*
Sadeghi, Farshid *engineering educator*
Salvendy, Gavriel *industrial engineer, educator*
Schwartz, Richard John *electrical engineering educator, researcher*
Shin, Yung Chul *engineering educator*
Sojka, Paul E. *engineering educator*
Taber, Margaret Ruth *retired engineering technology educator*
Thomas, Marlin Uluess *industrial engineer, academic administrator, educator*
Varma, Arvind *chemical engineering educator, researcher*
Viskanta, Raymond *mechanical engineering educator*
Wankat, Phillip Charles *chemical engineering educator*
Wasynczuk, Oleg *electrical engineer, educator*
Williams, Theodore Joseph *retired engineering educator*
Yao, Bin *mechanical engineering educator*
Yeo, Yoon *biomedical engineer, educator*

IOWA

Ames
Anderson, Robert Morris, Jr. *electrical engineer*
Baumann, Edward Robert *environmental engineering educator*
Black, James Robert *industrial engineer*
Buchele, Wesley Fisher *retired agricultural engineering educator*
Chang, Carl K. *engineering educator*
Cleasby, John LeRoy *civil engineer, educator*
Cormicle, Larry W. *engineering educator*
Kim, Sang Hyoun *environmental engineer, researcher*
Kim, Sunghwan *civil engineer, researcher*
Kushner, Mark Jay *engineering and physics educator, dean*
Larsen, William Lawrence *engineering educator*
Levitas, Valery *mechanics and materials educator, researcher*
Nair, Rajeev *engineering educator, researcher*
Okiishi, Theodore Hisao *mechanical engineering educator*
Reilly, Peter John *chemical engineer, educator*
Sanders, Wallace Wolfred, Jr. *civil engineer*
Tang, Lie *agricultural engineer, educator*
Ten, Chee-Wooi *electrical engineer, researcher*
Wickert, Jonathan Adam *engineering educator*
Wilder, David Randolph *retired materials engineer*

Bettendorf
Heyderman, Arthur Jerome *engineer, civilian military employee*

Cambridge
Colvin, Thomas Stuart *agricultural engineer, farmer*

Cedar Falls
Ghosh, Arindam *engineering educator, researcher*
Pecen, Recayi Reg *engineering educator*
Pedersen, Karen Sue *electrical engineer*
Posinasetti, Nageswara Rao *manufacturing engineering educator*

Cedar Rapids
Smith, Bruce Vaughn *electrical engineer*

Clear Lake
Brown, Robert Grover *engineering educator*

Davenport
Opar, Michael E. *engineering educator, department chairman*

Iowa City
Abdel-Malek, Karim A. *biomedical engineer, educator*
Boyle, Linda Ng *engineering educator*
Dasgupta, Soura *engineering educator*
Lonngren, Karl Erik *electrical and computer engineering educator*
Park, Joon Bu *biomedical engineer, researcher, educator*
Patel, Virendra Chaturbhai *mechanical engineer, educator*

Madrid
Handy, Richard Lincoln *civil engineer, educator*

Muscatine
Stanley, Richard Holt *consulting engineer*
Thomopulos, Gregs G. *consulting engineering company executive*

Orange City
Hancock, Albert Sidney, Jr. *engineering executive*
Zwiep, Donald Nelson *mechanical engineering educator, department chairman*

Ottumwa
Brookhiser, Randall L. *aviation educator*

West Des Moines
Conner, William Bruce *facility engineer, consultant*

KANSAS

Dodge City
Burns, Timothy Scott *welding instructor*

Emporia
Alshare, Khaled A. *information systems educator*

Garden City
Alam, A.N.M. Mahbub Ul *engineer, educator*

Kansas City
Albertini, David Fred *biomedical scientist, educator*
Liu, Wen *biomedical engineer, researcher*

Lawrence
Adams, Craig David *environmental engineering educator*
Benjamin, Bezaleel Solomon *structural engineer, educator*
Darwin, David *engineering educator, consultant*
Moore, Richard Kerr *electrical engineering educator*
Muirhead, Vincent Uriel *retired aerospace engineer*
Roskam, Jan *aerospace engineer*
Willhite, G. Paul *chemical engineer, petroleum engineer, educator*

Lenexa
Bona, Max *mechanical engineer, educator*

Manhattan
Ahmed, A.S.M. Sabbir *nuclear engineer, physicist*
Erickson, Larry Eugene *chemical engineering educator*
Gallagher, Richard Ray *engineering educator, dean*
Hutchinson, Stacy Lewis *environmental engineer, educator*
Johnson, William Howard *retired agricultural engineer, educator*
Lee, E(ugene) Stanley *engineering educator*
McCright, Paul R. *engineer, educator*
Schmidt, David A. *engineering educator*
Simons, Gale Gene *nuclear and electrical engineer, educator*

Mcpherson
Dickhudt, Gene Robert (Joe Dickhudt) *electrical engineer, college professor*

Overland Park
Karmeier, Delbert Fred *engineer, consultant, realtor*

Wichita
Emami, Tooran *electrical engineer, researcher*
McKee, George Moffitt, Jr. *retired civil engineer consultant*
Wilhelm, William Jean *civil engineering educator*

KENTUCKY

Campton
Drake, David Lee *electronics engineer*

Georgetown
Caroland, William Bourne *structural engineer*

Lexington
Baker, Merl *engineering educator*
Boone, Megan E. *engineer, director*
Brock, Louis Milton, Jr. *engineering educator, researcher*
Donohue, Kevin D. *computer engineer, educator*
Drake, Vaughn Paris, Jr. *electrical engineer*
Holsapple, Clyde Warren *decision and information systems educator*
Male, Alan Thomas *engineering educator, foundation administrator*

Louisville
Kantardzic, Mehmed M. *engineering educator*
Tran, Long Trieu *industrial engineer*

Murray
Ferreyra, Rafael Andres *agricultural and biological engineer, consultant, researcher*

LOUISIANA

Amite
Parish, Richard Lee *engineer, consultant*

Baton Rouge
Arman, Ara *civil engineering educator, dean*
Barbato, Michele *engineering educator*
Bengtson, Richard Lee *agricultural engineer, educator*
Bernhard, James M., Jr. *engineering executive*
Chen, Peter Pin-Shan *engineering, computer science educator, data processing executive*
Collier, John Robert *chemical engineer, educator*
Feldman, Martin *engineering educator*
Ferraioli, Brian K. *engineering executive*
Harris, Andres *manager*
Khonsari, Michael M. *mechanical engineering educator*
Lacy, Fred *engineering educator*
Pike, Ralph Webster *chemical engineer, educator, academic administrator*
Raghavendra, Amar *systems engineer*
Singh, Vijay Pal *civil engineer*
Tumay, Mehmet Taner *geotechnical engineering educator, researcher, consultant*
Valsaraj, Kalliat Thazhathuveetil *chemical engineering educator*
Woods, R. Clive *electrical engineer, educator*

Dubach
Straughan, William Thomas *structural engineering consultant, educator*

Harvey
Simon, Keith R. *safety engineer, petroleum engineer, radio personality*

Lafayette
Boukadi, Fathi Hamda *petroleum engineer, researcher*
Farshad, Fred F. *engineering educator*
Marshak, Alan Howard *electrical engineer, educator*

Lake Charles
Levingston, Ernest Lee *engineering company executive*

Metairie
Lourie, David E. *civil engineer, consultant*
Nicoladis, Michael F. *engineering company executive*

New Orleans
Colletti, Janet Sarradet *engineering educator*
Lannes, William Joseph III *electrical engineer*
Perrons, Robert K. *engineer, researcher*
Qiu, Meikang *engineering educator*

Ruston
Davis, Despina *engineering educator*
Fang, Ji *electrical engineer*
Genov, Dentcho Angelov *engineering educator*
Saber, Aziz *engineering educator*
Wasiuddin, Nazimuddin Mohammad *engineering educator*

Slidell
Stuart, Charles Edward *electrical engineer, oceanographer*
Tewell, Joseph Robert, Jr. *retired electrical engineer*

MAINE

Falmouth
Rohsenow, Warren Max *retired mechanical engineer, educator*

Fryeburg
Crane, Robert Kendall *engineering educator, researcher, consultant*

Oquossoc
Hughes, William Frank *mechanical and electrical engineering educator*

Orono
Abedi, Ali *engineering educator*
Dewhurst, Timothy Bruce *mechanical engineer educator*
Jianhui, Yue *computer engineer, researcher*

Portland
Edwards, Matthew William *systems engineer*

Waterville
Laurence, Robert Lionel *chemical engineering professor*

MARYLAND

Aberdeen Proving Ground
VanLandingham, Mark Reed *materials engineer*

Adelphi
Nguyen, Lam Huy *electronics engineer*

Annapolis
Criscimagna, Ned Henry *engineer*
Dawson, Thomas Henry *engineering educator*
Johnson, Bruce *engineering educator*
Rogers, David Freeman *aerospace engineering educator*
Salem, Thomas Eric *electrical engineer, educator*
Weese, John Augustus *retired mechanical engineer*

Baltimore
Acharya, Soumyadipta *engineer, researcher, physician, researcher, educator*
Alarcon, Cesar L *electrical engineer*
Amory, Reginald L. *civil engineer, educator*
Bardhan, Tridip K. *engineering educator, researcher*
Berkelman, Peter John *robotics researcher*
Carmi, Shlomo *mechanical engineering educator, research scientist*
Dalrymple, Robert Anthony III *civil engineering educator*
Ekekwe, Ndubuisi *electronics engineer, researcher*
Goldstein, Jerri Irene *industrial engineer*
Han, Jaeho *electrical engineer, researcher*
Jones, Nicholas Patrick *engineering educator*
Kang, Jin U. *engineering educator*
Katz, Joseph Louis *chemical engineer, educator*
Klimantov, Alexius George *engineering executive*
Kuo, Scot C. *engineering educator*
Lemer, Andrew Charles *engineer, economist*
Levchenko, Andre *biomedical engineer, educator*
Nathanson, Harvey Charles *electrical engineer*
Zhu, Weidong *engineering educator*

Beltsville
Wigand, Robert Charles, Jr. *retired civil engineer, retired aerospace engineer*

Bethesda
Burdeshaw, William Brooksbank *engineering executive*
Fields, Stephen Timothy *environmental engineer*
Kutemeyer, Peter Martin *industrial engineering executive*
Larsen-Basse, Jorn *mechanical and materials engineering educator, researcher, consultant*
Saville, Thorndike, Jr. *coastal engineer*

Boyds
Beach, Jeffrey E. *engineering educator, consultant*

Chevy Chase
Cheng, David Keun *engineering educator*
Lebow, Irwin Leon *communications engineering consultant*
Rockwell, Theodore *nuclear engineer*
Short, Steve Eugene *engineer*

College Park
Anderson, John David, Jr. *aerospace engineer*
Awad, Ehab *electronics engineer, computer engineer, researcher*
Barbe, David Franklin *electrical engineer, educator*
Chopra, Nikhil *systems engineer, researcher*
Farvardin, Nariman *engineering educator*
Gopalan, Gaurav *aerospace engineer, researcher*
Granatstein, Victor Lawrence *electrical engineer, educator*
Gupta, Ashwani Kumar *mechanical engineering educator*
Kang, Kyeongpyo *transportation engineer, researcher*
Levine, William Silver *electrical engineer, educator*
Mesgarani, Nima *electrical engineer, researcher*
Newcomb, Robert Wayne *electrical engineer, educator*
O'Shea, Patrick Gerard *engineering educator, department chairman*
Taylor, Leonard Stuart *engineering educator, consultant*
Tits, Andre Leon *electrical engineering educator*

Columbia
Straja, Sorin Radu *chemical engineer, mathematician, computer programmer*

Crofton
Laurenson, Robert Mark *mechanical engineer*
Vranish, John Michael *electrical engineer, researcher*

Fort Washington
Caveny, Leonard Hugh *mechanical engineer, aerospace scientist, consultant*

Gaithersburg
Cookson, Alan Howard *electrical engineer, researcher*
Fong, Jeffrey Tse-Wei *mechanical engineer*
LaVan, David *engineering executive*
Levine, Robert Sidney *retired chemical engineer*
Nedzelnitsky, Victor *electrical engineer, researcher*
Song, Junfeng John *engineer, researcher*
Wright, Richard Newport III *retired engineering executive, engineering educator*

Greenbelt
Amato, Deborah Douglass *aerospace engineer*
Ericsson, Aprille Joy *aerospace engineer*
Ferguson, Frank Thomas *chemical engineer*
Reupke, William Albert *engineer*
Rogers, Edward William *engineering company executive*

Hagerstown
Ksienski, Aharon Arthur *retired electrical engineer*

Hanover
Haque, Mohammed Nazmul *environmental engineer, researcher*

Kensington
Freeman, Ernest Robert *retired engineering executive*

La Plata
Zinn, Michael Wallace *aerospace engineer*

Lanham
Cheng, Jian-Yu *mechanical engineer, researcher, application developer*

Laurel
Biermann, Paul Joseph *materials engineer*
Eaton, Alvin Ralph, Jr. *aeronautical and systems engineer, applied physics executive*
Hudson, Patrick Jay *engineer, educator*
Land, Henry Bruce III *electronics engineer, researcher*
Levitt, Gerald Steven *engineering executive*
Weerackody, Vijitha *electrical engineer, researcher*

Linthicum
Metzel, Alan Barry *manufacturing engineer*

Linthicum Heights
Skillman, William Alfred *consulting engineering executive*

Patuxent River
Stroup, Darryl Ray *systems engineer*

Potomac
Williams, Peter MacLellan *nuclear engineer*

Queenstown
Corn, Morton *environmental engineer, educator*

Reisterstown
Broadbent, J. Streett *engineering executive*

Rockville
Abel, Dorothy B. *biomedical engineer*
Ashar, Hansraj G. *structural engineer, nuclear regulator*
McDonald, Capers Walter *biomedical engineer, manufacturing executive, entrepreneur, educator*
Seagle, Edgar Franklin *environmental engineer, consultant*

Silver Spring
Kainz, Wolfgang *electrical engineer*
Koltnow, Peter Gregory *engineer, consultant*
Mok, Carson Kwok-Chi *structural engineer*
Scipio, L. Albert, II, (Louis Albert Scipio II) *retired aerospace science engineering educator, historian*
Shalowitz, Erwin Emmanuel *civil engineer*
Smith, Michael Bryan *civil engineer*

Towson
Huang, Joseph Chen-Huan *civil engineer*

Westminster
Konigsberg, Robert Lee *retired electrical engineer*

MASSACHUSETTS

Acton
Hicks, Walter Joseph *electrical engineer*
Shah, Syed Faisal Ali *communications engineer*

Amherst
Franks, Lewis E. *electrical and computer engineering educator, researcher*
Ni, Daiheng *engineering educator*
Swift, Calvin Thomas *electrical and computer engineering educator*

Andover
Jakes, William Chester *electrical engineer*

Ashland
Sherr, Evan A. *biomedical engineer, consultant*

Auburndale
Drake, Elisabeth Mertz *chemical engineer, consultant*
Mark, Melvin *mechanical engineering educator, consultant*

Bedford
Greiner, Helen *mechanical engineer*
Jelalian, Albert V. *electrical engineer*

Belmont
Merrill, Edward Wilson *chemical engineering professor*

Billerica
Choi, Yong-Seok *device and materials scientist*
KuLesza, Frank William *chemical engineer*
Oluwole, Oluwayemisi Oluwi *chemical engineer, researcher*
Wu, Xuanhui *electrical engineer*

Bolton
Devgun, Jas S. *environmental engineer*

Boston
Adams, George Gabriel *mechanical engineering educator*
Baillieul, John Brouard *aerospace engineering and applied mathematics educator*
Beranek, Leo Leroy *acoustical engineer, consultant*
Caracoglia, Luca *civil engineer, educator*
De Luca, Carlo John *biomedical engineer, educator*
Director, Stephen William *electrical and computer engineering educator, academic administrator*
Frank-Kamenetskii, Maxim D. *biomedical engineer*
Fraser, Donald C. *engineering executive, educator*
Grenquist, Scott Anthony Francis *physicist, engineer*
Heimann, David Isidore *computer engineer, educator*
Jain, Rakesh K. *chemical engineering and tumor biology educator*
Knepper, Ronald William *computer engineer, educator*

Kowalski, Gregory J. *engineering educator, researcher*
Langer, Robert Martin *retired chemical engineering company executive, consultant*
Livingston, Frederic Holleyman *mechanical engineer*
Moore, Richard Lawrence *structural engineer, consultant*
Moustakas, Theodore D. *engineering educator, researcher*
Pierce, Allan Dale *engineering educator, researcher, editor*
Rappaport, Carey Milford *electrical engineering educator*
Sasani, Mehrdad *engineering educator*
Teich, Malvin Carl *electrical engineering educator*

Brookline
Pal, Uday B. *engineering educator, consultant*

Burlington
Chen, Chau-Chyun *chemical engineer*
Yang, Ming *engineering company executive, researcher*

Buzzards Bay
DiMassa, Diane D. *engineering educator*

Cambridge
Apostolakis, George E. *engineering educator, researcher*
Argon, Ali Suphi *mechanical engineering educator*
Armstrong, Robert C. *chemical engineer, educator*
Barnhart, Cynthia *engineering educator, researcher*
Battin, Richard Horace *aeronautical engineer*
Beér, János Miklós *engineering educator*
Belcher, Angela *engineering educator*
Berzin, Isaac *chemical engineer*
Bleris, Leonidas *electrical engineer, researcher*
Blumberg, Paul N. *mechanical engineer, consultant*
Bochicchio, James *project coordinator*
Bulovic, Vladimir *engineering educator*
Caplice, Christopher *engineering educator*
Clarke, David R. *materials engineer*
Colton, Clark Kenneth *chemical engineering professor*
Covert, Eugene Edzards *aerospace engineer, aeronautics professor*
Crandall, Stephen Harry *engineering educator*
de Neufville, Richard Lawrence *engineering educator*
de Weck, Oliver *engineering educator, researcher*
Dewey, Clarence Forbes, Jr. *engineering educator*
Drela, Mark *aeronautical engineer, educator*
Dugundji, John *aeronautical engineer*
Eagleson, Peter Sturges *civil and environmental engineer, educator*
Eltahir, Elfatih A.B. *engineering educator*
Fay, James Alan *mechanical engineering educator*
Flemings, Merton Corson *engineering educator, materials scientist*
Frey, Daniel D. *engineering educator, researcher*
Fujimoto, James G. *electrical engineering educator*
Goudey, Clifford A. *marine engineer, director*
Griffith(-Cima), Linda G. *biomedical and chemical engineer*
Hale, Patrick C. *engineering educator, director*
Hansen, Kent Forrest *nuclear engineering educator*
Hastings, Daniel E. *aeronautical engineer, educator*
Hunter, Ian W. *engineering educator, researcher*
Jensen, Klavs Flemming *chemical engineering educator*
Kazimi, Mujid Suliman *nuclear engineer, educator*
Kolachalama, Vijaya B. *mechanical engineer*
Ladd, Charles Cushing III *civil engineer, educator*
Langer, Robert Samuel, Jr. *chemical and biomedical engineering educator*
Markey, Winston Roscoe *aeronautical engineering educator*
McGarry, Frederick Jerome *civil engineering educator*
Milgram, Jerome H. *retired marine and ocean engineer, educator*
Moavenzadeh, Fred *engineering educator*
Narayanamurti, Venkatesh *engineering educator, physics professor*
Narayanamurti, Venkatesh *engineering professor, former dean*
Newman, Dava Jean *aerospace engineering educator, director*
Ochsendorf, John *structural engineer, educator*
Ortiz, Christine *engineering educator*
Penfield, Paul Livingstone, Jr. *electrical engineering educator*
Probstein, Ronald Filmore *mechanical engineering educator*
Rogers, Peter Phillips *environmental engineer, educator, urban planner*
Roos, Daniel *engineering educator*
Rose, Robert Michael *materials engineering educator*
Ruina, Jack Philip *electrical engineer, educator*
Russell, Kenneth Calvin *metallurgical engineering educator*
Samson, Leona D. *biological engineering educator, research center director*
Sankaranarayananan, Subramanian Krs *chemical engineer, researcher*
Schiller, Peter Harkai *biomedical engineering and physics educator*
Shapiro, Jeffrey Howard *electrical engineering professor, consultant*
Smida, Besma *engineering educator, researcher*
Smith, Amy B. *mechanical engineer, educator*
Smith, Henry Ignatius *engineering educator*
Smith, Kenneth Alan *chemical engineer, educator*
Staelin, David Hudson *electrical engineering educator, consultant*
Stevens, Kenneth Noble *electrical engineer, educator*
Suh, Nam Pyo *mechanical engineering educator*
Suresh, Subra *materials engineer, educator*
Sussman, Joseph *engineering educator, researcher*
Todreas, Neil Emmanuel *nuclear engineering educator*
Tomita, Masaru *engineering educator, researcher*
Triantafyllou, Michael Stefanos *engineering educator*
Trilling, Leon *aeronautical engineering educator*
Tsitsiklis, John N. *electrical engineering and computer science educator*
Ungar, Eric Edward *mechanical engineer*
Vander Velde, Wallace Earl *aeronautical and astronautical engineering educator*
White, David Calvin *electrical engineer, educator, energy executive, consultant*
Whitman, Robert Van Duyne *civil engineer, educator*
Williams, James Henry, Jr. *mechanical engineer, educator, consultant*
Wilson, David Gordon *mechanical engineering educator*
Wuensch, Bernhardt John *ceramic engineering educator*
Young, Laurence Retman *biomedical engineer, educator*
Zue, Victor W. *engineering educator*

Carlisle
Drew, Philip Garfield *retired engineering company executive, consultant*

Charlestown
Nahmias, Yaakov *biomedical engineer*
Ntziachristos, Vasilis *radiology, bioengineering educator*

Chelmsford
Bayat, Oguz *electrical engineer, educator*
Krishnan, Venkatarama *retired engineering professor*

Concord
Davidson, Frank Paul *retired macroengineer, retired lawyer*
Fowler, Charles Albert *electronics engineer*
Villers, Philippe *mechanical engineer*

Dedham
Ghosh, Asish *control engineer*

Fitchburg
Ifrim, Costin *electrical engineer, director*

Framingham
Crossley, Frank Alphonso *retired metallurgical engineer*

Holbrook
Crandlemere, Robert Wayne *engineering executive*

Hopkinton
Liang, Jin *engineer, consultant*

Hudson
Emer, Joel *computer engineer, educator*

Lexington
Bailey, Fred Coolidge *retired engineering consulting company executive*
Beusch, John Ulrich *engineer, researcher*
Brookner, Eli *electrical engineer*
Bussgang, Julian Jakub *electronics engineer, consultant*
Dinneen, Gerald Paul *electrical engineer, retired federal official*
Freed, Charles *engineering consultant, researcher*
Keicher, William Eugene *electrical engineer*
Kerekes, John Paul *electrical engineer*
Morrow, Walter Edwin, Jr. *electrical engineer, lab administrator*
Sheridan, Thomas Brown *mechanical engineering and applied psychology educator, researcher, consultant*
Zayhowski, John J. *electrical engineer, researcher*

Longmeadow
Lemnios, Andrew Zachery *aerospace engineer, educator, researcher*

Lowell
Kim, Byungki *engineering educator*
Luo, Yan *engineering educator*
Weitzen, Jay Allen *engineering educator*

Lynn
Chow, Humphrey Wai *mechanical engineer*

Marion
Landers, Donald Francis *mechanical engineer*

Marlborough
Bennett, C. Leonard *electrical engineer*

Maynard
Lindsay, Leslie *packaging engineer*

Medford
Abriola, Linda Marie *civil and environmental engineer*
Chapra, Steven Christopher *engineering educator, endowed chair*
Yi, Hyunmin *chemical engineer, educator*

Medway
Hoag, David Garratt *retired aerospace engineer*

Nantucket
Saperstein, Lee Waldo *mining engineering educator*

Natick
Berglund, Larry Glenn *mechanical engineer, educator*
Latanision, Ronald Michael *materials engineer*
Pokorny, Joseph Wenceslaus III *engineer*

Newton
Xiong, Renqiang *mechanical engineer, researcher*

North Chelmsford
Noto, John *engineering executive*

North Dartmouth
Law, Frederick Masom *structural engineering firm executive, educator*

Northampton
Ellis, Glenn W. *engineering educator*

Northborough
Lee, Sugjoon Joon *textile engineer, consultant*
Wang, Jun *process engineer, materials scientist*

Norwood
Sheingold, Daniel H. *electrical engineer*

Paxton
Clarke, Edward Nielsen *engineering science educator*

Peabody
Peters, Leo Francis *environmental engineer*

Pittsfield
Feigenbaum, Armand Vallin *systems engineer, information technology executive*
Shammas, Nazih Kheirallah *environmental engineer, consultant, engineering educator*

Reading
Tuttle, David Bauman *electrical engineer*

Shutesbury
Abbott, Douglas Eugene *engineering educator*

Stoughton
Wedig, Christopher P. *environmental engineer*

Swampscott
Kaufman, William Morris *electrical engineer, consultant*

Tewksbury
Faccini, Ernest Carlo *mechanical engineer*

Waltham
Gumpertz, Werner Herbert *structural engineering company executive*

Watertown
Joubert, Raymond Ernest *retired electrical engineer*

Wellesley
Weil, Thomas Alexander *retired electronics engineer*

Westborough
Gionfriddo, Maurice Paul *aeronautical engineer, research and development company executive*
Reza, Shahed *electrical engineer*

Weston
Katz, William Emanuel *retired chemical engineer*
Uhlir, Arthur, Jr. *retired electrical engineer, academic administrator*

Wilmington
Devarajan, Siddharth *electronics engineer*
Lagace, Paul Alfred *aeronautical engineering educator*

Woburn
Serfaty, Daniel *human systems engineer*

Worcester
DiIorio, Alexander L. *biomedical engineer, director*
Katz, Robert Nathan *ceramics engineer, educator*
Wilbur, Leslie Clifford *mechanical engineering educator*
Zalosh, Robert Geoffrey *engineering educator*

Wrentham
Bittenbender, Brad James *safety engineer*

Yarmouth Port
Stott, Thomas Edward, Jr. *retired engineering executive*

MICHIGAN

Allendale
Sun, Wanxiao *remote sensing educator*

Ann Arbor
Adriaens, Peter *environmental engineer, consultant*
Akcasu, Ahmet Ziyaeddin *nuclear engineer, educator*
Becher, William Don *retired electrical engineer, educator, writer*
Bhattacharya, Pallab Kumar *electrical engineering educator, researcher*
Burns, Mark *engineering educator*
Clark, John Alden *mechanical engineering educator*
Curl, Rane Locke *chemical engineering educator, consultant*
England, Anthony Wayne *engineering and science educator, dean*
Friedmann, Peretz Peter *aerospace engineer, educator*
Gibala, Ronald *metallurgical engineering educator*
Gilchrist, Brian E. *engineering educator, department chairman*
Grbic, Anthony *engineering educator*
Greenwood, Donald Theodore *retired aerospace engineering educator*
Hayes, John Patrick *electrical engineering and computer science educator, consultant*
He, Pingan *systems engineer*
Jarrahi, Mona *engineering educator, researcher*
Kozma, Adam *electrical engineer*
Kumon, Ronald Edward *biomedical engineer, researcher*
Kurabayashi, Katsuo *engineering educator*
Lee, John Chaeseung *nuclear engineering educator*
Lee, Juseop *electronics engineer, researcher*
Lyons, Harvey Isaac *mechanical engineering educator*
Martin, David Charles *materials science engineering educator*
Martin, William Russell *nuclear engineering educator*
Merte, Herman, Jr. *mechanical engineering educator*
Meyer, John Frederick *engineering educator*
Munson, David C. *computer engineer, educator, dean*
Parsons, Michael Gene *engineering educator*
Pehlke, Robert Donald *materials and metallurgical engineering educator*
Petrick, Ernest Nicholas *mechanical engineer, researcher*
Powell, Kenneth Grant *aerospace engineering educator*
Saitou, Kazuhiro *engineering educator*
Scott, Norman Ross *electrical engineering educator*
Senior, Thomas Bryan A. *electrical engineering educator, researcher, consultant*
Skerlos, Steven John *engineering educator*
Sobel, Alan *electrical engineer, physicist*
Steel, Duncan Gregory *engineering educator*
Ulsoy, Ali Galip *engineering educator*
Wilson, Richard Christian *engineering firm executive*
Wright, Steven Jay *environmental engineering educator, consultant*
Yagle, Andrew Emil *engineering educator*
Yang, Ralph Tzu-Bow *chemical engineer, educator*
Young, Edwin Harold *chemical and metallurgical engineering educator*
Young, Yin Lu *engineering educator*
Ziff, Robert Michael *engineering educator*

Auburn Hills
Beals, Randy S. *materials engineer*

Berrien Springs
Agoki, George Sammy *engineering educator, director*

Cass City
Reeder, Mike Fredrick *materials engineer, consultant*

Dearborn
Cairns, James Robert *mechanical engineering educator*
Essenmacher, Alan J. *engineering educator, researcher*
Kahveci, Nazli Eylem *electrical engineer, researcher*
Little, Robert Eugene *engineering educator*
Shen, Jie *engineering educator*

Detroit
Battah, Hammam Jamil *civil engineer, utilities executive*
Chou, Clifford Chi Fong *research engineering executive*
Das, Shuvra *engineering educator*
Kummler, Ralph H. *chemical engineer, educator, dean*
Mayeed, Mohammed *engineering educator, researcher*
McWhorter, Sharon Louise *engineering executive, inventor, consultant*
Rathod, Mulchand *mechanical engineering educator*
Rivin, Evgeny (Eugene) I. *engineering educator, researcher, inventor, consultant*
Ssemakula, Mukasa Emmanuel *engineering educator*
Wang, Caisheng *engineering educator*

Dexter
Zhang, Weiming *engineer*

East Lansing
Andersland, Orlando Baldwin *retired engineering educator*
Chan, Christina *chemical engineer, educator*
Cutts, Charles Eugene *retired engineering educator*
Foss, John Frank *mechanical engineering educator*
Goodman, Erik David *engineering educator*
Grotjohn, Timothy Allan *engineering educator*
Mitra, Joydeep *electrical engineer, educator*
Saul, William Edward *engineering educator*

Farmington
Subrahmanyam, Somashekar Ramachandran *mechanical engineer*

Farmington Hills
Hurd, Mary K. *civil engineer, writer*

Flushing
Bain, William David *electronics engineer, writer*

Grosse Pointe Shores
Burke, Thomas Joseph *civil engineer*
Holness, Gordon Victor Rix *engineering executive, mechanical engineer*

Houghton
Aleksandr, Sergeyev *engineering educator*
Lumsdaine, Edward *mechanical engineering educator, dean*
Miskioglu, Ibrahim *engineering educator*
Pandit, Sudhakar Madhavrao *engineering educator*

Jackson
Farooq, Umar *mechanical engineer*

Kalamazoo
Grantner, Janos L. *engineering educator*
Yehia, Sherif Abdel Aziz *civil engineer, educator*

Leland
Soutas-Little, Robert William *mechanical engineer, educator*

Livonia
Uicker, Joseph Bernard *retired engineering company executive*

Madison Heights
Peaslee, Robert Leon *metallurgical engineer, consultant*

Midland
Frank, Timothy Charles *chemical engineer, researcher*
Meister, Bernard John *retired chemical engineer*
Robbins, Lanny Arnold *chemical engineer*

Mount Pleasant
Lee, Roger Y. *engineering educator*
Yelamarthi, Kumar *engineering educator*

Niles
Marshall, Gerald Francis *optical engineer, consultant, physicist*

North Branch
Stevenson, James Laraway *engineering company executive, electronics, computer and communications engineer, educator*

Pontiac
Hampton, Philip Michael *consulting engineering company executive*
Singh, Avinash *mechanical engineer*
Wang, Yucong *engineering executive*

Rochester
Haskell, Richard Edmund *engineering educator*

Royal Oak
Fragomeni, James Mark *mechanical engineer, educator*

Shelby Township
Osuch, Debra K. *environmental engineer*

Southfield
Hettiarachchi, Chamil Hiroshan *civil engineer, educator*
McKeen, Alexander C. *retired engineering executive, foundation administrator*
Sliety, Mazin K. *engineering educator*
Song, Xubin *mechanical engineer, researcher*
Vantsevich, Vladimir V. *engineering educator, director*

Sterling Heights
Radzevich, Stepan Pavlovich *mechanical engineering educator*

Traverse City
Joshi, Ameet Vijay *engineering company executive, director*

Troy
Nefske, Donald Joseph *engineer*
Park, Won Chan *mechanical engineer*

University Center
Byam, Brooks Philip *mechanical engineer, educator*

Warren
Abd Elhamid, Mahmoud Hassan *engineer, researcher*
Caulk, David A. *engineering company executive, researcher*

Wixom
Huff, Alvin Edward *retired engineer*

Ypsilanti
Khan, Zafar U. *engineering educator*
Li, Zhang *engineering educator*

MINNESOTA

Bloomington
Ouyang, Jun *electrical engineer, researcher*

Coleraine
Iwasaki, Iwao *engineering educator*

Eden Prairie
Higgins, Robert Arthur *electrical engineer, educator, consultant*

Fairmont
Wolfgram, Kenneth Charles *retired agricultural engineer*

Lakeville
Setterholm, Jeffrey Miles *systems engineer*

Le Sueur
Yang, Mengyan *chemical engineer, research scientist*

Madison
Husby, Donald Evans *engineering company executive*

Maplewood
Thomas, Cristina Urdaneta *chemical engineer, researcher*

Minneapolis
Anderson, John Edward *mechanical engineering educator*
Avgoustiniatos, Efstathios S. *chemical engineer, educator*
Crouch, Steven L. *mining engineer, dean*
Fletcher, Edward Abraham *engineering educator*
Galambos, Theodore Victor *civil engineer, educator*
Goldstein, Richard Jay *mechanical engineer, educator*
Guzina, Bojan B. *engineering educator*
Johnson, Walter Kline *civil engineer*
Kvalseth, Tarald Oddvar *mechanical engineer, educator*
Lambert, Robert Frank *electrical engineer, educator, consultant*
Mwakabuta, Ndaga Stanslaus *electrical engineer*
Oriani, Richard Anthony *metallurgical engineer, educator*
Parhi, Keshab Kumar *electrical and computer engineering educator*
Pfender, Emil *mechanical engineering educator*
Sidebottom, Charles Benton *engineering executive*
Sparrow, Ephraim Maurice *engineer, educator*
Wollenberg, Bruce Frederick *electrical engineering educator, consultant*
Zapp, Kenneth Michael *engineering educator, department chairman*

North Oaks
Liu, Benjamin Young-hwai *engineering educator*

Plymouth
Kodali, Dharma Rao *engineering educator*

Saint Cloud
Hossain, Md Mahbub *engineering educator*
Petzold, Mark Carl *electrical engineer, educator*

Saint Paul
Greenwood, Stephen John *environmental engineer*
Stibbe, Craig Jule *engineer*

Shoreview
O'Dea, Thomas Joseph *clinical engineer, medical physicist*

Virginia
Blyckert, Judith A. *engineering educator*

Woodbury
Beck, Warren Randall *retired glass technologist*

MISSISSIPPI

Alcorn State
Aceil, Sam *engineering educator*

Biloxi
Brinsmade, Akbar Fairchild *chemical engineering consultant*

Booneville
Hawkins, Ricky Edward *engineering educator*

Hattiesburg
Buchanan, Randy *engineering educator*

Jackson
Blair, William Dodd *engineering educator, director*

Mississippi State
Cannayen, Igathinathane *agricultural engineer, educator*
Eksioglu, Burak *engineering educator*
Rais-Rohani, Masoud *aerospace and engineering mechanics educator*
Silva, Juan Luis *food processing engineer, educator*

Oxford
Costner, Charles Lynn *retired civil engineer*

Pascagoula
Wilkie, Barry James *manufacturing engineer*

Starkville
Eksioglu, Sandra Duni *industrial engineering educator*

University
Cheng, Alexander Hung-Darh *engineering educator, consultant*
Ding, Yan *engineering educator*
Ervin, Elizabeth K. *engineering educator*
Panickar, Praveen *aeronautical engineer, researcher*
Sadana, Ajit *chemical engineer, educator*
Zhang, Yaoxin *engineer, researcher*

Vicksburg
Kuljaca, Ognjen *engineering educator, researcher*
Martin, William A. *environmental engineer, researcher*

MISSOURI

Ballwin
Cornell, William Daniel *mechanical engineer*

Columbia
Creighton, Donald Louis *mechanical engineer, consultant*
Frisby, James Curtis *retired agricultural engineering educator*
Ho, Dominic KC *electrical engineering educator*
Islam, Naz E. *engineering educator, researcher*
Palaniappan, Kannappan *engineering educator*
Pringle, Oran Allan *mechanical and aerospace engineering educator*
Schuder, John Claude *retired biomedical engineer, educator*

Florissant
Tomazi, George Donald *retired electrical engineer*

Fulton
Hinchie, William Jules *nuclear engineer, director*

Kansas City
Acheson, Allen Morrow *retired engineering executive*
Eick, John David *materials engineer, educator*
Mathur, Naresh Chandra *retired engineering educator*

Raymore
Fairlie, Jeffrey Scott *engineering company executive*

Rolla
Bai, Baojun *engineering educator*
Banerjee, Arindam *engineering educator*
Cheng, Franklin Yih *civil engineering educator*
Look, Dwight Chester, Jr. *mechanical engineering educator, researcher*
Mishra, Rajiv Sharan *metallurgical engineer, educator*
Venayagamoorthy, Ganesh Kumar *electrical engineer, educator*
Xu, Bin *civil engineering researcher, educator*
Zawodniok, Maciej Jan *engineering educator*

Saint Louis
Byrnes, Christopher Ian *engineering educator*
Cosner, Raymond Robert *aeronautical engineer*
Dreifke, Gerald Edmond *electrical engineering educator*
Dudukovic, Milorad P. *chemical engineering educator, consultant*
Dugan, Timothy J. *electrical engineer, rancher*
Freeman, Terrence Lyle *engineering educator, consultant*
Groneck, Daniel *aerospace engineer*
Haas, Daniel Louis *structural engineer*
Izuchukwu, John Ifeanyichukwu *industrial and mechanical engineer*
Khomami, Bamin *chemical engineer, educator*
Oh, Jung Hun *computer engineer*
Orton, George Frederick *aerospace engineer*
Peters, David Allen *mechanical engineering educator, consultant*
Shrauner, Barbara Wayne Abraham *electrical engineer, educator*
Sutera, Salvatore Philip *mechanical engineer, educator*

Saint Peters
Dubé, George *optical equipment company executive*

Springfield
Dinwiddie, Keith E. *industrial engineer*
Newman, Earl E. *transportation engineer, consultant*

University City
Winter, David Ferdinand *electrical engineering educator, consultant*

MONTANA

Bozeman
Al-Kaisy, Ahmed *engineering educator, researcher*
Cokelet, Giles Roy *biomedical engineering educator*
McLeod, Bruce Royal *electrical engineering educator, consultant*
Sanks, Robert Leland *environmental engineer, retired educator*
Stanislao, Joseph *engineering educator, consultant*

Great Falls
Walker, Leland Jasper *civil engineer*

Harlem
Brekke, Alan Lee *industrial engineer*

Livingston
Schell, William Joseph, IV, *industrial engineer*

Pony
Anderson, Richard Ernest *agricultural engineer, consultant, rancher*

NEBRASKA

Hastings
Gompert, Daniel *electronics engineer, consultant*

Kimball
Kinnison, Daniel E. *manufacturing engineer*

Lincoln
Asgarpoor, Sohrab *engineering educator*
Bahar, Ezekiel *electrical engineering educator*
Edison, Allen Ray *electrical engineer, educator*
Edwards, Donald Mervin *systems engineer, educator, dean*
Jiang, Hong *engineering educator, researcher*
Pao, Yen-Ching *engineering educator, consultant*
Splinter, William Eldon *agricultural engineering educator*
Timm, Delmar C. *engineering educator, consultant*
Woollam, John Arthur *electrical engineering educator, physics professor*
Zaghloul, Abdel Rahman M. *electrical engineering educator, consultant, entrepreneur*

Omaha
Foster, Edward Terence, Jr. *engineering and technology educator, consultant*
Olney, Gisele Celeste *engineering educator, consultant*
Tunnicliff, David George *retired civil engineer*

NEVADA

Boulder City
Wyman, Richard Vaughn *engineering educator, company executive*

Dayton
Clements, Linda L. *innovator materials engineer, educator, journalist*

Henderson
Huang, Eugene Yuching *civil engineer, educator*
Wennerstrom, Arthur John *aeronautical engineer*

Incline Village
Thompson, David Alfred *industrial engineer*

Las Vegas
Culp, Gordon Louis *consulting engineer, management consultant*
Das, Biswajit *electrical engineer, educator*
Graebel, William Paul *engineering educator*
Massier, Paul Ferdinand *mechanical engineer*
Messenger, George Clement *engineering executive, consultant*
Neumann, Edward Schreiber *transportation engineering educator*
Palmieri, Frederick William *structural engineer*
Ramos, Albert A. *electrical engineer*
Reynolds, Douglas D. *mechanical engineer, educator*
Sanders, Charlotta Elisabeth *nuclear engineer, educator*
Singh, Sahjendra Narain *electrical engineering educator, researcher*

Minden
Yu, John Junyao *mechanical engineer, researcher*

North Las Vegas
Ackerman, Allan Joesph *computer engineer, educator*

Reno
Batchman, Theodore Earl *electrical engineering educator, researcher*
Carr, James Russell *engineering educator*
Coronella, Charles J. *chemical engineer, educator*
Danko, George *engineering educator*
Evrenosoglu, Cansin Yaman *electrical engineer, educator*
Fadali, Mohammed Sami *engineering educator*
Fuerstenau, M(aurice) C(lark) *metallurgical engineer*
Gunes, Mehmet H *engineering educator*
Kleppe, John Arthur *electrical engineer, educator, company executive*

Sparks
Lagasse, Bruce Kenneth *retired structural engineer*
Yuhara, Makoto *mechanical engineer*

NEW HAMPSHIRE

Durham
Ray, Ram Lakhan *civil engineer*
Thein, May-Win L. *mechanical engineer, educator*
White, Christopher *engineering educator*

Farmington
Panek, William Dominick *systems engineer executive*

Hanover
Garmire, Elsa Meints *electrical engineering educator, consultant*
Graves, Robert John *industrial engineering educator*
Queneau, Paul Etienne *retired metallurgical engineering educator*

Keene
Welkowitz, Walter *biomedical engineer, educator*

Lyme
Phetteplace, Gary *mechanical engineer*

Manchester
Kamen, Dean *biomedical engineer*

Merrimack
Yannone, Ronald Matthew *systems engineer, researcher*

Newmarket
McHose, Andre H. *industrial engineer*

Warner
Hunt, Everett Clair *engineering educator, researcher, consultant*

NEW JERSEY

Basking Ridge
Kim, Doh-Suk *electronics engineer*

Bedminster
David, Edward Emil, Jr. *electrical engineer, executive, management consultant*
Drewry, Don Neal *fire protection engineer*

Bridgewater
Dar, Yadunandan Lal *engineer*

Cherry Hill
Batterman, Steven Charles *engineering mechanics and bioengineering professor, consultant*
Fuentevilla, Manuel Edward *chemical engineer*

Cliffside Park
Samardzic, Veljko *engineering company executive, researcher*

Clifton
Shi, Qun *engineer*

Cranford
Hrycak, Peter *retired engineering educator*

East Brunswick
Daniel, Charles Timothy *transportation engineer, consultant*

Florham Park
O'Reilly, Gerard P. *engineering company executive*

Fort Monmouth
Perlman, Barry Stuart *electrical engineer, researcher, director*
Tse, Elizabeth Suet Hing *computer research engineer*

Freehold
Christ, Duane Marland *retired computer systems engineer*

Glassboro
Pillay, Gautam *chemical engineer, chemist, academic administrator*
Rusu, Adrian *engineering educator, director*
Savelski, Mariano J. *chemical engineer, educator*
Slater, C. Stewart *chemical engineering educator*

Highland Park
Spencer, Herbert Harry *structural engineer, researcher, computer analyst*

Hillsborough
Sun, Wei *electrical engineer*

Hoboken
Chassapis, Constantin *mechanical engineer, educator*
Fallah, M. Hosein *engineering management educator*
Fisher, Frank Thomas *engineering educator*
Griskey, Richard George *chemical engineering professor*
Rothberg, Gerald M. *materials engineer, educator*
Savitsky, Daniel *retired structural engineer, educator*
Wakeman, Thomas Herbert III *civil engineer, regional administrator*
Xing, Yiping *electrical engineer, researcher*

Holmdel
Foschini, Gerard J. *electrical engineer*
Lang, Howard Lawrence *electrical engineer*

Jackson
Tague, Charles Francis *retired engineering, real estate and construction company executive*

Jersey City
Wolchuk, Roman *engineering educator*

Kinnelon
Haller, Charles Edward *engineer, consultant*

Lake Hopatcong
Upadhya, Hiran S. *environmental engineer*

Little Egg Harbor Township
Hoden, Virginia *technology educator*

Livingston
Daman, Ernest Ludwig *mechanical engineer*

Mahwah
Rakotobe-Joel, Thierry *engineering educator, researcher, executive director*

Manasquan
Abate, John E. *electrical engineer, consultant*

Manchester
Madan, Deepak S. *engineering executive*

Matawan
Gemelos, Michael S. *engineer, consultant*

Mays Landing
Taggart, James Jeffrey *engineering educator*

Milltown
Liebowitz, Larry Arnold *electroceramics materials engineer*

Montclair
Eager, George Sidney, Jr. *electrical engineer, engineering executive*

Moorestown
Mulligan, James Christopher *safety and environmental engineer and manager*

Morris Plains
Bennett, John Charles *former engineering and construction executive*

Morristown
Kittelberger, Larry E. *engineering executive*
Lieberman, Lester Zane *engineering company executive*
Personick, Stewart David *electrical engineer*

New Brunswick
Awan, Ahmad Noor *civil engineer*
Jaluria, Yogesh *mechanical engineering educator, department chairman*
Weng, George Jueng-Cious *engineering educator*

Newark
Armenante, Piero M. *chemical engineering educator*
Aubry, Nadine Nina *mechanical engineering educator*
Bar-Ness, Yeheskel *electrical engineer, educator*
Bilgili, Ecevit Atalay *chemical engineer, researcher, assistant professor*
Brukh, Roman *engineer, educator, researcher*
Dhawan, Atam Prakash *engineering educator, dean*
Fleishman, Gregory D. *engineering educator*
Friedland, Bernard *electrical engineer, educator*
Hanesian, Deran *chemical engineer, environmental scientist, consultant, educator*
Marhaba, Taha Farouk *engineering educator*
Mendonca, David *engineering educator*
Rao, I. Joga *mechanical engineer, educator*
Rosato, Anthony Dominick *mechanical engineer, educator*
Saadeghvaziri, Mohamad Ala *civil engineering educator*
Spillers, William Russell *civil engineering educator*
Zhou, Mengchu *engineering educator*
Ziavras, Sotirios George *computer and electrical engineer, educator*

North Brunswick
Frenkiel, Richard Henry *retired systems engineer, consultant*
Marszalek, Wieslaw *electrical engineering educator*

Oakland
Azar, Fred S. *biomedical engineer, strategic opportunities researcher*

Ocean
Reich, Bernard *communications engineer*

Parsippany
Theiss, Richard Edward *electrical engineer, applications engineer*

Passaic
Lindholm, Clifford Falstrom, II, *engineering executive, mayor*

Pennington
Zhang, Hong (Rick) *design engineer, researcher*

Piscataway
Balaguru, Perumalsamy *civil engineering educator*
Baykal-Gursoy, Melike *engineering educator*
Cosandey, Frederic *engineering educator, researcher*
Ierapetritou, Marianthi G. *engineering educator*
Lacatus, Catalin *communications engineer*
Mazurek, Monica Ann *engineering educator*
Ozel, Tugrul *engineering educator, researcher*
Vieth, Wolf Randolph *chemical engineering educator*

Princeton
Billington, David Perkins *civil engineering educator*
Debenedetti, Pablo Gaston *chemical engineering professor*
Desai, Kalpit Vikrambhai *biomedical engineer, researcher*
Gillham, John Kinsey *chemical engineering professor*
Glassman, Irvin *mechanical and aeronautical engineering educator, consultant*
Gmachl, Claire *electrical engineer, educator*
Lam, Sau-Hai (Harvey) *aeronautical engineering educator*
Lechner, Bernard Joseph *consulting electrical engineer*
Leonard, Naomi Ehrich *aerospace engineer, educator*
Liu, Bede *electrical engineering educator*
Poor, Harold Vincent *engineering educator*
Powell, Warren B. *engineering educator*
Prevost, Jean Herve *civil engineer, educator*
Russel, William Bailey *engineering educator*
Soboyejo, Winston Oluwole *materials engineering educator, researcher*
Song, Zhen *electrical engineer, researcher*
Stengel, Robert Frank *engineering and applied science educator*
Tsui, Daniel C. *electrical engineer, physicist*
VanMarcke, Erik Hector *civil engineer, educator*
Wei, James *chemical engineering professor, academic dean*

Princeton Junction
Mandel, Andrea Sue *packaging engineer*
Vahaviolos, Sotirios John *electrical engineer, researcher, engineering executive*

Rahway
Truppo, Matthew David *biochemical engineer, researcher*

Red Bank
Kazovsky, Leonid Gregory *electrical engineer, educator*

Ridgewood
Farrell, Gregory Alan *biomedical engineer*

Sea Bright
Plummer, Dirk Arnold *chemical, electrical, and electronics engineer*

Short Hills
Wharton, Lennard *engineering company executive*

Somerset
Armstrong, David Francis *environmental engineer, consultant*

Somerville
Sivanesan, Sivaruban *mechanical engineer*

South Plainfield
Kennedy, John William *engineering company executive*

Summit
Fukui, Hatsuaki *retired electrical engineer, art historian*

Rosensweig, Ronald Ellis *chemical engineer, consultant*

Swedesboro
Lovell, Theodore *electrical engineer, consultant*

Teaneck
Ehrlich, Ira Robert *mechanical engineering consultant*
Reinish, Gloria Brooks *electrical engineer, educator*
Tan, Alfredo Cheng *engineering educator, director*

Titusville
Cooper, Paul *retired mechanical engineer, director, researcher*

Trenton
Barry, Robert Christopher *environmental engineer*
Mohr, Daniel Reed *electronics engineer*

Union
Newman, Stephen Alexander *chemical engineer*

Voorhees
Litman, Bernard *electrical engineer, consultant*
Schneider, Orren *environmental engineer, researcher*
Siskin, Edward Joseph *engineering and construction company executive*

Watchung
Michaelis, Paul Charles *engineering physicist executive*

Wayne
Geiger, David E. *engineer*

West New York
Gruenberg, Elliot Lewis *electronics engineer and company executive*

Westfield
Bhagat, Phiroz Maneck *mechanical engineer*

Whippany
Ascione, Al Neil *electrical engineer, educator*

NEW MEXICO

Albuquerque
Anderson, Lawrence Keith *electrical engineer, consultant*
Andrews, Jonathan R. *electrical engineer, researcher*
Ardelean, Emil Valentin *mechanical engineer, researcher*
Baum, Carl Edward *electrical engineer, researcher*
Clark, Arthur Joseph, Jr. *mechanical engineer, retired electrical engineer*
Dorato, Peter *electrical and computer engineering educator*
Efremov, Anatoly Ivanovich *mechanical engineer, educator*
Hall, Jerome William *research engineering educator*
Hulsbos, Cornie Leonard *civil engineering educator*
Jayaweera, Sudharman K. *engineering educator, researcher*
Vorobieff, Peter Vladimirovich *mechanical engineer, researcher*

Cerrillos
Lutz, Raymond Price *retired industrial engineer, educator*

Espanola
Fangyang, Shen *engineering educator*

Kirtland AFB
Pham, Khanh Dai *aerospace engineer, researcher*

Las Cruces
Ford, Clarence Quentin *mechanical engineer, educator*
Genin, Joseph *engineering educator, researcher*
Jauregui, David Villegas *civil engineer, educator*
Long, Richard Louis, Jr. *chemical engineer, educator*
Thode, Edward Frederick *chemical engineer, educator*
Zhang, Jie *engineering educator*

Las Vegas
Gallegos, Gil Roman *engineering educator*

Los Alamos
Dudziak, Donald John *nuclear engineer, educator*
Souto, Francisco Javier *nuclear engineer, researcher*
Stoddard, Stephen Davidson *ceramics engineer, retired state senator*

Mesilla Park
Baker, Kevin D. *agricultural engineer*

Placitas
Hidy, George Martel *chemical engineer, engineering executive*

Rio Rancho
Ives, John Milton *retired engineer*

Roswell
Sutton, Ferron *engineering educator*

Santa Fe
Kaman, Helen S. *retired aerospace engineer, artist*
Kaufman, Morris I. *mechanical engineer*
Morrison, Malcolm Cameron *engineering management professional*

Socorro
Deng, Baolin *environmental engineering educator*

Truth Or Consequences
Lederer, John Martin *retired aeronautical engineer*

NEW YORK

Albany
Fanuele, Frank John *engineering executive, electrical engineer*
Kaloyeros, Alain Elie *engineering educator, researcher*
Roy, Rob J. *biomedical engineer, anesthesiologist, educator*

Alfred
Jonchhe, Yogendra B. *mechanical engineer, educator*
Williams, John *engineering educator*

Amherst
Shaw, David Tai-Ko *electrical and computer engineering educator, academic administrator*

Bethpage
Conti, James Joseph *retired chemical engineer, educator*

Big Flats
Orsillo, James Edward *computer engineer, information technology executive*

Binghamton
Catalano, George Dominic *engineering educator*
Fowler, Mark L. *electrical engineer, educator*

Brewster
Ganguly, Adrish *materials engineer, researcher*
Nadel, Norman Allen *civil engineer*

Briarcliff Manor
Cavalcanti, Dave Alberto Tavares *electrical engineer*

Brockport
Anand, Vishal *engineering educator*

Bronx
Dunne, Kathleen Anne *structural engineer, educator*

Bronxville
Longobardo, Guy *biomedical engineer, consultant*

Brooklyn
Armenakas, Anthony Emmanuel *aerospace engineering educator*
Behzadan, Amir H. *engineering educator*
Birenbaum, Leo *retired engineering educator*
Daniels, Ellen Taxier *electrical advisor, computer engineer, educator*
Parlamis, Michael Frank *civil engineer, construction executive*
Tsygan, Leonid Iosifovich *civil engineer, writer*
Wei, Xinzhou *engineering educator*

Buffalo
Alexandridis, Paschalis *chemical engineer, educator*
Chang, Ching Ming (Carl) *engineering executive, mechanical engineer, educator, writer*
Jiang, Juan *chemical engineer*
Karwan, Mark Henry *engineering educator*
Kesavadas, Thenkurussi *mechanical engineering educator, researcher*
Luo, Hong *professor*
Meredith, Dale Dean *civil engineering educator*
Reismann, Herbert *engineer, educator*
Roberts, John S. *process engineer, researcher*
Ruckenstein, Eli *chemical engineering professor*
Tsai, Christina W. *civil engineer, educator*
Weber, Thomas William *chemical engineering professor*
Xu, Jinhui *engineering educator*
Zhuang, Jun *engineering educator, researcher*
Zirnheld, Jennifer L. *engineering educator, researcher*

Cold Spring
Pugh, Emerson William *electrical engineer*

Corning
Yuen, Po Ki *engineering company executive*

Dix Hills
Braun, Ludwig *retired engineering educator*

East Norwich
Rosen, Meyer Robert *chemical engineer*

East Syracuse
Ali, Amer *mechanical engineer*

Eastchester
Masucci, Carmine *retired electrical engineer*

Endicott
Chan, Benson *mechanical engineer*
Matienzo, Luis J. *chemical engineer*

Farmingdale
Bandyopadhyay, Amitabha *engineering educator*

Flushing
Goldenshteyn, Vladimir Lev *civil engineer*
Kopp, Ilya Zinovij *engineer, educator, researcher*
Stahl, Frank Ludwig *civil engineer*

Garden City Park
Radu, Bogdan *aerospace engineer*

Glenville
Anderson, Roy Everett *retired electrical engineer*

Greenlawn
Gorin, Brian A. *systems engineer*

Hauppauge
Buckley, Robert Matthew *electrical engineer*

Henrietta
Drummond, Malcolm McAllister *electronics engineer*

Huntington
Christiansen, Donald David *electrical engineer, publishing executive, consultant*
LaTourrette, James Thomas *retired electrophysics, electrical engineering and computer science educator*

Huntington Station
Agosta, Vito *mechanical and aerospace engineering educator*

Inwood
Chernov, Yuriy D. *engineering executive*

Irving
Greatbatch, Wilson *biomedical engineer*

Ithaca
Datta, Ashim Kumar *engineering researcher and educator*
De Boer, Pieter Cornelis Tobias *mechanical and aerospace engineering educator*
Dick, Richard Irwin *environmental engineer, educator*
Eastman, Lester Fuess *electrical engineer, educator*
Fuchs, W. Kent *engineering educator*
Hammer, David Andrew *nuclear science and engineering educator*
Harriott, Peter *chemical engineering educator*
Leibovich, Sidney *engineering educator*
Linke, Simpson *electrical engineering educator*
Loucks, Daniel Peter *environmental systems engineer*
Maxwell, William Laughlin *retired industrial engineering educator*
McGuire, William *civil engineer, educator*
Meyburg, Arnim Hans *transportation engineer, educator, consultant*
O'Rourke, Thomas Denis *civil engineer, educator*
Otani, Niels Fujio *electrical engineering educator*
Parlange, Jean-Yves *environmental engineer, educator*
Pope, Stephen Bailey *mechanical engineer, educator*
Rodríguez, Ferdinand *chemical engineer, educator*
Smith, Julian Cleveland, Jr. *chemical engineering professor*
Tiwari, Sandip *electrical and computer engineering educator*
Walter, Michael Todd *engineering educator*

Jericho
Shinners, Stanley Marvin *electrical engineer*

Katonah
Bashkow, Theodore Robert *electrical engineering consultant, former educator*

Kings Point
Butman, Boris S. *marine engineer, educator*

Latham
Eisman, Glenn Alan *engineering educator*

Liverpool
Hamlett, James Gordon *electronics engineer, management consultant, educator*

Melville
Olesen, Robert Lind Ole *electrical engineer*
Schmid, Charles Ernest *acoustical engineer, academic administrator*
Taub, Jesse J. *electrical engineering researcher*

Mineola
Newman, Malcolm *mechanical and civil engineering consultant*

Montrose
Reber, Raymond Andrew *chemical engineer*

Mount Sinai
Kopp, Richard Edgar *electrical engineer*

New Hyde Park
Hyman, Abraham *electrical engineer*

New York
Ahmad, Jameel *civil engineer, researcher, educator*
Bove, John Louis *chemistry and environmental engineering educator, researcher*
Brazinsky, Irv(ing) *chemical engineering educator, department chairman*
Briskman, Robert David *engineering executive*
Chevray, Rene *engineering educator*
Chowdhury, Shoaib *engineer*
Chung, Jung Git *retired aerospace engineer*
Clemente, Frank M., Jr. *civil engineer*
Cowin, Stephen Corteen *biomedical engineering educator, consultant*
Denn, Morton Mace *chemical engineering educator*
DiMaggio, Frank Louis *civil engineering educator*
Fawcett, Christopher Babcock *civil engineer, construction and water resources company executive*
Fogel, Irving Martin *consulting engineer*
Gambs, Gerard Charles *consulting engineer*
Gokhale, Nachiket Hemant *computer engineer, researcher*
Goldfarb, Donald *industrial engineering educator*
Gorevan, Stephen Paul *engineer, department chairman*
Griffis, Fletcher Hughes *civil engineering educator, engineering executive*
Guo, Xiang-Dong Edward *biomedical engineer, educator*
Habib, Ibrahim Wahby *computer engineer, educator*
Hielscher, Andreas Helmut *biomedical engineer*
Jarvik, Robert Koffler *biomedical research scientist*
Lai, W(ei) Michael *retired engineering educator*
Lammie, James Louis *engineering executive, retired military officer*
Lohez, Dening Suzanne *electrical engineer*
Manassah, Jamal Tewfek *electrical engineer, educator, management consultant*
Osgood, Richard Magee, Jr. *electrical engineering professor, researcher*
Paaswell, Robert Emil *civil engineer, educator*
Robertson, Leslie Earl *structural engineer*
Rubenstein, Leonard *engineering company executive*
Sadegh, Ali M. *mechanical engineering educator, researcher, consultant*
Schwartz, Mischa *electrical engineering educator*
Shinnar, Reuel *engineering educator, consultant*
Son, Young K. *engineering educator*
Sullivan, Kenneth Wayne *engineer*
Tomasetti, Richard L. *structural engineer*
Tsividis, Yannis P. *electrical engineering educator*
Tudor, Helen E. A. *materials engineer, consultant*
Vogelman, Joseph Herbert *scientific engineering company executive*
Weinstein, Herbert *chemical engineer, educator*
Wootton, David MacMullen *mechanical engineer, educator*
Yegulalp, Tuncel M. *mining engineer, educator*

Niskayuna
Happ, Harvey Heinz *electrical engineer, educator*
Kostedt, William, IV, *engineer, researcher*
Qu, Ronghai *electrical engineer*
Ruggiero, Eric John *mechanical engineer*
Sivasubramaniam, Kiruba Haran *engineer*
Tangirala, Venkat E. *aerospace engineer, researcher*

Norwood
Church, Richard Dwight *electrical engineer, scientist*

Oakdale
Srinivasan, Raghavan *engineering educator*

Oakland Gardens
Lee, Duk Gyoo *civil engineer*

Owego
Zendle, Howard Mark *systems engineer*

Pearl River
Skelly, Michael John *environmental engineer, consultant*

Peru
Schwartz, Richard Frederick *electrical engineering educator*

Plainview
Sangesland, Odd Einar *mechanical engineer, consultant*
Snyder, Joel Bennett *engineering executive*

Pomona
Haralick, Robert Martin *electrical engineering educator*

Potsdam
Chin, Der-Tau *chemical engineer, educator*
Fanelli, Timothy C. *engineering educator, application developer*
Hopke, Philip Karl *chemical engineering educator*
Krishnan, Sitaraman *engineering educator*
Qiu, Tong *engineering educator, consultant*
Sazonov, Edward Stanislavovich *computer engineer, researcher*

Poughkeepsie
Chu, Richard Chao-Fan *mechanical engineer*
Logue, Joseph Carl *electronics engineer, consultant*
Padegs, Andris *electrical engineer, company executive*
Simons, Robert Edward *mechanical engineer, consultant*

Riverdale
Leylegian, John C. *engineering educator*
Silverman, Gordon *engineering educator*

Rochester
Ampadu, Paul *engineering educator*
Carstensen, Edwin Lorenz *retired biomedical engineer, biophysicist*
Friedman, Eby G. *electrical engineer, educator*
Ghosh, Amitabha *engineering educator*
Kozak, Jeffrey D. *engineering educator*
Krispinsky, David George *engineering educator*
Kurdziel, Michael Thomas *engineering executive*
Lamkin-Kennard, Kathleen A. *engineering educator*
Lerner, Amy L. *engineering educator, researcher*
Parker, Kevin James *electrical engineer, educator, professor*
Stratton, John Alfred *electrical engineer, educator*
Tsouri, Gill R. *engineering educator, researcher, consultant*

Rosedale
Charles, William O. *electrical engineer*

Rye
Lehman, Lawrence Herbert *consulting engineering executive*

Saint James
Gambino, Richard Joseph *materials engineer, educator*

Scarsdale
Borg, Robert Frederic *civil engineer*

Schenectady
Davis, Lewis Berkley *mechanical engineer*
Goldmeer, Jeffrey S. *mechanical engineer, gas industry executive*
Ringlee, Robert James *retired consulting engineering executive*
Tchako, Abraham *engineering educator*
Zeng, Kai *biomedical engineer*

Smithtown
Rockensies, John William *mechanical engineer*

South Salem
Terman, Lewis Madison *retired electrical engineer, researcher, director*

Staten Island
Rizvi, Syed *engineering educator*

Stony Brook
Chiang, Fu-Pen *mechanical engineering educator, researcher*
Huang, Peisen Simon *mechanical engineer*
Sitharaman, Balaji *biomedical engineer, educator*
White, Henry J. *engineering educator, consultant*
Zemanian, Armen Humpartsoum *electrical engineer, mathematician*

Syracuse
Abaté, Charles Joseph *engineering educator*
Braiman, Mark Stephen *biomedical educator, researcher*
Fardad, Makan *engineering educator*
Fawcett, James Walter *computer engineer, educator*
Higuchi, Hiroshi *aerospace engineer, director*
Kadhikhaye, Sameer Pundlikrao *engineer, researcher*
Kim, Yong-Woo *engineer, educator, consultant*
La Graff, John Erwin *engineering educator*
Latham, Robert R., II, *engineering educator*
Sargent, Robert George *engineering educator*
Scott, Gary M. *engineering educator, department chairman*

Tappan
Cardenas, Raul Rodolfo, Jr. *engineering executive, educator, consultant*

Tonawanda
Drozdziel, Marion John *aeronautical engineer*
Rovison, John Michael, Jr. *chemical engineer*

Troy
Bergles, Arthur Edward *mechanical engineering educator*
Block, Robert Charles *nuclear engineering educator*
Chan, Wai Kin Victor *engineering educator*
Coppens, Marc-Olivier *chemical engineer, educator*
Dobry, Ricardo *engineering educator*
Dordick, Jonathan Seth *chemical engineer, educator*
Fleming, Edwards A. *engineering educator*
Gerhardt, Lester A. *engineering educator, dean*
Gill, William Nelson *chemical engineering professor*
Glicksman, Martin Eden *materials engineering educator*
Hajela, Prabhat *engineering educator, researcher*
Hsu, Cheng *decision sciences and engineering systems educator*
Hull, Maria-Catherine *engineering educator*
Lee, Moo-Yeal *chemical engineer, researcher*
Littman, Howard *chemical engineer, educator*
Sanderson, Arthur Clark *engineering educator*
Sharfstein, Susan T. *engineering educator*
Shur, Michael *electrical engineer, educator, consultant*
Woods, John William *electrical, computer and systems engineering educator, consultant*
Zimmie, Thomas Frank *civil engineer, educator*

Upton
Simos, Nikolaos *engineer, researcher*
Steinberg, Meyer *chemical engineer*

Utica
Dussault, Heather M.B. *electrical engineer, researcher*
Jones, Daniel Keane *engineering educator*
Lee, Hoseoup *engineering educator*

Watervliet
Elrahman, O. Abd *environmental and transportation engineer, educator*
Kathe, Eric *mechanical engineer*

Webster
McWilliams, C. Paul, Jr. *engineering executive*

Wellsville
Tezak, Edward George *mechanics educator*

West Hempstead
Cantilli, Edmund Joseph *safety engineer, educator, translator, writer, consultant*

Westhampton Beach
Ozero, Brian John *chemical engineer*

White Plains
Foster, John Horace *consulting environmental engineer*
Freed, Arthur *civil engineer*
Haines, Daniel Webster *engineering consultant, educator*

Williamsville
Kim, Jung Taek *electrochemical engineer*
Metzger, Ernest Hugh *aerospace engineer, research scientist*

Yorktown Heights
Das, Koushik K. *industrial research manager*
D'Emic, Christopher Peter *chemical engineer, researcher*
Dennard, Robert Heath *engineering executive, scientist*
Kim, Kyu-hyoun *electrical engineer, researcher*
Restle, Phillip J. *engineering company executive*

NORTH CAROLINA

Bald Head Island
Smith, Allie Maitland *retired engineering educator*

Cary
Conrad, Hans *materials science and engineering educator*
Vick, Columbus Edwin, Jr. *retired civil engineering design firm executive*

Chapel Hill
Green, Paul Eliot, Jr. *retired optical engineer*
Marchionini, Gary Joseph *information science educator*

Charlotte
Cooke, Steven John *chemical engineer, consultant, scientist*
Elanayar, Sunil K. *research and development engineer*
Kabengela, Lubambala Paul *engineering educator*
Merrifield, Jeffrey S. *engineering company executive, former commissioner*
Ozan, Erol *engineering educator, researcher*
Ramaprabhu, Praveen *engineering educator*
Valasquez, Joseph Louis *industrial engineer*
Xie, Jiang *engineering educator*
Zheng, Naiquan Nigel *mechanical engineer, educator*

Durham
Carter, Calvin H., Jr. *materials engineer*
Casey, H(orace) Craig, Jr. *electrical engineering educator*
Clark, Robert Lewis, Jr. *mechanical engineer, consultant, dean*
Crotty, Dominic *biomedical engineer*
Edmond, John *engineering company executive*
Goodwin, Frank Erik *materials engineer*
Petroski, Henry *engineering educator, writer*
Wilson, Blake Shaw *electrical engineer, researcher*
Yildirim, Huseyin *engineering educator*

Fayetteville
House, Terry C. *engineering educator*

Granite Falls
Humphreys, Kenneth King *engineer, professional society administrator, educator*

Greensboro
Bolick, Ronnie Lee *mechanical engineer*
Eromon, David Ighogboya *electronics engineer, educator*
Fujino, Michimasa *aeronautical engineer*
Kelkar, Ajit Dhundiraj *mechanical engineer, educator*
Lou, Jianzhong *chemical engineer, educator*
Mohan, Ram Vasu *engineering educator, researcher*
Oliver, Terry James *retired electronics engineer, communications engineer*

Mc Leansville
Taggart, Christopher Scott *systems engineer*

Montreat
Sprawls, Perry *biomedical engineer, educator*

New Bern
Moeller, Dade William *environmental engineer, educator*
Painter, Jack Timberlake *civil engineer*
Whitehurst, Brooks Morris *chemical engineer*

Raleigh
Agamloh, Emmanuel B. *systems engineer, consultant*
Beatty, Kenneth Orion, Jr. *chemical engineer, educator*
Bitzer, Donald Lester *electrical engineer, educator, retired lab administrator*
Carbonell, Ruben Guillermo *chemical engineering educator*
Doorn, Michiel Roelof Jan *environmental engineer, consultant*
Gardner, Robin Pierce *engineering educator*
Havner, Kerry Shuford *civil engineering and solid mechanics educator, scientist*
Healey, Christopher Graham *engineering educator*
Hinton, David Owen *retired electrical engineer*
Holton, William Coffeen *electrical engineering executive*
Kolbas, Robert Michael *electrical engineering educator*
Loboa, Elizabeth Grace *biomedical engineer, educator*
Murray, Raymond Le Roy *nuclear engineering educator*
Odum, Jeffery Neal *mechanical engineer*
Rizkalla, Sami *engineering educator*
Smetana, Frederick O. *aerospace engineer, educator, consultant*
Sneed, Ronald Ernest *retired project engineer, educator*
Terry, Stephen D. *mechanical engineer, educator*
Turinsky, Paul Josef *nuclear engineer, educator*
Wehring, Bernard William *nuclear engineering educator*
Williams, Hugh Alexander, Jr. *retired mechanical engineer, consultant*
Xu, Le *engineer*
Yim, Man-Sung *engineering educator, consultant*
Zorowski, Carl Frank *engineering educator, academic administrator*

Research Triangle Park
Everett, LaTonya Michelle *computer engineer*

Rockwell
Cobb, Tyrus Raymond, Jr., (Ty Cobb) *retired engineer, retired military officer*

Whispering Pines
Kuhn, Matthew *retired engineering company executive*

Winston Salem
Bourne, Henry Clark, Jr. *electrical engineer, educator, retired academic administrator*
Singleton, Teresa *engineering educator*

Winterville
Mayo, Calvin Jay *engineering executive*

NORTH DAKOTA

Fargo
Chinnam, Ratna Babu *industrial engineer, educator*
Li, Kam Wu *mechanical engineer, educator*
Reitan, Daniel Kinseth *electric and computer engineering educator*
Vinnakota, Bapeswara-Rao Venkata *engineering educator*
Yates, Janet Kathleen *civil engineering educator*
Yoon, Jaewan *civil engineering educator*

Grand Forks
Huang, Luke Hanming *engineering educator*
Ji, Yun *chemical engineer, researcher*
Kulkarni, Manohar Ramchandra *mechanical engineer, educator*
Lim, Yeo H. *engineering educator*

OHIO

Ada
Al-Olimat, Khalid Sulieman *electrical engineer, educator*
Estell, John K. *computer science and engineering educator, department chair*
Khorbotly, Sami *electrical engineer, educator*
Reza, Farhad *engineering educator*
Shen, Hui *engineering educator*
Srinivasa, Vemuru R. *engineering educator, researcher*
Yoder, John-David Samuel *mechanical engineer*

Akron
Brown, David Rupert *engineering executive*
Jana, Sadhan C. *engineering educator, researcher*
Pan, Ernian *engineering educator, researcher*
Phares, James Kenneth *retired electronics engineer*
Srivatsan, Tirumalai Srinivas *engineering educator*

Aurora
Kirchner, James William *retired electrical engineer*

Barberton
Kitto, John Buck, Jr. *mechanical engineer*

Bowling Green
Kolla, Sri R. *engineering educator, researcher*

Brookpark
Baumgartner, Kelli Ann Crews *aerospace engineer*

Cedarville
Tuinstra, Timothy Ryan *engineering educator*
Zavodney, Lawrence Dennis *mechanical engineer, educator*

Cincinnati
Agrawal, Dharma Prakash *engineering educator*
Ahn, Chong Hyuk *engineering educator, researcher*
Anand, Sam *engineering educator*
Anderson, William Edward *electrical engineer*
Bahnfleth, William Parry *mechanical engineering consultant*
Bahr, Donald Walter *retired chemical engineer*
Cabezas, Heriberto *chemical engineer, researcher*
Gan, Subhadeep *mechanical engineer, researcher*
Ghia, Kirti N. *fluid mechanics engineer, aerospace educator*
Greenberg, David Bernard *chemical engineering educator*
Hall, Ernest L. *electrical engineer, robotics educator*
Hantush, Mohamed M. *hydrologist, researcher*
Kinman, Riley Nelson *engineering educator*
Madson, Philip Ward *engineering executive, consultant*
Martin, John Bruce *chemical engineer*
Mihaescu, Mihai *engineering educator, researcher*
Minai, Ali *engineering educator*
Mital, Anil *engineering educator*
Morgan, William Richard *mechanical engineer*
Schafrik, Robert Edward *materials engineer, technology manager, information technologist*
Sinha, Sunil K. *aerospace engineer, consultant*
Smith, Leroy Harrington, Jr. *mechanical engineer, consultant*
Wei, Heng *engineering educator*
Weisman, Joel *retired engineering educator*

Cleveland
Angus, John Cotton *chemical engineering educator*
Bogie, Kath *biomedical engineer*
Burghart, James Henry *electrical engineer, educator*
Collin, Robert Emanuel *electrical engineering educator*
de Groh, Kim K. *materials engineer, researcher*
Deissler, Robert George *fluid dynamics researcher*
Hardy, Richard Allen *mechanical engineer, engineering executive*
Huang, Alex Yee-Chen *biomedical engineer, educator*
Keys, L. Ken *engineering educator*
Kirsch, James F. *materials executive*
Ko, Wen-Hsiung *electrical engineering educator*
Saada, Adel Selim *civil engineer, educator*
Slobozhanin, Lev Arkadievich *fluid mechanics engineer, researcher*
Sridhar, Nigamanth *engineering educator*
Taylor, Dawn M. *biomedical engineer, educator*
T'ien, James Shaw-Tzuu *engineering educator*
Wilson, Jack *aeronautical engineer*

Columbus
Alexander, Carl Albert *materials engineer, educator*
Altan, Taylan *engineering educator, director*
Anderson, Betty Lise *engineering educator*
Baeslack, William, III, (Bud) *engineering educator*
Bhushan, Bharat *mechanical engineer*
Bokhari, Shahid Hussain *electrical engineer, educator*
Brodkey, Robert Stanley *chemical engineering educator*
Chaudhari, Ajit Mohan Worthen *engineering educator, director*
Fan, Liang-Shih *chemical engineering educator*
Fenton, Robert Earl *electrical engineering educator*
Harris, Ronald David *chemical engineer*
Houser, Donald Russell *mechanical engineering educator, consultant*
Kennedy, Lawrence Allan *mechanical engineering educator*
Miller, Don Wilson *nuclear engineering educator*
Özbay, Hitay *electrical engineering educator*
Ozguner, Fusun *engineering educator*
Rapp, Robert Anthony *metallurgical engineering educator*
Sebo, Stephen Andrew *electrical engineer, educator, researcher, consultant*
Singh, Rajendra *mechanical engineering educator, director*
Smidts, Carol *mechanical engineer, educator*
Smith, Philip John *industrial and systems engineering educator*
Takeshita, Oscar Yassuo *engineering educator*
Vafai, Kambiz *mechanical engineering educator*
Yang, Yu-Ping *mechanical engineer*
Zakin, Jacques Louis *chemical engineering educator*

Dayton
Cooper, Thomas David *metallurgical engineer, consultant*
Eustace, Deogratias *civil engineer, educator*
Houpis, Constantine Harry *retired electrical engineering educator*
Huang, Hong-Hsin *engineering educator, researcher*
Joo, James Jinyong *mechanical engineering professor*
Kazimierczuk, Marian Kazimierczuk *electrical engineer, educator*
Loomis, John S. *engineering educator*
Malhas, Faris Amin *engineering educator*
Meyer, David Gilbert *engineering educator*
Mukhopadhyay, Sharmila Mitra *materials engineer, educator*
Phillips, Chandler Allen *biomedical engineer, human factors engineer*
Reynolds, David Burkman *biomedical engineer, department assistant chair*
Schmitt, George Frederick, Jr. *materials engineer*
Vukelich, Sharon Irene *aerospace engineer, consultant*
Wischgoll, Thomas *engineering educator*
Wolff, Mitch *engineering educator, researcher*
Zoghi, Manoochehr *civil engineering educator*

Delaware
Arnold, Jay *retired engineering executive, educator*

Dublin
De Vore, Paul Warren *technology educator*

Gahanna
Majtenyi, Steven Istvan *retired civil engineer, consultant*

Garrettsville
Chattopadhyay, Sudipta *engineer*

Gates Mills
Enyedy, Gustav, Jr. *chemical engineer*

Girard
Madgar, Adam Jason *engineering company executive*

Hudson
White, David Lawrence *mechanical engineer, marketing professional*

Lakeside Marblehead
Haering, Edwin Raymond *chemical engineering educator, consultant*

Mansfield
Sheridan, Mark William *mechanical engineer, financial planner*

Marietta
York, James Farnsworth *engineering educator, retired chemical engineer*

Maumee
Konopinski, Virgil James *retired safety engineer*

Mentor
Kaye, Christopher James *molding engineer*

Miamisburg
Louthain, James Allan *electrical engineer*

Middletown
Newby, John Robert *retired metallurgical engineer*

North Olmsted
Bluford, Guion Stewart, Jr. *engineering company executive*

Oxford
Morton, Yu Tong *electrical engineer, educator*

Rao, Dhananjai M. *engineering educator*
Ward, Roscoe Fredrick *engineering educator*

Rio Grande
Cornelius, E. Ronald *engineering educator*

Shaker Heights
Siegel, Robert *heat transfer engineer*

Solon
Malik, Masroor Rasheed *engineering executive*

Springboro
Saxer, Richard Karl *metallurgical engineer, retired military officer*

Toledo
Abron, James Arthur, Jr. *civil engineer, consultant, engineering educator*
Dismukes, John P. *engineering educator*
Koo, Benjamin Hai Chang *structural engineer, educator*
Springman, Richard Arthur *mechanical engineer, director*
Wolfe, Robert Kenneth *engineering educator*

West Chester
Tanov, Romil R. *mechanical engineer, researcher*

Worthington
Aggarwal, Gaurav *engineer*
Compton, Ralph Theodore, Jr. *electrical engineering educator*

Wright Patterson AFB
Goltz, Mark Neil *environmental engineer*
Palazotto, Anthony N. *aerospace engineering educator*

Yellow Springs
Trolander, Hardy Wilcox *engineering executive, consultant*

Youngstown
Islam, A.K.M. Anwarul *civil engineer, consultant*

OKLAHOMA

Bartlesville
Hankinson, Risdon William *retired chemical engineer*

Edmond
Morishige, Teruo Ted *engineering educator*

Medford
Robbins, Frankie *civil engineer*

Norman
Altan, M(ustafa) Cengiz *mechanical engineering educator*
Bert, Charles Wesley *mechanical and aerospace engineer, educator*
Campbell, John Morgan *retired chemical engineer*
Commuri, Sesh *electrical engineer, educator*
Diaz, Nina Isabel *industrial engineer*
Gollahalli, Subramanyam Ramappa *engineering educator*
Kang, Thomas H.-K. *engineering educator*
Khoury, Naji *engineering educator*
Lamb, Peter James *meteorology educator, researcher, consultant*
Mallinson, Richard Gregory *chemical engineering educator*
Ramseyer, Chris Charles Emil *engineering educator*
Zaman, Musharraf *civil engineering educator*

Oklahoma City
Miller, Herbert Dell *petroleum engineer*

Stillwater
Case, Kenneth Eugene *industrial engineering educator*
Hoberock, Lawrence Linden *mechanical engineer, educator*
Leuschen, Martin Leslie *engineer*
Mansy, Khaled *engineering educator, architect*
Mize, Joe Henry *industrial engineer, educator*
Rahnavard, Nazanin *engineering educator*
Thompson, David Russell *engineering educator, dean*

Tulsa
Azar, J. J. *engineering educator*
Bell, Stephen Scott *engineering educator*
Cobbs, James Harold *engineer, consultant*
Liu, Xiaofan Sophie *engineering educator*
Luks, Christi Patton *engineering educator*
Williams, John Horter *civil engineer, energy industry executive*

Weatherford
Fitzgerald, Brad W. *engineering educator, consultant*

OREGON

Beaverton
Gilbert, Barrie *electronics engineer, director*

Bend
Thompson, Douglas C. *engineer*

Corvallis
Byers, William D. *engineering executive*
Lee, Shiwoo *engineering educator*
Monkul, Mehmet Murat *geotechnical engineering researcher*
Temes, Gabor Charles *electrical engineering educator*

Eugene
Luu, Phan *engineering company executive*

Florence
Ericksen, Jerald Laverne *retired science engineering educator*

Hillsboro
Kocharyan, Varuzhan *electrical engineer, educator, researcher*
Koh, Kwang-Jin *electrical engineer*
Long, Men *computer engineer*

John Day
Tuttle, Kenneth Lewis *retired engineering educator, consultant, researcher*

Keizer
Stuivenga, Douglas R. *engineering educator*

Klamath Falls
Culler, David Earl *engineering educator, researcher*
Woodall, David Monroe *engineer, researcher, dean*

Lake Oswego
Gehrig, Edward Harry *electrical engineer, consultant*

Myrtle Point
Walsh, Don *engineer, consultant*

Newberg
Foster, Michael R. *engineering educator*

Portland
Kocaoglu, Dundar F. *engineering management educator, industrial engineer, civil engineer*
Lall, B. Kent *civil engineer, educator*
Martin, Kenneth E. *electrical engineer, consultant*
Prasad, Shalini *electrical and communications engineer*
Yamayee, Zia Ahmad *engineering educator, dean*

Salem
Butts, Edward Perry *civil engineer, environmental & water consultant*

Waldport
Smith, John William Hugh *civil engineer*

PENNSYLVANIA

Allentown
Gewartowski, James Walter *retired electrical engineer*

Ashland
Polyakov, Yuriy Sergeyevich *engineer, researcher*

Bethel Park
Korchynsky, Michael *metallurgical engineer*

Bethlehem
Bartoli, Filbert J. *electrical engineer, educator*
Christodoulides, Demetrios Nicolaou *electrical engineering educator*
El-Aasser, Mohamed S. *engineering educator, academic administrator*
Gardiner, Keith Mattinson *engineering executive, educator*
Michopoulos, John George *civil engineer, researcher*
Mirro, John *engineering company executive*
Neti, Sudhakar *mechanical engineering educator*
Pense, Alan Wiggins *metallurgical engineer, academic administrator*
Sengupta, Arup Kumar *engineering educator, researcher*
Tan, Gang *engineering educator*
Voloshin, Arkady *mechanical engineering and mechanics educator*

Blue Bell
Brownlowe, William Harold *engineer*

Boalsburg
Gettig, Martin Winthrop *retired mechanical engineer*

Bryn Mawr
Hegedus, L. Louis *chemical engineer, consultant, retired research and development company executive*

Chadds Ford
Isakoff, Sheldon Erwin *chemical engineer*

Cheltenham
Weinstock, Walter Wolfe *systems engineer*

Chester
Huang, Zhongping *engineering educator*
Nicosia, Mark *engineering educator*
Nippert, Charles *engineering educator, department chairman*

Coopersburg
Siess, Alfred Albert, Jr. *engineering executive, management consultant*

Coraopolis
Kay, George Paul *environmental engineer*

Downingtown
Deb, Arun Kumar *environmental engineer*

Erie
Zhao, Lin *engineering educator*

Glen Mills
Churchill, Stuart Winston *chemical engineering educator*

Greensburg
Ference, Edward W. *engineering executive, structural engineer*
Langer, Alois *biomedical engineer*

Grove City
Fair, Mark C. *engineering educator*

Hershey
Collins, Christopher Michael *engineering educator*

Homestead
Mandel, Herbert Maurice *civil engineer*

Huntingdon Valley
West, A(rnold) Sumner *chemical engineer*

Indiana
Maina, Joshua Y. *electronics engineer, researcher*

Irwin
Kuhn, Howard Arthur *engineering executive, educator*

Jamison
Touhill, C. Joseph *environmental engineer*

King Of Prussia
Lee, Robert *engineer*

Lansdale
Hargens, Charles William III *electrical engineer, consultant*

Leola
Chatterjee, Hem Chandra *electrical engineer*

Lewisburg
Mastascusa, Edward John *electrical engineering educator*

Lititz
Lehman, Richard William *electrical engineer*

Malvern
Mulford, Richard Albert *mechanical engineer, professional society administrator*

Media
Garrison, Walter R. *engineering executive, director*

Middletown
Clark, Shirley Elizabeth *engineering educator*

Murrysville
Yang, Wen-Ching *chemical engineer*

Nanticoke
Eddy, Carl F. *engineering educator*

New Holland
Wagner, Bradley Jeremiah *agricultural engineer*

New Kensington
Parks, Shannon Lynn Isovitsch *civil engineer*

Newtown
Rao, Sudhakar *aerospace engineer, researcher*

Newtown Square
Perrone, Nicholas *engineering company executive*

Nottingham
Sweeney, Richard Edward *biomedical engineer, consultant*

Philadelphia
Bilgutay, Nihat Mustafa *engineering educator, associate dean*
Bogen, Daniel *engineering educator*
Bordogna, Joseph *engineering educator, former science foundation executive*
Fegley, Kenneth Allen *systems engineering educator*
Fromm, Eli *engineering educator*
Glandt, Eduardo Daniel *chemical engineering educator*
Govindaraj, Muthu *engineering educator*
Guérin, Roch *systems engineer, educator*
Jaron, Dov *biomedical engineer, educator*
Kalghatgi, Sameer *engineering educator*
Kargbo, David M. *science & engineering educator*
Lang, Adam A. *computer engineer*
Lawley, Alan *materials engineer, educator*
Mao, Weidong *communications engineer, technology executive*
Pennoni, Celestino R. (Chuck Pennoni) *civil engineer, academic administrator*
Pillarisetti, Anand *mechanical engineer*
Ponte-Castañeda, Pedro *mechanical engineering educator*
Popovics, Sandor *civil engineer, educator, researcher*
Quinn, John Albert *chemical engineering professor*
Staley, Kenneth Bernard *civil engineer*
Vadigepalli, Rajanikanth *engineering educator*
Winey, Karen I. *engineering educator, researcher*
Yousuff, Ajmal *engineering educator*

Pittsburgh
Bloom, William Millard *furnace design engineer*
Boston, John Robert *electrical engineer, researcher*
Casasent, David Paul *electrical engineer, educator, data processing executive*
Charap, Stanley Harvey *electrical engineering educator*
Cho, Sangyeun *engineer*
Dutt, Varun *systems and software engineer*
Dzombak, David Adam *environmental engineering educator*
Farrell, Mark Oliver *engineering educator*
Grossmann, Ignacio Emilio *chemical engineering educator*
Harper, Robert William *engineering educator*
Hendrickson, Chris Thompson *civil and environmental engineering educator, researcher*
Hoburg, James Frederick *electrical engineering educator*
Jordan, Angel Goni *electrical and computer engineering educator*
Khosla, Pradeep Kumar *engineering educator*
Koepsel, Richard Robert *engineering educator*
Lejeune, Miguel *engineering educator*
Leney, George Willard *retired consulting engineer*
Li, Ching-Chung *electrical engineering educator*
Maly, Wojciech P. *engineering educator, researcher*
McAvoy, Bruce Ronald *engineer, consultant*
Mehalik, Matthew M. *industrial engineer, educator*
Mickle, Marlin Homer *electrical engineer, educator*
Milnes, Arthur George *electrical engineer, educator*
Morgan, M(illett) Granger *electrical engineering educator, researcher*
Morsi, Badie I. *engineering educator, researcher*
Narasimhan, Priya *engineering educator*
Neuman, Charles P. *electrical and computer engineering educator*
Nielsen, Paul Douglas *engineering executive, retired military officer*
O'Donnell, William James *engineering executive*
Oh, Chang Kook *civil engineer, researcher*
Park, Jeong-Heon *electronics engineer, researcher*
Peterson, Robert Scott *electrical engineer*
Pettit, Frederick Sidney *metallurgical engineering educator, department chairman*
Pittner, John R *electrical engineer, researcher*
Sirbu, Marvin Alan *engineering educator*
Srinivasan, Soundararajan *engineer, researcher*
Stahl, Laddie L. *engineering company executive*
Vidic, Radisav *engineering educator*
Wartmann, Michael Rudi *chemical engineer, researcher*
Woo, Savio Lau-Yuen *bioengineering educator*

Pottstown
Cross, Carole Ann *plastics engineer*

Reading
Moriarty, John Klinge *electrical engineer, consultant*

Schnecksville
Riola, Patricia Anne *computer engineer, educator*

Souderton
Silvestri, George Joseph, Jr. *retired thermodynamics engineer*

Spring Mills
Woodruff, Thomas Ellis *electronics consulting executive*

State College
Albright, Gifford Harry *retired architectural engineering educator, consultant*
Banks, Jeffrey Christopher *engineer, researcher*
Barnoff, Robert Mark *civil engineering educator*
Foderaro, Anthony Harolde *nuclear engineering educator*
Grimes, Dale Mills *physics and electrical engineering educator*
Olson, Donald Richard *mechanical engineering educator*
Reutzel, Edward William *mechanical engineer*

Swarthmore
Krendel, Ezra Simon *systems and human factors engineering consultant*
McGarity, Arthur Edwin *engineering educator, researcher*

University Park
Aplan, Frank Fulton *metallurgical engineering educator*
Bose, Nirmal Kumar *electrical engineer, mathematics educator*
Davids, Norman *engineering educator, researcher*
Grayson, Robert Larry *engineering educator, mining executive*
Irwin, Mary Jane (Janie) *engineering educator*
Modest, Michael Fritz *mechanical engineering educator*
Osseo-Asare, Kwadwo *engineering educator*
Purao, Sandeep *engineering educator*
Richard, Thomas Lehman *agricultural engineer, educator*
Todd Copley, Judith A. *engineering educator*
Vannice, M. Albert *chemical engineering professor, researcher*
Vrentas, James Spiro *chemical engineering professor*
Wormley, David Neal *engineering educator*

Villanova
Alaways, LeRoy Ward *mechanical engineer, educator*
McLaughlin, Philip VanDoren, Jr. *mechanical engineering educator, researcher, consultant*
Radhakrishnan, T. *engineering educator, educator*
Samanta, Biswanath *engineering educator*
Tomlinson, J. Richard *retired engineering services company executive*
Wu, Qianhong *engineering educator, researcher*

Warminster
Birnstiel, Charles *consulting engineer*

Wayne
DeBusk, Charles Richard *engineer, consultant*

West Grove
Fuller, Jack Glendon, Jr. *retired plastics engineer*

West Mifflin
Ardash, Garin *mechanical engineer*

West Point
Buckland, Barry Christopher *chemical engineer*

Wilkes Barre
Whitman, Brian E. *engineering educator*

Williamsport
Kinley, Kenneth James *engineering educator*

York
Horn, Russell Eugene *engineering executive, consultant*
Horn, Russell Eugene, Jr. *engineering executive*
Kennedy, Christopher Robin *ceramics engineer, director*

RHODE ISLAND

Bristol
Danzberger, Alexander Harris *retired chemical engineer, consultant*

Kingston
Barnett, Stanley M. *engineering educator*
Lee, Kang-Won Wayne *engineering educator*

Middletown
Ellison, William Theodore *marine engineer*

Newport
Harrison, Brian Francis *engineer, researcher*
Ruffa, Anthony Armand *mechanical engineer*

Providence
Breuer, Kenneth *engineering educator*
Glicksman, Maurice *engineering educator, retired dean, provost*
Hazeltine, Barrett *electrical engineer, educator*
Khrushchev, Sergei Nikitich *engineering educator*
Lawal, Taiwo Muniru *civil engineer*
Lysaght, Michael John *biomedical engineer, educator*
Medvedovski, Eugene *ceramics engineer, researcher*
Nurmikko, Arto Veikko *engineering educator*
Richman, Marc Herbert *engineer, forensic specialist, educator*
Suuberg, Eric Michael *chemical engineering educator*
Webster, Thomas Jay *engineering educator*
Weiner, Jerome Harris *mechanical engineering educator*

Wakefield
Boothroyd, Geoffrey *industrial and manufacturing engineering educator*

SOUTH CAROLINA

Beaufort
Pinkerton, Robert Bruce *mechanical engineer*

Bluffton
Jerger, Edward William *engineering educator, dean*

Charleston
Fei, James Robert *engineering executive, consultant*
Haemmerich, Dieter *biomedical engineer*

Clemson
Aziz, Nadim Mahmoud *engineering educator*
Chisman, James Allan *industrial engineering educator, consultant*
Greenstein, Joel Sandor *industrial engineering educator*
Jalili, Nader *mechanical engineer, educator*
Kimbler, Delbert Lee, Jr. *retired industrial engineering educator*
Kurz, Mary E. *engineering educator*
Luo, Jian *engineering educator, researcher*
Pang, Wei Chiang *civil engineer, educator*
Pursley, Michael Bader *engineering educator, communications systems researcher, consultant*
Ravichandran, Nadarajah *civil engineer, researcher*
Shappell, Scott Allen *engineering educator, consultant*
Walker, Ian David *engineering educator*
Xuan, Xiangchun *engineering educator*
Zumbrunnen, David Arnold *engineering educator*

Columbia
Chaudhry, M. Hanif *engineering educator, consultant, dean*
Fazzino, Paul *mechanical engineer*
Gibbons, Joseph Harrison *engineering educator, farmer*
Krishnan, Balakrishnan *engineering educator*
Papathanasiou, Thanasis D. *chemical engineer, educator*
Popov, Branko Nestor *engineering educator, educator*

Denmark
Goodman, Jonathan M., II, *engineering educator*

Florence
Goradia, Hrishikesh J. *engineering educator, researcher*

Greenville
Mears, Laine *engineering educator*
Zou, Tong *electrical engineer*

Greenwood
Towles, Elizabeth W. *engineering educator*

Greer
Hu, Yiping *metallurgical engineer*

Hartsville
Menius, Espie Flynn, Jr. *electrical engineer*

Hilton Head Island
Huckins, Harold Aaron *chemical engineer*
Windman, Arnold Lewis *retired mechanical engineer*

Myrtle Beach
Brogan, Richard Dennis *retired civil engineer*

Orangeburg
Brandes, Brian Todd *chemical engineer*
Hong, Jae-Dong *industrial engineering educator*

SOUTH DAKOTA

Pierre
Larsen, Wallace Lawrence *retired transportation engineer, county official*

Rapid City
Muci Küchler, Karim Heinz *mechanical engineering educator*
Patnaik, Anil Kumar *engineering educator, researcher*
Ramakrishnan, Venkataswamy *civil engineer, educator*
Scofield, Gordon Lloyd *mechanical engineer, educator*
Wynia, Steven *industrial technical educator*
Yoon, Myungkeun *engineering educator*

TENNESSEE

Arnold AFB
Davis, John William *government science and engineering executive*

Brentwood
Clevenger, William Thomas *electrical engineer*
Pulikollu, Rajasekhar Venkata *materials engineer, researcher*
Xu, Luoyu Roy *engineering educator*

Byrdstown
Willis, Keith Alan *energy scientist, engineer*

Chattanooga
Chopra, Prem Prem *engineering educator*
Ellis, Fredrick Vernon *metallurgical engineer, consultant*

Cookeville
Abdallah, Mohammed *engineering educator*
Chowdhuri, Pritindra *retired electrical engineer, educator*
Dainty, Helen Thompson *engineering educator*
Elkeelany, Omar *engineering educator, researcher*
Panchagnula, Mahesh *engineering educator*
Qiu, Robert Caiming *engineering educator, consultant*
Sissom, Leighton Esten *engineering educator, dean, consultant*

Crossville
Bell, Charles Eugene, Jr. *retired industrial engineer*
Hovmand, Svend *chemical engineer*

Greenbrier
Newell, Paul Haynes, Jr. *engineering educator*

Jackson
Cole, John Frankland *electrical engineer, educator*

Johnson City
Rahmani, Ramin Khosravi *mechanical engineer, researcher*

Kingsport
Tant, Martin Ray *chemical and biomedical engineer*

Knoxville
Alexeff, Igor *retired electrical engineering educator*
Beavers, James Earl *engineer, director, consultant*
Bose, Bimal Kumar *electrical engineering educator*
Brown, Donald Vaughn *retired engineer*
Burdette, Edwin Gordon *engineering educator, consultant*
Cummings, Peter Thomas *chemical engineering educator*
Irick, David Kim *engineering educator, consultant*
Kress, Tyler A. *biomedical engineer*
Mise, Jesse Sherden *structural engineer, consultant*
Paddison, Stephen John *engineering educator*
Prados, John William *retired engineering educator*
Richards, Stephen Harold *engineering educator*
Roth, John Reece *electrical engineer, educator, researcher, inventor*
Schuler, Theodore Anthony *retired civil engineer*
Scott, Bob (Robert Scott) *retired chemical engineer, educator*
Sorrells, Frank Douglas *retired mechanical engineer*
Xiang, Shu *civil engineer, researcher*

Maryville
Oakes, Lester Cornelius *retired electrical engineer, consultant*

Memphis
Maksi, Gregory Earl *engineering educator*
Marchetta, Jeffrey G. *mechanical engineer, educator*
Qi, Gang *mechanical engineer, educator*
Shiue, Yeu-Sheng Paul *mechanical engineer, educator*
Williams, Edward F(oster) III *retired environmental engineer*
Zeman, Herbert David *biomedical engineer*

Nashville
Galloway, Kenneth Franklin *engineering educator*
Hahn, George Thomas *materials engineering educator, researcher*
Hong, Liang *engineering educator*
Jiang, Xiaomo *engineering researcher*
Jordan, Benjamin T. *engineering educator*
LeVan, Martin Douglas *chemical engineering professor*
Morales-Paliza, Manuel Angel *electronic engineering educator*
Rababaah, Haroun R. *engineering educator, researcher*
Robinson, William H. *engineering educator*
Schnelle, Karl Benjamin, Jr. *chemical engineering professor, consultant, researcher*
Speece, Richard Eugene *civil engineer, educator*

Oak Ridge
Manges, Wayne William *electrical engineer, researcher*
Zinkle, Steven John *engineer, researcher*

Tullahoma
Hill, Susan Sloan *safety engineer*

Waverly
Hunter, William Michael *electrical engineer, civil engineer technician*

TEXAS

Allen
Hu, Rose Qingyang *communications engineer, educator*

Alpine
Kittlitz, Rudolf Gottlieb, Jr. *chemical engineer, researcher*

Amarillo
Von Eschen, Robert Leroy *electrical engineer, consultant*

Arlington
Bagcal, Orlando Raza *engineering educator*
Haji-Sheikh, Abdol Hossein *mechanical engineer, educator*
Liu, Hanli *biomedical engineer, educator*
Peterson, Lynn Meister *engineering educator*
Puppala, Anand Jagadeesh *engineering educator*
Rollins, Albert Williamson *civil engineer, consultant*
Shiakolas, Panos S. *mechanical engineer, educator*
Stevens, Gladstone Taylor, Jr. *retired industrial engineer, retired educator*
Wimberly, Clarence Ray *retired engineering educator*

Austin
Abraham, Jacob A. *computer engineering educator, consultant*
Baker, Lee Edward *biomedical engineering educator*
Biegalski, Steven Robert *nuclear engineer*
Borcherding, John David *civil engineer, educator*
Breen, John Edward *civil engineer, educator*
Bronaugh, Edwin Lee *retired electrical engineer*
Choi, Jinwoo *engineer, researcher*
Corsi, Richard *environmental engineer, educator*
Dougal, Arwin Adelbert *electrical engineer, educator*
Fair, James Rutherford, Jr. *engineering educator, consultant*
Fowler, David Wayne *architectural engineering educator*
Georgiou, George *chemical engineer, educator*
Goodenough, John Bannister *engineering educator, physicist, researcher*
Harris, Richard Lee *engineering executive, retired military officer*
Henderson, Terry Lee *electrical engineer, researcher*
Himmelblau, David Mautner *chemical engineer*
Hixson, Elmer L. *retired engineering educator*
Howell, John Reid *mechanical engineering educator, director*
Hughes, Thomas Joseph Robert *mechanical engineering educator, consultant*
Hull, David George *aerospace engineering educator, researcher*
Koen, Billy Vaughn *mechanical engineering educator*
Liljestrand, Howard Michael *environmental engineering educator*
Loo, Lynn (Yueh-Lin) *chemical engineer*
McGuffee, James W. *engineering educator*
Mc Ketta, John J., Jr. *chemical engineering professor*
Nichols, Steven Parks *mechanical engineer, educator, academic administrator, lawyer*
Oden, John Tinsley *engineering educator, mathematician, consultant*
Olsen, Richard Galen *biomedical engineer, consultant*
Patzek, Tadeusz W. *petroleum engineer, educator*
Peppas, Nicholas Athanassiou *chemical and biomedical engineering educator, consultant*
Reible, Danny David *environmental chemical engineer, educator*
Rylander, Henry Grady, Jr. *mechanical engineering educator*
Sanchez, Isaac Cornelius *chemical engineer, educator*
Sandberg, Irwin Walter *retired electrical and computer engineering educator*
Schechter, Robert Samuel *chemical engineer, educator*
Sciance, Carroll Thomas *chemical engineer, educator*
Stice, James Edward *chemical engineer, educator*
Stokoe, Kenneth H., II, *civil engineer, educator*
Swartzlander, Earl Eugene, Jr. *engineering educator, former electronics company executive*
Walton, Charles Michael *civil engineering educator*
Welch, Ashley James *engineering educator*
Willson, C. Grant *chemical engineering and chemistry professor*
Xie, Chi *transportation engineer, researcher*

Baird
Rodenberger, Charles Alvard *aerospace engineer, consultant*

Baytown
Cao, Chunshe (James) *chemical engineer*
Gilbert, Tatyana S. *engineering educator*
Thomas, Charles Edward *engineering educator*

Beaumont
Hopper, Jack Rudd *chemical engineering professor*
Jao, Mien *civil engineering educator*
Koehn, Enno *engineering educator, researcher*
Marquez, Alberto *industrial engineering educator, researcher*
Qian, Qin *engineering educator*
Tcheslavski, Gleb *engineering educator*

Beeville
Littlejohn, John Joseph *chemical engineer*

Bellaire
Cunningham, Robert Ashley *mechanical engineer*

Big Spring
Fryrear, Donald William *agricultural engineer, researcher*

Brownsville
Zhou, Yong *engineering educator*

Bryan
Bigham, Robert Eric *engineer*
Piper, Lloyd Llewellyn, II, *engineer, government and service industry executive*
Samson, Charles Harold, Jr., (Car) *retired engineering educator, consultant*

Bushland
Howell, Terry Allen *agricultural engineer*

Channelview
Dunn, Donald Glenn *electrical engineer, consultant*

College Station
Abu Al-Rub, Rashid Kamel *engineering educator*
Akin, Bilal *electrical engineer*
Annamalai, Kalyan *engineering educator*
Bennett, G(eorge) Kemble *engineering educator*
Benzerga, A. Amine *engineering educator*
Buchanan, Walter Woolwine *electrical engineer, educator, academic administrator*
Datta-Gupta, Akhil *engineering educator, consultant*
Daugherity, Walter C. *engineering educator*
Ehsani, Mehrdad (Mark) *electrical engineering educator, consultant*
Fletcher, Leroy Stevenson *mechanical engineer, educator*
Gegg, Brandon Christopher *engineering educator*
Hall, Kenneth Richard *chemical engineering professor, consultant*
Hann, Roy William, Jr. *civil engineer, educator*
Hueste, Mary Beth Deisz *engineering educator*
Hwang, Wonmuk *engineering educator*
Li, Ming-Han *engineer, educator*
Lowery, Lee Leon, Jr. *civil engineer*
Lu, Mi *computer engineer, educator*
Lytton, Robert Leonard *civil engineer, educator*
Makogon, Yuri F. *engineering educator*
Mathewson, Christopher Colville *engineer, geologist, educator*
Ntaimo, Lewis *engineering educator, researcher*
Page, Robert Henry *retired engineering educator, researcher*
Painter, John Hoyt *engineer*
Park, Yong Hun Sam *engineering company executive*
Patton, Alton DeWitt *electrical engineering consultant*
Radovic, Miladin *engineering educator, researcher*
Rasmussen, Bryan Philip *engineering educator*
Richardson, Herbert Heath *retired mechanical engineer, educator, dean, academic administrator*
Riskowski, Gerald Lee *engineering educator*
Roschke, Paul Norbert *engineering educator*
Saric, William Samuel *aerospace engineering educator*
Savari, Serap Ayse *engineering educator, researcher*
Zhao, Shengjie *electrical engineer, computer engineer*
Zollinger, Dan *engineering educator*

Dallas
Eberhart, Robert Clyde *biomedical engineering educator, researcher*
Etter, Delores M. *engineering educator, former political appointee*
Jester, Guy Earlscourt *enginneering consultant*
Kulkarni, Mak *electrical engineer*
Malouf, Mark E. *structural engineer, consultant*
Mohieldin, Ahmed Nader *electrical engineer*
Ray, Hillol Kumar *environmental engineer, poet*
Sermyagin, Konstantin *petroleum engineer*
Sims, Dale Benjamin *engineering educator*
Sundararajan, Vijay *systems engineer*
Szygenda, Stephen A. *electrical and computer engineering educator, researcher*
Waheed, Khurram *electrical and electronics engineer, educator*
Yang, Li *electronics engineer*

Denton
Needleman, Alan *mechanical engineering educator*
Scharf, Thomas W. *engineering educator*
Yuan, Xiaohui *engineering educator*

Edinburg
Abraham, John P. *computer engineer, educator*
Freeman, Robert Arthur *engineering educator*

El Paso
Biswas, Amitava *engineering educator*
Grieves, Robert Belanger *engineering and language educator*

Euless
Pascal, Tracey Michele *software engineer, director*

Fort Worth
Alvarez, Jill Lynn *mechanical engineer, management consultant*
Astrup, Jens Leo *retired civil engineer*
Cunningham, Atlee Marion, Jr. *aeronautical engineer*
Lewis, Frank Leroy *electrical engineer, educator, researcher*
Lewis, Leroy Frank *engineering educator*
Maldonado, Francisco Javier *electrical research engineer*
Mayyas, Mohammad A. *mechanical engineer, researcher*
Nichols, James Richard *civil engineer, consultant*

Freeport
Overton, Tim *chemical engineer*

Frisco
Holmes, William Larry *mechanical designer*

Galveston
Ingole, Sudeep Prabhakar *engineering educator, researcher*

Georgetown
Moore, Pat Howard *engineering and construction executive, educator*

Harker Heights
Bahr, Hubert Arthur *retired computer engineer*

Houston
Afify, Ahmed Aly *engineer*
Akers, William Walter *chemical engineering educator*
Antalffy, Leslie Peter *mechanical engineer*
Bensaoula, Abdelhak *engineering educator, consultant*
Bomba, John Gilbert *civil engineer, consultant*
Bovay, Harry Elmo, Jr. *retired engineering company executive*
Burrus, (Charles) Sidney *electrical engineering educator*
Byerly, Diane Leslie *aerospace engineer, researcher*
Cassimere, Brant *electrical engineer*
Cheatham, John Bane, Jr. *retired mechanical engineering educator*
Chowdhury, Shafkat Ahmed *aerospace engineer*
DeForest, Joanie *engineering educator*
Focht, John Arnold, Jr. *engineer*
Frank, Karen Denise *aerospace engineer*
Han, Choongyong *petroleum engineer, researcher*
Hasen, Michael *engineering company executive, civil engineer*
Henley, Ernest Justus *retired chemical engineering professor*
Hissong, Douglas Wayne *chemical engineer*
Horton, Thomas Edward, Jr. *mechanical engineering educator*
Hsu, Thomas Tseng-Chuang *civil engineer, educator*
Huang, Shawn Shaoping *engineer*
Kobayashi, Riki *retired chemical engineer, educator*
Koo, Weoncheol *ocean engineer*
Krause, William Austin *retired engineering executive*
Krishen, Kumar *research technologist*
Lienhard, John Henry, IV, *mechanical engineer, educator*
Love, Stanley Glen *scientist, astronaut*
Manzano-Ruiz, Juan José *mechanical engineer, researcher*
McLeod, Harry O'Neal, Jr. *retired petroleum engineer, consultant*
Miele, Angelo *engineering educator, researcher, consultant, author*
Mo, Yi-Lung *structural engineer, educator*
Morris, Owen Glenn *engineering corporation executive*
Peng, Liang-Chuan *mechanical engineer*
Powell, Alan *engineering educator, research scientist*
Prats, Michael *petroleum engineer, educator*
Putra, Erwinsyah *petroleum engineer*
Qiao, Fengxiang *transportation engineer, educator*
Sun, Yang *computer engineer*
Thorpe, Carlon Justine *engineering and operations executive*
Urthaler, Yetzirah Yksya *Subsea Engineer*
Yu, Aiting Tobey *engineering executive*

Humble
Brown, Samuel Joseph, Jr. *engineer, scientist*

Irving
Barnard, Ray F. *engineering and construction management company executive*
Boeckmann, Alan L. *engineering and construction management company executive*
Flowers, Garry W. *engineering and construction management company executive*
Gilbert, H. Steven *engineering and construction management company executive*
Hoops, Thomas *engineering educator*

Justin
Delashmit, Walter Howard, Jr. *engineering executive, researcher, consultant, application developer*

Kingsville
John, Kuruvilla *engineering educator*
Lee, Sangyong *engineering educator*
Li, Shuhui *engineer, educator*
Nekovei, Reza *engineering educator, researcher*
Sun, Dazhi *engineering educator*

Laredo
Ni, Qingwen *engineering educator*

League City
Kanuth, James Gordan *chemical engineer*

Levelland
Tackett, Billy John *electronics engineer, educator*

Livingston
Hayes, Gordon Glenn *retired civil engineer*

Lubbock
Kiesling, Ernst Willie *civil engineering educator*
Kristiansen, Magne *electrical engineer, educator*
Martin, Clyde F. *engineering educator*
Mitra, Sunanda Datta *engineering educator*

Mc Kinney
Gill, David bRIAN *electrical engineer, educator*

Mineral Wells
Mei, Anhua *mechanical engineer, researcher*

Mission
Gomez, Roberto *engineering executive*

Pflugerville
Upadhya, Girish *thermal mechanical engineer*

Plano
Hooper, Sandra *systems engineer*
Keathly, David Mark *electrical and computer engineer*

Prairie View
Cofie, Penrose *engineering educator, researcher*
Gyamerah, Michael *engineering educator*

Richardson
Henderson, Rashaunda *engineering educator*
Strieter, Frederick John *engineering executive*
Tang, Chinpei *mechanical engineer, researcher*

Rockport
Minor, Joseph Edward *civil engineer, educator*

Rosharon
Marya, Manuel Paul Claude *metallurgical and materials engineer, manager*

San Antonio
Abramson, Hyman Norman *engineering and science research executive*
Agaian, Sos Suien *electrical engineer, researcher*
Atchley, Curtis Leon *mechanical engineer*
Ayon, Arturo A. *electrical engineer, educator*
Emamian, Vahid *engineering educator*
Ghosh, Amitava *mining engineer*
Han, Hai-Chao *engineering educator*
Huang, Yufei *engineering educator*
Rezaie, Bahman *engineering educator, researcher*
Roberson, Dawnlee *engineering educator*

San Marcos
Stephan, Karl David *electrical engineering educator*
Stern, Harold Philip Elliott *electrical engineer, director*
Tate, Jitendra S. *engineering educator*

Stafford
Le, Duy-Loan *electrical engineer*

Sugar Land
Finch, Robert David *mechanical engineer, educator, consultant*

The Woodlands
Griffith, James William *systems engineer, consultant*

Tyler
Layton, Robert E., Jr. *retired aeronautical engineer*
Sathyamoorthy, Muthukrishnan *engineering educator, associate provost*

Victoria
McLain, Donald *engineering educator*

Waco
Farison, James Blair *electrical and biomedical engineer, educator*

Webster
Kobayashi, Herbert Shin *electrical engineer*

Weslaco
Yang, Chenghai *agricultural engineer, researcher*

UTAH

Corinne
Ahmad, Rashid Ahmad *mechanical engineer*

Logan
Baktur, Reyhan *engineering educator*
Bowles, David Stanley *engineering educator, consultant*
Hargreaves, George Henry *civil and agricultural engineer, researcher*
Keller, Jack *agricultural engineering educator, consultant*
Moon, Todd Kay *engineering educator*

Manti
Funk, William Henry *retired environmental engineering educator*

Ogden
Davidson, Thomas Ferguson *retired chemical engineer*
Milner, Robert Seaton *toolmaker, manufacturing engineer, graphics designer, educator*

Provo
Benzley, Steven E. *engineering educator*
Jackson, James F. *nuclear engineer, educator*
Jensen, Michael Allen *engineering educator*
Youd, T. Leslie *retired civil engineer*

Salt Lake City
Barney, Kline Porter, Jr. *engineering company executive, consultant*
Bhayani, Kiran Lilachand *environmental engineer, programs manager*
Bodson, Marc *engineering educator*
DeVries, Kenneth Lawrence *mechanical engineer, educator*
Gandhi, Om Parkash *electrical engineer*
Ghosh, Sambhunath (Sam) *environmental engineer, educator*
Ho, Chun-Hsing *civil engineer*
Janatova, Jarmila *biomedical investigator, educator*
Lee, Hosin *civil engineer, educator*
Sandquist, Gary Marlin *engineering educator, researcher, consultant, writer, military officer*
Sohn, Hong Yong *chemical and metallurgical engineer, educator*
Stringfellow, Gerald B. *engineering educator*
Yan, Xie *systems engineer*

Sandy
Sokolov, Yuri *engineer*

VERMONT

Burlington
Marshall, Jeffrey Scott *mechanical engineer, educator*
Pinder, George Francis *engineering educator, research scientist*

Essex Junction
Hook, Terence Blackwell *electrical engineer*

Grand Isle
Dufrene, Brian M. *engineering executive*

Shelburne
Anderson, Richard Louis *electrical engineer*

South Burlington
Outwater, John Ogden *mechanical engineering educator*

VIRGINIA

Afton
Anderson, Donald Norton, Jr. *retired electrical engineer*

Alexandria
Cook, Charles William *aerospace engineer, educator, consultant*
Gould, Phillip *engineer*
Harris, Dale William *systems engineer*
Karpiscak, John III *engineer, army officer*
Mack, Carl B. *engineering executive*
MacLaren, William George, Jr. *engineering executive*
Poehlein, Gary Wayne *retired chemical engineering professor*
Weisberg, Leonard R. *retired engineering executive, researcher*
Wilcox, David Eric *electrical engineering, educator, consultant, business owner*

Annandale
Ochs, Walter J. *civil engineer, consultant*

Arlington
Bement, Arden Lee, Jr. *engineering educator, government agency administrator*
Brighton, John A. *mechanical engineer, academic administrator*
Cox, Henry *engineer, researcher*
Hall, Carl William *agricultural and mechanical engineer*
Lala, Jaynarayan Hotchand *computer engineer*
Lee, Kangjin David *engineer*
Ng, Kam Wing *mechanical engineer, researcher*
Rahman, Muhammad Abdur *mechanical engineer*
Ren, Chiang H. *aerospace engineer*
Salmon, William Cooper *mechanical engineer, company executive*
Stevens, Donald King *retired aeronautical engineer, consultant*
Tang, William C. *electrical engineer*
Xuan, Jianhua Jason *engineering educator*

Ashburn
Nickle, Dennis Edwin *electronics engineer, consultant, deacon*

Big Stone Gap
Powers, Roy Daryl, Jr. *engineering educator*

Blacksburg
Agah, Masoud *electrical engineer, educator*
Aref, Hassan *fluid mechanics engineer, educator*
Baisden, Andrew Carson *electrical engineer, researcher*
Batra, Romesh Chander *engineering educator, researcher*
Benson, Richard Carter *mechanical engineer, educator, dean*
Brown, Gary Sandy *electrical engineering educator*
Disney, Ralph L(ynde) *retired industrial engineering educator*
Edwards, Marc A. *civil engineer, educator*
Ekkad, Srinath V. *engineering educator, researcher*
Gray, Festus Gail *electrical engineer, educator, researcher*
Hong, Dennis Wonsuh *engineering educator, researcher*
Mahmoodi, Seyed Nima *engineering educator*
Mitchell, James Kenneth *civil engineer, educator*
Pasupathy, Raghu *engineering educator*
Phadke, Arun G. *engineering educator*
Pickrell, Gary R. *engineering educator, director*
Price, Dennis Lee *industrial engineer, educator*
Randall, Clifford Wendell *civil engineer, educator*
Schetz, Joseph Alfred *aerospace engineer, educator*
Squires, Arthur Morton *chemical engineer, educator*
Stremler, Mark Andrew *engineering educator, researcher*
Thorp, James Shelby *electrical engineering educator*
Walker, Richard David *retired civil engineer*
Wang, Shuo *engineering researcher*
Yuan, Lijuan *engineering educator*

Blue Ridge
Elmore, Walter A. *electrical engineer, consultant*

Chantilly
Austin, Wanda Murry *systems engineer*

Charlottesville
Aylor, James Hiram *engineering educator*
Berger, Toby *electrical engineer, educator*
Dorning, John Joseph *nuclear engineering, applied physics and applied mathematics educator*
Fink, Lester Harold *retired engineering company executive, educator*
Fitzgerald, Mark *engineering educator*
Gaden, Elmer Lewis *retired engineering educator*
Garber, Nicholas Jack *civil engineer, educator*
Haimes, Yacov Yosseph *systems and civil engineering educator, consultant*
Hoel, Lester A. *civil engineering educator, department chairman*
Hudson, John Lester *chemical engineering professor*
Krzysztofowicz, Sir Roman *systems engineering and statistical science educator, consultant*
Li, Zuoping *biomedical engineer, researcher*
Maslen, Eric Harvey *engineering educator, researcher*
Park, Byungkyu (Brian Park) *engineering educator*
Townsend, Miles Averill *aerospace and mechanical engineering educator*
Untaroiu, Costin Daniel *engineering educator, researcher*
Wood, Houston G. *engineering educator, researcher*
Wulf, William Allan *engineering educator*

Edinburg
Trindal, Wesley Steele *mechanical engineer*

Fairfax
Agouris, Peggy *engineer, educator*
Boone, James Virgil *retired engineering executive, researcher*
Chen, Chun-Hung *engineering educator*
Cook, Gerald *electrical engineering educator*
Ganesan, Rajesh *industrial engineer, researcher*
Gertler, Janos John *electrical engineer, educator*
Houck, Mark Hedrich *engineering educator*
Klopfenstein, Rex Carter *retired electrical engineer*
Palmer, James Daniel *information technology educator*
Sage, Andrew Patrick *systems engineering and management educator*
Sikdar, Siddhartha *engineering educator*
Villarreal, Carlos Castañeda *engineering executive*

Fairfax Station
Duff, William Grierson *electrical engineer, educator*

Falls Church
Abou-Ellail, Mohsen Mohamed *engineering educator, researcher*
Jo, Kenneth Yoon *electronics engineer*
Jones, Russel Cameron *civil engineer, educator*
Lorenzo, Michael *engineer, real estate broker, government official*
Rahmandad, Hazhir *engineering educator*
Sveinsson, Linda Rodgers *engineering company executive*
Tether, Anthony John *aerospace executive*

Fort Belvoir
Gould, Jay William III *science and technology systems engineer, management development educator, lecturer, author, international consultant*

Fredericksburg
Hasenfus, Harold Joseph *retired mechanical engineer, naval technical director*
Medding, Walter Sherman *retired environmental engineer*

Hampton
Bai, Yingxin *optical engineer*
McAdaragh, Raymon Michael *aerospace engineer, researcher*
Nare, Otsebele E. *engineering educator, researcher*
Noor, Ahmed Khairy *engineering educator, researcher*
Refaat, Tamer F. *electrical engineer, researcher*
Sobieski, Jaroslaw *aerospace engineer*

Herndon
Akin, Jeffrey *human capital consulting executive*
Wang, Zhengang *civil engineer, researcher*
Young, Janet Cheryl *electrical engineer*

Lexington
Hyre, Matthew *engineering educator*

Lynchburg
Harvey, Aubrey Eaton III *retired industrial engineer*
Lewis, Edward *engineering educator*
Noronha, Silvester John *engineer, researcher*

Manassas
Haddad, Nadim Fawzi *engineer, researcher*

Mc Lean
Allen, David *systems engineer*
Carnicero, Jorge Emilio *aeronautical engineer, transportation executive*
Faga, Martin C. *engineer*

Ferrante, Frank Edward *telecommunications systems engineer*
Grasso, Alfred *engineering company executive, systems engineer*
Hashemi, Nastaran *research assistant professor*
Rosenbaum, David Mark *engineering executive, consultant, educator*
Shortal, Terence Michael *retired systems company executive*
Walsh, John Breffni *aerospace consultant*

Middleburg
Langley, Rolland Ament, Jr. *engineering and management consultant*

Montross
Fountain, Robert Roy, Jr. *retired engineering company executive, farmer, military officer*

Newport News
Hubbard, Harvey Hart *aeroacoustician, noise control engineer, consultant*

Norfolk
Bawab, Sebastian Y. *mechanical engineer, educator*
Donohue, David Patrick *retired engineering executive, military officer*
Geddis, Demetris L. *engineering educator, researcher*
Islam, Mohammed Nazrul *engineering educator, researcher*
Karim, Mohammad Ataul *electrical engineering educator, researcher*
Kunz, Donald Lee *aeronautical engineer*
Mohieldin, Taj Osman *engineering educator*
Popescu, Otilia *engineering educator*
Wiltse, James Clark *civil engineer*

Oakton
Felsburg, David F. *engineering executive, educator*

Petersburg
Slaughter, Gymama *engineering educator*

Reston
Jacyna, Garry Michael *research scientist*
Kahn, Robert E. *electrical engineer*

Richmond
Avrutin, Vitaliy *electrical engineer, researcher*
Compton, Olin Randall *consulting electrical engineer, researcher*
Gad-el-Hak, Mohamed *aerospace and mechanical engineering educator, researcher*
Jun, Jungwook *transportation engineer, researcher*
Mattauch, Robert Joseph *retired electrical engineering educator, retired dean*
Pidaparti, Ramana M. *engineering educator*

Roanoke
Landis, John William *retired engineering executive, consultant, government advisor*

Springfield
Ferrante, Jon Visconti *leadership and technology transfer executive, consultant*
Geiger, Richard Bernard *civil engineer, federal agency administrator*
Meikle, Philip G. *engineer, retired government agency executive*
Morsy, Mohamed Nageeb *electrical engineering educator, researcher*
Sonnemann, Harry *electrical engineer, consultant*

Vienna
Keiser, Bernhard Edward *engineering executive, communications engineer, consultant*

Virginia Beach
Spivak, Maurice Sidney *civil engineer, consultant*

Williamsburg
Coakley, Richard Walker *retired chemical engineer*
Denyes, James Richard *industrial engineer*
Lynn, Larry (Verne Lauriston Lynn) *engineering executive*

WASHINGTON

Anacortes
Pratt, David Terry *engineering consultant*

Bellevue
Cheevarunothai, Patikhom *transportation engineer*
Parks, Donald Lee *mechanical engineer, human factors engineer*

Bellingham
Jansen, Robert Bruce *consulting civil engineer*

Bothell
Gude, Veera Gnaneswar *civil engineer, researcher*

Brush Prairie
Edlich, Richard French *biomedical engineer, educator*

Coupeville
Goodman, William Lee *retired naval officer, aerospace engineer and commercial pilot*

Dupont
Pettit, Ghery St. John *electronics engineer*

Edmonds
Schmit, Lucien André, Jr. *retired structural engineer*

Issaquah
Evans, Ersel Arthur *engineering executive, consultant*
Reid, John Mitchell (Jack Reid) *biomedical engineer, researcher, consultant*

Kenmore
Guy, Arthur William *electrical engineering educator, researcher*

Lynnwood
Schein, Rodney M. *electronics engineer, educator*
Schneider, Robert Kerry *electric utility engineer*

Mountlake Terrace
Schweyen, Stephen Gregory *engineering company executive*

Mukilteo
Bohn, Dennis Allen *engineering executive*

Olympia
Sesonske, Alexander *nuclear and chemical engineer*

Pasco
Wyatt, Paige A. *mechanical engineer, educator*

Pullman
Bose, Susmita *engineering educator*
Ding, Jow-Lian *engineering educator*
Lawrence, Holder *engineering educator*
Tashman, Laith *civil engineer, educator*
Zbib, Hussein Mustapha *engineering educator*
Zhong, Weihong (Katie Zhong) *engineering educator*

Redmond
Michener, John Russell *electrical engineer*
Valencia Lavao, Jesus M. *electrical engineer, consultant*
Willard, H(arrison) Robert *electrical engineer*

Renton
Bengelink, Ronald Lee *aerodynamics engineer*

Richland
Cox, Gary Robert *engineer*
Doctor, Steven Richard *engineer*
Harutyunyan, Satenik *mechanical engineer*
Lu, Ning *electrical engineer, researcher*
Singhal, Subhash C. *engineer*
Westergard, Billie *project engineer*

Sammamish
Yocam, Eric Wayne *engineer*

Seattle
Bowen, Jewell Ray *chemical engineering professor*
Davis, Earl James *chemical engineering professor emeritus*
Dunbar, Bonnie J. *engineer, astronaut, museum administrator*
Ferrante, Antonino *aeronautical engineer, researcher*
Finlayson, Bruce Alan *retired chemical engineering professor*
Galloway, Patricia Denese *civil engineer*
Gaulke, Linda Strande *civil engineer, researcher*
Gilbert, Paul H. *engineering executive, consultant*
Hoffman, Allan Sachs *chemical engineer, educator*
Ishimaru, Akira *electrical engineering educator*
Jorgensen, Jens Erik *mechanical engineer, educator*
Kapur, Kailash Chander *industrial engineering educator*
Kim, Yongmin *electrical and biomedical engineer, educator*
Kobayashi, Albert Satoshi *mechanical engineering educator*
Lidstrom, Mary E. *chemical engineering and microbiology professor*
Liu, Chen-Ching *electrical engineering educator*
Mc Feron, Dean Earl *mechanical engineer, educator*
Montoya, Gonzalo *chemical engineer, educator*
O'Donnell, Matthew *electrical engineering, computer science educator, dean*
Oman, Henry *retired electrical engineer, engineering executive*
Pilat, Michael Joseph *engineering educator*
Popovic, Zoran *environmental engineer, educator*
Raese, David Senna *aerospace and mass properties engineer, consultant*
Rosen, Jacob *engineering educator*
Wenk, Edward, Jr. *civil engineer, educator, writer, policy analyst*

Vancouver
Kim, Dave Dae-Wook *engineering educator*

WEST VIRGINIA

Morgantown
Cheng, Yueming *engineering educator*
Cho, Eung Ha *engineering educator*
Choudhry, Muhammad Akram *engineering educator*
Eck, Ronald Warren *civil engineer, educator*
Etherton, John Richard *safety engineer*
Halabe, Udaya Bhatta *civil engineering educator, researcher*
Kemp, Emory Leland *civil engineering educator*
Peng, Syd S. *mining engineer, educator*

WISCONSIN

Dousman
Zettl, Gary T. *engineering educator*

Edgerton
Peck, David Blackman *electrical engineer*

Franklin
Graef, Luther William *civil engineer*

Green Bay
LaRue, Lillian Jayne *electrical engineer, educator*

Hartford
Aubuchon, Richard E. *engineering executive*

Janesville
Buechler, Dale *engineering educator*

La Crosse
Davy, Michael Francis *civil engineer, consultant*
Periyasamy, Kasilingam *engineering educator*

Madison
Beachley, Norman Henry *mechanical engineer, educator*
Bird, Robert Byron *chemical engineering educator, author*
Crone, Wendy Catherine *engineering educator*
Dietmeyer, Donald Leo *retired electrical engineering educator*
Emmert, Gilbert Arthur *retired engineering educator*
Haimson, Bezalel Cecil *engineering educator*
Hill, Charles Graham, Jr. *chemical engineering educator*
Huang, Ming-Huang *engineer, materials scientist*
Lewandowski, Gina *engineering educator*
Lightfoot, Edwin Niblock, Jr. *retired chemical engineering educator*
Long, Willis Franklin *electrical engineering educator, researcher*
Lovell, Edward George *mechanical engineering educator*
Ma, Zhenqiang *engineering educator*
Novotny, Donald Wayne *electrical engineer, educator*
Peercy, Paul Stuart *engineering educator*
Pfotenhauer, John M. *engineering educator, researcher*
Ramayya, Edwin Bosco *engineer, researcher*
Shi, Yu *engineer, researcher*
Webster, John Goodwin *biomedical engineering educator, researcher*

Menomonie
Asthana, Rajiv *engineering educator, researcher*

Milwaukee
Chen, Qinghua *engineering educator*
Cutler, Verne Clifton *engineering educator, consultant*
Gaggioli, Richard Arnold *mechanical engineering educator*
Garland, George Arthur *engineering educator, consultant*
Hassler, John Michael *engineering educator*
Heinen, James Albin *electrical engineering educator*
Jang, Jaejin *engineering educator, consultant*
Korn, Jeffrey Bernard *engineering educator*
Lu, Bin *electrical engineer, inventor, researcher*
Mehail, James Joseph *aerospace engineer, educator*
Meus, Jonathan A. *engineering educator*
Mossbrucker, Joerg *engineering educator*
Munson, Ethan Vincent *engineering educator*
Nasiri, Adel *retired engineering educator*
Stemper, Brian D. *biomedical engineer, educator*
Vairavan, Kasivisvanathan *electrical engineering and computer science educator*
Wentz, Blake E. *engineering educator*
Widera, Georg Ernst Otto *mechanical engineering educator, consultant*
Wrate, Glenn Thomas *engineering educator*

Pewaukee
Holtzman, Steven *engineering educator*

Plover
Drew, Richard Allen *retired electrical engineer*

Richland Center
Heinen, John Timothy *environmental engineer*

Soldiers Grove
Ewing, Brian Kim *retired engineering executive, writer*

Spooner
Frey, Paul Howard *chemical engineer, engineering consultants company executive*

Verona
Buelow, Frederick Henry *agricultural engineering educator*

WYOMING

Casper
Blesi, Jonathan W. *engineering educator*
Hinchey, Bruce Alan *environmental engineering company executive, state legislator, state legislator*

Lander
Field, Francis Edward *electrical engineer, educator*

Laramie
Mingle, John Orville *engineer, educator, lawyer, consultant*
Rechard, Paul Albert *retired civil engineering company executive, consultant*
Towler, Brian Francis *petroleum engineer, educator*

TERRITORIES OF THE UNITED STATES

PUERTO RICO

Gurabo
Kuruganty, Sastry Pratap *electrical engineering educator*

Mayaguez
Goyal, Vijay K. *engineering educator, researcher*
Perales-Perez, Oscar J. *engineering educator*
Suarez, Luis Edgardo *civil engineering educator*

VIRGIN ISLANDS

St Croix
Lee, Sidney Phillip *chemical engineer, state senator*

CANADA

ALBERTA

Calgary
Glockner, Peter G. *civil and mechanical engineering educator*
Lam, Galen Ka-Ron *electrical engineer*
Malik, Om Parkash *electrical engineering educator, researcher*

Edmonton
Beaulieu, Norman C. *engineering educator, writer*
Lock, Gerald Seymour Hunter *retired mechanical engineering educator*
Offenberger, Allan Anthony *retired electrical engineering educator*

BRITISH COLUMBIA

Lake Country
Muggeridge, Derek Brian *engineering executive, consultant*

Langley
Thomas, Howard Paul *civil engineer, consultant*

Vancouver
Salcudean, Martha Eva *mechanical engineer, educator*

Victoria
Antoniou, Andreas *electrical engineering educator*

West Kelowna
Wedepohl, Leonhard Martin *electrical engineering educator*

MANITOBA

Winnipeg
Cohen, Harley *engineering educator*
Mufti, Aftab A. *civil engineering educator*

ONTARIO

Burlington
Harris, Philip John *retired engineering educator*

Hamilton
Bandler, John William *electrical engineering educator, consultant*
Garland, William James *nuclear engineer, educator*
Wong, Kon Max *electrical engineer educator*

Kingston
Lewis, William John *aerospace engineer*

London
Inculet, Ion I. *electrical engineer, educator, science association director, consultant*

Mississauga
Gupta, Rajesh *engineer, consultant*

North York
Buzacott, John Alan *engineering educator*
Tse, Philip Kui *airport engineering maintenance consultant*

Oshawa
Zhang, Dan *engineering educator, researcher*

Ottawa
Altman, Samuel Pinover *mechanical engineer, research consultant*
Bozozuk, Michael *civil engineer*
Georganas, Nicolas D. *electrical engineering educator, academic administrator*
Shiari, Behrouz *mechanical engineer, researcher*

Toronto
Amon, Cristina Hortensia *mechanical engineering educator, researcher*
Davison, Edward Joseph *electrical engineering educator*
Janischewskyj, Wasyl *electrical engineering educator*
Piggott, Michael Rantell *chemical engineer, educator*
Salama, C. Andre Tewfik *electrical engineering educator*
Slemon, Gordon Richard *electrical engineering educator*
Smith, Peter William Ebblewhite *electrical engineer, educator, research scientist, physicist*
Venetsanopoulos, Anastasios Nicolaos *electrical engineer, educator*
Wonham, Walter Murray *electrical engineer, educator*

Waterloo
Anis, Mohab *engineering educator*
Penlidis, Alexander *chemical engineering professor*
Saini, Simarjeet Singh *electronics engineer*
Sedra, Adel Shafeek *engineering educator, academic administrator*
Vlach, Jiri *electrical engineering educator, researcher*

Windsor
Hackam, Reuben *electrical engineering educator*
Zhang, Guoqing *engineering educator*

QUEBEC

Montreal
Haccoun, David *electrical engineering educator*
Kamal, Musa Rasim *chemical engineer, consultant*
Ladanyi, Branko *civil engineer, educator*
Lamarre, Bernard *engineering executive*
Paidoussis, Michael Pandeli *mechanical engineering educator*
Pierre, Samuel J. *engineering educator*
Ramachandran, Venkatanarayana Deekshit *electrical engineering educator*
Selvadurai, Antony Patrick Sinnappa *civil engineer, mathematician, educator, consultant*

Varennes
Bartnikas, Raymond *electrical engineer, educator*

SASKATCHEWAN

Saskatoon
Billinton, Roy *engineering educator*

MEXICO

Baja California
Montero Alpírez, Gisela *chemical engineer, researcher*

Mexico City
Ramirez-Mireles, Fernando *electronics engineer, consultant*

Queretaro
Lesser-Carrillo, Luis Ernesto *civil engineer, educator*

Tlaquepaque
Cueva-Zepeda, Alfredo *mechanical engineer, educator*

AUSTRALIA

Adelaide
Sharma, Sanjeev *engineer, researcher*

Parkville
Boger, David Vernon *chemical engineer, educator*

AUSTRIA

Reutte
Knippscheer, Sven *mechanical engineer, materials scientist*

CHINA

Beijing
Deng, John (Zhonghan Deng) *electrical engineer, researcher*
Zhang, Chuhan *civil engineer, educator*

Guangzhou
Ren-Heidenreich, Lifen *engineering executive*

Hangzhou
Xiuzi, Ye *engineering educator*

Nanjing
Xie, Kai Ji *aeronautical engineering educator*

Xi'an
Yao, Xi *ceramics engineer, educator*

COLOMBIA

Bogota
Delgado, Alberto *engineering educator, researcher*

CZECH REPUBLIC

Olomouc
Merta De Velehrad, Jan *safety engineer, psychologist*

Prague
Kučera, Vladimír *control engineering educator*

Zlin
Kolomaznik, Karel *engineering educator*

DENMARK

Nordborg
Clausen, Jørgen Mads *engineering executive*

EGYPT

Alexandria
Noweir, Madbuli Hamed *chemical engineer, educator*

ENGLAND

Beaconsfield
Lindley, David *mechanical engineer*

Bedfordshire
Patel, Nildeep Mukundray *mechanical engineer, researcher*

Cambridge
Hawthorne, Sir William Rede *aerospace and mechanical engineer, educator*

Cardiff
Tumlinson, Alexandre Rex *biomedical engineer, researcher*

Coventry
Varghese, George *systems engineer*

London
Aguoru, Kingsley Chibuzor, Sr. *computer engineer, systems analyst, consultant*
Broers, Lord Alec Nigel *engineering educator*
Rees, David William Alan *engineering educator, researcher, writer*

Southampton
Brebbia, Carlos Alberto *engineering educator, consultant*

ESTONIA

Tartu
Voznesensky, Nikolay Boris *mechanical engineering educator*

FINLAND

Tampere
Salonen, Pekka Olavi *electrical engineer*

FRANCE

Blagnac
Joye, Jacky *flight test engineer*

Chevilly Larue
Chenay, Christian Jean-Marie *biomedical engineer*

Ecully
Comte-Bellot, Genevieve Marie *engineering educator*

Guyancourt
Criqui, Bernard Claude *materials processes engineer, researcher*

Le Vesinet
Fourt, Bernard-Francois P. *retired engineer*

Paris
Carlier, Bertrand *nuclear engineer*
Poloujadoff, Michel Eugene *electrical engineering educator*

Saint Cloud
Perrier, Piérre Claude *aeronautical engineer, researcher*

GERMANY

Aachen
Pischinger, Franz Felix *engineer, researcher, educator*

Berlin
Spur, Günter *engineering educator*
Tsatsaronis, George *mechanical engineering educator, researcher*

Freiberg
Zabecki, David Tadeusz *engineer, educator, military historian, military officer*

Meerbusch
Schulze, Juergen Helmut *engineering executive*

Munich
Heinzl, Joachim Lothar *engineering educator*
Schmidt, Stefan *mechanical engineer, economist*

Stuttgart
Warnecke, Hans-Jürgen *retired engineering educator*

GREECE

Athens
Zevgolis, Ioannis *geotechnical engineer, researcher*

Chania
Karystinos, George N. *engineering educator*
Lagoudakis, Michail G. *engineering educator*

Ptolemaida
Tsachouridis, Vassilios A. *electrical and control engineer, researcher*

HONG KONG

Hong Kong
Leung, Ka-Cheong *engineering educator*

Kowloon
Liu, Hugh *engineering company executive, electronics engineer*

HUNGARY

Budapest
Karpati, Attila *engineering educator, consultant, research scientist*
Michelberger, Pal *mechanical engineer, educator*

Sopron
Sitkei, György *engineer, educator*

ICELAND

Reykjavik
Wallevik, Jon Elvar *engineer, researcher*

INDIA

Bangalore
Rajuk, Venugopal Kuppanna *computer engineer, educator*

Kolkata
Kothari, Hemraj *mechanical engineer, management consultant*

Kurnool
Teegala, Brahmananda Reddy *electrical engineer, educator*

Noida
Jain, Prem Chand *mechanical engineer*
Mitra, Raja *electronics engineer*

IRAN

Shiraz
Ahmadizadeh, Mehdi *engineering educator, consultant*

ISRAEL

Be'er Sheva
Brosilow, Coleman Bernard *chemical engineering educator*

Jerusalem
Lehman, Meir (Manny Lehman) *computer scientist, software engineer, consultant*

ITALY

Povo
Palpanas, Themis *engineering educator, consultant*

JAPAN

Aichi
Hachisuka, Keisuke *mechanical engineer, researcher*

Bunkyo
Kasagi, Nobuhide *mechanical engineering educator*

Chigasaki
Hirota, Sadao *engineering educator, researcher*

Fukui
Taniguchi, Keiji *engineering educator*

Fukuoka
Ishibashi, Akira *mechanical engineer, educator*

Futtsu
Fujisaki, Keisuke *electrical researcher*

Hirosaki
Sato, Hiroyuki *materials engineer, researcher*

Kanagawa
Itako, Kazutaka *engineering educator, researcher*

Kasugai
Watanabe, Makoto *engineering educator*

Kinokawa
Yamawaki, Nobuyuki *engineering educator, biomedical engineer, researcher*

Kitakyushu
Noda, Nao-Aki *mechanical engineering educator, researcher*

Miyagi
Adachi, Saburo *electrical engineering educator, researcher*

Nagoya
Sakai, Toshihiko *engineer*
Sendo, Takeshi *mechanical engineering educator, researcher, writer*

Osaka
Kamitani, Takayuki *engineering educator*
Ohnami, Masateru *mechanical engineering educator*

Shizuoka
Anma, So *engineer, consultant*

Takasaki
Matsushiro, Nobuhito *engineering executive, researcher*

Tamano
Kunio, Saito *electronics engineer*

Tochigi
Ara, Katsutoshi *environmental engineer, researcher*

Tokyo
Aoyama, Hiroyuki *structural engineering educator*
Hori, Yukio *engineering educator, scientific association administrator, researcher*
Kuroyanagi, Noriyoshi *engineering educator*
Nagata, Minoru *retired electronics engineer*
Shibata, Tadashi *engineering educator*

KENYA

Nairobi
Kionga-Kamau, Stephen Githii *engineering executive, educator*

MALAYSIA

Johor
Wong, Kuan Yew *engineering educator, researcher*

NETHERLANDS

Delft
Buice, Eric Steve *mechanical engineer, researcher*

Eindhoven
Huiskes, Hendrik W.J. (Rik Huiskes) *biological engineer*

NIGERIA

Lekki Peninsula
Ogunlade, Abimbola Adegoke *systems engineer*

NORTHERN IRELAND

Belfast
McCanny, John Vincent *engineering educator, executive*

PAKISTAN

Lahore
Mahmood, Khalid *civil engineer, researcher, consultant, educator*

PHILIPPINES

Manila
Lohani, Bindu Nath *environmental engineer*

Marikina City
Salvador, Melchor Nepomuceno *engineering educator*

Mondaluyong City
Abiera, Roberto *mechanical engineer*

POLAND

Szczecin
Wierzcholski, Wunschik Christoph *mechanical engineer, mathematician, information scientist*

Warsaw
Klemens, Rudolf Henryk *mechanical engineer*

Wroclaw
Golinski, Joseph Antoni *mechanical engineer*

PORTUGAL

Lisbon
Portela, Antonio Gouvea *retired mechanical engineer, researcher*

REPUBLIC OF KOREA

Ansan
Kim, Insoo S. *electrical engineer, researcher*

Anyang
Kim, Pil Soo *automotive and electrical engineer, educator*
Kwak, Jin Sam *communications engineer*

Bucheon
Lee, Eun Seong *biomedical engineer*

Busan
Ha, Chang Sik *polymer science educator*
Kim, Kwang-Baek *engineering educator, researcher*
Lee, Heesoo *engineering educator*
Yang, Bo-Suk *mechanical engineering educator*

Changwon
Kim, Yeongchun *mechanical engineer, researcher*

Cheonan
Kim, Ki Young *engineering educator*
Oh, Seacheon *chemical engineer, educator*

Cheongju
Kim, Ung-Yong *civil engineer, education educator, researcher, sanitary engineer*

Chungnam
Kim, Byung-Gyu *electrical engineer*

Daegu
Cho, Jayoung *textile engineer, researcher*
Cho, Jin-Ho *biomedical engineer, educator, researcher*
Lee, Yong-Hyun *engineering educator*

Daejeon
Choi, Yong-Seok *communications engineer, researcher*
Chun, Dong Hyun *materials science engineer, researcher*
Hong, In Pyo *electronics engineer, researcher*
Kim, Manwoong *mechanical and nuclear engineer, educator, researcher*
Kim, Si-Moon *mechanical engineer, researcher*
Lee, Hak-Joo *mechanical engineer*
Park, Hyung Chul *electronics engineer, educator*
Yoon, Hosung *electronics engineer*

Goyang
Kim, Moon-Sang *aerospace engineering professor*

Gwangju
Kong, Changduk *aerospace engineering educator*
Lee, Jongjin *mechanical engineer, researcher*

Gyeonggi
Lyu, Myung Seok *engineer*

Gyeongsan
Jang, Ja-Soon *engineering educator*
Yeom, Seokwon (Sekwon) *engineering educator, researcher*

Incheon
Cho, Chongdu *mechanical engineer, educator*
Yang, Hoichang *engineering educator*

Jeju
Cho, Jungwon *computer engineer, educator, researcher*
Jung, Dong-Won *mechanical engineer, educator*

Kyonggi
Eun, In-Ung *mechanical engineer, educator*
Kim, Tae-Hoon *engineering educator, researcher*

Pocheon
Cho, Taejun *engineering educator*

Pohang
Lim, Tae-Gyoon *mechatronics engineer, consultant, researcher*

Seongnam
Ryim, Won-Gil *mechanical engineer, engineering executive*

Seoul
Baek, Ju-Yeoul *biomedical engineer, physicist*
Choi, Kyoung-Kyu *engineering educator*
Chun, Myoung-pyo *materials engineer, researcher*
Chung, Chang-Ho *engineering educator*
Jun, Hwandon *engineering educator*
Jung, Taeho *engineering educator, director*
Kim, Joo-Sik *environmental engineer, educator*
Ko, You-Chang *engineer*
Kwak, Ho-Young *mechanical engineer, educator*
Lee, Sang Hun *mechanical engineer, educator, researcher*
Noh, Kyoung Lae *electronics engineer, researcher*
Park, Chulhwan *chemical engineering educator, researcher*
Park, Koohyun *industrial engineer, professor*
Rhee, Gwang Hoon *mechanical engineer, educator*
Suh, Chang Ho *polymer engineer*

Suwon
Ahn, Kyung Seung *electronics engineer*
Choi, Hyohoon *electronics engineer*
Kang, Intae *telecommunications engineer, researcher*
Lee, Byoung-Kuk *engineering educator*
Park, Soohong *electrical engineer, researcher*
Shin, Woo C. *chemical engineer*
Won, Dongho *communications engineer, educator*
Won, Yong Sun *electronics engineer*

Uiwang
Park, Won-Hee *mechanical engineer, researcher*

Ulsan
Kwon, Soon-Yong *engineering educator*

Wonju
Jeon, Byong-Hun *engineering educator*

Yeongju
Kim, Sungwon *educator, researcher*

Yongin
Park, Sung *engineering educator, consultant*

Yuseung
Lee, Kwangil *electrical engineer, researcher*

Yusonggu
Cho, Dong-Ho *engineering and communication educator*

ROMANIA

Iasi
Horga, Vasile *electrical engineer*

RUSSIA

Ekaterinburg
Dmitriev, Andrey Nikolaevich *engineering educator*

Moscow
Kirpilenko, Grigory Grigor'evich *engineer, researcher*
Krikalev, Sergei Konstantinovich *flight engineer, cosmonaut, researcher*

Rostov-on-Don
Pogorelov, Vadim Alekseevich *engineer*

SINGAPORE

Singapore
Kong, Adams Wai Kin *electrical engineer, researcher*

SWEDEN

Kista
Fodor, Gabor Andras *electrical engineer, researcher*

SWITZERLAND

Windisch
Anderegg, Roland *mechanical engineer, researcher*

Zurich
Hogan, Joseph M. *engineering company executive*
Morari, Manfred *chemical engineer, educator*

TAIWAN

Chupei
Chou, Richard Chi-Chang *mechanical engineer*

Jhongli
Tseng, Dyi-Hwa *environmental engineer, educator, dean*

Keelung
An, John F. *engineering educator*
Wu, Jenq-Lang *engineering educator*

Taichung Hsien
Peng-Chi, Peng *metallurgical engineer*

Tainan
Huang, Ting-Chia *chemical engineering professor, researcher*

Taipei
Jan, Ming-Yie *biomedical engineer, consultant*
Lee, Lin-Shan *electrical engineering educator, research and development company executive*
Lin, Chia-Hsiang *electrical and electronics technologist*
Wu, Cheng-Hung *engineering educator, researcher*

TURKEY

Istanbul
Utku, Senol *civil engineer, computer science educator, mathematics professor*

Van
Tapan, Mucip *engineering educator, consultant*

UKRAINE

Kiev
Antonov, Alexander Alexandrovich *engineering executive, researcher*

VENEZUELA

Caracas
Chang-Mota, Roberto *electrical engineer*

ADDRESS UNPUBLISHED

Abdel-Hadi, Ali Ismail *engineer, educator*
Abetti, Pier Antonio *electrical engineer, management consultant, educator*
Abu-Khalaf, Murad *electrical engineer, computer scientist, educator*
Acar, Cenk *engineering company executive*
Adams, David Orin *aeronautical engineer*
Afon, Yinka *environmental engineer, consultant*
Agarwal, Pranab *engineering company executive*
Aguinsky, Richard Daniel *electrical engineer, engineering executive*
Ahmed, Walid Khairy Mohamed *electrical engineer*
Aipperspach, Ryan *computer engineer*
Akay, Hasan U. *engineering educator*
Akhavan, Farhad *electrical engineer*
Akinci, Necip Onder *structural engineer*
Aksamija, Zlatan *engineer, researcher*
Alasti, Hadi *electrical engineer, researcher*
Alfriend, Kyle Terry *aerospace engineer*
Altschaeffl, Adolph George *retired civil engineering educator*
Alvi, Mohammed Haroon *process engineer*
Amann, Charles Albert *mechanical engineer, researcher*
Amerasekera, Ekanayake Ajith *electronics engineer, director*
Amundson, John Kay *electrical engineer*
Anagnostou, Dimitris E. *engineering educator, researcher*
Anastasopoulos, Panagiotis Ch. *transportation engineer, economist*
Anderson, John Gaston *electrical engineer, consultant*
Andrawis, Alfred Samuel *engineering educator*
Andrea, Mario Iacobucci *retired engineer, scientist, gemologist, appraiser*
Ansari, Rashid *engineering educator*
Apsel, Alyssa *electrical and computer engineer*
Arciszewski, Tomasz Tadeusz *engineering educator*
Arif, Ronald *electronics engineer*
Armaingaud, Franck *engineer*
Asadorian, Diana C. *electrical engineer, educator*
Asamizu, Hirokuni *electronics engineer*
Asiabanpour, Bahram *engineering educator*
Avery, John Gates *retired engineering executive*
Axford, Roy Arthur *nuclear engineering educator*
Bakht, Baidar *civil engineer, researcher, educator*
Baktir, Selcuk *electrical and computer engineer, researcher*
Ball, Robert Edwin *engineering educator*
Ballhaus, William Louis *engineering executive*
Baltazzi, Evan Serge *retired engineering research consulting company executive*
Barbosa, Patricia R. *radar engineer*
Bar-Cohen, Avram *mechanical engineering educator*
Baron, Seymour *engineering and research executive*
Baron, Stanley N. *retired electrical engineer*
Basova, Yulia *chemical engineer, researcher*
Battaglia, Francine *mechanical engineering educator, researcher*
Bauer, Richard Carlton *nuclear engineer*
Bauhan, Hobart Baker *retired mining engineer, farmer*
Baum, Eleanor *electrical engineering educator*
Bayoumi, Hassan *engineer*
Beard, James K. *retired aeronautical engineer*
Beasley, James George *civil engineer*
Beckjord, Eric Stephen *nuclear engineer, researcher*
Bernath, John (Jack) Charles, Jr. *electronics and reliability engineer*
Bers, Abraham *electrical engineering and physics educator*
Bershad, Neil Jeremy *electrical engineering educator*
Beumer, Richard Eugene *retired engineering executive*
Bhada, Rohinton Khurshed *chemical engineering educator*
Bhanja, Sanjukta *engineering educator*
Bhatia, Rajan *engineer, physicist, researcher*
Binkley, David Martin *electrical engineer, educator, musician*
Bittner, David Michael *engineering educator and professional engineer*
Blaise, J. Harry *engineering educator*
Blizzard, James Michael *engineering educator*
Bloch, Erich *retired electrical engineer, science foundation director*
Bodycomb, Jeffrey Taylor *engineering company executive*
Bonds, Alfred B. III *engineering educator, consultant*
Bonnett, James W. *retired engineer*
Bontha, Srikanth *milling system engineer*
Boriboonsomsin, Kanok *transportation engineer*
Bowman, Bruce Alan *civil engineer*
Bowman, Craig Thomas *mechanical engineer, educator*
Braganza, Jennifer *engineering educator*
Brennan, Lawrence Edward *retired electronics engineer*
Brickell, Charles Hennessey, Jr. *marine engineer, retired military officer*
Bridger, Baldwin, Jr. *electrical engineer*
Briggs, William Benajah *retired aerospace engineer*
Brown, Steven Harry *engineering executive*
Brungraber, Robert J. *civil engineer, educator*
Buckman, Raymond William, Jr. *engineering educator*
Budgeon, Mark K. *mechanical engineer, consultant*
Budwig, Ralph Sanders *engineering educator, researcher*
Budynas, Richard Gordon *engineering educator, writer*
Bunch, Jennings Bryan, Jr. *retired electrical engineer*
Burchard, John Kenneth *retired chemical engineer*
Buritz, Robert Samson *retired electrical engineer*
Butler, Donald Philip *electrical engineer, educator*
Cai, Mei *materials engineer, researcher*
Cai, Ying *engineer, researcher*
Cai, Yuanfang *engineering educator*
Campbell, John *engineering educator*
Carbunar, Bogdan *engineer, researcher*
Carlson, Robert Codner *industrial engineering educator*
Carnahan, Brice *chemical engineer, educator*
Carnesale, Albert *engineering educator, former academic administrator*
Carsley, John E. *metallurgical engineer, researcher*
Carter, Thomas Allen *retired engineering executive*
Casazza, John Andrew *electrical engineer, energy executive*
Cathey, Wade Thomas *electrical engineering educator*
Cavaco, Sofia C.F.M. *engineering educator*
Celebi, M. Emre *engineering educator*
Cerny, Louis Thomas *civil and transportation engineer, consultant*
Cha, Soyoung Stephen *mechanical engineer, educator*
Chae, Moo Sung *electrical engineer*
Chakraborti, Rajat Kanti *engineer, consultant*
Chakravarty, Swapnajit *electrical engineer, researcher*
Challagulla, Venkata Udaya Bhaskar *computer engineer*
Chang, Ying Chih *engineering educator, researcher*
Charwat, Andrew Franciszek *engineering educator*
Chavan, Prithviraj Vasantrao *environmental engineer*
Cheah, Boon-Siang *electrical engineer*
Cheddie, Denver Faron *engineering educator, researcher*
Chen, Jiwei *computer engineer*
Chen, Nong *electronics engineer, researcher*
Chen, Shoei-Sheng *retired mechanical engineer*
Chen, Wei *mechanical engineer*
Cheng, Hefa *civil engineer, educator*
Cheng, Wan-Lee *mechanical engineer, educator*
Chiang, I-Ting *engineer*
Chidley, Matthew *optical engineer*
Chilingarian, George Varos (Chilingar) *petroleum, environmental educator*
Cho, Alfred Yi *electrical engineer*
Cho, Hyeonjoong *computer engineer, researcher*
Cho, Jaedong *engineering company executive, researcher*
Choi, David Kyu *electronics engineer*
Chou, Chung-Kwang *bio-engineer*
Chouery, Farid Alexandre *electrical and structural engineer, consultant*
Chow, Winston *engineering executive, researcher*
Chowdhury, Mashrur *engineering educator*
Chu, Jack J. (Zhu) *electrical engineer*
Chuah, Mooi Choo *electrical engineer*
Clancy, Mathew P. *chemical engineer, application developer*
Clark, Jack Ivor *civil engineer, researcher*
Cleave, Mary L. *environmental engineer, former astronaut*
Clough, Ray William, Jr. *civil engineering educator*
Collins, James Duffield *marine engineer, editor*
Connanghey, Mc. William Eugene *chemical engineer*
Connolly, Thomas Joseph *engineering educator*
Conway, Richard Ashley *environmental engineer*
Cormier, Jon *computer engineer*
Cortes Zavala, Luis Alberto *systems engineer, security researcher, consultant*
Crouch, Peter E. *engineering educator*
Crowl, Steven Craig *aerospace engineer*
Crume, Richard V. *engineering educator*
Cui, Hongliang *engineering company executive, researcher*
Cummins, Nancyellen Heckeroth *electronics engineer*
Cutsinger, Roger Lynn *engineering company executive*
'Dally, James William *mechanical engineering educator, consultant*
Dam, Q. Binh *engineering educator, researcher*
Damavandi, Nader *electrical engineer*
Das, Samik *research assistant*
Dastin, Samuel J. *aerospace engineer, consultant*
Day, Donald Lee *retired engineering educator*
Deabes, Wael Abdelrahman *electrical engineer, educator*
Dede, Ercan M. *mechanical engineer, researcher*
de Jong, Robert L. *chemical engineer*
Deng, Hai *engineering educator, researcher*
Deng, Weiling *chemical engineer*
Der Torossian, Papken *engineering executive*
de Soto, Simon *mechanical engineer*
Dhanda, Abhishek *engineering company executive*
Diakunchak, Ihor S. *retired mechanical engineer*
Dinwiddie, William James *environmental operator*
Dobson, Donald Alfred *retired electrical engineer*
Dolim, Henry Philip, Jr. *retired engineering educator*
Dolins, Steven Barnett *engineering educator*
Dong, Ren Guang *mechanical engineer*
Donohue, Marc David *chemical engineering professor*
Douglas, Karin Nadja *engineer*
Duan, Xiaochun *electrical engineer*
Duggirala, Rajesh *electrical engineer, researcher*
Dull, William Martin *retired engineering executive*
Dunlop, Matthew William *engineering educator*
Durrani, Sajjad Haidar *retired aerospace and communications engineer*
Dusan, Sorin *director of research*
Dutta, Achyut Kumar *electrical and electronics engineer*
Dutta, Anirban *biomedical engineer*
Eaglet, Robert Danton *electrical engineer, aerospace scientist, consultant, retired military officer*
Easton, John H. *engineering educator, consultant*
Eberstein, Arthur *former biomedical engineering educator, researcher*
Eccleston, Charles H. *environmental and nuclear consultant*
Edwards, David *engineering educator*
Edzwald, James K. *engineering educator*
Elam, Matthew *industrial engineer, educator*
Elgawady, Mohamed *structural engineer, researcher, educator*
El-Moursy, Magdy *electronics engineer*
Ergen, Mustafa *engineer*
Erpek, Tugba *electrical engineer*
Ertosun, Mehmet Günhan *electrical engineer*
Ettinger, Harry Joseph *retired industrial hygiene engineer, consultant*
Eustis, Steven M. *electrical engineer*

Richards, Earl Frederick *electrical engineer, educator*
Riofrio, José Antonio *electronics engineer*
Roa-Prada, Sebastian *engineering educator*
Robe, Thurlow Richard *retired engineering educator, dean*
Rode, Daniel L. *engineering educator*
Rogers, Hugh Daniel *electrical engineer, educator*
Rohatgi, Pradeep Kumar *engineering educator*
Romero Aguero, Julio Enrique *electrical engineer, educator*
Roosa, Stephen Allen *energy engineer*
Rose, James Turner *aerospace engineer, consultant*
Rosenthal, Lee *electrical engineer, educator*
Ross, Gerald Fred *electrical engineering executive, researcher*
Roy Chowdhury, Ayan *engineer*
Rubbert, Paul Edward *retired engineering executive*
Rudd, D(ale) F(rederick) *chemical engineering professor*
Rudi, Langston Cilibrasi *software engineer*
Russo, Roy Lawrence *retired electronics engineer*
Ruud, Clayton Olaf *engineering educator*
Sadjadi, Firooz Ahmadi *electrical engineer, consultant, researcher, lecturer*
Saeks, Richard Ephraim *engineering executive*
Safai, Nick M. *chemical engineer, director*
Sahin Sariisik, Asli *engineer*
Sahrakorpi, Seppo *senior research engineer*
Saint-Pierre, Guy *engineering executive*
Saldivar, Enrique *bioengineer, researcher*
Sami, Sedat *civil engineering, educator*
Sang-Sik, Yeo *civil engineer, consultant*
Sarkar, Joy *engineer, educator*
Saygili, Gokhan *civil engineer, researcher*
Schaelicke, Lambert *computer engineer*
Schaper, Leonard W. *retired engineering educator*
Schell, Allan Carter *retired electrical engineer*
Schmidt, David Kelso *engineering educator*
Schultz, Albert Barry *engineering educator*
Scott, Benjamin *retired electrical engineer*
Scott, Charles David *chemical engineer, consultant*
Seaden, George *civil engineer*
Seader, Junior DeVere (Bob Seader) *retired chemical engineering professor*
Secchiutti, Ronald *electrical engineering designer*
Sechrist, Chalmers Franklin, Jr. *electrical engineering educator*
Seible, Frieder *structural engineer, educator*
Seldner, Betty Jane *environmental engineer, aerospace transportation executive, consultant*
Sen, Alper *engineering educator*
Sendaula, Henry Musoke *engineering educator*
Sevier, Michael Christopher *engineer*
Shaffer, Bernard William *mechanical and aerospace engineering educator*
Shank, Maurice Edwin *aerospace engineer, consultant*
Shartle, Stanley Musgrave *engineering executive, consultant, surveyor*
Shaw, Judy Browder *engineer*
Shaw, Leonard Glazer *retired electrical engineering educator, consultant*
Sheaffer, Richard Allen *electrical engineer*
Shehab, Tariq *engineering educator, researcher*
Shim, Sang Eun *engineering educator*
Shiotsu, Masahiro *engineering educator*
Shrivastava, Amitesh *materials engineer*
Shulman, Yechiel *engineering educator*
Siegal, Rita Goran *engineering company executive*
Sieverts, Jorgen Francois *engineering executive*
Simpson, Murray *electrical engineer, consultant*
Singh, Chitranjan K. *electronics engineer*
Sinno, R. Ralph *civil engineer, educator*
Skeen, David Ray *systems engineer, consultant, engineering executive, educator*
Skelland, Anthony Harold Peter *chemical engineering professor*
Skov, Arlie Mason *petroleum engineer, consultant*
Skromme, Lawrence H. *consulting agricultural engineer*
Sliger, Rebecca North *mechanical engineer*
Smally, Donald Jay *consulting engineering executive*
Smith, Rita Rex *mechanical engineer*
Socolow, Robert Harry *engineering educator, physicist*
Somasundaran, Ponisseril *surface and colloid engineering educator*
Sommerfeld, Jude Thomas *chemical engineer, educator*
Song, Qi *electrical engineer*
Sridharan, Arvind *engineer*
Srinivasagupta, Deepak *chemical engineer, researcher*
Srinivasan, Vedanth *engineer*
Stancell, Arnold Francis *chemical engineering educator, retired oil industry executive*
Stapp, Joshua Paul *computer engineer*
Stewart, Albert Elisha *safety engineer, engineering executive*
Stiffler, Jack Justin *electrical engineer*
Stone, Brian *engineering educator*
Stone, Richie Eugene *engineering educator*
Strangman, Thomas *aerospace engineer*
Strieder, William Christian *chemical engineering educator, consultant*
Subramanian, Vijay *mechanical engineer*
Sudan, Ravindra Nath *electrical engineer, physicist, educator*
Sugiyama, Masano *chemical engineer, researcher*
Šulc, Vladimír *mechanical engineer*
Sullivan, Gregory Patrick *principal engineer*
Sullivan, Roy Michael *aerospace engineer, researcher*
Sun, Hongwei *mechanical engineer*
Sun, Hui *industrial engineer, operations research analyst*
Sun, Jie *R & D engineer*
Sun, Zuo *aerospace engineer, researcher*
Sundaram, Narayan *electrical engineer*
Sutton, George Paul *rocket propulsion engineer, writer, educator*
Svarovsky, Sergei A. *engineering educator*
Swalm, Thomas Sterling *aviations systems and weapons consultant, retired military officer*
Swayne, Kenneth E. *engineering educator*
Szabo, Barna Aladar *engineering educator*
Taheri, Saied *engineering educator*
Tamaro, George John *retired consulting engineer*
Tao, Jiang *engineering educator*
Taylor, Anthony Baldwin *civil engineer*
Teitelbaum, Michael Edward *electrical engineer*
Tejnil, Edita *engineering company executive*
Thackston, Edward Lee *civil engineering educator*
Thai, My T. *engineering educator*
Theophilou, Theophilos Sotiri *mechanical engineer*
Thodesen, Carl Christian *civil engineer*
Thomas, Donald Lee *construction technology educator*
Thornhill, Harlen Webster *retired aircraft engineer*
Thornton, Peter A. *engineering educator, consultant*
Tikalsky, Paul J. *civil engineering educator, structural engineer*
Tontiruttananon, Channarong *electrical engineer, researcher*
Tregub, Alexander (Alex Tregub) *electronics engineer*
Tsai, Chi Chun *engineering educator*
Tsoukalas, Lefteri H. *engineering educator, department chairman*
Turaga, Deepak Srinivas *electrical and computer engineer, researcher*
Ulate, Isai *engineering educator*
Upatnieks, Juris *retired optical engineer*
Vaidyanathan, Vijay V. *engineering educator*
Valentine, Ralph Schuyler *chemical engineer, director*
Vanek, Francis Michael *engineering educator, researcher*
Vayghan, Jamshid Abdollahi *architectural engineer*
Velev, Miroslav N. *electrical and computer engineer, educator, entrepreneur, inventor*
Velzy, Charles O. *mechanical engineer*
Venkatesh, Murali *engineering educator*
Vér, István László *acoustical engineer, consultant*
Viest, Ivan Miroslav *structural engineer, consultant*
Villforth, John Carl *engineer, health physicist*
Vohra, Amit *mechanical engineer*
Waaland, Irving T. *retired aerospace engineer*
Wagner, Karel *retired nuclear engineer, educator*
Waller, Steven R. *engineer*
Walsh, Michael P. *mechanical engineer*
Wan, Hung-da *mechanical engineer, educator*
Wang, Jin *engineering educator*
Wang, Lawrence K. *engineering educator*
Wang, Zhiyong *optical engineer, researcher*
Warey, Alok *diesel engineer*
Waxman, Ronald *computer engineer*
Weber, Larry Francis *retired electrical engineer*
Weil, Randolph Allen *executive*
Weingarten, Joseph Leonard *aerospace engineer*
Weiss, Alvin Harvey *chemical engineer, educator, research scientist, consultant*
Weitz, Lesley Anne *aerospace engineer, researcher*
Wells, Stephen Michael *engineering educator*
Wentz, William Henry, Jr. *aerospace engineer, educator*
Wettels, Nicholas Benjamin *biomedical engineer*
Wheeler, George Charles, Jr. *materials and process engineer*
White, Stanley Archibald *electrical engineer, researcher*
Wieselthier, Jeffrey E. *electronics engineer, researcher*
Wilde, Daniel Underwood *computer engineering educator*
Williams, Charles Wesley *retired engineering executive, consultant, researcher*
Williams, Howard Walter *aerospace engineer, engineering executive*
Williams, John Leicester *mechanical engineer, educator*
Williams, Michael Maurice Rudolph *nuclear engineering consultant*
Williams, Thomas W. *electrical engineer*
Willis, Selene Lowe *electrical engineer, application developer, consultant, information technology manager*
Wilson, Chester Goodwin *electrical engineer, educator*
Wilson, Melvin Edmond *retired civil engineer*
Winand, René Fernand Paul *retired metallurgy educator*
Woll, Harry J. *electrical engineer*
Woo, Derek *electrical and computer engineer*
Woodland, N. Joseph *retired optical engineer, retired mechanical engineer*
Woodward, Clinton Benjamin, Jr. *civil engineer, educator*
Wu, Huiquan *chemical engineer*
Wu, Xin *electrical engineer, researcher, educator*
Wu, Xingru *petroleum engineer*
Xingguo, Xiong *engineering educator*
Xu, Juncheng *engineer, researcher*
Xue, Yuan *engineering educator*
Yadavalli, Kameshwar *electronics engineer*
Yang, Bing-Shiang *engineering educator*
Yang, Bo *electrical engineer*
Yang, Jidong *transportation engineer*
Yang, Shujun *electrical engineer*
Yao, Yi *electrical engineer, researcher*
Yong, Raymond Nen-Yiu *civil engineering educator*
Yoon, Yeo-Sun *electronics engineer*
Young, Larry Allen *aerospace engineer*
Younkin, George Worthington *retired electrical engineer*
Yu, Chien-Ning *engineer, consultant*
Yuan, Zeng-Guang *mechanical engineer, researcher*
Yue, Alfred Shui-Choh *metallurgical engineer, consultant*
Yun, James Kyoon *electrical engineer*
Zabalawi, Salaheddin Aiman *electrical engineer*
Zanjacomo, Paulo Regis *engineering executive*
Zelby, Leon Wolf *electrical engineer, educator, consultant*
Zelinski, Joseph John *engineering educator, consultant*
Zhang, Harry X. *environmental engineer*
Zhang, Jianlong *engineer*
Zhang, Shibao *electrical engineer*
Zhao, Yongli *engineering educator*
Zhou, Dian *engineering educator*
Zhu, Yingxuan *engineering educator*
Zhu, Yongjie *engineer*
Zhu, Yun *engineer, researcher*
Zhu, Zhenyu *systems engineer*
Ziemba, Michael Robert *engineering educator*
Zimmerman, Marlin U., Jr. *chemical engineer*
Zunoubi, Mohammad R. *engineering educator*

FINANCE: BANKING SERVICES
See also **FINANCE: INVESTMENT SERVICES**

UNITED STATES

ALABAMA

Birmingham
Northen, Charles Swift III *retired bank executive*
Powell, William Arnold, Jr. *retired bank executive*

Dothan
Peterson, Roger *community bank executive, retired international investment banker, manufacturing executive, air force officer*

Montgomery
Lowder, Robert E. *bank executive*

ALASKA

Anchorage
Cuddy, Daniel Hon *bank executive*
Rasmuson, Edward Bernard *banker*
Reed, Frank Metcalf *bank executive, director*

ARIZONA

Paradise Valley
Unruh, James Arlen *bank executive*

Phoenix
Cappelli, Gregory W. *investment banker, Education Company Executive*
Edelstein, Charles Bruce *investment banker, education company executive*
Richardson, Judy McEwen *investment banker, consultant*

Scottsdale
Carpenter, Peter Rockefeller *retired bank executive*
Garfield, Ernest *bank executive, consultant*
Leonard, George Edmund *bank executive, credit manager, marketing professional*

Tucson
Abelt, Ralph William *bank executive*
Bradley, Gilbert Francis *retired bank executive*

ARKANSAS

Bentonville
Walton, Jim Carr *bank executive*

Fayetteville
Brooks, Mary Elizabeth *bank executive*

Little Rock
Bowen, William Harvey *bank executive, lawyer*
Smith, Susan *bank executive*

CALIFORNIA

Agoura Hills
Kurland, Stanford L. *mortgage company executive*

Arcadia
Ulrich, Peter Henry *banker*

Berkeley
Chirurg, James Thomas *financial holding company executive*

Beverly Hills
Goldsmith, Bram *banker*
Walker, William Tidd, Jr. *investment banker*

Burbank
Miller, Clifford Albert *merchant banker*

Calabasas
Desoer, Barbara Jean *mortgage company executive*

Carmel
Barton, Hugh Perry *bank executive*
Dobey, James Kenneth *banker*

Costa Mesa
Giannini, Valerio Louis *investment banker*
Harley, Halvor Larson *bank executive, lawyer*

Escondido
Newman, Barry Ingalls *retired bank executive*

Fresno
Smith, Richard Howard *banker*

Glendale
Cross, Richard John *bank executive*

Goleta
Nahra, Lynda J. *bank executive*

Irvine
Jamshidipour, Yousef *bank executive, economist, financial advisor*

La Jolla
Van Dine, Vance *investment banker*

La Mesa
Schmidt, James Craig *retired bank, savings and loan association executive*

Lafayette
Dethero, J. Hambright *banker*

Lake Arrowhead
Fitzgerald, John Charles, Jr. *investment banker*

Long Beach
Haller, Howard Edward *investment banker, real estate developer, filmmaker*
Hancock, John Walker III *banker*

Los Angeles
Barren, Bruce Willard (HRH The Duke de Serres) *merchant banker*
Cho, Eung-Rae (Brian) *bank executive*
Contreras-Sweet, Maria *bank executive*
Kang, Alvin *bank executive*
Kim, Min Jung *bank executive*
Mahmoodzadegan, Navid A. *investment banker*
Min, Soo Bong *bank executive*

Malibu
DeMieri, Joseph L. *retired bank executive*

Menlo Park
Grimes, Michael D. *investment banker*
Roberts, George R. *investment banker*
Schmidt, Chauncey Everett *banker, director*

Newport Beach
Casey, Thomas Clark *retired trust company executive, investment advisor*
Frederick, Dolliver H. *investment banker*
Prince, Thomas E. *bank executive*
Rinehart, Charles R. *savings and loan association executive*

Ontario
Myers, Christopher D. *bank executive*

Orinda
Trowbridge, Thomas, Jr. *mortgage company executive*

Palm Desert
Budzinsky, Armin Alexander *investment banker*

Pasadena
Freeman, Ralph Carter *investment banker, management consultant*
Ng, Dominic *bank executive*

San Diego
Rady, Ernest S. *thrift and loan association executive*
Reinhard, Christopher John *merchant banker, venture capitalist, biotechnologist, director*
Wiesler, James Ballard *retired banker*

San Francisco
Atkins, Howard Ian *bank executive*
August-deWilde, Katherine *banker*
Bee, Robert Norman *banker*
Boutros, George F. *investment banker*
Callahan, Patricia R. *bank executive*
Chan, Iris S. *bank executive*
Dellas, Robert Dennis *retired investment banker*
Gillette, Frankie Jacobs *retired savings and loan association executive, federal agency administrator, social worker*
Hoyt, David A. *bank executive*
Kinsell, Jeffrey Clift *investment banker*
Kovacevich, Richard Marco (Dick Kovacevich) *bank executive*
Lee, Pamela Anne *bank executive, accountant, financial analyst*
Levy, Richard D. *bank executive*
Loughlin, Michael J. *bank executive*
Matthews, Gilbert Elliott *investment banker*
McGettigan, Charles Carroll, Jr. *investment banker*
Modjtabai, Avid *bank executive*
Olds, John Theodore *banker*
Oman, Mark C. *bank executive*
Rhein, Kevin A. *bank executive*
Rosenberg, Richard Morris *banker*
Safreno, Casey *investment banker*
Starcher, Diana L. *bank executive*
Stumpf, John Gerard *bank executive*
Tolstedt, Carrie L. *bank executive*
Warner, Harold Clay, Jr. *banker, investment company executive*
White, Julie M. *bank executive*
Woo Ho, Doreen Woo *bank executive*
Yellen, Janet Louise *bank executive*

San Jose
Hall, Robert Emmett, Jr. *investment banker, realtor*

San Mateo
Douglass, Donald Robert *banker*

San Rafael
Djordjevich, Miroslav-Michael *bank executive*
Payne, David L. *bank executive*

Santa Ana
Piszel, Anthony S. (Buddy Piszel) *mortgage company executive*

Santa Barbara
Tilton, David Lloyd *savings and loan association executive*

Santa Monica
Heimbuch, Babette E. *bank executive*

Walnut Creek
Saavedra, Charles James *banker*

COLORADO

Denver
Grant, William West III *banker*
Nicholson, Will Faust, Jr. *bank executive*

Greenwood Village
Imhoff, Walter Francis *retired investment banker*

Lakewood
Orullian, B. LaRae *retired bank executive*

CONNECTICUT

Essex
Miller, Elliott Cairns *retired bank executive, lawyer*

Fairfield
Cooper, L.E. Butck, Jr. *bank executive, lawyer, writer*

Glastonbury
Fiszel, Geoffrey Lynn *investment banker, advisor*

Greenwich
Bedrosian, Gregory Ronald *investment banker*
Nevin, Crocker *investment banker*
Stockman, David Alan *investment banker, former US Representative from Michigan*

New Canaan
MacEwan, Nigel Savage *retired merchant banker*

Norwalk
Baylis, Robert Montague *investment banker, charity director*
Piper, Thomas Laurence III *banker*

Ridgefield
Mesznik, Joel R. *investment banker*

Stamford
Keane, Margaret *bank executive*

Washington Depot
Levine, Laurence Brandt *investment banker*

Weston
Zimmerman, Bernard *investment banker*

Westport
Donaldson, James Neill *banker*
Kelly, Paul Knox *investment banker*

DELAWARE

Hockessin
St. Clair, Jesse Walton, Jr. *retired savings and loan association executive*

Wilmington
Cecala, Ted Thomas, Jr. *banker, accountant*
Cohen, Betsy Z. *bank executive*
Porter, John Francis III *banker*
Struthers, Ric (Richard K. Struthers) *bank executive*

DISTRICT OF COLUMBIA

Washington
Bacon, Kenneth J. *mortgage company executive*
Benson, David C. *mortgage company executive*
Binder, Lisa B. *former bank executive*
Couper, William *bank executive*
Dallavecchia, Enrico *mortgage company executive*
Decker, Brett M. *bank executive*
Douglas, Leslie *investment banker*
Hisey, David C. *mortgage company executive*
Hochberg, Fred Philip *bank executive, former dean*
Johnson, David M. *mortgage company executive, former insurance company executive*
Laskawy, Philip Alan *mortgage company executive, retired accounting and management consulting firm executive*
Moreno, Luis Alberto *bank executive*
Pollock, Alexander John *banker*
Poole, William *retired bank executive*
Rotberg, Eugene Harvey *investment banker, lawyer*
Shaw, Michael *mortgage company executive*
Tomlinson, Alexander Cooper *investment banker, consultant*
Williams, Michael J. *mortgage company executive*
Wolfowitz, Paul Dundes *former President of the World Bank*
Zoellick, Robert Bruce *President of the World Bank, former federal agency administrator*

FLORIDA

Boca Raton
Spagnuolo, Louis D. *banker*
Tomasso, Anthony *banker*

Coral Gables
Brownell, Edwin Rowland *retired banker, civil engineer, land surveyor*
Weiner, Morton David *banker, insurance agent*

Dunedin
Rosa, Raymond Ulric *retired banker*

Englewood
Simis, Theodore Luckey *investment banker, information technology executive*

Fort Lauderdale
Leach, Ralph F. *banker*
Thayer, Charles James *investment banker*

Gainesville
Briggs-Simmons, Karen Elaine *bankruptcy firm executive*

Lake Wales
Mc Call, Julien Lachicotte *banker*

Lakewood Ranch
Piper, Mark Harry *retired banker*

Marco Island
Cooper, Thomas Astley *bank executive*

Miami
Abess, Leonard, Jr. *bank executive*

Naples
de Saint Phalle, Thibaut *investment banker, consultant*
Kley, John Arthur *banker*
Martinuzzi, Leo Sergio, Jr. *banker*

Pensacola
Stuart, Walter Bynum III *retired banker*

Ponte Vedra Beach
de Selding, Edward Bertrand *retired bank executive*
O'Brien, Raymond Vincent, Jr. *banker*

Punta Gorda
Haswell, Carleton Radley *banker*

Saint Petersburg
Godbold, Francis Stanley *investment banker, security firm executive*

Sarasota
Phillips, Howard William *investment banker*

Tampa
Johnson, Randall Clyde *mortgage company executive*

Tierra Verde
Stewart, John Murray *bank executive*

Vero Beach
Crosby, John Griffith *investment banker*

West Palm Beach
Addison, Ferguson Lofton Lightbourne *retired bank executive*

GEORGIA

Atlanta
Abbott, Gay O. *bank executive*
Breeden, Mimi *bank executive*
Chancy, Mark A. *bank executive*
Dierker, David F. *bank executive*
Dorfman, Richard *bank executive*
Dowling, Roderick Anthony *investment banker*
Freeman, Thomas E. *bank executive*
Joseph, Pamela A. *bank executive*
Kirby, C. Eugene, Jr. *bank executive*
Lockhart, Dennis P. *bank executive*
Patterson, Dennis M. *bank executive*
Reed, William R., Jr. *bank executive*
Rogers, William H., Jr. *bank executive*
Spiegel, John William *banker*
Sullivan, Timothy E. *bank executive*
Wells, James M. III *bank executive*

Columbus
Anthony, Richard E. *bank executive*
Carr, Leila S. *bank executive*

Flowery Branch
Monroe, Melrose *retired bank executive*

Hinesville
Smith, Barbara *bank executive*

Savannah
Clemmons, John B. *bank executive, director, retired mathematics educator*

IDAHO

Ketchum
McElhinny, Wilson Dunbar *banker*

ILLINOIS

Chicago
Bartter, Brit Jeffrey *investment banker*
Bobins, Norman R. *bank executive*
Bynoe, Peter Charles Bernard *investment banker, lawyer*
Citera, Peter M. *mortgage company executive*
Costello, Ellen M. *bank executive*
Dancewicz, John Edward *investment banker*
Evans, Charles L. *bank executive*
Feldman, Matthew R. *bank executive*
Fenton, Clifton Lucien *investment banker*
Hasten, Joseph Erwin *bank executive*
Mitchell, Lee Mark *private equity investor, executive*
Montgomery, Charles Howard *retired bank executive*
Reilly, Robert Frederick *investment banker*
Rieser, Richard M., Jr. *banker*
Schulte, David Michael *investment banker*
Steves Keiser, Susan *bank executive*
Stirling, James Paulman *investment banker*
Ward, Jonathan P. *investment banker*

Fox River Grove
Abboud, Alfred Robert *banker, investor, consultant, director*

Highwood
Brown, Lawrence Haas *retired banker*

Hinsdale
Fox, David Wayne *banker*

Lake Forest
Seaman, Irving, Jr. *banker*
Swift, Edward Foster III *investment banker*

Northbrook
Gratalo, John, Jr. *banker, small business owner*
Griffiths, Robert Pennell *banker*
Keehn, Silas *retired bank executive*

Palatine
Hershenhorn, Robert Gene *bank executive*

Winnetka
Klapperich, Frank Lawrence, Jr. *investment banker*

INDIANA

Columbus
Abts, Henry William *retired banker*

Indianapolis
Stitle, Stephen A. *bank executive*

La Porte
Bakwin, Edward Morris *banker*

Muncie
Anderson, Stefan Stolen *retired banker*

IOWA

Cedar Rapids
Wax, Nadine Virginia *retired bank executive*

Clinton
Kearney, Michael John *banker*

Des Moines
Heiden, Cara *mortgage company executive*

Mason City
Rodamaker, Marti Tomson *bank executive*

KANSAS

Liberal
Richard, Loren Dru *bank executive*

Pratt
Loomis, Howard Krey *banker, director*

Salina
Hale Carter, Mollie *bank executive*

Shawnee Mission
McEachen, Richard Edward *banker, lawyer*

Tonganoxie
Torneden, Connie Jean *banker*

Topeka
Bunten, William Daniel *retired banker*

KENTUCKY

Louisville
Thompson, Kathy C. *bank executive*

LOUISIANA

Covington
Blossman, Alfred Rhody, Jr. *banker*

Lafayette
Hail, Karen Lee *bank executive*

MAINE

Camden
Daly, Sean G. *bank executive*

Portland
Masrani, Bharat B. *bank executive*

MARYLAND

Annapolis
Schleicher, Nora Elizabeth *bank executive, treasurer, accountant*

Baltimore
Baldwin, Henry Furlong *banker*
Barnhill, Gregory Hurd *investment banker*
Dunn, Edward K., Jr. *banker*
Kent, Edgar Robert, Jr. *investment banker*
Liberto, Joseph Salvatore *retired bank executive*
Schaefer, Robert Wayne *banker*

Bethesda
Rosenbaum, Greg Alan *merchant banker, consultant*
Saul, B. Francis, II, *bank executive, director*

Centreville
Griffith, Alan Richard *retired banker*

Owings Mills
Sanner, George Bradley *bank executive*

MASSACHUSETTS

Andover
Yannalfo, Brett Conlon *bank executive*

Arlington
Smialowski, Joseph A. *former mortgage company executive*

Boston
Aquilino, Daniel *banker*
Finnegan, Neal Francis *retired banker*
Hill, Richard Devereux *retired banker*
Perrault, Paul A. *bank executive*
Pline, Jennifer Alice *trust company executive*
Rosengren, Eric S. *bank executive*
Vermilye, Peter Hoagland *banker*
Walters, Kirk W. *bank executive*

Cambridge
Edgerly, William Skelton *banker*

Dover
Aldrich, Frank Nathan *banker*

Gloucester
Fioravanti, Nancy Eleanor *retired banker*

Longmeadow
Lo Bello, Joseph David *bank executive*

Marblehead
Morton, Perry Williams *investment banker*

Reading
Burbank, Nelson Stone *investment banker*

Westwood
Riley, Henry Charles *banker*

Winchester
Brennan, Francis Patrick *banker*

MICHIGAN

Birmingham
Shields, Robert Emmet *merchant banker, lawyer*

Farmington Hills
Heiss, Richard Walter *retired bank executive, consultant, lawyer*

Frankfort
Foster, Robert Carmichael *banker*

Grand Rapids
Canepa, John Charles *banking consultant*
Van Dyke, Michelle *bank executive*

Grosse Pointe
Mengden, Joseph Michael *retired investment banker*

Saginaw
Evans, Harold Edward *retired banker*

MINNESOTA

Chanhassen
Severson, Roger Allan *bank executive*

Edina
Campbell, James Robert *retired bank executive*

Minneapolis
Cecere, Andrew *bank executive*
Davis, Richard K. *bank executive*
Nelson, Kenneth D. *bank executive*
Stern, Gary Hilton *bank executive*
Thormodsgard, Diane L. *bank executive*
Wunsch, John D. *former bank executive, financial consultant*

Wayzata
Rich, Willis Frank, Jr. *banker*

MISSISSIPPI

Gulfport
Thatcher, George Robert *banker, writer, columnist*

Tupelo
Patterson, Aubrey Burns, Jr. *banker*

MISSOURI

Independence
Barker, Keith Rene *investment banker*

Kansas City
Hoenig, Thomas M. *bank executive*
Kemper, Jonathan McBride *banker*

Reiter, Robert Edward *banker*

O Fallon
Das, Sanjiv *mortgage company executive*

Saint Louis
Bealke, Linn Hemingway *banker*
Bryant, Ruth Alyne *banker*
Bullard, James B. *bank executive*
Costigan, Edward John *retired investment banker*
Kling, S(tephen) Lee *banker*
Maurer, Frederic George III *bank executive*
Rasche, Robert Harold *banker, retired economics educator*
Stoecker, David Thomas *retired banker*

Saint Peters
Pring, Robert Bradford *banker, securities trader*

Walker
Martin, Phillip Dwight *bank consulting company executive, mayor*

NEBRASKA

Lincoln
Lundstrom, Gilbert Gene *bank executive, lawyer*
Young, Dale Lee *banker*

NEVADA

Logandale
Smiley, Robert William, Jr. *investment banker*

Reno
Binns, James Edward *retired banker*

NEW HAMPSHIRE

New Castle
Mapel, William Marlen Raines *retired bank executive*

Sanbornville
Berg, Warren Stanley *retired bank executive*

NEW JERSEY

Bay Head
O'Brien, Robert Brownell, Jr. *banker, consultant, yacht broker, opera company executive, museum director*

Guttenberg
Boss, Jeffrey *banker*

Jersey City
Goldberg, Arthur *merchant banker, financial consultant, educator*

Liberty Corner
Feeks, J. Michael *bank executive*

Morristown
Kearns, William Michael, Jr. *investment banker*

Mount Laurel
Verba, Linda *bank executive*

Paramus
Hermance, Ronald E., Jr. *bank executive*

Princeton
Ganoe, Charles Stratford *banker, consultant*
Mills, Bradford *merchant banker*

Ridgewood
Smethurst, E(dward) William, Jr. *investment banker*

Spring Lake
D'Luhy, John James *investment banker*

Summit
Lewis, Donald Emerson *banker*
Mueller, Paul Henry *retired bank executive*

Wood Ridge
Micco, Vincent *banker*

NEW MEXICO

Farmington
Schauer, Shelia I. *bank executive*

Santa Fe
Clyde, Larry Forbes *banker*
Dreisbach, John Gustave *investment banker*

NEW YORK

Albany
Dushensky, Jacqueline Amelia *banker, educator*

Bedford
Philip, Peter Van Ness *former trust company executive*

Bedford Hills
Dublon, Dina *former bank executive*

Brooklyn
Singer, Eric T. *investment banker*

Buffalo
Wilmers, Robert George *bank executive*

Cherry Valley
Humes, Graham *investment banker*

Elmont
Cusack, Thomas Joseph *retired banker*

Fire Island Pines
Herregat, Guy-Georges Jacques *retired banker*

Garden City
Sheinbaum, Marc X. *bank executive*

Harrison
Hurley, Dean C. *bank executive, lawyer*

Hartsdale
Katz, John *investment banker*

New York
Adams, John Brett *investment banker, pharmaceutical executive*
Agostinelli, Robert Francesco *investment banker*
Alemany, Ellen R. *bank executive*
Allen, Claxton Edmonds III *investment banker*
Anaya, Raul *bank executive*
Arlander, Bodil M. *bank executive*
Awad, George *bank executive*
Bagatelle, David Samuel *bank executive*
Bains, Leslie Elizabeth *banker*
Bakhshi, Suneel *bank executive*
Ballard, Charles Alan *investment banker*
Barry, Nancy Marie *bank executive*
Bellanger, Serge René *bank executive*
Berlinski, Milton R. *investment banking company executive*
Boardman, D(ennie) Dixon *investment banker*
Bober, Lawrence Harold *retired banker*
Brody, Kenneth David *investment banker*
Burke, James Joseph, Jr. *investment banker*
Carey, William Polk *investment banker*
Castle, John Krob *merchant banker*
Cephas, Derrick D. *bank executive, lawyer*
Clifford, Stewart Burnett *banker, director*
Cohn, Melissa Lynn *mortgage company executive*
Cromwell, Oliver Dean *investment banker*
David-Weill, Michel Alexandre *retired investment banker*
Davis, George Linn *banker*
Davis, Kimberly B. *bank executive*
Davis, Morty (J. Morton Davis) *investment banker*
Debs, Richard A. *investment banker*
DelliBovi, Alfred A. *bank executive, former federal agency administrator*
DeNunzio, David Ames *investment banker*
D'Erasmo, Diane *bank executive*
Deutsch, David Neil *investment banker*
Donnelly, John L. *bank executive*
Dooley, Douglas John *bank executive*
Drew, Ina R. *bank executive*
Dudley, William C. *bank executive, economist*
Duersten, Althea L. *bank executive*
Dwek, Cyril S. *bank executive*
Elliott, Steven G. *bank executive*
Epstein, Stuart Joel *investment banker*
Erdoes, Mary Callahan *bank executive*
Evangelisti, Joseph M. *bank executive*
FitzPatrick, Daniel M. *trust company executive, lawyer*
Flaherty, Pamela Potter *bank executive*
Forbes, Jim (James D. Forbes) *investment banker*
Fredericks, Ivy Lindstrom *investment banker*
Friedberg, Barry Sewell *investment banker*
Furman, Roy Lance *investment banker, theater producer*
Galant, Paul S. *bank executive*
Gamble, Theodore Robert, Jr. *investment banker*
Gant, Donald Ross *investment banker*
Garrett, Robert *investment banker, director*
Gellert, Michael Erwin *investment banker*
Gibbons, Thomas Patrick (Todd Gibbons) *bank executive*
Godridge, Leslie V. *bank executive*
Gold, Jeffrey Mark *investment banker*
Goldberg, Laurence *investment banker*
Goldmark, Peter Francis *banker*
Gossett, Robert Francis, Jr. *merchant banker*
Gramm, Phil (William Philip Gramm) *bank executive, former United States Senator from Texas*
Greenhill, Robert Foster (Bob Greenhill) *investment banker*
Greenthal, Jill A. *investment banker*
Hakala, Thomas John *private banker, financial planner, accountant*
Halpern, Merril Mark *retired investment banker*
Harmon, James Allen *bank executive*
Hassell, Gerald L. *bank executive*
Heaton, Eric *bank executive*
Heimann, John Gaines *investment banker*
Henry, Lawrence Charles (Lonny Henry) *investment banker*
Hersch, Dennis Steven *business executive, lawyer*
Hill, J(ames) Tomilson *investment banker*
Howard, Bonnie *bank executive*
Hricik, Lorraine E. *bank executive*
Ingrassia, Timothy J. *investment banker*
Janiak, Anthony Richard, Jr. *investment banker*
Johnson, Thomas Stephen *retired banker*
Johnston, Charles D. *bank executive*
Kaufmann, Mark Steiner *banker, director*
Keevil, Philip Clement *investment banker*
Kelly, Robert P. *bank executive*
Kravis, Henry R. *investment banker*
Krimendahl, Herbert Frederick, II, *investment banker*
Lane, Jeffrey Bruce *bank executive*
LeBlond, Richard Knight, II, *banker*
Leung, Firman *investment bank executive*
Levinson, Carl E. *bank executive*
Levy, Jack *investment banker*
Lieb, Richard Jay *investment banker*
Lincoln, Edmond Lynch *investment banker*
Lipper, Kenneth *investment banker, film producer, writer*
Lowman, David B. *mortgage company executive*
Macris, Achilles O. *bank executive*
Manges, James Horace *investment banker*
Masters, Blythe *bank executive*
Mathews, Michael Stone *investment banker*
Maxwell, Anders John *investment banker*
McDowell, Mary *bank executive*
McKinnon, Paul *bank executive, human resources specialist*
McMullan, William Patrick III *investment banker*
Meachin, David James Percy *investment banker*
Mendoza, Roberto G., Jr. *banker*
Menschel, Robert Benjamin *investment banker*
Merriss, Philip Ramsay, Jr. *banker*
Mills, William J. *bank executive*
Mintz, Norman Nelson *investment banker, educator, retired academic administrator*
Mnuchin, Alan Geoffrey *investment banker*
Monaco, Julie *bank executive*
Morrissey, Michael Joseph *finance executive*
Myerberg, Marcia *investment banker*
Needham, George Austin *investment banker*
Nemazee, Hassan *investment banker*
Obolensky, Ivan *investment banker, foundation administrator, writer*
Panagos, Steven Gregory *investment banker*
Paulson, John Alfred *hedge fund manager*
Peetz, Karen Bretherick *bank executive*
Peretsman, Nancy Beth *investment banker*
Perlmutter, Louis *investment banker, lawyer*
Petrie, Donald Joseph *banker*
Poll, Robert Eugene, Jr. *bank executive*
Porat, Ruth M. *investment bank executive*
Porter, Grant A. *investment banker*
Potter, William James *investment banker*
Price, Michael J. *investment banker*
Purse, Charles Roe *investment banker*
Rainis, Eugene Charles *bank executive*
Reyes, Diane S. *bank executive*
Rizzi, Joseph Vito *banker*
Rockefeller, David *banker*
Rogan, Brian G. *bank executive*
Roosevelt, Theodore, IV, *investment banker*
Rose, Robert Neal *investment banker*
Ross, Wilbur Louis, Jr. *investment banker*
Rubin, Robert Samuel *investment banker*
Sack, Brian P. *bank executive, economist*
Safra, Joseph *bank executive*
Salmans, Charles Gardiner *banker*
Sarkozy, Olivier (Pierre Olivier Sarkozy) *investment banker*
Schiff, David Tevele *investment banker*
Schneider, David C. *bank executive*
Schumacher, Robert Denison *banker*
Schupak, Donald *merchant banker, lawyer, strategic planner*
Scott, Margaret Simon *retired mortgage broker*
Sharma, Deepak *bank executive*
Shedlin, Gary Stephen *investment banker*
Shipley, Walter Vincent *retired bank executive*
Shohet, Zion *bank executive*
Slacik, Claudia *bank executive*
Slusser, William Peter *investment banker*
Smith, Hilary Cranwell Bowen *investment banker*
Smith, Phillips Guy *banker*
Smith, Raymond W. *investment banking executive*
Spielvogel, Sidney Meyer *retired investment banker*
Stakias, G. Michael *private equity*
Stein, Howard S. *retired banker*
Stern, James Andrew *investment banker*
Straton, John Charles, Jr. *investment banker*
Sutton, Cece (Cecilia Stewart Sutton) *bank executive*
Svenson, Charles Oscar *investment banker*
Tagliaferri, Lee Gene *investment banker*
Tanner, Harold *investment banker*
Taussig, Andrew Richard *investment banker*
Taylor, Richard William *investment banker, portfolio manager*
Thompson, George Kennedy (Ken Thompson) *retired bank executive*
Towbin, A. Robert *investment banker*
Tuft, Tom (Thomas Edwin Tuft) *investment banker*
Wadsworth, John (Jack) Spencer, Jr. *investment banker*
Wallace, William S. *bank executive*
Walters, Milton James *investment banker*
Warner, Miner Hill *investment banker*
Wasserstein, Bruce *investment banker*
Watters, Kevin *bank executive*
Weil, Frank A. *investment banker, lawyer*
Weiner, Elyse *bank executive*
Weintz, Jacob Frederick, Jr. *retired investment banker*
Wellin, Keith Sears *retired investment banker*
Wheeler, Jane *investment banker*
Whiting, Gordon James *investment banker*
Wit, Harold Maurice *retired investment banker, lawyer*
Witter, Jonathan W. *bank executive*
Wolff, William F. III *investment banker*
Wright, Deborah C. *bank executive*
Yancey, Richard Charles *investment banker*
Ybarra, Paco *bank executive*
Young, Robert Craig *banker*

Old Westbury
Ostrander, Thomas William *retired investment banker*

Oyster Bay
Schwab, Hermann Caspar *banker*
Walsh, Charles Richard *retired banker*

Rochester
Hanson, Karen Noble *financial holding company executive*
Wayland-Smith, Robert Dean *retired banker*

Saratoga Springs
Wait, Charles Valentine *banker*

Scarsdale
Abbe, Colman *investment banker*

Southampton
Brokaw, Clifford Vail III *investment banker*

Stamford
Bergleitner, George Charles, Jr. *investment banker*

Syracuse
Gray, Charles Augustus *banker*

Tonawanda
Haller, Calvin John *banker*

Wyandanch
Newman, Samuel *retired trust company executive*

Yonkers
Philipps, Edward William *former banker, real estate appraiser*
Singer, Cecile Doris *bank executive, former state legislator*

NORTH CAROLINA

Chapel Hill
Sewright, Charles William, Jr. *mortgage banking advisory services company executive*

Charlotte
Alphin, J. Steele *bank executive*
Banks, Keith *bank executive*
Baronoff, Steven A. *bank executive*
Bessant, Cathy (Catherine Pombier) *bank executive, marketing professional*
Chance, Gloria A. *bank executive*
Darnell, David Clark *bank executive*
Finucane, Anne M. *bank executive*
Jenkins, Benjamin P. III *bank executive*
Jones, Milton H., Jr. *bank executive*
Kelly, Stanhope A. *bank executive*
Lewis, Kenneth D. *bank executive*
Massey, Walter Eugene *bank executive, retired academic administrator*
McFayden, Shannon W. *bank holding company executive*
Montag, Thomas K. (Thomas Kell Montag) *bank executive*
Murray, Cindy *bank executive*
Preston, Margaret Mary V. *bank executive*
Price, Joe L. *bank executive*
Selig, Stefan M. *bank executive*
Smith, Wilburn Jackson, Jr. *retired bank executive*
Steel, Robert King *bank executive, former federal agency administrator*
Veyera, Jeffrey Alan *bank executive*
Zwiener, David Kenneth *bank executive*

Gastonia
Teem, Paul Lloyd, Jr. *bank executive*

Greenville
Wilkerson, William Holton *banker*

Hampstead
Snyder, Clair Allison *banker*

Highlands
Sheehan, Charles Vincent *investment banker*

Pinehurst
Rhody, Ronald Edward *bank, communications executive*

Raleigh
Hardin, Eugene Brooks, Jr. *bank executive*
Smith, Lanty Lloyd *bank executive, lawyer*

Winston Salem
Allison, John Andrew, IV, *bank executive*
Bible, Daryl N. *bank executive*
Henson, Christopher L. *bank executive*
King, Kelly S. *bank executive*
Medlin, John Grimes, Jr. *banker, director*
Wanders, Hans Walter *banker*

OHIO

Canton
Carpenter, Noble Olds *retired bank executive*

Cincinnati
Carmichael, Greg D. *bank executive*
Kabat, Kevin Thomas *bank executive*
Kari, Ross *bank executive*
Poston, Daniel T. *bank executive*
Westbrook, Lynda A. *bank executive*

Cleveland
Bibb, Paul E., Jr., (Buck Bibb) *bank executive*
Carter, E. Kennedy, Jr. *bank executive*
Clark, Paul G. *bank executive*
Crowl, Robert B. *bank executive*
DeKaser, Richard J. *bank executive*
Dunham, J. Andrew *bank executive*
Frate, Daniel J. *bank executive*
Glickman, Carl David *banker*
Goetz, Kenneth M. *bank executive*
Gorney, Jon L. *bank executive*
Grebenc, Jane *bank executive*
Gulick, James P. *bank executive*
Jelinek, Gregory M. *bank executive*
Kelly, Jeffrey D. *bank executive*
Khayat, Clark *bank executive*
Lathe, Timothy J. *bank executive*
Lyons, Janis E. *bank executive*
Manning, W. Robert, Jr. *bank executive*
McCartin, Joseph T. *bank executive*
McCrodden, Bruce A. *bank executive*
Mooney, Beth *bank executive*
Naraine, Chameli *bank executive*
Pianalto, Sandra *bank executive*
Pry, Carl G. *bank executive*

Rice, Philip L. *bank executive*
Richlovsky, Thomas Andrew *bank executive*
Rowe, Robert C. *bank executive*
Schecter, William H. *bank executive*
Seifert, Shelley Jane *bank executive*
Tengel, Jeffrey J. *bank executive*
Yanoti, Timothy *bank executive*

Columbus
Arvia, Anne L. *bank executive*
McCoy, John Bonnet *retired bank executive*
Steinour, Stephen D. *bank executive*

Newark
Busta, Paul Timothy *banker*
McConnell, William Thompson *bank executive*

Rocky River
O'Brien, John Feighan *investment banker*

Toledo
Kunze, Ralph Carl *retired savings and loan association executive*

OKLAHOMA

Bartlesville
Doty, Donald D. *retired bank executive*

Nichols Hills
Trost, Louis Frederick, Jr. *banker, financial planner*

Oklahoma City
Fiegel, Jacque R. *bank executive*
Reich, Richard Allen *bank executive*

Wewoka
Rains, Mary Jo *banker*

OREGON

Bend
Moss, Patricia L. *bank executive*

Lake Oswego
McKay, Laura L. *bank executive, consultant*

Portland
Pierson, Wayne George *trust company executive*
Rosencrantz, Lawrence *holding company executive, lawyer*

Sandy
Rosier, David Lewis *retired investment banker*

PENNSYLVANIA

Ambler
Carey, Francis James *investment banker*

Devon
Boehne, Edward George *banker*
Wilson, Malcolm Campbell *investment trust management executive*

Gibsonia
Groves, Michael *banker*

Gladwyne
Geisel, Cameron Meade, Jr. *retired bank executive*

Harleysville
Geraghty, Paul D. *bank executive*

Jenkintown
Mason, John Murwyn, Jr. *bank executive*

Lafayette Hill
Eagleson, William Boal, Jr. *banker*

Lansdale
Fawley, John Jones *retired banker*

New Holland
Roesch, Clarence Henry *banker*

New Hope
Hover, John Calvin, II, *banker*

Philadelphia
Johnson, Victor Lawrence *banker, director*
Plosser, Charles Irving *bank executive, economics professor*

Pittsburgh
Demchak, William Stanton *bank executive*
Gulley, Joan Long *banker*
Jefferson, Joseph Murray *banker*
Johnson, Richard J. *bank executive*
McLaughlin, Charlotte *bank executive*
Milsom, Robert Cortlandt *banker, director*
Rohr, James Edward (Jim Rohr) *bank executive*

Saint Davids
Sheftel, Roger Terry *merchant banker*

Sinking Spring
Bausher, Verne C(harles) *retired bank executive*

Souderton
Hoeflich, Charles Hitschler *banker*

Wayne
Coughey, Donna M. *bank executive*

RHODE ISLAND

Little Compton
Middendorf, J. William, II, *investment banker*

Newport
Sands, Harold Winthrop *banker, financial planner*

Providence
Fish, Lawrence Kingsbaker *bank executive*
Sherman, Merrill W. *bank executive*

SOUTH CAROLINA

Columbia
Boggs, Jack Aaron *retired banker, municipal government official*

Greenwood
Boxx, Rita McCord *retired banker*

North Myrtle Beach
Byrne, James Frederick *banker*

SOUTH DAKOTA

Sioux Falls
Sanford, T(homas) Denny *bank executive*

TENNESSEE

Knoxville
Lawson, Fred Raulston *banker*

Memphis
Jordan, D. Bryan *bank executive*

Murfreesboro
Ford, William F. *banker*

Nashville
Bottorff, Dennis C. *banker*
Burch, John Christopher, Jr. *investment banker*
Daane, James Dewey *banker*
Harrison, Clifford Joy, Jr. *banker*
Shell, Owen Gladstone, Jr. *retired bank executive*

TEXAS

Abilene
Bentley, Clarence Edward *savings and loan association executive*

Austin
Schneider, James M. *bank executive, former computer company executive*

Dallas
Babb, Ralph W., Jr. *bank executive*
Buttigieg, Joseph J. *bank executive*
Cochran, George Calloway III *retired bank executive, lawyer*
Fisher, Richard Welton *bank executive*
Reid, Langhorne III *merchant banker*
Stankunas, Edward Joseph *banker*

Fort Worth
Minton, Jerry Davis *retired banker, lawyer*

Houston
Anderson, D(arryl) Kent *bank executive*
Ball, George L. *investment banker*
Currie, John Thornton (Jack Currie) *retired investment banker*
Jordan, Carmen Angelle *bank executive*
King, Katrina *bank executive*
Neuhaus, Philip Ross *investment banker*
Trauber, Stephen M. (Steve Tauber) *investment banker*

Laredo
Gonzalez, Eugene Robert *investment banker*

New Braunfels
Pharis, Ruth McCalister *retired bank executive*

Pasadena
Moon, John Henry, Sr. *banker*

San Antonio
Duncan, A. Baker *investment banker*

UTAH

Salt Lake City
Chillingworth, Lori *bank executive*
Simmons, Harris H. *bank executive*
Smith, Cynthia M. *bank executive*
Urie, Alan T. *bank executive*

VERMONT

Lyndon Center
Dame, William Page III *bank executive, educational administrator*

Manchester
Carey, James Henry *banker*

Rutland
Haley, John Charles *retired bank executive*

VIRGINIA

Alexandria
Birely, William Cramer *investment banker*
Tucker, Howard McKeldin *investment banker, consultant*

Arlington
Leland, Marc Ernest *trust company executive, consultant, lawyer*
Ochoa-Brillembourg, Hilda Margarita *investment banker*
Rogers, James Frederick *banker, management consultant*

Ashburn
Pavsek, Daniel Allan *banker, educator*

Chantilly
Pocalyko, Michael Nicholas *investment banker, venture capitalist*

Charlottesville
Bull, George Albert *retired banker*

Falls Church
Bokhari, Mazhar Ali *bank executive*

Mc Lean
Boyd, Ralph F., Jr. *mortgage company executive, former federal agency administrator*
Cook, Patricia L. *mortgage company executive*
Fitzgerald, Peter Gosselin *bank executive, former United States Senator from Illinois*
George, Paul G. *mortgage company executive*
Haldeman, Ed (Charles Edgar Haldeman Jr.) *mortgage company executive, former investment company executive*
Koskinen, John Andrew *former mortgage company executive*
Perlman, Mike *mortgage company executive*
Pike, Lynn A. *bank executive*
Witherell, Bruce M. *mortgage company executive*

Reston
Blum, Edward Howard *investment banker*

Richmond
Black, Robert Perry *bank executive*
Lacker, Jeffrey Malcolm *bank executive, economist*
Moore, Andrew Taylor, Jr. *banker*
Talley, Charles Richmond *retired bank executive*

WASHINGTON

Coupeville
Piercy, Gordon Clayton *bank executive, educator*

Everett
Nelson, Carol Kobuke *bank executive*

Renton
Longbrake, William Arthur *bank executive*

Seattle
Andrew, Lucius Archibald David III *bank executive*
Campbell, Robert Hedgcock *investment banker, lawyer*
Rotella, Stephen J. *former bank executive*

Spokane
Horton, Susan Pittman *bank executive*
McWilliams, Edwin Joseph *banker*
Stanley, Heidi B. *bank executive*

Walla Walla
Purcell, Cynthia D. *bank executive*

WISCONSIN

Milwaukee
Lacy, William H. *retired mortgage company executive*
Murphy, Judith Chisholm *trust company executive*
Sims, Deloris *bank executive*

Racine
Baumgardt, George Francis *bank executive, musician, director*

WYOMING

Cheyenne
Knight, Robert Edward *bank executive, educator*

TERRITORIES OF THE UNITED STATES

GUAM

Agana
Flores, Philip Joseph *bank executive, former political organization administrator*

CANADA

ONTARIO

Niagara-on-the-Lake
Augustine, Jerome Samuel *merchant banker*

Toronto
Cefis, Alberta M. *bank executive*
Fullerton, R. Donald *banker*
Godsoe, Peter Cowperthwaite *retired banker*
Johnston, Colleen M. *bank executive*
Kumar, Subodh *investment banker*
MacDougall, Hartland Molson *retired bank executive*
Maidment, Karen E. *bank executive*
Nesbitt, Richard *bank executive, former stock exchange executive*
Stymiest, Barbara *bank executive*
Taylor, Allan Richard *retired banker*

QUEBEC

Montreal
Torrey, David Leonard *investment banker*

Mount Royal
Elie, Jean André *investment banker*

MEXICO

Districto Federal Mexico
Quiroz Robles, Fernando *bank executive*

Mexico City
Medina-Mora, Manuel *bank executive*
Zorilla Fullaondo, Enrique *bank executive*

ANGOLA

Luanda
Lavrador, Sebastiao Bastos *bank executive*

BELARUS

Minsk
Aleinikov, Gennady *bank executive*

BELGIUM

Beersel
Alfons Remi Emiel, Viscount Verplaetse *bank administrator*

Brussels
Ruding, Herman Onno *banker, former cabinet minister*

BULGARIA

Sofia
Harsev, Emil Manolov *bank executive*

CHINA

Hi-Tech Zone Xian
Leighton, Lawrence Ward *investment banker*

CYPRUS

Nicosia
Christodoulou, Christodoulos *business consultant*

DENMARK

Copenhagen
Hoffmeyer, Erik *former bank executive*

ENGLAND

London
Binney, Robert Harry *bank executive*
Collins, Paul John *banker*
Cowles, James C. *bank executive*
Evans, Richard C.S. *bank executive*
Fraser, Jane *bank executive*
Mosselmans, Carel Maurits *investment banker*
Oppenheimer, Deanna Watson *bank executive*
Quint, David Paul *investment banking executive*
Warner, Scott Dennis *investment banker*

Marlow
Le Blanc, Bart *banker*

HONG KONG

Chai, Nelson J. *bank executive, former stock exchange executive*

ICELAND

Reykjavik
Gunnarsson, Birgir Isleifur *bank executive, legislator*

JAPAN

Tokyo
Ogata, Shijuro *retired central banker*

KYRGYZSTAN

Bul Erkinduk
Sultanov, Marat *bank executive*

NETHERLANDS

Amsterdam
Groenink, Rijkman Willem Johan *bank executive*
Martinez, Arthur C. *bank executive, retired retail executive*

PHILIPPINES

Manila
Lee, Young-Hoi *bank executive*
Pholsena, Khempheng *finance and administration bank executive*

REPUBLIC OF KOREA

Seoul
Kang, Chung Won *bank executive*

RUSSIA

Moscow
Khokhlov, Vitaly Sergeyevich *bank executive*

SIERRA LEONE

Freetown
Swaray, Steven Mustapha *banker, economist*

SPAIN

Madrid
Botín, Ana Patricia *bank executive*

SURINAME

Paramaribo
Goedschalk, Henk Otmar *banker, educator*

SWEDEN

Stockholm
Hedelius, Tom Christer *banker*
Olsson, Curt Gunnar *banker*
Wallenberg, Peter *banker, investor*

SWITZERLAND

Geneva
Gueudet, Edouard Philippe *banker*

TAJIKISTAN

Dushanbe
Alimardonov, Murotali *bank executive*

UZBEKISTAN

Tashkent
Azimov, Rustam Sadikovich *bank executive*

ADDRESS UNPUBLISHED

Alper, Andrew Michael *former investment banker*
Atkins, Victor Kennicott, Jr. *private investor*
Baker, Henry S., Jr. *retired bank executive*
Bansak, Stephen A., Jr. *investment banker, financial consultant*
Barrow, Charles Herbert *investment banker*
Baxter, Nevins Dennis *bank consultant*
Birky, John Edward *banker, financial consultant*
Blake, Gerald Rutherford *retired banker*
Boykin, Robert Heath *retired banker*
Brillie, M. Scott *savings and loan association executive*
Brooks, Alfred R. *bank executive*
Brown, Edward J III *bank executive*
Buckels, Marvin Wayne *savings and loan association executive*
Burden, Ordway Partridge *investment banker*
Busse, Leonard Wayne *banker, financial consultant*
Campanelli, Joseph P. *former bank executive*
Carrion, Richard L. *bank executive*
Chase, Helen Louise *bank executive*
Christenson, Gregg Andrew *bank executive*
Clark, Thomas Carlyle *retired banker*
Cleghorn, John Edward *retired bank executive*
Clifton, Russell B. *retired mortgage company executive, consultant*
Cockrum, William Monroe III *investment banker, educator*
Cole, Stephen Mark *investment banker*
Cook, Charles Wilkerson, Jr. *retired bank executive, municipal official*
Corcoran, James B. *bank executive*
Cottrell, Mary-Patricia Tross *bank executive*
Crozier, William Marshall, Jr. *bank holding company executive*
Curry, John Michael *investment banker*
Czarnecki, Gerald Milton *investment banker, venture capitalist*
Dean, John Wesley III *investment banker, former federal official*
Dittenhafer, Brian Douglas *banker, economist*
Dixon-Nielsen, Judy E(arlene) *mortgage banker specialty in government lending, marketing professional, consultant*
Dodson, Samuel Robinette III *retired investment banker*
Donaldson, William Henry *investment banker, former federal agency administrator*
Douglass, Robert Royal *bank executive, lawyer*
Doyle, L. F. Boker *retired trust company executive*
Duteil, Hervé Pierre *bank executive, musician*
Fahringer, Catherine Hewson *retired savings and loan association executive*
Fetters, Norman Craig, II, *retired banker*
Finnessy, John P. *mortgage company executive, director*
Finocchiaro, Alfonso G. *bank executive*
Fix, John Neilson *banker*
Freeman, Richard Francis *banker*
Gaffney, Thomas *retired banker*
Gainor, Thomas Edward *bank executive*
Geithner, Paul Herman, Jr. *retired banker*
Giblin, Patrick David *retired bank executive*
Goldberg, David Alan *investment banker, lawyer*
Gonzales, Ernesto Luis B. *bank executive*
Gouw, Julia Suryapranata *bank executive*
Greer, K. Gordon *banker*
Grosland, Emery Layton *retired banker*
Hedstrom, Mitchell Warren *banker*
Hetland, James Lyman, Jr. *banker, lawyer, educator*
Hickey, Joseph Michael *investment banker*
Hoff, Charles Worthington III *retired banker*
Hogan, Robert Henry *trust company executive*
Holcomb, Gene Ann *federal loan officer*
Horvath, Debora D. *bank executive*
Howard, Donald Searcy *banker*
Hower, Frank Beard, Jr. *retired banker*
Huntington, Lawrence Smith *investment banker*
Ingersoll, Paul Mills *banker*
Jennings, Joseph Ashby *banker*
Jepson, Robert Scott, Jr. *bank executive*
Jesse, H. William, Jr. *investment banker*
Jones, Charles Hill, Jr. *banker*
Kaiser, Suzanne Billo *investment banker, writer*
Keith, Robert William *banker*
Kelly, Craig James *retired bank executive*
Killinger, Kerry Kent *retired bank executive*
Klett, Gordon A. *retired savings and loan association executive*
Lawer, Betsy *banker, small business owner, vintner, director*
Lee, Steve Chi Kong *bank executive*
Lewis, Perry Joshua *investment banker*
MacLellan, Steve *bank executive*
MacWilliams, Kenneth Edward *investment banker*
Mancera Aguayo, Miguel *retired banker*
McGee, Liam E. *former bank executive*
McGuinn, Martin Gregory *retired bank executive, lawyer*
McGuirk, Ronald Charles *retired bank executive, economic advisor*
Menaker, Ronald Herbert *retired bank executive*
Merchant, Rahul *former mortgage company executive*
Meyer, Henry Lewis III *bank executive*
Minehan, Cathy Elizabeth *retired bank executive*
Mistry, Percy Shiavak *investment banker*
Moffett, David McKenzie *former mortgage company executive, retired bank executive*
Moll, Lloyd Henry *retired bank executive*
Moore, Andrew Given Tobias, II, *investment banker, law educator*
Moriarty, Donald William, Jr. *bank executive*
Morris, Tammy Kay *bank executive*
Moskow, Michael Harold *retired bank executive*
Moyse, Hermann III *banker*
Mozilo, Angelo R. *retired mortgage company executive*
Murin, Joseph J. *former mortgage company executive*
Niculescu, Peter S. *former mortgage company executive*
Nuzzo, Anthony Gerald *bank executive*
Papademos, Lucas *bank executive*
Pefley, Norman Gordon *bank executive*
Perrotta, Antonio *trust company executive*
Poehner, Raymond Glenn *retired bank executive*
Porter, W. Thomas *retired bank executive*
Price, William James, IV, *investment banker*
Quinn, Kevin Anthony *investment banker*
Raines, Franklin Delano *former mortgage company executive*
Ramsey, Lloyd Brinkley *retired savings and loan executive, retired army officer*
Reifenheiser, Thomas V. *banker*
Reuber, Grant Louis *banking insurance company executive*
Rice, Joseph Albert *retired bank executive*
Riddell, Malcolm *investment banker*
Salamone-Kochowicz, Jean Gloria *retired bank executive*
Santomero, Anthony M. *financial consultant, former bank executive, public policymaker*
Schless, Phyllis Ross *investment banker*
Shah, Bipin Chandra *banker*
Shelton, James Douglas *banker*
Shinn, George Latimer *investment banker, consultant, finance educator*
Shuman, Stanley S. *investment banker*
Smith, Catherine H. *bank executive*
Sohn, Sung Won *former bank executive*
Stansell, Ronald Bruce *retired investment banker*
Stegenga, James Jay *senior compliance examiner*
Stephenson, Herman Howard *retired banker*
Stone, Edmund Crispen III *banker*
Stotter, Harry Shelton *banker, lawyer*
Swad, Stephen Mark *former mortgage company executive*
Swope, Donald Downey *retired banker*
Syron, Richard Francis *former mortgage company executive, economist*
Tatlock, Anne M. *retired trust company executive*
Thaler, Richard Winston, Jr. *investment banker*
Tyrrell, Gerald Gettys *banker*
Urkowitz, Michael *banker*
Vancastle, Robin *bank executive*
Vuoto, Anthony (Tony) F. *bank executive*
Walters, Glen Robert *retired banker*
Walton, Alice Louise *bank executive*
Watts, Anthony Lee *bank executive*
West, Rexford Leon *retired bank executive*
Whitehead, John Cunningham *former bank executive*
Whitney, Edward Bonner *retired investment banker*
Williams, Edward Joseph *banker*
Wilson, Paul Lowell *mortgage company executive, lawyer*
Winnowski, Thaddeus Richard (Ted Winnowski) *investment banker, consultant*
Wirth, Russell D. L., Jr. *investment and merchant banker*
Wolfensohn, James David *former President of the World Bank, diplomat*
Zauder, Gail S. *investment banker*
Zilkha, Ezra Khedouri *banker*

FINANCE: FINANCIAL SERVICES

UNITED STATES

ALABAMA

Albertville
Walker, Phillip *finance company executive, insurance company executive*

Birmingham
Hendley, Dan Lunsford *retired bank executive*
King, Alfreda L. *finance educator*
Newton, Don Allen *economic development consultant*
Ritter, C. Dowd *diversified financial services company executive*

Decatur
Michelini, Sylvia Hamilton *auditor*
Talley, Richard Woodrow *accountant*

Dothan
Lord, Jacqueline Ward *retired accountant, photographer, artist*

Hoover
Lanier, Mildred *finance educator*

Huntsville
Stewart, Verlindsey Laquetta *accounting educator*

Mobile
Ellzey, Wayne Ewell *retired accountant*

Monroeville
Hudson, Wanda Meadows *finance educator*

Tuscaloosa
Ray, Nelda Howton *financial consultant*
Taylor, Gary Kenneth *accountant, educator*
Zumpano, Leonard Vincent *finance educator*

Tuskegee
Cheng, William I. *business educator*

Tuskegee Institute
Siaway, Arthur T.G. *finance educator, educator*

ALASKA

Anchorage
Riendl, Robin W. *wealth advisor LPL branch manager*

Fairbanks
Charles, Dexter N. *finance educator*

ARIZONA

Bisbee
Page, Deborah J. *accountant*

Chino Valley
Norton, Douglas Ray *former auditor general*

Flagstaff
Wilburn, Nancy *accounting educator*

Goodyear
Eppen, Gary Dean *business educator*

Mesa
Linxwiler, Louis Major, Jr. *retired finance company executive*
Nganje, William Evange *finance educator*

Phoenix
Goorman, Brad *financial consultant*
Lemon, Leslie Gene *retired diversified financial services company executive, lawyer*
Marsh, Patricia A. *business educator*
Mullen, Daniel Robert *finance company executive*
Sanchez, Steven M. *financial executive*
Upson, Donald V. *retired corporate financial executive*
Van Fleet, David Dominic *management educator*

Scottsdale
Hathaway, Peter S. *corporate financial executive*
Huizingh, William *former accounting educator*
Washburn, Jerry Martin *accountant, corporate executive*

Sun City West
Schrag, Adele Frisbie *business education educator*

Surprise
Miller, James Rumrill III *finance educator*

Tempe
Bryan, Glynis A. *corporate financial executive*
Happel, Stephen Kent *business educator, dean*
Kaufman, Herbert Mark *finance educator*
Pany, Kurt Joseph *finance educator, consultant*
Reckers, Philip Merle *accountant, educator*
Roy, Asim *business educator*

Tucson
Cain, Vernon *retired diversified financial services company executive*
Carleton, Willard Tracy *retired finance educator*
Elger, William Robert, Jr. *accountant*
Fajardo, Sarah Elizabeth Johnson *financial consultant*
Hellon, Michael Thomas *tax specialist, political organization worker*
Horne, William McHenry *finance educator*
Seay, Suzanne *financial planner, educator*
Tuchi, Ben Joseph *retired finance educator*

Wickenburg
Daniel, James Richard *corporate financial executive*

ARKANSAS

Conway
Horton, Joseph Julian, Jr. *economics and finance educator*
McNew, Bennie Banks *retired finance educator*

Fayetteville
Setia, Pankaj *management educator*

Fort Smith
Hembree, Hugh Lawson III *diversified holding company executive*

Little Rock
Britt, Billy Jean *retired elementary school educator, economic education specialist*
Chapman, Alger Baldwin *financial services company executive, lawyer*
Waters, Zenobia Pettus *retired finance educator*

Searcy
Frazier, Allen Wayne *finance educator*

CALIFORNIA

Anaheim
Lano, Charles Jack *retired financial executive*

Atherton
Barker, Robert Jeffery *financial executive*

Berkeley
Rippe, Lynn E. *portfolio manager*
Staubus, George Joseph *finance educator*

Brea
Oh, Tai Keun *business educator, consultant*

Burbank
Murphy, Peter E. *corporate financial executive*

Calabasas
Goldfield, Emily Dawson *finance company executive, artist*
McLaughlin, Thomas Keith *diversified financial services company executive*
Sieracki, Eric P. *diversified financial services company executive*

Camarillo
Smith, David Michael *financial planner*

Campbell
Vincent, David Ridgely *financial consultant*

Carlsbad
Gillis, Christine Diest-Lorgion *retired certified financial planner, stockbroker*
Steele, Charles Glen *retired accountant*

Carmel
de Vos, Paula Francesca *finance company executive, investment advisor, consultant*

Carmichael
Speir, Marcia Ann *retired accountant*

Chula Vista
Sullivan, Patrick Allen *strategic management educator*

Cupertino
Mueller, Gerhard Gottlob *retired financial accounting standard setter, educator*

Davis
Biggart, Nicole Woolsey *management educator, former dean*

Fairfield
Schunke, Hildegard Heidel *accountant*

Fallbrook
Freeman, Harry Lynwood *retired accountant*
Hamilton, Robert *retired corporate financial executive, councilman*

Foster City
Lucio, Antonio J. *finance company executive*
Pollitt, Byron H., Jr. *finance company executive, former retail executive*
Sommer, Kenneth *finance company executive*

Fremont
Jensen, Paul Edward Tyson *business educator, consultant*

Fresno
Harris, Breck Anthony *business educator, writer, researcher*
Tellier, Richard Davis *management educator*

Fullerton
Foote, Paul Sheldon *business educator, administrator, consultant*

Glendale
Brestle, Daniel J. *corporate financial executive*
Levy, Murray *business educator*

Granada Hills
Lehtihalme, Larry K. (Lauri Lehtihalme) *financial planner*

Hayward
McKenzie, Brian Bruce *finance educator*

Irvine
Brandt, Eric K. *corporate financial executive*
Feldstein, Paul Joseph *management educator*
Gibson, Patrick Daniel *accountant, historian*
Graham, John Lawrence *finance educator, writer*
Rankin, James *finance company executive*

La Jolla
Schwartz, Donald A. *finance educator*

La Verne
Rossum, Constance *management and marketing educator, consultant*

Larkspur
Ramos, Charles Joseph (Joe Ramos) *wealth management consultant*

Lincoln
Dorn, Mary Ann *retired auditor*
Patten, Thomas Henry, Jr. *retired educator, personnel director*

Long Beach
Chapman, Lisa Ann *financial planner*
Metzger, Vernon Arthur *management educator, consultant*
Walker, Linda Ann *financial planner*

Los Angeles
Allen, Sharon *accounting firm executive*
Bennis, Warren Gameliel *business administration educator*
Berman, Geoffrey Louis *diversified financial services company executive*
Burke, Michael S. *corporate financial executive*
Chan, David Ronald *tax specialist, lawyer*
DePamphilis, Donald Michael *finance professor*
Goedde, Alan George *financial company executive*
Hakim, Sam *finance educator, consultant*
Harrison, William Burwell, Jr. *retired diversified financial services company executive*
He, Haihong *accounting educator*
McGagh, William Gilbert *financial consultant*
More, Philip Harvey Birnbaum *business administration educator*
Morrow, Winston Vaughan *financial executive*
Ramer, Lawrence Jerome *corporation executive*
Resnick, Lynda *corporate financial executive*
Roussey, Robert Stanley *accountant, educator*
Udvar-Hazy, Steven F. *leasing company financial executive*
Walendowski, George Jerry *accounting and business educator*
Westerfield, Randolph W. *finance educator, former dean*
Weston, John Frederick *business educator, consultant*
Wu, Vivian Y. *finance educator*

Los Gatos
McLaughlin, Glen *financial services company executive*

Malibu
Baskin, Otis Wayne *business educator*

Manhattan Beach
Allmon, Michael Bryan *accountant, financial consultant*

Menlo Park
McDonald, Warren George *accountant, mortage company, savings and loan association executive, consultant*
Scholes, Myron S. *financier, former law and finance educator*

Mill Valley
Mumford, Christopher Greene *corporate financial executive*

Montecito
Burford, Jerrad Dalon *corporate financial executive, writer*

Monterey
Hensel, Nayantara Diana *finance educator*

Moraga
Tom, Randolph L. *corporate financial executive, lawyer*

Napa
Hess, Donald Marc *diversified financial services company executive*

Newport Beach
Bruggeman, Terrance John *corporate financial executive*
Cote, Brian E. *financial executive*
Haussmann, Trudy Diane *financial planner*

Newport Coast
Pavony, William H. *financial and management consultant*

North Hollywood
Boulanger, Donald Richard *financial services executive*

Northridge
Ackerman, David Scott *finance educator*
Covrig, Vicentiu *finance educator*
Gunther, Richard Edward *operations management professor, consultant*

Novato
Bibeault, Donald Bertrand *corporate turnaround executive, investor*

Oakland
Lee, Jong Hyuk *accountant*
Smith, Christopher Allen *operations executive, financial executive*

Oceanside
Garfin, Louis *retired actuary*
Taverna, Rodney Elward *financial services company executive*

Pacific Palisades
Hagenbuch, Rodney Dale *finance educator, consultant*

Palo Alto
Horngren, Charles Thomas *finance educator*

Palos Verdes Peninsula
Manning, Christopher Ashley *finance educator, consultant*

Pasadena
Diallo, Laura Mann Willis *finance company executive, consultant*
Hunt, Hazel Analue Stanfield *retired accountant*
Norton, Karen Ann *accountant*

Paso Robles
Boxer, Jerome Harvey *accountant, management consultant, vintager*

Pittsburg
Williams-Thierry, Elizabeth A. *financial planner, consultant*

Pleasant Hill
Shahbazi, Shahbaz *finance and business educator*

Pleasanton
Call, John G. *corporate financial executive*
Edwards, Robert L. *corporate financial executive*

Pomona
Lin, Lianlian *management educator*

Redlands
Pick, James Block *business professor, writer*
Ryan, Jason K. *finance educator*

Rocklin
Dwyer, Darrell James *finance company executive*

Sacramento
Betts, Bert A. *retired treasurer, accountant*
Dear, Joseph Albert *pension fund administrator*
Gardner, Jerry Lee *financial consultant*
Ozcelik, Hakan *finance educator*
Palmer, William Joseph *accountant*
Stausboll, Anne *pension fund administrator*

Salinas
Stevens, Wilbur Hunt *accountant*

San Clemente
Petruzzi, Christopher Robert *business educator, consultant*

San Diego
Buska, Sheila Mary *chief financial officer, columnist, writer*
Gengor, Virginia Anderson *retired financial planning executive, educator*
Henne, Andrea Rudnitsky *business educator*
Markowitz, Harry Max *finance and economics educator*
Riedy, Mark Joseph *finance educator*
Sopp, Mark W. *corporate financial executive*
Stambaugh, Larry G. *strategic business consultant*
Turner, B. Russell *tax accountant, financial planner, real estate broker*
West, James Harold *finance company executive*

San Francisco
Barlow, William Pusey, Jr. *accountant*
Bauch, Thomas Jay *financial consultant, retired lawyer, apparel executive*
Carr-Ruffino, Norma *management educator*
Floum, Joshua R. *finance company executive, lawyer*
Fuller, James William *financial planner*
James, George Barker, II, *financial executive*
Patel, Bharat *financial executive*
Paterson, Richard Denis *corporate financial executive*
Sasaki, Robert J. *financial services executive*
Saunders, Joseph W. *finance company executive*
Shah, Premal *non-profit microloan company executive*
Simini, Joseph Peter *accountant, financial consultant, writer, former educator*
Sonneborn, William Charles *diversified financial services company executive*
Uri, George Wolfsohn *accountant*
Weihrich, Heinz *management educator*
Wilcke, Sam Lewis *financial analyst, consultant*

San Jose
Gilliss, David *finance educator*
Jiang, William Yuying *business educator, consultant, researcher*

San Marcos
Kagan, Stephen Bruce (Sandy Kagan) *corporate financial executive*

San Marino
Grantham, Richard Robert *financial consultant*

San Mateo
Johnson, Charles Bartlett *corporate financial executive*
Johnson, Gregory Eugene *diversified financial services company executive*
Johnson, Rupert Harris, Jr. *diversified financial services company executive*
Lewis, Kenneth Allan *diversified financial services company executive*

San Quentin
Hanna, Nessim *marketing educator*

Santa Ana
Kennedy, Parker S. *finance company executive*
Roberts, Hilda R. *business educator*

Santa Clara
Dillon, Adrian T. *financial executive*
Kim, Yongtae *accounting educator*

Santa Monica
Lempert, Robert Jay *Policy Analyst Educator*
Moses, Samuel B. *certified public accountant, consultant*
Teleki, Stephanie *policy analyst*

Santa Rosa
Biderman, Charles Israel *diversified financial services company executive*

Sherman Oaks
Ferguson, Lisa Beryl *accountant*

Sonora
Wheeler, Elton Samuel *financial executive*

Stanford
Duffie, Darrell *finance educator*
Holloway, Charles Arthur *public and private management educator*
McDonald, John Gregory *financial investment educator*
Montgomery, David Bruce *marketing educator*
Pfeffer, Jeffrey *business educator*

Stockton
Plovnick, Mark Stephen *business educator*
Post, Gerald V. *business educator*
Taylor, Francis Michael *auditor, municipal official*
Trager, Lorinda Adele *finance educator, legal association administrator*

Sunnyvale
Rivet, Robert J. *semiconductor company executive*

The Sea Ranch
Carter, Richard Duane *management educator*

Upland
Cullen, Robert John *financial planner, investment advisor*

Vista
Ferguson, Margaret Ann *tax specialist, consultant*

Walnut Creek
McCauley, Bruce Gordon *financial consultant*

West Sacramento
Anderson, William Wallace *financial executive*

Westlake Village
Belote, Lewis Rogers III *accountant*

Winnetka
Roberts, Teri Alane *finance educator, volunteer*

COLORADO

Arvada
Laidig, Eldon Lindley *financial planner*

Aurora
Klaus, Charlotte S. *finance company executive, director*

Boulder
Goeldner, Charles Raymond *retired business educator*
Melicher, Ronald William *finance educator*
Stanton, William John, Jr. *marketing educator, author*
Tarpeh-Doe, Linda Diane *retired controller*

Broomfield
Seabrook, Raymond J. *corporate financial executive*

Colorado Springs
Johnson, Melody Jacqueline *tax professional*
Moore, Donald L. *finance educator*

Conifer
Boese, Michelle Lynne *accountant, consultant*

Denver
Hall, Richard Murray, Jr. *finance executive, consultant*

Englewood
Clark, Ranjana B. *financial services company executive*
Flowers, David J. *corporate financial executive*

Fort Collins
Ewing, Jack Robert *accountant*
Kinnison, Robert Wheelock *retired accountant*

Golden
Wickesser, Thomas A. *finance company executive*

Grand Junction
Markham, Frank Bell *business educator*

Henderson
Reibold, Dorothy Ann *accountant, researcher*

Lakewood
Axley, Hartman *retired estate planner, underwriter*
Hadley, Marlin LeRoy *financial planner, consultant*
Nichols, Vicki Anne *financial consultant, librarian*

Littleton
Newell, Michael Stephen *finance company executive, protective services consultant*

Monument
McIver, Deborah Kay *tax specialist, entrepreneur, small business owner*

Morrison
Bowen, Peter Geoffrey *business educator, arbitrator*

Nederland
Thomas, Daniel Foley *retired diversified financial services company executive*

Steamboat Springs
Potter, William Bartlett *diversified financial services company executive*

CONNECTICUT

Avon
Mazur, Edward John, Jr. *financial planner*

Bethel
Tomasko, Edward A. *financial planner*

Danbury
Moskowitz, Stanley Adam *finance company executive*

East Hartford
Barredo, Rita M. *auditor*

Fairfield
Booth, George Keefer *corporate financial executive*
Cassidy, Kathryn A. *diversified financial services company executive*
Falconi, John J. *diversified financial services company executive*
Fitzsimons, Shane *diversified financial services company executive*
Fujimori, Yoshiaki *diversified financial services company executive*
Garwood, Jeff R. *diversified financial services company executive*
Heintzelman, Daniel C. *diversified financial services company executive*
Hewett, Wayne M. *diversified financial services company executive*
Ireland, Jay *diversified financial services company executive*
Ishrak, Omar S. *diversified financial services company executive*
Janki, Daniel C. *corporate financial executive*
Laopodis, Nick *finance educator*
Laxer, Richard *diversified financial services company executive*
Miller, Jamie S. *corporate financial executive*
Schauenberg, Trevor A. *corporate financial executive*
Sherin, Keith S. *corporate financial executive*
Stockton, Dmitri Lysander *diversified financial services company executive*
Whyte, Bruce Lincoln *management executive, Marketing Consultant*

Greenwich
Davidson, Thomas Maxwell *corporate financial executive*
Hewitt, Dennis Edwin *financial executive*
Macaulay, William Edward *financial executive*
Maxwell, Charles Thoburn *energy analyst*
Tarantino, Dominic A. *retired professional services firm executive*
von Braun, Peter Carl Moore Stewart *finance company executive*

Hamden
He, Xiaohong *finance educator*
Ibbotson, Roger G. *financial educator*
Laskin, Alexander V. *Investor Relations Educator*
Sheikh, Aamer *accounting educator*

Hartford
Cornell, James K. *diversified financial services company executive*

Litchfield
Martin, R. Keith *business and information systems educator, consultant*

New Canaan
Kamerschen, Robert Jerome *retired senior business executive, private investor, consultant*

New Haven
Spiegel, Matthew *finance educator*

Old Lyme
Fairfield-Sonn, James Willed *management educator, consultant*

Prospect
Powell, Raymond William *financial planner, school administrator*

Rocky Hill
Wilson, Karen Lynn *esthetician*

Southport
Fignar, Eugene Michael *finance company executive, lawyer*

Stamford
Brasser, William J. *finance company executive*
Cary, William H. (Bill Cary) *finance company executive*
Jason, J. Julie *portfolio manager, writer, lawyer*
McMahon, Robert Matthew *corporate financial executive*
Pansini, Michael Samuel *financial analyst, tax specialist*
Ressel, Teresa Mullett *diversified financial services company executive, former federal agency administrator*
Smith, Rodger Field *financial executive*

Storrs Mansfield
Eisdorfer, Assaf *finance educator*
Ghosh, Chinmoy *finance educator*

Waterford
Hinkle, Janet *financial analyst*

West Hartford
Sumukadas, Narendar *finance educator*

West Haven
Haley, George Thomas *marketing educator*

Westport
Hayden, Vern Clarence *financial planner*
McKane, David Bennett *business executive*
Ready, Robert James *finance company executive*
Sacchetta, Pasquale Joseph *financial services executive*

Windsor
Ferraro, John Francis *corporate executive*

DELAWARE

Dover
Kim, Dae Ryong *management information systems educator*

Newark
Sawyer, John Edward *management educator*

Wilmington
Copeland, Tatiana Brandt *accountant*
Fredrick, Susan Walker *tax company manager*
Hewitt, Cynthia A. *financial consultant, stockbroker*
Mand, Martin Gary *financial executive*
Rogoski, Patricia Diana *corporate financial executive*

DISTRICT OF COLUMBIA

Washington
Armstrong, Alexandra *financial planner*
Blakely, Robert T. *financial executive*
Collamore, Thomas Jones *corporate financial executive*
DiGanci, Todd T. *financial regulatory service executive*
Doran, Lynn Lanz *finance educator, director*
Droms, William George *finance educator, investment advisor*
Estefan, Nabil *finance and business executive*
Flügelman, Máximo Enrique *financier, composer*
Hale, Janet S. *accounting firm executive, former federal agency administrator*
Harper, Edwin Leland *corporate financial executive, manufacturing executive*
James, Otteson Roger *finance educator*
Ketchum, Richard Gardner *financial regulatory service executive*
Knight, Linda K. *financial company executive*
Kumar, Manmohan Singh *international monetary fund manager, researcher*
Malek, Frederic Vincent *finance company executive*
Mayo, John W. *finance educator*
Merrifield, Dudley Bruce *finance educator, federal official*
Merrill, Susan L. *financial regulatory service executive, lawyer*
Minow, Nell *financial analyst, editor*
Ord, Keith J. *finance educator*
Ouyang, Xiaomei O. *corporate financial executive*
Pollard, Daniel L. *financial analyst*
Rashid, Khadijat K. *finance educator*
Rieser, Joseph A., Jr. *tax specialist*
Rosebush, James Scott *financial services company executive, former government official*
Schloss, Howard Monroe *financial regulatory service executive*
Siddique, Akhtar *finance company executive*
Walker, David Alan *finance educator*
West, J. Robinson (Robin West) *petroleum finance company executive, former government official*
Zoeller, Jack Carl *diversified financial services company executive*

FLORIDA

Altamonte Springs
O'Connor, Sean M. *diversified financial services company executive*

Aventura
Fishel, Peter Livingston *finance company executive*
Kliger, Milton Richard *diversified financial services company executive*

Boca Raton
Dopkins, Leonard A(rnold) *accountant*
Freedman, Howard Martin *financial planner*
Grimaldi, David *financial advisor*
Hecht, William David *retired accountant*
Miller, Eugene *business educator, consultant*
Shah, Bimal *financial advisor, small business owner*
Sigel, Marshall Elliot *financial consultant*

Boynton Beach
Bartholomew, Arthur Peck, Jr. *accountant*

Bradenton
Hashmi, Sajjad Ahmad *finance educator, dean*

Clearwater
Crites, Richard Ray *financial planner, finance company executive, investment advisor*

Coral Gables
Banks, Russell *financial planner, consultant*

Coral Springs
Vasquez, William Leroy *business educator, consultant*

Crestview
Scott, George Gallmann *accountant*

Deerfield Beach
Siegel, Steven L. *finance company executive, consultant*

Fort Lauderdale
Shoemaker, William Edward *corporate financial executive*
Stephan, John *finance educator*

Gainesville
Shugan, Steven Mark *finance educator*

Hialeah
Laffitte-Reguera, Mary E. *finance executive*

Hobe Sound
Caspersen, Finn Michael Westby *diversified financial services company executive*

Jacksonville
Adams, Scott Leslie *accountant*
Edwards, Marvin Raymond *investment counselor, economical consultant*
Jaffe, Barbara Gefen *finance company executive*
Kennedy, Lee A. *financial services company executive*
Munoz, Oscar *corporate financial executive*
Tomlinson, William Holmes *management educator, retired military officer*
Vane, Terence G., Jr. *finance company executive, lawyer*

Kissimmee
Gowda, Narasimhan Ramaiah *financial consultant*

Lake City
Cummings, Charles Michael *finance educator*

Lake Wales
Connor, John Thomas, Jr. *portfolio manager*
Luing, Gary Alan *financial management educator*

Lakeland
Grossman, David Alan *finance educator*

Largo
Shillinglaw, Gordon *retired finance educator*

Lauderdale By The Sea
Kennedy, Beverly (Kleban) Burris *financial advisor, television and radio personality*

Miami
Birns, Ira Michael *corporate financial executive*
Capraro, Franz *accountant*
Coton, Carlos David *finance manager*
Freeman, Lewis Bernard *forensic accountant, lawyer*
Fuerst, Michael *finance educator, researcher*
Nunez-Lawton, Miguel G. *financial analyst*
Pomeranz, Felix *accounting educator*
Sanchez, Robert E. *corporate financial executive*

Miami Beach
Cohen, Philip Herman *accountant*
Howard, Melvin *financial executive*

Miami Shores
Diener, Betty Jane *business educator*

Naples
Brinker, Thomas Michael *retired finance company executive*
Hansen, Claire V. *financial executive*
Madigan, Joseph Edward *financial executive, director, consultant*
Ordway, John Danton *retired pension fund administrator, lawyer, accountant*
Schoen, William Jack *finance company executive*

Niceville
Litke, Donald Paul *acquisition executive, retired military officer*

North Miami Beach
Castro, Angel *accountant, author, educator*

North Palm Beach
Higgins, Jay F. *diversified financial services company executive*

Oviedo
Drummer, Donald Raymond *diversified financial services company executive, educator*

Pensacola
Apap, Antonio *finance educator, portfolio manager*

Saint Petersburg
Bryant, Timothy Clark *investment brokerage executive*
Freeburg, Richard Gorman *financial derivatives company executive*
Freeman, Corinne *financial analyst, retired mayor*
Meyer, Robert Allen *finance educator*
Naimoli, Vincent Joseph *diversified financial services company executive*

Sarasota
Bailey, Robert Elliott *financial executive*
Dryce, H. David *accountant, consultant*
Morris, Gordon James *financial company executive, consultant*
Schmalzried, Marvin Eugene *financial consultant*

Tallahassee
Bowen, Paul L. *information systems and accounting educator*
Cronin, Jerome Joseph, Jr. *marketing educator, consultant*
Nwabuzor, Augustine M. *global strategy educator, consultant*

Tampa
Alexander, William Olin *retired finance company executive*
Baumann, Martin F. *former finance company executive*
DeVane, Mindy Klein *financial planner*
Hernandez, Gilberto Juan *accountant, auditor, management consultant*
Hunter, Delroy M. *finance educator*
Lafferty, Barbara A. *finance educator*
Lebouitz, Martin Frederick *diversified financial services company executive, consultant*
Matulich, Erika *marketing educator*
Nord, Walter Robert *business administration educator, researcher, consultant*

Vero Beach
Chavez, Joseph *finance educator*
Conway, Earl Cranston *business educator, retired manufacturing company executive, educator*
Riefler, Donald Brown *financial consultant*

Wesley Chapel
Mendelsohn, Louis Benjamin *financial analyst*

West Palm Beach
Harper, Mary Sadler *wealth advisor and relationship manager*
Herrick, John Dennis *financial planner, consultant, retired food products executive*
Karmelin, Michael Allen *financial executive*
Livingstone, John Leslie *accountant, economist, management consultant, educator*
Siegel, Philip Harris *finance educator*

Weston
Holtzman, Gary Yale *retired diversified financial services company executive*

Winter Haven
Goodman, Karen Lacerte *retired financial services executive*

Winter Park
Matulich, Serge *accounting educator, writer*
Starr, Martin Kenneth *management educator*

GEORGIA

Alma
Murphy, Kenny R. *finance educator*

Athens
Miller, Herbert Elmer *accountant*

Atlanta
Blum, Terry Christine *management educator, former dean*
Charles, Sally Allen *financial consultant*
Douglas, Seymour Bentley *finance company executive, director*
Fleming, Stephen Richard *finance company executive, investor*
Hildreth, William Bartley *finance educator, consultant*
Hill, Scott A. *stock exchange executive*
Lobb, William Atkinson *financial services executive*
Malhotra, Naresh Kumar *marketing educator*
Metters, Richard *finance educator*
Parsons, Leonard Jon *marketing educator, consultant*
Slaughter, Sandra Ann *management educator*
Smith, Richard F. *financial services company executive*

Augusta
Schmidt, Buffie *finance educator*

Columbus
White, Lisa L. *diversified financial services company executive*

Decatur
Jones, Debbie Jo *finance educator*
Rodgers, Richard Malcolm *management accountant*

Gainesville
Lynn, Lois E. *finance educator*

Hinesville
Inman, Mitchell, II, *marketing educator*

Macon
Kitchens, William Charlie *accountant*

Milledgeville
Engerrand, Doris Dieskow *retired business educator*
Skinner, Marilynn Kearnes *finance educator*

Savannah
Gaines, Marion Saulsbury *accounting educator*
Smith, Elizabeth Mackey *retired financial consultant*

Watkinsville
Tate, Curtis E., Jr. *management educator*

Woodstock
Austin, John David *retired financial executive*

HAWAII

Hilo
Kojima, Sheri S. *high school business educator*

Honolulu
Bess, Henry David *management professor*
Betts, James William, Jr. *financial analyst, consultant*
Hirai, Craig Kazuo *accountant*
Hook, Ralph Clifford, Jr. *business educator*
Misawa, Mitsuru *finance educator*
Palia, Aspy Phiroze *marketing educator, researcher, consultant*
Solidum, James *finance and insurance executive*

IDAHO

Boise
Bahnson, Paul Richard *finance educator*
Ingram, Cecil D. *accountant, state legislator*

ILLINOIS

Belleville
Fietsam, Robert Charles *accountant*

Bloomington
Curry, Alan Chester *actuary*
Pana, Elisabeta *finance educator*

Bourbonnais
Vance, David A. *information systems educator*

Carbondale
Baker, Clora Mae *business educator*
Deng, Saiying *finance educator*

Centralia
Williams, Virginia Lee *finance educator*

Champaign
Brighton, Gerald David *retired finance educator*
Fang, Er *finance educator*
Hackbarth, Dirk *finance educator*
Perry, Kenneth Wilbur *finance educator*
Schoenfeld, Hanns-Martin Walter *accounting educator*

Chicago
Braun, Phillip A. *finance educator*
Brodsky, William J. *stock exchange executive*
Bujak, Denise A. *accountant, insurance company executive*
Christianson, Stanley David *finance company executive*
Chromizky, William Rudolph *accountant*
Classen, Timothy J. *finance educator*
Clayton, Mona M. *accountant*
Daley, William Michael *diversified financial services company executive, former United States Secretary of Commerce*
D'Souza, Rohit Michael *diversified financial services company executive*
Fedorova, Elena Albertovna *finance company executive, consultant*
Fisher, Randy *finance educator*
Fitzgerald, Robert Maurice *retired financial and bank executive*
Fleming, Richard H. *finance executive*
Goss, Howard S(imon) *financial executive*
Hiltz, Kenneth A. *corporate restructuring company executive*
Janecek, Lenore Elaine *healthcare and benefits specialist, consultant*

Kullberg, Duane Reuben *accounting firm executive*
Lorch, Robert K. *corporate financial executive*
Mayer, Raymond Richard *business administration educator*
McHugh, Miles William *corporate financial executive*
Nakata, Cheryl *finance educator*
Ravanas, Philippe Claude Dominique *management educator, consultant*
Schornack, John James *accountant*
Schueppert, George Louis *financial executive*
Schumann, William Henry III *corporate financial executive*
Tyler, W(illiam) Ed *finance company executive*
Waddell, Frederick H. (Rick Waddell) *finance company executive*
Weigand, Robert Eugene *university educator*

Deerfield
Boyd, Joseph Don *diversified financial services company executive*
Dammerman, Dennis Dean *finance company executive*
Heiman, Marvin Stewart *finance company executive*

Dekalb
Moorman, Ted *finance educator*

Edwardsville
Douglas, Thomas John *finance educator*

Elgin
Freeman, Corwin Stuart, Jr. *estate and financial consultant*

Elmhurst
Choyke, Phyllis May Ford (Mrs. Arthur Davis Choyke Jr.) *management executive, editor, poet*

Evanston
Chernev, Alexander *marketing educator, researcher*
Corey, Gordon Richard *financial advisor, former utilities executive*
Dranove, David Stuart *business educator, economist, consultant*
Jacobs, Donald P. *finance educator*
Kotler, Philip *marketing educator, writer*
Prince, Thomas Richard *accountant, educator*
Scott, Walter Dill *management educator*
Stern, Louis William *marketing educator, consultant*

Glen Ellyn
Kapoor, Jagdish R. (Jack Kapoor) *marketing educator, writer*

Glencoe
Silver, Ralph David *financial planner*

Glendale Heights
Cook, Doris Marie *retired accountant, educator*

Glenview
Levin, Donald Robert *business and finance executive, motion picture producer, professional sports team owner*
Mallory, Robert Mark *controller, retired finance company executive*

Greenville
Filby, Ivan Leonard *management educator*

Gurnee
Hall, Terry *accountant*

Kenilworth
Bott, Harold Sheldon *accountant, management consultant*

La Grange Park
Perkins, William H., Jr. *retired finance company executive*

Libertyville
Forester, Thomas H. *portfolio manager, investment advisor*

Lisle
Ruyle-Hullinger, Elizabeth Smith (Beth Ruyle) *municipal financial advisor, consultant*

Macomb
Bauerly, Ronald John *marketing educator*
Knod, Edward M., Jr. *finance educator*

Naperville
Tan, Li-Su Lin *accountant, insurance company executive, consultant, registered investment advisor representative*

Normal
Goodwin, Stephen Arthur *marketing educator*
MacMinn, Richard Dean *finance educator*

Northbrook
Afterman, Allan B. *accountant, educator, financial consultant, researcher*
Feibel, Frederick Arthur *financial consultant*
Newman, Lawrence William *financial executive*

Northfield
Shillestad, John Gardner *diversified financial services company executive*

Oakbrook Terrace
Keller, Dennis James *management educator*

Palatine
Bank, Martin Lee *finance company executive, director*
Spinner, Lee Louis *accountant*

Park Ridge
Russell, William Steven *finance executive*

Quincy
Mallory, Troy L. *accountant*

River Forest
Wolfe, Regina Wentzel *business ethics educator*

Riverwoods
Guthrie, Roy A. *finance company executive*
Hochschild, Roger C. *finance company executive*
Mandel, Karyl Lynn *accountant*
Nelms, David W. *finance company executive*
Offereins, Diane M. *finance company executive*

Robinson
Rahman, Gaziur *finance educator*

Schaumburg
Fitzpatrick, Edward J. *corporate financial executive*

Spring Grove
Garrigan, Richard Thomas *finance educator, consultant, editor*

Springfield
Kuhn, Kathleen Jo *accountant*
Travis, Lawrence Allan *accountant*

University Park
Cook, Constance A. *management educator*

Wilmette
Wishner, Maynard Ira *retired finance company executive, lawyer*

INDIANA

Bloomington
Belth, Joseph Morton *retired business educator*
Bonser, Charles Franklin *public administration educator*
Hustad, Thomas Pegg *marketing educator, association executive*
Perkins, William Clyde *business educator*
Wentworth, Jack Roberts *business educator, consultant*

Carmel
DeHayes, Daniel Wesley *business educator*
Goodwin, William Maxwell *financial executive, retired*
Pickens, Robert Bruce *retired accountant*

Columbus
Miller, William Irwin *finance company executive*

Fort Wayne
Boylan, Daniel H. *finance educator*
Gutreuter, Jill Stallings *financial consultant, planner*
Khamalah, Joseph N. *finance educator, researcher*
Moustafa Leonard, Karen *finance educator*

Gary
Strupeck, C. David *accounting educator*

Hobart
Arand, Frederick Francis *accountant, finance company executive*

Indianapolis
Fisher, Gene Lawrence *controller, accountant*
Furlow, Mack Vernon, Jr. *retired chief financial officer, treasurer*
Kaufman, Barton Lowell *financial services company executive*
Onochie, Florence N. *accountant*
Schmenner, Roger William *business educator*

Merrillville
Reitmeister, Noel *planner, advisor, insurance agent, mortgage consultant*

Muncie
Sundaram, Srinivasan *finance educator*

Notre Dame
Ackermann, Carl *finance educator*
Reilly, Frank Kelly *business educator*
Shannon, William Norman III *college educator, food service executive*

Portage
Schroeder, Marvis Lynn *accountant, artist*

Saint Mary Of The Woods
Wasmer, Donald J. *finance educator, director*

Santa Claus
Hoberg, Michael Dean *corporate financial executive, management analyst, educator*

South Bend
Agbetsiafa, Douglas Kofi *financial and management consultant, economics professor, department chairman*

Terre Haute
Steinbaugh, Robert P. *management and finance educator*

West Lafayette
Cooper, Arnold Cook *management educator, researcher*
Lewellen, Wilbur Garrett *management educator, consultant*
Moskowitz, Herbert *management educator*
Ro, Byung Tak *accounting educator*

IOWA

Ames
Kaufmann, Jeffrey Baer *finance educator*
Teas, Roy Kenneth *marketing educator*

Boone
Shirley, Donald Dean *appraiser*

Des Moines
Poppe, Pamela J. *accountant*
Smith, Diana Marie *business educator*
Vaughan, Therese Michele *insurance educator*

Dubuque
Muzinga, Laurent *finance educator*

Iowa City
Collins, Daniel W. *accountant, educator*
Riesz, Peter Charles *marketing educator, consultant*

Muscatine
Moorhead, Alan R. *internal auditor*

Ottumwa
Lang, Janelle J. *accountant*
Reed, Frank E., Jr. *finance educator*

Sioux Center
Vander Plaats, Gary Paul *accounting educator*

Waterloo
Mathys, Gordon D. *accountant, educator*

West Des Moines
Gleason, Robert Lyle *financial analyst, realtor*

KANSAS

Chanute
Watkins, Mark Charles Henry *finance educator*

Coffeyville
Nelson, Carolyn *auditor*

Elbing
Templin, Noreen *finance educator*

Emporia
Walters, George Kauffman *retired business educator*

Hillsboro
Kroeker, David Wayne *finance educator, coach*

Leawood
Dykes, Archie Reece *finance company executive*

Logan
Manion, Kay Daureen *financial and office manager*

Manhattan
Swanson, Diane Loraine *business management and economics educator, researcher*

Mission
Churchill, James Garton *retired finance company executive*

Overland Park
Stern, Carl Herbert *business educator*

Pittsburg
Muoghalu, Michael I. *finance educator*

Shawnee
Mustard, Mary Carolyn *financial executive*

Shawnee Mission
Johnson, Bradford McClure *financial consultant, investor*

Wichita
Feilmeier, Steve *corporate financial executive*

KENTUCKY

Campbellsville
Foster, Joseph Darrol *finance educator*

Frankfort
Obielodan, James Bolanle *management information systems educator*

Highland Heights
Mittal, Banwari *finance educator, entrepreneur*

Lexington
Labianca, Giuseppe *finance educator*

Louisville
Landan, Henry Sinclair *financial and business consultant*
McKim, Ruth Ann *financial planner*
Taylor, Robert Lewis *management educator*

Madisonville
Kington, Barry Clark *investor, consultant*

Pippa Passes
Mitchell, Kossuth Mayer *business educator*

Richmond
Maumbe, Blessing Mukabeta *finance educator*

LOUISIANA

Baton Rouge
Bedeian, Arthur George *business educator*
Crumbley, Donald Larry *accounting educator, writer*
Thomas, Jeffrey Cone *financial executive, consultant*

Covington
Aaron, Shirley Mae *retired tax specialist*
Doody, Louis Clarence, Jr. *retired accountant*

Grambling
Fields, Hall Ratcliff *retired finance educator*

Kenner
Scherich, Edward Baptiste *retired diversified company executive*

Metairie
Hussain, Mohammed Ershad *finance educator, researcher*

New Orleans
Barach, Jeffrey Alvan *management educator*
Cook, Victor Joseph, Jr. *business educator, consultant*
Manry, David L. *finance educator, consultant*

Pineville
Beall, Grace Carter *business educator*

Shreveport
Burton, George Aubrey, Jr. *accountant*

MAINE

Bangor
Erhardt, Niclas *finance educator*

Cumberland Foreside
Martin, Joseph Robert *retired corporate executive*

Lewiston
Aschauer, David Alan *finance educator*

MARYLAND

Adelphi
Sutherland, Alan Roy *business educator*

Annapolis
Gavian, Peter Wood *venture capitalist, securities executive, securities analyst*

Baltimore
Beasley, Robert Scott *financial executive*
Fetting, Mark R. *finance company executive*
Konar, Shameek *corporate financial executive*
Legum, Jeffrey Alfred *holding company executive*
Mason, Raymond Adams (Chip Mason) *diversified financial services company executive*
Phan, Phillip Hin Choi *business educator, consultant*

Bethesda
Castelli, Alexander Gerard *accountant*
Parrish, Edgar L. *financial services executive*

College Park
Fu, Michael C. *management science educator*
Shapiro, Debra L. *finance educator, consultant*

Gaithersburg
Johnson, George H. *finance company executive*
Ruth, James Perry *financial planner*

Germantown
South, Gail *business and mathematics professor*

Greenbelt
Skillern, Gwendolyn D. *accountant*

Hyattsville
Lovick, Norman *accountant*

Pasadena
Dubke, Marie E. *retired business educator*

Potomac
Rhode, Alfred Shimon *retired finance educator*

Princess Anne
Elobaid, Muna Elhag *computer instructor*
Sharma, Dinesh Kumar *management science educator*

Rockville
Cornelius, Maria G. *financial advisor*
Dineen, Thomas G. III *securities regulator, writer*
Edwards, Bert Tvedt *accountant*
McCann, S. Anthony *financial management consultant, former federal agency administrator*

Salisbury
Weer, Christy Harris *finance educator*

Stevenson
Hilgenberg, John Christian *retired corporate financial executive*

Takoma Park
Urciolo, John Raphael, II, *finance and real estate educator, developer*

Towson
Kues, Irvin William *financial planner*
Mangan, Michael D. *corporate financial executive*

Trappe
Blades, G(ene) Granville *accountant*

Upper Marlboro
Seibel, Charles Burgess *accountant, educator*

West River
Atkinson, Dorothy Scott *retired accountant*

Westminster
Konigsberg, Richard Lee *accountant*

Wye Mills
Schnaitman, William Kenneth *retired finance company executive*

MASSACHUSETTS

Allston
Mills, Daniel Quinn *business educator, consultant, author*

Ashfield
Gabriel, Peter Paul *business educator*

Ashland
Pettinella, Nicholas Anthony *corporate financial executive*

Barnstable
Temkin, Robert Harvey *accountant*

Bedford
Fairhead, Rona *financial information company executive*

Beverly
Ake, Margaret Sherrerd *finance educator*

Boston
Aber, John William (Jack) *finance educator, consultant*
Bower, Joseph Lyon *business administration educator*
Boyd, David Preston *business educator*
Brooke, Peter A. *corporate financial executive*
Bruns, William John, Jr. *business administration educator*
Carmany, George Walter III *finance company executive, consultant*
Christenson, Charles John *retired business educator*
Cody, Alan Morrow *financial consultant*
Deshpandé, Rohit *business educator*
Edmondson, Amy Claire *management professor*
Elfner, Albert Henry III *retired portfolio manager*
Gifford, Nelson Sage *finance company executive*
Gilmartin, Raymond Vincent *management educator, former pharmaceutical company executive*
Hayes, Robert Herrick *technology management educator*
Hayes, Samuel Linton III *business educator*
Heebner, Ken (George Kenneth Heebner) *portfolio manager*
Hudson, Bradford Taylor *management educator*
Ives, J. Atwood *financial executive*
Kanter, Rosabeth Moss *management educator, consultant, writer*
Kaplan, Robert Steven *management educator, investment banker*
Kaufmann, Patrick J. *business educator*
Latif, Nasreen *finance educator*
Lee, Jung Wan *Marketing Educator*
Lodge, George C(abot) *business administration educator*
McArthur, John Hector *business educator*
Murphy, Kathleen A. *diversified financial services company executive*
Park, William H(erron) *financial services executive*
Pell, Anthony Douglas *financial management company executive*
Pitts, James Atwater *finance company executive*
Sloane, Carl Stuart *corporate executive, educator, management consultant*
Stevenson, Howard Higginbotham *business educator*
Villalonga, Belen *finance educator, director*

Boxboro
Parmese, Gabriel J. *corporate financial executive*

Braintree
Sherman, Barnet *financial services executive*

Byfield
Baker, Charles Duane *business administration educator*

Cambridge
Allen, Thomas John *business educator*
Bilmes, Linda Jan *finance educator*
Chatterjee, Sharmila *marketing educator*
Cox, John Carrington *finance educator*
Ellison, Glenn *finance educator*
Freund, Robert *finance educator, consultant*
George, William Wallace (Bill George) *finance educator, former manufacturing executive*
Hauser, John Richard *marketing and management science educator*
Hax, Arnoldo Cubillos *management educator, industrial engineer*
Magnanti, Thomas L. *management and engineering educator*
Malone, Thomas W. *business educator, researcher*
Mora, Elizabeth *comptroller, academic administrator*
Pounds, William Frank *management educator*
Urban, Glen L. *management educator*
von Hippel, Eric Arthur *innovation educator*
Watts, Ross Leslie *finance educator*

Concord
Weiss, James Michael *financial analyst, portfolio manager*

Dudley
Downs, Lawrence Douglas *marketing educator, consultant*

Foxboro
Karelitz, Richard Alan *treasurer, lawyer*

Framingham
Komola, Christine T. *corporate financial executive*

Hingham
Riley, Robert Edward *financial services company executive*

Hopkinton
Teuber, William J., Jr. *corporate financial executive*

Lexington
Ackerman, Robert Wallace *private equity manager*

Marlborough
Norris, Richard Anthony *retired accountant*

Mattapan
Messam, Leroy Anthony *accountant*

Nantucket
Louderback, Peter Darragh *accountant, consultant*

North Dartmouth
Anderson, Michael Henning *finance educator*
Vasudevan, Gopala *finance educator*

Osterville
Silk, Alvin John *management educator, consultant*

Somerville
Levy, Elliott Stuart *accounting educator*

South Hadley
Fisher, William Thomas *business administration educator*

Sudbury
Meltzer, Donald Richard *retired treasurer*

Tewksbury
Black, Richard Bruce *corporate executive, consultant*

Waltham
Bayone, Edward *finance company executive, educator*
Campbell, Leland *marketing educator, consultant*
Cash, James Ireland, Jr. *retired business educator*
Farb, Thomas Forest *financial executive*
Levy, Elliott Stuart *accounting educator*
O'Connell, Jeanne *financial planner, insurance broker*
Shahrur, Husayn K. *finance educator*
Thamhain, Hans Jurgen *management educator*

Wellesley
Papageorgiou, John Constantine *management science educator*

Weston
Valente, Louis Patrick (Dan Valente) *financial planner, director*

Worcester
Greenberg, Nathan *accountant*
Pitcher, Stephen M. *finance company executive, museum director*

MICHIGAN

Alma
Baleja, Gregory *marketing educator*

Ann Arbor
Blome, Andrea *finance educator*
Kapuscinski, Roman *business educator*
Prahalad, C.K. *finance educator, corporate strategist*
Stecke, Kathryn Elizabeth *operations management educator*

Auburn Hills
Knight, Jeffrey Alan *corporate financial executive*

Bloomfield Hills
Poth, Stefan Michael *retired diversified financial services company executive*

Dearborn
Samfilippo, Chris Martin *finance educator, consultant*

Detroit
Datta, Sudip *finance educator*
de Molina, Alvaro G. *finance company executive, former bank executive*
Glowacki, David *finance educator*
Low, James Thomas *marketing educator*
Muir, William F. *finance company executive*

East Lansing
Kang, Jun-Koo *finance educator*
Luccock, Thomas Nelson *auditor, director*
Miracle, Gordon Eldon *advertising educator*
Wilson, R. Dale *marketing educator*

Farmington
Koziara, Michael *accountant, insurance company executive*

Farmington Hills
Smith, Isabel Francis *financial planner*

Fenton
Kruzan, James Brendan *financial planner*

Grand Rapids
Veazey, Richard Edward *accounting educator*

Livonia
McHard, James Lorin *corporate financial executive, freelance/self-employed composer, writer*
Valerio, Michael Anthony *diversified financial services company executive*

Maple City
Duff, James George *retired finance company and automotive executive*

Marquette
Camerius, James Walter *marketing educator, corporate researcher*

Midland
Boxwell, Barbara P. *finance educator*
Merszei, Geoffrey E. *corporate financial executive*
Spaulding, William Ellis *finance educator, consultant*

Muskegon
Behrens, Holly Marie *finance educator, researcher*

Oxford
Smith, Jay Lawrence *financial planning company executive*

Portage
Zhang, Charles C. *financial planner*

Royal Oak
Wagster, John Douglas *finance educator*

Southfield
Kern, Michael L. III *corporate financial executive*

University Center
Elfakhani, Said M. *finance educator*
Millikin, Marsha *finance educator*

Waterford
Gulda, Edward James *diversified financial services company executive*

West Bloomfield
Meyers, Gerald Carl *finance educator, retired automotive executive*
Rauwerdink, William Jay *accountant*

Ypsilanti
Tummala, V.M Rao *supply chain management and operations educator*

MINNESOTA

Eden Prairie
Reha, Rose Krivisky *retired finance educator*

Mankato
Park, Kwang Woo *financial planner, educator*

Marshall
Ibrayeva, Elina *management, international business educator*

Minneapolis
Avella, Joseph Ralph *university professor*
Berman, Walter S. *treasurer*
Berryman, Robert Glen *accounting educator, consultant*
Cracchiolo, James M. *diversified financial services company executive*
Goldberg, Luella Gross *diversified financial services company executive*
Hoffmann, Thomas Russell *business management educator*
Marano, Thomas *finance company executive*
Prestwich, Roger *educator*
Rudelius, William *marketing educator*
Weiss, Renee E. *accounting educator*

Minnetonka
Morisato, Susan Cay *actuary*

Nevis
Stibbe, Austin Jule *retired accountant*

North Mankato
Lee, Chan H. *finance educator*

Plymouth
Stranghoener, Larry W. *corporate financial executive*

Saint Cloud
Supanvanij, Janikan *finance educator*

Saint Paul
Heyman, William Herbert *financial services executive*

Winona
Haas, James Wayne *accountant*
Valluri, Chandrasekhar (Chandu Valluri) *marketing and international business educator*

MISSISSIPPI

Columbus
McClintock, Margaret Eleanor *finance educator*

Gulfport
Alston, Joanna *finance educator*

Jackson
Penn, William M. *finance educator, consultant*
Wooten, Kathy A. *finance educator, accountant*

Moorhead
Barr, Connie Buckels *finance educator, management consultant*

Natchez
Posey, Clyde Lee *business administration and accounting educator*

Poplarville
Foster, Delana Lynn *finance educator*

Tupelo
Nash, Henry Warren *marketing educator*

MISSOURI

Canton
Gaither, Kimberly Ann *finance educator*

Columbia
Nikolai, Loren Alfred *accounting educator*

Kansas City
Bloch, Henry Wollman *diversified financial services company executive*
Brandmaier, Jeff *diversified financial services company executive*
Graebner, Carol F. *diversified financial services company executive, lawyer*
Honley, Russell Loran *controller, accountant*
Jones, Charles Calhoun *estate and business planning consultant*
Pruitt, Stephen Wallace *finance educator*
Rowland, Landon Hill *diversified holding company executive*
Smyth, Russell P. *diversified financial services company executive, former food products executive*
Stevens, James Hervey, Jr. *retired financial planner*

Lees Summit
Foudree, Charles M. *financial consultant*

Maryland Heights
Hall, Jeffrey H. *corporate financial executive*

Neosho
Weber, Margaret Laura Jane *retired accountant*

Park Hills
Bayless, Alan Lee *finance educator*

Poplar Bluff
Smith, Terri C. *accountant, educator*

Rolla
Elrod, Cassandra C. *finance educator*

Saint Charles
Cannon, Douglas A. *retail merchandising educator*
Chilton, Kenneth Wayne *former business research director, educator*

Saint Louis
Armstrong, Theodore Morelock *corporate financial executive*
Arya, Bindu *finance educator*
Brockhaus, Robert Herold, Sr. *business educator, consultant*
Crider, Robert Agustine *international financier, protective services official*
Fitch, Rachel Farr *health policy analyst*
Frank, Terrence Dooley *diversified financial services company executive, director*
Hartley, Tom D. *corporate financial executive*
James, William W. *financial consultant*
Kadan, Ohad *finance educator*
Kamkwalala, Robert W. *finance educator*
Lock, Albert Larry, Jr. *financial services company executive*
Setser, Christie Elaine *auditor*
Smith, L. Douglas *business educator*
Snyder, William W. *corporate financial executive*
Thakor, Anjan V. *finance educator, consultant*
Tyree, Donald Andrew *financial educator, department chairman*
Wiggins, Dewayne Lee *financial executive*
Winter, Richard Lawrence *diversified financial services company executive*

Springfield
Manke, Dale R. *finance educator*

MONTANA

Bozeman
Davis, Nicholas Homans Clark *finance company executive*

Glendive
Holas, Marcia *finance educator*

Great Falls
Christiaens, Chris (Bernard Francis) *financial analyst, state legislator*

Helena
Toole, Joan Trimble *financial consultant*

NEBRASKA

Bellevue
Youssef, Carolyn Magdy *finance educator*

Blair
Udey, Susan S. *accounting educator*

Boys Town
DiBacco, T. Jay *financial services executive, retired military officer*

Dodge
Inman, Mitchell Lee, Jr. *accountant*

Fremont
Dunklau, Rupert Louis *financial planner, consultant*

Kearney
Hayes, Suzanne K. *finance educator*

Lincoln
Digman, Lester Aloysius *management educator*
Lee, Sang M. *management educator*
Olson, David Louis *management educator, researcher*
Sebora, Terrence *finance educator*
Trimi, Silvana *finance educator*

Omaha
Huq, Ziaul *finance educator, researcher*
Munger, Charles T. *diversified company executive*

NEVADA

Las Vegas
Danielson, Deborah Lee *financial analyst*
Duva-Mikhail, Donna Marie *financial executive*
Mellor, Eli *diversified financial services company executive, writer*
Park, Sung Min *finance educator*
Polovina, Gina Bri-Anne *casino gaming company executive*
Williams, Mary Irene *business education educator*

NEW HAMPSHIRE

Amherst
Atwater, Verne Stafford *finance educator*

Bedford
Steadman, David Rosslyn Ayton *corporate financial executive, director*

Brookline
Hemming, Walter William *retired CPA and business executive*

Hanover
French, Kenneth Ronald *finance educator*
Logue, Dennis Emhardt *finance educator, writer, banker, consultant*

Meredith
Lovett, Miller Currier *retired management educator, minister*

Nashua
Dehner, Frederick Thomas *business administration and mathematics educator, retired military officer*
Matarazzo, Maria C. *management educator, department chairman*
Perkins, George William, II, *financial services executive, film producer*

NEW JERSEY

Bernardsville
Flynn, Marie Cosgrove *retired portfolio manager, corporate financial executive*

Blackwood
O'Neal, Rondald Anson *finance educator*

Bloomfield
Conta, Richard Vincent *actuary*

Chatham
Earle, Jean Buist *finance executive*

Cherry Hill
Gorenberg, Charles Lloyd *finance company executive*

Edison
Pedescleaux-Muckle, Gail *retired business analyst, writer, consultant, model*
Romaguera, Allan E. (Al Romaguera) *credit manager*

Egg Harbor City
Earl, Donald W. *treasurer, executive secretary*

Florham Park
Bossen, Wendell John *retired financial planner*

Galloway
Newell, Eric James *financial planner, retired insurance company executive*

Hightstown
Darr, Walter Robert *financial analyst*

Jackson
Cohen, Walter Stanley *financial consultant*
Hagberg, Carl Thomas *financial executive*

Jersey City
Laski, John N. *finance educator*
Riotto, Joseph *finance educator*
Sangiuliano, Barbara Ann *tax director*

Kenilworth
Covert, Theresa M. *treasurer*

Livingston
Leone, Joseph M. *finance company executive*
Peek, Jeffrey M. *finance company executive*
Reilly, Christine L. *finance company executive*

Madison
Naadimuthu, Govindasami *finance educator*

Mahwah
Birnberg, Jack *financial executive*
Govindaluri, Srikrishna Madhumohan *management educator*

Medford
Micko, Alexander S. *corporate financial executive, educator, treasurer*

Metuchen
Cangemi, Michael Paul *accountant, author, consultant*

Middletown
Meyler, William Anthony *financial analyst*

Monmouth Beach
Herbert, LeRoy James *retired accounting firm executive*

Montclair
Luftglass, Murray Arnold *corporate financial executive*

Montvale
Galgano, Brenda M. *corporate financial executive*

Morristown
Cregan, Frank Robert *financial executive, consultant*
Kirby, Fred Morgan, II, *finance company executive*
Ross, Thomas J., Jr. *personal financial adviser*

Newark
Carbone, Richard J. *diversified financial services company executive*
Contractor, Farok *business and management educator*
Grier, Mark B. *diversified financial services company executive*
Lillard, Michael *diversified financial services company executive*
Strangfeld, John R., Jr. *diversified financial services company executive*
Xiong, Hui *finance educator*

Oradell
Geisst, Charles Robert *finance educator*

Parsippany
Langrana, Anita *financial analyst, personal trainer*
Winograd, Bernard B. *diversified financial services company executive*

Piscataway
Kim, Jin-Mo *finance educator*
Sopranzetti, Ben J. *finance educator, investment banker*

Princeton
Fan, Jianqing *finance educator, director*
Harvey, Norman Ronald *retired finance company executive*
Schreyer, William Allen *retired finance company executive*

Princeton Junction
Cohen, Florence Emery *retired financial services executive*

River Edge
Gass, Manus M. *accountant, construction executive*

Roseland
Golden, Robert Charles *finance company executive*
Morrison, Debra Lynn *financial planner*

Sea Isle City
Ramsey, George Bernard *retired financial planner*

Secaucus
Herndon, John Laird *accounting firm executive*

Short Hills
Alesio, Steven W. *financial services company executive*
Gibson, William Lee *financial consultant*
Hauck, Walter S. III *financial services company executive*
Mathew, Sara *corporate financial executive*
Mebane, William Black *controller, financial consultant*
Price, Michael F. *money management executive*

Somerville
Ferguson, Kevin P. *business development manager*

Spring Lake
O'Connor, Francis X. *financial executive*

Tinton Falls
Van Winkle, William *financial planner*

Upper Montclair
San Vicente Portes, Luis *finance educator*

Warren
Spiro, Richard Glenn *corporate financial executive*

NEW MEXICO

Albuquerque
Tchoumak, Adelina *corporate financial executive*

Las Cruces
Bell, M. Joy Miller *financial planner, real estate broker*
Constantini, Louis O. *financial consultant, stockbroker*
Peterson, Robin Tucker *marketing educator*

Portales
Hemley, David Dyson *finance educator*
Musonera, Etienne *finance educator, consultant*

Roswell
Winslow, Sandra Eileen *financial manager, professor*

Santa Fe
Thornburg, Garrett, Jr. *finance company executive*
Watkins, Stephen Edward *accountant, publishing executive*

Taos
Brown, David Warfield *management educator, lawyer, academic administrator*

NEW YORK

Albany
Blount, Stanley Freeman *marketing educator*
Dutta, Saurav K. *accountant, educator*
Mason, Jerry *finance educator, consultant*
Van Slyke, Rosemary *retired tax specialist*

Amherst
Jen, Frank Chifeng *finance and management educator*

Ardsley
Tognino, John Nicholas *diversified financial services company executive*

Baldwinsville
Wilson, Harold Batting *retired treasurer*

Bayside
Gerus, John Patrick *portfolio manager, retired educator*

Bronx
Lee, Dong Hwan *business administration educator*
Topyan, Kudret *finance educator*

Brooklyn
Fischman, Myrna Leah *accountant, educator*
Hechtman, Howard *financial analyst*
Kaplan, Jordan J. *management HRM educator*
Richardson, Alfonso Austin *accountant, financial services executive*
Wolitzer, Philip *accountant, educator*

Buffalo
Eagan, John Gayle *business educator*
Jacobs, Jeremy Maurice, Sr. *diversified financial services company and professional sports team executive*
Oliver, Dominick Michael *business educator*
Shick, Richard Arlon *finance educator*

Chittenango
Cassell, William Walter *retired accounting operations consultant*

Commack
Kurtz, Joel Barry *finance executive*

East Greenbush
Mucci, Patrick John *financial consultant, realtor, commercial loan broker*

Eden
Thomas, Jimmy Lynn *retired treasurer*

Fredonia
Aghazadeh, Seyed-Mahmoud *finance educator*

Glen Head
Stack, Edward William *diversified financial services company executive*

Hempstead
Aaron, Merik Roy *financial executive, lawyer, judge, educator*
Karagozoglu, Ahmet *finance educator*

Hicksville
Stein, Melvin A. *accountant*

Ithaca
Daouk, Hazem *finance educator*
Dyckman, Thomas Richard *accountant, educator*
Kadiyali, Vrinda *marketing & economics educator*
Lesser, William Henri *marketing educator*
Swieringa, Robert Jay *accounting educator, former dean*

Jericho
Bertucelli, Robert Edward *accountant, educator*
Corso, Frank Mitchell, Jr. *business management and business consultant*

Lakewood
Deppas, Louis Anthony *financial adviser*

Massena
Pollard, Fred Don *finance company executive, director*

Monroe
Fontana, John Arthur *employee benefits specialist*

Morrisville
Scalzo, Christopher M. *entrepreneurship and business educator*
Turner, Linda Fay *finance educator*

New York
Abdelnour, Gaby *diversified financial services company executive*
Aboaf, Eric W. *diversified financial services company executive*
Altfest, Lewis Jay *financial planner*
Assael, Henry *marketing educator*
Audet, Paul L. *diversified financial services company executive*
Ayres, Charles *diversified financial services company executive*
Bandera, Natalia *finance company executive*
Bash-Polley, Stacy *diversified financial services company executive*
Bateman, Paul T. *diversified financial services company executive*
Becker, Helane Renée *financial analyst, company executive*
Bender, Susan *financial advisor*
Bennett, Paul B. *stock exchange executive*
Berger, Stephen *finance company executive*
Bernstein, Richard *financial analyst, investment advisor*
Best, Tony (Anthony J. Best) *diversified financial services company executive*
Bhidé, Amarnath V. *business professor, writer*
Biglari, Hamid *diversified financial services company executive*
Bisignano, Frank J. *diversified financial services company executive*
Black, Steven D. *diversified financial services company executive*
Blankfein, Lloyd Craig *diversified financial services company executive*
Bleser, Philip F. *diversified financial services company executive*
Bovin, Denis Alan *diversified financial services company executive*
Bradley, John Francis *diversified financial services company executive*
Braunstein, Douglas Lee *diversified financial services company executive*
Brooke, Beth *diversified financial services company executive*
Brown, Clive Stuart *diversified financial services company executive*
Brustein, Lawrence *finance company executive*
Buckminster, Douglas E. *diversified financial services company executive*
Buttner, Jean Bernhard *diversified financial services company executive*
Calello, Paul *diversified financial services company executive*
Calio, Nicholas E. *diversified financial services company executive, lobbyist*
Callahan, Don *diversified financial services company executive*
Caputo, Lisa Maria *diversified financial services company executive*
Carpenter, Michael A. *diversified financial services company executive*
Cashin, Richard Marshall, Jr. *diversified financial services company executive*
Cavanagh, Michael J. *diversified financial services company executive*
Chakravarti, Amitav *finance educator*
Chang-Robbins, Joyce *diversified financial services company executive*
Chenault, Kenneth Irvine *finance company executive*
Chiarello, Guy *diversified financial services company executive*
Chinn, Adam D. *diversified financial services company executive, lawyer*
Claire, Thomas Andrew *financial executive, consultant, educator, writer*
Clark, Howard Longstreth, Jr. *finance company executive, director*
Clark, Robert Henry, Jr. *finance company executive*
Cohen, Abby Joseph *diversified financial services company executive*
Cohn, Bertram Josiah *portfolio manager*
Cohn, Gary D. *diversified financial services company executive*
Connolly, John P. *corporate financial executive*
Conway, E. Virgil *financial consultant, lawyer*
Corbat, Michael Louis *diversified financial services company executive*
Corrigan, Edward Gerald *diversified financial services company executive*
Craig, Charles Samuel *marketing educator*
Cramer, Jim (James J. Cramer) *financial information executive*
Crane, Charles Grant *financial analyst*
Crawford, Stephen S. *diversified financial services company executive*
Cribiore, Alberto *diversified financial services company executive*
Crockett, Andrew Duncan *diversified financial services company executive*
Davenport, Tim *diversified financial services company executive*
De, Prabal *finance educator*
de St. Paër, Jerry Michael *insurance executive*
Devlin, Robert Manning *diversified financial services company executive*
Dial, Teresa A. (Terri Dial) *diversified financial services company executive*
Dimon, Jamie (James L. Dimon) *diversified financial services company executive*
DiPiazza, Samuel A., Jr. *finance company executive*
Duch, Stephen *corporate financial executive*
Edelson, David Bick *diversified holding company executive*
Edward, Jeffrey N. *diversified financial services company executive*
Elmer, Russell S. *diversified financial services company executive, lawyer*
Emmerman, Michael N. *financial analyst*
Englander, Israel A. *financier*
Engle, Robert F. *finance educator*
Evans, Mary Johnston *corporate director*
Eveillard, Jean-Marie *finance company executive*
Farley, Thomas W. *stock exchange executive*
Feldstein, Eric A. *former finance company executive*
Ferguson, Roger Walter, Jr. *finance company executive*
Flynn, Timothy P. *accounting firm executive*
Foreman, James K. *risk management company executive*
Forese, James Anthony *diversified financial services company executive*
Freiberg, Steven J. *diversified financial services company executive*

Fridson, Martin Steven *finance company executive*
Friedman, Adena T. *stock exchange executive*
Frye, Clayton Wesley, Jr. *finance company executive*
Gallo, Martha Joan *diversified financial services company executive*
Gandhi, Mayank *financial analyst*
Gerspach, John Charles *diversified financial services company executive*
Gilligan, Edward P. *diversified financial services company executive*
Glenn, William Henry *diversified financial services company executive*
Goldstein, Jeffrey Alan *corporate financial executive*
Goodman, Roy Matz *corporate financial executive, former state senator*
Gorman, James P. *diversified financial services company executive*
Graf, Peter Gustav *accountant, lawyer*
Grebow, Edward *finance company executive*
Greenwald, Bruce Corman *finance educator*
Gregor, Andrew, Jr. *corporate financial executive*
Gubert, Walter Alexander *diversified financial services company executive*
Guernsey, Evelyn E. *diversified financial services company executive*
Gupta, Sanjay *finance company executive*
Havens, John Paul *diversified financial services company executive*
Hayes, John D. *diversified financial services company executive*
Heleniak, David William *diversified financial services company executive, lawyer*
Henderson, Edward Drewry, Jr. *finance company executive*
Henry, Daniel T. *diversified financial services company executive*
Henry, Emil William, Jr. *diversified financial services company executive, former federal agency administrator*
Hernandez, Carlos Mauricio *diversified financial services company executive*
Hintz, Brad (Charles Brad Hintz) *financial services company executive*
Hopkins, Deborah C. *diversified financial services company executive*
Horan, Anthony J. *diversified financial services company executive*
Jackson, Mike *finance company executive*
James, Hamilton Evans (Tony James) *private equity executive*
James, Kate *diversified financial services company executive*
Jariwala, Ashish *finance company executive*
Johnson, J. Chester *corporate financial executive, consultant, writer*
Joynt, Stephen W. *financial services company executive*
Kaden, Lewis B. *diversified financial services company executive*
Kalik, Robert M. *financial services executive*
Kapito, Robert S. *diversified financial services company executive*
Keegan, Peter W. *diversified holding company executive*
Kelleher, Colm (Thomas Colm Kelleher) *diversified financial services company executive*
Kelly, Alfred F., Jr. *diversified financial services company executive*
Kelly, Edward J., III, (Ned Kelly) *diversified financial services company executive*
Kennedy, Thomas Patrick *financial executive*
Kessinger, Kevin M. *diversified financial services company executive*
Kessler, Stuart *accountant, financial planner*
Ketterer, Gwyneth M. *finance educator, retired private equity firm executive*
Kilts, James M. *diversified financial services company executive, former consumer products company executive*
Kirsch, Arthur William *financial consultant*
Kirsch, Donald *financial consultant*
Koeppel, Noel Immanuel *financial planner, securities and real estate broker*
Kopelman, Richard Eric *management educator*
Kozlowski, Cheryl M. *fixed income analyst*
Ladjevardi, Hamid *portfolio manager*
Lamb, Robert Boyden *finance and management educator*
Layton, Donald Harvey *diversified financial services company executive*
Lazio, Rick (Enrico Anthony Lazio) *diversified financial services company executive, former United States Representative from New York*
Lee, James Bainbridge, Jr. *diversified financial services company executive*
Lessing, Brian Reid *actuary*
Leven, Ann Ruth *financial consultant*
Lewis, William M. *diversified financial services company executive*
Lin, Grace *financial analyst*
Linville, Judson C. *diversified financial services company executive*
Mack, John J. *diversified financial services company executive*
Maclin, Todd (Samuel Todd Maclin) *diversified financial services company executive*
Madden, Michael Daniel *finance company executive*
Malernee, James Kent, Jr. *financial consultant*
Mandelbaum, Jay Philip *diversified financial services company executive*
Marlas, James Constantine *diversified financial services company executive*
Martell, Terrence F. *stock exchange executive*
Mason, Alexander Taylor *finance company executive*
McCall, H. Carl *financial services firm executive, former state official*
McColgan, Ellyn A. *diversified financial services company executive*
McCormack, Richard Thomas Fox *diversified financial services company executive, former ambassador*
McDaniel, Raymond W., Jr. *financial information company executive*
McGuire, Raymond J. *diversified financial services company executive*
McQuade, Eugene M. (Gene McQuade) *diversified financial services company executive*
McWhinney, Deborah Doyle *diversified financial services company executive*
Mergenthaler, Frank *corporate financial executive*
Messier, Jean-Marie *corporate financial executive*
Miller, Heidi Goldberg *diversified financial services company executive*
Miscik, Jami A. *diversified financial services company executive, former federal agency administrator*
Molinaro, Samuel L., Jr. *diversified financial services company executive*
Moore, Melissa J. *diversified financial services company executive*
Morgan, David Raymond *financial consultant, retired bank executive*
Morse, Edward Lewis *energy economist, director*
Morton, Andrew J. *diversified financial services company executive*
Morwitz, Vicki Gail *finance educator*
Mosse, Peter John Charles *financial services executive*
Mudick, Stephanie B. *diversified financial services company executive, lawyer*
Muir, Christopher Bryant *financial analyst*
Mulford, David Campbell *finance company executive, former ambassador*
Murphy, John B. *portfolio manager*
Nally, Dennis Mathew *finance company executive*
Novick, Barbara *investment adviser*
Paddock, Anthony Conaway *financial consultant*
Pandit, Vikram Shankar *diversified financial services company executive*
Peppet, Russell Frederick *accountant*
Petach, Ann Marie *diversified financial services company executive*
Pincus, Lionel I. *financial executive, entrepreneur*
Portogallo, Richard V. *diversified financial services company executive*
Powell, Dina Habib *diversified financial services company executive, former federal agency administrator*
Powell, Scott E. *diversified financial services company executive*
Pruzan, Robert Alan *diversified financial services company executive*
Psoras, Andrea Marie *financial analyst*
Quigley, James B. *diversified financial services company executive*
Quigley, James H. *accounting firm executive*
Rebell, Arthur Leslie *diversified holding company executive*
Reiss, Dale Anne *corporate financial executive*
Rhodes, William Reginald (Bill Rhodes) *diversified financial services company executive*
Ritch, Kathleen *diversified financial services company executive*
Rocchi, Robin Henning *financial and automotive executive*
Roethenmund, Otto Emil *finance company and bank executive*
Rohatyn, Felix George *diversified financial services company executive, former ambassador*
Rosenberg, Alan David *accountant*
Rufeh, Mark *diversified financial services company executive*
Salzberg, Barry F. *accounting firm executive*
Sanzone, Thomas J. *diversified financial services company executive*
Savas, Emanuel S. *management educator, public official*
Scharf, Charles W. *diversified financial services company executive*
Scher, Peter Lawrence *diversified financial services company executive, lawyer*
Scherre, Clare R. *diversified financial services company executive*
Schick, Thomas *diversified financial services company executive*
Schoenhut, Frederick W. *stock exchange executive*
Schroeder, Alice Davey *diversified financial services company executive, writer*
Schueneman, Diane L. *diversified financial services company executive*
Schwartz, Alan David *diversified financial services company executive*
Schwartz, Robert *finance educator*
Segal, Martin Eli *retired actuarial and consulting company executive*
Sen, Kaustav *finance educator, consultant*
Shafir, Robert S. *finance company executive*
Sharma, Deven *financial information company executive*
Sharma, Gaurav *finance company executive*
Sharp, J(ames) Franklin *finance educator, portfolio manager*
Shenkman, Mark Ronald *investment and finance executive*
Simmons, John Derek *retired financial consultant*
Smith, Gordon A. *diversified financial services company executive*
Sobbott, Susan *diversified financial services company executive*
Squeri, Stephen *diversified financial services company executive*
Staley, Jes (James Edward Staley) *diversified financial services company executive*
Stein, Elliot, Jr. *business executive*
Steinhardt, Michael H. *diversified financial services company executive*
Taubman, Paul J. *diversified financial services company executive*
Thoman, G. Richard *corporate financial executive*
Tisch, Andrew Herbert *diversified holding company executive*
Tisch, James Solomon *diversified holding company executive*
Trinkaus, John William *management educator*
Turley, James S. *corporate financial executive*
Tutwiler, Margaret DeBardeleben *diversified financial services company executive, former stock exchange executive*
Updike, Helen Hill *wealth manager*
Veihmeyer, John Brady *public accounting firm executive*
Viniar, David Alan *diversified financial services company executive*
Volk, Norman Hans *financial executive*
Volk, Stephen Richard *diversified financial services company executive, investment banker, lawyer*
Voss, Linda L *finance company executive*
Warren, David P. *stock exchange executive*
Weaver, Richard Lindsay Newton *financial services executive*
Weill, Sandy (Sanford I. Weill) *retired diversified financial services company executive*
Weinberg, John Sidney *diversified financial services company executive*
Weingrow, Howard Louis *finance company executive*
Whiting, Anthony *executive search consultant*
Whitney, Meredith Ann *financial analyst*
Williams, Reba White *corporate financial executive, writer, researcher*
Wilson, Kendrick R. III *diversified financial services company executive*
Wolf, Robert *diversified financial services company executive*
Wood, Jerry (Jerome C. Wood) *diversified financial services company executive*
Wright, Joseph Robert, Jr. *corporate executive*
Young, George Haywood, III, (Woody Young) *investment banker*
Zand, Dale Ezra *business management educator*
Zubrow, Barry Lee *diversified financial services company executive*

Niagara Falls
Askins, Arthur James *accountant, auditor*

North Massapequa
Capone, Maryann *financial planner*

Northport
Donenfeld, Kenneth Jay *investor relations consultant*

Old Westbury
Boronico, Jess Stephen *management science educator, dean*

Pearl River
Bryant, Karen Worstell *financial advisor, investment company executive*

Pittsford
Snyder, Donald Edward *finance company executive*

Poughkeepsie
Ardalan, Kavous *finance educator*
Klingenberg, Beate *management educator, director*

Pound Ridge
Darcy, Keith Thomas *finance company executive, educator, not-for-profit developer*

Preston Hollow
King, Steven *financial services consultant*

Purchase
Banga, Ajay *finance company executive*
Heuer, Alan J. *finance company executive*
Hund-Mejean, Martina *finance company executive*
Kelly, Joan *financial services company executive*
Murdock, Wendy Jean *finance company executive*
Selander, Robert William *finance company executive*

Rochester
DuBrin, Andrew John *management and behavioral sciences educator, writer*
Golisano, B. Thomas (Tom Golisano) *financial services company and professional sports team executive*
Judge, Jonathan J. *financial services company executive*

Rye Brook
Berk, Alan S. *accountant*

Saratoga Springs
Dickinson, Richard Henry *accountant*

Scarsdale
Gladstone, William Louis *accountant*
O'Brien, Edward Ignatius *corporate financial executive, director, investor, lawyer*

Shelter Island
Shaw, Alan Roger *finance educator, retired company executive*

Staten Island
Clark, Sylvia Dolores *business educator*
Gelbein, Jay Joel *accountant*
Goodman, Robert Stanley *management educator*
Lo Re, Mary *finance educator*

Syracuse
Marcoccia, Louis Gary *accountant, academic administrator*
Yildirim, Yildiray *finance educator*

Tarrytown
Hyman, Leonard Stephen *financial consultant, economist, writer*

Valhalla
Christesen, John D. *business educator*
De Nicola, Peter Francis *tax executive*

Valley Stream
Ellis, Bernice *financial planner, investment advisor*

Wappingers Falls
Hogan, Edward Robert *financial services executive*

West Harrison
Ramos, Denise L. *corporate financial executive*

White Plains
Gillingham, Stephen Thomas *financial planner*
Prabhu, Vasant M. *corporate financial executive*
Sacco, John Michael *accountant*
Trapp, Peter Jarl Rudolf *investment manager*
Underwood, Steven Clark *financial services company executive*
Zuckerman, Marc Abraham *finance educator*

Windsor
Warner, Roberta Arlene *retired accountant, financial services executive*

Woodside
Hofmann, Herbert C. *diversified holding company executive*

Yonkers
Johansen, Robert Joseph *consulting actuary*

NORTH CAROLINA

Asheville
Horwitz, Bertrand Nathan *finance educator*
Letzig, Betty Jean *retired financial consultant*

Belmont
Rishel, Tracy D. *finance educator, director*

Boone
Sturgill, Brad *finance educator*

Chapel Hill
Brummet, Richard Lee *retired accounting educator*
Jones, W. S. (Steve Jones) *management educator, former dean*
Perreault, William Daniel, Jr. *business administration educator*
Ross, Coleman DeVane *accountant, insurance company executive*
Whybark, David Clay *business educator, researcher*

Charlotte
Anderson, Gerald Leslie *finance company executive*
Beams, Maliz *finance company executive*
Krawcheck, Sallie L. *diversified financial services company executive*
Kreimer, Michael Walter *financial planner, investment company executive*
Schnaper, Cara L. *diversified financial services company executive*
Thompson, Ronald L. *finance company executive, former manufacturing company executive*

Cullowhee
Moss, Hollye K. *finance educator*

Dallas
Conrad, Jamie Holleman *finance educator*

Durham
Bettman, James Ross *management educator*
Breeden, Douglas Tower *finance educator, consultant, former dean*
Conover, Christopher James *health policy analyst, educator*
Keller, Thomas Franklin *business administration educator*
Staelin, Richard *business administration educator*

Greensboro
Englar, John David *finance educator, textiles executive, lawyer*
Lowe, Kevin Brian *finance company executive*

Greenville
Hughes, Ralph Eugene *management educator*

Jefferson
Mitchell, Patricia *finance educator, director*

Lillington
Shull, Johnny Thomas *finance educator*

Mount Holly
Nutter, James Randall *management educator*

Pembroke
Gan, LooGeok Lydia *finance educator*

Raleigh
Jessen, David Wayne *retired accountant*
Moon, Sangkil *finance educator*
Padilla, Art *finance educator*
Stevenson, Denise L. *diversified financial services company executive, realtor, consultant*

Valdese
Denison, Cynthia Lee *accountant, tax specialist*

Winston Salem
Boone, Derrick S., Sr. *finance educator*
Cherikh, Moula *business educator*
Mecimore, Charles Douglas *retired accounting educator*
Patel, Ajay *finance educator*

Yanceyville
Webster, Hugh B. *accountant, former state legislator*

NORTH DAKOTA

Grand Forks
Dennis, Steven Allen *financial consultant*
Haskins, James P. *finance educator, consultant*
Patton, Gregory Kenneth *management educator*

Mayville
Skean, Mark Edgar *finance educator, consultant*

OHIO

Akron
Stephens, Rachel De-Vore *finance company executive, educator*

Amelia
Hayden, Joseph Page, Jr. *finance company executive*

Berea
Jacques, Kevin *finance educator*

Bowling Green
Guthrie, Mearl Raymond, Jr. *business administration educator*
Lunde, Harold Irving *retired management educator*
Varney, Glenn Herbert *finance educator*

Cincinnati
Anderson, Jerry William, Jr. *diversified financial services company executive, educator*
Conaton, Michael Joseph *diversified financial services company executive*
Gates, Katherine A. *accountant, writer*
Huenefeld, Thomas Ernst *financial consultant, retired banker*
Lawson, Randall Clayton, II, *finance company executive*
Lindner, Robert David *finance company executive*
Mantel, Samuel Joseph, Jr. *management educator, consultant*
McMullen, W. Rodney *financial officer*
Schiff, John Jefferson, Jr. *finance company executive*
Siekmann, Donald Charles *accountant*
Tuuk, Mary *diversified financial services company executive*
Wright, Shane M. *corporate financial executive*
Wulker, Laurence Joseph *portfolio manager, educator, financial planner*

Cleveland
Bajda, Andrew *finance educator*
Hennessy, Sean P. *corporate financial executive*
Hisrich, Robert Dale *business educator*
Hrivnak, Mary Wilson *educator*
Key, Helen Elaine *accountant, educator, consulting company executive*
Mayne, Lucille Stringer *finance educator*
Moise, Claudia *finance educator*
Venkateshan, Prahalad *Senior Financial Analyst*
Weiss, Zev *corporate financial executive*

Columbus
Anand, Jaideep *management educator, consultant*
Berry, William Lee *business administration educator*
Desai, Anand *finance educator*
LaLonde, Bernard Joseph *finance educator*
Raabe, William Alan *tax writer, business educator*
Sestina, John E. *financial planner*

Dayton
Hoge, Franz Joseph *accounting firm executive*
Singhvi, Surendra Singh *financial consultant*

Enon
Kankey, Roland Doyle *finance educator*

Fairfield
Stecher, Kenneth W. *financial corporation executive*

Findlay
Gamba, Maria V. *international business, economics, finance educator*
Gupta, Shiv K. *finance educator*

Harrison
Kocher, Juanita Fay *retired auditor*

Heath
Darst, David Earl *finance educator*

Kent
Ryans, John Kelley, Jr. *marketing educator*

North Canton
Secrest, Beth Anne *accounting educator*

Strongsville
Pinkerton, Richard LaDoyt *retired management educator, writer*

Toledo
Geisler, Nathan David *financial consultant*
HassabElnaby, Hassan *accounting educator*

University Heights
Murphy, Paul Regis, Jr. *business educator*

Willoughby
Brass, Ernest H. III *financial planner*

Youngstown
Edirisooriya, Gunapala *finance educator*

OKLAHOMA

Ada
Parham, Betty Ely *credit bureau executive*

Broken Arrow
Gaddis, Richard William *management educator*

Durant
Hrncir, Theresa June *accounting educator*

Langston
Mambula, Charles J. *finance educator, consultant*

Lawton
Davis, Ellen Marie *business educator*
Soylu, Ali *finance educator*

Moore
Lee, Myung Woo *accountant, financial secretary*

Okmulgee
Mitcham, Julius Jerome *accountant*

Seminole
Hamm, Dawna R. *accountant, educator*

Tonkawa
Allen, Bart W. *finance educator*

Tulsa
Davis, Tamra S. *business educator*
Huntley, Julie *business educator*
Kaiser, George B. *corporate financial executive*
O'Mealey, Jimmy Dee *finance educator*

OREGON

Eugene
Lindholm, Richard Theodore *economics and finance educator*
Miner, John Burnham *industrial relations educator, writer*
Starbuck, William Haynes *business management educator*

Grants Pass
Smith, Barnard Elliot *management educator*

Portland
Epperson, Eric Robert *finance executive, film producer*
Finley, Lewis Merren *financial consultant*
Goodson, Raymond Eugene *business educator, retired automotive executive*
Hagel, Shawn R. *corporate financial executive*
Watne, Donald Arthur *retired accountant, educator*
Weber, George Richard *financial and internet marketing executive, writer*

PENNSYLVANIA

Allentown
Balog, Ibolya *accountant*
Coyle, Charles A. *marketing educator*
Heitmann, George Joseph *business educator, consultant*

Allison Park
LaDow, C. Stuart *financial consultant*

Bala Cynwyd
Miller, L. Martin *accountant, financial planner*

Bethlehem
Barsness, Richard Webster *management educator, academic administrator*
Stella, John Anthony *financial executive*

Blue Bell
Haugen, Janet B. *corporate financial executive*

Bristol
McClain, John T. *corporate financial executive*

Bryn Mawr
Moyer, F. Stanton *financial executive*

Canonsburg
Varney, Jolene *corporate financial executive*

Chester
Saad, Germaine H. *business management professor, researcher*

Chesterbrook
Collis, Steven H. *corporate financial executive*
Cox, Karen Michelle *finance educator, computer company executive*
DiCandilo, Michael D. *corporate financial executive, accountant*

Clarks Summit
Evans, Lynn Susan *financial planner*

Flourtown
Christy, John Gilray *diversified financial services company executive*

Horsham
Harrison, Deborah Lynn *accountant, consultant*
Rassmann, Joel H. H. *corporate financial executive*

Indiana
Al-Shammari, Hussam A. *management educator*

Johnstown
Frye, Randy L. *finance educator*

King Of Prussia
Burda, Steven *financial analyst and manager*
Filton, Steve G. *corporate financial executive*
Gunn-Morton, Dawnell S. *auditor*

Lemoyne
Custer, John Charles *portfolio manager*

Lincoln University
Bradt, Donald James III *political science professor*

Malvern
Ferran, Carlos *finance educator*

Moon Township
Racic, Stanko *finance educator*

Newtown Square
Reiley, T(homas) Phillip *consultant*

Paoli
Gotshall, Jan Doyle *financial planner*

Philadelphia
Alexander, William Herbert *business educator, former construction executive*
Anderson, Rolph Ely *finance educator*
Avgiris, Catherine *financial executive*
Babbel, David Frederick *finance and insurance educator*
Blume, Marshall Edward *finance educator*
Choi, Jongmoo Jay *finance educator*
Di Benedetto, C. Anthony *marketing educator*
Eraslan, Hulya K. *finance educator*
Fisher, Marshall Lee *operations management educator*
Gopalan, Ram *finance educator*
Jiang, Pingjun *finance educator*
Joglekar, Prafulla Narayan *information systems management educator, consultant*
Kamp, R. Stephen *finance educator*
Keidat, Edward E. *finance educator*
Keim, Donald Bruce *finance educator*
Kimberly, John Robert *management educator, consultant*
Ksansnak, James Edward *diversified financial services company executive, accountant*
Levinthal, Daniel Alan *management educator*
Liebman, Andrew Michael *management educator*
Lodish, Leonard Melvin *marketing educator, entrepreneur*
Michel-Kerjan, Erwann O. *finance educator*
Ramani, Girish *marketing educator, researcher*
Rose, Jane A. *financial planner*
Rosenbloom, Bert *marketing educator, consultant, writer*
Rosenthal, Edward Charles *management science educator*
Schifter, Stephan Clay *retired finance educator*
Selles, Robert Hendrikus *retired actuary*
Siegel, Jeremy James *finance educator*
Wachter, Susan Melinda *finance educator*
Webber, Ross Arkell *management educator*
Ziegler, Donald Robert *cpa*

Pipersville
Ferrari, Robert Joseph *retired finance educator, bank executive*

Pittsburgh
Chieffe, Natalie *financial planner*
Guyaux, Joseph C. *corporate financial executive*
Ijiri, Yuji *finance educator*
McGuire, Timothy William *economics and management educator, dean, information technology executive*
Means, Dwight Bardeen, Jr. *financial consultant, educator*
Price, John Roy, Jr. *financial executive*
Ravi, R. *finance educator*
Spatt, Chester S. *finance educator*
Thiel, Glenn R. *finance educator*
Zoffer, H. Jerome *business educator, dean*

Reading
Chester, Mark Steven *finance educator*
McCullough, Eileen (Eileen McCullough LePage, Elli McCullough) *financial consultant, writer, editor, educator*
McVey, Diane Elaine *accountant*

Richboro
Higginbotham, Kenneth James *finance company executive*

Scranton
Comstock, Arthur *finance educator, consultant*

Sewickley
Bly, James Charles, Jr. *finance company executive*
Jehle, Michael Edward *financial advisor, lawyer*

Southampton
Christakis, Alexander N. *finance company executive*

University Park
Garud, Raghu *finance educator*
McKeown, James Charles *accounting educator, consultant*
Shane, Philip Barry *accounting educator*

Valley Forge
Phelizon, Jean Francois *finance company executive*

Villanova
Hanouna, Paul Emmanuel *finance educator*

Wayne
Sims, Robert John *financial planner*

West Chester
Blasiotti, Robert Vincent *accountant, consultant*
Brennan, Patricia Clark *financial planner*
Chu, Hung M. *finance educator*
Li, Huimin *finance educator*

West Conshohocken
Saul, Ralph Southey *diversified financial services company executive*
Schneider, John K. *financial advisor*

West Mifflin
Lindenfelser, Rodger William *finance educator*

Wilkes Barre
Hao, Qian *accountant, educator*
McHale, Maureen Bernadette Kenny *controller*

Williamsport
Hudock, Barbara Benner *financial consultant*

Wynnewood
Robinson, Robert L. *retired diversified financial services company executive, lawyer*
Sanyour, Michael Louis, Jr. *diversified financial services company executive*

York
Day, Ronald Richard *retired financial executive*

RHODE ISLAND

Cranston
Langlois, Michael A. *financial consultant*

Kingston
Mazze, Edward Mark *marketing educator, consultant*

Smithfield
Simons, Kathleen A. *accountant, educator*

Warwick
McNeil, Paul Joseph, Jr. *financial analyst*

West Warwick
Carter, Wilfred Wilson *retired finance company executive, controller*

SOUTH CAROLINA

Charleston
Donnem, Sarah Lund *financial analyst, non-profit and political organization consultant*
Lader, Philip *corporate director, lawyer, academic administrator, diplomat*
Pritchett, Samuel Travis *finance and insurance educator, researcher, consultant*

Clemson
Yang, Tina *finance educator*

Columbia
Hollis, Charles Eugene, Jr. *finance company executive*
Monahan, Thomas Paul *accountant*

Florence
Singletary, Eloise *business educator*

Greenville
Fallavollita, Paul *financial analyst*

West Columbia
Byars, Merlene Hutto *accountant, artist, writer*
Wheeler, Hoyt Noland *management educator, arbitrator*

Williamston
Alewine, James William *financial executive*

SOUTH DAKOTA

Sioux Falls
Rogers, David Hughes *banking and financial service professor, dean, real estate company executive*

TENNESSEE

Cleveland
Rhodes, Arthur Delano *benefits administrator*

Harriman
Glenn, Betty Jean *finance educator*

Jackson
Holt, Michael Kenneth *management and finance educator, consultant, city councilman*

Jellico
Walden, James William *accountant, educator*

Knoxville
Barnes, Samuel Coleman *Senior Technical Talent Advisor*
DeGennaro, Ramon P. *finance educator, researcher*

Martin
Phongkusolchit, Kiattisak *finance educator, researcher*
Williams-Boyd, Deborah Kay *finance educator*

Memphis
Brandon, Raymond Wilson *financial planner, securities principal*
Spahr, Ronald W. *finance educator, department chairman*
Sunderman, Mark A. *finance educator*
Umholtz, Clyde Allan *financial analyst*

Murfreesboro
Beckwith, Ruthie-Marie *financial consultant, director*

Nashville
Brophy, Jeremiah Joseph *retired finance company executive, military officer*
Clemens, Peter J., IV, *corporate financial executive*
Ford, Gerald J. (Jerry) *finance company executive*
Gore, Steven Lowell *accountant*
Ullestad, Merwin Allan *tax specialist, director*
Weingartner, H(ans) Martin *finance educator*

Rockford
Nesbit, Sandi Michelle *corporate financial executive*

Soddy Daisy
Randall, Kay Temple *accountant, retired real estate agent*

TEXAS

Abilene
Datta, Amlan *economics and business educator*

Argyle
Pettit, John Douglas, Jr. *management educator*

Arlington
Akpom, Uchenna Nwabufo *finance educator, consultant*
Swanson, Peggy Eubanks *finance educator*

Austin
Anderson, Urton Liggett *accounting educator*
Gau, George W. *finance educator, former dean*
Granof, Michael H. *finance educator, department chairman*
Graydon, Frank Drake *retired accounting educator, administrator*
Kimberlin, Sam Owen, Jr. *financial consultant*
Larson, Kermit Dean *finance educator*
Schloss, Hadassah *auditor*
Sialm, Clemens *finance educator*

Beaumont
Andes, Joan Keenen *tax specialist*

Brownwood
DeHay, Jerry Marvin *business educator, small business owner*

Burton
Knauss, Robert Lynn *corporate financial executive*

College Station
Mahajan, Arvind *finance educator*
Wichern, Dean William *business educator*

Cypress
Hlozek, Carole Diane Quast *finance company executive*

Dallas
Besio, Charles Arthur, Jr. *marketing educator*
Brooks, Carla Jo *financial services manager*
Grant, Joseph Moorman *finance company executive*
Guthrie, M. Philip *corporate financial executive*
Gyemant, Robert Ernest *diversified financial services company executive*
Hay, Jess Thomas *retired finance company executive*
Jobe, Larry Alton *finance company executive*
Keglevic, Paul *corporate financial executive*
Lemaster, Arthur James *educator*
Moore, Thomas Joseph *finance company executive*
Morgan, Gregory Paul *financial investment advisor*
Porter, Biggs C. *corporate financial executive*
Shimer, Daniel Lewis *finance company executive*
Vanderveld, John, Jr. *diversified financial services company executive*
Wright, Laura H. *corporate financial executive, air transportation executive*

Denton
Baker, Pamela Elaine *finance educator, consultant*
Bertine, Dorothy Wilmuth *retired accountant, artist, art educator, genealogist, writer*
Evangelopoulos, Nicholas E. *finance educator*
Hossain, Muhammad Muazzem *educator*
Newell, Charldean *public administration educator*
Salimath, Manjula S. *management educator*

Farmers Branch
Walsdorf, Marisa *finance educator*

Fort Sam Houston
Blueitt, Odis R. *financial analyst, military officer*

Fort Worth
Bass, Robert Muse *financier*
Berce, Daniel Eugene *financial services company executive, accountant*
Clark, Emory Eugene *diversified financial services company executive*
Rogers, Dale Craig *finance company executive*

Gainesville
McCormack, Lowell Ray *oil industry and corporate financial executive, consultant*

Garland
McGill, Maurice Leon *corporate financial executive*

Georgetown
Sellers, Fred Evans *accounting educator*

Hitchcock
Shaffer, Richard Paul *financial planner, real estate company executive, military officer*

Hockley
Williams, James Lee *finance company executive*

Houston
Ahearne, Michael *finance educator*
Arnold, Daniel Calmes *retired finance company executive, lawyer*
Braden, John Alan *accountant*
Cloninger, Dale Owen *retired finance educator, professor emeritus*
D'Agostino, James Samuel, Jr. *corporate financial executive*
Dorman, Margaret K. *corporate financial executive*
Harris, Venita Van Caspel *retired financial planner*
Horvitz, Paul Michael *finance educator*
Larkin, William Vincent, Jr. *corporate financial executive*
McMahon, Richard A. *finance educator*
Rauniar, Rupak *management educator*
Sarofim, Fayez Shalaby *finance company executive*
Serrato, Darlene B. *finance educator*

Hurst
Kaluya, Michael David *finance educator*

Laredo
Janamanchi, Balaji *operations management educator*
Liu, Shinhua *finance educator, researcher*
Nixon, Dennis E. *financial company executive*
Sagafi-nejad, Tagi *business educator*

Longview
Castro, Juan Ramon *finance educator*

Lubbock
Fullerton, Caren D. *finance educator*
Mitchell, Ronald K. *finance educator*

Midland
Groce, James Freelan *financial adviser*

Normangee
Cox, Jack Ronald, Jr. *business educator*

Palestine
Camp, Ronald Edward *accounting and economics educator*

Pasadena
Scott, William Floyd *accountant*

Plano
Day, Kevin Thomas *retired business executive, investment banker, foundation administrator*
Mahadeva, Manoranjan *financial executive, accountant*

Prairie View
wWheaton, Elizabeth M. *finance company executive, educator*

Quinlan
Smith, Patsy Juanita *retired financial executive*

Richardson
Burke, Thomas William *benefits compensation analyst*
Enthoven, Adolf Jan Henri *accounting educator*
Radhakrishnan, Suresh *finance educator*

Round Rock
Puri, Rajendra Kumar *business and tax specialist, consultant*

San Antonio
Darling, John Rothburn *business educator*
Forgione, Dana Anthony *accounting educator*
Fuhrmann, Charles J., II, *financial consultant, educator*
Jones, James Richard *business administration educator*
Lim, Seong Bae *business educator*

San Marcos
Suh, Taewon *marketing and business educator*

Sherman
Avard, Stephen Lewis *retired finance educator*
Simmons, Kevin Mark *finance educator*

Spring
Kehoe, John Kimball *finance educator, consultant*

Stephenville
Collier, Boyd Dean *finance educator, management consultant*

Tyler
Doty, Duane Harold *business educator*
Gainer, Lindsey Adams *finance educator, consultant*

Waco
Rose, John Thomas *finance educator*

Wimberley
Skaggs, Wayne Gerard *retired diversified financial services company executive*

UTAH

Orem
Hunt, H(arold) Keith *retired business management educator, marketing consultant*

Provo
Hill, Ned Cromar *finance educator, consultant, former dean*
Jensen, Robert J. *business strategy educator*
Stone, Bernell Kenneth *finance educator*

Saint George
Kohl, John Preston *retired finance educator, consultant*

Salt Lake City
Brady, Rodney Howard *diversified financial services and broadcast company executive, retired academic administrator, federal official*
Elkins, Glen Ray *retired diversified management services company executive*
Nelson, Roger Hugh *corporate financial executive, educator, consultant*

VERMONT

Quechee
Vitty, Roderic Bemis *retired financial planner, publishing executive*

VIRGINIA

Abingdon
Jones, Mary Trent *endowment fund trustee*

Alexandria
Hammad, Alam E. *international business consultant, author educator*

Arlington
Huff, Jimmy *finance company executive, director*
Page, Harry Robert *business administration educator*
Siegel, Laurie F. *accountant, painter*

Blacksburg
Moore, Laurence John *business educator*
Patterson, Douglas MacLennan *finance educator*
Uysal, Muzaffer Shamil *management educator*

Chantilly
Carlson, Robert Charles *financial planner, writer*

Charlottesville
Davis, Edward Wilson *business administration educator*
De Colle, Simone *finance educator, researcher*
DeMong, Richard Francis *finance and investments educator*
Mick, David Glen *finance educator*
Pinto, Jerald E. *financial analyst, director*
Sahr, Morris Gallup *financial planner*
Scott, Charlotte H. *business educator*
Shenkir, William Gary *business educator*
Sihler, William Wooding *finance educator*

Chesapeake
Barnes, Stacy Ray *finance educator, researcher*

Chesterfield
Garnett, Douglas Acree *financial analyst, researcher*

Danville
Martin, Marshall Wayne *finance educator*

Fairfax
Kravitz, David Albert *finance educator*

Falls Church
Mancuso, Michael John *corporate financial executive*

Glen Allen
Rajkowski, E. Mark *corporate financial executive*

Keswick
Pochick, Francis Edward *financial consultant*

Lexington
DeVogt, John Frederick *management science and business ethics educator, consultant*

Lynchburg
Gerdes, Darin L. *finance educator*
Gilmore, Philip Nathanael *finance educator, accountant*

Mc Lean
Bailar, Gregor S. *finance company executive*
Blisk, Brenda Pack *financial consultant*
Fairbank, Richard D. *diversified financial services company executive*
Goktepe, Janet Rose *retired financial analyst*
Kautt, Glenn Gregory *financial planner, consultant*
Perlin, Gary Laurence *diversified financial services company executive*

Melfa
Weitzel, Paul *finance educator*

Mineral
Mayo, Louis Allen *policy management counseling company executive*

Norfolk
Gopinath, Mahesh *finance educator*
McKee, Timothy Carlton *taxation educator*
Qian, Sun *finance educator*

Reston
Autor, Robert S. *finance company executive*
Clark, Jonathan C. *finance company executive*
Lord, Albert L. *finance company executive*
Palumbo, James Fredrick *finance company executive*
Polemitou, Olga Andrea *accountant*
Remondi, John F. (Jack Remondi) *finance company executive*
Terracciano, Anthony Patrick *finance company executive*
Young, Loretta Ann *auditor*

Richmond
Austin, John D. *corporate financial executive*
Gerner, John *financial consultant*
Harris, Ruth Hortense Coles *retired finance educator*
King, Robert Leroy *business administration educator*
Phillips, Thomas Edworth, Jr. *financial advisor, investment management consultant*
Salomon, Dalal Maria *financial consultant*

Virginia Beach
Oster, Gary Wayne *innovation and entrepreneurship educator*
Price, Alan Thomas *business and estate planner*

Weems
Martin, William Raymond *retired financial manager*

Williamsburg
Gottfried, Mark Ellis *accountant, consultant*
Holstein, William Kurt *business administration educator*
Kottas, John Frederick *business administration educator*
McLennan, Barbara Nancy *tax specialist*
Montgomery, Joseph William *financial consultant*
O'Connell, William Edward, Jr. *retired finance educator*
Paige, Hilliard Wegner *corporate executive, consultant*
Pearson, Roy Laing *business administration educator*

Winchester
Gouldey, Bruce K. *finance educator*

WASHINGTON

Bellevue
Graham, John Robert, Jr. *financial executive*

Bellingham
Wolters, Curt Cornelis Frederik *economic consultant, retired foreign service officer*

Edmonds
Monroe, James Walter *retired corporate financial executive*

Ellensburg
Takei, Hideki *business educator*

Issaquah
von Speyer, Jacques *financier*

Mukilteo
Brown, Bruce Baden *accountant*

Pullman
Kim, Hyun Jeong *tourism educator*

Seattle
Baker, Roland Jerald *finance educator*
Higgins, Robert *finance educator*
MacLachlan, Douglas Lee *marketing educator*
Szkutak, Tom *corporate financial executive*

Shelton
McNabb, David E. *educator, author*

Shoreline
Hanson, Kermit Osmond *business administration educator, retired dean*

Spokane
Beqiri, Mirjeta S. *operations management educator*
Cameron, Alex Brian *accountant, educator*
Friends, Todd Hart *finance educator*
Teets, Walter Ralph *accounting educator*

WEST VIRGINIA

Harpers Ferry
Boucher, Wayne Irving *policy analyst*

Institute
Bird, John D. *finance educator, consultant*

Morgantown
Griffith, Charles T. *accountant, consultant*
Sears, Robert Stephen *finance educator, former dean*

WISCONSIN

Appleton
Stellmacher, Jon Michael *corporate financial executive*

Eau Claire
Weil, D(onald) Wallace *business administration educator*

La Crosse
Ancius, Michael J. *corporate financial executive*
Graham, Lise N. *finance educator*

Madison
Aldag, Ramon John *management and organization educator*
Antonioni, David *professor, director*
Taber, Christopher Robert *finance educator*

Milwaukee
Bergmann, Thomas E. *corporate financial executive*
Culver, Curt S. *diversified financial services company executive*
Furlong, Mark Francis *diversified financial services company executive, bank executive*
Kuester, Dennis J. *diversified financial services company and bank executive*
Schnoll, Howard Manuel *financial consultant, investment company executive*
Szwarc, Wlodzimierz *operations research professor*
Zore, Edward John *financial services executive*

New Berlin
Gebhard, LaVerne Elizabeth *retired accounting educator*

Oconomowoc
Kneiser, Richard John *accountant*

Superior
Robek, Mary Frances *business education educator*

Waupun
Wendt, Thomas *finance company executive*

WYOMING

Cheyenne
Parrish, Denise Kay *regulatory accountant*

Laramie
Spiegelberg, Emma Jo *business education educator, academic administrator*

TERRITORIES OF THE UNITED STATES

PUERTO RICO

Hatillo
Santos, Isabel Rodriguez *marketing educator*

Mayaguez
Ruiz-Vargas, Yolanda *finance educator*

San Juan
Rosso de Irizarry, Carmen (Tutty Rosso de Irizarry) *finance executive*

CANADA

BRITISH COLUMBIA

Burnaby
Tung, Rosalie L. *business educator, consultant*

Vancouver
Mattessich, Richard Victor (Alvarus) *business administration researcher*

ONTARIO

London
Osbaldeston, Gordon Francis *finance educator, retired federal agency administrator*

Toronto
Are, Ayokunnu *financial advisor, investment banker*
Hore, John Edward *retired commodity futures educator*
Kerr, David Wylie *managing partner, director*
Mann, George Stanley *diversified financial services company executive, real estate company officer*
Mercier, Eileen Ann *pension fund chairman*
Morneau, William *pension and benefits company executive*
Poprawa, Andrew *diversified financial services company executive, accountant*
Price, Timothy R. *accountant*
Ronald, Thomas Iain *retired financial services executive*
Schwartz, Gerald Wilfred *business executive*

QUEBEC

Montreal
Desmarais, Paul *diversified management and holding company executive*
Gratton, Robert *diversified financial services company executive*
Laurin, Pierre *finance company executive*
Lessard, Michel M. *finance company executive*
Speirs, Derek James *diversified financial services company executive*

AUSTRALIA

Crawley
Sweeney, Jillian C. *marketing professor*

BERMUDA

Pembroke
Alexander, Barbara Toll *financial consultant*

CHINA

Beijing
Christianson, Wei Sun *diversified financial services company executive*

Hong Kong
Pacter, Paul Allan *accounting standards researcher*

Shantou
Leyden, Michael Joseph, II, (Lei Jie Ming) *business finance educator, entrepreneur, writer*

ENGLAND

Coventry
Thomas, Howard *business educator*

Henley-on-Thames
Bullock, Peter Bradley *company director, consultant*

London
Chammah, Walid A. *diversified financial services company executive*
Diederichs, Klaus *diversified financial services company executive*
Gyllenhammar, Pehr Gustaf *finance company executive, writer, retired automotive executive*
Ioannou, Constantinos Elia *accountant*
Lynch, Gary G. *diversified financial services company executive, lawyer*
Mantegazza, Sergio *finance company executive*
Pavlova, Anna *finance educator*
Sarkis, Ziad Joseph *private equity executive*
Sherwood, Michael S. *diversified financial services company executive*
Winters, William Thomas (Bill Winters) *diversified financial services company executive*

FRANCE

Fontainebleau
Hawawini, Gabriel Alfred *finance educator, former dean*

Le Chillou
Gourvest, Alain *retired finance educator*

Paris
Ricol, Rene Jean *accountant*
Vandame, Jean-Marie Richard *financial professional services firm executive*

GERMANY

Mannheim
Isaak, Robert Allen *international management and political economy educator, writer*

GREECE

Athens
Papadakis, Panagiotis Agamemnon *corporate financial executive*

HONG KONG

Central
Evans, J. Michael *diversified financial services company executive*
Roach, Stephen S. *diversified financial services company executive*

Wanchai
Wong, Albert Wing Kuen *finance educator*
Thomas, Owen D. *diversified financial services company executive*

IRELAND

Dublin
Cotter, John *finance educator*

ITALY

Milan
Zara, Claudio *finance educator, management consultant*

JAPAN

Hiratsuka
Ayano, Katsutoshi *management educator*

Kanagawa
Okada, Ellie *business educator*

Tokyo
Kobayashi, Noritake *business educator*
Suzuki, Tadao *retired corporate financial executive*

JORDAN

Amman
Batayneh, Malek Khaled *finance company executive, consultant*

NETHERLANDS

Breukelen
Uhlaner, Lorraine Marie *finance educator*

PHILIPPINES

Quezon City
Gokongwei, John Lim, Jr. *financial executive*

REPUBLIC OF KOREA

Cheongju
Na, Kwan-Sik *management information systems professor*

Gyeongbuk
Lee, Young-Chan *business professor*

Seoul
Park, Oh-Soo *finance educator, electronics executive*

SCOTLAND

St Andrews
Lee, Thomas Alexander *accountant, educator*

Stirling
Masocha, Walter *finance educator*

SPAIN

Zaragoza
Yadav, Prashant *economics educator*

SWITZERLAND

Alpnach
Bocker, Hans Jurgen *finance educator, editor-in-chief, consultant*

Hergiswil
Bröder, Ernst-Günther *financial executive, economist*

Zurich
Dougan, Brady W. *diversified financial services company executive*

TAIWAN

Hsinchu
Wang, David *finance educator*

Taichung
Chang, Pao-Long *management sciences educator, academic administrator*

Taipei
Tsung, Christine Chai-yi *financial executive, treasurer*

THAILAND

Pranakorn
Tepvorachai, Gorn *financial analyst*

ADDRESS UNPUBLISHED

Abbott, Edward Leroy *finance executive*
Abdelrahman, Talaat Ahmad Mohammad *financial executive*
Adler, Jack Saul *retired accountant*
Albano, Pasquale Charles *management educator, management consultant*
Aldridge, Adrienne Yingling *accountant, writer*
Almeida, Richard Joseph *finance company administrator*
Alper, Merlin Lionel *corporate financial executive*
Alvare, Charles Daguerre *financial advisor, educator*
Anderson, Maria Watkins *financial analyst*
Andrews, C.E. (Charles Elliot Andrews Jr.) *former finance company executive*
Arenberg, Julius Theodore, Jr. *retired accounting company executive*
Ashby, Franklin Charles, Jr. *corporate financial executive, educator*
Ashworth, Bessie *benefits compensation analyst, writer*
Atwood, Donna Elaine *retired financial manager*
Auerbach, David I. *health policy analyst*
Awazu, Yukika *corporate executive, researcher, consultant, writer*
Bains, Harrison MacKellar, Jr. *retired corporate financial executive*
Bákér, J. A., II, *executive management advisor and consultant, monetary architect, financial engineer emeritus*
Baranchuk, Nina *finance educator*
Bartlett, Shirley Anne *accountant*
Bauman, Winfield Scott *finance educator*
Bell, Angela Marie *accountant*
Belluomini, Frank Stephen *accountant*
Bennett, Peter Dunne *retired marketing educator*
Benson, Donald Erick *finance company executive*
Bhattacherjee, Anol *finance educator*
Biklen, Stephen Clinton *retired diversified financial services company executive*
Blencke, Carl Joseph *finance educator*
Blount, Vyren William *finance educator*
Bollon, Steven A. *financial analyst, educator*
Borum, Rodney Lee *corporate financial executive*
Boyer, Robert Allan *finance company executive*
Boyles, Robert Strickland, Jr. *financial consultant*
Braggs, Patricia *account manager*
Brdlik, Carola Emilie *retired accountant*
Brees, Michael Paul *controller*
Brenneman, Serena C. *finance educator*
Brewerton, Francis J. *business educator*
Broome, Oscar Whitfield, Jr. *finance educator*
Brown, James Nelson, Jr. *retired accountant*
Brown, Melvin F. *finance company executive*
Browne, John (Lord Browne of Madingley) *financial company executive, former oil industry executive*
Brown Klinger, Stephen *financial analyst*
Burman, Leonard Emanuel *tax specialist, director*
Butler, John Musgrave *financial consultant*
Carrasquilla, Kurt Frank *finance educator*
Cayne, James E. (Jimmy Cayne) *former diversified financial services company executive*
Chen, Chun-Da *finance educator*
Cittone, Henry Aron *hotel and restaurant management educator*
Clayton, Richard Reese *retired diversified financial services company executive*
Clemen, Robert T. *decision analysis educator*
Cohen, Rachel Rutstein *financial planner*
Colburn, Kenneth Hersey *retired financial executive*
Collette, Frances Madelyn *retired tax specialist, lawyer, consultant, advocate*
Conti, Indalicio Palomar *finance educator*
Cooper, Ken Errol *retired management educator*
Cosimano, Thomas Francis *finance educator*
Coulter, Jack Benson, Jr. *financial planner*
Crisci, Mathew G. *financial consultant and author*
Cruz, Zoe *diversified financial services company executive*
Cuffe, Stafford Sigesmund *business, technology, manufacturing and management consultant*
Culp, Mildred Louise *corporate financial executive*
Danforth, Arthur Edwards *finance executive*
Deng, Qian *finance company executive*
Denison, Dwight Val *finance educator*
Denn, Cyril Joseph *retired financial advisor*
DeWitt, Eula *retired accountant*
Dong, Beibei *finance educator*
Dorsey, Dolores Florence *retired corporate treasurer, finance company executive*
Doss, Jessica Yarina *incentive program manager*
Dossin, Ernest Joseph III *credit manager*
Dozier, Glenn Joseph *diversified financial services company executive*
Druskin, Robert A. *retired diversified financial services company executive*
Duncan, Robert Bannerman *finance educator, former dean*
Easton, Charles Clement, Jr. *corporate financial executive*
Eng, Adrienne Rose *corporate financial executive*
Ertugrul, Mine *finance educator*
Esmer, Burcu *finance educator*
Estrin, Herbert Alvin *financial consultant, film company executive*
Farrar, John Edson, II, *finance company executive, consultant, investment advisor*
Fassler, Kerin Irene *retired systems accountant*
Fetscherin, Marc Philippe *business educator*
Fitzpatrick, Lorraine *retired accountant*
Fletcher, Denise Koen *strategic and financial consultant*
Folz, Carol Ann *benefits compensation analyst*
Fox, Betty *financial services executive*
Fox, Edward Alan *retired finance company executive*
Frank, Edgar Gerald *retired finance company executive*
Frank, Ronald Edward *marketing educator*
Frankenstein, John *international management educator, consultant*
Friedman, Joan M. *retired accountant, educator*
Friedman, Tully Michael *finance company executive*
Furst, E. Kenneth *accountant*
Gaines, Brenda J. *retired financial services company executive*
Galda, Dwight William *finance company executive*
Gambrell, Luck Flanders *business executive*
Garcia-Granados, Sergio Eduardo *portfolio manager, writer, historian*
Garvey, Jane F. *diversified financial services company executive, former public relations firm executive*
Gehani, Ray R. *finance educator*
Giles, James Francis *financial executive*
Gines, Ernest *finance educator*
Gitelson, Susan Aurelia *corporate executive, philanthropist*
Goeltz, Richard Karl *finance company executive*
Goldberger, George Stefan *finance company executive*
Goodsell, Charles True *public administration educator, researcher*
Graham, Howard Lee, Sr. *finance company executive*
Graveline, Jeremy James *finance educator*
Greenberg, Alan Courtney (Ace Greenberg) *retired diversified financial services company executive*
Griffin, Carleton Hadlock *accountant, educator*
Griffith, Clark Dexter *corporate financial executive*
Groves, Ray John *accountant*
Gruver, William Rolfe (Bill Gruver) *finance educator, retired investment banker*
Guerrera, Lisa E. *financial planner*
Hamilton, Jean *financial services executive, e-commerce and software executive*
Handy, Edward Otis, Jr. *retired diversified financial services company executive*
Harper, James Weldon III *finance consultant*
Hartman, David G. *retired actuary*
Hayek, Carolyn Jean *financial consultant, retired judge*
He, Yi *marketing educator*
Healy, Steven Michael *accountant, city official*
Heineman, Ben Walter *corporation executive*
Heller, Robert *financial executive, economist*
Hendrix, Stephen C. *financial executive, consultant*
Hensley, Ralph Henry III *federal management analyst*
Herringer, Frank Casper *retired diversified financial services company executive*
Hicks, Greta Patterson *accountant, lecturer, writer*
Hildreth, Patricia Yvonne *retired finance company executive*
Hill, Lowell Dean *agricultural marketing educator*
Hines, Walter James *former stock exchange executive*
Hockin, Robert *business educator, consultant*
Hoel, Anne Kelly *finance educator, consultant*
Holloran, Thomas Edward *business educator*
Holton, Grace Holland *accountant*
Hooper, William Douglas *retired diversified financial services company executive, photographer, digital imaging artist*
Hubbe, Henry Ernest *financial forecaster, trading manager*
Huber, Wesley David *accountant, lawyer, financial planner, educator*
Hudak, Thomas F(rancis) *finance company executive*

Hueppi, Rolf *financial services executive*
Hull, Geordan *finance educator, director*
Hunger, J(ohn) David *business educator*
Hunter, Jeffrey Glen *finance educator, director*
Israel, Leo *accountant*
Jamison, John Callison *business educator, investment banker*
Johnson, Freda S. *financial analyst, consultant*
Johnson, Suzanne Nora *retired diversified financial services company executive, lawyer*
Kaehele, Bettie Louise *accountant*
Kamerick, Eileen Ann *financial executive, lawyer*
Kaplan, Leonard Eugene *accountant*
Karuna, Christo *finance educator*
Kavesh, Eden *fraud investigator, financial consultant*
Kercheval, John William III *finance professor, aerospace and defense executive, vulture capitalist, former investment banker*
Khuong, Loc Huu *finance educator*
Kilmann, Ralph Herman *business educator*
King, Alfred Meehan *financial executive*
King, Algin Braddy *retired marketing educator*
King, Ronald Lee *retired accountant, government agency administrator*
Kingsbery, Walton Waits, Jr. *retired accounting firm executive*
Kissinger, Henry Alfred *international consulting company executive, former United States Secretary of State*
Klein, Michael Stuart *former diversified financial services company executive*
Klemm, John Donald, Jr. *finance company executive, director*
Kohan, Dennis Lynn *finance educator*
Konola, Claudette June *consultant*
Kotter, John Paul *organizational behavior educator, management consultant*
Lamont, Alice *accountant, consultant*
Landeck, Carl *corporate financial executive*
Leibler, Kenneth Robert *finance company executive*
Leimkuhler, Gerard Joseph *diversified financial services company executive*
Lerner, Herbert J. *tax consultant*
Lester, Alicia Louise *financial analyst*
Levy, Louis Edward *retired accounting firm executive*
Lewin, Leif I. *finance executive*
Lewins, Steven *financial analyst, investment company executive, legislative staff member, retired military officer*
Lilien, Robert Jarrett (Jarrett Lilien) *former diversified financial services company executive*
Lippitt, Mary B. *finance company executive*
Loken, Barbara *marketing educator, social psychologist*
Loren, Allan Z. *former financial services company executive*
Maciewski, Bryan Jon *finance educator, consultant*
Madhavaram, Sreedhar *marketing educator*
Magnano, Salvatore Paul *retired finance company executive, treasurer*
Maheras, Thomas G. *former diversified financial services company executive*
Mankin, Robert Stephen *diversified financial services company executive*
Marciano, Sonia *finance educator*
Maruyama, Magoroh *business educator, researcher, consultant*
Maul, Kevin Jay *financial consultant, economist*
May, Phyllis Jean *financial executive*
McCann, Robert James *former diversified financial services company executive*
McClinton, Donald George *retired diversified holding company executive*
McDonough, William J. *diversified financial services company executive*
McFarlane, Donovan Anthony *finance educator, consultant*
McGill, Dan Mays *insurance business educator*
McKay, Patricia A. *corporate financial executive*
McNally, Regina C. *marketing educator*
Mednick, Robert *accountant*
Messmer, Donald Joseph *business management educator, marketing consultant*
Milch, Peter Stephen *retired finance educator*
Miller, Alan J. *retired financial company executive*
Miller, Richard Glen *financial planning executive*
Mitchem, Cheryl E. *accounting educator*
Mitroff, Ian I. *finance educator*
Moline, Jennifer M. *corporate financial executive*
Moore, Cornell Leverette *financial services executive, lawyer*
Morgan, William J. *independent director, leadership development consultant and retired accounting company executive*
Mossavar-Rahmani, Sharmin *diversified financial services company executive*
Moyer, R. Charles *finance company executive, educator, retired dean*
Mudry, Michael *pension and benefit consultant*
Myers, Phillip Fenton *corporate financial, technology executive*
Naoumova, Irina Yevgenievna *business educator, consultant*
Nawalkha, Sanjay K. *finance educator*
Needles, Belverd Earl, Jr. *accountant, educator*
Nehrt, Lee Charles *management educator*
Newell, Stephen *finance educator, department chairman*
Niehoff, Karl Richard Besuden *finance company executive*
Noonan, Patrick Sutton *author management educator*
Nutzell, Natalie *financial analyst*
Oladunni, Olutayo O. *consultant*
Ortiz-Walters, Rowena *management educator*
Osborn, Kenneth Louis *financial executive*
Osborne, John Edward *retired finance educator*
Ozzello, Lawrence Mural *accountant, educator*
Paige, Vivian Jo-Ann *accountant*
Pappas, Michael *payroll consultant*
Pappas-Speairs, Nina *financial planner, educator*
Parameswaran, Raju *accountant*
Park, Myung Seok *finance educator*
Parr, Janet Smyth *finance educator*
Parsons, Richard Dean (Dick Parsons) *diversified financial services company executive, former multimedia company executive*
Patmore, Kimberly S. *financial services executive*
Perry, Nancy Bland *accountant*
Petru, Suzanne Mitton *retired health care finance executive*
Prewitt, Lena Voncille Burrell *management educator*
Pyle, Robert Milner, Jr. *financial consultant*
Quant, Harold Edward *retired financial services company executive, rancher*
Raffegeau, Jean Michel *audit and consulting company executive*
Rai, Alexander K. *international affairs executive*
Rakes, Ganas Kaye *retired finance and banking educator*
Ray, Marjorie *retired financial planner*
Reed, John Shepard *retired diversified financial services company executive*
Reidy, Thomas Michael *financial executive*
Renouf, Anne *corporate financial executive, consultant*
Rinaldi, Emilia *finance educator*
Rizzo, Jeffrey F. *corporate and non-profit financial executive*
Robertson, A. Haeworth *actuary, foundation executive, benefits consultant*
Robertson, Jack Clark *accounting educator*
Rosenberg, Sheli Zysman *retired finance company executive*
Rubin, Robert Edward *former diversified financial services company executive, former United States Secretary of the Treasury*
Rumfolo, Marilu *financial analyst*
Rush, Richard Henry *finance company executive, educator, writer*
Rushing, John Alan *business educator*
Russell, Walter Dallas, Jr. *diversified financial services company executive*
Ryan, Arthur Frederick *retired diversified financial services company executive*
Ryan, Leo Vincent *business educator*
Saks, Stephen Howard *accountant, health organization executive*
Sanders, Heywood T. *finance educator*
Sanderson, Jihong W. *finance educator, consultant*
Saniga, Erwin Martin *educator, painter*
Saucier, Guylaine *corporate financial executive*
Sayles, Leonard Robert *management educator, consultant*
Schaap, James Ike *finance educator*
Scheel, Nels Earl *corporate financial executive, accountant*
Schein, Edgar Henry *management educator*
Schellenberger, Robert Earl *retired management educator, department chairman*
Scully, Robert William (Bob Scully) *retired diversified financial services company executive*
Seiple, John W., Jr. *corporate financial executive*
Seligson, Carl Harold *corporate financial executive*
Serrie, Hendrick *retired anthropology and international business educator*
Sharkey, Vincent Joseph *finance company executive*
Sharma, Divesh Shankar *finance educator*
Sharma, Vivek *finance educator*
Sheridan, Patrick Michael *retired finance company executive*
Sherman, Howard D. *financial consultant*
Sherrard, William Robert *retired operations management educator*
Shin, Shung Jae *management educators*
Shuchart, Eugene Joseph *retired accountant*
Shultis, Robert Lynn *finance educator, consultant, retired professional society administrator*
Siegel, Stanley *financial executive*
Simon, Donald John *financial planner, theta healer, small business owner*
Simon, Ronald Isaac *financial executive*
Slotkin, Todd *diversified financial services company executive*
Smith, Harold Charles *pension fund administrator*
Sollender, Joel David *accountant, consultant, financial executive*
Srinivasan, Venkataraman *marketing and management educator*
Staloff, Arnold Fred *financial services executive*
Stanfill, Dennis Carothers *corporate financial executive*
Steinback, Thomas R. *business management educator*
Strong, John Scott *finance educator*
Tang, Yue *financial analyst*
Tarleton, Jesse S. *retired business educator*
Tew, E. James, Jr. *management services company executive*
Thain, John Alexander *former diversified financial services company executive*
Thomson, Alexander Bennett, Jr. *financial planner, tax and management consultant*
Trachtenberg, Matthew J. *arts administrator, financial services executive, philanthropist*
Trent, Robert Harold *retired business educator*
Trubeck, William Lewis *former diversified financial services company executive*
Tu, Yufeng *business educator*
Turner, Henry Brown *finance company executive, director*
Valcic, Branka *finance educator*
Varjavand, Reza *finance educator*
Vaughn, John Rolland *retired auditor*
Vreeland, Russell Glenn *senior tax manager, accountant, consultant*
Vroom, Victor Harold *management consultant, educator*
Vu, Joseph Duong *financial educator*
Wagner, Harvey M. *finance educator, consultant*
Wall, M. Danny *retired finance company executive*
Walsh, John E., Jr. *business educator, consultant*
Warner, Douglas Alexander, III, (Sandy Warner) *retired diversified financial services company executive*
Wesselink, David Duwayne *finance company executive*
Wheatland, Richard, II, *fiduciary services executive, museum executive*
White, Luther G. *finance educator*
White, Ronald Leon *retired business executive*
Whitman, Martin J. *portfolio manager*
Widner, Roberta Ann *accountant, artist*
Wilhelmsen, Harold John *accountant*
Wilkinson, Harry Edward *management educator, consultant*
Williams, Alfred B. *retired management educator*
Wittbrodt, Edwin Stanley *financial planner, consultant, retired military officer*
Workman, John P., Jr. *marketing professor*
Wright, Judith Rae *retired accountant*
Wynne, Patricia M *finance company executive*
Yastine, Barbara A. *former diversified financial services company executive*
Zerom, Dawit *finance educator*
Zhang, Yan Anthea *finance educator*
Zimmerman, Helene Loretta *retired business educator*
Zuck, Alfred Miller *public administration educator*

FINANCE: INSURANCE

UNITED STATES

ALABAMA

Birmingham
Johns, John D. *insurance company executive, lawyer*

Fairhope
Norton, Margaret Sarah *retired insurance company executive*

Huntsville
Parker, Wayne, Jr. *insurance company executive*

ALASKA

Anchorage
Trevithick, Ronald James *underwriter*

ARIZONA

Paradise Valley
Tyner, Neal Edward *retired insurance company executive*

Rio Verde
Harding, John Hibbard *retired insurance company executive*

Scottsdale
Vairo, Robert John *insurance company executive*

Sun City
Reynolds, John Francis *insurance company executive*

Tucson
Haney, Robert Locke *retired insurance company executive*

CALIFORNIA

Castroville
Rhoades, Mark Matthew *risk management consultant, educator*

Cupertino
Knapp, George Griff Prather *retired insurance executive*

Encino
Parrott, Dennis Beecher *retired insurance industry executive*

Irvine
Matros, Richard K. *insurance company executive*

Los Angeles
Houston, Ivan James *insurance company executive*
Inman, James Russell *claims consultant*
Johnson, E. Eric *insurance company executive*
Joseph, George *insurance company executive*
Tirador, Gabriel *insurance company executive*

Marina Del Rey
Dexheimer, Henry Phillip, II, *insurance agency executive*

Menifee
Roark, Robert Cameron *insurance agent*

Newark
Gupta, Anju *risk management consultant*

Newport Beach
Cheever, Sharon Ann *insurance company executive, lawyer*
Fries, Arthur Lawrence *life and health insurance broker, disability claim consultant*
Marcoux, Carl Henry *former insurance company executive, writer, historian*
Morris, James T. *insurance company executive*
Tran, Khanh T. *insurance company executive*

Oakland
Halvorson, George Charles *healthcare insurance company executive*
Lancaster, Kathy *insurance company executive*

Rancho Mirage
Fromm, Erwin Frederick *retired insurance company executive*

Roseville
Carmen, Robert G. *insurance company executive*
Dodds, Larry D. *insurance company executive*
Rebok, Douglas E. *insurance company executive, accountant*

Sacramento
Fry, Patrick *insurance company executive*

San Diego
Baxter, Robert Hampton *insurance company executive*

San Francisco
Dean, Lloyd H. *insurance company executive*
Lamberson, John Roger *insurance company executive*
Martinez, Belinda *health insurance company executive*
Stewart, Richard Edwin *insurance consulting company executive*

San Rafael
Keegan, Jane Ann *insurance executive, consultant*

Santa Ana
Gilmore, Dennis J. *insurance company executive*
McMahon, Frank V. *insurance company executive*

Santa Barbara
Evans, Thomas Edgar, Jr. *title insurance agency executive*

Santa Monica
Schaeffer, Leonard David *health insurance company executive*

Santa Rosa
Farrell, Thomas Joseph *insurance company executive, consultant*

Whittier
Ross, Ami L. *insurance and finance company executive*

Woodland Hills
Berry, Carol Ann *insurance company executive*
Clarey, Patricia T. *health insurance company executive, former state official*

COLORADO

Aurora
Nelson, Marvin Ray *retired life insurance company executive*

Englewood
Hardy, Wayne Russell *insurance and investment broker*

CONNECTICUT

Bloomfield
Cordani, David M. *insurance company executive*

East Hartford
Lautzenheiser, Barbara Jean *insurance company executive*

Essex
Miller, Walter Neal *insurance company consultant*

Farmington
Herbert, Mickey *insurance company executive*

Goshen
Kaplan, Theodore Norman *insurance company executive*

Greenwich
Ballard, Eugene G. *insurance company executive*
Berkley, William Robert *insurance holding company executive*
Clements, Robert *insurance executive*
Fuller, Theodore *retired insurance executive*
Lederman, Ira Seth *insurance company executive, lawyer*

Hartford
Ayer, Ramani *insurance company executive*
Bertolini, Mark T. *insurance company executive*
Bombara, Beth Ann *insurance company executive*
Brubaker, Laurie *insurance company executive*
Campbell, Timothy R. *insurance company executive*
Casazza, William James *insurance company executive, lawyer*
MacDonald, Anne *insurance company executive*
Mathias, Michael G. *insurance company executive*
McGreevey, Greg *insurance company executive*
Sargent, Joseph Denny *insurance executive*
Scully, John Carroll *life insurance marketing research company executive*
Walters, John C. *insurance company executive*
Williams, Ronald A. *health insurance company executive*
Wright, Elease *insurance company executive*
Zlatkus, Lizabeth H. *insurance company executive*
Zubretsky, Joseph M. *insurance company executive*

Middletown
Bohan, Lawrence Stewart *retired insurance company executive*

New Canaan
Burns, John Joseph, Jr. *financial and insurance holding company executive*

Cohen, Richard Norman *insurance executive*

Stamford
Hudson, Harold Jordon, Jr. *retired insurance executive*
Montross, Franklin, IV, (Tad Montross) *reinsurance company executive*

Weston
Thompson, N(orman) David *insurance company executive*

DELAWARE

Wilmington
Phillips, Joyce A. *insurance company executive*

DISTRICT OF COLUMBIA

Washington
Merski, Richard P. *insurance company executive*
Nicely, Olza M. (Tony) *insurance company executive*
Pitt, Harvey Lloyd *risk management consultant, former federal agency administrator*

FLORIDA

Bonita Springs
Rainey, Barbara White *insurance company executive*

Coral Gables
Landon, Robert Kirkwood *philanthropist*

Coral Springs
Miller, Karl Frederick *insurance professional*

Delray Beach
Richardson, R(oss) Fred(erick) *insurance company executive, consultant*

Gainesville
Boothroyd, Herbert J. *insurance company executive*

Holiday
Peterson, George Folke *retired insurance company executive, writer*

Jacksonville
Bickett, Brent B. *insurance company executive*
Foley, William Patrick, II, *insurance company executive*
Lyon, Wilford Charles, Jr. *insurance executive*
Quirk, Raymond R. (Randy Quirk) *insurance company executive*
Stinson, Alan Lynn *insurance company executive*

Key Largo
Daenzer, Bernard John *insurance company executive, consultant*
Lynn, James Thomas *insurance company executive, lawyer, former United States Secretary of Housing and Urban Development*

Lake Mary
Swonger, Thomas K. H., Jr. *insurance company executive*

Miami
Gibson, William Shepard *retired insurance company executive*
Heggen, Arthur William *insurance company executive*
Shusterman, Nathan *underwriter, financial consultant*
Van Wyck, George Richard *insurance company executive*

Ormond Beach
Burt, Wallace Joseph, Jr. *insurance company executive*

Palm Harbor
Campos, Jackie C. *insurance agent*

Punta Gorda
McDaniel, Norwood Allan *insurance broker*

Sarasota
Bushey, Alan Scott *retired insurance holding company executive*

Spring Hill
Vanderburg, Paul Stacey *insurance executive, consultant*

Tallahassee
Gunter, William Dawson, Jr., (Bill Gunter) *insurance company executive, consultant*
Hunt, John Edwin *insurance company executive, consultant*

Tampa
Bishopric, Karl *insurance company executive, retired investment banker, real estate company executive, advertising executive*

GEORGIA

Atlanta
Gregory, Mel Hyatt, Jr. *retired insurance company executive*
Hilliard, Robert Glenn *insurance company executive, lawyer*
Peacock, George Rowatt *retired life insurance company executive*

Columbus
Amos, Daniel Paul *insurance company executive*
Amos, Paul Shelby *insurance company executive*
Amos, Paul Shelby, II, *insurance company executive*
Baker, Janet *insurance company executive*
Cloninger, Kriss III *insurance company executive*
Cox, Kermitt L. *insurance company executive*
Davis, Rebecca C. *insurance company executive*
Friou, Phillip J. (Jack Friou) *insurance company executive*
Hart, Angela *insurance company executive*
Janke, Kenneth S., Jr. *insurance company executive*
Jeffery, William Jeremy *insurance company executive*
Kirkland, Ronald E. *insurance company executive*
Ottman, Bob *insurance company executive*
Pringle, David L. *insurance company executive*
Rogers, Ralph A., Jr. *insurance company executive*
Shields, Gerald W. *insurance company executive*
Tillman, Audrey Boone *insurance company executive*
White, Teresa Lynne *insurance company executive*

Lagrange
Hudson, Charles Daugherty *insurance executive*

Savannah
Dodge, William Douglas *risk management consultant*

HAWAII

Honolulu
Noguchi, Hideo *insurance company executive*

ILLINOIS

Barrington
Karlin, Gary Lee *insurance executive*

Bloomington
Blackburn, John D. *insurance company executive*
Brunner, Kim M. *insurance company executive, lawyer*
Rust, Edward Barry, Jr. *insurance company executive, lawyer*
Rutrough, James E. *insurance company executive*

Chicago
Bartholomay, William C. *insurance brokerage company and professional sports team executive*
Case, Gregory C. *insurance company executive*
Davies, Christa *insurance company executive*
DeMoss, Jon W. *insurance company executive, lawyer*
Dorman-Rodriguez, Deborah *insurance company executive, lawyer*
Fernandez, Geno *insurance company executive*
Hemingway Hall, Patricia *health insurance company executive*
Hinkelman, Ruth Amidon *insurance company executive*
Lerner, Alexander Robert *insurance company executive*
Lorenz, Hugo Albert *retired insurance executive, consultant*
Manning, Frederick James *insurance company executive*
Meissner, Laurel G. *insurance company executive*
Peponis, Harold Arthur *insurance agent, portfolio manager*
Southwell, Donald G. *insurance company executive*
Tipsord, Michael L. *insurance company executive*
Vie, Richard Carl *insurance company executive*
Zucaro, Aldo Charles *insurance company executive*

Itasca
Gallagher, J. Patrick, Jr. *insurance company executive*

Lake Forest
Peterson, Donald Matthew *insurance company executive*

Naperville
Crawford, Raymond Maxwell, Jr. *management consultant*
Desch, Theodore Edward *retired insurance company executive, lawyer*
Dombeck, Harold Arthur *insurance company executive*

Northbrook
Brune, Catherine Spearman *insurance company executive*
Civgin, Donald E. *insurance company executive*
Cripe, Frederick F. *insurance company executive*
Cruikshank, John W. III *insurance agent*
Greffin, Judith *insurance company executive*
Mayes, Michele Coleman *insurance company executive, lawyer*
Richardson, Joseph J., Jr. *insurance company executive*
Roche, Michael J. *insurance company executive*
Ruebenson, George E. *insurance company executive*
Sorenson, Steven P. *insurance company executive*
Walker, Joan H. *insurance company executive*
Wilson, Thomas Joseph *insurance company executive*

Skokie
Hedien, Wayne Evans *retired insurance company executive*

Springfield
Dodge, Edward John *retired insurance company executive*
Simpson, William Arthur *insurance company executive*

Westmont
Friedrich, Charles William *insurance agent*

INDIANA

Carmel
Husman, Catherine Bigot *retired insurance company executive, consultant*
Prieur, C. James *insurance company executive*

Cicero
Howe, James Tarsicius *retired insurance company executive*

Indianapolis
Beer, Lori A. *health insurance company executive*
Boxer, Mark L. *healthcare insurance company executive*
Braly, Angela Fick *health insurance company executive, lawyer*
DeVeydt, Wayne S. *health insurance company executive*
Fluegel, Brad M. *health insurance company executive*
Glasscock, Larry Claborn *health insurance company executive*
Goulet, Kenneth R. *health insurance company executive*
Lewis, Dijuana K. *insurance company executive*
Lewis, Randall J. *healthcare insurance company executive*
McKinney, E. Kirk, Jr. *retired insurance company executive*
Miller, Cynthia S. *healthcare insurance company executive*
Nussbaum, Samuel R. *healthcare insurance company executive, medical educator*
Sassi, Brian A. *health insurance company executive*
Watts, John S., Jr. *insurance company executive*

Pendleton
Kischuk, Richard Karl *insurance company executive*

Schererville
Seward, John Edward, Jr. *insurance company executive*

IOWA

Des Moines
Brooks, Roger Kay *insurance company executive*
Griswell, J. Barry *insurance company executive*
Kelley, Bruce Gunn *insurance company executive, lawyer*
Lillis, Terry J. *insurance company executive*
Zimpleman, Larry Donald *insurance company executive*

West Des Moines
Hohmann, James E. *insurance company executive*

KANSAS

De Soto
Strubbe, Thomas R. *insurance industry executive*

KENTUCKY

Louisville
Hickey, Bobby Ray *underwriting assistant*
Jones, David A., Jr. *insurance company executive*
McCallister, Michael B. *insurance company executive*
Rosky, Theodore Samuel *insurance company executive*

MAINE

Augusta
Finnegan, John Vianney *insurance company executive, risk management consultant, educator*

Portland
Reid, Rosemary Anne *insurance agent*

MARYLAND

Adelphi
Turner, Marvin Wentz *insurance company executive*

Baltimore
Goodman, William Richard *insurance adjusting company executive*
Hecht, Alan Dannenberg *insurance executive*

Elkton
Jasinski-Caldwell, Mary L. *insurance company executive*

Laytonsville
Canapary, Herbert Carton *retired insurance company executive*

Reisterstown
Tirone, Barbara Jean *retired health insurance administrator*

Salisbury
O'Donnell, James Joseph *insurance company executive, economics professor*

MASSACHUSETTS

Boston
Brown, Stephen Lee *retired insurance company executive*
Bunker, Beryl H. *retired insurance company executive, volunteer*
Condrin, J. Paul III *insurance company executive*
Countryman, Gary Lee *retired insurance company executive*
Fallon, John A. *insurance company executive, physician*
Fontanes, A. Alexander *insurance company executive*
Kelly, Edmund Francis *insurance company executive*
Killingsworth, Cleve L., Jr. *insurance company executive*
Langwell, Dennis J. *insurance company executive*
Maltz, Allen P. *insurance company executive*
Morton, Edward James *insurance company executive*

Duxbury
Wangler, William Clarence *retired insurance company executive*

East Falmouth
Forte, Wesley Elbert *former insurance company executive, lawyer*

Needham
Rodman, Sumner *insurance company executive*

North Attleboro
Koussa, Harold Alan *insurance account executive*

Quincy
Moran, James Joseph, Jr. *insurance company executive*

Springfield
Crandall, Roger W. *insurance company executive*
Glavin, William Francis, Jr. *insurance company executive*
Johnson, Robert Allison *life insurance company executive*
Reese, Stuart Harry *insurance company executive*
Rollings, Michael Thomas *insurance company executive*
Sarsynski, Elaine A. *insurance company executive*

Watertown
Roosevelt, James, Jr. *insurance company executive, lawyer*

Webster
Fels, Gerald *insurance company executive*

Wellesley
Baker, Charles D. *health insurance company executive*

Worcester
Eppinger, Frederick H., Jr. *insurance company executive*

MICHIGAN

Detroit
Bartlett, Mark R. *insurance company executive*

Grand Rapids
Byrne, James *insurance company executive*
Hawkins, Gregory *insurance company executive*
Horn, Kimberly *insurance company executive*

Kalamazoo
Curry, John Patrick *insurance company executive, management consultant*

Lansing
Loepp, Daniel *insurance company executive*
Looyenga, Roger L. *insurance company executive*

Novi
Chadwick, Edward *insurance company executive*
Swedish, Joseph *insurance company executive*

Southgate
Torok, Margaret Louise *insurance company executive*

MINNESOTA

Bemidji
Bridston, Paul Joseph *strategic management consultant*

Coon Rapids
Bordner, Patricia Anne *insurance agent, writer*

Hibbing
Calligan, William Dennis *retired life insurance company executive*

Minneapolis
Boushek, Randy L. *insurance company executive*
Feldman, Nancy Jane *insurance company executive*
Keets, John David, Jr. *insurance company executive*
Mikan, G. Mike *healthcare services company executive, corporate financial executive*
Munsell, William A. *healthcare insurance company executive*
Nicholson, Bruce J. *insurance company executive*
Tuckson, Reed V. *physician, health insurance company executive*
Wichmann, David S. *health care services executive*

Minnetonka
Boudreaux, Gail K. *insurance company executive*
Penshorn, John S. *insurance company executive*
Rivet, Jeannine M. *health insurance company executive*
Robbins, Orem Olford *insurance company executive*
Sweere Komstadius, Lori *insurance company executive*

Saint Paul
Benet, Jay S. *insurance company executive*
Clarke, Charles J. *insurance company executive*
Ettinger, Irwin R. *insurance company executive*
Fishman, Jay Steven *insurance company executive*
MacLean, Brian W. *insurance company executive*
Senkler, Robert L. *insurance company executive*

MISSOURI

Saint Louis
Bryant, Donald L., Jr. *insurance and benefits company executive*
Winer, Warren James *insurance executive*

NEBRASKA

Holdrege
Hendrickson, Bruce Carl *life insurance company executive*

Omaha
Neary, Daniel P. *insurance company executive*

NEVADA

Henderson
Johnson, Joan Bray *insurance company consultant*

NEW HAMPSHIRE

Rochester
Dworkin, Gary Steven *insurance company executive*

NEW JERSEY

Augusta
Martin, Richard L. *retired insurance executive*

Branchville
Murphy, Gregory E. *insurance company executive*

Glen Rock
Mc Elrath, Richard Elsworth *retired insurance company executive*

Lumberton
Friedberg, Thomas Harold *insurance company executive*

Madison
Parker, Henry Griffith III *insurance executive*

Mountain Lakes
Cook, Charles Francis *insurance executive*

New Brunswick
Mills, George Marshall *risk management consultant*

New Vernon
McCormack, John Joseph, Jr. *insurance company executive*

Newark
Blount, Susan L. *insurance company executive, lawyer*
Marino, William J. *insurance executive*

Princeton
Sandman, Peter M. *risk management consultant*

Ridgewood
O'Leary, Paul Gerard *retired insurance company executive*

Short Hills
MacKinnon, Malcolm D(avid) *retired insurance company executive*

Summit
Gerathy, E. Carroll *retired insurance company executive, real estate developer*

Warren
Cox, Robert C. *insurance company executive*
Degnan, John J. *insurance company executive, lawyer*
Finnegan, John D. *insurance company executive*
Gerstman, Ned I. *insurance company executive*
Knight, James P. *insurance company executive*
Krump, Paul J. *insurance company executive*
McElwee, Andrew Allison, Jr. *insurance company executive*
Morrison, Harold L., Jr. *insurance company executive*
O'Reilly, Michael *insurance company executive*
Raines, Marjorie D. *insurance company executive*
Robusto, Dino E. *insurance company executive*
Tomlinson, Janice Meyer *insurance company executive*

Whitehouse Station
Fiscus, Philip Wayne *underwriter*

Wyckoff
Munson, William Leslie *insurance company executive*

NEW YORK

Albany
Cole, John Adam *insurance executive*

Amityville
Imbert, Richard Conrad *insurance company executive, real estate developer*

Armonk
Brown, Joseph Warner, Jr., (Jay Brown) *mortgage insurance company executive*

Binghamton
Best, Robert Mulvane *insurance company executive*

Brooklyn
Faison, Seth Shepard *retired insurance broker*

Dryden
Baxter, Robert Banning *insurance company executive*

Geneva
Vecchiotti, Tony V. *insurance agent*

Long Island City
Henrikson, C. Robert (Carl Robert Henrikson) *insurance company executive*

New York
Arning, Mark E. *insurance company executive*
Ashooh, Nicholas J. *insurance company executive*
Benmosche, Robert H. *insurance company executive*
Biggs, John Herron *retired insurance company executive*
Boccio, Frank M. *insurance company executive*
Broatch, Robert E. *insurance company executive*
Camacho, Philip Bruce *insurance company executive*
Chagnon, Kathleen *insurance company executive*
Clayton, Jon Kerry *insurance company executive*
Cloonan, Edward Thomas *insurance company executive*
Collesano, Stephen P. *insurance company executive*
Crystal, James William *insurance company executive*
D'Angelo, Charles H. *insurance company executive*
Davis, Karen *insurance company executive, educator*
Dooley, William N. *insurance company executive*
Duckett, Keith L. *insurance company executive*
Duperreault, Brian C. *insurance company executive*
Fattori, Ruth A. *insurance company executive*
Flynn, William Joseph *insurance company executive*
Frenkel, Jacob Aharon *insurance company executive*
Gender, Robert A. *insurance company executive*
Glaser, Daniel S. *insurance company executive*
Goodstein, Barbara *insurance company executive*
Harris, David Henry *retired life insurance company executive*
Herzog, David L. *insurance company executive*
Herzog, David Lawrence *insurance company executive*
Hohn, Harry George *retired insurance company executive, lawyer*
Hurd, Jeffrey J. *insurance company executive*
Hutchings, Peter Lounsbery *retired insurance company executive, director*
Jacobs, Philip M. *insurance company executive*
Jacobson, Robert P. *insurance company executive*
Johnson, L. Oakley (Oakley Johnson) *insurance company executive*
Kandarian, Steven A. *insurance company executive*
Kaslow, Andrew J. *insurance company executive, human resources specialist*
Kim, John Y. *insurance company executive*
Lewis, Robert E. *insurance company executive*
Machon, Monika Maria *insurance company executive, lawyer*
Manning, Dennis J. *insurance company executive*
Martin, Rodney O., Jr. *insurance company executive*
Mathas, Theodore A. (Ted Mathas) *insurance company executive, lawyer*
Mathieson, Garrett Alfred *insurance brokerage executive*
McGinn, Kevin B. *insurance company executive*
Melone, Joseph James *retired insurance company executive*
Moor, Kristian P. *insurance company executive*
Moran, Thomas J. *insurance company executive*
Morris, Maria R. *insurance company executive*
Mucci, Richard L. *insurance company executive*
Mullaney, William J. *insurance company executive*
Murray, Richard Maximilian *insurance company executive*
Nadler, David A. *professional services executive*
Neuger, Win Jay *insurance company executive*
Peninger, Michael J. *insurance company executive*
Pollock, Robert B. *insurance company executive*
Procope, Ernesta Gertrude *insurance company executive*
Roemer, Michael E. *insurance company executive*
Rosput Reynolds, Paula Gail *insurance company executive*
Schreiber, Brian T. *insurance company executive*
Shannon, Kathleen E. *insurance company executive*
Slevin, Eileen T. *insurance company executive*
Sproule, Michael E. *insurance company executive*
Sullivan, Martin J. *former insurance company executive*
Toppeta, William John *insurance company executive, lawyer*
Vidal, David Jonathan *insurance company executive, journalist*
Walsh, Nicholas C. *insurance company executive*
Watson, Teri L. *insurance company executive*
Weber, Lisa M. *insurance company executive*
Wendlandt, Gary E. *insurance company executive*
Wheeler, William J. *insurance company executive*
Willumstad, Robert B. (Bob Willumstad) *former insurance company executive, retired diversified financial services company executive*
Winans, Christopher D. *insurance company executive*
Wintrob, Jay S. *insurance company executive*
Wisner, Frank George *insurance company executive, former ambassador*
Wittman, Vanessa Ames *insurance company executive*
Wooster, John T., Jr. *insurance company executive*

Rochester
Combs, Thomas *insurance company executive*

Rye Brook
Barasch, Richard A. *insurance company executive*
Bryant, Gary Wayne *insurance company executive*

Saratoga Springs
Ford, Dexter *retired insurance company executive*

Schenectady
Braslow, Nelson M. *insurance company executive*

Staten Island
Gavrity, John Decker *retired insurance company executive*

Syosset
Kniffin, Paula Sichel *insurance sales executive*

NORTH CAROLINA

Camden
Hammond, Roy Joseph *reinsurance company executive*

Chapel Hill
Clark, Arthur Watts *insurance company executive*
Fine, J(ames) Allen *insurance company executive*

Greensboro
Soles, William Roger *insurance company executive, director*

Pinehurst
O'Loughlin, John Kirby *retired insurance executive*

NORTH DAKOTA

Grand Forks
Wogaman, George Elsworth *insurance company executive, financial consultant*

OHIO

Avon Lake
Lewis, Peter Benjamin *insurance company executive*

Canton
Schauer, Thomas Alfred *insurance company executive*

Cincinnati
Barrett, John F. *insurance company executive*
Hardy, Thomas Cresson *insurance company executive*
Klein, Jerry Emanuel *insurance and financial planning executive*
Lindner, Carl H. III *insurance company executive*
Lindner, Carl Henry, Jr. *insurance company executive, professional sports team owner*
Lindner, S(tephen) Craig *insurance company executive*

Cleveland
Chiricosta, Richard Alan (Rick) *insurance company executive*
Domeck, Brian C. *insurance company executive*
Douglas, Frank H., Jr. *insurance company executive*
Renwick, Glenn M. *insurance company executive*
Schader, Charles R. *insurance company executive*

Columbus
Duryee, Harold Taylor *insurance consultant*
Hilsheimer, Lawrence A. *insurance company executive*
Rasmussen, Stephen Scott *insurance company executive*
Thresher, Mark R. *insurance company executive*

Fairfield
Benoski, James E. *insurance company executive*

Newark
Lukco, Edward John *insurance company executive*

Powell
Emanuelson, James Robert *retired insurance company executive*

OKLAHOMA

Oklahoma City
Watson, Brenda Bennett *insurance company executive*

OREGON

Portland
Parsons, Eric E. *insurance company executive*

PENNSYLVANIA

Bala Cynwyd
Shepard, Geoffrey Carroll *insurance company executive*

Bushkill
Garretto, Leonard Anthony, Jr. *insurance company executive*

Camp Hill
Mead, James Matthew *insurance company executive*

Erie
Cavanaugh, Terrence W. *insurance company executive*
Ludrof, Jeffrey A. *insurance company executive*

King Of Prussia
Volpe, Ralph Pasquale *retired insurance company executive*

Newtown Square
Staats, Dean Roy *retired reinsurance executive*

Philadelphia
Glass, Dennis Robert *insurance company executive*
Hagan, Annmarie T. *insurance company executive*
Hanway, H. Edward *insurance company executive*
Murabito, John M. *insurance company executive*
Rohan, Karen S. *insurance company executive*
Stonecipher, David A. *insurance company executive*

Pittsburgh
DeTurk, Nanette *insurance company executive*
Gray, Robert C. *insurance company executive*
Melani, Kenneth R. *insurance company executive*

Radnor
Crawford, Frederick J. *insurance company executive*

Wayne
Ross, Roderic Henry *retired insurance company executive*
Yoskin, Jon William, II, *insurance company executive*

RHODE ISLAND

Johnston
Subramaniam, Shivan Sivaswamy *insurance company executive*

SOUTH CAROLINA

Camden
Pierce, Janis Vaughn *insurance executive, consultant*

Columbia
Drozda, Jeffery Allen *insurance company executive, former state legislator*

TENNESSEE

Athens
Trent, Henry Gibson, Jr. *insurance company executive, educator*

Chattanooga
Bishop, Liston, II, *insurance company executive*
Greving, Robert C. *insurance company executive*
McKenney, Richard P. *insurance company executive*
Watjen, Thomas Ros *insurance company executive*

Nashville
Howell, John Floyd *insurance company executive*

Seymour
Steele, Ernest Clyde *retired insurance company executive*

TEXAS

Austin
Payne, Tyson Elliott, Jr. *retired insurance executive*

Bedford
Blackburn, Wyatt Douglas *insurance executive*

Dallas
Cline, Bobby James *insurance company executive*
Weakley, Clare George, Jr. *insurance company executive, theologian, entrepreneur*

Flower Mound
Crosmer, Janie Lynn *insurance company executive*

Galveston
Moody, Robert Lee *insurance company executive*

Houston
Bramanti, Frank J. *insurance company executive*
Couch, Jesse Wadsworth *retired insurance company executive*
Hook, Harold Swanson *former management consulting executive*
Lindsey, John H. *former insurance agency executive*
Morris, Stewart, Jr. *title insurance company executive*
Poulos, Michael James *insurance company executive*

Livingston
Stovall, Jerry Coleman *insurance company executive*

Mc Kinney
McAndrew, Mark S. *insurance company executive*

North Richland Hills
Hildebrand, Phillip J. *insurance company executive*

San Antonio
Conklyn, Elizabeth D. *insurance company executive*
Garrison, David H. *insurance company executive*
Matus, Kristi Ann *insurance company executive*
Robles, Josue, Jr. *insurance company executive*
Strong, Wendi Ellen *insurance company executive*

UTAH

Bountiful
Clay, Orson C. *insurance company executive, director*

Ogden
Buckner, Elmer La Mar *retired insurance company executive*

VERMONT

Montpelier
MacLeay, Thomas H. *insurance company executive*

VIRGINIA

Charlottesville
Long, Charles Farrell *insurance company executive*

Glen Allen
Kirshner, Alan I. *insurance company executive*

Penhook
Hahn, John William *retired insurance company executive*

Richmond
Fraizer, Michael D. *insurance company executive*
Kelleher, Patrick B. *insurance company executive*
Knight, Wendy Diana *risk management officer*
Schutz, Pamela S. *insurance company executive*

Roanoke
DeVries, James D. *insurance company executive*

Williamsburg
Herrmann, Benjamin Edward *former insurance executive*

WASHINGTON

Kirkland
McDonald, Joseph Lee *insurance broker*

Seattle
Koster, John Frederick *insurance executive*

Spokane
Ogden, C(hester) Robert *insurance company executive*

Vancouver
Dettman, Donald Reese *loss control inspector*

Walla Walla
Perry, Louis Barnes *retired insurance company executive*

Woodland
Hansen, Walter Eugene *insurance executive*

WISCONSIN

Madison
Anderson, David R. *insurance company executive*
Post, Jeffrey H. *insurance company executive*
Salzwedel, Jack C. *insurance company executive*
Schultz, Daniel R. *insurance company executive*
Spencer, C. Stanley *insurance company executive*
Waldo, Robert Leland *retired insurance company executive*

Milwaukee
Carter, Michael G. *insurance company executive*
Poliner, Gary A. *insurance company executive*

Nashotah
Vincent, Norman L. *retired insurance company executive*

Stevens Point
Schuh, Dale R. *insurance company executive*

CANADA

NOVA SCOTIA

North Sydney
Nickerson, Jerry Edgar Alan *business executive*

CZECH REPUBLIC

Prague
Kočárnik, Ivan *insurance company executive*

FRANCE

Paris
Peugeot, Patrick *insurance executive*

ISRAEL

Givat Brener
Tritter, Richard Paul *strategic consultant*

JAPAN

Tokyo
Anderson, Ronald J. *insurance company executive*
Clyde, Robert W. *insurance company executive*

SOUTH AFRICA

Cape Town
Cleary, Sean Michael *risk management executive, founding chair, director*

SWITZERLAND

Zurich
Schiro, James Joseph *insurance company executive*

ADDRESS UNPUBLISHED

Adam, John, Jr. *insurance company executive emeritus*
Adams, John Carter, Jr. *retired insurance executive*
Alpert, Ann Sharon *retired insurance claims examiner*
Armstrong, F(redric) Michael *retired insurance company executive, consultant*
Bellamy, James Carl *retired insurance company executive*
Bennett, Alan M. *retired insurance company executive*
Bertrand, Frederic Howard *retired insurance company executive*
Bolger, David P. *former insurance company executive*
Bolnick, Howard Jeffrey *consultant, investor*
Borda, Richard Joseph *retired insurance company executive*
Browne, Ray *insurance agent, former United States Shadow Representative, DC*
Burkett, Lawrence V. *retired insurance company executive, lawyer*
Campbell, Judith E. *retired insurance company executive*
Carver, Kendall Lynn *insurance company executive*
Chilvers, Derek *insurance company executive*
Clark, Edgar Sanderford *insurance broker, expert witness, consultant*
Clemens, Alvin Honey *insurance company executive*
Conroy, Thomas Francis *insurance company consultant*
Cooper, Charles Gordon *retired insurance company executive*
Dackow, Orest Taras *insurance company executive*
D'Alessandro, Dominic *retired financial executive*
Denton, Ray Douglas *insurance company executive*
De Palma, Catherine S. *insurance adjuster, paralegal*
DiPiazza, Michael Charles *insurance company executive*
Emek, Sharon Helene *risk management consultant*
Ewald, Robert Frederick *insurance executive, consultant*
Fey, John Theodore *retired insurance company executive*
Froman, Michael Braverman *insurance company executive*
Goulet, Charles Ryan *retired insurance company executive*
Greenberg, Maurice Raymond (Hank Greenberg) *insurance company executive*
Hale, Margaret Smith *insurance company executive, educator*
Hincks, Marcia Lockwood *retired insurance company executive*
Holden, William Willard *insurance executive*
Hostovich, Teena Maria *insurance brokerage executive*
Impellizzeri, Anne Elmendorf *insurance company executive, non-profit executive*
Jacobson, James Bassett *retired insurance and financial services company executive*
Johnson, William Ray *insurance company executive*
Jones, Lupe Sirena *insurance agent*
Khan, Ahmed Mohiuddin *insurance company executive*
Krishna, Kiran *risk management consultant*
Ladd, Joseph Carroll *retired insurance company executive*
Lee, Katrina LaShawn *health insurance business consultant*
Lehmann, Noreen Veronica *insurance company executive*
Liddy, Edward M. *retired insurance company executive*
Maatman, Gerald Leonard *insurance company executive*
McCarthy, Harold Charles *retired insurance company executive*
McCaskey, Raymond F. *retired health insurance company executive*
McKenna, Terence Patrick *retired insurance company executive*
Millikan, Diane Linda *insurance company executive*
Motamed, Thomas Firouz *insurance company executive*
Moynahan, John Daniel, Jr. *retired insurance executive*
Nagler, Stewart Gordon *retired insurance company executive*
Nelson, Walter Gerald *retired insurance company executive*
Norris, Darell Forest *retired insurance company executive*
Papa, Vincent T. *insurance company executive*
Pearson, Paul Holding *insurance company executive*
Porter, Dixie Lee *retired insurance company executive, consultant*
Rein, Catherine Amelia *retired insurance company executive, lawyer*
Resnick, Myron Jay *retired insurance company executive, lawyer*
Ross, Donald Keith *retired insurance company executive*
Rowell, Lester John, Jr. *retired insurance company executive*
Ryan, James *insurance company executive*
Sanders, Franklin D. *retired insurance company executive*
Serag, Engy *claims consultant*
Shisler, Arden L. *insurance and transportation company executive*
Smith, Floyd Leslie *insurance company executive*
Snyder, William Burton *insurance company executive*
Stewart, Gordon Curran *retired insurance institute executive*
Strong, John David *insurance company executive*
Tresnowski, Bernard Richard *retired health insurance company executive*
Tringale, Anthony Rosario *insurance company executive*
Underhill, Jacob Berry III *retired insurance company executive*
Vasholz, Lothar Alfred *retired insurance company executive*
Volk, Austin N. *retired insurance company executive*
Wahweah, Linda McNeil *insurance agent, writer*
Weber, John Walter *insurance company executive*
Whiteley, Benjamin Robert *retired insurance company executive*
Wills, William Ridley, II, *retired insurance company executive, historian*
Young, Dona Davis Gagliano *retired insurance company executive, lawyer*
Zebroski, Edwin Leopold *risk management consultant*

FINANCE: INVESTMENT SERVICES

UNITED STATES

ALABAMA

Birmingham
Comer, Donald III *investment company executive*
Tucker, Thomas James *retired investment company executive*

ALASKA

Anchorage
Hickel, Walter Joseph *retired investment company executive, foundation administrator, former United States Secretary of the Interior governor of alaska*

ARIZONA

Phoenix
Stern, Richard David *investment company executive*
Taylor, Elizabeth Jane *investment advisor, real estate company and marketing executive*

Prescott
Sanderson, John Lewis *financial advisor*

Scottsdale
Doede, John Henry *investment company executive*
Kiyosaki, Robert Toru *investor, entrepreneur, author*
Parsons, Bob (Robert R. Parsons) *entrepreneur, domain register and web host company executive*
Samson, Allen Lawrence *investor, retired bank executive*

Tucson
Lomicka, William Henry *investor*

ARKANSAS

Cabot
Arbeene, Michael James *entrepreneur, business consultant*

Little Rock
Good, Mary Lowe *investment company executive, educator*
Light, Jo Knight *stockbroker*
Whiteside, Charles B. III *investment company executive*

CALIFORNIA

Atherton
Lynch, Charles Allen *investment company executive, director*

Belvedere Tiburon
Rayner, Arno Alfred *investment company executive, consultant*

Benicia
Szabo, Peter John *investment company executive, mining engineer, financial planner, lawyer*

Berkeley
Blume, James Beryl *investment advisor*

Beverly Hills
Covitz, Carl D. *investment company executive, federal and state official*
Eisner, Michael Dammann *investment and former entertainment company executive*
Evans, Louise *investor, retired psychologist*
Gambrell, Thomas Ross *investor, retired physician, surgeon*
Kerkorian, Kirk *investor, former motion picture company executive, consultant*
Seidel, Joan Broude *securities dealer, investment advisor*

Camarillo
Sullivan, Michael Evan *investment company executive*

Chino Hills
Ofner, William Bernard *investor, speechwriter*

Coronado
Smith, Albert Cromwell, Jr. *investment company executive, writer*

Costa Mesa
Kiang, Assumpta (Amy Kiang) *brokerage house executive*

El Segundo
Treat, John Elting *entrepreneur*

Foster City
Krikorian, Blake *entrepreneur, consumer electronics company executive*

Fremont
Grant, Alan J. *business executive, educator*

Fresno
Dauer, Donald Dean *investment company executive*

Huntington Beach
Macdonald, R. Fulton Smith *venture developer, business executive, educator, consultant*

Los Angeles
Angeloff, Dann Valentino *brokerage house executive*
Binder, Gordon M. *venture capitalist*
Gampel, Elaine Susan *investment company executive, consultant*
Johnson, Jeffrey M. *private equity company executive, former publishing executive*
Larkin, Thomas Ernest, Jr. *investment management company executive*
Matise, John J. *investment company executive*
Saban, Haim *investment company executive, television producer*
Spogli, Ronald Paul *private equity form executive, former ambassador*

Menlo Park
Byers, Brook *venture capitalist, investor*
Compton, Kevin R. *venture capitalist, professional sports team executive*
Davies, Paul Lewis III *venture capitalist*
Doerr, John (L. John Doerr III) *venture capitalist*
Fenton, Noel John *venture capitalist*
Giancarlo, Charles H. *investment company executive, former computer systems network executive*
Gordon, William Bingham (Bing Gordon) *venture capitalist, former software marketing executive*
Joy, Bill (William Nelson Joy) *venture capitalist, former computer software company executive*
Kramlich, C(harles) Richard (Dick) *venture capitalist*
Lucas, Donald Leo *investor*
Marquardt, David F. *venture capitalist*
Moritz, Michael J. *venture capitalist*
Perkins, Tom (Thomas James Perkins) *venture capital company executive*

Moraga
Gerber, Nicholas *investment advisor, entrepreneur*

Newport Beach
Arnott, Robert Douglas *investment company executive*
El-Erian, Mohamed A. *investment company executive*
Gross, Bill (William H. Gross) *investment company executive, financial analyst*
Thorp, Edward Oakley *investment management company executive*

North Hills
Iacocca, Lee (Lido Anthony) *venture capitalist, retired automotive executive*

Orange
Tuggle, Francis Douglas *entrepreneur, consultant, management educator, scientist*

Oxnard
Alexy, Kimberly E. *investment company executive*

Palm Desert
Hook, John Burney *investment company executive*

Palo Alto
Breyer, James W. (James William Breyer) *venture capitalist*
Cassidy, Sukhinder Singh *venture capitalist, former information technology executive*
Sculley, John *investment company executive, former computer company executive*

Pasadena
Fredericks, Ward Arthur *venture capitalist*

Pinedale
Falcone, Patricia Jeanne Lalim *investor, foundation administrator*

Sacramento
Ailman, Christopher J. *investment company executive*

San Diego
Batchelder, David H. *investment advisory firm executive*

San Francisco
Bettinger, Walter W., II, *investment company executive*
Dachs, Alan Mark *investment company executive*
Draper, William Henry III *venture capitalist*
Hagenbuch, John Jacob *investor*
Hellman, F(rederick) Warren *investor*
Levine, Alison *entrepreneur, leadership development consultant, adventurer*
Mahoney, Michael James *investment company executive*
Martinetto, Joseph R. *investment company executive*
Mullin, Hadley (Mary Hadley Mullin) *private equity firm executive*
Pottruck, David Steven *private equity firm executive*
Rienhoff, Hugh *venture capitalist, physician, geneticist*
Rock, Arthur *venture capitalist*
Rosenstein, Barry *hedge fund manager*
Schioldager, Amy Lee *investment company executive*
Schwab, Charles Robert, Jr., (Chuck Schwab) *investment company executive*
Steyer, Thomas Fahr *hedge fund manager*
Thiel, Peter Andreas *hedge fund manager*
Winblad, Ann *investment company executive*

San Marcos
Kumar, Chetan *entrepreneur, educator*

Santa Ana
Martinez, Rueben *entrepreneur*

Santa Barbara
Bartlett, James Lowell III *investment company executive*
Emmeluth, Bruce Palmer *investment company executive, venture capitalist*
Orfalea, Paul James *investment company executive, former printing company executive*
Vos, Hubert Daniel *investor*

Santa Clara
Dham, Vinod K. *Indo-US venture capitalist company executive*

Sausalito
Apatoff, Michael John *entrepreneur*

Sunnyvale
Rubin, Gary Andrew *entrepreneur, computer engineer*

Tarzana
Lauter, James Donald *retired stockbroker*

Thousand Oaks
Gregory, Calvin *real estate investor*

Torrance
Enright, Stephanie Veselich *investment company executive, financial consultant*

Woodland Hills
Feiman, Thomas E. *investment company executive*

Woodside
McCown, George E. *venture banking company executive*

COLORADO

Aurora
Ton, Paul *investor, educator*

Boulder
Mehalchin, John Joseph *entrepreneur, finance company executive*

Broomfield
Marr, James Joseph *venture capitalist*

Cherry Hills Village
Van Loucks, Mark Louis *venture capitalist, financial planner*

Denver
Case, Steve (Stephen M.) *healthcare investment company executive, former media and entertainment company executive*
Eppler, Jerome Cannon *investment advisor*
Ogard, Karen *investment advisor, financial planner*
Scheid, Steven L. *investment company executive*
Wagner, Judith Buck *investment firm executive*

Evergreen
Jackson, William Richard *entrepreneur*

Littleton
Lode, Trygve Tennyson *entrepreneur, actor*
Sutton, Robert Edward *investment company executive*

CONNECTICUT

Darien
Frey, Dale Franklin *financial investment company executive, manufacturing company executive*
Schiff, Peter David *investment advisor, economist*

Greenwich
Applegarth, Paul Vollmer *investment and development executive*
Asness, Clifford Scott *hedge fund executive*
Breeden, Richard C. *investment company executive, former federal agency administrator*
Foley, Thomas Coleman *investment company executive, former ambassador*
Ford, William E. *investment company executive*
Friedman, Stephen James *private equity firm executive, federal official*
Ganek, David Kent *hedge fund manager*
Halvorsen, Ole Andreas *hedge fund manager*
Hanson, Janet Tiebout *investment company executive*
Jones, Paul Tudor, II, *hedge fund manager*
Lampert, Edward S. *hedge fund manager*
Mandel, Stephen F., Jr. *hedge fund manager*
Owens, Bill (William Forrester Owens) *investment company executive, former governor*
Pados, Frank John, Jr. *investment company executive*
Schneider, John Arnold *investor*
Sternlicht, Barry Stuart *investment company executive, former hotel executive*
Tournillon, Nicholas Brady *investment company executive*

Litchfield
Booth, John Thomas *private investor*
Sherva, Dennis G. *retired investment company executive*

New Canaan
Bisbee, Gerald Elftman, Jr. *investment company executive*
Pike, William Edward *retired banking executive*

New Haven
Swensen, David Frederick *investment advisor*

Norwalk
Hudson, Thomas Richard, Jr. *hedge fund manager*
Tropin, Kenneth G. *hedge fund manager*

Sharon
Learsy, Raymond J. *private investor*

South Kent
Keehner, Michael Arthur Miller *investment banking executive*

Southport
Wilbur, E. Packer *investment company executive*

Stamford
Chilton, Richard L., Jr. *hedge fund manager*
Cohen, Steven A. *hedge fund manager*

Westport
Dalio, Raymond Thomas *hedge fund manager*
O'Keefe, John David *brokerage house executive*
Rudd, Nicholas *investor, consultant*
Stewart, Martha Kostyra *entrepreneur, lecturer, author*
Walton, Alan George *venture capitalist*

Wilton
Hawley, Frank Jordan, Jr. *venture capital executive*

DISTRICT OF COLUMBIA

Washington
Abizaid, John Philip *investment company executive, retired military officer*
Akerson, Daniel Francis *private equity firm executive, former telecommunications industry executive*
Coreth, Joseph Herman *investment advisor*
D'Aniello, Daniel A. *investment company executive*
Danilovich, John J. *investment company executive, former ambassador*
Fisher, Robert Dale *stockbroker, retired naval officer*
Forese, James John *investment company executive*
Franklin, Barbara Hackman *investment company executive, former United States Secretary of Commerce*
Goldsmith, Stephen *investment company executive, former mayor*
Johnson, James A. (Jim Johnson) *investment company executive*
Johnson, Sheila Crump *entrepreneur*
Kennard, William Earl *private equity firm executive, former federal agency administrator*
Kent, Jill Elspeth *entrepreneur, art appraiser, lawyer*
Macomber, John D. *investment company executive*
Nordlinger, Gerson *investor*
Powell, Michael Kevin *investment company executive, former federal official*
Quarles, Randal Keith *private equity firm executive, former federal agency administrator*
Rubenstein, David M. *investment company executive*
Shrier, Adam Louis *investment company executive, consultant*
Tanous, Peter Joseph *investment advisor*
Wheeler, Thomas Edgar *private equity executive*

FLORIDA

Boca Raton
Hampton, Benjamin Bertram *brokerage house executive*
Krouse, Rodger Russell *investment company executive*

Boynton Beach
Allison, Dwight Leonard, Jr. *investor*

Coral Gables
Nunez-Portuondo, Ricardo *investment company executive*

Fort Lauderdale
Huizenga, Wayne (Harry Wayne Huizenga) *entrepreneur, professional sports team owner*

Gainesville
Oliver, Robert Bruce *retired investment company executive*

Hobe Sound
Parker, H. Lawrence *retired investor, rancher, investment banker*

Jacksonville
Monsky, John Bertrand *investment company executive*
Schultz, Frederick Henry *investor, former government official*

Key Largo
Hawkins, Frank Nelson, Jr. *investor relations consultant, writer*

Maitland
DeWahl, Duncan Comrie *stockbroker*

Miami
Arison, Shari *investment company executive*
Batcheller, Joe Ann *entrepreneur*
Dorion, Robert Charles *entrepreneur, investor*
Rogers, Jim (James Beeland Rogers Jr.) *retired investment company executive*
Selin, Ivan *entrepreneur*

Naples
Frantzen, Henry Arthur *retired investment company executive*
Scott, Richard Lynn (Rick Scott) *investment company executive, former health and medical products company executive*

North Palm Beach
Dreyfoos, Alexander W., Jr. *investor, research scientist*

Palm Beach
McCarter, Thomas Nesbitt III *investment company executive, consultant*
Quick, Thomas Clarkson *brokerage house executive*

Palm Beach Gardens
Kleinberg, Lawrence H. *investor, consultant*
Mergler, H. Kent *investment counselor*

Pompano Beach
Grossman, Daniel V *investor*
Rifenburgh, Richard Philip *investment company executive*

Punta Gorda
Presley, Brian *investment company executive*

Saint Petersburg
Emerson, William Allen *retired investment company executive*
James, Thomas A. *investment company executive*

Sarasota
Balliett, John William *entrepreneur, real estate company executive*

Sebring
Littlewood, Douglas Burden *brokerage house executive*

Singer Island
Gad, Lance Stewart *investment advisor, lawyer, private investor*

Tampa
Hanford, Agnes Rutledge *retired investment advisor*
Sigety, Charles Birge *investment company executive*

Vero Beach
Bewkes, Eugene Garrett, Jr. *investment company executive, consultant*
Bigler, Harold Edwin, Jr. *retired investment company executive*

Village Of Golf
Birle, James Robb *investor*

West Palm Beach
Kulok, William Allan *entrepreneur, venture capitalist*

Windermere
Lewis, Joseph *investor, real estate development company executive*

GEORGIA

Alpharetta
Orr, Zellie *entrepreneur, educator, writer, researcher*

Atlanta
Green, Holcombe Tucker, Jr. *investment company executive*
Jackson, Geraldine *entrepreneur*
Keough, Donald Raymond *investment and former beverage company executive*
Lally, John Patrick *investment company executive*
Merkel-Moran, Christa Ilse *investor, linguist, educator*
Payne, William Porter (Billy Payne) *investment company executive*
Sprecher, Jeffrey C. *commodities exchange executive*

Saint Simons Island
Turbidy, John Berry *investor, management consultant*

HAWAII

Honolulu
Haight, Warren Gazzam *investor*

ILLINOIS

Chicago
Berghoef, Henry R. *investment company executive*
Bergonia, Raymond David *venture capitalist*
Block, Philip Dee III *retired investment company executive*
Canning, John Anthony, Jr. *private equity firm executive*
Carey, Charles P. *mercantile exchange executive*
Case, Donni Marie *investment company executive, consultant*
Cloonan, James Brian *investment company executive*
Cressey, Bryan Charles *venture capitalist*
Dan, Bernard W. *brokerage house executive, former commodities exchange executive*
Dias Griffin, Anne *investment advisor*
Donohue, Craig S. *mercantile exchange executive*
Duffy, Terrence A. *mercantile exchange executive*
Fagan, Shawn Francis *investment company executive*
Gardner, Chris(topher) *securities trader, entrepreneur*
Georgiadis, Margaret Hastings (Margo Georgiadis) *private equity firm executive, former finance company executive*
Gill, Phupinder *mercantile exchange executive*
Goldstein, William A. *investment counsel*
Griffin, Kenneth C. *hedge fund manager*
Grove, David L. *stock exchange executive*
Herron, David A. *stock exchange executive*
Hickey, Jerome Edward *investment company executive*
Hobson, Mellody *investment company executive*
Kelly, Arthur Lloyd *investment company executive*
Kerr, Michael H. *stock exchange executive, lawyer*
Miner, Thomas Hawley *entrepreneur*
Nygren, William C. *investment company executive*
Oliver, Harry Maynard, Jr. *retired brokerage house executive*
Osborn, William A. *investment company executive*
Pohl, Timothy R. *investment company executive, lawyer*
Pritzker, Penny Sue *investor*
Purcell, Philip James *investment company executive*
Ricketts, Thomas *investment company executive*
Rizzello, Joseph Samuel *stock exchange executive*
Rogers, John W., Jr. *investment company executive*
Rutledge, Edward K. *mortgage broker*
Schwertfeger, Timothy R. *investment company executive*
Slansky, Jerry William *investment company executive*
Stearns, Neele Edward, Jr. *investment company executive*
Underwood, Robert Leigh *venture capitalist*
Weinberg, David B. *investor*
Weiner, Gerald Arne *stockbroker*
Weston, Roger Lance *investment manager*
Whitney, Kent R.E. *securities trader*
Williams, Frederick Tyrone *entrepreneur, pastor*

Evanston
Wang, Sona *venture capitalist*

Highland Park
Uhlmann, Frederick Godfrey *securities trader*

Lake Bluff
Crotty, John T. *investment advisor*

Naperville
Penisten, Gary Dean *entrepreneur*
Vanagas, Rimantas Andrius (Ray Vanagas) *entrepreneur, real estate developer, real estate company executive*

Northbrook
Edelson, Ira J. *venture capitalist*

Oak Brook
Peckenpaugh, Robert Earl *investment advisor*

Park Ridge
Albert, Elizabeth Franz (Mrs. Henry B. Albert) *investor, artist, conservationist*

Westmont
Warner, H. Ty *entrepreneur, manufacturing executive*

Wilmette
Albright, Townsend Shaul *brokerage house executive, consultant*

Woodridge
Murray, Eileen K. *investment company executive*

INDIANA

Bloomington
Kuratko, Donald F. *entrepreneurial educator, consultant*

Carmel
Walsh, John Charles *investment company executive, director*

Evansville
Brill, Alan Richard *entrepreneur*

West Lafayette
Phillips, Terry LeMoine *investment advisor*

IOWA

Des Moines
Pappajohn, John G. *venture capitalist*

KANSAS

Shawnee Mission
Braude, Michael *commodities trader, researcher*

Topeka
Cripe, Elizabeth Ann (Betty) *investment company executive*

KENTUCKY

Lexington
Crooks, Peter Anthony *professor, researcher, entrepreneur*

LOUISIANA

New Orleans
Flower, Walter Chew III *investment counselor*

MAINE

Bryant Pond
Conary, David Arlan *investment company executive*

Fort Kent
Gauvin, Tony *entrepreneur, educator*

MARYLAND

Baltimore
D'Alfonzo, Samuel Donald *entrepreneur*
Ellenbogen, Henry Martin *investment company executive*
Himelfarb, Richard Jay *investment company executive*
Hopkins, Henry Holt *mutual fund attorney*
Kennedy, James Aloysius Charles *investment company executive*
Miller, Bill, III, (William Herbert Miller) *hedge fund manager*
Rogers, Brian Charles *investment company executive*

Bethesda
Allmon, Charles W. *investment advisor*
Ansary, Cyrus A. *investment company executive, lawyer*

Bowie
Gourdine-Tyson, Natachia *CIO, ladiez legacy*

Brookeville
Zehner, Lee Randall *entrepreneur, chemist*

Lutherville Timonium
Cappiello, Frank Anthony, Jr. *investment advisor*

Riverdale
Guetzkow, Daniel *technology company entrepreneur*

MASSACHUSETTS

Belmont
Lloyd, Boardman *investment company executive*

Boston
Antonellis, Joseph C. *investment company executive*
Carey, John Andrew *investment company executive*
Curran, Michael J. *stock exchange executive*
Daniels, Roanne Blythe *private equity firm executive*
de Burlo, Comegys Russell, Jr. *investment company executive, educator, retired treasurer*
Eckstein, Jens W. *venture capitalist, biotechnologist*
Estin, Hans Howard *retired investment company executive*
Hooley, Jay (Joseph L. Hooley) *investment company executive*
Johnson, Abigail Pierrepont *investment company executive*
Johnson, Edward Crosby, III, (Ned Johnson) *investment company executive*
Kaplan, Ilan Brett *brokerage house executive, researcher*
Klarman, Seth *hedge fund manager*
Lee, David Stoddart *retired investment company executive*
Levy, Stephen Raymond *venture capitalist*
Logue, Ronald E. *investment company executive*
Mendillo, Jane Lisa *investment manager*
Oates, William Armstrong, Jr. *investment company executive*
Peckham, John Munroe III *investment executive, author, lecturer*
Resch, Edward J. *investment company executive*
Reynolds, Robert L. *investment company executive*
Richardson, Duncan W. *investment company executive*

Cambridge
Goldberg, Marc Evan *healthcare venture capitalist*
Leiden, Jeffrey Marc *venture capitalist, molecular biologist, cardiologist*
Merrill, David *entrepreneur, researcher*
Read, Russell *investment company executive*

Concord
Schiller, Pieter Jon *retired venture capital executive*

Medford
Goldberg, Pamela Winer *entrepreneur, educator*

Siasconset
Albani, Thomas J. *investor*

South Dartmouth
Greene, William Caswell *investment company executive*

Taunton
Ricciardi, Louis Michael *brokerage house executive*

Waltham
Cox, Howard Ellis, Jr. *venture capitalist*
Manzi, Jim P. *investment company executive*
Metcalfe, Robert M. *venture capitalist, former science engineer, publishing executive, writer*
Spoon, Alan Gary *venture capital company executive*

West Roxbury
Lovell, Francis Joseph *retired investment company executive*

MICHIGAN

Farmington Hills
Ellmann, Sheila Frenkel *investment company executive*
Katzman, David *investment company executive*

Madison Heights
Janke, Kenneth *investment consultant*

Northville
Porcher, Robert III *entrepreneur, retired professional football player*

West Bloomfield
Mamut, Mary Catherine *retired entrepreneur*

MINNESOTA

Eagan
Bostock, Roy Jackson *investment company executive, air transportation executive*

Edina
Bagby, Robert L. *former investment company executive*

Minneapolis
Bagan, Mark G. *grain exchange executive*
Gallagher, Gerald Raphael *venture capitalist*
Pozen, Robert Charles *investment company executive*
Quam, Lois *investment company executive, former health insurance company executive*

Minnetonka
Pillsbury, George Sturgis *retired investment advisor*

Saint Paul
Rodriguez, Roberto Miguel *investment company executive, educator*
Rothmeier, Steven George *investment company executive*

Stillwater
Horsch, Lawrence Leonard *venture capitalist, corporate financial executive*

Waubun
Christensen, Marvin Nelson *venture capitalist*

MISSISSIPPI

Jackson
Molpus, Dick H. *investment company executive*

MISSOURI

Kansas City
Stowers, James Evans, Jr. *investment company executive*

Lees Summit
Korschot, Benjamin Calvin *retired investment company executive*

Saint Louis
Bickel, Floyd Gilbert III *investment counselor*
Keffler, Karl Joseph *private investor, lawyer, educator*
Skrainka, Alan Frederick *securities analyst*

Springfield
Cavner, Nadia *investment company executive*

MONTANA

Polson
Marchi, Jon *retired brokerage house executive, rancher, venture capitalist*

NEBRASKA

Omaha
Buffett, Warren Edward *entrepreneur, investment company executive*
Cross, Walter Thomas *investment company executive*
De Santiago-Young, Dena Kalene *investment company executive, writer*
Hamburg, Marc D. *investment company executive*
Moglia, Joseph H. *brokerage house executive*
Winter, Jimmy *entrepreneur, systems administrator*

NEVADA

Boulder City
Stephenson, Arthur Emmet, Jr. *investment company executive*

Carson City
Alexander, Judy Lynne *investor*

Las Vegas
Jalbert, Janelle Jennifer *entrepreneur, educator, social researcher*
Root, Wayne Allyn *entrepreneur, television producer, writer*

Reno
Harsh, Antoinette Mollett *investor*

Sparks
Holder, Harold Douglas, Sr. *investor, hotel executive*

NEW HAMPSHIRE

Dover
Parks, Joe Benjamin *entrepreneur visionary, state legislator*

NEW JERSEY

Avenel
Berg, Louis Leslie *investment executive*

Basking Ridge
Tamarelli, Alan Wayne *venture capitalist*

Chatham
Tepper, David Alan *hedge fund manager*

East Brunswick
Hurst, Gregory Squire *investment company executive, theater director and producer*

Fort Lee
Lippman, William Jennings *investment company executive*

Jersey City
Tomczyk, Fredric John *brokerage house executive*

Lincoln Park
Sichuk, George *entrepreneur, creator and builder mental analyst, writer, atomic scientist, biochemist, physiologist, transcendental academic theologian*

Little Falls
Shern, Stephanie Marie *investment company executive, accountant*

Mendham
Kirby, Allan Price, Jr. *investment company executive*
Pierson, Robert David *investor*

Montclair
Jones, Sylvia Calpurnia *investment company executive*

Morristown
Kirby, Jefferson W. *investment company executive*

Park Ridge
Giovannoli, Joseph Louis *entrepreneur, lawyer*

Princeton
Chamberlin, John Stephen *investor, consumer products company executive*
Gund, Gordon *venture capitalist, investment company executive*
Johnston, Robert Fowler *venture capitalist*

Red Bank
Hertz, Daniel Leroy, Jr. *entrepreneur*
Murphy, Philip D. *investment company executive, professional sports team executive*

Ridgewood
Hansmann, Ralph Emil *investment executive, director*

Skillman
Tenenbaum, Bernard Hirsh *entrepreneur, educator*

Teaneck
Fein, Lawrence Seth *investment advisor*

Tenafly
Insana, Ron (Ronald Gerard Insana) *investment company executive, financial analyst*

NEW MEXICO

Albuquerque
Green, Francis William *investment consultant, former missile scientist*

NEW YORK

Babylon
Brackett, Ronald E. *investment company executive, lawyer*

Bay Shore
Williams, Tonda *entrepreneur, consultant*

Bedford Corners
Singer, Craig *entrepreneur, inventor, executive*

Binghamton
Taylor, Kenneth Douglas *stockbroker, finance and computer consultant, educator*

Brooklyn
Griffin, John Anthony *hedge fund manager*
Ross, Randolph Ernest *investor*

Buffalo
Irwin, Robert James Armstrong *retired investment company executive*

East Setauket
Simons, James Harris *hedge fund manager*

Forest Hills
Flowers, Cynthia *investment company executive*

Great Neck
Appel, Gerald *investment advisor*

Harrison
Crawford, R. George *investment company executive, educator, filmmaker*

Holland
OBrien, Scott *entrepreneur*

Manhasset
Calvin, Donald Lee *stock exchange official*

Massapequa
Pettersen, Kevin Will *investment company executive*
Pettersen, Kjell Will *securities trader, consultant*

Mount Kisco
Kohlberg, James A. *venture capitalist*

New Hyde Park
Brun, Leslie Adolphe *investment advisor*
Richards, Bernard *investment company executive*

New York
Ackman, William Albert *hedge fund manager*
Ainslie, Lee S. III *hedge fund manager*
Allen, Herbert Anthony III *investment company executive*
Altman, Roger Charles *investment company executive, former federal agency administrator*
Andersen, K(ent) Tucker *investment executive*
Anderson, Dwight Walter *hedge fund manager*
Anderson, Fred D. *investment company executive, retired computer company executive*
Angelson, Mark Alan *investment company executive, retired printing company executive*
Arnaboldi, Nicole Sinek *investment company executive*
Aronson, Edgar David *venture capitalist*
Aronson, Jeffrey H. *private equity firm executive*
Bacon, Louis Moore *hedge fund manager*
Baha, Christian J. *hedge fund manager*
Barksdale, James Love *investment company executive*
Barry, Thomas Corcoran *investment advisor*
Beinecke, Frederick William *investment company executive*
Bell, Martin Allen *investment company executive*
Bellas, Albert Constantine *investment executive*
Belt, Bradley Deck *investment company executive, former pension fund administrator*
Berstein, Robert Laurance *investment company executive*
Beyman, Jonathan Eric *investment company executive*
Blalock, Sherrill *investment advisor*
Blavatnik, Leonard *investment company executive*
Boyd, Michael Alan *investment company executive, lawyer*
Bradley, Bill (William Warren Bradley) *investment company executive, former United States Senator from New Jersey, retired professional basketball player*
Brenneman, Gregory D. *private equity firm executive, former food service executive*
Britz Lotti, Diane Edward *investment company executive*
Brody, Alan Jeffrey *investment company executive*
Brosens, Frank Peter *hedge fund manager*
Brown, Thomas K. *hedge fund manager*
Browning, Candace *investment company executive*
Bruce, Duncan Archibald *investor, writer*
Buckles, Robert Howard *retired investment company executive*
Callan, Erin M. *investment company executive*
Carter, Marshall Nichols *stock exchange executive*
Chanos, James Steven *hedge fund manager*
Clark, Mayree Carroll *investment company executive*
Clark, Wesley Kanne *investment company executive, retired military officer*
Cloherty, Patricia M. *investment company executive*
Cohen, Alan M. *investment company executive, lawyer*
Cohen, Peter Anthony *investment company executive*
Cole, Carolyn Jo *brokerage house executive*
Cole, Christopher A. *investment company executive*
Coleman, Charles Payson, III, (Chase Coleman) *hedge fund manager*
Concannon, Christopher R. *trading company executive*
Conway, Richard Francis *investment company executive*
Cooper, Edith W. *investment company executive*
Cortez, Ricardo Lee *investment management executive*
Coulter, David Alan *private equity firm executive*
Cox, Archibald, Jr. *investor*
Crocker, Elaine (M. Elaine Crocker) *investment company executive*
Daniels, Randy A. *investment company executive, former state official*
Di Palma, Joseph Alphonse *investment company executive, lawyer*
Donohoe, Noel B. *investment company executive*
Dorsett, Burt *investment company executive*
Draddy, James J. *stock exchange executive*
Dubin, Glenn Russell *hedge fund manager*
Dunleavy, Kevin B. *investment company executive*
Durkin, Patrick J. *private equity firm executive*
Ehinger, Albert Louis, Jr. *securities trader*

Einhorn, David M. *hedge fund manager*
Einiger, Carol Blum *investment company executive*
Ercklentz, Alexander Tonio *investment company executive*
Fahey, James Edward *brokerage house executive*
Falcone, Philip Alan *hedge fund manager*
Feinberg, Stephen A. *hedge fund manager*
Feldberg, Meyer *investment advisor, university dean emeritus*
Filimonov, Mikhail Anatolyevitch *investment company executive*
Findakly, Hani K. *investment company executive*
Finerman, Karen *investment company executive*
Fink, Laurence D. (Larry Fink) *investment company executive*
Fisher, Peter R. *private equity firm executive, former federal agency administrator*
Flinn, Michael de Vlaming *investment company executive*
Flowers, J. Christopher (James Christopher Flowers) *private equity firm executive*
Forstmann, Ted (Theodore J. Forstmann) *private equity firm executive*
Fotiades, George L. *investment company executive*
Friedenberg, Daniel Meyer *investor, writer*
Friedman, Robert Laurence *investment company executive*
Gallogly, Mark Timothy *private equity firm executive*
Gelband, Michael R. *investment company executive*
Geltzeiler, Michael S. *stock exchange executive, former publishing executive*
Glauber, Robert R. *investment company executive, former financial regulatory service executive*
Gogel, Donald J. *investment company executive*
Goldfarb, David *investment company executive*
Golub, Harvey *private equity firm executive*
Golub, Steven J. *investment company executive*
Gotbaum, Joshua *hedge fund manager*
Gottesman, David Sanford *investment company executive*
Gottesman, Noam *hedge fund manager*
Gray, James L. *investment company executive*
Greenberg, Jeffrey Wayne *private equity firm executive, former insurance company executive*
Greenfield, Stefani *entrepreneur*
Greifeld, Robert *stock exchange executive*
Gribbin, D.J. (David James Gribbin IV) *investment company executive, former federal agency administrator*
Gutfreund, John Halle *investment company executive, consultant*
Hance, James Henry, Jr., (Jim Hance) *private equity firm executive, retired bank executive*
Handler, Richard B. *investment company executive*
Harper, Arthur Henry *investment company executive, former diversified technology and services company executive*
Hartman, Alan *investment company executive*
Haskell, John Henry Farrell, Jr. *investment company executive*
Herman, Darren *entrepreneur, marketing executive*
Herrmann, Lacy Bunnell *investment company executive, entrepreneur, venture capitalist*
Hessels, Jan-Michiel *stock exchange executive*
Hilzinger, Kurt John *investment company executive*
Hindery, Leo Joseph, Jr. *investment company executive*
Hochman, Richard H. *investment company executive*
Holland, Michael Francis *investment company executive*
Horn, Karen Nicholson *investment company executive, former bank executive*
Hutchins, Glenn H. *private equity firm executive*
Hyman, Morton Peter *private equity investment company executive*
Icahn, Carl Celian *investor*
Ilacqua, Rosario Salvatore *securities analyst*
Janney, Stuart Symington III *investment company executive*
Jepson, Hans Godfrey *investment company executive, director*
Jones, Alan Kent *investment company executive*
Katz, Gary *securities exchange executive*
Kinney, Gilbert Hart *investor*
Klinsky, Steven Bruce *investor*
Koplovitz, Kay *investment company executive*
Kovner, Bruce Stanley *hedge fund manager*
Kramer, Orin Stuart *hedge fund manager*
Kraus, Peter Steven *investment company executive*
Krell, David H. *securities exchange executive*
Kressel, Henry *venture capitalist*
Lamle, Hugh Roy *investment advisor, consultant*
Lamport, Anthony Matthew *venture capitalist*
Lasry, Marc *hedge fund manager*
Lasser, Joseph Robert *investment company executive*
Lauder, Ronald Stephen *investor*
Lawrence, Bryan Hunt *investment company executive*
Lee, Thomas H. *private equity firm executive*
Leitersdorf, Jonathan *investment company executive*
Lessing, Stephen M. *investment company executive*
Levitt, Arthur, Jr. *investment company executive, former federal agency administrator*
Lichtenstein, Warren G. *hedge fund manager*
Lifton, Robert Kenneth *entrepreneur*
Lockhart, James Bicknell III *investment company executive, former federal agency administrator*
Loeb, Daniel Seth *hedge fund manager*
Loeb, John Langeloth, Jr. *investment counselor, consultant*
Lowitt, Ian Theo *investment company executive*
Lukken, Walter L. *stock exchange executive, former commissioner*
Lutnick, Howard William *brokerage house executive*
Ma, Adrianna *private equity firm executive*
Mager, Ezra Pascal *investment company executive*
Magner, Marjorie J. (Marge Magner) *private equity firm executive*
Marron, Donald Baird, Sr. *venture capitalist*
Mayer, William Emilio *investor*
McGee, Hugh E. III *investment company executive*
McNulty, James J. *futures exchange executive*
Miller, Corbin Russell *investment company executive*
Miller, Jonathan F. *investment company executive, former Internet company executive*
Mindich, Eric M. *hedge fund manager*
Moltz, James Edward *brokerage house executive*
Morris, William Charles *investor*
Morse, Robert Parker *investment company executive*
Mudd, Daniel H. *investment company executive, former mortgage company executive*
Murphy, John Vincent *investment company executive*
Nabi, Stanley Andrew *brokerage house executive*
Nasser, Jacques *private equity firm executive, former automotive company executive*
Nazem, Fereydoun F. *venture capitalist, entrepreneur*
Neumark, Liz *entrepreneur*
Niederauer, Duncan L. *stock exchange executive*
Niederhoffer, Roy Gary *hedge fund manager*
Niemiec, David Wallace *investment company executive*
Novogratz, Michael E. *hedge fund manager*
Obernauer, Marne *securities company executive*
Och, Daniel S. *hedge fund manager*
O'Connor, Bridget *investment company technology officer*
Offit, Morris Wolf *investment company executive*
Palmer, Raquel Vargas *private equity firm executive*
Patricof, Alan Joel *venture capitalist*
Peltz, Nelson A. *investment company executive*
Perry, Richard Cayne *hedge fund manager*
Peterson, Peter George *retired investment company executive, former United States Secretary of Commerce*
Petno, Douglas B. *investment company executive*
Petrie, Thomas A. *investment company executive*
Pittman, Robert Warren *investor*
Pollack, Stephen J. *investment company executive, stockbroker*
Pollak, Dave J. *investment company executive, former political organization administrator*
Pouschine, John Laurence *private equity investment executive*
Proctor, Georganne C. *investment company executive*
Putnam, Jerry (Gerald D. Putnam) *stock exchange executive*
QNardelli, Robert Louis *private equity firm executive, former automotive executive*
Questrom, Allen I. *private equity firm executive, former retail executive*
Quirk, John James *investment company executive*
Rado, Patricia A. *stock exchange executive, retired electric power industry executive*
Rand, Lawrence Anthony *investor, finance company executive*
Reses, Jacqueline Dawn *private equity firm executive*
Robbins, Lawrence M. *hedge fund manager*
Robinson, James D. III *venture capitalist*
Rogers, Theodore Courtney *investment company executive*
Rosenblatt, Lief Dov *hedge fund manager*
Rosenbloom, Daniel *investment advisor, lawyer*
Saul, Andrew M. *investment company executive*
Schick, Harry Leon *investment company executive*
Schlosstein, Ralph L. *investment company executive*
Schwarzman, Stephen Allen (Steve Schwarzman) *private equity firm executive*
Scott, William Clement III *investor*
Sender, Adam D. *investment company executive, art collector*
Senor, Daniel Samuel *investment company and think-tank executive*
Shaffer Solovay, Susan *investment company executive*
Shapiro, Robert Frank *investment company executive*
Shaw, L. Edward, Jr. *investment company executive, lawyer*
Sica, Frank Vincent *investment company executive*
Siebert, Muriel (Mickie) *brokerage house executive, retired bank executive*
Silverman, Henry Richard *private equity firm executive*
Simpkins, Neil P. *investment and automotive company executive*
Smith, Malcolm Bernard *investment company executive*
Snow, John William (Jack Snow) *investment company executive, former United States Secretary of the Treasury*
Soros, George *hedge fund manager, entrepreneur, philanthropist*
Sorte, John Follett *investment firm executive*
Spier, Guy Selmar *investment advisor*
Stein, David Fred *investment company executive*
Steiner, Joshua Linder *private equity firm executive*
Sterling, Robert Lee, Jr. *investment company executive*
Stern, Walter Phillips *investment company executive*
Stewart, E(dward) Nicholson *investment management executive*
Sullivan, Hugh David *investment company executive*
Swieca, Henry Alexander *hedge fund manager*
Tamke, George William *venture capitalist*
Tananbaum, Steven Andrew *investment consultant*
Taylor, Diana Lancaster *investment company executive, former state official*
Taylor, John Read, Jr. *hedge fund manager*
Tendler, David *investment company executive*
Tenet, George John *investment company executive, former CIA director*
Thorne, Nathan C. *investment company executive*
Tosi, Laurence A. III *investment company executive*
Train, John *investment advisor, columnist*
Trotter, Lloyd G. *investment company executive, former diversified technology and services company executive*
Ule, Guy Maxwell, Jr. *stockbroker*
Virtue, Ted *investment company executive*
Vogelstein, John L. *venture capitalist*
Walker, George H. *investment company executive*
Walker, Jeffrey Clemens *venture capitalist*
Wall Spitzer, Silda Alice *hedge fund executive*
Wareham, Raymond Noble *investment advisor*
Weatherman, Elizabeth H. (Bess Weatherman) *private equity firm executive*
Wijnberg, Sandra S. *investment company executive*
Williams, Christopher J. *investment company executive*
Williams, Dave Harrell *investment company executive*
Winkler, Charles Howard *investment company executive*
Wittman, Thomas A. *stock exchange executive*
Wolf, Peter Michael *investment manager, consultant, writer*
Wright, Jason Howard Sebastian *private equity company executive*
Wright, Robert C. (Robert Charles Wright) *investment company executive, former media and entertainment company executive*
Zannino, Richard F. *private equity firm executive, former publishing executive*
Zarb, Frank Gustave *private equity firm executive*
Zeuschner, Erwin Arnold *brokerage house executive*
Zoullas, Deborah Decotis *investment company executive*

Ossining
Kelly, William Michael *investment company executive*

Purchase
Black, Leon David *private equity firm executive*
Olstein, Robert A. *investment company executive*
Wachenheim, Edgar III *investment company executive*

Riverhead
Orben, Jack Richard *investment company executive, director*

Ronkonkoma
Leventhal, Norman B. *entrepreneur*

Rye
Greenwald, Gerald (Jerry Greenwald) *private equity group executive*

Sag Harbor
Brody, Eugene David *investment company executive*

West Seneca
Humiston, Daniel J. *entrepreneur*

White Plains
Gottlieb, Lester M. *entrepreneur*

Woodstock
Ober, Stuart Alan *investment advisor, writer*

NORTH CAROLINA

Ararat
Marsh, Joseph Virgil *investment advisor, analyst, broker, consultant, research scientist*

Chapel Hill
Drutz, David Jules *venture capitalist*

Charlotte
Cummings, Stephen Emery *investment banking executive*
Moynihan, Brian T. *investment company executive, bank executive*
Noujaim, Fares Dourid *investment company executive*
Ragan, Robert Allison *private investment executive, financial consultant*

Greensboro
Johnson, Marshall Hardy *investment company executive*

Huntersville
Headd, Kevin *investment advisor*

Murphy
Pezzella, Jerry James, Jr. *investment and real estate company executive*

West End
Krallinger, Joseph Charles *entrepreneur, consultant, writer*

NORTH DAKOTA

Grand Forks
Gjovig, Bruce Quentin *entrepreneur, consultant*

OHIO

Athens
Wilhelm, David C. *venture capitalist*

Brookfield
Manos, Thomas G. *investment company executive*

Cincinnati
DeWitt, William O., Jr. *investor, professional sports team executive*
Lucke, Robert Vito *investment company executive*
Shipley, Tony L(ee) *investor, software company executive*

Cleveland
Brentlinger, Paul Smith *venture capital executive*
Charnas, Michael (Mannie) *investment company executive*
Morgenthaler, David Turner *venture capitalist*
Pollock, Lawrence Ira (Larry Pollock) *investment company executive*

Columbus
Barthelmas, Ned Kelton *brokerage house executive*
Kidder, Robert (Charles Robert Kidder) *private equity firm executive, automotive executive*
Shinkel, Bernie (Bernard Albert Shinkel) *investment advisor*

Delaware
Hamre, Gary Leslie William *retired entrepreneur*

Strongsville
Cameron, David Ronald *entrepreneur, historian, researcher*

OKLAHOMA

Lawton
Carraher, Shawn Michael *investment company executive, management educator*

Tulsa
Neas, John Theodore *investment company executive*

Yukon
Kang, Heesam *investment analyst, educator*

OREGON

Portland
Arthur, Michael Elbert *financial advisor, lawyer*
Rutherford, William Drake *investment executive*
Stott, Peter Walter *investment company executive*

PENNSYLVANIA

Berwyn
Hambrecht, William R. *investment banking firm executive*

Blue Bell
Giordano, Nicholas Anthony *brokerage house executive*

Lancaster
Carlisle, James Patton *entrepreneur*

Ligonier
Mellon, Seward Prosser *brokerage house executive*

Malvern
Brennan, Jack (John Joseph Brennan) *investment company executive*
McNabb, F. William, III, (Bill McNabb) *investment company executive*

Mechanicsburg
Owen, Tony Quinn *investment company executive, horse trainer*

Paoli
Denny, William Murdoch, Jr. *investment management executive*

Philadelphia
Frucher, Meyer S. (Sandy Frucher) *stock exchange executive*
Gowa, Andrew *investor, lawyer*
Nevels, James Edwin *investment company executive*
Palmer, Russell Eugene *investment company executive, retired dean*
Savitz, Samuel J. *actuarial consulting firm executive*
Woosnam, Richard Edward *venture capitalist, lawyer*

Pittsburgh
Bernt, Benno Anthony *entrepreneur, investor*
Druckenmiller, Stanley Freeman *hedge fund manager*
Heitzenroder, David August *investment advisor, investment banker*
Hillman, Henry Lea *investment company executive*
Walton, James Mellon *investment company executive*

Radnor
Buck, James Mahlon, Jr. *venture capitalist*
Hemphill, James S. *investment management executive, financial advisor*

Reading
Lehman, John F., Jr. *private equity firm executive*

Sewickley
Maurer, Richard Michael *investment company executive*

Valley Forge
Bogle, John Clifton (Jack Bogle) *investment company executive*

Wexford
Stover, Richard L. *investor*

Wilkes Barre
Hackett, Chris *entrepreneur*

Williamsport
McDonald, Peyton Dean *brokerage house executive*

York
White, Timothy Paul *brokerage house executive*

RHODE ISLAND

Narragansett
Stark, Dennis Edwin *private investor, retired bank executive and university administrator*

Providence
Joukowsky, Artemis A. W. *private investor*
Nelson, Jonathan M. *private equity firm executive*
Richardson, Julie G. *private equity firm executive*

Wakefield
Mason, Scott MacGregor *entrepreneur, inventor, consultant*

SOUTH CAROLINA

Clemson
Gartner, William B. *entrepreneur, educator*

Columbia
Brockelsby, Jeffrey Lind *investment executive*

Hilton Head
Drakeman, Donald Lee *venture capitalist*

Orangeburg
Dalton, Cheryl Renee *entrepreneur*

Ridgeland
Cameron, Thomas William Lane *investment company executive*

TENNESSEE

Chattanooga
Fossel, Jon S. *retired investment company executive*

Memphis
Hawkins, O. Mason *investment company executive*

Nashville
Bradford, James C., Jr. *brokerage house executive*
Byrd, Andrew Wayne *investment company executive*
Frist, Bill (William Harrison Frist) *investment company executive, Former United States Senator from Tennessee, thoracic surgeon*
Hanselman, Richard Wilson *entrepreneur*
Nelson, Edward Gage *brokerage house and bank executive, consultant*

TEXAS

Austin
Baumgartner, Robert *investment company executive, consultant*
Meredith, Thomas J. *investment company executive*

Dallas
Bayne, James Elwood *investor*
Brown, Benjamin A. *investment advisor*
Buchholz, Donald Alden *stock brokerage company executive*
Carrozza, Vincent A. *investment company executive*
Crockett, Dodee Frost *brokerage house executive*
Durham, Michael Jonathan *investment professional*
Kriscunas, Suzanne B. (Suzy Kriscunas) *private equity firm executive*
Lynch, William Wright, Jr. *investment company executive, engineer*
Meyerson, Morton Herbert *investor, real estate company executive*
Miller, David Bruce *investment company executive*
Muse, John R. *investment company executive*
Pickens, T. Boone (Thomas Boone Pickens Jr.) *hedge fund manager, former oil industry executive*
Rachofsky, Howard *retired investor, art collector, patron*
Simmons, Harold C. *investment and sugar company executive*
Stoffel, Paul T. *investment company executive*
Vest, Christina Weaver *private equity firm executive*
Wyly, Charles Joseph, Jr. *entrepreneur*

Fort Worth
Bass, Sid Richardson *investment company executive*
Bonderman, David *investment company executive, lawyer*

Heathridge
Vaughan, Joseph Lee, Jr. *entrepreneur, realtor, educational consultant*

Horseshoe Bay
Anderson, Kenneth Ward *investor, consultant*

Houston
Arnold, John Douglas *hedge fund manager*
Duncan, Charles William, Jr. *investor, former United States Secretary of Energy*
O'Connor, Ralph Sturges *investment company executive*
Patterson, William J. *investment company executive*
Ranieri, Lewis S. *investment company executive*
Richards, Leonard Martin *investment executive, consultant*
Vaughan, Eugene H. *investment company executive*
Wells, Damon *investment company executive*
Williams, Edward Earl, Jr. *entrepreneur, educator*

San Antonio
Terracina, Roy David *entrepreneur*

UTAH

Salt Lake City
Peterson, Joel C. *investment company executive*
Wallace, Matthew Walker *retired entrepreneur*

Sandy
Crittenden, Gary Lewis *private equity firm executive*

VERMONT

Montgomery Center
Sauvagnat, Henry Gabriel *entrepreneur, sales executive*

Montpelier
Thwaites, Christian William *investment company executive*

Quechee
DeRouchey, Beverly Jean *investment company executive*

VIRGINIA

Arlington
Choksi, Mary Claire *investment company executive*
Drayton, Bill (William Drayton) *social entrepreneur, lawyer, management consultant*
Muñoz, George *investment company executive, former federal agency administrator*
Scarborough, Robert Henry, Jr. *entrepreneur*

Bedford
Rasoul, Sam *entrepreneur*

Charlottesville
Gunter, Bradley Hunt *capital management executive*

Dutton
Washburn, John Rosser *entrepreneur*

Middleburg
Parkinson, James Thomas III *investment consultant*

Mount Vernon
Hartwell, Stephen *investment company executive*

Orange
Thompson, Louis Milton, Jr. *public investor relations consultant*

Richmond
Dehn, James Keith *investment company executive*

Springfield
Tian, Li *investment company executive, educator*

Stanardsville
Anns, Philip Harold *brokerage house and pharmaceutical executive*

Suffolk
Holloway, Christopher Matthew *brokerage house executive*

Vienna
Isaac, William Michael *brokerage house executive, retired federal official*

Virginia Beach
Melsheimer, Mel P(owell) *venture capitalist*

Warrenton
Day, Bill S., Jr. *entrepreneur*

Williamsburg
Gordon, Baron Jack *stockbroker*
Roberson, Robert S. *investment company executive*

WASHINGTON

Bellevue
Connors, John G. *venture capitalist, former computer software company executive*
Wells-Henderson, Ronald John *investment counselor*

Kirkland
Chapple, John H. *investment company executive*
Ryles, Gerald Fay *investor, finance company executive*

Redmond
Christie, Doug (Douglas Dale Christie) *entrepreneur, former professional basketball player*

Seattle
Alberg, Tom Austin *investment company executive, lawyer*
Heath, Richard Raymond *retired investment company executive*
McAndrews, Brian Patrick *venture capitalist, former computer software company executive*
McCaw, John Elroy, Jr. *investment company executive, professional sports team executive*
Milton, Catherine Higgs *entrepreneur*
Nelson, Allen F. *proxy solicitation company executive*
Ruckelshaus, William Doyle *investment company executive, former federal agency administrator*
Wright, Bagley *venture capitalist, entrepreneur, art collector*

Sequim
Kretschmer, Keith Hughes *investor*

WISCONSIN

Beloit
Gustafson, Jerry William *entrepreneur educator, economics professor*

Madison
Zinder, Newton Donald *investment advisor, consultant*

Mequon
Bloom, James Edward *sales and marketing director, commodity trading and financial executive*

Milwaukee
Weening, Richard William, Jr. *venture capitalist, media communications executive, entrepreneur*

WYOMING

Cheyenne
Myers, Rolland Graham *investment counselor*

Jackson
Hirschfield, Alan James *entrepreneur*
Trauner, Gary *entrepreneur*

Wilson
Chrystie, Thomas Ludlow *investor*
Davis, Shelby Moore Cullom *investment company executive, consultant*

TERRITORIES OF THE UNITED STATES

PUERTO RICO

Hato Rey
Ferrer, Miguel Antonio *brokerage house executive*

CANADA

BRITISH COLUMBIA

Vancouver
Aquilini, Francesco *investment company executive, professional sports team executive*

ONTARIO

Toronto
Dale, Robert Gordon *investment company executive*
Fox, Wayne C. *stock exchange and corporate financial executive*
Kloet, Thomas A. *stock exchange executive*
Leech, Jim (James William Leech) *investment company executive*
Lindsay, Roger Alexander (Baron of Craighall) *investment executive*

QUEBEC

Montreal
Cedraschi, Tullio *retired investment company executive*

AUSTRALIA

Clermont
Mepham, Derek John Amoore *business investor*

Melbourne
Fahour, Ahmed *investment company executive*

CHINA

Hong Kong
Ka-Shing, Li *international entrepreneur*

ENGLAND

Hull
Pettman, Barrie Owen *entrepreneur*

London
Blood, David *investment company executive*
Jourdren, Marc Henri *investment banking company executive*
Massenet, Natalie *internet entrepreneur*
Minnick, Mary E. *investment company executive, former beverage company executive*

HONG KONG

Wanchai
Suen, Stephen *investment company executive*

MONGOLIA

Ulaanbaatar
Mandel, Leslie Ann *investment advisor, writer*

SAUDI ARABIA

Riyadh
Alshareef, Fehied Fahad *government agency leader*

SLOVENIA

Ljubljana
Nabergoj, Andrej *entrepreneur*

SPAIN

Betlem
Cecchini, Leo *entrepreneur*

SWITZERLAND

Muttenz
L'Eplattenier, Francois *venture capitalist*

Zurich
Wassmer, Rudolf Andreas *entrepreneurial engineer*

UNITED ARAB EMIRATES

Dubai
Chohan, Gulshan-Naseem *office manager*

ADDRESS UNPUBLISHED

Ackerman, Melvin *investment company executive*
Albanese, Thomas *entrepreneur*
Albers, Charles Edgar *retired investment company executive*
Allen, Donald Vail *investment company executive, pianist*
Andreessen, Marc Lowell *venture capitalist, software company executive*
Aurin, Robert James *entrepreneur*
Bacharach, Melvin Lewis *venture capitalist*
Bahbah, Bishara Assad *investment company executive, consultant*
Bantry, Bryan *entrepreneur*
Beldock, Donald Travis *investor*
Berkley, Stephen M. *entrepreneur, investor*
Bertrand, Luc *former stock exchange executive*
Blum, Barbara Davis *investor*
Bowles, Barbara Landers *retired investment company executive*
Brady, Nicholas Frederick *investment company executive, former United States Secretary of the Treasury*
Brown, Herbert Graham *entrepreneur*
Burkle, Ronald W. *entrepreneur, retired food service executive*
Butte, Amy S. *former brokerage house executive*
Callard, David Jacobus *investment company executive*
Chase, Robin M. *entrepreneur*
Clawson, John Addison *investment company and retired chemicals executive*
Clay, John Peter *investment company executive*
Clemmensen, Larry P. *investment company executive*
Cohen, Claire Gorham *investment company executive*
Corbet, Kathleen A. *investment company executive, former financial information company executive*
Cormie, Donald Mercer *investment company executive*
Cottone, Anthony Matthew *investment advisor*
Culp, Michael Bronston *investor, writer, publisher*
Cunningham, Ronnie Walter *venture capitalist*
Daie, Jaleh *investment company executive*
Dean, Edwin Becton *entrepreneur*
De Lutis, Donald Conse *investment advisor, consultant*
Downing, Hudson Urquhart *retired securities trader, bank executive*
Drake, Rodman Leland *investment company executive, consultant*
Dunn, Richard Joseph *retired investment advisor*
Ellis, Laurel Glynn *retired entrepreneur*
Elman, Noel *entrepreneur, electrical engineer*
Estes, Jack Charles *entrepreneur, oil industry executive, research scientist*
Fakahany, Ahmass L. *retired investment company executive*
Falvey, Mark A. *entrepreneur*
Fitts, Catherine Austin *investment advisor*
Franklin, Edward Ward *international investment consultant, lawyer, actor*
Fuld, Richard Severin, Jr., (Dick Fuld) *former investment company executive*
Furash, Edward Elliott *investment company executive, banker, educator, writer, theater producer*
Gale, Michael Johnathan *entrepreneur*
Gerstner, Louis Vincent, Jr. *retired private equity firm executive*
Gilburne, Miles R. *venture capitalist*
Glasberg, Laurence Brian *investment company executive*
Godin, Seth Warren *entrepreneur, blog website writer, marketing professional*
Good, Walter Raymond *investment company executive*
Gundlach, Heinz Ludwig *doctor juris*
Hapner, Mary Lou *securities trader, writer*
Hertog, Roger *retired investment company executive*
Holte, Debra Leah *investment company executive, financial analyst*
Hourihan, Meg *entrepreneur, blog site host*
Howard, James Webb *brokerage house executive, engineer, lawyer*
Hudson, Donald J. *retired stock exchange executive*
Hull, Brian P. *former investment company executive*
Hunt, William W. *former investment company executive*
Hurt, William Holman *investment management company executive*

Ivester, M(elvin) Douglas *investment company executive, retired beverage company executive*
Johnson, Michael Warren *international relations specialist*
Joliat, Jay Frederick *venture capitalist, marketing consultant*
Jones, Abbott C. *investment company executive*
Jones, Frank Joseph *retired securities exchange executive*
Kahn, Herta Hess (Mrs. Howard Kahn) *retired investment company executive*
Kellogg, Peter R. *securities dealer*
Kiely, Dan Ray *fund manager, real estate company executive, consultant*
Kim, Dow *investment company executive*
Kolevar, Kevin M. *investment company executive, former federal agency administrator*
Kwitek, Benjamin Joseph *entrepreneur, consultant*
Landis, Kenneth H. *entrepreneur, private investor, venture capitalist*
Lasser, Lawrence J. *former investment company executive*
Leahy, T. Liam *business development and technology investor*
Level, Leon Jules *investor, director*
Levins, John Raymond *investment advisor, educator, management consultant*
Lewis, Hunter *investment advisor, writer*
Linde, Ronald Keith *investor*
Little, Arthur Dehon *investor*
Logan, Kent *retired securities industry executive*
Malin, Robert Abernethy *retired investment company executive*
Markopolos, Harry M. *financial investigator, former investment company executive*
Mayer, Anthony John *investment company executive*
McCausland, Thomas James, Jr. *retired brokerage house executive*
McClane, Robert Sanford *entrepreneur, bank executive*
McCormick, David Arthur *venture capitalist*
McMahon, Harry Thomas *investment company executive*
McNeill, Robert Patrick *investment advisor*
Mikeska, Noel Rhea *entrepreneur, health advocate*
Mikitka, Gerald Peter *brokerage house executive, consultant*
Mosbacher, Robert Adam, Jr. *former investment company executive*
Nadel, Elliott *investment company executive*
Neece, Olivia Helene Ernst *investment company executive, consultant*
Newsome, James Eugene *former mercantile exchange executive*
Nicholas, Lawrence Bruce *company executive*
Noto, Lucio A. *investment company executive, retired oil industry executive*
O'Keefe, James William, Jr. *investment manager and banker*
Olinger, Chauncey Greene, Jr. *investment company executive, editorial consultant*
Paladino, Albert Edward *venture capitalist*
Parker, Towana D. *entrepreneur, director*
Pauken, Thomas Weir *venture capital executive, mediator*
Petersen, Dorothy Virginia *investment company executive*
Peterson, Dawn Michelle *entrepreneur, writer*
Price, Steven *venture capitalist, communications executive, lawyer*
Quattrone, Frank P. *investment company executive*
Rappaport, Irving S. *entrepreneur, lawyer IP consultant*
Rattner, Steven Lawrence *former private equity firm executive*
Reilly, William Kane *private equity firm executive, preservationist, former federal agency administrator*
Renda, Patrick Blake *investment company executive*
Ridgway, Rozanne LeJeanne *corporate director, retired ambassador*
Roberts, David Glen *prospector, investor, ceo*
Robertson, Julian Hart, Jr. *hedge fund manager*
Robertson, Sara Stewart *investor, entrepreneur*
Robinson, Bob Leo *retired international investment service executive*
Rothstein, Gerald Alan *investment consultant*
Rydén, Bengt Gunnar *retired stock exchange executive*
Santry, Barbara Lea *venture capitalist*
Sells, Boake Anthony *private investor*
Snyder, Nathan *entrepreneur, investor*
Solberg, Ronald Louis *investment adviser, portfolio manager*
Stephens, Donald R(ichards) *investor*
Stewart, Thomas Clifford *investment company executive*
Stiles, Thomas Beveridge, II, *retired investment company executive*
Stuart, Gerard William, Jr. *investment company executive, alderman, city official*
Tarr, Kenneth J. *retired investment company executive*
Thomson, Todd Stuart *investment company executive*
Tilson, Whitney R. *investment company executive*
Trongale, Nicholas Albert *entrepreneur, researcher, educator*
Ulick, Susan E. *investment company executive*
Uys, Jurgen Peter Brinker *securities analyst*
Valentine, Gene C. *securities dealer*
Veselinovič, Draško *stock exchange executive*
Volkay, Chris John *investment company executive*
Wagner, Ron *entrepreneur*
Walsh, William Desmond *investor*
Welch, Martin E. III *investor, former rental company executive*
Whelan, James Robert *investor, mining company executive*
Wolkoff, Neal Lawrence *stock exchange executive*
Wong, Edward Vincent *investment company executive*
Wruble, Brian Frederick *investor*
York, Jerome B. *investment company executive*
Young, Ronald Faris *commodities trader*
Zeviar-Geese, Gabriole *stock market investor, lawyer*
Zwerling, Gary Leslie *retired investment company executive*

GOVERNMENT: AGENCY ADMINISTRATION

UNITED STATES

ALABAMA

Clanton
Baughman, Bruce Prentiss *state agency administrator*

Huntsville
Schumann, J. Paul *retired federal agency administrator*

Montgomery
Harrison, John D. *state banking agency administrator*
Wall, William Herbert *state coordinator student loan programs*
Williamson, Donald Ellis *state agency administrator, public health service officer*

Troy
Anderson, Rod L. *protective services official*

ALASKA

Anchorage
Burke, Marianne King *state agency administrator, finance executive, consultant*

Juneau
Hogan, William (Bill Hogan) *state agency administrator, public health service officer*
Hovanec, Lorie *state banking agency administrator*

ARIZONA

Goodyear
Carlson, Norman A. *retired federal agency administrator*

Phoenix
Chavez, Nelba R. *state and former federal agency administrator*
Humble, William *state agency administrator, public health service officer*
Karnas, Fred G., Jr. *poverty and homeless specialist*
Rotellini, Felecia A. *state banking agency administrator*

Scottsdale
Jarman, Beth S. *president FarSight group, author, former cabinet secretary, educator, consultant*

Tucson
Basefsky, Mitchell *public information officer*

ARKANSAS

Little Rock
Franks, Candace Ann *state banking agency administrator*
Halverson, Paul Kenneth *state agency administrator, public health service officer*

CALIFORNIA

Alpine
Oliverio, Ponzio *protective services official, educator*

Arroyo Grande
Willis, Ralph Walker *retired firefighter*

Bakersfield
Bernard, Alexander *protective services official*

Canyon Country
Catalani, Richard William *forensic specialist, writer*

Cardiff
Juskalian, Lee J. *former government official*

Carlsbad
Stenbit, John Paul *former federal agency administrator*

El Monte
Last, Marian Helen *public administration*

Fowler
Bowman, Joseph Paul *protective services official, writer, retired military officer*

Irvine
Hansen, William D. *former federal agency administrator*

La Jolla
Whaley, Storm Hammond *retired federal agency administrator*

Los Angeles
Bratton, Bill (William Joseph Bratton) *police chief*

Norco
McNeal, Phyllis Paulette *parole agent*

Sacramento
Belshé, Kimberly *state agency administrator, public health service officer*
Bornstein, Julie Ilene *state agency administrator*
Horton, Mark B. *state agency administrator, public health service officer*
Marin, Rosario *state agency administrator, former federal agency administrator*
Maxwell-Jolly, David *state agency administrator, public health service officer*
Myrrdin, Terry A. *state agency administrator*
Roberts, Paul Dale *state agency administrator, writer*

San Diego
Jarman, Tracy *fire chief*
Urquhart, Bruce *government agency administrator, engineering educator*

San Francisco
Gascón, George *police chief*
Haraf, William S. *state banking agency administrator*
Tarnoff, Peter *federal agency administrator, consultant*
Trounson, Alan Osbourne *state agency administrator, embryologist*

Santa Clarita
Neunhoffer, Steven Charles *protective services official*

Westlake Village
Seymour, Jeffrey Alan *governmental relations consultant*

COLORADO

Brighton
Wagner, Samuel Albin Mar *state agency administrator*

Centennial
Wilks, Dana Lyn *protective services official, writer*

Colorado Springs
Howard, Larry Bruce *forensic scientist*

Denver
Joseph, Fred J. *state banking agency administrator*
Mencer, Sue (Constance Suzanne Mencer) *former federal agency administrator*

Pueblo
Deasy, Irene M. *retired protective services official*

CONNECTICUT

Hartford
Galvin, J. Robert *state agency administrator, public health service officer*
Pitkin, Howard F. *state banking agency administrator*

Southbury
Foxworth, Johnnie Hunter *retired state agency administrator*

Suffield
Hanzalek, Astrid Teicher *public information officer, consultant*

DELAWARE

Dover
Britt, Maisha Dorrah *protective services official*
Danberg, Carl Christian *state agency administrator, former state attorney general*
Thomas Rattay, Karyl *state agency administrator, public health service officer*

DISTRICT OF COLUMBIA

Pentagon
Lynn, William James III *federal agency administrator*

Washington
Abbey, Robert Vernon (Bob Abbey) *federal agency administrator*
Adams, A. John Bertrand *public affairs consultant, director*
Adelstein, Jonathan Steven *federal agency administrator, former commissioner*
Ali, Russlynn *federal agency administrator*
Allison, Herbert Monroe, Jr. *federal agency administrator, former mortgage company executive*
Almquist, Katherine J. *federal agency administrator*
Alvillar-Speake, Theresa *federal agency administrator*
Ameri, Goli *federal agency administrator*
Aoki, Steven *federal agency administrator*
Appel, Peter H. *federal agency administrator*
Apple, Daina Dravnieks *federal agency administrator*
Ashley, Wiley Ross III *federal agency administrator*
Babbitt, Randy (Jerome Randolph Babbitt) *federal agency administrator, former pilot*
Bair, Sheila Colleen *federal agency administrator*
Baker, Roger W. *federal agency administrator*
Barofsky, Neil M. *federal agency administrator, former prosecutor*
Barr, Michael S. *federal agency administrator, law educator*
Barth, Richard C. *federal agency administrator*
Baruah, Sandy K. (Santanu Kumar Baruah) *former federal agency administrator*
Basham, W. Ralph *federal agency administrator*
Bateman, Paul William *federal agency administrator*
Beach, Gineen Bresso *federal agency administrator*
Beck, Andrew C. *federal agency administrator*
Becker, David M. *federal agency administrator, lawyer*
Beers, Rand *federal agency administrator, former think-tank executive*
Benjamin, Daniel *federal agency administrator*
Bernstock, Robert F. *postal service executive*
Berry, Matthew *federal agency administrator*
Birnbaum, S. Elizabeth (Liz Birnbaum) *federal agency administrator, lawyer*
Blake, Robert Orris, Jr. *federal agency administrator*
Bohigian, David Steele *federal agency administrator*
Bolden, Charles Frank, Jr. *federal agency administrator, retired astronaut, retired military officer*
Bomar, Mary Amelia *federal agency administrator*
Bonicelli, Paul J. *federal agency administrator*
Borzi, Phyllis Corinne *federal agency administrator*
Bostic, Raphael William *federal agency administrator, educator*
Boswell, Eric J. *federal agency administrator*
Bowman, John E. *federal agency administrator*
Boyd, April S. *federal agency administrator*
Brailer, David J. *federal agency administrator*
Branche, Christine M. *federal agency administrator, epidemiologist*
Brasseux, Barnaby L *federal agency administrator*
Brenner, Joel F. *federal agency administrator*
Breuer, Lanny Arthur *federal agency administrator, lawyer*
Bridges, Jerry *federal agency administrator, accountant*
Brimmer, Esther Diane *federal agency administrator*
Brinkman, William Frank *federal agency administrator, physicist*
Brown, Dana A. *federal agency administrator*
Brown, Harold *former United States Secretary of Defense*
Brown, Laurence G. *federal agency administrator, physician*
Brown, Mary Patrice *federal agency administrator*
Buck, Jennifer Cooney *federal agency administrator*
Burgess, Ronald L., Jr. *federal agency administrator, career military officer*
Burns, William Joseph *federal agency administrator, former ambassador*
Cabral, Anna Escobedo *former federal agency administrator*
Caliguiri, Laura M. *federal agency administrator*
Campbell, Kurt M. *federal agency administrator*
Carfine, Kenneth E., Jr. *federal agency administrator*
Carson, Johnnie *federal agency administrator, former ambassador*
Carter, Ashton Baldwin *federal agency administrator*
Caruso, Guy *federal agency administrator*
Castle, Anne *federal agency administrator, lawyer*
Chavarria, Adam *federal agency administrator*
Chellaraj, Rajkumar *federal agency administrator*
Chin, Curtis S. *federal agency administrator*
Christopherson, Charles (Chuck) Richard, Jr. *Sub Cabinet Official*
Chu, David S.C. *federal agency administrator, economist*
Chun, Shinae *federal agency administrator*
Ciccoella, Charles S. (Chick) *federal agency administrator*
Clapper, James R., Jr. *federal agency administrator, retired military officer*
Clark, John F. *federal agency administrator*
Cochran, Kelvin James *federal agency administrator*
Cohen, David S. *federal agency administrator, lawyer*
Connor, Chuck *federal agency administrator*
Connor, Michael Lee *federal agency administrator*
Corr, William V. (Bill Corr) *federal agency administrator, lobbyist*
Cox, John W. *federal agency administrator*
Cross, Gerald Marion *federal agency administrator*
Crowley, Philip J. (P.J. Crowley) *federal agency administrator*
Cruden, John Charles *federal agency administrator, lawyer*
Cunningham, Peter *federal agency administrator*
Curtin, Jeremy *federal agency administrator*
D'Agostino, Thomas Paul *federal agency administrator*
Daniels, Stephen M. *government official*
Davidson, Donetta Lea *federal agency commissioner, former state official*
Davis, Anselm G., Jr. *federal agency administrator*
Davis, Cameron *federal agency administrator, environmentalist*
Davis, Michele Aileen *federal agency administrator, former mortgage company executive*
de Baca, Luis C. *federal agency administrator*
DePass, Michelle J. *federal agency administrator*
Domenech, Edgar A. *federal agency administrator*
Donohue, Kenneth M. *federal agency administrator*
Downie, Richard Duncan *government agency administrator, retired military officer*
DuBester, Ernest William *federal agency administrator*
Duckworth, Tammy (Ladda Tammy Duckworth) *federal agency administrator, military officer*
Duffy, Michael F. *federal agency administrator*
Dugan, John Cunningham *federal agency administrator, lawyer*
Duke, Elaine Costanzo *federal agency administrator*
Dunn, Joseph A. *federal agency administrator*

Strickling, Lawrence E. (Larry Strickling) *federal agency administrator*
Suboleski, Stanley C. *federal agency administrator, mining engineer*
Suh, Rhea S. *federal agency administrator*
Sulick, Michael J. *federal agency administrator*
Sullivan, Mark J. *federal agency administrator*
Sumwalt, Robert Llewellyn III *federal agency administrator, pilot*
Sutton, William G., Jr., (Woody Sutton) *federal agency administrator, retired military officer*
Szabo, Joseph Clark *federal agency administrator*
Tangherlini, Daniel Mark *federal agency administrator*
Tauscher, Ellen O'Kane *federal agency administrator, former United States Representative from California*
Terpstra, A. Ellen *federal agency administrator*
Terry, James Philip *federal agency administrator*
Thorson, Eric Mines *federal agency administrator*
Tillman, Judith R. *federal agency administrator*
Tonsager, Dallas P. *federal agency administrator*
Trasviña, John David *federal agency administrator*
Triay, Inés R. *federal agency administrator*
Truscott, Carl Joseph *security firm executive, former federal agency administrator*
Tuerk, William F. *federal agency administrator, lawyer*
Varney, Christine Anne *federal agency administrator, lawyer*
Verma, Richard R. (Rahul Verma) *federal agency administrator, lawyer*
Verrilli, Donald B., Jr. *federal agency administrator, lawyer*
Vershbow, Alexander Russell (Sandy Vershbow) *federal agency administrator, former ambassador*
Vickers, Michael G. *federal agency administrator*
Vigilance, Pierre *state agency administrator, public health service officer*
Wahlquist, Brent T. *federal agency administrator*
Wallace, Kim N. *federal agency administrator*
Ward, Nancy L. *federal agency administrator*
Washington, Linda Jacobs *federal agency administrator*
Watson, Harlan L(eroy) *federal agency administrator, physicist, economist*
Webster, Douglas Wayne *federal agency administrator, management consultant*
Weich, Ronald Harris *federal agency administrator*
Weiner, Robert Stephen *federal agency administrator*
Weinstein, Kenneth N. *federal government administrator*
West, Tony (Derek Anthony West) *federal agency administrator, lawyer*
White, Scott *federal agency administrator*
Whiteside, Ruth A. *federal agency administrator*
Wieringa, Jeffrey A. *federal agency administrator, military officer*
Wilkinson, Winston *federal agency administrator, lawyer*
Williams, Aaron S. *federal agency administrator*
Williams, B. John, Jr. *retired federal agency administrator, lawyer*
Williams, Darlene F. *federal agency administrator*
Williams, James A. *federal agency administrator*
Wilson, John Silvanus, Jr. *federal agency administrator*
Wolanin, Thomas Richard *federal agency administrator, educator*
Wolff, Otto J. *federal agency administrator*
Wolin, Neal Steven *federal agency administrator*
Zarnikow, Eric R. *federal agency administrator*
Zinser, Todd J. *federal agency administrator*
Zoi, Catherine Radford (Cathy Zoi) *federal agency administrator*

FLORIDA

Fort Lauderdale
Carter Pereira, Claudine Renee *forensic specialist*

Fort Myers
Lounsbury, David Arthur *protective services official, educator*

Indian Rocks Beach
DeLucia, Gene Anthony *government administrator, computer company executive*

Jensen Beach
Peterson, David Frederick *retired government agency administrator*

Lake City
Gay, John Marion *retired federal agency administrator, financial analyst*

Lake Worth
Heessel, Eleanor Lucille Lea *retired state agency administrator*

Lakeland
Mahr, Aaron Lee *government agency administrator*

Largo
Hasen-Sinz, Susan Katherine *state agency administrator, actress*

Lithia
Richmond, Nancy Mason *retired state agency administrator*

Miami
Thorpe, Marion Dennis, Jr. *former state agency administrator*

North Miami
Plotkin, Sharon Lee *protective services official, educator*

Palm Coast
Swinburn, Carol Ditzler *retired state and municipal agency administrator*

Saint Petersburg
Bruni, Joseph Vincent, Jr. *protective services official, educator*

Tallahassee
Charity, Linda B. *state banking agency administrator*
Viamonte Ros, Ana M. *state agency administrator, public health service officer*

GEORGIA

Atlanta
Aiken, Vernoy Fred *government agency administrator*
Braswell, Robert M. *state banking agency administrator*
Donis, Ruben *federal agency administrator, researcher, virologist*
Ford, Sandra Elizabeth *state agency administrator, public health service officer*
Mecke, William Moyn *public information officer*
Medows, Rhonda M. *state agency administrator, public health service officer*
Schuchat, Anne *federal agency administrator*
Toomey, Kathleen Elizabeth *federal agency administrator*

Brunswick
Patrick, Connie L. *federal agency administrator*

Kennesaw
Paterson, Paul Charles *retired private investigator, security consultant*

Peachtree City
Ebneter, Stewart Dwight *utility industry management consultant*

Saint Simons Island
Williamson, Richard Hall *federal agency administrator*

HAWAII

Honolulu
Chapman, Duane Lee (Dog Chapman) *bail enforcement agent, television personality*
Fukino, Chiyome Leinaala *state agency administrator, public health service officer*
Griffin, Dominic B. III *state banking agency administrator*
Keogh, Richard John *firearms and explosives consultant*
Saiki, Patricia *federal agency administrator, congressman*

Mililani
Hunkele, Lester Martin III *retired federal agency administrator*

IDAHO

Boise
Armstrong, Richard *state agency administrator*

Idaho Falls
Rydalch, Ann *federal agency administrator, former state senator*

Ketchum
Nalen, Craig Anthony *federal agency administrator*

ILLINOIS

Chicago
Dart, Thomas J. *protective services official*
Weis, Jody P. (J.P. Weis) *police superintendent*

Flora
Shrum, John *equal rights officer*

Naperville
Nash, Donald Gene *retired federal investigator, economist*

Northlake
Haack, Richard Wilson *retired police officer*

Park Forest
Wheeler, Michael Joseph *protective services official, educator*

Springfield
Arnold, Damon Theodore *state agency administrator, public health service officer*
Schroeder, Joyce Katherine *state agency administrator, research analyst*
Solis, Jorge A. *state banking agency administrator*

INDIANA

Indianapolis
Gerdes, Ralph Donald *fire safety consultant*
Monroe, Judith A. *state agency administrator, public health service officer*
Ripley, Judith G. *state banking agency administrator*

South Bend
Hellyer, Timothy Michael *protective services officer*

West Lafayette
Geddes, Leslie Alexander *forensic engineer, educator, physiologist*

IOWA

Des Moines
Brickman, Kenneth Alan *state agency administrator*
Gronstal, Thomas B. *state banking agency administrator*
Nelson, Charlotte Bowers *retired public administrator*
Newton, Thomas *state agency administrator, public health service officer*

KANSAS

Topeka
Eberhart-Phillips, Jason *state agency administrator, public health service officer*
Thull, Tom (John Thomas Thull) *state banking agency administrator*

KENTUCKY

Frankfort
Hacker, William D. *state agency administrator, public health service officer*
Vice, Charles A. *state banking agency administrator*

Lexington
Calvert, C. Emmett *former state agency administrator*

Louisville
Adams, Robert Waugh *retired state agency administrator, economist, educator*

Madisonville
Veazey, Doris Anne *retired state agency administrator*

LOUISIANA

Alexandria
Phillips, Virginia *retired federal employee*

Baton Rouge
Ducrest, John P. *state banking agency administrator*
Levine, Alan *state agency administrator*
Parks, James William, II, *public facilities executive, lawyer*

New Orleans
Collins, Harry David *forensic, mechanical and nuclear engineer, claims consultant*

MAINE

Augusta
Harvey, Brenda M. *state agency administrator*
LaFountain, Lloyd P. III *state banking agency administrator*

MARYLAND

Baltimore
Abrams, Rosalie Silber *retired state agency official*
Bealefeld, Frederick Henry III *police commissioner*
Colmers, John M. *state agency administrator*
Crawford, Fred Lee *public information officer*
Koch, Edgar Frank *protective services official*
Mann, Cindy *federal agency administrator, healthcare educator*
O'Carroll, Patrick P., Jr. *federal agency administrator*
Raskin, Sarah Bloom *state banking agency administrator, lawyer*
Sharfstein, Joshua Moses *federal agency administrator, pediatrician*
Zerhouni, Elias Adam *former federal agency administrator, radiologist*

Bel Air
O'Bryon, James Fredrick *defense consultant*

Beltsville
Tso, Tien Chioh *federal agency administrator, agronomist, researcher*

Bethesda
Adler, Robert S. *federal agency administrator*
Aldridge, Edward Cleveland, Jr., (Pete Aldridge) *former federal agency administrator*
Alexander, Duane Frederick *federal agency administrator, pediatrician, researcher*
Alving, Barbara *federal agency administrator, hematologist*
Bachrach, Christine A. *federal agency administrator*
Battey, James F., Jr. *federal agency administrator, neurologist*
Berg, Jeremy Mark *federal agency administrator, biochemist, researcher*
Buscher, Leo F., Jr. *federal agency administrator*
Collins, Francis Sellers *federal agency administrator, geneticist*
Doroshow, James Halpern *federal agency administrator, oncologist*
Fauci, Anthony Stephen *federal agency administrator, allergist, immunologist*
Fraumeni, Joseph Francis, Jr. *federal agency administrator, epidemiologist*
Gallin, John I. *federal agency administrator, medical researcher*
Glass, Roger I. *federal agency administrator, research scientist*
Gottesman, Michael Marc *federal agency administrator, biomedical researcher*
Gottesman, Susan *federal agency administrator*
Grady, Patricia A. *federal agency administrator*
Greenwald, Peter *federal agency administrator, cancer prevention physician, epidemiologist, researcher*
Guttmacher, Alan Edward *federal agency administrator, physician, educator*
Haseltine, Florence Pat *federal agency administrator, gynecologist, obstetrician*
Hodes, Richard J. *federal agency administrator, immunologist, researcher*
Hrynkow, Sharon Hemond *federal agency administrator, neuroscientist, researcher*
Insel, Thomas R. *federal agency administrator, psychiatrist*
Jones, Jack F. (John Franklin Jones Jr.) *federal agency administrator*
Joyce, Bernita Anne *retired federal agency administrator*
Katz, Stephen Ira *federal agency administrator*
Kington, Raynard Stuart *federal agency administrator*
Kirschstein, Ruth Lillian *federal agency administrator, retired physician*
Kramer, Barnett Sheldon *federal agency administrator, oncologist*
Landis, Story Cleland *federal agency administrator, neurobiologist*
Lindberg, Donald Allan Bror *federal agency administrator, library director, pathologist*
Morgan, John Davis *government agency administrator, consultant*
Murrett, Robert B. *federal agency administrator, career military officer*
Nabel, Elizabeth Guenthner *federal agency administrator, cardiologist, researcher*
Niederhuber, John Edward *federal agency administrator*
Penn, Audrey S. *federal agency administrator*
Pettigrew, Roderic I. *federal agency administrator, radiologist, researcher*
Pinn, Vivian W. *federal agency administrator, pathologist*
Rabson, Alan Saul *federal agency administrator, pathologist, educator*
Richardson, John *retired international relations executive*
Rockey, Sally Jean *federal agency administrator*
Rodgers, Griffin Platt *federal agency administrator, researcher*
Ruffin, John *federal agency administrator, researcher*
Ruiz Bravo, Norka *federal agency administrator*
Scarpa, Antonio *federal agency administrator, physiologist, medical educator*
Sieving, Paul A. *federal agency administrator, ophthalmologist, educator*
Singer, Dinah S. *federal agency administrator, immunologist, researcher*
Stover, Ellen L. *federal agency administrator, health scientist*
Tabak, Lawrence A. *federal agency administrator, dentist*
Tenenbaum, Inez Moore *federal agency administrator, former school system administrator*
Volkow, Nora Dolores *federal agency administrator, medical researcher*
Warren, Kenneth R. *federal agency administrator*
Wellems, Thomas E. *federal agency administrator*
Wiltrout, Robert H. *federal agency administrator, medical researcher*

Chevy Chase
Broide, Mace Irwin *public information officer*

Clinton
Sander, Clarence Ellis, Jr. *retired protective services official*

College Park
Sundlof, Stephen Frederick *federal agency administrator, veterinarian*

Columbia
Young, Donald Alan *former Federal Agency Administrator*

Fort George G Meade
Alexander, Keith B. *federal agency administrator, career military officer*

Gaithersburg
Decker, Amy *forensic specialist, researcher*
Hertz, Harry Steven *government official*

Hanover
DeLeaver, Douglas *retired protective services official, telecommunications industry executive, Law Enforcement Association Administrator*

Kensington
Rosenthal, Alan Sayre *government official, lawyer*
Suraci, Charles Xavier, Jr. *retired federal agency administrator, air transportation executive, consultant*

La Plata
Martino, Paula L. *government agency administrator, art historian, educator*

Madison
Hoffman, Alicia Coro *retired federal executive*

Rockville
Barros, Colleen *federal agency administrator*
Clark, Harry Westley *federal agency administrator*
Cline, Terry L. *federal agency administrator*
Davis, Beverly Watts *federal agency administrator*
Duke, Elizabeth M. *federal agency administrator*
Dunham, Bernadette Margaret *federal agency administrator, veterinarian*
Garcia, Gregory T. (Greg Garcia) *federal agency administrator*
Gray, Paulette Styles *federal agency administrator, biologist*
Jaczko, Gregory Bela *federal agency administrator, physicist*

Johnson, Lenora *federal agency administrator, public health service officer*
McLellan, Thomas (Andrew Thomas McLellan) *federal agency administrator, psychology professor*
Power, A. Kathryn *federal agency administrator*
Telesetsky, Walter *federal agency administrator*
Torti, Frank Michael *federal agency administrator*
van Dyck, Peter Cuyler *federal agency administrator*
Whitescarver, Jack Edward *federal agency administrator*
Williams, Robert C. *federal agency administrator*
Woodcock, Janet *federal agency administrator*

Silver Spring
de Zafra Atwell, Dorothea Elizabeth *retired government agency administrator*
Dunnigan, John H. *federal agency administrator*
Ganley, Charles James *federal agency administrator, internist*
Hamburg, Margaret Ann (Peggy Hamburg) *federal agency administrator, former public health administrator*
Kline, Jerry Robert *retired administrative judge, ecologist*
Maas, Joe (Melvin Joseph Maas) *retired federal agency administrator*
Mathis, Lisa *federal agency administrator*
Mlay, Marian *retired government official*
Pollock, Martin L. *state agency administrator*
Spinrad, Richard William *federal agency administrator, oceanographer*
Ware, Thaddeus Van *retired government official*
Williams, Paul *retired federal agency administrator*

Upper Marlboro
Bune, Karen Louise *state agency administrator, legal assistant*

Woodbine
Uhl, Scott Mark *retired state agency administrator, consultant*

MASSACHUSETTS

Boston
Antonakes, Steven L. *state banking agency administrator*
Auerbach, John M. *state agency administrator, public health service officer*
Crimlisk, Jane Therese *probation officer*
Truta, Ioan *protective services official*

Cambridge
Dobriansky, Paula Jon *former federal agency administrator*
Donahue, John David *federal agency administrator, educator*
Hunt, Swanee Grace *public policy educator, former ambassador*
Mowatt-Larssen, Rolf *former federal agency administrator*
Tobey, William Hayward *former federal agency administrator*

Chatham
O'Connell, Brian *community organizer, educator, writer*

Watertown
Tompkins, Curtis Johnston *government agency administrator*

West Boylston
Perron, William Francis *retired protective services official*

MICHIGAN

Ann Arbor
Bierbaum, Rosina M. *federal agency administrator*

Detroit
Moss, Leslie Otha *homeland security specialist*

Lansing
Couto, C. Douglass *state agency administrator*
Olszewski, Janet *state agency administrator, public health service officer*
Ross, Ken *state banking agency administrator*

Midland
Adams, Thomas Walton *corrections official*

Muskegon
Ohst, Wendy Joan *government agency administrator, educator*

MINNESOTA

Elk River
Richardson, Mark P. *protective services official, educator*

Saint Paul
Magnan, Sanne *state agency administrator, public health service officer*
Murphy, Kevin M. *state banking agency administrator*

MISSISSIPPI

Jackson
Allison, John S. *state banking agency administrator*
Thompson, Ed *state agency administrator, public health service officer, epidemiologist, educator*

MISSOURI

Anderson
Coble, Mary Gloria *protective services official, rancher*

Brighton
Copus, Phyllis Lee *retired federal agency administrator*

Fort Leonard Wood
Collins, Pamela Marie *forensic specialist, educator*

Jefferson City
Donnelly, Margaret T. *state agency administrator, public health service officer, former state legislator*
Tackett, Natalie Jane *state administrator*
Weaver, Richard J. *state banking agency administrator*

Kansas City
Reynolds, Jerry (Gerald A. Reynolds) *federal agency administrator*

Saint Louis
Brown, Theodis (Ted), Sr. *fire chief*
King, Joseph, Jr. *federal agency administrator*

MONTANA

Helena
Goodwin, Annie M. *state banking agency administrator*
Whiting-Sorrell, Anna *state agency administrator*

Miles City
Coffman, Richard C. *retired protective services official*

NEBRASKA

Lincoln
Munn, John *state banking agency administrator*

Omaha
Bang, Michele Alene *protective services official*
Mactier, Ann Dickinson *state agency administrator*

NEVADA

Carson City
Whitley, Richard *state agency administrator*

Las Vegas
Burns, George E. *state banking agency administrator*
Smith, Jimmy Wayne, Sr. *forensic specialist*

Reno
Svahn, John Alfred *federal agency administrator*

NEW HAMPSHIRE

Concord
Cooney, Mary Ann *state agency administrator, public health service officer, community health nurse*
Hildreth, Peter C. *state banking agency administrator*
Mevers, Frank Clement *state agency administrator, archivist*
Montero, José Thier *state agency administrator, public health service officer*

Hanover
Koop, C. Everett (Charles Everett Koop) *former Surgeon General of the United States, educator*

NEW JERSEY

Brookside
Fairchild, Samuel Wilson *retired federal agency administrator, manufacturing and financial services executive*

East Rutherford
Robinson, Dennis R. *state agency administrator*

Fort Monmouth
Poulos, Andrew, Jr. *protective services official, director*

Montclair
Straten, Roland *retired protective services company executive*

Mount Holly
Chatzidakis, Larry *state agency administrator, former state legislator*

New Brunswick
Coscia, Anthony R. *state agency administrator, lawyer*

Princeton
McGowan, Angela Kay *public information officer*

Springfield
Weigele, Richard Sayre *police officer*

Tabernacle
DiBella, Russell Thomas *federal investigator*

Trenton
Howard, Heather *state agency administrator*
Jasey, Neil N. *state banking agency administrator, retired lawyer*

NEW MEXICO

Albuquerque
Jaramillo, Mari-Luci *retired federal agency administrator*
Varela, Alan Mark *state agency administrator, lawyer*
White, Darren P. *protective services official*

Las Cruces
Wedel, Voleen *police official*

Santa Fe
Verant, William J. *state banking agency administrator*
Vigil, Alfredo *state agency administrator*

NEW YORK

Albany
Bradley, Edward James *state official, computer programmer and analyst*
Menges, Susan Debra Favreau *retired protective services official, management consultant*

Chappaqua
Laun, Louis Frederick *government official*

Garden City
Laureano, Mari *government agency administrator, writer*

Jamaica
Reitnauer, Andrew Richard *forensic specialist*

Liverpool
Naum, Christopher John *fire protection, emergency management, training consultant, educator, firefighter safety advocate*

New York
Beausoleil, Doris Mae *retired federal agency housing specialist*
Falkenrath, Richard A. *protective services official*
Falt, Eric *government agency administrator*
Kelly, Raymond Walter *police commissioner*
Kirschner, Stuart Martin *forensic specialist, psychology professor*
Levin, Susan Bass *state agency administrator, lawyer*
Neiman, Richard H. *state banking agency administrator*
Noble, Ronald Kenneth *secretary general of Interpol*
Pack, Sandy (Sandra Lee Pack) *former federal agency administrator*
Rosenker, Mark Victor *former federal agency administrator*
Sheehan, Michael Andrew *former protective services official, former federal agency administrator*
Sorensen, Gillian Martin *United Nations official*
Talbot, Phillips *retired Asian affairs specialist*

Peekskill
Lalor, Kieran *protective services official*

Rochester
McCarthy, Michael E. *protective services official, director*
Phillips, Harold John III *protective services official, consultant*

Romulus
Ostrander, Robert Edwin *retired United Nations interregional advisor, petroleum company executive*

NORTH CAROLINA

Asheville
Ter Horst, Jerald Franklin *public affairs counselor, former White House press secretary*

Canton
Roberts, Bill Glen *retired protective services official*

Chapel Hill
Umminger, Bruce Lynn *government agency administrator, research scientist, educator, consultant*

Durham
Birnbaum, Linda S. *federal agency administrator, toxicologist*

Elizabeth City
Williams, Rita Carroll *protective services official, language educator, poet, librarian*

Moyock
Prince, Erik D. *protective services company executive*

Pinehurst
Denton, Estelle Rosemary *retired federal agency administrator*

Raleigh
Dornan, John Neill *public policy center professional*
Engel, Jeffrey P. *state agency administrator, public health service officer*
Freeman, Franklin Edward, Jr. *government agency administrator*
Smith, Joseph A., Jr. *state banking agency administrator*

NORTH DAKOTA

Bismarck
Dwelle, Terry *state agency administrator, public health service officer*
Karsky, Timothy J. *state banking agency administrator*

OHIO

Cleveland
Jettke, Harry Jerome *retired government official*

Columbus
Gillmor, Karen Lako *state agency administrator, state legislator*
Jackson, Alvin D. *state agency administrator, public health service officer*
Moncrief, Jacqueline C. *retired state agency administrator*
Reardon, John B. III *state banking agency administrator*

Delaware
Ciochetty, John Bryan *protective services official*

Dillonvale
Stobbs, Richard D. (Dick Stobbs) *protective services official*

Euclid
Ramsey, Charles *retired government agency administrator*

Independence
Grabow, Raymond John *mayor, lawyer*

Mount Vernon
Dailey, Fred L. *former state agency administrator*

North Canton
Dishong, Morris William *forensic specialist, nurse*

OKLAHOMA

Oklahoma City
McElvany, Rocky *state agency administrator*
Thompson, Mick *state banking agency administrator*

Wagoner
Hadley, Charline A. *protective services official*

OREGON

Portland
Kohn, Melvin A. *state agency administrator, public health service officer*

Salem
Tatman, David C. *state banking agency administrator*

PENNSYLVANIA

Easton
McConlogue, Terence R. *protective services official*

Gettysburg
Roach, James Clark *retired federal agency administrator*

Harrisburg
Gilhooley, Antoinette (Toni Gilhooley) *retired protective services official*
James, Everette *state agency administrator*
Kaplan, Steven *state banking agency administrator*
Reider, Victoria A. *state banking agency administrator*

Philadelphia
Akiyama, Cliff *forensic science educator, criminologist, researcher, gang specialist, consultant*
Emmett, Edward Anthony *medical practitioner, government executive*
Morisey, A. Alexander *government agency administrator*
Ramsey, Charles H. *police commissioner*

Unionville
De Marino, Donald Nicholson *federal agency administrator, diversified financial services company executive*

West Chester
Carter, Shawn David *protective services official*

RHODE ISLAND

Cranston
Cayouette, Steven L. *state banking agency administrator*

Providence
Gifford, David R. *state agency administrator, geriatrician*

Warren
Hedlund, Ellen Louise *administrator, educator*

SOUTH CAROLINA

Columbia
Hunter, C. Earl *state agency administrator, environmental services administrator*

Jacobs, Louie A. *state banking agency administrator*
Lloyd, Reginald Ivan *state agency administrator, former prosecutor*

SOUTH DAKOTA

Pierre
Hollingsworth, Doneen B. *state agency administrator*
Novotny, Roger *state banking agency administrator*

TENNESSEE

Chattanooga
Easter, Anthony James *protective services official, educator*

Johnson City
Freeman, Michael Byron *protective services official, consultant*

Mount Juliet
Chester, Thomas Wayne *state agency administrator*

Nashville
Cooper, Susan R. *state agency administrator*
Gonzales, Greg *state banking agency administrator*
Smith, Donnie Kay *state agency administrator, retired military officer*

TEXAS

Austin
Ashworth, Kenneth Hayden *public information administrator*
Cooper, Charles G. *state banking agency administrator*
Lakey, David L. *state agency administrator*

Beaumont
Lyons, Wilburn Franklin *college instructor, department chairman*

Dallas
Jackson, Jewel *retired state agency administrator*

Duncanville
Fewel, John Gerrard *government agency administrator, director*

San Antonio
Welch, Billy E. *retired government agency administrator, management consultant*

Tyler
Johnson, Thomas Allen *protective services official, educator*

Wharton
Maxfield, Rose Mary *retired government official*

UTAH

Salt Lake City
Leary, G. Edward *state banking agency administrator*
Sundwall, David N. *state agency administrator, public health service officer*

VERMONT

Burlington
Davis, Wendy Sue *state agency administrator, public health service officer*

Montpelier
Thabault, Paulette J. *state banking agency administrator*

Springfield
Putnam, Paul Adin *federal agency administrator*

VIRGINIA

Alexandria
Bynum, Gayela A. *public information officer*
Fryzel, Michael E. *federal agency administrator, lawyer*
Hark, William Henry *retired federal agency administrator, aerospace physician*
Hood, Rodney Eugene *federal agency administrator*
Hughes, Grace-Flores *federal agency administrator*
Hyland, Gigi (Christiane Hyland) *federal agency administrator*
Kappos, David J. *federal agency administrator*
Lang, William George, IV, *public policy administrator*
Leestma, Robert *retired federal agency and educational association administrator*
Leonhart, Michele Marie *federal agency administrator*

Annandale
Christianson, Geryld B. *government agency administrator, consultant*

Arlington
Baginski, Maureen A. *former federal agency administrator*
Covington, James Edwin *government agency administrator, psychologist*
Garcia, Eugene Ernest *federal agency administrator*
Harrison, Virginia M. *federal agency administrator*
McDonald, Bernard Robert *retired federal agency administrator*
Moore, Guy Will *retired public information officer, historian, writer*
Rossides, Gale D. *federal agency administrator*
Stickler, Richard E. *federal agency administrator*
Stoner, John Richard *federal agency administrator*
Walther, Larry Woodrow *federal agency administrator*

Ashburn
Harting, Harry Lloyd, Jr. *retired government agency administrator, military officer*

Chantilly
Large, Scott F. *federal agency administrator*

Charlottesville
Roseberry, Edwin Southall *retired state agency administrator*

Fairfax
Jones, George Fleming *international consultant*

Falls Church
Rooney, Kevin Davitt *federal agency administrator*

Fort Belvoir
Tegnelia, James A. *federal agency administrator*
Thompson, Alan S. *federal agency administrator, military officer*

Fort Lee
Sakowitz, Philip E. *federal agency administrator*

Great Falls
Turner, Stansfield *former CIA director, retired military officer*

Hampton
Roe, Lesa B. *federal agency administrator*

Keswick
Frazier, Henry Bowen III *retired federal agency administrator*

Mc Lean
Cannon, Mark Wilcox *retired government official*
Doyle, Frederick Joseph *retired government research scientist*
Mahan, Clarence *federal agency administrator, writer*
Malley, Raymond Charles *retired foreign service official, industrial executive*
Strom, Leland A. *federal agency administrator*
Thernstrom, Abigail *federal agency administrator, writer*

Mineral
Donald, James Robert *federal agency administrator, writer, economist*

Oakton
Entzminger, John Nelson, Jr. *federal agency administrator, electrical engineer*

Reston
Rosendhal, Jeffrey David *federal agency administrator, educator, astronomer, consultant*

Richmond
Blake, Peter A. *state agency administrator*
Face, E. Joseph, Jr. *state banking agency administrator*
Remley, Karen *state agency administrator, public health service officer*

Spotsylvania
Hill, Jimmie Dale *retired federal agency administrator*

Springfield
Herbst, Ellen *federal agency administrator*

Williamsburg
Gentry, James William *retired state agency administrator*
Towle, Leland Hill *retired federal agency administrator*

WASHINGTON

Gig Harbor
Meacham, Charles Harding *federal agency administrator*

Marysville
Bart, Rick *retired protective services official*

Olympia
Jarvis, Scott *state banking agency administrator*
Selecky, Mary C. *state agency administrator*

Poulsbo
Romaine, Grant Hirsch *retired protective services official*

Seattle
Krochalis, Richard F. *federal agency administrator*

Sequim
Huntley, James Robert *government official, international affairs scholar*

Vancouver
Ogden, Daniel Miller, Jr. *public official, educator*

WEST VIRGINIA

Charleston
Cline, Sara McLaughlin *state banking agency administrator*
Curtis, Chris *state agency administrator*
Walker, Martha Yeager *state agency administrator, former state senator*

Parkersburg
Zeck, Van *federal agency administrator*

WISCONSIN

Madison
Foldy, Seth Leonard *state agency administrator, public health officer, physician, educator*
Keating Heinemann, Lorrie T. *state banking agency administrator*

Sturtevant
Marschke, Sean M. *chief of police, emergency management director*

WYOMING

Cheyenne
Sherard, Brent D. *state agency administrator, physician*
Vogel, Jeffrey C. *state banking agency administrator*

TERRITORIES OF THE UNITED STATES

AMERICAN SAMOA

Pago Pago
Laumoli, Tuiasina Salamo *state agency administrator, public health service officer*

FEDERATED STATES OF MICRONESIA

Pohnpei
Akapito Skilling, Vita *state agency administrator*

GUAM

Barrigada
Ilagan, Artemio B. *territorial banking agency administrator*

Mangilao
Roberto, J. Peter *state agency administrator*

NORTHERN MARIANA ISLANDS

Saipan
Villagomez, Joseph K. *state agency administrator, public health service officer*

PUERTO RICO

San Juan
Padilla, Alfredo *territorial banking agency administrator*
Rivera-Dueño, Jamie *state agency administrator, public health service officer*

VIRGIN ISLANDS

St Thomas
Sheen-Aaron, Julia *state agency administrator, public health service officer*

MILITARY ADDRESSES OF THE UNITED STATES

EUROPE

APO
Carner, George *foreign service executive, economic strategist*

CANADA

BRITISH COLUMBIA

Kelowna
Basdeo, Sahadeo *government official, educator, politician*

NEWFOUNDLAND AND LABRADOR

Saint John's
Crosbie, John Carnell *retired Canadian government official, university administrator, lawyer*

ONTARIO

Markham
Tsubouchi, David H. *Canadian provincial official*

Ottawa
MacFarlane, John Alexander *retired federal agency administrator*

Toronto
Fraser, William Neil *retired government agency administrator*
Macdonald, Donald Stovel *public policy advisor*

GERMANY

Wyk-Wrixum
Friese, Brigitte *federal agency administrator*

SUDAN

Malakal
Wieu, Andrew W. Riang *government agency administrator*

ADDRESS UNPUBLISHED

Aamodt, Roger Louis *retired federal agency administrator*
Adams, Timothy D. *former federal agency administrator*
Adcock, Robert H., Jr., (Bunny Adcock) *former state banking agency administrator*
Allred, Stephen (Coral Stephen Allred) *former federal agency administrator*
Anderson, Wayne Carl *global public affairs officer, retired corporate executive*
Andrade, Joel T. *forensic specialist*
Arsht, Leslye Alene *retired federal agency administrator*
Baker, Gary Anthony *police officer and supervisor*
Baker, Jimmy H. *former state finance administrator*
Baker, Stewart Abercrombie *former federal agency administrator, lawyer*
Baquet, Charles R. III *former federal agency administrator, international studies educator*
Barnett, Patricia Ann *development professional*
Bell, Jack *federal agency administrator*
Benkert, Joseph A. *former federal agency administrator*
Bishop, C. Diane *state agency administrator, educator*
Blank, Rebecca Margaret *federal agency administrator, economist*
Boswell, Vivian Nicholson *protective services official*
Boucher, Richard A. *former federal agency administrator*
Brand, Rachel Lee *former federal agency administrator, lawyer*
Braswell, Jackie Boyd *state agency administrator*
Brown, Dale Susan *retired federal agency administrator, website manager, keynote speaker*
Brubaker, Crawford Francis, Jr. *federal agency administrator, aerospace scientist, consultant*
Bush, Frederick Morris *former federal agency administrator*
Cade, Gregory Brian *fireman, former federal agency administrator*
Cambone, Stephen Anthony *former federal agency administrator*
Campbell, Arthur Andrews *retired federal agency administrator*
Cantu, Jose Francisco *retired postal worker*
Capka, J. Richard (Joseph Richard Capka) *former federal agency administrator, retired military officer*
Chapman, Richard LeRoy *public affairs researcher*
Chealander, Steven Russell *former federal agency administrator*
Christie, Thomas Philip *former federal agency administrator*
Clark, Michell C. *former federal agency administrator*
Claytor, Richard Anderson *retired federal agency administrator*
Conner, Chuck (Charles F. Conner) *former federal agency administrator*
Conway, John Thomas *federal agency administrator, lawyer, engineer*
Crossley, Nancy Ruth *retired federal agency administrator*
Crowell, Craven H., Jr. *retired federal agency administrator*
Crumpton, Henry A. (Hank Crumpton) *former federal agency administrator*
Curie, Charles G. *former federal agency administrator*
Dailey, Dell Lee *former federal agency administrator, retired military officer*
Dale, Shana Leigh *former federal agency administrator*
Danzig, Richard Jeffrey *former federal agency administrator*
Dewey, Arthur Eugene *former federal agency administrator*
Doan, Lurita Alexis *former federal agency administrator*
Dominguez, Michael L. *federal agency administrator, former civilian military employee*
Edelman, Eric Steven *former federal agency administrator, former ambassador*
England, Gordon Richard *former federal agency administrator*
Farris, Ronald M. *retired intelligence officer*
Faulkner, Frances Mayhew *retired federal agency administrator*
Fort, Randall Martin *corporate executive*
Friday, Elbert Walter, Jr. *federal agency administrator, meteorologist*
Gaddy, Sidney Warren *government agency administrator*
Garman, David Kline *former federal agency administrator*

Gerberding, Julie Louise *former federal agency administrator*
Gioconda, Thomas F. *program manager, retired military officer*
Glassman, Cynthia Aaron *former federal agency administrator*
Glassman, James Kenneth *former federal agency administrator*
Gleichman, John Alan *protective services expert*
Goss, Porter Johnston *former CIA director, retired United States Representative from Florida*
Gregory, Frederick Drew *retired federal agency administrator*
Griffin, Richard J. *federal agency administrator*
Grim, Charles W. *former federal agency administrator*
Gurgulino de Souza, Heitor *government organization consultant*
Hall, Dale (Henry Dale Hall) *former federal agency administrator*
Harris, Stephanie L. *Government Agency Secretary*
Harvey, Thomas Edward *former federal agency administrator*
Hayes, Paula Freda *federal agency administrator*
Heyman, Ira Michael *federal agency administrator, law educator, museum executive*
Higgins, Kathryn O'Leary (Kitty Higgins) *former federal agency administrator, former consulting firm executive*
Hodel, Donald Paul *former United States Secretary of the Interior*
Hodsoll, Francis Samuel Monaise *government official*
Howard, Karrelldo J. *protective services official*
James, Randall S. *former state banking agency administrator*
Jameson, Patricia Marian *government agency administrator*
Jeffery, Michael *retired government agency administrator*
Jiler, Linda Cerise *retired fire and aviation program support specialist, fire emergency dispatcher, consultant, researcher, writer*
Johnson, Carl Thor *former federal agency administrator*
Johnson, David L. *federal agency administrator, retired military officer*
Johnson, Stephen L. *former federal agency administrator*
Joseph, Robert G. *former federal agency administrator*
Kearns, Merle Grace *state agency administrator*
Keenum, Mark Everett *former federal agency administrator*
Kernan, Barbara Desind *government agency administrator*
Keys, John W. III *former federal agency administrator*
Kimmitt, Mark (Mark Traecey Patrick Kimmitt) *former federal agency administrator, retired military officer*
Kincannon, Charles Louis (Louis Kincannon) *retired federal agency administrator*
Krieg, Kenneth Joseph *former federal agency administrator*
Krongard, Howard J. *former federal agency administrator, lawyer*
Kusserow, Richard Phillip *federal agency administrator, corporate financial executive*
Kutscher, Ronald Earl *retired federal agency administrator*
Lautenbacher, Conrad Charles, Jr. *former federal agency administrator, retired naval officer*
Laverty, Lyle (Robert Lyle Laverty) *former federal agency administrator*
Leonard, Bill (John William Leonard) *former federal agency administrator*
Leos, Kathleen *former federal agency administrator*
Lewis, Samuel Winfield *retired federal agency administrator, diplomat*
Li, Ting-Kai *retired federal agency administrator, biologist*
Lovell, Malcolm Read, Jr. *public information officer, educator, retired trade association administrator, federal official*
Luthi, Randall B. *former federal agency administrator*
Maco, Paul Stephen *securities and exchange administrator*
Mainella, Fran (Frances P. Mainella) *educator, former federal agency administrator*
Mansfield, Gordon Hall *former federal agency administrator*
McClain, Lena Alexandria *protective services official*
McCormack, Sean Ian *former federal agency administrator*
McCormick, Robert Junior *former federal agency administrator*
McLaughlin, John Edward *former federal agency administrator*
McLean, Walter Franklin *government agency administrator, business consultant, legislator, minister*
McManus, William Paul *police chief*
McSwain, Robert G. *former federal agency administrator*
McTaggart, Timothy Robert *state agency administrator, lawyer*
Middelhoek, André J. *retired international organization administrator, auditor*
Minners, Howard Alyn *federal agency administrator, researcher, preventive medicine physician*
Molholm, Kurt Nelson *retired federal agency administrator*
Molz, Redmond Kathleen *public affairs educator*
Murdock, Steven H. *former federal agency administrator*
Neal, Darwina Lee *retired federal agency administrator*
Negroponte, John Dimitri *former federal agency administrator, former Director of National Intelligence*
Nolan, Jeanada H. *retired state agency administrator, social worker, educator*
O'Donnell, F. Scott *former state agency administrator*
Oliver, Jerry Alton *former police chief*
Padden, Anthony Aloysius, Jr. *retired federal government official*
Parron, Delores L. *retired federal agency administrator*
Patino, Douglas Xavier *academic foundation and government agency administrator*
Paulison, Robert David *former federal agency administrator*
Pearson, W(illiam) Robert *former federal agency administrator, former ambassador*
Pitofsky, Robert *federal agency administrator, law educator*
Quintana-Allenson, Ana M. *government agency executive*
Rascon, Alfred V. *former federal agency administrator*
Reich, John M. *former federal agency administrator*
Rodgers, Bruce Alan *government agency administrator, psychologist*
Roe, Mary Ann *retired postmaster*
Rosenberg, Alison P. *retired public policy officer*
Scarlett, Lynn (Patricia Lynn Scarlett) *former federal agency administrator*
Schoenberger, James Edwin *retired federal agency administrator*
Schrader, Dennis R. *former federal agency administrator*
Schultz, Daniel G. *former federal agency administrator*
Schwartz, Carol Levitt *government official*
Scoppetta, Nicholas *fire commissioner*
Shasteen, Donald Eugene *retired government official, small business consultant*
Shinn, James Joseph (Jim Shinn) *former federal agency administrator*
Shorris, Anthony Ernest *former state agency administrator*
Silva, Robert Owen *retired protective service official*
Simon, Sandra Ruth Waldman *retired state agency administrator*
Skaff, Joseph John *state agency administrator, retired military officer*
Steffy, Marion Nancy *state agency administrator*
Steinberg, Andrew B. *former federal agency administrator, lawyer*
Sturgell, Robert Allan (Bobby Sturgell) *former federal agency administrator*
Swoap, David Bruce *government and state agency administrator, consultant, art director*
Taylor, Joel Sanford *retired government agency administrator, retired lawyer*
Thomas, Harry K., Jr. *former federal agency administrator*
Thompson, Philip Douglas *federal agency administrator, educator*
Tritten, James John *retired federal agency administrator*
Truesdale, John Cushman *federal agency administrator, lawyer*
Tschetter, Ronald Allen *former federal agency administrator*
Turner, John Freeland *former federal agency administrator, state legislator*
Uhler, Walter Charles *government official, writer*
Umpenhour, Ken Eugene *protective services official*
Utgoff, Kathleen Platt *former federal agency administrator*
Vandiver, Sara Elizabeth Sharp Rankin *retired postmaster*
Waidmann, Brian K. *former federal agency administrator*
Walz, Edward George *protective services official*
Warner, Susan *federal agency administrator*
Watters, Linda A. *former state banking agency administrator*
Weems, Kerry N. *former federal agency administrator*
Welch, C. David (Charles David Welch) *former federal agency administrator*
Wendt, E. Allan *international affairs consultant*
Werkman, Rosemarie Anne *former public relations professional, volunteer*
Widner, Ralph Randolph *retired public administrator*
Wilkie, Robert Leon, Jr. *former federal agency administrator*
Williams, Michael Richard *protective services official*
Winter, Roger Paul *former federal agency administrator*
Young, Edwin S. W. *federal agency official*
Young, Frank Edward *retired federal agency and religious organization administrator*
Young, John Jacob, Jr. *former federal agency administrator*
Yurechko, John Joseph *federal agency administrator, director*

GOVERNMENT: EXECUTIVE ADMINISTRATION

UNITED STATES

ALABAMA

Birmingham
Boomershine, Donald Eugene *bureau executive, development official*
Langford, Larry P. *Mayor, Birmingham, Alabama*

Huntsville
Battle, Thomas *Mayor, Huntsville, Alabama*

Mobile
Jones, Samuel L. *Mayor, Mobile, Alabama*

Montgomery
Bennett, James Ronald *Labor Commissioner, Alabama*
Chapman, Beth Killough *Secretary of State, Alabama*
Folsom, Jim, Jr., (James Elisha Folsom Jr.) *Lieutenant Governor of Alabama, former governor*
Ivey, Kay Ellen *state treasurer*
Jinright, Charles W. *acting Mayor, Montgomery, Alabama*
King, Troy *state attorney general*
Morton, Joseph *state official, school system administrator*
Riley, Bob (Robert Renfroe Riley) *Governor of Alabama*

Warrior
Johnson, Barbara L. *retired municipal official*

ALASKA

Anchorage
Brown, Dean Naomi *state official, geologist*
Campbell, Craig E. *Lieutenant Governor of Alaska*

Fairbanks
Murkowski, Frank Hughes *former Governor of Alaska*

Juneau
Burnett, Jerry *state treasurer*
LeDoux, Larry *state official, school system administrator*
Parnell, Sean *Governor of Alaska, former state legislator*
Sullivan, Daniel S. *state attorney general*

Kodiak
Selby, Jerome M. *mayor*

ARIZONA

Chandler
Dunn, Boyd W. *Mayor, Chandler, Arizona, lawyer*

Gilbert
Berman, Steven *Mayor, Gilbert, Arizona*

Glendale
Scruggs, Elaine M. *Mayor, Glendale, Arizona*

Marana
Davidson, Gilbert *city manager*

Mesa
Smith, Scott *Mayor, Mesa, Arizona, business, financial and legal consultant*

Phoenix
Bennett, Kenneth R. *state official, former state senator*
Brewer, Jan (Janice Kay Brewer) *Governor of Arizona*
England, Robert (Bob) *city health department administrator, epidemiologist*
Goddard, Terry *state attorney general*
Gordon, Phillip Bruce *Mayor, Phoenix*
Grumbles, Benjamin H. *state official, former federal agency administrator*
Horne, Thomas Charles *state official, school system administrator*
Martin, Dean *state treasurer*

Prescott
Edmondson, William Brockway *retired foreign service officer*

Quartzsite
Michel, Verlyn Lyle *mayor, consultant*

Scottsdale
Lane, W. James *Mayor, Scottsdale, Ariz., airline executive, CPA*
Quayle, Dan (James Danforth Quayle) *former Vice President of the United States*
Quayle, Marilyn Tucker *wife of former United States Vice President, lawyer*

Sun Lakes
Sharpless, Joseph Benjamin *retired county official*

Tempe
Hallman, Hugh *Mayor, Tempe, Arizona*

Tucson
Walkup, Robert E. *Mayor, Tucson*

ARKANSAS

Bella Vista
Medin, Myron James, Jr. *city manager*

Heber Springs
Rawlings, Paul C. *retired government official*

Little Rock
Beebe, Mike D. (Michael Dale Beebe) *Governor of Arkansas, former state attorney general, lawyer*
Cheek, James Richard *ambassador*
Daniels, Charlie L. *Secretary of State, Arkansas*
Halter, Bill (William A. Halter) *Lieutenant Governor of Arkansas*
Julian, Diana *state official, school system administrator*
McDaniel, Dustin *state attorney general*
Shoffner, Martha Ann *state treasurer*
Stodola, Mark Allen *Mayor, Little Rock, Arkansas, former prosecutor*

Weiss, Richard A. *state official*

CALIFORNIA

Anaheim
Pringle, Curt *Mayor, Anaheim, California*

Arroyo Grande
Benedict, Lawrence Neal *foreign service officer*

Berkeley
Taylor, John Lockhart *retired municipal official*

Carlsbad
Wollam, Jean Farr *retired diplomat*

Chula Vista
Cox, Cheryl *Mayor, Chula Vista, California*

Corona
Nolan, Steve *Mayor, Corona, California*

Felicity
Istel, Jacques Andre *Mayor, Felicity, California*

Folsom
Peck, Ellie Enriquez *retired state administrator*

Fontana
Nuaimi, Mark N. *Mayor, Fontana, California*

Fremont
Wasserman, Robert *Mayor, Fremont, California*

Fresno
Autry, Alan *Former Mayor, Fresno, California, film company executive, actor, former professional football player*
Swearengin, Ashley *Mayor, Fresno, California*

Garden Grove
Dalton, William J. *Mayor, Garden Grove, California*

Glendale
Drayman, John *Mayor, Glendale, California*

Huntington Beach
Bohr, Keith *Mayor, Huntington Beach, California*

Irvine
Kang, Sukhee *Mayor, Irvine, California*
Krom, Beth *former Mayor, Irvine, California*

La Jolla
Shakespeare, Frank *ambassador*

Laguna Woods
Hussey, William Bertrand *retired diplomat*

Littlerock
Haas, Sir Russell *ambassador*

Long Beach
Foster, Robert G. (Bob Foster) *Mayor, Long Beach, California*
Sato, Eunice Noda *former mayor, consultant*

Los Angeles
Baxter, Frank Edward *United States Ambassador to Uruguay, former brokerage executive*
Fielding, Jonathan Evan *county health department administrator, pediatrician*
Greuel, Wendy Jane *city official*
Gutierrez, Carlos Miguel *former United States Secretary of Commerce, former grocery manufacturing company executive*
Toman, Mary Ann *federal official*
Villaraigosa, Antonio Ramon *Mayor, Los Angeles*

Menlo Park
Lane, Laurence William, Jr. *retired ambassador, publisher*

Modesto
Ridenour, Jim *Mayor, Modesto, California*

Monterey Park
Smith, Betty Denny *county official, administrator, fashion executive*

Moreno Valley
Batey, William H., II, *Mayor, Moreno Valley, California*

Napa
Battisti, Paul Oreste *retired municipal official*

Oakland
Dellums, Ronald Vernie *Mayor, Oakland, California, retired congressman*
Heminger, Steve *city official*

Oceanside
Lyon, Richard *retired mayor, military officer*
Wood, Jim *mayor, Oceanside, California*

Ontario
Dastrup-Hamill, Faye Myers *city official*
Leon, Paul S. *Mayor, Ontario, California*

Oxnard
Holden, Thomas E. *Mayor, Oxnard, California*

Pasadena
Bogaard, William Joseph *mayor, lawyer, educator*

Pleasant Hill
Nelson, Douglas Swede Raymond *sheriff*

Pomona
Rothman, Elliott *Mayor, Pomona, California*

Rancho Cucamonga
Kurth, Donald James, Jr. *Mayor, Rancho Cucamonga, California, medical educator*

Richmond
Corbin, Rosemary MacGowan *former mayor*

Riverside
Loveridge, Ronald Oliver *Mayor, Riverside, California*

Sacramento
Bowen, Debra Lynn *Secretary of State, California, former state legislator*
Brown, Jerry, Jr., (Edmund Gerald Brown Jr.) *state attorney general, former mayor, governor*
Bustamante, Cruz M. *former lieutenant governor*
Chick, Laura Newman *state official, former city official*
Garamendi, John R. *Lieutenant Governor of California, former state legislator*
Hunter, Patricia Rae (Tricia Hunter) *state official*
Johnson, Kevin Maurice *Mayor, Sacramento, retired professional basketball player*
Lockyer, Bill (William Lockyer) *state treasurer*
Nichols, Mary D. *state official, former federal agency administrator*
O'Connell, Jack T. *state official, school system administrator*
Schwarzenegger, Arnold Alois *Governor of California*

Salinas
Mettee-McCutchon, Ila *municipal official, retired military officer*

San Bernardino
Morris, Patrick J. *Mayor, San Bernardino, California*

San Diego
Golding, Susan G. *former mayor*
Macchione, Nick *city health department director*
Sanders, Jerry *Mayor, San Diego, former social services executive*

San Francisco
Adams, Lisette *Sheriff*
Fischer, David Joseph *ambassador*
Gore, Al (Albert Arnold Gore Jr.) *former Vice President of the United States*
Hewitt, Conrad W. *former commissioner, accountant*
Newsom, Gavin Christopher *Mayor, San Francisco*

San Jose
Reed, Charles Rufus (Chuck Reed) *Mayor, San Jose, California, lawyer*

San Luis Obispo
Shlaudeman, Harry Walter *retired diplomat*

Santa Ana
Pulido, Miguel Angel *Mayor, Santa Ana, California*

Santa Monica
Aaron, David L. *diplomat, author*

Santa Rosa
Gorin, Susan *Mayor, Santa Rosa, California*

Solana Beach
Gildred, Theodore E. *former diplomat, real estate developer*

Stanford
Rumsfeld, Donald Henry *former United States Secretary of Defense*

Stockton
Johnston, Ann *Mayor, Stockton, California*

Valencia
Ferry, Frank *mayor, Santa Clarita, California, principal*

Walnut Creek
Walston, Roderick Eugene *federal official*

Yuba City
Kemmerly, Jack Dale *retired state official*

COLORADO

Aurora
Sheffield, Nancy *city agency administrator*
Tauer, Ed *Mayor, Aurora, Colorado*

Boulder
Minger, Terrell John *public administration and natural resource institute executive*

Buena Vista
Scott, Gerald Wesley *retired American diplomat*

Colorado Springs
Abbott, Gina *municipal government executive*
Rivera, Lionel *Mayor, Colorado Springs, Colorado*

Denver
Brown, Keith Lapham *retired ambassador*
Buescher, Bernard A. (Bernie Buescher) *state official, air transportation executive*
Cuba, Stanley L. *government official*
Hickenlooper, John W. *Mayor, Denver*
Jones, Dwight D. *state official, school system administrator*
Kennedy, Cary *state treasurer*
O'Brien, Barbara *Lieutenant Governor of Colorado*
Ritter, Bill (August William Ritter Jr.) *Governor of Colorado, former prosecutor*
Skaggs, David Evans *state official, former congressman*
Suthers, John William *state attorney general*

Pueblo
Occhiato, Michael Anthony *municipal official*

CONNECTICUT

Canton Center
Humphrey, Samuel Stockwell *town official, physicist*

Easton
Meyer, Alice Virginia *state official*

Hartford
Blumenthal, Richard *state attorney general*
Bysiewicz, Susan *Secretary of State, Connecticut*
Fedele, Michael Christian *Lieutenant Governor of Connecticut, computer company executive*
Margulies, Beth Zeldes *state attorney general*
McQuillan, Mark K. *state official, school system administrator*
Nappier, Denise L. *state treasurer*
Rell, Jodi (Mary Jodi Rell) *Governor of Connecticut*

Stamford
Malloy, Dannel Patrick *Mayor, Stamford, Connecticut*

DELAWARE

Dover
Bullock, Jeffrey W. *state official*
Denn, Matthew P. *Lieutenant Governor of Delaware*
Jones-Potter, Velda *state treasurer*
Lowery, Lillian M. *state official, school system administrator*
Markell, Jack A. *Governor of Delaware*

Newark
Woo, S. B. (Shien-Biau Woo) *retired state official, physicist, educator*

Wilmington
Biden, Beau (Joseph Robinette Biden III) *state attorney general, lawyer*

DISTRICT OF COLUMBIA

Washington
Abbott, Sherburne Bradstreet *federal official*
Abedin, Huma M. *federal official*
Abell, Richard Bender *federal judicial officer, lawyer*
Abrams, Elliott *former federal official*
Aguilar, Luis A. *commissioner*
Aguirre, Eduardo, Jr. *United States Ambassador to Spain and Andorra*
Alexander, Lewis Suverkrop *federal official, economist*
Allen, Bernadette *United States Ambassador to Niger*
Allgeier, Peter Frederick *federal official*
Aranoff, Shara Louise *federal official*
Archambault Gillette, Jodi *federal official*
Austin, Roy L. *United States Ambassador to Trinidad & Tobago*
Axelrod, David M. *federal official*
Ayalde, Liliana *United States Ambassador to Paraguay*
Ayres, Mary Ellen *federal official*
Baer, Kenneth S. *federal official, communications executive*
Baker, Meredith Attwell *commissioner*
Baldyga, Leonard J. *retired diplomat, consultant*
Bandler, Donald Keith *international consultant, former ambassador*
Bansal, Preeta D. *federal official, lawyer*
Barbosa, Rubens Antonio *former ambassador*
Barker, Constance S. *commissioner*
Barnes, Melody C. *federal official*
Barrett, Barbara McConnell *United States Ambassador to Finland*
Battista, Robert James *federal official, lawyer*
Bauer, Gary Lee *political action committee executive*
Bauerly, Cynthia Leora *commissioner, lawyer*
Beliveau, Emmett S. *federal official*
Bernanke, Ben Shalom *chairman board of governors of the Federal Reserve System*
Bernstein, Jared *federal official, economist*
Berry, John *federal official, former zoological park administrator*
Bersin, Alan Douglas *federal official, former county official*
Beyrle, John R. *United States Ambassador to Russia*
Bezner, Mark *United States Charge d'Affaires for Palau*
Biden, Jill Tracy Jacobs *Second Lady of the United States, literature and language professor*
Biden, Joe (Joseph Robinette Biden Jr.) *Vice President of the United States, former United States Senator from Delaware*
Bishop, Clyde *United States Ambassador to the Marshall Islands*
Blackman, Sir Courtney Newlands *diplomat*
Blackwell, Ken (John Kenneth Blackwell) *former state official, former mayor*
Blahous, Charles Paul (Chuck Blahous) *former federal official*
Blair, Dennis Cutler *Director of National Intelligence, retired military officer*
Block, John Rusling *former United States Secretary of Agriculture*
Bodde, Peter William *United States Ambassador to Malawi*
Booth, Donald E. *United States Ambassador to Zambia*
Bordonaro, Molly *United States Ambassador to Malta*
Bost, Eric M. *United States Ambassador to South Africa*
Boulware, Mark *United States Ambassador to Mauritania*
Bradtke, Robert A. *United States Ambassador to Croatia*
Brazeal, Aurelia Erskine *former ambassador*
Brennan, John Owen *federal official, former technical solutions company executive*
Brennan, Joseph Edward *federal official, former United States Representative from Maine*
Brewster, Robert Charles *diplomat, consultant*
Briggs, Kerri Layne *state official, school system administrator*
Broome, David *federal official*
Brown, Gayleatha Beatrice *United States Ambassador to Benin*
Browner, Carol Martha *federal official, consulting firm executive*
Brownfield, William R. *United States Ambassador to Colombia*
Browning, Steven Alan *United States Ambassador to Uganda*
Burk, Susan Flood *ambassador*
Burton, Bill *federal official*
Cabrera, Cesar B. *United States Ambassador to Mauritius and Seychelles*
Callahan, Robert J. *United States Ambassador to Nicaragua*
Carrión, Adolfo, Jr. *federal official, former city official*
Casey, Kathleen L. *commissioner*
Caulfield, John *United States Charge d'Affaires for Venezuela*
Chao, Elaine Lan *former United States Secretary of Labor*
Chaudhry, Asif J. *United States Ambassador to Moldova*
Chiles, Lisa *federal official*
Chilton, Bart (Bartholomew Hamilton Chilton) *commissioner*
Chopra, Aneesh Paul *federal official*
Chrisler, Tamara E. *federal official*
Chu, Steven *United States Secretary of Energy, physics professor*
Cianchette, Peter E. *United States Ambassador to Costa Rica*
Clinton, Hillary Rodham (Hillary Diane Rodham Clinton) *United States Secretary of State, former United States Senator from New York, former First Lady of United States*
Cloud, John Albert, Jr. *United States Ambassador to Lithuania*
Clyburn, Mignon L. *commissioner*
Collins, James Franklin *retired ambassador*
Coneway, Peter Richard *United States Ambassador to Switzerland and Liechtenstein*
Cook, Frederick B. *United States Ambassador to Central African Republic*
Copps, Michael Joseph *commissioner*
Cretz, Gene A. *United States Ambassador to Libya*
Crocker, Chester Arthur *diplomat, federal agency administrator*
Crowley, Jeffrey S. *federal official*
Crutchfield, Danielle M. *federal official*
Culbertson, James B. *United States Ambassador to The Netherlands*
Cumber, Sada *United States Special Envoy to the Organization of the Islamic Conference*
Cunningham, James Blair *United States Ambassador to Israel*
Curry, Thomas J. *federal official*
Cusick, Robert Irwin *federal official, lawyer*
Cutter, Stephanie *federal official*
Dawson, Horace Greeley, Jr. *former diplomat, government official*
Dean, Howard Brush III *former Governor of Vermont*
Debevoise, Eli Whitney, II, *federal official, lawyer*
Deese, Brian C. *federal official*
DeParle, Nancy-Ann Min *federal official, former private equity firm executive*
Derse, Anne E. *United States Ambassador to Azerbaijan*
de Souza Briggs, Xavier N. *federal official, sociology professor, writer*
Dieter, Robert J. *United States Ambassador to Belize*
Dillon, Patrick (Michael Patrick Dillon) *federal official*
Dinger, Larry M. *United States Charge d'Affaires to Myanmar (Burma)*
Dodaro, Gene (Eugene Louis Dodaro) *federal official*
Donilon, Thomas E. *federal official, lawyer*
Donovan, Joseph Richard, Jr. *United States Consul General in Hong Kong*
Donovan, Shaun L. *Secretary of Housing and Urban Development*
Douglas, Derek *federal official*
Dudley, Susan Elaine *federal official*
Duemling, Robert Werner *diplomat, museum director*
Duke, Elizabeth A. (Betsy Duke) *federal official, former bank executive*
Duncan, Arne *Secretary of Education, former school system administrator*
Duncan, Thomasenia P. *federal official*
Dunn, Anita Babbitt *federal official, political communications specialist*
Dunn, Michael V. *commissioner*
Dunn, Timothy J. *United States Chief of Mission for Netherlands Antilles and Aruba*
Du Pont, Pierre Samuel, IV, *former Governor of Delaware, lawyer*
Dye, Rebecca Feemster *commissioner*
Eaton, William A. *United States Ambassador to Panama, former federal agency administrator*
Elmendorf, Douglas William *federal official, economist*
Elwood, Patricia Cowan *city official, political scientist, consultant*
Emanuel, Rahm Israel *White House Chief of Staff, former United States Representative from Illinois*
English, Charles Lewis *United States ambassador to Bosnia and Herzegovina*
Ereli, Joseph Adam *United States ambassador to Kingdom of Bahrain*
Erickson, Nancy *federal official*
Fahmy, Nabil *ambassador*
Fannin, Paul Robert *United States Ambassador to the Dominican Republic*
Farrell, Diana *federal official*
Feinberg, Kenneth Roy *federal official, lawyer*
Fenty, Adrian M. *Mayor, Washington, DC*
Fleisher, Eric Wilfrid *retired foreign service officer*
Foley, April H. *United States Ambassador to Hungary*
Foley, James B. *federal official, former ambassador*
Ford, Christopher Ashley *federal official, lawyer*
Fox, Sam *United States ambassador to Belgium, manufacturing executive*
Fraker, Ford M. *United States Ambassador to Saudi Arabia*
Fried, Daniel *ambassador, former federal agency administrator*
Furman, Jason L. *federal official, economist*
Gaa, Willy C. *ambassador*
Gaffney, Glenn A. *federal official*
Gandhi, Natwar M. *city official*
Garcia, Frances *federal official, accountant*
Garthoff, Raymond Leonard *retired diplomat, diplomatic historian*
Garvey, Janet E. *United States Ambassador to Republic of Cameroon*
Gaspard, Patrick H. *federal official, former labor union administrator*
Gates, Robert Michael *United States Secretary of Defense, former academic administrator*
Geithner, Timothy Franz *United States Secretary of the Treasury*
Genachowski, Julius *federal official*
Gessaman, Donald Eugene *retired government executive*
Gfoeller-Volkoff, Tatiana C. *United States Ambassador to Kyrgyzstan*
Ghafari, Yousif Boutrous *United States Ambassador to Slovenia*
Gibbs, Robert L. *White House press secretary*
Glazer, Charles Louis *United States Ambassador to El Salvador*
Glendening, Parris Nelson *former governor, political science educator*
Gnehm, Edward W., Jr. *ambassador*
Godec, Robert F. *United States Ambassador to Tunisia*
Goolsbee, Austan Dean *federal official, economics professor*
Goosby, Eric Paul *ambassador, epidemiologist*
Gordon, Robert *federal official*
Graber, Richard William *United States Ambassador to Czech Republic, lawyer*
Grappo, Gary Anthony *United States Ambassador to Oman*
Gration, Scott (Jonathan Scott Gration) *diplomat, retired military officer*
Green, Mark Andrew *United States Ambassador to Tanzania, former congressman*
Griffin, Christine M. *federal official*
Gross, David Andrew *federal official, lawyer*
Grove, Brandon Hambright, Jr. *diplomat*
Gunderson, Brian F. *federal official*
Harbour, Pamela Jones *commissioner, lawyer*
Haslach, Patricia M. *ambassador*
Hill, Christopher Robert *United States Ambassador to Iraq*
Hoagland, Richard Eugene *United States Ambassador to Kazakhstan*
Hodges, Heather M. *United States Ambassador to Ecuador*
Hogan, Cynthia C. *federal official, lawyer*
Hoglander, Harry R. *federal official*
Holder, Eric Himpton, Jr. *United States Attorney General*
Holdren, John Paul *federal official, physicist, educator*
Horowitz, Herbert Eugene *retired diplomat*
Hughes, Miriam K. *United States Ambassador to Micronesia*
Hume, Cameron R. *United States Ambassador to Indonesia*
Hunter, Caroline C. *commissioner, lawyer*
Huntsman, Jon Meade, Jr. *United States Ambassador to China, former Governor of Utah*
Huso, Ravic R. *United States Ambassador to Laos*
Irving, Susan Jean *government executive*
Ishimaru, Stuart Jon *commissioner, lawyer*
Iskandar, Harris *attache*
Jackson, Jeanine E. *United States Ambassador to Burkina Faso*
Jacobson, Tracey Ann *United States Ambassador to Tajikistan*
Jarrett, Valerie Bowman *federal official*
Jawad, Said Tayeb (Said Tayeb Djawad) *ambassador, commentator, writer*
Jee, Justin Soonho *government official*
Jeffrey, James Franklin *United States Ambassador to Turkey*
Jenkins, Bonnie Denise *ambassador*
Johnson, Brenda LaGrange *United States Ambassador to Jamaica*
Johnson, Donald Crandall *United States Ambassador to Republic of Equatorial Guinea*
Johnson, Jennifer J. *federal official*
Johnson, Katie *federal official*
Jones, Deborah K. *United States Ambassador to Kuwait*
Jones, James Logan, Jr. *National Security Advisor, retired military officer*
Jones, James Robert *former White House chief of staff, ambassador, congressman*
Jones, John Melvin *US Ambassador to Guyana*
Jones, Van *federal official, lawyer*
Jurith, Edward Howard *federal official*
Kalil, Tom *federal official*
Kane, Robert *energy executive*
Kang, Eugene *federal official*
Kaplan, Stephen *federal official*
Kato, Ryozo *ambassador*

Katzen, Jay Kenneth *retired diplomat, state legislator, government agency administrator*
Kauzlarich, Richard Dale *retired ambassador, political scientist, consultant*
Keating, Francis Anthony, II, *Former Governor, Oklahoma, lawyer*
Keith, James *United States Ambassador to Malaysia*
Kelliher, Joseph Timothy *commissioner*
Kelly, Suedeen G. *commissioner*
Kennedy, Ambassador J. Christian *United States Special Envoy for Holocaust Issues*
Kenney, Kristie Anne *United States Ambassador to the Philippines*
Kerlikowske, R. Gil (Richard Gil Kerlikowske) *federal official, former police chief*
Killgore, Andrew Ivy *former ambassador*
Kim, Sung *United States Special Envoy for the Six-Party Talks*
Kirk, Ronald *federal official, former mayor*
Klain, Ronald Alan *federal official, former investment company executive*
Klemm, Hans G. *United States Ambassador to Timor-Leste*
Kohn, Donald L. *federal official, economist*
Korologos, Tom Chris *former ambassador*
Kosiak, Steven Michael *federal official*
Kostelnik, Michael Charles *commissioner, retired military officer*
Kovacic, William Evan *commissioner, law educator*
Kundra, Vivek *federal official*
LaHood, Ray H. *Secretary of Transportation, former United States Representative from Illinois*
Lane, Charlotte R. *Commissioner, United States International Trade Commission, lawyer*
Larson, Charles W., Jr. *United States Ambassador to Latvia*
Laudato, George A. *federal official*
Lavoy, Peter Rene *federal official*
Le Baron, Joseph Evan *United States Ambassador to Qatar*
Lefkowitz, Jay *United States Special Envoy for Human Rights in North Korea*
Leibowitz, Jon *commissioner, department chairman*
Lidinsky, Richard A., Jr. *commissioner*
Liebman, Jeffrey B. *federal official, economist*
Lippert, Mark William *federal official*
Llorens, Hugo *United States Ambassador to Honduras*
Locke, Gary Faye *Secretary of Commerce, former Governor of Washington*
Love, Reggie *federal official*
Lowe, Mary Frances *federal official*
Lowenstein, James Gordon *former diplomat, international consultant*
Lu, Christopher P. *federal official*
Lucas, James Walter *federal official*
Lundsager, Margrethe (Meg Lundsager) *federal official*
Lute, Douglas E. *federal official, career military officer*
Madras, Bertha Kalifon *federal official, neuroscientist, researcher*
Magee, Charles Thomas *international consultant, retired diplomat*
Manzanares, J. Robert *Permanent United States Representative to the Organization of American States*
Marantis, Demetrios J. *federal official*
Marquardt, R. Niels *United States Ambassador to the Comoros and Madagascar*
Marshall, Capricia Penavic *federal official*
Maruyama, Warren H. *federal official, lawyer*
Mason, David Marion *commissioner*
Mastromonaco, Alyssa *federal official*
Mathieu, Gail Dennise *United States Ambassador to Namibia*
Mazer, Roslyn A. *federal official, lawyer*
McCormick, William Paul *United States Ambassador to New Zealand and Samoa*
McDonough, Denis *federal official*
McDowell, Robert Malcolm *commissioner*
McEldowney, Nancy Eileen *United States Ambassador to Bulgaria*
McFarland, Stephen George *United States Ambassador to Guatemala*
McGahn, Donald F., II, *commissioner, lawyer*
McGann, C. Steven *United States Ambassador to Fiji, Nauru, Kiribati and Tonga and Tuvalu*
McGee, James D. *United States Ambassador to Zimbabwe*
McKinley, P. Michael (Peter Michael McKinley) *United States Ambassador to Peru*
McMahon Hawkins, Patricia *United States Ambassador to Togo*
McMullen, Ronald *United States Ambassador to Eritrea*
Mermoud, J. Frank *United States Special Representative, Commercial and Business Affairs*
Messina, Jim (James A. Messina) *federal official*
Michalak, Michael Walter *United States Ambassador to Vietnam*
Miller, William Green *former ambassador*
Milovanovic, Gillian Arlette *United States Ambassador to Republic of Mali*
Minton, Mark C. *United States Ambassador to Mongolia*
Mitchell, George John *diplomat, former United States Senator from Maine*
Moeller, Philip D. *commissioner*
Moller, Patricia Newton *United States Ambassador to Burundi*
Mombouli, Serge *ambassador*
Montgomery, Edward Bruce *federal official, former dean, economics professor*
Moore, Roderick W. *United State Ambassador to Montenegro*
Morales, Hector Elias, Jr. *ambassador, former bank executive*
Moriarty, James Francis *United States Ambassador to Bangladesh*
Mozena, Dan W. *United States ambassador to Angola*
Muñoz, Cecilia *federal official, civil rights advocate*
Munson, Alden V., Jr. *federal official*
Munter, Cameron *United States Ambassador to Serbia*
Myles, Marianne Matuzic *United States ambassador to Cape Verde*
Nabors, Robert Lee, II, *federal official*
Napolitano, Janet Ann *Secretary of Homeland Security, former Governor of Arizona*
Natsios, Andrew Stephen *diplomat, former federal agency administrator*
Nesbitt, Wanda L. *United States Ambassador to Cote d'Ivoire*
Newman, Sherryl Hobbs *former district secretary*
Nicholson, Marvin, Jr. *federal official*
Nickles, Peter *state attorney general*
Nigro, Louis J., Jr. *United States Ambassador to Republic of Chad*
Nolan, Robert B. *United States Ambassador to Lesotho*
Nolan, Stephen James *United States ambassador to Republic of Botswana*
Norland, Richard Boyce *United States Ambassador to Uzbekistan*
Norris, Jackie *federal official, history educator*
Obama, Barack Hussein, Jr. *44th President of the United States*
Obama, Michelle LaVaughn Robinson *First Lady of the United States, former hospital administrator*
Obsitnik, Vincent *United States Ambassador to Slovakia*
Okun, Deanna Tanner *federal official*
Olson, Richard Gustave *United States Ambassador to the United Arab Emirates*
Orszag, Peter Richard *federal official, economist*
Ourisman, Mary M. *United States Ambassador to Barbados and the Eastern Caribbean*
Owen, Henry *former ambassador, consultant*
Panetta, Leon Edward *CIA Director, United States Representative from California*
Paredes, Troy Allan *commissioner, law educator*
Parker, Maurice S. *United States Ambassador to Swaziland*
Pascual, Carlos Enrique *United States Ambassador to Mexico*
Pasi, Geeta *diplomat*
Patterson, Anne Woods *United States Ambassador to Pakistan*
Patterson, Mark Ainsley *federal official*
Pendleton, Miles Stevens, Jr. *diplomat*
Penn, Kal (Kalpen Suresh Modi) *federal official, actor*
Petersen, Matthew Spencer *commissioner, lawyer*
Pfeiffer, Daniel H. *federal official*
Pfeifle, Mark D. *federal official*
Phommahaxay, Phanthong *ambassador*
Pinkert, Dean A. *federal official*
Quainton, Anthony Cecil Eden *diplomat*
Ramirez, Saul N., Jr. *housing association executive*
Ranneberger, Michael E. *United States Ambassador to Kenya*
Reddick, Eunice *United States Ambassador to Gabon and Sao Tome & Principe*
Reed, John Hathaway *former ambassador*
Reeker, Philip Thomas *United States Ambassador to Macedonia*
Reynolds, Christina *federal official*
Richardson, Scott *federal official, researcher, writer*
Rickman, Gregg *United States Special Envoy to Monitor and Combat Anti-Semitism*
Riley, Thomas *United States Ambassador to Morocco*
Rivkin, Charles Hammerman *United States Ambassador to France and Monaco*
Roberts, Walter Ronald *retired diplomat*
Robinson, David M. *ambassador*
Rodley, Carol Ann *United States Ambassador to Cambodia*
Rodriguez, Rosemary E. *former municipal official, federal agency administrator*
Roemer, Timothy John *United States Ambassador to India, former United States Representative from Indiana*
Rogers, Desiree Glapion *federal official, former insurance company executive*
Rogers, Thomasina Venese *commissioner*
Romer, Christina Duckworth *federal official, economist*
Rooney, Daniel M. *United States Ambassador to Ireland, professional sports team executive*
Rosch, John Thomas (Tom) *commissioner, lawyer*
Rosenfeld, Arthur F. *federal official, lawyer*
Rouse, Cecilia Elena *federal official, economics and public affairs professor*
Rouse, Peter M. *federal official*
Rowe, Leslie V. *United States Ambassador to Papua New Guinea, Solomon Islands & Vanuatu*
Russell, Cathy (Catherine M. Russell) *federal official*
Salazar, Ken (Kenneth Lee Salazar) *Secretary of the Interior*
Sampas, Dorothy Myers *retired government official*
Sanders, Robin Renee *United States Ambassador to Nigeria*
Sanderson, Janet Ann *United States Ambassador to Haiti*
Sarros, P. Peter *diplomat, consultant*
Sarukhan, Arturo *ambassador*
Schieffer, J(ohn) Thomas (Tom) *United States Ambassador to Japan, former professional baseball team executive*
Schiliro, Philip M. *federal official*
Schlosser, Lisa *chief information officer*
Schneider, Cynthia Perrin *former ambassador, political science professor*
Schneider, Mark Lewis *foreign policy executive, retired government agency administrator*
Schreiber Hughes, Lisa Bobbie *United States Ambassador to Suriname*
Scott, Stephanie D. *city official*
Scowcroft, Brent *former national security advisor, retired military officer*
Sebelius, Kathleen Gilligan *Secretary of Health and Human Services, former Governor of Kansas*
Seche, Stephen A. *United States Ambassador to Yemen*
Sellin, Theodore *diplomat, consultant*
Shedd, David R. *federal official*
Shinseki, Eric Ken *Secretary of Veterans Affairs, retired military officer*
Simons, Paul E. *United States Ambassador to Chile*
Sison, Michele Jeanne *United States Ambassador to Lebanon*
Smalley, Robert Manning *retired diplomat*
Smith, Daniel B. *federal official*
Smith, Patricia Grace *federal official*
Snyder, Charles Robert *United States Senior Representative on Sudan*
Sobel, Clifford M. *United States Ambassador to Brazil*
Solis, Hilda Lucia *Secretary of Labor, former United States Representative from California*
Sommers, Jill Elaine *commissioner*
Sonnenfeldt, Helmut *former government official, educator, consultant, writer*
Speckhard, Daniel V. *United States Ambassador to Greece*
Spector, Melbourne Louis *retired foreign service officer*
Spellings, Margaret LaMontagne *former United States Secretary of Education*
Spitzer, Marc Lee *commissioner, former state legislator*
Stadtler, Walter Edward *diplomat*
Stephens, Kathleen (D. Kathleen Stephens) *United States Ambassador to South Korea*
Stephenson, Barbara J. *United States Ambassador to Panama*
Stephenson, Thomas F. *United States Ambassador to Portugal*
Stoltz, Joe *federal official*
Strautmanis, Michael (Michael A. Strautmanis) *federal official*
Summers, Larry (Lawrence Henry Summers) *federal official, economist, former United States Secretary of the Treasury*
Sunshine, Robert A. *federal official*
Susman, Louis B. *United States Ambassador to the United Kingdom, retired investment banker*
Sutley, Nancy Helen *federal official*
Sutphen, Mona K. *federal official*
Sutter, Eleanor Bly *retired diplomat*
Swan, James C. *United States Ambassador to Djibouti*
Swart, Susan *federal official*
Swimmer, Ross Owen *federal official*
Symington, W. Stuart, IV, (William Stuart Symington IV) *United States Ambassador to Rwanda*
Tahir-Kheli, Shirin *federal official*
Tapella, Robert Charles *federal official*
Tarullo, Daniel K. *federal official, law educator*
Taubman, Nicholas Frank *United States Ambassador to Romania*
Taylor, William B., Jr. *United States Ambassador to Ukraine*
Tchen, Christina M. (Tina Tchen) *federal official, lawyer*
Teare, Richard Wallace *retired foreign service officer*
Teehee, Kimberly Kay *federal official*
Tefft, John F. *United States Ambassador to Georgia*
Teitelbaum, Donald Gene *United States Ambassador to Ghana*
Thomas-Greenfield, Linda *United States Ambassador to Liberia*
Thompson, Horace A., III, (Topper Thompson) *commissioner, lawyer*
Thorne, David Hoadley *United States Ambassador to Italy and San Marino*
Timken, William Robert, Jr. *United States Ambassador to Germany, former manufacturing executive*
Urbancic, Frank Charles, Jr. *United States Ambassador to Cyprus*
van Voorst, Carol *United States Ambassador to Iceland*
Vela, Moe (Moises Vicente Vela Jr.) *federal official, communications executive*
Verveer, Melanne S. *ambassador*
Verville, Elizabeth Giavani *federal official*
Vilsack, Tom (Thomas James Vilsack) *Secretary of Agriculture, former Governor of Iowa*
Wagner, Ann Louise *United States Ambassador to Luxembourg, former political organization executive*
Walles, Jacob *Consul General in Jerusalem*
Walter, Elisse Barbara *commissioner*
Walther, Steven T. *commissioner, lawyer*
Warsh, Kevin Maxwell *federal official*
Watson, Arthur Dennis *federal official*
Wayne, Stephen J. *government educator, writer*
Weintraub, Ellen L. *commissioner*
Wellinghoff, Jon *commissioner*
Wells, Barry Leon *United States Ambassador to The Gambia*
Whitney, Benson K. *United States Ambassador to Norway*
Wilkins, David Horton *United States Ambassador to Canada, former state legislator*
Williamson, Clint (John Clint Williamson) *ambassador*
Williamson, Irving A. *federal official*
Winter, Melissa E. *federal official*
Withers, John Lovelle, II, *United States Ambassador to Albania*
Wood, Michael M. *United States Ambassador to Sweden*
Yamamoto, Donald Yukio *United States Ambassador to Ethiopia*
Yates, John Melvin *United States Special Envoy for Somalia*
Yovanovitch, Marie L. *United States Ambassador to Armenia*
Zarate, Juan Carlos *former federal official*
Zients, Jeffrey D. *federal official*
Ziglar, James W. *govt. official, investment banker, corporate, lawyer, educator*

FLORIDA

Aventura
Garcia, Marc Anthony *diplomat*

Boynton Beach
Warshaw, Stanley Irving *federal official, consultant*

Cape Coral
Burch, Jim *Mayor, Cape Coral, Florida*

Deerfield Beach
Johnson, Mary Margaret Dickens *governmental and commercial researcher, contract management educator, consultant*

Fernandina Beach
Smeeton, Thomas Rooney *government affairs consultant*

Fort Lauderdale
Burleigh, A. Peter *ambassador*
Gunzburger, Suzanne Nathan *municipal official, social worker*
Seiler, Jack P. *Mayor, Ft. Lauderdale, Florida, prosecutor*

Fort Myers
Lamach, Bernard D. *professional engineer, county commissioner*

Gainesville
Heflin, Martin Ganier *diplomat, political scientist*

Hialeah
Robaina, Julio *mayor, state representative*

Miami
Alvarez, Carlos *Mayor, Miami-Dade, Florida*
Diaz, Manny (Manuel Alberto Diaz) *Mayor, Miami, Florida*
Magrath, Kathleen Barry *retired municipal official*

Orlando
Dyer, John Hugh, Jr., (Buddy Dyer) *Mayor, Orlando, Florida, lawyer*

Palm Bay
Anderson, Richard Edmund *city manager, consultant*

Pensacola
Graves, Frederick David *state attorney general*

Port Saint Lucie
Christensen, Patricia *Mayor, Port St. Lucie, Florida*

Saint Petersburg
Baker, Rick (Richard M. Baker) *Mayor, St. Petersburg, Florida*
Mussett, Richard Earl *city official*

Sarasota
Morrow, William Earl *retired government official, law educator*

Sebastian
Eddy, Elsbeth Marie *retired government official, statistician*

Tallahassee
Browning, Kurt S. *Secretary of State, Florida*
Crist, Charlie (Charles Joseph Crist Jr.) *Governor of Florida, former state attorney general*
Marks, John R. III *mayor, Tallahassee, Florida, lawyer*
McCollum, Bill (Ira William McCollum Jr.) *state attorney general, former congressman*
Sink, Adelaide Alexander *state official*
Sink, Alex *state treasurer*
Smith, Eric J. *state official, school system administrator*

Tampa
Freedman, Sandra Warshaw *former mayor*
Iorio, Pam *mayor, Tampa*
Martinez, Bob *former federal official, former governor*
Platt, Jan Kaminis *former county official*

Trenton
Aderholt, David A. *state official*

GEORGIA

Atlanta
Baker, Thurbert E. *state attorney general*
Cagle, Casey *Lieutenant Governor of Georgia*
Carter, Jimmy (James Earl Carter Jr.) *39th President of the United States*
Carter, Rosalynn Smith (Eleanor Rosalynn Smith Carter) *former First Lady of the United States*
Cox, Kathy *state official, school system administrator*
Ebersole, W. Daniel *state treasurer*
Franklin, Shirley Clarke *Mayor, Atlanta*
Frieden, Thomas R. *federal official, epidemiologist*
Glover, Renée Lewis *city official*
Handel, Karen *Secretary of State, Georgia*
Laney, James Thomas *former ambassador, educator*
Perdue, George (Sonny Perdue) *Governor of Georgia*
Scott, Donald Lavern *city manager, librarian, former army officer*
Taylor, Mark *former lieutenant governor*

Augusta
Copenhaver, Deke *Mayor, Augusta-Richmond, Georgia*

Canton
Angulo, Charles Bonin *foreign service officer, lawyer*

Columbus
Wetherington, Jim *Mayor, Columbus, Georgia, former protective services official*

Saint Simons Island
Douglas, William Ernest *retired commissioner*

Tucker
Streeb, Gordon Lee *diplomat, economist*

HAWAII

Hilo
Kenoi, William P. *Mayor, Hilo, Hawaii*

Honolulu
Aiona, James R., Jr. *Lieutenant Governor of Hawaii*
Bennett, Mark J. *state attorney general*
Bronster, Margery S. *retired state attorney general, lawyer*
Hamamoto, Patricia *state official, school system administrator*
Hannemann, Mufi *Mayor, Honolulu*
Kawamura, Georgina K. *state treasurer, finance company executive*
Lingle, Linda *Governor of Hawaii*

IDAHO

Boise
Bieter, David H. *Mayor, Boise, Idaho*
Crane, Ron G. *state treasurer*
Little, Brad *Lieutenant Governor of Idaho, former state legislator*
Otter, Butch (C. L. Otter, Clement Leroy Otter) *Governor of Idaho, former United States Representative from Idaho*
Wasden, Lawrence *state attorney general*
Wilson, Jack Fredrick *retired federal government official*
Ysursa, Ben T. *Secretary of State, Idaho*

Idaho Falls
King, Ronald Amos *federal official, retired communications professional*

ILLINOIS

Aurora
Weisner, Tom *Mayor, Aurora, Illinois*

Carbondale
Cole, Brad *mayor*

Champaign
Semonin, Richard Gerard *retired state official*

Chicago
Daley, Richard Michael *Mayor, Chicago*
Dempsey, Mary A. *library commissioner, lawyer*
Enenbach, Mark Henry *community action agency executive, educator*
Madigan, Lisa *state attorney general*
Mason, Terry *city health department administrator, urologist*
Ocasio, Billy *state official, former alderman*
Topinka, Judy Baar *state official, political organization worker*
Trotter, Cortez *city official, former fire commissioner*
Wood, Patrick Henry III *former commissioner*

Downers Grove
Jacklin, William Thomas *retired county official, educator*

Glenview
Olson, Roy Arthur *retired government official*

Hinsdale
Mehuron, William Otto *retired federal official*

Machesney Park
Vaughn, Linda Marie *municipal official*

Rockford
Morrissey, Lawrence *Mayor, Rockford, Illinois*

Springfield
Giannoulias, Alexi *state treasurer*
Quinn, Patrick *Governor of Illinois*
White, Jesse *Secretary of State, Ill*

Urbana
Edgar, Jim *former governor*
Prussing, Laurel Lunt *mayor, economist*

INDIANA

Columbus
Herman, Alexis Margaret *former United States Secretary of Labor*

Fort Wayne
Henry, Thomas C. *Mayor, Fort Wayne, Indiana*
Lee, Timothy Earl *international agency executive, paralegal*

Indianapolis
Ballard, Gregory A. *Mayor, Indianapolis, retired military officer*
Bennett, Tony (Charles A. Bennett) *state official, school system administrator*
Caine, Virginia A. *city health department administrator*
Daniels, Mitchell Elias, Jr. *Governor of Indiana, former federal official*
Mourdock, Richard E. *state treasurer*
Nass, Connie Kay *state auditor*
Rokita, Todd *Secretary of State, Indiana*
Skillman, Becky Sue *Lieutenant Governor of Indiana, former state legislator*
Zoeller, Greg *state attorney general*

La Porte
Morris, Leigh Edward *former mayor, retired health facility administrator*

IOWA

Des Moines
Bergman, Bruce E. *municipal official*
Corning, Joy Cole *retired state official*
Cownie, TM Franklin *Mayor, Des Moines*
Culver, Chet (Chester John Culver) *Governor of Iowa*
Deluhery, Patrick John *retired state official*
Fitzgerald, Michael Lee *state treasurer*
Jeffrey, Judy *state official, school system administrator*
Judge, Patty Jean *Lieutenant Governor of Iowa, nurse*
Mauro, Michael Anthony *Secretary of State, Iowa*
Miller, Thomas J. *state attorney general*

Marion
Pate, Paul Danny *mayor*

Oelwein
McFarlane, Beth Lucetta Troester *retired mayor*

KANSAS

Hutchinson
Kerr, Dave *state official, marketing professional*

Overland Park
Gerlach, Carl R. *mayor, Overland Park, Kansas*

Pittsburg
Trent, Darrell M. *ambassador, academic administrator, transportation executive*

Pratt
Hayden, (John) Michael *state official, former Governor of Kansas*

Topeka
Findley, Troy Ray *Lieutenant Governor of Kansas, former state legislator*
Garner, Jim D. *state official, lawyer*
Parkinson, Mark Vincent *Governor of Kansas*
Posny, Alexa Emily *state official, school system administrator*
Six, Stephen N. *state attorney general, former judge*
Thornburgh, Ron E. *Secretary of State, Kansas*

Wichita
Brewer, Carl *Mayor, Wichita, Kansas*

KENTUCKY

Frankfort
Beshear, Steven Lynn *Governor of Kentucky, lawyer*
Conway, Jack W. *state attorney general*
Grayson, Trey (C.M. Grayson) *Secretary of State, Kentucky*
Hollenbach, Todd (L. J. Hollenbach IV) *state treasurer*
Holliday, Terry *state official, school system administrator*
Mongiardo, Daniel (Frank Daniel Mongiardo) *Lieutenant Governor of Kentucky, state senator, otolaryngologist*

Lexington
Miller, Pamela Gundersen *retired mayor*
Newberry, Jim *Mayor, Lexington, Kentucky*

Louisville
Abramson, Jerry E. *mayor, Louisville*
Henry, Stephen Lewis *retired lieutenant governor, orthopedic surgeon, educator*

LOUISIANA

Baton Rouge
Caldwell, James David, Jr., (Buddy Caldwell) *state attorney general*
Dardenne, Jay (John Leigh Dardenne Jr.) *Secretary of State, La, former state legislator*
Holden, Melvin Lee *Mayor-President, Baton Rouge, Louisiana*
Jindal, Bobby (Piyush Jindal) *Governor of Louisiana, former United States Representative from Louisiana*
Kennedy, John Neely *state treasurer*
Landrieu, Mitchell Joseph *Lieutenant Governor of Louisiana*
Pastorek, Paul G. *state official, school system administrator, lawyer*

New Orleans
Blakely, Edward James *city official, economics professor*
Nagin, Ray C. (Clarence Ray Nagin Jr.) *Mayor, New Orleans*

Shreveport
Glover, Cedric Bradford *Mayor, Shreveport, La*

MAINE

Augusta
Baldacci, John Elias *Governor of Maine*
Dunlap, Matthew Gordon *Secretary of State, Maine, former state legislator*
Gendron, Susan Ann *state official, school system administrator*
Lemoine, David G. *state treasurer*
Mills, Janet Trafton *state attorney general, former state representative*

Brunswick
King, Angus S., Jr. *former governor*

Castine
Kettis, Pär Axel *Swedish diplomat*

MARYLAND

Annapolis
Andrews, Archie Moulton *retired federal official*
Kopp, Nancy Kornblith *state treasurer*
McDonough, John Patrick *Secretary of State, Maryland*
O'Malley, Martin Joseph *Governor of Maryland, former mayor, lawyer*

Baltimore
Astrue, Michael James *commissioner, former pharmaceutical company executive*
Aumann, R. Karl *commissioner, former state official*
Brown, Anthony Gregory *Lieutenant Governor of Maryland, lawyer*
Dixon, Sheila Ann *Mayor, Baltimore*
Gansler, Douglas F. *state attorney general, former prosecutor*
Grasmick, Nancy S. *state official, school system administrator*
Miser, Ann *retired government researcher*
Perez, Thomas Edward *state official, law educator*

Bethesda
Bowsher, Charles Arthur *retired government official, financial executive*
Dennin, Joseph Francis *former government official, lawyer*
Harrop, William Caldwell *retired ambassador*
Laingen, Lowell Bruce *diplomat*
Moore, Thomas Hill *commissioner*
Morrison, Bruce Andrew *federal official, public affairs consultant*
Nord, Nancy Ann *commissioner*
North, William Haven *foreign service officer*
Northup, Anne Meagher *commissioner, former United States Representative from Kentucky*
Rowell, Edward Morgan *retired foreign service officer, educator*
Vest, George Southall *retired diplomat*

Chestertown
Meima, Ralph Chester, Jr. *retired diplomat, real estate company executive*

Chevy Chase
Albright, Raymond Jacob *federal official*
Cushwa, Patricia K. *commissioner*
Fulwood, Isaac, Jr. *federal official*
Mitchell, Cranston J. *commissioner*
Reilly, Edward Francis, Jr. *commissioner, former state senator*

Cockeysville
Barnes, Peter *retired federal official*

College Park
Benedick, Richard Elliot *diplomat*
Gansler, Jacques Singleton *public policy educator*

Columbia
Lok, Joan Mei-Lok *community affairs specialist, artist*

Easton
Shepard, William Seth *diplomat, writer*

Fort Washington
Smoot, Burgess Howard *federal official*

Gaithersburg
French, Judson Cull *federal official*
Ray, Charles Aaron *ambassador*

Hollywood
Newhouse, Alan Russell *retired federal official*

North Bethesda
Szabo, Daniel *federal official*

Rockville
Chiogioji, Melvin Hiroaki *retired federal official, entrepreneur*
Galson, Steven Kenneth *federal official*
Klein, Dale Edward *commissioner, engineering educator*
Lyons, Peter B. *commissioner*
Svinicki, Kristine L. *commissioner*

Silver Spring
Bassett, William, Jr. *geospatial intelligence officer*
Reinhardt, John Edward *former international affairs specialist*

MASSACHUSETTS

Amherst
Lupien, John Reilly *diplomat*

Boston
Bowles, Ian A., Jr. *state official*
Cahill, Timothy P. *state treasurer*
Coakley, Martha *state attorney general, former prosecutor*
Ferrer, Barbara *city health department executive director*
Galvin, William Francis *Secretary of the Commonwealth, Massachusetts*
Menino, Thomas M. *Mayor, Boston*
Patrick, Deval Laurdine *Governor of Massachusetts, lawyer*
Romney, Mitt (Willard Mitt Romney) *former Governor of Massachusetts*

Bridgewater
Heffernan, Peter John *state official*

Brockton
Fennel, John Andrew *state attorney general*
Sullivan, Brendan Paul *state official, consultant, communications educator*

Cambridge
Porter, Roger Blaine *federal official, educator*

Canton
Fuchs, Lawrence Howard *federal official, educator*

Dartmouth
Connors, Robert Leo *city official*

Malden
Chester, Mitchell Dan *state official, school system administrator*

Sherborn
Kennedy, Chester Ralph, Jr. *retired state official, art director*

Worcester
Lukes, Konstantina B. *Mayor, Worcester, Massachusetts, lawyer*

MICHIGAN

Ann Arbor
Davis, Robert Leach *retired federal official*
Ford, Betty Ann (Elizabeth Ann Ford) *former First Lady of the United States, health facility executive*
Levitsky, Melvyn *former ambassador*
Sheldon, Ingrid Kristina *retired mayor, controller*

Battle Creek
Baldwin, Susan Olin *commissioner, management consultant*

Detroit
Bing, David *Mayor, Detroit, metal products executive, retired professional basketball player*
Trent, Calvin R. *city health department director*

Farmington
Gordon, Arnold Mark *state attorney general, arbitrator, educator*

Fennville
Kamman, Curtis Warren *retired ambassador*

Grand Rapids
Donahue, Dennis Donald *foreign service officer*
Heartwell, George K. *Mayor, Grand Rapids, Michigan*
Logie, John Hoult, Sr. *former mayor, lawyer*

Lansing
Cherry, John D., Jr. *Lieutenant Governor of Michigan, former state senator*
Cox, Mike (Michael A. Cox) *state attorney general*
Flanagan, Michael P. *state official, school system administrator*
Granholm, Jennifer Mulhern *Governor of Michigan*
Kleine, Robert J. *state treasurer*
Land, Terri Lynn *Secretary of State, Michigan*

Pontiac
Pardee, Jeffrey Clark *county government official*

Sterling Heights
Binno, Joseph Michael *retired state attorney general*

Warren
Kolakowski, Diana Jean *economic development director*

MINNESOTA

Minneapolis
Carlson, Arne Helge *former governor*
Mondale, Joan Adams *wife of former Vice President of United States*
Mondale, Walter Frederick *former Vice President of United States, lawyer*
Rybak, R.T. *Mayor, Minneapolis*

Minnetonka
Anderson, Karen Jean *mayor, communications executive, researcher*

Northfield
Levin, Burton *diplomat*

Roseville
Seagren, Alice *state official, school system administrator, former state legislator*

Saint Paul
Coleman, Christopher B. *Mayor, St. Paul, Minnesota*
Hanson, Tom *state treasurer*
Molnau, Carol L. *Lieutenant Governor of Minnesota*
Pawlenty, Timothy James *Governor of Minnesota*
Ritchie, Mark *Secretary of State, Minnesota*
Swanson, Lori A. *state attorney general, lawyer*

MISSISSIPPI

Jackson
Barbour, Haley Reeves *Governor of Mississippi*
Bryant, Phil *Lieutenant Governor of Mississippi*

Hood, Jim *state attorney general*
Hosemann, Delbert (C. Delbert Hosemann Jr) *Secretary of State, Miss.*
Jordan, John W. *state official, school system administrator*
Reeves, Tate *state treasurer*
Winter, William Forrest *Former Governor, Miss, lawyer*

MISSOURI

Jefferson City
Carnahan, Robin *Secretary of State, Missouri*
Kinder, Peter D. *Lieutenant Governor of Missouri, former state senator*
Koster, Chris *state attorney general, former state senator*
Nicastro, Chris L. *state official, school system administrator*
Nixon, Jay (Jeremiah Nixon) *Governor of Missouri*
Zweifel, Clint *state treasurer*

Kansas City
Danner, Kathleen Frances Steele *federal official*
Davis, Richard Francis *city government official*
Funkouser, Mark *Mayor, Kansas City, Missouri*
Price, Charles H., II, *former ambassador*

Saint Charles
Gross, Charles Robert *county official, former state senator, former bank executive*

Saint Louis
Slay, Francis G. *Mayor, St. Louis*

Springfield
Carlson, Thomas Joseph *Mayor, Springfield, Missouri*

MONTANA

Billings
Larsen, Richard Lee *city manager, consultant, retired mayor, arbitrator*

Clancy
Ekanger, Laurie *retired state official, consultant*

Helena
Bohlinger, John C. *Lieutenant Governor of Montana, former state legislator*
Bullock, Steve *state attorney general*
Jergeson, Greg *Public Service Commissioner, Montana*
Juneau, Denise *state official, school system administrator*
Kelly, Janet Lee *state treasurer*
McCulloch, Linda Harman *state official, former school system administrator*
Schweitzer, Brian *Governor of Montana*

NEBRASKA

Lincoln
Beutler, Christopher John *mayor, Lincoln, Nebr., state legislator*
Breed, Roger *state official, school system administrator*
Bruning, Jon Cumberland *state attorney general*
Gale, John A. *Secretary of State, Nebraska*
Heineman, David Eugene *Governor of Nebraska*
Osborn, Shane *state treasurer*
Sheehy, Rick *Lieutenant Governor of Nebraska, former mayor*

Omaha
Fahey, Mike *Mayor, Omaha*

NEVADA

Carson City
Gibbons, Jim (James Arthur Gibbons) *Governor of Nevada, former United States Representative from Nevada*
Krolicki, Brian Keith *Lieutenant Governor of Nevada, former state official, state legislator*
Marshall, Kate *state treasurer*
Masto, Catherine Marie Cortez *state attorney general, former county official*
Miller, Ross James *secretary of state*
Rheault, Keith W. *state official, school system administrator*

Henderson
Gibson, James B. *mayor, Henderson, Nevada*

Las Vegas
Goodman, Oscar Baylin *Mayor, Las Vegas, lawyer*

North Las Vegas
Montandon, Michael *Mayor, North Las Vegas, Nevada*

NEW HAMPSHIRE

Concord
Barry, Virginia M. *state official, school system administrator*
Delaney, Michael A. *state attorney general*
Fitch, Orville Brewster, II, (Bud Fitch) *state official*
Gardner, William Michael *Secretary of State, New Hampshire*
Lynch, John H. *Governor of New Hampshire*
Provencher, Catherine A. *state treasurer*

Goffstown
Holden, Carol Helen *county official*

Nashua
Bergeron, Paul Robert *city clerk*
Pignatelli, Debora Becker *state official*

NEW JERSEY

Cape May Point
Fraser, Malcolm Cavanagh *former mayor*

Fort Lee
Mack, Earle Irving *former ambassador, real estate company executive*

Freehold
Guadagno, Kimberly McFadden *county official, former prosecutor*

Holmdel
Bateman, Alan R. *municipal official*

Irvington
Paden, Harry *municipal official*

Jersey City
Healy, Jerramiah *Mayor, Jersey City, New Jersey*

Morristown
Healey, Thomas J. *former government official, brokerage house executive*

Newark
Booker, Cory Anthony *Mayor, Newark, lawyer*
Pryor, Stefan I. *city manager, real estate developer*

Paterson
Torres, Jose (Joey) *mayor*

Princeton
Keevey, Richard Francis *federal and state official, educator*

Roseland
Byrne, Brendan Thomas, Sr. *former governor*

Sea Isle City
Tull, Theresa Anne *retired diplomat*

Trenton
Corzine, Jon Stevens *Governor of New Jersey*
Davy, Lucille E. *state official, school system administrator*
Milgram, Anne M. *state attorney general*
Palmer, Douglas Harold *Mayor, Trenton, New Jersey*
Rousseau, David R. *state treasurer*
Wells, Nina Mitchell *Secretary of State, New Jersey*

NEW MEXICO

Albuquerque
Cargo, David Francis *former Governor of New Mexico*
Chavez, Martin Joseph *Mayor, Albuquerque, lawyer*
Giller, Edward Bonfoy *retired government official, military officer*
Madrid, Patricia A. *former state attorney general*

Clovis
Bradley, Walter D. *lieutenant governor, real estate broker*

Santa Fe
Denish, Diane D. *Lieutenant Governor of New Mexico*
Garcia, Veronica C. *state official, school system administrator*
Herrera, Mary E. *Secretary of State, New Mexico*
King, Gary K. *state attorney general*
Lewis, James Beliven *state treasurer*
Richardson, Bill (William Blaine Richardson III) *Governor of New Mexico, former United States Secretary of Energy*

NEW YORK

Albany
Brewer, Aida M. *state treasurer*
Cortés-Vázquez, Lorraine *Secretary of State, New York*
Cuomo, Andrew Mark *state attorney general, former United States Secretary of Housing and Urban Development*
Daines, Richard F. *state health commissioner, former health services executive*
DiNapoli, Thomas Peter *state official, former state legislator*
Hogan, Michael F. *state official*
Huxley, Carole Frances Corcoran *former state official, school system administrator*
Jennings, Gerald D. (Jerry Jennings) *Mayor, Albany, New York*
Paterson, David Alexander *Governor of New York, former state legislator*
Rinckey, Greg T. *state attorney general*
Steiner, David Milton *state official, school system administrator, former dean*

Bronx
Diaz, Ruben, Jr. *city official*
Mendez, Ruben Policarpio *diplomat, educator, economist*

Brooklyn
Markowitz, Marty (Martin Markowitz) *city manager*

Buffalo
Brown, Byron William, Jr. *Mayor, Buffalo*

Fabius
Sweetland, Dale A. *former county official, former dairy farmer*

Greenport
Pedersen, Richard Foote *diplomat, academic administrator*

Kew Gardens
Marshall, Helen M. *city official*

Mineola
Martins, Jack M. *mayor*

Nedrow
Lyons, Oren *Native American chieftain, conservationist*

New York
al-Nasser, Nassir Abdulaziz *ambassador*
Arias, Ricardo Alberto *ambassador, lawyer*
Aswady, Adiyatwidi Adiwoso *diplomat*
Ataeva, Aksoltan *diplomat*
Blinken, Donald *ambassador, investment banker*
Bloomberg, Mike (Michael Rubens Bloomberg) *Mayor, New York City*
Brown, Carroll *retired diplomat, association executive, consultant*
Burian, Peter *ambassador*
Butagira, Francis *ambassador*
Christian, Leslie Kojo *ambassador*
Clinton, Bill (William Jefferson Clinton) *42nd President of the United States*
DiCarlo, Rosemary Anne *ambassador*
Eisenstadt, G. Michael *diplomat, writer, educator, researcher*
Farley, Thomas A. *city health department administrator, epidemiologist, pediatrician*
Ferraro, Geraldine Anne *attorney, former United States Representative from New York*
Gardner, Richard Newton *diplomat, lawyer, educator*
Gartner, Alan P. *municipal official*
Gibbs, Linda I. *city official*
Harris, Patricia E. (Patti Harris) *city official*
Heller Rouassant, Claude *ambassador*
Ikouebe, Basile *ambassador*
Ilkin, Baki *ambassador*
Kallstrom, James K. *state official*
Kouliev, Eldar *ambassador*
Kumalo, Dumisani Shadrack *ambassador*
Lefkowitz, Jay Philip *state attorney general*
Levin, Herbert *retired diplomat, foundation administrator*
Lieber, Robert C. *city official, former investment company executive*
Lucas, Sylvie *ambassador*
Marcus, Kenneth L. *federal official*
Mayr-Harting, Thomas *ambassador*
Murphy, Richard William *retired diplomat*
Ney, Edward N. *ambassador, advertising and public relations executive*
Okun, Herbert Stuart *diplomat, educator*
Omotoso, Edward *diplomat, author, journalist*
Platt, Nicholas *retired ambassador*
Reno, Janet *former United States Attorney General*
Rice, Susan Elizabeth *Permanent United States Representative to the United Nations*
Ripert, Jean-Maurice *ambassador*
Ross, Christopher Wade Stelyan *diplomat*
Sadik-Khan, Janette I. *city manager, former federal agency administrator*
Sawers, Sir John *ambassador*
Sheekey, Kevin J. *city official*
Skyler, Edward Gabriel *city official*
Spatafora, Marcello *ambassador*
Streator, Edward *retired diplomat, management consultant*
Stringer, Scott M. *city official, former state legislator*
Takasu, Yukio *ambassador*
Thompson, William Colridge, Jr., (Bill Thompson) *city official*
Urroz-Rapold, Patricia Julia S. *retired diplomat, writer*
Verbeke, Johan C. *ambassador*
Voto-Bernales, Jorge *ambassador*
Wang, Guangya *ambassador*
Weisfuse, Isaac Bram *city health department administrator*
Wolff, Alejandro Daniel *ambassador*
Wyzner, Eugeniusz *diplomat*

Rochester
Duffy, Robert John *Mayor, Rochester, New York*

Slingerlands
Herman, Robert S. *former state official, economist, author, educator*

Staten Island
Molinaro, James P. *city official*

Troy
McDermott, Robert J. *commissioner*

Watertown
Coe, Benjamin Plaisted *retired state official*

Yonkers
Amicone, Philip A. *Mayor, Yonkers, New York*

NORTH CAROLINA

Chapel Hill
Schoonover, Brenda B. *ambassador*

Charlotte
McCrory, Patrick *Mayor, Charlotte, North Carolina*

Durham
Bell, William (Bill) V. *Mayor, Durham, NC*
Joseph, James Alfred *retired ambassador, political scientist, educator*

Fayetteville
Chavonne, Anthony G. *Mayor, Fayetteville, North Carolina*

Greensboro
Johnson, Yvonne J. *Mayor, Greensboro, NC*

High Point
Pate, William Patrick *city manager*
Phillips, Stanley Davis (Dave) *United States Ambassador to Estonia*

Pittsboro
Cotter, Michael William *retired ambassador*

Raleigh
Cooper, Roy Asberry III *state attorney general*
Cowell, Janet *state treasurer*
Dalton, Walter H. *lieutenant governor*
Marshall, Elaine Folk *Secretary of State, NC*
Meeker, Charles C. *Mayor, Raleigh, North Carolina, lawyer*
Perdue, Beverly Eaves *Governor of North Carolina*

Winston Salem
Joines, Allen *mayor, Winston-Salem, North Carolina*

NORTH DAKOTA

Bismarck
Dalrymple, Jack *lieutenant governor*
Hoeven, John *Governor of North Dakota*
Jaeger, Al (Alvin A. Jaeger) *Secretary of State, North Dakota*
Sanstead, Wayne Godfrey *state official, school system administrator*
Schmidt, Kelly L. *state treasurer*
Stenehjem, Wayne Kevin *state attorney general, lawyer*

Minot
Watne, Darlene Claire *county official*

OHIO

Akron
Plusquellic, Donald L. *Mayor, Akron, Ohio*

Cincinnati
Mallory, Mark L. *Mayor, Cincinnati, former state legislator*

Cleveland
Jackson, Frank G. *Mayor, Cleveland*

Columbus
Boyce, Kevin L. *state treasurer*
Brunner, Jennifer Lee *Secretary of State, Ohio, lawyer*
Coleman, Michael Bennett *Mayor, Columbus, Ohio*
Delisle, Deborah S. *state official, school system administrator*
Fisher, Lee I. *Lieutenant Governor of Ohio, former state attorney general*
Lashutka, Gregory S. *mayor, lawyer*
Long, Teresa C. *city health department administrator*
Strickland, Ted *Governor of Ohio, former United States Representative from Ohio*

Dayton
Lashley, William Bartholomew *county official*
McLin, Rhine Lana *Mayor, Dayton, Ohio, former state legislator*
Taft, Bob (Robert Alphonso Taft II) *former governor, educator*

Mansfield
Converse, Sandra *city finance director, financial planner*

Medina
Ballard, John Stuart *retired mayor, lawyer, educator*

Toledo
Finkbeiner, Carlton S. (Carty Finkbeiner) *Mayor, Toledo*

Uniontown
Taylor, Mary *state official*

Worthington
Speck, Samuel Wallace, Jr. *federal official*

OKLAHOMA

Ada
Anoatubby, Bill *Governor of The Chickasaw Nation*

Oklahoma City
Askins, Jari *Lieutenant Governor of Oklahoma*
Cornett, Mick *Mayor, Oklahoma City*
Edmondson, Drew (William Andrew Edmondson) *state attorney general*
Garrett, Sandy Langley *state official, school system administrator*
Henry, Brad (C. Brad Henry) *Governor of Oklahoma*
Meacham, Scott *state treasurer*
Savage, Susan M. *Secretary of State, Oklahoma, former mayor*

Tulsa
Madison, Eddie Lawrence, Jr. *public relations consultant, editor, writer*
Taylor, Kathryn L. *Mayor, Tulsa*

OREGON

Cottage Grove
Clark-Bourne, Kathryn Orpha *retired consul*

Eugene
Bascom, Ruth F. *retired mayor*
Collas-Dean, Angela G. *retired state commissioner, small business owner*

Portland
Adams, Sam *Mayor, Portland, Oregon*
Katz, Vera *former mayor, college administrator, state legislator*
Lake, Joseph Edward *ambassador*
Myers, Hardy *former state attorney general*

Salem
Brown, Kate *state official, former state legislator*
Castillo, Susan *state official, school system administrator*
Kroger, John Richard *state attorney general, former prosecutor, law educator*
Kulongoski, Ted (Theodore Ralph Kulongoski) *Governor of Oregon, former state supreme court justice*
Taylor, Janet R. *Mayor, Salem, Oregon*
Westlund, Ben (Bernard John Westlund II) *state treasurer*

PENNSYLVANIA

Clearfield
McCracken, Mark B. *county official*

Harrisburg
Corbett, Thomas Wingett, Jr. *state attorney general, lawyer*
Cortés, Pedro A. *Secretary of the Commonwealth, Pennsylvania*
McCord, Robert M. *state treasurer*
Pizzingrilli, Kim *state official*
Rendell, Edward Gene *Governor of Pennsylvania, retired mayor, lawyer*
Scarnati, Joseph B. III *Lieutenant Governor of Pennsylvania, state legislator*
Wolfe, Gary Donald *commissioner, retired librarian*

Hazleton
Barletta, Louis *mayor*

Newtown
Brennan, Thomas John *city and state official, consultant, educator*

Philadelphia
Nutter, Michael Anthony *Mayor, Philadelphia, former councilman*
O'Connor, Charles Edward, Jr. *state government official, lawyer*
Schwartz, Donald F. *city health department administrator*
Schweiker, Mark S. *former governor*

Pittsburgh
Bloom, Ron A. *federal official, labor union administrator*
Kerber, Frank John *retired diplomat*
O'Neill, Paul Henry *former United States Secretary of the Treasury*
Ravenstahl, Luke R. *Mayor, Pittsburgh*
Simpson, Daniel H. *ambassador*

State College
Lamb, Robert Edward *retired diplomat, professional society administrator*

York
Wiles, William Wharton *retired federal government official*

RHODE ISLAND

Harmony
Fogarty, Charles Joseph *former lieutenant governor*

Kingston
Sundlun, Bruce *former governor*

Pawtucket
Doyle, James Ernest *mayor*

Providence
Caprio, Frank Thomas *state treasurer, lawyer*
Carcieri, Donald L. *Governor of Rhode Island*
Cicilline, David N. *Mayor, Providence, Rhode Island*
Gist, Deborah A. *state official, school system administrator*
Lynch, Patrick C. *state attorney general*
Mollis, A. Ralph *Secretary of State, Rhode Island, former mayor*
Roberts, Elizabeth H. *Lieutenant Governor of Rhode Island, former state legislator*

SOUTH CAROLINA

Columbia
Bauer, R. Andre *lieutenant governor*
Beasley, David Muldrow *former governor, consultant*
Chellis, Converse A., II, *state treasurer*
Hammond, Mark *state official*
McMaster, Henry Dargan *state attorney general*
Page, Randall *state official*
Rex, Jim *state official, school system administrator*
Sanford, Mark (Marshall Clement Sanford Jr.) *Governor of South Carolina, former United States Representative from South Carolina*

Pickens
Wyche, Sam David *county official, former professional football coach*

Sumter
Brown, Barbara Ann *county extension agent*

Walterboro
Workman, William Douglas III *town manager; retired mayor, gas industry executive*

SOUTH DAKOTA

Pierre
Daugaard, Dennis M. *lieutenant governor*
Larson, Vernon LeRoy *state treasurer*
Long, Larry *state attorney general*
Nelson, Chris A. *Secretary of State, South Dakota*
Oster, Tom (Thomas J. Oster) *state official, school system administrator*
Rounds, Mike (Marion Michael Rounds) *Governor of South Dakota*

Sioux Falls
Munson, David Roy *Mayor, Sioux Falls, South Dakota*

TENNESSEE

Brownsville
Banks, Webb Follin *mayor*

Chattanooga
Littlefield, Ron *Mayor, Chattanooga, Tennessee*

Fayetteville
Matlock, Jack Foust, Jr. *diplomat*

Knoxville
Haslam, Bill *Mayor, Knoxville, Tennessee*

Nashville
Bredesen, Philip Norman *Governor of Tennessee*
Cooper, Robert Elbert, Jr. *state attorney general*
Dean, Karl *Mayor, Nashville*
Gore, Tipper (Mary Elizabeth Gore) *wife of the former Vice President of the United States*
Hargett, Tre *state official*
Lillard, David H., Jr. *state treasurer*
Paul, William S. *city health department administrator*
Ramsey, Ronald L. *Lieutenant Governor of Tennessee*
Thomas, Hazel Beatrice *state official*
Webb, Timothy K. *state official, school system administrator*

Oak Ridge
Holloway, Jacqueline *county commissioner*

Springfield
Nutting, Paul John *city manager*

TEXAS

Amarillo
McCartt, Debra *Mayor, Amarillo, Texas*

Arlington
Cluck, Robert *Mayor, Arlington, Texas*

Austin
Abbott, Greg *state attorney general, former state supreme court justice*
Andrade, Hope (Esperanza Andrade) *Secretary of State, Texas*
Combs, Susan *state official*
Dewhurst, David *Lieutenant Governor of Texas*
Peacock, Penne Korth *ambassador*
Perry, Rick (James Richard Perry) *Governor of Texas*
Scott, Robert *state official, school system administrator*
Wynn, Will *Mayor, Austin, Texas*

Beaumont
Lord, Evelyn Marlin *mayor*

Brownsville
Ahumada, Patricio M., Jr. *Mayor, Brownsville, Texas*

Corpus Christi
Garrett, Henry *Mayor, Corpus Christi, Texas*

Dallas
Leppert, Thomas C. *Mayor, Dallas, former construction executive*
Thompson, Zachary *city health department administrator*

Denton
Homick, Michael Wayne *program manager, educator*

El Paso
Cook, John *Mayor, El Paso, Texas*

Fort Worth
Moncrief, Michael Joseph *Mayor, Fort Worth, former state legislator*

Garland
Jones, Ronald E. *mayor, Garland, Texas, assoc. pastor*

Giddings
Dismukes, Carol Jaehne *county official*

Grand Prairie
England, Charles *Mayor, Grand Prairie, Texas*

Harlingen
Matz, James Richard *municipal official*

Houston
Bush, George Herbert Walker *41st President of the United States*
Dinkins, Carol Eggert *federal official, lawyer*
Marcotte, Michael Steven *municipal official*
White, Bill (William Howard White) *Mayor, Houston*

Irving
Gears, Herbert A. *Mayor, Irving, Texas*

Laredo
Salinas, Raul G. *Mayor, Laredo, Texas*

Lubbock
Martin, Tom *mayor, Lubbock, Texas*

Mineola
Stevenson, David Wayne *municipal official*

New Braunfels
Krueger, Robert Charles *former ambassador, congressman, senator*

Plano
Evans, Pat *Mayor, Plano, Texas*

San Antonio
Hardberger, Phillip Duane *Mayor, San Antonio, judge, lawyer, journalist*
Henderson, Connie Chorlton *retired city planner, artist, writer*
Larson, Lyle Thomas *commissioner*

UTAH

Park City
Randt, Clark Thorp, Jr. *former ambassador, lawyer*

Saint George
Walker, Olene S. *former governor*

Salt Lake City
Allen, Ronald Carl *commissioner, artist, consultant, former state senator, computer company executive*
Anderson, Ross Carl *Mayor, Salt Lake City, Utah, lawyer, human rights advocate*
Becker, Ralph Elihu, Jr. *Mayor, Salt Lake City, Utah*
Bell, Gregory S. *Lieutenant Governor of Utah, former state legislator*
Ellis, Richard K. *state treasurer*
Herbert, Gary Richard *Governor of Utah*
Shumway, Larry K. *state official, school system administrator*
Shurtleff, Mark L. *state attorney general*

VERMONT

Burlington
Kunin, Madeleine May *former Governor of Vermont*

Montpelier
Douglas, Jim (James Holley Douglas) *Governor of Vermont*
Dubie, Brian E. *Lieutenant Governor of Vermont*
Markowitz, Deborah Lynn *Secretary of State, Vermont*
Sorrell, William H. *state attorney general*
Spaulding, Jeb (George B. Spaulding) *state treasurer*
Vilaseca, Armando *state official, school system administrator*

Peacham
Engle, James Bruce *ambassador*

Rochester
Eddy, John Joseph *diplomat*

South Londonderry
Spiers, Ronald Ian *diplomat*

VIRGINIA

Alexandria
Connell, Mary Ellen *diplomat*
Costagliola, Francesco *retired government official*
Fitton, Harvey Nelson, Jr. *former government official*
Gwadosky, Dan A. *former state official, federal agency administrator*
Havens, Harry Stewart *retired federal official, management consultant*
Helman, Gerald Bernard *diplomat*
Loren, Donald Patrick *federal official, retired military officer*
McNicol, David Leon *retired federal official, researcher*
Powell, Colin Luther *former United States Secretary of State, former chairman of the Joint Chiefs of Staff*
Smith, Elaine Diana *foreign service officer*
Tucker, Alvin Leroy *retired government official*

Annandale
Rogers, Stephen Hitchcock *retired ambassador*

Arlington
Aggrey, Orison Rudolph *former ambassador, consultant, academic administrator*
Bolster, Archie Milburn *retired foreign service officer*
Bowen, Stuart W., Jr. *federal official*
Chatfield, William Austin *federal official*
Galloway, William Jefferson *retired foreign service officer*
Krys, Sheldon Jack *retired diplomat*
Lenhardt, Alfonso Emanuel *federal official, retired career officer, foundation administrator*
Mc Donald, John Warlick *diplomat*
Ochmanek, David Alan *defense analyst*
Pendleton, Mary Catherine *retired foreign service officer*
Pyatt, Everett Arno *federal official*
Sundquist, M. Alexandra (Alix Sundquist) *diplomat, consultant*

Chesapeake
Krasnoff, Alan P. *mayor, Chesapeake, Virginia*
Myrick, Bismarck *diplomat, history professor*

Crozet
Reswick, James Bigelow *former government official, biomedical engineer*

Dulles
Beecroft, Robert Stephen *United States Ambassador to Jordan*
Eastham, Alan Walter, Jr. *United States Ambassador to the Republic of Congo, lawyer*
Mussomeli, Joseph Adamo *ambassador*
Perry, June Carter *United States Ambassador to Sierra Leone*
Ricciardone, Francis Joseph, Jr. *Deputy Ambassador to Islamic Republic of Afghanistan Kabul*
Wayne, Earl Anthony *ambassador*

Falls Church
Bingman, Charles Franklin *government executive, educator*
Ward, George Frank, Jr. *international programs executive, ambassador*

Fredericksburg
Jones, Harry Edward *diplomat, writer*

Great Falls
Minikes, Stephan Michael *ambassador, lawyer, banker*
Railton, W(illiam) Scott *retired commissioner*

Haymarket
Doolittle, Warren T. *retired federal official*

King George
Newhall, David III *retired federal official*

Lake Ridge
Stottlemyer, David Lee *federal official*

Lynchburg
Stephens, Bart Nelson *former foreign service officer*

Manassas
Crum, Charles Noel *state magistrate*
Storing, Paul Edward *retired foreign service officer*

Markham
Ojeda Eiseley, Jaime de *former Spanish ambassador, educator*

Mc Lean
Cahill, Harry Amory *diplomat, educator*
Card, Andy (Andrew Hill Card Jr.) *former White House chief of staff, former United States Secretary of Transportation*
Leiter, Michael E. *federal official*
Russell, Theodore Emery *diplomat*
Trout, Maurice Elmore *diplomat*

Newport News
Frank, Joe S. *Mayor, Newport News, Virginia, lawyer*

Norfolk
Fraim, Paul D. *Mayor, Norfolk, Virginia*

Oakton
Farwell, Albert Edmond *retired government official, consultant*

Reston
Grant, Carl Nothhaft III *business executive*

Richmond
Bolling, Bill (William T. Bolling) *Lieutenant Governor of Virginia*
Ganeriwala, Manju S. *state treasurer*
Hanley, Katherine Keith *Secretary of the Commonwealth, Virginia*
Jones, Dwight Clinton *Mayor, Richmond, Virginia*
Kaine, Timothy Michael *Governor of Virginia*
LeBlanc, Daniel G. *state official*
McDonnell, Bob (Robert Francis) *former state attorney general, state legislator*
Mims, William Cleveland *state attorney general, lawyer*
Wilder, Doug (Lawrence Douglas Wilder) *Mayor, Richmond, Virginia, former governor*
Wright, Patricia I. *state official, school system administrator*

Spotsylvania
Hardy, Dorcas Ruth *business and government relations executive*

Stanardsville
Keel, Alton Gold, Jr. *ambassador*

Suffolk
Walker, Dale Maxwell *city official*

Susan
Ambach, Dwight Russell *retired foreign service officer*

The Plains
Gibbons, John Howard (Jack, Jack Gibbons) *federal official, physicist*

Vienna
DeWitt, Charles Barbour *federal official*

Virginia Beach
Fraser, Ruth Hodges *city clerk*
Friedman, Andrew Mitchell *director housing and neighborhood preservation*
Sessoms, William D., Jr. *Mayor, Virginia Beach, Virginia, bank executive*

Williamsburg
Wilkerson, Lawrence B. *former federal official, retired military officer*

WASHINGTON

Battle Ground
Ezelle, Robert Eugene *diplomat*

Cosmopolis
Luark, Lillian *retired city clerk*

Mill Creek
O'Keefe, Kathleen Mary *state official*

Olympia
Dorn, Randy (Randolph I. Dorn) *state official, school system administrator*
Gregoire, Christine O'Grady *Governor of Washington, former state attorney general*
Kreidler, Myron (Mike) *State Insurance Commissioner of Washington, Fomer United States Representative, Washington, optometrist*
McIntire, James L. *state treasurer*
McKenna, Rob *state attorney general, former councilman*
Owen, Bradley Scott *Lieutenant Governor of Washington*
Reed, Sam *Secretary of State, Washington*

Redmond
Schneider, Roy Lester *former Governor of Virgin Islands*

Seattle
Fleming, David W. *city health department director*
Gouldthorpe, Kenneth Alfred Percival *state official, editor*
Johnson, Darryl Norman *former ambassador*
Nickels, Greg *Mayor, Seattle*
Rosellini, Albert D. *former governor*
Zumeta, William Mark *public policy educator*

Spokane
Verner, Mary *Mayor, Spokane, Washington*

Sumas
Hemry, Larry Harold *former federal agency official, writer, inventor*

Tacoma
Baarsma, Bill *Mayor, Tacoma*

Vancouver
Pollard, Royce *Mayor, Vancouver, Washington*

WEST VIRGINIA

Charleston
Douglass, Gus Ruben *Commissioner of Agriculture, West Virginia*
Hechler, Ken *retired state official, congressman, writer, political science professor*
Mc Graw, Darrell Vivian, Jr. *state attorney general*
Paine, Steven L. *state official, school system administrator*
Perdue, John D. *state treasurer*
Tennant, Natalie E. *state official*

WISCONSIN

Ashland
Smith, Jane Schneberger *retired city administrator*

Eau Claire
Frank, John LeRoy *commissioner, lawyer, educator*

Madison
Cieslewicz, David J. *Mayor, Madison, Wisconsin*
Doyle, Jim (James Edward) *Governor of Wisconsin, former state attorney general*
Earl, Anthony Scully *former governor, lawyer*
Evers, Tony (Anthony Evers) *state official, school system administrator*
La Follette, Douglas J. *Secretary of State, Wisconsin*
Lautenschlager, Peggy A. *former state attorney general*
Lawton, Barbara *Lieutenant Governor of Wisconsin*
Sass, Dawn Marie *state treasurer*
Thompson, Barbara Storck *state official*
Van Hollen, J(ohn) B(yron) *state attorney general, former prosecutor*

Milwaukee
Barrett, Thomas M. (Tom Barrett) *Mayor, Milwaukee, former United States Representative from Wisconsin*
Lucey, Patrick Joseph *former Governor of Wisconsin*

WYOMING

Cheyenne
Freudenthal, Dave (David D. Freudenthal) *Governor of Wyoming*
Maxfield, Max R. *Secretary of State, Wyoming*
Meyer, Joseph B. *state treasurer*
Salzburg, Bruce A. *state attorney general*
Thomson, Thyra Godfrey *former state official*
Woodhouse, Gay Vanderpoel *former state attorney general, lawyer*

Evanston
Harris, Mark W. *former mayor, lawyer*

Laramie
Dickman, Francois Moussiegt *former foreign service officer, educator*

TERRITORIES OF THE UNITED STATES

AMERICAN SAMOA

Pago Pago
Poumele, Claire Tuia *state official, school system administrator*
Ripley, Afa, Jr., (Fepulea'i A. Ripley Jr.) *attorney general*
Sunia, Ipulasi Aitofele Toese F. *Lieutenant Governor of American Samoa*
Tulafono, Togiola T.A. *Governor of American Samoa*

FEDERATED STATES OF MICRONESIA

Pohnpei
Falcam, Leo A. *former Micronesian government official*

GUAM

Hagatna
Camacho, Felix Perez *Governor of Guam*
Cruz, Michael W. *Lieutenant Governor of Guam, surgeon*
Limtiaco, Alicia Garrido *state attorney general, former prosecutor*

NORTHERN MARIANA ISLANDS

Saipan
Baka, Gregory *acting attorney general*
Fitial, Benigno Repeki *Governor of Northern Mariana Islands*
Inos, Eloy Songao *Lieutenant Governor of the Northern Mariana Islands*
Sablan, Rita Aldan *state official, school system administrator*

PUERTO RICO

San Juan
Fortuño, Luis Guillermo *Governor of Puerto Rico*
McClintock, Kenneth D. (Kenneth D. McClintock-Hernandez) *Puerto Rican secretary of state, former state legislator*
Sagardía, Antonio (Antonio Miguel Sagardía De Jesus) *attorney general*
Santini, Jorge A. *Mayor, San Juan, Puerto Rico*

VIRGIN ISLANDS

Christiansted
Francis, Gregory R. *Lieutenant Governor of US Virgin Islands*

St Thomas
de Jongh, John Percy, Jr. *Governor of the United States Virgin Islands, real estate company executive*
Frazer, Vincent F. *attorney general*
Turnbull, Charles Wesley *former governor*

MILITARY ADDRESSES OF THE UNITED STATES

EUROPE

APO
Marshall, Brian Laurence *federal official*

PACIFIC

Stanton, William Anthony *diplomat*

CANADA

BRITISH COLUMBIA

Vancouver
Austin, Jacob (Jack Austin) *retired Canadian government official*

MANITOBA

Winnipeg
Filmon, Gary Albert *Canadian provincial premier, civil engineer*

ONTARIO

Nobleton
Embleton, Tony Frederick Wallace *retired Canadian government official*

Ottawa
Armstrong, Henry Conner *former Canadian government official, consultant*
Buchanan, John MacLennan *Canadian provincial official*
Copps, Sheila *former Canadian government official, political journalist, commentator*
Fairbairn, Joyce *Canadian government official*
Hervieux-Payette, Céline *Canadian senator*
Malone, David Michael *diplomat, educator*
O'Connor, Gordon James *Canadian government official*
Penner, Keith *former Canadian government official*
Stanford, Joseph Stephen *diplomat, lawyer, educator*
Yalden, Maxwell Freeman *Canadian diplomat*
Yeomans, Donald Ralph *Canadian government official, consultant*

Toronto
Gotlieb, Allan E. *former ambassador*
Holyday, Douglas Charles *city councillor*
MacLaren, Roy *retired Canadian government official*
Mohler, Brian Jeffery *diplomat*

QUEBEC

Montreal
Gabbour, Iskandar *city and regional planning educator*
Mulroney, Brian (Martin Brian Mulroney) *former Prime Minister of Canada*

SASKATCHEWAN

Saskatoon
Blakeney, Allan Emrys *Canadian government official, lawyer, educator*

MEXICO

Mexico City
Cardenas Solorzano, Cuauhtemoc *Mexican government official*
Frenk, Julio Jose *minister of health for Mexico, health systems researcher, consultant*
Téllez Kuenzler, Luis *former government official, investment banker*

ALGERIA

Algiers
Bouteflika, Abdelaziz *President of Algeria*

El-Biar
Ford, Robert Stephen *United States Ambassador to Algeria*

ANTIGUA AND BARBUDA

St John's
Carlisle, James B. *former head of state*

ARUBA

Oranjestad
Oduber, Nelson Orlando *Prime Minister of Aruba*

AUSTRALIA

Barton
Evans, Gareth *Australian government and international official*

Camberwell
Peterson, Douglas Brian (Pete Peterson) *former ambassador, former United States Representative from Florida*

AUSTRIA

Vienna
Schulte, Gregory L. *United States Ambassador to United Nations, Vienna*
Finley, Julie Hamm *United States Ambassador to Organization for Security and Cooperation in Europe*

AZERBAIJAN

Baku
Garayev, Abulfas Mursal *government official*

BAHRAIN

Riffa
Al-Khalifa, Sheikh Hamad bin Isa *King of Bahrain*

BELARUS

Minsk
Prokopovich, Petr *federal official*

BELGIUM

Brussels
Albert II, King (Albert Félix Humbert Théodore Chrétien Eugène Marie) *Monarch of Belgium*
Daalder, Ivo H. *United States Permanent Representative to NATO*
Gray, C(layland) Boyden *federal official, former United States Ambassador to European Union, lawyer*

Habay-la-Neuve
Nothomb, Charles Ferdinand *Belgian government official, minister*

BELIZE

Belmopan
Young, Sir Colville *Belizean government official*

BRUNEI

Bandar Seri Begawan
Todd, William E. *United States Ambassador to Brunei Darussalam*

CAMBODIA

Phnom Penh
Chhang, Youk *Cambodian government official*

CAMEROON

Yaoundé
Biya, Paul *President of the Republic of Cameroon*

CHILE

Santiago
Wilkey, Malcolm Richard *retired ambassador, judge*

CHINA

Beijing
Jiabao, Wen *Chinese government official*

COSTA RICA

San José
Arias Sanchez, Oscar *President of Costa Rica*

COTE D'IVOIRE

Abidjan
Gbagbo, Laurent *President of Cote d'Ivoire*

CYPRUS

Nicosia
Evangelou, Alecos Costa *former Cyprian government official*

CZECH REPUBLIC

Prague
Dienstbier, Jiří *diplomat, writer, political scientist, journalist*

DEMOCRATIC REPUBLIC OF CONGO

Kinshasa
Garvelink, William John *United States Ambassador to the Democratic Republic of Congo*

DENMARK

Copenhagen
Petersen, Niels Helveg *Danish government official*

Lyngburg
Federspiel, Ulrik *diplomat*

DOMINICAN REPUBLIC

Santo Domingo
Fernandez Reyna, Leonel *President of The Dominican Republic*

EGYPT

Cairo
Marei, Mamdouh Mohey Eddine *Egyptian government official*

ENGLAND

London
Elizabeth II, (Elizabeth Alexandra Mary) *By the Grace of God of the United Kingdom of Great Britain and Northern Ireland and of Her Other Realms and Territories Queen, Head of the Commonwealth, Defender of the Faith*
Ischinger, Wolfgang *ambassador, diplomat*
LeBaron, Richard B. *ambassador*
Meyer, Sir Christopher J.R. *former ambassador*

Surrey
Weston, Sir John (Sir Philip John Weston) *retired diplomat*

ETHIOPIA

Addis Ababa
Simon, John Andrew *United States Ambassador to the African Union*
Wolde Giorgis, Girma *President of Ethiopia*

FIJI

Suva
Rabuka, Sitiveni Ligamamada *Fijian government official, army officer*

FINLAND

Raisio
Haavisto, Heikki Johannes *retired Finnish government official*

FRANCE

Paris
Egan, Christopher F. *United States Ambassador to the Organization for Economic Cooperation & Development*
Jeantelot, Charles Marcel Jean *retired French diplomat*
Jones, Richard Henry *international organization official, retired ambassador*
Kouchner, Bernard *French government official, humanitarian*
Lagarde, Christine *French government official, lawyer*
Myerson, Jacob Myer *retired diplomat*
Oliver, Louise V. *United States Ambassador to UNESCO*
Rocard, Michel Louis Léon *French politician*

Port-Fréjus
Crapon de Caprona, Count Noël François Marie *retired senior United Nations official*

GERMANY

Berlin
Stabreit, Immo Friedrich Helmut *diplomat*

Stuttgart
Yates, Mary Carlin *diplomat*

GREECE

Athens
Papoulias, Karolos *President of the Republic of Greece*
Tzannetakis, Tzannis *Greek government official*

HONG KONG

Central
Arculli, Ronald Joseph *Hong Kong government official*

Hong Kong
Wong, Joseph Wing Ping *Hong Kong government official*

HUNGARY

Budapest
Horn, Gyula *former Prime Minister of Hungary*

ICELAND

Mos
Hannibalsson, Jon Baldvin *Icelandic ambassador, politician*

Reykjavik
Oddsson, David *former Prime Minister of Iceland, bank executive*

INDIA

New Delhi
Dikshit, Sheila *state official*

INDONESIA

Manado
Sarundajang, Sinyo Harry *government official*

IRELAND

Derry
Hume, John *retired politician of Northern Ireland*

Dublin
Ahern, Dermot *Irish government official*
McDaid, Jim *government official*

ISRAEL

Jerusalem
Peres, Shimon *President of Israel*

ITALY

Rome
Berlusconi, Silvio *Prime Minister of Italy, professional sports team executive*
Khamzayev, Almaz N. *ambassador*
Vasquez, Gaddi H. *United States Ambassador to the United Nations, Rome*
Vento, Sergio *former ambassador*

JAPAN

Tokyo
Abe, Nobuyasu *ambassador*
Akihito, Emperor *Emperor of Japan*

JORDAN

Amman
Masri, Taher Nashat *Jordanian government official*

LATVIA

Riga
Ulmanis, Guntis *former President of Latvia*

LITHUANIA

Vilnius
Brazauskas, Algirdas Mykolas *Prime Minister Republic of Lithuania*

LUXEMBOURG

Senningerberg
Fulci, Francesco Paolo *former diplomat*

MALAWI

Lilongwe
Malewezi, Justin *Malawian government official*

MALTA

Valletta
Fenech, Joseph *former Maltese government official, lawyer*

MAURITIUS

Port Louis
Ramgoolam, Navinchandra *Prime Minister of the Republic of Mauritius*

MONTENEGRO

Podgorica
Vujanović, Filip *President of Republic of Montenegro*

NAMIBIA

Windoek
Nujoma, Sam Daniel *President of Namibia*

NETHERLANDS

Amsterdam
Momin, Alhaj Babul Ahmed *investigation bureau director, poet, writer*

The Hague
Beatrix, Her Majesty Queen (Beatrix Wilhelmina Armgard van Oranje-Nassau) *Queen of The Netherlands*
Tomka, Peter *diplomat, arbitrator, judge, lawyer*

NETHERLANDS ANTILLES

Willemstad
Saleh, Jaime *former Netherlands Antilles government official*

NORWAY

Oslo
Harald V, King *King of Norway*
Lodgaard, Sverre *nuclear disarmament researcher*
Vibe, Kjeld *ambassador*

PHILIPPINES

Makati
Ramos, Fidel V. (Eddie Ramos) *former president of The Philippines*

Pasay City
Romulo, Alberto G. *Philippine government official*

POLAND

Katowice
Messner, Zbigniew *former Prime Minister of Poland, politician, economist*

Warsaw
Oleksy, Jozef *former Prime Minister of Poland*

PORTUGAL

Cascais
Amaral, Diogo Freitas Do *former Portuguese government official, educator*

REPUBLIC OF KOREA

Seoul
Han, Seung-Soo *Prime Minister of South Korea*

RUSSIA

Moscow
Ushakov, Yury Viktorovich *Russian government official, former ambassador*

SAINT LUCIA

Castries
Louisy, Pearlette *governor general of Saint Lucia*

SAINT VINCENT AND THE GRENADINES

Bequia
Mitchell, Sir James Fitzallen *former Prime Minister of Saint Vincent and The Grenadines, agronomist, hotelier*

SAUDI ARABIA

Riyadh
Al-Shaikh, Abdallah Muhammad Ibrahim Al *Saudi Arabian government official*

SENEGAL

Dakar
Bernicat, Marcia Stephens Bloom *United States Ambassador to Republics of Senegal and Guinea-Bissau*
Wade, Abdoulaye *President of Senegal*

SERBIA

Belgrade
Milutinovic, Milan A. *former President of the Republic of Serbia*

SEYCHELLES

Victoria
Michel, Alix James *President of Seychelles*

SOUTH AFRICA

Mmabatho Northwest
Mangope, Lucas Manyane *tribal chief, politician*

SPAIN

La Gomera
Wells, Melissa Foelsch *retired ambassador*

Madrid
Juan Carlos, His Majesty , I, (Juan Carlos de Borbón y Borbón) *King of Spain*

SWEDEN

Stockholm
Gradin, Anita *former ambassador and European Commission member*
Wachtmeister, Count Wilhelm H.F. *retired diplomat*

SWITZERLAND

Berne
Blocher, Christoph *Swiss government official*

Geneva
Brown, Kent Newville *ambassador*
Tichenor, Warren W. *United States Ambassador to the United Nations, Geneva*

TAIWAN

Taipei
Chien, Fredrick Fu *Taiwan government official, foundation administrator*
Lee, Teng-Hui *Former President of Taiwan*
Lien Chan, *Chinese government official*

TAJIKISTAN

Dushanbe
Oqilov, Oqil Ghaybulloyevich *Prime Minister of Tajikistan*

THAILAND

Bangkok
John, Eric G. *United States Ambassador to Thailand*
McMillion, Margaret Kim *foreign service officer*
Suwat, Liptapanlop *Thailand government official*

TUNISIA

Tunis
Ben Ali, Zine El-Abidine *President of Tunisia*

TURKEY

Ankara
Gül, Abdullah *President of Turkey*

UNITED ARAB EMIRATES

Sharjah
al-Qasimi, Sheikh Sultan bin Muhammad (Sheikh Sultan bin Muhammad Al-Qasimi) *Emir of Sharjah*

ADDRESS UNPUBLISHED

Acevedo-Vilá, Aníbal *former Governor of Puerto Rico*
Adams, Edwin Melville *retired diplomat, actor, writer*
Adams, Weston *former diplomat, military officer, lawyer*
Addington, David S. *former federal official, lawyer*
Alholm, Björn-Olof Georg *diplomat*
Alter, Edward T. *former state treasurer*
Amato Chiaramonte Bordonaro, Baron Carlo Camillo *ambassador, consultant*
Andjaba, Martin *ambassador*
Arcos, Cresencio S. *ambassador*
Ash, Roy Lawrence *former federal official*
Ashe, Victor Henderson *former United States Ambassador to Poland, former mayor*
Atkins, Paul Stewart *former commissioner*
Atwater, Phyllis Y. *municipal official*
Ayotte, Kelly A. *former state attorney general*
Baca, Jim *mayor*
Bandar, Prince bin Sultan bin Abd al-Aziz Al Saud *former ambassador*
Bates, Barbara J. Neuner *retired municipal official*
Beard, Ann Southard *diplomat, oil industry executive*
Bellmon, Henry Louis *former Governor of Oklahoma*
Benson, Craig Robert *former governor*
Bergland, Robert Selmer *former United States Secretary of Agriculture*
Betti, John Anso *federal official, retired automotive executive*

Bierring, Ole *ambassador*
Bies, Susan Schmidt *former federal official*
Blagojevich, Rod R. (Milorad Blagojevich) *former Governor of Illinois, former United States Representatives from Illinois*
Blanco, Kathleen Babineaux *former governor*
Bliss, Donald Tiffany, Jr. *retired ambassador*
Bodman, Samuel Wright III *former United States Secretary of Energy*
Bolen, David Benjamin *former ambassador*
Bolten, Joshua Brewster *former White House chief of staff*
Bonardi De Bretignon, Claude-David *ambassador*
Bonilla, Fernando J. *former Puerto Rican government official*
Botelho, Bruce Manuel *mayor, retired state attorney general*
Bowen, Otis Ray *former United States Secretary of Health and Human Services, former Governor of Indiana*
Boyatt, Thomas David *retired ambassador*
Boyce, Ralph L., Jr., (Skip Boyce) *former ambassador*
Boyd, Alan Stephenson *retired United States Secretary of Transportation*
Bradbury, Bill (William Chapman Bradbury III) *former state official*
Bradley, Jennette B. *former state official, lieutenant governor*
Bremer, Paul (Lewis Paul Bremer III, Jerry Bremer) *former diplomat*
Brill, Kenneth C. *federal official, former ambassador*
Brock, William Emerson, III, (Bill Brock) *former United States Secretary of Labor*
Brook, Scott Jonathan Bradley *mayor, lawyer*
Brown, June Gibbs *retired government official*
Brown, Lee Patrick *retired mayor, former federal official*
Burchman, Leonard *federal official, journalist*
Bush, Barbara Pierce *former First Lady of the United States, volunteer*
Bush, George Walker *43rd President of the United States*
Bush, Jeb (John Ellis Bush) *former governor*
Bush, Laura Welch *former First Lady of the United States*
Butenis, Patricia Agatha *former ambassador*
Byrne, John Edward (JEB Byrne) *retired federal official*
Calderón, Sila Maria *former Governor of Puerto Rico*
Campbell, John *former ambassador*
Carlucci, Frank Charles III *former United States Secretary of Defense*
Carney, John C., Jr. *former Lieutenant Governor of Delaware*
Carney, Timothy Michael *ambassador*
Carter, Steve *former state attorney general*
Cason, James Caldwell *retired ambassador*
Chanos, George J. *former state attorney general*
Chem, Widhya *ambassador*
Cheney, Dick (Richard Bruce Cheney) *former Vice President of the United States, United States Secretary of Defense*
Cherry, Robert Steven III *municipal official*
Chien, Nguyen Tam *ambassador*
Chrétien, Raymond A.J. *retired ambassador*
Clamon, Christopher *state attorney general*
Clarke, Henry Lee *foreign service officer, ambassador*
Clayton, Raymond Edward *municipal official*
Clerides, Glafcos John *former President of Cyprus, lawyer*
Cockrel, Kenneth Vern, Jr. *former mayor*
Colberg, Talis James *mayor, former state attorney general*
Connor, Geoffrey Scott *former state official, lawyer*
Coop, Frederick Robert *retired city manager*
Coppie, Comer Swift *retired state official*
Cordray, Richard A. *state attorney general*
Cornell, Robert Arthur *retired federal official*
Cosman, Francene Jen *former government official*
Crocker, Ryan Clark *former ambassador*
Crvenkovski, Branko *former president of Macedonia*
Daglis, Lisa Genine *deputy attorney general*
Dailey, Jim *former mayor*
Dann, Marc E. *former state attorney general, former state senator*
Deily, Linnet Frazier *former ambassador*
Dell, Christopher William *United States Ambassador to the Republic of Kosovo*
Deming, Rust M. *ambassador, educator*
de Oliveira Maciel, Marco Antonio *former Brazilian Vice President*
Derwinski, Edward Joseph *former United States Secretary of Veterans Affairs*
de Schoutheete de Tervarent, Philippe *ambassador*
Devaney, Earl E. *federal official*
Dillon, Robert Sherwood *retired diplomat*
Dinallo, Eric Robert *former state official*
Dominguez, Cari M. *former federal official*
Dornbush, K. Terry *former ambassador, consulting company executive, educator*
Dozier, Therese Knecht *department of education advisor, former education association administrator*
Drue, Kerry Erica *former attorney general*
Duddy, Patrick Dennis *former ambassador*
Earp, Naomi Churchill *former federal official*
Easley, Michael Francis *former Governor of North Carolina*
Edwards, Randall *former state treasurer*
Egan, Wesley William *former ambassador*
Eisenhower, John Sheldon Doud *former ambassador, writer*
Ekeus, Rolf Carl *diplomat*
Eliasson, Jan Kenneth *former Swedish government official, former President of United Nations General Assembly and Minister for Foreign Affairs*
Eliot, Theodore Lyman, Jr. *former ambassador, consultant*
Elson, Edward Elliott *diplomat*
Emmons, Robert Duncan *diplomat*
Ewing, Raymond Charles *retired ambassador*
Fargo, Heather *Former Mayor, Sacramento, California*
Farren, J. Michael *former federal official, lawyer*
Fiddick, Paul William *public official, broadcast executive*
Fischer, David J. *retired mayor*
Fletcher, Ernie (Ernest Lee Fletcher) *Former Governor of Kentucky*
Ford, Charles A. *former ambassador*
Ford, Ford Barney *retired federal official*
Fraser, Donald MacKay *retired mayor, Former United States Representative, Minnesota*
Fratto, Tony (Salvatore Antonio Fratto) *former federal official*
Gardner, James Carson (Jim Gardner) *former lieutenant governor, congressman*
Gardom, Garde Basil *former lieutenant governor of British Columbia*
Garza, Ed *former mayor*
Gayoom, Maumoon Abdul *former president of Maldives*
Giulianti, Mara Selena *former mayor*
Glendon, Mary Ann *US Ambassador to the Holy See, law educator*
Grady, Wayne Joseph *retired government official*
Gribbin, Robert E. III *diplomat*
Guhin, Michael Alan *ambassador*
Guinn, Kenny C. (Kenneth Carroll Guinn) *former governor*
Gumppert, Karella Ann *federal government official*
Hadley, Stephen John *former National Security Advisor*
Haig, Alexander Meigs, Jr. *former United States Secretary of State, retired military officer*
Hanmer, Stephen Read, Jr. *retired federal official*
Hannah, John Peter *former federal official*
Harder, Robert Clarence *state official*
Hardie Boys, Sir Michael *former New Zealand governor general*
Harris, Jeremy *former mayor*
Harris, Joe Frank *former governor*
Haskett, Dianne Louise *retired mayor, lawyer, consultant*
Healey, Kerry Murphy *former lieutenant governor*
Heckler, Margaret Mary *former ambassador, former United States Secretary of Health & Human Services*
Heed, Peter W. *former state attorney general*
Heimbold, Charles Andreas, Jr. *former ambassador*
Hennessey, Keith B. *former federal official*
Herbold, Patricia Louise *retired ambassador*
Herenton, Willie W. *retired mayor*
Hermannsson, Steingrimur *former Prime Minister of Iceland*
Hester, Nancy Elizabeth *county government official*
Higginbottom, Heather A. *federal official*
Hillman, Jennifer Anne *international official*
Hinds, Sallie Ann *retired township official*
Holbrooke, Richard Charles Albert *diplomat*
Holiday, Edith Elizabeth *former presidential adviser, cabinet secretary*
Holmes, Henry Allen *diplomat, educator*
Howard, Robert Elliott *former federal official, consultant, educator*
Huckabee, Mike (Michael Dale Huckabee) *former Governor of Arkansas*
Huddle, Franklin Pierce, Jr. *diplomat*
Huddleston, Vicki Jean *former ambassador*
Hull, Jane Dee *former governor, state legislator*
Hunt, Lorraine T. *former lieutenant governor*
Ireland, Betty *former state official*
Isaac, Teresa Ann *former mayor, lawyer*
Jackson, Alphonso Roy *former United States Secretary of Housing and Urban Development*
Jackson, Barry Steven *former federal official*
Jacobsen, Diane DeMell *foreign policy specialist*
James, William Hall *former state official, educator*
Javits, Eric Moses *ambassador, lawyer*
Jennings, Toni (Antoinette Lee Jennings) *former lieutenant governor, former state senator*
Johnson, Brad *former state official*
Johnson, Bruce E. *former lieutenant governor, state legislator*
Johnson, Clay III *former federal official*
Johnson, Gary Earl *former governor*
Kaplan, Richard Alan *government official*
Katzenbach, Nicholas deBelleville *former United States Attorney General*
Kay, Joshua B. *attorney, educator*
Keegan, John Charles *former mayor, retired military officer, former state legislator*
Kempthorne, Dirk Arthur *former United States Secretary of the Interior*
Kendig, William Lamar *retired federal official, financial manager*
Kerr, Donald MacLean, Jr. *federal official, physicist*
Khalilzad, Zalmay Mamozy *former Permanent United States Representative to the United Nations*
Kim Jong Il, *Democratic People's Republic of Korea Supreme Leader*
Knowles, Tony (Anthony Carroll Knowles) *former governor*
Konwinski, Lisa Michele *federal official, lawyer*
Koplan, Stephen *former federal official*
Kottkamp, Jeffrey Dean *Lieutenant Governor of Florida, lawyer*
Kulstad, Guy Charles *public works official*
Lahoud, Émile Jamil *former president of Lebanon, retired military officer*
Laird, Melvin Robert, Jr. *former United States Secretary of Defense*
Langdale, Mark *former ambassador, former hotel executive*
Leavitt, Michael Okerlund *former United States Secretary of Health and Human Services*
Ledogar, Stephen J. *retired diplomat*
Le Pensec, Louis *French government official*
Levitte, Jean-David *former ambassador*
Levy, Leah Garrigan *federal official*
Lewis, Andrew Lindsay, Jr., (Drew Lewis) *former United States Secretary of Transportation*
Loiello, John Peter *diplomat, international consultant*
Loy, Frank Ernest *retired federal official diplomat*
Lozančić, Niko *former President of Federation of Bosnia and Herzegovina*
Luti, Bill (William Joseph Luti) *federal official, retired military officer*
MacAulay, Lawrence A. *former Canadian government official, member of Parliament*
Macedo de la Concha, Rafael *former Mexican government official*
Maisto, John F. *former ambassador*
Manning, David Geoffrey *former ambassador*
Marburger, John Harmen III *former federal official*
Marine, Michael W. *former ambassador*
Marshall, Freddie Ray *former United States Secretary of Labor*
Martin, Edwin Wilson *mayor*
Martin, Kevin Jeffrey *former federal official*
Martin, Lynn Morley *former United States Secretary of Labor*
Martin, Paul *former Prime Minister of Canada*
Masekela, Barbara Joyce Mosima *former ambassador*
Mathews, Mary Kathryn *retired government official*
Mattingly, Mack Francis *former ambassador, Former United States Senator, Georgia, entrepreneur*
Mazankowski, Donald Frank *Canadian government official*
McBride, Anita Bevacqua *former federal official*
McCallum, Robert Davis, Jr. *former ambassador*
McCaw, Susan Rasinski *former ambassador*
McClennen, Miriam J. *former state official*
McConnell, Mike (John Michael McConnell) *former Director of National Intelligence, retired military officer*
Mc Coy, Tidal Windham *former government official*
McDougall, Donald Blake *retired provincial official, librarian*
McMillin, Stephen Scott *former federal official*
McNamara, Thomas Edmund (Ted) *federal official, former ambassador*
Millane, Lynn *retired municipal official*
Miller, Jonathan S. *former state treasurer*
Miller, Laura M. *former mayor, journalist*
Mills, Richard Paul *former state official, school system administrator*
Minner, Ruth Ann *former Governor of Delaware*
Moe, Lonn Andre *state revenue official*
Mogae, Festus Gontebanye *former president of Botswana*
Moloney, William J. *former state official, school system administrator*
Montgomery, Betty Dee *former state attorney general, state legislator*
Moore, John Eddy *former lieutenant governor*
Morris, Robert Gemmill *retired foreign service officer*
Morrison, Paul J. *former state attorney general, prosecutor*
Muluzi, Elson Bakili *former President of Malawi*
Murphy, Gerald *retired federal official*
Murphy, Michael Joseph *former state treasurer*
Murphy, Remington Morris *clerk*
Murray, Timothy Patrick *Lieutenant Governor of Massachusetts, former mayor*
Nelson, Norman Daniel *government official*
Nemfakos, Charles Panagiotis *defense industry executive, strategic consultant*
Norton, Jane Ellen Bergman (Jane Bergman) *former lieutenant governor*
Nuland, Victoria J. *former United States permanent representative to NATO*
Obermann, Richard Michael *governmental technology and policy analyst*
Oberndorf, Meyera E. *Former Mayor, Virginia Beach, Virginia*
Obiozor, George Achulike *former ambassador*
O'Neill, Beverly Lewis *former mayor, college president*
Ong, John Doyle *former ambassador, retired manufacturing executive*
Palin, Sarah Heath *former Governor of Alaska*
Paulson, Hank (Henry Merritt Paulson Jr.) *former United States Secretary of the Treasury*
Peake, James Benjamin *former United States Secretary of Veterans Affairs, retired military officer*
Pearce, Drue *federal official, former state legislator*
Pearl, Laurence Dickson *retired federal government executive*
Pederson, Sally J. *former lieutenant governor*
Peters, Mary Elizabeth *former United States Secretary of Transportation*
Petrequin, Harry Joseph, Jr. *foreign service officer*
Peyton, John *Mayor, Jacksonville, Florida*
Placke, James Anthony *retired diplomat*
Powell, Donald E. *former federal official*
Powell, J. Braxton *retired state treasurer*
Preston, Steven C. *former United States Secretary of Housing and Urban Development*
Price, Daniel Martin *federal official, lawyer*
Pridmore, Roy Davis *retired federal official*
Qualls, Roxanne *mayor*
Quinn, Eugene Frederick *diplomat, minister*
Randolph, Virgella *retired federal official*
Reagan, Nancy Davis (Anne Francis Robbins) *former First Lady of the United States, volunteer*
Redd, Scott (John Scott Redd) *former federal official, retired military officer*
Rickert, Jonathan Bradley *retired foreign service officer*
Ricks, Mark G. *former lieutenant governor, state senator*
Ries, Marcie Berman *former ambassador*
Rivers, Beverly D. *former district secretary*
Rocca, Christina B. *ambassador, former federal agency administrator*
Rosenthal, James D. *retired federal official, retired ambassador*
Ross, Dennis B. *diplomat, writer*
Rossin, Lawrence George *ambassador*
Rowe, G. Steven *former state attorney general*
Rudin, Anne *retired mayor, nursing educator*
Russack, John A. *federal official*
Sanchez-Ramos, Roberto J. *former attorney general*
Satterfield, David Michael *federal official*
Schafer, Ed (Edward Thomas Schafer) *former United States Secretary of Agriculture, former Governor of North Dakota*
Schlicher, Ronald Lewis *former ambassador*
Scobey, Margaret *former ambassador*
Sentenne, Justine *corporate ombudsman consultant*
Silverberg, Kristen Lee *former ambassador*
Sims, Dale *former state treasurer*
Siv, Sichan Aun *former ambassador*
Slutz, Pamela Jo Howell *former ambassador*
Smith, Robert Powell *former ambassador, retired foundation administrator*
Snider, L. Britt *federal official*
Soderberg, Nancy *former ambassador*
Sonego, Ian G. *retired assistant attorney general*
Spencer, John Daniel *former mayor*
Stapleton, Craig Roberts *former ambassador*
Stevens, Kenneth Allen *retired defense department worker*
Stevenson, Deborah L. *government official, educator*
Street, John Franklin *former mayor*
Stridiron, Iver Allison *former attorney general*
Stroup, Kala Mays *former education commissioner, educational alliance administrator*
Stumpe, Warren Robert *county official, retired engineering executive*
Swett, Richard Nelson (Dick) *former ambassador, former congressman*
Tambs, Lewis Arthur *diplomat, historian, educator*
Tate, Deborah Taylor *former commissioner*
Thomas, Ralph Charles III *attorney*
Thomas, Regena L. *former state official*
Townsend, Fran (Frances Fragos Townsend) *former federal official*
Townsend, Kathleen Kennedy *former lieutenant governor*
Tuck, Amy *former lieutenant governor*
Tuttle, Robert Holmes *former ambassador*
Usery, Willie J., Jr. *former United States Secretary of Labor*
Ushijima, Jean M. *retired city official*
Valeri, Tony *Canadian government official, small business owner*
Valles, Judith *president, former mayor, retired academic administrator*
Ventura, Jesse (James Janos, "The Body") *former Governor of Minnesota, retired professional wrestler*
Vike-Freiberga, Vaira *former President of Latvia*
Villarosa, Shari *former ambassador*
Volker, Kurt Douglas *former United States permanent representative to NATO*
von Moltke, Gebhardt *retired diplomat*
Walker, George Herbert III *former ambassador, retired investment banking company executive*
Walker, Gordon Davies *government official, writer, lecturer, consultant*
Wallace, Nicolle (Nicolle Devenish) *former federal official*
Ware, Marilyn *former ambassador, former utilities company executive*
Watkins, James David *former United States Secretary of Energy, retired military officer*
Webster, Christopher White *foreign service officer*
Weisberg, Robert Irving *former ambassador*
Wheaton, Douglas B. *city manager, lawyer*
Whitney, Jane *foreign service officer*
Wilson, Joseph Charles, IV, *former ambassador*
Wilson, Ross *former ambassador*
Windsor, Harriet Smith *former state official*
Wolf, Dale Edward *former Governor of Delaware*
Wood, Corinne Gieseke *former lieutenant governor*
Zischke, Douglas Arthur *foreign service officer*

GOVERNMENT: LEGISLATIVE ADMINISTRATION

UNITED STATES

ALABAMA

Abbeville
Baker, Locy (Sonny) L. *state legislator*

Anniston
Boyd, Barbara Bigsby *state legislator*
Fite, Lea *state legislator*

Bessemer
Dunn, Priscilla *state legislator*

Birmingham
Allen, Maryon Pittman *former senator, clothing designer, journalist*
Coleman, Merika *state legislator*
Hilliard, Earl Frederick *Former United States Representative, Alabama, lawyer*

Brewton
Baker, Alan *state legislator*

Carbon Hill
Guin, James Kenneth (Ken Guin) *state legislator*

Clayton
Beasley, Billy *state legislator*

Cusseta
Bridges, DuWayne *state legislator*

Fairhope
Faust, Teddy Joe, Sr., (Joe Faust) *state legislator*

Florence
Curtis, Mike *state legislator*

Gadsden
Ford, Craig *state legislator*

Galliher, Blain *state legislator*

Geneva
Beck, Warren Harris *state legislator*

Hanceville
Fields, James C., Jr. *state legislator*

Hartselle
Grantland, Ronald *state legislator*

Huntsville
Ball, Mike A. *state legislator*
Hall, Laura *state legislator*

Irvington
Collier, Spencer *state legislator*

Leeds
Drake, Owen *state legislator*

Mobile
Bonner, Josiah Robins, Jr., (Jo Bonner) *United States Representative from Alabama*
Buskey, James E. *state legislator*
Edwards, Jack *former congressman, lawyer*
Gaston, Henry Victor (Victor Gaston) *state legislator*
Gordon, James O. *state legislator*

Montgomery
Barton, James E., Jr. *state legislator*
Canfield, Greg *state legislator*
Davis, Randy *state legislator*
DeMarco, Paul J. *state legislator*
Dixon, Larry Dean *state legislator*
Graham, Betty Carol *state legislator, retired academic administrator*
Greeson, Todd *state legislator*
Grimes, David G. III *state legislator*
Hilliard, Earl F. *state legislator, lawyer*
Hubbard, Mike *state legislator, political organization administrator*
Love, Jay *state legislator*

Opelika
Bandy, George C. *state legislator*

Ozark
Clouse, Steve *state legislator*

Prattville
Gipson, H. Mac, Jr. *state legislator*

Semmes
Fincher, Chad *state legislator*

Troy
Boothe, Alan C. *state legislator*

Tuscaloosa
Allen, Gerald *state legislator*
Bentley, Robert J. *state legislator, dermatologist*
England, Chris (Christopher John England) *state legislator*

Tuscumbia
Black, Marcel *state legislator*

ALASKA

Anchorage
Begich, Mark P. *United States Senator from Alaska, former mayor*
Sturgulewski, Arliss *state legislator*

Eagle River
Dyson, Fred *state legislator*

Juneau
Davis, Bettye Jean *state legislator*
Johansen, Kyle *state legislator*
Kelly, Timothy Donahue *former state legislator*
Kerttula, Beth *state legislator*
Wilson, Peggy *state legislator*

ARIZONA

Phoenix
Baier, Maria *Councilwoman*
Bee, Timothy S. *state legislator*
Brown, Jack A. *state legislator, rancher, real estate broker*
Campbell, Cloves C., Jr. *state legislator*
DiCiccio, Sal *Councilman*
Fleming, Patricia V. *state legislator*
Johnson, Michael *councilman*
Kyl, Jon Llewellyn *United States Senator from Arizona*
Mattox, Claude *councilman*
Neely, Peggy *councilwoman*
Nowakowski, Michael *Councilman*
Salmon, Matt *Former United States Representative, Arizona, communications executive*
Simplot, Tom *Councilman*
Williams, Thelda *Councilwoman*

Tucson
Bartlett, David Carson *state legislator*
Kany, Judy C(asperson) *retired state senator*

ARKANSAS

Carlisle
Glover, Bobby L. *state legislator*

Cedarville
Whitaker, Ruth Reed *state legislator, retired publishing executive*

Conway
Baker, Gilbert R. *state legislator*

Gravette
Hendren, Kim *state legislator*

Greenwood
Walters, Bill *retired state senator*

Jonesboro
Bookout, Paul *state legislator*

Little Rock
Altes, Robert Dennis (Denny) *state legislator*
Broadway, Shane *state legislator*
Bryles, Steve M. *state legislator*
Capps, John Paul *state legislator*
Elliott, Joyce *state legislator*

Malvern
Faris, Steve *state legislator*

Rogers
Bledsoe, Cecile H. *state legislator*

Widener
Crumbly, Jack *state legislator*

CALIFORNIA

Arroyo Grande
Lagomarsino, Robert John *former congressman*

City Of Industry
Calderon, Ronald Steven *state legislator*

Glendale
Weaver, Dave *Councilman*

Huntington Beach
Coerper, Gil *Councilman, Huntington Beach, California*

Los Angeles
Cardenas, Tony *councilman*
Garcetti, Eric *councilman*
Hahn, Janice *councilwoman*
Huizar, Jose *councilman*
LaBonge, Tom *councilman*
Parks, Bernard *councilman*
Perry, Jan *Councilwoman*
Reyes, Ed P. *councilman*
Rosendahl, Bill *councilman*
Smith, Greig Louis *councilman*
Wesson, Herb J. *councilman*
Zine, Dennis P. *councilman*

Pacoima
Alarcón, Richard *councilman*

Pomona
Torres, Norma *state legislator*

Sacramento
Ashburn, Roy *state legislator*
Chesbro, Wesley *state legislator*
Kuehl, Sheila James *state board member*
Yee, Leland Y. *state legislator*

San Diego
DeMaio, Carl *councilman*
Emerald, Marti *councilwomen, reporter*
Faulconer, Kevin *councilman*
Frye, Donna *councilwoman*
Gloria, Todd *councilman*
Hueso, Ben *councilman*
Lightner, Sherri *councilwoman, mechanical engineer*
Young, Tony *councilman*

San Francisco
Alioto-Pier, Michela *city supervisor*
Avalos, John *city supervisor*
Campos, David *city supervisor, lawyer*
Chiu, David *city supervisor, lawyer*
Chu, Carmen *city supervisor*
Daly, Chris *city supervisor*
Dufty, Bevan *city supervisor*
Elsbernd, Sean R. *city supervisor*
Mar, Eric Lee *city supervisor, college professor*
Maxwell, Sophenia (Sophie) *city supervisor*
Mirkarimi, Ross *city supervisor*

San Jose
Campos, Nora *Councilwoman*
Chirco, Judy *Councilwoman*
Chu, Kansen *councilman*
Constant, Pete *councilman*
Herrera, Rose A. *councilwoman*
Kalra, Ash *councilman*
Liccardo, Sam T. *councilman*
Nguyen, Madison *councilwoman*
Oliverio, Pierluigi *councilman*
Pyle, Nancy *Councilwoman*

San Juan Capistrano
Wyland, Mark *state legislator*

Saratoga
Konnyu, Ernest Leslie *former congressman*

Stockton
Singleton, Marvin Ayers *state legislator, otolaryngologist*

West Covina
Torres, Esteban Edward *former congressman, trade association administrator*

COLORADO

Colorado Springs
Lamborn, Douglas L. *United States Representative from Colorado*

Denver
Cadman, Bill Lee *state legislator*
Carroll, Terrance D. *state legislator, lawyer*
Faatz, Jeanne Ryan *councilwoman*
Frangas, K. Jerry *state legislator*
Judd, Joel Stanton *state legislator, lawyer*
Labuda, Jeanne *state legislator*
McGihon, Anne Lee *state legislator, lawyer*
Meiklejohn, Alvin J., Jr. *state legislator, lawyer, accountant*
Pommer, John (Jack Pommer) *state legislator*

Fort Collins
Schaffer, Robert W. (Bob Schaffer) *former congressman*

Grand Junction
Bishop, Tilman Malcolm *state legislator*

Lakewood
Armstrong, William L. *former senator*

Westminster
Udall, Mark *United States Senator from Colorado*

CONNECTICUT

Danbury
Cappiello, David J. *state legislator*

Hartford
Giannaros, Demetrios Spiros *state legislator, economist, educator*
Godfrey, Robert Douglas *state legislator, lawyer*
Meyer, J. Edward *state legislator*

New Britain
Murphy, Christopher S. *United States Representative from Connecticut, former state senator*

New Haven
Dyson, William R. *state legislator*

Riverside
Powers, Claudia McKenna *state legislator*

Stafford Springs
Guglielmo, Anthony *state legislator*

Stonington
Simmons, Robert Ruhl *former congressman*

Vernon Rockville
Courtney, Joe (Joseph D. Courtney) *United States Representative from Connecticut*

Westport
Mioli, Joseph S. *state legislator*

DELAWARE

Dover
Amick, Steven Hammond *state legislator, lawyer*

Newark
Neal, James Preston *state senator, project engineer*

DISTRICT OF COLUMBIA

Washington
Abercrombie, Neil *United States Representative from Hawaii*
Abrams, Edgar M. (Mac Abrams) *legislative staff member*
Ackerman, Gary Leonard *United States Representative from New York*
Adams, Michelle T. *legislative staff member*
Aderholt, Robert B. *United States Representative from Alabama, lawyer*
Adler, John Herbert *United States Representative from New Jersey, former state legislator*
Ahouse, Daniel J. *legislative staff member*
Akaka, Daniel Kahikina *United States Senator from Hawaii*
Akin, Todd (William Todd Akin) *United States Representative from Missouri, former state legislator*
Albee, Luke S. *legislative staff member*
Alexander, Rodney M. *United States Representative from Louisiana*
Alexander, Stacey Anne *legislative staff member*
Altmire, Jason *United States Representative from Pennsylvania*
Amaral, Johnny A. *legislative staff member*
Anderson-Lee, Michelle D. *legislative staff member*
Andrews, Robert Ernest *United States Representative from New Jersey, lawyer*
Anuzis, Andrius A. *legislative staff member*
Arcuri, Michael Angelo *United States Representative from New York*
Asselbaye, Amy Brinkmeyer *legislative staff member*
Ates, Katherine A. (Kerry Ates) *legislative staff member*
Atkin, James *legislative staff member*
Austin, Lisa A. *legislative staff member*
Austria, Steve *United States Representative from Ohio, former state senator*
Baca, Joe *United States Representative from California*
Bachmann, Michele *United States Representative from Minnesota, former state legislator*
Bachus, Spencer T. III *United States Representative from Alabama, lawyer*
Baird, Brian N. *United States Representative from Washington*
Baldwin, Tammy *United States Representative from Wisconsin, lawyer*
Barlow, Michelle L. *legislative staff member*
Barrasso, John Anthony *United States Senator from Wyoming, orthopedic surgeon*
Barrett, James Gresham *United States Representative from South Carolina*
Barrow, John Jenkins *United States Representative from Georgia, lawyer*
Barry, Marion Shepilov, Jr. *city councilman, former mayor*
Bartheld, Elizabeth L. *legislative staff member*
Bartlett, Roscoe G. *United States Representative from Maryland*
Bartlett, Steve (Harry Steven Bartlett) *former congressman, mayor*
Barton, Joe Linus *United States Representative from Texas*
Battles, Caroline Pelot *legislative staff member*
Baucus, Max Sieben *United States Senator from Montana*
Bauleke, Howard Paul *legislative staff member, lawyer*
Bayh, Evan (Birch Evan Bayh III) *United States Senator from Indiana*
Bean, Melissa *United States Representative from Illinois*
Beard, Daniel P. *legislative staff member*
Beard, Jean-Louise *legislative staff member*
Becerra, Xavier *United States Representative from California, lawyer*
Becker, Tim *legislative staff member*
Beeton, Jonathan *legislative staff member*
Benczkowski, Brian Allen *legislative staff member, lawyer*
Bennet, Michael Farrand *United States Senator from Colorado*
Bennett, Barry P. *legislative staff member*
Bennett, Robert F. *United States Senator from Utah*
Benzing, Sarah Ruth *legislative staff member*
Berardini, Christopher F. *legislative staff member*
Bergreen, Timothy S. *legislative staff member*
Bergren, Eric *legislative staff member*
Berkley, Shelley (Rochelle Levine Berkley) *United States Representative from Nevada, lawyer*
Berman, Howard Lawrence *United States Representative from California, lawyer*
Bernhardt, W. Bret *legislative staff member*
Berry, Marion *United States Representative from Arkansas*
Biggert, Judith Borg *United States Representative from Illinois, lawyer*
Bilbray, Brian Patrick *United States Representative from California*
Bilirakis, Gus Michael *United States Representative from Florida, lawyer*
Bingaman, Jeff (Jesse Francis Bingaman Jr.) *United States Senator from New Mexico*
Birman, Igor *legislative staff member*
Bishop, Robert *United States Representative from Utah*
Bishop, Sanford Dixon, Jr. *United States Representative from Georgia, lawyer*
Bishop, Timothy H. *United States Representative from New York*
Bjornstad, Jeff *legislative staff member*
Blackburn, Marsha *United States Representative from Tennessee*
Blanchard, Denise *legislative staff member*
Blanco, Cesar *legislative staff member*
Blunt, Roy D. *United States Representative from Missouri*
Blustein, Gideon D. *legislative staff member*
Boccieri, John A. *United States Representative from Ohio, former state senator*
Bock, Paul S. *legislative staff member*
Boehner, John Andrew *United States Representative from Ohio*
Boerckel, Winfield A., Jr. *legislative staff member*
Bogdanovich, Michele L. *legislative staff member*
Bolar, Lucas J. *legislative staff member*
Bond, Christopher Samuel (Kit Bond) *United States Senator from Missouri, lawyer*
Bonfiglo, Joseph *legislative staff member*
Bonior, David Edward *former congressman, educator*
Bonlender, Brian N. *legislative staff member*
Bono Mack, Mary Whitaker *United States Representative from California*
Bonyun, Sean C. *legislative staff member*
Boozman, John *United States Representative from Arkansas*
Bordallo, Madeleine Zeien (Mrs. Ricardo Jerome Bordallo) *Delegate to United States House Representative from Guam*
Boren, David Daniel *United States Representative from Oklahoma*
Borntrager, Randy *legislative staff member*
Boswell, Leonard L. *United States Representative from Iowa*
Boucher, Rick (Frederick Carlyle Boucher) *United States Representative from Virginia, lawyer*
Bourke, Jaron *legislative staff member*
Boustany, Charles W., Jr. *United States Representative from Louisiana, surgeon*
Bowen, David *legislative staff member*
Bowser, David G. *legislative staff member*
Boxer, Barbara *United States Senator from California*
Boyd, F. Allen, Jr. *United States Representative from Florida, farmer*
Brady, Kevin Patrick *United States Representative from Texas*
Brady, Robert A. *United States Representative from Pennsylvania*
Braley, Bruce *United States Representative from Iowa*
Brand, Adam G. *legislative staff member, lawyer*
Brandell, Jim (James F. Brandell) *legislative staff member*
Branton, Brian E. *legislative staff member*
Brickman, Blake *legislative staff member*

Hilleary, Van (William Vanderpool Hilleary) *former congressman, lawyer*

Himes, Jim (James A. Himes) *United States Representative from Connecticut, former nonprofit organization executive*

Hinchey, Maurice D. *United States Representative from New York*

Hinojosa, Rubén *United States Representative from Texas*

Hinz, Jean *legislative staff member*

Hodes, Paul William, II, *United States Representative from New Hampshire, lawyer*

Hoeflich, Scott J. *legislative staff member*

Hoekstra, Peter *United States Representative from Michigan, manufacturing executive*

Holden, Tim (Thomas Timothy) *United States Representative from Pennsylvania*

Holder, Nicholas *legislative staff member*

Holt, Rush D. *United States Representative from New Jersey*

Honda, Michael M. (Mike Honda) *United States Representative from California*

Hoyer, Steny Hamilton *United States Representative from Maryland*

Hugya, John A. *legislative staff member*

Humphrey, Connie J. *legislative staff member*

Hunter, Duncan Duane *United States Representative from California, military officer*

Husband, Shelley H. *legislative staff member*

Hutchison, Kay Bailey (Kathryn Ann Bailey Hutchison) *United States Senator from Texas*

Hyder, Rebecca J. *legislative staff member*

Inglis, Bob (Robert Durden) *United States Representative from South Carolina*

Ingram, Thomas J. *legislative staff member*

Inhofe, James Mountain *United States Senator from Oklahoma*

Inouye, Daniel Ken *United States Senator from Hawaii*

Inslee, Jay Robert *United States Representative from Washington*

Irvine, Mary M. *legislative staff member*

Isakson, Johnny (John Hardy Isakson) *United States Senator from Georgia*

Israel, Steven Jay *United States Representative from New York*

Issa, Darrell E. *United States Representative from California*

Jablon, Ann M. *legislative staff member*

Jackson, Jesse Louis, Jr. *United States Representative from Illinois*

Jackson, Rhonda Ann *legislative staff member*

Jackson Lee, Sheila *United States Representative from Texas*

Jafari, Beth *legislative staff member*

Jenkins, Lynn M. *United States Representative from Kansas*

Johanns, Michael Owen *United States Senator from Nebraska, former United States Secretary of Agriculture*

Johnson, Eddie Bernice *United States Representative from Texas*

Johnson, Eric *legislative staff member*

Johnson, Jace *legislative staff member*

Johnson, Nancy Lee *former congresswoman*

Johnson, Samuel (Sam Johnson) *United States Representative from Texas*

Johnson, Timothy Peter *United States Senator from South Dakota*

Johnson, Timothy Vincent *United States Representative from Illinois, lawyer*

Johnston, Kimberly D. *legislative staff member*

Jones, Ashley *legislative staff member*

Jones, Walter Beaman, Jr. *United States Representative from North Carolina*

Jordan, Jim (James D. Jordan) *United States Representative from Ohio, former state legislator*

Joseph, Meg (Margaret Joseph) *legislative staff member*

Joyner, Christopher *legislative staff member*

Kagen, Steven L. *United States Representative from Wisconsin, physician*

Kanjorski, Paul Edmund *United States Representative from Pennsylvania, lawyer*

Karvelas, Dave (David M. Karvelas) *legislative staff member*

Kassiday, Joel David *legislative staff member*

Katich, Steve J. III *legislative staff member*

Katz, Daniel E. *legislative staff member*

Kaufman, Ted (Edward E. Kaufman) *United States Senator from Delaware*

Keefe, Maura *legislative staff member*

Keiser, Andy (Andrew J. Keiser) *legislative staff member*

Kennan, Stephanie Ann *senior policy advisor*

Kennedy, Patrick Joseph, II, *United States Representative from Rhode Island*

Kennedy, Ted (Edward Moore Kennedy) *United States Senator from Massachusetts*

Kerry, John Forbes *United States Senator from Massachusetts*

Keyser, Timothy Kent *legislative staff member*

Kildee, Dale Edward *United States Representative from Michigan*

Kilpatrick, Carolyn Cheeks *United States Representative from Michigan*

Kilroy, Mary Jo *United States Representative from Ohio, former county official*

Kincaid, Trevor *legislative staff member*

Kind, Ronald James *United States Representative from Wisconsin, lawyer*

King, Crystal A. *legislative staff member*

King, Sophia Atlee *legislative staff member*

King, Steve *United States Representative from Iowa*

Kingston, Jack *United States Representative from Georgia*

Kirincich, John G., Jr. *legislative staff member*

Kirk, Mark Steven *United States Representative from Illinois*

Kirkpatrick, Ann L. *United States Representative from Arizona, lawyer*

Kissell, Larry (Lawrence Webb Kissell) *United States Representative from North Carolina, former social studies educator*

Klein, Ronald Jay *United States Representative from Florida, lawyer*

Klessig, Margaret J. *legislative staff member*

Kline, John Paul *United States Representative from Minnesota*

Klobuchar, Amy Jean *United States Senator from Minnesota, lawyer*

Knox, Wendy *legislative staff member*

Knutson, Karen Y. *legislative staff member*

Kohl, Herbert H. *United States Senator from Wisconsin, professional sports team owner*

Kohl, Jennifer D. *legislative staff member*

Koromilas, Alec J. *legislative staff member*

Koski, James E. *legislative staff member*

Kosmas, Suzanne M. *United States Representative from Florida, former real estate company executive*

Kouters, Angela M. *legislative staff member*

Krahe, Julia Louise *legislative staff member*

Kratovil, Frank Michael, Jr. *United States Representative from Maryland, lawyer*

Krieger, William C. *legislative staff member*

Krupnick, Dan *legislative staff member*

Lackey, Miles M. *legislative staff member*

Lance, Leonard *United States Representative from New Jersey, former state legislator*

Landrieu, Mary Lorretta *United States Senator from Louisiana*

Lane, Jeff A. *legislative staff member*

Langevin, James R. (Jim Langevin) *United States Representative from Rhode Island, former state official*

Larsen, Richard Ray (Rick Larsen) *United States Representative from Washington*

Larson, John Barry *United States Representative from Connecticut, insurance company executive*

Latham, Tom *United States Representative from Iowa*

Latta, Robert Edward (Bob Latta) *United States Representative from Ohio*

Leahy, Patrick Joseph *United States Senator from Vermont*

Leavandosky, Stacey E. *legislative staff member*

Lee, Barbara Jean *United States Representative from California*

Lee, Christopher J. *United States Representative from New York, former manufacturing executive*

LeMieux, George S. *United States Senator from Florida, lawyer*

Leone, Katherine C. *legislative staff member*

Leopold, Patrick R. *legislative staff member*

Levin, Carl Milton *United States Senator from Michigan*

Levin, Michael *legislative staff member*

Levin, Sander Martin *United States Representative from Michigan, lawyer*

Lewis, Charles Jeremy (Jerry Lewis) *United States Representative from California*

Lewis, John Robert *United States Representative from Georgia*

Lewis, Muffy (Lucille Miraim Lewis) *legislative staff member*

Lieberman, Joe (Joseph Isadore Lieberman) *United States Senator from Connecticut*

Lierman, Terry L. *legislative staff member*

Lightfoot, Karen *legislative staff member*

Lincoln, Blanche Lambert *United States Senator from Arkansas*

Linde, Jason P. *legislative staff member*

Linder, John E. *United States Representative from Georgia, dentist*

Lipinski, Daniel *United States Representative from Illinois*

Lira, José A. *legislative staff member*

Little, Corey *legislative staff member*

Lizardo, Thomas Charles *legislative staff member*

Loebsack, Dave *United States Representative from Iowa, former political science professor*

Lofgren, Zoe *United States Representative from California*

Lovelace, Telly *legislative staff member*

Loveng, Jeffrey R. (Jeff Loveng) *legislative staff member*

Luetkemeyer, Blaine *United States Representative from Missouri*

Lugar, Dick (Richard Green Lugar) *United States Senator from Indiana*

Lujan, Ben Ray, Jr. *United States Representative from New Mexico, former state official*

Lummis, Cynthia Marie *United States Representative from Wyoming, former state official, lawyer*

Lungren, Daniel Edward *United States Representative from California, former state attorney general*

Lungren-McCollum, Kelly *legislative staff member*

Lydon, Kathleen *legislative staff member*

Lydon, Timothy *legislative staff member*

Lyles, David S. *legislative staff member*

Lynch, Christopher W. *legislative staff member*

Lynch, Michael Lee *legislative staff member*

Lynch, Stephen F. *United States Representative from Massachusetts*

Macias, Linda C. *legislative staff member*

Mack, Connie, IV, *United States Representative from Florida*

Macomber, Marshall C. *legislative staff member*

Maffei, Daniel B. *United States Representative from New York, former investment company executive*

Magary, Adam J. *legislative staff member*

Magnuson, Rachel *legislative staff member*

Mahler, Jason M. *legislative staff member*

Maloney, Carolyn Bosher *United States Representative from New York*

Mamaux, Lale M. *legislative staff member*

Maness, Theodore E. (Ted Maness) *legislative staff member*

Manzullo, Donald A. *United States Representative from Illinois, lawyer*

Marchant, Kenny *United States Representative from Texas*

Marchio, Sam *legislative staff member*

Markey, Betsy (Elizabeth Helen Markey) *United States Representative from Colorado*

Markey, Edward John *United States Representative from Massachusetts*

Marshall, Jim (James Creel Marshall) *United States Representative from Georgia*

Marston, Michelle Presson *legislative staff member*

Martin, Jay (Robert Joseph Martin) *legislative staff member*

Massa, Eric J.J. *United States Representative from New York, retired military officer, former congressional aide*

Massimino, Julia A. *legislative staff member, lawyer*

Matheson, James David (Jim) *United States Representative from Utah*

Matsui, Doris Okada *United States Representative from California*

McAvoy, Susan A. *legislative staff member*

McBride, William R. *legislative staff member*

McCain, John (John Sidney McCain III) *United States Senator from Arizona*

McCann, Tim *legislative staff member*

McCannell, Christopher *legislative staff member*

McCarthy, Carolyn *United States Representative from New York*

McCarthy, Kevin *United States Representative from California, former state legislator*

McCarty, Mary Colleen *legislative staff member*

McCaskill, Claire C. *United States Senator from Missouri*

McCaul, Michael T. *United States Representative from Texas*

McClintock, Tom (Thomas Miller McClintock II) *United States Representative from California, former state senator*

McCollum, Betty *United States Representative from Minnesota*

McConnaughey, Flip *legislative staff member*

McConnell, Mitch (Addison Mitchell McConnell) *United States Senator from Kentucky, lawyer*

McCotter, Thaddeus George *United States Representative from Michigan*

McCreary, Robert J. *legislative staff member*

McCullough, Mary T. (Terri McCullough) *legislative staff member*

McDermott, James A. *United States Representative from Washington, psychiatrist*

McDonald, Ed *legislative staff member*

McFaul, Daniel F. *legislative staff member*

McGinley, Matthew S. *legislative staff member*

McGovern, James P. *United States Representative from Massachusetts*

McHenry, Patrick Timothy *United States Representative from North Carolina*

McIntyre, Mike (Douglas Carmichael McIntyre II) *United States Representative from North Carolina*

McKenney, Kerry B. *legislative staff member*

McKeon, Howard Phillip (Buck McKeon) *United States Representative from California*

McMahon, Michael E. *United States Representative from New York, former city councilman*

McMorris-Rodgers, Cathy *United States Representative from Washington*

McNerney, Jerry (Gerald M. McNerney) *United States Representative from California, engineer*

Meachum, Pete (Charles Peterson Meachum) *legislative staff member*

Mecher, Greg *legislative staff member*

Meek, Kendrick B. *United States Representative from Florida*

Melancon, Charles *United States Representative from Louisiana*

Menendez, Robert (Bob Menendez) *United States Senator from New Jersey*

Metwalli, April Beeman *legislative staff member*

Mica, John L. *United States Representative from Florida*

Michaud, Michael Herman *United States Representative from Maine*

Middleton, Victoria J. *legislative staff member*

Mikulski, Barbara Ann *United States Senator from Maryland*

Miller, Brad (Ralph Bradley Miller) *United States Representative from North Carolina*

Miller, Candice S. *United States Representative from Michigan*

Miller, Chris J. *legislative staff member*

Miller, Gary G. *United States Representative from California*

Miller, George III *United States Representative from California*

Miller, Jeff *United States Representative from Florida*

Miller, Scott Eugene *legislative staff member*

Min, James B. *legislative staff member*

Minnick, Walter Clifford *United States Representative from Idaho, former building materials company executive*

Mitchell, Harry E. *United States Representative from Arizona, former state legislator*

Mitchell, Peter J. *legislative staff member*

Mitchell, Todd (James Todd Mitchell) *legislative staff member*

Mobley, Dawn Kelly *legislative staff member*

Moe, Kari J. *legislative staff member*

Mollohan, Alan Bowlby *United States Representative from West Virginia*

Mondello, Lisette McSoud *legislative staff member, former federal agency administrator*

Montano, Gloria I. *legislative staff member*

Moore, Dennis *United States Representative from Kansas*

Moore, Gwendolynne S. (Gwen Moore) *United States Representative from Wisconsin*

Moore, Steven E. *legislative staff member*

Moran, Jerry *United States Representative from Kansas*

Moran, Jim (James Patrick Moran Jr.) *United States Representative from Virginia, stock broker*

Morris, Brad *legislative staff member*

Morris, Martin W. *legislative staff member*

Morris, Melanie R. *legislative staff member*

Moskowitz, Jedd I. *legislative staff member*

Mosychuk, Susan *legislative staff member*

Muñoz, Leo R. *legislative staff member*

Munson, Lester *legislative staff member*

Murat, William M. *legislative staff member*

Murkowski, Lisa Ann *United States Senator from Alaska*

Murphy, Ryan *legislative staff member*

Murphy, Scott (Matthew Scott Murphy) *United States Representative from New York*

Murphy, Timothy F. *United States Representative from Pennsylvania*

Murray, Liz *legislative staff member*

Murray, Patty (Patricia Lynn Murray) *United States Senator from Washington*

Murtha, John Patrick, Jr. *United States Representative from Pennsylvania*

Mushnick, Ashley *legislative staff member*

Myers, Mindy *legislative staff member*

Myrick, Gary *legislative staff member*

Myrick, Sue Wilkins *United States Representative from North Carolina, former mayor*

Nadler, Jerrold Lewis *United States Representative from New York, lawyer*

Nagle, Thomas W. *legislative staff member*

Napolitano, Grace Flores *United States Representative from California*

Nardi Riddle, Clarine *chief staff, lawyer*

Natonski, Dave *legislative staff member*

Neal, Richard Edmund *United States Representative from Massachusetts, former mayor*

Nelson, (Earl) Ben(jamin) *United States Senator from Nebraska, former governor, lawyer*

Nelson, Bill (Clarence William Nelson) *United States Senator from Florida*

Nelson, Karen *legislative staff member*

Neugebauer, Dale *legislative staff member*

Neugebauer, Randy (Robert R. Neugebauer) *United States Representative from Texas*

Neville, J. Gabriel *legislative staff member*

Nicholson, Kristin E. *legislative staff member*

Nickson, Julie L. *legislative staff member*

Noble, John W. *legislative staff member*

Norton, Eleanor Holmes *Delegate to United States House Representative from District of Columbia, lawyer, educator*

Novascone, Todd *legislative staff member*

Nunes, Devin *United States Representative from California*

Nussle, Jim (James Allen Nussle) *former United States Representative from Iowa*

Nye, Glenn Carlyle III *United States Representative from Virginia*

Oberstar, James Louis *United States Representative from Minnesota*

Obey, David Ross *United States Representative from Wisconsin*

O'Black, Sean *legislative staff member*

O'Brien, Danny *legislative staff member*

O'Connell, Dawn C. Myers *legislative staff member*

O'Connor, Gail *legislative staff member*

O'Donnell, Amy L. *legislative staff member*

O'Donnell, Tom *legislative staff member*

Olson, Pete *United States Representative from Texas, former congressional aide*

Olver, John Walter *United States Representative from Massachusetts*

O'Neill, Maura Louise *legislative staff member, environmentalist*

Ortiz, Solomon Porfirio, Sr. *United States Representative from Texas*

Otis, Bud (Harold F. Otis) *legislative staff member*

Oursler, Tara Linnehan *legislative staff member*

Pagano, Edward *legislative staff member*

Pallone, Frank, Jr. *United States Representative from New Jersey, lawyer*

Panetta, Michael *Shadow Representative to US Congress from DC*

Park, Phil W. *legislative staff member*

Parker, Scott Benson *legislative staff member*

Pascrell, William J., Jr. *United States Representative from New Jersey*

Pastor, Edward *United States Representative from Arizona*

Paul, Ronald Ernest *United States Representative from Texas*

Paulsen, Erik *United States Representative from Minnesota, former state legislator*

Payne, Donald Milford *United States Representative from New Jersey*

Pelosi, Nancy Patricia *United States Representative from California*

Pence, Mike (Michael Richard Pence) *United States Representative from Indiana*

Perlmutter, Ed (Edwin George Perlmutter) *United States Representative from Colorado, former state legislator, lawyer*

Perriello, Tom (Thomas Stuart Price Perriello) *United States Representative from Virginia*

Perry, Richard S. *legislative staff member*

Peters, Gary Charles *United States Representative from Michigan*

Peterson, Collin Clark *United States Representative from Minnesota*

Petri, Thomas Evert *United States Representative from Wisconsin*

Pewen, William F. *legislative staff member*

Pfaff, Bruce *legislative staff member*

Philbin, Christopher R. *legislative staff member*

Phillips, Clay Thomas *legislative staff member*

Pierluisi, Pedro R. *Resident Commissioner from Puerto Rico, United States House of Representatives*

Pignatelli, Donna M. *legislative staff member*

Pingree, Chellie M. (Rochelle M. Pingree) *United States Representative from Maine*

Piper, William H. (Billy Piper) *legislative staff member*

Platts, Todd Russell *United States Representative from Pennsylvania, state legislator*

Poe, Amy Field *legislative staff member*

Poe, Ted *United States Representative from Texas, former judge*

Pohl, Zack *legislative staff member*

Policelli, Maura *legislative staff member*

Poling, Parker Hamilton *legislative staff member*

Polis, Jared Schutz *United States Representative from Colorado, entrepreneur, philanthropist*

Pollner, Leslie *legislative staff member*

Pomeroy, Earl Ralph *United States Representative from North Dakota, retired commissioner*

Ponder, Jacqueline A. *legislative staff member*

Poole, Todd W. *legislative staff member*

Poppleton, Janet Waters *legislative staff member*

Porter, Amy M. *legislative staff member*

Posey, Bill (William J. Posey) *United States Representative from Florida*
Powden, Mark E. *legislative staff member*
Powell, Leanne *legislative staff member*
Pratt, Jack *legislative staff member*
Price, David Eugene *United States Representative from North Carolina, education educator*
Price, Thomas E. *United States Representative from Georgia*
Primus, Robert E. *legislative staff member*
Primus, Wendell *legislative staff member*
Prosienski, Lisa *legislative staff member*
Protic, Paul B. *legislative staff member*
Pryor, Mark Lunsford *United States Senator from Arkansas*
Putnam, Adam Hughes *United States Representative from Florida, farmer, rancher*
Quaranta, Michael J. *legislative staff member*
Quigley, Ellen White *legislative staff member*
Quigley, Mike *United States Representative from Illinois, former county commissioner*
Quinn, Jack (John Francis Quinn) *former congressman, English language educator*
Rabin, Ethan M. *legislative staff member*
Racalto, Joseph *legislative staff member*
Radanovich, George P. *United States Representative from California*
Radovich Piper, Danielle *legislative staff member*
Rahall, Nick Joe, II, (Nick Rahall) *United States Representative from West Virginia*
Ramey, David *legislative staff member*
Ramirez, Angela *legislative staff member*
Ramseur, David *legislative staff member*
Ramsey-Cook, Heather *legislative staff member*
Rangel, Charlie (Charles Bernard Rangel) *United States Representative from New York*
Rasley, George, Jr. *legislative staff member*
Raymond, Joshua H. *legislative staff member*
Reagan, Paul *legislative staff member*
Reed, Jack (John Francis Reed) *United States Senator from Rhode Island*
Rehberg, Dennis R. *United States Representative from Montana*
Reichert, David G. (Dave Reichert) *United States Representative from Washington*
Reid, Harry Mason *United States Senator from Nevada*
Reilly, James Dalton *legislative staff member*
Reilly-Hudock, Patricia A. (Trish Reilly) *legislative staff member*
Renteria, Amanda A. *legislative staff member*
Reyes, Silvestre *United States Representative from Texas*
Reynolds, Thomas M. *former United States Representative from New York*
Ribeiro, Catherine McKenna *legislative staff member*
Rich, Benjamin Jacobs *legislative staff member*
Richard, Bill *legislative staff member*
Richardson, Laura A. *United States Representative from California*
Ridgway, R. Hunter *legislative staff member*
Risch, Jim (James Elroy Risch) *United States Senator from Idaho, former Governor of Idaho*
Ritvo, Jacob *legislative staff member*
Roberts, Charles Patrick (Pat Roberts) *United States Senator from Kansas*
Roberts, Craig A. *legislative staff member*
Roberts, Russell L. (Rusty Roberts) *legislative staff member*
Robinson, Josh *legislative staff member*
Robison, Matthew L. *legislative staff member*
Rockefeller, Jay (John Davison Rockefeller IV) *United States Senator from West Virginia*
Rodriguez, Ciro Davis *United States Representative from Texas*
Roe, Jamie A. *legislative staff member*
Roe, Phil (David Phillip Roe) *United States Representative from Tennessee, former vice-mayor*
Rogers, Harold Dallas (Hal) *United States Representative from Kentucky*
Rogers, Hayden *legislative staff member*
Rogers, Mike (Michael J. Rogers) *United States Representative from Michigan*
Rogers, Mike D. *United States Representative from Alabama*
Rohrabacher, Dana T. *United States Representative from California*
Rooney, Tom *United States Representative from Florida, lawyer*
Roper, Wayne R. *legislative staff member*
Rosenbaum, Sidney J. (Jerr Rosenbaum) *legislative staff member*
Ros-Lehtinen, Ileana Carmen *United States Representative from Florida*
Ross, Mike *United States Representative from Arkansas*
Rothman, Steven R. *United States Representative from New Jersey*
Rothrock, John G. *legislative staff member*
Roybal-Allard, Lucille *United States Representative from California*
Royce, Ed (Edward Randall Royce) *United States Representative from California*
Ruckert, Kyle *legislative staff member*
Rudolph, Kimberly *legislative staff member*
Ruppersberger, Charles Albert, III, (Dutch) *United States Representative from Maryland*
Rush, Bobby L. *United States Representative from Illinois*
Russell, Robert A. *legislative staff member*
Rutkin, Amy B. *legislative staff member*
Ryan, Paul *United States Representative from Wisconsin*
Ryan, Robert Kevin *legislative staff member*
Sablan, Gregorio Camacho (Gregorio Kilili Camacho Sablan) *Delegate from the Northern Mariana Islands*
Sagely, Matt (Christopher Matthew Sagely) *legislative staff member*
Sajery, Algene T. *legislative staff member*
Sakai, James K. *legislative staff member*
Salazar, John Tony *United States Representative from Colorado*
Samuelson, Drey *legislative staff member*
Sánchez, Linda T. *United States Representative from California*
Sánchez, Loretta *United States Representative from California*
Sanders, Bernard (Bernie Sanders) *United States Senator from Vermont, former congressman*
Sandlin, Stephanie Herseth *United States Representative from South Dakota, lawyer*
Sandy, John A. *legislative staff member*
Sarbanes, John Peter Spyros *United States Representative from Maryland, lawyer*
Satcher, Daraka E. (Dok) *legislative staff member*
Scalise, Steve (Stephen Joseph Scalise) *United States Representative from Louisiana, former state legislator*
Schakowsky, Janice *United States Representative from Illinois*
Schauer, Mark Hamilton *United States Representative from Michigan*
Schiappa, David S. *legislative staff member*
Schiff, Adam Bennett *United States Representative from California, lawyer*
Schloegel, Scott P. *legislative staff member*
Schmidt, Jean *United States Representative from Ohio*
Schock, Aaron Jon *United States Representative from Illinois, former state legislator*
Schrader, Kurt *United States Representative from Oregon, former state senator*
Schreiber, Sara *legislative staff member*
Schubert, Brian *legislative staff member*
Schumer, Chuck (Charles Ellis Schumer) *United States Senator from New York*
Schwartz, Allyson Y. *United States Representative from Pennsylvania*
Schwartz, Michael *legislative staff member*
Scott, David Albert *United States Representative from Georgia*
Scott, Makeda *legislative staff member*
Scott, Robert Cortez *United States Representative from Virginia, lawyer*
Selib, Jonathan *legislative staff member*
Sensenbrenner, Frank James, Jr. *United States Representative from Wisconsin*
Serrano, José Enrique *United States Representative from New York*
Sessions, Jeff (Jefferson Beauregard Sessions III) *United States Senator from Alabama, former state attorney general*
Sessions, Pete (Peter Anderson Sessions) *United States Representative from Texas*
Seum, Jack F. *legislative staff member*
Shadegg, John Barden *United States Representative from Arizona*
Shafroth, Frank H., Jr. *legislative staff member*
Shapiro, Jeffrey A. *legislative staff member*
Shea-Porter, Carol *United States Representative from New Hampshire, social worker*
Shelby, Richard Craig *United States Senator from Alabama*
Sherman, Bradley James *United States Representative from California*
Shields, Christopher D. *legislative staff member*
Shimkus, John Mondy *United States Representative from Illinois*
Shooshan, Alyssa *legislative staff member*
Siggins, Robert G. *legislative staff member*
Simmons, Ronnie (Elias R. Simmons) *legislative staff member*
Simpson, Michael K. *United States Representative from Idaho*
Sires, Albio *United States Representative from New Jersey, former state legislator*
Skelton, Ike (Isaac Newton Skelton IV) *United States Representative from Missouri*
Slaughter, Louise McIntosh *United States Representative from New York*
Smith, Adam *United States Representative from Washington*
Smith, Adrian M. *United States Representative from Nebraska, real estate agent*
Smith, Amy D. *legislative staff member*
Smith, Bradley W. *legislative staff member*
Smith, Christopher Henry *United States Representative from New Jersey*
Smith, Cori Elizabeth *legislative staff member*
Smith, Lamar Seeligson *United States Representative from Texas*
Smith, William *legislative staff member*
Smith, William A. *legislative staff member*
Snowbarger, Vince *former congressman*
Snowe, Olympia J. *United States Senator from Maine*
Snyder, Vic *United States Representative from Arkansas, physician*
Solarz, Stephen Joshua *former congressman*
Souder, Mark Edward *United States Representative from Indiana*
Souders, Patrick J. *legislative staff member*
Sours, David A. *legislative staff member*
Sozan, Michael L. *legislative staff member*
Space, Zack (Zachary T. Space) *United States Representative from Ohio*
Spear, Susan *legislative staff member*
Specter, Arlen *United States Senator from Pennsylvania*
Speier, Jackie (Karen Lorraine Jacqueline Speier) *United States Representative from California, former state senator*
Spencer, Alan C. *legislative staff member*
Speth, Andrew D. *legislative staff member*
Spira, Michael *legislative staff member*
Spiro, Peter M. *legislative staff member*
Spratt, John McKee, Jr. *United States Representative from South Carolina, lawyer*
Stabenow, Deborah Ann *United States Senator from Michigan, former congresswoman*
Staley, Michael *legislative staff member*
Stallings, Tommy Ray *legislative staff member*
Stampley, Stephen M. *legislative staff member*
Stanley, Elizabeth G. *legislative staff member*
Stark, Fortney Hillman (Pete Stark) *United States Representative from California*
Stearns, Clifford Bundy *United States Representative from Florida*
Sterlin, Shrita D. *legislative staff member*
Stoddard, Andrew T. *legislative staff member*
Strauss, Paul *Shadow Senator to US Congress from DC*
Struble, Wayne T. *legislative staff member*
Stupak, Bart (Bartholomew Thomas Stupak) *United States Representative from Michigan, lawyer*
Sullivan, John A. *United States Representative from Oklahoma*
Sutton, Betty *United States Representative from Ohio, lawyer*
Swindell, Russell A., II, *legislative staff member*
Sypolt, Jennifer Lynn *legislative staff member*
Tagen, Julie *legislative staff member*
Tameron, Alexis C. *legislative staff member*
Tanner, John S. *United States Representative from Tennessee, lawyer*
Tantillo, Andrew M. *legislative staff member*
Tateishi, Peter *legislative staff member*
Taub, Robert G. *legislative staff member*
Taylor, Gene (Gary Eugene Taylor) *United States Representative from Mississippi*
Teague, Harry *United States Representative from New Mexico*
Terry, Adam *legislative staff member*
Terry, Lee Raymond *United States Representative from Nebraska, lawyer*
Tester, Jon(athan) *United States Senator from Montana, former state legislator, farmer*
Teuber Moore, Terri *legislative staff member*
Thomas, Bill (William Marshall Thomas) *Former United States Representative from California*
Thomas, Brian C. *legislative staff member*
Thompson, Bennie G. *United States Representative from Mississippi*
Thompson, Christopher *legislative staff member*
Thompson, Darrel L. *legislative staff member*
Thompson, Glenn W., Jr. *United States Representative from Pennsylvania, former health facility administrator*
Thompson, Mike (C. Michael Thompson) *United States Representative from California*
Thompson, Ryan D. *legislative staff member*
Thornberry, Mac (William McClellan Thornberry) *United States Representative from Texas*
Thune, John Randolph *United States Senator from South Dakota*
Tiahrt, Todd (W. Todd Tiahrt) *United States Representative from Kansas, former state senator*
Tierney, John F. *United States Representative from Massachusetts, lawyer*
Tighe, William (Bill Tighe) *legislative staff member*
Titus, Alice Costandina (Dina Titus) *United States Representative from Nevada, former state legislator*
Tomberlin, Michael *legislative staff member*
Tonko, Paul David *United States Representative from New York, former state agency administrator*
Towns, Edolphus (Ed Towns) *United States Representative from New York*
Trevena, Anthony *legislative staff member*
Tsongas, Niki (Nicola S. Tsongas) *United States Representative from Massachusetts, former dean*
Turner, Michael R. *United States Representative from Ohio*
Udall, Thomas S. (Tom) *United States Senator from New Mexico*
Upton, Frederick Stephen *United States Representative from Michigan*
Urey, Richard *legislative staff member*
Van Hollen, Christopher, Jr. *United States Representative from Maryland*
Vaught, Laura E. *legislative staff member*
Velázquez, Nydia Margarita *United States Representative from New York*
Videnieks, Barbara J. *legislative staff member*
Viers, Hillary Wicai *legislative staff member*
Visclosky, Peter John *United States Representative from Indiana, lawyer*
Vitter, David Bruce *United States Senator from Louisiana, former congressman*
Voinovich, George Victor *United States Senator from Ohio*
Wade, David Eckels *legislative staff member*
Walden, Greg *United States Representative from Oregon*
Walker, John Stanley *legislative staff member*
Walker, Kristin *legislative staff member*
Walker, Mark Alan *legislative staff member*
Walker, Matthew Vincent *legislative staff member*
Walker, Ryan P. *legislative staff member*
Walsh, Bridget (Mary Bridget Walsh) *legislative staff member*
Walsh, Jennifer Fitzgerald *legislative staff member*
Walz, Tim (Timothy J. Walz) *United States Representative from Minnesota, former social science educator*
Wamp, Zachary Paul *United States Representative from Tennessee*
Ward, Stephen D. *legislative staff member*
Warner, Mark Robert *United States Senator from Virginia, former governor*
Wasserman-Schultz, Debbie *United States Representative from Florida*
Waters, Maxine *United States Representative from California*
Watkins, Stanley *legislative staff member*
Watkins, Yelberton R. (Yebbie Watkins) *legislative staff member*
Watson, Diane Edith *United States Representative from California*
Watt, Melvin Luther *United States Representative from North Carolina, lawyer*
Waxman, Henry Arnold *United States Representative from California*
Way, Kristi *legislative staff member*
Webb, Jim (James Henry Webb Jr.) *United States Senator from Virginia*
Webb, Nate *legislative staff member*
Weinberg, Thomas *legislative staff member*
Weiner, Anthony David *United States Representative from New York*
Weiss, Daniel *legislative staff member*
Weitz, William F. (Bill Weitz) *legislative staff member*
Welch, Peter F. *United States Representative from Vermont, former state legislator*
Werner, Sharon *legislative staff member, lawyer*
Westmoreland, Lynn A. *United States Representative from Georgia*
Wexler, Robert *United States Representative from Florida*
Wheeler, Sharon *legislative staff member*
Whelan, Andrew T. *legislative staff member*
White, Dorinda *legislative staff member*
White, John D. *legislative staff member*
White, Stanley V. *legislative staff member*
Whitehouse, Sheldon *United States Senator from Rhode Island, former state attorney general*
Whitener, Jeanette (Jeanette Penny Forcash Whitener) *legislative staff member*
Whitfield, Edward (Wayne) *United States Representative from Kentucky*
Whitman, Shawn R. *legislative staff member*
Whitt, John J. *legislative staff member*
Wicker, Roger Frederick *United States Senator from Mississippi*
Williams, Clarence *legislative staff member*
Williams, David B. *legislative staff member*
Williams, Lisa M. *legislative staff member*
Williams, Tonya *legislative staff member, lawyer*
Willis, Arlene M. *legislative staff member*
Wilson, Charles A., Jr. *United States Representative from Ohio, funeral director*
Wilson, Joe (Addison Wilson) *United States Representative from South Carolina, former senator, lawyer*
Witte, Eric *legislative staff member*
Wittman, Robert J. *United States Representative from Virginia, former state legislator*
Wolf, Frank Rudolph *United States Representative from Virginia, lawyer*
Wolpe, Howard Eliot *former Congressman, political scientist*
Womack, Todd *legislative staff member*
Woodall, William Robert *legislative staff member*
Woolley, Leslie Ann *legislative staff member*
Woolsey, Lynn C. *United States Representative from California*
Wormmeester, Justin T. *legislative staff member*
Wright, Ron *legislative staff member*
Wyatt, John *legislative staff member*
Wybensinger, Netonis (Tonnie Wybensinger) *legislative staff member*
Wyden, Ron(ald) (Lee) *United States Senator from Oregon*
Yarmuth, John Allan *United States Representative from Kentucky*
Yonkura, Raymond *legislative staff member*
Young, Bill (Charles William Young) *United States Representative from Florida*
Young, David *legislative staff member*
Young, Donald Edwin *United States Representative from Alaska*
Young, Todd Dean *legislative staff member*
Zabel, Matthew L. *legislative staff member*
Zamore, Michael Seth *legislative staff member*
Zody, John C. *legislative staff member*

FLORIDA

Brooksville
Brown-Waite, Virginia (Ginny Brown-Waite) *United States Representative from Florida*

Daytona Beach
Lynn, Evelyn Joan *state legislator*

Jacksonville
Bishop, William *Councilman*
Brown, Reginald L. *Councilman*
Clark, Richard *Councilman*
Corrigan, Michael *Councilman*
Crescimbeni, John R. *Councilman*
Davis, Daniel *Councilman*
Fussell, Ronnie *Councilman*
Gaffney, Johnny A.
Graham, Arthur (Art) *Councilman*
Holt, Ray *Councilman*
Hyde, Kevin *Councilman*
Johnson, Glorious J. *Councilwoman*
Jones, Warren A. *Councilman*
Joost, Stephen C. *Councilman*
Lee, E. Denise *Councilwoman*
McBurney, Charles Walker, Jr. *state representative, lawyer*
Redman, Don *Councilman*
Shad, Arthur (Art) *councilman*
Webb, Jack D. *Councilman*
Yarborough, Clay *Councilman*

Miami
Margolis, Gwen *former state legislator*

Miami Lakes
Graham, Bob (Daniel Robert Graham) *former United States Senator from Florida*

Saint Augustine
Proctor, William Lee *state legislator, academic administrator*

Sarasota
Fitzgerald, Keith *state legislator, political science professor*

Tampa
Castor, Kathy *United States Representative from Florida*
Culp, Faye Berry *state legislator*
Davis, Helen Gordon *retired state senator*

GEORGIA

Americus
Hooks, George Bardin *state legislator, insurance company executive*

Athens
McBee, Mary Louise *state legislator, academic administrator*

Atlanta
Cleland, Max (Joseph Maxwell Cleland) *former United States Senator from Georgia*
Miller, Zell Bryan *former senator, governor*

Augusta
Barnard, Druie Douglas, Jr. *former congressman, bank executive*

Columbus
Harbison, Ed *state legislator, broadcast journalist, motivational speaker*
Smyre, Calvin *state legislator*

Decatur
Mobley, Barbara Jean *former state legislator, lawyer*

Jonesboro
Tanks, Ashley *legislative staff member*

Lawrenceville
Wall, Clarence Vinson *state legislator*

Lithonia
Johnson, Henry C. (Hank Johnson) *United States Representative from Georgia, lawyer*
McKinney, Cynthia Ann *former United States Representative from Georgia*

Marietta
Manning, Judith Hubert *state legislator, real estate company executive*

Rincon
Purcell, Ann Rushing *state legislator, human services manager*

Smyrna
Atkins, William Austin, Sr., (Bill Atkins) *former state legislator*

HAWAII

Honolulu
Goto Sabas, Jennifer *legislative staff member*
Hanabusa, Colleen W. *state legislator, lawyer*
Hirono, Mazie Keiko *United States Representative from Hawaii, former lieutenant governor*
Inouye, Lorraine R. *state legislator*
Sakamoto, Norman Lloyd *state legislator, civil engineer*
Takumi, Roy Mitsuo *state legislator*

IDAHO

Boise
Bell, Maxine Toolson *state legislator*
Black, Pete *retired state legislator, educator*
LaRocco, Larry *former congressman*

Ketchum
Stennett, William Clinton (Clint) *state legislator, entrepreneur*

Meridian
McKague, Shirley *state legislator*

ILLINOIS

Bloomingdale
Roskam, Peter James *United States Representative from Illinois, former state legislator, lawyer*

Chicago
Allen, Thomas R. *alderman*
Austin, Carrie *alderwoman*
Balcer, James A. *alderman*
Banks, William J.P. *alderman*
Beale, Anthony *alderman*
Berman, Arthur Leonard *state legislator*
Brookins, Howard, Jr. *alderman*
Burke, Edward Michael *alderman*
Burnett, Walter, Jr. *alderman*
Cardenas, George A. *alderman*
Carothers, Isaac Sims (Ike Carothers) *alderman*
Cochran, Willie B. *alderman*
Colon, Rey *alderman*
Daley, Vi *alderwoman*
Dixon, Sharon Denise *alderwoman*
Doherty, Brian Gerard *alderman*
Dowell, Pat *alderwoman*
Fioretti, Robert William *lawyer*
Flores, Manuel *alderman*
Foulkes, Toni *Alderwoman*
Hairston, Leslie *alderwoman*
Harris, Gregory Scott *state legislator*
Harris, Michelle A. *alderwoman*
Jackson, Sandra (Sandi Jackson) *alderwoman*
Jones, Emil III *state legislator*
Lane, Lona *alderwoman*
Laurino, Margaret *alderwoman*
Levar, Patrick J. *alderman*
Lyle, Freddrenna M. *alderwoman*
Madigan, Michael Joseph *state legislator, political organization administrator*
Mell, Richard F. *alderman*
Mitts, Emma *alderwoman*
Moore, Joseph Arthur *alderman, lawyer*
Muñoz, Ricardo *alderman*
O'Connor, Patrick J. *alderman*
Olivo, Frank J. *alderman*
Pope, John A. *alderman*
Preckwinkle, Toni *alderwoman*
Reboyras, Ariel E. *alderman*
Reilly, Brendan *alderman*
Rugai, Virginia A. (Ginger Rugai) *alderwoman*
Schulter, Eugene C. *alderman*
Shiller, Helen *alderwoman*
Smith, Ed H. *alderman*
Smith, Mary Ann *alderwoman*
Solis, Daniel S. *alderman*
Stone, Bernard Leonard *alderman, vice mayor*
Suarez, Ray (Regner Suarez) *alderman*
Thomas, Latasha R. *alderwoman*
Thompson, JoAnn *Alderwoman*
Tunney, Thomas M. *alderman, restaurant owner*
Waguespack, Scott *Alderman*
Zalewski, Michael R. *alderman*

Jacksonville
Findley, Paul *former congressman, author, educator*

Springfield
Cullerton, John James *state legislator*
Currie, Barbara Flynn *state legislator*
Davis, Jack *former congressman*
Davis, Monique D. (Deon Davis) *state legislator*
Hannig, Gary L. *state legislator, state legislator*
Jefferson, Charles E. *state legislator*
Klingler, Gwendolyn Walbolt *state representative*
Kosel, Renée *state legislator*
Martinez, Iris *state legislator*

West Chicago
Fortner, Michael R. *state legislator, physics professor*

West Frankfort
Gray, Kenneth J. *former congressman*

INDIANA

Beech Grove
Day, N. Susie *councilwoman*

Indianapolis
Bateman, Paul C., Jr. *councilman*
Brown, Vernon *councilman*
Cain, Virginia J. *councilwoman*
Cardwell, Jeff *Councilman*
Cockrum, Bob *councilman*
Coleman, Edward *councilman*
Evans, Jose M. *Councilman*
Gray, Monroe, Jr. *councilman*
Hunter, Benjamin *Councilman*
Lewis, Maggie *councilwoman*
Lutz, Robert *councilman*
Mahern, Brian *Councilman*
Mahern, Dane *councilman*
Malone, Barbara *councilwoman*
Mansfield, Angela *councilwoman*
McHenry, Janice *councilwoman*
McQuillen, Michael J. *Councilman*
Minton-McNeill, Doris *councilwoman*
Moriarty Adams, Mary Bridget *councilwoman, human resources specialist*
Nytes, Jackie (M. Jacqueline Nytes) *councilwoman*
Oliver, William *councilman*
Pfisterer, Marilyn *councilwoman*
Plowman, Lincoln *councilman, protective services official*
Sanders, Joanne *councilwoman*
Scales, Christine *Councilwoman*
Smith, Kent B. *councilman*
Speedy, Mike *councilman, real estate consultant*
Vaughn, Ryan *councilman*
Wilson, Richard Harry, Jr. *congressional chief of staff*

Jeffersonville
Sodrel, Michael Eugene *former congressman, small business owner*

West Lafayette
Scholer, Sue Wyant *state legislator*

IOWA

Bettendorf
Hartsuch, David *state legislator*

Des Moines
Bukta, Polly *state legislator*
Quirmbach, Herman Charles *state legislator*
Smith, Neal Edward *former congressman, lawyer*

Sioux City
Andersen, Leonard Christian *former state legislator, real estate investor*

KANSAS

Hutchinson
O'Neal, Michael Ralph *state legislator*

Lawrence
Ryun, Jim (James Ronald Ryun) *former congressman*

Overland Park
Vratil, John Logan *state legislator*

Shawnee
Jordan, Nick M. *state legislator*

Shawnee Mission
Sader, Carol Hope *former state legislator*

Topeka
Carlin, Sydney *state legislator*
Gordon, Lana G. *state legislator*
Holmes, Carl Dean *state legislator*
Horst, Deena Louise *state legislator*
McKinney, Dennis *state treasurer*
Schmidt, Derek Larkin *state legislator*

Wichita
Betts, Donald, Jr. *state legislator*
Pottorff, Jo Ann *state legislator*

KENTUCKY

Frankfort
Carroll, Julian Morton *state legislator, former Governor of Kentucky, lawyer*
Stumbo, Gregory D. *state legislator, former state attorney general*

Owensboro
Boswell, David E., Sr. *state legislator*

Shelbyville
Miller, Mary Helen *retired state government administrator*

LOUISIANA

Lafayette
Cravins, Donald R., Jr. *state legislator*

Lake Charles
Mount, Willie Landry *state legislator*

New Orleans
Boggs, Corinne Claiborne (Lindy Boggs) *Former United States Representative, La*
Irons, Paulette Riley *state legislator, lawyer*

MAINE

Augusta
Martin, John Lewis *state legislator*
Mitchell, Elizabeth H. (Libby Mitchell) *state legislator*

Hallowell
Douglass, Neria Gay *state legislator, lawyer*

Windham
Diamond, G. William *state legislator*

MARYLAND

Annapolis
Clagett, Virginia Parker *state legislator*
Doory, Ann Marie *state legislator*
Frosh, Brian Esten *state legislator, lawyer*
Harris, Andrew Peter *state legislator*
Kelley, Delores Goodwin *state legislator*

Bethesda
Reed, Miriam Bell *legislative staff member*

MASSACHUSETTS

Boston
Binienda, John J., Sr. *state legislator*
Canavan, Christine Estelle *state legislator*
Chandler, Harriette Levy *state legislator, management consultant, educator*
Creedon, Geraldine *state legislator*
Creem, Cynthia Stone *state legislator, lawyer*
Finegold, Barry R. *state legislator, lawyer*
Moore, Richard Thomas *state legislator*
Stanley, Harriett Lari *state legislator*
Walrath, Patricia A. *state legislator*
Wolf, Alice Koerner *state legislator, former mayor*

Chelmsford
Cleven, Carol Chapman *state legislator*

Springfield
Melconian, Linda Jean *state senator, lawyer, educator*

MICHIGAN

Detroit
Cockrel, Sheila M. *Councilwoman*
Collins, Barbara-Rose *Councilwoman*
Kenyatta, Kwame *councilman*
Reeves, Martha *Councilwoman*
Tinsley-Talabi, Alberta *Councilwoman*
Watson, JoAnn *Councilwoman*

East Lansing
Jones, Brenda *Councilwoman*

Farmington Hills
Dolan, Jan Clark *former state legislator*

Lansing
Hoffman, Philip Edward *legislative consultant*
Hoogendyk, Jacob William, Jr., (Jack Hoogendyk) *state legislator*

MINNESOTA

Excelsior
Oliver, Edward Carl *state legislator, insurance company executive, small business owner*

Mankato
Salsbery, Meredith A. *legislative staff member*

Minneapolis
Penny, Timothy Joseph *former congressman*

Saint Paul
Kiffmeyer, Mary *state legislator*
Pappas, Sandra Lee *state legislator*

MISSISSIPPI

Fulton
Miles, William Trice *state legislator*

MISSOURI

Cape Girardeau
Haynes, Joshua *legislative staff member*

Columbia
Klippenstein, Brian *legislative staff member*

Jefferson City
Griesheimer, John Elmer *state legislator*
Walton Gray, Rochelle LaJoyce *state legislator*

Springfield
Champion, Norma Jean *state legislator, communications educator*
Hancock, Mel *former congressman*

MONTANA

Helena
Cooney, Michael Rodman *state legislator*
Peterson, James Erling *state legislator*

NEBRASKA

Lincoln
Avery, William Paul *state legislator, political scientist, educator*
Council, Brenda Joyce *state legislator*
Dierks, Merton Lyle *state legislator, retired veterinarian*
Harms, John N. *state legislator*
Landis, David Morrison *state legislator*
Schimek, DiAnna Ruth Rebman *state legislator*

Omaha
Ellis, Lisa *legislative staff member*

NEVADA

Carson City
Raggio, William John *state legislator, lawyer*
Wiener, Valerie *state senator, communications executive, writer*

Elko
Heller, Dean *United States Representative from Nevada, former state official*

NEW HAMPSHIRE

Concord
Bradley, Paula E. *former state legislator*
Clemons, Jane Andrea *state legislator*
Cote, David Edward *state legislator*
DiFruscia, Anthony R. *state legislator, lawyer*
Foster, Linda Timberlake *state legislator*
Gile, Mary Stuart *state legislator*
Larsen, Sylvia B. *state legislator*
Norelli, Terie Thompson *state legislator*
Nowe, Ronald John *state legislator, small business owner*
Pilliod, James P. *state legislator*

Derry
Katsakiores, George Nicholas *state legislator, retired food service executive*

Hanover
Crory, Elizabeth Lupien *state legislator*

Manchester
Shaheen, Jeanne *United States Senator from New Hampshire, political scientist, former governor*

Moultonborough
Patten, Betsey Leland *state legislator*

Wolfeboro
Bradley, Jeb E. (Joseph E. Bradley) *state legislator*

NEW JERSEY

Clifton
Giblin, Thomas Patrick *state legislator, labor union administrator*

Matawan
Thompson, Samuel D. *state legislator*

Mays Landing
LoBiondo, Frank A. *United States Representative from New Jersey*

Newark
Lautenberg, Frank Raleigh *United States Senator from New Jersey*

Ocean City
Hughes, William John *former congressman, diplomat*

Paterson
Pou, Nelida (Nellie) *state legislator*

Piscataway
Smith, Bob *state legislator, lawyer*

Short Hills
Ogden, Maureen Black *state legislator*

Trenton
Baroni, Bill (William E. Baroni Jr.) *state legislator*
Codey, Richard James (Dick Codey) *state legislator*
Green, Gerald B. *state legislator*
Vitale, Joseph F. *state legislator*

Union
Cryan, Joseph P. *state legislator, political organization administrator*

Westfield
Kean, Thomas H., Jr., (Thomas Howard Kean Jr.) *state legislator*

NEW MEXICO

Albuquerque
Rutherford, Thomas Truxtun, II, *state legislator, municipal official*

Hobbs
Reagan, Gary Don *state legislator, lawyer*

NEW YORK

Albany
Canestrari, Ronald J. *state legislator*
Smith, Ada LaVerne *state legislator*
Smith, Malcolm A. *state legislator*
Volker, Dale Martin *state legislator, lawyer*

Bayside
Avella, Tony *city councilman*

Bronx
Arroyo, Maria del Carmen *City Councilwoman*
Baez, Maria *city councilwoman*
Foster, Helen Diane *city councilwoman, lawyer*
Koppell, G. Oliver *city councilman, former NY State Atty. Gen., lawyer*
Palma, Annabel *city councilwoman*
Rivera, Joel *city councilman*
Seabrook, Larry B. (Lawrence B. Seabrook) *city councilman, former state legislator*
Vacca, James *city councilman*

Brooklyn
Barron, Charles *city councilman*
Dilan, Erik Martin *city councilman*
Eugene, Mathieu *city councilman*
Felder, Simcha *city councilman*
Fidler, Lewis A. *city councilman, lawyer*
Gentile, Vincent Joseph *city councilman, former state legislator*
Gonzalez, Sara M. *city councilwoman*
Mealy, Darlene *city councilwoman*
Nelson, Michael Chaim *city councilman*
Recchia, Domenic M., Jr. *city councilman*
Reyna, Diana *city councilwoman*
Stewart, Kendall *city councilman, podiatrist*
Vann, Albert *city councilman, former state legislator*
Yassky, David S. *City Councilman, Brooklyn, New York, lawyer*

Derby
Pordum, Francis J. *supervisor, former state legislator, educator, marketing professional*

Far Rockaway
Ulrich, Eric A. *city councilman*

Flushing
Stavisky, Toby Ann *state legislator*

Forest Hills
Katz, Melinda R. *city councilwoman, former state legislator*

Glendale
Maltese, Serphin Ralph *state legislator, lawyer*

Jamaica
Flake, Floyd Harold *former United States Representative from New York*
Meeks, Gregory Weldon *United States Representative from New York*

Massapequa Park
King, Peter Thomas *United States Representative from New York, lawyer*

Middle Village
Crowley, Elizabeth S. *city councilwoman*

New York
Brewer, Gale A. *city councilwoman*
de Blasio, Bill *city councilman*
Dickens, Inez Elizabeth *city councilwoman, real estate executive*
Farrell, Herman D., Jr., (Denny Farrell) *state legislator*
Garodnick, Daniel R. *city councilman, lawyer*
Gerson, Alan J. *city councilman, lawyer*
Jackson, Robert *city councilman*
James, Letitia *city councilwoman, lawyer*
Kostmayer, Peter Houston *former congressman, community organization administrator*
Lappin, Jessica S. *city councilwoman*
Mark-Viverito, Mellisa *Councilwoman*
Mendez, Rosie *city councilwoman*
Quinn, Christine Callaghan *city councilwoman*
Silver, Sheldon *state legislator*

Ossining
Galef, Sandra Risk *state legislator*

Queens
Comrie, Leroy G. *city councilman*
Gennaro, James F. *city councilman*
Gioia, Eric N. *city councilman, lawyer*
Liu, John C. *city councilman*
Sanders, James, Jr. *city councilman*
Sears, Helen *city councilwoman*
Vallone, Peter F. *city councilman, lawyer*
Weprin, David I. *city councilman, lawyer*

Rego Park
Lowey, Nita Melnikoff *United States Representative from New York*

Rochester
John, Susan V. *state legislator*

Rockville Centre
Skelos, Dean George *state legislator*

South Ozone Park
White, Thomas, Jr. *city councilman*

Staten Island
Ignizio, Vincent *city councilman*
Oddo, James S. *city councilman, lawyer*

Syracuse
DeFrancisco, John Anthony *state legislator, lawyer*

Watertown
McHugh, John Michael *United States Representative from New York*

NORTH CAROLINA

Advance
Cochrane, Betsy Lane *former state senator*

Asheville
Mumpower, Carl III *councilman*
Shuler, Heath (Joseph Heath Shuler) *United States Representative from North Carolina, retired professional football player*

Burlington
Holt, Bertha Merrill *state legislator*

Charlotte
Clodfelter, Daniel Gray *state legislator, lawyer*

Clemmons
Foxx, Virginia Ann *United States Representative from North Carolina, small business owner*

Fayetteville
Rand, Anthony Eden *state legislator, lawyer*

Greensboro
Shaw, Robert Gilbert *state legislator, food service executive*

Hickory
Ballenger, Thomas Cass *former congressman, retired plastics company executive*

Raleigh
Hagan, Kay Ruthven *United States Senator from North Carolina*
Hunt, Neal Kemp *state legislator, real estate company executive*
Kinnaird, Eleanor Gates *state legislator, lawyer*
Lancaster, H(arold) Martin *Former United States Representative, NC, academic administrator*
Stevens, Richard Yates *state legislator*
Sutton, Ronnie Neal *state legislator, lawyer*

Southern Pines
Funderburk, David Britton *Former United States Representative, NC, ambassador, consultant*

NORTH DAKOTA

Bismarck
Klemin, Lawrence R. *state legislator, lawyer*
Nelson, Carolyn *state legislator*

Fargo
Mathern, Tim *state legislator*

Grand Forks
Glassheim, Eliot Alan *state legislator*

Minot
Tollefson, Ben C. *state legislator, retired utilities executive*

Osnabrock
Monson, David Carl *state legislator*

Venturia
Kretschmar, William Edward *state legislator, lawyer*

OHIO

Aurora
Herington, Leigh Ellsworth *state legislator, lawyer*

Beachwood
Budish, Armond David *state legislator, lawyer, journalist*

Cleveland
Drake, Grace L. *retired state senator, cultural organization administrator*

Columbus
Beatty, Joyce *state legislator*
Buehrer, Stephen *state legislator*
Chandler, Kathleen Leone *state legislator, former mayor, educator*
Craig, Hearcel F. *city councilman*
Ginther, Andrew J. *city councilman*
Glenn, John Herschel, Jr. *former senator, retired astronaut*
Mentel, Michael C. *city council president, lawyer*
Miller, A. Troy *city councilman, information technology executive*
Paley, Eileen Y. *city councilwoman, lawyer*
Schuring, J. Kirk *state legislator*
Stivers, Steve *state legislator*
Tavares, Charleta B. *city councilwoman*
Tiberi, Patrick Joseph *United States Representative from Ohio, former state legislator*
Trakas, James Peter *state legislator*
Tyson, Priscilla R. *city councilwoman*

Lakewood
Kucinich, Dennis John *United States Representative from Ohio*

Napoleon
Wachtmann, Lynn R. *state legislator*

Painesville
LaTourette, Steven C. *United States Representative from Ohio*

Toledo
Kaptur, Marcia Carolyn (Marcy Kaptur) *United States Representative from Ohio*

Warren
Ryan, Timothy J. *United States Representative from Ohio*

OKLAHOMA

Durant
Gumm, Jay Paul *state legislator, association executive*

Oklahoma City
Fallin, Mary Copeland *United States Representative from Oklahoma, former lieutenant governor*
Jones, Tad *state legislator*
Rice, Andrew *state legislator*

Stillwater
Lucas, Frank D. *United States Representative from Oklahoma*

OREGON

Albany
Oakley, Carolyn Le *state legislator, city manager, director*

Mcminnville
Nelson, Donna Gayle *state legislator*

Portland
Blumenauer, Earl *United States Representative from Oregon*
Furse, Elizabeth *Former United States Representative, Oregon, small business owner*
Hatfield, Mark Odom *former senator*
Kardon, Joshua R. *legislative staff member*
Merkley, Jeffery A. *United States Senator from Oregon*
Wu, David *United States Representative from Oregon*

Salem
Burdick, Ginny Marie *state legislator*
Carter, Margaret Louise *state legislator*
Hunt, David G. *state legislator, coalition executive*

PENNSYLVANIA

Bethlehem
Dent, Charles Wieder (Charlie Dent) *United States Representative from Pennsylvania*

Bristol
Murphy, Patrick Joseph *United States Representative from Pennsylvania*

Chalfont
Wilson, Jean Louise *state legislator*

Cranberry Township
Hart, Melissa Anne *former congresswoman*

Harrisburg
Bishop, Louise Williams *state legislator*
Dinniman, Andrew Eric *state legislator, international studies and history professor*
O'Brien, Dennis M. *state legislator*
Pileggi, Dominic F. *state legislator*
Williams, Constance *state legislator*
Williams, Jewell *state legislator*

Hollidaysburg
Shuster, William (Bill Shuster) *United States Representative from Pennsylvania*

Media
Sestak, Joe (Joseph A. Sestak Jr.) *United States Representative from Pennsylvania, retired military officer*

Philadelphia
Blackwell, Jannie L. *councilwoman*
Brown, Blondell Reynolds *councilwoman*
Clarke, Darrell L. *councilman*
DiCicco, Frank J. *councilman*
Goode, W. Wilson, Jr. *councilman*
Green, William Joseph, IV, (Bill Green) *councilman, lawyer*
Greenlee, William K. *councilman*
Jacobs, Jonathan Mark *parliamentary consultant*
Jones, Curtis, Jr. *councilman*
Kelly, John P. (Jack Kelly) *councilman*
Kenney, James F. *councilman*
Krajewski, Joan L. *councilwoman*
Margolies-Mezvinsky, Marjorie *former congresswoman, political organization worker*
Miller, Donna Reed *councilwoman*
O'Neill, Brian J. *councilman*
Quiñones-Sánchez, Maria D. *councilwoman*
Tasco, Marian B. *councilwoman*
Verna, Anna Cibotti *councilwoman*

Unionville
Pitts, Joseph R. (Joe Pitts) *United States Representative from Pennsylvania*

RHODE ISLAND

Middletown
Gibbs, June Nesbitt *state legislator*

Pawtucket
Doyle, James E., II, *state legislator*

Providence
Ajello, Edith H. *state legislator*
Algiere, Dennis Lee *state legislator*
Connors, Daniel Paul *state legislator*

SOUTH CAROLINA

Columbia
Courson, John Edward *state legislator, insurance company executive*
Leatherman, Hugh Kenneth, Sr. *state legislator, engineering executive*
McLeod, Walton James III *state legislator, lawyer*
Sellers, Bakari T. *state legislator*
Weeks, J. David *state representative, lawyer*

Greenville
DeMint, Jim (James Warren DeMint) *United States Senator from South Carolina, former congressman*

Mc Cormick
Clayton, Verna Lewis *state legislator*

Saint Helena Island
Googins, Sonya Forbes *state legislator, retired banker*

SOUTH DAKOTA

Mud Butte
Ingalls, Marie Cecelie *former state legislator, retail executive*

Pierre
Gray, Bob *state legislator, political organization administrator*
Lucas, Larry James *state legislator*

Wall
Pederson, Gordon Roy *retired state legislator, military officer*

TENNESSEE

Athens
Higdon, Linda Hampton *congressional staff*

Knoxville
Griffitts, Bobby R. *legislative staff member*

Mason
Wilder, John Shelton *state legislator, former lieutenant governor*

Nashville
Alexander, Lamar (Andrew Lamar Alexander) *United States Senator from Tennessee, former United States Secretary of Education*
Brown, Tommie Florence F. *state legislator, social work educator*

TEXAS

Austin
Noriega, Rick (Richard Joel Noriega) *state legislator*
Wentworth, Earl Jeffrey *state legislator, lawyer*

Beaumont
Brooks, Jack Bascom *former congressman*

Dallas
Allen, Jerry R. *Councilman*
Atkins, Tennell *Councilman*
Caraway, Dwaine R. *Councilman*
Davis, Carolyn R. *Councilwoman*
García, Elba *city councilwoman, dentist*
Hartnett, Will Ford *state legislator, lawyer*
Hill, Vonciel Jones *Councilwoman*
Hunt, Angela *city councilwoman*
Kadane, Sheffield A. *city councilman, investment company executive, real estate agent*
Koop, Linda *city councilwoman*
Medrano, Pauline *city councilwoman, ESL educator*
Natinsky, Ron *city councilman, entrepreneur*
Neumann, David A. *city councilman, small business owner*

Rasansky, Mitchell *city councilman*
Salazar, Steve *Councilman*

Garland
Driver, Joe Luther *state legislator, insurance agent, consultant*

Houston
Adams, Wanda *city councilwoman*
Brown, Peter *city councilman, architectural firm executive*
Clutterbuck, Anne *city councilwoman*
Holm, Pam *city councilwoman*
Johnson, Jarvis *city councilman*
Jones, Jolanda F. *city councilwoman, lawyer*
Khan, M.J. *city councilman, real estate developer*
Lawrence, Toni *city councilwoman, small business owner*
Lovell, Sue *city councilwoman*
Noriega, Melissa *city councilwoman, educator*
Rodriguez, James G. *city councilman*
Sullivan, Mike *city councilman, small business owner*

Lubbock
Duncan, Robert Lloyd *state legislator, lawyer*

San Antonio
Cibrian, Diane G. *Councilman*
Cisneros, Mary Alice P. *Councilwoman*
Clamp, John G. *Councilman*
Cortez, Philip A. *Councilman*
Galvan, Lourdes *Councilwoman*
Herrera, Delicia *councilwoman*
McNeil, Sheila D. *Councilwoman*
Ramos, Jennifer V. *Councilwoman*
Rodriguez, Justin *Councilman*
Rowe, Louis E. *Councilman*

UTAH

Provo
Valentine, John Lester *state legislator, lawyer*

Salt Lake City
Black, Wilford Rex, Jr. *state legislator*
Carnahan, Orville Darrell *state legislator, academic administrator*
Davis, Gene *state legislator*
Shepherd, Karen *former congresswoman*
Walker, Carlene Martin *state legislator*

VERMONT

Barre
Koch, Thomas F. *state legislator*

Montpelier
Keenan, Kathleen *state legislator, nurse*
Nuovo, Betty A. *state legislator, lawyer*
Paquin, Edward H., Jr. *state legislator, not-for-profit developer*

Rutland
Ferraro, Betty Ann *retired state senator*

VIRGINIA

Alexandria
Collins, Cardiss *retired congresswoman*

Arlington
Musgrave, Marilyn Neoma *former United States Representative from Colorado*
Wheat, Alan Dupree *former Congressman, political consultant*

Fairfax
Miller, Emilie F. *former state senator, consultant*

Herndon
Allen, George Felix, Jr. *former United States Senator from Virginia, former Governor of Virginia*

Richmond
Griffith, Howard Morgan *state legislator, lawyer*

WASHINGTON

Olympia
Long, Jeanine Hundley *state legislator*

Port Angeles
Kessler, Lynn Elizabeth *state legislator*

Renton
Thomas, Brian Chester *retired state legislator, engineer*

Seattle
Evans, Daniel Jackson *former senator, management consultant*
Pedersen, Jamie D. *state legislator, lawyer*

Spanaway
Campbell, Thomas J. *state legislator, chiropractor*

WEST VIRGINIA

Charleston
Barth, Elizabeth Anne *former aide*
McCabe, Brooks Fleming, Jr. *state legislator*
Tomblin, Earl Ray *state legislator, Lieutenant Governor of West Virginia*

Huntington
Jenkins, Evan H. *state legislator*

Shinnston
Spears, Jae *state legislator*

WISCONSIN

Green Bay
Gard, John *state legislator*

Madison
Albers, Sheryl Kay *state legislator*
Darling, Alberta Helen *state legislator*
Whitney, Lori Ann *legislative staff member*

WYOMING

Casper
Fagan, Tucker *legislative staff member, former state agency administrator*

Cheyenne
Johnson, Wayne Harold *state legislator*
Kunz, April Brimmer *state legislator, lawyer*

Laramie
Hansen, Matilda *former state legislator*
Maxfield, Peter Charles *state legislator, lawyer, educator*

Riverton
Bebout, Eli Daniel *state legislator*

TERRITORIES OF THE UNITED STATES

VIRGIN ISLANDS

St Thomas
Berry, Lorraine Ledee *state senator*
Donastorg, Adlah, Jr., (Foncie Donastorg) *territorial legislator*

CANADA

BRITISH COLUMBIA

Vancouver
McWhinney, Edward Watson *Canadian government legislator*

ONTARIO

Ottawa
Bacon, Lise *Canadian senator*
Dryden, Ken *legislator, former sports team executive, retired professional hockey player*

Toronto
Eyton, John Trevor *business executive*

QUEBEC

Montreal
Demers, Jacques *legislator, sports analyst, former professional hockey coach*

Saint-Laurent
Dion, Stéphane *Canadian legislator*

NEPAL

Kathmandu
Rana, Pashupati S.J.B. *legislator*

ADDRESS UNPUBLISHED

Abey, Kathy Michele *district representative, retired congressional caseworker*
Allard, Wayne (Alan Wayne Allard) *retired US Senator from Colorado, veterinarian*
Armey, Dick (Richard Keith Armey) *former United States Representative from Texas*
Bass, Charles Foster *former United States Representative from New Hampshire*
Beauprez, Bob (Robert L. Beauprez) *former congressman*
Bilbray, James Hubert *Former United States Representative from Nevada, lawyer, consultant*
Bilirakis, Michael *former congressman, lawyer, corporate financial executive*
Boyda, Nancy E. *former United States Representative from Kansas*
Burns, Max *former congressman*
Callahan, Vincent Francis, Jr. *state legislator, retired publishing executive*
Cannon, Christopher Black *former United States Representative from Utah, lawyer*
Carson, Brad Rogers *former congressman*
Carstairs, Sharon *legislator*
Case, Edward Espenett *former United States Representative from Hawaii, lawyer*
Cazayoux, Don (Donald J. Cazayoux Jr.) *former United States Representative from Louisiana*
Chabot, Steven Joseph *former United States Representative from Ohio, lawyer*
Churchill, Robert Wilson *state legislator, lawyer*
Coleman, Norman, Jr. *former United States Senator from Minnesota, mayor*
Cox, Christopher (Charles Christopher Cox) *former United States Representative from California*
Cubin, Barbara Lynn *former United States Representative from Wyoming*
Daschle, Tom (Thomas Andrew Daschle) *former United States Senator from South Dakota*
Davis, David Lee *former United States Representative from Tennessee*
Dayton, Mark Brandt *former senator*
DeLay, Tom (Thomas Dale DeLay) *former United States Representative from Texas*
DeWine, Mike (Richard Michael DeWine) *former senator, lawyer*
Dole, Elizabeth Hanford *former United States Senator from North Carolina*
Domenici, (Pete) Vichi *retired United States Senator from New Mexico*
Doolittle, John Taylor *former United States Representative from California*
Dowdy, Charles Wayne *former United States Representative from Mississippi*
Drake, Thelma Day *former United States Representative from Virginia*
Dunnam, James Robert *state legislator, lawyer*
Dymally, Mervyn Malcolm *retired state legislator*
English, Philip Sheridan *former United States Representative from Pennsylvania*
Evans, Lane Allen *Former United States Representative, Ill*
Everett, Terry (Robert Terry Everett) *retired United States Representative from Alabama*
Federing, Eric K. *legislative staff member, public information officer, business executive*
Feeney, Tom (Thomas Charles Feeney III) *former United States Representative from Florida, lawyer*
Ferguson, Michael A. (Mike) *former United States Representative from New Jersey*
Foley, Mark Adam *former congressman*
Forbes, Michael Patrick *former congressman*
Fossella, Vito John, Jr. *former United States Representative from New York*
Frelinghuysen, Peter Hood Ballantine, Jr. *Former United States Representative, New Jersey*
Ganske, J. Greg *former congressman, plastic surgeon*
Garton, Robert Dean *state legislator*
Geren, Pete (Preston M. Geren III) *former United States Representative from Texas*
Gibbons, Sam Melville *former United States Representative, Florida, government agency administrator*
Gilchrest, Wayne Thomas *former United States Representative from Maryland, secondary school educator*
Goode, Virgil Hamlin, Jr. *former United States Representative from Virginia*
Gravel, Mike (Maurice Robert Gravel) *former United States Senator from Alaska*
Greenfield, Lee *state legislator*
Gutknecht, Gil (Gilbert William Gutknecht Jr) *former congressman, former state legislator*
Hagel, Chuck (Charles Timothy Hagel) *retired United States Senator from Nebraska*
Hall, Tony P. *retired congressman, former ambassador*
Hammerschmidt, John Paul *former United States Representative, Arkansas, lumber company executive*
Hawkins, Mary Ellen Higgins *state legislator, public relations executive*
Hayes, Robin (Robert Cannon Hayes) *former United States Representative from North Carolina*
Hayworth, J.D. (John David Jr.) *former congressman*
Hearn, Joyce Camp *retired state legislator, educator, consultant*
Hill, Richard Allan (Rick Hill) *former congressman*
Hollings, Fritz (Ernest Frederick) *former senator*
Hooley, Darlene Kay Olson *former United States Representative from Oregon*
Hostettler, John Nathan *former congressman*
Hulshof, Kenny Charles *former United States Representative from Missouri*
Hunter, Duncan Lee *retired United States Representative from California*
Ipsen, Grant Ruel *state legislator, insurance and investments professional*
Istook, Ernest James, Jr., (Jim) *former congressman, lawyer*
Jeffords, James Merrill *former United States Senator from Vermont*
Kastenmeier, Robert William *former Congressman*
Kennedy, Mark Raymond *former congressman*
Keys, Martha Elizabeth *former congresswoman*
Knollenberg, Joseph Castl (Joe Knollenberg) *former United States Representative from Michigan*
Kolbe, Jim (James Thomas Kolbe) *former United States Representative, Arizona*
Kuhl, Randy (John R. Kuhl Jr.) *former United States Representative from New York, lawyer*
Lampson, Nick (Nicholas Valentino Lampson) *former United States Representative from Texas*
Lewis, Ron (Ronald E. Lewis) *former United States Representative from Kentucky*
Mahoney, Tim (Timothy Edward Mahoney) *former United States Representative from Florida*
Martinez, Mel (Melquiades Rafael Martinez) *former United States Senator from Florida, former United States Secretary of Housing and Urban Development*
McCarthy, Karen P. *former congresswoman, state legislator*
McCormack, Mike *former congressman*
McGovern, George Stanley *former United States Senator from South Dakota*
McNulty, Michael Robert *former United States Representative from New York*
Meshel, Harry *former state senator, political party official*
Mogilnicki, Eric J. *legislative staff member*
Morella, Constance Albanese *former United States Representative from Maryland*
Munt, Janet Staples *state senator*
Owens, Major Robert Odell *former congressman*
Pascoe, Patricia Hill *former state legislator*
Patterson, Elizabeth Johnston *Former United States Representative, South Carolina*
Pearce, Steve (Stevan Edward Pearce) *former United States Representative from New Mexico*
Pease, Edward A. *former congressman*
Pendleton, Florence Howard *former shadow senator*
Peterson, John E. *former United States Representative from Pennsylvania*
Pettis-Roberson, Shirley McCumber *former US Representative, California*
Petzold, Carol Stoker *state legislator*
Pevear, Roberta Charlotte *state legislator*
Pickering, Chip (Charles Willis Pickering Jr.) *former United States Representative from Mississippi*
Pombo, Richard William *former congressman, rancher, farmer*
Poos, Jacques Francois *former foreign minister, member of European Parliament*
Pressler, Larry *former senator, lawyer*
Pryce, Deborah Denine *former United States Representative from Ohio*
Ramstad, James Marvin (Jim Ramstad) *former United States Representative from Minnesota, lawyer*
Redfield, Pamela A. *state legislator*
Redwine, John Newland *state legislator, physician*
Regula, Ralph Straus *former United States Representative from Ohio, lawyer*
Renzi, Rick (Richard George Renzi) *former United States Representative from Arizona*
Rogeness, Mary Speer *retired state legislator*
Rudy, Ruth Corman *former state legislator*
Russell, Carol Ann *city council member, retired company executive*
Sabo, Martin Olav *former congressman*
St. Germain, Fernand Joseph *Former United States Representative, Rhode Island*
Sali, Bill (William Thomas Sali) *former United States Representative from Idaho*
Sarbanes, Paul Spyros *former United States Senator from Maryland*
Sasser, James Ralph *former United States Senator from Tennessee*
Saucier, Gene Duane *state legislator, import/export company executive*
Saxton, Jim (Hugh James Saxton) *former United States Representative from New Jersey*
Schexnayder, Charlotte Tillar *state legislator*
Schwarz, Joe (John J.H. Schwarz) *former congressman, physician*
Searle, Rodney Newell *state legislator, farmer, insurance agent*
Shays, Christopher H. *former United States Representative from Connecticut*
Sinagra, Jack G. *former state senator*
Skinner, Patricia Morag *state legislator*
Smith, Linda Gene (Gene Smith) *former legislative staff member*
Smith, Nick H. *former congressman, archivist, farmer*
Snelling, Barbara W. *retired state legislator*
Stevens, Ted (Theodore Fulton Stevens) *former United States Senator from Alaska*
Stickney, Jessica *former state legislator*
Stuhr, Elaine Ruth *former state legislator*
Sununu, John Edward *former United States Senator from New Hampshire*
Sweeney, John E. *former United States Representative from New York*
Talent, James Matthes *former United States Senator from Missouri*
Tancredo, Tom (Thomas Gerard Tancredo) *retired United States Representative from Colorado*
Taylor, Charles Hart *former United States Representative from North Carolina*
Tenorio, Pedro Agulto *former Resident Representative from Northern Mariana Islands*
Thompson, Jill Lynette Long *former congressman*
Toomey, Patrick Joseph *former United States Representative from Pennsylvania*
Torkildsen, Peter Gerard *former United States Representative from Massachusetts*
Vellenga, Kathleen Osborne *state legislator*
Walberg, Tim (Timothy Lee Walberg) *former United States Representative from Michigan, former state legislator*
Wallach, Patricia *councilman, retired mayor*
Weaver, James Howard *former Congressman*
Weldon, David Joseph, Jr. *former United States Representative from Florida*
Weller, Gerald C. (Jerry Weller) *former United States Representative from Illinois*
Wilson, Heather Ann *former United States Representative from New Mexico*
Wojahn, R. Lorraine *retired state senator*
Youngquist, Arvid Tadao *legislation advocate, public servant*

HEALTHCARE: DENTISTRY

UNITED STATES

ALABAMA

Birmingham
Bottino, Marco Cicero *dentist*

ARIZONA

Scottsdale
Bassett, Joyce *dentist*
Winkler, Sheldon *dentist, educator*

Tucson
Hawke, Robert Francis *dentist*

ARKANSAS

Jonesboro
Rowe, William Johnston, Jr. *dentist*

CALIFORNIA

Agoura Hills
Ziv, Jonathan *cosmetic dentist*

Beverly Hills
Frey, David S. *cosmetic dentist*
Sands, Kevin B. *cosmetic dentist*

Carlsbad
Langland, Olaf Elmer *retired dental educator*

Danville
Pescatore, Christopher *cosmetic dentist*

Fullerton
Choi, John U. *periodontist, educator*

Irvine
Yehezkel, Shaul *orthodontist*

Loma Linda
Lee, Sean S. *dentist, researcher*

Los Angeles
Bogen, George *endodontist, educator*
Chugal, Nadia *dental educator, director*
Dorfman, William M. (Bill Dorfman) *dentist*
Dummett, Clifton Orrin *dentist, educator*
Kupferman, Steven Barry *oral & maxillofacial surgeon*
Mobasser, Anthony *cosmetic dentist*
Shi, Songtao *dentist, educator*

Los Banos
Yoshizumi, Donald Tetsuro *dentist*

Manteca
Tonn, Elverne Meryl *pediatric dentist, dental benefits consultant, forensic odontologist*

Northridge
Logan, Lee Robert *orthodontist, department chairman*

Pasadena
Mc Carthy, Frank Martin *oral surgeon, educator*

San Diego
Ingle, John Ide *dental educator*

San Francisco
Atrouni, Marwan *dentist*
Azarinfar, André *dentist*
Bensinger, David August *dentist, dean*
Cornehl, Jarrod *dentist*
Gekelman, Diana *dentist, dental educator, researcher*
Greenspan, Deborah *dental educator*
Hamsayeh, Niloufer G. *dentist*
Hwang, Helen *orthodontist*
Lam, Peter *orthodontist*
Le, Caroline M. *dentist*
Levi, Nick *dentist*
Mosavian, Parisa *dentist*
Shen, David *orthodontist*
Tomer, Britta *orthodontist, educator*
Urick, James R. *dentist*
Wescott, William Burnham *oral maxillofacial pathologist, educator*

San Rafael
Greene, John Clifford *dentist, retired dean*
Gryson, Joseph Anthony *orthodontist*

Santa Ana
Elo, Jeffrey A. *oral and maxillofacial surgeon*

Santa Clarita
Goodrick, Dell Ariel *dentist*

Santa Rosa
Klim, James D. *dentist*

Tustin
Zahrowski, James J. *orthodontist*

COLORADO

Golden
Christensen, Robert Wayne *oral maxillofacial surgeon, minister*

Littleton
Scrabeck, Jon Gilmen *retired dental educator*

Lone Tree
Grant, Nancy C. *dentist*

CONNECTICUT

Brookfield
Cohen, Mark Steven *dentist*

Fairfield
Zerella, Joseph A. *endodontist*

Farmington
Burstone, Charles *dental educator, researcher*
Nichols, Frank C. *dental educator*

Southbury
Hopf, Frank Rudolph *retired dentist*

West Hartford
Hall, Robert Stevens *retired dentist*

DELAWARE

Hockessin
Ulmer, William H., Sr. *dentist*

DISTRICT OF COLUMBIA

Washington
Calhoun, Noah Robert *retired oral maxillofacial surgeon, educator*
Richeson, James Grady, Jr. *dentist*

FLORIDA

Aventura
Rosenbluth, Morton *periodontist, educator*

Boca Raton
Lerner, Theodore Raphael *dentist*

Bradenton
Engelman, Melvin Alkon *retired dentist, dental products executive*

Davie
Kang, Taeheon *dentist*

Gainesville
Lundgren, Tord *dental educator, researcher*
Magnusson, Ingvar *periodontist, educator*

Hernando
Manhold, John Henry *dental educator, consultant*

Jacksonville
Halil, Susan Terrell *dental hygienist*

Miami
Iver, Robert Drew *dentist*

North Miami Beach
Abbo, Bill *dentist, educator*

Sarasota
Mohl, Norman David *dental educator*

Tampa
Pasetti, Louis Oscar *retired dentist*

Winter Park
McKean, Thomas Wayne *retired dentist, military officer*

GEORGIA

Atlanta
Flax, Hugh *dentist*
Freedman, Louis Martin *dentist*
Hoskyns, William A. *dentist*
King, Debra Gray *cosmetic dentist*
Weathers, Dwight Ronald *dental educator*

Augusta
Baker, Philip Steven *dentist, educator*
Lapp, Carol Anne *oral biology educator*
Londono, Martinez Jimmy *dentist*
Rogers, Michael Bruce *orthodontist*
William, W. Brackett *dentist, educator*

Fort Gordon
Goksel, Tamer *oral surgeon, director*

HAWAII

Honolulu
Nishimura, Pete Hideo *oral surgeon*

IDAHO

Idaho Falls
Gaffner, Vernon *dentist*

Ketchum
Mazzola, Chris *dentist*

ILLINOIS

Bloomington
Chrisman, Jay W. *cosmetic dentist*

Chicago
Barr, Sanford Lee *dentist*
Graber, Thomas M. *orthodontist, researcher*
Hardaway, Ernest, II, *oral and maxillofacial surgeon, public health service officer*
Johnson, Bradford R. *endodontist, researcher*
Licari, Frank William *dentist, educator*
O'Loughlin, Kathleen T. *dental association administrator*
Santangelo, Mario Vincent *retired dentist*
Wigdor, Harvey Alan *dentist, educator*

Elgin
Lodding, Dean W. *dentist*

Elmhurst
Valcarenghi, Ivan *dentist*

Geneva
Lazzara, Dennis Joseph *orthodontist*

Lake Forest
Jones, Gordon Kempton *dentist, retired military officer*

Lake In The Hills
Shirazi, Eman Ali *dentist*

Lincolnwood
Glenner, Richard Allen *dentist, dental historian*

Park Ridge
Kenney, John Patrick *dentist*

Riverwoods
Douglas, Bruce Lee *oral and maxillofacial surgeon, occupational and geriatric health educator, consultant*

Westmont
Schefdore, Ronald L. *dentist*

INDIANA

Indianapolis
Christen, Arden Gale *dental educator, researcher, consultant*
Hancock, Everett Brady *retired periodontist*
Tellman, William C. *dentist*

Terre Haute
Roshel, John Albert, Jr. *orthodontist*

IOWA

Ankeny
Weigel, Ollie J *dentist, former mayor*

Iowa City
Bishara, Samir Edward *orthodontist*
Olin, William Harold *orthodontist, educator*

Solon
Schneider, Robert *prosthodontist, educator*

West Des Moines
Thomas, Phelan R. *dentist*

KENTUCKY

Brandenburg
Bowen, Patricia Lederer *dental educator*

Lexington
Arnold, J. Fred III *cosmetic dentist*
Hartsfield, James Kennedy, Jr. *orthodontist, geneticist*
Justice, Laura L. *dentist*
Pearson, Cheryl A. *dentist*

Louisville
Alpert, Brian *oral surgeon, educator*
Parkins, Frederick Milton *dental educator, dean*
Schaefer, David A. *dentist*

LOUISIANA

Lafayette
Malone, Mike *dentist*

Metairie
Roussos, Christopher Wayne *dental association administrator*

MAINE

Kennebunkport
Mulvihill, James Edward *periodontist, educator, health center administrator*

MARYLAND

Bethesda
Baum, Bruce J. *dentist, medical geneticist*
Kruger, Gustav Otto, Jr. *retired oral surgeon, educator, department chairman*

Simpsonville
Altschuler, Bruce Robert *research dentist*

Timonium
Zeren, Karl Joseph *dentist, educator*

Woodstock
Hargadon, Michael T. *dentist*

MASSACHUSETTS

Boston
Nunn, Martha Elizabeth *dental educator, director*
Sachdeo, Amit *dentist, researcher*
Samet, Nachum *retired dental educator*
Stipho, Huda D. *dentist, educator*
Teles, Flavia R.F. *clinical investigator, dental educator*

Dedham
Miner, Robert Matthew *orthodontist, educator*

Fitchburg
Shemmeri, Thafur *pediatric dentist*

Newton Center
Peck, Sheldon *orthodontist, educator, dental anthropologist*

Worcester
Ayers, David C. *orthodontist, educator*

MICHIGAN

Ann Arbor
Eber, Robert Michael *dental educator, periodontist*

East Lansing
Spagnuolo, Mark Mario *retired dentist*

MINNESOTA

Minneapolis
Shapiro, Burton Leonard *dentist, maxillofacial pathologist, geneticist, educator*
Young, Lynda Jeanne *dental educator, director*

MISSISSIPPI

Flowood
Byrd, Joyce Marie *dentist*

MISSOURI

Chesterfield
Selfridge, George Dever *retired dentist, retired military officer*

Kansas City
Crain, Geralyn D. *dental educator*
Eick, J. David *dental educator, department chairman*
Hong, Liang *dentist, educator*
Mobley, James Robert *dentist*
Reed, Michael John *dentist, dean, educator*

NEBRASKA

Lincoln
Sullivan, Robert Emmett *pediatric dentist, educator*

Omaha
Zaiman, K(oichi) Robert *dentist*

NEW JERSEY

Cedar Grove
Mandel, Irwin Daniel *dentist*

Hackettstown
Wiedemann, Charles Louis *dentist*

Livingston
Ehrenkranz, Howard *dentist, educator*

Voorhees
Lampert, S. Henry *retired dentist*

Woodbridge
Galkin, Samuel Bernard *orthodontist*

NEW YORK

Bellmore
Lederman, Gary *dentist*

Brooklyn
Ogle, Orrett E. *oral surgeon*
Schweikert, Edgar Oskar *dentist*

Buffalo
Casey, David Michael *prosthodontist*

Grand Island
Hennigar, William Grant, Jr. *dentist*

New York
Apa, Michael *cosmetic dentist*
Denmark, Stanley Jay *orthodontist*
Glassman, Debra *dentist*
Glassman, Steven *dentist*
Greenberg, Alex Michael *oral and maxillofacial surgeon*
Kahn, Norman *dental educator, pharmacologist*
Linhart, Jan *cosmetic dentist*
Lituchy, Gregg *dentist*
Lowenberg, Marc Gregory *dentist*
Marder, Michael Zachary *dental educator, researcher*
Rosenthal, Larry W. *cosmetic dentist*
Rozenberg, Lana *cosmetic dentist*
Russell, Stefanie Luise *dental educator*
Sendax, Victor Irven *dentist, educator, dental implant researcher*
Smigel, Irwin *dentist*
Wank, Gerald Sidney *periodontist, educator*

Ossining
Maloney, William James *dentist, educator*

Rochester
Bowen, William Henry *dental researcher, educator*
Pogal, Meredith A. *dentist*
Sussman, Paul I. *dentist*

Schenectady
DeLuke, Dean M. *oral surgeon*

Shelter Island
Moran, Daniel Thomas *dentist, poet*

Troy
Medicus, Hildegard Julie *retired dentist, orthodontist, educator*

Williamsville
Zahn, Cindy Mae *dental educator*

Yonkers
Torrese, Dante Michael *prosthodontist, educator*

NORTH CAROLINA

Chapel Hill
Patton, Lauren L. *dentist, researcher*
Proffit, William Robert *orthodontics educator*
White, Raymond Petrie, Jr. *dentist, educator, dean*

Matthews
Twisdale, Harold Winfred *dentist*

OHIO

Beachwood
Robertson, Ned *dentist*

Beavercreek
Notestine, Greg *dentist*

Cincinnati
Robinson, David M. *dentist*

Cleveland
Palomo, Juan Martin *dental educator, director, orthodontist*
Tetelman, Evan David *dentist, educator*

Columbus
Brantley, William Arthur *dental educator, educator*
Buchsieb, Walter Charles *orthodontist, director*
Jolly, Daniel Ehs *dental educator*

Cuyahoga Falls
Barsan, Robert Blake *dentist*

OKLAHOMA

Norman
Spurgeon, Jim D. *dentist*
Williams, Ronald L. *dentist*

Oklahoma City
Shillingburg, Herbert Thompson, Jr. *dental educator*

PENNSYLVANIA

Clarion
Foreman, Thomas Alexander *dentist*

Erdenheim
Schiff, Lawrence Alan *dentist*

Fayetteville
Scarlata, Paul Anthony *oral surgeon*

Lansdale
Strohecker, Leon Harry, Jr. *orthodontist*

Perkasie
Ohama, Gary Louis *dental ceramist*

Philadelphia
Fielding, Allen Fred *oral and maxillofacial surgeon, educator*
Pappas, Charles Nicholas III *dentist, educator*
Vanarsdall, Robert Lee, Jr. *orthodontist, educator*

Pittsburgh
Collins, Bobby McManus, II, *dental educator*

Yardley
Marus, Robert *dentist*

RHODE ISLAND

Riverside
Rawlinson, Kenneth J. *dentist*

Warren
Mehlman, Edwin Stephen *endodontist*

SOUTH CAROLINA

Columbia
Witherspoon, Walter Pennington, Jr. *orthodontist*

Kiawah Island
Andria, Louis Matthew *orthodontist*

TENNESSEE

Brentwood
Wells, Dennis J. *dentist*

Knoxville
McGuire, John Albert *dentist*

Memphis
Butts, Herbert Clell *retired dentist, educator*
Slagle, William F. *dental educator, dean*

Nashville
Martin, James Larence *dentist, educator*

TEXAS

Austin
Matthews, Dan *dentist*
Sweeney, Mark *dentist*

Bellaire
Frazar, Kathy *cosmetic dentist*

Cedar Hill
Potter, Joe W. *dentist*

Corsicana
Harper, Richard Patrick *oral and maxillofacial surgeon*

Dallas
Ajlouni, Raed Fakhry *dentist, educator*

Flower Mound
Kolodny, Stanley Charles *oral surgeon, retired military officer*

Fort Sam Houston
Kulild, James Clinton *dentist, army officer*

Houston
Ellis, Eric *dentist*
Lyons, Lillian Carmina *periodontist, educator*
McGuire, Michael K. *periodontist*
Scheyer, Eric Todd *dentist, periodontist, surgeon, educator*

Mount Pleasant
McCauley, Dan Paul *dentist*

Plano
Findley, John Sidney *dentist*

VERMONT

Rutland
Carroll, LaShun La Rue *dentist*

VIRGINIA

Fredericksburg
Liewehr, Frederick Russell *endodontist, educator*

Richmond
Laskin, Daniel M. *oral and maxillofacial surgeon, educator*

Springfield
Bilodeau, John Edward *dental educator, consultant*

WASHINGTON

Bellevue
Page, Roy Christopher *periodontist, scientist, educator*

East Wenatchee
Fluegge, Matthew W. *dentist*

Everett
Oliver, William Donald *orthodontist*

Seattle
Baker-Johnson, Marcia J. *dental hygienist*
Berman, Robert G. *dentist*
Hollender, Lars Gösta *dental educator*
Rubenstein, Jeffrey Elliot *prosthodontist, professor*

Spokane
Bulan, Liana *dentist*

WISCONSIN

Beloit
Green, Harold Daniel *dentist*

River Falls
Hammarback, Bernt J. *dental association administrator*

Sun Prairie
Amstadt, James R. *cosmetic dentist*

WYOMING

Casper
Keim, Michael Ray *dentist*

Sheridan
Korsch, Tobin Anne *dental hygienist, educator*

CANADA

ONTARIO

London
Perinpanayagam, Hiran *dental educator*

ENGLAND

MacClean, Walter Lee *dentist*

FRANCE

Morlaix
Baillet, Gilles Pierre *orthodontist*

GERMANY

Witten
Gaengler, Peter Wolfgang *dentist, researcher*

ITALY

Rimini
Mazza, Domenico *orthodontist*

REPUBLIC OF KOREA

Gwangju
Hwang, Hyeon-Shik *orthodontist, educator, dean*
Kim, Su-Gwan *dental educator, oral surgeon, medical researcher*

Jeonju
Byun, June-Ho *oral and maxillofacial surgeon, educator*

Seoul
Choi, Yongchang *dentist, educator*

TAIWAN

Taipei
Sun, Andy *dentist*

ADDRESS UNPUBLISHED

Abdelkarim, Ahmad *dentist, educator*
Barkmeier, Wayne W. *dentist, researcher, educator*
Beagrie, George Simpson *dentist, educator, retired dean*
Bentley, Kenneth Chessar *oral and maxillofacial surgeon, educator*
Braun, Stanley *orthodontist, educator*
Brooke, Ralph Ian *dental educator*
Christiansen, Richard Louis *orthodontist, educator, dean*
Collins, Frank, Jr. *dentist, educator*
Geistfeld, Ronald Elwood *retired dental educator*
Goldstein, Leonard Barry *dentist*
Hammer, Wade Burke *retired oral and maxillofacial surgeon, educator*
Herman, David Jay *orthodontist*
Hoffman, Jerry Irwin *retired dental educator*
Houk, Irene Miller *dentist*
Huja, Sarandeep *orthodontist, educator*
Ismail, John Y. H. *dentist, prosthodontist*
Kaslick, Ralph Sidney *dentist, educator*
Khosla, Ved Mitter *oral and maxillofacial surgeon, educator*
Lee, Jeong Keun *oral, maxillofacial surgeon, director*
Little, James W. *retired dental educator*
Magne, Michel Jaques *dental educator, ceramist*
Marcello, Patrick Ryan *dentist*
Martens, Leslie Vernon *retired dentistry educator, consultant*
Meffert, Roland Matthew *retired periodontist*
Mele, Joanne Theresa *dentist*
Molinaro, Joseph Daniel *dentist, director*
Morley, Jeffrey Joshua *dentist, educator*
Newbrun, Ernest *oral biology and periodontology educator*
Nigwekar, Sagar U. *dentist, researcher*
Rehak, James Richard *orthodontist*
Rippert, Eric Theodore *oral and maxillofacial surgeon, healthcare consultant, author, writer*
Roche, James Richard *pediatric dentist, university dean*
Rodin, Howard Alan *periodontist*
Rogers, E. Kennedy *dentist*
Rose, Ernst *dentist*
Sabeti, Mike A. *endodontist, periodontist, educator*
Sedghizadeh, Parish Paymon *dentist, oral and maxillofacial pathologist, educator*
Sinkford, Jeanne Craig *dental association administrator, retired dentist, dean, educator*
Slaughter, Freeman Cluff *retired dentist*
Taylor, John Calvin *dentist*

HEALTHCARE: HEALTH SERVICES

UNITED STATES

ALABAMA

Auburn University
Simmons, Karla Peavy *researcher, educator*

Birmingham
Casazza, Krista *dietician, researcher*
Cates, Marshall E. *pharmacist, medical educator*
Cooper, Karen René *health facility and nursing administrator*
Grinney, Jay *health facility company executive*
Lowman, John D., Jr. *physical therapist, researcher*
Mohon, Earlene Mann *counselor*
Monk-Tutor, Mary R. *pharmacist, educator*
Perry, Helen *medical/surgical nurse, secondary school educator*
Roth, William Stanley *hospital foundation executive*
South, Lisa *nursing educator*

Daphne
Curreri, Peter William *health facility administrator, consultant*

Evergreen
Jackson, Eula *nursing educator*

Lafayette
Woody, Mary Florence *nursing educator, academic administrator*

Livingston
Cannon, Marsha A. *nursing educator*

Mobile
Clark, Jack *retired health facility administrator*
Wisner, Pamela L. *social worker*

Montgomery
Joan, Perl *nurse, educator*
Munson, Edward Harry, Jr. *medical investigator*

Opelika
Smith-Sanders, Carol Ann *physical therapist, music therapist, psychologist*

Semmes
Dockery, Herbert Donald *health and rehabilitation company executive*

Theodore
Hollis, Julia Ann Roshto *critical care, medical, and surgical nurse*

Tuscaloosa
Farahat, Medhat S. *researcher*
Orcutt, Ben Avis *retired social work educator*

Tuskegee Institute
Cooley, Fannie Richardson *counselor, educator*

ALASKA

Anchorage
Kasmar, Marilyn Walsh *health facility administrator, nurse*
Kincaid, Karen Owers *nursing educator*
Mandsager, Richard *hospital administrator*
Stohl, Sharon Aline *art therapist*

Bethel
Turner, Kathy Ann *special education services professional, director*

Big Lake
Gillette, Muriel Delphine *nurse*

Juneau
Butler, Jay C. *public health service officer*

Palmer
Lawler, Marita A. *therapist*
Young-Campbell, Laura L. *speech pathology/audiology services professional*

Soldotna
Moore, Hubert, Jr. *retired addictions counselor, consultant*

ARIZONA

Casa Grande
McGillicuddy, Joan Marie *psychotherapist, consultant*

Fort Defiance
Morgan, Leon Terrell *environmental health services specialist*

Fort Huachuca
Sleeper, Nancy JoAnn *mental health services professional*

Fountain Hills
Magazine, Cynthia Penrose *retired health care consultant*

Glendale
Cacciatore, Joanne *thanatologist and social worker*
Mahrous, Hisham *pharmacist, educator*
McNatty, Danny *pharmacist*

Hereford
Schenk, Quentin Frederick *retired social work educator, psychologist, mayor*

Mesa
Ahearn, Geraldine *medical/surgical nurse, writer, poet*
David, Susan Holcombe *child and family therapist*

Peoria
Nelson, Mary Kathryn *bilingual counselor, small business owner, real estate and insurance agent, artist*

Phoenix
Farmer, Kenneth Lloyd, Jr. *health system administrator, retired military officer*
Garcia, Ernest G. *audiologist, technologist*
Johnson, Elizabeth Misner *health services executive*
Meyer, Hermann Belton Perrin *retired neonatologist, health facility administrator, bioethicist*

Mitchell, Wayne Lee *retired health administrator*
Richardson, Mary L. *psychotherapist*
Sidora-Arcoleo, Kimberly Joan *nursing educator*
Tritle, Bradley *health facility administrator*
Welker, Kristina Diane *psychotherapist*

Prescott
Blaess, Donna Adele *psychotherapist, educator, counseling administrator*

Rio Verde
Ramsey, David Selmer *retired health facility administrator*

Scottsdale
Brown, Frederick Lee *health facility administrator*
Jayaraman, Ganapathi Subramaniam *healthcare industry executive*
Lasys, Joan *medical/surgical nurse, educator*
Meyers, Marlene O. *retired hospital administrator*
Timmons, Evelyn Deering *pharmacist*
Valdivieso, Angelica *physical therapist*
Weaver, Linda Marie *pharmacist, education educator*

Sedona
Catterton, Marianne Rose *occupational therapist*

Sun City
Arbogast, Susan D. *nursing educator*

Tempe
Crowe, Barbara J. *recreational therapist, educator*

Tucson
Barrette-Mozes, Susan Jean *counselor, psychotherapist*
Carmona, Richard Henry *health facility administrator, former Surgeon General of the United States*
Diáz, Elena R. *community health nurse*
Dyer-Raffler, Joy Ann *retired special education diagnostician, educator*
Effken, Judith A. *nursing educator*
Glueck-Rambaldi, Mary Audrey *retired psychiatric and mental health nurse*
Howell, Wanda H. *dietician, educator*
Pitpitan, Consuelo Lopez *pharmacist, educator*
Shropshire, Donald Gray *hospital executive*
Troxell, Mary Theresa (Terry Troxell) *geriatrics services professional*
Vincent, Deborah *nursing educator*

Wickenburg
Brooks, Donna Jean *retired counselor, educator*

Young
Burke, Karen A. *medical/surgical nurse*

Yuma
Houggard, Santa Carol Hall *family nurse practitioner, consultant*

ARKANSAS

Bentonville
Peerson, Michael B. *pharmacist, director*

Harrison
Holtslander, Dorothy Brock *counselor, educator, author, reporter*

Little Rock
Bates, Jonathan R. *hospital administrator*
Brown, Larry Douglass *research consultant, writer*
Smith, G. Richard *psychiatry educator*

Marion
Lodor, Marci Ann *dietitian*

Searcy
Willmore, Catherine Bernadette *pharmacist professor, research scientist*

CALIFORNIA

Agoura Hills
Canatsey, Ken *nurse*
Gilbert, Jane H. *health science association administrator*

Anaheim
Lee, Donna Jean *retired nurse*

Aptos
White, Elizabeth Nichole *lab administrator, educator*

Arcadia
Anderson, Holly Geis *health facility administrator, educator, commentator*

Arleta
Kelley, Frances A. *occupational therapist, consultant*

Berkeley
Enoch, Jay Martin *optometrist, research scientist, educator*
Gilbert, Neil Robin *social work educator, writer, consultant*
Gumbs, Pam *pharmacist*
Harris, Michael Gene *optometrist, lawyer, educator*
Kindblad, Nina Claire *educational therapist*
Remer, Lillian Gladys *public health researcher*
Ruzer, Lev Solomon *lab administrator, researcher*
Westheimer, Gerald *optometrist, educator*
Zhang, Hui *researcher*

Beverly Hills
Rinsch, Maryann Elizabeth *occupational therapist*

Canyon Country
Alvarez, Neisy Virginia *physician assistant*

Cardiff By The Sea
Epstein, Robert *psychologist, consultant*

Carlsbad
Benjamin, Theresa Mary *retired psychotherapist*

Carmel
Reamy, Michaelin *marriage and family therapist, educator, consultant*

Carson
El-Ahraf, Amer M. *health facility administrator, educator*

Cathedral City
Berry, Ester Lorée *vocational nurse*

Channel Islands
Steinorth, Christina Enni *psychotherapist, author*

Claremont
Martin, Jay Herbert *psychoanalyst, literature professor, political science professor*

Clovis
Von Prince, Kilulu Magdalene *retired occupational therapist, sculptor*

Costa Mesa
McCarthy, Mary Ann *counselor, educator*

Davis
Stern, Judith Schneider *nutritionist, researcher, educator*
Stroeve, Pieter *chemical engineering researcher and educator*

Desert Hot Springs
Zarres, Sharon L. *marriage and family therapist, health facility administrator*

Downey
Orozco, Jorge *rehabilitation hospital administrator*

Duarte
Riggs, Arthur D. *health facility administrator, research scientist*

Emeryville
Chang, Ying-Lan *technologist*

Encino
House, Karen House Milburn *nursing consultant*

Escondido
Bakko, Orville Edwin *retired health facility administrator*

Fair Oaks
Weston, Louanne C. *marriage and family therapist*

Fairfield
Dabeck, Donna *nursing administrator*

Fountain Valley
Montgomery, Thom Mathew *health program administrator, counselor*

Frazier Park
Edwards, Sarah Anne *social worker, psychologist*

Fresno
Corless, Dorothy Alice *nursing educator*

Glendale
Shou, Sharon Louise Wikoff *vocational rehabilitation counselor*

Hawthorne
Fila, John Charles *psychoanalyst*

Highland
Fangerow, Kay Elizabeth *nurse*
Tacal, Jose Vega, Jr. *retired public health official, veterinarian*

Huntington Beach
Herron, Harriette A. *retired occupational health nurse*

Imperial
Plascencia, Jose J. *social worker, consultant*

Irvine
Grossman, Barbara Robinson *marriage and family therapist*
Jones, Joie Pierce *physicist, acoustician, writer, educator*
Miller, Crystal Ann *respiratory therapist*

La Jolla
Johnson, Gayle Ann *cardiology nurse*
Morello, Candis Marguerite *pharmacist, educator*
Snyder, Lisa *social worker, consultant*

Ladera Ranch
Nguyen, Monique M. *optometrist, educator*

Lafayette
Nolan, Janiece Simmons *retired health system administrator, consultant*

Laguna Beach
Arnold, John David *management counselor*

Laguna Hills
Banuelos, Betty Lou *rehabilitation nurse*

Laguna Woods
Leonard, Elizabeth Adney *social worker*

Lake Elsinore
Young, Patricia Janean *speech pathology/audiology services professional*

Lake View Terrace
McCraven, Eva Stewart Mapes *health service administrator*

Lincoln
Helzer, James Dennis *retired health facility administrator*

Loma Linda
Molnar, Violet *mental health nurse*
Tanyi, Ruth A. *family practice nurse practitioner, lifestyle diseases consultant*

Lompoc
Wagner, Geraldine Marie *nursing educator, consultant*

Long Beach
Mathieu, Susan Leifer *recreational therapist, educator*
Smeal, Kemp Leslie *psychotherapist, musician*

Los Angeles
Boyajian, Timothy Edward *public health officer, educator, consultant*
Breslow, Lester *public health physician, educator*
Cordova, Richard D. *hospital administrator*
Corley, Constance *social worker, professor*
Epstein, Marsha Ann *public health physician*
Feinberg, David T. *hospital administrator*
Gong, William C. *pharmacist, educator*
Gutierrez, Mary Alice *pharmacist, educator*
Katzin, Carolyn Fernanda *nutritionist, consultant*
McCabe, Edward R. B. *hospital administrator, educator, physician*
Noce, Walter William, Jr. *hospital administrator*
Obert, Jeanne L. *alcohol/drug abuse services professional, director*
Oh, Soon Young *researcher*
Oster, Marcia Rebecca *mental health services professional*
Que Hee, Shane Stephen *environmental health educator*
Rice, Thomas Howard *healthcare educator*
Silverstein, Suzanne *art therapist*
Territo, Mary C. *health facility administrator, hematologist, educator*
van Dam, Heiman *psychoanalyst*
Ver Steeg, Donna Lorraine Frank *nurse, sociologist, educator*

Lower Lake
Garcia, Beatrice Maude *social worker, director*

Modesto
Robinson, Tonya Louise *nursing educator, director*

Monterey
Kolar, Ramesh *technologist, educator*

Moraga
Allen, Richard Garrett *healthcare educator*

Morro Bay
LaLanne, Jack (François Henri LaLanne) *physical fitness specialist, entrepreneur*

Murrieta
Rose, Norma Louise *retired human services manager*

Newbury Park
Knutzen, Robert *health science association administrator, educator*

Newhall
Stone, Susan Foster *mental health services professional*

Northridge
Gehart, Diane Rebecca *marriage and family therapist, educator*

Oakland
Bouska Lee, Carla Ann *nursing and healthcare educator*
Hafey, Joseph Michael *retired health association executive*
Howatt, Sister Helen Clare *human services administrator, director, retired school librarian*

Ontario
Chavez, Virginia *bilingual counselor*
Hanner, Jean P. *retired state civil servant*

Palm Desert
Adelman, Bayla Ann *occupational therapist*

Palo Alto
Brodell, Anne Rayne *psychotherapist, consultant*
Dawes, Christopher *hospital administrator*

Panorama City
Lugg, Marlene Martha *immunization coordinator, health information systems specialist, health planner*

Pasadena
Brotman, Richard Dennis *counselor*
Nackel, John George *health venture capital executive*
Omery, Anna *nursing administrator*

Pittsburg
Gustafson, Sally Ann *counselor, cosmetologist, educator*

Pomona
Chung, Eunice P. *pharmacist, educator*
Gupta, Eric K. *pharmacist, educator*
Holmes, Louis Ira *retired physician assistant, educator, photojournalist*
Nguyen, Megan *pharmacist, educator*

Poway
Farrell, Peter Craig *health care company executive*

Rancho Mirage
Lange, Gary F. *psychotherapist, educator*

Reedley
Jones, Steven D. *academic counselor*

Reseda
Hoover, Pearl Rollings *nurse*

Roseville
Netto, Paul V. *critical care nurse*

Sacramento
Brotman, Martin *health care services executive, gastroenterologist*
Burks, Rocky Alan *disability access manager and consultant*
Drachnik, Catherine Meldyn *recreational therapist, artist, counselor*
Phipps, Shawn Christopher *occupational therapist*
von Friederichs-Fitzwater, Marlene Marie *researcher*

San Andreas
Cretan, Donna *neonatal nurse, consultant*

San Bernardino
Robinson, James Sidney *public health service officer*

San Bruno
Edwards, Kassandra Bennett *psychotherapist, consultant*

San Clemente
Renk, Pamela Jean *counselor, psychotherapist, small business owner*

San Diego
Astroth, Margo Foltz *mental health nurse, nurse psychotherapist*
Atayee, Rabia Samady *pharmacist, educator*
Georgeson, Jacquelyn J. *audiologist, director*
Lee, Christian C. *pharmacist, researcher*
Lewis, Shirley Jeane *retired therapist, educator*
Novotny, Thomas Edward *healthcare educator, consultant*
Roth, Jonathan David *pharmacist, researcher*
Ruth, Dianne *personal growth and prosperity coach, holistic counselor*
Stahovich, Marcia *nurse*

San Dimas
Flores, Frank Cortez *public health researcher, educator, administrator*

San Fernando
Salkin, Barbara Ruth *social worker*

San Francisco
Aweeka, Francesca Teresa *pharmacist, educator*
Beaulieu, Richard Joseph *pediatric nurse practitioner*
Beitel, Karl *researcher*
Browner, Warren Seth *hospital administrator, internist, educator*
Feachem, Richard George Andrew *health science association administrator*
Green, Lawrence Winter *public health educator*
Laret, Mark R. *hospital administrator*
Lynn, Paul *health facility administrator*
Phoenix, Bethany Joyce *healthcare educator*
Rutherford, George Williams III *public health association administrator, educator*
Sadée, Wolfgang *pharmacy educator*
Speidel, John Joseph *public health professional, educator*
Strawbridge, William J. *healthcare educator*

San Jose
Ha, Kiet Tuan *hospital administrator*
Li, Mike Peng *technologist*
Poyadue, Florene Stewart *nurse, foundation administrator*

San Marcos
Gentile, Robert Dale *optometrist, consultant*

San Marino
Hong, Kurt *nutritionist, director*

San Rafael
Amada, Gerald *retired psychotherapist*
Friesecke, Raymond Francis *health company executive, president*
Malifrando, Frank *healthcare executive, theater producer, consultant, film producer, international real estate investor, publisher*

Santa Barbara
Steckel, Julie Raskin *psychotherapist, lecturer, consultant*
You, Sukkyung *research faculty*

Santa Monica
Besson, Nicole Marie Archambault *speech pathology/audiology services professional*
McGlynn, Elizabeth A. *health policy analyst*

Santa Paula
Broughton, Margaret Martha *mental health nurse*

Santa Ynez
O'Grady, Barbara Vinson *retired community health nurse, administrator*

Saratoga
Greenleaf, John Edward *human research consultant*

Simi Valley
Erzinger, Kathy McClam *credential nurse educator*

Sonoma
Markey, William Alan *health facility administrator, consultant*

South San Francisco
Lee, Leonard S. *health facility administrator*

Spring Valley
Siddiqui, Razia Sultana *retired psychotherapist, educator*

Stanford
Henriksen, Thomas Hollinger *researcher*
Mc Namara, Joseph Donald *researcher, retired protective services official*

Studio City
Childs, Erin Therese *psychotherapist*
Weiner, Sandra Samuel *critical care nurse, consultant*

Sunol
Rebello, Marlene Munson *speech pathologist, consultant*

Temecula
Keenan, Retha Ellen Vornholt *retired nursing educator*

Toluca Lake
Merchant, Roland Samuel, Sr. *retired health facility administrator, educator*

Tomales
Oman, Doug *healthcare educator*

Torrance
Wise, Joyce Kathryn *nursing educator*

Truckee
Todd, Linda Marie *nutrition researcher, circulation facilitator, financial consultant, pilot*

Vallejo
Toms, Kathleen Moore *nurse*

Van Nuys
Dea, Fay Suey *counselor, educator*

Victorville
Truelove, Terry N. *nursing educator*

Visalia
Gray, Kris Diane *nursing consultant, forensic specialist*

Walnut Creek
Mackay, Patricia McIntosh *psychotherapist*

West Hills
Cheney, Anna Marie Jangula *retired medical/surgical nurse*

Westminster
Pitts-Cutler, Melissa Anne *counselor, social worker*

Woodland
Bauer, Cynthia Renae *nurse*
Butler, Patricia *psychiatric and mental health nurse, educator, consultant*

Woodland Hills
Brandewie, Richard Anthony *laser and optics consultant*
Pettit, John W. *health facility administrator*

Woodside
Potter, Myrtle Stephens *healthcare consulting company executive, retired pharmaceutical executive*

Yuba City
Price, Ardythe Bernadeane *registered nurse*

COLORADO

Aurora
Biester, Doris J. *hospital administrator*
Golightly, Larry K. *pharmacist, educator*
Morrow, Caroline Donovan *retired social worker*
Nuffer, Monika *pharmacist, educator*

Boulder
Holdsworth, Janet Nott *women's health nurse*
Princeton, Joy Carol *retired nursing educator*

Centennial
Frame, Roger Everett *school psychologist*

Colorado Springs
Baldvins, Lynn Ann *medical/surgical nurse, army officer*
Lokken, Steven Lee *chiropractor, internist, nutritionist*
McChesney, Jean Angeline *community health nurse*
Strickland, Sylvia Raye *social worker*
Weslin, Anna Therese *clinical nurse specialist, dance consultant*

Denver
Barber, Patricia Louise *nurse practitioner*
Calonge, Bruce Nedrow (Ned Calonge) *public health service officer*
Edelman, Joel *health facility administrator*
Jennett, Shirley Shimmick *health facility administrator*
LaGanga, Linda Rose *health facility administrator, educator, researcher*
McCollum, Marianne *pharmacist, educator, medical researcher*
Plummer, Ora Beatrice *nursing educator, consultant*
Rael, Henry Sylvester, Sr. *retired health administrator, financial and management consultant*

Englewood
Fordyce, Michael *rehabilitation hospital administrator*

Federal Heights
Adams, Judith Ann *school nurse practitioner*

Fort Collins
Savage, Eldon Paul *retired environmental health educator*

Grand Junction
Coffin, Kelly Faye *nurse, educator*
Hoagland, Christina Gail *occupational therapist, industrial drafter*

Greeley
Linde, Lucille Mae (Lucille Jacobson) *motor-perceptual specialist*

Mead
Jones, Beverly Ann Miller *nursing administrator, retired patient services administrator*

Montrose
Modrell, Corey John *educator*

CONNECTICUT

Avon
Lerer, René *health services company executive*

Bridgeport
Macdonald, Karen Crane *occupational therapist, geriatrics services professional*
Trefry, Robert J. *health facility administrator*

Clinton
Douglas, Hope M. *psychotherapist, forensic specialist*

Glastonbury
Cassotto, Mary Lou Grace *counselor, educator, librarian*

Greenwich
Krauser, Robert Stanley *healthcare executive*

Hamden
Jansson, Maija *text editor*

Hartford
Abrahams, Ronald *pharmacist*

Milford
Muth, Eric Peter *optician, consultant*

New Haven
Baker, Deanna Louise *technologist*
Benfer, David William *hospital administrator*
De Rose, Sandra Michele *psychotherapist, coach, educator, administrator*
Dubrow, Ro D. *public health service officer, educator*
Grey, Margaret *nursing educator*
Lord, Ruth *researcher, writer, philanthropist*
Savoye, Mary *dietician, researcher*

New London
Tassinari, Melissa Sherman *teratologist, developmental toxicologist*

Newington
Reynolds, Patricia Jean *psychiatric social worker, songwriter*

North Haven
Hogan, James Carroll, Jr. *public health administrator, research biologist*

Norwalk
Fish, James *healthcare administrator*
Hammer, Warren *chiropractor*

Plainfield
Brown, Philip Henry *psychiatric social worker*

South Windsor
Mulé, Lisa Nystrom *speech pathology/audiology services professional*

Stamford
Bostin, Marvin Jay *hospital and health services consultant*

Storrs Mansfield
Basu, Joysurya *technologist, researcher*
Petrovic, Kimberly Ann *nursing researcher, educator*
Wang, Fei *pharmacist, educator*

Suffield
Bianchi, Maria *critical care specialist, acute care nurse practitioner, consultant*

Waterbury
Lum, Johnny *physician assistant, consultant*
Zasada, Mary Eileen *nursing administrator*

DELAWARE

Dagsboro
Wallach, Harold Charles *health policy and health services research administrator, educator*

Dover
Rubino, Joelle L. *physical therapist, athletic trainer*

Greenville
McDonough, Kenneth Lee *pharmaceutical company medical administrator*

Hockessin
Croyle, Barbara Ann *health facility administrative executive*

Lewes
Fried, Jeffrey Michael *health care administrator*

Newark
McNutt, John Glenn *educator*

Wilmington
Miranda-Evans, Valetta Lee *social worker, human services manager*
Netta-Turner, Denise *nurse*
Schacter, Bernice Zeldin *biotechnology consultant, researcher*

DISTRICT OF COLUMBIA

Washington
Alleyne, Sir George A.O. *public health administrator, educator*
Alward, Ruth Rosendall *nursing consultant*
Anderson, Norman B. *health science association administrator, psychologist, educator*
Behney, Clyde Joseph *health science association administrator, researcher*
Brown, Laurence George *medical director*
Burris, James Frederick *federal healthcare administrator, educator*
Day, Carol R.T. *nursing educator, director*
Delbanco, Suzanne F. *human services administrator*
Ebrahim, Shahul Hameed *health science association administrator*
Eckenhoff, Edward Alvin *health facility administrator, educator*
Erickson, Chris *counselor, educator*
Eshkevari, Ladan *nursing educator*
Fineberg, Harvey Vernon *health science association administrator*
Gary, Lawrence Edward *social work educator*
Ginsburg, Paul B. *health facility administrator*
Hansen, Jennie Chin *nursing educator, association executive*
Hartmann, Robert Sankey *health facility administrator, not-for-profit fundraiser*
Holland, Joy *health care facility executive*
Johnson, Eric H., Sr. *special education services professional*
Jones, Stanley Boyd *retired researcher*
Lewis, Prudence Fox *Christian science practitioner*
McCarter, Katherine Sauter *association executive*
McQueen, Lynn *public health service officer, information scientist, administrator*
Michnich, Marie E. *health policy analyst, consultant, educator*
Pierce, John Randall *medical inspector, pediatrician*
Pollack, Ronald Frank *healthcare organization executive, lawyer*
Porter, John Weston *counselor, consultant, administrator*
Rouson, Vivian Reissland *alcohol/drug abuse services professional, consultant, journalist*
Ruoff, Janis Kaye *human services administrator*
Salisbury, Dallas L. *researcher, director*
Sanchez-Way, Ruth Dolores *public health administrator*
Seims, La Rue K. *public health service officer*
Shadow, Ruby L. Wesley *nursing educator, administrator, researcher*
Spieler, Jeff *public health service officer*
Tipre, Dnyanesh Nishikant *pharmacist, researcher*
Walker, Audrey Thayer *clinical social worker, psychotherapist*
Weber, Deanne *health science association administrator*
Yarwood, Bruce *health science association administrator*
Zechman, Edwin Kerper, Jr. *medical facility administrator*

FLORIDA

Boca Raton
Alpert, Martin Jeffrey *chiropractic physician*
Foreman, Barbara Blatt *healthcare facility administrator*
Raines, Deborah A. *neonatal/perinatal nurse specialist, educator, nursing researcher, consultant*
Richman, Joseph Herbert *retired public health service officer*
Rothberg-Blackman, June Simmonds *retired nursing educator, psychotherapist*

Bokeelia
Donlon, Josephine A. *diagnostic and evaluation counseling therapist, educator*

Bradenton
Anderson, Ruth McClendon *nursing educator*
Harris, Judith Ann White *occupational health nurse, educator*

Clearwater
Barry, Joyce Alice *dietician, consultant*
Bauwin, Roberta Elizabeth *counselor, director*
Halsey, Jean Michele *nursing educator*

Coral Gables
Siegel, Jeanne Hinton *occupational health nurse practitioner, educator*

Coral Springs
Brill, Janet Bond *nutritionist, educator*

Crawfordville
Simmons, Sharon Ritchey *counselor*

Davie
Ambris, Everiste *social worker, educator*

Daytona Beach
Cardwell, Harold Douglas, Sr. *retired rehabilitation services professional*

Deerfield Beach
Gambino, S(alvatore) Raymond *lab administrator, educator*
Solomon, Barry J. *human services administrator, consultant*

Delray Beach
Ellsweig, Phyllis Leah *retired psychotherapist*

Deltona
Bondinell, Stephanie *counselor, academic administrator*

Doral
Brioso-Mesa, Maureen Diane *mental health services professional*

Ellenton
Edson, Herbert Robbins *retired foundation and hospital executive, military officer*

Fernandina Beach
Kurtz, Myers Richard *retired hospital administrator*

Fort Lauderdale
Adams, Nancy R. *nurse, retired military officer*
Benavides, Sandra *pharmacist, educator*

Fort Myers
Danneffel-Mandelkorn, Mary Beth *nursing consultant*

Gainesville
Acholonu, Wilfred W., Jr. *clinical pharmacy specialist, educator*
Bzoch, Kenneth Rudolph *speech and language educator, department chairman*
Chiara, Toni *physical therapist*
Conrad, Joseph Henry *animal nutrition educator*
Dougherty, Molly Crocker *nursing educator, researcher*
Jia, Huanguang *health scientist, researcher*
Jin, Bumsub *researcher*
Wharton, Arthur Emrie *pharmacist, director*

Hillsboro Beach
Marshall, Jo Taylor *social worker*

Hollywood
Scott, Mimi Koblenz *psychotherapist, actress, journalist, playwright*

Jacksonville
Chen, Lei-Shih *healthcare educator*
Mack, Jeannette Ana *medical technician*
Rine, Rose Marie *physical therapist, educator*
ScarborougH, Marion Nichols *nutritionist, recreational facility executive*
Tripodi, Tony *retired social worker, dean, editor, writer*

Largo
Bush, Debra W. *occupational health nurse*
Hamlin, Robert Henry *public health service officer, educator, management consultant*

Leesburg
Osborne, Glenna Jean *health facility administrator*

Miami
Auerbach, Ethel Louise *retired healthcare facility administrator*
Chisholm, Martha Maria *dietitian*
Clark, Ira C. *hospital administrator, educator*
Himburg, Susan Phillips *dietician, educator*
Newton, Terry Fernando *health facility specialist, writer*
Osinski, Martin Henry *healthcare consultant*
Schafer, Marie *nurse, educator*
Suarez, Mildred *speech pathology/audiology services professional, educator*
Teicher, Morton Irving *social worker, anthropologist, educator*
Yaziji, Hadi *lab administrator*

Miami Beach
Bredemeier, Mary Elizabeth *counselor, educator*

Miami Springs
Neasman, Annie Ruth *health facility administrator*

Mount Dora
Crone, Eugene N. *addictions specialist, retired educator*

Naples
Mavrides, Elaine *retired mental health services professional, social worker*
Newsome, Gary D. *hospital operations company executive*
Seavey, Christopher Gordon *psychotherapist, alcohol/drug abuse services professional*

Ocala
Ettinger, Penny A. *medical/surgical nurse*

Orange Park
Rice, Ronald James *hospital administrator*

Orlando
Capraun, Lynn W. *chairperson respiratory care*
Cramer, Stephen John *paramedic, educator*
Forbes, Wanda Iris *nurse*
Fottler, Myron David *health services educator*
Kent-Walsh, Jennifer E. *speech pathology/audiology services professional, educator*
O'Shaughnessy, Rosemarie Isabelle Rao *clinical nutritionist*
Zhang, Ning Jackie *lab administrator, consultant*

Osprey
Schirber, Annamarie Riddering *retired speech and language pathologist, educator*

Palm Beach Gardens
Holloway, Edward Olin *human services manager*

Palm Harbor
Rivelli, Susan Veronica *nurse*

Panama City Beach
Nelson, Edith Ellen *dietician*

Parkland
Harris, Jacqueline Myers *speech/language pathology services professional*

Pembroke Pines
Alber, Oro Linda *healthcare educator, consultant*
Reynolds, Felicia *technologist educator, consultant*

Pensacola
Brewer, Dale *healthcare educator*

Plant City
Henry, J. Myrle *retired pharmacist*

Plantation
Gonshak, Isabelle Lee *nurse, volunteer*

Saint Petersburg
Jordan, William Reynier, Sr. *retired therapist, poet*
Macauley, Karen Elizabeth *nursing administrator, emergency nurse practitioner*

Sanford
Mena, Michele M. *counselor, therapist*

Sarasota
Hanson, Virginia A. *human services administrator*
Middleton, Norman Graham *social worker, psychotherapist*
Tucci, Steven Michael *health facility administrator, physician, recording industry executive*

Sebring
Hixon, Andrea Kaye *health science association administrator*

Tallahassee
Blair, Maudine *psychotherapist, communications executive, management consultant*
Ford, Ann Suter *family practice nurse practitioner, consultant*
Kandimalla, Karunya Kumar *pharmacist, educator*
Lambert, Nathaniel M. *researcher*
Reichert, Philip E. *health science association administrator*
Toran, Eric James *physical therapist, director*

Tamarac
Krause, John L. *retired optometrist*

Tampa
Andersen, Jc *physical therapist, director*
Boutros, Linda Nelene Wiley *medical/surgical nurse*
Brault, Rose *healthcare administrator, educator*
Price, Douglas Armstrong *chiropractor*
Russell, Diane Elizabeth Henrikson *career counselor*

Tarpon Springs
Georgiou, Ruth Schwab *retired social worker*

Venice
Barritt, Evelyn Ruth Berryman *nurse, educator, dean*
Belok, Carol Jean *nurse, alcohol/drug abuse services professional*

Vero Beach
McCrystal, Ann Marie *community health nurse, administrator*

West Palm Beach
Bernhardt, Marcia Brenda *mental health counselor*
Chahine, Elias B. *pharmacist, educator*
Koslow, Stephen Hugh *health science association administrator, pharmacologist, neuroscientist*

Weston
Gordon, Lori Heyman *psychotherapist, author, educator*

Winter Park
Haendiges, Anne R. *retired marriage and family therapist*

Winter Springs
San Miguel, Sandra Bonilla *social worker*

Zephyrhills
Walton, Shirley Dawn *retired medical technician*

GEORGIA

Alpharetta
Bunker, Kimberly LeAnn *critical care nurse, emergency nurse practitioner*

Americus
Barnetson, Katherine Olson *nursing educator*

Atlanta
Bailey, Stephanie B.C. *public health service officer*
Baird, Marianne Saunorus *critical care clinical nurse specialist, administrator*
Baldwin, Dee M. *nursing educator*
Barker, William Daniel *hospital administrator*
Bevington, Paula Lawton *principal*
Bradley, Rebekah *healthcare educator, lab administrator*
Brooks, Durado *health science association administrator, oncologist*
Foege, William Herbert *public health administrator, educator*
Hodges, Helen Frishe *nurse, professor*
Honaman, J. Craig *health facility administrator*
Hopkins, Donald Roswell *public health physician*
Johanson, Marie A. *physical therapist, educator*
Kachur, Stephen Patrick *health science association administrator*
Martin, David Edward *health sciences educator*
Polhamus, Barbara *behavioral scientist*
Salmon, Daniel Aryeh *public health policy fellow*
Satcher, David *public health service officer, former Surgeon General of the United States*
Seffrin, John Reese *health science association administrator, educator*
Ulicny, Gary R. *rehabilitation center executive*
Weed, Roger Oren *rehabilitation services professional, educator*

Augusta
Barab, Patsy Lee *nutritionist, realtor*
Gillespie, Edward Malcolm *hospital administrator*
Logan, Betty Mulherin (Elizabeth Carson Logan) *human services specialist*

Austell
Anderson, Barbara Allen *alcohol/drug abuse services professional, archivist*

Brunswick
Riner, Deborah Lillian *mental health services professional*

Canton
Yarbrough, Kathryn Davis *public health nurse*

Clarkston
Peiffer, Jerri Ann *lab administrator, educator*

Columbus
Simmons, Lynda Teel *nurse, healthcare executive*

Covington
Sigh, Robert Virgil *public health physician*

Dahlonega
Thornton, Anita Lyn *family nurse practitioner*

Decatur
Hagood, Susan Stewart Hahn *dietician*
Hinman, Alan Richard *public health physician, epidemiologist*
Kelly, Karen Deloris *addiction counselor, administrator*
Polensek, Sharon Hartman *speech pathology/audiology services professional*
Rosenberg, Mark L. *health facility administrator*

Demorest
Schick, Barbara Jean *medical technician, educator*

Evans
Feldman, Elaine Bossak *medical nutritionist, educator*

Fayetteville
Cokuslu, Lynda Elizabeth McCord *medical assistant*

Fort Gordon
Whittemore, Ronald Paul *hospital administrator, retired army officer, nursing educator*

Gainesville
Lee, Kathleen Mary *health facility administrator, nursing executive*

Jasper
Keating, Thomas Patrick *health care administrator, educator*
Ledford, Shirley Louise *practical nurse*

Kingsland
Barlow, Paula C. *nurse*

Lawrenceville
Swanson, Lynnette Sue *special olympics coordinator, special education educator*

Marietta
Petit, Parker Holmes *health care corporation executive*

Moultrie
Cox, Carol Yvonne *counselor*

Ringgold
Muerth, Cherie Anne *retired social worker*

Rock Spring
Spivey, Karen *nursing educator*

Savannah
Kincaid, Scott Edward *pharmacist, educator*
Tackett, Kimberly Lynn *pharmacist, educator*

Snellville
Dodd, Violet M. *nursing educator, dance therapist, counselor*

Statesboro
Bartels, Jean Ellen *nursing educator*

Union City
Riley, Francena *nurse, retired non-commissioned officer*

Warner Robins
Cox, Lorna Diane *medical technician, director*

HAWAII

Haleiwa
Shigemasa, Teresa *mental health services professional, educator*

Hilo
Pezzuto, Mimi *pharmacist, educator*

Honolulu
DeWeert, Michael James *technologist*
Fischer, Joel *social work educator*
Kadohiro, Jane K. *nurse, educator, consultant*
Kennedy, Faye *retired social worker, author*
Morris, Joseph Wesley *physician assistant*

Kaaawa
Maris, Margaret Atma *psychotherapist, educator*

Kaneohe
Downing, Hazel Lawrence *nursing educator*
Feagai, Hobie Etta *family practice nurse practitioner, educator*

Makawao
Tanner, Barbara Ann *pediatrics nurse*

IDAHO

Boise
Brownson, Mary Louise *counselor, educator, artist*
Nadelson, Sandra G. *nursing educator*

Ketchum
Parry, Janet *retired health facility administrator*

Moscow
Fischer, Jerome M. *rehabilitation services professional*

Pocatello
Owens, Christopher Taft *pharmacist, educator*

Rexburg
Pearson, Fred Ross *healthcare educator, consultant*

Sagle
Groth-Marnat, Gabrielle *counselor*

ILLINOIS

Arlington Heights
Telleen, Judy *counselor*

Belleville
Shim, Sang Koo *mental health services professional*

Berwyn
Hudik, Martin Francis *hospital administrator, educator, consultant, writer*

Bolingbrook
Price, Theodora Hadzisteliou *mental health services professional*

Carbondale
Kawewe, Saliwe Moyo *social work educator, researcher*
Malkin, Marjorie J. *recreational therapist, educator*

Chicago
Ailey, Sarah Herrink *nursing educator*
Alexander, Kenneth Ross *scientist, educator*
Andreoli, Kathleen Gainor *nurse, educator, dean*
Barnhart, Mary C. *health facility administrator*
Benson, Irene M. *nurse*
Dawson, Caron *medical and legal consultant*
Gonzalez, William G. *healthcare advisor*
Gulati, Martha *health facility administrator, cardiologist*
Heltne, Paul Gregory *researcher, museum director*
Hong, Philip Young P. *social worker, educator*
Krishnamurthy, Kathiravan *research assistant professor engineer*
Lal, Anil *health facility administrator*
Leeper, Mary Ann *health science association administrator*
Lerner, Wayne M. *hospital administrator*
Logemann, Jerilyn Ann *speech pathologist, educator*
Lubawski, James Lawrence *businessman and consultant*
Magoon, Patrick Michael *hospital administrator*
Meccia, Francis (Frank) Anthony *physician assistant*
Mirza, Mansha Parven Qamar Husain *public health service officer, consultant*
Nielsen, Nancy H. *health organization executive, medical educator*
Nobles-Knight, Dolores *pharmacist, educator*
Raby, Theri Greigo *health facility administrator, internist*
Rublee, Dale Allan *researcher*
Sagraves, Rosalie *pharmacy practice educator, former dean*
Schaaf, Linda Ann *nurse, educator*
Shafiro, Valeriy *audiologist, educator*
Sheean, Patricia M. *nutritionist, educator*
Simmons, Barbara *nursing educator, director*
Smith, Joanne C. *health facility administrator*
Spergel, Irving Abraham *social worker, researcher*
Szerlag, Chester Theodore *health care executive*
Wicks, Sheila M. *hospital administrator, research scientist, educator*
Zhang, James Xuejie *healthcare educator*

Crystal Lake
Schaefer, Mary Ann *health facility administrator, consultant*

Decatur
Mayfield, Peggy Lee *counselor, educator*

Deerfield
Shakno, Robert Julian *hospital and social services administrator*

Dekalb
Bukonda, Ngoyi K. Zacharie *health care management educator*
Crosser, Carmen Lynn *marriage and family therapist, social worker, consultant*
Henry, Beverly Weidinger *dietician, educator*

Des Plaines
D'Anca, John Arthur *psychotherapist, educator*

Downers Grove
Klausner, Eytan A. *pharmacist, educator*

Edwardsville
Madison, Grace Lenore *retired medical/surgical nurse, psychologist, educator*
McCullough, Theresa Marie *pharmacist, director*
Newland, Pamela Kay *nursing educator*
Norris, Sandra Love *occupational therapy assistant*

Elgin
Beyer, Karen *social worker*

Elmhurst
Jaramillo, Andres *lab administrator, researcher*

Evanston
Hughes, Edward F. X. *healthcare educator, preventive medicine physician*
Li, Shifeng *technologist*
Thomas, Eugene *social worker*

Freeport
Weaver, Michael Glen *pharmacist*

Galena
Alexander, Barbara Leah Shapiro *clinical social worker*

Galesburg
Kehoe, Peter Herbert *optometrist*

Glen Ellyn
Greer, Julianna Patterson *health and human services executive*

Glenview
Underwood, Catherine H. *healthcare association administrator*

Godfrey
Kessler, William Eugene *retired healthcare executive*

Ingleside
D'Andrea, Dana M. *medical/surgical nurse, lawyer*

Kankakee
Smith, Joanne Genevieve *nursing educator*

Lincolnshire
Fradin, Russell P. *human resources company executive, former computer company executive*

Lisle
Arnold, Catherine Leona Stein *nutritionist, educator, department chairman, researcher*

Lombard
Holgers-Awana, Rita Marie *electrodiagnosis specialist*

Macomb
Hopper, Stephen Rodger *hospital administrator*

Maywood
Barbato, Anthony L. *hospital administrator, medical educator*

Mount Prospect
Catizone, Carmen A. *health science association administrator, secretary*

Niles
Roepenack, Dwight Elmer *public health service officer*

Northbrook
Kahn, Sandra S. *psychotherapist*

Oak Forest
MacMullen, Nancy Jane *critical care nurse, department chairman*

Park Ridge
Campbell, Bruce Crichton *hospital administrator*

Peoria
Perrilles, Angela Terese *physical therapist*

Plainfield
Schinderle, Robert Frank *retired hospital administrator*

Quincy
Reynolds, Judith Amy *nutritionist, animal scientist, consultant, educator*

Rock Island
Blackmer, Michelle A. *women's health nurse, educator*

Rockford
Walters, Mary Lynn *nursing educator*

Rockton
Pennell, Danny Joe *social worker*

Skokie
Guillermo, Linda *clinical social worker*
Langguth, Margaret Witty *health facility administrator*

Springfield
Coulson, Elizabeth Anne *physical therapist, educator, Illinois State Representative*

Urbana
Baker, David Hiram *nutritionist, educator*
Chow, Poo *wood technologist*

Westmont
Lucas, Wes W. *relocation company executive*

Wheaton
Lawrence-Water, Bette Ann *community health leader*

Willowbrook
Thomas, Leona Marlene *retired healthcare educator*

Wilmette
Citrin, Judith *counselor, artist, educator*

INDIANA

Anderson
Bracken, Linda Darlene *medical/surgical nurse*

Bloomington
Bullard, Thomas Eddie *researcher*
Engs, Ruth Clifford *health educator, historian*
Wigley, Diana Gail *respiratory therapist*

Bluffton
Brockmann, William Frank *retired health facility administrator*

Indianapolis
Baird, Carol Lynne *nursing educator*
Campo, Gabrielle Nicole *social worker*
Davis, Edgar Glenn *healthcare executive, educator*
Fink, Daniel L. *hospital administrator*
Handel, David Jonathan *health facility administrator*
Harden, Anita Joyce *nurse*
Moelhman, Amy Jo *social worker*
Schroyer, Michael Kevin *healthcare consultant, hospital executive*
Stern, Phyllis Noerager *nursing educator*
VanTyle, Jeanne Hawkins *pharmacy educator, consultant*
Von Ah, Diane Marie *nursing researcher, educator*

Jeffersonville
Walburn, John Clifford *retired mental health services professional*

Kokomo
Coppock, Janet Elaine *retired mental health nurse*

Lafayette
Geddes, LaNelle Evelyn *nurse, physiologist*
McBride, Angela Barron *nursing educator*

Middlebury
Stiver, James Frederick *retired pharmacist, health physicist, administrator, scientist*

Mishawaka
Haley, David Alan *healthcare executive*

Muncie
Hoffman, Mary Catherine *retired nurse, anesthetist*

New Castle
Pierce, Terry Jo *medical/surgical nurse*

Notre Dame
Kominkiewicz, Frances Bernard *social worker, educator, director*

Rockport
Davis, Karen Sue *hospital nursing supervisor*

Seymour
Norrell, Mary Patricia *nursing educator*

Terre Haute
Thomas, Anne C. *nursing researcher, nurse practitioner*

West Lafayette
Avery, George H. *healthcare educator*
Belcastro, Patrick Frank *pharmacist, researcher*
Chang, Karen C.K. *nursing educator*
Christian, John Edward *health science association administrator, educator*
Clifton, Christopher W. *researcher, educator*
Ferruzzi, Mario G. *nutritionist, food scientist, educator*
Kirksey, Avanelle *nutrition educator*
Morré, Dorothy Marie *nutrition educator, researcher*
Peck, Garnet Edward *pharmacist, educator*
Shaw, Stanley Miner *retired pharmacist, educator*

IOWA

Altoona
Berkenes, Joyce Marie Poore *social worker, director*

Bettendorf
Dittmer, Julie J. *nursing educator*

Council Bluffs
Alley, Mary Lou Vande Woude *retired medical/surgical nurse*

Des Moines
Oren, Glenn M. *healthcare educator, consultant*
Ramsden, Mary Catherine *substance abuse specialist*
Walters, Clayton William *health facility administrator, rehabilitation services professional, consultant*

Glenwood
Campbell, William Edward *mental hospital administrator, psychologist, psychotherapist*

Iowa City
Anderson, Rachel L. *healthcare educator, researcher*
Bream-Rouwenhorst, Heather R. *pharmacist*
Densen, Paul Maximillian *retired health facility administrator*
Kates, Kenneth P. *hospital administrator*
Muir, Ruth Brooks *alcohol/drug abuse services professional, consultant*

Oskaloosa
Gleason, Carol Ann *mental health nurse, educator*

Sheldon
Eichmann, Harold D. *laboratory administrator*

Walford
Brooks, Debra L. *healthcare executive, neuromuscular therapist, artist*

West Des Moines
Goldsmith, Janet Jane *pediatric nurse practitioner*
Matthews, Alexander *health facility administrator*
Owens, Fredric Newell *animal nutritionist, educator*

KANSAS

Fort Scott
Wassenberg, Evelyn M. *retired medical/surgical nurse, educator*

Hays
Caprez, Judith V. *social worker, director*

Kansas City
Godwin, Harold Norman *pharmacist, educator*
Guenther, Sheldon *chiropractor, educator*
Jerome, Norge Winifred *nutritionist, anthropologist, educator*
Kumm, Sharon Kay *critical care nurse*
Richards, Lorie Gage *occupational therapist, educator*

Lawrence
Mc Coin, John Mack *social worker*

Manhattan
Shanklin, Carol W. *dietician, educator*

Mission
Bonci, Andrew S. *chiropractor*

Russell
Harrington, Joan Kathryn *counselor*

Shawnee Mission
Breen, Katherine Anne *speech and language pathologist*

Topeka
Khan, Lori Marie *physical therapist*
Varner, Charleen LaVerne McClanahan *nutritionist, educator, dietician*

Wichita
Budnicki, Michael J. *nurse*
Da'Luz Vieira-Jones, Lorraine Christine C. *acupuncturist, researcher*
Dorr, Stephanie Tilden *psychotherapist*
Guthrie, Diana Fern *nursing educator*
Holaday, Bonnie Jean *nursing educator*

KENTUCKY

Berea
Cornette, Robert E. *pediatric nurse practitioner, educator*
Frazier, Joy A. *retired nurse*

Brooksville
Dorton, Truda Lou *medical/surgical and geriatrics nurse*

Edgewood
Kalos, Alan V. *health planning administrator*

Elizabethtown
Lassanske, Donna J. *nurse, educator*

Georgetown
Patton, Mary Ritchie *retired pediatric nurse practitioner, consultant*

Henderson
Logan, John A. III *hospital administrator*

Lexington
Bennett, Victoria Elizabeth *rehabilitation nurse, dialysis nurse and technician*
DeLuca, Patrick Phillip *pharmacist, medical association administrator, educator*
Garman, Ray Fillmore *occupational physician, director*
Huberfeld, Nicole Lauren *healthcare educator*

Louisville
Ansong, Miriam Adjoa *pharmacist, educator*
Bloem, James H. *managed health care executive*
Dahl, Marilyn Gail *psychotherapist*
Eighmey, Douglas Joseph, Jr. *hospital administrator*
Hathcock, Bonita Catherine (Bonnie Hathcock) *managed health care company executive*
Huber, Ruth *social worker*
Hutti, Marianne Hopkins *nursing educator*
Kehrt, Bettie F. *medical transcriptionist*
Kuntz, Edward Lawrence *healthcare executive*
Mather, Elizabeth Vivian *healthcare executive*
Mountz, Wade *retired healthcare executive*
Murray, James E. *managed health care company executive*
Musacchio, Marilyn Jean *nurse midwife, educator*
Noland, Thomas Turley, Jr. *managed healthcare company executive*

Pikeville
Hunter, Trudy Pearl *surgical nurse*

Radcliff
Cole, Jessie Mae *nursing assistant, freelance/self-employed writer*

Richmond
Hall, Kathy *health facility administrator*

Russellville
Harper, Shirley Fay *nutritionist, educator, consultant, lecturer*

LOUISIANA

Alexandria
Mathews, Peggy Anne *nurse*

Baton Rouge
Francois, M. Rony *public health service officer*
Guidry, Jimmy *public health service officer*
Iqbal, Javed *lab administrator*
Kight, Dawn Ventress *technologist, consultant*

Mandeville
Pittman, Jacquelyn *retired mental health nurse, nursing educator*
Treuting, Edna Gannon *retired nursing administrator, educator*

Morganza
Williams, Ella *healthcare educator*

New Orleans
Brock, Cori M. *pharmacist, educator*
Carlson, Robert Marshall *health facility administrator*
Culbertson, Richard Allen *healthcare educator, health facility administrator*
Echeverri, Margarita *researcher, educator*
Gage, Anastasia Jessica *healthcare educator, researcher*
Higgins, Oleda Jackson *retired medical and surgical nurse*
Raj, Madhwa Hg *healthcare educator*
Strength, Catherine Bush *nursing educator*

Pearl River
Thiel, David Brian *physician assistant*

Pineville
Thorn, Shannon H. *hospital administrator, consultant*

Shreveport
Powell, Thomas William *speech and language pathology educator*
Sutton, G. Katherine Hallett *nurse*

MAINE

Bangor
Ballesteros, Paula Mitchell *nurse*
Rich, Karen Verna Stonebridge *nursing educator*

Dresden
Iserbyt, Charlotte Thomson *researcher, writer, educational consultant*

East Boothbay
Eldred, Kenneth McKechnie *acoustician, consultant*

Ellsworth
Young, Lucia Patat *psychotherapist*

Fort Fairfield
Shapiro, Joan Isabelle *lab administrator, medical/surgical nurse*

Portland
Morgan, Patricia Ann *nursing educator*

MARYLAND

Adamstown
Munson, John Christian *acoustician*

Arnold
Gagné, Doreen Frances *nurse practitioner, educator*

Baltimore
Bleich, Sara *healthcare educator, researcher*
Buccino, Daniel L. *psychotherapist, consultant*
Cheskin, Lawrence J. *healthcare educator, director*
Costa, Paul Theodore, Jr. *lab administrator, researcher*
Fall-Dickson, Jane Murray *oncology nurse*
Feller-Kopman, David *hospital administrator*
Henderson, Donald Ainslie *public health service officer*
Hilton, Adriel Adon *researcher*
Hollinger, Paula Colodny *associate director*
Hong Smith, Vicki YuKyung *ESOL educator*
Kass, Nancy *bioethicist, public health educator*
Kent, Vicky P. *nursing educator*
Klejnot, Getha Jean *school nurse practitioner, music educator*
Lawson, Edward Earle *neonatologist*
Massie, Maribeth Leigh *nursing educator*
Meltzer, Arthur Adam *researcher*
Merritt, Betty L. *medical/surgical and mental health nurse*
Ostrand-Rosenberg, Suzanne *immunology researcher*
Ruknudin, Abdul M. *health program administrator*
Simpson, Mildred Kathleen *health facility administrator*
Truong, Hoai-An *pharmacist, director*

Bethesda
Freeman, Robert Charles *health scientist administrator*
Gaarder, Marie *speech pathologist*
Guertin, Shawn M. *health facility administrator*
Hausman, Steven Jack *health science association administrator*
Jonas, Gary Fred *healthcare executive*
Longacre, Lisa Schwartz *health scientist administrator*
Ludlow, Christy Leslie *speech pathologist, scientist*
Nightingale, Stuart Lester *public health consultant*
Obrams, Gunta Iris *clinical research administrator*
Oddis, Joseph Anthony *health associations executive*
Sich, Jeffrey John *health education analyst*
Taylor, Lindsay David, Jr. *health care executive, bank executive, federal agency administrator*
Tracy, Thomas Miles *international health organization official*
Williams, Marni Dianne *pharmacist*
Wise, Allen F. *health care company executive*

Bowie
Staples, Lola Roebuck *healthcare educator*

Chevy Chase
Pedersen, Wesley Niels M. *public relations and public affairs counselor*

Cockeysville
Howard, Bettie Jean *retired surgical nurse*
Selway, Janet Small *family nurse practitioner*

College Park
Gordon-Salant, Sandra *audiology educator*
Vanderveen, John E. *nutritionist, federal agency administrator*

Columbia
Abel, Florence Catherine Harris *social worker*
Piou-Brewer, Magalie *psychotherapist, educator, small business owner*

Damascus
Styer, Joanne Louise *retired dietician*

Elkton
Mayer, Margaret Ellen *medical coding specialist*

Ellicott City
Cox, Pierre Napoleon *health and safety education consultant*

Frederick
Daniel, J. Christopher *health facility executive, family medicine physician, military officer*
De Jong, Marla J. *nurse, researcher*

Gaithersburg
Ramalingam, Murugan *researcher*

Hagerstown
Harrison, Lois Smith *hospital executive, educator*
Williams, Patricia C. *nursing educator*

Manokin
Miles, Elizabeth Jane *social worker*

Mitchellville
Kendall, Katherine Anne *social worker*

Owings Mills
Ryan, Judith W. *geriatrics nurse, educator*

Rockville
Chiacchierini, Richard Philip *healthcare consultant*
Menikoff, Jerry Alan *health facility administrator, law educator*
O'Donnell, James Francis *retired health scientist administrator*
Oyler, Anne *audiologist*
Parham-Hopson, Deborah *health programs administrator*
Scully, Martha Seebach *speech and language pathologist*

Severna Park
Rheinstein, Peter Howard *healthcare company executive, physician, lawyer*

Silver Spring
Arvin, Linda Lee *counselor*
Mashin, Jacqueline Ann Cook *health facility consultant*
Patton, Rebecca M. *nursing administrator*
Weinel, Pamela Jean *nurse consultant*
Young, Jay Alfred *chemical safety and health consultant, editor, writer*

Stevensville
Keever, Kathy Jo Bertelsen *nurse midwife, educator*

The Kentlands
Moody, Mary Elizabeth *speech pathology/audiology services professional*

MASSACHUSETTS

Amherst
Backes, Ruth Emerson *counseling psychologist*

Andover
Govern, Frank Stanley *health facility and research administrator, healthcare educator, writer*

Arlington
Junger, Miguel Chapero *retired acoustics researcher*
Stein, Miriam *social worker, training services executive*
Zimmer, Anna Held *retired social worker*

Auburndale
Kibrick, Anne *retired nursing educator, dean*

Belmont
Hanfling, Suki *social worker*

Billerica
Barnes, Shirley Moore *retired psychiatric social worker, genealogist*

Boston
Cohen, Alan Barry *researcher, educator*
Corless, Inge Baer *nursing educator and researcher*
Curtis, Marah A. *social worker, educator*
Dwyer, Johanna Todd *nutritionist, educator*
Fava, Maurizio *hospital administrator, researcher*
Frank, Richard G. *healthcare educator*
Gura, Kathleen Marie *pediatric pharmacist, educator*
Hanser, Suzanne Blottner *recreational therapist, department chairman*
Holick, Michael Francis *nutritionist*
Lowenstein, Arlene Jane *nursing educator, health facility administrator*
Lowenstein, Nancy *occupational therapist, educator*
Mandell, James *health facility executive, urologist, educator*
Mongan, James John *healthcare system administrator*
Olson, Cheryl Kay *public health consultant, educator*
Reinherz, Helen Zarsky *social worker, researcher*
Slavin, Peter L. *hospital administrator*
Tammaro, Kelly Ann *pharmacist, researcher*
Taylor, Allen *nutritionist, educator*
Tirella, Linda Grey *occupational therapist*
Wall, Conrad III *lab administrator, researcher*
Zaleznik, Abraham *psychoanalyst, management specialist, educator*

Boylston
Larson, Roland Elmer *health facility administrator*

Brockton
Moore, Mary Johnson *retired community health nurse*

Buzzards Bay
Cirillo, Jeannine L. *pharmacist*

Cambridge
Burns, Virginia *social worker*
Orfield, Antonia Marie *optometrist, researcher*
Sapirie, Stephen Alan *international public health consultant*

Canton
Bihldorff, John Pearson *hospital director*
Sawtelle, Carl S. *psychiatric social worker*

Centerville
Condon, Ann Blunt *staff training and development*
Williams, Ann Meagher *retired hospital administrator*

Chestnut Hill
Mahoney, Kevin J. *social worker, educator*

Concord
Barney, Beverly Garrett *social worker, consultant*

Dover
Bonis, Laszlo Joseph *consultant, executive, chemist*

Fairhaven
Merolla, Michele Edward *chiropractor, broadcaster*

Greenfield
Young, Elizabeth V. *social worker*

Harwich
Diggs, Walter Whitley *health science facility administrator*

Holyoke
Dearborn, Maureen Markt *speech and language clinician*

O'Leary, Mary Elizabeth *retired nursing educator, college dean*

Longmeadow
Kenefick, Amy Laufer *nurse midwife, nurse practitioner, consultant*

Natick
Wallace, Elizabeth *medical/surgical nurse*

Needham
Ryan, Una Scully *health science association administrator, medical educator*

Newtonville
Mullen, Maureen Ann *social worker*

Northampton
Anastas, Jeane Wiener *social work educator*

Rockland
Dunne, Myra Schley *nurse, consultant*

Shrewsbury
Watanabe, Mark David *pharmacist, educator*

Somerville
Berlet, John Foster *researcher*

South Hamilton
Nemeskal, Natalie Ann *massage therapist*

Sudbury
Ames, Lois Winslow Sisson *social worker, educator, writer*
Henderson, Ernest III *healthcare executive*

Tewksbury
Tabea, Emile Victor *health facility administrator*

Waltham
Fleming, Samuel Crozier, Jr. *healthcare executive*

Wareham
Nolan, Marilyn Ann *health facility administrator*

Woods Hole
Speck, William T. *former physician, health facility administrator*

Worcester
Amory, Francis Inman *social worker, educator*
Harper, Doreen C. *nursing educator*
Stempsey, William Edward *medical philosopher*

MICHIGAN

Adrian
McGuire, Sharon, Sr. *nursing educator*

Ann Arbor
Beeton, Alfred Merle *lab administrator, director, biologist, educator, environmentalist*
Dormire, Sharon Lee *nurse, nursing educator*
El-Kattan, Ayman Fawzi *pharmacist, researcher*
Hinshaw, Ada Sue *nursing educator, former dean*
Ketefian, Shaké *nursing educator*
Oakley, Deborah Jane *educator*
Pescovitz, Ora Hirsch *health facility administrator, medical educator*
Romani, John Henry *health science association administrator, educator*
Strong, Douglas L. *health facility administrator*
Villaruel, Antonia M. *nursing educator*

Bloomfield Hills
Bauser, Nancy *social worker, disability life coach*

Dearborn
Irving, Patrice Marie *nursing educator*

Detroit
Cacace, Anthony T. *audiologist, educator*
Campbell, Margaret L. *adult nurse practitioner, researcher*
Cleveland, Sandra D. *nursing educator*
Fussell, Karen Marie *social worker, protective services official*
Genest, Theresa Joan *lab technician*
Gray, Herman B. *hospital administrator*
Jackson, Linda Shorter *nutritionist, educator*
Redman, Barbara Klug *nursing educator*
Ruckdeschel, John Charles *health facility administrator*
Schlichting, Nancy Margaret *hospital administrator*
Sloane, Bonnie Fiedorek *pharmacology and cancer biology educator, researcher*

Dexter
Hanamey, Rosemary T. *nursing educator*

East Lansing
Noel, Mary Margaret *nutritionist, educator*

Flint
Williams-Latnie, Veronica Myres *psychotherapist, social worker*

Franklin
Sax, Mary Randolph *speech and language pathologist*

Grand Ledge
Evert, Sandra Florence (Sandra Wheeler) *medical/surgical nurse, consultant*

Grand Rapids
Hoogenboom, Barbara Jo *physical therapist, educator*

Grosse Pointe
Marshall, Douglas William *health research administrator, educator*

Grosse Pointe Park
Knapp, Mildred Florence *retired social worker*

Jonesville
Corwin, Danny Willard *rehabilitation services professional, director*

Kalamazoo
Bennett, Arlie Joyce *clinical social worker*
Lander, Joyce Ann *retired nursing educator, medical/surgical nurse*
Price, Kim Denise *counselor*

Lansing
Nicholas, Caroline Jean *retired nurse, consultant*

Livonia
Gepford, Barbara Beebe *retired nutrition educator*

Mattawan
Magrath, Shari Marie *healthcare educator*

Mount Clemens
Robinson, Earl, Jr. *nanotechnologist, marketing, transportation executive, educator, retired air force officer*

Novi
Begley, Heidi Marie *nurse, entrepreneur*

Oak Park
Coleman, Dorothy Charmayne *nurse*

Owosso
McKean, Sherry Lynn *neurodiagnostic technologist*

Royal Oak
Grines, Cindy Lee *health facility administrator, cardiologist*

Southfield
Martin, Marcella Edric *retired community health nurse*
Torraco, Pamela Louise *psychotherapist*

Sterling Heights
Forkan, Eveleen *counselor, educator, researcher*
Robatchka-Walters, Janice Marie *medical/surgical and critical care nurse*

Traverse City
Anderson, Carol Lynn *social worker, educator*
Walker, Dorothea Leigh (Thea Walker) *art therapist, educator*

Trout Creek
Bruno, Judyth Ann *chiropractor*

Watervliet
Watkins, M(artha) Anne *family practice nurse practitioner*

Wixom
Welch, Cherie Lynn *healthcare educator*

Ypsilanti
Ervin, Naomi Estalee *nurse, educator*

MINNESOTA

Alexandria
Capp, Cheryl L. *nurse, educator*

Bemidji
Martinson, Ida Marie *retired medical/surgical nurse, physiologist*

Burnsville
Foss, Emma Thoren *retired social worker*

Faribault
Collins, Ruth Ann *special education services professional, director*

Golden Valley
McMahan, Robert *pharmacist, director*
Zabinski, Richard A. *pharmacist*

Granite Falls
Alness, Mae Christine *retired medical/surgical nurse*

Maplewood
Erhardt, Rhoda P. *occupational therapist*

Minneapolis
Appel, William Frank *pharmacist*
Blewett, Lynn A. *healthcare educator*
Burke, Richard T., Sr. *healthcare company executive, former professional sports team executive*
Drake, Dallas Sumner *researcher*
Hemsley, Stephen J. *healthcare company executive*
John, Charles J. *public health service officer, educator*
Kane, Robert Lewis *public health service officer, educator*
Larson, Sheryl Ann *social worker, researcher, writer*
Remmel, Rory Patrick *pharmacy educator*
Steen-Hinderlie, Diane Evelyn *social worker, musician*
Stevens, Simon *healthcare company executive*
Welters, Anthony *health services executive*

Rochester
Cortese, Denis A. *healthcare executive, medical educator*

Gervais, Sister Generose *hospital consultant*
Mrazek, David Allen *child and adolescent psychiatrist*
Robbins, Thomas Landau *researcher, editor*
Tescher, Ann Noreen *nurse*

White Bear Lake
Bruhn, JoAnn Marie *radiologic technologist, writer, speaker*

MISSISSIPPI

Brandon
Hall, Breda Faye Kimbrough Inman *counselor, educator*

Centreville
Nelson, Janie Rish *health facility administrator*

Columbus
Jones, Carol A. *nutritionist, artist*

Gautier
Block, Paul Conrad *registered respiratory therapist*

Hattiesburg
Dunaway, Melissa Faye *pediatrics nurse*
Vincent, Sharon Elaine *nursing educator*

Jackson
Heitman, Elizabeth *healthcare educator, anesthesiologist*
Tchounwou, Paul Bernard *environmental health specialist, toxicologist, educator*
Uzodinma, Minta LaVerne Smith *retired nursing administrator, nurse midwife*

Mayhew
Emerson, Tonsha Loranda *nursing educator*

Moss Point
Bolton, Betty J. *medical/surgical nurse, poet*

Mound Bayou
Robinson, Oliver Dale *counselor, pastor*

Pass Christian
Henrion, Rosemary Provenza *psychotherapist, educator*

Shaw
Garner, Mable Tecola *health facility administrator*

Tupelo
Zurawski, Jeanette *rehabilitation services professional*

University
Beebe, Stephanie H. *speech pathology/audiology services professional*
Lowe, Rebecca *audiologist, educator*

MISSOURI

Arnold
Porter, Kathy Lee *marriage and family therapist, minister*

Branson West
McCall, Charles Barnard *retired health facility administrator*

Cape Girardeau
Langenfeld, Mark E. *healthcare educator*

Chesterfield
Ashworth, Ronald Broughton *health facility executive, accountant*

Columbia
Gysbers, Norman Charles *counselor, educator*
Hensley, Elizabeth Catherine *nutritionist, educator*
Sable, Marjorie R. *social worker, educator*
Von Holt, Lael Powers *psychotherapist, psychiatric social worker*

Independence
Sturges, Sidney James *pharmacist, educator, investment and development company executive*

Kansas City
Krieg, Nancy Kay *social worker, poet, musician*
McKelvey, John Clifford *mental health services professional*
Norris, Ruth Ann Fink *social worker*
Oliver, Thornal Goodloe *retired health facility administrator*

Liberty
Samuel, Robert Thompson *optometrist*

Mansfield
Cotrone, Janice Lynne *nursing consultant*

O Fallon
Gross, Stanley Merhl *chiropractor*

Poplar Bluff
Wilson, Terrilyn Louella *nursing educator*

Rolla
Sin, Yong Wook *researcher, educator*

Saint Charles
Tabaka, Sandra Lee *retired medical/surgical nurse*

Saint Louis
Baum, M(ary) Carolyn *occupational therapist*
Becvar, Dorothy Stroh *family therapist*
Bennett, Edward Strachan *optometrist*

Carpenter, Brian D. *psychotherapist, educator*
Dias, Konrad Joseph *physical therapist, educator*
Fetter, Lee F. *hospital administrator*
Frandsen, Geralyn Marie *nursing educator*
Kotrba, Camilla Anne *dietician, consultant*
Loughrey, Thomas James *health and wellness professor*
Maposa, Sithokozile *nursing researcher*
Pryor, David Bram *health science association administrator*
Sabbert, Anne Ward *vision therapist, consultant*
Schoenhard, William Charles, Jr. *health system executive*
Wilbanks, Donnie Jo *healthcare educator*

Springfield
Amtower, Debra Lynn *nursing consultant*
Pedigo, Justin B. *audiology services professional, media consultant*

Wentzville
Saran, Shailee *dietician*

Wildwood
Drucker, Barry Jules *environmental health specialist*

MONTANA

Missoula
Dent, Larry A. *pharmacist, educator*
Roy, Tom McKim *social worker*
Stratton, Timothy Patrick *pharmacy educator*

Pablo
Lambert, Lorelei Anne *nursing educator*

Polson
Lenau, Laura Arline *retired nursing educator*

NEBRASKA

Lincoln
Campbell-Grossman, Christie Kay *nursing educator*
Havlicek, Kathy L. *family practice nurse practitioner, counselor, nurse, health facility administrator*
Schaefer, Joann *public health service officer*
Zempleni, Janos *nutritionist, educator*

Omaha
DeSimone, Edward Mario, II, *pharmacist, educator*
Hachten, Richard Arthur, II, *healthcare system executive*
Nailon, Regina Eileen *nurse*

Scottsbluff
Shoemaker, Troy *hazardous materials response team coordinator, fire captain*

NEVADA

Henderson
Bhakta, Ragini S. *pharmacist, educator*
Van Noy, Terry Willard *health care executive*

Las Vegas
Duke, Edward Marion, III, (Mickey) *health facility administrator, consultant*
Emerson, Shirley *retired professor counseling*
Gilchrist, Ann Roundey *medical/surgical nurse*
Meiner, Sue Ellen Thompson *nurse, consultant, gerontologist, author, writer*
Wakefield, Marie A. *counselor, educational association administrator*

North Las Vegas
Brown, Angela Khristin *lab administrator, educator*

Pahrump
Lubbers, Alice Dianne *operating room nurse*

Reno
Bonaldi-Moore, Lorraine Kay *nursing educator*
Middlebrooks, Deloris Jeanette *retired nursing educator*
Pinson, Larry Lee *pharmacist, state agency administrator*

NEW HAMPSHIRE

Bedford
Demers, Nancy Kae *nursing educator*

Concord
MacKay, James Robert *psychiatric social worker, mayor, educator*

Derry
Craft, Katie Ann *health facility administrator*

Hanover
Sekula, David Joseph *lab administrator, researcher*

Jackson
Baker, Mary Jane *clinical social worker*

Littleton
Lucas, Kurt John *health facility director*

Londonderry
Parten, Priscilla M. *medical and psychiatric social worker, educator*

Nashua
Martel, Marci *mental health services professional*

Ossipee
Bartlett, Diane Sue *counselor*

Plymouth
Gorin, Stephen H. *social worker, educator*

Sunapee
Springer, John Kelley *hospital administrator*

Tilton
Wolf, Sharon Ann *psychotherapist*

NEW JERSEY

Belle Mead
Sarle, Charles Richard *health facility executive*

Belvidere
Walsh, John Alfred *retired social worker*

Bridgewater
Weingast, Marvin *laboratory executive*

Burlington
Rowlette, Henry Allen, Jr. *social worker, counseling psychologist*

Camden
Grazel, Regina M. *medical/surgical nurse*

Chatham
Murphy, Joseph James *chiropractic physician*

Cherry Hill
Blakney, Juanita Mosley *psychotherapist*

East Orange
Hudson-Zonn, Eliza *nurse, psychologist*

East Rutherford
Cathey, Gertrude Brown *retired medical/surgical nurse*

Edgewater Park
Mednick, Sheldon Ira *pharmacist*

Edison
Winter, Robin Okner *health facility administrator*

Elizabeth
Rauh, Linda Ann *rehabilitation services professional, counselor*

Hackensack
Alvarez, Manuel *hospital executive, medical educator and news correspondent*
Ferguson, John Patrick *health facility administrator*

Holmdel
Levanda, Matthew *pharmacist, director*

Jersey City
Mahood, Marie I. *counselor, educator*

Kenilworth
Ehrenthal, Herb *health care company executive, marketing professional*

Livingston
Pansini, Jill Anne *medical/surgical nurse, consultant*

Madison
Ellenbogen, Leon *nutritionist, biochemist, retired pharmaceutical executive*

Mahwah
Hailparn, Diana Finnegan *psychotherapist, writer*

Medford
Kang, Jie *healthcare educator*

Metuchen
Macarin-Mara, Lynn *psychotherapist, consultant*

Millville
Caldwell, Linda E. *critical care nurse*

Monmouth Junction
Kaminker, Marcia Kahn *physical therapist*

Monroe Township
Stein, Florence Taub *retired social worker*

Montclair
Brock-Murray, Raymond *psychotherapist*

Morristown
Prince, Leah Fanchon *lab administrator, executive secretary*

Mount Laurel
Gray-Miceli, Deanna Lynn *geriatric nurse practitioner, educator, researcher*

Mountainside
Mansue, Amy *hospital administrator*

Neptune
Bediguian, Mariamig Jinx *operating room nurse*

New Brunswick
Bindra, Dilbir S. *pharmacist*
Brilliant, Eleanor Luria *retired social work educator*

New Providence
Sniffen, Michael Joseph *hospital administrator*

Newfield
Dreher, Frank H., Jr. *retired optician*

North Haledon
Latner, Selma *retired psychoanalyst*

Pennington
Harkness, Joan Ann V. *retired health educator*

Princeton
Logue, Judith Felton *psychoanalyst, educator*
Marks, James S. *public health service administrator*
Weinman, Steven Alan *emergency nurse practitioner, educator, writer, health facility administrator*

Randolph
Whildin, Leonora Porreca *retired nursing educator*

Red Bank
Brown, Valerie Anne *psychotherapist, social worker, educator*
Carmody, Margaret Jean *retired social worker*
Gutentag, Patricia Richmand *social worker, family counselor, occupational therapist*

Ridgewood
Clements, Lynne Fleming *marriage and family therapist, application developer*

Roseland
Malafronte, Donald *health planning consultant*

Rutherford
Suarez, Sally Ann Tevis *health facility administrator, nurse, consultant*

Sicklerville
Browna, Jo McIntyre *nurse*

South Orange
Hansell, Phyllis Shanley *nursing educator, administrator, researcher, consultant*

Teaneck
Alperin, Richard Martin *social worker, psychoanalyst*

Teterboro
Hagemann, Robert A. *health care company executive*
Mohapatra, Surya N. *laboratory executive*

Titusville
Jain, Reema *pharmacist, pharmaceutical executive*

Trenton
Ritchey, Kenneth William *human services administrator*

Vauxhall
Jacobs-Smith, Ruby Eudora *retired medical/surgical nurse, public health service officer*

Warren
Yang, Tsong-Toh (T.T.) *pharmacist, researcher*

Wayne
D'Andrea, Kathleen Claire *speech therapist*

West Caldwell
Schiff, Robert *healthcare consulting company executive*

West New York
Schmidt, Nancy Anne *psychotherapist*

West Orange
Bornstein, Lester Milton *retired health facility administrator*
De Lisa, Joel Alan *rehabilitation physician, research executive*
Jacobs, Fred M. *hospital administrator, former state agency administrator*

West Trenton
Farajollahi, Ary *health facility administrator*

NEW MEXICO

Albuquerque
Adams, Mary Elizabeth *counselor, psychotherapist, writer*
Darbro, Nancy M. *nursing administrator*
Davidge, K. Genevieve *clinical social worker*
Erickson, Sue Alice *health educator, consultant, nurse*

Carlsbad
DeFeo, Dayna Jean *researcher*
Goad, Faith *nursing educator*

Las Cruces
Little, Karen J. *counselor*

Roswell
Buldra, Gina *physical therapist*

Santa Fe
Davis, Marcie L. *public health and human services consultant*
Howell, Vicky Sue *health data analyst*
Jordan, James *psychotherapist, educator*

Truth Or Consequences
Rush, Domenica Marie *health facilities administrator*

NEW YORK

Albany
DeNuzzo, Rinaldo Vincent *pharmacy educator*
Kennett, Ellen L. *lab administrator, pharmacist*

Apalachin
Linder, Fannie Ruth *psychotherapist, concert soprano*

Bayside
Kennedy, Mary Theresa *mental health services professional*

Bayville
Calodny, Alan Lee *retired pharmacist*

Binghamton
Lawrence, Karen Roseman *special education services professional, educator*
Terriquez-Kasey, Laura Marie *emergency nurse*

Bronx
Flores, Guillermo *health science association administrator*
Hilliard, Carol *nurse, educator, consultant, researcher*
Safyer, Steven Michael *hospital administrator*
Wylie-Rosett, Judith *dietician, educator*

Brooklyn
Austin, Denise *dietician*
Brier, Pamela Sara *health facility administrator*
Brines, Seymour *psychotherapist, consultant, educator*
Gonsalves, Patricia E. *surgical nurse*
Gulstone, Jacqueline *nurse*
Halley-Boyce, Jamesetta A. *hospital administrator*
Lockey, James Peter *public health service officer*
Najib, Jadwiga S. *pharmacist, educator*
Peters, Mercedes *psychotherapist*
Toranzo, Nilsa Caridad *special education services professional*
Wilkow, Brian Richard *hospital administrator and clinician*
Wilson, Nancy Esther *social worker*
Wrotten, Marylean *medical coordinator, counselor*

Buffalo
Aquilina, Suzanne *pediatric nurse practitioner, educator*
Blane, Howard Thomas *alcohol/drug abuse services professional, researcher*
Germain, Pamela *health facility administrator, educator*
Gibson, Judith W. *retired psychotherapist*
Gingher, Merlene C. *occupational therapist, educator*
Hoffman, Faith Louise *social worker*
Wicher, Camille Phyllis *nursing administrator*
Wright, Dana Jace *retired emergency nurse practitioner*
Wu, Changxu *researcher, consultant*
Zittel-Palamara, Kimberley *social worker, educator*

Byron
Ruck, Rosemarie Ulissa *retired social worker, freelance/self-employed writer*

Camillus
Thompson, Mary Cecilia *nurse midwife*

Centerport
Yadeka, Theophilus Adeniyi *hospital administrator*

Cortland
Brush, Florence Clapham *kinesiologist, exercise physiologist, physical education educator*

Dunkirk
Strychalski, Elizabeth Arlene *nanotechnologist, physicist, researcher*

Eastchester
Giuliano, Robert Paul *pharmacist*

Flushing
Kim, Sun-Hae *retired medical/surgical nurse, writer, nurse midwife, physical therapist*

Franklin Square
Maffia, Jason *health services administrator*

Haverstraw
Eidelman, Sharon (Sherry) R. *marriage and family therapist*

Hewlett
Cohen, Lawrence Alan *health facility administrator*

Horseheads
Halm, Brian Thomas *technologist, educator*

Huntington
Hofmann, Jennifer *physician assistant, educator*

Huntington Station
Williams, Una Joyce *retired psychiatric social worker*

Ithaca
Habicht, Jean Pierre *public health educator*
Wills, Michael Stephen *nutritionist, quality assurance professional, photographer*

Jamaica
Geffner, Donna Sue *speech pathology/audiology services professional, audiologist, educator*
Morrill, Joyce Marie *social worker, educator, photographer*

Kew Gardens
Reddick, Deirdre Shadeia *physician assistant*

Lewiston
Moraca-Sawicki, Anne Marie *oncology nurse*

Middletown
Ojeda, Joseph A. *psychotherapist*

Mineola
Yeh, James Kuen-Jann *nutritionist*

New York
Abbatiello, Geraldine A. *geriatric nurse practitioner*
Barrett, Elizabeth Ann Manhart *psychotherapist, consultant, nursing educator*
Batavia, Mitchell *physical therapist, educator*
Bauer, Joy *nutritionist, consultant*
Beaton, Ann R. *educator*
Boufford, Jo Ivey *health science association administrator, educator*
Camp, Sharon L. *reproductive health organization administrator*
Cardinale, Kathleen Carmel *retired health facility administrator*
Caroff, Phyllis M. *social work educator*
Clemens, Rosemary A. *foundation and health facility administrator*
Coleman, Jo-Ann S.E. *social worker*
Daniel, Samuel J. *hospital administrator, medical educator*
Darnton-Hill, Ian *public health physician, nutrition consultant*
Drayer, Burton Paul *hospital administrator, neuroradiologist*
Ethan, Carol Baehr *psychotherapist, psychoanalyst*
Fagin, Claire Mintzer *nursing administrator, educator*
Fenchel, Gerd Hermann *psychoanalyst*
Garcia, Minerva Melinda *human resources manager, director of diversity*
Gaudreau, Nicolas P. *social worker, director*
Giordano, Bill A. *psychotherapist*
Goodwin, Beatrice *nursing educator, consultant*
Gourguechon, Prudence Leib *psychoanalyst*
Greenblatt, Michael Noel *hospital administrator, primary care internist*
Gure, Anna Valerie *retired social worker, consulting psychotherapist*
Hill, Marjorie Jean *health association administrator, psychologist*
Kamerman, Sheila Brody *social work educator*
Kapoor, Neera *optometrist, research scientist*
Kassel, Catherine M. *community, maternal, and women's health nurse, consultant*
Kaufman, Michele Beth *clinical pharmacist, educator, writer, editor, consultant*
Keathley, Wayne E. *hospital administrator*
Kent, Deborah Warren *hypnotherapist, consultant, lecturer*
Kove, Miriam *psychotherapist*
Kuttler, Judith Esther *retired psychotherapist*
Leitman, I. Michael *health facility administrator*
Levinson, Rascha *psychotherapist*
Levitt, Harry *speech and hearing scientist*
Lieberman, Alan J. *paramedic, consultant*
Low, Ronald Bruce *hospital administrator*
Matheson, Linda *retired social worker*
Mayeux, Richard *hospital administrator, neurologist*
McCaughey, Betsy (Elizabeth P. McCaughey) *health policy advocate, former lieutenant governor*
McGinn, Eileen *public health service officer, researcher*
McGonagle, Duncan Francis *mental health nurse, substance abuse counselor*
Mitchell, Mary Jenkins *public health service officer*
Moffat Salant, Marilyn *physical therapist, educator*
Moore, Brian P. *health care professional*
Moskowitz, Randi Zucker *nurse*
Nasser, Jennifer Ann *nutritionist, researcher, healthcare educator*
Nickitas, Donna Marie *nursing educator, researcher*
Novick, Richard Paul *research scientist, public health institute administrator*
O'Neil Mundinger, Mary *nursing educator*
Packer, Linda S. *geriatric care manager*
Pakter, Jean *maternal and child health consultant*
Pandolfi, Frances *health facility administrator*
Pardes, Herbert *health facility executive, psychiatrist, educator*
Pennisi, Liz *women's health nurse*
Rackow, Eric C. *health care company executive*
Rees, Ellen *psychoanalyst, psychiatrist*
Richards, Cecile *healthcare network executive*
Rude, Eric John *public health service officer, researcher*
Shapiro, Louis A. *hospital administrator*
Sochet, Mary Allen *psychotherapist, educator, writer*
Tahir, Rabia *pharmacist, educator*
Turo, Joann K. *psychoanalyst, psychotherapist, consultant*
Varmus, Harold Eliot *health science administrator, educator, science researcher*
Watson, Anthony L. *health facility executive*
Zolla-Pazner, Susan *hospital administrator, biologist, biomedical researcher*

Niskayuna
Laskaris, E(vangelos) Trifon *technologist, researcher*

Old Westbury
Seelow, David D. *family therapist*

Olean
McGovern-Scaturo, Diane Joan *psychotherapist*

Orchard Park
Askew, Gloria Yarbrough *dietician*

Orient
Cochran, Judy Anne *psychiatric nurse practitioner*

Ossining
Robinson, Karen Vajda *dietician*

Patchogue
Lombardo, Robin Ann *therapeutic recreation director, educator*
McPherson, Sherry Lynn *social worker*

Penfield
Hamilton, Candis Lee *counselor*

Poughkeepsie
Deiters, Sister Joan Adele *psychoanalyst, nun, chemistry professor*
Heller, Mary Bernita *psychotherapist*

Ravena
Coye, Mary P. *counselor*

Rochester
Aydelotte, Myrtle Kitchell *retired nursing administrator*
Braley, Oleta Pearl *community health nurse, writer*
Chiverton, Patricia Ann *nursing educator*
Hurlbut, Robert Harold *health care services executive*
Jain, Manish *researcher*
Mitchell, Lance Bernard *social worker*
Sammler, Anne Michelle *healthcare educator*
Tantillo, Mary Darlene *nurse*

Rome
Anderson, Nora *retired nurse*

Roslyn
Aptekar, Doris Mae Weinberg *psychotherapist, school psychologist, hypnotherapist*
Rosen, Sarah Perel *social worker*

Rye
Megalli, Maguid Ramzi *retired health facility administrator, urologist*
Newburger, Howard Martin *psychoanalyst*
Wilmot, Irvin Gorsage *former hospital administrator, educator, consultant*

Saranac Lake
Caguiat, Carlos Jose *health facility administrator, priest*

Scarsdale
Glickenhaus, Sarah Brody *speech therapist*

Schenectady
Oliker, David William *healthcare management administrator*

Sleepy Hollow
Resnick, Adrienne Jo *clinical social worker, psychotherapist*

Southampton
Kapenhas-Valdes, Edna *hospital administrator*

Staten Island
Gaeta, Rosemarie *psychotherapist*

Syracuse
Fitzgerald, Harold Kenneth *social work educator, consultant*
Kalman, Melanie Beth *nursing educator, researcher*
Salerno, Sister Maria *advanced practice nurse, educator*
Walsh-Hunt, Linda Ann *social worker, consultant, poet*

Tuckahoe
Thornton, Elaine Seretha *oncology clinical nurse specialist*

Valhalla
Iatropoulos, Michael John *health research executive, pathology educator*

Valley Stream
Gustin, Mark Douglas *retired healthcare executive*

West Harrison
Gutheil, Irene A. *social work educator, researcher*

White Plains
Fowlkes, Nancy Lanetta Pinkard *social worker*
Russo, Donna Lee *social worker*
Schandler, Jon B. *hospital administrator*

Williamsville
Perry, J. Warren *health facility administrator, educator*

NORTH CAROLINA

Boiling Springs
Walker, Vickie Elaine *nursing educator*

Burlington
King, David Paul *health services executive, lawyer*
Powell, James Bobbitt *health facility administrator, pathologist*

Carrboro
Jones-Smith, Jessica Claire *dietician*

Chapel Hill
Baker, Edward L., Jr. *public health physician*
Gordon-Larsen, Penny *nutritionist, educator, researcher*
Johnson, Lucie Jenkins *retired social worker*
MacRae, Elizabeth (Elizabeth MacRae Halsey) *counselor, actor*
Zeisel, Steven H. *nutritionist, scientist, educator*

Charlotte
Crawford, Juanita Gatewood *nursing technician*
Johnson, Constance Green *health facility administrator*
Laditka, Sarah Beth *healthcare educator*
Prabha, Karan *lab administrator*
Schorr, Alvin Louis *social worker, educator*

Concord
Faw, Ernie M. *healthcare educator*

Durham
Fulkerson, William *hospital administrator, pulmonologist*
Merson, Michael Howard *public health physician, epidemiologist, educator*
Snyder, Denise *nutritionist, researcher*
Vaughan, Cathy Ann *pharmacist*

Elizabeth City
Griffin, Gladys Bogues *critical care nurse, educator*

Fairmont
Spencer, Melissa Johanna *psychotherapist, special education educator*

Fayetteville
Jansen, Michael John *health facility administrator*

Greensboro
Allen, Jesse Owen III *organizational behavior specialist*
Dollahite, David Curtis *family science educator*
Harris-Offutt, Rosalyn Marie *counselor, consultant, mental health nurse, consultant, writer*
Knesel, Ernest Arthur, Jr. *health facility administrator, chemicals executive*
Mozell, Herbert Lee *mental health services professional*
Penley, Virginia Long *social worker*
Schwenn, Lee William *retired health facility administrator*

Greenville
Dickerson, Anne Elizabeth *educator*

Hendersonville
Jefferson, Letitia Gibson *rehabilitation counselor*
Weeks, Sandra Kenney *nursing administrator*

Lenoir
Bailey-Day, Kay Lynn *psychotherapist*
Caknipe, Christopher Howard *substance abuse services professional*

Raleigh
Hughes, Barbara Ann *dietician, public health administrator*
Slaton, Joseph Guilford *social worker*

Rutherfordton
Crummie, Ann Vaughn *mental health services professional*

Thomasville
Johnson, Kathie Anne *hospital administrator*

Wentworth
Evans, Jonathan Christopher *social worker*

Wilson
Morris, Sharon Louise Stewart *emergency medical technician, paramedic*

Wingate
Alston, Gregory Lloyd *pharmacist, educator*

Winston Salem
Cook, Sharon Warren *social worker, educator*
Harper-Harrison, Alfreda Denise *nursing educator, researcher*
Preslar, Len Broughton, Jr. *hospital administrator*

Zebulon
Maness, Eleanor Palmer *researcher*

NORTH DAKOTA

Fargo
Friesner, Daniel *pharmacist, educator*

Grand Forks
Nielsen, Forrest Harold *research nutritionist*

OHIO

Akron
West, Michael Alan *retired hospital administrator*

Ashtabula
Hornbeck, Harold Douglas *psychotherapist*

Barnesville
Kelley-Hall, Maryon Hoyle *retired social worker*

Canfield
Weiss, Susan Ellen *adult nurse practitioner, educator*

Centerville
Appelbaum, Bernardine *cardiovascular nurse*

Cincinnati
Anderson, James Milton *hospital administrator*
Besier, James Louis *pharmacist, educator*
Chernus, Linda A. *psychoanalytic psychotherapy educator, social worker*
Curtin, Leah Louise *publisher, nurse, educator*
De Witt, Jeanette Marie *physical therapist*
Hensgen, Herbert Thomas *medical technologist*
Lang, Jackie Ann *nursing consultant*
Stinson, Mary Florence *retired nursing educator*
Worthen, Dennis Brent *researcher, educator*

Cleveland
Adams, Kathryn Betts *social worker, educator*
Brouhard, Ben Herman *hospital administrator, nephrologist*
Gallagher, Lisa Marie *music therapist*
Gary, Faye *nursing educator*
Kalina, Eunice Goldstein *human services director*
Kohn, Mary Louise Beatrice *nurse*
Rothstein, Fred C. *health facility administrator*
Threats, Travis T. *speech-language pathologist*
Wynd, Christine Anne *nursing service administration*
Zhang, Amy Yanyun *cancer and health services researcher*

Columbus
Buffington, C. A. Tony *nutritionist, educator*
Duckworth, Winston Howard *researcher*
Fawcett, Sherwood Luther *lab administrator*
Herron, Holly Lynn *critical care nurse, educator*
Medeiros, Denis Michael *nutrition educator*
Mendell, Jerry R. *hospital administrator*
Murden, Robert A. *medical administrator, physician*
Nahata, Milap Chand *pharmacy educator*
Sims, Richard Lee *retired hospital administrator*
Stebbins, Barry Steven *educational technologist*
Winters, Jane A. *nurse, educator*

Copley
Smith, Joan H. *retired women's health nurse, educator*

Coshocton
McGinnis, Tammy Marie *health services manager*

Dayton
Nixon, Charles William *retired acoustician*
Stalter, Ann Marie *nursing educator*
Todd, Dianna Kaye *nursing administrator, educator*

Dover
Haggis, Mary Ripley *nurse, genealogist*

East Palestine
Miller, Darren John *social worker*

Eaton
Kisling, Fanny *counselor, educator*

Elyria
Myers, John T. *physical therapist, educator*

Findlay
Hotaling, Cynthia Ann *nursing administrator, educator*

Hamilton
Fein, Linda Ann *nurse anesthetist, consultant*

Hudson
Wooldredge, William Dunbar *health facility administrator*

Independence
Van Kirk, Robert John *nursing clinical manager, educator*

Kent
Sonnhalter, Carolyn Therese *physical therapist, consultant*

Lancaster
Varney, Richard Alan *health facility administrator*

Mason
Clements, Michael Craig *health services consulting executive, retired renal dialysis technician*
Goldstein, Sidney *pharmacist*
Lawson, Stephen C. *lab administrator*

Miamisburg
Perry, William Francis *nurse, educator*

North Olmsted
Semple, Jane Frances *health facility director*

Orrville
Roncone, John Edward *health educator*

Owensville
Seifert, Caroline Hamilton *community health nurse*

Ravenna
Turcotte, Margaret Jane *retired nurse*

Rootstown
Bhatia, Deepak *pharmacist, educator*

Sandusky
Runner, Jack Charles *health facility executive*

Sidney
Leffler, Carole Elizabeth *retired women's and mental health nurse*
Menz, Robert L. *psychotherapist, minister*

Toledo
Ormond, Paul A. *healthcare company executive*
Trendel, Jill A. *pharmacist, educator*
Weikel, Malcolm Keith *healthcare company executive*

Urbana
Meyers, Marsha Lynn *retired social worker*

Westlake
Schroth, Joyce Able *social worker*

Worthington
Bernhagen, Lillian Flickinger *retired school health consultant*

Wright Patterson AFB
Meccia, Neil Rocco *health facility administrator, physician*

Youngstown
Itts, Elizabeth Ann Dunham *retired psychotherapist, consultant*

Miller, Kenneth Lee *counselor, educator*
Pintar, Jennifer A. *healthcare educator*
Valenta, Janet Anne *substance abuse professional*

OKLAHOMA

Ada
Emrich, Paul M. *psychotherapist, educator*
Schubert, Geri M. *psychotherapist*

Bethany
Alexander, Patrick Byron *hospital administrator*
Arbuckle, Averil Dorothy (Cookie Arbuckle) *healthcare facility administrator*
Campbell Detrixhe, Dia D. *nursing educator*
Dorough, Carol *nursing educator*

Broken Arrow
Muller, Patricia Ann *nursing administrator, educator*

Edmond
Laughlin, Monique Myrtle Weant *mental health counselor, retired*
Lewis, Gladys Sherman *university professor*

Frederick
Stone, Voye Lynne *women's health nurse practitioner*

Lamont
Covalt, Edna Irene *retired medical/surgical nurse*

Oklahoma City
Boutsen, Frank R. *healthcare educator*
Dailey, Patrick R. *health facility administrator*
Forni, Patricia Rose *nursing educator*
Lynn, Thomas Neil, Jr. *retired medical center administrator, physician*
McClellan, Mary Ann *pediatric nurse practitioner*
Mustion, Alan Lee *pharmacist*
Resman-Targoff, Beth Holly *pharmacist, educator*
Spencer, Melvin Joe *retired health facility administrator, lawyer, consultant*

Sayre
Clifton, E. Roxann *lab administrator*

Stillwater
Basu, Arpita *dietician, educator*

Tulsa
Bransford-Young, Angharad Ann *counselor, educator*
Jurgensen, Monserrate *clinical nurse, consultant*

Weatherford
Blatnick, Tammy D. *nursing educator*

Wilburton
Carey, Levenia Marie *counselor*

OREGON

Ashland
Love, John M. *policy researcher*

Coos Bay
Hockman, Catherine *counselor, educator*

Corvallis
Oldfield, James Edmund *retired nutrition educator*

Eugene
Acker, Martin Herbert *psychotherapist, educator*

Florence
Van Horn, O. Frank *retired counselor, consultant*

Lebanon
Griswold, Elaine C. *nurse, consultant*

Newport
Goudy, Josephine Gray *social worker*

North Bend
Hudson, Mary Anne *public health nurse*

Pendleton
Smiley, Richard Wayne *researcher*

Phoenix
Dodd, Darlene Mae *retired nurse, retired military officer*

Portland
Cereghino, James Joseph *health facility administrator, neurologist*
Cherala, Ganesh *healthcare educator, researcher*
Korb, Christine Ann *music therapist, researcher, educator*
Seymour, B(arbara) J(ean) *social worker*
Wrightman, Caroline Anne McGhee *nursing educator*

Redmond
Dey, Charlotte Jane *retired community health nurse*

Sandy
Jensen, Judy Dianne *psychotherapist, consultant*

Stayton
Zumwalt, Roger Carl *healthcare accreditation consultant*

PENNSYLVANIA

Allentown
Gammon, Sally (Sara T. Gammon) *hospital administrator, physical therapist*

Bala Cynwyd
Peret, Karen Krzyminski *health facility administrator*

Bloomsburg
Oman, Terina Louise *nursing educator*

Camp Hill
Mazzolla, D. Patrick *healthcare services executive*

Devon
Quinn, Lois Marie *health service innovator*

Export
Carter, Linda Whitehead *oncological nurse, educator*

Hanover
Davis, Ruth Carol *pharmacist, educator*

Harrisburg
Bailey, Diandrea Michelle *rehabilitation services professional*
Cadieux, Roger Joseph *geriatrics services professional*
Kreidie, Marwan *human services administrator*
Schneider, Nina Michelle *nursing educator*

Hershey
Paz, Harold Louis *hospital administrator, internist, educator*

Horsham
Cohen, Michael R. *health facility administrator, pharmacist*

Hulmeville
Jackson, Mary L. *health services executive*

Johnstown
Ondrejcak, Sally Suzanne *psychotherapist*

King Of Prussia
Goldsmith, Eleanor Jean *retired hospital administrator*
Miller, Alan B. *hospital management executive*
Souney, Paul Frederick *pharmacist*

Lancaster
Bell, Frances Louise *medical technologist*

Lansdale
Bierman, Arnold *optometrist*

Levittown
Ferraro, Ronald Louis *health facility administrator*

Lincoln University
Norris, JoAnne Wareham *school counselor*

Lititz
Gingerich, Naomi R. *emergency room nurse*

Moon Township
Maurer, Cheryl *lab administrator, researcher*

Mount Pleasant
Morgan, Joyce Kaye *social worker*

Northern Cambria
Fisher, Connie Marie *physical therapist*

Oaks
Snyder, Jeffrey Scott *chiropractor*

Orwigsburg
Mason, Joan Ellen *nurse*

Philadelphia
Altschuler, Steven M. *health facility executive, pediatrician, gastroenterologist*
Butler, Marie Gladys *nursing educator*
Carroll, Jack Adien *rehabilitation hospital administrator*
Charney, Natalie J. *behavioral health services professional, researcher, clinician*
Fuchs, Barry D. *hospital administrator*
Geifman-Holtzman, Ossie *health science association administrator*
Hynes, Virtner Gilmore *rehabilitation services professional*
Joseph, Andrea Stein *pharmacist, educator*
McFadden, Cori Erin *psychotherapist, educator*
Mc Ghan, William Frederick *pharmacist, educator*
Morgan, Elizabeth K. *retired critical care nurse*
Muller, Ralph W. *hospital administrator*
Newman, Bernie Sue *social worker, educator*
Rosenberg, Robert Allen *psychology professor*
Seiden, Michael V. *hospital administrator, physician*
Shapiro, Paula *retired maternal/women's health nurse*
Silberstein, Stephen David *health facility administrator, neurologist*
Silfies, Sheri *physical therapist, educator*
Solomon, Phyllis Linda *social work educator, researcher*
Williams, Sankey Vaughan *health services researcher, internist*
Wray, Matt *healthcare educator*

Pittsburgh
Dato, Virginia Marie *public health physician*
Friede, Samuel A(rnold) *healthcare executive*
Gorge, John Anthony *health corporation executive*
Kapucu, Naim *researcher*
Kowalski Trakofler, Kathleen Madland *psychotherapist, researcher*
Lenhart, Cheryl Hayes *nursing administrator, consultant*
Mark, Scott M. *pharmacist, director, healthcare educator*
Mitchell, Ann Margaret *psychiatric nurse practitioner, educator*
Moore, Pearl B. *retired nursing educator*
Oxendale, Roger A. *hospital administrator*
Pennell, Daniel Mark *researcher*
Perel, James Maurice *pharmacology and healthcare educator, researcher*
Shin, Sungjae *nutritionist*
Shvedova, Anna Alexandrovna *nutrition research manager, consultant*
Wilson, Frances Helen *retired occupational therapist*
Xie, Xiang-Qun Sean *pharmacist, educator*
Zanardelli, John Joseph *healthcare organization executive*

Port Matilda
Holt, Frieda M. *nursing educator, retired academic administrator*

Reading
Shultz, Lois Frances Casho *nursing supervisor*

Richboro
Maholic, Nancy L. *nurse*

Scranton
McKenna, Ann K. *nutritionist, educator*
Turock, Jane Parsick *nutritionist*

Spring House
van Steenwyk, John Joseph *healthcare plan consultant*

Uniontown
Halfhill, Terry Ray *researcher, educator*

University Park
Mayers, Stanley Penrose, Jr. *public health service officer, educator*
Rolls, Barbara Jean *nutritionist, educator, director*

Villanova
Capolupo, Joan M. Novelli *counselor, educator*
Zhang, Yimin *researcher*

Warminster
Bleam, Laura Jane *pediatrics nurse, educator*

Washington Boro
Snyder, John Jacob *researcher*

West Chester
Clarkin, John Francis *health care management executive*
Gunter, Cheryl Darcel *speech pathology/audiology services professional, educator*

West Mifflin
Rosko, Maryann A. *nurse*

West Point
Grabenstein, John Douglas *pharmacist, military officer*

Willow Street
Keiser, Paul Harold *retired hospital administrator*
Wesbury, Stuart Arnold, Jr. *health science association administrator, educator*

Wynnewood
Anyanwu, Chukwuma Uchenna *clinical pharmacist, biomedical researcher*

Wyomissing
Gordon, Mildred Harriet Gross *hospital executive*

York
Alcon, Sonja L. *retired medical social worker*
Bartels, Bruce Michael *health facility administrator*
Pucino, Carrie *critical care nurse*

RHODE ISLAND

Cranston
Lisi, Deborah Jeanne *performance improvement coordinator*

Newport
Woods, Donald E. *healthcare executive*

Pawtucket
Cheever, James Jefferson *counselor*

Providence
Kenna, George Anthony *pharmacist, researcher*
Price, William Walley, Jr. *counselor, artist*
Viner-Brown, Samara I. *public health administrator*

Warwick
Richards, Priscilla Ann *medical/surgical nurse*

SOUTH CAROLINA

Aiken
Jefferson, Helen Butler *health protection technician*

Charleston
Madory, James Richard *hospital administrator, retired military officer*

Columbia
Amidon, Roger Lyman *public health service officer, educator*
McLendon, Brian Andrew *lab administrator, educator*
Moskowitz, Jay *health science association administrator, educator, dean*
Seigler, Ruth Queen *college nursing administrator, educator, consultant*

Easley
Howe, Linda Arlene *nursing educator, writer*

Gaffney
Griffin, Penni Oncken *social worker, educator*

Greenville
Johnson, Jane Elizabeth *medical technician*
Riordan, Michael C. *hospital administrator*

Hilton Head Island
Kearney-Nunnery, Rose *nursing administrator, educator, consultant*
Wesselmann, Glenn Allen *retired health facility administrator*

Myrtle Beach
Lowes, Sandra Elaine *chiropractor, educator*

Newberry
McDowell, Betsy M. *critical care nurse, educator*

Orangeburg
Manson, Bonita Yvonne *nutritionist, educator*

Spartanburg
Jones, William Osborne, II, *physician assistant, nephrologist*

Summerville
Burke, Rhonda Williams *counselor*
Deavers, James Frederick *optometrist, clinical nutritionist*

SOUTH DAKOTA

Brookings
Dalaly, Basil *nutritionist, educator*

Pierre
Weyer, Dianne Sue *health facility administrator*

Rapid City
Brookes, Leslie Joan *retired maternal/surgical nurse*
Corwin, Bert Clark *optometrist*

Vermillion
Sevening, Diane Kay *alcohol/drug abuse studies educator, researcher*

Yankton
Jorgensen, Katherine Lange *nursing educator*

TENNESSEE

Brentwood
Carpenter, William F. III *hospital management company executive, lawyer*

Franklin
Fink, Robert Michael *pharmacist*
Miller, Dennis Edward *health medical executive*
Smith, Wayne Thomas *healthcare company executive*

Gallatin
Loerakker, Jo Ann Katherine *retired chiropractor*

Goodlettsville
Harper, Jewel Benton *pharmacist*

Harrogate
McGuire, Sandra Lynn *nursing educator*

Jackson
Jones, Dalan Dee *nursing educator*

Jellico
Hausman, Keith Lynn *health facility administrator, physical therapist*

Johnson City
Henry, Robin Michelle *pharmacist, director*

Knoxville
Airee, Anita *pharmacist*
Fender, Allison Jean *physical therapist, personal trainer*
Haren, Elizabeth Gaye *counselor*
Lee, Jan Louise *nursing educator*
Mc Hargue, Carl Jack *lab administrator*
Reynolds, Marjorie Lavers *nutritionist, educator*
Trout, Monroe Eugene *health facility administrator*

Martin
Parrish, Alissa Renee *nursing educator*

Memphis
Bargagliotti, Lillian Antoinette *nursing educator*
Bhattacharya, Sujoy *scientist, researcher*
Boucher, Bradley Albert *pharmacist, educator*
Bowles, Grover Cleveland, Jr. *pharmacist, educator*
Crain, Frances Utterback *retired dietitian*
Evans, William Edward *hospital administrator, pharmacist, researcher*
Ramsdell, Heather L. *speech pathology/audiology services professional, researcher*
Smith, Karen Ann *nutritionist*
Suda, Katie Joy *pharmacist, educator*

Nashville
Cannon, Sharon M. *health facility administrator*
Dalton, James Edgar, Jr. *health facility administrator*
Frist, Thomas Fearn, Jr. *hospital management company executive*
Johnson, R. Milton *healthcare executive*
Kaiser, Allen Bernard *health facility administrator*
McNutt, Mona Belle *retired clinical social worker*

Perlin, Jonathan Brian *health services company executive, former federal agency administrator*
Shelton, Amy Elizabeth *health facility administrator*
Stiles, Renee A. *hospital administrator, educator*
Watts, Carolyn Sue *nurse*

Oak Ridge
Jones, Virginia McClurkin *retired social worker*

Somerville
Macdonald, Sally Polk Bowers *retired addictions therapist*

Union City
Crist, Marilyn I. *social worker*

TEXAS

Abilene
Morrison, Shirley Marie *retired nursing educator*

Addison
Goldmann, James Allen *healthcare consultant*

Amarillo
Reed, Katherine (Kathy) E. *nursing educator*

Arlington
Basham, Randall E. *social worker, educator*
McCuistion, Robert Wiley *hospital administrator, management consultant, lawyer*
Oehler, Judith Jane Moody *retired counselor*
O'Quinn, Josie Lu *nursing educator*

Austin
Adams, Mary Louise *nursing educator, researcher*
Barrera, Elvira Puig *retired counselor, academic administrator*
Cankar, Paul Anthony *physical therapist, director*
Fleming, Francine Faye *legal nurse consultant*
Gimson, William H., III, (Bill Gimson) *health facility administrator*
Lansford, James Lowell *technologist*
Larkam, Beverley McCosham *clinical social worker, marriage and family therapist*

Baytown
Soileau, Veronica Demoruelle *counselor, educator*

Big Spring
Warner, William Dee *nursing consultant*

Bulverde
Lamoureux, Gloria Kathleen *nurse, consultant, retired military officer*

Carrollton
Withrow, Lucille Monnot *nursing home administrator*

Coleman
Smith, Eva Joyce *retired counselor, social worker*

College Station
Rimer, Mendell de Jesus *healthcare educator*

Dallas
Bradley, John Andrew *health facility administrator*
Brown, Nancy A. *health science association administrator*
Brown, Stephen F. *health facility administrator*
Durovich, Christopher J. *hospital administrator*
Fetter, Trevor *healthcare industry executive*
Focht, Michael Harrison *health care industry executive*
France, Newell Edwin *retired health facility administrator*
Gwinn, Robert Allen *technologist, director*
Hitt, David Hamilton, Sr. *retired health facility administrator*
Kangas, Edward A. *healthcare company executive*
Miller, Jo Carolyn Dendy *family and marriage counselor, educator*
Naziruddin, Bashoo *lab administrator, director*
Newman, Steven L. *health care executive*
Schecter, Arnold Joel *public health physician, researcher*
Schochet, Barry P. *health care executive*
Skinner, Jon *rehabilitation hospital administrator*
Taulbee, Thomas Lester *psychotherapist, educator*
Wassenich, Linda Pilcher *retired health policy analyst, social worker*
Watson, Claude Armstead *counselor*
Wells, Melanie Kay *marriage and family therapist, director*

Denison
Bredberg, Kathleen Hope *nursing administrator, director*

Denton
Surprise, Juanee *chiropractor, nutrition consultant*

Dickinson
Fotsch, George Bernard III *chemical addiction counselor*

Duncanville
Timpa, Vicki Ann *government health program administrator*

Edinburg
Leal, Hector *lab administrator*
Wilson, Bruce Keith *consultant in men's health issues*

El Paso
Edmonds, Velma McInnis *nursing educator*
Jordan, Shannon Collen *medical/surgical nurse*
Juarez, Antonio *psychotherapist, counselor, consultant, educator*
Mitchell, Paula Rae *nursing educator, dean*
Moya, Eva M. *health services executive*

Fort Sam Houston
Todd, Reeder Allen *pharmacist*

Fort Worth
Adams, Lavonne Marilyn Beck *critical care nurse, educator*
Dunn, Connie *lab administrator, educator*
Hong, Xin *optometrist*
Isik, Tela Mae *obstetrical/gynecological nurse practitioner*
Pettit, George Hunter *lab administrator, researcher*
Thomas, Frank Nelson *family therapist*
Wall, G. Michael *medical chemist*

Galveston
Munsell, Debra S. *physician assistant, educator*
Nash, Kathleen *nursing educator*
Protas, Elizabeth J. *physical therapist, academic administrator*

Garland
Kemp, Pamela Jean *marriage and family therapist*

Georgetown
Smitheram, Margaret Etheridge *health facility administrator, director*

Grand Prairie
Solomon, Arthur Charles *pharmacist*

Harlingen
Llerandi Phipps, Carmen Guillermina *nutritionist and dietitian*

Helotes
Rojo, Ruth M. *nutritionist, consultant, director*

Hereford
Fangman, Karen Walker *school nurse practitioner*

Houston
Aboul-Enein, Faisal H. *family practice nurse practitioner, educator*
Arafat, Raouf Raafat *public health service officer*
Bahl, Saroj Mehta *nutritionist, educator*
Battin, R. Ray (Rosabell Harriet Ray) *audiologist, neuropsychologist*
Bryan Green, Meva *hospital administrator, educator*
Callender, Norma Anne *counselor, public relations executive*
Demory-Luce, Debby Kay *dietitian, consultant*
Engebretson, Joan C. *nursing educator*
Fine, David Jeffrey *hospital administrator, educator*
Girotto, Ronald G. *hospital administrator*
Gunn, Joan Marie *health facility administrator*
Hanneman, Sandra K. Goodnough *nursing educator, researcher*
Hanrahan, Lawrence Martin *healthcare consultant*
Hawkins, Barbara Reed *mental health nurse*
Hempfling, Linda Lee *nurse*
Holmes, Harry Dadisman *health care administrator*
Jhin, Michael Kontien *healthcare executive*
Johnson, Sandra Ann *counselor, educator*
Josehart, Carl *rehabilitation hospital administrator*
Kajander, John *hospital administrator*
Lewis, Russell E. *pharmacist, educator*
Montgomery, Denise Karen *nurse*
Peabody, Arlene L. Howland Bayar *retired enterostomal therapy nurse*
Potluri, Venkateswara Rao *medical facility administrator*
Reed, Kathlyn Louise *occupational therapist, educator*
Robbins, Susan Paula *social work educator*
Schultze, Deborah *healthcare educator*
Shaffer, Anita Mohrland *counselor, educator*
Shiao, Shyang-Yun Pamela K. *nursing educator, researcher*
Simon-Campbell, E'Loria *nursing educator*
Spikes, Patricia White *medical technologist*
Wagener, Christine Elizabeth *psychotherapist, educator*
Wallace, Mark Allen *hospital administrator*

Joaquin
Gill, Madeline Kay *counselor*

Keene
Taroy-Valdez, Lolita B. *nursing educator*

Laredo
Cepeda, Carmen Griselda *nurse*
Chavez, Mary Rose *counselor, educator*

Lubbock
Ashcraft, Alyce Smithson *nursing educator*
Valle-Garcia, Esteban *social worker*
Yoder-Wise, Patricia Snyder *nursing educator*

Mcallen
Arredondo, Jenna Dolores *speech pathology/audiology services professional*
Countryman, Karen Sue *nurse, educator*

Midland
Fredrickson, Mark Allan *health facility administrator, physiatrist*
Syed, Elizabeth Chance *health facility administrator, critical care nurse*

Missouri City
Starnes, Katie Gerard *retired community health nurse*

Normangee
Rector, M. Eugene *community pharmacist*

Odessa
Kipple, Mary Elizabeth *nursing educator*

Panhandle
Sherrod, Lloyd Bruce *retired nutritionist*

Pasadena
Kenagy, Cheri Lynn *nurse*

Plainview
Pitts, Sharon Ann Gammage *nursing director*

Plano
Becker, Doreen Doris *medical/surgical nurse*
Shelton, James D. (Denny Shelton) *hospital investment company executive*

Red Oak
Jones, Genia Kay *critical care nurse, consultant*

Richardson
Byrd, Ellen Stoesser *school nurse practitioner*
Kaplan-Thornton, Karen Ellen *speech pathology/audiology services professional, educator*

Rowlett
Openshaw, Linda Leek *social worker, educator*

San Angelo
Chatfield, Mary Van Abshoven *independent researcher*

San Antonio
Avant, Patricia Kay *nursing educator*
Bellanger, Renee A. *pharmacist, educator*
Crabtree, Ben C. *neuromuscular therapy clinic director*
Downing, Jane Katherine *psychiatric nurse, lawyer*
Durbin, Richard Louis, Sr. *health facility administrator, consultant*
Fisher, Dierdre Denise *mental health nurse, administrator, educator*
Gonzalez, Hector Hugo *nursing educator*
Lin, Ai-Ling *medical physicist, researcher in neuroscience and neuroimaging*
Nelson, James Harold *health sciences administrator*
Ramirez, Amelie G. *health facility administrator, director*
Ratliff, Dan A. *marriage and family therapist, educator*
Robertson, Samuel Luther, Jr. *psychotherapist, educator*
Skelley, Dean Sutherland *clinical laboratory administrator*
Vadlamudi, Ratna K. *healthcare educator*
Walsh, Nicolas Eugene *rehabilitation services professional, educator*

San Marcos
Nauert, Rick *healthcare educator, consultant*

Snyder
Barnes, Maggie Lue Shifflett (Mrs. Lawrence Barnes) *nurse*

Spur
Warren, Jennifer Elizabeth *family nurse practitioner*

Sugar Land
Heitzenrater, James F. *hospital administrator*
Kakkanatt, George Mathew *psychotherapist, consultant*
Wagner, Donald Bert *health facility administrator*

Temple
Furst, Cari Michelle *nursing educator*
Northrup, Jason *marriage and family therapist*

Texarkana
Bertrand, Betty Harleen *nurse*

Tyler
Mastern, Dean Scott *personal growth and development consultant*

Waller
Evans, Nancy Peltier *behavioral specialist, educator*

Woodway
Packard, Joyce Hornaday *retired counselor*

UTAH

Centerfield
Parkin, Fern Agnes Marvel *medical/surgical nurse, educator*

Orem
Takke, Karyn Coppock *social worker, educator*

Salt Lake City
Hull, Grafton Hazard, Jr. *social work educator*
Melton, Arthur Richard *public health administrator*
Speer, William Dale *lab administrator, biology professor*

West Jordan
Gutman, Lucy Toni *social worker, educator*

VERMONT

Brattleboro
Smiley, Carol Anne *health facility administrator, sculptor*

Burlington
Carew, Lyndon B., Jr. *nutritionist, educator*
Drizo, Aleksandra *researcher, educator*

Putney
Gill, Jane Roberts *retired psychotherapist, clinical social worker*

VIRGINIA

Alexandria
Ebi, Kristie L. *consultant*
Hausner, Laurence *health science association administrator*
Pastin, Mark Joseph *health science association administrator, educator*
Shern, David L. *mental health services professional, former dean*

Arlington
Hickman, Elizabeth Podesta *retired counselor*
Kerns, Wilmer Lee *researcher*
Stombler, Robin *health science association administrator*

Blacksburg
Serrano, Elena Lidia *nutritionist, educator*

Charlottesville
Wiggins, Barbara Sue *pharmacist, educator*

Chesapeake
Hudgins, Paul Granville *health facility administrator*

Clifton Forge
Miller, Catherine H. *nursing administrator, property manager*

Crozet
Detmer, Don Eugene *health informatics, management and policy researcher*

Culpeper
Goddard, Frances Byrd *clinical social worker*

Daleville
Kinzie, Brenda Asburry *counselor*

Fairfax
Dutch, Nicole M. *researcher*

Fairfax Station
Barringer, Joan Marie *counselor, educator, artist, writer*

Farmville
Terry, Wayne Gilbert *healthcare educator, hospital administrator*

Hampton
Barrow, Irene Marie *speech pathology educator*
Wechsler, Toni *healthcare educator, writer*

Harrisonburg
Johnson, Kia Noelle *speech pathology/audiology services professional, educator*

Lynchburg
Pursley, Frank James *retired personal development specialist*

Mc Lean
Filerman, Gary Lewis *healthcare educator*

Purcellville
Grob, George Frederick *independent program evaluator*

Reston
Brown, Dudley Earl, Jr. *retired health science association and federal agency administrator, retired military officer*

Richlands
Sullivan, Sheila C. *critical care nurse, educator*

Richmond
Ballentine, Ron *pharmacist, educator*
Balster, Robert Louis *Alcohol/Drug Abuse Educator Researcher*
Bovender, Jack Oliver, Jr. *hospital management company executive*
Gandy, Gerald Larmon *rehabilitation counseling educator, psychologist, writer*
Glasser, Wolfgang Gerhard *science researcher, educator*
Izyumskaya, Natalia *researcher*
Marshall Traino, Heather M. *researcher*
Neal, Gail Fallon *physical therapist, educator*
Shall, Mary Snyder *physical therapist, educator*

Roanoke
Dagenhart, Betty Jane Mahaffey *nursing educator, administrator*

Springfield
Dake, Marcia Allene *retired nursing educator, dean*
Shoemake, Angela Nichole *nursing educator*
Williams, Cecilia Lee Pursel *optometrist*

Verona
Grizzel, Patsy (Pat) Pauline *human services administrator*

Virginia Beach
Carlson, James G. *healthcare services executive*
Chalk, Barbara Ann *surgical nurse*

Williamsburg
Farrar, John Thruston *health facility administrator*
Ringlesbach, Dorothy Louise *retired nurse, writer*

Winchester
Rahman, Ateequr *pharmacist, educator*

Woodbridge
Flori, Anna Marie DiBlasi *health facility administrator, nurse, anesthesiologist*

WASHINGTON

Bellevue
Lynch, Juneann M. *medical/surgical nurse, nursing educator*
Swailes, Heidi Robin *counselor*

Camano Island
Hartley, Celia Love *author, consultant, retired nursing educator, administrator*

Centralia
Gimbel, Hervey Willis *public health physician, medical administrator*

Federal Way
Blywise, Barbara *mental health services professional*

Issaquah
Curre, Cora Lee *medical laboratory manager*

Kent
Dumitrescu, Cristina M. *intensive care nurse*

Langley
Cammermeyer, Margarethe *retired medical/surgical nurse*

Lynnwood
Sandahl, Bonnie Beardsley *nursing administrator*

Oak Harbor
Miller, Robert Scott *clinical social worker, project manager*

Olympia
Hayes, Maxine Delores *public health service officer, physician, pediatrician*

Pullman
Campbell, R. Keith *pharmacist, educator*
Espinola-Arredondo, Ana *researcher*
McNamara, John Patrick *nutritionist, educator*
Shen, Shihui *research assistant*

Redmond
Hardin, Bryan David *occupational safety and health specialist*

Seattle
Berni, Rosemarian Rauch *rehabilitation and oncology nurse*
Dear, Ronald Bruce *retired social work educator*
Hansen, Thomas Nanastad *hospital administrator, pediatrician*
Hansten, Philip Douglas *pharmacist, educator*
Kates, Carolyn Louise *physical therapist*
Lynass, Lori *researcher*
Nelson, Arleen Bruce *social worker*
Neuhouser, Marian L. *nutritionist, researcher*
Ramsey, Scott D. *researcher, educator*
Sin, Mo-Kyung *nurse*
Smith-DiJulio, Kathleen *psychosocial clinical nurse specialist*
Woods, Nancy Fugate *nursing educator*
Zieniewicz, Stephen *hospital administrator*

Snohomish
Hill, Valerie Charlotte *nurse*

Spokane
Robinson, Herbert Henry III *psychotherapist, educator*

Tacoma
Houston, Phillip Thomas *social worker*
McGraw, Leigh Kyle *family practice nurse practitioner, researcher*

Wenatchee
Reilly, Joan *nursing educator*

WEST VIRGINIA

Charleston
Alkhateeb, Fadi Mohammad Ali *pharmacist, educator*

Elkins
Cruz, Lora N. *mental health nurse, educator*

Hedgesville
Boland, Gerald Lee *health facility administrator*

Huntington
Confer, Jennifer *pharmacist, educator*
Wietholter, Jon Patrick *pharmacist, educator*

Martinsburg
Foley, Diana Kay Teets *mental health nurse, educator*

Morgantown
Collins, James William *health science association administrator, epidemiologist, mechanical engineer*
Stout, Nancy Ann *health science association administrator, director*

Parkersburg
Wilson, Roberta Bush *retired psychotherapist, accountant*

Ranson
Rudacille, Sharon Victoria *medical technician*

West Liberty
Domyan, Steve Richard *audiologist, educator*

White Sulphur Springs
Henry, Cynthia Ann *retired gerontology nurse, educator*

WISCONSIN

Brookfield
Rooney, Carol Bruns *dietitian*

Eau Claire
Brill, Donald Maxim *researcher, educator*
Kirkhorn, Lee-Ellen Charlotte *community health nurse, educator*

Franklin
Stenzel, Mary Francis *social worker*
Tittl, Matthew Paul *medical technician, educator*

La Crosse
Byom, Carolyn E. *lab administrator*

Land O Lakes
Sharpee, Rhoda Anderson *social worker*

Madison
Derzon, Gordon M. *hospital administrator*
Jacobsen, Kendra *health facility administrator*
Johnson, Jean Elaine *nursing educator*
Katen-Bahensky, Donna *health facility administrator*
Marlett, Judith Ann *nutritional sciences educator, researcher*

Marinette
Ceccarelli, Michael Paul *technologist*

Marshfield
Balz, Jean Arlynn *physician assistant*

Milwaukee
Eshetu, Gwendelbert Lewis *retired social worker*
Stoffel, Virginia Carroll *occupational therapist, educator*
Winters, Jill Mary *nursing educator, director*

New Berlin
Winkler, Dolores Eugenia *retired health facility administrator*

Oshkosh
Turnmeyer, Denise L. *pediatrics nurse, educator*

Pewaukee
Johnson, Patricia Lynn *nursing educator*

Racine
Baker, Joyce Mildred *medical/surgical nurse, volunteer*

Watertown
Schott, Katharine Sue *nursing educator*

Whitewater
Choi, Sang D. *researcher, educator*

WYOMING

Casper
Hartsock, Jane Marie *nurse, educator*

Laramie
Schatz, Mona Claire Struhsaker *social worker, educator, consultant, researcher*

Rock Springs
Thompson, Josie *nurse*

Wilson
Hall, Zach Winter *former scientist and research administrator*

TERRITORIES OF THE UNITED STATES

GUAM

Tamuning
Cahinhinan, Nelia Agbada *retired public health nurse, health facility administrator*

PUERTO RICO

San Juan
Almodovar, Edna *pharmacist, educator*
Ortiz, Alexis *physical therapist, educator*

Santa Isabel
Lugo-Paoli, Luz Minerva *counselor, educator*

VIRGIN ISLANDS

Charlotte Amalie
Garfield, Winifred L. *nursing administrator*

Christiansted
Christian, Cora L.E *health facility administrator, physician*

CANADA

ONTARIO

Etobicoke
Scholefield, Peter Gordon *health facility administrator*

Toronto
Turnbull, John Cameron *retired pharmacist, consultant*
Doolittle-Romas, Monique *health science association administrator*

QUEBEC

Montreal
Limperopoulos, Catherine *occupational therapist, researcher*

MEXICO

Alvaro Obregon
Sepúlveda Amor, Jaime *public health service officer*

AUSTRALIA

New Farm
Ward, Megan Mae *yoga therapist*

BAHRAIN

Manama
Al-Salman, Jameela M.R. *public health service officer, consultant*

BRAZIL

Ribeirao Preto
Roque, Eliana Mendes S. Teixeira *social worker, educator*

São Paulo
Riecken, Claudia *researcher, director*

CHINA

Dalian
Zhao, Zhongkui *researcher*

ENGLAND

London
de Savorgnani, Adriane Aldrich *healthcare administrator, nurse*

FRANCE

Amiens
Barpanda, Prabeer *researcher*

INDIA

Chennai
Punnoose, A. John *hospital administrator*

JAPAN

Kyoto
Tsuji, Toshizo *hospital administrator, educator*

LATVIA

Riga
Lācis, Aris *health facility administrator, cardiac surgeon*

PAKISTAN

Karachi
Khan, Nadeem Kamal Mustafa *health facility administrator, accountant*

PHILIPPINES

Quezon City
Maglacas, A. Mangay *nursing researcher, educator*

REPUBLIC OF KOREA

Cheongju
Yeun, Eunja *nursing educator, director*

Gyungsangnamdo Masan
Seo, Yoo-jin *occupational health educator*

Seoul
Yoo, Vak Yeong *health facility administrator*

Uiwang
Hwang, Jong-Gyu *researcher, electrical engineer*

SINGAPORE

Singapore
Aung, Naing Naing *technologist, researcher*

SWITZERLAND

Bern
Shaha, Maya *nursing educator*

Bulle
Haeusler, Jean-Marc C. *global medical director*

ZAMBIA

Nangoma
Hansen, Florence Marie Congiolosi (Mrs. James S. Hansen) *social worker*

ADDRESS UNPUBLISHED

Abdellah, Faye Glenn *retired public health service officer*
Acheampong, Joseph Kofi *pharmacist, researcher*
Ackermann, Barbara Bogel *counselor*
Adair, Irmalee Traylor *social worker*
Ader, Pauletta *technologist*
Adesogan, Adegbola *nutritionist, educator*
Aehlert, Barbara June *health facility administrator*
Agar, Beatrice Arlene *nutritionist, educator*
Aigen, Betsy P. *psychotherapist*
Alford, Renee Marie *speech pathology/audiology services professional, educator*
Alvarez-Galloso, Roberto C. *mental health professional*
Anderson, Allamay Eudoris *retired health educator, home economist*
Anderson, Linda Jean *critical care nurse, psychiatric nurse practitioner*
Aon, Frank Joseph Garcia *lab administrator, materials scientist*
Aouizerat, Bradley Eric *nursing educator*
Arcus, Sam George *social worker, educator, author and writer*
Arif, Sally A. *pharmacist, educator*
Arking, Lucille Musser *nurse, epidemiologist, consultant*
Armbruster, Paula *social worker, director, child mental health educator*
Arnold, Janet Nina *health facility administrator, consultant*
Avinor, Eleanor Zeitlen *marriage and family therapist*
Baier, Edward John *retired public health service officer, industrial hygiene engineer, consultant*
Bailey, Margaret Elizabeth *nurse, retired military officer*
Bain, Kevin T. *pharmacist, educator*
Baker, Bonnie *nursing educator*
Baker, John David *health facility administrator, not-for-profit fundraiser, real estate agent*
Baldwin, William Russell *optometrist, foundation administrator*
Balish, Ruth Reitz *retired community health nurse*
Ball, John Robert *healthcare executive*
Barker, Virginia Lee *nursing educator*
Bass, Lynda D. *retired medical/surgical nurse, nursing educator*
Bates, Gwen Lee *health facility administrator, consultant*
Batman, Keith *healthcare educator*
Baymiller, Lynda Doern *social worker*
Bear, Geraldine M. *nursing assistant, poet*
Becker, Nancy May *nursing educator*
Beckerman, Nancy Lisa *psychotherapist, educator*
Bell, Susan Jane *nurse*
Benyshek, Denita Maree *psychotherapist, educator, artist*
Berardi, John M. *nutritionist, educator*
Berman, Richard Angel *health facility administrator*
Berra, Kathy *rehabilitation nurse, researcher*
Berry, Sharon *medical/surgical nurse, legal nurse consultant*
Beyer, Norma H. *nursing educator*
Biegel, David Eli *social worker, educator*
Binnie, Nancy Catherine *retired nurse, educator*
Bircher, Andrea Ursula *retired psychiatric mental health clinical nurse specialist*
Bishop, Anne Hughes *retired nursing educator*
Blacher, Joan Helen *psychotherapist, educator*
Blake, Kimberly Bosworth *pharmacist*
Blumberg, Mark Stuart *health service researcher, scientist, director*
Bockius, Ruth Bear *nursing educator*
Bohanon, Kathleen Sue *neonatologist*
Bollinger, Sharon Moore *psychotherapist*
Boone, Donna Clausen *physical therapist, statistician, researcher*
Botkin, James W. *leadership and executive coach*
Bowman, Ned David *medical administrator*
Boyd, Mary Frances *retired school nurse, pastor*
Boyer, Albert Bruce *optometrist, educator*
Boyte, Harry Chatten *social worker, director*
Braun, Mary Lucile Dekle (Lucy Braun) *psychotherapist, counseling administrator, educator*
Brayer, Edith Marie *marriage and family therapist, consultant*

Brewer, Barbara Bagdasarian *nursing administrator*
Broughton, Hazel Callen *rehabilitation counselor, consultant*
Brown, Alberta Mae *nurse*
Brown, Barbara June *hospital and nursing administrator*
Brown, Geraldine *nurse, freelance writer*
Brown, Laima Adomaitis *art therapist, artist, writer*
Brown, Viseeta *health science association administrator*
Bryant, Bertha Estelle *retired medical/surgical nurse*
Buckley, John Joseph, Jr. *healthcare executive*
Burgher Schweppe, Pauline Menefee *retired marriage and family therapist*
Burgstaler, Edwin Allen *medical technologist*
Bussabarger, Mary Louise *mental health services professional*
Buzard, James Albert *biomedical start-up consultant*
Campbell, Charles Edward *scientist, opthalmic consultant*
Campbell, Judy *medical/surgical nurse, educator*
Campbell, Reginna Gladys *medical/surgical nurse*
Canny, Priscilla Forney *senior vice president*
Carpenter, Denise A. *social worker*
Carpentieri, Sarah C. *neuropsychologist, researcher, clinical psychologist*
Carr, Mindy Lea *healthcare educator*
Carr, Patricia Ann *community health nurse*
Carson, Regina E. *healthcare administrator, geriatric specialist*
Carter, Melva Jean *retired medical technician*
Cason, Nica Virginia *retired nursing educator*
Cassagnol, Manouchkathe *pharmacist, educator*
Centafont, Lucy Ann Alexander *occupational therapist, consultant*
Chalikian, Alice Beatrice *chiropractor*
Chang, Yun Kyung *researcher*
Charles, Luenda E. *public health service officer, researcher*
Chase, Sandra Lee *clinical pharmacist, consultant*
Chodorow, Nancy Julia *psychoanalyst, educator*
Cholewka, Patricia Anne *nursing educator*
Choo, Christie *pharmacist, educator*
Chow, Rita Kathleen *nursing consultant*
Cianciosa, Carolyn Lucy *radiologic technologist, educator*
Ciesielka, Debbie *nurse, educator*
Clarkson, Charles Eugene *medical technician*
Coleman, Jean Black *nurse, physician assistant*
Collins, Terry *health educator*
Collins-McNeil, Janice *nursing professor, researcher*
Compton, Diane Groat *professional counselor, researcher*
Condry, Robert Stewart *retired hospital administrator*
Conte, Julie Villa *nurse, administrator*
Cooper, Eugene Bruce *speech pathology/audiology services professional, educator*
Cooperman, Jack Morris *nutrition educator*
Couch, Daniel Michael *healthcare executive*
Cowles, Lois Anne Fort *social worker, educator, poet*
Cox, Tiffany L. *researcher*
Craig, Carol Mills *marriage, family and child counselor*
Crawford, Mallory *counselor*
Cromwell, Florence Stevens *occupational therapist*
Crowder, Heather Elizabeth *mental health services professional, consultant*
Cruz, Theresa Lavaina *mental health services professional, educator*
Cunningham, Terence Thomas III *hospital administrator*
Daniels, Lydia M. *health care administrator*
Davis, Donald Robert *nutritionist, researcher, consultant*
Davis, Katherine Sarah *physical therapist*
Davis, Linda Lennon McConnell *critical care nurse*
Davis, Samuel *hospital administrator, educator, consultant*
De Antoni, Edward Paul *retired lab administrator*
DeBrincat, Susan Jeanne *nutritionist*
Decker, Josephine I. *health clinic official*
Dee, Brian Michael *pharmacist*
Deiro, Judith Anne *chemical dependency educator*
DeLapp, Tina Davis *retired nursing educator*
Deng, Shaoping *lab administrator, director*
Dickens, Joyce Rebecca *retired addictions therapist, educator*
DiCristino, Dia *health facility administrator*
DiLiberto, Frank E. *physical therapist*
Dimaira, Ann B. *medical/surgical nurse*
Dincecco, Jennie Elizabeth Williams Swanson *healthcare administrator, mentor, educator, volunteer*
Doberenz, Alexander R. *retired nutrition educator, chemist*
Dodgen, Daniel W. *health policy advisor, psychologist*
Dohn, Julianne *child protective services specialist*
Donna, Stewart *researcher*
Doten, David R. *social worker*
Dow, William Hatfield *healthcare educator*
Drews, Jürgen *pharmaceutical researcher*
Duerksen, George Louis *music therapist, educator*
Dumas, Sandra Lee *medical technician, microbiologist*
Dunn, Patricia C. *retired social work educator*
Durkee, Dianna *medical/surgical nurse*
Dye, Sharon Elizabeth Herndon *speech pathologist*
Dyer, Wayne Walter *psychologist, writer, radio and television personality*
Dy-Liacco, Gabriel S. *psychotherapist, social sciences educator*
Earhart, Gammon M. *physical therapist, researcher*
Eaton, Shirley M. *medical/surgical nurse*
Edelsberg, Sally Comins *retired physical therapist, educator*
Eick-Gamm, Kimberly Marie *social worker*
Eimers, Jeri Anne *retired counselor*
Eisenberg, Patricia Lee *medical/surgical nurse*
Elkins, Kathryn Marie *alcohol/drug abuse services professional, recreational therapist*
Eltayeb, Emil *pharmacist, researcher*
English, Patricia Dorzell *women's health nurse practitioner*
Ewing, Mary Eileen *radiologic technologist*
Farber, Roselee Cora *counselor*
Farrington, Bertha Louise *retired nursing administrator*
Ferencz, Nicholas *pharmacist, educator*
Ferguson, Jeannette E. *research technician*
Fields, Velma Archie *retired medical/surgical nurse*
Fierman, Ella Yensen *retired psychotherapist*
Finley, Sarah Maude Merritt *retired social worker*
Fischbach, Cheryl L. *nursing educator*
Fischer, Carl Robert *retired health facility administrator*
Flanagan, Nancy A. *nursing educator, researcher*
Floyd, William R. *former health facility administrator*
Fogelman, Ann Florence *nutrition consultant, educator, researcher*
Fondiller, Shirley Hope Alperin *nursing educator, journalist, historian*
Foreman, Spencer (Spike Foreman) *retired hospital administrator, pulmonologist*
Forest, Eva Brown *retired nursing home supervisor, composer*
Foster, Deborah Megivern *counselor, consultant*
Fralix Gold, Carolyn M. *medical/surgical nurse, educator, consultant*
Frederick-Mairs, T(hyra) Julie *administrative health services official*
Fuhr, Patti Sue Wimbs *optometrist, director*
Garcia y Carrillo, Martha Xochitl *pharmacist*
Gardenhire, Douglas Shawn *health facility administrator*
Garland, Elsie M. *adolescent and family violence counselor*
Garner, Algean, II, *healthcare company administrator, consultant*
Garrido, Terhilda *health science association administrator, consultant*
Garza, Cutberto *nutrition educator*
Gaudio, Maxine Diane *biofeedback therapist, stress management consultant*
Gelman, Deborah *healthcare educator*
Geraci, Matthew James *pharmacist*
Giberson, Joan Alyne *retired school nurse*
Giles, Melva Theresa *nursing educator*
Gimenes, Sonia Regina Rosendo *family therapist, psychologist*
Gladden, Vivianne Cervantes *healthcare consultant, writer*
Glover, Sherry Register *nursing educator*
Goldberg, Edwin *rehabilitation specialist, interfaith clergyman*
Goldberg, Lois D. *health facility administrator, disability analyst*
Good, Laurance Frederic *retired hospital administrator*
Gottlieb, Gary L. *hospital administrator, psychiatrist*
Grachek, Marianna Kern *healthcare administrator*
Graham, Jewel Freeman *social worker, lawyer, educator*
Graham, Joy Francine *pediatric clinical nurse specialist*
Graham, Olive Jane *retired medical/surgical nurse*
Grant, Richard Earl *retired medical and legal consultant*
Greene, Lynne Jeannette *wellness consultant, artist*
Grenier, Laura Margiotta *medical/surgical nurse*
Griffith, Douglas *research scientist*
Hadley, Susan *health educator*
Hammond, Robie Lee *health science association administrator*
Harbaugh, Janice M. *counselor, consultant*
Harms, Nancy Ann *nursing educator*
Harrell, Richard Godwin *alcohol/drug abuse services professional*
Harris, Erica Renee *researcher*
Hartling, Linda M. *human services administrator, researcher*
Harwell, Denise *researcher*
Hayden, Paul Allan *speech pathology educator, consultant, researcher*
Haynes, Kevin *pharmacist, researcher*
Heatherley, James Lawrence *psychotherapist, educator*
Heck, Jennifer Leigh *neonatal clinical nurse specialist, educator*
Hedrick, Amy *health facility administrator, educator*
Henley, Richard James *health facility administrator*
Herlihy-Chevalier, Barbara Doyle *retired mental health nurse*
Hickman, Lucille *physical therapist*
Hicks, Allen Morley *retired hospital administrator*
Hines, Colleen M. *clinical nurse specialist*
Hofmann, Paul Bernard *healthcare consultant*
Homer, Melodie Antonette *clinical nursing instructor*
Horvath, Annette *home care administrator*
Hot, Aliya *optometrist, educator*
Houtz, Duane Talbott *hospital administrator*
Howard, John W.S. *mental health services professional, alcohol/drug abuse services professional, theology studies educator*
Howe, John Prentice III *health facility administrator, physician*
Howell, Embry Martin *researcher*
Huey, Constance Anne Berner *mental health counselor*
Hunt, Andrea Wheaton *nurse*
Hutchinson, Edna M. *home care nurse*
Iles, Warthell Browne *retired nursing educator, consultant*
Iriart, Celia Beatriz *public health specialist, consultant, researcher, sociologist*
Isaac, Carol A. *physical therapist, researcher*
Ivey, Mary Bradford *counselor, vice president*
Jacobs, Arthur Dietrich *health services executive, educator, researcher*
Jacoby, Erika *social worker*
Janczewski, Colleen *social worker*
Janke, Norma E. *legal nursing consultant*
Jenai, Marilyn *psychotherapist*
Jensen, Eva Marie *medical/surgical nurse*
Johnson, Hazel Winifred *nurse, retired army officer*
Johnson, Nichole Sharese *school nurse practitioner, basketball coach*
Johnson, Patricia B. *retired surgical and mental health nurse*
Johnson, Sally A. *nurse, educator*
Johnson-Ferrell, June Alexis *counselor, social worker*
Jones, Lisa Maria Draper *counselor*
Jones, Wayne Allen *psychotherapist, publisher*
Jordan, Deovina Nasis *nursing administrator, educator*
Kacines, Juliette Rosette *dialectical behavior therapist*
Kamel, Haidy Nasr *pharmacist*
Kaminski, Patricia Joyce *lab administrator*
Karp, Rosanne *oncology and women's health nurse*
Katazkos, Victoria Elena *nurse*
Kelly, Lucie Stirm Young *retired nursing educator*
Kendrick, Beverly Ann *medical/surgical nurse, small business owner*
Kennan, Dan *counselor*
Kerr, Frederick Hohmann *retired health facility and academic administrator*
Kezlarian, Nancy Kay *marriage and family therapist*
King, Sheldon Selig *health facility administrator, educator*
Kirsch, Nancy Rosenthal *physical therapist, educator*
Kline, Leona Ruth *nurse, volunteer*
Knefel, Ann Margaret *researcher*
Knies, Robert Carl, Jr. *critical care nurse*
Kohn, Jean Gatewood *retired health facility administrator, pediatrician*
Koperski, Nanci Carol *legal nurse consultant, women's health nurse*
Kroske, Mary Louise *family practice nurse practitioner*
Kuhler, Deborah Gail *grief therapist, former state legislator*
Kuo, Chun-Fang Frank *counselor, educator*
Lachapelle, Cleo Edward *retired social worker, real estate broker*
Laird, Cheryl F. *mental health services professional, paralegal*
Lancaster, Carroll Townes, Jr. *health services executive*
Landgarten, Helen Barbara *art psychotherapist, educator*
Langenkamp, Sandra Carroll *retired human services administrator*
Lanterman, Jennifer L. *researcher, educator*
Lass, Diane *marriage and family therapist*
Latta, George Haworth III *neonatal/perinatal nurse practitioner*
Leath, Mary Elizabeth *medical/surgical nurse*
Lebowitz, Charlotte Meyersohn *social worker*
Lee, Jongdoo *researcher*
Lenden-Holt, Jessica Marie *speech pathology/audiology services professional*
Leon, Nellie *health educator*
Lev, Elise L. *nursing educator*
Lilly-Hersley, Jane Anne Feeley *nursing researcher*
Lindstrom, Rosetta Arline *retired medical technician*
Lofton, Kevin Eugene *medical facility administrator*
Lovvorn, Audrey Marie *mental health therapist*
Lubic, Ruth Watson *health facility administrator, nurse midwife*
Luddy, Paula Scott *nursing educator*
Lutz, Tamara Jean *nursing consultant*
Lysne, Allen Bruce *laboratory director*
Mackay, Leo Sidney, Jr. *healthcare company executive, former federal agency administrator*
MacKenzie, Donald Murray *health facility administrator*
Madrid, Cirilo L. *health facility administrator*
Magee, Elaine *dietician, consultant*
Magnan, Morris Allen *nursing researcher, educator*
Malks, Betty F. *social worker*
Manner, Jennifer Fouse *social worker*
Maplesden, Carol Harper *marriage and family therapist, music educator*
Markel, Anna *pharmacist, educator*
Martin, William Collier *hospital administrator*
Materia, Kathleen Patricia Ayling *nurse*
Mates, Lawrence A., II, *medical company executive, consultant*
Matterson, Joan McDevitt *physical therapist*
Mazak, Arlene Patricia *marriage and family therapist*
McCormick, Joseph B. *healthcare educator*
McCuistion, Peg Orem *retired health facility administrator*
Mc Donald, Shirley Peterson *social worker*
McGee, Stacie *social worker, educator*
McKay, Michael Kevin *nurse, priest, chaplain*
McKay, Paul Patrick *healthcare educator*
McKeever-Thompson, Claire L. *nurse, educator, consultant, human services manager*
McLaughlin, Frank E. *nursing educator*
McNulty, Kathleen Anne *social worker, consultant, psychologist*
McPhearson, Geraldine June *retired medical/surgical nurse*
Meacham, Susan *dietician, educator*
Mecklenburg, Gary Alan *retired hospital administrator*
Medders, Emily Anna *speech pathology/audiology services professional*
Medina, Sandra *social worker, educator*
Meredith, Thomas Brian *healthcare consultant*
Mersfelder, Tracey *pharmacist, educator*
Mestel, Sherry Y. *social worker, school psychologist, art therapist*
Meyer, Charlotte Lois *medical geriatric social worker, consultant*
Meyer, Dorothy Jean *nursing consultant, director*
Michael, Jerrold Mark *public health service officer, educator, retired dean*
Michel, Mary Ann Kedzuf *retired nursing educator*
Mick, Diane Joan *nurse*
Milnor, Hazel *nurse*
Milunas, J. Robert *health care organization executive*
Milway, Phyllis Louise *human services manager*
Miracle, Doris Jean *retired medical/surgical nurse*
Misrack, Tana Marie *counselor, minister, writer*
Mitchell, Carol Ann *nursing educator*
Moenssens, Sandra Birkelbach *licensed marriage and family therapist, licensed mental health counselor*
Monsen, Elaine Ranker *nutritionist, educator, editor*
Moon, Loretta Marie *recreational therapist*
Mooney, Robert Thurston *healthcare educator*
Moore, Jean E. *social worker, academic administrator, educator, radio personality*
Mulvey, Victoria A. *counselor*
Muñoz Dones De Carrascal, Eloisa (Eloise Munoz Dones) *hospital administrator, pediatrician, educator*
Munro, Barbara Hazard *retired nursing educator, dean, researcher*
Murphy, Stacia *former health service association executive*
Murray, Julia Kaoru (Mrs. Joseph E. Murray) *occupational therapist*
Naes, Jennifer Le *medical technologist*
Nelson, Alice Carlstedt *retired nursing educator*
Nelson, Delores Privette *nurse*
Neumann, Forrest Karl *retired health facility administrator*
Norbeck, Jane S. *retired nursing educator*
Norkin, Cynthia Clair *retired physical therapist*
Oakes, Ellen Ruth *psychotherapist, health facility administrator*
O'Baire-Kark, Marika *nurse, educator, writer*
Obot, Isidore Silas *public health scholar*
O'Brien, Denise Diane *medical/surgical nurse, perianesthesia nurse*
O'Connor, R. D. *retired healthcare executive*
Oerter, Cynthia Lynn *medical technologist*
Olgin, Gregory B. *pharmacy technician, educator*
Ongkingco, Florence Kagahastian *health facility educator*
Paparella, Leon Ralph *psychotherapist, consultant*
Paps, Betty Lou *nursing educator*
Parker, Joel L. *nursing administrator*
Parks, Jean Anne *retired acute care nurse*
Paskawicz, Jeanne Frances *pain specialist*
Paudel, Kalpana S. *pharmacist, educator*
Pavone, Shirley A.
Pelham, Judith *health system administrator*
Pelletier, Elise M. *Director Health Economics & Outcames Reaserch*
Penrod, Marian Penuel *wellness consultant, retired school librarian*
Peper, Charlotte Ann *psychotherapist*
Pereiras, Maribel Alvara *pharmacist, educator*
Peringian, Lynda Ann *dietician, writer*
Peters, Douglas Alan *appeals nurse supervisor*
Peterson, Steven W. *neonatal nurse*
Phansalkar, Shobha *health facility administrator, researcher*
Phillips, Caroline L. *lab administrator*
Pickett, Eugenia Valdivia *retired social worker*
Plauche, Nancy Caroline *retired counselor*
Plumb, Marjorie Jane *social worker, consultant*
Podkul, Theodore B., Jr. *healthcare executive*
Poirier, Therese Irene *pharmacist, pharmacy educator*
Poulos, Clara Jean *retired nutritionist*
Prema, Nitya *marriage and family therapist, artist*
Quiala, Maribel *psychotherapist, consultant*
Rahming, Etta Lorraine *social worker, psychotherapist, school psychologist, consultant*
Raju, Minnie M. *application analyst, critical care nurse*
Ralston, Martha Jane *retired medical/surgical nurse*
Rand, Joella Mae *retired nursing educator, counselor*
Raphael, Carol *health care administrator*
Rastogi, Anjali *health care executive*
Rasu, Rafia S. *pharmacy and nursing educator researcher*
Raucher, Gary M. *psychotherapist, educator*
Ray, Marilyn Anne *nursing educator, researcher*
Reck, Elizabeth Torre *social worker, educator*
Rehth, Ann *counselor*
Reid, Dolores B. *retired social services administrator, consultant*
Reilly, Dinah *physical therapist*
Remkus, Connie Elaine *nutritional consultant*
Resnick, Elaine Bette *psychotherapist, licensed clinical social worker*
Ribley-Borck, Joan Grace *medical/surgical rehabilitation nurse*
Rice, Claretha Mayes *medical/surgical nurse, educator*
Rich, Karen *nursing educator*
Ritman, Barbara Ellen *counselor*
Robinson, Gail Patricia *retired mental health counselor*
Robinson, William Andrew *retired health service executive, physician*
Rogalski, Lois Ann *speech and language pathologist*
Rogers, Elizabeth London *retired geriatrics services professional*
Rollins, Diann Elizabeth *retired occupational health nurse, primary school educator, activist and advocator*
Romano, Joseph Anthony *healthcare education and marketing consultant*
Rosenthal, Howard Gary *psychotherapist, educator, author*
Royce, Paul Chadwick *healthcare administrator*
Rubin, Phyllis Getz *health association executive*
Rundquist, Elizabeth Ann *art therapist*
Sabatini, Nelson John *healthcare executive*
Sadow, Harvey S. *healthcare company executive*
Samolyk, Keith Andrew *cardiovascular perfusionist, director*
Sanders, Marion Yvonne *retired geriatrics nurse*
Santina, Dalia *nutritionist, writer, skin care specialist*
Savoy, Suzanne Marie *nursing educator*
Sawyer-Morse, Mary Kaye *nutritionist, educator*
Scala, James *health facility administrator, consultant, writer*
Scherer, Ronald Callaway *voice scientist, educator*
Schmidtke, Suzanne de Fine *retired social worker*
Schneider, Catherine Chemin *occupational therapist, consultant, writer*

Schneider, Phillip Harry Leonard (Phil Schneider) *healthcare organization executive*
Schroeder, LaVerne *medical/surgical nurse*
Sciuva, Margaret W. *counselor*
Scollard, Patrick John *hospital executive*
Scott-Battle, Gladys Natalie *retired social worker*
Sears, Sandra Jones *medical/surgical nurse, consultant*
Seymour, Daniel Keith *human services administrator*
Shannon, Mary Lou *adult health nursing educator*
Shaughnessy, Allen F. *pharmacist, educator*
Sheaffer, Suzanne Frances *geriatrics nurse*
Shen, Zheng-Xuan *researcher*
Shihabi, Zak K. *lab administrator, director*
Shilling, Lilless McPherson *healthcare educator*
Silver, Audrey Wilma *nurse, educator, writer*
Simon, Bernece Kern *retired social worker*
Simpson, Jack Benjamin *medical technologist, business executive*
Skarecky, Douglas William *lab administrator*
Sliesoraitis, Sarunas *pharmacist, educator*
Smith, Monica *chiropractor, researcher*
Somes, Joan Marie *emergency nurse practitioner*
Spottswood, Lydia Carol *nurse, health facility administrator*
Stadler, Selise McNeill *laboratory and x-ray technician, medical assistant*
Staivisky, Jeanne Louise *counselor, alcohol/drug abuse services professional*
Stein, Sandra Therese *pharmacist*
Stittich, Eleanor Maryann *retired nursing educator*
Stohlman, Connie Suzanne *neonatal intensive care unit nurse, obstetrical gynecological nurse*
Stoiber, Susanne A. *health science association administrator*
Storm, J. Reni *nurse, consultant*
Strange, Donald Ernest *healthcare company executive*
Stratton, Mariann *retired military nursing executive*
Sung, Kyu-Taik *social worker, gerontologist, educator, researcher*
Svoboda, Janice June *nurse*
Swann, Charena Rai *psychotherapist, social worker*
Talmadge, Mary Christine *nursing educator administrator*
Tanyuk, Kathryn Mary *medical/surgical nurse, educator*
Taylor, Cora Hodge *social worker*
Taylor, Edna Jane *retired employment program counselor*
Taylor, Nathalee Britton *retired nutritionist, freelance/self-employed writer*
Taylor-Dunn, Corliss Leslie *marriage and family therapist*
Terry, Frances Jefferson *retired psychiatric nurse practitioner*
Thacker, Patricia Ann *nursing educator*
Thrasher, Rose Marie *critical care and community health nurse*
Thurman, Cynthia Denise *former human services administrator, writer*
Tingstrum, Nancy Ash *dietitian*
Tocco, Elaine Kay *technical expert*
Torrie, Jane Marie *chiropractor, secondary school educator*
Townsend, Frances (Fran Townsend) *healthcare educator, writer*
Tyson, Lucille R. *health facility administrator, geriatrics nurse*
Upenieks, Valda V. *nursing educator*
Van Arsdale, Sharon A. *nurse*
Van de Bogart, Debra Scherwerts *medical/surgical nurse, researcher*
Van Dyke, Debbie K. *special education services professional*
Van Hoey, Nicole *pharmacist, writer*
Varner, Joyce McCullers *geriatric nurse practitioner, educator*
Vaughn-Daniels, Kymberly Louise *healthcare educator, consultant*
Vendé, Sandra *lab administrator*
Vladeck, Bruce Charney *healthcare consultant, former academic administrator*
Vogel, H. Victoria *psychotherapist, educator, writer, stress disorder and addiction recovery counselor*
Vohs, James Arthur *health plan administrator*
Vyas, Deepti *pharmacist*
Vyn, Eleanor Mears *physical therapist*
Wacker, Kelly Lynn *audiologist, educator*
Waddill, Cynthia Kay *orthopaedic nurse practitioner*
Walker, Philip Chamberlain, II, *retired health facility administrator*
Wall, Sonja Eloise *nursing administrator*
Wallerstein, Betty Cooper *clinical social worker, family therapist*
Walter, Patricia L. *psychotherapist, consultant*
Walters, Farah M. *health services company administrator, former hospital administrator*
Ward, Jacqueline Ann Beas *nurse, healthcare administrator, legal nurse consultant*
Warfel, M(artha) Kay *speech pathology/audiology services professional*
Warren, Daniel Churchman *health facility administrator*
Warwick, Margaret Ann *retired health science facility administrator, consultant*
Watson, Robert Joe *retired health facility administrator, retired career officer*
Webb, Katharine *counselor*
Weickert, Wanda Opal *child welfare and attendance counselor, psychotherapist, educator*
Weil, Thomas P. *retired health services consultant*
Weiss, Joan Oppenheimer *social worker, educator*
Weng, Daniella *pharmacist, researcher*
Wetherbe, Herbert John *pharmacist*
Wheeler, Cass (M. Cass. Wheeler) *healthcare consultant, former health science association administrator*
White-Means, Shelley *healthcare educator*
Williams, Barbara Kitty *nursing educator*
Williams, Elizabeth *human services administrator*
Williams, Freda Videll *speech pathology/audiology services professional*
Williams, Jatika *social worker, educator*
Williams, Patricia Badia *retired counselor, academic administrator, mathematics educator*
Williams, Shannon Renee *mental health services professional*
Wirebaugh, Amy *physical therapist, educator*
Wish, LeslieBeth Berger *psychotherapist, writer, management consultant*
Wolf, Dale B. *former health care company executive*
Wolfberg, Melvin Donald *optometrist, educational association administrator, consultant*
Woteki, Catherine Ellen *nutritionist*
Wright, Dell *residential care and treatment facility executive*
Yale (Yeleyenide-Yale), Melpomene Fotine *researcher, anthropologist, archaeologist, art historian, conservator*
Yu, Boas J. *nursing educator*
Zavala, Pedro Jose *pharmacy educator*
Zhou, Ji-Xun *ocean acoustics physicist, acoustician*
Zhu, Carolyn Wei *healthcare educator*
Zhuravenko, Igor N. *health services administrator, physician*
Zimmerman, D. Patrick *psychotherapist, health facility administrator*
Zimmerman, Jo Ann *retired health science association administrator, educator, retired lieutenant governor*
Zuck, Rosemary *social worker, educator*

HEALTHCARE: MEDICINE

UNITED STATES

ALABAMA

Athens
Bebin, Martina *pediatrician, neurologist*

Bayou La Batre
Benjamin, Regina Marcia *physician, health facility administrator*

Birmingham
Andrews, James R. *orthopedic surgeon*
Arnett, Donna K. *epidemiologist, educator*
Arnoletti, Juan Pablo *oncologist, educator*
Bittner, Vera *cardiologist*
Bloomer, Joseph Robert *physician, educator*
Bonatz, Ekkehard *hand surgeon*
Boyd, Gwendolyn Louise *anesthesiologist, educator*
Briggs, Dick Dowling, Jr. *physician, educator*
Bueschen, Anton Joslyn *physician, educator*
Caulfield, James Benjamin *pathologist, educator*
Chattopadhyay, Debasish *medical educator, researcher*
Diethelm, Arnold Gillespie *surgeon*
Dugan, Byrdena DeeAnn *medical educator*
Ferniany, William (Isaac William Ferniany) *health system administrator*
Finley, Wayne House *medical educator*
Foft, John William *physician, educator*
Gaggar, Amit *medical educator, researcher*
Gavino, Alde Carlo Patdu *dermatologist*
Hahn, Beatrice H. *biomedical researcher, medical educator*
Hedden, William James *plastic surgeon*
Huechtker, Edward Darrell *department chairman*
Johnston, Carden *emergency physician, pediatrician, educator*
Kimberly, Robert Parker *medical educator*
Markland, Alayne Denise *geriatrician, educator*
Meezan, Elias *pharmacologist, educator*
Nanda, Navin Chandar *cardiologist, educator*
Ness, Timothy John *anesthesiologist, researcher*
Omura, George Adolf *medical oncologist*
Oparil, Suzanne *cardiologist, educator, researcher*
Pappas, Dennis G. *otolaryngologist*
Pasche, Boris Claude Roger *physician*
Pass, Robert *pediatrician*
Pittman, Constance Shen *endocrinologist, educator*
Pittman, James Allen, Jr. *endocrinologist, educator*
Russell, Richard Olney, Jr. *retired cardiologist*
Sanderson, Ralph *medical educator*
Shawn, Gilbert R. *orthopedist, educator*
Siegal, Gene Philip *pathology educator*
Singh, Satinder P. *medical educator, director*
Stevenson, Edward Ward *retired otolaryngologist, surgeon*
Trigg, Jack Walden, Jr. *retired physician*
Volanakis, John Emmanuel *immunologist, rheumatologist*
Young, Carlton Joseph *abdominal transplant kidney and pancreas surgeon, educator*

Dothan
Zloty, Peter *ophthalmologist*

Huntsville
Edmonson, Brenda *ophthalmologist*

Mobile
Abi-Saleh, Bernard S. *cardiologist*
Brogdon, Byron Gilliam *radiologist, educator*
Frye, Karen Ernst *surgeon*
Guarino, Anthony Michael *pharmacologist, educator, consultant, counselor*
Littleton, Jesse Talbot III *radiology educator*
Ponnambalam, Ananthasekar *pediatrician, gastroenterologist*
Rodning, Charles Bernard *surgeon*
Scantlebury, Velma Patricia *surgeon*
Smith, Jesse Graham, Jr. *dermatologist, educator*

Montgomery
Kerr, Kim *medical educator*

Orange Beach
Conrad, Marcel Edward *hematologist, oncologist, educator*

Tuscaloosa
Keeton, J. E. *retired psychiatrist*
Lumpkin, Thomas Riley *retired physician*
Pieroni, Robert Edward *internist, educator, military officer*
Rand, Elizabeth Hartmann *psychiatrist*
Sinclair, Robert Ewald *retired physician*

Tuskegee Institute
Casimire-Etzioni, Athema Louise *veterinary pathologist*

Vestavia
Nuckols, Frank Joseph *psychiatrist*

ALASKA

Anchorage
Arnold, Robert Wendell *ophthalmologist*
Galloway, Christopher George *oncologist, director*
Mills, William James, Jr. *orthopedist, surgeon, researcher*
Plant, Randall Leslie *otolaryngologist*

Fort Wainwright
McWilliams, Grant *osteopath*

ARIZONA

Anthem
Guerra, Aldo Benjamin *plastic and cosmetic surgeon*

Chandler
Zavala-Alarcon, Edgardo Donato *medical association administrator, director*

Glendale
Teague, Robert Cole *physician*

Goodyear
Brunk, Samuel Frederick *oncologist*
Nixon, Daniel Walker *oncologist, researcher*

Green Valley
Bachman, David Christian *orthopedic surgeon*
Ford, Neville F. *clinical pharmacologist*
Moser, Robert Harlan *internist, educator, writer*
Reichlin, Seymour *endocrinologist, educator*

Kingman
Ramadan, Mohamed Ibrahim *psychiatrist*
Rebik, James Michael *otolaryngologist*

Mesa
Cooley, Jack Crain *cardiovascular surgeon*
Cox, Heidi Pinkerton *pediatric surgeon*
Janik, Joseph S. *pediatrician*
Kronenfeld, Michael Reed *medical librarian*

Oracle
Mueller, Timothy I. *psychiatrist*

Oro Valley
Abbassian, Assad *urologist*

Paradise Valley
Lorenzen, Robert Frederick *ophthalmologist*
Sharma, Virender *medical educator, director*
Targovnik, Selma E. Kaplan *dermatologist*

Peoria
Nicchi, Vincent, Jr. *cardiologist*

Phoenix
Agudo, Mercedes Engracia *psychiatrist*
Bennett, Peter Howard *retired medical researcher*
Chambliss, Linda R. *obstetrician, consultant*
Charlton, John Kipp *pediatrician*
Cole, Daniel John *anesthesiologist, educator*
Cornella, Jeffrey Lynn *surgeon*
da Fonte, Mauro Valente *medical educator*
Feldman, Jeremy Phillip *pulmonologist*
Jason, Philip Caplan *psychiatrist*
Johnson, Mystie L. *obstetrician, gynecologist, department chairman*
Khan, Mohammed Yousuf *physician, consultant*
Laufer, Nathan *cardiologist*
Lovett, William Lee *surgeon*
Malhotra, Ashish *medical researcher*
Martinez-Conde, Susana *neurologist, researcher*
Pershad, Ashish *cardiologist*
Reed, Wallace Allison *anesthesiologist*
Rekate, Harold Louis *neurosurgeon*
Schwartz, Eric Alexander *biomedical researcher, educator*
Shishov, Michael *rheumatologist*
Swafford, Leslie Eugene *physician assistant, consultant*
Von Hoff, Daniel Douglas *oncologist, researcher*
Wait, Scott D. *neurosurgeon*
Wright, Richard Oscar III *pathologist, educator, clinical ethicist*
Zerella, Joseph T. *retired pediatric surgeon*

Prescott
Garcia-Buñuel, Luis *neurologist*
Sagman, Arthur M. *radiologist*

Rio Verde
Culligan, John Austin *thoracic surgeon*

Scottsdale
Arora, Sandeep *cardiologist*
Dahl, Mark Victor *dermatologist, educator*
Fowler, R. Stuart *gynecologist*
Friedland, Jack Arthur *plastic surgeon*
Gregory, Robert Erb *surgeon*
Haas, Ingrid Elizabeth *physician*
Harrison, Nedra Joyce *surgeon*
Hinni, Michael L. *otolaryngologist*
Khandheria, Bijoy K. *cardiologist*
Mikhael, Joseph *hematologist*
Orford, Robert Raymond *physician, consultant*
Parish, James Michael *medical educator*
Reznick, Richard Howard *pediatrician*
Roarke, Michael Charles *medical educator, nuclear medicine physician*
Sanderson, David R. *physician*
Sengupta, Partho P. *cardiologist, educator*
Sheridan, Donald Charles *orthopedist, hand surgeon*
Underwood, Paul Lester *cardiologist*
Watkins, Eugene Leonard *surgeon, educator*

Sedona
Briney, Allan King *retired radiologist*
Hawkins, David Ramon *psychiatrist, writer, researcher, spiritual teacher*
Metzner, Richard Joel *psychiatrist, psychopharmacologist, educator*

Sells
Ostrum, Robert F. *orthopaedic surgeon*

Sun City
Buchman, Elwood *internist, former pharmaceutical executive, director*

Tempe
Anand, Suresh Chandra *physician*
Schneller, Eugene Stewart *health administration and policy educator*

Tucson
Ablin, Richard Joel *immunologist, educator*
Alberts, David Samuel *physician, pharmacologist, educator*
Allred, Kendall S. *emergency physician*
Alpert, Joseph Stephen *cardiologist, educator*
Babcock-Parziale, Judi L. *medical researcher, psychology professor*
Banerjee, Bhaskar *gastroenterologist, medical educator*
Becker, Gary J. *radiologist, health science association administrator*
Ben-Asher, M. David *physician*
Chutkow, Lee Robinson *retired physician*
Corrigan, James John, Jr. *pediatrician, dean, educator*
Cunniff, Christopher M. *pediatrician, educator*
Dalen, James Eugene *cardiologist, educator*
Enright, Paul Lewis *pulmonologist*
Ewy, Gordon Allen *cardiologist, researcher, educator*
Fishkind, William J. *ophthalmologist*
Foley, Louise *medical educator, retired military officer*
Fulcher, Claire E *psychotherapist, organization consultant*
Goldfarb, Robert Paul *neurological surgeon*
Goldman, Steven *cardiologist, researcher*
Goshima, Kaoru Ruth *surgeon, educator*
Graham, Anna Regina *pathologist, educator*
Grana, William A. *orthopedist, surgeon*
Greenfield, Russell Howard *physician, educator*
Harris, David Thomas *immunology educator*
Hattery, Robert Ralph *radiologist, educator*
Houser, Harold Byron *epidemiologist*
Katakkar, Suresh Balaji *hematologist, oncologist*
Khouzam, Rami Nadim *physician*
Kischer, Clayton Ward *human embryologist, educator*
Leon, Luis R. *surgeon*
Levenson, Alan Ira *psychiatrist, physician, educator*
Marcus, Frank Isadore *cardiologist, educator*
Menick, Frederick J. *plastic surgeon*
Morgan, Wayne Joseph *medical educator, medical association administrator*
Parthasarathy, Sairam *pulmonologist*
Rogers, Lee Frank *radiologist*
Russell, Findlay Ewing *physician*
Shahidullah, Mohammad *medical researcher, educator*
Thal, Sergio Gustavo *cardiologist, director, medical educator*
Weil, Andrew Thomas *physician, educator*
Woolfenden, James Manning *nuclear medicine physician, educator*
Zheng, Wenxin *gynecologist, pathologist*

Yuma
Anderson, John Albert *physician*

ARKANSAS

Fayetteville
Fink, William James *retired surgeon*
Parker, Lee Bryan *retired physician*

Fort Smith
Snider, James Rhodes *radiologist*

Hot Springs
Kamel, Hosam Kamal *medical educator, researcher, geriatrician*

Jefferson
Wolff, George Louis *biomedical researcher*

Jonesboro
Jones, Kenneth Bruce *surgeon*

Little Rock
Anand, Kanwaljeet Singh *pediatrician, researcher*
Bruce, Thomas Allen *physician, educator*
Campbell, Gilbert Sadler *surgeon, educator*
Elbein, Alan David *medical science educator*
Emanuel, Peter D. *medical educator, director*
Ferguson, Alesia C. *medical educator*
Fiser, Debra H. *pediatrician, educator, dean*

Hart, Ronald Wilson *radiobiologist, educator, toxicologist, business adviser*
Jansen, G. Thomas *dermatologist*
Lucy, Dennis Durwood, Jr. *neurologist, educator*
Mehta, Jawahar Lal *cardiologist*
O'Brien, Mark Stephen *pediatric neurosurgeon*
Olden, Kevin William *medical researcher*
Patil, Naveen *preventive medicine physician*
Raza, Asim *psychiatrist*
Sotomora-von Ahn, Ricardo Federico *pediatrician, educator*
Suva, Larry John *orthopedic researcher*
York, John Lyndal *medical educator*

North Little Rock
Komoroski, Richard Andrew *medical sciences educator, spectroscopy researcher*

Scranton
Uzman, Betty Ben Geren *retired pathologist*

Springdale
Rosenschein, Guy Raoul *pediatric and visceral surgeon, airline pilot*

CALIFORNIA

Agoura Hills
Barker, Wiley Franklin *surgeon, educator*
deCiutiis, Alfred Charles Maria *oncologist, television producer*

Alameda
Whorton, M. Donald *physician, epidemiologist*

Alhambra
Sussman, Steven Yale *preventive medicine and psychology educator*

Anaheim
Glazer, Sidney *physician, director*
Jolley, Weldon Bosen *surgery educator, research executive*
Matallana, Lynne *patient advocacy association administrator*

Aptos
Miura, Masako Kusayanagi *retired dermatologist*

Arcadia
Sathyavagiswaran, Lakshmanan *pathologist, county official*

Auburn
Henrikson, Donald Merle *forensic pathologist*

Bakersfield
Sharma, Sanjiv *cardiologist*
Sio, Jimmy Ong *embryologist*

Bellflower
Henry, Harold M. *obstetrician, gynecologist, maternal-fetal medicine*
Lee, Paul Yue-Yan *surgeon*
Maples, Karen Elizabeth *obstetrician, gynecologist*

Belvedere Tiburon
Fishman, Robert Allen *retired neurologist, educator, department chair*
Hoffman, Julien Ivor Ellis *pediatrician, cardiologist, educator*

Berkeley
Budinger, Thomas Francis *radiologist, educator*
Grossman, Elmer Roy *pediatrician*
Ivey, Susan Lee *health services researcher, educator*
Orbison, James Archer, Jr. *cardiologist, surgeon*
Pugsley, Michael Kenneth *cardiac pharmacologist, research scientist*
Rundall, Thomas Gene *medical educator*
Tempelis, Constantine Harry *immunologist, educator*
Winkelstein, Warren, Jr. *physician, educator*

Beverly Hills
Alter, Gary *plastic and reconstructive surgeon, urologist*
Amron, David M. *plastic surgeon*
Bao, Katherine Sung *pediatric cardiologist*
Caster, Andrew Ian *ophthalmologist*
Catz, Boris *endocrinologist, educator*
Diamond, Jason Brett *plastic surgeon*
Diaz, John *plastic surgeon*
Fein, William *ophthalmologist*
Fisher, (Donald) Garth *plastic surgeon*
Jarrahnejad, Payam *plastic surgeon*
Jeong, Jae Hoon *physician*
Kadz, Bruce B. *plastic surgeon*
Kamrava, Michael M. *reproductive endocrinologist*
Karpman, Harold Lew *cardiologist, educator, writer*
Klein, Arnold William *dermatologist*
Kotler, Robert *cosmetic surgeon*
Li, Linda (Linda Jian-Yuh Li) *plastic surgeon*
Marshak, Harry *plastic surgeon*
Moelleken, Brent Roderick Wilfred *plastic surgeon*
Nassif, Paul S. *facial plastic and reconstructive surgeon*
Omidi, Michael M. *plastic surgeon*
Ordon, Andrew Paul (Drew Ordon) *plastic surgeon*
Perlman, Jon Arthur *plastic surgeon*
Rey, Robert M. *plastic surgeon*
Salz, James Joseph *medical association administrator*
Tabak, Steven William *cardiologist*
Yuan, Robin Tsu-Wang *plastic surgeon*

Bloomington
Ojo-Amaize, Emmanuel Ade *immunologist*

Borrego Springs
Strong, John Oliver *plastic surgeon, educator*

Burbank
Renner, Andrew Ihor *surgeon*
Schlaerth, John Burr *oncologist, gynecologist*
Zhao, Chonghao *neurologist, educator*

Burlingame
Rosenfield, Lorne King *plastic surgeon*

Canyon Country
Rivero, Luis Raul *aerospace physician, military officer*

Canyon Lake
Sparks, Dale Boyd *allergist, health facility administrator*

Capistrano Beach
Sears, Jim (James M. Sears) *pediatrician*
Sears, William *pediatrician*

Carlsbad
Chopra, Deepak *preventive medicine physician, writer*
Kizer, Kenneth Wayne *physician, executive, educator*

Cerritos
Lee, Jhemon Hom *physician*

Chico
Ritter, Dale William *obstetrician, gynecologist*

Chula Vista
Cohen, Elaine Helena *pediatrician, cardiologist, educator*

Claremont
Johnson, Jerome Linné *cardiologist, educator*
Tang, Yao Liang *medical educator, researcher, surgeon*

Corona
Haynes, Moses Alfred *physician*
Silva, A. R. *surgeon, educator*

Corona Del Mar
Tobis, Jerome Sanford *physician*

Coronado
Mock, David Clinton, Jr. *internist*

Culver City
Muller, Jenny Helen *physician, psychiatrist*

Daly City
Dunlap, Robert William *internist, cardiologist, educator*
So, Samuel Cho Yee *therapeutic radiological physicist, physician*

Dana Point
Fisher, Delbert Arthur *pediatric endocrinologist, educator, retired health facility administrator*

Davis
Bodine, Sue Carol *medical educator*
Cardiff, Robert Darrell *pathology educator*
Gardner, Murray Briggs *pathologist, educator*
Halsted, Charles Hopkinson *internist*
Jensen, Hanne Margrete *pathologist, educator*
Palmer, Philip Edward Stephen *radiologist*
Rhode, Edward Albert *veterinary medicine educator, veterinary cardiologist*
Richman, David Paul *neurologist, educator, researcher*
Siegler, Richard Louis *pediatric nephrologist, educator*

Del Mar
Iverson, Gilbert Michael *retired immunologist*

Delano
Salmassi, Sadegh *physician*

Downey
Bessman, Alice Neuman *internist, educator*
Hackney, Jack Dean *physician*
Perry, Jacquelin *orthopedist, surgeon*

Duarte
Chu, David Z.J. *surgeon, oncologist, research scientist*
Figlin, Robert Alan *hematologist, oncologist*
Grannis, Frederic Winslow, Jr. *thoracic surgeon*
Reckamp, Karen *medical educator*

El Dorado Hills
Sparks, Robert Dean *medical administrator, gastroenterologist*

El Segundo
Nissenson, Allen Richard *physician, educator*

Elk Grove
Forbes, Kenneth Albert Faucher *retired urological surgeon*

Emeryville
Fields, Howard Lincoln *neurologist, physiologist, educator*
Witbrodt, Jane Ann *medical researcher*

Encino
Lesavoy, Malcolm Alan *plastic surgeon*

Escondido
McCarberg, Bill Harold *physician*

Fair Oaks
Haugen, David Lee *surgeon*

Fairfield
Chen, William T. *plastic surgeon*

Folsom
Ewing, Russell Charles, II, *physician*

Foster City
Liang, Yu *biomedical researcher*

Fresno
Warwick, Tanya C. *neurologist, educator, researcher*

Fullerton
Sugarman, Michael *physician, rheumatologist*

Goleta
Zuk, Carmen Veiga *psychiatrist*

Grass Valley
Ely, Parry Haines *dermatologist, educator*

Greenbrae
Eisenberg, Peter David *internist, oncologist*
Parnell, Francis William, Jr. *otolaryngologist*
Poulos, Stanley *plastic surgeon*
Rosbe, Kristina W. *pediatric otolaryngologist, surgeon*

Gualala
Ring, Alice Ruth Bishop *retired preventive medicine physician*

Half Moon Bay
Robertson, Abel L., Jr. *pathologist*

Hayward
Bachicha, Joseph Alfred *physician, educator*

Hemet
Mata, David Joseph *physician*

Huntington Beach
Horowitz, Jed H. *plastic surgeon, reconstructive surgeon*

Inglewood
Dorr, Lawrence Douglas *orthopedic surgeon*

Irvine
Bic, Zuzana *medical educator*
Bose, Swaraj *ophthalmologist, educator*
Clayman, Ralph Victor *urologist, medical educator, dean*
Detrano, Robert *medical educator*
Duckles, Sue Piper *pharmacologist, educator*
Friedenberg, Richard Myron *radiologist, physician, educator*
Gupta, Sudhir *immunologist, educator*
Hubbell, Floyd Allan *internist, educator*
Kuppermann, Baruch D. *ophthalmologist, educator*
McEligot, Archana Jaiswal *epidemiologist, educator*
Molloi, Sabee *medical educator*
Nelson, Edward Lee *biomedical researcher, educator*
Noymer, Andrew *medical educator, researcher*
Qin, Yufen *immunologist, researcher*
Quilligan, Edward James *retired obstetrician, gynecologist, educator*
Ramzy, Ibrahim *medical educator*
Simmons, Peter A. *medical researcher*
Werlin, Lawrence B. *obstetrician, gynecologist, reproductive endocrinologist*
Wong, Brian Jet-Fei *surgeon*
Wong, Nathan Donald *medicine and epidemiology researcher, educator*

Kentfield
German, Donald Frederick *physician*

La Canada Flintridge
Byrne, George Melvin *physician*

La Crescenta
Riccardi, Vincent Michael *pediatrician, educator, entrepreneur*

La Honda
Jahn, Thomas M. *medical educator*

La Jolla
Adamson, John William *hematologist*
Akiskal, Hagop Souren *psychiatric researcher, educator*
Al-Delaimy, Wael *medical educator*
Blantz, Roland C. *nephrologist, educator*
Bokoch, Gary Michael *immunology research scientist*
Carethers, John Michael *physician, gastroenterologist, researcher*
Carmichael, David Burton *physician*
Coutts, Richard David *surgeon*
Dandan, Randa Hilal *pharmacologist, researcher*
Dang, Qun *pharmacologist*
Daniels, Lori B. *cardiologist*
Dimsdale, Joel Edward *psychiatry educator*
Edgington, Thomas S. *pathologist, molecular and vascular biologist, educator*
Fukuda, Minoru *cancer research scientist*
Gardner, Humphrey Athelstan Roy *pathologist*
Garland, Cedric Frank *epidemiologist, educator*
Golomb, Beatrice Alexandra *physician, medical researcher*
Goltz, Robert William *retired dermatologist*
Hamburger, Robert N. *pediatrician, educator, consultant*
Hofmann, Alan Frederick *biomedical researcher, educator*
Horner, Anthony Adam *pediatrician, educator*
Jones, Kenneth Lyons *pediatrician, birth defects researcher*
Jorgensen, Judith Ann *psychiatrist, educator*
Kalichman, Michael *neuropathologist*
Kono, Dwight *medical educator*
Korn, Bobby *ophthalmologist, educator*
Liddington, Robert C. *biomedical researcher, educator*
Lowy, Andrew M. *oncologist, surgeon*
MacRae, Ian John *medical educator, researcher*
Mendoza, Stanley Atran *pediatric nephrologist, educator*
Moossa, A. R. *surgeon, educator*
Mundt, Arno J. *oncologist, department chairman*
Nakamura, Robert Motoharu *pathologist*
Nyhan, William Leo *pediatrician, educator*
Oldham, Sean Michael *medical educator, consultant*
Rapaport, Samuel I. *educator, physician*
Rubenstein, Howard S. *physician, writer*
Rubin, Lewis Joseph *physician, researcher*
Schatz, Richard A. *cardiologist*
Schneider, Gerald L. *plastic surgeon*
Schooley, Robert T. *medical educator*
Silver, Dee Edward *physician, neurologist*
Singer, Robert *plastic surgeon*
Sirotin, Nicole Ashley *physician*
Steinberg, Daniel *biomedical scientist*
Tan, Eng Meng *immunologist, biomedical researcher*
Teirstein, Paul Shepherd *cardiologist, educator*
Thompson, Charlotte Ellis *pediatrician, educator, writer*
Tsuang, Ming Tso *psychiatrist, educator*
Walker, Richard Hugh *orthopaedic surgeon*
Zhang, Dong-Er *medical educator*
Zhou, Quansheng *medical researcher*

La Quinta
Pitkin, Roy Macbeth *retired obstetrician, educator*

Lafayette
Kang, Isamu Yong *retired nuclear medicine physician*

Laguna Beach
Barr, Ronald Jeffrey *dermatologist, pathologist*

Lake Forest
Larsen, Robert Ray *healthcare executive, surgeon*

Lake Isabella
Fraser, Eleanor Ruth *radiologist, administrator*

Lakewood
Gelb, Arthur Franklin *pulmonologist, educator*

Lancaster
Khanal, Sanjaya *cardiologist, educator*

Larkspur
Strunk, Brian L. *medical educator*

Lincoln
Chong, Vernon *retired surgeon, military officer*
Rockwell, Don Arthur *retired psychiatrist*

Livermore
Seward, James Pickett *internist, educator*

Loma Linda
Bailey, Leonard Lee *surgeon*
Bull, Brian Stanley *pathologist, educator*
Chan, Philip J. *medical educator*
Chinnock, Richard *pediatrician, educator*
Coggin, Charlotte Joan *cardiologist, educator*
Condon, Stanley Charles *gastroenterologist*
Herrmann, Paul C. *physician, chemist*
Llaurado, Josep G. *nuclear medicine physician, researcher*
Lohman, Everett III *medical educator, director*
Ojogho, Okechukwu N. *surgeon, educator*
Singh, Pramil Nand *epidemiologist, educator*
Slater, James Munro *radiation oncologist*
Strother, Allen *biochemical pharmacologist, researcher*
Wareham, Ellsworth Edwin *cardiothoracic surgeon, educator*
Williams, Paul Allen *biomedical engineer, researcher*
Wood, Virchel Edgar *orthopedist, surgeon, educator*

Long Beach
Kwaan, Jack Hau Ming *retired physician*
Macer, George Armen, Jr. *orthopedic hand surgeon*
Marks, Melvin I. *physician, educator, hospital administrator, consultant*
Molina, Joseph Mario (Mario Molina) *medical administrator*
Sassoon, Catherine *pulmonologist, educator*
Worcester, Howard Lester *internist*
Wu, Sing-Yung *physician, researcher*

Los Altos
Kaiman, Sarah *retired physician*

Los Angeles
Agus, David Bernard *oncologist, researcher, medical educator*
Akhtari, Massoud *medical educator*
Alkalay, Arie L. *neonatologist*
Alkon, Ellen Skillen *physician*
Anderson, Martin Mathew *pediatrician, educator*
Ansell, Benjamin Jesse *physician*
Apt, Leonard *pediatric ophthalmologist*
Apuzzo, Michael Lawrence John *neurological surgeon*
Askanas-Engel, Valerie *neurologist, educator, researcher*
Avidan, Alon Y. *physician*
Azen, Stanley Paul *medical educator*
Baker, Craig J. *surgeon, department chairman*
Bazargan-Hejazi, Shahrzad *medical researcher*
Beart, Robert W., Jr. *colon and rectal surgeon, educator*
Berman, David Albert *pharmacologist, educator*
Bernstein, Sol *cardiologist, educator*
Black, Keith Lanier *neurosurgeon, educator*
Blahd, William Henry *nuclear medicine physician, director*

Borenstein, Daniel Bernard *psychiatrist, educator*
Brent, Gregory *endocrinologist, educator*
Caren, Jeffrey F. *cardiologist, educator*
Casillas, Jacqueline Nieto *hematologist, oncologist, educator*
Chandor, Stebbins Bryant *pathologist*
Chang, Tom Shio min *ophthalmologist*
Cherry, James Donald *pediatrician*
Chhetri, Dinesh Khatri *surgeon, educator*
Chopra, Inder Jit *endocrinologist*
Clemente, Carmine Domenic *anatomist, educator*
Coates, Thomas Duane *pediatrician, hematologist, educator*
Conklin, Jeffrey L. *medical educator, director*
Cook, Ian Ainsworth *psychiatrist, researcher, educator*
Cordasco, Kristina M. *medical researcher, educator*
Cummings, Jeffrey L. *neurologist, educator*
Currier, Jesse *cardiologist*
Czer, Lawrence S.C. *internist*
Daley, Melita *psychiatrist, director*
Danoff, Dudley Seth *surgeon, urologist*
Davidson, Ezra C., Jr. *obstetrician, gynecologist, academic administrator, educator*
Detels, Roger *epidemiologist, retired dean*
Deville, Jaime Gerardo *medical educator*
Don, Manuel *medical researcher*
Dubeau, Louis *medical educator, researcher*
Duel, Barry P. *urologist, pediatrician*
Edgerton, Bradford Wheatly *plastic surgeon*
Ellenbogen, Richard *plastic surgeon*
Engel, Jerome, Jr. *neurologist, neuroscientist, psychiatry professor*
Engel, William King *neurologist, educator*
Enstrom, James Eugene *epidemiologist*
Eo, SuRak *plastic surgeon, educator*
Escarce, José J. *medical educator*
Ettenger, Robert Bruce *physician, pediatric nephrologist*
Feig, Stephen Arthur *pediatrician, hematologist, oncologist, educator*
Ferrell, Bruce Allen *medical educator*
Fincher, Edgar Franklin *dermatologic surgeon*
Fleming, Arthur Wallace *physician, surgeon*
Fodor, Peter Bela *plastic surgeon, educator*
Fonarow, Gregg Curtis *cardiologist, educator*
Fonkalsrud, Eric Walter *pediatric surgeon, educator*
Forrester, James Stuart *cardiologist, medical educator*
Gabriel, Ronald Samuel *child neurologist*
Ganz, Patricia Anne *medical educator, physician*
Garban, Hermes J. *biomedical researcher, educator*
Gatti, Richard A. *medical geneticist, educator*
Geller, Kenneth Allen *otolaryngologist*
Geller, Stephen Arthur *pathologist, educator*
Gewertz, Bruce Labe *surgeon, educator*
Ginsberg, David *medical educator*
Glaspy, John *hematologist and oncologist, cancer researcher*
Goin, Marcia Kraft *physician*
Gorney, Roderic *psychiatrist, educator*
Grody, Wayne William *physician, educator*
Guevara, Ramon Emmanuel *epidemiologist*
Guzy, Peter Michael *cardiologist, educator*
Haas, Mark *pathologist*
Hachamovitch, Rory *cardiologist, consultant*
Harber, Philip *preventive medicine physician, educator*
Harrison, Rick E. *pediatrician*
Haywood, L. Julian *cardiologist, educator*
Hecht, Joel Randolph *oncologist*
Henderson, Brian Edmond *preventive medicine physician, educator, former dean*
Henriksen, Eva Hansine *retired anesthesiology educator*
Herrmann, Christian, Jr. *medical educator*
Herschman, Harvey Roy *medical educator, researcher*
Hirai, Denitsu *surgeon*
Hoang, Duc Van *pathologist, educator*
House, John William *otolaryngologist*
Hubbell, Wayne Lester *ophthalmologist, chemist, educator*
Hyde, Manly Richard *thoracic surgeon*
Ignarro, Louis J. *pharmacology educator*
IsHak, Waguih William *psychiatrist*
Jadvar, Hossein *nuclear radiologist, biomedical engineer*
Jalali, Behnaz *psychiatrist, educator*
Jamieson, Beth D. *medical educator, director*
Jelliffe, Roger Woodham *cardiologist, pharmacologist*
Jobe, Frank Wilson *orthopedic surgeon*
Johnson, Cage Saul *hematologist, educator*
Kar, Saibal *cardiologist*
Karlan, Beth Young *gynecologic oncologist*
Karp, Harvey Neil *pediatrician*
Katz, Roger *pediatrician, allergist, immunologist, educator*
Kaul, Sanjay *cardiologist*
Kaunitz, Jonathan Davidson *physician*
Kelly, Arthur Paul *physician*
Keyes, Geoffrey Robin *plastic surgeon*
Kim, Kwang-Jin *medical educator*
King, Bryan Harry *neuropsychiatrist, medical educator and researcher*
Kirsch, Claudia Françoise *radiologist*
Klitzner, Thomas S. *pediatric cardiologist*
Kobashigawa, Jon Akira *internist, cardiologist, researcher, educator*
Kramer, Barry Alan *psychiatrist, educator*
Lawrence, Sanford Hull *physician, immunochemist, author*
Lehrer, Robert Irving *medical educator*
Lekovic, Gregory Punisa *surgeon, lawyer*
Lipshutz, Gerald S. *medical educator, researcher*
MacAlpin, Rex Nere *physician, educator*
Macavinta-Tenazas, Gemorsita *physician*
Maloney, Robert Keller *ophthalmologist, medical educator*
Martinez, Miguel Acevedo *urologist, consultant, lecturer*
Martins, David *medical researcher*
Matlock, David Louis *obstetrician, gynecologist, reconstructive surgeon*
McCurdy, Deborah K. *pediatric rheumatologist*
McFadden, P. Michael *physician, surgeon*
McGough, James John *psychiatrist*
Mendez Ashla, Mario *neurologist, educator, internist*
Mihan, Richard *retired dermatologist*
Miller, Lee Todd *pediatrician, educator*
Mishra, Shri Kant *neurologist, educator, neuroscientist*
Mitsuyasu, Ronald T. *physician, researcher, medical educator*
Mondino, Bartly J. *ophthalmologist*
Moore, Wesley Sanford *vascular surgeon*
Morgan, Jean Elizabeth *plastic surgeon*
Motykie, Gary *plastic surgeon*
Moxley, John Howard III *internist*
MoY, Ronald Leonard *dermasurgeon*
Nathwani, Bharat N. *pathologist, educator*
Navab, Mohamad *cardiologist, educator*
Nishi, Gregg K. *surgeon, educator*
Noble, Ernest Pascal *pharmacologist, biochemist, educator, psychiatrist*
Olsen, Jørn *epidemiology educator, researcher*
Parmelee, Arthur Hawley, Jr. *pediatric medical educator*
Paulson, Richard John *obstetrician, gynecologist, educator*
Perloff, Joseph Kayle *cardiologist, educator*
Pi, Edmond Hsin-Tung *psychiatry educator*
Prins, Robert Michael *medical educator*
Qiao, Jian-Hua *pathologist, researcher*
Raja, Rajalingam *immunologist, educator*
Ramanathan, Rangasamy *pediatrician*
Rao, Narsing A. *ophthalmologist, pathologist, educator*
Reiter, Robert E. *urologist, educator*
Richman, Michael F. *thoracic surgeon, consultant*
Rimoin, David Lawrence *medical geneticist*
Rosenbaum, Arthur L. *ophthalmologist*
Roven, Alfred Nathan *surgeon*
Roy-Burman, Pradip *molecular biology and virology educator*
Rubin, Robert Terry *psychiatrist, researcher, educator*
Sahai Srivastava, Soma *neurologist, educator*
Salusky, Isidro B. *pediatric nephrologist, educator*
Samet, Jonathan Michael *epidemiologist, educator*
Sankar, Raman *pediatric neurologist*
Sarma, Radha J. *cardiologist, educator*
Sarnat, Bernard George *plastic surgeon, educator, researcher*
Scheibel, Arnold Bernard *psychiatrist, educator, research director*
Schelbert, Heinrich Ruediger *nuclear medicine physician*
Schneider, Edward Lewis *medicine educator, research administrator*
Schneider, Paul Leonard *internist*
Schwarz, Ernst Ruediger *cardiologist, researcher*
Selby, Robert Rick *surgeon*
Shafipour, Pouya *physician, dermatologist*
Shah, Prediman K. *cardiologist, educator*
Shemin, Richard Jay *cardiothoracic surgeon, educator*
Shields, William Donald *physician, educator*
Shivkumar, Kalyanam *cardiologist, consultant*
Siegel, Michael Elliot *nuclear medicine physician, educator*
Siegel, Stuart Elliott *pediatric oncologist, educator*
Skaggs, David L. *orthopedist, educator*
Sofroniew, Michael Victor *medical educator*
Stiehm, E. Richard *pediatrician, educator*
Straatsma, Bradley Ralph *ophthalmologist, educator*
Streeter, Oscar Edward, Jr. *radiation oncologist*
Sullivan, Stuart Francis *anesthesiologist, educator*
Svehlak, Steven Andrew *plastic surgeon*
Tabachnick, Norman Donald *psychiatrist, educator*
Tachdjian, Raffi *pediatrician*
Tolstrup, Kirsten *cardiologist, educator*
Trento, Alfredo A. *thoracic surgeon, educator*
Vega, William A. *psychiatrist, educator*
Vo, Ashley *medical association administrator*
Vojdani, Aristo *medical association administrator, researcher*
Watson, Karol Elizabeth *internist, educator*
Weiss, Martin Harvey *neurosurgeon, educator*
Whybrow, Peter Charles *psychiatrist, educator, director, author*
Wilkinson, Alan Herbert *nephrologist, educator*
Wilson, Miriam Geisendorfer *retired physician, educator*
Wincor, Michael Z. *psychopharmacology educator, clinician, researcher, director*
Withers, Hubert Rodney *radiotherapist, radiobiologist, educator*
Woodley, David Timothy *dermatology educator*
Yamaguchi, Dean Takao *medical educator, researcher*
Yamauchi, Paul Steven *dermatologist, researcher*
Yamini, Daniel *plastic surgeon*
Yang, Allen S. *medical educator*
Yazdani, Shahram *pediatrician*
Yiu, Samuel Chi-Hung *ophthalmologist, researcher*
Young, Ronald Frederick *neurosurgeon*
Yu, John Sun *neurosurgeon, immunologist*
Zeltzer, Lonnie K. *pediatrician, educator*

Lower Lake
Hodgkin, John E. *pulmonologist*

Malibu
Morgenstern, Leon *surgeon*

Marina Del Rey
Parks, D. Gene *gynecologist*
Stevens, William Grant (Grant Stevens) *plastic surgeon*
Stoker, David Allen *plastic surgeon*
Watkins, Robert G *surgeon*

Menifee
Uhl, Suzanne M. *educator*

Menlo Park
Harris, Edward Day, Jr. *physician*
Kovachy, Edward Miklos, Jr. *psychiatrist, consultant*

Singh, Kuldev *medical educator*

Milpitas
Chiu, Peter Yee-Chew *physician*

Modesto
Jensen, Ronald D. *podiatrist*
Khanna, Kanwal *rheumatologist*

Mountain View
Abel, Elizabeth Ann *dermatologist*
Brilliant, Larry (Lawrence Brent Brilliant) *preventive medicine physician, entrepreneur*
Golden, Neville Hylton *pediatrician*
Tang, Paul C. *medical administrator, educator*
Warren, Richard Wayne *obstetrician, gynecologist*

Murrieta
Miller, Stephen Herschel *surgeon, educator*

Napa
Kanaan, Samer Azzam *cardiothoracic surgeon*
Zimmermann, John Paul *plastic surgeon*

Newbury Park
Bleiberg, Leon William *surgeon, podiatrist*

Newport Beach
Aiello, William Philip *plastic surgeon*
Batniji, Rami K. *facial plastic surgeon*
Brant-Zawadzki, Michael *radiologist, director*
Chiu, John Tang *physician*
Connolly, John Earle *surgeon, educator*
Daniel, Rollin Kimball *plastic surgeon*
Grover, Sanjay *plastic surgeon*
Heinrichs, Harvey L. *plastic surgeon, educator*
Lambros, Val (Vasilios S. Lambros II) *plastic surgeon*
Paul, Malcolm David *plastic and reconstructive surgeon*
Seify, Hisham *plastic surgeon, researcher*
Zubrin, Jay Ross *surgeon*

North Hills
Fujikawa, Denson Gen *neurologist, researcher*

Novato
Bredesen, Dale Eric *neurologist, director*

Oakland
Brindis, Ralph *cardiologist, consultant, medical educator*
Cary, Alice Shepard *retired physician*
Feusner, James *oncologist, director*
Gruber, Ronald P. *plastic surgeon, researcher*
Harken, Alden Hood *thoracic surgeon*
Herring, Bernard Duane *physician*
Iribarren, Carlos *epidemiologist*
Killebrew, Ellen Jane (Mrs. Edward S. Graves) *cardiologist, educator*
Magloire, Alix J. (Magloire) *internist*
Ng, Lawrence Ming-Loy *pediatrician*
Roy-Burman, Arup *pediatrician*
Singh, Amandeep *emergency physician*
Vichinsky, Elliott P. *pediatrician, director*

Oceanside
Curtin, Thomas Lee *ophthalmologist*

Orange
Alkire, Michael T. *anesthesiologist, researcher*
Amin, Alpesh N. *internist*
Batra, Anjan S *medical educator*
Berman, Michael Leonard *gynecologic oncologist*
Borghei, Peyman *medical researcher*
Bota, Daniela Annenelie *neurologist, educator*
Chang, Jae Chan *hematologist, oncologist, educator*
Crumley, Roger Lee *surgeon, educator, otolaryngologist*
DiSaia, Philip John *obstetrician, gynecologist, radiology educator*
Djalilian, Hamid *neurosurgeon, director*
Evans, Gregory Randolph Dean *plastic surgeon, educator*
Finley, David Scott *surgeon*
Fruehauf, John Paul *oncologist, director*
Gatcliffe, Troy Antony *gynecologic oncologist, researcher*
Goodwin, Scott Craig *interventional radiologist*
Hoyt, David Butler *surgeon, department chairman*
Kobayashi, Mark Robert *plastic surgeon, educator*
Liao, Solomon *geriatrician, educator*
Lott, Ira Totz *pediatric neurologist*
Morgan, Beverly Carver *pediatrician, educator*
Muhonen, Michael Gordon *neurological surgeon*
Najm, Wadie I. *geriatrician, educator*
Pare, Laura *neurosurgeon, educator*
Rowen, Marshall *radiologist*
Saremi, Farhood *radiologist*
Simjee, Aisha *ophthalmologist, educator*
Smith, Ronald Edward *ophthalmologist*
Vaziri, Nosratola Dabir *internist, nephrologist, educator*
Wirth, Garrett Andrew *plastic surgeon*
Yu, Jen *medical educator*
Zetin, Mark I. *psychiatrist*

Pacific Palisades
Beck, John Christian *physician, educator*
Claes, Daniel John *physician*
Rachelefsky, Gary Stuart *medical educator*

Palo Alto
Adamson, Geoffrey David *reproductive endocrinologist, surgeon*
Bensch, Klaus George *pathology educator*
Bertaccini, Edward J. *anesthesiologist, educator*
Bohman, Bryan *anesthesiologist, hospital administrator*
Chen, Stephen Shi-hua *pathologist, biochemist*
Commons, George W. *plastic surgeon*
de Waal Malefyt, Rene *immunologist*
Dubin, Anne *medical educator*
Fries, James Franklin *internal medicine educator*
Galel, Susan Alpert *transfusion medicine physician*
Hays, Marguerite Thompson *nuclear medicine physician, educator*
Holman, Halsted Reid *physician, educator*
Jeng, Michael Raymond *medical educator*
Lee, Gordon *plastic surgeon, educator*
Marina, Neyssa *pediatrician, educator*
Mitchell, Beverly Shriver *hematologist, oncologist, educator*
Ohayon, Maurice Moyses *medical educator, director*
Rose, Jessica *medical educator*
Salvatierra, Oscar, Jr. *transplant surgeon, urologist, educator*
Schendel, Stephen Alfred *surgeon, educator*
Schrier, Stanley Leonard *hematologist, educator*
Schurman, David Jay *orthopedic surgeon, educator*
Shuer, Lawrence Mendel *neurosurgery educator, dean*
Silverman, Norman Henry *cardiologist, educator*
Strober, Samuel *immunologist, educator*
Urquhart, John *medical researcher, educator*
Westphal, Lynn Marie *obstetrician, gynecologist*
Wu, Lin *cardiologist, researcher*

Palos Verdes Peninsula
Thomas, Claudewell Sidney *psychiatrist, educator*
Van Der Meulen, Joseph Pierre *neurologist*

Panorama City
Bass, Harold Neal *pediatrician, medical geneticist*
Fleisher, Arthur A., II, *physician*
Lieberthal, Allan Stuart *pediatrician, educator*
Sue, Michael Alvin *allergist*

Pasadena
Glovsky, Myron Michael *medical educator*
Harvey, Joseph Paul, Jr. *orthopedist, educator*
Lake, Kevin Bruce *medical association administrator*
Opel, William *medical research administrator*
Shaw, Anthony *pediatric surgeon, retired educator*
Short, Elizabeth M. *internist, educator, retired federal agency administrator*

Piedmont
Montgomery, Theodore Ashton *physician*
Reich, Stanley Benjamin *radiologist, medical educator*

Pleasant Hill
Dixon, Martha Lee *anatomist, physiologist, educator*
Hollister, Arthur Clair, Jr. *epidemiologist, consultant, retired public health service officer*

Pomona
Gambone, Joseph Charles *medical educator, consultant*
Huang, Ying *medical educator*
Khasawneh, Fadi T. *medical educator, researcher*
Rodriguez, Jose L. *neurosurgeon, educator*

Porterville
Neal-Parker, Shirley Anita *obstetrician, gynecologist*

Portola Valley
Fogarty, Thomas James *surgery educator*
Hafkenschiel, Joseph Henry, Jr. *retired cardiologist*

Rancho Mirage
Atiba, Joshua Olajide Oluwabunmi *internist, philanthropist, oncologist, educator, pharmacologist*
Chuang, Tsu-Yi *dermatologist, epidemiologist, educator*
Cone, Lawrence Arthur *medical educator*
Leydorf, Mary Malcolm *physician, writer*
Shaeffer, Charlie Willard, Jr. *cardiologist*
Shen, Alfred C. *neurosurgeon*
Stone, Richard Alan *medical educator*

Rancho Palos Verdes
Chlebowski, Rowan Thomas *oncologist, educator*
Kwan, Benjamin Ching Kee *ophthalmologist*
Neilan, Aidan Joseph *radiologist*

Rancho Santa Fe
Affeldt, John Ellsworth *retired physician*
Carr, David Turner *physician*
Haddad, Gabriel G. *pediatrician, educator*
Nadler, Henry Louis *pediatrician, educator, geneticist*
Rockoff, S. David *radiologist, physician, educator*

Rancho Santa Margarita
Bunkis, Juris *plastic surgeon*

Redding
Renard, Ronald Lee *allergist*

Redlands
Kohli, Gurmander Singh *plastic surgeon*
Skoog, William Arthur *retired oncologist*

Redondo Beach
Grollman, Julius Harry, Jr. *cardiovascular and interventional radiologist*

Redwood City
Deresinski, Stanley C. *epidemiologist*
Fredericson, Michael *physiatrist*
Palmer, Pamela Pierce *anesthesiologist*

Richmond
Arnon, Stephen Soulé *physician, research scientist*
Windham, Gayle C. *epidemiologist*

Riverside
Bricker, Neal S. *physician, educator*
Jung, Timothy Tae Kun *otolaryngologist*
Su, Kenneth C. H. *gynecologist*

Rolling Hills Estates
Bellis, Carroll Joseph *surgeon, educator*

Roseville
Liu, Davis *physician, writer*
Murray, Michael *gynecologist, department chairman*

Sacramento
Albertson, Timothy E. *physician, educator*
Bogren, Hugo Gunnar *radiology educator*
Chamie, Karim *urologist*
Chapman, Michael William *orthopedist, educator*
Cunningham, Mary Elizabeth (Mary Cunningham-Lusby) *physician*
de Vere White, Ralph *urologist, educator*
Donald, Paul James *otolaryngologist*
Flamm, Melvin Daniel, Jr. *cardiologist*
Fung, Maxwell Alexander *medical educator*
Gilbert, William McBeath *physician, perinatologist*
Hales, Robert Ernest *psychiatrist, educator*
Jackson, Richard Joseph *epidemiologist, educator, pediatrician, preventive medicine physician*
Katzberg, Richard Wier *radiologist, researcher*
Khatri, Vijay Pranjivan *surgeon, researcher, educator*
Kon, Alexander A. *pediatrician, educator*
Lara, Primo *medical educator*
Laslett, Lawrence J. *physician, educator*
Lim, Alan Young *plastic surgeon*
Lin, Lily Koo *ophthalmologist*
Lloyd, William C. III *ophthalmologist*
Low, Reginald Inman *cardiologist*
Lynch, Peter John *retired dermatologist*
Makker, Sudesh Paul *physician*
Maverakis, Emanual *dermatologist, educator*
Nagy, Stephen Mears, Jr. *physician, allergist*
Olson, Steven Arthur *orthopaedic surgeon*
Rab, George T. *pediatric orthopedic surgeon*
Robinson, Muriel Cox *psychiatrist*
Wolfman, Earl Frank, Jr. *surgeon, educator*
Wolkov, Harvey Brian *oncologist, researcher*
Wun, Ted *medical educator*
Zusman, Edie Ellen *neurosurgeon*

Salinas
Castro, Robert *pediatrician, educator*

San Bernardino
De Haas, David Dana *emergency physician*

San Clemente
Betts, Andres Betkowsky *anesthesiologist*
Kim, Edward William *ophthalmic surgeon*

San Diego
Achar, Suraj Arthur *medical educator*
Barrett, Kim Elaine *medical educator*
Benirschke, Kurt *retired pathologist, educator*
Bigby, Timothy D. *medical educator*
Bloom, Floyd Elliott *internist, neuroscientist*
Bot, Adrian Ion *immunologist*
Chambers, Henry George *orthopedic surgeon*
DeMaria, Anthony Nicholas *cardiologist, educator*
Doherty, Joni K. *neurologist, educator*
Friedman, Paul Jay *retired radiologist*
Greenberg, Barry H. *cardiologist, medical educator*
Harris, Jeffrey Paul *otolaryngologist*
Herrera, Fernando A. *physician*
Horgan, Santiago *surgeon*
Jamieson, Stuart William *surgeon, educator*
Jeste, Dilip Vishwanath *psychiatrist, researcher*
Kahn, Bruce S. *obstetrician, gynecologist*
Kane, Christopher J. *urologist, educator*
Kaplan, George Willard *urologist*
Kellogg, Huston Glenn *pediatrician, medical educator*
Kim, Choll W. *spine surgeon*
Koka, Prasad S. *biomedical researcher*
Kung, Faith Hilda *pediatrician, educator*
Langenberg, Bret James *surgeon*
Lavine, Joel Edward *physician, medical educator*
Levy, Jerome *dermatologist, retired military officer*
Nahm, Walter K. *dermatologist, researcher*
Parthemore, Jacqueline Gail *internist, educator, hospital administrator*
Pathan, Nuzhat *medical researcher*
Pitt, William Alexander *cardiologist*
Ray, Albert *physician, educator*
Reid, Robert Tilden *medical association administrator, internist*
Resnik, Robert *medical educator*
Roizen, Michael F. *anesthesiologist, medical educator, writer*
Ross, John, Jr. *cardiologist, educator*
Sabbagh, Marwan Noel *physician, researcher*
Schallhorn, Steven *ophthalmologist*
Schmidt, Joseph David *urologist*
Talamini, Mark A. *surgeon, department chairman*

San Dimas
Deliman, Robert Michael *surgeon*

San Francisco
Abbas, Abul K. *pathologist, educator*
Alpert, Bernard Stephen *plastic surgeon, educator*
Amend, William John Conrad, Jr. *physician, educator*
Bainton, Dorothy Ford *pathologist, educator*
Barondes, Samuel Herbert *psychiatrist, educator*
Baskin, Laurence Seth *pediatrician, educator*
Becker, David Kenneth *pediatrician, educator*
Behrens, M. Kathleen *medical researcher*
Beinfield, Harriet *medical association administrator*
Benet, Leslie Zachary *pharmacologist, educator*
Bernstein, Harold Seth *pediatric cardiologist, molecular geneticist*
Bibbins-Domingo, Kirsten Beatrice *internist*
Bikle, Daniel David *research physician*
Bodenheimer, Thomas Siegmund *physician, educator*
Boles, Roger *otolaryngologist*
Botvinick, Elias H. *nuclear medicine physician, researcher, medical educator*
Bourne, Henry R. *pharmacology professor, department chairman, researcher*
Brook, Michael Morris *cardiologist, educator*
Bryant, Allison S. *obstetrician, educator*
Buncke, Gregory M. *plastic surgeon*
Buntic, Rudy F. *plastic surgeon*
Burchard, Esteban Gonzalez *physician, educator*
Chambers, Henry F. *epidemiologist, educator*
Chatterjee, Kanu *cardiologist, educator*
Chin-Hong, Peter Vincente *medical educator*
Chiu, Cynthia S. *ophthalmologist, educator*
Church, Gwynne D. *pediatrician, educator*
Clever, Linda Hawes *physician*
Cobbs, Price Mashaw *social psychiatrist*
Crawford, J. Brooks *ophthalmologist, educator*
Crawford, Michael Howard *cardiologist, educator, researcher*
Dae, Michael W. *cardiologist, medical educator, researcher*
Darney, Philip Dempsey *gynecologist, educator*
Deicken, Raymond Friedrich *neuropsychiatrist, neuroscientist*
Delgado, Eliana *orthopedic surgeon*
Diab, Mohammad *orthopedic surgeon*
Dolev, Jacqueline *physician, researcher*
El-Sayed, Ivan Homer *otolaryngologist, researcher*
Epstein, Charles Joseph *pediatrician, geneticist, biochemist, educator*
Epstein, John Howard *dermatologist*
Erskine, John Morse *surgeon*
Esserman, Laura Jean *oncologist, educator*
Facchini, Francesco Stefano *internist, researcher, nephrologist, researcher*
Farmer, Diana Lee *pediatric surgeon*
Feldman, Mitchell Dean *medical educator*
Ferriero, Donna M. *pediatric neurologist*
Fessel, Walford Jeffrey *rheumatologist*
Finberg, Laurence *pediatrician, educator, dean*
Foster, Elyse *cardiologist, educator*
Foster-Barber, Audrey Elizabeth *neurologist, educator*
Frick, Oscar Lionel *pediatrician, educator*
Frieden, Ilona Josephine *pediatric dermatologist*
Friedman, Gary *plastic surgeon*
Friedman, Suzanne *holistic medical practitioner*
Gellin, Gerald Alan *dermatologist*
Giudice, Linda Carmen *obstetrician, gynecologist, biochemist, reproductive endocrinologist*
Goldschlager, Nora Fox *internist, cardiologist, educator*
Goode, Erica Tucker *internist*
Goodman, Daniel F. *ophthalmologist*
Greenblatt, Ruth Martha *medical educator, researcher*
Greene, Warner Craig *medical educator, administrator*
Greenspan, Francis S. *physician*
Greenspan, Louise Catherine *pediatrician*
Grumbach, Melvin Malcolm *pediatrician, educator*
Havel, Richard Joseph *physician, educator*
Henderson, Isaac Craig *oncologist, researcher*
Heyman, Melvin Bernard *pediatric gastroenterologist*
Higashida, Randall Takeo *radiologist, neurosurgeon, medical educator*
Hodgson, John Graeme *medical researcher*
Hoffman, William Yanes *plastic surgeon, educator*
Hsu, Chi-yuan *nephrologist, researcher*
Ikeda, Clyde Junichi *plastic and reconstructive surgeon*
Jampolis, Melina Beth *internist, physician nutrition specialist*
Jonsen, Albert R(upert) *medical ethics educator*
Kan, Yuet Wai *hematologist, educator*
Katzung, Bertram George *pharmacologist*
Kaymen, Amelia *dermatologist*
Kessler, David Aaron *medical educator, writer, former federal agency administrator, dean*
Kim, David Woojin *plastic surgeon, educator*
King, Talmadge E. *physician*
Kline, Howard Jay *cardiologist, educator*
Koda-Kimble, Mary Anne *pharmacologist, educator, dean*
Koo, John Ying Ming *psychiatrist, dermatologist*
Kriegstein, Arnold *neurologist, educator*
Krishnan, Suneeta *epidemiologist, educator*
Kunwar, Sandeep *neurosurgeon*
Lattanza, Lisa *orthopedist, consultant*
Leard, Lorriana E. *medical educator*
Lee, Charles K. *plastic surgeon, educator*
Levy, Jay A. *medical educator*
Low, Randall *internist, cardiologist*
Lucia, Marilyn Reed *physician*
Lustig, Lawrence Robert *medical educator*
Maa, John *surgeon*
Maas, Corey S. *plastic surgeon*
Mahadevan, Uma *physician*
Marten, Timothy James *plastic surgeon*
Mason, Dean Towle *cardiologist*
Mathias, Robert S. *pediatric nephrologist*
McAninch, Jack Weldon *urological surgeon, educator*
Miller, Arthur Joseph *neurophysiology and craniofacial biology researcher*
Miller, Bruce Lawrence *neurologist, educator*
Miller, Carol A. *pediatrician, educator*
Mustacchi, Piero *preventive medicine physician, educator*
Neylan, Thomas Coogan *psychiatrist*
Nobuhara, Kerilyn *medical educator*
Ousterhout, Douglas Kenneth *plastic surgeon*
Owsley, John Quincy, IV, *plastic surgeon, educator*
Pantell, Robert Howard *pediatrician, educator*
Patti, Marco Giuseppe *surgeon, educator*
Peterlin, Boris Matija *physician*
Petrakis, Nicholas Louis *epidemiologist, medical researcher, educator*
Phillips, Theodore Locke *radiologist, educator*
Prusiner, Stanley Ben *neurologist, educator, biochemist*
Ptacek, Louis John *medical educator, medical researcher*
Raffin, Thomas Alfred *physician, educator, venture capitalist*
Redberg, Rita Fran *cardiologist*
Reijo Pera, Renee A. *reproductive science director, educator*
Ristow, Brunno *plastic surgeon*
Robbins, Elizabeth *pediatric hematologist, oncologist*
Rosenthal, Philip *gastroenterologist*
Rosinski, Edwin Francis *medical educator*
Rudolph, Abraham Morris *pediatrician, educator*
Sawaya, George F. *obstetrician, gynecologist, educator*
Schmidt, Robert Milton *preventive medicine physician, educator, medical association administrator*
Schroeder, Steven Alfred *medical educator*
Schuberth, John M. *surgeon*
Seebach, Lydia Marie *physician*
Shaw, Richard Eugene *cardiovascular researcher*
Sherr, Elliott Harold *neurologist, researcher*
Smith, David Elvin *physician*
Smith, Lloyd Hollingsworth *physician*
Soifer, Scott Jay *pediatrician*
Somsouk, Ma *gastroenterologist*
Speight, Joycelyn *oncologist*
Spivey, Bruce E. *ophthalmologist, educator, health facility administrator*
Stamper, Robert Lewis *ophthalmologist, educator*
Stoller, Marshall *urologist, educator*
Strober, Jonathan Bret *neurologist, educator*
Su, Hua *medical educator*
Suh, Sang Won *medical educator*
Taekman, Michael Seymour *neurological surgeon*
Takemoto, Steven Kan *medical educator*
Tanagho, Emil Abdelsayed *urologist, eductor*
Terr, Lenore Cagen *psychiatrist, writer*
Tihan, Tarik *pathologist, educator*
Uba, Alan Keith *pediatrician, educator*
Vail, Thomas Parker *orthopaedic surgeon*
Varanasi, Venu Gopal *biomedical researcher*
Varma, Madhulika G. *colon and rectal surgeon*
Volberding, Paul Arthur *academic physician*
Volpe, Peter Anthony *surgeon*
Way, E(dward) Leong *pharmacologist, toxicologist, educator*
Weinstein, Philip *neurosurgeon, educator*
Woeber, Kenneth Alois *physician*
Wolters, Paul John *medical educator*
Ying, Weihai *biomedical researcher, educator*
Zhang, Yu *medical researcher*
Zippin, Calvin *epidemiologist, educator*

San Gabriel
Chen, John Calvin *retired psychiatrist, educator*

San Jose
Huynh, Minh Quan *physician*
Lippe, Philipp Maria *neurosurgeon, academic administrator, educator*
Nelson, Lionel M. *otolaryngologist*
Sajjadi, Hamed *otolaryngologist*
Stein, Arthur Oscar *retired pediatrician*
Stevens, David Alec *medical educator*

San Juan Capistrano
Zalta, Edward *otolaryngologist, physician*

San Leandro
Zeller, Scott L. *psychiatrist*

San Luis Obispo
Pinkel, Donald Paul *pediatrician*

San Marino
Sadun, Alfredo Arrigo *neuro-ophthalmologist, scientist, educator*

San Mateo
Chabra, Anand *public health physician, epidemiologist*
Sutherland, Vanna Rae *psychiatrist*
Van Kirk, John Ellsworth *retired cardiologist*

San Rafael
Hoffman, Charles Louis *physician*

San Ramon
Litman, Robert Barry *physician, writer, television and radio commentator*

Sanger
Patton, Jack Thomas *family practice physician*

Santa Ana
Connell, Bruce F. *plastic surgeon*
Myers, Marilyn Gladys *pediatric hematologist, oncologist*
Sporty, Lawrence Douglas *psychiatrist*

Santa Barbara
Avery, Robert Logan *ophthalmologist*
Behrman, Richard Elliot *pediatrician, dean*
Bischel, Margaret DeMeritt *physician, consultant*
Campagna, Jason Adam *anesthesiologist*
Fisher, Steven Kay *neurobiology educator*
Jovanoviè, Lois *medical researcher*
Kohn, Roger Alan *surgeon*
Mathews, Barbara Edith *gynecologist*
Ray, Charles Dean *neurosurgeon, spine surgeon, bioengineer, inventor*
Suh, Wonsuk Warren *radiation oncologist*
Wittenstein, George Juergen *retired surgeon, retired educator*
Wollman, Glenn David *physician, medical guide*

Santa Cruz
Shorenstein, Rosalind Greenberg *internist*

Santa Monica
Alpern, Harvey L. *cardiologist*
Bilchik, Anton Joel *surgeon*
Giuliano, Armando Elario *surgical oncologist, educator, author*
Jain, John Kumar *medical educator, health facility administrator*
Kawamoto, Henry Katsumi, Jr. *plastic surgeon*
Malphus, Edward Wilson *pediatric gastroenterologist*
Mandelbaum, Bert Roland *orthopedist*
Masterson, Lisa M. *gynecologist, obstetrician*
McGuire, Michael Francis *plastic surgeon*
Meier, Steven W. *orthopedist, surgeon, consultant*
O'Connor, Edward Joseph *neurologist*
Oppenheim, William L. *pediatric orthopedist*
Parker, William Howard *obstetrician-gynecologist*
Porter, Verna R. *neurologist, educator*
Resnick, Jeffrey I. *plastic surgeon*
Schultz, Victor M. *physician*
Singer, Frederick Raphael *medical researcher*
Soule, Howard R. *medical association administrator*
Spooner, Sharon Nau *pediatric ophthalmologist*
Stern, Walter Eugene *neurosurgeon, educator*
Teitelbaum, Steven *plastic surgeon*
Tompkins, Ronald K. *retired surgeon, educator*
Wang, Jeffrey C. *surgeon*
Zarem, Harvey Alan *plastic surgeon*

Santa Paula
Edwards, Samuel Roger *retired internist*

Santa Rosa
Cohn, Joseph David *surgeon*
Lewis, Alvin Edward *pathology educator*
McAvoy, John Martin *plastic surgeon*

Sausalito
Keeffe, Emmet Britton *medical educator*
Ornish, Dean *medical association administrator and educator*

Scotts Valley
Cassidy-Eagle, Erin Lynne *social science researcher, director*
Pletsch, Marie Eleanor *plastic surgeon*

Sepulveda
Yano, Elizabeth Martin *epidemiologist, researcher*

Sherman Oaks
Eisenkop, Scott *oncologist*
Handel, Neal *plastic surgeon, researcher, educator*
Stein, Kira D. *psychiatrist*

Sonoma
Emery, John Edward *plastic surgeon, vintner*

Sonora
Duensing, Lennie *medical association administrator*

South San Francisco
Humphrey, Patrick Paul *pharmacologist*
Hurst, Deborah *pediatric hematologist*

Stanford
Abrams, Herbert LeRoy *radiologist, educator*
Ardehali, Reza *cardiologist*
Berek, Jonathan Samuel *surgeon, gynecologic oncologist, writer*
Blau, Helen Margaret *pharmacology educator*
Brock-Utne, John *medical educator*
Brodsky, Jay Barry *medical educator*
Chase, Robert Arthur *surgeon, educator*
Chertow, Glenn M. *internist, nephrologist, researcher*
Clarke, Michael F. *oncologist, educator*
Donaldson, Sarah Susan *radiologist*
Egbert, Peter Roy *ophthalmologist, educator*
Farquhar, John William *physician, educator*
Fearon, William *cardiologist*
Fire, Andrew Z. *pathologist, geneticist, educator*
Fisher, George Albert, Jr. *internist, oncologist*
Fredrick, Douglas Robert *pediatric ophthalmologist*
Galli, Stephen Joseph *biomedical researcher*
Gambhir, Sanjiv Sam *nuclear medicine physician, educator*
Garber, Alan Michael *internist, educator, economist*
George, Tracy I. *pathologist, educator*
Goodman, Stuart B. *medical educator*
Guilleminault, Christian *neurologist*
Hammer, Gregory Benson *anesthesiologist, pediatrician, educator*
Henderson, Victor Warren *behavioral and geriatric neurologist, epidemiologist, researcher, educator*
Hillard, Paula J. Adams *gynecologist, educator*
Hlatky, Mark Andrew *cardiologist, researcher*
Horwitz, Ralph Irving *internist, epidemiologist, educator, former dean*
Hunt, Sharon Ann *cardiologist*
Jardetzky, Oleg *retired medical educator, researcher*
Katznelson, Laurence *medical educator, researcher*
Krensky, Alan Michael *pediatrician, educator*
Levy, Ronald *medical educator, researcher*
Longaker, Michael T. *plastic surgeon, educator*
Lorenz, Hermann Peter *plastic surgeon*
Mansour, Tag Eldin *pharmacologist, educator*
Mark, James B. D. *surgeon, educator*
Marmor, Michael Franklin *ophthalmologist, educator*
McQuillen, Michael Paul *neurologist, educator*
Mignot, Emmanuel *medical researcher*
Miller, D. Craig *cardiovascular surgeon*
Momeni, Arash *plastic surgeon*
Morton, John M. *surgeon, consultant*
Negrin, Robert S *medical educator*
Oberhelman, Harry Alvin, Jr. *surgeon, educator*
Parsonnet, Julie *medical educator*
Perreau Guimaraes, Marcos *medical researcher*
Reddy, Vadiyala Mohan *cardiothoracic surgeon*
Reitz, Bruce Arnold *cardiac surgeon, educator*
Robbins, Robert Clayton *surgeon*
Robert, Herfkens John *medical educator*
Rosenberg, Saul Allen *oncologist, educator*
Rubenstein, Edward *physician, educator*
Schatzberg, Alan Frederic *psychiatrist, researcher*
Shortliffe, Linda Marie Dairiki *urology educator, researcher*
Skirboll, Stephen Lance *neurosurgeon*
So, Samuel Kai Sum *surgeon, researcher*
Sokol, Eric Russell *urogynecologist, reconstructive surgeon, educator*
Stamey, Thomas Alexander *urologist, educator*
Steinberg, Gary K. *neurosurgeon, educator*
Tam, See-Ying Sebastian *biomedical researcher, consultant, entrepreneur*
Valantine, Hannah A. *cardiologist, educator*
Whyte, Richard Ian *surgeon*
Zarins, Christopher Kristaps *surgeon, educator*

Stevenson Ranch
Wick, Mitchell A. *physician*

Stockton
Guo, Xin *medical educator, researcher*
Matuszak, Alice Jean Boyer *pharmacy educator*

Sylmar
Kamangar, Nader *physician, pulmonologist, director, researcher, educator*
Koretz, Ronald Lee *medical educator*
Wong, Andrew L. *rheumatologist, educator*

Templeton
Abernathy, Shields B. *allergist, immunologist, internist*

Thousand Oaks
Dussault, Isabelle *medical researcher*
Eisenberg, Paul Richard *cardiologist, consultant, educator*
Farshidi, Ardeshir B. *cardiologist, educator*
Solomon, David Harris *geriatrician, educator*

Torrance
Brass, Eric Paul *internal medicine and pharmacology educator, academic administrator*
Budoff, Matthew Jay *cardiologist*
Daar, Eric Steven *medical educator*
Dauphine, Christine E. *surgeon*
Emmanouilides, George Christos *physician, educator*
Hammer, Terence Michael *physician*
Hansen, James Edward *medical educator, researcher*
Isenberg, Sherwin Jay *pediatric ophthalmologist*
Kalantar-Zadeh, Kamyar *pediatrician, nephrologist*
Kopple, Joel D. *medical educator, researcher*
Mason-Lipton, Holli Marie *pathologist, educator*
Omari, Bassam O. *cardiothoracic surgeon*
Rajfer, Jacob *urologist, educator*
Stabile, Bruce Edward *surgeon*
Swerdloff, Ronald S. *physician, educator, researcher*
Tanaka, Kouichi Robert *hematologist, educator*
White, Rodney *surgeon*

Tustin
Herdeg, Howard Brian *retired physician*
Neutel, Joel *medical educator, director*

Ukiah
McClintock, Richard Polson *dermatologist*

Valencia
Faris, Mary *medical researcher, director*

Vallejo
Towne, Sarah Patton *physician*

Ventura
Abul-Haj, Suleiman Kahil *pathologist*
Villaveces, James Walter *allergist, immunologist, consultant*

Visalia
Riegel, Byron William *ophthalmologist*

Walnut Creek
Carson, Jay Wilmer *pathologist, educator*
Collen, Morris Frank *retired medical administrator, physician, consultant, researcher*
Gershony, Gary *cardiologist*
Man, Pang Ling *retired psychiatrist*

West Los Angeles
Bohn, Paul Bradley *psychiatrist, psychoanalyst*

West Sacramento
Liu, Fu-Tong *biomedical researcher, dermatologist*

Westminster
Luong, Khanh Vinh Quoc *nephrologist, researcher*

Whittier
Arenowitz, Albert Harold *psychiatrist*
Kirsch, Scott Douglas *family practice physician, director*
Prickett, David Clinton *physician*

Yuba City
Dhillon, Davinder Pal Singh *pulmonologist*

COLORADO

Arvada
Eickhoff, Theodore Carl *infectious disease physician, epidemiologist*
Schrier, Robert William *physician, educator*

Aurora
Arend, William Phelps *medical researcher*
Balasubramaniam, Vivek *pediatrician, educator*
Battaglia, Frederick Camillo *physician*
Connick, Elizabeth *medical educator, researcher*
Crawford, E. David *urologist, surgeon, researcher*
Crowley, Thomas James *psychiatry educator*
Degruy, Frank V. III *physician*
Deitrich, Richard Adam *pharmacology educator*
Eckel, Robert H. *endocrinologist, educator*
Fennessey, Paul Vincent *pediatrics and pharmacology educator, researcher*
Furuta, Glenn Tsuyoshi *physician*
Galinkin, Jeffrey *pediatric anesthesiologist*
Green, Larry Alton *physician, educator*
Grover, Theresa R. *pediatrician, educator*
Haas, Robert Lance *surgeon, consultant*
Jenkins, Herman Arthur *otologic educator, otolarynologist*
Johnston, Richard Boles, Jr. *pediatrician, educator, biomedical researcher*
Jones, M. Douglas, Jr. *pediatrician, educator*
Kappy, Michael Steven *pediatrics educator*
Kingdom, Todd T. *otolaryngologist, educator*
Koyle, Martin Allan *surgeon, educator*
Krugman, Richard David *pediatrician, academic administrator, educator*
La Rosa, Francisco Guillermo *pathologist, researcher, educator*
Leehey, Maureen A. *neurologist, researcher*
Lindenfeld, JoAnn *physician, educator*
Mandell, Mercedes Susan *anesthesiologist, educator*
Nora, Audrey Hart *physician*
Patel, Vikas *orthopedist, educator*
Ridgway, Eli Chester *medical educator*
Ringel, Steven Peter *neurology educator*
Rothman, Micol Sara *medical educator*
Said, M. Sherif A. *pathologist, consultant*
Schmitt, Barton Douglas *pediatrician, educator*
Serkova, Natalie Julia *medical educator, researcher*
Shore, James H(enry) *psychiatrist*
Wilson, Shandra Sheppard *urologist*
Younoszai, Adel K. *pediatrician, director*

Boulder
Bock, S. Allan *physician, educator*
McFarland, Robert Bruce *physician*
Schulz-Heik, R. Jay *medical researcher*
Van Guilder, Gary Preston *medical researcher*

Colorado Springs
Barber, Michael J. *cardiologist, educator*

Denver
Accurso, Frank Joseph *physician, educator*
Anderson, Benjamin Olney *surgeon*
Appel, Alicia Lynn *medical educator*
Cochran, John Howard *plastic and reconstructive surgeon*
Curiel, Tyler Jay *immunologist, educator*
Dinarello, Charles A. *medical educator*
Durairaj, Vikram David *plastic surgeon*
Friesen, Robert Hattan *anesthesiologist*
Gabow, Patricia Anne *internist, health facility executive*
Glanz, Jason *epidemiologist, researcher*
Golitz, Loren Eugene *dermatologist, pathologist, medical association administrator*
Grover, Frederick Lee *cardiothoracic surgeon*
Guber, Myles Stuert *surgeon*
Hoffman, Murray Stanley *internist, educator, cardiologist*
Johnson, Candice Elaine Brown *pediatrician, educator*
Kassan, Stuart S. *rheumatologist*
Keep, Marcus Floyd *neurosurgeon*
Kendig, Lynne E. *physician*
Kim, Fernando J. *urologist, director*
Krikos, George Alexander *pathologist, educator*
Larsen, Gary Loy *physician, researcher*
Lazarus, Jeremy A. *psychiatrist*
Leung, Donald Y. M. *pediatric allergist*
Lewis, Evan Larson *urologist*
Lin, Eugene *radiologist, nuclear medicine physician*
Marrack, Philippa Charlotte *immunologist, researcher*
Martin, Richard Jay *medical educator*
McIntyre, Robert C., Jr. *surgeon, critical care consultant*
Mehler, Philip S. *internist*
Morin, Christopher Joseph *vascular surgeon*
Ogsbury, James Stanley III *neurosurgeon, educator*
Parikh, Chirag R. *physician scientist*
Pearlman, David Samuel *allergist*
Petty, Thomas Lee *internist, educator*
Pomerantz, Marvin *thoracic surgeon*
Porreco, Richard Patrick *physician*
Price, David W. *physician, educator, reseachrer*
Price, David William *physician, educator, researcher*
Rainer, William Gerald *cardiac surgeon*
Schwartz, David A. *genetics, environmental sciences and pulmonology medicine physician, former federal agency administrator*
Sparks, John Wesley *physician*
Stamm, Carol Ann *obstetrician, gynecologist*
Szefler, Stanley James *pediatrics and pharmacology educator*
Taylor, Edward Stewart *obstetrician, educator*
Wang, Cecilia Chiacheh Low *internist, educator*
Washington, Reginald Louis *pediatric cardiologist*
Weatherley-White, Roy Christopher Anthony *surgeon, consultant*

Edwards
Prather, William Ronald *medical association administrator*

Englewood
Fillmore, Joseph H. *physiatrist*
Kelly, Jason Lincoln *radiologist*
Knize, David Maurice *plastic surgeon*
Shah, Manish Harikant *plastic surgeon*
Whiteneck, Gale *medical researcher*

Fort Collins
Aboellail, Tawfik A. *pathologist, educator*
Phemister, Robert David *veterinary medical educator*
Rash, John Edward *medical educator*
Rhyan, Jack C. *pathologist*
Wang, Tian *immunologist, educator*

Glenwood Springs
Jaffrey, Ira *oncologist, educator*

Golden
Grossman, Terry Alan *medical association administrator, director*

Greeley
Cook, Donald Evan *pediatrician, educator*

Lafayette
Mehl, Albert L. *pediatrician, poet, composer*
Thornbury, John Rousseau *radiologist, physician*

Lakewood
Eikleberry, Lois Schillie *physician*

Littleton
Forstot, Stephan Lance *ophthalmologist*

Louisville
Bluestein, Eve *plastic surgeon*
Pneuman, Linda Jackson *retired physician*

Montrose
Boice, Judith Lynette *physician, writer, educator*

Sterling
Mitchell, Stacy Marie *medical transcriptionist*

Vail
Bevan, William Arnold, Jr. *emergency physician*
Millett, Peter J. *orthopedist*
Philippon, Marc Joseph *orthopaedic surgeon*

Wheat Ridge
Fleischaker, Gordon Henry, Jr. *pediatrician*

Wolcott
Flacke, Joan Wareham *physician, anesthesiologist, educator*

CONNECTICUT

Ansonia
Dvoretzky, Israel *dermatologist*

Bethany
Niederman, James Corson *retired internist, educator*

Bridgeport
Abdelsayed, George Gabriel *gastroenterologist*
Atweh, Nabil A. *surgeon, department chairman*
Choi, Young J. *pathologist, educator*
Lobdell, David Hill *retired pathologist*
Maiocco, Kenneth Joseph *dermatologist*
Mcpherson, Craig A. *cardiologist, educator*
Moss, Jeremy Ethan *dermatologist*
Salam, Adil *pulmonary critical care physician*

Danbury
Belsky, Joseph L. *endocrinologist*
Leebens, Patricia Kay *psychiatrist*

Derby
Katz, David Lawrence *preventive medicine physician, researcher*

Fairfield
Burd, Robert Meyer *hematologist, oncologist, educator*
Stanton, Robert Alan *orthopaedic surgeon*

Farmington
Bluestein, Paul A. *physician, insurance company executive*
Deckers, Peter John *surgeon, former dean*
Donaldson, James Oswell III *neurologist, educator*
Fortinsky, Richard Harold *medical educator*
Grant-Kels, Jane Margaret *dermatologist, educator*
Grunnet, Margaret Louise *retired pathologist, educator*
Hussain, Naveed *neonatologist & pediatrician*
Kaplan, Andre Albert *physician*
Liebowitz, Neil Robert *psychiatrist*
Mazzocca, Augusta D. *surgeon*
McCawley, Austin *psychiatrist, educator*
Rosinski, David J. *cardiovascular parfusionist*
Rothfield, Naomi Fox *physician*
Runowicz, Carolyn Dilworth *gynecologist, oncologist, researcher*
Scaniffe, Joseph Albert *anesthesiologist, consultant*
Wand, Martin *ophthalmologist, educator*
White, William B. *medical educator, researcher*

Glastonbury
Singer, Paul Richard *retired ophthalmologist*

Greenwich
Blumberg, Joel Myron *cardiologist*
Bonheim, Nelson Alfred *gastroenterologist, educator*
Grant, Ronald Alfred *psychiatrist, pastoral counselor, psychoanalyst*

Hamden
Nuland, Sherwin *surgeon, writer*

Hartford
Duffy, James Desmond *neopsychiatrist, palliative care physician*
Dworkin, Paul Howard *pediatrician*
Gould, Bruce Elliott *physician, academic administrator, educator*
Jahiel, Rene Ino *physician*
Klimek, Joseph John *physician, educator*
Ramanan, Sundaram V. *internist, hematologist, oncologist*
Rosenberg, Ronald J. *radiologist, director*
Schechter, Neil Lawrence *pediatrician, educator*
Sundaram, V. Ramanan *hematologist, educator*
Zempsky, William Todd *physician*

Lakeville
Lipton, Lester *ophthalmologist, entrepreneur*

Madison
Snell, Richard Saxon *anatomist*

Meriden
Horton, Paul Chester *psychiatrist*
Shapiro, Philip Edwin *dermatologist, dermatopathologist, educator*

Middlebury
Keggi, Kristaps J. *orthopedist, educator*

Milford
Friedman, Lloyd N. *medical educator*
Lee, Sin Hang *pathologist, educator*

New Canaan
Ackerman, Sigurd Howard *psychiatrist*
Coughlin, Francis Raymond, Jr. *surgeon, educator, lawyer*
Hugo, Norman Eliot *retired plastic surgeon, educator*
Klenk, Rosemary Ellen *pediatrician, educator*

New Haven
Akkoyunlu, Mustafa *physician, scientist*
Altice, Frederick L. *epidemiologist, director*
Andiman, Warren Alan *epidemiologist, educator*
Baltimore, Robert Samuel *pediatrician, epidemiologist*
Berland, Gretchen K. *medical educator, filmmaker*
Bloomgarden, Gary Michael *neurosurgeon*
Boyer, James Lorenzen *internist, educator*
Braverman, Irwin Merton *dermatologist, educator*
Burtness, Barbara Ann *medical educator, oncologist*
Cha, Charles *surgical oncologist, hepatobiliary surgeon*
Chhieng, Cheung David *pathologist, educator*
Cohen, Lawrence Sorel *internist, educator*
Collins, William F., Jr. *neurosurgery educator*
Comer, James Pierpont *psychiatrist, educator*
Curtis, Jeptha P. *cardiologist, educator*
Dardik, Alan *surgeon, educator*
Ehrenkranz, Richard Allan *pediatrician*
Floch, Martin Herbert *physician*
Forget, Bernard G. *hematologist, educator*
Foster, Roger Sherman, Jr. *surgeon, educator, health facility administrator*
Funai, Edmund F. *gynecologist*
Genel, Myron *pediatrician, educator*
Goodrich, Isaac *neurosurgeon, educator*
Grauer, Jonathan Newman *orthopedist, educator*
Gross, Ian *academic pediatrician, neonatologist*
Gusberg, Richard Jefferson *surgeon, educator*
Hostetter, Margaret K. *pediatrician, medical educator*
Hsiao, Allen L. *physician, educator*
Igarashi, Peter *nephrologist, educator, nephrologist, researcher*
Jatlow, Peter I. *pathologist, medical educator, researcher*
Jordt, Sven-Eric *pharmacologist, researcher*
Kalyanpur, Arjun *radiologist*
Kashgarian, Michael *pathologist, educator*
Kawano, Tsutomu *medical researcher*
Kim, Jung H. *medical researcher, educator*
Kim, Young Shin *psychiatrist, educator*
King, Robert Alan *psychiatrist, educator*
Krause, Peter James *pediatrician, researcher, educator*
Krumholz, Harlan Marc *cardiologist, internist, educator*
Kushlan, Samuel Daniel *internist, educator, hospital administrator*
Lampert, Rachel *cardiologist, educator*
Leffell, David Joel *dermatologist, surgeon, writer, photographer, medical school administrator, educator*
Levine, Robert John *internist, medical educator, ethicist*
Lytton, Bernard *urology educator*
Meier, George Henry *vascular surgeon*
Mercurio, Mark R. *pediatrician, educator*
Miller, I. George *physician, educator, researcher*
Modd, Lawrence R. *surgeon*
Musto, David Franklin *medical researcher, educator, historian, consultant*
Patrizio, Pasquale *reproductive endocrinologist, andrologist, and infertility specialist*
Patwa, Huned S. *neurology educator*
Persing, John Arthur *surgeon*
Pieribone, Vincent Allen *medical researcher, educator*
Risch, Harvey A. *epidemiologist, educator*
Roberts, Kurt Eric *medical educator, director*
Rose, Aron D. *ophthalmologist, educator*
Ryder, Robert Winsor *medical epidemiologist*
Sartorelli, Alan Clayton *pharmacologist, educator*
Sasaki, Clarence Takashi *surgeon, educator*
Scoutt, Leslie M. *medical educator*
Seashore, Margretta Reed *physician, educator*
Shapiro, Eugene David *pediatrician, epidemiologist, educator*
Shaw, Albert Cheng-gin *medical educator, researcher*
Smith, Brian Richard *hematologist, oncologist, pathologist*
Srihari, Vinod Hiremagalur *psychiatrist*
Stack, Gary Edward *medical educator*
Stahl, Richard Sheldon *surgeon*
Stern, Robert *psychiatrist*
Strauss, John Steaven *psychiatrist, educator*
Tinetti, Mary E. *geriatrician, educator*
Volkmar, Fred Robert *psychiatrist, educator, director*
Webster, Tashonna *health services researcher*
Weiss, Robert M. *urologist, educator*
Zaret, Barry Lewis *cardiologist, medical educator*

New London
Schoenberger, Steven Harris *physician, research consultant*
Urbanetti, John Sutherland *internist, consultant*

Niantic
Douglas, Robert Gordon, Jr. *physician*

Norwalk
Falsone, Jack Joseph *physician*
Littman, Edward *physician*

Old Greenwich
Lorefice, Laurence Santo *psychiatrist*

Orange
Liu, Chuanju *orthopedist, educator*

Oxford
Hayes, Arthur Hull, Jr. *physician, clinical pharmacology educator, medical school dean, business executive, consultant*

Putnam
Day, John Anthony, Jr. *pulmonologist*

Ridgefield
Yang, Jianfei *immunologist*

Shelton
Aferzon, Mark *otolaryngologist*
Spivack, Barney S. *physician*

Southington
Byeff, Peter David *hematologist, oncologist*

Southport
Cutler, Kenneth B., Jr. *dermatologist, educator*
Yach, Derek *epidemiologist, health policy analyst*

Stamford
Cook, Colin Burford *psychiatrist*
Erichson, Robert B. *hematologist, oncologist*
Goodhue, Peter Ames *obstetrician, gynecologist, educator*
Klein, Neil Charles *physician*
Nitowsky, Harold Martin *physician, educator*
Rosenstock, Arthur Richard *plastic surgeon, educator*
Simon, Scott *neurosurgeon, director*
Walsh, Thomas Joseph *ophthalmologist*

Storrs Mansfield
Shapiro, Eve Ilana *medical researcher*

Stratford
Feinberg, Dennis Lowell *dermatologist*
Mahoney, Maurice Jeremiah *medical educator*

Torrington
Kathuria, Nirmal Bhatia *psychiatrist*

Trumbull
Bernstein, Larry Howard *clinical pathologist*

Vernon Rockville
Marmer, Ellen Lucille *pediatrician, cardiologist*

Wallingford
Kryger, Meir *medical educator, researcher*
Lelas, Snjezana *pharmacologist, researcher*

Waterbury
Chabria, Shiven B. *physician, educator*
DeFrancesco, Mark Stephen *physician*
Dudrick, Stanley John *surgeon, research scientist, educator*
Garsten, Joel Jay *gastroenterologist*
Renda, Joseph L. *nephrologist, educator*
Silbert, Jonathan E. *ophthalmologist, educator*

Waterford
Pierson, Anne Bingham *physician*

West Hartford
Silver, Herbert *physician*

Westport
Clausman, Gilbert Joseph *retired medical librarian*
Sacks, Herbert Simeon *psychiatrist, educator, consultant*

Wilton
Radin, Alan Mervyn *physician*

Woodbridge
Mason, John Wayne *psychoneuroendocrinologist, retired medical educator*

DELAWARE

Newark
Dempsey, Kandie *medical researcher, director*
Gardner, Timothy Joseph *surgeon, educator*
Kee, Chandra A. *psychiatrist, director*
Lemole, Gerald Michael *surgeon*
Nomura, Jason T. *emergency physician*

Wilmington
Dadmarz, Kewmars Ebrahim *physician, educator*
Euganeo, Kathleen *radiologic technologist, educator*
Feingold, Ellen *pediatrician, medical writer*
Frelick, Robert Westcott *physician, consultant*
Harcke, Howard Theodore *diagnostic radiologist*
Hsia, Judith Ann *physician*
Ikeda, Satoshi *thoracic and cardiovascular surgeon*
Malatack, James Jeffrey *pediatrician, liver transplant specialist*
Pell, Sidney *epidemiologist*
Pizarro, Christian *surgeon, department chairman*
Saruk, Michael *dermatologist, educator*
Shah, Udayan Kanaiyalal *surgeon*
Teng, Renli *pharmacologist, director*
Wilson, Samuel Earl *anesthesiologist*

DISTRICT OF COLUMBIA

Washington
Adams-Campbell, Lucile L. *epidemiologist, oncologist, educator*
Ahlgren, James David *oncologist*
Ahmed, Atif Ali *pathologist*
Alster, Tina S. *dermatologist, educator*
Anthony, Virginia Quinn Bausch *medical association executive*
Ascensão, João Luis Afonso *physician, researcher, educator*
Aulisi, Edward Fiore *neurosurgeon*
Barnet, Robert Joseph *cardiologist, philosopher*
Batshaw, Mark Levitt *pediatrician, director*
Benjamin, Georges Curtis *medical association administrator, emergency physician, consultant*
Bennett, Stephen *medical association administrator*
Benoit, Marilyn B. *psychiatrist, consultant*
Bielamowicz, Steven A. *otolaryngologist, educator*
Borenstein, David Gilbert *internist, writer, rheumatologist*
Bourne, Peter Geoffrey *physician, educator, writer*
Bruce, Stephanie Robin *geriatrician*
Callaway, Clifford Wayne *physician*
Callender, Clive Orville *surgeon*
Catoe, Bette Lorrina *pediatrician, educator*
Chamberlain, John Loomis III *retired pediatrician, educator*
Chase, Thomas Newell *neurologist, researcher, educator, entrepreneur*
Chatoor-Koch, Irene *child psychiatrist*
Cheng, Tsung O. *cardiologist, educator*
Chester, Alexander Campbell III *physician*
Chiu, Arthur Oi-Shui *pathologist, toxicologist*
Collea, Joseph Vincent *perinatologist, educator*
Collins, Robert Ellwood *surgeon*
Cooper, Byron Stanley *internist, educator*
Delahay, John N. *orthopedist, surgeon*
Desai, Mehul J. *physician, director*
Deshmukh, Vivek R. *neurosurgeon, medical educator*
Ducic, Ivica *medical educator*
Earll, Jerry Miller *internist, educator, endocrinologist*
Eden, Guinevere F. *neurologist, educator*
Edwards, Willarda V. *medical association administrator, internist*
Ein, Daniel *allergist*
Ellis, Jennifer Lynn *thoracic surgeon*
Epps, Roselyn Elizabeth Payne *pediatrician, educator*
Erdtmann, Frederick J. *physician, retired military officer*
Etzel, Ruth Ann *pediatrician, epidemiologist, educator*
Faden, Alan Ira *neurology educator*
Fishbein, Thomas Marlon *general surgeon, transplant surgeon*
Fornace, Albert J., Jr. *medical researcher*
Gaillard, William Davis *physician*
Garcia, Jorge Mance *cardiologist*
Gardner, William Albert, Jr. *pathologist, medical products executive*
Gehrig, Leo Joseph *retired surgeon*
Giannini, Margaret Joan *pediatrician, federal agency administrator*
Glassman, Leonard M. *radiologist*
Grandi, Edward *medical association administrator*
Gray, Sheila Hafter *psychiatrist, researcher*
Harter, Donald Harry *neurologist, medical educator*
Hayes, Daniel Fleming *oncologist, educator*
Hoffman, Eric P. *medical geneticist, educator*
Hong, Y. Mark *urologist*
Hussain, Syed Taseer *biomedical researcher, educator*
Isaacs, Claudine Janet Diana *internist*
Johnston, Gerald Samuel *physician, educator*
Jonas, Richard Andrew *medical educator*
Jordan, V. Craig *endocrine pharmacologist, educator*
Jose, Pedro A. *physician*
Kalfoglou, Andrea Lynn *medical educator, researcher*
Katz, Ira R. *psychiatrist, mental health services administrator*
Kennedy, Richard Odell *physician*
Kirch, Darrell Gene *medical association administrator, former dean*
Korn, David *pathologist, educator*
Labbok, Miriam Harriet *physician, educator*
Laredo, James *surgeon, educator*
Latham, Patricia S. *physician*
Lauerman, William *medical educator*
Leffall, LaSalle Doheny, Jr. *surgeon, educator*
Lessin, Lawrence Stephen *hematologist, oncologist, educator*
Lewin, John Calvert *medical association administrator*
Lo, Shyh-Ching *pathologist*
Longnecker, David Eugene *anesthesiologist, educator*
Lynn, D. Joanne *physician, researcher*
Makhlouf, Hala R. *pathologist, educator*
Mandel, Harold George *pharmacologist, educator*
Manderson, Easton L. *orthopedist, surgeon*
Maniscalco-Theberge, Mary Elizabeth *surgeon, medical educator*
Mann, Oscar *retired physician, internist, educator*
Marshall, John Lindsay *medical educator*
Marshall, Margaret Blair *thoracic surgeon*
McGinnis, James Michael *physician*
Mishra, Lopa *gastroenterologist, educator*
Murray, Robert Fulton, Jr. *physician*
Nass, Sharyl Jeanne *medical educator*
Nesti, Leon J. *orthopedist, educator*
Novitch, Mark *physician, retired pharmaceutical executive*
Nsouli, Talal Mounir *physician, allergist, immunologist*
Oertel, Yolanda Castillo *pathologist, educator*
Olding, Michael *plastic and reconstructive surgeon*
Paulson, Jerome Avrom *pediatrician*
Pellegrino, Edmund Daniel *internist, educator, retired academic administrator*
Perkins, Jeremy Goodrich *hematologist, oncologist, researcher*
Pichard, Augusto D. *cardiologist, medical educator*
Potter, John Francis *oncologist, surgeon*
Raines, C. Fay *medical association administrator, dean*
Randolph, Linda A. *medical association administrator*
Rayner, Victoria Leigh *medical educator, consultant*
Reaman, Gregory Harold *pediatric hematologist, oncologist*
Robinowitz, Carolyn Bauer *psychiatrist, educator, director*
Rodriguez, Jorge Jacinto *psychiatrist*
Rubenstein, Lisa V. *medical association administrator, educator*
Ruckman, Roger Norris *pediatric cardiologist*
Ruehle, Charles Joseph *pathologist, military officer*
Schechter, Geraldine Poppa *hematologist*
Shaffer, Benjamin Scott *surgeon*
Shanahan, Sheila Ann *pediatrician, educator*
Shanmugam, Victoria Kate *medical educator*
Siegel, Robert Steven *internist, oncologist, educator*
Simon, Gary Leonard *internist, educator*
Sivasubramanian, Kolinjavadi Nagarajan *neonatologist, educator*
Sly, Ridge Michael *pediatrician, allergist, immunologist, educator*
Smith, Lee Elton *surgery educator, retired military officer*
Spagnolo, Samuel Vincent *internist, pulmonary specialist, educator*
Spear, Scott Lawrence *plastic surgeon*
Starr, Dorothy Anne *retired psychiatrist*
Stepp, Mary Ann *medical educator*
Thompson, Terry Lamar *orthopedist, educator*
Toretsky, Jeffrey A. *physician, researcher, educator*
Valachovic, Richard William *medical association administrator*
Wartman, Steven A. *medical association administrator*
Witorsch, Philip *internist, educator*
Wolfe, Sidney Manuel *physician*

FLORIDA

Alachua
Yang, Li-Xia *biomedical researcher, scientist, educator*

Amelia Island
Schiebler, Gerold Ludwig *pediatrician, educator*

Atlantic Beach
Walker, Richard Harold *pathologist, educator*

Bartow
Etheredge, Edward Ezekiel *retired surgeon*

Bay Pines
Jewell, Vanessa Yoder *surgical physician assistant*
Law, David Hillis *physician*

Boca Raton
Buchbinder, Ligaya H. *dermatologist*
Calabrese, Carlo *naturopathic physician*
Fagien, Steven *ophthalmologist, consultant*
Garrod, Kenneth J. *orthopedist, surgeon*
Haugen, Christine *plastic surgeon*
Jahanzeb, Mohammad *oncologist, hematologist*
Johr, Robert Henry *dermatologist*
Man, Daniel *plastic surgeon*
Parra-Davila, Eduardo *surgeon, educator*
Pasternack, Stefan Alan *psychiatrist, psychoanalyst*
Penhollow, Tina Marie *health science researcher, educator*
Ripps, Harris *ophthalmologist, educator*
Sperry, Len Thomas *psychiatrist and preventive medicine educator*
Weiner, Howard Marc *physician*

Bonita Springs
Kopf, George Michael *retired ophthalmologist*

Boynton Beach
Chalal, Joseph B. *orthopedist, surgeon*
Glickman, Franklin Sheldon *dermatologist, educator*
Pataky, Paul Eric *ophthalmologist*

Bradenton
Vereb, Teresa B. *psychiatrist*

Cape Canaveral
Carrick, Frederick Robert *neurologist, researcher*

Cape Coral
Martin, Benjamin Gaufman *ophthalmologist*

Clearwater
Bailey, Robin Keith *medical educator*

Coconut Grove
Stuzin, James M. *plastic surgeon*

Coral Gables
Brandt, Frederic Sheldon *dermatologist*
Owens, Michael Howard *otolaryngologist*
Perez, Josephine *psychiatrist, educator*
Wolf, Aizik Loft *neurosurgeon*

Davie
Lenchus, Joshua David *physician, pharmacist*

Daytona Beach
Bower, Roger Harrison *endocrinologist, director*
Dineen, Martin Kevin *urologist*
Duma, Richard Joseph *epidemiologist, microbiologist, pathologist, physician, researcher, educator*
Regnier, Nancy Mae *medical educator*

Deland
Blais, Michael Roland *retired urologist*
Goldberg, Paul Bernard *gastroenterologist, clinical researcher*

Delray Beach
Belizon, Avraham *colon and rectal surgeon, researcher*
Rosenfeld, Steven Ira *ophthalmologist*

Doral
Badia, Alejandro *orthopedist*

Englewood
Sanders, W(illiam) Eugene, Jr. *retired internist*

Fernandina Beach
Barlow, Anne Louise *pediatrician, medical researcher*

Fort Lauderdale
Das, Sudip Kumar *pharmaceutical scientist*
Droege, Marcus *medical educator, researcher*
Fleisher, Jay M. *medical educator*
Glick, Richard Stephen *internist, rheumatologist*
Lichtinger, Moises *obstetrician, gynecologist*
Lodwick, Gwilym Savage *radiologist, educator*
Parker, Sasha Smilka *medical educator, nurse, consultant*
Rubinson, Howard Alan *physician*
Shen, Michael Yue-Hua *cardiologist*
Tristano, Antonio Gino *medical researcher*
Velez, Ines *oral pathologist, educator*
Whitmore, Douglas Michael *physician*
Winner, Paul Kevin *medical educator, researcher*

Fort Myers
Gorovoy, Mark S. *physician*
Mandelkorn, Robert Marc *ophthalmologist*
Meng, Gunter Richard *retired surgeon*

Gainesville
Baz, Maher Afif *internist, educator, medical director lung transplant program*
Behnke, Marylou *pediatrician, educator*
Berns, Kenneth Ira *physician*
Copeland, Edward Meadors III *surgeon, educator*
Denardo, Scott Jeffrey *cardiologist*
Dharnidharka, Vikas R. *pediatrician*
Drago, Valeria *neurologist, researcher*
Drummond, Willa Hendricks *neonatologist, educator, information technology executive*
Forsmark, Chris E. *medical educator*
Freund, Gerhard *retired medical educator*
Good, Michael Lowell *anesthesiologist, educator, dean*
Greer, Melvin *medical educator*
Heilman, Kenneth Martin *neurologist, educator*
Herzog, Roland W. *medical educator*
Huang, Emina Hui-na *surgeon, educator*
LeVeen, Robert Frederick *radiologist*
LeVine, Ann Marie *medical educator, director*
Lynn, Romrell John *medical educator*
Mazzaferri, Ernest Louis *endocrinologist, educator*
Modell, Jerome Herbert *anesthesiologist, educator*
Mubarak, Kamal K. *pulmonologist, intensivist*
Neiberger, Richard Eugene *pediatrician, nephrologist, educator*
Neims, Allen Howard *pediatrician, educator, dean, researcher*
Pepine, Carl John *physician, educator*
Pfaff, William Wallace *medical educator*
Rhoton, Albert Loren, Jr. *neurosurgeon, educator*
Rubin, Melvin Lynne *ophthalmologist, educator*
Shanklin, Douglas Radford *physician*
Silverstein, Janet Hope *pediatrician, educator*
Small, Parker Adams, Jr. *pediatrician, educator*
Suzuki, Howard Kazuro *retired anatomist, educator*
Tisher, Charles Craig *nephrologist, educator, former dean*
Tonelli, Adriano R. *cardiologist*
Toskes, Phillip Paul *gastroenterologist, educator, researcher*
Tuli, Sonal *medical educator*
Vincent, Kevin Robert *physician, educator*
Wagner, Mary *medical educator*
Walsh, Katherine Jean *physician*
Wheat, Myron William, Jr. *cardiothoracic surgeon*
Wingard, John Reid *medical educator*
Yuan, Zhen *biomedical researcher*
Zhou, YiLi *physician*

Hallandale
Braverman, Stanley Deems *ophthalmologist*

Hialeah
Sosa, Jorge Luis *surgeon*

Hollywood
Constantinescu, Alex R. *pediatrician, nephrologist*
Duffner, Lee R. *ophthalmologist*
Sofman, Michael S. *dermatologist*

Jacksonville
Aldana, Philipp Roque *neurosurgeon*
Armitage, Faye *medical researcher*
Berquist, Thomas H. *radiologist, educator*
Bosworth, William Posey *physician, physical education educator*
Cheshire, William Polk, Jr. *neurologist*
Edwards, Fred Hayden *cardiologist*
Erasmus, David B. *pulmonologist, consultant*
Kusumoto, Fred *cardiologist, director*
Mai, Martin *nephrologist, consultant*
Mass, Myron Frank *allergist, immunologist*
Mazur, John M. *orthopedist, educator*
Mooradian, Arshag Dertad *internist, educator*
Moreno-Aspitia, Alvaro *physician, researcher*
Nussbaum, Michael Scot *physician, medical educator*
Olney, Robert Caldwell *pediatrician, researcher*
Radisky, Derek Charles *biomedical researcher, educator*
Sands, Michael Lee *infectious diseases physician*
Siragusa, Daniel *radiologist, educator*
Stein, Keith Lance *health system administrator*
Talley, Nicholas Joseph *medical educator, research scientist, physician*
Woodward, Timothy Andre *gastroenterologist*

Jupiter
Ernst, Calvin Bradley *retired vascular surgery educator*
Zelnick, Ronald Stuart *surgeon*

Lady Lake
Pflum, William John *retired physician*

Lakeland
Kottke, Bruce A. *internist*

Largo
Brown, Warren Joseph *physician*
Grove, Jeffrey Scott *family practice physician*
Krolick, Merrill A. *cardiologist*
Ristow, George Edward *neurologist, educator*

Leesburg
Moore, Wistar *cardiovascular surgeon*

Longboat Key
Howell, Robert S. *retired pathologist*
McCollough, Newton Clark III *orthopaedic surgeon*

Loxahatchee
Wisnicki, Jeffrey Leonard *plastic surgeon*

Lutz
Cualing, Hernani Del Mundo *physician, researcher*

Marco Island
Sundberg, Ruth Dorothy *hematologist, educator*

Melbourne
Grenevicki, Lance Francis *surgeon*
Magee, Thomas Henry *radiologist, educator*
Pocoski, David John *cardiologist*

Miami
Abitbol, Carolyn Larkins *pediatrician, nephrologist, educator*
Albini, Thomas A. *ophthalmologist*
Arnold, David Jack *surgeon, educator*
Asensio, Juan A. *medical association administrator*
Baker, Thomas J., Jr. *plastic surgeon*
Bandstra, Emmalee S. *physician, pediatrician, researcher, educator*
Beck, Morris *allergist*
Benyunes, Abraham Joseph *pediatrician*
Blechman, Wilbur Jordan *medical educator*
Block, Norman Louis *oncologist, educator*
Burke, George William III *surgery educator*
Burke, Redmond Paul *cardiologist, surgeon*
Cabrera DeBuc, Delia *medical researcher, educator*
Campos, Michael *medical educator*
Castro, Jose Guillermo *infectologist, educator*
Chernow, Bart *critical care physician*
Chiron, Harlan S. *orthopedic surgeon, educator*
Colon, Ennio M. *pediatrician*
Culbertson, William W. *ophthalmologist, educator*
DeChurch, Stephanie J. *pediatrician*
Duchesne, Carlos A. *epidemiologist, military officer*
Eftekhari, Nasser *physiatrist*
Elsas, Louis Jacob, II, *physician, educator*
Escalon, Maricer *medical educator*
Espinoza, Luis Alberto *medical educator, researcher*
Freshwater, Michael Felix *hand surgeon, educator*
Fukata, Masayuki *gastroenterologist, hematologist*
Furst, Alex Julian *thoracic and cardiovascular surgeon*
Gebhard, Ralf Erich *anesthesiologist*
Ginsberg, Myron David *neurologist*
Goldschmidt, Clermont Pascal J. *medical educator, cardiologist, dean*
Green, Barth *neurosurgeon*
Hare, Joshua Michael *cardiologist, educator*
Harper, Thomas Wayne *ophthalmologist*
Hershberger, Ray E. *cardiologist, educator*
Hochstein, Leonard Mark *plastic surgeon*
Howell, Ralph Rodney *pediatrician, geneticist, educator*
Ichii, Hirohito *surgeon, educator*
Kaiser, Robert Mark *geriatrician, educator*
Kessler, Kenneth Michael *cardiologist*
Khurana, Seema Rani *osteopath, educator*
Kim, Hee Kee *medical researcher*
Kurlansky, Paul Alan *cardiovascular and thoracic surgeon*
Labbie, Andrew Scott *pediatric urologist, surgeon*
Landy, Howard Jay *medical educator*
Lemberg, Louis *cardiologist, educator*
Levine, Jay Alan *cardiologist*
Lew, John I. *surgeon, educator*
Lippman, Marc Estes *oncologist, educator, medical researcher*
Messiah, Sarah Elizabeth *medical researcher*
Nahab, Fatta B. *neurologist, educator*
Nahmad, Michel Henry *thoracic surgeon*
Neville, Holly Leigh *pediatrician, surgeon*
Nguyen, Dao Minh *thoracic surgeon, director*
O'Brien, Christopher Blackburn *gastroenterologist, director*
Page, Larry Keith *neurosurgeon, educator*
Panthaki, Zubin Jal *medical educator, plastic surgeon*
Pavlow, Shara Toursh *professor, medical administrator*
Pericak-Vance, Margaret A. *medical geneticist, educator, health facility administrator*
Persoff, Myron Mayer *plastic surgeon*
Pham, Si Mai *cardiothoracic surgeon*
Porter, Wayne Randolph *dermatologist*
Raez, Luis Estuardo *physician*
Rao, Cv *medical educator*
Richton, Samuel M. *pediatric endocrinologist*
Ricordi, Camillo *surgeon, researcher*
Rodriguez, René F. *orthopedic surgeon*
Rossi, Anthony Fred *cardiologist*
Rubell, Donald *gynecologist, hotel executive, art collector*
Sanders, Lee Michael *medical association administrator, educator*
Schally, Andrew Victor *endocrine oncologist, researcher*
Schulman, Carl *surgeon, educator*
Scully, Sean Patrick *orthopaedic surgeon, educator*
Sheremata, William A. *neurologist, educator*
Skyler, Jay S. *medical educator, consultant*
Smiddy, William Earl *ophthalmologist*
Smith, Stanley Bertram *clinical and anatomic pathologist, allergist, immunologist*
Struhl, Theodore Roosevelt *surgeon*
Swaminathan, Sethuraman *pediatrician, cardiologist*
Thaller, Seth Ray *plastic surgeon*
Vogt-Lowell, Robert W. *pediatric cardiologist*
Wang, Michael Y. *neurosurgeon*
Weed, Donald T. *otolaryngologist, educator*
Wheeler, Steve Dereal *neurologist*
Wolfson, Aaron Howard *radiation oncologist, educator*
Young, Mark Philip *allergist*
Zaydon, Thomas John, Jr. *plastic surgeon*

Miami Beach
Agatston, Arthur Stephen *cardiologist, educator*
Gagner, Michel *surgeon, educator*
Justiniani, Federico Roberto *internist, educator*
Katz, Brian Jeffrey *dermatologist*
Koffler, Karen *internist*
Lopera, Gustavo Adolfo *cardiologist, electrophysiologist*
Mandy, Stephen Howard *dermatologist, educator*
Sackner, Marvin Arthur *physician*
Shaw, Jon Angus *psychiatrist*

Naples
Blumenberg, Robert Murray *retired surgeon, educator*
Carneiro, Ronaldo Dos Santos *surgeon*
Carrick, Lee *retired dermatologist*
Gaskins, William Darrell *ophthalmologist*
Gehring, David Austin *cardiologist, physician, health facility administrator*
Greene, David *surgeon, researcher*
Hogg, Virginia Lee *retired medical educator*
Pfister, Raymond Lawrence *otolaryngologist*
Randall, Neil Warren *gastroenterologist*
Schwartz, Stephen Gregory *ophthalmologist*
Temple, Donald *retired allergist, dermatologist*

Neptune Beach
Perniciaro, Charles Vincent *dermatologist, educator, entrepreneur*

North Miami
Ferro, Alejandro F. *obstetrician, gynecologist*

North Miami Beach
Soto, Jose Antonio *family medicine physician*

Ocala
Cunha, Tim *biological researcher, entrepreneur*

Oldsmar
Gambone, Victor, Jr. *internist, geriatrician*

Orlando
Badhwar, Vinay *thoracic surgeon, researcher*
DeCampli, William Michael *surgeon, researcher*
Nathanson, Ian Thomas *pediatric pulmonologist*
Nykanen, David Gordon *pediatrician, cardiologist, consultant*
Peters, Calvin Ronald *plastic and reconstructive surgeon*
Price, Charles Turner *surgeon*
Pyrsopoulos, Nikolaos T. *medical educator, director*
Taitt, Earl Paul *psychiatrist, military officer*

Ormond Beach
Hewes, Robert Charles *radiologist*

Palm Bay
Burgio, Michael *medical researcher*

Palm Beach
Guthrie, Randolph Hobson, Jr. *plastic surgeon, consultant*
Simon, Harold *radiologist*

Palm Beach Gardens
Grewal, Dilraj S. *ophthalmologist, researcher*
Kapnick, Samuel Jason *oncologist*
Kershner, Robert *ophthalmologist, educator*
Krathen, Richard Andrew *dermatologist*
Latimer, Michael C. *medical educator*

Panama City Beach
Reading, Anthony John *retired psychiatrist, educator*

Pensacola
Canady, Alexa Irene *pediatric neurosurgeon, educator*
Gill, Becky Lorette *retired psychiatrist*
Ricketson, George Manning III *retired surgeon*
Sharma, Venkatanarayanan *professor*
Vuksta, Michael Joseph *surgeon*

Placida
Prabhudesai, Mukund M. *physician, educator, health facility and academic administrator, researcher*

Plantation
Latta, Loren Lee *orthopaedic research educator*
Morris, James Bruce *internist*

Port Charlotte
Asperilla, Marianito O. (Mark) *epidemiologist*

Punta Gorda
Hollinshead, Ariel Cahill *oncologist, educator, researcher*

Royal Palm Beach
Cutler, Jonathan M. *podiatrist*

Saint Leo
Ondrovic, Leo E. *medical researcher, educator*

Saint Petersburg
Betzer, Susan Elizabeth Beers *physician, geriatrician*
Buckspan, Randy Jay *plastic surgeon*
Gilbert, Gordon Joel *neurologist, electroencephalographer*
Linask, Kersti K. *medical educator*
Linhart, Joseph Wayland *retired cardiologist, educational administrator*
MaCris, Jack Achilles *surgeon*
Root, Allen William *pediatrician, educator*
Rosenblum, Martin Jerome *ophthalmologist*
Wallach, Stanley *medical educator, consultant, administrator*

Sanford
Drewry, Marcia Ann *physician*
Shub, Harvey Allen *surgeon*

Sarasota
Aull, Susan *physician*
Bowers, Charles Richard *surgeon*
Cavanagh, Denis *gynecologist, obstetrician, gynecological oncologist, educator*
Cummings, Martin Marc *physician, educator, academic administrator*
El Shahawy, Mahfouz *internist, cardiologist, educator*
Iverson, Robert Louis, Jr. *retired internist, physician*
Jelks, Mary Larson *retired pediatrician*
O'Malley, Thomas Anthony *gastroenterologist, internist*
Runge, Paul E. *ophthalmologist, educator*

South Miami
Ballen, Ann E. *ophthalmologist*
Rossi, Patricio *radiologist*

Stuart
Maldonado, Carlos Manuel *surgeon*
Moran, Michael E. *urologist*

Sunny Isles Beach
Harezi, Ilonka Jo *medical technology research executive*

Sunrise
Adams, Nelson L. III *obstetrician, gynecologist*

Tallahassee
Cavanagh, James Ellsworth, Jr. *medical educator*
Deeb, Larry Charles *pediatric endocrinologist, epidemiologist*
Hercule, Hantz C.P. *physician, research scientist*
Hernandez, Jose Yolando Balagtas *surgeon*
Hernandez, Minerva Cuadrante *physician, consultant*
Maguire, Charlotte Edwards *retired pediatrician*
Rahman, Saleh Mahmudur *medical educator*
Williams, Charles D. *radiologist*

Tampa
Acs, Geza *medical educator, surgical pathologist*
Afield, Walter Edward *psychiatrist, health facility administrator, educator*
Barness, Lewis Abraham *physician*
Boyce, H. Worth *gastroenterologist, educator*
Branch, William Terrell *urologist, educator*
Eichberg, Rodolfo David *physiatrist, educator*
Gallagher, Scott Farrell *surgeon, researcher*
Gerhard, H. John *orthopaedic surgeon, retired military officer*
Gilbert-Barness, Enid F. *pathologist, educator*
Greenfield, George B. *radiologist*
Greenwald, Daniel Paul *plastic surgeon*
Hoffmann, Michael *neurologist*
Howlett, Lee Ann *medical librarian, writer*
Jacobson, Howard Newman *obstetrics and gynecology educator, researcher*
Kazem, Ismail *radiation oncologist, educator, health facility administrator*
Kirby, Russell Stephen *epidemiologist, geographer, researcher*
Knox, Michael Dennis *medical educator, research center administrator*
List, Alan *medical educator*
Lockhart, Jorge Luis *urologist, educator*
McIlwain, Harris H. *physician, researcher*
Muroff, Lawrence Ross *nuclear medicine physician, educator*
Nagera, Humberto *psychiatrist, psychoanalyst, educator, writer*
Older, Jay Justin *ophthalmic plastic surgeon*
Olson, Robert Eugene *physician, biochemist, educator*
Orlowski, James Phillip *pediatrician*
Pedowitz, Robert Alan *orthopaedic surgeon, researcher*
Pfeiffer, Eric Armin *psychiatrist, gerontologist, writer*
Powers, Pauline Smith *psychiatrist, educator, researcher*
Rentos, Peter George *medical educator*
Rowlands, David Thomas *pathology educator*
Saba, Hussain Ismail *hematologist, researcher*
Sanberg, Paul Ronald *medical educator*
Sexton, Wade J. *oncologist, educator*
Shenefelt, Philip David *dermatologist*
Shephard, Bruce Dennis *obstetrician, educator, medical writer*
Silbiger, Martin L. *radiologist, educator, dean*
Smith, David John, Jr. *plastic surgeon*
Spellacy, William Nelson *obstetrician, gynecologist, educator*
Sullebarger, John Thompson *internist, cardiologist, educator*
Tebbi, Cameron K *hematologist, oncologist*
Vale, Fernando Luis *medical educator*
Vesely, David Lynn *medical educator, research scientist*
Volicer, Ladislav *physician, educator*
Watkins, Joan Marie *retired osteopath, physician*
Wolfson, Jay *medical educator, consultant, lawyer*

The Villages
Mirkin, Gabe Baron *physician, medical educator, writer, radio personality*

Titusville
Duffy, John Charles *psychiatrist, educator, consultant*

Valrico
Palmer, Louis Thomas *pathologist*

Venice
Abernathy, George Thomas *cardiologist, consultant*
Hrachovina, Frederick Vincent *retired osteopathic physician*

Vero Beach
Christopher, Robert Paul *retired physical medicine physician*
Hilker, Robert Reuben John *medical educator, researcher, administrator, consultant*
Schwarz, Berthold Eric *psychiatrist*

Weeki Wachee
Finney, Roy Pelham, Jr. *urologist, surgeon, inventor*

West Palm Beach
Brumback, Clarence Landen *physician*
Cooney, Gail Austin *medical association administrator*
Gonzalez, Faustino Agustin *preventive medicine physician, director*
Levin, Ronald Mitchell *geriatrician*
Newmark, Emanuel *ophthalmologist*
Pottash, A. Carter *psychiatrist, hospital executive*
Stashenko, Vetaley *anatomist, educator*
Whitfield, Graham Frank *orthopedic surgeon*

Weston
Galvez-Jimenez, Nestor *neurologist*
Ghoniem, Gamal M. *urologist*
Lazar, Marioara *psychiatrist*
Malave, Andres *pharmacologist, educator*

Winter Haven
Okun, Neil Jeffrey *vitreoretinal surgeon*

Winter Park
Baker, James L., Jr. *plastic surgeon, educator*
Kolin, Irving Seymour *psychiatrist*
Wilson, Cecil Bruce *internist*

GEORGIA

Acworth
Oloni, Anthony Olushegun *medical association administrator, director*

Atlanta
Albee, Robert Bruce *gynecologist, endoscopic laser surgeon*
Arias, Ileana *psychiatrist, educator*
Ashizawa, Annette Eiko *epidemiologist, researcher*
Barnett, Crawford Fannin, Jr. *internist, educator, cardiologist, travel medicine specialist*
Barrow, Daniel Louis *neurosurgeon*
Berkelhamer, Jay Ellis *pediatrician*
Besser, Richard Eric *pediatrician, federal agency administrator*
Blumenthal, Daniel Sender *medical educator*
Boden, Scott David *orthopedic surgeon, spine surgeon, educator*
Brandenburg, David Saul *gastroenterologist, educator*
Brandes, Johann Christoph *oncologist*
Branson, Bernard M. *medical association administrator, director*
Bremner, James Douglas *psychiatrist, researcher, education educator*
Brigham, Kenneth Larry *medical educator*
Brown, William Virgil *internal medicine educator*
Burrows, Nilka Rios *epidemiologist*
Clearo, Kellie Anne *internist, pharmacist, psychiatrist*
Codner, Mark Allen *plastic surgeon*
Cooper, Gerald Rice *clinical pathologist*
Cooper, William A. *cardiothoracic surgeon, medical educator*
Cooper-Ruspoli, Annie Nataf *psychiatrist, director*
Coughlin, Steven Scott *epidemiologist*
Davis, Lawrence William *radiation oncologist*
Davis, Michael *medical educator*
DeLong, Mahlon R. *neurologist, educator*
De Rosa, Christopher Thomas *biomedical researcher*
Dhawan, Saurabh *physician, educator*
Dietz, William Harry *pediatrician*
Din-Dzietham, Rebecca L.P. *cardiologist, educator*
Dobes, William Lamar, Jr. *dermatologist, educator*
D'Orsi, Carl Joseph *medical educator, radiologist, researcher*
Douglas, John Simonton, Jr. *cardiologist, educator*
Dutt, Kamla *medical educator*
Elliott, Lester Franklyn *plastic surgeon*
Fajardo, Geroncio Cagigas *epidemiologist*
Falk, Henry *pediatrician, epidemiologist, researcher*
Fenton, Kevin Andrew *epidemiologist, educator*
Ferdinand, Keith C. *cardiologist*
Frias, Jaime Luis *retired pediatrician, clinical geneticist, educator*
Frumkin, Howard *epidemiologist, educator*
Ganaway, George Kenneth *psychiatrist, psychoanalyst, educator, researcher*
Gayle, Helene D. *pediatrician, public health service officer*
Gibbons, Gary Hugh *cardiologist, educator*
Gordon, Frank Jeffrey *medical educator*
Grossniklaus, Hans E. *ophthalmologist, educator*
Gupta, Sanjay *neurosurgeon, educator, medical correspondent, journalist*
Gutman, Julie Rae *pediatrician*
Guyton, Robert A. *cardiothoracic surgeon, medical educator*
Hall, Wilbur Dallas, Jr. *medical educator*
Hao, Chunhai *pathologist, researcher*
Harrison, David Glenn *medical educator, cardiologist*
Hatcher, Charles Ross, Jr. *surgeon, health facility administrator*
Helmick, Charles Gardiner III *epidemiologist*
Hester, Thomas Roderick, Jr. *plastic surgeon, educator*
Higginbotham, Eve Juliet *ophthalmologist, educator, dean*

Hug, Carl Casimir, Jr. *pharmacology and anesthesiology educator, medical ethics educator*
Igietseme, Joseph Ugbodaga *biomedical researcher, educator*
Israili, Zafar Hasan *pharmacologist, educator*
Jurkiewicz, Maurice John *surgeon, educator*
Kalogeropoulos, Andreas P. *cardiologist*
Karp, Herbert Rubin *neurologist, educator, geriatrician*
Kauten, James Richard *cardiothoracic surgeon*
Keyserling, Harry L. *pediatric infectious disease physician, researcher*
King, Spencer Bidwell III *cardiologist, educator, medical educator*
Klippel, John H. *medical association administrator, physician*
Kohler, James J. *medical researcher*
Kushner, Howard I. *public health and history of medicine educator*
Lapu-Bula, Rigobert *cardiologist, medical educator, researcher*
Lubin, Michael Frederick *physician, educator*
Mackay, Gregory James *plastic surgeon*
Mayberg, Helen Susan *neurologist, educator*
McCord, Clinton D., Jr. *oculoplastic surgeon*
McDonald, L. Clifford *epidemiologist*
Meador, Kimford Jay *neurologist, researcher*
Mezencev, Roman *arms control expert, consultant, translator*
Milton, Micah H. *medical researcher*
Minneman, Kenneth Paul *pharmacology educator*
Morris, Douglas Claude *cardiologist, educator*
Murphy, Douglas A. *cardiothoracic surgeon*
Nahai, Foad *plastic surgeon, educator*
Namnoum, Anne Brawner *obstetrician, gynecologist*
Namnoum, James Daniel *plastic surgeon*
Newport, D. Jeffrey *psychiatrist, researcher*
Nunn, Donald Ray *plastic surgeon*
O'Regan, Ruth *oncologist, educator*
Parks, John Scott *pediatric endocrinologist*
Patel, Pragna *epidemiologist*
Pickering, Larry Kenneth *pediatrician, researcher*
Podewils, Laura Jean *epidemiologist, researcher*
Puskas, John Daniel *cardiothoracic surgeon, medical educator*
Ramalingam, Suresh S *oncologist*
Reed, James Whitfield *internist, educator, endocrinologist*
Ressler, Kerry *psychiatrist, educator*
Rust, George S. *physician, educator*
Sands, Jeff Michael *medical educator*
Saslow, Debbie L. *cancer control specialist, director*
Shah, Nikhil L. *urologist, surgeon*
Siffel, Csaba *medical epidemiologist*
Singh, Narendra *cardiologist, researcher, medical educator*
Smith, Robert A. *medical association administrator*
Smith, Robert Boulware III *vascular surgeon, educator*
Steinberg, James Paul *infectious diseases physician, educator*
Steinhaus, John Edward *retired anesthesiologist, educator*
Stevens, Judy A. *epidemiologist*
Stillwagon, Gary Bouldin *radiation oncologist*
Stowe, Zachary Neil *psychiatrist, researcher*
Sullivan, Louis Wade *medical educator, former United States Secretary of Health & Human Services*
Taliaferro, Sumayah Jamila *dermatologist*
Taylor, Andrew T., Jr. *radiologist, educator*
Thacker, Stephen Brady *medical association administrator, epidemiologist*
Thattassery, Emil George *cardiologist*
Tiwari, Tejpratap S. P. *epidemiologist*
Toledo, Andrew Anthony *obstetrician, gynecologist*
Udoff, Eric Joel *diagnostic radiologist*
Vaccarino, Viola *professor medicine*
Vogel, Victor Gerald *medical educator, researcher*
Ward, Elizabeth *medical association administrator, director*
Waring, George Oral III *ophthalmologist, surgeon*
Wenger, Nanette Kass *cardiologist, medical researcher, educator*
Weyand, Cornelia Maritta *medical educator*
White, Perry Merrill, Jr. *orthopedic surgeon*
Wickliffe, Charles Walton *cardiologist*
Williams, Ifor R. *immunologist, director*
Yancey, Asa G., Sr. *physician, educator*

Auburn
Hutchinson, Leslie Julian *preventive medicine physician*

Augusta
Albo, Daniel *surgeon, researcher*
Atteberry, Linda Rose *surgeon, retired military officer*
Bhatia, Jatinder J. S. *pediatrician*
Bittner, James Graham *surgeon*
Borke, James L. *medical educator*
Carroll, James Edwin *child neurologist, researcher*
Chamberlain, Sherman *gastroenterologist, educator*
Chandler, Arthur Bleakley *pathologist, educator*
Cresci, Gail *surgeon, educator, nutritionist*
Dodani, Sunita *physician, educator*
Fincher, Ruth Marie Edla *medical educator, dean*
Gamboa, Gloria Mabel *plastic surgeon, educator*
Given, Kenna Sidney *surgeon, educator*
Hepburn, Iryna Sophia *physician*
Hooks, Vendie Hudson III *surgeon*
Horuzsko, Anatolij *medical researcher*
Johnson, William Michael *physician*
Kapuku, Gaston Kakota *medical educator*
Kumar, Vijay *urologist, researcher*
Lee, Gregory Price *neuropsychology educator*
Luxenberg, Malcolm Neuwahl *ophthalmologist, educator*
Nesbit, Robert Raymond, Jr. *surgeon*
Ownby, Dennis Randall *pediatrician, allergist, educator, researcher*
Prisant, Louis Michael *cardiologist, educator*
Raja, Dayal Davis *endocrinologist*
Ryan, James Walter *physician, researcher*
Talledo, Oscar Eduardo *medical educator*
Ustun, Celalettin *hematologist, educator, bone marrow transplant specialist*
Wray, Betty Beasley *allergist, immunologist, pediatrician*

Austell
Halwig, J. Michael *allergist*
Tissue, Mike *medical educator, respiratory therapist*

Buford
Byrd, Larry Donald *behavioral pharmacologist*

Columbus
Chan, Philip *retired dermatologist, military officer*

Decatur
Henderson, Ralph Hale *physician*
Ioachimescu, Octavian Cosmin *medical educator*

Dublin
Giannini, A. James *psychiatrist, educator, researcher, author*

Fort Stewart
Warner, Christopher Hugh *psychiatrist*

Lagrange
Copeland, Robert Bodine *internist, cardiologist*
West, John Thomas *retired surgeon*

Lawrenceville
Fetner, Robert Henry *radiobiologist*

Macon
Elliott, Richard Laurence *psychiatrist, educator*
Lauterbach, Edward Charles *psychiatric educator*
Robinson, Joe Sam *neurosurgeon, educator*
Scheetz, Allison Paige *medical educator*
Seale, James Paul *medical educator, researcher*
Young, Henry E. *tissue engineering medical educator*
Zalups, Rudolfs Karlis *medical educator, director*

Marietta
Mahle, William T. *pediatric cardiologist, educator*
Ranu, Harcharan Singh *biomedical scientist, administrator, orthopaedic biomechanics educator*
Schell, Norman Barnett *preventive medicine physician, consultant*

Martinez
Colborn, Gene Louis *anatomy educator, researcher*
Nesbitt, Robert Edward Lee, Jr. *physician, educator, research scientist, writer, poet*

Rome
Bushnell, Brandon DuBose *orthopedist*

Roswell
McCloud, Melody T. *obstetrician, gynecologist, surgeon, media consultant, health care strategist*

Savannah
Andrus, Jennifer Gail *otolaryngologist, surgeon, educator, educational consultant*
DeVaro, John Michael *ophthalmologist*
Fetterman, James William, Jr. *medical educator*
Fishburne, John Ingram, Jr. *retired obstetrician/gynecologist, educator*
Klein, Benjamin Daniel Berrigan *medical educator, consultant*
Krahl, Enzo *retired surgeon*
Lindley, James Gunn, Jr. *neurosurgeon*
Zoller, Michael *otolaryngologist, head and neck surgeon, educator*

Smyrna
Jeffords, Keith (Kelland Keith Jeffords Jr.) *plastic surgeon*

Statesboro
Fitzmorris, Kari Beth *medical educator*
Sturges, Diana *medical educator*

Stockbridge
Friedman, Robert Barry *neurosurgeon*

Stone Mountain
Gotlieb, Jaquelin Smith *pediatrician*

Tifton
Dorminey, Henry Clayton, Jr. *allergist*

Valdosta
Beal, John M. *surgeon, medical educator*
Morgan, Joe Leland *physician, psychiatrist*

Warner Robins
Gayton, Johnny Lee *ophthalmologist, recreational facility executive, educator*

HAWAII

Honolulu
Brady, Stephen R. P. K. *physician*
Curb, Jess David *medical educator, researcher*
Diamond, Milton *anatomy and reproductive biology educator*
Fitz-Patrick, David *endocrinologist, educator*
Flowers, Robert Swaim *medical educator, surgeon*
Fong, Bernard W.D. *physician, educator*
Goldstein, Sir Norman *dermatologist*
Goodhue, William Walter, Jr. *pathologist, military officer, educator*
Guerrero, Reuben Castro *oncologist, internist*
Ho, Reginald Chi Shing *medical educator*
Kane, Thomas Jay III *surgeon, educator*
Lau, H. Lorrin *obstetrician, gynecologist*
Lau, William Kienki *medical educator*
Lee, Yeu-Tsu Margaret *surgeon, educator*
Parsa, Fereydoun Don *plastic surgeon*
Schatz, Irwin Jacob *cardiologist, educator*
Sharma, Santosh Devraj *obstetrician, gynecologist, educator*
Sugiki, Shigemi *ophthalmologist, educator*
Withy, Kelley *medical educator*
Yew, David *physician, director*

Kamuela
Morgan, Andrew Lane *urologist, educator*

Koloa
Donohugh, Donald Lee *physician*

Lahaina
Percy, Helen Sylvia *physician*

Mililani
Gardner, Sheryl Paige *gynecologist*
Okita, George Torao *retired pharmacologist*

Waikoloa
Copman, Louis *radiologist*

IDAHO

Coeur D' Alene
Jain, Sachin *medical educator*

Idaho Falls
Lee, Glenn Richard *medical association administrator, educator*

Pocatello
Guo, Ruiling *medical librarian, educator*

Post Falls
Owsley, Frederick Mark *plastic surgeon*

Sandpoint
Bird, Forrest M. *retired medical inventor*

Sun Valley
Pesch, LeRoy Allen *physician, educator, health and hospital consultant, business executive*

ILLINOIS

Abbott Park
Hui, Yu-Hua *pharmaceutical researcher*
Martin, Ruth L. *pharmacologist*

Alden
Tayloe, David T., Jr. *pediatrician*

Anna
Srinivasaraghavan, Jagannathan *forensic psychiatrist*

Arlington Heights
Placik, Otto Joseph *plastic surgeon*
Ruder, John Regan *physician*

Bloomington
Trefzger, Richard Charles *surgeon*

Bolingbrook
Malicay, Manuel Alaban *physician*

Buffalo Grove
Dunn, Jonathan *orthopedist, surgeon*

Carbondale
McKinnies, Richard Charles *radiation therapist, assistant professor*

Carthage
Aanenson, Marian Ham *medical educator*

Champaign
Freedman, Philip *internist, educator*
Gold, Paul Ernest *psychology and behavioral neuroscience educator*

Chicago
Abecassis, Michael *medical educator*
Abelson, Herbert Traub *pediatrician, educator*
Akhter, Shahab A. *Cardio Thoracic Surgeon*
Alaraj, Ali *neurosurgeon*
Albrecht, Ronald Frank *retired anesthesiologist*
An, Howard S. *physician, educator*
Andersen, Burton Robert *immunologist, educator, medical historian*
Andersson, Gunnar Bengt Johan *orthopedist, educator*
Anzia, Joan Meyer *psychiatrist*
Arruda, Jose *nephrologist*
Babjak, Patricia M. *medical association administrator*
Bach, Bernard R., Jr. *orthopedist, educator*
Bailey, Robert Converse *epidemiologist, anthropologist, educator*
Bakay, Roy Arpad Earle *neurosurgeon, educator*
Bakris, George L. *nephrologist, educator, clinical researcher, hypertension specialist*
Baldwin, DeWitt Clair, Jr. *physician, educator*
Baron, Joseph Mandel *hematologist*
Baroody, Fuad *pediatrician, educator*
Barton, John Joseph *obstetrician, gynecologist, administrator, educator, researcher*
Basu, Anirban *medical educator*
Beam, Craig Allen *biomedical researcher, educator, director*
Becker, Michael Allen *internist, rheumatologist, educator*
Bell, Carl Compton *psychiatrist, researcher*
Bendok, Bernard R. *neurosurgeon, researcher*
Benson, Al Bowen III *oncologist, educator*
Benzon, Honorio Tabal *anesthesiologist*
Boggs, Joseph Dodridge *pediatric pathologist, educator*
Bogolub, David Louis *physician*
Bonow, Robert Ogden *cardiologist, educator*
Bowman, James Edward *pathologist, educator*
Brauner, Daniel *geriatrician, educator, rheumatologist*
Burget, Gary Crites *plastic surgeon*
Burton, Barbara K. *medical geneticist, pediatrician, educator*
Bush-Joseph, Charles A. *orthopedist*
Buttin, Barbara M. *oncologist, educator*
Cabay, Robert John *physician, dentist, author, researcher*
Campbell, Tracy M. *dermatologist*
Caro, William Allan *physician, educator*
Celesia, Gastone Guglielmo *neurologist*
Chan, Lawrence Siu-Yung *dermatologist, educator*
Charbel, Fady Toufic *neurosurgeon, educator*
Charrow, Joel *pediatrician, geneticist, educator, director*
Chatterton, Robert Treat, Jr. *reproductive endocrinology educator*
Chlewicki, Lukasz Krzysztof *immunologist, educator*
Chunprapaph, Boonmee *physician, educator*
Coe, Fredric L. *internist, educator, researcher*
Cohen, Mark S. *orthopedist, medical educator*
Cohen, Russell *gastroenterologist*
Cohran, Valeria *pediatrician, educator*
Cole, Brian Jared *orthopedist, educator*
Cook, Edwin H., Jr. *psychiatrist, educator*
Cook, John Q. *plastic surgeon*
Curry, Raymond Howard *physician*
Davidson, Michael H. *cardiologist, researcher*
Dayal, Vijay Shanker *physician, educator*
Della Valle, Craig J. *orthopedist, medical educator*
DeMay, Richard Mac *pathologist*
Deutsch, Thomas Alan *ophthalmologist, educator, dean*
Diamond, Seymour *physician*
Dilley, Kimberley Jo *pediatrician, educator*
Downham, Max C. *medical association administrator*
Du, Pan *biomedical researcher, educator*
Dulcan, Mina K. *psychiatrist, educator*
Dumanian, Gregory A. *surgeon*
Dunea, George *nephrologist, educator*
Eastman, Charmane I. *medical researcher*
Elliott, William John *clinical pharmacology educator*
Espat, N. Joseph *surgeon*
Feingold, Daniel Leon *anesthesiologist, consultant*
Fernandez, John J. *orthopedist*
Fetzer, April M. *orthopedist*
Few, Julius Warren, Jr. *surgeon*
Fine, Neil A. *surgeon*
Flaherty, Emalee Gottbrath *pediatrician*
Frederiksen, Marilynn C. *physician*
Friedman, Michael *surgeon*
Galante, Jorge Osvaldo *orthopedic surgeon, educator*
Gerber, Diane *plastic surgeon*
Gitelman, Darren Ross *neurologist, educator*
Gittler, Michelle S. *physiatrist*
Glassroth, Jeffrey *internist, educator*
Goetz, Christopher Graves *neurologist, educator*
Goldberg, Arnold Irving *psychoanalyst, educator*
Goldberg, Edward Jay *orthopaedic surgeon*
Golomb, Harvey Morris *hematologist, oncologist, educator*
Gorbien, Martin John *medical educator, geriatrician*
Gossett, Dana Rigsby *gynecologist, director*
Greenberger, Paul Allen *allergist, immunologist, educator*
Gregory, Stephanie Ann *hematologist, educator*
Gundeti, Mohan Saheb *urologist, educator*
Hahn, Yoon Sun *pediatric neurosurgeon, educator*
Hambrick, Ernestine *retired colon and rectal surgeon*
Harris, Gerald David *surgeon*
Hatsopoulos, Nicholas G. *biomedical researcher, educator*
Head, Louis Rollin, II, *surgeon*
Heckman, Charles Jackson, II, *medical educator*
Hellman, Samuel *radiologist, educator*
Herbst, Arthur Lee *obstetrician, gynecologist*
Hershow, Ronald C. *epidemiologist, educator*
Hill, Carlotta H. *physician*
Hirano, Ikuo *gastroenterologist*
Holinger, Lauren Drake *surgeon*
Honig, George Raymond *pediatrician*
Hou, Wanqiu *immunologist, microbiologist*
Huckman, Michael Saul *neuroradiologist, educator*
Hughes, John Russell *neurologist, educator*
Inan, Zabrin *psychiatrist*
Ivankovich, Anthony D. *anesthesiologist, educator*
Iyer, Kishore *transplant surgeon*
Jacobs, Joshua J. *orthopaedic surgeon*
Jensen, Donald Milton *hepatologist*
Jilhewar, Ashok *gastroenterologist*
Johnson, Timothy Patrick *health and social researcher*
Kadish, Alan Howard *internist, educator, researcher*
Kahana, Madelyn D. *pediatric anesthesiologist*
Kahrilas, Peter James *medical educator, researcher*
Kamin, Carol *medical educator*
Kane, Sunanda Vinayak *internist, gastroenterologist*
Kao, Johnny *radiologist, oncologist*
Kataria, Tripti Caday *anesthesiologist*
Katz, Mark Harold *urologist*
Kavey, Rae-Ellen Webb *pediatric cardiologist*
Ke, Yunbo *medical educator, researcher*
Keith, Louis Gerald *medical educator*
Khuntia, Anjana (Annie Khuntia) *pediatrician, educator*
Kilpatrick, Sarah J. *obstetrician, gynecologist, educator*
Kirsner, Joseph Barnett *physician, educator*
Kittle, Charles Frederick *surgeon*
Kraft, Sumner Charles *physician, educator*
Kuiken, Todd Alan *medical researcher, rehabilitation services professional, educator*
Landsberg, Lewis *endocrinologist, medical researcher, former dean*
Lauderdale, Diane S. *epidemiologist, educator*
Lee, Raphael Carl *plastic surgeon, biomedical engineer*
Lee, Simon *orthopedist*
Leff, Alan Richard *medical educator, researcher*
Leventhal, Bennett Lee *psychiatry and pediatrics educator, academic administrator*
Li, An *medical educator*

Lichtor, Terry *neurosurgeon, neuro-oncologist*
Liptay, Michael Justin *surgeon*
Luchins, Daniel Jonathan *psychiatrist*
Lurain, John Robert III *gynecologist*
Lussier, Yves A. *biomedical researcher, medical educator, physician*
Mahaffey, John Christopher *medical association executive*
Malkinson, Frederick David *dermatologist, educator*
Mathew, James M. *immunologist, educator*
Maves, Michael Donald *medical association executive*
Maxwell, Sarz *psychiatrist, educator*
McCarthy, Patrick M. *surgeon*
McDermott, Raymond, Jr. *physician*
McKoy, June Marcia *medical educator, researcher, lawyer*
Meadow, William Lee *medical educator*
Mellott, Ann L. *hematologist, oncologist*
Mendelsohn, Janis S. *pediatrician, educator*
Metz, Charles Edgar *radiology educator*
Millichap, Joseph Gordon *neurologist, educator*
Millikan, Keith William *surgeon, educator*
Morgan, Elaine R. *hematologist, oncologist, medical educator*
Moss, Gerald S. *medical educator*
Nachman, James Burt *pediatric hematologist-oncologist*
Nahrwold, David Lange *surgeon, educator*
Naithani, Rajesh *oncologist*
Nam, Ellis K. *orthopedist*
Narahashi, Toshio *pharmacology educator*
Nayar, Ritu *pathologist, educator*
Newman, Steven B. *hematologist, oncologist*
Nicholson, Greg Powell *orthopedist*
Nordli, Douglas R. *neurologist*
O'Connell, John Bernard, Jr. *medical educator, department chairman*
Olson, Jack Conrad, Jr. *geriatrician*
Olson, Steven Thomas *medical researcher*
Pahl Schuette, Elfriede *pediatric transplant cardiologist*
Paller, Amy S. *pediatric dermatologist, educator*
Paprosky, Wayne G. *orthopedist*
Pensler, Jay Michael *plastic surgeon, educator*
Perambakam, Supriya *medical educator*
Phillips, Frank m. *orthopedic surgeon*
Poznanski, Andrew Karol *pediatric radiologist*
Prinz, Richard Allen *surgeon*
Pugh, Carla M. *surgeon, educator*
Putterman, Allen Michael *surgeon, oculofacial plastic surgeon*
Racker, Darlene Katie *cardiovascular anatomist, electrophysiologist*
Rafeyan, Roueen *psychiatrist, educator*
Ramsey-Goldman, Rosalind *physician*
Replogle, Robert Lee *cardiovascular and thoracic surgeon*
Robertson, William Wright, Jr. *orthopedist, educator*
Robinson, June Kerswell *dermatologist, educator*
Rogers, Eugene Jack *retired medical educator*
Roitberg, Ben Zion *neurosurgeon, educator*
Romeo, Anthony Albert *orthopedic surgeon*
Rosen, Steven Terry *medical professor, oncologist, hematologist*
Rosenberg, Aaron Glen *orthopedist, educator*
Rosenson, Robert Sidney *cardiologist, researcher*
Rosseau, Gail L. *neurosurgeon, educator*
Rowley, Janet Davison *physician*
Russell, Thomas R. *medical association administrator*
Sabelli, Hector Carlos *psychiatrist, neuropharmacologist, writer*
Sadikot, Ruxana T. *internist, educator*
Salant, Talya *medical researcher*
Sandler, Richard H. *pediatric gastroenterologist*
Saps, Miguel *pediatrician, gastroenterologist*
Sarwark, John Francis *orthopaedic surgeon, educator*
Scarse, Olivia Marie *cardiologist, consultant*
Scheiber, Stephen Carl *psychiatrist*
Scheiner, David Lawrence *internist*
Schilsky, Richard Lewis *oncologist, researcher*
Schink, Julian C. *oncologist, director*
Schroeder, James W., Jr. *otolaryngologist*
Schwab, Joel Gerson *pediatrician, educator*
Schwartzberg, Joanne Gilbert *physician*
Sciarra, John J. *obstetrician, gynecologist, educator*
Scommegna, Antonio *obstetrician, gynecologist, educator*
Seeler, Ruth Andrea *pediatrician, educator*
Sha, Beverly E. *medical educator*
Shah, Anil R. *plastic surgeon*
Shaw, John M. *oncologist*
Sheinkop, Mitchell *orthopedist, surgeon, educator*
Shields, Thomas William *surgeon, educator*
Shikanov, Sergey *urologist*
Shore, Richard M. *radiologist, educator*
Short, Marion Priscilla *neurogenetics educator*
Sidle, Douglas M. *medical educator*
Siegler, Mark *internist, educator*
Silverstein, Jonathan Charles *surgeon, researcher*
Smith, Earl Charles *nephrologist, educator*
Smith, Lewis J. *medical educator, researcher*
Smith, Michael Cremin *neurologist, director*
Socol, Michael Lee *obstetrician, gynecologist, educator*
Song, David *plastic surgeon, medical educator*
Sparberg, Marshall Stuart *gastroenterologist, educator*
Spargo, Benjamin H. *renal pathologist, educator*
Stamler, Jeremiah *medical professor, researcher*
Stayner, Leslie Thomas *epidemiologist*
Stone, James Leland *surgical neurologist, educator*
Stone, Neil Joseph *cardiologist, educator*
Strassner, Howard Taft, Jr. *obstetrician, educator*
Straus, Francis Howe *pathologist, educator*
Sugar, Joel *ophthalmologist*
Surendra, Basti *ophthalmologist, educator*
Tanna, Angelo Peter *ophthalmologist, educator, researcher*
Tatar, Arnold Marshall *internist, educator*
Telfer, Margaret Clare *internist, hematologist, oncologist*
Tellez, Claudia *hematologist, oncologist, educator*
Tharp, Michael D. *medical educator*
Thomas, J. Regan *plastic surgeon, educator*
Toig, Randall Marc *obstetrician, gynecologist*
Toriumi, Dean Michael *facial, plastic and reconstructive surgeon, educator*
Umbdenstock, Richard J. *medical association administrator*
Urayama, Shiro *internist*
Valle, Rafael F. *obstetrician, gynecologist, educator*
Vartanian, A. John *otolaryngologist, researcher*
Vassallo, Brett Joseph *gynecologist, surgeon*
Vaughan, Douglas Eugene *medical association administrator, department chairman*
Verma, Nikhil *orthopedist*
Videnovic, Aleksandar *medical educator*
Vigneswaran, Wickii Thambiah *cardiothoracic surgeon, educator*
Vitullo, Dolores *cardiologist, director*
Wagner, Annette M. *dermatologist, surgeon*
Walton, Robert Lee *plastic surgeon*
Wang, Ting *biomedical researcher*
Ward, R. Parker *cardiologist, educator*
Wayne, Jeffrey D. *surgeon*
Weber, Kathleen M. *sports medicine physician, orthopedist*
Webster, James Randolph, Jr. *physician*
Weese-Mayer, Debra Ellyn *pediatrician, educator*
Weinstein, Robert A. *physician, medical educator, director, medical researcher*
Weissbluth, Marc *pediatrician, educator*
Wershil, Barry Kent *pediatrician*
Whitington, Peter Frank *pediatric hepatologist, educator*
Wied, George Ludwig *physician*
Williams, Philip Copelain *obstetrician, gynecologist*
Williams, Stephanie F. *oncologist*
Willoughby, William Franklin, II, *retired physician, scientist, military officer*
Yang, Benson Pin-Sheng *neurosurgeon*
Yudkowsky, Rachel *medical educator*
Zhou, Xiaofeng *biomedical researcher, medical geneticist*

Darien
Kulkarni, Bidy *reproductive endocrinologist, biomedical researcher, consultant*

Deerfield
Ben-Shir, Rya Helen *medical librarian*
Sanner, John Harper *retired pharmacologist*

Des Plaines
Johnson, Peter E. *plastic surgeon*
Quintanilla, Antonio Paulet *retired physician, educator*
Wilson, Elizabeth M. *medical association administrator*

Downers Grove
Allin, Edgar Francis *retired anatomist*
Bastian, Robert W. *otolaryngologist*
Dahdal, Wafa Y. *pharmacologist, educator*
Nelson, Paul D. *podiatrist*
Rembos, Steven *podiatrist*
Richardson, Brent Earl *otolaryngologist*

Elk Grove Village
Alden, Errol R. *medical association administrator*
David, Tayloe T., Jr. *pediatrician, medical association administrator*

Elmhurst
Banich, Francis Edward *surgeon*
Blain, Charlotte Marie *internist, educator*
Eckhardt, Richard Dale *retired physician, educator*
Evrard, Marilyn L. *oncologist, internist*
Lyster, Michael T. *oncologist, hematologist*
Rosi, David R. *internist, oncologist, hematologist*

Elmwood Park
Tiesenga, Marvin Francis *surgeon*

Evanston
Anderson, Kenneth Paul *nephrologist, administrator*
Awad, Issam Abdullah *neurosurgeon, educator*
Bloomer, William David *radiologist, oncologist, educator*
Braithwaite, Susan Shapiro *endocrinologist, educator*
Brendler, Charles Burgess *urologist, educator*
Bro, William Price *medical association administrator*
Crawford, James Weldon *psychiatrist, educator, administrator*
Cvetanovic, Ivana *medical educator, editor*
Fenninger, Leonard Davis *medical educator, consultant*
Gaiha, Vishnu Das *cardiologist*
Good, Andrew Evans *obstetrician*
Karaikovic, Eldin *surgeon, educator*
Koh, Jason *orthopedic surgeon*
Mustoe, Thomas Anthony *physician, plastic surgeon*
Peterson, Lance Robert *physician*
Schwartz, Neena Betty *endocrinologist, educator*
Sener, Stephen Francis *oncologist, surgeon*
Sprang, Milton LeRoy *obstetrician, gynecologist, educator*
Stumpf, David Allen *pediatric neurologist*
Traisman, Howard Sevin *retired pediatrician*
Weiss, Kevin Barton *epidemiologist, medical association administrator*

Galena
Bezkorovainy, Anatoly *medical educator, retired biochemist*

Galesburg
Gupta, Madan Lal *cardiologist*
Tourlentes, Thomas Theodore *retired psychiatrist*

Geneva
Mehta, Vishal M. *orthopedist*

Glen Ellyn
Dieter, Raymond Andrew, Jr. *physician, thoracic general and vascular surgeon*

Glencoe
Milloy, Frank Joseph, Jr. *surgeon*

Glenview
Casas, Laurie Ann *plastic surgeon*
Haddad, Steven L. *orthopaedic surgeon*
Haebich, Arthur T. *retired thoracic surgeon*
Hafner, Arthur Wayne *author, information scientist, academic librarian*

Godfrey
King, Ordie Herbert, Jr. *oral pathologist*

Greenville
Junod, Daniel August *podiatrist*

Hazel Crest
Williamson, Wayne C. *internist, geriatrician*

Herrin
Gauto, Nelson Fernando *plastic surgeon, consumer products company executive*

Highland Park
Miller, Albert J. *cardiologist, internist*

Hines
Joehl, Raymond Joseph *surgeon, consultant*

Hinsdale
Bardfield, Steven *orthopedist*
Brueschke, Erich Edward *physician, researcher, educator*
Chassin, Eric *orthopedist*
Chudik, Steven *orthopedist*
Collins, Michael J. *orthopedist*
Daley, Robert *orthopedist*
Durkin, Michael C. *orthopedist*
Dworsky, Brad *orthopedist*
Gilligan, William J. *orthopedist*
Kirincic, Marie *orthopedist*
Kuhlman, Geoffrey S. *orthopedist*
Lorenz, Mark A. *orthopedist*
Louis, Steven *orthopedist*
Shiffman, Kenneth *orthopedist, surgeon*
Trksak, Paul M. *orthopedist*
Vargo, Robyn *orthopedist, surgeon*
Wiet, Richard James *otolarygnologist*
Zindrick, Michael R. *orthopedist*

Indian Head Park
Johnson, (Mary) Anita *physician, medical association administrator*

Joliet
Ring, Alvin Manuel *pathologist, educator*

Lake Forest
Levy, Nelson Louis *immunologist, educator, surgeon*
Salter, Edwin Carroll *retired pediatrician*
Terrasse, Anthony P. *plastic surgeon*
Wilbur, Richard Sloan *medical association administrator, physician*

Libertyville
Bush, Eugene Nyle *retired pharmacologist, pharmacist*

Lincolnshire
Erickson, James Clifford III *anesthesiologist, educator*

Lombard
Cisneros, Laura E. *internist, hematologist, oncologist*
Henkin, Robert Elliott *nuclear medicine physician*

Long Grove
Ausman, Robert K. *surgeon, research and development company executive*

Macomb
Dexter, Donald Harvey *surgeon, educator*

Maywood
Albain, Kathy S. *oncologist*
Aranha, Gerard V. *surgeon*
Biller, Jose *neurologist, educator*
Flanigan, Robert Charles *urologist, educator*
Gianopoulos, John George *obstetrician*
Hatch, David A. *urologist*
Miele, Lucio *physician, medical researcher, pharmacologist*
Moran, John Francis *cardiologist*
Nand, Sucha *medical educator*
Origitano, Thomas Charles *neurological surgeon*
Samarel, Allen Mark *physician, biochemistry and cell biology educator*
Shoham, David A. *epidemiologist, educator*
Sizemore, Glen William *medical educator*
Stiff, Patrick Joseph *internist, hematologist, oncologist, educator*
Varma, Niraj *cardiologist, physiologist, researcher*
Warpeha, Raymond Leonard *surgeon, educator*
Wheeler, John S., Jr. *urologist*

Mc Gaw Park
Bernardo, Angelito Alday *nephrologist, medical products executive*

Melrose Park
Banerji, Manatosh *oncologist, hematologist*
Klein, Lloyd William *cardiologist, researcher*
Rossof, Arthur Harold *internal medicine educator*
Shanes, Jeffrey Glenn *cardiologist*

Mount Carroll
Akar, Joseph G. *medical educator*

Mount Prospect
Martin, David Julian *medical association administrator*

Naperville
Bufalino, Vincent John *cardiologist, medical administrator*
Cholkeri-Singh, Aarathi *gynecologist, surgeon*
Folk, Frank Anton *surgeon, educator*
Miller, Charles E. *gynecologist*

North Chicago
Chedid, Antonio *pathologist, educator, researcher*
Gall, Eric Papineau *internist, educator*
Hawkins, Richard Albert *medical educator, administrator*
Khraisat, Ahmad *internal medicine, adult cardiovascular medicine*
Kim, Yoon Berm *immunologist, educator*
Nair, Velayudhan *pharmacologist, educator, academic administrator*
Schneider, Arthur Sanford *medical educator*
Sierles, Frederick Stephen *psychiatrist, educator*
Singh, Sarabjeet *cardiologist*

Northbrook
Cucco, Ulisse P. *retired obstetrician, gynecologist*

Oak Brook
Christian, Joseph Ralph *physician*
Dmowski, W. Paul *obstetrician, gynecologist, educator, endocrinologist, researcher*
Serry, Cyrus *medical educator*

Oak Lawn
elZein, Chawki Fayez *pediatrician, surgeon*
Hayani, Ammar *pediatrician, director*

Oak Park
Matsuda, Takayoshi *surgeon, educator, biomedical researcher*

Oakbrook Terrace
Gruft, James Harris *physiatrist, educator*

Orland Park
Evans, Wayne *obstetrician, perinatologist*

Park Ridge
Bitran, Jacob David *internist*
Novey, Donald W. *physician, health facility administrator*
White, John Vincent *surgeon, consultant*

Peoria
de Alarcon, Pedro Antonio *pediatric oncologist, educator*
Fukuchi, Ken-ichiro *medical educator, researcher*
Geiss, Roger William *pathologist, medical educator*
Masi, Alfonse Thomas *medical educator*
Meriden, Terry *physician*
Mongkolrattanothai, Kanokporn *medical educator*
Pearl, Richard H. *surgeon*

Pinckneyville
Cawvey, Clarence Eugene *retired physician*

River Forest
Mason, George Robert *retired surgeon, educator*

Rochester
Myers, Phillip Ward *retired otolaryngologist*

Rockford
Heerens, Robert Edward *physician*
Johanson, John F. *gastroenterologist, researcher*
Olson, Stanley William *physician, educator, dean*
Pryor, Landon Scott *plastic surgeon*

Rushville
Dohner, Russell Rowland *physician*

Saint Charles
Best, William Robert *internist, educator, dean*

Skokie
Turowski, Gregory *plastic surgeon*

Springfield
Bhat, Shyam Khandige *psychiatrist, internist, educator*
Brozoski, Thomas J. *otolaryngologist, researcher*
Callahan, Charles Daniel *physiatrist, director*
Godwin, John E. *hematologist, oncologist*
Holland, John Madison *retired family practice physician*
Poole, Connie *medical librarian*
Woodson, Gayle Ellen *otolaryngologist*
Yaffe, Stuart Allen *physician*
Zook, Elvin Glenn *plastic surgeon, educator*

Sterling
Tóth, Peter Paul *physician, researcher*

Tinley Park
John, Thomas *ophthalmologist*

Urbana
Kaufman, Jerome Benzion *retired neurosurgeon*
Krock, Curtis Josselyn *pulmonologist*
Novak, Michael *physician, otologist*
O'Morchoe, Charles Christopher Creagh *anatomist, surgeon, educator*

Vernon Hills
Kim, Jung *physician, health facility administrator*
Morcott, Scott M. *physician, health facility administrator*
Zamyatin, Alexander *medical researcher*

West Chicago
Paulissen, James Peter *retired pediatrician, county official*

Westchester
Berger, Richard A. *orthopedist*
Holmes, George B., Jr. *orthopedist*

Zhang, Yejia (Zhang Yejia) *physiatrist*

Wheaton
Pak, John *plastic surgeon*

Wilmette
Hier, Daniel Barnet *neurologist*

Winfield
Sporer, Scott M. *orthopedist, surgeon*

Winnetka
Rossi, Ennio C. *internist, educator*
Rubnitz, Myron Ethan *pathologist, educator*

INDIANA

Alexandria
Irwin, Gerald Port *physician*

Bedford
Hunter, Harlen Charles *orthopedic surgeon*

Bloomington
Chen, Yu *medical educator*
Moore, Ward Wilfred *medical educator*

Carmel
Cohen, Marlene Lois *pharmacologist*
Frazer, Margaret L. *neurologist, director*

Chesterton
Martino, Robert Salvatore *orthopedic surgeon*

Corydon
Kelty, Paul David *obstetrician, educator*

Fishers
Thomas, John Arlen *pharmacologist, educator, science administrator*

Fort Wayne
Bacchus, Harold Mustapha *physician*
Lee, Shuishih Sage *pathologist*
Richardson, Joseph Hill *physician, medical educator*
Salam, Gohar Azam *physician, director*

Greenfield
Hunter, Robert Paul *pharmacologist, senior research scientist*

Greenwood
Greenbaum, Larry Marc *rheumatologist*
Koch, Michael Oscar *urologist*

Indianapolis
Albrecht, Willard Harold *retired medical educator*
Allen, Stephen D(ean) *pathologist, microbiologist*
Applegate, Kimberly Elaine *radiologist*
Bowyer, Suzanne Louise *pediatrician, educator*
Brandt, Ira Kive *pediatrician, geneticist*
Brater, Donald Craig *medical educator, dean*
Bright, John J. *medical researcher*
Brown, Edwin Wilson, Jr. *preventive medicine physician, educator*
Broxmeyer, Hal Edward *medical educator*
Bull, Marilyn Jean *pediatrician, educator*
Cheng, Liang *pathologist*
Cleary, Robert Emmet *gynecologist, infertility specialist*
Coleman, John Joseph III *plastic surgeon, educator*
Conley, Robert R. *psychiatrist, educator*
Crabb, David William *medical educator, researcher*
Dalsing, Michael Cletus *surgeon, educator*
Daly, Walter Joseph *medical educator*
DiMeglio, Linda A. *pediatrician, endocrinologist, researcher*
Durell, Todd *psychiatrist, medical researcher*
Dyken, Mark Lewis, Jr. *neurologist, educator*
Einhorn, Lawrence Henry *oncologist, medical educator*
Fitzgerald, Joseph Francis *pediatric gastroenterologist*
Foster, Richard Scott *urologist, educator*
Fridell, Jonathan Aaron *transplant surgeon*
Gaffney, Margaret Mary *dermatologist, educator*
Ghetti, Bernardino Francesco *neuropathologist, educator*
Goggins, William Christopher *surgeon, director*
Grosfeld, Jay Lazar *surgeon, educator*
Gunderman, Richard B. *medical educator*
Halum, Stacey Leigh *otolaryngologist, researcher*
Hansell, Richard Stanley *obstetrician, gynecologist, educator*
Havlik, Robert John *plastic surgeon*
Helveston, Eugene McGillis *pediatric ophthalmologist, educator*
Hughes, Charles E. III *plastic surgeon*
Hurd, William Ward *obstetrician, gynecologist*
Hynes, Martin Dennis III *pharmacologist, toxicologist*
Irwin, Glenn Ward, Jr. *medical educator, physician, academic administrator*
Johnston, Cyrus Conrad, Jr. *medical educator*
Knoebel, Suzanne Buckner *cardiologist, educator*
Konger, Raymond Lloyd *pathologist*
Kroenke, Kurt *medical educator, researcher*
Lemberger, Louis *pharmacologist*
MacDougall, John Duncan *thoracic surgeon*
Manders, Karl Lee *neurosurgeon*
Marinkovic, Serge Peter *urologist, educator, surgeon*
Moore, David Harry *medical educator*
Norins, Arthur Leonard *dermatologist, educator*
O'Neil, Joseph *pediatrician*
Pande, Prakash Narain *cardiologist, educator, consultant*
Pawaskar, Manjiri D. *medical researcher*
Rogers, Robert Ernest *medical educator*
Ross, Edward *cardiologist*
Roth, Lawrence Max *pathologist, educator*
Sachs, Greg Alan *preventive medicine physician*
Sadove, Alan Michael *plastic surgeon*
Saxena, Romil *pathologist, educator*
Schmetzer, Alan David *psychiatrist*
Smith, James Warren *pathologist, educator, microbiologist, parasitologist*
Sutton, Gregory Paul *obstetrician, gynecologist*
Taskonak, Burak *medical educator, dentist*
Watanabe, August Masaru *physician, educator, retired pharmaceutical executive*
Weber, George *oncology and pharmacology educator, researcher*
Williams, Eric S. *cardiologist, educator*
Woolling, Kenneth Rau *vascular internist*
Yao, Yongxue *immunologist*
Zipes, Douglas Peter *cardiologist, researcher*

Lafayette
Hamdi, Hamid S. *neurologist, neurorehabilitation specialist, consultant, researcher*
Langston, Edward Lee *physician, pharmacist*

Marion
Fisher, Pierre James, Jr. *physician*

Merrillville
Nguyen, Thach Ngoc *cardiologist*
Wang, Josephine L. Fen *physician*
Yu, Peter Legaspi *rehabilitation physician*

Muncie
Nanko, Raymond S. *physician*
Roch, Lewis Marshall, II, *ophthalmic surgeon, medical entrepreneur*

Richmond
Howanitz, E. Paul *thoracic surgeon*
Murray, Kevin Dennis *surgeon*

Schererville
Galante, Gustavo E. *plastic surgeon*

Scottsburg
Kho, Eusebio *surgeon*

South Bend
Davis, Glen Anthony *pediatrician*
Yergler, Willard G. *orthopedist*

Valparaiso
Kobak, Alfred Julian, Jr. *obstetrician, gynecologist*

Walton
Chu, Johnson Chin Sheng *retired physician*

West Lafayette
Borowitz, Joseph Leo *pharmacologist, educator*
Cramer, William Anthony *biochemistry and biophysics researcher, educator*
Poulos, James Thomas *endocrinologist, educator*
Rutledge, Charles Ozwin *pharmacologist, educator*
Stob, Martin *retired physiology educator*
Svensson, Craig Karl *pharmaceutical sciences educator, dean*

IOWA

Ames
Randic, Mirjana *retired neurologist*
Roth, James A. *medical educator, director*

Cedar Rapids
Houmes, Blaine V. *emergency physician*
Maikon, Marc Steven *podiatrist*

Clive
Neis, Arthur Veral *healthcare and development company executive*

Coralville
Aly, Al Said *plastic surgeon, otolaryngologist*

Des Moines
Bevilacqua, Nicholas J. *podiatrist, educator*
Clark, Craig Boyd *cardiologist*
Habib, Shahid *medical association administrator*
Song, Joseph *pathologist, educator*
Wattleworth, Roberta Ann *physician*

Iowa City
Abboud, Francois Mitry *physician, educator*
Ali, Saad *radiologist*
Andreasen, Nancy Coover *psychiatrist, educator, neuroscientist*
Atkins, Dianne L. *pediatrician, educator*
Brophy, Patrick David *pediatrician, researcher*
Buckwalter, Joseph Addison *orthopedic surgeon, educator*
Clifton, James Albert *physician, educator*
Cooper, Christopher S. *urologist, educator*
Cooper, Reginald Rudyard *orthopedic surgeon, educator*
Cornell, Robert Aaron *embryologist, educator*
Cowdery, John Stewart *physician*
Diekema, Daniel James *epidemiologist, educator*
Dietz, Frederick R. *orthopaedic surgeon*
Fellows, Robert Ellis *medical educator, researcher*
George, Weiner *medical researcher, director*
Grose, Charles Frederick *pediatrician, epidemiologist*
Hammond, Harold Logan *oral and maxillofacial pathologist, retired educator*
Hawtrey, Charles Edward *urologist, educator*
Heistad, Donald Dean *cardiologist*
Johnson, Chris Alan *ophthalmology educator*
Kerber, Richard E. *cardiologist*
Konety, Badrinath R. *surgeon, researcher*
Kwitek, Anne E. *medical educator*
Laxmisan, Archana *medical researcher*
Magboul, Magboul M. *anesthesiologist, educator*
Mason, Edward Eaton *surgeon*
Moritani, Toshio *radiologist, educator*
Morriss, Frank Howard, Jr. *pediatrics educator*
Niebyl, Jennifer Robinson *obstetrician, gynecologist, educator*
Sandlow, Jay Ira *urologist, researcher*
Sindt, Christine W. *medical educator*
Smoker, Wendy Rue Kartinos *neuroradiologist, consultant, educator*
Snyder, Peter M. *medical educator, medical researcher*
Staggs, Susan Hettie *medical educator*
Tsalikian, Eva *physician, educator*
Van Beek, Edwin Jacques Rudolph *radiologist, researcher*
Vandenberg, Byron F. *cardiologist*
Weiner, George Jay *internist*
Williams, Richard Dwayne *physician, educator, urologist*
Wolf, Brian R. *orthopedist, educator*
Zaheer, Asgar *medical educator*
Ziegler, Ekhard Erich *pediatrics educator*

Marshalltown
Davison, James A. *surgeon*
Thomas, David Llewellyn *physician*

Orange City
Vander Aarde, Stanley Bernard *retired otolaryngologist*

Ottumwa
Miller-Meeks, Mariannette Jane *ophthalmologist*

Polk City
Gaylor, James Leroy *biomedical research educator*

Sioux City
Ayi, Bertha Serwa *infectious disease specialist, internist*
Nwanegbo, Edward *epidemiologist, researcher*

West Des Moines
Alberts, Marion Edward *retired physician*

KANSAS

Fairway
O'Leary, Dennis Sophian *accrediting body executive*

Garden City
Malik, Abid *psychiatrist*

Hays
Novotorov, Andrew *educator*
Tsereteli, Zurab *surgeon*

Hutchinson
Crater, Timothy Andrews *internist*

Kansas City
Anderson, Harrison Clarke *pathologist, educator, biomedical researcher*
Arakawa, Kasumi *physician, educator*
Berenbom, Loren David *cardiologist*
Duchene, David Arthur *urologist, educator*
Dunn, Marvin Irvin *physician*
Griebling, Tomas Lindor *urologist, educator*
Holzbeierlein, Jeffery *medical educator*
Hudson, Robert Paul *medical educator*
Huet, Raul *psychiatrist*
Kim, Samuel S. *endocrinologist, educator*
Lawrence, Walter Thomas *plastic surgeon*
Lee, Kyo Rak *radiologist, educator*
Lukert, Barbara P. *medical educator*
Meyers, David George *internist, cardiologist, educator*
Mohn, Melvin Paul *anatomist, educator*
Perez, Victor Manuel *physician, plastic surgeon*
Rawitch, Allen Barry *medical educator, academic administrator*
Schloerb, Paul Richard *surgeon, educator*
Thrasher, J. Brantley *urologist*
Xiao, Zhousheng *pharmacologist, bone biologist*

Leawood
Epperly, Ted *physician, medical association administrator*

Louisville
Jabbar, Abdul *physician, educator, gastroenterologist*

Manhattan
Chapes, Stephen Keith *immunologist, educator*
Durkee, William Robert *retired internist*

Olathe
Luetje, Charles Marion, II, *otolaryngologist*
Monzon, Carlos Manuel *physician*

Overland Park
Blim, Richard Don *retired pediatrician, health facility administrator*
Butrick, Charles W. *gynecologist*
Landry, Mark Edward *podiatrist, researcher*

Pittsburg
Morgan, Lyle Warner, II, *medical educator*

Prairie Village
Fairchild, Robert Charles *pediatrician*
Mainster, Martin Aron *ophthalmologist, educator*

Shawnee Mission
Bell, Deloris Wiley *physician*
Fleming, Michael O. *physician*
Henley, Douglas E. *medical association administrator*
Price, James Gordon *physician, educator*
Thomas, Christopher Yancey III *surgeon, educator*

Topeka
Menninger, William Walter *psychiatrist*
Roy, William Robert *physician, lawyer, former congressman*

Westwood
Bodensteiner, David Carl *medical educator*

Wichita
Bloom, Barry Theil *pediatrician, researcher*
Yang, Shang-You *medical educator*

KENTUCKY

Ashland
Ali, Arshad *cardiologist, medical researcher*

Berea
Lamb, Irene Hendricks *medical researcher*

Buckner
Kelley, Michael *internal medicine and pediatric physician*

Danville
Nickens, Harry Carl *medical association administrator*

Edgewood
Dick, Barry Lee *surgeon*

Elizabethtown
Rahman, Rafiq Ur *oncologist, educator*

Elkton
Manthey, Frank Anthony *physician, director*

Grand Rivers
Young, Lucy Cleaver *retired physician*

Lexington
Al-Hasan, Majdi N. *medical educator, researcher*
Anderson, James Wingo *physician*
Ballard-Croft, Cherry *medical educator, researcher*
Campbell, Charles Larry, Jr. *cardiologist*
Chance, Kenneth Bernard, Sr. *endodontist educator, academic administrator*
Clawson, David Kay *orthopedic surgeon*
Colbert, Marvin Jay *retired internist, educator*
Davey, Diane Davis *pathologist, educator*
Fleischman, Roger Alan *medical educator, researcher*
Fragneto, Regina *anesthesiologist*
Gedaly, Roberto *surgeon, educator*
Hagen, Michael Dale *family physician educator*
Herberth, Johann *nephrologist, educator*
Holsinger, James Wilson, Jr. *cardiologist, physician*
Hoven, Ardis Dee *epidemiologist, medical educator*
Kibler, William Benjamin *orthopedist, surgeon*
Lain, Kristine Yoder *medical educator*
Means, Robert Taylor, Jr. *hematologist, educator, researcher*
Moliterno, David J. *cardiologist, educator*
Mukherjee, Debabrata *cardiologist, researcher*
Panayiotis, Zavos Michael *retired medical educator*
Paruchuri, Jithendra Kumar *signal processing researcher*
Puffer, James C. *sports medicine physician, educator, medical association administrator*
Randall, David Clark *medical educator, researcher*
Reynolds, Eric William *medical educator*
Roberts, Kenneth Boyett *pharmacy educator, former dean*
Smith, Charles Dennis *neurologist, researcher*
Stack, Steven J. *emergency physician*
Strup, Stephen Edward *urologist, educator*
Sun, LuZhe *pharmacology educator, researcher*
Waid, Thomas Henry *physician, researcher, educator*
Woodring, John Howell *radiologist*

Louisville
Amin, Mohammad *urology educator*
Andrew, Lane N. *medical researcher, educator*
Andrews, Billy Franklin *pediatrician, educator*
Aronoff, George Rodger *medicine and pharmacology educator*
Ballew, Laurie K. *psychiatrist*
Bodduluri, Haribabu *medical educator, researcher*
Breidenbach, Warren Conrad III *plastic surgeon, hand surgeon*
Buell, Joseph F. *surgeon, director*
Callen, Jeffrey Phillip *dermatologist, educator*
Chagpar, Anees Bahadurali *surgeon*
Chien, Sufan *surgeon, educator*
Danzl, Daniel Frank *emergency physician*
DeMunbrun-Harmon, Donne O'Donnell *retired family physician*
Elin, Ronald John *pathologist, educator*
Farman, Allan George *radiologist, pathologist, educator*
Foulks, Gary Neal *ophthalmologist, educator*
Gall, Stanley Adolph *immunologist, researcher*
Gleis, Linda Hood *physician*
Harkema, Susan *medical researcher, director*
Helm, Cyril William *physician, medical educator, researcher*
Holt, Homer Anthony, Jr. *urologist, educator*
Houghton, David Jeffery *neurologist, educator*
Ildstad, Suzanne T. *transplant surgeon, immunologist, educator*
Kaplan, Henry Jerrold *ophthalmologist, educator*
Kutz, Joseph Edward *hand surgeon, educator*
Levinson, Stanley S. *pathologist, educator*
Lin, Ji-Tzuoh *energy harvesting researcher*
Miller, Donald Max *medical association administrator*
Moore, Joseph Patrick *medical researcher, educator*
Neustadt, David Harold *physician*
Perez-Abadia, Gustavo A. *medical educator*
Ravindra, Kadiyala V *medical educator, director*
Richardson, James David *surgeon*
Scott, David Albert *biomedical researcher, dental educator*
Scott, Ralph Mason *retired radiologist, educator*
Shields, Christopher Brian *neurosurgeon*
Sumanasekera, Wasana Kumarihamy *medical educator*

Syed, Ibrahim Bijli *medical educator, physicist*
Talwalkar, Sameer S. *pathologist, researcher*
Tsai, Tsu-Min *surgeon*
Waddell, William Joseph *pharmacologist, toxicologist*
Wright, Jesse Hartzell *psychiatrist, educator*

LOUISIANA

Alexandria
Freedman, Robert J. *cardiologist, educator*
Hanley, Henry Gorman *cardiologist*

Baton Rouge
Bray, George August *internist, researcher, educator*
DiBenedetto, Robert Lawrence *retired obstetrician, retired gynecologist, retired insurance company executive*
Gettys, Thomas Wigington *medical researcher*
Gibbons, William *reproductive endocrinologist*
Kastin, Abba Jeremiah *endocrinologist, researcher*
Puyau, Francis Albert *retired radiology educator, physician*
Spencer, Fitzgerald *medical educator*

Covington
Metzner, David Mark *plastic and reconstructive surgeon*

Denham Springs
Ishler, Harold LeRoy, Jr. *retired physician*

Doyline
Willis, Gladden Williams *retired pathologist, scientific photographer, tree farmer*

Hammond
Kraemer, Robert R. *health educator, researcher*

Kenner
Farber, George Allan *dermatologist, educator*

Lafayette
Appley, Alan J. *neurosurgeon*
Lipstate, Linda *endocrinologist, educator*
Meza, Luis Alberto *internist, researcher*

Lake Charles
Drez, David Jacob, Jr. *orthopedic surgeon, educator*
Gunderson, Clark Alan *orthopedic surgeon*

Mandeville
Desper, Beatrice S. *obstetrician, gynecologist*

Marrero
Kushner, Frederick Gary *cardiologist, medical educator*

Metairie
Colon, Gustavo Alberto *plastic surgeon*
Edisen, Clayton Byron *physician*
Farris, Patricia K. *dermatologist, educator*
Jacobs, Benjamin Franklin *cardiologist*

Minden
Kemmerly, James Robert *obstetrician, gynecologist*

Monroe
Cooksey, John Charles *ophthalmologist, former congressman*

New Orleans
Agrawal, Krishna Chandra *pharmacology educator*
Ali, Juzar *medical educator, director*
Beck, David Edward *surgeon*
Bennett, James Toliver *pediatric orthopedist*
Berenson, Gerald Sanders *physician*
Bidima, Jean Godefroy *medical educator, researcher, Philosophy Professor*
Blonde, Lawrence *endocrinologist, director*
Botros, Fady T. *medical educator*
Bowers, Cyril Y. *endocrinologist, educator*
Chiu, Ernest Sai-Yun *plastic and reconstructive surgeon, educator*
Cohn, Isidore, Jr. *surgeon, educator*
Cui, Yan *medical educator, researcher*
Easson, William McAlpine *psychiatrist, educator*
Fisher, James William *pharmacologist, medical educator*
Frohlich, Edward David *medical educator*
Fuselier, Harold Anthony, Jr. *urologist, director, educator*
Gould, Harry J. III *neurology educator*
Hill, James *medical educator, researcher*
Hobden, Jeffery Andre *medical researcher, educator*
Hollier, Larry Harold *vascular surgeon, hospital administrator, dean*
Hu, Jennifer J. *epidemiologist, researcher*
Hyslop, Newton Everett, Jr. *infectious disease specialist*
Incaprera, Frank Philip *internist*
Jenkins, James Stephen *internist*
Joshi, Virendra *medical educator*
Kolinsky, Michael Allen *emergency physician*
Kruse-Jarres, Rebecca *medical educator*
Laborde, James Monroe *orthopedist*
Lavie, Carl J. *cardiologist, researcher*
Lichtveld, Maureen Yvette *medical educator, department chairman*
Locke, William *retired endocrinologist*
Magnus, Jeanette H. *medical educator*
Martin, David Hubert *internist, epidemiologist, educator*
McMullan, Paul *cardiologist*
Millikan, Larry Edward *dermatologist*
Moulder, Peter Vincent *cardiovascular surgeon, educator*
Navar, Luis Gabriel *physiology educator, director, researcher*
Nichols, Ronald Lee *surgeon, educator*
Nuss, Daniel Wehrmann *surgeon, educator*
Ochsner, John Lockwood *thoracic-cardiovascular surgeon*
Pankey, George Atkinson *internist, educator, researcher*
Porter, George Homer III *physician, medical foundation executive*
Richardson, Donald Edward *neurosurgery educator*
Riddick, Frank Adams, Jr. *physician, healthcare administrator*
Sacks, Joel Gerald *ophthalmologist, educator*
Summer, Warren R. *pulmonologist, director*
Tender, Gabriel Claudiu *neurosurgeon, consultant*
Threefoot, Sam Abraham *physician, educator*
Timmcke, Alan Edward *colon and rectal surgeon*
Tracy, Richard E. *medical educator*
Van Dyke, Russell Barrett *medical educator*
Zimmerman, Robert S. *internist, endocrinologist*

Opelousas
Lafleur, Kenneth Charles *ophthalmologist*

Pineville
Webb, Watts Rankin *surgeon*

Shreveport
Blondin, Joan *nephrologist educator*
Brannon, Guy Emilio *psychiatrist*
Chung, Jun *medical educator*
Conrad, Steven Allen *critical care and emergency physician, biomedical engineer, educator*
El-Haddad, Ghassan *nuclear medicine physician, researcher*
Jawahar, Ajay *neurosurgeon, educator*
Jones, Kenneth B., Jr. *surgeon*
Misra, Raghunath Prasad *physician, educator*
Parish, Roy Clayton *medical researcher*
Reddy, Pratap Chandupatla *cardiologist, educator, researcher*
Shelby, James Stanford *surgeon, researcher*
Stucker, Fred Joseph *otolaryngology educator*
Vachharajani, Tushar Jitendra *nephrologist, researcher*
Wall, Simeon Heninger, Jr. *plastic surgeon*
Wilson, John T. *pediatrics and pharmacology educator*

Slidell
McBurney, Elizabeth Innes *dermatologist, physician, educator*

Sulphur
Toniette, Sallye Jean *physician*

MAINE

Augusta
Davis, George Edward *internist*

Bangor
Davis, Bruce Hewat *pathologist, researcher*
Martin, Thomas Charles *pediatrician*

Biddeford
Ford, Charles Willard *medical educator*

Lewiston
Coleman, Laurel *geriatrician, internist*
Singh, Abhay Kumar *psychiatrist, department chairman*

Lubec
Hayes, Ernest M. *podiatrist*

Portland
McAfee, Robert Elwood *retired surgeon*
Wilkinson, Barbara J. *pediatrician, educator*

Scarborough
Clark, Gordon Hostetter, Jr. *physician*

South Portland
Wheeler, Hewitt Brownell *surgeon, educator*

Southport
Gibson, Edgar Thomas *retired surgeon, educator*

Topsham
Arnold, Charles Burle, Jr. *retired physician*

MARYLAND

Aberdeen Proving Ground
Jones, Bruce Hovey *physician, researcher*
Sagripanti, Jose-Luis *biomedical scientist*

Annapolis
Halpern, Joseph Alan *physician*
Welch, Robert Bond *ophthalmologist, educator*

Arnold
Lee, Yu-Jin *retired military physician*

Baltimore
Abadir, Peter M. *physician, educator*
Achuff, Stephen Charles *cardiologist*
Agre, Peter Courtland *medical institute executive, educator, researcher*
Ahuja, Nita *medical educator*
Aneja, Alka *child psychiatrist*
Appel, Lawrence John *physician, educator*
Appleby, Brian Stephen *psychiatrist*
Aucott, Susan Wright *medical educator, researcher*
Aurelian, Laure *medical sciences educator*
Bahrami, Hossein *epidemiologist, physician*
Baker, R. Robinson *surgeon*
Baker, Timothy Danforth *physician, educator*
Baumgartner, William Anthony *cardiac surgeon*
Belzberg, Allan Joel *neurosurgery educator*
Black, Betty Smith *psychiatrist*
Blumenthal, Roger Scott *cardiologist*
Bollinger, Mary Elizabeth *immunologist*
Brant, Steven Ross *medical educator*
Brasic, James Robert *psychiatrist*
Brenner, Joel I. *cardiologist, educator*
Brieger, Gert Henry *medical educator*
Brodie, Angela M. *biomedical researcher, educator*
Brody, Eugene Bloor *psychiatrist, educator, editor*
Brookmeyer, Ronald *medical educator*
Canto-Soler, Valeria *medical educator, researcher*
Cao, Dengfeng *pathologist*
Carrier, France *medical educator*
Carson, Benjamin Solomon *neurosurgeon*
Castellani, Rudolph Joseph *pathologist*
Celnik, Pablo Ariel *neurologist*
Chaudhry, Vinay *medical educator*
Childs, Barton *retired physician, educator*
Christopher-Stine, Lisa *rheumatologist*
Civin, Curt Ingraham *oncologist*
Cohen, Bernard A. *pediatric dermatologist*
Cole, John W. *neurologist*
Colomer, Veronica *medical educator, researcher*
Conway, Janet Donohue *surgeon*
Cooper, Lisa Angeline *internist, medical educator*
Cooper, Matthew *surgeon, educator*
Cullen, Kevin Joseph *oncologist, educator*
Czinn, Steven J. *pediatrician, department chairman*
Dannenberg, Arthur Milton, Jr. *experimental pathologist, immunologist, educator*
Davidson, Nancy Ellen *oncologist*
DeLateur, Barbara Jane *medical educator*
DePaulo, J. Raymond, Jr. *psychiatrist, researcher*
DeWeese, Theordore L. *radiation oncologist*
Dietz, Harry C. *pediatrician, educator*
Dobs, Adrian Sandra *endocrinologist, educator*
Dover, George Joseph *pediatric oncologist*
Drachman, Daniel Bruce *neurologist, educator*
Dutton, Richard P. *anesthesiologist, educator*
Eakle, A. Jonathan *medical educator, director*
Eberhart, Charles George *medical educator*
Eggleston, Peyton Archer *allergist, immunologist*
Eisenberg, Howard Michael *neurosurgeon*
El-Kamary, Samer S. *pediatrician, educator*
Erozan, Yener Sahir *pathologist, educator*
Ettinger, David Seymour *oncologist*
Ezeugwu, Camellus O. *cardiologist, director*
Fahy, Brenda G. *medical educator, anesthesiologist*
Feinberg, Andrew P. *medical geneticist, oncologist, educator*
Feldman, Leonard Samuel *medical educator*
Fox, Harold Edward *obstetrician, researcher, gynecologist, educator*
Freeman, John Mark *pediatric neurologist*
Gamaldo, Charlene Edie *medical educator*
Georgiades, Christos *medical educator*
Gerstenblith, Gary *medical educator, cardiologist*
Gimenez, Luis Fernando *physician, educator*
Godenne, Ghislaine Dudley *physician, psychotherapist, educator*
Goldberg, Morton Falk *ophthalmologist, educator*
Goldman, Lynn Rose *medical educator*
Goldman, Stuart Miles *podiatrist*
Goodman, Steven N. *medical educator*
Gordis, Leon *physician*
Gorelick, David *medical educator*
Gorospe, Emmanuel Cruz *physician, medical researcher*
Gott, Vincent Lynn *physician*
Gray, Ronald H. *medical educator*
Greenough, William Bates III *medical educator*
Griffin, Diane Edmund *research physician, virologist, educator*
Griffith, Lawrence Stacey Cameron *cardiologist, educator*
Grossman, Stuart Alan *oncologist, medical educator*
Harris, James Carol Overton, Jr. *psychiatrist, pediatrician*
Hatef Naimi, Elham *medical researcher*
Helfaer, Mark Allen *anesthesiologist*
Helrich, Martin *anesthesiologist, educator*
Hess, Allan Duane *medical educator*
Hoffman, Elmer *surgeon*
Hofkin, Gerald Alan *gastroenterologist*
Hungerford, David Samuel *orthopedic surgeon, educator*
Hurley, Robert W. *anesthesiologist, educator*
Jeffrey, Janofsky S. *psychiatrist, educator*
Johns, Richard James *physician, educator*
Johnson, Kenneth Peter *neurologist, researcher*
Kalloo, Anthony *gastroenterologist, educator*
Kastor, John Alfred *cardiologist, educator*
Kelemen, Mark David *cardiologist, hospital administrator*
Kelen, Gabor David *emergency physician*
Kerr, Douglas Anthony *neurologist, researcher*
Kessler, Irving Isar *epidemiologist, consultant*
Knapp, David Allan *pharmaceutical educator, researcher, former dean*
Krasna, Mark Jonathan *thoracic surgeon, researcher*
Labrique, Alain Bernard *epidemiologist, educator*
Ladenson, Paul *endocrinologist*
Lawrence, Robert Swan *physician, educator*
Lazarus, Gerald Sylvan *dermatologist, educator, dean*
Levien, David Harold *surgeon*
Lima, João A.C. *cardiologist, educator*
Litrenta, Frances Marie *psychiatrist*
Loeb, Stacy *physician*
Longo, Dan Louis *internist, researcher, oncologist*
Macko, Richard Frank *medical educator*
Maguire, Brian J. *medical educator*
Manheimer, Eric *medical researcher*
Manson, Paul Nellis *plastic surgeon, educator*
McHugh, Paul R. *psychiatrist, neurologist, educator*
McMillan, Julia A. *pediatrician, educator*
Meeker, Alan Keith *biomedical researcher, educator*
Mehra, Mandeep Rajinder *cardiologist*
Mezey, Esteban *internist, gastroenterologist, educator*
Migeon, Claude Jean *pediatrics educator*
Miller, Edward Doring *anesthesiologist, hospital administrator, dean*
Miller, Michael *physician, educator*
Mirski, Marek Alexander *anesthesiologist, educator*
Montaner, Silvia *medical educator, researcher*
Montgomery, Robert Avery *transplant surgeon*
Nahabedian, Maurice Y. *plastic surgeon*
Nelkin, Barry David *oncology researcher and educator*
Neu, Alicia Mallare *pediatric nephrologist*
North, Richard Boydston *neurological surgery educator*
Nuzzo, Jenniffer Bronwyn *epidemiologist*
O'Toole, Tara Jeanne *medical educator, former federal agency administrator*
Paige, David Martin *pediatrician, educator*
Palmer, Jeffrey Bruce *physiatrist, researcher*
Parsa, Cameron Farrokh *ophthalmologist, educator*
Pass, Carolyn Joan *dermatologist*
Pearlson, Godfrey David *psychiatrist, researcher, educator*
Pereira, Kevin *pediatrician, director*
Perler, Bruce Alan *vascular surgeon*
Petri, Michelle *medical educator*
Philosophe, Benjamin *surgeon*
Pollin, Toni I. *endocrinologist, educator*
Pronovost, Peter J. *anesthesiologist, health facility administrator, medical educator*
Quigley, Harry Alan *ophthalmologist, medical professor*
Quinn, Thomas Charles *medical researcher, educator*
Quiñones-Hinojosa, Alfredo *neurosurgeon, educator*
Rayson, Glendon Ennes *internist, preventive medicine specialist, writer*
Rose, Noel Richard *immunologist, microbiologist, educator*
Rumbaugh, Jeffrey Arlin *neurologist, neuroscientist*
Russell, Stuart Dean *cardiologist, educator*
Schoenrich, Edyth Hull *internist, preventive medicine physician*
Sham, James S.K. *medical educator*
Shamsuddin, AbulKalam Mohammed *medical educator*
Shuldiner, Alan Rodney *endocrinologist, educator*
Silbergeld, Ellen Kovner *epidemiologist, toxicologist, researcher*
Silverman, Ronald *plastic surgeon*
Simpkins, Cuthbert Ormond *surgeon, educator, writer*
Simpson, Elizabeth B. *medical association administrator, management consultant*
Slezak, Sheri *plastic surgeon*
Smith, Seth Aaron *medical educator*
Sommer, Alfred *ophthalmologist, medical educator, researcher*
Spence, Robert James *plastic surgeon*
Starfield, Barbara Helen *pediatrician, educator*
Stark, Walter J. *ophthalmologist, educator*
Strauch, Eric David *surgeon*
Talalay, Paul *pharmacologist, educator*
Tamargo, Rafael J. *neurological surgeon, educator*
Tchantchou, Flaubert *medical researcher*
Vogelstein, Bert *oncology educator*
Wachtel, Lee Elizabeth *psychiatrist, educator*
Wahl, Richard Leo *radiologist, educator, nuclear medicine physician, researcher*
Walkup, John Timothy *psychiatrist, educator*
Walsh, Patrick Craig *urologist*
Wang, Jian *medical researcher, educator*
Weiner, Jonathan P. *health policy and management educator*
Weisfeldt, Myron Lee *cardiologist, educator*
Weiss, James Lloyd *cardiology educator*
Wilson, Donald Edward *internist, educator, former dean*
Winkelstein, Jerry Allen *retired pediatrician*
Wong, Dean *radiologist, educator*
Wood, Robert A. *pediatrician, allergist, educator*
Xing, Michael Mingzhao *endocrinologist, educator*
Yang, Vincent Wen-shan *gastroenterologist, educator, researcher*
Young, Barbara *psychiatrist, educator, photographer, psychoanalyst*
Zandi, Peter P. *medical educator*
Ziessman, Harvey A. *nuclear medicine physician, medical association administrator*
Zimmerman, Andrew *pediatrician, neurologist*

Bethesda
Akhondi, Hossein *internist, researcher*
Alter, Harvey J. *hematologist, educator*
Anderson, George Kenneth *physician, retired military officer, foundation administrator*
Arai, Andrew E. *cardiologist*
Ashwell, Jonathan D. *medical researcher*
Berzofsky, Jay A. *medical researcher*
Buetow, Kenneth H. *medical geneticist*
Campbell, William Wesley *medical educator, department chairman*
Camphausen, Kevin A. *oncologist, researcher*
Cantor, Kenneth P. *epidemiologist, researcher*
Cao, Jie Jane *cardiologist, researcher*
Celi, Francesco Saverio *geriatrician, endocrinologist*
Chan, Leighton *physiatrist, educator*
Chew, Emily Ying *epidemiologist, director*
Choyke, Peter L. *radiologist, researcher*
Cohen, Robert Abraham *retired physician*
Cohen, Sheldon Gilbert *physician, historian, immunologist*
Cruz, Wilhelmina Mangahas *critical care physician*
Datiles, Manuel Bernaldes III *ophthalmologist, researcher*
De Cherney, Alan Hersh *obstetrics and gynecology educator*
Dietrich, Robert Anthony *pathologist, consultant, medical association administrator*
Emanuel, Ezekiel J. *oncologist, bioethicist*
Farci, Patrizia *medical educator, researcher*
Farley, John Hall *medical educator*
Fine, Howard A. *medical researcher*
Fradkin, Judith Elaine *endocrinologist, director*
Fukunaga, Masaki *medical researcher*
Gastwirth, Glenn Barry *medical association administrator*
Giaccone, Giuseppe *oncologist, researcher*
Goldstein, Murray *medical epidemiologist and research administrator*
Goldstein, Rise Belle *medical researcher*
Gonzalez, Frank J. *medical researcher*
Goodman, Wayne K. *psychiatrist, researcher*
Gress, Ronald E. *oncologist, medical researcher*
Gulley, James Leonard *internist, oncologist*
Guttman, Helene Nathan *biomedical consultant, transpersonal counselor*
Hallett, Mark *neurologist, educator, researcher*

Hance, Kenneth William *immunologist, researcher*
Harlan, Linda Carol *epidemiologist*
Harris, Curtis Craig *medical researcher*
Harvey, John Collins *internist, educator*
Hejtmancik, James Fielding *medical researcher*
Helman, Lee J. *medical researcher*
Herman, Mary Margaret *neuropathologist*
Hingson, Ralph W. *medical educator*
Holland, Steven M. *epidemiologist*
Hsia, Chu Chieh *medical researcher*
Hutton, John Evans, Jr. *surgeon, educator, retired military officer*
Jaffe, Elaine Sarkin *pathologist, researcher*
Johnson, Joyce Marie *psychiatrist, public health service officer, epidemiologist*
Joy, Robert John Thomas *medical educator*
Kapikian, Albert Zaven *physician, epidemiologist*
Kataoka, Tatsuki R. *pathologist, researcher*
Kelly, Kathleen *medical researcher*
Klee, Claude Blanc *medical researcher*
Koroshetz, Walter J. *neurologist, educator*
Kotin, Robert Michael *biomedical researcher*
Krause, Richard Michael *medical scientist, government official, educator, researcher*
Kuehl, W. Michael *medical researcher*
Kunos, George *pharmacologist*
Lane, H. Clifford *internist*
Lauer, Michael Solon *cardiologist, director*
Lee, Jongho *medical researcher*
Levine, Mark A. *endocrinologist*
Levine, Zachary Thomas *neurosurgeon*
Li, Qingdi Quentin *physician, research scientist, medical educator*
Libutti, Steven Kenneth *medical researcher*
Lichtenberg, Joseph David *psychiatrist*
Linehan, William Marston *urologist, researcher*
Lipman, David J. *medical association administrator, researcher*
Lowy, Douglas Ronald *oncologist, researcher*
Lumelsky, Nadya L. *medical researcher, director*
Mackall, Crystal L. *medical researcher*
Malech, Harry Lewis *immunologist, researcher*
Manolio, Teri A. *physician*
Martensen, Robert Lawrence *emergency physician, educator, historian, ethicist, writer*
Masur, Henry *internist*
McCurdy, Harry Ward *otolaryngologist*
Merlino, Glenn T. *medical researcher*
Mitchell, James B. *medical researcher*
Morens, David Michael *epidemiologist, tropical medicine investigator*
Murphy, Philip M. *biomedical researcher*
Oberholtzer, J. Carl *pathologist, researcher*
Ognibene, Frederick Peter *internist*
Park, Yikyung *epidemiologist, oncologist*
Pastan, Ira Harry *medical researcher*
Paul, William Erwin *immunologist*
Perlin, Seymour *psychiatrist, educator*
Peterson, Charles Marquis *medical educator*
Phillips, Terence Martyn *immunologist*
Pollard, Harvey B. *medical educator, neuroscientist*
Pommier, Yves Georges *medical researcher*
Puri, Raj K. *medical researcher, director*
Quinnan, Gerald Vincent, Jr. *medical educator*
Rapoport, Judith *psychiatrist*
Rennert, Owen Murray *pediatrician, geneticist, educator*
Reynolds, Herbert Young *internist*
Rice, Charles Lane *surgeon, educator*
Rider, Lisa G *pediatric rheumatologist, researcher*
Rosenberg, Steven Aaron *surgeon, medical researcher*
Saffiotti, Umberto *pathologist*
Samelson, Lawrence Elliot *medical researcher*
SanGiovanni, John Paul *ophthalmic epidemiologist, eye and vision researcher*
Schechter, Alan Neil *medical researcher*
Schrump, David Stuart *medical association administrator, researcher*
Shapeero, Lorraine G. *physician, researcher, educator*
Shevach, Ethan Menahem *physician*
Shortliffe, Edward Hance *internist, medical educator, computer scientist*
Shulman, Lawrence Edward *biomedical researcher, rheumatologist*
Simons-Morton, Denise G. *medical researcher*
Singer, Alfred *immunologist, researcher*
Smoller, Bruce Melvyn *psychiatrist*
Sneiderman, Charles Alan *medical researcher*
Sobel, Mark Esar *pathologist, researcher*
Song, Byoung-Joon *pharmacologist, biochemist*
Stetler-Stevenson, Maryalice *cytologist, director*
Stratton, Pamela *gynecologist*
Sturtz, Donald Lee *surgeon, military officer, educator*
Thorgeirsson, Snorri Sveinn *medical researcher*
Udey, Mark C. *dermatologist, researcher*
Ursano, Robert Joseph *psychiatrist*
Vonderhaar, Barbara K. *medical researcher*
Wahl, Sharon Marie *immunologist*
Waldmann, Thomas Alexander *medical researcher, physician*
Wassermann, Eric M. *neurologist, department chairman*
Watanabe, Kazuhide *medical researcher*
Watashi, Koichi *medical educator, researcher*
Watson, Michael S. *medical geneticist, educator*
Weinstein, Lee S. *endocrinologist*
Wells, Samuel Alonzo, Jr. *surgeon, educator*
Wright, Pamela Ann *surgeon*
Wu, Carl *medical researcher*
Yuspa, Stuart Howard *oncologist, researcher*

Bowie
Pearse, Warren Harland *obstetrician, gynecologist, medical association administrator*

Chevy Chase
Croft, Joseph David *medical educator*
Dufresne, Craig Roger *plastic surgeon, educator*
Emsellem, Helene *medical association administrator*
Feldman, Bruce Allen *otolaryngologist*
Goldstein, Lawrence Steven *medical professor and investigator*
Goodwin, Frederick King *psychiatrist*
Hahn, Marc B. *physician, educator, former dean*
Hani, Antoine George *psychiatrist, psychoanalyst*
Harlan, William Robert, Jr. *internist, educator, researcher*
Hersh, Stephen Peter *psychiatrist, psycho-oncologist, chronic pain expert, educator*
Khairalla, Eric William *plastic surgeon*
Knable, Michael *medical researcher*
Lyons, Jonathan Spencer *ophthalmologist*
Pogue, John Marshall *physician*
Resnik, Harvey Lewis Paul *psychiatrist*

College Park
Katz, Ronald Alan *dermatologist*

Columbia
Campbell-Alston, Deirdre Adina *anatomist, physiologist, researcher*
Hyman, Lawrence Robert *psychiatrist*
Jani, Sushma Niranjan *pediatric psychiatrist*
Strahlman, Richard Scott *pediatrician*

Darnestown
Cohen, Sanford Irwin *physician, educator*

Easton
Rever, George Wright *psychiatrist, health facility administrator*

Frederick
Belard, J-Louis Hubert *medical researcher*
Blumenthal, Robert P. *medical researcher*
Bobe, Gerd *medical researcher*
Byrd, R. Andrew *medical researcher*
Colburn, Nancy Hall *medical researcher*
Hanna, Michael George, Jr. *immunologist, pharmaceutical executive*
Keefer, Larry Kay *medical researcher*
Le Grice, Stuart F.J. *senior investigator*
Malin, Howard Gerald *podiatrist*
Marquez, Victor E. *medical researcher*
McMahon, James Brislin *medical researcher*
Morrison, Deborah K. *medical researcher*
Oppenheim, Joost J. *allergist, immunologist, researcher*
Ortaldo, John R. *immunologist, researcher*
Perantoni, Alan O. *medical researcher*
Sharifi, Nima *oncologist, researcher*
Strathern, Jeffrey N. *medical researcher*
Trinchieri, Giorgio *medical researcher*
Weissman, Allan M. *medical researcher*
Wlodawer, Alexander *medical researcher*
Zimmer-Galler, Ingrid E. *ophthalmologist, educator*

Gaithersburg
Brodine, Charles Edward *physician*
Hegyeli, Ruth Ingeborg Elisabeth Johnsson *pathologist, federal official*
Schwartzberg, Allan Zelig *psychiatrist, educator*

Garrett Park
Elwood, William *medical educator*

Germantown
Adamson, Richard Henry *pharmacologist*
Fountos, Barrett Nicholas *epidemiologist, researcher*
Stevceva, Liljana *medical educator, researcher*

Greenbelt
Obamogie, Mercy A. *physician*
Weltz, Martin David *hematologist*

Hyattsville
Gillum, Richard Frank *epidemiologist*

Kensington
Mavilio, Domenico *medical researcher, physician*

Laurel
Calvert, Richard John *medical researcher*

Lutherville
Baramki, Theodore Atallah *gynecologist, reproductive endocrinologist*
Berg, Wendie *radiologist*
Chuck, Roy S. *surgeon*
Elma, Bayani Borja *physician*
O'Brien, Terrence P. *ophthalmologist, educator*

Lutherville Timonium
Auwaerter, Paul Gisbert *physician, educator*
Meyer, Jon Keith *psychiatrist, psychoanalyst, educator*
Park, Lee Crandall *psychiatrist, physician*

North Bethesda
Kreling, Barbara Bartholf *medical educator*

Owings Mills
Heck, Albert Frank *retired neurologist*
Rose, Stephen *medical researcher*

Pikesville
Sokol, Marian *medical association administrator*

Potomac
Gaston, Marilyn Hughes *physician, administrator, public health expert, author*
Howe, Edmund Grant III *psychiatrist, educator*

Rockville
Banfield, William Gethin *physician*
Barker, Lewellys Franklin *medical association administrator*
Bautista, Abraham Parana *immunologist*
Birns, Mark Theodore *physician*
Bough, Kristopher *pharmacologist*
Chretien, Paul Bernard *oncologist, medical researcher*
Clancy, Carolyn M. *internist, federal agency administrator*
Crout, J. Richard *pharmacologist, researcher*
DuPont, Robert Louis *psychiatrist, physician*
Fink, Kenneth Stuart *physician, researcher*
Goodman, Jesse *physician, director, public health facility administrator, research scientist*
James, Eric Robert *medical educator*
Kroner, Barbara L *epidemiologist*
Leach, Berton Joe *medical educator*
Leventhal, Carl M. *neurologist, consultant, retired government agency administrator*
Malik, Waheed Ahmad *cardiologist*
Mallak, Craig T. *pathologist*
McMurry, James Finley, Jr. *endocrinologist, researcher*
Ralph, Robert Alan *ophthalmologist, educator*
Sullivan, Marian Toth *epidemiologist, researcher*
Tabor, Edward *medical researcher*
Toro, Jorge R. *dermatologist, researcher*
Yaes, Robert Joel *radiologist, educator*

Silver Spring
Beard, Lillian B. McLean *pediatrician, consultant*
Bergmann-Leitner, Elke S. *immunologist, researcher*
Eliot, John *psychologist, educator*
Eydelman, Malvina *ophthalmologist*
Gilbert, Charles Richard Alsop *obstetrician, gynecologist, surgeon, educator*
Heppner, Donald Gray, Jr. *immunology research physician, army officer*
Magill, Alan Jon *preventive medicine physician*
Mosholder, Andrew Donald *psychiatrist*
Ohrt, Colin *pharmacologist, department chairman*
Supanich, Barbara Ann *physician*
Waldrop, Francis Neil *physician*

Stevenson
Hendler, Nelson Howard *physician, health facility administrator, director*

Takoma Park
Ndeumeni, Charles Dechateau *medical educator*
Wagner, Marsden Grigg *medical educator, director*

Timonium
Forrester, Alfred Whitfield *psychiatrist, educator*

Towson
Adams, Joseph Andrew *internist, health facility administrator, educator*
Corcoran, Paul John *physician*
Sills, Edward M. *pediatric rheumatologist*
Spodak, Michael Kenneth *forensic psychiatrist*

Upper Marlboro
Jones-Lukács, Elizabeth Lucille *physician*

Waldorf
Wiggins, Stephen Edward *physician*

Wheaton
Kaliner, Michael Aron *physician, researcher*
White, Martha Vetter *allergist, immunologist*

Woodbine
Mc Indoe, Darrell Winfred *retired nuclear medicine physician*

MASSACHUSETTS

Acton
Benz, Edward John, Sr. *clinical pathologist*
Ziegler, Robert George *psychiatrist, family therapist*

Amesbury
Heyman, Joseph Martin *gynecologist*

Amherst
Braun, Barry *kinesiologist*
Palmer, John Derry *physiology educator*
Zilberberg, Marya *epidemiologist, researcher*

Belmont
Cohen, Bruce Michael *psychiatrist, educator, scientist, health facility administrator*
Coyle, Joseph Thomas *psychiatrist*
de Marneffe, Francis *psychiatrist, hospital administrator*
Forester, Brent Peter *psychiatrist*
Onesti, Silvio Joseph *psychiatrist*
Pope, Harrison Graham, Jr. *psychiatrist, educator*

Boston
Abrahm, Janet Lee *hematologist, oncologist, educator, palliative care specialist*
Abularrage, Christopher Joseph *surgeon*
Abu-moustafa, Adel H. *medical educator, dean*
Adelstein, S(tanley) James *radiologist, educator*
Adler, Dale Steven *internist, cardiologist*
Aisenberg, Alan C. *physician, educator, researcher*
Akins, Cary Willard *cardiac surgeon*
Albert, Martin Lawrence *behavioral neurologist, writer, educator, researcher*
Albright, Eric D. *medical librarian, director*
Alpert, Joel Jacobs *pediatrician, educator*
Anderson, Ana Carrizosa *neurologist, educator*
Anderson, Kenneth Carl *physician, educator*
Anderson, William Stanley *neurosurgeon*
Angelo, E. Joanne *child, adolescent and adult psychiatrist*
Antman, Elliott Marshall *cardiologist, educator*
Antman, Karen Hamm *oncologist, educator, dean*
Anversa, Piero *medical educator*
Ardison, Matthew Tanner *physician assistant*
Aronson, Mark David *medical educator*
Atkinson, David *medical educator*
Audette, Joseph F. *medical educator, physician*
Austen, W(illiam) Gerald *surgeon, educator*
Avorn, Jerry L. *epidemiologist, educator*
Azadzoi, Kazem M. *urologist, educator*
Bacha, Emile A. *surgeon*
Bae, Donald S. *orthopedist*
Bailin, Michael Traherne *physician*
Bandipalliam, Prathap V. *oncologist, researcher*
Banks, Henry H. *orthopedist, educator, dean*
Barouch, Dan Hung *physician, scientist, educator*
Barsky, Arthur Joseph III *physician, researcher*
Bates, David Westfall *internist, educator, medical researcher*
Baughman, Kenneth Lee *cardiologist, educator*
Becker, James Murdoch *surgeon, educator*
Belkin, Michael *vascular surgeon*
Benacerraf, Baruj *pathologist, educator*
Benz, Edward John, Jr. *hematologist, educator, health facility administrator*
Bernhard, William Francis *thoracic and cardiovascular surgeon*
Bernstein, Edward *medical educator, director*
Berson, Eliot Lawrence *ophthalmologist, medical educator*
Bistrian, Bruce Ryan *internist, educator*
Black, Paul Henry *medical educator, researcher*
Black, Peter *neurosurgeon, educator*
Blacklow, Robert Stanley *internist, educator*
Blinderman, Craig D. *physician*
Bolman, R. Morton, III, (Chip Bolman) *surgeon, educator*
Borus, Jonathan Frederick *psychiatrist, educator*
Braunwald, Eugene *physician, educator*
Brenner, Barry Morton *physician*
Brenner, Gary Jay *medical association administrator*
Brenner, Michael Barry *rheumatologist, educator*
Brown, Florence M. *endocrinologist, educator*
Buchmiller, Terry Lynn *pediatrician, surgeon*
Busse, Paul Martin *oncologist, researcher*
Buxbaum, Robert C(ourtney) *internist*
Canellos, George Peter *hematologist, oncologist, educator*
Caplan, Louis Robert *neurologist, educator*
Carey, Martin Conrad *gastroenterologist, molecular biophysicist, educator, medical geneticist*
Carter, Bob S. *neurosurgeon, educator*
Cavazos, Lauro Fred *medical educator, former United States Secretary of Education*
Celi, Leo Anthony G. *intensivist, infectious disease specialist, internist, informaticist, researcher*
Chatzizisis, Yiannis S. *physician, researcher*
Chobanian, Aram *medical educator, cardiologist, former academic administrator*
Choo, Sin H. *neurosurgeon*
Christakis, Nicholas Alexander *internist, social scientist, educator*
Christen, William G. *epidemiologist, educator*
Ciraulo, Domenic Anthony *psychiatrist, educator*
Cobey, Frederick Carpinter *anesthesiologist*
Coffin, John Miller *medical researcher, biology professor*
Cohen, Alan Seymour *internist*
Cohen, Lee Stuart *psychiatrist, educator*
Cohn, Lawrence H. *cardiothoracic surgeon*
Crosby, Steven Joseph *medical educator*
Cypess, Aaron M. *endocrinologist*
Daffner, Kirk Reid *neurologist, researcher*
Daley, George Quentin *hematologist, biomedical research scientist*
Davidoff, Ravin *cardiologist*
DeCamp, Malcolm M., Jr. *thoracic surgeon*
Dedeoglu, Fatma *pediatrician, educator*
Demling, Robert Hugh *surgeon, researcher*
DeSanctis, Roman William *cardiologist, educator*
Dluhy, Robert George *physician*
Drappatz, Jan *neuro-oncologist*
Drazen, Jeffrey Mark *medical educator*
Duda, Rosemary Bernadette *surgeon*
Dvorak, Harold Fisher *retired pathologist*
Eder, Joseph Paul, Jr. *physician*
Egdahl, Richard Harrison *surgeon, educator, health science association administrator*
Egorina, Elena *medical researcher*
Eisenberg, Leon *psychiatrist, educator*
Eisenberg, Ronald Lee *radiologist*
Eliopoulos, George Miltiades *epidemiologist*
Ellis, Franklin Henry, Jr. *surgeon, educator*
Engelman, Alan *medical educator*
Epler, Gary Robert *physician, author, educator*
Epstein, Arnold M. *medical educator*
Erban, John Kalil III *medicine educator, cancer specialist, researcher*
Estrada, Carlos R. *urologist*
Fan, Xiaoduo *psychiatrist*
Farraye, Francis Anthony *gastroenterologist*
Faxon, David Parker *cardiologist*
Fazio, Sara *medical educator*
Felson, David *epidemiologist, educator, rheumatologist*
Ferber, Richard Allen *neurologist, educator*
Field, Alison E. *medical educator*
Flaherty, Alice Weaver *neurologist*
Fleisher, Gary Robert *pediatrician, educator*
Fletcher, Robert Hillman *medical educator*
Frigoletto, Fredric David, Jr. *physician*
Fuhlbrigge, Robert Conrad *pediatric rheumatologist, medical educator*
Galaburda, Albert Mark *neurologist, researcher, educator*
Garber, Jeffrey Richard *endocrinologist*
Gates, Jonathan Dean *surgeon, educator*
Gawande, Atul A. *surgeon, writer*
Gazelle, G. Scott *radiologist, researcher*
Gaziano, J. Michael *cardiovascular epidemiologist, geriatrician, educator*
Geha, Raif Salim *immunologist, allergist, pediatrician*
Gelman, Simon *anesthesiologist, educator*
Ghaemi, S. Nassir *psychiatrist, educator*
Gilliland, Gary *oncologist, researcher*
Gitlin, David *psychiatrist, director*
Giugliano, Robert Patrick *physician*
Golby, Alexandra Jacqueline *neurosurgeon, educator*
Goldberg, Irving Hyman *molecular pharmacology and biochemistry educator*
Goldhaber, Samuel Zachary *cardiologist, educator*
Goldie, Sue J. *health service researcher*
Gordon, Gregory Aaron *physician*
Gottlieb, Alice B. *dermatologist, rheumatologist*
Greco, Frank A. *physician, research scientist*
Greenblatt, David J. *pharmacologist*
Gregory, Shawn Alen *cardiologist, physician, researcher*
Grillone, Gregory Angelo *otolaryngologist, educator*
Grinspoon, Steven Kyle *medical educator, director*

Groopman, Jerome *medical educator*
Grundfast, Kenneth Martin *otolaryngologist*
Guinan, Eva C. *hematologist, director*
Halamka, John D. *emergency physician, information technology executive*
Hall, Ferris M. *radiologist, educator*
Hamrah, Pedram *ophthalmologist, scientist*
Harris, Mitchel Brion *orthopedist, surgeon*
Hedley-Whyte, John *anesthesiologist, educator*
Heier, Jeffrey S. *ophthalmologist, consultant*
Hendler, Gail Y. *medical librarian*
Herndon, James Henry *orthopedic surgeon, educator*
Hettmer, Simone *hematologist, oncologist*
Hiatt, Howard H. *internist, educator*
Hickey, Paul Robert *anesthesiologist, educator*
Hochberg, Fred *neurologist*
Hoffmann, Udo *radiologist, educator*
Howley, Peter Maxwell *pathology educator*
Hutchinson, Bernard Thomas *ophthalmologist*
Iosifescu, Dan V. *psychiatrist*
Jacobs, Alice Kaufman *cardiologist, educator*
Jaff, Michael Ritt *osteopath, internist*
Jeyapalan, Suriya *neurooncologist*
Kaelin, William George, Jr. *oncologist*
Kakkar, Rahul *cardiologist, researcher*
Kang, Jing X. *medical researcher, educator*
Kaplan, Gary B. *psychiatrist, researcher*
Kassirer, Jerome Paul *medical educator*
Kaye, Kenneth Marc *physician, educator, scientist*
Kelsey, Karl Timothy *medical educator*
Kesari, Santosh *neurologist, oncologist, neuroscientist*
Kiang, Nelson Yuan-sheng *medical educator*
Kieran, Mark W. *pediatric oncologist*
Kim, Daniel *epidemiologist*
Kim, David Hanwuk *surgeon, orthopedist, researcher*
Kim, Ducksoo *radiologist, inventor, educator*
Kircher, Moritz Florian *radiologist, researcher*
Kitz, Richard John *anesthesiologist, educator*
Kleinman, Ronald Ellis *pediatrician*
Kocher, Mininder Singh *pediatric orthopaedic surgeon, epidemiologist*
Kolodny, Gerald M. *radiologist, director*
Komaroff, Anthony Leader *physician*
Kupper, Thomas S. *dermatologist, scientist, educator*
Kyriakos, Walid Elias *medical educator*
Lapidus, Mariana *medical librarian*
Laufer, Marc R. *gynecologist*
Lazar, Harold Lee *cardiothoracic surgeon*
LeBoff, Meryl Susan *physician, medical educator*
Lee, Charles *cytologist*
Lee, I-Min *epidemiologist*
Lee, Thomas Henry *internist, cardiologist, healthcare executive*
Liang, Marilyn G. *dermatologist*
Liao, James Kuang-Jan *cardiologist, educator*
Libby, Peter *cardiologist, medical researcher*
Lin, Nancy U. *oncologist, educator*
Little, John Bertram *radiologist, educator, researcher*
Livingston, David Morse *internist, biomedical researcher*
Loeffler, Jay Steven *physician, educator*
Loscalzo, Joseph *cardiologist, biochemist*
Loui, Psyche *medical educator*
Ludwig, David S. *endocrinologist*
MacGillivray, Thomas E. *cardiothoracic surgeon*
Mahan, Susan Thayer *orthopedist*
Maisel, William Howard *cardiologist, internist*
Malchau, Henrik *orthopedist*
Mandelbrot, Didier A. *physician, internist, educator*
Manson, JoAnn Elisabeth *endocrinologist*
Mantzoros, Christos Socrates *internist*
Marasco, Wayne A. *oncologist, educator*
Maratos-Flier, Eleftheria *physician, educator*
Martin, Joseph Boyd *neurologist, educator, retired dean*
Maryniuk, Melinda Downie *medical educator, director*
Mason, Joel Bernard *internist, gastroenterologist*
Mason, Keira *anesthesiologist*
Matheson, Jean King *neurologist, educator*
Mathisen, Douglas J. *thoracic surgeon*
May, James Warren, Jr. *plastic surgeon*
Mayer, Robert J. *oncologist, gastroenterologist, educator*
McCormick, Marie Clare *pediatrician, educator*
McDougal, William Scott *urology educator*
McGowan, Francis X. *anesthesiologist, educator*
McNeil, Barbara Joyce *radiologist, educator*
McNicol, Ewan *medical educator, director*
Meara, John Gerard *plastic surgeon*
Meehan, William Paul *pediatrician, educator*
Melnitchouk, Serguei *physician*
Merk, Frederick Bannister *biomedical educator, researcher*
Meyerhardt, Jeffrey Abraham *internist, oncologist*
Mihm, Martin Charles, Jr. *pathologist, educator*
Milne, Christopher-Paul *medical association administrator*
Mitchell, Susan Lisa *geriatrician*
Moellering, Robert Charles, Jr. *internist, educator*
Mooney, David Patrick *surgeon*
Morgan, James Philip *pharmacology and cardiology educator*
Mostafavi Abdolmaleky, Hamid *psychiatrist, researcher*
Mudge, Gilbert H., Jr. *cardiologist*
Mukamal, Kenneth J. *internist*
Murphy, George Francis *dermatopathologist, educator*
Myers, Jeff L. *surgeon*
Nelson, Caleb P. *urologist, educator*
Newburger, Jane Wimpfheimer *pediatric cardiologist*
Nurko, Samuel *gastroenterologist, researcher*
Nuss, Roger Charles *otolaryngologist, director*
Oaklander, Anne Louise *medical educator*
Odze, Robert D. *pathologist*
Oettgen, J. Peter *cardiologist, researcher*
O'Gara, Patrick Thomas *internist, cardiovascular physician*
Oh, William Kyu *oncologist*
Oken, Emily *physician, educator*
Ono, Santa Jeremy *immunologist, educator, administrator*
Otu, Hasan Huseyin *medical researcher, educator*
Pallotta, Johanna Antonia (Johanna Stephen) *endocrinologist, educator*
Pavlakis, Martha *medical association administrator, researcher*
Pearce, Elizabeth Niewoehner *endocrinologist, researcher*
Perrimon, Norbert Jean Paul *medical geneticist, educator*
Pienaar, Rudolph *biomedical researcher*
Pieretti, Rafael Vicente *urologist, pediatrician*
Plummer-D'Amato, Prudence *medical educator*
Pochi, Peter Ernest *physician*
Polizzotti, Brian David *medical researcher*
Polyak, Kornelia *oncologist, researcher*
Pomahac, Bohdan *plastic surgeon, educator*
Poussaint, Alvin Francis *psychiatrist, educator*
Pribaz, Julian Joseph *plastic surgeon, medical educator*
Quickel, Kenneth Elwood, Jr. *physician, medical center executive*
Rabkin, Mitchell Thornton *physician, educator, hospital administrator*
Radmanesh, Alireza *medical researcher*
Ramoni, Rachel Badovinac *medical educator*
Rao, Sowmya R. *medical educator*
Rathmell, James P. *anesthesiologist, educator*
Rauch, Paula *psychiatrist*
Relman, Arnold Seymour *physician, editor, educator*
Rennke, Helmut G. *pathologist, educator*
Richardson, Martha (Marcie) Kirk *obstetrician, gynecologist*
Ridker, Paul M. *cardiologist, medical educator*
Rigotti, Nancy *medical educator*
Riley, Laura E. *obstetrician, gynecologist*
Robertson, Edwin Malcolm *psychology educator*
Rockoff, Mark Alan *pediatric anesthesiologist*
Ronan, Laurence Joseph *internist, pediatrician*
Rosen, Harold *medical association administrator*
Rosenblatt, Michael *internist, dean, educator*
Rosman, Samantha L. *pediatrician, emergency physician*
Rota, Marcello *medical educator*
Roth, Sanford Irwin *pathologist, educator*
Roubenoff, Ronenn *medical educator, researcher*
Russell, Paul Snowden *surgeon, educator*
Ryan, Daniel Patrick *pediatrician*
Sachs, David Howard *surgeon, immunologist, educator*
Sadeghi-Nejad, Abdollah *pediatrician, educator*
Sahin, Mustafa *neurologist, educator*
Samuels, Martin Allen *neurologist*
Sanchez, Teresa *medical educator*
Sargent, John *psychiatrist*
Sawicki, Gregory *pulmonologist*
Scadden, David Thomas *hematologist, oncologist, research scientist*
Schlossman, Stuart Franklin *physician, educator, researcher*
Schneeweiss, Sebastian *medical educator, pharmacoepidemiologist*
Schouten, Ronald *psychiatrist, educator*
Schuppan, Detlef *medical educator, researcher*
Schwartz, John Henry *physician, educator*
Scott, Crouter *medical educator*
Scott, James Arthur *radiologist, educator*
Seddon, Johanna Margaret *ophthalmologist, epidemiologist*
Seibel, Machelle Mayer *gynecologist, educator*
Selkoe, Dennis Jesse *neurologist, researcher, educator*
Sellke, Frank William *cardiothoracic surgeon, researcher*
Shaik, Shavali *medical researcher*
Shay, Jonathan *psychiatrist, writer*
Sheth, Kevin Navin *neurologist, researcher*
Shields, Lawrence Thornton *orthopaedic surgeon, educator*
Shore, Miles Frederick *psychiatrist, educator*
Silbersweig, David Alan *physician*
Singh, Ajay Kumar *nephrologist, educator*
Slack, Warner Vincent *medical educator, researcher*
Sodroski, Joseph G. *medical educator*
Souza, Frederico Ferreira *radiologist*
Sparrow, Joshua D. *child psychiatrist*
Sperling, Reisa A. *neurologist, researcher*
Spiegel, Jeffrey H. *plastic surgeon*
Springer, Timothy Allan *health researcher, immunology educator*
Stair, Thomas Osborne *physician, educator*
Stecker, Michael S. *interventional radiologist*
Steere, Allen Caruthers, Jr. *physician, educator*
Stevenson, Lynne W. (Lynne Leslie Warner Stevenson) *cardiologist, educator*
Stewart, Elizabeth AnNella *gynecologist, researcher*
Stone, Peter Howard *cardiologist, educator*
Stossel, Thomas Peter *medical educator, researcher, director*
Streeter, Chris Conway *psychiatrist, educator*
Surman, Owen Stanley *psychiatrist*
Swartz, Morton Norman *medical educator*
Sykes, Megan *immunologist*
Tabatabaei, Shahin *urologist, educator*
Tachado, Souvenir D. *medical educator*
Tang, Xiaolei *immunologist*
Tavakkolizadeh, Ali *surgeon*
Tenner, Scott *physician, researcher*
Theoharides, Theoharis Constantin *pharmacologist, physician, educator*
Thompson, Christopher C. *gastroenterologist*
Thrall, James Hunter *radiologist, educator*
Thwin, Soe Se *medical researcher*
Toth, Thomas Louis *medical educator, director*
Tracy, Erin Elizabeth *obstetrician, gynecologist*
Trichopoulos, Dimitrios Vassilios *epidemiologist, educator*
Trier, Jerry Steven *gastroenterologist, educator*
Tritos, Nicholas Angelos *internist*
Turner, Christopher D. *pediatrician, director*
Tworetzky, Wayne *cardiologist*
Udelson, James Eric *cardiologist, educator*
Vacanti, Joseph Philip *pediatric and transplant surgeon*
Vadivel, Nidyanandh *nephrologist*
Vallet, Sonia *hematologist, researcher*
van Dam, Robert M. *epidemiologist, educator*
Van Etten, Richard A. *hematologist, researcher*
Vassilev, Peter Mihailov *biomedical researcher*
Viguera, Adele Casals *psychiatrist, researcher*
Viswanathan, Akila *oncologist*
Volpe, Joseph John *pediatrician, neurologist, educator*
Volpe, MaryAnn Vitoria *pediatrician*
Wang, Zhi *biomedical researcher*
Warth, James Arthur *physician, researcher*
Weiss, Earle Burton *physician*
Werchniak, Andrew Eugene *dermatologist, educator*
White, Augustus Aaron III *orthopaedic surgeon*
Whittemore, Anthony Dunster *vascular surgeon, chief medical officer*
Willett, Walter Churchill *epidemiologist, educator*
Winer, Eric P. *hematologist, oncologist, educator*
Wong, Richard Chi Kit *gastroenterology*
Wood, Malissa J. *cardiologist, educator*
Woolf, Alan *pediatrician*
Wozniak, Janet *psychiatrist*
Wu, Jim S. *radiologist*
Wu, Julian K. *neurosurgeon*
Xie, Zhongcong *anesthesiologist, educator*
Yuan, Junying *medical educator, researcher*
Zai, Adrian *medical researcher, director*
Zeitels, Steven Marc *surgeon, educator*
Zon, Leonard Ira *pediatrics educator, researcher*
Zusman, Randall Mark *physician*

Boylston
Hanshaw, James Barry *pediatrician, educator*

Brighton
Lathi, Ellen S. *neurologist*

Brockton
Carlson, Desiree Anice *pathologist*

Brookline
Golan, Yoav *physician*
Goldsmith, Gary Norman *psychiatrist, psychoanalyst*
Jakab, Irene *psychiatrist*
Lipsitt, Don Richard *psychiatrist, educator*
Pearlman, Justin D. *medical educator*
Seltzer, Benjamin *neurologist, educator*
Slavin, Sumner Andrew *plastic surgeon*
Tyler, H. Richard *physician*

Burlington
Beamis, John Francis *pulmonologist*
Cosgrove, Garth Rees *neurosurgeon*
Hughes, Kevin Steven *surgeon*
Hurd, Joseph Kindall, Jr. *obstetrician, gynecologist*
McQuillen, Daniel Paul *infectious diseases physician, medical educator*
Mourtzinos, Arthur *urologist*
Nicholas, Lynn B. *medical association administrator*
Schoetz, David John, Jr. *colon and rectal surgeon, educator*
Shils, Jay Lawrence *neurologist, researcher*
Soto-Wright, Valena *gynecologist, director*

Cambridge
Abelmann, Walter H. *internist, educator*
Bisognano, Maureen A. *medical association administrator*
Bortnick, Rachel Anne *medical researcher*
Brusch, John Lynch *physician, educator, hospital administrator*
Burkle, Frederick Martin, Jr. *physician, educator*
Cady, Blake *surgical oncologist*
Chen, Lincoln Chin-ho *medical educator*
Dawson, Steven Lee *radiologist, researcher*
Demirci, Utkan *medical educator*
Djousse, Luc *epidemiologist, educator, medical researcher*
Eisen, Herman Nathaniel *immunology researcher, medical educator*
Feldman, Joel J. *plastic surgeon*
Foster, Charles Stephen *surgeon*
Friedman, Jeffrey Robert *psychiatrist, educator*
Guarente, Leonard P. *medical geneticist, educator*
Havens, Leston Laycock *retired psychiatrist, educator*
Herr, Hugh Miller *biomechatronics researcher, educator*
Hirsch, Martin Stanley *internist, epidemiologist, researcher*
Liberman, M. Charles *otolaryngologist, educator*
Lim, Kok-Seong *medical researcher*
London, Irving Myer *physician, educator*
Mathews, Joan Helene *pediatrician*
McCunney, Robert Joseph *physician*
Melcher, Jennifer *otolaryngologist, educator*
Mootha, Vamsi Krishna *biomedical researcher, educator*
Nathanson, Larry *medical educator*
Padmanabhan, Bharani *neurologist, educator*
Sauzier, Maria Consuela *psychiatrist, educator*
Telingator, Cynthia J. *psychiatrist, director*
Tsai, Li-Huei *pathologist, researcher*
Vernillet, Laurent *pharmacologist, researcher*
Wacker, Warren Ernest Clyde *internist, educator*

Charlestown
Isselbacher, Kurt Julius *internist, educator*
Kegel, Kimberly B. *neurologist, educator*
Leaf, Alexander *preventive medicine physician, epidemiologist*
Potts, John Thomas, Jr. *physician, educator*
Schneeberger, Eveline Elsa *pathologist, cell biologist, educator*
Sharma, Nutan *neurologist, educator*
Zamecnik, Paul Charles *oncologist, medical researcher*

Chelmsford
Menitoff, Paul Alan *psychiatrist*

Chestnut Hill
Arndt, Kenneth Alfred *dermatologist, educator*
Dahlben, Salin Abraham *neuropsychiatrist*
Flax, Martin Howard *pathologist, retired educator*
Gottlieb, Marise Suss *epidemiologist*
Hyman, Albert Lewis *cardiologist, educator*
Kraus, Frederick Thier *pathologist*
Sykiotis, Gerasimos *biomedical researcher, geneticist*
Thier, Samuel Osiah *physician, educator*

Clinton
Lanza, Robert Paul *medical scientist*

Concord
Andrews, Joseph Lyon, Jr. *internist, pulmonologist, medical educator, writer*
Boger, William Pierce III *ophthalmologist*
Coles, Robert *child psychiatrist, educator, writer*

Dover
Buyse, Marylou *pediatrician, geneticist, medical administrator*

East Boston
Patinkin, Terry Allan *physician*

Fall River
Medeiros, Antone Arruda *retired medical educator*

Framingham
Bern, Murray Morris *hematologist, oncologist*
Capobianco, Anthony G. *physician*
Castelli, William Peter *cardiovascular epidemiologist, educator*
Kannel, William Bernard *cardiovascular epidemiologist*
Klapholz, Henry *obstetrician, gynecologist, educator*
Nivarthi, Raju Naga *anesthesiology educator*

Gardner
Du Buske, Lawrence Michael *immunologist, rheumatologist*

Gloucester
White, Harold Jack *pathologist*

Harvard
Barrie, Joseph Rollin *retired surgeon*

Harwich
Barton, Alice *physician, educator*

Hyannis
Cochrane, Paul Hollis *general practice physician*

Jamaica Plain
Pierce, Chester Middlebrook *retired psychiatrist, educator*

Lexington
Wada, Yumiko *pharmacologist*
Waksman, Byron Halsted *immunologist, educator, medical association administrator*

Lynn
Copeland, Paul Michael *endocrinologist*

Manchester
Prout, Curtis *internist, educator*

Marlborough
Johannes, Richard Scott *medical association administrator*

Mattapoisett
Mazer, Mike *cardiologist, retired nephrologist, artist*

Melrose
Desforges, Jane Fay *retired internist, hematologist, educator*

Natick
Gottlieb, Michael Norman *internist, educator, health facility administrator*

Needham
Cowell, Henry Richard *orthopaedic surgeon, journal editor*
Osser, David Neal *psychiatrist, educator*

Needham Heights
Gelfand, Jeffrey Alan *physician, educator*

Newburyport
Wilner, Eric Mark *radiologist*

Newton
Bassuk, Ellen Linda *psychiatrist*
Garcia, Eduardo *neurologist, consultant*
May, Harold Louis *retired surgeon, not-for-profit developer*
Sasahara, Arthur Asao *cardiologist, educator, researcher*

Newton Center
Eichler, Marc *neurosurgeon*

Newtonville
Dews, P(eter) B(ooth) *retired pharmacology educator, physician*

North Dighton
Cserr, Robert *psychiatrist, physician, hospital administrator*

Northborough
FitzGerald, Thomas Jeffrey *medical educator, department chairman*
Fulmer, Hugh Scott *physician, educator*
Yao, Wei-Dong *medical educator, researcher*

Norwood
Berliner, Allen Irwin *dermatologist*
Howell, Michael Dwight *physician, director*

Oxford
Schur, Walter Robert *physician*

Peabody
Birdsall, Melinda R. *gynecologist*
Lipman, Richard Paul *pediatrician*

Petersham
Chivian, Eric Seth *psychiatrist, environmental scientist, educator*

Pittsfield
Johnson, Rebecca L. *pathologist*

Rockland
Blethen, Sandra Lee *pediatric endocrinologist*
Tredway, Donald Ray *endocrinologist, educator*

Salem
Jacobson, Joseph O. *oncologist, department chairman*

Somerville
Holmes, Lewis B. *pediatrician, medical geneticist*

South Wellfleet
Blau, Monte *retired radiology educator*

South Weymouth
Young, Michael Chung-En *allergist, immunologist, pediatrician*

Southampton
Borowsky, Claude David *sports medicine physician*

Springfield
Farkas, Paul Stephen *gastroenterologist*
Friedmann, Paul *surgeon, educator, research and development company executive*
Kottamasu, Mohan Rao (K.V.R. Mohan Rao) *physician, health facility administrator*
Liptzin, Benjamin *psychiatrist*
McGee, William Tobin *internist*
Petrone, William Francis *pediatrician, microbiologist, corporate executive*
Romero, Ricardo Vicente *gastroenterologist*

Sterling
Antonelli, Richard Christopher *pediatrician, educator*

Stockbridge
Kenny, Charles *orthopedist*
Shapiro, Edward Robert *psychiatrist, educator, health facility administrator, psychotherapist*

Stoughton
Joseph, Anthony Barnett *psychiatrist*

Sudbury
Lamont-Havers, Ronald William *retired physician, medical association administrator*

Waban
Rogoff, Jerome Howard *psychiatrist, psychoanalyst, forensic expert*
Schuntermann, Peter Paul *psychiatrist*
Shklar, Gerald *pathologist, periodontist, educator*

Waltham
Landaw, Stephen Arthur *physician, educator*
Leach, Robert Ellis *orthopedist, surgeon, educator*
Xue, Fei *epidemiologist*

Wayland
Edelman, Stuart Edward *psychiatrist*
Moncure, Ashby Carter *surgeon, educator*

Webster
Keller, David Martin *pediatrician*

Wellesley
Murray, Joseph Edward *retired plastic surgeon*
Twitchell, Thomas Evans *neurologist, educator*
Zhou, Li *medical researcher*

West Falmouth
Holz, George G., IV, *medical educator, research scientist*

West Springfield
Desai, Veena Balvantrai *obstetrician, gynecologist, educator*

Weston
Mannick, John Anthony *surgeon*

Wilmington
Lang, Elvira Valentina *radiologist, educator, medical products executive*

Woods Hole
Laster, Leonard *internist, gastroenterologist, academic administrator, educator, writer, researcher*
Prendergast, Robert Anthony *pathologist educator*

Worcester
Benjamin, Sheldon *psychiatrist, educator*
Bernhard, Jeffrey David *dermatologist, educator, editor*
Drachman, David Alexander *neurologist*
Felice, Marianne Elizabeth *pediatrician, educator*
Irwin, Richard Stephen *physician, scientist, educator*
Kothare, Sanjeev Vithal *pediatrician*
Mello, Craig C. *molecular medicine educator, researcher*
Morse, Leonard J. *epidemiologist, public health service officer*
Newburger, Peter E. *hematologist, oncologist*
Savageau, Judith A. *epidemiologist, researcher*
Selin, Lisa K. *physician*
Swanson, Richard Sprague *oncologist, surgeon*
Young, Stephen Bernard *urogynecologist, surgeon*
Zurier, Robert Burton *rheumatology educator*

Yarmouth Port
Gordon, Benjamin Dichter *pediatrician, health facility administrator, educator*

MICHIGAN

Ada
Mason, James Hamilton *surgeon*

Ann Arbor
Abrams, Gerald David *pathologist, educator*
Akin, Cem *internist, allergist, medical researcher*
Ansbacher, Rudi *physician*
Bacon, George Edgar *retired pediatrician*
Baker, Shan Ray *medical educator*
Baler, Blanche Kimoto *retired child psychiatrist*
Barsan, William George *emergency physician*
Bates, Eric Randolph *physician, educator*
Berguer, Ramon *medical educator*
Bloom, David Alan *pediatric urology educator, department chairman*
Bloom, Jane Maginnis *emergency physician*
Blum, James Marlow *medical educator, researcher*
Bolling, Steven Fredric *cardiac surgeon, educator*
Bowdler, Anthony John *internist, educator*
Boxer, Laurence Alan *physician, research educator*
Burdi, Alphonse Rocco *anatomist*
Carey, Thomas E. *medical educator, researcher*
Carlson, Bruce Martin *anatomist*
Carlson, Martha Diane *neurologist*
Casey, Kenneth Lyman *neurologist*
Charpie, John *medical educator*
Chervin, Ronald David *neurology educator*
Chey, William D *physician, researcher*
Chinnaiyan, Arul M. *pathologist, researcher*
Clemens, J. Quentin *urologist, educator*
Dick, Macdonald, II, *pediatrician*
Dickinson, Chris John *gastroenterologist, director*
DiMagno, Matthew J. *medical educator*
Domino, Edward Felix *physician, clinical pharmacologist, educator*
Doyle, Constance Talcott Johnston *physician, medical association administrator, educator*
Elder, James Tilford *dermatologist, educator*
Fajans, Stefan Stanislaus *retired internist*
Farmer, Cheryl Christine *internist, industrial hygienist*
Fetters, Michael Derwin *medical educator, director*
Fox, David Alan *rheumatologist, immunologist*
Garton, Hugh J.L. *neurosurgeon, educator*
Gelehrter, Thomas David *medical educator, geneticist*
Ghaziuddin, Mohammad *psychiatrist, educator*
Gikas, Paul William *medical educator*
Gilman, Sid *neurologist*
Gross, Barry H. *radiologist, educator*
Harlow, Siobán D. *medical educator, consultant*
Helvie, Mark Alan *radiologist, educator*
Hollenberg, Paul Frederick *pharmacology educator*
Holoshitz, Joseph *medical educator*
Horowitz, Samuel Boris *biomedical researcher, educational consultant*
Humes, Harvey David *nephrologist, educator, director*
Hurvitz, Edward A. *physiatrist*
Hyzy, Robert Curtis *medical educator*
Kahana, Alon *ophthalmologist, educator*
Kakarala, Madhuri *oncologist*
Kaminski, Mark Stefan *medical educator*
Kasapis, Christos *cardiologist*
Keshamouni, Venkateshwar G. *medical educator*
Kitko, Carrie L. *medical educator*
Kuhl, David Edmund *nuclear medicine physician, educator*
Lawrence, Theodore S. *oncologist, educator*
Levine, John E. *pediatrician, director*
Lichter, Paul Richard *ophthalmology educator*
Lok, Anna Suk-Fong *medical educator*
Ludgate, Mathew William *medical educator*
Magee, John C. *surgeon, educator*
Margolis, Philip Marcus *psychiatrist, educator*
Markel, Howard *physician, educator*
McKenna, Barbara J. *clinical pathologist*
Menon, Ram Kumar *neurosurgeon, consultant*
Merchant, Juanita Lynne *gastroenterologist, educator*
Mian, Shahzad *ophthalmologist*
Mitchiner, James C. *emergency physician*
Modell, Stephen Mark *medical researcher, educator*
Monto, Arnold Simon *epidemiology educator*
Moyer, Jeffrey S. *plastic surgeon, educator*
Napolitano, Lena Marie *surgeon, educator*
Newman, Lisa Ann *surgical oncologist*
Oliver, William John *pediatrician, educator*
Orringer, Jeffrey S. *dermatologist, educator*
Patil, Parag G. *neurosurgeon, educator*
Pitt, Bertram *cardiologist, educator, consultant*
Platt, Jeffrey Louis *experimental surgeon, immunologist, pediatric nephrologist, educator*
Powsner, Edward Raphael *physician*
Rees, Riley *medical educator*
Rosenthal, Amnon *pediatric cardiologist*
Sagher, Oren *neurosurgeon*
Saper, Joel R. *neurologist, educator*
Sasson, Comilla *medical researcher*
Schottenfeld, David *retired epidemiologist, educator*
Schwenk, Thomas L. *physician*
Shah, Rajal B. *pathologist*
Shanley, Thomas Patrick *medical educator*
Shewach, Donna S. *pharmacologist, educator*
Sloan, Herbert Elias *physician, surgeon*
Smith, Donald Cameron *retired preventive medicine physician*
Solomon, Richard *pediatrician*
Sowers, MaryFran *epidemiologist, gynecologist, educator*
Stanley, James Charles *vascular surgeon*
Strang, Ruth Hancock *pediatrician, cardiologist, priest, educator*
Taylor, Stephan F. *psychiatrist, educator*
Thompson, Norman Winslow *surgeon, educator*
Todd, Robert Franklin III *oncologist, educator*
Tosney, Kathryn W. *embryologist, biology educator*
Turke, Paul William *pediatrician, anthropologist*
Weg, John Gerard *physician*
Wei, John Thomas *urologist, educator*
Wicha, Max S. *oncologist, educator*
Wong, Sandra Lynn *oncologist, educator*
Zivin, Kara *psychiatry professor, researcher*

Beverly Hills
Castle, Maurice Emmett *orthopedist, surgeon*

Bingham Farms
Giles, Conrad Leslie *ophthalmic surgeon*

Birmingham
Edwards, Michael Gerard *physician*
Hammami, Mouhanad *pediatrician*

Bloomfield Hills
Brent, Robert Lewis *urologist*
Coburn, Ronald Murray *ophthalmologist, surgeon*
Mathog, Robert Henry *otolaryngologist, educator*
O'Hara, John Paul III *orthopedic surgeon*

Brighton
Clark, Robert Thomas *ophthalmologist*

Detroit
Abramson, Hanley Norman *pharmacy educator*
Auner, Gregory *medical educator*
Baugh, Reginald Franz *otolaryngologist*
Besarab, Anatole *internist*
Bluth, Martin H. *medical association administrator*
Elder, Jack S. *urologist, educator*
Elisevich, Kost *neurosurgeon*
Hashimoto, Ken *dermatologist, educator*
Hudgel, David William *allergist, immunologist, educator*
Jarvis, James Nelson *pediatrician, rheumatologist*
Kelley, Mark Albert *physician, educator, health products executive*
Khalid, Imran *physician*
Koo, Winston *medical educator, pediatrician*
Levine, Steven Richard *neurology educator, medical facility administrator*
Lewis, Richard Alan *neurologist, educator*
Lim, Henry Wan-Peng *dermatologist*
Lin, Ho-Sheng *surgeon, educator*
Lisak, Robert Philip *neurologist, researcher, educator*
LoRusso, Patricia M. *medical educator, director*
Lupulescu, Aurel Peter *medical educator, researcher, physician*
Maiese, Kenneth *neurologist, neuroscientist*
Mari, Giancarlo *obstetrician, gynecologist, educator*
Marsh, Harold Michael *anesthesiologist*
Mehta, Ruby *pediatric gastroenterologist*
Meier, Frederick Augustus *physician, director*
Menon, Mani *urological surgeon, educator*
Miller, Orlando Jack *obstetrician, gynecologist, educator, geneticist*
Mittal, Sandeep *neurosurgeon, director*
Munkarah, Adnan R *medical educator, department chairman*
Nathanson, Saul David *oncologist, surgeon, educator*
Nordstrom, Cheryl K. *epidemiologist, researcher*
O'Sullivan, Nancy Louise *immunologist, educator*
Pappas, Athina *pediatrician, educator*
Prasad, Ananda Shiva *medical educator*
Romero, Roberto J. *perinatologist, educator*
Ryu, Samuel *surgeon*
Schiffer, Charles Alan *oncologist, educator*
Schweitzer, Vanessa Gayl *otorhinolaryngologist*
Shade, George Henry, Jr. *obstetrician, gynecologist, educator*
Smith, Wilbur Lazear *radiologist, educator*
Sokol, Robert James *obstetrician, gynecologist, educator*
Sosne, Gabriel *ophthalmologist, educator*
Spanaki, Marianna V. *neurologist, educator*
Tancer, Manuel E. *psychiatrist*
Tyburski, James Gerard *surgeon*
Tzivion, Guri *medical educator*
Uberti, Joseph P. *oncologist, educator*
Vander Heide, Richard Stuart *pathologist, educator, research scientist*
Weaver, W(ayne) Douglas *cardiologist, researcher, medical educator*
Whitehouse, Fred Waite *endocrinologist, researcher*
Wiener, Joseph *pathologist, educator*
Wong, Henry Keung *dermatologist, educator*
Yaremchuk, Kathleen *otolaryngologist, department chairman*
Zemlicka, Jiri *medical educator, researcher*

East Lansing
Gangur, Venu *medical educator*
Gottschalk, Alexander *radiologist, educator*
Gulick, Peter Gregory *medical educator*
Monson, Carol Lynn *osteopath, psychotherapist*
Perlstadt, Harry *medical sociology educator*
Pervaiz, Mohammad Hassan *cardiologist*
Pysh, Joseph John *neurologist, neuroanatomist*
Rosenman, Kenneth D. *medical educator*
Watson, Ralph Edward *internist, educator*

Farmington Hills
Blumberg, Seth N. *medical association administrator*
Bojrab, Dennis Issac *otologist, neurotologist, skull base surgeon*
Luby, Elliot Donald *psychiatrist, educator*

Fife Lake
Knecht, Richard Arden *family practitioner*

Flint
Iddings, Douglas Matthew *oncologist, researcher*

Grand Rapids
Abdel-Mageed, Aly S. *medical association administrator*
Bengtson, Bradley *plastic surgeon*
Daniels, Joseph *neuropsychiatrist*
Forzley, Gregory *physician, medical association administrator*
Hammond, Dennis Clyde *plastic surgeon, educator*
Karayil, Diljit Bahuleyan *physician, consultant*
Reifler, David Martin *ophthalmologist*
Verdier, David D'Ooge *ophthalmologist, educator*
Wendt, Vernon Earl *internist, cardiologist*

Grosse Ile
Stryker, Joan Copeland *retired obstetrician, gynecologist, educator*

Grosse Pointe
Appleyard, Jennifer *allergist, immunologist*
Koo, Winston Wun Kwong *neonatologist, researcher, educator*
Rosman, Howard S. *cardiologist, educator*

Grosse Pointe Shores
Sphire, Raymond Daniel *anesthesiologist, educator*

Holland
Zuidema, George Dale *surgeon, educator*

Kalamazoo
Bricker, Lee Alan *medical educator*
Feinberg, Arthur Norman *medical educator*
Fischell, Tim Alexander *cardiologist*
Gonzales, Andrea *biomedical researcher*

Lake Angelus
Kresge, Bruce Anderson *retired physician*

Lansing
Kepros, John Paul *trauma surgeon*
Maio, Ronald Frank *emergency medicine physician*

Midland
Collins, James J. *epidemiologist*

Milford
Oliveri, Eugene Alfred *gastroenterologist*

Niles
Gibbs, Denis Laurel *radiologist*

Northport
Schultz, Richard Carlton *plastic surgeon*

Northville
Nasr, Samya Z. *pediatric pulmonologist*

Petoskey
Meengs, William Lloyd *cardiologist*

Pontiac
Stein, Paul David *cardiologist*

Richland
Atkinson, Arthur John, Jr. *pharmacologist, educator, consultant*

Rochester
Reygaert, Wanda C. *medical educator*
Spears, James Richard *cardiologist*
Youn, Anthony Sungjin *plastic surgeon*

Royal Oak
Britt, Stephen Thomas *medical educator*
Drenser, Kimberly *ophthalmologist*
Ernstoff, Raina Marcia *neurologist*
Hassan, Tarek S. *ophthalmologist*
Peters, Kenneth Michael *urologist, researcher*
Ryan, Jack *physician, retired hospital corporation executive*

Saginaw
Hammel, Iriana Simona *geriatrician*

Southfield
Levine, Robert-Bob Alter *biomedical researcher, educator*
Monsell, Edwin *otolaryngologist, educator*
Perez-Cruet, Mick Jorge (Miguelangelo Jorge Perez-Cruet) *neurosurgeon, educator*
Pieper, Daniel Roy *neurosurgeon*

Sterling Heights
Rizk, Maged *cardiologist, researcher*

Sturgis
Reiff, James Stanley *osteopathic physician, addictions and psychiatric physician, surgeon*

Traverse City
Drake, Daniel H. *thoracic surgeon*

Troy
Duffy, Michael Charles *physician, director*
Schafer, Sharon Marie *anesthesiologist*

Warren
Teitge, Robert A. *medical association administrator*

Ypsilanti
Benedek, Elissa Leah *psychiatrist*
Gillard, Montgomery *dermatologist*
Smith, Phil *medical educator, director*

MINNESOTA

Austin
Rioux, Pierre August *psychiatrist*

Bloomington
Wilhelm, Gary Bretz *physician*

Burnsville
Lakin, James Dennis *allergist, immunologist, director*

Duluth
Aufderheide, Arthur Carl *pathologist*
McKee, David Charles *neurologist*

East Gull Lake
Simons, John Nelson *surgeon, consultant*

Edina
Rucker, Richard Douglas, Jr. *emergency physician*
Tagatz, George Elmo *retired obstetrician, gynecologist, educator*

Excelsior
Anderson, William Robert *retired pathologist educator*

Minneapolis
Aamoth, Gordon M. *medical association administrator*
Almquist, Adrian K. *clinical cardiac electrophysiologist*
Anand, Inder S. *medical educator, director*
Bache, Robert James *physician, educator*
Balfour, Henry Hallowell, Jr. *medical educator, researcher, physician, writer*
Berry, Susan A. *pediatrician, educator*
Bhavsar, Abdhish Raman *ophthalmologist, researcher*
Buchwald, Henry *surgeon, educator, researcher*
Chavers, Blanche Marie *pediatrician, educator, researcher*
Church, Timothy Robert *medical educator, researcher*
Cohn, Jay N. *cardiologist, educator*
Craig, James Lynn *physician, health services administrator*
Dykstra, Dennis Dale *physiatrist*
Fisch, Robert Otto *medical educator*
Freese, Andrew *neurosurgeon, educator*
Georgieff, Michael Kara *medical educator, researcher*
Gerberich, Susan Goodwin *epidemiologist, educator, medical researcher*
Gruessner, Rainer W.G. *surgeon, educator*
Haines, Stephen John *neurosurgeon*
Hanson, Arthur Stuart *physician, consultant*
Hays, Thomas S. *medical educator, researcher*
Ibrahim, Hassan N. *nephrologist, educator*
Israni, Ajay *medical educator, researcher*
Joseph, Marilyn Susan *gynecologist*
Judson, Patricia Lynn *obstetrician, gynecologist, oncologist*
Kaufman, Stephen Charles *ophthalmologist, clinician and surgeon*
Keenan, Joseph *retired medical educator, consultant, emergency physician*
Kennedy, William Robert *neurologist, educator*
Kjellstrand, Carl Magnus *physician, educator*
Kratzke, Robert Arthur *oncologist, educator*
Kumra, Sanjiv *psychiatrist, educator*
Leon, Arthur Sol *research cardiologist, exercise physiologist*
Leppik, Ilo E. *neurologist, educator*
Litman, Theodor James *medical educator*
Loh, Horace H. *pharmacology educator*
Luepker, Russell Vincent *epidemiology educator*
Maheshwari, Aditya V. *orthopedist, educator*
Malmquist, Carl Phillip *psychiatrist*
Mandel, Sheldon Lloyd *dermatologist, educator*
Menge, David Maina *biomedical researcher*
Moller, James Herman *pediatrician, educator*
Monga, Manoj *medical educator*
Morita, Norimasa *otolaryngologist, researcher*
Najarian, John Sarkis *surgeon, educator*
Osterholm, Michael T. *epidemiologist, public health service officer*
Pambuccian, Stefan E. *cytologist, educator*
Phibbs, Clifford Matthew *surgeon, educator*
Polly, David W., Jr. *surgeon*
Powell, Deborah Elizabeth *pathologist, dean*
Quie, Paul Gerhardt *pediatrician, educator*
Salerno, Salvatore *medical educator*
Sielaff, Timothy David *oncologist, department chairman*
Stauffer, William Moyer *medical educator, director*
Stenwick, Michael William *retired internist, geriatrician, consultant*
Sutherland, David E.R. *surgeon*
Sweet, Robert Marten *urologic surgeon, medical simulation scientist/administrator*
Swiontkowski, Marc Francis *orthopedist*
Thompson, Theodore Robert *pediatric educator*
Toscano, James Vincent *medical foundation president*
Ugurbil, Kamil *radiologist, neuroscientist, educator*
Ulstrom, Robert A. *retired pediatrician*
Vuchetich, John Patrick *psychiatrist*
Weir, Edward Kenneth *cardiologist, educator*
Wild, John Julian *surgeon, researcher, medical educator*
Yuan, Jian-Min *epidemiologist*
Zlowodzki, Michal Pawel *surgeon, researcher*

Minnetonka
Sandy, Lewis Gordon *physician, healthcare executive*

Olivia
Cosgriff, James Arthur *physician*

Richfield
Mayberry, Shawna *preventive medicine physician, educator*

Rochester
Abel, Martin D. *anesthesiologist*
Arnold, Phillip Gordon *plastic surgeon*
Asirvatham, Samuel J. *physician*
Bartholomew, Lloyd Gibson *physician*
Bartley, George B. *ophthalmologist, oculoplastic, surgeon*
Brewer, Jerry Dewayne *dermatologic surgeon, researcher*
Brown, Arnold Lanehart, Jr. *pathologist, educator, dean*
Charles, Erlichman *oncologist, educator*
Cicek, Muzaffer *medical researcher*
Cofield, Robert Hahn *orthopedic surgeon, educator*
Cullinane, Daniel Christopher *surgeon, educator*
Daly, Richard C. *director of heart transplantation*
Danielson, Gordon Kenneth, Jr. *cardiovascular surgeon, educator*
DeRemee, Richard Arthur *retired internist, educator, researcher*
Douglass, Bruce E. *physician*
Driscoll, David John *pediatric cardiologist*
Engel, Andrew George *neurologist*
Fervenza, Fernando C. *nephrologist, educator*
Forstrom, Lee Arthur *physician*
Frye, Robert Leo *medical educator, cardiologist*
Fye, W. Bruce III *cardiologist*
Garcia Franco, Carlos Enrique *thoracic surgeon*
Giannini, Caterina *neurologist, educator*
Gibbons, Raymond John *cardiologist*
Gloviczki, Peter *surgeon*
Goetz, Matthew P. *oncologist, educator*
Gorman, Colum Alphonsus *retired endocrinologist*
Haddy, Francis John *internist, educator*
Hammill, Stephen Charles *cardiologist, medical educator*
Hartmann, Lynn C. *physician, educator*
Herman, David Christopher *ophthalmologist, consultant*
Hurley, Daniel L. *physician, consultant*
Inwards, David James *hematologist, educator*
Jensen, Michael Dennis *endocrinologist, researcher*
Johnson, Charles Daniel *radiologist*
Kantarci, Kejal *radiologist, researcher*
Karpyak, Victor M. *psychiatrist, researcher*
Katipamula Malisetti, Rajini *hematologist*
Knopman, David S. *neurologist*
Kovtun, Irina V. *medical researcher, consultant*
Kyle, Robert Arthur *medical educator, hematologist*
Li, James Tung Chieh *physician*
Loprinzi, Charles Lawrence *oncologist, educator*
Lucas, Alexander Ralph *child psychiatrist, educator, writer*
Malkasian, George Durand, Jr. *obstetrician, educator*
McGoon, Michael Douglas *cardiologist, educator*
McGregor, Christopher George Aloysius *surgeon, educator, consultant*
Naina, Harris V.K. *hematologist*
Neel, Harry Bryan III *surgeon, scientist, educator*
Nivatvongs, Santhat *colorectal surgeon*
Oh, Jae Kuen *cardiologist, consultant, medical educator, director*
Petersen, Ronald C. *neurologist, educator*
Phillips, Sidney Frederick *gastroenterologist, educator*
Piepgras, David G. *neurosurgeon, educator*
Pittelkow, Mark Robert *physician, dermatologist, educator, researcher*
Poland, Gregory A. *medical professor, researcher*
Riggs, Byron Lawrence, Jr. *physician, educator*
Rizza, Robert Allan *physician*
Rogers, Roy Steele III *dermatologist, educator, dean*
Sanchez-Sotelo, Joaquin *surgery consultant*
Sartori-Valinotti, Julio *medical educator*
Schaff, Hartzell Vernon *surgeon*
Scott, John Paul *medical educator*
Seferian, Edward G. *medical educator*
Selcen, Duygu *physician*
Siddiqui, Mustaqeem Ahmad *physician*
Siekert, Robert George *retired neurologist, educator*
Sim, Franklin H. *orthopedic surgery educator*
Sit, Arthur J. *ophthalmologist, researcher*
Stickler, Gunnar Brynolf *pediatrician*
Syed, Imran Shafi *cardiologist, consultant*
Tangalos, Eric G. *internist, geriatrician, educator*
Thomas, Randal J. *cardiologist*
Truty, Mark *surgeon*
Ward, Louis Emmerson *retired physician*
Warner, Mark A. *anesthesiologist*
Wass, C(harles) Thomas *anesthesiologist*
Whisnant, Jack Page *neurologist*
Wood, Douglas Lynn *medical educator*
Woods, John Elmer *plastic surgeon*

Saint Cloud
Olson, Barbara Ford *physician*

Saint Louis Park
Beecher, Lee Hewitt *psychiatrist*
Saliterman, Steven S. *internist, educator*

Saint Paul
Burton, Charles Victor *neurosurgeon*
Cavert, Henry Mead *retired physician, educator*
Mammel, Mark Crawford *pediatrician, researcher*
Michael, Alfred Frederick, Jr. *physician, medical educator*
Swaiman, Kenneth Fred *pediatric neurologist, educator*
Weigelt, John August *surgeon*
Westermeyer, Joseph John *psychiatrist*
Wexler, Deborah Lee *physician*

Stillwater
Asch, Susan McClellan *pediatrician*

Virginia
Knabe, George William, Jr. *pathologist, educator*

Willmar
Sheehan, William Patrick *psychiatrist, astronomer*

Woodbury
McGary, Carl Thomas *pathologist*

MISSISSIPPI

Brandon
Wilson, Floyd *pathologist, educator*

Flowood
Das, Suman Kumar *plastic surgeon, researcher*

Jackson
Cruse, Julius Major, Jr. *pathologist, educator*
deShazo, Richard Denson *medical educator, academic administrator*
Geissler, William Bennett *orthopaedic surgeon*
Harisdangkul, Valee *physician*
Hughson, Michael Donald *pathologist, researcher, medical educator*
Izevbigie, Ernest B. *biomedical researcher*
Jones, Daniel Wayne *physician, medical educator*
Marshall, Gailen Daugherty, Jr. *allergist, educator*
Moll, George William *pediatrician, educator*
Munera, Pedro Antonio *child and adolescent psychiatrist*
Muzny, Christina A. *infectious diseases physician*
Nix, J. Elmer *retired orthopedist, surgeon*
Porter, Scott E. *orthopedist*
Savoie, Felix Henry III *orthopaedic surgeon*
Thigpen, James Tate *oncologist, educator*
Vance, Ralph Brooks, Sr. *oncologist, educator*
Yanes, Licy Lorena *medical educator*
Yates, Anne Bridges *allergist, immunologist, educator*

Laurel
Lindstrom, Eric Everett *ophthalmologist*

Ocean Springs
Austin, Claude Lidell *retired surgeon*

Oxford
Murthy, Narasimha S. *pharmaceutical scientist, researcher*

Whitfield
Montgomery, John Harold *psychiatrist*

MISSOURI

Ballwin
Pierce, John Albert *retired medical educator*

Cape Girardeau
Caragine, Louis Philip, Jr. *neurosurgeon*
Sacha, Robert Frank *osteopath, educator*

Caruthersville
Puangsuvan, Somporn *surgeon, consultant*

Chesterfield
Qazi, Mujtaba A. *ophthalmologist*
Silber, Sherman J. *urologist, consultant*

Columbia
Anderson, Ralph Robert *endocrinologist, educator*
Barnes, Stephen L. *surgeon*
Churchill, Robert Joseph *radiologist, educator, dean*
Colwill, Jack Marshall *physician, educator*
Cunningham, Milamari Antoinella *retired anesthesiologist*
Eggers, George William Nordholtz, Jr. *anesthesiologist, educator*
Forte, Leonard Ralph *pharmacologist, educator*
James, Elizabeth Joan Plogsted *pediatrician, educator*
Khojasteh, Ali *medical oncologist, hematologist*
König, Peter *pediatrician, educator*
Nolph, Georgia Bower *physician*
Perry, Michael Clinton *internist, academic administrator, educator*
Sethi, Yash Pal *radiologist, consultant*
Sowa, Grzegorz *pharmacologist, educator*
Stephenson, Hugh Edward, Jr. *retired surgeon*
Tarnove, Lorraine *medical association executive*
Tobias, Joseph Drew *pediatric anesthesiologist*
Twardowski, Zbylut Józef *nephrologist, educator*
Wakefield, Mark Richard *urologist, educator*
Yerram, Preethi *physician*

Festus
Ducharme, Nicole Marie *endocrinologist*

Florissant
Tanphaichitr, Kongsak *rheumatologist, allergist, immunologist, internist*

Hazelwood
Rajagopalan, Raghavan *medical researcher*

Hillsboro
Schuessler, Thomas Frederick *medical educator*

Joplin
Daus, Arthur Steven *neurological surgeon*

Kansas City
Abdou, Nabih I. *physician, educator*
Alon, Uri S. *pediatrician, nephrologist*
Bjerke, H. Scott *surgeon*
Carver, Terrence Wayne, Jr. *pediatrician, educator*
Deng, Hong-Wen *medical educator, researcher*
Dimond, Edmunds Grey *medical educator*
Drees, Betty *medical educator, dean*
Friedlander, Edward Robert *pathologist*
Hagan, John Charles III *ophthalmologist*
Harper, Diane M. *medical educator, researcher*
Heymach, George John III *physician, educator, health facility administrator, consultant*
Holcomb, George Whitfield *pediatrician, surgeon, educator*
Kindred, Lynn Herbert *cardiologist*
Lofland, Gary Kenneth *cardiac surgeon*
Long, Edwin Tutt *surgeon*
McCallister, Ben D. *internist, cardiologist, educator*
McGregor, Douglas Hugh *pathologist, educator*
McPhee, Mark Steven *gastroenterologist, educator*
Molteni, Agostino *pathology educator*
Muffly, Tyler *medical educator*
Nguyen, Trung Hieu *internist*
O'Brien, James Edward *surgeon*
Olitsky, Scott Eric *ophthalmologist*
Piepho, Robert Walter *pharmacy educator, researcher*
Rada, David Charles *dermatologist*
Raghuveer, Geetha *pediatrician, educator*
Schwend, Richard Michael *orthopedist, educator*
Spielberg, Stephen Paul *pediatrician, medical educator, former dean*
Thakre, Tushar P. *physician, scientist*
Truog, William Edward III *pediatrician, educator, researcher*
Walsh-Kelly, Christine Mary *pediatrician, educator*

Kearney
Waltz, James Richard *physician*

Kirksville
Darmani, Nissar Ahmad *pharmacologist, educator*
Holman, Charles Raymond *osteopathic physician*

Lees Summit
Cil, Akin *orthopedic surgeon*

Moberly
Fleming, David Avery *internist*

Rolla
Stoecker, William Van *physician, computer scientist*

Saint Joseph
Malani, Ashok K. *physician*

Saint Louis
Achilefu, Samuel *biomedical educator director*
Agarwal, Banke *gastroenterologist, educator*
Alpers, David Hershel *gastroenterologist, educator*
Bach, Richard Gordon *internist, cardiologist, educator*
Bacon, Bruce Raymond *physician*
Ballinger, Walter Francis *surgeon, educator*
Belshe, Robert *epidemiologist, educator*
Bhavsar, Neelima G. *educator*
Bierut, Laura J. *psychiatrist, educator*
Bjerregaard, Preben *cardiologist, educator*
Boswell, C.B. *plastic surgeon*
Botteron, Kelly Nicole *psychiatrist, educator*
Brandt, Keith E. *plastic surgeon, educator*
Branham, Gregory Harris *facial plastic surgeon*
Bridwell, Keith Happ *orthopedic surgeon*
Burke, William *neurologist*
Chaplin, Hugh, Jr. *preventive medicine physician, educator*
Cheng, Steven Chih-nung *nephrologist, educator*
Cloninger, Claude Robert *psychiatrist, epidemiologist, educator, researcher*
Constantino, John Nicholas *medical educator, researcher*
Correa-Perez, Juan Ramon *andrologist, embryologist, researcher*
Crim, Courtney *physician, educator*
Cross, Dewitte Talmadge III *radiologist*
Cryer, Philip Eugene *endocrinologist*
DeBaun, Michael R. *pediatrician, educator*
Dewald, Paul Adolph *psychiatrist, educator*
Di Bisceglie, Adrian Michael *pathologist, department chairman*
DiPersio, John F. *oncologist*
Dougherty, Charles Hamilton *pediatrician*
Eckstein, Julie *healthcare administrator, former state agency administrator*
Ellis, Matthew James *oncologist, educator*
Faro, Albert *pediatric pulmonologist*
Farria, Dione Marie *radiologist, educator*
Felthous, Alan Robert *psychiatrist*
Fitch, Coy Dean *internist, educator*
Fleshman, James W. *medical association administrator*
Flye, M. Wayne *surgeon, immunologist, educator, writer*
Frater, John Lawrence *medical educator*
Frey, Sharon Elizabeth *internist, adult infectious disease physician*
Friedman, William Hersh *otolaryngologist, educator*
Goldberg, Anne Carol *physician, educator*
Goldberg, Mark Paul *neurologist*
Gordon, Jeffrey Ivan *gastroenterologist, educator, molecular biologist, researcher*
Grossberg, George Thomas *psychiatrist, educator*
Grubb, Robert L., Jr. *neurosurgeon*
Haines, Cindy D. *physician, consultant*
Hammerman, Marc Randall *nephrologist, educator*
Heiken, Jay Paul *physician*
Heuckeroth, Robert O. *pediatrician, educator*
Hirose, Keiko *otolaryngologist, educator*
Hoft, Daniel Fredric *immunologist, director*
Holmes, Nancy Elizabeth *pediatrician*
Holtzman, David Michael *neurologist*
Hyers, Thomas Morgan *internist, biomedical researcher*
Inder, Terrie Eleanor *pediatrician, educator*
Kale, Sushant P. *neurologist*
Kienstra, Kathleen O. *radiation therapist professor, program director*
Knutsen, Alan Paul *pediatrician, immunologist, allergist*
Kouchoukos, Nicholas Thomas *surgeon*
Lai, H. Henry *urologist*
Lasala, John M. *cardiologist, medical educator*
Lewis, Lawrence M. *emergency physician, researcher*
Lewis, Robert David *ophthalmologist, educator*
Ley, Timothy James *hematologist, molecular biologist*
Li, Ping *pharmacologist, educator, researcher*
Ludmerer, Kenneth Marc *medical educator*
Mackinnon, Susan *plastic surgeon*
Majerus, Philip Warren *physician*
Manary, Mark John *pediatrician*
Mazuski, John Edward *surgeon, researcher*
Middelkamp, John Neal *pediatrician, educator*
Mohanakumar, Thalachallour *medical educator, director*
Momtahen, Amir Javad *radiologist*
Moore, Terry Lynn *physician, researcher*
Morley, John Edward *physician*

Morris, John Carl *neurologist, educator, researcher*
Myerson, Robert J. *radiologist, educator*
Neely, John Gail *otolaryngologist*
Neidorff, Michael F. *health care executive*
Nelson, D. Michael *gynecologist, educator*
Newcomer, John Whitney *psychiatrist, researcher, educator*
Nunley, Ryan M. *orthopaedic surgeon*
Oliver, George Charles *medical educator, cardiologist*
Owens, William Don *anesthesiology educator*
Prensky, Arthur Lawrence *pediatric neurologist, educator*
Purkerson, Mabel Louise *physician, physiologist, educator*
Rednam, Krishna Rao Venkata *ophthalmologist*
Riew, K. Daniel *cervical spine surgeon*
Rodin, Miriam B. *medical educator*
Rosenbaum, Herbert Edwin *neurology educator*
Sachdeva, Ashutosh *pulmonologist, director*
Schonfeld, Gustav *medical educator, researcher, administrator*
Schwartz, Alan Leigh *pediatrician, educator*
Siegel, Barry Alan *radiologist*
Sita, Michael John *pharmacy educator*
Smith, Kenneth Rupert, Jr. *neurosurgeon, educator*
Smith, Morton Edward *ophthalmology educator, dean*
Spector, Gershon Jerry *otolaryngologist, educator, researcher*
Stenson, William Frederick *gastroenterologist*
Stone, Christian Diaz *medical educator*
Strunk, Robert Charles *physician*
Suen, Hon Chi *thoracic surgeon*
Ternberg, Jessie Lamoin *pediatric surgeon, educator*
Tiefenbrunn, Alan James *medical educator*
Tollefsen, Douglas Meyer *medical educator*
Unanue, Emil Raphael *immunopathologist*
Walsh, David Joseph *pediatric neurologist, educator*
Wedner, H. James *physician, researcher*
Whyte, Michael P. *genetics educator, researcher, director*
Yokoyama, Wayne Makoto *medical educator, researcher, rheumatologist*
Young, Paul Andrew *anatomist*
Young, Vernon Leroy *plastic surgeon, researcher*

Saint Peters
Wang, William Weiqi *physician*

Town And Country
Levin, Marvin Edgar *physician*

West Plains
Dreckman, Dale P. *medical educator*

MONTANA

Big Sky
Strickler, Jeffrey Harold *pediatrician*

Billings
Glenn, Guy Charles *pathologist*
Knapp, Howard Raymond *internist, clinical pharmacologist*

Bozeman
Pardue, A. Michael *retired plastic and reconstructive surgeon*

Missoula
Grimes, Mark Lindsay *medical educator, researcher*

NEBRASKA

Bennington
Burgher, Louis William *physician, educator, academic administrator*
Fleming, William Hare *surgeon*

Hastings
Dungan, John Russell, Jr., (12th Viscount Dungan of Clane, Hereditary Prince of Fermoy and Arra) *anesthesiologist, health facility administrator*

Lincoln
Holguin, Adelina *biomedical researcher*
Koszewski, Bohdan Julius *retired internist, medical educator*
Michels, Dale E. *physician*
Spry, Leslie Allen *nephrologist, director*
Voigt, David William *surgeon, director*
Wilson, Charles Stephen *cardiologist, educator*

Omaha
Agrawal, Sandeep K. *pharmacologist, educator*
Allen-Gipson, Diane S. *assistant professor, scientist*
Alnouti, Yazen M. *medical educator*
Baltaro, Richard J. *pathologist, medical educator*
Benson, John Alexander, Jr. *internist, educator*
Bewtra, Chhanda *pathologist, educator*
Bracciano, Alfred Gerald *medical educator, occupational therapist*
Casale, Thomas Bruce *medical educator*
Casey, Murray Joseph *physician, educator*
Dvorak, Allen Dale *radiologist*
Enarson, Cam Edwin *medical educator, dean*
Fernandes, Praveen Paul *psychiatrist, educator*
Freeman, Thomas L. *medical educator*
Fritzsch, Bernd *comparative neuroembryologist*
Garvin, Kevin L. *surgeon, educator*
Godfrey, Maurice *biomedical scientist*
Hinder, Ronald Albert *surgeon, researcher*
Hodgson, Paul Edmund *surgeon, department chairman*
Howard, Woodward Randal *orthopedist*
Huurman, Walter William *pediatric orthopaedic surgeon, educator*
Imray, Thomas John *radiologist, educator*
Khoynezhad, Ali *surgeon, educator*
Korbitz, Bernard Carl *hematologist, consultant*
Leopold, Donald A. *medical educator*
Lynch, Thomas Gerald *surgeon, educator*
Margalit, Eyal *ophthalmologist, educator*
Maurer, Harold Maurice *pediatrician*
Mohiuddin, Syed Maqdoom *cardiologist, educator*
Murrin, Leonard Charles, II, *pharmacology educator, researcher*
O'Brien, Richard L(ee) *physician, educator, academic administrator*
Pipinos, Iraklis Ilias *surgeon*
Porter, Thomas R. *cardiologist*
Rizzo, William Bradley *pediatrician, educator*
Rogan, Eleanor Groeniger *oncologist, educator*
Sankaranarayanan, Jayashri *medical educator, researcher*
Schlessinger, Joel *dermatologist, researcher, entrepreneur*
Shilling, Kay Marlene *psychiatrist*
Skoog, Donald Paul *retired pathologist, educator*
Sooriyaarachchi, Gamini Sarathchandra *oncologist, hematologist, educator*
Stageman, James Henry *physician*
Thorson, Alan Glen *surgeon*
Upadhyaya, Prashant Kudigram *surgeon*
Vandenberg, Edward V. *geriatrician, educator*
Vinogradov, Serguei V. *medical educator*
Ward, Vernon Graves *retired internist*
Wigton, Robert Swift *medical educator*
Wyatt, Todd A. *medical educator*
Zetterman, Rowen Kent *gastroenterologist, hepatologist, dean*

Plattsmouth
Fusaro, Ramon Michael *dermatologist, preventive medicine physician, researcher*

Scottsbluff
Kabalin, John Nicholas *urologist*

NEVADA

Glenbrook
Goldsmith, Harry Sawyer *surgeon, educator*

Henderson
Duong, Hon-Vu Quang *ophthalmologist, educator*
Gollard, Russell Patrick *hematologist*
Kebede, Kebret Theodore *medical educator*

Las Vegas
Ahmad, Shamoon *hematologist, oncologist, consultant*
Gremse, David Albert *pediatrician, educator*
Hoepfner, Mark Thomas *surgeon*
Hrabal, Antonin *physician, educator*
Kline, Ronald Michael *pediatrician, hematologist*
Kurlinski, John Parker *physician*
McCann, Biff (Raymond Biff McCann) *plastic surgeon*
Moritz, Timothy Bovie *psychiatrist*
Noback, Richardson Kilbourne *medical educator*
Speck, Eugene Lewis *internist*
Wheeler, Darren Thomas *pathologist*

North Las Vegas
El-Husseini, Randa A. *physician*
Webber, Robert *medical researcher*

Reno
Akiyama, Toshio *cardiologist, educator, researcher, director*
Crognale, Michael Anthony *medical educator, neuroscientist, consultant*
Guneyi, Umit Ahmet *physician, consultant*
MacKintosh, Frederick Roy *oncologist*
Pixley, John Seymour *immunology educator*
Sanders, Kenton Morris *medical educator*
Small, Elisabeth Chan *psychiatrist, educator*

NEW HAMPSHIRE

Bartlett
Pomfret, David B. *medical educator, internist*

Campton
Scrimshaw, Nevin Stewart *physician, nutritionist, educator*

Concord
Bagan, Merwyn *neurological surgeon*
Stadelmann, Wayne Karl *plastic surgeon*
Vidaver, Robert Maxwell *medical educator*

Durham
Finkelhor, David *medical researcher, director*
Taylor, Robert Lawrence, Jr. *medical educator*

Franconia
Chen, Andrew Lawrence *orthopedist, surgeon, sports medicine specialist*

Hanover
Beisswenger, Paul James *medical educator, researcher*
Chapman, Robert James *psychiatrist, educator*
Green, William R. *medical educator, researcher, dean*
Rolett, Ellis Lawrence *cardiologist, educator*
Weinstein, James Neil *orthopaedic surgeon*

Lebanon
Bernat, James Lawrence *neurologist, educator*
Bernstein, Henry H. *pediatrician, educator*
Brinckerhoff, Constance Elizabeth *medical educator, researcher*
Chertoff, Jocelyn D. *radiologist, department chairman*
Cohen, Jeffrey Allen *neurologist, educator*
DeLong, Peter *medical educator*
Fanciullo, Gilbert J. *physician, educator*
Ferrell, Richard Bradley *neuropsychiatrist*
Gallagher, John D. *anesthesiologist, educator*
Glass, Donald David *anesthesiologist*
Holmes, Gregory Lawrence *pediatrician, educator, neurologist*
Kantor, Stephen Richard *orthopedic surgeon*
Longnecker, Daniel Sidney *pathologist, researcher*
Mirza, Sohail K. *orthopedist, educator*
Nugent, William C. *cardiothoracic surgeon*
Oxman, Thomas Elliot *psychiatrist*
Plehn, Jonathan Freeman *internal medicine and cardiology educator*
Sateia, Michael John *psychiatrist, educator*
Shaker, Marcus Sidney *pediatrician*
Shu, Jennifer A. *pediatrician, writer*
Silberfarb, Peter Michael *psychiatrist, educator*

Lincoln
Seletz, Jules M. *surgeon*

Lyme
Cornwell, Gibbons Gray III *retired internist, educator*
McIntyre, Oswald Ross *physician*

Manchester
Lavery, Robert Michael *internist, cardiologist*

Mirror Lake
Culleton, James Frederick *neurologist*

Nashua
Constantian, Mark Barbour *plastic surgeon, educator*
Knights, Edwin Munroe *pathologist*
Siroty, William Charles *physician*

Peterborough
Cahill, George Francis, Jr. *physician, educator*

Rye
Wilson, Ralph Sloan *retinal surgeon*

West Lebanon
Sox, Harold Carleton, Jr. *physician, educator, editor*

NEW JERSEY

Belle Mead
Goodnick, Paul Joel *psychiatrist*

Belleville
Wagner, Rudolph Steven *ophthalmologist, educator*

Berkeley Heights
Momeni, Reza *plastic surgeon*

Bernardsville
Louria, Donald Bruce *retired medical educator*

Brick
Kaufman, Nathan *oncologist*

Bridgewater
Bernson, Marcella S. *psychiatrist*
Cohen, Marc *cardiologist, educator*

Browns Mills
Cha, Se Do *internist*
Moore, Roger Addison *pediatrician, anesthesiologist*

Camden
Ances, I. G(eorge) *obstetrician, gynecologist*
Jean, Smith *biomedical researcher, director*
Parra, Raul O. *urologist, educator*
Parrillo, Joseph Edison, Jr. *allergist, immunologist, cardiologist*
Rajaram, Sri-Sujanthy *internist, educator*
Ross, Steven Elliot *surgeon*

Cedar Knolls
Hariri, Robert Joseph *neurosurgeon, researcher*

Cherry Hill
Goldberg, Jack *hematologist*
Swibinski, Edward Thomas *internist, endocrinologist, educator*
Werbitt, Warren *gastroenterologist, educator*

Closter
Minikes, Neil Ira *pediatrician, allergist, immunologist*

Cranford
Mendelson, Joel Stuart *allergist, immunologist*

Demarest
Dornfest, Burton Saul *anatomy educator scientist*

East Brunswick
Kaufman, Matthew *plastic surgeon*
Kirshner, Jacob *physician*
Milgraum, Sandy *surgeon, educator*

East Orange
Agarwal, Shashi Kant *cardiologist*

Edison
Gizzi, Martin Sherman *neurologist, neurophysiologist*

Elizabeth
Sananman, Michael Lawrence *neurologist*

Elmwood Park
Weisberger, James David *hematopathologist*

Englewood
Bloomenstein, Richard B. *plastic surgeon*
D'Amico, Richard *plastic surgeon*
Elias, Steven *surgeon*
Frieden, Faith Joy *obstetrician*
Goldweit, Richard Scott *cardiologist*
Herman, Steven Douglas *cardiothoracic surgeon, educator*
Shammash, Jonathan *medical educator*
Tobias, Geoffrey *otolaryngologist, plastic surgeon*
Wuhl, Charles Michael *psychiatrist*

Fair Lawn
Namerow, David Mark *pediatrician*

Flanders
Huang, Jacob Chen-ya *physician, educator, city health official*

Flemington
Rushton, Alan R. *physician, medical researcher, historian*
Taylor, Duncan Paul *pharmacologist, researcher*

Fort Lee
Huang, Jianzhong *biomedical researcher*
Li, Tien-Shun *obstetrician, gynecologist, educator*

Glen Ridge
Zbar, Lloyd Irwin Stanley *otolaryngologist, educator*

Glen Rock
Goldstone, Robert Allen *orthopaedic surgeon*

Guttenberg
Wright, Jane Cooke *oncologist, educator, consultant*

Hackensack
Agress, Harry, Jr. *radiologist, nuclear medicine physician*
Ashinoff, Robin *dermatologic surgeon*
Bhattacharyya, Pritish *hematologist, director*
Davies, Richard John *surgical oncologist*
Gardin, Julius Markus *cardiologist, educator*
Gross, Peter Alan *epidemiologist, researcher*
Haines, Kathleen Ann *pediatrician, educator*
Kim, Richard Young Jin *plastic surgeon, educator*
Kimura, Yukiko *pediatric rheumatologist, educator*
Pecora, Andrew Louis *hematologist, oncologist*
Stagnaro-Green, Alex *medical educator*

Hackettstown
Singh, Harjit *medical educator, artist*

Haddonfield
Capelli, John Placido *nephrologist, educator*
Fisher, George Ross III *physician, educator*
Gatti, Eugene Anthony *immunologist, pediatrician*
Jensh, Ronald Paul *retired anatomist*

Haledon
Ishiguro, Hiroki *psychiatrist, geneticist, researcher*

Hamilton
Sporn, Aaron Adolph *physician, educator*

Hammonton
Adetunji, Babatunde Abayomi *forensic psychiatrist*

Harrisonville
Stallone, George R. *neurophysiologist*

Hillsdale
Copeland, Lois Jacqueline *physician*

Holmdel
Kane, Michael Joel *physician*

Hopewell
Jaffe, Russell Merritt *pathologist, research director*

Jersey City
Greenberg, William Michael *psychiatrist*

Kenilworth
Waskin, Hetty Anne *epidemiologist, director*

Lakewood
Marchese, Michael James, Jr. *radiation oncologist*

Lawrenceville
Rosenthal, Albert Lester *dermatologist, educator*
Witte, Arnold Stewart *neurologist*

Linden
Bukosky, Richard J. *allergist*

Little Silver
Marcus, Abir A. *psychiatrist*

Livingston
Conde, Miguel A. *hematologist, oncologist*
Samojlik, Eugeniusz *medical educator, health facility administrator*

Long Branch
Checton, John Burt *cardiologist*
Luria, Martin Jay *endocrinologist*

Lumberton
Campagnolo, Mary Frances *physician*

Madison
Culligan, Patrick John *obstetrician, urogynecologist, surgeon, researcher*

Mahwah
Lee, Reginald K. *orthopedist, researcher*

Maplewood
Shuttleworth, Anne Margaret *psychiatrist*
Silverman, Martin Arnold *psychiatrist*

Margate City
Trocki-Videll, Cyla *psychiatrist, healthcare administrator*
Videll, Jared Steven *cardiologist*

Medford
Lawson-Ndu, Ovunda A. *emergency physician, surgeon*

Merchantville
Li, Christopher L. *epidemiologist, educator*

Monroe Township
Wallach, Jacques Burton *pathologist, educator*

Montclair
Downie, Jeanine B. *dermatologist*
Rosen, Allen David *plastic surgeon*

Moorestown
Cervantes, Luis Augusto *neurosurgeon*
Saouaf, Sandra J. *immunologist, consultant*

Morris Plains
Goldenberg, David Milton *experimental pathologist, oncologist*

Morristown
Adler, Kenneth R. *oncologist, hematologist*
Colizza, Wayne Anthony *orthopaedic surgeon*
De Rosa, William Thomas *internist, hematologist, oncologist*
Fiel, Stanley Bruce *internist, pulmonologist, educator*
Finkel, Marion Judith *internist, pharmaceutical administrator*
Parr, Grant Van Siclen *surgeon*
Rogachefsky, Arlene Sandra *dermatologist*
Rogido, Marta Raquel *medical educator*
Smart, Frank Wilson *physician*
Timins, Julie Kelter *radiologist*
Zaubler, Thomas Scot *psychiatrist, educator*

Neptune
Laraya-Cuasay, Lourdes Redublo *pediatrician, pulmonologist, educator*
Rice, Stephen Gary *pediatrician, sports medicine physician, educator*
Stumpf, Paul George *obstetrician-gynecologist*

New Brunswick
Aisner, Joseph *oncologist, medical educator*
Bertino, Joseph Rocco *oncologist, educator*
Boyarsky, Andrew Harold *surgeon, educator*
Coromilas, James *cardiologist*
Day-Salvatore, Debra Lynn *medical geneticist*
Dhib-Jalbut, Suhayl S. *physician*
Drachtman, Richard Allan *pediatrician, educator*
Gibbon, Darlene G. *medical educator*
Golbe, Lawrence Ingram *neurologist*
Goldberg, Michael Ira *obstetrician, gynecologist*
Goldrich, Michael Seth *otolaryngologist*
Greenwald, Alfred Emanuel *retired cosmetic surgeon*
Kaufman, Kenneth Roland *psychiatrist, educator*
Kostis, John Basil *cardiologist*
Laouar, Amale *immunologist, educator*
Lepore, Frederick Everett *neurologist, educator*
Leventhal, Elaine A. *internist*
Lowry, Stephen Frederick *surgeon, educator*
Lu-Yao, Grace *epidemiologist*
Makhija, Mohan *nuclear medicine physician*
Mann, Richard Alan *physician, educator*
Moreyra, Abel E. *medical educator*
Nissenblatt, Michael Jeffrey *medical oncologist*
Nosko, Michael Gerrik *neurosurgeon, educator*
Pinals, Robert Stanton *physician*
Pitchumoni, Capecomorin Sankar *gastroenterologist, educator*
Raska, Karel Frantisek Julian, Jr. *pathologist, virologist, educator*
Reiss, Michael *medical oncologist, researcher*
Roth, Daniel B. *ophthalmologist, researcher*
Salas, Max *pediatrician, educator*
Schneider, Stephen Harley *medical educator*
Scholz, Peter M. *surgeon, director*
Selby, Ronald M. *orthopedic surgeon*
Tallia, Alfred F. *physician, educator*
Trooskin, Stanley Z. *surgeon*
Upton, Arthur Canfield *experimental pathologist, educator*
Weinstein, Melvin Phillip *physician educator*

Newark
Ahmed, Shaikh Sultan *cardiologist, educator*
Baker, Herman *medical educator, writer*
Carmel, Peter W. *neurosurgeon*
Cherniack, Neil Stanley *pulmonologist, educator*
Connolly, Mark W. *thoracic surgeon*
Cook, Stuart Donald *neurologist, educator*
Donahoo, James Saunders *cardiothoracic surgeon*
Evans, Hugh E. *pediatrician, educator*
Goldstein, Ira Morris *neurosurgeon*
Granick, Mark S. *plastic surgeon, medical educator*
Iffy, Leslie *medical educator*
Kirmani, Jawad F. *neurologist, surgeon, researcher*
Kirschner, Marvin A. *retired endocrinologist*
Kou, Victoria *medical educator*
Little, Alan Brian *gynecologist, educator*
Liu, Qinyue (Sherry Liu) *physician, consultant*
Maqsood, Ahsan *cardiologist, researcher*
Mitchell, Jason Wayne *interventional radiologist*
Prestigiacomo, Charles Joseph *neurosurgeon, educator*
Reichman, Lee Brodersohn *physician*
Ryan, Lisa Kathleen *environmental and medical science educator*
Schleifer, Steven J. *psychiatrist, educator*
Sifri, Ziad C. *emergency physician, educator*
Weiss, Gerson *endocrinologist, educator*

Northfield
Margolis, Thomas Ira *vitreoretinal ophthalmologist*

Nutley
Mostillo, Ralph *medical association administrator*

ORADELL
Azmi, Hooman *neurosurgeon*

Paramus
Hochstein, Martin Alan *endocrinologist*

Paterson
DeFilippi, Vincent J(ohn) *cardiac surgeon*
Fink, David Leonard *surgeon*

Peapack
Eddey, Gary Erwin *physician, administrator, educator*

Pennington
Fong, Donald P. *psychiatrist*
Sun, Jianxin *medical educator, researcher*

Phillipsburg
Burke, John F. *retired surgeon*
Drago, Joseph Rosario *urologist, educator*

Piscataway
Colaizzi, John Louis *medical educator*
Conney, Allan Howard *pharmacologist, researcher*
Johnson, William Gessner *neurologist, educator*
Mardikian, Jackie *medical librarian*
Menza, Matthew A. *psychiatrist*
Nowakowski, Richard Stanley *medical educator, director*
Sahota, Amrik *medical researcher, educator, lab administrator*
Volfson-Doubova, Elena *psychiatrist, researcher*

Plainsboro
Brolin, Robert Edward *physician, surgeon*
Chau, Wai Yip *surgeon*

Princeton
Carr, Marcus Eugene, Jr. *internist*
Carver, David Harold *retired pediatrician*
Engel, J. Mark *ophthalmologist*
Grover, Gary James *pharmacologist*
Kang, Yibin *medical educator, researcher*
Lavizzo-Mourey, Risa Juanita *medical foundation administrator*
Lee, Francis Y. *pharmacologist*
Lumpkin, John Robert *public health physician, state official*
Mueller, Peter Sterling *psychiatrist, educator*
Notterman, Daniel A. *pediatrician, educator*
Putukian, Margot *sports medicine physician*
Rosenzweig-Lipson, Sharon Joy *pharmacologist*
Sierocki, John Stanley *oncologist*
Sigal, Leonard H. *physician*
von der Schmidt, Edward III *neurosurgeon, veterinarian*

Princeton Junction
Amenta, Peter Sebastian *pathologist, dean*

Rahway
Xu, Jinyou *medical researcher*

Randolph
Strutin, Millard Desmond *surgeon*

Red Bank
Braddom, Randall Lee *physiatrist, educator*
Clever, Marcia Sue *psychiatrist*
Scaccia, Frank John *facial surgeon, otolaryngologist*

Ridgewood
Baddoura, Rashid Joseph *emergency physician*
Brizzio, Mariano E. *thoracic surgeon, educator*

Roseland
Panagides, John *pharmacologist*

Sewell
DePace, Nicholas Louis *physician*

Short Hills
Chaiken, Bernard Henry *internist, gastroenterologist*

Shrewsbury
Rose, Michael Ian *plastic surgeon*

Somerset
De Salva, Salvatore Joseph *retired pharmacologist, toxicologist*
Ilogu, Noel Obiajulu *physician*

South Plainfield
Kwon, Ik Hyun *internist*

Spring Lake
De Pinies, Felix *retired physician*
Harrigan, John Thomas, Jr. *physician, obstetrician, gynecologist*

Springfield
Kerner, Michael Bernard *gastroenterologist*

Stratford
Kosciuk, Mary C. *medical researcher, educator*
Levitas, Andrew Stephen *child psychiatrist, educator*

Summit
Carniol, Paul J. *plastic and reconstructive surgeon, otolaryngologist*
Duberstein, Joel Lawrence *internist, pulmonologist, educator*
Greenberg, Rosalie *child psychiatrist*
Halperin, John Jacob *neurology educator, researcher*
Oppenheimer, John Jacob *allergist, immunologist*
Wang, Er-Jia *drug safety researcher*

Teaneck
Goldfarb, Joel Peter *internist, gastroenterologist*
Ladenheim, Jules Calvin *neurosurgeon*
Novogroder, Michael *pediatric endocrinologist*
Scotti, Dennis Joseph *educator, researcher, consultant*

Tenafly
Gerst, Paul Howard *physician*
Golomb, Frederick Martin *surgeon, educator*

Tinton Falls
Macdonald, Donald Arthur, Jr. *physician, surgeon*

Titusville
Girgis, Suzette *clinical pharmacologist, researcher*

Trenton
Fares, Louis George *surgeon, educator*
Gomez, William *orthopedist*
Zanna, Martin Thomas *physician*

Vineland
Clinton, Lawrence Paul *psychiatrist*

Voorhees
Glasofer, Eric David *allergist, immunologist, pediatrician, educator*
Schwartz, Bennett K. *dermatologist*
Somer, Robert A. *physician, educator*

Wall
Monaco, Robert Anthony *radiologist*

Washington
Massimo, Anna Georgieva *medical educator*

Wayne
Gollance, Robert Barnett *ophthalmologist*
Wise, Jeffrey Bruce *plastic surgeon, educator*

West Orange
Brodkin, Roger Harrison *dermatologist, educator*
Casella, Anthony John *cardiologist*
Gans, Bruce Merrill *physiatrist, educator, health facility administrator*
Gehl, Raymond Harold *psychiatrist, educator*
Ghali, Anwar Youssef *psychiatrist, educator*
Hill, George James *physician, educator*
Langsner, Alan Michael *pediatric cardiologist*
Martin, Boston Faust *neurosurgeon*
Rogal, Gary Jeffrey *cardiologist*
Whang, Matthew Ihn Seong *urologist*

Westwood
Landzberg, Joel Serge *cardiologist*

Wyckoff
Gartner, Joseph John, II, *obstetrician, gynecologist*
Marcus, Linda Susan *dermatologist*

NEW MEXICO

Albuquerque
Berwick, Marianne *epidemiologist, educator*
Brown, Lee Kelvin *pulmonary, critical care and sleep medicine physician, researcher*
Burge, Mark R. *physician, educator*
Chand, Hitendra S. *medical educator*
Chang, Barbara Karen *medical educator, director*
Chilton, Lance Alix *pediatrician*
Clarke, Gray B. *psychiatrist*
Eldredge, Jonathan DeForest *medical librarian, educator, social informaticist*
Fry, Donald Edmund *surgeon*
Gordon, Larry Jean *sanitarian, environmental health consultant*
Kempaiah, Prakasha *pathologist, researcher*
Knospe, William Herbert *medical educator*
Lin, Henry C. *physician, researcher*
Lindeman, Robert Dean *medical educator, researcher, consultant*
Mapel, Douglas Wayne *epidemiologist, educator, pulmonologist, critical care specialist*
Martino, Sal *medical association administrator*
McCarthy, Denis M. *medical educator*
Omer, George Elbert, Jr. *retired orthopaedic surgeon, educator*
Phillips, John P. *neurologist, educator*
Rayburn, William Frazier *obstetrician, gynecologist, educator*
Rivero, Dennis P. *orthopedist*
Scott, Bobby Randolph *biomedical researcher, writer*
Tzamaloukas, Antonios Helias *nephrologist*
Uhlenhuth, Eberhard Henry *psychiatrist, educator*
Waitzkin, Howard Bruce *internist, sociologist, educator*

Las Cruces
Jacobs, Kent Frederick *dermatologist*
wwRupp, Michael Richard *immunologist*

Los Alamos
Smith, Fredrica Emrich *rheumatologist, internist*

Rio Rancho
Melendez, Robert F. *ophthalmologist*

Santa Fe
Alfidi, Ralph Joseph *retired radiologist, educator, researcher, administrator*
Hoffmann, Louis Gerhard *immunologist, educator*
Kingsmore, Stephen Francis *physician, research scientist*
Schiller, William Richard *surgeon*
Williams, Ralph Chester, Jr. *physician, educator*

Tesuque
Bornstein, Paul *medical educator, biochemist*

NEW YORK

Albany
Carl, Allen Laurence *surgery educator*
Cavaliere, Ludovico Frank Roland *rheumatologist*
Davis, Paul Joseph *endocrinologist*
Farber, Martha J. (Marty Farber) *ophthalmologist, medical association administrator*
Gibbons, Vincent Paul *pediatric neurologist, educator*
Gruenthal, Michael *neurologist, department chairman*
Hoffmeister, Jana Marie *cardiologist*
Kanwar, Vikramjit Singh *pediatrician, educator, oncologist*
Lepow, Martha Lipson *pediatric educator, consultant*
Mehta, Manish *surgeon*
Metzger, Dennis W. *medical educator, immunologist, researcher*
Molho, Eric Steven *neurologist, researcher*
Pinheiro, Joaquim Manuel Bernardino *pediatrician, educator*
Sell, Stewart *pathologist, immunologist, educator*
Shapshay, Stanley M. *otolaryngologist, educator*
Tepper, Clifford *allergist, immunologist, educator*
Veille, Jean-Claude *obstetrician, educator*
Zimmerman, Earl Abram *neurologist, educator*

Amherst
Butsch, John Lord *surgeon, educator*
Granger, Carl V. *physician, educator*
Monte, Scott Vincent *medical researcher, director*

Amityville
Upadhyay, Yogendra Nath *physician, educator*

Amsterdam
Castro, Michael *oncologist*

Armonk
Bakalar, Richard S. *physician*

Bath
White, Richard Thomas *radiologist*

Bayside
Ellerton, Sharon Speiser *biomedical researcher, science educator*
Miller, Albert *physician, researcher*

Bedford
Tischler, Gary Lowell *psychiatrist, educator*

Bedford Hills
Pappas, George Demetrios *retired anatomist, cell biologist, educator*

Briarcliff Manor
Pousada, Lidia *physician*

Bronx
Abbott, Ira Richmond, III, (Rick) *pediatric neurosurgeon, educator*
Alderman, Elizabeth *pediatrician, educator*
Bark, Nigel Martyn *psychiatrist*
Barzilai, Nir Jacob *geriatrician, educator*
Blaufox, Morton Donald *hypertension specialist, nuclear medicine physician, educator*
Brandt, Lawrence Jay *internist, gastroenterologist, educator*
Chambers, Earle *epidemiologist, educator*
Cohen, Herbert Jesse *pediatrician, educator*
Cosgrove, John Morgan *surgeon, department chairman*
Dam, Tarun *biomedical researcher, educator*
Das, Ashoke Kumar *internist, consultant*
DeAnda, Abelardo *thoracic surgeon, educator*
De Blasio, Maria P. *physician*
Deitrick, George Albert III *physician, surgeon*
Djukic, Aleksandra *medical educator, director*
Dolich, Barry H. *plastic surgeon, educator*
Drepaul, Loris Omesh *internist, infectious diseases physician*
Dutcher, Janice Jean Phillips *oncologist*
Fine, Eugene Jonathan *nuclear medicine physician, educator*
Fisher, John Devens *cardiologist, educator*
Frater, Robert William Mayo *surgeon, educator*
Freeman, Leonard Murray *radiologist, nuclear medicine physician, educator*
Garg, Madhur *oncologist*
Goldfischer, Sidney Leo *pathologist, educator, dean*
Goldstein, Daniel J. *thoracic surgeon, medical educator*
Gonzalez, Angela E. *obstetrician, gynecologist*
Goodman, Robert L. *internist, epidemiologist, educator*
Greenstein, Stuart Mark *surgical educator*
Gross, Susan *obstetrician, department chairman*
Gruson, Konrad *orthopedist, educator*
Guha, Sushovan *physician, researcher*
Hait, Gershon *pediatric cardiologist*
Heagarty, Margaret Caroline *retired pediatrician*
Kahn, Thomas *medical educator*
Kalnicki, Shalom *radiologist, educator*
Kalpana, Ganjam V. *biomedical researcher*
Kaushik, Sashank *psychiatrist, researcher*
Kennedy, Gary J. *psychiatrist*
Khan, Amir Maqbul *physician*
Khodakhah, Kamran *medical educator*
Kim, Soo G. *medical educator, lab administrator*
Koss, Leopold G. *pathologist, educator*
Lopez, Leo *cardiologist*
Melamed, Michal L. *epidemiologist*
Melman, Arnold *urologist*
New, Antonia S. *psychiatrist, educator*
Oertel, Michael *researcher, medical educator*
Oktay, Maja Hrzenjak *medical educator*
Owen, Randall P. *surgeon, researcher*
Pranevicius, Mindaugas *anesthesiologist, educator*
Radel, Eva *pediatrician, hematologist*
Raman, Shankar *surgeon*
Reichgott, Michael Joel *medical educator, dean, physician*
Rohan, Thomas E. *epidemiologist, educator*
Rosenstreich, David Leon *medical educator, immunologist, allergist*
Rubinstein, Arye *pediatrician, microbiologist, immunologist, educator*
Sable, Robert Allen *gastroenterologist*

Schaumburg, Herbert Howard *neurology educator*
Shafritz, David Andrew *physician, research scientist*
Shinnar, Shlomo *pediatric neurologist, educator*
Spitzer, Adrian *pediatrician, educator*
Stein, Cy Aaron *oncologist, pharmacologist*
Stein, Ruth Elizabeth Klein *physician*
Strassberg, Barbara Esther *pediatrician, educator*
Tan, XiangLin *epidemiologist, researcher*
Tong, Tommy R. *surgeon, pathologist*
Veith, Frank J. *vascular surgeon, researcher, educator*
Whyte, Mary Christina *pediatrician*
Zou, Yiyu *medical educator*

Bronxville
Bent, John *otolaryngologist, educator*
Bertles, John Francis *physician, educator*

Brooklyn
Abott, Michael Larry *physician*
Abrol, Sunil *thoracic surgeon, director*
Ackerman, Jacob Lewis *ophthalmologist*
Adachi, Masazumi *pathologist*
Astrow, Alan B. *oncologist, hematologist*
Bandler, Martin *physician*
Barone, Frank C. *researcher and medical educator*
Behm, Dutsi *physician*
Biro, Laszlo *dermatologist*
Bodis-Wollner, Ivan Gyorgy *neurologist, educator*
Brown, Evrick H. *medical educator*
Butt, Mohammad Zaman *internist, geriatrician, researcher*
Cohen, Carl I. *psychiatrist, educator*
Coplan, Jeremy David *psychiatrist, researcher*
Cracco, Roger Quinlan *neurologist, educator*
D'Ayala, Marcus *surgeon*
Erber, William Franklin *gastroenterologist*
Friedman, Eli A. *nephrologist, educator*
Gerber, Donald Albert *medical educator*
Ghevariya, Vishal *internist*
Giusti, Robert John *pulmonologist, pediatrician*
Green, William Larimore *physician*
Hammerschlag, Margaret Rosenblum *pediatrician, educator*
Huang, Yiwu *hematologist, oncologist, educator*
Jacobowitz, Israel Jacob *cardiothoracic surgeon*
Joy, Mark Kelly *physician*
Kazachkov, Mikhail *pediatric pulmonologist*
Kilanko, Oyenike Eunice *obstetrician, gynecologist*
Kugler, Anne *medical educator*
Lakhi, Nisha Amarlal *obstetrician, gynecologist*
Lichstein, Edgar *cardiologist*
Luka, Bishoy *pharmacologist, educator*
Mirra, Suzanne Samuels *pathologist*
Mittman, Neal *nephrologist, medical educator*
Nazaire, Michel Harry *physician*
Nemazie, Siamack *nephrologist, consultant*
Norstrand, Iris Fletcher *psychiatrist, neurologist, educator*
Plotz, Charles Mindell *physician, educator*
Poludasu, Shyam Sunder *cardiologist*
Price, Ely *dermatologist*
Purvin, Jack Mitchell *physician*
Savits, Barry Sorrel *surgeon*
Sawyer, Philip Nicholas *surgeon, educator, health science facility administrator*
Schwarz, Richard Howard *obstetrician, gynecologist, educator*
Shalita, Alan Remi *dermatologist*
Sharma, Bhavneesh K. *internist, researcher*
Shelov, Steven Patrick *pediatrician, educator*
Shulman, Abraham *otolaryngology educator, hospital administrator*
Turitto, Gioia *physician*
Weber, Michael A. *physician, researcher*
White, Suzanne Marie *medical educator*
Wolintz, Arthur Harry *neurologist, ophthalmologist*
Zhong, Jun *medical educator*

Buffalo
Ambrus, Clara Maria *physician*
Ambrus, Julian L. *physician, educator*
Ballow, Mark *immunologist, educator*
Batt, Ronald Elmer *gynecologist, historian, biomedical research scientist*
Bhattacharya, Arup B. *Homeopathy*
Cao, Shousong *medical researcher, educator*
Chandel, Anil *endocrinologist*
Creaven, Patrick Joseph *pharmacologist*
Cropp, Michael W. *physician, insurance company executive*
Deshmukh, Hitesh *medical researcher*
Donahue, Richard P. *epidemiologist, educator*
Genco, Robert Joseph *immunologist, periodontist, educator, scientist*
Halbreich, Uriel Morav *psychiatrist, educator*
Judelsohn, Richard *pediatrician, consultant*
Lele, Amol Shashikant *obstetrician, gynecologist*
Lema, Mark Joseph *anesthesiologist, educator*
Mindell, Eugene Robert *surgeon, educator*
Naughton, John Patrick *cardiologist, educator*
Nolan, James Paul *internist, educator, researcher*
Piver, M. Steven *gynecologic oncologist*
Popat, Saurin Rajnikant *oncologist, surgeon*
Simpson, George True, II, *surgeon, educator*
Springate, James Edward *pediatrician*
Vladutiu, Adrian O. *physician, educator*

Canandaigua
Beal, Myron Clarence *osteopath*
Wormer, Thomas Andrew *surgeon*

Cherry Creek
Lee, Tat-Sum *physician*

Chester
Amelar, Richard Daniel *urologist*

Chestnut Ridge
Day, Stacey Biswas *physician, educator*

Cooperstown
Bordley, James, IV, *surgeon*
Resnick, Steven David *pediatric dermatologist, educator*

Sauer, Leonard Austin *retired medical researcher*

Elmhurst
Masci, Joseph Richard *physician*

Elmira
Graham, David Richard *orthopedic surgeon*

Elmsford
Demopoulos, Harry Byron *retired pathologist, pharmaceutical researcher*
Panitz, Lawrence *physician*

Farmingdale
Temple, Donald Edward *medical association administrator*

Fishkill
Brocks, Eric *ophthalmologist, surgeon*

Flushing
Dalal, Aman K. *infectious diseases specialist*
Hon, John Wingsun *physician*
Kim, Mi Suk *medical educator*
Nussbaum, Michel Ernest *physician*
Rahal, James Joseph, Jr. *medical educator*

Forest Hills
Eden, Alvin Noam *pediatrician, writer*

Fresh Meadows
Amram, Laura *psychiatrist*
Godfrey, Philip M. *plastic surgeon*

Garden City
Douglas, Barry K. *plastic surgeon*

Garrison
Callahan, Daniel John *biomedical researcher*

Glen Oaks
Malhotra, Anil *psychiatrist, educator*

Gouverneur
Kuehl, Alexander Edward *physician, health facility administrator, educator, writer*

Great Neck
Brownstein, Martin Herbert *retired dermatopathologist*
Dines, David Michael *surgeon, educator*
Dines, Joshua S. *orthopedist, sports medicine physician*
Gold, Alan H. *plastic surgeon*
Goldman, Ira Steven *gastroenterologist*
Jacobson, Marc Stephen *pediatrician, educator*
Jacono, Andrew A. *plastic surgeon*
Kechijian, Paul *dermatologist, educator*
Samuel, Paul *retired cardiologist*
Scherr, Lawrence *internist, healthcare educator, historian*
Shons, Alan Rance *plastic surgeon, surgical oncologist, educator*
Silber, Jeff Scott *physician, educator*
Wolff, Edward *physician*

Hamburg
Calkins, Evan *physician, educator*

Hampton Bays
Jacobs, George Braun *neurosurgeon*

Harrison
Silverman, Amy Jocelyn *psychiatrist*
Weinstein, Carol *psychiatrist*

Hartsdale
Chait, Maxwell Mani *physician*

Hastings On Hudson
Rosch, Paul John *internist, educator*

Hawthorne
McClung, John Arthur *cardiologist*
Pianka, George *orthopedic surgeon*
Taneja, Indu *medical educator, researcher*

Hempstead
Waterman, Jason *pediatrician*

Herkimer
Gay, Douglas MacKenzie *pharmacologist*

Hewlett
Steinfeld, Philip Sheldon *pediatrician*

Huntington
Joseph, Richard Saul *cardiologist, educator*

Ithaca
Dietert, Rodney Reynolds *immunology and toxicology educator*
Whitaker, Susanne Kanis *veterinary medical librarian*

Jamaica
Kemeny, M. Margaret *oncologist, surgeon, hospital administrator, educator*
Merlino, Joseph P. *psychiatrist, director*
Satyan, Shyama *ophthalmologist*
Sharma, Jayendra *pediatrician, cardiologist*
Trombetta, Louis D. *medical educator, department chairman*

Jamestown
DJang, Arthur H.K. *pathologist, preventive medicine physician*

Katonah
Bauman, Jonathan Hugh *psychiatrist*
Stillman, Michael Allen *dermatologist*

Kenmore
Elibol, Tarik *gastroenterologist, educator*

Lake Success
Handelsman, John Ellis *pediatric orthopedist, surgeon*
Schlesinger, Irwin D. *neurologist*

Larchmont
Rockland, Lawrence Howard *psychiatrist, educator*
Sklarew, Robert Jay *biomedical research educator, consultant*

Latham
Litchmore, Trevor Alexander *physician*

Lockport
Carr, Edward Albert, Jr. *pharmacologist, educator, physician*
Lanham, Richard J. *oncologist, educator*

Lynbrook
Good, Larry Irwin *gastroenterologist, educator*

Malverne
Van Bosse, Harold J.P. *orthopedic surgeon*

Mamaroneck
Halpern, Abraham Leon *psychiatrist*
McLarnon, Mary Frances *neurologist*

Manhasset
Bernstein, David *gastroenterologist*
Bosworth, Jay L. *radiation oncologist*
Budman, Cathy Linda *psychiatrist, physician*
Catanzaro, John N. *cardiologist*
Doddamani, Sanjay *cardiologist, educator*
D'Olimpio, James Thomas *oncologist*
Esposito, Rick Anthony *thoracic surgeon*
Kandel, Anuj R. *surgeon*
Marchant, Donna *cardiologist, director*
Menzin, Andrew *gynecologist*
Milhorat, Thomas Herrick *neurosurgeon*
Ovadia, Marc *pediatric cardiologist, educator*
Pogo, Gustave Javier *cardiothoracic surgeon, educator*
Rochelson, Burton L. *obstetrician*

Manlius
Vick, Dana James *physician*

Massapequa
Ruotolo, Charles J. *orthopedist, department chairman*
Zwanger, Jerome *physician*

Melville
Copperman, Stuart Morton *pediatrician, educator*

Miller Place
Gresser, Mark Geoffrey *podiatrist*

Mineola
Brand, Donald Albert *medical researcher, educator*
Burakoff, Robert *gastroenterologist, educator*
Ente, Gerald *pediatrician*
Harris, Henry William *physician*
Ilowite, Jonathan *pulmonologist*
Niederman, Michael Steven *physician, educator*
Ortiz, Orlando *radiologist, department chairman*
Roberts, Jon *pulmonologist*

Morrisville
Rusch, Lisa Marie *medical educator*

Mount Kisco
Cameron, Daniel *internist, medical researcher*
Hayworth, Scott David *physician*
Powell, Jeffrey Scott *endocrinologist*
Schneider, Robert Jay *oncologist*

Mount Sinai
Feinberg, Sheldon Norman *pediatrician, educator*

New City
Esser, Aristide Henri *psychiatrist*

New Hyde Park
Blaufox, Andrew D. *medical educator*
Brock, William Alton *pediatric urologist*
Goilav, Béatrice Sarah *internist, educator*
Heller, Keith S. *surgeon*
Ilowite, Norman T. *pediatric rheumatologist*
Kamler, Kenneth Mark *microsurgeon*
Mehta, Ashesh *neurologist*
Mittler, Mark A. *neurosurgeon*
Muscat, Joshua Ethan *epidemiologist*
Palestro, Christopher J. *physician*
Schneider, Steven Jack *neurosurgeon*
Shanies, Stanley Alvin *cardiologist*

New Rochelle
Eaton, Richard Gillette *retired surgeon, educator*
Gerardi, Paul *cardiologist, educator*
Gitler, Bernard *cardiologist, critical care specialist*
Kumar, Anil *physician*
Lobach, Katherine S. *retired pediatrician*
Newsome, Frederick V. *medical educator*
Thomson, Gerald Edmund *physician, educator*

New Windsor
Mandel, Joel Emanuel *orthopedist*

New York
Abdel Dayem, Hussein Mahmoud *nuclear medicine physician, radiology educator*
Abramovitz, Robert *psychiatrist, director*
Adams, David H. *cardiac surgeon, educator*
Adlersberg, Jay Ben *internist*
Ahn, Jaimo *orthopedist, director*
Akin, Oguz *radiologist, educator*
Akinboboye, Olakunle Olaniran *cardiologist, educator*

Alderson, Philip Otis *radiologist, educator*
Alexiades-Armenakas, Macrene Renee *dermatologist, scientist, researcher, educator, consultant*
Alexis, Andrew F. *dermatologist*
Alikhani, Zoubin *internist, molecular biologist, researcher*
Alizadeh, Kaveh *plastic surgeon, educator*
Allen, Jeffrey C. *pediatric neurologist, educator*
Allison, James Patrick *immunology educator, medical association administrator*
Altman, Lawrence Kimball *physician, journalist*
Altman, Roy Peter *pediatric surgeon*
Amerling, Richard *nephrologist, educator*
Ames, Richard Pollard *physician, educator, lecturer*
Anderer, Erich Gen *neurosurgeon*
Andersen, Holly Sue *cardiologist, educator*
Antell, Darrick Eugene *plastic surgeon, educator*
Appel, Gerald Bernard *physician, nephrologist, educator*
Appel, Norman *ophthalmologist, educator, real estate and import/export company executive*
Appelbaum, Paul Stuart *psychiatrist, medical educator, department chairman*
Armenakas, Noel Anthony *medical educator*
Aron, Alan Milford *pediatric neurology educator*
Aronne, Louis J. *internist*
Ascherman, Jeffrey Alan *plastic and reconstructive surgeon*
Aston, Sherrell Jerone *plastic surgeon, educator*
Aufses, Arthur Harold, Jr. *surgeon, educator*
Axel, Richard *pathology and biochemistry educator*
Baden, Michael M. *pathologist, educator*
Baker, Daniel Clifton III *plastic surgeon, educator*
Bank, Arthur *physician*
Barchas, Jack David *psychiatrist, medical researcher, educator, behavioral molecular neurobiologist*
Barker, Barbara Ann *ophthalmologist*
Barondess, Jeremiah Abraham *physician*
Bartholomew, Lincoln Edwin *physician*
Bauer, Joel J. *surgeon, educator*
Beal, M. Flint *neurologist*
Beard, John *medical educator, researcher*
Beldner, Steven *orthopedist, surgeon*
Belgorod, Barry Miles *surgeon, educator*
Ben-Avi, Simon Stephen *biomedical researcher, educator*
Beraka, George Joseph *plastic surgeon*
Berenstein, Alejandro *neuro-radiologist, educator*
Bergman, Donald Arthur *endocrinologist, educator*
Berman, Carol Wendy *psychiatrist*
Bernstein, Robert M. *dermatologic surgeon*
Berson, Anthony M. *oncologist*
Bessey, Palmer Quintard *surgeon*
Bessler, Marc *surgeon, educator*
Bhargava, Peeyush *nuclear medicine physician*
Bholat, Omar *surgeon*
Bickers, David Rinsey *dermatologist, educator, department chairman, health facility administrator*
Bird, Hector Ramón *child psychiatrist, psychoanalyst, educator*
Black, Henry Richard *physician*
Blaser, Martin Jack *medical educator, researcher*
Blitzer, Andrew *otolaryngologist, educator, research scientist, writer*
Bogdonoff, Morton David *internist, educator*
Borer, Jeffrey Stephen *cardiologist*
Bosl, George Joseph *physician, oncologist*
Brauner, Gary Jules *dermatologist, cosmetic laser surgeon*
Breinin, Goodwin M. *physician*
Brennan, Murray Frederick *surgeon, oncologist*
Brill, Paula Wolfe *radiologist, educator*
Brodie, Jonathan David *psychiatrist, educator*
Brodman, Michael Lewis *gynecologist, educator*
Broumand, Stafford R. *plastic surgeon*
Brown, Arthur Edward *physician*
Brown, Jason Walter *neurologist, educator, researcher*
Brown, Robert Stephen, Jr. *physician*
Brust, John Calvin Morrison *neurologist, educator*
Bryan, Katherine Byram *healthcare executive*
Bussel, James Bruce *pediatrician, obstetrician, gynecologist, educator*
Butler, Vincent Paul, Jr. *internist, educator*
Butts, Hugh Florenz *physician, psychiatrist, psychoanalyst*
Buxton, Douglas Francisco *ophthalmologist, educator*
Bystryn, Jean-Claude *dermatologist, educator*
Cammarata, Angelo *surgical oncologist*
Campbell, Magda *retired child psychiatrist, researcher, educator*
Campolattaro, Brian Nicholas *ophthalmologist, educator*
Cancro, Robert *psychiatrist, educator*
Canetti, Alexandra *psychiatrist*
Cantor, Richard Ira *physician, corporate health executive*
Carroll, William Larkin *medical researcher*
Carucci, John A. *physician*
Casden, Andrew Michael *orthopedist*
Case, David Bartlett *internist, educator*
Case, Robert Brown *physician*
Catalano, Robert Anthony *ophthalmologist, hospital administrator, writer*
Cayne, Neal Scott *surgeon*
Cerfolio, Nina Estelle *psychiatrist, educator*
Chabot, John Anthony *surgeon*
Chandrasekhar, Sujana S. *otologist, educator, neurotologist*
Chang, Stanley *ophthalmologist*
Charash, Bruce D. *cardiologist, educator*
Charlton, Brittany Michelle *public health researcher*
Charon, Rita *internist, medical educator, writer*
Chaudhry, Farooq A. *cardiologist*
Cheema, Faisal Habib *surgeon, researcher*
Chen, Jonathan M. *thoracic surgeon, educator*
Chiu, David Tak Wai *surgeon*
Choe, Won-Taek *neurologist, educator*
Chutorian, Abe M. *pediatrician, educator*
Clark, Sheryl Diane *physician*
Close, Lanny Garth *otolaryngologist, educator*
Coffey, Barbara Jane *psychiatrist*

Cohen, Howard A. *cardiologist*
Cohen, Noel Lee *otolaryngologist, educator*
Cohen, Seymour Martin *oncologist, hematologist, educator*
Coleman, Donald Jackson *ophthalmologist, educator*
Coleman, Morton *oncologist, educator*
Coleman, Sydney Reese *plastic surgeon, educator*
Colen, Helen Sass *plastic surgeon*
Colen, Stephen R. *plastic and reconstructive surgeon*
Coller, Barry Spencer *internist, pathologist, hematologist, educator, department chairman*
Compte, Maria Emilia *physician, educator, administrator*
Constantinides, Minas Spiros *otolaryngologist, plastic surgeon, educator*
Cooney, Michael J. *ophthalmologist*
Cooper, Rubin Seymour *pediatric cardiologist*
Coplan, Neil Lawrence *cardiologist*
Cordeiro, Peter Gabriel *plastic surgeon, medical educator*
Craig, Edward Vincent *orthopedic surgeon, educator*
Crane, Stephen Charles *medical association executive*
Crystal, Ronald G. *medical geneticist, educator*
Cucin, Robert Louis *plastic surgeon, lawyer*
Cunningham-Rundles, Charlotte *physician, educator*
Cuttner, Janet *hematologist, educator*
Davis, Owen Kidder *physician, reproductive endocrinologist*
Debiec, Jacek *psychiatrist, research scientist, educator*
Debrovner, Charles Howard *obstetrician, gynecologist, educator*
Delauney, Sophie *medical relief organization executive*
Del Pizzo, Joseph J. *urologist, educator*
Dermksian, George *cardiologist*
Desloge, Rosemary Byrne *otolaryngologist, educator*
Devinsky, Orrin *neurologist, medical educator*
De Vivo, Darryl Claude *pediatrician, neurologist*
Diaz, Angela *pediatrician, educator*
Diktaban, Theodore *plastic surgeon*
DiMaio, Mary F. *pediatrician*
DiMichele, Donna *medical educator, researcher*
Disa, Joseph James *plastic surgeon*
Dohrenwend, Bruce Philip *epidemiologist, social sciences educator*
Dorfman, Howard David *pathologist, educator*
Downey, Susan E. *plastic surgeon*
Doyle, Eugenie Fleri *pediatrician, cardiologist, educator*
Dreyer, Benard Philip *pediatrician, educator*
Dubois, Michel *anesthesiologist*
Du Mont, Nicolas *psychiatrist, educator*
Dworetzky, Murray *retired physician, educator*
Eddleman, Keith Arnold *obstetrician-gynecologist*
Edelstein, Barbara A. *radiologist*
Eichenfield, Andrew Howard *pediatric rheumatologist*
Einstein, Andrew J. *cardiologist, educator*
Elgert, Paul A. *cytotechnologist*
El-Sadr, Wafaa Mahmoud *epidemiologist, medical educator*
English, Joseph Thomas *psychiatrist, medical administrator*
Epstein, Gerald N. *psychiatrist, educator*
Erlenmeyer-Kimling, L. *psychiatrist, researcher*
Errico, Thomas *neurosurgeon, educator*
Fahey, Thomas *surgeon, educator*
Fahn, Stanley *neurologist, educator*
Felderman, Lenora I. *physician*
Field, Steven Philip *medical educator*
Figgie, Mark Phillips *surgeon*
Fink, Matthew E. *neurologist*
Finlay, Jonathan Lester *pediatric oncologist, educator*
Fins, Joseph Jack *internist, medical ethicist*
First, Michael Bruce *psychiatrist, educator*
Fischer, Avi *medical educator*
Fisher, Edward Abraham *cardiologist, educator*
Fisher, Laura Lani *physician, educator*
Flanagan, Steven *physiatrist*
Flynn, Patrick Alex *pediatric cardiologist*
Foster, Craig Allen *plastic surgeon*
Fox, Arthur Charles *cardiologist, educator*
Frantz, Andrew Gibson *endocrinologist, educator, dean*
Freedman, Michael Leonard *geriatrician, educator*
Freeman, Harold Paul *oncologist, educator, director*
Freire, Maria C. *medical association administrator*
Friedman, Jeffrey M. *medical researcher, educator*
Friedman, Richard Alan *psychiatrist*
Frumkin, William Ira *cardiologist*
Funk, Mark Eugene *medical librarian*
Fuster, Valentin *cardiologist, educator*
Gabrilove, Jacques Lester *physician*
Gadsden, Jeff Charles Frederick *anesthesiologist, director*
Galanter, Marc *psychiatrist, educator*
Gallagher, Mary Patricia *pediatric endocrinologist, researcher*
Gallin, Pamela Frances *pediatric ophthalmologist*
Gandy, Sam *neurologist, neuroscientist, educator*
Garzon, Maria C. *pediatric dermatologist*
Gaynor, Mitchell *oncologist, consultant*
Gebbie, Kristine Moore *medical educator*
Gelmann, Edward Paul *oncologist, educator*
Genden, Eric Michael *otolaryngologist*
Gendler, Ellen *dermatologist*
Germano, Isabelle Margherita *neurosurgeon*
Gersony, Welton Mark *pediatrician, cardiologist, educator*
Gerst, Scott Richard *radiologist, photographer*
Gertler, Menard M. *physician, educator*
Ghesani, Munir *radiologist*
Giardina, Elsa Grace Vonna *cardiologist, educator*
Gilligan, James F. *psychiatrist, educator*
Glasberg, H(erbert) Mark *psychiatrist, educator*
Glasberg, Scot Bradley *plastic surgeon*
Glass, Ronald Bernhard Jacob *radiologist*
Glassman, Alexander Howard *psychiatrist, researcher*
Glesby, Marshall Jay *physician, educator*
Glickman, Robert Morris *medical educator, former dean*
Glickstein, Julie Sue *pediatric cardiologist*
Gliklich, Jerry *physician, educator*
Gobin, Y. Pierre *radiologist, educator*
Godfrey, Norman V. *plastic surgeon*
Gold, Arnold P. *neurologist*
Goldberg, Elkhonon *medical association administrator, educator*
Goldberg, Ira Jay *internist, educator*
Goldberg, Nieca *cardiologist, educator*
Goldfrank, Lewis Robert *physician*
Goldman, Martin Elliot *cardiologist*
Goldsmith, Stanley Joseph *nuclear medicine physician, educator*
Goldstein, Marc *surgeon, urologist, health facility administrator, educator*
Goldstein, Martin S. *obstetrician, gynecologist, educator*
Gordon, Marsha L. *dermatologist*
Grafstein, Bernice *physiology and neuroscience educator, researcher*
Graham, Philip Lamar *epidemiologist, physician*
Granstein, Richard David *dermatologist*
Grant, Alfred David *orthopaedic surgeon, educator*
Green, Wayne Hugo *psychiatrist, psychoanalyst*
Greenwald, Bruce Michael *pediatrician*
Griffiths, Sylvia Preston *physician, educator*
Grifo, James (Jamie) A. *obstetrician, gynecologist*
Grossman, Melanie *dermatologist*
Gruen, Alison Brett *dermatologist*
Grunebaum, Amos *obstetrician, gynecologist*
Guida, Robert Anthony *otolaryngologist, plastic surgeon*
Haddad, Heskel Marshall *ophthalmologist, educator*
Haddad, Joseph, Jr. *pediatric otolaryngologist*
Hadjiangelis, Nicos Pavlos *medical educator, consultant*
Haight, David Hulen *ophthalmologist*
Hamburg, Beatrix Ann *medical educator, researcher*
Hamburg, David A. *psychiatrist, foundation administrator*
Hann, Lucy E. *radiologist, educator*
Harpaz, Noam *medical educator*
Harris, Matthew Nathan *surgeon, educator*
Hartl, Roger *physician, researcher*
Hawkins, Katherine Ann *hematologist, educator, lawyer*
Healey, John Henry *orthopaedic surgeon, researcher*
Henchcliffe, Claire *neurologist, educator*
Henderson, Christopher *pathologist, educator, neuroscientist*
Henschke, Claudia Ingrid *physician, radiologist*
Hensle, Terry W. *pediatric urologist*
Herr, Harry Wallace *medical researcher, educator, surgeon, urologist*
Hertzig, Margaret E. *psychiatrist*
Hidalgo, David Arthur *plastic surgeon*
Hirsch, Jules *physician, researcher*
Hirschhorn, Kurt *pediatrics educator*
Ho, David D. (Da-i Ho) *research physician, virologist, scientific organization director*
Hochberg, Mark Stefan *surgeon*
Hochman, Judith Sheryl *cardiologist, researcher*
Hochster, Howard S. *oncologist*
Hoffman, Lloyd Alan *plastic surgeon*
Holland, Jimmie C. *psychiatrist, educator*
Holt, Peter Rolf *gastroenterologist, educator*
Holzman, Ian Ronald *pediatrician, educator*
Hoppenstein, Reuben *neurosurgeon, healthcare executive*
Horovtiz, Len *internist, pulmonologist*
Hoskins, William John *obstetrician, educator, gynecologist*
Howe, Louise R. *medical educator*
Hsu, Daphne T. *pediatrician, educator*
Hudis, Clifford Alan *internist, oncologist*
Hyman, Bruce Malcolm *ophthalmologist*
Hyman, Joshua E. *pediatric orthopaedic surgeon*
Imber, Gerald *plastic surgeon*
Imparato, Anthony Michael *vascular surgeon, educator, researcher*
Ioachim, Harry L. *pathologist, educator*
Isaacson, Steven Robert *surgeon*
Isom, O(ttis) Wayne *thoracic surgeon, educator*
Jabs, Douglas Alan *ophthalmology professor, chairman, dean*
Jacobs, Stacy *radiologist*
Jacobson, Julius H., II, *vascular surgeon, writer*
Jallo, George Issa *physician*
Jan, Dominique Michel *surgeon, educator*
Jarecki, Henry George *physician, financial planner*
Javitt, Norman B. *medical educator, researcher*
Jelks, Glenn William *plastic surgeon*
Jessell, Thomas M. *medical educator*
Jetter, Robert Bruce *plastic surgeon*
Johnson, Horton Anton *pathologist*
Johnson, Valerie Lynne *pediatric nephrologist, educator*
Jonas, Saran *neurologist, educator*
Josephson, Jordan Stuart *otolaryngologist*
Josephson, Stephen C. *psychiatrist, educator*
Kacker, Ashutosh *medical educator*
Kalsner, Stanley *pharmacologist, physiologist, educator*
Kanick, Virginia *retired radiologist*
Kapelman, Barbara Ann *hepatologist, gastroenterologist, educator*
Kappas, Attallah *physician*
Karasu, T(oksoz) Byram *psychiatrist, educator, writer*
Karp, Nolan Serge *plastic surgeon*
Kato, Tomoaki *surgeon*
Katz, Bruce Elliot *dermatologist*
Kaufman, David Marc *pediatric neurologist*
Kaufmann, Horacio Carlos *professor of neurology, medicine and pediatrics*
Kelly, Patrick Joseph *neurosurgeon, educator*
Kerman, Jules *psychiatrist, educator*
Kim, Chun Ki *radiology and nuclear medicine educator*
Kleber, Herbert David *psychiatrist, educator*
Klein, Donald Franklin *psychiatrist, research scientist, educator*
Klein, Harvey *medical educator*
Klimstra, David S. *pathologist*
Knapp, Albert Bruce *gastroenterologist*
Knapp, Robert Charles *retired obstetrics and gynecology educator*
Kobylarz, Erik Joseph *neurologist, educator*
Kolker, Adam Ross *plastic surgeon, educator*
Kolodny, Edwin Hillel *neurologist, geneticist, director*
Komisar, Arnold *otolaryngologist, educator*
Kopenhaver, Patricia Ellsworth *podiatrist*
Korein, Julius *neurologist*
Kosofsky, Barry E. *pediatric neurologist*
Kourides, Ione Anne *endocrinologist, researcher, educator*
Krieger, Karl Hemingway *cardiothoracic surgeon*
Kuppin, Sara *postdoctoral fellow*
Kushner, Brian Harris *oncologist*
Lahita, Robert George *immunologist*
Lalwani, Anil Kumar *otolaryngologist*
Landreth, Barbara Horan *pediatrician, educator*
Landrigan, Philip John *epidemiologist*
Landry, Donald William *physician, educator, scientist*
Langer, David J. *neurological surgeon*
LaQuaglia, Michael Patrick *pediatric surgeon, neuroblastoma researcher*
Laragh, John Henry *physician, scientist, educator*
Laufer, Ira Jerome *physician*
Laufman, Harold *surgeon, consultant*
Laurence, Jeffrey Conrad *immunologist, educator*
Lawson, William *otolaryngologist, educator*
Lazarus, Herbert *pediatrician, educator*
Lederman, Stephanie *medical association administrator*
Ledger, William Joe *obstetrician, gynecologist, educator*
Leeman, Eve *psychiatrist*
Lefkovits, Albert Meyer *dermatologist*
Legato, Marianne *internist, educator*
Leon, Martin Bert *cardiologist, educator*
Lepor, Herbert *urologist*
Lesesne, Carroll Boutell (Cap Lesesne) *plastic surgeon*
Lessnau, Klaus-Dieter Karl *pulmonologist, director, medical educator*
Levin, Bernard *physician*
Levin, Frances R. *psychiatrist, educator*
Levine, Robert H. *medical educator, psychiatrist*
Levy, Albert *physician*
Levy, Joseph *physician, pediatric gastroenterologist*
Lewis, Blair Seth *gastroenterologist*
Lewis, Jonathan Joseph *surgical oncologist, molecular biologist, educator, entrepreneur*
Lewy, Robert Max *physician*
Libby, Daniel M. *pulmonologist*
Liebowitz, Michael Robert *psychiatrist, educator*
Ligh, Jonathan Kennard *ophthalmologist*
Lincoff, Harvey Allen *ophthalmologist*
Lindsey, Robert J. *medical association administrator*
Lipkin, Martin *medical scientist and educator*
Lipkin, W. Ian *epidemiologist, neurologist, educator*
Lobo, Rogerio Arnaldo *obstetrician, gynecologist*
Lodge, Henry Sears *physician*
Loeb, John Nichols *physician, educator*
Loft, Lloyd Mark *otolaryngologist*
Loo, Marcus Hsieu-Hong *urologist, physician, educator*
Lopez, Ralph Ivan *pediatrics educator*
Loughlin, Gerald M. *pediatrician, educator*
Luntz, Maurice Harold *ophthalmologist*
Lusskin, Shari I. *psychiatrist, educator*
Madhrira, Machaiah M. *nephrologist*
Magramm, Irene *ophthalmologist*
Malkin, Stanley Lee *neurologist*
Manger, William Muir *internist, educator, writer, research scientist*
Marcus, Eric Robert *psychiatrist*
Marin, Deborah B. *psychiatrist, educator*
Marks, Paul Alan *oncologist, cell biologist, educator*
Marx, Robert G. *orthopedic surgeon, educator*
Maslak, Peter George *hematologist*
Masterson, James Francis *psychiatrist*
Matarasso, Alan *plastic and reconstructive surgeon*
Matera, Cristina m *gynecologist, educator*
Mazza, David S. *pediatric allergist, immunologist*
McCance, Sean E. *orthopedist*
McCarthy, Edith A. *pediatrician, educator*
McCarthy, Joseph Gerald *plastic surgeon, educator*
McClelland, Shearwood Junior *orthopaedic surgeon*
McCullough, Andrew Richard *physician*
McDowell, David Michael *psychiatrist, educator, researcher*
Meier, Diane Eve *geriatrician, researcher, medical educator*
Meller, Jose *cardiologist*
Mellins, Robert B. *pediatrician, educator*
Meltzer, Jay Ivan *medical educator*
Merrell, Woodson C. *integrative medicine specialist*
Michelassi, Fabrizio *surgeon*
Michelis, Michael Frank *nephrologist*
Michels, Robert *psychiatrist, educator*
Michelsen, Christopher Bruce Hermann *surgeon*
Middlesworth, William *pediatric surgeon*
Mildvan, Donna *infectious diseases physician*
Milrod, Barbara *psychiatrist*
Mintz, Douglas N. *radiologist*
Mirowski, Piotr *medical researcher*
Mitelman, Serge A. *researcher*
Mohr, Jay Preston *neurologist, educator*
Moline, Jacqueline *occupational physician*
Moore, Anne *physician*
Morrow, Monica *medical educator*
Mortiz, Jacques *obstetrician, gynecologist, educator*
Moses, Jeffrey Warren *cardiologist, educator*
Moss-Salentijn, Letty (Aleida) *anatomist, educator*
Muchnick, Richard Stuart *ophthalmologist, educator*
Murphy, Ramon J.C. (Ramon Jeremiah Castroviejo Murphy) *pediatrician, physician, educator*
Myskowski, Patricia Lois *dermatologist*
Nachamie, Mark Spencer *cardiologist, educator*
Naftolin, Frederick *gynecologist, educator*
Nahas, Gabriel Georges *pharmacologist, educator, writer*
Naidich, Thomas Paul *neuroradiologist, educator*
Naqvi, Nasir Hasnain *psychiatrist, neuroscientist*
Narayanan, Kumaran *medical educator*
Neuwirth, Robert Samuel *obstetrician, gynecologist, educator*
New, Maria Iandolo *pediatrician, educator*
Newhouse, Jeffrey H. *radiologist, educator*
Nho, Shane Jay *surgeon*
Nicholas, Stephen J. *orthopedic surgeon, sports medicine physician*
Nimer, Stephen David *physician, leukemia researcher*
Nimkarn, Saroj *endocrinologist, researcher*
Norton, Larry *oncologist, researcher*
Novick, Nelson Lee *dermatologist, internist, consultant, cosmetic dermasurgeon, writer*
Nussenzweig, Michel Claudio *immunologist, educator*
Oberfield, Sharon Elefant *pediatric endocrinologist*
Oettgen, Herbert Friedrich *physician*
Olsson, Carl Alfred *urologist, department chairman*
Omura, Yoshiaki *medical educator*
Oratz, Ruth *physician*
Ordorica, Steven Anthony *obstetrician, gynecologist, educator*
O'Reilly, Richard John *pediatrician*
Orkin, Louis Richard *physician, educator*
Orlow, Seth J. *dermatologist*
Oz, Mehmet Cengiz *cardiac surgeon*
Palusci, Vincent John *physician, researcher*
Panicek, David *radiologist*
Park, Chae Gyu *immunologist, educator*
Parness, Ira Allen *pediatric cardiologist*
Pastores, Stephen M. *internist*
Paul, Edward Mark *psychiatrist, educator*
Pavlick, Anna Catherine *oncologist, hematologist*
Pearlman, Steven Jay *otolaryngologist, surgeon, educator*
Pedley, Timothy Asbury, IV, *neurologist, educator, researcher*
Perelstein, Eduardo M. *pediatric nephrologist*
Perin, Noel I. *neurosurgeon*
Peter, Bach *epidemiologist, pulmonologist*
Pfeifer, Tracy M. *plastic surgeon*
Phillips, Gerald Baer *internal medicine scientist, educator*
Phillips, Holly L. *internist, medical reporter*
Pierson, Richard Norris, Jr. *medical educator*
Pitman, Gerald H. *plastic surgeon*
Pomp, Alfons *medical educator*
Posner, Jerome Beebe *neurologist, educator*
Post, Martin Roger *cardiologist*
Powell, Simon N. *medical researcher*
Prasad, Mukesh *otolaryngologist*
Prasad, Vinod K. *bone marrow transplantation physician, researcher*
Quackenbush, Margery Clouser *psychoanalyst, researcher*
Quaegebeur, Jan Modest *pediatric thoracic surgeon*
Rabinowitz, Jack Grant *radiologist, educator*
Radevic, Miroslav Rade *pathologist*
Ragnarsson, Kristjan Tomas *physiatrist*
Ramsay, David Leslie *physician, dermatologist, educator*
Rapaport, Robert *pediatric endocrinologist*
Raynor, Richard Benjamin *neurosurgeon, educator*
Reed, Lawrence Samuel *plastic surgeon, medical educator*
Reidenberg, Marcus Milton *physician, educator*
Reisberg, Barry *geriatric psychiatrist, neuropsychopharmacologist*
Reiss, Carol Shoshkes *immunology educator*
Richert, John Rolin *neuroimmunologist, educator*
Rifkind, Arleen B. *pharmacologist, researcher, educator*
Rigel, Darrell Spencer *dermatologist, educator, skin cancer researcher*
Ritch, Robert Harry *ophthalmologist, educator*
Robins, Perry *dermatologist, educator, foundation administrator*
Roland, J. Thomas *surgeon, researcher*
Romano, John Francis *dermatologist*
Romita, Mauro Charles *plastic surgeon*
Rose, Eric Allen *cardiothoracic surgeon*
Rosenbaum, Michael A. *pediatrician, educator*
Rosenblum, Jay Alan *neurologist*
Rosenfeld, Isadore *cardiologist, educator*
Rosenfeld, Suzanne *pediatrician*
Rosner, Ingrid K. *pediatric allergist*
Ross, Joseph Solomon *physician investigator*
Rothe, Desider J. *gynecologist-obstetrician*
Rothschild, Michael Alan *pediatric otolaryngologist, educator*
Roven, Robert Bochner *cardiologist, educator*
Rowland, Lewis Phillip *neurology educator, editor, clinical investigator*
Roye, David P., Jr. *pediatric orthopaedic surgeon*
Rozbruch, S. Robert *orthopedist, researcher*
Rubin, Theodore Isaac *psychiatrist, writer*
Rudloff, Udo *surgeon, researcher*
Rusch, Valerie Williams *thoracic surgeon*
Ruzal-Shapiro, Carrie B. *pediatric radiologist, educator*
Sacco, Ralph Lewis *neurologist*
Sachar, David Bernard *gastroenterologist, educator*
Sacks, Oliver Wolf *neurologist, writer*
Sadick, Neil Scott *dermatologist*
Salgo, Peter Lloyd *internist, writer, anesthesiologist, journalist, commentator*
Salky, Barry A. *surgeon*
Salvati, Edwardo A. *surgeon*
Sampson, Hugh Albert, Jr. *medical educator*
Samson, C. Michael A. *ophthalmologist*
Samuel, Selesnick H. *otolaryngologist, educator*
Saphir, Richard Louis *pediatrician*
Sarnoff, Deborah Susan *dermatologist, educator*
Satlin, Lisa M. *pediatrician, educator*
Savitz, David A. *epidemiologist*
Sawyers, Charles L. *oncologist, hematologist, educator*
Saxena, Brij B. *endocrinologist, biochemist, educator*
Sceusa, Nicholas A. *pharmacologist*
Schachter, Edwin Neil *pulmonologist, educator*
Schafer, Andrew I. *hematologist, department chairman*
Schaffer, Julie V. *pediatric dermatologist, researcher*
Schaffner, Bertram Henry *psychiatrist*

Schiano, Thomas Dominic *hepatologist, director*
Schiff, Howard Irwin *urologist*
Schiff, Nicholas D. *neurologist*
Schlegel, Peter Niles *urologist, educator*
Schlesinger, Sarah Jane *medical educator, researcher*
Schley, William Shain *otolaryngologist*
Schuster, Carlotta Lief *psychiatrist*
Schwartz, Allan *cardiologist*
Schwartz, Theodore H. *neurosurgeon*
Sclafani, Anthony Paul *plastic surgeon, educator, biomedical researcher*
Sclafani, Lisa *surgeon, educator*
Scott, Susan Craig *plastic surgeon*
Sculco, Thomas Peter *surgeon*
Sealey-Laragh, Jean E. *emeritus medical educator, researcher*
Seely, Robert Daniel *cardiologist, medical association administrator*
Serulle, Yafell *medical researcher*
Shah, Jatin Premanand *head and neck surgeon, educator*
Shapiro, Theodore *psychiatrist, educator*
Sharma, Samin Kumar *internist, interventional cardiologist, educator*
Sharma, Vanshdeep *psychiatrist*
Shepherd, Gillian Mary *physician*
Sherman, John Eric *plastic surgeon*
Sherman, Spencer E. *ophthalmologist*
Shupack, Jerome Leonard *dermatologist, educator*
Sicherer, Scott H. *pediatric allergist, researcher*
Siebert, John Weston *plastic surgeon*
Sigal, Samuel Harold *gastroenterologist*
Siller, Keith A. *neurologist, psychiatrist*
Silver, Richard Tobias *oncologist, educator, hematologist*
Sitarz, Anneliese Lotte *pediatrician, educator*
Skolnik, Richard Alan *plastic surgeon*
Smith, Craig Richey *cardiothoracic surgeon*
Smith, Michael W. *physician, medical editor*
Snyderman, Nancy *surgeon, journalist*
Sobel, Howard D. *dermatologist*
Sockolow, Robbyn Ellen *pediatrician*
Softness, Barney *pediatrician, educator*
Som, Peter M. *radiologist*
Soto, Claudio *medical educator*
Spector, Jason A. *plastic surgeon, educator*
Sperber, Alan B. *urologist*
Spinelli, Henry Michael *plastic surgeon*
Springfield, Dempsey Stewart *physician, educator*
Srichai-Parsia, Monvadi Barbara *cardiologist, educator*
Steele, Mark A. *pediatric ophthalmologist*
Stein, Joel *physiatrist*
Stein, Marvin *psychiatrist, historian*
Stein, Richard Alan *cardiologist, educator*
Steinberg, Jonathan S. *cardiologist, educator*
Steinglass, Peter Joseph *psychiatrist, educator*
Steinman, Ralph M. *medical educator*
Stelwagon, Jennifer Cooper *psychiatrist*
Stelzer, Paul *thoracic surgeon, educator*
Stern, Nathalie M. *pediatrician*
Stieg, Philip *neurosurgeon*
Stifelman, Michael D. *surgeon, director*
Stimmel, Barry *cardiologist, internist, dean, educator*
Stock, Richard John *cardiologist*
Stolar, Charles J.H. *pediatrician, surgeon, educator*
Stone, Michael Howard *psychiatry educator*
Stoopler, Mark Benjamin *physician*
Strauchen, James Arthur *medical educator, pathologist*
Strauss, Eric Jason *orthopedist*
Strome, Marshall *otolaryngologist, educator*
Strongwater, Allan *orthopedist, director*
Stübgen, Joerg-Patrick *neurologist*
Su, Edwin *orthopedist*
Sultan, Mark R. *plastic surgeon*
Swift, Ronnie Gorman *psychiatrist, educator*
Swistel, Daniel George *surgeon*
Tabbal, Nicolas G. *plastic surgeon*
Taha, Assad M. *surgeon*
Talmor, Mia *plastic surgeon*
Tan, Chin-Tuan *medical educator, engineering educator, consultant*
Tancredi, Laurence Richard *medical educator, psychiatrist*
Tehrany, Armin M. *orthopedic surgeon, educator*
Teirstein, Alvin Stanley *physician*
Tenenbaum, Joseph *cardiologist*
Thebner, Lisa Ilene *pediatrician*
Thorne, Charles Hedges McKinstry *plastic surgeon*
Tilson, M(artin) David III *surgeon, scientist, educator*
Tolchin, Joan Gubin *psychiatrist, educator*
Tortolani, Anthony John *surgeon, educator*
Trestman, Robert Lee *psychiatrist, educator, administrator*
Tuhrim, Stanley *physician, neurologist*
Turino, Gerard Michael *internist, educator*
Turk, Jon Branden *plastic surgeon*
Turtil, Lawrence Charles *psychiatrist*
Tzimas, Nicholas Achilles *orthopedic surgeon, educator*
Urban, Nina B.L. *psychiatrist, psychotherapist, researcher*
Vaughan, Edwin Darracott, Jr. *urologist, surgeon*
Véronneau-Troutman, Suzanne *retired ophthalmologist*
Vilcek, Jan Tomas *immunologist, medical educator*
Vlahov, David *epidemiologist*
Vogel, James M. *hematologist, oncologist*
Walden, Jennifer Lee *plastic surgeon*
Walsh, Joseph Brennan *ophthalmologist*
Waner, Milton *otolaryngologist, pediatric facial plastic surgeon*
Wang, Frederick Mark *pediatrician, ophthalmologist, educator*
Ward, Robert F. *pediatric otolaryngologist*
Warren, Michelle Palmieri *internist, endocrinologist*
Warren, Russell Frederick *orthopedist*
Warren, Stephen Michael *plastic surgeon*
Wayne, Michael G. *surgeon*
Weiss, Carol Juliet *psychiatrist*
Weiss, Paul Richard *plastic surgeon*
Wells, John Timothy *pediatric neurologist*
Werman, David Sanford *psychiatrist, psychoanalyst*
West, Alexander Brian *pathologist*
Westhoff, Carolyn Louise *obstetrician, gynecologist, epidemiologist, educator*
Westrich, Geoffrey Howard *orthopaedic surgery*
Wexler, Leonard Howard *pediatric oncologist*
Wexler, Patricia Susan *dermatologist, surgeon*
Whang, William *cardiologist*
Wharton, Ralph Nathaniel *psychiatrist, educator*
Widmann, Roger Franklin *Pediatric Orthopaedic Surgeon*
Winawer, Sidney J. *physician, educator*
Winchester, James Frank *medicine educator*
Winick, Myron *nutrition professor, physician*
Winn, H. Richard *surgeon*
Winston, Arnold *psychiatrist, educator*
Wolden, Suzanne Leesa *pediatric radiation oncologist*
Wolf, Carl F.W. *retired pathologist, consultant*
Wolk, Michael Jay *cardiologist, educator*
Wood-Smith, Donald *plastic surgeon*
Worman, Howard Jay *internist, educator*
Yankelevitz, David F. *radiologist, educator*
Yeh, Hsu-Chong *radiology educator*
Youm, Thomas *orthopedist, surgeon*
Young, Bruce Kenneth *obstetrician, gynecologist, educator*
Young, Estelle Irene *dermatologist, educator*
Yurt, Roger William *surgeon, educator*
Yutaka, Nibu *medical educator*
Zaidi, Mone *endocrinologist, educator*
Zeichner, Joshua A. *dermatologist*
Zhuge, Jian *medical educator, researcher*
Zimbler, Marc S. *plastic surgeon, director*
Zinn, Keith Marshall *ophthalmologist, educator*
Zitrin, Arthur *physician*
Zucker-Franklin, Dorothea *internist, educator*
Zuckerman, Joseph D. *orthopedist, surgeon*

Newburgh
Grossman, Stanley Lawrence *surgeon*

Niskayuna
Asma, Evren *medical imaging researcher*

Northport
Adyanthaya, Rohit *ophthalmologist, researcher*
Graber, Mark L. *internist*
Lake-Bakaar, Gerond Vidal *gastroenterologist*

Oceanside
Zimmerman, Thomas Glenn *physician, educator*

Old Westbury
Dedkov, Eduard I. *medical educator*

Orangeburg
Basavarajappa, Balapal *medical researcher, educator*
Levine, Jerome *psychiatrist, educator*
Nixon, Ralph Angus *psychiatrist, educator, research neuroscientist*

Orchard Park
Lee, Richard Vaille *internist, educator*

Pawling
Caplan, Ronald Mervyn *obstetrician, gynecologist*

Penfield
Chen, Alice W. *mycologist biomedical researcher*

Pittsford
Faloon, William Wassell *physician, educator*

Plainview
Kelemen, John *neurologist, educator*

Plattsburgh
Bedworth, David Albert *health educator*

Port Jefferson
Ahmad, Arif *surgeon*

Port Washington
Rogatz, Peter *retired physician*

Poughkeepsie
Hansraj, Kenneth Karamchand *surgeon, research scientist*

Purchase
Frost, Elizabeth Ann McArthur *physician*

Queensbury
De Pan, Harry McCarthy *retired surgeon*

Rego Park
Davidov, Ludmila G. *psychiatrist*
Robbins, Michael J. *cardiologist*

Rhinebeck
Crum, Albert B. *psychiatrist, consultant*

Richmond Hill
Gintautas, Jonas *physician, scientist, administrator*

Riverdale
Klampfer, Lidija *medical educator*

Riverhead
Pearson, John William *cardiologist*
Scherzer, Alfred L. *developmental pediatrician*

Rochester
Abu-Baker, Asim Mohammed *medical educator*
Apostolakos, Michael John *medical educator, director*
Baumhaver, Judith Ford *surgeon*
Bidlack, Jean Marie *pharmacologist, educator, researcher*
Blumberg, Neil *hematologist, educator*
Brody, Bernard B. *internist, educator*
Burton, Richard Irving *orthopedist, educator*
Bushinsky, David Allen *nephrologist, educator, researcher*
Chen, Guangchun *medical researcher*
Chey, William Yoon *physician*
Cohen, Nicholas *immunologist, educator*
Corsetti, James Pasquale *pathologist, medical educator*
Deveikis, John P. *radiologist*
Dolan, William A. *orthopedist, medical educator*
Dreyfuss, Eric Martin *allergist*
Farmer, Richard Gilbert *academic physician, foundation administrator*
Finkelstein, Jacob Noah *pediatrics and toxicology educator*
Ghazle, Hamad *medical educator, director*
Goepp, Julius George Konrad *pediatrician, consultant*
Guo, Hailong *immunologist, researcher*
Hall, Caroline Breese *pediatrician, educator*
Haywood, Anne Mowbray *pediatrician, educator*
Hyman, Susan L. *pediatrician, educator*
Jean-Pierre, Pascal *oncologist, educator*
Jiang, Rulang *biomedical researcher, educator*
Kashyap, Randeep *surgeon*
Khorana, Alok Anand *oncologist, medical researcher*
Kurlan, Roger *neurologist, educator*
Langstein, Howard Neil *plastic surgeon*
Lichtman, Marshall Albert *hematologist, medical educator, research scientist*
Liptak, Gregory Stephen *pediatrician, educator*
Logigian, Eric L. *neurologist*
Lyness, Jeffrey Marc *psychiatrist, educator*
Marshall, Frederick J. *neurologist, educator*
McDonald, Joseph Valentine *neurosurgeon*
McMeekin, Thomas Owen *dermatologist*
Moss, Arthur Jay *physician*
Nazarian, Lawrence Fred *pediatrician*
Notter, Robert H. *biomedical researcher, educator*
Palis, James *pediatrician*
Pearson, Thomas Arthur *epidemiologist, educator*
Phillips, Gordon Leigh, II, *oncologist*
Porsteinsson, Anton P. *medical educator, director*
Powers, James Matthew *neuropathologist, educator, researcher*
Pryhuber, Gloria Salvini *pediatrician, educator*
Ritchlin, Christopher Trevor *rheumatologist*
Schneider, Sandra McEwen *emergency physician educator*
Shortell, Cynthia K. *vascular surgeon*
Shoulson, Ira *neurologist, pharmacologist, educator*
Sparks, Charles Edward *pathologist, educator*
Sparks, Janet Lindsay Dehoff *pathologist, educator*
Suchman, Anthony Lee *physician, consultant*
Utell, Mark Jeffrey *medical educator*
White, Ann Marie *medical educator*
Williams, Marc Adrian *medical educator, scientist, researcher*
Williams, Thomas Franklin *physician, educator*

Rockville Centre
Teyan, Frederick Gene *pediatrician*

Roslyn
Greenberg, Steven M. *physician*
Hartman, Nancy Lee *physician*
Mazlen, Roger Geoffrey *internist, pharmacologist*
Robinson, Newell Bruce *cardiothoracic surgeon*
Shlofmitz, Richard Alan *cardiologist*

Rye
Barker, Harold Grant *surgeon, educator*
Curtin, Brian Joseph *retired ophthalmologist*
Waltz, Joseph McKendree *neurosurgeon, educator*

Sands Point
Lear, Erwin *anesthesiologist, educator*

Scarsdale
Jacobs, Theodore Joseph *psychiatrist, educator*
Lipman, Marvin Matthew *physician, medical educator, editor, writer*
Mercando, Anthony Dominic *cardiologist*
Moser, Marvin *physician, educator, author*
Rovit, Richard Lee *neurosurgeon*
Soley, Robert Lawrence *plastic surgeon*

Schenectady
Depan, Harry John *cardiothoracic surgeon*
Schenck, John Frederic *physician*

Scotia
de la Rocha, Carlos A. *retired physician*

Slingerlands
Ipsen, Carol Anne *psychiatrist, educator*

Smithtown
Tuzel, Suzanne L. *psychiatrist*

Somers
Bauman, William Allen *pediatrician, educator, health systems consultant*
Reznick, Steven Michael *orthopedic surgeon, educator*
Rubin, Samuel Harold *internist, consultant*

Staten Island
Bruckstein, Alex Harry *internist, gastroenterologist, geriatrician*
Ferzli, George Salem *surgeon*
Israeli, Ron Samuel *urologist*
Popler, Kenneth *behavioral health services administrator, psychologist*
Sheka, Kedambady P. *surgeon*
Winter, Steven *internist, cardiologist*

Stony Brook
Andriola, Mary Repole *neurologist, pediatrician*
Badalamente, Marie Ann *orthopedist, educator*
Baker, David A. *obstetrician, gynecologist, educator*
Corman, Marvin Leonard *surgeon, educator*
Dagum, Alexander B. *plastic surgeon*
Fine, Richard Nisan *pediatrician, educator, dean*
Fritts, Harry Washington, Jr. *retired internist, educator*
Gelato, Marie Catherine *physician, clinical investigator, educator*
Glass, Peter Stanley Abraham *anesthesiologist, educator*
Hurst, Lawrence *orthopedic surgeon*
Jaber, Rajaa *physician, educator*
Jasiewicz, Ronald Clarence *anesthesiologist, educator, osteopath*
Jonas, Steven *preventive medicine physician, author*
Kuchner, Eugene Frederick *neurosurgeon, neuroscientist, educator*
Landman, Ursula N. *anesthesiologist*
Liang, Jerome Zhengrong *radiology educator*
Meliker, Jaymie R. *medical educator*
Meltzer, Donna *medical educator*
Meyers, Morton Allen *radiologist, educator*
Miller, Frederick *pathologist*
Monheit, Alan Goodman *obstetrician, gynecologist*
Rosengart, Todd Kenneth *cardiothoracic surgeon, researcher, neurosurgeon, consultant*
Seifert, Frank C. *thoracic surgeon*
Shroyer, Kenneth Reed *medical educator, department chairman*
Steigbigel, Roy Theodore *epidemiologist, educator, research scientist*
Tassiopoulos, Apostolos K. *vascular surgeon*
Varadaraj, Kulandaiappan *medical researcher, educator*
Weisbrot, Deborah Marcia *psychiatrist*
Williams, Peter C. *medical association administrator*
Wittpenn, John Ryder *ophthalmologist, consultant*

Suffern
Codispoti, Andre John *allergist, immunologist*

Syracuse
Badawy, Shawky Z.A. *gynecologist, educator*
Baker, Bruce Edward *orthopedic surgeon, consultant*
Becker, Lorne Arthur *family physician*
Caldicott, Catherine V. *medical educator, researcher*
Canute, Gregory William *neurosurgeon*
Carey, Robert J. *medical educator*
Choudhary, Madhuchhanda *epidemiologist, educator*
Cusato, Karen *medical educator*
Fortune, John B. *medical educator*
Gold, Joseph *medical researcher*
Hodge, Charles Joseph, Jr. *neurosurgeon, educator*
Kane, Peter Bayard *physician*
Kaplan, Eugene Alken *psychiatry professor, department chairman*
King, Robert Bainton *neurosurgeon, educator*
McCabe, John B. *emergency physician, health science association administrator*
Phillips, Paul Everard *medical educator, rheumatologist*
Rabuzzi, Daniel D. *medical association administrator*
Streeten, Barbara Wiard *ophthalmologist, medical educator*
Szasz, Thomas Stephen *psychiatrist, educator, writer*
Williams, William Joseph *retired hematologist, educator*
Wolff, L. Thomas *physician, educator*

Tarrytown
Field, Barry Elliot *internist, gastroenterologist*
Sullivan, Janet Nelson *dermatologist, department chairman, health facility administrator*

Tonawanda
Stall, Robert *geriatrician*

Troy
Kaye, Gordon Israel *pathologist, educator, waste management consultant*

Tuxedo Park
Dai, Wei *biomedical researcher*
Regan, Ellen Frances (Mrs. Walston Shepard Brown) *ophthalmologist, educator*
Zelikoff, Judith Terry *medical educator, consultant*

Upton
Hamilton, Leonard Derwent *physician, molecular biologist*
Henn, Fritz Albert *psychiatrist*

Valhalla
Aronow, Wilbert Solomon *physician, educator*
Cohen, Martin Bruce *physician*
Del Guercio, Louis Richard Maurice *surgeon, educator*
Golombek, Sergio Gustavo *pediatrician, educator, neonatologist*
Inchiosa, Mario Anthony, Jr. *pharmacologist*
Kline, Susan Anderson *internist, dean, educator*
Lerner, Robert Gibbs *internist, hematologist, educator*
Liu, Delong *oncologist, hematologist*
Marks, Stephen J. *neurologist, educator*
McGoldrick, Kathryn Elizabeth *anesthesiologist, educator, writer*
Palaniswamy, Chandrasekar *surgeon, researcher*
Parton, Lance A. *pediatrician, educator*
Quilley, John *medical educator, researcher*
Recchia, Fabio Anastasio *medical educator*
Reed, George Elliott *surgeon, educator, dean*
Safai, Bijan *physician, investigator*
Selman, Jay E. *neurologist*
Weinstein, Arthur *rheumatologist, educator*
Williams, Gary Murray *pathologist, educator*
Yang, Yang-Ming *medical educator*

Vestal
Grinberg, Raul *internist*

Wantagh
Luchs, Jodi Ian *ophthalmologist*

Washingtonville
Casazza, Sharen *pediatrician*

Water Mill
Hagstrom, Jack Walter Carl Kling *retired pathology educator*

West Harrison
Boczko, Judd *urologist, educator*

West Islip
Cokinos, Stephan George *cardiologist*
Rifkin, Matthew D. *radiologist*

White Plains
Baran, Xiaolei Yu *physician, psychiatry professor*
Bernard, Robert William *plastic surgeon*
Blass, John Paul *physician, biochemist*
Eil, Lois Helen *retired physician*
Fleischman, Alan Robert *medical educator, administrator*
Katz, Michael *pediatrician, educator*
Kirschenbaum, Ira H. *orthopedist*
Marano, Anthony Joseph *cardiologist*
Morello, Daniel Conway *plastic surgeon*
Munich, Richard Lee *psychiatrist*
Narins, Rhoda S. *dermatologist, educator*
Pfeffer, Cynthia Roberta *psychiatrist, educator*
Shamoian, Charles Anthony *psychiatrist, educator*
Streisand, Robert L. *thoracic surgeon*
Weisburger, John Hans *retired medical researcher*

Williamsville
Neiman, Joseph Bruce *dermatologist, educator*
Ogra, Pearay L. *pediatrician, educator*
Reisman, Robert E. *allergist, educator*
Rekate, Albert C. *physician*

Woodbury
Greenberg, Stephen Todd *plastic surgeon*

Yorktown Heights
Mayer, Gerard J. *physician*

NORTH CAROLINA

Advance
Guth, Caryl Joy *retired anesthesiologist*

Arden
Leacock, Rodney Owen *neurologist, educator*

Banner Elk
Hutcheson, James Sterling *retired physician, allergist*

Black Mountain
Blackwell, Anna Nelle *medical educator, medical technician*

Burlington
Brennan, Michael W. *ophthalmologist*
Wilson, William Preston *retired psychiatrist*

Camp Lejeune
Kuhn, Michael A. *orthopedist*

Carrboro
Prather, Donna Lynn *psychiatrist*

Cary
Dreyer, Duane Arthur *medical educator*
Kennedy, Andrew Scott *nuclear medicine physician, educator*

Chapel Hill
Atashili, Julius *epidemiologist*
Ballard, David Eugene *anesthesiologist*
Barrett, Stephen *psychiatrist, educator, consultant*
Bender, Deborah E. *medical educator*
Benjamin, John Tabb *retired pediatrician*
Bennett, Peter Brian *medical researcher, educator*
Bernard, Stephen Alan *oncologist*
Buse, John Bernard *physician, educator*
Callahan, Leigh Fleming *medical educator, researcher*
Campion, Edmund Ronan *orthopedist, educator*
Carey, Lisa Anne *oncologist, educator*
Carson, Culley Clyde III *urologist, educator*
Cohen, Myron *epidemiologist*
Collier, Albert M. *pediatrician, educator, director*
D'Ercole, Augustine Joseph *pediatrician, educator*
Dohlman, Henrik Gunnar *medical educator, department vice chairman*
Drake, Amelia F. *otolaryngologist*
Drossman, Douglas Arnold *medical investigator, gastroenterologist, educator*
Egan, Thomas Michael *surgeon, educator*
Escolar, Maria L. *pediatrician, educator*
Feins, Richard Harry *thoracic surgeon*
Fletcher, Suzanne Wright *epidemiologist, medical educator, editor*
Fordham, Lynn Ansley *pediatric radiologist*
Fowler, W. Craig *ophthalmologist, educator*
Frantz, Elman G. *pediatric cardiologist, surgeon*
Garbutt, James C. *psychiatrist, educator*
Gold, Stuart Harrison *pediatrician*
Goldberg, Richard Miles *physician, medical oncologist*
Goldsmith, Lowell Alan *medical educator*
Goyer, Robert Andrew *pathology educator*
Greenwood, Robert Samuel *pediatric neurologist*
Greganti, Mac Andrew *physician, educator*
Gregory, Patricia Caroline *medical educator*
Hadler, Nortin Marvin *rheumatologist, clinical investigator, educator*
Hamrick, Harvey J. *pediatrician*
Henry, G. William *pediatrician*
Henson, O'Dell Williams, Jr. *retired anatomy educator*
Hines, Ian Neil *immunologist, educator*
Hirsch, Philip Francis *pharmacologist, educator*
Hulka, Jaroslav Fabian *obstetrician, gynecologist*
Hurwitz, Shepard Raphael *orthopaedic surgeon, educator*
Kakoki, Masao *medical educator*
Kampov-Polevoi, Alexei Boris *psychiatrist, educator*
Kaufman, David Gordon *medical educator*
Lohr, Jacob Andrew *pediatrician, educator*
Margolis, David Michael *medical educator*
Martikainen, A(une) Helen *retired health specialist educator*
Miller, C. Arden *physician, educator*
Moll, Stephan *medical educator*
Morrell, Dean Scott *pediatric dermatologist*
Muss, Hyman Bernard *oncologist, educator*
Peacock, Erle Ewart, Jr. *surgeon, lawyer, educator*
Peterson, Herbert Bryson *obstetrician, gynecologist, educator*
Pillsbury, Harold Crockett III *otolaryngologist*
Pisano, Etta D. *radiologist, educator*
Piven, Joseph *psychiatrist, educator*
Retsch-Bogart, George Z. *pediatric pulmonologist, surgeon*
Runyan, Desmond Kimo *medical educator, researcher*
Schrock, Robert D., Jr. *retired orthopaedic surgeon, educator*
Shaheen, Nicholas J. *epidemiologist, educator*
Sheldon, George Frank *medical educator*
Smith, Sidney Crawle, Jr. *cardiologist, educator*
Sorenson, James Roger *public health educator*
Sparling, Philip Frederick *medical educator*
Spencer, Roger Felix *psychiatrist, educator*
Stockman, James Anthony III *pediatrician*
Stouffer, George Andrew *cardiologist, educator*
Taft, Timothy Ned *orthopedist, surgeon, sports medicine physician*
Thomas, Colin Gordon, Jr. *surgeon, medical educator*
Thorp, John Mercer, Jr. *physician*
Tie, Jian-Ke *medical educator*
Tolley, Aubrey Granville *psychiatrist, health facility administrator*
von Allmen, Daniel *pediatric surgeon*
Weinberg, Richard J. *medical educator*
Weiner, Timothy M. *pediatric surgeon*
West, Alisha Nicole *otolaryngologist, surgeon*
Wilfert, Catherine M. *medical association administrator, pediatrician, epidemiologist, educator*
Williams, Mark Edward *geriatrician*
Wilson, Frank Crane, Jr. *orthopedist*
Winfield, John Buckner *rheumatologist, educator*

Charlotte
Al-Ruzzeh, Sharif *cardiothoracic surgeon*
Eaves, Felmont Farrell III *plastic surgeon*
Hall, James Bryan *gynecologist, oncologist*
Hunstad, Joseph Paul *plastic surgeon, educator*
Jacobs, Gordon Waldemar *surgeon, educator*
Schafermeyer, Robert William *emergency physician, educator, health policy consultant*
Thompson, John Albert, Jr. *dermatologist*

Concord
Langford, Francis Page Johns *otolaryngologist*
Peterson, Ralph E. *endocrinologist, researcher*

Durham
Albala, David Mois *urologist, educator*
Amaya-Jackson, Lisa *psychiatrist*
Anderson, William Banks, Jr. *ophthalmology educator*
Anlyan, William George *surgeon, educator, academic administrator*
Anscher, Mitchell Steven *physician, educator*
Asrani, Sanjay *ophthalmologist*
Bashore, Thomas Michael *cardiologist, educator*
Bennett, Charles Lee *medical educator*
Berchuck, Andrew *gynecologic oncologist, educator*
Blazer, Dan German, II, *psychiatrist, epidemiologist*
Bollinger, Ralph Randal *surgeon, researcher*
Bordley, William Clayton (Clay) *pediatrician, educator*
Borges-Neto, Salvador *radiologist, cardiologist, educator*
Bradford, William Dalton *pathologist, educator*
Bravender, Terrill (Terry) D. *pediatrician*
Brodie, Harlow Keith Hammond *psychiatrist, educator*
Buckley, Rebecca Hatcher *allergist, immunologist, pediatrician, educator*
Califf, Robert McKinnon *cardiologist, educator*
Chang, Zheng *medical educator*
Cohen, Harvey Jay *geriatrician, hematologist, oncologist, educator*
Colvin, O. Michael *medical association administrator, educator*
Cook-Deegan, Robert Mullan *physician, educator*
Coppridge, Alton James *urological surgeon*
Cushman, Ian *biomedical researcher*
Desjardins, Annick *medical educator*
Donatucci, Craig F. *urologist, educator*
Douglas, Pamela Susan *physician, researcher, educator*
Edwards, Christopher Levon *medical association administrator*
Elmore, Susan A. *pathologist*
Fairbank, John A. *psychiatrist, educator*
Falletta, John Matthew *pediatrician, educator*
Fitch, Robert D. *orthopedic surgeon*
Foreman, John William *pediatrician, educator*
Freedland, Stephen Jay *urologist*
Freedman, Sharon Fridovich *opthalmologist*
Friedman, Allan Howard *neurosurgeon*
Frothingham, Thomas Eliot *pediatrician*
Gainetdinov, Raul Radikovich *pharmacologist, researcher*
Garst, Jennifer *oncologist*
Georgiade, Gregory Stephen *plastic surgeon, educator*
Giannopoulos, Athina *physician, surgeon*
Greenfield, Joseph Cholmondeley, Jr. *physician, educator*
Gutman, Robert Allan *nephrologist*
Hammond, Charles Bessellieu *obstetrician, gynecologist, educator*
Hardaker, William Thomas *orthopedist, director*
Harrington, Robert A. *cardiologist*
Harrison, Dean Thomas *medical educator*
Haynes, Barton Ford *medical educator*
Isaacs, Robert Eric *neurosurgeon*
James, Sherman Athonia *epidemiologist, educator*
Jennings, Robert Burgess *experimental pathologist, medical educator*
Jirtle, Randy *medical educator, geneticist*
Katz, Samuel Lawrence *pediatrician, researcher*
Kirkpatrick, John Paxton *oncologist, educator*
Kishnani, Priya Sunil *medical geneticist*
Koepke, John Arthur *hematologist, clinical pathologist*
Krishnan, Krishnaswamy Ranga Rama R. *psychiatry educator*
Lefkowitz, Robert Joseph *biomedical researcher, educator*
Levin, Lawrence Scott *plastic surgeon*
Lopes, Renato Delascio *cardiologist, researcher*
Lyman, Gary Herbert *epidemiologist, cancer researcher, educator*
MacIntyre, Neil Ross, Jr. *medical educator*
Marcom, Paul Kelly *oncologist*
Masand, Prakash S. *psychiatrist, researcher*
Matchar, David B. *physician, researcher*
Michener, James Lloyd *medical educator*
Murphy, Thomas Miles *pediatrician, educator*
Newgard, Christopher B. *medical educator*
Nicandri, Gregg Thomas *orthopedist*
O'Connor, Christopher M. *cardiologist*
Ohman, E. Magnus *cardiologist, educator*
Ostbye, Truls *medical researcher, educator*
Parkerson, George Robert, Jr. *medical educator*
Pizzo, Salvatore Vincent *pathologist*
Preminger, Glenn Michael *urologist, surgeon*
Prose, Neil Stuart *pediatric dermatologist*
Rao, Sunil V. *cardiologist, educator*
Raynor, Eileen Margolies *otolaryngologist, educator*
Robboy, Stanley J. *pathologist, educator*
Sampson, John Howard *neurosurgeon, educator*
Sanders, Donald Benjamin *neurologist, educator*
Shelburne, John Daniel *pathologist*
Smith, Peter K. *cardiothoracic surgeon*
Stacy, Mark Allen *neurologist*
Svetkey, Laura Pat *nephrologist*
Swamy, Geeta K. *obstetrician, gynecologist*
Syn, Wing-Kin *gastroenterologist, hepatologist, researcher*
Taekman, Jeffrey Marc *anesthesiologist*
Tcheng, James Enlou *physician*
Tedder, Thomas Fletcher *immunology educator, researcher*
Thompson, William Moreau *radiologist, educator*
Ulshen, Martin Howard *pediatric gastroenterologist, researcher*
Vaslef, Steven Nicholas *surgeon*
Vredenburgh, James Joseph *medical educator*
Wilkins, Robert Henry *neurosurgeon, editor, educator*
Williams, Redford Brown *medical educator*
Wilson, Joanne A.P. *gastroenterologist, educator*
Young, Terri L. *ophthalmologist*
Zenn, Michael Robert *plastic and reconstructive surgeon*

Elizabeth City
Khan, Sultana Ahmed *medical educator, director*

Ellerbe
Rankin, Pressley Robinson, Jr. *physician*

Fayetteville
Greene, Walter Blair *pediatric orthopedist*

Flat Rock
Weill, Hans *medical educator*

Four Oaks
Jordan, Lyndon Kirkman *physician*

Greensboro
Bratton, Teresa Sue *pediatrician*
Brodie, Bruce Rogers *cardiologist*
Houston, Frank Matt *dermatologist*
Roberts, Kenneth Barry *pediatrician*

Greenville
Allison, Ron *oncologist, researcher*
Babb, Joseph Dolby *physician*
Ferguson, Thomas Bruce, Jr. *cardiothoracic surgeon*
Habal, Nizar *oncologist, surgeon, educator*
Lee, Kenneth Stuart *neurosurgeon, educator*
Lewis, Michael Justin *medical educator*
Newton, Edward R. *obstetrician, educator*
Painter, Jane A. *medical educator*
Perkin, Ronald Murray *pediatrician, educator*
Pories, Walter Julius *surgeon, educator*
Steinweg, Kenneth K. *medical educator, department chairman*
Waugh, William Howard *physician, research scientist*

Henderson
Serafin, Donald *plastic surgeon, educator*

Hendersonville
Roberts, James Allen *retired urologist, educator*

Hickory
Lefler, Wade Hampton, Jr. *ophthalmologist*

High Point
Bardelas, Jose Antonio *allergist*
Draelos, Zoe Diana *dermatologist, consultant*
Kandt, Raymond S. *neurologist*

Hillsborough
Johnston, William Webb *pathologist, educator*

Huntersville
Atrak, Taisser M. *pediatrician, director*

Lenoir
Warrick, Paul David *otolaryngologist*

Monroe
Taylor, Jimmy Lynn *retired family practice physician, administrator*

Morganton
Hawkins, Seth C. *physician*

Morrisville
Wiegerink, Robin L. *medical association administrator*

Murphy
Jordan, Barbara Moore *retired psychiatrist*

New Bern
McKee, Francis John *medical association consultant, lawyer*

Pine Knoll Shores
Graham, Gloria Flippin *dermatologist*

Pittsboro
Herman-Giddens, Marcia Edwina *physician associate*

Raleigh
Barish, Charles Franklin *internist, gastroenterologist, researcher*
Bateman, Angela Anderson *anesthetist*
Gordon, Morris Aaron *medical mycologist*
Hardison, Cynthia Ann Stoltze *retired hematologist, oncologist*
Parsons, William Jonathan *cardiologist*
Riviere, Jim Edmond *pharmacologist, toxicologist, educator*
Shea, Katherine Marie *physician, consultant*
Speer, Kevin Paul *surgeon*

Research Triangle Park
Gavin, Norma Irene *medical researcher*
Waters, Michael Dee *corporate scientific officer, consultant*

Salisbury
Crowe, John Albert, Jr. *surgeon*

Southern Pines
Warren, Donald William *medical and dental educator*

Tryon
Mellberg, James Richard *retired dental research chemist*

Waxhaw
Edwards, Irene Elizabeth (Libby Edwards) *dermatologist, educator, researcher*

Wilmington
Boyle, Joseph Hugh *psychiatrist*
Gonzalez, Jorge Jose *medical educator*

Wilson
Kushner, Michael James *neurologist, consultant, educator*
Ladwig, Harold Allen *neurologist*

Winston Salem
Atala, Anthony John *surgeon*
Baillie, John (Nmn) *gastroenterologist*
Dean, Richard Henry *surgeon, educator*
Dyer, Raymond B. *diagnostic radiology physician*
Eldridge, J. Charles *endocrinologist, educator, researcher*
Ellis, Thomas L. *neurosurgeon, educator*
Hammon, John William, Jr. *medical educator, thoracic surgeon*
Hill, Ivor Dennis *pediatrician, educator*
James, Francis Marshall III *anesthesiologist*
Jeevanantham, Vinodh *medical educator, researcher*
Kaur, Mandeep *dermatologist, educator*
Kohut, Robert Irwin *otolaryngologist, educator*
Kritchevsky, Stephen Bennett *epidemiologist, educator*
Loeser, Richard Frank, Jr. *medical researcher, director*
Marks, Malculm Wernick *plastic surgeon, educator*
Maynard, Charles Douglas *radiologist*
Mclorie, Gordon Arthur *urologist, educator*
Moody, Dixon McGuire *radiologist*
Murray, Nial Patrick *retired anesthesiologist educator*
O'Donovan, Cormac A. *neurologist, educator*
O'Steen, Wendall Keith *anatomist, neurologist, educator*
Podgorny, George *emergency physician*
Powell, Bayard Lowery *oncologist, educator*
Schwartz, Robert Paul *pediatric endocrinologist*
Simon, Jimmy Louis *pediatrician, educator*
Slaughter, Thomas Freeman *anesthesiologist, educator, physician*
Soliman, Elsayed Z. *cardiologist, educator*
Stein, Barry Edward *medical educator*
Tatter, Stephen Bradley *neurosurgeon, educator*
Toole, James Francis *medical educator*
Vachharajani, Vidula T. *emergency physician*
Weller, Robert Stephen *anesthesiologist*
Yentzer, Brad A. *medical researcher*
Zhang, Zhu-ming *medical educator*

NORTH DAKOTA

Fargo
Mistry, Bhargav Mangaldas *surgeon, director*

Grand Forks
Gaul, Gerald *ophthalmologist*
Jackson, Jon *medical educator, consultant*
Sticca, Robert P. *surgeon*
Wakefield, Mary Katherine *medical association administrator, medical educator*
Yoshida, Glen Yoshio *otolaryngologist*

Williston
Adducci, Joseph Edward *obstetrician, gynecologist*

OHIO

Akron
Emmett, John Colin *retired inventor, consultant*
Gil, Karen M. *medical researcher, director*
Hopkins, Michael Patrick *obstetrician, oncologist, surgeon*
Lavin, Justin Paul, Jr. *obstetrician, gynecologist, perinatologist*
Moser, James Michael *medical educator*
Seiwald, Robert J. *retired inventor*

Aurora
Allen, Marc Kevin *emergency physician, educator*

Avon Lake
Hrinczenko, Borys Walter *oncologist, hematologist, medical educator, medical researcher, consultant*

Beachwood
Moskowitz, Roland Wallace *internist*

Bexley
Yashon, David *neurosurgeon, educator*

Bowling Green
Danilov, Evgeny *medical researcher, director*

Bratenahl
Jones, Trevor Owen *biomedical industry executive, management consultant*

Bryan
Carrico, Virgil Norman *physician*

Canton
Howland, Willard J. *radiologist, educator*
Nadas, John Adalbert *psychiatrist, educator*
Starchman, Dale Edward *medical educator*

Chagrin Falls
Lingl, Friedrich Albert *psychiatrist*

Chardon
Kellis, Michael John *osteopathic physician*

Cincinnati
Ahmad, Syed *surgeon*
Alexander, James Wesley *surgeon, educator*
Altug, Cetinkaya *oculo-plastic surgeon ophthalmologist*
Baker, Raymond Charles *pediatrician, educator*
Balistreri, William Francis *pediatric gastroenterologist, educator*
Baughman, Robert Phillip *physician, educator*
Beary, John Francis III *rheumatologist, clinical pharmacologist, medical researcher, naval officer*
Bommireddy, Ramireddy *immunologist, researcher*
Boyd, Deborah Ann *pediatrician*
Butsch Kovacic, Melinda *epidemiologist, medical researcher*
Ching, Ho *surgeon*
Choo, Daniel *otolaryngologist, educator*
Chung, Eugene Sejin *cardiologist, director*
Cotton, Robin T. *pediatric otolaryngologist, surgeon*
Daniel, J. Lovell *pediatrician, educator*
de Courten-Myers, Gabrielle Marguerite *retired neuropathologist*
DeWitt, Thomas G. *pediatrician*
Feinberg, Judith *physician, medical researcher, educator*
Frenck, Robert W., Jr. *pediatrician, educator, epidemiologist*
Gaitonde, Krishnanath *urologist, educator*
Gass, Margery Stoops *obstetrician, gynecologist*
Geller, James Ian *pediatrician, oncologist*
Geracioti, Thomas Dino, Jr. *psychiatry, researcher*
Gerson, Myron Craig *cardiologist, researcher*
Haswani, Dinesh K. *medical researcher*
Heimlich, Henry J. *physician, surgeon, educator*
Hess, Evelyn Victorine *medical educator*
Hiratzka, Loren F. *surgeon*
Holland, Edward J. *ophthalmologist, surgeon*
Hom, David Brian *surgeon*
Inge, Thomas *pediatric surgeon*
Jobe, Alan Hall *pediatrician, educator*
Joseph, Patricia Maxwell *pulmonologist, educator*
Keck, Paul E., Jr. *psychiatrist*
Kereiakes, Dean James *cardiologist*
Khurana Hershey, Gurjit *pediatrician, pulmonologist, educator*
Kircher, Christopher *neurologist, consultant, medical researcher*
Kukielka, Gilbert Leon *physician*
Kuntz, Charles, IV, *neurosurgeon*
Lehmann, Corinne E. *medical educator*
Levinson, Joseph E. *retired internist, rheumatologist, educator*
Lichtin, Leon (Judah Leon Lichtin) *retired pharmaceutical educator*
Liggett, Stephen B. *pharmacologist, educator*
Loggie, Jennifer Mary Hildreth *retired physician, educator*
Lower, Elyse E. *physician, educator*
Malik, Punam *medical educator*
Maltz, Robert *surgeon*
Mattner, Jochen *medical educator, researcher*
McMurray, James Scott *pediatric otolaryngologist*
Merrill, Walter Hilson *surgeon*
Munir, Muhammad *pain medicine physician, director*
Nakata, Akinori *epidemiologist, psychologist, researcher*
Nasrallah, Henry Ata *psychiatry researcher, educator*
O'Hara, Sara Marie *radiologist*
Pathak, Sanjeev *psychiatrist, researcher*
Porembka, David Thomas *anesthesia and surgery educator*
Ritschel, Wolfgang Adolf *medical educator, sculptor, artist*
Safdi, Alan V. *gastroenterologist, director*
Samy, Ravi *otolaryngologist*
Sarembock, Ian Joseph *internist, cardiologist*
Siegel, Robert M. *pediatrician, educator*
Strauss, Arnold Wilbur *pediatrician, educator*
Supp, Dorothy M. *medical educator, researcher*
Swank, Michael Lawson *orthopedist*
Talaska, Glenn *medical educator*
Visscher, Marty Orrico *biomedical researcher*
Wells Wulsin, Victoria *epidemiologist*
Welsh, George Franklin *plastic surgeon, educator*
Wexler, Laura F. *cardiologist, academic administrator*
Wiot, Jerome Francis *radiologist*

Cleveland
Anderson, Michael Robert *pediatrician, educator*
Arnold, James E. *pediatrician, educator*
Awais, George Musa *obstetrician, gynecologist*
Baker, Mark Early *radiology educator*
Baker, Saul Phillip *geriatrician, cardiologist, internist*
Barksdale, Edward Metz, Jr. *pediatrician, educator*
Bause, George Stephen LoneRaven *anesthesiologist*
Berger, Nathan Allen *medical educator, academic administrator*
Berman, Brian William *pediatrician, educator*
Bodner, Donald Roger *urologist, medical educator*
Bolwell, Brian J. *oncologist, director*
Bowerfind, Edgar Sihler, Jr. *retired medical association administrator, internist, educator*
Boyd, Arthur Bernette, Jr. *surgeon, clergyman, beverage company executive*
Brody, Robert *dermatologist, educator*
Brooks, Elizabeth B. *rheumatologist, educator*
Bruner, William Evans, II, *ophthalmologist, educator, researcher*
Castele, Theodore John *radiologist*
Cerqueira, Manuel DeCastro *nuclear medicine physician*
Church, James Michael *surgeon*
Citardi, Martin Jason *medical educator*
Connors, Alfred Francis *internist, researcher*
Cooper, Gregory Scott *epidemiologist, gastroenterologist, educator*
Copelan, Edward A. *medical educator*
Cowan, Dale Harvey *internist, lawyer*
Daniel, Thomas Mallon *medical educator, researcher*
Daroff, Robert Barry *neurologist, educator*
Davis, Pamela Bowes *pediatric pulmonologist, dean*
Dell, Michael S. *pediatrician*
Djohan, Risal *plastic surgeon*
Dobyns, Brown McIlvaine *retired surgeon, educator*
Dunlap, Mark Evans *cardiologist*
Eiben, Robert Michael *pediatric neurologist, educator*
Ellis, Lloyd H., Jr. *emergency physician, art historian*
Eng, Charis Eu Li *oncologist, geneticist*
Faiman, Charles *endocrinologist*
Flocke, Susan A. *medical educator, director*
Francis, Gary S. *cardiologist, educator*
Furman, Lydia M. *pediatrician, educator*
Glazer, John Prescott *psychiatrist*
Goldberg, Victor M. *orthopedist*
Goldman, Steven Andrew *plastic surgeon, educator*
Gorman Koch, Colleen *anesthesiologist, educator*
Griffin, Brian Pius *cardiologist*
Gubitosi-Klug, Rose Anne *pediatrician*
Haaga, John R. *radiologist*
Hajj-Ali, Rula Adel *rheumatologist, researcher*
Harding, Clifford Vincent III *medical educator*
Heman-Ackah, Yolanda Denise *otolaryngologist, director*
Hermann, Robert Ewald *retired surgeon*
Hertzer, Norman Ray *surgeon*
Hoffman, Gary Stewart *rheumatologist*
Huang, David *ophthalmologist, medical educator*
Isaacson, J. Harry *medical educator*
Kaouk, Jihad H. *urologist*
Kapadia, Samir R. *cardiologist, educator*
Kass, Lawrence *hematologist, oncologist, educator*
Kenagy, David Neil *pediatrician*
Klein, Eric Alan *surgical oncologist, urologist*
Kumar, Ajay *physician, director*
Kumar, Mary Louise *physician, educator*
Lass, Jonathan Herschel *ophthalmologist*
Lefferts, William Geoffrey *internist, educator*
Lenkoski, Leo Douglas *retired psychiatrist, educator*
Lietman, Steven Andrea *physician*
Lindsay, Bruce Duncan *cardiologist*
Lytle, Bruce Whitney *cardiovascular surgeon*
Maciunas, Robert Joseph *medical educator, researcher*
Macklis, Roger Milton *physician, educator, researcher*
Malangoni, Mark Alan *surgeon, educator*
Marcus, Randall Evan *orthopaedic surgery educator*
Mays, MaryAnn *neurologist*
McHenry, Martin Christopher *physician, educator*
Minai, Omar Ahmad *physician*
Misra-Hebert, Anita Diana *physician*
Modic, Michael *radiologist, educator*
Montague, Drogo K. *urologist*
Murthy, Sudish C. *thoracic surgeon*
Myers, Stephen *preventive medicine physician*
Neuhauser, Duncan vonBriesen *medical educator*
Nissen, Steven Evan *cardiologist, researcher*
Olness, Karen Norma *medical educator*
Patel, Sanjay *pulmonologist, educator*
Payne, Michael Cordell *medical researcher*
Pesek, Todd *physician, director*
Petterson, Gosta *surgeon*
Post, Anthony Benjamin *gastroenterologist, director*
Raaf, John Hart *retired surgeon, educator, health facility administrator*
Remick, Scot Clifton *oncologist, clinical investigator, educator*
Rezai, Ali *neurosurgeon, educator*
Roham, Masoud *biomedical researcher*
Ruff, Robert Louis *neurologist, physiologist, researcher*
Schauer, Philip R. *surgeon*
Shrestha, Nabin K. *physician, researcher*
Siemionow, Maria *microsurgeon*
Stanton-Hicks, Michael D'Arcy *anesthesiologist, pain medicine specialist*
Starling, Randall Carson *cardiologist, educator*
Stavitsky, Abram Benjamin *immunologist, educator*
Steinemann, Thomas L. *ophthalmologist, educator*
Stephenson, Andrew J. *urologist*
Stewart, William James *cardiologist*
Strosaker, Robyn Heather *pediatrician, educator*
Stulberg, Bernard Nathan *orthopaedic surgeon, research scientist*
Talanow, Roland *radiologist*
Taylor, Harris C. *endocrinologist, consultant*
Tomashefski, Joseph Francis, Jr. *pathologist, educator*
Tuzcu, Emin Murat *cardiologist, educator*
Utian, Wulf Hessel *gynecologist, endocrinologist*
Videtic, Gregory *physician*
Waldo, Albert Leon *cardiologist, educator*
Walsh, R. Matthew *surgeon, gastroenterologist*
Wang, Bingcheng *oncologist, researcher*
Webster, Leslie Tillotson, Jr. *pharmacologist, educator*
Wiersma, Susan Renee *pediatrician*
Williams, Wesley Montgomery *medical researcher*
Wish, Jay Barry *nephrologist, specialist*
Wolinsky, Emanuel *internist, educator*
Yao, Qingping *rheumatologist*
Yetman, Randall John *plastic surgeon*
Young, Jess Ray *retired internist*
Zahka, Kenneth George *pediatrician, cardiologist, educator*
Zaidat, Osama O. *neurologist*

Cleveland Heights
Zakaria, Asma *neurologist*

Columbus
Abaza, Ronney *surgeon, director*
Allen, Hugh Daryl *pediatric cardiologist, educator*
Balcerzak, Stanley Paul *retired hematologist, oncologist, director, medical educator*
Barth, Rolf Frederick *pathologist, educator*
Batisky, Donald Lee *pediatrician, educator*
Berlet, Gregory Charles *surgeon*
Berntson, Gary Glen *psychiatry, psychology and pediatrics educator*
Billings, Charles Edgar *physician*
Bloomfield, Clara Derber *oncologist, educator, medical institute administrator*
Blum, William George *hematologist, clinical researcher educator*
Bullock, Joseph Daniel *pediatrician, educator*
Chen, Chun-Liang *oncologist*
Christoforidis, A. John *radiologist, educator*
Clark, K. Reed *medical geneticist, pediatrician*
Corrigan, John Dudley *physiatrist*
Coury, Daniel *pediatrician, educator*
DiLorenzo, Carlo *pediatrician, gastroenterologist, educator*
Ellison, Edwin Christopher *surgeon, educator*
Falcone, Robert Edward *surgeon*
Fraker, Theodore D'Eston, Jr. *cardiologist, educator*
Galantowicz, Mark Edward *cardiothoracic surgeon*
Haque, Malika Hakim *pediatrician*
Hasan, Ayesha *cardiologist, educator*
Higgins, Gloria C. *pediatrician*
Hitchcock, Charles L. *pathologist, educator*
Jones, Jeffrey Alan *physician, researcher*
Kim, Do Gyoon *biomedical researcher*
Lander, Ruth A. *medical association administrator*
Leier, Carl Victor *internist, cardiologist*
Long, Sarah Elizabeth Brackney *physician*
Marsh, Clay Braden *pulmonologist, researcher*
Mayr, Nina A. *medical educator*
Metrione, Lara *biomedical researcher*
Mueller, Charles Frederick *radiologist, educator*
Needham, Glen Ray *entomology and acarology educator, researcher*
Newton, William Allen, Jr. *pediatrician, pathologist*
Nwomeh, Benedict C. *pediatric surgeon*
Pacht, Eric Reed *pulmonary and critical care physician*
Paskett, Electra *epidemiologist, oncologist, educator*
Pease, William Stoess *physiatrist, educator*
Ramaswamy, Bhuvaneswari *medical educator, researcher*
Rund, Douglas Andrew *emergency physician*
Sayers, Martin Peter *pediatric neurosurgeon*
Shah, Kaushal J. *thoracic surgeon*
Shroff, Ness *medical educator, researcher*
Sood, Namita *medical educator*
Souba, Wiley William, Jr. *medical educator, researcher, dean*
Stawicki, Stanislaw Peter *surgeon, medical researcher*
Taylor, Benjamin Craig *orthopedist*
Virk, Subhdeep *psychiatrist*
Vogel, Thomas Timothy *surgeon, educator, lay worker*
Wasserman, Deborah L. *medical researcher*
Weinstein, Samuel *thoracic surgeon, pediatrician, researcher*
Yeager, Nicholas D. *pediatrician, educator*
Yu, Chack Yung *pediatrics educator, molecular biologist*

Dayton
Ambalavanan, Siva *nephrologist, educator*
Chin, Hong Woo *oncologist, educator, researcher*
Forbis, Shalini G. *pediatrician, educator*
Gillig, Paulette Marie *psychiatry educator, researcher*
Hitch, David Charles *surgeon*
Laughlin, Richard T. *orthopedist, educator*
Mohler, Stanley Ross *preventive medicine physician, educator*
Monk, Susan Marie *pediatrician, educator*
Mossman, Douglas *psychiatrist, educator*
Pascoe, John M. *pediatrician, educator*
Ruegsegger, Donald Ray, Jr. *radiological physicist, educator*
Siddiqi, Munawar *anesthesiologist, consultant*
Syed, Mubin Isaac *interventional radiologist, neuroradiologist*
Termuhlen, Paula *oncologist, surgeon*
Wilson, William Campbell McFarland *gastroenterologist*

Dublin
Smith, Stephen Puntenney *plastic surgeon, educator*

Galena
Berggren, Ronald Bernard *surgeon, retired educator*

Gates Mills
van Heeckeren, Anna M. *biomedical researcher, veterinarian*

Grove City
Kilman, James William *surgeon, educator*

Harrison
West, Clark Darwin *pediatric nephrologist, educator*

Independence
Chapa, Jeffrey *obstetrician, gynecologist*

Kent
Ference-Valenta, Mary Jean *osteopath, health facility administrator*

Lyndhurst
Guyuron, Bahman *plastic surgeon, educator*

Mansfield
Houston, William Robert Montgomery *ophthalmologist, surgeon*

Massillon
Vaughn, Lisa Dawn *physician, educator*

Middleburg Heights
Shatila, Ahmad Hussain *surgeon, oncologist*

North Canton
Di Simone, Robert Nicholas *radiologist, educator*

Oberlin
Salter, Robin S. *immunologist, educator*

Oxford
Biran Weinberger, Mia *mental health educator*

Port Clinton
Woodson, Riley Donald *thoracic and cardiovascular surgeon, lawyer*

Rootstown
Sutariya, Vijaykumar Bhadabhai *medical educator*

Salem
Madison, John Robert *surgeon*

Solon
Rosen, Michael Joshua *surgeon*

Springdale
Schreiner, Albert William *internist, educator*

Sylvania
Burkhart, Craig Garrett *dermatologist, researcher*

Toledo
Comerota, Anthony James *vascular surgeon, biomedical researcher*
Ferguson Rayport, Shirley Martha *psychiatrist*
Goodenday, Lucy Sherman *cardiologist, educator*
Hasan, Rashed A. *pediatrician, educator*
Heiney, Jake P. *orthopedist*
Homolka, Linda Mary *radiographer, educator*
Mrak, Robert Emil *neuropathologist, educator*
Mulrow, Patrick Joseph *medical educator*
Rees, Michael A. *urologist*
Rejent, Marian Magdalen *retired pediatrician*
Shaikh, Bahu Sultan *physician, educator*
Siddiqui, Fouzia *neurologist*
Talmage, Lance Allen *obstetrician, gynecologist, military officer*

Wadsworth
Aragon, Lynn D. *retired physician*

Westerville
St. Pierre, Ronald Leslie *public health and medical educator, academic administrator*

Wooster
Zink, Harry A. *ophthalmologist*

Worthington
Winter, Chester Caldwell *surgeon, educator, historian, writer*

Youngstown
Barr, Richard Gary *radiologist, chemist*

OKLAHOMA

Claremore
Wittenberg, Henry Taylor, Jr. *physician, surgeon*

Edmond
Adams, Donald E. *physiatrist*
Halverstadt, Donald Bruce *urologist, educator*
Lester, Richard Garrison *radiologist, educator*

Kingfisher
Buswell, Arthur Wilcox *physician, surgeon*

Konawa
Jabeen, Seema *internist*

Lawton
Perez-Cruet, Jorge *geriatric psychiatrist, researcher*

Muskogee
Kent, Bartis Milton *retired physician*

Norman
Berkowitz, Ari *medical educator, director*
Dille, John Robert *retired physician*

Oklahoma City
Abid, Farida *neurologist, pediatrician*
Andrews, Mitchell Dewayne *internist, dean, educator*
Aravindan, Natarajan *medical educator*
Bamgbola, Oluwatoyin Fatai *pediatric renal physician, researcher*
Bogardus, Carl Robert, Jr. *radiologist, educator*
Bozalis, John Russell *physician*
Claflin, James Robert *pediatrician, allergist*
Collins, William Edward, Jr. *aeromedical administrator, psychologist, researcher*
Comp, Philip Cinnamon *medical researcher*
Couch, James Russell, Jr. *neurology educator*
Culkin, Daniel Joseph *urologist, educator, department chairman*
Escobedo, Marilyn Barnard *physician, educator*
Filley, Warren Vernon *allergist*
George, James Noel *hematologist, oncologist, educator*
Gilchrist, John Mark *otolaryngologist*
Hampton, James Wilburn *hematologist, oncologist*
Harley, John Barker *rheumatologist*
Harolds, Jay Alan *radiologist, nuclear medicine physician*
Jacobs, Eric J. *epidemiologist, researcher*
Keddissi, Jean I. *medical educator*
Kreth, Jens *medical educator*
Lazzara, Ralph *cardiologist*
Loftus, Christopher Miranda *neurosurgeon*
McCaffree, Mary Anne Wight *pediatrician, neonatal-perinatal specialist, educator*
McKee, Patrick Allen *physician*
McNall-Knapp, René Yvonne *pediatrician, educator*
McShan, William Michael *medical educator*
Meyer, William H. *pediatrician, educator*
Mold, James William *geriatrician, preventive medicine physician, educator*
Oehlert, William Herbert, Jr. *cardiologist, administrator, educator*
Ozer, Howard *oncologist, hematologist*
Parke, David Wilkin, II, *ophthalmologist, educator, health facility administrator*
Plafker, Scott *medical educator*
Postier, Russell Glen *surgeon*
Rabadi, Meheroz Hoshang *neurologist, consultant*
Raj, Tilak D. *anesthesiologist, educator*
Rhoades, Everett Ronald *medical educator*
Ruffin, Richard A. *orthopedic surgeon*
Sawalha, Amr *medical educator*
Thadani, Udho *physician, cardiologist*
Tuggle, David W. *pediatric surgeon*
West, Eileen C. *general internal medicine physician, educator*
Wolraich, Mark Lee *pediatrician, educator*
Wong, Carson *surgeon, educator*

Stillwater
Cooper, Donald Lee *physician*
Giddens, Cheryl LeAnn *medical educator*

Tulsa
Hoskison, Thomas Karl *medical educator*
Kaul, Rashmi *immunologist, educator*
LaButti, Ronald Stephan *orthopedist*
McCullough, Robert Dale, II, *osteopath*
Nettles, John Barnwell *obstetrics and gynecology educator*
Say, Burhan *retired physician*

OREGON

Bend
Peters, Gerald Eugene, Jr. *dermatologist, surgeon*
Singletary, DeJuan Theresa *child and adolescent psychiatrist*

Corvallis
Baird, William McKenzie *chemical carcinogenesis researcher, biochemistry professor*

Eugene
Jewell, Mark Laurence *plastic surgeon*
Loescher, Richard Alvin *retired gastroenterologist*
Roe, Thomas Leroy Willis *retired pediatrician*

Lake Oswego
Hutchens, Tyra Thornton *pathologist, educator*
Julien, Robert Michael *anesthesiologist, writer*

Medford
Shekhar, Stephen S. *obstetrician, gynecologist*

Milwaukie
Sklovsky, Robert J. *naturopathic physician, pharmacist, educator*

Newberg
Koler, Robert Donald *medical educator*

Portland
Andresen, Michael Christian *biomedical research scientist*
Ball, Melvyn *medical educator*
Beckerman, James Gregg *cardiologist*
Beer, Tomasz M. *physician*
Bennett, William Michael *internist, educator, nephrologist*
Blank, Eugene *pediatrician, radiologist, educator*
Burchiel, Kim James *neurosurgeon*
Campbell, John Richard *pediatric surgeon*
Casey, Daniel E. *psychiatrist, educator*
Daneshmand, Siamak *urologist*
Druker, Brian Jay *medical educator, researcher*
Filip, Gregory Michael *forest pathologist*
Fraunfelder, Frederick Theodore *ophthalmologist, educator*
Grady-Weliky, Tana Annette *psychiatrist, educator*
Jacob, Stanley Wallace *surgeon, educator*
Kaufman, John Andrew *radiologist*
Kendall, John Walker, Jr. *internist, researcher, dean*
Krol, Alfons *dermatologist, educator*
Mandel, Gail *immunologist*
Maziarz, Richard Thomas *hematologist, educator*
Patterson, James Randolph *physician*
Poehlein, Christian Heinrich *medical researcher*
Reich, Jerome Mark *pulmonologist, consultant*
Sandler, Alan Bart *oncologist*
Scott, John D. *pharmacologist*
Shangraw, Robert Edward *medical educator, researcher*
Smith, Dennis B. *neurologist, educator*
Starr, Albert *thoracic surgeon, educator, research scientist*
Sussman, Michael David *orthopedic surgeon*
Sutherland, Donald Wood *retired cardiologist*
Swanstrom, Lee Leray *surgeon*
Taylor, Robert Brown *physician, educator, writer*
Westbrook, Gary L. *neurologist*
Wildin, Robert *medical geneticist*
Wilson, William Harwell *psychiatrist, educator*
Zerbe, Kathryn Jane *psychiatrist*

Roseburg
Oliphant, Charles Romig *retired physician*

Tualatin
Tongue, John Richard *orthopedist*

PENNSYLVANIA

Allentown
Arangio, George A. *orthopedist, educator*
Barraco, Robert Don *surgeon*
Gaylor, Donald Hughes *surgeon, educator*
Maffeo, Alphonse A. *anesthesiologist*
Smulian, John C. *obstetrician*

Altoona
Gurman, Andrew William *orthopedist, educator*

Ambler
Kim, Junghoon *medical researcher, educator*

Ardmore
Goodrich, Edward (Ned) Olin *surgeon, educator*
Honebrink, Ann Louise *gynecologist, educator*
Weiss, Marisa C. *breast cancer oncologist, non-profit breast cancer organization executive*

Bakerstown
Beachley, Michael Charles *radiologist*

Bensalem
Carruthers, Catherine Douglas *surgeon*

Broomall
Fras, Christian Ivan *orthopedist*

Bryn Mawr
Bernstein, Eric Ferenc *dermatologist, educator*
Brunt, Manly Yates, Jr. *psychiatrist*
Godinez, Marye H. *anesthesiologist*
Huth, Edward Janavel *internist, educator, editor*
Levitt, Robert E. *gastroenterologist*
Noone, Robert Barrett *plastic surgeon*
Thompson, Geraldine Kelleher Richter *retired orthopedist*
Webber, John Bentley *orthopedic surgeon*

Camp Hill
Tokuhata, George K. *retired medical educator, epidemiologist, consultant*
Yates, James Arthur *plastic surgeon*

Carlisle
Vickery, Jon Livingstone *neurologist*

Center Valley
Risher, William Henry *cardiothoracic surgeon, educator*

Cheltenham
Fleisher, Linda *medical researcher, director*

Coatesville
Ainslie, George William *psychiatrist*

Danville
Blankenship, James Colegrove *cardiologist*
Maroon, Michele Senga *dermatologist*
Pierce, James Clarence *surgeon, educator*
Sidorov, Jaan Erik *physician, researcher*
Steele, Glenn Daniel, Jr. *oncologist, healthcare system executive*
Toms, Steven A. *neurosurgeon, researcher*

Darby
Eiser, Arnold Robert *physician executive, bioethicist, nephrologist, internist, medical educator*

Dillsburg
Jackson, George Lyman *retired nuclear medicine physician*

Downingtown
Scheer, R. Scott *physician*

Easton
Grunberg, Robert Leon Willy *nephrologist, educator*
Trigiano, Lucien Lewis *physician*

Elkins Park
Esquenazi, Alberto *physiatrist*

Erie
Brunner-Martinez, Kirstin Ellen *pediatrician, psychiatrist*
Kondylis, Philip Demetrios *colon and rectal surgeon*
Mason, Gregg Claude *orthopedic surgeon, researcher*
Michaelides, Doros Nikita *internist, medical educator*

Gaines
Beller, Martin Leonard *retired orthopaedic surgeon*

Garnet Valley
Chirinos, Julio Alonso *physician, researcher*

Gibsonia
Krause, Helen Fox *retired otolaryngologist*

Gladwyne
Kaye, Donald *internist, educator*
Morrison, Gail *internist, nephrologist, educator*

Glen Mills
Goldberg, Morton Edward *pharmacologist*

Glenolden
Malykhina, Anna P. *medical educator*

Glenside
Reiss, George Russell, Jr. *physician*

Hallstead
Remakus, Bernard Leo *physician, medical educator, writer, medical journalist*

Harrisburg
Chernicoff, David Paul *osteopathic physician, educator*
Rudy, Frank R. *pathologist*

Haverford
Aronson, Carl Edward *pharmacology and toxicology educator*

Hershey
Berlin, Cheston Milton, Jr. *pediatrician, educator*
Bixler, Edward O. *psychiatrist, educator*
Caputo, Gregory Michael *internist, educator*
Davis, Dwight *cardiologist, educator*
Eyster, Mary Elaine *hematologist, educator*
Fedok, Fred G. *plastic surgeon, educator*
Ghossaini, Soha Nadim *medical educator*
Hauck, Randy Milton *surgeon, educator*
Janicki, Piotr K. *anesthesiologist, educator*
Kauffman, Gordon Lee, Jr. *surgeon, educator*
Krieg, Arthur Frederick *pathologist*
Lynch, Scott Alan *orthopedist, educator*
Madewell, John Edward *radiologist*
Marks, James Garfield, Jr. *dermatologist*
Naeye, Richard L. *pathologist, educator*
Ostrov, Barbara E. *physician*
Pierce, William Schuler *cardiac surgeon*
Planas-Silva, Maricarmen Delia *cancer researcher*
Schuller, Diane Ethel *allergist, immunologist, educator*
Severs, Walter Bruce *pharmacology educator, researcher*
Shope, Timothy Robert *medical educator*
Tan, Tjiauw-Ling *psychiatrist, educator*
Thomas, Patrick Robert Maxwell *oncologist, educator, academic administrator*
Uhde, Thomas Whitley *psychopharmacology, psychiatrist*
Vesell, Elliot Saul *pharmacologist, educator*
Waldhausen, John Anton *retired surgeon, editor*
Wassner, Steven Joel *pediatric nephrologist, educator*
Zelis, Robert Felix *cardiologist, educator*

Horsham
DeHoratius, Raphael Joseph *rheumatologist*

Hummelstown
Biebuyck, Julien Francois *physician, anesthesiologist, medical administrator, educator*

Irwin
Brown, Donald Clyde *surgeon*

Jenkintown
Sadoff, Robert Leslie *psychiatrist, educator*

Kennett Square
Harrington, Anne Wilson *medical librarian*
Hinz, Carl Frederick, Jr. *immunologist, educator*
Richardson, Dean Wheeler *equine surgeon, veterinary educator*

King Of Prussia
Katolik, Leonid I. *surgeon, educator*

Lancaster
Burlingame, Mark Wayne *cardiothoracic surgeon*

Langhorne
Manyak, Michael John *urologist, educator, researcher*

Lansdale
Sensenig, David Martin *retired surgeon*

Lower Gwynedd
Pendleton, Robert Grubb *pharmacologist*

Malvern
Hallenbeck, Paul Leon *medical researcher, director*

Media
Behbehanian, Mahin Fazeli *surgeon*

Middletown
Walters, Marian R. *research administrator*

Monongahela
Yovanof, Silvana *physician*

Narberth
Strom, Brian Leslie *internist, educator*

New Hope
Ecker, Sidney Wolf *urologist, consultant*
Raabe, Gerhard Karl *epidemiologist*

Newtown Square
Cordes, Eugene Harold *retired pharmacy and chemistry educator*
de Rivas, Carmela Foderaro *retired psychiatrist, health facility administrator*
Lawrence, Theodore *retired physician*

Norristown
Colcher, Robert Ely *surgeon*

North Wales
Calder, Robert Austin *preventive medicine physician, administrator*
Gorby-Schmidt, Martha Louise *pharmacologist, researcher*
Musliner, Thomas Allen *cardiologist, director*
Nguyen, Bach-Yen T. *medical association administrator*

Paoli
Burget, Dean Edwin, Jr. *plastic surgeon*

Philadelphia
Acker, Michael A. *thoracic surgeon, educator*
Albert, Todd James *orthopedist*
Allen, Julian Lewis *pediatric pulmonologist, medical educator*
Ances, Beau M. *neurologist*
Anjan, Chatterjee *neurologist, educator*
Arce, A. Anthony *psychiatrist, educator*
Asbury, Arthur Knight *neurologist, educator*
Bagley, Demetrius H. *urologist, educator, researcher*
Ballweg, Jean A. *pediatrician, educator*
Barker, Clyde Frederick *surgeon, educator*
Baron, David A. *neuropsychiatric researcher, educator*
Bartlett, Scott Paul *plastic surgeon*
Baum, Stanley *radiologist, educator*
Beck, Aaron Temkin *psychiatrist, educator*
Beck, John Robert *pathologist, information scientist*
Becker, Lance B. *medical educator*
Bennett, Jean *ophthalmologist, educator*
Bibbo, Marluce *physician, educator*
Bigelow, Douglas C. *otolaryngologist*
Bing, Zhanyong *medical educator*
Boden, Guenther *endocrinologist*
Bove, Alfred Anthony *medical educator*
Brady, Luther W., Jr. *radiation overlogist, educator*
Bridges, Charles R. *cardiologist, surgeon*
Brighton, Carl Theodore *orthopedic surgery educator*
Brooks, John Samuel Joseph *pathologist, researcher*
Brucker, Alexander J. *ophthalmologist, educator*
Bucky, Louis P. *plastic surgeon, educator*
Bucurescu, Gabriel *neurologist*
Callahan, James Michael *physician, educator*
Campbell, Robert Murray, Jr. *surgeon, researcher*
Casale, Pasquale *urologist, consultant, researcher*
Charkes, N. David *nuclear medicine physician, educator*
Chen, Xiaoli *pathologist*
Chen, Yibai *mass spectrometrist*
Chung, Esther Kyunghi *pediatrician*
Clearfield, Harris Reynold *physician*
Colman, Robert Wolf *hematologist, educator*
Cooper, Edward Sawyer *retired cardiologist, internist, educator*
Cooper, Joel David *physician, medical educator*
Daly, John M. *surgeon, educator*
D'Angio, Giulio John *radiologist, educator*
Dasgupta, Indranil *physician, educator*
Daskalaki, Irini *medical educator*
Deschler, Daniel Gert *otolaryngologist, educator*
Dichter, Marc Allen *physician*
DiMarino, Anthony J., Jr. *gastroenterologist, educator*
DiPalma, Joseph Rupert *pharmacology educator, dean*
Dominici, Paul G. *emergency physician*
Dormans, John Paul *surgeon, educator*
Doty, Richard L. *medical researcher*
Driscoll, Deborah Anne *gynecologist, obstetrician*
Ehrlich, George Edward *rheumatologist, consultant*
Eisen, Howard Joel *internist, researcher*
Engstrom, Paul F. *oncologist, medical educator*
Epstein, Jonathan A. *medical educator, researcher*
Eskin, Bernard Abraham *obstetrics and gynecology educator, researcher*
Feldman, Arthur M. *cardiologist*
Fishman, Alfred Paul *physician*
Fleisher, Lee Alan *anesthesiologist, educator*
Forbes, Brian John *pediatrician, orthopedist*
Frank, Barbara Balis *gastroenterologist, educator*
Friedberg, Joseph Stewart *surgeon*
Friedenberg, Frank K. *medical educator*
Friedman, Harvey Michael *infectious diseases educator*
Gallagher, Rollin M. *psychiatrist, anesthesiologist*
Ganley, Theodore *orthopedist*
Garcia, Fernando Uriel *pathologist, educator*
Gausas, Roberta Elisabeth *oculoplastic and orbital surgeon*
Gavrin, Jonathan Robert *medical educator, internist*
Gearhart, John D. *obstetrician, gynecologist, medical educator, developmental geneticist*
Gerner, Edward William *medical educator*
Glick, John H. *oncologist, medical educator*
Gonzalez-Scarano, Francisco Antonio *neurologist, virologist*
Grady, M. Sean *neurosurgeon*
Greenstein, Jeffrey Ian *neurologist*
Gueson, Emerita Torres *obstetrician, gynecologist*
Gyulai, Laszlo *psychiatrist, educator*
Herling, Irving Marc *internal medicine educator, cardiologist*

High, Katherine Ann *physician, researcher*
Hogarty, Michael David *pediatrician*
Humphreys, Tatyana *medical educator, director*
Jessup, Mariell L. *cardiologist, educator*
Jimenez, Sergio A. *internist, educator, rheumatologist*
Johnson, Philip Rudolph, Jr. *pediatrician, epidemiologist*
Kaji, Hideko *pharmacology educator*
Kamen, Leonard Bert *osteopath*
Kang, Ju-Seop *medical educator, consultant, medical researcher*
Kang, Yoogoo *anesthesiologist, educator*
Kaufman, Russel Eugene *hematologist, oncologist*
Kazazian, Haig Hagop, Jr. *pediatrician, researcher, educator*
Kefalides, Nicholas Alexander *physician, educator*
Kelley, William Nimmons *physician, educator, science administrator, dean*
Kennedy, David William *otolaryngologist, medical administrator, educator*
Klein, Michael Elihu *physician*
Klein-Szanto, Andres J. P. *pathologist*
Klumpp, Thomas Russell *bone marrow transplant physician, educator*
Knudson, Alfred George, Jr. *medical geneticist*
Koretzky, Gary Alan *rheumatologist, educator*
Kresh, J. Yasha *cardiovascular researcher, educator*
Kujubu, Dean Akira *physician, educator*
Lange, Beverly J. *pediatric oncologist*
Langer, Jill E. *radiologist, educator*
Lazar, Mitchell Avery *physician, educator*
Lee, David Inkoo *urologist*
Lee, Virginia M. -Y. *medical educator, health science association administrator*
Leist, Paul Thomas *neurologist, director*
Lemanski, Larry Fredrick *medical educator, academic administrator*
Le Roux, Peter David *neurosurgeon*
Leventhal, Lawrence Jay *rheumatologist, educator*
Levitt, Jerry David *medical educator*
Lewis, Frank Russell, Jr. *surgeon*
Li, Weiye *ophthalmologist, educator, biochemist*
Lippa, Carol Frances *neurologist*
Litzky, Leslie Anne *pathologist, educator*
Long, Sarah Sundborg *pediatrician, educator*
Ludwig, Stephen *pediatrics and emergency medicine educator*
Mahmud, Jamal *psychiatrist*
Maitin, Ian *physiatrist*
Malkowicz, Stanley Bruce *urologist*
Mancall, Elliott Lee *retired neurologist, educator*
Maqbool, Asim *pediatrician, gastroenterologist*
Marcotte, Paul John *neurosurgeon, educator*
Margo, Katherine Lane *family physician, educator*
Meisel, Zachary Franklin *emergency physician, educator*
Melvin, John Lewis *physical and rehabilitation physician, educator, administrator*
Meropol, Neal J. *oncologist, researcher*
Meucci, Olimpia *medical educator*
Ming, Si-Chun *pathologist, educator*
Montone, Kathleen T. *pathologist*
Moxon, Karen Anne *medical educator*
Mraovic, Boris *medical educator, researcher*
Muravchick, Stanley *anesthesiologist, educator*
Nathanson, Katherine L. *medical geneticist, educator*
Newschaffer, Craig J. *epidemiologist, educator*
Nikonova, Elena Vladimirovna *physician, scientist*
Nowell, Peter Carey *pathologist, educator*
Offit, Paul Allan *pediatrician*
Parveen, Zahida *medical educator, researcher*
Parvizi, Javad *orthopedist, educator*
Pasquariello, Patrick S., Jr. *pediatrician*
Piccoli, David Anthony *pediatrics educator*
Pien, Grace *medical educator*
Piltz-Seymour, Jody Robin *ophthalmologist*
Pinto-Martin, Jennifer Anne *epidemiologist, educator*
Plimack, Elizabeth R. *oncologist*
Potsic, William Paul *otolaryngologist, educator*
Rader, Daniel J. *cardiologist, educator*
Rickels, Karl *psychiatrist, educator*
Ritchie, Wallace Parks, Jr. *retired surgeon, educator*
Ritter, Deborah Elizabeth *anesthesiologist, educator*
Rogers, Fred Baker *medical educator*
Rorke-Adams, Lucy Balian *pathologist, educator*
Rossman, Milton David *medical educator, director*
Rubesin, Steohen E. *radiologist*
Rubin, Stephen Curtis *gynecologic oncologist, educator*
Ruggieri, Michael Raymond *pharmacologist, educator*
Russo, Irma Haydee Alvarez de *pathologist*
Schotland, Donald Lewis *retired medical educator, neurologist*
Schumacher, H(arry) Ralph *internist, rheumatologist, medical educator, researcher*
Schwartz, Gordon Francis *surgeon, educator*
Schwartz, J. Sanford *internist, educator*
Schwartz, Marshall Zane *pediatric surgeon*
Segal, Bernard Louis *cardiologist, educator*
Shaffer, Thomas H. *medical educator, consultant*
Silberberg, Donald H. *neurologist*
Slupianek, Artur *medical educator*
Spaeth, George Link *ophthalmologist, educator, writer*
Spiegel, Joseph *medical educator*
Spinner, Nancy Bettina *medical educator, director*
Steinberg, Marvin Edward *orthopaedic surgeon, educator*
Stunkard, Albert James *psychiatrist, educator*
Suh, Byungse *medical educator*
Suzuki, Jon Byron *medical educator, periodontist, microbiologist*
Talerman, Aleksander *pathologist, educator*
Tannen, Richard Laurence *nephrology educator*
Tchou, Julia *surgeon, educator*
Torg, Joseph Steven *orthopedic surgeon, educator*
Tourtellotte, Charles Dee *internist, rheumatologist, educator*
Tran, Judith Thuha *psychiatrist*
Trerotola, Scott Oakley *intervention radiologist, division chief*
Truant, Allan L. *medical educator, laboratory scientist, health science administrator*
Tüzün, Erdem *neurologist, consultant*
Uzzo, Robert G. *physician, consultant*
Van Decker, William Arthur *cardiologist*
Vetter, Victoria L. *pediatric cardiologist, educator*
Wapner, Keith Leslie *orthopedic surgeon, educator*
Webb, Gary Douglas *cardiologist*
Weitz, Howard Hy *cardiologist, educator*
Weller, Elizabeth Boghossian *child and adolescent psychiatrist*
Whitaker, Linton Andin *plastic surgeon*
Willi, Steven Matthew *physician, educator, researcher*
Williams, Gerald Ross *orthopedist, surgeon*
Wolfson, Marla R. *medical educator*
Wu, Hong *pathologist*
Yanoff, Myron *ophthalmologist*
Yeo, Charles John *surgery educator*
Young, Donald Stirling *clinical pathology educator*
Zderic, Stephen Anthony *urologist, surgeon*
Zweiman, Burton *allergist, immunologist, educator*

Pittsburgh
Aggarwal, Shushma *anesthesiologist, educator*
Ahluwalia, Ajit Singh *physician, educator*
Alonso, Laura Cristina *endocrinologist*
Anoosh, Farhad *surgeon*
Bartoletti, Stefano C. *radiologist*
Becker, Dorothy J. *pediatrician, educator*
Belani, Chandra Prakash *oncologist*
Bluestone, Charles D. *otolaryngologist*
Boninger, Michael Lee *physiatrist*
Caritis, Steve Nick *obstetrician, gynecologist, educator*
Carty, Sally E. *endocrine surgeon*
Caserio, Rebecca JoAnn *dermatologist, educator*
Caushaj, Philip *surgeon*
Chelly, Jacques E. *anesthesiologist*
Cockerham, Kimberly Peele *ophthalmologist, educator*
DeGroat, William Chesney *pharmacology educator*
Detre, Thomas *psychiatrist, educator*
Dillavou, Ellen D. *thoracic surgeon*
Doft, Bernard Harvey *ophthalmologist*
Dohar, Joseph *pediatrician, educator*
Duncan, Steven Ray *pulmonologist, immunologist, educator*
Epstein, Barbara A. *medical librarian*
Fernstrom, John Dickson *pharmacology and nutrition researcher, educator*
Fireman, Philip *pediatrician, allergist, immunologist*
Fisher, Bernard *surgeon, educator*
Fontes, Paulo A. *surgeon, educator*
Friday, Gilbert Anthony, Jr. *pediatrician*
Geskin, Larisa *dermatologist, researcher*
Girnita, Alin Lucian *medical educator, researcher*
Hardesty, Robert Lynch *surgeon, educator*
Heckler, Frederick Roger *plastic surgeon*
Horwitz, Mara *medical educator*
Huq, Mohammed Saiful *medical educator, director*
Jarrett, Fredric *surgeon, educator*
Jenkins, Frank *pathologist, educator*
John, Robert Hotchkiss *medical educator*
Joyce, Judith Marie *radiologist*
Kanal, Emanuel *radiologist*
Kassam, Amin B. *neurosurgeon, educator*
Kaye, Robin D. *pediatric radiologist, educator*
Kochanek, Patrick Michael *pediatrician, educator*
Kondziolka, Douglas *neurosurgeon*
Landreneau, Rodney J. *surgeon*
Lee, W.P. Andrew *plastic surgeon*
Levine, Macy Irving *physician*
Lin, Ridwan *neurologist*
Lunsford, Lawrence Dade *medical educator*
Lyjak Chorazy, Anna Julia *retired pediatrician, retired health facility administrator*
McCafferty, Leo Raymond *plastic surgeon*
Mcmahon, Patrick J. *orthopedist*
Minshew, Nancy J. *neurologist, educator*
Mosesso, Vincent Nicholas, Jr. *emergency physician*
Mountz, James Michael *radiologist, educator, biomedical researcher*
Muder, Robert Richard *physician, epidemiologist*
Mullen, Charles Frederick *health educator*
Myers, Eugene Nicholas *otolaryngologist, educator*
Nash, David Reinthal *pediatrician*
Nichols, Larry *medical educator*
Palevsky, Paul Marc *nephrologist, educator*
Parness, Jerome *medical educator*
Perlmutter, David H. *physician, educator*
Pilewski, Joseph Mark *medical and cell biology educator*
Pirris, Stephen Montgomery *neurosurgeon*
Pollack, Ian Fredric *physician, researcher*
Rastogi, Priya *medical educator*
Reed, Douglas Scott *immunologist*
Roth, Loren H. *psychiatrist*
Rubin, J. Peter *plastic surgeon*
Salter, Russell David *medical educator, researcher*
Schmidt, Christopher C. *orthopedist*
Servan-Schreiber, David *psychiatrist*
Siker, Ephraim S. *anesthesiologist*
Silveira, Fernanda de Pinho *infectious diseases physician, educator*
Simmons, Richard L. *surgeon*
Slivka, Adam *medical educator*
Smith, Kenneth J. *medical educator, researcher*
Starzl, Thomas Earl *physician, educator*
Strollo, Patrick J., Jr. *medical educator, researcher*
Talbott, Evelyn Eleanor *epidemiologist, educator*
Tao, Ran *immunologist, researcher*
Thase, Michael E. *psychiatrist*
Wald, Niel *public health educator*
Wang, Bing *medical educator*
Wholey, Mark H. *radiologist, director*
Winter, Peter Michael *anesthesiologist, educator*
Winters, Sharon Beth *medical researcher, director*
Xu, Juan *medical researcher*
Yonas, Howard *neurosurgeon, neuroscientist*
Zelle, Boris Alexander *orthopedist, researcher*
Zuley, Margarita *radiologist, educator*

Plymouth Meeting
Nobel, Joel J. *biomedical researcher*

Radnor
Raju, T. Shantha *medical researcher*

Reading
Pumariega, Andres Julio *medical administrator, educator, researcher*

Rydal
Johnson, Waine Cecil *dermatologist, educator*

Sayre
Moody, Robert Adams *neurosurgeon*

Scottdale
Tavoularis, Marjorie Osterwise *psychiatrist*

Scranton
Rhiew, Francis Changnam *radiologist, physician*

Springfield
Sing, Robert Fong *physician*

Strasburg
Morton, D. Holmes *physician*

Stroudsburg
Finch, Alberta May *retired pediatrician*

Sugarloaf
Waldron, Theodore Charles *physician*

Swarthmore
Carey, William Bacon *pediatrician, educator*

Thorndale
Hodess, Arthur Bart *cardiologist*

University Park
Underwood, Robyn M. *medical researcher*

Upper Saint Clair
Raymond, Bruce Allen *retired surgeon, medical association administrator*

Warminster
Leinweber, Bruce Kornblatt *obstetrician, gynecologist, educator*

Wayne
Earley, Laurence Elliott *retired medical educator*

Waynesboro
Cryer, Theodore Hudson *ophthalmologist, educator*
Kirk, Daniel Lee *retired physician, consultant*

West Conshohocken
Templeton, John Marks, Jr. *retired pediatric surgeon, foundation administrator*

West Grove
Snow, James Byron, Jr. *otolaryngologist, research administrator, educator*

Wilkes Barre
Casale, Alfred Stanley *thoracic and cardiovascular surgeon*
Feerick, John Paul *neurologist, researcher, military officer*
Nikam, Shivprasad *vascular and endovascular surgeon*

Williamsport
Martin, Thomas John *pediatrician, sports medicine physician*

Windber
Hu, Hai *biomedical researcher, director*

Wyndmoor
Brown, Gary Christian *ophthalmologist, director*

Wynnewood
Alter, Milton *retired neurologist*
Benz, Robert L. *internist*
Clarke, John Rodney *surgeon*
Frankl, William Stewart *cardiologist, educator*
Marks, Gerald *surgeon, educator*
Rosefsky, Jonathan Benensohn *pediatrician*
Shems, Estherina *retired child psychiatrist*
Ying, Gui-shuang *ophthalmologist, educator*
Zhang, Li *medical researcher*

Wyomissing
Hildreth, Eugene A. *physician, educator*

Yardley
Basil, Biju *psychiatrist, researcher*
Fraser, David William *epidemiologist*

RHODE ISLAND

Barrington
Carpenter, Charles Colcock Jones *internist, educator*

Newport
Rous, Stephen Norman *urologist, educator*

North Providence
Stankiewicz, Andrzej Jerzy *physician, biochemistry educator*

Pawtucket
Crowley, James Patrick *hematologist, medical educator, immunologist*
Glicksman, Arvin S(igmund) *radiation oncologist*
La Bresh, Kenneth Albert *cardiologist*
McCool, Franklin Dennis *pulmonologist, researcher*

Providence
Aronson, Stanley Maynard *physician, educator*
Biron, Christine Anne *medical science educator, researcher*
Buka, Stephen L. *epidemiologist, educator*
Davis, Robert Paul *retired physician, educator*
DeGiorgis, Joseph Alan *medical educator*
Degroot, Leslie Jacob *medical educator*
Donahue, John Edward *physician*
Easton, J(ohn) Donald *neurologist, educator*
Fritz, Gregory Kenneth *psychiatrist*
Gilchrist, James Manning *neurologist, researcher, educator*
Gilmore, Judith Marie *physician*
Gravenstein, Stefan *medical educator, director*
Green, Andrew *orthopedist, educator*
Guggenheim, Frederick Gibson *psychiatrist, educator*
Hamolsky, Milton William *retired physician*
Hennessey, James Vincent *physician, educator*
Hochberg, Leigh Robert *neurologist, neuroscience educator*
Hoy, Erik Alexander *plastic surgeon*
Jackson, Benjamin Taylor *retired surgeon, educator, health facility administrator*
Jacobson, Sandra A. *medical educator, physician*
Kadin, Marshall Edward *hematopathologist, educator*
Kane, Agnes Brezak *pathologist, educator*
Keefe, David Lawrence *medical doctor & infertility specialist, biomedical researcher*
Knopf, Paul Mark *immunologist*
Kramer, Peter David *psychiatrist, educator*
LaFrance, William Curt Phillip, Jr. *neuropsychiatrist, educator, medical researcher*
Lewis, David Carleton *medical educator, academic administrator*
Liu, Paul Yu *plastic surgeon, educator*
Mandelbaum, David Ezra *pediatric neurologist*
Mc Donald, Charles J. *dermatologist, educator*
Merlino, Anthony Frank *orthopedist*
Oh, William *physician*
Pueschel, Siegfried M. *pediatrician, educator*
Rhodes, Ramona Lagiers *medical educator, researcher*
Richman, Jesse *ophthalmologist, researcher*
Risica, Patricia *medical researcher, educator*
Sweeney, Patrick J. *medical educator*
Treaba, Diana Olguta *physician*
Triche, Elizabeth W. *epidemiologist, educator*
Vezeridis, Michael Panagiotis *surgeon, educator*
Weinstock, Martin Arthur *dermatologist, epidemiologist, educator*
Weitberg, Alan Barry *physician, researcher, dean*
Williams, David Owen *cardiologist*
Wing, Edward Joseph *biomedical researcher, educator, dean*
Zhou, Linda Hua *dermatologist, educator*
Zienowicz, Richard Joseph *plastic surgeon*

Riverside
Lekas, Mary Despina *retired otolaryngologist*
Thayer, Walter Raymond *retired internist*

Woonsocket
Brennan, Troyen A. *physician, retail pharmacy company executive*
Wanebo, Harold J. *surgeon, educator*

SOUTH CAROLINA

Aiken
Bransome, Edwin Dagobert, Jr. *internal medicine educator*

Anderson
Chipman, Dennis Clarence, Jr. *forensic psychiatrist, consultant*
Lummus, William Faulkner *retired physician*

Charleston
Allen, Robert Johnson *plastic surgeon, educator*
Ballenger, James C. *psychiatrist, researcher*
Barbour, John Richard *plastic surgeon*
Bell, Norman Howard *retired endocrinologist, educator*
Chi, Angela *pathologist, educator*
Chiaramida, Salvatore *cardiologist, educator, health facility administrator*
Colwell, John Amory *physician*
Cooper, George, IV, *cardiologist, educator*
Crawford, Fred Allen, Jr. *cardiothoracic surgeon, educator*
Daniell, Herman Burch *pharmacologist*
Frankel, Bruce Michael *neurosurgeon, researcher*
Garnovskaya, Maria N. *medical educator, researcher*
Garr, David Ross *physician, educator*
Glassman, Armand Barry *physician, educator, scientist, administrator, pathologist*
Greenberg, Charles Steven *hematologist*
Gross, Richard H. *surgeon, educator*
Gupta, Monika *nephrologist, researcher*
Hulsey, Thomas C. *epidemiologist, researcher*
Jaffa, Ayad A. *medical educator, researcher*
Jaffe, Murray Sherwood *retired surgeon*
Key, Lester Lyndon, Jr. *pediatrician, director*
Leman, Robert Burton *cardiology educator*
Malcolm, Robert James *psychiatrist, educator, clinical investigator*
Mallin, Robert *medical educator*
Maria, Bernard L. *pediatric neurologist*
McConnell, Bright III *orthopaedic surgeon*
McCurdy, Layton *medical educator*
Metcalf, John Stevenson *surgical pathologist, dermatologist*
Mohr, Lawrence Charles *physician*
Newhard, James Michael Lloyd *medical educator*
Oates, James Caldwell *rheumatologist, physician, research scientist*
Osguthorpe, John David *otolaryngologist, educator*
Othersen, Henry Biemann, Jr. *surgeon, physician, educator*
Reed, Carolyn E. *thoracic surgeon*
Reves, Joseph Gerald (Jerry Reves) *anesthesiology educator, dean*

Rousseau, Paul Charles *geriatrician, palliative care physician, educator*
Sahn, Steven Alan *internist, educator*
Solomon, Kerry D. *ophthalmologist, surgeon, consultant*
Stuart, Robert Kenneth *internist, hematologist, oncologist, educator*
Tolliver, Bryan K. *psychiatrist, educator*
Underwood, Paul Benjamin *gynecologist, oncologist, educator*
Waller, John Louis *anesthesiologist, educator*
Wingo, Marshall Scott *urologist*

Columbia
Almond, Carl Herman *surgeon, physician, educator*
Bostick, Robert Maner *epidemiologist, family physician*
Donald, Alexander Grant *psychiatrist, educator*
Flanagan, Clyde Harvey, Jr. *psychiatrist, psychoanalyst, educator*
Gaffney, Thomas Edward *physician*
Hooker, Steven P. *sports medicine physician, educator*
Humphries, John O'Neal *cardiologist, educator, dean*
Lindley, Lisa L. *medical educator*
McGuire, Franklin Riley *pulmonologist, educator*
McKeown, Robert E. *epidemiologist, educator*
Nottingham, James M. *surgeon, educator*
Piper, Crystal Nicole *medical researcher*
Sheppe, Joseph Andrew *surgeon*
Still, Charles Neal *retired neurologist, medical educator, consultant*
Thiruvanamalai, Valarmathi Mani *pathologist, educator*
Tripathi, Ramesh Chandra *ophthalmologist, researcher, educator*
Waldron, Robert Leroy, II, *radiologist, educator*
Wright, Harry Hercules *psychiatrist*

Conway
McMillan, Michael Reid *retired orthopedic surgeon*

Florence
DeMichele, Domenic John *neurologist, neuroradiologist*
Imbeau, Stephen Alan *allergist*

Georgetown
Ahearn, Arthur Mason *orthopedist, surgeon, consultant*

Greenville
Bonner, Jack Wilbur III *psychiatrist, educator, administrator*
Brownlee, Noel Anderson *pathologist, consultant*

Greenwood
Schwartz, Charles E. *medical geneticist, medical association administrator*

Hilton Head Island
Burns, C(harles) Patrick *hematologist, oncologist*
Engelman, Karl *physician*
Field, James Bernard *internist, educator*
Jarvis, William Robert *epidemiologist, educator*
Roehrig, C(harles) Burns *internist, consultant*

Inman
Fogarty, Charles Michael *pulmonologist, researcher*

Isle Of Palms
Elliott, Larry Paul *radiologist, educator*

Mount Pleasant
Esnaola, Nestor F. *surgeon, director*
Maize, John Christopher *dermatologist, educator*
Weininger, Markus *radiologist*

Myrtle Beach
Favaro, Mary Kaye Asperheim *pediatrician, writer*
Schwartz, Steve Wendelin *physician*

Orangeburg
Smoak, Randolph Duncan, Jr. *surgeon*

Spartanburg
Dille, Brice *ophthalmologist*
Richard, Orr Kenneth *oncologist, educator*

Sullivans Island
Selby, John Bayne, Sr. *retired radiologist, medical educator*

Sumter
Barrow, Tawana Walker *psychiatrist, consultant*
Leavell, Elizabeth Boykin *retired pediatrician*

West Columbia
Klutzow, Friedrich Wilhelm *neuropathologist*
Phillips, Karen Diane *surgeon*

SOUTH DAKOTA

Aberdeen
Anderson, Esther Elizabeth *retired pediatrician, educator*

Jefferson
Gitter, Richard *thoracic surgeon*

Rapid City
White, Ronald Joseph *biomedical researcher, physiologist, educator*

Sioux Falls
Casas-Melley, Adela Teresa *pediatrician, surgeon*
Jaqua, Richard Allen *pathologist*
Wegner, Karl Heinrich *retired pathologist, educator, farmer*

Vermillion
Burton, Maureen B. *medical educator*

TENNESSEE

Chattanooga
Cofer, Joseph Broaddus *surgeon*
Marshall, Willis Henry *psychiatrist*
Santos, Benjamin Guzman *physician, anesthesiologist*
Segler, Christopher Paige *surgeon, researcher*
Wessels, Izak Frederick *ophthalmologist*

Columbia
Fleming, Emma Kae Brock *radiography educator*

Cookeville
Smolenski, Lisabeth Ann *physician*

Franklin
Petrie, William Marshall *psychiatrist*

Germantown
Beaty, James Harold *pediatric orthopaedic surgeon*
Ling, Frank W. *obstetrician, gynecologist*

Gray
Combs, Stephen Paul *pediatrician, health facility administrator*

Hendersonville
Burt, Alvin Miller III *anatomist, cell biologist, writer, educator*

Jackson
Nord, Keith Douglas *surgeon, director*
Swaim, Mark Wendell *physician, molecular biologist, hepatologist, essayist, gastroenterologist, photographer*

Johnson City
Adebonojo, Festus O. *medical educator*
Cupp, Horace Ballard *surgeon, educator*
Giorgadze, Tamar Alfred *pathologist, physician*
Hamdy, Ronald Charles *geriatrician*
Kao, Race Li-Chan *medical educator*
Olsen, Martin E. *obstetrician, educator*
Pandian, Shantha G. *psychiatrist*
Taylor, Grant David *urologist*

Knoxville
Byrd, Debbie Curtis *medical educator*
Filston, Howard Church *pediatric surgeon*
Kliefoth, A. Bernhard III *neurosurgeon*
White, Wesley Matthew *urologist*

Maryville
Howard, Cecil Byron *retired pediatrician*

Memphis
Adams-Graves, Patricia E. *medical educator*
Allen, David Mark *psychiatrist, educator, director*
Beranova-Giorgianni, Sarka *biomedical researcher, educator*
Chesney, Russell Wallace *pediatrician, educator*
Clarke, Dave F. *neurologist, educator*
Cohen, Harris L. *diagnostic radiologist, consultant*
Cox, Clair Edward, II, *urologist, medical educator*
Currey, Thomas Arthur *ophthalmologist*
Eason, James David *surgeon*
Egidi, Maria Francesca *transplant physician*
Freire, Amado X. *pulmonary physician, clinical researcher*
Gerald, Barry *retired radiology educator, neuroscientist*
Green, Daniel Michael *pediatric oncologist*
Heimberg, Murray *pharmacologist, biochemist, physician*
Helton, Kathleen Jacobson *neuroradiologist*
Herrod, Henry Grady III *pediatrics professor, allergist, immunologist*
Hoffer, Fredric Alan *pediatric radiologist*
Hughes, Walter Thompson *pediatrician, educator*
Hunt, James Calvin *physician, academic administrator*
Johnson, Karen C. *epidemiologist, researcher*
Karcioglu, Zeynel A. *ophthalmologist, educator*
Kitabchi, Abbas Eqbal *medical educator*
Korones, Sheldon Bernarr *pediatrician, educator*
Kutteh, William H. *medical educator, director*
Lewis, James Bryant, Jr. *physician*
Mallett, Veronica T. *medical educator, director*
Mansbach, Charles *gastroenterologist, researcher*
Morreim, E. Haavi *medical ethics educator*
Osarogiagbon, Ray Uyiosa *oncologist, educator*
Patay, Zoltán *radiologist, educator*
Razzouk, Bassem Ibrahim *hematologist, oncologist*
Schwartzberg, Lee S. *internist, oncologist, hematologist*
Shan, Zuyao *medical researcher*
Shochat, Stephen Jay *pediatrician, surgeon*
Tonkin, Ina Lynn Dyer *physician, cardiovascular radiologist, educator*
Van Middlesworth, Lester *physiology, biophysics and medicine educator, internist*
Wilcox, Harry Hammond *retired anatomist*
Zhao, Wei *medical researcher*

Murfreesboro
Coleman, Jack Andrew, Jr. *otolaryngologist*

Nashville
Abou-Khalil, Bassel William *neurologist, epileptologist*
Allison, Fred, Jr. *internist, retired medical educator*
Arteaga, Carlos Luis *medical researcher, director*
Aschner, Judy Lynn *pediatrician, educator*
Baldwin, Harold Scott *pediatrician, educator*
Bates, George William *obstetrician, gynecologist, educator*
Beauchamp, Robert Daniel *surgeon, educator*
Berlin, Jordan D. *gastrointestinal oncologist, healthcare educator*
Bernard, Louis Joseph *surgeon, educator*
Boothby, Mark R. *immunologist*
Brill, Aaron Bertrand *nuclear medicine educator*
Brock, John William III *surgeon, urologist, educator*
Burnett, Lonnie Sheldon *obstetrics and gynecology educator*
Byrne, John G. *surgeon*
Capdevila, Jorge H. *medical educator, biochemistry educator*
Carroll, Frank Edward, Jr. *radiologist, researcher*
Chang, Sam S. *urologist, surgeon, educator*
Crowe, James Earl, Jr. *pediatrician, educator*
Davis, Stephen N. *endocrinologist*
Delbeke, Dominique *nuclear medicine physician, educator*
Dmochowski, Roger *urologist, educator*
Edwards, Kathryn Margaret *physician, researcher, educator*
Epps, Anna Cherrie *immunologist, educator, dean interim president*
Feng, Hua-Jun *medical educator, researcher*
Fields, James Perry *dermatologist, dermatopathologist, allergist, pharmacologist, pharmacist*
Fisher, Jack *medical educator, plastic surgeon*
Fleischer, Arthur C. *medical educator, radiologist*
Fonseca, Ricardo B. *nuclear medicine physician*
Gingrass, Mary Katherine *plastic surgeon*
Greelish, James P. *cardiologist, surgeon, educator*
Greer, John P. *medical educator*
Hays, Stephen Robert *pediatrician, anesthesiologist*
Head, David R. *pathologist, educator*
Helderman, J. Harold *transplant physician, immunologist, educator*
Hickson, Gerald Bennett *pediatrician*
Hildreth, James E.K. *pharmacology and molecular science educator, dean*
Hong, Charles C. *cardiologist, medical educator*
Jackson, Gretchen Purcell *surgeon, educator*
Jarquin Valdivia, Adrian Alberto *internist, neurologist, researcher*
Jennings, Henry Smith III *cardiologist*
Johnson, David Horton *oncologist*
Joo, Myungsoo *immunologist, researcher*
Lagrange, Andre Hollis *neurologist, educator*
Lee, Donald Han *surgeon, orthopedist*
Linton, MacRae Fort *internist, educator*
Lynch, John Brown *plastic surgeon, educator*
Marney, Samuel Rowe, Jr. *retired allergist, immunologist, educator*
Maron, David Joel *cardiologist, educator*
Martin, Peter Robert *psychiatrist, pharmacologist*
Martin, William H. *medical educator, director*
Masys, Daniel Richard *medical educator, department chairman*
Mathew, Revi Puthenpurackal *pediatrician, educator*
Melvin, Willie Valentenia *surgeon, educator*
Melzer, Peter *neuroanatomist, educator, research scientist*
Morris, John Albert *medical educator*
Neilson, Eric Grant *physician, educator, health facility administrator*
Oates, John Alexander III *medical educator*
Pagnani, Michael Joseph *orthopaedic surgeon*
Pham, Wellington *radiologist, educator*
Pinson, Charles Wright *surgeon, educator, academic administrator*
Polk, David Brent *pediatrician, educator*
Ray, Wayne Allen *epidemiologist, educator*
Roberts, John Robert *cardiothoracic surgeon, consultant*
Robertson, David *physician, pharmacologist, educator*
Robinson, Nathaniel David, Jr. *physician, consultant*
Rojas, Mario Augusto *pediatrician, director*
Rollins-Smith, Louise Ann *immunologist, educator*
Ross, Joseph Comer *pulmonologist, educator, academic administrator*
Schaffner, William *medical educator*
Shack, Robert Bruce (Bruce Shack) *plastic surgeon, department chairman*
Smith, Bradley E. *anesthesiologist*
Stahlman, Mildred Thornton *pediatrician, pathologist, educator, researcher*
Stork, Travis Lane *emergency physician*
Trochtenberg, David Scott *medical educator, director*
Vermund, Sten Halvor *epidemiologist, educator*
Walters, Arthur Scott *neurologist, educator, clinical research scientist*
Whitlock, James Alan *pediatrics educator*

Oak Ridge
Spray, Paul Ellsworth *retired surgeon*

Ooltewah
Birch, Lorna May *geriatrician*

Talbott
Gresham, Chip *physician, researcher*

Williamsport
Dysinger, Paul William *preventive medicine physician, educator*

TEXAS

Abilene
Morgan, Clyde Nathaniel *dermatologist*

Amarillo
Laur, William Edward *retired dermatologist*
Marupudi, Sambasiva Rao *surgeon, educator*
Parker, Gerald M. *osteopath, researcher*
Saadeh, Constantine Khalil *internist, educator, health facility administrator*
Siddiqui, Afzal A. *medical educator*
Wilson, Golder North *medical educator*

Arlington
Ahmed, M. Basheer *psychiatrist, educator*
Tingley, Floyd Warren *retired internist*

Austin
Aldrich, Richard W. *biomedical researcher, neurobiology professor*
Annis, Joseph P. *anesthesiologist, educator*
Crismon, Miles Lynn *clinical psychopharmacologist, dean, educator*
Elequin, Cleto, Jr. *retired physician*
Fleeger, David Clark *colon and rectal surgeon*
Ivy, John L. *medical educator, researcher*
Langlois, Peter Hayes *epidemiologist*
Leslie, Steven W. *pharmacologist, educator, former dean*
Mukai, Ai *physiatrist*
Neavel, Celia Beth *medical association administrator*
Painter, Theophilus Shickel, Jr. *internist, allergist*
Sutton, Beverly Jewell *psychiatrist*
Thompson, Sanna J. *medical educator*

Baytown
Williams, Drew Davis *surgeon*

Beaumont
Lozano, Jose *nephrologist*
Luviano, Damien M. *ophthalmologist*
Soudi, Matthew M. *retired surgeon*
Tinsley, Judith Anne *sonographer, program director*

Bellaire
Haywood, Theodore Joseph *physician, educator*

Boerne
Wittmer, James Frederick *preventive medicine physician, educator*

Brooks City-Base
Balldin, Ulf Ingemar *medical researcher*

College Station
Carlton, Paul Kendall, Jr. *physician*
Colenda, Christopher Columbus III *psychiatrist, dean*
Hawes, Catherine *medical educator, director*
Kier, Ann B. *pathology educator*
Samollow, Paul B. *medical educator, researcher*
Wenger, Scott Andrew *orthopedist, surgeon*

Coppell
Khan, Amir Manzoor *orthopedist*

Corpus Christi
Al-Akash, Samhar I. *pediatrician, nephrologist*
Blankenship, Billy Jim *surgeon*
Lim, Alexander Rufasta *neurologist, clinical investigator and neurophysiologist, educator, writer*
Sisley, Nina Mae *physician, public health service officer*

Dallas
Adams, William Peter, Jr. *plastic surgeon, educator*
Aggarwal, Nalini K. *ophthalmologist, educator*
Alexander, Gail Susan *psychiatrist*
Anwar, Azam *cardiologist*
Ashfaq, Raheela *pathologist, educator*
Barnes, Madge Lou *physician*
Barton, Fritz Engel, Jr. *plastic surgeon, educator*
Bergstresser, Paul Richard *dermatologist, educator*
Bidic, Sean Michael *plastic surgeon, orthopedist*
Bonte, Frederick James *radiologist, educator, physician*
Boswell, George Marion, Jr. *orthopedist, health facility administrator*
Buchanan, George R. *oncologist, hematologist, educator*
Byrd, Steve (Henry Stephenson Byrd) *plastic surgeon, educator*
Caetano, Raul *psychiatrist, educator*
Cavanagh, Harrison Dwight *ophthalmologist, educator*
Chinnakotla, Srinath *surgeon, director*
Connolly, John E. *immunologist, educator*
Cowling, Terianne *medical researcher*
Cox, Rody P(owell) *internist, educator*
Devous, Michael David, Sr. *radiologist, educator*
Einspruch, Burton Cyril *psychiatrist*
Eugene, Phillip Frenkel *hematologist*
Ewalt, David Harris *pediatrician, urologist*
Fenves, Andrew Zoltan *nephrologist*
Flatt, Adrian Ede *surgeon*
Fordtran, John Satterfield *physician*
Frenkel, Eugene Phillip *physician*
Friedberg, Errol Clive *pathology educator, researcher*
Fyfe, Alistair Ian *cardiologist, scientist, educator*
González-Boles, Cristina M. *medical educator*
Goodenberger, Daniel Marvin *medical educator*
Grammer, John Colquitte *cardiologist*
Gross, Gary Neil *allergist, physician*
Gruchalla, Rebecca Sue *medical researcher, educator*
Guleserian, Kristine Jane *surgeon, thoracic surgeon, educator*
Gunter, Jack Pershing *plastic surgeon, otolaryngologist*
Haley, Barbara Jean *oncologist, hematologist*
Hamra, Sameer T. *plastic surgeon, educator*
Hardy, R. Doug *epidemiologist, educator*
Hinnant, Jerry Herbert *surgeon*
Hobar, P. Craig *plastic surgeon, educator*
Holman, James *allergist*
Hurd, Eric Ray *rheumatologist, internist, educator*
Hurwitz, Jodie Linda *cardiologist*
Isaacson, Brandon *medical educator*
Janis, Jeffery E. *plastic surgeon, educator*
Jeyarajah, Dhiresh Rohan *surgeon*
Johnson, Robert Lee, Jr. *physician, educator, researcher*
Kaiser, Fran Elizabeth *endocrinologist, gerontologist*
Kenkel, Jeffrey Miller *plastic surgeon, educator*
Kernie, Steven Gerard *pediatrician, educator*
Kogan, Inna *psychiatrist, educator*
Lenkovsky, Fima *anesthesiologist*
Lerman, Mark Jeffrey *nephrologist, medical administrator*

Lewis, Jerry M. *psychiatrist, educator*
Lichliter, Warren Eugene *surgeon, educator*
Lister, George *pediatrician*
Liu, George Tye *surgeon, educator*
Maddrey, Willis Crocker *medical educator, internist, academic administrator, consultant, researcher*
Mc Clelland, Robert Nelson *surgeon, educator*
Menter, M(artin) Alan *dermatologist*
Mitchell, Teddy Lee *physician*
Moddelmog, Hala *medical association administrator*
Moore, Hugh Leslie *retired pediatrician*
Myers, Larry Leonard *otolaryngologist, educator*
Naylor, Rebekah Ann *surgeon, educator*
Noguchi, Hirofumi *surgeon*
Odom, Floyd Clark *surgeon*
O'Shaughnessy, Joyce Ann *oncologist, director*
Parkey, Robert Wayne *radiology and nuclear medicine educator, research radiologist*
Phillips, Joseph Theodore, Jr. *neurologist, educator*
Ring, W(illiam) Steves *thoracic and cardiovascular surgeon*
Rohrich, Rod(ney) James *plastic surgeon, educator*
Rosenberg, Roger Newman *neurologist, educator, department chair*
Sagalowsky, Arthur I. *urologist, educator*
Saint-Cyr, Michel *plastic surgeon*
Silverstein, Russell L. *physician*
Stastny, Peter *medical educator*
Stewart, William C. *medical researcher, director*
Stone, Marvin Jules *hematologist, oncologist, educator*
Sucato, Daniel J. *orthopaedic surgeon*
Suter, Robert Eduard *emergency physician, educator*
Tebbetts, John Beryl *plastic surgeon*
Tran, Quoc-Hung *psychiatrist*
Trotter, James *physician*
Waddell, Douglas Howard *family physician*
Wallace, Charles Alan *plastic surgeon*
Wildenthal, C(laud) Kern *physician, educator*
Wilson, Jean Donald *endocrinologist, educator*
Wolford, Larry M. *surgeon*
Xie, Yang *medical educator*
Yancy, Clyde Warren, Jr. *cardiologist, educator*
Yaradanakul, Alp *biomedical researcher*
Yu, Gang *medical educator, researcher*

El Paso
Adams, Bruce Douglas *physician, researcher*
Hanbali, Fadi *neurosurgeon, educator*
Kuczkowski, Krzysztof Marek *anesthesiologist, department chairman*
Martinez-Lopez, Jorge Ignacio *internist, educator, cardiologist, consultant*
Mulla, Zuber *epidemiologist*
Sozer, Sadri Ozan *plastic surgeon*
Taber, David O. *urological surgeon*

Enchanted Oaks
Melton, Kathy A. *medical transcription educator*

Fort Sam Houston
Givens, Melissa Lousie *emergency physician*
Hewitson, William Craig *physician, career officer*

Fort Worth
Bailey, Susan Rudd *physician*
Choudhary, Adil Mushtaq *gastroenterologist*
Cox, James Sidney *physician*
Dubin, Bruce *medical educator, dean*
Hey, Wayne Albert *urologic surgeon, medical association executive*
Jones, Harlan Pierre *medical educator*
Jurgensen, Warren Peter *retired psychiatrist, educator*
Kowalski, Debra Atkisson *physician*
Lichtman, David Michael *orthopedist, health facility administrator, educator, retired military officer*
Matsumoto, Shinichi *surgeon, researcher*
Motley, Travis *surgeon*
Tobey, Martin Alan *cardiologist*

Galveston
AL-Hendy, Ayman *gynecologist, obstetrician*
Ashizawa, Tetsuo *neurologist, educator*
Bytautiene, Egle *medical educator*
Dawson, Earl Bliss *medical educator*
Duarte, Alexander *medical educator*
Gonzalez, Emilio Bustamante *rheumatologist, educator*
Goodwin, Jean McClung *psychiatrist*
Gugala, Zbigniew *medical educator*
Gwak, Young Seob *biomedical researcher*
Hankins, Gary D.V. *medical educator*
Harirah, Hassan M. *medical educator*
Hawkins, Hal K(enneth) *pathologist*
Hirschfeld, Robert M.A. *psychiatrist*
James, Thomas Naum *cardiologist, educator*
Klein, Gordon Leslie *pediatrician, educator*
Kumar, Santosh *medical educator, research scientist*
Malloy, Michael Howard *pediatrician*
McKendall, Robert Roland *neurologist, virologist, educator*
Mohanty, Aaron *neurosurgeon, educator*
Nguyen-Oghalai, Tracy Uyentrang *medical educator, researcher*
Oberhauser, Andres F. *medical educator, researcher*
Pyles, Richard B. *medical educator*
Rosanio, Salvatore *cardiologist, educator*
Rose, Robert M. *consultant interdisciplinary research netwoks*
Sahu, Gautam K. *medical educator*
Sandstead, Harold Hilton *physician, researcher, educator, director*
Savidge, Tor *medical educator*
Simmons, Anthony *virology educator, physician, researcher*
Smith, David English *pathologist, educator*
Theiler, Regan *obstetrician, gynecologist, educator*
Townsend, Courtney M. *surgeon*
Zhu, Bao Ting *pharmacologist, toxicologist, researcher*

Georgetown
Manning, Robert Thomas *internist, educator*
Parker, Lynda Michele *psychiatrist*
Tegtmeier, Ronald Eugene *physician, surgeon*

Grapevine
Ghaffar, Faryal *pediatrician, infectious disease specialist, educator*

Harlingen
Cohn, Aaron I. *anesthesiologist, educator*
Salcedo-Dovi, Hector Eduardo *anatomist, educator, surgeon*

Houston
Abdalla, Eddie K. *surgeon, educator*
Alam, Mahboob *internist*
Aldape, Ken *pathologist, researcher*
Alexanian, Raymond *hematologist*
Alford, Bobby Ray *otolaryngologist, academic administrator, educator*
Allred, D. Craig *pathologist, educator*
Alt, Eckhard U. *physician, educator*
Appel, Stanley Hersh *neurologist, educator*
Arjomand, Bijan *medical educator*
Ayus, Juan Carlos *nephrologist*
Bailey, Harold Randolph *surgeon, educator*
Baldwin, Bonnie *physician*
Ball, Valdesha LeChante' *physician*
Ballo, Matthew T. *radiation oncologist, educator*
Barrett, Bernard Morris, Jr. *plastic and reconstructive surgeon*
Barshes, Neal Ryan *surgeon*
Bast, Robert Clinton, Jr. *medical researcher, educator*
Batsakis, John George *pathology educator*
Berg, Stacey Lynn *pediatric oncologist*
Bidani, Akhil *biomedical researcher, educator*
Bodey, Gerald Paul *retired medical educator*
Bou Aram, Boura'a Abdul Karim *pediatrician, researcher*
Boutros, Sean *plastic surgeon*
Braiteh, Fadi *physician*
Braun, Michael C. *nephrologist, educator*
Brener, Daniel Michael *psychiatrist*
Brenner, Malcolm K. *pediatric and medical educator*
Brewer, Eileen D. (L. Eileen Doyle Brewer) *nephrologist, educator*
Brown, Powel H. *oncologist, educator*
Bryan, Nathan Scott *medical educator*
Buja, L. Maximilian *pathologist, academic administrator, educator*
Bungo, Michael William *cardiologist, educator, administrator*
Burzynski, Stanislaw Rajmund *internist*
Buster, John Edmond *obstetrician, researcher*
Buzdar, Aman U. *internal medicine educator*
Cantor, Scott Brian *medical educator*
Casscells, Samuel Ward III *cardiologist, educator, former federal agency administrator*
Catlin, Francis Irving *physician*
Caviness, Alison Chantal *pediatrician, educator*
Chaiyarat, Walailuk *medical researcher*
Chemaly, Roy F. *physician*
Chen, Eric *ophthalmologist*
Cheung, Min Rex *medical educator*
Chevray, Pierre M. *medical educator*
Chiou-Tan, Faye *physician, educator*
Cocanour, Christine Susan *surgery educator, researcher*
Cohn, William Ettlinger *cardiologist, thoracic surgeon, product designer*
Corriere, Joseph N., Jr. *urologist, educator*
Cortes, Jorge *oncologist*
Couch, Robert Barnard *physician, scientist, microbiologist, educator*
Daiger, Stephen P. *ophthalmologist, educator*
Dinney, Colin P. *surgeon, urologist*
Dodd, Gerald Dewey, Jr. *radiologist, educator*
DuBois, Raymond N. *medical educator, researcher*
DuPont, Herbert Lancashire *medical educator, researcher*
Durand, Jean-Bernard *cardiologist, researcher*
Eichenwald, Eric *pediatrician, director*
Eissa, Mona Ah *pediatrician, researcher, educator*
El-Zein, Randa *medical educator*
Engelhardt, Hugo Tristram, Jr. *physician, educator*
Ertan, Atilla *medical educator, physician, researcher, health facility administrator*
Evans, Harry Launius *pathology educator*
Ewer, Michael S. *medical educator*
Fadul, Nada Abdellatif *medical researcher*
Fakhri, Samer *otolaryngologist, educator*
Feigon, Judith Tova *ophthalmologist, surgeon, educator*
Ferrendelli, James Anthony *neurologist, educator*
Fischer, Craig Peter *surgeon*
Fishman, Marvin Allen *pediatric neurologist, educator*
Fornage, Bruno Denis *radiologist, educator*
Freireich, Emil J *hematologist, educator*
Gabbard, Glen Owens *psychiatrist, psychotherapist*
Gershenson, David Marc *oncology educator, university administrator*
Gertzbein, Stanley David *orthopedic surgeon*
Giardino, Angelo Peter *pediatrician, director*
Gigli, Irma *dermatologist, academic administrator, educator*
Gilbert, Mark R. *neuro-oncologist, educator*
Ginsberg, Lawrence David *psychiatrist, researcher*
Goldman, Stanford Milton *medical educator*
Goldstein, Stuart Leonard *pediatrician, educator*
Gong, Yun *cytologist, educator*
Gonzalez-Angulo, Ana Maria *medical educator*
Goss, John Alan *surgeon, educator*
Gould, Lance K. *medical scientist, professor*
Graves, Daniel Edward *medical association administrator, researcher*
Grigore, Alina M. *anesthesiologist*
Grossman, Herbert Barton *urologist, researcher*
Grossman, Robert George *neurosurgeon, department chairman*
Gunn, Albert Edward, Jr. *internist, health facility administrator, lawyer, educator*
Gupta, Monesha *pediatrician, educator*
Hall, Robert Joseph *internist, educator*
Hamid, Basem *neurologist, consultant*
Hamilton, Carlos Robert, Jr. *endocrinologist, academic administrator, consultant*
Hamilton, Steven M. *plastic surgeon*
Handy, Beverly C. *medical educator*
Hankins, Christopher Lovell *plastic surgeon*
Hanna, Ehab Y. *otolaryngologist, educator*
Hayes-Jordan, Andrea Anita *surgeon, educator*
Haymond, Morey William *pediatrician, endocrinologist*
Haynie, Thomas Powell III *physician*
He, Renjie *medical researcher*
Heird, William Carroll *pediatrician, educator*
Hellerstein, Lewis Jan *hematologist, oncologist, consultant*
Holsinger, Floyd Christopher *surgeon*
Hsu, Sylvia *dermatologist, educator*
Hurwitz, Richard Louis *medical sciences educator*
Hutchens, Jerome Enos *psychiatrist*
Hwang, Rosa F. *oncologist, educator*
Hwu, Patrick *oncologist*
Jabbour, Elias *hematologist, oncologist, educator*
Jaeckle, Kurt Alfred *neuro-oncologist, neurologist, educator*
Jankovic, Joseph *neurologist, educator*
Jefferies, John Lynn *cardiologist, educator*
Jneid, Hani *interventional cardiologist, researcher*
Jones, Dan *medical educator*
Jones, Dan Brigman *ophthalmologist, educator*
Jones, Edith Irby *internist*
Kahan, Barry Donald *surgeon, educator*
Kaiser, Larry Robert *thoracic surgeon*
Kaplan, Alan Leslie *gynecology educator, oncologist, department chairman*
Katrana, David John *retired plastic and reconstructive surgeon, director*
Kaufman, Raymond Henry *physician, educator*
Keyomarsi, Khandan *medical educator*
Kim, Daniel H. *neurosurgeon*
Klish, William John *pediatrician, educator*
Kone, Bruce C. *medical educator, nephrologist, scientist, former dean*
Kosten, Thomas Richard *psychiatrist, educator*
Kraft, Irvin Alan *retired psychiatrist*
Kraus, Gary Edward *neurosurgeon*
Kundra, Vikas *radiologist, educator*
Lally, Kevin P. *Pediatric Surgeon, Department Chairman*
Lang, Frederick F. *medical educator*
Langston, Claire *pathologist, educator*
Lawrie, Gerald Murray *cardiovascular and thoracic surgeon, educator*
Le, Weidong *neurologist, educator, neuroscientist*
Leeds, Norman E. *medical educator, radiologist*
Letsou, George Vasilios *cardiothoracic surgeon*
Lewis, Dorothy E. *medical educator*
Lewis, Valerae Olive *surgeon, educator*
Lindsey, John William *neurologist, educator*
Lippman, Scott Michael *oncologist, educator*
Liu, Jing *pathologist, educator*
Liu, Jinsong *pathologist*
Lopez, Jose Aron *hematologist*
Lypka, Michael Alexander *surgeon, dentist*
Mallory, George B. *pulmonologist, educator*
Mancias, Peedro *pediatrician*
Mann, Douglas Lowell *cardiologist*
Marangell, Lauren Beth *psychiatrist, researcher*
Margulis, Vitaly *urologist*
Massin, Edward Krauss *physician*
McFarlin, Brian Keith *medical educator, researcher*
McKechnie, John Charles *gastroenterologist, educator*
McKenzie, Laurie Jane *medical association administrator*
McPherson, Alice Ruth *ophthalmologist, educator*
McPherson, David D. *cardiologist, educator*
Mentz, Henry A. III *plastic surgeon*
Milam, John Daniel *pathologist, educator*
Miles, Brian John *urologist*
Miller, Gary Evan *psychiatrist, mental health services professional*
Miller, Robert Harold *otolaryngologist, educator*
Milosavljevic, Aleksandar *medical geneticist, educator*
Mintz-Hittner, Helen Ann *physician, researcher*
Moise, Kenneth Joseph, Jr. *medical educator*
Moore, Robert H. *pediatrician, educator*
Moran, Cesar A. *pathologist, educator*
Munk, Zev Moshe *physician, researcher*
Murad, Ferid *physician*
Murphy, William Alexander, Jr. *diagnostic radiologist, educator*
Musher, Daniel Michael *medical educator, researcher, epidemiologist, director*
Nebgen, Denise R. *physician, researcher*
Nelson, Flavia *neurologist, professor, researcher, consultant*
Neul, Jeffrey Lorenz *medical educator, researcher*
Ng, Chaan S. *radiologist, educator*
Nosé, Yukihiko *surgeon, educator*
Oldham, John Michael *physician, psychiatrist, educator*
Onn, Amir *medical educator, researcher*
Orengo-Nania, Silvia *ophthalmologist*
Ornstein, David *urologist*
Osborne, C. Kent *oncologist, educator*
Osborne, Charles Kent *oncologist, researcher*
Pan, Hui-Lin *medical educator*
Paniagua, David *physician*
Perrier, Nancy *endocrinologist, educator*
Persse, David *emergency physician, director*
Petropoulos, Dimitrios *oncologist, hematologist, educator*
Phung, Nguyen Dinh *medical educator*
Quiros-Tejeira, Ruben Eloy *pediatrician, educator, researcher*
Qureshi, Waqar A. *medical educator*
Raad, Issam I. *medical educator, researcher*
Raijman, Isaac *gastroenterologist, educator*
Rapini, Ronald Peter *dermatology educator*
Rappaport, Norman Harvey *plastic surgeon*
Rasekh, Abdi *cardiologist*
Rhoads, Jon Marc *pediatric gastroenterologist, educator*
Ribble, John Charles *medical educator*
Riley, William John *neurologist*
Risin, Semyon Aaron *pathologist, educator*
Rivenes, Shannon Marie *pediatric cardiologist*
Rivera, Victor M. *medical educator, director*
Robb, Geoffrey Lawrence *plastic surgeon*
Ross, Patti Jayne *obstetrics and gynecology educator*
Safdar, Amar *medical educator, researcher*
Salem, Philip Adeeb *medical educator*
Sanderson, Mary Louise *medical association administrator*
Sawaya, Raymond *neurosurgeon*
Sazama, Kathleen *pathologist, lawyer*
Schachtel-Green, Barbara Harriet Levin *retired epidemiologist*
Scharold, Mary Louise *psychoanalyst, psychiatrist, educator*
Selber, Jesse Creed *plastic surgeon, researcher*
Sellin, Joseph Henry *gastroenterologist*
Shearer, William Thomas *pediatrician, educator*
Shen, Ying H. *medical educator*
Sherman, Steven I. *endocrinologist, educator*
Sherman, Vadim *surgeon, director*
Shulman, Robert Jay *pediatrician, nutritionist, gastroenterologist, educator*
Smirnakis, Stelios Manolis *medical educator*
Smythe, Cheves McCord *internist, geriatrician, educator, dean*
Sood, Anil K. *oncologist, researcher*
Sostman, Dirk *physician, clinical researcher, medical educator*
Speer, Michael Emery *neonatologist, educator*
Stal, Samuel *plastic surgeon, educator*
Stasney, C. Richard *otolaryngologist, director*
Stewart, David James *oncologist, educator*
Suarez-Almazor, Maria E. *rheumatologist, educator*
Subramanian, Shyam *sleep physician director*
Sugimoto, Mitsushige *medical association administrator, researcher*
Suki, Dima *epidemiologist*
Sutton, Jeffrey Paul *physician, scientist, administrator*
Swick, Todd J. *medical association administrator*
Swisher, Stephen G. *thoracic surgeon*
Toy, Eugene C. *gynecologist*
Traber, Peter George *medical educator, former academic administrator*
Tweardy, David John *physician, educator*
Vallbona, Carlos *physician*
Vallejo, Jesus G. *medical educator*
Varma, Datla G.K. *radiologist, researcher*
Vierling, John Moore *physician*
Walker, William Easton *surgeon, educator, lawyer*
Waymire, Jack Calvin *medical educator*
Willerson, James Thornton *cardiologist, researcher, medical educator*
Wong, Kwong-Kwok *medical educator*
Woodward, Wendy Ann *radiation oncologist*
Yeh, Edward Tu-Hsing *cardiologist, educator, medical researcher*
Yeoman, Lynn Chalmers *medical educator*
Yu, Peirong *plastic surgeon, educator*
Zacharias, Nikolaos Marios *obstetrician, gynecologist, perinatologist*
Zarrin-Khameh, Neda *pathologist*
Zoghbi, William Antoine *cardiologist, educator*

Humble
Trowbridge, John Parks *physician*

Huntsville
Conwell, Halford Roger *physician*

Irving
Natour, Nahille I. *obstetrician, gynecologist*

Katy
Puig, Carlos J. *plastic surgeon*

Kingsville
Nutan, Mohammad Tawhidul Haque *pharmacy educator, researcher*
Sethi, Rajat *cardiologist, educator*

Lackland AFB
Fadare, Oluwole *pathologist, researcher, director*
Sabanegh, Edmund Sami, Jr. *urologist*

Lubbock
Bagdure, Satish Ramesh *epidemiologist*
Beck, George Preston *anesthesiologist, educator*
Buesseler, John Aure *ophthalmologist, management consultant*
Frezza, Eldo E. *surgeon, educator*
Gill, Gurdev S. *orthopaedic surgeon*
Halldorsson, Ari *cardiologist*
Kanu, Adaobi *pediatrician, educator*
Kumar, Ashwani *cardiologist*
Laski, Melvin Edward *nephrologist, educator*
May, Donald Robert Lee *ophthalmologist, educator, academic administrator, farmer*
Sabatini, Sandra *physician*
Shabaneh AlTamimi, Hamed A. *medical educator, consultant*
Wachtel, Mitchell Steven *pathologist*

Magnolia
Girard, Louis Joseph *retired ophthalmologist, educator*

Marshall
Sudhivoraseth, Niphon *pediatrician, immunologist, allergist*

Mcallen
Casso, Ramiro Raul *physician, academic administrator*

Meadowlakes
Nussbaum, Paul Stowell *retired urologist*

Pasadena
Mullins, Jack Allen *cardiologist, educator*
Shapiro, Edward Muray *dermatologist*

Pearland
Hammond, Raymond William *pharmacotherapy specialist*
Horton, Terzah Marie *pediatrician*

Plano
Gajraj, Noor *anesthesiologist, educator*
Guyer, Richard *surgeon*
Hu, Mei Melvin *interventional physiatrist*
Miller, Waenard Livingston *cardiologist*
Tong, John *ophthalmic plastic surgeon, pediatric ophthalmologist, educator*

Red Oak
Shaw, Sue Ann *medical transcriptionist*

Rockport
Johnson, Marilyn *retired obstetrician, gynecologist*

Rockwall
Kotas, Robert Vincent *pediatrician, educator*

San Angelo
Fischer, Duncan Kinnear *neurosurgeon*

San Antonio
Aust, Joe Bradley *surgeon, educator*
Baker, Floyd Wilmer *surgeon, retired military officer*
Becker, Quinn Henderson *orthopedic surgeon, military officer*
Borron, Stephen W. *medical educator*
Corrigan, Helen González *retired cytologist*
Dumitru, Daniel *physiatrist*
Feldman, Marc D. *cardiologist, biomedical engineer, physiologist*
Hare, Henry Phillip, Jr. *psychiatrist*
Harrison, Stephen A. *gastroenterologist*
Henao, Andres Felipe *internist*
Hermann, Robert Charles, Jr. *neurologist, educator*
Horton, Granville Eugene *occupational medicine physician, retired air force officer*
Kasinath, Balakuntalam S. *medical researcher*
Lefeber, Edward James, Jr. *internist, educator*
Leon, Robert Leonard *psychiatrist, educator*
McFee, Arthur Storer *physician*
McGill, Henry Coleman, Jr. *pathologist, educator, researcher*
Mortensen, Eric Michael *medical researcher*
Mulrow, Cynthia Diane *internist, editor*
Ognibene, Andre John *internist, educator, retired military officer*
O'Rourke, Robert A. *cardiologist, educator*
Padmanabhan, Swaminathan *hematologist, oncologist, researcher*
Parekh, Dipen *medical educator*
Patterson, Jan Evans *epidemiologist, educator*
Pestana, Carlos *surgeon, retired dean, educator*
Pruitt, Basil Arthur, Jr. *surgeon, retired military officer*
Ramsinghani, Sushma *medical educator*
Restrepo, Ruben Dario *physician, educator*
Reuter, Stewart Ralston *retired radiologist*
Schenker, Steven *internist, educator*
Shanfield, Stephen B. *psychiatrist, educator*
Shanklin, Kenneth Dale *plastic surgeon*
Shireman, Paula K. *medical educator*
Smith, Reginald Brian Furness *retired anesthesiologist, educator*
Trichopoulos, Nikolaos *ophthalmologist*
Williams, Thomas Eugene *pediatric hematologist and oncologist, pharmaceutical executive*
Williams Adams, Annette Lynn *emergency physician*
Wolf, Steven E. *surgeon, educator*
Zilveti, Carlos Benjamin *preventive medicine physician, pediatrician*

Seabrook
Fischer, Craig Leland *physician*
Patten, Bernard Michael *neurologist, writer, educator*

Southlake
Bogdan, Michael Andrew *plastic surgeon*

Sugar Land
Schulze, Keith E. *dermatologist, surgeon*

Temple
Bennett, Daniel D *preventive medicine physician*
Butler, David Ford *dermatologist*
Dehmer, Gregory Joseph *cardiologist*
Frankel, Arthur E. *oncologist, educator*
Gaglani, Manjusha *medical educator*
Holleman, Vernon Daughty *internist, educator*
Mahabir, Raman Chaos *plastic surgeon, educator*
Rohack, John James *cardiologist*
Rosa, Robert H., Jr. *ophthalmologist, medical educator, researcher*
Sawyer, William Dale *internist, educator, dean, foundation administrator*
Smythe, William Roy *surgeon*

The Woodlands
Bethea, Louise Huffman *allergist*
Desjardins, Raoul *medical association administrator, financial consultant*
Shannon, Thomas O. *plastic surgeon*

Tyler
Gould, Tracy *medical educator*
Wrenn, Christopher Jay *physician*

Waco
Richie, Rodney Charles *critical care and pulmonary medicine physician*

Willis
Rappaport, Martin Paul *internist, nephrologist, educator*

Woodway
Kunert, Holly Leigh *medical educator*

Yoakum
Watson, David H. *physician*

UTAH

Mapleton
Hillyard, Ira William *retired pharmacologist, educator*

Park City
Cooley, Vernon Jackman *orthopedic surgeon*

Provo
Bott, Jay Cordell *oncologist, hematologist*
Hwang, Chun *cardiologist*
Sudweeks, Sterling N. *medical educator*

Salt Lake City
Agarwal, Neeraj *medical educator, researcher*
Anderson, Jeffrey Lance *cardiologist, educator*
Antommaria, Armand Herbert Matheny *pediatrician, educator*
Bauer, A(ugust) Robert, Jr. *surgeon*
Bloom, Sherman *retired pathology educator, photographer*
Bruggers, Carol S. *pediatrician, educator*
Burke, John Patrick *internist, educator*
Capecchi, Mario Renato *genetics educator*
Carey, John Clayton *pediatrician, educator, medical geneticist*
Foster, Carol Marvel *pediatric endocrinologist*
Fujinami, Robert Shin *pathologist, researcher*
Futrell, Nancy Nielson *neurologist*
Gleich, Gerald Joseph *immunologist, researcher, educator*
Gray, Douglas D. *child and adolescent psychiatrist*
Grosser, Bernard Irving *psychiatrist, educator*
Janát-Amsbury, Margit Maria *gynecologist, educator*
Kishore, Bellamkonda Krishna *biomedical researcher, educator*
Kolb, Helga Ellen *retired medical educator*
Matlak, Michael Edward *pediatric general surgeon*
Meyers, Rebecka Louise *pediatric general surgeon*
Middleton, Anthony Wayne, Jr. *urologist, educator*
Moser, Royce, Jr. *preventive medicine physician, educator*
Nelson, Russell Marion *surgeon, educator*
Pace, Nathan Leon *anesthesiologist, educator*
Palmer, David Keith *otolaryngologist*
Patel, Amit N. *surgeon, researcher*
Reddy, Chakravarthy B. *pulmonologist, educator*
Rodgers, George Marion *hematologist*
Saltz, Renato *plastic surgeon*
Shipman, Jean Pugh *medical librarian*
Sorensen, John B. *surgeon*
Spangrude, Gerald John *hematologist, researcher*
Tani, Lloyd Yasuo *pediatrician, educator*
Wallis, M. Chad *medical educator*
Wolf, Harold Herbert *pharmacy educator*
Wright, Larry Jan *epidemiologist*

VERMONT

Brattleboro
Agallianos, Dennis Dionysios *psychiatrist*

Burlington
Cooper, Sheldon Mark *immunologist, rheumatologist, educator, researcher*
First, Lewis Richard *pediatrician*
Gennari, F(rank) John *medical educator*
Gogo, Prospero Barquero *cardiologist, director*
Grunberg, Steven Marc *medical educator*
Lidofsky, Steven David *medical educator*
Lucey, Jerold Francis *pediatrician*
Naylor, Magdalena Raczkowska *psychiatrist, educator*
Riddick, Daniel Howison *obstetrician, gynecologist, priest*
Tampas, John P. *radiologist*

Colchester
Sobel, Burton Elias *cardiologist, educator*

Dorset
Bamford, Joseph Charles, Jr. *gynecologist, obstetrician, educator, medical missionary, author*

Jacksonville
Dell, Ralph Bishop *retired pediatrician, researcher*
Hein, Karen Kramer *pediatrician, epidemiologist*

Norwich
Katz, Arnold Martin *medical educator*
Parker, H. Worth *medical association administrator*

Shelburne
Mead, Philip Bartlett *retired obstetrician, healthcare administrator, educator*

South Burlington
Gerson, William Thomas *pediatrician*
Shinozaki, Tamotsu *retired physician, anesthesiologist*

Underhill
Danforth, Elliot, Jr. *medical educator*

White River Junction
Berman, Stephen Alan *neurologist*
Wallace, Amy Elizabeth *psychiatrist*

VIRGINIA

Afton
McCoy, Sue *retired surgeon, biochemist, bioethicist*

Alexandria
Balch, Charles M. *surgeon, educator*
Fisher, Donald Wayne *medical association administrator*
Flynn, Arlene A. *pharmacy association administrator*
Jonas, Wayne B. *physician, researcher*
Kaplowitz, Lisa Glauser *physician, educator*
Kolesnikov, Evgeni *surgeon, scientist, consultant*
Lichter, Allen S. *oncologist, medical association administrator*
McAndrews, Lawrence A. *medical association administrator*
Puscheck, Elizabeth Ella *physician*
Rayman, Russell Barry *physician*

Annandale
Gorsen, Robert Marc *neurosurgeon*
Kim, Stephen S. *surgeon, educator*
Shamburek, Roland Howard *physician*

Arlington
Ferraz, Francisco Marconi *neurological surgeon*
Gabelnick, Henry Lewis *medical research administrator*
Hariadi, John Wesley *otolaryngologist, surgeon*
Jarris, Paul *medical association administrator, former state agency administrator, physician*
Lundeen, William Bruce *radiologist*
Nirschl, Robert Phillip *orthopedic surgeon*
Sanz, Luis E. *gynecologist, educator*
Watkins, Deborah Karen *epidemiology investigator, educator*

Ashburn
Green, James *medical educator*

Charlottesville
Aldrich, Clarence Knight *physician, educator*
Balogun, Rasheed Abiodun *physician and medical educator*
Beller, George A. *cardiologist, educator*
Cantrell, Robert Wendell *otolaryngologist, head and neck surgeon, educator*
Carey, Robert Munson *physician, educator*
Carter, Bruce Thomas *ophthalmologist*
Cherry, Kenneth Jerome, Jr. *surgeon*
Chevalier, Robert Louis *nephrologist, educator, medical researcher*
Drake, David Bartleson *medical educator*
Epstein, Robert Marvin *anesthesiologist, educator*
Flickinger, Charles John *anatomist, educator*
Galazka, Sim Stevens *medical educator, department chairman*
Guise, Theresa A. *endocrinologist, educator*
Gwaltney, Jack Merrit, Jr. *physician, educator, scientist*
Hostler, Sharon Lee *pediatrician, educator*
Hunt, William B. *pulmonologist*
Johnston, Karen Chodack *neurologist, educator*
Kattwinkel, John *pediatrician, educator*
Keats, Theodore Eliot *radiologist, educator*
Kesser, Bradley W. *otolaryngologist, educator*
Lobo, Peter Issac *physician*
Marshall, John Crook *internal medicine educator, researcher*
Matherne, G. Paul *medical educator*
Matsumoto, Alan H. *radiologist, educator*
McCall, Anthony Leo *medical educator, researcher*
McGahren, Eugene Dewey III *surgeon*
Mintz, Paul David *pathologist*
Modesitt, Susan Carnall *oncologist, director*
Morgan, Raymond F. *plastic surgeon*
Nolan, Stanton Peelle *surgeon, educator*
Oldfield, Edward Hudson *neurosurgeon, researcher*
Owen, John Atkinson, Jr. *internist, educator*
Platts-Mills, Thomas Alexander Evelyn *immunologist, educator, researcher*
Ragosta, Michael *cardiologist*
Rehm, Patrice Koch *radiologist, educator*
Rheuban, Karen Schulder *pediatric cardiologist, educator*
Rodgers, Bradley Moreland *pediatric, thoracic surgeon*
Rogol, Alan David *pediatric endocrinologist*
Rowlingson, John Clyde *anesthesiologist, physician, educator*
Russell, Mark A. *dermatologist*
Saller, Devereux Nathaniel *medical educator, director*
Saulsbury, Frank T. *pediatric immunologist and rheumatologist*
Scheld, William Michael *internist, educator*
Selfe, Terry Kit *medical researcher*
Shi, Weibin *medical educator*
Strayer, Scott Merle *medical educator*
Sutphen, James L. *pediatrician*
Walker, William F. *medical educator*
Weary, Peyton Edwin *retired medical educator*

Chesapeake
Jackson, Cynthia Ann *medical association administrator, health consultant*

Fairfax
Gerber, Naomi Lynn Hurwirtz *physiatrist, educator*
McKnight, Patrick E. *medical educator, consultant*
Schulman, Joseph Daniel *physician, health facility administrator, medical geneticist, educator*

Falls Church
Barakat, Amin J. *pediatrician, pediatric nephrologist*
Borman, Karen Renee *surgeon*
Evans, Peter Yoshio *ophthalmologist, educator*
Kurtzke, John Francis, Sr. *neurologist, epidemiologist*
Lefrak, Edward Arthur *cardiovascular and thoracic surgeon*
Mukherjee, Dipankar *surgeon*
Nguyen-Dinh, Thanh *internist, geriatrician, acupuncturist*
Wah, Robert M. *reproductive endocrinologist, obstetrician, gynecologist*

Gainesville
Lee, Won Jay *radiologist*
Lukowsky, Gerhard Hans *internist*

Glen Allen
Hossain, Deloar *pathologist, director*

Hampton
Enriquez, Manuel Hipolito *physician*
Redwanski, John *medical educator*

Harrisonburg
Dalton, Claudette Ellis Harloe *anesthesiologist, educator, dean*

Herndon
Hazel, William A., Jr. *orthopedist*

Lancaster
Kingsbury, Ellen Ann Dagon *anesthesiologist, general practitioner*

Locust Grove
Gulya, Aina Julianna *otolaryngologist*

Lynchburg
Solyom, Antal Endre *retired psychiatrist*

Manassas
Cooper, James Nelson *medical educator*

Manquin
Osgood, Nancy Jean *medical educator, writer*

Mc Lean
Wallace, Robert Bruce *retired surgeon*
Wright, William Evan *physician, consultant*

Mechanicsville
Silver, Timothy Milton *physician, educator*

Merrifield
Bumgarner, Robert L. *pathologist, retired military officer*

Midlothian
Friedel, Robert Oliver *physician*

Monterey
Tabatznik, Bernard *retired cardiologist*

Newport News
Forbes, Sarah Elizabeth *gynecologist, real estate company officer*
Shwayder, James Mark *obstetrician-gynecologist*

Norfolk
Faulconer, Robert Jamieson *pathologist, educator*
Fisher, Randall G. *pediatrician, educator*
Han, Joseph Khristian *medical association administrator*
Johnson, David Allan *internist, gastroenterologist, educator*
Lo, Bruce Mingyung *emergency physician*
Okeke, Constance O. *ophthalmologist, educator*
Pariser, David Michael *dermatologist, educator*
Platsoucas, Chris Dimitrios *immunologist*
Strasnick, Barry *otolaryngologist, health facility administrator, educator*
Taylor-Fishwick, David *immunologist, educator*
Werner, Eric James *pediatrician, director*
Wolcott, Hugh Dixon *obstetrics and gynecology educator*

North Garden
Moses, Hamilton III *neurologist, hospital administrator, consultant, author*

Oakton
Levin, Warren Mayer *family practice physician*

Portsmouth
DeMaio, Marlene *orthopedist, surgeon*
Wolf, Jeffrey Stephen *physician*
Yarbrough, Terry Pinckney *physician*

Reston
Harrison, William Henry *retired medical educator*
Hughes, Lauren *medical association administrator*
Sharara, Fady Ihsan *reproductive endocrinologist, infertility specialist*

Richmond
Atkinson, Richard Lee, Jr. *internal medicine educator*
Bartle, Samuel Thomas *pediatrician*
Bates, Hampton Robert, Jr. *pathologist*
Blair, Robert E. *medical educator, researcher*
Blumberg, Michael Zangwill *allergist*
Boudinot, F. Douglas *medical educator*
Corey, Linda Ann *medical educator, researcher*
Cuttino, Laurie Wright *medical educator*
Hardy, Richard Earl *rehabilitation counseling educator*
Hayes, Curtis W. *radiologist, director*
Kendler, Kenneth S. *medical educator*
Kornstein, Susan G. *medical educator*
Kukreja, Rakesh C. *medical educator*
Lawrence, Walter, Jr. *surgeon, educator*
Merrell, Ronald Clifton *surgeon, educator*
Mollen, Edward Leigh *pediatrician, allergist, clinical immunologist*
Natarajan, Ramesh *medical educator*
Nestler, John Edwin *endocrinology educator*
Nixon, J.V. *cardiologist, educator*
Ornato, Joseph P. *emergency physician, educator*
Owen, Duncan Shaw, Jr. *internist, retired educator*
Richardson, David Walthall *cardiologist, educator, consultant*
Sirica, Alphonse Eugene *pathology educator*
Strauss, Jerome Frank III *medical researcher, educator*
Svikis, Dace Susan *medical educator*
Takabe, Kazuaki *surgeon, research scientist*
Torres Filho, Ivo *medical educator*
Vetrovec, George Wayne *cardiologist, medical researcher, educator*

Roanoke
Hess, Darla Bakersmith *cardiologist, educator*

Hutcheson, Jack Robert *hematologist, medical oncologist*
Johnson, Cynda Ann *physician, educator*

Roseland
Stemmler, Edward Joseph *physician, retired health facility administrator, dean*

Salem
Brown, Gerald LaVonne *psychiatrist*

South Hill
Huot, Rachel Irene *biomedical educator, research scientist, physician*

Spotsylvania
Singleton, Tanya *nursing educator*

Springfield
Furst, Eric Jonathan *physician, surgeon*

Vienna
Schwartz, Richard Harvey *pediatrician*

Virginia Beach
Carraway, James H. *plastic surgeon*
Choe, Kyle Seung *facial plastic surgeon*
Schreiber, Mark Traudt *psychiatrist*

Ware Neck
Tabb, Waller Crockett *retired allergist, immunologist*

Williamsburg
Connell, Alastair McCrae *physician*
Jacoby, William Jerome, Jr. *internist, retired military officer*
Maloney, Milford Charles *retired internal medicine educator*
Schwartz, Miles Joseph *retired cardiologist*
Voorhess, Mary Louise *pediatric endocrinologist*

Winchester
Bechamps, Gerald Joseph *surgeon*
Helentjaris, Diane *physician*
Roberts, Charles Stewart *surgeon*

WASHINGTON

Bellevue
Brockenbrough, Edwin Chamberlayne *surgeon*
Hackett, Carol Ann Hedden *physician*
Hackett, John Peter *dermatologist*
Khan, Arif *psychiatrist, educator*
Rand, Richard Pierce *plastic surgeon*
Shifrin, Donald Lee *pediatrician*

Bellingham
Howe, Warren Billings *physician*

Bothell
Hauser, Robert G. *cardiologist, medical products executive*
Oflazoglu, Ezogelin *oncologist, science administrator*

Burien
Risse, Guenter Bernhard *physician, historian, educator*

Clyde Hill
Condon, Robert Edward *surgeon, educator, consultant*

Colville
Gray, Edmund Wesley *physician*

Coupeville
Mayhew, Eric George *medical researcher, educator, consultant*

Everett
Valentine, Mark Conrad *dermatologist*

Fairchild Air Force Base
Files, Douglas Scott *flight surgeon, military officer*

Friday Harbor
Geyman, John Payne *physician, educator*

Issaquah
Barchet, Stephen *obstetrician, gynecologist, retired military officer*

Kirkland
Barto, Deborah Ann *physician*
Dunn, Jeffrey Edward *neurologist*
Scranton, Pierce Edward *orthopedist, department chairman*

Lacey
Fett, James D. *epidemiologist, director*

Liberty Lake
Mielke, Clarence Harold, Jr. *hematologist*

Mercer Island
Dunner, David Louis *medical educator*
Elgee, Neil Johnson *retired internist, endocrinologist, educator*
Reed, May J. *medical educator*

Mountlake Terrace
Baxter, Richard Alan *plastic surgeon, educator*

Mukilteo
White, Lowell Elmond, Jr. *retired medical educator*

Olympia
Fisher, Nancy Louise *pediatrician, geneticist, retired nurse*

Port Angeles
Andrew, Louise Briggs *emergency physician, medical legal consultant*

Port Orchard
Thoman, Mark Edward *pediatrician*

Pullman
Klavano, Paul Arthur *veterinary pharmacologist, anesthesiologist, educator*
Meier, Kathryn Elaine *pharmacologist, educator, academic administrator*

Richland
Bair, William J. *retired radiobiologist*

Seattle
Ansell, Julian S. *urologist, educator*
Anzai, Yoshimi *radiologist, director*
Appelbaum, Frederick Ray *oncologist*
Backous, Douglas D. *otolaryngologist, director*
Baker, K. Scott *pediatrician, educator*
Bevan, Michael J. *immunologist, educator, researcher*
Bishop, Michael Joshua *medical educator*
Boucek, Robert Joseph, Jr. *pediatrician, educator*
Bowden, Douglas McHose *neuropsychiatric scientist, neuroinformaticist*
Brentnall, Teresa A. *gastroenterologist, educator*
Buck, Linda B. *medical educator*
Burke, Wylie *medical geneticist*
Carithers, Robert L. *medical educator*
Collier, Ann *epidemiologist, researcher*
Corey, Lawrence *medical educator*
Dale, David C. *physician, educator*
Davis, James *physician, educator*
Davydow, Dimitry *psychiatrist, educator*
Dawson, Patricia Lucille *surgeon*
Day, Robert Winsor *preventive medicine physician, researcher*
Eddy, Allison *nephrologist, educator*
Emery, Helen Margaret *pediatric rheumatologist*
Feldman, Kenneth W. *pediatrician*
Gassner, Holger Guenther *surgeon, consultant*
Giblett, Eloise Rosalie *retired hematologist*
Glomset, John Asbjorn *medical educator*
Golden, Matthew *epidemiologist*
Goldin, Adam *medical educator*
Goodkin, Robert *neurosurgeon, educator*
Gralow, Julie Ruth *physician*
Groudine, Mark Terry *oncologist*
Guntheroth, Warren Gaden *pediatrician, educator*
Harlan, John Marshall *medicine educator*
Hazzard, William Russell *geriatrician, educator*
Hellström, Ingegerd *medical researcher*
Henderson, Maureen McGrath *medical educator*
Hornbein, Thomas Frederic *anesthesiologist*
Isik, Frank *plastic surgeon*
Kahn, Steven Emanuel *medical educator*
Karl, Mike O. *medical researcher*
Kharasch, Evan David *physician*
Kimball, Harry Raymond *medical association administrator, educator*
Klebanoff, Seymour Joseph *medical educator*
Kliot, MIchel *neurosurgeon*
Kraft, George Howard *physician, educator*
Krohn, Kenneth Albert *radiologist, educator*
Larson, Anne M. *internist*
Larson, Eric B. *medical educator, director, internist*
Lehman, Constance Dobbins *radiologist, researcher*
Loeb, Lawrence A. *medical educator, director*
Maier, Ronald Vitt *surgeon, educator*
Martin, Thomas Reed *medical educator, medical association administrator*
Marty, Raymond *nuclear physician*
Matsen, Frederick Albert III *orthopedic educator*
Matsuoka, Yoky *medical educator*
McClure, R. Dale *physician*
McLaughlin, John F. *pediatrician, educator*
Meehan, John J. *pediatrician, educator*
Mills, Richard Pence *ophthalmologist*
Moore, Daniel Charles *retired anesthesiologist*
Mostaghel, Elahe A. *medical educator*
Motulsky, Arno Gunther *internist, geneticist, educator*
Murray, Christopher J.L. *medical educator*
Neal, Joseph M. *anesthesiologist, educator*
Neligan, Peter C. *plastic surgeon, educator*
Nelson, James Alonzo *radiologist, educator*
Neppe, Vernon Michael *neuropsychiatrist, behavioral neurologist, psychopharmacologist, writer, phenomenologist, conciousness researcher, forensic specialist, philosopher*
Nghiem, Paul T. *dermatologist, educator*
O'Brien, Kevin D. *medical educator*
Ostrow, Jay Donald *gastroenterology educator, researcher*
Otto, Catherine Mary *cardiologist, educator*
Page, Richard Leighton *cardiologist, medical educator, researcher*
Pagon, Roberta Anderson *pediatrician, educator*
Parikh, Jay R. *radiologist*
Perkins, James D. *surgeon*
Perrin, Edward Burton *biomedical researcher, public health educator*
Rabak, David William *retired family practice physician, educator, consultant*
Rabinovich, Regina *pediatrician, epidemiologist, director*
Ravenholt, Reimert Thorolf *epidemiologist, researcher*
Rivara, Frederick Peter *pediatrician, educator*
Saneto, Russell Patrick *pediatric neurologist, epileptologist, neurobiologist*
Sathyanarayana, Sheela *pediatrician, educator*
Schimmelbusch, Werner Helmut *psychiatrist*
Sidbury, Robert *pediatrician*
Simon, Gregory E. *psychiatrist, researcher*
Skerrett, Shawn Joseph *physician*
Sobel, Michael *vascular surgeon, researcher*
Song, Kit M. *orthopedist, educator*
Stapleton, F. Bruder *pediatric nephrologist, academic administrator*
Stenchever, Morton Albert *obstetrician, gynecologist*
Stolov, Walter Charles *medicine physiatrist, educator*
Thirlby, Richard Coller *surgeon*
Thomas, Edward Donnall *internist, hematologist, retired medical educator*
Thomas, Herbert Cushing, Jr. *physician, educator*
Tonelli, Mark R. *cardiologist, educator*
Townes, David Andrew *medical educator*
Trier, William Cronin *retired medical educator, plastic surgeon*
True, Lawrence *pathologist, educator*
Vater, Youri L. *medical educator*
Vedder, Nicholas Blair *plastic surgeon, educator*
Wagner, Edward Harris *epidemiologist, educator*
Waterston, Robert Hugh *medical educator, researcher, medical geneticist, department chairman*
Weaver, Lois Jean *physician, educator*
Wessells, Hunter *urologist, researcher*
Yashruti, Salah Hadi *retired surgeon*
Yee, Cassian K. *oncologist, researcher*
Yue, Agnes Kau-Wah *otolaryngologist*

Shoreline
Merendino, K. Alvin *surgeon, educator*

Spokane
Cohen, Arnold Norman *gastroenterologist*
Krizan, Kelly Joe *physician, leather craftsman*
Lee, Hi Young *physician, acupuncturist*
Powell, Darren D. *medical educator*
Saha, Sandeep Ajoy *medical educator, researcher*

Tacoma
Flemming, Stanley Lalit Kumar *physician, mayor, state legislator*

Vancouver
Karmy-Jones, Riyad Caradog *surgeon, educator*
Lenfant, Claude Jean-Marie *physician, director*

Walla Walla
McIlvaine, Patricia Morrow *physician*

Wenatchee
Primm, Richard Kirby *physician*

Woodinville
Couser, William Griffith *nephrologist, academic administrator, educator*

WEST VIRGINIA

Charleston
Boland, James Pius *surgeon, educator*
Udall, John Nicholas, Jr. *medical educator, researcher*

Daniels
Buratynski, Theresa Joan *physician*

Frankford
Mazzio-Moore, Joan L. *retired radiology educator, physician*

Gandeeville
Hameed, Omar *pathologist*

Huntington
Cocke, William Marvin, Jr. *plastic surgeon, educator*
Delidow, Beverly *medical educator*
Foster, Earl James *orthopedist*
Jude, David C. *medical educator*
Mufson, Maurice Albert *infectious diseases physician, educator*
Petrany, Stephen Michael *medical educator, director*

Kingwood
Moyers, Sylvia Dean *retired medical librarian*

Morgantown
Albrink, Margaret Joralemon *medical educator*
Bang, Ki Moon *epidemiologist, professor*
Fleming, William Wright, Jr. *retired pharmacology professor*
Glover, Douglas Dennis *obstetrics, gynecology and pharmacology educator*
Kurian, Sobha *medical educator*
Lambert, H. Wayne *medical educator, researcher*
Nugent, George Robert *neurosurgeon*
Prabhu, Vikram Clifford *physician*
Rao, Katikineni Murali Krishna *medical researcher*
Zhang, Yadong *medical researcher*

Ronceverte
Hooper, Anne Dodge *pathologist, educator*

Shepherdstown
Abbrecht, Peter Herman *medical educator*

Wheeling
Akhavan-Heidari, Mehdi *cardiothoracic surgeon*

WISCONSIN

Appleton
Boren, Clark Henry, Jr. *general and vascular surgeon*
Luther, Thomas William *retired dermatologist*

Egg Harbor
Schultz, Richard Otto *ophthalmologist, educator*

Fitchburg
Gurkow, Helen J. *retired physician*

Fond Du Lac
Treffert, Darold Allen *psychiatrist, writer, hospital administrator*

Grafton
Stock, E. Lee *ophthalmologist, consultant*

Green Bay
Edgar, Terence S. *pediatric neurologist*

La Crosse
Lenards, Nishele Dyan *medical educator*
Rademacher, Dana Ellis *urologist*
Webster, Stephen Burtis *dermatologist, educator*

Madison
Albert, Daniel Myron *ophthalmologist, educator*
Allen, David Bruce *endocrinologist, educator*
Arndt, George Arthur *anesthesiologist, consultant*
Barrett, Bruce *medical educator, researcher*
Burgess, Richard Ray *oncologist, biotechnologist, educator*
Connors, Kenneth Antonio *retired pharmacy educator*
Crow, James Franklin *retired genetics educator*
Dempsey, Robert J. *neurosurgeon*
Eichelman, Burr Simmons, Jr. *psychiatrist, researcher, educator*
Fahien, Leonard August *physician, educator*
Farrell, Philip M. *pediatrician, medical educator, former dean*
Hansen, Sherri M. *psychiatrist*
Heatley, Gregg Alan *ophthalmologist*
Hetsko, Cyril Michael *internist*
Javid, Manucher J. *retired neurosurgeon, educator*
Jefferson, James Walter *psychiatrist, educator*
Ji, Li Li *biomedical researcher*
Johnson, Maryl Rae *cardiologist*
Julian, Thomas Michael *gynecologic surgeon, educator*
Knechtle, Stuart Johnston *medical educator, transplant immunologist*
Kudsk, Kenneth Allan *surgeon*
Laessig, Ronald Harold *preventive medicine and pathology educator, state official*
Landry, Gregory L. *pediatrician, educator*
Mahoney, Jane E. *medical educator, director*
Maki, Dennis G. *epidemiology educator*
Mostaghimi, Ladan *psychiatrist*
Nordby, Eugene Jorgen *orthopedic surgeon*
Pitot, Henry Clement III *pathologist, educator*
Ranallo, Frank N. *medical researcher*
Reynolds, Ernest West *retired internist, educator*
Roberts, Leigh Milton *psychiatrist*
Sondel, Paul Mark *pediatric oncologist, educator*
Stein, James Howard *medical educator, researcher*
Wald, Arnold *gastroenterologist*
Wenger, Ronald David *surgeon*
Westman, Jack Conrad *child psychiatrist, educator*
Whiffen, James Douglass *surgeon, educator*

Manitowoc
Trader, Joseph Edgar *orthopedic surgeon*

Marshfield
Islam, Tasbirul *physician*
Kuehner, Marvin Ernest *surgeon*
Okon, Tomasz R. *palliative medicine physician, educator*

Mequon
Terry, Leon Cass *neurologist, educator*

Middleton
Olive, David L. *endocrinologist, educator*

Milton
Enlow, Donald Hugh *retired anatomist, dean*

Milwaukee
Ali, Omar *medical educator*
Ball, Elizabeth Fikenscher *gynecologist*
Beard, Daniel Andrew *medical educator*
Beilke, Mark A. *medical educator*
Bohn, Michael J. *psychiatrist, director*
Brodwin, Paul Eric *medical educator*
Chan, Carlyle Hung-lun *psychiatrist, educator*
Diaz, Luis Alberto *dermatologist, educator*
Earing, Michael G. *cardiologist, director*
Gennarelli, Thomas A. *neurosurgeon, consultant*
Gudausky, Todd *cardiologist, educator*
Henrickson, Kelly John *pediatrician, medical educator*
Hernandez, Lyndon Joseph DeVera *medical educator*
Hur, Su-Ryong *physician, anesthesiologist*
Johnson, Sheri *medical educator, former state agency administrator*
Jordan, Ruth Ann *retired physician*
Kochar, Mahendr Singh *physician, health facility administrator, research scientist, educator, writer, consultant*
Kroft, Steven Howard *hematopathologist, medical educator*
Kwiatt, James T. *physician*
LaDosa, John *medical researcher*
Layde, Joseph Bernard *psychiatrist, educator*
Massey, Patrick Baber *internist, health facility administrator*
Namdari, Bahram *surgeon*
Nattinger, Ann B. *internist, researcher, medical educator*
Neuner, Joan Marie *medical educator*
Olds, Glenn Richard *medical educator, department chairman*
Pagel, Paul Stanley *cardiac anesthesiologist*
Peoples, Robert William *biomedical researcher*
Rilling, William S. *radiologist*
Rosenberg, Lucille Glicklich *retired child psychiatrist*
Santo Tomas, Linus Hipolito *pulmonologist*
Shetty, Kaup Rajmohan *endocrinologist, educator*
Soergel, Konrad Hermann *physician*
Suster, Saul *medical educator, director*
Talano, Julie M. *medical educator*
Wang, Marjorie *medical educator*
Whelan, Harry T. *neurologist, educator*
Yancey, Kim Bruce *dermatology researcher*
Zhu, Shankuan *epidemiologist, educator*

Nashotah
Hollister, Winston Ned *pathologist*

New Berlin
Kumar, Gagan *physician, educator*

Onalaska
Waite, Lawrence Wesley *osteopathic physician, educator*

Oshkosh
Cheng, Theresa *neurosurgeon*
Cooper, Janelle Lunette *neurologist, educator*
McLaughlin, Jeffrey R. *orthopedist, director*

Racine
Stewart, Richard Donald *internist, educator, writer*

Wauwatosa
Kalogjera, Ikar Jaksa *psychiatrist, educator*

Weyauwega
Maasch, Lloyd Palmer *physician*

WYOMING

Casper
Bennion, Scott Desmond *physician*
Prypchan, Lida D. *psychiatrist*
Scaling, Sam T. *obstetrician, gynecologist*

TERRITORIES OF THE UNITED STATES

NORTHERN MARIANA ISLANDS

Saipan
Lamkin, Celia Belocora *physician*

PUERTO RICO

Bayamon
Cabrera-Otero, Sylvia *physician*
Carro, Eric F. *neurosurgeon*

Mayaguez
Sahai, Hardeo *medical statistics educator*

Mercedita
Perez-Nieves, Roberto *plastic surgeon, educator*

Ponce
Rivera-Amill, Vanessa *medical educator*

San Juan
Bonilla-Felix, Melvin A. *pediatrician, educator*
Cordero, Jose Fernando *pediatrician, dean*
Joshipura, Kaumudi Jinraj *epidemiologist*
Pérez-Cardona, José Manuel *cardiologist*
Santos Pico, Jose V. *neurosurgeon*
Valcárcel, Marta Iris *pediatric educator*

VIRGIN ISLANDS

Christiansted
Centeno, Robert Francis *plastic surgeon*

MILITARY ADDRESSES OF THE UNITED STATES

EUROPE

APO
Leibrecht, Murl Edwin *preventive medicine physician, consultant, retired military officer*

CANADA

ALBERTA

Calgary
Smith, Eldon *cardiologist, physiologist, educator*

Edmonton
Gyenes, Gábor *physician, educator*
Halloran, Philip Francis *nephrologist, immunologist*
Oberg, Lyle *physician, academic administrator*

BRITISH COLUMBIA

Parksville
Weir, Bryce Keith Alexander *neurosurgeon, neurologist, educator*

Vancouver
Baird, Patricia Ann *physician, educator*
Friedman, Sydney M. *anatomist, educator, medical researcher*
Hardwick, David Francis *pathologist*
McGeer, Edith Graef *retired neurological science educator*
Mizgala, Henry F. *physician, consultant, retired medical educator*
Schaller, Jane Green *pediatrician*

MANITOBA

Winnipeg
Haworth, James Chilton *pediatrics educator*

NOVA SCOTIA

Halifax
Langley, George Ross *medical educator*
Murray, Thomas John (Jock Murray) *physician, neurologist, educator*

Mahone Bay
Collins, John Alfred *retired obstetrician, gynecologist, educator*

ONTARIO

Hamilton
Hirsh, Jack *medical researcher*

Kingston
Low, James A. *physician*

London
Marotta, Joseph Thomas *medical educator*

Manotick
Osmond, Dennis Gordon *anatomist, researcher, medical educator*

Ottawa
de Bold, Adolfo J. *pathologist, educator, physiologist, researcher*
Hurteau, Gilles David *retired obstetrician, gynecologist, educator, dean*
Lavoie, Lionel A. *physician, health science association administrator*
Vassilyadi, Michael *pediatric neurosurgeon*

Toronto
Angel, Aubie *endocrinologist, academic administrator*
Dick, John E. *medical geneticist, educator*
Goodwin, Pamela J. *oncologist, educator*
Kaufman, Nathan *retired pathologist, educator*
Mc Culloch, Ernest Armstrong *internist, educator*
Nguyen, San Duy *psychiatrist, educator*
Ogilvie, Richard Ian *clinical pharmacologist*
Pollock, Bruce Godfrey *psychiatrist, educator*
Sole, Michael Joseph *cardiologist*

Windsor
Ferguson, John Duncan *medical research educator*

QUEBEC

Montpellier
Poirier, Louis Joseph *neurology educator*

Montreal
Burgess, John Herbert *cardiologist, educator*
Cruess, Richard Leigh *orthopedic surgeon, dean*
Franco, Eduardo L.F. *epidemiologist, educator*
Freeman, Carolyn Ruth *oncologist*
Genest, Jacques *nephrologist, clinical scientist, science administrator*
Gold, Phil *immunologist, educator, researcher*
Goldbloom, Victor Charles *pediatrician*
Goltzman, David *endocrinologist, educator, researcher*
Jones, Barbara Ellen *neurologist, educator*
Kramer, Michael Stuart *pediatric epidemiologist*
Mac Lean, Lloyd Douglas *surgeon*
Mulder, David S. *cardiovascular surgeon*
Nattel, Stanley *cardiologist, research scientist*
Ohayon, Maurice M. *research center administrator, psychiatrist*
Pasternac, André *cardiologist, educator*
Scriver, Charles Robert *medical researcher, human geneticist, retired medical educator*
Snell, Linda S. *internist, educator*
Wainberg, Mark Arnold *medical educator, director*

MEXICO

Tijuana
Chayet, Arturo S. *ophthalmologist, surgeon, consultant*

ARGENTINA

Buenos Aires
Bergel, Meny *physician, researcher*
Montes, Leopoldo Feliciano *dermatologist, educator*

AUSTRALIA

Clayton
Tonge, Bruce John *psychiatrist*

Darwin
Rao, Akkinepalli Badri Narayan *physician, educator*

Melbourne
Denton, Derek Ashworth *medical researcher, foundation administrator*
Rosenfeld, Jeffrey Victor *neurosurgeon*

Nedlands
Oxnard, Charles Ernest *anatomist, anthropologist, biologist, educator*

Rankin Park
Chapman, Barry Lloyd *retired cardiologist, educator, army officer*

Sydney
Huckstep, Ronald Lawrie *traumatic and orthopaedic surgery educator, consultant*

Townsville
Ho, Yik Hong *colon and rectal surgeon*

Victoria
Johnston, Colin Ivor *medical educator, researcher*

AUSTRIA

Grossgmain
Mueller, Christa *radiologist*

Salzburg
González, Ricardo *surgeon, educator*

Wien
Hornykiewicz, Oleh *retired biochemical pharmacologist*

BANGLADESH

Dhaka
Alam, Nazmul *medical researcher*
Brooks, W. Abdullah *pediatrician, researcher*

BELGIUM

Brussels
Boon, Thierry *biomedical researcher*
Ciarka, Agnieszka *cardiologist*
Godfraind, Theophile Joseph *pharmacologist, educator*
Lengele, Benoît G. *surgeon, educator*
Maisin, Jean René Simon *medical researcher, educator*

BRAZIL

São Paulo
Dini, Gal Moreira *plastic surgeon, researcher, university teacher*
Lopes, Maria-Cecilia *pediatrician*

CHINA

Beijing
Sheng, Zhi (Chih) Yong *surgeon, educator*

Wuhan
Li, Chaoying *biomedical researcher, researcher*

COLOMBIA

Bogota
Reina, Carrillo José Gabriel *physician, surgery educator*

CROATIA

Rijeka
Bosnar, Alan *medical university administrator, physician*

Zagreb
Drazancic, Ante *obstetrician, gynecologist, educator*

CUBA

Havana
Gonzalez, Gisela *immunologist, researcher*

CZECH REPUBLIC

Prague
Neuzil, Petr *cardiologist, researcher*
Potmesil, Petr *pharmacologist*
Tuma, Stanislav Josef *radiologist*

DENMARK

Aarhus
Gjedde, Albert Hellmut *neurology educator, neurobiology researcher*

Frederiksberg
Buch, Jan *retired medical research administrator, director*

EGYPT

Cairo
Hamza, Ahmed Mohamed *pediatrician, researcher*

ENGLAND

Hertfordshire
Bishop, Malcolm Graham Hamilton *medical essayist, dental surgeon*

London
Butler, Peter E. *plastic surgeon*
Hakim, Nadey Subhy *surgeon*
Janossy, George *immunologist, educator*
Maini, Sir Ravinder Nath *rheumatologist, educator*
Muir-Taylor, Douglas James *ophthalmologist*
Powles, Trevor James *physician, oncologist*
Rutter, Michael Llewellyn *child psychology educator*

Oxford
Peto, Sir Richard *medical researcher*

Redhill
Donaldson, David *pathologist*

Salford
Madan, Vishal *dermatologist*

Wigan
Talapatra, Indrajit *endocrinologist*
Stern, Claudio Daniel *medical educator, embryological researcher*

FINLAND

Helsinki
Liewendahl, Bo Kristian *retired pathologist, nuclear medicine physician*

FRANCE

Fontenay-aux-Roses
Dauguet, Julien Charles *computational biomedicine researcher, educator*

Gif-sur-Yvette
Le Bihan, Denis *radiologist*

Hénin Beaumont
Fournier, Eric *internist, pulmonologist*

Paris
Mercadal, Lucile *nephrologist*

Saint Cloud
Atassi, Ghanem *retired oncologist*

Toulouse
Sarramon, Jean-Pierre Fernand Louis *urologist, educator*

Tours
Barthelemy, Jean-Paul Francois *orthopedic surgeon*

GERMANY

Berlin
Holzmann, Ruth Dorothee *dermatologist*
Jahnke, Kristoph *internist, hematologist, oncologist, researcher*

Bielefeld
Brock, Norbert *retired pharmacologist*

Bremen
Fahle, Manfred *ophthalmology researcher*

Duisburg
Kumm, Dietmar Alfred *orthopedist, consultant, surgeon*

Freiberg
Van Calker, Dietrich O. *psychiatrist, educator*

Furth im Wald
Rau, Magda *ophthalmologist*

Halle
Schmoll, Hans Joachim *hematology and oncology educator*

Hanau
Rink, Thomas *nuclear medicine physician*

Munich
Heywang-Koebrunner, Sylvia H. *radiologist, educator*
Schwarz, Markus J. *psychoneuroimmunologist, neurochemist*

Regensburg
Eisenmann-Klein, Marita *plastic surgeon*

Seeheim-Jugenheim
Halama, Niels *physician, researcher*

Tübingen
Nüsslein-Volhard, Christiane *medical researcher*

Wuppertal
Schubert, Guenther Erich *pathologist*

GREECE

Athens
Boudoulas, Harisios *cardiologist, researcher, medical educator*

Brilakis, Harry Stylianos (Harilaos Stylianos Brilakis) *ophthalmologist*
Lapatsanis, Petros Dimitris *pediatrician*

Larissa
Zacharoulis, Dimitris *surgeon, researcher*

Thessaloniki
Baloyannis, Stavros Joannis *neurologist, educator, researcher*

GUATEMALA

Guatemala City
Mishaan, Emilio *transplant surgeon, educator*

INDIA

Haryana
Katariya, Kushagra *cardiothoracic surgeon, educator, healthcare developer, stratigist*

Hyderabad
Gummaraju, Srinivas Chakravarthy *oncologist, hematologist*

Kolkata
Moideen, Rafeeq *dermatologist, consultant*

Trivandrum
Valiathan, Marthanda Varma Sankaran *cardiac surgeon*

ISRAEL

Be'er Sheva
Glick, Shimon Michael *medical educator*

Jerusalem
Hazboun, Viveca *psychiatrist*
Merrick, Joav *pediatrician, government agency administrator, researcher*
Page, Ernest *retired medical educator*

Maale Efraim
Gur, Itzhak *physician, researcher*

Rehovot
Arnon, Ruth *immunologist, educator, researcher*
Sela, Michael *immunologist, chemist*

ITALY

Florence
Nicolodi, Maria *neuropharmacologist, medical researcher*

Milan
Goldwurm, Gian Franco *psychiatrist, psychologist, psychotherapist*
Tonon, Giovanni *medical researcher*

Monza
Lanzetta, Marco *hand surgeon, microsurgeon*

Palermo
Fiumara, Ettore *neurosurgeon*

JAPAN

Chiba
Suzuki, Makoto *thoracic surgeon*

Hamamatsu
Kaneko, Masao *radiology educator, researcher, specialist*

Hirakata
Shigemitsu, Toshiro *ophthalmologist, researcher*

Hirosaki
Fukui, Atsushi *gynecologist, immunologist, physician*
Sakai, Takehiro *surgeon*

Kagoshima
Arima, Eitoku *surgeon*

Kashihara
Tsujimoto, Tatsuhiro *gastroenterologist, researcher*

Koriyama
Goto, Noboru *neuroanatomist, neuropathologist*

Kureshiki
Oiwa, Hiroshi *surgeon*

Kushimoto
Akura, Junsuke *ophthalmologist, researcher*

Miyagi
Tan, Masaki *surgeon, director*

Nagasaki
Tsurumoto, Toshiyuki *orthopaedic surgeon, researcher*

Nagoya
Kasuya, Hideki *medical researcher, surgeon*

Niigata
Suzuki, Noriyasu *physician, psychologist, journalist*
Takizawa, Hideaki *gastroenterologist*

Okayama
Morooka, Hiroshi *neurosurgeon*

Okinawa
Nishihara, Minoru *surgeon*

Osaka
Otsuka, Ryo *medical educator*
Shindo, Katsuhisa *surgeon*
Usami, Masahisa *physician, director*

Saitama
Furuya, Kenichi *reproductive endocrinologist, gynecologic surgeon*

Sendai
Hozawa, Atsushi *medical educator*

Shiga
Matsuda, Wakoto *neurosurgeon, researcher*

Shinjuku
Morikawa, Shunichi *medical educator*

Suita
Iida, Norihiko *physiatrist, educator*

Tochigi
Honma, Koichi *pathologist, researcher*
Hyodo, Haruo *radiologist, educator*

Tokorozawa
Nakamura, Hiroshi *urology educator*

Tokyo
Akiyama, Shinichiro *oncologist, hematologist, researcher*
de la Fuente Ramirez, Juan Ramon *psychiatrist, former academic administrator*
Fukuyama, Yukio *child neurologist, pediatrics educator*
Hirai, Makiko *physician*
Jyoji, Yoshizawa *medical educator*
Kawakami, Masaya *medical educator*
Kumagai, Takashi *physician, researcher*
Sasaki, Akihiko *cardiologist*
Watanabe, Takahiro *medical educator*

Tsukuba
Shiotani, Seiji *diagnostic radiologist*

Yatomi
Sakai, Yu *pathologist*

Yonago
Maeda, Kazuo *obstetrician, gynecologist, educator*

JORDAN

Amman
Habboushe, Mudhafer Petros *orthopedist, educator*
Saadeh, Sherif Nabil *gastroenterologist, hepatologist, researcher*

KUWAIT

Safat
Alazmi, Waleed *medical educator*

LEBANON

Beirut
Hamdan, Abdul-latif H. *otolaryngologist, educator*
Khatib, Rustom Atfat *gynecologist, endocrinologist, researcher, consultant*
Shehadi, Sameer Ibrahim *plastic surgeon*

Byblos
Sheikh-Taha, Marwan *medical educator, researcher*

MALAYSIA

Putrajaya
Omar, Salem *physician, gastroenterologist, researcher*

Selangor
Azer, Samy Aziz *gastroenterologist, educator*

MONGOLIA

Ulaanbaatar
Nymadawa, Pagbajabyn *physician, public health administrator*

MOROCCO

Rabat
Rafi, Mostafa *ophthalmologist*

NETHERLANDS

Maastricht
Van Praag, Herman Meir *psychiatrist, educator, researcher*

Vlaardingen
Smith, Arlan Robert *plastic and reconstructive surgeon*

NEW ZEALAND

Auckland
Sims, Francis Harding *retired medical researcher*

NIGERIA

Enugu
Ozumba, Benjamin Chukwuma *obstetrician, gynecologist, educator*

NORWAY

Oslo
Winnem, Bjørn Magne *anesthesiologist*

PHILIPPINES

Quezon City
Macalalag, Eufemio Vera, Jr. *urologist, researcher*
Padlan, Eduardo Agustin *retired immunologist*

POLAND

Cracow
Kowalczyk, Maciej Stanislaw *obstetrician, gynecologist, sexologist*

Warsaw
Ruzyllo, Edward Emil *medical educator*

PORTUGAL

Lisbon
Ferreira-Coelho, José Manuel Martins *surgeon, urologist, educator*

REPUBLIC OF KOREA

Busan
Lee, Young Woo *neurosurgery educator*
Roh, Myung Hwan *medical educator*
Sung, Gyung Tak *urologist, department chairman*

Daegu
Choi, Youn Seok *gynecologist, educator*
Park, Eui-Soo *dermatologist, consultant*
Yim, Man Bin *neurosurgeon, educator*

Daejeon
Duck-Hwan, Kim *medical educator*
Shin, Eui-Cheol *medical researcher*

Gwangju
Kim, Kwang Seog *plastic and reconstructive surgeon, professor*

Gyeongbuk
Lim, Hyun-Sul *medical educator*

Jeongju
Jeong, Hwan-Jeong *nuclear medicine physician, educator*

Jeonju
Oh, Hong Keun *medical educator, physician*

Kyonggi
Park, In Suh *internist, educator*

Namdong
Yang, Hyuk Jun *emergency physician*

Seoul
Chi, Je Geun *retired pathologist*
Choe, Jin *obstetrician, gynecologist, biomedical researcher*
Han, Jin Suk *medical educator, researcher*
Jee, Won-Hee *radiologist, educator*
Kang, Seong-Woong *physiatrist, educator*
Kim, Hun-Soo *psychiatrist, educator, researcher*
Kim, Jin Wang *plastic surgeon, educator*
Kim, Sae-Chul *urologist, educator*
Kim, Sungjoo *transplant surgeon*
Kwon, DoHoon *neurosurgeon, medical educator*
Lee, Il-Ok *anesthesiologist, education educator*
Lee, Jong-Min *oncologist, gynecologist, medical researcher*
Park, Moon Suh *otolaryngologist*
Yoon, Hana *urologist, educator*

Suwon
Choi, Sangdun *biomedical educator*

Taegu
Kim, Sang-Ha *retired ophthalmology educator*

Ulsan
Ko, Sang-Hun *orthopedist, educator*

RUSSIA

Moscow
Bockeria, Leo Antonovich *cardiac surgeon*

SAINT KITTS AND NEVIS

Basseterre
Mohammed, Hamish *epidemiologist, educator*

SAUDI ARABIA

Al Madinah
Molla, Ahmed Abdin *surgeon*

Riyadh
Wagoner, Michael D. *ophthalmologist*

SCOTLAND

Edinburgh
Tsirikos, Athanasios Ioannis *orthopedist, spinal surgeon, educator*

SINGAPORE

Singapore
Low, Cze Hong *ophthalmologist*
Swain, Judith Lea *cardiologist, educator*

SOUTH AFRICA

Bloemfontein
Stulting, Andries Andriessen *ophthalmologist*

Witbank
Jansen van Rensburg, Dirkie Johanna *physician, medical researcher*

SPAIN

Barcelona
Vilardell, Francisco *gastroenterologist, educator*

Zaragoza
Hernandez Altemir, Francisco *surgeon*

SWEDEN

Stockholm
Gustafsson, Jan-Åke *molecular endocrinologist, medical nutritionist*

SWITZERLAND

Aargau
Bodis, Stephan B. *radiologist, oncologist, educator*

Basel
Eriksen, Erik Fink *endocrinologist, internist, researcher*
Nidecker, Andreas Cornelis *radiologist, educator*

Busingen
Friede, Reinhard L. *neuropathologist, educator*

Hinterkappelen
Reuter, Harald *pharmacologist*

Langenthal
Maleck, Wolfgang Helmut *anesthesiologist*

Versoix
Mahler, Halfdan Theodor *physician, health organization executive*

TAIWAN

Kaohsiung
Wang, Gwo Jaw *orthopedic surgery educator*

Taichung
Chuo, Liang-Jen *psychiatrist, researcher*
Wang, Matthew Nai-Hwei *surgeon, educator*

Taipei
Chao, Hsia Fu *gastroenterologist, administrator*
Chen, Chien-Jen *epidemiologist, Minister of Health, Minister of Science*
Chu, Tzong-Shinn *physician scientist, medical educator*
Huang, Song-Yuan *health educator*
Tsai, Ming-Hung *internist, researcher*

THAILAND

Bangkok
Bovornkitti, Somchai *internist*
Intuwongse, Chai-Sit *orthopedist, consultant*
Meensook, Charoen *physician, consultant*
Warrasak, Sukhuma *ophthalmologist*

UNITED ARAB EMIRATES

Dubai
Jarade, Elias Fares ophthalmologist

WALES

Aberystwyth
Lairikyengbam, Shyam Kishore Singh cardiologist

Jeffreyston
Woodman, Grey Musgrave psychiatrist

ADDRESS UNPUBLISHED

Abanilla, Patricia Karen Amarillas psychiatrist
Abdollahian, Mark medical educator
Abelin, Theodor retired medical educator, epidemiologist
Abiose, Ademola cardiologist, educator
Abrams, Arthur Jay retired physician
Abrams, Fredrick Ralph physician, clinical ethicist
Achord, James Lee retired gastroenterologist
Adair, Stefan Rene plastic surgeon
AdamLichtman, Adam David medical educator, director
Adams, Forrest H. retired pediatrician
Adams, James Thomas surgeon
Addae-mensah, Kweku biomedical researcher
Adelstein, Robert S. medical researcher
Adeyemi, Oluwadamilola Adebola infectious diseases physician
Adler, Brent H. radiologist
Adrogue, Horacio Esteban nephrologist, educator
Aduen, Javier Francisco physician, researcher
Adzamli, Kofi radiologist scientist & patent agent
Agrawal, Amit medical educator, researcher
Ahmed, Ali epidemiologist, researcher
Aiyer, Meenakshy K. medical educator
Alasio, Teresa Marie pathologist, educator
Alessio, Adam medical educator, researcher
Alexander, Jessica Aronow anesthesiologist
Alexander, Jonathan cardiologist, consultant
Ali, Asem Computer Vision Researcher
Almas, Tabish medical researcher
Altekruse, Joan Morrissey retired preventive medicine physician
Altenburger, Karl Marion allergist
Althoff, Robert R. psychiatrist, educator
Altshuler, Kenneth Z. psychiatrist, educator
Amacher, Arthur Loren neurosurgeon
Ambrose, John Anthony cardiologist, educator
Amiel, Howard ophthalmologist, corneal surgeon
Amis, Edward Stephen, Jr. radiologist, retired military officer
Ammanamanchi, Sudhakar cancer biologist, educator
Amylon, Michael David physician, educator
Anderson, Geraldine Louise medical researcher
Anderson, Porter Warren, Jr. retired pediatrics educator
Andreeva, Valentina A. medical researcher
Andreoli, Thomas Eugene physician
Andrews, David Wallace medical educator
Andrews, William Cooke physician
Andriole, Vincent Thomas medical educator, researcher
Anis, Munazza radiologist, educator
Anstee, Jaime Lee Kelly medical researcher
Antich, Peter radiologist, educator
Apfelbach, George Leonard, Jr. urologist
Appenzeller, Otto neurologist, researcher
Applebaum, Edward Leon otolaryngologist, educator
Aranguri, Cesar internist, cardiologist, educator
Argiris, Athanassios oncologist, researcher
Arriaga, Moises Alberto biomedical researcher, educator
Artis, LaToya CheRee medical researcher
Atkinson, Holly Gail physician, journalist, educator, human rights activist, writer
Atlee, John Light retired physician, consultant
Augenstein, Ralf Gerald physician
August, Gilbert Paul pediatrician, educator
Augustine, Samuel Charles medical educator, consultant
Austin, John H.M. retired radiologist
Auyang, Edward D. surgeon
Avery, Mary Ellen pediatrician, educator
Aziz, Noreen oncologist, senior program director
Babar, Sardar Ijlal pulmonologist
Baertschi, Steven W. Pharmaceutical Researcher
Bagshaw, Malcolm A. radiation oncologist, educator
Bahl, Tracy L. healthcare executive
Baker, Augustus L., Jr. retired surgeon
Baker, Paul Scott ophthalmologist
Baldwin, John Charles surgeon, researcher
Baliga, Ragavendra Ramakrishna cardiologist, researcher
Ball, Carroll Raybourne anatomist, researcher, medical educator
Bankhurst, Arthur Dale medical educator, researcher
Banta, James Elmer epidemiologist, educator, dean
Barbo, Dorothy Marie obstetrician, gynecologist, educator
Barish, Matthew Adam radiologist
Barnett, Benjamin Lewis, Jr. retired physician, educator
Baron, Jeffrey retired pharmacologist
Barrett, Austin John hematologist, researcher
Barricks, Michael Eli retinal surgeon
Bartlett, Eugene Fred retired surgeon
Bartlett, Heather cardiologist, educator
Barzilay, Joshua Israel endocrinologist, educator
Bascom, John Upton retired surgeon
Bauer, Natalie Renee medical educator
Baugh, Charles Milton biochemistry educator, dean
Baum, Jules Leonard ophthalmologist, educator
Baxter, John Darling internist, endocrinologist, educator, health facility administrator
Beaven, Michael Anthony biomedical researcher
Beckett, Victoria Ling physician
Beckson, Mace psychiatrist
Bednoff, Stuart Leon obstetrician, gynecologist, educator
Bencardino, Jenny Teresa musculoskeletal radiologist
Benfield, John Richard surgeon, educator
Benjamin, Latanya T. dermatologist
Bennett, Edward Virdell, Jr. surgeon
Benoit, Danielle Sw medical researcher
Bercu, Barry Bernard pediatric endocrinologist
Beredjiklian, Pedro Kirkor physician
Berger, Michael physician, educator
Berger, Stuart medical educator
Berglund, Robin G. psychiatrist, management consultant
Berry, Gail W. psychiatrist, educator
Beshai, John cardiologist, educator
Besur, Siddesh V. medical educator
Bielory, Leonard allergist, immunologist, medical school administrator
Bigby, JudyAnn medical educator
Birder, Lori A. medical educator
Blankfein, Robert Jerome retired neurologist
Bleck, Phyllis Claire surgeon
Bloodworth, Glen Alexander nuclear medicine physician
Blount, Benroe Wayne physician, department chairman
Blume, Sheila Bierman retired psychiatrist
Blumencranz, Peter William surgeon
Blumenfeld, Thomas Jefferson orthopedist
Blumenthal, Susan Jane physician, psychiatrist, educator
Boggs, Charles Harmon, Jr. retired surgeon
Boothby, Richard Alfred gynecologist, educator
Borden, Ernest Carleton oncologist, educator
Borgman, Matthew pediatrician
Boris, Neil Walden psychiatrist, consultant
Bos, Gary D. orthopedist
Botsford, Mary Henrich retired ophthalmologist
Boudoulas, Olga dermatologist
Bougas, James Andrew physician, surgeon, educator
Bourguignon, Lilly Y. medical educator, researcher
Bourke, Anthony Thomas Conal retired medical researcher, microbiologist
Boyle, Michael Dermot medical educator
Boynes, Sean G. dental anesthesiologist, researcher
Braasch, John William retired surgeon, consultant
Brady, Rebecca medical educator
Brandom, Barbara Wendeborn anesthesiologist, consultant
Brandon, Kathryn Elizabeth Beck pediatrician
Brasher, George Walter physician, consultant
Braude, Robert Michael retired medical librarian
Brawley, Otis Webb oncologist, educator
Brega, Kerry Elizabeth physician, researcher
Brenes, Jeremy homeopath, researcher
Brennan, Mark Joseph physiatrist
Brenner, Dean Elliott medical oncology and pharmacology educator
Brent, Robert Leonard medical educator
Brent, Thomas Peter retired molecular pharmacologist
Brewer, Timothy Francis III retired cardiologist
Brewster, Abenaa Marcia oncologist, educator
Brin, Foster Blake psychiatrist
Brizio-Molteni, Loredana surgeon, educator
Brody, Alan Samuel radiologist, researcher
Broome, Claire Veronica epidemiologist, researcher
Brott, Walter Howard retired cardiac surgeon, educator, military officer
Brown, Ronald Delano endocrinologist
Brownlee, Robert Calvin pediatrician, educator
Bruzoni, Matias physician
Bubrick, Melvin Phillip surgeon
Buchanan, J(ohn) Robert physician, educator
Buchman, Craig otolaryngologist
Buck, Louise Bryden psychiatrist
Buck, Martina medical researcher
Budimirovic, Dejan B. academic child psychiatrist
Bui, Yen Kim pediatrician, researcher
Buist, Neil Robertson MacKenzie pediatric educator, medical association administrator
Burk, Raymond Franklin, Jr. internist, educator, researcher
Burket, John McVey retired dermatologist
Burrow, Gerard Noel internist, educator
Bursten, Stuart Lowell physician, biochemist
Buschke, Herman neurologist
Butchko, Harriett Hays physician
Butman, John Anthony radiologist
Buttner, Edgar Arnold medical educator
Buzard, Kurt Andre ophthalmologist
Bynes, Frank Howard, Jr. physician
Calderwood, Stuart Keith medical educator, consultant
Calvert, William Preston radiologist
Campbell, Andrew William immunotoxicology physician
Canady, John W. medical educator
Cansev, Mehmet physician, researcher
Canter, Maria P. gynecologist
Canty, John M., Jr. medical educator, researcher
Caplovitz, Coleman David retired physician
Carl, Schanbacher F. dermatologist, director
Carling, Tobias John Eric surgeon, research scientist
Carpenter, Robert J. epidemiologist
Carroll, Karen Colleen pathologist, infectious diseases specialist
Carswell, Jane Triplett retired family physician
Cassell, Eric Jonathan physician
Cassiani Ingoni, Riccardo medical researcher
Cassidy, Carl Eugene physician
Castel, Amanda Derryck pediatrician
Castellino, Ronald Augustus Dietrich radiologist, educator
Caston, J(esse) Douglas retired medical educator
Castro, Maria Graciela medical educator, geneticist, researcher
Catalano, Louis William, Jr. neurologist
Catalano, Patrick M. medical educator, researcher
Censullo, Michael radiologist
Cesarman, Ethel physician scientist
Chaban, Victor medical educator, consultant
Chahinian, A(ram) Philippe oncologist
Chaiyasate, Kongkrit surgeon
Chakrabarti, Anjan K. preventive medicine physician
Chalif, Ronnie medical association co-founder, artist
Chambers, Setsuko gynecologic oncologist
Chandler, James John surgeon, educator
Chang, David Z. oncologist
Chang, Hernan Robert infectious disease consultant
Chang, John B. surgeon
Chang, Kevin Jeffrey radiologist, educator
Chang, Victor Tsu-Shih oncologist, researcher, educator
Chao, Ronald Philip plastic surgeon
Chaplin, Tara M. medical researcher
Chapman, Daniel P. epidemiologist
Chasnoff, Ira Jay pediatrician
Chassin, Jameson Lewis retired surgeon
Chawla, Soni Chander medical educator, consultant
Cheetham, Jonathan surgeon, researcher
Chen, Kuen Hai physician
Cheng, Boyle C. medical educator
Cheng, Yiling J. epidemiologist
Chernoff, Amoz Immanuel hematologist, consultant
Chiang, Michael Fred physician
Chloros, George surgeon
Choi, Samuel medical researcher
Chollet, Philippe Jean Marie oncologist, educator
Chretien, Jane Henkel internist
Christie, Laurence Glenn, Jr. surgeon, educator
Christy, Nicholas Pierson physician
Chung, Benjamin Inbeh urologist
Chung, Kevin C. medical educator
Clemendor, Anthony Arnold obstetrician, educator, gynecologist, educator
Cline, Carolyn Joan plastic and reconstructive surgeon
Cloonan, Yona Keich epidemiologist
Coakley, Erin Louise internist
Cobabe, Alvin Fred retired surgeon, small business owner
Cobb, John Candler medical educator
Cochran, Robert Carter surgical educator
Cohen, Burton Jack otolaryngologist, educator
Cohen, William Nathan radiologist
Collins, Ronald Leslie Leopold neurosurgeon
Colman, Jenny Meyer psychiatrist
Colonnier, Marc Leopold retired anatomist
Connor, Daniel F. child and adolescent psychiatrist, researcher
Conomy, John Paul neurologist, educator, lawyer
Conrad, Harold Theodore psychiatrist
Cooley, Denton Arthur surgeon, educator
Cordes, Brett McCormack otolaryngologist
Correa-de-Araujo, Rosaly Lia medical researcher, educator
Courtnay, Wiliam Gerard osteopathic physician
Covintree, George E. retired anesthesiologist
Cox, William Andrew cardiovascular thoracic surgeon
Crary, Michael A. medical educator
Crino, Marjanne Helen anesthesiologist
Cronce, Paul Calvin retired dermatologist
Cruciani, Ricardo Alberto physician
Cuetter, Albert Cayetano neurologist
Cunniff, Suzanne surgical technician
Cunningham, Kimberly Ellen medical transcriptionist
Curry, Nancy S. radiologist, educator
Curtis, George Clifton psychiatrist, educator, researcher
Curtis, James L. psychiatrist
da Cruz, Eduardo M. cardiologist, educator
Daher, Edouard cardiologist
Dalessandri, Kathie Marie surgeon, educator
Daley, Jennifer internist, educator
Daly, Miriam Shamer retired family physician
Danilov, Alexey V. hematologist
Danse, Ilene Homnick Raisfeld physician, educator, toxicologist, sculptor
Date, Elaine Satomi physiatrist, educator
Davidson, Mayer B. endocrinologist, educator, researcher
Davis, Mary Helen psychiatrist, educator
Davis, Mellar Pilgrim oncologist
Dawson, Geraldine medical educator, social worker
Debbie, Gipson S. pediatrician, educator
Decker, Mark Jonathan radiologist
Decker, Wyatt W. emergency physician, educator
DeDio, Robert otolaryngologist
Degann, Sona Irene obstetrician, gynecologist, educator
Degos, Laurent hematology professor, public health administrator
Dehm, Scott M. medical educator, researcher
De La Zerda, David Joseph internist
Delgado, Roger Rodriguez surgeon, educator
DellaVecchia, Michael Anthony ophthalmologist, pathologist educator, scientist
DeMille, Dale Esther LPN director
Deneve, Jeremiah Lee surgeon
Denniston, George Clinton medical activist, medical association administrator
DePalma, Ralph George surgeon, educator, medical administrator
Der Kaloustian, Vazken Movses pediatrics and medical genetics educator
Desbiens, Norman A. medical educator, researcher
DeSilvey, Dennis Lee cardiologist, educator, academic administrator
DeSousa, Maria Ab immunologist, educator
DeStafeno, John J. ophthalmologist
Deverts, Denise Janicki health psychology researcher
Dewji, Nazneen N. medical educator, small business owner
Dezube, Bruce Jeffrey internist, oncologist, hematologist
Dhoble, Abhijeet internist
Diao, Xiumin medical researcher
Dicksheet, Sharadkumar plastic surgeon
Dickson, James Francis III surgeon
Diehl, Louis F. hematologist
Dimancescu, Mihai D. neurosurgeon, researcher, educator
Dincer, Umit Deniz pharmacologist, researcher
Ding, Jinwen biomedical researcher
DiPasqua, Aimee Dora physician
Djalilian, Hamid Reza medical educator, neurologist
Djang, David S.W. physician
Doherty, Peter Charles immunologist
Doncarlos, Lydia medical educator
Doria, Cataldo transplant surgeon
Dow, David Sontag retired ophthalmologist
Downey, John Alexander physician, educator
Drance, Stephen Michael ophthalmologist, educator
Draper, Edgar psychiatrist
Dreskin, Stephen Charles immunologist, allergist
Dreyer, Nancy Ann epidemiologist, researcher
Drucker, Carol R. medical educator
Druz, Regina Shmukler cardiologist, researcher
Dryman, Amy epidemiologist
Dubin, Howard Victor dermatologist
Dubuque, Theodore Julien, Jr. retired surgeon
Duchesne, Juan Carlos surgeon, director
Dumont, Allan Eliot retired physician, educator
Dunaway, Frank Rosser III emergency physician
Dunn, Jack Newton urologist
Dunn, Linda Kay retired physician
Durell, Jack psychiatrist
Duro, Debora gastroenterologist
Dyar, Kathryn Wilkin pediatrician
Dybul, Mark Richard immunologist, former ambassador
Dyck, Walter Peter gastroenterologist, educator, academic administrator
Dykewicz, Mark Steven physician
Dziewanowska, Zofia Elizabeth pharmaceutical executive
Eagle, Kim Allen cardiologist
Ebell, Mark Herbert physician, researcher
Ebraheim, Nabil Anwar orthopedist, surgeon
Eckel, Christine Marie medical educator
Edelman, David A. surgeon
Edwards, Bruce George retired ophthalmologist, military officer
Edwards, Larry David internist, educator, dean
Egger-Halbeis, Christoph B. (Chris Egger-Halbeis) medical educator, director
Eglinton, Daniel Thomas orthopedist
Ehigie, Benjamin Odion radiographer, technologist
Ehlers, Kathryn Hawes (Mrs. James D. Gabler) physician
Ehtesham, Moneeb neurologist, educator
Eisenberg, Carola psychiatrist, educator
Eisenstat, Theodore Ellis colon and rectal surgeon, educator
Eisold, John Francis physician
el-Azhary, Rokea Adel dermatologist, educator
Elfenbein, Gerald Jay physician, scientist, educator
Ellender, Timothy James emergency physician, educator
Ellis, Lawrence Dobson internist, educator
Ellison, Lois Taylor internist, educator, medical association administrator
El-Serag, Hashem Beshir gastroenterologist, educator
Eltahawy, Hazem A. neurosurgeon, educator
Engelhardt, Jeffery Allen pathologist
Enhorning, Goran obstetrician, gynecologist
Epps, Charles Harry, Jr. retired orthopaedic surgery educator, dean
Erkonen, William Edward radiologist, medical educator
Ertel, Karen epidemiologist, researcher
Ettinger, Lawrence Jay pediatric hematologist, oncologist, educator
Eviatar, Lydia pediatrician, neurologist
Ewing, Scott Edwin physician, psychiatrist, educator
Eyzaguirre, Eduardo Javier medical educator, researcher
Fabunan, Ruben G. physician, research scientist, inventor
Fan, Zihong J. epidemiologist
Faris, James Vannoy cardiologist, educator, health facility administrator
Fariss, Bruce Lindsay endocrinologist, consultant
Farr, Barry Miller physician, epidemiologist
Feinstein, Robert P. dermatologist
Feldman, Eva Lucille neurology educator
Feldman, Marc David psychiatrist
Felgar, Raymond Eugene pathologist, educator
Feng, Lei medical researcher
Ferencz, Charlotte retired pediatrician, epidemiologist
Fernandes, Marlos Ramalho physician, researcher
Ferstenfeld, Julian Erwin internist, educator
Fietsam, Robert, Jr. physician
Figueroa, Yolanda cardiologist
Filley, Christopher Mark neurologist, researcher
Fink, Raymond medical educator
Finkelstein, Daniel ophthalmologist
Fitch, Frank Wesley pathologist, immunologist, educator
Fleishman, Philip Robert internist
Fogel, Evan Lloyd gastroenterologist
Foley, Kevin Thomas neurosurgeon, educator
Fontes, Manuel Lopes medical educator, researcher
Fornari, Victor M. psychiatrist
Fornoni, Alessia medical educator
Fountain, Karen Schueler retired physician
Fournier, Dudley John surgeon
Fox, Karen C. medical educator, health science association administrator
Fraenkel, Liana rheumatologist, researcher
Francis, Warren William retired surgeon, educator
Franco, Sharone Elizabeth psychiatrist
Frank, Philippe G. medical educator
Franklin, Renty B. medical educator
Frederick, Peter J. medical researcher
Freedman, Aaron David retired medicine and biochemistry educator, dean
Freedman, Brett Arthur orthopedist, surgeon
Freedman, Gerald Stanley radiologist, educator, healthcare administrator
Freeman, Phillip psychiatrist
Freeman, Theodore Monroe physician
Friedensohn, Henry retired physician
Friedman, Richard Joel orthopaedic surgeon
Friedman, Samuel Robert HIV/AIDS epidemiologist
Frush, Donald Paul radiologist

Fulcher, Samuel F.A. *medical educator*
Furnas, David William *plastic surgeon, educator*
Galbraith, William Bruce *internist, educator*
Gale, Stanley William *psychiatrist*
Galvin, Matthew Reppert *psychiatry educator*
Gan, Quan *medical researcher*
Ganley, James Powell *retired ophthalmologist*
Ganske, Ingrid *medical researcher*
Gardner, Bernard *surgeon, educator*
Gardner, John Howland III *neurologist*
Garrett, Marshall Lee *anesthesiologist, educator*
Gartner, Lawrence Mitchell *pediatrician, medical educator*
Gaylin, Willard *physician, educator*
Geha, Alexander Salim *cardiothoracic surgeon, educator*
Genieser, Nancy Branom *radiologist*
Genkins, Gabriel *physician*
George, Rohini *medical physicist*
Gerald, Michael Charles *pharmacy educator, dean*
Gewitz, Michael Harold *pediatric cardiologist*
Gharabawi Garibaldi, George Milad *psychiatrist, neuroscientist*
Gibson, Milton Eugene *cardiologist*
Gilchrist, Gerald Seymour *pediatric hematologist, oncologist, educator*
Gill, Thomas James III *pathologist, educator*
Ginossar, Tamar *medical researcher, educator*
Ginsberg-Fellner, Fredda *retired pediatric endocrinologist, researcher*
Girgis, Michael M. *physician*
Glaser, Robert Joy *retired internist, foundation administrator*
Glass, Dorothea Daniels *physiatrist, educator*
Glassheim, Jeffrey Wayne *allergist, immunologist, pediatrician*
Glick, Jane Mills *retired biomedical researcher*
Goffman, Thomas Edward *radiation oncologist*
Gogbashian, Andrew *surgeon, researcher*
Gold, Judith Hammerling *psychiatrist*
Goldberg, Burton David *pathologist, researcher, educator*
Goldberg, Mark Arthur *neurologist*
Goldberg, Martin *internist, educator*
Goldberg, Michael Ellis *neurologist, neuroscientist*
Golden, Gerald Samuel *retired national medical board executive*
Golden, Robert Neal *psychiatrist, researcher, dean, medical educator*
Goldmann, Morton Aaron *cardiologist, educator*
Goldsmith, Jay Paul *pediatrician, educator*
Goldsmith, Michael Allen *oncologist, educator*
Goldstein, Avram *pharmacology educator*
Goldstein, Burton Jack *psychiatrist*
Goldstein, Dora Benedict *pharmacologist, educator*
Gonnering, Russell Stephen *ophthalmic plastic surgeon*
Gonwa, Thomas Arthur *nephrologist, educator*
Gonzalez, Caleb *ophthalmologist, educator*
Goodfellow, Robin Irene *surgeon*
Gooding, Charles Arthur *radiologist, physician, educator*
Goodman, Cynthia Diane *public health physician*
Gorfe, Alemayehu A. *medical educator*
Gorodeski, George *medical educator*
Gorodeski, George I. *medical educator*
Gottlieb, H. David *podiatrist*
Gottlieb, Klaus T. *gastroenterologist, educator*
Gotto, Jamie L. *medical educator*
Graham, David G. *preventive medicine physician, psychiatrist*
Graham, James Herbert *retired dermatologist*
Grant, Gerald A. *neurosurgeon*
Gray, Mary Jane *retired obstetrician, gynecologist*
Graziano, Michael Steven Anthony *medical educator*
Grdina, David John *radiation biologist, educator*
Green, David *hematologist*
Green, Louis Harry *retired surgeon*
Green, Morris *retired pediatrician, educator*
Greenberg, Carolyn Phyllis *retired anesthesiologist*
Greenblatt, Hellen Chaya *immunologist, microbiologist*
Greene, Donald Richard *dermatologist, educator*
Greenfield, Val Shea *ophthalmologist*
Greenspan, Robert Edward *physician*
Greer, Robert Bruce III *orthopedist, educator*
Gregory, Daniel Hayes *gastroenterologist*
Gresham, Glen Edward *physician*
Griffith, B(ezaleel) Herold *retired plastic surgeon, educator*
Grijalva, Carlos Gabriel *medical educator*
Grimmer, Johannes Fredrik *otolaryngologist, educator*
Grosso, Sue Jane Rivas *radiologist*
Grow, Daniel R. *gynecologist*
Grunt, Jerome Alvin *retired pediatric endocrinologist*
Gulbrandsen, Patricia Hughes *physician*
Gupta, Abhay *plastic and reconstructive surgeon, medical educator*
Gupta, Amit *physician, consultant*
Gurudu, Suryakanth R. *gastroenterologist, educator*
Guth, Amber Azniv *surgeon, educator*
Gutman, David Andrew *psychiatrist*
Habibi, Reza *radiologist, researcher*
Haddady, Shirin *physician*
Haddy, Theresa Brey *pediatrician, hematologist, oncologist, educator*
Haggerty, Robert Johns *pediatrician, educator*
Hales, Charles Albert *physician, educator*
Hall, Courtney D. *medical educator, researcher*
Halliday, William Ross *retired physician, speleologist, writer*
Hamilton, James William *psychiatrist, writer, artist*
Hammel, Ernest Martin *medical educator, academic administrator*
Hammond, Graeme Lord *surgeon, educator*
Hancock, John C. *pharmacologist*
Hand, Ivan Leslie *pediatrician, researcher*
Hand, Roger *physician, educator*
Hanna, Duke Ellsworth *retired neurological surgeon*
Hansell, John Royer *retired pathologist*
Hardaway, Robert Morris III *retired surgeon*
Harford, Robert R. *dermatologist*
Harmatuk, Frances A. *retired psychiatrist, anesthesiologist*
Harmel, Merel Hilber *anesthesiologist, educator*
Harper, Cynthia Channing *medical researcher, educator*
Harrigan, Rosanne Carol *medical educator*
Harrington, John Tolan *internist, nephrologist, educator, retired dean*
Harris, Elaine K. *medical consultant*
Harris, Randall Edward *preventive medicine physician*
Harrop, Daniel Smith III *psychiatrist*
Hart, Cecil William Joseph *otolaryngologist, surgeon*
Hatami, Mehrangiz *obstetrician, gynecologist, researcher*
Hatton, Caroline Kim *sports anti-doping scientist*
Hayanga, Awori Jeremiah *surgeon*
H'Doubler, Francis Todd, Jr. *surgeon*
Heckadon, Robert Gordon *plastic surgeon*
Hecker, Scott Jonathan *pharmaceutical research director*
Hegde, Vinod R. *medical association administrator, researcher*
Heggers, John Paul *retired surgery, immunology and microbiology educator*
Heileman, John Phillip *endocrinologist*
Heiner, Douglas Cragun *pediatrician, educator, immunologist, allergist*
Heitman, Kristin *medical educator*
Helfand, Arthur Erwin *podiatrist*
Hellerstein, David Joel *psychiatrist, researcher, writer*
Henderson, Melford J. *epidemiologist, molecular biologist, chemist*
Hendry, Jean Sharon *psychopharmacologist*
Hennessey, William Joseph *physician*
Henney, Christopher Scot *immunologist*
Heptinstall, Robert Hodgson *physician*
Herzberger, Eugene E. *retired neurosurgeon*
Higginbotham, Edith Arleane *radiologist, researcher*
Hildebrandt, Friedhelm *medical educator, researcher*
Himes, John Harter *medical researcher, educator*
Hinterbuchner, Catherine N. *physician, medical educator*
Hirose, Teruo Terry *surgeon educator, essayist, medical writer*
Hirsch, Lawrence Leonard *physician, retired educator*
Hodge, Jacqueline Celeste *freelance/self-employed radiologist*
Hoffman, Lucas Raphael *medical educator*
Hofseth, Lorne John *medical researcher, educator*
Holifield-Kennedy, Linda R. *physician*
Hollowell, John W. *retired urologist*
Holmes, David Richard, Jr. *cardiologist*
Holmes, Larry *epidemiologist, educator*
Holtzman, Robert Neil Nehemiah *neurosurgeon, neurologist*
Homayoon, Kaveh *urologist*
Hood, William Boyd, Jr. *cardiologist, educator*
Horswill, C. Weir *retired obstetrician-gynecologist, photographer*
Houston, Alma Faye *retired psychiatrist*
Howard, Terry Thomas *obstetrician, gynecologist*
Howards, Stuart S. *pediatric urologist*
Howell, Della *hematologist, oncologist*
Howell, Joel DuBose *internist, educator*
Hricak, Hedvig *radiologist*
Hsu, Hugo Y. *ophthalmologist, educator*
Hughes, Francis P. *medical association administrator*
Hunt, Oliver Raymond, Jr. *thoracic and cardiovascular surgeon*
Huntoon, Marc Alan *anesthesiologist, educator*
Hutcheon, Duncan Elliot *physician educator*
Hutter, Adolph Matthew, Jr. *cardiologist, educator*
Huvos, Andrew *internist, cardiologist, educator*
Hwynn, Julie Huynh *internal medicine physician*
Ilag, Liza Luna *endocrinologist, educator*
Illanes, Katarina *nephrologist*
Imperato, Pascal James *physician, healthcare administrator, writer, historian*
Imperiale, Michael *medical educator*
Ingelfinger, Julie R. *physician, researcher*
Ingle, James Newell *oncologist, consultant*
Iqbal, Shahed *epidemiologist*
Irwin, Peter John *orthopaedic surgeon*
Iserson, Kenneth Victor *bioethicist, writer, medical educator*
Islam, Saleem *pediatric surgeon, researcher*
Jacobs, Gretchen Huntley *physician, psychiatrist*
Jacobs, Laurence Stanton *physician, educator*
Jaffe, Norman *oncologist, educator*
Jain, Sudhanshu *emergency physician, educator*
Jalba, Mihai Sergiu *epidemiologist, pulmonologist, physician, researcher*
Janicak, Philip Gregory *psychiatrist, educator*
Jansen, Koen *medical association administrator*
Jarrett, David G. *emergency physician*
Jason, Hilliard *physician, educator*
Jauhar, Sandeep *physician, director*
Javitt, Daniel C. *psychiatrist, researcher*
Javitt, Jonathan C. *ophthalmologist*
Jegga, Anil G. *medical educator*
Jemal, Ahmedin *epidemiologist*
Jiao, Guansheng *medical researcher*
Jindal, Rohit *medical researcher*
Johnson, Charles Felzen *retired medical educator*
Johnson, Frank Edward *surgeon educator*
Johnson, Leonard Morris *retired pediatric surgeon*
Johnson, Martin Clifton, Sr. *retired physician*
Jones, Cecil Paul *retired surgeon*
Jones, Kellie *medical educator*
Jones-Webb, Rhonda Jean *epidemiologist, educator*
Jordan, Richard Charles *pathologist, educator*
Joseph, Ramon Rafael *internist, educator*
Jun, Soojin *medical educator, researcher*
Jung, Rodney C. *internist, academic administrator*
Kaakaji, Wayel *neurosurgeon, educator*
Kaback, Michael *medical educator*
Kaddoum, Roland *anesthesiologist, researcher*
Kalaany, Nada Y. *biomedical researcher*
Kalbfleisch, John McDowell *retired cardiologist*
Kamarajan, Chella *medical researcher*
Kandula, Praveen *medical educator*
Kane, Frank Lester *physician*
Kang, Steven S. *surgeon*
Kang, Un Jung *neurologist, educator*
Kaplan, Aaron Val *cardiologist, educator*
Kaplan, Gabriela Diana *radiologist*
Kaplan, Harriet Smith *psychiatrist, educator*
Kaplan, Justin *medical educator*
Kaplowitz, Neil *gastroenterologist, educator*
Kashyap, Purna Chandra *gastroenterologist*
Kass, Mary Elizabeth *pathologist, hospital administrator*
Kastenbaum, Robert Jay *life course educator, researcher*
Kaufman, Stephen Lawrence *radiologist, educator*
Kaul, Sanjeev A. *urologist, consultant*
Kaur, Judith Salmon *oncologist*
Kaushal, Shalesh *ophthalmologist, biochemist*
Kaushik, Prashant *rheumatologist, educator*
Kaza, Aditya K. *physician*
Keeney, Virginia T. *retired child psychiatrist*
Keill, Stuart Langdon *psychiatrist*
Kemp, Aaron Shane *neuropsychiatry, researcher*
Kern, Eugene Barton *plastic surgeon, director*
Kettelkamp, Donald Benjamin *retired orthopedist*
Khachemoune, Amor *physician*
Khan, Ahsan Yaqoob *psychiatrist, educator*
Khan, Fareesa Ghousia *gynecologist*
Khan, Mohamed K. *oncologist, educator*
Kim, Caroline Choi *dermatologist, director*
Kim, Deok-Ho *biomedical researcher*
Kim, Hee-Young *otolaryngologist*
Kim, Sarang *medical educator*
Kimball, Alexa Boer *dermatologist*
Kimes, Alane S. *medical researcher*
Kim-Farley, Robert James *epidemiologist, educator*
Kindberg, Shirley Jane *pediatrician*
King, Hueston Clark *retired otolaryngologist, educator*
King, Paul J. *orthopedist*
Kingdon, Henry Shannon *retired internist, biochemist, science administrator*
Kinrys, Gustavo *psychiatrist, director*
Kinzie, Jeannie Jones *radiation oncologist, nuclear medicine physician*
Kirkland, Rebecca Trent *endocrinologist*
Kirkpatrick, Charles Harvey *immunologist, researcher*
Kiryluk, Krzysztof *nephrologist, researcher*
Kitridou, Rodanthi C. *medical educator*
Kivikoski, Asko Ilmari *retired obstetrician, gynecologist*
Kizilisik, Aydin Tarik *surgeon, researcher*
Klimo, Paul *neurosurgeon*
Kline, Frank Menefee *psychiatrist*
Knobloch, Ferdinand J. *psychiatrist, educator*
Kobashigawa, Suzan *educator*
Kobayashi, Koichi S. *immunologist, educator*
Kohrman, Arthur Fisher *pediatrics educator*
Koletsky, Alan Jared *oncologist, educator*
Koller, Loren D. *veterinary medicine educator*
Kornel, Ludwig *medical educator, physician, scientist*
Kothary, Nishita *radiologist, consultant*
Kramer, Richard Jay *gastroenterologist, educator*
Kreider, Clement Horst, Jr. *neurosurgeon*
Kremer, Michael *surgeon*
Kronman, Andrea C. *medical educator*
Kudo, Toshifumi *surgeon, researcher*
Kumar, Vivek *urologist, surgeon*
Kundel, Harold Louis *radiologist, educator*
Kunkler, Arnold William *retired surgeon, educator*
Kunz, Alexandra Cavitt *physician, anthropologist, researcher*
Kuppermann, Nathan *emergency physician*
Kurnick, Nathaniel Bertrand *retired oncologist, hematologist*
Kuwajima, Shirou *physician*
Kuwayama, S. Paul *physician, immunologist, allergist*
Kwon, Jeff Soonchuel *physician*
Kyle, Jeffrey A. *medical educator*
La Gamma, Edmund Francis *pediatrician*
Lagunoff, David *pathologist, educator*
Lai, Yurong *medical researcher*
Lal, Geeta *surgeon*
Lambert, George H. *physician, director*
Landau, Judith *psychiatrist*
Lane, Richard Allan *preventive medicine physician, educator*
Laowattana, Somchai *neurologist, educator*
Laroche, Helena Hillman *medical researcher*
Larson, Richard Smith *pathologist, researcher*
Lasher, Lara Elaine *epidemiologist, researcher*
Lau, David L-C. *cardiologist*
Lavelle, John Paul *urologist*
Law, Shek Hang *medical educator*
Lawless, Michael Rhodes *pediatrics educator*
Lawrence, Christine *physician*
Layfield, Lester James *pathologist, educator*
Layke, John C. *plastic surgeon, researcher*
Layton, Robert Glenn *radiologist*
Lazo, Mariana *epidemiologist, researcher*
Lederer, William Jonathan *medical association administrator, educator*
Lee, David B.N. *internist, educator, nephrologist, consultant*
Lee, Heung-Man *otolaryngologist, educator*
Lee, Thomas Tehwen *neurosurgeon*
LeFante, Carolyn J. *medical association administrator*
Legters, W. Matthew *medical educator*
LeMaistre, Charles Aubrey *internist, epidemiologist, educator*
Lenert, Petar S. *medical researcher*
Lepore, Natasha *medical researcher*
Lesnewski, Ruth *physician, director*
Lester, Mark Charles *neurosurgeon*
Levin, Alan Scott *pathologist, allergist, immunologist, lawyer*
Levin, Steven Jonathan *physician*
Levitt, Seymour Herbert *radiologist, educator*
Levy, Norman B. *psychiatrist, educator*
Lichtenstein, Lawrence Mark *immunologist, allergist, educator*
Lichtman, Emily Ann *radiologist*
Liebowitz, Daniel S.F. *retired medical educator*
Lifton, Robert Jay *psychiatrist, author*
Lillehoff, Piper *psychiatrist*
Lin, David C. *biomedical researcher*
Lin, Xi *medical educator*
Lincicome, David Richard *biomedical scientist, animal scientist*
Lindell, Dennis Michael *medical educator*
Linz, Anthony James *osteopathic physician, consultant, educator*
Lipkowitz, George S. *surgeon, director*
Lipton, Glenn E. *orthopaedic surgeon*
Liu, Songtao *medical researcher*
Liu, Te Hua *retired neuroradiologist*
Lobue, Ange *psychiatrist, author*
Loewald, Elizabeth Longshore *retired psychiatrist*
Logan, Latania K. *physician scientist*
Logue, James Nicholas *epidemiologist*
Lohmann, George Young, Jr. *neurosurgeon, health facility administrator, artist*
Long, Mary E. *medical researcher*
Lonsdale, Howard Charles *physician*
Looney, Gerald Lee *medical educator, administrator*
Lowe, John C. *medical researcher, director*
Lubaroff, David Martin *immunologist, educator*
Luce, Edward Andrew *plastic surgeon*
Luedeman, Gerald Warren *radiologist*
Luke, Robert George *nephrologist, medical educator*
Lynch, Dennis James *retired plastic surgeon*
Lyon, Gholson *psychiatrist*
MacLeod, Gordon C. *surgeon*
Maeda, Kenji *medical researcher*
Maeda, Koichi *pathologist*
Magnes, Harry Alan *physician*
Magro, Cynthia Maria *pathologist*
Mahajan, Anita *oncologist, educator*
Maher, Cormac Oliver *neurosurgeon, pediatrician, researcher*
Mahesh, Virendra Bhushan *endocrinologist*
Mahmood, Nafeesa F. *physician, consultant*
Mak, Linda L. *dermatologist*
Makdisi, Tony *medical educator*
Maksem, John Adelbert *pathologist*
Mala, Theodore Anthony *physician, consultant*
Malach, Monte *physician*
Malhotra, Madhu Bala *psychiatrist*
Malluche, Hartmut Horst *nephrologist, medical educator*
Mandell, Gerald A. *nuclear medicine physician*
Mandell, Gerald Lee *internist, educator*
Mangalpally, Kiran Kumar Ramchander *medical researcher*
Mangano, Salvatore Nicholas *retired surgeon*
Mangla, Sundeep *radiologist, research scientist*
Manjunath, Prashanth *anesthesiologist, researcher*
Manning, John Warren III *retired surgeon, medical educator*
Mannino, J(oseph) Robert *medical educator*
Mansergh, Gordon Dwight *health maintenance and prevention researcher*
Manyam, Bala Venkatesha *medical researcher, neurology educator*
Marc, David Tischler *cardiologist, director*
Marcdante, Karen Jean *medical educator*
Margulis, Alexander Rafailo *physician, educator*
Mariano, Ana Virginia *retired pathologist*
Mari Aparici, Carina *nuclear medicine physician*
Mariash, Cary Norman *medical educator, researcher*
Markham, Charles Henry *neurologist*
Marrin, Charles Ainsworth Staveley *cardiovascular and thoracic surgeon, educator*
Marshall, Wayne Keith *anesthesiology educator*
Martin, Daniel C. *surgeon, gynecologist, educator*
Martin, Kathryn A. *endocrinologist*
Martino, Silvana *osteopath, medical oncologist*
Mashberg, Arthur *medical educator*
Massey, Robert Unruh *internist, educator, dean*
Matarasso, Seth L. *dermatologic surgeon*
Mates, Susan Onthank *physician, educator, musician, writer*
Maxwell, George Patrick *plastic surgeon*
Mayfield-Clarke, Ann Bernadette *speech, language pathologist*
Mbulaiteye, Sam *medical researcher*
McCartney, David L. *ophthalmologist, department chairman*
McClelland, Shearwood III *physician*
McCullough, Laurence Bernard *medical educator, consultant*
Mc Dermott, John Francis *psychiatrist, physician*
McGlashan, Thomas Hamel *psychiatrist, educator*
McGrath, Mary Helena *plastic surgeon, educator*
McGregor, John M. *medical educator*
McInerney, Elaine F. *medical educator*
McKinney, Bart *orthopedist, researcher*
McKinney, Brett *medical educator*
McLaurin, Lambert Paschal *retired medical educator*
McLawhon, Ronald William *pathology educator, biochemist*
Mclendon, Roger Edwin *neuropathologist, educator*
McLeskey, Charles Hamilton *anesthesiologist, educator, pharmaceutical executive*
McMahan-Woneis, Celestine *integrative medical educator, health psychologist, educator, educational therapist, health psychology educator*
McNeal, Monica Malone *medical educator, director*
Meadows, Gwendolyn Joann *retired behavioral disorders educator*
Meerschaert, Joseph Richard *retired physician*
Meilman, Edward *physician*
Mejico, Luis J. *neurologist, educator*
Mellerick-Dressler, Dervla M. *medical association administrator*
Mellinkoff, Sherman Mussoff *medical educator*
Mellins, Harry Zachary *radiologist, educator*
Mendels, Joseph *psychiatrist, educator*
Meredith, Andrea L. *medical educator*
Merkin, Albert Charles *pediatrician, allergist*
Merrill, Joseph Melton *medical educator*
Messa, Charles Angelo III *plastic surgeon*
Messerle, Judith Rose *retired medical librarian, public relations executive*
Meurer, William Joseph *emergency physician, educator*
Meyer, Theo E. *cardiologist*
Meyerhoff, James Lester *medical researcher*

Michael, Mark Alber *cardiologist, researcher*
Michael, Simon R. *physician scientist, educator*
Milan, Stojanovic P. *medical educator, director*
Millar, John Donald *physician, occupational & environmental health services consultant, musician*
Miller, Anthony Bernard *physician, researcher*
Miller, Jack David R. *radiologist, physician, educator*
Miller, Mark David *orthopedist, surgeon, educator*
Miller, Ross Hays *retired neurosurgeon*
Miskimen, Theresa Marie *psychiatrist, educator*
Mitchell, William Marvin *pathology educator*
Mladick, Richard Anthony *plastic surgeon*
Modisher, Melvin Wayne *obstetrician, gynecologist, educator*
Modny, Cynthia Jean *dermatologist*
Mohaideen, A. Hassan *surgeon, consultant, health products executive*
Mohamadi, Masoud *retired surgeon*
Montgomery, Hubert Theron, Jr. *physician, health care administrator*
Montgomery, John Richard *pediatrician, educator*
Moore, Donnica Lauren *physician, medical writer*
Moore, William Henry *radiologist*
Moore, William Vegh *sports medicine physician*
Moossy, John *neurologist, consultant, pathologist*
Morgan, Oliver WC *epidemiologist*
Morgenstern, Kenneth E. *plastic surgeon*
Mosier, William Arthur *psychiatrist, psychotherapist, director, medical educator, researcher*
Moss, Marc *medical educator*
Motto, Jerome Arthur *psychiatrist, educator*
Mounasamy, Varatharaj *orthopedist, educator*
Movahedzadeh, Farahnaz *medical researcher, educator*
Mower, Morton Maimon *cardiologist*
Mueller-Heubach, Eberhard *medical educator*
Mulcahy, Gabriel M. *pathologist*
Mullins, Charles Brown *physician, academic administrator*
Munver, Ravi *urologist*
Murat, Yusef J. *plastic surgeon*
Murphey, Sheila Ann *infectious diseases physician, educator, researcher*
Murry, J. Warren *surgeon, educator*
Myerowitz, P(aul) David *cardiac surgeon, educator, writer*
Myers, Allen Richard *rheumatologist*
Naik, Rupali K. *researcher*
Najjar, Samer S. *internist, educator*
Naval, Neeraj *medical educator*
Nelson, Christopher Grant *dermatologist*
Nelson, John Woolard *neurology educator, physician*
Nelson, Kristin Schad *otolaryngology, facial plastic surgeon*
Nelson, Nancy Eleanor *retired pediatrician, educator*
Newsome, Lisa Testa *anesthesiologist, educator*
Nguyen, Khanh Gia *medical educator*
Nicholls, Richard Aurelius *retired obstetrician, gynecologist*
Nicholson, Henry Hale, Jr. *retired surgeon*
Nieto, Juan Manuel *emergency medicine physician*
Niloff, Paul Hyman *surgeon, educator*
Nistala, Ravi *nephrologist*
Nkoy, Flory Lumu *medical educator*
Noonan, Jacqueline Anne *pediatrician, educator*
Nora, James Jackson *physician, writer, educator*
Norrid, Henry Gail *osteopathic physician and surgeon, researcher, educator, healthcare facility administrator*
Novack, Alvin John *physician*
Novak, James Edmund *nephrologist*
Novello, Antonia Coello *pediatric nephrologist, former state health commissioner, former United States Surgeon General*
Nuchtern, Jed G. *surgeon, educator*
Nyirjesy, Istvan *retired obstetrician, gynecologist*
Oktem, Ozgur *medical doctor, researcher*
Olds, Jacqueline *psychiatrist, educator*
Olearchyk, Andrew *cardiothoracic surgeon, educator*
Omidi, C. Julian *plastic surgeon*
Orlando, Lori Ann *medical researcher, educator, physician*
Orr, Robert David *clinical ethicist, educator, physician*
Orth, David Nelson *endocrinologist, educator, sculptor, potter*
Ory, Steven Jay *physician, educator*
Osborn, June Elaine *pediatrician, microbiologist, educator, foundation administrator*
Osborn, Lucy Morin *pediatrician, educator*
Ossoff, Robert Henry *otolaryngologist, surgeon*
Otto, Randal Allen *otolaryngologist, educator*
Pachter, Lee M. *pediatrician*
Pacifico, Albert Dominick *cardiovascular surgeon*
Packard, John Mallory *physician, researcher*
Pahuja, Madhuri (Pahujaa) *scientist, educator*
Paniello, Randal C. *otolaryngologist, educator*
Pao, Lincoln K. *oncologist, educator*
Papadonikolakis, Anastasios *orthopedist, surgeon*
Papoiu, Alexandru Dragos Petru *medical researcher, chemist*
Parasuraman, Ravi Kumar *nephrologist*
Parikh, Rahul Kedar *physician*
Park, Eun-Young *medical educator*
Park, In-Seop *orthopedist, researcher*
Park, John K. *neurosurgeon*
Park, Myung Kun *medical educator*
Parker, Brent Mershon *retired medical educator, internist, cardiologist*
Parmley, Richard Turner *pediatric hematologist, oncologist*
Passos, Maria de Lourdes *psychological researcher*
Patchin, Rebecca J. *anesthesiologist, educator, administrator*
Patel, Alpa V. *epidemiologist, director*
Patel, Niketa *medical researcher*
Patel, Uptal Dinesh *nephrologist, researcher*
Paul, Norman Leo *psychiatrist, educator*
Pauly, John Edward *retired anatomist*
Paz-Filho, Gilberto Jorge *endocrinologist*
Pearson, William S. *epidemiologist*
Pecora, David Victor *retired surgeon*
Peden, Eric Kevin *thoracic surgeon, educator*
Pederson, William Christopher *plastic surgeon*
Peixoto Neto, Jose Ulysses *internist, researcher*
Pellegrino, Peter *retired surgeon*
Pereira, Marcia Elisa *pathologist*
Perez, Edith Adaljisa *physician*
Perez, Louis Anthony *radiologist*
Perkins, Robert Mitchell, Jr. *pediatrician*
Perl, Harold *neonatologist, pediatrician*
Pero, Colin Daniel *facial plastic surgeon researcher*
Perry, William Brian *colorectal surgeon*
Pesola, Gene Raymond *physician*
Peszke, Michael Alfred *psychiatrist, writer*
Peters, Todd *psychiatrist*
Peterson, Alfred Edward *retired family physician*
Peterson, Ann Sullivan *physician, consultant*
Petriashvili, Marina *physician*
Petrovic, Bojan D *diagnostic radiologist*
Pflum, Barbara Ann *retired allergist*
Phillips, John P(aul) *retired neurosurgeon*
Phillips, Katharine Anne *psychiatrist*
Phillips, Melannie *medical educator*
Phillips, Peggie L. *medical educator*
Phitayakorn, Roy *surgeon*
Pick, Donald Lowell *urologist*
Piedimonte, Giovanni *pediatrician*
Pierangeli, Silvia Susana *medical educator, consultant*
Pierce, Donald Shelton *retired orthopedic surgeon, educator*
Pierce, Michael Norman *internist*
Pimiento, Jose Mario *physician*
Pineda, Albert Anthony *obstetrician, gynecologist, educator*
Pinter, Gabriel George *retired physiology educator*
Pirodsky, Donald Max *psychiatrist, educator*
Pirro, Alfred Anthony, Jr. *emergency physician*
Pitcock, James Allison *retired pathologist*
Pittman, Roy Clinton, Jr. *neurosurgeon, theologian, lawyer, philosopher*
Plews-Ogan, Margaret L. *pediatrician, department chairman*
Plotkin, Horacio *pediatric endocrinologist, orthopedic surgeon, educator*
Podichetty, Vinod Kumar *medical researcher*
Poehling, Katherine *pediatrician*
Pokala, Naveen *urologist*
Polfliet, Sarah Jean *physician*
Poppers, Paul Jules *anesthesiologist, educator*
Powell, John Livingston *retired obstetrician and gynecologist*
Powell, Matthew *oncologist, educator*
Powers, Scott *medical association administrator*
Prabhakar, Swaroop *medical educator*
Prange, Hilmar Walter *neurology educator*
Prasad, Navin *ophthalmologist*
Prchal, Josef Tomas *hematologist, researcher*
Price, Jack F. *cardiologist*
Prilipko, Olga *medical researcher*
Prince, Martin Raymond *radiologist*
Promod Kumar, Ramachandran Pillai *neurosurgeon, educator*
Propst, Michael Truman *pathologist*
Pryor, Carol Graham *retired obstetrician, gynecologist*
Pust, Ronald E. *physician, educator*
Qiang, Mei *biomedical researcher, educator*
Qin, Xiaofa *medical educator, research scientist*
Qiu, Shenfeng *medical researcher*
Quencer, Robert Moore *neuroradiologist, researcher*
Quillian, Warren Wilson, II, *pediatrician, educator*
Quintero, Elias Matthew *biomedical researcher*
Quock, Raymond Mark *pharmacologist, health sciences educator, biomedical researcher*
Race, George Justice *pathology educator*
Ragins, Herzl *retired surgeon*
Raichle, Marcus Edward *radiology and neurology educator*
Raines, Jeff *biomedical scientist, medical research director*
Ram, Chitta Venkata *physician*
Ramirez-Rivera, Jose *physician*
Rammohan, Kottil Walappil *neurologist, educator*
Rampersad, Sally Elizabeth *anesthesiologist*
Randall, Peter *retired plastic surgeon*
Rangappa, Sunil *cardiologist*
Ranney, Helen Margaret *retired internist, hematologist, educator*
Ranney, Richard Raymond *periodontist educator, researcher, dean*
Rapolu, Praveen *physician*
Raval, Ma Florena Tenazas *retired pathologist*
Ravdin, Peter Marcus *internist, educator, oncologist*
Ravindran, Cholapurath Nishal *physician*
Rawnsley, Howard Melody *pathologist, educator*
Rebhun, Joseph *allergist, immunologist, medical educator*
Reddy, Chakradhar M. *gastroenterologist, educator*
Reddy, Ravinder *medical educator, director*
Refaat, Marwan *lebanon cardiology fellow*
Regan, Peter Francis III *physician, medical educator*
Regatte, Ravinder R. *medical educator*
Reid, Robert Alfred *physician*
Reinsmoen, Nancy Louise *medical educator, director*
Reinus, William R. *radiology educator*
Reiss, Robert Francis *physician*
Ren, Shunlin *medical educator*
Ren, Xing Jian *physician*
Ren-Patterson, Renee Feng *neuropathologist, neuroscientist*
Restrepo, Humberto *gynecologist, obstetrician, educator*
Rewcastle, Neill Barry *neuropathologist*
Rhodes, Linda Jane *psychiatrist*
Richard, A. Kerber *medical educator*
Richardson, Willie Forrest, Jr. *physician, consultant*
Rifkin, Stephen *nephrologist*
Rigg, Charles Andrew *pediatrician*
Riggins, Tracy *neurologist, educator*
Rincon, Fred *neurologist, researcher*
Rinker, Charles F., II, *surgeon*
Risin, Diana *biomedical researcher*
Ritter, Ann Marie *pediatric neurosurgeon*
Rivadeneira, David Edward *colon and rectal surgeon, researcher*
Rizza, Frank Alfonso *retired surgeon, educator*
Robbins, Richard James *endocrinologist, researcher*
Roberts, Melville Parker *neurosurgeon*
Robinson, Mary Jo *pathologist*
Robinson, Rebecca Lynne *medical researcher*
Rodgers, Lawrence Rodney *internist, educator*
Rodriguez-Cintron, William *pulmonologist*
Rolland, Jannick P. *medical educator*
Rollins, Faye Lorraine *medical transcriptionist*
Rollins, Lisa Kay *medical educator, director*
Romero-González, Mauricio *psychiatrist, educator, consultant*
Roscoe, Kevin Jay *radiologist, physician*
Rosen, Paul Peter *pathologist*
Ross, Gerald Harvey *family practice and environmental medicine physician*
Roth, Karl Sebastian *retired pediatrician*
Rothenberg, Albert *psychiatrist, educator*
Rothman, Kenneth Jay *epidemiologist*
Rotman, Marvin *radiation oncologist, radiologist, educator*
Rottenberg, Hagai *medical educator*
Rotunda, Adam Michael *dermatologist*
Rouman, James Christ *anesthesiologist*
Rouphael, Nadine G. *physician*
Roy, Sanjoy *health outcomes researcher*
Rubin, Alan *physician*
Rubin, Bruce Kalman *medical professor, researcher*
Rubin, Robert Joseph *internist, nephrologist, consultant*
Rudolph, Andrew Henry *retired dermatologist, educator*
Rufanova, Victoriya *medical researcher*
Runge, Marschall Stevens *cardiologist, educator*
Runge, Val Murray *medical educator*
Russo, Jose *pathologist*
Russo, Vincent Joseph *surgeon*
Ryan, John Joseph *physician*
Sabharwal, Sunil *emergency physician*
Saeed, Shehzad *pediatrician, educator*
Sahota, Puneet *medical researcher*
Salazar, Omar Mauricio *radiation oncologist, educator*
Saltz, Leonard Bruce *oncologist*
Saltzman, Brian *physician, surgeon, educator*
Salyer, Kenneth E. *surgeon*
Samardjiev, Ivan Jordanov *medical researcher*
Samkoff, Lawrence Mark *neurologist, educator*
Sampram, Ellis Senanu Kojo *physician*
Sanders, Joe Maxwell, Jr. *pediatrician*
Sangster, Paul Edward *retired radiologist*
Saravolatz, Louis Donald *epidemiologist, medical educator*
Sargent, William Winston *retired anesthesiologist*
Satpathy, Ruby *cardiologist, researcher*
Sawczuk, Ihor S. *urologist*
Schaffner, Adam David *plastic surgeon*
Scharschmidt, Bruce Frederick *physician*
Schauf, Victoria *pediatrician, educator*
Schenker, Marc Benet *preventive medicine physician, medical educator, department chairman*
Scherger, Joseph Edward *family physician, educator*
Schiff, Martin *physician, surgeon*
Schneck, Stuart Austin *retired neurologist, educator*
Schneider, Calvin *physician*
Schneider, Jan *retired obstetrics and gynecology educator*
Schoen, Robert Taylor *rheumatologist*
Scholz, Thomas *plastic surgeon, researcher*
Schulman, Harold *obstetrician, gynecologist*
Schulman, Sidney *neurologist, educator*
Schwartz, George R. *physician, researcher*
Schwartz, Judy Ellen *thoracic surgeon*
Schwarz, M. Roy *retired physician, administrator*
Segars, Kelly Scott, Sr. *physician, banker*
Seli, Emre Utku *reproductive endocrinology and infertility specialist, physician researcher*
Seller, Robert Herman *cardiologist, physician*
Seltser, Raymond *epidemiologist, educator, preventive medicine physician*
Seltzer, Vicki Lynn *obstetrician, gynecologist*
Selvaraju, Raghuram *medical researcher*
Semler, William Ludwig *retired obstetrician, retired gynecologist*
Sena, Charalena *dental office executive*
Sepehr, Ali *physician*
Sessions, Roy Brumby *otolaryngologist, educator*
Sever, John Louis *medical researcher, educator*
Sewell, Daniel D. *psychiatrist, educator*
Seyoum, Berhane *medical educator*
Shabot, Myron Michael *hospital administrator*
Shader, Richard Irwin *psychiatrist, pharmacologist, educator*
Shaffer, Kitt *radiologist, educator*
Shagan, Bernard Pellman *endocrinologist, educator*
Shane, John Marder *endocrinologist*
Sharifi, Neda A. *scientist*
Sharma, Sushil K. *medical educator*
Sharp, Dan Steven *epidemiologist*
Shaw, Ronald Ahrend *physician, educator*
Shedd, Donald Pomroy *surgeon*
Sheldon, Stephen *pediatric sleep medicine educator, researcher*
Shepard, Richard Blount *surgeon, educator*
Sher, Leo *psychiatrist*
Sherman, John Foord *biomedical consultant*
Sherris, David Allan *surgeon, researcher, educator*
Shihab, Fuad Said *medical educator, researcher*
Shils, Maurice Edward *physician, educator, research scientist*
Shlimovich, Pavel *internist*
Shoemaker, Lawrence R. *pediatrician, educator*
Shoul, Melvin I. *retired surgeon*
Shoupe, Donna *obstetrician-gynecologist, educator*
Shulman, Bernard H. *psychiatrist, educator*
Shuster, Frederick *retired internist, gastroenterologist*
Siffert, Robert Spencer *orthopedic surgeon*
Sigmon, J. Lewis, Jr. *medical educator*
Silva, Omega Logan *physician*
Silver, Malcolm David *pathologist, educator*
Simmons, Richmond Hogle *retired obstetrician, gynecologist*
Singer, Jack Wolfe *medical educator*
Sivak-Callcott, Jennifer A. *ophthalmologist*
Slachta, Gregory Andrew *urologist*
Slavit, David Hal *otolaryngologist*
Slesnick, Timothy *cardiologist, educator*
Slim, Michel S. *surgeon, educator, health facility administrator*
Sloan, Michael Allan *neurologist*
Slockett, Deena *medical educator*
Smith, Darvin Scott *internist*
Smith, Martin Henry *retired pediatrician*
Smith, Phillip Walton *retired surgeon*
Smith, Raymond Leigh *plastic surgeon*
Smith, Russell B. *surgeon*
Smith, Stuart Lyon *psychiatrist, corporate financial executive*
Smith, Thomas F. *immunologist*
Sobin, Leslie Howard *pathologist, educator*
Sobkowicz, Hanna Maria *retired neurologist*
Soe, Kyaw K. *medical educator*
Sokol, Ronald Jay *pediatric gastroenterologist, researcher*
Soltero-Harrington, Luis Rubén *retired surgeon, educator*
Sontag, James Mitchell *oncologist, researcher*
Soran, Z. Ozlem *medical educator*
Sosa, Julie A. *medical educator*
Sotos, John George *cardiologist, writer*
Sourial, Alfy Saif *surgeon*
South, Michael Shane *oncologist*
Spackman, Thomas James *radiologist*
Spaulding, Anne C. *epidemiologist, educator*
Speicher, Carl Eugene *pathologist*
Spellman, Mitchell Wright *surgeon, academic administrator, educator*
Squires, Kathleen Elaine *internal medicine educator*
Stallworth, Monica Lavaughn *geriatrician*
Steier, Michael Edward *cardiac surgeon*
Steinbach, Lynne Susan *radiologist, educator*
Steinberg, Russell Max *behavioral pediatrician, educator*
Stemerman, David H. *radiologist*
Stewart, Michael Glenn *otolaryngologist, educator*
Stewart, S. Evelyn *child psychiatrist, researcher*
Stimpson, Jim P. *medical educator*
Stock, Wendy *physician, educator*
Stolier, Alan J. *surgeon*
Stollerman, Gene Howard *internist, educator*
Stolley, Paul David *medical educator, researcher*
Storer, Thomas W. *medical educator*
Strain, James Ellsworth *pediatrician, educator, retired medical association administrator*
Strauch, Berish *plastic surgeon, hand and cosmetic surgeon*
Strongin, Jonathan David *physician*
Sullivan, Colleen Anne *anesthesiologist, educator*
Summers, David Stewart *neurologist, consultant*
Sun, Changquan Calvin *medical researcher, educator*
Sundaram, Senthil K. *pediatrician, educator*
Sunde, Douglas *plastic surgeon*
Suneja, Manish *physician*
Sung, Kyongje *medical researcher*
Supino, Phyllis Gail *medical researcher, educator*
Surawicz, Borys *physician, educator*
Surbone, Antonella *medical oncologist, bioethics researcher*
Sutnick, Alton Ivan *internist, dean, educator, researcher, consultant*
Swerdlow, Martin Abraham *retired pathologist, educator*
Swift, Michael Ronald *internist, educator*
Szakal, Andras Kalman *immunologist, anatomist, educator*
Tagiuri, Consuelo Keller *child psychiatrist, educator*
Talamo, Jonathan Haskell *ophthalmologist, educator*
Talor, Zvi *nephrologist*
Tan, Dongfeng *pathologist, educator*
Tandon, Rajiv *psychiatrist, educator*
Tang, Xiaoli *medical educator*
Taplin, Mary-Ellen *medical educator*
Tasto, James P. *orthopedist, educator*
Taylor, Alice P. *medical researcher*
Taylor, Peyton Troy, Jr. *oncologist, educator*
Taylor, Sarah Ann *oncologist, educator*
Taylor, William Colton *physician, educator*
Taylor-Clark, Kalahn Alexandra *medical researcher*
Taype, Carmen Amelia *physician*
Teman, Elly *medical researcher*
Teodorescu, Victoria Jean *surgeon*
Tepper, Lloyd Barton *occupational and preventive medicine physician, educator*
Teresi, Jeanne A. *medical researcher, director*
Terris, Susan *physician, cardiologist, researcher*
Therrell, Bradford Leon, Jr. *medical researcher*
Thomas, Forsthuber G. *immunologist, educator*
Thompson, Dennis Peters *plastic surgeon*
Thoms, Norman Wells *retired cardiovascular and thoracic surgeon*
Thornton, James F. *plastic surgeon, former military officer*
Thornton, Yvonne Shirley *obstetrician, writer, musician*
Thorsen, Marie Kristin *radiologist, educator*
Tiedge, Henri *medical educator, researcher*
Tiefenbrun, Jonathan *surgeon*
To, Kenneth Kin Wah *medical educator, researcher*
Tobacman, Joanne Kramer *medical educator, researcher*
Tolia, Vasundhara K. *pediatric gastroenterologist, educator*
Top, Franklin Henry, Jr. *physician, researcher*
Tourtellotte, Wallace William *neurologist, educator*
Towfighi, Amytis *neurologist*
Tranquada, Robert Ernest *retired internist, educator*
Trevathan, Edwin *neurologist, educator*
Trindade, Arvind Julius *internist, researcher*
Tropez-Sims, Susanne *pediatrician, educator*
Trumbull, William Ernest *retired surgeon, educator*
Tsay, Ching Sow *retired anesthesiologist*
Tsuang, John *psychiatrist*
Turk, Richard Errington *retired psychiatrist*
Turndorf, Herman *anesthesiologist, educator*
Turner, Harry Spencer *preventive medicine physician, educator*

Turner, John Sidney, Jr. *retired otolaryngologist, educator*
Twenhafel, Nancy Ann *pathologist, director*
Tyler, Carl Walter, Jr. *retired epidemiologist, health science association administrator*
Unger, Gere Nathan *emergency physician, lawyer*
Unger, Roger Harold *physician, research scientist*
Uscinski, Ronald Henry *medical educator*
Vakili, Bahman Fakhimi *urologist*
Valentine, William Newton *retired physician, educator*
Vallabhan, Girish C. *urologist*
Vanderwagen, W. Craig (William Craig Vanderwagen) *physician, former federal agency administrator*
Van Ha, Thuong G. *radiologist, educator*
Van Heertum, Ronald Lanny *physician*
VanItallie, Theodore Bertus *physician*
van Nagell, John Rensselaer *oncologist, gynecologist*
Vasquez, Margarita M. *pediatrician, educator*
Vasudev, Brahm Sarup *nephrologist*
Velazquez, Omaida Caridad *vascular surgeon, researcher*
Velisek, Libor *medical educator*
Vest, Gayle Southworth *obstetrician, gynecologist*
Vicencio, Alfin Gemil *pediatrician*
Victor, John C. *epidemiologist*
Vinkey, Rachel Burdick *psychiatrist*
Vittetoe, Marie Clare *retired clinical laboratory science educator*
von Eschenbach, Andrew C. *oncologist, former federal agency administrator*
Voorhis, Brenda Heath Jacobsen *retired psychiatrist*
Wagner, Michael *medical researcher, educator*
Walker, David H. *medical educator*
Walker, Joae Brooks *retired psychiatrist*
Wallace, Joyce Irene Malakoff *internist*
Waller-Niewold, Marilyn J. *podiatric surgeon*
Wallerstein, Robert Solomon *retired psychiatrist*
Wang, Nancy *pathologist, educator*
Ward, Chester Lawrence *physician, consultant*
Watanabe, Kyoichi A(loysius) *pharmacology educator, chemist*
Waterhouse, Keith *urologist, educator, retired surgeon*
Waters, William Carter III *retired internist, educator*
Watson, Donald Charles, Jr. *cardiothoracic surgeon, educator*
Waugh, Theodore Rogers *orthopedic surgeon*
Wax, Martin Bruce *ophthalmologist*
Way, Barbara Haight *retired dermatologist*
Weber, Randal Scott *head and neck surgeon, educator*
Wei, Maria L. *dermatologist, educator*
Weil, Richard III *surgeon, medical educator*
Weiler, John M. *physician, educator, executive*
Weinberg, Richard M. *internist, pulmonary and critical care physician, consultant*
Weiner, Louis Marc *oncologist*
Weingarten, Michael S. *surgeon, educator*
Weinshenker, Naomi Joyce *clinical psychiatrist, educator, researcher*
Weisman, Leonard E. *medical educator*
Weiss, Avery H. *ophthalmologist, educator*
Weiss, Lyn Denise *physician*
Welmaker, Gregory S. *medical researcher*
Welsh, Christabel Jane *neuroimmunologist*
Weltman, Joel Kenneth *immunologist*
Welzel, Tania M. *physician*
Wenk, Robert E. *pathologist*
Wessel, Morris Arthur *retired pediatrician*
Westernoff, Trent H. *surgeon*
White, Kerr Lachlan *retired physician, foundation administrator*
Whitman, Gregory Theodore *neurologist*
Whitsell, John Crawford, II, *general surgeon*
Wieland, Gilbert Darryl *medical researcher, anthropologist, gerontologist*
Wiernik, Peter Harris *oncologist, educator*
Wilk, Ronald *physician*
Wilkins, Fred Clayton *physician, educator, engineer*
Williams, James Buchanan *retired surgeon*
Williams, Kim Allan *cardiologist, educator*
Williams, Robert Leon *retired psychiatrist, neurologist, educator*
Wilson, James Miller, IV, *cardiovascular surgeon, educator*
Wilson, Lynn Deyo *radiation oncologist*
Wilson, Mary Elizabeth *epidemiologist, physician, educator*
Wilson, Myron Robert, Jr. *retired psychiatrist*
Winer, Karen K. *endocrinologist*
Winneker, Richard Craig *pharmacologist, researcher*
Wira, Charles Ryan *physician, educator*
Wishnick, Marcia Margolis *pediatrician, geneticist, educator*
Wisniewski, P. Michelle *retired obstetrician, gynecologist*
Wolanskyj, Alexandra *hematologist*
Woldman, Sherman *pediatrician*
Wolfersteig, Jean Lois *retired medical association administrator*
Wong, Albert J. *medical educator*
Woo, Kenneth Roger *urologist*
Wood, Maurice *medical educator*
Woods, Jason C. *medical educator*
Woolston-Catlin, Marian *retired psychiatrist*
Worner, Theresa Marie *internist, educator*
Worrell, Richard Vernon *orthopedic surgeon, dean*
Wu, Yu-Chien *medical researcher*
Wyman, Milton *ophthalmologist*
Wyngaarden, James Barnes *retired physician*
Xi, Yutao *medical researcher*
Xia, Guohua *scientist, psychiatrist, psychologist*
Yadavalli, Gopala Krishna *medical educator*
Yalam, Arnold Robert *allergist, immunologist, consultant*
Yalamanchili, Praveen Raj *nephrologist*
Yamamoto, Joe *retired psychiatrist, educator*
Yamamoto, Nobuto *immunologist, director*
Yan, Xin *preventive medicine physician, educator*
Yang, Bin *pathologist, molecular biologist*
Yang, Weibin *physician*
Yarchoan, Robert *clinical immunologist, researcher*
Ye, Weilan *scientist*
Yehia, Baligh R. *physician*
Yielding, K. Lemone *physician*
Yildizhan, Ahmet *neurosurgeon, educator*
Yock, Paul Godo *biomedical researcher, educator*
Yodaiken, Ralph E. *pathologist, occupational health physician, educator*
Youmans, Julian Ray *neurosurgeon, educator*
Young, Alfred Byron *neurosurgeon*
Yu, Hannah *medical researcher*
Yu, Kelly Jen-Yi *epidemiologist*
Zabetakis, Paul Michael *nephrologist, educator*
Zaets, Sergey *medical researcher, consultant, director*
Zalavras, Charalampos *orthopedic surgeon*
Zarins, Bertram *orthopedic surgeon*
Zawacki, Bruce Edwin *surgeon, educator, ethicist*
Zawadzki, Robert J. *ophthalmologist, educator*
Zeidenweber, Carlo M. *cardiologist*
Zha, Jiping *pathologist*
Zhan, Xianquan *medical educator*
Zhang, Ming *medical educator*
Zhang, Song *computer science educator*
Zhou, Pengbo *medical educator*
Zoumalan, Richard Abraham *otolaryngologist*
Zuhdi, Nazih *retired surgeon*
Zumwalt, Ross Eugene *forensic pathologist, educator*
Zuna, Rosemary Elizabeth *pathologist*
Zwass, Maurice S. *medical educator*

HUMANITIES: LIBERAL STUDIES

UNITED STATES

ALABAMA

Auburn
Amacher, Richard Earl *retired literature educator*

Birmingham
Allen, Lee Norcross *historian, educator*
Benditt, Theodore Matthew *humanities educator*
Crocker, Carolyn Robertson *language educator*
Ledgerwood, Mikle Dave *language educator*
Lester, V. Markham *history professor*
Sansom, Dennis Lee *philosopher, educator*
Whitaker, Elaine Emanuel *humanities educator*
Workman, Charles Thomas *language educator*

Hanceville
Buckelew, Kathy *literature and language professor*
Davis, Robert Scott *history professor*

Huntsville
Cachán, Manuel *Spanish language educator*
Lang, Sharon *historian*

Jacksonville
Spector, Daniel Earl *historian, educator*

Livingston
Davis, Debbie Dawson *literature and language professor*

Loachapoka
Schafer, Elizabeth Diane *historian, writer*

Mobile
Donalson, Malcolm Drew *classics educator*
Kargleder, Charles Leonard *language educator*
Miller, Harrison Stewart *history professor*
Roddy, Harry Louis, Jr. *language educator*
Thomason, Michael V.R. *retired history professor*

Monroeville
Estill, Donna Rae *literature and language professor, director*

Montevallo
Stoops, Rosa Maria *language educator*

Montgomery
Cornett, Lloyd Harvey, Jr. *retired historian*
Miller, John Winfield *language educator, researcher*
Rose, Shirley Kelly *retired language educator*

Normal
Vaughn, Michael Oscar *history professor*

Ramer
Napier, John Hawkins III *historian*

Troy
Mitchell, Norma Taylor *history professor*

Tuscaloosa
Adams, Hilda J. *English language educator*
Hocutt, Max Oliver *retired philosophy educator*
Jennings, Thomas Steven *history professor*
Pass, Charlotte Louise *literature educator, consultant*

ALASKA

Anchorage
Craig, Robert Dean *historian, educator*

Fairbanks
Kan, Rosalind J. *highway design engineer and language educator*

Gakona
Ainsworth, Cynthia Lee *folklorist*

ARIZONA

Arizona City
Landers, Patricia Glover *language educator*

Flagstaff
Price, Nicole Denise *literature and language professor*
Reese, Marilya Veteto *literature and language professor*

Glendale
Eyres, Beth Kathleen *literature educator*

Green Valley
Brewington, Arthur William *retired English language educator*

Holbrook
Lawson, Michael J. *history and anthropology educator*
O'Hop, Suzanne Elizabeth *educator*

Laveen
Meneses (Gonzales), Diana Marina *history professor*

Phoenix
Carpenter-Olney, Tami Anne *Spanish elementary language educator*
David, Christian Rubi *language educator*
Haberman, lidia W. *literature and language professor*
Rister, Gene Arnold *humanities educator*
Schiffner, Adrienne Anita *art historian, educator*

Prescott
Cook, K. L. *literature educator*
Glidden, Moses *language educator*

Safford
Kaliher, Michael Dennis *historian, librarian*

Scottsdale
Land, George Ainsworth *philosopher, consultant, writer*

Sierra Vista
Bates, Norman Walter *literature educator, department chairman*
Bordelois, Martha *language educator*
Mutchler, J.C. *history professor*

Sun City
Oppenheimer, Max, Jr. *foreign language educator, consultant*

Surprise
Clark, Lloyd *historian, writer, educator*

Tempe
Burg, Barry Richard *history educator, writer*
Duncan, Kate Corbin *art historian, educator*
Hendrickson, Suzanne Bader *language educator*
Iverson, Peter James *historian, educator*
Jagos, Vic Bruce *history professor*
MacKinnon, Stephen R. *Asian studies administrator, educator*
Richard, Thelma Shinn *literature and language professor*
Vanden Heuvel, Michael John *literature educator*
VanderMeer, Philip R. *history professor*

Thatcher
Raines, Ken S. *literature and language professor*
Wilton, Marilyn Jean Mueller *literature and language professor*

Tucson
Alfie, Fabian Roberto *language educator*
Baca, Damian *language educator*
Brescia, Michael M. *historian, educator*
Coleman, Jane Candia *writer, English educator*
Cortés-Torres, Mayra E. *language educator*
Herrnstadt, Richard Lawrence *American literature educator*
Hunter, Leslie Gene *history educator*
Jerez, Marco A. *language educator*
Jurkowitz, Lisa Amy *language educator*
Kellogg, Frederick *historian*
Mills, Jan-Ruth *history professor*
Modica, Robert I., IV, *humanities educator*
Rabuck, Donna Fontanarose *English writing educator*
Rousos, Linda *language educator*
Schulz, Renate Adele *German studies and second language acquisition educator*
Wright, George Thaddeus *humanities educator*

Yuma
Martínez, Martha C. *language educator*

ARKANSAS

Arkadelphia
Graves, John William *historian*

Beebe
Knapp, Stephen John *language educator*

Bentonville
Hubbard, Mary Miller *literature and language professor*

Conway
Monty, Julie Anne *language educator*
Ziegler, John Alan *historian, political scientist, educator*

Fayetteville
Candido, Joseph Dominic *literature and language professor*
Cochran, Robert Brady *literature and language professor*
Levine, Daniel Blank *classical studies educator*

Fort Smith
Colbert, Alice Taylor *history professor*
Siler, Dennis James *literature and language professor*

Jonesboro
Elkins, Francis Clark *historian, educator, director*

Little Rock
Recken, Stephen Louis *history professor*
Vinikas, Vincent *historian, educator*
Yoder, R. Paul *literature and language professor*

Magnolia
Mallory, Kathleen Norris Brown *literature and language professor*
Terry, Robert Arthur *literature and language professor, director*

Mena
Eddleman, Floyd Eugene *retired language educator*

Monticello
Babin, Claude Hunter *history professor*

North Little Rock
Robbins, Dorothy Ann *retired foreign language educator*

Russellville
Jenkins, Ellen Janet (Jan) *history professor*

Searcy
Harris, Julie E. S. *history professor*
Love, Joli Gibbs *language educator*

Siloam Springs
Himes, Jonathan Bryant *literature and language professor*

State University
Cave, Eric Macdonald *philosopher, educator*
Milner, Clyde A., II, *historian*

Stuttgart
Layne, Allen *historian, educator*

CALIFORNIA

Aliso Viejo
La Marca, Jeffry Peter *language educator, consultant*
Williams, James Dale *language educator, researcher*

Aptos
Robles, Félix *retired language educator, dean*

Arcadia
Yen, Wen-Hsiung *language and music professional, educator*

Azusa
Griesinger, Emily Ann *literature and language professor*
Rojas-González, Marcela *language educator*

Bakersfield
Burns, Sarah Chloe *historian, educator*
Flachmann, Michael Charles *English language educator*
Kegley, Jacquelyn Ann *philosophy educator*
Meyers, Christopher *humanities educator, consultant*

Berkeley
Alter, Robert Bernard *literature educator, critic*
Anderson, William Scovil *classics educator*
Bloom, Robert *language educator*
Booth, Stephen Walter *language educator*
Chihara, Charles Seiyo *philosophy educator*
Chytry, Josef V. *humanities educator*
Costa, Gustavo *Italian studies scholar*
Frede, Dorothea Aline *philosopher, educator*
Herr, Richard *history professor*
Hollinger, David Albert *historian, educator*
Janmohmed, Abdul Raheman *language educator*
Kay, Paul de Young *linguist*
Lakoff, George *linguistics professor*
Litwack, Leon Frank *historian, retired educator*
Lloyd, Elisabeth Anne *philosophy educator*
Middlekauff, Robert Lawrence *historian, educator, academic administrator*
Murgia, Charles E. *retired classicist*
Partridge, Loren Wayne *art historian, educator*
Rauch, Irmengard *linguist, educator*
Rex, Walter Edwin III *humanities educator*
Richmond, Hugh Macrae *English language educator*
Selz, Peter Howard *art historian, educator*
Shannon, Thomas Frederic *German language educator*
Slezkine, Yuri *history professor*
Tansman, Alan *language educator*
Zwerdling, Alex *language educator*

Beverly Hills
Novak, Maximillian Erwin *retired English literature professor*

Carmel
Chung, Kyung Cho *Korean history specialist, writer, educator*

Carpinteria
Li, Winston Zai-Yang *language educator*

Chula Vista
Capehart, Bonnie *language educator*

Claremont
Ackerman, Gerald Martin *art historian, consultant, author*
Atlas, Jay David *philosopher, consultant, linguist, educator*
Blitz, Mark *philosopher*
Boucquey, Thierry *literature and language professor*
Burns, Richard Dean *historian, educator, writer*
Davis, Nathaniel *humanities educator*
Deese, E(thel) Helen *retired literature and language professor*
Lofgren, Charles Augustin *historian, educator*
McKirahan, Richard Duncan *classics and philosophy educator*
Moss, Myra Ellen (Myra Moss Rolle) *philosophy educator*
Neumann, Harry *philosophy educator*
Petropoulos, Jonathan George *history professor*
Rachlin, Nathalie *language educator*
Wall, Helena M. *historian, educator*
Wheeler, Geraldine Hartshorn *historian, writer*
Woodress, James Leslie, Jr. *language educator*
Young, Howard Thomas *foreign language educator*

Clovis
Contreras, Carlos Arturo *retired history professor*

Coalinga
Tincher, Chris Michael *history professor*

Colma
Papakonstantino, Stacy *language educator*

Davis
Blodgett, Harriet *retired language educator*
Hoffman, Michael Jerome *humanities educator*
Lazzara, Michael James *literature and language professor*
Torrance, Robert Mitchell *comparative literature educator*
Waddington, Raymond Bruce, Jr. *language educator*
Williamson, Alan Bacher *literature educator, poet, writer*
Willis, Frank Roy *historian, educator*

El Cerrito
Crompton, Louis William *English literature educator*

Folsom
Ritzi-Marouf, Viviane Cosette *language educator, department chairman*

Fountain Valley
Crecelius, Daniel Neil *history professor*

Fremont
Lemon, Deborah *literature and language professor, dancer*

Fresno
Chang, Sidney H. *history professor*
Contreras, Luis A. *literature and language professor*
Ryan, Judy *literature and language professor*
Siroky, Allen James *history professor*

Fullerton
Bjorklund, Nancy Basler *history professor*
Druon, Michele Valentine *language educator*
Loupe, Leleua Laurita *history professor*
Praitis, Irena *literature and language professor*

Garden Grove
Cochrum, Ellen Joan *language educator*

Glendale
de Grassi, Leonard *art historian, educator*

Hacienda Heights
Dodson, Arleen Cecilia *language educator*

Hayward
Garcia, Richard Amado *history professor, writer*
Henig, Gerald S. *history professor*
Paz, Marcelo *literature and language professor*
Reichman, Henry Frederick *history educator*
Weiss, Jessica *history professor*

Hemet
Culverwell, Albert Henry *historian*

Huntington Beach
Winterowd, Walter Ross *language educator*

Imperial
Cormier, Judy Ann *literature and language professor*

Irvine
Boyd, Carolyn Patricia *history professor*
Folkenflik, Robert *retired literature and language professor*
Garb, Paula Jean *humanities educator, researcher*
Hine, Robert V. *historian, educator*
Leonard, Karen Isaksen *anthropology professor*
Schwegler, Armin *language educator*
Wilentz, Amy *literature educator*

Kentfield
Fitzpatrick, Mary Patricia *language educator, writer*

La Jolla
Gere, Cathy *history professor*
Kluender, Robert E. *linguist, educator*
Langacker, Ronald Wayne *linguistics educator*
Lerer, Seth *literature professor, writer*
McDonald, Marianne *classicist*
Olafson, Frederick Arlan *philosophy educator*
Oreskes, Naomi *science historian*
Rahimi, Babak *literature and language professor*
Wright, Andrew *English literature educator*
Zentella, Ana Celia *retired language educator*

Lafayette
Lichterman, Martin *history professor*

Laguna Beach
Toliver, Harold Earl *retired English language professional*

Lancaster
Zamudio, Celia Isabel *language educator*

Livermore
Raymond, Kristy Lynn *language educator*

Long Beach
Hinton, Marie-Laure *language educator, researcher*
Mandolini-Pesaresi, Massimo *classicist, educator*
Ross, Melvin Lee *history professor*
Zitzer-Comfort, Carol *literature and language professor*

Los Altos
Nivison, David Shepherd *language educator, philosopher*

Los Angeles
Allen, Michael John Bridgman *language educator*
Alpers, Edward Alter *history professor*
Baehr, Jason *philosopher, educator*
Bahr, Ehrhard *Germanic languages and literature educator*
Birge, Bettine *history professor*
Bradshaw, Murray Charles *musicologist, educator, composer*
Caram, Eve La Salle *language educator, writer*
Cohen, S(tephen) Marshall *philosophy educator*
Ezaki, Motoko *literature and language professor*
Friedlander, Saul *historian, educator*
Hayes, Timothy Kai *language educator*
Hundley, Norris Cecil, Jr. *historian, educator*
Keenan, Edward L. *linguist, educator*
Kelly, Henry Ansgar *language educator*
Kolve, V. A. *English literature educator*
Lanham, Richard Alan *retired English language educator, literary critic*
Lauerhass, Ludwig, Jr. *history professor*
Levine, Philip *classics educator*
Lionnet, Francoise *French and comparative literature educator*
Parsons, Terence Dwight *linguist, educator*
Pecora, Vincent Pitt *English educator*
Porter, Theodore Mark *history educator*
Ramos, Francisco *language educator*
Rouse, Richard Hunter *historian, educator*
Shuger, Debora Kuller *humanities educator*
Silverman, Debora Leah *history professor*
Sonnenfeld, Albert *retired French literature and comparative literature educator, food historian*
Stockwell, Robert Paul *linguist, educator*
Stone, Marla Susan *history professor*
Tongson, Karen *language educator*
Trenton, Patricia Jean *art historian*
Tritle, Lawrence Alan *history professor*
Troy, Nancy J. *art history educator*

Malibu
Langford, Michèle K. *language educator*
Larson, Edward John *history and law professor*
Lorenzi, Paola *literature and language professor, writer*
Marshall, Donald Glenn *English language and literature educator*

Marina Del Rey
Rimer, John Thomas *language educator, academic administrator, writer*

Menlo Park
Bales, Royal Eugene *retired philosophy educator*
Cohn, Robert Greer *literary arts educator*

Merced
Amussen, Susan Dwyer *history professor*
Shirley, Kahlert *literature and language professor*

Modesto
Nicholson, Coy Lee *language educator, writer*

Montclair
Haage, Robert Mitchell *retired history professor, cultural organization administrator*

Monterey
Peet, Phyllis Irene *art historian, women's studies educator*

Moraga
Gorsch, Robert E. *literature and language professor, department chairman*
Malary, Claude Rheal *language educator*

Napa
Rosselli, Denise Louise *literature and language professor, department chairman*

National City
Becerra, David *language educator*

Newport Beach
Brown, Giles Tyler *history professor, lecturer*
Mc Culloch, Samuel Clyde *history professor*

Northridge
Bouguarche, Ahmed *language educator, researcher*
Falk, Heinrich Richard *humanities and theater educator*
Omatsu, Glenn *Asian American studies professor*
Parker, David Miller *history professor, retired advertising executive*
Perez, Pamela Lindsey *language educator*
Sefton, James Edward *history professor*
Swenson, Patricia J. *literature and language professor*

Norwalk
Ernest, Roger Craig *language educator*
Haas, John Henry *history professor*
Jaime, Jennie H. *literature and language professor*

Oakland
Sheldon, Marianne Buroff *history professor*

Orange
Barb Mingo, Arturo *romance literature and languages educator*
de Souza, Marcela *educator*
Williams, Danna Beth *reading specialist, educator*

Oroville
Gantt, Ileana Maria *language educator*

Pacific Palisades
Perloff, Marjorie Gabrielle *literature educator*

Palmdale
Kilanowski, Dana Marcotte *historian, writer, filmmaker, archaeologist*

Palo Alto
Knoles, George Harmon *history educator*
Mommsen, Katharina *retired literature and language professor, foundation administrator*

Palos Verdes Peninsula
Alkon, Paul Kent *language educator*

Pasadena
Gregory, Timothy Peter *historian, consultant*
O'Brien, Grace Wilhelmina Ehlig *genealogical consultant, psychologist, retired educational administrator, writer*
Parr, James Allan *literature professor*
Williams, Bradley Bennett *historian*
Zwicky, Barbarina Exita *humanities educator, researcher*

Paso Robles
Gerstung, Estella Rose Baker *literature professor*
Judd, Dennis Paul *history professor*

Pebble Beach
Dallmann, William Charles *speech educator, writer*

Piedmont
Putter, Irving *retired French language educator*

Placerville
Leland, Kathryn Ann *literature and language professor*

Pleasant Hill
Ashby, Denise Stewart *speech educator, communications consultant*
George, Brian Thomas *historian*
Mikolavich, Daniel Keith *literature and language professor, consultant*

Pomona
Morsberger, Robert Eustis *English language educator*
Wohlcke, Anne Elizabeth *historian, educator*

Porterville
Benander, Kathryn Marie *literature and language professor*
Hargis, Jay Jackson *history professor*

Portola Valley
Carnochan, Walter Bliss *retired humanities educator*

Rancho Cucamonga
Tirado, Victoria *language educator*

Rancho Santa Fe
Ruiz, Ramón Eduardo *history professor*

Randsburg
Ramirez Gelpi, Ana Sofia *language educator, consultant*

Redlands
Gonzalez, Olga Carreras *language educator*
Lu, Hongwei *literature and language professor*

Riverside
Barkin, Kenneth David *history professor*
Brinkerhoff, Dericksen Morgan *art historian, educator*
Grimm, Reinhold *humanities educator*
Head, Randolph Conrad *history professor*
MacDougall, Diana E. *interpreter, educator, social sciences educator*
Ross, Delmer Gerrard *historian, educator*
Rudolph, Conrad *medieval art history educator*
Salzman, Michele Renee *historian, educator*
Snyder, Henry Leonard *historian, educator, writer*

Rocklin
Bowen, Brenda Denise *literature and language professor*

Rohnert Park
Wautischer, Helmut *philosophy educator*

Sacramento
Carr, Gerald Francis *language educator*
Katranis Fotopoulos, Kathy Ekaterini Christou *ancient language educator, social sciences educator*
Masuyama, Kazue *literature and language professor*
Palermo, Joseph Anthony *history professor*
Singh, Amrik *literature and language professor*
Takanikos-Quiñones, John Nicholas *history professor*

Saint Helena
Yates, Donald Alfred *retired literature educator*

San Diego
Blum, Edward James *history professor*
Brandes, Raymond Stewart *historian, educator, dean*
Browne, John Robert *education and African studies educator, educational consultant*
Dunlop, Marianne *retired language educator*
Estrada, Jaime Olalde *language educator, department chairman*
Haddad, Jiryes Michael *language educator*
Peffer, Rodney Gene *philosopher, educator*
Rasih, Buu-Van AjareyaJemir *language and culture expert*
Rohatyn, Dennis *philosopher, educator*
Schilz, Jodye Lynn Dickson *history professor*
Wawrytko, Sandra Ann *humanities educator*
Weldele, Edda Hilda Temoche *language educator*
Withee, Diana Keeran *art historian, art dealer, educator*

San Francisco
Arnold, Lauren *art historian, writer*
Cherny, Robert Wallace *historian, educator*
Costa-Zalessow, Natalia *foreign language educator*
Dennehy, Raymond Leo *philosopher, educator*
Hansen, Carol Louise *literature and language professor*
Kelley, Michael Garhart Roosevelt *historian, educator, writer*
Kidner, Frank L. *retired history professor*
Neaman, Elliot Yale *history professor*
Needleman, Jacob *philosophy educator, writer*
Satin, Joseph *language educator, retired dean*
Schramm, Darrell G.H. *literature and language professor*
Stahr, Celia Suzanne *art historian, educator*
Stump, David James *philosopher, educator*
Wonder, John Walder *classicist, educator*

San Jose
Alldis, Phung *language educator, director*
Mou, Bo *philosopher, educator*
Nava, Elizabeth M. *history professor*
Nguyen-Wong, Khanh-Hoa Thi *literature and language professor*
Stewart, Denise Margaret *ESL educator, consultant*
Thompson, Jan Newstrom *art historian, educator*

San Marcos
Anover, Veronica *language educator*
Mohamed, Jabari *language educator*
Rolle-Rissetto, Silvia *foreign languages educator, writer, artist*
Scaduto, Provvidenza *language educator*
Sepinwall, Alyssa *history professor*
Velasco, Martha *literature and language professor*

San Marino
Zall, Paul Maxwell *language educator, consultant*

Santa Barbara
Abbott, Horace Porter *English literature educator*
Athanassakis, Apostolos N. *classics educator*
Chafe, Wallace LeSeur *linguist, educator*
Del Chiaro, Mario Aldo *art historian, archaeologist, etruscologist, educator*
Erickson, Robert Allen *English literature educator*
Fingarette, Herbert *philosopher, educator*
Göllner, Marie Louise *musicologist, retired educator*
Gordon, Helen Heightsman *language educator, publishing executive, writer*
Hoffmeister, Gerhart *German language educator*
Lomeli, Francisco A. *language educator, department chairman*
Mahlendorf, Ursula Renate *literature educator*
McGee, James Sears *historian, educator*
Rickels, Laurence Arthur *foreign language educator*
Rock, David Peter *history professor*
Rose, Mark Allen *humanities educator*
Russell, Jeffrey Burton *historian, educator*
Wilkins, Burleigh Taylor *philosophy educator*

Santa Clara
Le, Son Minh *philosophy educator*

Santa Cruz
Basu, Dilip Kumar *history professor, film company executive, director*
Hankamer, Jorge *linguistics educator*
Lasar, Matthew *History Instructor*
Leicester, Henry Marshall, Jr. *literature and language professor*
Stevens, Stanley David *historian, researcher, retired librarian, archivist*

Santa Maria
Isaacson, Robert Anton *language educator, researcher*

Santa Monica
See, Carolyn *English language educator, writer, book critic*

Santa Paula
Lattimore, Steven *classicist, educator*

Santa Rosa
Aman, Reinhold Albert *philologist, writer*
Gleason, Ken Bell *historian, educator, journalist*
Schwartz, Marine Lenore *humanities educator*

Seaside
Krasnyanskaya, Elena *language educator*
Tringali, Maria Rosaria *language educator*
Zielina, Maria C. *literature and language professor*

Sherman Oaks
Howe, Daniel Walker *historian, educator*

Snelling
Jones, Mabel Bennett *retired history professor*

Spring Valley
Madigan, William Charles *literature and language professor, consultant*

Stanford
Baker, Keith Michael *history professor*
Brooks, Helen Bousky *literature and language professor, performing arts educator*
Dekker, George Gilbert *literature professor, writer, former academic administrator*
Duus, Peter *retired historian*
Felstiner, John *literature educator, translator*
Fleishman, Lazar *literature educator*
Gelpi, Albert Joseph *language educator, department chairman, critic*
Hanson, Victor Davis *historian, educator, writer*
Harrison, Robert Pogue *literature educator*
Kennedy, David Michael *historian, educator*
Loftis, John (Clyde), Jr. *language educator*
Martin, Richard Peter *classics educator, consultant*
Robinson, Paul Arnold *historian, educator, writer*
Sag, Ivan A. *linguist, educator*
Salti, Ramzi *literature and language professor*
Sheehan, James John *historian, educator*
Stansky, Peter David Lyman *historian, writer, retired professor*
Traugott, Elizabeth Closs *linguist, educator, researcher*
van Benthem, Johan Franciscus Abraham Karel *philosophy, mathematics and computer science educator*

Stockton
Camacho, Manuel *language educator*
Krise, Thomas Warren *academic administrator, literature and language professor, retired military officer*
Limbaugh, Ronald Hadley *retired historian, cultural organization administrator*

Sylmar
Pursley, Mark R. *philosopher, educator*

Topanga
Waldron, Jill Genevieve *retired language educator*

Torrance
Anderson, Marilyn Wheeler *English language educator*
Cummings, Anne *language educator*

Turlock
Regalado, Samuel *history professor*

Vallejo
Brown, Earl Kent *historian, minister*
Paine-Clemes, Bunny Lee *humanities educator*

Van Nuys
Zucker, Alfred John *English and history educator, academic administrator, historian*

Venice
Padilla, Mario René *literature educator, writer*

Ventura
Armstrong, Dianne Owens *retired language educator*
Sanchez, Tomas David *history professor*

Victorville
Davis-Butros, Tracy L. *history professor*

Visalia
Sense, Edgar H. *language educator*

Woodland Hills
Dompe, Rudy F. *literature and language professor*

Yucaipa
Lardy, Leonard Anthony *English educator*

COLORADO

Boulder
Barbosa, Francisco Javier *history professor*
Brand, Charles Macy *history professor*
Colwell, James Lee *humanities educator*
Cowell, James Andrew *language educator*
Hall, Joan Lord *literature and language educator*
Keister, Jay Davis *musicologist, educator*
Limerick, Patricia Nelson *history professor*
Motte, Warren F., Jr. *literature and language professor*
Widmann, R L. *literature and language professor*

Breckenridge
Mosher, Joyce Devlin *literature and language professor*

Cherry Hills Village
Conroy, Mary Elizabeth *history professor*

Colorado Springs
Barton, Ruth *retired language educator*
Brosman, Catharine Savage *retired language educator, poet*
Cramer, Owen Carver *classics educator, department chairman*
Hilberry, Jane Elizabeth *literature and language professor*
Jiang, Hong *language educator*
Murphy, Jane Holt *history professor*
von Dassanowsky, Robert *literature and film professor, writer, producer*
Watts, Linda K. *language educator*
Yaney, George *retired history professor*

Cripple Creek
MacKell, Jan *historian, writer*

Denver
Castro, Obdulia *language educator, researcher*
Gellan, Kebede Gobena *literature and language, international law professor*
Luna, Sheryl Alison *literature and language professor*
MacDonald, Lunden Eschelle *language educator*
Owen, Elizabeth Marie *art historian, educator*

Fort Collins
Huffman Proctor, Jeremy Werner *literature and language professor*
Kennedy, George Alexander *classicist, educator*
McComb, David Glendinning *history professor*
Murphy, Robert James *language educator, consultant, pianist, pipe organ performer*

Glenwood Springs
Ketzenbarger, Gary C. *speech educator, director*
Wadyko, Michael Anthony *historian, educator*

Golden
Dickinson, Carol Rittgers *art historian, cconsultant, writer*
Pegis, Anton George *retired language educator*

Grand Junction
Bruch, Julie *linguistics and language professor*
Fay, Abbott Eastman *history professor*
Schulte, Steven C. *history professor*

Greeley
Downey, Matthew T. *history professor, writer*
Perl, Don A. *literature and language professor*

Greenwood Village
Chico, Beverly Ann *history professor, humanities educator*

Highlands Ranch
Cherno, Melvin *humanities educator*

La Junta
Keith, RuAnn Rae *humanities educator*

Pueblo
Farwell, Hermon Waldo, Jr. *parliamentarian and speech educator*

Saguache
Sanchez, Karla Ann *language educator*

Westminster
Heideman, Anthony Jon *history professor*

CONNECTICUT

Branford
Whitaker, Thomas Russell *English literature educator*

Bridgeport
London, Samuel Gene, Jr. *history professor*
Psarras, Mary Auten *language educator, tax specialist*

Colebrook
McNeill, William Hardy *retired historian, writer*

Essex
Hieatt, Constance Bartlett *English language educator*

Fairfield
Miller, Frederick Edwin, Jr. *history professor, government agency administrator*
Newton, Lisa Haenlein *philosopher, educator*

Farmington
Reeves, John Drummond *retired English language professional, writer*

Guilford
Colish, Marcia Lillian *history professor*

Hamden
Kagan, Donald *historian, educator*
McClellan, Edwin *literature educator*
Valone, David Andrew *history professor*

Hartford
Bilston, Sarah Rosemary *novelist, college professor*
Fisher, Sheila Marie *literature and language professor*
Riggio, Milla C. *language educator, researcher*

Ivoryton
Osborne, John Walter *historian, educator, author*

Litchfield
Phillips, Kevin Price *political historian, writer*

Middletown
Buel, Richard Van Wyck, Jr. *retired history professor, editor, writer*
Coryell, May M. *language educator*
Gillmor, Charles Stewart *historian, researcher, educator*
Gruen, Lori *philosopher, educator*
Mark, Peter A. *history professor*
Meyer, Priscilla Ann *literature and language professor*
Miel, Jan *humanities educator*
Pomper, Philip *historian, educator*
Reed, Joseph Wayne *American studies educator, artist*
Schwarcz, Vera *historian, poet, educator*
Slotkin, Richard Sidney *literature educator*
Wensinger, Arthur Stevens *literature and language professor, writer, translator*

New Britain
Chung, Inkie *language educator*

New Haven
Abramson, Arthur Seymour *linguistics educator, researcher*
Bloom, Harold *humanities educator, writer*
Borroff, Marie *English language educator*
Bynum, Terrell Ward *humanities educator, consultant*
Clark, Katerina *literature and language professor*
Dimock, Wai Chee *literature and language professor*
Gendler, Tamar Szabo *philosopher, educator*
Gilbert, Creighton Eddy *art historian*
Goffart, Walter André *history professor*
Hallo, William Wolfgang *literature and language professor, writer*
Harries, Karsten *philosophy educator, researcher*
Henderson, Timothy John *history educator*
Hollander, John *humanities educator, poet*
Kastan, David Scott *literature educator, writer*
Kevles, Daniel Jerome *historian, educator, writer*
Kiernan, Benedict Francis *historian, educator*
Lord, George deForest *language educator*
Manley, Lawrence G. *literature educator*
Marcus, Ruth Barcan *philosopher, educator, writer, lecturer*
Patterson, Lee *language educator*
Prochaska, Alice *historian, librarian*
Prown, Jules David *art historian, educator*
Quint, David Louis *literature and language professor*
Rawson, Claude Julien *literature and language professor*
Robinson, Fred Colson *language educator*
Sammons, Jeffrey Leonard *foreign language educator*
Semmel, Stuart *historian*
Smith, John Edwin *philosophy educator*
Snowden, Frank Martin III *history professor*
Stepto, Robert Burns *literature and language professor*
Sussman, Henry Stephen *literature and language professor*
Turner, Frank Miller *historian, educator*
Underdown, David Edward *historian, educator*
Wandycz, Piotr Stefan *historian, educator*
Winroth, Anders *historian, educator*
Winter, Jay Murray *history professor*
Yeazell, Ruth Bernard *English language educator*

New London
Paxton, Frederick S. *history professor*

Newington
Chiarenza, Frank John *language educator*

North Branford
Blum, John Morton *retired historian*

Norwalk
Nelson, Paula Morrison Bronson *retired reading specialist*

Norwich
Ringel, Faye Joyce *retired literature educator*

Old Lyme
Willauer, George Jacob *American literature educator*

Orange
Davis, David Brion *historian, educator*

Rocky Hill
Decker, Robert Owen *history professor, clergyman*

Salisbury
Kilner, Ursula Blanche *genealogist, educator, writer*

Southport
Herzog, John E. *numismatist*

Storrs Mansfield
Azimi, Fakhreddin *history professor*
Brown, Richard David *history professor*
Caner, Daniel Folger *classicist, history professor*
Cazel, Fred A., Jr. *history professor*
Charters, Ann *literature educator*
Coons, Ronald Edward *historian, educator*
Gross, Robert Alan *history professor*
Irizarry, Guillermo B. *language educator*
Moynihan, William Trumbull *educator*
Orringer, Nelson Robert *Spanish and comparative literature educator*
Reed, Howard Alexander *retired historian, educator*
Simons, Doreen Lee *language educator, researcher*

Torrington
Gradowski, Kristine Shepard *language educator*

Washington
Leab, Daniel Joseph *history professor*

Waterbury
Donahue, Linda Wheeler *retired humanities educator, writer*
MacLeod, Glen Gary *language educator*

West Hartford
Collins, Alma Jones *language educator, writer*
Ealy, Nicholas *language educator*

West Haven
Corraro, Dominic J. *language educator*

West Simsbury
Rockas, Leo *English educator*

Westport
Demakis, Louise Ward *archivist historian, writer*

Windsor
Auten, Arthur Herbert *history professor*

Woodbridge
Dupré, Louis *retired philosopher, educator*
Ecklund, Constance Cryer *French language and literature educator*
Kleiner, Diana Elizabeth Edelman *art historian, educator, academic administrator*

DELAWARE

Hockessin
Valbuena-Briones, Angel Julian *retired language educator, author*

Newark
Day, Robert Androus *literature and language professor, retired library director, editor, publisher*
Frassetto, Michael *history professor*
Halio, Jay Leon *language educator*
Lathrop, Thomas Albert *language educator, publisher*
Quintus, John Allen *English professor*
Thibault, Bruno *literature and language professor*
Weintraub, Stanley *arts and humanities educator, writer*
Wolters, Raymond *historian, educator*

Wilmington
Kneavel, Ann Callanan *humanities educator, communications consultant*

DISTRICT OF COLUMBIA

Fort McNair
Raines, Edgar Frank, Jr. *historian*

Washington
Albrecht, Kathe Hicks *art historian, visual resources manager*
Alexander, Adele Logan *history professor*
Asike, Joseph Ike *philosopher, educator*
Berdahl, Robert Max *history professor, association and former academic administrator*
Biesenbach-Lucas, Sigrun *language educator, consultant*
Breitman, Richard David *historian, educator, writer*
Broun, Elizabeth *art historian, curator*
Cheney, Lynne Vincent *humanities educator, writer, former Second Lady of the United States*
Cubeta, Paul Marsden *English literature educator*
Dawley, Edward Armistead III *language educator*
Dick, Steven J. *historian*
Dougherty, Jude Patrick *philosopher, educator, dean*
Durfee, Harold Allen *philosophy educator*
Eigler, Friederike *literature and language professor*
Farr, Judith Banzer *retired literature educator, writer, lecturer*
Foss, Clive Frank Wilson *history professor*
Franklin, Paige Elizabeth *literature and language professor*
Hager, Jenna (Jenna Welch Bush) *language educator, writer, volunteer, former first daughter*
Ham, Debra Newman *historian, educator*
Hartig, Rachel Mildred *literature and language professor, writer*
Heelan, Patrick Aidan *philosophy educator*
Helal, Gamal *interpreter, diplomat*
Hilton, Alison *art historian, educator*
Hirsh, John Campion *literature and language professor*
Hsiao, Juei-chen *language educator*
Hughes, Ellen Roney *historian, curator, educator*
Kamwangamalu, Nkonko Mudipanu *language educator*
Kass, Leon Richard *humanities educator*
Kazin, Michael *historian, writer*
Kelley, David Christopher *philosopher*
Kim-Renaud, Young-Key *linguist, educator*
Lavine, Thelma Zeno *philosophy educator*
Livingston, Robert Gerald *historian, journalist*
Logan, Paul Ellis *language educator, consultant*
Marder, Michael V. *philosopher, educator*
Marr, Phebe Ann *retired historian, educator*
Miller, Jeanne-Marie Anderson (Mrs. Nathan J. Miller) *language educator, academic administrator*
Mujica, Barbara Louise *language educator, writer*
Neville, Leonora Alice *history professor*
Olesko, Kathryn Mary *historian*
Payne-Jackson, Arvilla Chapin *linguist, anthropologist, consultant*
Perett, William Gregory *historian*
Randall, Willard Sterne *biographer, historian*
Robb, James Willis *Romance languages educator*
Roberts, Jeanne Addison *retired literature educator*
Roberts, John W. *historian, federal agency official*
Rojer, Olga Elaine *German studies educator, translator*
Rosenblatt, Jason Philip *literature and language professor*
Salamon, Linda Bradley *retired English literature scholar*
Segraves, Jamie Nicole *language educator*
Severino, Roberto *language educator, academic administration executive*
Simko, Jan *English, foreign language and literature educator*
Svoboda, Patricia Helen *art historian*
Taavila, Pia Seija *literature and language professor*
Trisco, Robert Frederick *church historian, educator*
Veatch, Robert Marlin *philosopher, researcher*
Voll, John Obert *history professor*
Winston, Michael Russell *historian*

FLORIDA

Belleair Bluffs
Alexander, Christina Anamaria *translator, performing company executive*

Big Pine Key
Fleischer, Roland Edward *art history professor*

Boca Raton
Collins, Robert Arnold *literature and language professor*
Dickenson, Katharine Horn *historic preservationist*
Diffine, Suzanne Michele *language educator*
Kollander, Patricia *history professor*
McFarland, Thomas *English literature educator*
Mitchell, Carmencita C. *literature and language professor*
Shusterman, Richard Marc *philosophy educator*
Strother, Judith Dianne Banks *linguistics educator*

Bradenton
Grieneisen, Jeff *literature and language professor*
Ruffner, Courtney Judith *literature and language professor*
Stewart, Priscilla Ann Mabie *art historian, educator*

Clearwater
Knoop, Maggie Pearson *language educator*

Clermont
Ortiz Aponte, Sally *retired literature and language professor*

Cocoa
Mihai, Florin Marius *language educator*

Coconut Creek
Romero, Dora Y. Marron *language educator*

Cooper City
Maugere, Dennis Paul *historian, educator*

Coral Gables
Galang, M. Evelina *literature and language professor*
Negueruela-Azarola, Eduardo *linguist, educator*
Spivey, Donald *history professor*

Davie
Wang, Xiao *language educator*

Daytona Beach
Duval, Cynthia *art historian, museum administrator, curator, consultant*
Kruse, Marylin Lynn *retired language educator*
Sanzenbacher, Richard *humanities educator*
West, Carolyn Christensen *literature and language professor*
Zenkovsky, Betty Jean *modern languages educator*
Zurstadt, William John *history professor*

Deland
Markham, Reed B. *speech communication professor*

Fort Lauderdale
Shaw, Andrea Elizabeth *literature and language professor, director*

Fort Myers
Curtin, Constance O'Hara *language educator, writer*
Halloran, William Frank *English educator*

Fort Pierce
Pino, Veronica Woodard *humanities educator*

Fort Walton Beach
Register, Annette Rowan *literature educator*

Gainesville
Bullivant, Keith *modern German literature educator*
Curta, Florin *historian, educator*
Gentry, Robert Bryan *humanities educator, writer*
Hulvey, S. Yumiko *literature educator*
Kushner, David Zakeri *musicologist*
Liner, James *literature and language professor*
Link, William Allen *history educator*
New, Melvyn *retired literature and language professor*
Pleasants, Julian McIver *history educator, summer school director*
Ulmer, Gregory Leland *literature and language professor*
Valladares, Maria Elena *language educator*

Hillsboro Beach
O'Connell, Richard (James) *English literature educator, poet*

Jacksonville
Barrett, J. Lynn *literature and language professor*
Carpenter, JoAnn Deakin *history professor*
Clarke, Joseph Calvitt III *retired history professor*
Reams-Johnson, Ansa *history professor*

Jasper
Rehberg, Shirley M. *literature and language professor*

Jupiter
Vazquez, Miguel Angel *literature and language professor*

Key Biscayne
Ross, Marilyn J. *language and communications educator*

Lake Worth
Wilson, William J. *language educator*

Lakeland
Cotton, Rickey Allen *literature and language professor, department chairman*
Crutchfield, Drucella *language educator*

Lakewood Ranch
Domonkos, Leslie S. *history professor, researcher*

Land O Lakes
Loewe, Barbara *speech educator, theater educator, humanities educator*

Lighthouse Point
Hampares, Katherine James *retired foreign language educator*

Marathon
Wiecha, Joseph Augustine *language educator*

Marianna
Dunkle, J. Robert *humanities educator*

Melbourne
Patterson, Gordon M. *history professor*
Renee, Cheryl *literature and language professor*

Miami
Bello, Milagros *art historian, educator*
Falco-Leshin, JoAnna M. *literature and language professor*
Istifan, Jamil *language educator*
Neu, Charles Eric *historian, educator*
Orro, Margarita B. *language educator*
Parks, Arva Moore *historian*
Paulson, Michael George *foreign language educator*
Taddeo, Annette *language services professional*
Vazquez, America *language educator*

Miami Shores
Missick, Lamont S. *literature and language professor*

Mulberry
Bowman, Hazel Lois *retired English language educator*

Niceville
Lopez Morgan, Maria Helena *literature and language professor*

North Palm Beach
Gaudieri, Alexander V.J. *art historian, museum director, educator*

Oldsmar
Thompson, Mack Eugene *historian, educator*

Opa Locka
Thevenin, Rose Carine *history professor*

Orlando
Garcia, Martha *language educator*
Murphrey, Elizabeth Hobgood *history professor, librarian*
Vanryckeghem, Martine *speech language professional, educator*

Pembroke Pines
Nightingale, Barbra Lynne *English language educator, poet*

Pensacola
Brown, Susan Louise *philosopher, educator*
Mayo, Ned Henderson *retired physics professor*

Plant City
Lawson, Kara L. *history professor*

Port Charlotte
Winters, Stanley B. *history professor, consultant, writer*

Ruskin
Chase, Don *reading and English teacher*

Saint Augustine
Goldthwait, John Turner *emeritus humanities educator*
Lidh, Todd *literature and language professor, department chairman*
Voguit, Steve George *humanities educator*

Saint Leo
McTague, John J. *history professor*
Vicas, Astrid *philosopher, educator*

Saint Petersburg
Brooker, Jewel Spears *literature educator*
Chabrier, Christina Ferree *literature and language professor*
Empric, Julienne H. *literature educator, consultant*
Meese, George Philip Elman *literature and rhetoric professor, consultant*

Sanford
Fitzgerald, J. Patrick *philosopher, educator, film producer*

Sarasota
Benowitz, June Melby *historian, educator*
Doenecke, Justus Drew *history professor*
Dungy, Kathryn R. *humanities educator*
Snyder, Lee Daniel *historian, educator*
Taplin, Winn Lowell *historian, retired federal agency administrator*

Stuart
Gilbert, Glenn Gordon *retired linguistics educator*

Summerfield
Gates, Elena Miranda *language educator*

Tallahassee
Bartlett, Richard Adams *historian, writer, retired history professor*
Coldiron, A. E. B. *language educator*
Fulkerson, Laurel *humanities educator*
Golden, Leon *classicist, educator*
Halpern, Paul G. *retired history professor*
Hunt, Mary Alice *retired humanities educator*
Laird, Doris Anne Marley *retired humanities educator, musician*
Leiber, Justin *philosophy educator, writer*
McMahon, Darrin Michael *history professor*
Mele, Alfred R. *philosophy educator*
Oliver, Andrea LaKaye *history professor*
Rai, Amitabh Shambhu *humanities educator*
Taylor, Gary *literature and language professor*
Trujillo, Evelyn Franquiz *language educator, consultant*
Zimmerman, Kenneth Jay *humanities educator*

Tampa
Anton, John Peter *philosopher, educator*
Gurrie, Christopher Timothy *speech educator, director*
Mitchell, Mozella Gordon *language educator, minister*
Perry, James Frederic *philosophy educator, writer*
Tunstall, Graydon Allen *history professor, professional society administrator*
Turner, Stephen Park *philosopher, sociologist, educator*

Temple Terrace
Crispell, Brian Lewis *history professor, dean of students*

Winter Park
Seymour, Thaddeus *language educator*
Wilson, Robley Conant, Jr. *language educator, editor, writer*

GEORGIA

Albany
Gassel, Elizabeth Marie *literature and language professor*
Grey, Charles Robert *literature and language professor*
Melton, Maurice K. *history professor*

Americus
Adler, Brian Ungar *language educator, director*
Isaacs, Harold *history professor*

Andersonville
Boyles, Frederick Holdren *historian*

Athens
Brooks, Linda Marie *humanities educator*
Correa-Diaz, Luis Alberto *language educator*
Covington, Michael Aaron *computation linguist*
Hutchinson, Amelia M. *literature and language professor*
Klein, Jared Stephen *linguist, educator*
Kretzschmar, William Addison, Jr. *language educator*
Menke, Richard *literature and language professor*
Miller, Ronald Baxter *language educator, writer*
Poss, C. Thomas *ancient language educator*
Waters, John Caldwell *historic preservation professor*
Winship, Michael P. *history professor*

Atlanta
Bakewell, Peter John *history educator*
Benario, Herbert William *classicist, educator*
Bennington, Geoffrey Peter *language educator, writer*
Brown, Lorene B(yron) *retired library educator*
Burns, Thomas Samuel *history professor*
de Sousa Sheppard, Dalila *history professor*
Hallen, Barry *philosopher, educator*
Hartfield-Méndez, Vialla *language educator*
Kuntz, Marion Lucile Leathers *classicist, historian, educator*
Li, Hong *language educator*
Lu, Hanchao *humanities educator, writer*
Luce, Willard Ray *historian, director*
Murray, Janet Horowitz *humanities educator, multimedia designer*
Nana, Georges *language educator*
Pindle, Arthur Jackson, Jr. *philosopher, researcher*
Reynolds, Douglas R. *history professor*
Velásquez, Lucía E. *language educator, researcher*
Welp, Herrad Susanne *language educator*
Zboray, Ronald John *history educator*

Augusta
Dyer, James Harold, Jr. *language educator*

Avondale Estates
Rouse, Jacqueline Anne *historian, educator*

Bainbridge
LaFace, Betty *language educator, consultant*

Barnesville
Parsons, Gail PaT *history professor*

Brooklet
Warrick, Kimberley Kaye *language and social studies educator*

Carrollton
Blair, John *language educator, director*
MacKinnon, Aran Stuart *history professor*

College Park
Oliver-Warren, Mary Elizabeth *retired library science educator, library and information scientist*

Dahlonega
Murray, Heather M. *history professor*
Torres-Calderon, Alvaro Martin *language educator*
Williams, Linda Stallworth *literature and language professor*

Decatur
Dillingham, William Byron *literature educator, author*
MacEwen, Sally *ancient language educator*
Manley, Frank *language educator, writer*
Pepperdene, Margaret Williams *English educator*
Showers Johnson, Violet Mary-Ann Iyabo *history professor*

Dunwoody
Roddy, Kathleen *literature and language professor*

Fayetteville
Addison, Maria José *literature and language professor*

Flowery Branch
Kilinski, April Conley *language educator*

Griffin
Henderson, Gloria Mason *retired literature and language professor*

Grovetown
Monassar, Hisham M.A. *language and linguistics educator*

Hinesville
Etheridge, James Ralph *history professor*

Hoschton
Sneed, Larry Allan *history professor*

Jackson
Beasley, Anita Claire *reading specialist, consultant*

Kennesaw
Huang, Yuling *art historian, educator*
Simon, Robert *language educator*
Thompson, Eva M. *humanities educator*
Vladimirov, Katya *history professor*

Lookout Mountain
Dennison, William D. *interdisciplinary educator*

Macon
Glance, Jonathan Carlyle *literature and language professor, director*
Huffman, Joan Brewer *history professor*
Klingelhofer, Eric Charles *history professor, archaeologist*

Milledgeville
Bailey, Anne J. *history professor*
Vess, Deborah Lynn *history professor*
Wang, Huaihyu *philosopher, educator*

Mount Berry
Gregoire, Vincent Maric-Luc *language educator*

Oxford
Galle, Jeffrey Wayne *literature and language professor, academic administrator*

Reidsville
Dees, Louise Mitchell *language educator*

Robins AFB
Head, William Pace *historian, educator*

Savannah
Fertig, Barbara Conway *history professor*
Hales, Kevin Joseph *history professor, researcher*
Morris, Tony Ray *literature and language professor, writer*
Stanton, Kamille Stone *literature and language professor*
Yagami, Kazuo *historian*

Tifton
McGruder, Larry *history professor*

Villa Rica
Blevins, Ernest Everett *genealogist, researcher, historian, preservationist*

Waco
House, Myron Wade *retired professor & special collections librarian*

Waycross
Keeler, Margaret Alexandra Sandy *history professor*

Winder
Ouzts, Karl Claybourne *history educator*

HAWAII

Honolulu
Bender, Byron Wilbur *linguistics educator*
Blust, Robert *linguist, educator*
Forbis, Deborah Anne *history professor*
Higgins, Christina Michael *applied linguist*
Hoffmann, Kathryn Ann *humanities educator*
Hoonchamlong, Yuphaphann *literature and language professor*
Jordan, Amos Azariah, Jr. *foreign affairs educator, retired military officer*
Kipnis, Kenneth *philosopher, educator*
Moore, Willis Henry Allphin *history educator*
Ning, Cynthia Yumei *language educator*
Niyekawa, Agnes Mitsue *foreign language professor*
Rapson, Richard L. *history professor*
Schweizer, Niklaus R. *German educator*
Shinagawa, Satoru *language educator*
Stephan, John Jason *historian, educator*

Laie
Richardson, Timothy Wayne *language educator*

Pearl City
Fujita, James Hiroshi *history educator*

IDAHO

Boise
Sloan, Nina *language educator*

Post Falls
Chojnowski, Peter Edward *philosopher, educator*

Rexburg
Coates, Lawrence G. *history professor*
Ivers, John Joseph *language educator, dean*
Kumferman, Edwin C. *literature and language professor*

Twin Falls
Ricketts, Virginia Lee *historian, researcher*

ILLINOIS

Bloomington
Bridges, Roger Dean *historian*
Callahan, Christopher John *literature and language professor, interpreter*
Laurenti, Joseph Luciano *language educator, writer*
Prandi, Julie Diane *retired literature and language professor*

Carbondale
Sasse, Mary Hawley *retired language educator, editor*

Champaign
Douglas, George Halsey *language educator, writer*
Hurd, Heidi M. *humanities and law educator*
McGlathery, James Melville *retired foreign language educator*
Melka, Tomi *language educator, historian*
Watts, Emily Stipes *retired English language educator*

Charleston
Leddy, Michael *english educator*

Chicago
Battle, Stephanie *literature and language professor*
Bevington, David Martin *English literature educator*
Biggs, Robert Dale *Near Eastern studies educator*
Boyer, John William *history professor, dean*
Briggs, Jennifer K. *literature and language professor*
Brinkman, John Anthony *historian, educator*
Carson, Thomas Lee *philosopher, educator*
Cohen, Ted *philosopher, educator*
Cullen, Charles Thomas *historian, librarian*
De Armas, Frederick Alfred *foreign language educator*
Debus, Allen George *historian, educator*
Dembowski, Peter Florian *foreign language educator*
D'Emilio, John *humanities educator, writer*
Fennell, Frank L. *literature and language professor, dean*
Fitzpatrick, Sheila Mary *historian, educator*
Fortmann, Patrick *literature and language professor*
Garrigan, Kristine Ottesen *English literature educator*
Gatti, Alberta *language educator, director*
Geyer, Michael *history professor*
Ghazzal, Zouhair *history professor, researcher*
Goldsmith, John Anton *linguist, educator*
Gomberg, Paul *philosopher, educator*
Gossett, Philip *musicologist*
Grant, Robert McQueen *humanities educator*
Gray, Hanna Holborn *historian, educator*
Hamp, Eric Pratt *linguist*
Hast, Adele *historian, editor, writer*
Hillocks, George, Jr. *language educator, researcher*
Hung, Wu *art historian, educator*
Johnson, Janet Helen *literature educator*
Kaegi, Walter Emil *history professor*
Kang, Soo Yun *art historian, educator*
Keenan, James George *classics educator*
Knight, Alrick Clauson, Jr. *language educator*
Knight, Cranston S. *history professor*
Kulczycki, John Jacob *retired historian*
Liebenow, Franklin Eastburn, Jr. *English literature educator*
Long, Jacqueline Flint *classicist, educator*
Mahowald, Mary Briody *humanities educator*
McCloskey, Deirdre Nansen *economics and history educator*
Niebylski, Dianna C. *Latin American and comparative literature professor*
Odishoo, Sarah A. *literature and language professor, writer, poet*
Phillips, Gene Daniel *language educator*
Pippin, Robert B. *philosopher, educator*
Remini, Robert Vincent *historian*
Rosales, Veronica *language educator*
Roy, David Tod *literature educator*
Spargo, R. Clifton *literature and language professor*
Villa-Flores, Javier *history professor*
Yartz, Frank Joseph *retired professor, author*

Colchester
Combs, William Lee *history professor emeritus*

Danville
Hantz, Charles Anthony *humanities educator*

Decatur
Cabrera, Eduardo C. *literature and language professor*

Deerfield
Fratt, Steven D. *humanities educator*

Dekalb
Fehrenbach, Heide *historian, educator*
Leang, Kheang *language educator*
Phares, Dee Anna *literature and language professor*
Ryan, Timothy Andrew *literature and language professor*
Stahl, Norman A. *literature and language professor, department chairman*

Des Plaines
Page, Helen (Lyn) Bard Ward *literature educator*

Elmhurst
Ford, Russell Clarke *philosopher, educator*

Stanger, John Goodman *literature and language professor, archivist*

Evanston
Carroll, Peter James *history professor*
Gourianova, Nina *art and literary historian*
Hayford, Charles W. *historian, educator*
Hine, Darlene Clark *history educator, administrator*
Reiss, Lenore Ann *language educator, retired secondary school educator*
Sheridan, James Edward *history professor*
Wills, Garry *historian*
Wright, John *classics educator*

Freeport
Giaimo, Paul Sebastian *English and philosophy educator*

Galesburg
Gold, Penny Schine *history professor*
Hamilton, Konrad M. *history professor*
Hellenga, Robert Riner *language educator, writer*

Glen Ellyn
Georgalas, Robert Nicholas *English language educator*
Wu, Jane Jiajing *history professor, consultant*

Grayslake
Hopkins, Leslie Huntress *humanities educator, choreographer*

Homewood
Schillings, Denny Lynn *retired history professor, educational and grants consultant*

Jacksonville
Jerry, E. Claire *history professor, communications educator*

Joliet
Yarrow, William Paul *literature and language professor*

Lake Bluff
Sweetser, Marie-Odile Gauny *retired language educator*

Lincoln
Franz, Karin *humanities educator*

Macomb
Brice, Lee L. *history professor*
Karlowicz, Sarah Hanks *musicologist*
Key, Barclay Taylor *history professor*

Mattoon
Francis, Sue *humanities educator*

Moline
McFarland, David Alexander *literature and language professor*

Monmouth
Cordery, Stacy A. *history professor, writer*

Mount Vernon
Hall, Sharon Gay *retired language educator, artist*

Normal
Hoy, Jessica De May *language educator*
Huff, Cynthia Anne *English educator*
Kim, In-Sop *speech professional, educator*
Lord, Timothy Charles *philosophy educator*
Segelcke, Elke *literary scholar*
Shields, John Charles *literature educator*
Trouille, Mary Seidman *foreign language educator*

Oak Park
Shaw, Leroy Robert *retired language educator, writer*

Palatine
Hernandez, Ana Lucia *language educator*
Hull, Elizabeth Anne *retired English language educator*
Middleton-Kaplan, Richard Edward *literature and language professor*

Palos Park
Walther, Daniel Joseph *historian*

Pearl City
Kostallari, Adrian A. *language educator*

Peoria
Guzman, Gregory G. *retired history professor*
Katz, Seth Robert *literature and language professor*
Williams, John Alexander *history professor*

River Forest
Davlin, Mary Clemente *literature and language professor, dominican sister*
Jackson, William Vernon *Latin American studies and library science educator*
Keberlein Gutierrez, Douglas Robert *history professor*

Robinson
Wolven, Ann Reed *literature and language professor, journalist*

Rock Island
Goebel, Catherine Carter *art history professor, department chairman*
Vivian, Kim *language educator*

Rockford
Hoshaw, Lloyd *retired historian, educator*
Porterfield, Susan Azar *literature and language professor*
Sytsma, David Allen *history professor, department chairman*

Romeoville
Hoppe, Elizabeth Anne *philosopher, educator*

Saint Charles
Thorsen, Denise *language educator*

Seymour
Carringer, Robert *film and language educator*

Springfield
Burkhardt, Barbara Ann *literature and language professor, writer*
Jackson, Jacqueline Dougan *literature educator, writer*
Seney, Ronald Joe *speech educator, theater educator*
Temple, Wayne Calhoun *historian, writer*

Streator
Tyne, Gerald Robert *history professor*

Sugar Grove
Iacopetti, Rebecca *language educator*

Sycamore
Whisenhunt, Donald Wayne *retired historian, dean, educator*

Urbana
Arnstein, Walter Leonard *retired historian*
Haile, H. G. *German language and literature educator*
Hendrick, George *retired English language educator*
Hlongwa, Tholani *language educator*
Hoxie, Frederick Eugene *history professor*
Kaufmann, Urlin Milo *English literature educator*
Koshy, Susan *literature and language professor*
Lasersohn, Peter Nathan *linguist, educator*
Love, Joseph LeRoy *history professor, former cultural studies center administrator*
Mainous, Bruce Hale *foreign language educator*
McKay, John Patrick *history professor*
Nichols, J(ohn) Alden *retired history professor*
Puri, Vandana *linguist, educator*
Reagan, Leslie Jean *history professor, writer*
Schoeps, Karl Heinz Joachim *German language educator*
Solberg, Winton Udell *historian, educator*
Some-Guiebre, Wen-Yam Esther *language educator*
Stillinger, Jack Clifford *language educator*
Talbot, Emile Joseph *French language educator*

Wadsworth
Young, Susan Jean *music specialist*

Westchester
Masterson, John Patrick *retired language educator*

Wheaton
Talbot, Mark Ross *philosophy educator*

Wilmette
Lopez, Tania *literature educator*
Monter, E. William *retired history professor*

INDIANA

Anderson
Shrock, Joel D. *history professor*

Bloomington
Anderson, Judith Helena *English language educator*
Assensoh, Akwasi Bretuo *historian, educator*
Bernhardt-Kabisch, Ernest Karl-Heinz *English and comparative literature educator*
Choksy, Jamsheed Kairshasp *historian, religious scholar, humanities educator, language educator*
Dunn, Jon Michael *logician, dean emeritus, consultant*
Eisenberg, Paul David *philosophy educator*
El-Shamy, Hasan M. *philosopher, educator*
Hanson, Karen *philosopher, educator*
Hertz, David Michael *literature and arts educator*
Johnson, Owen Verne *historian, educator*
Lebano, Edoardo Antonio *foreign language educator*
Mickel, Emanuel John *foreign language educator*
Newman, Paul *linguist, educator*
Peterson, M. Jeanne *historian, educator*
Port, Robert Frederick *linguist*
Ransel, David Lorimer *history professor*
Rosenberg, Samuel Nathan *French and Italian language educator*
Shapshay, Sandra Lynne *philosopher, educator*
Sinor, Denis *history professor, linguist*
Stoeltje, Beverly June *liberal studies educator*
Valdman, Albert *language and linguistics educator*
Watts, Edward Jay *history professor*

Carmel
Sukapdjo, Wilma Irene *language educator*

Columbus
Spector, Judith Ann *retired english educator*

Crawfordsville
Barnes, James John *historian, educator*

Donaldson
Buchanan, Thomas Wayne *history professor*

Evansville
Bone, Paul *literature and language professor*

Fort Wayne
Camara, Esperanca Maria *art historian, educator*
Smith, Matthew Joseph *literature and language professor*

Franklin
Colburn-Alsop, Sara Noelle *language educator*

Granger
Cook, Pamela Margaret *French educator*

Greencastle
Belyavski-Frank, Masha *literature and language professor, linguist*
Dittmer, John Avery *history professor*
Spicer, Harold Otis *retired English language educator, communications educator*
Weiss, Robert Orr *speech educator*

Hammond
Detmer, David *philosopher, educator*

Hanover
Aguilar-Monsalve, Luis Antonio *language educator, writer*
Dalka, Laverne Barbara *language educator*

Indianapolis
Baetzhold, Howard George *retired language educator*
Bodenhamer, David Jackson *historian, educator*
Boling, Joseph Edward *numismatist, retired military officer*
Connor, Ulla M. *linguistics educator*
Krasean, Thomas Karl *retired historian*
Lindseth, Erik Lars *humanities educator*
Lucchi-Riester, Elisa *literature and language professor*
Mason, Thomas Alexander *historian, educator, author*
Musgrave Moosbrugger, Megan *literature and language professor*
Tezanos-Pinto, Rosa *Hispanic American literature educator*

Muncie
Fritz, Robert Karl *language educator*
Hudson, Kevin Roy *language educator*
Suppe, Frederick *historian, educator*

Nashville
Wills, Katherine V. Tsiopos *language educator*

Notre Dame
Bloomer, W. Martin *classicist, educator*
Bruns, Gerald L. *English literature educator*
Hosle, Vittorio Giovanni *philosopher, educator*
Lanzinger, Klaus *language educator*
MacCormack, Sabine Gabriele *history educator*
McInerny, Ralph Matthew *philosopher, educator, writer*
Noble, Thomas Francis *history professor, department chairman*
Noll, Mark A. *history professor*
O'Rourke, William Andrew *literature and language professor, writer*
Perry, Catherine *language educator*
Raymer, John David *literature and language professor*
Schoen, Suzanne *English educator*
Sloan, Phillip Reid *liberal studies educator*
Taccheri, Umberto *language educator*
Walker, Clint B. *Russian language and literature educator*

Richmond
Passet, Joanne Ellen *history professor, writer*

Saint Meinrad
Hagan, Harry *ancient language educator*

South Bend
Nilsen, Micheline Celestine *art historian, educator*
Sheapentukh, Dmitry V. *history professor*
Shlapentokh, Dmitry Vladimir *history educator*
van Inwagen, Peter Jan *philosophy educator*

Terre Haute
Baker, Ronald Lee *folklore educator*
De Marr, Mary Jean *English language educator*
Grcic, Joseph *philosophy educator*
Mehrens, Christopher Emile *musicologist, music librarian*

Upland
Ringenberg, William Carey *historian, minister*
Satterlee, Thom *literature educator, director*

Valparaiso
Parroquin, Rachel Rivers *language educator*
Peters, Howard Nevin *foreign language educator*

West Lafayette
Bergmann, Michael *philosophy professor*
Bertolet, Rodney Jay *philosophy educator*
Brennan, Akiko Ohashi *language educator*
Broden, Thomas Francis III *French language educator*
Contreni, John Joseph, Jr. *humanities educator*
Dawuda, Alhassan *language educator*
Francis, Elaine J. *linguist, educator*
Hearden, Patrick Joseph *history professor*
Larson, John Lauritz *history professor*
Lein, Clayton David *literature and language professor*
May, Robert E. *history professor*
Mc Bride, William Leon *philosopher, educator*
Platt, Donald Oliver *literature and language professor*
Rankine, Patrice D. *literature and language professor*
Rowland, Herbert *language educator*
Woodman, Harold David *historian, educator*

Westfield
Hayashi, Tetsumaro *retired literature educator, writer, editor*

IOWA

Ames
Courteau, Joanna *foreign language educator*
Cravens, Hamilton *history professor*

Maxwell Dial, Eleanore *foreign language educator*
Monroe, John Warne *history professor*
Silet, Charles Loring Provine *emeritus literature and language professor*

Cedar Falls
Schnucker, Robert Victor *historian, educator*
Shepardson, Donald Eugene *history professor*

Davenport
Holleran, Karen Elaine *literature and language professor*

Decorah
Christianson, John Robert *historian, educator*
Tejada, Rita María *literature and language professor*

Des Moines
Duffy, Kathryn Ann Pohlmann *musicologist, educator*

Fairfield
Rogers, Benjamin Franklin *retired history professor*

Forest City
Biggs, Douglas Lee *historian, educator*

Grinnell
Kintner, Philip L. *history professor*
Michaels, Jennifer Tonks *foreign language educator*
Nyden, Tammy Marie *philosopher, educator*

Indianola
Dinesen, Tracy A. *language educator*

Iowa City
Addis, Laird Clark, Jr. *philosopher, educator, musician*
Aspel, Paulene Violette *retired language educator*
Díaz-Duque, Ozzie Francis *literature and language professor*
Ertl, Wolfgang *German language and literature educator, artist*
Folsom, Lowell Edwin *language educator*
Gelfand, Lawrence Emerson *historian, educator*
Green, Peter Morris *classics educator, writer, translator*
Guentner, Wendelin Ann *literature and language professor*
Hawley, Ellis Wayne *historian, educator*
Heath, Richard *language educator*
Hornsby, Roger Allen *classics educator*
Kerber, Linda Kaufman *historian, educator*
Kostina, Irina S. *language educator*
Kramer, Paul Alexander *history professor*
Laronde, Michel Serge *language educator*
Leone, Leah Elizabeth *language educator*
Lutgendorf, Philip *language educator*
Mazurkewycz, Christine A. *literature and language professor*
McKee, Christopher Fulton *historian, educator*
Percas-Ponseti, Helena *foreign language and literature educator*
Raeburn, John Hay *language educator*
Solbrig, Ingeborg Hildegard *retired literature educator, writer*

Lamoni
Casey, Michael S. *humanities educator*

Mount Vernon
Gruber-Miller, John C. *humanities educator*

Oskaloosa
Porter, David Lindsey *history and political science professor, writer*
Robbins, Janet Linda *language and citizenship educator*

Ottumwa
Ford, Ruston C. *language educator*
Luman, Richard Gordon *retired historian*

Pella
Den Adel, Raymond Lee *classics educator*

Sioux City
Oggel, Ynés M. *language educator, director*

Waverly
Blair, Rebecca Sue *English educator*
Schneider, Richard John *literature and language professor*

West Burlington
Evans, James Richard *history professor*

KANSAS

Atchison
Lane, Elizabeth Ann *genealogist, researcher*
Newton, Lloyd Alfred *philosopher, educator*

Chanute
Dillard, Dean Innes *retired English language educator*

Dodge City
Burke, Larry Keith *history professor*

Emporia
Riegler, Roxane *language educator, researcher*

Fort Leavenworth
King, Curtis Steeble *history professor*

Fort Scott
Bailey, Ronda Wyckoff *literature and language professor*

Hays
Bovee, David Steven *historian, educator*

Hillsboro
Kyle, Richard Granville *history professor, religion educator*

Lawrence
Boyd, Beverly *English literature educator*
Brundage, James Arthur *historian, educator*
Caminero-Santangelo, Marta Maria *literature and language professor*
Cienciala, Anna Maria *history professor*
De George, Richard Thomas *philosophy educator*
Eldredge, Charles Child III *art history educator*
Gunn, James Edwin *language educator*
Hardin, Richard Francis *language educator*
Harvey, Douglas Scott *historian, educator*
Hemenway, Robert E. *history professor, former academic administrator*
Kelly, Mary Byrd *language educator*
Levin, Eve *history professor*
Pasco, Allan Humphrey *literature educator*
Saleebey, Dennis *humanities educator*
Saul, Norman Eugene *historian, educator*
Tuttle, William McCullough, Jr. *history professor*
Weber, Jennifer Lee *historian, educator*
Woelfel, James Warren *philosophy and humanities educator*
Worth, George John *retired English literature educator*

Leawood
Zell, Valerie *art historian, educator*

Lindsborg
Homan, Delmar Charles *English educator*
Lewis, Linda M. *humanities educator*

Manhattan
Higham, Robin *historian, editor, publisher*

North Newton
Sprunger, Keith L. *historian, educator*

Olathe
Anderson, Joshua M. *speech educator*

Onaga
Dillinger, Susan Alice *instructor*

Overland Park
Burger, Henry G. *vocabulary scientist, anthropologist, writer*
Hillen, James Joseph *language educator*
Hoare, Timothy Douglas *humanities educator*
Paulsen, Ruth Ann *French and Spanish language educator*
Pribyl, Rick R. *English language educator*

Salina
Ackerman, Patricia Elizabeth *language educator*

Topeka
Hoogenakker, Jim L. *literature and language professor*
Pruitt, Virginia Diane *literature and language professor*
Sheldon, Roy Albert *literature and language professor*

Wichita
Bakken, Linda *Developmental And Social Psychology Professor*
Gythiel, Anthony Paul *history professor*

KENTUCKY

Barbourville
Wood, Andelys *literature and language professor*

Bowling Green
Endres, Nikolai *literature educator*
Pertusa, Inmaculada *language educator*

Columbia
Senters, Melinda *history professor*

Crestwood
Hanson, Richard Harris *language educator*

Danville
Allen, John Jay *Spanish language educator*
Bradshaw, Richard Albert *historian, consultant*
Levin, William Robert *art historian*

Elsmere
Miller, Jackie Dean, I, *genealogist, historian*

Georgetown
Klotter, James C. *historian, educator*

Lexington
Anderson, Terri Diane *history professor*
Coffman, Edward McKenzie *retired history professor*
Pickens, Rupert Tarpley III *French language educator*
Santí, Enrico Mario *humanities educator*
Shawcross, John Thomas *English educator*
Svarlien, John E. *classicist, educator*
Thelin, John Robert *historian, educator, researcher*
Tribble, Joan Lucille (Joan Farnsley Tribble) *retired literature and language professor, writer*

Louisville
Barnes, Brian Glen *philosopher, educator, researcher*
Bosley, Gabriele W. *language educator, director*
Lopez, Nelson *theatre literature professor*
McLeod, John Edmond *history professor*

Morehead
Kiffmeyer, Thomas Joseph *history professor*

Owensboro
Barrette, Craig Richard *literature and language professor*
Moffett, Joe *literature and language professor*

Paducah
Craig, Berry Franklin III *history professor*

Richmond
Day-Lindsey, Lisa *literature and language professor*
Huch, Ronald Kind *historian, educator*
Sweely, Gay Caryll *art historian, educator*

Southgate
Glenn, Jerry Hosmer, Jr. *retired language educator*

Williamsburg
Pilant, Charles Alan *history professor*

LOUISIANA

Alexandria
Vanderslice, Stephen J. *literature and language professor*

Baton Rouge
Arceneaux, William *historian, educator, association administrator*
Byrd, Lidia María *language educator*
Cooper, William James, Jr. *history professor*
Doty, Gresdna Ann *theatre historian, educator*
Hardy, John Edward *language educator, writer*
Leupin, Alexandre *language educator*
Lott, Bret *literature and language professor, writer*
Ricapito, Joseph Virgil (Giuseppe Ricapito) *literature educator*
Sasek, Gloria Burns *English language and literature educator*

Hammond
Ostarly-Ulfers, Lori Ann *history professor*

Lafayette
Brasseaux, Carl Anthony *historian, educator, academic administrator, curator*
Carstens, Jane Ellen *retired library science educator*
Honegger, Mark Andrew *language educator*
Raffel, Burton Nathan *novelist, poet, translator*

Lake Charles
Cook, Nancy J. *language educator*
Walsh, Louise Jaquelyn *literature and language professor*

Metairie
Toups, Kim G. *language educator, department chairman*

Natchitoches
LeBreton, Marietta M. *history professor*

New Orleans
Bischof, Günter Josef *history professor*
Brumfield, William Craft *Slavic studies educator, photographer, writer*
Dorris, Ronald *humanities educator, literature and language professor*
Frystak, Shannon Lee *historian, researcher*
Hall, Gwendolyn Midlo *historian, educator*
Hasselbach, Karlheinz *retired literature educator*
Kilroy, James Francis *humanities educator*
Luza, Radomir Vaclav *retired historian, educator*
McAllister, James Anthony *literature and language professor*
McClay, Wilfred Mark *history educator, writer*
Mitchell, Mary Niall *history professor*
Paolini, Gilberto *literature educator*
Poesch, Jessie Jean *art historian*
Qian, Zhaoming *literature educator, critic*
Reck, Andrew Joseph *philosopher*
Salm, Steven J. *history professor*
Saloy, Mona Lisa *literature and language professor*
Schalow, Frank Hickey *philosopher, educator*
Sloan, Dauphine de Montlaur *literature and language professor*

Ruston
de Mattos, Rudy *language educator*

Shreveport
Mikaberidze, Alexander *history professor, researcher*
Pleasant, John Ruffin, Jr. *retired literature and language professor*

MAINE

Boothbay
Kaplan, Fred *literature educator, biographer*

Brunswick
Hodge, James Lee *German language educator*

Castine
Berleant, Arnold *philosopher*

Dresden
Turco, Lewis Putnam *writer, English educator*

Farmington
Frary, John Newton *history professor*

Fort Kent Mills
Paradis, Roger *history & folklore professor, researcher*

Harpswell
Ford, Elaine *english educator*

Long Island
Chassen-López, Francie R. *history professor*

Orono
Crouch, Terrell Hunter *literature and language professor*

Portland
Chapkis, Wendy Lynn *women's studies educator, sociologist*
Schwanauer, Francis *philosopher, educator*

Rockport
Goodwin, Doris Helen Kearns *historian, writer*

Sanford
Allan, Jonathan David *autograph dealer, pop culture historian, writer*

Scarborough
Sadik, Marvin Sherwood *art historian, consultant, retired museum director*

Waterville
Bassett, Charles Walker *retired literature and language professor*
Simon, David L. *art historian*

MARYLAND

Annapolis
Abels, Richard Philip *history professor, department chairman*
Brann, Eva Toni Helene *philosophy educator*
Burt, Clarissa C. *literature and language professor*

Baltimore
Baldwin, John Wesley *history professor*
Bell, David Avrom *humanities educator*
Chapelle, Suzanne Ellery Greene *history professor*
Cooper, Jerrold Stephen *historian, educator*
Elfenbein, Jessica I. *historian, educator*
Hsieh, Rebecca Tung *language educator, interpreter*
Irwin, John Thomas *humanities educator*
Johnson, Michael Paul *historian, educator*
Judson, Horace Freeland *history professor, writer*
Kessler, Herbert Leon *art historian, educator, academic administrator*
Kim, Dong-Won *historian, educator*
Kimbrough, Natalie *history professor*
Lidtke, Vernon LeRoy *history professor*
McCarthy, Patricia Anne *reading educator*
Ranum, Orest Allen *historian, educator*
Savell, Catherine *humanities educator*
Stephens, Walter *language educator*
Terborg-Penn, Rosalyn Marian *historian, educator*
Williams, Michael J. *philosopher, educator*
Ziff, Larzer *literature and language professor*

Bel Air
Lu, David John *historian, writer*

Beltsville
Merriam, Diane Louise *ESL educator*

Bethesda
Blackmore, John Thomas *historian, philosopher*
Child-Olmsted, Gisèle Alexandra *retired language educator*
Fee, Elizabeth *medical historian, administrator*
Highfill, Philip Henry, Jr. *retired language educator*
Ludlow, Gregory *language educator*
van der Linden, Frank Morris *historian*

Betterton
Kohl, Benjamin Gibbs *historian, educator*

Bowie
LeCounte, Lola Houston *literature and language professor, educational consultant*
Sterling, Richard Leroy *English and foreign language educator*

Catonsville
Oden, Gloria *language educator, poet*

Chevy Chase
Cline, Ruth Eleanor Harwood *translator*
Fern, Alan Maxwell *art historian, retired museum director*

College Park
Hallett, Judith Peller *classical studies educator*
Odell, Stanley Jack *retired philosopher professor*
Oster, Rose Marie Gunhild *foreign language professional, educator*
Panichas, George Andrew *language educator, critic, editor*
Pasch, Alan *philosopher, educator*
Soergel, Philip Mark *history professor*
Spear, Richard Edmund *art history educator*
Turner, Mark Bernard *English language educator*
Weart, Spencer Richard *historian*

Columbia
Mitchell, Helen Buss *philosophy educator*

Cumberland
Riggs, Robert Meldrum *French educator*

Ellicott City
Loerke, William Carl *art historian, educator*

Emmitsburg
Merrill, Charles J. *language educator*

Frederick
Course, Didier Jean *literature and language professor, writer*

Gaithersburg
Rodgers, Mary Columbro *literature educator, writer, academic administrator*

Germantown
Kronstadt, Jill *literature and language professor*
Naake, Joan Murray *English professor*

Hagerstown
Clark, Ann Maureen *literature and language professor*

Hyattsville
Golden, Marita *literature educator, writer, foundation administrator*

La Plata
Brantley, David H. *literature and language professor, department chairman*
Layer, Marianne Elizabeth *literature and language professor, department chairman*
Stephanic, Barbara Jean *art historian, writer, curator, researcher*

Lusby
Eshelman, Ralph Ellsworth *historian, consultant, paleontologist*

Mitchellville
Embree, Ainslie Thomas *history professor*
Griffen, Clyde Chesterman *retired historian*
Heald, Morrell *humanities educator*

Ocean Pines
Fullerton, Jean Leah *retired language educator, researcher, census researcher*

Pasadena
De Pauw, Linda Grant *historian, educator, writer*

Pikesville
Rosen, Leslie Smith *humanities educator, director*

Potomac
Cohen, Warren I. *historian*

Rockville
Hare, John L. *literature and language professor*
Hewlett, Richard Greening *historian*
LeCompte, Andrew C. *freelance/self-employed interpreter*
Medina, Eduardo Jose *language educator*

Saint Marys City
Wilson, Bruce Matthew *literature and language professor*

Severna Park
Schick, Edgar Brehob *language educator*

Silver Spring
Borkovec, Vera Z. *literature and language professor*
Doherty, William Thomas, Jr. *historian, retired educator*
Edwards, Kamala Doris *humanities educator*
Papas, Irene Kalandros *English language educator, poet, writer*
Rothberg, Morey David *historian, editor*

Smithsburg
Gift, Edward Lee *history professor*

Takoma Park
Luna-Escudero-Alie, María-Elvira *language educator*

Towson
Baker, Jean Harvey *history professor*
Heaney, Steven *literature and language professor*
Kurth, Lieselotte *foreign language educator*

Tracys Landing
Smith, Elbert Benjamin *historian, educator*

Wye Mills
Tecce, Anita Mercedes *literature, language and theatre professor*

MASSACHUSETTS

Amherst
Baker, Lynne Rudder *philosophy educator*
Benson, Lucy Wilson *historian, consultant*
Bricker, Phillip *philosopher, educator*
Brooks, A. Taeko *historian*
Higginson, John Edward *history professor*
Kinney, Arthur Frederick *humanities educator, writer*
Minear, Richard Hoffman *history professor*
Oates, Stephen Baery *retired historian*
Taubman, Jane Andelman *literature and language professor*
Wyman, David Sword *retired historian, educator*

Auburndale
Lindgren, Charlotte Holt *language educator*
Scheffler, Israel *philosopher, educator*

Belchertown
Kitchell, Kenneth Francis, Jr. *classical studies educator*

Belmont
Dohanian, Diran Kavork *art historian, educator*

Beverly
Gangle, Rocco *philosopher*

Boston
Bacevich, Andrew J. *international relations and history professor, writer*
Blakely, Allison *history professor*
Boskin, Joseph *history professor*
Child, Christopher Challender *genealogist*
Diamandopoulos, Peter *philosophy professor*
Glick, Thomas F. *history educator*
Henry, DeWitt Pawling, II, *literature educator, art association administrator, writer*
Hintikka, Jaakko *philosopher, educator*
Kafker, Frank A. *historian, educator*
Kleiner, Fred Scott *art historian, archaeologist, educator, editor*
Kline, Thomas Jefferson *foreign language educator*
Lyons, David Barry *philosophy and law educator*
Mc Carthy, Joseph Michael *historian, educator*
Musselman, Cecelia Anne *linguist, educator*
Properzio, Paul J. *classicist, educator*
Robbins, David Lee *history professor, educator*
Rosellini, Jay Julian *language educator*
Rosen, Stanley Howard *humanities educator*
Samons, Loren J., II, *classicist*
Scanlon, Dorothy Therese *history professor*
Wermuth, Paul Charles *retired language educator*

Bridgewater
Crowe, Margaret Isabella Roxburgh *history professor*

Brookline
Binion, Rudolph *history professor*
Connolly, Thomas Francis *English language educator, theatre scholar*
Epstein, Leslie *literature educator, writer*
Michopoulos, Aristotle V. *humanities educator, researcher*
Moon, John Ellis van Courtland *retired historian*

Cambridge
Afsaruddin, Asma *Arabic language educator*
Arteta, Jorge *foreign language educator, consultant*
Asani, Ali S. *foreign language and religious studies educator*
Bailyn, Bernard *historian, educator*
Barnet, Sylvan *English literature educator*
Bleichmar, Daniela *history professor*
Bolster, Arthur Stanley, Jr. *history professor*
Browne, Janet *historian, educator*
Brustein, Robert Sanford *literature and language professor, theater director, writer*
Chomsky, Noam (Avram Noam Choamsky) *linguistics and philosophy educator*
Ciarlo, David Michael *history professor*
Cott, Nancy F. *history professor, writer*
Craig, Albert M. *history professor, researcher*
Damrosch, Leopold, Jr., (Leo Damrosch Jr.) *English educator*
Dupree, Anderson Hunter *historian, educator*
Elkins, Caroline M. *history professor, writer*
Engell, James Theodore *language educator, department chairman*
Fanger, Donald Lee *Slavic language and literature educator*
Ferguson, Niall Campbell Douglas *history professor, writer*
Fisher, Philip J. *English language and literature educator*
Flier, Michael Stephen *Slavic languages educator*
Gates, Henry Louis, Jr. *literature and language professor, historian*
Graham, Loren Raymond *historian, educator*
Greenblatt, Stephen Jay *literature and language professor, writer*
Guthke, Karl Siegfried *language educator*
Hanan, Patrick Dewes *foreign language professional, educator*
Handlin, Oscar *historian, educator*
Iriye, Akira *historian, educator*
Keller, Evelyn Fox *philosophy of science professor*
Keyser, Samuel Jay *linguist, educator*
Kirby, William C. *historian, former dean*
Koester, Helmut Heinrich *history professor*
Laiou, Angeliki Evangelos *history professor*
Liebmann, Matthew Joseph *history professor*
Maier, Charles Steven *history professor*
Malmstad, John Earl *literature and language professor*
Mazlish, Bruce *historian, educator*
McDonald, Christie Anne *literature and language professor, writer*
Monson, Ingrid *musicologist*
Mugane, John Muratha *literature and language professor*
O'Neil, Wayne *linguist, educator*
Owen, Edward Roger John (E. Roger Owen) *Middle Eastern studies professor, writer*
Perdue, Peter C. *history professor*
Pesetsky, David Michael *linguist*
Pipes, Richard Edgar *historian, educator*
Rehding, Alexander *musicologist*
Ritvo, Harriet *historian*
Rosenberg, Charles Ernest *historian, educator*
Rotberg, Robert Irwin *historian, political scientist, educator, academic administrator*
Sevcenko, Ihor *history and literature professor*
Simpson, W. James *literature and language professor*
Smith, Merritt Roe *history professor*
Stauffer, John William *cultural historian*
Tapscott, Stephen *literature educator*
Tarrant, Richard J(ohn) *classicist, educator*
Trumpbour, John *historian, researcher, director*
Vanger, Milton Isadore *historian, educator*
Vendler, Helen Hennessy *literature educator, poetry critic*
Ware, Susan W. *historian*
Watson, Nicholas James *literature and language professor*
Weitzman, Arthur Joshua *language educator*
Ziolkowski, Jan Michael *medievalist educator, library director*

Chelmsford
DiPillo, Patricia Anne *language educator, researcher*

Chelsea
Burds, Jeffrey *history professor*

Chestnut Hill
Bicks, Caroline *language educator*
Blanchette, Oliva *philosophy educator*
Cardona, Rodolfo *Spanish language and literature educator*
Davarian, Baldwin L. *history professor*
Hachey, Thomas Eugene *British and Irish history educator*
Kearney, Richard Marius *philosopher, educator, writer, poet*
Leone, Stephanie C. *history professor*
Reed, James Eldin *historian, consultant, educator*
Resler, Michael *literature and language professor*
Taylor, E. Dennis *English language educator, editor*
Valette, Rebecca Marianne *Romance languages educator*

Dartmouth
Larkosh, Christopher *language educator*

Dudley
Lambert, Paul Edward *history educator*

Fitchburg
Gim, Lisa *English professor*
Williams, Ian *English literature professor*

Gloucester
Basile, Celestino *language educator*

Granby
Ingham, Norman William *literature educator, genealogist*

Leicester
Statkus, Daryl Anne *literature and language professor*

Lexington
Simon, Eckehard (Peter) *foreign language educator*

Lowell
Kaufman, Whitley Robert Peters *humanities educator*
Marshall, Bridget *literature and language professor*

Medford
Bedau, Hugo Adam *philosophy educator*
Caviness, Madeline Harrison *art history educator, researcher*
Fyler, John Morgan *language educator*
Kaiser-Lenoir, Claudia *literature and language professor*
Mazzotti, José Antonio *humanities educator, researcher*
Wilson, Jonathan Michael *literature educator, writer*

Milton
Frazier, Marie Dunn *speech professional, public relations executive, human resources specialist*

Needham
Engels, Donald Whitcomb *history educator*

Newton
Marshall, Robert Lewis *musicologist, educator*
Steinberg, Roberta Gail *language educator*

North Adams
Bishoff, Robert Earl, Jr. *literature educator*

North Dartmouth
Borim, Dario, Jr. *literature educator*
Yoken, Mel B(arton) *language educator, writer, radio personality*

North Easton
Varella, Hazel L. *historian, educator*

Northampton
Vaget, Hans Rudolf *language professional, educator*
Von Klemperer, Klemens *historian, educator*

Norton
Mayer, Reinhard Albert *language educator*

Paxton
Heslinga, Virginia *literature and language professor*

Revere
Paananen, Victor Niles *language educator*

Salem
Gozemba, Patrica Andrea *women's studies and English language educator, writer*
Rhodes, Karin T. *language educator*

Sharon
Eiland, Howard Avery *literature educator*

Sherborn
Cushing, Steven *linguist, educator, writer, researcher, consultant*

Shutesbury
Creed, Robert Payson, Sr. *retired literature educator*

South Hadley
Brownlow, Frank Walsh *literature and language professor*
Burns, Michael Thornton *historian, educator, farmer*
Farnham, Anthony Edward *language educator, department chairman*
Gundermann, Christian *language educator*
Horsnell, Margaret Eileen *retired historian*
Van Handle, Donna *language educator*

Springfield
Habermehl, Lawrence LeRoy *philosophy educator*
Miller, Leroy Paul, Jr. *language educator*
Wyzik, Susan Aldrich *history professor*

Stoughton
Hall, Roger Lee *musicologist, composer, educator*

Sunderland
Baritz, Loren *history professor*

Taunton
Nunes, Anthony S. *language educator*

Waban
Black, Eugene Charlton *historian, educator*

Waltham
Burt, John D. *literature and language professor*
Fischer, David Hackett *historian, educator*
Jankowski, Paul Felix *history professor*
Marques, Nadejda *language educator, interpreter*
Pages-Rangel, Roxana *language educator*
Sachs, Murray *French language and literature educator, researcher*
Schrecker, John *historian, educator*
Spack, Ruth Karten *literature educator*
Whitfield, Stephen Jack *history educator*

Wellesley
Bidart, Frank *English educator, poet*
Cummings, Cathleen Ann *art historian, educator*
Dougherty, Carol *humanities educator*
Lefkowitz, Mary Rosenthal *ancient language educator*
Mistacco, Vicki E. *foreign language educator*
Zimmerman, Eve Kathleen *literature and language professor*

Wenham
Flint-Ferguson, Janis Deane *English language and literature educator*
Thuswaldner, Gregor *literature and language professor*

West Barnstable
Martin, Kate M. *history professor*

Westfield
Cleaton-Ruiz, Christin *history professor*

Weston
Higgins, Sister Therese *literature educator, former college president*

Williamstown
Bell, Robert *literature educator*
Dalzell, Robert Fenton, Jr. *historian, educator*
Dew, Charles Burgess *historian, educator*
Fuqua, Charles John *retired classicist*
Graver, Suzanne Levy *English literature educator*
Oakley, Francis Christopher *historian, educator*
Pistorius, George *language educator*
Rudolph, Frederick *history professor*
Shepard, James Russell *literature and language professor*
Siniawer, Eiko Maruko *history professor*

Worcester
Bastien, Louis A. *literature and language professor*
Billias, George Athan *historian, educator*
D'Lugo, Carol Clark *language educator*
Hangen, Tona J. *history professor*
McAvey, Marion Sheila *college professor, editor*
Schmitt, Richard *philosopher, educator*
Vaughan, Alden True *history professor*
Vicuña, Maximo Quintiliano *retired language educator*
Zeugner, John Finn *historian, educator, writer*

Yarmouth Port
Weiner, Charles *historian, educator*

MICHIGAN

Albion
Myers, Perry W. *language educator*

Allendale
Alexander, John K. *philosopher, educator*
Benjamin, Craig Gordon *history professor*
Rayor, Diane Jill *classics educator*

Alpena
Walchak, Karol Lynn *literature and language professor, department chairman*

Ann Arbor
Asso, Paolo *ancient language educator*
Blouin, Francis Xavier, Jr. *history professor*
Brick, Howard *historian*
Brown, Miranda Dympna *language educator*
Chambers, Leigh Ross (Ross Chambers) *French and comparative language educator*
Chang, Chun-Shu *historian, educator, writer*
Cowen, Roy Chadwell, Jr. *language educator*
Curley, Edwin Munson *philosophy educator*
Delbanco, Nicholas Franklin *language educator, writer*
Dunnigan, Brian Leigh *historian, curator*
Eisenstein, Elizabeth Lewisohn *historian, educator*
Ferrell, Robert Hugh *historian, educator*
Feuerwerker, Albert *historian, educator*
Forsyth, Ilene Haering *art historian*
Hackett, Roger Fleming *historian, educator*
Izzo, Herbert John *language and linguistics educator, researcher*
Janko, Richard Charles Murray *humanities educator*
Knott, John Ray, Jr. *language educator*
Kucich, John Richard *English language educator*
McCarus, Ernest Nasseph *retired language educator*
Mersereau, John, Jr. *literature and language professor*
Mizruchi, Mark Sheldon *sociology professor, business administration professor*
Munro, Donald Jacques *philosopher, educator*
Nelson, Roy Jay *retired French educator*
Rabkin, Eric S. *English educator*

Reed, Joseph Duffield *ancient language educator*
Rodríguez, María Isabel *literature and language professor*
Thoburn, Elisabeth Z. *humanities educator*
Thornton, Jonathan Mills *history professor*
Trautmann, Thomas Roger *history professor, anthropology educator*

Auburn Hills
Bembas, Catherine Hagan *literature and language professor*

Berrien Springs
Bryson, Jeanette Patricia *literature and language professor, director*
O'Reggio, Trevor Evan *history professor*

Beulah
Tanner, Helen Hornbeck *historian, consultant*

Dearborn
Claerr, Thomas A. *language educator*
Papazian, Dennis Richard *retired historian, educator, commentator*
Rahman, Ahmad A. *history professor, writer*

Dearborn Heights
Jordan, Theresa Anne Rose *language educator*

Detroit
Covensky, Edith *language educator, poet*
DeSilvio, David Michael *history professor*
Elster, William Lawrence *history professor*
Hyde, Charles Keith *historian, educator*
Joost-Gaugier, Christiane Louise *art history educator*
Martin, Michael Thomas *humanities educator, writer*
Mueckenheim, Robert Carl *literature and language professor*
Rashid, Frank Damian *literature and language professor*
Small, Melvin *historian, educator*
Torres Cancel, Lourdes Ivelisse *philosopher, educator*

East Lansing
Anderson, David Daniel *retired humanities educator, writer, editor*
Fisher, Alan Washburn *historian, educator*
Natoli, Joseph *language educator*
Prestel, David Kirk *literature and language professor, department chairman*
Schoenl, William James *history professor*
Tzitsikas, Helene *retired literature educator*

Flint
Knight, Suzanne Dee *literature and language professor*
Marinucci, Ronald E. *history professor*

Grand Rapids
Gunnoe, Charles D. *history professor*
Pichot, Michel *language educator, department chairman*
Pinheiro, John C. *historian, educator*
Vande Kopple, William John *literature and language professor*
Van Vugt, William E. *history professor*

Grosse Pointe
Hendrie, Janice Ellen *language educator*

Holland
Catel, Mylène Jeanne *French educator, poet*
Johnson, Freddie Lee III *history professor*
Swierenga, Robert *humanities educator, researcher*

Jackson
Feldmann, Judith Gail *language professional, educator*

Jenison
Wooster, Stephanie Lynne *art historian, artist*

Jerome
Dillon, Merton Lynn *historian, educator*

Kalamazoo
Berto, Luigi Andrea *history professor*
Breisach, Ernst A. *historian, educator*
Desroches, Vincent *language educator*
Dybek, Stuart *language educator, writer*
Larrieu, Gloria Lynn *language educator*
Maier, Paul Luther *history professor, minister, writer*
Rivara, Sara *language educator*
Sauret, Martine *French educator*

Livonia
Holtzman, Roberta Lee *French and Spanish language educator*
Malalahalli, Jayalakshmi S. *history professor*

Marquette
Sotiropoulos, Carol Strauss *language educator*

Mount Pleasant
Doyle, Randall Jordan *history professor*
Meixner, John B. *philosopher, educator*
Torgersen, Eric *literature and language professor*

Muskegon
Wible, Andy *philosopher, educator*

Okemos
Huddleston, Eugene Lee *retired American studies educator*

Portage
Gregory, Ross *retired history professor, writer*

Rochester
Cole, Natalie Bell *literature and language professor*
Hoffiz, Benjamin Theodore *literature and language professor*

Spring Arbor
Moore-Jumonville, Kimberly *literature educator*

University Center
Clark, Basil Alfred *language educator*
Fogarty, Julia T. *language educator*

Warren
Henning, Billie Harrold *retired speech educator*

West Bloomfield
Goldsmith, Arnold Louis *American literature educator*
Stern, Guy *German language and literature educator, writer*
Williamson, Marilyn Lammert *literature educator, academic administrator*

Ypsilanti
Cere, Ronald Carl *languages educator, consultant, researcher*

MINNESOTA

Alexandria
Scholer, Catherine Rochelle *language educator*

Bloomington
Bigalk, Kristina *writing professor*

Coon Rapids
Klamm-Doneen, Kristin Irene *philosopher, educator*

Duluth
Hodapp, William F. *literature and language professor*
Schroeder, Fred Erich Harald *humanities educator*

Edina
Farah, Caesar Elie *retired language educator, historian*

Mankato
Janc, John J. *language educator*
Longwell, Patricia Anne *language educator*
Tomany, Maria-Claudia Christine *language educator, director*

Marshall
Pichaske, David Richard *language educator*

Mendota Heights
McMullin, Ernan Vincent *retired philosophy educator*

Minneapolis
Bashiri, Iraj *Central Asian studies educator*
Erickson, Gerald Meyer *classical studies educator*
Firchow, Evelyn Scherabon *German language and literature educator, writer*
Firchow, Peter Edgerly *language professional, educator, writer*
Hellman, Geoffrey P. *philosopher, educator*
Plomondon, John Edmund *literature and language professor*
Reini-Grandell, Lynette Eileen *literature and language professor, writer*
Ross, Donald, Jr. *language educator, academic administrator*
Seidel, Robert Wayne *science historian, educator*
Tracy, James Donald *historian, educator*
Weiss, Gerhard Hans *German language educator*

Moorhead
Buckley, Joan N. *retired literature and language professor*
Gargurevich, Eduardo *language educator*
Shoptaugh, Terry Lee *historian, archivist*
Smemo, Irwin Kenneth *history professor*

New Ulm
Czer, Lawrence Joseph *literature and language professor*

Northfield
Clark, Clifford Edward, Jr. *history professor*
Iseminger, Gary Hudson *philosophy educator*
Kucera, Karil J. *Ancient History Professor*
Soule, George Alan *literature educator*
Yandell, Cathy Marleen *language educator*

Roseville
Gross, Alan Gerald *rhetoric educator*

Saint Cloud
Hofsommer, Donovan Lowell *history professor*

Saint Paul
Capello, Ernesto *history professor*
DeRouchie, Jason S. *ancient language educator*
Huzar, Eleanor Goltz *historian, educator*
Keillor, Steven James *historian, educator*
Mather, Richard Burroughs *retired Chinese language and literature educator*
Monson, Dianne Lynn *literacy educator*
Weiner, Carl Dorian *retired historian*
Younoszai, Barbara B. *literature and language professor, researcher*

Vadnais Heights
Polakiewicz, Leonard Anthony *foreign language and literature educator*

Winona
Rabuse, Lynne Marie *language educator*

MISSISSIPPI

Brandon
Terrell, Elise I. *humanities educator*

Cleveland
Boschert, Thomas Neville *historian, educator*

Clinton
Potts, James B. III *literature and language professor*
Randle, Jonathan Thomas *language educator*

Decatur
Crenshaw, Phillip *history professor*

Fulton
Lowe, Robin Monaghan *language educator*

Gulfport
Harvey, Cathy Chance *literature and writing professor*
Swetman, Glenn Robert *literature and language professor, poet*

Hattiesburg
Chambers, Douglas Brent *history professor*
Mitchell, Geoffrey Scott *Spanish language educator*

Jackson
Daniels, Patsy Jean *English professor*
Gardner, Bonnie Bowie *history professor*

Kosciusko
Cox, Howard Andrew *English educator*

Macon
Barge, Laura Inez *literature and language professor*

Mississippi State
Lowery, Charles Douglas *historian, dean, educator*
Marcus, Alan I. *historian, educator*

Oxford
Landon, Michael de Laval *retired history professor*
Laurenzo, Frederick E. *retired history professor*

Raymond
Scifres, Denise Celia Le Blanc *historian, educator*

Senatobia
Banham, Sandra Rodgers *language educator*

Tougaloo
Ray, Larry L. *language educator*

University
Field, Lester L., Jr. *historian, educator*
Gussow, Adam *literature and language professor*
Manson, Neil Alan *philosopher, educator*

MISSOURI

Branson
Ford, Jean Elizabeth *retired language educator*

Branson West
Zank, Virginia *retired literature and language professor, educational consultant*

Cape Girardeau
Stepenoff, Bonnie Marie *history professor*

Columbia
Bien, Joseph Julius *philosophy educator*
Fulweiler, Howard Wells *language professional*
Horner, Winifred Bryan *humanities educator*
Keown, Linda Jane *language educator*
Mullen, Edward John, Jr. *Spanish language educator*
Schwartz, Richard Brenton *English language educator, dean, writer*
Strickland, Arvarh Eunice *history professor*

Gainesville
Sayles, Wayne Gerald *numismatist, writer, publisher*

Hillsboro
Everett, Gabrielle *history professor*
Loomis, Trish *literature and language professor*

Jefferson City
Greene, Debra Foster *history professor*
Heermance, J. Noel *literature and language professor*

Kansas City
Hoffmann, Donald *architectural historian*
Katz, Milton S. *humanities educator*
Oldani, Louis Joseph *literature educator*

Kirksville
Hanley, Mark Young *historian, educator, researcher*
Ling, Huping *history professor*
Maldonado-Class, Joaquin *language educator*
Rose, (M.) Lynn *history professor*

Knob Noster
Resch, Tonda Rae *language educator*

Liberty
Nore, Nano Ann *Art History Professor*

Mount Vernon
Shelton, Charity Faith *speach language pathologist*

Neosho
Wallace, Richard Le Roy Wayne *language educator*

Point Lookout
Blake, John Tyler *literature and language professor*

Saint Charles
Hurst, Spencer Eugene *literature and language professor, writer*
Tretter, Sue Ann *literature and language professor*
Whaley, Michael Joseph *history professor*

Saint Joseph
Adkins, Kaye *rhetoric and writing professor*
Morris, Stephen *philosopher, educator*

Saint Louis
Allen, Garland Edward *historian of science, professor, writer*
Balogh, María Teresa *language educator*
Barmann, Lawrence Francis *historian, educator*
Blalock, Kay J. *history professor*
Bornstein, Daniel E. *history professor, religious studies educator*
Bregni, Simone *language educator, researcher*
Bush, Harold K. *literature and language professor*
Casaregola, Vincent Gerard *literature and language professor*
Clark, Mark A. *language educator, director*
Eckelkamp, Elizabeth Bremer *literature and language professor*
Floyd, Richard D. *historian, writer*
Gillingham, John Rowley III *history professor, writer*
Gordon, Brian G. *history professor*
Hendrickson, William Lee *retired French language educator*
Herbert, Kevin Barry John *classics educator*
Hurley, Andrew J. *historian*
Kavadlo, Jesse *literature and language professor*
Krukowski, Lucian *philosopher, educator, artist*
Lawton, David Arthur *literature and language professor*
Lemons, Shelly L. *history professor*
Llewellyn, Kathleen Marie *language educator*
López, Oscar R. *language educator, researcher*
Messbarger, Rebecca Marie *literature and language professor*
Pegg, Mark Gregory *historian, educator*
Piccinini, Gualtiero *philosopher, educator*
Revard, Stella Hill Purce *English literature educator*
Rowan, Steven William *history professor*
Ruland, Richard Eugene *literature educator, critic, historian*
Sale, Merritt *classicist, educator, comparatist*
Schwarz, Egon *language educator, writer, critic*
Uraizee, Joya *literature and language professor*
van den Berg, Sara Jane *language educator*
Weixlmann, Joseph Norman, Jr. *language educator, academic administrator*
Wellman, Carl Pierce *philosophy educator*

Saint Peters
Long, Lydia Ann *literature and composition professor*

Springfield
Bartee, Wayne C. *retired history professor*
Bodo, Bela *historian, educator*
Burgess, Ruth Lenora Vassar *speech and language educator*
Burt, Larry W. *history professor, researcher*
Easley, June Ellen Price *genealogist*
Giglio, James Nicholas *humanities educator, writer*
Nugent, Pauline *ancient language educator*

Trenton
Cowling, Linda Sue *literature and language professor*

Union
Henderson, Russell J. *history professor*

Windyville
Condron, Barbara O'Guinn *philosopher, educator, academic administrator, writer*

MONTANA

Billings
Schaffer, Deborah Beth *English language educator*

Crow Agency
Crow, Joseph Medicine (Joe Crow) *Native American chief, historian*

Dillon
Krank, Sarah Cleland *humanities educator*

Kalispell
Voronina, Valeriya *language educator, consultant*

Missoula
Auge', Cynthia Riley *humanities educator*
Bitar, Samir I. *language educator*
Kittredge, William Alfred *humanities educator*

Poplar
Abbott, Margaret Ann *literature and language professor*

NEBRASKA

Dalton
Kandel, Sue Ellen *English language educator*

Kearney
Arrieta, Mariela *language educator*

Lincoln
Caramagno, Thomas Carmelo *English educator*
Curry, Dawne Yvette *history professor*
Hayden-Roy, Priscilla Ann *language educator*
Leinieks, Valdis *classicist, educator*
Mach, Jan Ellen Walkenhorst *literature educator, editor*
Mennard, Mike *literature and language professor*

Rader, Benjamin Gene *history educator*
Sawyer, Robert McLaran *historian, educator*

Omaha
Eikenberry, Angela M. *public administration professor*
Johanningsmeier, Charles *literature and language professor*
Knopp, Lisa *literature and language professor*
Lund, Jan Louise *art historian, educator*
Mordaunt, Owen Glen *literature and language professor, director*
Pasley, Anthony J. *history professor*
Reilly, Hugh Joseph *humanities educator, writer*
Stephens, William Olen *humanities educator, consultant*

York
McNeese, Beverly Diane *language educator*

NEVADA

Las Vegas
Barnes, H. Lee *English and creative writing educator, writer*
Clayson, William S. *history professor*
Erwin, Daniel Timothy *literature and language professor*
Gafford, Mary May Grimes *retired humanities educator*
Tanenhaus, David Spinoza *historian, educator*

North Las Vegas
Eliopulos, Tina Dawn Ann *language educator*
Williams, Richard L. *literature and language professor*

Reno
Glotfelty, Cheryll *literature and language professor*

NEW HAMPSHIRE

Concord
Tolles, Bryant Franklin, Jr. *retired history and art history professor*

Derry
Willard-Wotring, Sheila Duram *retired English language and humanities educator*

Dover
Johnson, Verdenal Hoag *English language educator, art and copy editor, writer*

Durham
Gould, Eliga H. *historian, educator*
Hapgood, Robert Derry *language educator*
Lofty, John Sylvester *English education and literature professor*
Ramadanovic, Petar *literature and language professor, writer*
Simic, Charles *language educator, poet*

Hanover
Bien, Peter Adolph *language educator, writer*
Daniell, Jere Rogers, II, *retired historian*
Doenges, Norman Arthur *retired classics educator*
Garthwaite, Gene Ralph *historian, educator*
Luxon, Thomas Hyatt *language educator, director*
Mansell, Darrel Lee, Jr. *language educator*
Oxenhandler, Neal *literature educator, writer*
Pease, Donald Eugene *humanities educator, department chairman*
Russell, Robert Hilton *Romance languages and literature educator*
Scherr, Barry Paul *foreign language educator*
Sheldon, Richard Robert *retired literature and language professor*
Shewmaker, Kenneth Earl *history professor*
Wright, James Edward *historian, educator, former academic administrator*

Laconia
Kenney, Kathleen *literature and language professor, department chairman*

Meredith
Heald, Bruce Day *English and music educator, historian*

New London
Anderson, Patrick D. *humanities educator*

Portsmouth
Harter, Hugh Anthony *foreign language educator*

NEW JERSEY

Atlantic Highlands
Levine, George Lewis *literature and language professor, critic*

Avon By The Sea
Potter, Emma Josephine Hill *language educator*

Belle Mead
Brown, Elizabeth Schmeck *fashion historian*

Bordentown
Zeitz, Joshua *history professor, writer*

Camden
Soll, Jacob *history professor*

Cape May
Savage, Maureen Walls *retired history professor*
Turner, Almon Richard *retired art historian, educator*

Chester
Lynch, Beverly Love *language educator*

Cranford
Russell, John Joseph *English educator*

East Brunswick
Zatlin, Phyllis *language educator, translator*

Edison
Granuzzo, Nanette *language educator*

Ewing
Kentengian, Isabel *language educator*
Taylor, James Stacey *philosopher, educator*

Glassboro
Blanck, Emily Vanessa *history professor*
Hasit, Cindi *literacy educator*
Heinzen, James Warren *history professor*
Hottle, Andrew D. *art historian*
Jorgensen, Donna W. *literature and language professor, department chairman*
Korieh, Chima J. *history professor*
Wiltenburg, Joy *history professor*

Hackettstown
Holt, John R. *literature and language professor*

Highland Park
Safir, Ken *linguist, educator*

Hightstown
Schorske, Carl Emil *historian, educator*

Lakewood
Bennett, Scott H. *history professor*
Rader, Pamela J. *literature and language professor*

Lincroft
Zigo, Paul Edward *historian, educator*

Lodi
McParland, Robert Patrick *literature educator, writer*
Vecchio, Maria Theresa *history professor*

Madison
Bazán-Figueras, Patricia *literature and language professor*
Benson, Peter *literature and language professor*
Rosales Herrera, Raúl Joaquin *language educator*

Mahwah
Martin, Sandra Hancock *language educator*

Maplewood
Knight, Nathaniel *history professor*

Montclair
Afzal-Khan, Fawzia *literature and language professor*
Dufour, Josette Isabelle *language educator*
Lapp, Benjamin N. *history professor*
Obydol-Alexandre, Kareen *literature and language professor*

New Brunswick
Adickes, Sandra Elaine *language educator, writer*
Gillette, William *historian, educator*
Grob, Gerald N. *historian, educator*
Jenkins, Reese V. *historian, educator*
O'Neill, William Lawrence *retired history professor*
Rowsell, Jennifer *literature and language professor*
Schrepfer, Susan R. *history professor, director*
Wailoo, Keith Andrew *historian, educator*

Newark
Chukunta, Ndubuisi (Niki) Konyeaso Onuoha *literature and language professor*
Cowans, Jon *history professor*
Langhorne, Richard Tristan Bailey *history professor*
Lynch, Jack *literature and language professor*
Price, Clement Alexander *historian, educator*
Schweizer, Karl Wolfgang *historian, educator, author*

North Brunswick
Moon, Kathleen K. *language arts educator*

Nutley
Marée, Kathleen Nancy *retired language educator*

Piscataway
Zhilina, Irina *language educator*

Pomona
Jacobson, Kristin J. *literature educator*
Lubenow, William Cornelius *historian, educator*

Princeton
Aarsleff, Hans *linguistics educator*
Bermann, Sandra Lekas *English language educator*
Bishop, George Reginald, Jr. *foreign language educator*
Bowersock, Glen Warren *retired historian, educator*
Brombert, Victor Henri *literature educator, author*
Brooks, Peter (Preston) *literature educator, department chairman, writer*
Brown, Leon Carl *historian, educator*
Brown, Peter Robert Lamont *historian, history professor*
Cooper, John Madison *philosophy educator*
Corngold, Stanley Alan *language educator, writer*
Deming, James C. *history professor*
Ermolaev, Herman Sergei *Slavic languages educator*
Fleming, John Vincent *humanities educator*
Ford, Andrew Laughlin *ancient language educator*
Grafton, Anthony Thomas *history professor*
Harman, Gilbert Helms *philosophy educator*
Hollander, Robert B., Jr. *retired romance languages educator*
Howarth, William (Louis) *literature and language professor, writer*
Howell, David Luke *history professor*
Hynes, Samuel *language educator, writer*
Israel, Jonathan I. *history professor*
Itzkowitz, Norman *history professor*
Jeffery, Peter Grant *musicologist, fine arts educator*
Jordan, William Chester *historian, educator*
Keeley, Edmund LeRoy *literature educator, writer, translator*
Knoepflmacher, Ulrich Camillus *literature educator*
Koepplin, Leslie W. *historian*
Mc Pherson, James Munro *history professor*
Moote, A. Lloyd *history professor*
Nehamas, Alexander *philosophy educator*
Paret, Peter *historian*
Rodgers, Daniel Tracy *historian, educator*
Rubin, Dorothy Molly *language educator, writer*
Scott, Joan Wallach *historian, educator*
Shimizu, Yoshiaki *art historian*
Walter, Hugo Günther *humanities educator, poet*
Weigert, Laura *history professor*
West, Cornel Ronald *humanities educator, writer*
White, Morton Gabriel *philosopher, writer, historian, retired educator*
Wilentz, Sean *historian, educator, writer*
Wilmerding, John *art historian, educator, curator*
Ziolkowski, Theodore Joseph *literature educator, writer*

Sewell
Brookins, Birdena *literature and language professor*

South Orange
Molesky, Mark *history professor*

Stewartsville
Busch, Beverly Gail *English and literature educator, dean*

Teaneck
Brownridge, Sonia Marie *language educator*
Brudner, Helen Gross *history professor, political science professor*
Gordon, Lois G. *language educator*
Wiener, Joel Howard *historian, educator*
Williams, John Alfred *educator, author*

Tenafly
Rudy, Dorothy Lucille *poet, educator*

Toms River
Bosley, Karen Lee Foley *language and communications educator*
Lauro, Dana *literature and language professor*

Trenton
George, Emery Edward *foreign language and studies educator, writer*

Union
DeMarco, Michael R. *history professor, writer*
Shaw, Thomas M. *art historian, educator*

Wall
Mudd, Mary Michaels *historian*

Wayne
Rogoff, Paula Drimmer *English and foreign language educator*

West Long Branch
Gardner, Burdett Harmon *English language educator*
Lake, Elsa Taboada *retired language educator*

West Paterson
Varley, Herbert Paul *Japanese language and cultural history educator*

Woodbury
Donahue, Mary Lee *American English language professor, editor and author*

NEW MEXICO

Albuquerque
Croft, William Albert *linguistics educator*
Davies, Thomas Mockett, Jr. *history professor*
Hannan, Barbara Ellon *philosophy educator, lawyer*
Hutton, Paul Andrew *historian, educator, writer*
Lange, Dale Lowell *language educator, researcher*
Pabisch, Peter Karl *literature and language professor, humanities educator*
Peña, Juan José *retired interpreter*
Richter, Harvena *retired literature educator, poet*
Spidle, Jake W. *history professor*
Szasz, Ferenc M. *historian, educator*

Clovis
Johnson, Janett *literature and language professor*

Farmington
Peterson Gerstner, Janet *English professor*

Gallup
Edgewater, Virginia Lynn *language educator*

Hobbs
Connell, Linda Evans *literature and language professor*
Sumruld, Bill *history professor*

Las Cruces
Barquet, Jesus Jose *literature and language professor, writer*
Laroche, Jacques M. *language educator*
Neves, Aexandra Moreira *language educator*

Las Vegas
Simpson, Dorothy Audrey *retired speech educator*

Los Lunas
Melzer, Richard Anthony *historian, educator*

Portales
Elder, Donald Cameron *history professor, broadcast executive*

Roswell
Gallagher, Bill *history professor*

Santa Fe
Lehmberg, Stanford Eugene *historian, educator*
Peters, Margaret Annette *English language educator*

Silver City
Fritz, Scott *history professor*
Toth, Bill D. *literature and language professor*

Socorro
Lara-Martínez, Rafael *humanities educator*

Taos
Bolls, Imogene Lamb *English language educator, poet*

NEW YORK

Albany
Acosta-Belén, Edna *literature and language professor*
Armour-Garb, Bradley Philip *philosopher, educator*
Chan, May Caroline *language educator*
Howell, Robert Charles *philosopher, educator*
Joris, Pierre *literature and language professor*
Lenardon, Robert Joseph *classics educator*
Magnus, P.D. *philosopher, educator*
Olmstead, Lucinda Sue *English professor*
Reese, William Lewis *philosophy educator*
Steinbock, Bonnie *philosophy educator*
Ungar, Barbara Louise *literature and language professor*
Ziamandanis, Claire M. *language educator*

Alfred
Anderson, Martha G. *history professor*
Eaklor, Vicki Lynn *history professor*
Newsome, William Brian *history professor*

Amherst
Kurtz, Paul *philosopher, educator, writer, publisher*

Annandale On Hudson
Ashbery, John Lawrence *language educator, poet, playwright, art critic*
Morrow, Bradford *novelist. editor, educator*

Aurora
Farnsworth, Beatrice Brodsky *history professor*

Bellvale
Murnion, William Edward *philosopher, theologian*

Binghamton
Brinker-Gabler, Gisela *literature educator*
Corley, Scott Anthony *history professor, academic service provider*
Einhorn, Lois J. *rhetoric and communication professor, writer*
Gaddis Rose, Marilyn *literature educator, translator*
Kadish, Gerald Edwin *history professor*
Polachek, Dora Eisenberg *humanities educator*
Sklar, Kathryn Kish *historian, educator*

Brockport
Bucholz, Arden *historian, educator*
Leslie, William Bruce *history professor*
O'Brien, Kenneth Paul *historian, educator*
Ortiz, Joseph M. *literature and language professor, writer*
Rossi, Frank Dominick *language educator*
Wakefield, Wanda Ellen *historian, educator, sports association executive*

Bronx
Alcaide, Juan Abraham *literature and language professor*
Balestra, Dominic J. *philosopher, educator*
Bonelli, Vincent Francis *history professor*
Bullaro, Grace Russo *literature, film and foreign language educator, critic*
Dean, Nancy *literature educator, retired playwright*
Hallett, Charles Arthur, Jr. *language educator, humanities educator*
Hermalyn, Gary Douglas *historian, publisher, educator*
Himmelberg, Robert Franklin *historian, educator*
Kirsch, George Benson *history professor*
Newman, Zelda Kahan *linguist*
Penella, Robert Joseph *ancient language educator*
Ray, Carina *history professor*
Rosenthal, Bernice Glatzer *history professor*
Spatt, Hartley Steven *humanities educator*
Ultan, Lloyd *historian, educator*
Wabuda, Susan *historian, educator*
Zubeck, Jacqueline Ann (Nina Zubeck) *literature and language professor*

Bronxville
Peters, Sarah Whitaker *art historian, writer*
Pollin, Burton Ralph *language educator*

Brooklyn
Asekoff, Louis S. *literature and language professor, director*
Childers, William P. *literature and language professor*
Edelheit, Abraham J. *history professor*
Flam, Jack Donald *art historian, educator*
Forsberg, Suzanne *humanities educator*
Hoogenboom, Ari Arthur *retired history professor*
Infante-Voelker, Josefina *literature and language professor, writer*

King, Margaret Leah *history professor*
Kriftcher, Noel N. *humanities educator, science director*
Lobron, Barbara L. *speech educator, editor, photographer, writer*
Lopate, Phillip *language educator, writer*
Miller, Walter James *retired literature educator, writer*
Molina_Figueroa, Sintia E. *language educator*
Reeves, William *language educator*
Renner, Bernd *literature and language professor*
Rosenthal, Abigail Laura *philosophy educator*
Sanua, Marianne Rachel *historian, educator*
Swaminathan, Srividhya *literature and language professor*
Tague, Gregory Frank *literature and language professor*
Trefousse, Hans Louis *history professor*

Buffalo
Bachman, Charles R. *literature and language professor*
Cohen, Richard *philosopher, educator*
Conte, Joseph Mark *literature and language professor*
Ellis, Richard Emanuel *historian, educator*
Fuller, David Randall *musicologist*
Gazzo, Arthur D., Jr. *history professor*
Iggers, Georg Gerson *history professor*
Jurasek, Barbara S. *language educator*
McKee, Eliane *retired literature and language professor*
Merini, Rafika *humanities and foreign languages educator, writer*
Milligan, John Drane *retired historian, educator*
Paterson, Eleanor Cohen *language educator, director*
Peradotto, John Joseph *retired classics educator, editor*
Ross, Gary Earl *writing educator*
Siedlecki, Peter Anthony *English language and literature educator*
Twagilimana, Aimable *language educator, writer*
Wölck, Wolfgang Hans-Joachim *linguist, educator*
Woolverton, Diane Marie *literature language and education professor*

Canton
Goldberg, Rita Maria *foreign language educator*
Nouryeh, Christopher *humanities educator*

Charlton
Kekes, John *philosopher, educator*

Corning
Guzzy, Mary Elizabeth *humanities educator, director*

Cortland
Anderson, Donna Kay *musicologist, educator*
Weaver, Wesley James III *literature and language professor*

Dobbs Ferry
Poian, Edward Licio *historian*

East Aurora
Perry, Marion J.H. *English educator*

Elmira
Leveen, Pauline *retired history professor, government professor*

Endicott
Cocozzella, Peter *retired language educator*
Conlon, Michael James *literature and language professor*

Flushing
Alcalay, Ammiel *literature and language professor, writer*
Bird, Thomas Edward *foreign language and literature educator*
Khalil, Andrea Flores *literature and language professor*
Lonigan, Paul Raymond *language professional, educator*
Rabassa, Gregory *language educator, translator, poet*
Sungolowsky, Joseph *literature educator*
Tytell, John *literature educator, writer*
Winter, Amy *art historian, critic*

Forest Hills
Kra, Pauline Skornicki *French language educator*

Fredonia
Jarvis, Joseph Anthony *history professor*
McVicker, Jeanette *literature and language professor*
Stinson, John Jerome *literature and language professor*
Wescott, Howard Blakely *retired humanities educator*
Zlotchew, Clark Michael *Spanish educator*

Freeport
Ledkovsky, Marina *retired Slavic languages and literature educator*

Fresh Meadows
Duckett, Lila Wheeler *retired language educator, writer*

Garden City
Bouchard, Wendy Ann Borstel *language educator*
Brett, Laurel *literature and language professor*
Jenkins, Kenneth Vincent *literature educator, writer*
McNair, Marcia L. *language educator, writer, editor*
Okoampa-Ahoofe, Kwame *language educator, historian*

Gardiner
Mabee, Carleton *historian, educator*

Geneseo
Cook, William Robert *history professor, religious studies educator*
Evans, Beverly Jean *literature and language professor*
Herzman, Ronald B. *literature and language professor*
Scalzo, Joseph *history professor*

Greenvale
Dircks, Phyllis Toal *language educator*

Hamilton
Bien, Gloria *Chinese educator*
Knuth-Klenck, Deborah Jane *English and women's studies educator*
McIntyre, Lee Cameron *philosophy educator*
Rotter, Andrew Jon *history educator*

Hancock
Senia, Grace Melanie *language and music educator*

Hempstead
Galofaro, Manuel *language educator*
Zhou, Zuhan *literature educator*

Highland Falls
Combs, Farah *ancient language educator*

Hillsdale
Parmet, Herbert Samuel *historian, writer*

Holley
Lepkowski, Suzanne Joy *language educator*

Huntington
Anzalone, Robert S. *history professor*
Williams, Charles Theodore *language educator*

Ithaca
Abrams, Meyer Howard *language educator*
Colby-Hall, Alice Mary *language educator*
Deinert, Herbert *German language, literature and history educator*
Dimitrova, Nora Mitkova *classics scholar*
Eddy, Donald Davis *language educator*
Hohendahl, Peter Uwe *German language and literature educator*
Hull, Isabel Virginia *history professor*
Kammen, Michael *historian, educator*
LaCapra, Dominick Charles *historian, educator*
LaFeber, Walter Frederick *historian, educator, writer*
Laquatra, Joseph *humanities educator*
McDougal, Stuart Yeatman *comparative literature educator, author*
O'Connor, Stanley James *Asian studies educator*
Radzinowicz, Mary Ann *language educator*
Silbey, Joel Henry *history professor*
Sukle, Robert J. *language educator*
Zaslaw, Neal *musicologist*

Jamaica
Coppa, Frank John *historian, educator*
Ekbatani, Glayol *language educator, director, writer*
Eltabib, Sarah *history professor*
Kinkley, Jeffrey C. *historian*
Parmet, Robert David *historian, educator*
Ramlal, Derek *history professor, personal trainer*

Johnson City
Bernardo, Aldo Sisto *retired foreign language educator*

Kingston
Davila, Elisa *language and literature educator*

Long Island City
Coogan, Timothy Christopher, II, *history professor, researcher*

Loudonville
Barbir, Karl K. *history professor*
Davies, Julian A. *philosopher, educator, archivist*
Fiore, Peter Amadeus *English educator, priest*
Teepe, Christopher John *literature and language professor*

Melville
Levin, Richard Louis *retired language educator*

Middletown
Wright, Kathleen M. *literature and language professor*

New Hyde Park
Low, Frederick Emerson *language educator*

New Paltz
Brown, Peter David Gilson *German language educator*

New Rochelle
Buonanno, Elda *literature and language professor*
Morgan, Joseph Gerard *history professor*

New York
Achinstein, Peter Jacob *philosopher, educator*
Anderson, Bonnie S. *history professor, writer*
Bagnall, Roger Shaler *history professor, director*
Baker, Paul Raymond *historian, educator*
Belknap, Robert Lamont *literature educator*
Bender, Thomas *historian, educator*
Berghahn, Volker Rolf *history professor*
Bernard, Claudie *literature educator*
Bertram, Paul Benjamin *language educator*
Billows, Richard A. *history professor*
Bishop, Thomas Walter *French language and literature educator*
Block, Ned *philosopher, educator*
Bonfante, Larissa *classics educator*
Brinkley, Alan David *historian, educator, former academic administrator*
Brown, Jonathan *art historian, educator*
Butz, William Fortune *literature and language professor*
Cahn, Steven Mark *philosopher, educator*
Calotychos, Vangelis *literature and cultural studies, language professor*
Caro, Robert Allan *historian, writer*
Cavallo, Jo Ann *language educator*
Caws, Mary Ann *literature and language professor*
Chapman, Herrick Eaton *historian, educator*
Coatsworth, John Henry *history professor, writer, dean*
Cohen, Morton Norton *English educator, writer*
Collins, Nancy Walbridge *historian, educator*
Cook, Blanche Wiesen *historian, educator, journalist*
Cornelio, Maria A. *language educator*
Dawson, Philip *history professor*
de Grazia, Victoria *historian, educator, writer*
Del Risco, Enrique A. *language educator*
de Menil, Lois Pattison *historian, philanthropist*
den Dikken, Marcel *language educator*
Driver, Martha Westcott *literature educator, researcher, writer*
Duberman, Martin *historian, gay activist, educator*
Fine, Kit *philosophy educator*
Flescher, Sharon *art historian, educator*
Flint, Aili *retired literature and language professor*
Foner, Eric *historian, educator*
Gasman, Daniel E. *retired history professor, writer*
Gay, Peter *historian, educator, writer*
Ginter, Valerian Alexius *urban historian, educator*
Gluck, Carol *history professor*
Gordon, Linda *history educator*
Gromada, Thaddeus V. *historian, academic administrator*
Haahr, Joan Gluckauf *English language educator*
Haft, Adele J. *classicist, educator*
Harris, Katherine Safford *speech and hearing educator*
Hartman, Joan Edna *retired literature educator, dean, provost*
Harvey, David W. *humanities educator*
Heffner, Richard Douglas *historian, educator, communications consultant, television producer*
Helly, Dorothy Oxman *historian, educator*
Hirsch, Edward Mark *language educator, poet*
Hoeflin, Ronald Kent *philosopher, writer*
Holquist, James Michael *literature educator, department chairman*
Hovde, Carl Frederick *language professional, educator*
Howe, Florence *literature educator, writer, publisher*
Hyman, Arthur *philosopher, educator*
Jackson, Kenneth Terry *historian, academic administrator*
Jackson, Robert L. *literature and language professor*
Kaiser, Walter *language educator*
Karsen, Sonja Petra *retired literature educator*
Katz, Esther *historian, educator*
Kaur, Harminder *language educator*
Kerz, Louise (Louise Hirschfeld) *historian*
Kimber, Karen Beecher *ESL educator*
Krinsky, Carol Herselle *art historian, educator*
Kroeber, Karl *language educator*
Leibowitz, Herbert Akiba *literature and language professor, writer*
Levi, Isaac *philosophy educator*
Lindo-Fuentes, Hector *history professor*
Lippman, Sharon Rochelle *art historian and therapist, filmmaker*
Ludden, David Ellsworth *history professor*
Malin, Irving *language educator, critic*
Manthorne, Katherine E. *art historian, educator*
Matteson, John Thomas *English educator, lawyer*
May, Gita *literature educator*
Maynard, John Rogers *language educator*
Mehta, Linn Cary *literature educator*
Oakes, James *history professor*
Odenweller, Robert Paul *philatelist, trade association administrator, retired pilot*
Oppenheimer, Paul *literature educator, poet*
Papalia, Diane Ellen *humanities educator*
Patterson, Remington Perrigo *retired English language educator*
Paxton, Robert Owen *historian, educator*
Plottel, Jeanine Parisier *foreign language educator*
Prescott, Anne Lake *English language educator*
Quigley, Austin Edmund *literature and language professor, former dean*
Quiñones Keber, Eloise *art historian, educator*
Quiroz, Alfonso Walter *history professor*
Rabassa, Clementine Christos *humanities educator, translator*
Randall, Francis Ballard *retired historian, educator, writer*
Ravitch, Diane Silvers *historian, writer, government official, educator*
Regalado, Nancy Freeman *language educator*
Rheins, Carl Jeffrey *historian, educator*
Romero, Raul Enrique *literature and language professor*
Rosand, David *art historian, educator*
Rothman, David J. *historian, educator*
Rozencvaig, Perla *language educator*
Ruch, Barbara *Japanese literature and culture educator emerita*
Scheindlin, Raymond Paul *professor Hebrew literature*
Schiffer, Stephen *philosopher, educator*
Schirokauer, Conrad *history professor*
Scribner, Charles III *art historian, writer*
Seigel, Jerrold Edward *historian, writer*
Selig, Karl-Ludwig *literature and language professor*
Shao, Qiuxia *literature and language professor*
Sherry, Lee Francis *literature and language professor*
Shires, Linda M. *English educator, writer*
Siraisi, Nancy Gillian *historian, writer, educator*
Stade, George Gustav *humanities educator*
Stadler, Eva Maria *literature and language professor*
Stern, Fritz Richard *historian, educator*
Stevens, Rosemary Anne *medicine and public health historian, artist*
Stimpson, Catharine Rosalind *literature educator, writer*
Tanselle, George Thomas *language educator, foundation administrator*
Taran, Leonardo *classicist, educator*
Tusiani, Joseph *foreign language educator, author*
Unger, Peter Kenneth *philosophy educator*
von Hagen, Mark Louis *history professor, director*
Wakeman, Rosemary *history professor*
Waldhorn, Arthur *literature educator, researcher, scriptwriter*
Wasser, Henry *retired American literature and sociology educator*
Weil-Garris Brandt, Kathleen (Kathleen Brandt) *art historian*
Weinberg, H. Barbara *art historian, educator, curator*
Weinstein, Barbara *history professor*
Wixom, William David *art historian, museum administrator, educator*
Wortman, Marlene Stein *historian*
Wortman, Richard S. *historian, educator*
Wyschogrod, Edith *philosophy educator*
Younts, Shane-Ann *speech educator*

Newark
Biddle, Jane Lammert *retired English educator*

Newburgh
Adams, Barbara *literature and language professor, poet, writer*

Niagara Falls
Wos, Paul M. *music educator, infosystems specialist, educator*

North Collins
Bowman, Georgianne *historian, reporter*

Oakland Gardens
Polak, Emil Joseph *history professor, researcher*

Old Westbury
Hegde, Narayan *language educator*
Hobson, Christopher Z. *literature and language professor*
Watson, Denton L. *history professor*

Oneonta
Doughty, Amie A. *language educator*
Eluwawalage, Damayanthie *assistant professor, researcher, costume historian*

Orangeburg
Dolgin, Ellen Ecker *English and gender studies professor*

Oswego
Bishop, Rand *retired humanities educator*
Smiley, Marilynn Jean *musicologist*

Pittsford
French, Henry Pierson, Jr. *retired historian, educator*

Pleasant Valley
Ghedini, Gloria Maryann *language educator*

Pleasantville
Benton, Janetta Rebold *art historian, professor, writer*
Meisel, Martin *retired English and comparative literature educator*
Mirakian-Escobar, Rachel Ann *language educator*

Port Washington
Williams, George Leo *historian, retired secondary school educator, landmark director*

Potsdam
Casper, Stephen Trevor *historian, educator*

Poughkeepsie
Bartlett, Lynn Conant *English literature educator*
Church, Jennifer *philosopher, educator*
Daniels, Elizabeth Adams *English language educator*
Gregio, Marcus D. *literature and language professor*
Hathaway, Richard Dean *retired language educator*
Olsen, Barbara A. *literature and language professor, classicist, educator*
Pohl, Michaela *historian, educator*
Qiu, Peipei *language educator*
Russell, Paul Elliott *literature and language professor*
Sharp, Ronald Alan *language educator, writer, former dean*

Purchase
Hartmann, Van Charles *literature and language professor*

Queensbury
Gallipeo, Paul *literature and language professor*

Rochester
Berman, Milton *history professor*
Black, Candace Regan *language educator*
Caton, Scott Brenon *history professor*
Chiarenza, Carl *art historian, critic, artist, educator*
Gordon, Dane Rex *philosophy educator, minister*
Griffin, Oliver *history professor*
Hauser, William Barry *historian, educator*
Herminghouse, Patricia Anne *foreign language educator*
Johnson, Bruce Marvin *language educator*
Joyce, John Joseph *language educator*
Lansky, Lewis *history professor*
Meconi, Honey *musicologist, writer*
Niu, Greta Aiyu *language educator*
Nolasco, Lori D. *literature and language professor*

Paauw, Scott H. *linguist, educator*

Rockville Centre
Fitzgerald, Janet Anne *philosophy educator, academic administrator*

Saint Bonaventure
Cellini, Alva V. *language educator, women's studies, translator*
Mazon, Margaret Fausold *language educator*

Saratoga Springs
Caruso, Adrienne Iorio *retired language educator*

Scarsdale
Brilliant, Richard *art historian, educator*
Graff, Henry Franklin *historian, educator*
Johnson, William Alexander *philosophy and theology educator, clergyman*

Schenectady
Heinegg, Peter *literature and language professor, writer*

Seaford
González del Real, Rodolfo Antonio *language educator*

Selden
Busby, Robert Wilson *history professor*
West, Norman R. *history professor*

Skaneateles
Vetrano, Anthony Joseph *foreign language and literature professor*

Slingerlands
Zacek, Joseph Frederick *historian, educator*

Snyder
Levine, George Richard *language educator*

Staten Island
Anderson, Robert Mapes *history professor*
Hensley, Donald Melton *literature and language professor*
Mbah, Emmanuel Mbah *history professor*

Stony Brook
Aronoff, Mark H. *linguistics educator, writer, consultant*
Fontanella, Luigi *literature and language professor, writer*
Grim, Patrick Neal *philosopher, educator, logician*
Ihde, Don *philosopher, educator*
Kuspit, Donald Burton *art historian, critic, educator*
Mignone, Mario B. *language educator*
Olster, Stacey Michele *literature and language professor*
Silverman, Hugh J. *philosophy educator*
Simpson, Louis Aston Marantz *language educator, writer*

Suffern
Bierman, Mara-Lee *language educator*
Mitchell, Shamika Ann *literature and language professor*

Syracuse
Carnes, Jeffrey Scott *ancient language educator*
Carter Grosso, Erika *language educator*
Chamorro Galán, María Gloria *language educator*
Eisele, Kathleen L. *composition, literature educator*
Ende, Mark L. *language educator*
García-Calderón, Myrna *language educator*
Greenberg, Gerald R. *language educator, dean*
Langdon, John W. *history professor*
Powell, James Matthew *history professor*
Prettyman, John A. *language educator*
Sternlicht, Sanford *literature educator, writer*
Waddy, Patricia A. *art historian, retired architecture educator*

Troy
Ahlers, Rolf Willi *philosopher, theologian*

Utica
Boylan, Kristina A. *history professor*
Gifford, James J. *literature and language professor*
Liang, Yixiong *language educator*
Vendetta, Constance Joan *language educator*
Wagner, Frederick Reese *retired language educator*
Zogby, William Joseph *history professor, management consultant*

Valhalla
Leone, Stephen Joseph *language educator, computer technician, consultant*

Vestal
Donnelly, Mary Elizabeth *language educator*
Oggins, Robin S. *history professor*

Wantagh
Smits, Edward John *historian, consultant*

Watertown
Palmer, Ronald R *history professor*

Watkins Glen
LaMoreaux, Kathleen Ann Warner *English educator*

Webster
Warford, Mark Kellison *language educator, consultant*

West Hempstead
Chciuk-Celt, Alexandra M. *language educator*

West Point
Czajkoski, Christina Marie *language educator*
Gentile, Gian P. *history professor*

White Plains
Barrera-Tobon, Carolina *language educator, researcher*

Williamsville
Garton, Charles *classics educator*

Wyandanch
Fonseca, Alejandra *language educator*

NORTH CAROLINA

Andrews
Fonda, Ronald Alan *epistemologist*

Boiling Springs
Cox, Tamara *language educator*
Vanderburg, Timothy Warren *history professor*

Boone
Cox, Victoria Kathleen *humanities educator*
Frindethie, Martial Kokroa *literature and language professor*

Chapel Hill
Binotti, Lucia *language educator*
Brown, Michael L. *language educator*
Browning, Christopher R. *historian, educator*
Caldwell, Kia Lilly *humanities educator*
Davis, Sarah Irwin *retired language educator*
Flora, Joseph M(artin) *language educator*
Grendler, Paul Frederick *historian, educator*
Gura, Philip Francis *English and American literature educator*
Kohn, Richard H. *historian, educator*
Li, Wendan *literature and language professor, researcher*
Nelson, Philip Francis *musicologist, consultant, conductor*
Pérez, Louis A., Jr. *history professor*
Rabil, Albert, Jr. *humanities educator*
Radding, Cynthia *historian, educator*
Riess, Werner *ancient history and classics professor*
Sherman, Daniel James *art history professor*
Strauss, Albrecht Benno *retired language educator, editor*
Summers, Sandra Lindemann *language educator*
Visser, Robin *humanities educator*
Watson, Harry L. *history professor, director*
West, III, William Custis *retired ancient language educator*
Williamson, Joel Rudolph *humanities educator, writer*
Yow, Valerie Raleigh *historian, writer, counselor*

Charlotte
Aydin, Cemil *history professor*
Crickenberger, Heather Marcelle *literature and language professor*
Goldfield, David *history professor, writer*
Munroe, Jennifer *literature and language professor*
Myers, Robert Manson *language educator, writer*

Dallas
Neuman, Deborah *language educator*

Davidson
Cole, Richard Cargill *language educator*

Dublin
Sellers, Ella Jo *literature and language professor*

Durham
Armstrong, Nancy *literature and language professor*
Baxter, Stephen Bartow *retired historian*
Brothers, Thomas *musicologist, educator*
Budd, Louis John *language educator*
Butters, Ronald Richard *language educator*
Clay, Diskin *classical studies educator*
Colton, Joel *historian, educator*
Davis, Calvin De Armond *historian, educator*
Holley, Irving Brinton, Jr. *historian, educator*
Randall, Dale Bertrand Jonas *English language educator*
Scales, Jean Norris *retired English language educator*
Scott, Anne Byrd Firor *history professor*
Smith, Grover C(leveland) *language educator*
Williams, George Walton *language educator*

Elkin
Casper, Rick D. *literature and language professor*

Elon
de Lama, Mayte *language educator*

Fayetteville
Ajani, Timothy T. *language educator*
Curry, Virginia Frances *retired language educator*
Morley, James Thomas *philosopher, educator*

Fearrington Village
Cell, Gillian Townsend *retired historian, educator*

Franklin
Johnson, Herbert Alan *historian, lawyer*

Gerton
Whitt, Margaret Earley *retired literature and language professor*

Goldsboro
Bass, Tara Thompson *literature and language professor, director*

Greensboro
Fonge, Fuabeh P. *history professor*
Gorden, Richard *history faculty, associate director*
Hunter, Phyllis Whitman *history professor*
Israel, Adrienne Manns *history professor*
Levy, Michele Frucht *literature and language professor*
Miller, Don Maz *literature and language professor*
Nieman, Valerie Gail *writer, language educator, journalist*
Penninger, Frieda Elaine *retired literature educator*
Schweninger, Loren *history professor*

Greenville
Beers, Burton Floyd *historian, educator*
Daneri, Juan J. *literature and language professor*
Deena, Seodial Frank *language educator*
Palmer, Michael A. *history professor*
Romer, Frank E. *literature and language professor, department chairman*
Stevens, John A. *classicist, educator*
Twark, Jill E. *language educator*

Hendersonville
Harris, James Braxton *retired humanities educator, freelance/self-employed writer*
Pierard, Richard Victor *history educator*

High Point
Chavis, Glenn Romero *retired historian, writer*

Jacksonville
Kimball, Lynn Jerome *historian*

Kings Mountain
Depew, Ellie *language educator, writer*

Matthews
Black, Albert George *English language educator*

Montreat
Hernandez, Horacio Antonio *literature and language professor*

Mooresville
Turner, Michael G. *history professor*

Mount Olive
Charles, Asselin *literature and language professor*

Pinehurst
Nordloh, David Joseph *literature and language professor, dean*

Raleigh
Kiec, Kate Smolko *literature and language professor*
LaMonte, Jennifer Adams Emnett *history professor*
Larsen, Jamie Strauss *technical and professional writing educator, consultant*
Moore, Nancey Fay *history educator*
Morrison, James Emerson *English language educator*
Rhodes, Donald Robert *musicologist, educator, retired electrical engineer*
Riddle, John Marion *retired humanities educator*
Ruark, Gibbons *retired literature and language professor*
Slattery, Michael G. *humanities educator*
Tague, Fanella *language educator*
Welch, Milton Lamont *literature and language professor*

Rocky Mount
Holmes, Marbeth Hunt *humanities educator*

Roxboro
Gates, Rosalie Prince *history professor*

Salisbury
Freeze, Gary Richard *historian*

Sanford
Watson, David Riddle *literature and language professor*

Shelby
Zamora, Bobbie Jean *literature and language professor*

Supply
Pontious, Robert Ronald *literature and language professor*

Wilmington
Stanfield-Maddox, Elizabeth *language educator, writer, translator, library advocate*

Winston Salem
Barnett, Richard Chambers *historian, educator*
Covey, Cyclone *history professor*
Forrest-Carter, Audrey Faye *literature and writing professor*
Hendricks, J(ames) Edwin *retired historian, educator, consultant, author*
Margitić, Milorad R. *language educator, researcher*
May, Darlene Rae *language educator*
Miller, Richard Harry *philosopher, educator*
Shapere, Dudley *philosophy educator*

NORTH DAKOTA

Bismarck
Camp, Gregory Scott *history professor*
Newborg, Gerald Gordon *retired state archives administrator*
Rettig, Pam *literature educator*

Dickinson
Johnson, Bonnie Tunnicliff *History Instructor*
Laman, Barbara *retired literature and language professor*
Larson, Carl Frederick William *retired literature and language professor*

Grand Forks
Berger, Albert Isaac *historian, consultant*
Handy-Marchello, Barb *history educator, researcher*
Wolfe, Eric Andrew *literature and language professor*

Jamestown
Joy, Mark Stephen *history professor, department chairman*

Mayville
Brunsdale, Mitzi Louisa Mallarian *language educator, critic*
McMahon, Dalton Edward *history professor, social sciences educator, department chairman*

Minot
Henderson, Liana Solorzano *language educator*

Wahpeton
Reubish, Gary Richard *English language educator*

OHIO

Akron
Fant, J. Clayton *classical studies professor*
Knepper, George W. *historian, educator*
Williams, William Proctor *literature educator*

Ashland
Moser, John Evan *history professor*

Athens
Borchert, Donald Marvin *philosopher, educator*
Deguchi, Ayako *language educator*
Ehrlich, Philip *philosophy educator*
Marks, Emilia Alonso *language educator, researcher*
Matthews, Jack (John Harold Matthews) *language educator, writer*
Ulbrich, David J. *history professor*
Whealey, Lois Deimel *humanities scholar*
Wrage, William *retired language educator*

Avon Lake
Douglas, Carolyn Grace *language educator*

Beachwood
Davis, Ben, Jr. *literature and language professor*

Bowling Green
Browne, Ray Broadus *popular culture educator*
Grunden, Walter Eugene *history professor*

Brecksville
Pappas, Effie Vamis *language educator, finance educator, writer, poet, artist*

Canton
Armentrout, Allison *literature and language professor*
Vazzano, Frank Paul *historian, educator*

Cedarville
Mach, Thomas S. *history professor*
Wood, Michelle Gaffner *language educator*

Chillicothe
Reiger, John Franklin *history professor, researcher*

Cincinnati
Alexander, John Kurt *history professor*
Bleznick, Donald William *Romance languages educator*
Chekour, Adam *interpreter, educator*
Ciani, Alfred Joseph *dean*
Harmon, Patrick *historian, retired editor, commentator*
Kamesar, Adam *literature educator*
Phillips, Christopher *history professor, researcher*
Prince, Susan Hukill *ancient language educator*
Sauer, Matthew James *history professor*
Schrier, Arnold *historian, educator*

Cleveland
Borowitz, Helen Osterman *art historian*
Dancyger, Ruth *art historian*
Engelking, Tama Lea *language educator, department chairman*
Greppin, John Aird Coutts *philologist, editor, educator*
Miller, Genevieve *retired medical historian*
Moutafakis, Nicholas James *philosopher, educator*
Nanfito, Jacqueline *literature and language professor*
Nelson, Sue Grodsky *humanities educator, consultant*
Pizot-Haymore, Fabienne *language educator, translator*
Salomon, Roger Blaine *retired language educator*
Workman, Deborah S. *literature and language professor, director*
Young, Henry Walthall, Jr. *speech educator*

Columbus
Battersby, James Lyons, Jr. *language educator*
Boyle, Kevin Gerard *historian, educator, writer*
Coulson, Frank Thomas *humanities educator*
Graff, Harvey J. *history and humanities educator*
Hahm, David Edgar *classics educator*
Hanawalt, Barbara Ann *British history educator, consultant*
Hartmann, Susan M. *history professor*
Jarvis, Gilbert Andrew *humanities educator, writer*
Jeffries, Hasan Kwame *history professor*
Kern, Stephen Roger *history educator*
Kuhn, Albert Joseph *language educator*
Lehiste, Ilse *retired language educator*
Peterson, Gale Eugene *historian*
Scanlan, James Patrick *philosophy and Slavic studies educator*
Stebenne, David Lawler *historian, educator*
Stephan, Alexander Friedrich *German language and literature educator*
Williams, Susan Shidal *literature and language professor*

Concord
Ulsenheimer, Dean *language educator*

Dayton
Harden, Oleta Elizabeth *literature educator, academic administrator*
Miyasaki, Donovan *philosopher, educator*
Serrano Guerra, Damaris Elizabeth *language educator*
Slade, R. Andrew *literature and language professor*
Swanson, Donald Roland *retired English literature and language educator*
Vice, Roy Lee *history professor*
Winkler, Jonathan Reed *historian, educator*

Delaware
Fratantuono, Lee Michael *philatelist, educator*
Vedder, Debra Scott *language educator*

Elyria
Dryden, Jonathan Norton *literature and language professor*

Findlay
Van Vorhis, Andrea Christine *literature and language professor*

Granville
Lisska, Anthony Joseph *humanities educator, philosopher*
Santoni, Ronald Ernest *philosophy educator*

Huron
Saunders, Patrick Reed *history professor*

Kent
Beer, Barrett Lynn *historian*
Hassler, Donald Mackey, II, *English language educator, writer*
Koby, Geoffrey Stanhope *language and translation studies professor*
Marovitz, Sanford Earl *English language and literature educator*
M'Baye, Babacar *black literature educator*
Mitchell, Pamela R. *speech professional, educator*
Remley, R. Dirk *English educator, consultant*
Scarnecchia, Timothy *history professor*
Shreve, Gregory Monroe *language educator, department chairman*
Williams, Christopher T. *history professor*

Lakewood
Pangrace, Ruth A. *history professor*

Lyndhurst
Harper, Williard Flemmett *language educator*

Marietta
Abbott, Mary Ann *literature and language professor*
Krawczyk, Carl Michal *history professor*
Torbett, David James *religion professor*
Wilbanks, Jan Joseph *retired philosopher*

Middletown
Camara, Babacar *literature educator*

New Philadelphia
Li, Hongshan *history professor*

North Canton
Norton-Smith, Thomas Michael *humanities educator*

Oberlin
Volk, Steven S. *history professor*

Oxford
Baird, Jay Warren *historian, educator*
Frazier, Nishani *history professor*
Harwood, Britton James *literature and language professor, department chairman*
Hedrick, Linnea S. (fka Dietrich) *retired art historian*
Pratt, William Crouch, Jr. *literature and language professor, writer*
Rahman, Jacquelyn *language educator, researcher, director*
Yamauchi, Edwin Masao *history professor emeritus*

Painesville
McQuaid, Kim *historian, educator, writer*

Parma
Redles, David *history professor*

Portsmouth
Feight, Andrew Lee *history professor*
Spradlin, Patricia C. *literature and language professor*

Shaker Heights
Weinberg, Helen Arnstein *retired literature and art educator*

Solon
Gallo, Donald Robert *retired literature educator*

Springfield
Cantrell, John L. *language educator*
Fleissner, Robert F. *retired English language educator*
Reed, Don Collins *philosopher, educator*
Smith, James Fitzpatrick *literature educator*
Taylor, Thomas Templeton *history professor*

Sylvania
Stockwell, Mary Elizabeth *history professor*

Toledo
Brown, Nancy J. *literature educator*
Campbell, James *philosopher, educator*
Glaab, Charles Nelson *historian, educator*
Phelps, Carmen Lanette *literature educator*
Van Ness, Mary Beth *literature and language professor*

University Heights
Langenfus, William Louis *philosopher, educator*

Urbana
Phillips, Julieanne Appleson *history professor*

Wilberforce
Onwudiwe, Ebere *humanities educator, writer*

Yellow Springs
Seon, Yvonne *retired cultural educator, minister*

Youngstown
Bowers, Bege Kaye *literature and communications educator, academic administrator*
Brown, Steven Ray *language professional*

Zanesville
Giannandrea, Beatrice *language educator*
Holdren, Susan *literature and language professor, foundation administrator*

OKLAHOMA

Ada
Daniel, Arlie V. *speech education educator*

Alva
Steed, Patricia L. *literature and language professor*

Beaver
Hodges, Vivan Pauline *educator and consultant*

Lawton
Thomlinson, Vivian Aytes *literature and language professor*

Norman
DeSpain, Matthew Stanley *history professor*
Fears, Jesse Rufus *historian, academic dean, educator*
Keppel, Ben *history professor*
Levy, David William *history educator*
Lowitt, Richard *history professor*
Savage, William Woodrow, Jr. *historian, consultant, social sciences educator*
Sellars, Nigel Anthony *historian, writer*

Oklahoma City
Carlisle, Jeffrey Deward *history professor*
Hooper, Marie E. *history professor*

Stillwater
Fischer, LeRoy Henry *historian, educator*
Jones, Edward John *literature and language professor*
Luebke, Neil Robert *philosophy educator*
Max, Elizabeth *english language educator*

Tulsa
Buckley, Thomas Hugh *historian, educator*
Chew, Pamela Christine *language educator*
Farnsworth, David *language educator*
Garrison, Beverly Mustain *history professor*
Hayden, Donald Eugene *retired emeritus English language educator*
Latham, Sean *literature and language professor*
Swails, John Washington III *history professor, director*

Weatherford
Craig, Viki Pettijohn *language educator*

OREGON

Ashland
Harrison, Robert Thomas *history professor*

Corvallis
Farber, Vreneli Regula *retired linguist*
Rudinsky, Norma Leigh *English language educator, translator*
Stehr, Christian Peter *literature and language professor*

Eugene
Pascal, C(ecil) Bennett *classics educator*

Forest Grove
Garcia, Sandra Pearl *language educator*

Gresham
Barnes, James Keener *retired history professor*

Keizer
Dmytryshyn, Basil *historian, educator*

Madras
Ramsey, Jarold William *literature and language professor, writer*

Medford
Gill, Gudrun *retired language educator*

Monmouth
Rector, John Lawrence *history professor*

Newport
Pavlish, Catherine Ann *language educator, writer*

Portland
Basci, Pelin *literature and language professor*
Beckham, Stephen Dow *history educator*
Bentley-Quintero, Sarah Catherine *language educator*
Faller, Thompson Mason *philosophy educator*
Hayashi, Satomi *language educator*
McDowell, Michael J. *literature and language professor*
Meyer, Paulette Ann *history professor*
Morgan, Douglas F. *public service educator*
Steinman, Lisa Malinowski *English literature educator, writer*
Trimble, Anmarie *language educator, editor*
Underwood, Jan Marie *language educator*
Vaughan, Thomas James Gregory *historian, writer*

Salem
Loftus, Ronald Phelps *literature and language professor*

PENNSYLVANIA

Allentown
Brunner, John Wilson *foreign language educator*

Bala Cynwyd
Dorwart, Bonnie Brice *historian, retired rheumatologist*
Murphey, Murray Griffin *history professor*

Berwyn
Bluestone, Ellen Hope *literature, writing, and women's studies professor, writer*

Bethlehem
Parmet, Harriet Abbey L. *literature educator*
Pavlock, Barbara R. *literature and language professor*
Saeger, James Schofield *history professor, writer*
Trautmann, Nancy E. *language educator*

Bloomsburg
Decker, Mark Tingey *literature and language professor*

Blue Bell
Lazar, Stanley William *history professor*
Raskin, Anna Viktorovna (Roper Raskin) *history professor*
Roden, Carol Looney *retired language educator*

Boyertown
Fortes, Brenda Joyce *English language educator*

Bradford
Frederick, Richard George *history professor*

Bryn Athyn
Henderson, Brian D. *history professor*

Bryn Mawr
Dudden, Arthur Power *historian, educator*
Gaisser, Julia Haig *classics educator*
Harte, Tim *history professor*
Krausz, Michael *philosopher, educator*
Lane, Barbara Miller (Barbara Miller-Lane) *humanities educator*
Lang, Mabel Louise *classics educator*
McCabe, Louise Beachboard *language educator*
Thompson, Wayne Wray *historian*

Canonsburg
Southern, David W. *history professor*

Carlisle
Crane, Conrad C. *history professor*
Fox, Arturo Angel *Spanish language educator*
Shrader, Charles Reginald *historian*

Chambersburg
O'Connor, John Morris III *retired humanities educator*

Chester
Buck, Lawrence Paul *history professor, former academic administrator*
Thompson, Jayne Marie *literature and language professor*

Cheyney
Gaffin, Virgilette Nzingha *language educator, department chairman*

Clarks Green
Bourcier, Richard Joseph *retired French language and literature educator*

Dallas
Betterly, Richard Douglas *historian, educator*

East Petersburg
Pedrow, Brenda M. *retired language educator*

East Stroudsburg
Meyers, Ronald J. *literature and language professor*
Squeri, Lawrence *history professor*
Switzer, Sharon Cecile *language educator, researcher*

Easton
Lamb-Faffelberger, Margarete Barbara *foreign language educator*
Schlueter, June Mayer *literature educator, writer*

Edinboro
Bemko, Ihor Jurij Tadej *history professor*

Elizabethtown
Mead, Dana Gulling *literature and language professor*

Elkins Park
Davidson, Abraham Aba *art historian, educator, photographer*

Erie
Baker, Parris Jerome *humanities educator*
Giannelli, Mariagrazi Licia *language educator*

Fairfield
Freund, John Richard *former English educator*

Ford City
Smits, Ronald Francis *retired language educator, poet*

Gettysburg
Harman, Troy D. *history professor*
Snively, Carolyn S. *ancient language educator, archaeologist*

Grantham
LaGrand, James B. *history professor*

Greensburg
Greenfield, Sayre Nelson *literature and language professor*

Grove City
Dixon, James George III *literature and language professor, department chairman, theater director*
Spradley, Garey B. *philosopher, educator, rancher, theologian*
Tinkey, Patricia A. *literature and language professor*
Trammell, Catherine Louise *language educator*

Harrisburg
Boswell, James Aurthur, Jr. *English language educator*
Cockeram, Paul D. *humanities educator*
Smith, Eric Ledell *historian*

Haverford
Castillo Sandoval, Roberto *literature and language professor*
Gutwirth, Marcel Marc *literature educator*
Kitroeff, Alexander *history professor*

Hershey
Hufford, David J. *humanities educator*

Huntingdon
Rosell, Karen J. *art history professor*

Huntingdon Valley
Gryminska, Teresa Lidia *literature and language professor, interpreter*

Indiana
Alkhatnai, Mubarak H. *language educator*
Mannard, Joseph Gerard *history professor*
Sherwood, Kenneth W. *language educator*

Johnstown
Dewey, Joseph Owen *literature and language professor*

Kennett Square
van der Veur, Paul W. *humanities educator*

Kutztown
Meyer, Susan Moon *speech pathologist, educator*

La Plume
White, Sara Kathryn *literature and language professor*

Lancaster
Binkley, Luther John *philosophy educator*
Hanahoe-Dosch, Patricia *language educator*
Joseph, John *historian, educator*
Schuyler, David P. *historian, educator*
Steiner, Robert Lisle *retired language educator*

Lansdowne
Purcell, Mary Hamilton *speech educator*

Lewisburg
Delgado-Morales, Manuel *language educator*
Edgerton, Mills Fox *retired foreign language educator*
Payne, Michael David *English language educator*
Siewers, Alfred Kentigern Karlson *literature educator*

Ligonier
Vogelsang, Eric R. *language educator, basketball and soccer coach*

Lock Haven
Satya, Laxman D. *history professor*
Story, Julie Ann *language educator*

Loretto
Jareb, Jerome *history professor, researcher, retired*

Lykens
Sultzbaugh, John Stephan *retired historian, educator, researcher*

Mansfield
Gaskievicz, Andrew *history professor, department chairman*
Keeth, William P. *language educator*
Washington, Edward T. *literature and language professor*

Meadville
Helmreich, Jonathan Ernst *history professor*
Stewart, Anne Williams *historian, writer, researcher*

Media
Ginsberg, Robert E. *philosophy educator, editor*
Robertson, James Henry *history professor*

Millersville
Gaudry-Hudson, Christine M. *literature and French language professor*
Himmele, Persida *language educator, consultant*

Miller, Steven Max *humanities educator*
Rineer, Carla Mary *literature and language professor*
Shin, Duckhee *literature and language professor*

Millville
Gilmore, Stephen R. *retired ancient language educator*

Moon Township
Eckman, Robin Jean *literature and language professor*

Nanticoke
Kashatus, William Charles *history professor*

New Freedom
Sedlak, Valerie Frances *retired English language and literature educator, academic administrator*

Newtown
Loughran, Richard David *history professor*
Strauss, John *literature and language professor*

Newtown Square
DeLuca, Jennie M. *language educator*

Philadelphia
Betancourt, Philip P. *art historian, archaeologist, educator*
Blaszczyk, Regina Lee *historian, writer*
Blyn-LaDrew, Roslyn *language educator*
Davis, Allen Freeman *history professor, writer*
Dawid, Sister Doloretta *literature and language professor*
DiCapua, Christopher *literature and language professor*
Ellman, Norman Stephen *language educator*
Fusco, Richard *English literature educator*
Giammarco, Maurizio Mercedes *literature educator, director*
Godfrey, Joseph John *philosophy professor, priest*
Hackney, (Francis) Sheldon *history professor, former academic administrator*
Haller, Mark H. *history professor, researcher*
Knauer, Georg Nicolaus *philologist*
Mair, Victor Henry *language and literature educator*
Mitchell-Boyask, Robin Norman *classics educator*
Moss, Roger William *historian, writer, administrator*
Pavuk, Alexander *history professor*
Quann, Joan Louise *French language educator, real estate broker*
Rabaté, Jean-Michel *literature and language professor*
Ren, Huizhen *language educator*
Rogers, Carmen Villegas *language educator*
Rossi, John Patrick *retired history professor*
Sachs, Katherine Stein *art historian*
Schiffman, Harold Fosdick *Asian language educator*
Sebold, Russell Perry III *romance languages educator, writer*
Sokol, Jason *historian*
Stow, George *history professor*
Sugrue, Thomas J. *history and social sciences professor*
Webb, Helen *literature and language professor*
Zuckerman, Michael *history professor*

Phoenixville
Lukacs, John Adalbert *historian, retired educator*

Pittsburgh
Arac, Jonathan *literature and language professor*
Clack, Jerry *classics educator*
Donnorummo, Bob Pepe *history professor, department chairman*
Drescher, Seymour *historian, educator, writer*
Gale, Robert Lee *retired literature educator, critic*
Goldstein, Donald Maurice *historian, educator*
Grünbaum, Adolf *philosophy educator, writer*
Gupta, Anil K. *philosophy professor*
Harris, Ann Birgitta Sutherland *art historian*
Hounshell, David Allen *history professor*
Jannetta, Ann Bowman *retired history professor*
McDuffie, Keith A. *literature educator*
Miller, David William *historian, educator*
Paulston, Christina Bratt *linguistics educator*
Rescher, Nicholas *philosopher, author, educator*
Sheon, Aaron *art historian, educator*
Sieg, Wilfried *philosophy educator*
Tarr, Joel Arthur *historian, educator*
Thomason, Sarah Grey *linguistics educator*
Trotter, Joe William, Jr. *history professor, writer*
Weingartner, Rudolph Herbert *philosophy educator*
West, Michael Davidson *English educator*
Wilson, Mark Lowell *philosopher, educator*

Pottstown
Kensicki, Marybeth *literature and language professor*
Nestler, Patricia C. *English professor*

Reading
DeMeo, Marybeth *literature and language professor*

Saint Davids
Boehne, Patricia Jeanne *foreign languages educator, department chairman*

Schnecksville
Foulsham, Christopher *retired language educator*
Gerken, Joanne D. *literature and language professor*

Scranton
Conover, Willis M. *history professor*
Lawhon, Patricia Patton *literature, language and writing professor*

Slippery Rock
Cosgrove, Cornelius *composite and literature professor, middle state coordinator*
McIlvaine, Robert Morton *literature educator*
Peacock, Joan Sunita *literature and language professor*
White, Frederick *literature and language professor, researcher*

State College
Brault, Gerard Joseph *French language educator*
Goldschmidt, Arthur Eduard, Jr. *retired educator, historian, writer*
Redford, Donald Bruce *historian, archaeologist*
Schmalstieg, William Riegel *retired Slavic languages educator*
You, Xiaoye *literature and language professor*

Sunbury
Cafiso, Bonna R. *retired language educator*

Swarthmore
DuPlessis, Robert Saint-Cyr *history professor*
North, Helen Florence *classicist, educator*
Ostwald, Martin *retired classicist*
Pagliaro, Harold Emil *language educator*

Tamaqua
Cardimona, Kimberly Marie *language educator*

Thorndale
Gougher, Ronald Lee *retired language educator*

University Park
Ebitz, David MacKinnon *art historian, educator, museum director*
Grosholz, Emily Rolfe *philosopher, educator, poet*
Halsey, Martha Taliaferro *Spanish language educator*
Lima, Robert *language educator*

Villanova
Bergquist, James Manning *history professor*
Helmetag, Charles Hugh *foreign language educator*
Meltzer, Gary Stephen *ancient language educator*
Mires, Charlene *historian, educator*
Omran, Elsayed M. *language educator, consultant*
Poeta, Salvatore J. *literature and language professor*

Wayne
Tatta, Joseph *language educator*

West Chester
Hipple, Walter John *language educator*
Myrsiades, Kostas Yannis *literature educator*
Pauly, Rebecca Mehl *foreign languages educator*
Ramanathan, Geetha *literature and language professor*
Scythes, James Michael *history professor*
Tartar Esch, Stacy *literature and language professor*
Varricchio-Di Vito, Andrea *language educator*

Wilkes Barre
Hepp, John Henry, IV, *historian, lawyer*
Wenger, Diane E. *history professor*

Williamsport
Beaston, Lawrence Keith *literature and language professor*

York
Avillo, Philip J., Jr. *history professor*

RHODE ISLAND

Cumberland
Clemente, Alice Rodrigues *language educator*

Greenville
Lemons, James Stanley *history professor*

Jamestown
Wright, Harrison Morris *historian, educator*

Kingston
Kim, Yong Choon *philosopher, theologian, educator*

Newport
Haas, William Paul *humanities educator, retired academic administrator*
Petro, Allison N. *language educator*

North Kingstown
Mellor, Kathy *English as a second language educator*

Providence
Abbotson, Susan Claire Whitfield *literature and language professor*
Ackerman, Felicia Nimue *philosophy educator, writer*
Barbour, Brian *English professor*
Blasing, Mutlu Konuk *English language educator*
Cohen, Deborah Anne *historian*
Donovan, Bruce Elliot *literature educator, dean*
Enteman, Willard Finley *retired philosopher*
Espinosa, David *history professor*
Ferguson, Simone D. *literature and language professor*
Fornara, Charles William *historian, classicist, educator*
Grace, Richard John *history professor*
Harleman, Ann *literature educator, writer*
Kim, Jaegwon *philosophy educator*
Konstan, David *classics and comparative literature professor, researcher*
Lesko, Leonard Henry *historian, educator, writer, publisher*
Marks, Sally Jean *historian, educator*
Nieto Hernández, María de la Purificación *language educator*
Putnam, Michael Courtney Jenkins *classics educator*
Raaflaub, Kurt Arnold *classics educator*
Ribbans, Geoffrey Wilfrid *language educator*
Rohr, Donald Gerard *history professor*
Saint-Amand, Pierre Nemours *humanities educator*
Schulz, Juergen *art historian, educator*
Senerchia, Rory Elizabeth *language educator*
Wideman, John Edgar *English literature educator, novelist*
Wood, Gordon Stewart *historian, educator, writer*

Saunderstown
Waters, Chris Harold *literature and language professor, poet*

Smithfield
Litoff, Judy Barrett *history professor*
Reedy, Walter Jay *history professor*

Tiverton
Kamm, Lewis *language educator*

Warwick
Madden, Cheryl Ann *history professor*

SOUTH CAROLINA

Aiken
Geyer, Andrew *literature and language professor*
Sykes, Richard Nesbit *retired history professor, department chairman*

Anderson
Palacios, Conny *language educator, writer*

Beaufort
Hunt, Rosemary Richardson *language educator*
Mauriocourt, Gregory *history professor*

Blythewood
Turfa, Arthur William *literature and language professor*

Charleston
Barrett, Michael Baker *historian, educator*
Colomina-Garrigos, Maria D. *language educator*
Grantham, Todd *philosopher, educator*
Knapp, Keith Nathaniel *history professor*
Peek, Pamela *language educator*
Simon, Kindra Lee *language educator, translator*
Sinisi, Kyle Scott *history professor*

Clemson
An, Yanming *philosopher, literature and language professor*
Bailey, Beatrice Naff *language educator, researcher*
Barfield, Ray Elliott *literature and language professor*
Bartley, Abel Alphonso *history professor*
Cranston, Philip Edward *foreign language professional*
Underwood, Richard Allan *English language educator*

Clinton
Skinner, James Lister III *retired language educator*

Columbia
Bates, Carol Henry *musicologist, music educator*
Briggs, Ward Wright *classics educator*
Edgar, Walter Bellingrath *historian, educator*
Franklin, Benjamin, V, *English language educator*
Long, Eugene Thomas III *philosophy educator, academic administrator*
Synnott, Marcia Graham *history professor*
Turnage, Scott E. *history professor*

Conway
Bachman, Maria K. *English professor*
Melcher, Martha Elena *language educator*

Donalds
Carlock, John Bruce, Jr. *retired language educator*

Greenville
Blackwell, Christopher William *literature educator*
Crabtree, John Henry, Jr. *retired English educator*
Rowe, Karen D. *literature and language professor*
Schoolfield, Brenda Thompson *history professor*

Greenwood
Cushing, Sara Elizabeth *language educator, writer*
Phillips, Robert Kenney *retired english literature and language professor*
Witherspoon, Kevin B. *history professor*

Hartsville
Cuppett, Cathleen G. *literature and language professor*

Indian Land
Pettus, Mildred Louise *retired history professor, writer*

Nesmith
Pressley, Deloris N. *retired literacy educator*

North Charleston
Hartnett, Richard James *literature and language professor, artist*

Orangeburg
Dees Grevious, Annette *speech educator, actress*
Konate, Dior *history professor*
Silvestry, Ruben *philologist, educator*
Wallace, Nathaniel Owen *English language educator*

Spartanburg
Cann, Katherine Davis *history professor*
Harris, Carmen *history professor*
Kay, Charles D. *philosophy educator*
Krick-Aigner, Kirsten Andrea *language educator*
Pollack, Elisa Erali *language educator*

Sumter
Fulcher, James P. *language educator*

Tigerville
Gonzalez, Jorge Ivan *language educator*
Shin, Hiewon *literature and language professor*

Travelers Rest
Bailey, Helen McShane *historian, consultant*

Trenton
Mims, Julian L. III *history professor, archivist*

Whitmire
Kibler, James Everett, Jr. *English language educator, writer*

Winnsboro
Meyer, Jack Allen *historian, consultant*

SOUTH DAKOTA

Brookings
Brooks, April Ahlers *history professor*
Funchion, Michael F. *historian, educator*

Eagle Butte
Eisenbraun, Monica T. *language educator*
Houston, Pamela Jo *humanities educator*

Madison
John, Laflin H. *literature and language professor*

Rapid City
Comcally, Tillian *historian, educator*

Rosholt
Swier, Carol Ann *English educator*

Sioux Falls
Huseboe, Arthur Robert *American literature educator*
Staggers, Kermit LeMoyne, II, *history and political science professor, state legislator, municipal official*

Spearfish
King, Vincent Allan *literature and language professor*
Meyers, Kent *literature and language professor, writer*

Vermillion
Balakier, James J. *literature and language professor*
Bucklin, Steven Jay *history professor*
DiMond, Patricia Rae *literature and language professor*
Hilderbrand, Robert Clinton *history professor*
Hoover, Herbert Theodore *historian, educator*
Knutson, Wayne Shafer *retired theater and English educator*
Schlarman, Julie Jo *history professor, consultant*

Yankton
Lofthus, Richard *history professor*

TENNESSEE

Chattanooga
Gartman, Max Dillon *language educator*
Henderson, Joel Bridges *literature and language professor*
Long, Kathy Lynne *history professor*
Resnick, Irven Michael *philosophy educator*
Stifler, William L., Jr. *literature and language professor*

Cleveland
Hoffman, Daniel Lee *history professor, researcher*
Wilkins, James D. *language educator*

Columbia
Curry, Beatrice Chesrown *retired English educator*
Gardner, Hoyt Devane, Jr. *history professor*
Gidcomb, Barry Doyle *history professor*

Cookeville
Campana, Phillip Joseph *German language educator*
Rios, Marjorie Evans *language educator*

Dayton
Boling, Paul C. *philosopher, educator*
Ketchersid, William Lester *history professor*

Dyersburg
Northcutt, William Marion *English literature educator*
Strong, David A., Jr. *history professor*

Gallatin
Douglas, Joseph C. *history professor*
Durham, Walter Thomas *historian, researcher*
Schipper, Jan D. *language educator*

Jackson
Blanca, Acosta *literature and language professor, translator*
Hudacek, Vivian Susan *literature and language professor*
Lindley, W. Lindley *history professor*

Jefferson City
Austin, David Brian *philosopher, educator*
Baumgardner, James Lewis *history professor*
Moffat, Charles Gordon *history professor, department chairman*

Johnson City
Drinkard-Hawkshawe, Dorothy Lee *historian, educator, writer*
Mwinyelle, Jerome Banaya *language educator*
Storie, Melanie *history professor*
Waage, Frederick Oswin *English educator*

Knoxville
Adabra, Kodjo *language educator*
Allington, Richard Lloyd *literacy studies educator*
Ash, Stephen Vaughan *history professor, writer*
Burman, Thomas Earl *history professor*
Easterly, Joan Elizabeth *language educator*
Gale, Richard Milton *retired philosopher*
Koch, Erec R. *literature and language professor*
Koester, Rudolf *educator*
Rubenstein, Jay *history professor, writer*
Trotter, Donald Wesley *history professor*

Madisonville
Allen, Robert Howard *language educator*

Martin
Bradshaw, Charles Callis *literature and language professor*
Jarmon, Laura C. *retired literature and language professor*
Parker, Henry Herbin *humanities educator*

Memphis
Russell, Thomas Arthur *humanities educator, religious studies educator, researcher*
Smallwood, Arwin Doremus *history professor*
Tabachnick, Stephen Ely *English literature educator*

Morristown
Knowles, David L. *history professor*
McLain, Chippy A. *language educator*
Rouse, Viki Dasher *literature and language professor*

Murfreesboro
Baily, Carol Ann *language educator*
Bynum, Thomas L. *history professor*
Corlew, Robert Ewing *history professor, academic administrator*

Nashville
Compton, John Joseph *philosophy educator*
Dayan, Colin (A.K.A. Joan Dayan) *professor of comparative literature, legal history and religion, writer*
Dickerson, Dennis Clark, Sr. *historian, educator*
Girgus, Sam B. *English literature educator*
Hassel, Rudolph Christopher *language educator*
Hearn, Matthew Galen *literature and language professor*
Jarman, Mark Foster *language educator*
Lachs, John *philosopher, educator*
Lee, Douglas A. *musicologist*
Maurer, Christopher Herman *foreign language educator*
Pickard, Robert Evins *history professor*
Sevin, Dieter Hermann *literature and language professor*
Voegeli, Victor Jacque *historian, educator, dean*

Sevierville
Austin, Birgit Kuban *language educator*

Sewanee
Perry, Charles Richard *history professor*
Poe, George Wilkinson *literature, culture and language professor*
Ridyard, Susan J. *history professor*
Williamson, Samuel Ruthven, Jr. *historian, educator*
Winton, Calhoun *literature educator*

Shiloh
Allen, Stacy Dale *historian, parks director*

TEXAS

Abilene
Alcorta, Joe H. *literature and language professor*
Woodfin, Carol Gale *history professor*

Alpine
Antrim, Nancy Mae *linguistics professor, consultant*

Alvin
Guess, Ann H. *literature and language professor, director*

Amarillo
Gladstein, John G. *language educator*

Arlington
Alfaro, Ashley Barden *speech educator*
Nussbaum, Charles Oliver *philosopher, educator*
Trevino, Roberto Rosalez *historian, educator*

Athens
Estep, William Merl *history educator*
Leeper, Marianne *history professor*

Austin
Arens, Katherine Marie *language educator*
Brown, Norman Donald *history professor*
Divine, Robert Alexander *history professor*
Farrell, Edmund James *retired English language educator, writer*
Freeman, Robert Schofield *musicologist, pianist, educator*
Friedman, Alan Warren *humanities educator*
Galinsky, Gotthard Karl *classicist, educator*
Harms, Robert Thomas *linguist, educator*
Hopkins, Antony Gerald *history professor*
Jaimes, Becky S. *Spanish language professor*
Kane, Robert Hilary *philosophy educator*
Lockett, Landon Johnson *retired linguist*
Louis, William Roger *historian*
Middleton, Christopher *Germanic languages and literature educator*
Miller, Richard Owen *history professor*
Moag, Rodney Frank *language educator, country and bluegrass singer, musician, record producer*
Oshinsky, David M. *history professor, writer*
Rich, John Martin *humanities educator, researcher*
Stoff, Michael B. *history professor*
Vacchio, Rene *language educator*
Whitbread, Thomas Bacon *language educator, writer*
Wink, Amy L. *literature and language professor*

Baytown
Britt, Johjn Carrigan *history professor, academic administrator*

Beaumont
Needham, Keith Alan *language educator*

Beeville
Past, Kay Cude *language educator*

Belton
Peterson, Brady *literature and language professor*

Bertram
Albert, Susan Wittig *writer*

Brenham
Coston, Carrie Allen *history professor*
Neill, Lisa *literature and language professor*
Richarz, Charisse Elaine *language educator*

Brownsville
Harris, William *literature and language professor*
Langerbein, Helmut *history professor, department chairman*
Sinha, Aum C. *language educator*
Stephenson, Mimosa Summers *literature and language professor*

Bryan
Bryant, Keith Lynn, Jr. *history professor*

Castroville
Wurn, Kathleen Marie *English educator*

Cedar Park
Golden, John Thomas *language educator, consultant*

College Station
Adams, Ralph James Quincy *historian, educator*
Cannon, Garland *linguist, educator*
Dethloff, Henry Clay *historian, educator*
Galdo, Juan Carlos *literature and language professor*
Harner, James Lowell *language educator*
Hoagwood, Terence Allan *English educator*
Loving, Jerome MacNeill *biographer*
Matthews, Pamela R. *literature and language professor, dean*
Wang, Di *historian*

Commerce
Linck, Charles Edward, Jr. *English language educator*
Moseley, Ann *retired literature and language professor*

Corinth
England, Barbara Jane *history professor*

Corpus Christi
Cain-Calloway, Jonizo *literature and language professor*
Crowson, Sue *literature and language professor*
Oden, Derek *history professor*
Wooster, Robert *history professor*

Dallas
Chavez, John Richard *historian, educator*
Chawner, Lucia Martha *language educator*
Comini, Alessandra *art historian, educator*
Crain, John Walter *historian, educator*
Creamer, Barry Kenneth *humanities educator*
Crossland, Mary Helen *language educator*
Davis, Daisy Sidney *history professor*
Fagin, Stephen Andrew *historian*
Lowry, Sharon Kathleen *history professor*
Nabors, Marion Carroll *retired English educator*
Newton, Pauline T. *humanities educator*
Parker, Stephen G. *linguist, consultant*
Ritchey, Kathy J. *history professor*
Smits, Jasper *humanities educator*
Weber, David J. *history educator*
Wu, John Guoqiang *literature and language professor*

Denton
Cassella, Dean Marcel *language educator*
Greer, Russell Alan *literature and language professor*
Gunter, Pete A.Y. *philosophy educator*
Hurley, Alfred Francis *historian, academic administrator emeritus, retired air force officer*
Kesterson, David Bert *language educator, academic administrator*
Morton, Sophie *literature and language professor*
Munshi, Sadaf *linguistics professor, researcher*
Pollack, Eunice G. *history professor*
Rozzi, Ricardo *philosopher, ecologist*
Snapp, Harry Franklin *historian, educator*

Edinburg
Anderson-Mejias, Pamela L. *applied linguistics professor*
Ayala, Kara J. *speech educator, researcher*

El Paso
Cuartas, Beatriz H. *humanities educator*
Lujan, Rosa Emma *bilingual specialist, trainer, consultant, assistant principal*
Salinas, Carlos Dominic *literature and language professor, consultant*
Tabuenca-Moyer, Rosamaria *language educator*

Flint
Young, Earle Michael III *history professor*

Fort Worth
Araujo, Ilka Vasconcelos *musicologist, pianist*
Boller, Paul Franklin, Jr. *retired American history educator, writer*
Gilderhus, Mark Theodore *historian, educator*
Johnson, Abbie Mae *language educator*
Reuter, Frank Theodore *historian, educator*
Rich, Harold W. *history professor*
Robin, Clara Nell (Claire Robin) *English language educator*

Fredericksburg
Miller, Charles Wallace *historian, retired environmental geologist, educator*

Galveston
Bloomfield, Maxwell Herron III *retired history and law professor*
Willett, Donald *historian*

Georgetown
Browning, Grayson Douglas *philosophy educator*
Proctor, Claude Oliver *Russian language educator*

Grapevine
Stack, George Joseph *philosopher, writer*

Hillsboro
Hyles, Vernon Ross *literature and language professor*

Houston
Achenbaum, W(ilbert) Andrew *historian, gerontologist*
Baggétt, Antrece Lynette *historian, educator*
Belk, Joan Pardue *language and literature educator*
Brinkley, Douglas G. *historian, writer, educator*
Chance, Jane *English literature educator*
Drew, Katherine Fischer *history professor*
Ehrmann, Susanna *language educator, photographer, writer*
Espree, Mildred Michelle *language educator, writer*
García, Ricardo Thomas *language educator*
Giacchetti, Claudine A. *language educator*
Goux, Jean-Joseph Claude *humanities educator, writer*
Hattaway, Karen Ann *literature and language professor*
Lamb, Sydney MacDonald *linguistics educator*
Leguillon, Rolande Lucienne *French educator*
Markos, Louis A. *language educator*
Martin, James Kirby *historian, educator*
Minter, David Lee *English literature educator*
Patten, Robert Lowry *language educator*
Petrovich, Alisa Vladimira *historian, educator*
Pryor, William Daniel Lee *humanities educator*
Rolnik, Claire Yvette *literature and language professor*
Schnoebelen, Anne Mary *musicologist, educator*
Sher, George Allen *philosophy educator*
Tran, Qui-Phiet *English educator*
Vallbona, Rima-Gretel Rothe *retired foreign language educator, writer*
Wright, Madeleine Elaine Pate *humanities educator*
Yampey-Jorg, Gloria Leonor *language educator*

Huntsville
Gutermuth, Mary Elizabeth *retired foreign language educator*
Huntsman, Silvia A. *literature and language professor*

Hurst
Gallagher, Eddye Skillern *language educator, director*
Wisdom, Rita Parker *literature and language professor*

Irving
Bodily, Brett Hogan *literature and language professor*
Dupree, Robert Scott *literature and language professor, library director*
Elmore, Phyllis Pearson *literature and language professor*
Sommerfeldt, John Robert *historian, educator*
Vega, Vanessa Leigh *English educator*

Jacksonville
Heflin, David Duane *literature and language professor*

Kingsville
Melendy, Brenda *history professor, department chairman*
Vela Córdova, Roberto J. *literature and language professor*

Kingwood
Heineman, Angela Gail *history professor*
Hullar, Leonard Earl *history professor*

Lake Jackson
Tarrant, Sasha Ranae Adams *history professor*

Lakeway
Carlson, Lewis Herbert *history professor*

Lancaster
Rolling, Lincoln Curtis *history professor*

Laredo
Seitel, Alan Lewis *speech pathology educator*

Levelland
Carden, Ronald M. *history professor, department chairman*

Lubbock
Ketner, Kenneth Laine *philosopher, educator*
Miller, Paul Allen *literature educator*
Oberhelman, Harley Dean *retired educator*
Spurgeon, Sara Louise *literature and language professor*
Vieth, Ronja *literature and language professor*

Lufkin
Rankin, Daniel F., Jr. *humanities educator*

Marshall
Alonzo, Jose Alfredo *language educator*
Falke, Cassandra Marie *literature and language professor*

Mc Kinney
Collins, Larry D. *history professor*

Mcallen
Lopez, Nereida *literature and language professor*

Mesquite
Budd, Rose Antoinette *language educator*
Fox-Balli, Christina Maria *language educator, translator*
Huston, Elizabeth *literature professor*
Sharp, Robert Gene *history professor*

Midland
Hinton, Diana Davids *history professor, consultant*

Missouri City
de Kanter, Ellen Ann *retired English and foreign language educator*

Mount Pleasant
Vaughn, William Preston *retired historian, educator*

Nacogdoches
Doyle-Anderson, Ann *language educator*
Kroll, Charles Elliot *literature language and cinema studies professor*

Odessa
León, Ana E. *humanities educator*
McMinn, J. B. *retired philosophy educator, composer*
Richardson, Todd H. *literature and language professor*

Pasadena
LeMaster, David James *literature and language professor*
Shelton, Hal Terry *history professor*
Thornburg, John N. *literature and language professor*

Plainview
Ray, Thomas M. *history professor*

Plano
Brown, Peggy Ann *language educator, writer*
Coulter, Matthew Ware *history professor, writer*
Cullen, David O'Donald *history professor*

Prairie View
Goodwin, Ronald E. *history professor*
Howell, Kenneth Wayne *history professor*

Richardson
Redman, Timothy Paul *language educator, writer*
Roemer, Nils H. *history professor*

Richmond
Cox, Dorothy M. *language educator*
O'Shea, Joyce Burnett *English educator*

San Angelo
Cody, Karen *linguistics professor*
Dewar, David P. *humanities educator*
Ellery, Jon Christopher *literature and language professor*
Schonberg, Jeff Brett *literature and language professor, researcher*
Zheng, Guoqiang *history professor*

San Antonio
Acosta, Carlos L. *history professor, researcher*
Aguirre, Javier Ramos *historian, educator*
Buitron, Richard Arthur *literature and language professor*
Daniels, Bruce C *history professor, author*
Focht-Hansen, Jane *literature and language professor*
Gardner, Kirsten Elizabeth *history professor*
Gower, Patricia E. *history professor*
Grimshaw, James Albert, Jr. *retired language educator*
Kellman, Steven G. *literature educator, author*
Klugman, Craig M. *humanities educator*
Lanehart, Sonja Lanehart *language educator*
Lárraga, Maribel *language educator*
Lonchar, Patricia Paulette *English educator*
McCracken, Richard Joseph *English educator, college administrator*
Mustain, Megan Rust *philosopher, educator*
Myers, Ellen Howell *historian, educator*
Nath, Lopita *history professor*
Newhauser, Richard Gordan *Medieval philology educator*
Passty, Jeanette Nyda Mendelssohn *literature and language professor, writer, editor*
Rollin, Michael Fredrick *history professor*
Salvucci, Linda *history professor*
Sebastian, Thomas *language educator*
Vinson, Audrey Lawson *retired literature and language professor*
Walker, William Oliver, Jr. *retired humanities educator, dean*
Ward, Michael T. *classicist, educator*
Weinberg, Florence May *retired modern language and literature educator*

San Marcos
Garner, Lydia M. *history professor*
Mejía, Jaime Armin *language educator*
Skerpan-Wheeler, Elizabeth Penley *English language educator*
Yazedjian, Ani *humanities educator*

Sherman
Melancon, Glenn *history professor*

Stephenville
Christopher, Joe Randell *retired language educator*
Quazi, Moumin Manzoor *literature educator, consultant*
Schmelzer, Janet L. *history professor, researcher*

Tyler
Ross, Catherine Elizabeth *literature and language professor*

Waco
Dooley, Bill *language educator*
Roldan-Figueroa, Rady *philosopher, educator*
SoRelle, James *history professor*

Waxahachie
Lewis, Diane Dunn *literature and language professor, department chairman*

Weslaco
Wyatt, Debra Sue *speech educator*

Wichita Falls
McClintock, Stuart *language educator*

UTAH

Cedar City
Blodgett, Terry Marvin *language educator*
Ping, Larry Lee *history professor*

Orem
McDonald, Richard Blaise *literature and language professor*

Provo
Anderson, Neil J. *literature and language professor*
Christianson, Frank Quinn *literature and language professor*
Cooper, Glen M. *history professor*
Cutchins, Dennis R. *literature and language professor*
Fox, Frank Wayne *retired history professor*
Hauglid, Brian Michael *ancient language educator*
Johnson, Mark Joseph *art historian, educator*
Peer, Larry Howard *literature educator*
Tanner, Stephen Lowell *retired literature educator*
York, Neil Longley *history professor*

Saint George
Bondanella, Peter *literature and language professor, writer*

Salt Lake City
Bausset Page, Ana *language educator*
Dole, Janice Gail Arnold *literacy educator*
Madsen, Brigham Dwaine *history professor*
Newman, Lance B. *literature and language professor*
Notarianni, Philip Frank *historian, program coordinator*

Sandy
Gentry, Jeffery Scott *history professor*

VERMONT

Burlington
Daniels, Robert Vincent *history professor, former state senator*
Hutton, Patrick H. *retired history professor*
Kahn, Robbie Pfeufer *humanities educator*
Rodgers, Robert Howard *ancient language educator*

Colchester
Umanzor-Yashimura, Marta A. *literature educator*

East Calais
Low, Anthony *language educator*

Middlebury
Albers, Jan Maria *historian, museum director*
Jacobs, Travis Beal *historian, educator*
Katz, Michael Ray *Slavic languages educator*
McWilliams, John Probasco, Jr. *English literature educator*
Moss, Kevin *literature and language professor*
Vail, Van Horn *German language educator*

Montpelier
Facos, James Francis *language educator*

Norwich
Stamelman, Richard Howard *French and humanities educator*

South Burlington
Hauptman, Robert *retired humanities educator*

Strafford
Manheim, Michael *English literature educator*

Williston
Laskarzewski, Debra Sue *language educator*

VIRGINIA

Alberta
Walker, Stephen D. *history professor*

Alexandria
Duncan, Richard Ray *history professor*

Arlington
Allard, Dean Conrad *historian, retired historical center director*
Langley, Harold David *historian, retired educator*
Salter, Mark *speechwriter*
Smith, Louis John *historian*
Wilcox, Shirley Jean Langdon *genealogist*

Ashland
Inge, Milton Thomas *American literature and culture educator, author*

Blacksburg
Doswald, Herman Kenneth *language educator, retired academic administrator*
Farmer, Ted Anthony *history professor*

Bridgewater
Elick, Catherine Lilly *literature and language professor*

Callao
Freeman, Anne Hobson *language educator, writer*

Centreville
De Gennaro, Eida Mendoza *interpreter, real estate agent*

Charlottesville
Abbot, William Wright *history professor*
Battestin, Martin Carey *retired literature and language professor*
Belanger, Terry *historian, educator*
Colker, Marvin Leonard *classics educator*
Crabtree, Loren William *history professor, former academic administrator*
Crackel, Theodore Joseph *historian*
Daugherty, Leo *literature and language educator*
Davidson, Hugh MacCullough *French language and literature educator*
Forbes, John Douglas *architectural and economic historian*
Gasman, Lydia Casto *art historian, educator*
Graebner, Norman Arthur *historian, educator*
Haines, Gerald Kenneth *retired historian*
Hirsch, Eric Donald, Jr. *language educator*
Humphreys, Paul William *philosophy educator, consultant*
Lane, Ann Judith *history and women's studies educator, director*
Levenson, Jacob Clavner *language educator*
Lichtenstein, Nelson *history educator*
Little, Wm. A. (William Alfred Little) *language educator, researcher, musicologist*
McGann, Jerome John *language educator*
Megill, Allan *historian*
Mikalson, Jon Dennis *classics educator*
Nohrnberg, James Carson *language educator*
Peterson, Merrill Daniel *historian, educator*
Pope, Randolph D. *literature and language professor*
Rini, Joel *language educator, linguist*
Rubin, David Lee *humanities educator, critic, editor*
Schuker, Stephen Alan *historian, educator*
Sedgwick, Alexander *retired historian, educator*
Shaw, Donald Leslie *Spanish language educator*
Spearing, Anthony Colin *English literature educator*
Stocker, Arthur Frederick *classics educator*
Thomas, Mark Francis *history professor, economics professor, researcher*
Zinberg, Cecile *retired history professor*
Zunz, Olivier Jean *history professor*

Chester
Brooks, Marty Frances *language educator*

Emory
Denham, Robert Dayton *language educator*

Fairfax
Brown, Lorraine A. *literature educator*
Horton, Lois Elaine *history professor*
Hutcheon, Wallace Schoonmaker *retired historian*
King, James Cecil *retired language and literature educator, medievalist*
Ramos-Pellicia, Michelle Frances *linguist, educator*
Smith, Richard Norton *historian, former library director*

Farmville
Etheridge, Elizabeth Williams *history professor*
Smith, Shawn *language educator*

Fort Belvoir
Fyfe, Laura Jane *language educator*

Fredericksburg
Dorman, John Frederick *genealogist*
Noel, Nancy W. *literature and language professor*
Rotter, Marcel Paul *literature and language professor*

Hampton
Barnes, Paula Cassandra *literature and language professor*
Halabuk, Michael Patrick *language educator*
Khawaja, Mabel Masuda *English composition and literature educator*
Lohourou-Digbeu, Jacques *language educator, consultant*
Lowery, Alicia Carmen *language educator*

Hardyville
White, Gordon Eliot *historian, writer*

Harrisonburg
Congdon, Lee Walter *retired history professor*
Geary, Robert Francis, Jr. *English educator*
Tkac, John Anthony *language educator*
White, Christopher Todd *language educator, anthropologist*

Keysville
Lloyd, Judy M. *literature and language professor*

Lexington
Benefiel, Rebecca Ruth *ancient language educator*
Dellinger, Mary Ann *language educator*
Stephens, Laurence David, Jr. *linguist, investor, oil industry executive*

Lovettsville
Foard, Douglas W. *historian*

Lynchburg
Akubue-Brice, Dorothy A. *history professor, researcher*
Henderson, Horace Edward *World War II historian, peace advocate*
Partie, David John *language educator*

Mc Lean
Salem, Rhonda Ziadeh *language and special education educator*

Melfa
Grewe, Kim E. *literature and language professor*

Midlothian
Parrott, Neva *language educator*
Seay, William Claude, Jr. *history professor, geography educator*

Newport News
Hurst, Rebecca McNabb *language educator*

Norfolk
Byrne, William Andrew *historian, educator*
Habib, Imtiaz H. *language educator*
Heller, Dana A. *literature and language professor, director*
Wilson, Harold Stacy *history professor, writer*

North
Fang, Joong *philosopher, mathematician, educator*

Petersburg
Garrott, Carl Lee *foreign language educator*
Kabia, Mohamed Saidu *literature and language professor*
Philipsen, Dirk Peter *history professor, consultant*
Proenza-Coles, Christina *history professor*
Rissel, Hildegard *language educator*
Townsel, A. Sylviane *language educator*

Portsmouth
Jackson, Cheryl K. *English educator*
Paquette, William Arthur *historian, educator*

Radford
Barris, Roann *art historian, educator*

Reston
Holdheim, William Wolfgang *retired comparative literature educator*

Rice
Hildebrandt, Susan A. *language educator*

Richmond
Cornis-Pope, Marcel Horatiu *literature educator, literary critic, program director*
Daniel, Wilbon Harrison *retired history professor*
Fuller-Seeley, Kathryn Helgesen *historian, educator*
Givens, Terryl L. *literature educator*
Glass, Carmen Cecilia *language educator*
Hall, James H(errick), Jr. *philosophy educator, writer*
Hylton, Raymond Pierre *history professor, researcher*
Levit, Héloïse B. (Ginger Levit) *art historian, journalist, art dealer, consultant*
Munro, George E. *history professor*
Nadal, Anita *language educator*
Rilling, John Robert *history professor*
Sterling, Keir Brooks *historian, educator*

Ridgeway
Martin, Leland Morris (Pappy) *historian, educator*

Roanoke
Doan, Ruth Alden *history professor*
Kurtz, Jenifer *literature and language professor*
Sebolt, Stephanie Ann *literature and language professor*

Salem
Bañuelos-Montes, Jose F. *language educator*
Gathercole, Patricia May *modern foreign languages educator*
Talbot, Lynn K. *language educator*

Springfield
Murri, Luella Davis *personnel and language professional*

Stafford
Mezo, Richard Eugene *literature and language professor, writer*

Staunton
Arnold, Albert James *retired foreign language educator, consultant*

Sterling
Cooper, Cinder S. *literature and language professor*

Sumerduck
McCamy, Sharon Grove *English educator*

Sweet Briar
Piepho, Lee (Edward Lee Piepho) *humanities educator*

Tappahannock
McGuire, Lillian (Elizabeth) Hill *historian, researcher, retired education educator, writer*

Vienna
Cook, Jane Hampton *author, speaker, historian, commentator*
Drumheller, Linda Blocher *language educator*

Virginia Beach
Grimsley, Joseph Wayne *history professor*
Reece-Porter, Sharon Ann *international human rights educator*

Warrenton
Bobbitt, David Carroll *history professor*

Williamsburg
Al-Shalchi, Olla Najah *language educator*
Axtell, James Lewis *history professor*
Chappell, Miles Linwood, Jr. *art historian, educator*
Crapol, Edward P. *history professor*
Esler, Anthony James *historian, novelist, educator*
Fauvel, Maryse *language educator*
Goldman, Alan H. *philosophy educator*
Hoffman, Ronald *historian, educator*
Landen, Robert Geran *retired historian, academic administrator*
McGiffert, Michael *retired historian*
Nettels, Elsa *English language educator*
Prokhorova, Elena V. *language educator*
Sherman, Richard Beatty *historian, educator*
Wallach, Alan *art historian, educator*

Winchester
Schweitzer, Petra *literature and language professor*

Wise
Ponce - Ortiz, Esteban *literature and language professor*

Woodbridge
Figueroa, Carmen R. *language educator, assistant dean*
Hood, Ronald Chalmers III *historian, writer*

Yorktown
Henney, Frederic Allison *retired English language educator*

WASHINGTON

Bainbridge Island
Berg, Walter Louis *retired history professor*
Brians, Paul Edward *retired literature and language professor*

Bellevue
Ellison, Herbert Jay *retired historian, educator*
Stewart, Anne Matsumoto *language educator*

Bellingham
Gogröf-Voorhees, Andrea Elizabeth *foreign language educator*
Johnston, Robert M. *retired literature and language professor*
Thompson, Roger Roy *history professor*
Vajda, Edward J. *literature and language professor*

Bothell
Watts, Linda Susan *humanities educator*

Burien
Burgess, Charles Orville *history professor*

Cheney
Smith, Grant William *language educator, volunteer*
Steiner, Henry-York *English language and literature educator*

Colville
Monroe, John B. *history professor*

Coupeville
Menzel, Paul Theodore *philosopher, educator*

Lake Forest Park
Adams, Hazard Simeon *retired language educator, writer*

Olympia
Coontz, Stephanie Jean *history professor, writer*

Pasco
Cruz, Antonio *language educator*

Pullman
Condon, William Francis, Jr. *literacy educator*
Moss, Jeffrey P. *language educator*

Seattle
BonJour, Laurence Alan *philosopher, educator*
Coldewey, John Christopher *English literature educator*
Estes, Kenneth William *history professor, military officer*
Fine, Arthur I. *philosopher, educator*
Harmon, Daniel Patrick *classics educator*
Heer, Nicholas Lawson *language educator*
Iyer, Nalini *literature and language professor*
Keyt, David *philosophy and classics educator*
Korg, Jacob *English literature educator*
Matchett, William H(enry) *English literature educator*
Pressly, Thomas James *history professor*
Taylor-Brochet, Andrea *language educator*
Thomas, Carol Guggenheim *history professor, writer*
Yee, Shirley Jo-Ann *history professor*

Spokane
Carriker, Robert Charles *history professor*

Lamon, Laurie JoAnne *literature and language professor*
Migliazzo, Arlin C. *history professor*
Stackelberg, John Roderick *history professor*

Tacoma
Nelson, Eric Dolaine *literature educator, consultant*

Vancouver
Diggs, Marylynne *literature and language professor*
Donovan, Thomas John *retired humanities educator*

Walla Walla
Carlsen, James Caldwell *retired systematic musicologist*

Wenatchee
Hall-Thur, Celia Marie *history professor*
Howard, Nancy D. *literature and language professor*

WEST VIRGINIA

Athens
O'Haynes, Delilah Ferne *literature and language professor*

Bluefield
Cochran, Dana Stoker *literature and language professor*

Buckhannon
Waggoner, Eric *literature and language professor*

Charles Town
Na, Tsung Shun (Terry Na) *Chinese studies educator, writer*

Huntington
Chrol, E. Del *classicist, educator*
Kawada, Ikuyo *language educator*
Woodward, David Reid *retired history professor*

Martinsburg
Radosh, Ronald *history professor*

Morgantown
Blaydes, Sophia Boyatzies *English language educator*
Ernest, John Richard *literature and language professor*
McCluskey, Stephen C. *retired history professor*
Tauger, Mark Bernard *historian*
Vehse, Charles Theodore *humanities educator*

Parkersburg
Notturno, Mark Amadeus *philosopher*

West Liberty
Hattman, John William *literature and language professor*
Thomas, David Joseph *literature and language professor*

Wheeling
Whelton, Beverly Jean *philosopher, educator*

WISCONSIN

Appleton
Chaney, William Albert *retired history professor*
Goldgar, Bertrand Alvin *literary historian*

De Pere
Crowley, Karlyn *educator*
Humphrey, Nicolas Scott *literature and language professor*
Risden, Edward L. *literature and language professor*

Eau Claire
Berg-Peck, Catherine *literature and language professor*
Bogstad, Janice Marie *Literature & Language Professor Women Studies, Academic Librarian*

Ferryville
Tedeschi, John Alfred *historian, librarian, educator*

Hales Corners
McNally, Vincent Joseph *historian, educator*

Janesville
Fingerson, Kyle R. *history professor*

Kenosha
Kulke, Erik C. *language educator*
Kummings, Donald Dale *language educator*
Morales, Maria Isabel *language educator*
Renaud, Christine *classicist, educator*
Udry, Stephen Potter *history professor*

La Crosse
Kooiman, Barbara Marlene *historian*
Smuksta, Michael J. *history professor*

Madison
Auerbach, Emily K. *language educator, director*
Berg, William James *language educator, writer, translator*
Berghahn, Klaus Leo *German and Jewish studies educator*
Bogue, Allan George *historian, educator*
Ciplijauskaite, Birute *humanities educator*
Cronon, William *history professor*
Dubrow, Heather *literature educator*
Frykenberg, Robert Eric *historian, educator*
Hamerow, Theodore Stephen *historian, educator*
Hannouchi, Said *language educator*
Kleinhenz, Christopher *foreign language educator, researcher, director*
Knowles, Richard Alan John *language educator*
Kutler, Stanley Ira *historian, lawyer, educator*
Leavitt, Judith Walzer *history of medicine educator*
Madureira, Luis Manuel *literature and language professor*
Martin-Berg, Laurey *literature and language professor*
Meisner, Maurice J. *history professor*
Misran, Jennifer *language educator*
Powell, Barry Bruce *classicist, educator*
Rao, Velcheru Narayana *south asian professor*
Sonnedecker, Glenn Allen *pharmaceutical historian, educator*
Vowles, Richard Beckman *literature educator*
Weinbrot, Howard David *language educator*
Wiesenfarth, Joseph John *retired literature educator*
Zell, Josephine May *retired language educator*

Menomonie
Schuler, Robert Jordan *language educator, writer*

Mequon
Krueger, Doreen *language educator*
Menuge, Angus Jl *philosopher, educator*
Stephens, Carolyn King *retired literature and language professor*

Milwaukee
Alred, Gerald James *writing and language professor*
Amster, Ellen Jean *history professor*
Benoit, Edward A. III *researcher*
Flamboe, Jennifer M. *language educator, interpreter*
Forner, Sean A. *historian, educator*
Gallop, Jane (Jane Anne Gallop) *women's studies educator, writer*
Lea, Filomena *English language educator, writer*
McCaw, Robert John *language educator*
Siegel, Robert Harold *English literature educator, writer*
Swanson, Roy Arthur *classicist, educator*
Theoharis, Athan George *history professor*
Trattner, Walter Irwin *humanities educator, educator*
Ullman, Pierre Lioni *retired Spanish literature and language educator*
Vanderheyden, Jennifer Sue *language educator*
Vang, Chia Youyee *history professor*

Mukwonago
Breeden, David Marion *Parish minister, English language educator, writer*

Orfordville
Griffin, Julie Marie *literature educator*

Platteville
Tigerman, Kathleen *humanities educator*

Plymouth
Albrinck, Meg *literature and language professor*

Richland Center
Zorea, Aharon W. *history professor*

Ripon
Reed, Timothy Peter *language educator*

River Falls
Pavlov, Vladimir Grigorievich *language educator*
Schneider-Rebozo, Lissa Price *literature and language professor*

Stevens Point
Francis, Edgar Walter, IV, *history professor*
Mertz, Paul Eric *retired history professor, writer*

Sturgeon Bay
Maher, Virginia Jones *art historian, educator*

Watertown
Midcalf, Randall *language educator, director*

Waukesha
Kelly, Lori Duin *literature and language professor*

Wausau
Sexauer, Cornelia F. *history professor*
Veninga, James Frank *humanities educator, editor, writer*

WYOMING

Cheyenne
Breen, Nathan David (Nate Breen) *historian, educator*

Cody
Garry, James B. *historian, naturalist, storyteller, writer*

Laramie
Hind, Emily *language educator*
Nye, Eric W. *English language and literature educator*
Williams, Roger Lawrence *historian, educator*

Powell
Myers, Rex Charles *historian, educator, retired dean*

Torrington
Nesbitt, John Dunville *literature and language professor, writer*

TERRITORIES OF THE UNITED STATES

PUERTO RICO

Bayamon
Morales-Zeno, Ana J. *literature and language professor*

CANADA

BRITISH COLUMBIA

Burnaby
Kitchen, John Martin *historian, educator*

North Saanich
Saddlemyer, Ann (Eleanor Saddlemyer) *humanities educator, critic, theater historian*

Richmond
Durrant, Geoffrey Hugh *retired language educator*

Vancouver
Conway, John S. *history professor*
Newmeyer, Frederick Jaret *linguist, educator*
Overmyer, Daniel Lee *humanities educator*
Pacheco-Ransanz, Arsenio *language educator, historian, educator*
Unger, Richard Watson *history professor*

MANITOBA

Winnipeg
Rozumnyj, Jaroslav *literature educator*

NEW BRUNSWICK

Saint John
Condon, Thomas Joseph *university historian*

NOVA SCOTIA

Halifax
Gray, James *English literature educator*

ONTARIO

Brampton
Paikeday, Thomas M. *lexicographer, linguistic consultant*

Kingston
Wall, Wendy Lynn *history professor, writer*

London
Gerber, Douglas Earl *classics educator*

Nepean
Kallmann, Helmut Max *musicologist, retired librarian*

North York
Adelman, Howard *philosophy educator*
Thomas, Clara McCandless *retired literature educator*

Ottawa
Dray, William Herbert *philosophy educator*
Labarge, Margaret Wade *medieval history professor, historian, writer*
Squire, Anne Marguerite *retired humanities educator*
Staines, David McKenzie *language educator*

Toronto
Blewett, David Lambert *English literature educator*
Granatstein, Jack Lawrence *historian*
Millgate, Michael (Henry) *retired literature educator*
Morey, Carl Reginald *musicologist*
Pickren, Wade Edward *historian*

Windsor
Bertman, Stephen Samuel *languages, literatures and civilizations educator, writer*

PRINCE EDWARD ISLAND

Charlottetown
Sanborn, George Freeman, Jr. *genealogist*

QUEBEC

Montreal
Kinsley, William Benton *literature educator*
Normore, Calvin *philosophy professor*

North Hatley
Jones, Douglas Gordon *retired literature educator*

AUSTRALIA

Melbourne
MacKinnon, Dolly *historian, music educator*

BELGIUM

Antwerp
Saal, Ilka *literature and language professor*

BOSNIA-HERZEGOVINA

Sarajevo
John, C. Dayton *literature and language professor*

CHINA

Dongguan
McIlvain, Peter James *literature and language professor*

CROATIA

Split
Buble, Nikola *musicologist, conductor*

DENMARK

Copenhagen
Parrott, Jeffrey Keith *linguist, researcher*

Farum
Larsen, Poul Steen *retired information science educator*

ENGLAND

Ashford
Prickett, Stephen *retired literature and language professor*

Cambridge
Garrow, David Jeffries *historian, author*

London
Abu-Deeb, Kamal Mikha'il *humanities educator*
Jeet, Surjit Singh (Surjit Singh) *historian, research scholar*
Lowenthal, David *historian, geographer*

Newcastle
De Jong, Nanette *musicologist, educator*

Oxford
Morpurgo Davies, Anna Elbina *philologist, educator*
Thomas, Keith Vivian *historian, former college president*

FRANCE

Dissay
Marchessou, Helene Daisy *English and American literature educator*

Paris
Kouymjian, Dickran *art historian, educator*
Le Roy Ladurie, Emmanuel Bernard *historian, educator*

GEORGIA

Tbilisi
Gamkrelidze, Thomas Valerian *linguist, educator*

GERMANY

Berlin
Kocka, Juergen *history professor*
Piper, Adrian Margaret Smith *philosopher, artist, educator*

Bremen
Bathrick, David *foreign language educator, academic administrator*

Münster
Spevack, Marvin *language educator*

Nuremberg
Doerries, Reinhard René *historian, educator*

Würzburg
Keil, Gundolf *medical historian*

HONG KONG

Pokfulam
Gould, Gaye *linguist, educator*

ITALY

Padua
Beatrice, Pier Franco *humanities educator*
Shea, William Rene *historian, history and philosophy professor*

Pisa
Most, Glenn Warren *classics professor*

Verona
Pozzo, Riccardo *philosophy educator*

JAPAN

Kashiwara
Hori, Keiko *English literature educator*

Mitaka
Kazama, Toshio *retired humanities educator*

Osaka
Akase, Masako *humanities educator*
Nagae, Yoshio *English educator*

Tsukuba
Imaizumi, Yoko (Ima-Izumi) *literature and film educator*

MOLDOVA

Floresti
Palii, Larisa P. *language educator*

MOROCCO

Sale
Hamzaoui, Ahmed *literature and language professor*

NETHERLANDS

Groningen
Holz, Hans Heinz *philosophy educator*

RUSSIA

Moscow
Bylinskaya, Tatiana Georg *history professor*

SCOTLAND

Fife
Roff, William Robert *historian, educator, writer*

Stirling
Lenman, Bruce Philip *historian, educator*

SLOVENIA

Ljubljana
Bernik, France *literature educator*

SPAIN

Badajoz
Gómez Galán, José *historian, philosopher, writer, theologian, educator*

Madrid
Abellan, José Luis *humanities educator*

SWEDEN

Goteborg
Martinovski, Bilyana *language educator, researcher*

Lerum
Borei, Sven Hans Emil *translator, writer, educator*

SWITZERLAND

Waldenburg
Hamm, Palma *art historian, writer, researcher, art expert, educator, art collector*

ADDRESS UNPUBLISHED

Abate, Carol Elizabeth *humanities educator, writer*
Abdul-Aziz, Rana *language educator*
Adams, David Parrish *historian, epidemiologist, educator*
Adams, Phyllis Yewell *foreign language educator*
Adamson, Lynda G. *literature educator, writer*
Adegbile, Isaiah Olanipekun *history professor, poet*
Adesola, Oluseye *language educator*
Adler, Raphael *retired humanities educator, speech pathology/audiology services professional*
Agan, Cami D. *literature and language professor*
Akers, Sharron Loella *language educator*
Alam, Nadia M. *language educator, researcher*
Alban-Salazar, Miguel F. *language educator*
Aleinikov, Andrei Grigoryevich *linguist, educator*
Alia, Valerie *humanities educator, writer*
Allan, Sarah Katherine *Oriental studies educator*
Al-Tonsi, Abbas Ahmed *language educator, consultant*
Alvarez, Veronica Iris *language educator*
Amatulli, Rosa *literature educator*
Anderson, Nona Louise *literature and language professor*
Angell, Richard Bradshaw *philosophy educator*
Angle, Thomas E. *history professor*
Annen, Margaret T. *language educator*
Ansbro, John Joseph *philosopher, educator*
Antebi, Guy *language educator*
Armour, Robert Alexander *literature and language professor, researcher*
Armstrong, James Francis III *retired language educator, writer*
Arnold, Marygwen Suella *language educator, medical/surgical nurse*
Asirvatham, Sulochana Ruth *philologist, educator*
Askay, Richard R. *philosopher, educator*
Attebery, Louie Wayne *language educator*
Bader, William Banks *historian, former corporate executive, foundation executive*
Bagnall, Joseph Albert *history professor*
Bailey, Charles-James Nice *retired linguistics educator*
Baird, Alice Knar *retired language educator*
Baker, Ian Archbald *explorer, educator, writer, photographer*
Baker, Ronald James *language educator, academic administrator*
Bannister, Robert Corwin, Jr. *historian, educator*
Bardaglio, Peter Winthrop *humanities and sustainability educator, former academic administrator*
Barry, John M. *historian, writer*
Basnett, Margaret G. *reading and language arts educator, consultant*
Bates, Kim *history professor*
Baym (Stillinger), Nina *literature educator, researcher, writer, editor*
Becker, Lawrence Carlyle *philosopher, educator, writer*
Beecher, Graciela Fernandez *language educator, writer*
Belieu, Erin *literature educator*
Belk, Leotis S. *language educator*
Belnap, Nuel Dinsmore, Jr. *philosophy educator*
Benjamin, Croxton G. *history professor*
Benton, Malu *language educator*
Bercovitch, Sacvan *English language professional, educator*
Berlin, Robert Harry *historian, educator*
Bertolet, Jennifer L. *historian*
Beschloss, Michael *historian, writer, lecturer, commentator*
Bess, Michael Demaree *history professor*
Biasin, Giovanni *language educator*
Bird-Soto, Nancy I. *language educator*
Black, Kathleen Marie *literature and language professor*
Blackbourn, David Gordon *history professor*
Blackmun, Barbara Winston *art historian, educator, academic administrator*
Blake, King Charles *humanities educator, writer*
Blissett, William Frank *English literature educator*
Bobzien, Susanne *philosopher, educator*
Bodman, Helene Dunn *musicologist, arts administrator*
Bohstedt, John *retired history professor*
Bolsterli, Margaret Jones *English professor, farmer*
Boly, Lillian Byronell *retired language educator*
Bonekemper, Edward Henry III *history professor*
Bonilla-Ríos, Daniel Cecilio *ancient language educator*
Bordelon, Suzanne Mackie *writing and rhetoric educator*
Bosmajian, Haig Aram *speech communication educator*
Boterbloem, Kees *humanities educator*
Bounds, Sarah Etheline *historian*
Bowen, Bonnie T. *literature and language professor*
Bowser, Osen Felton *literature and language professor*
Boyer, Dale Kenneth *English educator*
Brack, O. M., Jr. *language educator*
Brant, Nataliya Borisovna *language educator*
Bremer, Ronald Allan *genealogist, editor*
Brentegani, Teresa E. *language educator*
Brewster, Elizabeth Winifred *literature educator, poet, writer*
Briggs, Martijna Aarts *language educator*
Broady, Christel H. *language educator*
Brock, Geoffrey *literature and creative writing professor*
Brody, Saul Nathaniel *retired English literature educator*
Brown, Beth A. *language educator*
Brown, Marvin Thomas *philosopher, educator*
Brown, Stephen Ira *mathematics and philosophy of education professor emeritus*
Bruckert, Vincent *literature and language professor, playwright*
Brunner, Kathleen Marie *humanities educator*
Bryant, Paul Thompson *language educator*
Buck, David R. *history professor*
Buckner, Sally Beaver *literature and language professor, writer*
Buell, Lawrence Ingalls *language educator*
Burger, Glenn Douglas *literature and language professor*
Bush, Sarah Lillian *retired historian*
Byrne, Edmund Francis *philosophy educator*
Byrne, Lawrence John *literature and language professor*
Calleo, David Patrick *history professor, political economy international relations*
Calvert, Berta Alicia *language educator*
Campbell, Joyce S. *language educator, department chairman*
Canaday, Steven *literature and language professor*
Cantero-Exojo, Monica *language educator*
Carney, Amy Beth *history instructor*
Carpenter, Lynn *language educator*
Carpenter, Marlene *retired philosopher, educator*
Castellarin, John Stephen *literature and language professor*
Castelloes, Frederico Lemos *language educator*
Cawley, Joseph Douglas *retired reading professor*
Cerutti, Steven Matthew *ancient language educator*
Chambers, Bettye Thomas *language educator*
Chaney, Laura D. *humanities educator*
Chappell, Fred Davis *language educator, poet*
Chastain, Kenneth Duane *retired foreign language educator, writer*
Chen, Zu-yan *language educator*
Cher-Killigm, Beatrice M. *history professor, art educator*
Chesson, Michael Bedout *history professor, writer*
Choi, Young Eui *English language professor*
Cintron-Laguna, Pilar Teresa *language educator*
Civetta, Peter Joseph *literature and language professor, researcher*
Clark, Eve Vivienne *linguist, educator*
Clayton, Glenn N. *literature and language professor*
Clogan, Paul Maurice *English language and literature educator*
Clough, Patricia G. *literature and language professor*
Clow, Richmond L. *professor*
Cohen, Alvin P. *language educator*
Colfax, Toyoko Suzuki *language educator*
Collins, Martha *English language educator, writer*
Collmer, Robert George *retired language educator*
Cook, Hardy Merrill III *retired literature and language professor*
Cook, Lisa Connelly *historian, educator*
Cook, Martha E. *retired language educator*
Cook, Sharki Jo *humanities educator*
Corbett, Donna M. *historian*
Cordero-Román, Arnaldo *humanities educator*
Cordova, Ruben Charles *art historian, curator, photographer*
Cornejo-Patterson, Deanna Hortensia *language educator*
Cornelius, Nathalie *language educator*
Corrigan, Brian Jay *literature educator, writer*
Courington, Leigh Ann *history professor*
Courtenay, William James *historian, educator*
Courtés, Joseph Jean-Marie *humanities educator, writer*
Courtney, Edward *retired classics educator*
Coyle, Mary Bridget *humanities educator*
Cravens, Thomas D. *literature and language professor*
Crossley, Pamela Kyle *history professor, writer*
Csikszentmihalyi, Mark *language educator*
Cullingford, Elizabeth *literature and language professor, department chairman*
Culp, Courtney Ann *history professor*
Cutler, Deborah *literature and language professor*
Dabbagh, Mahmoud *language educator, linguist, researcher*
Dallek, Robert *historian, writer*
D'Angelo, Lawrence M. *humanities educator*
Dattolo, Alphonse A. *language educator*
Daugherity, Brian James *historian, educator, historian, writer*
Davis, Kate K. *literature and language professor*
De Cou-Landberg, Michelle V. *retired language educator*
Defever, Susanna Ethel *retired language educator*
de la Torre, Otto J. *language educator, minister*
Del Corso, Robert Engel *retired history professor*
Delgadillo, Maria Lorena *language educator, translator*
Delgado-Norris, Evelyne Mattie *language educator*
Demskis, Erinn Elisabeth *language educator*
Denecker, Christine *language educator*
Dennis-Bay, Laura *language educator*
Derbyshire, William Wadleigh *language educator, translator*
Der-Houssikian, Haig *retired linguist, educator*
Dickstein, Morris *language educator, writer*
Diefendorf, Jeffry M. *history professor*
Di Palma, Sunday Lynn *retired humanities educator*
Ditta, Joseph Michael *literature and language professor*
Djordjevic, Dimitrije *historian, educator*
Dofflemyer, Leonard *retired history professor*
Dollinger, Marc Lindsey *historian*
Doolittle, Deborah Hope *language educator, writer*
Dorel, Theresa Garfield *humanities educator, department chairman*
Downs, Dorothy Rieder *art historian, consultant, writer*
Drew, Fraser Bragg Robert *language educator*
Duhl, Olga Anna *literature educator, researcher*
Duley, Margot Iris *historian, educator*
Dummett, Sir Michael Anthony Eardley *philosopher, educator*
Duran, Victor Manuel *literature and language professor*
Ebert, Robert Peter *German language professor*
Eckstein, Jerome *philosopher, retired educator*
Edmonds, Crystal D. *language educator, department chairman, distance learning coordinator*
Edson, Evelyn *history professor, writer*
Eich, Jennifer L. *literature educator*
Eire, Carlos *historian, educator, writer*
Eisler, Colin Tobias *art historian, curator*
Eisner, Sigmund *retired English language educator*
El-Attar, Heba Ahmed Nabil *language educator*
Elbert, Sarah *retired history professor*
Elderfield, John *art historian, museum curator*
Elmore, Kimberly Pruett *literature and language professor*
Elrick, Donald *retired literature educator*
Elstun, Esther Nies *foreign language educator*
Emerson, Alex Louise *literature and language professor*
Emmett, Rita *professional speaker*
English, Bertis Deon *history professor*
Erickson, Carol Jean *literature and language professor*
Fabre, Niza Elsie *African studies and hispanic literature educator*
Fagan, Drew Stephen *language educator*
Farrington, Carole Chaney *literature and language professor*
Fatemi, Faramarz Saifpour *history and political science professor, consultant*
Feal, Gisele Catherine *foreign language educator*
Feeney, Matthew Edward *linguist, educator*
Fehler, Timothy *history professor*
Feinstein, Amy *literature and language professor*
Felos, Kimberly *humanities educator*
Felstiner, Mary Lowenthal *retired history professor*
Ferraro, Cristiana S. *language educator, interior designer*
Flint, John E. *retired historian*
Fofana, Amadou Tidiane *literature and language professor*
Fogu, Claudio *literature and language professor*
Foote, Beverly Alice *language educator*
Forslund, Catherine *history professor*
Forster, Merlin Henry *foreign languages educator, writer, researcher*
Foster, Virginia Ramos *language educator*
Freeman, Margaret Helen *language educator*
French, Shelley *language educator*
Froberg, Brent Malcolm *classics educator*
Fuller, Anne Elizabeth Havens *English language and literature educator, consultant*
Gall, Robert Stephen *philosophy educator*
Gandal, Keith *literature and language professor*
Gasque, Thomas James *retired English educator*
Gatewood, Willard Badgett, Jr. *retired historian, writer*
Gaustad, Edwin Scott *historian, educator*
Geiger, Melissa S. *art history professor*
Gerlach, Jeanne Elaine *English language educator*
Ghazvinian, John H. *historian, writer*
Gibson, Donald Bernard *literature educator, educator*
Gillespie, Gerald Ernest Paul *comparative literature educator, writer*
Gillett, Mary Caperton *military historian*
Glick, Ruth Burtnick *literature educator, writer*
Goduti, Philip Anthony, Jr. *history professor*
Gofferje, Hadwig *retired language educator*
Goodlett, David Eugene *history professor*
Gordon, Leonard H(erman) D(avid) *history educator*
Graham, Clarence E., Jr., (Jay Graham) *humanities educator, literature and language educator*
Graham, Lanier *art historian, curator*
Grant, Kathleen J. *history professor*
Grant, Ken A. *history professor*
Gray, Phebe Xu *language educator*
Green, Keith DeWayne *humanities educator*
Grigorian, Siran *language educator*
Grisham, Therese Elizabeth *humanities educator*
Gromen, Richard John *historian, educator*
Gross, Deborah Anne *literature and language professor*
Gruber, Ira Dempsey *historian, educator*
Haas-Belluz, Sigrid Charlotte *literature and language professor, director*
Hadda, Janet Ruth *language educator, lay psychoanalyst*
Hain, Pamela Chase *historian, writer*
Halliburton, Lloyd *retired Romance philology educator*
Hamadeh, Shirine *history professor, researcher*
Hamelin, Marcel *historian, educator*
Hamilton, Mark Wade *literature educator*
Hamilton, Virginia Van der Veer *historian, educator*
Handy, Rollo Leroy *philosopher, researcher*
Hanes, Carol Louise *language educator*
Hanfelt, Peggy Jean *speech educator*
Hannau, Lucia *literature and language professor*
Hannon-Odom, Roxanne Denise *literature and language professor, department chairman*
Hansen, Cory Cooper *literature educator*
Hardin, James Neal *language educator, publisher*
Hardy, Nat W. *literature and language professor*
Haring, Ellen Stone *philosophy educator*
Harkins, Thomas Edward *literature educator*
(Reyes) Harrington, Sandra J. *translator, educator*
Harris, Alice *linguist, educator*
Harris, Frederick John *foreign language and literature educator*
Hart, Robert Lee *retired English educator*
Harwell, Xenia Srebrianski *language educator, researcher*
Hawkins, Kellye Danielle *language educator*
Hawthorne, Margaret Rush *historian, director*
Hearn, Fil *retired architectural history professor*
Heath, Kevin Kevin *literature and language professor*
Heffernan, James Anthony Walsh *language and literature educator*
Hendrix, Mary Elizabeth *assistant professor in education, language educator, researcher*
Herbst, Jurgen *historian, educator*
Heredia, Juanita *language educator*
Herrera, Enrique *language educator*
Hicks, Lewis Edward *history professor, political science professor, department chairman*
Hodgen, Maurice Denzil *retired history professor, writer*
Hoerder, Dirk *history educator*
Hoffman, Daniel (Gerard Hoffman) *literature educator, poet*
Hokenson, Jan Walsh *literature and language professor*
Holli, Melvin George *retired history professor*
Holowchak, Mark *philosopher, educator*
Hootman, Harry Edward *English professor, retired nuclear engineer*
Horward, Donald David *retired history professor*
Houshiar, Bobbie Kay *retired language arts educator*
Hubnik, Sandi J. *literature and language professor*
Huegel, Donna Marie *historian, author*
Hughes-Hallett, Karen P. *language educator*
Hull, Richard Thompson *retired philosophy educator, not-for-profit executive*
Huppert, George *historian*
Iglesias, Maria Estrella *language educator, writer*
Ingham, John Norman *retired history professor*
Ison, John Montgomery *language educator, writer*
Ivers, Louise H. *retired art history professor*
Izadi, Behnaz *language educator*
Janelli, Roger L. *literature and language professor*
Jaynes, Mike *literature and language professor*
Jennings, Sister Vivien *retired literature and language professor*
Johnson, Dale Arthur *church history professor*
Johnson, Janet Hovey *English language educator*
Johnson, John Prescott *retired philosophy educator*

Jones, Leander Corbin *history professor, media specialist*
Jones, Peter d'Alroy *historian, writer, retired educator*
Jones, Suejette Albritton *basic skills educator*
Joseph, Elizabeth *literature and language professor*
Juliá, Mercedes *literature and language professor*
Kalbacken, Joan Muriel *foreign language educator, author*
Kambach, Bel *travel & tourism educator*
Kaminsky, Alice Richkin *retired literature educator*
Kaplan, Robert B. *linguistics educator, consultant, researcher*
Kastor, Frank Sullivan *language educator*
Katers, Nicholas *history professor*
Kauffman, B. Suzanne *historian, genealogist*
Kearney, John D. *history professor*
Kehler, Dorothea Faith *retired English educator*
Keith, Kelly Ann *language educator*
Kennedy, Cynthia Carolyn Marshall *language educator*
Kennedy, Jonny D. *language educator*
Kennett, Lee Boone, Jr. *historian, educator*
Khokhar, M. Inam *language educator*
Kim, Soonhyang *literature and language professor*
Kinder, Suzanne Fonay Wemple *retired historian, educator*
Kingdon, Robert McCune *historian, educator*
Klinghoffer, Judith Apter *historian, consultant*
Kohn, Liberty Lee *language educator*
Kolaitis, Marinna Mallis *language educator, writer*
Kolb, Harold Hutchinson, Jr. *language educator*
Kopp, Achim *language educator*
Koszarski, Richard *film historian, curator*
Kramer, Dale Vernon *retired language educator*
Kravitz, Ellen King *musicologist, educator*
Kuehn, Lucille M. *retired humanities educator*
Kultermann, Udo *architectural and art historian, educator, writer*
Labor, Earle Gene *literature and language professor*
LaHood, Marvin John *retired language educator*
Laird, Gwendolyn Ann *history professor, bank executive*
Lantzer, Jason Scott *historian, educator*
Laqueur, Walter *history professor, writer*
Lash, Barbara Platten *art historian, educator*
Laurent, Pierre-Henri *retired history professor*
Lawhon, Tommie Collins Montgomery *humanities educator*
Lawson, Carolina-Donadio *language educator, translator*
Lee, Alvin A. *literary educator, scholar, author*
Lee, Karen An-hwei *english professor, poet*
Lehtola, Lori A. *history professor*
Leinweber, David Walter *history professor*
Lesser, Ruth *language educator*
Levine, Susan Beth *history professor*
Levinsky, Frieda Libby *language educator*
Levy, Stephen H. *philosopher, logician computer scientist, author*
Lewis, David Charles *historian, educator*
Lewis, Douglas *retired art historian*
Lewis, Emanuel Raymond *historian, psychologist, retired librarian*
Limouze, Henry S. *literature and language professor, department chairman*
Lin, Hsiu Ling *literature and language professor*
Lisio, Donald John *historian, educator*
Lobo, Lucía *language educator*
Loftin, Craig Michael *history professor*
Logan, Robert Alexander *literature and language professor*
Longsworth, Robert Morrow *language educator*
Lopes, Jacqueline Cunha *language educator*
Lovelle, William *language educator*
Lowenthal, Constance *art historian, consultant*
Lubich, Frederick Alfred *language educator*
Luther, Nicole *language educator*
Lyons, John David *literature and language professor*
Lyons-Hunt, Jennifer K. *history professor*
Mackin, Randal Thomas *literature and language professor*
Maehl, William Harvey *retired historian*
Mahoney, John L. *English literature educator*
Mahoney, Michael Robert Taylor *art historian, educator*
Mansfield, Jerry W. *literature and language professor*
Manso, Leira A. *Latin American literature educator, poet, translator*
Mapp, Edward Charles *speech educator*
Marion, Marjorie Anne *literature and language professor, educational consultant*
Martin, Tony *retired humanities educator*
Martinez, Ronald L. *literature and language professor*
Marx, Michael William *language educator, writer*
Massey, Keith Andrew *language educator*
Mathews, E. Anne Jones *retired library educator, academic administrator*
Mauskopf, Seymour Harold *history professor*
Mayfield, Sandra J. *literature and language professor*
Mazzola, Marjorie Ellen *humanities educator*
McAfee, Noelle Claire *philosopher, educator*
McAndrews, Lawrence John *history professor*
McCarthy, Jeanne *literature and language professor*
McClintock, Anne *literature and language professor*
McCormick, John Owen *retired comparative literature educator*
McDermott, Agnes Charlene Senape *philosophy educator*
McDiarmid, Lucy *literature educator, writer*
McDonough, Richard Michael *philosophy educator*
Mc Fadden, Joseph Michael *historian, educator*
McGann, Lisa B. Napoli *language educator*
McGuire, Vail H. *literature and language professor*
McKee, Betty Davis *English language educator*
McKenna, Erin Nicole *history professor*
McKnight, Lee Holland *literature and language professor*
McLauchlin, Vera Ann *history professor*
McLure, Victoria *literature and language professor*
McMaster, Juliet Sylvia *English language educator*
McNally, Mark Thomas *history professor*
McPherson, Naemi Tanaka *language educator*
Mejia, Sister Cristel *language educator*
Meloy, Judith Marie *retired humanities educator*
Merino, Adriana Graciela *language educator*
Metallo, Claudine *language educator*
Mick III, Leonard Silas *language educator*
Midelfort, Hans Christian Erik *retired history professor*
Migaj, David *language educator*
Miguda, Edith Atieno *history professor*
Miley, Bryan S. *language educator, real estate broker*
Miller, Dale Eugene *philosopher, educator*
Miller, Elizabeth Gamble *literature and language professor, translator*
Mindlin, Paula Rosalie *retired reading educator*
Mohan, Jyoti *history professor*
Monaco, Chris *historian, writer, documentary filmmaker*
Mongo, Karen Mathis *speech educator*
Morgan, Edmund Sears *retired history professor*
Morgan, Jeff *literature and language professor*
Morrell, Ayako M. *language educator*
Morrissey, Charles Thomas *historian, educator*
Mugambi, Helen Nabasuta *literature educator*
Murphy, Francis *language educator*
Nagel, Thomas *philosopher, lawyer, educator*
Napier, Cameron Mayson Freeman *historic preservationist*
Nashat, Guity *historian, education educator, researcher*
Naumer, Carola *art historian, educator*
Neill, Debra R. *history professor*
Nesanovich, Stella Ann *literature educator, poet*
Newman, Richard *history professor*
Newmark, Leonard Daniel *linguistics educator*
Nicholas, Lynn Holman *historian, researcher, writer*
Nitzarim, Yoel David *language educator*
Nochman, Lois Wood Kivi (Mrs. Marvin Nochman) *retired literature educator*
Nolles, Niki *literature and language professor*
Noor, Ronny *language educator, writer*
Norberg, Arthur Lawrence, Jr. *historian, physicist, educator*
Norden, Ernest Elwood *retired foreign language educator*
Nugent, Helen Jean McClelland *history professor*
Nugent, Walter Terry King *historian*
Nunis, Doyce Blackman, Jr. *historian, educator*
Odenigbo, Innocent Chukwunwike *linguist, writer, consultant*
O'Driscoll, Seamas Stiofan *literature and language professor*
Oehler, Michael Glenn *humanities educator, social sciences educator, researcher, administrator*
Ogawa, Ayako *language educator, writer*
Olson, Keith Waldemar *historian, educator*
Onofre-Madrid, Maria de los Santos *language educator*
Ortiz-Taylor, Sheila *retired English language educator*
Osbey, Brenda Marie *literature and language professor*
Osborne, Edward C. *history professor*
Oster, Sharon B. *literature and language professor*
Overman, Linda Rader *literature and language professor, writer*
Palmer, Marilyn Joan *English composition educator*
Palmieri, Dora Ann *retired language educator*
Palter, Robert Monroe *humanities educator*
Panzer, Mary Caroline *historian, museum curator*
Parascandola, John Louis *science historian*
Parker, Janet *language educator*
Parrish, Carl E. *liberal arts professor, director*
Paterson, Craig *philosopher, researcher*
Pauley, Bruce Frederick *retired history professor*
Pearson, Lon *Spanish educator, translator*
Pearson, Patricia Annette *history professor*
Peck, Abraham Joseph *historian*
Pegman, Andrew J. *literature and language professor*
Pensa, Mariana *language educator*
Penuel, Suzanne *literature and language professor*
Pepples, Jason John *language educator*
Perdigó, Luisa Marina *foreign language and literature educator*
Perkins, John N. *history professor*
Perkins, Leeman Lloyd *musicologist, educator*
Perkowski, Jan Louis *language, literature and folklore educator*
Perlingieri, Ilya Sandra *art historian, writer*
Persico, Joseph Edward *historian*
Peters, Rosemary Alison *literature and language professor*
Peterson, Barbara Ann Bennett *history professor, television personality*
Peterson, Betty W. *language educator, writer*
Peterson, Keith Stanley *literature and language professor*
Pettener, Emanuele *literature and language professor*
Pettit, Marilyn Hilley *historian, educator, archivist, consultant*
Pham, Lee *literature and language professor, consultant*
Pickett, Terry Hill *language professional educator*
Pickrel, Paul *language educator*
Piecuch, Jim *history professor, writer*
Pinero, Maria Anabel *language educator*
Porras, Vicki *language educator*
Portocarrero, Melvy R. *language educator*
Pospisil, JoAnn *historian, archivist*
Post, Gaines, Jr. *retired history professor, dean, academic administrator*
Potts, Christopher Gerard *language educator*
Potts, Rebecca *literature and language professor*
Privett, Ronna *literature and language professor*
Propst, Christopher M. *literature and language professor*
Puig, Steve *ancient language educator*
Pulitzer, Emily Rauh (Mrs. Joseph Pulitzer Jr.) *art historian, consultant*
Ramos, Marta *language educator*
Rangaswamy, Padma *historian, director, author, interculturist*
Ransom, Roger L. *retired history professor*
Rebay, Luciano *language educator, literary critic*
Reed, Mark Lafayette III *retired humanities educator*
Reid, Ivonne Figueroa *language educator*
Reiman, Donald Henry *language educator*
Reisenauer, Eric Michael *humanities educator*
Ress, Regina *story telling and language professor, actor*
Reuszer, Diane Curtis *humanities educator*
Reznikov, Vladimir Lvovich (Vadim Lesnikov) *historian, playwright*
Riasanovsky, Nicholas Valentine *retired historian, educator*
Rice, Mary Kathleen *literature and language professor*
Richards, David Gleyre *German language educator*
Richardson, Robert Dale, Jr. *language educator*
Riche, Dennis M. *retired history professor*
Richey, James D., Jr. *literature and language professor*
Ricks, Thomas Miller *retired historian, faculty researcher, academic administrator, independent scholar*
Robins, Linda Carol *language educator*
Robinson, Mary Elizabeth Goff *retired historian, researcher*
Rodriguez, Timothy Allen *language educator*
Rojas-Primus, Constanza *language educator*
Rolle, Andrew *historian, writer*
Rosenberg, David Alan *military historian, strategic analyst*
Ross-Nazzal, James *history professor*
Rouman, John Christ *classics educator*
Roy, Thomas Fredrick *history professor*
Roy, Valeria Acosta *language educator*
Ruan, Jiening *language and literacy professor, director, writer*
Rubin, Jay *retired literature and language professor*
Rubin, Louis Decimus, Jr. *retired language educator, writer, publishing executive*
Ruffin, Herbert George, II, *history professor*
Ryan, Marleigh Grayer *language educator*
Sadek, Sanaa Mounir *literature and language professor*
Sadler, Irene Constance *retired language educator*
Sadock, Geoffrey Johnston *English professor*
Saha, Santosh Chandra *history educator*
Saint-Jacques, Bernard *linguistics educator*
Salama, Aman *language educator*
Salama, Mohammad *literature and language professor*
Salcedo, Claudia S. *language educator, lab administrator*
Sanders, Patricia Smith *language educator, consultant*
Sandford, Virginia Adele *retired motivational speaker, writer*
Sanjian, Ara *history professor*
Santana, Suzette M. *language educator*
Santos, Santos V. *literature and language professor, researcher*
Sapienza, Madeline *historian, researcher*
Sawai, Dahleen Emi *language educator*
Saxon, Burton Roy *humanities educator*
Scarlett, Elizabeth Ann *foreign language educator*
Schadow, Karen E. *public speaking trainer, educator*
Scheidel, Walter *historian*
Schlagel, Richard H. *retired philosophy educator*
Schmider, Mary Ellen Heian *American studies educator, academic administrator*
Schmitz, Dennis Mathew *retired language educator*
Schneewind, Sarah Katherine *history professor*
Schneider, Amanda E. *literature and language professor*
Schneider, Duane Bernard *English literature educator*
Schneider, Valerie Lois *retired speech educator*
Schofield, Robert E. (Robert Edwin Schofield) *historian, educator, academic administrator*
Schroeder, Brian S. *philosopher, educator, theologian*
Schwartz, Brian Michael *philosopher, think-tank executive*
Schwartz, Leon *foreign language educator*
Schwarz, Jan *literature and language professor*
Scott, Karen N. *language educator*
Seary, Jennifer *language educator*
Seidenman, Neil Arnold *interpreter*
Sens, Alexander *classicist, educator*
Shaktini, Namascar *language educator*
Sheffey, Ruthe T. *language educator*
Sheppard, Jennifer Modlin *genealogist, retired government employee*
Shillingburg, Constance Joanne *historian, retired history professor*
Shindle, William Richard *retired musicologist, educator*
Shoji, Kakuko *language educator*
Shumate, David John *literature and language professor*
Sieben, J(ohn) Kenneth *retired humanities educator, writer, editor*
Sieburth, Richard *literature educator, interpreter*
Silverman, Kenneth Eugene *language educator, writer*
Sinclair, Patricia White *language educator*
Skalsky, Askold *retired literature and language professor*
Skinner, Frederick William *retired history professor*
Sljivic-Simsic, Biljana B. *retired Slavic and Baltic languages educator*
Slocum, Kay Brainerd *history professor, musician*
Smith, Ellen Louise *retired language educator*
Smither, Howard Elbert *musicologist, educator*
Smock, Raymond William *historian*
Sosa, Ernest *philosopher, educator*
Spadafora, David Charles *historian, educator*
Spangler, Beulah Stark (Bes Spangler) *retired literature and language professor*
Speelman, Patrick J. *history professor*
Sprague, Esther Sparks *art history educator*
Squibb, John R. *history professor*
Sreenivas, Mytheli *history professor*
Stabler, Scott Lawrence *historian, educator*
Staley, Thomas Fabian *literature and language professor, museum director*
Steiner, Elizabeth *philosopher, psychologist, educator*
Stendahl, Brita Kristina *humanities and social studies educator*
Stephens, Robert Oren *retired English language educator*
Stevenson, Marshall Field, Jr. *history professor*
Stewart, Rod *retired literature and language professor*
Stiebing, William Henry, Jr. *retired history professor*
Stiritz, Marette McCauley *English language educator, consultant*
Stockdale, Nancy L. *historian, educator*
Stocker, Christine Marie *language educator*
Stolarik, M. Mark *history professor*
Stone, Jin *language educator*
Story, Joyce Ann *retired language educator*
Street, John Charles *linguistics educator*
Sullivan, Mary Rose *retired English language educator*
Sutton, Julia *musicologist, dance historian*
Suzuki, Yukiko *language educator*
Taar, Mireille *language educator, interpreter*
Taifi, Mohamed *language educator, researcher*
Tarantino, Cheryl *literature and language professor*
Tayler, Irene *retired English literature educator*
Taylor, Henry Splawn *retired literature educator, poet*
Taylor, James C. *language educator*
Taylor, Marisa *literature and language professor*
Teaford, Jon Christian *retired history professor*
Thernstrom, Stephan *historian, educator*
Thomas, Lynnell L. *language educator*
Thomason, James Brant *history professor*
Thompson, Edleeca Payne *humanities educator*
Thompson, Ewa M. *foreign language educator*
Thomson, Virginia Winbourn *humanities educator, writer*
Thornton, Richard C. *history professor*
Thorson, Connie Capers *library educator*
Thursby, Jacqueline Schuster *literature and language professor, director*
Tise, Larry Edward *historian, cultural organization administrator*
Titcomb, Caldwell *music and theatre historian*
Tkach, Dianne *educator*
Todd, William Mills III *literature educator*
Tomlinson, Susan Elizabeth *language educator*
Toplin, Robert Brent *history professor, television producer*
Torda, Elinor A. *language educator*
Tran, Tammie *language educator*
Trelease, Allen William *historian, educator*
Trinchet, Jorge *language educator*
Tubb, Gary Alan *humanities educator*
Tucker, Thomas Deane *humanities educator*
Turk, Eleanor Louise *history professor*
Tutt, Karl Fleming *literature and language professor*
Ugalde, Arantza *language educator*
Ullestad, Charles Lee *humanities educator*
Ulloa, Leonor Alvarez de *language educator*
Unterberger, Betty Miller *retired history professor*
Urbano, Arthur Peter *historian, theologian*
Urofsky, Melvin Irving *historian, educator, director*
Vailakis, Ivonne G. *literature educator*
Valdez, Patricia *language educator*
Valencia, Margarita *Spanish language educator*
van der Marck, Jan *art historian*
Velikanova, Olga *historian, educator*
Venema, Jeremy *literature and language professor*
Vernon, Alex *literature and language professor*
Villarrubia, Glenda Boone *reading specialist and coordinator, educator, consultant*
Voloshin, Beverly R. *literature and language professor*
von Bothmer, Bernard Nicholas *history professor*
Vuong, Joseph Trung *humanities educator*
Vuong, Lynette Dyer *literature and language professor*
Wakefield, Sarah Rebecca *literature and language professor*
Walker, James Edward *humanities educator*
Walker, Philip Doolittle *retired literature and language professor, composer*
Walker, Rachel Brady *retired literature and language professor*
Walker, Ruth Charlotta *language educator, real estate broker*
Walker, Steven Charles *literature and language professor*
Walsh, Michael Thomas *historian, musician*
Wang, Richard G. *literature educator*
Wang, Youru *philosopher, educator*
Wax, Alan S. *language educator*
Weinberg, Gerhard Ludwig *history professor, writer*
Weintraub, Sam *retired reading educator*
Weir, Jeffrey Michael *history professor, consultant*
Wheeler, Burton M. *language educator, dean*
Whitburn, Merrill Duane *English literature educator*
White, Charles Sidney John *retired humanities educator*
Wiebenson, Dora Louise *architectural historian, editor, writer*
Williams, Rachel D. *literature and language professor*
Wills, John Elliot, Jr. *retired historian, writer*
Winter, Judy Elaine *author, speaker*
Wiswall, Dorothy Roller *language educator*
Wizda, Christine Anne *history professor*
Wolfe, Margaret Ripley *historian, educator, consultant*
Woloch, Isser *history educator*
Woodring, Carl *English language educator*
Woodside, Lisa Nicole *retired humanities educator*
Woodward, Ralph Lee, Jr. *retired historian, educator*
Wright, Josephine Rosa Beatrice *musicologist, educator*
Wu, Fengtao *language educator*
Yannella, Donald *literature and language professor*
Yarbrough, Robert Allen *literature and language professor*
Yepes, Enrique *language educator*

Yerushalmi, Yosef Hayim *historian, educator*
Young, David *language educator*
Young, MaryAnn *humanities educator*
Zazueta, Dolores Manrique *language educator*
Zhang, Qing *language educator*
Zimmermann, Thomas Callander Price *retired historian, educator*
Zubieta, Maria Jose *language educator*

HUMANITIES: LIBRARIES

UNITED STATES

ALABAMA

Auburn University
MacEwan, Bonnie *librarian, dean*

Birmingham
Sirmans, Barbara C. *library director*
Stephens, Jerry Wayne *librarian, director*

Gardendale
McKay, Marie Conyers *librarian, writer*

Huntsville
Abram, Stephen *librarian, writer*

Jacksonville
Hubbard, William James *library director*

Mobile
Bahr, Alice Harrison *librarian*
Parsley, Brantley Hamilton *librarian*

Montgomery
Owes, Jaunita *library director*

Northport
Stephens, Annabel Kuykendall *retired library and information scientist*

Selma
Carstarphen, Minnie Lee *library director*

Troy
Stewart, Henry R. *library director*

Tuscaloosa
Grimes, Deborah Jeanne *library director*
Osburn, Charles Benjamin *retired librarian, dean*

ALASKA

Fairbanks
Knutsen, Deborah May *librarian*

Juneau
Schorr, Alan Edward *librarian, publishing executive*
Thibodeau, Linda *state librarian*

ARIZONA

Chandler
Brown, Brenda *library director*

Cottonwood
Oneill, John Robert *library director*

Glendale
Honsa, Vlasta *retired librarian*

Lake Havasu City
Mahan, James E. *archivist, educator*

Mesa
Schneider, Rebecca *librarian*
Wolf, Heather *library director*

Phoenix
Roof, Sally Jean-Marie *library and information scientist, educator*
Willocks, Robert Max *retired librarian*

Scottsdale
Hamilton, Rita *library director*

Sun City
Williams, William Harrison *retired librarian*

Tempe
Duvernay, Jennifer *librarian*
Gabbard, Ralph Barnhart *user services officer*
Metros, Mary Teresa *librarian*
O'Clair, Katherine Clemens *library and information scientist*
Schmidt, Sherrie *library director, dean*

Tucson
White, Herbert Spencer *library and information scientist, educator, dean*

ARKANSAS

Beebe
Russ, Ronald Steven *librarian*

El Dorado
Arn, Nancy Lynn *library director*

Fort Smith
Van Arsdale, Dennis G. *librarian*

Little Rock
Ashcraft, Carolyn *state librarian*
Garner, Terri *library and museum director*
Mulkey, Jack Clarendon *retired library director*

Monticello
Vincent, Angelia Annette *librarian*

CALIFORNIA

Aptos
Heron, David Winston *librarian*

Bakersfield
Asher, Curtis Martin *librarian*

Berkeley
Buckland, Michael Keeble *librarian, educator*
Leonard, Thomas C. *librarian, dean*

Cupertino
Fletcher, Homer Lee *librarian*

Danville
Gold, Anne Marie *library consultant*

Davis
Sharrow, Marilyn Jane *library administrator*
Stevens, Robert David *librarian, educator*

Downey
Todd, Margaret Donnellan *library director*

Fontana
Higgins, Rosemarie Lorraine *librarian*

Fremont
Bray, Richard Daniel *librarian*
Hofacket, Jean *library director*

Fullerton
Ayala, John L. *retired librarian, dean*
Johnson, Carolyn Elizabeth *librarian*

Glendale
Michelson, Lillian *librarian, researcher*

Gustine
Ramirez, Nola Marie *librarian*

Lafayette
Morehouse, Valerie Jeanne *librarian*

Laguna Beach
Anderson, Elizabeth Carmal (Bette Anderson) *librarian, writer*

Long Beach
Proust, Joycelyn Ann *retired librarian*
Schmidt, Eleanore *library director*

Los Angeles
Bates, Marcia Jeanne *information scientist educator*
Chang, Henry C. *library administrator*
Cheng, Hong *library and information scientist*
Cuadra, Carlos Albert *library and information scientist, consultant*
Custen, Barbara S. *library director*
Quinlan, Catherine *library director*
Richardson, John Vinson, Jr. *library and information science professor*
Shank, Russell *librarian, educator*
Song, Yongyi *librarian*
Starr, Kevin *librarian, educator*

Menlo Park
White, Cecil Ray *librarian, consultant*

Merced
Near, Delia Mary *librarian*

Mill Valley
Dillon, Richard Hugh *librarian, author*

Monterey
Reneker, Maxine Hohman *librarian*

Monterey Park
Wilson, Linda *librarian*

Mountain View
Di Muccio, Mary-Jo *retired librarian*
Healy, Jodi *library services manager*

Northridge
Duran, Karin Jeanine *librarian*
Finley, Mary Margaret *librarian*

Oakland
Coaston, Shirley Ann Dumas *librarian*
Green, David Edward *retired librarian, priest, translator*
Lee, Ella Louise *librarian, educator*
Price, Gary *librarian*
Rubin, Rhea Joyce *library consultant*
Woo, Janice *librarian*

Oceanside
Lange, Clifford Elmer *retired librarian*

Palm Springs
Conover, Robert Warren *retired librarian*

Palo Alto
Schmidt, Cyril James *librarian*

Port Hueneme Cbc Base
Nichols, Gina Lynn *archivist, writer*

Redlands
Burgess, Larry Eugene *library director, historian, educator*

Sacramento
Jimenez, Regina Ann *librarian*

San Bernardino
Burgess, Michael (Robert Reginald) *librarian, writer*

San Diego
Barrow, Deborah *library director*
Sauer, David Andrew *librarian, writer*
Schon, Isabel *library science specialist, educator*

San Francisco
Aldrich, Michael Ray *library curator, health educator*
Bocobo-Balunsat, Dalisay *librarian, journalist*
Poitras, Gilles Lee *librarian*

San Jose
Chase, Joy Doris *librarian*
Light, Jane Ellen *library director*

San Luis Obispo
Dowell, David Ray *library administrator*

San Mateo
Gómez, Martín *library director*
Johnson, Victoria L. *library director*

Santa Barbara
Gartrell, David Christian *archivist*
Johnson, Brenda L. *university librarian*

Santa Clara
Hopkinson, Shirley Lois *library and information scientist, educator*
Karas, Timothy *library director*
Ostwald, Venice Eloise Varner *librarian, educator, minister, writer*

Santa Monica
Levin, Barry Raymond *rare book dealer, film producer*

Santa Rosa
Rosaschi, Jim *librarian*

Sebastopol
Sabsay, David *retired library director*

Simi Valley
Blackwood, (R.) Duke *library and museum director*

Stanford
Derksen, Charlotte Ruth Meynink *librarian*
Keller, Michael Alan *librarian, musicologist*

Stockton
Gertler, Fred *librarian, dean*
Hawbaker, A. Craig *librarian*
Wong, Patricia M.Y. *library director*
Yamashita, Kenneth Akira *library administrator, librarian*

Susanville
Brown, Rosanna Maria Nelson *library director*

Thousand Oaks
Brogden, Stephen Richard *library director*

Torrance
Grigsby, Alice Burns *librarian*

Turlock
Parker, John Carlyle *retired librarian and archivist, editor*

Whittier
Weismiller, Eleanor Kovacs *library director*

Woodland Hills
Zeitlin, Eugenia Pawlik *librarian, educator, writer*

Yorba Linda
Naftali, Timothy J. *library director, historian, educator, writer*

COLORADO

Boulder
Bintliff, Barbara Ann *library director, law educator*
O'Brien, Elmer John *librarian, educator*
Wertheimer, Marilyn Lou *librarian, educator*

Canon City
Cochran, Susan Mills *research librarian*

Colorado Springs
Miller, Paula J. *library director*

Denver
Ahern, Arleen Fleming *retired librarian*
Amore, Shirley C. *library director*
Garcia, June Marie *librarian*
White, Joyce Louise *librarian*

Fort Collins
Mc Clellan, William Monson *retired library director*

Grand Junction
Bragdon, Lynn Lyon *library administrator*

Greeley
Chaudhuri, Jayati *librarian*

Lakewood
Knott, William Alan *library director*

Longmont
Salberg, Anne Scholberg *retired librarian*

Louisville
Maddock, Jerome Torrence *library and information scientist*

Westminster
Dockerty, Katherine *librarian, educator*

CONNECTICUT

Danbury
Hasskarl, Mark P. *library director*

Fairfield
Bryan, Barbara Day *retired librarian*

Glastonbury
Bailey, Barbara *library director*

Hartford
Antonucci, Carl Anthony *library director, educator*
Kaimowitz, Jeffrey Hugh *librarian*

Middletown
Klare, Diane G. *librarian*

New Haven
Heister, Carla Gayle *librarian*
Okerson, Ann Shumelda Lillian *librarian*
Stuehrenberg, Paul Frederick *librarian*

Niantic
Deakyne, William John *library director, musician*

Plainville
Chase, Peter *library director*

Simsbury
Roberts, Celia Ann *librarian*

Storrs Mansfield
Franklin, Brinley *library director*

Waterbury
McSweeney, J. Emmett *library director*

Wilton
Poundstone, Sally Hill *library director*

DELAWARE

Wilmington
Williams, Richmond Dean *library consultant and appraiser*

DISTRICT OF COLUMBIA

Washington
Adamson, Jeremy E. *library director*
Beall, Julianne *librarian*
Billington, James Hadley *librarian, historian*
Cooper, Ginnie *library director*
Cylke, Frank Kurt *librarian*
Dixson, Diane Elizabeth *library congress docent retired,acquisitions librarian, tax preparation business owner visitors service office retired senior acquisitions librarian, financial counselor*
Emperado, Mercedes Lopez *librarian*
Guyton, Clara L. *librarian*
Haley, Roger Kendall *librarian*
Harlem, Susan Lynn *librarian*
Henry, Charles Jay *library and information scientist*
Kadis, Averil Jordan *retired librarian*
Lippincott, Joan K. *library director*
Lowry, Charles Bryan *librarian, dean*
Missar, Charles Donald *retired librarian*
Player, Thelma B. *librarian*
Rovelstad, Mathilde V(erner) *retired library and information scientist, educator*
Smith, George Vinal *librarian*
Stevens, Roberta A. *librarian*
Turtell, Neal Timothy *librarian*

FLORIDA

Deland
Caccamise, Genevra Louise Ball (Mrs. Alfred E. Caccamise) *retired librarian*

Destin
Burns, Jurate *library director*
Deel, Frances Quinn *retired librarian*

Englewood
McCall, Gene William *conservator, sculptor, artist, furniture designer*

Fort Lauderdale
Acosta, Lydia M. *library director*
Beach, Cecil Prentice *librarian*
Cannon, Robert Eugene *library director*

Fort Myers
Miller, Kathleen Fairbrother *librarian*

Gainesville
Russell, Judith *librarian, dean*

Jacksonville
Lee, Hwa-Wei *librarian, educator, consultant*

Jensen Beach
Lowrie, Jean Elizabeth *librarian, educator*

Juno Beach
Terwillegar, Jane Cusack *retired librarian, educator*

Lakeland
Reich, David Lee *library director*

Leesburg
Morse, Barbara Jeanne *library director*

Lighthouse Point
Gauthier, Doreen Ann *librarian*

Madison
Hiss, Sheila Mary *librarian*

Miami
Lehman, Douglas Kent *librarian*
Santiago, Raymond *library director, educator*

Miami Beach
King, Sky V. *librarian*

Naples
Hall, Beverly Barton *librarian*

North Miami
Downs, Antonie *librarian*

Ocala
Tesmer, Nancy Ann Stutler *retired librarian*

Orlando
Allison, Anne Marie *retired librarian*
Hodel, Mary Anne *library director*

Palm Bay
Anderson, Deborah F. *librarian, educator*

Saint Leo
Neuhofer, Mary Dorothy *archivist, librarian*
Van Kampen, Doris J. *librarian, educator*

Saint Petersburg
Kent, Allen *library and information sciences professor*

Sarasota
Brandhorst, Wesley Theodore *retired library and information scientist*
De Gennaro, Richard *retired library director*
Retzer, Mary Elizabeth Helm *retired librarian*

Sun City Center
Willard, Louis Charles *retired librarian*

Tallahassee
Doffek, Pamala Jean *library director*
Goldstein, Julia Sonia *librarian*
McClure, Charles Robert *library and information science educator, consultant*
Ring, Judith A. *state librarian*
Thompson, Jean Tanner *retired librarian*
Zachert, Martha Jane *retired librarian*

Tampa
Barron, Elizabeth Lee *librarian*
Keach, Michael Andrew *library and information scientist*

University Park
Compain, Rita *librarian*

Venice
Asp, William George *librarian*

Winter Park
Bloodworth, Velda Jean *librarian, educator*
Murray, Susan Lyons *library director*
Rogers, Rutherford David *librarian*

GEORGIA

Albany
McLaughlin, LaVerne Laney *library director*

Athens
Donovan, James M. *librarian, anthropologist*
Nicewarner, Metta Lee *library director, artist*

Atlanta
Fox, Robert E., Jr. *library director*
Hakes, Jay Edward *library director, former federal agency administrator*
McDavid, Sara June *librarian*
Meier, Gayle M. *library director*
Roberts, Edward Graham *librarian*
Wallace, Gladys Baldwin *retired librarian*

Barnesville
Anderson, Nancy Dixon *librarian*
Hollingsworth, Edna Diane *librarian*

Clarkston
Barrow, Ellen *librarian, educator*

Cleveland
Edwards, John Carver *retired archivist*

Evans
Rowland, Arthur Ray *librarian*

Fayetteville
Neal, Joan Burkes *retired librarian*

Fort Valley
Mahitab, Frank *librarian, director*

Griffin
Bunnell, David Paul *library director*

Kennesaw
Hansen, Jon *librarian*

Rome
Doyle, James Donald, Jr. *librarian*

Statesboro
Hamilton, Ann Hollingsworth *library director*
Mitchell, Wilfrid Bede *librarian, library association executive*
Skewis, Charles Arthur *librarian*

Thomaston
Adams, Cynthia Ann *librarian, media specialist, language educator*

Thomasville
Tillinghast, Nancy *library director*

Warner Robins
Bunn, Dumont C. *academic library director, educator, consultant*
Merk, P. Evelyn *retired librarian*

HAWAII

Honolulu
Mochida, Paula T. *library director*
Yee, Florence *library director*

Kahului
Tolliver, Dorothy *library director*

Kailua
Wright, John Cotton *archivist, consultant*

IDAHO

Idaho Falls
Gray, Catherine Jean *librarian*

Kimberly
Owings, Vickie Ann *librarian*

ILLINOIS

Addison
Medjo Me Zengue, Mary *library director*

Arlington Heights
Giannini, Evelyn Louise *retired library consultant*

Bloomington
Olson, Rue Eileen *retired librarian*

Calumet City
Muñoz, Romeo Solano *audio visual curator*

Carbondale
Bauner, Ruth Elizabeth *library director*
Carlson, David Harold *library director, dean*

Champaign
Richardson, Selma Katherine *retired library and information scientist*
Ruan, Lian Jin *library director*

Chicago
Ashton, Rick James *librarian*
Bentley, Carol Ligon *retired library and information scientist*
Brown, Richard Holbrook *library director, historian, researcher*
Choldin, Marianna Tax *librarian, educator*
Funk, Carla Jean *library association director*
Gerdes, Neil Wayne *library director, educator*
Hagan, Kate (Kathryn T. Hagan) *library director, editor*
Martin, Kristin Emily *librarian*
Nadler, Judith *library director*
Parr, Virginia Helen *retired librarian*
Seal, Robert A. *library director*
Sullivan, Peggy *librarian, consultant*
Zelenka, H. Dayle Kendall *librarian*

Dekalb
Hamilton, David Arnold *retired librarian*

Downers Grove
Bowen, Christopher Frank *library director*

East Peoria
Bell, Lori (Lorelei Junot) *library director, library and information scientist*
Pope, Kitty *library director*

Elmhurst
Willis, Kathleen A. *librarian*

Evanston
Bethel, Kathleen Evonne *librarian*
Bishop, David Fulton *retired library administrator*
Crawford, Susan *library director, educator, editor, writer*
Pritchard, Sarah Margaret *library director*

Freeport
Vogt, Lorna Corrine *retired librarian, small business owner*

Galesburg
Coatney, Louis Robert *librarian, historian*

Glen Ellyn
Slusar, Linda *library and information scientist*

Indian Head Park
Bamberger, Mary Ann *archivist, consultant*

Jacksonville
Gallas, Martin Hans *librarian*

Lincolnwood
Bodi, Sonia Ellen *library director, educator*
DeBock, Cynthia Marie *archivist, researcher*

Lisle
DeGreve, Luann *library assistant director*
Kroll, Mark Alan *librarian*

Morton
Andrews, Cynthia Kay *librarian*

Oak Park
Burnette, Mark C. *librarian*

Peoria
Corpuz, Laura Balatbat *library coordinator*

Quincy
Tyer, Travis Earl *librarian, consultant*

Red Bud
Light, David Mark *retired librarian, retired musician*

Riverside
Van Cura, Joyce Bennett *librarian*

Roselle
Hanrath, Linda Carol *librarian, archivist*

Rosiclare
Largent, Judy *library director*

Schaumburg
Adrianopoli, Barbara Catherine *librarian*
Davis, Joseph Dean *librarian*

Skokie
Anthony, Carolyn Additon *librarian*
Bush, Gail *librarian, educator, writer*

South Beloit
Dunbar, Ortus Lee *librarian*

South Holland
Connolly, Carla Marie *librarian*

Springfield
Craig, Ann *library director*
Roberts, Ryan M. *librarian, educator, webmaster*

Urbana
Bennett, Scott Boyce *retired librarian, consultant*
Brichford, Maynard Jay *archivist*
O'Brien, Nancy Patricia *librarian, educator*
Watson, Paula D. *retired librarian*
Weissinger, Thomas *librarian, educator*

Westmont
Kuhn, Christine Marie *library director*

Wheaton
Thompson, Bert Allen *retired librarian*
Tucker, Beverly Sowers *library and information scientist*

Wheeling
Long, Sarah Ann *librarian*

Wilmette
Hansen, Andrew Marius *retired library director*

Zion
Hilyard, Nann Blaine *librarian*

INDIANA

Bloomington
Dalmau, Michelle *library and information scientist*
Meho, Lokman I. *library and information scientist, educator*
Rudolph, Lavere Christian *library director*
Studwell, William Emmett *librarian, writer*

Columbus
Schmidt, Steven Jameson *library director*

Fort Wayne
Krull, Jeffrey Robert *library director*

Indianapolis
Bramble, Laura *library director*
Gnat, Raymond Earl *librarian*
Irwin, Marilyn M. *librarian, educator*
Turner-Wright, Marie Annetta *retired librarian*

Lafayette
Mobley, Emily Ruth *library director, educator, dean*

Muncie
Dolak, Fritz *librarian, information administrator*
Schaefer, Patricia *retired librarian*
Yeamans, George Thomas *librarian, educator*

Seymour
Aker, Julia Kathleen *library director*

Valparaiso
Katich, Janet *librarian*

West Lafayette
Markee, Katherine Madigan *librarian, educator*
Nixon, Judith May *librarian*

IOWA

Davenport
Roudebush, LaWanda Carpenter *library director*
Runge, Kay Kretschmar *library consultant*

Des Moines
Wegner, Mary *state librarian*

Dubuque
Lathrop, Carolynne Sue *librarian*

Iowa City
Baker, Nancy L. *university librarian, educator*
Bentz, Dale Monroe *retired librarian*
Huttner, Sidney Frederick *librarian*
McCartney, David Farnham *archivist, educator*

Newton
Padilla, Sue Ann *librarian*

Spirit Lake
Spriester, Rebecca Groen *librarian*

West Branch
Mather, Mildred Eunice *retired archivist*
Walch, Timothy George *library director*

KANSAS

Abilene
Holt, Daniel D. *library director*

Fort Leavenworth
Barker, Ray Todd *archivist, writer*

Hugoton
Schroeder, Eunice M. *library director*

Hutchinson
Kelly, Robert, IV, *library director*

Lawrence
Crowe, William Joseph *librarian*
Haricombe, Lorraine *library director, dean*

Manhattan
Trussell, Alice J. *library director, department chairman*

Parsons
Zollars, Scotty M. *library director*

Pittsburg
Lee, Earl Wayne *library science educator*

Wichita
Berner-Harris, Cynthia Kay *library director*

KENTUCKY

Bowling Green
Forrest, Dan *librarian*
Foster, Connie L. *librarian*

Campbellsville
Burch, John Russell, Jr. *library director, historian, writer*

Danville
Pappas, Marjorie L. *library studies educator*

Frankfort
Gibbons, Judith A. *librarian*
Hampton-Norphlet, Dantrea RayAnn *librarian*
Hecker, Margaret Prentice *academic librarian*

La Grange
Morgan, Mary Dan *librarian*

Lexington
Imhoff, Kathleen Ruth Tostrud *library administrator*
Mason, Ellsworth Goodwin *retired librarian*
Sineath, Timothy Wayne *librarian, educator, dean*

Louisville
Deering, Ronald Franklin *librarian, minister*

Middlesboro
Ahlstedt, Lisa Anne *librarian*

Morehead
Pritchard, Elsie Tomlinson *librarian*

Paducah
Kirk, Terri G. *library media specialist*

Williamsburg
Bay, Mark Twitchell *librarian*

LOUISIANA

Baton Rouge
Hamilton, Rebecca L. *state librarian*
Lusk, Glenna Rae Knight *librarian*

Bossier City
Brantley, Brenda Bradford *librarian*

Grambling
King, Gennice Williams *librarian*

Lafayette
Triche III, Charles Walter *librarian, director*

Lake Charles
McNeill, Joseph Peele *librarian*

Paris, Margaret G. *librarian*
Sawyer, Michael E. *library director*

Metairie
Dickerson, Lon Richard *library administrator*

Napoleonville
Maggio, Theresa Griffin (Terri Maggio) *librarian*

New Orleans
Bender, Thomas Benton, IV, *librarian*

New Roads
Hymel, Melissa K. *librarian*

Pineville
Martin, W. Terry *librarian*

Ponchatoula
Kuechmann, Christopher Robert *library director*

Shreveport
Timm, Donna Faye *librarian*

MAINE

Bangor
Rea, Ann W. *librarian*

Lewiston
Speer, Richard Allan *library director*

Orono
Richard, Hollinger Vernon *archivist, historian*

MARYLAND

Baltimore
Bluh, Pamela M. *library associate director*
Bradley, Wanda Louise *librarian*
Hayden, Carla Diane *library director, educator*
Tabb, Winston *library director*

Beltsville
Young, Peter Robert *library director*

Bethesda
Conger, Lucinda *retired librarian*
Knachel, Philip Atherton *librarian*
Ostell, James M. *library and information scientist, biotechnologist*
Yang, Key Paik *librarian, archivist*

Bowie
Wardrip, Elizabeth Jane *retired librarian*

Chestertown
Rather, Lucia Porcher Johnson *library administrator*
Shoge, Ruth Casandra *library director*

Chevy Chase
Basa, Enikö Molnár *retired librarian*

College Park
Lowell, Howard Parsons *archivist, federal agency administrator*
Weinstein, Allen *archivist*

Columbia
Gruhl, Andrea Morris *librarian*
Klein, Sami Weiner *librarian*

Forestville
Moore, Virginia Bradley *librarian*

Gaithersburg
Broderick, John Caruthers *librarian, educator*

Germantown
Lewis, Robert John Cornelius Koons *retired library director*

Glen Burnie
Mc Cabe, Gerard Benedict *retired library administrator*

Hagerstown
Feagin, James R.H. *librarian, director*

La Plata
Johnson, Diane Jones *librarian*

Potomac
Webster, Duane Ernes *retired librarian*

Princess Anne
Brooks, Sharon Denise *librarian*

Rockville
Hamilton, Parker *library director*
Renninger, Mary Karen *retired librarian*

Saint Leonard
Seifert, Betty L. *conservator, consultant*

Salisbury
Wolter, John Amadeus *librarian, federal official*

Springdale
Keith, Patricia *multi-media specialist*

Towson
Tull, Willis Clayton, Jr. *retired librarian*

MASSACHUSETTS

Amherst
Schafer, Gerald Lewis (Jay Schafer) *library director*
Trumble, Paul *librarian*

Boston
Armstrong, Rodney *librarian*
Christopher, Irene *librarian, consultant*
Cloonan, Michele V. *library director*
Putnam, Thomas J. *library and museum director*
Reid-Cunningham, James *conservator*
Ryan, Amy E. *library director*
Wakeling, William Michael *librarian, director*
Warab, Kristi *librarian*

Brookline
Brenner, Robin E. *librarian*

Cambridge
Darnton, Robert Choate *library director, historian, educator*
Steins, Janet L. *librarian, consultant*
Stoddard, Roger Eliot *scholar*
Wolpert, Ann J. *library director*

Canton
Kelley, Irene W. *retired librarian, musician, artist*

Carver
Neubauer, Richard A. *library science educator, consultant*

Chatham
Gillies, Irene B. *library director*

Chestnut Hill
Hebard, Barbara Adams *conservator*

Cohasset
Wendorf, Richard Harold *library director, scholar*

Dover
Peirce, Bonnie *librarian*

Heath
Howland, Margaret E.C. *retired librarian*

Lexington
Freitag, Wolfgang Martin *retired librarian*

Lincoln
Bracken, (Myra) Jeanne Munn *librarian, writer*

Marstons Mills
Martin, Susan Katherine *librarian*

Medford
Michalak, Jo-Ann *library director*

Natick
Rendell, Kenneth William *rare and historical documents dealer, consultant*

Newton
Glick-Weil, Kathy *library director*

North Adams
Gross, Marcia R. *library director, educator*

Northampton
Piccinino, Rocco Michael *librarian*

Shirley Center
Holden, Harley Peirce *retired archivist*

Springfield
Spencer, Estelle Heidi *library director*

Wenham
Schirer-Suter, Myron *library director*

Williamstown
Pilachowski, David M. *library director*

Woods Hole
Gifford, Prosser *retired library administrator*

Worcester
Dunlap, Ellen S. *library administrator*
McCorison, Marcus Allen *librarian, cultural organization administrator*

MICHIGAN

Adrian
Geyer, Richard Douglas *librarian, editor, poet*

Allendale
Murray, Diane Elizabeth *librarian*

Ann Arbor
Beaubien, Anne Kathleen *librarian*
Blumenthal, Jane Leonardi *library director*
Buckley, Francis J., Jr. *librarian*
Daub, Peggy Ellen *library administrator*
Didier, Elaine K. *library and museum director, educator*
Dougherty, Richard Martin *library and information science professor*
Dunlap, Connie *librarian*

Big Rapids
Konovalov, Yuri *librarian, educator*

Birmingham
Custer, Martha Lou *library director*

Clinton Township
Rybicki, Stephen (Steve Rybicki) *librarian*

Dearborn
Powell, Ronald Rowe *retired library science educator*

Detroit
Godzak, Roman Paul *archivist*
Hudson, Anne Laurie *librarian*
Mika, Joseph John *library and information scientist, educator*
Skowronski, Nancy *library director*
Spyers-Duran, Peter *librarian, educator*
Yee, Sandra Gayle Brown *library director, dean*

East Lansing
Baclawski, Diane Kay *librarian, researcher*
Haka, Clifford Hughey *library director*

Grand Rapids
Ingersoll, Patricia Lee *library director*

Grosse Pointe
Casey, Genevieve M(ary) *librarian, educator*

Harsens Island
Woodford, Arthur MacKinnon *library director, historian*

Hillsdale
Pierson, Diana Lee *librarian, educator*

Holt
Smith, Betty W. *librarian*

Kalamazoo
Grotzinger, Laurel Ann *librarian, educator*
Nowicki, Stacy A. *library director*

Lansing
Franklin, James J. *librarian*

Midland
Potts, Sandra *library director*

Mount Pleasant
Lorenzen, Michael Gary *librarian, researcher*
Messick, Frederic Morton *librarian*

Plymouth
Berry, Charlene Helen *librarian, musician*

Port Huron
Miller, Theresa L. *library director*
Wu, Harry Pao-Tung *retired librarian*

Redford
Karpinski, Huberta *library trustee*

Rochester
Keller, Alison E. *library director*

Trenton
Sanak, Francene Elizabeth *librarian*

West Bloomfield
Morgan, Jane Hale *retired library director*

MINNESOTA

Bemidji
Conely, Patrice Erin *librarian*

Breezy Point
Anderson, Gail Marie *retired librarian*

Duluth
Pearce, Donald Joslin *retired librarian*

Good Thunder
Bothmann, Robert *librarian*

Hopkins
Young, Margaret Labash *librarian, information consultant, editor*

Minneapolis
Hadley, Katherine G. (Kit) *library director*
Johnson, Margaret Ann (Peggy) *library administrator*
Ostrem, Walter Martin *librarian, educator, consultant*

Northfield
Christensen, Beth Elaine *music librarian*
Edwins, Jennifer *librarian*

Rochester
Key, Jack Dayton *librarian*
Lange, Elizabeth Ann *retired librarian*

Roseville
Miller, Suzanne Marie *library director, educator*

Saint Paul
Huggins, Melanie *library director*
Wagner, Mary Margaret *library and information scientist, educator*

Saint Peter
Haeuser, Michael John *library administrator*

Winona
Beth, Sandra A. *library director*

MISSISSIPPI

Alcorn State
Yu, May Huang *librarian, educator*

Gulfport
Lipscomb, Robert McBride *library director, educator*

Jackson
Smith, Sharman Bridges *state librarian*

Natchez
McLemore, Joan Meadows *librarian, consultant*

Raymond
Hilkert, Judith Rene *librarian*

MISSOURI

Bolivar
Brown, Sandra L. *librarian, educator*

Chesterfield
Kohnen, Carol Ann *librarian*

Columbia
Almony, Robert Allen, Jr. *librarian*
Caruthers, Janet *library director*
Cogswell, James A. *library director*
Cogswell, Jim *library director*
Pinkerton, Marjorie Jean *retired librarian*

Greenwood
Zeller, Marilynn Kay *retired librarian*

Hermann
Wilson, C. Daniel, Jr. *library director*

Independence
Devine, Michael J. *library and museum director, educator*

Joplin
Nodler, Charles Edward, Jr. *archivist, history professor*

Kansas City
Nelson, Freda Nell Hein *librarian*

Parkville
Schultis, Gail Ann *library director*

Saint Louis
Berger, David Otto *library director, educator*
Brown, Bettye *librarian, educator*
Cann, C. J. *librarian*
McCaslin, Sharon *librarian*
Pace, Charles *library director*
Verbeck, Alison *librarian*

Springfield
Horny, Karen Louise *library administrator*

MONTANA

Billings
Cochran, William Michael *librarian*

Havre
Jestrab, Carol A. *librarian*

Livingston
Cummins, Milla Lattan *library director*

Poplar
Scheetz, Anita A. *library director*

NEBRASKA

Boys Town
DiBacco, Nadine Louise *retired library director, photographer, writer*

Kearney
Hardesty, Larry Lynn *librarian*

Lincoln
Giesecke, Joan Ruth *librarian, dean*
Wagner, Rod *library director*

Omaha
Bernardi, John Vincent *librarian*
Sass, Rivkah K. *library director*

Plattsmouth
Hunt, Stephen Lynn *library director*

York
Carlock, Ruth Marie *librarian, educator*
Ratliff, Ramona *librarian*

NEVADA

Reno
Cummings, Nancy *library director*
Ross, Robert Donald *library director*

NEW HAMPSHIRE

Berlin
Doherty, Katherine Mann *librarian, writer*

Concord
York, Michael Charest *librarian*

Durham
Young, Arthur Price *librarian, educator*

Exeter
Thomas, Jacquelyn May *librarian*

Goffstown
Wajenberg, Arnold Sherman *retired librarian, educator*

Hanover
Horrell, Jeffrey Lanier *library director*

Milton
Edelman, Hendrik *library and information science professor*

NEW JERSEY

Allentown
Van Hise, Yvonne *librarian*

Blackwood
Getaz, Joan *library director*

Browns Mills
Clarke, Betty Ann *librarian, minister*

Cape May Court House
Hsu, Hsiu-hsiang *retired librarian*

Edgewater
Berliner, Barbara *retired librarian, consultant*

Fort Lee
Altomara, Rita Ecke *library director, writer*

Glassboro
Wright, William Cook *archivist, director*

Glen Rock
Savoie, Brietta Dolores Giger *retired librarian*

Hoboken
Widdicombe, Richard Palmer *librarian*

Jersey City
Bulaong, Grace F. *library director*
Smith, Frederick Augustus *librarian*

Linden
Purves, Dennis Patrick *library director*

Madison
Rubinstein, Ernest *librarian, educator*
Scrimgeour, Andrew David *library director*

Mahwah
Knight, Shirley Delores *librarian*

Middletown
O'Neal, Susan *library director*

New Brunswick
Anderson, James Doig *library and information science educator*
Denda, Kayo *librarian*
Gaunt, Marianne I. *university librarian*
Lesk, Michael E. *library and information science educator*
Marker, Rhonda Joyce *librarian*

Oakland
Reutty, Michele Marie *library director*

Plainfield
Da Rold, Joseph Hugh *library director, museum director*

Plainsboro
Baeckler, Virginia Van Wynen *librarian, writer*

Point Pleasant
Greene, Ellin *library service educator*

Princeton
Burger, Leslie B. *library director, library association executive*
Fox, Mary Ann Williams *librarian*
Gray, Nancy Wicklund *librarian, educator*
Hermann, Janie L. *librarian*
Trainer, Karin A. *librarian*

Princeton Junction
Butorac, Frank George *librarian, educator*

South Orange
Bao, Xue-Ming *librarian, educator*
Loesch, Martha M. *academic librarian*

Teaneck
Stein-Smith, Kathleen *librarian, foreign language educator*
Weiss, Mitchell Joseph *librarian*

Tenafly
Wechtler, Stephen Robert *library director*

Trenton
Blake, Norma E. *library director*
Russell, Joyce Anne Rogers *retired librarian*

Union
Rogge, Rena Wolcott *librarian*

Vineland
Schmid, Patti A. *library director*

Voorhees
Brahms, William Bernard *librarian, publisher, writer*

Wayne
Pardo, Janette M. *archivist, librarian*

NEW MEXICO

Albuquerque
Clarke, Julia L. *library director*
Freeman, Patricia Elizabeth *multi-media specialist, educational consultant*
Lewis, Linda Kathryn *librarian*

Farmington
Mathers, Margaret *senior copy editor*

Gallup
Fellin, Octavia Antoinette *retired librarian, historical researcher*

Los Alamos
Ramsey, Margie *librarian*

Portales
Walker, Melveta *librarian, director*

Silver City
Ortego, Gilda Baeza *library director, educator*

NEW YORK

Albany
Aceto, Vincent John *librarian, educator*
Ebert, Loretta Caren *librarian*
Ritter, Philip Wayne *library administrator*

Alfred
Johnson, Carla Conrad *library dean*

Annandale On Hudson
Dougall, Jane *librarian*

Bellmore
Andrews, Charles Rolland *library administrator*

Brightwaters
Kavanagh, Eileen J. *librarian*

Brockport
Hacker, Linda Wessels *librarian*

Bronx
Alvarez, Michael *librarian*
Cohen, Selma *retired librarian*
Fazal, Shafeek *assistant director*
James, Gesille *librarian*
Munch, Janet Butler *librarian*
Padnos, Mark *library administrator, translator*

Brooklyn
Loum, Anthony Webster *librarian*
Mack-Harvin, Dionne L. *library director*
Thomas, Lucille Cole *librarian*

Buffalo
Bobinski, George Sylvan *librarian, educator*
Camhi, Rebecca Ann *librarian, writer*
Mahaney, Michael C. *library director*

Cold Spring Harbor
Crosson, Helen M. *librarian, director*

Corona
Jackson, Andrew Preston *library director*

Dansville
Dearing, Teresa Allison *librarian*

East Islip
Edwards, Guy Paul *library director*

Guilderland
Nichols Randall, Barbara Lee *library director, educator*

Hempstead
Freese, Melanie Louise *librarian, educator*

Hyde Park
Koch, Cynthia M. *library and museum director*

Ithaca
Perry, Margaret *librarian, writer*

Jamaica
Galante, Thomas W. *library director*
Garcia-Febo, Loida *librarian*

Nassau
Benamati, Dennis Charles *librarian, editor, consultant*

New Hartford
Anthony, Donald Charles *librarian, educator*

New Paltz
Nyquist, Corinne Elaine *librarian*

New York
Balaban, Vivian *librarian, elementary school educator*
Belliveau, Gerard Joseph, Jr. *librarian*
Berger, Pearl *librarian, dean*
Berner, Andrew Jay *library director, writer*
Ferriero, David S. *library administrator*
Fletcher, Harry George III *curator and library director*
Freedman, Jenna *librarian*
Gonzalez, Luis J. *librarian, educator*
Hewitt, Vivian Ann Davidson (Mrs. John Hamilton Hewitt Jr.) *retired librarian*
Kadel, Andrew Gordon *library director, priest*
Kent, Susan *library director, consultant*
Khalil, Mounir A. *librarian, educator*
LeClerc, Paul *library director*
LoSchiavo, Linda Bosco *library director*
Lubetski, Edith Esther *librarian*
Margalith, Helen Margaret *retired librarian*
Meyerhoff, Erich *librarian, educator*
Miller, Barbara Kenton *retired librarian*
Niss, Barbara Joyce *archivist*
Palmer, Robert Baylis *librarian*
Rachow, Louis A(ugust) *librarian*
Root, Nina J. *librarian, writer*
Sharify, Nasser *librarian, educator, writer*
Sloan, Elaine Frank *librarian*
Swan, Philip George *librarian, educator, director, artist*
Thomas, Dorothy *indexing consultant, writer*
Vilchez, Ricardo S. *library director*
Whittingham, Charles Arthur *library director, publishing executive*

Oakdale
Pope Robbins, Laura E. *librarian*

Oneonta
Johnson, Richard David *retired librarian*

Poughkeepsie
Van Zanten, Frank Veldhuyzen *library director*

Rexford
Nitecki, Joseph Zbigniew *librarian*

Rochester
Cohen, Ann Ellen *librarian*
Frontz, Stephanie J. *librarian*
Gibbons, Susan Lynn *library director*
Traub, Adam *librarian*

Rye
Harrington, Diane *librarian, writer*

Saint Bonaventure
Tenglund, Ann M. *librarian*

Saratoga Springs
Chen, Dung-Lan *librarian*

Schenectady
Mancuso, J(ohn) James *librarian*

Stony Brook
Filstrup, (E.) Christian *library director, dean*

Syracuse
Stam, David Harry *librarian*
Verheyen, Peter David *librarian, conservator*

Tarrytown
Osborne, Robin *library and information scientist*

West Nyack
Fogelman, Rita Tavel *library director*

White Plains
Manville, Stewart Roebling *archivist*
Marino, Jane B. *library director*
Scott-Williams, Wendy Lee *library and information scientist*

Whitestone
Wingate, Constance Blandy *retired librarian*

Williamsville
Cloudsley, Donald Hugh *retired library administrator*

Woodside
Sfiroudis, Gloria Tides *library and information scientist, educator*

NORTH CAROLINA

Burlington
Ellington, Beth Elder *librarian*

Chapel Hill
Jones, Houston Gwynne *archivist, history professor*
Pruett, James Worrell *librarian, educator, musicologist*

Charlotte
Jordan, Carol Walker *librarian, educator*
Rhue, Monika Rivera *archivist*
Sintz, Edward Francis *librarian*

Cove City
Hawkins, Elinor Dixon (Mrs. Carroll Woodard Hawkins) *retired librarian*

Davidson
Park, Leland Madison *retired librarian*

Durham
Auld, Skip (Hampton Auld) *library director*
Canada, Mary Whitfield *retired librarian*

Elizabeth City
Andrews, Alice K. *librarian*

Gastonia
Burns, Judith O'Dell *library assistant, educator*

Greenville
Greenstein, Patricia *librarian, director*

Hendersonville
Snyder, William *library director*

Mount Olive
Ryberg, Susan Gribble *librarian*

Pembroke
Power, June Lynn LaVoie *librarian*

Pittsboro
Boyce, Emily Stewart *retired library and information scientist, educator*

Raleigh
Boone, Mary L. *library director*
Littleton, Isaac Thomas III *retired library director*
Nutter, Susan K. *librarian, academic administrator*

Winston Salem
Levine, Cynthia Oglesby *librarian*
Sutton, Lynn Sorensen *librarian*

NORTH DAKOTA

Bismarck
Ott, Doris Ann *librarian*

Fargo
Postema, Beth E. *librarian, director*

Grand Forks
Stolt, Wilbur A. *library director*

Mayville
Karaim, Betty June *retired librarian*

Minot
Iversen, David Stewart *librarian*

OHIO

Barberton
Vernacotola, Joseph N. *librarian*

Bellaire
Kniesner, John Thomas *librarian*

Bluffton
Dudley, Durand Stowell *retired librarian*

Canal Winchester
Roddy, Carol Lynn *library director*

Canfield
Yurchekfrodl, Patricia *librarian*

Canton
Oliver, Kenton L. *library director*

Cincinnati
Abate, Anne Katherine *librarian, consultant, educator*
Brehm-Heeger, Paula *library director, library association executive*
Everson, Jean Watkins Dolores *librarian, media consultant, educator*
Fender, Kimber L. *library director, educator*
Montavon, Victoria A. *university librarian, dean*

Cleveland
Gardner, Richard Kent *retired librarian, editor, educator*
Neal, Carolyn V. *librarian*
Thomas, Felton, Jr. *library director*
Thornton, Glenda Ann *librarian*

Columbus
Branin, Joseph J. *library director*
Brown, Rowland Chauncey Widrig *library and information scientist, consultant*
Budler, Joanne *library director*
El-Sherbini, Magda A. *librarian, educator*
Losinski, Patrick A. *library director*
Studer, William Joseph *library director*
Swarlis, Linda *library and information scientist*

Dayton
Kaylor, Douglas N. *library director*

Delaware
Jin, Xudong *associate library director*
Schlichting, Catherine Fletcher Nicholson *librarian, educator*

Dublin
Jordan, Robert (Jay) L. *computer library service and research organization executive*
Needham, George Michael *library consultant*

Fremont
Hill, Rebecca Baker *librarian*

Galloway
Pelz, Carol E. *library director, consultant*

Hubbard
Trucksis, Theresa A. *retired library director*

Kent
Weber, Mark W. *library director, dean*
Zampini, Carmen C. *library director*

Lima
Bohle, Shannon Denise *archivist*
Shafer, Scott L. *library director*

Marion
Blankenship, Betsy Lee *library director*

Mount Healthy
Scheffel, Kenneth Paul *retired archivist*

Oberlin
English, Ray *library administrator*
Moore, Jane Ross *librarian, educator*

South Euclid
Zoller, Karen Ann *library and art gallery director*

Steubenville
Rekowski, Lois Thompson *library director*

Sylvania
Rutkowski, Sandra L. *library director*

Tiffin
Hillmer, Margaret Patricia *retired library director*

Toledo
Scoles, Clyde Sheldon *library director*

University Heights
Milota, Marcella D. *librarian*

Wickliffe
Fisher, Nancy DeButts *library director*

OKLAHOMA

Hodgen
Brower, Janice Kathleen *library and information scientist*

Holdenville
Cook, Francile *retired library director*

Lawton
Bonnell-Mihalis, Pamela Gay Scoggins *library director*

Mcalester
Hanway, Wayne Edward *library director*

Muskogee
Hinshaw, Marilyn L. *retired library director*

Norman
Lee, Sul Hi *library administrator, dean*
Lester, June *library and information scientist, educator*
Lura, Susan *librarian*
Masters, Anne *library director*
Van Fleet, Connie Jean *library and information scientist, educator*

Stillwater
Leech, Robin *librarian*

Tulsa
Clement, Evelyn Geer *librarian, educator*

OREGON

Astoria
LaMear, Arline Joan *librarian, writer*

Beaverton
Pond, Patricia Brown *library and information science educator*

Corvallis
Sapon-White, Richard E. *librarian*

Eugene
Edwards, Ralph M. *librarian*

Portland
Browne, Joseph Peter *retired librarian*

Salem
Scheppke, Jim *library director*

PENNSYLVANIA

Allentown
Sacks, Patricia Ann *librarian, consultant*

Allison Park
Howe, Eleanor B. *librarian, educator*

Beaver Falls
Miller, Albert Jay *retired library director*

Bethlehem
Taggart, Bruce M. *library administrator*

California
Pokol, Albert Ronald *librarian*

Carlisle
Darr, Jonelle Prether *librarian*

Coplay
Norbeck, Jack Carl *library exhibitor*

Cranberry Township
Lorenz, John George *librarian, consultant*

Erie
Maxted, Lawrence Richard *librarian*
Wise, Penelope M. *librarian*

Greensburg
Duck, Patricia Mary *librarian*

Greenville
Morrill, Allen S. *library director*

Harrisburg
Zales, Mary Clare *library director*

Hughesville
Kuhar, Deborah Ann *librarian*

Lancaster
Shelley, Leo Eugene *retired librarian*

Lock Haven
Fulton, Tara Lynn *library director, academic administrator*

Loretto
Balough, Sandra A. *library director*

Mansfield
DiMarco, Scott R. *library director*

New Holland
Fanus, Pauline Rife *librarian*

New Kensington
Gilley, Jennifer R. *librarian*

Philadelphia
Alford, Larry P. *university librarian*
Davidoff, Joanne Malatesta *multi-media specialist*
Mancall, Jacqueline Cooper *library and information scientist, educator*
Reardon, Siobhan A. *library director*
Rogers, Carton (H. Carton Rogers III) *library director*

Pittsburgh
Jenkins, Georgann Klaus *librarian*
Lugar, Gary Lance *librarian*
Miller, Rush Glenn, Jr. *library director*
Minnigh, Joel Douglas *library director*
St. Clair, Gloriana Strange *librarian, dean*
Wohleber, Lynne Farr *archivist, librarian*

Punxsutawney
Dinsmore, Roberta Joan Maier *library director*

Reading
Mack, Sara Rohrbach *librarian, educator*

Riegelsville
Banko, Ruth Caroline *retired library director*

Sidman
Miller, Noelle Christine *librarian*

Springfield
Boyer, Harold Norman, Sr. *library director, educator*

State College
Pisciotta, Henry Andrew *librarian, researcher*

University Park
Eaton, Nancy Ruth Linton *librarian, dean*
Joyce, William Leonard *librarian*

Wayne
Garrison, Guy Grady *librarian, educator*

Wilkes Barre
Mech, Terrence Francis *library director*

RHODE ISLAND

Kingston
Caldwell, Naomi Rachel *library and information scientist, educator, writer*
Gilton, Donna Louise *library and information scientist, educator*

Portsmouth
Fontaine, David G. *librarian, education educator, consultant*

Providence
Hamerly, Michael T. *librarian, historian*
Nacheman, Elinor Laurie *librarian*

Riverside
Schwegler, Nancy Ann *librarian, writer*

Wakefield
Alexander, Jacqueline Peterson *retired librarian*

SOUTH CAROLINA

Bluffton
Cann, Sharon Lee *retired health science librarian*

Charleston
Seaman, Sheila Lynne *librarian*

Columbia
Rawlinson, Helen Ann *librarian*
Warren, Charles David *library consultant*

Darlington
Ladson, Brenda Lee *librarian*

Georgetown
Bazemore, Trudy McConnell *librarian*

Hardeeville
Kadar, Karin Patricia *librarian*

Lexington
MacNeill, Daniel Scott *library director*

Orangeburg
Byers, Keith Thomas *librarian*

SOUTH DAKOTA

Pierre
Siebersma, Daniel *state librarian*

Sioux Falls
Hagemeier, Deborah Anne *library director*
Thompson, Ronelle Kay Hildebrandt *library director*

TENNESSEE

Cleveland
Hunt, Andrew L. *library director*

Dayton
Fitsimmons, Gary N. *library director, writer*

Greeneville
Smith, Myron John, Jr. *librarian, author*

Jackson
Hoyle, Shetina Yevette *librarian*

Johnson City
Scher, Rita Ann *librarian*

Kingsport
Smith, JoAnn Carroll *library and information scientist*

Knoxville
Dewey, Barbara I. *librarian, dean*
Felder-Hoehne, Felicia Harris *librarian, researcher*

Maryville
Tabor, Curtis Harold, Jr. *retired librarian, minister*

Memphis
Pourciau, Lester John, Jr. *retired librarian*
Wallis, Carlton Lamar *librarian*

Nashville
Alvin, Glenda Marie *assistant director*
Craiglow, Hilary A. *librarian*
Radcliff, Joyce B. *librarian*
Shockley, Ann Allen *librarian, writer*
Stewart, David Marshall *librarian*
Sugg, Jeanne D. *library director*
Wilson, Carolyn Taylor *librarian*

Parsons
Economos, Cora Matheny *librarian*

TEXAS

Arlington
Siegfried, Cary Ann *library director*

Austin
Billings, Harold Wayne *retired library director, editor, writer*
Flowers, Betty Sue *library director, educator*
Heath, Fred Milton *library director, educator*
Neely, Stephanie *librarian*
Payne, John Ross *archivist, educator, library and information scientist*
Roy, Loriene *library and information scientist, association executive*
Smith, John Brewster *library administrator*
Smith, Patricia H. *library association director*
Tuohy, Patricia Anne *library director, consultant*
Warren, Karen Cohen *librarian*
Wassenich, Red *librarian*

Blanco
Holleman, Curt Paul *librarian*

Brownwood
Weeks, Patsy Ann Landry *librarian, educator*

Canyon Lake
Bowden, Virginia Massey *librarian*

Carrollton
Jacobson, Carrie *librarian*

Cedar Hill
Hickman, Traphene Parramore *retired library director, consultant, storyteller*

Cedar Park
Lam, Pauline Poha *library director*

College Station
Cook, C. Colleen *librarian, dean*
Finch, Warren Luenberg, Jr. *library and museum director, archivist*
Piscitelli, Felicia Ann *librarian, musician, musicologist*

Denton
Poole, Eva Duraine *librarian*
Snapp, Elizabeth *librarian, educator*
Swigger, Keith *library and information scientist, educator*

El Paso
Brey-Casiano, Carol A. *library director*
Gardner, Kerry Ann *librarian*

Fort Worth
Ard, Harold Jacob *library administrator*
de Tonnancour, Paul Roger Godefroy *library administrator*
Ford, Jeanette White *archivist, educator*
Robinson, Gleniece Armstrong *library director*
Sikes, Mary Taggart *librarian*

Galena Park
Fierro, Robert, Jr. *librarian*

Garland
Burns, George Franklin *archivist, retired English language educator*

Harlingen
Rendon, Jose Ruben *library director*

Houston
Bigwood, David P. *librarian, writer*
Boule, Michelle L. *librarian, writer*
Garner, Madelyn C. *librarian*
Henington, David Mead *retired library director*
James, Dean *librarian, writer*
Lawson, Rhea Brown *library director*
Lowman, Sara Allison *library director*
Miller, Sabrina Wares *librarian*
Radoff, Leonard Irving *retired librarian, consultant*
Russell, John Francis *retired librarian*
Witmer, John Richard *librarian*

Hurst
Davidsson, John Paul *librarian*

Kingsville
Schueneman, Bruce R. *librarian*

Lake Jackson
Alcorn, JoAnne Miller *librarian*

Laredo
Maxstadt, John M. *librarian*

Lewisville
Lowe, Alan Conner *policy director*
Simpson, Carol Mann *librarian, editor, educator, attorney*

Longview
Geer, Caroline L. *librarian*

Lubbock
Clausen, Jane *library director*

Marshall
Adams, Venesia Yevette *library director*
Magrill, Rose Mary *library director*
Peterson, Cynthia Lynn *library director, educator*

Mcallen
McGee, William Howard John *retired library director*

Midland
Dawkins, Diantha Dee *librarian*

Mission
Guajardo, Graciela *librarian*

Nacogdoches
Oswald, Tina Atkinson *librarian*

Palestine
Williams, Franklin Cadmus, Jr. *bibliographer*

Plano
Shubert, Joseph Francis *librarian*

Richardson
Sall, Larry David *library director*
Snow, Linda E. *librarian*

Round Rock
Ricklefs, Dale Lynne *library director*

San Antonio
Brewster, Olive Nesbitt *retired librarian*
Duesterhoeft, Diane M. *librarian*
Hood, Sandra Dale *librarian*
Newton, Virginia *archivist, historian, librarian*
Odom, Marjorie Mildred Morgan *retired librarian*

Tyler
Albertson, Christopher Adam *librarian*
Dubre, Vandy *librarian*
Pyle, Jeanne *library director*

Waco
Karney, James A. *library director*

Weslaco
Fogarty, Elizabeth Jordan *retired librarian, researcher*

Wichita Falls
Parker, Eva Annette *retired librarian*

UTAH

Logan
Clement, Richard Wolcott *librarian, educator*

Moab
Tallman, Eve *library director*

Orem
Hall, Blaine Hill *retired librarian*

Provo
Jensen, Richard Dennis *librarian*

Salt Lake City
Morris, Donna Jones *library director*
Watt, Ronald G. *archivist*

VERMONT

Burlington
Kascus, Marie Annette *librarian*

Middlebury
Raum, Hans L. *librarian*

Montpelier
McShane, Sybil Brigham *retired library director, librarian*

Northfield
Petrusa, Joshua H. *librarian*

VIRGINIA

Alexandria
Berger, Patricia Wilson *retired librarian*
Gernand, Bradley Elton *archivist, librarian*
Knechtmann, James Allen *archivist, researcher*
Manson, Connie Jeane *librarian*

Arlington
Bromley, Marilyn Modlin *librarian*
Stone, Stuart Lee Morrison *librarian, language educator*

Blacksburg
Bailey, Annette F. *librarian*

Charlottesville
Onega, Esther E. *librarian*

Chesapeake
Stillman, Margaret (Peggy Stillman) *library director*

Fairfax
Clay, Edwin S. III *library director*
Hurt, Charlene Schmidt *library director*
Mann, Wendy *librarian*

Farmville
Howe, Patricia Anne *librarian*

Fredericksburg
Edmunds, Jeffrey Garth *librarian*
Raspen, Janice Ann *librarian, educator*
Van Neste, Karen Lane *librarian, editor*

Gainesville
Cochran, Radeen M. *librarian*

Hampton
Gibson, Barbara S. *librarian*

Harrisonburg
Gill, Gerald Lawson *librarian*
Palmer, Forrest Charles *librarian, educator*

Independence
Webb, Adam Paul *librarian*

Lexington
Gaines, James Edwin, Jr. *retired librarian*
Leach, Maurice Derby, Jr. *librarian, educator*

Mc Lean
Murphy, Mary *retired librarian*

Middleburg
Tourney, Michele Marie *archivist, historian*

Poquoson
Tai, Elizabeth Shi-Jue Lee *library director*

Portsmouth
Monroe, Evelyn Jones *retired librarian*

Radford
Hayes, David Lavern *librarian*

Rapidan
Grimm, Ben Emmet *library director, consultant*

Reston
Bradley, Murray L(ee) *librarian*

Richmond
Coalter, Milton J., Jr. *library director, educator*
Henderson, Harriet *librarian, director*
Kozlowski, Ronald Stephan *retired librarian*
Miah, Abdul Jalil *library director*
Treadway, Sandra Gioia *library director*
Yelich, Nolan T. *library director*

Springfield
Heise, Dorothy Hilbert *retired librarian, government agency administrator*

Suffolk
Burd, Joyce Ann *librarian*

Verona
MacTavish, Susanne Hanna *retired library and information scientist*

Virginia Beach
Johnson, Janice Sims *library director*

Washington
Arbelbide, C(indy) L(ea) *librarian, historian, author*

Williamsburg
Brooks, Philip Coolidge, Jr. *archivist, curator, historian*

WASHINGTON

Bainbridge Island
Harrison, Cynthia L. *librarian*

Grandview
Verhoeven, Linda Stransky *librarian, educator*

Issaquah
Ptacek, William H. *library director*

Lummi Island
Hanson, Polly (Pauline) Mae Early *librarian*

Oak Harbor
Shaw, Kathleen M. Troutner *retired librarian*

Olympia
Hutchins, Diane Elizabeth Rider *librarian*
Walsh, Jan *library director*

Seattle
Bishop, Virginia Wakeman *retired librarian, humanities educator*
Boylan, Merle Nelson *librarian, educator*
Hildreth, Susan *library director*
Hill, Chrystie R. *library and information scientist*
Mason, Marilyn Gell *retired library administrator, writer, consultant*
McCracken, Peter H. *librarian*
Shadle, Steven Curtis *librarian*
Whisner, Mary *librarian*

Spokane
Bender, Betty Wion *librarian*
Bynagle, Hans Edward *library director, philosophy educator*
Murray, James Michael *librarian, lawyer*
Wirt, Michael James *library director*

Tumwater
Mallory, Tim *librarian*

Vancouver
Bridgewater, Rachel *library and information scientist*

Wenatchee
Daling, LaiLee T. *librarian*

WEST VIRGINIA

Athens
Turnbull, Robert B. *librarian*

Glenville
Tubesing, Richard Lee *library director*

Huntington
Pratt, Mary Louise *librarian, writer*

Morgantown
Pyles, Rodney Allen *archivist, county official*

Parkersburg
Heiss, Harry Glen *archivist*

Shepherdstown
Elliott, Jean Ann *retired library director*

WISCONSIN

Eau Claire
Tiefel, Virginia May *librarian*

Hortonville
Habeck, Carolyn R. *library director*

Madison
Bunge, Charles Albert *library science educator*
Dimick, Barbara L. *library director*
Hawkinson, Lorraine A. *librarian*
Horning, Kathleen T. *library director*
Kresse, Kerry L. *library director*

Milwaukee
Little, Robert David *library science professor*
Mandernack, Scott Bryan *librarian*

Richland Center
Gollata, James Anthony *library director, educator*

River Falls
Montgomery, Karen E. *retired library and information scientist*

Sheboygan
Weinhold, David *library director*

Superior
Nordgren, Debra *librarian, educator*

Thiensville
Roselle, William Charles *librarian*

Whitewater
Bren, Barbara R. *librarian*

WYOMING

Casper
Anderson, Kevin Stuart *archivist, librarian*

TERRITORIES OF THE UNITED STATES

PUERTO RICO

Ponce
Toro Vargas, Cirilo *library director, educator*

CANADA

BRITISH COLUMBIA

Vancouver
Piternick, Anne Brearley *librarian, educator*
Rothstein, Samuel *librarian, educator*

Victoria
Richards, Vincent Philip Haslewood *librarian*

NOVA SCOTIA

Dartmouth
Horrocks, Norman *librarian, educator, editor*

ONTARIO

Guelph
Land, Reginald Brian *library administrator*

Hamilton
Etches-Johnson, Amanda *library and information scientist*

Ottawa
Scott, Marianne Florence *retired librarian, educator*
Sylvestre, Jean Guy *former national librarian*

Toronto
Bryant, Josephine Harriet *library executive*
Moore, Carole Irene *librarian*

QUEBEC

Montreal
Large, John Andrew *library and information service professor*

SASKATCHEWAN

Saskatoon
Kennedy, Marjorie Ellen *librarian*

ARMENIA

Yerevan
Sargsyan, Davit *library director*

AUSTRALIA

Sydney
Bishop, Rosalinda Matubis *information manager*

CZECH REPUBLIC

Prague
Kalkus, Stanley *librarian, administrator, consultant*

DENMARK

Copenhagen
Nielsen, Erland Kolding *library director*

ENGLAND

Oxford
Shaw, Dennis Frederick *former library director, chartered physicist, consultant*
Vaisey, David George *librarian, archivist*

ESTONIA

Tartu
Eeber, Ludmilla *acquisition librarian*

FRANCE

Paris
Cagle, William Rae *retired librarian*

GERMANY

Lübeck
Fligge, Jörg *librarian, library director*

Stuttgart
Geh, Hans-Peter *retired library director, consultant*

GUATEMALA

Antigua
Rodgers, Frank *librarian*

JAPAN

Ibaraki
Taniguchi, Shoichi *library and information scientist, educator*

LUXEMBOURG

Niederkorn
Meder, Cornel *retired archivist, director*

QATAR

Doha
Warro, Edward A. *library director, dean*

REPUBLIC OF KOREA

Cheongju
Kim, Nam-Soo *library and information scientist, director*

SWEDEN

Stockholm
Lidman, Tomas Erik *national archivist*

ADDRESS UNPUBLISHED

Abulhab, Saad Dean *librarian, Information Technology Director & Type Designer*
Aho, Melissa Kay *librarian, educator, writer*
Allen, Patricia J. *retired library director*
Anderson, Herschel Vincent *retired librarian*
Anderson, Rachael Keller (Rachael Keller) *retired library director*
Aust-Keefer, Mary Beth *library administrator*
Baker, Carolyn Simmons *library director, consultant, researcher*
Baker, Zachary Moshe *librarian*
Barkley, Terrell Wayne *archivist, curator, school librarian*
Beatty, Virginia Lewis *librarian, archivist, environmental education & urban horticulture consultant*
Berman, Miriam Naomi *librarian*
Birdsall, William Forest *retired librarian*
Blalock, Louise *librarian, public administrator, executive coach*
Bowen, Jean *retired librarian, consultant*
Brady, Jean Stein *retired librarian*
Brechtel, Unda Jurka *retired library director*
Brown, Barbara *librarian, educator*
Brown, Carol Ann *librarian, director*
Brown, Elizabeth Eleanor *retired librarian*
Budington, William Stone *retired librarian*
Bundy, Annalee Marshall *retired library director*
Burnette, Brandon R. *librarian*
Burson, Betsy Lee *librarian*
Busch, Annie *retired library director*
Campbell, Henry Cummings *librarian*
Carlock, Barbara E. *librarian*
Carmack, Mona *library administrator*
Carr, E. Barbara *librarian*
Carter, Yvonne Breaux *retired librarian*
Caspers, Jean S. *librarian*
Cassell, Kay Ann *librarian*
Chen, Xiaotian *librarian, educator*
Chirico-Elkins, Ursula *retired librarian*
Chow, Judy *library and information scientist, educator*
Chu, Ellin Resnick *librarian, consultant*
Clauson, Kathleen Jo *writer, library operations associate*
Clement, Yvonne Madeline *librarian*
Collins, Brian David *archivist*
Cooper, Jacquelyn Barber *librarian*
Cottam, Keith M. *librarian, educator, administrator*
Crahan, Elizabeth Schmidt *librarian*
Crawford, Sheila Jane *librarian, reading specialist retired*
Daffron, MaryEllen *retired librarian*
deBear, Richard Stephen *library planning consultant*
Desnoyers, Megan Floyd *retired archivist, educator*
Dickinson, Donald Charles *library science professor*
Dickinson, Gail Krepps *library science educator*
Dow, Ronald F. *librarian, dean*
Drake, Miriam Anna *retired librarian, educator, writer, consultant*
Drazan, Joseph Gerald *retired librarian*
Drescher, Judith Altman *library director*
Dye, Michele Yvette *librarian*
Dyson, Allan Judge *retired librarian*
Edmonds, Anne Carey *librarian*
Elder, Mary Louise *retired librarian*
Eller, Christina Hull *librarian*
Else, Carolyn Joan *retired library director*
Elwood-Akers, Virginia Edythe *librarian, retired archivist*
Emry, Betsy *librarian*
Engelson, Leslie *librarian*
Erickson, Alan Eric *librarian*
Erwin, Linda McIntosh *retired librarian*
Estes, Elaine Rose Graham *retired librarian*
Euster, Joanne Reed *retired librarian*
Fasick, Adele Mongan *library and information scientist, educator*
Fawcett, John Thomas *archivist*
Figueredo, Danilo H. *librarian, writer*
Ford, Barbara Jean *librarian, educator*
Fountain, Joanna Fraser *library consultant, business owner*
Frank, Larry James *library director*
Frantz, Ray William, Jr. *retired librarian*

Fredeman, Betty Coley (Betty Coley) *retired librarian, editor*
Freeman, Rosalind Alter *retired library and information scientist*
Fricker, Janet S. *library director*
Frost, Michelle *librarian*
Gainey, Lilah Leigh *librarian*
Gatch, Milton McCormick, Jr. *library director, clergyman, educator*
Gaulke, Mary Florence *retired library administrator*
Gold, Leonard Singer *librarian, translator, curator*
Gould, Martha Bernice *retired librarian*
Gregor, Dorothy Deborah *retired librarian*
Gundersheimer, Werner Leonard *library director*
Hainsworth, Melody May *library and information scientist, researcher*
Hoffmann, Frances Porter *librarian*
Hoke, Sheila Wilder *retired librarian*
Howard, Joseph Harvey *retired librarian*
Hughes, Sue Margaret *retired librarian*
Hutchinson, Barbara Jane *retired library director, history educator*
Ibach, Robert Daniel, Jr. *retired library director*
Jenkins, Darrell Lee *librarian*
Johnson, Donald Clay *retired librarian, curator*
Jones-Eddy, Julie Margaret *retired librarian*
Kallenberg, John Kenneth *retired librarian*
Karetzky, Stephen *library director, educator, writer, researcher*
Kaser, David *retired librarian, educator, consultant*
Kiser, Nagiko Sato *retired librarian*
Klein, Susan Elaine *librarian*
Klinck, Cynthia Anne *retired library director*
Knight, Margaret L. *librarian, educator*
Koenigstein, David *librarian, educator*
Kordish, Heike Christiane *retired library director*
Korenic, Lynette Marie *librarian*
Kreitzburg, Marilyn June *academic librarian*
Kunselman, JoAn Dorothy *librarian, educator, editor, writer*
Lee, Harrison Hon *librarian, consultant*
Lee, Pali Jae *retired librarian, writer*
Lehner-Quam, Alison Lynn *library administrator*
Leonhardt, Thomas Wilburn *librarian, library director*
Lewis, Frederick A. *library director*
Liegl, Dorothy M. *retired library director*
Lindgren, William Dale *librarian*
Logsdon, Vicki Dianne *librarian, director*
Lucker, Jay *library consultant*
MacDonald, Alan Hugh *academic administrator*
Marcum, James Walton *library director, educator*
Margolis, Bernard Allen *library administrator*
Margoshes, Miriam Kagan *information specialist*
Massey, Stephen Charles *rare book dealer, consultant*
Matthews, Waide Kareem *librarian*
McBurney, Margot B. *retired librarian*
McGlothlen, John M. *librarian*
McKowen, Dorothy Keeton *educator, librarian*
McManus, Alesia *librarian*
Metz, T(heodore) John *librarian, educator*
Miller, Beverly A(nn) *reference librarian, professor*
Miller, Jacqueline Winslow *library director*
Miller, Marilyn Lea *library and information scientist, educator*
Morton, Donald John *librarian*
Muñoz-Solá, Haydeé Socorro *retired library administrator*
Murphy, Marilyn Jane *library director*
Pearlstein, Toby *retired librarian, archivist*
Pearson, Roger Lee *library director*
Pierce, Charles Eliot, Jr. *retired library director, educator*
Pitman, LaVern Frank *librarian*
Raphael, Molly (Mary E. Raphael) *retired library director*
Rayward, Warden Boyd *librarian, educator*
Renfro, Patricia Elise *library director, academic administrator*
Repinski, Sara *library director*
Rhoads, James Berton *archivist, consultant, federal official, educator*
Rickard, Margaret Lynn *library director, consultant*
Roark, Barbara Ann *librarian*
Roll, Todd M. *library director*
Rosenthal, Susan Barbara *retired librarian*
Rouse, Roscoe, Jr. *retired librarian, educator*
Rusaw, Sally Ellen *librarian*
Sager, Donald Jack *librarian, consultant, retired publishing executive*
Sawyers, Elizabeth Joan *retired librarian, director*
Scales, Pat R. *retired library association executive, director*
Schindler, Jo Ann *retired library director*
Schlesinger, Deborah Lee *retired librarian*
Scott, Catherine Dorothy *library and information scientist, consultant*
Settles, Jeanne Dobson *retired librarian*
Shelton, Kathryn H. *retired librarian*
Shipman, Barbara Lowther *librarian*
Slavens, Thomas Paul *library science educator*
Smelser, June *librarian*
Smith, Barbara Jeanne *retired librarian*
Snell, Patricia Poldervaart *retired librarian, consultant*
Soules, Aline *librarian, writer*
Sprince, Leila Joy *retired librarian*
Stewart, Dorothy K. *librarian*
Strait, Viola Edwina Washington *librarian*
Stubbs, Kendon Lee *retired librarian*
Summers, Lorraine Dey Schaeffer *retired librarian*
Suput, Ray Radoslav *librarian*
Swenson, Sara *librarian, educator*
Thiele, Gloria Day *librarian, small business owner*
Thomason, Christia R. *librarian*
Topper, Elisa Freiden *former librarian, consultant*
Trezza, Alphonse Fiore *librarian, educator*
Triipan, Maive *library director*
Turock, Betty Jane *retired library and information science professor*
VanMeter, Vandelia L. *retired library director*
Van Orden, Phyllis Jeanne *librarian, educator*
Van Valkenburgh, Holly Viola *librarian, consultant*
Varner, Joyce Ehrhardt *retired librarian*
Vernon, Lawrence Gordon *librarian*
von Hake, Margaret Joan *librarian*
Wade, Heather A. *archivist, educator*
Wallot, Jean-Pierre *archivist, historian*
Wang, Chen-ku *retired library director*
Warwick, Shelly *library director, researcher*
Weaver, John B. *library director*
Weiherer, Patricia Dee *retired librarian*
Weingand, Darlene Erna *librarian, educator*
Welles, Ferne Bingham Malcolm *retired archivist*
Wertsman, Vladimir Filip *librarian, writer, library and information scientist, translator*
Wightman, Sharon Leilani *retired librarian*
Wilkins, Barratt (George Wilkins) *librarian*
Willis, Paul Allen *retired librarian, dean*
Wilson, Patricia Potter *library and information science educator*
Winn, Carolyn Pautke *librarian, consultant*
Wise, Ronnie W. *retired library director*
Wolfram, Dietmar *Information Scientist Educator*
Woodrum, Patricia Ann *librarian*
Wynar, Bohdan Stephen *retired librarian, writer, editor*
Yavarkovsky, Jerome Harold *university librarian emeritus*
Yiotis, Gayle *archivist, researcher, anthropologist, writer*
Yu, Ying *librarian, educator*
Zack, Daniel Gerard *library consultant*
Zaleski-Vegazo, Ilene *librarian*

HUMANITIES: MUSEUMS

UNITED STATES

ALABAMA

Anniston
Bragg, Cheryl H. *museum director*

Birmingham
Andrews, Gail *museum director*
Pijeaux, Lawrence J., Jr. *museum director*

Huntsville
Bass, Clayton *museum director*

Mobile
Alsobrook, David Ernest *museum director, archivist, historian*
Richelson, Paul William *curator*
Schenk, Joseph Bernard *museum director*

Montgomery
Johnson, Mark Matthew *museum director, curator*

Tuscaloosa
Gaddy, Kenneth C. *museum director*

ALASKA

Anchorage
Pepper Henry, James *museum director*

Fairbanks
Jonaitis, Aldona Claire *museum director, art historian*

Haines
Clarke, Jerrie *museum director, researcher*

Homer
Beggs, Heather *museum director*

Juneau
Kato, Bruce H. *curator*

Kodiak
Haakanson, Sven *museum director, anthropologist*

ARIZONA

Bisbee
Gustavson, Carrie *museum director*

Flagstaff
Breunig, Robert Glass *museum director*

Glendale
Almstead, Sheila Louise *art gallery owner*

Green Valley
Lusk, Harlan Gilbert *national park superintendent, business executive*

Mesa
Wilson, Thomas H. *museum director*

Phoenix
Ballinger, James K. *museum director*
Goodyear, Frank H(enry), Jr. *museum director*
Loscher, Tricia Diane *curator, director*

Portal
Zweifel, Richard George *curator*

Prescott
Langellier, John *museum director*

Tucson
Guerin, Charles Allan *museum director, artist*
King, James Edward *retired museum director, consultant*
Knight, Robert E. *museum director*
Lomawaima, Hartman H. *museum director*

ARKANSAS

Fayetteville
Barnes, Jeffrey K. *curator*

Little Rock
Plummer, Ellen *museum director*
Selz, Nan *museum director*

State University
Allen, Marti Lu *museum director*

CALIFORNIA

Bakersfield
Enriquez, Carola Rupert *museum director*

Berkeley
Alesander, Terry Pink *museum director*
Benedict, Burton *retired museum director, anthropologist*
Day, Lucille Lang *museum administrator, educator, writer*
Grossman, Bonnie *art gallery director*

Carmel Valley
Wolfe, Maurice Raymond *retired museum director, educator*

Carson
Zimmerer, Kathy Louise *museum director*

Claremont
Moreno, William A. *museum director*

Fresno
Martinez, Carlos *museum director*
Monaghan, Kathleen M. *art museum director*

Irvine
Stern, Jean *museum director*

La Jolla
Beebe, Mary Livingstone *curator*
Davies, Hugh Marlais *museum director*

Long Beach
Myers, Robert *museum director*

Los Angeles
Barron, Stephanie *curator*
Berns, Marla C. *museum director*
Brand, Michael *museum director*
Byrnes, James Bernard *museum director, consultant*
Govan, Michael James *museum director*
Gray, John L. *museum director*
Hooks, Rosie Lee *museum director, actor, filmmaker*
May, Rabbi Meyer H. *museum director*
Pisano, Jane G. *museum administrator*
Santelli, Robert *museum director, historian*
Strick, Jeremy *curator, museum director*

Los Olivos
Knowles, Elizabeth Pringle *museum director*

Monterey
Whittington, E. Michael *museum director*

Oakland
Fogarty, Lori *museum director*
Zwissler, Alexander *museum director*

Palm Springs
Hammond, Michael *museum director*
Nash, Steven Alan *museum director, curator, art historian*
Stearns, Robert Leland *curator*

Pasadena
Bosley, Edward Richmond *historical site administrator*

Rancho Palos Verdes
Yassin, Robert Alan *museum director, curator*

Riverside
Green, Jonathan William *museum director, educator, artist, writer*

Sacramento
Jones, Lial A. *museum director*

Salinas
Hoffman, Steven *museum administrator*

San Diego
Cartwright, Derrick *museum director*
Hager, Michael W. *museum director*
Salvador, Mari Lyn C. *museum director*
Sidner, Robert Brown *museum director*
Teagle, Rachel *museum director*
Wilson, John Human III *museum director, art historian*

San Francisco
Bartels, Dennis M. *museum director*
Benezra, Neal *museum director, curator*
Buchanan, John Edward, Jr. *museum director*
Farrington, Gregory C. *museum director, former academic administrator*
Hertz, Betti-Sue *curator, art gallery director*
Leviton, Alan Edward *curator*
Shank, J. William *art conservator*
Xu, Jay Jie *museum director*

San Jose
Friess, Peter *museum administrator*
Hernandez, Jo Farb *museum director, curator, professor, consultant*
Krane, Susan *museum director, curator*

San Marino
Murdoch, John *museum director*

Santa Barbara
Feinberg, Larry J. *museum director, curator*
Hutterer, Karl Leopold *museum director*
Kanjo, Kathryn *museum director*

Santa Clara
Schapp, Rebecca Maria *museum director*

Santa Cruz
DeWald, Celeste *museum director*

Santa Maria
DeLaurier, Roger Darren *conservator, director*

Stanford
Siekierski, Maciej M. *curator*

The Sea Ranch
Baas, Jacquelynn *museum director, art historian*

COLORADO

Aspen
Zuckerman Jacobson, Heidi *museum director*

Boulder
Sheldon, Sara A. *museum director, writer*

Colorado Springs
Raintree, Shawn *museum administrator, former insurance company executive*

Denver
Downey, Tom *museum director, former lawyer*
Heinrich, Christoph *curator*
Sharp, Lewis Inman *museum director, curator*
Sparks, George *museum administrator*

Littleton
Nimz, Timothy J. *museum director*

Parker
Smartt, Richard A. *museum director*

Pueblo
Divelbiss, Maggie (Margaret G. Divelbiss) *museum director*

CONNECTICUT

Bridgeport
Maher, Kathy *museum director*

Hartford
Talbott, Susan Lubowsky *museum director, curator, arts administrator*

Litchfield
Fields, Catherine K. *museum director*

Mashantucket
Hatcher-White, Kimberly *museum director*

Mystic
Teeson, Douglas H. *museum director*

New Haven
Hickey, Leo Joseph *museum curator, educator*
Meyers, Amy *museum director*
Trumble, Angus A. G. *curator, writer*

Norwalk
Herring, Jennifer E. *museum administrator*

Old Lyme
Andersen, Jeffrey W. *museum director*

Ridgefield
Ramírez-Montagut, Mónica *curator*

Stamford
Mulrooney, Melissa Hutchens *museum director*

Storrs Mansfield
Goldich, Terri Jean *curator*
Harty, Leanne Kennedy *museum director*

West Hartford
Faude, Wilson Hinsdale *museum director, consultant*
Sullivan, Kevin B. *museum administrator, former lieutenant governor, state legislator*

DELAWARE

Wilmington
Gaiber, Maxine *museum director*
Halfpenny, Geoffrey *museum director*
Rice, Danielle *museum director*
Spruance, Halsey *museum director*

Winterthur
Bowman, Leslie Greene *museum director*

DISTRICT OF COLUMBIA

Washington
Abramowitz, Michael *museum program director*
Bell, Ford Watson *museum association administrator*
Bertin, Margaret A.H *museum administrator*

Bloomfield, Sara J. *museum director*
Bretzfelder, Deborah May *retired museum staff member*
Brougher, Kerry *curator*
Bunch, Lonnie III *museum director*
Carr, Carolyn Kinder *art gallery director, museum director*
Clough, G. Wayne (Gerald Wayne Clough) *museum administrator, former academic administrator*
Cole, Johnnetta Betsch *museum director, former academic administrator*
Conroy, Amy *museum director*
Dailey, John Revell *museum director, retired military officer*
Glass, Brent D. *museum director*
Gover, Kevin *museum director, former federal agency administrator*
Hand, John Oliver *museum curator*
Harvey, Eleanor Jones *museum curator*
Hollins, Hunter *museum administrator*
Kelly, Franklin Wood *museum curator, educator*
Ketchum, James Roe *curator*
Kornicker, Louis Sampson *museum curator*
Koshalek, Richard *museum director, former academic administrator*
Kosinski, Dorothy M. *museum director*
Larson, Judy L. *museum director, curator*
Launius, Roger D. *museum administrator*
Legro, Patrice *museum director*
McKinney, David Duane *museum director, architectural historian*
Noe, Adrianne *museum administrator*
Norton, Susan E.S. *museum director*
Pachter, Marc *retired museum director*
Patton, Sharon F. *retired museum director*
Raby, Julian *art gallery director*
Samper, Cristián *museum director*
Sullivan, Martin Edward *museum director*
Talley, Vernon Andrew *museum administrator*
Urschel, Joe *museum director, former news executive*
Vaccarello, Janine *museum administrator*

FLORIDA

Boca Raton
Bolge, George Stephen *museum director*

Clewiston
Osceola, Tina *museum director*

Coral Gables
Lane, Christina M. *curator, educator*

Daytona Beach
Atherholt, Wayne David *museum director*
Libby, Gary Russell *museum director emeritus, writer*

Eglin AFB
Jones, George W. *museum director, military officer*

Fort Lauderdale
Cavendish, Kim L. Maher *museum administrator*

Gainesville
Nagy, Rebecca Martin *museum director*
Wing, Elizabeth Schwarz *museum curator, educator*

Jacksonville
Peter, Jack E. *museum administrator*

Lakeland
Stetson, Daniel Everett *museum director*

Miami
Buergel, Roger M. *curator, art historian, educator*
Dursum, Brian A. *museum director, art educator*
Hoffman, Joel M. *museum director*
Riley, Terence *curator, architect*

Miami Beach
Camber, Diane Woolfe *association president*
Cubiñá, Silvia Karman *museum director, curator*

Ocala
McClea, Robin Muse *museum director, painter*

Orlando
Morrisey, Marena Grant *museum director*

Palm Beach
Blades, John Michael *museum director*

Pensacola
Rasmussen, Robert L. *museum director, military officer*
Spencer, Vivian L. *gallery director*

Saint Augustine
Harper, Robert Walter III *museum director*

Saint Petersburg
Connelly, David O'Brien *museum administrator, journalist*
Schloder, John E. *museum director*

Sarasota
Montrose-Graem, Douglass *poet-painter, music-man, museum director, bank executive*
Wetenhall, John *museum director*
Zahn, Carl Frederick *museum program director, photographer, graphics designer*

Tallahassee
Brunson, Jeana *museum director*
Palladino-Craig, Allys *museum director, educator*

Tampa
de Quesada, Alejandro Manuel *film and museum consultant, writer*
Ostrenko, Wit *museum administrator*

Vero Beach
Gedeon, Lucinda Heyel *museum director*

GEORGIA

Athens
Eiland, William U. *museum director*

Atlanta
Cilella, Salvatore George, Jr. *museum director*
Galina, Brenda Moss *museum director*
King, Linda Orr *museum director, consultant*
Shapiro, Michael Edward *museum director*
Speed, Bonnie Anne *museum director*
Vigtel, Gudmund *retired museum director*

Augusta
Glaser, Nancy Jane *museum director*

Cartersville
Hopkins, Seth M. *museum director*

Columbus
Butler, Charles Thomas *museum director, curator*

Fort Benning
Hanner, Z. Frank *museum director*

Macon
Ambrose, Andy *museum director*

Robins AFB
Wolfe, Sarah Catharine *curator*

Savannah
High, Steven Samuel *museum director*

HAWAII

Honolulu
Johns, Timothy E. *museum director*

Mililani
Magee, Donald Edward *retired national park service administrator*

IDAHO

Coeur D' Alene
Dahlgren, Dorothy *museum director*

Pocatello
Jackson, Allen Keith *retired museum administrator*

ILLINOIS

Champaign
Harleman, Kathleen Towe *museum director*

Chicago
Balzekas, Stanley, Jr. *museum director*
Cuno, James *museum director*
Czestochowski, Joseph Stephen *administrator, publisher, investor*
Grynsztejn, Madeleine *museum director, curator*
Hankewych, Jaroslaw J. *museum administrator*
Jacob, Mary Jane *curator*
Knappenberger, Paul Henry, Jr. *science museum director*
Lorys, Jan M. *museum director*
Lumbsch, Helge Thorsten *curator*
Mc Carter, John Wilbur, Jr. *museum executive*
Mosena, David R. *museum administrator*
Murphy, Patricia M. *art gallery director*
Nordland, Gerald *museum administrator, historian, consultant*
Rabineau, Phyllis *museum administrator*
Rosen, Rhoda *museum director*
Von Klan, Laurene *museum administrator*
Voris, Harold K *curator*

Edwardsville
Barnett, Eric B. *museum director*

Evanston
Danilov, Victor Joseph *museum administrator, educator, writer*
Robertson, David Alan *museum director, educator*

Peoria
Richerson, James J. *museum administrator, consultant*

Petersburg
Hallmark, Donald Parker *retired museum director, educator*

Princeton
Collins, N. Dana *art gallery owner, consultant, retired art educator*

Springfield
Styles, Bonnie W. *museum director, archaeologist*

INDIANA

Bloomington
Gealt, Adelheid Maria *museum director*

Crawfordsville
Catlin-Legutko, Cinnamon *museum director*

Evansville
Streetman, John William III *museum director*

Fort Wayne
Flinspach, Joan L. *museum administrator*

Indianapolis
Anderson, Maxwell L. *museum director*
Dressel, Barry *museum director*
Easter, Jeanmarie *conservator*
Gantz, Richard Alan *museum administrator*
Patchen, Jeffrey Hart *museum director, music educator*
Vanausdall, John *museum director*
Villers, Lynne M. *curator*

Michigan City
Saxton, Carolyn Virginia *museum director*

Muncie
Blume, Peter Frederick *museum director*

Notre Dame
Loving, Charles Roy *museum director, curator*

South Bend
Bonham, Rebecca June *museum director, educator*

Terre Haute
Vollmer, David L. *museum director*

Zionsville
Hatfield, Tiffany Clellan *museum director and curator*

IOWA

Cedar Falls
Taylor, Darrell Richard *art gallery director, artist*

Cedar Rapids
Moore, Thomas *museum director, retired accountant*
Pitts, Terence Randolph *museum director, consultant*

Davenport
Findlay, Kim *museum administrator*

Dubuque
Enzler, Jerome Anthony *museum director*

KANSAS

Chanute
Froehlich, Conrad Gerald *museum director, researcher*

Hutchinson
Orwoll, Christopher D. *museum administrator, military officer*

Iola
Toland, Clyde William *historic site director, lawyer*

Kansas City
Porter, Marty *museum director*

Lawrence
Hardy, Saralyn Reece *museum director*

North Newton
Pannabecker, Rachel K. *museum director, social sciences educator*

Pleasanton
Earnest, Ola May *curator*

Salina
Ferrell, Heather A. *museum director, curator*

Topeka
Chinn, Jennie *museum director*

Wichita
Jones, Schuyler *museum director, anthropologist*
McDonnell, Patricia Joan *museum director*

KENTUCKY

Lexington
Henrich, Sarah E. *museum director*
Walsh-Piper, Kathleen A. *museum director*

Louisville
O'Brien, Kevin James *museum director*
Venable, Charles L. *museum director*

Owensboro
Hood, Mary Bryan *museum director, painter*

LOUISIANA

Baton Rouge
Gikas, Carol Sommerfeldt *museum director*
Livesay, Thomas Andrew *museum director, educator*

Deridder
Mallory, Patricia Jody *museum curator*

Donaldsonville
Hambrick-Jackson, Kathe *museum director*

New Orleans
Bullard, Edgar John III *museum director*
Casellas, Joachim *art gallery executive*
Fagaly, William Arthur *curator*
Gruber, J. Richard *museum director*
Kahn, David M. *museum director*
Schehr, Kevin John *art gallery owner*

Slidell
Dearing, Reinhard Josef *curator, retired city official*

MAINE

Augusta
Phillips, Joseph Robert *museum director*

Brunswick
Kline, Katy *museum director*

Hancock
Silvestro, Clement Mario *museum director, historian*

Portland
D'Abate, Richard *museum director, historian*
O'Leary, Daniel E. *museum program director*

Rockland
Urbanelli, Lora *museum director*

South Portland
Thompson, Mark R. *museum director*

MARYLAND

Annapolis
Harmon, J. Scott *museum director*

Baltimore
Bolger, Doreen *museum director*
Gibbons, Michael Louis *museum director, educator*
Lee, Steven Xavier *museum director, artist, educator and environmentalist*
Reiner, Van R. *museum administrator*

Clinton
Whittington, Ralph Edward *retired curator, librarian*

College Park
Quick, Edward Raymond *museum director, educator, curator*

Friendship
Clagett, Diana Wharton Sinkler *museum docent*

Landover
Luchs, Alison *curator, art historian*

Mitchellville
Marsh, Caryl Amsterdam *retired curator, psychologist*

Rockville
Kennedy, Roger George *museum program and parks director*

Saint Michaels
Parnes, Stuart L. *museum director*

Silver Spring
Pisney, Raymond Frank *international consulting services executive*

Solomons
Alves, C. Douglass, Jr. *museum director*

Thurmont
Schuettinger, Bruce Michael *conservator*

MASSACHUSETTS

Acton
Judd, Michael W. *museum director*

Amherst
Barker, Elizabeth E. *museum director, curator*

Boston
Cronin, Bonnie Kathryn Lamb *museum director*
Fiori, Dennis A. *museum director*
Hills, Patricia Gorton Schulze *curator, art historian*
Miaoulis, Ioannis Nikolaos *museum director, mechanical engineer, educator*
Nold, Carl Richard *museum administrator*
Robinson, Jeri *museum program director*
Rogers, Malcolm Austin *museum director, art historian*
Shackelford, George T. M. *curator*
Wu, Tung *curator, artist, art historian, educator*
Zannieri, Nina *museum director*

Cambridge
Durant, John R. *museum director, educator*
Ellis, David Wertz *retired museum director, academic administrator, consultant, arbitrator*
Francis, Carl A. *museum director, educator*
Gaskell, Ivan George Alexander De Wend *art museum curator, educator*
Lentz, Thomas W. *museum director, curator*
Slive, Seymour *museum director, art educator*
Tucker, Louis Leonard *retired historical society administrator*

Clinton
Russell, Kent dur *museum administrator*

Concord
Caldwell, Desiree *museum director*

Dennis
Hunter, Elizabeth Ives-Valsam *museum director*

Fitchburg
Jareckie, Stephen Barlow *museum curator*

Lexington
Ott, John Harlow *museum administrator*

Lincoln
Capasso, Nicholas John *curator, art historian, public art expert*
Kois, Dennis *museum director*

Marblehead
Peterson, Pam M. *museum director*

Milton
Randall, Lilian Maria Charlotte *museum curator*

North Adams
Thompson, Joseph C. *museum director*

Northampton
Holbert, Kelly McKay *exhibition coordinator, art historian*

Pepperell
Holmes, Jean Louise *museum director, humanities educator*

Salem
Monroe, Dan L. *museum director*

Springfield
Haskell, Heather R. *museum director*

Stockbridge
Moffatt, Laurie Norton *museum director, curator*

Sudbury
Pitman, Ursula Wall *curator, educator*

Waltham
Arena, Albert A. *museum director*

Williamstown
Conforti, Michael Peter *museum director, art historian*

Worcester
Welu, James A. *museum director*

MICHIGAN

Ann Arbor
Steward, James Christen *museum director, educator*

Bloomfield Hills
Wittkopp, Gregory Mark *museum director*

Charlevoix
Miles, David Loren *museum director*

Dearborn
Ameri, Anan *museum director*
Mooradian, Patricia *museum administrator*

Detroit
Beal, Graham William John *museum director*
Darr, Alan Phipps *curator, historian*
Moore, Juanita *museum administrator*
Peck, William Henry *curator, archaeologist, educator*
Prihod, Kevin F. *museum administrator*

East Lansing
Bandes, Susan Jane *museum director, educator*
Dewhurst, Charles Kurt *museum director, curator, language educator*

Grand Rapids
Adams, Celeste *museum director*
Lee, Mary Esther *museum director*

Kalamazoo
Bridenstine, James Aloysius *museum director*
Norris, Richard Patrick *museum director, historian, educator*
Rose, William N. (Bill Rose) *museum administrator*

Owosso
Schneider, Don (Charles Schneider) *museum administrator*

MINNESOTA

Minneapolis
Alexander, Darsie *curator*
Crippen, John Raymond *museum director*
Feldman, Kaywin *museum director, curator*
King, Lyndel Irene Saunders *museum director*
Viso, Olga *museum director*

Saint Paul
Jolly, Eric J. *museum director*

MISSISSIPPI

Biloxi
Gowdy, Marjorie E. *museum director*

Jackson
Bradley, Betsy *museum director*

MISSOURI

Columbia
Barker, Alex W. *museum director, educator*
Kremer, Gary R. *museum director, historian, educator*

Fredericktown
Sudmeyer, Alice Jean *art gallery owner*

Hannibal
Faden, Regina *museum director*

Independence
Potts, Barbara Joyce *retired historic site director*

Kansas City
Carroll, Gregory A. *museum director, educator, musician*
Cozad, Rachael Blackburn *museum director*
Leitch, Christopher *museum director, artist*
Wilson, Marc Fraser *art museum director*

Saint Joseph
Chilcote, Gary M. *museum director, reporter*
Oldham, Terry L. *museum director*

Saint Louis
Benjamin, Brent R. *museum director*
Goldblatt, Peter *curator*
King, Douglas R. *museum administrator*
Yatskievych, George Alfred *curator, educator*

MONTANA

Billings
Peterson, Robyn Gayle *museum director*

Missoula
Brown, Robert Munro *museum director*
Millin, Laura Jeanne *museum director*

West Yellowstone
Shea, Paul *museum association administrator, curator*

NEBRASKA

Ashland
McLean, John Mac *museum director*

Boys Town
Lynch, Thomas Joseph *museum director*

Chadron
Lecher, Belvadine (Belvadine Reeves) *museum curator*
Polak, Sarah *museum association administrator, educator*

Grand Island
Black, Joe *museum director, curator*

Omaha
Joyner, John Brooks *museum director*
Smith, Leo W., II, *museum director*

NEVADA

Carson City
Barmore, James Gilbert *museum director, curator*

Las Vegas
Herridge, Elizabeth *museum director*
Lumpkin, Libby *museum director*

NEW HAMPSHIRE

Concord
Balla, Wesley G. *museum curator, historian*

Hanover
Kennedy, Brian P. *museum director*

Meredith
Lane, Sophia *art gallery director*

Portsmouth
Nylander, Jane Louise *museum director, educator, writer*
Yerdon, Lawrence J. *museum administrator*

NEW JERSEY

Holmdel
Smith, Sibley Judson, Jr. *historic site administrator, educator*

Jersey City
Koster, Emlyn Howard *museum administrator, geologist, educator*

Morristown
Butera, Virginia Fabbri *art gallery director, educator*
Call, Denise Hodgins *curator, artist*
Miller, Steven H. *museum director*

Newark
Buck, Rebecca A. *museum administrator, registrar*
Connor, Holly Pyne *curator, art historian*
Price, Mary Sue Sweeney *museum director*

Ramsey
Libin, Laurence Elliot *retired curator*

Ridgewood
Fox, Ingrid *curator*

Somerville
O'Brien, Walter John *retired artist management executive, writer*

NEW MEXICO

Alamogordo
Hayes, Randall *museum director*

Albuquerque
Baker, Laura Kay *art gallery owner, writer*
Solimon, Ronald James (Ron Soliman) *museum administrator*
Wright, Cathy L. *museum director*

Las Cruces
Reynolds, Terry Ray *curator, anthropologist, educator*

Placitas
Smith, Richard Bowen *retired national park superintendent*

Roswell
Rufe, Laurie J. *museum director*

Ruidoso Downs
Smith, Jay S. *museum director*

Santa Fe
Bol, Marsha C. *museum director*
Ice, Joyce *museum director*
Levine, Frances *museum director*
Tisdale, Shelby Jo-Anne *museum director, consultant*

Taos
Witt, David L. *curator, writer*

NEW YORK

Albany
Miles, Christine Marie *museum director*
Siegfried, Clifford A. *museum director*

Bethel
Lawrence, Wade *museum director*

Blue Mountain Lake
Welsh, Caroline Mastin *museum director, curator, art historian*

Bronx
Block, Holly *museum director*

Brooklyn
Desmarais, Charles Joseph *museum director, writer*
Enseki, Carol *museum director*
Lehman, Arnold Lester *museum director, art historian, educator*
Zuther, Simone Margrietha *curator*

Buffalo
Dreishpoon, Douglas Scott *curator, art historian*
Jackson-Forsberg, Eric M. *curator, educator*
Pietrzak, Ted S. *art gallery director*

Centerport
Mallamo, J. Lance *museum director*

Cold Spring Harbor
DeOrsay, Paul *museum director*
MacKay, Robert Battin *museum director*

Corning
Spillman, Jane Shadel *curator, writer, researcher*
Swain, Kristin A. *museum director*
Whitehouse, David Bryn *museum director*

Corona
Finkelpearl, Tom *museum director*

Cortland
Parks, Paul Joseph *curator, educator*

East Hampton
Appelhof, Ruth Stevens *museum director, curator, art historian*
Strassfield, Christina Mossaides *museum director, chief curator*

Glens Falls
Setford, David F. *museum director*

Hamilton
Moynihan, William J. *museum executive*

Hempstead
Levinthal, Beth Ellen (Kuby Levinthal) *museum director*

Ithaca
Allmon, Warren D. *museum director, educator*
Ferri, Laurent *curator, educator*
Robinson, Franklin Westcott *museum director, art historian*

Katonah
Simpson, William Kelly *curator, Egyptologist, educator*

Long Island City
Heiss, Alanna *museum director*

New York
Armstrong, Richard A. *museum director, curator*
Bailey, Colin Barry *curator*
Barnett, Vivian Endicott *curator*
Basquin, Mary Smyth (Kit Basquin) *museum administrator*
Beck, Martha Ann *curator, director*
Bothmer, Dietrich Felix von *curator, archaeologist*
Bull, David *fine art conservator*
Campbell, Thomas P. *museum director, curator*
Conelli, Maria Ann *museum director, art educator*
Cooke, Lynne Catherine *curator*
de Montebello, Philippe Lannes *retired museum director, art educator*
Draper, James David *art museum curator*
Ferber, Linda S. *museum director*
Fitzpatrick, Robert John *museum director*
Flynn, John J. *museum curator*
Foster, Carter *curator*
Freed, Stanley Arthur *retired museum curator*
Fung, Lance Michael *curator, art gallery director*
Futter, Ellen Victoria *museum administrator*
Golden, Thelma *museum director, curator*
Grasselli, Margaret Morgan *curator*
Griswold, William M. *museum director, curator*
Gumpert, Lynn *gallery director*
Gund, Agnes *retired museum administrator*
Halbreich, Kathy *museum director*
Haskell, Barbara *curator*
Hays, Helen *museum program director*
Hotchner, Holly *museum director, curator, conservator*
Hoving, Thomas *museum director, consultant, writer*
Howat, John Keith *retired museum executive*
Ilse-Neuman, Ursula *curator*
Joo, Eungie *curator*
Kallir, Jane Katherine *art gallery director, author*
Kardon, Janet *museum director*
Kramer, Linda Konheim *curator, art historian*
Krens, Thomas *museum administrator*
Kuchta, Ronald Andrew *museum director, editor, curator*
Lai, Charles *museum director*
Lerner, Martin *museum curator*
Levai, Pierre Alexandre *art gallery executive*
Levine, Louis D. *museum administrator, archaeologist*
Lowry, Glenn David *art museum director*
Marenoff, Susan *museum director, former professional athletics manager*
Mayo, Paula *museum director*
Mertens, Joan R. *museum curator, art historian*
Messer, Thomas Maria *museum director*
Mitchell, Patricia Edenfield *broadcast museum administrator*
Momin, Shamim *curator*
Murdock, Robert Mead *curator*
Myer, Keats *museum director*
Phillips, Linda *museum director*
Phillips, Lisa *museum director*
Platnick, Norman I. *curator, entomologist*
Poulet, Anne Litle *museum director, art historian*
Powell, Earl Alexander III *art museum director*
Prather, Marla *curator*
Rafferty, Emily Kernan *museum administrator*
Rosenbaum, Joan Hannah *museum director*
Simon, Ronald Charles *curator, educator*
Spector, Nancy *curator*
Stanley, John Slusarski *art museum administrator*
Steglitz, Marc H. *museum administrator*
Sutton, Karen E. *museum director*
Temkin, Ann *curator*
Thompson, Paul Warwick *museum director*
Toll, Barbara Elizabeth *art gallery director*
Wardropper, Ian Bruce *museum curator, educator*
Weinberg, Adam D. *museum director*
Zugazagoitia, Julian *museum director*

Purchase
Collins, Thom *museum director*
Posner, Helaine J. *museum curator*

Rochester
Adams, G. Rollie *museum executive*
Bannon, Anthony Leo *museum director*
Bennett, Kate *museum director*
Ravines, Patrick C. *conservator, researcher*

Rye
Sollins, Susan *curator, television producer*

Sands Point
Olian, JoAnne Constance *curator, art historian*

Southampton
Sultan, Terrie Frances *museum director*

Stony Brook
Stone, Gaynell *museum director, educator*

Tupper Lake
Welsh, Peter Corbett *museum director, historian*

Utica
Schweizer, Paul Douglas *museum director*

West Point
Reel, David Mark *curator, museum director*

Yonkers
Botwinick, Michael *museum director*

NORTH CAROLINA

Asheville
Rickman, Ellen Erwin *museum administrator*

Chapel Hill
Kass, Emily *museum director*
Riggs, Timothy Allan *museum curator*

Charlotte
Kline, Phil *museum director*
Zimmern, Emily Fairchild *museum director*

Durham
Rorschach, Kimberly *museum director*
Van Deman, Barry Alan *museum administrator*

Gastonia
Tippitt, Ann *museum director*

Greensboro
Dobrogosz, Glenn D. *museum director*

Raleigh
Bennett, Betsy M. *museum director*
Howard, Kenneth B. *museum director*
Kuhler, Renaldo Gillet *retired museum director, medical illustrator*
Wheeler, Lawrence Jefferson *museum director*

Wilmington
Seapker, Janet Kay *museum administrator, architectural historian, consultant*
Velders, Deborah *museum director*

Winston Salem
Rauschenberg, Bradford Lee *retired museum program director*
Sanford, Beverly Shaw *museum director*
Whittington, Stephen Lunn *museum director*

NORTH DAKOTA

Bismarck
Paaverud, Merlan E., Jr. *museum director*

Fargo
Pauley, Edward E. *museum administrator*
Ryan, Mark A. *museum staff member*

OHIO

Canton
Perry, Stephen A. *museum administrator, former federal agency administrator*

Cincinnati
Betsky, Aaron *museum director*
Brown, Daniel *curator, executive secretary*
Crew, Spencer *museum administrator*
Long, Phillip Clifford *retired museum director*
McDonald, Douglass Wayne *museum administrator*
Platow, Raphaela *museum director, curator*

Cleveland
Davis, Gainor Buckingham *museum administrator*
Edmonson, James Milton *museum director*
Latimer, Bruce M. *museum director, anthropologist, educator*
Mann, C. Griffith *curator*
Rub, Timothy F. *museum director*
Stewart, Terry *museum administrator*

Columbus
Maciejunes, Nannette V. *museum director*

Dayton
Driesbach, Janice T. *museum director, curator*
Meister, Mark Jay *museum director, professional society administrator*

Groveport
Motts, Warren Earl *museum director*

Oberlin
Wiles, Stephanie *museum director*

Oxford
Wicks, Robert S. *museum director, educator*

Toledo
Bacigalupi, Don *museum director*

University Heights
Cook, Alexander Burns *curator, artist, educator*

Wright Patterson AFB
Metcalf, Charles David *museum director, retired military officer*

Youngstown
Zona, Louis Albert *museum director*

OKLAHOMA

Norman
Censky, Ellen Joan *curator, biologist, museum director*

Oklahoma City
Granger, Brenda Ann *museum director*
Otto, Donald R. *museum director*
Plummer, William Hamilton III *museum director, editor*
Schroeder, Charles P. (Chuck Schroeder) *museum director*

Ripley
Chlouber, Dale Edward *curator*

Shawnee
Pollei, Dane F. *museum director*

Tulsa
Suffolk, Randall *museum director, curator*

OREGON

Bend
Upp, Janeanne A. *museum administrator*

Jacksonville
Enders, John *museum administrator, former journalist*

Pendleton
Reese, Julie *museum director, association administrator*

Portland
Ferriso, Brian J. *museum director*
Stueber, Nancy *museum director*
Taylor, J(ocelyn) Mary *museum director, educator, zoologist*

Salem
Olbrantz, John Paul *museum director, art historian*

PENNSYLVANIA

Allentown
Perry, Gregory J. *museum director*

Altoona
Moffitt, Charles William *owner servello gallery art*

Chadds Ford
Duff, James Henry *museum director, environmental services administrator*

Erie
Vanco, John L. *art museum director*

Grantham
Mark, Kenneth Dean *museum director, educator*

Harrisburg
Franco, Barbara Alice *museum director*
Leighow, Jack (John C. Leighow, Jr.) *museum director*
Mahey, John Andrew *retired museum director*

Merion Station
Gillman, Derek A. *museum director, academic administrator*

Philadelphia
Beck, Tracey Rae *museum director*
Brigham, David R. *museum director*
Brown, William Yancey *museum administrator*
Dreher, Derick *museum director*
Goodman, Gwen Ducat *museum director*
Gould, Claudia *museum director*
Hodges, Richard Andrew *museum director, archaeologist, educator*
Hough, Melissa Ellen *curator, museum director*
Kolb, Nancy Dwyer *museum director*
Rech, Lori Dillard *museum administrator*
Shoemaker, Innis Howe *art museum curator*
Smith, Sharon A. *museum administrator*
Wint, Dennis Michael *museum director*

Pittsburgh
Bodine, William Beekman, Jr. *museum director*
Dawson, Mary Ruth *curator, educator*
Gancas, Ronald S. *museum administrator, historian*
Haas, Joanna E. *museum director*
Hillenbrand, David M. *museum administrator*
King, Elaine A. *curator, art historian, critic*
Lippincott, Louise *museum director, curator*
Masich, Andrew Edward *museum director, historian*
Rolla, Maureen J. *museum director*
Sokolowski, Thomas William *museum director*
Werner, Jane *museum administrator*
Zelevansky, Lynn *museum director*

Reading
Dietrich, Bruce Leinbach *museum administrator, astronomer, educator*
Roth, Ronald C. *museum director*

Rector
Smith, David A. *museum director*

Sewickley
Kornetchuk, Elena *curator, art dealer*

South Williamsport
Ogurcak, Janice L. *museum director, educator*

Strasburg
Dunn, David W. *museum director*
Lindsay, George Carroll *former museum director*

Titusville
Zolli, Barbara Turk *museum director*

University Park
Muhlert, Jan Keene *art museum director*

RHODE ISLAND

Providence
Alswang, Hope *museum director*
Fishman, Bernard Philip *museum director*

Saunderstown
Leavitt, Thomas Whittlesey *retired museum director, educator*

SOUTH CAROLINA

Charleston
Brumgardt, John Raymond *museum director*
Richardson, Anne Worsham *art gallery owner, artist*
Smith, J. Roy *museum director, education educator*
Smith, Todd D. *museum director*

Columbia
Brosius, Karen *museum director*

Mount Pleasant
Macdonald, Robert Rigg, Jr. *retired museum director*

Pawleys Island
Matelic, Candace Tangorra *museum director, educator, organizational consultant*

Salmon, Robin Robertson *museum curator, editor*

West Columbia
Harmon, Horace Elmer, Jr. *retired museum director, cultural history consultant*

TENNESSEE

Chattanooga
Kret, Robert A. *museum director*

Crossville
Buechel, Eric *art gallery owner, visual artist*

Johnson City
Gerhardt, E. Alvin, Jr. *retired museum director*

Knoxville
Butler, David *museum director*
Chapman, Jefferson *museum director*

Memphis
Hackett, Richard Cecil *museum director, former mayor*
Kitchin, Cameron (L. Cameron Kitchin) *museum director*
Lyons, Al(pha) L. *museum director, retired manufacturing executive*

Nashville
Duvenhage, Susan B. *museum administrator*
Riggins-Ezzell, Lois *museum administrator*

TEXAS

Austin
Theriot, Edward C. *museum director*

Canyon
Frederickson, Mary Christine *conservator*
Trela, Richard Joseph *conservator, educator*
Vanderpool, Guy Clifton *museum director*

Dallas
Brice, Wanda R. *museum administrator*
Hoffman, Marguerite Steed *former art gallery director*
Longford, Nicola *museum director*
Pitman-Gelles, Bonnie Louise *museum administrator, educator*

El Paso
Sipiora, Leonard Paul *retired museum director, art appraiser*

Fort Worth
Auping, Michael G. *curator*
Lee, Eric McCauley *museum director, art historian*
Scott, Janice Wilkie *museum director*
Tyler, Ronnie Curtis *museum director, art historian*

Fredericksburg
Manhart, Marcia Y(ockey) *retired art museum director*

Houston
Bartsch, Joel A. *museum administrator, curator*
Marzio, Peter Cort *museum director*
Shearer, Linda *museum director*

Lubbock
Baker, Robert J. *museum director, science educator, researcher*

Mc Kinney
Bahm, Matt Anthony *museum administrator, consultant*

Post
Neff, Marie Taylor *museum director, artist*

San Antonio
Barilleaux, Rene Paul *curator*
Drutt, Matthew J. W. *museum director*
Rubin, David Stuart *curator, art critic*

UTAH

Salt Lake City
Dee, David L. *museum director*
Olsen, Steven Lloyd *museum administrator, educator*

VERMONT

Bennington
Franklin, Jamie *curator, consultant*
Williams, Robert Joseph *retired museum director, educator*

Manchester
Kouwenhoven, Gerrit Wolphertsen *retired museum director*

Windsor
Gilbert-Smith, Alma *museum director*

VIRGINIA

Alexandria
Lundeberg, Philip Karl Boraas *curator, historian*
Mackay, James Cobham *museum director*

Arlington
Demetrion, James Thomas *retired museum director, consultant*

Charlottesville
Hartz, Jill *museum director*

Hampton
Courtney, Vernon S. *museum director, Museum Association Administrator*

Lynchburg
Elson, James Martin *retired landmark director*

Martinsville
Gette, Timothy J. *museum director*

Mc Lean
Forman, Lee Lavinthal *museum administrator*

Newport News
Hightower, John Brantley *retired museum administrator*

Norfolk
Hennessey, William John *museum director*

Richmond
Conti, Richard C. *museum director*
Nyerges, Alexander Lee *museum director*
Rawls, S. Waite III *museum director, investment company executive*

Sterling
Friedheim, Jerry Warden *museum consultant*

Tazewell
Weeks, Ross Leonard, Jr. *museum executive*

Williamsburg
Christison, Muriel Branham *retired museum director, art history educator*
Emerson, Philip G. *historic site director*
Sullivan, Timothy Jackson *museum administrator, retired academic administrator, educator*

WASHINGTON

Bellevue
Warren, James Ronald *retired museum director, journalist*

Bellingham
Clark-Langager, Sarah Ann *curator, academic administrator*

Goldendale
Skillern, Michael Phillip *museum administrator*

Kennewick
Camp, Kimberly N. *museum administrator, artist*

Redmond
Sobey, Edwin J. C. *museum director, oceanographer, consultant*

Seattle
Callan, Josi Irene *museum director*
Garfield, Leonard *museum director*
Stein, Julie K. *museum director, educator*

Tacoma
Nicandri, David L. *museum director*
Stebich, Stephanie A. *museum director*
Wimberger, Peter Hans *museum director, educator*

WEST VIRGINIA

Charleston
Hodges, Adam *museum director*

Harpers Ferry
Kodak, Don *museum director*

WISCONSIN

Green Bay
Telzrow, Michael E. *museum director, historian*

Kenosha
Joyce, Daniel James *curator*

Madison
Fleischman, Stephen *museum director*
Garver, Fanny P. *art gallery owner*
Garver, Thomas Haskell *curator, consultant, writer*
Koski, Ann Louise *museum director*
Panczenko, Russell *museum director*
Pillaert, E(dna) Elizabeth *museum director*

Milwaukee
Boie, Charles A. *museum administrator*
Finley, Daniel Mark *museum administrator, former county official*
Green, Edward Anthony *museum director*
Keegan, Daniel T. *museum director*
Peltz, Cissie Jean *art gallery director, cartoonist*
Quirk, James *museum director*

Racine
Pepich, Bruce Walter *museum director, curator*

WYOMING

Cody
Donoghue, Ann Marie *museum administrator, consultant*

Jackson Hole
McNutt, James Charles *museum director*

CANADA

ALBERTA

Canmore
Janes, Robert Roy *museum director, archaeologist, editor, consultant*

BRITISH COLUMBIA

Victoria
Finlay, James Campbell *retired museum director*

ONTARIO

London
Poole, Nancy Geddes *art gallery curator, writer*

Ottawa
McAvity, John Gillis *museum director, association executive, museologist*

PRINCE EDWARD ISLAND

Belfast
Weber, Jean Macphail *retired museum director*

ENGLAND

London
Penny, Nicholas Beaver *museum director*

SWEDEN

Stockholm
Cavalli-Björkman, Görel *professor*

ADDRESS UNPUBLISHED

Abram, Ruth Jacobeth *museum founder*
Adams, Margaret Bernice *retired museum official*
Ahrens, Kent *museum director, art historian*
Andrews, Richard Otis *former art gallery director, curator*
Becker, Gail Roselyn *museum director*
Bishop, Budd Harris *retired museum director*
Bolas, Gerald Douglas *museum director, art historian, educator*
Booker, Nana Laurel *art gallery owner, honorary consul*
Carter, John Swain *retired museum director*
Castile, Rand (Jesse Randolph III) *retired museum director*
Cikovsky, Nicolai, Jr. *retired curator, art historian, educator*
Consey, Kevin Edward *museum administrator*
Crusan, Ronald L. *retired museum director*
Damon, Shirley Stockton *art gallery owner*
Deutsch, James I. *curator*
Ebie, William D. *retired museum director*
Edmar, Désirée Anna Elisabeth *retired museum director*
Elam, Leslie Albert *retired museum director*
Emerson, Anne Devereux *retired museum administrator*
Feisthammel, Audrey Marie *museum director, educator*
Fri, Robert Wheeler *retired museum director*
Friedman, Richard Everett *curator, art appraiser*
Gates, Jay Rodney *retired museum director*
Gates, Mimi Gardner *retired museum director*
Gear, Emily *museum director, curator*
Glenn, Constance White *art museum director, educator, consultant*
Godbille, Lara *museum director*
Gorelick, Ellen Catherine *museum executive director, chief curator, artist, educator, civic volunteer, retired*
Gribbon, Deborah *museum director*
Grinell, Sheila *museum director, consultant*
Hartfield, Elizabeth Ann (Libby Hartfield) *museum director*
Hasse, John Edward *music curator*
Hayes, Charles Franklin III *retired museum director*
Hellmers, Norman Donald *retired historic site director*
Jacobowitz, Ellen Sue *curator, museum administrator*
Johnston, Phillip Michael *retired museum director, curator*
Kahn, James Steven *retired museum director*
Mandle, Roger *museum administrator, former academic administrator*
Maples, Philip G. *retired museum director*
Melder, Keith E. *retired curator*
Metcalf, William Edwards *museum curator, educator*
Millard, Charles Warren III *retired museum director, writer*
Nasgaard, Roald *museum curator*
Newman, Bruce Murray *retired antiques gallery owner*
Organ, Rita C. *museum administrator, consultant*
Pal, Pratapaditya *curator*
Parris, Nina Gumpert *curator, writer, researcher, photographer*
Perrot, Paul Norman *museum director*
Petersen, Martin Eugene *curator*
Phillips, Laughlin *retired museum director, editor*
Potts, Timothy F. *former museum director*
Rich, Andrea Louise *former museum administrator*
Rifkin, Ned *former museum director*
Robertson, Charles James *museum director emeritus*
Rollins, Ken (Quinton C. Rollins) *museum director*
Rosenthal, Nan *curator, educator, author*
Rouse, Terrie Suzitte *museum director*
Ryskamp, Charles Andrew *museum director, educator*
Sanchez-Kennedy, Maria *museum director*
Schlageter, Robert William *museum administrator*
Schneider, Janet M. *museum administrator, painter, curator*
Segger, Martin Joseph *museum director, educator, art historian*
Shakespeare, Valerie Monroe *curator, director, art gallery owner*
Shaw, Nancy Rivard *museum curator, art historian, consultant*
Shestack, Alan *retired museum administrator*
Shimoda, Jerry Yasutaka *retired national historic park manager*
Sims, Lowery Stokes *museum curator, administrator, writer, educator*
Skramstad, Harold Kenneth, Jr. *museum consultant*
Small, Lawrence M. *former museum executive*
Steadman, David Wilton *retired museum director, deacon*
Steele, Valerie Fahnestock *museum director, writer, educator*
Stryker, Richard Ripley, Jr. *museum director*
Stuart, Joseph Martin *museum administrator*
Summerfield, John Robert *textile curator*
Sutton, Peter Campbell *museum director*
Taragin, Davira Spiro *curator*
Tobin, Paul Edward, Jr. *museum director, retired admiral*
Trop, Sandra *former museum director*
Trutor, Genevieve Williamson *museum director*
Walker, Roslyn Adele *retired museum director*
Way, Jacob Edson III *museum director*
West, W. Richard, Jr. *retired museum director*
Wilson, Karen Lee *museum staff member, researcher*

INDUSTRY: MANUFACTURING
See also **FINANCE: FINANCIAL SERVICES**

UNITED STATES

ALABAMA

Birmingham
Bennett, Joe Claude *pharmaceutical executive*
Breitfeld, Philip Paul *pharmaceutical executive, oncologist*
Cohen-DeMarco, Gale Maureen *pharmaceutical executive*
Dean, Joseph Oral, Jr. *retired pharmaceutical executive*
Gorrie, M. Miller *construction executive*
Hall, Robert Alan *construction company executive*
James, Donald M. *construction materials executive*
Neal, Phil Hudson, Jr. *retired manufacturing executive*
Sklenar, Herbert Anthony *industrial products manufacturing company executive*
Styslinger, Lee Joseph, Jr. *manufacturing executive*

Gadsden
Farr, Dwayne Louis *automotive executive*

Huntsville
Anwer, Khursheed Nadeem *research and development company executive*

Mobile
Rummel, Harold Edwin *construction executive*

Opelika
Jenkins, Richard Lee *manufacturing executive*

ALASKA

Anchorage
Choudhury, Raj Deo *global energy industry executive*

Haines
Kaufman, David Graham *construction executive*

ARIZONA

Carefree
Wearly, William Levi *retired manufacturing executive*

Chandler
Kim, James Joo-Jin *electronics company executive*

Mesa
DeRosa, Francis Dominic *chemical company executive*

Phoenix
Altmann, Jon Christopher *research and development company executive*
Church, Steve *electronics executive*
Dewane, John Richard *retired manufacturing executive, small business owner*
Giedt, Bruce Alan *paper company executive*
Giltner, Phil (F. Phillips Giltner III) *food distributing executive*
Hamada, Rick *electronics executive*
Kamins, Edward *electronics executive*
Mondry, Lawrence N. *automotive executive*
Phillips, Steve *electronics executive*
Sadowski, Raymond *electronics executive*
Vallee, Roy A. *electronics executive*
White, Edward Allen *electronics executive*

Prescott
Forth, Kevin Bernard *beverage distributing industry consultant*

Scottsdale
Farley, James Newton *retired manufacturing executive, electrical engineer*
Freedman, Stanley Marvin *manufacturing executive*
Grenell, James Henry *retired manufacturing company executive*
Howard, William Gates, Jr. *electronics company executive*
Jesky, T. J. *pharmaceutical products executive*
Levine, Stanley Walter *chemical company executive*
Lloyd, Eugene Walter *retired construction company executive*
Rethore, Bernard Gabriel *manufacturing and mining company executive, consultant*
Walsh, Edward Joseph *food products and cosmetics executive*

Surprise
Lazar, Max Seymour *retired pharmaceutical company executive*

Tucson
Francesconi, Louise L. *defense equipment manufacturing company executive*
Jeffe, Sidney David *automotive executive, engineer*

ARKANSAS

Little Rock
Bell, Richard Eugene *agricultural products executive, state official*

Springdale
Leatherby, Dennis *food products executive*
Tollett, Leland Edward *food products executive*
Tyson, John H. *food products executive*
Van Bebber, David L. *food products executive, lawyer*

CALIFORNIA

Alamo
Liggett, Lawrence Melvin *vacuum equipment manufacturing company executive*

Aliso Viejo
Morrison, Patricia B. *former electronics executive*

Anaheim
Palfenier, David *food products executive*

Atherton
Goodman, Sam Richard *electronics executive*

Beverly Hills
Kardashian, Kim (Kimberly Noel Kardashian) *apparel retailer, television personality*
Winthrop, John *wines and spirits company executive*

Burbank
Joseff, Joan Castle *manufacturing executive*
Raulinaitis, Pranas Algis *electronics executive, consultant*

Burlingame
Wright, Ian M. *automotive executive, electrical engineer*

Calabasas
Asscher, Jean-Claude *electronics executive*
Dreier, R. Chad (Robert Chad Dreier) *construction and mortgage company executive*
Nicholson, Larry T. *construction executive*

Carlsbad
Crooke, Stanley Thomas *pharmaceutical executive*

Carmel Valley
Kasson, James Matthews *electronics executive*

Carson
Heiser, James S. *manufacturing executive*

Claremont
Forti, William Bell *manufacturing executive*

Clovis
Turner, Eugene Andrew *manufacturing executive*

Colusa
Carter, Jane Foster *agricultural industry executive*

Concord
Amies, Christopher Jude *medical products executive*

Corona
Chao, Allen Y. *pharmaceutical executive*

Coronado
Sack, Edgar Albert *electronics company executive*

Costa Mesa
Hazewinkel, Van *manufacturing executive*

Culver City
Leve, Alan Donald *electronics executive*

Cupertino
Bernhardt, Richard Bruce *electronic company executive*
Gong, Yihong *research and development company manager*

El Segundo
Thiry, Kent J. *health products executive*
Whitney, Richard K. *health products executive*

Emeryville
O'Dea, Patrick J. *food products executive*
Renton, Hollings C. *health products executive*
Robb, Walter *food products executive*

Escalon
Barton, Gerald Lee *farming company executive*

Foster City
Alton, Gregg H. *pharmaceutical executive, lawyer*
Denny, James M. *pharmaceutical and former retail executive*
Lucier, Gregory Thomas *medical technology executive*
Martin, John C. *pharmaceutical company executive*
Tretton, Jack *electronics executive*

Fountain Valley
Wilhite, Steve *automotive executive*

Fremont
Alsborg, Thomas C. *electronics executive*
Bagley, James W. *semiconductor equipment company executive*
Huang, Robert T. *electronics executive*
Murai, Kevin M. *electronics executive*
Newberry, Stephen G. *semiconductor equipment company executive*
Polk, Dennis *electronics executive*
Zimmer, George A. *men's apparel executive*

Fullerton
Garrett, Scott T. *medical products executive*
Miller, Arnold *electronics executive*

Glendale
Harris, John J. *food products executive*

Hillsborough
Keller, John Francis *retired food products executive, mayor*

Hollywood
Parks, Robert Myers *appliance manufacturing company executive*

Huntington Beach
McKnight, Robert B., Jr. *sporting goods manufacturing executive*

Irvine
Alspach, Philip Halliday *manufacturing executive*
Baumgartner, Anton Edward *automotive sales professional*
Broadhurst, Norman Neil *food products executive*
Fisker, Henrik *automobile designer and company executive*
Khalifeh, Ala F. *research and development company researcher*
Mussey, Joseph Arthur *health and medical product executive*
Peterson, Jeffrey V. *construction executive*
Pyott, David Edmund Ian *pharmaceutical executive*

La Jolla
Geckler, Richard Delph *retired metal products executive*

Lafayette
Romanowski, Bill (William Thomas Romanowski) *nutrition company executive, retired professional football player, actor*

Lake Forest
Higby, Lawrence M. *medical products executive*

Los Angeles
Adler, Fred Peter *retired electronics company executive*
Borneman, John Paul *pharmaceutical executive*
Charney, Dov *apparel executive*
dePaolis, Potito Umberto *food company executive*
Golleher, George *food company executive*
Hannah, David H. *metal products executive*
Hedley, Mary Lynne *biopharmaceutical executive*
Hutchins, Joan Morthland *manufacturing executive, farmer*
Lewis, Karla R. *metal products executive*
Marciano, Georges G. *apparel executive*
Marciano, Maurice *apparel executive*
Marciano, Paul L. *apparel executive*
Mezger, Jeffrey T. *construction executive*
Mollins, Gregg J. *metal products executive*
Murdock, David H. *food products executive*
Resnick, Stewart Allen *diversified company executive*

Marina Del Rey
Bennett, Joel Herbert *construction executive*

Menlo Park
Carlson, Curtis R. *electronics research industry executive*
Marks, Michael E. *electronics executive*
Okarma, Thomas Bernard *biotechnology company executive*
Saifer, Mark Gary Pierce *pharmaceutical executive*
Taft, David Dakin *chemicals executive*
Westcott, Brian John *manufacturing executive*

Milpitas
Hasler, William Albert *electronics executive*
Roddick, David Bruce *construction company executive*

Mission Viejo
Sganga, John B. *retired furniture holding company executive*

Montecito
Meghreblian, Robert Vartan *manufacturing executive, physicist*
Purl, O. Thomas *retired electronics company executive*

Monterey
Hanlon, James Allison *confectionery company executive*

Napa
Ali, Yusuf *research and development company executive*

Newport Beach
Bennett, Bruce W. *retired construction executive, civil engineer*

Oakland
Heinrich, Daniel J. *chemicals executive*

Oceanside
Montgomery, Michael Davis *research and development company executive, real estate investor*

Palm Desert
Epstein, Marvin Morris *retired construction company executive*

Palo Alto
Bennett, Alan Jerome *electronics executive, physicist*
Guertin, Timothy E. *medical products executive*
Morris, Arlene Myers *biopharmaceutical company executive*
Sager, Philip Travis *pharmaceutical executive, cardiologist, researcher*
Seethaler, William Charles *high technology manufacturing executive*
Shetty, Jay K. *research and development company executive, researcher*
Sledd, Robert C. *food products executive*
Smith, Julie Ann *pharmaceutical executive*
Staprans, Armand *electronics executive*

Palos Verdes Peninsula
Grant, Robert Ulysses *retired manufacturing executive*
Leone, William Charles *retired manufacturing executive*
Wilson, Theodore Henry *retired electronics executive, aerospace engineer*

Pasadena
Bishop, Robert Calvin *pharmaceutical company executive*
Davidson, Robert C., Jr. *manufacturing executive*
Hunter, Milton *construction company executive, retired career military officer*
Kresa, Kent *manufacturing executive, retired aerospace executive*
Marlen, James S. *chemical, plastics and building materials manufacturing company executive*
Smith, Howard Russell *manufacturing executive, director*
Watson, Noel G. *construction executive*

Playa Del Rey
Mishelevich, David Jacob *medical products executive*

Pleasanton
Bond, David F. *food products executive*
Ching, David T. *food products executive*
Weiss, Robert Stephen *medical manufacturing company operating executive*

Portola Valley
Graham, William James *packaging company executive*

Rancho Dominguez
Janura, Jan Arol *apparel manufacturing executive*

Rancho Santa Fe
Jordan, Charles Morrell *retired automotive designer*
Step, Eugene Lee *retired pharmaceutical executive*

Redwood City
Pleasants, John F. *electronics executive*
Wang, Chen Chi *electronics, real estate and diversified financial services company executive*

Rio Vista
Azarnoff, Daniel Lester *pharmaceutical executive, consultant*

Riverside
Chamberlain, Willard Thomas *retired metal products executive*
Smith, Elden Leroy *recreational vehicle and manufactured housing company executive*

Sacramento
Aldrich, Thomas Albert *former brewing executive, consultant*
Baccigaluppi, Roger John *agricultural products executive*

San Anselmo
Chiaverini, John Edward *construction company executive*

San Carlos
Eberhard, Martin *automotive executive, electronics engineer*
Lund, Victor L. *healthcare company executive*

San Clemente
Clark, Earnest Hubert, Jr. *tool company executive*

San Diego
Jamali, Hamadi *research and development company executive*
Kessler, Armin M. *retired pharmaceutical company executive*
Lundy-Slade, Bettie B. *retired electronics worker*
Mollica, Joseph A. *pharmaceutical executive*
Rice, Clare I. *electronics company executive*
Rolland, Alain P. *pharmaceutical executive*
Savall, Brad M. *pharmaceutical executive, researcher*
Spanos, Alexander Gus *construction and professional sports team executive*

San Francisco
Anderson, R. John *apparel executive*
Campbell, Jeffrey C. *health products executive*
Hammergren, John H. *health products executive*
Jorgensen, Blake J. *apparel company executive, former Internet company executive*
Julian, Paul C. *health products executive*
Kneen, Simon *apparel executive*
Lyon, David William *retired research executive*
Mahoney, David L. *former pharmaceutical wholesale and healthcare management company executive*
Mellor, Robert E. *building materials company executive, lawyer*
Owen, Marc E. *health products executive*
Rogers, T. Gary *apparel company executive, former food products company executive*
Shackley, Douglas John *fire alarm company executive*
Simmons, Sabrina L. *apparel executive*
Slipsager, Henrik C. *building services company executive*
Spratt, Randall N. *healthcare services and information technology executive*
Turek, Paul John III *construction executive*
Wolford, Richard G. *food products executive*
Wyatt, Tom (John Thomas Wyatt) *apparel executive*
Zellerbach, William Joseph *retired paper company executive*

San Jose
Bermudes, Louis David *construction executive*
Bronson, Joseph R. *manufacturing executive*
Hill, Richard S. *manufacturing executive*
Inani, Anand *manufacturing executive, director*
Koo, Yido *electronics executive*
Maekawa, Koji Ogura *technology company administrator*
Pausa, Clements Edward *electronics company executive*
Pillai, Hari *electronics executive*
Rodgers, T(hurman) J. *semiconductor company executive*
Sola, Jure *electronics executive*
Zaro, Brad A. *research and development company executive, biologist*

San Luis Obispo
Sullivan, Thomas James *retired manufacturing company executive*

San Mateo
Kennedy, W(ilbert) Keith, Jr. *retired electronics executive, transportation executive*
Washington, Robin L. *pharmaceutical executive*

San Pedro
Hamai, James Yutaka *manufacturing executive*

Santa Ana
Washburn, Lawrence Robert *manufacturing executive*

Santa Barbara
Coffin, Dwight Clay *retired grain company executive*

Santa Clara
Cundy, Kenneth Charles *pharmaceutical executive*
Davis, George S. *manufacturing executive*
Halla, Brian L. *electronics executive*
Huang, Jen-Hsun *electronics executive*
Maloney, Sean M. *electronics company executive*
Moore, Gordon E. *electronics executive, researcher*
Morgan, James C. *retired manufacturing executive*
Otellini, Paul Stevens *electronics company executive*
Pinto, Mark R. *manufacturing executive*
Shaw, Jane Elizabeth *electronics company executive, retired pharmaceutical company executive*
Solomon, Darlene J.S. *electronics executive*
Splinter, Michael R. *manufacturing executive*
Sullivan, William P. *electronics executive*

Santa Monica
Bush, William Glenn *manufacturing company executive, engineer*
Kanouse, David Earl *research and development company executive*
Rosensweig, Daniel L. *video gaming company executive*
Weden, Margaret *research and development company executive*

Santa Rosa
Jackson, Jess S. *vintner*

Saratoga
Houston, Joseph Brantley, Jr. *optical instrument company executive*
Rollo, F. David *healthcare company executive, cardiologist*

Sherman Oaks
Reiner, Thomas Karl *manufacturing executive, engineering scientist*

Simi Valley
Davenport, Alfred Larue, Jr. *manufacturing executive*

Lewis, Richard B. *manufacturing and logistics executive*

Soquel
Cureton, Glen *pharmaceutical executive*

South San Francisco
Schenk, Dale Bernard *pharmaceutical executive, neuroscientist*
Soriot, Pascal *pharmaceutical executive*

Stanford
Elliott, David Duncan III *science company executive*
Miller, William Frederick *research and development company executive, educator, financial consultant*

Sunnyvale
Doluca, Tunc *electronics executive*
Rusch, Thomas William *manufacturing executive*

Sylmar
Tutor, Ronald N. *construction executive*

Thousand Oaks
Birren, James Emmett *research and development company executive*
Bonanni, Fabrizio *medical products executive*
Bradway, Robert *medical products executive*
Flanagan, Thomas James *medical products executive*
McNamee, Brian *medical products executive*
Morrow, George J. *medical products executive*
Perlmutter, Roger *medical products executive*
Sharer, Kevin W. *medical products executive*

Torrance
Ismail, Alexandre *diversified technology and manufacturing company executive*
Lentz, James E. III *automotive executive*
Mendel, John W. *automotive executive*

Tustin
Hester, Norman Eric *chemical company technical executive, chemist*

Ukiah
Newell, Barbara Ann *coatings company executive*

Ventura
Barber, Jerry Randel *retired medical device company executive*

Villa Park
Hawe, David Lee *manufacturing consultant, venture capitalist*

Watsonville
Dorey, William G. *construction executive*

West Covina
Cheng, Bridget *agricultural products executive*

Westlake Village
DeLorenzo, David A. *food products executive*

Willits
Handley, Margie Lee *manufacturing executive*

Woodland Hills
Capezza, Joseph C. *health insurance company executive*
Gellert, Jay M. *health and medical products executive*
Greaves, Roger F. *health and medical products executive*
Mayhew, Karin D. *health and medical products executive*
Scheff, Jonathan H. *health and medical products executive*
Sivori, John P. *health and medical products executive*
Woys, James E. *health and medical products executive*

Woodside
Gates, Milo Sedgwick *retired construction company executive*

COLORADO

Boulder
Clark, Melvin Eugene *chemical company executive*

Broomfield
Hayes, John A. *packaging company executive*
Hoover, R. David *packaging company executive*

Castle Rock
Albright, Jeffrey R. *pharmaceutical executive*

Colorado Springs
Stanley, David John *research and development company executive*

Denver
Alvarado, Linda G. *construction executive*
Boyer, William Joseph *food products executive*
Brakken, William *construction executive*
Glendinning, Stewart *food products executive*
Hylbert, Paul W. *construction executive*
Leydon, Debra Jean *food products executive*
Livingston, Johnston Redmond *manufacturing executive*
Mizel, Larry A. *housing construction company executive*
Oakes, Terry Louis *resident real estate broker*
Swinburn, Peter *brewery company executive*

Englewood
Gertz, David Lee *homebuilding company executive*

Fort Collins
Jaouen, Stephen H. *construction executive, educator*

Golden
Coors, Peter Hanson *brewery company executive*

Jefferson
Maatsch, Deborah Joan *manufacturing executive*

Littleton
Battilega, John A. *research and development company executive*

Longmont
Davies, David Huw *electronics and engineering company executive*

Niwot
Duerden, John H. *apparel executive*

Wellington
Grant, Lewis O. *agricultural products executive, meteorology educator*

CONNECTICUT

Bloomfield
Hermann, Robert Jay *former manufacturing executive, consultant*

Branford
Rothberg, Jonathan M. *medical products executive, researcher*

Bristol
Barnes, Carlyle Fuller *manufacturing executive*
Barnes, Wallace *manufacturing executive*

Broad Brook
Kement, Isabella Viniconis *retired construction company executive*

Danbury
Angel, Stephen F. *chemicals executive*
Sawyer, James S. *chemicals executive*

Darien
Dordelman, William Forsyth *food company executive*
Sprole, Frank Arnott *retired pharmaceutical executive, lawyer*

Dayville
Funk, Michael S. *food products executive*
Spinner, Steven L. *food products executive*

Fairfield
Beccali-Falco, Ferdinando *manufacturing executive*
Daley, Pamela *diversified services, technology and manufacturing company executive*
Dineen, John C. *health products executive*
Johnsen, Walter Craig *manufacturing executive*
Pressman, Ronald R. *manufacturing executive*
Schweikert, Timothy J. *industrial equipment company executive*
Vachon, Mark L. *manufacturing executive*
Wanchoo, Vishal K. *electromedical equipment company executive*
Worrell, Brian *manufacturing executive*

Farmington
Michaud-Daniel, Didier *manufacturing executive*

Greenwich
Dettmer, Robert Gerhart *retired beverage company executive*
May, William Frederick *manufacturing executive*

Hartford
Bellemare, Alain M. *manufacturing executive*
Bousbib, Ari *manufacturing executive*
Bowler, J. Thomas, Jr. *manufacturing executive*
Brown, William M. *manufacturing executive*
Chênevert, Louis R. *manufacturing executive*
Darnis, Geraud *manufacturing executive*
David, George Alfred Lawrence *manufacturing executive*
Doucette, John J. *manufacturing executive*
Drake, Eileen *manufacturing executive*
Geisler, James E. *manufacturing executive*
Hayes, Gregory James *manufacturing executive*
Hess, David P. *manufacturing executive*
McQuade, J. Michael *manufacturing executive*

Hebron
Kauffman, Scot R. *medical supply company executive*

Lyme
Bloom, Barry Malcolm *research and development company executive, consultant*

Madison
Cohen, Gordon S. *health products executive*
Golembeski, Jerome John *manufacturing executive*

Naugatuck
Flannery, Joseph Patrick *manufacturing executive, director*

New Canaan
Burns, Ivan Alfred *grocery products and industrial company executive*

New Haven
Jacob, Deirdre Ann Bradbury *manufacturing executive, finance educator, consultant*

New London
Dunne, Michael William *research and development company executive*

North Branford
Ingram, George *manufacturing executive*

Norwalk
Guzzi, Anthony J. *construction executive*
Harris, Holton Edwin *plastics machinery manufacturing executive*
MacInnis, Frank T. *construction and holding company executive, securities trader*
Pompa, Mark A. *construction executive*

Plainville
Glassman, Gerald Seymour *metal products executive*

Ridgefield
Hilbrich, Lutz *physician, pharmaceutical executive*
Levine, Paul Michael *paper company executive, consultant*

Riverside
Deering, Allan Brooks *retired soft drink company executive*

Somers
Blake, Stewart Prestley *retired ice cream company executive*

South Kent
Samartini, James Rogers *retired appliance company executive*

Stamford
Allott, Anthony J. *packaging industry executive*
Buzzard, James A. *paper, packaging and chemical company executive*
Caldwell, Philip *retired automobile manufacturing and finance company executive*
Faraci, John Vincent, Jr. *paper company executive*
Fast, Eric Carson *manufacturing executive*
Gladstone, Herbert Jack *manufacturing executive*
Gross, Ronald Martin *forest products executive, consultant*
Horrigan, D. Gregory *packaging products executive*
Lesko, Newland A. *paper company executive*
Levitan, Gutman *research and development company executive, communications engineer*
Martin, Murray D. *manufacturing executive*
Monahan, Michael *manufacturing executive*
Munera, Gerard Emmanuel *manufacturing executive*
Silver, R. Philip *packaging products executive*

Stratford
Jonas, Tina Westby *helicopter manufacturing company executive, former federal agency administrator*
Pino, Jeffrey P. *manufacturing executive*

Thomaston
Mühlanger, Erich *ski manufacturing company executive*

Wallingford
Loeffler, Martin H. *electronics executive*
Norwitt, Richard Adam *manufacturing executive*

Waterbury
Moon, Lloyd N. *chemicals executive*
Rogerson, Craig Allan *manufacturing executive*

West Hartford
Doran, James Martin *retired food products company executive*
Raffay, Stephen Joseph *manufacturing executive, director*
Visconti, Joseph B. *contractor, small business owner*

Westport
Breitbarth, S. Robert *manufacturing executive*
Defeo, Ronald M. *machinery manufacturing executive*
Gans, Eugene Howard *cosmetic and pharmaceutical company executive, consultant*
Riordan, Thomas J. *manufacturing executive*
Widman, Phillip C. *machinery manufacturing executive*

DELAWARE

Greenville
Miller, Duane King *health and beauty care company executive*

Milford
Konowitz, Herbert Henry *retired textile company executive*

Newark
Gantzer, Mary Lou *medical products executive*

Rockland
Rubin, Alan A. *pharmaceutical and biotechnology consultant*

Wilmington
Anton, David L. *research and development company executive, biotechnologist, researcher*
Bills, David G. *chemicals executive*
Borel, James Calvin *chemical company executive*
Connelly, Thomas M., Jr. *chemicals executive*
Goodmanson, Richard R. *chemicals executive*
Gulyas, Diane H. *manufacturing executive*
Holliday, Chad (Charles O. Holliday Jr.) *chemicals executive*
Holtzman, Arnold Harold *chemical company executive*
Keefer, Jeffrey L. *chemicals executive*
Kullman, Ellen Jamison *chemicals executive*
Lassen, John Kai *financial instruments executive*
McLeer Free, Laureen Dorothy *drug development and pharmaceutical professional*
Rose, Selwyn H. *chemicals executive*
Sager, Thomas Lauck *chemical company executive, lawyer*
Uffner, Michael S. *automotive executive*

DISTRICT OF COLUMBIA

Washington
Barnette, Curtis Handley *retired metal products executive, lawyer*
Becker, Brenda L. *medical products executive, former federal official*
Beier, David *medical products executive*
Brown, Lester Russell *research and development company executive*
Comas, Daniel L. *manufacturing executive*
Culp, H. Lawrence *manufacturing executive*
Engler, John M. *manufacturing executive, former governor*
Lorell, Beverly H. *medical products executive, consultant*
Moore, Robert Madison *food products executive, lawyer*
Paliwal, Dinesh C. *electronics executive*
Persinger, Del Louis *pharmaceutical company executive*
Principi, Anthony Joseph *pharmaceutical company executive, former United States Secretary of Veterans Affairs*
Rales, Mitchell P. *automotive parts company executive*
Rales, Steven M. *automotive parts company executive*

FLORIDA

Altamonte Springs
Kaplan, Judith Helene *manufacturing executive*

Amelia Island
Adelman, Robert Paul *retired construction executive, lawyer*

Bartow
Kincart, Robert Owen *technological executive*

Boca Raton
Clarke, Kenneth Kingsley *retired electronics executive*

Bonita Springs
Costley, Gary Edward *food company executive*
Sargent, Charles Lee *manufacturing executive*

Boynton Beach
Goldenberg, George *retired pharmaceutical executive*
Jensen, Reuben Rolland *former automotive company executive*

Bradenton
Barnebey, Kenneth Alan *food products executive*
Carnes, James Edward *retired electronics executive*
Price, Edgar Hilleary, Jr. *manufacturing executive, consultant*

Cape Coral
Stuart, Robert *container manufacturing executive*

Clearwater
Chisholm, William DeWayne *retired contractor*
Kiehl, E. Robert *manufacturing executive, consultant*
Sebring, Marjorie Marie Allison *former home furnishings company executive*
Smith, Marion Pafford *retired avionics company executive*

Coral Gables
Burini, Sonia Montes de Oca *apparel manufacturing and public relations executive*

Daytona Beach
Scott, John Brooks *retired research and development company executive*
Tribble, Dennis Anthony *pharmaceutical executive*

Deerfield Beach
Brown, Colin *automotive executive*

Englewood
Richard, Edward H. *manufacturing executive, retired municipal official*

Fort Lauderdale
Faraone, Antonio *electronics executive*
Jackson, Michael J. *automotive retail company executive*
Maroone, Michael E. *automotive executive*
Rojas, Jesus Jon *health products executive, researcher*
Short, Michael J. *automotive executive*

Fort Myers
Edmonds, Scott A. *apparel executive*
Haug, Warren R. *research and development consultant*
Wendeborn, Richard Donald *retired manufacturing executive*

Heathrow
Darbelnet, Robert Louis *automobile association executive*

Highland Beach
Frager, Albert S. *retired food products executive*

Hobe Sound
Casey, Edward Paul *manufacturing executive*

Hollywood
Isenberg, Abraham Charles *shoe manufacturing company executive*

Holmes Beach
Kaiser, Albert Farr *manufacturing executive*

Homestead
Willner, Eugene Burton *food and liquor company executive*

Islamorada
Gates, Richard Daniel *retired manufacturing executive*

Jacksonville
Bodkin, Lawrence Edward *inventor, essayist, research and development company executive, consultant*
McKinney, James Clayton *electronics executive, electrical engineer*
Nussbaum, Bennett L. *food products executive*
Smith, David A. *medical services executive*

Jupiter
Feinberg, Herbert *wine company executive*
Garfinkel, Harmon Mark *retired specialty chemicals company executive*

Lady Lake
Akins, Zane Vernon *agricultural products executive*

Lakeland
Hatten, William Seward *manufacturing executive, consultant*
Mutz, Oscar Ulysses *manufacturing and distribution executive*

Longboat Key
Dalgleish, Stuart McNaught *retired manufacturing executive*

Marco Island
Guerrant, David Edward *retired food company executive*
Moore, Faye Halfacre *jewelry manufacturer*

Melbourne
Buchanan, Richard Kent *electronics company executive*

Merritt Island
Roub, Bryan R(oger) *electronics executive*

Miami
Becker, Steven Richard *beverage corporation executive*
Beckwitt, Richard *construction executive*
Borkan, William Noah *electronics executive, biomedical engineer, entrepreneur*
Braman, Norman *automotive and former sports team executive*
Carbonell, Josefina G. *healthcare company executive, former federal agency administrator*
Frigo, James Peter Paul *industrial hardware company executive*
Frost, Phillip *pharmaceutical executive, dermatologist*
Miller, Stuart A. *construction executive*
Nahmad, Albert H. *manufacturing executive*
Zubieta, Alberto Aleman *construction executive*

Miami Beach
Lanzkron, Rolf Wolfgang *manufacturing executive*

Naples
Askins, Wallace Boyd *manufacturing executive*
Butler, Frederick George *retired drug company executive*
Gade, Marvin Francis *retired paper company executive*
Garratt, Reginald George *electronics executive*
LaRusso, Anthony Carl *company executive, lecturer, consultant*
Salentine, Thomas James *pharmaceutical executive*
Sampson, John Eugene *food products executive, consultant*
Sekowski, Cynthia Jean *health products executive, medical consultant*
Swanson, Donald Frederick *retired food company executive*
von Arx, Dolph William *food products executive*

New Port Richey
Lake, Victor Hugo *former manufacturing company executive*
Maysilles, Daniel Bruce *pharmaceutical services executive*

Orlando
Brownlee, Thomas Marshall *manufacturing executive*
Smyth, Joseph Vincent *manufacturing executive*

Osprey
Feder, Allan Appel *retired food products executive*

Palm Beach
Pearlman, Jerry Kent *electronics company executive*

Palm Beach Gardens
Jaffe, Jeff Hugh *retired food products executive*
Staub, W. Arthur *health care products executive*

Palm City
Conklin, George Melville *retired food products executive*
Wishart, Ronald Sinclair *retired chemical company executive*

Palm Harbor
Bennett, John Joseph *electronics executive*

Pembroke Pines
Seidel, James P. *manufacturing executive*

Reddick
Corwin, Joyce Elizabeth Stedman *construction company executive*

Saint Petersburg
Alexander, Forbes I.J. *electronics executive*
Main, Timothy L. *electronics company executive*
Mills, William Harold, Jr. *construction executive*
Mondello, Mark T. *electronics executive*

Sanford
Davis, Darrell L. *retired automotive executive*

Sarasota
Daoust, Donald Roger *pharmaceutical executive, microbiologist, cosmetics executive*
Jellison, Brian D. *manufacturing executive*
Miranda, Carlos Sa *food products company executive*
Mullane, John Francis *pharmaceutical executive*
Venit, William Bennett *electrical products company executive, consultant*
Wadsworth, Dyer Seymour *minerals executive*
West, Bob *pharmaceutical executive*

Summerfield
McNulty, Carrell Stewart, Jr. *retired manufacturing executive, architect*

Tampa
Adams, Rex M. *health products executive, former telecommunications executive*
Berg, Charles G. *health products executive*
Dvorchik, Barry H. *pharmaceutical executive*
Flom, Edward Leonard *retired metal products executive*
Schiesser, Heath *health products executive*
Tran, Thomas L. *health products executive*

Tavares
Gross, Paul Allan *health products executive*

The Villages
Graham, David Bolden *food products executive*

Vero Beach
Anderson, Raymond Quintus *diversified company executive*
Janicki, Robert Stephen *retired pharmaceutical executive*
Reed, Sherman Kennedy *chemicals executive, consultant*
Standish, John Spencer *textile manufacturing company executive*
Wilcox, Harry Wilbur, Jr. *retired manufacturing executive*

Wesley Chapel
Revelle, Donald Gene *manufacturing and health care company executive, consultant*

West Palm Beach
Brown, Paul A. *medical services executive*
Furlaud, Richard Mortimer *pharmaceutical executive*
Jenkins, Ruben Lee *chemicals executive*

Windermere
Hahn, Dowon *pharmaceutical researcher, educator*

Winter Park
Merrill, Harvie Martin *retired manufacturing executive*
Whitworth, Hall Baker *forest products company executive*

Zephyrhills
Shea, Bernard Charles *retired pharmaceutical executive*

GEORGIA

Alpharetta
Adams, Kenneth Francis *automotive executive*
Brands, James Edwin *medical products executive*

Atlanta
Allan, Alexander R.C. (Sandy Allan) *food products executive*
Armstrong, Sarah Madden *beverage company executive*
Beazer, Brian C. *construction executive*
Blystone, Lawrence K. *machinery and equipment company executive*
Bostic, James E., Jr. *paper company executive*
Brock, John F. *beverage company executive*
Carrico, Paul D. *chemical company executive*
Corr, James Vanis *furniture manufacturing executive, accountant*
Douglas, J. Alexander M. (Sandy) *beverage company executive*
Douglas, William W. *food products executive*
Fayard, Gary P. *beverage company executive*
Finan, Irial *beverage company executive*
Gallagher, Thomas C. *diversified manufacturing executive*
Hyland, Gregory E. *manufacturing executive*
Isdell, Neville (Edward Neville Isdell) *retired beverage company executive*
Joung, Yeun-Ho *research and development company executive*
Kelley, Brian P. *beverage and former relocation services company executive*
Kent, Muhtar *beverage company executive*
Liebmann, Seymour W. *construction executive, consultant*
McCarthy, Ian J. *construction executive*
Mildenhall, Jonathan *beverage company executive*
Moeller, Joseph W. *forest products company executive, former chemicals executive*
Nagel, Vernon J. *chemicals and electronics executive*
Nix, Jerry W. *automotive executive*
Parker, John R., Jr. *food products executive, lawyer*
Tripodi, Joseph V. *beverage company executive*
Zaghloul, Yasser A. *research and development company executive*

Ball Ground
Tucker, Robert Dennard *health care products executive*

Calhoun
Boykin, Frank H. *textiles executive*
Lorberbaum, Jeffrey S. *textiles executive*
Lucke, James T. *textiles executive*

Cartersville
Swanson, William Fredin III *manufacturing executive*

Duluth
Beck, Andrew H. *farm equipment manufacturing executive*
Brody, Aaron Leo *food and packaging consultant*
Kuper, Debra E. *manufacturing executive, lawyer*
Richenhagen, Martin H. *manufacturing executive*

Lawrenceville
Bannick, Janice Carol *automotive dealerships executive*
Schoen, Marc Alan *pension and employee benefits executive*

Marietta
Hill, Stephen A. *pharmaceutical executive*
Mutisya, Elizabeth M. *pharmaceutical executive*
Scheible, David W. *paper company executive*

Norcross
Rubright, James Alfred *paperboard and packaging company executive*

Roswell
Abernathy, Robert E. *health products executive*
Bauer, Joanne B. *health products executive*
Gottung, Lizanne C. *health products executive*
Spencer, Jan B. *health products executive*

Savannah
Cartledge, Raymond Eugene *retired paper company executive*
Craib, Kenneth Bryden *research and development company executive, physicist, economist*
Spitz, Seymour James, Jr. *retired fragrance company executive*
Sprague, William Wallace, Jr. *retired food company executive*

Thomasville
Deese, George E. *food products company executive*

Woodstock
Hudson, Roy Davage *retired pharmaceutical executive*

HAWAII

Kaneohe
Vincent, Thomas James *retired manufacturing executive*

IDAHO

Boise
Appleton, Steven R. *electronics executive*
Benson, Kenneth Victor *manufacturing executive, lawyer*
Carlile, Thomas E. *paper company executive*
Cleary, Edward William *retired diversified forest products company executive*
Ditali, Akram *manufacturing executive*
Foster, Ronald C. *electronics executive*
Lewis, Roderic W. *electronics executive, lawyer*
McDougall, Duane C. *manufacturing executive*
Washington, Dennis R. *contracting company executive*

ILLINOIS

Abbott Park
Ashley, Richard W. *pharmaceutical executive*
Freyman, Thomas C. *pharmaceutical executive*
Liepmann, Holger A. *pharmaceutical executive*
Nemmers, Joseph M., Jr. *pharmaceutical executive*
White, Miles D. *pharmaceutical executive*

Arlington Heights
Li, Norman N. *chemicals executive*

Barrington
Burrows, Brian William *retired research and development company executive*
Nadig, Gerald George *retired manufacturing executive*

Carol Stream
Back, Robert Wyatt *investment company and pharmaceutical executive, consultant*

Chester
Welge, Donald Edward *food manufacturing executive*

Chicago
Antler, Steven David *manufacturing executive, economics professor*
Barnes, Brenda C. *food products executive*
Borenstine, Alvin Jerome *search company executive*
Bosowski, Edward M. *manufacturing executive*
Brake, Cecil Clifford *retired diversified manufacturing executive*
Cline, William Chambers *automotive executive*
Cooper, Charles Gilbert *cosmetics executive*
Crown, Lester *manufacturing executive*
Edlis, Stefan T. *plastics company executive*
Feitler, Robert *shoe company executive*
Gamoran, Reuben *candy company executive*
Giesen, Richard Allyn *business executive*
Heisley, Michael E., Sr. *manufacturing executive, professional sports team owner*
Hinrichs, Charles A. *paper company executive*
Jezuit, Leslie James *manufacturing executive*
Klinger, Steven J. *paper company executive*
McKee, Keith Earl *manufacturing technology executive*
Metcalf, James S. *manufacturing executive*
Moore, Patrick J. *paper company executive*
Moseley Braun, Carol Elizabeth *food products executive, former United States Senator from Illinois*
Murphy, Michael Emmett *retired food company executive*
Novak, John G. *construction executive*
Novich, Neil S. *metals distribution company executive*
Perez, William D. (Bill Perez) *candy company executive, former sports apparel company executive*
Senior, Richard John Lane *linen and uniform services executive*
Stack, Stephen S. *manufacturing executive*
Steinfeld, Manfred *furniture manufacturing executive*
Umans, Alvin Robert *manufacturing executive*
Urban, Jeff *food products executive*
Walsh, Matthew M. *construction executive*
Williams, Richard Lucas III *electronics executive, director, lawyer*
Wrigley, William, Jr., (Bill Wrigley Jr.) *candy company executive*

Crystal Lake
Anderson, Lyle Arthur *retired manufacturing executive*

Decatur
Mills, Steven R. *agricultural company executive, accountant*
Rice, John D. *agricultural products executive*
Woertz, Patricia Ann *agricultural company executive, retired oil company executive*

Deerfield
Ahlbrandt, Robert Alan *pharmaceutical executive*
Amundson, Joy A. *pharmaceutical and health products executive*
Davis, Robert M. *medical products executive*
Parkinson, Robert L., Jr. *medical products executive, health facility administrator*
Quinn, Donal *diagnostic equipment company executive*

Dekalb
Troyer, Alvah Forrest *agricultural products executive, horticulturist*

Des Plaines
Frank, James S. *automotive executive*

Downers Grove
Fraleigh, Christopher J. *food products executive*
Nolan, James W. *food products executive*

Evanston
Menke, Allen Carl *retired manufacturing executive*

Frankfort
Burhoe, Brian Walter *automotive executive*

Franklin Park
Simpson, Michael *retired metals service center executive*

Glen Ellyn
Barrett, Carolyn Hernly *manufacturing executive*

Glenview
Bruns, Nicolaus, Jr. *retired agricultural products executive, lawyer, educator*
Eck, Robert J. *electronics executive*
Gillis, Marvin Bob *retired chemical executive, consultant*
Golsby, Stephen W. *pharmaceutical executive*
Hickey, John Thomas *retired electronics executive*
Speer, David Blakeney *chemicals executive*

Highland Park
Korzenski, Robert M. *manufacturing executive*
Rudo, Milton *retired manufacturing executive*

Lake Forest
Begley, Christopher B. *pharmaceutical executive*
Carroll, Barry Joseph *manufacturing and real estate executive*
Hamilton, Peter Bannerman *manufacturing executive, lawyer*
Hammar, Lester Everett *retired manufacturing executive*
Knight, Lester B. *healthcare company executive*
Leemputte, Peter G. *manufacturing executive*
McCoy, Dustan Elwood *manufacturing executive, lawyer*
O'Mara, Thomas Patrick *manufacturing executive*
Romans, Donald Bishop *manufacturing executive*
Sherrill, Gregg M. *automotive executive*
Trammell, Kenneth R. *automotive executive*

Lake Villa
Anderson, Milton Andrew *chemicals executive*

Lincolnshire
Simes, Stephen Mark *pharmaceutical executive*

Lisle
Krehbiel, Frederick August, II, *electronics executive*
Krehbiel, John H., Jr. *electronics company executive*
Slark, Martin P. *electronics executive*

Melrose Park
Boswell, Gina R. *cosmetics executive*
Wechter, Clari Ann *manufacturing executive*

Moline
Allen, Samuel R. *farm equipment manufacturing executive*
Field, James M. *farm equipment manufacturing executive*
Lane, Robert W. *farm equipment manufacturing executive*
Mack, Michael J., Jr. *farm equipment manufacturing executive*

Naperville
Katai, Andrew Andras *chemical company executive*
Nieto, Lou *food products executive*
Stall, Alan David *manufacturing executive*

Northfield
Carlin, Donald Walter *retired food products executive, consultant*
Firestone, Marc *food products executive, lawyer*
Hadley, Stanton Thomas *manufacturing executive, director, lawyer*
Rosenfeld, Irene B. *food products company executive*
Smeds, Edward William *retired food company executive*
Stepan, Frank Quinn *chemicals executive*
Stepan, Frank Quinn, Jr., (F. Quinn Stepan Jr.) *chemical company executive*
West, Mary Beth *food products executive*

Oak Brook
Alvarez, Ralph *food products executive*
Bensen, Peter J. *food products executive*
Dillon, Mary N. *food products executive*
Skinner, James A. *food products executive*
Thompson, Don *food products executive*

Park Ridge
Barber, Edward Bruce *medical products executive*

Peoria
Burritt, David B. *manufacturing executive*
Lavin, Richard P. *manufacturing executive*
Levenick, Stuart L. *manufacturing executive*
Oberhelman, Douglas Ray *tractor company executive*
Owens, James W. (Jim Owens) *manufacturing executive*
Rapp, Edward J. *manufacturing executive*
Vittecoq, Gerard R. *manufacturing executive*
Wunning, Steven H. *manufacturing executive*

Prospect Heights
Byrne, Michael Joseph *manufacturing executive*

Rockford
O'Donnell, William David *retired construction firm executive*

Rosemont
Meinert, John Raymond *apparel executive, investment banker*
Reyes, J. Christopher *food products distribution executive*

Schaumburg
Delaney, Eugene A. *electronics executive*
Moloney, Daniel M. *electronics executive*
Soon-Shiong, Patrick *pharmaceutical executive*

Summit Argo
Trumbore, David C. *retired building materials executive. consultant*

Westchester
Gordon, Ilene *food products executive*

Wheeling
Keats, Glenn Arthur *manufacturing executive*

Wilmette
Coughlan, Gary Patrick *pharmaceutical executive*

INDIANA

Anderson
Carrell, Terry Eugene *manufacturing executive*

Batesville
Classon, Rolf Allan *pharmaceutical company executive*
Soderberg, Peter H. *health products executive*

Bloomington
Webb, Lisa Michelle *regulatory affairs manager*

Brownstown
Robertson, Joseph Edmond *grain processing company executive*

Carmel
Shoup, Charles Samuel, Jr. *chemicals and materials executive*

Columbus
Blackwell, Jean Stuart *manufacturing executive*
Boll, Charles Raymond *engine company executive*
Linebarger, Thomas (Norman Thomas Linebarger) *manufacturing executive*
Satterthwaite, Tony *manufacturing executive*
Solso, Theodore M. *manufacturing executive*
Wall, John C. *manufacturing executive*
Ward, Patrick J. *manufacturing executive*

East Chicago
Chukwulebe, Bernard Obioma *manufacturing executive, consultant*

Elkhart
Lawson, William Hogan III *electrical motor manufacturing executive*
Mathias, Margaret Grossman *manufacturing company executive, leasing company executive*
Mischke, Frederick Charles *retired manufacturing executive*

Evansville
Koch, Robert Louis, II, *manufacturing company executive, mechanical engineer*
Muehlbauer, James Herman *manufacturing and distribution executive*

Fort Wayne
Busse, Keith E. *manufacturing executive*

Frankfort
LeBlanc, John Keith *manufacturing executive*

Indianapolis
Boor, Anthony W. *electronics executive*
Dunayevich, Eduardo *pharmaceutical executive*
Hubbard, Allan Brooks *chemical company executive, former federal official*
King, J. B. *medical device company executive, lawyer*
Lacy, Andre Balz *industrial executive*
Lechleiter, John C. *pharmaceutical executive*
Lugar, Thomas R. *manufacturing executive*
Mahony, Susan *pharmaceutical company executive*
Mc Farland, H. Richard *food products executive*
Paul, Steven M. *pharmaceutical executive*
Peribere, Jerome A. *agricultural products executive*
Peterson, Bart R. (Barton R. Peterson) *pharmaceutical company executive, former mayor*
Ralston, Ronald Lee *retired manufacturing tradesman*
Rice, Derica W. *pharmaceutical executive*
Santini, Gino *pharmaceutical executive*
Stewart, Paul Arthur *pharmaceutical company executive*

Middlebury
Corson, Thomas Harold *retired manufacturing executive*
Guequierre, John Phillip *manufacturing executive*

Mishawaka
Rubenstein, Pamela Silver *manufacturing executive*

Plainfield
Laikin, Robert J. *electronics executive*

Portage
Popp, Joseph Bruce *manufacturing executive*

Warsaw
Binder, Jeffrey R. *medical products executive*
Dvorak, David C. *medical products executive, lawyer*
McGoldrick, John Lewis *medical products executive, lawyer*
Throdahl, Mark Crandall *medical products executive*

IOWA

Cedar Falls
Power, Daniel Joseph *business educator*

Cedar Rapids
Jones, Clayton M. *electronics company executive*

Davenport
Gildehaus, Thomas Arthur *manufacturing executive, museum director*
Juckem, Wilfred Philip *manufacturing executive*

Des Moines
Zgarrick, David Paul *pharmaceutical executive*

Dubuque
Crahan, Jack Bertsch *retired manufacturing executive*

Johnston
Oestreich, Dean *manufacturing executive*

Muscatine
Askren, Stan A. *manufacturing executive*
Housh, E. William *manufacturing executive*

Pella
Dout, Anne Jacqueline *manufacturing and sales company executive*

Sioux City
Bennett, Michael L. *agricultural products executive*

KANSAS

Mission
Bresky, Steven J. *agricultural products executive*

Olathe
Kao, Min H. *manufacturing executive*

Shawnee Mission
Gamet, Donald Max *appliance company executive*

KENTUCKY

Bardstown
Sutton, Brian K. *construction executive*

Bellevue
Carpenter, Woodrow Wilson *manufacturing executive, ceramics engineer*

Bowling Green
Holland, John Ben *clothing manufacturing company executive*

Covington
Chambers, Lamar M. *chemical company executive*
Froesel, David W., Jr. *medical products executive*
Gemunder, Joel Frank *healthcare company executive*
O'Brien, James J. *manufacturing executive*

Highland Heights
Foley, Sean P. *construction executive, educator*
Kenny, Gregory B. *industrial equipment executive*

Louisville
Brolick, Emil J. *food products executive*
Diaz, Paul J. *health products executive*
Eaton, Roger *food products executive*
Heiden, Charles Kenneth *metal products executive, consultant, retired military officer*
Pottinger, Ronald Wayne *food products executive*
Varga, Paul C. *beverage products executive*

LOUISIANA

Baton Rouge
Calabrese, Michael Raphael *manufacturing executive, lawyer, consultant*

New Orleans
Cospolich, James Donald *electronics executive, consultant*

MAINE

Andover
Kaltsos, Angelo John *electronics executive, educator, photographer*

Falmouth
Cabot, Lewis Pickering *manufacturing company executive, art consultant*

Kennebunk
Damon, Edmund Holcombe *retired plastics company executive*

Kennebunkport
Featherman, Bernard *steel company executive*

New Vineyard
Smith, Frederick Orville, II, *agricultural products executive, retired military officer*

Scarborough
Shire, Donald Thomas *retired chemicals executive, lawyer*

South Portland
Thompson, Mark S. *electronics executive*

Westbrook
Lee, Shepard *automobile dealership owner*

MARYLAND

Baltimore
Hackerman, Willard J. *construction executive*
Plank, Kevin A. *apparel executive*

Bethesda
Forster, Peter C. *construction executive*
Manasse, Henri Richard, Jr. *pharmaceutical executive*
Spector, Eleanor Ruth *manufacturing executive*

Chevy Chase
Bissinger, Frederick Lewis *retired manufacturing executive*
Ewing, Frank Marion *lumber company executive, real estate developer*

Columbia
Aiken, Robert B. *food products executive*
Festa, (Al)Fred E. *chemicals executive*
La Force, Hudson III *chemicals executive, former federal agency administrator*

Frederick
Lin, George *research and development company executive, biomedical researcher*

Gaithersburg
Nabors, Gary Scott *medical products executive*

Hunt Valley
Hiremath, Praveen S. *pharmaceutical executive, researcher*

Rockville
Altmeyer, Mark P. *pharmaceutical executive*
Landon, John Campbell *research and development company executive*
Miller, Kenneth Michael *electronics executive, director*

Saint Michaels
Peck, Charles Edward *retired construction and mortgage executive*

Silver Spring
Batra, Hitesh *research and development company executive*
Khan, Mansoor A. *pharmaceutical science executive, director*

Sparks
Wilson, Alan D. *food products executive*

Temple Hills
Ourisman, Mandell Jack *automotive executive*

MASSACHUSETTS

Billerica
Kolb, Charles Eugene *research and development company executive*

Boston
Franko, Lawrence George *business educator/investment advisor*
Glass, Milton Louis *retired manufacturing company executive*
Hoskins, William Keller *pharmaceutical executive, lawyer, mediator, arbitrator*
Leaman, J. Richard, Jr. *paper company executive*
Macomber, John D. *former construction executive*
Prevost, Patrick M. *chemicals executive*

Burlington
Sproull, Robert Fletcher *research and development company executive*

Cambridge
Berke, Neal S. *research and development company executive*
DiStefano, Peter S. *pharmaceutical executive*
Dunsire, Deborah *pharmaceutical executive*
Emmens, Matthew W. *pharmaceutical executive*
Forney, G(eorge) David, Jr. *retired electronics executive*
Frosch, Robert Alan *retired automobile manufacturing executive, physicist*
Galakatos, Nick *pharmaceutical executive*
Holtzman, Steven H. *pharmaceutical executive*
Lewis, Henry Rafalsky *manufacturing executive*
Li, Yuexian *Research And Development Company Scientist*
Matsui, Connie L. *pharmaceutical executive*
Riva, Carlos *pharmaceutical executive*
Schaub, Robert George *pharmaceutical executive*
Termeer, Henricus Adrianus *pharmaceutical executive*

Charlestown
English, Todd *food company executive, chef*

Danvers
Dolan, John Ralph *retired electronics executive*
Waite, Charles Morrison *food products executive*

Easthampton
Perkins, Homer Guy *manufacturing executive*

Falmouth
Litschgi, Richard John *computer manufacturing company executive*

Framingham
Lesser, Richard G. *retired apparel executive*

Haverhill
Bigelow, Peter *electronics executive*

Hingham
Scarpa, Michael *former apparel executive*
Sullivan, Trudy (Gertrude Fulham Sullivan) *apparel company executive*
Zetcher, Arnold B. *apparel executive*

Lexington
Bahcall, Safi R. *pharmaceutical executive*
Baron, Sheldon *research and development company executive*
Goell, James Emanuel *electronics executive*
McGirr, David William John *pharmaceutical executive*
Sandage, Bobby, Jr. *pharmaceutical executive*
Smith, Robert Louis *construction company executive*
Williams, Anthony *pharmaceutical executive*
Zhang, Mei *pharmaceutical executive, researcher*

Longmeadow
Gallup, John Gardiner *retired paper company executive*

Mashpee
Wasiele, Harry W., Jr. *diversified electrical manufacturing company executive*

Natick
Elliott, Ray (J. Raymond Elliott) *biomedical device manufacturing company executive*
LaViolette, Paul A. *former medical products executive*
Leno, Samuel R. *biomedical device manufacturing company executive*
McConnell, William F., Jr. *medical products executive*
Nicholas, Peter M. *medical products executive*

North Andover
Gelb, Harold Seymour *retired manufacturing executive, entrepreneur, consultant*
Jannini, Ralph Humbert III *electronics executive*

North Chatham
Wilson, E. B. *manufacturing executive, consultant, writer*

Norwood
Li, Chiang J. *pharmaceutical executive, physician scientist*

Orange
Rivers, Robert Alfred *microwave company executive*

Pittsfield
Begley, Charlene *manufacturing executive*

Quincy
Levin, Robert Joseph *food products executive*
Young, Richard William *chemicals executive*

Southborough
Lavin, Philip Todd *medical executive*

Springfield
Winn, Janice Gail *food products administrator*

Waltham
Bernstein, Stanley Joseph *manufacturing executive*
Best, Lawrence C. *retired medical products executive*
Casper, Marc Nolan *scientific instrument company executive*
Dekkers, Marijn E. *electronics executive*
Friel, Robert F. *electronics executive*
Swanson, William Henry *defense equipment manufacturing company executive*
Wajsgras, David C. *manufacturing executive*
Wilver, Peter M. *electronics executive, accountant*

Wellesley
DiCamillo, Gary Thomas *manufacturing executive*
Gailius, Gilbert Keistutis *manufacturing executive*

Wellesley Hills
Marcus, William Michael *rubber and vinyl products manufacturing company executive*

Weston
Saad, Theodore Shafick *retired microwave company executive*

Winchester
Jackson, Francis Joseph *research and development company executive*

Woburn
Andriano, Kirk Patrick *biotechnology executive*
Kang, Yun *pharmaceutical executive*

MICHIGAN

Ann Arbor
Cole, David Edward *automotive executive, educator*
Decker, Raymond Frank *chemicals and metal products executive*
Desai, Kashappa Goud *pharmaceutical executive, researcher*
McCormack, Terry R. *automotive executive*
Wolf, Timothy Van de Wint *food products executive*

Auburn Hills
Accavitti, Michael J. *automotive executive*
Boag, Simon *automotive executive*
Campi, John Paul *automotive executive*
Ebeid, Russell Joseph *glass manufacturing executive*
Ewasyshyn, Frank Joseph *automotive executive*
Farrar, Stephen Prescott *glass products manufacturing executive*
Fong, Peter L. *automotive executive*
Gerson, Ralph Joseph *manufacturing executive*
Gorlier, Pietro *automotive executive*
Manganello, Timothy M. *auto parts company executive*
Manley, Michael *automotive executive*
Meyer, Deborah Wahl *automotive executive*
Press, Jim (James E. Press) *automotive executive*
Rae, Nancy Ann *automotive executive*
Unger, Susan J. *automotive executive*

Battle Creek
Bryant, John A. *food products executive*
Jenness, James M. *food products executive*
Mackay, David (A.D. David Mackay) *food products executive*
Pilnick, Gary H. *food products executive, lawyer*

Belleville
Quigley, William G. *automotive supplier company executive*
Stebbins, Donald J. *car parts manufacturing company executive*

Benton Harbor
Brown, Mark E. *manufacturing executive*
Fettig, Jeff M. *manufacturing executive*
Templin, Roy W. *manufacturing executive*
Todman, Michael A. *manufacturing executive*

Beulah
Edwards, Wallace Winfield *retired automotive executive*

Birmingham
Foxen, Richard William *manufacturing executive*
Maxwell, Jack Erwin *manufacturing executive*
Sharf, Stephan *automotive executive*

Bloomfield Hills
Cregg, Roger A. *construction executive*
Dugas, Richard J., Jr. *construction executive*
Eller, Timothy R. *construction and real estate company executive*
Ellinghausen, James R. *construction executive*
Keane, Peter J. *construction executive*
Kurnick, Robert H., Jr. *automotive executive, lawyer*
Lapadot, Sonee Spinner *retired automobile manufacturing company official*
O'Shaughnessy, Robert T. *automotive executive*
Petruska, Steven C. *construction executive*
Pickard, William Frank *plastics company executive*
Pulte, William J. *retired construction executive*

Brooklyn
Vischer, Harold Harry *manufacturing executive*

Cass City
Althaver, Lambert Ewing *manufacturing executive*

Dearborn
Bakaj, Joseph *automotive executive*
Bannister, Michael E. *automotive executive*
Biegun, Stephen E. *automotive executive*
Booth, Lewis W.K. *automotive company executive*
Brown, Thomas K. (Tony Brown) *automotive executive*
Cischke, Susan Mary *automotive executive*
Czubay, Ken *automotive executive*
Daniel, Peter J. *automotive executive*
Day, Raymond F. *automotive executive*
Farley, James D. (Jim Farley) *automotive executive, marketing professional*
Fields, Felicia J. *automotive executive*
Fields, Mark *automotive executive*
Ford, Bill (William Clay Ford Jr.) *automotive company executive*
Ford, Elena (Elena Anne Ford-Niarchos) *automotive industry executive*
Ford, William Clay *automotive and professional sports team executive*
Fowler, Bennie W. *automotive executive*
Graziano, Robert *automotive executive*
Hazel, Darryl Barton *automotive executive*
Hinrichs, Joseph R. *automotive executive*
Kuzak, Derrick M. *automotive executive*
Leitch, David G. *automotive executive, lawyer*
Macfarlane, Ken *automotive executive*
Mascarenas, Paul A. *automotive executive*
Mays, J. C. *automotive executive*
Mulally, Alan R. *automotive company executive, former aerospace company executive*
Mulloy, Martin J. *automotive executive*
Ohtani, Hiroko *automotive professional*
Samardzich, Barb *automotive executive*
Schloss, Neil M. *automotive executive*
Schmidt, Gerhard *automotive executive*
Shanks, Robert L. *automotive executive*
Spender, Philip G. *automotive executive*
Sviggum, Ingvar *automotive executive*
Tetreault, James *automotive executive*

Detroit
Barclay, Kathleen S. *automotive executive*
Barra, Mary Teresa *automotive industry executive*
Borst, Walter G. *automotive executive*
Browning, Jonathan *automotive executive*
Burns, Lawrence D. *automotive executive*
Buttermore, John R. *automotive executive*
Clarke, Troy Allen *automotive executive*
Cole, Kenneth W. *automotive executive, lobbyist*
Coombs, Martyn *pharmaceutical executive*
Cowger, Gary L. *automotive executive*
Cyprus, Nicholas Stanley *automotive executive, accountant*
Dauch, Richard E. *automotive executive*
Everett, Nancy C. *automotive executive*
Forster, Carl-Peter *automotive executive*
Gillum, Roderick D. *automotive executive*
Hancock, Daniel M. *automotive executive*
Harris, Steven Jay *automotive executive*
Henderson, Fritz (Frederick A. Henderson) *automotive executive*
Huber, Chester A., Jr., (Chet Huber) *automotive executive*
Kempston-Darkes, Maureen *automotive executive*
Koerner, Edward C. *automotive executive*
LaNeve, Mark R. *automotive executive, marketing professional*
Lauckner, Jonathan J. *automotive executive*
Lee, Timothy Eby *automotive executive*
Lieblein, Grace D. *automotive executive*
Lowery, Elizabeth A. *automotive executive*
Lutz, Robert Anthony (Bob Lutz) *automotive executive*
Mooney, Dennis M. *automotive executive*
Polis, Nancy E. *automotive executive*
Powell, William E. *automotive executive*
Reilly, David N. (Nick Reilly) *automotive executive*
Reuss, Mark *automotive executive*
Slym, Karl *automotive executive*
Smith, John F. *automotive executive*
Stephens, Thomas G. *automotive executive*
Szygenda, Ralph J. *automotive executive*
Tremblay, Diana D. *automotive executive*
Wale, Kevin E. *automotive executive*
Whitacre, Edward E., Jr. *automotive executive, retired telecommunications industry executive*
White, Gary A. *automotive executive*
Williams, Kevin W. *automotive executive*
Young, Ray G. *automotive executive*

Farmington Hills
Fluharty, David Arthur *automotive manager, statistician, consultant*

Fraser
Veryser, Harry Cornelius *manufacturing executive, educator*

Grand Rapids
Baker, Hollis MacLure *furniture manufacturing company executive*
Currie, William G. *forest products executive*
Glenn, Michael B. *forest products executive*
Hackett, James P. *manufacturing executive*
Sadler, David G(ary) *manufacturing executive*
Secchia, Peter F. *forest products executive, former United States ambassador to Italy*

Grosse Pointe
Wilkinson, Warren Scripps *manufacturing executive*

Houghton
Utt, Glenn S., Jr. *retired medical products executive*

Kalamazoo
Hartman, Curt *health products executive*
MacMillan, Stephen P. *health products executive*

Livonia
Cantie, Joseph S. *automotive executive*
Lake, Peter J. *automotive executive*
Lunn, Steven *automotive executive*
Malcolm, Mark M. *automotive executive*

Marchuk, Neil *automotive executive*
Plant, John Charles *automotive executive*

Midland
Banholzer, William F. *chemical company executive*
Burns, Stephanie A. *chemicals executive*
Fasone Holder, Julie *chemicals executive*
Freiwald, Gregory M. *chemical company executive*
Gambrell, Michael R. *chemicals executive*
Haller, Heinz *chemicals executive*
Hampton, Leroy *retired chemical company executive*
Kepler, David E., II, *chemicals executive*
Kresge, Charles T. *chemicals executive*
Liveris, Andrew N. *chemical company executive*
Schmidt, William C. *retired chemicals executive*
Veurink, Gary R. *chemicals executive*

Milford
Bennur, Mallikarjuna *automotive executive*

Monroe
Darrow, Kurt L. *manufacturing executive*

Northville
Clawson, Curtis J. *manufacturing executive*

Novi
Hasler, Edward A. *automotive executive*
McElya, James S. *automotive executive*

Plymouth
Vlcek, Donald Joseph, Jr. *food products executive, wholesale distribution executive, writer*

Portage
Bergy, Dean H. *health products executive*
Brown, John Wilford *health products executive*
Fox-Smith, Andrew G. *health products executive*

Reed City
Rautiola, Norman A. *manufacturing executive*

Rochester Hills
Denton, Lawrence A. *automotive executive*

Royal Oak
Cook, Noel Robert *manufacturing executive*

Saint Joseph
King, George Raleigh *retired manufacturing executive*

Southfield
Alapont, José Maria *automotive executive*
Brackenbury, James M. *manufacturing executive*
Rossiter, Robert E. *manufacturing executive*
Salvatore, Louis R. *manufacturing executive*
Scott, Raymond E. *manufacturing executive*
Simoncini, Matthew J. *manufacturing executive*
Vandenberghe, James H. *manufacturing executive*

Taylor
Yaggi, W. Timothy *manufacturing executive*

Troy
Craig, Jeffrey A. *automotive executive*
Donlon, James D. III *automotive executive*
McClure, Charles G. *automotive executive*
Miller, Robert Stevens, Jr., (Steve Miller) *automotive parts company executive*
O'Neal, Rodney *automotive company executive*
Sheehan, John D. *automotive executive*
Weber, Mark R. *automotive executive*

Warren
Deeb, Edward *food products executive*
Ferman, Martin A. *research and development company executive*
Schmieg, Steven Jeffrey *research and development company executive, researcher*

Whitehall
Squier, David Louis *manufacturing executive*

Zeeland
Walker, Brian C. *manufacturing executive*

MINNESOTA

Austin
Binder, Steven G. *food products executive*
Ettinger, Jeffrey M. *food products executive, lawyer*
Feragen, Jody H. *food products executive*

Bloomington
Buhrmaster, Robert C. *manufacturing executive*

Eagan
Clemens, T. Pat *manufacturing executive*

Eden Prairie
Henningsen, Peter, Jr. *manufacturing executive*
Murphy, Daniel J., Jr. *aerospace and defense manufacturing company executive, military officer*

Edina
Brown, Charles Eugene *retired electronics company executive*
Lapadat, Paul *food products executive*

Golden Valley
Hogan, Randall J. *manufacturing and electronics executive*

La Crescent
Gelatt, Charles Daniel *manufacturing executive*

Lindstrom
Messin, Marlene Ann *plastics company executive*

Mankato
Kunz, Alan Leonard *automotive executive, educator*

Mendota Heights
Frechette, Peter Loren *medical products executive*

Minneapolis
Cook, William M. *manufacturing executive*
Curler, Jeffrey H. *packaging manufacturing executive*
Dallas, H. James *medical products executive*
Dimond, Robert B. *food products executive*
Durkin, G. Michael *food products executive*
Ellis, Gary *medical products executive*
Ferrari, Giannantonio *electronics executive*
Hale, Roger Loucks *manufacturing executive, director*
Hawkins, William A. III *medical products executive*
Hoffman, Michael J. *manufacturing executive*
Jacobs, Irwin Lawrence *diversified corporate executive*
Lumpkins, Robert L. *food products executive*
Mackay, Harvey B. *paper company executive, writer*
Mansfield, William L. *manufacturing executive*
Morrison, John Lewis *former food company executive, investor*
Ni, Jessie H.-T. *research and development company executive, director*
Oesterle, Stephen N. *medical products executive, cardiologist, educator*
Page, Gregory R. *agricultural products and diversified services company executive*
Spoor, William Howard *food products executive*
Wurtele, Christopher Angus *paint and coatings company executive*

Minnetonka
Erlandson, Patrick J. *health products executive*

Plymouth
Kahler, Herbert Frederick *manufacturing executive*
Nagler, Lorna E. *apparel executive*
Prokopanko, James T. *agricultural products executive*

Saint Paul
Buckley, George W. *manufacturing executive*
Campbell, Patrick D. *manufacturing executive*
Debertin, Jay D. *energy and food products executive*
Johnson, John D. *energy and food products executive*
Kluempke, Patrick M. *energy and food products executive*
Knutson, Dan *food products executive*
Larson, Thomas D. *energy and food products executive*
Meline, David W. *manufacturing executive*
Palmquist, Mark L. *energy and food products executive*
Policinski, Chris *food products executive*
Schmitz, John *energy and food products executive*
Starks, Daniel J. *medical technology and services executive*
Westbrock, Leon E. *energy and food products executive*
Wiltz, James W. *medical products executive*

Wayzata
Blodgett, Frank Caleb *retired food company executive*
Johnson, Sankey Anton *manufacturing executive*
Luthringshauser, Daniel Rene *manufacturing executive*
Sullivan, Austin Padraic, Jr. *retired diversified food company executive*

Winona
Oberton, Willard D. *industrial supply company executive*

MISSISSIPPI

Hattiesburg
Chain, Bobby Lee *electrical contractor, former mayor*

MISSOURI

Bridgeton
Andrews, William Frederick *manufacturing executive*

Carthage
Flanigan, Matthew C. *manufacturing executive*
Haffner, David S. *manufacturing executive*

Chesterfield
Carpenter, Will Dockery *chemicals executive*
Winter, William Earl *retired beverage company executive*

Clayton
Rupp, Joseph D. *metal products executive*

Excelsior Springs
Schroeder, Horst Wilhelm *food products executive*

Kansas City
Bass, Lee Marshall *food products company executive*
Berkley, Eugene Bertram (Bert Berkley) *envelope company executive*
Johnson, Richard Dean *pharmaceutical consultant, educator*
Jung, Craig D. *food products executive*
Smith, Richard P. *dairy product company executive, lawyer*

Lebanon
Russell, Doug *manufacturing executive, former political organization administrator*

Lees Summit
Henley, Joseph Oliver *manufacturing executive*

Maryland Heights
Holmes, Michael *health products executive*
Ignaczak, Edward B. *health products executive*
McNamee, Patrick *health products executive*
Paz, George *health products executive*
Porter, Douglas W. *health products executive*
Rey-Giraud, Agnès *health products executive*
Steward, David L. *technology company executive*

Saint Louis
Baker, W. Randolph *brewery company executive*
Browde, Anatole *electronics company executive, consultant*
Crews, Terrell K. *agricultural products executive*
Edison, Bernard Alan *retired apparel executive*
Farr, David N. *electronics executive*
Fromm, Ronald A. *apparel executive*
Galvin, Walter J. *electrical equipment manufacturing executive*
Grant, Hugh *agricultural products executive*
Gupta, Surendra Kumar *chemicals executive*
Harvey, David R. *chemical company executive*
Hirsch, Raymond Robert *chemicals executive, lawyer*
Hunt, Kevin J. *food products executive*
Joffrion, James L., Jr. *pharmaceutical executive*
Lowenberg, David A. *pharmaceutical executive*
McCann, Melinda Camille *agricultural professional*
Monroe, Thomas Edward *business and financial executive*
Monser, Edward L. *electronics executive*
Nagarkatti, Jai Prakash *chemical company executive*
Peacock, David A. *brewery company executive*
Peters, Charles A. *electronics executive*
Quinn, Jeffry N. *chemicals executive, lawyer*
Reynolds, Robert A., Jr. *electric distributor executive*
Skarie, David P. *food products executive*
Snively, David Frederick *agricultural products company executive, lawyer*
Stearley, Robert Jay *retired packaging company executive*
Stokes, Patrick T. *brewery company executive*
Swain, David O. *manufacturing executive*
Weldon, Virginia V. *retired food products executive, pediatrician*

Springfield
Henslee, Gregory L. *automotive executive*

MONTANA

Big Sky
Ryan, Raymond D. *retired steel and insurance company executive*

Bozeman
Minton, Dwight Church *manufacturing executive*

NEBRASKA

Elkhorn
Regan, Timothy James *grain company executive*

Lincoln
Fisher, Calvin David *food products executive*
Qingping, Tao *research and development company executive*

Omaha
Bolles, Al *food products executive*
Chow, Joan K. *food products executive*
Gehring, John F. *food products executive*
Grewcock, Bruce E. *construction and mining executive*
Hardy, Jim, Jr. *food products executive*
Hawaux, André J. *food products executive*
Heckman, Gregory A. *food products executive*
Knudsen, Doug *food products executive*
McCook, Jacqueline K. Heslop *food products executive*
Perez, Peter Michael *food products executive*
Pouw, King T. *food products executive*
Rodkin, Gary M. *food products executive*
Stinson, Kenneth E. *construction and mining company executive*
Teer, Diane *food products executive*

NEVADA

Carson City
Burns, Dan W. *manufacturing executive*

Henderson
Goode, John Martin *manufacturing executive*

Incline Village
Strack, Harold Arthur *retired electronics executive, military officer, financial consultant, musician, writer*

Las Vegas
Arell, Bobby Ray, Jr. *pharmaceutical executive, management consultant*
Derrick, William Dennis *retired physical plant administrator, consultant*
Jakopec, Carl Thomas *pharmaceutical executive*

Reno
Jacobson, Raymond Earl *electronics executive*
Tedford, Jack Nowlan III *construction executive, small business owner*

NEW HAMPSHIRE

Bennington
Verney, Richard Greville *paper company executive*

East Andover
Gould, Donald Everett *retired chemical company executive, consultant*

Keene
Cohen, Richard B. *grocery company executive*
Miller, Rita *die-casting company executive, personnel consultant*

Milford
Morison, John Hopkins *casting manufacturing company executive*

Nashua
Egan, John Frederick *retired electronics executive*

New London
Condict, Edgar Rhodes *manufacturing executive, minister*

North Hampton
Taylor, Donald *retired manufacturing executive*

Portsmouth
Breen, Edward Deveaux *manufacturing executive*

NEW JERSEY

Basking Ridge
Conklin, Donald Ransford *retired pharmaceutical executive*

Bridgeton
Howell, James Burt III *retired agricultural products company sales consultant*

Bridgewater
Irace, Gregory *pharmaceutical executive*
Maynard, Kenneth Irwin *pharmaceutical executive, medical educator, researcher*

Camden
Britt, Irene Chang *food products executive*
Conant, Douglas R. *food products executive*
Connolly, Sean *food products executive*
Driscoll, Jennifer Kay *food products executive*
Linder, Maureen *food products executive, marketing professional*
Morrison, Denise M. *food products executive*
Owens, B. Craig *food products executive*
Reardon, Nancy Anne *food products executive*

East Brunswick
Wildnauer, Richard Harry *pharmaceutical executive*

East Hanover
Wen, Hong *pharmaceutical executive*

Eatontown
Bouchard, Gilles *manufacturing executive*

Edison
Alexander, John Charles *pharmaceutical executive, preventive medicine physician*

Elmwood Park
Kelsey, David H. *manufacturing executive*

Englewood
Rotondi, Nicholas John *automotive executive*

Englewood Cliffs
Lawrence, James A. *food products executive*
Neis, Arnold Hayward *pharmaceutical company executive*

Fair Haven
McKissock, David Lee *retired manufacturing company executive*

Farmingdale
Schluter, Peter Mueller *electronics executive*

Fort Monmouth
Schwering, Felix Karl *electronics executive, researcher*
Thornton, Clarence Gould *electronics executive, civilian military employee*

Franklin Lakes
Considine, John R. *pharmaceutical company executive*
Elkins, David V. *medical products executive*
Forlenza, Vincent A. *medical products executive*
Klepper, Kenneth O. *healthcare executive*
Ludwig, Edward J. *medical technology executive*
Rubino, Richard J. *pharmaceutical executive*
Snow, David B., Jr. *pharmaceutical executive*

Hainesport
Sylk, Leonard Allen *manufacturing executive, real estate developer*

Jersey City
Perhach, James Lawrence *pharmaceutical executive*

Kendall Park
Hershenov, Bernard Zion *research and development company executive*

Kenilworth
Bertolini, Robert J. *pharmaceutical executive*
Cox, Carrie S. *pharmaceutical executive*
Dodsworth, Roy W. *pharmaceutical executive*
Hassan, Fred *pharmaceutical executive*

Little Falls
Fleming, Shane D. *plastic products company executive*

Madison
Dohlsten, Mikael *pharmaceutical executive, researcher*
Poussot, Bernard Jean *pharmaceutical executive*

Mahwah
Gerstein, David Brown *manufacturing and professional sports team executive*

Maplewood
Zoss, Abraham Oscar *chemical company executive*

Medford
Springer, Douglas Hyde *retired food products executive, lawyer*

Montville
Boudes, Pol Francis *pharmaceutical executive, researcher*

Morristown
Anderson, David J. *diversified technology and manufacturing company executive*
Brown, Adriane McClenny *diversified technology and manufacturing company executive*
Cameron, Nicholas Allen *manufacturing executive*
Cote, David M. *diversified technology and manufacturing company executive*
Fradin, Roger Brent *manufacturing executive*
Kramvis, Andreas Constantinos *chemicals company executive*
Martelet, Francois R. *pharmaceutical executive*
Sperber, Martin *pharmaceutical company executive, pharmacist*
Williams, Joseph Dalton *pharmaceutical executive*

Murray Hill
Ring, Timothy Michael *pharmaceutical executive*

New Brunswick
Deyo, Russell C. *health products executive, lawyer*
Foster-Cheek, Kaye I. *health products executive*
Goggins, Colleen A. *health products executive*
Gorsky, Alex *pharmaceutical executive*
Larsen, Ralph S(tanley) *retired pharmaceutical executive*
McCoy, Sherilyn S. *pharmaceutical executive*
Weldon, William Conrad *pharmaceutical executive*

New Providence
Chatterji, Debajyoti *retired manufacturing executive*
Dolch, Gary D. *health products executive*
McCaffrey, Robert Henry, Jr. *retired manufacturing company executive*

Northvale
Di Mino, André Anthony *manufacturing executive, consultant*

Ocean City
Juliana, James Nicholas *manufacturing executive*

Park Ridge
Douglas, Elyse *automobile rental and leasing company executive*
Frissora, Mark P. *automobile rental and leasing company executive*

Parsippany
Garbarini, William Nicholas *pharmaceutical executive*
Newman, Mark S. *electronics company executive*

Pennington
McBride, Anthony *pharmaceutical executive*

Pompton Plains
Shrem, Charles Joseph *metals corporation executive*

Princeton
Bergman, Richard Isaac *health information executive*
Campbell, Robert Emmett *retired health products executive*
Cavanaugh, James Henry *health products executive, retired federal official*
Dovey, Brian Hugh *health care products company executive, venture capitalist*
Ghasemi, Seifi *chemicals executive*
Mittleberg, Eric Michael *pharmaceutical executive*
Pien, Howard *pharmaceutical executive*

Rahway
Bloomfield, Daniel Mark *pharmaceutical executive*
Haupt, Richard M. *pharmaceutical executive*

Raritan
Fischer, Seth H.Z. *pharmaceutical executive*
Tortoriello, William Joseph *pharmaceutical executive*

Red Bank
Sorsby, James Larry *home building company executive*

Ridgewood
Healey, Frank Henry *retired chemicals executive*

Riverton
O'Brien, James Jerome *construction management consultant*

Saddle Brook
Hickey, William V. *manufacturing executive*

Secaucus
Liao, Paul Foo-Hung *electronics executive*
Weil, Laura A. *apparel executive*

Skillman
Rai, Sanjiv *research and development company executive, educator*

Springfield
Mamidwar, Sachin Sureshrao *medical products executive*

Summit
Zachary, Louis George *chemical company consultant*

Teaneck
Feinberg, Robert S. *plastics company executive, marketing professional*
Woerner, Alfred Ira *medical device manufacturer, educator*

Totowa
Schady, Kathleen *pharmaceutical executive*

Trenton
Viscomi, Frank Joseph *pharmaceutical executive*

Union
Franklin, William George *manufacturing executive*

Wayne
Bess, Alan L. *pharmaceutical executive, Physician Author*
Friedman, Martin Burton *retired chemicals executive*
Heyman, Samuel J. *chemical manufacturing company executive*

Whitehouse Station
Anstice, David W. *pharmaceutical executive*
Clark, Richard T. *pharmaceutical company executive*
Deese, Willie A. *pharmaceutical executive*
Frazier, Kenneth C. *pharmaceutical executive, lawyer*
Kellogg, Peter Newman *pharmaceutical executive*
McGuire, John Lawrence *pharmaceutical executive*
Scalet, J. Chris (James Christopher Scalet) *pharmaceutical executive*

NEW MEXICO

Albuquerque
Friberg, George Joseph *electronics company executive, entrepreneur*
Korman, Nathaniel Irving *research and development company executive*
Roberts, Dennis William *retired construction executive*

Sandia Park
Wilczynski, Janusz S. *manufacturing executive, retired physicist*

Santa Fe
Robinson, Charles Wesley *boat design company executive*

NEW YORK

Albany
Heshmat, Hooshang *manufacturing executive*
Walton, James Farley *research and development company executive*

Astoria
DiGiovanni, Eleanor Elma *scaffold installation company executive*

Baldwin
Chopra, Samir *pharmaceutical and real estate company executive*

Barneveld
Hanna, Richard L. *construction executive*

Belle Harbor
Re, Edward Domenic, Jr. *construction executive*

Bohemia
Rudolph, Scott *pharmaceutical executive*

Briarcliff Manor
Bingham, J. Peter *electronics research executive*

Buffalo
Collins, Christopher Carl *manufacturing executive*
Rich, Robert E., Jr. *frozen foods company executive*
Starks, Fred William *chemicals executive*

Cazenovia
Carlson, William Clifford *retired defense industry executive, military officer*

Corning
Behm, Forrest Edwin *retired glass manufacturing company executive*
Volanakis, Peter F. *manufacturing executive*

Cross River
Lang, Robert Mays, Jr. *manufacturing and not-for-profit executive*

East Amherst
Watson, Stewart Charles *construction executive*

East Hampton
Karp, Harvey Lawrence *metal products executive*

East Northport
Kehoe, Thomas J. *food products executive*

Elma
Hawk, George Wayne *retired electronics company executive*

Fayetteville
Pachter, Irwin Jacob *pharmaceutical consultant*

Glen Cove
Burnham, Harold Arthur *pharmaceutical executive, physician*

Great Neck
Arams, Frank Robert *electronics executive*

Greenvale
Krasnoff, Eric *health products executive*

Hartsdale
Martin, Daniel Richard *pharmaceutical executive*

Hauppauge
Hausman, Howard *electronics executive*

Hopewell Junction
Ouyang, Xu *research and development company executive*

Ithaca
Cottrell, G. Walton *manufacturing executive*

Jericho
Blau, Harvey Ronald *manufacturing executive*
Kramer, Ronald J. *manufacturing executive*

Larchmont
Cavanna, Dino Francesco *chemicals executive*
Hinerfeld, Norman Martin *manufacturing executive*

Long Island City
Rosenfeld, Edward R. *apparel executive*

Mamaroneck
Mizrahi, Abraham Mordechay *retired health products executive, pediatrician*

Melville
Bergman, Stanley M. *health products executive*
Boehlke, Charles *industrial machinery company executive*
Breslawski, James P. *health products executive*
Kissinger, Walter Bernhard *retired automotive executive*
Long, Michael J. *electronics executive*
McMahon, John P. *electronics executive*
Mitchell, William Edmund *electronics executive*
Morris, M. Catherine *electronics executive*
Paladino, Steven *health products executive*
Reilly, Paul J. *electronics executive*
Waddell, John Comer *electronics executive*

Monroe
Dierna, Joseph Biagio *construction company executive, land development consultant*

New Rochelle
Tassone, Gelsomina (Gessie) *metal products executive*

New York
Andreotti, Lamberto *pharmaceutical executive*
Armen, Garo H. *research and development company executive*
Axelrod, Norman N *optical electro-optical and imaging consultant*
Azria, Max *apparel executive*
Bagger, Richard Hartvig *pharmaceutical executive*
Barton, Lewis *food products executive, consultant*
Beattle, E. Scott *cosmetics executive*
Bernsohn, Randall *construction executive, real estate developer*
Bernstein, Richard Allen *food products executive*
Boddewyn, Jean J. *RETIRED business educator*
Breen, Thia *cosmetics company executive*
Bresani, Federico Fernando *manufacturing executive*
Brown, Bobbi *cosmetics executive*
Casey, Gerard William *retired food products executive, lawyer*
Cazala, Béatrice *pharmaceutical executive*
Celentano, John E. *pharmaceutical executive*
Chang, Nancy T. *pharmaceutical executive*
Cheung, Raymond Yan Ling *pharmaceutical executive, director*
Chirico, Emanuel *apparel executive*
Cole, Kenneth D. *apparel company executive*
Cornelius, James Milton *pharmaceutical company executive*
Cramb, Charles W. *cosmetics executive*
D'Amelio, Frank Anthony *pharmaceutical executive, former telecommunications industry executive*
Demsey, John D. *cosmetics executive*
Denmark, Bernhardt *manufacturing executive*
de Notaristefani, Carlo *pharmaceutical executive*
Devitre, Dinyar S. *tobacco company executive*
Deyrmenjian, Liza (Liza D.) *fashion consultant, film producer*
Dixon, Wendy L. *pharmaceutical executive*
Earl, Christopher D. *health products executive*
Engel, Amy J. *tobacco company executive*
Ennis, Alan T. *cosmetics company executive*
Farber, John J. *chemical company executive*
Freda, Fabrizio *cosmetics executive*
Geckle, Robert Alan *manufacturing executive*
Glaubinger, Lawrence David *retired manufacturing company executive*
Goodale, Toni Krissel *research and development company executive*
Gould, Harry Edward, Jr. *paper company executive*
Granoff, Jill *apparel executive*
Greenberg, David I. *tobacco company executive*
Gromek, Joseph R. *apparel executive*
Gunn, Tim (Timothy M. Gunn) *apparel executive*
Hardwick, Charles Leighton *pharmaceutical executive, former state legislator*
Holsenbeck, George Penn *tobacco company executive, lawyer*
Hooper, Anthony C. *pharmaceutical executive*
Huet, Jean-Marc *pharmaceutical executive*
Johnson, John H. *medical products executive*
Jung, Andrea *cosmetics company executive*
Katen, Karen L. *retired pharmaceutical company executive*
Kennedy, David L. *cosmetics company executive*
Kindler, Jeffrey B. *pharmaceutical company executive, lawyer*
Kleinfeld, Klaus *metal products executive, former electronics executive*
Koch, David Hamilton *chemical company executive*
Krill, Kay (Katherine Lawther Krill) *apparel executive*
Kuhbach, Robert Gerdes *manufacturing executive*
Kunes, Richard W. *cosmetics executive*
Langhammer, Fred H. *cosmetics company executive*
Lauder, Aerin Rebecca (Aerin Lauder Zinterhofer) *cosmetics executive*
Lauder, Evelyn H. *cosmetics executive*
Lauder, Leonard Alan *retired cosmetic and fragrance company executive*
Lauder, William P. *cosmetics executive*
Leung, Sandra *pharmaceutical executive, lawyer*
Levinson, Robert Alan *textiles executive*
Lewis-Hall, Freda C. *pharmaceutical executive*
Livingston, Robert A. *manufacturing executive*
Lord, Marvin *apparel executive*
Mackay, Martin *pharmaceutical executive*
Mallis, Fern J. *fashion industry executive*
McComb, William L. *apparel company executive*
McFadden, Mary Josephine *fashion industry executive*
McKinnon, Floyd Wingfield *textile executive*
McLane, Charles D., Jr. *metal products executive*
McLeod, Mary S. *pharmaceutical executive*
Monaghan, Craig Thomas *automotive executive*
Moore, Charles Hewes, Jr. *manufacturing executive*
Morrison, Briggs *pharmaceutical executive*
Mullen, Robert W. *construction executive*
Mulligan, John J. *tobacco company executive*
Munroe, George Barber *retired mining and manufacturing company executive*
O'Connor, Rory *pharmaceutical company executive, medical director*
Oglesby, Charles R. *automotive executive*
Pietruski, John Michael, Jr. *pharmaceutical executive*
Read, Ian C. *pharmaceutical executive*
Reitan, Bernt *metal products executive*
Rosen, Andrew W. *apparel executive*
Rosenberg, Robert Charles *housing corporation executive*
Rothwell, Timothy *pharmaceutical executive*
Rubin, Joel Edward *theatre consulting executive*
Schell, J. Michael *metal products executive, lawyer*
Schulhof, Michael Peter *electronics company executive*
Schulman, Amy Weinfeld *pharmaceutical company executive, lawyer*
Sigal, Elliott C. *pharmaceutical executive*
Slavin, Rosanne Singer *textile converter*
Smith, Elizabeth A. (Liz Smith) *cosmetics company executive*
Solomon, Howard *pharmaceutical executive*
Sosnow, Lawrence Ira *health care company executive*
Stringer, Sir Howard *electronics company executive*
Susman, Sally S. *pharmaceutical executive, former cosmetics executive*
Szymanczyk, Michael E. *tobacco products executive*
Tiesi, Joseph A. *tobacco company executive*
Tishman, Daniel R. *construction executive*
Underhill, Paco *market research and consulting company executive, environmental psychologist*
von der Heyden, Karl Mueller *retired manufacturing executive*
Warren, Andrew C. *apparel executive*
Weber, Mark *apparel executive*
Whiting, Susan Dickinson *media research company executive*
Wieser, Helmut *metal products executive*
Wolgemuth, Richard Lee *pharmaceutical executive*
Wu, Jason *apparel executive*
Zabar, Eli *food products executive*
Zito, Robert Thomas *pharmaceutical executive*
Zlateva, Gergana P. *pharmaceutical executive, director*

Niskayuna
Arik, Mehmet *research and development company executive*
Little, Mark M. *manufacturing executive*

Pittsford
Green, Martin Lincoln *retired medical products executive*

Plainview
Stalzer, Frank Joseph *electronics company executive*

Poughkeepsie
Slade, Bernard Newton *electronics executive*

Purchase
Beraud, Jill *food products executive, marketing professional*
Compton, John C. *food products executive*
D'Amore, Massimo Fasanella *food products executive*
Goodman, Richard *food products executive*
Johnston, Hugh Francis *food products executive*
Nooyi, Indra Krishnamurthy *food products executive*
Wallach, Kenneth L. *paper company executive*
White, Michael Dennis *food products executive*

Rochester
Bouyoucos, John Vinton *retired research and development company executive*
Dobbs, Herbert Hotaling *automotive executive, consultant, research scientist, retired military officer*
Duke, Charles Bryan *electronics executive, physicist, educator*
Ostrov, Gerald Martin *pharmaceutical executive*
Sieg, Albert Louis *photographic company executive*
Sklarsky, Frank S. *manufacturing executive*
Zarrella, Ronald L. *retired pharmaceutical executive*

Roslyn Heights
Guthart, Leo A. *electronics executive*

Rye
Finnerty, Louise Hoppe *food products executive*

Rye Brook
Kuntzman, Ronald *research and development company executive*

Sands Point
Wurzel, Leonard *retired candy manufacturing company executive*

Scarsdale
Blitman, Howard Norton *construction executive*
Johnson, Boine Theodore *manufacturing executive, mayor*

Schenectady
Sternlicht, Beno *research and development company executive*

Seaford
Setzler, William Edward *retired chemicals executive*

Sidney
Werner, David A. *paper company executive*

Skaneateles Falls
Shimer, Julie A. *health products executive*

Utica
Antzelevitch, Charles *research and development company executive*

Victor
Sands, Richard E. *food products executive*
Sands, Robert *food products executive*

Wantagh
Blum, Melvin *chemical company executive, researcher*

Webster
Curtis, Deana A. *electronics executive, small business owner*

West Harrison
Loranger, Steven R. *industrial manufacturing company executive*
Reichelderfer, Brenda L. *manufacturing executive*

West Seneca
Bidlack, Jerald Dean *manufacturing executive*

White Plains
Fisher, Jerome *apparel executive*

Woodbury
Guttenplan, Harold Esau *retired food company executive*

Yonkers
Holtz, Gilbert Joseph *steel company executive*

Youngstown
Alpert, Norman *chemical company executive*

NORTH CAROLINA

Beaufort
Cullman, Hugh *retired tobacco company executive*

Cary
Grubb, Gary S. *pharmaceutical executive*
Lawson, William, Jr., (B.J. Lawson) *medical products executive*

Chapel Hill
Cummings, Sandra Eileen *medical products executive*

Charlotte
Aycock, Hugh David *steel manufacturing company executive*
Belk, Thomas Milburn, Jr., (Tim) *apparel executive*
Corvi, Carolyn *manufacturing executive*
Cosper, David P. *automotive executive*
Dickson, Thomas Walter *textile company executive*
DiMicco, Daniel R. *manufacturing executive*
Ferriola, John J. *manufacturing executive*
Kearney, Christopher J. *manufacturing executive, lawyer*
Kuechle, Scott E. *manufacturing executive*
Larsen, Marshall O. *manufacturing executive*
Lea, Scott Carter *retired packaging company executive*
Lisenby, Terry S. *manufacturing executive*
Lott, Hamilton, Jr. *manufacturing executive*
Martin, James Grubbs *healthcare consultant, Former United States Representative, NC*
Morgan, James H. *food services company executive, former investment company executive*
O'Leary, Patrick J. *manufacturing executive*
Parrish, D. Michael *manufacturing executive*
Peacock, A(lvin) Ward *textile company executive*
Roberts, David A. *manufacturing executive*
Rutkowski, Joseph A. *manufacturing executive*
Siegel, Samuel *metals company executive*
Slater, Charles James *construction company executive*
Smith, B. Scott *automotive executive*
Smith, O. Bruton *automotive company executive*
Spangler, Clemmie Dixon, Jr. *construction company executive*
Sulg, Madis *manufacturing executive, entrepreneur*

Durham
Gillings, Dennis B. *medical products executive*

Gastonia
Lawson, William David III *retired cotton company executive*

Greensboro
Barnett, Sharron Hogan *animal health technical director,parasiticides*
Choplin, Melody L. *manufacturing executive, educator*
Roberts, Jeffrey Owayne *builder, renovator, consultant*
Shearer, Robert K. *apparel executive*
Wiseman, Eric C. *apparel executive*

Hertford
Johnson, Donald Lee *retired agricultural materials company executive, product consultant*

High Point
Fenn, Ormon William, Jr. *furniture company executive*

Kitty Hawk
Sjoerdsma, Albert *research and development company executive*

Morrisville
Harrison, Pete (Robert E. Harrison) *tobacco company executive*

Mount Airy
Woltz, Howard Osler, Jr. *retired metal products executive*

Pisgah Forest
Dixit, Ajit Suresh *chemicals executive, research scientist*

Raleigh
Sloan, O. Temple, Jr., (Temple Sloan) *automotive equipment executive*
Zelnak, Stephen P., Jr. *construction materials company executive*

Research Triangle Park
Connelly, Deirdre P. *pharmaceutical executive*

Sapphire
Lewis, William Headley, Jr. *manufacturing executive*

Weldon
Barringer, Paul Brandon, II, *lumber company executive*

Winston Salem
Adams, Thomas R. *tobacco company executive*
Chaden, Lee A. *apparel and former food products executive*
Gentry, Jeffery S. *tobacco company executive*
Ivey, Susan M. *tobacco company executive*
Maselli, John Anthony *food products executive*
Noll, Richard A. *apparel executive*

NORTH DAKOTA

Minot
Weinmann, Ronald Vincent *business educator*

OHIO

Akron
Gingo, Joseph Michael *chemicals company executive*
Keegan, Robert J. *manufacturing executive*
Kihn, Jean-Claude *automotive executive*
Kramer, Richard J. *manufacturing executive*
Ruocco, Joe *manufacturing executive*
Rzonzef, Michel *manufacturing executive*
Wells, Darren R. *manufacturing executive*

Avon Lake
Newlin, Stephen Dore *chemicals executive*

Beachwood
Demetriou, Steven J. *metal products executive*
Stack, Sean M. *metal products executive*

Bellville
Hooker, James Todd *manufacturing executive*

Boardman
Skinner, William Philip, Jr. *manufacturing executive*

Canton
Griffith, James W. *manufacturing executive*
Swidarski, Thomas W. *manufacturing executive*
Timken, Ward J., Jr. *manufacturing executive*

Chagrin Falls
Brophy, Jere Hall *manufacturing executive*
Heckman, Henry Trevennen Shick *retired steel executive*

Cincinnati
Aguirre, Fernando *food products executive*
Christensen, Paul Walter, Jr. *retired gear manufacturing company executive*
Farmer, Richard T. *uniform rental and sales executive*
Farmer, Scott D. *apparel executive*
Holloman, J. Phillip *apparel executive*
Lundgren, Terry (Terrence J. Lundgren) *apparel company executive*
Schlotman, J. Michael *food products executive*

Cleveland
Arnold, Craig *manufacturing executive*
Christopher, William F. *metal products executive*
Connor, Christopher M. *manufacturing executive*
Cutler, Alexander MacDonald *manufacturing executive*
Decker, John William *metal products executive*
Fearon, Richard H. *manufacturing executive*
Gross, Thomas S. *manufacturing executive*
Jameson, J(ames) Larry *chemical company executive*
Jenson, Jon Eberdt *metal products executive*
Luke, Randall Dan *retired manufacturing executive, lawyer*
Mandel, Jack N. *manufacturing executive*
McFadden, John Volney *retired manufacturing company executive*
Morikis, John G. *manufacturing executive*
Pistell, Timothy K. *manufacturing executive*
Pugh, David L. *manufacturing executive*
Thomas, Richard Stephen *construction executive*
Washkewicz, Donald E. *manufacturing executive*
Weiss, Morry *greeting card company executive*

Columbus
Carter, William H. *chemicals executive*
Daab-Krzykowski, Andre *pharmaceutical and nutritional manufacturing company administrator*
Filliol, Olivier A. *manufacturing executive*
McConnell, John P. *metal products executive, professional sports team executive*
Milford, Frederick John *retired research and development company executive*
Morrison, Craig O. *chemicals executive*
Pfening, Frederic Denver III *manufacturing executive*
Robinson, David *manufacturing executive*
Spoerry, Robert F. *manufacturing executive*
Wadsworth, Jeffrey *research and development institute executive, metallurgist*
Wexner, Abigail *apparel executive*
Wigington, Ronald Lee *retired chemical information services executive*

Dayton
Duval, Daniel Webster *electronics executive*
Isaacson, Milton Stanley (Jim) *research and development company executive, engineer*

Delaware
Huml, Donald Scott *manufacturing executive*

Delta
Leavitt, Bradley S. *steelworker*

Dublin
Barrett, George S. *health products executive*
Bird, Shelley *health products company executive, corporate communications specialist*
Clark, R. Kerry (R. Kerry Clark) *health products executive*
Duffy, Michael A., Jr. *health products company executive*
Henderson, Jeffrey W. *health products executive*
Jain, Vivek *health products company executive*
Kaufmann, Michael *health products executive*
Lynch, Michael A. *health products executive*
Morford, Craig S. *health products executive, former prosecutor*
Rosenbaum, Mark E. *health products executive*
Schlotterbeck, David L. *health products executive*
Troup, Gordon A. *health products executive*
Walter, Robert D. *health products executive*
Winstead, Dwight *medical products executive*

Elyria
Mixon, Aaron Malachi III *medical products executive*

Findlay
Armes, Roy V. *manufacturing executive*

Gates Mills
Veale, Tinkham, II, *retired chemicals executive, engineer*

Hilliard
Rahal, Robert Woodward (Bobby Rahal) *automotive company and race car team executive, retired professional race car driver*

Jackson Center
Thompson, Wade Francis Bruce *manufacturing executive*

Mansfield
Gorman, James Carville *manufacturing executive*

Mason
Kohlhepp, Robert J. *apparel executive*

Mayfield Heights
Rankin, Alfred Marshall, Jr. *manufacturing executive*

Medina
Smith, Richey *manufacturing executive*
Sullivan, Frank C. *manufacturing executive*
Sullivan, Thomas Christopher *coatings company executive*

Mentor
Callsen, Christian Edward *health products executive*

Miamisburg
Suwyn, Mark A. *paper company executive*

Middletown
Wainscott, James Lawrence *steel industry executive*

Milan
Henry, Joseph Patrick *chemicals executive*

New Albany
Jeffries, Michael S. (Mike Jeffries) *apparel executive*

North Canton
Lynham, C(harles) Richard *manufacturing executive*

North Ridgeville
Stewart, Arden Ruth *retired automotive executive*

Orrville
Smucker, Richard K. *food products executive*
Smucker, Timothy P. *food products executive*

Ottawa Hills
Bryant, Martin *automotive executive*
Levin, Marc S. *manufacturing company executive, lawyer*

Perrysburg
White, Edward C. *chemicals executive*

Randolph
Pecano, Donald Carl *automotive manufacturing executive*

Solon
Rosica, Gabriel Adam *retired manufacturing executive, electrical engineer*

Toledo
Convis, Gary L. *automotive parts company executive*
Devine, John Martin *automotive parts company executive*
Romanoff, Milford Martin *retired building contractor*
Sweetnam, James E. *automotive executive*
Thaman, Michael H. *building material systems executive*
Yost, James A. *automotive parts company executive*

West Chester
Mack, Mark Philip *chemical company executive*

Wickliffe
Cooley, Charles P. *chemicals executive*
Hambrick, James L. *chemicals executive*

Youngstown
Powers, Paul J. *manufacturing executive*

OKLAHOMA

Bristow
Primeaux, Henry III *automotive executive, author, speaker*

Oklahoma City
Murray, James William III *manufacturing executive, lawyer*

Tulsa
Thomas, Robert Eggleston *retired manufacturing executive*
Thompson, Scott L. *automotive executive*
Wyant, Clyde W., Jr. *manufacturing executive*

OREGON

Albany
Smith, Steve *pharmaceutical executive*

Beaverton
Azuma, Mitsuyoshi *pharmaceutical executive*
Bird, Lewis L. III *apparel executive*
Blair, Donald W. *apparel executive*
Clarke, Thomas E. *apparel executive*
Denson, Charles D. *apparel executive*
DeStefano, Gary M. *apparel executive*
Jackson, Jeanne Pellegren *apparel executive, former investment company executive*
Knight, Philip Hampson *apparel executive*
Parker, Mark G. *apparel executive*

Eugene
Woolley, Donna Pearl *lumber company executive*

Klamath Falls
Wendt, Richard L. *manufacturing executive*

Medford
De Boer, Sidney B. *automotive executive*

Portland
Carter, John D. *metal products executive*
Donegan, Mark *metal products executive*
Larsson, William Dean *metal products executive*
Lundgren, Tamara L. *metal products executive*
Pamplin, Robert Boisseau, Jr. *manufacturing company executive, minister, writer*
Watkins, Charles Reynolds *medical equipment company executive*

PENNSYLVANIA

Allentown
Huck, Paul E. *chemicals company executive*
Hutton, William Michael *technology & consulting executive*
Lovett, John Robert *retired chemical company executive*
McGlade, John E. *chemicals executive*

Avondale
Friel, Daniel Denwood, Sr. *manufacturing executive*

Belle Vernon
Wapiennik, Carl Francis *manufacturing executive, planetarium and science institute administrator*

Bethlehem
Hartmann, Robert Elliott *retired manufacturing executive*
Marsh, Robert Harry *chemicals executive*

St. John, Anthony Paul *retired manufacturing executive*

Blue Bell
Agersborg, Helmer Pareli K. *pharmaceutical company executive, researcher*
Gregson, Nigel Christopher *pharmaceutical executive, consultant*

Boalsburg
Gardner, James Richard *retired pharmaceutical company executive, investor*

Bristol
Card, Wesley Roy *apparel and footwear company executive*
Kimmel, Sidney *apparel company executive, film producer*

Canonsburg
Bresch, Heather M. *pharmaceutical executive*
Coury, Robert J. *pharmaceutical executive*

Chambersburg
Rumler, Robert Hoke *agricultural products executive, consultant, retired trade association administrator*

Chesterbrook
Gozon, Richard C. *pharmaceutical executive, retired paper distribution executive*

Collegeville
Mahady, Joseph Michael *pharmaceutical executive*

Conshohocken
Barry, Michael F. *chemicals company executive*
Naples, Ronald James *manufacturing executive*
Spaeth, Karl Henry *retired chemicals executive, lawyer*

Denver
Milner, Charles Fremont, Jr. *manufacturing executive*

Devon
Porter, Roger John *research and development company executive, neurologist, pharmacologist*

Doylestown
Manion, Tom *pharmaceutical executive*

Easton
Sun, Robert Zu Jei *manufacturing company executive, inventor, educator*

Eighty Four
Magerko, Margaret Hardy (Maggie) *lumber company executive*

Emmaus
Bowers, Klaus D(ieter) *electronics executive, researcher*

Erie
Renkis, Alan Ilmars *plastics formulating company executive*

Frazer
Baldino, Frank, Jr. *biopharmaceutical executive*

Greentown
Forcheskie, Carl S. *former apparel company executive*

Hanover
Kline, Donald *food company executive*

Hershey
Buck, Michele G. *food products executive*
West, David J. *food products executive*

Hollidaysburg
Bloom, Lawrence Stephen *retired clothing company executive*

Horsham
Christian, Mildred Stoehr *health products executive*
Sachs, Keith L. *manufacturing executive*
Toll, Robert Irwin *home construction company executive*

King Of Prussia
Turner, Peter *biopharmaceutical company executive*
Waterworth, Dawn Marie *research and development company executive, director*

Lancaster
High, S. Dale *construction executive*
Lockhart, Michael D. *manufacturing executive*

Langhorne
Caruso, Dominic J. *pharmaceutical executive*

Latrobe
Cardoso, Carlos M. *metal products executive*
Dur, Philip Alphonse *retired shipbuilding executive, military officer*
McLevish, Timothy R. *food products executive*

Levittown
Henshaw, Jonathan Cook *retired manufacturing executive*

Ligonier
Pilz, Alfred Norman *manufacturing executive*

Limerick
Black, Jeffrey P. *manufacturing executive*

Malvern
Espe, Matthew J. *manufacturing executive*
Paul, Gerald D. *electronics executive*
Roggio, Bob *retired manufacturing executive*
Zandman, Felix *electronics executive*

Marion Center
Purdy, David Lawrence *medical products executive*

Mc Murray
Langenberg, Frederick Charles *manufacturing executive*

Mechanicsburg
Ortenzio, Robert A. *health and medical products executive*
Ortenzio, Rocco Anthony *health products executive*

New Kensington
Zaidi, Mohammad A. *metal products executive*

Newtown
Ross, Edwin William *rubber company executive*

Newtown Square
Ranganathan, Natarajan *research and development company executive*

North Wales
Fletcher, William A. *pharmaceutical executive*
Kim, Peter Sungbai *pharmaceutical and research and development company executive, educator*
Marth, William S. *pharmaceutical executive*

Paoli
Hardin, John Wesley *electronics executive*
Hermance, Frank S. *electronics executive*

Philadelphia
Brondeau, Pierre R. *chemicals executive*
Conway, John W. *manufacturing executive*
Croisetiere, Jacques M. *chemicals executive*
Donahue, Timothy J. *manufacturing executive*
Gupta, Rajiv Lochan *chemicals executive*
Katherine, Robert Andrew *chemicals executive*
Neubauer, Joseph *food services company executive*
Sutherland, L(ewis) Frederick *food products executive*
Witty, Andrew *pharmaceutical executive*

Pipersville
McNutt, Richard Hunt *manufacturing executive*

Pittsburgh
Belda, Alain J. P. *metal products executive*
Bunch, Charles E. *manufacturing executive*
Edelman, Harry Rollings III *engineering and construction company executive*
Engel, John J. *electronics executive*
Frank, Alan I W *manufacturing executive*
Goodish, John H. *metal products executive*
Haggerty, Gretchen R. *metal products executive*
Haley, Roy W. *electronics executive*
Harrell, Edward Harding *wine festival executive*
Harshman, Richard J. *metal products executive*
Hassey, L. Patrick *metal products executive*
Heilman, Marlin Stephen *medical products executive*
Hernandez, William H. *chemical company executive*
Huntington, James Cantine, Jr. *retired equipment manufacturing company executive*
Johnson, William R. *food products executive*
Kahle, Charles F., II, *manufacturing executive, chemist*
Kutka, J. James, Jr. *metal products executive*
Lego, Paul Edward *retired manufacturing executive*
Lohr, David H. *metal products executive*
Paul, Robert Arthur *steel company executive*
Sterling, Thomas W. *metal products executive*
Straub, Terrence D. *metal products executive*
Surma, John P., Jr. *metal products executive*
Thomas, Paul D. *metal products executive, human resources specialist*
Van Oss, Stephen A. *electronics executive*
Winkleblack, Arthur B. *food products executive*

Saint Marys
Johnson, J. M. Hamlin *manufacturing executive*

Schaefferstown
Skamangas, Anna Lynn *manufacturing executive, educator*

Sewickley
Bouchard, James Paul *metal products executive*

State College
Byrom, Fletcher Lauman *chemical manufacturing company executive*
Huck, John Lloyd *pharmaceutical executive*

Valley Forge
Dachowski, Peter Richard *manufacturing executive*

Warminster
Hull, Lewis Woodruff *manufacturing executive*

Warrendale
O'Donnell, James V. *apparel executive*

Wayne
Yost, R. David (David Yost) *pharmaceutical executive*

West Chester
Gadsby, Robin Edward *chemicals executive*
Heaps, Marvin Dale *retired food services company executive*

West Point
Schoepp, Darryle D. *pharmaceutical executive, researcher*

Wexford
Rastogi, Anil Kumar *health products executive*

Whitehall
Mansell, Danny Eugene *construction executive*

Willow Street
Coleman, Ernest Albert *plastics and materials consultant*

Wyomissing
Stevens, Anne L. *metal products executive, retired automotive executive*
Ziolkowski, Andrew T. *metal products executive*

York
Knowlton, Warren D. *plastics company executive*
Wills, Richard Andrew *materials handling equipment company executive*
Wise, Bret W. *chemical company executive*

RHODE ISLAND

Cranston
Papitto, Ralph Raymond *manufacturing executive*

North Kingstown
Novich, Bruce Eric *chemicals executive*

Pawtucket
Goldner, Brian D. *toy company executive*

Providence
Bready, Richard Lawrence *manufacturing executive*
Donnelly, Scott C. *manufacturing executive*
Lapczyk, Ireneusz *research and development company researcher*

Woonsocket
Denton, David M. *pharmaceutical executive*
Foulkes, Helena B. *pharmaceutical executive*
McGuigan, Stuart M. *pharmaceutical executive*
McLure, Howard A. *pharmaceutical executive*
Roberts, Jonathan C. *pharmaceutical executive*
Ryan, Thomas Michael (Tom Ryan) *pharmaceutical company executive*

SOUTH CAROLINA

Beaufort
Ivy, Conway Gayle *paint company executive*

Charleston
Geentiens, Gaston Petrus, Jr. *former construction management consultant company executive*
Martin, Roblee Boettcher *retired cement manufacturing executive*
Torras, Joseph Hill *pulp and paper company executive*

Clemson
Petzel, Florence Eloise *textiles educator*

Clinton
Cornelson, George Henry, IV, *retired textile company executive*

Columbia
Duggan, Carol Cook *research and development company executive*

Hartsville
DeLoach, Harris E.(Eugene), Jr. *manufacturing executive, lawyer*

Hilton Head
Harty, James D. *former manufacturing company executive*

Hilton Head Island
Cunningham, William Henry *retired food products executive*
Lewis, Gene Evans *retired medical equipment company executive*
Rulis, Raymond Joseph *manufacturing executive, consultant*
Russell, Allen Stevenson *retired metal products executive*
Wright, Marshall *manufacturing executive, diplomat*

Marion
Harrelson, Nancy *construction and real estate development company executive*

Spartanburg
Milliken, Roger *textile and chemical company executive*

SOUTH DAKOTA

Rapid City
Lien, Chris *construction executive*
Voyles, C. Robert *electronics executive*

Sioux Falls
Christensen, David Allen *retired manufacturing executive*

TENNESSEE

Bartlett
Huffman, Delton Cleon, Jr. *pharmacy association executive*

Brentwood
Wright, James F. *agricultural products executive*

Bristol
Markison, Brian A. *pharmaceutical executive*

Collegedale
McKee, Ellsworth R. *food products executive*

Dandridge
Bowers, Timothy J. *automotive executive*

Franklin
Carolin, Brian *automotive executive*
Lankford, Monty J. *medical products executive*
White, David R. *healthcare company executive*

Kingsport
Coover, Harry Wesley *manufacturing executive*
Espeland, Curtis E. *chemicals executive*
Ferguson, J. Brian *chemicals executive*
Head, William Iverson, Sr. *retired chemical company executive*
Rogers, James P. *chemicals executive*

Knoxville
Cecil, William Thomas *health products executive, director*

Memphis
Nicholls, Tim S. *paper company executive*
Pileggi, Dominic J. *electronics executive*
Rhodes, William C. III *automotive executive*

Morristown
Comer, Evan Philip *manufacturing executive*

Nashville
Bracken, Richard M. *healthcare company executive*
Cook, E. Gary *manufacturing executive*
Frost, Richard W. *manufacturing executive*
Frost, Rick *manufacturing executive*
Harris, J(acob) George *health products executive*
Martin, Charles Neil, Jr. *health care management company executive*
Pantelides, Sokrates Theodore *research scientist*
Wire, William Shidaker, II, *retired apparel and footwear manufacturing company executive*

Oak Ridge
Deiterding, Ralf *research and development company executive*
Poutsma, Marvin L. *retired chemical research administrator*

TEXAS

Addison
Peiser, Robert Alan *turnaround executive*
Wellborn, W. Christopher *construction executive*

Angleton
Fu, Cary T. *electronics executive*

Arlington
Mc Keen, Chester M., Jr. *retired manufacturing executive*

Austin
Beyer, Richard Michael *manufacturing executive*
Derrickson, William Borden *manufacturing executive*
Gallo, A.C. *food products executive*
Lang, Roberta Lynn *food products company executive, lawyer*
Mackey, John P. *food products executive*
Sullivan, Jerry Stephen *electronics executive*
Thornton, Joseph Scott *research and development company executive, materials scientist*

Boerne
Richmond, James Ellis *retired restaurant company executive*

Carrollton
Illes, George Maximilian *retired food products executive*

Conroe
Steed, Theresa Jean *manufacturing executive*

Coppell
McCally, Charles Richard *construction company executive, consultant, mathematician, educator*

Corpus Christi
Samocha, Tzachi Matzliach *research and development company executive, director*

Dallas
Angelilli, Lawrence *construction executive*
Black, Robert W. *executive*
Bosch, Joseph A. *construction executive*
Bradford, William Edward *manufacturing executive*
Buthman, Mark A. *health products executive*
Callahan, Jack F., Jr. *food products executive*
Delagi, Greg *electronics executive*
Engles, Gregg L. *food products executive*
Ethridge, Joseph Alfred *manufacturing executive*
Falk, Thomas J. *health products executive*
George, Arthur L. *electronics executive*
Guerin, Dean Patrick *metal products executive*
Hames, Michael J. *electronics executive*
Heacock, David *electronics executive*
Hirsch, Laurence Eliot *construction executive*
Kemp, Mark D. *construction executive*
Leedom, John Nesbett *manufacturing executive, state legislator*
Lovett, Melendy *electronics executive*
Lowe, Gregg A. *electronics executive*
March, Kevin P. *electronics executive*
McElvain, David Plowman *retired manufacturing, finance company executive*
McKelvey, Gregory A. *food products executive*
Murphy, John Joseph *manufacturing executive*
Palmer, Anthony J. *health products executive*
Pearce, Ronald *retired cosmetic company executive*
Ritchie, Kevin *electronics executive*

Roach, John D. *building products company executive*
Robertson, Beverly Carruth *retired steel company executive*
Rosson, Glenn Richard *building products and furniture company executive*
Roth, James Frank *chemicals executive, chemist*
Stewart, Robert S. *construction executive*
Templeton, Richard K. *electronics executive*
Tucker, J. Walter, Jr. *manufacturing executive*
Van Scoter, John C. *electronics executive*
Wallace, Timothy R. *manufacturing executive*
Weidman, David N. *chemicals executive*
West, Teresa L. (Terri West) *electronics executive*
Whitaker, Darla *electronics executive*

Dripping Springs
Thompson, Larry Flack *nanotechnology and semiconductor process company executive*

El Paso
Czacki, Stanislas T. *manufacturing executive, consultant, retired automotive executive*

Fort Worth
Dwyer, Stacey H. *construction executive*
Horton, Donald R. *construction executive*
Tomnitz, Donald J. *construction executive*
Wheat, Bill W. *construction executive*

Georgetown
Gerding, Thomas Graham *medical products executive*

Granbury
Adams, Christopher Steve, Jr. *retired electronics executive, military officer*

Houston
Boren, William Meredith *manufacturing executive*
Byreddy, Chakradhar R. *research and development company executive*
Carroll, Chuck (Charles A. Carroll) *manufacturing executive*
Chao, Albert *chemicals executive*
Delaney, William J. III *food products executive*
DeNicola, T. Kevin *construction executive*
De Wree, Eugene Ernest *manufacturing executive*
Giadrossi, Nicoletta *manufacturing company executive*
Gonçalves, C. Lourenço *metal products executive*
Helland, George Archibald, Jr. *manufacturing executive, federal official*
Huff, Danny W. *paper products executive*
Klausmeyer, David Michael *scientific instruments manufacturing company executive*
Menscher, Barnet Gary *steel company executive*
Mozzato, Luciano *manufacturing company executive*
Munisteri, Joseph George *construction executive*
Nichols, Michael Cooper *food products executive, lawyer*
Pourgol-Mohammad, Mohammad *manufacturing executive*
Pulliam, Larry G. *food products executive*
Rickel, John C. *automotive executive*
Riedel, Alan Ellis *manufacturing executive, lawyer*
Rock, Douglas Lawrence *manufacturing executive*
Ross, R. Dale *medical products executive*
Smith, Dan F. *chemicals executive*
Spitler, Kenneth F. *food products executive*
Swift, David L. *manufacturing executive*
Usher, Thomas James *metal products executive*
Utt, William P. (Bill Utt) *construction executive*
Wilkinson, Bruce W. *construction executive*
Wilson, Carl Weldon, Jr. *construction company executive, civil engineer*
Yearwood, John *manufacturing executive*

Irving
Kling, Lewis M. *multi-industry executive*
Larson, William B. *metal products executive*
McClean, Murray R. *metal products executive*

Pasadena
Gross, Cynthia Sue *petrochemicals manufacturing executive*

Pittsburg
Cogdill, Richard A. *food products executive*
Jackson, Donald *food products executive*
Pilgrim, Lonnie (Bo Pilgrim) *food products executive*

Plano
Bain, Travis Whitsett, II, *manufacturing and retail executive*
Naor, Daniel *food products executive*

Richardson
Bluedorn, Todd M. *manufacturing executive*
Goodspeed, Linda A. *manufacturing executive*
Richards, Frederick Francis, Jr. *manufacturing executive, consultant*
Schjerven, Robert E. *retired manufacturing executive*

Rockwall
Fisher, Gene Jordan *retired chemical company executive*

San Antonio
Cisneros, Henry Gabriel *construction executive, former United States Secretary of Housing & Urban Development*
McGuire, William Dennis *healthcare consultant*
Wang, Lindsay L. *research and assessment director, principal*
Wood, Thomas Willard *retired health industry executive, retired military officer*

Seguin
Robinson, Ronald Alan *manufacturing executive*

Spring
Cox, Geoffrey F. *pharmaceutical executive*

The Woodlands
Barker, Sam L. *pharmaceutical executive*
Broussard, Bruce D. *medical products executive*
Sands, Arthur T. *biopharmaceutical executive, medical geneticist*
Stolle, Russell Robert *chemicals executive*

Waco
Bassett, Randy L. *chemicals executive, director*

Whitewright
Burg, John Parker *construction panel executive*

UTAH

Orem
Segelman, Alvin Burton *pharmaceutical executive, educator, research scientist*

Salt Lake City
Beauchamp, Christine Marie *apparel executive*
Dew, Bill *construction executive*
Esplin, J. Kimo *chemicals executive*
Frank, Thomas *construction executive, management and design executive*
Hankins, Anthony P. *chemicals executive*
Hulme, Paul G. *chemicals executive*
Huntsman, Jon Meade, Sr. *chemicals company executive*
Huntsman, Peter R. *chemicals executive*
Keenan, Thomas J. *chemicals executive*
Kern, Michael J. *chemicals executive*
Ninow, Kevin J. *chemicals executive*
Ridd, Brian V. *chemicals executive*
Stanutz, Donald J. *chemicals executive*

VERMONT

Brownsville
Olderman, Gerald *retired medical device company executive*

South Burlington
Pizzagalli, James *construction and real estate company executive*

VIRGINIA

Alexandria
Crundwell, Duncan James *electronics executive*

Arlington
Culligan, Thomas M. *electronics executive*
Franklin, Jude Eric *electronics executive*
Junker, Bobby Ray *research and development company executive, physicist*
O'Keefe, Sean Charles *manufacturing executive, former academic administrator*
Rabbitt, Linda D. *construction executive*
Wagner, Caroline S. *research and development company executive*

Bassett
Spilman, Robert Henkel *furniture company executive*

Charlottesville
Jolly, Bruce Dwight *manufacturing executive*
Wolcott, John Winthrop III *retired manufacturing executive*

Deltaville
Koedel, John Gilbert, Jr. *retired metal products executive*

Falls Church
Chabraja, Nicholas D. *equipment manufacturing executive, lawyer*
Hall, Charles M. *manufacturing executive*
Heebner, David K. *manufacturing executive, retired military officer*
Johnson, Jay L. *manufacturing executive, retired military officer*
Redd, L. Hugh *manufacturing executive*

Glen Allen
Luke, John Anderson, Jr. *paper, packaging and chemical company executive*

Herndon
Hall, John Reginald, II, *electronics company executive, retired army officer*
Ward, Jeri *automotive company executive, marketing professional*

Mc Lean
Barbiero, Victor Kelvin *health products executive, educator*
Dempsey, James Raymon *manufacturing executive*
Mars, Forrest E., Jr. *candy company executive*
Mars, John Franklyn *candy company executive*
Michaels, Paul S. *food products executive*

Mechanicsville
Bierman, James L. *health products executive*
Hinkle, Barton Leslie *retired electronics company executive*
Minor, George Gilmer III *drug and hospital supply company executive*
Smith, Craig R. *health products executive*

Powhatan
Eberle, Charles Edward *paper and consumer products executive*

Reston
Saville, Paul C. *construction executive*
Schar, Dwight C. *construction executive*

Richmond
Beran, David R. *food products executive*
Browning, Keith D. *automotive executive*
Bunzl, Rudolph Hans *retired manufacturing executive*
Folliard, Thomas J. *automotive executive*
Gottwald, Floyd Dewey, Jr. *chemicals executive, director*
Harlow, John T. *electronics company executive*
Helwig, Arthur Woods *retired chemical company executive*
Holm, George L. *food products executive*
Johnson, Craig A. *tobacco company executive*
Nelson, John Robert, Jr. *manufacturing executive*
Parrish, Steven C. *tobacco company executive*
Rohr, Mark C. *chemicals executive*
Willard, Howard A. III *food products executive*

Roanoke
Brouillard, Jack (John Charles Brouillard) *automotive parts company executive*
Freeland, Kevin Paul *automotive executive*
Jackson, Darren Richard *automotive parts company executive*
Norona, Mike *automotive parts company executive*
Wade, Jim L. (Jimmie L. Wade) *automotive executive*

Smithfield
Cole, Michael H. *food products executive, lawyer*
Luter, Joseph Williamson III *meat packing and processing company executive*
Manly, Robert W., IV, *food products executive*
Pope, C. Larry *food products executive*
Zadeh, Mansour T. *food products executive*

Williamsburg
Freeman, Rowland Godfrey III *retired manufacturing executive, military officer, consultant*

Winchester
Holland, James Tulley *retired plastics company executive*

WASHINGTON

Bellevue
Cardillo, James G. *automotive executive*
Cremin, Robert W. *manufacturing executive*
Gangl, Kenneth R. *automotive executive*
Lepore, Dawn Gould *Internet pharmaceutical company executive*
Pigott, Mark C. *automotive executive*
Plimpton, Thomas E. *automotive executive*
Tembreull, Michael A. *automotive executive*

Camano Island
Clowes, Garth Anthony *electronics executive, consultant*

Cheney
Wainwright, Paul Edward Blech *construction company executive*

Clinton
Holtby, Kenneth Fraser *retired manufacturing executive*

Coupeville
Thom, Richard David *retired electronics executive*

Edmonds
Daum, David Ernest *machinery manufacturing company executive*

Federal Way
Bedient, Patricia M. *paper company executive*
Fulton, Daniel S. *paper company executive*
Gideon, Thomas F. *paper company executive*

Gig Harbor
McClung, J(ames) David *corporate executive, lawyer, academic administrator*

Kent
Booth, Pieter *research and development company executive, consultant*
Goo, Abraham Meu Sen *retired manufacturing executive*
Hebeler, Henry Koester *retired electronics executive, aerospace engineer*

Maple Valley
Brown, Thomas Andrew *retired aircraft and weaponry manufacturing executive*

Medina
Schlotterbeck, Walter Albert *manufacturing executive, lawyer*

Mercer Island
Gould, Alvin R. *manufacturing executive*

Mill Creek
Aagard, Todd Allen *electronics company executive*

Oak Harbor
Daugherty, Kenneth Earl *research company executive, educator*

Redmond
Panke, Helmut *retired automotive executive*

Seattle
Albrecht, Richard Raymond *retired manufacturing executive, lawyer*
Denson, Nikkole E. *beverage company executive, film producer*
Holley, Rick R. *lumber company executive*
Kilpatrick, John Aaron *construction and development company executive*
Lincoln, Howard *manufacturing company and sports team executive*
Schoenfeld, Walter Edwin *manufacturing executive*
Seidl, R(obert) Bryce *museum director, former manufacturing company executive, city official*

Spokane
Siegel, Louis Pendleton *retired forest products executive*

WISCONSIN

Appleton
Boldt, Oscar Charles *construction executive, director*
Grayson, David S. *paper company executive*

Beloit
Knueppel, Henry W. *manufacturing executive*

Fitchburg
Kaus, Michael *research and development company executive*

Fort Atkinson
Jones, Alan Porter, Jr. *food manufacturing executive*

Glendale
Sterner, Frank Maurice *manufacturing executive*
Wright, Mary Ann *automotive components company executive*

Kenosha
Pinchuk, Nicholas Thomas *manufacturing executive*

Kohler
Kohler, Herbert Vollrath, Jr. *diversified manufacturing company executive*

Madison
Linton, William A., Jr. *medical products executive*
Shain, Irving *retired chemicals executive, academic administrator*

Manitowoc
Tellock, Glen E. *manufacturing executive*

Markesan
Chamberlain, Robert Glenn *retired tool manufacturing executive*

Milwaukee
Beals, Vaughn Le Roy, Jr. *retired motorcycle manufacturing executive*
Bleustein, Jeffrey L. *motorcycle company executive*
Boyd, Colin *manufacturing executive*
Colbert, Virgis W. *food products executive*
Davis, Susan F. *manufacturing executive*
Jones, Paul W. *manufacturing executive*
Josyula, Kanth V. *research and development company executive*
Koss, John Charles *consumer electronics products manufacturing company executive*
Manning, Kenneth Paul *specialty chemical company executive*
McDonald, R. Bruce *manufacturing executive*
Nosbusch, Keith D. *multi-industry high-technology company executive*
Roell, Stephen A. *manufacturing executive*
Shiely, John Stephen *manufacturing executive, lawyer*
Strayer, Jacqueline F. *manufacturing executive*
Sutherlin, Michael W. *paper company executive*
Wandell, Keith E. *motorcycle company executive*

Neenah
Theisen, Henry J. *manufacturing executive*

Oconomowoc
Peebles, Allene Kay *retired manufactured housing company executive*

Pleasant Prairie
Morrone, Frank *electronics executive*

Racine
Burke, Thomas A. *manufacturing executive*
Johnson, H(erbert) Fisk *manufacturing executive*
Konz, Gerald Keith *retired manufacturing executive*
Wambold, Richard Lawrence *manufacturing executive*

Sheboygan
Yurk, Todd Michael *retired health products executive*

South Milwaukee
Kitzke, Eugene David *research and development company executive*

Sturtevant
Johnson, S. Curtis *chemicals executive*
Lonergan, Edward F. *manufacturing executive*

Sussex
Stromberg, Gregory *printing ink company executive*

West Bend
Schaefer, Gordon Emory *food products executive*

Wisconsin Rapids
Engelhardt, LeRoy A. *retired paper company executive*

WYOMING

Wilson
Gordon, Stephen Maurice *manufacturing company executive, rancher*

TERRITORIES OF THE UNITED STATES

PUERTO RICO

Dorado
Spector, Michael Joseph *agribusiness executive*

CANADA

ALBERTA

Edmonton
Katz, Daryl A. *pharmaceutical executive, entrepreneur, professional sports team executive*

MANITOBA

Winnipeg
MacKenzie, George Allan *company director*

NEW BRUNSWICK

Fredericton
Grotterod, Knut *retired paper company executive*

NOVA SCOTIA

Stellarton
Sobey, David Frank *food company executive*

ONTARIO

Aurora
Lanthier, Ronald Ross *retired manufacturing executive*

Cambridge
White, Joseph Charles *manufacturing and retailing company executive*

Kingston
Gerson, Donald Franklin *pharmaceutical executive*

Mississauga
Dempsey, William G. *pharmaceutical executive*

Nepean
Chudobiak, Walter James *electronics executive*

Oshawa
Elias, Arturo S. *automotive executive*

Ottawa
Beare-Rogers, Joyce Louise *retired research and development executive*

Rexdale
Kraemer, Philipp *retired manufacturing company executive, inventor*

Toronto
Connell, Philip Francis *food industry executive*
Tanenbaum, Larry (Lawrence Tanenbaum) *construction executive, professional sports team executive*
Wleugel, John Peter *manufacturing executive*

QUEBEC

Montreal
Molson, Geoffrey Eric *brewery company executive*
Paterson, David J. *paper company executive*
Rolland, Lucien Gilbert *paper company executive, director*
Williams, John D. *paper company executive*

MEXICO

Garza Garcia
Zambrano, Lorenzo H. *manufacturing executive*

Mexico City
Aramburúzabála De Garza, Maria Asunción *food products executive*
Goeser, Louise K. *retired automotive executive*
Vargas Legaspi, Juan *manufacturing executive*

AUSTRALIA

Melbourne
Prescott, John Barry *resource industry executive*

Milsons Point
Foster, Milo George *manufacturing executive*

North Ryde
Selley, Michael L. *pharmaceutical company executive*

North Sydney
Dienst, Daniel W. *metal products executive*

BELGIUM

Brussels
Buysse, Paul Henri Maria *manufacturing executive*

CHINA

Beijing
Dingman, Michael David *manufacturing executive, investor*

Pudong
Wan, Zehong *research and development company executive*

Shanghai
Cheng, Mei Wei *automotive executive*

DENMARK

Bagsvaerd
Erhardtsen, Elisabeth *pharmaceutical executive*

ENGLAND

Beckenham
Lader, Malcolm Harold *pharmaceutical consultant*

Brentford
Bondy, Rupert *pharmaceutical executive, lawyer*

Cheshunt
Leahy, Sir Terry *food products executive, marketing professional*

Gloucester
Angus, Sir Michael Richardson *chemical company executive*

London
Ahrendts, Angela J. *apparel executive*
Baird, Dugald Euan *automotive executive*
Brennan, David R. *pharmaceutical executive*
Lindahl, Göran *manufacturing and engineering executive*
Mellon, Tamara *apparel executive*
Walsh, Paul S. *beverage executive*

Uxbridge
Dere, Willard Honglen *medical products executive*

Wiltshire
Dyson, Sir James *manufacturing executive, inventor*

FRANCE

Clichy
Attal, Laurent *cosmetics executive*

Lyon
Gardner, David *electronics executive*

Paris
Beffa, Jean-Louis Guy Henri *manufacturing executive*
Choay, Patrick Henri *pharmaceutical executive*
Lahrs, Claus-Dietrich *apparel executive*
Nehmé, Paul J. *beverage company executive*
Payri, Joel *pharmaceutical marketing executive*
Tribouillard, Daniel Jean Louis *fashion executive*

Suresnes
Monnet, Jacques Charles Louis *automotive executive*

GERMANY

Bad Homburg
Klatten, Susanne Quandt *pharmaceutical executive*

Düsseldorf
Schulz, Ekkehard D. *metal products executive*

Frankfurt
Maucher, Helmut Oswald *food products executive*

Herzogenaurach
Schaeffler, Maria-Elisabeth *manufacturing executive, small business owner*

Holzkirchen
George, Jeff *pharmaceutical executive*

Kunzelsau
Würth, Reinhold *manufacturing executive*

Ludwigshafen
Strube, Juergen F. *chemical company executive*

Rüsselheim
Demant, Hans Henrich *automotive executive*

Schleusingen-Gethles
Frank, Dieter *retired chemicals executive*

Stuttgart
Zetsche, Dieter *automotive executive*

GREECE

Athens
Larounis, George Philip *manufacturing executive, director*

HONG KONG

Shatin
Ding, Quan Long *research and development company executive*

ITALY

Firenze
Santiago, Claudi *manufacturing executive*

Milan
Del Vecchio, Leonardo *manufacturing executive*

JAPAN

Aichi
Toyoda, Shuhei *automotive executive*

Hamamatsu
Suzuki, Osamu *automotive executive*

Kobe
Mizukoshi, Koshi *metal products executive*

Nagoya
Nakanishi, Kiyoshi *retired automotive executive*

Osaka
Morita, Katsura *chemical company executive*

Otawara
Tatsuro, Baba *health products executive, medical educator*

Tokyo
Aihara, Hironori *electronics executive*
Hagiwara, Toshitaka *manufacturing executive*
Ichikawa, Yoshio *wood trade company executive*
Karatsu, Osamu *research and development company executive*
Mitarai, Fujio *electronics company executive*
Nomakuchi, Tamotsu *electronics executive*
Ohga, Norio *retired electronics executive*
Takenaka, Toichi *pharmaceutical executive*

Toyota
Toyoda, Eiji *automotive executive*
Toyoda, Tatsuro *automobile company executive*

NETHERLANDS

Rotterdam
Gallogly, James Lawrence (Jim Gallogly) *chemical company executive, retired oil industry executive*

Zaandam
Vuursteen, Karel *beverage industry executive*

PORTUGAL

Leiria
Vieira, Carlos Jose *construction equipment company president*

REPUBLIC OF KOREA

Incheon
Grimaldi, Michael J. *automotive executive*

Yongin
Kim, Dongwook *research and development company executive*

RUSSIA

Moscow
Gubbey, Chris *automotive executive*

SINGAPORE

Singapore
McNamara, Michael *electronics executive*

SPAIN

Madrid
Feltenstein, Harry David, Jr. *chemicals executive*

SWEDEN

Stockholm
Ax:son Johnson, Antonia Margaret *industrial, marketing and trading company executive*
Johnson, Antonia Ax:son *food products executive*

SWITZERLAND

Hinwil
Sala, Marzio Giuseppe *research and development company executive*

Hunenberg
Buehler, Kevin J. *pharmaceutical executive*

Lausanne
Camilleri, Louis Carey *tobacco company executive*
Wall, Charles R. *tobacco company executive, lawyer*

Schaffhausen
Poses, Frederic M. *manufacturing executive, former engineering company executive*

Zurich
Dewar, Brent (Walter William Brent Dewar) *automotive executive*
Stevens, Eric R. *automotive executive*

TAIWAN

Taipei
Ling, Chung-Mei *pharmaceutical executive*

TRINIDAD AND TOBAGO

San Fernando
Mahabir, Errol Edward *company executive*

UNITED ARAB EMIRATES

Dubai
Rabbat, Guy *electronics executive, consultant*

ADDRESS UNPUBLISHED

Abbas Borhan, Richat *research and development company executive*
Acerra, Michele (Mike Acerra) *engineering and construction company executive*
Aggarwal, Sanjeev *manufacturing executive, director*
Alden, Ingemar Bengt *pharmaceuticals executive*
Alexander, Judd Harris *retired paper company executive*
Allemang, Arnold A. *chemicals executive*
Alm, John Richard *beverage company executive*
Anderer, Joseph Henry *textile company executive*
Anderson, Joseph Norman *retired food products executive, academic administrator*
Anderson, Russell *research and development company executive*
Andersson, Bo I. *automotive executive*
Andersson, Craig Remington *retired chemical company executive*
Ando, Yushi *chemicals executive*
Archibald, Nolan D. *household and industrial products company executive*
Aschauer, Charles Joseph, Jr. *retired health products executive*
Atchison, Joseph Edward *pulp and paper industry consultant*
Au, Howard *manufacturing executive*
Autrey, Wesley James *construction worker*
Bainton, Donald J. *diversified manufacturing company executive*
Barca, George Gino *international winery executive, financial investor, consultant*
Batts, Warren Leighton *retired manufacturing executive*
Beck, Albert *manufacturing executive*
Bekkali, Younes *pharmaceutical executive, director*
Beracha, Barry Harris *retired food products executive*
Berkoff, Charles Edward *pharmaceutical and biotech consultant*
Bern, Dorrit J. *former apparel executive*
Bernthal, Harold George *health products executive, director*
Berry, Robert Vaughan *retired electrical manufacturing company executive*
Bestwick, Warren William *retired construction company executive*
Bevington, Edmund Milton *electrical machinery manufacturing company executive*
Bhanot, Sanjay *pharmaceutical executive, researcher*
Bikoff, J. Darius *beverage company executive*
Bishop, Charles Joseph *retired manufacturing executive*
Bishop, Kim Irene *pharmaceutical consultant, cognitive psychopharmacologist*
Blanchard, Richard Frederick *construction executive*
Blickwede, Donald Johnson *retired metal products executive*
Blumenthal, W. Michael (Werner Michael Blumenthal) *retired manufacturing company executive, former United States Secretary of the Treasury*
Bollenbacher, Herbert Kenneth *steel company official*
Bonner, David Calhoun *chemical company executive*
Bossidy, Larry (Lawrence Arthur) *pharmaceutical company and former industrial manufacturing executive*
Bowers, Richard Philip *manufacturing executive*
Brancato, Leo John *manufacturing executive*
Brandeis, Barry *retired apparel executive*
Bravo, Rose Marie *former apparel company executive, food products executive*
Brewster, Daryl G. *former food services company executive*
Britt, Ronald Leroy *retired manufacturing company executive*

Brody, Arthur *industrial executive*
Bronfman, Edgar Miles, Sr. *retired liquor company executive*
Brown, Jerry Milford *health products executive*
Browning, Peter Crane *manufacturing executive*
Bru, Abelardo E. *retired food products executive*
Bucy, J. Fred, Jr. *retired electronics company executive*
Bull, Bergen Ira *retired equipment manufacturing company executive*
Burns, Michael J. *former automotive parts company executive*
Busch, August Anheuser III *retired brewery company executive*
Busch, August Anheuser, IV, *former brewery company executive*
Bush, Norman *research and development company executive*
Calarco, Vincent Anthony *specialty chemicals company executive*
Caldwell, William Mackay, IV, *cloning and stem cell research company executive*
Campbell, James P. *manufacturing executive*
Candlish, Malcolm *manufacturing executive*
Cash, W. Larry *health products executive*
Cassidy, James Mark *construction company executive*
Castaldi, David Lawrence *health products executive*
Catling, Douglas George *product development company executive*
Chaykin, Robert Leroy *manufacturing and marketing executive*
Chen, Di *electronics executive, optical engineer, consultant*
Chen, Yue *research and development company executive, director*
Chihorek, John Paul *electronics company executive*
Chmielinski, Edward Alexander *retired electronics company executive*
Chubb, Stephen Darrow *health products executive*
Cicolani, Angelo George *research and development company executive, operating engineer*
Clark, Wesley M. *manufacturing executive*
Cook, William Alfred *medical products executive*
Cooper, Norton J. (Sky) *liquor, wine and food company executive*
Cornish, Jay (Thelbert Bernard Cornish Jr.) *research and development company executive, former internet company executive*
Correll, Alston Dayton, Jr., (Pete) *forest products company executive*
Cotting, James Charles *manufacturing executive, director*
Covalt, Robert Byron *chemicals executive*
Cox, John Francis *retired cosmetic company executive*
Coyne, Brian J(oseph) *pharmaceutical researcher*
Craft, Edmund Coleman *retired manufacturing executive*
Culwell, Charles Louis *retired manufacturing executive*
D'Andrade, Hugh A(lfred) *retired pharmaceutical company executive, lawyer*
Darrow, William Richard *retired pharmaceutical company executive, consultant*
Dattilo, Thomas A. *retired manufacturing executive*
Davis, John Ripoll *manufacturing executive*
DeMane, Michael F. *former medical products executive*
Dent, Frederick Baily *retired textiles executive, former United States Secretary of Commerce*
Derbes, Daniel William *retired manufacturing executive*
Deromedi, Roger K. *food products executive*
DiGregorio, Amanda Elizabeth *medical products executive*
Dohrmann, Russell William *retired manufacturing executive*
Dollens, Ronald W. *pharmaceutical executive*
Doyle, Irene Elizabeth *retired electronic sales executive, retired nurse*
Dragon, William, Jr. *footwear and apparel company executive*
Dressler, David Charles *retired construction materials executive*
Duclos, Laura M. *research and development company executive, director*
Durr, Robert Joseph *construction executive, mechanical engineer*
Dusevich, Vladimir M. *electronics executive, researcher*
Egloff, Fred Robert *manufacturers representative, writer, historian*
Elliott, J. Raymond *medical products executive*
Elverum, Gerard William *retired electronics and aerospace transportation executive*
Engels, Lawrence Arthur *retired metal products executive*
Evans, Barton, Jr. *retired analytical instrument company executive*
Faggin, Federico *electronics executive*
Farrell, W. James *retired metal products manufacturing company executive*
Fein, Seymour Howard *pharmaceutical executive*
Fell, Samuel Kennedy (Ken) *retired infosystems executive*
Finlay, Robert Derek *food products executive*
Fischer, Joseph L. *pharmaceutical executive*
Fitch, Robert McLellan *research and development company executive, consultant*
Flanders, Donald Hargis *manufacturing executive*
Flitcraft, Richard Kirby, II, *former chemical company executive*
Fogg, Richard Lloyd *food products executive*
Foote, William Chapin *manufacturing executive*
Frieling, Gerald Harvey, Jr. *specialty steel company executive*
Frisco, Louis Joseph *retired electronics executive, electrical engineer*
Fritz, Rene Eugene *manufacturing executive*
Garnier, Jean-Pierre *retired pharmaceutical executive*
Gassaway, William Brooks *retired manufacturing executive, writer*
Gilbert, Allan Arthur *retired manufacturing executive*
Gloyd, Lawrence Eugene *retired diversified manufacturing company executive*
Goldberg, Lee Winicki *furniture company executive*
Graham, Ginger L. *pharmaceutical executive*
Graham, Stuart Edward *construction company executive*
Graham, Wallace Karl *chemicals executive*
Gray, Richard Alexander, Jr. *retired chemical company executive*
Greenberg, Jack M. *former food products executive*
Greetham, Elizabeth M. *former health products executive*
Grove, Richard Charles *retired power tool company executive*
Gurfein, Jared L. *wine and spirits executive, lawyer*
Haas, Frederick Carl *retired paper company and chemicals executive*
Haas, Howard Green *retired bedding manufacturing company executive*
Habicht, Frank Henry *retired manufacturing executive*
Hagenlocker, Edward E. *retired automobile company executive*
Hake, Ralph F. *former appliance manufacturing executive*
Halle, Bruce T. *automotive products company executive*
Halperin, Jerome Arthur *retired pharmaceutical executive*
Harrison, Alonzo *construction executive*
Hartmann, George Herman *retired manufacturing executive*
Hayes, John Patrick *retired manufacturing company executive*
Heimbinder, Isaac *lawyer*
Heininger, S(amuel) Allen *retired chemical company executive*
Henning, George Thomas, Jr. *retired steel company executive*
Herbert, Gavin Shearer *health care products company executive*
Herzfeld, Siegfried *manufacturing executive, consultant*
Hesterberg, Earl J. *automotive executive*
Hiatt, Arnold *apparel and retail executive*
Hind, Harry William *pharmaceutical company executive*
Hirai, Kazuo (Kaz) *electronics executive*
Hirsch, Horst Eberhard *metal products executive, consultant*
Hitchcock, Frederick E., Jr., (Fritz) *automotive company executive*
Hook, Jerry B. *pharmaceutical consultant*
Houghton, James Richardson *retired manufacturing executive*
Hudson, Franklin Donald *manufacturing executive, consultant*
Hurd, Richard Nelson *pharmaceutical executive*
Hushen, John Wallace *manufacturing executive*
Hyde, Lawrence Henry, Jr. *manufacturing executive*
Ivanchenko, Lauren Margaret Dowd *pharmaceutical executive*
Ix, Robert Edward *food products executive*
Jackson, John Wyant *biotechnology company executive*
Jackson, William Elmer, Jr. *retired packaging company administrator*
Johnson, Irving Stanley *pharmaceutical executive, biomedical research consultant*
Johnston, Lawrence R. (Larry Johnston) *retired food products executive*
Johnstone, John William, Jr. *retired chemical company executive*
Jones, Christine Massey *retired furniture company executive*
Jones, Robert Henry *automotive distribution executive*
Kallay, Michael Frank, II, *medical products executive*
Karchov, Michael *electronics executive*
Kavli, Fred *retired manufacturing and engineering executive, physicist*
Keeler, James Leonard *food products executive*
Kelly, Anthony Odrian *textiles executive*
Kern, Irving John *retired food company executive*
Keyes, James Henry *retired manufacturing executive*
Khersonsky, Yuri *retired research and development company executive*
Killian, William Paul *manufacturing executive*
Kimura, Suguru Roy *pharmaceutical executive, researcher*
Kirsch, Nathan C. *retired pharmaceutical executive, consultant*
Klaehne, Eberhard O.W. *pharmaceutical executive, chemist*
Knight, Herbert Borwell *manufacturing executive*
Kogan, Richard J. *former pharmaceutical company executive*
Kohrt, Carl Fredrick *former research and development institute executive*
Kolb, Gloria Ro *medical products executive*
Krenicki, John, Jr. *manufacturing executive*
Krominga, Lynn *cosmetics executive, lawyer, director*
Kuo, Hong-Hsiang (Harry Kuo) *automotive executive, researcher*
Labrecque, Richard Joseph *retired industrial executive*
Lala, Dominick Joseph *manufacturing executive*
Lane, William W. *electronics executive*
Langbo, Arnold Gordon *retired food products company executive*
Langer, Dennis Henry *pharmaceutical company executive*
Laskey, Richard Anthony *biomedical device executive*
LeBlanc, Leonard Joseph *retired electronics company executive*
Leff, Joseph Norman *yarn manufacturing company executive*
Leveille, Gilbert Antonio *food products executive*
Lew, Roger Alan *manufacturing executive*
Lewis, Martin R. *paper company executive, consultant*
Lewis, Rita Hoffman *plastic products manufacturing company executive*
Liberati, Maria Theresa *lifestyle company executive, writer, chef*
Lippincott, Philip Edward *retired paper company executive*
Lohman, Gordon Russell *retired manufacturing executive*
Luke, David Lincoln III *retired paper company executive*
Lynch, Charles Andrew *chemicals executive*
MacAvoy, Thomas Coleman *manufacturing executive, educator*
Madden, Richard Blaine *forest products executive*
Magee, John Francis *research and development company executive*
Mahoney, Robert William *electronic and security systems manufacturing executive*
Manchester, Kenneth Edward *electronics executive, consultant*
Mangold, John Frederic *manufacturing executive, retired military officer*
Manning, William Dudley, Jr. *retired specialty chemical company executive*
Margolis, Jay M. *former apparel company executive*
Martin, Albert Charles *manufacturing executive, lawyer*
Mason, Frank Henry III *automotive and rental company executive*
Maxwell, Jerome Eugene *corporate executive*
May, Kenneth Nathaniel *retired food industry consultant*
McCurdy, Larry Wayne *automotive parts company executive*
McDonald, William Henry *venture capitalist*
McGregor, Theodore Anthony *chemical company executive*
McIlroy, Alan F. *manufacturing executive*
McKennon, Keith Robert *chemical company executive*
McKinnell, Hank (Henry A. McKinnell Jr.) *retired pharmaceutical executive*
McNamee, Lawrence Ross, Jr. *manufacturing executive*
McNitt, Willard Charles *food products executive*
Meilan, Celia *food products executive*
Mikhelashvili, Tim *pharmaceutical executive*
Miller, Harold Edward *retired manufacturing conglomerate executive, consultant*
Montero, Sylvia *former pharmaceutical executive*
Montrone, Paul Michael *former scientific instruments company executive*
Moore, John Ronald *manufacturing executive*
Moore, Malcolm Frederick *manufacturing executive*
Morcott, Southwood Jelks (Woody Morcott) *retired automotive parts company executive*
Moretti, August Joseph *pharmaceutical executive, lawyer*
Morgenstein, William *shoe company executive*
Morris, G. Ronald *automotive executive*
Morrison, Robert Scheck *former manufacturing executive, former food products executive*
Morton, James Carnes, Jr. *retired automotive executive*
Mosemann, Lloyd Kenneth, II, *retired research and development company executive*
Motheral, Brenda R. *health products executive*
Mott, Rodney B. *metal products executive*
Mueller, Robert Louis *manufacturing executive*
Navetta, Christopher J. *metal products executive*
Nelson, Glen David *health products executive, physician*
Nemirow, Arnold Myles *paper company executive*
Newman, R. Donald *retired paper company executive*
Niu, Feng *research and development company executive*
Noe, Elnora (Ellie) *retired chemicals executive*
O'Donnell, Kevin *retired metal products executive*
O'Neill, Harry William *retired research market and opinion company executive*
Ordal, Caspar Reuben *retired executive*
Osborne, Robert Stephen *automotive executive, lawyer*
Oster, Lewis Henry *manufacturing executive, industrial engineer, consultant*
O'Sullivan, Daniel John *research and development company executive*
Padilla, James Jerome (Jim Padilla) *retired automotive executive*
Parrish, Overton Burgin, Jr. *pharmaceutical corporation executive*
Pattillo, Gary A. *beverage distribution executive*
Peapples, George Alan *retired automotive executive*
Pearce, Paul Francis *retired electronics executive, aerospace engineer*
Peck, Arthur John, Jr. *retired manufacturing executive, lawyer*
Peterson, Carl Eric *metal products executive, banker*
Peterson, Robert Austin *retired manufacturing executive*
Philips, Laura Alma *former pharmaceutical executive*
Ponturo, Anthony T. (Tony Ponturo) *former brewery company executive*
Potts, Gerald Neal *manufacturing executive*
Powell, Thomas Edward III *biological supply company executive, physician*
Preston, Seymour Stotler III *chemicals executive*
Pruis, John J. *manufacturing executive*
Pure, Pamela J. *former health products executive*
Pyatt, Kedar Davis, Jr. *research and development company executive*
Pylipow, Stanley Ross *retired manufacturing company executive*
Qualls, Robert L. *manufacturing and bank executive, educator, retired state official*
Queen, James E. *automotive executive*
Rachor, Jeffrey C. *former automotive supplies company executive*
Rao, Rama Krishna R. *pharmaceutical company executive*
Ray, Jane Zimrude *retired machine shop executive*
Regelbrugge, Roger Rafael *steel company executive*
Reigel, Marissa M. *research and development company executive*
Reinhard, Joao Pedro *chemicals company executive*
Reyes, M. Jude *food products distribution executive*
Rhodes, Peter Edward *label company executive*
Richman, Peter *electronics executive*
Risdon, Michael Paul *manufacturing executive*
Risi, Louis James, Jr. *manufacturing executive*
Roesner, Peter Lowell *manufacturing executive*
Rooke, David Lee *retired chemical company executive*
Rooney, Francis (Laurence Francis Rooney III) *construction executive, former ambassador*
Roorda, John Francis, Jr. *manufacturing executive, consultant*
Rosenberg, Rudy *chemical company executive*
Ross, Dennis E. *retired automotive executive, lawyer*
Rudy, Raymond Bruce, Jr. *retired food company executive*
Rukeyser, Robert James *manufacturing executive*
Rutsky, Lester *retired textiles executive, writer*
Ryan, George William *manufacturing executive*
Rymar, Julian W. *manufacturing executive, director*
Salathe, John, Jr. *retired manufacturing executive*
Sapoff, Meyer *retired electronics executive*
Serenbetz, Robert *manufacturing executive, financial planner*
Shaheen, Gerald L. *retired manufacturing executive*
Shea, Christopher *chemicals executive, director*
Shorter, Walter Wyatt *paper company executive*
Shuster, Robert G. *electronics executive, consultant*
Siegel, Jack Morton *retired pharmaceutical executive*
Silverman, Stanley Wayne *chemical company executive*
Simeral, William Goodrich *retired chemical company executive*
Simonelli, Lorenzo *manufacturing executive*
Singh, Kunwar Pal *manufacturing executive, researcher*
Sipowicz, Sharie *pharmaceutical executive, researcher*
Sloan, Hugh Walter, Jr. *automotive executive*
Smith, Frederick Coe *retired manufacturing executive*
Smith, John Francis, Jr., (Jack Smith) *retired automotive executive*
Smith, Orin Robert *chemical company executive*
Smith, Robert Hugh *retired engineering construction company executive*
Smith, Ronald Lynn *health system executive*
Somers, Louis Robert *retired food company executive*
Song, Byung Youn *electronics executive, consultant*
Sorensen, Carl Edward *manufacturing executive*
Southerland, S. Duane *manufacturing executive*
Stadelman, William Ralph *chemicals executive*
Stavropoulos, William S. *retired chemical company executive*
Stein, Robert Alan *electronics executive*
Stern, Arthur Paul *electronics executive*
Stone, Alan John *manufacturing and real estate company executive*
Stratton, Robert *retired electronics executive*
Sui, Lei *technical leader*
Sullivan, Eugene John Joseph *manufacturing executive, director*
Sun, Wei *pharmaceutical executive, researcher*
Szydlowski, Ralph *retired metal products engineer*
Tallett, Elizabeth Edith *biopharmaceutical company executive*
Talley, Robert Morrell *aerospace company executive*
Tane, Susan Jaffe *retired manufacturing company executive*
Tannenberg, Dieter E.A. *retired manufacturing executive*
Tarrance, Vernon Lance, Jr. *research and development company executive*
Taylor, Robert Morgan *electronics executive*
Temsch, Richard *research and development company executive, consultant*
Teplow, Theodore Herzl *retired valve company executive*
Thomas, Tom *retired plastics company executive*
Thompson, Ralph Newell *former chemical corporation executive*
Thompson, Richard Leon *pharmaceutical executive, lawyer*
Thorp, Benjamin A. III *retired paper company executive*
Tobin, James Robert (Jim Tobin) *retired biomedical device manufacturing company executive*
Tollenaere, Lawrence Robert *retired industrial products company executive*
Tombros, Peter George *pharmaceutical executive*
Torbica, Zeljko Marko *construction executive, educator*
Toupin, Harold Ovid *retired chemical company executive*
Troy, Daniel E. *pharmaceutical executive, lawyer*
Tse, Charles Yung Chang *pharmaceutical executive, lawyer*
Uffelman, Malcolm Rucj *electronics executive*
Ulsh, Gordon A. *battery manufacturing company executive*
Van Houten, G. David, Jr. *beverage company executive*
Vanzura, Liz (Elizabeth K. Vanzura) *automotive executive*
Vitt, David Aaron *health products executive*
Volkhardt, John Malcolm *retired food products executive*
Wagoner, Rick (George Richard Wagoner Jr.) *former automotive executive*
Watkins, Dean Allen *electronics executive, educator*
Watts, Wendy Hazel *wine consultant*
Wavle, James Edward, Jr. *pharmaceutical company executive, lawyer*
Waxman, Allen Perry *former pharmaceutical executive, lawyer*
Weaver, William Charles *manufacturing executive*
Weiswasser, Stephen *electronics executive*
Welburn, Edward T. *automotive executive*
White, Gerald Andrew *retired chemical company executive*
White, Ralph Paul *automotive executive, consultant*
White, Tony L. *former health and medical products executive*

Wiesen, Donald Guy *retired diversified manufacturing company executive*
Wilds, Daniel O. *health products executive*
Wiley, Carl Ross *timber company executive*
Willauer, Whiting Russell *retired manufacturing executive, systems engineer*
Williams, Linda Frances *public nutrition administrator*
Wilson, James Lawrence *retired chemical company executive*
Winn, Joseph Lampher *retired electronics executive*
Witt, Hugh Ernest *manufacturing executive, consultant*
Wollert, Gerald Dale *retired food products executive, securities trader*
Wright, David L. *food and beverage company executive*
Yeager, Kurt Eric *research and development company executive*
Yontz, Kenneth Fredric *medical and chemical company executive*
Zajac, John *semiconductor equipment company executive*
Zeffren, Eugene *cosmetics executive*
Zeng, Sheng *research and development company executive*
Zhang, Shishan *researcher*

INDUSTRY: SERVICE

UNITED STATES

ALABAMA

Athens
Lafevor, Kimberly Ann *human resources specialist, educator*

Birmingham
Harris, Aaron *management consultant*
Tonkery, Dan *Internet company executive*

Decatur
Miles, Mary Ellen *retired human resources specialist*

Gadsden
Grimm, James R. (Ronald) *management consultant*

Huntsville
Ivy, Joan Carol *data processing executive*

Mobile
Hart, Eric Mullins *consumer products company executive*

Montgomery
Luna, Patricia Adele *marketing executive*

Trussville
Spahn, James Francis *marketing professional*

ALASKA

Anchorage
Porcaro, Michael Francis *advertising executive*

Fairbanks
Thompson, Daniel Emerson *vending machine service company executive*

ARIZONA

Chandler
Brunello-McCay, Rosanne *sales executive*
Powers, Ronald George *management consultant*
Williams, James Eugene *management consultant*

Flagstaff
Bolin, Richard Luddington *industrial development specialist, consultant*
Evans, Ronald Allen *lodging chain executive*

Green Valley
Ragan, James Thomas *communications executive*

Mesa
Gottry, Steven Roger *communications executive, scriptwriter*
Luth, William Clair *geochemist, retired research manager*
Murphy, Edward Francis *sales executive*

Peoria
Gould, Dorothy Mae *executive secretary, soprano*
Schindler, William Stanley *retired public relations executive*
Willis, Edward Oliver *management consultant, state agency administrator*

Phoenix
Feldberg, Harley *marketing professional*
Slager, Donald W. *waste management executive*
Zillmer, John J. *waste management administrator*

Rio Verde
Scott, Louis Edward *advertising executive*

Scottsdale
Grier, James Edward *hotel executive, lawyer*
Milanovich, Norma JoAnne *training services executive*
Quigley, Jerome Harold *management consultant*
Schleifer, Thomas C. *management consultant, author, lecturer*
Stambaugh, Armstrong A., Jr. *restaurant and hotel executive*
Strock, James Martin *author, speaker, executive educator, sustainability leadership development*
Woods, Duane C. *waste management executive*

Sun City West
Berkenkamp, Fred Julius *management consultant*
Stevens, George Richard *business consultant, public information officer*

Tempe
Laybourne, Stanley *computer technology company executive*

Tucson
Barton, Stanley Faulkner *retired management consultant*
Cooper, Corinne *communications consultant, lawyer*
Jones, Frank Wyman *management consultant, director, mechanical engineer*
Lewis, Wilbur H. *educational management consultant*
Pedersen, Arlene *web design company executive*

Williams
Calley, Tranquil Hudson *retired travel consultant, educator, counselor*

ARKANSAS

Bentonville
Ohm, Seong K. *consumer products company executive*
Quinn, Stephen F. *marketing executive*
Young, Wanda *marketing executive*

Conway
Hatcher, Joe Branch *management consultant*

Fayetteville
Kester, Cheryl L. *management consultant*

Little Rock
Gardner, Jeffrey R. *communications executive*

Magnolia
Davis, La'Tricia Danyelle *administrative assistant*

Pine Bluff
Long, Edward Arlo *management consultant, retired manufacturing executive*

CALIFORNIA

Agoura Hills
Gressak, Anthony Raymond, Jr. *sales executive*

Alameda
Blackmore, Peter *computer company executive*

Alamo
Whalen, John Sydney *management consultant*

Aliso Viejo
Blum, Scott Allen *Internet company executive*
Harder, Wendy Wetzel *communications executive*

Aptos
Trounstine, Philip John *communications consultant, online publisher*

Arcadia
Jemelian, John Nazar *management consultant*

Atherton
Baran, Paul *computer executive*

Berkeley
Klaus, Peggy Louise *consultant, communication and leadership coach*
Waters, Alice L. *executive chef, restaurant owner, writer*

Beverly Hills
Berger, Adam *Internet company executive*
Brown, Paul J. *travel company executive*
Hart, Matthew J. *hotel and recreation executive*
Hefter, Lee *chef*
Hill, Chandra *Internet company executive*
Hilton, (William) Barron *hotel executive*
Isaacs, Cheryl Boone *marketing executive, consultant*
Kozberg, Joanne Corday *public affairs consultant*
Malhotra, Neil *computer game company executive*
Marks, Howard *computer game company executive, information technology executive*
Nassetta, Christopher J. *hotel executive*

Brea
Vargas, Louis F. *marketing executive, author, speaker*

Burbank
Caouette, David Paul *public relations executive*

Camarillo
Cobb, Shirley Ann Dodson *public relations consultant, journalist*

Cambria
Morse, Richard Jay *human resources and organizational development specialist, consultant*

Carlsbad
Ritchie, Doris Lee *executive secretary*

Carmel
Smith, Gordon Paul *management consultant*

Carpinteria
Morgan, Alfred Vance *management consulting company executive*

Citrus Heights
Leisey, Donald Eugene *learning materials executive*

Corona
White, Joy Mieko *retired communications executive*

Corona Del Mar
Fabricant, Jill Diane *technology company executive*
O'Brien, John William, Jr. *management consultant*

Corte Madera
Mindel, Laurence Brisker *restauranteur*
Tate, John William *consumer products company executive, former food products executive*

Coto De Caza
Kishel, Patricia Gunter *management consultant, writer*

Culver City
Van Galder, Valerie *marketing executive*

Cupertino
Cook, Timothy D. *computer company executive*
Cooperman, Daniel *computer company executive, lawyer*
DeSouza, Francis *software company executive*
Fadell, Tony (Anthony M. Fadell) *computer company executive*
Jobs, Steve (Steven Paul Jobs) *computer company executive*
Johnson, Ron *computer company executive*
Oppenheimer, Peter *computer company executive*
Papermaster, Mark D. *computer company executive*
Schiller, Philip W. *computer company executive*

Danville
Winer, David M. *computer software company executive, software developer, blogger*

El Dorado Hills
Alexander, Candice M. *sales executive*

El Segundo
Brown, Lorraine Ann *founder, event coordinator, minister*
DeBuck, Donald G. *computer company executive*
Eckert, Robert A. *consumer products company executive*
Farr, Kevin M. *consumer products executive*
Gieselman, Jon *advertising executive*
Kilpatrick, Frank Stanton *marketing executive*
Laphen, Michael W. *computer services company executive*

Folsom
Yang, Dan *marketing executive, researcher*

Foster City
Liu, Leonard *software services company executive*
Lutvak, Mark Allen *computer company executive*
Yan, Martin *celebrity chef*

Fullerton
Sheridan, Christopher Frederick *human resources executive*

Glendale
Hughes, Bradley Wayne *storage company executive*
Reppen, Kyra E. *Internet company executive*
Stewart, Julia A. *food service executive*

Healdsburg
Keane, Douglas *chef*

Hillsborough
Westerfield, Putney *management consulting executive*

Hollywood
Batt, Anthony *Internet company executive*
Cintron, Alan *Internet company executive*
Goldman, Tyler *Internet company executive, lawyer*

Huntington Beach
Goldman, Henry Howard *management consultant*

Indian Wells
Jennings, Richard Milburn *resort developer*
Kelley, John Paul *communications consultant*

Indio
Garra, Raymond Hamilton, II, *marketing executive*

Irvine
Elsasser, Gary *computer company executive*
Karlovic, Martin Stephen *marketing executive, electrical engineer*
McGregor, Scott A. *broadband communications company executive*
Ovens, David *food service executive, marketing professional*
Seller, Gregory Erol *marketing executive, consultant, writer*
Snyder, Rick (Richard D. Snyder) *computer company executive*

Joshua Tree
Hope, Harry Joe (Joeseph) *retired corporate communications specialist, writer*

Kentfield
Edgar, James Macmillan, Jr. *management consultant*

La Habra
Chase, Cochrane *advertising agency executive*

La Jolla
Bardwick, Judith Marcia *management consultant*
Katinsky, Steven B. *communications company executive*
Vallbona, Marisa *public relations counselor*

Lake Forest
Coyne, John F. *computer company executive*
Earhart, Donald Marion *management consultant, health care company executive*

Livermore
Tripodes, James G. *nuclear safety and environmental regulatory affairs professional*
Zalk, David Mark *industrial hygienist, EHS manager occupational health researcher*

Long Beach
Brown, Roxanne (Jerene Roxanne Brown) *sales executive*
Halili, Antonio Marquez *facilities maintenance mechanic*

Los Angeles
Benson, Michael *marketing executive*
Cecere, Domenico *homebuilding company executive*
Cooper, Stephen F. *management consultant, film company executive*
Cora, Cat *chef*
Dayton, Sky *telecommunications company executive*
Dotolo, Vinny *chef*
Faber, George Donald *retired communications executive*
Feldman, Robert C. (Bob) *public relations executive*
Feniger, Susan *chef, television personality, writer*
Geoffrion, Arthur Minot *management scientist*
Giffin, Margaret Ethel (Peggy Giffin) *management consultant*
Gottfried, Ira Sidney *management consulting executive*
Hack, Bruce *computer game and music company executive*
Harris, Godfrey *public policy consultant*
Hartsough, Gayla Anne Kraetsch *management consultant*
Hateley, J. Michael *human resources executive*
Hill, Bonnie Guiton *consulting company executive*
Hull, LeAnne von Neumeyer *public relations and communications executive, research consultant, writer*
Jensen, David Gram *management consultant*
Kalis, Murray *advertising agency executive, writer*
Kline, Richard Stephen *communications and public affairs executive*
Krieger, Ellie *chef, dietitian, TV personality*
Levine, Michael *public relations executive, author, television and radio personality*
Linton, Mike *marketing executive*
Mathias, Alice Irene *business management consultant*
Messick, Andrew *marketing executive*
Milliken, Mary Sue *chef, television personality, writer*
Nadler, Gerald *management consultant, educator*
Nazarian, Sam *hotel executive, film producer*
Palevsky, Max *industrialist, director*
Provencio, Marla *marketing executive*
Quinn, Tom *communications executive*
Rong, Yue *environmental services administrator*
Schultz, Louis Michael *advertising agency executive*
Shook, Jon *chef*
Silverton, Nancy *chef*
Sitrick, Michael Steven *public relations executive*
Small, Stacy H. *luxury travel company executive, former magazine editor*
Tardio, Thomas A. *public relations executive*
Torres, Cynthia Ann *marketing professional*
White, Jennifer Elizabeth Belk *corporate training specialist*

Manhattan Beach
McQuillin, Richard Ross *management consultant*

Manteca
Talmage, Kenneth Kellogg *consumer products company executive*

Marina Del Rey
Gold, Carol Sapin *international management consultant, speaker, writer*
Jeffrey, John Orval *Internet company executive, lawyer*
Will, Peter Milne *computer and robotics research executive*

Menlo Park
Eslambolchi, Hossein *communications executive*
Lanzone, Jim *Internet company executive*
Messmer, Harold Maximilian, Jr., (Max Messmer) *consulting company executive*
Waddell, M. Keith *consulting company executive*

Mill Valley
Hargrave, Sarah Quesenberry *consulting company and training executive*

Milpitas
Harari, Eli *computer company executive*
Talwalkar, Abhi Y. (Abhijit Y. Talwalkar) *computer company executive*

Moorpark
Viviani, Fabio *chef*

Moss Beach
Glauthier, T. J. *management consultant*

Mountain View
Blackwell, Trevor *Internet company executive*
Brown, Shona L. *Internet company executive*
Campbell, William V. *computer company executive*
Cook, Scott David *computer software company executive*
Engeström, Jyri *Internet company executive*

Fried, Benjamin Cecil *Internet company executive*
Golub, Ben *Internet company executive*
Graham, Paul *Internet company executive, writer*
Hoffman, Reid *Internet company executive*
Huang, Charles *computer game company executive*
Huang, Kai *computer game company executive*
Koponen, Petteri *Internet company executive*
Lewin, Dan'l *computer software company executive*
Livingston, Jessica *Internet company executive*
Masonis, Todd *Internet company executive*
Price, Penry *advertising executive*
Qureishi, A. Salam *computer company executive*
Ring, Cameron *Internet company executive*
Smarr, Joseph *Internet company executive*
Sumner, Kelly *computer game company executive*
Tyabji, Hatim Ahmedi *computer systems company executive*
Vaillant, Jean-Luc *Internet company executive*
Weiner, Jeff *Internet company executive*

Newport Beach
Fargo, Brian *computer game company executive*
Findley, Matthew *computer game company executive*
Shonk, Albert Davenport, Jr. *advertising executive*

Newport Coast
Evanoff, George C. *retired consumer products company executive*

North Hollywood
Wadsworth, Steve *Internet company executive*

Northridge
Stark, Martin J. *international management consultant*

Novato
Doris, Robert J. *computer video company executive*
Habiger, Dave *computer video company executive*

Oak View
Tennant, John Randall *management consultant*

Oakland
Buttimer, Jessica *consumer products company executive, marketing professional*
Knauss, Donald R. *consumer products company executive*
Lebda, Douglas R. *Internet company executive*
Parker, Melissa Bernice *advertising executive*
Stetler, Russell Dearnley, Jr. *investigator*
Williams, Carol H. *advertising executive*

Oceanside
Hoff, Bernadine Ryan *management consultant*
Klaas, Nicholas Paul *management consultant*

Pacific Palisades
Humphreys, Robert Lee *advertising executive*

Palm Springs
Arnold, Stanley Norman *management consultant, educator*
Scott, Walter, Jr. *business consultant*

Palmdale
Yore, Joseph N. *communications executive*

Palo Alto
Amdahl, Gene Myron *computer company executive*
Banerjee, Prith *computer company executive, computer engineering professor*
Bianchini, Gina L. *Internet company executive*
Bocian, Peter *computer company executive*
Bradley, Todd (Richard Todd Bradley) *computer company executive*
Dillman, Linda M. *computer company executive, former retail executive*
Donatelli, David *computer company executive*
Ebersman, David A. *Internet company executive*
Flaxman, Jon E. *computer company executive*
Fruchterman, James Robert, Jr. *computer company and not-for-profit executive*
Grantham, Donald *computer company executive, former computer systems network executive*
Hurd, Mark Vincent *computer company executive*
Joshi, Vyomesh I. *computer company executive*
Lesjak, Catherine A. *computer company executive*
Livermore, Ann Martinelli *computer company executive*
Lyons, Cathy *computer company executive*
Maritz, Paul *computer software company executive*
McAniff, Richard *computer software company executive*
Mendenhall, Michael *computer company executive*
Moskovitz, Dustin Aaron *Internet company executive, entrepreneur, application developer*
Mott, Randy (Randall D. Mott) *computer company executive*
Nishar, Dipchand (Deep Nishar) *Internet company executive*
Perez de Alonso, Marcela *human resources specialist, information technology executive*
Ressi, Adeo (Adeo Gregory Ressi di Cervia) *Internet company executive*
Robison, Shane V. *computer company executive*
Sandberg, Sheryl Kara *Internet company executive*
Spohn, Nor Rae *computer company executive*
Zuckerberg, Mark Elliot *Internet company executive, entrepreneur, programmer*

Pasadena
Caine, Stephen Howard *data processing executive*
Gillespie, Harry Robinson *management consultant*
Hernandez, Enrique, Jr., (Rick Hernandez) *security firm executive*
Kaplan, Gary *executive recruiter*
O'Bryant, Daniel R. *consumer products company executive*
Steiner, Greg *Internet company executive*
Stevens, Roy W. *sales and marketing executive*
Waldorf, Gregory *Internet company executive, venture capitalist*

Warren, Neil Clark *Internet company executive, psychologist*
Watkins, John Francis *management consultant*

Piedmont
Welch, John *computer game company executive*

Pleasanton
Burd, Steven A. *food service executive*
Dietz, Diane M. *marketing executive*
Gordon, Robert Allen, Jr. *food service executive, lawyer*
Jackson, Russell M. *food service executive*
Plaisance, Melissa C. *consumer products company executive*

Pomona
Abedini, Kamran *management consultant*
Lee, Myong Jae *educator*

Rancho Mirage
Misa, Kenneth Franklin *management consultant*

Rancho Palos Verdes
Curtis, Carole Ortale *executive recruiter, consultant*
Douglass, Craig Bruce *computer technology executive*

Rancho Santa Fe
Best, Jacob Hilmer, Jr. *retired hotel chain executive*

Rancho Santa Margarita
Lawson, Thomas Cheney *marketing executive*
Parth, Frank R. *consulting company executive, educator*

Redlands
Roberts, Katharine Adair *retired bookkeeper*

Redwood City
Adelman, Barnet Reuben *management consultant*
Penner, Susanne Mary *communications executive*
Poole, Will *computer company executive*
Schappert, John Conrad *computer software company executive*
Sim, Judith *marketing executive*

Rutherford
Staglin, Garen Kent *computer services company executive, venture capitalist*

Sacramento
Franz, Jennifer Danton *public opinion and marketing researcher*
Schmidt, Steve (Stephen E. Schmidt) *public relations executive*
Swatt, Stephen Benton *communications executive, consultant*
Tract, Larry Scott *construction management consultant*

Saint Helena
Kostow, Christopher *chef*
Sone, Hiro *chef, restaurant owner, writer*

Salinas
Jeffries, Russell Morden *communications company official*

San Bernardino
Martinez, Benjamin Ray *security firm executive, public relations executive, retired military non-commissioned officer*

San Bruno
Chen, Steve Shih *Internet company executive*
Grove, Steve *Internet company executive*
Hurley, Chad Meredith *Internet company executive*

San Carlos
Eby, Michael John *marketing research and technology consultant*
Vanderryn, Jack *environmental services administrator*

San Clemente
Konney, Paul Edward *health products executive, lawyer*

San Diego
Adams, Loretta *marketing executive*
Altman, Steven *education company executive, academic administrator*
Cady, Joseph Howard *management consultant*
Comrie, Sandra Melton *human resources executive*
Gilbertson, Oswald Irving *marketing executive*
Jacobs, Irwin Mark *communications executive*
Jacobs, Paul E. *communications company executive*
Jagoda, Barry Lionel *communications executive, writer*
Lang, Linda A. *food service executive*
Larson, Mark Devin *communications executive*
Padovani, Roberto *communications executive*
Rosenberg, Donald Jay *communications company executive, lawyer*
Russo, Anthony Joseph *public relations professional*
Wertheim, Robert Halley *national security consultant*

San Francisco
Adelson, Jay Steven *Internet company executive*
Appleman, Nate *chef*
Bancel, Marilyn *fund raising management consultant*
Benioff, Marc *Internet company executive*
Bernstein, Gerald William *management consultant, researcher*
Caldwell, Dalton *Internet company executive, application developer*
Carpenter, Steven A. *Internet company executive*
Coburn, Lawrence *Internet company executive*
des Jardins, Traci *chef, restaurant owner*
Dorman, David W. *management consultant, former telecommunications industry executive*

Edelman, Brad *computer game company executive*
Figueredo, Jorge L. *human resources specialist*
Freeman, Matt *advertising executive*
Gardner, Sue *Internet company executive, journalist*
Garg, Akash *Internet company executive*
Goodby, Jeffrey *advertising agency executive*
Gossman, Bill *Internet company executive*
Gravelle, Stephanie *Internet company executive*
Hickerson, Glenn Lindsey *leasing company executive*
Jones, Stanton William *management consultant*
Kahle, Brewster *communications executive*
Kertzman, Mitchell E. *former software company executive, venture capitalist*
Kimber, Richard B. *Internet company executive*
Klammer, Joseph Francis *retired management consultant*
Kroenert, Rob *Internet company executive, marketing professional*
Kunz, Heidi *healthcare company executive*
Lindstrom, Kent J. *Internet company executive*
Mendlin, Ronald C. *employment specialist, writer*
Munson, Alexander Lee *management consultant*
Nash, Jill *communications executive*
Newmark, Craig Alexander *Internet company executive*
Pritzker, John A. *leisure services executive*
Reed, Doug *Internet company executive*
Rheingold, Ted *Internet company executive*
Saeger, Rebecca *advertising executive*
Schleier-Smith, Johann *Internet company executive*
Sharkey, Tina *Internet company executive*
Silverstein, Richard *advertising agency executive*
Spanier, Joshua *advertising agency executive, director*
Stoppelman, Jeremy *Internet company executive, entrepreneur*
Torme, Margaret Anne *public relations executive, management consultant*
Tseng, Greg *Internet company executive*
Vars, John *Internet company executive*
Wernick, Sandra Margot *meeting event planner and public relations executive*
Williams, Evan *Internet company executive*
Yalamanchi, Ramu *Internet company executive*

San Jose
Bostrom, Susan L. *marketing executive*
Calderoni, Frank A. *computer company executive*
Carges, Mark Thomas *Internet company executive*
Cobb, William C. (Bill Cobb) *Internet company executive*
Donahoe, John Joseph, II, *Internet company executive*
Elfrink, Wim *computer company executive*
Justice, Richard J. *computer company executive*
Liu, Derek *Internet company executive*
Lynch, Kevin *computer software company executive, application developer*
Malloy, Tom *computer company executive*
Norrington, Lorrie M. *Internet company executive*
Omidyar, Pierre M. *Internet company executive*
Pond, Randy *computer company executive*
Roelandts, Willem P. *data processing executive*
Sherman, Craig *Internet company executive*
Silverman, Josh *communications executive*
Swan, Robert H. *Internet company executive*
Wallace, Richard P. *computer company executive*
Warnock, John Edward *computer company executive*
Yang, Stanley *computer company executive*

San Marcos
Barnes, Howard G. *communications executive, film producer*

San Mateo
Helfert, Erich Anton *management consultant, writer, educator*
Sisson, Kathy B. *chef*
Tobisawa, Hiroshi *computer game company executive*
Tsujimoto, Kenzo *computer game company executive*
Zander, Edward J. *retired communications executive*

San Pedro
Gaines, Frank, Jr. *retired management consultant*

San Rafael
Bass, Carl *computer software company executive*
Finkelstein, James Arthur *management consultant*
Hinners, Billy *computer software company executive*

San Ramon
Laymon, Joe W. *human resources specialist*

Santa Ana
Tanaka, Richard I. *computer company executive*
Torrez, Caroline Herminia *human resources specialist, director, actress, musician, singer, dancer*

Santa Barbara
Schultz, Arthur Warren *retired communications executive*

Santa Clara
Baker, Robert J. *computer company executive*
Bhagat, Nancy *marketing executive*
Bray, Tim(othy) (William) *computer company executive, software developer*
Bryant, Andy D. *computer company executive*
Culbertson, Leslie S. *computer company executive*
Halloran, Jean M. *human resources specialist*
Holt, William M. *computer company executive*
Li, Lihong *Internet company researcher*
Lin, Frank C. *computer company executive*
Perlmutter, David (Dadi) *computer company executive*
Scott, Edward William, Jr. *retired computer company executive & philanthropist*
Smith, Stacy J. *computer company executive*
Sodhani, Arvind *computer company executive*

Santa Monica
Blankley, Tony *public relations executive, columnist, radio personality*
Constan, Sandy *marketing and advertising executive*
Griffith, Huw *advertising executive*
Hirschhorn, Jason *Internet company executive*
Jones, Michael *Internet company executive*
Kelly, Brian *computer game company executive, accountant, lawyer*
Ovitz, Michael S. *communications executive*
Patel, Chandra Kumar Naranbhai *communications executive, educator, entrepreneur, researcher*
Tinsley, Jeffrey *Internet company executive*
Van Natta, Owen Thomas *Internet company executive*

Saratoga
Syvertson, Clarence Alfred *management consultant, engineer*

Scotts Valley
Crandell, Kenneth James *management consultant, entrepreneur*
Luczo, Stephen James *computer hardware company executive*

Sherman Oaks
Merritt, Jean *consulting firm executive, psychotherapist*
Yasnyi, Allan David *communications company executive*

Soquel
Tomash, Erwin *retired computer company executive*

South Pasadena
Echeveste, John Anthony *public relations consultant*

Stanford
Allen, Richard Vincent *international business consultant, former national security advisor*
Baumard, Philippe Nicolas *strategic management educator*

Stockton
Hackley, Carol Ann *public relations educator, consultant*

Studio City
Laba, Marvin *management consultant*
La Cava, Donald Leon *communications executive*
Silverman, Bruce Gary *advertising executive, consultant*

Sun Valley
Miller, Flemon Marshall *public works manager*

Sunnyvale
Baldwin, Penny *Internet company executive, marketing professional*
Bartz, Carol Ann *Internet company executive*
Bradford, Joanne K. *Internet company executive*
Butterfield, Stewart *Internet company executive*
Claflin, Bruce L. *software company executive*
Fake, Caterina *Internet company executive*
Filo, David *Internet company executive*
Flaherty, Lauren Patricia *marketing executive*
Morse, Timothy R. *Internet company executive*
Ratchev, Boris A. *high technology executive*
Rubinstein, Jonathan J. *communications executive, former computer company executive*
Sartain, Libby *Internet company executive*
Schneider, Hilary A. *Internet company executive*
Steele, Elisa Anne *Internet company executive, marketing professional*

Sutter Creek
Sanders, Elizabeth Anne Weaver (Betsy Sanders) *management consultant, coach, writer*

Tarzana
Lantz, Kenneth Eugene *consulting firm executive*

Tehachapi
Smith-Thompson, Patricia Ann *public relations consultant, educator*

Thousand Oaks
Fulton, Michael L. *optical company executive, researcher*

Torrance
Sugra, Cynthia Mariel *marketing executive*

Tracy
Kiggins, Mildred L. *marketing professional*

Universal City
Kay, Christopher K. *travel company executive, lawyer*

Vallejo
Davis, William Albert *parks director*

Ventura
Bierly, Shirley Adelaide *communications executive*

Victorville
Yochem, Barbara June (Runyan) *sales executive, lecturer*

Villa Park
Britton, Thomas Warren, Jr. *retired management consultant*

Walnut
Johnson, Keith Liddell *management consultant, retired chemicals executive*

Walnut Creek
Henshaw, Guy Runals *management consultant*

West Hollywood
Braverman, Alan Michael *Internet company executive*
Sacks, David O. *Internet company executive, film production company executive*

Westlake Village
Berkowitz, Steven *Internet company executive*
Long, W. Michael *Internet company executive*
Power, J.D., III, (James David Power III) *marketing executive*
Smyth, Glen Miller *management consultant*
Troxell, Lucy Davis *management consultant*

Woodland Hills
Ennis, Thomas Michael *management consultant*
Goldston, Mark R. *Internet company executive*
McArthur, Steven B. *Internet company executive*
Morishita, Akihiko *trading company executive*

Yountville
Keller, Thomas A. *chef*

COLORADO

Aurora
Ritchie, Coy Doyle *management consultant*

Boulder
Burns, Daniel Hobart *management consultant*
Collins, Jim *management researcher, author*
Langer, Steven *human resources specialist, consultant, psychologist*

Broomfield
Berte, Lucia Marie *quality management professional, consultant*
Crowe, James Quell (Jim) *communications executive*
Hobbs, John Neil *communications executive*

Colorado Springs
Sciorsci, Adam Q. *sales executive*
Yanney, Patrick Steven *human resources specialist*

Denver
Anderson, William (Albion), Jr. *management consultant*
Blatter, Frank Edward *travel company executive*
Crystal, Darren *Internet company executive, application developer*
Dunham, Joan Roberts *administrative assistant*
Euteneuer, Joseph John *communications executive*
Goebel, Karey Lyn *marketing professional, director*
Johnston, Gwinavere Adams *public relations consultant*
Karsh, Philip Howard *retired advertising executive*
LaMendola, Walter Franklin *technology business executive, educator*
Meister, Ryan Edward *marketing executive*
Myhren, Trygve Edward *communications company executive*
Osberg, Gregory John *mobile video company executive, former publishing executive*
Purcell, Scott *Internet company executive, publishing executive*
Welch, Alex *Internet company executive, application developer*
Woodward, Jackie *marketing professional*

Durango
Foster, James Henry *advertising and public relations executive*

Englewood
Barnes, David G. *data processing company executive*
Bracken, Charles H.R. *communications executive*
Case, Paul Watson, Jr. *communications executive*
Dvorak, Bernard G. *communications executive*
Fries, Michael T. *communications executive*
Gold, Christina A. *data processing company executive*
Han, Bernard L. *communications executive*
Maffei, Gregory B. *media company executive, former computer software company executive*
Malone, John C. *media company executive*
Stockdale, Stewart A. *data processing company executive*

Golden
Olson, Marian Katherine *management consultant*

Greeley
Miller, Diane Wilmarth *retired human resources director*

Greenwood Village
Benson, Robert Craig III *business consultant*

Lakewood
Martinen, John A. *travel company executive*

Littleton
Ergen, Charles W. (Charlie Ergen) *communications executive*
Kullas, Albert John *management consultant, systems engineer*

Longmont
Newman, Dean Gordon *community volunteer*

Morrison
Lutsky, Sheldon Jay *financial and marketing consultant, writer*

Sedalia
Cooley, Andrew Lyman *computer company executive*

Snowmass Village
Strand, Curt Robert *hotel executive*

CONNECTICUT

Bloomfield
Tortorello, Nicholas John *public opinion and market research company executive*

Cos Cob
Murphy, R. Blair *management consulting company executive*

Cromwell
Izzo, Lucille Anne *sales representative*

Danbury
Mann, Richard O. *public relations consulting company executive*

Darien
McKim, Paul Arthur *management consultant, retired gas industry executive*

Fairfield
Hamilton, Gretchen Worley *retired public relations executive, management consultant*
Henson, Daniel S. *marketing executive*
Luther, David Byron *management consultant*
Lynch, John F. *human resources specialist*
Orris-Modugno, Michele Marie *public relations, marketing and advertising consultant*
Peters, Susan P. *human resources specialist*

Farmington
Trani, John M. *former consumer products company executive*

Greenwich
Ball, John Fleming *advertising and film company executive*
Bara, Jean Marc *finance and communications executive, artist*
Carmichael, William Daniel *management consultant, educator*
Henkelmann, Thomas *chef*
Kessler, Murray S. *consumer products company executive*
Kneeland, Michael J. *rental company executive*
Kucic, Joseph Banrer *banker, management consultant, industrial engineer, network engineer, information security specialist*
Paulson, Paul Joseph *advertising executive*
Perless, Ellen *advertising executive*
Plummer, William B. *rental company executive, former publishing executive*
Srere, Benson M(ortimer) *communications executive, consultant*
Wyman, Ralph Mark *multifamily office firm executive*

Kent
Friedman, Frances *public relations executive*

New Britain
Lundgren, John F. *consumer products company executive*

New Canaan
Crossman, William Whittard *retired wire cable and communications executive*
Grace, Julianne Alice *retired investor relations executive*
White, Richard Booth *management consultant*

New Haven
Huwiler, Joan P. *public relations executive, consultant*

Newtown
Cole, Richard John *marketing executive*

Norwalk
Gold, Richard N. *management consultant*
Nightingale, William Joslyn *management consultant*
Yeosock, Michael Michael *funeral director, civil engineer*
Zimmerman, Lawrence A. *printing company executive*

Old Saybrook
Norcia, Stephen William *advertising executive*
Phillips, William E. *advertising agency executive*

Redding
Kobak, James Benedict *management consultant*

Riverside
Geismar, Richard Lee *communications executive*

Salisbury
Dresser, James van Benschoten *retired management consultant*

Sandy Hook
Rosenblatt, Stephen Paul *marketing and sales promotion company executive*

Southbury
Welton, Sharon Marie *food service executive*

Stamford
Burns, Ursula M. *copier company executive*
Burston, Richard Mervin *marketing executive*
Burton, Robert Gene *printing company executive*
Dell, Warren Frank, II, *management consultant*
Dolan, Thomas J. *printing company executive*
Fernandez, Manual A. *information technology consulting executive*
Firestone, James A. *printing company executive*
Mac Donald, Michael C. *printing company executive*
Martin, John K. *communications executive*
Mulcahy, Anne Marie *copier company executive*
Nazemetz, Patricia M. *printing company executive*
Pappas, Alceste Thetis *consulting company executive, educator*
Thompson, Fred *public relations executive, former medical association administrator*
Vandebroek, Sophie Verdonckt *printing company executive*
Walker, Jay Scott *media company executive*

Stratford
Linder, Anthony *marketing executive*

Waterbury
Carrington, Virginia Gail (Vee) *marketing professional, consultant*
Swiech, Alan M. *human relations executive*

West Hartford
Glasser, Joseph *management consultant, educator*

Weston
Falber, Harold Julius *marketing professional*
Murray, Thomas J. *advertising executive*

Westport
Blau, Barry *marketing professional, financial consultant*
Lewis, Margaret Mary *marketing professional*

Willimantic
Mitchell, Homer *marketing executive*

Wilton
Nickel, Albert George *advertising agency executive*
Pethley, Lowell Sherman *retired management consultant*

Woodbridge
Alvine, Robert *industrialist, entrepreneur, world business leader, philanthropist, business owner*

Woodbury
Feskoe, Gaffney Jon *management consultant*

DELAWARE

Greenville
DeWees, Donald Charles *security firm executive*

Newark
Aristigueta, Maria Pilar *public relations executive, educator*

Wilmington
Bloom, David Andrew *communications operations director*
Fisher, Linda J. *consumer products company executive, former federal agency administrator*
Freeh, Louis Joseph *consulting firm executive, former FBI director*
Peterson, Russell Wilbur *environmental services administrator, Former Governor, Del*
Shipley, Samuel Lynn *advertising and public relations executive*
Weisenfeld, Carol Ann Trimble *marketing executive, consultant*

DISTRICT OF COLUMBIA

Washington
Abraham, Spencer (Edward Spencer Abraham) *consulting company executive, former United States Secretary of Energy*
Albright, Madeleine Korbel *consulting firm executive, political science professor, former United States Secretary of State*
Allbaugh, Joe M. (Joseph Marvin Allbaugh) *consulting firm executive, former federal agency administrator*
Andrés, José *chef*
Baer, Donald Aaron *public relations executive*
Beckström, Rod Allen *internet security company executive, former federal agency administrator*
Berger, Sandy (Samuel Richard Berger) *financial consulting firm executive, former national security advisor*
Boorstin, Robert Olsan *Internet company executive, political consultant*
Brown, Michael DeWayne *consulting firm executive, former federal agency administrator*
Chertoff, Michael *consulting firm executive, lawyer, former United States Secretary of Homeland Security*
Clifton, James K. (Jim Clifton) *consulting company executive*
Cogman, Don V. *public relations executive*
Cohen, William Sebastian *consultant, former United States Secretary of Defense*
Collender, Stanley E. *communications executive, columnist*
Comerford, Cristeta *chef*
Compton, Mary Beatrice Brown *public relations executive, writer*
Cook, Frances D. *management consultant*
Corso, John Anthony *management consultant, educator*
Dawson, Mimi Weyforth *public policy consultant*
Dean, Robert J. *funeral director*
Dezenhall, Eric B. *management consultant, writer*
Downey, Mortimer Leo III *consulting firm executive, former transportation executive*
Drapeau, Mark David *defense contractor*
Eskew, Carter *public relations executive*
Fanning, Fred Eldridge *public administrator*
Farrow, Elizabeth Oliver *public and government relations consultant*
Feldman, Michael *public relations executive*
Fields, Stuart Howard *labor relations specialist*
Fishel, Andrew S. *managing director*
Ford, Carl W., Jr. *consulting firm executive, former federal agency administrator*
Fuller, Edwin Daniel *hotel executive*
Gordon, David F. *consulting firm executive, former federal agency administrator*
Grant, Carl N. *communications and sales executive*
Gray, William Herbert III *consulting firm executive, Former United States Representative, Pennsylvania*
Greenspan, Alan *consulting firm executive, former Chairman of the Board of Governors of the Federal Reserve System*
Griffin, Kelly Ann *public relations executive, consultant*
Grigsby Queen, Sharlyn Ann *human resources specialist*
Harrington, Anthony Stephen *consulting firm executive, former ambassador*
Hasselmo, Ann Hayes Die *executive recruiter, psychologist, academic administrator, consultant, educator*
Helm, Lewis Marshall *communications executive*
Higgins, James Henry III *marketing executive*
Howard, Jack *industrial relations specialist, consultant*
Howe, Fisher *management consultant, retired foreign service officer*
Ickes, Harold McEwen *public relations executive, former federal official*
Jones, A. Elizabeth *corporate communications specialist, former federal agency administrator*
Jones, Brian (William Brian Jones) *public affairs executive*
Kaludis, George *management consultant, publishing executive, educator*
Killefer, Nancy *consulting firm executive, former federal agency administrator*
Krump, Gary Joseph *marketing executive, lawyer, judge*
Lackey, Gerald Francis *management consultant*
Leibach, Dale William *government relations and public affairs executive*
Lindemann, Adam *communications executive*
Lockhart, Joe (Joseph P. Lockhart) *public relations firm executive, former White House press secretary*
Lubic, Benita Joan Alk *travel company executive*
Ludwig, Eugene Allan *financial consulting firm executive*
Mansfield, Edward Patrick, Jr. *advertising executive*
Marriott, John W. III *hotel executive*
Marriott, John Willard, Jr. *lodging and senior living executive*
McBride, Jonathan Evans *governance consultant, director*
McClellan, Scott *consulting company executive, former White House press secretary*
McCue, Susan M. *communications executive*
McLarty, Mack (Thomas F. McLarty III) *leasing company executive, former White House chief of staff*
McQuillan, Laurence Joseph *communications consultant, educator*
Mederos, Carolina Luisa *public policy consultant*
Melton, Carol A. *communications executive*
Mineta, Norman Yoshio *consulting firm executive, former United States Secretary of Commerce and Transportation*
Moore, Bob Stahly *communications executive*
Nason, David George *financial consulting firm executive, former federal agency administrator*
Nelson, Terry A. *public relations executive*
O'Connor, Tom *corporate executive, management consultant*
Pals, Tony Mitchel *public relations executive, director*
Palumbo, Benjamin Lewis *public relations executive, consultant*
Papuchis, Matthew J. *communications executive, journalist*
Payne, Lewis Franklin, Jr., (L.F. Payne) *management consultant, former congressman*
Pearson, Christina H. *public relations executive, former federal agency administrator*
Perino, Dana Marie *public relations executive, former White House press secretary*
Pines, Wayne Lloyd *public relations executive, author*
Prince, Charles O., III, (Chuck Prince) *financial consulting firm executive, retired diversified financial services company executive*
Pyle, Robert Noble *public relations executive*
Raymond, David Alan *business executive, former government official*
Reed, Travis Dean *public relations executive*
Rice, Lois Dickson *retired computer company executive*
Ridge, Tom (Thomas Joseph Ridge) *consulting company executive, former United States Secretary of Homeland Security*
Rose, George Andrew *Internet information systems specialist*
Rothkopf, David Jochanan *consulting firm executive, former federal agency administrator*
Rotunda, Donald Theodore *public relations consultant*
Seats, Peggy Chisolm *public affairs executive*
Shapiro, Robert Jacob *economic advisory firm executive*
Shear, Natalie Pickus *conference and event management executive*
Sherman, Wendy Ruth *consulting firm executive, former federal agency administrator*
Skol, Michael *counter-money laundering consultant*
Smith, Dean *communications advisor, arbitrator*
Smith, Esther Thomas *communications executive*
Sullivan, James M. *hotel executive*
Tate, Sheila Burke *public relations executive*
Terzian, Grace Paine *communications executive*
Timmons, William Evan *retired consulting firm executive*
Vandaele, Bart *chef*
Ventimiglia, Vincent J., Jr. *consulting firm executive, former federal agency administrator*
Vickery, Raymond Ezekiel, Jr. *international business consultant, lawyer*
Villarreal, June Patricia *retired sales executive*
Walcott, John L. *communications executive*
Weaver, John *political strategist*

Williams, Steven A., Jr. *environmental services administrator, former federal agency administrator*
Witt, James Lee *management consultant, former federal agency administrator*

FLORIDA

Amelia Island
Freeman, Neal Blackwell *communications corporation executive*

Arcadia
Spangler, Colleen Ann *marketing professional*
White, Will Walter III *public relations consultant, writer*

Aventura
Schwartz, Gerald *public relations and fundraising agency executive*

Bascom
Hart, James Whitfield, Jr. *retired public relations executive, lawyer*

Boca Raton
Brown, Charles E. *consumer products company executive*
Dorfman, Allen Bernard *international management consultant*
Dunhill, Robert *advertising executive*
Ellis, Martin F. *computer company executive*
Langbort, Polly *retired advertising executive*
Luechtefeld, Monica *consumer products company executive*
Odland, Steve *consumer products company executive*
Rubin, Chuck (Carl Rubin) *consumer products company executive*
Vanderlinde, Daisy *consumer products company executive*
Yoder, Patricia Doherty *public relations executive*

Bonita Springs
Gillis, James R. *consumer products company executive*
Tuchman, Alan *consumer products company executive*

Bradenton
Seavers, Dean S. *security firm executive*

Casselberry
Pantuso, Vincent Joseph *food service consultant*

Clearwater
Baker-Bowens, Helen L. *administrative assistant, genealogy researcher*
Dutkowsky, Robert M. *computer company executive*
Howells, Jeffrey P. *computer company executive*
Raymund, Steven A. *computer company executive*

Coconut Grove
Softness, John *public relations executive*

Coral Gables
Cole, Todd Godwin *management consultant transportation*
Gould, Taffy *Internet company executive, real estate executive*
Hertz, Arthur Herman *communications executive*
Lomonosoff, James Marc *marketing professional*
Miville, Nina DeCario *management consultant, educator*

Delray Beach
Charyk, Joseph Vincent *retired satellite telecommunications executive*
Ehrlich, Geraldine Elizabeth *management consultant*
Hardiman, Joseph Raymond *security firm executive*

Eustis
King, Robert Howard *marketing professional*

Fernandina Beach
Britt, David Van Buren *retired educational communications executive*

Fort Lauderdale
Cantwell, John Walsh *advertising executive*
Carroll, Chris *marketing executive*
Fine, Howard Alan *management consultant*
Hinson, Robert William *advertising executive, consultant*
Jotcham, Thomas Denis *marketing communications consultant*
Kjellmark, Eric William, Jr. *management consultant, performing company executive*
Krause, Roy G. *office staffing firm executive*
O'Connor, James E. *waste management executive*

Fort Myers
Blanchard, Richard Emile, Sr. *retired management services executive, consultant*
Goyak, Elizabeth Fairbairn *retired public relations executive*
Taylor, Kenneth Brooks *retired marketing executive*

Gainesville
Puckett, Ruby Parker *food service executive, writer, dietician*

Hallandale Beach
Duffy, Earl Gavin *hotel executive*

Highland Beach
Upbin, Hal J. *consumer products company executive*

Hollywood
Sundel, Martin *management consultant, psychologist, educator*

Hypoluxo
DeBow, Jay Howard Camden *public relations executive*

Jacksonville
Craft, Mary Faye *public relations executive, consultant, television producer*

Jacksonville Beach
Saltzman, Irene Cameron *consumer products company executive*

Juno Beach
Nelson, Bruce (Murray Bruce Nelson) *former consumer products company executive*

Jupiter
Baum, Herbert Merrill *consumer products company executive*
Eskandarian, Edward *advertising executive*
Gerson, Irwin Conrad *advertising executive*

Key Biscayne
Cardozo, Richard Nunez *marketing professional, educator, entrepreneur*
Evans, Peter Kenneth *advertising executive*

Lake Buena Vista
Biggar, Jim (James Biggar) *hotel executive*
Garfield, Randy Alan *marketing executive*

Lake City
Irwin, Byron *management executive*

Lake Worth
Saffir, Leonard *public relations executive*

Lakeland
Jenkins, Howard M. *supermarket executive*
Meads, Walter Frederick *communications executive, consultant, writer*
Phillips, David P. *grocery company executive*

Largo
Stover, Brian Allan *advertising executive, marketing professional*

Longwood
Bernabei, Raymond *management consultant*

Lutz
Miller, Bonnie Sewell *marketing professional, writer*

Marco Island
Kelly, Robert Donald *management consultant*

Melbourne
Koenig, Harold Paul *management consultant, ecologist, evangelist, writer*
Lance, Howard L. *communications executive, industrial engineer*

Miami
Amos, Betty Giles *food service executive, accountant*
Arison, Micky *cruise line company executive, professional sports team owner*
Bogusky, Alex *advertising executive*
Chidsey, John W. *food service executive*
Ehrlich, Morton *marketing executive, management consultant*
Gonzalez, Eddie *advertising executive*
Klein, Russell B. *fast food company executive, marketing professional*
Kosel, Tiffany *advertising executive*
Neuman, Susan Catherine *public relations and marketing consultant*
Omohundro, William Addison *research marketing executive*
Porter, Charles King *advertising executive*
Schriesheim, Chester Arthur *management educator*
Sherman, Beatrice Ettinger *hotel executive*
Vasquez, Jennifer *marketing and public relations executive, researcher*

Miami Beach
Todd, Christopher Michael *marketing executive, consultant*

Mount Dora
Hensinger, Margaret Elizabeth *real estate, horticultural and agricultural advertising and marketing executive*

Naples
Berman, Robert S. *marketing consultant*
Gilman, John Richard, Jr. *retired management consultant, sculptor*
Kozitka, Richard Eugene *retired consumer products company executive*
Meyers, Christine Laine *marketing and media executive, consultant*
Synnott, William Raymond *retired management consultant*

North Miami
Martinez, Raul L. *public relations executive*

Ocala
Sostilio, Robert Francis *office equipment marketing consultant*

Oldsmar
Brunner, George Matthew *management consultant, retired manufacturing executive*

Orlando
Brouillard, Robert Paul *maintenance planning manager*
Dawson, Leslie Naryne *quality assurance professional*
Goings, Everett Vernon (Rick) *consumer products company executive*
Madsen, Andrew H. (Drew Madsen) *food service executive*
Otis, Clarence, Jr. *restaurant executive*
Williams, Thomas L. *recreational facility executive*
Yesawich, Peter Charles *advertising executive*

Osprey
Dyche, David Bennett, Jr. *management consultant*

Palm Beach
Fisher, Fenimore *business development consultant*
Flanagan, Joseph Patrick *advertising executive*
Rumbough, Stanley Maddox, Jr. *industrialist*
Tiefel, William Reginald *hotel company executive*

Palm Beach Gardens
Mendelson, Richard Donald *former communications company executive*

Ponte Vedra Beach
Leek, Jay Wilbur *management consultant*
Linnen, Thomas Francis *international strategic management consulting executive*

Port Charlotte
Reynolds, Helen Elizabeth *management consultant*

Saint Petersburg
Davis, Christopher J. *management consultant, educator*
Engel, John Jacob *communications executive*

Sarasota
Beck, Robert Alfred *hotel executive, educator*
Fendrick, Alan Burton *advertising consultant*
Honner Sutherland, B. Joan *advertising executive*
Huppe, Alex *public relations executive*
Landis, Edgar David *business consultant*
Mattran, Donald Albert *management consultant, educator*
Schlegel, John Frederick *management consultant, personal trainer*
Shulman, Arthur *communications executive*
Stickler, Daniel Lee *health care management consultant*

Seminole
Evans, Thomas Passmore *management consultant*

Sunny Isles Beach
Edelcup, Norman Scott *management and financial consultant*

Tallahassee
Nasser, Joseph Yousef *public safety administrator, consultant*
Spooner, Donna *management consultant*

Tampa
Ferree, Patricia Ann *quality assurance professional*
Studer, William Allen *security consultant, retired military officer*

Tarpon Springs
Crismond, Linda Fry *public relations executive*

Titusville
Stewart, David Witherington *business consultant*

Venice
Bluhm, Barbara Jean *communications agency executive*
Dodderidge, Richard William *retired marketing executive*

Vero Beach
Fisher, Andrew *retired management consultant*
Leonsis, Ted *media and professional sports team executive*
McNamara, John J(oseph) *advertising executive, writer*
Spivak, Alvin A. *retired public relations executive*

West Palm Beach
Ronan, William John *management consultant*

Weston
Gómez Martinez, Juan Carlos *senior executive and consultant*

Winter Haven
Cover, Norman Bernard *retired electronic data processing administrator*

Winter Park
Leslie, John William *public relations and advertising executive*

GEORGIA

Alpharetta
Winegar, Albert Lee *computer company executive*

Athens
Golembiewski, Robert Thomas *management consultant, educator*

Atlanta
Bayne, Katie J. (Katherine J. Bayne) *marketing executive*
Bifulco, Frank P. *marketing executive*
Blake, Frank (Francis Stanton Blake) *consumer products company executive, lawyer*
Bremer, Karen Ingrid *food service executive*
Carey, Matthew *consumer products company executive*
Chasen, Sylvan Herbert *data processing executive, financial planner*
Clark, Wendy *advertising executive*
Costello, John H. III *business and marketing executive*
Crow, Tim *consumer products company executive*
Crump-Caine, Lynn *management consultant, former food service executive*
Daley, Sharon R. *human resources specialist*
Darden, Claibourne Henry, Jr. *marketing research professional*
Davis, Stephen H. *food service executive, marketing professional*
DeAngelo, Joseph J. *consumer products company executive*
Deason, Stephen Earl *computer company executive*
Dobrzyn, Janet Elaine *quality assurance professional*
Flanders, Karen *consumer products company executive*
Forte, Judy *parks director*
Gephardt, Dick (Richard Andrew Gephardt) *consulting company executive, former United States Representative from Missouri, lawyer*
Gordon, Helen Tate *program assistant, nurse*
Harrison, Clifford *chef, small business owner*
Holly, Timothy Arnold *security firm executive*
Hopkins, Linton *chef*
Hussey, Kent J. *consumer products company executive*
Johnson, F. Ross (Frederick Ross Johnson) *international management advisory company executive*
Ketchum, Mark D. *consumer products company executive*
Levy, David Ruben *advertising and broadcasting executive*
Lunsford, Mike (Michael Cameron Lunsford) *Internet company executive*
Marohn, William D. *consumer products company executive*
Massey, Charles Knox, Jr. *advertising agency executive*
Parker, Dan *human resources executive*
Quatrano, Anne *chef, restaurant owner*
Raper, Charles Albert *retired management consultant*
Robinson, J. Patrick *consumer products company executive*
Schoen, Scott Alan *corporate executive*
Schulze, Horst H. *hotel company executive*
Smith, Joanne *marketing executive*
Smith, Roland C. *food service company executive*
Stormont, Richard Mansfield *hotel executive*
Suciu, James N. *sales executive*
Tomé, Carol Buchenroth *consumer home products company executive*
Verrill, F. Glenn *advertising executive*
Wald, Michael Leonard *public relations executive*
Winograd, Audrey Lesser *retired advertising executive*
Young, Andrew Jackson, Jr. *consulting firm executive, former mayor, former United States Representative from Georgia*

Brunswick
Fowler, Mary A. *administrative assistant*

Buford
Jondahl, Terri Elise *supply chain management, distribution and manufacturing executive*

Carrollton
Kelley, Patricia *marketing representative*

Clarkesville
Dowden, Thomas Clark *telecommunication executive*

Decatur
Barnett, Rebecca Lynn *communications executive*
Terry, Elizabeth Hudson *personal care industry executive, realtor*

Duluth
Reed, Ralph Eugene, Jr. *political consultant, former political organization administrator*

Franklin Springs
Benson, Jennifer Lester *communications executive*

Griffin
Marshall, Allen Wright III *communications executive, financial consultant*

Marietta
McKenzie, Kay Branch *public relations executive*
Smith, Baker Armstrong *management executive, lawyer*
Spann, George William *management consultant*
Wenk, Michael Scott *environmental services administrator*

Milton
Tomaszewski, Richard Paul *market representation executive*

Norcross
Chell, Beverly C. *retired media company executive, lawyer*
Cramer, James Perry *management strategist, author, educator*
Metz, Robert C. *media company executive*

Pine Mountain
Callaway, Howard Hollis *resort executive, former congressman*

Roswell
Hill, Donald Dee *management consultant, educator, writer*
Rogers, Richard Hilton *hotel executive*

Savannah
Otter, John Martin III *retired television advertising consultant*

Smyrna

Lnenicka, Wade Sheridan *purchasing agent, councilman, consultant*

HAWAII

Honolulu

Kelley, Richard Roy *hotel executive*

O'Neill, Charles Kelly *marketing professional, retired advertising executive*

Kahului

Osgood, Christopher Mykel *radio sales manager*

Kapaau

Ralston, Joanne Smoot *public relations executive*

IDAHO

Eagle

McCahill, Barry Winslow *public relations executive*

Idaho Falls

Barbe, Betty Catherine *marketing professional, retired financial analyst*

Ketchum

Ziebarth, Robert Charles *management consultant*

ILLINOIS

Addison

Christopher, Doris K. *consumer products company executive*

McDonald, David Eugene *transportation operator*

Algonquin

Shaw, Cecelia *retired chef*

Barrington

Murphy, Robert *executive recruiter, consultant*

Ross, Frank Howard III *management consultant*

Stephens, Norval Blair, Jr. *marketing consultant*

Belleville

Gale, Neil Jan *Internet company executive, computer scientist, consultant*

Bloomingdale

Flaherty, John Joseph *quality assurance company executive*

Bloomington

Dietz, William Ronald *corporate management professional*

Burr Ridge

Bottom, Dale Coyle *marketing executive, director, management consultant*

Champaign

Moore, Jerry Jay *sales executive, retired archaeologist*

Chicago

Achatz, Grant (Grant Sherman Achatz Jr.) *chef*

Allen, Belle *management consulting firm and communications executive*

Bailey, Robert, Jr. *advertising executive*

Bayless, Rick *chef*

Bensinger, Peter Benjamin *consulting firm executive*

Bernardin, Thomas L. *advertising executive*

Bernatowicz, Frank Allen *management consultant*

Bess, Ronald W. *advertising executive*

Bowles, Graham Elliot *chef*

Brandt, William Arthur, Jr. *consulting executive*

Brown, Jeremy Earle *advertising executive*

Brown, Peter C. *video game company executive, former movie theater company executive*

Cesario, Robert Charles *marketing executive*

Cornelious, Vida *marketing executive*

Cox, Allan James *management consultant*

Diefendorf, Jeanenne Marie *travel company executive*

Draft, Howard Craig *advertising executive*

Fisher, Eugene *marketing professional, community leader*

Furcon, John Edward *management and organizational consultant*

Gand, Gale *chef, restaurateur*

Gardner, Howard Alan *travel company executive, writer, editor*

Geller, Laurence S. *hotel executive*

Glasser, James J. *retired leasing company executive*

Goldring, Norman Max *marketing professional*

Gordon, Howard Lyon *advertising and marketing executive*

Haffner, Charles Christian III *retired printing company executive*

Hansen, Carl R. *management consultant*

Harford, Barney *travel company executive*

Hofrichter, David Alan *management consultant*

Hollis, Donald Roger *management consultant*

Hoplamazian, Mark Samuel *hotel executive*

Huggins, Lois M. *human resources specialist, consumer products company executive*

Kindzred, Diana *communications company executive*

Kobs, James Fred *direct marketing consultant*

Koernig, Stephen K. *marketing professional, educator*

Kornick, Michael *chef*

Krivkovich, Peter George *advertising executive*

Kunda, Dolores A. *marketing executive*

Lewis, Aylwin B. *food service executive, former retail executive*

Lowry, James Hamilton *management consultant*

McCallister, Richard Anthony *business consulting company executive*

McClain, Shawn *chef*

McConnell, E. Hoy, II, *advertising and public policy executive*

McCullough, Richard Lawrence *advertising executive*

Melamed, Leo *global consulting firm executive*

Nelson, Harry Donald *telecommunications executive*

Newman, Bruce Ira *marketing professional*

Paloian, John R. *printing company executive*

Paul, Ronald Neale *management consultant*

Pincus, Theodore Henry *public relations executive*

Plotkin, Manuel D. *management consultant, educator, former corporate executive, government official*

Poggenpohl, Teresa Loyola *marketing executive*

Porowski, Anne M. *management consultant*

Posner, Kathy Robin *retired communications executive*

Pritzker, Thomas Jay *hotel executive*

Quinlan, Thomas J. III *printing company executive*

Rabin, Joseph Harry *marketing research company executive*

Raphaelson, Joel *retired advertising agency executive*

Reitman, Jerry Irving *advertising agency executive*

Rich, S. Judith *public relations executive*

Rooney, John Edward *communications company executive*

Salah, Greg *marketing executive*

Samuelson, Peter A. *management consultant*

Sive, Rebecca Anne *public relations executive*

Skiko, Marla *communications executive*

Small, Richard Donald *travel company executive*

Stead, James Joseph, Jr. *security firm executive*

Stern, Carl William, Jr. *management consultant*

Swinand, Andrew *advertising executive*

Talbot, Pamela *public relations executive*

Trotter, Charlie *chef*

Tyson, Kirk W. M. *management consultant*

Van Den Hende, Fred J(oseph) *human resources executive*

Weinfurter, Daniel Joseph *business services executive*

Williams, Marsha C. *travel company executive*

Wolf, Stephen M. *consumer products company executive, former air transportation executive*

Deerfield

Carbonari, Bruce A. *consumer products company executive*

Chawla, Sona *consumer products company executive*

Feil, Kimberly Lynn *marketing executive*

Gochnauer, Richard Wallis *consumer products company executive*

Lezak, Carol Spielman *communications executive, editor, writer, design consultant, medical librarian*

Omtvedt, Craig P. *consumer products executive*

Pugh, Bryan *retail company marketing executive*

Reich, Victoria J. *consumer products company executive*

Wesley, Norman H. *consumer products company executive*

Dekalb

Li, Lan *educator*

Des Plaines

Kaczor, Diane L. *marketing professional, researcher*

Downers Grove

Kent, Geoffrey *travel company executive*

Morgan-Grenville, George S. *travel company executive*

Dundee

Carlini, James *management consultant*

Edwardsville

Dietrich, Suzanne Claire *communications consultant, researcher, museum director*

Elburn

Hansen, H. Jack *management consultant*

Elgin

Robinson, Lois Hart *retired public relations executive*

Rogers, Carleton Carson, Jr. *trade show and convention executive*

Elmhurst

Boggs, William Norman, Jr. *marketing professional, educator*

Evanston

Larson, Paul William *public relations executive*

Fairview Heights

Walter, Arenstein Alan *environmental services administrator*

Glen Ellyn

Conti, Paul Louis *management consulting company executive*

Glencoe

Isaacs, Roger David *public relations executive*

Glenview

Franklin, Lynne *corporate communications specialist, writer*

Mukoyama, James Hidefumi, Jr. *security firm executive*

Highland Park

Cohen, Burton David *food service executive, lawyer*

Harris, Thomas L. *public relations executive*

Hinsdale

Whitney, William Elliot, Jr. *advertising agency executive*

Hoffman Estates

Gerstein, Richard *marketing and retail company executive*

Lee, Gregory A. *human resources specialist*

Snyder, Mark A. *marketing executive*

Winckler, Alicia Jean *human resources vice president*

Joliet

Williams, Jennifer Ann *public relations executive*

Kenilworth

Weaver, Donna Rae *winery executive*

Lake Bluff

Griem, John Michael *management consultant*

Lake Forest

Brewer, Paul Huie *advertising executive, artist, portrait painter*

Carter, Donald Patton *retired advertising executive*

Mohr, Roger John *retired advertising agency executive*

Stecko, Paul T. *packaging company executive*

Libertyville

Bramhall, Robert Richard *management consultant*

Maczulski, Margaret Louise *marketing professional*

Lincolnshire

Keller, Robert J. *consumer products company executive*

Lincolnwood

Lebedow, Aaron Louis *consulting company executive*

Lisle

Skweres, Thomas W. *sales executive, advertising executive, public relations executive, investor, entrepreneur*

Litchfield

Talley, Hayward Leroy *communications executive*

Lombard

Anderson, Phyllis Reinhold *management consultant*

Harris, Jeff M. *waste management executive*

Melrose Park

Bernick, Carol Lavin *consumer products company executive*

Moline

Schwiebert, Deborah Johnson *marketing executive*

Mount Prospect

Sayers, Gale *computer company executive, retired professional football player*

Naperville

Fritz, Roger Jay *management consultant*

Thacker, Robert George (Bob Thacker) *marketing executive*

Niles

Beton, John Allen *communications company executive*

Normal

Devinatz, Victor Gary *industrial relations specialist, educator*

Northbrook

Clarey, John Robert *executive recruiter, consultant*

Moser, Larry Edward *marketing professional*

Sudbrink, Jane Marie *sales and marketing executive*

Wajer, Ronald Edward *management consultant*

Northfield

Vilim, Nancy Catherine *advertising executive*

Oak Brook

Carroll, Anja Morrisson *marketing professional, food service executive*

Coudreaut, Dan *chef*

DeLorey, John Alfred *printing company executive*

Fenton, Tim *food service executive*

Fields, Janice L. *food service executive*

Floersch, Richard R. *food service executive, human resources specialist*

Golden, Neil B. *marketing executive*

Nelson, Robert Eddinger *retired management consultant*

Proud, Dayna *public relations executive*

Wells, Karen *food service company executive*

Oak Park

Cannon, Patrick Francis *public relations executive*

Devereux, Timothy Edward *advertising executive*

Peoria

Banwart, Sidney C. *human resources executive*

Prospect Heights

Lynch, William Thomas, Jr. *advertising executive*

Rockford

Albert, Janyce Louise *human resources specialist, retired business educator, banker, consultant*

Romeoville

Carey, John Patrick *broadcasting executive and educator*

Rosemont

Blake, Norman Perkins, Jr. *computer company executive*

Schaumburg

Brown, Gregory Q. *communications executive*

Conrado, Eduardo *marketing executive*

Hill, Raymond Joseph *packaging company executive*

Jha, Sanjay K. *communications executive*

Springfield

Harris, Linda C. *training services executive*

Vernon Hills

Gambill, Mark J. *marketing executive*

Powers, Anthony Richard, Jr. *educational sales professional*

Wauconda

Meehan, Jean Marie Ross *human resources, occupational health and safety management consultant*

Willowbrook

Foley, Joseph Lawrence *sales executive*

Winnetka

Cole, Kathleen Ann *advertising executive, social worker*

Thomas, John Thieme *management consultant*

Woodridge

O'Connor, William Michael *search company executive*

INDIANA

Bloomington

Hawley, Kimra *computer company executive*

Carmel

Mahoney, Margaret Ellis *advertising executive*

Columbus

Tucker, Thomas Randall *public relations executive*

Indianapolis

Brown, Randy L. *human resources specialist, health insurance company executive*

Buranello, Raymond Terrence *quality assurance executive, chemist*

Gilman, Alan B. *restaurant company executive*

Harden, Annette C. *recreation director*

Kirkpatrick, Robert Hugh *communications executive*

Slaymaker, Gene Arthur *public relations executive*

Spanogle, Robert William *marketing and advertising company executive, association administrator*

Liberty

Pringle, Lewis Gordon *marketing professional, educator*

Munster

Larson, Dean Roy *management consultant, educator*

Valparaiso

Ziegler, Jennifer Anne *management consultant, educator*

Wabash

Scales, Richard Lewis *retired sales executive*

West Lafayette

Schendel, Dan Eldon *management consultant, finance educator*

IOWA

Ames

Bonomi, Ferne Gater *public relations executive*

Davis, Wayne Pitman *public relations executive*

Atlantic

Johnson, Joan (Jan) Hope Voss *communications and public relations executive, photojournalist*

George

Symens, Maxine Brinkert Tanner *retired marketing professional*

KANSAS

Chanute

Fewins, David W. *marketing executive*

Junction City

Werts, Merrill Harmon *retired management consultant*

Lawrence

Tull, Pamela M. *public relations executive*

Leawood

King, Barbara Sackheim *travel company executive*

Mooney, Justin David *motel executive, consultant*

Vanatta, Chester B. *management consultant, educator*

Overland Park

Green, John Lafayette, Jr. *strategic planning executive, academic administrator*

Shawnee Mission

Putman, Dale Cornelius *management consultant, lawyer*

Wagner, Robert Wayne *management consultant*

Wichita

Gallardo, Cheryl K. *administrative assistant*

Herr, Peter Helmut Friederich *sales executive*

Koch, Charles de Ganahl *industrial company executive*

KENTUCKY

Hawesville
Curry, Michael Jason *human resources specialist*

Hopkinsville
Neville, Thomas Lee *food service company executive*

Louisville
Novak, David C. *restaurant company executive*

Richmond
Whitt, Marcus Calvin *marketing executive, public relations executive*

LOUISIANA

Baton Rouge
Davis, Hall L., IV, *funeral director*

Metairie
Grimm, John Lloyd *marketing professional*

New Orleans
Brennan, Ella *restaurant manager*
Lagasse, Emeril *chef, restaurant owner, television show host, writer*
Ryu, Kisang *educator*
Schnoebelen, Ian *chef*
Snyder, Sharon Veta *management consultant, educator*

Ruston
Hudnall, Jarrett, Jr. *management consultant, educator, marketing professional*

MAINE

Bangor
Fletcher, Francis Stephen *marketing and management consultant*

Brooklin
Schmidt, Klaus Dieter *marketing professional, management consultant, educator*

Hollis Center
Kaake, Norman Bradford *quality assurance professional*

Portland
Spalding, Tim *Internet company executive*

Sumner
Rudd, David William *management consultant, chemical engineer*

MARYLAND

Annapolis
Branand, Claire Diane *advertising executive, writer*
Lombardo, David Domenic *human resources professor and consultant*

Baltimore
Battista, Stephen J. *marketing executive*
Brotman, Phyllis Block *advertising and public relations executive*
Dickinson, Jane W. *retired executive secretary, volunteer*
Howes, James Guerdon *communication and transportation executive*
Kerriem, Rasheed T. *human resources specialist, educator*
Robinson, Florine Samantha *marketing executive*
Talbot, Donald Roy *management consultant*

Beltsville
Miller, Ted Robert *management consultant*

Bethesda
Allnutt, Robert Frederick *management consultant, lawyer*
Beecher, William Manuel *management consultant*
Berquist, Carl Thomas *hotel executive, accountant*
Cody, Thomas Gerald *management consultant, writer*
Harvey, Larry K. *hotel executive*
Marriott, Richard Edwin *hotel and contract services executive*
McClure, Brooks *management consultant*
Mc Gurn, Barrett *communications executive, writer*
Neill, Denis Michael *management consultant*
Shaw, William J. *hotel executive*
Sorenson, Arne M. *hotel executive*
Terragno, Paul James *information industry executive*
Walter, W. Edward *hotel and corporate financial executive*

Bozman
Wyatt, Wilson Watkins, Jr. *public relations executive, writer*

Cambridge
Tyagi, Punam *environmental services administrator*

Catonsville
Diggs, Carol Beth *marketing professional*

Chevy Chase
Baruch, Jordan Jay *retired management consultant*
Bisconti, Ann Stouffer *public opinion research company executive*
Michaelis, Michael *management and technical consultant*

Cockeysville
Bracey, Esi Eggleston *consumer products company executive, marketing professional*

Cockeysville Hunt Valley
Elkin, Lois Shanman *business systems company executive*
Whitehurst, William Wilfred, Jr. *management consultant*

Columbia
Van Buiten, Robert D. *management consultant, career planner*

Ellicott City
Estin-Klein, Libbyada *advertising executive, writer*

Fort Washington
Satterthwaite, George, II, *security firm executive*

Gaithersburg
Landel, Michel *food service and management company executive*

Gibson Island
Forster, William Hull *management consultant*

Hagerstown
Higgins, M. Eileen *management consultant, educator*

Hanover
Henderson Hall, Brenda Ford *computer company executive*

Potomac
Medin, A. Louis *computer company executive*
Owen, Harrison Hollingsworth *management consultant*

Rockville
Klosson, Michael *public policy director*
Levitt, Mark Howard *sales executive*

Silver Spring
Altschul, b j *public relations counselor*
Carter-Johnson, Jean Evelyn *management consultant*
Joyce, Stephen P. *hotel executive*
Madison, Anne Conway *marketing, public relations professional*
Shih-Carducci, Joan Chia-mo *food service executive, medical technologist, biochemist, writer, educator*

Solomons
Harrington, John Vincent *retired communications executive, engineer, educator*

Sudlersville
Covington, Donald Kingsley, Jr. *plywood sales executive*

Towson
Filmore, Jacquelyn V. *marketing professional*
Passano, E. Magruder, Jr. *management consultant*

MASSACHUSETTS

Andover
Chao, Shirley Y.L. *food service executive*

Belmont
Bingham, George Walter Chandler *retired sales executive*

Beverly
Barger, Richard Wilson *hotel executive*

Boston
Adams, Jody *chef, restaurant owner*
Berger, Jerome Morris *communications executive*
Burnham, David Henderson *management consultant*
Connors, Jack, Jr., (John M. Connors, Jr.) *retired advertising executive*
Dowd, Peter Jerome *public relations executive*
Hamersley, Gordon *food service executive*
Hamlin, Pam *marketing executive*
Hayes, Andrew Wallace, II, *consumer products company executive*
Hudson, Dawn Emily *former food service company executive*
Hunter, Durant Adams *executive search company executive*
Kaplan, Karen *marketing and communications executive*
Kelly, Francis J. III *global marketing company executive*
Luongo, C. Paul *public relations executive*
Lynch, Barbara *chef, restaurant owner*
Maffeo, Pino *chef*
McGovern, Patrick J. *communications executive*
Onishi, Anna Tokiko *marketing professional*
Oringer, Kenneth M. *chef, restaurant owner*
Peirce, Georgia Wilson *public relations executive*
Reese, C. Richard *data processing executive*
Rosen, David Michael *public relations administrator, public affairs consultant*
Ross, Elizabeth *advertising executive*
Saunders, Donald Leslie *hotel executive, real estate developer*
Schlow, Michael *food service executive*
Shapiro, Eli *business consultant, educator, economist*
Tierney, Susan Fallows *consulting company executive, former federal agency administrator*
Whouley, Michael J. *communications specialist, political strategist*

Braintree
Driscoll, Megan *executive recruiter*

Brookline
Kliman, Sylvia Stern *communications executive*

Burlington
Wysopal, Chris *software company executive*

Cambridge
Bloom, Kathryn Ruth *public relations executive*
Godfrey, Victoria *rental company executive, marketing professional*
Little, John Dutton Conant *management scientist, educator*
Maiden, Barry *chef*
Palestrant, Daniel *Internet company executive*
Pytka, Stephen Milton *office equipment executive*
Yea, Sehoon *consumer electronics industry executive, researcher*

Canton
Allen, Frances L. *marketing executive*
Judson, Arnold Sidney *management consultant*
Luther, Jon L. *food service executive*
Travis, Nigel *food service executive*

Charlestown
White, John P. *consulting firm executive, public policy educator*

Chatham
Rhinesmith, Stephen Headley *leadership consultant*

Chelmsford
Fulks, Robert Grady *computer company executive*

Chelsea
Jenkins, Alexander III *consumer products company executive, consultant*

Chestnut Hill
O'Block, Robert Paul *management consultant*

Cohasset
Rabstejnek, George John *healthcare executive*

Concord
Parrish, Thomas Kirkpatrick III *marketing consultant*

Dedham
Redstone, Shari Ellin *amusement company executive*

Duxbury
Woods, Reginald Foster *management consulting executive*

Eastham
Birch, Eleanor Mansfield *management educator*

Framingham
DeWerth, Gordon Henry *management consultant*
Meador, Charles Lawrence *management and systems consultant, educator*
Torres, Maryellen *marketing executive*

Gloucester
Littlefield, Paul Damon *retired management consultant*

Lexington
Brick, Donald Bernard *software company executive*
Daltas, Arthur John *management consultant, software services manager*
Dougherty, Richard Hamlen *management and healthcare consultant*
Fray, Lionel Louis *management consultant*
Kasputys, Joseph Edward *corporate executive, economist*

Marlborough
Murray, R. Scott *computer software company executive*

Needham
Grasso, James Anthony *public relations executive, educator*

New Bedford
Soares, Carl Lionel *quality assurance professional, metrologist*

Newton
Benner, Mary Wright *program director, the conference board*

Norwell
Case, David Knowlton *management consultant*

Norwood
Fishman, Jerald G. *semiconductor executive*

Peabody
Gordon, Bernard M. *computer company executive*
Southwick, Paul *retired public relations executive*

Quincy
Hall, John Raymond, Jr. *fire protection executive*

Rockport
Wiberg, Lars-Erik *occupational compatibility consultant*

Sherborn
Hancock, William Frank, Jr. *management consultant*

South Yarmouth
Tracey, William Raymond *international management consultant*

Southbridge
Anderson, Ross Barrett *healthcare environmental services manager*

Vineyard Haven
Schmetterer, Robert Allen *advertising executive*

Waltham
Nye, Dan *former internet company executive*

Wellesley Hills
Doorley, Thomas Lawrence III *management consultant*

Westford
Nottenburg, Richard N. *former communications executive*

Williamstown
Robinson, Hobart Krum *management consulting company executive*
Sprague, John Louis *management consultant*

Worcester
Heman, Robert Jerome, Jr. *printing company executive, retired association executive*

MICHIGAN

Ada
Lyall, Lynn *consumer products company executive*
Weiss, Joseph Joel *consulting company executive*

Allen Park
Bizon, Emma Djafar *management consultant*

Ann Arbor
Belcher, Louis David *marketing professional, retired mayor*
Brandon, David A. *food service executive*
Foley, Daniel Ronald *retired personnel director, lawyer*
Lindsay, June Campbell McKee *communications executive*
Martin, Claude Raymond, Jr. *marketing consultant, educator*
Mounts, L. David *food service executive*

Benton Harbor
Binkley, David A. *human resources specialist*

Beulah
Auch, Walter Edward *security firm executive*

Bloomfield Hills
Adams, Charles Francis *advertising and real estate company executive*
Berline, James H. *advertising and public relations executive*
Sandy, William Haskell *training and communication systems executive*
Trojniak, Duane *marketing executive, consultant*

Detroit
Banko, Bernadette Illona *advertising executive*
Bassett, Tina *communications executive*
Brake, Willie Edward *computer company executive, educator*
Karmanos, Peter, Jr. *computer company executive, professional sports team executive*
Novak, Raymond Francis *environmental services administrator, pharmacology educator*

Farmington
Werba, Gabriel *public relations consultant*

Glen Arbor
Wagner, Bruce Stanley *marketing professional*

Grand Rapids
Dykstra, William Dwight *management executive, consultant*
Spaulding, Dan *public relations executive*

Grosse Pointe
Moran, Justin Louis *retired management consultant*

Grosse Pointe Park
Krebs, William Hoyt *industrial hygienist, health science association administrator*

Hastings
Jones, Kensinger *advertising executive, author, educator*

Hillsdale
Bachelder, Cheryl Anne *former food service company executive*

Holland
Garlough, William Glenn *marketing executive*

Kentwood
Purchase-Owens, Francena *marketing professional, consultant, educator, scholar*
Roberts-Brown, Arlene Maria *executive assistant*

Lansing
Lobenherz, William Ernest *consumer products company executive, trade association administrator, lawyer*

Livonia
Maibach, Ben C., Jr. *consumer products company executive*

Midland
Rocks, Patti Temple *marketing executive*

Southfield
Barnett, Marilyn *advertising executive*
Caponigro, Jeffrey Ralph *public relations counselor*

Taylor
DeMarie, Donald J., Jr. *consumer products company executive*
Manoogian, Richard Alexander *consumer products company executive*

Wadhams, Timothy *consumer products company executive*

Troy
Adderley, Terence Edward *human resources executive*
Camden, Carl T. *human resources company executive*
Chalil, Joseph Mathew *sales executive, consultant, liver disease specialist, medical products executive*
Corona, George S. *recruiting company executive*

Walled Lake
Gillespie, J. Martin *sales and distribution company executive*

West Bloomfield
Lewis, Harold Allen *childcare company executive*

MINNESOTA

Farmington
Wurdeman, Lew Edward *Internet company executive, consultant*

Lake Crystal
Pawlitschek, Donald Paul *management consultant*

Mahtomedi
Brainerd, Richard Charles *human resources executive, consultant, educator*

Marshall
Varcoe, Jeffrey John *food service executive*

Minneapolis
Agyenkwah, Kennedy Seth *communications executive*
Brosseau, Lisa M. *industrial hygienist, educator*
Fallon, Patrick R. *advertising executive*
Finkelstein, Paul D. *personal care industry executive*
Grimes, David Lynn *communications executive*
Johnson, Lola Norine *retired advertising and public relations executive, educator*
Kelly, Charles Harold *advertising executive*
Marinello, Kathryn V. *human resources company executive*
McKee, Tim *chef*
Mulligan, Donal L. *consumer products company executive*
Palmore, Rick (Roderick A. Palmore) *consumer products company executive, lawyer*
Pohlad, Robert C. *consumer products company executive*
Powell, Ken (Kendall J. Powell) *consumer products company executive*
Spong, Douglas K. *public relations executive*
Sullivan, Michael Patrick *food service executive*
Veblen, Thomas Clayton *management consultant*
Wangberg, Larry W. *business consultant*
Wickesberg, Albert Klumb *retired management consultant*
Woodman, Stewart *chef*
Yourzak, Robert Joseph *management consultant, educator, engineer*

Minnetonka
Gillies, Donald Richard *marketing and advertising consultant, educator*
Joly, Hubert Bernard *hotel and travel company executive*
Nelson, Marilyn Carlson *hotel and travel company executive*

North Mankato
Taylor, Glen A. *printing, direct mail and technology executive, professional sports team owner*

Northfield
Immel, Cynthia Luanne *medical sales specialist*

Rochester
Hiniker, LuAnn *management consultant, educator, researcher, grants consultant*
Nevling, Harry Reed *human resources consultant*

Saint Paul
Baker, Douglas M., Jr. *service industry executive*
Courtney, Eugene Whitmal *computer company executive*
Fritze, Steven L. *service industry executive*

Shakopee
Eibeler, Paul G. *former computer game company executive*

Wayzata
Waldera, Wayne Eugene *crisis management executive*

MISSISSIPPI

Biloxi
Love, James Sanford III *communications executive*

Columbus
Labensky, Sarah Ross *culinary educator*

Holly Springs
Moyo, Debayo R. *communications executive*

Mississippi State
Kellermanns, Franz Willi *management consultant, educator*

Ocean Springs
Culberson, Gary Michael *hotel manager*

MISSOURI

Blue Springs
Page, Leslie Andrew *retired consumer products company executive*

Bolivar
Smith, Sharina *marketing executive, writer*

Cape Girardeau
Smallwood, Glenn Walter, Jr. *utility marketing management executive*

Chesterfield
Stork, Donald Arthur *advertising executive*

Independence
Evans, Margaret Ann *human resources administrator, business owner*

Kansas City
Baker, Ronald Phillip *service company executive*
Courson, Marna B.P. *public relations executive*
Dwyer, William Michael *health care company advisor*
Hall, Donald Joyce, Jr. *consumer products company executive*
Lawson, Melanie Kay *retired management administrator, early childhood consultant*
Lopez, Gerardo Isaac *movie theater company executive*
Robertson, Leon H. *management consultant, educator*
Tio, Celina *chef*

Richmond Heights
Shaich, Ronald M. *food service executive*

Saint Louis
Bachmann, John William *security firm executive*
Black, Dale R. *hotel and gaming company executive*
Cornelius, Charles H. *recruitment company executive*
Crooks, Carol Yvonne *power systems sales engineer*
Cropf, Robert Allan *department chairman*
Curran, Michael Walter *management scientist*
Davis, Irvin *advertising, public relations and broadcast executive*
Ferguson, Gary Warren *retired public relations executive*
Handelman, Alice Samuels *public relations professional, writer*
Klein, Ward M. *consumer products company executive*
Kornblet, Donald Ross *communications company executive*
Kwak, No Kyoon *business administration educator*
Nicholson, Pamela M. *rental and leasing company executive*
Riley, Michael Robert *marketing and business development executive*
Rosen, Fred *travel company executive*
Ross, Donald L. *rental and leasing company executive*
Schmitz, Eloise E. *communications executive*
Schremp, Ted W. *communications executive*
Sibbald, John Ristow *management consultant*
Siemer, Paul Jennings *public relations executive*
Tapp, Shelley Raye *marketing educator*
Taylor, Andrew C. *rental and leasing company executive*
Taylor, Jack Crawford *rental and leasing company executive*
Tyler, William Howard, Jr. *advertising executive, educator*

Springfield
Kim, Kee S. *management consultant, educator*

Warrenton
Dapron, Elmer Joseph, Jr. *communications executive*

NEBRASKA

Blair
Conlon, Thomas James *marketing executive*

Lincoln
Bauer, Daryl L. *environmental services administrator*

Omaha
Caggiano, Joseph *retired advertising executive*
Eggers, James Wesley *executive search consultant*
Hedren, Paul Leslie *retired parks director, historian*
Khots, Dmitriy *data mining executive*
Mew, Calvin Marshall *advertising executive*
Roskens, Ronald William *management consultant, retired academic administrator*

NEVADA

Boulder City
Spadafor, Christine J. *management consultant*

Henderson
Cohan, George Sheldon *advertising and public relations executive*
McNeal, Ralph LeRoy, Sr. *management consultant, financial executive*
Ryan, Shelli Ann *public relations executive*

Las Vegas
Adelson, Sheldon Gary *hotel and gaming company executive*
Arce, Phillip William *hotel and casino executive*
Atwood, Charles L. *hotel and gaming company executive*
Bai, Billy *hospitality and tourism educator*
Bartolotta, Paul Wenzel *chef*
Beeman, Karl Joseph, Jr. *warehouse manager*
Boyd, William S. *hotel and gaming company executive*
Brock, Holly Melinda *marketing professional*
Griesche, Robert Price *hospital purchasing executive*
Halkyard, Jonathan S. *entertainment industry executive*
Hardie, George Graham *casino executive*
Isidori, Joe *chef*
Kay, Kenneth Jeffrey *hotel executive*
Leven, Michael Alan *hotel and gaming company executive*
Loveman, Gary W. *hotel and gaming company executive*
McCaw, Craig Oliver *communications executive*
Moonen, Rick *chef, restaurant owner*
Murren, James Joseph *hotel corporation executive*
Satre, Philip Glen *casino entertainment executive, lawyer*
Sillerman, Robert F. X. *communications executive, banker*
Smith, Keith E. *hotel and gaming company executive*
Sorrell, Michael E. *consulting company and hospitality management executive*
Stark, S. Daniel, Jr. *casino and gaming resort company executive*
Wynn, Steve Alan (Stephen A. Wynn) *hotel and gaming company executive*

Reno
Adams, Kenneth Robert *gaming analyst, writer, historian, consultant*
Ford, Victoria *retired public relations executive, writer, oral historian*
Frank, Lillian Gorman *human resources executive, management consultant*

NEW HAMPSHIRE

Bedford
Hall, Pamela S. *environmental consulting services executive*

Center Harbor
Shaw, Robert William, Jr. *management consultant, venture capitalist*

Concord
Roberts, George Bernard, Jr. *management and government relations consultant, former state legislator*

Dublin
Vecchiotti, Robert Anthony *management and organizational consultant*

Grantham
Hansen, Herbert W. *management consultant, educator*

Hampstead
Hargreaves, David William *retired communications company executive*

Litchfield
Darlington, David William *management consultant*

Merrimack
Gallup, Patricia *computer company executive*

Mirror Lake
Phillips, Tyler Bradstreet *retired business executive*

Waterville Valley
Saenger, Bruce Walter *consulting firm executive*

NEW JERSEY

Atlantic City
Irvine, Robert *chef*

Basking Ridge
Moden, Joleen *communications executive*
Perez, Glad M. *marketing executive*
Schmidt, William Max *management consultant, marketing and business development executive*

Bedminster
Bailye, John E. *software company executive*
Gardner, David John *communications executive, sound recording engineer*

Bernardsville
Dixon, Richard Wayne *retired communications company executive*

Bloomfield
Bunin, Jeffrey Howard *management consultant*

Boonton
Bona, Frederick Emil *public relations executive*
Ward, Solveig Maria *marketing professional*

Brick
Roache, Patrick Michael, Jr. *management consultant*

Bridgewater
Sethi, Shyam Sunder *management consultant*

Cape May
Kurkowski, David *marketing professional*

Clifton
Burke, Bruce Lowell *consumer products company executive*
DiNicola, Robert J. *consumer products company executive*
Gries, Michael F. *consumer products company executive*

Dover
Derr, Debra Hulse *advertising executive, writer*

East Rutherford
Kempner, Michael W. *public relations executive*

Englewood
Fay, Toni Georgette *communications executive*

Englewood Cliffs
Clift, Simon *consumer products company executive, marketing professional*
Master, Robert Jeffery *consumer products company executive, marketing professional*
Polk, Michael B. *consumer products company executive*

Fair Haven
Wyndrum, Ralph William, Jr. *communications consultant*

Florham Park
Naimark, George Modell *marketing and management consultant*

Fort Dix
Boyd, Larry Chester *colonel*

Franklin Lakes
Williams, Edward David *information technology management consultant*

Glen Ridge
Agnew, Peter Tomlin *employee benefit consultant*

Green Village
Swift, John Francis *retired health care advertising company executive*

Hackettstown
Van Campen, Stephen Bernard *executive recruiter, consultant*

Haddonfield
Baltake, Susan *marketing and communications professional*
Bauer, Raymond Gale *sales professional*

Hoboken
Bostwick, Randell Armour *retired food service executive*
Fassoulis, Satiris Galahad *communications executive, director*

Lawrenceville
Coleman, Wade Hampton III *management consultant, mechanical engineer, retired banker*
Cox, Teri Polack *public relations executive*
Weaver, Charles Lyndell, Jr. *marketing executive, educational consultant*

Little Falls
Margaritis, John Paul *advertising and public relations executive*

Madison
Byrd, Stephen Fred *human resource consultant*
O'Brien, Mary Devon *communications executive, consultant*

Mahwah
Gibbons, Robert Philip *management consultant, director*

Matawan
Amato, Vincent Vito *marketing and business consultant*

Medford
Kaser, Richard Todd *communications executive*

Mendham
Hambleton, George Blow Elliott *retired management consultant*

Millburn
Bablin, Mark Edward *security administrator, mortgage consultant*

Monroe Township
Cushman, Helen Merle Baker *retired management consultant*

Montclair
Dubrow, Marsha Ann *management consultant, musicologist*
Greenwald, Robert *public relations executive*
Zhang, Yanli *management consultant, educator*

Montvale
Lamach, Michael W. *diversified industrial company executive*

Moorestown
Bennington, William Jay *management consultant*
Schwerin, Horace S. *marketing research consultant*

Morristown
Weidenkopf, Thomas W. *human resources specialist*

Mount Laurel
Klein, Gerhart Leopold *public relations executive*

Murray Hill
Chen, Jingdong *communications executive*

New Brunswick
Heller, Bridgette P. *marketing executive*
Perkins, Brian D. *consumer products company executive*

New Providence
Del Tiempo, Sandra Kay *sales executive*

Newark
Courter, James A. (Jim) *communications executive, former United States Representative, New Jersey*
Jonas, Howard S. *communications executive*
Sommer, Bob (Robert G. Sommer) *public relations executive, lobbyist*

North Bergen
Archbold, Michael G. *consumer products company executive, former retail executive*

North Brunswick
Bern, Ronald Lawrence *management consultant, writer*

North Plainfield
Dunbar, Holly Jean *communications executive, public relations executive*

Oak Ridge
Kieren, Thomas Henry *management consultant & architectural photographer*

Parsippany
Ferguson, Thomas George *retired healthcare advertising agency executive*
Gros, Simon Charles *travel company executive, former federal agency administrator*
Holmes, Stephen P. *hotel executive*
Nelson, Ronald L. *travel services company executive, former film company executive*
Salerno, F. Robert *travel company executive*
Wyshner, David B. *travel company executive*

Pennington
Czach, Gabriela Bozena *personal care industry executive*

Plainsboro
Devine, Hugh James, Jr. *retired marketing executive*
Spiegel, Phyllis *public relations consultant, journalist*

Princeton
Craigie, James R. *consumer products and former sports equipment apparel company executive*
Crossley, Helen Martha *public opinion analyst, research consultant*
Davies, Robert Abel III *consumer products company executive*
Kenny, Jane M. *environmental and energy policy consulting executive*
Khan, Sajid A. *management consultant, entrepreneur*
Leetmaa, Ants *environmental services administrator, educator*
Morris, Mac Glenn *advertising executive*
Pfister, Marc *consumer products company executive, physician, researcher*
Whitman, Christine Todd (Christie Whitman) *consulting firm executive, former federal agency administrator, former governor*

Randolph
Charm, Joel Barry *management consultant*
Chen, Kevin S. *management executive, consultant, educator*

Red Bank
Meyer, Robert Alan *management consultant*

Ridgefield Park
Cook, Steven *marketing executive*

Ridgewood
Warner, John Edward *advertising executive*

Roseland
Butler, Gary C. *computer company executive*
Martone, S. Michael *computer company executive*
Reidy, Christopher R. *computer company executive*

Scotch Plains
Lipton, Bronna Jane *marketing communications executive*

Short Hills
Harwood, Jerry *market research executive*
Schaefer, Charles James III *advertising executive, consultant*

Somerset
Brophy, Joseph Thomas *computer company executive*
Wallfesh, Henry Maurice *communications executive, writer*

Summit
Fuess, Billings Sibley, Jr. *advertising executive*

Teaneck
Connola, Donald Pascal, Jr. *management consultant*
Lafer, Fred Seymour *data processing executive*

Toms River
Kanarkowski, Edward Joseph *data processing company executive*

Trenton
Fischer, Pamela Shadel *public relations executive*
Marcus, Alan C. *public relations consultant*

Upper Montclair
Tintle, Carmel Joseph *public relations executive*

West Caldwell
Dixon, Jo-Ann Conte *management consultant*
Page, Frederick West *retired business consultant*

West Orange
Kyle, Corinne Silverman *management consultant*

Westfield
Davoren, Steven Michael *marketing professional, psychologist*

Whitehouse Station
Graddick-Weir, Mirian *human resources specialist*

Wyckoff
Lavery, Daniel P. *management consultant*

NEW MEXICO

Albuquerque
Hayo, George Edward *management consultant*
Rehder, Robert Richard *business management educator, management consultant*
Stevenson, Bradford Allen *management consultant*
Westwood, Albert Ronald Clifton *management consultant, researcher*

Las Cruces
Reynolds, Collins James III *management consultant*

Sandia Park
Greenwell, Ronald Everett *communications executive*

Santa Fe
Brandt, Richard Paul *communications and entertainment company executive*
Mercer, James Lee *management consultant*
Merrin, Seymour *computer company executive*
Miller, Dwight Richard *professional hair care industry executive, cosmetologist, consultant*
Welch, Jasper Arthur, Jr. *security company executive, consultant*

NEW YORK

Armonk
Greene, Jesse J., Jr. *computer company executive*
Iwata, Jon C. *computer company executive*
Loughridge, Mark *computer company executive*

Bedford
Husted, William Armstrong *sales executive*

Bethpage
Dolan, James L. *communications executive*
Huseby, Michael P. *communications executive*
Rutledge, Thomas M. *communications executive*
Seibert, Gregg George *communications executive, former investment company executive*

Brewster
Shepard, Lance Hastings *marketing professional, consultant, newscaster*

Bronxville
Ellinghaus, William Maurice *communications executive*

Brooklyn
Allison, Eric William *management consultant, historic preservationist*
Allison, Mary Ann *consulting company executive, writer, speaker*
Carswell, Lois Malakoff *botanical garden executive, consultant*
Galatianos, Gus A. *computer company executive, consultant, real estate developer, educator*
Hendra, Barbara Jane *public relations executive*
Heron, Earl D. *communications executive*
Krukowski, Jan *communications executive*
Laverty, Marilyn T. *public relations executive, media consultant*
MacKay, Malcolm *executive search consultant*
Reichel, Walter Emil *advertising executive*

Buffalo
Fryer, Appleton *sales executive, diplomat*
Pegels, C. Carl *management consultant, educator*

Canaan
Hooper, Ian (John Derek Glass) *retired marketing communications executive*

Carle Place
McCann, Jim (James F. McCann) *consumer products company executive*

Centerport
Stratigos, William Narge *computer company executive*

Chatham
Light, Lisa *travel company executive*

Cheektowaga
Ganz, Howard *consumer products company executive*

Chester
Mackerodt, Fred *public relations specialist*

Claverack
Barrett, William Gary *advertising and marketing executive*

Croton On Hudson
Plotch, Walter *management consultant, fund raising counselor*

Delmar
Button, Rena Pritsker *public relations executive*

East Hampton
Mencher, Stuart Alan *sales and marketing executive*
Nash, Edward L. *advertising executive*

East Northport
Schlam, Mark Howard *international marketing executive*

Elmont
Butera, Ann Michele *consulting company executive*

Far Rockaway
Epstein, Samuel Abraham *sales executive*

Flushing
Washington, Mario R. *computer company executive*

Garden City
Conlon, Brian Thomas *promotion executive*
Doucette, Mary-Alyce *computer company executive*

Geneseo
Zuckerman, Mary Ellen Waller *marketing educator*

Glen Cove
Mansi, Joseph Anneillo *public relations company executive*

Hancock
DeLuca, Ronald *former advertising agency executive, consultant*

Hartsdale
Greenawalt, Peggy Freed Tomarkin *advertising executive*
Pell, Arthur Robert *human resources specialist, consultant, writer*

Hauppauge
Rupp, Katherine M. *marketing executive*

Honeoye Falls
Hillabrandt, Larry Lee *service industry executive*

Hurley
Smith, Lewis Motter, Jr. *retired advertising and direct marketing executive*

Hyde Park
Ryan, L. Timothy *chef, educator, academic administrator*

Irvington
Sherman, Norman Mark *advertising agency executive*

Islandia
Handal, Kenneth V. *computer software company executive, lawyer*
Swainson, John A. *software company executive*

Ithaca
Park, Roy Hampton, Jr. *advertising executive*

Jamestown
O'Brian, Jonathan D. *recreation director, story educator, language educator, educator*

Jericho
Edson, Andrew Stephen *public relations executive*
Rosen, Robert Arnold *management consultant, real estate owner, manager, developer, investor, farmer*

Katonah
Morris, Stephen Burritt *marketing information company executive*

Lake Luzerne
Goldstein, Manfred *retired management consultant*

Lancaster
Neumaier, Gerhard John *environmental services administrator, consultant*

Larchmont
Greenwald, Carol Schiro *professional services marketing research executive*
Plumez, Jean Paul *advertising executive, consultant*

Latham
Schwartz, Robert William *management consultant*
Wilkes, Brent Ames *management consultant*

Locust Valley
Fletcher, Mary Lee *retired marketing professional*

Manlius
der Boghosian, Paula *retired computer business consultant*

Mount Kisco
Novak, Gregory *marketing professional*

New Hyde Park
Weinbach, Arthur Frederic *retired computer company executive*

New Rochelle
Johnson, John William, Jr. *business advisor*

New York
Abruzzo, Joseph *media communications company executive, director*
Adler, David A. *communications executive*
Agisim, Philip *advertising and marketing executive*
Albert, Adrienne *real estate marketing executive*
Alecia, Suzanne Bussart *advertising executive*
Allen, Alice *communications and marketing executive*
Alschuler, Steven *public relations executive, writer, consultant*
Alvarez, Antonio C., II, *restructuring company executive, former food products executive*
Amen, Robert M. *consumer products company executive*
Anderson, Arthur Allan *management consultant*
Anderson, Sunny *chef, television personality*
Andolsen, Alan Anthony *management consultant*
Andree, Tim *advertising executive*
Arnell, Peter Eric *advertising executive, photographer, writer*
Aronstam, Neil Lee *media marketing firm executive*
Arpaia, Donatella *restaurateur*
Axthelm, Nancy *advertising executive*
Banikarim, Maryam *marketing executive*
Barber, Dan *chef, restaurant owner*
Bartow, Diane Grace *marketing professional, sales executive*
Baruch, Ralph M. *communications executive*
Bastholm, Lars *interactive marketing executive*
Bastianich, Lidia Matticchio (Lidia Motika) *chef, food service executive*
Batali, Mario Francis *chef*
Beason, Steve W. *computer company executive*
Beaven, Richard *media strategy and marketing company executive*
Becker, Susan Kaplan *management and marketing communication consultant, presentation coach, educator*
Beinecke, William Sperry *retired consumer products company executive*
Beleson, Robert Brian *marketing executive*
Bell, David Arthur *retired advertising agency executive*
Benenson, Joel R. *political consultant, pollster*
Bennett, James Marvin *consulting company executive*
Berlin, Andrew Mark (Andy Berlin) *advertising agency executive*
Bernard, David George *retired management consultant*
Bernbach, John Lincoln *marketing professional*
Berndt, Andy *advertising executive*
Bewkes, Jeffrey Lawrence *multi media company executive*
Biederman, Barron Zachary (Barry) *advertising agency executive*
Binz-Scharf, Maria Christina *management consultant, educator*
Bishop, Susan Katharine *executive search company executive*
Blatt, Gregory R. *Internet company executive, lawyer*
Bloomfield, April *chef*
Boice, Craig Kendall *management consultant*
Bologna, Anne *advertising executive*
Bolton, Roger *public relations executive*
Boulud, Daniel *chef, restaurant owner*
Brady, Adelaide Burks *public relations agency executive, giftware catalog executive*
Braverman, Robert Jay *management consultant, educator*
Brien, Nick *advertising and marketing company executive*
Brod, Jon *Internet company executive*
Brooke, Linda Hundley *retired human resources specialist*
Brooks, Gary *crisis management and family business consultant*
Brunson, Curtis *communications systems company executive*
Brymer, Chuck (Charles Edward Brymer) *advertising executive*
Burke, David *corporate and executive chef*
Burns, M. Michele *management consulting firm executive*
Burson, Harold *public relations executive, director*
Burton, Peggy *advertising and marketing executive*
Butler, David T. III *communications systems company executive*
Calabrese, Rosalie Sue *management consultant, writer*
Call, Neil Judson *management consultant*
Cameron, Ewen *advertising executive*
Carmellini, Andrew *chef*
Carroll, Tom *advertising executive*
Casella, Cesare *chef, educator*
Cenedella, Marc *Internet company executive*
Chambrello, Michael R. *computer company executive*
Chang, David *chef*
Cheney, Richard Eugene *public relations executive, psychoanalyst*
Civiello, Mary *communications executive, journalist*
Clarke, Frank William *communications executive*
Clow, Lee *advertising agency executive*
Cohen, Alan L. *advertising executive*
Cohn, Theodore *management consultant*
Coleman, Gregory G. *Internet company executive, former magazine publisher*
Colicchio, Tom *chef, food service executive*
Comstock, Beth (Elizabeth J. Comstock) *marketing executive*
Cook, Ian M. *consumer products company executive*
Cortese, Edward *marketing and public relations executive*
Cox, L. Kevin *human resources specialist*
Coyne, Nancy Carol *advertising executive*
Craig, Elizabeth Coyne *marketing executive*
Craig, Pamela J. *management consulting firm executive*
D'Ambrosio, Ralph G. *communications systems company executive*
Daniel, David Ronald *management consultant*
Dart, Leslee *public relations company executive*
Daum, Julie Hembrock *executive recruiter*
David, Miles *marketing executive*
Davidson, Donald William *advertising executive*
D'Elia, Valarie *travel writer and commentator*
DePalma, Gina *chef*
Desmond, Laura *advertising executive*
Deutsch, Donny (Donald Jay Deutsch) *advertising executive, business commentator*
Devine, Jack *consulting firm executive, former federal agency administrator*
DiFebo, Valerie *advertising executive*
Diller, Barry *Internet company executive*

Dimling, John Arthur *marketing executive*
Doctoroff, Daniel L. *communications executive, former city manager*
Dooner, John Joseph, Jr. *advertising executive*
Doyle, Lee *marketing and communications executive*
Dru, Jean-Marie Paul *advertising executive*
Drzik, John P. *management consulting firm executive*
Dubuc, Nancy *communications executive*
Ducasse, Alain *chef*
Dufresne, Wylie *chef, food service executive*
Dunn, James W. *communications systems company executive*
Edelman, Richard Winston *public relations executive*
Edlow, Kenneth Lewis *security firm executive*
Eisler, Susan Krawetz *advertising executive*
Ellig, Janice Reals *marketing professional, human resources specialist*
Ernst, John Louis *management consultant*
Evans, Alfred Lee, Jr. *advertising executive*
Faber, Neil *advertising executive*
Feder, Benjamin *computer game company executive*
Feldman, Allan Roy *corporate development and marketing executive*
Feldman, Stuart I. *Internet company executive*
Fernandez de Cordova, Sergio Alonso *advertising and publishing executive*
Fili-Krushel, Patricia *media company executive*
Fine, Jo Renée *management consultant*
Finley, Skip *communications executive*
Finn, Peter *public relations executive*
Flaherty, Clementina Santi *corporate communications specialist, writer*
Flay, Bobby (Robert William Flay) *chef, restaurateur*
Fleischer, Ari (Lawrence Ari Fleischer) *public relations executive, former White House press secretary*
Fleischman, Barbara Greenberg *public relations consultant*
Fluhr, Howard *consulting firm executive*
Fogelson, Susie *marketing and broadcast executive*
Foster, Richard Norman *management consultant*
Frank, William Fielding *computer company executive, consultant*
Frankfort, Lew *consumer products company executive*
Furman, Anthony Michael *public relations executive*
Gallay, Barbara *travel company executive*
Gardiner, E. Nicholas P. *personnel director*
Gatfield, Stephen J. *advertising executive*
Gay, Richard *communications executive*
Geier, Philip Henry, Jr. *advertising executive*
Geller, Robert James *advertising executive*
Gerard-Sharp, Monica Fleur *communications executive*
Gerzema, Mary *advertising executive*
Gianinno, Susan McManama *advertising executive*
Gill, Linda A. *advertising executive*
Ginsburg, Sigmund G. *management and executive search consultant*
Goldschmidt, Charles *advertising agency executive*
Goldsmith, Clifford Henry *retired consumer products company executive*
Goldstone, Steven F. *former consumer products company executive*
Gosen, David *computer game company executive*
Gottlieb, Jerrold Howard *advertising executive*
Graves, Valerie Jo *advertising executive*
Gray, Bill *advertising executive*
Greco, John A., Jr. *marketing executive*
Greenland, Leo *advertising executive*
Grossman, Lawrence Kugelmass *former communications and advertising executive*
Gumbinner, Paul S. *advertising and executive recruitment agency executive*
Gunning, Paul *advertising and marketing agency executive*
Gupta, Rajat Kumar *management consultant*
Haas, Thomas F. *marketing executive*
Haberman, Seth *advertising executive*
Hammond, Lou Rena Charlotte *public relations executive*
Hara, Eric *chef*
Haselmann, John Philip *management consultant*
Hatheway, John Harris *advertising agency executive*
Hauser, Francesca (Fran) *media communications executive*
Heekin, Jim (James Robson Heekin III) *advertising executive*
Heimann, Gail *public relations executive*
Hemsing, Josephine Claudia *public relations executive*
Hill, Nancy *advertising association executive*
Hiller, John *Internet company executive*
Holzer, Harold *museum and marketing executive, historian, writer*
Hopson, Craig *chef*
Horvath, Robert G. *advertising executive*
Houser, Dan *computer game company executive*
Houser, Sam *computer game company executive*
Hudes, Nana Brenda *marketing professional*
Ilson, Bernard *public relations executive, writer*
Isay, Joshua D. *political consultant*
Jacoby, Robert Harold *management consulting executive*
James, Robert Leo *advertising executive, director*
Jeffrey, Robert (Bob) *advertising executive*
Johnson, Harold Earl *human resources specialist*
Jones, David *advertising executive*
Josell, Jessica (Wechsler) *public relations executive*
Just, Gemma Rivoli *retired advertising executive*
Karalekas, George Steven *advertising agency executive, political consultant*
Karp, Martin Everett *management consultant*
Kassel, Terry *human resources specialist*
Kaufman, Elaine *restaurant owner*
Keenan, Kerry *marketing and advertising executive*
Keenan, Michael Edgar *marketing professional*
Kelmenson, Leo-Arthur *advertising executive*
Khanna, Vikas *chef*
Kiger, Kris *advertising executive*
Kins, Gloria *public relations executive, photojournalist, writer, editor*
Kleisner, Frederick J. *hotel executive*
Klores, Dan (Daniel Aaron Klores) *public relations executive*
Koplik, Michael R. *sales representation company executive*
Kotuk, Andrea Mikotajuk *public relations executive, writer*
Kreuther, Gabriel *chef*
Krinsky, Robert Daniel *consulting firm executive*
Kummel, Eugene H. *advertising agency executive*
Kuperman, Robert Ian *retired advertising agency executive*
Kyriakou, Linda Grace *communications executive*
Lakshmi-Ratan, Ramnath Ayyan *marketing professional*
Lang, George *restaurateur*
Lannamann, Richard Stuart *executive search consultant*
Lawlor, Norah *public relations executive*
Lazarus, Shelly (Rochelle) *advertising executive*
Le Dû, Jean-Luc *Wine Shop Owner*
Leubert, Alfred Otto Paul *management consultant*
Levy, Tara Walpert *advertising executive*
Liebrandt, Paul *chef*
Lindblad, Lisa *travel company executive, anthropologist, writer*
Lindstrom, Martin *marketing professional, writer*
Liodice, Robert D. *advertising executive*
Lipman, Ira Ackerman *security service company executive*
Lipton, Charles *public relations executive*
Lipton, Joan Elaine *advertising executive*
Lo, Anita M. *chef*
Lockwood, Molly Ann *communications company executive*
Loeb, Larry Morris *communications company executive*
Logan, Don *communications industry executive*
Longobardi, David *executive vice president, chief content officer*
Lorber, Barbara Heyman *communications executive*
Lubars, David Charles *advertising executive*
Lyne, Susan Markham *Internet sales company executive, former multi-media company executive*
Maas, Jane Brown *advertising executive*
Maccioni, Sirio *restaurant manager*
Makovsky, Kenneth Dale *public relations executive*
Malgieri, Nick *food service executive, educator, chef, writer*
Manoff, Richard Kalman *advertising executive, writer, public health service officer, consultant*
Marcosson, Thomas I. *management consultant, advertising executive*
Marsal, Bryan Paul *restructuring company executive*
Martínez-López, Carmen Leonor *management consultant, educator*
Masi, Jane Virginia *marketing and sales consultant*
Masters, Jon Joseph *corporate governance specialist, management consultant*
Matsuhisa, Nobuyuki *chef, restaurant owner*
McCabe, Jim *Internet company executive*
McCabe, Mary F. *marketing professional*
McCarthy, Joseph D. *advertising agency executive*
McCaslin, Teresa Eve *human resources specialist*
McGinnis, Arthur Joseph, Jr. *public relations executive*
McGrath, Michael G. *management consulting firm executive*
McGuire, Maureen A. *marketing executive*
McInerney, Thomas J. *Internet company executive*
McLennan, Hamish *advertising executive*
Meehan, Sandra Gotham *communications and creative consultant, writer*
Mehlman, Ken (Kenneth Brian Mehlman) *public relations executive*
Meyer, Danny *restaurateur*
Miller, Alan *computer company executive, management consultant*
Miller, Ernest Charles *management consultant*
Miller, Neil Stuart *advertising executive*
Miller, Robert *advertising executive*
Minson, Arthur *Internet company executive*
Moreira, Marcio Martins *advertising executive*
Murphy, James Edward *public relations and marketing executive*
Nadler-Hurvich, Hedda Carol *public relations executive*
Neff, Thomas Joseph *search firm executive*
Nieporent, Drew A. *restaurant owner*
Nisenholtz, Martin Abram *telecommunications executive, educator*
Olafsson, Olaf *communications executive*
Oppenheim, Robert *beauty industry executive*
O'Sullivan, Eugene Henry *retired advertising executive, management consultant*
Parkes, Jacqueline Dale *marketing executive*
Patrick, Stephen C. *consumer products company executive*
Pearlstine, Norman *communications executive, consultant, former editor*
Penn, Mark J. *public relations executive, pollster, political strategist*
Perelman, Ronald Owen *consumer products company executive*
Poe, Randall Ellsworth *public relations executive, author*
Pompadur, I. Martin *communications executive*
Portale, Alfred *chef, restaurant owner*
Price, Paul *marketing and communications company executive*
Price, Robert *media and communications executive, investment banker, lawyer*
Pyne, George *marketing executive*
Radice, Frank J. *communications executive*
Rauch, Arthur Irving *management consultant*
Ray, Rachael Domenica *chef, television personality*
Reges, Marianna Alice *marketing executive*
Reynolds, James *management consultant*
Ripert, Eric Frank *chef*
Robbins, John Clapp *management consultant*
Roberts, Francis Stone *advertising executive*
Roberts, Kevin *advertising executive*
Robertson, Andrew J. *advertising executive*
Robinson, Peter M. *business association executive*
Roche, Gerard Raymond *management consultant*
Roldan, Kenneth Arroyo *executive recruiter, lawyer*
Rosenshine, Allen Gilbert *retired advertising agency executive*
Roskin, William A. *communications executive*
Roth, Michael I. *marketing executive*
Rothenberg, Robert Philip *public relations counselor*
Rubenstein, Howard Joseph *public relations executive*
Ruder, William *public relations executive*
Ruhanen, Troy *advertising agency executive*
Rutcofsky, Barry *computer game company executive, lawyer*
Samuelsson, Marcus (Kasshun Tsegie) *food service executive*
Sansone, Guy *restructuring company executive*
Sawyer, Linda *advertising executive*
Scarpelli, Bob (Robert) *advertising executive*
Schafer, Charles J. *communications systems company executive*
Schatz, Gary Stewart *marketing professional*
Schrager, Ian *hotel executive*
Schupak, Leslie Allen *public relations company executive*
Schwab, Frank, Jr. *management consultant*
Schwartz, Alan Victor *advertising executive*
Seaman, Alfred Jarvis *retired advertising agency executive*
Secunda, Eugene *marketing professional, educator*
Seiden, Steven Arnold *executive search consultant*
Serra, Matthew D. *consumer products company executive*
Shapiro, Mark S. *theme park company executive*
Shapiro, Marvin Lincoln *communications company executive*
Shepard, Thomas Rockwell III *advertising executive*
Sherman, Eugene Jay *retired marketing professional, bank executive, economist*
Shinder, Marcella Marie *marketing executive*
Siegel, Herbert Jay *communications executive, director*
Siegel, Lucy Boswell *public relations executive*
Siewert, Jake (Richard L. Siewert Jr.) *communications executive, former White House press secretary*
Silverstein, Scott A. *trading card company executive*
Sinclair, Daisy *communications executive*
Softness, Donald Gabriel *marketing professional, manufacturing executive*
Sohm, Aldo *Sommelier*
Souham, Gérard *communications executive*
Stahl, Sandra Michelle *communications executive*
Steves, Gale C. *marketing professional, writer, editor-in-chief, publishing executive*
Stotsky, Adam *communications executive*
Stoute, Stephen *marketing executive, entrepreneur*
Stover, Annette Birgit *advertising and public relations executive*
Strear, Joseph D. *public relations executive*
Strianese, Michael T. *communications systems company executive*
Stroock, Mark Edwin, II, *public relations company executive*
Swid, Stephen Claar *communications executive, director*
Tangney, Michael J. *consumer products company executive*
Tarter, Fred Barry *advertising executive*
Terkelsen, Brian J. *entertainment marketing executive*
Thorne, John Watson III *advertising and marketing executive*
Tisch, Jonathan Mark *hotel company executive*
Torrenzano, Richard *public relations executive*
Tortorici, Peter *marketing executive*
Trabocchi, Fabio *chef*
Tusk, Bradley *communications specialist*
Underwood, Joanna DeHaven *environmental services administrator*
Vidal, Manolo (Manny) *marketing communications agency executive*
Volk, Kristin *advertising agency executive*
von Baillou, Astrid *executive search consultant*
Vongerichten, Jean-Georges *food service executive, chef*
Wasow, Omar *Internet company executive*
Waters, Donald Joseph *data processing executive*
Weil, A. Lorne *computer company executive*
Weinstein, Sharon Schlein *corporate communications executive, educator*
Weisenburger, Randall J. *advertising executive*
Weiss, Myrna Grace *management consultant*
Werfelman, William Herman, Jr. *public relations executive*
Willett, Roslyn Leonore *public relations executive, food service consultant, writer, editor*
Wishart, George *marketing and media information company executive*
Wolff, Richard Joseph *public relations executive, consultant, historian*
Wolfson, Howard L. *corporate communications specialist, political analyst*
Wren, John D. *advertising executive*
Yeo, Patricia *chef*
Young, Antony *marketing and communications company executive*
Young, Miles *advertising executive*
Zelnick, Strauss *entertainment company executive*

Nyack
Karp, Peter Simon *marketing executive*

Ossining
Dolmatch, Theodore Bieley *management consultant*
Gilbert, Joan Stulman *retired public relations executive*

Palisades
Lenton, Roberto Leonardo *environmental services administrator*

Pelham
Hearle, Douglas Geoffrey *public relations consultant*
Tolliver, Lisa Marie *management consultant, educator*

Pleasantville
Eschweiler, Peter Quintus *planning consultant*
Radin, Amy Janine *marketing executive, publishing executive*

Port Chester
Ailloni-Charas, Dan *marketing executive*
Rosenberg, William Mark *chef, restaurant owner*

Port Washington
Leeds, Richard *computer marketing executive*

Poughkeepsie
Darrow, Emily M. *public relations executive, writer*
VanBuren, Denise Doring *corporate communications executive*

Purchase
Carey, Albert P. *retail sales professional*
Hilado, Tessa *beverage company executive*
Kempczinski, Chris *marketing executive*

Quogue
Burkhardt, Ronald Robert *advertising executive, filmmaker, artist, writer*

Rochester
Bachison, Justine *customer service administrator*
Berman, Robert L. *imaging company executive*
Cisney, Jennifer *photography and printing company executive, blogger*
Faraci, Philip J. *imaging company executive*
Goldberg-Schaible, Jocelyn Hope Schnier *market research professional*
Harris, Diane Carol *merger and acquisition consulting firm executive*
Hayzlett, Jeffrey Wayne *marketing executive*

Rockville Centre
Beyer, Suzanne *advertising agency executive*

Roslyn
Ulanoff, Stanley M. *communications executive*

Rye
Franklin, Martin E. *consumer products company executive*
Kaulakis, Arnold Francis *management consultant*
Moore, Mechlin Dongan *communications executive, marketing consultant*
Pearson, Nathan Williams *communications and investment executive*

Rye Brook
Mariam, Thomas Fred *public relations executive, radio producer*

Saint Huberts
Neilson, Winthrop Cunningham III *retired communications executive, financial consultant, photographer*

Saint Regis Falls
Gaggin, Warren William *personnel director, special education administrator*

Scarsdale
Kaufman, Robert Jules *communications consultant, lawyer*
Laufer, Leonard Justin *management consultant*

Sleepy Hollow
Schmidt, Klaus Franz *advertising executive*

Somers
Berisford, John L. *consumer products company executive*
Bronzo, Neal A. *consumer products company executive*
Crawford, Victor L. *consumer products company executive*
Drewes, Alfred H. *consumer products company executive*
Foss, Eric J. *consumer products company executive*
Franks, Brent J. *consumer products company executive*
King, Robert C. *consumer products company executive*

Staten Island
Fafian, Joseph, Jr. *management consultant*

Syosset
Cordaro, Joanne *human resources specialist, director*

Syracuse
Cooper, John Ambrose *management consultant, marketing professional*
Newman, David *environmental services administrator, educator*

Tappan
Fox, Muriel *retired public relations executive*

Thornwood
Bassett, Lawrence C. *management consultant*

White Plains
Duncan, Bruce W. *hotel and retired real estate company executive*
Gofman, Alex J. (Alexander Gofman) *marketing executive, author*
Klein, Ross A. *hotel executive*
Lukaszewski, James Edmund *communications executive*
Park, John *Internet company executive*
van Paasschen, Frits *hotel executive*

Yonkers
Capodilupo, Elizabeth Jeanne Hatton *public relations executive, writer*

NORTH CAROLINA

Arden
Baker, Kerry Allen *management consultant*

Asheboro
Sanders, William Eugene *marketing executive*

Asheville
Mundt, Barry Maynard *management consultant*

Chapel Hill
Conley, Patrick *clinic administrator*
Lochridge, Julie Deane *retired communications executive*

Charlotte
Austin, Margaret Gibson *public relations executive*
Bass-Hollis, Cynthia Gibson *environmental services administrator*
Eppes, Thomas Evans *advertising and public relations executive*
Hauser, David L. *communications executive*
Lee, Joseph William *sales executive*
Van Alstyne, Vance Brownell *management consultant*

Cullowhee
Jensen, Donald A., Jr. *management consultant, educator*

Davidson
Henkel, Herbert Ludwig *diversified industrial products company executive*

Durham
Barker, Ben *chef, restaurant owner*
Barker, Karen *restaurant owner, chef*
Mela, Carl Frederick *marketing educator*
Otterbourg, Robert Kenneth *public relations consultant, writer*

Elon
Powell, William Council, Sr. *service company executive*

Flat Rock
Childress, Richard Thomas *international business consultant, author*

Greensboro
Staab, Thomas Robert *consumer product company financial executive*

Hayesville
Turner, Lisa Phillips *human resources executive*

Hendersonville
Carney, Robert Arthur *restaurant executive*

Lake Toxaway
Raynolds, Elaine Spalding *sales executive, photojournalist*

Lumberton
Dent, Eric B. *management consultant*

Mars Hill
Sime, Donald Rae *retired business administration educator*

Mooresville
Johnston, James Wesley *retired consumer products company executive*
Mabry, Joseph M.(Mike), Jr. *consumer products company executive*
Niblock, Robert A. *consumer home products company executive*

Morrisville
Amelio, Bill (William J.) *computer company executive*
Indursky, Mike *consumer products company executive, marketing professional*
Ward, Stephen M., Jr. *computer company executive*

New Bern
Naumann, William Carl *consumer products company executive*

North Wilkesboro
Stone, Larry Dean *consumer products company executive*

Pinehurst
Rees, Clifford Harcourt, Jr., (Ted Rees) *consulting company executive, retired trade association administrator, military officer*
Stevenson, Josiah, IV, *management consultant*

Raleigh
Burton, Troy *parks director, museum association administrator*
Eberly, Harry Landis *retired communications company executive*
Leak, Robert Edwards *economic development consultant*
Lucht, John Charles *management consultant, writer*

Sanford
Brown, Eva Everlean *business executive*
Sodini, Peter J. *food service executive*

Southern Pines
Owings, Malcolm William *retired management consultant*

Wilkesboro
Bridgeford, Gregory M. *consumer products company executive*
Hull, Robert F., Jr., (Bob Hull) *consumer products company executive*

Winston Salem
Lambeth, Judy (E. Julia Lambeth) *tobacco company executive, lawyer*

OHIO

Akron
Liu, Liping *management consultant, educator*

Cincinnati
Bateman, Sharon Louise *corporate philanthropist*
Brown, Bruce *consumer products company executive*
Brown, Dale Patrick *retired advertising executive*
Daley, Clayton Carl, Jr. *consumer products company executive*
Dillon, David Brian *retail grocery executive*
Dougherty, David Francis *business process outsourcing executive*
Goodwin, John P. *consumer products company executive*
Hawkins, Lawrence Charles *management consultant, educator*
Healey, Melanie Liddle *consumer products company executive, marketing professional*
Lafley, A.G. (Alan George Lafley) *consumer products company executive*
List, Teri L. *consumer products company executive*
Majoras, Deborah Platt *consumer products company executive, former commissioner*
McDonald, Robert Alan (Bob McDonald) *consumer products company executive*
Moeller, Jon R. *consumer products company executive*
Odeen, Philip A. *communications executive*
Otto, Charlotte R. *consumer products company executive*
Peterson, Randy *consumer products company executive, information technology professional*
Pritchard, Marc S. *consumer products company executive*
Shirley, Edward D. *consumer products company executive*
Sommer, Scott William *control systems integrator manager*

Cleveland
Cook, Susan J. *human resources specialist, manufacturing executive*
Danco, Léon Antoine *management consultant, educator*
Dunbar, Mary Asmundson *retired communications executive, investor relations and public relations consultant*
Henry, Edward Frank *retired data processing executive*
Perkovic, Robert Branko *retired international management consultant*
Roop, James John *public relations executive*
Stauffer, Thomas George *retired hotel executive*
Taw, Dudley Joseph *sales executive, director*

Columbus
Davis, Steven A. *restaurant company executive*
Hobson, David Lee *consulting firm executive, former United States Representative from Ohio*
James, Donna Anita *consulting firm executive*
Mahoney, Kimberly Lynne *event and facility executive*
Ress, Charles William *management consultant*

Dayton
Massetti, Tony J. *computer services company executive*
Mitakides, Jane *corporate communications specialist*
Nuti, William R. *computer services company executive*

Dublin
Smith, K(ermit) Wayne *computer company executive*
Wang, Andrew Hsing-Jen *marketing professional, information technology executive, journalist, librarian*
Watkins, Carole S. *human resources specialist, medical products executive*

Fostoria
Howard, Kathleen *computer company executive*

Garrettsville
Diskin, Michael Edward *consumer products and plastics company executive, construction executive*

Gates Mills
Reitman, Robert Stanley *management consultant, not-for-profit advisor*

Germantown
Fetzer, Ronald Charles *communications and business educator, consultant*
Lansaw, Charles Ray *rendering industry executive*

Kent
Bissler, Richard Thomas *mortician*

Lancaster
Katlic, John Edward *management consultant*
Phillips, Edward John *consulting firm executive*

Lyndhurst
Lipson, Renée Sue *organization development consultant*

Mansfield
Pesec, David John *data systems executive*

Marysville
Hagedorn, James *landscape company executive*

Mason
Tracy, Allen Wayne *management consultant*

Mayfield Heights
Newman, Joseph Herzl *advertising executive, consultant*

Miamisburg
Ringler, James M. *computer services company executive*

Middletown
Carroll, Mike *steelworker*
Turpin, Richard E. *sales executive*

New Albany
Duggan, Thomas Patrick *management consultant*

North Canton
Fountain, Ronald Glenn *management consultant, corporate financial executive, entrepreneur, educator, investor*

Olmsted Falls
Faller, Dorothy Anderson *training services executive, consultant*

Orange Village
Stauderman, Bruce Ford *advertising executive, writer*

Rocky River
Hosek, John Jude *planning organization executive*

Salem
Fehr, Kenneth Manbeck *retired computer company executive*

Strongsville
Potter, David *sales executive*

Toledo
Block, Allan James *communications executive*
Paquette, Jack Kenneth *management consultant, author, historian*
Stroucken, Albert P. L. *consumer products company executive, former chemical company executive*

Troy
Puls, Sarah *marketing executive*
Tipton, Clyde Raymond, Jr. *communications and resources development consultant*

Warrensville Heights
Simmons, Clinton Craig *human resources executive*

Westlake
O'Brien, Thomas M. *travel company executive*
Rebholz, Andrew J. *hospitality company executive*

Xenia
Nutter, Zoe Dell Lantis *retired public relations executive*

Youngstown
Estrin, Melvyn J. *computer products company executive*
Hudak, Cheryl C. *travel company executive*

OKLAHOMA

Cleveland
Henry, Kathleen Marie *marketing executive*

Enid
Marquardt, Shirley Marie *retired management consultant*
Taveggia, Thomas Charles *retired management consultant, educator*

Oklahoma City
Greiner, Kenneth Donald, Jr. *retired management consultant, health facility administrator*
LaMotte, Janet Allison *retired management consultant*
Vargo, Stephen Louis *travel company executive*

Tulsa
Gentry, Bern Leon, Sr. *management consultant*

OREGON

Beaverton
Dima, Smolyansky *marketing executive*

Brookings
Kovach, Robin *environmental services administrator*

Clackamas
Thomas, Sonia *provider specialist, trainer*

Eugene
Cawood, Elizabeth Jean *public relations executive*

Jacksonville
Hennion, Reeve Lawrence *communications executive*

Lake Oswego
Parrick, Gerald Hathaway *communications and marketing executive*

Medford
Entorf, Richard Carl *retired management consultant*

Monmouth
Chong, Che *marketing executive*

Portland
Barbeau, Monique Andrée *chef*
Conkling, Roger Linton *management consultant, business administration educator, retired utilities executive*
Hinckley, Gregory Keith *software industry executive*
Linstone, Harold Adrian *management consultant, educator*
Pomeroy, Naomi *chef*

Tualatin
Hick, Kenneth William *marketing executive*

PENNSYLVANIA

Allentown
Borger, Ann Work *computer and communications professional*

Beach Lake
Chatlos, William Edward *management consultant*

Bethel Park
Willard, John Gerard *communications executive, consultant, writer, educator*

Blue Bell
Evans, John Derelc *marketing executive*

Bryn Mawr
Eiser, Barbara J.A. *management consultant, executive coach*

Canonsburg
Cashman, James E. III *engineering software company executive*
Smith, Peter J. *engineering software company executive*

Chambersburg
Elias, Janilyn *student personnel director*

Conshohocken
Spiers-Lopez, Pernille (Pernille Lopez) *consumer products company executive*
Thompson, Pamela Padwick *public relations executive*

Drexel Hill
Tirado, Janet A. *advertising marketing and public relations communications executive*

Fairless Hills
Frazier, Brett W. *waste management executive*

Gettysburg
Hallberg, Budd Jaye *retired management consulting firm executive*

Kennett Square
Hennes, Robert Taft *former management consultant, investment executive*

King Of Prussia
Clauson, Sharyn Ferne *consulting company executive, educator*

Lafayette Hill
Edwards, JoAnn Louise *human resources executive*

Lancaster
Kelly, Robert Lynn *advertising executive*

Manns Choice
Braendel, Douglas Arthur *hotel executive*

Mechanicsburg
Harper, Diane Marie *retired corporate communications specialist*

Media
Barnett, Samuel Treutlen *consultant*
Garvin, Florence Ward *management consultant*

Narberth
Newhall, John Harrison *retired business executive, management consultant*

New Hope
Cook, Geoff *Internet company executive*

Newtown
Morrill, Nancy Porter *management consultant*

Nottingham
White, Richard Edmund *human resources specialist*

Oaks
Marland, Alkis Joseph *leasing company executive, computer scientist, educator, financial planner*

Paoli
Brundage, Russell Archibald *retired data processing executive*

Philadelphia
Angelakis, Michael J. *communications executive*
Arnold, Anne Katrin *communication researcher, international development civil servant*
Banse, Amy L. *communications executive, lawyer*
Benson, Romona A. Riscoe *marketing executive, museum administrator*
Block, Arthur R. *communications executive, lawyer*
Burke, Jim *chef*
Carrig, Kenneth J. *human resources specialist*
Cohen, David Louis *communications executive*
Coulson, Zoe Elizabeth *retired consumer marketing executive*
Finney, Graham Stanley *management consultant*
Liebermann, Dan A. *cancer investigator, medical educator*

Logue-Kinder, Joan *public relations consultant*
McDade, Sean *market research company executive*
McKee, Lynn B. *human resources specialist, food products executive*
Morimoto, Masaharu *chef, television personality*
Roberts, Brian L. *communications executive*
Roth Rogers, Sheryl Lynn *marketing professional*
Showalter, Michael *marketing executive*
Starr, Stephen *restaurant owner*
Tuan, Kailin *management consultant, educator*
Vetri, Marc *chef*
Walter, William G. *consumer products company executive*
Wicks, Judy *restaurant manager*
Xu, Yao L *marketing professional, consultant*

Pittsburgh
Burger, Herbert Francis *retired advertising agency executive*
Dempsey, Jerry Edward *retired service company executive*
Ferrara, Albert E. *corporate executive*
Franklin, Kenneth Ronald *management consultant*
George, Carole A. *usability specialist*
Kilkeary, Kevin P. *hospitality executive*
Neel, John Dodd *cemetery executive*
Peterman, Donna Cole *communications executive*
Radakovich, Daniel I. *communications executive, consultant*
Rathke, Sheila Wells *strategic planning and marketing executive*
Reichblum, Audrey Rosenthal *public relations and publishing executive*
Wabby, James Patrick *quality assurance professional, educator*

Port Royal
Wert, Jonathan Maxwell, II, *management consultant*

Radnor
Paier, Adolf Arthur *management consultant*

Reading
Kraras, Gust C. *hotel executive*

Ridley Park
Walls, William Walton, Jr. *management consultant*

Rydal
Boreen, Henry Isaac *computer company executive*

Sadsburyville
Gellman, Gloria Gae Seeburger Schick *marketing professional*

Sewickley
Swann, Lynn Curtis *management consultant, retired professional football player*
Woody, Carol Clayman *data processing executive*

Southeastern
Rassbach, Herbert David *marketing executive*

State College
Subler, Edward Pierre *advertising executive*

Steelton
Zimmerman, Connie Ann *public administrator*

Sunbury
Weis, Robert Freeman *supermarket company executive*

Swarthmore
Krizek, Edwin John *marketing professional*

Valley Forge
LaBoon, Lawrence Joseph *human resources specialist, consultant*

Wallingford
Adamiec, Jean Kraus *retired advertising executive*

Wayne
Carroll, Robert W. *retired management consultant*
Conde, Cristobal I. *computer company executive*

West Chester
Hanna, Colin Arthur *management consultant, political consultant*
Murray, Lawrence *management consultant*

West Conshohocken
Mullen, Eileen Anne *human resources executive*

Willow Grove
Schiffman, Louis F. *management consultant*

Willow Street
Blevins, William Edward *management consultant*

Wyndmoor
Barrett, James Edward, Jr. *management consultant*

Wyomissing
Carlino, Peter M. *gaming company executive*
Wilmott, Timothy J. *gaming company executive*

Yardley
Makadok, Stanley *management consultant*
Minter, Philip Clayton *retired communications company executive*
Weaver, William Clair, Jr., (Mike Weaver) *human resources development executive*

York
Livingston, Pamela A. *corporate image and marketing management consultant*

RHODE ISLAND

Barrington
Mihaly, Eugene Bramer *management consultant*

Middletown
Leighton, Charles Milton *retired specialty consumer products executive*

North Kingstown
Kullberg, Gary Walter *advertising agency executive*

Pawtucket
Hargreaves, David D. *toy company executive*
Hassenfeld, Alan Geoffrey *retired toy company executive*
Thomas, Deb *toy company executive*
Verrecchia, Alfred Joseph *toy company executive*

Providence
Archer, William M. *marketing executive*
Szostak, (M.) Anne *consulting firm executive, former bank executive*

Saunderstown
Zaccaria, Mark Stuart *marketing professional*

Wakefield
Frostic, Frederick Lee *strategic planning and defense policy consultant*

Woonsocket
Frappier, Pearl Peters *retired bookkeeper*

SOUTH CAROLINA

Bluffton
Reuben, Alvin Bernard *communications and entertainment executive*

Charleston
Barickman, Donald *chef*
Ketner, Linda *consulting company executive, civic worker*
Martin, Thomas Rhodes *communications executive, writer, educator*

Columbia
Barnum, Mary Ann Mook *information management manager*
Barnum, William Douglas *retired communications executive*
Beyer, Christine E. *academic standards and assessment consultant*
Grimball, Caroline Gordon *retail sales professional*

Greenville
Dorman, D. Douglas *human resources specialist, hospital administrator*

Greer
Sundstrom, Harold Walter *public relations executive*

Hilton Head Island
Conn, Margaret Elbow *human resources specialist*
McKeldin, William Evans *management consultant*
Patton, Joseph Donald, Jr. *management consultant*

Myrtle Beach
Sugishita, Jonea Gene *marketing executive, copywriter*

North Charleston
Perry, Evelyn Reis *communications company executive*

Pawleys Island
Bodie, Joseph Russell *environmental services administrator*
Grubb, William Francis Xavier *consumer products company executive, marketing professional*

Seneca
Strong-Tidman, Virginia Adele *marketing professional*

Spartanburg
Chmiel, Mark E. *marketing professional, food service company executive*
Marchioli, Nelson Jerome *restaurant chain executive*
Smithart-Oglesby, Debra Lynn *restaurant chain executive*

Sunset
Brodbeck, William Jan *marketing professional*

SOUTH DAKOTA

Sioux Falls
Hildebrand, Steve C. *consulting firm executive, political strategist*
Murdock, Rebecca Therese *management consultant, director*

TENNESSEE

Bristol
Overstreet, Catherine Ann *sales executive*

Crossville
Frazier, June Marie *retired public relations executive*

Gallatin
Bradley, Nolen Eugene, Jr. *retired personnel executive, educator*

Kingston
Shacter, John *technology management and education consultant*

Knoxville
Campbell, Michael L. *theatre company executive*
Cox, Anna Lee *retired administrative assistant*
Dunn, Gregory W. *theatre company executive*
Miles, Amy E. *theatre company executive*
Ownby, David H. *theatre company executive*
Sansom, William B. *consumer products executive*
Whiteside, Joan Robinson *administrative assistant, music educator*

Lebanon
Cochran, Sandra Brophy *restaurant chain company executive*
Woodhouse, Michael A. *restaurant holdings company executive*

Lenoir City
Edwards, C. Karen *consultant company executive*

Memphis
Abston, Dunbar, Jr. *management consultant*
Bollheimer, (Cecilia) Denise *marketing professional, finance company executive*
English, Kelly *chef*
Krieger, Robert Lee, Jr. *human resource/management consultant, educator, writer, travel/meeting planner, political analyst, internet marketing consultant*
Tucker, Laurie A. *marketing executive*

Mount Juliet
Donovan, Gerard *management consulting company executive*

Nashville
Dobbs, George Albert *funeral director, embalmer*
Hartley, Michael J. *travel company executive*
Hillenmeyer, Henry Reiling, Jr. *restaurant company executive*
Reed, Colin V. *hotel company executive*
Reynolds, Doris Elizabeth *management consultant, poet*
Rose, Michael David *hotel company executive*
Seigenthaler, John Michael *public relations executive, former newscaster*
Van Mol, Louis John, Jr. *public relations executive*

Puryear
Hedges, Patrick Armand *security firm executive*

Shelbyville
Nelson, Clara Singleton *human resources consultant*

TEXAS

Arlington
Butte, Norine *marketing executive*
English, Marlene Cabral *management consultant*
Sawyer, Dolores *motel chain executive*

Austin
Bartlett, Dan (Daniel Joseph Bartlett) *consulting firm executive, former federal official*
Dessau, Nigel *computer company executive*
Dowd, Matthew John *communications executive, political consultant*
Garza, Antonio Oscar, Jr., (Tony Garza) *consulting firm executive, former ambassador*
Green, Shirley Moore *retired communications executive, public information officer*
Gurasich, Stephen William, Jr. *advertising executive*
Hughes, Karen Parfitt *public relations executive, former federal agency administrator*
Irgang, Carole A. *marketing executive*
Kallman, James William *management consultant, educator*
Mathias, Reuben Victor (Vic Mathias) *organization executive, real estate investor*
McKinnon, Mark David *consulting firm executive*
Spence, Roy Milam, Jr. *advertising executive*
Trabulsi, Judy *advertising and marketing executive*
Wahl, William Bryan *marketing professional, real estate company officer*
Whitney, Bret Meyers *travel company executive*
York, Candace A. *marketing professional, writer*

Carrollton
Owen, Cynthia Carol *sales executive*

College Station
Gunn, Clare Alward *travel consultant, writer, retired educator*
Hise, Richard Todd *marketing professional, educator, consultant*
Solymosy, Edmond Sigmond Albert *marketing professional, retired military officer*

Dallas
Brooks, Douglas H. *food service executive*
Bryant, L. Gerald *management consultant*
Byas, Teresa Ann Uranga *customer service administrator, interior designer, consultant*
Campbell, Raymond III *publication director*
Crusemann, F(rederick) Ross *advertising agency official*
Dawson, Edward Joseph *merger and acquisition executive*
Dozier, David Charles, Jr. *advertising and public relations executive*
Dykeman, Alice Marie *public relations executive*
England, Julie Spicer *computer company executive*
Fairbairn, Ursula Farrell *human resources executive*
Ghormley, Jason Grant *sales executive*
Gleason, Sean *marketing executive*
Hegi, Frederick B., Jr. *consumer products company executive*
Heslin, Peter A. *management consultant, researcher, educator*
Horchow, S. Roger *marketing consultant*
Joyner, Oscar A. *communications executive*
Koeppel, Peter Stafford *advertising executive*
Levenson, Stanley Richard *public relations and advertising executive*
Lilyhorn, Gregory Dean *security firm executive*
May, Kenneth Austin *former consumer products company executive*
Migdol, Marvin Jacob *public relations and marketing executive, consultant*
Pace, Carolina Jolliff *communications executive, investor*
Parks, J. Michael *data processing executive*
Pearson, Robert Lawrence *executive recruiter*
Quinoy, Melisa *marketing and advertising executive*
Sabat, Hemant Kumar *communications and information technology industry leader*
Smith-Becker, Nancy Woolverton *public relations executive, art appraiser*
Spiegel, Lawrence Howard *advertising executive*
Zeitlin, Laurie *printing company and information technology executive*

Del Rio
Prather, Gerald Luther *management consultant, retired judge, military officer*

El Paso
Roberts, Ernst Edward *marketing consultant*

Fairview
Hansen, Elizabeth (Beth) Stevens *human resources consultant*

Flower Mound
Ross, Lesa Moore *quality assurance professional*

Fort Worth
Appel, Bernard Sidney *marketing professional, consultant, retired electronics executive*

Frisco
Forêt, Randy Blaise *public relations executive, insurance company executive*
Hawk, Phillip Michael *service corporation executive*

Georgetown
Maxfield, Louise Fonda Gribble *executive secretary*

Grapevine
Carlson, David W. *computer software company executive*
DeMatteo, Daniel A. *computer game company executive*
Fontaine, R. Richard *computer game company executive*
Morgan, Steven R. *computer game company executive*
Raines, J. Paul *computer company executive*
Smith, Catherine R. *computer software company executive*

Houston
Aardsma, David A. *waste management executive*
Burnett, Susan Walk *personnel service company owner*
Caddell, Lynn M. *waste management executive*
Caldwell, Barry H. *waste management executive*
Caswell, Bryan *chef*
Farrow, Anthony Raymond *management consultant*
Flato, William Roeder, Jr. *software development company executive*
Gilbert, Jill Barson *management consultant*
Mays, Randall T. *communications company executive*
McCollam, Marion Andrus *consulting firm executive, educator*
Myers, A. Maurice *waste management executive*
Myers, James Clark *advertising and public relations executive*
Noland, Mary Richerson *management consultant*
O'Donnell, Lawrence III *waste management executive*
Romans, Jay *waste management executive*
Ryan, Thomas L. *funeral company executive*
Saizan, Paula Theresa *business consultant*
Simpson, Robert G. *waste management executive*
Smith, Stephen F. *food service executive*
Steiner, David P. *waste management executive*
Stephens, Sidney Dee *human resources specialist, retired chemical manufacturing company executive*
Wiglesworth, Michael Bland *advertising executive*

Hurst
Bishara, Amin Tawadros *management and consulting firm executive*

Irving
Caldwell, James D. *hotel executive*
Deitemeyer, Michael J. *hotel executive*
Hawkins, William David *marketing executive*
Potter, Robert Joseph *technical and business executive*
Wicks, William Withington *retired public relations executive*

Junction
Evans, Jo Burt *communications executive, rancher*

Keller
Patterson, Ronald R(oy) *management consultant*

Kosse
Nicholas, Nickie Lee *retired industrial hygienist*

Lubbock
Dennison, Daniel Thomas *environmental compliance and lab administrator*
Jugenheimer, Donald Wayne *advertising executive, communications educator, academic administrator*

Mesquite
Cloud, Kevin *computer game company executive*
Hollenshead, Todd *computer game company executive*
Willits, Tim *computer game company executive*

New Caney
Hayes, Ann Carson *computer company executive*

Odonnell
Stephens, Stephanic Mica *executive secretary, educator*

Plano
Dillon, Donald Ward *management consultant*
Heller, Jeffrey M. *data processing executive*
Scott, Terry Lee *communications executive*
Speese, Mark E. *rental company executive*
Trebilcock, James R. *marketing executive*

Port Arthur
Munoz, Andrea Lee *human resources specialist*

Richardson
Madden, Marie Frances *marketing professional*

Round Rock
Bell, Paul D. *computer company executive*
Clarke, Jeffrey W. *computer company executive*
Dell, Michael Saul *computer company executive*
Garriques, Ronald G. *computer company executive*
Gladden, Brian T. *computer company executive*
Nelson, Erin Mulligan *computer company executive, marketing professional*
Schuckenbrock, Steve (Stephen Francis Schuckenbrock) *computer company executive, former information technology executive*

San Antonio
Butt, Charles Clarence *food service executive*
Garcia, Henry Frank *supply and project management consultant*
Mays, Mark Pitman *communication company executive*
Schembri, Chris *communications company executive, media specialist*

Southlake
Peluso, Michelle *Internet and travel company executive*
Sorge, Karen Lee *printing company executive, consultant*

Spring
Ciancimino, Joseph Andrew *data processing executive*

Spring Branch
Barban, Arnold Melvin *advertising executive, educator, writer*

Texas City
Hodges, Richard Dean *instrument and electrical technician*

The Woodlands
Glenn, Gerald Marvin *marketing, engineering and construction executive*
Morrison, Scott David *management consultant, small business owner*

Waco
Sorrels, Carolyn Jean *assistant to CIO*

Willis
Snider, Robert Larry *management consultant*

UTAH

Midway
Zenger, John Hancock *training company executive*

Orem
Sawyer, Thomas Edgar *management consultant*

Park City
Milner, Harold William *hotel executive*

Salt Lake City
Davis, Loyd Evan *defense industry marketing professional*
Shipko, Janet M. *human resources specialist*

Sandy
Phillips, Ted Ray *advertising executive*

VERMONT

Burlington
Shaw, Naomi *sales consultant, insurance agent, management consultant*

Putney
Keil, John Mullan *advertising executive, artist*

Vergennes
Kamman, Alan Bertram *retired communications consulting company executive*

Waitsfield
Esty, David Cameron *marketing and communications executive*

Wilmington
Little, Thomas M. *public relations executive*

Woodstock
Hoyt, Coleman Williams *postal consultant*
Matlins, Stuart M. *management consultant, publisher*

VIRGINIA

Abingdon
Ramos-Cano, Hazel Balatero *caterer, chef, innkeeper, restaurateur, entrepreneur*

Alexandria
Anderson, Maynard Carlyle *security firm executive*
Armstrong, Cathal *chef*
Beales, Char *marketing executive*
Braun, Michael A. *securities firm executive, retired federal agency administrator*
Coons, Barbara Lynn *public relations executive, librarian*
Falcon, Armando J., Jr. *consulting firm executive*
Fosdick (Beebe), Cora Prifold *management consultant*
Foster, Robert Francis *communications executive*
Frommer, Lawrence Julian *retired travel company executive*
Gage, Alex P. *marketing consultant*
Gallagher, Anne Porter *communications executive*
Harris, David Ford *management consultant, retired federal official*
Laurent, Lawrence Bell *communications executive, retired journalist*
Lightner, Candy (Candace Lynne Lightner) *non-profit management consultant, advocate*
McMillan, Charles William *consulting company executive*
Nelson, David Leonard *business executive*
Quirk, Frank Joseph *management consulting company executive*
Saunders, Steven R. *international public policy specialist*
Shirley, Craig P. *public relations executive, writer*
Stone, Ann Elizabeth *marketing agency executive, entrepreneur, volunteer, consultant*
Verburg, Edwin Arnold *management consultant*
Walker, Edward Keith, Jr. *retired management consultant, military officer*
Winkenwerder, William, Jr. *consulting firm executive, former federal agency administrator*

Annandale
Greinke, Everett Donald *management consultant*

Arlington
Adams, Jimmie Vick *communications systems company executive, retired military officer*
Armitage, Richard Lee *consulting firm executive, former federal agency administrator*
Clarke, Richard Alan *management consultant, former federal official*
Claussen, Eileen Barbara *environmental services administrator, former federal agency administrator*
DeFeo, Charles Joesph *Internet company executive*
Erwin, Frank William *human resources consultant*
Fay, Kevin J. *public relations executive*
Harrison, Emmett Bruce, Jr. *corporate communications counselor*
Helm, Roger Charles *environmental services administrator*
Luchok, Joseph Alan *communications executive, consultant*
Magrath, Michael P. *marketing executive, director*
McCaffrey, Barry Richard *consulting firm executive, retired military officer*
Newburger, Beth Weinstein *communications executive*
Potvin, William Tracey *management consultant*
RisCassi, Robert W. *communications systems company executive, retired military officer*
Vuono, Carl E. *communications systems company executive, retired military officer*
Zorthian, Barry *communications executive*

Chantilly
Fimian, Keith *property inspection company executive*

Charlottesville
Brown, Holmes *public relations executive*
Colley, John Leonard, Jr. *management consultant, educator, writer*

Cobbs Creek
Crum, John Kistler *management consultant*

Dulles
Armstrong, Tim *Internet company executive*
Parker, Ira H. *Internet company executive, lawyer*

Fairfax
Baker, Daniel Richard *computer company executive*
Saverot, Pierre-Michel *nuclear waste management company executive*
Witek, James Eugene *retired public relations executive*

Falls Church
Cherkasky, Michael Griffin *security firm executive, former insurance company executive*
Hays, Sharon Lynn *consulting company executive, former federal official*

Fredericksburg
Harrod, Audrey Hunter *retired executive secretary*

Glen Allen
Gulling, Mark V. *consumer products company executive*

Great Falls
Bachner, John Philip *business consultant*

Harrisonburg
Adams, Tom *foreign language services executive*

Lake Ridge
Ingrassia, Anthony Frank (Tony) *human resource specialist*

Leesburg
Lobanov-Rostovsky, Oleg *management consultant*
Strasser, Gabor *management consultant*

Lorton
Jackson, Gary Lee *security consultant*

Manassas
Locigno, Paul Robert *public relations executive*

Mc Lean
Dempsey, Joan Avalyn *consulting firm executive, former federal agency administrator*
Estren, Mark James *communications executive, television producer, writer, editor*
Ford, Nelson M. *consulting firm executive*
Harbach, Ed (Frank Edwin Harbach) *management and technology consulting executive*
Jayne, Edward Randolph, II, *executive search consultant*
Orkand, Donald Saul *management consultant*
Rose, Susan Porter *management and governmental affairs consultant*
Saylor, Michael J. *computer software company executive*
Shrader, Ralph William *consulting firm executive*
Watson, Jerry Carroll *advertising executive*

Middleburg
McNichols, Gerald Robert *consulting company executive*

Midlothian
Wadsworth, Robert David *advertising executive*

Norfolk
Blount, Robert Haddock *management consultant, retired military officer*
Miller, Christine Marie *sales, marketing and public relations executive*

Reston
Maher, David Willard *Internet company executive*
Pendergraft, David *lean six sigma consultant*
Sarreals, Sonia *data processing executive, consultant*
Witt, Ruth Hutt *management consultant*

Richmond
Brewer, W. Keith *tobacco company executive*
Dan, Michael T. *security firm executive*
Freeman, George C. III *tobacco company executive, lawyer*
Hughes, Mike *advertising executive*
Jacobs, Harry Milburn, Jr. *advertising executive*
Moore, David C. *tobacco company executive*
Peebles, Robert M. *tobacco company executive*
Woodley, John Paul, Jr. *consulting firm executive, former civilian military employee*

Round Hill
Schleede, Glenn Roy *marketing professional, consultant*

Seaford
Jenkins, Margaret Bunting *human resources executive*

Springfield
Bruen, John Dermot *management consultant*

Suffolk
Hall, Wayne Michael *management consultant*

Vienna
Monroe, Robert Rawson *national security consultant*
Olson, Walter Justus, Jr. *management consultant*

Virginia Beach
Alexander, William Powell *business advisor*
Wick, Robert Thomas *retired supermarket executive*

Washington
O'Connell, Patrick *chef*

Williamsburg
Finn, A. Michael *corporate communications specialist*

Winchester
Bonometti, Robert John *technology management and strategy executive*
Engelage, James Roland *commercial property manager*

Woodbridge
Zhao, Tong *management consultant*

WASHINGTON

Anacortes
Hoffmann, Manfred Walter *consulting company executive*

Arlington
Gerwick, Madeline Carol *marketing and timing professional*

Bellevue
Hall, Eleanor Williams *public relations executive*
Khosrowshahi, Dara *travel company executive*
McReynolds, Neil Lawrence *management consultant*
Myhrvold, Nathan P. *technology executive*

Federal Way
Hooper, John A. *human resources specialist*

Gig Harbor
Stover, Miles Ronald *management consultant*

Hunts Point
Ebsworth, Barney A. *retired travel company executive*

Issaquah
Matthews, John *human resources specialist, wholesale distribution executive*

Kennewick
Brewton, Wesley Hopkins (Wes Brewton) *retired chef, retired real estate manager*

Lacey
Caplan, Frank *retired management consultant, educator*

Medina
Dagnon, James Bernard *human resources executive*

Mercer Island
Dykstra, David Charles *management executive, consultant, accountant, author, educator*
Hilst, Glenn Rudolph *environmental sciences administrator, researcher*

Parkland
Johnson, LuAn K. *disaster management consultant*

Port Ludlow
Krugman, Stanley Lee *international management consultant*

Redmond
Abu-Hadba, Walid *computer software company executive*
Allard, J. *computer software company executive*
Andersen, Klaus Holse *computer software company executive*
Anderson, Brad *computer software company executive*
Anderson, Nancy J. *computer software company executive, lawyer*
Arbogast, Brian *computer company executive*
Ayala, Orlando *computer software company executive*
Bach, Robert J. (Robbie Bach) *computer software company executive*
Ballmer, Steven Anthony *computer software company executive*
Belfiore, Joe *computer software company executive*
Bevington, Sue *computer software company executive*
Brod, Frank H. *computer software company executive, accountant*
Brooks, Brad *computer software company executive*
Brummel, Lisa E. *computer software company executive*
Burt, Thomas William *computer software company executive, lawyer*
Capossela, Chris *computer software company executive*
Charney, Scott *computer software company executive, lawyer*
Chrapaty, Debra J. *computer software company executive*
Crozier, Alain *computer software company executive*
Davis, T. Ronald *marketing professional*
DelBene, Kurt *computer software company executive*
Delman, Michael *computer software company executive*
DeVaan, Jon S. *computer software company executive*
Domeniconi, Robin *computer company executive, former publishing executive*
Dunaway, Cammie *marketing executive*
Eisler, Craig *computer software company executive*
Elop, Stephen A. *computer software company executive*
Fathi, Ben *computer software company executive*
Ferguson, Donald *computer software company executive*
Flake, Gary William *computer software company executive*
Flowers, Melvin *computer software company executive*
Gates, Bill (William Henry Gates III) *computer software company executive*
George, Grant *computer software company executive*
Gibbons, Tom *computer software company executive*
Golden, L. Michael *computer software company executive*
Gounares, Alexander *computer software company executive*
Guggenheimer, Steve *computer software company executive*
Gupta, Anoop *computer software company executive*
Guthrie, Scott *computer software company executive*
Gutiérrez, Horacio E. *computer software company executive*
Hey, Tony *computer software company executive*
Higuchi, Yasuyuki *computer software company executive*
Ho, Roz *computer software company executive*
Hogan, Kathleen *computer software company executive*
Holland, Todd *computer software company executive*
Homldahl, Todd *computer software company executive*
Huston, Darren *computer software company executive*
Jeffress, Rusty *computer company executive*
Jha, Rajesh K. *computer software company executive*
Jones, Chris *computer software company executive*
Jorgensen, Erik *computer software company executive*
Kaplan, Rich *computer software company executive*
Kelly, Bob *computer software company executive*
Kennedy, William *computer software company executive*
Khaki, Jawad *computer software company executive*
Kim, Shane *computer software company executive*

Kimishima, Tatsumi *computer game company executive*
Klein, Peter *computer software company executive*
Koch, Mitchell L. *computer software company executive*
Kummert, Ted *computer software company executive*
Laing, Bill *computer software company executive*
Larson-Green, Julie *computer software company executive*
Leblond, Antoine *computer software company executive*
Lees, Andrew *computer software company executive*
Leung, Simon *computer software company executive*
Lichtman, Moshe *computer software company executive*
Liddell, Christopher P. *computer software company executive*
Liffick, Steve *computer software company executive*
Lu, Qi *computer software company executive*
MacDonald, Brian *computer software company executive*
Markezich, Ron *computer software company executive*
Mathews, Mich *computer company executive*
Mattrick, Donald A. *computer software company executive*
Matz, Joseph S. *computer software company executive*
Mehdi, Yusuf *computer software company executive*
Mital, Amit *computer software company executive*
Mitchell, William H. *computer software company executive*
Mount, Mindy (Melinda J. Mount) *computer software company executive*
Muglia, Bob (Robert L. Muglia) *computer software company executive*
Mulinder, Austen *computer software company executive*
Mundie, Craig James *computer software company executive*
Myerson, Terry *computer software company executive*
Nackman, Lee *computer software company executive*
Nadella, Satya *computer software company executive*
Nash, Mike *computer software company executive*
Nelson, Kimberly Terese *computer software company executive, former federal agency administrator*
Neupert, Peter *computer software company executive*
Numoto, Takeshi *computer software company executive*
Ozzie, Ray (Raymond E. Ozzie) *computer software company executive*
Pall, Gurdeep Singh *computer software company executive*
Paolucci, Umberto *computer software company executive*
Park, Michael S. *computer software company executive*
Parthasarathy, Sanjay *computer software company executive*
Passman, Pamela S. *computer software company executive*
Phelps, Marshall C., Jr. *computer software company executive*
Pitasky, Scott *computer software company executive*
Porter, David *computer software company executive*
Rashid, Richard F. *computer software company executive*
Reed, Daniel A. *computer software company executive*
Reller, Tami *computer software company executive*
Ritchie, J. *computer software company executive*
Rodriguez, Enrique *computer software company executive*
Rosini, Eduardo B. *computer software company executive*
Roskill, Jon *computer software company executive*
Rudder, Eric D. *computer company executive, information technology executive*
Schiro, Steve *computer software company executive*
Scott, Tony *computer software company executive*
Shaw, Frank X. *computer software company executive*
Sheldon, Jeanne *computer software company executive*
Shum, Harry *computer software company executive*
Sinofsky, Steven J. *computer software company executive*
Smith, Bradford Lee *computer software company executive, lawyer*
Snapp, Mary E. *computer software company executive, lawyer*
Somasegar, Sivarama Kichenane *computer software company executive*
Srivastava, Amitabh *computer software company executive*
Taneja, Rajat *computer software company executive*
Teper, Jeffrey Allen *computer software company executive*
Thompson, David M. *computer software company executive*
Thompson, Rick *computer software company executive*
Tobey, Brian *computer software company executive*
Treadwell, David *computer software company executive*
Turner, Kevin (B. Kevin Turner) *computer software company executive*
van der Kooi, Rik *computer software company executive*
Vaskevitch, David *computer software company executive*
Veghte, Bill *computer software company executive*
Vigil, Henry P. *computer software company executive*
Wahbe, Robert *computer software company executive*
Watson, Allison L. *computer software company executive*
Westlake, Blair *computer software company executive*
Witts, Simon *computer software company executive*
Youngjohns, Robert H. *computer software company executive*
Zecher, Linda *computer software company executive*
Zhang, Ya-Qin *computer software company executive*
Zinn, George *computer software company executive*

Seattle
Alstead, Troy *food service executive*
Barton, Richard N. *computer company executive*
Beren, Steve *Internet marketing professional*
Culver, John *food service executive*
Elgin, Ron Alan *advertising executive*
Eller, Marlin *security firm executive*
Fuller, Mark *chef*
Gass, Michelle Petkers *beverage service company executive, marketing executive*
Heinsen, Kaare *computer game company executive, application developer*
Sasenick, Joseph Anthony *health care company executive*
Schultz, Howard D. *beverage service company executive*

Spokane
Chamberlain, Barbara Kaye *communications executive*

Tacoma
Bartlett, Norma Thyra *retired administrative assistant*

Vancouver
Ogden, Valeria Munson *management consultant, state representative*

WEST VIRGINIA

Bluefield
Gearheart, Gary *sales executive*

Ravenswood
Barber, Donald Gene, Jr. *supply chain professional*

WISCONSIN

Algoma
Golomski, William Arthur Joseph *consulting company executive*

Brookfield
Dillon, Donald F. *data processing executive*
Yabuki, Jeffrey W. *data processing company executive, former accounting company executive*

Darien
Miller, Malcolm Henry *manufacturing sales executive, real estate developer*

Lomira
Kittelson, Roger *marketing professional*

Menomonee Falls
Lanier, Bob *promotional products company executive, retired professional basketball player*

Mequon
Elias, Paul S. *retired marketing executive*

Middleton
Lee, Leslie Warren *marketing executive, educator*

Milwaukee
Arbit, Bruce *direct marketing executive, consultant*
Barnett, Robert L. *retired communications executive*
Baumann, Roxanne Lee *industrial products international executive*
Bowles, Jacqueline Moore *marketing executive*
Hagerman, Douglas M. *consumer products company executive, lawyer*
Joerres, Jeffrey A. *employment services executive*
Kerr, Dorothy Marie Burmeister *marketing executive, consultant*
Schoenfeld, Howard Allen *management consultant, lawyer*

Plymouth
Gentine, Lee Michael *marketing professional*

Racine
Johnson-Leipold, Helen P. *outdoor recreation company executive*
Klein, Gabriella Sonja *retired communications executive*

Waterford
Karraker, Louis Rendleman *retired corporate executive*

Wausau
Wadzinski, Mary Beth *administrative assistant*

WYOMING

Jackson
Herrick, Gregory Evans *computer company executive*

Yellowstone National Park
Lewis, Suzanne *parks director*

TERRITORIES OF THE UNITED STATES

AMERICAN SAMOA

Pago Pago
Langkilde, Fagafaga Daniel *communications executive, political organization administrator*

PUERTO RICO

Manati
Martinez, Heriberto *human resources and management professional*

CANADA

BRITISH COLUMBIA

Kelowna
Krysko, Dave *Internet company executive*
Merrifield, Lane *Internet company executive*
Priebe, Lance *Internet company executive, application developer*

Victoria
Nuttall, Richard Norris *management consultant, physician*
Singleton-Wood, Allan James *communications executive*

ONTARIO

Chatham
McKeough, William Darcy *retired supply company executive*

Freelton
Sonnenberg, Hardy *data processing executive, researcher, electrical engineer*

Ottawa
Courtois, Bernard Andre *communications executive*
McLure, John Douglas *management consultant, former Canadian government official*
Silverman, Ozzie *consulting strategist*

Toronto
Bandeen, Robert Angus *management consultant*
Cowan, Benson *travel company executive, lawyer*
Curlook, Walter *management consultant*
Fatt, William Robert *hotel executive*
Fierheller, George Alfred *retired communications executive*
MacDonald, Brian Scott *management consultant*
Taylor, Kathleen P. *hotel executive*

QUEBEC

Leclercville
Morin, Pierre Jean *retired management consultant, social services administrator*

Montreal
Beauregard, Luc *public relations executive*
Molson, Andrew T. *management consultant*

Rosemere
Hopper, Carol *trade association administrator*

Saint-Faustin-Lac-Carre
Des Marais, Pierre, II, *communications holding company executive*

Whistler
Rae, Barbara Joyce *staging company*

AUSTRALIA

Footscray Victoria
Wheeler, Tony (Anthony Ian Wheeler) *travel publishing executive*

North Sydney
Scott, Brian Walter *management consultant*

AUSTRIA

Steinerkirchen
Handel, Norbert Erasmus Freiherr van *marketing professional*

CHINA

Beijing
Ma (Xuezheng), Mary *retired computer company executive*

CZECH REPUBLIC

Frenstat
Kusin, Vladimir Victor *retired communications executive*

Prague
Dostál, Jan *hotel, tourist and gaming industry executive*

ENGLAND

Berkshire
Everitt-Newton, Katherine Evelyn *international management consultant, business coach*

Bradford
Morrison, Kenneth Duncan *retired retail grocery executive*

Edgware
Walji, Jabir Mohamed *strategist, futurist and systematic innovation consultant*

London
Amaechi, John *motivational speaker, retired professional basketball player*
Bremer, J. Marco *Internet company executive, director*
Greener, Sir Anthony *computer company executive, director*
Hallissey, Michael *retired management consultant*
Hegarty, John F., Jr. *advertising executive*
Leaf, Robert Stephen *public relations executive*
Oliver, Jamie *chef, television personality*
Romano, Fernanda (Fefa Romano) *advertising executive*
Slootweg, Caroline *marketing executive*
Sorrell, Martin Stuart *advertising and marketing executive*
Zennström, Niklas *Internet company executive, entrepreneur*

Middlesex
Bonfield, Sir Peter Leahy *international business executive*

Stroud
Robinson, John Beckwith *development management consultant*

FINLAND

Espoo
Watson, Gregory Harriss *consulting company executive*

FRANCE

Issy Les Moulineaux
Pouzilhac, Alain Duplessis de *advertising executive*

Marseille
Boutterin, Emmanuel *public relations executive*

Paris
Arnault, Bernard Jean Etienne *consumer products company executive*
Chiquet, Maureen *consumer products company executive*
Courtois, Jean-Philippe *computer software company executive*
Marcus, Claude *advertising executive*

GERMANY

Fulda
Beckman, James Wallace Bim *management consultant, educator*

Neu Isenburg
Hoare-Temple, Piers Howard *building maintenance executive*

GREECE

Marousi
Joannou, Dakis *businessman*

HONG KONG

Kwun Tong
Tunkey, James Peter *security firm executive*

INDIA

Chandigarh
Chhabra, Tarlok Singh *advertising executive*

New Delhi
Machan, Polly Joseph *hotel manager*

ITALY

Milan
Bisiachi, Irene Maria Giulia *press office consultant*

Rome
Flood, Gregory Charles *human resources management specialist retired*

JAPAN

Tokyo
Kitajima, Yoshitoshi *printing company executive*
Suzuki, Yoichiro *retired asset management company executive*

MALAYSIA

Selangor
Manaf, Mohammed Zaini *management consulting company executive*

REPUBLIC OF KOREA

Ulsan
Suh, Keun Tae *management consultant, educator*

SINGAPORE

Singapore
Bompard, Julien *chef*
Henretta, Deborah A. *consumer products company executive*

SOUTH AFRICA

Port Alfred
Stocks, Rundell Kingsley *management, construction, education and general consultant*

SWEDEN

Helsingborg
Kamprad, Ingvar *former consumer products company executive*

Linköping
Spaeth, Mary Shepard *marketing communications executive*

SWITZERLAND

Chambésy
Helland, Douglas Rolf *retired intergovernmental organization computer executive*

Geneve
Dubrule, Paul Jean-Marie *hotel and restaurant company executive, vintager*

Lausanne
Chakravarthy, Balaji Srinivasan *strategic management educator, consultant*

Verbier
Gyll, John Sören *marketing executive*

ADDRESS UNPUBLISHED

Abraham, Francine Dinneen *sales executive, banker*
Ackerman, Raymond Basil *advertising executive*
Alderfer, Clayton Paul *professor, organizational consultant, writer*
Alderson, Vanessa *administrative assistant*
Alexander, Icie Mae *communications executive*
Allbritton, Cliff *personal and organizational consultant*
Allen, Bennie Carnel *employee relations specialist*
Allen, Charles E. *consulting firm executive, former federal agency administrator*
Allen, Louis Alexander *management consultant*
Amatangelo, Nicholas S. *retired financial printing company and document management executive, educator*
Anderson, Lance Eric *management consultant*
Anderson, Mark Robert *data processing executive, biochemist*
Anderson, Mary Ann Grasso *business executive*
Anderson, Paul Irving *management executive*
Anderson, Tom *former Internet company executive*
Andre, Anthony D. *management consultant*
Anschutz, Philip F. *communications and professional sports team executive*
Anthony, Tisi Paul *recreational facility executive*
Anthony, Wilma Tylinda *retired customer service administrator*
Appell, Louise Sophia *retired consulting company executive*
Arkless, David *employment services executive*
Arnold, George Lawrence *retired advertising company executive*
Askins, Nancy Ellen Paulsen *training services executive*
Avrett, Roz (Rosalind Case) *writer*
Babauta, Darlyn Salas *customer service associate*
Bainbridge, Dona Bardelli *marketing professional*
Baldwin, Irene S. *hotel executive, real estate developer*
Bamberger, Gerald Francis *plastics marketing consultant*
Barad, Jill Elikann *former family products company executive*
Barasch, Marc Ian *writer*
Barger, William James *management consultant, educator*
Barr, Michael Charles *research director, lawyer*
Barrett, Beverly Frances *public relations specialist*
Barr-Marinetti, Shannon Evette *management consultant*
Bauer, Barbara Ann *marketing consultant*
Beasley, Barbara Starin *sales executive, marketing professional*
Beck, Barbara J. *employment services executive*
Beers, Charlotte Lenore *retired advertising executive, former federal agency administrator*
Belinger, Harry Robert *retired business executive*
Bell, Jeff *former computer software marketing executive*
Bennett, Stephen M. *former computer software company executive*
Benney, Douglas Mabley *direct marketing executive, consultant*
Benoit, Philip Grosvenor *communications executive, educator, writer*
Berger, Frank Stanley *management consultant*
Berman, Jeff *former Internet company executive*
Berman, Sandra Rita *retired personnel director*
Bernard, Cathy S. *management corporation executive*
Bernstein-Siegel, Debra Lynn *marketing administrator, dance educator*
Berrien, James Stuart *environmental news and information web site executive, former magazine publisher*
Biondi, Frank J., Jr. *entertainment company executive*
Birch, Michael *Internet company executive, application developer*
Birk, John Richard *management consultant*
Bishop, William Peter *management consultant, rancher, musician*
Black, Kris Susan Lynn *marketing company executive, speaker, author, poet*
Blaine, Davis Robert *valuation consultant, investment banker*
Blanchard, Townsend Eugene *retired service companies executive*
Blatz, Linda Jeanne *sales executive*
Blum, Bradley Dickerson *restaurant chain executive*
Bolton, Caroline Joy *retired quality assurance professional*
Bonates, Tiberius Oliveira *management consultant*
Bonnie, Shelby W. *Internet company executive*
Boone, Earle Marion *marketing executive, investor*
Botkin, Monty Lane *computer company executive*
Boudreaux, John *marketing and public relations executive*
Bourdain, Anthony *chef, writer*
Bow, Stephen Tyler, Jr. *business executive*
Bowick, Susan D. *retired computer company executive*
Braddock, Richard S. *Internet company executive*
Bradley, Melvin LeRoy *communications executive*
Brady, Donna Elizabeth *sales, marketing and performing company executive*
Brennan, Donna Lesley *public relations company executive*
Brennen, Stephen Alfred *management consultant*
Brotman, Stuart Neil *management consultant, law educator, communications executive*
Burch, Michael Ray *computer company executive*
Burgdoerfer, Jerry J. *marketing and distribution executive*
Burge, John Wesley, Jr. *management consultant*
Burnett, Iris Jacobson *corporate communications specialist*
Burnham, J. V. *retired sales executive*
Burwick, David A. *marketing executive*
Busquet, Anne M. *Internet company executive*
Butler, Robert Thomas *retired advertising executive*
Butterfield, Bruce Scott *executive, editor, author, educator, consultant*
Cage, Jack Hays *executive search consultant*
Calcanis, Jason McCabe *Internet company executive*
Calvin, Robert Joseph *professor, author, management consultant*
Cantor, Alan Bruce *management consultant, application developer*
Cantus, H. Hollister *marketing and government relations consultant*
Carder, Paul Charles *retired advertising executive*
Cardno, Donald Barry *retired personnel director*
Carpenter-Mason, Beverly Nadine *quality assurance professional*
Cartwright, Talula Elizabeth *leadership consultant, educator*
Carty, Donald J. *former computer company executive, former air transportation executive*
Catelan, Paolo *environmental services administrator*
Cavanagh, Richard Edward *corporate chairman, director*
Cedeno, Amy A. *regulatory affairs, quality assurance professional*
Chamberlain, William Edwin, Jr. *management consultant*
Chandler, Robert Leslie *public relations executive*
Chang, Edward H. *consulting and marketing company executive*
Chaseman, Joel *communications consultant*
Chauvette, Claude R. *retired executive secretary*
Chen, Philip Minkang *strategic consultant*
Chernin, Peter F. *former multimedia company executive*
Child, Margaret Smillie *retired consultant, former government official*
Chrisanthopoulos, Peter *advertising executive*
Clarke, Cordelia Kay Knight Mazuy *management consultant, artist*
Clarke, Janet Morrison *marketing executive*
Clarke, Logan, Jr. *management consultant*
Cohen, Jay M. *consulting firm executive, former federal agency administrator, retired military officer*
Cohen, Larry *computer software company executive*
Coker, Donald William *banking, management and economic consultant*
Coleman, Claire Kohn *public relations executive*
Collins, Richard Stratton (Dick Collins) *retired public relations executive*
Colwell, Howard Otis *advertising executive*
Conaway, Edward C. *corporate communications specialist*
Connell, Carol Matheson *corporate communications specialist, consultant*
Connell, Shirley Hudgins *public relations professional*
Conway, David Antony *marketing professional*
Cormier, Joseph Bowman *private investigator, consultant*
Cortese, Richard Anthony *computer company executive*
Cotter, Robert F. *hotel executive*
Craig, Larry Edwin *consulting company executive, former United States Senator from Idaho*
Crawford, Bruce Edgar *advertising executive*
Crawford, William Walsh *retired consumer products company executive*
Criswell, Kimberly Ann *executive coach, communications consultant, performance artist*
Cuddihy, Robert Vincent, Jr. *finance and marketing executive*
Curry, Catharine Terrill *marketing and sales corporate executive*
Curtis, Drew *Internet company executive*
Dangoor, David Ezra Ramsi *consumer goods company executive*
DaVerne, Steven Richard *advertising director, artist, illustrator*
David, Clive *events executive*
Davidson, Rick *employment services executive*
Davis, Frederic Emery *corporate executive*
Davis, Robert W. *computer company executive*
Deacon, David Emmerson *advertising executive*
Dean, Leslie Alan (Cap Dean) *international economic, social and political development consultant, interagency and defense analyst*
DeBow, Thomas Joseph, Jr. *advertising executive*
Decker, Susan Lynne *former Internet company executive*
DeGroff, Dale *food service executive*
De Laurentiis, Giada *chef*
de Margitay, Gedeon *acquisitions and management consultant*
De Sofi, Oliver Julius *data processing executive*
DeVaney, Carol Susan *management consultant*
deWilde, David Michael *management consultant, lawyer, finance company executive, retired recruiter*
DeWolfe, Christopher T. *former Internet company executive*
Diamond, Susan Zee *management consultant*
DiDomenico, Mauro, Jr. *communications executive*
Diederichs, Janet Wood *public relations executive*
Diehl, Stephen Anthony *human resources consultant*
Di Massa, Ernani Vincenzo, Jr. *communications executive, television producer, writer*
Dirvin, Gerald Vincent *retired consumer products company executive*
Dobler, Donald William *retired procurement and materials executive, dean*
Doering, Kelly Bell Scribner *marketing executive*
Donald, James Lloyd (Jim Donald) *former beverage service company executive*
Drozdeck, Steven Richard *management consultant*
Duff, Gill *advertising executive*
Duke, Robin Chandler Tippett *retired public relations executive, former ambassador*
Dulski, Jennifer *Internet company executive*
Dumont, Mary *chef*
Dunne, Diane C. *marketing professional*
Dyson, Tim *public relations executive*
Dzhandzhulyan, Lev *business analyst, consultant*
Echols, Mary Evelyn *motivational speaker and business consultant, writer*
Ecton, Donna R. *business executive*
Ellig, Bruce Robert *retired personnel director*
Elliot, Jared *financial management consultant*
Ellis, Steven George *public relations and corporate communications executive*
Emerling, Carol G. *corporate governance consultant*
Emerson, Daniel Everett *retired communications company executive*
Enraght-Moony, Thomas *former internet company executive*
Esposito, Bonnie Lou *marketing professional*
Evans, Charlotte Mortimer *communications consultant, writer*
Evans, Pamela R. *sales and marketing executive*
Falcon, Yvonne *management consultant*
Farrell, Brian J. *computer game company executive*
Fay, Conner Martindale *retired marketing executive*
Fay, Sarah *former advertising executive*
Feigin, Barbara Sommer *marketing consultant*
Feld, Carole Leslie *marketing executive*
Feller, Robert William Andrew *public relations executive, retired professional baseball player*
Fenimore, George Wiley *management consultant*
Ferguson, Gary Lee *public relations and security management executive*
Ferreira, Jo Ann Jeanette Chanoux *management consultant, delivery service executive*
Fink, Daniel Julien *management consultant*
Fischer, Russell Leonard *public relations executive*
Fleisher, Frederic Elliott *communications executive*
Flock, Kelly *computer game company executive*
Foresman, George W. *consulting company executive, former federal agency administrator*
Forrester, Jay Wright *management consultant, educator*
Fudge, Ann Marie *former advertising executive*
Gadiesh, Orit *management consulting executive*
Gallagher, Michael Robert *retired consumer products company executive*
Gardner, Meredith Lee *communication consultant*
Gasser, Michael J. *consumer products company executive*
Geller, Scott A. *management consultant*
Geschke, Charles M. *computer company executive*
Gianturco, Delio Emanuele *management consultant, educator, author*
Gimple, W. Thomas *sales executive*
Glass, Kenneth Edward *management consultant*
Gleaves, Leon Rogers *marketing and sales executive*
Glick, J. Leslie *management consultant*
Goldberg, Victor Joel *retired data processing company executive*
Goldfarb, Muriel Bernice *marketing and advertising consultant*
Goldsmith, Jeff Charles *management consultant*
Goldstein, Alfred George *consumer products company executive*
Goldstein, Burton Benjamin, Jr. *university professor*
Golemon, Patricia Lynn *marketing professional, educator, writer*
Gorman, Marcie Sothern *retired personal care industry executive*
Gorsline, Stephen Paul *security specialist*
Gottlieb, Alan Merril *advertising, fundraising and broadcasting executive, writer*
Grace, Marcia Bell *advertising executive*
Greaser, Constance Udean *communications executive, researcher*
Greene, Alvin *management consultant*
Growick, Philip *advertising executive*
Grunder, Fred Irwin *retired industrial hygienist, consultant*
Gugel, Craig Thomas *research and planning executive*
Gunderson, Ted Lee *security consultant*
Gurwitch, Arnold Andrew *communications executive*
Gutheinz, Jean *public relations executive*
Haas, Edward Lee *management consultant*
Hackett, John Byron *retired advertising executive, lawyer*
Hagel, John III *management consultant*
Haines, David Harry *consulting executive*
Halaska, Terrell Lynn *consulting firm executive, former federal agency administrator*
Hall, Hansel Crimiel *communications executive*
Hall, John N. *news service executive*
Hamlin, Sonya B. *communications specialist*
Hannaford, Peter Dor *public relations executive, writer*
Hansen, B. J. (Bobby J. Hansen) *management consultant, real estate investor and developer*
Harrington, Gerard III *marketing and communications executive, business consultant*
Harrington, Robert Dudley, Jr. *retired printing company executive*
Harris, Robert Norman *advertising executive, educator*
Hartger, Barbara J. *marketing professional*
Hartsock, Linda Sue *retired management consultant*
Hausdorfer, Gary Lee *management consultant*
Hauser, Joyce Roberta *marketing professional*
Haver-Allen, Ann *communications director*
Hayden, Michael Vincent *consulting firm executive, former CIA Director, retired military officer*
Hayes, Janet Gray *retired management consultant, mayor*
Hazard, Robert Culver, Jr. *retired hotel executive*
Hearl, Peter R. *former food service executive*
Heaton, Larry Cadwalder *estate planner, security firm executive*
Heller, Arthur *advertising executive*
Hendrickson, William George *business executive*
Hergenhan, Joyce *communications executive*
Herz, Irene Laurel *web site design company executive, librarian*
Heuer, Martin Frederick *retired human resources specialist*
Heyer, Steven J. *former hotel and beverage company executive*
Hickey, Kevin Francis *software company executive*
Hicks, Wayland R. *rental company executive*
Hillman, Gracia M. *former management consultant, federal agency administrator*
Hochhalter, Gordon Ray *advertising communications executive*
Hochschild, Carroll Shepherd *computer company and medical equipment executive, educator*
Hoffman, Darnay Robert *management consultant*
Hoog, Thomas W. *public relations executive*
Hooper, Josh *advertising executive, speaker, writer, director*
Houghtaling, Pamela Ann *communications consultant, writer*
Houston, Stanley Dunsmore *retired public relations executive*
Hudson, Sharon Marie *communications executive*
Hudson, Stanton Harold, Jr. *public relations, development executive, academic administrator, educator*
Hundt, Reed Eric *management consultant, former federal agency administrator*
Ignatius, Roger *educator, consultant*
Immel, Barbara Kay Kephart *management consultant*
Irving, Jeffrey Alan *management consultant, educator, lawyer*
Irwin, Linda Belmore *public relations/marketing consultant*
Isbell, Marcia Annette *management consultant*
Jackson, Phillip Ellis *marketing executive, writer*
Jacobs, Bradley S. *former rental company executive*
James, Louis Meredith *personnel executive*
Jetley, Karun *software company executive, consultant*
Jiang, Tianyi *computer company executive*
Joanou, Phillip *advertising executive, artist*
Johns, Tammy *employment services executive*
Johnson, Camille *media executive*
Johnson, Craig N. *management consultant*
Johnson, Herbert Frederick *sales executive, retired academic administrator, librarian*
Johnson, Laymon, Jr. *management analyst*
Jones, Gerre Lyle *marketing and public relations consultant*
Jones, Thomas Owen *computer company executive*
Juliber, Lois D. *retired consumer products company executive*
Kalafatoglu, Tugba *marketing and public relations professional, business and political communications consultant*
Kane, Karen Marie *public affairs consultant*
Kanuk, Leslie Lazar *management consultant, educator*
Kapur, Amit *former Internet company executive*
Karalis, John Peter *computer company executive, lawyer*
Karim, Jawed *Internet company executive, application developer*
Kasi, Vijay *management consultant*
Keala, Francis Ahloy *security executive*
Kelleher, Kathleen *marketing professional*

Keller, Paul *retired advertising executive researcher*
Kelly, Sue W. (Susan Weisenbarger Kelly) *consulting firm executive, former congresswoman*
Kendrick, Peter Murray *communications executive, investor*
Kennedy, Karen Syence *advertising agency executive*
King, Philip Gordon *public relations counselor*
Kirk, Carmen Zetler *data processing executive and science fiction writer*
Klein, Bernard Joseph *management specialist*
Klein, Charlotte Conrad *public relations executive*
Klein, Chuck *retired private investigator, writer*
Knickrehm, Glenn Allen *management executive*
Knight, Francine *administrative assistant, economics professor*
Koelmel, Lorna Lee *data processing executive*
Komisarjevsky, Christopher P.A. *retired public relations executive*
Koo, George Ping Shan *business consultant*
Korologos, Ann McLaughlin *communications executive, former United States Secretary of Labor*
Kovach, Andrew Louis *human resources specialist, consultant*
Krakower, Bernard Hyman *management consultant*
Kramer, Peter Robin *computer company executive, artist*
Krupp, James Arthur Gustave *management consultant*
Kushner, Harvey David *management consultant*
Kusterer, Thomas *program director*
LaMantia, Charles Robert *management consulting company executive*
Lambert, Kirsten Schnoor *public relations executive, writer*
LaMotta, Connie Frances *public relations agency owner*
Lampert, Eleanor Verna *retired human resources specialist*
Landau, Ellis *hotel executive*
Langton, Cleve Swanson *author, advertising executive*
Lanni, Terry (Joseph Terrence Lanni) *retired hotel corporation executive*
Larson, Charles Fred *management consultant*
Lauria, Rita Marie *attorney, media and communications researcher, consultant*
Lavidge, Robert James *marketing research executive*
Lawrence, Margery H. (Margery Hulings Lawrence) *marketing consultant*
Layton, William George *consultant, retired human resources and import/export company executive*
LeBar, Mark *computer products company executive*
Lee, Richard Kenneth *software company executive*
Leeds, Douglas Brecker *advertising executive, theater producer*
Leff, Ilene J(afnel) *management consultant, social sector organization and companies corporate executive, federal official*
Lempert, Philip *advertising executive, writer, news correspondent*
Levick, Richard Scott *communications executive, lawyer, consultant, educator*
Levy, Arthur James *public relations executive, writer*
Levy, Robert Edward *retired management consultant*
Lewis, David L. *security firm executive, consultant*
Li, Charlene *market trend analyst, media strategist*
Ligon, Demond L., Sr. *sales executive*
Lilley, William III *business executive*
Linda, Gerald *advertising and marketing executive*
Lindberg, Francis Laurence, Jr. *management consultant*
Linton, Michael Alan *Internet company executive*
Litou, Hendry *Internet company executive, researcher*
Littman, Earl *advertising and public relations executive*
Livingstone, Susan Morrisey *management consultant, former federal agency administrator*
Lochner, Philip Raymond *retired communications executive, former commissioner*
Lockwood, Robert W. *management consultant*
Longaberger, Tami *home decor accessories company executive*
Lorelli, Michael Kevin *consumer products company executive*
Losi, Maxim John *medical communications executive*
Lotas, Judith Patton *advertising executive*
Lotz, George Michael *retired computer company executive, graphics designer, photographer*
Luttner, Edward F. *consulting company executive*
Mac Alister, Robert James *executive recruiter*
MacNeill, James William *environmental energy and management consultant*
Malkan, Stacy *communications executive, director*
Mallison, Howard Danford *retired corporate communications specialist*
Malone, Claudine Berkeley *management consultant*
Malphurs, Roger Edward *biomedical marketing executive*
Maneker, Roberta S(ue) *frelance writer*
Mark, Reuben *retired consumer products company executive*
Marolda, Anthony Joseph *management consulting company executive*
Marone, Anthony F., Jr. *quality assurance professional*
Marsh, Don Ermal *supermarket executive*
Marshall, Robert Charles *computer company executive*
Marshall, Robert Norman *hotel executive*
Martin, James Kay *policy and management consultant*
Massoudi, Bahram Barry *management consultant*
Matschullat, Robert W. *former consumer products company executive*
Matthew, Lyn *sales executive, consultant, marketing professional*
Maupin, Michael Dennis *quality assurance professional*
Maxwell, W(ilbur) Richard *retired management consultant*
Mayer, Allan *public relations executive, consultant*
McCandless, Carolyn Keller *retired human resources executive*
McCann, Renetta *former advertising executive*
McCarthy, Daniel William *management consultant*
McCloskey, J(ohn) Michael *retired environmental policy organization manager*
McDade, James Russell *management consultant*
McElwreath, Sally Chin *corporate communications executive*
McGee, Patrick Edgar *postal service clerk*
McGuire, John W., Sr. *advertising executive, marketing professional, writer*
McPherson, Donald Scott *labor and employment arbitrator/mediator*
Meads, Donald Edward *management services company executive*
Meigher, S. Christopher III *communications and media executive, publisher*
Mikiewicz, Anna Daniella *marketing and international business export manager*
Miles, Laveda Ann *advertising executive*
Miller, Brenda *Johrei practitioner*
Miller, Ellen S. *marketing executive*
Mitchell, John Charles *marketing professional*
Mobley, William Hodges *management consultant, educator, writer, researcher*
Moffat, MaryBeth *consulting company executive*
Mok, Samuel Tinsing *management consultant, former federal agency administrator*
Monroe, William Lewis *human resources executive*
Montague, Brian John *consulting company executive*
Montelongo, Michael D. *marketing executive, former civilian military employee*
Montford, John Thomas *communications executive, lawyer, former state legislator*
Moradi, Ahmad F. *software company executive*
Moran, Charles A. *security firm executive, educator*
Morden, John Reid *security-international relations consultant*
Motroni, Hector John *retired printing company executive*
Mracky, Ronald Sydney *marketing executive, tourism consultant, media specialist*
Mulcahy, Robert Edward *management consultant*
Mustard, Lewis Williams *management consultant, educator*
Nason, Dolores Irene *computer company executive, social services administrator, minister*
Neel, Judy Murphy *management consultant*
Nelson, Dean B. *media company executive*
Neslund, Scott *former marketing and communications company executive*
Nicholson, Cie (Cynthia Nicholson) *marketing professional*
Nissen, Varina *employment services executive*
O'Brien, Morgan Edward *communications executive, lawyer*
O'Brien, Robert John, Jr. *public relations executive, former government official, air force officer*
O'Byrne, Michael *retired management consultant*
Olins, Robert Abbot *communications research executive*
Olson, Dale C. *public relations executive*
O'Neal, Kathleen Len *communications executive, writer, management speaker, financial consultant*
Oppedahl, Phillip Edward *computer company executive*
O'Shea, Catherine Large *marketing and public relations consultant*
Ostberg, Henry Dean *marketing executive*
Ostrow, Joseph W. *advertising executive*
O'Sullivan, Paul Kevin *management and instructional systems consultant*
Papay, Lawrence T. *management consultant, retired engineer*
Paresky, David S. *travel company executive*
Parra, Ro (Rosendo G. Parra) *former computer company executive*
Parsons, Vinson Adair *retired computer company executive*
Paulraj, Antony *management consultant, educator*
Peden, Keith J. *human resources specialist*
Pennington, Robert Michael *marketing professional, consultant, communications educator, consultant*
Penny, Roger Pratt *retired management consultant*
Pépin, Jacques G. *chef*
Pepper, Jonathon L. *communications executive*
Perez, Antonio M. *imaging company executive*
Perlmutter, Barbara S. *retired public relations executive*
Perlov, Dadie *management and executive search consultant*
Perry, James Benn *former hotel and gaming company executive*
Pfuntner, Walter Alan, Jr. *marketing executive, educator*
Platt, Robert L. *retired industrial hygienist, consultant*
Pocock, J. Michael *communications executive*
Pomeroy, Heather Aline *sales and marketing executive*
Poppel, Harvey Lee *management consultant, investment banker*
Portway, Patrick Stephen *telecommunications consulting company executive, educator*
Post, Richard Bennett *retired human resources executive*
Potash, Stephen Jon *public relations executive*
Potter, James Earl *retired international hotel management company executive*
Power, Katherine *Internet company executive*
Poza, Ernesto *management consultant, educator*
Preudhomme, Marcia Denrique *marketing executive, writer*
Prising, Jonas *employment services executive*
Puck, Wolfgang *chef*
Pulwers, Jack Edward *public affairs specialist, news executive, writer, historian, journalism educator, lecturer, broadcaster*
Purcell, Steven Richard *international management consultant, engineer, economist*
Railsback, Sherrie Lee *management consultant, educator*
Rainey, Jean Osgood *public relations executive*
Rallo, James Gilbert *retired management company executive*
Ray, Paul Richard, Jr. *executive recruiter, consultant*
Reed, Anne F. Thomson *management consultant*
Reisman, Judith Ann Gelernter *media communications executive, educator*
Reynolds, John Hughes, IV, *retired research and development executive*
Rhodes, Eric Foster *employee relations consultant, writer*
Robertson, Michael *Internet company executive*
Robinson, Hugh Granville *consulting management company executive*
Robinson, Linda Gosden *communications executive*
Roehm, Julie Ann *marketing executive*
Roman, Kenneth *business consultant, corporate communications executive*
Rook, Vicki Lynn *safety specialist*
Rose, (Robert) Kevin *Internet company executive, blogger*
Roseman, Jack *computer services company executive*
Rosen, Arthur Marvin *advertising executive*
Rosenfield, James Harold, Sr. *communications executive*
Rosensaft, Lester Jay *management consultant, lawyer*
Rothwell, Robert Alan *investing and consulting company executive, writer*
Ruggles, Rudy Lamont, Jr. *international security advisor*
Russ, Edmond Vincent, Jr. *marketing professional*
Ryan, Melbagene T. *retired food service and nutrition director*
Rydholm, Ralph Williams *advertising executive*
Sacks, Temi J. *public relations executive*
Saligman, Harvey *retired consumer products and services company executive*
Sanders, Walter Jeremiah, III, (Jerry Sanders) *retired computer company executive*
Sanger, Stephen W. *retired consumer products company executive*
Sasso, John *advertising and public strategies executive*
Scerno, Joseph Benedict *management consultant executive, arbitrator*
Schlafly, Hubert Joseph, Jr. *communications executive*
Schonberg, Alan Robert *personnel director*
Schott, John Robert *international consultant, educator*
Schramm, Bernard Charles, Jr. *retired advertising agency executive*
Schreckinger, Sy Edward *advertising executive, consultant*
Schubert, Helen Celia *public relations executive*
Schuessler, John T. (Jack Schuessler) *retired food service executive*
Schultz, Harley *consulting company executive*
Schwartz, Michael Robinson *management consultant*
Sease, Gene Elwood *communications executive*
Seelig, Gerard Leo *management consultant*
Selkowitz, Arthur *retired advertising executive*
Semel, Terry S. *retired Internet company executive*
Shaker, William Haygood *marketing professional, public policy reformer*
Sharp, William *retired advertising executive*
Shaw, Jack Allen *communications company executive*
Sheehan, Robert James, II, *retired management and market research consultant*
Shikuma, Eugene Yujin *travel company executive*
Shirley, Jon Anthony *former computer software company executive*
Siegel, George Henry *management consultant*
Siegel, Herbert Bernard *management consultant*
Simecka, Betty Jean *marketing executive*
Simmons (Neumann), Sylvia *advertising executive, writer*
Simpson, Andrea Lynn *communications executive*
Sincoff, Michael Z. *human resources and marketing executive, educator*
Singer, David Michael *marketing and public relations executive*
Slosberg, Mike *advertising executive*
Smith, John W(esley), Jr. *data processing executive, retired municipal official*
Sorensen, Jack *computer game company executive*
Sorstokke, Ellen Kathleen *marketing executive, educator*
Spainhour, J. Patrick (James Patrick Spainhour) *outsourcing company executive, former apparel executive*
Speer, Richard John *security consultant*
Spivak, Joan Carol *communications executive*
Stark, Diana *public relations executive*
Starkweather, Frederick Thomas *retired data processing executive*
Stebel, Michael David *marketing professional, consultant*
Stein, Daniel *hotel and resort operations executive*
Stengel, James R. *retired consumer products company executive*
Stengel, Ronald Francis *management consultant*
Stern, S(eesa) Beatrice *executive secretary, medical/surgical nurse*
Stevens, Art *public relations executive*
Stevens, Berton Louis, Jr. *data processing executive*
Stevenson, Earl *communications executive, entrepreneur*
Stone, James Howard *management consultant*
Stone, Susan Ridgaway *marketing educator*
Stott, Terri Jeuan *residential services director*
Strem, Ryan David *educator*
Strother, Patrick Joseph *public relations executive*
Strubel, Richard Perry *Internet company executive*
Stults, Walter Black *management consultant, trade association administrator*
Sturges, John Siebrand *management consultant*
Sudarsky, Jerry M. *industrialist*
Sullivan, John Louis, Jr. *retired search company executive*
Sullivan, Owen *employment services executive*
Sussberg, Milton Joel *marketing professional*
Swan, Mara E. *employment services executive*
Sweet, Chad Creighton *consulting firm executive, former federal official*
Tandy, Karen Pomerantz *communications executive, former federal agency administrator*
Tarbutton, Lloyd T. *hotel executive, consultant*
Tarr, Curtis W. *management consultant, educator*
Tate, Kristopher *Internet company executive*
Taviss, Patricia Ann *management consultant, library association executive*
Taylor, Volney *retired information company executive*
Temerlin, Liener *advertising executive*
Tersine, Brenda L. *funeral director*
Thomas, Joe Carroll *retired human resources director*
Thompson, Craig Snover *corporate communications executive*
Thompson, Dean M., II, *knowledge management and learning executive*
Thornton, Felicia D. *food service company executive*
Tomlin-Houston, Lisa *executive, career coach workforce strategist*
Tramonto, Rick *chef*
Trevathan, James E. *waste management executive*
Tribus, Myron *management consultant, educator*
Troop, Paul Melvin *public relations executive, journalist*
Tucci, Oscar Maximillian *restauranteur, radio host, writer, philanthropist*
Tuft, Mary Ann *executive search firm executive*
Unwin, Stephen Forman *advertising executive, educator*
Van der Horst, Brian Christopher *communications consultant, author, educator*
Van Dine, Alan Charles *advertising agency executive, writer*
Van Handel, Michael J. *employment services executive*
Vine, Kimberly Ann *public relations executive*
Wadley, M. Richard *consumer products executive*
Wales, Jimmy Donal (Jimbo Wales) *Internet company executive*
Walk, Barbra Denise *customer service administrator, tutor*
Walker, Gloria Lee *training services executive*
Walsh, William Albert *management consultant, retired military officer*
Walter, Carmel Monica *security consultant, writer*
Wangsness, Genna Stead *retired hotel executive, innkeeper*
Warner, John Hilliard, Jr. *technical services company executive*
Weathersby, George Byron *management company executive*
Weber, Donald B. *advertising executive, marketing professional*
Weil, Lynne Amy *communications executive, writer*
Weinbach, Lawrence Allen *computer services company executive, private equity managing director*
Weiner, Richard *public relations executive*
Weismantel, Gregory Nelson *management consultant, computer company executive*
Weizmann, Howard Charles *consulting firm executive, former federal agency administrator*
Welter, William Michael *marketing and advertising executive*
Wendlinger, Robert Matthew *communications and memory consultant*
Wentz, Jeffrey Lee *information systems executive*
Werner, Stuart Lloyd *computer services company executive*
Wheeler, Barbara J. *management consultant*
Whitman, Meg (Margaret Cushing Whitman) *former Internet company executive*
Wicks, David O., Jr. *communications executive*
Wikina, Suanu Bliss *human resources specialist*
Williams, Louis Clair, Jr. *public relations executive*
Williams, Nicole Leann *human resources specialist, director*
Williams, Paul Stratton *executive recruiter*
Williams, Terrie Michelle *public relations executive*
Wimpress, Gordon Duncan, Jr. *management consultant, foundation administrator*
Winkler, Agnieszka M. *marketing executive*
Witcher, Michael H. *homeland and national security expert*
Wojcik, Cass *decorative supply company executive, retired municipal official*
Worboys, Roger Dick *retired communications executive*
Wright, Jeanne Elizabeth Jason *retired advertising executive*
Wright, Tony *advertising executive*
Yang, Jerry *former Internet company executive*
Yocam, Delbert Wayne *retired software products company executive*
Yopconka, Natalie Ann Catherine *secretary officer, computer specialist, educator, entrepreneur, small business owner*
Youst, David Bennett *career development educator*
Zalewa, Donald Andrew *management consultant, educator*
Zeller, Joseph Paul *advertising executive*
Zhang, Ming *business and management consultant*
Zimmern, Andrew *chef, television personality*
Zipf, Jennifer E. *marketing professional*

INDUSTRY: TRADE

UNITED STATES

ALABAMA

Birmingham

George, Frank Wade *small business owner, antiquarian book dealer*
Pizitz, Richard Alan *retail executive, real estate company officer*

Madison
Bogard, Eileen Judith *investor, retired small business owner, education administrator*

Mobile
Jones, Joseph Seymour *small business owner, poet*

ALASKA

Anchorage
Schnell, Roger Thomas *small business owner, retired state official, military officer*

Wrangell
Smith, Kimmie Christine *small business owner*

ARIZONA

Clarkdale
Tod, Martha Ann *retired small business owner*

Goodyear
McBride, Janet Marie *small business owner*

Phoenix
Francis, Philip L. *retail executive*
Moran, Robert F. *retail executive*
Steckler, Phyllis Betty *business owner*

Scottsdale
Williams-De Silva, Lisa Annette *small business owner, adult nurse practitioner*

Sun City
Thompson, Betty Jane *retired small business owner*

Tucson
Betteridge, Frances Carpenter *small business owner, retired lawyer, mediator*
Fay, Mary Anne *retail executive*

ARKANSAS

Bentonville
Agwunobi, John Oderah *retail executive, former federal agency administrator*
Castro-Wright, Eduardo *retail executive*
Chambers, Susan (M. Susan Chambers) *retail executive*
Cornell, Brian Christian *retail executive*
Curran, Patricia A. *retail executive*
Dach, Leslie Alan *retail executive, former public relations company executive*
Dobbs, Johnnie C., Jr. *retail executive*
Duke, Mike (Michael Terry Duke) *retail executive*
Fleming, John E. *retail executive*
Ford, Rollin L. *retail executive*
Gearhart, Jeffrey J. *retail executive, lawyer*
Hefner, Linda P. *retail executive*
Holley, Charles Murphy, Jr. *retail company executive*
Hyde, Thomas D. *retail executive, lawyer*
McMillon, Doug (Carl Douglas McMillon) *retail executive*
Mora, Alberto J. *retail executive, lawyer*
Schoewe, Thomas M. *retail executive*
Scott, Lee (Harold Lee Scott Jr.) *retail executive*
Simon, William S. *retail executive*
Sinclair, Jack L. *retail executive*
Spragg, Gregg E. *retail executive*
Trius, Vicente *retail executive*
Walton, (Samuel) Rob(son) *discount department store chain executive*
Weir, Rita Mary *retail executive*
Westling, John T. *retail executive*
Whaley, Steven P. *retail executive*
Zorn, Eric Stuart *retail executive*

Little Rock
Dillard, William, II, *department store chain executive*
Freeman, James I. *retail department store company executive*

CALIFORNIA

Aliso Viejo
Purdy, Alan MacGregor *financial executive*

Berkeley
Rosenthal, Bernard Michael *small business owner*

Carmel
Aurner, Robert Ray, II, *retail development executive*

Cathedral City
Jackman, Robert Alan *retail executive*

City Of Commerce
Plamann, Alfred A. *wholesale distribution executive*

Encinitas
Shields, Patricia Allene *retail executive*

Encino
Joy, Alexa *small business owner, artist, educator*

Fresno
Winslow, Norman Eldon *small business owner*

Los Angeles
Hawley, Philip Metschan *retired retail executive, management consultant*
Roeder, Richard Kenneth *business owner, lawyer*
Sinay, Joseph *retail executive*

Menlo Park
VanHook, Tracie Lynnette *small business owner*

Newport Beach
Wade, Michael Robert Alexander *import/export company executive*

Orange
Busby, Nita June *small business owner*

Pacific Palisades
Diehl, Richard Kurth *retail executive, consultant*

Palos Verdes Peninsula
Slayden, James Bragdon *retired retail executive*

Petaluma
Gervais, Cherie Nadine *small business owner*

Pleasanton
Balmuth, Michael A. *retail executive*
Cribb, Gary L. *retail executive*
Everette, Bruce L. *retail executive*
Ferber, Norman Alan *retail executive*
LeHocky, Mark *retail executive, lawyer*
Renda, Larree M. *retail executive*
Shachmut, Kenneth Michael *retail executive*
Stern, David R. *retail executive*
Tidwell, Jerry *retail executive*
Wright, Donald P. *retail executive*

Riverside
White, Clara Jo *small business owner, consultant*

San Bernardino
Brown, Jack H. *supermarket company executive*

San Diego
Hawkins, Rey *shop owner, educator*
Mooney, Patricia Kathryn *business owner, video producer, writer, philanthropist*
Saito, Frank Kiyoji *import and export firm executive*

San Francisco
Calhoun, John Joseph (Jack) *retail executive*
Fisher, Donald G. *retail executive*
Fisher, Doris *retail executive*
Fogarty, James P. *retail executive, corporate financial executive*
Folkman, David H. *retail, wholesale and consumer products consultant*
Hansen, Marka *retail executive*
Harriss, Cynthia Therese (Cynthia Therese Clarke) *retail executive*
Lenk, Edward C. (Toby) *retail executive*
Lester, W. Howard *retail executive*
McCollam, Sharon L. *retail executive*
Murphy, Glenn T. *retail executive*
Peck, Art *retail executive*
Sage-Gavin, Eva Marie *retail executive*
Tasooji, Michael B. *retail executive*

Santa Rosa
Monk, Diana Charla *small business owner*
Smith, Betty L. *small business owner, educator*

South San Francisco
Walsh, J. Michael *wholesale distribution executive*

Venice
Johnson, Cheryl *small business owner*

Walnut Creek
Brown, William E. *retail executive*

COLORADO

Boulder
Johnson, Maryanna Morse *business owner*

Colorado Springs
Noyes, Richard Hall *bookseller*

Denver
Cheris, Elaine Gayle Ingram *business owner*
Clinch, Nicholas Bayard III *small business owner*
Newberry, Elizabeth Carter *greenhouse and floral company owner*
Sullivan, William E. *wholesale distribution executive*

CONNECTICUT

Darien
Charron, Paul Richard *consultant, former retail executive*

Enfield
Del Vecchio, Claudio *retail executive*

Essex
Thompson, George Lee *retail executive, consultant*

Greenwich
Rudy, Kathleen Vermeulen *small business owner*

Old Greenwich
Robertson, Dawn H. *former retail executive*

DISTRICT OF COLUMBIA

Washington
Tetelman, Alice Fran *small business owner*

FLORIDA

Boca Raton
Maguire, Kim D. *retail executive*
Newman, Michael D. *retail executive*

Bradenton
Beall, Robert Matthews, II, *retail executive*
Rutstein, Stanley Harold *apparel retailing company executive*

Clearwater
Maxwell, Richard Anthony *retail executive*
Turley, Stewart *retired retail company executive*

Jacksonville
Lynch, Peter L. *retail executive*

Key Biscayne
de la Cruz, Carlos *wholesale distribution executive*

Lakeland
Barnett, Hoyt R. (Barney Hoyt) *supermarket company executive*
Jones, Todd *retail executive*

Miami
Rawl, Arthur Julian (Lord of Cursons) *corporate director, retail executive, consultant, accountant, writer*

Miramar
Catalano, Carl Philip *small business owner*

Naples
Hutson Councell, Janet Kern *retired small business owner, retired educator*
Ludwig, Richard Joseph *small business owner*

Palm Beach
Radner, Sidney Hollis *retired retail executive*

Palm Beach Gardens
Runge, Donald Edward *food wholesale company executive*

Palm Coast
Slatner, Thomas Allen *bookseller*

Panama City Beach
Jenkins, Frances Owens *retired small business owner*

Pembroke Pines
Feldman, Jacqueline *retired small business owner*
Schaefer, Bonnie (E. Bonnie Schaefer) *retail executive*

Port Saint Lucie
LaHowchic, Nicholas John *consulting company executive*

Saint Petersburg
Grossman, Mindy *retail executive*

San Antonio
Beverland, Jack Edwin *retired retail executive, folk artist*

Tampa
Eddy, Colette Ann *aerial photography studio owner, photographer*

University Park
Walker, Jane Stewart *small business owner, publishing executive, educator*

West Palm Beach
Lynch, Edward J. *small business owner, contractor*

Winter Park
Alfond, Theodore B. *retired shoe company executive*
Smetanka, Sally S. *small business owner*

GEORGIA

Atlanta
Campbell, Ann-Marie *retail executive*
Judd, George R. *wholesale distribution executive*
Kalafut, George Wendell *retired distribution company executive, retired naval officer*
Ridley, Clarence Haverty *retail executive*

Social Circle
Penland, John Thomas *retired import/export and development company executive*

Union City
Malcolm, Gloria J. *small business owner*

Valdosta
Halter, Henry James, Jr., (Diamond Jim Halter) *retail executive*

HAWAII

Hilo
Ornellas, Lorraine B. (Lori Ornellas) *small business owner*

IDAHO

Boise
Herbert, Kathy J. *retail executive*

ILLINOIS

Chicago
Nickell, Jake *internet retail executive, apparel designer*
Vrablik, Edward Robert *import/export company executive*

Decatur
Bradshaw, Billy Dean *retired retail executive*

Deerfield
Blaylock, Stanley B. *retail executive*
Green, Dana I. *retail executive, lawyer*
McNally, Alan G. *retail executive*
Miquelon, Wade D. *retail executive*
Riedl, George J. *retail executive*
Rudolphsen, William M. *retail executive*
Wagner, Mark A. *retail executive*
Wasson, Gregory D. *retail executive*
Watts, Colin F. *retail executive*
Zavada, Jeffrey J. *retail executive*

Glen Ellyn
Baloun, John Charles *retired wholesale distribution executive*

Glencoe
Nebenzahl, Kenneth *rare book and map dealer, author*

Glenview
Letham, Dennis J. *wholesale company executive*

Hoffman Estates
Austin, Karen A. *retail executive*
Coe, Nick *retail executive*
Collins, Michael D. *retail executive, accountant*
Crowley, William C. *retail executive*
de Bruin, Jerry Mark *retail executive*
Freidheim, Scott J. *retail executive*
Froman, John W. *retail executive*
Israel, Craig M. *retail executive*
Johnson, W. Bruce *retail executive*
Moore, Douglas T. *retail executive*
Pearlman, Michelle *retail executive*
Reed, Stuart C. *retail executive, former communications executive*
Trieb, Guenther *retail executive*

Hoopeston
Hicks, Carol Ann *small business owner, educator*

Itasca
Duncan, Sam K. *retail executive*

Lake Bluff
Ochsner, Othon Henry, II, *importer, restaurant critic*

Lake Forest
Jadin, Ronald L. *wholesale distribution executive*
Keyser, Richard Lee (Dick Keyser) *wholesale distribution executive*
Loux, P. Ogden *distribution company executive*
Ryan, James T. *wholesale distribution executive*
Ysasi-Diaz, Gloria *wholesale distribution executive*

Lisle
Thierer, Mark A. *retail executive*

Naperville
Besanko, Bruce H. *retail executive*

Niles
Renner, Jacqueline Marie *industrial and wholesale supply company executive*

Northbrook
Warchol, Judith Marie *small business owner*

Oak Brook
McKenna, Andrew James *wholesale distribution, printing company executive, sports association executive*

Saint Charles
LaHood, Julie Ann *small business owner*

IOWA

Ankeny
Myers, Robert J. *retail executive*

Cedar Rapids
Baldwin, George Koehler *retired retail executive*

Waterloo
Johannsen, Sonia Alicia *retired small business owner*

KANSAS

Topeka
Cantrell, Duane L. *retail executive*
Rubel, Matthew Evan *retail executive*

KENTUCKY

Eubank
Karriker, Danny Allen *small business owner, protective services official*

Lexington
Novak, Camille *small business owner, consultant*

Owensboro
Thomas-Löwe, Christine L. *small business owner*

Winchester
Book, John Kenneth (Kenny) *retail store owner*

LOUISIANA

Baker
Baker, Otis McDowell *small business owner*

Coushatta
Wiggins, Mary Ann Wise *small business owner, educator*

Covington
Perez de la Mesa, Manuel Jose *swimming pool company executive*

Lafayette
Menutis, Ruth Ann *small business owner*

New Orleans
DeFelice, Frances Radosta *retired restaurateur*

MAINE

Cumberland
Jamison, Elizabeth Alease *executive director*

MARYLAND

Baltimore
Hug, Richard Ernest *small business owner*

Brandywine
Richards, Madge Marie *business owner, professor, consultant, recruiter, professional fundraiser*

Laurel
Buffkins, LeRachel Harombe *small business owner*

Pikesville
Stein, Bernard Alvin *retail executive, consultant*

Potomac
Shapiro, Richard Gerald *retail executive, consultant*

Rockville
Cohan, June Elizabeth *small business owner*

Takoma Park
Miller, Kendra Danette *art services business owner*

MASSACHUSETTS

Framingham
Barron, Arnold S. *retail executive*
Butka, Paul C. *retail executive*
Cammarata, Bernard *retail executive*
Campbell, Donald G. *retail executive*
Chande, Amee *retail executive*
Doody, Joseph G. *retail executive*
Feldberg, Sumner Lee *retired retail executive*
Flores, Greg *retail executive*
Gilbert, John F. *retail executive*
Goodman, Shira D. *retail office and business products executive*
Herrman, Ernie *retail executive*
Lindenmeyer, Peter W. *retail executive*
Mahoney, John J. *office supply company executive*
Meyrowitz, Carol M. *retail executive*
Miles, Michael A., Jr. *retail executive*
Naylor, Jeffrey Gordon *retail executive*
Parneros, Demos *retail executive*
Rossi, Jerome R. *retail executive*
Sargent, Ronald L. *retail office and business products executive*
Sherr, Richard *retail executive*
Sweetenham, Paul *retail executive*
Tripathy, Nirmal K. *retail executive*

Medfield
McQuillen, Jeremiah Joseph *distribution executive*

Natick
Forward, Frank D. *wholesale distribution executive*
Povich, Lon F. *wholesale distribution executive*
Sen, Laura J. *wholesale distribution executive*
Zarkin, Herbert J. *wholesale distribution executive*

Newburyport
Lessard, Arnold Fred *international business executive*

Worcester
Candib, Murray A. *retail executive, consultant*

MICHIGAN

Ann Arbor
Armstrong, Kenneth Howard *retail executive*
Bierley, Mark Russell *retail executive*
Kramer, Elke *small business owner*
Kubek, Anne Marie *retail executive*
Marshall, Ron *retail executive*
McGuire, Richard (Mick McGuire) *retail executive*
Smith, Daniel T. *retail executive*

Bad Axe
Sullivan, James Gerald *small business owner*

Bloomfield Hills
Robinson, Jack Albert *retail executive*

Grand Rapids
Eidson, Dennis *retail executive*
Meijer, Hank *retail company executive*
Sturken, Craig C. *retail executive*

Harbor Beach
Falkenberg, Mary Elaine *small business owner*

Rothbury
Fischer, Dorothy Virginia *retired small business owner*

Troy
Koch, Albert Acheson *music distribution company executive, management consultant*
Strome, Stephen *former music distribution company executive*

MINNESOTA

Chanhassen
Froemming, Herbert Dean *retired retail executive*

Eden Prairie
Herkert, Craig R. *grocery retail and supply chain service company executive*
Knous, Pamela K. *wholesale distribution executive*
Noddle, Jeffrey *retail and food distribution company executive*
Van Helden, Peter J. *grocery company executive*

Edina
Covington, Alec C. *retail executive*

Minneapolis
Dunn, Brian J. *retail executive*
Francis, Michael R. *retail executive*
Griffith, John D. *retail executive*
Hale, James Thomas *retail executive, lawyer*
Kozlak, Jodeen A. *retail executive*
Mammel, Russell Norman *retired food distribution company executive*
Paulu, Frances Brown *retired international center administrator*
Risch, Troy H. *retail executive*
Schulze, Richard M. *retail executive*
Scovanner, Douglas A. *retail executive*
Scully, Terrence J. *retail executive*
Steinhafel, Gregg William *retail executive*
Tesija, Kathee (Kathryn A. Tesija) *retail executive*
Trestman, Frank D. *distribution company executive, director*
Ulrich, Robert J. (Bob Ulrich) *retired retail executive*

Richfield
Anderson, Brad (Bradbury H. Anderson) *retail executive*
Ballard, Shari Lynn *retail executive*
Muehlbauer, James L. *retail executive*

Saint Paul
Nash, Nicholas David *retail executive*

MISSISSIPPI

Greenwood
Jones, Carolyn Ellis *retired employment agency owner*

MISSOURI

Charleston
Cassell, Lucille Richardson *small business owner*

Cuba
Work, Bruce Van Syoc *small business owner, consultant*

Independence
Francis, Mary Frances Van Dyke *small business owner, real estate company executive, retired editor*
Lundy, Sadie Allen *small business owner*

Kingsville
Stimac, John Anthony *small business owner, poet, cartoonist, inventor*

Overland
Clark, Maxine *retail executive*

Saint Louis
Bridgewater, Bernard Adolphus, Jr. *retired retail executive*

NEBRASKA

Sidney
Highby, Dennis *retail executive*
Millner, Thomas L. *retail executive*

NEVADA

Henderson
Marcovitz, Leonard Edward *retail executive*

NEW HAMPSHIRE

Campton
Benton, Geraldine Ann *preschool owner, director*

New Castle
Friese, George Ralph *retail executive*

Wolfeboro
Baker, David Arthur *retired small business owner, manufacturing executive*

NEW JERSEY

Belle Mead
Dyer, Hugh Nelson III *management company owner*

Burlington
Kingsbury, Tom (Thomas A. Kingsbury) *retail executive*

Edison
Kijowski, Rosemary Joan *small business owner, retired music educator*

Elizabeth
Gellert, George Geza *food importing company executive*

Monroe Township
Zelin, Jerome *retired retail executive*

Montvale
Claus, Eric *retail executive*
Haub, Christian W.E. *retail executive*

New Milford
Walsh, Joseph Michael *magazine distribution executive*

Park Ridge
Ciannella, Joeen Moore *small business owner*

Pennington
Donnelly, Gerard Kevin *marketing and retail executive*

Princeton
Hochschwender, Karl Albert *international trade and government relations consultant*

Secaucus
Crovitz, Charles K. *former retail executive*
Syms, Marcy *retail executive*

Union
Castagna, Eugene A. *retail executive*
Eisenberg, Warren *retail executive*
Feinstein, Leonard *retail executive*
Temares, Steven H. *retail executive*

Wayne
Babrowski, Claire Harbeck *retail executive*
Boire, Ron *retail executive*
Creasey, F. Clay *retail executive*
Derby, Deborah *retail executive*
Storch, Gerald L. (Jerry Storch) *retail executive*

Whiting
Foster, Eric Harold, Jr. *retail executive*

NEW MEXICO

Albuquerque
East, Daniel K. *small business owner*

Santa Fe
Tinsley, Edward *small business owner, rancher*

NEW YORK

Bellport
Regalmuto, Nancy Marie *small business owner, consultant*

Ghent
Rao, Natti Sreerama *small business owner, consultant*

New York
Brizel, Michael Alan *retail executive, lawyer*
Catsimatidis, John Andreas *retail executive*
Daniels, Edward M. *small business owner, paralegal*
D'Arezzo, David W. *retail executive*
Drexler, Mickey (Millard Steven) *retail executive*
Farah, Roger N. *retail company executive*
Gilhart, Julie Lynn *retail executive*
Hailey, V. Ann (Vera Ann Hailey) *retail executive*
Hicks, Ken Carlyle *retail executive*
Holtz, Diane *retail executive*
Klipper, Mitchell S. *retail executive*
Kowalski, Michael J. *retail products executive*
Lederer, John A. *retail executive*
Lombardi, Joseph J. *retail executive*
Meads, Mindy *retail executive*
Michelson, Gertrude Geraldine *retired retail executive*
Obler, Geri *small business owner, artist, educator*
Quint, Ira *retail executive*
Riggio, Leonard *book store company executive*
Riggio, Stephen *book store company executive*
Riley, William *wholesale distribution executive, writer, conservationist*
Sadove, Stephen Irving *retail executive*
Schwarz, David *retail executive*
Toulantis, Marie J. *former retail bookseller executive, consultant*
Travis, Tracey Thomas *retail executive*
Washburn, Joan Thomas *small business owner*

Sands Point
Cohen, Ida Bogin (Mrs. Savin Cohen) *import/export company executive*

Southampton
Moneypenny, Edward William *retail executive*

NORTH CAROLINA

Black Mountain
Ingle, Robert P. *retail executive*

Charlotte
Belk, Irwin *retail executive*
Gambrell, Sarah Belk *retail executive*
Kelly, R. James *retail executive*
Levine, Howard R. *retail executive*
Macadam, Stephen E. *wholesale distribution executive*
Smith, Kenneth T. *retail executive*

Durham
Lieberman, Rochelle Phyllis *small business owner*

Greensboro
Jin, Byoungho *retail educator*

Hickory
Lynn, Tony Lee *import company executive*

Highlands
Shaffner, Randolph Preston *shop owner, educator, writer, publisher*

Salisbury
Candler, Faxon David *small business owner*

Wilkesboro
Brown, Michael K. *retail executive*
Canter, Charles W. (Nick) *retail executive*

Winston Salem
Strickland, Robert Louis *retired retail executive*

OHIO

Beachwood
Fufuka, Natika Njeri Yaa *retail executive*

Chesterland
Aster, Ruth Marie Rhydderch *business owner*

Cincinnati
Cody, Thomas Gerald *retail executive, lawyer*
Cole, Thomas L. *retail executive*
Gould, Michael *retail executive*
Grove, Janet E. *retail executive*
Hanson, Amy *retail company executive*
Hoguet, Karen M. *retail executive*
Kronick, Susan D. *retail executive*
McGeorge, Don W. *retail executive*
Reardon, Martine *department store executive, marketing professional*
Sachse, Peter *retail executive*

Cleveland
Crosby, Fred McClellan *retail executive*

Columbus
Burgdoerfer, Stuart *retail executive*
Fishman, Steven S. *retail executive*
Redgrave, Martyn Robert *retail executive*
Turney, Sharen Jester *retail executive, cosmetics executive*
Wexner, Leslie Herbert *retail executive*

Dayton
Jenefsky, Jack *wholesale company executive*

Hudson
Webb, Darrell D. *retail executive*

New Albany
Stevens, Kenneth T. *retail executive*

Newark
Black, Boyd Carson *small business owner*

Norwalk
Mays, George Francis *small business owner*

Reynoldsburg
McDonald, Camille Ann *retail executive*

Youngstown
Catoline-Ackerman, Pauline Dessie *small business owner*

OKLAHOMA

Oklahoma City
Peace, H. W., II, *small business owner, retired oil industry executive*

OREGON

Bend
Lemas, Noah *small business owner*

Forest Grove
Fuiten, Helen Lorraine *small business owner*

Salem
Robertson, Marian Ella (Hall) *small business owner, handwriting analyst*

Tualatin
Peters, Robert Wayne *small business owner*

PENNSYLVANIA

Allentown
Bennett, Siobhan L. (Sam Bennett) *small business owner*

Bensalem
Rosskamm, Alan D. *retail executive*

Berwyn
Fry, Clarence Herbert *retired retail executive*

Camp Hill
Cardinale, Gerald P. (Jerry Cardinale) *retail executive*
Davis, Don P. *retail executive*
Donley, Douglas E. *retail executive*

Hall, Christopher S. *retail executive*
Keough, Philip J., IV, *retail executive*
Learish, John *retail executive*
Lester, Wilson A., Jr. *retail executive*
Martindale, Kenneth Allen *retail executive*
Mastrian, James P. *retail executive*
Miller, Robert G. *drug store chain company executive*
Rugen, Karen *retail executive, corporate communications specialist*
Sammons, Mary Frances *retail executive*
Shirtliff, Bryan *retail executive*
Standley, John T. *retail executive*
Vitrano, Frank G. *retail executive*

Eighty Four
Hardy, Joseph A., Sr. *wholesale distribution executive*

Erie
Hagen, Thomas Bailey *business owner, former state official, retired insurance company executive*

Gap
Slater, Bruce *small business owner*

Mercer
DaCosta, Caroline Lee *small business owner*

Pittsburgh
Fortunato, Joseph *retail executive*
Stack, Edward W. *retail executive*

Shiremanstown
Nesbit, William Terry *small business owner, consultant*

Silverdale
Carney, Shannon Maureen *small business owner, educator*

West Chester
Ballbach, John M. *wholesale distribution executive*
Watts, Claire A. *retail executive*

York
Bergren, Byron L. *retail executive*

RHODE ISLAND

Woonsocket
Bodine, Chris W. *retail executive*
Ferdinandi, V. Michael *retail executive*
Merlo, Larry J. *retail executive*
Rickard, David B. *retail executive*
Sgarro, Douglas A. *retail executive, lawyer*

SOUTH CAROLINA

Hilton Head Island
Davis, Mary Martha (Marty Davis) *small business owner, consultant*

Yemassee
Olendorf, William Carr, Jr. *small business owner*

TENNESSEE

Gallatin
Ellis, Joseph Newlin *retired wholesale distribution executive*

Goodlettsville
Dreiling, Richard W. (Rick Dreiling) *retail executive*
Tehle, David M. *retail executive*

Memphis
Giles, William (Bill) T. *retail executive*
Hayes, Michael J. *retail executive*

Nashville
Zibart, Michael Alan *wholesale book company executive*

Waynesboro
Morris, Randy G. *small business owner*

TEXAS

Austin
Wilson, Margaret Scarbrough *retail executive*

Brenham
Lubbock, Mildred Marcelle (Midge Lubbock) *former small business owner*

Corpus Christi
Finley, George Alvin III *wholesale and oil industry executive*

Dallas
Augur, Marilyn Hussman *distribution executive*
Bush, Jack Eugene *retail executive*
Hall, Neva L. *retail executive*
Katz, Karen W. *retail executive*
Menzer, John Bruce *retail executive*
Mortensen, Pamela S. *retail executive*
Ross, Roman *retail executive*
Skinner, James E. *retail executive*
Stordahl, Ann M. *retail executive*
Tansky, Burton M. *department store executive*

Fort Worth
Brister, Gloria Nugent *small business owner, elementary school educator*
Day, Julian C. *retail executive*
Roberts, Leonard H. *retail executive*

Horseshoe Bay
Simpson, H. Richard (Dick Simpson) *retail merchandiser*

Houston
Levit, Max *wholesale distribution and food service executive*
Nesbitt, DeEtte DuPree *small business owner, investor*
Wike, D. Elaine *small business owner*
Woodhouse, John Frederick *retired wholesale distribution executive*

Irving
Goldberg, Neal *retail executive*

Lago Vista
Thompson, Dayle Ann *small business owner, consultant*

Plano
Boylson, Michael J. *retail executive, marketing professional*
Cavanaugh, Robert B. *department store executive*
Ullman, Myron Edward, III, (Mike Ullman) *retail executive*

San Antonio
Condrill, Jo Ellaresa *small business owner, writer, consultant*
Jary, Mary Canales *business owner*
Keck, Judith Marie Burke *business owner, retired career officer*
Williams, Docia Schultz *small business owner*

Selma
Kent, Jeff (Jeffrey Franklin Kent) *business owner, retired professional baseball player*

Snyder
Gray, Donna Lea *small business owner*

Tyler
Edwards, D. M. *retail, wholesale distribution and real estate company executive*

Wichita Falls
Waun, Roger *small business owner, minister*

UTAH

Saint George
Day, John Denton *small business owner, american quarter horse breeder*

VERMONT

Danby
Peel, Harris *retired small business owner*

Vergennes
Grant, Edwin Randolph *retail and manufacturing executive*

VIRGINIA

Arlington
Russell, William Trower III *small business owner*
Walcher, Greg E. *small business owner*

Bristow
Schrock, Simon *wholesale executive*

Charlottesville
Crutchfield, William Gayle, Jr. *retail executive*

Chesapeake
Sasser, Robert *retail executive*

Fairfax
Pugh, Arthur James (Jay Pugh) *retired retail executive*
Solomon, Ellen Joan *business owner, consultant*

Fairfax Station
Szczublewski, Wendy Sue *small business owner, musician, freelance/self-employed writer*

Falls Church
Bruck, Bill *business owner*

Midlothian
Cauthen, Charles Edward, Jr. *retired retail executive, management consultant*

Newport News
Williams, Cynthia Ann *small business owner, pediatrics nurse, writer, model, mentor*

Occoquan
Nemecek, Albert Duncan, Jr. *retail executive, investment banker, management consultant*

Richmond
Casini, Jane Sloan *wholesale distribution executive*
Dias, Fiona P. *retail executive*
Dunn, Philip J. *retail executive*

Salem
Brand, Edward Cabell *retail executive*

Upperville
Powell Gebhard, Joy Lee (Bok Sin Lee) *small business owner*

Vienna
Edwards, Phillip Milton *retired import/export company executive*

WASHINGTON

Bellevue
Fiske, Neil S. *retail executive*

Everett
Olsen-Estie, Jeanne Lindell *golf course owner*

Issaquah
Brotman, Jeffrey H. *wholesale distribution executive*
DiCerchio, Richard D. *wholesale distribution executive*
Galanti, Richard A. *wholesale business executive*
Sinegal, James D. (Jim Sinegal) *wholesale distribution executive*

Seattle
Bridge, Herbert Marvin *retail executive*
Jassy, Andrew R. *retail sales company executive*
Koppel, Michael G. *retail executive*
Leale, Olivia Mason *small business owner, import marketing executive*
Nordstrom, Blake W. *retail executive*

Spokane
Sines, Randy D. *retail executive*

Tacoma
Frantz, Dale Nelson *automobile import processing company executive*

Yakima
Phillips, Kathleen Gay *small business owner*

WEST VIRGINIA

Martinsburg
Ayers, Anne Louise *small business owner, consultant, counselor*

WISCONSIN

Brookfield
Pottebaum, Sharon Mitchell *farm manager, retired health educator*

Eau Claire
Menard, John R., Jr. *home improvement retail executive*
Stark, Paul *small business owner*

Menomonee Falls
Brennan, Donald A. *retail executive*
Eskenasi, Peggy *retail executive*
Gardner, Julie *retail executive*
Jeffries, Telvin *retail executive*
Mansell, Kevin B. *retail executive*
McDonald, Wesley S. *retail executive*
Montgomery, Larry (R. Lawrence Montgomery) *retail executive*
Worthington, John M. *retail executive*

Mequon
Kopfmann, Beverly Jean *small business owner*

Wausau
Builer, Dorothy Marion *business owner*

WYOMING

Jackson
Law, Clarene Alta *small business owner, state legislator*

ENGLAND

London
Habgood, Anthony John *corporate executive*

GHANA

Kumasi
Jafar, Muhammad Mamun *non governmental organization executive*

JAPAN

Tokyo
Sasaki, Mikio *trading company executive*

MALDIVES

Malé
Deen, Mohamed Waheed *small business owner*

SCOTLAND

Shetland
Kynastone, Vivien Rebecca *export company executive*

SWEDEN

Stockholm
van den Bosch, Margareta *apparel company executive*

VENEZUELA

Caracas
Cisneros, Gustavo Alfredo *retail executive*

ADDRESS UNPUBLISHED

Aved, Barry *retail executive, consultant*
Baker, Edward Kevin *retail executive*
Banks, Charles Augustus III *distribution executive*
Barth, David Keck *retired wholesale distribution executive, consultant*
Bell, Sharon Kaye *small business owner*
Bersell, Sean Devlin *trade association executive*
Bishop, Claire DeArment *small business owner, retired librarian*
Blackwell, Vickie Jan *small business owner*
Blagden, Susan Lowndes *retired small business owner*
Blizard, Marjorie Claire *small business owner*
Blum, Gerald Henry *retired retail executive*
Bryant, Warren F. *former retail executive*
Busch, Joyce Ida *small business owner*
Castagna, Vanessa J. *retired retail executive*
Castro, Teresa Jacira *small business owner*
Chevalier, Paul Edward *retired retail executive, lawyer*
Claus, Carol Jean *small business owner*
Connolly, Violette M. *small business owner*
Cope, Kenneth Wayne *retail executive*
Criscuolo, Esperanza *retail executive*
Cullen, Fergus P. *small business owner, former political organization administrator*
Degn, Douglas J. *retired retail executive*
Delaney, Marnie Patricia *retail executive*
DeVivo, Ange *retired small business owner*
Donley, Russell Lee III *small business owner, former state legislator*
Dufour, Jack Edward *retired small business owner, special education educator, athletic director, coach*
Dwight, Harvey Alpheus *retired small business owner*
Easley, Robert J. *retail executive*
Edwards, Patrick Ross *retail executive, lawyer, management consultant*
Eyler, John H., Jr. *retail toy and game company executive*
Farr, Ivanne Estelle *small business owner, artist, consultant*
Fields, Douglas Philip, Sr. *real estate and investment company executive*
Finnigan, Robert Emmet *retired small business owner*
Goldberg, Nancy G. *business owner, community volunteer*
Goldner, Sheldon Herbert *retired import/export company executive*
Goldstein, Norman Ray *international trading company executive, consultant*
Grantham, Joyce Carol *small business owner, music educator*
Greenstein, Merle Edward *import/export company executive*
Guzman, Carole L. *small business owner*
Hamed, Martha Ellen *retired federal government official, small business owner*
Jenkins, Charles H., Jr. *retail company executive*
Johnston, Gregory L. *retail executive*
Jones, George L. *retail executive*
Jourdan, Toni Christina *small business owner, actress, writer*
Kipper, Barbara Levy *wholesale distribution executive*
Lang, William Charles *retail executive*
Lanphear, AErin Marie *school system administrator*
Lazarus, Adrienne B. *retail executive*
Legault, Pierre *retail executive, pharmaceutical executive*
Lipsey, Joseph, Jr. *retired wholesale distribution executive*
Masten, Jacqueline Gwendolyn *small business owner*
Matthews, Norman Stuart *retail executive*
McKlenshaw, Irvin Lee *retired small business owner, advocate*
Meek, Forrest Burns *retired trading company executive*
Mench, John William *retail executive, electrical engineer*
Nemiroff, Maxine Celia *small business owner, art historian*
Nicolas, Kenneth Lee *import/export company executive*
Nishimura, Joseph Yo *retired retail executive, accountant*
Orenstein, Fran M. *small business owner, writer, editor*
Paterson, Robert E. *retail executive*
Raskin, Michael A. *retail executive, director*
Raymond, Ural Wayne *retired retail executive*
Reece, Karyn Lynn *business owner, consultant*
Richards-Vital, Claudia *small business owner, recreational facility executive*
Ritchey, Samuel Donley, Jr. *retired retail executive*
Rodbell, Clyde Armand *retired distribution executive*
Rodman, Sue A. *wholesale company executive, artist, writer*
Ross, Molly Owings *small business owner, sculptor*
Ruland, Mildred Ardelia *retired retail executive and buyer*
Schoonover, Philip J. *former retail executive*
Shapiro, Marc Robert *retail executive*
Sherman, Jeffrey Barry *retired retail executive*
Simms, Maria Kay *small business owner, writer, artist, publisher*
Strom, Victoria *small business owner*
Terry, Carole Cosgrove *retired small business owner, historian, researcher*
Tielke, James Clemens *retired retail and manufacturing executive*
Torson, Dianna May *retired small business owner*
Turner, Natalie A. *retired consultant*

Twomey, Kevin *retail executive*
Vernon, Carl Atlee, Jr. *retired wholesale food distributor executive*
West, Catherine G. *former retail executive*
Willingham, Mary Maxine *fashion retailer*

INDUSTRY: TRANSPORTATION

UNITED STATES

ALABAMA

Abbeville
Anderson, Ruth T. *retired air traffic controller*

Anniston
Huddleston, Tim *aerospace industry executive*

Gulf Shores
Wallace, John Loys *retired aviation services executive*

ALASKA

Anchorage
Shively, John Terry *cruise line executive*
Sullivan, George Murray *transportation executive, consultant, retired mayor*

ARIZONA

Phoenix
Gillette, Robert J. *aerospace transportation executive*
Isom, Robert D., Jr. *air transportation executive*
Moyes, Jerry C. *transportation executive, professional sports team executive*

Tempe
Kerr, Derek J. *transportation executive*
Kirby, J. Scott *air transportation executive*
Lakefield, Bruce R. *air transportation executive*
Parker, Doug (William Douglas Parker, W. Douglas Parker) *air transportation executive*

Tucson
Mercker, Mary Alice *aviation school administrator*

ARKANSAS

Bentonville
Pogue, William Reid *retired astronaut, foundation administrator, aerospace scientist, consultant*

Fort Smith
Davidson, Robert A. *trucking executive*

Lowell
Thompson, Kirk *transportation executive*

CALIFORNIA

Concord
Uremovich, Michael Elliot *transportation company executive*

Coto De Caza
Bezar, Gilbert Edward *retired aerospace company executive, volunteer*

Edwards AFB
Fritz, Matthew T. *pilot*

El Segundo
Musk, Elon *aerospace transportation executive*

Fremont
Smith, Bernald Stephen *retired pilot*

Gilroy
Borton, George Robert *retired airline captain*

Hermosa Beach
Kokalj, James Edward *retired aerospace administrator*

Huntington Beach
Burson, Thomas Daniel *retired aerospace executive*

La Jolla
Drake, Hudson Billings *aerospace and electronics executive*

La Mesa
Hansen, Grant Lewis *retired, aerospace executive*

Los Altos
Bergrun, Norman Riley *aerospace executive*

Los Angeles
Bush, Wesley G. *aerospace transportation executive*
Ervin, Gary W. *aerospace transportation executive*
Livanos, Alexis C. *aerospace transportation executive*
Mager, Artur *retired aerospace executive*
Mills, Linda A. *aerospace transportation executive*
Palmer, James F. *aerospace transportation executive*
Sugar, Ronald D. *aerospace transportation company executive*

Marina Del Rey
Gregg, Lucius Perry, Jr. *aerospace executive*

Mojave
Melvill, Michael W. *aircraft company executive, experimental test pilot*
Witt, Stuart O. *aerospace transportation executive*

Montague
Downs, Floella McIntyre *retired ferry pilot, instructor, flight examiner*

Newbury Park
Lindsey, Joanne M. *flight attendant, poet*

Oakland
Haskell, Arthur Jacob *retired water transportation executive*

Oceanside
Miller, Donald Eugene *retired air traffic controller*

Orange
Dearden, John Duncan *aircraft manufacturing executive*

Palos Verdes Estates
Smith, Stephen Randolph *aerospace executive*

Palos Verdes Peninsula
Slusser, Robert Wyman *aerospace transportation executive*

Poway
Sirangelo, Mark N. *aerospace transportation executive*

Ramona
Hoffman, Wayne Melvin *retired airline official*

Rancho Santa Fe
Arledge, Charles Stone *former aerospace executive, entrepreneur*

Redlands
Skomal, Edward Nelson *aerospace company executive, electromagnetic environments consultant*

Redondo Beach
Freeland, Pete *aerospace transportation executive, consultant, actor*

Sacramento
Acree, G. Hardy *airport executive*

San Diego
Butterfield, Alexander Porter *air transportation executive, former federal official*
Mc Kinnon, Clinton Dan *aerospace transportation executive*

San Francisco
Royer, Kathleen Rose *pilot*

San Mateo
Stotlar, Douglas W. *transportation executive*

Saratoga
Reagan, Joseph Bernard *retired aerospace executive, management consultant*

Simi Valley
Eberhard-Neveaux, Christine *aviation and dispute resolution executive*

West Hollywood
Brace, Frederic F. (Jake Brace) *retired air transportation executive*

COLORADO

Aurora
Gault, Paul Ryan *air transportation executive*

Denver
McMorris, Jerry *transportation company, sports team executive*
Menke, Sean E. *air transportation executive*

CONNECTICUT

Stamford
Barker, James Rex *water transportation executive, director*

DISTRICT OF COLUMBIA

Washington
Altschul, Alfred Samuel *airline executive*
Boardman, Joseph H. *rail transportation executive*
Carmody, Carol Jones *transportation executive, former federal agency administrator*
Cox, Rebecca Gernhardt *air transportation executive*
Donovan, George Joseph *transportation executive, consultant*
Downs, Thomas Michael (Tom Downs) *transportation executive*
Howell, Mary L. *multi-industry company executive*
Oh, Jung Eun Jen *transportation executive, researcher*

FLORIDA

Boca Raton
Garelick, Martin *retired transportation executive*
Iacobucci, Edward E. *air transportation and former software company executive*

Fort Lauderdale
Baldanza, Ben (Basil Ben Baldanza) *air transportation executive*

Jacksonville
Gerkens, Henry H. *trucking executive*
Kneller, Michael K. *transportation services executive*
Scanlon, George Patrick *transportation services executive, accountant*
Ward, Michael J. *rail transportation executive*

Miami
Fain, Richard David *cruise line executive*
Goldstein, Adam M. *cruise line executive*
Hanrahan, Daniel J. *cruise line executive*
Swienton, Gregory T. *transportation company executive*

Naples
Myers, Robert Jay *retired aerospace executive*

Orlando
Breazeale, Will *pilot, military officer*
Davis, H. Alan *retired airline captain, consultant*
Fornaro, Robert L. *air transportation executive*

Plantation
Fellows, John *delivery service executive*

Ponte Vedra Beach
Hamilton, William Berry, Jr. *retired transportation executive*

Saint Petersburg Beach
Mason, Phillip Howard *aircraft company executive, retired military officer*

Sanibel
Hasselman, Richard B. *retired rail transportation executive*

Satellite Beach
Loney, Mary Rose *former airport administrator, aviation industry consultant*

Tallahassee
Thagard, Norman E. *astronaut, physician, engineer, educator*

Vero Beach
Ingwersen, Martin Lewis *water transportation executive*

GEORGIA

Alpharetta
Chatlen, Stanley Lee *transportation executive*

Atlanta
Abney, David P. *delivery service executive*
Anderson, Richard H. *air transportation executive*
Barnes, David A. *delivery service executive*
Bastian, Edward H. *air transportation executive*
Brutto, Daniel J. *delivery service executive*
Campbell, Michael H. *air transportation executive*
Carp, Daniel Allen *air transportation executive, former consumer products company executive*
Davis, D. Scott (D. Scott Davis) *delivery service executive*
Gershenhorn, Alan *delivery service executive*
Gorman, Stephen E. *air transportation executive*
Halter, Hank *air transportation executive*
Hauenstein, Glen W. *air transportation executive*
Hill, Allen Edward *delivery service executive*
Kirchner, Eric W. *delivery service executive*
Kuehn, Kurt P. *delivery service executive*
Loewy, Robert Gustav *aerospace executive, engineering educator*
Macenczak, Lee Andrew *air transportation executive*
McDevitt, John *delivery service executive*
Owens, Christine M. *delivery service executive*
Stoffel, Robert E. *delivery service executive*
Torok, Ken *delivery service executive*

Greensboro
Campbell, Charles Alton *transportation executive*

Marietta
Clarkson, Lawrence William *air transportation executive*

Savannah
Lombardo, Joseph T. *aerospace transportation executive*

HAWAII

Honolulu
Doane, W. Allen *water transportation executive*

IDAHO

Boise
Ilett, Frank, Jr. *trucking executive, educator*

ILLINOIS

Arlington Heights
Halbert, Keith *air transportation executive*

Chicago
Andolino, Rosemarie S. *transportation executive*
Bell, James A. *aerospace transportation executive*
Burkhardt, Edward Arnold *rail transportation executive*
Hagin, Joseph Whitehouse, II, *aircraft maintenance company executive, former federal official*
Hill, Shepard W. *air transportation executive*
Luttig, J. Michael (John Michael Luttig) *aerospace transportation executive, former federal judge*
McDonald, Peter D. *air transportation executive*
McNerney, James, Jr., (W. James McNerney) *aerospace transportation executive, former manufacturing executive*
Mikells, Kathryn Ann *air transportation executive*
Nord, Henry J. *transportation executive*
Rodriguez, Richard L. *transportation executive*
Stephens, Richard *aerospace transportation executive*
Tague, John Patrick *air transportation executive*
Tilton, Glenn F. *air transportation executive*

Downers Grove
Yeager, David P. *transportation executive*

Oak Brook
Goodwin, James E. (Jim Goodwin) *retired air transportation executive*

Park Ridge
Carr, Gilbert Randle *retired railroad executive*

Urbana
Neogi, Natasha Anita *astronaut, educator*

Warrenville
Ustian, Daniel C. *trucking executive*

KANSAS

Overland Park
Zollars, William D. *freight company executive*

KENTUCKY

Louisville
Hayes, William Meredith *pilot, retired military officer*

MARYLAND

Baltimore
Glassman, Jon David *aerospace executive*

Bethesda
Comey, James B., Jr. *aerospace company executive, lawyer, former federal agency administrator*
Heath, Ralph D. *aerospace transportation executive*
Kubasik, Christopher E. *aerospace transportation executive*
Maguire, Joanne M. *aerospace transportation executive*
Tanner, Bruce L. *aerospace transportation executive*
Webber, Derek *aerospace executive, space tourism entrepreneur*

Owings Mills
Colussy, Dan Alfred *aviation executive*

Potomac
Fthenakis, Emanuel John *aerospace transportation and communications executive*

Rockville
Zinni, Anthony Charles *global defense company executive, retired military officer*

MASSACHUSETTS

Boston
Hasan, Masroor *transportation executive, consultant*
Klotz, Charles Rodger *water transportation and investment company executive*

Brookline
Frankel, Ernst Gabriel *shipping and aviation business executive, educator*

Cotuit
Ballou, Kenneth Walter *retired business executive, university dean*

Falmouth
McInnes, Donald Gordon *rail transportation executive*

MICHIGAN

Ann Arbor
Bruffett, Stephen L. *trucking executive*
Drake, John Warren *aviation consultant*

Detroit
Newman, Andrea Fischer *air transportation executive*

Grand Rapids
Auwers, Stanley John *motor carrier executive*

Waterford
Randall, Karl W. *air transportation executive, lawyer*

MINNESOTA

Eagan
Bauer, Kris *air transportation executive*
Becker, Michael J. *air transportation executive*

Davis, David M. *air transportation executive*
Friedel, Jim *air transportation executive*
Griffin, J. Timothy *air transportation executive*
Haan, Philip C. *air transportation executive*
Hirst, Richard B. *air transportation executive, lawyer*
Knotek, Crystal *air transportation executive*
Matthews, Daniel B. *air transportation executive*
Rainey, Timothy J. *air transportation executive*
Roberts, Andrew C. *air transportation executive*
Wise, Theresa *air transportation executive*

Eden Prairie
Lindbloom, Chad M. *transportation executive*
Satterlee, Scott A. *trucking executive*
Wiehoff, John P. *trucking executive*

Minneapolis
Harper, Donald Victor *retired transportation and logistics educator, consultant*
Nyrop, Donald William *air transportation executive*
Olson, James Richard *retired transportation executive*

North Oaks
Engle, Donald Edward *retired rail transportation executive, lawyer*

MISSOURI

Kansas City
Baisden, Eleanor Marguerite *retired airline compensation executive, consultant*
Haverty, Michael R. *rail transportation executive*
Starling, David L. *rail transportation executive*

Saint Louis
Graff, George Stephen *aerospace transportation executive*
Griggs, Leonard LeRoy, Jr. *air transportation executive, consultant*

NEBRASKA

Omaha
Duffy, Dennis J. *rail transportation executive*
Eisele, Charles R. *rail transportation executive*
Knight, Robert M., Jr. *rail transportation executive*
Koraleski, John J. *rail transportation executive*
McClish, Richard R. *transportation executive*
Schaefer, Barbara W. *rail transportation executive*
Tennison, Lynden *rail transportation executive*
Turner, Robert W. *rail transportation executive*
Werner, Clarence L. *transportation executive*
Werner, Gregory L. *transportation executive*
Young, James R. *rail transportation executive*

NEVADA

Las Vegas
Bigelow, Robert Thomas *aerospace transportation executive*

Nellis AFB
Malachowski, Nicole *pilot*

Reno
Shoen, Edward Joseph *transportation and insurance companies executive*

Sparks
Trabitz, Eugene Leonard *aerospace company executive*

NEW JERSEY

Cherry Hill
Gooden, Linda R. *aerospace transportation executive*

Edgewater
Pohan, Armand *transportation executive, professional hockey club executive, lawyer*

Flemington
Kettler, Carl Frederick *airline executive*

Moorestown
Myers, Christopher D. *defense company executive*

Morristown
Olcott, John Whiting *air transportation executive*

Newark
Baer, Susan M. *airport executive*

Piscataway
Boile, Maria *transportation executive, educator*

Roseland
Sugahara, Byron Masahiko *transportation executive*

Trenton
Kelly, Quentin Thorn *water and power company executive, writer*

Union
White, Robert Leslie Gordon, Jr. *aerospace transportation executive*

Wharton
Krosser, Howard S. *aerospace transportation executive*

NEW MEXICO

Albuquerque
Figueroa, Francisco Armando *aerospace defence executive, chief financial officer*
Masefield, Oliver Leslie Peter *aerospace transportation executive, aerospace engineer*
Raburn, Vern L. *air transportation executive, former Internet company executive*
Weh, Allen Edward *aviation executive*

NEW YORK

Albany
Joyce, William George, Jr. *transportation executive*

Buffalo
Cart, Stuart Edwin *air transportation executive, consultant*

Centerport
Trotta, Ric Charles *aerospace transportation executive, consultant*

Forest Hills
Barger, David J. *air transportation executive*
Barnes, Edward A. *air transportation executive*
Battaglia, Alex *air transportation executive*
Maruster, Robert Alan *air transportation executive*

Greenvale
Coutts, Robert B. *retired aerospace transportation executive*

Lindenhurst
Boltz, Mary Ann *aerospace materials and travel company executive*

New Windsor
Heinecke, John Kevin *military pilot, educator, researcher*

New York
Armstrong, Neil Alden *retired astronaut*
Chao, James Si-Cheng *maritime executive*
Hemmerdinger, Dale (Henry Dale Hemmerdinger) *transportation executive*
Rome, Todd M. *air transportation executive*
Thayer, Russell III *air transportation executive*
Treitel, David Henry *aviation executive*
Ward, Christopher O. *transportation executive, director*
Williams, Helena E. *rail transportation executive*

Northport
Reinertsen, Norman *retired air transportation executive*

Oyster Bay
Smith, Pamela Rosevear *air transportation executive*

Peekskill
Harte, Andrew Dennis *transportation company executive*

Queensbury
Mainwaring, Thomas Lloyd *transportation executive, director*

Troy
Holguin-Veras, Jose Ernesto *transportation researcher*

NORTH CAROLINA

Chapel Hill
Moellering, John Henry *aviation maintenance company executive*

Charlotte
Handy, John W. *shipping company executive, retired military officer*

Cherryville
Mayhew, Kenneth Edwin, Jr. *retired transportation executive*

Greensboro
Sink, Harry Lee *transportation executive*

Kannapolis
Thigpen, Alton Hill *transportation executive*

Raleigh
Whitehurst, Jim (James M. Whitehurst) *former air transportation executive*

OHIO

Cincinnati
Joyce, David L. *air transportation executive*

Columbus
Mason, Raymond E., Jr. *distributing company executive*

Painesville
Luhta, Caroline Naumann *airport manager, flight educator, museum administrator*

Xenia
Bigelow, Daniel James *aerospace executive*

OKLAHOMA

Grove
Trippensee, Gary Alan *retired aerospace executive*

Tulsa
Collins, John Roger *transportation company executive*

OREGON

Portland
Erickson, Mike *transportation executive*

PENNSYLVANIA

Allentown
Doughty, George Franklin *airport administrator*

Charleroi
Lekse, William John *water transportation executive*

Red Lion
Hartman, Charles Henry *transportation and not-for-profit executive, educator*

Washington
Kastelic, Robert Frank *aerospace transportation executive*

RHODE ISLAND

Providence
Adu-Gyamfi, R. Siisi *multi-industry company executive*
Bohlen, Kenneth C. *multi-industry company executive*
Butler, John D. *multi-industry company executive*
Campbell, Lewis B. *multi-industry company executive*
Yates, Richard L. *multi-industry company executive*

SOUTH CAROLINA

Columbia
Conrad, Paul Ernest *transportation consultant*

Easley
Dyer, Jane Ballard *pilot*

TENNESSEE

Chattanooga
Quinn, Patrick *transportation executive*

Memphis
Carter, Robert B. *delivery service executive*
Felix, Cheryl A. *air transportation executive*
Glenn, T. Michael *delivery service executive*
Graf, Alan B., Jr. *delivery service executive*
Reid, Karen Denise *aerospace transportation executive, writer*
Richards, Christine P. *delivery service executive, lawyer*
Smith, Frederick Wallace *delivery service executive*

Morristown
Johnson, Evelyn Bryan *airport terminal executive*

TEXAS

Austin
Aadnesen, Christopher *rail transportation executive, consultant*
Howell, Jefferson Davis, Jr. *aerospace transportation executive, educator, retired military officer*

Dallas
Adams, John Lewis *transportation executive*
Arpey, Gerard J. *air transportation executive*
Kelly, Gary Clayton *air transportation executive*
Philips, Brian D. *delivery service executive*
Ricks, Ron *air transportation executive*
Van de Ven, Michael G. *air transporation company executive*

Denton
Alatzas, George *delivery service company executive*

Desoto
Ennis, Rodney Craig *pilot*

Fort Worth
Frizzell, Roger C. *air transportation industry executive*
Garton, Daniel P. *air transportation executive, marketing professional*
Horton, Thomas W. *air transportation and former telecommunications company executive*
Hund, Thomas N. *rail transportation executive*
Ice, Carl R. *rail transportation executive*
Kennedy, Gary F. *air transportation executive, lawyer*
Lanigan, John P., Jr. *rail transportation executive*
Nober, Roger *rail transportation executive, lawyer*
Reding, Robert W. *air transportation executive*
Rose, Matthew K. *rail transportation executive*

Houston
Acaba, Joseph M. *astronaut*
Anderson-Lehman, Ron *air transportation executive*
Antonelli, Dominic A. *astronaut*
Archambault, Lee Joseph *astronaut*
Ashby, Jeffrey S. *astronaut*
Barratt, Michael Reed *astronaut*
Bergsrud, Mark *air transportation executive*
Boe, Eric A. *pilot, astronaut*
Bonds, Michael P. *air transportation executive*
Bowen, Stephen G. *astronaut*
Brandenstein, Daniel Charles *astronaut, retired military officer*
Chamitoff, Gregory Errol *astronaut, aerospace engineer*
Chiao, Leroy *astronaut*
Compton, James E. *air transportation executive*
Doi, Takao *astronaut*
Erwin, Mark A. *air transportation executive*
Eyharts, Leopold *astronaut*
Ferguson, Christopher J. *astronaut*
Foreman, Michael J. *astronaut*
Fossum, Michael E. *astronaut*
Frick, Stephen N. *astronaut*
Garan, Ronald J., Jr. *astronaut*
Grizzle, J. David *air transportation executive*
Grunsfeld, John M. *astronaut, astronomer*
Ham, Kenneth T. *astronaut, military officer*
Hilfman, David L. *air transportation executive*
Hoshide, Akihiko *astronaut*
Kellner, Larry (Lawrence Wesley Kellner) *air transportation executive*
Kelly, Mark E. *astronaut*
Kimbrough, Robert S. *astronaut*
Kopra, Timothy L. *astronaut*
Laderman, Gerald *air transportation executive*
Linnehan, Richard M. *astronaut, veterinarian*
Lopez-Alegria, Michael Eladio *astronaut*
Magnus, Sandra H. *astronaut*
Marshburn, Thomas H. *astronaut, emergency physician*
Meehan, William A. *air transportation executive*
Melroy, Pamela Ann *astronaut*
Melvin, Leland D. *astronaut*
Moran, Mark J. *air transportation executive*
Nyberg, Karen L. *astronaut*
Parazynski, Scott E. *astronaut*
Passonno Stott, Nicole *astronaut*
Pettit, Donald R. *astronaut, flight engineer, researcher*
Phillips, John L. *astronaut*
Poindexter, Alan *astronaut*
Qisheng, Pan *transportation executive, educator*
Ream, James B. (Jim Ream) *air transportation executive*
Rowe, Zane Conrad *air transportation executive*
Runco, Mario, Jr. *astronaut, meteorologist, researcher*
Schlegel, Hans *astronaut*
Shannon, Holden E. *air transportation executive*
Smisek, Jeffery A. *air transportation executive*
Stefanyshyn-Piper, Heidemarie M. *astronaut*
Sturckow, Frederick W. (Rick) *astronaut*
Swanson, Steven R. *astronaut*
Tani, Daniel M. *astronaut*
Thirsk, Robert Brent *astronaut*
Wakata, Koichi *astronaut*
Walheim, Rex J. *astronaut, military officer*
Walker, John E. (Ned Walker) *air transportation executive*
Wheelock, Douglas H. *astronaut, military officer*
Zamka, George D. *astronaut*

Irving
Plaskett, Thomas George *transportation executive, director*

New Braunfels
Rush, W.M. (Rusty) *trucking executive*

San Antonio
Rush, W. Marvin *trucking executive*
Weinstein, Martin *aerospace transportation and manufacturing executive, materials scientist*

Zavalla
Devlin, Cynthia M. *air transportation executive, consultant*

UTAH

Orem
Snow, Marlon O. *trucking executive, state agency administrator*

Saint George
Atkin, Jerry C. *air transportation executive*

VERMONT

Manchester Center
Carr, Gerald Paul *retired astronaut, engineer, marketing professional, military officer*

VIRGINIA

Alexandria
Crum, Richard *air transportation executive*

Arlington
Graves, Bill (William Preston Graves) *transportation association executive, former Governor of Kansas*
Hullin, Tod Robert *aerospace transportation executive*
Wahlquist, Andrew Folkman *government affairs executive*

Catlett
Broderick, Anthony James *air transportation executive*

Chesterfield
Congdon, John Rhodes *transportation executive*

Gainesville
Levell, Edward, Jr. *retired airport director, aviation consultant*

Mc Lean
Taylor, George Peach, Jr. *aerospace transportation executive, retired military officer*

Norfolk
Goode, David Ronald *retired transportation company executive*
Manion, Mark D. *rail transportation executive*
Moorman, Charles W. *transportation executive*
Phillips, Richard *cargo ship captain*
Squires, James A. *rail transportation executive*

Poquoson
Holloway, Paul Fayette *retired aerospace transportation executive*

Reston
Kreyling, Edward George, Jr. *retired railroad executive*

Richmond
Watkins, Hays Thomas *retired railroad executive*

Sterling
Thompson, David Walker *astronautics company executive*

Vienna
Anderson, Eric C. *aerospace transportation executive*
Beyer, Barbara Lynn *transportation executive, consultant*
Rogers, Raymond Jesse *retired federal railroad associate administrator*

Williamsburg
Spitzer, Cary Redford *avionics consultant, electrical engineer*
Starry, Donn Albert *retired aerospace corporate executive, retired military officer*

WASHINGTON

Belfair
Hager, Robert Worth *retired aerospace executive*

Ellensburg
Hoover, Amy Lynn *pilot, educator*

Seattle
Albaugh, James F. *aerospace transportation executive*
Ayer, William S. *air transportation executive*
Beighle, Douglas Paul *aerospace transportation executive*
Bezos, Jeffrey Preston *mail order services company executive*
Carson, Scott E. *aerospace transportation executive*
Delavar, Michael *pilot*
Gates, R. Jordan *delivery service executive*
Hirschmann, Franz Gottfried *aerospace executive*
Rose, Peter J. *delivery service executive*

Vancouver
Robertson, Joel Thomas *railroad executive*

WISCONSIN

Appleton
Petinga, Charles Michael *transportation executive*

Oshkosh
Bohn, Robert G. *transportation company executive*
Sagehorn, David M. *transportation company executive*
Szews, Charles *transportation executive*

WYOMING

Worland
Woods, Lawrence Milton *airline company executive*

CANADA

ONTARIO

Ottawa
Coleman, John Morley *transportation engineering executive*

QUEBEC

Montreal
Rochette, Louis *water transportation executive*

Saint Hubert
Payette, Julie *astronaut, electrical engineer, computer engineer*

AUSTRALIA

Springfield
Spalvins, Janis Gunars *steamship company executive*

BRAZIL

Varginha
Pereira, Renato Claudio Costa *air transportation executive*

DENMARK

Copenhagen
Moller, Maersk Mc-Kinney *shipowner*

ENGLAND

London
Kallakis, Ambassador Achilleas Michalis S. (His Excellency Ambassador Achilleas M. Kallakis of the Republic of *transportation executive, real estate company executive*

FRANCE

Roissy
Spinetta, Jean-Cyril *airline executive*

ITALY

Rome
Guarguaglini, Pier Francesco *aerospace transportation executive*

JAPAN

Tokyo
Kaneko, Isao *air transportation executive*
Kusakari, Takao *transportation executive*
Ohashi, Yoji *air transportation executive*

RUSSIA

Moscow
Perminov, Anatoly *aerospace agency executive*

SWEDEN

Solna
Ljøstad, Torstein Torberg *retired airline company executive*

SWITZERLAND

Rolle
Aaronson, Robert Jay *air transportation executive*

ADDRESS UNPUBLISHED

Aldrin, Buzz *retired astronaut*
Arnold, James Oliver *aerospace executive, researcher*
Baddour, Anne Bridge *pilot*
Bain, Douglas G. *retired aerospace transportation executive, lawyer*
Bielucke, Edward Anthony III *transportation executive, writer*
Brand, Vance Devoe *astronaut, director*
Brown, Donald Douglas *transportation executive, consultant, retired military officer*
Carpenter, Scott (Malcolm Scott Carpenter) *retired astronaut, oceanographer*
Carter, Thomas Smith, Jr. *retired rail transportation executive*
Checchi, Alfred A. *air transportation executive, financial consultant*
Christopher, Alexander George *transportation company executive*
Cohen, Neal Stuart *air transportation executive*
Collins, Eileen Marie *astronaut*
Cook, Richard Kelsey *aerospace transportation executive*
Dely, Steven *retired aerospace company executive*
Dewar, James McEwen *marketing, aerospace and defense executive, developing nations consultant*
Duelfer, Charles Alfred *aerospace transportation executive, weapons inspector, director*
Evans, James Hurlburt *retired transportation and natural resources executive*
Ferguson McGinnis, Kathryn Joan (Kathy Ferguson McGinnis) *flight attendant*
Fischbach, Charles Peter *rail transportation executive, consultant, lawyer, arbitrator, mediator, government official*
Fish, Howard Math *aerospace transportation executive*
Forgeard, Noël *retired aerospace and defence company executive*
Gasich, Welko Elton *retired aerospace defense executive, management consultant*
Gitner, Gerald L. *air transportation executive, investment banker*
Goldstein, Bernard *metal recycling, transportation and casino executive*
Graebner, James Herbert *transportation executive*
Gray, Richard Arden *retired transportation executive*
Grossman, Robert Allen *retired transportation executive*
Gulcher, Robert Harry *aerospace transportation executive*
Hahn, Virginia Lynn *reservations agent*
Hertrich, Rainer *aerospace and defense company executive*
Higginbottom, Samuel Logan *retired air transportation executive*
Keenan, Anthony Lee *trucking executive*
Kelleher, Herbert David *retired air transportation executive, lawyer*
Kennard, Lydia H. *former airport terminal executive*
Knight, Eric A. *aerospace executive, entrepreneur, inventor*
Knutsen, Gregg Evan *transportation executive*
Lewis, Martin Edward *transportation executive, oil trader, foreign government concessionary*
Lovell, James Arthur, Jr. *retired astronaut*
Malishenko, Timothy Peter *retired aerospace company executive*
Marshall, Charles Noble *rail transportation executive*
Masiello, Rocco Joseph *air transportation executive, consultant*
Matsuda, Masatake *former rail transportation executive*
McCarthy, Paul Fenton *aerospace transportation executive, retired military officer*
McCarty, Shirley Carolyn *retired aerospace executive*
Myers, Donald Alan *transportation executive*
O'Brien, Raymond Francis *transportation executive*
Parker, James Francis *former air transportation executive, lawyer*
Pickering, Thomas Reeve *retired aerospace transportation executive*
Pope, John Charles *former airline company executive*
Rivkind, Perry Abbot *federal railroad agency administrator*
Saleh, Brian Behrooz *aerospace transportation executive*
Sander, Elliot Gene (Lee Sander) *former transportation executive*
Savitz, Maxine Lazarus *retired aerospace transportation executive*
Schaupp, Joan Pomprowitz *trucking executive, writer*
Seymour, Joseph John *air transportation executive*
Shockley, Edward Julian *retired air transportation executive*
Sitomer, Richard Allen (Ricky Sitomer) *air transportation executive*
Snowden, Lawrence Fontaine *retired air transportation executive, retired military officer*
Stapleton, Beverly Cooper *aerospace executive*
Steenland, Douglas M. *former air transportation executive*
Stevens, Robert J. *aerospace transportation executive*
Sullenberger, Chesley Burnett, III, (Sully Sullenberger) *pilot, airline safety consulting company executive*
Swinburn, Charles *retired rail transportation executive*
Thorne, James Dana *astronautical engineer, researcher*
Wallace, F. Blake *retired aerospace transportation executive, retired mechanical engineer*
Washburn, Donald Arthur *retired business executive, investor*
Yeager, Phillip Charles *transportation company executive*
Zeidlik, Thomas Richard *pilot, educator*

INDUSTRY: UTILITIES, ENERGY, RESOURCES

UNITED STATES

ALABAMA

Birmingham
Johnson, Wylie Pierson *electric utility executive*

Foley
St. John, Henry Sewell, Jr. *utility company executive*

ALASKA

Fairbanks
Beistline, Earl Hoover *mining consultant*

ARIZONA

Phoenix
Adkerson, Richard C. *mining executive*
Quirk, Kathleen L. *mining executive*

Scottsdale
Trimble, Thomas James *retired utilities executive, lawyer*

Sedona
Dansby, John Walter *retired oil industry executive*

Show Low
Pershing, Robert George *retired telecommunications industry executive*

Sun City
Black, Robert Frederick *retired gas industry executive*

Tempe
Hickson, Robin Julian *mining company executive*

Tucson
Heller, Frederick *retired mining executive*
Peeler, Stuart Thorne *oil industry executive, consultant*
Peters, Charles William *nuclear energy industry executive*

ARKANSAS

El Dorado
Fitzgerald, Kevin Gerard *oil industry executive*
Nolan, William C., Jr. *oil industry executive*
Wood, David M. *oil industry executive*

Little Rock
Ford, Scott T. *telecommunications industry executive*

CALIFORNIA

Alameda
Lu, Hong Liang *telecommunications industry executive*

Alamo
Shiffer, James David *retired utilities executive*

Berkeley
Baack, Lawrence James *energy executive, history professor*

Calabasas
Bhatnagar, Atul *telecommunications industry executive*
Ginsberg, Errol *telecommunications industry executive*

Calistoga
Savage, Michael John Kirkness *oil industry, performing arts company executive and winegrower*

Carmel
Hamilton, Lyman Critchfield, Jr. *telecommunications industry executive*

La Jolla
Rinaker, Samuel Mayo, Jr. *retired utilities executive*

Lake Forest
Pardun, Thomas E. *telecommunications industry executive*

Los Angeles
Chazen, Stephen I. *oil industry executive*
Irani, Ray R. *oil, gas and chemical company executive*
Lienert, James M. *oil industry executive*

Mill Valley
Premo, Paul Mark *oil industry executive*

Mountain View
Koopmans, Chris *telecommunications industry executive*

Newport Coast
Swan, Peer Alden *public utility executive*

Pacific Palisades
Mulryan, Henry Trist *mining executive, consultant*

Palo Alto
Agassi, Shai *alternative energy company executive, former application developer*
Cohen, Karl Paley *nuclear energy consultant*
Loewenstein, Walter Bernard *nuclear energy industry executive*
O'Donnell, John Setel *energy executive*

Palos Verdes Peninsula
Christie, Hans Frederick *retired utilities executive*

Pasadena
White-Thomson, Ian Leonard *retired mining executive*

Rosemead
Craver, Theodore F., Jr. *utilities and energy executive*
Featherstone, Diane L. *utilities executive*
Gault, Polly L. *utilities executive*
House, Cecil R. *utilities executive*
Parsky, Barbara J. *utilities executive*
Scilacci, W. James, Jr. *utilities executive*
Yazdi, Mahvash *utilities executive*

Sacramento
Shewry, Sandra *telehealth company executive*

San Diego
Altman, Steven R. *telecommunications executive*
Felsinger, Donald E. *utilities corporation executive*
Hutcheson, S. Douglas *telecommunications industry executive*
Lauer, Len J. *telecommunications industry executive*
Schmale, Neal E. *utilities company executive*
Snell, Mark A. *utilities executive*

San Francisco
Barcon, Barbara L. *utilities executive*
Darbee, Peter A. *utilities executive*
Dickinson, Wade *oil industry executive, educator*
Goldstein, David Baird *energy executive, physicist*
Harvey, Kent M. *utilities executive*
Johns, Christopher P. *utilities executive*
McFadden, Nancy Elizabeth *utilities executive*
Rosenberg, Rand L. *utilities executive*
Simon, John R. *utilities executive*
Sproul, John Allan *retired utilities executive*

San Jose
Fusco, Jack A. *energy executive*
Guthrie, Laura D. *energy executive, human resources specialist*
Prasad, Neil A. *telecommunications industry executive, computer company executive*

San Ramon
Beebe, Lydia I. *oil industry executive, lawyer*
Bethancourt, John E. *oil industry executive*
Breber, Pierre R. *oil industry executive*
Gass, John D. *oil industry executive*
Humphrey, Mark A. *oil industry executive*
Kirkland, George L. *oil industry executive*
McDonald, John W. *oil industry executive*
O'Reilly, David J. *oil industry executive*
Pryor, Jay R. *oil industry executive*
Schuttish, Thomas R. *oil industry executive, lawyer*
Siegele, Paul K. *oil industry executive*
Taylor, Charles A. (Chuck Taylor) *oil industry executive*
Watson, John S. *oil industry executive*
Wirth, Michael K. (Mike Wirth) *oil company executive*
Yarrington, Patricia E. *oil industry executive*
Zygocki, Rhonda I. *oil industry executive*

Santa Ana
Laurance, Dale R. *oil company executive*

Santa Cruz
Kahn, Philippe *telecommunications industry executive, entrepreneur*

Santa Rosa
Wagner, Harold A. *retired gas industry executive*

South Pasadena
Finnell, Michael Hartman *mining executive*

Sunnyvale
Sundberg, Carl-Erik Wilhelm *telecommunications executive, researcher*

Westwood
Sull, Wonhee *telecommunications industry executive*

COLORADO

Broomfield
Patel, Sunit *telecommunications industry executive*

Denver
Clevenger, Jeffrey Griswold *mining company executive*
Hall, Larry Dean *utilities executive, lawyer*
Kruger, Paula *telecommunications industry executive*
Larson, Randall J. *energy executive*
Lewis, Jerome A. *petroleum company executive, investment banker*
Macey, William Blackmore *oil industry executive*
Mogg, Jimmy W. *gas industry executive*
Mueller, Edward A. *telecommunications industry executive*
O'Brien, Richard T. *mining executive*
O'Connor, Thomas C. *energy executive*
Taylor, Teresa A. *telecommunications industry executive*
Thornton, Roland *telecommunications industry executive*
Tregemba, Robert D. *telecommunications industry executive*
Trueblood, Harry Albert, Jr. *oil industry executive*
Yost, Dan *telecommunications industry executive*

Englewood
Bennett, Robert R. *telecommunications company executive*
Dodge, R. Stanton *energy executive*
Schleyer, William T. *cable company executive*

Golden
Ding, Shi-You *energy executive, researcher*
von Roedern, Bolko Graf *energy executive, researcher*

CONNECTICUT

Fairfield
Begor, Mark W. *energy executive*
Bolze, Stephen *energy executive*
Bornstein, Jeffrey S. *energy executive*

Greenwich
Alonzo, Martin Vincent *mining and aluminum company executive, investor, financial consultant*

Guilford
Morgan, Leon Alford *retired utilities executive*

Hartford
McHale, David R. *utilities executive*
Olivier, Leon J. *utilities executive*

Madison
Kay, Herbert *retired energy executive*

New Canaan
McIvor, Donald Kenneth *retired petroleum company executive*

Orange
Powers, Timothy H. *electric power industry executive*

South Windsor
van Dokkum, Jan *electric power industry executive*

Southport
Damson, Barrie Morton *oil and gas exploration company executive*

Stamford
Mc Kinley, John Key *retired oil company executive*
Walsh, Kevin P. *energy executive, financial services executive*

Waterbury
Shivery, Charles W. *utilities executive*

Westport
Hall, Andrew J. *oil industry executive*

DELAWARE

Rockland
Cosgrove, Howard Edward, Jr. *utilities executive*

DISTRICT OF COLUMBIA

Washington
Barry, Paul H. *utilities executive*
Buchan, Douglas Charles *gas industry executive, government agency administrator*
DeGraffenreidt, James H., Jr. *gas company executive*
Emge, Kirk J. *electric power industry executive, lawyer*
Fraulino, Philip Samuel *telecommunications industry executive*
Friedman, Gregory H. *energy administrator*
Friend, William L. *retired engineering/construction industry executive*
Giusti, Luis E. *gas industry executive*
Largent, Steven Michael *telecommunications industry executive, former congressman, retired professional football player*
Marks, Ronald Anthony *communications industry executive*
Moler, Elizabeth Anne *utilities executive*
Raymond, Lee R. *retired oil company executive*
Rigby, Joseph M. *utilities executive*
Sant, Roger W. *retired energy executive*
Yulish, Charles Barry *retired energy and environmental consultant, public relations executive*

FLORIDA

Boca Raton
Gralla, Eugene *natural gas company executive*

Clearwater
Spiegel, Colleen *electric power industry executive*

Deerfield Beach
Laser, Charles, Jr. *oil company executive*

Indian River Shores
Wiegner, Edward Alex *financial and energy executive*

Juno Beach
Hay, Lewis III *utilities executive*
Litchfield, R. Wade *energy executive*
Robo, James L. *utilities executive*

Longwood
Cirello, John *utility and engineering company executive*

Miami
Kasbar, Michael J. *energy executive*
Pimentel, Armando *energy executive*
Stebbins, Paul H. *energy executive*

Naples
Gelfand, Neal *oil industry executive*
Marienthal, George *telecommunications industry executive*
Marino, William Francis *telecommunications industry executive, consultant*

North Palm Beach
Sieving, Charles E. *energy executive, lawyer*
Stall, John A. *energy executive*

Orlando
Wei, Lei *telecommunications educator*

Palm Beach Gardens
Harnett, Joseph Durham *oil industry executive*

Pensacola
Story, Susan N. *utilities executive*

Ponte Vedra
Wood, Quentin Eugene *oil industry executive*

Saint Petersburg
Fleming, William Sloan *energy and computer company executive*

Saint Petersburg Beach
Garnett, Stanley Iredale, II, *utilities executive, lawyer*

Sarasota
Torrey, Richard Frank *retired utilities executive*

Stuart
Kirkpatrick, Harold (Kirk) Wayne *telecommunications industry executive*

Tampa
Brown, Troy Anderson, Jr. *retired electric power industry executive*
Hudson, Sherrill W. *energy executive*

Vero Beach
Bennett, Jack Franklin *oil industry executive*

Village Of Golf
Allen, Robert Eugene *retired telecommunications industry executive*

GEORGIA

Atlanta
Arroyo, F. Thaddeus *telecommunications industry executive*
Bolch, Carl Edward, Jr. *oil industry executive, lawyer*
Bowers, W. Paul *utilities executive*
Carbonell, Joaquin R. III *telecommunications industry executive, lawyer*
Carter, Stephen M. *telecommunications manufacturing industry executive*
Dawson, Robert G. *telecommunications industry executive*
Dearman, Andrew J. III *utilities executive*
Ellis, James O., Jr. *nuclear energy industry executive, retired military officer*
Fanning, Thomas Andrew *utilities executive*
Garrett, Michael D. *utilities executive*
Gilligan, Bob *energy executive*
Johnson, Marsha Sampson *utilities executive*
Martin, C. Alan *utilities executive*
McCrary, Charles D. *utilities executive*
Muller, Edward Robert *energy executive, lawyer*
Nagel, Jeffrey A. *energy executive*
Ramsey, Ira Clayton *retired petroleum industry executive*
Ratcliffe, David M. *utilities executive*
Somerhalder, John W., II, *energy executive*
Womack, Christopher C. *utilities executive*
Yaccarino, Linda *telecommunications industry executive, marketing professional*

Duluth
McCracken, William Henry *retired mining executive*

HAWAII

Honolulu
Lau, Constance H. (Connie Lau) *electric power industry executive*
Rosenblum, Richard Mark *utilities executive*
Wilson, William Hall, Jr. *retired telecommunications executive*

Kaneohe
Amioka, Wallace Shuzo *retired petroleum company executive*

Waikoloa
Calvert, Delbert William *retired energy executive*

IDAHO

Coeur D' Alene
Wheeler, Dennis Earl *mining company executive, lawyer*

ILLINOIS

Argonne
Ban, Stephen Dennis *gas industry executive*

Chicago
Brooker, Thomas Kimball *oil industry executive*
Carlson, LeRoy Theodore, Jr. *telecommunications industry executive*
Clark, Frank M. *utilities executive*
Crane, Christopher M. *utilities executive*
Gillis, Ruth Ann M. *utilities executive*
Hilzinger, Matthew F. *utilities executive*
McLean, Ian P. *utilities executive*
Meyers, Kenneth Raymond *telecommunications industry executive*
Morrow, Richard Martin *retired oil company executive*
O'Leary, Joseph P. *energy executive*
Rowe, John William *utilities executive*
Schrock, Charles A. *energy executive*
Zopp, Andrea Lynne *energy company executive, lawyer*

Deerfield
Zywicki, Robert Albert *retired electric power industry executive*

Joliet
Easton, Kenneth Glenn *retired utilities executive*

Maryville
Bonneville, Richard Briggs *retired gas industry executive*

Naperville
Burken, Ruth Marie *utilities executive*
Pullen, Robert W. *telecommunications industry executive*
Strobel, Russ M. *gas industry executive, lawyer*

Warrenville
Yoon, Seong-Hoon *energy executive, researcher*

West Frankfort
Williams, Joseph Scott *energy and natural resources company executive, former city commissioner*

INDIANA

Evansville
Ellerbrook, Niel Cochran *gas industry executive*

Indianapolis
Grube, F. William *refining company executive*

Merrillville
O'Donnell, Michael W. *energy company executive*
Skaggs, Robert C., Jr. *utilities executive, lawyer*
Smith, Stephen P. *utilities executive*

IOWA

Des Moines
Abel, Gregory E. *utilities company executive*
Sokol, David Lee *utilities company executive*

KANSAS

Overland Park
Alves, Paget L. *telecommunications industry executive*
Betts, Gene M. *telecommunications industry executive*
Ferrell, James Edwin *nuclear energy industry executive*
Gerke, Thomas A. *telecommunications industry executive, lawyer*
Morgan, William (Bill) *telecommunications industry executive*
Patterson, James *telecommunications industry executive*
Toussaint, Claudia S. *telecommunications industry executive, lawyer*

Pittsburg
Nettels, George Edward, Jr. *retired mining executive*

Topeka
Moore, William B. *energy executive*
Spencer, William Edwin *retired telecommunications industry executive, engineer*

Wichita
Cadman, Wilson Kennedy *retired utilities executive*

KENTUCKY

Crescent Springs
Chellgren, Paul Wilbur *energy industry executive*

Lexington
Boyd, James Robert *energy executive*

Louisville
Ronald, Peter *utilities executive*

LOUISIANA

Baton Rouge
Longwell, Harry J. *retired oil industry executive*

Lacombe
Harlan, Jim *energy executive*

Monroe
Post, Glen Fleming III *telecommunications industry executive*

New Orleans
Lind, Thomas Otto *barge transportation company executive*
Moffett, James Robert *mining executive*
Sloan, Robert D. *energy executive, lawyer*

MAINE

Casco
Brown, Ronald Osborne *telecommunications and computer systems consultant*

Portland
von Schack, Wesley W. *utilities executive*

Yarmouth
Haynes, Peter Lancaster *retired utilities executive*

MARYLAND

Baltimore
Barron, Henry B., Jr., (Brew) *energy executive*
Brady, Thomas F. *energy executive*
Brooks, Thomas V. *energy executive*
Collins, John R. *energy executive*
Connaughton, James Laurence *energy executive, former federal official*
Hyle, Kathleen W. *energy executive*
Ihrie, Robert *oil, gas and real estate company executive*
Rzepkowski, James Edward *energy executive*
Shattuck, Mayo Adams III *utilities executive*
Thayer, Jonathan W. *energy executive*
Wallace, Michael J. *energy executive*

Bethesda
McMurphy, Michael Allen *energy company executive, lawyer*
Olmsted, Jerauld Lockwood *telephone company executive*
Starkey, Russell Bruce, Jr. *energy executive*
Welch, John Kirtland *nuclear energy industry executive*

Columbia
Gilbert, Douglas Brainerd *telecommunications industry executive*

Frederick
Safavian, S. Rasoul *telecommunications industry executive*

Gaithersburg
Delgado, Dwighd D(ubied) *electric power industry executive*

Glen Arm
Jackson, Theodore Marshall *retired oil industry executive*

Rockville
Griffith, Jerry Dice *energy executive, management consultant*

Severna Park
Kumm, William Howard *energy products company executive*

Silver Spring
Jacobs, George *broadcast engineering consulting company executive*

MASSACHUSETTS

Boston
Kennedy, Joseph Patrick, II, *utilities executive, former United States Representative from Massachusetts*
May, Thomas J. *electric company executive*
Stobaugh, Robert Blair *professor emeritus*

Centerville
Anderson, Gerald Edwin *retired utilities executive*
Scherer, Harold Nicholas, Jr. *electric power industry executive*

Needham
Cogswell, John Heyland *retired telecommunications industry executive, financial consultant*

Newton
Petrowski, Joseph H. *oil industry executive*

Plymouth
Staszesky, Francis Myron *electric power industry executive, consultant*

Waltham
Bok, Joan Toland *utilities executive*
Hollister, Thomas J. *oil industry executive*
Malis, Andrew Gary *telecommunications industry executive*
Slifka, Eric *oil industry executive*

Westborough
Catell, Robert Barry *gas industry executive*

Weston
Goldstein, Arthur Louis *retired utilities executive*

MICHIGAN

Ann Arbor
White, Dawn Roberta *energy executive*

Detroit
Anderson, Gerard M. *energy executive*
Earley, Anthony Francis, Jr. *utilities company executive, lawyer*
Ellyn, Lynne *energy executive*

Jackson
Joos, David W. *energy executive*
Webb, Thomas J. *utilities executive*
Whipple, Kenneth *utilities executive*

MINNESOTA

Burnsville
O'Brien, Gerald James *utilities executive*

Eden Prairie
Switz, Robert E. *telecommunications executive*

Minneapolis
Bonavia, Paul J. *energy executive*
Hartwell, Kimberly S. *telecommunications industry executive*
Kelly, Richard C. *energy executive*
Nicholson, Hilton M. *telecommunications industry executive*
O'Brien, Patrick D. *telecommunications industry executive*
Olson, John Richard *power industry electrician*
Parran, Richard B., Jr. *telecommunications industry executive*
Sparby, David M. *energy executive*
Wilks, David M. *energy executive*

MISSISSIPPI

Gulfport
Topazi, Anthony J. *utilities executive*

Jackson
Denault, Leo P. *energy executive*
Leonard, J. Wayne *energy executive*
Smith, Richard J. *energy executive*

Ocean Springs
Braumiller, Allen Spooner *gas industry executive, geologist*

MISSOURI

Kansas City
Baker, John Russell *utilities executive*
Chesser, Michael J. *gas and electric power industry executive*
Potter, George William, Jr. *mining executive*
Riggins, William G. *electric power industry executive*

Lake Sherwood
Torbett, Gary Burl *retired telephone company executive*

Saint Louis
Baxter, Warner L. *electric power industry executive*
Boyce, Gregory H. *energy executive*
Crews, Michael C. *energy executive*
Leer, Steven F. *mining executive*
Lyons, Martin J., Jr. *electric power industry executive*
Navarre, Richard A. *energy executive*
Rainwater, Gary L. *electric power industry executive*
Smit, Neil *telecommunications industry executive*
Stroup, John S. *high speed electronic industry executive*
Voss, Thomas R. *electric power industry executive*
Yaeger, Douglas Harrison *gas industry executive*

Springfield
Jura, James J. *electric utility executive*

NEBRASKA

Omaha
Crouse, Jerry K. *energy company executive*
Hawks, Howard L. *energy executive*
Scott, Walter, Jr. *telecommunications industry executive*
West, Mary E. *telecommunications industry executive*

NEVADA

Las Vegas
Shaw, Jeffrey William *gas industry executive*
Yackira, Michael William *electric power industry executive*

Reno
Gundersen, Wayne Campbell *energy executive, consultant*

Winnemucca
Hesse, Martha O. *gas industry executive*

NEW JERSEY

Basking Ridge
D'Ambrosio, Louis J. *telecommunications industry executive*
Mason, Michael A. *telecommunications industry executive, former FBI agent*
Matthews, Craig Gerard *retired energy executive*
McAdam, Lowell C. *telecommunications industry executive*
Ruesterholz, Virginia P. *telecommunications industry executive*
Schenker, Leo *retired utilities executive*

Bedminster
Strigl, Dennis F. *telecommunications industry executive*

Belmar
Downes, Laurence M. *gas industry executive*

Holmdel
Winzer, Peter J. *telecommunications industry executive, researcher*

New Providence
Carapezzi, William R., Jr. *telecommunications industry executive, lawyer*
Kim, Jeong H. *telecommunications industry executive, communications engineer*
Morgan, Dennis R. *telecommunications industry executive*

Newark
Byrd, Stephen C. *utilities executive*
Dorsa, Caroline D. *utilities company executive, former software company executive*
Izzo, Ralph *utilities executive*
LaRossa, Ralph *utilities executive*
Levis, William *utilities executive*
Lopriore, Richard P. *utilities executive*
Moran, Eileen A. *utilities executive*
Pego, Margaret M. *utilities executive*
Quinn, Kevin J. *utilities executive*
Simpson, Elbert C. *utilities executive*

Peapack
Walsh, Philip Cornelius *retired mining executive*

Piscataway
Chynoweth, Alan Gerald *retired telecommunications industry executive*

Princeton
Bodman, Richard Stockwell *telecommunications executive*
Crane, David W. *energy executive*
Flexon, Robert C. *energy executive*
Freeland, Clint *energy executive*
Murphy, J. Andrew (Drew Murphy) *energy executive, lawyer*
Ragan, John W. *energy executive*

Roseland
Fuller, S(heri) Marce *energy executive*

NEW MEXICO

Albuquerque
Ofte, Donald *retired nuclear energy industry executive*
Sterba, Jeffry E. *energy executive*
Yates, Harvey E. *oil industry executive, political organization administrator*

High Rolls Mountain Park
Ellison, Luther Frederick *oil industry executive*

Los Alamos
Dienes, John Kalman *energy executive*

Roswell
Anderson, Donald Bernard *oil industry executive*

Santa Fe
Duhaime, Nina Lee *retired energy and research and development company executive*

NEW YORK

Binghamton
Carrigg, James A. *retired utility company executive*

Brooklyn
Bishar, John Joseph, Jr. *utilities executive, lawyer*
Donohue, Alfred F. *retired telecommunications supervisor*
Fani, Robert J. *gas industry executive*

Farmingdale
Mason, James Eliot *energy executive, director*

Greenvale
Cordaro, Matthew Charles *energy and utility executive, educator*

Irvington
Carey, Edward John *utilities executive*

New York
Bartlett, Thomas A. *telecommunications industry executive*
Berkett, Neil *telecommunications industry executive*
Brown, Edward James, Sr. *utilities executive*
Burke, Kevin *utilities executive*
Casey, Thomas Jefferson *clean energy industry executive and entrepreneur, environmental activist*
Delaney, Robert Vincent *former gas company executive, economic development consultant*
Diercksen, John W. *telecommunications industry executive*
Grillo, Kathleen M. *telecommunications industry executive*
Hess, John B. *oil industry executive*
Hill, Gregory Paul *oil industry executive*
Hoglund, Robert N. *utilities executive*
Killian, John F. *telecommunications industry executive*
Lataille, Ronald H. *telecommunications industry executive*
Leidheiser, Kathleen H. *telecommunications industry executive*
Limpe, Stephen T. *oil industry executive*
Lynch, Richard J. *telecommunications industry executive, communications engineer*
Lyons, John Matthew *telecommunications industry, broadcast executive*
Mead, Daniel S. *telecommunications industry executive*
Milch, Randal S. *telecommunications industry executive, lawyer*
Osborne, Richard de Jongh *mining and metals company executive*
Reed, Marc C. *telecommunications industry executive, human resources specialist*
Rielly, J(ohn) P. *oil industry executive*
Seidenberg, Ivan G. *telecommunications industry executive*
Stratton, John G. *telecommunications industry executive, marketing professional*
Tauke, Thomas Joseph *telecommunications company executive, former United States Representative from Iowa*
Turner, Michael R. *energy executive*
Walker, F(rank) Borden *oil industry executive*
Webster, Catherine T. *telecommunications industry executive*

Niskayuna
Mangan, John Leo *retired electric power industry executive, international trade specialist*

Rochester
Sollecito, Larry A. *energy executive*
VanderLinden, Camilla Denice Dunn *telecommunications industry executive*

Rye
Lawi, David Steven *utilities executive, merchant banker*

Schenectady
Robb, Walter Lee *retired electric and management company executive, consultant*

Scotia
Buhrmaster, James R. *energy executive*

Wadhams
Foley, Matthew William *electric power industry executive*

White Plains
Underweiser, Irwin Philip *mining executive, lawyer*

Williamsville
Ackerman, Philip Charles *gas industry executive*

NORTH CAROLINA

Asheville
Haynes, John Mabin *retired utilities executive*

Charlotte
Good, Lynn J. *energy executive*
Jamil, Dhiaa M. *energy executive*
Janson, Julia S. *energy executive*
Roche, Cathy *energy executive*
Rogers, James Eugene (Jim Rogers) *energy executive*
Rolfe, Christopher C. *energy executive*
Shaw, Ruth G. *energy company executive*
Skains, Thomas E. *gas industry executive*
Turner, James Lee *energy executive*

Raleigh
Johnson, William Dean *electric power industry executive*
McArthur, John R. *utilities executive, lawyer*
Mulhern, Mark F. *electric power company executive*
Smith, Sherwood Hubbard, Jr. *retired electric utilities executive*

Southern Shores
Kegel, William George *mining company executive*

NORTH DAKOTA

Bismarck
Hildestad, Terry D. *energy executive*

OHIO

Akron
Alexander, Anthony J. *electric power industry executive*
Grigg, Richard R. *energy executive*
Marsh, Richard H. *energy executive*
Smart, George M. *energy executive, former packaging company executive*

Chagrin Falls
Miller, John Robert *oil industry executive*

Cleveland
Carrabba, Joseph A. *mining executive*
Stropki, John M., Jr. *electric power industry executive*

Columbus
Akins, Nicholas K. *electric power industry executive*
English, Carl L. *electric power industry executive*
Koeppel, Holly Keller *electric power industry executive*
McCellon-Allen, Venita *utilities executive*
Morris, Michael G. *electric power industry executive*
Powers, Robert P. *electric power industry executive*
Tierney, Brian X. *utilities executive*
Tomasky, Susan *electric power industry executive*
Welch, Dennis E. *electric power industry executive*

Dublin
Vassell, Gregory S. *electric utility consultant*

Lima
Pranses, Anthony Louis *retired electric power industry executive*

Perrysburg
Williamson, John Pritchard *retired utilities executive*

OKLAHOMA

Bartlesville
Berney, Rand C. *oil industry executive*
Silas, Cecil Jesse *retired petroleum company executive*

Enid
Ward, Llewellyn Orcutt III *oil industry executive*

Jennings
Nixon, Arlie James *gas and oil company executive*

Oklahoma City
Delaney, Peter B. *energy executive*
Dixon, Steven *energy executive*
Hefner, William Johnson, Jr., (W. John Hefner Jr.) *oil and gas industry executive*
McClendon, Aubrey K. *energy executive*
Richels, John *energy executive, lawyer*
Rowland, Marcus C. *energy executive*

Tulsa
Chappel, Donald R. *petroleum pipeline company executive*
Dinan, Curtis L. *gas industry executive*
Dotson, George Stephen *retired oil industry executive*
Gibson, John W. *gas industry executive*
Helmerich, Hans Christian *oil industry executive*
Horkey, William Richard *retired oil industry executive*
Ingram, Charles Clark, Jr. *energy executive*
Kneale, James C. *gas company executive*
Kronfeld, Edwin *natural gas company executive*
Kyle, David L. *gas industry executive*
Lawhorn, Caron A. *gas industry executive*
Malcolm, Steven J. *petroleum pipeline company executive*
Nedom, H. Arthur *petroleum consultant*

OREGON

Newport
Morrow, James Thomas *energy executive*

Portland
Bacon, Vicky Lee *lighting services executive*

Tualatin
West, Michael G. *electric power industry executive*

PENNSYLVANIA

Allentown
Farr, Paul A. *electric power industry executive*
Miller, James H. *electric power industry executive*
Spence, William H. *electric power industry executive*

Bryn Mawr
Braha, Thomas I. *oil industry executive*

Camp Hill
Fazzolari, Salvatore D. *mining products executive*

Canonsburg
Harvey, J. Brett *energy executive*

Coraopolis
Koepfinger, Joseph Leo *retired utilities executive*

Gladwyne
Patten, Lanny Ray *gas industry executive*

Greensburg
Evanson, Paul John *utilities executive*

King Of Prussia
Greenberg, Lon Richard *energy executive, lawyer*
Walsh, John L. *energy executive*

Philadelphia
Adawi, Nadia Sharon *business consultant*
Calman, Robert Frederick *mining executive*
Delaney, Terence (Terry) P. *oil industry executive*
Elsenhans, Lynn Laverty *oil industry executive*
Fischer, Bruce G. *oil industry executive*
Harris, Isiah, Jr. *former telecommunications industry executive*
Hennigan, Michael J. *oil industry executive*
Kelley, Vincent J. *oil industry executive*
Krott, Joseph P. *oil industry executive, comptroller*
Kuritzkes, Michael S. *oil industry executive, lawyer*
MacDonald, Brian P. *oil industry executive*
Mulé, Ann C. *oil industry executive*
O'Brien, Denis P. *utilities executive*
Owens, Robert W. *oil industry executive*
Roberts, Ralph Joel *telecommunications industry and cable broadcast executive*
Thomson, Michael J. *oil industry executive*
Zeleny, Dennis *oil industry executive, human resources specialist*

Pittsburgh
Bartley, Burnett Graham, Jr. *oil industry executive*
Stirewalt, John Newman *coal company executive*

Presto
Moeller, Audrey Carolyn *retired energy company executive, corporate secretary*

Valley Forge
Kelly, Peter *energy executive*

Wilkes Barre
Lindemann, George L. *gas industry executive*

RHODE ISLAND

Providence
Blase, William A., Jr. *telecommunications industry executive*

SOUTH CAROLINA

Columbia
Timmerman, William B. *utilities executive, accountant*

Jackson
Smith, Mark Eugene *nuclear engineering service company executive*

Pawleys Island
Justice, Franklin Pierce, Jr. *oil industry executive*

TENNESSEE

Knoxville
Jones, Sherman J. *non profit organization executive, financial consultant, educator*
Kilgore, Tom D. *electric power industry executive*
Moore, Richard Wayne *electric power industry executive, former prosecutor*

Nashville
Adams, Kenneth Stanley, Jr., (Bud Adams) *energy and professional sports team executive*

TEXAS

Austin
Galloway, Gale Lee *oil and gas executive, rancher*
Groten, Barnet *energy executive*
Haas, Joseph Marshall *retired petroleum consultant*

Corpus Christi
Paulson, Bernard Arthur *oil industry executive, consultant*
Susser, Sam L. *oil industry and consumer products company executive*

Dallas
Baker, Tom *utilities executive*
Best, Robert Wayne *gas transmission company executive, lawyer*
Blessing, Edward Warfield *petroleum company executive*
Carson, Virginia Hill *oil and gas executive*
Clifton, Matthew P. *petroleum refining company executive*
Cocklin, Kim Roland *gas industry executive, lawyer*
Davis, Barry E. *energy executive*
Fielder, Charles Robert *retired oil industry executive*
Hoglund, Forrest Eugene *retired petroleum company executive*
Hunt, Ray Lee *petroleum company executive*
Lake, Charlene Farrell *telecommunications industry executive*
Linquist, Roger D. *telecommunications industry executive*
McCrea, Marshall S. III *energy executive*
Meisenheimer, Fred E. *gas industry company executive*
Moore, Christopher Robertson Kinley *energy industry consultant*
Rabun, Daniel W. *oil and gas industry executive*
Salinas, Martin *energy executive*
Sell, Clay (Jeffrey Clay Sell) *energy company executive, former federal agency administrator*
Sizer, Phillip Spelman *retired oil and gas industry executive*
Spears, Ronald E. *telecommunications industry executive*
Warren, Kelcy L. *energy executive*
Young, John F. *energy executive*

El Paso
Dalke, Gary R. *oil industry executive*
Foster, Paul L. *oil industry executive*
Stevens, Jeff A. *oil industry executive*

Fair Oaks
Regan, William Joseph, Jr. *energy company executive*

Fort Worth
Hutton, Keith A. *energy executive*
Hyde, Clarence Brodie, II, *oil industry executive*
Simpson, Bob R. *energy executive*

Fredericksburg
Malec, William Frank *utilities company executive*

Frisco
Malik, Imtiaz *telecommunications industry executive, educator*

Horseshoe Bay
Jorden, James Roy *oil industry executive, consultant*

Houston
Anderson, Paul Milton *energy executive*
Archibald, Lawrence E. (Larry Archibald) *oil industry executive*
Armstrong, Greg L. *oil industry executive*
Aron, Doug *oil industry executive*
Barham, Stephen R. *oil industry executive*
Barracano, Henry Ralph *retired oil company executive, management consultant*
Bartling, Phyllis McGinness *oil company executive*
Batchelder, Gene (Eugene Lewis Batchelder) *oil industry executive*
Bay, Annell R. *oil industry executive, geologist*
Bookout, John Frank, Jr. *oil industry executive*
Bowles, James L. *oil industry executive*
Brand, Stephen R. *oil industry executive*
Bullock, William L., Jr. *oil industry executive*
Burke, Michael Donald *oil and gas company executive*
Campbell, Eileen M. *oil industry executive*
Carameros, George Demitrius, Jr. *natural gas company executive*
Carrig, John A. *oil industry executive*
Carroll, Milton *oil industry executive*
Cavaney, Red (Byron M. Cavaney Jr.) *oil industry executive, lobbyist*
Cazalot, Clarence P., Jr. *oil industry executive*
Chalmers, David B. *petroleum executive*
Chiang, W.C.W (Willie Chiang) *oil industry executive*
Clark, Janet F. *oil industry executive*
Clayton, Benjamin J. *oil industry executive*
Colson, John R. *electric power industry executive*
Conway, C.W. *oil industry executive*
Cornelius, Sigmund L. (Sig Cornelius) *oil industry executive*
Creel, Michael Allen *energy executive*
Crum, John A. *energy executive*
Cunningham, Ralph Sanford *energy executive*
Dang, Kimberly Allen *energy executive*
Davidson, Charles D. *energy executive*
Deaton, Chad C. *oil and gas industry executive*
DeVault, John Lee *oil industry executive, geophysicist*
Dice, Bruce Burton *gas industry executive*
Dobson, Rick *energy executive*
Dreyer, Alec Gilbert *electric power industry executive*
Drury, Leonard Leroy *retired oil company executive*
Duncan, Dan L. *energy executive*
Ebel, Gregory L. *energy executive*
Eichler, Rodney J. *energy executive*
Erikson, Sheldon R. *oil industry executive*
Esrey, William Todd *telecommunications company executive*
Farris, G. Steven *energy executive*
Flesher, Robert G. *oil industry executive*
Foshee, Douglas L. *gas industry executive*
Fowler, W. Randall *energy executive*
Fredin, Todd W. *oil industry executive*
Frost, John Elliott *minerals company executive*
Fulwiler, Robert Neal *oil industry executive*
Gaille, Shelby Scott *oil industry executive*
Gibbs, James R. *oil industry executive*
Goff, Gregory J. *oil industry executive*
Goodman, Herbert Irwin *petroleum company executive*
Gould, Andrew *oil industry executive*
Hassler, Robert J. *oil industry executive*
Heim, Michael A. *energy executive*
Heminger, Gary R. *oil industry executive*
Hinchman, Steven B. *oil industry executive*
Howard, Jerry *oil industry executive*
Irwin, John Robert *oil and gas industry executive*
Jacobs, Mark M. *energy executive*
Jaffe, Amy Myers *energy executive, educator*
Jennings, Michael C. *oil industry executive*
Johnson, Wayne D. *gas industry executive*
Jones, Darren C. *oil industry executive*
Joyce, Rene R. *energy executive*
Kean, Steven J. *energy executive*
Kelly, Janet Langford *oil industry executive, lawyer*
Kinder, Richard Dan *natural gas pipeline, oil and gas company executive*
Kinnear, Peter D. *energy executive*
Kliewer, Keith A. *oil industry executive*
Knesek, Michael John *energy executive*
Knickel, Carin S. *oil industry executive*
Knudsen, J.R. (Jim Knudsen) *oil industry executive*
Kramer, Phillip D. *oil industry executive*
Krohn, Tracy W. *oil industry executive, gas industry executive*
Kuntz, Hal Goggan *petroleum exploration company executive, rancher*
Lance, Ryan M. *oil industry executive*
Lesar, David J. *oil industry executive*
Lowe, John E. *oil industry executive, accountant*
Luigs, Charles Russell *retired gas and oil drilling industry executive*
Lyons, A. Roy *oil industry executive*
McClanahan, David M. *energy executive*
McCollum, Mark A. *oil industry executive*
McKay, Lamar *oil industry executive*
McParland, Jeffrey J. *energy executive*
Messier, Luc J. *oil industry executive*
Meyer, Ernst A. *oil industry executive, consultant*
Meyers, Kevin Omar *oil industry executive*
Miller, Merrill Anthony, Jr. *energy executive*
Miller, Steven L. *oil industry executive*
Miller, W. Thaddeus *energy executive*
Moore, Jack B. *oil industry executive*
Mosbacher, Robert Adam, Sr. *oil and gas industry executive, political organization executive, former United States Secretary of Commerce*
Mulva, James Joseph *oil industry executive*
Neumann, Henry W., Jr. *energy executive*
Odum, Marvin E. *oil industry executive*
Ordemann, William *energy executive*
Papa, Mark Gary *oil and gas industry executive*
Pefanis, Harry N. *oil industry executive*
Perkins, Joe Bob *energy executive*
Plank, Roger B. *energy executive*
Probert, Tim *oil industry executive*
Ragauss, Peter A. *oil industry executive*
Ralls, W. Matthew *gas and oil industry drilling executive*
Raspino, Louis A. *energy executive*
Rauf, Zamir *energy executive*
Reasor, Clayton (Craig Clayton Reasor, C.C. Reasor) *oil industry executive*
Reddy, J. Patrick *former energy executive*
Reinbolt, Paul C. *oil industry executive*
Ridge, Robert A. *oil industry executive*
Roberts, David E., Jr. *oil industry executive*
Rodríguez, Félix M. *oil industry executive*
Roff, J(ohn) Hugh, Jr. *energy executive*
Schwarz, Glenda M. *oil industry executive*
Shaper, C. Park *energy executive*
Sheets, Jeff W. *oil industry executive*
Skelly, Michael *energy executive*
Sledge, Charles M. *oil industry executive*
Sneed, Thomas K. *oil industry executive*
Snider, Stephen A. *oil industry company executive*
Staff, Joel V. *energy executive*
Stewart, J.W. *energy executive, lawyer*
Sullenbarger, Daniel James *oil industry executive, lawyer*
Swanson, Al *oil industry executive*
Taylor, Cindy B. *oil industry executive*
Thompson, Jon L. *retired oil industry executive*
Trice, David A. *oil industry executive*
Vallejo, Frances M. *oil industry executive*
Van Dyke, Gene *oil industry executive*
Whitlock, Gary L. *energy executive*
Williams, Clay C. *energy executive*
Williamson, Bruce A. *gas industry executive*
Wilson, Edward Converse, Jr. *oil and natural gas production company executive*
Wilson, Floyd C. *oil industry executive*
Wuori, Stephen J. *energy executive*
Ziemba, Lawrence M. *oil industry executive*

Ingleside
Vaden, William R. *oil industry executive, councilman*

Irving
Albers, Mark W. *oil industry executive*
Cavanaugh, Lucille J. *oil industry executive*
Cejka, A. Tim *oil industry executive*
Cohen, Kenneth P. *oil industry executive, lawyer*
Dingle, Philip *retired oil industry executive*
Dolan, Michael J. *oil industry executive*
Duffin, Neil W. *oil industry executive*
Glass, Sherman J., Jr. *oil industry executive*
Hubble, Henry H. *oil industry executive*
Humphreys, Donald D. *oil industry executive*
Kelly, Alan J. *oil industry executive*
Kruger, Richard M. *oil industry executive*
Luxbacher, Roberta *oil industry executive*
Matthews, Charles W., Jr. *oil industry executive, lawyer*
Mulva, Patrick T. *oil industry executive*
Pisarczyk, Richard V. *oil industry executive*
Pryor, Stephen D. *oil industry executive*
Sheffield, Scott D. *oil industry executive*
Stuewer, Sherri K. *oil industry executive*
Swales, Larry D. *oil industry executive*
Swiger, Andrew P. *oil industry executive*
Tillerson, Rex W. *oil company executive*
Walters, Thomas R. *gas and power company executive*

Midland
Grover, Rosalind Redfern *oil and gas company executive*
Robertson, Melanie Anne *oil industry executive*

Pottsboro
Hanning, Gary William *utilities and water transportation executive, consultant*

Salado
Parks, Lloyd Lee *oil industry executive*

San Antonio
Arthur, Gary L., Jr. *energy executive*
Browning, Jay D. *energy executive, lawyer*
Callaway, James W. (Jim) *telecommunications industry executive*
Ciskowski, Michael S. *energy executive*
Coughlin, Catherine M. *telecommunications industry executive*
Coughlin, Katherine M. *telecommunications industry executive*
Crownover, Mike *energy executive*
de la Vega, Ralph *telecommunications industry executive*
Donovan, John *telecommunications industry executive*
Edwards, S. Eugene *energy executive*
Finnerty, William J. *oil industry executive*
Fisher, Eric A. *energy executive, lawyer*
Flagg, C.A. (Chuck Flagg) *oil industry executive*
Gilbert, Steve *energy executive, lawyer*
Gorder, Joseph W. *energy executive*
Haywood, J. William *oil industry executive*
Killinger, Clayton *energy executive*
Klaerner, Curtis Maurice *gas industry executive*
Lewis, Everett D. *oil industry executive*
Lindner, Richard G. (Rick Lindner) *telecommunications industry executive*
Marcogliese, Richard J. *energy executive*
McCoy, Joseph G. *oil industry executive*
Miller, Forrest E. *telecommunications industry executive*
Monroe, Joseph M. *oil industry executive*
Moreau, Claude P. *oil industry executive*
Pawel, Nancy Emma Ray *oil industry executive, educator, artist*
Porter, Daniel J. *oil industry executive*
Rice, Chris *telecommunications industry executive*
Schwethelm, Otto C. *oil industry executive*
Smith, Bruce Alfred *oil industry executive*
sStankey, John T. *telecommunications industry executive*
Stankey, John T. *telecommunications industry executive*
Stephenson, Randall L. *telecommunications industry executive*
Titzman, Donna M. *energy executive*
Watts, D. Wayne *telecommunications industry executive, lawyer*
Westfall, Lynn D. *oil industry executive*
Wilkins, Rayford, Jr. *telecommunications industry executive*
Wright, Gregory A. *oil industry executive*
Zesch, Hal *energy executive*

Spring
Corbett, Luke R. *former energy company executive*

Sugar Land
Lipinski, John J. (Jack) *oil industry executive*
Morgan, Edward A. *oil industry executive*
Riemann, Stanley A. *oil industry executive*

The Woodlands
Gwin, Robert G. *oil industry executive*
Hackett, James T. *oil industry executive*
Walker, R. A. *oil industry executive*
Wilcox, Raymond I. *oil industry executive*

Wichita Falls
Fowler, Robert Martin, Jr. *oil industry executive, consultant*

UTAH

Ogden
Adams, J. Phillip *oil industry executive*

Park City
Edwards, Howard Lee *retired oil and gas industry executive, lawyer*

Salt Lake City
Holding, R(obert) Earl *oil industry executive*
Rattie, Keith O. *gas industry executive*
Sigal, Jill Lea *nuclear energy industry executive, former federal agency administrator*

VERMONT

Barnard
Larson, John Hyde *retired utilities executive*

Dorset
Hittle, Richard Howard *oil and gas industry executive, consultant*

Springfield
Guité, J. C. Michel *telephone company owner*

VIRGINIA

Abingdon
Quillen, Michael J. *energy executive*

Alexandria
Hirsch, Robert Louis *energy analyst, consultant*

Arlington
Gluski, Andrés R. *electric power industry executive*
Hackenson, Elizabeth *electric power industry executive*
Hanrahan, Paul Thaddeus *electric power industry executive*
Harker, Victoria D. *electric power industry executive*

Bridgewater
Siders, David L. *oil industry executive, educator*

Chesterfield
Love, Dana Francis Ignatius *telecommunications industry executive*

Fairfax
Cramer, H. R. (Hal Cramer) *oil industry executive*

Reston
Brust, Robert H. *telecommunications industry executive*
Conway, William E., Jr. *telecommunications industry executive, venture capitalist*
Cowan, Keith O. *telecommunications industry executive*
Dears, Donn Dougherty *electric power industry executive*
Dziak, Jack *telecommunications industry executive*
Foosaner, Robert Stephen *telecommunications industry executive, lawyer*
Gude, Atish *telecommunications industry executive*
Hesse, Daniel Ryan *telecommunications industry executive*
LeFave, Richard T.C. *telecommunications industry executive*
Redden, Shelton Dennis *telecommunications industry executive*
West, Barry J. *telecommunications industry executive*

Richmond
Blankenship, Don L. *energy executive*
Chewning, Thomas N. *energy executive*
Christian, David A. *energy executive*
Doswell, Mary Cummings *energy executive*
Farrell, Thomas Francis, II, *energy executive*
Hetzer, G. Scott *energy executive*
Koonce, Paul D. *energy executive*
McGettrick, Mark F. *energy executive*
Poma, John M. *mining company executive, lawyer*
Rogers, Steven A. *energy executive*
Sanderlin, James L. *energy executive, lawyer*

Suffolk
Hines, Angus Irving, Jr. *petroleum marketing executive*

WASHINGTON

Bellevue
Post, Denny Marie *telecommunications industry executive, marketing professional*
Reynolds, Stephen Philip *utility company executive*
Williamson, Charles R. *retired energy company executive*

Olympia
Oberbillig, Molly Castleman *utilities executive*

Spokane
Eliassen, Jon Eric *retired corporate financial and utilities executive*
Ely, Gary G. *utilities company executive*

WEST VIRGINIA

Charleston
Bennett, Robert Menzies *retired gas pipeline company executive*

WISCONSIN

Green Bay
Weyers, Larry Lee *energy executive*

La Crosse
Rude, Brian David *utilities executive*

Madison
Harvey, William D. *utilities executive, lawyer*

Milwaukee
Klappa, Gale E. *energy executive*

WYOMING

Casper
Stroock, Thomas Frank *oil and gas company executive*

TERRITORIES OF THE UNITED STATES

VIRGIN ISLANDS

St Thomas
Prior, Cornelius Bernard, Jr. *utilities executive, financial consultant*

CANADA

ALBERTA

Calgary
Bird, J. Richard *energy executive*
Daniel, Patrick D. *energy executive*
Maier, Gerald James *gas industry executive*
Southern, Nancy C. *utilities executive*

Red Deer
Donald, Jack C. *oil industry executive*

BRITISH COLUMBIA

Vancouver
Keevil, Norman B. *mining executive*
Lyons, Terrence Allan *mining executive*

Winfield
Horton, William Russell *retired utilities executive*

ONTARIO

Brockville
Spalding, James Stuart *retired telecommunications industry executive*

North York
Blundell, William Richard Charles *retired electric company executive*

Richmond Hill
Fong, Maryanne T.P. *telecommunications industry executive, researcher*

Toronto
Martin, Robert William *retired utilities executive*
Munk, Peter *mining executive*
Wilson, Lynton Ronald *telecommunications industry executive, academic administrator*

QUEBEC

Montreal
Cyr, J. V. Raymond *telecommunications industry executive*

BERMUDA

Hamilton
Pitman, Gary Robert *oil industry executive*

BULGARIA

Rousse
Loukantchevsky, Milen *telecommunications industry executive*

CHINA

Beijing
Yan, Gao *power company executive*

ENGLAND

London
Carroll, Cynthia B. *mining executive*
Duffy, Simon P. *telecommunications industry executive*
Mooney, James F. *telecommunications industry executive*
Sukawaty, Andrew J. *telecommunications industry executive*

FINLAND

Helsinki
Ollila, Jorma Jaakko *telecommunications industry executive*

FRANCE

Paris
Roussely, Francois *electric power industry executive*
Tufano, Paul J. *telecommunications industry executive*
Weymuller, Bruno *oil and gas industry executive*

ITALY

Rome
Brachetti Peretti, Aldo Maria *gas industry executive*
Poli, Roberto *oil industry executive*

JAPAN

Nagoya
Kawaguchi, Fumio *electric power industry executive*

Yokohama
Ito, Noboru *electric power industry executive*

KUWAIT

Safat
Al-Turki, Abdul Aziz Abdallah *oil industry association executive*

LATVIA

Riga
Kabashkin, Igor *telecommunications industry executive*

NETHERLANDS

Amsterdam
Dahan, Rene *retired oil industry executive*

Rijswijk
Pickard, Ann *oil industry executive*

Rotterdam
van Wachem, Lodewijk Christiaan *petroleum company executive*

NORWAY

Tananger
Warwick, Paul C. *oil industry executive*

THAILAND

Bangkok
Narayan, Amarendra *telecommunications executive*

ADDRESS UNPUBLISHED

Ahuja, Sanjiv *telecommunications industry executive*
Alramahi, Bashar *oil industry researcher*
An, Chungming *telecommunications industry executive*
Arlidge, John Walter *retired utilities executive*
Arthur, John Morrison *retired utilities executive*
Barham, Charles Dewey, Jr. *electric power industry executive, lawyer*
Barnes, Wesley Edward *energy and environmental executive*
Barr, James III *telecommunications company executive*
Barrow, Thomas Davies *retired oil and mining company executive, consultant*
Baumgartner, John H. *gas industry executive*
Beavers, Roy Lackey *retired utilities executive, volunteer, writer*
Berry, William Willis *retired utilities executive*
Bijur, Peter I. *retired petroleum company executive*
Bodensteiner, Lisa M. *former utilities executive, lawyer*
Bowling, Woodrow Wilson *telecommunications industry executive, insurance company executive*
Brothers, John Alfred *retired oil company and chemicals executive*
Brown, Stephen S. *telecommunications industry executive*
Bryan, J(ames) P(erry), Jr. *energy executive*
Burrow, Harold *retired gas industry executive*
Capra, Frances M. *retired telecommunications industry executive*
Carron, Ronald Joseph *retired electric power industry executive*
Carter, James E. *mining company executive*
Chaturvedi, Anil Dass *telecommunications executive, researcher*
Chelle, Robert Frederick *electric power industry executive, educator*
Clark, Philip Raymond *nuclear utility executive, engineer*
Coffin, Bertha Louise *retired telecommunications industry executive*
Conger, Harry Milton *mining company executive*
Connelly, Sharon Rudolph *nuclear energy industry executive*
Cook, Linda Z. *former oil industry executive*
Cullen, James G. *telecommunications industry executive*
Cummings, Blake *landsman*
Dahan, Andre *telecommunications industry executive*
Dea, Peter Allen *gas industry executive, geologist*
Derr, Kenneth Tindall *retired oil industry executive*
Di Giovanni, Anthony *retired coal mining company executive*
Di Martino, Rita *utility company executive, government representative*
Dragoumis, Paul *electric utility company executive*
Draper, E(rnest) Linn, Jr. *retired electric utility executive*
Drechsel, Edward Russell, Jr. *retired utilities executive*
Drosdick, John Girard *retired oil industry executive*
Dunham, Archie Wallace *retired oil industry executive*
Ellis, James D. *retired telecommunications industry executive, retired lawyer*
English, Floyd Leroy *telecommunications industry executive*
Evans, John Derby *telecommunications industry executive*
Fagin, David Kyle *mining executive*
Fowke, Benjamin G.S. III *energy executive*
Frank, Stephen Edward *retired electric power industry executive*
Fuller, Sandra Vivian *oil and gas industry executive*
Gadomski, Robert Eugene *gas industry executive*
Gardiner, Hobart Clive *petroleum company executive*
Gerard, Roy Dupuy *retired oil company executive*
Gottschalk, Charles M. *international energy consultant*
Grigg, William Humphrey *utilities executive*
Gurian, Mal *telecommunications executive*
Heiney, John Weitzel *former utilities executive*
Helton, Sandra Lynn *telecommunications industry executive*
Herron, Edwin Hunter, Jr. *energy consultant*
Hines, Andrew Hampton, Jr. *utilities executive*
Hofmeister, John D. *retired oil industry executive*
Huffman, James Thomas William *oil industry executive*
Hughes, Nicholas Melvin *mining company executive*
Humke, Ramon Lyle *utilities executive*
Hyland, Geoffrey Fyfe *retired energy executive*
Isaacs, Jonathan William *oil industry executive*
Jackson, Robert William *retired utilities executive*
Kaiser, Robert A. *telecommunications industry executive*
King, William Collins *retired oil industry executive*
Klesse, William R. (Bill Klesse) *energy executive*
Leet, Richard Hale *oil industry executive*
Lewis, Albert James, Jr. *energy executive, director*
Lewis, Floyd Wallace *former electric utility executive*
Lilly, Edward Guerrant, Jr. *retired utilities executive*
Limbacher, Randy L. *oil industry executive*
Loh, Wai Kiew *oil industry executive*
Loveland, Eugene Franklin *retired gas industry executive*
Lutz, Matthew Charles *oil industry executive, geologist*
Manlove, Benson *retired gas industry executive, secondary school educator*
Mauch, Robert Carl *energy and financial services executive*
Mc Carthy, Walter John, Jr. *retired utilities executive*
McGee, Robert Merrill *oil industry executive*
McSweeny, William Francis *petroleum company executive, author*
Mokhatab, Saeid *gas industry technical consultant*
Montgomery, Roy Delbert *retired gas industry executive*
Munsey, Virdell Everard, Jr. *retired utilities executive*
Myers, Franklin *oil industry executive*
Narumanchi, Sreekant Venkat Jagannath *energy executive*
Nicholson, Leland Ross *retired utilities executive, energy consultant*
Noski, Charles H. *former telecommunications executive*
Nurenberg, David *retired oil company executive*
Nyberg, Donald Arvid *oil industry executive*
O'Connor, James John *retired utility company executive*
O'Hare, James Raymond *energy executive*
Olson, Robert Edward *coal mining executive*
Owens, William Arthur (Bill Owens) *telecommunications industry executive, retired military officer*
Perry, George Wilson *oil and gas company executive*
Portal, Gilbert Marcel Adrien *oil industry executive*
Prabhu, Krish Anant *former telecommunications industry executive, educator*
Pryor, Richard Walter *telecommunications executive, retired air force officer*
Quenon, Robert Hagerty *retired mining consultant and holding company executive*
Rawson, Richard J. *telecommunications industry executive, lawyer*
Richman, Paul *semiconductor industry executive, educator*
Roberts, Lawrence Gilman *telecommunications industry executive*
Roe, Thomas Coombe *former utility company executive*
Rogers, Justin Towner, Jr. *retired utility company executive*
Russo, Patricia F. *former telecommunications company executive*
St. Clair, Thomas McBryar *mining and manufacturing company executive*
Saleh, Paul N. *former telecommunications executive*
Samuels, John Stockwell III *mining company executive, financier*
Schenck, Jack Lee *retired electric utility executive*
Serkes, Jeffrey D. *former energy executive*
Shindler, Steven M. *telecommunications industry executive*
Shirilau, Mark Steven *utilities executive*
Shoup, Andrew James, Jr. *retired oil industry executive*
Sigman, Stanley T. *retired telecommunications industry executive*
Simon, J. Stephen *retired oil industry executive*
Smith, Elmer *telecommunications industry executive*
Smith, Paul Vergon, Jr. *retired gas industry executive*
Strobel, Pamela B. *former energy executive*
Tamura, Shigemi *electric power industry executive*
Terry, John David *telecommunications industry executive, educator*
Thomas, Kenneth Glyndwr *mining executive*
Thompson, Jack Edward *mining company executive*
Thompson, Jerry E. *oil industry executive*
Thorn, Terence Hastings *energy executive, consultant, writer*
Tillinghast, John Avery *utilities executive*
Todd, Zane Grey *retired utilities executive*
Travis, Vance Kenneth *petroleum business executive*
Tucker, H. Richard *oil industry executive*
Vermylen, Paul Anthony, Jr. *oil industry executive*
Weaver, William Schildecker *retired electric power industry executive*
Weeks, William Rawle, Jr. *oil industry executive*

Whisler, James Steven *retired mining executive, lawyer, rancher*
Williams, Neville *solar power company executive*
Wilson, Walter Clinton *retired oil and gas industry executive*
Wood, Willis Bowne, Jr. *retired utilities executive*
Wright, David John *telecommunications systems specialist, educator*
Wrobel, Bruce J. *energy and utilities company executive*
Wu, Xianren *telecommunications industry executive, researcher*
Yu, Jie *researcher*

INFORMATION TECHNOLOGY
See also SCIENCE: MATHEMATICS AND COMPUTER SCIENCE

UNITED STATES

ALABAMA

Auburn
Sankar, Chetan Subramanian *management information systems educator*

Florence
Foote, Avon Edward *web developer/producer, communications educator*

Huntsville
Libutti, Frank *information technology company executive, retired military officer*

Mobile
McCleery, Winston Theodore *information technology executive*

ARIZONA

Scottsdale
Friesen, Oris Dewayne *software engineer, historian*
Stott, Brian *software company executive, consultant*

Tempe
Crown, Timothy A. *information technology executive*
Fennessy, Richard A. *information technology executive*

Tucson
Donoghue, John Charles *application developer, consultant*
Fredericksen, Dick Hartman *retired computer programmer*

ARKANSAS

Little Rock
Mahabhashyam, Sai Rajesh *application developer*

CALIFORNIA

Aliso Viejo
Dutile, Robert Arthur *information technology manager*
Schultz, E. Eugene, Jr. *information security engineer*

Antelope
Nenov, Ivo P. *mathematical and software researcher*

Aptos
Griffin, James Bernard, Jr. *application developer, educator*

Berkeley
Karp, Richard Manning *computer science educator*
Séquin, Carlo H. *computer science educator*
Sikder, Abdur R. *information technology executive, director*
Wieczorek, John Richard *application developer, systems analyst*

Brisbane
Daniels, Caroline *information services executive*

Cupertino
Bregman, Mark *information technology executive*
Ive, Jonathan *information technology executive, product designer*
Salem, Enrique T. *information technology executive*
Serlet, Bertrand *information technology executive*
Tamaddon, Sina *information technology executive*
Thompson, John Wendell *information technology executive*

Danville
Bergsten, James Robert *computer technology architect*

El Segundo
Barram, David J. *information technology executive, former federal agency administrator*

Folsom
Bahbah, Amr G. *application developer, consultant*
Haga, Enoch John *retired computer educator, writer, editor*

Foster City
Milligan, John F. *information technology executive*

Fremont
Tang, John *network technician, information scientist, educator*
Yang, Di *systems administrator*

Glen Ellen
Hurlbert, Roger William *information technology executive*

Hemet
Clark, Harold L. *technology company executive, consultant*

Irvine
Morhaime, Mike *video game company executive*
Silverman, Louis E. *information technology executive*

Lafayette
Lewis, Sheldon Noah *technology consultant*

Laguna Niguel
Cooper, Roger Merlin *information technology executive, federal agency and school system administrator*

Los Angeles
Boehm, Barry William *computer science educator*
Feuerstein, William Michael *application developer*
Halloran, John Alan *information technology executive*
Trivedi, Abhishek *application developer*
Urzhumov, Yaroslav Aleksandrovich *application developer, researcher*

Martinez
Tong, Siu Wing *computer programmer*

Menlo Park
Bechtolsheim, Andy (Andreas von Bechtolsheim) *information technology executive*
Dubinsky, Donna L. *information technology executive*
Patterson, Anna *information technology executive*

Modesto
Kushar, Kent *information technology executive*

Mountain View
Baker, Mitchell *computer software developer, foundation administrator*
Bloch, Joshua J. *software designer*
Brin, Sergey Mihailovich *information technology executive*
Cerf, Vinton Gray *information technology executive*
Coughran, William M., Jr. *information technology executive, researcher*
Denzel, Nora Manley *information technology executive*
Drummond, David C. *information technology executive, lawyer*
Eustace, Alan *information technology executive*
Halvorsen, Per-Kristian *software company executive, former educator, researcher*
Mayer, Marissa Ann *information technology executive*
Page, Larry (Lawrence E. Page) *information technology executive*
Pan, Junfeng *application developer, researcher*
Pichette, Patrick *information technology company executive*
Reicher, Dan William *information technology executive, former federal agency administrator*
Rubin, Andrew E. (Andrew E. Rubin) *technology product developer*
Schmidt, Eric Emerson *information technology executive*
Tan, Chade-Meng *application developer, educator*
Woodside, Dennis *information technology executive*

Newport Beach
Fielding, Roy Thomas *software scientist*

Oakland
Safka, Jim *information technology executive, investment services company executive*

Orange
Ahlquist, John B. *application developer*

Redondo Beach
Sloan, Michael Dana *information systems specialist, management consultant*

Redwood City
Block, Keith *computer software company executive*
Burkhardt, Roger *information technology executive*
Danielson, David Robert *information technology manager, consultant*
Kurian, Thomas *computer software company executive*
Lee, V. Paul *entertainment software company executive*
Parameswaran, Rupa *software security developer*
Phillips, Charles E., Jr. *computer software company executive*
Polese, Kim *software company executive*
Probst, Lawrence F. III *interactive software/gaming executive*
Riccitiello, John S. *interactive software and gaming executive, venture capitalist*
Rottler, Juergen *computer software company executive*
Rozwat, Charles *computer software company executive*

Redwood Shores
Catz, Safra Ada *computer software company executive*
Ellison, Larry (Lawrence Joseph Ellison) *computer software company executive*

Epstein, Jeffrey Emanuel *computer software company executive*
Henley, Jeffrey O. *computer software company executive*

San Diego
Alving, Amy Elsa *information technology executive*
Fricke, Martin Paul *science company executive*
Goldstein, Mark Kingston Levin *information technology executive, researcher*
Rastetter, William H. *biotechnology company executive*
Simpson, William *information technology manager, consultant*
Tom, Lawrence *technology executive*

San Francisco
Buckmaster, Jim *online community bulletin board company executive*
Cohen, Bram *web programmer*
Dodge, Geoffrey A. *information technology executive, former publishing executive*
Dorsey, Jack *software architect*
Kapor, Mitchell David *application developer, foundation administrator*
Kingdon, Mark *computer software company executive*
Kumar, Deept *information technology manager*
Mullenweg, Matt(hew) (Charles) *software developer, blogger*
Rosedale, Philip E. *computer software company executive*
Stone, Issac (Biz Stone) *application developer, consultant*
Templeton, Brad *information technology executive, software engineer, entrepreneur*
Torvalds, Linus Benedict *application developer*
Trott, Mena *application developer*

San Jose
Bazzi, Samer *software developer, consultant*
Belluzzo, Rick E. (Richard) *information technology and former computer software company executive*
Chambers, John Thomas *computer systems network executive*
Chandler, Mark D. *computer systems network executive, lawyer*
Chizen, Bruce R. *computer software company executive*
Chuang, Alfred Sze *information technology executive*
Emmett, Brian *software developer*
Gong, Zhenxiang *application developer*
Grandison, Tyrone Wilberforce André *systems administrator*
Kumar, Sailesh *network technician, researcher*
Lloyd, Robert L. *computer systems network executive*
Loiacono, John P. *information technology executive*
Narayen, Shantanu *computer software company executive*
Pham, Christopher Hoang *application developer, educator*
Sueltz, Patricia C. *information technology executive*
Warrior, Padmasree Y. *computer systems network executive*

San Mateo
Fu, Dan *information technology manager*

San Rafael
Faden, Glenn *application developer*

San Ramon
Schofield, James Roy *computer programmer*

Santa Ana
Boyd, Larry C. *information technology executive, lawyer*
Humes, William D. *information technology executive*
Monié, Alain *information technology executive*
Patel, Paresh *application developer*
Salem, Karen E. *information technology executive*
Spierkel, Gregory M. *information technology executive*

Santa Barbara
Boehm, Eric Hartzell *information technology executive*

Santa Clara
Benson, Jon H. *information technology executive*
Beveridge, Crawford W. *information technology executive*
Bolin, Christopher *software security company executive*
Bryant, Diane M. *information technology executive*
Bucklin, Christine B. *information technology executive*
Fowler, John *information technology executive*
Gadre, Anil *information technology executive*
Green, Rich *information technology executive*
Hall, William Spencer *software engineer*
Harris, David M. *information technology executive*
Heel, Joe *information technology executive*
Iyar, Subrah S. *information technology executive*
Lehman, Michael Evans *information technology executive*
MacGowan, Bill *information technology executive*
McCabe, Eugene *information technology executive*
McNealy, Scott Glenn *information technology executive*
Miller, Dan *information technology executive*
Papadopoulos, Gregory Michael *information technology executive*
Robel, Chuck (Charles J. Robel) *computer software company executive*
Ryan, Peter *computer systems network executive*
Schwartz, Jonathan Ian *information technology executive*
Stern, Hal *information technology executive*
Sutphin, Brian *information technology executive*
Tremblay, Marc *information technology executive*
Van Den Hoogen, Ingrid *information technology executive*

White, Ian *information technology executive*
Worrall, Robert *information technology executive*
Yen, David *information technology executive*

Santa Monica
Kotick, Robert Andrew *computer software company executive*

Sausalito
Jepsen, Mary Lou *information technology executive*

Stanford
Feigenbaum, Edward Albert *retired computer science educator*

Sunnyvale
Balogh, Aristotle N. *information technology executive*
Hawkins, Jeff *information technology company executive*
Johnson, Kevin *information technology executive, former computer software company executive*
Kispert, John H. *information technology executive*
Kraft, Reiner *information technology manager*
Kriens, Scott Gregory *information technology executive*
McCoy, Thomas M. *information technology executive*
Meyer, Dirk (Derrick R. Meyer) *information technology executive*
Orr, Dominic P. *information technology company executive*
Ruiz, Hector de Jesus *information technology executive*
Shanbhag, Abhijit G. *semiconductor company executive*
Xie, Liang *application developer*

Venice
Museth, Ken *application developer, educator*

West Sacramento
Glaholt, William Edward *information technology manager*

Westlake Village
Borenstein, Lorna M. *information technology executive*

COLORADO

Boulder
Kenney, Belinda Jill Forseman *information technology executive*

Colorado Springs
Thor, Paul Viets *computer science educator*

Denver
Labrecque, Joseph *application developer*
Rodriguez, Juan Alfonso *information technology executive*

Greenwood Village
Capellas, Michael D. *information technology executive*
Wall, Phil *information technology executive*

Littleton
Marion, John Martin *instructional technology educator*
Spalding, Robert Steele, II, *systems administrator*

CONNECTICUT

Danbury
Collar, Emilio, Jr. *information systems consultant*

Fairfield
Immelt, Jeffrey Robert *diversified technology and services company executive*
Neal, Michael A. *diversified technology and services company executive*
Reiner, Gary M. *diversified technology and services company executive*
Rice, John G. *diversified technology and services executive*

New London
Carpenter, Bruce William *information technology manager, director*

Newtown
Coates, John Peter *technical executive*

Norwalk
Alvey, Brian *blogger*
Carlucci, David R. *information technology executive*

Norwich
Pudlo, Steven Edward *computer technician*

Stamford
Wilderotter, Maggie (Mary Agnes Wilderotter) *software company executive, former cable television executive*

Trumbull
Lang, James Richard *software designer, magician*

DISTRICT OF COLUMBIA

Washington
Black, Duncan Bowen *political blogger*
Dale, Adrianne Marie *information technology executive, consultant*
Gross, Patrick Walter *information technology executive*
Hungate, Joseph Irvin III *government executive*

Meyer, Paul *information technology executive*
Russell, Clara B. *information technology manager*
Shields, Christopher Andrew *website director*
Wertheim, Mitzi Mallina *information technology executive*
Young, Darlene H. *information system security officer*

FLORIDA

Boca Raton
Breakstone, Robert Albert *information technology and consumer products company executive, consultant*

Celebration
Johnson, Derrick M. *information technology executive*

Clearwater
Osbourn, Joseph A. *information technology executive*

Jacksonville
Chambers, Jack Allen *application developer, educator*
Payne, Timothy D. *information technology executive*
Portell, Keith S *application developer, consultant*

Land O Lakes
McGrew, Kelly Calhoun *training services executive, systems engineer*

Miami
Clemence, Cheryl Lynn *systems administrator*

Naples
Thomas, Gary Lynn *information technology executive*

Newberry
Thornton, J. Ronald *technology consultant*

Ocala
Strait, William Robert *computer technician*

Ormond Beach
Burke, Marguerite Jodi Larcombe *application developer, consultant*

Punta Gorda
Ott, Walter Richard *information technology executive, writer*

Riverview
Alvarez, Jorge *application developer*

Sanibel
Trevor, Alexander Bruen *information technology consultant*

Tampa
Bedgood, Alvin J. *information technology manager, director*

GEORGIA

Atlanta
Blalock, Rebecca A. *information technology specialist*
DeRodes, Robert P. *information technology executive*
Tanteh, Victor Nkangami *information technology educator*

Canton
Wilson, Brian Andrew *computing performance consultant, educator, writer, editor*

Swainsboro
Watt, (Arthur) Dwight, Jr. *computer programming and microcomputer specialist*

Warner Robins
Gibson, John Robert *software engineer*

HAWAII

Honolulu
Owen, Cathy Hesse *nanotechnology company executive*

IDAHO

Boise
Kirklin, Vance Lane *software company executive*

Rathdrum
Dickinson, Linda Mary *web designer, graphics designer, art educator*

ILLINOIS

Burr Ridge
Rosenberg, Robert Brinkmann *information technology executive*

Champaign
McConnell, William Stewart *application developer*

Chicago
Balasa, Florin *software engineer, mathematician*
Larson, Nancy Celeste *information technology manager*
Sviokla, John Julius *technology consultant*

Deerfield
Gershteyn, Yefim *application developer, researcher*

Effingham
Fatheree, Joseph G. *information technology educator*

Evanston
Fisher, Andrew Taylor *computer software developer*

Urbana
Le, Hieu Khac *information technology executive, researcher*

Vernon Hills
Edwardson, John Albert *information technology executive*
Klein, Barbara A. *information technology executive*
Richards, Thomas Edward *information technology executive, former telecommunications industry executive*
Stevens, Jonathan J. *information technology executive*

Winnetka
Sick, William Norman, Jr. *technology company executive*

Woodridge
Puthenpurakal, Joseph Mathew *information technology executive*

INDIANA

Bloomington
Henson, Jane Elizabeth *information management professional, adult education educator*
Smith, Janet Sue *systems process specialist*

Fort Wayne
Carroll, Betty Jean *retired application developer*

Terre Haute
Frey, Susan M. *information specialist*

KANSAS

Claflin
Lewis, Robert V., Jr. *computer programmer*

Kansas City
Olofson, Tom William *technology company executive*

Overland Park
Shoemaker, Scott David *network consultant, educator*
Thompson, Mary Elizabeth *retired application developer*

KENTUCKY

Lexington
Canales, Denise Niles *software company executive*
Curlander, Paul Joseph *technology executive*

Louisville
Martin, David Allen *application developer, computer scientist*

Prospect
Kehlbeck, Joseph H. *software developer, consultant*

MAINE

Yarmouth
Grover, Mark Donald *software developer, town councilor, computer scientist*

MARYLAND

Baltimore
Park, Mary Woodfill *information consultant, librarian, writer*
Strull, Gene *technology consultant, retired manufacturing executive*

Beltsville
Basinger, William Daniel *computer programmer*

Bethesda
Karev, Georgiy Petrovich *application developer*

College Park
Frank, Howard *information technology educator, former dean*
Miller, Raymond Edward *computer science educator*

Columbia
Armstrong, T. Paul *information technology executive*
Giannopoulos, A.L. (Tom Giannopoulos) *information technology executive*
Miller, Andrea R. *application developer, educator*

Crofton
Dey, Saikat *information technology manager*

Frederick
Merrill, Daniel A. *program manager*

Havre De Grace
Sweatman, Kelly *information technology executive*

Hyattsville
Asongu, Januarius Jingwa *business executive*

Rockville
Haber, Margaret Wilson *informatics specialist, director*
MacArthur, Diana Taylor *advanced technology executive*
Proffitt, John Richard *information technology executive, educator, public official*
Rodriguez-Cambero, Rafael Luis *project manager*

Salisbury
Kutchen, John E. *information technology manager*

Silver Spring
Tobe, Barbara Gaines *information technology executive*

MASSACHUSETTS

Beverly
Smith, Derek Armand *information technology executive*

Boston
Kumar, Vikram Sheel *information technology executive*
Stallman, Richard Matthew *software developer*

Boxborough
Devor, Jonathan *application developer*

Cambridge
Berners-Lee, Sir Timothy John *inventor of world wide web, research scientist, writer*
Brooks, Rodney Allen *information technology executive, educator*
Egozy, Eran *video game development company executive*
Gagliardi, Ugo Oscar *systems software architect, educator*
Goentzel, Jarrod *information technology executive, director*
Liskov, Barbara Huberman *software engineering educator*
Mandl, Robert *application developer*
Mullen, James C. *biotechnology company executive*
Rigopulos, Alexander Peter *video game development company executive*
Sagan, Paul *information technology executive*
Teevan, Jaime *application developer, researcher*

Chelmsford
Ain, Aron J. *information technology executive*
Ain, Mark Stuart *information technology executive*
George, Peter *information technology executive*
Lacy, Paul *information technology executive*

Duxbury
Zachmann, William Francis *computer and communications industry market research company executive*

Foxboro
Martin, Peter Gerard *computer technician, consultant, secondary school educator*

Hopkinton
Goulden, David *information technology executive*
Tucci, Joseph M. *information technology executive*

Lynn
D'Entremont, Edward Joseph *application developer, educator*

Mashpee
Kilmartin, Joseph Francis, Jr. *information technology executive*

Natick
Dang, Pritpal S. *application developer*

Needham Heights
Joseph, Nevil Elliot *application developer*

Newton
Bagalay, John Earl *information technology executive, venture capitalist, consultant*

Newton Highlands
Bricklin, Daniel *software designer, consultant*

Sudbury
McCree, Paul William, Jr. *systems design and engineering company executive*

Waltham
Hovsepian, Ronald W. *network management software company executive*

Woburn
Mehra, Raman Kumar *aerospace and defense technology executive, automotion and control engineering researcher*

MICHIGAN

Ann Arbor
Vielmetti, Edward Marshall *webmaster*

Bloomfield Hills
Weil, John William *technology management consultant*

Detroit
Kruse, Ronia *information technology executive*

Holland
Albert, Stephen Wayne *information technology executive, manufacturing executive*

West Bloomfield
Cox, Clifford Ernest *information systems consulting executive, former academic administrator*

Ypsilanti
Boone, Morell Douglas *information technology educator*

MINNESOTA

Buffalo
Moon, James Russell *retired technology education educator*

Elk River
McClure, Alvin Bruce *watchmaker*

Minnetonka
Tao, Li *application developer*

Oakdale
Russomanno, Frank P. *information technology executive*

Roseville
El-Hilali, Oussama *application developer*

Saint Paul
Gouin, Warner Peter *information technology consultant*

MISSOURI

Kansas City
McDonnell, Thomas A. *information technology executive*
West, Marc *information technology executive*

Rolla
Datz, Israel Mortimer *information systems specialist*

Saint Louis
Elliott, Susan Spoehrer *information technology executive*
Fryman, Bill *information technology manager, educator*
Pollack, Seymour Victor *computer science educator*
Wafapoor, Farzad *information technology executive, educator*

MONTANA

Missoula
Howe, Scott E. *information technology executive*

NEBRASKA

Omaha
Barker, Thomas B. *information technology executive*
Gupta, Vinod (Vin Gupta) *information database company executive*
Hopkins, Charles L., III, (Hop Hopkins) *information technology executive, former federal agency administrator*

NEVADA

Las Vegas
Stanley, Tim *information technology executive*

Reno
Matthews, Thomas J. *game company executive*
Ragavan, Anpalaki Jeyabalasinkham *software developer, researcher*

NEW HAMPSHIRE

Franconia
Schaffer, David Edwin *retired systems administrator*

NEW JERSEY

Bedminster
Johnson, Garry D. *information technology executive*
Ripp, Joseph Allen *information technology executive*

Cherry Hill
Schelm, Roger Leonard *information systems specialist*

Hackensack
Mavrovic, Paul J. *information technology executive*

Lake Hiawatha
Wyka, Tom *information technology manager*

Monmouth Junction
Kolan, Prakash Reddy *information technology manager*

New Providence
Bruch, Ruth E. *information technology executive*

Newark
Edwards, Samuel Lawrence, II, *information technology executive, writer*
Nash, Alicia Lardé *application developer, physicist*

Princeton
Yang, Hua *video coding expert*

South Orange
Hoffert, Eric Michael *application developer, information technology executive*
Long, Philip Lee *information systems executive*

Sparta
Bhattacharyya, Dev *information technology executive, consultant*

Teaneck
D'Souza, Francisco B. *information technology executive, consultant*

NEW MEXICO

Albuquerque
Alexis, Tracy L. *project manager*
Orona, Joseph Ryan *information technology executive*

Las Cruces
Kilmer, Neal Harold *application developer*

Taos
Garen, Kenneth Bruce *software designer, company executive*

NEW YORK

Armonk
Daniels, Michael E. *information technology executive*
Kavanaugh, James J. *information technology executive*
Kelly, John E. III *information technology executive*
Kern, Franklin R. *information technology executive*
Palmisano, Samuel J. *information technology executive*
Rometty, Ginny (Virginia Maria Rometty) *information technology executive*
Schroeter, Martin J. *information technology executive*
Shaughnessy, Timothy S. *information technology executive*

Chatham
Yale, John Paul *computer systems developer*

Corning
Flaws, James B. *technology executive*

Endicott
Markovich, Voya R. *information technology executive*

Hauppauge
Doucette, David Robert *information technology executive*

Haverstraw
Alpert, Revell Judith *retired information technology executive*

Hawthorne
Russell, Jim *application developer*

Hicksville
Yen, Henry Chin-Yuan *computer systems programmer, software engineer, consulting company executive*

Islandia
Christenson, Michael J. *management software technology company executive*
McCracken, William E. *information technology executive*
Nugent, Alan F. *software company executive*

Ithaca
Howell, Debra Lynne *information technology executive*
Jeong, JongMin *systems administrator, researcher*

Jamaica
Chropufka, Mark A. *information technology executive, poet*

Latham
Bruno, Joseph L. *information technology executive, retired state senator*

Massapequa
Roberts, Kathleen Joy Doty *technology staff developer, educational consultant, supervisor*

Melville
Settle, Mark *information technology executive*

New York
Bahash, Robert J. *information technology executive*
Calhoun, David L. *information and media company executive*
Caponnetto, Marianne *information technology executive*
Chang, Mona Mei-Hsuan *computer programmer, analyst*
Cooke, Phil *application developer*
Danic, Robert Ian *application developer*
Gorton, Mark Howard *information technology executive, entrepreneur*
Kheradpir, Shaygan *information technology executive*
Kozik, Susan S. *information technology executive*
Maia, Tiago Vaz *researcher*
McGraw, Harold W., III, (Terry McGraw) *information company executive*
Morgan, Suann Lee *information technology manager, consultant*
O'Connor, Kevin *computer programming executive*
Pierce, David *information technology executive*
Powell, Timothy Wood *information executive, consultant*
Rubin, Harry Meyer *software industry executive*
Shaw, Steven A. *information technology executive*
Widlund, Olof Bertil *computer science educator, mathematician*
Zúñiga, Markos Moulitsas *political blogger, social activist*

Niskayuna
Huening, Walter Carl, Jr. *retired consulting application engineer*

Pittsford
Herge, Henry Curtis, Jr. *information technology executive, consultant*

Rochester
VanGelder, Kim E. *information technology executive*

Somers
Adkins, Rodney Carl *information technology executive*
Sanford, Linda S. *information technology executive*

Syracuse
Gartner, Joseph Charles *retired systems administrator*

Troy
Demertzoglou, Pindaro Epaminonda *system administrator, clinical assistant professor*
Hendler, James Alexander *computer science educator, consultant*

Wappingers Falls
Khare, Mukesh V. *information technology manager*

White Plains
Moffat, Robert W., Jr. *information technology executive*

Yorktown Heights
Joshi, Rajiv V. *information technology manager, researcher*

NORTH CAROLINA

Cary
Capps, Michael *video game company executive*
Goodnight, James H. *software company executive*
Sweeney, Tim *computer game developer, programmer*

Raleigh
Cox, David E. *application developer*
Szulik, Matthew J. *information technology executive*

Winston Salem
Hanes, Ralph Philip, Jr. *network technician*

OHIO

Athens
Kurz, David Bryan *web site designer*

Beavercreek
Pasupuleti, Venumadhav *information technology executive*

Cincinnati
Laney, Sandra Eileen *information technology executive*
Passerini, Filippo *information technology executive*

Columbus
Taylor, Celianna Isley *information systems specialist*

Dublin
Davids, Jody R. *information technology executive*

Newark
Sharrock (Wrentmore), Anita Kay *information technology specialist*

Troy
Platfoot, Christopher W. *systems administrator, information technology executive*

Westlake
Whitehouse, John Harlan, Jr. *systems software consultant, diagnostician*

OKLAHOMA

Ada
Baker, Judith Ann *retired computer technician*

Stillwater
Sharda, Ramesh *management science-information systems educator*

Tulsa
Oliver, Georgianna White *technology consulting company executive*

OREGON

Beaverton
Kamenev, Boris V. *applications developer, materials scientist, metrologist, engineer, researcher*
McKenney, Paul E. *application developer*
Monalisa, Mitali *application developer*

PENNSYLVANIA

Blue Bell
Coleman, J. Edward (Ed Coleman) *information technology executive, former computer company executive*

Dallas
Filipiak, Stephen *web programmer, educator*

Gap
Burton, Mary Louise Himes *retired information technology executive*

Glen Mills
Kaufman, Antoinette Dolores *information technology manager*

King Of Prussia
Swank, Annette Marie *software designer*

Langhorne
Day, Melvin Sherman *retired information and telecommunications company executive*

Newtown Square
McDermott, William R. *information technology executive*

Philadelphia
Dougherty Buchholz, Karen *systems administrator*

Reading
Shin, Dong-Hee *communication technology educator*

Williamsport
Gorka, Sandra *information technology executive, educator*

RHODE ISLAND

Providence
Canning, Deborah *technology educator*
Savage, John Edmund *computer science educator, researcher*

SOUTH CAROLINA

Columbia
Duggan, Kevin *information technology professional*
Hudson, Carolyn Brauer *application developer, educator*

Greenville
Baur, Michael L. *information technology executive*

SOUTH DAKOTA

Spearfish
Ellis, Mary Louise Helgeson *retired healthcare technology company executive*

TENNESSEE

Memphis
Griffin, Clement M. *information technology executive*

TEXAS

Abilene
Weller, David Allen *information technology executive, poet*

Arlington
Fouse, David Jesse *sr. web application developer*

Austin
Anand, Vaijayanthimala K. *software engineer*
Knowles, Harry Jay *Internet personality, blogger, film critic*
Lam, Simon Shin-Sing *computer science educator*

Bandera
Bartley, Dee Gray *information technology executive*

Beaumont
Smith-Sterling, Carolyn Leola *technology educator*

Conroe
Johnson, Raymond K. *information technology manager*
Kramm, Deborah Ann *retired information technology executive*

Dallas
Beer, James A. *information technology executive, former air transportation executive*
Blodgett, Lynn R. *information technology company executive*
Burlin, Tom *information technology executive*
Deason, Darwin *information technology executive*
Kruse, Ann Gray *computer programmer*
Kyser, Kevin *information technology executive*
Panos, Tas *information technology executive, lawyer*

Denton
Garcia, Oscar Nicolas *computer science educator*

Fort Worth
Hodgkins, W. Grant *supply chain improvements manager, project management professional, consultant*

Grapevine
Blizzard, Linda Kay *software engineer, consultant*

Houston
Barnea, Dan *information technology executive*
Beauchamp, Robert E. *information technology executive*
Cupp, B. Garland *information technology executive*

Katy
Smith, Theodore Glenn *technology educator, researcher*

Keene
Miller, Rebecca Lynn *software engineer*

Plano
Dougherty, F(rancis) Kelly *application developer*
Jordan, Michael Hugh *information technology executive*
Musser, Cherri M. *information technology executive*
Rittenmeyer, Ronald Allen *information technology executive*
Ryu, Manho *application developer*
Vargo, Ronald Paul *information technology executive*
Wyman, Richard Thomas *information technology manager, researcher*

San Antonio
Frazier, Eric David *information technology manager, consultant*

Stephenville
Bane, Alma Lynn *data research administrator*

Sugar Land
Kulkarni, Sachin Rameshchandra *application developer*

UTAH

Salt Lake City
Mendenhall, Robert W. *education technology executive*

VIRGINIA

Alexandria
Nodeen, Janey Price *information technology executive*

Annandale
Khim, Jay Wook *information technology executive*

Arlington
Calland, Albert M. III *information technology executive, former federal official, retired military officer*
Cofoni, Paul Michael *information technology executive*
Jacoby, Lowell Edwin (Jake Jacoby) *information technology executive, retired military officer*
Kang, Mikyung *application developer, researcher*
Kneuer, John M.R. *information technology executive, former federal agency administrator*
London, J. Phillip (Jack London) *information technology executive*
McKenzie, Walter L., Jr. *information technology executive, consultant*

Big Stone Gap
Moore, Rosa-lee *information technology executive*

Fairfax
Golden, James Leslie *information technology executive, retired military officer*

Falls Church
DeMuro, Gerard J *information technology executive*
McCue, David J. *information systems specialist, entrepreneur*

Fort Belvoir
DuBrow, Alexander Alan *information technology executive, consultant*

Harrisonburg
Duncan, Cheryl J. (Cheri Duncan) *systems administrator, librarian*

Herndon
O'Connor, Christopher John *information technology manager, consultant*

Leesburg
Macfarlane, David Gordon *defense systems design and development executive*

Norfolk
Maly, Kurt John *computer science educator*

Reston
Christian, Eliot Jordan *information technology manager, consultant*

Richmond
McDermid, Margaret E. (Lyn McDermid) *information technology executive, engineer*
Weistroffer, Heinz Roland *information systems professional, educator*

Springfield
Greer, Mark Francis *information technology executive*

WASHINGTON

Bellevue
Tian, Hongqi *application developer, researcher*

Carnation
Burner, Darcy *application developer*

Everett
Byrne, Patrick J. *information technology executive*

Kenmore
Gilleland, John Rogers *technology company executive*

Pullman
O'Fallon, Andrew Steven *software engineer, educator*

Redmond
Blakeley-Perez, Jose Alfredo *software architect*
Cutler, David Neil, Sr. *software engineer*
Nan, Fei *application developer*
Niehaus, Michael *application developer, consultant*
Tatarinov, Kirill *computer software industry expert*
Ul-Mustafa, Raza *application developer, researcher*

Seatac
Wells, Roger Stanley *software engineer*

Seattle
Crenshaw, Edward Lee, Sr. *aviation electronics technician*
Desouza, Kevin Clyde *application developer, educator*
Hills, Regina J. *web manager*
Lazowska, Edward Delano *computer science educator*
Mayo, Robert N. *computer science researcher*
Shankaran, Nishanth *application developer*
Simonyi, Charles *software engineer*

WISCONSIN

Brookfield
Jones, Richard K. *information technology executive*

Franksville
Palecek, Michael R. *information technology manager*

Milwaukee
Liu, Qingmin *software engineer, materials engineer*

Racine
Schneider, David Alan *information technology manager*

CANADA

ONTARIO

Ottawa
Campbell, Don *information technology executive*
Silvestri, Claudio *information technology executive*
Zambonini, Ron (Renato Zambonini) *information technology executive*

Waterloo
Balsillie, Jim *information technology executive*
Lazaridis, Mike *information technology executive, entrepreneur*

AUSTRALIA

Altona
Daniel-Dreyfus, Susan B. Russe *information technology executive*

Melbourne
Wolfram, David Anthony *information technology executive*

EGYPT

Alexandria
Eldakar, Youssef I. *software engineer*

ENGLAND

London
Wyn-Jones, Alun (William Wyn-Jones) *software developer, mathematician*

ITALY

Rome
Stigliano, Jose Maria *information technology executive, computer scientist*

JAPAN

Tokyo
Harada, Norio *software engineer, researcher, educator*

REPUBLIC OF KOREA

Seoul
Lee, Ki-Tae *information technology executive*

SOUTH AFRICA

Johannesburg
Pesic, Ratnik Josip *application developer, management consultant, mathematician, educator*

ADDRESS UNPUBLISHED

Alexander, Nancy A. *information technology manager, director*
Ali, Mohammed Zamshed *information technology executive, researcher*
Bass, Steven Craig *computer science educator*
Batchu, Ravi Venkata *software engineer, researcher*
Bennett, Robert LeRoy *computer software development company executive*
Bleszinski, Cliff (Clifford Michael) *game designer*
Bonnell, Bruno *information technology executive*
Bramhall, Debra A. *information technology manager, consultant*
Callaway, Matthew Stephen *application developer*
Castle, James Cameron *information technology executive*
Castor, Jon Stuart *technology executive*
Clarizio, Lynda M. *former information technology advertising executive, lawyer*
Constantine, Larry L. *software designer, design and consulting company executive*
Cron, Kenneth D. *former interactive software and gaming executive*
Cui, Minghao *application developer, researcher*
Culleeney, Maureen Ann *information technology executive, educator*
Dalzell, Rick *information technology executive*
Davis, Ruth Margaret *information technology executive*
DiPentima, Renato Anthony *information technology executive*
Duffield, David A. *application developer, former computer software company executive*
Elix, Douglas Thorne *retired information technology executive*
Etheridge, Diana Carol *Internet business executive*
Faison, Edmund "Ted" Winston, Jr. *software architect*
Franklin, William Price *information technology manager*
Frase, Katharine *information technology executive*
Fuller, Dale L. *software security company executive*
Ganguly, Arijit *software engineer*
Gareau, Jean L. *application technology executive*
Gibbs, Johnie Elizabeth *information technology manager, educator, consultant*
Godhardt, Karen *information technology executive*
Goel, Tushar *application developer, researcher*
Goldberger, Arthur Earl, Jr. *information technology executive*
Goldfarb, Eric Daniel *information technology executive*
Gomes, Kevin *application developer*
Granville, Richard Scott *information technology executive*
Greene, Diane B. *information technology executive*
Gupta, Ram *software company executive*
Ha, Chong Wan *information technology executive*
Hashimoto, Sozo *information technology executive*
Hemann, Raymond Glenn *research company executive*
Heng, Iem H. *application developer, educator*
Hill, Patricia Francine *information technology executive, educator*
Holt, George, Jr. *information technology executive*
Hornby, Kenneth Peter *self-employed*
Hu, Weigang *software engineer*
Huang, Rick Y. *application developer*
Huang, Yun *application developer, research scientist*
Hubona, Geoffrey Stuart *information systems educator, computer scientist*
Huffman, Brenda S. *information technology executive*
Ihrig, Colin J. *application developer*
Ishaque, Mashhood *application developer, researcher*
Javed, Faizan *application developer*
Jiang, Wei *application developer*
Jing, Xiangpeng *information technology manager*
Jones, Carleton Shaw *information technology executive, lawyer*
Kadel, Lee A. *information security analyst*
Kleinlein, Kathy Lynn *training and development executive*
Kramp, Suzan Marie *systems programmer*
Krishnaswamy, Mukunda *information technology executive, entrepreneur*
Kubilus, Norbert John *information technology executive*
La Blanc, Robert Edmund *information technology executive*
Larson, Janice Talley *application developer*
Le, Hung Qui *application developer*
Levy, Leslie Ann *application developer*
Liang, Jian *application developer*
Lyles, Mark Bradley *advanced technology company executive, military officer*
Lyons, Susanne D. *information technology executive*
Ma, Wenjing *application developer*
MacDonald, J. Randall *information technology executive, human resources specialist*
Manyame, Comfort *systems administrator*
McCausland, Peter *technology company executive*
Menon, Jai M. *information technology manager*
Mills, Steven A. *information technology executive*
Minshall, Greg *computer programmer*
Morgan, M. Jane *computer systems consultant*
Mueller, Gary Alfred *software engineer*
Nam, Seung Yeob *network technician, researcher*
Nicoll, Edward J. *information technology company executive*
Nolff, Susan D. *web site designer, small business owner*
O'Connor, John Joseph *information technology manager*
Pallapa, Gautham *webmaster*
Papathomas, Georgia Nikolakopoulou *technology executive*
Payne, Velma L. *application developer*
Persad, Chadee *information technology manager*
Phipps, Robert Lee *information technology manager*
Rada, Mihai Catalin *application developer*
Raley, Beverly Spickelmier *retired systems administrator, writer*
Reece, David Bryson *information systems administrator*
Rich, Jeffrey A. *former information technology company executive*
Rohde, James Vincent *medical devices company executive*
Rose, Paul Edward *systems administrator, educator*
Sacco, Louis John *software design architect*
Salisbury, Alan Blanchard *information technology officer*
Schloter, Philipp *information technology executive*
Schreiber, Horst *information technology manager*
Secretan, Jimmy *application developer, researcher*
Sedighi, Artin *application developer, researcher*
Segrove, David Anthony *information technology manager*
Sen, Dipankar *technology manager, principal*
Sia, Ka Cheung *application developer*
Sills, Scott E. *nanotechnologist*
Smith, Anne Marie Schoefer *application developer*
Smith, Leonard R. *information technology executive, educator*
Smyth, Ellen Gray Menees *systems support specialist*
Still, Homer Ibson *information technology executive*
Sweeney, James *application developer*
Tanachaiwiwat, Sapon *information technology manager*
Tang, Wei *software engineer*
Tesler, Lawrence Gordon *technology company executive*
Thompson, Kenneth *software engineer*
Udupi, Yathiraj Bhat *software engineer*
Vazacopoulos, Alkis *application developer, educator*
Vaze, Shilpa Arun *software, firmware, modeling engineer*
Visocki, Nancy Gayle *information services consultant*
Wang, Haibin *systems administrator, consultant*
Wilhelmi, Cynthia Joy *business and information technology manager, information scientist executive consultant*
Woods, Dan *information technology manager, consultant*
Wu, Yongjun *application developer*
Yu, Xunqi *software engineer*
Zehring, Karen *information executive*
Zhao, Yong *application developer, researcher*
Zhu, Xianjin *application developer*
Zucker, David F. *former information technology executive*

INTERNET *See* INFORMATION TECHNOLOGY

LAW: JUDICIAL ADMINISTRATION

UNITED STATES

ALABAMA

Ashland
Ingram, Kenneth Frank *retired state supreme court justice*

Birmingham
Houston, James Gorman, Jr. *retired state supreme court justice*
Pryor, William Holcombe, Jr. *federal judge, former state attorney general, educator*

Mobile
Butler, Charles Randolph, Jr. *federal judge*
Cox, Emmett Ripley *federal judge*
Graddick, Charles Allen *judge*
Granade, Callie Virginia Smith *federal judge*
Howard, Alex T., Jr. *federal judge*

Montgomery
Bolin, Michael F. *state supreme court justice*
Carnes, Edward E. *federal judge*
Cobb, Sue Bell *state supreme court chief justice*
Dubina, Joel Fredrick *federal judge*
Maddox, Alva Hugh *retired state supreme court justice*
Murdock, Glenn *state supreme court justice*
Parker, Tom *state supreme court justice, lawyer*
Shaw, James Gregory (Greg) *state supreme court justice*
Smith, Patricia M. (Patti Smith) *state supreme court justice*
Steele, Rodney Redfearn *judge*
Stuart, Lyn (Jacqueline Lyn Stuart) *state supreme court justice*
Woodall, Thomas A. *state supreme court justice*

ALASKA

Anchorage
Burgess, Timothy M. *federal judge, former prosecutor*
Christen, Morgan *state supreme court justice*
Eastaugh, Robert L. *state supreme court justice*
Fabe, Dana Anderson *state supreme court justice*
von der Heydt, James Arnold *federal judge*
Winfree, Daniel Edward *state supreme court justice, lawyer*

Fairbanks
Kleinfeld, Andrew J. *federal judge*

Juneau
Carpeneti, Walter L. *state supreme court justice*

ARIZONA

Phoenix
Anderson, Lawrence Ohaco *federal judge, lawyer*
Bales, W. Scott *state supreme court justice*
Berch, Rebecca White *state supreme court justice, lawyer*
Broomfield, Robert Cameron *federal judge*
Canby, William Cameron, Jr. *federal judge*
Carroll, Earl Hamblin *federal judge*
Gaines, Francis Pendleton III *judge*
Hawkins, Michael Daly *federal judge*
Hurwitz, Andrew D. *state supreme court justice*
McNamee, Stephen M. *federal judge*
Pelander, John *state supreme court justice*
Ryan, Michael D. *state supreme court justice*
Schroeder, Mary Murphy *federal judge*
Silverman, Barry G. *federal judge*
Snow, G. Murray *federal judge*
Strand, Roger Gordon *federal judge*
Weisenburger, Theodore Maurice *retired judge, poet, educator*
Winthrop, Lawrence Fredrick *judge*

Tempe
Arkfeld, Louraine C. *judge*

Tucson
Brammer, J. William, Jr. *judge, lawyer*
Cooper, Jean Saralee *retired judge*
Miller, Leslie Beth *judge*

ARKANSAS

Batesville
Harkey, John Norman *retired judge*

El Dorado
Barnes, Harry Francis *federal judge*

Fayetteville
Smith, Lavenski Roy *federal judge*

Little Rock
Arnold, Morris Sheppard *federal judge*
Bird, Samuel N. *judge*
Corbin, Donald L. *state supreme court justice*
Danielson, Paul E. *state supreme court justice*
Gunter, James Houston, Jr. *state supreme court justice*
Hannah, James *state supreme court chief justice*
Imber, Annabelle Clinton *state supreme court justice*
Miller, Brian Stacy *federal judge*
Wills, Elana Cunningham *state supreme court justice*
Wright, Susan Webber *federal judge*

Searcy
Hughes, Thomas Morgan III *circuit judge*

Texarkana
Stroud, John Fred, Jr. *judge*

CALIFORNIA

Alameda
Bartalini, C. Richard *judge*

El Segundo
Smith, Milan Dale, Jr. *federal judge*

Irvine
Crawford, Susan Jean *federal judge*

Long Beach
Tucker, Marcus Othello *judge*

Los Angeles
Alarcón, Arthur Lawrence *federal judge*
Highberger, William Foster *lawyer*
Johnson, Earl, Jr. *retired judge, author*
Manella, Nora Margaret *judge*
Mosk, Richard Mitchell *judge*
Pfaelzer, Mariana R. *federal judge*
Timlin, Robert J. *judge*
Wu, George H. *federal judge*
Zelon, Laurie Dee *judge*

Mendocino
Masterson, William A. *retired judge*

Oakland
Jensen, D. Lowell *federal judge*
Newsome, Randall Jackson *judge*

Pasadena
Boochever, Robert *federal judge*
Fernandez, Ferdinand Francis *federal judge*
Fisher, Raymond Corley *federal judge*
Goodwin, Alfred Theodore *federal judge*
Hall, Cynthia Holcomb *federal judge*

Johnson, Barbara Jean *retired judge, lawyer*
Kozinski, Alex *federal judge*
Nelson, Dorothy Wright *federal judge*
Paez, Richard A. *federal judge*
Rymer, Pamela Ann *federal judge*
Tashima, Atsushi Wallace *federal judge*
Wardlaw, Kim A. McLane *federal judge*

Pauma Valley
Lewis, Gerald Jorgensen *judge*

Point Richmond
Herron, E. Patricia *retired judge*

Ramona
Marquez, Alfredo C. *federal judge*

Redwood City
Grandsaert, John Leo *judge*

Sacramento
Callahan, Consuelo Maria *federal judge*
Mendez, John Anthony *federal judge*
Moulds, John F. *judge*
Van Camp, Brian Ralph *judge*

San Diego
Anello, Michael M. *federal judge*
Bowie, Peter Wentworth *judge, educator*
McKeown, Mary Margaret *federal judge*
Sammartino, Janis Lynn *federal judge*
Thompson, David Renwick *federal judge*
Thompson, Gordon, Jr. *federal judge*
Wallace, J. Clifford *federal judge*

San Francisco
Baxter, Marvin Ray *state supreme court justice*
Bea, Carlos Tiburcio *federal judge*
Berzon, Marsha S. *federal judge*
Browning, James Robert *federal judge*
Chin, Ming W. *state supreme court justice*
Corrigan, Carol A. *state supreme court justice*
Fletcher, William A. *federal judge, educator*
George, Ronald M. *state supreme court chief justice*
Ikuta, Sandra Segal *federal judge*
Jarvis, Donald Bertram *judge*
Kennard, Joyce L. *state supreme court justice*
Kolkey, Daniel Miles *former judge, lawyer*
Moreno, Carlos R. *state supreme court justice*
Noonan, John T., Jr. *federal judge, educator*
Walker, Vaughn R. *federal judge*
Werdegar, Kathryn Mickle *state supreme court justice*

San Marino
Mortimer, Wendell Reed, Jr. *retired judge*

Santa Ana
Guilford, Andrew John *federal judge*
Stotler, Alicemarie Huber *federal judge*

Santa Barbara
Aldisert, Ruggero John *federal judge*

Studio City
Gold, Arnold Henry *judge*

Woodland Hills
Mund, Geraldine *judge*
Pregerson, Harry *federal judge*

COLORADO

Black Hawk
Rodgers, Frederic Barker *judge*

Denver
Arguello, Christine Marie *federal judge*
Bender, Michael Lee *state supreme court justice*
Brimmer, Philip A. *federal judge*
Coats, Nathan B. *state supreme court justice*
Daniel, Wiley Young *federal judge*
Ebel, David M. *federal judge*
Eid, Allison Hartwell *state supreme court justice*
Felter, Edwin Lester, Jr. *judge*
Gorsuch, Neil McGill *federal judge, lawyer*
Hobbs, Gregory James, Jr. *state supreme court justice*
Keithley, Roger Lee *judge*
Lucero, Carlos *federal judge*
Martinez, Alex J. *state supreme court justice*
McWilliams, Robert Hugh *federal judge*
Mullarkey, Mary J. *state supreme court chief justice*
Porfilio, John Carbone *federal judge*
Rice, Nancy E. *state supreme court justice*
Rovira, Luis Dario *state supreme court justice*
Tymkovich, Timothy Michael *federal judge*

Littleton
Erickson, William Hurt *retired state supreme court justice*

Westminster
Scott, Gregory Kellam *former state supreme court justice, lawyer*

CONNECTICUT

Bridgeport
Shiff, Alan Howard William *judge*

Cheshire
Ross, Michael Frederick *judge, lawyer*

Danbury
Yamin, Dianne Elizabeth *judge*

Hartford
Bieluch, William Charles *judge*
Bryant, Vanessa Lynne *federal judge, lawyer*
Katz, Joette *state supreme court justice*
Killian, Robert Kenneth, Jr. *judge, lawyer*
McLachlan, C. Ian (Charles McLachlan) *state supreme court justice*
Newman, Jon O. *federal judge*
Norcott, Flemming L., Jr. *state supreme court justice*
Palmer, Richard N. *state supreme court justice*
Peters, Ellen Ash *retired judge*
Rogers, Chase Theodora *state supreme court chief justice*
Squatrito, Dominic J. *judge*
Vertefeuille, Christine Siegrist *state supreme court justice*
Wright, Douglass Brownell *retired judge, lawyer*
Zarella, Peter T. *state supreme court justice*

New Haven
Cabranes, José Alberto *federal judge*
Calabresi, Guido *federal judge, educator*
Dorsey, Peter Collins *federal judge*
Silbert, Jonathan E. *judge*
Walker, John Mercer, Jr. *federal judge*
Winter, Ralph Karl, Jr. *federal judge*

Waterbury
Sullivan, William J. *state supreme court justice*
Upson, Thomas Fisher *judge, retired state senator, lawyer*

DELAWARE

Dover
Ridgely, Henry duPont *state supreme court justice*

Wilmington
Ambro, Thomas L. *federal judge*
Berger, Carolyn *state supreme court justice*
Jacobs, Jack Bernard *state supreme court justice*
Jordan, Kent A. *federal judge*
Parsons, Donald Francis *judge*
Roth, Jane Richards *federal judge*
Stapleton, Walter King *federal judge*
Steele, Myron Thomas *state supreme court chief justice*

DISTRICT OF COLUMBIA

Washington
Alito, Samuel Anthony, Jr. *United States supreme court justice*
Allegra, Francis M. *federal judge, retired federal official*
Archer, Glenn LeRoy, Jr. *federal judge*
Bacon, Sylvia *judge, educator*
Baker, James Edgar *federal judge, educator*
Bartnoff, Judith *judge*
Barton, Robert Leroy, Jr. *judge, educator*
Bates, John D. *federal judge*
Bayly, John Henry, Jr. *judge*
Beghe, Renato *federal judge*
Belson, James Anthony *Senior Judge, DC Court of Appeals*
Blackburne-Rigsby, Anna *Associate Judge, DC Court of Appeals*
Block, Lawrence J. *federal judge*
Breyer, Stephen Gerald *United States supreme court justice*
Brown, Janice Rogers *federal judge, former state supreme court justice*
Bruggink, Eric G. *federal judge*
Bryson, William Curtis *federal judge*
Burnett, Arthur Louis, Sr. *judge*
Bush, Lynn Jeanne *federal judge*
Carr, William B., Jr. *retired judge*
Chabot, Herbert L. *federal judge*
Clevenger, Raymond Charles III *federal judge*
Cohen, Mary Ann *federal judge*
Colvin, John O. *federal judge*
Damich, Edward John *federal judge*
Darden, William Horace *federal judge*
Davis, Robert Nolan *federal judge, educator*
Dawson, Howard Athalone, Jr. *federal judge*
Dean, John F. *federal judge*
Dyk, Timothy Belcher *federal judge*
Edwards, Harry Thomas *federal judge*
Effron, Andrew S. *federal judge*
Epstein, Anthony Charles *judge*
Erdmann, Charles Edgar (Chip Erdmann) *federal judge, former state supreme court justice*
Farrell, Michael W. *Senior Judge, DC Court of Appeals*
Ferren, John Maxwell *Senior Judge, DC Court of Appeals*
Firestone, Nancy B. *federal judge*
Fisher, John R. *Associate Judge, DC Court of Appeals*
Foley, Maurice B. *federal judge*
Friedman, Daniel Mortimer *federal judge*
Futey, Bohdan A. *federal judge*
Gajarsa, Arthur J. *federal judge*
Gale, Joseph H. *federal judge*
Garland, Merrick Brian *federal judge*
Gerber, Joel *federal judge*
Gierke, Herman Fredrick, III, (Sparky Gierke) *federal judge*
Ginsburg, Douglas Howard *federal judge*
Ginsburg, Ruth Bader *United States supreme court justice*
Glickman, Stephen H. *judge*
Goeke, Joseph Robert *federal judge, lawyer*
Goldberg, Stanley Joshua *federal judge*
Greene, William P., Jr. *federal judge*
Griffith, Thomas Beall *federal judge*
Gustafson, David Douglas *federal judge*
Hagel, Lawrence B. *federal judge*
Haines, Harry Allen *federal judge*
Halpern, James S. *federal judge*
Henderson, Karen LeCraft *federal judge*
Hewitt, Emily Clark *federal judge, minister*
Hodges, Robert H., Jr. *federal judge*
Holmes, Mark V. *judge*
Horn, Marian Blank *federal judge*
Irving, Alfred S., Jr. *judge*
Jacobs, Julian I. *federal judge*
Kasold, Bruce Edward *federal judge, lawyer*
Kavanaugh, Brett Michael *federal judge*
Kennedy, Anthony McLeod *United States supreme court justice*
Kern, John Worth III *Senior Judge, DC Court of Appeals*
King, Warren R. *Senior Judge, DC Court of Appeals*
Kollar-Kotelly, Colleen *federal judge*
Kramer, Noël Anketell *Associate Judge, DC Court of Appeals*
Kroupa, Diane Lynn *federal judge*
Lamberth, Royce C. *federal judge*
Lance, Alan George *federal judge, former state attorney general*
Laro, David *federal judge*
Lettow, Charles Frederick *federal judge*
Lourie, Alan David *federal judge*
Mack, Julia Cooper *retired judge*
Margolis, Lawrence Stanley *federal judge*
Marvel, L. Paige *federal judge*
Mayer, Haldane Robert *federal judge*
Mencher, Bruce Stephan *judge*
Merow, James F. *federal judge*
Michel, Paul Redmond *federal judge*
Miller, Christine Odell Cook *federal judge*
Moore, Kimberly Ann *federal judge*
Moorman, William A. *federal judge, retired career military officer*
Morrison, Richard Thane *federal judge*
Nebeker, Frank Quill *Senior Judge, DC Court of Appeals*
Newman, Pauline *federal judge*
Nims, Arthur Lee III *federal judge*
Oberly, Kathryn Anne *judge*
Pan, Florence Y. *judge*
Panuthos, Peter J. *federal judge*
Paris, Elizabeth Crewson *federal judge*
Plager, S. Jay *federal judge*
Prost, Sharon *federal judge*
Pryor, William C. *Senior Judge, DC Court of Appeals*
Rader, Randall Ray *federal judge*
Randolph, A(rthur) Raymond *federal judge*
Reid, Inez Smith *Associate Judge, DC Court of Appeals, lawyer, educator*
Rives, Jack L. *judge, career military officer*
Roberts, John Glover, Jr. *United States supreme court chief justice*
Robertson, James *federal judge*
Rogers, Judith Ann Wilson *federal judge*
Rothstein, Barbara Jacobs *federal judge*
Ruiz, Vanessa *Associate Judge, DC Court of Appeals*
Ruwe, Robert Paul *federal judge*
Ryan, Margaret A. *federal judge*
Scalia, Antonin Gregory *United States supreme court justice*
Schall, Alvin Anthony *federal judge*
Schoelen, Mary Jeanette *federal judge*
Schwelb, Frank Ernest *Senior Judge, DC Court of Appeals*
Sentelle, David Bryan *federal judge*
Smith, Loren Allan *federal judge*
Smith, Roy Philip *judge*
Sotomayor, Sonia *United States supreme court justice*
Steadman, John Montague *Senior Judge, DC Court of Appeals*
Stevens, John Paul *United States supreme court justice*
Stucky, Scott Wallace *federal judge, lawyer*
Sweeney, Margaret Mary *federal judge*
Swift, Stephen Jensen *federal judge*
Tatel, David Stephen *federal judge*
Terry, John Alfred *Senior Judge, DC Court of Appeals*
Thomas, Clarence *United States supreme court justice*
Thompson, Phyllis D. *Associate Judge, DC Court of Appeals, lawyer*
Thornton, Michael B. *federal judge*
Urbina, Ricardo Manuel *judge*
Vasquez, Juan Flores *federal judge*
Vittone, John Michael *federal judge*
Wagner, Annice McBryde *Senior Judge, DC Court of Appeals*
Wagner, Curtis Lee, Jr. *judge*
Wald, Patricia McGowan *retired federal judge*
Walton, Reggie Barnett *federal judge*
Washington, Eric T. *judge*
Wells, Thomas B. *federal judge*
Whalen, Laurence J. *federal judge*
Wheeler, Thomas Craig *federal judge*
Wherry, Robert Allen, Jr. *federal judge, lawyer*
Wiese, John Paul *federal judge*
Williams, Mary Ellen Coster *federal judge*
Williams, Stephen Fain *federal judge*
Wolski, Victor J. *federal judge, lawyer*
Yock, Robert John *federal judge*
Yoder, Ronnie A. *judge*

FLORIDA

Boynton Beach
Bernstein, Edwin S. *judge*

Destin
Robinson, Wilkes Coleman *retired federal judge*

Fort Lauderdale
Gonzalez, Jose Alejandro, Jr. *federal judge*
Ray, Raymond B. *federal judge*
Seltzer, Barry S. *federal judge*

Fort Myers
Schoonover, Jack Ronald *senior judge*

Jacksonville
Hill, James Clinkscales *federal judge*
Howard, Marcia Morales *federal judge*
Melton, Howell Webster, Sr. *federal judge*
Schlesinger, Harvey Erwin *judge*
Tjoflat, Gerald Bard *federal judge*

Longboat Key
Morse, Marvin Henry *retired judge*

Miami
Barkett, Rosemary *federal judge*
Cristol, A. Jay *federal judge*
Davis, Edward Bertrand *retired federal judge, lawyer*
Highsmith, Shelby *federal judge*
Marcus, Stanley *federal judge*
Siegel, Paul *judge*
Wilson, Thomas Strong, Jr., (Tam Wilson) *judge*

Ocala
Hodges, William Terrell *federal judge*

Orlando
Fawsett, Patricia Combs *federal judge*
Scriven, Mary Stenson *federal judge*
Thorpe, Janet Claire *judge*
Young, George Cressler *federal judge*

Panama City
Smith, Larry Glenn *retired state judge*

Pensacola
Vinson, Clyde Roger (Roger Vinson) *federal judge*

Safety Harbor
Dail, Joseph Garner, Jr. *retired judge*

Saint Petersburg
Chipman, Marion Walter *retired judge*

Seminole
Carrere, Charles Scott *judge, educator*

Tallahassee
Benton, Robert Tyrie, II, *judge*
Canady, Charles Terrence *state supreme court justice, former congressman*
Grimes, Stephen Henry *retired state supreme court justice*
Labarga, Jorge *state supreme court justice, lawyer*
Lewis, R. Fred *state supreme court justice*
McCord, Guyte Pierce, Jr. *retired judge*
Pariente, Barbara J. *state supreme court justice*
Perry, James E.C. *state supreme court justice*
Polston, Ricky L. *state supreme court justice*
Quince, Peggy A. *state supreme court chief justice*
Strickland, Delphene Coverston *judge*
Webster, Peter David *judge*

Tampa
Wilson, Charles Reginald *federal judge*

GEORGIA

Atlanta
Benham, Robert *state supreme court justice*
Birch, Stanley Francis, Jr. *federal judge*
Carley, George H. *state supreme court justice*
Deane, Richard Hunter, Jr. *former federal judge, lawyer*
Duffey, William Simon, Jr. *federal judge, former prosecutor*
Edmondson, J.L. (James Larry Edmondson) *federal judge*
Evans, Orinda D. *federal judge*
Hines, Preston Harris *state supreme court justice*
Hull, Frank Mays *federal judge*
Hunstein, Carol *chief justice*
Melton, Harold D. *state supreme court justice*
O'Kelley, William Clark *federal judge*
Thompson, Hugh P. *state supreme court justice*
Ward, Horace Taliaferro *federal judge*

Augusta
Hall, James Randal *federal judge*
Wood, Lisa Godbey *federal judge, former prosecutor*

Columbus
Laney, John Thomas III *federal judge*

Macon
Anderson, Robert Lanier III *federal judge*
Hershner, Robert Franklin, Jr. *judge*
Phillips, John Taylor *judge*

Marietta
Smith, George Thornewell *retired state supreme court justice*

Newnan
Drake, W. Homer, Jr. *federal judge*

Rome
Murphy, Harold Loyd *federal judge*

Roswell
Feldman, Joel Martin *retired judge*

Savannah
Edenfield, Berry Avant *federal judge*

HAWAII

Honolulu
Acoba, Simeon Rivera, Jr. *state supreme court justice, educator*
Clifton, Richard Randall *federal judge*
Duffy, James Earl, Jr. *state supreme court justice*
Moon, Ronald T.Y. *state supreme court chief justice*
Nakayama, Paula Aiko *state supreme court justice*
Recktenwald, Mark E. *state supreme court justice*

IDAHO

Boise
Burdick, Roger S. *state supreme court justice*
Eismann, Daniel T. *state supreme court chief justice*
Horton, Joel D. *state supreme court justice*
Jones, James Thomas *state supreme court justice, former state attorney general*
Jones, Warren Eugene *state supreme court justice*
McDevitt, Charles Francis *retired judge, lawyer*
Nelson, Thomas G. *federal judge*
Trott, Stephen Spangler *federal judge*

Pocatello
Smith, Norman Randy *federal judge*

ILLINOIS

Chicago
Aspen, Marvin Edward *federal judge*
Bauer, William Joseph *federal judge*
Bower, Glen Landis *judge, lawyer*
Burke, Anne M. *state supreme court justice*
Castillo, Ruben *federal judge*
Cudahy, Richard D. *federal judge*
Dow, Robert Michael, Jr. *federal judge*
Easterbrook, Frank Hoover *federal judge*
Fitzgerald, Thomas Robert *state supreme court chief justice*
Flaum, Joel Martin *federal judge*
Garman, Rita B. *state supreme court justice*
Gottschall, Joan B. *judge*
Hart, William Thomas *federal judge*
Kilbride, Thomas L. *state supreme court justice*
Leighton, George Neves *retired judge*
Leinenweber, Harry D. *federal judge*
Norgle, Charles Ronald, Sr. *federal judge*
Pallmeyer, Rebecca Ruth *judge*
Posner, Richard Allen *federal judge*
Rovner, Ilana Kara Diamond *federal judge*
Sonderby, Susan Pierson *federal judge*
Thomas, Robert R. *state supreme court justice*
Williams, Ann Claire *federal judge*
Wood, Diane Pamela *federal judge*
Zagel, James Block *federal judge*

Downers Grove
McGarr, Frank James *retired federal judge, consultant*

Nashville
Karmeier, Lloyd A. *state supreme court justice*

Peoria
Heiple, James Dee *retired state supreme court justice*

Rockford
Kapala, Frederick J. *federal judge*

Rolling Meadows
Roti, Thomas David *judge*

Skokie
Fein, Roger Gary *judge*

Springfield
Evans, Charles H. *federal judge*
Mills, Richard Henry *federal judge*

Wheaton
Leston, Patrick John *judge*

INDIANA

Boonville
Campbell, Edward Adolph *judge, electrical engineer*

Franklin
Hamner, Lance Dalton *judge*

Hammond
Van Bokkelen, Joseph Scott *federal judge, former prosecutor*

Indianapolis
Boehm, Theodore Reed *state supreme court justice*
Carlisle, Sheila A. *judge*
Dickson, Brent E. *state supreme court justice*
Foster, Kennard P. *magistrate judge*
Hamilton, David Frank *federal judge*
Lawrence, William T. *federal judge*
McKinney, Larry J. *federal judge*
Rucker, Robert D. *state supreme court justice*
Shepard, Randall Terry *state supreme court chief justice*
Sullivan, Frank, Jr. *state supreme court justice*

Kokomo
Stein, Eleanor Bankoff *retired judge*

Lafayette
Kanne, Michael Stephen *federal judge*

Lagrange
Brown, George E. *judge, educator*

New Albany
Orth, Susan Lynn *judge*

South Bend
Manion, Daniel Anthony *federal judge*
Miller, Robert L., Jr., (Bob Miller) *federal judge*
Ripple, Kenneth Francis *federal judge*
Tinder, John Daniel *federal judge*

IOWA

Cedar Rapids
Hansen, David Rasmussen *federal judge*
Melloy, Michael J. *federal judge*

Des Moines
Appel, Brent Robert *state supreme court justice, lawyer*
Baker, David L. *state supreme court justice*
Cady, Mark S. *state supreme court justice*
Carter, James Harvey *retired state supreme court justice*
Colloton, Steven M. *federal judge*
Hecht, Daryl L. *state supreme court justice*
Jarvey, John Alfred *federal judge*
Larson, Jerry Leroy *state supreme court justice*
Streit, Michael J. *state supreme court justice*
Ternus, Marsha K. *state supreme court chief justice*
Walters, Ross A. *federal judge*
Wiggins, David Stewart *state supreme court justice*
Wolle, Charles Robert *judge*

Ida Grove
Snell, Bruce M., Jr. *judge*

KANSAS

Kansas City
Lungstrum, John W. *federal judge*
Vratil, Kathryn Hoefer *federal judge*
Waxse, David John *judge*

Lawrence
Briscoe, Mary Beck *federal judge*
Tacha, Deanell Reece *federal judge*

Topeka
Beier, Carol Ann *state supreme court justice*
Biles, Dan *state supreme court justice*
Crow, Sam Alfred *judge*
Davis, Robert Edward *state supreme court chief justice*
Johnson, Lee Alan *state supreme court justice*
Luckert, Marla Jo *state supreme court justice*
Marquardt, Christel Elisabeth *judge*
Nuss, Lawton R. *state supreme court justice*
Rogers, Richard Dean *federal judge*
Rosen, Eric S. *state supreme court justice*

Wichita
Brown, Wesley Ernest *federal judge*
Melgren, Eric Franklin *federal judge, former prosecutor*

KENTUCKY

Bowling Green
Huddleston, Joseph Russell *retired judge, mediator, arbitrator*

Frankfort
Cunningham, Bill *state supreme court justice*
Minton, John Dean, Jr. *state supreme court chief justice*
Schroder, Wil *state supreme court justice*
Scott, Will T. *state supreme court justice*
Venters, Daniel Joseph *state supreme court justice*

Lexington
Noble, Mary C. *state supreme court justice*
Thapar, Amul R. *federal judge, former prosecutor*
Varellas, Sandra Motte *judge*

London
Siler, Eugene Edward, Jr. *federal judge*

Louisville
Boggs, Danny Julian *federal judge*
Heyburn, John Gilpin, II, *federal judge*
Hughes Abramson, Lisabeth *state supreme court justice*
Martin, Boyce Ficklen, Jr. *federal judge*

Madisonville
Spain, Thomas B. *retired state supreme court justice*

Paducah
Foreman, James Louis *retired judge*

Richmond
Chenault, James Stouffer *judge*

Wickliffe
Shadoan, William Lewis *retired judge*

LOUISIANA

Baton Rouge
Cole, Luther Francis *former state supreme court associate justice*
Riedlinger, Stephen C. *federal judge*

Lafayette
Davis, William Eugene *federal judge*

New Orleans
Beer, Peter Hill *federal judge*
Brown, Jerry A. *federal judge*
Clement, Edith Brown *federal judge*
Dennis, James Leon *federal judge*
Guidry, Greg G. *state supreme court justice*
Johnson, Bernette Joshua *state supreme court justice*
Kimball, Catherine D. *state supreme court chief justice*
Knoll, Jeannette Theriot *state supreme court justice*
Traylor, Chet D. *state supreme court justice*
Victory, Jeffrey Paul *state supreme court justice*
Weimer, John L. *state supreme court justice*
Wiener, Jacques Loeb, Jr. *federal judge*

Ponchatoula
Kuhn, James Edward *judge*

Shreveport
Shemwell, Robert H. *federal judge*
Stewart, Carl E. *federal judge*

MAINE

Auburn
Clifford, Robert William *state supreme court justice*

Bangor
Silver, Warren M. *state supreme court justice*

Portland
Alexander, Donald G. *state supreme court justice*
Bradford, Carl O. *judge*
Glassman, Caroline Duby *state supreme court justice*
Gorman, Ellen A. *state supreme court justice*
Levy, Jon D. *state supreme court justice*
Lipez, Kermit V. *federal judge*
McKusick, Vincent Lee *retired chief justice, arbitrator, lawyer, mediator*
Mead, Andrew M. *state supreme court justice*
Saufley, Leigh Ingalls *state supreme court chief justice*

Rockland
Collins, Samuel W., Jr. *retired judge*

MARYLAND

Accokeek
Beddow, Richard Harold *retired judge*

Annapolis
Battaglia, Lynne Ann *Judge, Maryland Court of Appeals*
Greene, Clayton, Jr. *judge, Maryland Court of Appeals*
Nolan, Theresa A. *retired judge, mediator, arbitrator*
Zarnoch, Robert Anthony *judge, lawyer, educator*

Baltimore
Bell, Robert M. *Chief Judge, Maryland Court of Appeals*
Gauvey, Susan Kathryn *judge*
Harvey, Alexander, II, *retired federal judge*
Motz, Diana Gribbon *federal judge*
Motz, John Frederick *federal judge*
Niemeyer, Paul Victor *federal judge*
Rodowsky, Lawrence Francis *retired state judge*

Bethesda
Harris, Stanley S. *retired judge*

Greenbelt
Chasanow, Howard Stuart *retired judge, mediator*
Messitte, Peter Jo *federal judge*
Titus, Roger Warren *judge*

Rockville
Barbera, Mary Ellen *state appeals court judge*

Salisbury
Adkins, Sally D. *Judge, Maryland Court of Appeals*

Towson
Murphy, Joseph F. *Judge, Maryland Court of Appeals*

Upper Marlboro
Harrell, Glenn T., Jr. *judge*

MASSACHUSETTS

Boston
Botsford, Margot *state supreme court justice*
Boudin, Michael *federal judge*
Collings, Robert Biddlecombe *judge*
Connolly, Thomas Edward *judge*
Cordy, Robert J. *state supreme court justice*
Cowin, Judith Arnold *state supreme court judge*
Dreben, Raya Spiegel *judge*
Gants, Ralph D. *state supreme court justice*
Gorton, Nathaniel M. *federal judge*
Ireland, Roderick L. *state supreme court justice*
Lasker, Morris E. *judge*
Lynch, Sandra Lea *federal judge*
Marshall, Margaret Hilary *state supreme court chief justice*
Spina, Francis X. *state supreme court justice*
Stahl, Norman H. *federal judge*
Tauro, Joseph Louis *federal judge*
Torruella, Juan R. *federal judge*
Woodlock, Douglas Preston *judge*
Zobel, Rya Weickert *federal judge*

Cambridge
Kaplan, Benjamin *judge*

Harwich Port
Smith, Ralph Wesley, Jr. *retired federal judge*

Longmeadow
Keady, George Cregan, Jr. *judge*

Springfield
Neiman, Kenneth Paul *judge*

MICHIGAN

Ann Arbor
Guy, Ralph B., Jr. *federal judge*

Bay City
Ludington, Thomas Lamson *federal judge*

Detroit
Callahan, J(ohn) William (Bill Callahan) *judge*
Corrigan, Maura Denise *state supreme court justice*
Cox, Sean F. *federal judge*
Edmunds, Nancy Garlock *federal judge*
Feikens, John *federal judge*
Keith, Damon Jerome *federal judge*
Kennedy, Cornelia Groefsema *federal judge*
Murphy, Stephen Joseph III *federal judge, former prosecutor*
Rosen, Gerald Ellis *federal judge*
Ryan, James Leo *federal judge*
Taylor, Anna Diggs *federal judge*
White, Helene Nita *federal judge*

Grand Rapids
Brenneman, Hugh Warren, Jr. *judge*
Jonker, Robert James *federal judge*
Neff, Janet T. *federal judge*
Quist, Gordon Jay *federal judge*

Kalamazoo
Enslen, Richard Alan *federal judge*
Maloney, Paul Lewis *federal judge*

Lansing
Cavanagh, Michael Francis *state supreme court justice*
Harrison, Michael Gregory *judge*
Hathaway, Diane Marie *state supreme court justice*
Kelly, Marilyn *state supreme court justice*
Markman, Stephen J. *state supreme court justice*
McKeague, David William *federal judge*
Suhrheinrich, Richard Fred *federal judge*
Young, Robert P., Jr. *state supreme court justice*

Pontiac
Andrews, Steven Nicholas *judge*

Saint Clair Shores
Hausner, John Herman *retired judge*

Traverse City
Weaver, Elizabeth A. *state supreme court justice*

Warren
Binkowski, Don *retired judge, writer*

MINNESOTA

Eden Prairie
Arthur, Lindsay Grier *retired judge, editor, writer*

Lake Elmo
Tomljanovich, Esther M. *retired judge*

Minneapolis
Alton, Ann Leslie *judge, lawyer, educator*
Doty, David Singleton *federal judge*
Hanson, Samuel Lee *former state supreme court justice*
Lebedoff, Jonathan Galanter *retired judge, mediator*
Loken, James Burton *federal judge*
Murphy, Diana E. *federal judge*
Noel, Franklin Linwood *judge*
Rosenbaum, James Michael *federal judge*

Minnetonka
Rogers, James Devitt *judge*

Plymouth
Willis, Bruce Donald *retired judge*

Saint Paul
Alsop, Donald Douglas *federal judge*
Anderson, G. Barry *state supreme court justice*
Anderson, Paul Holden *state supreme court justice*
Dietzen, Christopher J. *state supreme court justice*
Gildea, Lorie Skjerven *state supreme court justice*
Magnuson, Eric J. *state supreme court chief justice*
Meyer, Helen M. *state supreme court justice*
Page, Alan Cedric *state supreme court justice*

MISSISSIPPI

Aberdeen
Aycock, Sharion *federal judge*
Davidson, Glen Harris *federal judge*

Batesville
Carlson, George Clarence, Jr. *state supreme court justice*

Jackson
Banks, Fred Lee, Jr. *former state supreme court justice, lawyer*
Barksdale, Rhesa Hawkins *federal judge*
Chandler, David A. *state supreme court justice*
Dickinson, Jess H. *state supreme court justice*
Graves, James E. *state supreme court justice, educator*
Jolly, E. Grady *federal judge*
Kitchens, James W. *state supreme court justice*
Lamar, Ann Hannaford *state supreme court justice*
Lee, Tom Stewart *judge*
Pierce, Randy G. *state supreme court justice*
Randolph, Michael K. *state supreme court justice*
Southwick, Leslie Harburd *federal judge, lawyer*
Sugg, Robert Perkins *retired judge*
Waller, William Lowe, Jr. *state supreme court chief justice*

MISSOURI

Cape Girardeau
Limbaugh, Stephen Nathaniel, Jr. *federal judge, former state supreme court judge*

High Ridge
Karll, Jo Ann *retired judge, lawyer*

Jefferson City
Breckenridge, Patricia *state supreme court judge*
Fischer, Zel M. *state supreme court judge*
Price, William Ray, Jr. *state supreme court chief judge*
Russell, Mary Rhodes *state supreme court judge*
Stith, Laura Denvir *state supreme court judge*
Teitelman, Richard B. *state supreme court judge*
Wolff, Michael A. *state supreme court judge*

Kansas City
Benton, William Duane *federal judge*
Bowman, Pasco Middleton, II, *federal judge*
Gibson, John Robert *federal judge*
Kays, David Gregory *federal judge*
Whipple, Dean *federal judge*
Wright, Scott Olin *federal judge*

Saint Louis
Gruender, Raymond W. *federal judge, former prosecutor*
Hamilton, Jean Constance *judge*
Limbaugh, Stephen Nathaniel *retired federal judge*
Litz, Arthur *retired judge*
Noce, David D. *judge*
Rendlen, Charles Earnest, III, (Sketch Rendlen) *federal judge, lawyer*

Springfield
Parrish, John Edward *state appellate judge*

MONTANA

Billings
Fagg, Russell *judge, lawyer*
Thomas, Sidney R. *federal judge*

Glendive
McDonough, Russell Charles *retired state supreme court justice*

Helena
Cotter, Patricia O'Brien *state supreme court justice*
Leaphart, W. William *state supreme court justice*
McGrath, Mike *state supreme court chief justice, former state attorney general*
Morris, Brian *state supreme court justice*
Nelson, James C *state supreme court justice*
Rice, Jim *state supreme court justice*
Warner, John Arnan *state supreme court justice*

Polson
Turnage, Jean Allen *retired state supreme court chief justice*

NEBRASKA

Lincoln
Beam, Clarence Arlen *federal judge*
Connolly, William M. *state supreme court justice*
Gerrard, John M. *state supreme court justice*
Heavican, Michael G. *state supreme court chief justice*
McCormack, Michael *state supreme court justice*
Miller-Lerman, Lindsey *state supreme court justice*
Stephan, Kenneth C. *state supreme court justice*
Urbom, Warren Keith *federal judge*
Wright, John F. *state supreme court justice*

Omaha
Riley, William Jay *federal judge*
Strom, Lyle Elmer *judge*

NEVADA

Carson City
Agosti, Deborah Ann *retired senior justice*
Cherry, Michael A. *state supreme court justice*
Gibbons, Mark *state supreme court justice*
Hardesty, James W. *state supreme court chief justice*
Parraguirre, Ronald David *state supreme court justice*
Pickering, Kristina *state supreme court justice*
Saitta, Nancy M. *state supreme court justice*
Springer, Charles Edward *retired judge*

Las Vegas
Bybee, Jay Scott *federal judge, former federal agency administrator*
Douglas, Michael Lawrence *state supreme court justice*
Pro, Philip Martin *judge*
Rawlinson, Johnnie Blakeney *federal judge*

Reno
Brunetti, Melvin T. *federal judge*
Hug, Procter Ralph, Jr. *federal judge*
Sandoval, Brian Edward *federal judge, former state attorney general*

NEW HAMPSHIRE

Concord
Broderick, John T., Jr. *state supreme court chief justice*
Conboy, Carol Ann *state supreme court justice*
Dalianis, Linda Stewart *state supreme court justice*
DiClerico, Joseph Anthony, Jr. *federal judge*
Duggan, James E., Jr. *state supreme court justice*
Hicks, Gary Ellis *state supreme court justice*
Howard, Jeffrey R. *federal judge*
Laplante, Joseph Normand *federal judge*

NEW JERSEY

Atlantic City
Knight, Edward R. *judge, psychologist, law educator*

Camden
Brotman, Stanley Seymour *federal judge*
Hillman, Noel L. *federal judge, former prosecutor*
Laskin, Lee B. *judge, state senator*
Simandle, Jerome B. *federal judge*

Egg Harbor Township
Lashman, Shelley Bortin *retired judge*

Flemington
Buchsbaum, Peter A. *judge*

Jersey City
Curran, Barbara A. *superior court judge*

Millburn
Kuttner, Bernard A. *retired judge, lawyer, arbitrator*

Newark
Barry, Maryanne Trump *federal judge*
Cavanaugh, Dennis M. *federal judge*
Debevoise, Dickinson Richards *federal judge*
Fuentes, Julio M. *federal judge*
Garth, Leonard I. *federal judge*
Greenaway, Joseph Anthony, Jr. *judge*

Somerville
Albin, Barry Todd *state supreme court justice*

Trenton
Cowen, Robert E. *federal judge*
Greenberg, Morton Ira *federal judge*
Hoens, Helen E. *state supreme court justice*
LaVecchia, Jaynee *state supreme court justice*
Long, Virginia *state supreme court justice*
Rabner, Stuart *state supreme court chief justice, former state attorney general*
Rivera-Soto, Roberto A. *state supreme court justice*
Wallace, John E. *state supreme court justice*

NEW MEXICO

Albuquerque
Conway, John E. *federal judge*
Hansen, Curtis LeRoy *federal judge*
Hartz, Harris L *federal judge*
Parker, James Aubrey *federal judge*

Roswell
Baldock, Bobby Ray *federal judge*

Santa Fe
Chavez, Edward L. *state supreme court chief justice*
Daniels, Charles Wesley *state supreme court justice, lawyer, educator*
Kelly, Paul Joseph, Jr. *federal judge*
Maes, Petra Jimenez *state supreme court justice*
Serna, Patricio *state supreme court justice*
Vázquez, Martha Alicia *federal judge*

NEW YORK

Albany
Devine, Eugene Peter *supreme court justice*
Donohue, Mary O. *judge, former lieutenant governor*
Graffeo, Victoria A. *state appeals court judge*
Jones, Theodore T., Jr. *state appeals court judge*
Levine, Howard Arnold *judge*
Meader, John Daniel *judge*
Miner, Roger Jeffrey *federal judge*
Pigott, Eugene F., Jr. *state appeals court judge*
Read, Susan Phillips *state appeals court judge*
Smith, Robert Sherlock *state appeals court judge*

Binghamton
Peckham, Eugene Eliot *judge, lawyer*
Regenbogen, Adam *judge*

Bronx
Stadtmauer, David *judge*

Brooklyn
Block, Frederic *judge*
Garaufis, Nicholas G. *federal judge*
Glasser, Israel Leo *federal judge*
Korman, Edward Robert *federal judge*
Mann, Roanne L. *federal judge*
Matsumoto, Kiyo Ann *federal judge*
Mauskopf, Roslynn R. *federal judge, former prosecutor*
Raggi, Reena *federal judge*
Ryan, Leonard Eames *judge*
Trager, David G. *federal judge*
Vitaliano, Eric Nicholas *federal judge*
Weinstein, Jack Bertrand *federal judge*

Buffalo
Bucki, Carl Leo *judge*
Skretny, William Marion *federal judge*

Central Islip
Boyle, E. Thomas *federal judge*
Platt, Thomas Collier, Jr. *federal judge*

Garden City
Harwood, Stanley *retired judge, lawyer, arbitrator, mediator*

Mineola
Sher, Denise Linda *judge*

New York
Andrias, Richard T. *judge*
Aquilino, Thomas Joseph, Jr. *federal judge, educator*
Barzilay, Judith Morgenstern *federal judge*
Blinder, Albert Allan *judge*
Carman, Gregory Wright *federal judge*
Cedarbaum, Miriam Goldman *federal judge*
Ciparick, Carmen Beauchamp *state appeals court judge*
Cyganowski, Melanie L. *federal judge*
Eaton, Richard Kenyon *federal judge*
Feinberg, Wilfred *federal judge*
Freedman, Helen E. *judge*
Gardephe, Paul G. *federal judge*
Gerber, Robert Evan *judge*
Goldberg, Richard W. *federal judge*
Gordon, Leo Maury *federal judge*
Griesa, Thomas Poole *federal judge*
Gropper, Allan Louis *judge*
Hall, Peter W. *federal judge*
Hardin, Adlai Stevenson, Jr. *retired judge*
Jacobs, Dennis G. *federal judge*
Kaplan, Lewis A. *federal judge*
Katzmann, Robert Allen *federal judge*
Kearse, Amalya Lyle *federal judge*
Keenan, John Fontaine *federal judge*
Koeltl, John George *federal judge*
Lebovits, Gerald *judge*
Leisure, Peter Keeton *federal judge*
Leval, Pierre Nelson *federal judge*
Lippman, Jonathan *chief judge*
Livingston, Debra Ann *federal judge, educator*
Lynch, Gerard E. *federal judge*
Marrero, Victor *federal judge, lawyer*
McLaughlin, Joseph Michael *federal judge*
Meron, Theodor *judge, educator, researcher*
Musgrave, R. Kenton *federal judge*
Patterson, Robert Porter, Jr. *federal judge*
Pogue, Donald Carl *federal judge*
Rakoff, Jed Saul *federal judge, author*
Restani, Jane A. *federal judge*
Ridgway, Delissa Anne *federal judge*
Sack, Robert David *federal judge, educator*
Seibel, Cathy *federal judge*
Stanceu, Timothy Charles *federal judge*
Straub, Chester John *federal judge*
Sullivan, Richard Joseph *federal judge*
Swain, Laura Taylor *federal judge*
Tsoucalas, Nicholas *federal judge*
Wallach, Evan Jonathan *federal judge, educator*
Wesley, Richard C. *federal judge*
Wood, Kimba Maureen *federal judge*

Poughkeepsie
Dolan, Thomas Joseph *judge*
Rosenblatt, Albert Martin *retired state appeals court judge*

Rochester
Siragusa, Charles J. *judge*

Rye
Carey, John *judge*

Syracuse
McCurn, Neal Peters *federal judge*
Pooler, Rosemary S. *federal judge*
Scullin, Frederick James, Jr. *federal judge*
Suddaby, Glenn T. *federal judge, former prosecutor*

Utica
Cardamone, Richard J. *federal judge*

White Plains
Parker, Barrington D., Jr. *federal judge*

NORTH CAROLINA

Asheville
Reidinger, Martin Karl *federal judge*
Thornburg, Lacy Herman *federal judge*

Charlotte
Conrad, Robert J., Jr. *federal judge*
Horn, Carl III *retired federal judge, lawyer*
Mullen, Graham Calder *federal judge*
Whitney, Frank DeArmon *federal judge, former prosecutor*

Elizabeth City
Boyle, Terrence W. *federal judge*

Greensboro
Osteen, William Lindsay, Sr. *federal judge*
Osteen, William Lindsay, Jr. *federal judge*
Stocks, William L. *federal judge*

Greenville
Howard, Malcolm Jones *federal judge*

Raleigh
Brady, Edward Thomas *state supreme court justice*
Eagles, Sidney Smith, Jr. *retired judge*
Edmunds, Robert Holt, Jr. *state supreme court justice*
Hudson, Robin E. *state supreme court justice*
Leonard, J. Rich *federal judge, educator*
Martin, John Charles *judge*
Martin, Mark D. *state supreme court justice*
Newby, Paul Martin *state supreme court justice*
Parker, Sarah Elizabeth *state supreme court chief justice*
Timmons-Goodson, Patricia *state supreme court justice*

Randleman
Jordan, Lillian B. *judge*

Winston Salem
Eliason, Russell Allen *retired judge*
Schroeder, Thomas D. *federal judge, lawyer*

NORTH DAKOTA

Bismarck
Crothers, Daniel John *state supreme court justice*
Kapsner, Carol Ronning *state supreme court justice*
Maring, Mary Muehlen *state supreme court justice*
Sandstrom, Dale Vernon *state supreme court justice*
VandeWalle, Gerald Wayne *state supreme court chief justice*

Fargo
Bright, Myron H. *federal judge*
Bye, Kermit Edward *federal judge, lawyer*

OHIO

Akron
Bell, Samuel H. *federal judge, educator*

Chagrin Falls
O'Neill, William M. (Bill O'Neill) *former appellate judge*

Cincinnati
Clay, Eric L. *federal judge*
Cook, Deborah L. *federal judge, former state supreme court justice*
Griffin, Richard Allen *federal judge*
Hopkins, Jeffery P. *federal judge*
Kethledge, Raymond Michael *federal judge*
Perlman, Burton *judge*
Rogers, John Marshall *federal judge*
Sutton, Jeffrey S. *federal judge*
Weber, Herman Jacob *federal judge*

Cleveland
Aldrich, Ann *judge*
Boyko, Christopher Allan *federal judge*
Burke, Lillian Walker *retired judge*
Knapp, Christian Jakob *judge*
Markus, Richard M. *judge, arbitrator*
Moore, Karen Nelson *federal judge*
Rhew, Perry James *federal judge*
Wells, Lesley *federal judge*
White, Gregory A. *federal judge, former prosecutor*

Columbus
Cole, Ransey Guy, Jr. *federal judge*
Cupp, Robert Richard *state supreme court justice, former state senator, attorney*
Frye, Richard Arthur *judge*
Holschuh, John David *federal judge*
Lanzinger, Judith Ann *state supreme court justice*
Mc Cormac, John Waverly *judge*
Moyer, Thomas J. *state supreme court chief justice*
Norris, Alan Eugene *federal judge*
O'Connor, Maureen *state supreme court justice*
O'Donnell, Terrence *state supreme court justice*
Pfeifer, Paul E. *state supreme court justice*
Smith, George Curtis *judge*
Stratton, Evelyn Lundberg *state supreme court justice*

Dayton
Knapp, James Ian Keith *judge*
Petzold, John Paul *judge*

Kettering
Porter, Walter Arthur *retired judge*

Lima
Derryberry, Glenn Hollis *judge*

Lucasville
Reno, Ottie Wayne *former judge*

Sandusky
Stacey, James Allen *retired judge*

Toledo
Carr, James Gray *federal judge*
Potter, John William *federal judge*

Warren
Nader, Robert Alexander *retired judge, lawyer*

OKLAHOMA

Lawton
Moore, Roy Dean *retired judge*

Norman
Trimble, Preston Albert *retired judge*

Oklahoma City
Colbert, Thomas *state supreme court justice*
DeGiusti, Timothy D. *federal judge*
Edmondson, James E. *state supreme court chief justice*
Hargrave, Rudolph *state supreme court justice*
Henry, Robert Harlan *federal judge, former attorney general*
Holloway, William Judson, Jr. *federal judge*
Kauger, Yvonne *state supreme court justice*
Lavender, Robert Eugene *former state supreme court justice*
Leonard, Timothy Dwight *federal judge*
Moser, Eleanor T. Pendell *federal administrative law judge*
Opala, Marian Peter *state supreme court justice*
Reif, John F. *state supreme court justice*
Russell, David L. *federal judge*
Taylor, Steven W. *state supreme court justice*
Watt, Joseph Michael *state supreme court justice*
West, Lee Roy *federal judge*
Winchester, James R. *state supreme court justice*

Tulsa
Frizzell, Gregory Kent *federal judge*
Gabbard, Douglas, II, (James Gabbard) *judge*
Goodman, Jerry L(ynn) *judge*

Holmes, Jerome A *federal judge*
Kern, Terry C. *judge*
Seymour, Stephanie Kulp *federal judge*

OREGON

Eugene
Walters, Martha Lee *state supreme court justice*

Portland
Beatty, John Cabeen, Jr. *judge*
Dunn, Randall Lawson *judge*
Fisher, Ann Lewis *judge*
Graber, Susan P. *federal judge*
Jones, Robert Edward *federal judge*
Leavy, Edward *federal judge*
Mosman, Michael W. *federal judge, former prosecutor*
O'Scannlain, Diarmuid Fionntain *federal judge*
Redden, James Anthony *federal judge*
Skopil, Otto Richard, Jr. *federal judge*
Sullivan, Donal D. *federal judge*
Van Hoomissen, George Albert *state supreme court justice*

Salem
Balmer, Thomas Ancil *state supreme court justice*
De Muniz, Paul J. *state supreme court chief justice*
Durham, Robert Donald, Jr. *state supreme court justice*
Gillette, W. Michael *state supreme court justice*
Kistler, Rives *state supreme court justice*
Linde, Hans Arthur *state supreme court justice*
Linder, Virginia Lynn *state supreme court justice*
Peterson, Edwin J. *retired judge, mediator, educator*

Troutdale
Unis, Richard L. *judge*

PENNSYLVANIA

Allentown
Platt, William Henry *judge*

Duncansville
Smith, D. Brooks *federal judge*

Easton
Van Antwerpen, Franklin Stuart *federal judge*

Harrisburg
Saylor, Thomas G. *state supreme court justice*

Lansdowne
Tolliver, Elkin, Jr. *judge*

Mechanicsburg
Eakin, J. Michael *state supreme court justice*

Philadelphia
Buckwalter, Ronald Lawrence *federal judge*
Castille, Ronald D. *state supreme court chief justice*
Chagares, Michael Arthur *federal judge*
Coleman, Gerald Charles *judge, educator*
Goldberg, Mitchell Steven *federal judge*
Hardiman, Thomas Michael *federal judge*
Jones, C. Darnell, II, *federal judge, law educator*
Ludwig, Edmund Vincent *federal judge*
McCaffery, Seamus P. *state supreme court justice*
McKee, Theodore A. *federal judge*
McLaughlin, Mary A. *Federal Judge*
Nygaard, Richard Lowell *federal judge*
Reed, Lowell A., Jr. *federal judge*
Rendell, Marjorie O. *federal judge*
Scirica, Anthony Joseph *federal judge*
Shapiro, Norma Sondra Levy *federal judge*
Slomsky, Joel Harvey *federal judge*
Sloviter, Dolores Korman *federal judge*

Pittsburgh
Baer, Max *state supreme court justice*
Brosky, John G. *retired judge*
Cohill, Maurice Blanchard, Jr. *federal judge*
Diamond, Gustave *federal judge*
Fischer, Nora Barry *federal judge, lawyer*
Fisher, D. Michael *federal judge*
Fitzgerald, Judith Klaswick *federal judge*
Flaherty, John Paul, Jr. *chief justice emeritus*
Greenspan, Jane Cutler *state supreme court justice*
Ross, Eunice Latshaw *retired judge*
Standish, William Lloyd *judge*
Todd, Debra *state supreme court justice*
Weis, Joseph Francis, Jr. *federal judge*
Ziegler, Donald Emil *retired federal judge*

Scranton
Blewitt, Thomas Michael *federal judge*
O'Malley, Carlon Martin *judge*

West Chester
Griffith, Edward *judge*

Wilkes Barre
Schwartz, Roger Alan *judge*

Williamsport
McClure, James Focht, Jr. *federal judge*
Muir, Malcolm *federal judge*

RHODE ISLAND

Providence
Flaherty, Francis Xavier *state supreme court justice*
Goldberg, Maureen McKenna *state supreme court justice*
Hagopian, Jacob *federal judge*
Lagueux, Ronald Rene *federal judge*
Robinson, William Philip III *state supreme court justice*
Selya, Bruce Marshall *federal judge*
Suttell, Paul Allyn *state supreme court justice*
Williams, Frank J. *retired state supreme court chief justice, historian, writer*

Riverside
Weisberger, Joseph Robert *retired state supreme court justice*

SOUTH CAROLINA

Charleston
Sanders, Alexander Mullings, Jr. *judge*

Columbia
Beatty, Donald W. *state supreme court justice*
Currie, Cameron McGowan *federal judge*
Hamilton, Clyde Henry *federal judge*
Hearn, Kaye Gorenflo *state judge*
Kittredge, John Williamson *state supreme court justice*
Pleicones, Costa M. *state supreme court justice*
Shedd, Dennis W. *federal judge*
Toal, Jean Hoefer *state supreme court chief justice*
Waller, John Henry, Jr. *state supreme court justice*

Greenville
Simmons, Charles Bedford, Jr. *judge*
Traxler, William Byrd, Jr. *federal judge*

Greenwood
Moore, James E. *former state supreme court justice*

Myrtle Beach
Harwell, David Walker *retired judge*

Pauline
Burnett, E. C. III *former state supreme court justice*

SOUTH DAKOTA

Brookings
Gienapp, David Ray *judge*

Pierre
Gilbertson, David *state supreme court chief justice*
Konenkamp, John K. *state supreme court justice*
Meierhenry, Judith Knittel *state supreme court justice*
Severson, Glen Arthur *state supreme court justice*
Zinter, Steven L. *state supreme court justice*

Sioux Falls
Piersol, Lawrence L. *federal judge*
Wollman, Roger Leland *federal judge*

TENNESSEE

Chattanooga
Franks, Herschel Pickens *judge*
Mattice, Harry Sandlin, Jr. *federal judge, former prosecutor*

Jackson
Anderson, Stanley Thomas *federal judge*
Boswell, G(eorge) Harvey *federal judge*
Todd, James Dale *federal judge*

Knoxville
Jordan, Robert Leon *judge*
Lee, Sharon Gail *state supreme court justice, lawyer*
Murrian, Robert Phillip *retired federal judge, educator*
Wade, Gary R. *state supreme court justice*

Memphis
Broffitt, Joyce Cassandra *judge*
Donald, Bernice B. *judge*
Gibbons, Julia Smith *federal judge*
Gilman, Ronald Lee *federal judge*
Holder, Janice Marie *state supreme court justice*

Nashville
Brown, Joe Blackburn *judge*
Clark, Cornelia A. *state supreme court justice*
Daughtrey, Martha Craig *federal judge*
Echols, Robert L. *federal judge*
Koch, William C., Jr. *state supreme court justice*
Merritt, Gilbert Stroud *federal judge*
Trauger, Aleta Arthur *judge*
Wiseman, Thomas Anderton, Jr. *federal judge*

Signal Mountain
Cooper, Robert Elbert *state supreme court justice*

TEXAS

Austin
Benavides, Fortunato Pedro (Pete Benavides) *federal judge*
Brister, Scott Andrew *state supreme court justice*
Garwood, William Lockhart *federal judge*
Green, Paul Warren *state supreme court justice*
Greenhill, Joe Robert *retired judge, lawyer*
Hecht, Nathan Lincoln *state supreme court justice*
Higginbotham, Patrick Errol *federal judge*
Jefferson, Wallace B. *state supreme court chief justice*
Johnson, Philip Wayne *state supreme court justice*
Justice, William Wayne *federal judge*
Medina, David *state supreme court justice*
O'Neill, Harriet *state supreme court justice*
Owen, Priscilla Richman *federal judge, former state supreme court justice*
Pope, Andrew Jackson, Jr., (Jack Pope) *retired judge*
Ray, Cread L., Jr. *retired judge*
Wainwright, Dale V. *state supreme court justice*
Willett, Don R. *state supreme court justice*
Williams, Mary Pearl *judge*

Corpus Christi
Head, Hayden Wilson, Jr. *federal judge*

Dallas
Fish, A. Joe *federal judge*
Haynes, Catharina D. *federal judge, lawyer*
O'Connor, Reed Charles *federal judge*
Price, Robert Eben *judge*

Driftwood
Miller, Charles E. (Chuck Miller) *judge*

El Paso
Briones, David *judge*

Fort Worth
King, Steve Mason *judge, lawyer*
McBryde, John Henry *federal judge*
Means, Terry Robert *federal judge*

Houston
Atlas, Nancy Friedman *judge*
Bue, Carl Olaf, Jr. *retired federal judge*
DeMoss, Harold Raymond, Jr. *federal judge*
Elrod, Jennifer Walker *federal judge*
Hanks, George Carol, Jr. *state judge*
Hinde, Dan *judge*
Hittner, David *federal judge*
Hunter, Jack E. *Senior District Judge*
King, Carolyn Dineen *federal judge*
Miller, Gray Hampton *federal judge, lawyer*
Reavley, Thomas Morrow *federal judge*
Smith, Jerry Edwin *federal judge*
Sondock, Ruby Kless *retired judge*
Werlein, Ewing, Jr. *federal judge*

Kaufman
Tygrett, Howard Volney, Jr. *judge, lawyer*

Laredo
Kazen, George Philip *federal judge*

Mcallen
Hinojosa, Ricardo H. *federal judge*

Richmond
Elliott, Brady Gifford *judge*

San Angelo
Walther, Barbara Ann Lane *judge, former lawyer*

San Antonio
Butler, Edward Franklyn *administrative law judge, educator*
Clark, Leif Michael *federal judge*
Furgeson, William Royal *federal judge*
Garza, Emilio Miller *federal judge*

Temple
Clawson, James F., Jr. *judge, arbitrator, mediator*

Tyler
Guthrie, Judith K. *federal judge*

UTAH

Salt Lake City
Anderson, Stephen Hale *federal judge*
Benson, Dee Vance *federal judge*
Durham, Christine Meaders *state supreme court chief justice*
Durrant, Matthew B. *state supreme court justice*
Greene, John Thomas *judge*
Jenkins, Bruce Sterling *federal judge*
McConnell, Michael W. *federal judge, law educator*
McKay, Monroe Gunn *federal judge*
Murphy, Michael R. *federal judge*
Nehring, Ronald E. *state supreme court justice*
Parrish, Jill Niederhauser *state supreme court justice*
Sam, David *federal judge*
Switzer, Kathleen Henderson *administrative law judge, clinical nurse specialist*
Waddoups, Clark *federal judge*
Warner, Paul Michael *federal judge, former prosecutor*
Wilkins, Michael Jon *state supreme court justice*

VERMONT

Burlington
Sessions, William K. III *federal judge*

Montpelier
Burgess, Brian Louis *state supreme court justice*
Dooley, John Augustine III *state supreme court justice*
Gibson, Ernest Willard III *retired state supreme court justice*
Johnson, Denise Reinka *state supreme court justice*
Reiber, Paul L. *state supreme court chief justice*
Skoglund, Marilyn *state supreme court justice*

Woodstock
Billings, Franklin Swift, Jr. *federal judge*

VIRGINIA

Abingdon
Jones, James Parker *federal judge*

Alexandria
Barry, Lance Leonard *judge*
Bostetter, Martin V. B., Jr. *federal judge*
Ellis, Thomas Selby III *federal judge*
Hilton, Claude Meredith *federal judge*
O'Grady, Liam *federal judge*
Trenga, Anthony John *federal judge*

Charlottesville
Goodrich, George Herbert *retired judge*
Wilkinson, J(ames) Harvie III *federal judge*

Chesterfield
Davis, Bonnie Christell *judge*

Lynchburg
Burnette, Ralph Edwin, Jr. *judge*

Norfolk
Bonney, Hal James, Jr. *federal judge*
Davis, Mark S. *federal judge*

Richmond
Agee, G(eorge) Steven *federal judge, former state supreme court justice*
Carrico, Harry Lee *retired judge*
Dohnal, Dennis William *judge*
Goodwyn, S. Bernard *state supreme court justice*
Gregory, Roger Lee *federal judge*
Hassell, Leroy Rountree, Sr. *state supreme court chief justice*
Keenan, Barbara Milano *state supreme court justice*
Kinser, Cynthia D. *state supreme court justice*
Koontz, Lawrence L., Jr. *state supreme court justice*
Lacy, Elizabeth Bermingham *state supreme court justice*
Lemons, Donald W. *state supreme court justice*
Millette, LeRoy F., Jr. *state supreme court justice*
Tice, Douglas Oscar, Jr. *federal judge*
Williams, Richard Leroy *federal judge*

Roanoke
Turk, James Clinton *federal judge*

Staunton
Cochran, George Moffett *retired judge*

Williamsburg
O'Connor, Sandra Day *retired United States supreme court justice*

WASHINGTON

Bellevue
Andersen, James A. *retired state supreme court justice*

Olympia
Alexander, Gerry L. *state supreme court chief justice*
Chambers, Thomas Jefferson *state supreme court justice*
Fairhurst, Mary E. *state supreme court justice*
Johnson, Charles William *state supreme court justice*
Johnson, James Martin *state supreme court justice, lawyer*
Madsen, Barbara A. *state supreme court justice*
Owens, Susan *state supreme court justice*
Sanders, Richard Browning *state supreme court justice*
Smith, Charles Z. *retired state supreme court justice*
Stephens, Debra L. *state supreme court justice*

Seattle
Coughenour, John Clare *federal judge*
Dimmick, Carolyn Reaber *federal judge*
Fletcher, Betty Binns *federal judge*
Gould, Ronald Murray *federal judge*
Jones, Richard A. *federal judge*
Tallman, Richard C. *federal judge, lawyer*
Weinberg, John Lee *federal judge*
Zilly, Thomas Samuel *federal judge*

Spokane
Grant, William Joseph *retired judge*
Quackenbush, Justin Lowe *federal judge*

Tacoma
Bryan, Robert J. *federal judge*
Settle, Benjamin Hale *federal judge*

Tukwila
Talmadge, Philip Albert *retired judge, state senator*

Yakima
Suko, Lonny Ray *judge*

WEST VIRGINIA

Charleston
Benjamin, Brent D. *state supreme court chief justice, lawyer*
Brewer, Lewis Gordon *judge, educator*
Davis, Robin Jean *state supreme court justice*
Ketchum, Menis E., II, *state supreme court justice*
King, Robert Bruce *federal judge*
McHugh, Thomas Edward *state supreme court justice, lawyer*
Michael, M. Blane *federal judge*
Workman, Margaret Lee *state supreme court justice, lawyer*

Elkins
Maxwell, Robert Earl *federal judge*

Wheeling
Bailey, John Preston *federal judge, lawyer*
Johnston, Thomas E. *judge*
Stamp, Frederick Pfarr, Jr. *federal judge*

WISCONSIN

Appleton
Froehlich, Harold Vernon *judge, retired congressman*

Madison
Abrahamson, Shirley Schlanger *state supreme court chief justice*
Bradley, Ann Walsh *state supreme court justice*
Crooks, Neil Patrick *state supreme court justice*
Gableman, Michael J. *state supreme court justice*
Martin, Robert David *judge, educator*
Prosser, David Thomas, Jr. *state supreme court justice, former state legislator*
Roggensack, Patience Drake *state supreme court justice*
Shabaz, John C. *judge*
Ziegler, Annette Kingsland *state supreme court justice*

Milwaukee
Evans, Terence Thomas *federal judge*
Kessler, Joan F. *judge, lawyer*
Shapiro, James Edward *judge*
Stadtmueller, Joseph Peter *federal judge*
Sykes, Diane S. *federal judge, former state supreme court justice*

WYOMING

Cheyenne
Brimmer, Clarence Addison *federal judge*
Brorby, Wade *federal judge*
Burke, E. James *state supreme court justice, lawyer*
Golden, T. Michael *state supreme court justice*
Hill, William U. *state supreme court justice, former state attorney general*
Kite, Marilyn S. *state supreme court justice, lawyer*
O'Brien, Terrence Leo *federal judge*
Voigt, Barton R. *state supreme court chief justice*

Powell
Patrick, H. Hunter *retired judge, lawyer*

TERRITORIES OF THE UNITED STATES

AMERICAN SAMOA

Pago Pago
Kruse, F. Michael *Chief Justice, American Samoa High Court*
Richmond, Lyle L. *Associate Justice, American Samoa High Court*

GUAM

Hagatna
Carbullido, F. Philip *Associate Justice, Guam Supreme Court*
Maraman, Katherine Ann *associate justice, Guam Supreme Court*
Torres, Robert J., Jr. *Chief Justice, Guam Supreme Court*
Unpingco, John Walter Sablan *federal judge*

NORTHERN MARIANA ISLANDS

Saipan
Castro, Alexandro Cruz *commonwealth supreme court justice*
Demapan, Miguel S. *commonwealth supreme court justice*
Manglona, John A. *commonwealth supreme court justice*

PUERTO RICO

San Juan
Acosta, Raymond Luis *federal judge*
Fiol Matta, Liana *territorial supreme court justice*
Hernández Denton, Federico *territorial supreme court justice*
Kolthoff Caraballo, Erick V. *territorial supreme court justice*
Martinez Torres, Rafael L. *territorial supreme court justice*
Pabon Charneco, Mildred G. *territorial supreme court justice*
Rivera Pérez, Efraín E. *territorial supreme court justice*
Rodriguez, Annabelle *territorial supreme court justice, former attorney general*

Viejo San Juan
Casellas, Salvador E. *judge*

VIRGIN ISLANDS

Charlotte Amalie
Barnard, Geoffrey W. *judge*

Christiansted
Finch, Raymond Lawrence *judge*

St Croix
Cannon, George W., Jr. *United States Magistrate Judge, VI District Court*

St Thomas
Cabret, Maria *territorial supreme court justice*
Gomez, Curtis V. *Chief Judge, United States District Court of VI*
Hodge, Rhys S. *territorial supreme court chief justice*
Swan, Ive Arlington *territorial supreme court justice*

CANADA

ALBERTA

Calgary
Major, John Charles *judge*

Edmonton
Stevenson, William Alexander *retired justice of Supreme Court of Canada*

NEW BRUNSWICK

Fredericton
Strange, Henry Hazen *judge*

NOVA SCOTIA

Halifax
Glube, Constance Rachelle *retired judge*

ONTARIO

Bracebridge
Evans, John David Daniel *judge*

Ottawa
Binnie, William Ian Corneil *judge*
Margeson, Theodore Earl *judge*
McLachlin, Beverley *Canadian supreme court chief justice*
Strayer, Barry Lee *retired judge*

Toronto
Boland, Janet Lang *judge*
McMurtry, R. Roy *federal judge*

QUEBEC

Montreal
Bisson, Claude *retired Chief Justice of Quebec*

SASKATCHEWAN

Regina
Bayda, Edward Dmytro *retired chief justice*

MEXICO

Mexico City
Azuela Güitrón, Mariano *judge*

ARGENTINA

Buenos Aires
Petracchi, Enrique Santiago *judge*

AUSTRALIA

South Yarra
Stephen, Ninian Martin *judge*

Sydney
Brennan, Hon. Sir Gerard *judge*

CHANNEL ISLANDS

Saint Helier
Bailhache, Sir Philip Martin *judge*

ENGLAND

Norfolk
Roberts, Sir Denys (Tudor Emil) *judge*

Temple
Bingham, Thomas Henry (Lord Bingham of Cornhill) *judge*

IRELAND

Dublin
Murray, John Loyola *judge*

ITALY

Rome
Bile, Franco *judge*

MAURITIUS

Port Louis
Glover, Sir Victor Joseph Patrick *former chief justice*

NETHERLANDS

The Hague
Allison, Richard Clark *judge*
Buergenthal, Thomas *international judge*
Higgins, Dame Rosalyn *judge*
Jiuyong, Shi *judge*
Kaul, Hans-Peter *international judge*
Koroma, Abdul G. *judge*
Kourula, Erkki *international judge*
Owada, Hisashi *judge*
Parra-Aranguren, Gonzalo *judge*
Ranjeva, Raymond *judge*

REPUBLIC OF KOREA

Seoul
Song, Sang-Hyun *judge, law educator, consultant*

SPAIN

Madrid
Santiago, Francisco José Hernando *judge*

ADDRESS UNPUBLISHED

Ablard, Charles David *administrative judge*
Aboussie, Marilyn *retired judge*
Albritton, William Harold III *federal judge*
Amestoy, Jeffrey Lee *former state supreme court chief justice, educator*
Anderson, Russell A. *former state supreme court justice*
Anthony, Joan Caton *administrative judge*
Astwood, Sir James Rufus *court administrator*
Austin, John DeLong *retired judge*
Baca, Joseph Francis *retired judge*
Baer, Harold, Jr. *federal judge*
Barr, James Norman *retired federal judge*
Bartell, Angela Gina Baldi *retired judge*
Batchelder, Alice M. *federal judge*
Baynes, Thomas Edward, Jr. *retired judge, lawyer, mediator, educator*
Beezer, Robert Renaut *federal judge*
Biester, Edward George, Jr. *judge, former congressman*
Birch, Adolpho A., Jr. *retired state supreme court justice*
Black, Susan Harrell *federal judge*
Borden, David M. *former state supreme court justice*
Bosson, Richard Campbell *state supreme court justice*
Boudreau, Daniel J. *retired state supreme court justice*
Bridge, Bobbe Jean *former state supreme court justice*
Bristow, Walter James, Jr. *retired judge*
Brown, Frank R. *judge*
Brown, Michael John *retired judge*
Brown, Robert Laidlaw *state supreme court justice*
Bryner, Alexander O. *former state supreme court justice*
Buckingham, David Cowan *judge*
Butler, Louis Bennett, Jr. *former state supreme court justice*
Callow, William Grant *retired judge*
Campbell, Levin Hicks *federal judge*
Cathell, Dale Roberts *former Judge, Maryland Court of Appeals*
Chapman, Robert Foster *federal judge*
Chiechi, Carolyn Phyllis *federal judge*
Coan, Patricia A. *retired judge*
Cobb, Kay Beevers *retired state supreme court justice, state senator*
Coffey, John Louis *federal judge*
Colaianni, Joseph Vincent *judge*
Cooper, William S. *retired state supreme court justice*
Costes, George T. *retired state judge*
Couvillion, David Irvin *retired federal judge*
Cyr, Conrad Keefe *federal judge*
Dela Cruz, Jose Santos *retired commonwealth supreme court justice*
de Puget, Albert Borg Olivier *magistrate judge*
Ditter, J. William, Jr. *federal judge*
Duncan, Allyson K. *federal judge*
Edward, Sir David Alexander Ogilvy *retired judge*
Engel, Albert Joseph *retired federal judge*
Enoch, Craig Trively *retired judge*
Epstein, Judith Ann *judge*
Fagg, George Gardner *retired federal judge*
Farris, Jerome *federal judge*
Fay, Peter Thorp *federal judge*
Fitzgerald, James J. III *former state supreme court justice*
Freeman, Charles E. *state supreme court justice*
García-Valdecasas Y Fernández, Rafael *judge*
Gebelein, Richard Stephen *judge, former state attorney general*
Godbold, John Cooper *federal judge*
Gorence, Patricia Josetta *judge*
Grant, Isabella Horton *retired judge*
Gray, Karla Marie *retired state supreme court chief justice*
Grévisse, Fernand *judge*
Hamblen, Lapsley Walker, Jr. *retired judge*
Hammond, Glenn Barry, Sr. *judge, electrical engineer*
Harris, Dale Hutter *retired judge*
Hightower, Jack English *retired judge, former congressman*
Hodge, Verne Antonio *judge*
Holdaway, Ronald M. *retired federal judge*
Holland, Randy James *state supreme court justice*
Holman, Dixon Wade *retired judge*
Holmes, Dallas Scott *judge, educator*
Ingram, George Conley *judge*
Ivers, Donald Louis *retired federal judge*
Johnstone, Douglas Inge *retired state supreme court justice, lawyer*
Jones, Edith Hollan *federal judge*
Jones, Phyllis Gene *judge*
Jordan, Michelle Denise *judge*
Kehoe, L. Paul *state judge*
Kenworthy, William Eugene *judge*
Kiser, Jackson L. *federal judge*
Kline, Norman Douglas *retired judge*
Kooijmans, Pieter Hendrik *former judge*
Korinek, Karl *retired judge, law educator*
Kramer, Kenneth Bentley *retired federal judge, former congressman*
Kravitch, Phyllis A. *federal judge*
Kunkle, William Joseph *judge, lawyer*
Kyle, Richard House *federal judge*
Lake, I. Beverly, Jr. *retired state supreme court chief justice*
Lambert, Joseph Earl *retired state supreme court chief justice*
Linn, Richard *federal judge*
Lioi, Sara Elizabeth *judge*
Low, Harry William *judge*
Lyons, Champ, Jr. *state supreme court justice*
Manglona, Ramona V. *judge, former attorney general*
Mason, Thomasine Grayson *judge*
McAnulty, William E., Jr. *former state supreme court justice*
McKee, Roger Curtis *retired federal judge*
Myers, Robert David *judge*
Nelson, David Aldrich *retired federal judge*
Newbern, William David *retired state supreme court justice*
Newman, Theodore Roosevelt, Jr. *Senior Judge, DC Court of Appeals*
Nottingham, Edward Willis, Jr. *former federal judge*
Papadakos, Nicholas Peter *retired state supreme court justice*
Patterson, John Malcolm *judge, former Governor of Alabama*
Payne, Mary Libby *retired judge*
Phillips, James Dickson, Jr. *retired federal judge*
Pierce, Lawrence Warren *retired federal judge*
Pokras, Sheila Frances *retired judge*
Porter, James Morris *retired judge*
Prado, Edward Charles *federal judge*
Prather, Lenore Loving *former state supreme court chief justice*
Quillen, William Tatem *retired judge, lawyer, educator*
Raker, Irma S. *retired Judge, Maryland Court of Appeals*
Rebollo López, Francisco *retired Associate Justice, PR Supreme Court*
Reinhardt, Stephen Roy *federal judge*
Resnick, Alice Robie *retired state supreme court justice*
Rose, Robert Edgar *retired state supreme court justice*
Schwab, Howard Joel *retired judge*
Schwarzer, William W. *federal judge*
Shearing, Miriam *retired state supreme court chief justice*
Shepherd, Bobby E. *federal judge*
Shubb, William Barnet *judge*
Silberman, Laurence Hirsch *federal judge*
Sinclair, Virgil Lee, Jr. *judge, writer*
Souter, David Hackett *retired United States supreme court justice*
Spector, Rose *former state supreme court justice*
Stafford, William Henry, Jr. *federal judge*
Stanton, Louis Lee *federal judge*
Stewart, Annette *retired lawyer*
Sullivan, Eugene Raymond *federal judge*
Sypolt, Diane Gilbert *retired judge*
Thompson, Ralph Gordon *retired federal judge*
Thurmond, George Murat *judge*
Trout, Linda Copple *former state supreme court justice*
Vacchelli, Robert Francis *judge*
Waldon, Alton Ronald, Jr. *judge*
Walsh, Joseph Thomas *retired state supreme court justice*
Watson, Jack Crozier *retired state supreme court justice*
Wilson, Ronald A. *judge*
Wintersheimer, Donald Carl *retired state supreme court justice*
Wittig, Don *judge*
Wroble, Arthur Gerard *judge*

LAW: LAW PRACTICE AND ADMINISTRATION

UNITED STATES

ALABAMA

Andalusia
Fuller, William Sidney *lawyer*

Anniston
Klinefelter, James Louis *retired lawyer*

Birmingham
Alexander, James Patrick *lawyer, educator*
Baker, David Remember *lawyer*
Balch, Samuel Eason *lawyer*
Blan, Ollie Lionel, Jr. *retired lawyer*
Carmody, Richard Patrick *lawyer*
Carruthers, Thomas Neely *lawyer*
Clark, William Northington *lawyer, retired military officer*
Cohen, Ross Neil *lawyer*
Coleman, Brittin Turner *lawyer*
Cooper, N. Lee *lawyer*
Corliss, Deane Kenworthy *lawyer*

Denson, William Frank III *lawyer*
Donahue, Timothy Patrick *lawyer*
Ely, Bruce Peter *lawyer*
Farley, Joseph McConnell *lawyer*
Garner, Robert Edward Lee *lawyer*
Givhan, Robert Marcus *lawyer*
Haskell, Wyatt Rushton *lawyer*
Hawley, Gregory H. *lawyer*
Hinton, James Forrest, Jr. *lawyer*
Irons, William Lee *lawyer*
Jones, D. Paul, Jr. *lawyer, retired bank executive*
Lacy, Alexander Shelton *retired lawyer*
Langum, David John *law educator, historian*
Long, Deborah Joyce *lawyer*
Long, Thad Gladden *lawyer*
Mc Millan, George Duncan Hastie, Jr. *lawyer, former state official*
McWhorter, Hobart Amory, Jr. *lawyer*
Mills, William Hayes *lawyer*
Molen, John Klauminzer *lawyer*
Newton, Alexander Worthy *lawyer*
Palmer, Robert Leslie *lawyer*
Powell, Jerry W. *lawyer*
Rogers, Ernest Mabry *lawyer*
Rountree, Asa *lawyer*
Selfe, Edward Milton *lawyer*
Small, Clarence Merilton, Jr. *lawyer*
Stabler, Lewis Vastine, Jr. *lawyer*
Trimmier, Charles Stephen, Jr. *lawyer*
Vance, Joyce White *prosecutor*
Vinson, Laurence Duncan, Jr. *lawyer*
Warburton, Reed Thomas *lawyer*
Weaver, Dennis Russell *lawyer*
Wells, Huey Thomas, Jr. *lawyer*
Wilson, James Charles, Jr. *lawyer*
Wrinkle, John Newton *lawyer*
Wyatt, James Alexander III *lawyer*

Camden
Fendley, George W. III *lawyer*

Dothan
Baxley, Wade H. *lawyer*
Shimoda, Nick Yoshinari *lawyer*

Florence
Parker, Tina M. *lawyer*

Jacksonville
Bundrum, Kenneth Owen *lawyer, writer*

Jasper
Sparks, Nicholas B. *lawyer*

Mobile
Armbrecht, William Henry III *retired lawyer*
Braswell, Louis Erskine *lawyer*
Harris, Benjamin Harte, Jr. *lawyer*
Helmsing, Frederick George *lawyer*
Holland, Lyman Faith, Jr. *lawyer*
Pierce, Donald Fay *lawyer*
Reeves, W. Boyd *lawyer*
Roedder, William Chapman, Jr. *lawyer*

Montgomery
Beasley, Jere Locke *lawyer*
Byrne, Bradley Roberts *lawyer*
Campbell, Maria Bouchelle *lawyer, consultant*
Canary, Leura Garrett *prosecutor*
Dees, Morris Seligman, Jr. *lawyer*
Hamner, Reginald Turner *lawyer*
Hester, Douglas Benjamin *lawyer*
Kloess, Lawrence Herman, Jr. *retired lawyer*
Lawson, Thomas Seay, Jr. *lawyer, actor*
Leslie, Henry Arthur *lawyer, retired bank executive*
Lewis, Joseph Brady (Jay Lewis) *lawyer*
McElvy, James Douglas *lawyer*
McFadden, Frank Hampton *lawyer, former judge*
Northcutt, Robert F. *lawyer*
Segall, Robert D. *lawyer*
Wood, James Jerry *lawyer*

Opelika
Samford, Yetta Glenn, Jr. *lawyer, director*

Point Clear
Holt, Thaddeus *lawyer*

Rainsville
Huntley, Daphne White *lawyer*

Troy
Moten, Sebrena R. *law educator*

Tuscaloosa
Cook, Camille Wright *retired law educator*
Smalley, Donna Wesson *lawyer, educator*
Smith, Ralph Harrison, II, *lawyer*
Weeks, Lillian Durrett *law librarian*
Wilson, William Roberts, Jr., (Bob Wilson) *lawyer*

ALASKA

Anchorage
Berkowitz, Ethan A. *lawyer, former state representative*
Brown, Keith E. *lawyer*
Butler, Rex Lamont *lawyer*
Cantor, James Elliot *lawyer*
Claman, Matthew W. *lawyer, acting Mayor, Anchorage*
De Lisio, Stephen Scott *lawyer, director, pastor*
Ealy, Jonathan Bruce *lawyer*
Fleischer, Hugh William *lawyer*
Grahame, Heather H. *lawyer*
Katcher, Jonathon A. *lawyer*
Kendall-Miller, Heather *lawyer*
Lerman, Averil *lawyer, historian*
Loeffler, Karen Louise *prosecutor*
Roberts, John Derham *lawyer*

Bethel
Owen, Lauri J. *lawyer*

Kodiak
Jamin, Matthew Daniel *lawyer, judge*

ARIZONA

Bisbee
Moreno, Patricia Frazier *lawyer*

Carefree
Putney, Mark William *lawyer, utilities executive*
Whittington, Thomas Lee *lawyer*

Flagstaff
Pickett, A. Dean *lawyer*

Fountain Hills
Berg, Madelaine R. *lawyer*

Kingman
Basinger, Richard Lee *lawyer*

Marana
O'Shaughnessy, James Patrick *lawyer, consultant*

Paradise Valley
Tubman, William Charles *lawyer*

Phoenix
Allen, Robert Eugene Barton *lawyer*
Atkinson, Joseph Matthew *lawyer*
Baker, William Dunlap *lawyer*
Bakker, Thomas Gordon *lawyer*
Beauchamp, David George *lawyer*
Begam, Robert George *lawyer*
Birk, David R. *lawyer, electronics executive*
Bivens, Donald Wayne *lawyer, political organization administrator*
Bodney, David Jeremy *lawyer*
Burke, Timothy John *lawyer*
Case, David Leon *lawyer*
Coghill, William Thomas, Jr. *retired lawyer*
Cohen, Jon Stephan *lawyer*
Comus, Louis Francis, Jr. *lawyer*
Conant, Paul Allen *lawyer*
Crozier, Scott A. *lawyer*
Davies, David George *lawyer, educator*
Dawson, John Joseph *lawyer*
Derdenger, Patrick *lawyer*
Donovan, Timothy R. *lawyer*
Ehmann, Anthony Valentine *lawyer*
Everroad, John David *lawyer*
Falck, David Phillip *lawyer, utilities executive*
Fellows, Gerald Lee *lawyer*
Fenzl, Terry Earle *lawyer*
Galbut, Martin Richard *lawyer*
Gallagher, Michael L. *lawyer*
Goldstein, Stuart Wolf *lawyer*
Gomez, David Frederick *lawyer*
Grant, Merwin Darwin *lawyer*
Grimwood, Helen Perry *lawyer*
Halpern, Barry David *lawyer*
Hardwick, Catherine R. *lawyer*
Harrison, Mark I. *lawyer*
Hay, John Leonard *lawyer*
Hayden, William Robert *lawyer*
Hicks, William Albert III *lawyer*
Hoecker, Thomas Ralph *lawyer*
Howard, William Matthew *arbitrator, lawyer, writer*
Huntwork, James Roden *lawyer*
Itkin, Robert Jeffrey *lawyer*
Jakubczyk, John Joseph *lawyer*
James, Charles E., Jr. *lawyer*
Jirauch, Charles W. *lawyer*
Johnson, Christopher D. *lawyer*
Kant, Robert S. *lawyer*
Klahr, Gary Peter *retired lawyer*
Klausner, Jack Daniel *lawyer*
Knoller, Guy David *lawyer*
Kurn, Neal *lawyer*
LaVoy, Christopher Alan *lawyer*
Levetown, Robert Alexander *lawyer*
Lubin, Stanley *lawyer*
Martori, Joseph Peter *lawyer*
Mast, Gregory Lewis *lawyer*
McAuliffe, Daniel Joseph *lawyer*
McKellips, Gordon Wayne, Jr. *lawyer, land developer*
McMillan, Lee Richards, II, *lawyer, mining executive*
McRae, Hamilton Eugene III *lawyer*
Mitchell, Robert D. *lawyer*
Olsen, Alfred Jon *lawyer*
O'Steen, Van *lawyer*
Perry, Lee Rowan *retired lawyer*
Petitti, Michael Joseph, Jr. *lawyer*
Pietzsch, Michael Edward *lawyer*
Placenti, Frank Michael *lawyer*
Platt, Warren E. *lawyer*
Price, Charles Steven *lawyer*
Rathwell, Peter John *lawyer*
Refo, Patricia Lee *lawyer*
Rivera, Jose de Jesus *lawyer*
Rose, David L. *lawyer*
Rudolph, Gilbert Lawrence *lawyer*
Sanders, Barry R. *lawyer*
Sherk, Kenneth John *lawyer*
Short, Dean C., II, *lawyer*
Silverman, Alan Henry *lawyer*
Simes, Michael Louis *lawyer*
Storey, Norman C. *lawyer*
Tennen, Leslie Irwin *lawyer, consultant*
Thompson, Terence William *lawyer*
Ulrich, Paul Graham *lawyer, writer, editor*
Wall, Donald Arthur *lawyer*
Wilenchik, Dennis I. *lawyer*
Williams, Quinn Patrick *lawyer*
Wirken, Charles William *lawyer*
Wolf, G. Van Velsor, Jr. *lawyer*
Yarnell, Michael Allan *mediator, arbitrator, law educator*

Scottsdale
Buri, Charles Edward *lawyer*
Calise, Nicholas James *lawyer*
Crawford, Robert F. *lawyer*
Everett, James Joseph *lawyer*
Hittner, George J. *lawyer*
Hutchison, Stanley Philip *retired lawyer*
Inman, William Peter *lawyer*
Krupp, Clarence William *lawyer, health facility administrator*
Lindgren, D(erbin) Kenneth, Jr. *retired lawyer*
Lord, Robert James *lawyer*
Lowry, Edward Francis, Jr. *lawyer*
Marks, Merton E. *lawyer, international arbitrator, mediator, consultant*
Overgaard, Cordell Jersild *lawyer, rancher, director*
Peshkin, Samuel David *retired lawyer*
Smith, David Burnell *lawyer, state legislator*
Walker, Richard K. *lawyer*

Sun City
Keesling, Karen Ruth *lawyer*

Sun Lakes
Glein, Richard Jeriel, Sr. *lawyer*

Surprise
Hayes, Ray, Jr. *lawyer*

Tempe
Andrews, Steven R. *lawyer*
Gaffney, John T. *lawyer*
Johnson, Stephen L. *lawyer, transportation executive*
Matheson, Alan Adams *law educator*
Spritzer, Ralph Simon *lawyer, educator*

Tucson
Amhowitz, Harris J. *lawyer, educator*
Bainton, Denise Marlene *lawyer*
Blackman, Lee L. *lawyer*
Christiano, Thomas Dominic *law educator*
Dobbs, Dan Byron *lawyer, educator*
Esposito, Joseph Louis *lawyer*
Feldman, Stanley George *lawyer*
Froman, Sandra Sue *lawyer*
Gantz, David Alfred *law educator, academic administrator*
Grand, Richard D. *lawyer*
Kozolchyk, Boris *law educator, consultant*
Kuklin, Susan Beverly *lawyer, librarian, educator*
Mc Donald, John Richard *lawyer*
Meehan, Michael Joseph *lawyer*
Morrow, James Franklin *lawyer*
Noonan, James C. *lawyer, mediator, arbitrator*
O'Leary, Thomas Michael *lawyer*
Pace, Thomas M. *lawyer*
Rose, Carol Marguerite *law educator*
Samet, Dee-Dee *lawyer*
Schorr, S. L. *lawyer*
Spaeth, Jan Mills *jury consultant*
Staubitz, Arthur Frederick *retired lawyer, health products executive*
Strong, John William *lawyer, educator*
Sweeney, Joseph Dudley *law educator, political organization worker*
Tindall, Robert Emmett *lawyer, educator*
Weiss, Stephen M. *lawyer*

Yuma
Hossler, David Joseph *lawyer, educator*
Smith, Jimmie Dee *lawyer*

ARKANSAS

Ashdown
Finley, John Cyrus III *lawyer, judge*

Benton
Krueger, Marlo Bush *retired lawyer*

Conway
Johnson, James Douglas (Jim Johnson) *lawyer*

El Dorado
Cossé, Steven A. *lawyer, oil industry executive*

Fayetteville
Epley, Lewis Everett, Jr. *lawyer*
Kester, Charles Melvin *lawyer*

Fort Smith
Cooper, Richard F. *lawyer*
Horton, William Gene *lawyer*
Meadors, C. Brian *lawyer*

Helena
Roscopf, Charles Buford *lawyer*

Hot Springs
Drake, Joshua *lawyer*
Miller, Gary C. *lawyer*

Hot Springs National Park
Schnipper, Don Martin *lawyer*

Jonesboro
Deacon, John C. *lawyer*

Little Rock
Allen, H(enry) William *lawyer*
Anderson, Philip Sidney *lawyer*
Boe, Myron Timothy *lawyer*
Burchfield, Jessie Wallace *law librarian*
Cross, J. Bruce *lawyer*
Duke, Jane W. *prosecutor*
Eubanks, Gary Leroy, Sr. *lawyer*
Gunter, Russell Allen *lawyer*
Haught, William Dixon *lawyer, writer*
Hoover, Paul Williams, Jr. *lawyer*
Lemke, Judith A. *lawyer*
Lipe, Linda Bon *lawyer*
Massey, Richard N. *lawyer, telecommunications industry executive*
May, Ronald Alan *lawyer*
Murphey, Arthur Gage, Jr. *law educator*
Nelson, Edward Sheffield *lawyer, retired utilities executive*
Prince, David Cannon *lawyer*
Schroeder, Paul J., Jr. *lawyer*
Sherman, William Farrar *lawyer, former state legislator*
Stockburger, Jean Dawson *lawyer*
Terry, William Leake *lawyer*
Trice, William Henry III *lawyer*
Ursery, Frederick Stanley *lawyer*
Witherspoon, Carolyn Brack *lawyer*

Malvern
Dodd, Jerry Lee *lawyer*

Monticello
Ball, William Kenneth *lawyer*

North Little Rock
Patty, Claibourne Watkins, Jr. *lawyer*
Welch, Morgan E. *lawyer*

Pine Bluff
Sims, David Lloyd *lawyer*
Strode, Joseph Arlin *lawyer*

Rogers
Balfe, Robert Cramer III *lawyer, former prosecutor*

Searcy
Hughes, Teresa Lee *lawyer, educator*

Warren
Claycomb, Hugh Murray *lawyer, writer*

CALIFORNIA

Agoura Hills
Lingl, James Peter *lawyer, mediator*

Alameda
Stonehouse, James Adam *lawyer*

Alamo
Madden, Palmer Brown *lawyer*
Schreiber, John T. *lawyer*

Alhambra
Determan, John David *lawyer*

Alta Loma
Klein, Henry *lawyer*

Arroyo Grande
Saari, David John *retired law educator*

Atascadero
Colamarino, Katrin Belenky *lawyer, consultant*

Atherton
Ferris, Robert Albert *lawyer, venture capitalist*

Belvedere Tiburon
Stotter, Lawrence Henry *lawyer*

Berkeley
Arguedas, Cristina Claypoole *lawyer*
Berring, Robert Charles, Jr. *law educator, librarian, association administrator*
Buxbaum, Richard M. *lawyer, educator*
Campbell, Tom *law and business professor, former dean, congressman*
Caron, David Dennis *lawyer, educator*
Choper, Jesse Herbert *law educator, dean*
Ginger, Ann Fagan *lawyer*
Halbach, Edward Christian, Jr. *law educator*
Haley, George Patrick *lawyer*
Kadish, Sanford Harold *law educator*
Kay, Herma Hill *law educator*
McNulty, John Kent *lawyer, educator*
Meador, Ross DeShong *lawyer*
Moran, Rachel *law educator*
Scheiber, Harry N. *law educator, historian*
Seligman, Brad *lawyer*
Traynor, J. Michael *retired lawyer*
Wolfram, Charles William *law educator*
Woodhouse, Thomas Edwin *lawyer, trust company administrator*
Yoo, John Choon *law educator, former federal agency administrator*
Zimring, Franklin E. *lawyer, educator*

Beverly Hills
Blumenfeld, Eli *lawyer*
Bordy, Michael Jeffrey *lawyer*
Brockovich-Ellis, Erin *legal researcher*
Burns, Marvin Gerald *lawyer*
Clark, Marcia Rachel *former prosecutor*
Donaldson, Michael Cleaves *lawyer*
Hogan, Steven L. *lawyer*
Jaffe, F. Filmore *lawyer, retired judge*
Kaufman, Robert *lawyer*
Newman, Jeanne *lawyer*
Opri, Debra Ann *lawyer*
Ramer, Bruce M. *lawyer*
Schiff, Gunther Hans *lawyer*
Sobelle, Richard E. *lawyer*

Bodega Bay
Sorensen, Linda *lawyer*

Burbank
Brandis, Bernardine *lawyer*
Braverman, Alan N. *lawyer*

Burlingame
Cotchett, Joseph Winters *lawyer, writer*
McCloskey, Pete (Paul Norton McCloskey Jr.) *lawyer, former congressman*

Calabasas
Geckle, Timothy J. *lawyer*

Samuels, Sandor Eli *lawyer, diversified financial services company executive*
Tarr, Ralph William *lawyer, former federal government official*
van Schoonenberg, Robert G. *lawyer, consumer products company executive*

Carlsbad
Hanscom, Eric Alan *lawyer*
Mezzullo, Louis Albert *lawyer*

Chico
Jacobs, Douglas Bram *law educator, attorney*

Chino Hills
Lipinsky, Daren H. *lawyer*

City Of Industry
Padilla, James G. *paralegal*

Claremont
Ansell, Edward Orin *lawyer*
Ferguson, Cleve Robert *lawyer, educator*
Kury, Bernard Edward *lawyer*

Clayton
Rainey, William Joel *lawyer*

Coachella
Trover, Ellen Lloyd *lawyer, rancher, art dealer*

Coalinga
Frame, Ted Ronald *lawyer*

Concord
Borson, Daniel Benjamin *lawyer, educator*
Moyal, Maurice *lawyer, former accounting and business law educator*

Corona Del Mar
Allen, Russell G. *lawyer*

Coronado
Herman, Stephen Charles *lawyer*
Herring, Charles David *lawyer, educator*
Raushenbush, Walter Brandeis *retired law educator*

Costa Mesa
Anderson, Jon David *lawyer*
Caldwell, Courtney Lynn *lawyer, real estate consultant*
Daniels, James Walter *lawyer*
Jones, H(arold) Gilbert, Jr. *lawyer*
Marshall, Ellen Ruth *lawyer*
Mooradian, George T. *lawyer*
Samet, Jack I. *lawyer*
Schaaf, Douglas Allan *lawyer*

Crescent City
Owen, Thomas Sumner *lawyer*

Culver City
Nicholas, Frederick M. *lawyer*
Roberts, Virgil Patrick *lawyer, judge*

Cupertino
Courville, Arthur F. *lawyer*
Jelinch, Frank Anthony *lawyer*
Svalya, Phillip Gordon *lawyer*
Wildman, Iris J. *retired law librarian*

Cypress
Olschwang, Alan Paul *lawyer, crossword and variety puzzle author*

Dana Point
Mallory, Frank Linus *lawyer*

Danville
Candland, D. Stuart *lawyer*

Darwin
Palazzo, Robert Paul *lawyer, accountant*

Davis
Bruch, Carol Sophie *law educator*
Feeney, Floyd Fulton *law educator*
Imwinkelried, Edward John *law educator*
Perschbacher, Rex Robert *law educator*
Poulos, Joan Graham *lawyer*
Wydick, Richard Crews *lawyer, educator*

Del Mar
Seitman, John Michael *arbitrator, mediator, lawyer*

Diablo
Burnison, Boyd Edward *lawyer*

Diamond Bar
Knox Rios, Delilah Jane *lawyer*

East Palo Alto
Bates, William III *lawyer*
Schelling, Donald Lawrence *lawyer*

El Cajon
Graf, Sheryl Susan *lawyer*

El Segundo
Muhlbach, Robert Arthur *lawyer*
Normile, Robert J. *lawyer, consumer products company executive*
Pruetz, Adrian Mary *lawyer*

Encino
Lambirth, Timothy A. *attorney*
Rose, I. Nelson *lawyer, educator*
Smith, Selma Moidel *lawyer, composer*

Escondido
Guinn, Stanley Willis *retired lawyer*

Fair Oaks
Betts, Barbara Lang *lawyer, real estate agent, rancher*

Foster City
Karnazes, Elizabeth Marie Barnson *lawyer, photojournalist travel agency owner*

Fremont
Chien-Hale, Elizabeth *lawyer*
Leung, Simon *lawyer, electronics executive*
Stinnett, Terrance LLoyd *lawyer*

Fresno
Berman, Richard P. *lawyer*
Lagle, John Franklin *retired lawyer*
Lambe, James Patrick *lawyer*
Reinhardt, LeRoy Jacob *lawyer*

Fullerton
Frizell, Samuel *law educator*
Steinmeyer, Robert Jay *retired lawyer*

Glendale
Hoffman, Donald M. *lawyer*
Jones, William Allen *retired lawyer*
Kazanjian, Phillip Carl *lawyer, educator*
Martinetti, Ronald Anthony *lawyer*
Stevens, Steve J. *lawyer*

Gold River
Andrew, John Henry *lawyer, writer*

Grass Valley
Sutton, John Paul *lawyer*

Greenbrae
Bonapart, Alan David *lawyer*

Half Moon Bay
Lambert, Frederick William *lawyer, educator*

Hayward
Beck, Edward William *lawyer*

Hercules
Richards, Gerald Thomas *lawyer, educator, writer*

Hillsborough
Mitchell, Bruce Tyson *lawyer*

Hollywood
Luti, Anthony Ngula *lawyer*

Huntington Beach
Baroni, Michael L. *lawyer*
Garrels, Sherry Ann *lawyer*
Jensen, Dennis Lowell *lawyer*

Imperial Beach
Merkin, William Leslie *retired lawyer*

Indian Wells
McDermott, Thomas John, Jr. *lawyer*
Reuben, Don *lawyer*

Irvine
Aitken, Ashleigh E. *lawyer*
Bastiaanse, Gerard C. *lawyer*
Chong, Arthur *lawyer*
Christensen, Becky Vanderhoof *lawyer*
Dull, David A. *lawyer*
Grabowski, Richard Joseph *lawyer*
Huang, Wendy Wan-Juoh *lawyer*
Ingram, Douglas Stephen *lawyer*
Lowe, Kathlene Winn *lawyer*
Re, Joseph R. *lawyer*
Rooklidge, William Charles *lawyer*
Specter, Richard Bruce *lawyer*
Sunshine, Steven H. *lawyer*
Tachner, Leonard *lawyer*
Wine, Mark Philip *lawyer*
Wintrode, Ralph Charles *lawyer*

Jamul
Newmeyer, Robert J. *lawyer*

La Canada Flintridge
Costello, Francis William *lawyer*

La Jolla
Buchholz, Debby *lawyer*
Kirchheimer, Arthur E(dward) *lawyer, business executive*
Mayer, James Hock *lawyer, mediator*
Morgens, Warren Kendall *retired lawyer*
Wilkins, Floyd, Jr. *retired lawyer*
Wilson, Bonnie Jean *lawyer, educator, investor*
ZoBell, Karl *lawyer*

Lafayette
Davies, Paul Lewis, Jr. *retired lawyer*
Freeman, Tom M. *lawyer*
Sherrer, Charles William *lawyer, writer*

Laguna Beach
Simons, Barry Thomas *lawyer*

Laguna Hills
Beard, Ronald Stratton *lawyer*
DeGrave, Douglas Michael *lawyer*
Reinglass, Michelle Annette *lawyer, mediator, arbitrator*

Laguna Niguel
Pollock, John Phleger *retired lawyer*

Lake Forest
Bukaty, Raymond M. *lawyer*

Larkspur
Greenberg, Myron Silver *lawyer*

Ratner, David Louis *retired law educator*

Long Beach
Calhoun, John R. *lawyer*
Deukmejian, George *lawyer, Former Governor, California*
Fradella, Henry F. *law educator*
Schultz, Gary David *lawyer*
Wise, George Edward *lawyer*

Los Altos
Miller, Thormund Aubrey *lawyer*
Yang, Roxana Hwu *lawyer, investor*

Los Angeles
Abrams, Norman *retired law educator, former academic administrator*
Adams, Thomas Merritt *lawyer*
Adell, Hirsch *lawyer*
Adler, Erwin Ellery *lawyer*
Allred, Gloria Rachel *lawyer*
Alves, Rodney Almeida *lawyer, consultant*
Anderson, Joshua E. *lawyer*
Aronoff, Vera *law librarian*
Aronzon, Paul S. *lawyer*
Austen, Karl Ramsdell *lawyer*
Azad, Susan Stott *lawyer*
Bakaly, Charles George, Jr. *lawyer, mediator*
Barrett, Jane Hayes *lawyer*
Barton, Alan Joel *lawyer*
Baum, Michael Lin *lawyer*
Baumann, Richard Gordon *lawyer*
Baumgarten, Ronald Neal *lawyer*
Bender, Charles William *lawyer*
Bendix, Helen Irene *lawyer*
Bennett, Fred Gilbert *lawyer*
Berk, Blair *lawyer*
Berman, Myles Lee *lawyer*
Bibicoff, Hillary Sue *lawyer*
Biele, Hugh Irving *retired lawyer*
Blencowe, Paul Sherwood *lawyer, private investor*
Bloom, Alan *lawyer*
Bodkin, Henry Grattan, Jr. *lawyer*
Bonesteel, Michael John *lawyer*
Bonner, Robert Cleve *lawyer*
Borkowski, George Myron *lawyer*
Boxer, Lester *lawyer*
Boyle, Kevin Richard *lawyer*
Bradley, Lawrence D., Jr. *lawyer*
Branca, John Gregory *lawyer, consultant*
Braun, Harland W. *lawyer*
Bressan, Paul Louis *lawyer*
Bryan, Greyson *lawyer*
Bugliosi, Vincent T. *lawyer, writer*
Burch, Robert Dale *lawyer*
Burke, Robert Bertram *lawyer, political scientist, lobbyist*
Butler, James Robertson, Jr. *lawyer*
Byrd, Christine Waterman Swent *lawyer*
Capron, Alexander Morgan *lawyer, educator, bioethicist*
Carr, Willard Zeller, Jr. *retired lawyer*
Carrey, Neil *lawyer, educator*
Castro, Leonard Edward *lawyer*
Chadwick, William Jordan *lawyer*
Chang, Cyndie Marie *lawyer*
Chen, Tony Dong *lawyer*
Chiate, Kenneth Reed *lawyer*
Christol, Carl Quimby *lawyer, political science professor*
Christopher, Warren Minor *lawyer, former United States Secretary of State*
Chu, Morgan *lawyer*
Clark, R(ufus) Bradbury *lawyer, director*
Cohen, Cynthia Marylyn *lawyer*
Collier, Charles Arthur, Jr. *lawyer*
Cooley, Steve *prosecutor*
Cooper, Robert E. *lawyer*
Coupe, James Warnick *lawyer*
Coyne, Joseph Francis, Jr. *lawyer*
Crabtree-Ireland, Duncan *lawyer*
Curtiss, Thomas, Jr. *lawyer*
Daniels, John Peter *lawyer*
Darden, Christopher Allen *lawyer, writer*
Davis, Gray (Joseph Graham Davis) *lawyer, former governor*
De Brier, Donald Paul *lawyer, oil industry executive*
Decker, Richard Jeffrey *lawyer*
Demoff, Marvin Alan *lawyer*
Denham, Robert Edwin *lawyer*
Diamond, Stanley Jay *lawyer*
Dienes, Louis Robert *lawyer*
Dinel, Richard Henry *lawyer*
Dodd, Jan Eve *lawyer*
Drooyan, Richard E. *lawyer*
Eatman, Louis Perkins *lawyer*
Edelman, Scott Alan *lawyer*
Fairbank, Robert Harold *lawyer*
Farmer, Robert Lindsay *lawyer*
Feigen, Brenda S. *lawyer, film producer, writer*
Fein, Ronald Lawrence *lawyer*
Feldman, Larry Robert *lawyer*
Feldman, Lewis G. *lawyer*
Felker, Patti C. *lawyer*
Fenning, Lisa Hill *lawyer, mediator, retired judge*
Fields, Bertram Harris *lawyer*
Finnegan, Michael J. *lawyer*
Fisher, Ruth E. *lawyer*
Foley, Martin James *lawyer*
Follick, Edwin Duane *law educator, dean, chiropractor*
Foust, Lawrence L. *lawyer*
Fragner, Matthew Charles *lawyer*
Francis, Merrill Richard *lawyer*
Freier, Elliot G. *lawyer*
Fujie, Holly J. *legal association administrator, lawyer*
Galton, Stephen Harold *lawyer*
Garbacz, Gregory A. *lawyer*
Garofalo, Ellyn S. *lawyer*
Geragos, Mark John *lawyer*
Gest, Howard David *lawyer*
Girardi, Thomas Vincent *lawyer*
Glaser, Patricia L. *lawyer*
Goldman, Allan Bailey *lawyer*
Goldman, Donald Aaron *lawyer*
Goldman, Ronald L.M. *lawyer*
Goldsman, Melvin Saul *lawyer*
Goodman, Max A. *lawyer, educator*
Gorman, Joseph Gregory, Jr. *lawyer*
Graves, Anna Marie *lawyer*
Green, William Porter *lawyer*
Greenberg, Gordon Alan *lawyer*
Grobe, Charles Stephen *lawyer, accountant*
Gurfein, Peter J. *lawyer*
Halberstadter, David *lawyer*
Halkett, Alan Neilson *lawyer*
Hansell, Dean *lawyer*
Hanson, John J. *retired lawyer*
Harkness, Nancy P. *lawyer*
Havel, Richard W. *lawyer*
Heinke, Rex S. *lawyer*
Heller, Philip *lawyer*
Hemminger, Pamela Lynn *lawyer*
Hinojosa, Lynard Chris *lawyer*
Holliday, Thomas Edgar *lawyer*
Holscher, Mark Charles *lawyer*
Holtzman, Robert Arthur *lawyer*
Hooper, Patric *lawyer*
Hufstedler, Shirley Mount *lawyer, former United States Secretary of Education*
Husar, Linda S. *lawyer*
Hyman, Ursula H. *lawyer*
Irwin, Philip Donnan *lawyer*
Jackson, Alan Jay *prosecutor*
Johnson, Jonathan Edwin, II, *lawyer*
Jordan, Robert Leon *lawyer, educator*
Kagan Bierman, Ivy *lawyer*
Kamine, Bernard S. *lawyer*
Kanoff, Mary Ellen *lawyer*
Kanter, Sandra May *lawyer*
Kaplan, Mark Vincent *lawyer*
Karst, Kenneth Leslie *law educator*
Katzenstein, Andrew M. *lawyer*
Kieffer, George David *lawyer*
Kiley, Anne Campbell *lawyer*
Kirkland, John C. *lawyer*
Klein, Deborah L. *lawyer*
Klinger, Marilyn Sydney *lawyer*
Krupka, Robert George *lawyer*
Kveton, Kyle *lawyer*
Langan, Kenneth J. *lawyer*
Lappen, Chester I. *lawyer*
Latham, Joseph Al, Jr. *lawyer*
Lawler, Jean Marie *lawyer*
Layne, Jonathan K. *lawyer*
Lesser, Joan L. *lawyer*
Letwin, Leon *law educator*
Leung, Frankie Fook-Lun *lawyer*
Levine, Marci Robyn *lawyer*
Levy, Seth David *lawyer*
Lichter, Linda *lawyer*
Lindholm, Dwight Henry *lawyer*
Lipsig, Ethan *lawyer*
Long, Gregory Alan *lawyer*
MacLaughlin, Francis Joseph *lawyer*
Mancino, Douglas Michael *lawyer*
Marder, John Adam *lawyer*
Margo, Rod David *lawyer*
Marmorstein, Victoria E. *lawyer*
Martinez, Vilma Socorro *lawyer*
McKinzie, Carl Wayne *lawyer*
McLane, Frederick Berg *lawyer*
McLurkin, Thomas Cornelius, Jr. *lawyer*
McNevin, Christopher J. *lawyer*
Meaders, Donald W. *lawyer*
Medearis, Miller *lawyer*
Melby, Donna D. *lawyer*
Mesereau, Thomas Arthur, Jr. *lawyer*
Meshki, Hamed *lawyer*
Metzger, Robert Streicher *lawyer*
Meyer, Bruce D. *lawyer*
Meyer, Michael Edwin *lawyer*
Midler, Laurence H. (Larry) *lawyer, real estate company executive*
Millard, Neal Steven *lawyer, educator*
Miller, Milton Allen *lawyer*
Modabber, Zia F. *lawyer*
Morrissey, J. Richard *lawyer*
Murray, Anthony *lawyer*
Nachshin, Robert Jay *lawyer*
Neiter, Gerald Irving *lawyer*
Newman, Michael Rodney *lawyer*
Nicholas, William Richard *lawyer*
Nochimson, David *lawyer*
Nordlinger, Stephanie G. *lawyer*
O'Brien, Robert Charles *lawyer*
O'Brien, Thomas Peter *lawyer, former prosecutor*
Ochoa, Arthur J. *lawyer, hospital administrator*
O'Connell, Kevin *lawyer*
O'Leary, Prentice Lee *retired lawyer*
Oliver, Dale Hugh *lawyer*
Olson, Ronald Leroy *lawyer*
Oppenheim, Charles B. *lawyer*
Oppenheimer, Randy (Mark Randall Oppenheimer) *lawyer*
Ordin, Andrea Sheridan *lawyer*
Owen, Michael Lee *lawyer*
Owens, Stephen Thomas *lawyer*
Palmieri, Victor Henry *lawyer, director, investment advisor*
Panish, Brian Joseph *lawyer*
Parsky, Gerald Lawrence *lawyer*
Pascotto, Alvaro *lawyer*
Pasich, Kirk Alan *lawyer*
Perlis, Michael Fredrick *lawyer*
Perron, Edward Adrian *lawyer*
Perry, Ralph Barton III *lawyer*
Pesta, Ben W., II, *lawyer, writer*
Peterson, Kurt C. *lawyer*
Petrocelli, Daniel M. *lawyer*
Phillips, Stacy D. *lawyer*
Pircher, Leo Joseph *lawyer, director*
Porter, Verna Louise *lawyer*
Power, John Bruce *lawyer*
Pugsley, Robert Adrian *law educator*
Quinn, John B. *lawyer*
Quinn, John J. *lawyer*
Racine, Scott H. *lawyer*
Rath, Howard Grant, Jr. *lawyer*
Renwick, Edward S. *lawyer*
Richland, Kent Lewis *lawyer*

Riff, Lawrence P. *lawyer*
Rigole, Rose Hickman *lawyer*
Rishwain, James Michael, Jr. *lawyer*
Rosenthal, Sol *lawyer*
Rosett, Arthur Irwin *lawyer, educator*
Ross, Bruce Shields *lawyer*
Rothenberg, Alan I. *lawyer, professional sports association executive*
Rustand, Kay *lawyer*
Ruthberg, Miles N. *lawyer*
Sager, Kelli L. *lawyer*
Saxe, Deborah Crandall *lawyer*
Schwartz, Robert M. *lawyer*
Seto, Theodore Paul *lawyer, educator*
Shacter, David Mervyn *lawyer*
Shapiro, Robert L. *lawyer*
Sheehan, Lawrence James *lawyer*
Sheller, John Willard *lawyer*
Sherrell, John Bradford *lawyer*
Sherwood, Arthur Lawrence *lawyer*
Shiba, Wendy C. *lawyer*
Shortz, Richard Alan *lawyer*
Shostak, S. Richard *lawyer*
Shultz, John David *lawyer*
Siemens, Reynold (Rene Siemens) *lawyer*
Silbergeld, Arthur F. *lawyer*
Singer, Martin Dori *lawyer*
Sloan, Sheldon Harold *lawyer*
Snider, Darryl *lawyer*
Stamm, Alan *lawyer*
Stein, Laurence Jay *lawyer*
Stinehart, William, Jr. *retired lawyer*
Strong, George Gordon, Jr. *lawyer, management consultant*
Sun, Brian A. *lawyer*
Sweeney, Paul W., Jr. *lawyer*
Thoren-Peden, Deborah Suzanne *lawyer*
Title, Gail Migdal *lawyer*
Tobisman, Stuart Paul *lawyer*
Treister, George Marvin *lawyer*
Trope, Sorrell *lawyer*
Trygstad, Lawrence Benson *lawyer*
Ukropina, James R. *lawyer*
Umberg, Thomas John *lawyer*
Van de Kamp, John Kalar *lawyer*
Varat, Jonathan D. *law educator, dean*
von Kalinowski, Julian Onesime *lawyer*
Wagner, Darryl William *lawyer*
Walcher, Alan Ernest *lawyer*
Warren, Robert Stephen *lawyer*
Wasser, Dennis Matthew *lawyer*
Wasser, Laura Allison *lawyer*
Wayte, Alan (Paul) *lawyer*
Weatherup, Roy Garfield *lawyer*
Weiner, Perrie M. *lawyer*
Weiss, Walter Stanley *lawyer*
White, Robert Joel *lawyer*
Williams, Harold Marvin *lawyer, retired foundation, academic and federal agency administrator*
Williams, Norma Jean *lawyer*
Williams, Richard Thomas *lawyer*
Woodsome, Edwin Valentine, Jr. *lawyer*
Wright, Kenneth Brooks *lawyer*
Yang, Debra Wong *lawyer, former prosecutor*
Yslas, Stephen Daniel *lawyer*
Ziffren, Kenneth *lawyer*

Lynwood
Sterling, Arthur James *retired legal assistant*

Malibu
Cihak, Herbert Earl *law librarian, educator*
Davenport, David *lawyer, educator, academic administrator*
Factor, Max III *arbitrator, mediator*
Nelson, Grant Steel *law educator*

Manhattan Beach
Rae, Matthew Sanderson, Jr. *lawyer*

Menlo Park
Chao, Howard H. *lawyer*
Crawford, Roy Edgington III *lawyer*
Dyer, Charles Arnold *lawyer*
Fisher, Ora T. *lawyer*
Hearst, William Randolph III *lawyer, former newspaper publisher*
Hockett, Christopher Burch *lawyer*
Karel, Steven *lawyer*
Kaufman, Christopher Lee *lawyer*
Kelly, Daniel Grady, Jr. *lawyer*
Kennelly, Dennis L. *lawyer*
Kirk, Cassius Lamb, Jr. *retired lawyer, investor*
Madison, James Raymond *lawyer*
Mendelson, Alan Charles *lawyer*
Radlo, Edward John *lawyer, mathematician*
Yang, Joseph *lawyer*

Merced
Lashley, Lenore Clarisse *lawyer*

Mill Valley
Nemir, Donald Philip *lawyer*
Schwartzbach, M. Gerald *lawyer*

Mission Viejo
Ruben, Robert Joseph *lawyer*
Tuohey, Conrad Gravier *lawyer*

Monterey
Duran, June Clark *legal research company executive*
Gaver, Frances Rouse *lawyer*

Monterey Park
Grasse, Wanda Gene *lawyer, writer*

Mountain View
Kraw, George Martin *lawyer, writer*
Nash, Horace Lyons *lawyer*
Pasahow, Lynn Harold *lawyer*
Spang-Hanssen, Henrik Stakemann *lawyer, researcher*

Napa
Cahill, Richard Frederick *lawyer*
Thomas, William Scott *lawyer*

Newport Beach
Baskin, Scott David *lawyer*
Borges, Fredrick Mario *lawyer*
Duncan, John Alexander *lawyer*
Fehner, Michael Richard *lawyer*
Goldstein, Michael Gerald *lawyer, director*
Harlan, Nancy Margaret *lawyer*
Herron, J. Jay *lawyer*
Hueston, John Charles *lawyer*
Millar, Richard William, Jr. *lawyer*
Schnapp, Roger Herbert *lawyer, consultant*
Wentworth, Theodore Sumner *lawyer*
Yoder, Michael G. *lawyer*

North Hollywood
Ajalat, Sol Peter *lawyer*

Northridge
Avsharian, Roupen *prosecutor, academic administrator*
Runquist, Lisa A. *lawyer*

Oak Park
Vinson, William Theodore *lawyer*

Oakland
Berry, Phillip Samuel *lawyer*
Bryant, Arthur H. *lawyer*
Cannady, Walter Jack *lawyer*
Deming, Willis Riley *retired lawyer*
Fleming, Jayne Elizabeth *lawyer*
Johnson, Kenneth F. *lawyer*
Kazan, Steven *lawyer*
Kohn, Steven M. *lawyer*
Quinby, William Albert *lawyer, arbitrator, mediator*
Reese, Charles Woodrow, Jr. *lawyer, real estate developer*
Stein, Laura *lawyer, consumer products company executive*
Wallis, Eric G. *lawyer*
Wood, James Michael *lawyer*

Oceanside
Sullivan, Patrick James *lawyer*

Orange
Batchelor, James Kent *lawyer*
Rotunda, Ronald Daniel *law educator, consultant*
Steiner, Ronald Lee *lawyer, educator, director*

Orinda
Hetland, John Robert *law educator*

Oxnard
Sands, Velma Ahda *lawyer*

Pacific Palisades
Cale, Charles Griffin *lawyer, real estate and corporate financial company executive*
Flattery, Thomas Long *lawyer, administrator*
Jones, Edgar Allan, Jr. *lawyer, arbitrator, educator*
Share, Richard Hudson *lawyer*

Palm Desert
Goldberg, Martin Stanford *retired lawyer*

Palm Springs
Kimberling, John Farrell *retired lawyer*

Palo Alto
Abrams, William F. *lawyer*
Baron, Frederick David *lawyer*
Baum, Brandon *lawyer, educator*
Benton, Lee F. *lawyer*
Bradley, Donald Edward *lawyer*
Climan, Richard Elliot *lawyer*
Feldman, Boris *lawyer*
Flaum, Keith Avery *lawyer*
Fordis, Jean Burke *lawyer*
Furbush, David Malcolm *lawyer*
Gaither, James C. *lawyer*
Gorman, Maureen J. *lawyer*
Greco, Joseph A. *lawyer*
Halluin, Albert Price *lawyer*
Hinman, Harvey DeForest *lawyer*
Hiscox, Frank S. *lawyer*
Hoak, Jonathan S., Sr. *lawyer*
Holston, Michael Joseph *lawyer, computer company executive*
Ivey, Thomas J. *lawyer*
King, Kenton J. *lawyer*
Laurie, Ronald Sheldon *lawyer*
McCall, Jennifer Jordan *lawyer*
Michels, Dirk *lawyer*
Neal, Stephen Cassidy *lawyer*
Nopar, Alan S. *lawyer*
Nuchi, Lior O. *lawyer*
Petkanics, Donna M. *lawyer*
Radcliffe, Mark Flohn *lawyer*
Roos, John Victor *lawyer*
Shi, Qin *lawyer, technologist*
Smith, Glenn A. *lawyer*
Sonsini, Larry W. *lawyer*
Tiffany, Joseph Raymond, II, *lawyer*

Palos Verdes Estates
DeLuce, Richard David *lawyer*

Pasadena
Buck, Jonathan Frederick *lawyer*
Call, Merlin Wendell *lawyer*
Calleton, Theodore Edward *lawyer, educator*
D'Angelo, Robert William *lawyer*
Haight, James Theron *lawyer*
Hunt, Gordon *lawyer*
Leeson, Peter J., IV, *lawyer*
Logan, Francis Dummer *retired lawyer*
Markley, William C. *lawyer*
Miller, Susan Calabrese *lawyer, consumer products company executive*
Mosher, Sally Ekenberg *lawyer, musician*
Mueth, Joseph Edward *lawyer*
Myers, R(alph) Chandler *lawyer*
Solis, Carlos *lawyer*
Sullivan, William Francis *lawyer*
Wyatt, Joseph Lucian, Jr. *lawyer, writer*
Yohalem, Harry Morton *lawyer*

Petaluma
Archer, Richard Joseph *lawyer*

Pleasanton
Askanas, Mark S. *lawyer*
Fine, Marjorie Lynn *lawyer*
Opperwall, Stephen Gabriel *lawyer*

Point Richmond
Edginton, John Arthur *lawyer*

Rancho Mirage
Leydorf, Frederick Leroy *lawyer*
Pierno, Anthony Robert *lawyer*

Rancho Palos Verdes
Haile, Lawrence Barclay *lawyer*
Schimmenti, John Joseph *lawyer*

Rancho Santa Fe
Woolley, Roger Swire *lawyer*

Redwood City
Bell, Frank Ouray, Jr. *lawyer*
Coddington, Clinton Hays *lawyer*
Daley, Dorian Estelle *lawyer, computer software company executive*
Gunderson, Robert Vernon, Jr. *lawyer*
McLaughlin, David Michael *lawyer*
Pape, Glenn Michael *lawyer, retired financial planner*
Powers, Matthew Douglas *lawyer*
Wilhelm, Robert Oscar *lawyer, civil engineer*
Winters, Vernon Michael *lawyer*

Richmond
Dolberg, David Spencer *lawyer*
Jenkins, Everett Wilbur, Jr. *lawyer, writer, historian*

Riverside
Darling, Scott Edward *lawyer*
Heiting, James Otto *lawyer*

Rosemead
Adler, Robert L. *lawyer, utilities executive*

Running Springs
Marcus, John Richard *lawyer*

Sacramento
Bell, Wayne S. *lawyer, state agency official*
Bleckley, Jeanette A. *lawyer*
Brown, Lawrence George *prosecutor*
Burton, Randall James *lawyer*
Day, James McAdam, Jr. *lawyer*
Friedman, Morton Lee *retired lawyer*
Hernandez, James, Jr. *criminal justice educator*
Houpt, James Edward *lawyer*
Huh, Joan *lawyer*
Kelso, J(ohn) Clark *law educator, consultant*
Manson, H. Craig (Harold Craig Manson) *law educator, former federal agency administrator, former judge*
McGrath, William Arthur *arbitrator, mediator, lawyer, real estate broker*
Scott, McGregor W. *lawyer, former prosecutor*
Taylor, Joseph Evans *law educator*
Taylor, Walter Wallace *retired lawyer*

Saint Helena
Seavey, William Arthur *lawyer, vintner*

San Anselmo
Truett, Harold Joseph, III, (Tim) *lawyer*

San Diego
Allen, P. Blake *lawyer*
Bell, Robert Jeffrey *lawyer*
Boggs, William S. *lawyer*
Brooks, John White *lawyer*
Brownlie, Robert William *lawyer*
Cannon, Gary Curtis *lawyer, publishing executive*
Chaudhri, Javade *lawyer, utilities executive*
Cohn, Marjorie F. *law educator, legal association administrator*
Corbett, Luke Robinson *lawyer*
Dollarhide, Mary C. *lawyer*
Doppelt, Roy Martin *lawyer*
Dorne, David J. *lawyer*
Eigner, William Whitling *lawyer*
Gerber, Robert Scott *lawyer*
Gomez, John Hamilton *lawyer*
Hagarty, Mark *lawyer*
Heidrich, Robert Wesley *lawyer*
Hewitt, Karen Peckham *prosecutor*
Insogna, Anthony M. *lawyer*
Jacobs, Ginger Elaine *lawyer*
Klinedinst, John David *lawyer*
Lam, Carol Chien-Hua *lawyer*
Lathrop, Mitchell Lee *lawyer*
Levine, Harvey Robert *lawyer*
McCoy, Lilys D. *lawyer*
McGinnis, Robert E. *lawyer*
McMahon, Gerald Lawrence *lawyer*
Mebane, Julie S. *lawyer*
Minteer, Daniel C. *lawyer*
Mittermiller, James Joseph *lawyer*
Payne, Margaret Anne *lawyer*
Pharies, Stephen Andrew *lawyer*
Plourd, Christopher John *lawyer, consultant*
Pray, Ralph Marble III *lawyer*
Pugh, Richard Crawford *lawyer, educator*
Rains, Cameron Jay *lawyer*
Roseman, Charles Sanford *lawyer*
Scott, Douglas Edward *lawyer*
Shapiro, Philip Alan *lawyer*
Shepherd, Bruce P. *lawyer*
Shippey, Sandra Lee *lawyer*
Smith, Steven Ray *law educator*
Song, Jane Inyoung *lawyer*
Thorud, Jeffrey Scott *lawyer, legal studies director*
Vitek, Reg(inald) A. *lawyer*
Wagner, Sandra M. *lawyer*
Weaver, Michael James *lawyer*
Wolfe, Deborah Ann *lawyer*

San Francisco
Abbott, Barry Alexander *lawyer*
Anderson, Edward Virgil *lawyer*
Bancroft, James Ramsey *lawyer*
Banks, Michelle *lawyer, retail executive*
Barbagelata, Robert Dominic *lawyer*
Baysinger, Kara *lawyer*
Bennett, James Patrick *lawyer*
Berning, Paul Wilson *lawyer*
Bleich, Jeffrey Laurence *lawyer, educator*
Blohm, Kenneth E. *lawyer*
Bondoc, Rommel *lawyer*
Borowsky, Philip *lawyer*
Bostwick, James Stephen *lawyer*
Boven, Douglas George *lawyer*
Brandel, Roland Eric *lawyer*
Briscoe, John *lawyer*
Brosnahan, James Jerome *lawyer*
Brown, Donald Wesley *lawyer*
Bruen, James A. *lawyer*
Burns, Brian Patrick *lawyer*
Burton, Joseph M. *lawyer*
Cabraser, Elizabeth Joan *lawyer*
Callan, Terrence A. *attorney*
Cartmell, Nathaniel Madison III *lawyer*
Casey, Bernard J. *lawyer*
Chapman, William B. *lawyer*
Chung, Eric C. *lawyer*
Clowes, John Howard *lawyer*
Cohn, Cindy A. *lawyer*
Coleman, Thomas Young *lawyer*
Cominos, Dion Nicholas *lawyer*
Coombe, George William, Jr. *lawyer, retired bank executive*
Cranston, Mary Bailey *lawyer*
Curran, Mary *lawyer*
Danoff, Eric Michael *lawyer*
Davis, Roger Lewis *lawyer*
Dell, Robert Michael *lawyer*
DeMuro, Paul Robert *lawyer*
Dolinko, Robert A. *lawyer*
Dryden, Robert Eugene *lawyer*
Dubreuil, Francis W. *lawyer*
Durdik, Paul A. *lawyer*
Durie, Daralyn J. *lawyer*
Dwyer, Carrie Elizabeth *lawyer, investment company executive*
Edwards, Robin Morse *lawyer*
Falk, Jerome B., Jr. *lawyer*
Feldman, Robert Paul *lawyer*
Fergus, Gary Scott *lawyer*
Finberg, James Michael *lawyer*
Finck, Kevin William *lawyer*
Fisher, Kathleen V. *lawyer*
Folberg, Harold Jay *lawyer, educator, dean, mediator*
Fong, Kevin Murray *lawyer*
Foster, David Scott *lawyer*
Friedman, K. Bruce *lawyer*
Friese, Robert Charles *lawyer*
Garvey, Joanne Marie *lawyer*
Getto, Ernest John *lawyer*
González, Arturo J. *lawyer*
Gonzalez, Matt *lawyer*
Goodwin, David B. *lawyer*
Gordon, Andrew K. *lawyer*
Gresham, Zane Oliver *lawyer*
Guggenhime, Richard Johnson *lawyer*
Haas, Raymond P. *lawyer*
Haber, Scott R. *lawyer*
Harris, Kamala D. *prosecutor*
Havian, Eric R. *lawyer*
Hazard, Geoffrey Cornell, Jr. *law educator*
Heilbron, David Michael *lawyer, arbitrator, mediator*
Henson, Ray David *law educator, consultant*
Hernandez, Gary A. *lawyer*
Hernandez, Jennifer Lynn *lawyer*
Highman, Bruce James *lawyer*
Hilton, Stanley Goumas *lawyer, educator, writer*
Hirsch, (William) Reece *lawyer*
Hisert, George Arthur *lawyer*
Hofmann, John Richard, Jr. *retired lawyer*
Holden, Frederick Douglass, Jr. *lawyer*
Howard, Carl *retired lawyer*
Hubbell, Robert B. *lawyer*
Huhs, John I. *international lawyer*
Juster, Kenneth Ian *lawyer*
Keker, John Watkins *lawyer*
Kelly, J. Michael *lawyer*
Kennedy, Raoul Dion *lawyer*
Kern, Brad D. *lawyer*
Koeppel, John A. *lawyer*
Krevans, Rachel *lawyer*
Kuhl, Paul Beach *lawyer*
Lane, Fielding H. *retired lawyer*
Larrabee, Matthew Lloyd *lawyer*
Larson, John William *lawyer*
Lee, Richard Diebold *lawyer, educator*
Leshy, John David *lawyer, solicitor, educator*
Little, Jan Nielsen *lawyer*
Livermore, Samuel Morgan *lawyer*
Livsey, Robert Callister *lawyer*
Lowell, Frederick K. *lawyer*
MacNeil, Justin W. *lawyer*
Maier, Peter Klaus *lawyer*
Maly, Michael Kip *lawyer*
Mann, Bruce Alan *lawyer, investment banking executive*
Manning, Jerome Alan *retired lawyer*
Marshall, Patrick C. *lawyer*
Martel, John Sheldon *lawyer, writer, musician*
Masters, Joseph *lawyer, engineering company executive*
Matthews, Philip Richard *lawyer*
McGinnis, James Landon *lawyer*
Miller, William Napier Cripps *lawyer*
Minnick, Malcolm David *lawyer*
Mooney, Brian Joseph *lawyer*

Morrissey, John Carroll, Sr. *lawyer*
Murray, Kathleen Anne *lawyer*
Nelson, Paul Douglas *lawyer*
Odgers, Richard William *lawyer*
Okeke, Christian Nwachukwu *law educator*
Olson, Robert Howard *lawyer*
Palmer, Venrice Romito *lawyer, educator*
Park, Hyun *lawyer, utilities executive*
Paxton, Jay L. *lawyer*
Perry, E. Lynn *lawyer*
Pickett, Donn Philip *lawyer*
Popofsky, Melvin Laurence *lawyer*
Pringle, Paul C. *lawyer*
Pringle, Robert Bernard *lawyer*
Reding, John Anthony, Jr. *lawyer*
Rice, Denis Timlin *lawyer*
Richards, Norman Blanchard *lawyer*
Robinson, Ralph W. *lawyer*
Rogan, Richard A. *lawyer*
Rosen, Sanford Jay *lawyer*
Rosenfeld, Robert A. *lawyer*
Ross, Jeffrey S. *lawyer*
Rowland, John Arthur *lawyer*
Russoniello, Joseph Pascal *prosecutor, lawyer*
Ryan, Kevin Vincent *lawyer, former prosecutor*
Sanders, Joel Steven *lawyer*
Savage, Mark Randall *lawyer*
Schenkkan, Dirk McKenzie *lawyer*
Schickman, Mark Isaac *lawyer*
Seabolt, Richard L. *lawyer*
Seeger, Laureen E. *lawyer, health products executive*
Serota, Gilbert Ross *lawyer*
Shepherd, John Michael *lawyer*
Shiffman, Michael A. *lawyer*
Shostak, Linda E. *lawyer*
Silk, Thomas *lawyer*
Singer, Allen Morris *lawyer*
Siniscalco, Gary Richard *lawyer*
Skaggs, Sanford Merle *lawyer*
Smegal, Thomas Frank, Jr. *lawyer*
Snow, Tower Charles, Jr. *lawyer*
Snyder, Darin W. *lawyer*
Soberon, Presentacion Zablan *state bar administrator*
Sparks, Thomas E., Jr. *lawyer*
Staring, Graydon Shaw *lawyer*
Story, Joan H. *lawyer*
Street, Paul Shipley *lawyer*
Stromberg, Ross Ernest *lawyer*
Strother, James M. *lawyer*
Sugarman, Myron George *lawyer*
Sugarman, Paul William *lawyer*
Sullivan, Robert Edward *lawyer*
Taylor, William James (Zak) *lawyer*
Thayer, M. Patricia *lawyer*
Thompson, Patrick S. *lawyer*
Vazquez-Azpiri, A. James *lawyer*
Veaco, Kristina *lawyer*
Venning, Robert Stanley *lawyer*
Wald, Peter Allen *lawyer*
Wang, William Kai-Sheng *law educator*
Weber, Arnold I. *lawyer*
Weinberg, Doron *lawyer*
Whitehead, David Barry *lawyer*
Wild, Nelson Hopkins *lawyer*
Wong, Ray L. *lawyer*
Wood, Robert Warren *lawyer*
Wyle, Frederick S. *lawyer*
Yost, Nicholas Churchill *lawyer*
Young, Bryant Llewellyn *lawyer*
Young, Douglas Rea *lawyer*

San Jose
Denver, Thomas HR *lawyer*
Gallo, Joan Rosenberg *lawyer*
Hernández, Fernando Vargas *lawyer*
Jacobson, Michael R. *lawyer, Internet company executive*
McManis, James *lawyer*
Mitchell, David Walker *lawyer*
Stein, John C. *lawyer*
Stutzman, Thomas Chase, Sr. *lawyer*
Tyler, Michael Robert *lawyer*

San Juan Capistrano
Graves, Patrick Lee *lawyer*
Suzuki, Yasuhiko *retired law educator*

San Luis Obispo
Daly, John Paul *lawyer*

San Marino
Galbraith, James Marshall *lawyer, corporate executive*
Tomich, Lillian *lawyer*

San Mateo
O'Reilly, Terence John *lawyer*
Pileggi, Jennifer Wendy *lawyer, transportation services executive*
Tyle, Craig S. *lawyer, investment company executive*

San Rafael
Busterud, John Armand *lawyer, consultant*
Chilvers, Robert Merritt *lawyer*
Cortés, Antonio Luis *lawyer*
Drexler, Kenneth *lawyer*

San Ramon
Garten, David Burton *lawyer*
Haynes, William James, II, *lawyer*
James, Charles Albert *lawyer, oil industry executive*
Pate, R. Hewitt (Robert Hewitt Pate III) *lawyer, oil industry executive*

Santa Ana
Aitken, Wylie A. *lawyer*
Capizzi, Michael Robert *lawyer, former prosecutor*
DeGiorgio, Kenneth D. *lawyer, insurance company executive*
Digorgio, Kenneth *lawyer*
Dillard, John Martin *lawyer, pilot*
Storer, Maryruth *law librarian*

Santa Barbara
Braun, David A(dlai) *lawyer*
Cappello, A. Barry *lawyer*
Reed, Frank Fremont, II, *retired lawyer*
Ziegler, R. W., Jr. *lawyer, consultant*

Santa Clara
Dillon, Michael A. (Mike) *lawyer, information technology executive*
DuChene, Todd Michael *lawyer*
Glancy, Dorothy Jean *lawyer, educator*
Hsieh, Marina Cing *lawyer, educator*
Nordlund, Donald Craig *lawyer, electronics executive*
Sewell, D. Bruce (Bruce Sewell, Durward Bruce Sewell) *lawyer*
Sweeney, Joseph J. *lawyer, manufacturing executive*

Santa Cruz
Seligmann, William Robert *lawyer, author*

Santa Monica
Chapman Holley, Shawn Snider *lawyer*
Cooper, Jay Leslie *lawyer*
Cowan, Jeffrey Wrubel *lawyer*
Geiser, Thomas Christopher *lawyer, insurance company executive*
Grossman, Marshall Bruce *lawyer*
Handzlik, Jan Lawrence *lawyer*
Heller, Lawrence Howard *lawyer*
Hinerfeld, Robert Elliot *lawyer*
Levin, Marvin Eugene *lawyer*
Morgan, Kermit Johnson *lawyer*
Risman, Michael *lawyer, real estate developer, broker*
Soodik, Lynn *lawyer*
Tunney, John Varick *lawyer, former United States Senator from California*
Weitzman, Howard L. *lawyer, former film company executive*

Saratoga
Liccardo, Salvador A. *lawyer*

Sausalito
Berkman, William Roger *lawyer, retired major general army*
Gordon, Robert Eugene *lawyer*

Scotts Valley
Hudson, William L. *lawyer, electronics executive*

Seal Beach
Denson-Low, Wanda K. *lawyer, aerospace transportation executive*

Sebastopol
Greiner, Robert Philip *lawyer, real estate broker*
Rappaport, Stuart Ramon *lawyer*

Sherman Oaks
Crump, Gerald Franklin *retired lawyer*
Joyce, Stephen Michael *lawyer*
Mersel, Marjorie Kathryn Pedersen *lawyer*

Sonoma
Obninsky, Victor Peter *lawyer*

Stanford
Casper, Gerhard *law educator, retired academic administrator*
Cohen, William *law educator*
Franklin, Marc Adam *law educator*
Friedman, Lawrence M. *law educator*
Gould, William Benjamin, IV, *law educator*
Grundfest, Joseph Alexander *law and business educator*
Karlan, Pamela Susan *law educator*
Kelman, Mark Gregory *law educator*
Klausner, Michael David *law educator*
Lemley, Mark Alan *law educator*
Lessig, L. Lawrence III *law educator, writer*
Petersilia, Joan *law educator, criminologist*
Rhode, Deborah Lynn *law educator*
Scott, Kenneth Eugene *lawyer, educator*
Sofaer, Abraham David *lawyer, former federal judge, educator, consultant*

Stockton
Parish, William Henry *lawyer*

Sunnyvale
Callahan, Michael John *lawyer*
McReynolds, Stephen Paul *lawyer*
Wehde, Albert Edward *lawyer*

Thousand Oaks
Gentile, Joseph F. *lawyer, educator*
Kuelbs, John Thomas *lawyer*
Scott, David J. *lawyer, medical products executive*

Tiburon
Tobin, James Michael *lawyer*
Widman, Gary Lee *lawyer*

Torrance
Bryan, Sharon Ann *lawyer*
Carlson, Terrance L. *lawyer, aerospace transportation executive*
Hahn, Elliott Julius *lawyer*
Moore, Christopher M. *lawyer*
Petillon, Lee Ritchey *lawyer*

Turlock
Werling, Robert Lewis *law educator*

Tustin
Madory, Richard Eugene *lawyer*

Universal City
Golper, John Bruce *lawyer*

Valley Village
Davis, Edmond Ray *lawyer*

Van Nuys
Arabian, Armand *arbitrator, mediator, lawyer*

Visalia
Crowe, John T. *lawyer*

Walnut
McKee, Catherine Lynch *lawyer, educator*

Walnut Creek
Ginsburg, Gerald J. *lawyer, management consultant*
Hanschen, Peter Walter *lawyer*
Ogilby, Barry Ray *lawyer*
Pagter, Carl Richard *lawyer*

West Covina
Ebiner, Robert Maurice *lawyer*
Galen, Albert John *retired lawyer*
McHale, Edward Robertson *retired lawyer*

Westlake Village
Strote, Joel Richard *lawyer*

Woodland Hills
DeSantis, Richard A. *lawyer*
Mroz, Erik Shane *lawyer*
Tiano, Linda V. *lawyer, insurance company executive*

Yorba Linda
McCune, Brenda L. *lawyer*

COLORADO

Alamosa
Garcia, Castelar Medardo *lawyer*

Aurora
Katz, Michael Jeffery *lawyer*

Basalt
Shipp, Dan Shackelford *lawyer*

Boulder
Carrigan, Jim R. *arbitrator, mediator, retired judge*
Deaktor, Darryl Barnett *lawyer*
Fenster, Herbert Lawrence *lawyer*
Fiflis, Ted James *lawyer, educator*
Flowers, William Harold, Jr. *lawyer*
Getches, David Harding *lawyer, educator, dean*
Iatridis, Asimakis D. *lawyer, educator*
Moses, Raphael Jacob *lawyer*
Nehls, Richard Charles *lawyer*
Peterson, Courtland Harry *law educator*
Porzak, Glenn E. *lawyer*
Purvis, John Anderson *lawyer, educator*
Steuben, Norton Leslie *lawyer, educator*
Stevens, Glenn H. *lawyer*
Yee, Sienho *law educator*

Broomfield
Baker, Charles E. *lawyer*

Cherry Hills Village
Tisdale, Douglas Michael, Sr. *lawyer*

Colorado Springs
Adams, Deborah Rowland *lawyer*
Deeny, Raymond M. *lawyer*
Evans, Paul Vernon *retired lawyer*
Haskins, Thomas Marston III *lawyer*
Kraemer, Sandy Frederick *lawyer*
Millman, Robert A. *lawyer*
Sargent, Walter Harriman, II, *lawyer*

Denver
Aro, Edwin Packard *lawyer*
Austin, H(arry) Gregory *lawyer*
Bader, Gerald L., Jr. *lawyer*
Baer, Richard N. *lawyer, telecommunications industry executive*
Bain, Donald Knight *lawyer*
Banks, Britt D. *lawyer*
Bartlit, Fred Holcomb, Jr. *lawyer*
Benton, Auburn Edgar *lawyer*
Berry, Robert Worth *lawyer, retired military officer, educator*
Bess, Charles Wayne *lawyer*
Blitz, Stephen M. *lawyer*
Blum, Gary Bernard *lawyer*
Brady, William John, Jr. *lawyer*
Breeskin, Michael Wayne *lawyer*
Brega, Charles Franklin *lawyer*
Briggs, Steve Clement *lawyer*
Bruce, Teresa Mary *lawyer, educator*
Butler, David *lawyer*
Cain, Douglas Mylchreest *lawyer*
Campbell, William J. *lawyer*
Carlson, Erik B. *lawyer*
Clark, Phillip R. *lawyer*
Cooper, Paul Douglas *lawyer*
Cope, Thomas Field *lawyer*
Dauer, Edward Arnold *law educator*
Davis, R. Steven *lawyer, telecommunications industry executive*
Dean, James Benwell *lawyer*
Dempsey, Stanley (Howard Stanley Dempsey) *lawyer, mining and investment company executive*
Deutsch, Harvey Elliot *lawyer*
Dorr, Robert Charles *lawyer*
Dowdle, Patrick Dennis *lawyer*
Duffy, William J. *lawyer*
Eckstein, Max *law educator, director*
Eid, Troy A. *lawyer, former prosecutor*
Eklund, Carl Andrew *lawyer*
Elston, Frank *law educator, consultant*
Farber, Steven W. *lawyer*
Featherstone, Bruce Alan *lawyer*
Gehres, James *retired lawyer*
Grant, Patrick Alexander *lawyer*
Green, Jersey Michael-Lee *lawyer*
Haddon, Harold Alan *lawyer*
Hale, Allan L. *lawyer*
Harris, Dale Ray *lawyer, arbitrator, mediator*
Hendrix, Lynn Parker *lawyer*
Holme, Richard Phillips *lawyer*
Hopfenbeck, George Martin, Jr. *lawyer*
Houghtaling, Walter Nicholas *lawyer*
Houtsma, Peter C. *lawyer*
Irwin, R. Robert *lawyer*
Jacobs, Paul Alan *lawyer*
Jestrab, Frank F. *retired lawyer*
Jones, Richard Michael *lawyer*
Juárez, José Roberto, Jr. *law educator, former dean*
Kahn, Edwin Sam *lawyer*
Katz, Martin Jonathan *law professor*
Kerwin, Mary Ann Collins *lawyer*
Kintzele, John Alfred *lawyer*
Krendl, Cathy Stricklin *lawyer*
Low, Andrew M. *lawyer*
Low, John Wayland *lawyer*
Lutz, John Shafroth *lawyer*
Lyons, James M. *lawyer*
Mackey, Pamela Robillard *lawyer*
Major, Alice Jean *lawyer*
Marquess, Lawrence Wade *lawyer*
Mathis, Karen J. *lawyer, legal association administrator*
Mauro, Richard Frank *retired lawyer, investment company executive*
McCabe, John L. *lawyer*
McIntosh, Carolyn Leigh *lawyer*
McMichael, Donald Earl *lawyer*
Merker, Steven Joseph *lawyer*
Miller, Gale Timothy *lawyer*
Miller, Robert Nolen *lawyer*
Mitchem, Allen P. *lawyer*
Murane, William Edward *lawyer*
Newcom, Jennings Jay *lawyer, director*
Norton, Gale Ann *lawyer, former United States Secretary of the Interior*
Olsen, M. Kent *lawyer, educator*
Osman, Lee R. *lawyer*
Palmer, David Gilbert *lawyer*
Petkun, Richard Michael *lawyer*
Piché, Gregory Russell *lawyer*
Pozner, Larry S. *lawyer, educator*
Rench, Stephen Charles *lawyer*
Rothrock, Lindsey Nichole *lawyer*
Samuels, Donald L. *lawyer*
Seawell, Donald Ray *lawyer, performing company executive*
Shepherd, John Frederic *lawyer*
Staelin, Earl Hudson *lawyer*
Steefel, David Simon *lawyer*
Thomasch, Roger Paul *lawyer*
Ulrich, Theodore Albert *lawyer*
Walker, Samuel David *lawyer*
Weber, Matthew George *lawyer*
Wheeler, Malcolm Edward *lawyer, educator*
Williams, Michael Anthony *lawyer*
Wohlgenant, Richard Glen *lawyer, director*
Woodward, Lester Ray *lawyer*
Wunnicke, Brooke *lawyer*

Durango
Burnham, Bryson Paine *retired lawyer*

Englewood
Markowski, Elizabeth M. *lawyer*
Moskowitz, David K. *lawyer*
Tanabe, Charles Y. *lawyer*

Evergreen
Prichard, Vincent Marvin *lawyer*

Fort Collins
Johnson, Donald Edward, Jr. *lawyer*
Ray, Steven Billy *lawyer*
Schwartz, Allen R. *lawyer*

Frisco
Helmer, David Alan *lawyer*

Golden
Kopel, David Benjamin *lawyer*
Phillipson, Donald E. *lawyer*

Greenwood Village
Blank, Alan Robert *lawyer*
Davis, Tracy A. *lawyer*
Dewald, Bruce Wayne *lawyer*
Lidstone, Herrick Kenley, Jr. *lawyer*
Money, David R. *lawyer, information technology executive*
Poe, Robert Alan *lawyer*
Rairdon, James Lee *paralegal, educator*
Ramsey, John Arthur *lawyer*
Schlapbach, David *lawyer*

Howard
Hopkins, Donald J. *retired lawyer*

Lakewood
Guyton, Samuel Percy *retired lawyer*
Humphrey, Charles Edward, Jr. *lawyer*

Littleton
Meyer, Milton Edward, Jr. *retired lawyer, artist*

Lone Tree
Morrow Campbell, Juliette Michelle *lawyer*
Spelts, Richard John *lawyer*

Loveland
Clark, Roger Earl *lawyer*

Norwood
Reagan, Harry Edwin III *lawyer*

Pueblo
Farley, Thomas T. *lawyer*
Humes, James Calhoun *lawyer, communications consultant, writer, educator*

Steamboat Springs
Moylan, James Joseph *lawyer*

Windsor
DiFalco, John Patrick *lawyer, arbitrator*
Downey, Arthur Harold, Jr. *lawyer, mediator*

CONNECTICUT

Avon
Harrison, Thomas Flatley *lawyer, environmental consultant*

Bridgeport
Bowen, Patrick Harvey *lawyer, consultant*

Cos Cob
Bruder, George Frederick *retired lawyer*

Danbury
Bassett, Robert Andrews *lawyer*
Breedlove, James T. (Jim Breedlove) *lawyer*

Darien
Kaynor, Sanford Bull *lawyer*
Michalski, Paul Peter *lawyer*
Prince, Kenneth Stephen *lawyer*
Rucci, Joseph J., Jr. *lawyer*

Derby
McEvoy, Sharlene Ann *law educator*

Fairfield
Bhatia, Karan Krishna *lawyer, former federal official*
Caruso, Daniel F. *lawyer, judge, former state legislator*
Denniston, Brackett Badger III *lawyer*
Klee, Ann Renee *lawyer*
Samuels, John *lawyer*
Ury, Frederic Stephen *lawyer*
Wales, Gwynne Huntington *retired lawyer*

Farmington
Grafstein, Joel M. *lawyer*

Greenwich
Atkins, Ronald Raymond *lawyer*
Brandrup, Douglas Warren *lawyer*
Coleman, Joel Clifford *lawyer*
Gelfman, Robert William *retired lawyer*
George, Cynthia Coulter *lawyer*
Gover, Alan Shore *lawyer*
More, Douglas McLochlan *lawyer*
Nemser, Earl Harold *lawyer*
Nimetz, Matthew *lawyer, investment company executive*
Paul, Roland Arthur *lawyer*
Schoonmaker, Samuel Vail III *lawyer*
Schwed, Roger E. *lawyer, rental company executive*
Selby, Leland Clay *lawyer*
Storms, Clifford Beekman *lawyer*

Guilford
Dubin, Brock Thomas *lawyer*

Hamden
Margulies, Martin B. *lawyer, educator*

Hartford
Alfano, Charles Thomas, Sr. *lawyer*
Anthony, Julian Danford, Jr. *lawyer*
Berall, Frank Stewart *lawyer*
Blumberg, Phillip Irvin *law educator*
Butler, Gregory B. *lawyer, utilities executive*
Cain, George Harvey *lawyer, association administrator*
Casey, Coleman Hampton *lawyer*
Chesman, Michael Richard *lawyer*
Flaschen, Evan Daniel *lawyer*
Garabedian, Todd Evan *lawyer*
Gill, Charles D. *lawyer*
Kreczko, Alan James *lawyer, insurance company executive*
Leonhardt, Clifton Andrew *lawyer, public information officer*
Lloyd, Alex *lawyer*
Lotstein, James Irving *lawyer*
Louden, Wm. Bruce *lawyer*
Lyon, James Burroughs *lawyer*
O'Connor, Kevin James *lawyer, former federal agency administrator*
O'Donnell, Edward Francis, Jr. *lawyer*
O'Connor, Kevin J. *lawyer, former federal agency administrator*
Pepe, Louis Robert *lawyer, educator*
Richter, Donald Paul *lawyer*
Ryan, David Thomas *lawyer*
Sorokin, Ethel Silver *lawyer*
Strasser, Kurt Albert *law educator, researcher, author*
Tancredi, James J. *lawyer*
Taylor, Allan Bert *lawyer*
Voigt, Richard *lawyer*

Lakeville
Cook, Charles David *international lawyer, arbitrator, consultant*
Jerome, John James *lawyer*
Jones, Ronald David *retired lawyer*

Litchfield
Fiederowicz, Walter Michael *lawyer*
Fishman, Mitchell Steven *lawyer*

Milford
Berchem, Robert Lee, Sr. *lawyer*
Hogan, John W., Jr. *lawyer*

New Britain
Pearl, Helen Zalkan *lawyer*

New Canaan
Ferro, Guy (Gaetano Ferro) *lawyer*
Nichols, Ralph Arthur *retired lawyer*
Steinmetz, Richard Bird, Jr. *lawyer*
Wiechmann, Eric Watt *lawyer*

New Haven
Bagley, Constance Elizabeth *lawyer, educator*
Behling, Paul Lawrence *lawyer, educator*
Brilmayer, R. Lea *lawyer, educator*
Burt, Robert Amsterdam *lawyer, educator*
Carter, Stephen Lisle *law educator*
Clark, Elias *law educator*
Dannehy, Nora R. *prosecutor*
Days, Drew S. III *lawyer, educator*
Del Negro, John Thomas *lawyer*
Duke, Steven Barry *law educator*
Durham, John H. *prosecutor*
Ellickson, Robert Chester *law educator*
Errante, Steven James *lawyer*
Fiss, Owen M. *law educator*
Fleming, Gregory James *law educator, former diversified financial services company executive*
Gastwirth, Donald Edward *lawyer, literary agent*
Gildea, Brian Michael *lawyer*
Graetz, Michael J. *law educator*
Hansmann, Henry Baethke *law educator*
Johnstone, Quintin *law educator*
Langbein, John Harriss *lawyer, educator*
Priest, George L. *law educator*
Robinson, Dorothy K. *lawyer*
Rose-Ackerman, Susan *law and political economy educator*
Schuck, Peter Horner *lawyer, educator*
Siegel, Reva B. *law educator*
Simon, John Gerald *law educator*
Stapleton, James Francis *lawyer*
Stith-Cabranes, Kate *law educator*
Sullivan, Shaun Stuart *lawyer*
Thaw, David Bernard *law educator*
Wagoner, Walter Dray, Jr. *lawyer*

New London
Asselin-Connolly, John Thomas *lawyer*
Reardon, Robert Ignatius, Jr. *lawyer*

Newtown
Sanetti, Stephen Louis *lawyer*

Norfolk
Jessup, Philip Caryl, Jr. *retired lawyer*

North Stonington
Svengalis, Kendall Frayne *law librarian, publishing executive, educator, writer*

Norwalk
Cammaker, Sheldon Ira *lawyer*
Reilly, Edward Arthur *lawyer*
Walker, Kellye L. *lawyer*

Orange
Davies, Richard Warren *lawyer*

Redding
Quinn, Andrew Peter, Jr. *lawyer, retired insurance company executive*

Ridgefield
Ingram, Samuel William, Jr. *retired lawyer*

Simsbury
Eisenmann, Carl D. *lawyer*
Long, Michael Thomas *lawyer, manufacturing executive*

South Glastonbury
Schroth, Peter William *lawyer, management, educator*

Southbury
Russell, Allan David *lawyer*

Stamford
Bainton, J(ohn) Joseph *lawyer*
Burton, David K. *lawyer*
Certilman, Steven Andrew *lawyer*
Della Rocco, Kenneth Anthony *lawyer*
duPont, Augustus Irénée *lawyer*
Dupont, Ralph Paul *lawyer, educator*
Glassman, Hilary E. *lawyer, communications executive*
Gold, Steven Michael *lawyer*
Krutter, Forrest Nathan *lawyer*
Leader, Leonard *lawyer*
Liu, Don H. *lawyer, printing company executive*
McGrath, Richard *lawyer*
McKenna, Matthew Morgan *lawyer*
O'Meara, Vicki A. *lawyer*
Perle, Eugene Gabriel *lawyer*
Pickel, Alan Scott *lawyer*
Rose, Richard Loomis *lawyer*
Shanman, James Alan *lawyer*
Sherman, Mickey (Michael Sherman) *lawyer*
Skidd, Thomas Patrick, Jr. *lawyer*
Staab, Diane D. *lawyer*
Teitell, Conrad Laurence *lawyer, writer*
Weitzel, William Conrad, Jr. *lawyer*
Willkie, Wendell Lewis, II, *lawyer*

Stonington
Cole, Richard A. *retired lawyer*

Storrs Mansfield
Tucker, Edwin Wallace *law educator*

Stratford
O'Rourke, James Louis *lawyer*

Torrington
Lippincott, Walter Edward *law educator*
Wall, Robert Anthony, Jr. *lawyer*

Waterbury
Dost, Mark W. *lawyer*
Flaherty, Billie S. *lawyer, chemicals executive*
Lipshaw, Jeffrey Marc *lawyer, chemicals executive, educator*

West Hartford
Bonee, John Leon III *lawyer*
Herzog, Brigitte *retired lawyer*
Wolman, Martin *lawyer*

Weston
Aibel, Howard James *arbitrator, mediator*
Murray, Stephen James *lawyer*

Westport
Barberi, Robert Obed *lawyer*
Carr, Cynthia *lawyer*
Cohen, Eric I. *lawyer*
Cramer, Allan P. *lawyer*
Daw, Harold John *lawyer, director*
Fried, Burton Theodore *lawyer*
Heyman, Ronnie Feuerstein *lawyer*
Margolis, Emanuel *lawyer, educator*
Razzano, Pasquale Angelo *lawyer*
Sheiman, Ronald Lee *lawyer*
Wolson, Craig Alan *lawyer*

Wilton
Adams, Thomas Tilley *lawyer*
Duke, Robert Dominick *lawyer*
Fricke, Richard John *lawyer*
Healy, James Casey *lawyer*
Ziegler, William Alexander *lawyer*

Windsor Locks
Hoffman, Lee D. *prosecutor*

Woodbridge
Haering, Margaret Elaine *lawyer*

Woodbury
Giuliano, Rosemary E. *lawyer*

DELAWARE

Dover
Ennis, Bruce Clifford *retired lawyer*

Greenville
Stone, F. L. Peter *lawyer*

Milton
Carrow, Milton Michael *law educator*

Newark
Elson, Charles Myer *law educator*
Mangone, Gerard J. *international maritime law educator*

Rehoboth Beach
Stokes, Richard Francis *lawyer*

Wilmington
Baumann, Julian Henry, Jr. *lawyer*
Chehi, Mark *lawyer*
DiLiberto, Richard Anthony, Jr. *lawyer*
Fenton, Wendell *lawyer*
Finkelstein, Jesse Adam *lawyer*
Green, James Samuel *lawyer*
Herdeg, John Andrew *lawyer*
Johnston, William David *lawyer*
Jolles, Janet K. Pilling *lawyer*
Kirkpatrick, Andrew Booth, Jr. *lawyer*
Klayman, Barry Martin *lawyer*
Kristol, Daniel Marvin *retired lawyer*
Mekler, L. Arlen *lawyer, chemist*
Nolen, Samuel Augustus *lawyer*
Paschetto, John J. *lawyer*
Reed, Thomas James *law educator*
Salinger, Frank Max *lawyer*
Semple, James William *lawyer*
Stargatt, Bruce M. *lawyer*
Sullivan, Lawrence Matthew *lawyer*
Tumas, Michael B. *lawyer*
Waisanen, Christine M. *lawyer, writer*
Ward, Rodman, Jr. *lawyer, director*
Winslow, Helen Littell *lawyer*
Zahralddin-Aravena, Rafael Xavier *law educator*

DISTRICT OF COLUMBIA

Washington
Aaronson, David Ernest *lawyer, educator*
Abbott, Alden Francis *lawyer, federal official*
Acheson, David Campion *retired lawyer, policy analyst, writer*
Ackerson, Nels J(ohn) *lawyer*
Adams, Frances Grant, II, *lawyer*
Adamson, Terrence Burdett *lawyer*
Adler, Howard Bruce *lawyer*
Agrast, Mark David *lawyer*
Ain, Sanford King *lawyer*
Alberg, James L. *lawyer*
Albrecht, Ralph P. *lawyer*
Aldock, John Douglas *lawyer*
Alexander, Clifford Joseph *lawyer*
Alvarez, Scott G. *lawyer*
Ambrose, Myles Joseph *lawyer*
Anderson, Frederick Randolph, Jr. *lawyer, educator*
Anderson, James E. *lawyer*
Anderson, John Bayard *lawyer, former United States Representative from Illinois*
Anderson, Thomas D. *lawyer, former prosecutor*
Andrew, Joseph Jerald *lawyer*
Andrews, Bruce *lawyer, former automotive executive*
Andrews, Mark Joseph *lawyer*
Andril, David T. *lawyer*
Anthony, Stephen Pierce *lawyer*
Apple, James Glenn *lawyer, educator*
Aronica, Joseph J. *lawyer*
Asbill, Henry W. (Hank Asbill) *lawyer*
Attridge, Daniel F. *lawyer*
Atwood, James R. *lawyer*
Avil, Richard Daniel, Jr. *lawyer*
Axelrod, Jonathan Gans *lawyer*
Ayer, Donald Belton *lawyer*
Azcuenaga, Mary Laurie *lawyer*
Babbitt, Bruce Edward *lawyer, former United States Secretary of the Interior*
Babby, Lon S. *lawyer*
Badillo, Alejandro *lawyer*
Baer, William J. *lawyer*
Baker, David Harris *lawyer*
Baker, Howard Henry, Jr. *lawyer, former US Senator from Texas, White House chief of staff*
Baker, P. Jean *lawyer, mediator*
Baldrate, Brian Christopher *lawyer*
Ball, Markham (Robert Ball) *lawyer, arbitrator, educator*
Bank, Rita M. *lawyer*
Banks, Vanita M. *lawyer*
Barcella, Ernest Lawrence, Jr. *lawyer*
Barclay, George N. *lawyer*
Barnes, Donald Michael *lawyer*
Barnes, Mark James *lawyer*
Barnett, Helaine M. *legal association administrator, lawyer*
Barnett, Robert Bruce *lawyer*
Barnett, Thomas Overton *lawyer, former federal agency administrator*
Barron, Jerome Aure *law educator*
Barry, Dennis M. *lawyer*
Barshefsky, Charlene *lawyer, former federal official*
Barton, R. Joseph *lawyer*
Barusch, Ronald Charles *lawyer*
Battle, Michael A. *lawyer, former federal agency administrator, prosecutor*
Bauer, Robert F. *lawyer*
Baum, Lynne Miriam *lawyer*
Baumann, Linda Adriene *lawyer*
Bayh, Birch (Birch Evans Bayh Jr.) *lawyer, former senator*
Bea Roberts, Barbara Ann *legal secretary*
Beckwith, Edward Jay *lawyer*
Behan, Kathleen A. (Kitty Behan) *lawyer*
Beiro Farabow, Sara *lawyer*
Bell, Stephen Robert *lawyer*
Beller, Herbert N. *lawyer*
Bellinger, John B. III *lawyer, former federal official*
Benner, C. Jonathan *lawyer*
Bennett, Alexander Elliot *lawyer*
Bennett, Robert Stephen *lawyer*
Ben-Veniste, Richard *lawyer*
Berenson, Bradford A. *lawyer*
Beresford, Douglas Lincoln *lawyer*
Bergner, Jane Cohen *lawyer*
Berlack, Evan Raden *lawyer*
Berlin, Kenneth *lawyer*
Bernabei, Lynne Ann *lawyer*
Berner, Frederic George, Jr. *lawyer*
Bernhardt, David Longly *lawyer, former federal agency administrator*
Bernstein, Mitchell Harris *lawyer*
Berrington, Craig Anthony *lawyer*
Best, Judah *lawyer*
Bial, Joseph J. *lawyer, consultant*
Bierman, James Norman *lawyer*
Birnkrant, Henry Joseph *lawyer*
Bishop, James Dodson *lawyer, mediator*
Black, Stephen Franklin *lawyer, writer*
Blair, Robert Allen *lawyer*
Blalack, K. Lee *lawyer*
Blanchard, Charles Alan *lawyer*
Blanchard, James Johnston *lawyer, former Governor of Michigan*
Blazek-White, Doris *lawyer*
Bloch, Susan Low *law educator*
Blumenfeld, Jeffrey *lawyer, educator*
Blumenthal, William *lawyer*
Bodine, Susan Parker *lawyer, former federal agency administrator*
Bodner, John, Jr. *lawyer*
Boehm, Steven Bruce *lawyer*
Bogard, Lawrence Joseph *lawyer*
Boggs, George Trenholm *lawyer*
Boland, Christopher Thomas, II, *lawyer*
Bolton, John Robert *lawyer, former ambassador*
Bonvillian, William Boone *lawyer*
Born, Brooksley Elizabeth *retired lawyer*
Borsari, George Robert, Jr. *lawyer, commentator*
Boskey, Bennett *lawyer*
Boss, Lenard Barrett *lawyer*
Bowker, David William *lawyer*
Boyd, Thomas Marshall *lawyer*
Braden, Gregory C. *lawyer*
Bradfield, Michael *lawyer*
Brecher, Mitchell Fredrick *lawyer*
Bregman, Arthur Randolph *lawyer, educator*
Brenner, Janet Maybin Walker *lawyer*
Bresnahan, Pamela Anne *lawyer, mediator, arbitrator*
Brody, Peter Martin *lawyer*
Bromwich, Michael Ray *lawyer*
Bronstein, Alvin J. *lawyer*
Brower, Charles Nelson *lawyer, judge*
Brown, Barbara Berish *lawyer*
Brown, Lisa (Elizabeth Merrill Brown) *lawyer*
Brown, Preston *lawyer*
Browne, Richard Cullen *lawyer*
Bruce, Carol Elder *lawyer*
Bruce, Estel Edward *lawyer*
Bruemmer, Russell John *lawyer*
Brunsvold, Brian Garrett *lawyer, educator*
Buckley, Jeremiah Stephen *lawyer*
Buffon, Charles Edward *lawyer*
Bui, Hung H. *lawyer*
Burchfield, Bobby Roy *lawyer*
Burck, William Anthony *lawyer*
Burka, Robert Alan *lawyer*
Burnley, James Horace, IV, *lawyer, former United States Secretary of Transportation*
Burns, Stephen Gilbert *lawyer*
Burt, Jeffrey Amsterdam *lawyer*
Burton, Robert Arnold *lawyer*
Busby, David *lawyer*
Butler, Mary K. *prosecutor*
Butler, Michael Francis *lawyer*
Butler, Paul William *lawyer*
Butts, Cassandra Quin *lawyer*
Cabrera, Orlando Jose *lawyer*
Calamaro, Raymond Stuart *lawyer*
Callery, T. Grant (Grant Callery) *lawyer*

Calvani, Terry lawyer
Cameron, Donald B., Jr. lawyer
Campbell, Nancy Duff lawyer
Campos, Roel Clark lawyer, former commissioner
Caplin, Mortimer Maxwell lawyer, educator
Carey, Sarah Collins lawyer
Carlisle, Linda Elizabeth lawyer
Carneal, George Upshur lawyer
Carr, Lawrence Edward, Jr. lawyer
Carter, Barry Edward law educator
Carter, William Joseph lawyer
Cary, George S. lawyer
Cashen, Henry Christopher, II, lawyer, government agency administrator
Casserly, James Lund lawyer
Cassidy, Robert Charles, Jr. lawyer
Chabot, Elliot Charles lawyer
Chandler, James Phillip III law educator
Chang, Sam Hsien-Cheng lawyer
Chanin, Michael Henry lawyer
Chanin, Robert Howard lawyer
Chaplin, Peggy Louie lawyer
Chopko, Mark E. lawyer
Chorba, Timothy A. lawyer, former ambassador
Choukas-Bradley, James Richard lawyer, musician
Christian, Betty Jo lawyer
Christian, Ernest Silsbee, Jr. lawyer
Clark, Julia L. Akins lawyer
Clayton, Carol A. lawyer
Clayton, Michael F. lawyer
Clement, Paul Drew lawyer, former federal agency administrator
Coats, Daniel Ray lawyer, former ambassador, Former United States Senator, Ind
Cobb, Ty lawyer
Cobbs, Nicholas Hamner lawyer, judge
Coffina, Scott A. lawyer
Cohen, Louis Richard lawyer
Cohn, Sherman Louis lawyer, educator
Cole, John Pope, Jr. lawyer
Cole, Robert Theodore lawyer
Coleman, William Thaddeus, Jr. lawyer, former United States Secretary of Transportation
Colley, Mark Douglas lawyer
Collins, Daniel Francis lawyer
Collinson, Dale Stanley lawyer
Colson, Earl Morton lawyer, educator
Comstock, Robert Francis lawyer
Condrell, William Kenneth lawyer
Connelly, Warren E. lawyer
Conner, Frank M. (Rusty) III lawyer
Conrad, Robin S. lawyer
Cook, Bryson Leitch lawyer
Cook, Elisebeth Collins lawyer, former federal agency administrator
Cook, Harry Clayton, Jr. lawyer
Cook, Michael Harry lawyer
Cooper, Charles Justin lawyer, former federal agency administrator
Cooper, Ronald Stephen lawyer
Corn-Revere, Robert lawyer
Cortese, Alfred William, Jr. lawyer, consultant
Coston, William Dean lawyer
Covucci, George E. lawyer
Cox, M. Carolyn lawyer
Cox, Robert Haymes lawyer
Coyne, Patrick Joseph lawyer
Craft, Robert Homan, Jr. lawyer
Craig, Gregory Bestor lawyer
Crocker, Thomas Edward lawyer
Crosby, William Duncan, Jr. lawyer
Cross, Meredith B. lawyer
Crump, John lawyer
Culvahouse, Arthur Boggess, Jr. lawyer
Cummings, Frank lawyer
Curtin, Peter J. lawyer
Daley, Henry J. lawyer
Damelin, Harold D. lawyer, former federal agency administrator
Dana, Jonathan M. lawyer
Davidson, Daniel Ira lawyer
Davidson, Daniel Morton lawyer
Davidson, Tom William lawyer
Davis, William E. lawyer
Davison, Calvin retired lawyer
Deal, Jill B. lawyer
Deckelbaum, Nelson lawyer
Deese, Pamela McCarthy lawyer
deKieffer, Donald Eulette lawyer
de Leon, Sylvia A. lawyer
Dell'Orto, Daniel Joseph lawyer
Dembling, Paul Gerald lawyer, former government official
Denison, Mary Boney lawyer
Deutsch, Peter R. former congressman
Dienelt, John F. lawyer
Diercks, Walter Elmer lawyer
diGenova, Joseph E. lawyer
Dinh, Viet D. law educator
Disheroon, Fred Russell lawyer
Dolan, Michael William lawyer
Dolin, Mitchell F. lawyer
Donegan, Charles Edward lawyer, educator
Doolittle, Jesse William, Jr. lawyer
Dorfman, Marc lawyer
Doty, James Robert lawyer
Dowd, John Maguire lawyer
Dowley, Joseph Kyran lawyer
Downs, Clark Evans lawyer
Dribinsky, Leonard lawyer
Dudas, Jon W. lawyer, former federal agency administrator
Duff, James C. lawyer
Duncan, John Dean, Jr. lawyer
Durney, Michael Cavalier lawyer
Durnil, Gordon Kay lawyer, arbitrator, diplomat
Dwyer, Maureen Ellen lawyer
Eastment, Thomas James lawyer
Easton, John Jay, Jr. lawyer
Edelman, Peter Benjamin lawyer, educator
Edmisten, Jane Moretz lawyer, educator
Efros, Ellen Ann lawyer
Eggleston, W. Neil lawyer
Ehrenhaft, Peter David lawyer
Eizenstat, Stuart Elliot lawyer, former federal agency administrator
Ellett, Ted (E. Tazewell Ellett) lawyer
Ellicott, John LeMoyne lawyer
Ellis, Courtenay lawyer
Elmer, Brian Christian lawyer
Elrod, Eugene Richard lawyer
Ensenat, Donald Burnham lawyer, former ambassador
Epstien, Jay Alan lawyer
Espy, Mike (Alphonso Michael Espy) lawyer, former United States Secretary of Agriculture, former United State Representative from Mississippi
Evans, David C. lawyer
Ewing, Kenneth Patrick Ky lawyer
Fairbanks, Richard Monroe III lawyer, educator, retired ambassador
Fedders, John Michael lawyer
Feder, Samuel L. lawyer
Feffer, Gerald Alan lawyer
Feinstein, Deborah L. lawyer
Feith, Douglas Jay lawyer, former federal agency administrator
Feldman, Clarice Rochelle lawyer
Feldman, Elliot Jay lawyer
Fennell, Stephen A. lawyer
Ferguson, Lewis Hamilton III lawyer
Ferris, Charles Daniel lawyer, former government official
Fiedler, Marc lawyer, advocate
Field, Andrea Bear lawyer
Fielding, Fred Fisher lawyer
Fields, Wendy Lynn lawyer
Finkel, Eugene Jay lawyer
Firestone, Charles Morton lawyer, educator
Fishburne, Benjamin Postell III lawyer
Fisher, Alice Stevens lawyer, former federal agency administrator
Fisher, Bart Steven lawyer, educator, investment banker
Fisher, Benjamin Chatburn lawyer
Fitzpatrick, James Franklin lawyer
Flagg, Ronald Simon lawyer
Flanigan, Timothy Elliott lawyer, former federal official
Flannery, Ellen Joanne lawyer
Fleischman, Aaron I. lawyer
Fong, Ivan Kenneth lawyer, former health products executive
Ford, Ann K. lawyer
Ford, Harold Eugene, Jr. law educator, former United States Representative from Tennessee
Forester, John Gordon, Jr. lawyer
Forrest, Herbert Emerson lawyer
Fortuno, Victor M. lawyer
Foscarinis, Maria lawyer
Foster, C(harles) Allen lawyer
Frank, Richard Asher lawyer, health products executive
Frank, Theodore David lawyer
Freedman, Jay Weil lawyer
Fried, Bruce Merlin lawyer
Friedrich, Dabney Langhorne lawyer, commissioner
Friedrich, Matthew Wilhelm lawyer, former federal agency administrator
Frost, Martin, III, (Jonas Martin Frost III) lawyer, former congressman
Fu Claffe, Lily lawyer
Fulton, Scott Colton lawyer
Gable, Edward Brennan, Jr. lawyer
Gallagher, Michael David lawyer, former federal agency administrator
Gallas, Philip S. lawyer
Gallo, Kenneth A. lawyer
Gardiner, Kent A. lawyer
Garr, Sally D. lawyer
Garre, Gregory G. law educator, former federal agency administrator
Garrett, Theodore Louis lawyer
Garrish, Theodore John lawyer
Garza, Deborah A. lawyer, former federal agency administrator
Gazzola, Robert Allen lawyer
Geller, Kenneth Steven lawyer
Geniesse, Robert John lawyer
Gerson, Stuart Michael lawyer
Gerstell, Glenn Steven lawyer
Gibbs, Lawrence Blair lawyer
Gideon, Kenneth Wayne lawyer
Gidley, J. Mark lawyer
Gilmore, James Stuart III lawyer, former governor
Ginsberg, Benjamin L. lawyer
Ginsburg, Martin David lawyer, educator
Glancz, Ronald Robert lawyer
Gleklen, Jonathan Ian lawyer
Glick, Leslie Alan lawyer
Glynn, Edward F., Jr. lawyer
Goewey, David W. lawyer
Gold, Peter Frederick lawyer
Goldberg, Fred T., Jr. lawyer
Goldberg, Jolande Elisabeth law librarian
Goldberg, Seth A. lawyer
Goldsmith, Barry Richard lawyer
Goldstein, Frank Robert lawyer
Goldstein, Michael B. lawyer
Goodman, Alfred Nelson lawyer
Gorelick, Jamie Shona lawyer
Gorrell, J. Warren, Jr. lawyer
Gottfried, Keith Evan lawyer
Gottschalk, Thomas A. lawyer, retired automotive executive
Graefe, Frederick H. lawyer
Graham, Jonathan P. lawyer
Grant, Paula DiMeo lawyer, mediator, nursing educator
Gray, Edward Wesley lawyer
Green, Donald Hugh lawyer
Green, Thomas Charles lawyer
Greenberger, Marcia Devins lawyer
Gross, Charles R. prosecutor
Gross, Kenneth Andrew lawyer
Gulland, Eugene D. lawyer
Gunn, Will A. lawyer, retired military officer
Gutman, Harry Largman lawyer, educator
Guttman, Egon law educator
Hackett, Susan J. legal association administrator, lawyer
Hagner, John D. lawyer
Halbert, Gary L. lawyer
Halloran, Michael James lawyer
Halvorson, Newman Thorbus, Jr. lawyer
Hand, Lloyd N. lawyer
Hanlon, William R. lawyer
Hansen, Kenneth lawyer
Hanzlik, Rayburn DeMara lawyer
Harper, Emery Walter lawyer
Harper, Keith M. lawyer
Harris, Don Victor, Jr. lawyer
Harris, Jeffrey lawyer
Harris, Scott Blake lawyer
Harrison, Earl David lawyer, real estate company officer
Hartman, Michael Ross lawyer
Hassett, Joseph Mark lawyer
Hastings, Douglas Alfred lawyer
Hausfeld, Michael D. lawyer
Havens, Charles William III retired lawyer
Hawke, John Daniel, Jr. lawyer, former federal official
Haynes, R. Michael lawyer
Heffernan, James Vincent lawyer
Hefferon, Thomas Michael lawyer
Heintz, John Edward lawyer
Helfer, Michael Stevens lawyer
Heller, Jack Isaac lawyer
Heller, John Roderick III lawyer, corporate financial executive
Henderson, Douglas Boyd lawyer
Henke, Michael John lawyer, educator
Herman, Anthony lawyer
Herzog, Richard Barnard lawyer
Herzstein, Robert Erwin lawyer
Hewitt, Paul Buck lawyer
Hill, David R. lawyer, former federal agency administrator
Hills, Carla Anderson lawyer, former United States Secretary of Housing and Urban Development
Hills, Roderick M. lawyer, former government official
Hirschhorn, Eric Leonard lawyer
Hobbs, J. Timothy, Sr. lawyer
Hobelman, Carl Donald lawyer
Hochman, Nathan Joseph lawyer, former federal agency administrator
Hoffinger, Adam Steven lawyer
Hoffman, E. Leslie lawyer
Hoffman, Joel Elihu lawyer
Hoffman, Richard Bennett court administrator
Hollingsworth, Joe Gregory lawyer
Hollis, Sheila Slocum lawyer
Holmstead, Jeffrey Ralph lawyer, former federal agency administrator
Horahan, Edward Bernard III lawyer
Horn, Charles M. lawyer
Horowitz, Philip Martin lawyer
Howard, Glen Scott lawyer, consultant
Howard, Jeffrey Hjalmar lawyer
Howard, Roscoe Conklin, Jr. lawyer, former prosecutor
Howell, Beryl A. lawyer, commissioner
Hoyt, Robert F. lawyer
Huberman, Richard Lee lawyer
Huddleson, Edwin Emmett III lawyer
Huge, Harry lawyer
Hughes, Elizabeth R. (Beth Hughes) lawyer
Hughes, Marija Matich law librarian
Hunnicutt, Charles Alvin lawyer
Hutchinson, James S. (Jamie Hutchinson) lawyer
Hutt, Peter Barton lawyer
Huttler, Stephen B. lawyer
Hyman, Lester Samuel lawyer
Ihnen, Jeffrey L. lawyer
Irving, Thomas L. lawyer
Isbell, David Bradford lawyer, educator
Ives, Stephen Bradshaw, Jr. retired lawyer
Iwry, J. Mark lawyer
Jackson, Darryl W. lawyer, former federal agency administrator
Jackson, John Howard lawyer, educator
Jacobson, David Edward lawyer
Jacobson, Richard Lee lawyer, educator
Jakes, J. Michael lawyer
Jeffress, William Horace, Jr. lawyer
Johnson, Broderick D. lawyer, lobbyist
Johnson, Jeh Charles lawyer
Johnson, Oliver Thomas, Jr. lawyer
Johnson, Philip McBride lawyer
Johnston, Alan Cope lawyer
Jolly, Thomas R. lawyer, lobbyist
Jonas, John Francis lawyer
Jones, Aidan Drexel lawyer
Jones, Allen, Jr. lawyer
Jones, Brian Wesley lawyer
Jones, George Washington, Jr. lawyer
Jones, Kelsey A. law educator, law administrator
Jones, Michael D. lawyer
Jordan, Robert Elijah III lawyer
Kabalkin, Barry E. lawyer
Kabel, Robert James lawyer, political organization administrator
Kafka, Gerald Andrew lawyer
Kahn, Thomas S. lawyer
Kanovsky, Helen Renee lawyer
Kantor, Mickey (Michael Kantor) lawyer, former United States Secretary of Commerce
Kaplan, Elaine D. lawyer
Kaplan, Gilbert B. lawyer
Kaplan, Paul A. lawyer
Kaplan, Steven lawyer
Kapp, Robert Harris lawyer
Kappel, Brett Guthrie lawyer, lobbyist
Kappler, Ann M. lawyer, finance company executive
Kass, Benny Lee lawyer
Katz, John W. lawyer, state official
Katz, Sherman E. lawyer
Katzman, Scott H. lawyer
Kaufman, Joshua Jacob lawyer
Kaufman, Thomas Frederick lawyer, educator
Keeney, John Christopher lawyer
Keeney, John Christopher, Jr. lawyer
Keisler, Peter Douglas lawyer, former federal agency administrator
Kelly, Thomas J., Jr. lawyer
Kennard, Mary Elizabeth lawyer
Kennedy, Victoria Reggie lawyer, not-for-profit executive
Kent, M. Elizabeth lawyer
Kepplinger, Gary L. lawyer
Kerry, Cameron Forbes lawyer
Kiko, Philip George lawyer
Kilberg, William Jeffrey lawyer, director
Kim, Sukhan lawyer
Kim, Wan J. lawyer, former federal agency administrator
Kimmitt, Robert Michael lawyer, former federal official
Kingham, Richard Frank lawyer
Kirsch, Laurence Stephen lawyer
Kiser, Chérie R. lawyer
Kissel, Peter Charles lawyer
Kittrell, Steven Dan lawyer
Kittrie, Nicholas international lawyer, writer
Klarfeld, Peter James lawyer
Klawiter, Donald Casimir lawyer
Klein, Roger A. lawyer
Kline, Thomas R. lawyer
Knowles, Jeffrey D. lawyer
Kohn, Stephen Martin lawyer
Kolasky, William Joseph, Jr. lawyer
Korb, Donald L. lawyer
Korth, Fritz-Alan lawyer
Kramer, Andrew Michael lawyer
Kramer, William David lawyer
Krasnow, Erwin Gilbert lawyer
Kriesberg, Simeon M. lawyer
Kroener, William Frederick III lawyer
Kushner, Gary Jay lawyer
Kutler, Alison L. lawyer
Kyhos, Thomas Flynn lawyer
Lake, William Truman lawyer
Lambert, Jeremiah Daniel lawyer, educator
Lambert, Steven Charles lawyer
Lamken, Jeffrey A. lawyer
Lamm, Carolyn Beth lawyer
Landry, Brock R. lawyer
Lane, Bruce Stuart lawyer
Lane, John Dennis lawyer
Lapidus, Lawrence Searle lawyer
Laporte, Gerald Joseph Sylvestre lawyer
Larroca, Raymond G. lawyer
Latham, Patricia Horan lawyer
Latham, Peter Samuel lawyer
Latham, Weldon Hurd lawyer
Latimer, Katharine Ruth lawyer
Laughlin, Felix B. lawyer
Laughlin, James Harold, Jr. lawyer
Lavelle, Joseph P. lawyer
Lavine, Henry Wolfe lawyer
Law, Steven James lawyer, former federal agency administrator
Lawler, William E. III lawyer
Lazarus, Arthur, Jr. lawyer
Lazarus, Kenneth Anthony lawyer
Lee, Ronald Derek lawyer
Leibold, Arthur William, Jr. lawyer
Levin, Edward M. lawyer
Levine, Henry David lawyer
Levinson, Lawrence Edward lawyer
Levinstein, Mark Steven lawyer, educator
Levy, Gregg H. lawyer
Levy, Mark Irving lawyer
Lewis, Eleanor Roberts lawyer
Lewis, Guy A. prosecutor
Lewis, Mark K. lawyer
Lewis, William Henry, Jr. lawyer
Lewris, Basil J. lawyer
Lichtenstein, Elissa Charlene legal association executive
Liebeskind, Richard lawyer
Lindsey, Seth Mark lawyer
Liptak, Adam lawyer, reporter
Litt, Robert S. lawyer
Livingston, Donald Ray lawyer
Livingston, Douglas Mark lawyer
Locklear, Arlinda Faye lawyer
Loepere, Carol Colborn lawyer
Loftus, Carroll Michael (Michael Loftus) lawyer
Loots, James Mason lawyer
Lopatin, Alan G. lawyer
Low, Daniel L. lawyer
Lowell, Abbe David lawyer
Lupo, Raphael V. lawyer
Luque, Nancy lawyer
Lurensky, Marcia Adele lawyer
Luskin, Robert David lawyer
Luxton, Jane Charlotte lawyer
Lybecker, Martin Earl lawyer
Lyons, Dennis Gerald lawyer
Lyons, Mona lawyer
MacBeth, Angus lawyer
Machen, Ronald C. lawyer
Macleod, John Amend lawyer
Madden, Thomas James lawyer, educator
Magielnicki, Robert L. lawyer
Mahoney, Maureen E. lawyer
Manatt, Charles Taylor lawyer
Mancuso, Mario lawyer, former federal agency administrator
Manning, Michael J. lawyer
Manthei, John Richard lawyer
Marcuss, Stanley Joseph lawyer
Margeton, Stephen George law librarian
Marks, Herbert Edward lawyer
Marshall, Alison Buell lawyer
Martella, Roger Romulus, Jr. lawyer, former federal agency administrator
Martin, David Alan lawyer, law educator
Martin, David Briton Hadden, Jr. lawyer
Martin, Guy lawyer
Martin, Thomas Stephen lawyer
Martin, William R. (Billy Martin) lawyer
May, Timothy James lawyer
Mayers, Daniel Kriegsman lawyer
Mayo, George Washington, Jr. lawyer
Mayopoulos, Timothy J. lawyer, mortgage company executive
Mays, Janice Ann lawyer
Mazo, Mark Elliott lawyer
McCann, Clifton Everett lawyer

Zaucha, Jerome J. *lawyer*
Zax, Leonard A. *lawyer*
Zeidman, Philip Fisher *lawyer*
Zentay, John H. *lawyer*
Zimmerman, Edwin Morton *lawyer*
Zwick, Kenneth Lowell *lawyer, director*
Zwillinger, Marc J. *lawyer*

FLORIDA

Alachua
Gaines, Weaver Henderson *lawyer*

Altamonte Springs
Hoogland, Robert Frederics *lawyer*

Anna Maria
Hoffmann, Carl Konrad *retired lawyer*

Arcadia
Hall, Miles Lewis, Jr. *lawyer*

Aventura
McKenna, Peter Dennis *lawyer*

Bascom
Brooten, Kenneth Edward, Jr. *lawyer, author, writer, rancher*

Bay Harbor Islands
Solomon, Michael Bruce *lawyer*

Boca Raton
Beber, Robert H. *lawyer, diversified financial services company executive*
Buckstein, Mark Aaron *lawyer, mediator, educator*
Cowen, Edward S. *lawyer, consultant*
Garcia, Elisa Dolores *lawyer*
Godofsky, Stanley *lawyer*
Gortz, Albert W. *lawyer*
Gracin, Hank *lawyer*
Kitzes, William Fredric *lawyer, advocate, researcher*
Marcus, Andrea Candace Sills *lawyer*
Martin, James Russell *lawyer*
Reinstein, Joel *lawyer*
Roselli, Richard Joseph *lawyer*
Schechterman, Lawrence *lawyer, chef, business consultant*
Silver, Barry Morris *lawyer*
Smith, Yoshimi O. *lawyer*
Wolf, Jerome L. *lawyer*

Bonita Springs
Crutcher, Michael Bayard *lawyer, retired consumer products company executive*
Dignan, Thomas Gregory, Jr. *retired lawyer*
Hastings, Vivien N. *lawyer*

Boynton Beach
Altman, Allan *lawyer*
McNair, Russell Arthur, Jr. *lawyer*

Bradenton
Brenner, Frank *lawyer*
Shapiro, Richard Michael *lawyer*

Brooksville
Cario, Jeffrey Peter *lawyer*

Celebration
Schroeder, James White *retired lawyer*

Clearwater
Pope, Fred Wallace, Jr. *lawyer*
Tragos, George Euripedes *lawyer*
Vetter, David R. *lawyer*
Weidemeyer, Carleton Lloyd *lawyer*
Zschau, Julius James *lawyer*

Coconut Grove
Tein, Michael *lawyer*

Coral Gables
Buell, Rodd Russell *lawyer*
Coe, Jack Martin *lawyer, consultant*
Dady, Robert Edward *lawyer*
Graham, H. Dillon III *lawyer*
Green, Stephanie *lawyer*
Hernandez, Eugenio *lawyer*
Klock, Joseph Peter, Jr. *lawyer*
Moss, Ambler Holmes, Jr. *lawyer, educator, former ambassador*
Murai, Rene Vicente *lawyer*
Pérez Damera, Myra M. *lawyer*
Saleh, Anis Nouhad *lawyer*

Dade City
Brennan, Thomas Emmett *lawyer*

Davie
Richmond, Gail Levin *law educator*

Daytona Beach
Barker, Robert Osborne (Bob Barker) *mediator, retired educator*
Del Rosario, Romeo Rey *lawyer*
Harris, Christy Franklin *lawyer*
Neitzke, Eric Karl *lawyer*
Vasilaros, Steven Thomas *lawyer*

Deerfield Beach
Lenoff, Michele Malka *lawyer*

Delray Beach
Reichart, Stuart Richard *lawyer*

Destin
Havens, Jason Edward *lawyer*

Englewood
Van Leuven, Robert Joseph *lawyer*

Estero
Morgan, Dennis Richard *lawyer*

Fort Lauderdale
Adams, S.C. Chase *lawyer, writer, speaker, radio and television commentator, financial consultant*
Barre, Steven Craig *lawyer*
Bogenschutz, J. David *lawyer*
Bunnell, George Eli *lawyer*
Bustamante, Nestor *lawyer*
Dressler, Robert A. *lawyer*
Ferrando, Jonathan P. *lawyer, automotive executive*
Franz, William Mathew *lawyer*
Goldberg, Alan Joel *lawyer*
Haliczer, James Solomon *lawyer*
Hargrove, John Russell *lawyer*
Hirsch, Jeffrey Allan *lawyer*
Jarvis, Robert Mark *law educator*
Kuehne, Benedict P. *lawyer*
Litman, Donna Carol *law educator*
Meeks, William Herman III *lawyer*
Moss, Stephen Bruce *lawyer*
Nyce, John Daniel *lawyer*
O'Brien, Patrick T. *lawyer*
Picazio, Kim Lowry *lawyer*
Polish, Sheldon S. *lawyer*
Russell, Terrence Joseph *lawyer*
Sanders, Dale R. *lawyer*
Sherr, Brian J. *lawyer*
Sullivan, Edward Delano *lawyer, investor*
Turner, Hugh Joseph, Jr. *lawyer*
Wright, Blandin James *lawyer*

Fort Myers
Colasurd, Richard Michael *retired lawyer*
Medvecky, Robert Stephen *lawyer*
Rice, J. Jeffrey *lawyer*
Stanley, Bruce McLaren, Sr. *lawyer*
Sturgis, Kathy Ann *lawyer*

Fort Pierce
Conklin, Howard Lawrence *lawyer*

Gainesville
Boyes, Patrice Flinchbaugh *lawyer*
Criser, Marshall M. *lawyer, retired academic administrator*
Hiers, Richard Hyde *lawyer, educator, writer*
Maurer, Virginia Gallaher *law educator*
O'Donnell, Bernard Joseph, Jr. *lawyer*
Price, Mary Kathleen *law librarian, educator*
Probert, Walter *retired law educator*
Smith, David Thornton *lawyer, educator*
Van Alstyne, W. Scott, Jr. *lawyer, educator*

Hernando
Keyser, Frank Ray, Jr. *lawyer, Former Governor, Vermont*

Hobe Sound
Markoe, Frank, Jr. *lawyer, health facility administrator*

Hollywood
Phillips, Gary Stephen *lawyer*
Rogovin, Lawrence H. *lawyer*

Homestead
Ireland, Patricia *lawyer*

Jacksonville
Ansbacher, Barry Barnett *lawyer*
Appel, Laurence Bruce *lawyer, retail executive*
Beytagh, Francis X. *law educator*
Boyer, Tyrie Alvis *lawyer*
Bradford, Dana Gibson, II, *lawyer*
Bryan, Joseph Shepard, Jr. *lawyer*
Bullock, Bruce Stanley *lawyer, mediator*
Cavendish, Michael Robert *lawyer*
Cobb, James E. *lawyer*
Coker, Howard Coleman *lawyer*
Commander, Charles Edward *lawyer, real estate consultant*
Coxe, Henry M. III *lawyer*
Farnell, Robert Henry, II, *lawyer*
Fitzsimmons, Ellen Marie *lawyer*
Gabel, George DeSaussure, Jr. *lawyer*
Israel, Kimberly Held *lawyer*
Kelso, Linda Yayoi *lawyer*
Kent, John Bradford *lawyer*
Killea, Michael F. *lawyer*
Main, James L. *lawyer*
Mc Carthy, Edward, Jr. *retired lawyer*
Milton, Joseph Payne *lawyer*
Moseley, James Francis *lawyer*
Rinaman, James Curtis, Jr. *lawyer*
Sadowski, Peter T. *lawyer*
Sheppard, William J. *lawyer*
Weaver, Dianne Jay *lawyer*
White, Edward Alfred *lawyer*

Jacksonville Beach
Mahorner, James G. *lawyer*
McWilliams, John Lawrence III *lawyer*

Juno Beach
Knapp, George M. *lawyer*
Tancer, Edward F. *lawyer, utilities executive*

Jupiter
Click, David Forrest *lawyer, investment advisor*
Solomon, Stephen L. *lawyer*

Key Largo
Mattson, James Stewart *lawyer, environmental scientist, educator*

Key West
MacDougall, Peter *retired lawyer*

Lake Mary
Silver, Elaine Terry *lawyer*

Lake Placid
Adams, Herbert Ryan *publishing executive, retired minister*

Lakeland
Attaway, John A., Jr. *lawyer*
Cooper, James Russell *retired law educator*
Wendel, John Fredric *lawyer, consultant*

Lakewood Ranch
Fetterman, James Charles *lawyer*

Largo
Hult, Catherine Day *lawyer*

Lecanto
Goss, Richard Henry *lawyer*

Leesburg
Austin, Robert Eugene, Jr. *lawyer*
Fechtel, Vincent John *legal administrator*

Longwood
Tomasulo, Virginia Merrills *retired lawyer*

Lutz
Wester, J. Meredith *lawyer*

Maitland
Wilder, Charles David *lawyer*

Marco Island
Kerstetter, Wayne Arthur *law educator*

Melbourne
Brown, Seymour R. *retired lawyer*
Cacciatore, S. Sammy *lawyer*
Cavallucci, Eugene S. (Gene Cavallucci) *lawyer*
Hament, Andrew Stanton *lawyer*

Miami
Alvarez, Cesar L. *lawyer*
Anderson, Terence James *law educator*
Arsht, Adrienne *lawyer, broadcast and bank executive*
Astigarraga, Jose I(gnacio) *lawyer*
Baena, Scott Louis *lawyer*
Baumberger, Charles Henry *lawyer*
Beckham, Walter Hull, Jr. *law educator*
Berman, Bruce Judson *lawyer*
Black, Roy *lawyer*
Bloom, Mark David *lawyer*
Blumberg, Edward Robert *lawyer*
Brodie, Steve Jeffrey *lawyer*
Burnett, Henry *lawyer*
Cardenas, Alberto R. *lawyer, lobbyist*
Connor, Terence Gregory *lawyer*
David, Christopher Mark *lawyer*
Dienstag, Cynthia Jill *lawyer*
Dunn, Richard M. *lawyer*
Eaton, Joel Douglas *lawyer*
Engel, Tala *lawyer*
England, Arthur Jay, Jr. *lawyer, former state justice*
Epstein, Gary M. *lawyer*
Essen, Richard Joel *lawyer*
Fatovic, Robert Dean *lawyer*
Fleming, Joseph Z. *lawyer*
Gang, Robert C. *lawyer*
Gong, Edmond Joseph *lawyer*
Greenleaf, Walter Franklin *lawyer*
Gross, Leslie Jay *lawyer, real estate broker, investment banker*
Grossman, Robert Louis *lawyer*
Hall, Andrew Clifford *lawyer*
Hartz, Steven Edward Marshall *lawyer, educator*
Hoffman, Larry J. *lawyer*
Houlihan, Gerald John *lawyer*
Humphrey, Christine M. *lawyer*
Jhabvala, Farrokh *lawyer*
Jimenez, Marcos Daniel *former prosecutor*
Landy, Burton Aaron *lawyer*
Leibowitz, Mark Alan *lawyer*
Levine, Robert Jeffrey *lawyer*
Lipoff, Norman Harold *lawyer*
Lynch, Dennis O. *law educator, former dean*
Martinez, Walfrido (Wally Martinez) *lawyer*
Martinez-Fraga, Pedro J. *lawyer*
Mehta, Eileen Rose *lawyer*
Mena, Daniel *lawyer, arbitrator*
Menéndez Cambó, Patricia *lawyer*
Mudd, John Philip *lawyer*
Murphy, Timothy James *lawyer*
Nachwalter, Michael *lawyer*
Norris, Timothy Jon *lawyer*
Nuernberg, William Richard *lawyer*
Orlin, Karen J. *lawyer*
Papy, Charles C. III *lawyer*
Poston, Rebekah Jane *lawyer*
Pratt, John Patrick *lawyer*
Quentel, Albert Drew *lawyer*
Rossman, Stephen F. *lawyer*
Rubin, Steven D. *lawyer*
Saldana, Alfonso Manuel *lawyer*
Samole, Myron Michael *lawyer, management consultant*
Schulman, Clifford A. *lawyer*
Sears, John Patrick *lawyer*
Sirvén, José E. *lawyer*
Skolnick, S. Harold *lawyer*
Sonberg, Steven *lawyer*
Sonnett, Neal Russell *lawyer*
Thornburg, Frederick Fletcher *lawyer executive, educator*
Tifford, Arthur W. *lawyer*
Traurig, Robert Henry *lawyer*
Upshaw, Anthony N. *lawyer*
Vento, M. Thérèse *lawyer*
Walton, Rodney Earl *lawyer, historian*
Weiner, Lawrence *lawyer*
Weinger, Steven Murray *lawyer*
Weinstein, Alan Edward *lawyer*
Wing, James David *lawyer*
Zack, Stephen Neal *lawyer*
Zeydel, Diana S. C. *lawyer, former professional ballet dancer*

Miami Beach
Ryce, Donald Theodore, Jr. *lawyer*

Miami Gardens
Ersek, Gregory Joseph Mark *lawyer*
Light, Alfred Robert *law educator*

Naples
Adams, John Marshall *lawyer*
Anderson, John Thomas *lawyer*
Bruce, Jackson Martin, Jr. *lawyer*
Cox, Joe Bruce *lawyer*
Crehan, Joseph Edward *lawyer*
Doub, William Offutt *lawyer*
Ericson, Roger Delwin *lawyer, forest resource company executive*
Faison, William Franklin, II, *lawyer, retired manufacturing corporation executive*
Gardner, George Victor *lawyer*
Goldman, Joel J. *retired lawyer*
Heindl, Phares Matthews *lawyer*
Lowery, William Herbert *lawyer*
Norton, Elizabeth Wychgel *retired lawyer*
Peck, Bernard Sidney *lawyer*
Petersen, David L. *lawyer*
Root, Stanley William, Jr. *retired lawyer*
Smith, Numa Lamar, Jr. *lawyer*
Strauss, Jerome Manfred *lawyer, bank executive*
Westman, Carl Edward *lawyer*

Neptune Beach
Mantle, Raymond Allan *lawyer*

North Fort Myers
Miller, William Charles *lawyer*

North Palm Beach
Brophy, Gilbert Thomas *lawyer*

Orlando
Ahlers, Glen-Peter, Sr. *law library director, educator, consultant*
Arkin, J. Gordon *lawyer*
Brumby, Andrew M. *lawyer*
Christiansen, Patrick T. *lawyer*
Clem, Alexander Murphree *lawyer*
Courtright, Paul Eric *lawyer*
deBeaubien, Hugo H. *lawyer*
Eagan, William Leon *lawyer*
Frey, Louis, Jr. *lawyer, federal official*
Gangitano, James J. *lawyer*
Gerber, Daniel J. *lawyer*
Gilbert, Suzanne E. *lawyer*
Gray, J. Charles *lawyer, former cattle rancher*
Handley, Leon Hunter *lawyer*
Kelaher, James Peirce *lawyer*
Leonhardt, Frederick Wayne *lawyer*
Mock, Frank Mackenzie *lawyer*
Nadeau, Robert Bertrand, Jr. *lawyer*
Pierce, John Gerald (Jerry) *lawyer*
Ragland, Robert Allen *lawyer*
Rounsaville, Keith Eugene *lawyer*
Russ, James Matthias *lawyer*
Sheaffer, William Jay *lawyer*
Shives, Paula J. *lawyer, food service executive*
Sims, Roger W. *lawyer*
Skambis, Christopher Charles, Jr. *lawyer*
Sloane, Jeremy Stanton *lawyer*
Snively, Stephen Wayne *lawyer*
Spaulding, Karla Rae *lawyer*
Weiss, Christopher John *lawyer*
Wells, Charles Talley *lawyer, retired state supreme court justice*
Yates, Leighton Delevan, Jr. *lawyer*

Ormond Beach
Hayes, Larry B. *retired lawyer*
Logan, Sharon Brooks *lawyer*

Osprey
Partoyan, Garo Arakel *lawyer*

Palm Beach
Adler, Frederick Richard *lawyer, corporate financial executive*
Canary, Nancy Halliday *lawyer*
Crawford, Sandra Kay *lawyer*
Parker, Ellis Jackson III *lawyer, broadcaster*

Palm Beach Gardens
Auerbach, Paul Ira *lawyer*
Freedman, Warren *lawyer, educator, judge*
Newman, Stephen Michael *lawyer*
O'Brien, Thomas George III *lawyer*
Savrann, Richard Allen *lawyer*
Tauber, Mark J. *retired lawyer*

Palm Coast
Duncan, Donald William *lawyer*

Palm Harbor
Richeson, Hugh Anthony, Jr. *lawyer*

Palmetto Bay
O'Connor, Kathleen Mary *lawyer*

Panama City
Patterson, Christopher Nida *lawyer*

Patrick AFB
McAlwee, Martin Frederick *lawyer*

Pensacola
Bookman, Alan B. *lawyer*
Bozeman, Frank Carmack *lawyer*
Geeker, Nicholas Peter *lawyer, judge*
Levin, Fredric Gerson *lawyer*
Papantonio, Mike (James Michael Papantonio) *lawyer, talk radio host*
Soloway, Daniel Mark *lawyer*
Windham, John Franklin *lawyer, educator*

Plant City
Buchman, Kenneth William *lawyer*

Sparkman, Steven Leonard *lawyer*

Pompano Beach
Gude, Nancy Carlson *lawyer*

Ponte Vedra Beach
Davis, Wendell, Jr. *lawyer*

Port Saint Lucie
Lambert, George Robert *lawyer, realtor*

Punta Gorda
Bailey, F. Lee (Francis Lee Bailey) *lawyer*

Saint Augustine
Brady, James Joseph *labor arbitrator*
Poland, Richard Clayton *law educator*

Saint Petersburg
Bairstow, Frances Kanevsky *arbitrator, mediator, educator*
Battaglia, Anthony Sylvester *lawyer*
Escarraz, Enrique III *lawyer*
Glass, Roy Leonard *lawyer*
Higham, Frederick A. *lawyer*
Jacob, Bruce Robert *law educator*
Janney, Oliver James *lawyer*
Lang, Joseph Hagedorn *lawyer*
Lousberg, Peter Herman *former lawyer*
Mann, Sam Henry, Jr. *retired lawyer*
Matecki, Paul L. *lawyer*
Mayhall, Clifford Wesley *lawyer*
Moody, Lizabeth Ann *lawyer, educator*
Paver, Robert L. *lawyer*
Zacur, Richard Aaron *lawyer*

Sanford
Capps, James Leigh, II, *lawyer, military officer*

Sanibel
Rothschild, Donald Phillip *retired lawyer, arbitrator*

Sarasota
Blucher, Paul Arthur *lawyer*
Ehrlich, Bernard Herbert *lawyer, trade association administrator*
Freeman, Richard Merrell *retired lawyer*
Garland, Richard Roger *lawyer*
Greenfield, Robert Kauffman *retired lawyer*
Heitler, George *lawyer*
Herb, Frank Steven *lawyer*
Knickerbocker, Robert Platt, Jr. *lawyer, consultant*
Raimi, Burton Louis *lawyer*
Tachna, Ruth C. *retired lawyer*

Sea Ranch Lakes
Gore, George Henry *lawyer*

Sebring
McCollum, James Fountain *lawyer*

South Miami
Keedy, Christian David *lawyer*

Stuart
Bowdish, James L.S. *lawyer*
Gary, Willie E. *lawyer*

Tallahassee
Aurell, John Karl *lawyer*
Baggett, Fred W. *lawyer*
Barnett, Martha Walters *lawyer*
Buck, Thomas Randolph *retired lawyer, diversified financial services company executive*
Carson, Leonard Allen *lawyer*
Curtin, Lawrence N. *lawyer*
Ervin, Robert Marvin *lawyer*
Gievers, Karen A. *lawyer*
Harper, Robert Augustus *lawyer*
Holcomb, Lyle Donald, Jr. *retired lawyer*
Johnson, Kelly Overstreet *lawyer*
Kerns, David Vincent *lawyer*
Kirwin, Thomas F. *prosecutor*
Kitchen, E.C. Deeno *lawyer*
Miller, Gregory R. *retired prosecutor*
Miller, Morris Henry *lawyer*
Minnick, Bruce Alexander *lawyer*
Phipps, Benjamin Kimball, II, *lawyer*
Reid, Sue Titus *law educator*
Simpson, Larry Dean *lawyer*
Terry, Anne Curtis *lawyer, writer*
Waas, George Lee *lawyer*
Walker, Karen D. *lawyer*
Zaiser, Kent Ames *lawyer*

Tampa
Albritton, Arthur Dallas *lawyer*
Albritton, Brian (A. Brian Albritton) *prosecutor*
Barbas, Stephen Michael *lawyer*
Barkin, Marvin E. *lawyer*
Barton, Bernard Alan, Jr. *lawyer*
Bedke, Michael A. *lawyer*
Black, Caroline Kapusta *lawyer*
Campbell, Richard Bruce *lawyer*
Christian, Terry Clifton *lawyer*
Corcoran, Clement Timothy III *lawyer, mediator, retired judge*
Cury, Bruce Paul *lawyer, magistrate, educator*
Davidson, Charles Thomas *lawyer*
Davis, Jim *lawyer, former congressman*
Diehr, Beverly Hunt *lawyer*
Doliner, Nathaniel Lee *lawyer*
Garrett, Howard Leon *lawyer*
Gilbert, Leonard Harold *lawyer*
Gonzalez, Joe Manuel *lawyer*
Grammig, Robert James (Bob Grammig) *lawyer*
Gunn, Lee Delton, IV, *lawyer*
Hamilton, William F. *lawyer*
Humphries, J. Bob *lawyer*
Jamieson, Michael Lawrence *lawyer*
Koren, Edward Franz, Jr. *lawyer*
Lane, Robin R. *lawyer*
LaRussa, Rudy G. *lawyer*
Martin, Gary Wayne *lawyer*
McAdams, John Pope *lawyer*
McDevitt, Sheila Marie *retired lawyer, energy executive, business consultant*
Mulholland, Jason Christopher *lawyer*
O'Neill, Albert Clarence, Jr. *lawyer*
O'Neill, Robert E. *prosecutor*
Pankau, Barbara Ropes *lawyer*
Pellett, Jon Michael *lawyer*
Robinson, John William, IV, *lawyer*
Rydberg, Marsha Griffin *lawyer*
Smith, William Reece, Jr. *lawyer*
Susanin, Timothy Scott *lawyer, health products executive*
Taub, Theodore Calvin *lawyer*
Thomas, Gregg Darrow *lawyer*
Thomas, Wayne Lee *lawyer*
Unhjem, Michael Bruce *lawyer*
Wagner, Frederick William (Bill Wagner) *lawyer*
Waller, Edward Martin, Jr. *lawyer*
Watson, Roberta Casper *lawyer*
Weinberg, Morris (Sandy Weinberg) *lawyer*
Whatley, Jacqueline Beltram *lawyer*
Yerrid, C. Steven *lawyer*

Venice
Clarke, Edward Owen, Jr. *lawyer*
Miller, Allan John *retired lawyer, oil industry executive*

Vero Beach
Geiman, J. Robert *lawyer*
Higgs, John H. *lawyer*
Ughetta, William Casper *lawyer, manufacturing executive, director*

Village Of Golf
Sutter, William Paul *lawyer*

Wellington
Behren, Robert Alan *lawyer, accountant*

West Palm Beach
Ackerman, David P. *lawyer*
Beall, Kenneth Sutter, Jr. *lawyer*
Beasley, James W., Jr. *lawyer*
Chopin, L. Frank *lawyer*
Coyle, Dennis Patrick *lawyer, retired utilities executive*
Damsel, Charles H., Jr. *lawyer*
Gildan, Phillip Clarke *lawyer*
Henry, Thornton Montagu *lawyer*
Hill, Thomas William, Jr. *lawyer, educator*
Kelley, Craig I. *lawyer, educator*
Lamb, Kevin Thomas *lawyer*
Lane, Matthew Jay *lawyer*
Link, Scott J. *lawyer*
Loring, Arthur *lawyer, diversified financial services company executive*
Moore, George Crawford Jackson *lawyer*
Mrachek, Lorin Louis *lawyer*
Roshkind, Robin *divorce lawyer*
Royce, Raymond Watson *lawyer, rancher, citrus grower, investor*
Schneider, Lisa A. *lawyer*
Spillias, Kenneth George *lawyer*
Strolla, Cory C. *lawyer*
Vilchez, Victoria Anne *lawyer*
Zeller, Ronald John *lawyer*

Weston
Blandon, Elizabeth Rose *lawyer*

Winter Park
Ackert, T(errence) W(illiam) *lawyer*
Builder, J. Lindsay, Jr. *lawyer*
Dempsey, Bernard Hayden, Jr. *lawyer*
Hadley, Ralph Vincent III *lawyer*
Heinle, Richard Alan *lawyer*
Helms, Roger D. *lawyer*
Jontz, Jeffry Robert *lawyer*
Kittleson, Henry Marshall *lawyer*
Morgan, Mary Ann *lawyer*
Swann, Richard Rockwell *lawyer, banker*
Troutman, Holmes Russell *lawyer*
Vila, Adis Maria *lawyer, educator, business government executive*

GEORGIA

Athens
Carlson, Ronald Lee *law educator*
Chaffin, Verner Franklin *lawyer, educator*
Ellington, Charles Ronald *lawyer, educator*
Hellerstein, Walter *lawyer*
Huszagh, Fredrick Wickett *lawyer, information technology executive, educator*
Kurtz, Paul Michael *law educator*
Puckett, Elizabeth Ann *law librarian, educator*
Tolley, Edward Donald *lawyer*

Atlanta
Abrams, Harold Eugene *lawyer*
Albert, Ross Alan *lawyer*
Alexander, Kent B. *lawyer*
Alexander, Miles Jordan *lawyer*
Altman, Robert *lawyer*
Antonino, Lauren Slepin *lawyer*
Barr, Robert Laurence, Jr., (Bob Barr) *lawyer, former United States Representative from Georgia*
Bassett, W. Randall *lawyer*
Beckham, Walter Hull III *lawyer*
Beerman, Joel I. *lawyer, chemical manufacturing company executive*
Bird, Wendell Raleigh *lawyer*
Blake, Elizabeth K. *lawyer*
Blank, A(ndrew) Russell *lawyer*
Bonds, John Wilfred, Jr. *lawyer*
Booth, Gordon Dean, Jr. *lawyer*
Bowden, Henry Lumpkin, Jr. *lawyer*
Bratton, James Henry, Jr. *lawyer*
Brecher, Armin George *lawyer*
Byrne, Granville Bland III *lawyer*
Cadenhead, Alfred Paul *lawyer*
Carpenter, David Allan *lawyer*
Carter, Dudley Rochelle *lawyer*
Chilivis, Nickolas Peter *retired lawyer*
Ciucci, Joseph A. *lawyer*
Clarke, Thomas Hal *lawyer*
Cohen, Ezra Harry *lawyer*
Cohen, George Leon *lawyer*
Cohen, Lori G. *lawyer*
Cohen, N. Jerold *lawyer*
Conboy, Kevin Patrick *lawyer*
Cook, Philip Carter *lawyer*
Croft, Terrence Lee *lawyer, mediator, arbitrator*
Curtis, J. Vaughan *lawyer*
Dalton, John Joseph *lawyer*
Darden, George Washington, III, (Buddy Darden) *lawyer, former United States Representative from Georgia*
Davis, Benjamin Alando *lawyer*
Davis, Frank Tradewell, Jr. *lawyer*
Denny, Richard Alden, Jr. *retired lawyer*
Domby, Arthur H. *lawyer*
Douglas, John Lewis *lawyer*
Driver, Walter W., Jr. *lawyer*
Dunlevie, Steven S. *lawyer*
Durrett, James Frazer, Jr. *retired lawyer*
Eckl, William Wray *lawyer*
Edwards, Stephen Allen *lawyer*
Egan, Michael Joseph *retired lawyer, state legislator*
Finnerty, Terry P. *lawyer*
Fleming, Julian Denver, Jr. *lawyer*
Forry, Robert H. *lawyer*
Fortin, Raymond D. *lawyer, bank executive*
Foulke, Edwin Gerhart, Jr. *lawyer, former federal agency administrator*
Gambrell, David Henry *lawyer*
Gary, Kenneth J. *lawyer*
Gaudet, Matthew C. *lawyer*
Genberg, Ira *lawyer*
Gerakitis, Richard *lawyer*
Girth, Marjorie Louisa *lawyer, educator*
Glaser, Arthur Henry *lawyer, mediator*
Goldstein, Elliott *retired lawyer, director*
Gomes, Matthew Trainor *lawyer*
Grady, Kevin E. *lawyer*
Greer, Bernard Lewis, Jr., (Ben Greer) *lawyer*
Groton, James Purnell *lawyer, arbitrator*
Harkey, Robert Shelton *retired lawyer*
Hasson, James Keith, Jr. *lawyer, educator*
Hatcher, James A. *lawyer*
Hawks, Barrett Kingsbury *lawyer*
Hay, Peter Heinrich *law educator*
Hays, Richard R. *lawyer*
Healy, Bridget M. *lawyer*
Hinchey, John William *lawyer*
Hinkel, Daniel Farris *lawyer, writer, investment company executive*
Hinson, H. Douglas *lawyer*
Hobby, Scott M. *lawyer*
Hoff, Gerhardt Michael *lawyer, insurance company executive*
Holland, George Edison, Jr., (Ed) *lawyer, utilities executive*
Hopkins, John David *lawyer*
Howard, Harry Clay *lawyer*
Howell, Arthur *lawyer*
Ide, Roy William III *lawyer*
Izard, John *lawyer*
Jameson, Louis Norwood (L. Norwood 'Woody' Jameson) *lawyer*
Janney, Donald Wayne *lawyer*
Jenkins, Albert Felton, Jr. *lawyer*
Johnson, Benjamin F(ranklin) III *lawyer*
Johnson, John H. *lawyer*
Jones, Glower Whitehead *lawyer*
Jordak, John A., Jr. *lawyer*
Katz, Joel Abraham *lawyer*
Kaufman, Mark David *lawyer*
Kaufman, Mark Stuart *lawyer*
Kaywood, Sam K., Jr. *lawyer*
Kelly, Geoffrey J. *lawyer, beverage company executive*
Kelly, James Patrick *lawyer*
Kennedy, Dorian Bruce *lawyer*
Kessler, Richard Paul, Jr. *lawyer*
Khoury, Kenneth F. *lawyer, air transportation executive*
Kilgore, Cada T. III *lawyer*
Killorin, Robert Ware *lawyer*
Kitchens, William H. *lawyer*
Kneisel, Edmund M. *lawyer*
Knowles, Marjorie Fine *law educator, dean*
Kung, Lisa *lawyer*
Lackland, Theodore Howard *lawyer*
Lamberth, James A. *lawyer*
Lamberth, Rebecca M. *lawyer*
Landau, Michael B. *law educator*
Landon, James Henry *lawyer*
Latham, John L. *lawyer*
Leach, Karen Kay *lawyer*
Leet, Alan C. *lawyer*
Leonard, David Morse *lawyer*
Lester, Charles Turner, Jr. *lawyer*
Lewis, Stephen E. *lawyer*
Linch, Keth *commercial real estate and partnership lawyer*
Linkous, William Joseph, Jr. *lawyer*
Lipshutz, Robert Jerome *lawyer, former government official*
Litman, Seth Adam *lawyer*
Looby, Brian William *lawyer, lobbyist*
Loveland, L. Joseph, Jr. *lawyer*
Lower, Robert Cassel *lawyer, educator*
Marshall, John Treutlen *lawyer, educator*
Marvin, Charles Arthur *law educator*
Matschullat, Dale Lewis *lawyer*
McAlpin, Kirk Martin *lawyer*
McClure, Teri Plummer *lawyer, delivery service executive*
McNeill, Thomas Ray *lawyer*
Meachum, Daniel Ray *lawyer*
Mercer, John T.W. *lawyer*
Miller, Douglas Linn *lawyer*
Mize, Gerald L., Jr. *lawyer*
Mobley, John Homer, II, *lawyer*
Moeling, Walter Goos, IV, *lawyer*
Mones, Stuart Matthew *lawyer*
Moore, Rodney Gregory *lawyer*
Nahmias, David E. *prosecutor*
Newton, Floyd Childs III *lawyer*
Norman, Albert George, Jr. *lawyer*
Owens, Laura Lewis *lawyer*
Pelypenko, Elizabeth *lawyer*
Persons, (W.) Ray (W. Ray Persons) *lawyer, legal association administrator*
Petrik, Michael Thomas *lawyer*
Phillips, Barry *lawyer*
Pike, Larry Samuel *lawyer*
Pilcher, James Brownie *lawyer*
Pottle, Steven L. *lawyer*
Quittmeyer, Peter Charles *lawyer*
Raby, Kenneth Alan *lawyer, retired military officer*
Rafuse, Nancy E. *lawyer, director*
Reed, Glen Alfred *lawyer*
Reeder, Joe Robert *lawyer, former federal official*
Reinhardt, Daniel Sargent *lawyer*
Remar, Robert Boyle *lawyer*
Rhodes, Thomas Willard *lawyer*
Riggs, Gregory Lynn *lawyer*
Rogers, C. B. *lawyer*
Rogers, DeWitt Ralph *lawyer*
Roseborough, Teresa Wynn *lawyer*
Rusche, Mark C. *lawyer*
Sanders, Carl E. *lawyer, former Governor of Georgia*
Schroder, Jack Spalding, Jr. *lawyer*
Schulte, Jeffrey Lewis *lawyer*
Shapiro, George Howard *retired lawyer*
Smith, Edward Kendrick *lawyer*
Smith, Jeffrey Michael *lawyer*
Smith, Sidney Oslin, Jr. *lawyer*
Stallings, Ronald Denis *lawyer*
Stein, Douglas Warren *lawyer*
Stephenson, Mason Williams *lawyer*
Stockton, David A. *lawyer*
Sweeney, Neal James *lawyer*
Swift, Frank Meador *lawyer*
Taylor, George Kimbrough, Jr. *lawyer*
Taylor, Roger Dale *lawyer*
Thomas, Lizanne *lawyer*
Thompson, Philip C. *lawyer, investment advisor, private equity fund manager, educator, journalist*
Thrower, Randolph William *lawyer*
Travis, Robert M. *lawyer*
VanWoerkom, Jack A. *lawyer, consumer products company executive*
Varner, Chilton Davis *lawyer*
Volentine, Richard J., Jr. *lawyer*
Weathersby, Michael Nelson *lawyer*
Wellon, Robert G. *lawyer*
Whitley, Joe Dally (Joe Dally Whitley) *lawyer*
Williams, Neil, Jr. *retired lawyer*
Williamson, R. Mark *lawyer*
Wilson, Brent Lawrence *lawyer, mediator*
Wilson, James Hargrove, Jr. *lawyer*
Wood, L. Lin, Jr. *lawyer*
Wright, Peter Meldrim *lawyer*
Zealey, Sharon Janine *lawyer*

Augusta
Hyder, James Davis, Jr. *lawyer*

Calhoun
Perillo, Salvatore J. *lawyer*

College Park
Patterson, P(ickens) Andrew *lawyer*

Columbus
Brinkley, Jack Thomas *lawyer, former United States Representative, Georgia*
Hatcher, Samuel F. *lawyer, diversified financial services company executive*
Johnson, Walter Frank, Jr. *lawyer*
Loudermilk, Joey M. *lawyer, insurance company executive*
Patrick, James Duvall, Jr. *lawyer*
Poydasheff, Robert Stephen *lawyer*
Wooten, Joel Orba, Jr. *lawyer*

Decatur
Williams, Rita Tucker *lawyer*

Duluth
Chandler, Elizabeth Brannen *lawyer*
Lupton, Stephen D. *lawyer*
Sloan, Donnie Robert, Jr. *lawyer*

Dunwoody
Callison, James W. *retired lawyer, air transportation executive*

Jasper
Marger, Edwin *lawyer*

Macon
Dantzler, Deryl Daugherty *lawyer, educator, dean*
Jones, Frank Cater *retired lawyer*
Robinson, W. Lee *lawyer*

Madison
DuBose, Charles Wilson *lawyer*

Marietta
Bentley, Fred Douglas, Sr. *lawyer*
Braun, Michael Rene *lawyer*
Hellrung, Stephen Andrew *lawyer*
Nowland, James Ferrell *lawyer*
Powell, Richard Lynn *lawyer*

Moultrie
Collum, Rick Daniel *lawyer*

Norcross
Koman, Alan James *lawyer, educator*

Roswell
Birmingham, Richard Gregory *lawyer*
Nilsen, Arthur Christian *lawyer*

Saint Simons Island
Taylor, Philip Raymond *lawyer*

Thau, William Albert *lawyer*

Sandy Springs
Owen, Robert Hubert *lawyer, real estate broker*

Savannah
Berry, Jack K. *lawyer*
Booth, Edmund A., Jr. *prosecutor*
Bowman, Catherine McKenzie *lawyer*
Dickey, David Herschel *lawyer, accountant*
Forbes, Morton Gerald *lawyer*
McCracken, Eugene Luke *lawyer*
Searcy, William Nelson *lawyer, director*
Stillwell, Walter Brooks III *lawyer*

Sea Island
Revoile, Charles Patrick *lawyer*

Sky Valley
Wilkinson, Albert Mims, Jr. *lawyer*

Smyrna
Seigler, Michael Edward *lawyer, librarian*

Statesboro
Edenfield, Gerald M. *lawyer*
Franklin, James Burke *lawyer*
Wilson, LeVon Edward *lawyer, educator*

Tifton
Reinhardt, George Robert *lawyer*

Valdosta
Dodd, Roger J. *lawyer*
Sinnott, John Patrick *lawyer, educator*

Watkinsville
Wright, Robert Joseph *lawyer*

HAWAII

Honolulu
Akiba, Lorraine Hiroko *lawyer*
Akinaka, Asa Masayoshi *lawyer*
Ariyoshi, George Ryoichi *lawyer, business consultant, former governor*
Bloede, Victor Carl *lawyer, consultant, director*
Boas, Frank *retired lawyer*
Callies, David Lee *lawyer, educator*
Case, James Hebard *lawyer*
Char, Vernon Fook Leong *lawyer*
Cowan, Stuart Marshall *lawyer*
Dang, Marvin S.C. *lawyer*
Deaver, Phillip Lester *lawyer*
Devens, Paul *retired lawyer*
Fong, Peter C. K. *lawyer, judge*
Fukumoto, Leslie Satsuki *lawyer*
Gay, E(mil) Laurence *lawyer*
Gelber, Don Jeffrey *lawyer*
Godbey, Robert Carson *lawyer*
Hazlett, Mark A. *lawyer*
Heller, Ronald Ian *lawyer*
Hipp, Kenneth Byron *lawyer*
Katayama, Robert Nobuichi *retired lawyer*
Kim, Gregory Robert *lawyer, entrepreneur*
Kubo, Edward Hachiro, Jr. *prosecutor*
Lacy, John Robert *lawyer*
Lee, Dale W. *lawyer*
Lilly, Michael Alexander *lawyer, writer*
Louie, David Mark *lawyer*
Ma, Alan Wai-Chuen *lawyer*
Mau-Shimizu, Patricia Ann *lawyer*
Miller, Richard Sherwin *law educator*
Nakata, Gary Kenji *lawyer*
Nasky, H(arold) Gregory *lawyer*
Okinaga, Lawrence Shoji *lawyer*
Potts, Dennis Walker *lawyer*
Reber, David James *lawyer*
Sakamoto, Ronald Rikio *lawyer, construction executive*
Sato, Glenn Kenji *lawyer*
Sumida, Gerald Aquinas *lawyer*
Woo, Vernon Ying-Tsai *lawyer, real estate developer*

Kapolei
Zabanal, Eduardo Olegario *lawyer*

Kihei
Burns, Richard Gordon *retired lawyer, writer, consultant*

Kula
Rohlfing, Frederick William *lawyer, retired judge, political scientist*

Wailuku
Goldsmith, Stephen Ernest *lawyer*

IDAHO

Boise
Craig, Hemmens *law educator, director*
Geston, Mark Symington *lawyer*
Hunter, Forrest Walker *lawyer*
Leroy, David Henry *lawyer*
McGown, John, Jr. *lawyer*
Meyer, Christopher Hawkins *lawyer*
Moss, Thomas E. *prosecutor*
Park, William Anthony (Tony Park) *lawyer*
Shurtliff, Marvin Karl *lawyer*

Caldwell
Kerrick, David Ellsworth *lawyer*

Coeur D' Alene
Reed, Scott W. *lawyer*

Hailey
Hogue, Terry Glynn *lawyer*
Roark, Keith (R. Keith Roark) *lawyer, political organization administrator*

Idaho Falls
Hopkins, C. Timothy (Tim Hopkins) *lawyer*

Kamiah
Mills, Lawrence *lawyer, business and transportation consultant*

Ketchum
Holland, Robert James *retired lawyer*

Lewiston
Tait, John Reid *lawyer*

Pocatello
Nye, W. Marcus W. *lawyer*

Potlatch
Severns, Karen S. *family court services administrator*

Twin Falls
Berry, L. Clyel *lawyer*

ILLINOIS

Abbott Park
Schumacher, Laura J. *lawyer, pharmaceutical executive*

Arlington Heights
Blomquist, Ernest Richard III *lawyer*

Barrington
Lee, William Marshall *lawyer*
Wyatt, James Frank, Jr. *lawyer*

Belleville
Gossage, Roza B. *lawyer, educator*
Hess, Frederick J. *lawyer*
Ripplinger, George Raymond, Jr. *lawyer*

Bourbonnais
McClure, Thomas Edward *lawyer*

Burr Ridge
Decker, Richard Knore *lawyer*

Calumet City
Oyeyemi, Olusola Olayinka *lawyer*
Scullion, Annette Murphy *lawyer, educator*

Carbondale
Clemons, John Robert *lawyer*
Dahlen, Michael F. *lawyer*
Lee, Mark Richard *lawyer, educator*

Carol Stream
Larson, Ward Jerome *lawyer, retired banker*

Carrollton
Strickland, Hugh Alfred *lawyer*

Carthage
Glidden, John Redmond *lawyer*

Champaign
Boyle, Francis Anthony *law educator*
Kindt, John Warren *lawyer, educator*
Krause, Harry Dieter *law educator*
Maggs, Peter Blount *lawyer, educator*
Mamer, Stuart Mies *lawyer*
Nowak, John E. *law educator*

Chatham
Post, Alan Richard *lawyer*

Chicago
Abrams, Lee Norman *lawyer*
Acker, Ann E. *lawyer*
Adelman, Stanley Joseph *lawyer*
Adelman, Steven Herbert *lawyer*
Alexander, Ann *lawyer*
Allen, Henry Sermones, Jr. *lawyer*
Allen, Thomas Draper *lawyer*
Anderson, Kimball Richard *lawyer*
Angst, Gerald L. *lawyer*
Anthony, Michael Francis *lawyer*
Antonio, Douglas John *lawyer*
Anvaripour, M. A. *lawyer*
Appel, Nina Schick *law educator, dean, academic administrator*
Aronson, Virginia L. *lawyer*
Athas, Gus James *lawyer*
Avery, Robert Dean *lawyer*
Babcock, Sandra L. *lawyer, educator*
Badel, Julie *lawyer*
Baer, John Richard Frederick *lawyer*
Baird, Douglas Gordon *law educator, dean*
Baird, James *lawyer*
Baker, Bruce Jay *lawyer*
Baldwin, Shaun McParland *lawyer*
Banoff, Sheldon Irwin *lawyer*
Barden, Larry A. *lawyer*
Barner, Sharon Ruth *lawyer*
Barr, John Robert *retired lawyer*
Barron, Harold Sheldon *lawyer*
Barron, Howard Robert *lawyer*
Bart, Susan Therese *lawyer*
Bashwiner, Steven Lacelle *lawyer*
Beck, Philip S. *lawyer*
Beem, Jack Darrel *retired lawyer*
Bellows, Laurel Gordon *lawyer*
Bennington, Thomas Francis *lawyer, county official*
Berens, Mark Harry *lawyer*
Berenzweig, Jack Charles *lawyer*
Berger, Robert Michael *lawyer*
Berkoff, Adam T. *lawyer*
Berkoff, Mark Andrew *lawyer*
Berkowitz, Sean M. *lawyer*
Bernstein, Charles Bernard *lawyer*
Bernstein, H. Bruce *lawyer*
Berolzheimer, Karl *retired lawyer*
Bettman, Suzanne S. (Sue Bettman) *lawyer*
Bixby, Frank Lyman *retired lawyer*
Bleiweiss, Shell J. *lawyer*
Block, Neal Jay *lawyer*
Blount, Michael Eugene *lawyer*
Bodenstein, Ira *lawyer*
Boehnen, Daniel A. *lawyer*
Boho, Dan L. *lawyer*
Bowe, William J(ohn) *lawyer*
Bowen, Stephen Stewart *lawyer*
Boyer, Bruce A. *law educator, director*
Boykin, Richard Renarda *lawyer, former legislative staff member*
Boykins, Michael L. *lawyer*
Bramnik, Robert Paul *lawyer*
Brice, Roger Thomas *lawyer*
Brizzolara, Charles Anthony *lawyer, director*
Bro, Ruth Hill *lawyer*
Bromley, Richard *lawyer*
Brown, Alan Crawford *lawyer*
Brown, Gregory K. *lawyer*
Brown, Matthew S. *lawyer*
Bruner, Philip Lane *arbitrator, mediator*
Bulger, Brian Wegg *lawyer*
Burke, Thomas Joseph, Jr. *lawyer*
Burns, James B. *prosecutor*
Busey, Roxane C. *lawyer*
Calabresi, Steven G. *law educator*
Callahan, Michael R. *lawyer*
Carlin, Dennis J. *lawyer*
Carlson, Walter Carl *lawyer*
Carpenter, David William *lawyer*
Carr, Jeffrey W. *lawyer, manufacturing executive*
Carr, Walter Stanley *lawyer*
Carroll, William Kenneth *lawyer, educator, psychologist, theologian*
Cascino, Anthony Elmo, Jr. *lawyer, insurance company executive*
Ceko, Theresa C. *lawyer, educator*
Chafetz, Barry Richard *lawyer*
Chandler, Kent, Jr. *lawyer*
Chatfield, Lloyd C. *lawyer*
Chemers, Robert Marc *lawyer*
Cherney, James Alan *lawyer*
Chizewer, David J. *lawyer*
Chomicz, Thomas E. *lawyer, consultant*
Cicero, Frank, Jr. *lawyer*
Clark, Michael A. *lawyer*
Clemens, Richard Glenn *lawyer*
Clinton, Edward Xavier *lawyer*
Cohen, Frederick H. *lawyer*
Cole, Thomas Amor *lawyer*
Collen, John *lawyer, educator*
Comiskey, Michael Peter *lawyer*
Congalton, Christopher William *lawyer*
Conklin, Thomas William *lawyer*
Conway, Michael Maurice *lawyer*
Copeland, Edward Jerome *lawyer*
Costello, John William *lawyer*
Crane, Edward M. *lawyer*
Craven, George W. *lawyer*
Cremin, Susan Elizabeth *lawyer*
Crossan, John Robert *lawyer*
Crull, Jan, Jr. *lawyer, investment banker, consultant*
Csar, Michael F. *lawyer*
Cummings, Andrea J. *lawyer*
Cummings, Daniel *lawyer*
Cunningham, Robert James *lawyer*
Cusack, John Thomas *lawyer*
Custer, Charles Francis *lawyer*
Daley, Michael Joseph *lawyer*
Dam, Kenneth W. *law educator, former federal agency administrator*
D'Amato, Anthony *law educator*
Davis, Muller *lawyer*
Davis, Scott Jonathan *lawyer*
Dechene, James Charles *lawyer*
Deitrick, William Edgar *lawyer*
Delp, Wilbur Charles, Jr. *lawyer*
Dent, Thomas G. *lawyer*
D'Esposito, Julian C., Jr. *lawyer*
Devine, Richard A. (Dick DeVine) *lawyer, former prosecutor*
Ditelberg, Joshua L. *lawyer*
Dockterman, Michael *lawyer*
Domanskis, Alexander Rimas *lawyer*
Dondanville, Patricia *lawyer*
Donlevy, John Dearden *lawyer*
Donohue, Richard Harney *lawyer*
Downs, Robert K. *lawyer*
Drymalski, Raymond *lawyer*
DuCanto, Joseph Nunzio *lawyer, educator*
Duncan, John Patrick Cavanaugh *lawyer*
Dunn, Edwin Rydell *lawyer*
Durchslag, Stephen P. *lawyer*
Eaton, Maja Campbell *lawyer*
Egan, Kevin James *lawyer*
Eggert, Russell Raymond *lawyer*
Eimer, Nathan Philip *lawyer*
Elden, Gary Michael *lawyer*
Elson, John S. *law educator*
Erens, Jay Allan *lawyer*
Esrick, Jerald Paul *lawyer*
Evanich, Kevin Reese *lawyer*
Fahner, Tyrone C. *lawyer, former state attorney general*
Fazio, Peter Victor, Jr. *lawyer*
Feinstein, Fred Ira *lawyer*
Fellows, Jerry Kenneth *lawyer*
Felsenthal, Steven Altus *lawyer*
Ferguson, James Richard *lawyer, educator*
Ferguson, Stanley Lewis *lawyer*
Filip, Mark Robert *lawyer, former federal agency administrator*
Findlay, Donald Cameron *lawyer, former federal agency administrator, insurance company executive*
Finke, Robert Forge *lawyer*
Finnegan, Sheila *lawyer*
Fitzgerald, Patrick J., Jr. *prosecutor*
Fort, Jeffrey C. *lawyer*
Foudree, Bruce William *lawyer*
Fox, Paul T. *lawyer*
Franklin, Richard Mark *lawyer*
Frederick, Thomas James *lawyer*
Freehling, Daniel Joseph *lawyer, consultant*
Freeman, Lee Allen, Jr. *lawyer*
Freeman, Louis S. *lawyer*
Friedman, Lawrence Milton *lawyer, finance company executive*
Fross, Roger Raymond *lawyer*
Furlane, Mark Elliott *lawyer*
Gabric, Ralph J. *lawyer*
Gaggini, John Edmund *lawyer*
Garber, Samuel B. *lawyer, retail executive*
Gavin, John Neal *lawyer*
Gecker, James M. *lawyer*
Gelman, Andrew Richard *lawyer*
Genson, Edward Marvin *lawyer*
Georges, Mara Stacy *lawyer*
Geraldson, Raymond I., Jr. *lawyer*
Gerber, Dean N. *lawyer*
Gersh, Deborah Louise *lawyer*
Gerstein, Mark Douglas *lawyer*
Ginsburg, Allen J. *lawyer*
Glieberman, Herbert Allen *lawyer*
Golan, Stephen Leonard *lawyer*
Goldblatt, Stanford Jay *lawyer*
Gralen, Donald John *lawyer*
Grant, Robert Nathan *lawyer*
Greenbaum, Lewis *lawyer*
Greenberg, Richard T. *lawyer*
Grossman, Robert Mayer *lawyer*
Grund, David Ira *lawyer*
Guthman, Jack *lawyer*
Gutstein, Solomon *lawyer*
Hahn, Arthur W. *lawyer*
Hammond, Celeste M. *law educator*
Hannah, Wayne Robertson, Jr. *lawyer*
Hannay, William Mouat III *lawyer*
Hanson, Ronald William *lawyer*
Hardgrove, James Alan *lawyer*
Harmon, Teresa Wilton *lawyer*
Harrington, Carol A. *lawyer*
Harrington, James Timothy *lawyer*
Harris, Donald Ray *lawyer*
Harrison, Holly A. *lawyer*
Harrold, Bernard *lawyer*
Hartz, Michael O. *lawyer*
Hayes, David John Arthur, Jr. *legal association executive*
Hayward, Thomas Zander, Jr. *lawyer*
Heatwole, Mark M. *lawyer, director*
Heinz, John Peter *lawyer, educator*
Heinz, William Denby *lawyer*
Heisler, Quentin George, Jr. *lawyer*
Heller, Stanley J. *lawyer, physician, educator*
Helman, Robert Alan *lawyer*
Helmholz, R(ichard) H(enry) *law educator*
Henning, Joel Frank *lawyer, writer*
Henrick, Michael Francis *lawyer*
Herald, J. Patrick *lawyer*
Herbert, William Carlisle *law educator*
Hess, Sidney J., Jr. *lawyer*
Hilliard, David Craig *lawyer, educator*
Hilliker, Donald Beckstett *lawyer*
Hirsh, Bobbe *lawyer, accountant*
Hodes, Scott *lawyer*
Hofer, Roy Ellis *lawyer*
Hoff, John Scott *lawyer*
Hoffman, Richard Bruce *lawyer*
Hoffman, Valerie Jane *lawyer*
Homburger, Thomas Charles *lawyer*
Horwich, Allan *lawyer*
Hoskins, Richard Jerold *lawyer*
Howe, Jonathan Thomas *lawyer*
Howell, R(obert) Thomas, Jr. *lawyer, former food company executive*
Hummel, Gregory William *lawyer*
Hunt, Craig A. *lawyer, paper company executive*
Ismail, Tarek *lawyer*
Jachino, Daneen L. *legal administrator*
Jacobson, Marian Slutz *lawyer*
Jacoby, John Patrick *lawyer*
Jaconetty, Thomas Anthony *lawyer*
Jacover, Jerold Alan *lawyer*
Jager, Melvin Francis *lawyer*
Jahns, Jeffrey *lawyer*
Jennings, Jonathan Scott *lawyer*
Johnson, Garrett Bruce *lawyer*
Johnson, Richard Fred *lawyer*
Junewicz, James J. *lawyer*
Kallick, David A. *lawyer*
Kamin, Kim *law educator*
Kaminsky, Richard Alan *lawyer*
Kaplan, Howard Gordon *lawyer*
Katz, Avrum Sidney *lawyer*
Kaufman, David J. *lawyer*
Kawitt, Alan *lawyer, arbitrator*
Kellman, Barry S. *law educator, consultant*
Kerwin, Brian P. *lawyer*
Kikoler, Stephen Philip *lawyer*
Kim, Michael Charles *lawyer*
King, Sharon Louise *retired lawyer*
Kiriakos, Thomas Sam *lawyer*
Kissel, Richard John *lawyer*
Kite, Steven B. *lawyer*
Klenk, James Andrew *lawyer*
Knight, Christopher Nichols *lawyer*
Knuepfer, Robert Claude, Jr. *lawyer*
Kolek, Robert Edward *lawyer*
Kopelman, Ian Stuart *lawyer*
Kozak, John W. *lawyer*
Kramer, Andrea S. *lawyer*
Kriss, Robert J. *lawyer*
Kroll, Barry Lewis *retired lawyer*
Kroot, Jason M. *lawyer*
Krueger, Herbert William (Bert Krueger) *lawyer*
Landes, William M. *law educator*
Landow-Esser, Janine Marise *lawyer*
Laner, Richard Warren *lawyer*
Latimer, Kenneth Alan *lawyer*
Learner, Howard Alan *lawyer*
Lefco, Kathy Nan *law librarian*
LeRoy, Spencer III *lawyer*
Levi, John G. *lawyer*
Levin, Charles Edward *lawyer*
Levin, Jack S. *lawyer*
Levin, Lawrence Daniel *lawyer*
Levy, Peter A. *lawyer*
Levy, Susan C. *lawyer*
Lewis, Charles B. *lawyer*

Lieb, Peter *lawyer*
Liggio, Carl Donald *lawyer*
Litwin, Burton Howard *lawyer*
Lochbihler, Frederick Vincent *lawyer*
Lockwood, Gary Lee *lawyer*
Loesch, William R. *lawyer*
Lona, Marie A. *lawyer*
Looman, James R. *lawyer*
Lopez, Joseph R. *lawyer*
Lorch, Kenneth F. *lawyer*
Lovejoy, Paul Robert *lawyer, air transportation executive*
Lowinger, Frederick Charles *lawyer*
Lubin, Donald G. *lawyer*
Lufrano, Michael Richard *lawyer*
Lurie, Paul Michael *lawyer*
Luscombe, George A., II, *lawyer*
Lutter, Paul Allen *lawyer*
Lyerla, Bradford Peter *lawyer*
Lynn, Nicholas J. *lawyer*
Macaulay, Susan Jane *lawyer, educator*
MacCarthy, Terence Francis *lawyer*
Maher, John M. *lawyer*
Malinowski, Arthur Anthony *lawyer, arbitrator*
Malkin, Cary Jay *lawyer*
Malovany, Howard *lawyer, food products executive*
Mancoff, Neal Alan *lawyer*
Manning, Amy B. *lawyer*
Mansfield, Karen Lee *lawyer*
Manzo, Edward David *lawyer*
Martin, Arthur Mead *lawyer*
Martin, Laura Keidan *lawyer*
Mascherin, Terri Lynn *lawyer*
Matis, Nina B. *lawyer*
McClure, James Julius, Jr. *lawyer, former city official*
McCracken, Thomas James, Jr. *lawyer*
McCue, Judith W. *lawyer*
McDermott, John H. *lawyer*
McDonald, Thomas Alexander *lawyer*
McGowan, Michael Jeremy *lawyer*
McKenzie, Robert Ernest *lawyer*
McKittrick, William Wood *lawyer*
McLaren, Richard Wellington, Jr. *lawyer*
McLaughlin, T. Mark *lawyer*
McVisk, William Kilburn *lawyer*
Mehlman, Mark Franklin *lawyer*
Melbinger, Michael S. *lawyer*
Melton, David Reuben *lawyer*
Menchetti, David Barry *lawyer*
Mendelsohn, David Edward *lawyer*
Michaels, Richard Edward *lawyer*
Mikva, Abner Joseph *lawyer, retired judge*
Miller, Kenneth W. *lawyer*
Miller, Ronald Stuart *lawyer*
Miller, Stephen Ralph *lawyer*
Minichello, Dennis *lawyer*
Minow, Newton Norman *lawyer, educator*
Montgomery, Charles Barry *lawyer*
Montgomery, William Adam *lawyer*
Morency, Paula J. *lawyer*
Morgan, Betsy Stelle *lawyer*
Morgan, Donna Evensen *lawyer*
Morrison, Portia Owen *lawyer*
Motherway, Nicholas J. *lawyer*
Muller, Kurt Alexander *lawyer*
Murdock, Charles William *lawyer, educator*
Murray, Daniel Richard *lawyer*
Myers, Lonn William *lawyer*
Natarus, Burton F. *lawyer, former city alderman*
Neff, David M. *lawyer*
Neumeier, Matthew Michael *lawyer, educator*
Newlin, Charles Fremont *lawyer*
Nicklin, Emily *lawyer*
Nijman, Jennifer T. *lawyer*
Nitikman, Franklin W. *lawyer*
Notz, John Kranz, Jr. *arbitrator, mediator, retired lawyer*
Novak, Mark *lawyer*
Novotny, David Joseph *lawyer*
Nowacki, James Nelson *lawyer*
Nowak, Patricia Cari *lawyer*
O'Brien, James Phillip *lawyer*
Oesterle, Eric Adam *lawyer*
O'Hagan, James Joseph *lawyer*
Olian, Robert Martin *lawyer*
O'Malley, John Daniel *lawyer, educator, banker*
O'Neil, Michael C. *lawyer*
Orpett, Mitchell A. *lawyer*
O'Toole, William George *lawyer*
Palmer, John Bernard III *lawyer*
Palmer, Robert Towne *lawyer, bank executive*
Partridge, Mark Van Buren *lawyer, author, professional speaker, educator, mediator*
Pascal, Roger *lawyer*
Pavalon, Eugene Irving *lawyer*
Pedersen, Peer *lawyer*
Pelton, Russell Meredith *lawyer*
Perzek, Philip John *lawyer*
Petersen, Donald Sondergaard *lawyer*
Peterson, Kenneth Allen, Jr. *lawyer*
Peterson, Ronald Roger *lawyer*
Pflaum, Steven F. *lawyer*
Power, Joseph Aloysius, Jr. *lawyer*
Presser, Stephen Bruce *lawyer, educator*
Price, Charles T. *lawyer*
Price, Paul L. *lawyer*
Prochnow, Douglas Lee *lawyer*
Quaini, Duane C. *lawyer*
Ragan, Charles Ransom *lawyer*
Rankin, James Winton *lawyer*
Rappaport, Richard J. *lawyer*
Raskin, Richard D. *lawyer*
Ratner, Gerald *lawyer*
Redish, Martin Harris *law educator*
Reed, Keith Allen *lawyer*
Reich, Allan J. *lawyer*
Reicin, Ronald Ian *lawyer*
Reidy, Daniel Edward *lawyer*
Reiter, Michael A. *lawyer, educator*
Relias, John Alexis *lawyer*
Resnick, Donald Ira *lawyer*
Reum, James Michael *lawyer*
Reyes, Victor H. *lawyer*
Rhind, James Thomas *lawyer*
Richard, Howard M. *lawyer*
Richman, John Marshall *lawyer, food products executive*
Richman, Lawrence I. *lawyer*
Riley, James B., Jr. *lawyer*
Ritchie, William Paul *lawyer*
Rizzo, Ronald Stephen *lawyer*
Roberts, John Charles *law educator*
Rooney, Matthew A. *lawyer*
Roper, Harry Joseph *lawyer*
Ropski, Gary Melchior *lawyer*
Rosenbloom, Lewis Stanley *lawyer*
Rosenfeld, Howard H. *lawyer*
Ruder, David Sturtevant *lawyer, educator, former federal agency administrator*
Rudnick, Lewis G. *lawyer*
Rundio, Louis Michael, Jr. *lawyer*
Rupert, Donald William *lawyer*
Rutkoff, Alan Stuart *lawyer*
Ruxin, Paul Theodore *lawyer*
Ryan, Thomas F. *lawyer*
Sanders, Richard Henry *lawyer*
Sathy, Anup *lawyer*
Saunders, George Lawton, Jr. *lawyer*
Sawyier, Michael Tod *lawyer, director*
Schaffner, Howard Sheldon *lawyer*
Scharf, Stephanie A. *lawyer*
Schiller, Donald Charles *lawyer*
Schimberg, A(rmand) Bruce *retired lawyer*
Schink, James Harvey *lawyer*
Schmidt, John R. *lawyer*
Schneider, Robert Jerome *lawyer*
Schopf, William Grant *lawyer*
Schoumacher, Bruce Herbert *lawyer*
Schriver, John T. III *lawyer*
Schulz, Keith Donald *corporate lawyer, writer*
Schwab, Stephen Wayne *lawyer*
Scogland, William Lee *lawyer*
Scriven-Young, David Joseph *lawyer*
Seaman, Scott M. *lawyer*
Selander, Larry *lawyer*
Selman, Russell Bertram *lawyer, department chairman*
Sennet, Charles Joseph *lawyer*
Sennett, Michael *lawyer*
Sergi, Vincent A.F. *lawyer*
Serritella, James Anthony *lawyer*
Serritella, William David *lawyer*
Shapiro, Keith J. *lawyer*
Shapiro, Stephen Michael *lawyer*
Shapo, Marshall Schambelan *lawyer, educator*
Sheffield, Jeffrey T. *lawyer*
Sherman, Ian Matthew *lawyer*
Sherman, Jeremy P. *lawyer*
Shields, Thomas Charles *lawyer*
Silverman, Michael J. *lawyer*
Silverman, Ross O. *lawyer*
Simon, John Bern *lawyer*
Skinner, Samuel Knox *lawyer, retired transportation executive, former United States Secretary of Transportation*
Smedinghoff, Thomas J. *lawyer*
Smith, Arthur B., Jr. *lawyer*
Smith, Mary L. *lawyer*
Smolen, Lee M. *lawyer*
Snider, Rowe Winston *lawyer*
Solovy, Jerold Sherwin *lawyer*
Solow, Michael Barry *lawyer*
Sorosky, Sheldon M. *lawyer*
Spector, David M. *lawyer*
Spellmire, George W. *lawyer*
Spiotto, James Ernest *lawyer*
Sprayregen, James H.M. *lawyer, former diversified financial services company executive*
Sproger, Charles Edmund *retired lawyer*
Stack, Paul Francis *lawyer*
Stallworth, Stanley B. *lawyer*
Stanhaus, James Steven *lawyer*
Starkman, Gary Lee *lawyer*
Steinberg, Morton M. *lawyer*
Sternstein, Allan J. *lawyer*
Stevens, Stanley M. *lawyer*
Stevenson, Adlai Ewing III *lawyer, former United States Senator, Illinois*
Stillman, Nina Gidden *lawyer*
Stone, Susan A. *lawyer*
Sullivan, Barry *lawyer, educator*
Sullivan, Marcia Waite *lawyer*
Sullivan, Thomas Patrick *lawyer*
Swartzman, Daniel *lawyer, educator*
Swibel, Steven Warren *lawyer*
Swiger, Elinor Porter *lawyer*
Sykes, Alan O'Neil *lawyer, educator*
Tabin, Julius *lawyer, physicist*
Theobald, Edward Robert *lawyer*
Thomas, Frederick Bradley *lawyer*
Thomas, Stephen Paul *lawyer*
Thompson, James Robert, Jr. *lawyer, former governor*
Tobin, Craig Daniel *lawyer*
Trio, Edward Alan *lawyer, accountant*
Trost, Eileen Bannon *lawyer*
Truskowski, John Budd *lawyer*
Tryban, Esther Elizabeth *lawyer*
Turilli, M. Louise *lawyer*
Ungaretti, Richard Anthony *lawyer*
Valukas, Anton Ronald *lawyer, former prosecutor*
Van Gorp, Jon D. *lawyer*
Van Hoene, William, Jr. *lawyer, utilities executive*
Veverka, Donald John *lawyer*
Vezeau, Timothy J. *lawyer*
Vojcanin, Sava Alexander *lawyer*
von Ohlen, Robert Charles *lawyer*
Wakschlag, Milton Samuel *lawyer*
Wander, Herbert Stanton *lawyer*
Webb, Dan K. *lawyer*
Weinberg, Walter S. *lawyer*
Weiss, John Robert *lawyer*
Weiss, Steven Allan *lawyer*
Weissenberger, Glen *law educator, former dean*
Weissman, Michael Lewis *lawyer*
Welsh, Kelly Raymond *lawyer, investment company executive*
Werner, Raymond J. *lawyer*
Westerberg, Gary W. *lawyer*
White, Henry F., Jr. *legal association administrator, retired military officer*
White, Linda Diane *lawyer*
Williamson, Richard Salisbury *lawyer, former ambassador*
Wise, William Jerrard *lawyer*
Witcoff, Sheldon William *lawyer*
Wolf, Charles Benno *lawyer*
Wolf, Neal Lloyd *lawyer*
Wolfe, David Louis *lawyer*
Wood, Mark D. *lawyer*
Woodford, Peter C. *lawyer*
Wright, Judith Margaret *law librarian, educator, dean*
Yeager, Mark Leonard *lawyer*
Yelin, David B. *lawyer*
Zagel, Margaret Maxwell *lawyer*

Crystal Lake
Rozovics, Michelle Janeen *lawyer*
Thoms, Jeannine Aumond *lawyer*
Wade, Edwin Lee *lawyer, writer*

Decatur
Smith, David James *lawyer*

Deerfield
Blanchard, Eric Alan *lawyer*
Lichtenstein, Susan R. *lawyer, medical products executive*
Roche, Mark A. *lawyer, consumer products company executive*
Scott, John Joseph *lawyer*

Downers Grove
Hart, Brett J. *lawyer, food products executive*

Edwardsville
Hawkins, Deborah Anne *lawyer*
Rikli, Donald Carl *lawyer*

Elmwood Park
Spina, Anthony Ferdinand *lawyer*

Evanston
Bitner, John Howard *lawyer*
Morrison, John Horton *lawyer, arbitrator*
Nechin, Herbert Benjamin *lawyer*

Fairview Heights
Cox, A. Courtney *prosecutor, lawyer*

Flossmoor
Garrison, Ray Harlan *lawyer*

Galesburg
Mustain, Douglas Dee *lawyer*

Geneva
Tyler, Lloyd John *retired lawyer*

Genoa
Cromley, Jon Lowell *lawyer*

Glen Ellyn
O'Connell, Daniel James *lawyer*
Sandrok, Richard William *lawyer*
Ulrich, Werner *retired lawyer*

Glencoe
Cohen, Melanie Rovner *lawyer*
Hollins, Mitchell Leslie *lawyer*

Glenview
Dul, John A. *lawyer, electronics executive*
Hagy, James C. *lawyer*
Hunt, Lawrence Halley, Jr. *lawyer*
Knox, James Edwin *lawyer*
Marmet, Gottlieb John *lawyer*
Wooten, James H., Jr. *lawyer, engineering executive*

Granite City
Rarick, Philip Joseph *lawyer, retired state supreme court justice*

Hanover
Bleveans, John *lawyer*

Highland Park
Karol, Nathaniel H. *lawyer, consultant*
Nelson, Richard David *lawyer*
Reed, Jan Stern *lawyer*
Schindel, Donald Marvin *retired lawyer*

Hoffman Estates
Dziezak, Judie D. *lawyer*
Harker, William R. *lawyer*

Joliet
Taylor, Jeffrey Scott *lawyer*

Kenilworth
Feng, Paul Yen-Hsiung *lawyer, chemist*
Weaver, Clifford Lee *retired lawyer, winery owner*

La Grange
Kerr, Alexander Duncan, Jr. *lawyer*
Kohlstedt, James August *lawyer*
Smith, Arthur Edward, Jr. *lawyer*

Lake Forest
Coleman, Kristin M. *lawyer*
Emerson, William Harry *retired lawyer*
Howard, John Lawrence *lawyer*
Palmer, Ann Therese Darin *lawyer*
Sikorovsky, Eugene Frank *retired lawyer*
Wardell, David A. *lawyer, automotive executive*

Lake In The Hills
Franks, David Brian *lawyer*

Lincolnshire
Michalik, John James *legal association administrator*

Lincolnwood
Alexander, Cyrus A. *lawyer, arbitrator*
Carroll, Howard William *state legislator*
Kamensky, Marvin *lawyer*
Martin, Siva *lawyer*

Long Grove
Obert, Paul Richard *lawyer, manufacturing executive*

Marengo
Franks, Herbert Hoover *lawyer*

Melrose Park
Schmidt, Gary P. *lawyer, personal care industry executive*

Moline
Cleaver, William Lehn *lawyer*
Jenkins, James Robert *lawyer, manufacturing executive*

Morris
Rooks, John Newton *lawyer*

Mount Vernon
Harvey, Morris Lane *lawyer*

Naperville
Broad, Matthew *lawyer*
Larson, Mark Edward, Jr. *lawyer, educator, financial planner*
Nortell, Bruce *lawyer*
Tibble, Douglas Clair *lawyer*

New Lenox
Field, Robert Edward *lawyer*

Normal
Bender, Paul Edward *lawyer*

Northbrook
Lapin, Harvey I. *lawyer*
Levenfeld, Milton Arthur *lawyer*
Rosemarin, Carey Stephen *lawyer*
Sernett, Richard Patrick *lawyer*

Oak Brook
Barnes, Karen Kay *lawyer*
Congalton, Susan Tichenor *lawyer, business executive*
Ring, Leonard M. *lawyer, writer*
Santona, Gloria *lawyer, food products executive*

Oak Park
Schubert, Blake H. *lawyer*
Sengpiehl, Paul Marvin *lawyer, retired state official*

Palatine
Victor, Michael Gary *lawyer, physician*
Zamarin, Ronald George *lawyer*

Park Forest
Goodrich, John Bernard *consultant*
Pryor, Vikki Lynn *lawyer*

Park Ridge
Hegarty, Mary Frances *lawyer*
LaRue, Paul Hubert *retired lawyer*

Peoria
Bertschy, Timothy L. *lawyer*
Buda, James B. *lawyer, manufacturing executive*
Parsons, Richard Hugo *lawyer*

Riverwoods
Gold, Deidra D. *lawyer*
McNamara Corley, Kelly *lawyer*
Vollen, Robert Jay *lawyer*

Rock Island
Wallace, Franklin Sherwood *lawyer, director*

Rockford
Johnson, Thomas Stuart *lawyer*
Reno, Roger *lawyer*
Tuite, Gerald Francis *lawyer, commercial real estate manager*

Rolling Meadows
Giampietro, Wayne Bruce *lawyer*

Rosemont
Nichols, Robert Hastings *lawyer*

Round Lake Beach
Harter, Jeremiah Steven *lawyer*

Schaumburg
Lawson, A. Peter *lawyer*
Marshall, John David *lawyer*
Nehs, (William) Scott *lawyer*

Shorewood
Heaphy, John Merrill *lawyer*

Springfield
Heaton, Rodger A. *prosecutor*
Kerr, Gary Enrico *lawyer, educator, musician*
LeBlang, Theodore Raymond *law educator, lawyer*
Londrigan, Thomas Foster *lawyer*
Mathewson, Mark Stuart *lawyer, editor*
Morse, Saul Julian *lawyer*
Reed, Robert Phillip *lawyer*
Van Meter, Abram DeBois *lawyer, retired banker*

Sterling
Pace, Ole Bly III *lawyer*

Streamwood
Bailey, Robert Short *retired lawyer*

Taylorville
Austin, Daniel William *lawyer*

Toledo
Prather, William C. III *lawyer, writer*

Urbana
Frederick, Robert George *lawyer*
Grossman, Margaret Rosso *law educator*
Rich, Robert F. *law and political science professor*
Thies, Richard Leon *lawyer, director*

Vernon Hills
Leahy, Christine A. *lawyer, information technology executive*

Warrenville
Boardman, Robert A. *retired lawyer*
Covey, Steven K. *lawyer*
Johnson, Douglas Wells *lawyer*

Waukegan
Stone, Jed *lawyer*

Western Springs
Hanson, Heidi Elizabeth *lawyer*

Willowbrook
Walton, Stanley Anthony III *lawyer*

Wilmette
Anderson, J. Trent *retired lawyer*
Atkinson, Jeff John Frederick *lawyer, educator, writer*
Bunge, Jonathan Gunn *lawyer*
Cherry, Daniel Ronald *lawyer*

Winnetka
Berner, Robert Lee, Jr. *lawyer*
Crowe, Robert William *lawyer, mediator*
Greenblatt, Ray Harris *lawyer*
Hales, Daniel B. *lawyer*
Hickman, Frederic W. *retired lawyer*
McWhirter, Bruce J. *retired lawyer*
Webster, David Macpherson *lawyer*

Woodridge
Farrug, Eugene Joseph, Sr. *retired lawyer*

INDIANA

Anderson
Scott, John Toner *retired lawyer*

Angola
Cain, Tim J. *lawyer*

Bloomington
Baude, Patrick Louis *law educator*
Johnsen, Dawn E. *law educator, former federal agency administrator*

Carmel
Burkett, Robert E., Jr. *lawyer, insurance company executive*

Columbus
Harrison, Patrick Woods *lawyer*
Rose, Marya Mernitz *lawyer*

Connersville
Brooks, Susan W. *lawyer, academic administrator, former prosecutor*

Elkhart
Gassere, Eugene Arthur *lawyer, investment company executive*
Treckelo, Richard M. *lawyer*

Evansville
Harrison, Joseph Heavrin *lawyer*
Hayes, Philip Harold *lawyer*
Shoulders, Patrick Alan *lawyer, educator*
Wallace, Paul J. *lawyer*

Fort Wayne
Anderson, Kathleen Marie *lawyer*
Colvin, Sherrill William *lawyer*
Helmke, Paul (Walter Paul Helmke Jr.) *lawyer, former mayor*
Logan, Thomas D. *lawyer*
Pope, Mark Andrew *lawyer, academic administrator*
Tourkow, Joshua Isaac *lawyer*

Fowler
Weist, William Bernard *lawyer*

Greenwood
Van Valer, Joe Ned *lawyer, real estate developer*

Hammond
Capp, David A. *prosecutor*
Diamond, Eugene Christopher *lawyer, health facility administrator*

Indianapolis
Albright, Terrill D. *lawyer*
Allen, David James *lawyer*
Armitage, Robert Allen *lawyer, pharmaceutical executive*
Avery, Melissa J. *lawyer*
Badger, David Harry *lawyer*
Beckwith, Lewis Daniel *lawyer*
Blythe, James David, II, *lawyer*
Boldt, Michael Herbert *lawyer*
Born, Samuel Roydon, II, *retired lawyer, practicing mediator and arbitrator*
Cannon, John III *lawyer, insurance company executive*
Choplin, John M., II, *lawyer*
Drentlicher, David *lawyer, educator, physician*
Dutton, Stephen James *lawyer*
Elberger, Ronald Edward *lawyer*
Ewbank, Thomas Peters *lawyer, retired banker*
Fels, James Alexander *lawyer, mediator*
FitzGibbon, Daniel Harvey *lawyer*
Fruehwald, Kristin Gail *lawyer*
Funk, David Albert *retired law educator*
Gilliland, John Campbell, II, *lawyer*
Hammons, Timothy A. *lawyer*
Henderson, Ronald Sherman *lawyer*
Hovde, F. Boyd *lawyer*
Jegen, Lawrence A. III *law educator*
Kappes, Philip Spangler *lawyer*
Kemper, James Dee *lawyer*
Kerr, William Andrew *lawyer, educator*
Kinney, Eleanor De Arman *law educator*
Knebel, Donald Earl *lawyer*
Lobley, Alan Haigh *retired lawyer*
Lofton, Thomas Milton *lawyer*
McCarthy, Kevin Bart *lawyer*
McKinney, Dennis Keith *lawyer*
Mead, Susanah M. *law educator*
Morrison, Timothy M. *prosecutor*
Neff, Robert Matthew *lawyer, finance company executive*
Newman, Norman Richard *lawyer*
Padgett, Gregory Lee *lawyer*
Paul, Stephen Howard *lawyer*
Petersen, James L. *lawyer*
Reuben, Lawrence Mark *lawyer*
Reynolds, Robert Hugh *lawyer*
Roberts, William Everett *lawyer*
Russell, David Williams *lawyer*
Ryder, Henry Clay *lawyer*
Scaletta, Phillip Ralph III *lawyer*
Schlegel, Fred Eugene *lawyer*
Scism, Daniel Reed *lawyer*
Shula, Robert Joseph *lawyer*
Stayton, Thomas George *lawyer*
Strain, James Arthur *lawyer*
Swhier, Claudia Versfelt *lawyer*
Tabler, Norman Gardner, Jr. *lawyer*
Thurston, Kathy Lynn *paralegal*
Vorndran-Jones, MaCharri *lawyer, chemist*
White, James Patrick *law educator*
Wishard, Gordon Davis, Sr. *lawyer*

Jeffersonville
Hoehn, Elmer Louis *lawyer, state and federal agency administrator, educator, consultant*

Kokomo
Maugans, John Conrad *lawyer*

Lafayette
Emerick, William E. *lawyer*
McBride, John Kuhns *lawyer*
McCully, Thomas Richardson *lawyer*

Merrillville
Compton, Clyde D. *lawyer*
Gioia, Daniel August *lawyer*
Hightman, Carrie J. *lawyer, former telecommunications company executive*
Miller, Richard Allen *lawyer*

Muncie
Kelly, Eric Damian *lawyer, educator*
Smith, Gregory Butler *lawyer*

Notre Dame
Blakey, G. Robert (George Robert Blakey) *law educator*
O'Hara, Patricia Anne *law educator, former dean*
Robinson, John Hayes *law educator*
Rodes, Robert Emmet, Jr. *law educator*

Plainfield
Cavanaugh, Eric Maurice *lawyer*
Fivel, Steven Edward *lawyer, communications executive*

Seymour
Pardieck, Roger L. *lawyer*

Shelbyville
Lisher, James Richard *lawyer*
McNeely, James Lee *lawyer*

South Bend
Reinke, William John *lawyer*
Seall, Stephen Albert *lawyer*
Shaffer, Thomas Lindsay *lawyer, educator*
Vogel, Nelson J., Jr. *lawyer*

Terre Haute
Bopp, James, Jr. *lawyer*
Britton, Louis Franklin *lawyer*

Vincennes
Emison, Ewing Rabb, Jr. *lawyer*

IOWA

Burlington
Hoth, Steven Sergey *lawyer, educator*

Cedar Rapids
Chadick, Gary Robert *lawyer*
Davis, Michael A. *lawyer*
Dummermuth, Matt M. *prosecutor*
Riley, Tom Joseph *lawyer*
Wilson, Robert Foster *lawyer*

Clear Lake
Enabnit, Ted *retired lawyer*

Clinton
Smith, Lauren Ashley *lawyer, clergyman, physicist, journalist*

Coralville
Coulter, Charles Roy *lawyer*
Hobart, Thomas D. *lawyer*

Davenport
Dettmann, David Allen *lawyer*

Des Moines
Begleiter, Martin David *law educator, consultant*
Conlin, Roxanne Barton *lawyer*
Critelli, Nicholas *lawyer, barrister*
Crook, Charles Samuel III *lawyer*
Devine, Michael Buxton *attorney, barrister, educator*
Fisher, Thomas George *lawyer, retired media company executive*
Frederici, C. Carleton *lawyer*
Graziano, Craig Frank *lawyer*
Hansell, Edgar Frank *lawyer*
Harris, Charles Elmer *retired lawyer*
Hill, Luther Lyons, Jr. *lawyer*
Jensen, Dick Leroy *lawyer*
Koehn, William James *lawyer*
Kruidenier, Elizabeth Stuart *lawyer*
Norris, Glenn L. *lawyer*
Peddicord, Roland Dale *lawyer*
Schmett, Kim D. *lawyer*
Shaff, Karen E. *lawyer, insurance company executive*
Simpson, Lyle Lee *lawyer*
Trout, Brett Joseph *lawyer*
Whitaker, Matthew George *prosecutor*

Dubuque
Hammer, David Lindley *lawyer, writer, investor*

Harlan
Salvo, J. C. *lawyer*

Indianola
Ouderkirk, Mason James *lawyer*

Iowa City
Bonfield, Arthur Earl *law educator*
Gallanis, Thomas P. *law educator*
Hines, Norman William *law educator, retired dean*
Holland, Charles Joseph *lawyer*
Hovenkamp, Herbert *law educator*
Kurtz, Sheldon Francis *lawyer, educator*
Trca, Randy Ernest *lawyer*
Wing, Adrien Katherine *law educator*

Marshalltown
Brennecke, Allen Eugene *lawyer*

Mason City
Funkhouser, David Edward *lawyer*
Winston, Harold Ronald *lawyer*

Muscatine
Lande, Roger Lee *lawyer*
Nepple, James Anthony *lawyer*

Nevada
Countryman, Dayton Wendell *lawyer*

Ottumwa
Krafka, Mary Baird *lawyer*

Sioux City
Madsen, George Frank *lawyer*

West Des Moines
Hockenberg, Harlan David *lawyer*
Johnson, John Paul *lawyer, judge*
Power, Joseph Edward *lawyer*
Tully, Robert Gerard *lawyer*

KANSAS

Berryton
Schroer, Gene Eldon *lawyer*

Emporia
Helbert, Michael Clinton *lawyer*

Garden City
Loyd, Ward Eugene *lawyer*

Girard
Gayoso, Michael, Jr. *lawyer*

Grantville
Hodges, Edna (Lee) Elizabeth *retired lawyer, educator*

Hutchinson
Swearer, William Brooks *lawyer*

Lawrence
Casad, Robert Clair *legal educator*
Dickinson, Martin Brownlow, Jr. *law educator*
Turnbull, H. Rutherford III *lawyer, educator*
Winter, Winton Allen, Jr. *lawyer, state legislator*

Leavenworth
Crow, Michael P. *lawyer*

Lincoln
Crangle, Robert D. *lawyer, management consultant, entrepreneur*

Olathe
Eichholz, Mark Joseph (Mick) *lawyer*
Kline, Phillip D. *prosecutor, former state attorney general*
McVey, Walter Lewis *retired lawyer, educator*

Overland Park
Churay, Daniel J. *lawyer*
Keplinger, Bruce (Donald Keplinger) *lawyer*
Murray, Thomas Veatch *lawyer*
Stanton, Roger D. *lawyer*
Walker, H. Reed *lawyer*
Woods, Richard Dale *lawyer*
Wunsch, Charles Robert *lawyer*

Shawnee Mission
Badgerow, John Nicholas *lawyer*
Becker, David M. *lawyer*
Nulton, William Clements *retired lawyer*
Snyder, Willard Breidenthal *lawyer*
Starrett, Frederick Kent *lawyer*

Topeka
Elrod, Linda Diane Henry *lawyer, educator*
Griffin, Ronald Charles *law educator*
Hayse, Richard Franklin *lawyer*
Monk, Carl Colburn *law educator, former legal association administrator*
Stratton, Wayne Thomas *lawyer*

Wichita
Ayres, Ted D. *lawyer*
Badger, Ronald Kay *lawyer*
Docking, Thomas Robert *lawyer, former state lieutenant governor*
Holden, Mark V. *lawyer*
Johnson, Kevin Blaine *lawyer, educator*
Parker, Marietta *prosecutor*
Parks, Linda S. *lawyer*
Stephenson, Richard Ismert *lawyer*
Winkler, Dana John *lawyer*

KENTUCKY

Campbellsville
Creason, Larry Dean *law educator*

Catlettsburg
Nixon, Ronda Lynn *paralegal*

Covington
Hausrath, David L. *lawyer*
Kobasuk, Mark G. *lawyer, pharmaceutical executive*
Sloan, David B. *lawyer*

Eastwood
Snyder, Ronald R. *lawyer*

Florence
Robinson, William T. III *lawyer*

Frankfort
Palmore, John Stanley, Jr. *retired lawyer*

Lexington
Fryman, Virgil Thomas, Jr. *lawyer*
Larson, Jon S. *lawyer*
Lester, Roy David *lawyer*
Piper, George Chilton *lawyer*
Todd, James Marion *retired lawyer*
Zerhusen, James A. *prosecutor*

London
Keller, John Warren *lawyer*

Louisville
Ballantine, John Tilden *lawyer*
Barr, James Houston III *lawyer*
Campbell, Christian Larsen *lawyer, food service executive*
Carucci, Richard T. *lawyer*
Conner, Stewart Edmund *lawyer*
Davidson, Gordon Byron *lawyer*
Dudley, George Ellsworth *lawyer*
Gilfert, Justin Scott *lawyer*
Gilman, Sheldon Glenn *lawyer*
Herrington, Alice Elizabeth *associate lawyer*
Herrington, E. Paul III *lawyer*
Jones, Frances Brooks *lawyer, bank executive*
Lavelle, Charles Joseph *lawyer*
Lay, Norvie Lee *law educator*
McClain, Tim S. *lawyer*
Mellen, Francis Joseph, Jr. *lawyer*
Metzmeier, Kurt X. *legal association administrator*
Northern, Richard *lawyer*
Osborn, John Simcoe, Jr. *lawyer*
Pence, Stephen Beville *lawyer, former lieutenant governor*
Riedman, Mary Suzanne *lawyer*
Rothstein, Laura *law educator, former dean*
Runyon, Keith Leslie *lawyer, editor*
Skees, William Leonard, Jr. *lawyer*
Talbott, Ben Johnson, Jr. *lawyer*
Todoroff, Christopher M. *lawyer, insurance company executive*
Vish, Donald H. *lawyer, writer, photographer*
Welsh, Sir Alfred John *lawyer, investment advisor*
Westberry, Robert Kent *lawyer*

Newport
Siverd, Robert Joseph *lawyer*

Owensboro
Moore, Charles Edward *lawyer, political organization administrator*

Prospect
Aberson, Leslie Donald *lawyer*

Scottsville
Secrest, James Seaton, Sr. *lawyer*

LOUISIANA

Baton Rouge
Blackman, John Calhoun, IV, *lawyer*
Brewer, Ralph Wright, Jr. *lawyer, writer*
Casey, Robert Reisch *lawyer*
Costonis, John J. *law educator, former academic administrator*
Crawford, William Edward *law educator*
Dugas, David Roy *prosecutor*
Elkins, Gary J. *lawyer*
Graphia, Gary P. *lawyer*
Grey, Emily Black *lawyer*
Hobbs, Betty Juanita *executive legal secretary*

Hymel, L(ezin) J(oseph) *lawyer, former prosecutor*
Johnson, Joseph Clayton, Jr. *lawyer*
King, Katherine Wright *lawyer*
McKay, Michael Wendell *lawyer*
Moréteau, Olivier *law educator*
Pugh, George Willard *law educator*
Rankin, Cliff (Clifton S. Rankin) *lawyer*
Rubin, Michael Harry *lawyer, educator*
Stapp, Dan Ernest *retired lawyer, utilities executive*
Taylor, John McKowen *lawyer*
Whittington, Christopher L. *lawyer, political organization administrator*
Wisbar, Rebecca Kittok *lawyer*

Chalmette
Mumphrey, J. Wayne *lawyer*

Covington
Rice, Winston Edward *lawyer, priest*
Snyder, Charles Aubrey *lawyer*

Destrehan
Griffith, Steven Franklin, Sr. *lawyer, insurance agent*

Jennings
Marcantel, Bernard Norman *lawyer, judge*

Kaplan
LeMoine, Frank Eugene *lawyer, judge*

Lafayette
Angers, Winston Thomas *lawyer, publishing executive*
Davidson, James Joseph III *lawyer*
Judice, Marc Wayne *lawyer*
Neuner, Frank X., Jr. *lawyer*
Roy, James Parkerson *lawyer*
Skinner, Michael David *lawyer, lobbyist, consultant*

Mandeville
Deano, Edward Joseph, Jr. *lawyer, state legislator*
Ewen, Pamela Binnings *retired lawyer*

Marksville
Riddle, Charles Addison III *district attorney, former state legislator*

Metairie
Burns, William Glenn *lawyer*
Nehrbass, Seth Martin *lawyer*
Rosen, Charles, II, *retired lawyer*

Monroe
Sartor, Daniel Ryan, Jr. *lawyer*

New Orleans
Abaunza, Donald Richard *lawyer*
Acomb, Robert Bailey, Jr. *lawyer, educator*
Alsobrook, Henry Bernis, Jr. *lawyer*
Barry, Francis Julian, Jr. *lawyer*
Beisenherz, Nona Kay *law librarian*
Benjamin, Edward Bernard, Jr. *lawyer*
Bieck, Robert Barton, Jr. *lawyer*
Cheatwood, Roy Clifton *lawyer*
Childress, Steven Alan *law educator*
Combe, John Clifford, Jr. *lawyer*
Conroy, David Jerome *lawyer*
Conroy, Patrick *legal educator, department chairman*
Crusto, Mitchell Ferdinand *lawyer, educator*
Duggan, James Edgar *law professor and law librarian*
Force, Robert *law educator*
Foti, Charles C., Jr. *lawyer, former state attorney general*
Fraiche, Donna DiMartino *lawyer*
Goins, Richard Anthony *lawyer, educator*
Hardin, Harry S. III *lawyer*
Healy, George William III *lawyer, mediator*
Hoffman, Donald Alfred *lawyer*
Hurley, Grady Schell *lawyer*
Jones, Philip Kirkpatrick, Jr. *lawyer*
Kern, Clifford Harold, Jr. *retired lawyer*
Lemann, Thomas Berthelot *lawyer*
Letten, James B. *prosecutor*
Lowe, Robert Charles *lawyer*
Marcus, Bernard *lawyer, arbitrator, mediator*
Osakwe, Christopher *lawyer, educator*
Ostendorf, Lance Stephen *lawyer, financial consultant, educator, importer exporter entrepreneur*
Pyburn, Keith McBride, Jr. *lawyer*
Rodriguez, Antonio Jose *lawyer*
Schnabel, Marta-Ann *lawyer*
Simon, H(uey) Paul *lawyer*
Smith, Juanita Bérard *lawyer, artist*
Steeg, Moise S., Jr. *lawyer*
Talley, Patrick A., Jr. *lawyer*
Trostorff, Danielle M. *lawyer*
Vaudry, J. William, Jr. *lawyer*
Weinmann, John Giffen *lawyer, ambassador*
Wolfe, Richard Peel *lawyer*
Worley, Robert Bruce, Jr. *lawyer*

River Ridge
Didriksen, Caleb H. III *lawyer*

Shreveport
Bryant, J(ames) Bruce *lawyer*
Carmody, Arthur Roderick, Jr. *lawyer, director, author*
Carmouche, Paul J. *lawyer*
Cox, John Thomas, Jr. *lawyer*
Goodman, Robert Uhle *lawyer*
Payne, Roy Steven *lawyer*
Washington, Donald W. *prosecutor*

Slidell
Singletary, Alvin D. *lawyer*

MAINE

Augusta
Cragin, Charles Langmaid *lawyer*
Johnson, Phillip Edward *lawyer*

Bangor
Bickford, Meris J. *lawyer, bank executive*

Brunswick
Owen, H. Martyn *retired lawyer*

Castine
Wiswall, Frank Lawrence, Jr. *lawyer, educator*

Georgetown
Chapin, Richard *trustee*

Jefferson
MacKinnon, Victor Stuart *retired law educator*

Kennebunkport
Picavet, Robert Clement *retired lawyer*

Orrs Island
Nelson, Robert Louis *lawyer*

Portland
Altshuler, Kenneth Paul *lawyer*
Dana, Howard H., Jr. *lawyer, retired state supreme court justice*
Graffam, Ward Irving *lawyer*
Hunt, David Evans *lawyer*
Jones, Blair Anthony *lawyer*
Kayatta, William J., Jr. *lawyer*
Lancaster, Ralph Ivan, Jr. *lawyer*
LeBlanc, Richard Philip *lawyer*
Silsby, Paula D. *prosecutor*
Stauffer, Eric P. *lawyer*
White, Jeffrey Munroe *lawyer*
Zarr, Melvyn *lawyer, educator*

Raymond
Coughlan, Patrick Campbell *lawyer, mediator*

Tenants Harbor
Bates, John Cecil, Jr. *lawyer*

Wells
Carleton, Joseph George, Jr. *lawyer, state legislator*

MARYLAND

Annapolis
Lillard, John Franklin III *lawyer*
Marchant, Byron Frank *lawyer, foundation administrator*
Perkins, Roger Allan *lawyer*
Poe, Luke Harvey, Jr. *lawyer*

Annapolis Junction
Koplow, Ellen Lori Saltzman *lawyer, brokerage house executive*

Arnold
Green, John Cawley *lawyer*

Baltimore
Baker, Constance H. *lawyer*
Baker, William Parr *lawyer*
Bartlett, James Wilson III *lawyer*
Berardesco, Charles A. *lawyer, energy executive*
Berlage, Jan Ingham *lawyer*
Blakeslee, Wesley Daniel *lawyer, consultant, director*
Carbine, James Edmond *lawyer*
Carlin, Paul Victor *legal association executive*
Carney, Stephen Patrick *lawyer, retired insurance company executive*
Civiletti, Benjamin Richard *lawyer, former United States Attorney General*
Coppel, Lawrence David *lawyer*
Crowe, Thomas Leonard *lawyer*
Devan, Deborah Hunt *lawyer*
DeVries, Donald Lawson, Jr. *lawyer*
Dewey, Joel Allen *lawyer*
DiBiagio, Thomas Michael *lawyer, former prosecutor*
Dunn, Jeffrey A. *lawyer*
Eisner, Jonathan David *lawyer*
Ellin, Marvin *lawyer*
Fergenson, Arthur Friend *lawyer*
Finnerty, Joseph Gregory, Jr. *lawyer*
Finney, Jervis Spencer *lawyer, former prosecutor*
Fisher, Morton Poe, Jr. *lawyer*
Frenkil, Steven David *lawyer*
Friedman, Louis Frank *lawyer*
Gately, Mark Donohue *lawyer*
Gillece, James Patrick, Jr. *lawyer*
Goldman, Brian Arthur *lawyer, certified public accountant*
Goldman, Meir *lawyer*
Golomb, George Edwin *lawyer*
Gonzales, Louise Michaux *lawyer*
Gray, Frank Truan *lawyer*
Guben, Jan K. *lawyer*
Hafets, Richard Jay *lawyer*
Hanks, James Judge, Jr. *lawyer*
Hirsh, Theodore William *lawyer*
Honemann, Daniel Henry *lawyer*
Iverson, Kelly Hughes *lawyer*
Jones, John Martin, Jr. *lawyer*
Kandel, Nelson Robert *lawyer*
Kremen, Richard M. *lawyer*
Levin, Edward Jesse *lawyer*
Levine, Richard E. *lawyer*
Liebmann, George W. *lawyer*
Loucks, Allen Frazier *prosecutor, lawyer*
Lundy, Audie Lee, Jr. *lawyer*
Lurie, Jerald B. *lawyer*
Mareiniss, Darren Peter *lawyer, physician*
McClung, A(lexander) Keith, Jr. *retired lawyer*
McPherson, Donald Paxton III *lawyer*
McWilliams, John Michael *lawyer*
Miller, Decatur Howard *lawyer*
Mogol, Alan Jay *lawyer*
Nathans, Larry Allen *lawyer*
Nemphos, George J. *lawyer*
Nilson, George Albert *lawyer*
Orman, Leonard Arnold *lawyer*
Plant, Albin MacDonough *lawyer*
Pollak, Mark *lawyer*
Putzel, Constance Kellner *retired lawyer*
Radding, Andrew *lawyer*
Reno, Russell Ronald, Jr. *lawyer*
Reynolds, William Leroy *lawyer, educator*
Rochlin, Paul R. *lawyer*
Rosenstein, Rod J. *prosecutor*
Rosenthal, William J. *lawyer*
Rothenberg, Karen H. *law educator, former dean*
Scheeler, Charles P. *lawyer*
Schlaff, Barbara E. *lawyer*
Schochor, Jonathan *lawyer, educator*
Scriggins, Larry Palmer *lawyer, director*
Shapiro, Harry Dean *lawyer*
Shea, James L. *lawyer*
Shepherd, Kevin L. *lawyer*
Short, Alexander Campbell *lawyer*
Silverman, Steven Donald *lawyer*
Sirota, Wilbert H. *lawyer*
Smith, Lisa J. *lawyer*
Smith, Robert W., Jr., (Jay) *lawyer*
Snell, Steven Layne *lawyer, consultant*
Somer-Greif, Penny Lynn *lawyer*
Sykes, Melvin Julius *lawyer*
Taylor, Frances O'Connell *lawyer*
Tiburzi, Paul A. *lawyer*
Tyler, Ralph Sargent III *lawyer*
Walker, Irving Edward *lawyer*
Wasserman, Richard Leo *lawyer*
White, Pamela Janice *lawyer*
Wilson, Thomas Matthew III *lawyer*
Winn, James Julius, Jr. *lawyer*

Bel Air
Helfrich, Cornelius David *lawyer*
Miller, Max Dunham, Jr. *lawyer*

Bethesda
Abdoo, Elizabeth A. *lawyer*
Aisenberg, Irwin Morton *retired lawyer*
Baird, Bruce Allen *lawyer*
Bauersfeld, Carl Frederick *lawyer*
Bebchick, Leonard Norman *lawyer*
Berman, Marshall Fox *lawyer*
Calhoun, Carol Victoria *lawyer*
Cox, Kenneth Allen *retired lawyer, communications executive, consultant*
Daniels, Michael Paul *lawyer*
Downey, Arthur Thomas III *lawyer*
English, William deShay *lawyer, director*
Ewing, Ky Pepper, Jr. *lawyer*
Faley, R(ichard) Scott *lawyer*
Feuerstein, Donald Martin *lawyer*
Hannan, Myles *lawyer*
Horne, Michael Stewart *retired lawyer*
Mogel, William Allen *lawyer*
Nelson, William Eugene *lawyer*
Padgett, Nancy Weeks *retired law librarian, lawyer, consultant*
Pipkin, James Harold, Jr. *lawyer*
Schifter, Richard *lawyer*
Silver, David *lawyer*
Weinberger, Alan David *lawyer, business executive*
Zielinski, Thomas C. *lawyer, insurance company executive*

Catonsville
Hubbard, Herbert Hendrix *lawyer*

Chevy Chase
Coerper, Milo George *lawyer, priest*
Curzan, Myron Paul *lawyer*
Gildenhorn, Joseph Bernard *lawyer, real estate company executive, retired diplomat*
Murphy, John Condron, Jr. *lawyer*
Pollard, Michael Ross *lawyer, health science association administrator*

College Park
Petraitis, Karel Colette *lawyer*

Columbia
Closson, Walter Franklin *child support prosecutor*

Crownsville
Irish, Leon Eugene *lawyer, non-profit organization executive, educator*

Dickerson
Duncan, Jack G. *lawyer*

Easton
Maffitt, James Strawbridge *lawyer*

Ellicott City
Pairo, Preston Abercrombie, Jr. *lawyer*

Forest Hill
Wolf, Martin Eugene *lawyer, educator*

Fort George G Meade
Robertson, Alonzo Morrell *lawyer, educator*

Fort Washington
Alexander, Gary R. *lawyer, state legislator, lobbyist*

Frederick
Hogan, Ilona Modly *lawyer*

Gaithersburg
Gordon, Michael Robert *lawyer, state legislator*
Lastra, Carlos Mariano *lawyer*
McCann, Joseph Leo *lawyer, former government official*
McDowell, Donna Schultz *lawyer, educator*

Glen Arm
Blanton, Edward Lee, Jr. *lawyer*

Glen Echo
Levinson, Peter Joseph *retired lawyer*

Glyndon
Renbaum, Barry Jeffrey *lawyer*

Greenbelt
Billingsley, Lance W. *lawyer*
Brennan, William Collins, Jr. *lawyer*
Fax, Charles Samuel *lawyer*

Hagerstown
Berkson, Jacob Benjamin *lawyer, writer*

Hunt Valley
Everton, Angus R. *lawyer*

Kensington
Dauster, William Gary *lawyer, economist*

Landover
Levy, David Lawrence *retired lawyer, legal association administrator*

Linthicum
Ehrlich, Bob (Robert Leroy Ehrlich Jr.) *lawyer, Former Governor, Maryland*

Lutherville
Freeland, Charles *lawyer, accountant*

Lutherville Timonium
Howell, Harley Thomas *lawyer*

Mount Airy
Quarles, Steven Princeton *lawyer*

Parkville
Hill, Milton King, Jr. *retired lawyer*

Pasadena
Asti, Alison Louise *lawyer*

Potomac
Hall, William Darlington *lawyer*
Meyer, Lawrence George *lawyer*
Peter, Phillips Smith *lawyer*
Redding, Robert Ellsworth *lawyer*
Schmeltzer, Edward *lawyer*
Schwartz, Gregory John *international business lawyer, business and investments transactions specialist*
Troffkin, Howard Julian *lawyer*

Princess Anne
Seabrook, Renita L. *criminal justice professor*

Randallstown
Holt, John J. *mediator, arbitrator, retired human resources specialist*

Rockville
Avery, Bruce Edward *lawyer*
Barkley, Brian Evan *lawyer, political consultant*
Berryman, Richard Byron *lawyer*
Conroy, J. Michael *lawyer, judge*
De Jong, David Samuel *lawyer*
Dragga, Patrick W. *lawyer*
Frye, Roland Mushat, Jr. *lawyer*
Hepfer, Cheryl Lynn *lawyer*
Kadish, Richard L. *lawyer*
Karp, Ronald Alvin *lawyer*
Karson, Emile *lawyer*
Katz, Steven Martin *lawyer, accountant*
Kerxton, Alan Smith *lawyer*
Lehman, Leonard *retired lawyer, consultant*
Lessenco, Gilbert Barry *retired lawyer*
Provorny, Frederick Alan *lawyer, educator*
Rothenberg, Alan David *lawyer*
Senger, Jeffrey M. *lawyer*
Thompson, James Lee *lawyer*
Tomar, Richard Thomas *lawyer*
Zaphiriou, George Aristotle *lawyer, educator*

Saint Michaels
Brown, Omer Forrest, II, *lawyer*

Silver Spring
Berns, Peter Vernon *lawyer*
Calvert, Gordon Lee *retired legal association executive*
Craig, Paul Max, Jr. *retired lawyer*
Lipstein, Robert A. *lawyer*
Sapienza, John Thomas *retired lawyer, director*

Sparks Glencoe
Carpenter, W. Geoffrey *lawyer, food products executive*

Towson
Carney, Bradford George Yost *lawyer, educator*
Fenton, Charles E. *lawyer*
Gilliss, Edward Johnson *lawyer*
Proctor, Kenneth Donald *lawyer*

Trappe
Paul, James Caverly Newlin *law educator, retired dean*

West Bethesda
Scully, Roger Tehan, II, *lawyer*

Westminster
Dulany, William Bevard *lawyer*
Preston, Charles Michael *lawyer*
Staples, Lyle Newton *lawyer*

MASSACHUSETTS

Amherst
Schimmel, David M. *law educator*

Andover
Dyleski-Najjar, Debra *lawyer*

Arlington
Keshian, Richard *lawyer*

Barnstable
Paquin, Thomas Christopher *lawyer*
Perry, Blair Lane *lawyer*

Belmont
Greer, Gordon Bruce *retired lawyer, writer*

Boston
Abbott, William Saunders *lawyer*
Abrams, Roger Ian *lawyer, educator*
Ajemian, Marianne *lawyer*
Aman, Alfred Charles, Jr. *law educator*
Apjohn, Nelson George *lawyer*
Aresty, Jeffrey M. *lawyer*
Balliro, Joseph James, Sr. *lawyer*
Benjamin, William Chase *lawyer*
Bennett, Richard Edward *lawyer*
Berube, Brian A. *lawyer, chemicals executive*
Bines, Harvey Ernest *lawyer, educator, writer*
Birmingham, Thomas F. *lawyer, former state legislator*
Bodner, Randall Wayne *lawyer*
Bok, John Fairfield *retired lawyer*
Bonauto, Mary *lawyer*
Bornheimer, Allen Millard *lawyer*
Brody, Richard Eric *lawyer*
Bromberg, Lee Carl *lawyer*
Brown, Margaret A. *lawyer*
Buchanan, Robert McLeod *lawyer*
Burleigh, Lewis Albert *lawyer*
Burns, Thomas David *lawyer*
Byer, David J. *lawyer*
Carp, Jeffrey N. *lawyer, investment company executive*
Carroll, James Edward *lawyer*
Cellucci, Paul (Argeo Paul Cellucci) *lawyer, Former Governor of Massachusetts*
Cohn, Andrew Howard *lawyer*
Cronin, Philip Mark *lawyer*
Curley, Robert Ambrose, Jr. *lawyer*
Curtin, John Joseph, Jr. *lawyer*
Cutrell, Charles C. III *lawyer*
Daley, Paul Patrick *lawyer*
Daynard, Richard Alan *law educator*
De Amicis, Don S. *lawyer*
DeBevoise, Charles Henry *lawyer*
Delaney, John White *lawyer*
de Rham, Casimir, Jr. *lawyer*
Dickie, Robert Benjamin *lawyer, educator*
Di Cola, Joan Barbara *lawyer*
Dillon, James Joseph *lawyer*
Dineen, John K. *lawyer*
Ebb, Peter L. *lawyer*
Engel, David Lewis *lawyer*
Eurich, Richard Rex *lawyer*
Everett, Jonathan Jubal *lawyer*
Fischer, Eric Robert *lawyer, educator*
Fischer, Mark Alan *lawyer*
Fishman, Robert A. *lawyer*
Fitzgerald, Warren Franklin *lawyer*
Floor, Richard Earl *lawyer*
Fortier, Albert Mark, Jr. *lawyer*
Foster, James J(ohn) *lawyer*
Fox, Francis Haney *lawyer*
Frank, Jason D. *lawyer*
Fraser, Robert Burchmore *lawyer*
Freishtat, Harvey W. *lawyer*
Gaff, Brian Michael *lawyer*
Gaudreau, Russell A., Jr. *lawyer, educator*
Gault, Robert Mellor *lawyer*
Gelb, Richard Mark *lawyer*
Gill, Robert Tucker *lawyer*
Gleason, Daniel J. *lawyer*
Glosband, Daniel Martin *lawyer*
Gonson, S. Donald *lawyer*
Goodman, Louis Allan *lawyer*
Gottfried, Michael R. *lawyer*
Green, Karen F. *lawyer*
Hall, David *law educator, dean, department chairman*
Hall, Henry Lyon, Jr. *lawyer*
Halston, Daniel William *lawyer*
Halström, Frederic Norman *lawyer*
Handly, Kevin J. *lawyer, educator*
Harrington, John Michael, Jr. *lawyer*
Harvey, Christopher P. *lawyer*
Hayes, Robert Francis *lawyer*
Heigham, James Crichton *lawyer*
Hieken, Charles *lawyer*
Hoort, Steven Thomas *lawyer*
Howe, Janice W. *lawyer*
Jesse, Sandra L. *lawyer, insurance company executive*
Johnston, Susan A. *lawyer*
Jones, Jeffrey Foster *lawyer*
Jordan, Alexander Joseph, Jr. *lawyer*
Kalkstein, Joshua Adam *lawyer*
Karelitz, Robert N(elson) *lawyer*
Keating, Michael Burns *lawyer, educator*
Kehoe, William Francis *lawyer*
Keller, Stanley *lawyer*
Kenney, Raymond Joseph, Jr. *lawyer*
Kirchick, William Dean *lawyer*
Kirsch, Robert L. *lawyer*
Klem, Christopher A. *lawyer*
Knag, Paul Everett *lawyer*
Kociubes, Joseph Leib *lawyer*
Kopelman, Leonard *lawyer*
Last, Michael P. *lawyer*
Lee, William F. *lawyer*
Lepore, Ralph Thomas III *lawyer*
Licata, Arthur Frank *lawyer*
Litwin, Paul Jeffrey *lawyer*
Loder, John Mark *lawyer*
Looney, William Francis, Jr. *lawyer*
Loria, Martin A. *lawyer*
Lyons, Paul Vincent *lawyer*
Macdonald, Peter J. *lawyer*
MacLeish, Roderick, Jr. *lawyer*
Malt, Ronald Bradford *lawyer*
Manekas, Jason Arthur *lawyer*
Mansfield, Christopher Charles *lawyer*
Marett, Louis J. *lawyer*
Markey, John K. *lawyer*
Martin, Gina Lynn *lawyer*
Martin, Stanley Allen *lawyer*
Matuschak, Mark G. *lawyer*
Mayer, William P. *lawyer*
McAuliffe, Rosemary *lawyer*
McLaughlin, Michael J. *lawyer*
Menna, Gilbert G. *lawyer*
Merrill, Stephen *lawyer, consultant, Former Governor, New Hampshire*
Meserve, William George *lawyer*
Mikels, Richard Eliot *lawyer*
Milstein, Richard Sherman *lawyer*
Miner, Tracy A. *lawyer*
Minot, Winthrop Gardner *lawyer*
Mirabito, Anthony Jason *lawyer, educator*
Montgomery, John T. *lawyer*
Mooney, Michael Edward *lawyer*
Moore, Paul D. *lawyer*
Moriarty, George Marshall *lawyer*
Motenko, Neil Philip *lawyer*
Muldoon, Robert Joseph, Jr. *lawyer*
Mundy, Patricia Wall *lawyer*
Newberg, Joseph H. *lawyer*
Notopoulos, Alexander Anastasios, Jr. *lawyer*
Novack, Kenneth Joseph *lawyer*
Nunnally, Allen C. *lawyer*
O'Connell, Mary-Kathleen *lawyer*
O'Donnell, Thomas Lawrence Patrick *lawyer*
O'Neill, Philip Daniel, Jr. *lawyer, arbitrator, educator*
Pappalardo, A. John *former prosecutor, lawyer*
Park, William Wynnewood *law educator*
Partan, Daniel Gordon *lawyer, educator*
Patterson, John de la Roche, Jr. *lawyer*
Pearlman, Ronald Alan *lawyer, educator*
Peckham, Thomas Elwood *lawyer*
Perera, Lawrence Thacher *lawyer*
Pierce, Daniel Robert *lawyer*
Polito, Anthony Peter *law educator*
Pomeroy, Robert Corttis *lawyer*
Popeo, R. Robert *lawyer*
Porter, Jeffrey R. *lawyer*
Preston, Jerome, Jr. *retired lawyer*
Price, Robert F. *lawyer*
Raish, David Langdon *lawyer*
Reardon, Frank Emond *lawyer*
Remis, Robin E. *lawyer*
Remz, Sanford F. *lawyer*
Renehan, Richard William *lawyer*
Rich, Patricia R. *lawyer*
Richmond, Alice Elenor *lawyer*
Roberts, Bronwyn L. *lawyer*
Rudavsky, Dahlia C. *lawyer*
Rudman, Jeffrey B. *lawyer*
Ryan, Allan Andrew, Jr. *lawyer, director, educator, writer*
Sawyer, William C. *lawyer*
Sears, John Winthrop *lawyer*
Shapiro, Sandra *lawyer*
Sheehan, Gregory D. *lawyer*
Shilepsky, Nancy Sue *lawyer*
Shulkin, Martin B. *lawyer*
Sigel, John D. *lawyer*
Singer, Steven D. *lawyer*
Sinnott, William F. *lawyer*
Sirkin, Joel H. *lawyer*
Smith, Craig R. *lawyer*
Smith, Edwin Eric *lawyer*
Smith, Philip Jones *lawyer*
Snyder, Richard Joseph *lawyer*
Soden, Richard Allan *lawyer*
Solet, Maxwell David *lawyer*
Southard, William G. *lawyer*
Speer, Brownlow Main *lawyer*
Steinberg, Laura *lawyer*
Stern, Donald Kenneth *lawyer*
Stillwell, R. Newcomb *lawyer*
Storey, James Moorfield *lawyer*
Sugarman, Paul Ronald *lawyer, educator, academic administrator*
Sunstein, Bruce David *lawyer*
Surkin, Elliot Mark *lawyer*
Swope, Jeffrey Peyton *lawyer*
Tarantino, Louis Gerald *lawyer, management consultant*
Taylor, Thomas William *lawyer*
Touster, Saul *law educator*
Trimmier, Roscoe, Jr. *lawyer*
Troupe, William Harold *lawyer*
Tse, Marian A. *lawyer*
Tuchmann, Robert *lawyer*
Vaughan, Herbert Wiley *retired lawyer*
Walek, David B. *lawyer*
Walsh, Joseph Hayes *lawyer*
Weiner, Stephen Mark *lawyer*
Weitzel, John Patterson *lawyer*
White, Barry Bennett *lawyer*
White, Dennis J. *lawyer*
Whitters, James Payton III *lawyer, educator*
Wilcox, Steven Alan *lawyer*
Winslow, Daniel B. *lawyer*
Woodburn, Ralph Robert, Jr. *lawyer*
Yurko, Richard John *lawyer*
Zack, Arnold Marshall *lawyer, mediator, arbitrator, judge*
Zarutskie, Jennifer Anne *lawyer*

Brookline
Bander, Edward Julius *lawyer, librarian emeritus*

Cambridge
Alexander, Susan H. *lawyer, pharmaceutical executive*
Bebchuk, Lucian Arye *law and finance educator*
Cogan, John Francis, Jr. *lawyer*
Dershowitz, Alan Morton *law educator*
Fisher, Roger Dummer *negotiation expert, law educator*
Freitas, Mark R. *lawyer*
Goldsmith, Jack Landman III *law educator, former federal agency administrator*
Heineman, Benjamin Walter, Jr. *lawyer*
Hostage, John Brayne Arthur *law librarian*
Jackson, Howell Edmunds *law educator, dean*
Kaplow, Louis *law educator*
Kaufman, Andrew Lee *law educator*
Kennedy, Duncan McLean *law educator*
King, William Bruce *retired lawyer*
Kober, Jane *lawyer*
Mahoney, Kevin J. *lawyer*
Ogletree, Charles J., Jr. *law educator*
Parker, Richard Davies *law educator*
Patton, Bruce M. *law educator, management consultant*
Sander, Frank Ernest Arnold *law educator*
Sapers, Carl Martin *lawyer, educator*
Scott, Hal S. *law educator*
Shapiro, David Louis *law educator*
Shavell, Steven M. *law educator*
Steiner, Henry Jacob *law and human rights educator*
Stuntz, William John *law educator*
Sunstein, Cass Robert *law educator*
Tribe, Laurence Henry *law educator*
Vagts, Detlev Frederick *law educator*
Warren, Alvin Clifford, Jr. *law educator*
Warren, Elizabeth Ann *law educator*
Wirth, Peter *lawyer*
Wolfman, Bernard *lawyer, educator*
Zittrain, Jonathan L. *law educator*

Chatham
Popkin, Alice Brandeis *lawyer*

Chestnut Hill
Batchelder, Samuel Lawrence, Jr. *retired corporate lawyer*
Vance, Verne Widney, Jr. *retired lawyer*

Concord
Perkins, John Allen *lawyer*

Danvers
Haber, Frederic *lawyer*

Dedham
Fabiano, Mark G. *lawyer*

Dennis Port
Singer, Myer R(ichard) *lawyer*

Dover
Craver, James Bernard *lawyer*
Edwards, Carl Norman *lawyer*

Duxbury
Schwartz, Edward Arthur *lawyer*

Framingham
Campbell, Kristin A. *lawyer, retail executive*
McCauley, Ann *lawyer, retail executive*
Rikleen, Lauren Stiller *lawyer*
Vrabel, Joseph P. *lawyer*

Gloucester
Birchfield, John Kermit, Jr. *lawyer*

Holyoke
Resnic, Burton S. *lawyer*

Hopkinton
Dacier, Paul T. *lawyer, information technology executive*

Hull
Medalie, Richard James *lawyer*

Hyannis
Attea, Paul J. *lawyer*
Segersten, Robert Hagy *lawyer, investment banker*

Ipswich
Getchell, Charles Willard, Jr. *lawyer, publisher, foundation executive*

Lexington
Kent, Robert Brydon *law educator*

Lincoln
Gnichtel, William Van Orden *lawyer*

Lowell
Curtis, James Theodore *lawyer*
Martin, William Francis, Jr. *lawyer*
O'Donnell, Kathleen Marie *lawyer*

Lynnfield
McGivney, John Joseph *lawyer*

Marblehead
McAndrews, Robert Kiernan *lawyer, social work educator*

Medford
Berman, David *lawyer, poet*
Jacobs, Mary Lee *lawyer*
Rubin, Alfred Peter *law educator, educator*
Salacuse, Jeswald William *lawyer, educator*

Nantucket
Rauch, George Washington *lawyer, director*

Natick
Grassia, Thomas Charles *lawyer, educator, writer*
Oulton, Donald Paul *lawyer*
Pratt, Timothy *lawyer*

Needham
Bohnen, Michael J. *lawyer, foundation administrator*

New Bedford
Benoit, Richard Armand *lawyer, retired police chief*

Newton
Baron, Charles Hillel *lawyer, educator*
Coquillette, Daniel Robert *lawyer, educator*
Frankenheim, Samuel *retired lawyer*
Glazer, Donald Wayne *lawyer, corporate financial executive, educator*
Isselbacher, Rhoda Solin *lawyer*
Weisz, Virginia Graves *law educator*

Newton Center
Friedman, David Samuel *lawyer*
Snyder, John Gorvers *lawyer*

Newtown
Wilson, Paul Holliday, Jr. *lawyer*

Northampton
Santopietro, Albert Robert *lawyer*

Norwell
Mullare, T(homas) Kenwood, Jr. *lawyer*

Prides Crossing
Crowley, Ann V. *lawyer*
Garcia, Adolfo Ramon *lawyer, director*

Quincy
Hayes, Mary Dianne Wixted *lawyer*

Randolph
Johnson, Laurence Michael *lawyer*

Rockland
Durant, Leigh-Ann Margaret *lawyer*

Salem
Moran, Philip David *lawyer*
Rabchenuk, Paul Thomas *lawyer*

Sandwich
Troy, Robert Sweeney, Sr. *lawyer*

Southborough
Kriegsman, Edward Michael *lawyer*

Springfield
Dibble, Francis Daniel, Jr. *lawyer*
Oldershaw, Louis Frederick *retired lawyer*
Parke, David Alan *lawyer*
Roellig, Mark D. *lawyer, insurance company executive*
Weiss, Ronald Phillip *lawyer*

Stoughton
Gabovitch, Steven Alan *lawyer, accountant*

Truro
Chaplin, Ansel Burt *lawyer*

Waltham
Chory, John H. *lawyer*
Faneuil, Edward J. *lawyer*
Stephens, Jay B. *lawyer, defense technologies company executive*
Storey, Mimi Ellis *lawyer*

Watertown
Kaloosdian, Robert Aram *lawyer*
Young, Raymond Henry *lawyer*

Wellesley
Burstein, Harvey *lawyer, educator*
Clapp, Jennifer *lawyer*
Silberman, Robert A. S. *lawyer*

Wellesley Hills
Peabody, Laura S. *lawyer, insurance company executive*

West Falmouth
Carlson, David Bret *retired lawyer*

Weston
Lashman, L. Edward *arbitrator, mediator, consultant*
McDaniel, James Alan *lawyer*
Thomas, Roger Meriwether *lawyer*

Westwood
Partnoy, Ronald Allen *lawyer*

Windsor
Leaf, Martin Norman *lawyer*

Winthrop
Brown, Patricia Irene *retired law librarian, lawyer*

Worcester
Donnelly, James Corcoran, Jr. *lawyer*
Huber, J. Kendall *lawyer, insurance company executive*
Mirick, John O. *lawyer*
Uhl, Christopher Martin *lawyer*
Van Nostrand, Richard Charles *lawyer*

MICHIGAN

Ada
Mohr, Michael Arthur *lawyer*

Alpena
Hunter, Mark John *lawyer, photographer*

Ann Arbor
Adams, James Charles *lawyer*

Allen, Layman Edward *law educator, research scientist*
Anderson, Austin Gothard *lawyer, consultant, academic administrator*
Buesser, Anthony Carpenter *lawyer*
Carney, Thomas Daly *lawyer*
Cooper, Edward Hayes *lawyer, educator*
Darlow, Julia Donovan *lawyer*
DeVine, Edmond Francis *retired lawyer*
Duquette, Donald Norman *law educator*
Eggertsen, John Hale *lawyer*
Ellmann, Douglas Stanley *lawyer*
Garris, Michael Jack *lawyer*
Gray, Whitmore *lawyer, educator*
Joscelyn, Kent Buckley *lawyer*
Kahn, Douglas Allen *law educator*
Kamisar, Yale *lawyer, educator*
Kauper, Thomas Eugene *lawyer, educator*
Keppelman, Nancy *lawyer*
Krier, James Edward *law educator, writer*
Laycock, Harold Douglas *law educator, writer*
MacKinnon, Catharine Alice *lawyer, educator, writer*
Miller, William Ian *law educator*
Radin, Margaret Jane *law educator*
Reed, John Wesley *lawyer, educator*
Regan, Donald H. *law educator*
Ryan, Marianne Elizabeth *lawyer*
St. Antoine, Theodore Joseph *retired law educator, arbitrator*
Sandalow, Terrance *law educator*
Scott, Rebecca J. *law and history educator*
Simpson, A.W. Brian *law educator*
Stein, Eric *retired law educator*
Sullivan, Teresa Ann *law and sociology educator, academic administrator*
Theut, C. Peter *lawyer*
Vining, (George) Joseph *law educator*
Waggoner, Lawrence William *law educator*
White, James Boyd *law educator*

Auburn Hills
Gasparovic, John J. *lawyer*
Leese, Holly Elisabeth *lawyer, automotive company executive*

Bay City
Boylan, Winnifred Padden *lawyer*
Powers, David Louis *lawyer*

Benton Harbor
Hopp, Daniel Frederick *lawyer, manufacturing company executive*

Bingham Farms
Goren, Steven Eliot *lawyer*

Birmingham
Elsman, James Leonard, Jr. *lawyer*
Kienbaum, Thomas Gerd *lawyer*

Bloomfield Hills
Banas, C(hristine) Leslie *lawyer*
Birnkrant, Sherwin Maurice *lawyer*
Bogas, Kathleen Laura *lawyer*
Burstein, Richard Joel *lawyer*
Charla, Leonard Francis *lawyer, publishing executive*
Clippert, Charles Frederick *lawyer*
Cook, Steven M. *lawyer, construction executive*
Dawson, Stephen Everette *lawyer*
Galante, Jerome Anthony *lawyer*
Googasian, George Ara *lawyer*
Haynes, Jeffrey Kennard *lawyer*
Kanter, Alan Michael *lawyer*
Kasischke, Louis Walter *lawyer*
Kirk, John MacGregor *lawyer*
Ledwidge, Patrick Joseph *lawyer*
LoPrete, James Hugh *lawyer*
Meyer, George Herbert *lawyer*
Norris, John Hart *lawyer, director*
Rader, Ralph Terrance *lawyer*
Robinson, Logan Gilmore *lawyer*
Simon, Evelyn *lawyer*
Smith, H(arold) Lawrence *lawyer*
Snyder, George Edward *lawyer*
Solomon, Mark Raymond *lawyer, educator*
Spradlin, Shane M. *lawyer, automotive executive*

Brighton
McDonald, Patrick Allen *lawyer, educator, arbitrator*
Wallack, Rina Evelyn *lawyer*

Dearborn
Harris, John Fitgerald *lawyer*
Kahn, Mark Leo *arbitrator, educator*
Nelson, Alison R. *lawyer*

Detroit
Archer, Dennis Wayne *lawyer, former mayor*
Berg, Terrence G. *prosecutor*
Bilstrom, Jon Wayne *lawyer*
Calkins, Stephen *lawyer, educator*
Candler, James Nall, Jr. *lawyer*
Charfoos, Lawrence Selig *lawyer*
Cohen, Norton Jacob *lawyer*
Cothorn, John Arthur *lawyer*
Cranmer, Thomas William *lawyer*
Deason, Herold McClure *lawyer*
DeMoss, Lisa S. *lawyer, insurance company executive*
Drutchas, Gregory G. *lawyer*
Dudley, Arthur, II, *lawyer*
Dunn, William Bradley *lawyer*
Hampton, Verne Churchill, II, *lawyer*
Howbert, Edgar Charles *lawyer*
Kessler, Philip Joel *lawyer*
Krsul, John Aloysius, Jr. *lawyer*
Lawrence, John Kidder *lawyer*
Leuchtman, Stephen Nathan *lawyer*
Lewis, David Baker *lawyer*
Lockman, Stuart M. *lawyer*
Mamat, Frank Trustick *lawyer*
McKim, Samuel John III *lawyer*
Miller, Bruce Abraham *lawyer*
Millikin, Michael P. *lawyer, automotive executive*
Raymond, Richard Gerard, Jr. *lawyer*
Saxton, William Marvin *lawyer*
Schwartz, Alan Earl *lawyer, director*
Sedler, Robert Allen *law educator*
Shapiro, Michael Bruce *lawyer*
Smith, S. Kinnie, Jr. *lawyer*
Solomon, William B., Jr. *lawyer, finance company executive*
Sparrow, Herbert George III *lawyer, educator*
Thelen, Bruce Cyril *lawyer*
Valade, Alan Michael *lawyer*
Volz, William Harry *lawyer, educator*
Wexler, Raymond P. *lawyer, automotive executive*
Wittlinger, Timothy David *lawyer*
Wyrick, Jermaine Albert *lawyer*
Zuckerman, Richard Engle *lawyer, educator*

East Lansing
Johnson, Clark Cumings *lawyer, educator, dean*
Lashbrooke, Elvin Carroll, Jr. *law educator, consultant, dean*
Wilkinson, William Sherwood *lawyer*

Farmington
Shaevsky, Mark *lawyer*

Farmington Hills
Fenton, Robert Leonard *lawyer, writer, film producer*
Meyer, Philip Gilbert *lawyer*

Fenton
Gilbert, Ronald Rhea *lawyer*

Frankfort
Gerberding, Miles Carston *lawyer*

Grand Rapids
Barnes, Thomas John *lawyer*
Brinkmeyer, Scott S. *lawyer*
Davis, Henry Barnard, Jr. *retired lawyer*
Deems, Nyal David *lawyer, mayor*
Hall, William Wesley *lawyer*
Hooyenga, Judith Waara *lawyer*
Jennette, Noble Stevenson III *lawyer*
McCallum, Charles Edward *lawyer*
Mears, Patrick Edward *lawyer*
Sytsma, Fredric A. *lawyer*

Grosse Pointe
Amsden, Ted Thomas *lawyer*
Maurer, David Leo *lawyer*

Grosse Pointe Farms
Thurber, Peter Palms *lawyer*

Grosse Pointe Park
Centner, Charles William *lawyer, educator*
Mogk, John Edward *law educator, association executive, consultant*

Harbor Springs
Smith, Wayne Richard *lawyer*

Harper Woods
Mitseff, Carl *lawyer*

Holland
Murphy, Max Ray *lawyer*

Inkster
Bullock, Steven Carl *lawyer*

Jackson
Brunner, James Edwin *lawyer*
Marcoux, William Joseph *lawyer*

Kalamazoo
Gordon, Edgar George *retired lawyer*
Van Slambrouck, John G. *lawyer*

Lake Orion
Robinson, Marietta S. *lawyer*

Lansing
Baker, Frederick Milton, Jr. *lawyer*
Cawthorne, Dennis Otto *lawyer*
Ewert, Quentin Albert *lawyer, consultant*
Fink, Joseph Allen *lawyer*
Foster, Joe C., Jr. *lawyer*
Hess, Steven Charles *lawyer*
Marvin, David Edward Shreve *lawyer*
Rogers, Paulleto *researcher, writer, delegate*
Rooney, John Philip *law educator*
Stockmeyer, Norman Otto *law educator, consultant*
Yeutter, Clayton Keith *lawyer, former United States Secretary of Agriculture*

Livonia
Bialosky, David L. *lawyer, automotive executive*
Hoffman, Barry Paul *lawyer*

Manistee
Broberg, Leonard Eliot *lawyer*

Marquette
Osstyn, Randolph Beier *lawyer*

Midland
Kalil, Charles James *lawyer, chemicals executive*

Monroe
Lipford, Rocque Edward *lawyer*

Muskegon
McKendry, John H., Jr. *lawyer*
Nehra, Gerald Peter *lawyer*

New Buffalo
Stassen, John Henry *retired lawyer*

Northville
Leavitt, Martin Jack *lawyer*

Novi
Bullard, Willis Clare, Jr. *lawyer, public official*
Darke, Richard Francis *lawyer*
Hale, Daniel G. *lawyer, insurance company executive*

Pinckney
Britton, Clarold Lawrence *lawyer, consultant*

Plymouth
Martina, Carlo Jack *lawyer*

Portage
Hall, Curtis E. *lawyer, health products executive*

Riverview
Ward, George Edward *lawyer, law educator*

Rockford
Grady, Kenneth Alan *lawyer, corporate secretary*

Royal Oak
Wise, John Augustus *lawyer, director*

Sault Sainte Marie
France, Jennifer Jean *lawyer, educator*

South Haven
Waxman, Sheldon Robert *lawyer*

Southfield
Andreoff, Christopher Andon *lawyer*
Bassey, Ronald D. *tax attorney*
Darling, Robert Howard *lawyer*
Dawson, Dennis Ray *lawyer, manufacturing executive*
Fieger, Geoffrey Nels *lawyer*
Katz, Robert L. *lawyer*
Larkin, Terrence B. *lawyer*
Low, James William *lawyer*
Morganroth, Mayer *lawyer*
Porter, Thomas W.B. *lawyer*
Ritchie, Alexander Buchan *lawyer*
Thurswell, Gerald Elliott *lawyer*
Toll, Sheldon Samuel *lawyer*

Sylvan Lake
Derdarian, Christine Anne *lawyer*

Taylor
Leekley, John Robert *lawyer, consumer products company executive*

Traverse City
Kubiak, Jon Stanley *lawyer, casino and hotel industry executive*

Troy
Alterman, Irwin Michael *lawyer*
Baker, Vernon G., II, *lawyer, automotive executive*
Branigan, Thomas Patrick *lawyer*
Castelli, Ralph Anthony, Jr. *lawyer*
Cunningham, Gary H. *lawyer*
Haron, David Lawrence *lawyer*
Hilton, Michael E. *lawyer*
Kruse, John Alphonse *lawyer*
Lis, Daniel T. *lawyer*
Navarro, Monica *lawyer*
Pearce, Harry Jonathan *lawyer, manufacturing executive*
Sherbin, David M. *lawyer*
Thoms, David Moore *lawyer*

Van Buren Township
Donofrio, John *lawyer*

Wyandotte
Pentiuk, Randall Alan *lawyer*

Ypsilanti
Barr, John Monte *lawyer*

MINNESOTA

Austin
Cavanaugh, James W. *lawyer*

Bemidji
Kief, Paul Allan *lawyer*

Bloomington
Mooty, John William *lawyer*

Chatfield
Opat, Matthew John *lawyer*

Detroit Lakes
Stowman, David L. *lawyer*

Duluth
Balmer, James Walter *lawyer*
Burns, Richard Ramsey *lawyer*

Eden Prairie
Gernander, Barton Carl *lawyer*

Edina
Bakken, Eric Allen *lawyer*
Barden, Robert Christopher *lawyer, psychologist, educator, writer*
Neff, Fred Leonard *lawyer*
Schulze, Chad William *lawyer*

Golden Valley
Schlichting, William Henry *lawyer, writer*

Hopkins
Zotaley, Byron Leo *lawyer*

Kenyon
Peterson, Franklin Delano *lawyer*

Mankato
Levin, Daniel A. *law educator*

Maple Grove
Oh, Allen James *lawyer*

Mendota Heights
Deans, Thomas Seymour *lawyer*

Minneapolis
Anderson, Eric Scott *lawyer*
Baer, Timothy R. *lawyer, retail executive*
Baillie, James Leonard *lawyer*
Ballintine, Daniel John *lawyer*
Berens, William Joseph *lawyer*
Borger, John Philip *lawyer*
Branson, Timothy E. *lawyer*
Bress, Michael E. *retired lawyer*
Brink, David Ryrie *lawyer*
Busdicker, Gordon Gene *retired lawyer*
Caplan, Allan Hart *lawyer*
Carlson, Thomas David *lawyer*
Cattanach, Robert Edward, Jr. *lawyer*
Champlin, Steven Kirk *lawyer*
Ciresi, Michael Vincent *lawyer*
Clary, Bradley G. *lawyer, educator*
Cole, Phillip Allen *lawyer*
Connelly, Michael C. *lawyer, energy executive*
Constantine, Katherine A. *lawyer*
Eck, George Gregory *lawyer*
Finch, Frederick Earl *lawyer*
Flom, Gerald Trossen *lawyer*
Flynn Peterson, Kathleen A. *lawyer*
Garon, Philip Stephen *lawyer*
Garton, Thomas William *lawyer*
Greener, Ralph Bertram *lawyer*
Gross, David J.F. *lawyer*
Hamel, Mark Edwin *lawyer*
Hansen, Robyn L. *lawyer*
Haynsworth, Harry Jay, IV, *law educator*
Hayward, Edward Joseph *lawyer*
Heffelfinger, Thomas Backer *lawyer, former prosecutor*
Heiberg, Robert Alan *lawyer*
Helsene, Amy L. *lawyer*
Hendrixson, Peter S. *lawyer*
Herman, John Hughes *lawyer*
Hibbs, John Stanley *lawyer*
Holden, Susan M. *lawyer*
Jarboe, Mark Alan *lawyer*
Jones, B. Todd (Byron Todd Jones) *prosecutor*
Joyce, Joseph M. *lawyer, retail executive*
Junek, John C. *lawyer, finance company executive*
Kahn, Jonathan *law educator*
Kaplan, Sheldon *lawyer, director*
Keene, Lonnie *lawyer*
Kelley, Douglas A. *lawyer*
Kelly, A. David *lawyer*
Keppel, William James *lawyer, educator, writer*
Keyes, Jeffrey J. *lawyer*
Kirtley, Jane Elizabeth *law educator*
Klaas, Paul Barry *lawyer*
Koneck, John Michael *lawyer*
Lancaster, Peter McCreery *lawyer*
Lavik, Bricker L. *lawyer*
Lebedoff, David Miller *lawyer, writer*
Lillehaug, David Lee *lawyer*
Lindgren, Jay Randolph *lawyer, former state senator*
Lindsay, Michael Anthony *lawyer*
Lucke, Stephen P. *lawyer*
Lueck, Martin R. *lawyer*
Magill, Frank J., Jr. *prosecutor*
Magnuson, Roger James *lawyer*
Mahoney, Kathleen Mary *lawyer*
Martin, Phillip Hammond *lawyer*
Martinson, Bradley James *lawyer*
Matheson, John H. *lawyer, educator*
Maynard, Hugh M. *lawyer*
McDonald, John J., Jr. *lawyer*
McGunnigle, George Francis *lawyer, judge*
McLaughlin, Patrick J. *lawyer*
Melendez, Brian *lawyer, political organization administrator*
Meshbesher, Ronald I. *lawyer*
Mitau, Lee R. *lawyer, bank executive*
Morrison, Fred LaMont *law educator*
Novak, Leslie Howard *lawyer*
Ort, Shannon *lawyer*
Painter, Richard William *lawyer, educator*
Palmer, Deborah Jean *lawyer*
Parsons, Charles Allan, Jr. *lawyer*
Payne, William Bruce *lawyer, director*
Pfau, James Michael *lawyer*
Pflaum, Jeffrey D. *lawyer*
Pratte, Robert John *lawyer*
Price, Joseph Michael *lawyer*
Radmer, Michael John *lawyer, educator*
Raskind, Leo Joseph *law educator*
Rasmussen, Teresa J. *lawyer, insurance company executive*
Ratchye, Boyd Havens *lawyer*
Rosenbaum, Robert A. *lawyer*
Rosenblatt, Cynthia Schaffer *lawyer*
Saeks, Allen Irving *lawyer*
Safley, James Robert *lawyer*
Santana, Lymari Jeanette *lawyer*
Sawicki, Zbigniew Peter *lawyer*
Sawyer, Charles F. *lawyer*
Schutz, Ronald James *lawyer*
Shnider, Bruce Jay *lawyer*
Short, Marianne Dolores *lawyer*
Simonson, James S. *lawyer*
Sippel, William Leroy *lawyer*
Sisk, Gregory Charles *lawyer, educator*
Sortland, Paul Allan *lawyer*
Stageberg, Roger V. *lawyer*
Stein, Robert Allen *lawyer, educator, former legal association administrator*
Stern, Leo G. *lawyer*
Stoeri, William R. *lawyer*
Struthers, Margo S. *lawyer*
Swanson, David P. *lawyer*
Tanick, Marshall Howard *lawyer, educator*

Torgerson, Paul M. *prosecutor*
Trucano, Michael *lawyer*
Van Brunt, William A. *lawyer*
Wahoske, Michael James *lawyer*
Whelpley, Dennis Porter *lawyer*
Windhorst, John William, Jr. *lawyer*
Winer, Edward L. *lawyer*
Woods, Robert Edward *lawyer*
Younger, Judith Tess *law educator*

Northfield
Lundergan, Barbara Keough *lawyer*

Plymouth
Mack, Richard L. *lawyer, software company executive*
Saville, Derric James *lawyer*

Rochester
Orwoll, Gregg S.K. *lawyer*

Saint Paul
Allison, John Robert *lawyer*
Bell, Lawrence T. *lawyer*
Daly, Joseph Leo *law educator*
Galvin, Michael John, Jr. *lawyer*
Garon, Jon M. *law educator, dean*
Geis, Jerome Arthur *lawyer, educator*
Janzen, Peter S. *lawyer, food products executive*
Johnson, Paul Oren *lawyer*
Kastelic, David Allen *lawyer, energy and food products executive*
Kelly, Patrick J. *lawyer*
Kirwin, Kenneth Francis *law educator*
Krop, Pamela Sue *lawyer*
Leighton, Robert Joseph *lawyer*
Pugh, Thomas Wilfred *lawyer*
Schnitzer, Alan D. *lawyer*
Seymour, McNeil Vernam *lawyer*
Smith, Marschall Imboden *lawyer*
Spence, Kenneth F. III *lawyer, insurance company executive*
von Geldern, James Robert *law educator*
Zibell, Donald Fredrick *lawyer*

Waseca
Deike, Keith Lawrence *lawyer*

Wayzata
Bergerson, David Raymond *lawyer*
Feuss, Linda Anne Upsall *lawyer*
Heckt, Melvin Dean *lawyer*
Palmer, Brian Eugene *retired lawyer*
Reutiman, Robert William, Jr. *lawyer*
Schnobrich, Roger William *lawyer*

MISSISSIPPI

Bay Saint Louis
Bernstein, Joseph *lawyer*

Greenwood
Swayze, Charles J., Jr. *lawyer*

Gulfport
Phifer-Starks, Kim D. *paralegal, educator*
Phillips, Joy Lambert *lawyer, banker*

Hattiesburg
Adelman, Michael Schwartz *lawyer*

Jackson
Ables, Jackson Henderson III *lawyer*
Corlew, John Gordon *lawyer*
Drinkwater, William Wayne *lawyer*
Hafter, Jerome Charles *lawyer*
Harkins, Patrick Nicholas III *lawyer*
Henegan, John C(lark) *lawyer*
Houston, Jamie Giles III *lawyer, accountant*
Hughes, Byron William *oil industry executive*
Hutchison, Mark Stevenson *lawyer*
Kennedy, Kristi D. *lawyer*
Langston, Rebecca McRae *lawyer*
Martinez, Eduardo Vidal *lawyer*
McIntyre, James G. *lawyer*
Montjoy, Richard Wilson, II, *lawyer*
Roberts, Richard Charlton III *lawyer*
Scanlon, Pat H. *lawyer*
Travis, Jay A. III *lawyer*
Welch, W(alter) Scott III *lawyer*

Madison
McDavid, John Sanford *lawyer*

Mooreville
Franks, Jamie (James R. Franks Jr.) *lawyer, political organization administrator*

Olive Branch
Carnall, George Hursey, II, *lawyer*

Oxford
Greenlee, Jim Ming *prosecutor*
Howorth, David Bishop *retired lawyer*
Knox, James Marshall *lawyer*
Scruggs, Richard F. (Dickie Scruggs) *lawyer*

Philadelphia
Duncan, Mark *prosecutor*

Tylertown
Mord, Irving Conrad, II, *lawyer*

University
Bradley, John Robin, Jr. *law educator*

Vicksburg
Bailess, Robert R. *lawyer*

MISSOURI

Ballwin
Luberda, George Joseph *lawyer, educator*

Belton
Taylor, Reginald L. *lawyer, consultant*

Cape Girardeau
McManaman, Kenneth Charles *lawyer*

Carthage
Jett, Ernest Carroll, Jr. *lawyer*

Cassville
Cole, David A. *lawyer, political organization administrator*

Chesterfield
Canis, Randy Lawrence *lawyer, educator*
Gerard, Jules Bernard *law educator*
Hier, Marshall David *lawyer*
Wood, Donald Euriah *retired lawyer*

Clayton
Kolker, Scott Lee *lawyer*
Mohan, John J. *lawyer*
Pain, George H. *lawyer*
Tremayne, Eric Flory *lawyer*

Columbia
Easton, Stephen Douglas *lawyer, educator*
Esbeck, Carl H. *law educator*
Moore, Mitchell Jay *lawyer, educator*
Phillips, Walter Ray *law educator*
Westbrook, James Edwin *law educator*

Dexter
Ringer, John William *lawyer*

Independence
Albano, Michael Santo John *lawyer*
Shomin, Janet L. *paralegal*

Jefferson City
Bandré, David George *lawyer*
Bartlett, Alex *lawyer*
Chapel, Nimrod T., Jr. *lawyer, government agency administrator*
Covington, Ann K. *lawyer, former state supreme court justice*
Deutsch, James Bernard *lawyer*
Mitten, L. Russell *lawyer, former telecommunications industry executive*
Tettlebaum, Harvey M. *lawyer*

Kansas City
Atkinson, David Neal *law educator*
Balloun, Joseph Eugene *lawyer*
Beck, William G. *lawyer*
Beckett, Theodore Charles *lawyer*
Beihl, Frederick *retired lawyer*
Berkowitz, Lawrence M. *lawyer*
Blanton, W. C. *lawyer*
Brous, Thomas Richard *lawyer*
Clarke, Milton Charles *lawyer*
Crawford, Randy M. *lawyer*
Cross, William Dennis *lawyer*
Davis, John Charles *lawyer*
Deacy, Thomas Edward, Jr. *lawyer*
Doan, Kirk Hugh *lawyer*
Egan, Charles Joseph, Jr. *lawyer, consumer products company executive*
Foster, Mark Stephen *lawyer*
Freeman, Frederick Roe *lawyer*
Frisbie, Charles *retired lawyer*
Geroe, Michael R. *lawyer*
Gorman, Gerald Warner *lawyer*
Graves, Todd Peterson *lawyer, former prosecutor*
Handley, Gerald Matthew *lawyer, educator*
Harris, Charlie J., Jr. *lawyer*
Hindman, Larrie C. *lawyer*
Johnson, Mark Eugene *lawyer*
Johnston, John Steven *lawyer*
Kaplan, Harvey L. *lawyer*
Kilroy, John Muir *lawyer*
Kilroy, William Terrence *lawyer*
Klamann, John Michael *lawyer*
Kobach, Kris William *law educator, former political organization administrator*
Koerner, Wendell Edward, Jr. *lawyer, mediator*
Langworthy, Robert Burton *lawyer*
Litan, Robert Eli *lawyer, economist*
Magill, Kent B. *lawyer*
Martucci, William Christopher *lawyer*
Matheny, Edward Taylor, Jr. *lawyer*
McManus, James William *lawyer*
Milton, Chad Earl *lawyer*
Moore, Stephen James *lawyer*
Mordy, James Calvin *retired lawyer*
Murphy, John F. *lawyer*
Newsom, James Thomas *lawyer*
Northrip, Robert Earl *lawyer*
Pelofsky, Joel *lawyer*
Price, James Tucker *lawyer*
Prugh, William Byron *lawyer*
Redfearn, Paul L. III *lawyer*
Robb, Gary Charles *lawyer*
Sampson, William Roth *lawyer*
Shaw, John W. *lawyer*
Spalty, Edward Robert *lawyer*
Stoup, Arthur Harry *lawyer*
Tyler, John Edward III *lawyer*
Van Dyke, Thomas Wesley *lawyer*
Vering, John Albert *lawyer*
Versfeld, Leon *lawyer*
Viani, James Laurence *retired lawyer*
Ward, R. Lawrence *lawyer*
Whisler, Joe B. *lawyer*
Willy, Thomas Ralph *lawyer*
Wirken, James Charles *lawyer*
Woody, Teresa Ann *lawyer*
Woolley, Brian N. *lawyer*
Wrobley, Ralph *lawyer*
Wyrsch, James Robert *lawyer, educator, writer*

Marshfield
Knust, Daniel Max *lawyer*

Saint Charles
Rollings, Dale Linn *lawyer*

Saint Joseph
Kranitz, Theodore Mitchell *lawyer*
Taylor, Michael Leslie *lawyer*

Saint Louis
Appleton, R. O., Jr. *lawyer*
Arnold, Fred English *lawyer*
Arnold, John Fox *lawyer*
Aylward, Ronald Lee *lawyer*
Baldwin, Edwin Steedman *lawyer*
Ball, Dan H. *lawyer*
Baum, Gordon Lee *lawyer, non-profit organization administrator*
Becker, David Mandel *law educator, author, consultant*
Blanke, Richard Brian *lawyer*
Bodnar, John Charles *lawyer*
Boggs, Beth Clemens *lawyer*
Bonacorsi, Mary Catherine *lawyer*
Bretton, Randolph H. *lawyer, researcher*
Brickler, John Weise *lawyer*
Burke, Thomas Michael *lawyer*
Carp, Larry *lawyer*
Carr, Gary Thomas *lawyer*
Clear, John Michael *lawyer*
Copeland, Douglas Allen *lawyer*
Cornfeld, Dave Louis *lawyer*
Cornfeld, Richard Steven *lawyer*
Cullen, James D. *lawyer*
Danforth, John Claggett *lawyer, former ambassador, Former United States Senator, Missouri*
DeVoto, Thomas C. *lawyer*
Doody, Gregory L. *lawyer, former energy executive*
Dorwart, Donald Bruce *lawyer*
Dowd, Edward L., Jr. *lawyer, former prosecutor*
Downey, Michael Patrick *lawyer*
Duesenberg, Richard William *lawyer*
Duesenberg, Robert H. *retired lawyer*
Elliott, Howard, Jr. *lawyer, gas industry executive*
Epstein, Robert Harry *lawyer*
Falk, William James *lawyer*
Fogle, James Lee *lawyer*
Fox, G. Richard *lawyer*
Gilster, Peter Stuart *lawyer*
Goldner, Jesse Alan *law educator*
Gray, Charles Elmer *lawyer, rancher, investor*
Greenley, Beverly Jane *lawyer, educator*
Guarigila, Dale A. *lawyer*
Guerri, William Grant *lawyer*
Hackmann, Frank H. *lawyer*
Hansen, Charles *lawyer*
Harris, Whitney Robson *lawyer, military officer, volunteer, educator*
Hayman, Randy E. *lawyer*
Hermeling, Caroline L. *lawyer*
Immel, Vincent Clare *retired law educator*
Inkley, John James, Jr. *lawyer*
Jaudes, Richard Edward *lawyer*
Johnson, E. Perry *lawyer*
Joley, Lisa Annette *lawyer, brewery company executive*
Kohn, Alan Charles *lawyer*
Kortenhof, Joseph Michael *lawyer, educator*
Kraft, Carl David *lawyer*
Kuhlmann, Fred Mark *lawyer*
Lause, Michael Francis *lawyer*
Lebowitz, Albert *lawyer, writer*
Lents, Don Glaude *lawyer*
Lonsberg, John V. *lawyer*
Lowenhaupt, Charles Abraham *lawyer*
Lucchesi, Lionel Louis *lawyer*
Lynch, Robert Martin *lawyer, consultant*
Madsen, Matthew J. *lawyer*
Mandelstamm, Jerome Robert *lawyer*
McCarter, Charles Chase *lawyer*
McDaniel, James Edwin *lawyer*
McKinnis, Michael Bayard *lawyer*
Meehan, John Justin *lawyer*
Merrill, Charles Eugene *lawyer*
Metcalfe, Walter Lee, Jr. *lawyer*
Meyer, David Alan *lawyer*
Michenfelder, Albert A. *lawyer*
Moore, McPherson Dorsett *lawyer*
Mulligan, Michael Dennis *lawyer*
Neville, James Morton *retired lawyer, consumer products company executive*
Newman, Charles *lawyer*
Oberlander, Michael I. *lawyer, consumer products company executive*
O'Keefe, Michael Daniel *lawyer*
O'Malley, Kevin Francis *lawyer, educator, writer*
Palans, Lloyd Alex *lawyer*
Peper, Christian Baird *lawyer*
Petruska, Paul Eric *lawyer*
Phoenix, G. Keith *lawyer*
Raclin, Grier C. *lawyer, telecommunications industry executive*
Riddle, Veryl Lee *lawyer*
Ringkamp, Stephen H. *lawyer, educator*
Roodman, David A. *lawyer*
Rose, Albert Schoenburg *lawyer, educator*
Rubenstein, Jerome Max *lawyer*
Sachs, Alan Arthur *lawyer*
Schoch, Alexander C. *lawyer, energy executive*
Schramm, Paul Howard *retired lawyer*
Searls, Eileen Haughey *retired lawyer, librarian, educator*
Sestric, Anthony James *lawyer*
Sherby, Kathleen Reilly *lawyer*
Smith, Arthur Lee *lawyer*
Stoneman, Mark L. *lawyer*
Sullivan, Steven R. *lawyer*
Teasdale, Kenneth Fulbright *lawyer*
Temporiti, John J. *lawyer, former political organization administrator*
Underwood, Anthony Paul *lawyer*
Van Fleet, Lisa A. *lawyer*
Wagner, Raymond Thomas, Jr. *lawyer*
Walker Tucker, Dana *lawyer*
Walsh, Thomas Charles *lawyer*
Weiss, Charles Andrew *lawyer*
Wells, W. David *lawyer*
Wheelock, Bryan King *lawyer, educator*
Wilkinson, Robert F. *lawyer*
Williamson, Keith Harvey *lawyer*
Wolff, Frank Pierce, Jr. *lawyer*

Sedalia
Rice, James Briggs, Jr. *lawyer*

Springfield
Baird, C. Ronald *lawyer*
Christian, John Catlett, Jr. *lawyer*
Hamra, Sam F. *lawyer, restauranteur*
Hosmer, Craig William *lawyer, political organization administrator*
Pratt, John S. *lawyer*
Sanders, Bryan Howard *law educator, consultant*
Schnake, Richard Lane *lawyer*

Stockton
Hammons, Brian Kent *executive lawyer*

Town And Country
Fagerberg, Roger Richard *lawyer*

MONTANA

Billings
Dalthorp, George Carrol *lawyer*
Mercer, William W. *prosecutor*
Sites, James Philip *lawyer*
Thompson, James William *lawyer*
Towe, Thomas Edward *lawyer*

Bozeman
Conover, Richard Corrill *lawyer*

Columbia Falls
Chisholm, Dean D. *lawyer*

Havre
Maristuen, Keith A. *lawyer*

Helena
Hunt, William Edward, Sr. *lawyer, retired state supreme court justice*
Meadows, Judith Adams *law librarian, educator*
Morrison, John Martin *lawyer, State Auditor Montana*

Missoula
Bowman, Jean Louise *lawyer, civic worker*
Doherty, Steve *lawyer, state legislator*
Willey, Charles Wayne *lawyer*

Whitehall
Bernard, Donald Ray *retired law educator*

NEBRASKA

Broken Bow
Sennett, John O. *lawyer*

Chadron
Bump, Bevin B. *lawyer*

Columbus
Schumacher, Paul Maynard *lawyer*

Lincoln
Covalt, Victor E. III *lawyer, political organization administrator*
Crump, Linda R. *lawyer*
Fahleson, Mark A. *lawyer, political organization administrator*
Guthery, John M. *lawyer*
Johnson, Douglas Blaikie *lawyer*
Lichty, Warren Dewey, Jr. *lawyer*
Perry, Edwin Charles *lawyer*
Rembolt, James Earl *lawyer*
Rowe, David Winfield *lawyer*

Omaha
Achelpohl, Steven Edward *lawyer*
Batcheler, Colleen *lawyer, food products executive*
Caporale, D. Nick *lawyer*
Creigh, James Carey *lawyer*
Dahlk, Thomas Harlan *lawyer*
Daub, Hal (Harold John Daub Jr.) *lawyer*
Dittrick, William G. *lawyer*
Fellman, Richard Mayer *retired lawyer*
Gleason, James Mullaney *lawyer, insurance company executive*
Hamann, Deryl Frederick *lawyer, bank consultant*
Hemmer, J. Michael *lawyer, rail transportation executive*
Jensen, Sam *lawyer*
Koley, James L. *lawyer, corporate director*
Lieben, Thomas Geoffrey *lawyer*
Mark, Wayne Joseph *lawyer*
Quandahl, Mark C. *lawyer, former political organization administrator*
Reiser, Richard Scott *lawyer*
Rock, Harold L. *lawyer*
Schropp, Tobin *lawyer*
Sharpe, Robert Francis, Jr. *lawyer, food products executive*
Smal, Luba Dmitrievna *lawyer*
Stecher, Joe W. *prosecutor*
Stenberg, Donald B. *lawyer*
Vosburg, Bruce David *lawyer*
Wells, Roger W. *lawyer*

NEVADA

Henderson
Berns, Philip Allan *lawyer*

Ogg, Wilson Reid *lawyer, retired judge, poet, curator, publishing executive*
Schwartz, Richard *retired lawyer*

Lamoille
Vaughan, Robert Oren *lawyer*

Las Vegas
Anderson, Dominica C. *lawyer*
Barker, James Michael *lawyer*
Bernhard, Peter C. *lawyer, state agency administrator*
Brammell, Stephen Harrison *lawyer*
Bridges, B. Ried *lawyer*
Brower, Gregory A. *prosecutor, lawyer*
Browning, Laura Ellen *lawyer*
Consul, Vincent A. *lawyer*
Curran, William P. *lawyer*
Faiss, Robert Dean *lawyer*
Goodwin, John Robert *lawyer, educator, writer*
Gubler, John Gray *lawyer*
Hilbrecht, Norman Ty *lawyer*
Hill, Judith Deegan *retired lawyer*
Jacobs, Gary N. *lawyer, hotel executive*
Kamer, Gregory Jay *lawyer*
Kardum, Karmen Ana *lawyer*
Kennedy, Margaret Alexis *law educator, researcher*
Mansfield, Lorraine J. *lawyer*
McNulty, James Francis, Jr. *lawyer, consultant*
Miller, Robert Joseph *lawyer, former governor*
Morgan, Richard J. *law educator, dean*
Moss, Gary Curtis *lawyer*
Rapoport, Nancy B. *law educator*
Solomon, Jack Avrum, Jr. *lawyer, automotive executive, art dealer*
Stein, Stephen *lawyer*

Reno
Carlson, Severin A. *lawyer*
Goodenow, Rew R. *lawyer*
Hardy, Del *lawyer*
Hibbs, Loyal Robert *lawyer*
Hill, Earl McColl *lawyer*
Pagni, Albert Frank *lawyer*
Santos, Herbert Joseph, Jr. *lawyer*
White, John, Jr. *lawyer*

NEW HAMPSHIRE

Concord
Heard, Charles Wolfe *lawyer, consultant*
Kacavas, John P. *prosecutor*
Potter, Fred Leon *lawyer, retired insurance company executive*
Uchida, Richard Y. *lawyer*

Hanover
Gardner, Peter Jaglom *lawyer*
Isaacs, Robert Charles *retired lawyer*
Lundquist, Weyman Ivan *lawyer*
Mannix, Charles Raymond *law educator*

Keene
Bell, Ernest Lorne III *retired lawyer*

Littleton
Merritt, Thomas Butler *lawyer*

Manchester
Dugan, Kevin F. *lawyer*
Haffer, Edward Anthony *lawyer*
Hood, James Calton *lawyer*
Middleton, Jack Baer *lawyer*

Orford
Martin, Allen *retired lawyer*

Portsmouth
Abelson, Elias *lawyer*
Doleac, Charles Bartholomew *lawyer*
Tober, Stephen Lloyd *lawyer*
Volk, Kenneth Hohne *lawyer*

NEW JERSEY

Basking Ridge
Craven, Pamela F. *lawyer*

Bayonne
Fitzpatrick, Harold Francis *lawyer*

Bloomfield
Lordi, Katherine Mary *lawyer*

Bridgewater
Dreier, William Alan *lawyer*
Gallagher, Jerome Francis, Jr. *lawyer*
Sponzilli, Edward George *lawyer*
Wood, J(oshua) Warren III *lawyer, arbitrator, mediator*

Budd Lake
Webb, John Gibbon III *lawyer*

Burlington
Tang, Paul C. *lawyer*

Caldwell
Castano, Gregory Joseph *lawyer*

Camden
Kaden, Ellen Oran *lawyer, consumer products company executive*
Pomorski, Stanislaw *lawyer, educator*

Cape May Court House
Fineberg, Robert Alan *lawyer*

Cedar Grove
Voynick, John S., Jr. *lawyer*

Chatham
Zegas, Alan Lee *lawyer*

Cherry Hill
Brooks, Gilbert L. *lawyer*
Caldwell, Wesley Stuart III *lawyer, lobbyist*
D'Alfonso, Mario Joseph *lawyer*
Folkman, Benjamin *lawyer*
Kole, Janet Stephanie *lawyer, writer*
Myers, Daniel William, II, *lawyer*
Rochester, Andrew Lawrence *lawyer*
Rose, Joel Alan *legal consultant*

Clifton
Feinstein, Miles Roger *lawyer*
Lieb, L. Robert *lawyer*

Cranbury
Testa, James A. *lawyer*

Cranford
McCreedy, Edwin James *lawyer*

East Brunswick
Zaun, Anne Marie *lawyer*

Edison
Vercammen, Kenneth Albert *lawyer, prosecutor*

Elmwood Park
Mangano, Louis *lawyer*
White, H. Katherine *lawyer*

Fairfield
Connell, William Terrence *lawyer, judge*

Flemington
Lenagh, Thomas Hugh *lawyer, financial advisor*

Florham Park
Chase, Eric Lewis *lawyer*
Elias, John M. *lawyer*
Hardin, William Downer *retired lawyer*
Kahn, Richard *lawyer*
Kandravy, John *lawyer*
Laulicht, Murray Jack *lawyer*
Long, Stephen R. *lawyer*
Malone, Robert K. *lawyer*
Nittoly, Paul Gerard *lawyer*
O'Connell, Daniel Francis *lawyer*
Reid, Charles Adams III *lawyer*
Ridley, John A. *lawyer*
Rosenberg, Paul I. *lawyer*
Tallmadge, Mark Myron *lawyer*

Fort Lee
Goldberg, Harry Finck *lawyer, business consultant*
Weiss, Simona *retired paralegal*

Franklin Lakes
Moriarty, Thomas M. *lawyer*
Sherman, Jeffrey Scott *lawyer*

Garfield
Herpst, Robert Dix *lawyer, optical materials company executive*

Hackensack
Bronson, Meridith J. *lawyer*
Caminiti, Donald Angelo *lawyer*
Deener, Jerome Alan *lawyer*
Forman, Michael H. *lawyer*
Greenberg, Steven Morey *lawyer*
Hetherington, Robert Alexander *lawyer*
Latimer, Stephen Mark *lawyer*
Mullin, Patrick Allen *lawyer*
Rose, Arthur *lawyer*
Stein, Gary S. *lawyer, retired state supreme court justice*
Vort, Robert A. *lawyer*
Zucker, Arthur *lawyer*

Hackettstown
Kobert, Joel A. *lawyer*

Haddonfield
Iavicoli, Mario Anthony *lawyer*
Spevak, Eric Scott *lawyer*

Hampton
Nevins, Arthur Gerard, Jr. *lawyer*

Ho Ho Kus
Bryan, Thomas Lynn *lawyer, educator*

Hoboken
Sommers, George R. *lawyer*

Holmdel
Colmant, Andrew Robert *lawyer*

Iselin
Dornbusch, Arthur A., II, *lawyer*

Jersey City
DeCicco, John *law educator*
Filler, Ronald Howard *lawyer*
Guarini, Frank Joseph *lawyer, real estate developer, former congressman*
Nilsen, Martin John *lawyer*
Ott, Gilbert Russell, Jr. *lawyer*
Turula, Joseph *lawyer*

Kearny
Dunne, Frederick R., Jr. *lawyer*

Keyport
McLeod, Robert E. *lawyer*

Lebanon
Sabatino, Thomas Joseph, Jr. *lawyer, pharmaceutical executive*

Little Silver
Schmidt, Daniel Edward, IV, *lawyer, arbitrator*

Livingston
Ingato, Robert Joseph *lawyer*
Wolfe, Jonathan W. *lawyer*

Lyndhurst
Prevoznik, Michael E. *lawyer*

Madison
Brown, Paulette *lawyer*
Jibilian, Gerald Arsen *lawyer, manufacturing corporation executive*
Lach, Eileen Marie *lawyer*
Rosen, David M. *law educator*
Sawma, Gabriel M. *law educator*
Stein, Lawrence V. *lawyer*

Mahwah
Bear, Larry Alan *retired lawyer, educator*

Manalapan
Stone, Fred Michael *lawyer*

Marlboro
Bass, David Steven *law educator, arbitrator, mediator*

Mendham
Tramutola, Joseph Louis *lawyer, educator*

Millburn
Diamond, Richard S. *lawyer*

Montvale
Falcon, Raymond Jesus, Jr. *lawyer*

Montville
Heller, Hanes Ayres *lawyer*

Moorestown
Buckman, William H. *lawyer*
Garrigle, William Aloysius *lawyer*
Hyland, William Francis *retired lawyer*

Morris Plains
Pluciennik, Thomas Casimir *lawyer, former assistant county prosecutor*

Morristown
Adams, Katherine Leatherman *lawyer, diversified technology and manufacturing company executive*
Aspero, Benedict Vincent *lawyer*
Bromberg, Myron James *retired lawyer*
Coleman, James H., Jr. *lawyer, former state supreme court justice*
Gillen, James Robert *lawyer, insurance company executive*
Humick, Thomas Charles Campbell *lawyer*
Jacobs, Andrew Robert *lawyer*
Korf, Gene Robert *lawyer*
O'Grady, Dennis Joseph *lawyer*
Pollock, Stewart Glasson *lawyer, state supreme court justice*
Rose, Robert Gordon *lawyer*
Stanton, Patrick Michael *lawyer*

Mountain Lakes
Daniel, Royal Thomas III *lawyer, mechanical engineer, accountant*

Mountainside
Helander, Robert Charles *lawyer, arbitrator, contributing editor*

New Brunswick
Biribauer, Richard Frank *lawyer*
Miller, Lynn Fieldman *lawyer*
Yorke, Marianne *lawyer, real estate executive*

New Providence
McCarthy, G. Daniel *lawyer*

New Vernon
Kushen, Allan Stanford *retired lawyer, corporate executive*

Newark
Alexander, Mark C. *law educator, policy advisor*
Aron, Lester *lawyer*
Ashley, Thomas R. *lawyer*
Askin, Frank *law educator*
Bizub, Johanna *law librarian*
Blumrosen, Alfred William *law educator*
Bruno, Rosemary Joan *lawyer*
Cahn, Jeffrey Barton *lawyer*
Colón, Melinda *lawyer*
Crawford, Marjorie E. *law librarian, educator*
Cummis, Clive Sanford *lawyer*
Cunningham, LeeAnn *assistant prosecutor*
Day, Edward Francis, Jr. *lawyer*
Dee, Francis X. *lawyer*
Deutsch, Stuart Lewis *law educator, former dean*
Fishman, Paul J. *lawyer*
Foran, Margaret M. (Peggy Foran) *lawyer, financial services executive*
Freilich, Irvin Mayer *lawyer*
Garde, John Charles *lawyer*
Gibbons, John Joseph *lawyer, retired federal judge*
Goldstein, Marvin Mark *lawyer*
Green, Stuart Paul *law educator*
Haring, Eugene Miller *lawyer*
Kott, David Russell *lawyer*
Krovatin, Gerald *lawyer*
La Rocco, Anthony P. *lawyer*
Lorell, Jeffrey W. *lawyer*
McCarthy, Kathleen Jane *law educator, school librarian*
McGuire, William B(enedict) *lawyer*
McLean, David J. *lawyer*
Mehrberg, Randall Eric *lawyer, utilities executive*
Perez, John D. *lawyer*
Reilly, William Thomas *lawyer*
Risinger, D. Michael *lawyer, educator*
Rothschild, Gita F. *lawyer*
Selover, R. Edwin *lawyer, utilities executive*
Siegal, Joel Davis *lawyer*
Tischman, Michael Bernard *lawyer*
Vajtay, Stephen Michael, Jr. *lawyer*
Warren Ellison, Tasheaya L. *lawyer, director*
Zazzali, James R. *lawyer, retired state supreme court chief justice*
Zuckerman, Herbert Lawrence *lawyer*

Newton
Cox, William Martin *lawyer, educator*

North Bergen
Gilbert, Stephen Alan *retired lawyer, organization executive*

Northfield
Zlotnick, Norman Lee *lawyer*

Ocean City
Kyriazis, Arthur John (Athanasios Ioannis Kyriazis) *lawyer, molecularbiologist, patent attorney*

Oradell
Blakeslee, Edward Eaton *lawyer, insurance company executive*
Mavroudis, John M. *lawyer*

Park Ridge
Zimmerman, J. Jeffrey *lawyer, automotive executive*

Parsippany
Cox, Melvin Monroe *lawyer*
Deones, Jack E. *lawyer, broadcast executive*
Ewan, David E. *lawyer*
Sclafani, Karen C. *lawyer*
Wasser, Marilyn J. *lawyer, real estate company executive*

Pennington
Bustin, George Leo *lawyer*

Piscataway
Gustafsson, Mary E. *lawyer*
Nachtigal, Patricia *lawyer*

Pitman
Cloues, Edward Blanchard, II, *lawyer*

Plainfield
Ellington II, Michael L. *lawyer*

Pomona
Latourette, Audrey Wolfson *law educator*

Princeton
Anderson, Ellis Bernard *retired lawyer, pharmaceutical executive*
Bergman, Edward Jonathan *lawyer, educator*
Bramnick, Michael Richard *lawyer, energy executive*
Connor, Geoffrey Michael *lawyer*
Gibbons, Francis Clifford *lawyer, writer*
Kaplowitz, Karen (Jill) *lawyer, consultant*
Katz, Stanley Nider *law educator*
Keephart, Lydia Fabbro *lawyer, mediator*
Law, Stuart A., Jr. *lawyer*
Louka, Elli *lawyer, consultant*
Luchak, Frank Alexander *lawyer*
Mulchinock, David Steward *lawyer*
Scott, David Rodick *retired lawyer, educator*
Sullivan, Diane P. *lawyer*
Theivakumar, Jeyakumary Ruby *lawyer*

Randolph
Zelante, Thomas Andrew *lawyer*

Red Bank
Reinhart, Peter Sargent *lawyer*

Ridgewood
Harris, Micalyn Shafer *lawyer, arbitrator, mediator, educator, consultant*
Nachman, David Howard *lawyer*
Seigel, Jonas Kearney *prosecutor*

Riverton
Rabil, Mitchell Joseph *lawyer*

Roseland
Bennett, John K. *lawyer*
Benson, James Bracken *lawyer, computer company executive*
Brody, Jane L. *lawyer*
Cummis Sandlaufer, Deborah Gwen *lawyer*
Cutler, Laurence Jeffrey *lawyer*
Eakeley, Douglas Scott *lawyer*
Eichler, Burton Lawrence *lawyer*
Farber, Zulima V. *lawyer, former state attorney general*
Mazie, David A. *lawyer*
McMahon, Edward Richard *lawyer*
Positan, Wayne John *lawyer*
Post, John N. *lawyer*
Smith, Wendy Hope *lawyer*
Taylor, Lisa Deitsch *lawyer, arbitrator, mediator*
Vanderbilt, Arthur T., II, *lawyer*
Yun, Edward Joon *lawyer*

Saddle Brook
Cohn, Albert Linn *lawyer*

Scotch Plains
Klock, John Henry *lawyer*
Shaw, Alan *lawyer*

Sewell
Crouse, Farrell R. *lawyer*

Short Hills
Hazlehurst, Robert Purviance, Jr. *lawyer*

Schirmeister, Charles F. *retired lawyer*
Siegfried, David Charles *retired lawyer*

Shrewsbury
Michaelson, Peter Lee *lawyer*

Somerville
Fleischman, Joseph Jacob *lawyer*
Hutcheon, Peter David *lawyer*
Ligorano, Michael Kenneth *lawyer*

Sparta
McMeen, Elmer Ellsworth III *lay minister, musician, retired lawyer*
McMeen, Sheila Taenzler *retired lawyer*

Springfield
Mytelka, Arnold Krieger *lawyer*

Summit
Caming, H. W. William *retired lawyer, consultant*
Kenyon, Edward Tipton *lawyer*
Lijoi, Peter Bruno *lawyer*
Macioce, Frank Michael *lawyer, financial services company executive*
Pfaltz, Hugo Menzel, Jr. *lawyer*
Woller, James Alan *lawyer*

Teaneck
Cowan, Wallace Edgar *retired lawyer*

Trenton
Bigham, William J. *lawyer*
Blackburn, Audrey Peyton *lawyer*
Corman, Randy *lawyer*
Jones, Dale Edwin *public defender*

Union
Bottitta, Joseph Anthony *lawyer*
Rauch, Allan N. *lawyer*

Vineland
Coant, Charles Ian *lawyer*

Wall
Dugan, Mariellen *lawyer*
Nucciarone, A. Patrick *lawyer*

Warren
Brundage, Maureen A. *lawyer, insurance company executive*
Ventantonio, James Bartholomew *lawyer*

Wayne
Schwartz, David Jay *lawyer*

West Orange
Jordan, Leo John *lawyer*
McKinney, John Adams, Jr. *lawyer*
Richmond, Harold Nicholas *lawyer*
Samson, David *lawyer*

West Paterson
Smith, Roy (R. Smith) *lawyer*

Westwood
Parish, J. Michael *lawyer, mutual fund executive, writer*

Whitehouse Station
Feingold, Mark Howard *lawyer*
Kuhlik, Bruce Neil *lawyer*

Woodbridge
Barcan, Stephen Emanuel *lawyer*
Brown, Morris *lawyer*
Gill, Raymond A., Jr. *lawyer*
Lepelstat, Martin L. *lawyer*

Woodcliff Lake
Pell, Elliott Louis *lawyer*

NEW MEXICO

Alamogordo
Wills, Kimberly Kay *legal association administrator, educator*

Albuquerque
Aurbach, Robert Michael *legal executive, lawyer, consultant, photographer*
Beach, Arthur O'Neal *lawyer*
Bova, Vincent Arthur, Jr. *lawyer, consultant, photographer*
Caruso, Mark John *lawyer*
Chávez, Carmela Bernadette *lawyer, consultant*
Colón, Brian S. *lawyer, political organization administrator*
Dugan, Virginia Ruth *lawyer*
Fouratt, Gregory J. *prosecutor*
Hart, Frederick Michael *law educator*
Keleher, Michael Lawrence *lawyer*
Lasater, W(illiam) Robert, Jr. *lawyer*
Long, Stephen Carrel Mike *lawyer*
Martz, Clyde Ollen *retired lawyer*
Mays, G. Larry *criminal justice educator*
O'Brien, Daniel J. *lawyer*
Orraj, Craig Allen *lawyer*
Ortiz, Patrick T. *lawyer*
Ramo, Roberta Cooper *lawyer*
Robb, John Donald, Jr. *lawyer*
Roehl, Jerrald J. *lawyer*
Salazar, John Paul *lawyer*
Schuler, Alison Kay *lawyer*
Sisk, Daniel Arthur *lawyer*
Slade, Lynn *lawyer*
Vigil, Charles J. *lawyer*

Bayard
Foy, Thomas Paul *lawyer, retired state legislator, bank executive*

Corrales
Arkin, Michael Barry *lawyer, arbitrator, writer*
Campion, Kathleen Francis *lawyer, gifted and talented educator*

Deming
Cilento-Foran, Deborah *lawyer, bank executive*

Farmington
Perry, Mark Bradley *lawyer, minister*
Titus, Victor Allen *lawyer*

Las Cruces
Lutz, William Lan *lawyer*

Lovington
Crutchfield, Carl Barry *lawyer*

Placitas
Schoen, Stevan Jay *lawyer*

Sandia Park
Rager, Rudolph Russell *retired lawyer*

Santa Fe
Aarons, Stephen D. *lawyer*
Adams, Mark Kildee *lawyer*
Casey, Patrick Anthony *lawyer*
Dodds, Robert James III *lawyer*
Farber, Steven Glenn *lawyer*
Justice, Jack Burton *retired lawyer, writer*
McClaugherty, Joe L. *lawyer, educator*
Pound, John Bennett *lawyer*
Schwarz, Michael *lawyer*
Wertheim, John V. *lawyer, former political organization administrator*
Wolkoff, Eugene Arnold *lawyer*

Seneca
Monroe, Kendyl Kurth *retired lawyer*

Socorro
Bejnar, Thaddeus Putnam *law librarian*

NEW YORK

Albany
Alessi, Robert Joseph *lawyer, real estate developer, pharmacist*
Barsamian, John Albert *lawyer, arbitrator, criminologist, judge, educator*
Bonventre, Vincent Martin *lawyer, educator*
Cogen, Richard M. *lawyer*
Everett, James W., Jr. *lawyer*
Finnessey, Samuel J., Jr. *lawyer*
Koff, Howard Michael *lawyer*
Novotny, F. Douglas *lawyer*
Picotte, Susan Carroll *lawyer*
Rostow, Charles Nicholas *lawyer, educator*
Sheehan, Deborah Hardick *lawyer*
Tully, Mathew B. *lawyer*
Winner, George Henry *lawyer, state legislator*
Yanas, John Joseph *lawyer, director*
Zambri, Melissa Marie *lawyer, educator*

Albertson
Berlin, Mark A. *lawyer*

Alden
Pajak, David Joseph *lawyer, consultant*

Amherst
Kryzan, Alice J. *retired lawyer*
Walsh, Laurie Ann *law educator*

Ardsley On Hudson
Stein, Milton Michael *retired lawyer*

Armonk
Boies, David *lawyer*
O'Donnell, Daniel E. *lawyer, information technology executive*
Rosenberg, Michael *lawyer*
Weber, Robert Carl *lawyer*
Wertheim, Ram D. *lawyer*

Ballston Spa
Brown, Ifigenia Theodore *retired lawyer*

Batavia
Van Rees, Cornelius S. *lawyer*

Bath
BetzJitomir, Susan Marie *lawyer, educator, judge, policy analysis researcher*

Bethpage
Schwartz, Jonathan D. *lawyer*

Binghamton
Gouldin, David Millen *lawyer*
Madigan, Kathryn Grant *lawyer*

Briarcliff Manor
Bernstein, Nadia Jacqueline *lawyer*
Bower, Thomas Michael *lawyer*

Bronx
Balka, Sigmund Ronell *lawyer*
Cornfield, Melvin *lawyer, director*
Richman, Murray W. *lawyer*
Richman, Stacey Gayle *lawyer*
Yunen, Jose R. *surgical intensivist, director, epidemiologist*

Bronxville
Fuller, David Otis, Jr. *lawyer*
Hagendorn, William Hull *lawyer*

Brooklyn
Barabash, Claire *lawyer, special education services professional, psychologist*
Bloomfield, David Charles *lawyer, educator, school district government official, not-for-profit public executive*
Campbell, Benton Jay *prosecutor*
Josephson, William Howard *retired lawyer*
Kamins, Barry Michael *lawyer*
Kanwar, Vivek Vik *law educator, consultant*
Karmel, Roberta Segal *lawyer, educator*
Leamer, Robert Eldon *lawyer, hospital administrator*
Moran, Marissa J. *law educator*
Pearsall, Otis Pratt *retired lawyer*
Poser, Norman Stanley *law educator*
Roth, Robert *lawyer, journalist*

Buffalo
Barber, Janice Ann *lawyer*
Brown, Lawrence Charles *lawyer*
Brydges, Thomas Eugene *lawyer*
Day, Donald Sheldon *lawyer*
Doren, Robert Alan *lawyer*
Flynn, Terrance Patrick *lawyer, former prosecutor*
Freedman, Maryann Saccomando *lawyer*
Gardner, Arnold Burton *lawyer*
Glanville, Robert Edward *lawyer*
Goldberg, Neil Alan *lawyer*
Grasser, George Robert *lawyer, real estate developer, consultant*
Greene, Robert Michael *lawyer*
Halpern, Ralph Lawrence *lawyer*
Headrick, Thomas Edward *lawyer, educator*
Kristoff, Karl W. *lawyer*
Lippes, Gerald Sanford *lawyer*
Lukasik, Daniel T. *lawyer*
Manning, Kenneth Alan *lawyer*
Mehltretter, Kathleen M. *prosecutor*
Mucci, Gary Louis *lawyer*
Odza, Randall M. *lawyer*
O'Loughlin, Sandra S. *lawyer*
Olsen, R. Nills *law educator, former dean*
Rachlin, Lauren David *lawyer*
Sahlem, James Robert *law librarian*
Segalla, Thomas Francis *lawyer*
Wisbaum, Wayne David *lawyer*
Wiswall, Thomas S. *lawyer*

Camillus
Armani, Frank Henry *retired lawyer*

Canaan
Pennell, William Brooke *lawyer*

Canandaigua
Chapple, Thomas Leslie *lawyer*

Carmel
Laporte, Cloyd, Jr. *retired lawyer, manufacturing executive*
Lowe, Edwin Nobles *retired lawyer*

Cazenovia
Shattuck, George Clement *retired lawyer*

Cedarhurst
Schonfeld, Esther Miriam *lawyer*
Taubenfeld, Harry S. *lawyer*

Central Islip
Morris, Jeffrey Brandon *law educator*

Chappaqua
Romney, Richard Bruce *lawyer*

Chatham
Weiner, Jack H. *lawyer*

Chautauqua
Schmidt, Edward Craig *lawyer*

Clifton Park
Hilts, Earl T. *lawyer, government official, educator*

Commack
Steindler, Walter G. *retired lawyer*

Corning
Hatton, Vincent Paul *lawyer*
Hauselt, Denise Ann *lawyer*

Cortland
Taylor, Leland Baridon *lawyer*

Croton Falls
Curtis, Frank R. *lawyer*

Dobbs Ferry
Juettner, Diana D'Amico *lawyer, educator*
Meyer, Mark Alan *lawyer*

East Greenbush
McConville, Edward Patrick *lawyer*

East Hampton
Ehren, Charles Alexander, Jr. *lawyer, educator*
Wainwright, Carroll Livingston, Jr. *retired lawyer*

East Meadow
Adler, Ira Jay *lawyer*
Hyman, Montague Allan *lawyer, educator*

East Northport
Juliano, John Louis *lawyer*

East Norwich
Busner, Philip H. *retired lawyer, judge*

East Syracuse
Oot, Michael P. *lawyer*

Fairport
Bartlett, Cody Blake *retired lawyer*

Far Rockaway
Helfgott, Samson *lawyer*

Floral Park
Corbett, William John *lawyer, public relations executive, minister, consultant*
Giuffré, John Joseph *lawyer*

Flushing
Farago, John Michael *law educator, consultant*
Schwartz, Estar Alma *lawyer*

Forestville
Adams, Lee Towne *lawyer*

Franklin Square
Vanora, Jerome Patrick *lawyer*

Freeport
Berg, Alan *lawyer, arbitrator*

Fresh Meadows
Greenberg, Robert Jay *law educator*

Garden City
Calamari, Joseph August *legal educator*
Cook, George Valentine *lawyer, consultant*
Fishberg, Gerard *lawyer*
Freedman, Monroe Henry *lawyer, educator*
Kaplan, Joel Stuart *lawyer*
Klein, Arnold Spencer *lawyer*
Paterson, Basil Alexander *lawyer*
Persons, John Wade *lawyer*
Riordan, Sean Patrick Josep *lawyer, educator*
Rosenberg, Lee *lawyer*

Glen Cove
Hoynes, Louis LeNoir, Jr. *lawyer*

Glen Oaks
Hanoverian, Susan Michelle *lawyer*

Glens Falls
Bartlett, Richard James *lawyer*

Gouverneur
Leader, Robert John *lawyer*

Greenlawn
Robinson, Kenneth Patrick *lawyer, electronics executive*

Greenvale
Halper, Emanuel B(arry) *lawyer, real estate developer, consultant, law educator, writer, real estate broker*
Manzari, Laura Lynn *law educator*

Hamburg
Hargesheimer, Elbert III *lawyer*
Wiltse, Peter Christian *lawyer*

Hamilton
Dallal, Shawkat Jamil (Shaw Dallal) *law educator*

Harrison
Kramer, Alan Sharfsin *lawyer*

Hastings On Hudson
Edelman, Paul Sterling *lawyer*
Goldstein, Alvin *lawyer*
Thornlow, Carolyn *law firm administrator, consultant*

Hempstead
Mahon, Malachy Thomas, Sr. *lawyer, educator*
Sharifov, Rovshan Chingiz *lawyer*

Hicksville
Lieberman, Douglas Mark *lawyer*

Hillsdale
Lunde, Asbjorn Rudolph *lawyer*

Hollis
Jairam, Khelanand Vishvaykanand *lawyer*

Hornell
Pulos, William Whitaker *lawyer*

Hudson
Agata, Burton C. *lawyer, educator*

Huntington
German, June Resnick *lawyer*
Hochberg, Ronald Mark *lawyer*
Tucker, William P. *lawyer, writer*

Irvington
Jackson, Thomas Gene *lawyer*

Islandia
Pruzansky, Joshua Murdock *lawyer*

Ithaca
Alexander, Gregory Stewart *law educator*
Barcelo, John James III *law educator*
Clermont, Kevin Michael *law educator*
Cramton, Roger Conant *lawyer, educator*
Gold, Michael Evan *law educator*
Roberts, E. F. *law educator*
Schneiderman, Anne Mercedes *lawyer, neurobiologist*
Sherwin, Emily *law educator*

Jamaica
Angione, Howard Francis *lawyer, retired editor*
Brown, Kenneth Lloyd *lawyer*
Traub, Barbara Gellis *law librarian*

Jamestown
Idzik, Martin Francis *lawyer*

Jamesville
DeCrow, Karen *lawyer, educator, writer*

Jericho
Beal, Carol Ann *lawyer*
Chaiet, Clifford Paul *lawyer*
Minicucci, Richard Francis *lawyer, former hospital administrator*
Schatkin, Andrew James *lawyer*

Katonah
Bandon, William Edward III *lawyer*

Lake Success
Lee, Brian Edward *lawyer*

Larchmont
Berridge, George Bradford *retired lawyer*
Bloom, Lee Hurley *lawyer, consultant, retired consumer products company executive*
Burkett, Bradford Charles *lawyer*
McSherry, William John, Jr. *lawyer, consultant*
White, Thomas Edward *lawyer*

Lawrence
Bursky, Herman Aaron *lawyer*

Livingston Manor
Root, Stuart Dowling *lawyer, retired government agency administrator, banker*

Lockport
Penney, Charles Rand *lawyer, civic worker*

Manhasset
Wachtler, Sol *lawyer, educator*

Mattituck
Palumbo, Anthony Howard *lawyer*

Melville
Brown, Peter Stewart *lawyer, electronics executive*
Ettinger, Michael Saul *lawyer*
Lane, Arthur Alan *lawyer*
Reardon, George Martin *lawyer*
Schoenfeld, Michael P. *lawyer*

Middletown
Kossar, Ronald Steven *lawyer*

Mineola
Bartlett, Clifford Adams, Jr. *lawyer*
Halloran, Daniel James *lawyer*
Lynn, Robert Patrick, Jr. *lawyer*
Schaffer, David Irving *lawyer*
Zeldin, Lee M. *lawyer*

Montauk
Kahn, Richard Dreyfus *lawyer*

Mount Kisco
Curran, Maurice Francis *lawyer*
Kilbourn, Joseph A. *lawyer*
Zimmerman, Jean *lawyer*

Mount Vernon
Weisman, Richard Scott *lawyer*

New Hyde Park
Offner, Eric Delmonte *lawyer*
Pegalis, Steven E. *lawyer*
Sweetbaum, Marshall David *lawyer*

New York
Aaron, Stewart D. *lawyer*
Abrahams, Robert M. *lawyer*
Abramowitz, Elkan *lawyer*
Abrams, Floyd *lawyer, educator*
Abrams, Robert *lawyer, state attorney general*
Adams, George Bell *lawyer*
Addison, Linda Leuchter *lawyer, commentator, columnist*
Agranoff, Gerald Neal *lawyer*
Ahrens, Mary Elizabeth *attorney*
Aidinoff, M(erton) Bernard *retired lawyer*
Aksen, Gerald *arbitrator, mediator, lawyer*
Albert, Garett J. *lawyer*
Alden, Steven Michael *lawyer*
Allen, Leon Arthur, Jr. *lawyer*
Almon, Lorie *lawyer*
Alter, Eleanor Breitel *lawyer*
Amdur, Martin Bennett *retired lawyer*
Amsterdam, Anthony Guy *law educator*
Amsterdam, Mark Lemle *lawyer*
Andrews, Gordon Clark *lawyer*
Angland, Joseph *lawyer*
Anthoine, Robert *lawyer, educator*
Appel, Albert M. *lawyer*
Appelbaum, Ann Harriet *lawyer*
Aquila, Francis Joseph *lawyer*
Arenson, Gregory K. *lawyer*
Arkin, Stanley S. *lawyer*
Arlen, Jennifer Hall *law educator*
Armbrust, Joseph W., Jr. *lawyer*
Arouh, Jeffrey Alan *lawyer*
Arquit, Kevin James *lawyer*
Arrow, Allen H. *lawyer*
Atkins, Peter Allan *lawyer*
Auslander, Mitchell J. *lawyer*
Aviles, Alan D. *lawyer, insurance company executive*
Axinn, Stephen Mark *lawyer*
Bach, Thomas Handford *lawyer, investor*
Bachelder, Joseph Elmer III *lawyer*
Badertscher, David Glen *law librarian, consultant*
Bahler, Gary M. *lawyer*
Bahlke, Conrad George *lawyer*
Baity, John Cooley *lawyer*
Baker, Mark M. *lawyer, law educator*
Bamberger, Michael Albert *lawyer, educator*
Bancroft, Margaret Armstrong *lawyer*
Barandes, Robert *lawyer*
Barasch, Clarence Sylvan *lawyer*
Barasch, Mal Livingston *lawyer*
Barist, Jeffrey *lawyer*
Barnard, Kevin Francis *lawyer*
Barr, William Pelham *lawyer, former United States Attorney General*
Barrett, David A. *lawyer*
Barrie, John Paul *lawyer, educator*
Barry, Desmond Thomas, Jr. *lawyer*
Bason, George R., Jr. *lawyer*
Bassen, Ned Henry *lawyer*
Bauer, Douglas F. *retired lawyer*
Baum, Stanley David *lawyer*
Baumgardner, John Ellwood, Jr. *lawyer*
Baumgarten, Sidney *lawyer*
Baumrin, Bernard Stefan Herbert *lawyer, educator*
Beattie, Richard Irwin *lawyer*
Beck, Andrew James *lawyer*
Becker, Brandon *lawyer, insurance company executive*
Beekman, William B. *lawyer*
Beerbower, John Edwin *lawyer*
Beeson, Ann *lawyer*
Behr, Alan Andrew *lawyer, writer, photographer*
Behrendt, John Thomas *lawyer*
Beinecke, Candace Krugman *lawyer*
Bell, Jonathan Robert *lawyer*
Beller, Gary A. *lawyer, former insurance company executive*
Ben-Ami, Leora *lawyer*
Bender, Susan L. *lawyer*
Benenson, Mark Keith *lawyer*
Benjamin, Harvey E. *lawyer, sports association executive*
Benjamin, Jeff *lawyer, pharmaceutical executive*
Bennett, Scott Lawrence *lawyer*
Berg, Andrew N. *lawyer*
Berger, George *lawyer*
Bergmann, Peter George *lawyer*
Berke, Barry H. *lawyer*
Berney, Elizabeth A. *lawyer*
Bernstein, Daniel Lewis *lawyer*
Bernstein, David William *lawyer*
Bernstein, Robert Jay *lawyer*
Bernstein, Warren J. *lawyer*
Beshar, Peter Justus *lawyer, insurance company executive*
Beshar, Robert Peter *lawyer*
Beslow, William S. *lawyer*
Bharara, Preet *prosecutor*
Bialkin, Kenneth Jules *lawyer, director*
Bicks, David Peter *lawyer*
Bienenstock, Martin J. *lawyer*
Birnbaum, Edward Lester *lawyer*
Birnbaum, Sheila L. *lawyer, educator*
Black, Barbara Aronstein *legal history educator*
Black, James Isaac (Jib) III *lawyer*
Black, Jerry Bernard *lawyer*
Blackman, Kenneth Robert *lawyer*
Blair, William McCormick, Jr. *lawyer*
Blanc, Roger David *lawyer*
Blasband, David *lawyer*
Blassberg, Franci J. *lawyer*
Blivaiss, David Harvey *lawyer, accountant*
Block, Dennis Jeffrey *lawyer*
Blue, Catherine Anne *lawyer*
Bockstein, Herbert *lawyer*
Bodine, Susan H. *lawyer*
Boehner, Leonard Bruce *lawyer*
Bogdanos, Matthew F. *lawyer, reserve military officer, writer*
Booth, Mitchell B. *retired lawyer*
Borchard, William Marshall *lawyer*
Boulhosa, Michael L. *lawyer*
Bowers, William Charles *lawyer*
Boxer, Leonard *lawyer*
Brach, Richard S. *lawyer*
Bradley, E. Michael *lawyer*
Bradley, Phillip Alden *lawyer, retail executive*
Brafman, Benjamin *lawyer*
Braun, Jeffrey Louis *lawyer*
Brecker, Jeffrey Ross *lawyer, educator*
Breglio, John F. *lawyer*
Breslow, Stephanie R. *lawyer*
Brett, Barry J. *lawyer*
Briskman, Louis Jacob *lawyer, broadcast executive*
Broadwater, Douglas Dwight *lawyer*
Brock, Charles Lawrence *lawyer, diversified financial services company executive*
Broder, Douglas Fisher *lawyer*
Brodsky, David Michael *lawyer*
Brome, Thomas Reed *retired lawyer*
Broude, Richard Frederick *lawyer, educator*
Browdy, Joseph Eugene *lawyer*
Brown, Loren H. *lawyer*
Brown, Paul M. *lawyer*
Brown, Ralph Sawyer, Jr. *retired lawyer*
Brownwood, David Owen *lawyer*
Brozman, Andrew P. *lawyer*
Brumm, James Earl *lawyer, import/export company executive*
Bruner, Jerome S. *law educator*
Bryan, Barry Richard *lawyer*
Budd, Thomas Witbeck *lawyer*
Burak, H(oward) Paul *lawyer*
Burgess, Lynne Anne *lawyer*
Burgman, Dierdre Ann *lawyer*
Burgweger, Francis Joseph Dewes, Jr. *lawyer*
Burns, Arnold Irwin *lawyer*
Burrell, Lizabeth Lorie *lawyer*
Burrows, Kenneth David *lawyer*
Burrows, Michael Donald *lawyer*
Burstein, Judd *lawyer*
Burton, Eve Bradley *lawyer*
Bushnell, George Edward III *lawyer*
Butler, Samuel Coles *lawyer*
Buttenwieser, Lawrence Benjamin *lawyer*
Byowitz, Michael H. *lawyer*
Cailteux, Konrad Lee *lawyer*
Calbert, Michael M. *lawyer*
Caldwell, Leslie Ragon *lawyer, former prosecutor*
Califano, Joseph Anthony, Jr. *lawyer, former United States Secretary of Health Education and Welfare*
Cambria, Christopher C. *lawyer, communications systems company executive*
Camera, Nicholas J. *lawyer*
Canellos, Peter C. *lawyer*
Cannell, John Redferne *lawyer*
Cappuccio, Paul T. *lawyer, communications executive*
Carb, Stephen Ames *lawyer*
Carnell, Richard Scott *law educator*
Carter, James Hal, Jr. *lawyer*
Carter, Zachary W. *lawyer*
Caulfield, Jerome Joseph *lawyer*
Cayea, Donald Joseph *lawyer*
Caytas, Ivo George *lawyer*
Cendali, Dale Margaret *lawyer*
Chapin, Julie Kurtz *lawyer*
Chappell, John Charles *lawyer*
Chatillon, Devereux *lawyer*
Chen, Wesley *lawyer*
Chesler, Evan Robert *lawyer*
Chiang, Yung Frank *law educator*
Chiarchiaro, Frank John *lawyer*
Chin, Sylvia Fung *lawyer*
Christensen, Henry III *lawyer*
Chromow, Sheri P. *lawyer*
Chused, Richard Harris *law educator*
Clair, Bernard E. *lawyer*
Clark, James Joseph *lawyer*
Clary, Richard Wayland *lawyer*
Cliff, Walter Conway *lawyer*
Coffee, John Collins, Jr. *legal educator*
Cohen, Edmund Stephen *lawyer*
Cohen, Harriet Newman *lawyer*
Cohen, Henry Rodgin (H. Rodgin Cohen) *lawyer*
Cohen, Joshua Robert *lawyer*
Cohen, Robert Stephan *lawyer*
Cohen, Robin L. *lawyer*
Cohn, Joshua D. *lawyer*
Cole, Lewis George *lawyer*
Coleman, Charles Payson, Jr., (Payson Coleman) *lawyer*
Coleman, Stuart H. *lawyer*
Coll, John Peter, Jr. *lawyer*
Collazo, Salvador *lawyer*
Collins, J. Barclay, II, *lawyer, oil industry executive*
Collins, John F. *lawyer*
Conason, Robert *lawyer*
Conboy, Kenneth *lawyer, retired federal judge*
Conston, Henry Siegismund *lawyer*
Cook, Michael Lewis *lawyer*
Cooney, John Patrick, Jr. *lawyer*
Cooper, Michael Anthony *lawyer*
Cooper, Stephen Herbert *retired lawyer*
Corbin, Sol Neil *lawyer*
Cornell, John Robert *lawyer*
Corwin, Leslie D. *lawyer*
Cotton, Richard *lawyer*
Cox, Edward Finch *lawyer*
Craft, Randal Robert, Jr. *lawyer*
Cramer, Edward Morton *lawyer, music company executive*
Crames, Michael J. *lawyer*
Crane, Benjamin Field *lawyer*
Crews, Kenneth Donald *law educator, consultant, librarian, academic administrator*
Critchlow, Charles Howard *lawyer*
Culhane, Stephen (David Stephen King Culhane) *lawyer*
Cundiff, Victoria Anne *lawyer*
Cunha, Mark Geoffrey *lawyer*
Cuomo, Mario Matthew *lawyer, former governor*
Cutler, Bruce *lawyer*
Cutler, Stephen M. *lawyer, former federal agency administrator*
Czepiel, Lori Anne *lawyer*
Dadakis, John D. *lawyer*
Daniels, Jennifer M. *lawyer*
Dannhauser, Stephen J. *lawyer*
Darrell, Norris, Jr. *lawyer*
Darrow, Jill E(llen) *lawyer*
Dassin, Lev L. *prosecutor*
David, Reuben *lawyer*
Davidson, Douglas E. *lawyer*
Davidson, George Allan *lawyer*
Davidson, Robert Bruce *retired lawyer*
Davidson, Sheila Kearney *lawyer, insurance company executive*
Davis, Evan Anderson *lawyer*
Davis, Michael Steven *lawyer*
Davis, Trayton M. *lawyer*
Debo, Vincent Joseph *lawyer, director, manufacturing executive*
Della Rocca, Steven *lawyer*
Del Tufo, Robert J. *lawyer, former state attorney general*
DeMarco, Jennifer C. *lawyer*
Denno, Deborah W. *law educator*
DeOrchis, Vincent Moore *lawyer*
de Ravel d'Esclapon, Pierre F. *lawyer*
DeRoma, Nicholas John *lawyer, metal products executive*
Derzaw, Richard Lawrence *lawyer*
De Sear, Edward Marshall *lawyer*
Desmarais, John M. *lawyer*
Detjen, David Wheeler *lawyer*
Deutsch, Irwin Frederick *lawyer*
Diamond, Bernard Robin *lawyer*
Diamond, Brian *lawyer*
Diaz-Cruz, Mario III *lawyer*
DiLorenzo, Louis Patrick *lawyer*
DiSciullo, Alan Michael *lawyer*
Diskant, Gregory L. *lawyer*
Dombroff, Robert Michael *lawyer*
Donovan, Maureen Driscoll *lawyer*
Donovan, Richard Edward *lawyer*
Dopf, Glenn William *lawyer*
Dorkey, Charles E., III, (Trip Dorkey) *lawyer*
Dorsen, Norman *lawyer, educator*
Douglas, James McCrystal *lawyer*
Douglas, Peter Roderick *lawyer*
Douglas, Preston J. *lawyer*
Doyle, Joseph Anthony *retired lawyer*
Drebsky, Dennis Jay *lawyer*
Drost, Marianne *lawyer, telecommunications industry executive*
Drucker, Richard Allen *lawyer*
Dubbs, Thomas Allan *lawyer*
Dubin, James Michael *lawyer*
Duff, William Brandon *lawyer*
Duffy, W. Leslie *lawyer*
Dugan, James Connolly *lawyer*
Dunham, Wolcott Balestier, Jr. *lawyer*
Dworkin, Ronald Myles *law educator*
Eakins, William Shannon *lawyer*
Edelson, Gilbert Seymour *lawyer*
Edgar, Harold Simmons Hull *legal educator*
Edlin, Richard A. *lawyer*
Ehrenkranz, Joel S. *lawyer*
Einstein, Steven Henry *lawyer, investment banker*
Eisen, Robert L. *lawyer*
Eisenberg, Barbara Anne K. *lawyer*
Eisenberg, Herbert *lawyer*
Eisert, Edward Gaver *lawyer*
Elkin, Judith *lawyer*
Elkin, Michael S. *lawyer*
Ellenhorn, David N. *lawyer*
Elliot, Cameron Robert *lawyer*
Elsen, Sheldon Howard *lawyer*
Emmerich, Adam Oliver *lawyer*
Engel, Ralph Manuel *lawyer*
English, Thomas Francis *lawyer*
Entwistle, Andrew John *lawyer, consultant*
Epling, Richard Louis *lawyer*
Epstein, Melvin *lawyer*
Epstein, Michael Alan *lawyer*
Ercklentz, Enno Wilhelm, Jr. *lawyer*
Estreicher, Samuel *lawyer, educator*
Evans, Douglas Hayward *lawyer*
Evans, John Thomas *lawyer*
Evans, Martin Frederic *lawyer*
Faber, Peter Lewis *lawyer*
Fasman, Zachary Dean *lawyer*
Fass, Peter Michael *lawyer, educator*
Fastow, Jay N. *lawyer*
Fawbush, Andrew Jackson *lawyer*
Feder, Arthur A. *lawyer, association administrator*
Feder, Saul E. *lawyer*
Feerick, John David *law educator*
Feigelson, Jonathan *lawyer*
Feiler, William S. *lawyer*
Feit, Glenn Martin *lawyer*
Felder, Raoul Lionel *lawyer*
Feldman, Franklin *retired lawyer, printmaker*
Fenster, Marvin *lawyer, retail executive*
Fensterstock, Blair Courtney *lawyer*
Ferber, Laurie R. *lawyer*
Fernandez, Jose Walfredo *lawyer, department chairman*
Fine, Drew S. *lawyer*
Fink, Robert Steven *lawyer, writer, educator*
Finkelstein, Stuart M. *lawyer*
Finley, John G. *lawyer*
Finnerty, Joseph Gregory III *lawyer*
Firestone, Louise *lawyer*
Fischer, Mark David *lawyer*
Fishbein, Peter Melvin *lawyer*
Fisher, Robert I. *lawyer*
Fishman, Ellen Beth *lawyer*
Fishman, Fred Norman *lawyer*
Fiske, Robert Bishop, Jr. *lawyer, former prosecutor*
FitzPatrick, James A., Jr. *lawyer*
Fleischer, Arthur, Jr. *lawyer*
Fleischman, Edward Hirsh *lawyer, consultant*
Fletcher, Anthony Lee *lawyer*
Flint, George Squire *lawyer*
Flom, Joseph Harold *lawyer*
Florescue, Leonard George *lawyer*
Flumenbaum, Martin *lawyer*
Ford, Jack *lawyer, news correspondent, news correspondent*
Ford, Ralph A. *lawyer, moving and relocation company executive*
Forrest, Katherine B. *lawyer*
Forstadt, Joseph Lawrence *lawyer*
Fox, David *lawyer*
Fragomen, Austin T. *lawyer*
Frank, Lloyd *lawyer, director, retired chemicals executive*
Frankel, Adam B. *lawyer*
Franklin, Blake Timothy *lawyer*
Fredericks, Wesley Charles, Jr. *lawyer*
Freeman, David John *lawyer*
Freilicher, Morton *lawyer, educator*
French, John III *lawyer, director*
Freund, Fred A. *retired lawyer*
Frey, Andrew Lewis *lawyer*
Fricklas, Michael David *lawyer, broadcast executive*
Fried, Donald David *lawyer*
Fried, Richard L. *lawyer*
Friedman, Alan Roy *lawyer*
Friedman, Bart *lawyer*
Friedman, George *lawyer*
Friedman, Jeff J. *lawyer*
Friedman, Samuel Selig *lawyer*
Frischling, Carl *lawyer*
Frommer, William S. *lawyer*
Frumkin, Joseph B. *lawyer*
Fry, Morton Harrison, II, *lawyer*
Fuzesi, Stephen, Jr. *lawyer, communications executive*
Gallagher, Brian John *lawyer*
Galvis, Sergio J. *lawyer*
Ganz, David L. *lawyer*
Ganz, Howard Laurence *lawyer*
Garbus, Martin Solomon *lawyer*
Garcia, Michael J. *lawyer, former prosecutor*
Gardner, Stephen David *lawyer, educator*
Garfinkel, Barry Herbert *lawyer*
Garland, David William *law and sociology educator*
Garson, Andrew S. *lawyer*
Garson, Gary Wayne *lawyer, diversified holding company executive*
Garvey, Richard Anthony *retired lawyer*
Gaughan, Eugene Francis *lawyer, retired accountant*
Gauster, Stephen Wilhelm *lawyer, corporate financial executive*
Gelb, Judith Anne *lawyer*
Geoghegan, Patricia *lawyer*
Gerard, Whitney Ian *lawyer*
Gerspach, Thomas Joseph *lawyer*
Getnick, Neil Victor *lawyer*
Ghani, Cyrus *lawyer*
Giannetti, Thomas Leonard *lawyer*
Gifford, William C. *lawyer, educator*

Gill, E. Ann *lawyer*
Gillers, Stephen *law educator*
Gillespie, George Joseph III *lawyer*
Gitter, Max *lawyer*
Giuliani, Rudy (Rudolph William Louis Giuliani III) *consultant, lawyer, former mayor*
Glekel, Jeffrey Ives *lawyer*
Glickstein, Steven *lawyer*
Glusband, Steven Joseph *lawyer*
Goetz, Maurice Harold *lawyer*
Golanski, Alani *lawyer*
Gold, Martin Elliot *lawyer, educator*
Gold, Simeon *lawyer*
Gold, Stuart Walter *lawyer*
Goldberg, Jay *lawyer*
Golden, Arthur F. *lawyer*
Golden, Daniel H. *lawyer*
Goldman, Charles Norton *retired corporate lawyer*
Goldman, Lawrence Saul *lawyer*
Goldman, Louis B. *lawyer*
Goldman, Steven M. *lawyer, former commissioner*
Goldschmid, Harvey Jerome *law educator, former commissioner*
Goldsmith, Willis Jay *lawyer*
Goldstein, Charles Arthur *lawyer*
Goldstein, Howard Sheldon *lawyer*
Goldstein, Howard Warren *lawyer*
Goldstein, Linda C. *lawyer*
Goldstein, Marcia Landweber *lawyer*
Goldstein, Sandra Cara *lawyer*
Golick, Toby *law educator, legal services administrator*
Goodale, James Campbell *lawyer, television producer, columnist, educator*
Goodell, Timothy B. *lawyer, oil industry executive*
Goodman, Gary A. *lawyer*
Goodridge, Allan D. *lawyer*
Goott, Alan F(ranklin) *lawyer*
Gordon, Jeffrey Neil *law educator*
Gordon, Jennifer Lynn *lawyer, law educator*
Gordon, Stephen Louis *lawyer*
Gordon, Stuart A. *lawyer*
Gordon-Reed, Annette *law educator, historian*
Gotthoffer, Lance *lawyer*
Gotts, Ilene Knable *lawyer*
Gourevitch, David U. *private practice lawyer*
Grad, Frank Paul *lawyer, educator*
Granito, Frank Henry III *lawyer*
Granoff, Gary Charles *lawyer, investment company executive*
Grassi, Joseph F. *lawyer, mediator, arbitrator*
Green, Alvin *lawyer, consultant*
Green, Mark Joseph *lawyer, author*
Greenawalt, Robert Kent *lawyer, educator*
Greenberg, Ira George *lawyer*
Greenberg, Jack *lawyer, educator*
Greenberger, Howard Leroy *lawyer, educator*
Greene, Bernard Harold *lawyer*
Greene, Ira S. *lawyer*
Greenspon, Robert Alan *lawyer*
Greiner, Stephen W. *lawyer*
Griffin, Michael F. *lawyer*
Griffith, William R. *lawyer*
Grohman, Michael D. *lawyer*
Gross, Ari Michael *lawyer*
Gross, Christina *lawyer*
Gross, Steven Ross *lawyer*
Grossman, Dan Steven *lawyer*
Grubin, Sharon Ellen *lawyer, former federal judge*
Grubman, Allen J. *lawyer*
Grushkin, Jay D. *lawyer*
Guedry, James Walter *lawyer, retired manufacturing executive*
Guggenheim, Martin Franklin *lawyer, educator*
Gupta, Paul R. *lawyer*
Gurevich, Alexander J. *lawyer, real estate developer*
Gurfein, Richard Alan *lawyer*
Gustafson, Albert Katsuaki *lawyer, engineer*
Gutman, Henry B. *lawyer*
Haffner, F. Kinsey *lawyer*
Haig, Robert Leighton *lawyer*
Hall, Bryan H. *lawyer*
Hall, John Herbert *lawyer*
Hall, Thomas J. *lawyer*
Hallake, Marcello *lawyer*
Halliday, Joseph William *lawyer*
Halvey, John K. *lawyer*
Hamburg, Charles Bruce *lawyer*
Hamm, David Bernard *lawyer*
Handelsman, Lawrence Marc *lawyer*
Handler, Arthur M. *lawyer*
Handley, Siobhan A. *lawyer*
Hanisch, Toula *legal assistant*
Hanks, Kendyl T. *lawyer*
Hannon, Gerard V. *lawyer*
Hansen, Kristopher M. *lawyer*
Hanson, Jean Elizabeth *lawyer*
Haracz, Stephen M. *lawyer*
Harbison, James Wesley, Jr. *lawyer*
Harkrider, John David *lawyer*
Harlow, Ruth *lawyer*
Harper, Gerard Edward *lawyer*
Harris, Adam C. *lawyer*
Harris, Arlene *lawyer*
Harris, Joel B. (Joel Bruce Harris) *lawyer*
Hart, Robert M. *lawyer*
Hartnett, William M. *lawyer*
Hartzell, Andrew Cornelius, Jr. *retired lawyer*
Hasday, Robert Joel *lawyer*
Hass, Lawrence Joel *lawyer*
Hathaway, Gerald Thomas *lawyer*
Hauser, Rita Eleanore Abrams *retired lawyer*
Hawke, Roger Jewett *lawyer*
Hayden, Raymond Paul *lawyer*
Hayes, Eddie (Edward W. Hayes) *lawyer*
Hayes, Ellen Louise *lawyer*
Hayes, Gerald Joseph *lawyer*
Hazan, Scott L. *lawyer*
Head, Elizabeth *lawyer, arbitrator, mediator*
Headley, Mark J. *lawyer*
Healy, J. Kevin *lawyer*
Hearn, George Henry *lawyer, water transportation executive*
Hebert, Jay Howell *lawyer*
Heim, Robert G. *lawyer*
Heisler, Stanley Dean *lawyer*
Heitner, Kenneth Howard *lawyer*
Held, Huyler Clark *lawyer*
Hellenbrand, Samuel Henry *lawyer*
Heller, Robert Martin *lawyer*
Hellerer, Mark R. *lawyer*
Henderson, Donald Bernard, Jr. *lawyer*
Hendry, Andrew Delaney *lawyer, consumer products company executive*
Henry, Sally McDonald *lawyer*
Henze, William F., II, *lawyer*
Herbst, Todd L. *lawyer*
Herman, Kenneth Beaumont *lawyer*
Herman, Susan N. *legal association administrator, law educator*
Hershcopf, Gerald Thea *retired lawyer*
Herz, Andrew Lee *lawyer*
Herzeca, Lois Friedman *lawyer*
Hess, Michael David *lawyer*
Hewitt, William Joseph *lawyer*
Hiden, Robert Battaile, Jr. *lawyer*
Hill, Alfred *law educator*
Hirshman, Michele S. *lawyer, former prosecutor*
Hirshowitz, Melvin Stephen *lawyer*
Hogan, Mary Beth *lawyer*
Holley, Steven Lyon *lawyer*
Holman, Bud George *lawyer*
Holtzman, Elizabeth *lawyer*
Holtzmann, Howard Marshall *lawyer, judge*
Hooker, Wade Stuart *lawyer*
Hopkinson, R. Ronald *lawyer*
Horowitz, Steven Gary *lawyer*
Howe, Richard Rives *lawyer*
Hritz, George F. *lawyer*
Hruska, Alan J. *lawyer, filmmaker*
Huck, L. Francis *lawyer*
Huebner, Marshall Scott *lawyer*
Hulbert, Richard Woodward *lawyer*
Hunt, Franklin Griggs *lawyer*
Hupper, John Roscoe *retired lawyer*
Hurley, Lawrence Joseph *lawyer*
Hurlock, James Bickford *lawyer*
Huston, Barry Scott *lawyer*
Hutton, G. Thompson *lawyer*
Hyde, David Rowley *lawyer*
Hyman, Jerome Elliot *lawyer*
Hynes, Patricia M. *lawyer*
Iannuzzi, John Nicholas *lawyer, author, educator*
Ichel, David W. *lawyer*
Insel, Michael S. *lawyer*
Intriligator, Marc Steven *lawyer*
Isquith, Fred Taylor *lawyer*
Issler, Harry *lawyer*
Jackson, Mark H. *lawyer, publishing executive*
Jacob, Edwin J. *lawyer*
Jacobs, Arnold Stephen *lawyer*
Jacobs, Paul *lawyer*
Jacobs, Robert Alan *lawyer*
Jacobson, Jerold Dennis *lawyer*
Janklow, Morton Lloyd *lawyer, literary agent*
Janowitz, James Arnold *lawyer*
Jassy, Everett Lewis *lawyer*
Jenner, Jesse Jacob *lawyer*
Jock, Paul F., II, *lawyer*
Joffe, Robert David *lawyer*
Johnson, David J., Jr. *lawyer*
Johnson, Peter James, Jr. *lawyer, legal analyst*
Johnston, Rita Rodin *lawyer*
Jordan, Vernon Eulion, Jr. *lawyer*
Joseph, Gregory Paul *lawyer*
Joseph, Leonard *lawyer*
Juceam, Robert E. *lawyer*
Kafin, Robert Joseph *lawyer*
Kahn, Alan Edwin *lawyer*
Kailas, Leo George *lawyer*
Kalik, Mildred *lawyer*
Kalish, Arthur *lawyer*
Kalish, Myron *lawyer*
Kaltzer, Albert *lawyer, educator*
Kamin, Sherwin *retired lawyer*
Kandel, William Lloyd *lawyer, arbitrator, mediator*
Kanter, Carl Irwin *retired lawyer*
Kanzer, Alan *lawyer*
Kaplan, Mark Norman *lawyer*
Kaplan, Paul Michael *lawyer, educator*
Karelis, Kathleen E. *lawyer, communications systems company executive*
Karls, John Spencer *lawyer, accountant*
Karmali, Rashida A. *lawyer*
Karp, Brad S. *lawyer*
Kartiganer, Joseph *retired lawyer*
Kasi, Srinandan Ramamurthi *lawyer*
Katsh, Salem Michael *lawyer*
Katz, Jerome Charles *lawyer*
Katz, Robert James *lawyer*
Katz, Ronald Scott *lawyer*
Katz, Stuart Z. *lawyer*
Kaufman, Robert Max *lawyer, director*
Kaufman, Stephen Edward *lawyer*
Kavaler, Thomas J. *lawyer*
Kavoukjian, Michael Edward *lawyer*
Kaye, Judith Smith *lawyer, retired state appeals court chief judge*
Kayser, Leo III *lawyer*
Kean, Hamilton Fish *lawyer*
Kelley, David Noel *lawyer, former prosecutor*
Kelly, Anastasia Donovan (Stasia Kelly) *lawyer, insurance company executive*
Kelly, Thomas Michael *lawyer*
Keltner, Thomas Nethery, Jr. *lawyer*
Kende, Christopher Burgess *lawyer, educator*
Keneally, Kathryn Marie *lawyer*
Kenney, John Joseph *lawyer*
Kenney, Robert J. *lawyer*
Kern, George Calvin, Jr. *lawyer*
Kersh, Candace L. *lawyer*
Kerwick, Colleen *lawyer, actress*
Kiernan, John S. *lawyer*
Kies, David M. *lawyer*
Kiessling, B. Robbins *lawyer*
Kim, Michael S. *lawyer*
Kimball, John Devereux *lawyer*
King, Alison *lawyer*
King, Henry Lawrence *lawyer*
King, Stephen C. *lawyer, commissioner, educator*
Kinney, Stephen Hoyt, Jr. *lawyer*
Kinzler, Thomas Benjamin *lawyer*
Kirby, John Joseph, Jr. *lawyer*
Kirschbaum, Myron *lawyer*
Klapper, Richard H. *lawyer*
Klausner, Peter L. *lawyer*
Kleckner, Robert George, Jr. *retired lawyer*
Klein, Eleazer *lawyer*
Klein, Martin I. *lawyer*
Kleinberg, Norman Charles *lawyer*
Klemann, Gilbert Lacy, II, *lawyer*
Kline, Eugene Monroe *lawyer*
Klinger, Alan Mark *lawyer*
Klipstein, Robert Alan *lawyer*
Kobak, James Benedict, Jr. *lawyer, educator*
Kobi, Daniel Casey *lawyer*
Kobrin, Lawrence Alan *lawyer*
Koch, Ed (Edward Irving Koch) *lawyer, former mayor*
Koegel, William Fisher *lawyer*
Koen, Robert G. *lawyer*
Kohn, Immanuel *lawyer*
Koob, Charles Edward *lawyer*
Koral, Alan Max *lawyer*
Kornberg, Alan William *lawyer*
Kornreich, Edward Scott *lawyer*
Korotkin, Michael Paul *lawyer*
Krane, Steven Charles *lawyer*
Kreitzman, Ralph J. *lawyer, mayor*
Krieger, Sanford *lawyer*
Kroll, Sol *lawyer*
Krupman, William Allan *lawyer*
Krupp, Fred D. *lawyer, environmental services administrator*
Kubek, Gary W. *lawyer*
Kuby, Ronald Lawrence *lawyer*
Kuntz, Lee Allan *lawyer*
Kuntz, William Francis, II, *lawyer, educator*
Kurtz, Jerome *lawyer, educator*
Kurz, William Charles Frederick *lawyer*
Kurzweil, Harvey *lawyer*
LaBarre, Dennis W. *lawyer*
Lack, Robert Joel *lawyer*
Lacovara, Philip Allen *lawyer*
Lacy, Robinson Burrell *lawyer*
Lambert, Judith A. Ungar *lawyer*
Lampen, Richard Jay *lawyer, investment banker*
Lanchner, Bertrand Martin *lawyer, advertising executive*
Langan, Richard F., Jr. *lawyer*
Langer, Bruce Alden *lawyer*
Larose, Lawrence Alfred *lawyer*
La Rossa, James Michael *lawyer*
Latza, William D. *lawyer*
Lauer, Eliot *lawyer*
Lavin, Howard S. *lawyer*
Lawrence, Robert Cutting III *lawyer*
Lawrence-Apfelbaum, Marc *lawyer, broadcast executive*
Lechner, Alfred James, Jr. *lawyer, former federal judge*
Lederman, Lawrence *lawyer, writer, educator*
Lee, Jerome G. *lawyer*
Lefcourt, Gerald B. (Gerry Lefcourt) *lawyer*
LeFevre, David E. *lawyer, business executive*
Lefkowitz, David S. *lawyer*
Lenobel, Jeffrey A. *lawyer*
Leonard, Edwin Deane *lawyer*
Lerman, Bradley E. *lawyer*
Lerner, Marni Jo *lawyer*
Lesk, Ann Berger *lawyer*
Lesser, Lori Ellen *lawyer*
Levi Caroti, Gisella *lawyer*
Levie, Joseph Henry *lawyer, banker*
Levin, Michael Joseph *lawyer*
Levine, Robert Jay *lawyer*
Levine, Ronald Jay *lawyer*
Levitan, David M(aurice) *lawyer, educator*
Levitan, Steve *lawyer*
Levy, Stanley Herbert *lawyer*
Lewin, Robert *lawyer*
Lewyn, Thomas Mark *lawyer*
Li, Tze-chung *lawyer, educator*
Lieberman, Nancy Ann *lawyer*
Liebmann, Jeff S. *lawyer*
Liman, Lewis Jeffrey *lawyer*
Lindsay, George Peter *lawyer*
Link, Robert O., Jr. *lawyer*
Linker, Arthur S. *lawyer*
Lipscomb, James Louis *lawyer, insurance company executive*
Lipton, Martin *lawyer*
Litman, Jack Theodore *lawyer*
Lloyd, William Frederick *lawyer*
Lobenfeld, Eric Jay *retired lawyer*
Lobl, Herbert Max *lawyer, writer*
Lobrano, John D. *lawyer*
Logan, Kenneth Richard *lawyer*
Lotwin, Stanford Gerald *lawyer*
Lowenfeld, Andreas Frank *law educator*
Lowenfels, Lewis David *lawyer*
Lowy, George Theodore *lawyer*
Lunding, Christopher Hanna *lawyer*
Lupert, Leslie Allan *lawyer*
Luria, Mary Mercer *lawyer*
Luxenberg, Arthur Martin *lawyer*
Lynch, Kyle Thomas *lawyer*
Lyon, Carl Francis, Jr. *lawyer*
Lytton, William Bryan *lawyer, former manufacturing company executive*
Macan, William Alexander, IV, *lawyer*
MacCrate, Robert *lawyer*
MacRae, Cameron Farquhar III *lawyer*
Macris, Michael *lawyer*
Madden, John J. *lawyer*
Madden, John Patrick *lawyer*
Madsen, Stephen Stewart *lawyer*
Maidman, Richard Harvey Mortimer *lawyer*
Mailman, Stanley *lawyer*
Maitland, Guy Edison Clay *lawyer*
Malkin, Peter Laurence *lawyer, investor*
Mallin, Joel *lawyer*
Mallow, Matthew J. *lawyer*
Maneker, Morton M. *lawyer*
Manewitz, Mark Lee *lawyer*
Maney, Michael Mason *lawyer*
Mann, Pamela A. *lawyer*
Mantel, Allan David *lawyer*
Marcus, Maria Lenhoff *lawyer, educator*
Mariani, Michael Matthew *lawyer*
Markel, Gregory Arthur *lawyer*
Marks, Ramon Paul *lawyer*
Marks, Theodore Lee *lawyer*
Martin, Malcolm Elliot *lawyer*
Martinez, Lucy *lawyer*
Martone, Patricia Ann *lawyer*
Marx, Owen Cox *lawyer*
Mason, Christopher May *lawyer*
Massad, Timothy G. *lawyer*
Materna, Joseph Anthony *lawyer*
Matteson, William Bleecker *lawyer*
Matus, Wayne Charles *lawyer*
Maxfield, Guy Budd *lawyer, educator*
Mayer, Carl Joseph *prosecutor, lawyer, educator*
Mayer, Christopher *lawyer*
Mayer, Theodore V.H. *lawyer*
McCabe, David J. *lawyer*
McCaffrey, Judith Elizabeth *lawyer*
McCarthy, Robert Emmett *lawyer*
McCaw, Robert Bruce *lawyer*
McGowen, Lorraine S. *lawyer*
McGrath, Thomas John *lawyer, writer, film producer*
McKeefry, Mark *attorney, director*
McMahon, James Charles *lawyer*
McMillan, L. Londell *lawyer*
McNamara, J. Donald (John Donald McNamara) *retired lawyer, business executive*
McTiernan, Charles E., Jr. *lawyer, energy executive*
Mehler, Gordon *lawyer, former federal prosecutor*
Melton, Howell Webster, Jr. *lawyer*
Menton, Tanya Lia *lawyer, educator*
Merow, John *lawyer*
Merrill, George Vanderneth *lawyer, investment executive*
Michaelson, Arthur M. *lawyer*
Mikumo, Akiko *lawyer*
Miller, Arthur Madden *lawyer, investment banker, brokerage house executive*
Miller, Charles Hampton *lawyer*
Miller, Harvey R. *lawyer, bankruptcy reorganization specialist*
Miller, J. Allen *lawyer*
Miller, Michael Campion *lawyer*
Miller, Paul Samuel *lawyer*
Miller, Sam Scott *lawyer*
Miller, Theodore Norman *lawyer*
Millstein, Ira M. *lawyer, educator*
Milmoe, J. Gregory, Jr. *lawyer*
Minkel, Herbert Philip, Jr. *lawyer*
Minkowitz, Martin *lawyer, former state government official*
Modlin, Howard S. *lawyer*
Moerdler, Charles Gerard *lawyer*
Moloney, Thomas Joseph *lawyer*
Moore, Thomas A. *lawyer*
Moore, Thomas Ronald (Lord Bridestowe) *lawyer*
Morak, Glenn H. *lawyer*
Morales, Carlos M. *lawyer*
Morgenthau, Robert Morris *prosecutor*
Morphy, James Calvin *lawyer*
Mortimer, Peter Michael *lawyer*
Morvillo, Robert Guy *lawyer*
Moskin, Morton *lawyer, director*
Moskowitz, Ellen Hope *lawyer*
Moss, Sara E. *lawyer, cosmetics executive*
Mourning, Paul W. *lawyer*
Mueller, Thomas M. *lawyer*
Mukasey, Marc L. *lawyer*
Mukasey, Michael Bernard *lawyer, former United States Attorney General*
Muller, Scott William *lawyer*
Mulligan, Jeremiah T. *lawyer*
Mundheim, Robert Harry *law educator*
Murase, Jiro *lawyer*
Murphy, Arthur William *lawyer, educator*
Muscato, Andrew *lawyer*
Myerson, Toby Salter *lawyer*
Naftalis, Gary Philip *lawyer, educator*
Nance, Allan Taylor *retired lawyer*
Napolitano, Andrew P. *lawyer, former judge*
Nassau, Michael Jay *lawyer*
Nathan, Frederic Solis *lawyer*
Neff, Daniel A. *lawyer*
Neidell, Martin H. *lawyer*
Neiman, Shirah *prosecutor*
Neufeld, Peter J. *lawyer*
Neuwirth, Gloria S. *lawyer*
Neveloff, Jay A. *lawyer*
Newman, Kenneth E. *lawyer*
Newman, Lawrence Walker *lawyer*
Newman, Thomas Rubin *lawyer*
Nicholas, Robert A. *lawyer*
Niemeth, Charles Frederick *lawyer*
Nigam, Hemanshu *lawyer, Internet company executive*
Nimkin, Bernard William *retired lawyer*
Ninivaggi, Daniel A. *lawyer, manufacturing executive*
Niño, Deanna Hollye *lawyer*
Nix, Kelsey I. *lawyer*
Noble, Kenneth Eric *lawyer*
North, Steven Edward *lawyer, educator*
Nusbacher, Gloria Weinberg *lawyer*
Oberman, Michael Stewart *lawyer*
O'Brien, Clare *lawyer*
O'Brien, Michael J. *lawyer, advertising executive*
Oechler, Henry John, Jr. *lawyer*
O'Grady, John Joseph III *lawyer*
Ohlemeyer, William S. *lawyer*
Olick, Philip Stewart *lawyer*
Oliveri, Paul Francis *lawyer*
Oltarsh, Kenneth S. *lawyer*
O'Neil, John Joseph *lawyer*
O'Neill, Charles K. *lawyer*
Orce, Kenneth W. *lawyer*
Ordway, Eric *lawyer*
O'Rorke, James Francis, Jr. *lawyer*
Ortner, Charles B. *lawyer*
Osborn, Donald Robert *lawyer*
Ostrager, Barry Robert *lawyer*
O'Sullivan, Thomas J. *lawyer*
Padnick, Jennifer C. *lawyer*
Pagano, Vincent, Jr. *lawyer*
Page, Kenneth R. *lawyer*

Palm, Gregory K. *lawyer, diversified financial services company executive*
Palme, Deryck A. *lawyer*
Panken, Peter Michael *lawyer*
Papernik, Joel Ira *lawyer*
Parcher, L. Peter *lawyer*
Parent, Louise Marie *lawyer, corporate financial executive*
Passer, Juliette Mayabelle *lawyer*
Pataki, George Elmer *lawyer, former governor*
Patrikis, Ernest T. *lawyer*
Paul, Herbert Morton *lawyer, accountant, educator*
Paul, Robert Carey *lawyer*
Payton, John *legal association administrator, lawyer*
Pearce, Alan S. *lawyer*
Peet, Charles D, Jr. *lawyer*
Peloso, John Francis Xavier *lawyer*
Peluso, John *lawyer, insurance company executive*
Pennoyer, Paul Geddes, Jr. *retired lawyer*
Pennoyer, Robert M. *lawyer*
Penzer, Michèle Olivier *lawyer*
Peppers, Jerry P. *lawyer*
Perkins, Roswell Burchard *lawyer*
Perlmuth, William Alan *lawyer*
Pershan, Richard Henry *lawyer*
Petrow, George J. *lawyer*
Pettibone, Peter John *lawyer*
Pfeffer, David H. *lawyer*
Phillips, Pamela Kim *lawyer*
Picard, Irving H. *lawyer*
Pickholz, Jason R. *lawyer*
Pickholz, Marvin G. *lawyer*
Pidot, Whitney Dean *retired lawyer*
Piel, Eleanor Jackson *lawyer*
Pierce, Morton Allen *lawyer*
Pietrzak, Alfred Robert *lawyer*
Pildes, Richard H. *law educator*
Pinczower, Kenneth Ephraim *lawyer*
Pittoni, Luke M. *lawyer*
Plevan, Bettina B. *lawyer*
Plotkin, Loren H. *lawyer*
Polak, Vivian Louise *lawyer*
Polevoy, Nancy Tally *lawyer, social worker, genealogist*
Pollack, Stanley P. *lawyer*
Pollan, Stephen Michael *lawyer, life coach, finance expert, journalist*
Pomerantz, Mark F. *lawyer, former prosecutor*
Portier, Guido Marcel *lawyer*
Posner, Michael Hoffman *lawyer*
Post, Steven M. *lawyer, communications systems company executive*
Poulson, Richard Jasper Metcalfe *lawyer*
Pratt, William *lawyer*
Prins, Richard T. *lawyer*
Profusek, Robert Alan *lawyer*
Puccio, Thomas Phillip *lawyer*
Puleo, Frank Charles *lawyer*
Quale, Andrew Christopher, Jr. *lawyer*
Quigley, Thomas John *lawyer*
Quinlan, Guy Christian *lawyer*
Quinn, Francis Flaherty *lawyer*
Quinn, Yvonne Susan *lawyer*
Raab, Sheldon *lawyer*
Rabin, Jack *lawyer*
Radke, Kirk August *lawyer*
Rado, Peter Thomas *lawyer*
Radon, Jenik Richard *lawyer*
Raisler, Kenneth Mark *lawyer*
Ralli, Constantine Pandia *lawyer*
Rankin, Clyde Evan III *lawyer*
Rapoport, Bernard Robert *lawyer*
Rappaport, Charles Owen *lawyer*
Rappaport, Linda Ellen *lawyer*
Ravitch, Richard *lawyer, former city official*
Raylesberg, Alan Ira *lawyer*
Reich, Larry Sam *lawyer*
Reid, Edward Snover III *lawyer*
Reid, John Phillip *law educator*
Reifler, Stewart *lawyer*
Reinthaler, Richard Walter *lawyer*
Reiss, Steven Alan *lawyer, educator*
Reitzas, Joshua T. *lawyer, venture capitalist*
Reitzfeld, Alan D. *lawyer*
Reynard, Muriel Joyce *lawyer*
Reynolds, Michael Timothy *lawyer*
Rice, Donald Sands *lawyer*
Rice, Joseph Lee III *lawyer*
Rice, Thomas Charles *lawyer*
Rich, Tracy Leon *lawyer, insurance company executive*
Richards, David Alan *lawyer*
Richieri, Kenneth A. *lawyer, publishing executive*
Richman, Daniel Charles *law educator*
Richman, Martin Franklin *lawyer*
Riesel, Sheila Ginsberg *lawyer*
Rifkind, Robert S. *lawyer*
Rigolosi, Elaine La Monica *lawyer, educator*
Rikon, Michael *lawyer*
Rikoon, Jonathan J. *lawyer*
Riley, Thomas Edward *lawyer*
Ringel, Dean *lawyer*
Ritter, Ann L. *lawyer*
Roberts, Burton Bennett *lawyer, retired judge*
Robertson, Edwin David *lawyer*
Robertson, Hugh (Elihu F.) *lawyer*
Robinson, Barbara Paul *lawyer*
Robinson, Irwin Jay *lawyer*
Rocklen, Kathy Hellenbrand *lawyer*
Rodriguez, Vincent Angel *lawyer, director*
Roe, Bonnie Jean *lawyer*
Roehrs, Christopher Scott *lawyer*
Rogers, Theodore Otto, Jr. *lawyer*
Rolfe, Ronald Stuart *lawyer*
Romans, John Niebrugge *lawyer*
Romero, Anthony D. *legal association administrator*
Rooney, Paul C., Jr. *retired lawyer*
Rosell, Kurt F. *lawyer*
Rosen, Jeffrey J. *lawyer*
Rosen, Michael N. *lawyer*
Rosen, Richard Lewis *lawyer, real estate developer*
Rosenberg, Alan Stewart *lawyer*
Rosenberg, Marc Steven *lawyer*
Rosenblum, Scott S. *lawyer*
Rosenfeld, Steven B. *lawyer*
Rosensaft, Menachem Zwi *lawyer, writer, foundation administrator*
Rosenzweig, Charles Leonard *lawyer*
Ross, Barry C. *lawyer*
Ross, Matthew *lawyer*
Rossen, Jordan *lawyer*
Rothberg, Glenda Fay Morris *lawyer*
Rothenberg, Laraine S. *lawyer*
Rothman, Henry Isaac *lawyer*
Rovine, Arthur William *international arbitrator*
Rowen, Andrew S. *lawyer*
Roznovschi, Mirela *law librarian, writer*
Rubenstein, Joshua Seth *lawyer*
Rubin, Herbert *lawyer*
Rubinstein, Aaron *lawyer*
Rubinstein, Javier H. *lawyer*
Rucker, Kim K.W. *lawyer, cosmetics executive*
Rudenstine, David *law educator, former dean*
Rudoff, Sheldon *lawyer*
Rusmisel, Stephen Raymond *lawyer*
Russo, Thomas Anthony *lawyer, former investment company executive*
Rutkowski, Lawrence *lawyer*
Ryan, Lisa *lawyer*
Sabel, Bradley Kent *lawyer*
Saeed, Faiza J. *lawyer*
Saft, Stuart Mark *lawyer*
Samuels, Leslie B. *lawyer*
Sanocki, Edward John, Jr. *lawyer*
Sanseverino, Raymond Anthony *lawyer*
Satine, Barry Roy *lawyer*
Saunders, Paul Christopher *lawyer*
Savrin, Louis *lawyer*
Schaab, Arnold J. *lawyer*
Schaffer, Seth Andrew *lawyer*
Schallert, Edwin Glenn *lawyer*
Schapiro, Donald *lawyer*
Scheiman, Eugene R. *lawyer*
Scheler, Brad Eric *lawyer*
Schiffman, Daniel *lawyer, arts advocate*
Schizer, Zevie Baruch *lawyer*
Schler, Michael Lawrence *lawyer*
Schlesinger, Sanford Joel *lawyer*
Schmertz, Eric Joseph *lawyer, educator, commissioner*
Schmidt, Benno Charles, Jr. *lawyer*
Schmidt, Joseph W. *lawyer*
Schmolka, Leo Louis *law educator*
Schneider, Willys Hope *lawyer*
Schneiderman, Irwin *lawyer*
Schofield, Lorna Gail *lawyer*
Schreyer, Leslie John *lawyer*
Schueller, Thomas George *lawyer*
Schulhofer, Stephen Joseph *law educator*
Schumacher, Harry Richard *lawyer*
Schwab, Harold Lee *lawyer*
Schwartz, Barry Fredric *lawyer, diversified holding company executive*
Schwartz, Bart *lawyer*
Schwartz, Herbert Frederick *lawyer*
Schwartz, Jordan M. *lawyer*
Schwartz, Marvin *lawyer*
Schwartz, Renee Gerstler *lawyer*
Schwartz, Wallace L. *lawyer*
Schwartz, William *lawyer, educator*
Schwarz, Frederick A.O., Jr. *lawyer*
Seidler, B(ernard) Alan *lawyer*
Seifert, Thomas Lloyd *lawyer*
Seiff, Eric A. *lawyer*
Seigel, Stuart Evan *lawyer*
Selver, Paul Darryl *lawyer*
Senzel, Martin Lee *lawyer*
Serbaroli, Francis J. *lawyer, educator, writer*
Serchuk, Ivan *lawyer*
Serota, James Ian *lawyer*
Serota, Susan Perlstadt *lawyer, educator*
Setrakian, Berge *lawyer*
Seward, George Chester *lawyer*
Seymour, Everett Hedden, Jr. *lawyer*
Seymour, Karen Patton *lawyer, former prosecutor*
Shainwald, Sybil *lawyer*
Shannon, Careen Brett *lawyer, educator, writer*
Shapiro, Isaac *lawyer*
Shapiro, Meryl *lawyer*
Shapiro, Michael *lawyer*
Shapiro, Steven R. *legal association administrator*
Shargel, Gerald L. *lawyer*
Sharkey, Catherine Moira *law educator*
Shea, Edward Emmett *lawyer, educator, writer*
Shecter, Howard Lee *lawyer*
Sheehan, Robert C. *lawyer*
Shen, Michael *lawyer*
Shepard, Robert M. *lawyer, investment banker, engineer*
Sheresky, Norman M. *lawyer*
Shientag, Florence Perlow *lawyer*
Shinkle, John Thomas *lawyer*
Shorter, James Russell, Jr. *lawyer*
Shoss, Cynthia Renée *lawyer*
Shutran, Richard *lawyer*
Shyer, John D. *lawyer*
Sidamon-Eristoff, Constantine *lawyer*
Siegel, Edward M. *lawyer*
Siegel, Jeffrey Norton *lawyer*
Siegel, Stanley *lawyer, educator*
Siffert, John Sand *lawyer, educator, writer*
Silberberg, Richard Howard *lawyer*
Silberman, John Alan *lawyer*
Silkenat, James Robert *lawyer*
Siller, Stephen I. *lawyer*
Silverberg, Michael Joel *lawyer*
Silverman, Arthur Charles *lawyer*
Silverman, Eric F. *lawyer*
Silverman, Moses *lawyer*
Simmons, Peter Lawrence *lawyer*
Simone, Joseph R. *lawyer*
Simons, Albert III *lawyer*
Sinsheimer, Warren Jack *lawyer*
Sirkin, Michael S. *lawyer*
Siskind, Arthur Michael *lawyer*
Siskind, Donald Henry *lawyer*
Sklyar, Adelina M. *lawyer*
Sladkus, Harvey Ira *lawyer*
Slotnick, Barry Ivan *lawyer*
Small, Jonathan Andrew *lawyer, consultant*
Smith, Brian D. *lawyer*
Smith, Edward Paul, Jr. *lawyer*
Smith, Jason A. B. *lawyer*
Smith, Robert Everett *lawyer*
Smoak, Evan L. *lawyer*
Snyder, Leslie Crocker *lawyer*
Solano, Henry L. *lawyer*
Solomon, Andrew P. *lawyer*
Solomon, Terri Marcia *lawyer*
Sorensen, Ted (Theodore Chaikin Sorensen) *lawyer, former federal official*
Sorkin, David James *lawyer*
Sorkin, Ira Lee (Ike Sorkin) *lawyer*
Sorkin, Laurence Truman *lawyer*
Sorter, George Hans *accounting and law educator, consultant*
Soussloff, Andrew D. *lawyer*
Sovern, Michael Ira *law educator*
Spatt, Robert Edward *lawyer*
Spear, Harvey M. *lawyer*
Spelfogel, Evan J. *lawyer, educator*
Spellman Sweet, Julie T. *lawyer*
Spencer, Michael C. *lawyer*
Spillane, Dennis Kevin *lawyer*
Spinner, Marina A. *lawyer*
Squire, Walter Charles *lawyer*
Srulowitz, Marvin *lawyer*
Standard, Kenneth G. *lawyer*
Starer, Brian Douglas *lawyer*
Starr, Michael *lawyer*
Stecher, Esta E. *lawyer, investment company executive*
Stein, Ronald J. *lawyer*
Stein, Stephen William *lawyer*
Steinberg, Arthur Jay *lawyer*
Steinberg, Debra Brown *lawyer*
Steinberg, Howard Eli *lawyer, diversified financial services company executive*
Stephenson, Alan Clements *lawyer*
Stern, Donald Allan *lawyer*
Stern, Jeffrey Ross *lawyer*
Sternman, Joel W. *lawyer*
Sterns, William S. III *lawyer*
Steuer, Richard Marc *lawyer*
Stewart, Geoffrey S. *lawyer*
Stewart, Lynne F. *former lawyer*
Stillman, Charles Allen *lawyer*
Stoll, Neal Richard *lawyer*
Stone, Merrill Brent *lawyer*
Straniere, Robert A. *lawyer, restaurant owner*
Strauss, Peter L(ester) *law educator*
Strickon, Harvey Alan *lawyer*
Strom, Milton Gary *lawyer*
Struve, Guy Miller *lawyer*
Sturman, Deborah Muscha *attorney*
Sullivan, Kathleen Marie *lawyer, educator*
Suydam, John J. *lawyer*
Synnott, Aidan John *lawyer*
Taber, Kenneth W. *lawyer*
Tacopina, Joseph *lawyer*
Tahbaz, Christopher K. *lawyer*
Tallackson, Jeffrey Stephen *lawyer*
Tanenbaum, Edward *lawyer*
Tanenbaum, William Alan *lawyer*
Tanner, Douglas Alan *lawyer*
Tarnoff, Jerome *lawyer*
Taylor, Errol Bancroft *lawyer*
Taylor, Jeffrey A. *lawyer, former prosecutor*
Teiman, Richard Barry *lawyer*
Terrell, J. Anthony *lawyer*
Terry, Frederick Arthur, Jr. *lawyer*
Testa, Michael Harold *lawyer*
Thal, Steven Henry *lawyer, consultant*
Thalacker, Arbie Robert *lawyer, director*
Thomas, Jeremiah Lindsay III *lawyer*
Thomas, Roger Warren *lawyer*
Thompson, Lawrence Bigelow *lawyer*
Thompson, Timothy Lewis *lawyer*
Thoyer, Judith Reinhardt *lawyer*
Tierney, James Edward *law educator, former state attorney general*
Tilewick, Robert *lawyer*
Tillinghast, David Rollhaus *lawyer*
Todd, Ronald Gary *lawyer*
Toumey, Donald Joseph *lawyer*
Tracey, Dennis Henry III *lawyer*
Tramontine, John Orlando *retired lawyer*
Treadway, James Crispin Curran Corbett *lawyer, brokerage house executive, investor, federal official*
Trepper, Myron *lawyer*
Tuchmann, Eric P. *lawyer*
Tung, Ko-Yung *lawyer*
Turner, E. Deane *lawyer*
Turner, Roger D. *lawyer*
Tusk, Claude M. *lawyer*
Tween, Douglas M. *lawyer, former prosecutor*
Underberg, Mark Alan *lawyer*
Unger, Sydney Elliott *lawyer*
Uram, Gerald Robert *lawyer*
Urowsky, Richard J. *lawyer*
Vachss, Andrew Henry *lawyer, writer, juvenile justice and child abuse consultant*
Valente, Peter Charles *lawyer*
Vance, Cyrus Roberts, Jr. *lawyer*
Varet, Michael A. *lawyer*
Vassallo, John A. *lawyer*
Verkuil, Paul Robert *law educator, lawyer, former dean*
Versfelt, David Scott *lawyer*
Victor, A. Paul *lawyer*
Vig, Vernon Edward *lawyer*
Vinegrad, Alan *prosecutor*
Vingoe, D. Grant *lawyer*
Vitkowsky, Vincent Joseph *lawyer*
Vittor, Kenneth Mark *lawyer*
von Mehren, Robert Brandt *retired lawyer*
Wachsberger, Chaim *lawyer*
Waddell, Mark E. *lawyer*
Wahlquist, Andrea K. *lawyer*
Wailand, George *lawyer*
Wald, Bernard Joseph *lawyer*
Waldman, Michael *lawyer*
Wallace, Nora Ann *lawyer*
Wallach, Eric Jean *lawyer*
Wang, Xinsheng *lawyer*
Warden, John Lehman *lawyer*
Warnke, Gordon E. *lawyer*
Warren, William Bradford *lawyer*
Waxenberg, Jay David *lawyer*
Waybourn, Kathleen Ann *lawyer, consultant*
Weinberg, Jeffrey J. *lawyer*
Weiner, Andrew Jay *lawyer*
Weiner, Earl David *lawyer*
Weiner, Michael S. *lawyer, labor union administrator*
Weiner, Stephen Arthur *lawyer*
Weingarten, Marc *lawyer*
Weinschel, Alan Jay *lawyer*
Weinstock, Leonard *lawyer*
Weisbrod, Carl *lawyer, public official*
Weiss, Lawrence N. *lawyer*
Weissmann, Andrew *lawyer, former prosecutor*
Weithorn, Stanley Stephen *lawyer*
Weitz, Perry *lawyer*
Weld, Jonathan Minot *lawyer*
Weld, William F. *former governor*
Welikson, Jeffrey Alan *lawyer*
Wellington, Harry Hillel *lawyer, educator*
Wells, Theodore V., Jr., (Ted Wells) *lawyer*
Welshimer, Mark J. *lawyer*
Weltman, Edward S. *lawyer*
Wenig, Cindy L. *lawyer*
Werder, Richard I., Jr. *lawyer*
Werner, Robert L. *lawyer, consultant*
Wesely, Edwin Joseph *lawyer*
Wesely, Marissa Celeste *lawyer*
West, Stephen Kingsbury *lawyer, director*
Wetmore, Keith Chidester *lawyer*
Wexelbaum, Michael *lawyer*
Whitaker, G(eorge) Warren *lawyer*
White, John Patrick *lawyer*
White, Mary Jo *lawyer, former prosecutor*
White, W. Christopher *lawyer*
Whitmer, Frederick Lee *lawyer*
Wilcox, John Caven *lawyer, financial executive*
Wilkinson, John Hart *lawyer*
Willett, John A. *lawyer*
Williams, William John, Jr. *lawyer*
Willis, William Ervin *lawyer*
Wilson, Peter Scott *lawyer*
Windels, Paul, Jr. *lawyer*
Winfield, Richard Neill *lawyer*
Winterer, Philip Steele *lawyer*
Wise, Aaron Noah *lawyer*
Witkin, Eric Douglas *lawyer*
Witmeyer, John Jacob III *lawyer*
Wohl, Frank Harold *lawyer*
Wolf, Barry M. *lawyer*
Wolfe, James Ronald *retired lawyer*
Woods, John Maynard *lawyer*
Wynne, William Francis *lawyer*
Yamin, Michael Geoffrey *lawyer*
Yankwitt, George B(ruce) *lawyer*
Yelenick, Mary Therese *lawyer*
Young, Jonathan *lawyer*
Young, Nancy *lawyer*
Youngwood, Alfred Donald *lawyer*
Zabel, William David *lawyer*
Zager, Steven Mark *lawyer*
Zagorin, Janet Susan *legal firm administrator, marketing professional*
Zaitzeff, Roger Michael *lawyer*
Zammit, Joseph Paul *lawyer*
Zauderer, Mark Carl *lawyer*
Zedrosser, Joseph John *lawyer*
Ziegler, Richard Ferdinand *lawyer*
Zifchak, William C. *lawyer*
Zimand, Harvey Folks *lawyer*
Zimmerman, Diane Leenheer *law educator*
Zimmett, Mark Paul *lawyer, educator*
Zinberg, David J. *lawyer*
Zito, Robert John Amadeus *lawyer*
Zoogman, Nicholas Jay *lawyer*
Zornow, David Merrill *lawyer*
Zuckerman, Paul Herbert *lawyer*
Zukerman, Michael *lawyer*
Zweibel, Joel Burton *retired lawyer*

Nyack
Tirana, Bardyl Rifat *lawyer*

Old Chatham
Severs, Charles A. III *lawyer*

Orangeburg
Rivet, Diana Wittmer *lawyer, farmer*

Orchard Park
Sullivan, Mortimer Allen, Jr. *lawyer*

Ossining
Hall, H(erbert) Glen *lawyer*

Oyster Bay
Coates, Winslow Shelby, Jr. *lawyer*

Pearl River
Meyer, Irwin Stephan *lawyer, accountant*
Riley, James Kevin *lawyer*

Pelham
Gaffney, Mark William *lawyer*

Penn Yan
Mathewson, George Atterbury *retired lawyer*

Pittsford
Buzard, A. Vincent *lawyer*
Hampson, Thomas Meredith *lawyer*
Stonehill, Eric *lawyer*
Turri, Joseph A. *lawyer*
Willett, Thomas Edward *lawyer*

Pleasant Valley
Vasti, Thomas Francis III *lawyer*

Pleasantville
DeCaro, Shana *lawyer*

Port Washington
Andriola, Rocco F. *lawyer, diversified financial services company executive*

Rush, Curt Stefan *lawyer*
Ullman, Leo Solomon *lawyer*

Purchase
Gioffre, Bruno Joseph *lawyer*
Hanft, Noah Jonathan *lawyer*
Kelly, Edmund Joseph *lawyer, investment banking executive*
Thompson, Larry Dean *lawyer, former federal agency administrator, food products executive*
Ughetta, James C. *lawyer*

Rensselaerville
Fletcher, Raymond Russwald, Jr. *lawyer*

Rhinebeck
Aarons, Jonas *arbitrator, mediator*
Melley, Steven Michael *lawyer*

Rochester
Buckley, Michael Francis *lawyer*
Dolin, Lonny H. *lawyer*
Haag, Joyce P. *lawyer, imaging company executive*
Kurland, Harold Arthur *lawyer*
Law, Michael R. *lawyer*
Lundback, Staffan Bengt Gunnar *lawyer*
McCrory, John Brooks *retired lawyer*
Moore, James Conklin *lawyer*
Morrison, Patrice Burgert *lawyer*
Palermo, Anthony Robert *lawyer*
Paley, Gerald Larry *lawyer*
Payment, Kenneth Arnold *lawyer*
Price, Richard Edward *lawyer*
Rosenbaum, Richard Merrill *lawyer*
Rosenhouse, Michael Allan *lawyer, editor, consultant, columnist*
Rosner, Leonard Allen *lawyer*
Samar, Vincent Joseph *lawyer*
Stewart, Sue S. *lawyer*
Tyler, John Randolph *lawyer*
Vigdor, Justin Leonard *lawyer*
Waite, Stephen Holden *lawyer*

Rome
Simons, Richard Duncan *lawyer, retired judge*

Rosedale
Charrington, Karen Hillary *lawyer, consultant*

Rye
Capps, John Edward *lawyer, consumer products company executive*

Saint James
Maggipinto, V. Anthony *lawyer*

Sanborn
Mezhir, James A. *law educator*

Scarsdale
Angel, Dennis *lawyer*
Belasco, Steven Ronald *lawyer*
Beuchert, Edward William *lawyer*
Bosses, Stevan J. *mediator, arbitrator*
Van Gundy, Gregory Frank *retired lawyer*

Schenectady
Levine, Sanford Harold *lawyer*
Teff, Justin Samuel *lawyer*

Scottsville
Williams, Henry Ward, Jr. *lawyer, writer*

Seaford
Furey, Raymond Joseph *lawyer*

Smithtown
Spellman, Thomas Joseph, Jr. *lawyer*

Somers
Rapp, Steven M. *lawyer, consumer products company executive*
Reiman, Richard J. *lawyer*

South Richmond Hill
Scheich, John F. *lawyer*

South Salem
Cowles, Frederick Oliver *lawyer*

Southampton
Lopez, David *lawyer*
Platt, Jonathan James *lawyer*

Staten Island
Humphries, Edward Francis *lawyer*
Prince, Andrew Steven *lawyer, retired government agency administrator*

Syracuse
Baldwin, Robert Frederick, Jr. *lawyer*
Barclay, H. Douglas (Hugh Douglas Barclay) *lawyer, legislator, diplomat*
Baxter, Andrew Thomas *prosecutor*
Cirando, John Anthony *lawyer*
Fitzpatrick, James David *lawyer*
Gaal, John *lawyer*
Givas, Thomas Peter *lawyer*
Hayes, David Michael *lawyer*
Lee, David Ames *lawyer, banker*
Luchsinger, John Francis, Jr. *lawyer*
McLaughlin, Robert S. *lawyer*
O'Connor, Michael E. *lawyer*
Philippone, David J. *lawyer*
Pinsky, Roy David *lawyer*
Richardson, M. Catherine *lawyer*
Roberson, Michael Lee *lawyer*

Tarrytown
Garen, Daniel Joseph *lawyer*
Pollak, Martin Marshall *lawyer, training company executive*

Troy
Jones, E. Stewart, Jr. *lawyer*
LaMarche, George E. III *lawyer*
Lang, Valerie Anne *educator*

Uniondale
Berzow, Harold Steven *lawyer*
Duffy, James Raymond *lawyer*
Kotula, Michael Anthony *lawyer*
Lemle, Robert Spencer *lawyer*
Levy, Robert S. *lawyer*
Pratt, George Cheney *law educator, retired judge*

Victor
Mullin, Thomas J. *lawyer, food products executive*

Wantagh
Petris, Elli *bankruptcy case manager*

Waterford
Glavin, A. Rita Chandellier (Mrs. James Henry Glavin III) *lawyer*

West Harrison
Maffeo, Vincent Anthony *lawyer, director*

Westbury
Boes, Lawrence William *lawyer*

White Plains
Atnally, Edward Vincent *lawyer*
Berlin, Alan Daniel *lawyer, real estate company officer, consultant*
Bodnar, Peter O. *lawyer*
Carlisle, Jay Charles, II, *lawyer, educator*
Carlucci, Joseph P. *lawyer*
Culleton, James J. *lawyer, former prosecutor*
Feder, Robert *lawyer*
Greenawalt, William Sloan *lawyer*
Greenspan, Leon Joseph *lawyer*
Greenspan, Michael Evan *lawyer*
Halpern, Philip Morgan *lawyer*
Jimenez, Frank R. *lawyer*
Kelly, Regina Fogel *lawyer*
Landa, Howard Martin *lawyer, management consultant*
Levine, Steven Jon *lawyer*
Milone, Lydia A. *lawyer*
Munneke, Gary Arthur *law educator, consultant*
Null, William Seth *lawyer*
Payson, Martin F. *lawyer*
Robinson, Nicholas Adams *law educator, department chairman*
Ryan, Robert Davis *lawyer*
Sheehan, Timothy J. *lawyer*
Siegel, Kenneth S. *lawyer*
Sloan, F(rank) Blaine *retired law educator*
Steccato, Carl L. *lawyer*
Whittemore, Gail Farnsworth *law librarian*

Williamsville
Farrell, Mark G. *lawyer, judge*
Pearson, Paul David *lawyer, arbitrator, mediator*

Woodbury
Heath, David Lewis *lawyer*

Yonkers
Kilsch, Gunther H. *lawyer*

NORTH CAROLINA

Asheville
Davis, Roy Walton, Jr. *lawyer*
Elmore, Bruce Alexander, Jr. *lawyer*
Lavelle, Brian Francis David *lawyer*
Martin, Harry Corpening *lawyer, retired state supreme court justice*

Bryson City
Miller, Gary H. *lawyer*

Carthage
Gebhardt, Robert Charles *lawyer*

Cary
Montgomery, Charles Harvey *lawyer*

Chapel Hill
Boger, John Charles *law educator, dean*
Brophy, Alfred Laurence III *law educator*
Corrado, Michael Louis *law educator*
Fitzpatrick, Whitfield Westfeldt *lawyer*
Freedman, Irving Melvin *lawyer*
Hardin, Paul III *law educator*
Klinefelter, Anne *law librarian, educator*
Lawrence, David Michael *lawyer, educator*
Loeb, Ben Fohl, Jr. *retired law educator*
Moore, Albert Cunningham *lawyer, insurance company executive*
Nichol, Gene Ray, Jr. *law educator, former academic administrator*
Southern, Robert Allen *lawyer*
Wegner, Judith Welch *lawyer, educator, dean*

Charlotte
Ayscue, Edwin Osborne, Jr. *lawyer*
Blanchfield, Francis J., Jr. *lawyer*
Brackett, Martin Luther, Jr. *lawyer*
Buchan, Jonathan Edward, Jr. *lawyer*
Buckley, Charles Robinson III *lawyer*
Coss, Stephen K. *lawyer*
Cramer, Robert W. *lawyer*
Dunn, Jackson Thomas, Jr. *lawyer, educator*
Erdman, David Williams *lawyer*
Gage, Gaston Hemphill *lawyer*
Goldstein, Stuart N. *lawyer*
Gunson, Douglas R. *lawyer*
Hankins, Irvin W. III *lawyer*
Hanna, George Verner III *lawyer*
Hatcher, James Gregory *lawyer*
Jackson, Gary Walker *lawyer*
Kelley, Janet Godsey *lawyer*
Knox, Frances S. *lawyer*
Lilly, Kevin L. *lawyer, manufacturing executive*
Linnert, Terrence Gregory *lawyer*
Manly, Marc Edward *lawyer, energy executive*
Mauney, Gary Vance *lawyer*
McBryde, Neill Gregory *lawyer*
McCoy, Michael D. *lawyer*
McGill, John Knox *lawyer*
Mehta, Kiran H. *lawyer*
Nedzbala, Michael *lawyer*
Raper, William Cranford *lawyer*
Rawlins, Donald Ray *lawyer*
Sherburne, Jane C. *lawyer, bank executive*
Snyder, James C., Jr. *lawyer, consumer products company executive*
Summa, Philip *lawyer*
Thompson, Sydnor, Jr., (Charles William Sydnor Thompson Jr.) *lawyer, mediator, arbitrator*
Trent, B. Keith *lawyer, energy executive*
Van Allen, William Kent *lawyer*
Van Hoy, Philip Marshall *lawyer*
Vinroot, Richard Allen *lawyer, mayor*
Wood, William McBrayer *lawyer*
Wyche, James Ramage *lawyer*

Cherryville
Huffstetler, Palmer Eugene *lawyer*

Clinton
Davis, William Maxie, Jr. *lawyer*

Durham
Baker, Robert Flowers *lawyer, mediator and arbitrator*
Bartlett, Katharine Tiffany *law educator, former dean*
Bernard, Pamela Jenks *lawyer*
Carrington, Paul DeWitt *lawyer, educator*
Christie, George Custis *lawyer, educator, writer*
Cox, James D. *law educator*
Dellinger, Walter Estes III *law educator*
Demott, Deborah Ann *law educator*
Havighurst, Clark Canfield *law educator*
Holder, Angela Roddey *retired law educator*
Horowitz, Donald Leonard *lawyer, arbitrator, political scientist, educator*
Jenkins, Richard Erik *lawyer*
Maxwell, Richard Callender *retired lawyer, educator*
McMahon, John Alexander *law educator*
Robertson, Horace Bascomb, Jr. *retired law educator*
Schwarcz, Steven Lance *lawyer, educator*
Tigar, Michael Edward *law educator*

Fayetteville
Townsend, William Jackson *lawyer*

Fletcher
Seagle, J. Harold *lawyer*

Gastonia
Stott, Grady Bernell *lawyer*

Greensboro
Bullock, Frank William, Jr. *lawyer, retired federal judge*
Clark, David McKenzie *lawyer*
Cummings, Candace S. *lawyer, apparel company executive*
Davis, Ferd Leary, Jr. *law educator, consultant*
Davis, Herbert Owen *lawyer*
Floyd, Jack William *lawyer*
Gumbiner, Kenneth Jay *lawyer*
Hunter, Bynum Merritt *retired lawyer*
Koonce, Neil Wright *lawyer*
McGinn, Max Daniel *lawyer*
Melvin, Charles Edward, Jr. *lawyer*
Slaughter, James H. *lawyer*
Swan, George Steven *law educator*
Wagoner, Anna Mills S. *prosecutor*
Ward Black, Janet *lawyer*

Greenville
Colombo, Michael Allen *lawyer*

Hendersonville
Mitchell, William P. (Billy) *arbitrator*

Hickory
Johnson, Daniel *lawyer*

Kitty Hawk
Tucker, Don Eugene *retired lawyer*

Laurinburg
Sojka, Nickolas Joseph, Jr. *lawyer*

Lexington
Snyder, James Eugene, Jr. *lawyer*

Marion
Burgin, Charles Edward *retired lawyer*

Mc Leansville
Miles, John Benjamin *lawyer*

Mooresville
McCanless, Ross William *lawyer, retail executive*

Morganton
Simpson, Daniel Reid *lawyer, mediator*

Murphy
Bata, Rudolph Andrew, Jr. *lawyer*

New Bern
Davis, James Lee *lawyer*
Overholt, Hugh Robert *lawyer, retired military officer*

North Wilkesboro
Keener, Gaither McDonald, Jr. *corporate lawyer*

Raleigh
Bar, Roselyn R. *legal association administrator, executive secretary*
Bills, Jennifer Leah *lawyer*
Boyette, Richard T. *lawyer*
Cain, James Palmer *lawyer, former ambassador*
Carlton, Alfred Pershing, Jr. *lawyer*
Carter, Jean Gordon *lawyer*
Case, Charles Dixon *lawyer*
Cunningham, Michael *lawyer*
Davis, Egbert Lawrence III *retired lawyer*
Dorsett, James K. III *lawyer*
Edwards, Elizabeth (Mary Elizabeth Edwards) *lawyer, writer*
Ellis, Lester Neal, Jr. *lawyer*
Gailor, Frank Robert *lawyer*
Hargrove, Wade Hampton *lawyer*
Holding, George E.B. *prosecutor*
Hunt, James Baxter, Jr. *lawyer, former governor*
Jordan, John Richard, Jr. *lawyer*
Joyner, Gary Kelton *lawyer*
Kapp, Michael Keith *lawyer*
Lilliston, Andrew Wilson, Jr. *lawyer*
Markoff, Brad Steven *lawyer*
McNish, Susan Kirk *retired lawyer*
Meek, Jerry (Gerald Francis Meek) *lawyer, former political organization administrator*
Millberg, John C. *lawyer*
Miller, Robert James *lawyer*
Mitchell, Burley Bayard, Jr. *lawyer*
Patterson, William S. *lawyer*
Philbeck, John Heydt *lawyer*
Roach, Wesley Linville *lawyer, insurance executive*
Simpson, Steven Drexell *lawyer*
Spearman, Robert Worthington *lawyer*
Spruill, W. Murray *lawyer*
Suhr, Paul Augustine *lawyer*
Taylor, Raymond Mason *lawyer, educator, former government official*
Valois, Robert Arthur *lawyer*
Weisel, Michael Lloyd *lawyer, educator*
Yearwood, Douglas Lyman *legal association administrator, researcher*

Research Triangle Park
Meigs, Joseph Timothy *lawyer*
Welborn, Reich Lee *lawyer*
Whichard, Willis Padgett *lawyer, retired educator, judge*

Rocky Mount
Zipf, Robert Eugene, Jr. *medical laboratory director, legal medicine consultant, pathologist*

Tabor City
Jorgensen, Ralph Gubler *lawyer, accountant*

Tarboro
Davis, Robert Christopher *law educator*
Hopkins, Grover Prevatte *lawyer*

Trinity
Walker, Kenneth Lynn *lawyer*

Willow Spring
Valvo, Barbara-Ann *lawyer, surgeon*

Wilmington
McCauley, Cleyburn Lycurgus *lawyer*
Medlock, Donald Larson *lawyer*

Winston Salem
Adams, Alfred Gray *lawyer*
Adams, Reid C., Jr. *lawyer*
Barnhill, Henry Grady, Jr. *lawyer*
Blynn, Guy Marc *retired lawyer*
Chilson, John A. *lawyer, military officer*
Davis, Linwood Layfield *lawyer*
Edwards, Charles Archibald *lawyer*
Foy, Herbert Miles III *lawyer, educator*
Graham, William Thomas *lawyer*
Greason, Murray Crossley, Jr. *lawyer*
Gunter, Michael Donwell *lawyer*
Holton, Walter Clinton, Jr. *lawyer*
Humphrey, Dudley *lawyer*
King, Roberta B. *lawyer*
Leonard, R. Michael *lawyer*
Loughridge, John Halsted, Jr. *lawyer*
Moser, Kenneth Allen *lawyer*
Oldaker, Guy Brooklyn III *lawyer*
Oliver, Patricia *lawyer*
Osborn, Malcolm Everett *lawyer*
Quick, Elizabeth L. *lawyer*
Ray, Michael Edwin *lawyer*
Sandridge, William Pendleton, Jr. *lawyer*
Schollander, Wendell Leslie, Jr. *lawyer*
Schollander, Wendell Wes III *lawyer*
Sharpe, Keith Yount *retired lawyer, writer*
Taylor, Daniel Russell, Jr. *lawyer*
Vaughan, Keith W. *lawyer*
Vaughn, Robert Candler, Jr. *lawyer*
Walker, George Kontz *law educator*
Walsh, Robert K. *law educator, former dean*
Wilson, Grover Gray *lawyer*
Womble, William Fletcher *lawyer*

Zebulon
O'Neal, Cynthia Ann *lawyer*

NORTH DAKOTA

Bismarck
Moore, Sherry Mills *lawyer*
Murry, Charles Emerson *lawyer, federal official*
Sandness, Paul K. *lawyer, energy executive*

Fargo
Herman, Sarah Andrews *lawyer*
Williams, Michael James *lawyer*
Wrigley, Drew H. *prosecutor, lawyer*

Grand Forks
Davis, W. Jeremy *retired lawyer, dean*

Myers, Bradley Kevin *lawyer, educator*
Widdel, John Earl, Jr. *lawyer*

Mandan
Bair, Bruce Blythe *lawyer*

OHIO

Ada
Fenton, Howard Nathan III *lawyer, educator*

Akron
Belsky, Martin Henry *law educator, dean*
Bishop, Christy B. *lawyer*
Cherpas, Christopher Theodore *lawyer*
Fisher, James Lee *lawyer*
Harvie, Crawford Thomas *lawyer*
Lombardi, Frederick McKean *lawyer*
Reilly, Elizabeth Ann *law educator, dean*
Richert, Paul *law educator*
Schrader, Alfred Eugene *lawyer*
Taylor, E. Jane *lawyer*
Tipping, Harry A. *lawyer*
Trotter, Thomas Robert *lawyer*
Vespoli, Leila L. *lawyer, energy executive*
Wolfe, John Leslie *lawyer*

Beachwood
Braverman, Herbert Leslie *lawyer*
Clegg, Christopher R. *lawyer*
Pearlman, Samuel Segel *lawyer, educator*
Zambie, Allan John *retired lawyer*

Bellevue
Aigler, William Frank *lawyer*

Bryan
Shaffer, Wayne Eugene *lawyer*

Canton
Barnhart, Gene *lawyer*
Bell, Lee J. *lawyer*
Burkhart, William R. *lawyer*
Tyburski, Charles J. *lawyer*

Centerville
Giffen, Daniel Harris *lawyer, educator*

Cincinnati
Adams, Edmund John *lawyer*
Albainy-Jenei, Stephen R. *lawyer*
Anthony, Thomas Dale *lawyer*
Bahlman, William Thorne, Jr. *retired lawyer*
Bridgeland, James Ralph, Jr. *lawyer*
Broderick, Dennis John *lawyer, retail executive*
Burke, Timothy Michael *lawyer, educator*
Chesley, Stanley Morris *lawyer*
Christenson, Gordon A. *law educator*
Cioffi, Michael Lawrence *lawyer*
Cissell, James Charles *lawyer*
Cobey, John Geoffrey *lawyer, consultant*
Coffaro, Steven C. *lawyer*
Combs, Eric K. *lawyer*
Cruz, A. B., III, (Anatolio Benedicto Cruz III) *lawyer, multimedia company executive*
Cunningham, Pierce Edward *lawyer, city planner*
Dehner, Joseph Julnes *lawyer*
DeLong, Deborah *lawyer*
Desai, Deepak K. *lawyer*
Diller, Edward Dietrich *lawyer*
Dornette, W(illiam) Stuart *lawyer, educator*
Faller, Susan Grogan *lawyer*
Fink, Jerold Albert *lawyer*
Friedman, Penny *lawyer, not-for-profit developer*
Gettler, Benjamin *lawyer, manufacturing company executive*
Goodman, Stanley *lawyer*
Hardy, William Robinson *lawyer*
Harris, Irving *lawyer*
Heldman, James Gardner *lawyer*
Heldman, Paul W. *lawyer, food service executive*
Hermanies, John Hans *retired lawyer*
Hill, Thomas Clark *lawyer*
Hoefle, H. Frederick *lawyer*
Hoffheimer, Daniel Joseph *lawyer*
Jemison, Steven W. *lawyer, consumer products company executive*
Jones, Nathaniel Raphael *lawyer, retired federal judge*
Kelley, John Joseph, Jr. *lawyer*
Kindt, Monica V. *lawyer*
Kordons, Uldis *lawyer*
Kyle, Kimberly *lawyer*
Lawrence, James Kaufman Lebensburger *lawyer*
Lindberg, Charles David *lawyer*
Longenecker, Mark Hershey, Jr. *lawyer*
Mann, David Scott *lawyer, former congressman*
Maxwell, Robert Wallace, II, *lawyer*
McClain, William Andrew *lawyer*
McGavran, Frederick Jaeger *lawyer*
Meister, Julia B. *lawyer*
Meyers, Karen Diane *lawyer, educator*
Meyers, Pamela Sue *lawyer*
Mulvey, William J. *lawyer*
Nechemias, Stephen Murray *lawyer*
Oberhaus, Geoffrey Luther *lawyer*
O'Reilly, James Thomas *lawyer, educator, writer*
Parker, R. Joseph *lawyer*
Petrie, Bruce Inglis *lawyer*
Porter, Robert Carl, Jr. *lawyer*
Portman, Robert Jones *lawyer, former United States Representative from Ohio*
Reichert, David *lawyer*
Reuter, Mark F. *lawyer*
Reynolds, Paul L. *lawyer, bank executive*
Rich, Robert Edward *lawyer*
Richardson, Eric W. *lawyer*
Ross, Lori A. *lawyer*
Rucker, Fanon A. *lawyer*
Ruh, Michael A., Jr. *lawyer*
Ruwe, Bradley N. *lawyer*
Schuck, Thomas Robert *lawyer, farmer*
Shore, Thomas Spencer, Jr. *retired lawyer*
Silbersack, Mark Louis *lawyer*
Stern, Noah J. *lawyer*
Swigert, James Mack *lawyer*
Thompson, James E. *lawyer, food products executive*
Tobias, Paul Henry *lawyer*
Travis, Lawrence F. *law educator*
Vander Laan, Mark Alan *lawyer*
Vogel, Cedric Wakelee *lawyer*
Wales, Ross Elliot *lawyer*
Weeks, Steven Wiley *lawyer*
Weisenberger, Andrew *lawyer*
Wilson, Christopher J. *lawyer*
Woodside, Frank C. III *lawyer, educator, physician*
Wuebbling, Donald J. *lawyer, insurance company executive*
Zimmerman, James M. *lawyer*

Cleveland
Adamo, Kenneth Robert *lawyer*
Adams, Albert T. *lawyer*
Ashmus, Keith Allen *lawyer*
Austin, Arthur Donald, II, *lawyer, educator*
Bacon, Brett Kermit *lawyer*
Bays, James C. *lawyer*
Berick, James Herschel *lawyer*
Boukis, Kenneth *lawyer*
Bravo, Kenneth Allan *lawyer*
Brennan, Maureen *lawyer*
Brucken, Robert Matthew *lawyer*
Burge, David Alan *lawyer, writer*
Burke, Kathleen B. *lawyer*
Calkins, Benjamin *lawyer*
Callahan, Thomas James *lawyer*
Carson, Van *lawyer*
Chandra, Subodh *lawyer*
Clarke, Charles Fenton *lawyer*
Coleman, Deborah Ann *lawyer*
Collin, Thomas James *lawyer*
Coquillette, William Hollis *lawyer*
Currivan, John Daniel *lawyer*
Dampeer, John Lyell *retired lawyer*
DeMetz, Kathleen Susan *lawyer*
Demitrack, Thomas *lawyer*
DiSilvio, Marilena *lawyer*
Duncan, Ed Eugene *lawyer*
Duvin, Robert Phillip *lawyer*
Edwards, William J. *prosecutor*
Emrick, Charles Robert, Jr. *lawyer*
Fabens, Andrew Lawrie III *lawyer*
Fay, Regan Joseph *lawyer*
Fletcher, Robert *retired lawyer*
Friedman, Avery S. *lawyer*
Friedman, Harold Edward *lawyer*
Gentile Sachs, Valerie Ann *lawyer*
Glaser, Robert Edward *lawyer*
Gold, Gerald Seymour *lawyer*
Goldfarb, Bernard Sanford *lawyer*
Goler, Michael David *lawyer*
Gray, R. Benton *lawyer*
Groetzinger, Jon, Jr. *lawyer, pharmaceutical executive, educator*
Grossman, Theodore Martin *lawyer*
Haiman, Irwin Sanford *lawyer*
Harris, Paul N. *lawyer*
Hochman, Kenneth George *lawyer*
Horst, J. Robert *lawyer*
Horvitz, Michael John *lawyer*
Jacobs, Leslie William *lawyer*
Janke, Ronald Robert *lawyer*
Jorgenson, Mary Ann *lawyer*
Kahrl, Robert Conley *lawyer*
Karp, Marvin Louis *lawyer*
Katz, Lewis Robert *law educator*
Kestner, Robert Steven *lawyer*
Kilbane, Thomas Stanton *lawyer*
Kohn, William Irwin *lawyer*
Kramer, Edward George *lawyer*
Lawniczak, James Michael *lawyer*
Leavitt, Jeffrey Stuart *lawyer*
Leiken, Earl Murray *lawyer*
Lennox, Heather *lawyer*
Lewis, John Francis *lawyer*
Liebson, Matthew Edward *lawyer*
Linetsky, Tanya M. *lawyer*
Lowe, James Allison *lawyer, educator*
Matia, Paul Ramon *lawyer*
Mc Cartan, Patrick Francis *lawyer*
McCarthy, Mark Francis *lawyer*
McGuire, Mark M. *lawyer, manufacturing executive*
McKee, Thomas Frederick *lawyer*
McLaughlin, Patrick Michael *lawyer*
Mehlman, Maxwell Jonathan *law educator*
Messinger, Donald Hathaway *lawyer*
Meyer, G. Christopher *lawyer*
Millisor, Kenneth Ray *lawyer*
Millstone, David Jeffrey *lawyer*
Moore, Kenneth Cameron *lawyer*
Newman, John M., Jr. *lawyer*
Okada, Ronald Shig *lawyer*
O'Keefe, Francis Ronald *lawyer*
Perry, George Williamson *lawyer*
Pietrzen, Julie Lynn *lawyer*
Piraino, Thomas Anthony, Jr. *lawyer*
Podboy, Alvin Michael, Jr. *law librarian, director*
Pogue, Richard Welch *lawyer*
Pollock, R. Jeffrey *lawyer*
Putka, Andrew Charles *lawyer*
Rains, M. Neal *lawyer*
Rawson, Robert H., Jr. *lawyer*
Roberts-Mamone, Lisa A. *lawyer*
Rosenbaum, Jacob I. *retired lawyer*
Ruben, Alan Miles *law educator*
Sanislo, Paul Steve *lawyer*
Schreiber, Svetlana J. *lawyer*
Shapiro, Fred David *lawyer*
Sicherman, Marvin Allen *lawyer*
Simson, Gary Joseph *law educator*
Sogg, Wilton Sherman *lawyer*
Solomon, Randall Lee *lawyer*
Stanley, Hugh Monroe, Jr. *lawyer*
Stellato, Louis Eugene *lawyer*
Stokes, Louis *lawyer, former congressman*
Stone, James Merrill *lawyer*
Strimbu, Victor, Jr. *lawyer*
Stuhan, Richard George *lawyer*
Summers, William Lawrence *lawyer*
Swartzbaugh, Marc L. *lawyer*
Thimmig, Diana Marie *lawyer*
Thomas, Dynda A. *lawyer*
Toomajian, William Martin *lawyer*
von Mehren, George M. *lawyer*
Waldeck, John Walter, Jr. *lawyer*
Wallach, Mark Irwin *lawyer*
Watson, Richard Thomas *lawyer*
Weiler, Jeffry Louis *lawyer*
Whitney, Richard Buckner *lawyer*
Wong, Margaret Wai *lawyer*
Young, James Edward *lawyer*
Zoeller, David Louis *lawyer, bank executive*

Cleveland Heights
Chilcote, Lee A. *lawyer*

Columbus
Bailey, Daniel Allen *lawyer*
Blackburn, John D(avid) *lawyer, educator*
Brooks, Richard Dickinson *lawyer*
Brubaker, Robert Loring *lawyer*
Buchenroth, Stephen Richard *lawyer*
Carnahan, John Anderson *retired lawyer*
Chappelear, Stephen Eric *lawyer*
Chester, John Jonas *lawyer, educator*
Cvetanovich, Dan L. *lawyer*
Dunlay, Catherine Telles *lawyer*
Fahey, Richard Paul *lawyer*
Fay, Terrence Michael *lawyer*
Gall, John Ryan *lawyer*
Gibson, Rick J. *lawyer*
Gross, James Howard *lawyer*
Grotenrath, Mary Jo *lawyer, writer*
Hardymon, David Wayne *lawyer*
Harmon, Phillip Louis *lawyer*
Hatler, Patricia Ruth *lawyer, insurance company executive*
Haubiel, Charles W., II, *lawyer, retail executive*
Hollenbaugh, H(enry) Ritchey *lawyer*
Hutson, Jeffrey Woodward *lawyer*
Johnson, Mark Alan *lawyer*
Keane, John B. *lawyer, electric power industry executive*
Kinzer, Allen Shawn *lawyer*
Kuehnle, Kenton Lee *lawyer*
Liston, Jefferson Edward *lawyer*
Mann, William Craig *lawyer*
McConnaughey, George Carlton, Jr. *retired lawyer*
McCutchan, Gordon Eugene *retired lawyer, insurance company executive*
McDermott, Kevin R. *lawyer*
McKenna, Alvin James *lawyer*
McNealey, J. Jeffrey *lawyer, corporate executive*
Miller, Terry Morrow *lawyer*
Minor, Robert Allen *lawyer*
Mirman, Joel Harvey *lawyer*
Moloney, Thomas E. *lawyer*
Mone, Robert Paul *lawyer*
Moul, William Charles *lawyer*
Nigh, Joseph Aaron *lawyer*
Oman, Richard Heer *retired lawyer*
Patmon, William Wesley III *lawyer*
Petricoff, M. Howard *lawyer, educator*
Phillips, James Edgar *lawyer*
Quigley, John Bernard *law educator*
Radnor, Alan T. *lawyer*
Ramey, Denny L. *bar association executive director*
Ray, Frank Allen *lawyer*
Rector, Susan Darnell *lawyer*
Ridgley, Thomas Brennan *lawyer*
Robol, Richard Thomas *lawyer*
Rogers, Nancy Hardin *law educator, former dean, former state attorney general*
Saad, Michael D. *lawyer*
Saxbe, William Bart *lawyer, former United States Attorney General, former United States Senator from Ohio*
Schmidt, Robert James, Jr. *lawyer*
Shane, Peter Milo *law educator*
Sidman, Robert John *lawyer*
Sites, Richard Loren *lawyer, educator*
Sowald, Heather Gay *lawyer*
Stern, Geoffrey *lawyer*
Sully, Ira Bennett *lawyer*
Swift, David A. *lawyer*
Taggart, Thomas Michael *lawyer*
Tait, Robert E. *lawyer*
Tarpy, Thomas Michael *lawyer*
Thompson, Harold Lee *lawyer*
Tyack, Thomas Michael *lawyer*
Warner, Charles Collins *lawyer*
Whipps, Edward Franklin *lawyer*
Wightman, Alec *lawyer*
Willcox, Roderick Harrison *lawyer*

Dayton
Faruki, Charles Joseph *lawyer*
Furry, Richard Logan *lawyer*
Hadley, Robert James *lawyer*
Jenks, Thomas Edward *lawyer*
Johnson, C. Terry *lawyer*
Kirby, Tami Hart *lawyer*
Lockhart, Gregory Gordon *prosecutor*
Macklin, Crofford Johnson, Jr. *lawyer*
Mues, Robert Leighton *lawyer*
Saul, Irving Isaac *lawyer*
Swartz Neuhardt, Sharen *lawyer*
Vaughn, Noel Wyandt *lawyer*

Dublin
Tenuta, Luigia *lawyer*

Eastlake
Balester, Vivian Shelton *retired lawyer, consultant*

Findlay
Kline, James Edward *lawyer*

Gambier
Leech, Charles Russell, Jr. *lawyer*

Howard
Lee, William Johnson *lawyer*

Hudson
Merwin, John David *lawyer, former Governor of the Virgin Islands*

Independence
Kola, Arthur Anthony *lawyer*
Maser, Douglas James *legal and governmental operations lawyer*

Jackson
Lewis, Richard M. *lawyer*

Kettering
Eubank, David Lynn *lawyer, consultant*

Lakewood
Greenman, Frederick F., Jr. *lawyer*

Lancaster
Libert, Donald Joseph *retired lawyer*

Marietta
Fields, William Albert *lawyer*

Marysville
Hamilton, Robert Otte *lawyer*

Maumee
Fallat, Dale William *lawyer*
Marsh, Benjamin Franklin *lawyer*
Tuschman, James Marshall *lawyer*
Witherell, Dennis Patrick *lawyer*

Mayfield
Jarrett, Charles Elwood *lawyer, insurance company executive*

Miamisburg
Byrd, James Everett *lawyer*

Middletown
Horn, David C. *lawyer*
Rathman, William Ernest *retired lawyer, minister*

Newark
Mencer, Jetta *lawyer*

North Canton
Dettinger, Warren Walter *lawyer*

Orange Village
Pace, Stanley Dan *lawyer*

Orrville
Harlan, Mary Ann *lawyer*

Pepper Pike
Martin, Aric Doyle *lawyer*

Perrysburg
Baehren, James W. *lawyer*
Skiver, Stephen Allen *lawyer, physician*

Portsmouth
Gerlach, Franklin Theodore *lawyer*

Saint Marys
Kemp, Barrett George *lawyer*

Sheffield Village
Kolczun, Lee S. *lawyer*

Springfield
Lagos, James Harry *lawyer, small business owner*

Terrace Park
Naylor, Paul Donald *retired lawyer*

Toledo
Anspach, Robert Michael *lawyer*
Dalrymple, Thomas Lawrence *retired lawyer*
Jackson, Reginald Sherman, Jr. *lawyer, educator*
Krull, Stephen Keith *lawyer*
O'Connell, Maurice Daniel *lawyer*
Pletz, Thomas Gregory *lawyer*
Webb, Thomas Irwin, Jr. *lawyer, director*
Wicklund, David Wayne *lawyer*

Troy
Puthoff, Mark Allen *lawyer*

Warren
Rossi, Anthony Gerald *lawyer*

Westerville
Helvey, Edward Douglas *lawyer*
Young, Sheldon Mike *lawyer, author*

Westlake
Skulina, Thomas Raymond *lawyer*
Young, Mark R. *lawyer, hospitality company executive*

Wickliffe
Bauer, Joseph W. *lawyer, chemicals executive*
Kidder, Fred Dockstater *retired lawyer*

Willoughby
Driggs, Charles Mulford *lawyer*

Wooster
Kennedy, Charles Allen *lawyer*

Worthington
Fisher, Fredrick Lee *lawyer*
Minton, Harvey Steiger *lawyer*

OKLAHOMA

Claremore
Steidley, Juan Dwayne *lawyer, judge*

Edmond
Angel, Steven Michael *retired lawyer*
Lester, Andrew William *lawyer*
Loving, Susan Brimer *lawyer, former state official*
Powell, Courtney Davis *lawyer*
Wilson, Julia Ann Yother *lawyer*

Enid
Jones, Stephen *lawyer*

Frederick
Evans, Michael D. *lawyer*

Guthrie
Davis, Frank Wayne *lawyer*

Kingfisher
Elsener, G. Dale *lawyer*

Mcalester
Cornish, Richard Pool *lawyer*

Muskogee
Robinson, Adelbert Carl *lawyer, judge*
Sperling, Sheldon J. *prosecutor*

Norman
Elkouri, Frank *law educator*
Miller, Fred Heins *lawyer, retired educator*
Robertson, Lindsay Gordon *law educator*

Oklahoma City
Beveridge, Norwood Pierson *law educator*
Court, Leonard *lawyer, educator*
Elder, James Carl *lawyer*
Fenton, Elliott Clayton *lawyer*
Ford, Michael Raye *lawyer*
Homsey, Joseph Richard, Jr. *lawyer*
Hood, Henry J. *lawyer, energy executive*
Legg, William Jefferson *lawyer*
Lowe, Lyle Justin *lawyer*
McCampbell, Robert Garner *lawyer, former prosecutor*
McMillin, James Craig *lawyer*
Moler, Edward Harold *retired lawyer*
Nelon, Robert Dale *lawyer*
Ogle, James David *lawyer*
Paul, William George *lawyer*
Perry, Steven L. *lawyer*
Richter, John Charles *prosecutor*
Rockett, D. Joe *lawyer, director*
Ross, William Jarboe *lawyer*
Schuster, E. Elaine *lawyer*
Smith, (Carl) Michael *lawyer, former federal agency administrator*
Steinhorn, Irwin Harry *lawyer, corporate financial executive, educator*
Stewart, Robert D., Jr. *lawyer*
Stong, Roger Alan *lawyer*
Stringer, L. E. (Dean) *retired lawyer*
Taylor, Lyndon Clint *lawyer, energy executive*
Towery, Curtis Kent *lawyer*
Walsh, Lawrence Edward *lawyer*
Woods, Harry Arthur, Jr. *lawyer*

Ponca City
Northcutt, Clarence Dewey *lawyer*
Raley, John Wesley, Jr. *lawyer*

Sayre
Brooks, David Eugene *lawyer*

Stillwater
DeLacerda, Melissa Griner *lawyer*

Tulsa
Arrington, John Leslie, Jr. *lawyer*
Barker, John Roy *lawyer, gas industry executive*
Bender, James J. *lawyer, oil industry executive*
Biolchini, Robert Fredrick *lawyer*
Bryant, Hubert Hale *lawyer*
Cooper, Richard Casey *lawyer*
Daniel, Samuel Phillips *lawyer*
Farrell, John L., Jr. *lawyer, consultant, corporate financial executive*
Frey, Martin Alan *lawyer, educator*
Gaberino, John Anthony, Jr. *lawyer*
Gardner, Dale Ray *lawyer*
Givens, Jack Rodman *lawyer*
Hatfield, Jack Kenton *lawyer, accountant*
Haynie, Tony Wayne *arbitrator, lawyer, mediator*
Howard, Gene Claude *lawyer, retired state senator*
Huckin, William Price, Jr. *prosecutor*
Johnson, Cornelius Raymond *lawyer*
Luthey, Graydon Dean, Jr. *lawyer, educator*
Marlar, Donald Floyd *lawyer*
O'Meilia, David E. *prosecutor, lawyer*
Strecker, David Eugene *lawyer*
Williamson, Walter Bland *lawyer*

OREGON

Astoria
Haskell, Donald McMillan *lawyer*

Aurora
Ringle, Philip Hamilton, Jr. *lawyer*

Beaverton
Carter, James C. *lawyer, apparel executive*
Houser, Douglas Guy *lawyer*
Mc Cray, Ronald David *lawyer, apparel executive*

Brookings
Maxwell, William Stirling *retired lawyer*

Central Point
Richardson, Dennis Michael *lawyer, educator*

Corvallis
Frohnmayer, John Edward *lawyer, writer*

Dayton
Anderson, Herbert Hatfield *lawyer, farmer*

Eugene
Aldave, Barbara Bader *lawyer, educator*
Scoles, Eugene Francis *lawyer, educator*

Jacksonville
O'Connor, Karl William (Goodyear Johnson) *retired lawyer*

Keizer
Stevens, Sharon Cox *lawyer*

Lake Oswego
Byczynski, Edward Frank *lawyer, corporate financial executive*
Owen, Berniece Marie *law librarian, director*
Rasmussen, Richard Robert *lawyer*

Lincoln City
Arant, Eugene Wesley *lawyer*

Medford
Carter, William G. *lawyer*
Deatherage, William Vernon *lawyer*

Oregon City
Lounsbury, Steven Richard *lawyer*

Portland
Abravanel, Allan Ray *lawyer*
Backlar, Byron *lawyer*
Brenneman, Delbert Jay *lawyer*
Cable, John Franklin *lawyer*
Cook, Nena *lawyer*
Cooke, Roger Anthony *lawyer, manufacturing executive*
Crowell, John B., Jr. *lawyer, former government official*
English, Stephen Francis *lawyer*
Epstein, Edward Louis *lawyer*
Ferris, Kassim M. *patent lawyer*
Feuerstein, Howard M. *lawyer*
Foley, Ridgway Knight, Jr. *lawyer, writer*
Hanna, Harry Mitchell *lawyer*
Harnden, Edwin A. *lawyer*
Hinkle, Charles Frederick *lawyer, educator*
Hirshon, Robert Edward *lawyer*
Jarvis, Peter R. *lawyer*
Johnston, David Frederick *lawyer*
Jolles, Bernard *lawyer*
Josephson, Richard Carl *lawyer*
Kanter, Stephen *lawyer, educator, dean*
Kester, Randall Blair *lawyer*
Klonoff, Robert Howard *lawyer, educator*
Larpenteur, James Albert, Jr. *retired lawyer*
Love, William Edward *lawyer*
Maloney, Robert E., Jr. *lawyer*
Menashe, Albert Alan *lawyer*
Miller, William Richey, Jr. *lawyer*
Mowe, Gregory Robert *lawyer*
Murphy, Timothy E. *lawyer*
O'Neil, Katherine Huff *lawyer*
Richardson, Campbell *retired lawyer*
Richter, Peter Christian *lawyer*
Rosen, Steven O. *lawyer*
Ryan, John Duncan *lawyer*
Shertz, Laurie *lawyer*
Simpson, Robert Glenn *lawyer*
Stone, Richard James *lawyer*
Sullivan, Edward Joseph *lawyer*
Swenson, Constance Rae *lawyer*
Tucker, Roy W. *lawyer*
Van Valkenburg, Edgar Walter *lawyer*
Waggoner, James Clyde *lawyer*
Westwood, James Nicholson *lawyer*
White, Douglas James, Jr. *lawyer*
Williamson, Charles Ready III *lawyer*
Wilson, Owen Meredith, Jr. *lawyer, mediator, arbitrator*
Wood, Marcus Andrew *lawyer*
Zalutsky, Morton Herman *lawyer*

Salem
Breen, Richard F., Jr. *law librarian, educator*
Brown, Eden Rose *lawyer*
Clark, David Scott *law educator, consultant*
Dubanevich, Keith Scott *lawyer*
Gangle, Sandra Smith *arbitrator, mediator*
Haselton, Rick Thomas *lawyer*
Mannix, Kevin Leese *lawyer*
Nafziger, James Albert Richmond *law educator*

PENNSYLVANIA

Abington
Bildersee, Robert Alan *lawyer*

Allentown
Brown, W(illiam) Douglas *lawyer*
Grey, Robert J. (Bob Grey) *lawyer, electric power industry executive*
Holt, Leon Conrad, Jr. *lawyer, chemicals executive*
Jones, Stephen J. *lawyer, chemicals company executive*

Allison Park
Ewalt, Henry Ward *lawyer*
Herrington, John David III *retired lawyer, director*
Rulis, Christopher C. *lawyer*

Bala Cynwyd
Garrity, Vincent Francis, Jr. *lawyer*
Manko, Joseph Martin, Sr. *lawyer*
Mattison, Priscilla Jane *lawyer*
Wiener, Thomas Eli *lawyer*

Bensalem
Osterhout, Richard Cadwallader *lawyer*
Segal, Robert Martin *lawyer*

Berwyn
Huffaker, John Boston *lawyer*
Seidel, Arthur Harris *lawyer*
Watters, Edward McLain III *lawyer*

Bethlehem
Hemphill, Meredith, Jr. *retired lawyer*
Rambo, Kelly Clifford *lawyer*

Blue Bell
Blazey, Douglas R. *lawyer*
Elliott, John Michael *lawyer*
Rounick, Jack A. *lawyer, clothing retail executive*
Sundheim, Nancy Straus *lawyer, computer company executive*
Swansen, Samuel Theodore *lawyer*

Bryn Mawr
Frick, Benjamin Charles *lawyer*
Phillips, Stephen S. *lawyer*

Camp Hill
Mackin, Charles Philip, Jr. *lawyer*
Strassler, Marc A. *lawyer, retail executive*

Canonsburg
Richey, P. Jerome *lawyer, energy executive*

Carlisle
Butler, William Elliott *lawyer, educator*

Chesterbrook
Chou, John G. *lawyer*

Downingtown
Wusinich, Joseph F. III *lawyer, educator*

Doylestown
Elliott, Richard Howard *lawyer*

Drexel Hill
Williams, W. Craig *prosecutor*

Dunmore
Marino, Thomas A. *lawyer, former prosecutor*

Easton
Brown, Robert Carroll, Jr. *lawyer*
Milgrim, Roger Michael *lawyer*
Murphy, Bruce Allen *government and law educator, writer*

Erie
Tanous, James Joseph *lawyer, insurance company executive*

Exton
Bertolino, Dean A. *lawyer*

Fayetteville
Molitor, Graham Thomas Tate *lawyer*

Feasterville Trevose
Kats, Marina *lawyer*

Frazer
Pappert, Jerry (Gerald J. Pappert) *lawyer, former state attorney general*

Gibsonia
Benson, Stuart Wells III *lawyer*

Gladwyne
Acton, David *lawyer*
Booth, Harold Waverly *lawyer, finance company executive*

Glenshaw
Vogrin, Joseph Edward III *lawyer*

Glenside
Mermelstein, Jules Joshua *lawyer, educator, commissioner*

Greensburg
Demosky, Lou Anne *lawyer*
Gounley, Dennis Joseph *lawyer*

Harrisburg
Adams, Barbara *lawyer*
Angino, Richard Carmen *lawyer*
Diehm, James Warren *lawyer, educator*
Fine, David R. *lawyer*
Fontana, Mark Allan *lawyer*
Gornish, Gerald *lawyer*
Kane, Yvette *lawyer, judge*
Kelly, Robert Edward, Jr. *lawyer*
Lappas, Spero Thomas *lawyer*
Meilton, Sandra L. *lawyer*
Sheldon, J. Michael *lawyer, educator*
Sullivan, John Cornelius, Jr. *lawyer*
Warshaw, Allen Charles *lawyer*
West, James Joseph *lawyer*
Weston, R. Timothy *lawyer, government administrator*

Haverford
Brown, William Hill III *lawyer*
Palmer, Richard Ware *retired lawyer*
Stiller, Jennifer A. *lawyer*
Stroud, James Stanley *retired lawyer*

Hershey
Snyder, Burton Harold *lawyer*

Horsham
Best, Franklin Luther, Jr. *lawyer*

Huntingdon Valley
Krzyzanowski, Richard L. *lawyer*

Jenkintown
Bales, John Foster III *retired lawyer*

Johnstown
Kaharick, Jerome John *lawyer*

Kennett Square
Conard, Alfred Fletcher *legal educator*

King Of Prussia
Gilbert, Bruce Rits *lawyer*

Lake Harmony
Polansky, Larry Paul *legal association administrator*

Lancaster
Burkholder, Michele Stawinski *lawyer*
Nast, Dianne Martha *lawyer*
Rigas, John Nicholas *lawyer*
Zimmerman, Donald Patrick *lawyer*

Lansdale
Geiger, Alexander *lawyer*

Latrobe
Greenfield, David W. *lawyer*

Lemoyne
Stewart, Richard Williams *lawyer*

Lewisburg
Fernsler, John Paul *lawyer*

Lewistown
Levin, Allen Joseph *lawyer*

Malvern
Cameron, John Clifford *lawyer, health science association administrator*
Dohan, Andrew H. *lawyer*

Mc Keesport
Kessler, Steven Fisher *lawyer*
Micale, Frank Jude *lawyer*

Media
Durham, James W. *lawyer*
Emerson, Sterling Jonathan *lawyer*

Mendenhall
Reinert, Norbert Frederick *lawyer, retired chemicals executive*

Moon Township
Alstadt, Lynn Jeffery *lawyer*

Murrysville
Creenan, James William *lawyer*
Ferri, Karen Lynn *lawyer*

New Kensington
Wallace, Henry Jared, Jr. *lawyer*

Newtown
Godwin, Robert Anthony *lawyer*

Newtown Square
Bower, Ward Alan *management consultant, lawyer*
Kendall, Robert Louis, Jr. *lawyer*

Norristown
Aman, George Matthias III *lawyer*

Philadelphia
Abramowitz, Robert Leslie *lawyer*
Adamany, David Walter *law and political science educator, former academic administrator*
Adams, Jonathan Craig *business immigration attorney*
Ammon, Gary D. *lawyer*
Anders, Jerrold P. *lawyer*
Angel, Marina *law educator*
Auten, David Charles *lawyer*
Auten, Donald R. *lawyer*
Barbour, John A. (Jack Barbour) *lawyer*
Barnett, Bonnie Allyn *lawyer*
Barrett, John J(ames), Jr. *lawyer*
Beck, Stuart Edwin *lawyer*
Berger, Harold *lawyer, electrical engineer*
Berger, Lawrence Howard *lawyer*
Berkley, Emily Carolan *lawyer*
Bernard, John Marley *lawyer, educator*
Bernheim, Daniel S. *lawyer*
Bershad, Jack R. *retired lawyer*
Bersoff, Donald Neil *lawyer, psychologist, educator*
Black, Allen Decatur *lawyer*
Black, Creed C., Jr. *lawyer*
Blume, Fred *lawyer*
Bogdanoff, Charles Jay *lawyer*
Boggia, Eugene Stephen *lawyer*
Bogutz, Jerome Edwin *lawyer, educator*
Bonovitz, Sheldon Michael *lawyer*
Boss, Amelia Helen *lawyer, educator*
Bovaird, Brendan Peter *lawyer*
Bressler, Barry E. *lawyer*
Bricknell, Sarah M. *lawyer*
Briscoe, Jack Clayton *lawyer*
Brookman, Marc D. *lawyer*
Browne, Stanhope Stryker *lawyer*
Buccino, Ernest John, Jr. *lawyer*
Buchholz, Carl M. *lawyer*
Budin, Beverly R. *lawyer*
Burbank, Stephen Bradner *law educator*
Calvert, Jay H., Jr. *lawyer*
Casper, Charles B. *lawyer*
Chang, Howard Fenghau *law educator, consultant*
Cherken, Harry Sarkis, Jr. *lawyer*
Clark, Peter S., II, *lawyer*
Clark, William H., Jr. *lawyer*
Clauss, Peter Otto *lawyer*
Coleman, Robert J. *lawyer*
Collings, Robert L. *lawyer*
Comisky, Hope A. *lawyer*

Connolly, Colm F. *lawyer, former prosecutor*
Cooney, J(ohn) Gordon, Jr. *lawyer*
Cooper, Frank G. *lawyer*
Cox, Roger Frazier *lawyer*
Coyne, Charles Cole *lawyer*
Cramer, Harold *lawyer*
Crawford, James Douglas *lawyer*
Cross, Milton H. *lawyer*
Damsgaard, Kell Marsh *lawyer*
D'Angelo, Christopher Scott *lawyer*
DeBunda, Salvatore Michael *lawyer*
Del Raso, Joseph Vincent *lawyer*
Devlin, John Gerard *lawyer, writer*
Diaz, Nelson A. *lawyer*
Diaz, Romulo L., Jr. *lawyer*
Donner, Henry Jay *lawyer*
Donohue, James J. *lawyer*
Donohue, John Patrick *lawyer*
Dorfman, John Charles *lawyer*
Dougherty, Brian James *lawyer*
Drake, William Frank, Jr. *lawyer*
Efstratiades, Anastasius *lawyer*
Elliott, Homer Lee *lawyer*
Esser, Carl Eric *lawyer*
Fala, Herman Camillo *lawyer*
Fickler, Arlene *lawyer*
Fiebach, H. Robert *lawyer*
Finkelstein, Joseph Simon *lawyer*
Flanagan, Joseph Patrick, Jr. *retired lawyer*
Floyd, Michael O'S. *retired lawyer*
Fox, Richard L. *lawyer*
Frank, George Andrew *lawyer*
Fritton, Karl Andrew *lawyer*
Gallagher, William T. *lawyer, manufacturing executive*
Garcia, Rudolph *lawyer*
Genkin, Barry Howard *lawyer*
Gilberg, Kenneth Roy *lawyer*
Giles, James T. *lawyer, retired federal judge*
Girard-diCarlo, David Franklin *lawyer, former ambassador*
Goldberg, Joseph *lawyer*
Goldberg, Richard Robert *lawyer*
Goodman, Stephen Murry *lawyer*
Gough, John Francis *lawyer*
Grant, M. Duncan *lawyer*
Greenberg, Stephen Jay *lawyer*
Grove, David Lavan *lawyer*
Haimm, Neil Keith *lawyer*
Haines, Clifford E. *lawyer*
Haley, Vincent Peter *retired lawyer*
Hamilton, Stephen David Derwent *lawyer*
Harkins, John Graham, Jr. *lawyer*
Harmelin, Stephen Joseph *lawyer*
Harvey, Gregory Merrill *lawyer*
Henrich, William Joseph, Jr. *lawyer*
Hoelscher, Robert James *lawyer*
Howard, David Miles *lawyer*
Hunter, James Austen, Jr. *lawyer*
Jones, Robert Jeffries *lawyer*
Kahn, James Robert *lawyer*
Kaier, Edward John *lawyer*
Kapur, Drew K. *lawyer*
Keene, John Clark *lawyer, educator*
Kessler, Alan Craig *lawyer*
Klasko, Herbert Ronald *lawyer, educator, writer*
Klein, Howard Bruce *lawyer, educator*
Kline, Thomas Richard *lawyer*
Knoll, Michael Steven *law educator*
Koc, Lorraine K. *lawyer*
Kopp, Charles Gilbert *lawyer*
Kormes, John Winston *lawyer*
Kraeutler, Eric *lawyer*
Kupperman, Louis Brandeis *lawyer*
LaCheen, Stephen Robert *lawyer*
Laguzzi, Carina *lawyer*
Lasher, Lori L. *lawyer*
Lavorgna, Gregory Joseph *lawyer*
Ledwith, John Francis *lawyer*
Leech, Noyes Elwood *lawyer, educator*
Leonard, Thomas *lawyer*
Lesser, Bruce R. *lawyer*
Levin, Murray Simon *lawyer*
Levy, Michael L. *lawyer*
Lewis, John Hardy, Jr. *lawyer*
Libonati, Michael Ernest *law educator, writer*
Liebenberg, Roberta D. *lawyer*
Lipman, Frederick D. *lawyer, educator, writer*
Loder, David E. *lawyer*
Lombard, John James, Jr. *lawyer, writer*
Lonergan, Robert A. *lawyer, chemicals executive*
Magargee, W(illiam) Scott III *lawyer*
Malloy, Michael Patrick *lawyer*
Mann, Theodore R. *lawyer*
Mathes, Stephen Jon *lawyer*
Mattoon, Peter Mills *lawyer*
McCabe, James J. *lawyer*
McConnell, Stephen John *lawyer*
McHugh, James Joseph, Jr. *lawyer*
McKeever, John Eugene *lawyer*
McQuiston, Robert Earl *lawyer*
Meigs, John Forsyth *lawyer*
Meyer, Dianne A. *lawyer*
Milbourne, Walter Robertson *lawyer*
Miller, Henry Franklin *lawyer*
Mistrano, Joseph *lawyer*
Momjian, Arthur James *lawyer*
Morris, Roland *lawyer*
Moss, Arthur Henshey *lawyer*
Mustokoff, Michael Mark *lawyer*
Newman, Sandra Schultz *lawyer, former state supreme court justice*
Oley, Jodi Dyan *lawyer*
Ominsky, Harris *lawyer*
Pagliaro, James Domenic *lawyer*
Parks, J. Manly *lawyer*
Parry, William DeWitt *lawyer and speech-language pathologist, speech pathology/audiology services professional*
Petrelli, Thomas J. *lawyer*
Petren, Carol Ann *lawyer, insurance company executive*
Pokotilow, Manny David *lawyer, educator*
Pomerantz, Nora E. *lawyer*
Price, Robert Stanley *lawyer*
Promislo, Daniel *lawyer, small business owner*
Putnam, Alfred W., Jr. *lawyer*
Rachofsky, David J. *lawyer*
Rackow, Julian Paul *lawyer*
Ramsey, Natalie D. *lawyer*
Raymond, Fred Douglas III *lawyer*
Redeker, James Russell *lawyer*
Reed, Michael Haywood *lawyer*
Reich, Abraham Charles *lawyer*
Reinstein, Robert J. *law educator, former dean*
Reiss, John Barlow *lawyer*
Reiter, Joseph Henry *lawyer, retired judge*
Reitz, Curtis Randall *lawyer, educator*
Roberts, Carl Geoffrey *lawyer*
Rosenbloom, Morey Stephen *lawyer*
Rosenstein, James Alfred *lawyer, mediator, negotiation facilitator*
Ross, Daniel R. *lawyer*
Russakoff, Nina L. *lawyer*
Samuel, Ralph David *lawyer*
Satinsky, Barnett *lawyer*
Scher, Howard Dennis *lawyer*
Schmuhl, Thomas Roeger *lawyer*
Schorling, William Harrison *lawyer*
Segal, Jonathan A. *lawyer*
Servodidio, Thomas Gerard *lawyer*
Shay, Kathleen M. *lawyer*
Sheils, Denis Francis *lawyer*
Shestack, Jerome Joseph *lawyer*
Siegel, Bernard L. *lawyer*
Sigman, Scott P. *lawyer*
Simpson, Colleen Healy *lawyer*
Smith, John Francis III *lawyer*
Solano, Carl Anthony *lawyer*
Soroko, John J. *lawyer*
Spaeth, Edmund Benjamin, Jr. *retired lawyer, retired law educator, former judge*
Spolan, Harmon Samuel *lawyer*
Steinberg, Robert Philip *lawyer*
Stock, William August *lawyer*
Stone, Antoinette R. *lawyer*
Strasbaugh, Wayne Ralph *lawyer*
Strickler, Matthew M. *lawyer*
Sykes, David Terrence *lawyer*
Taney, Francis Xavier, Jr. *lawyer*
Taylor, Matthew A. *lawyer*
Toomey, David Charles *lawyer*
Tumola, Thomas Joseph *lawyer*
Vaira, Peter Francis *lawyer*
Virelli, Louis James, Jr. *lawyer*
Vogel, Warren *lawyer*
Wajert, Sean Peter *lawyer*
Webb, William Yerick *lawyer*
Weisberg, Morris L. *retired lawyer*
Whiteside, William Anthony, Jr. *retired lawyer*
Williams, R. Seth *lawyer*
Wittels, Barnaby Caesar *lawyer, writer*
Wolff, Deborah H(orowitz) *lawyer*
Wright, Minturn Tatum III *retired lawyer*

Pittsburgh
Albert, Lorrie Kay *lawyer*
Allen, Rachel Lorey *lawyer*
Aronson, Mark Berne *retired lawyer, advocate*
Baldwin, Cynthia Ackron *lawyer, former state supreme court justice*
Basinski, Anthony Joseph *lawyer*
Beck, Paul A. *lawyer*
Bissoon, Cathy *lawyer*
Bobby, Theodore N. *lawyer, food products executive*
Booker, Daniel I. *lawyer*
Boswell, William Paret *lawyer*
Brown, James Benton *lawyer*
Brownlee, David A. *lawyer*
Buchanan, Mary Beth *prosecutor*
Candris, Laura A. *lawyer, mediator*
Cheever, George Martin *lawyer*
Cohen, Nelson P. *prosecutor*
Colen, Frederick Haas *lawyer*
Coney, Aims C., Jr. *lawyer, labor-management negotiator*
Connors, Eugene Kenneth *lawyer, educator*
Cowan, Barton Zalman *lawyer*
Daniel, Robert Michael *lawyer*
Davis, Lewis U., Jr. *lawyer*
Doty, Robert Walter *lawyer*
Dugan, John F. *lawyer*
Ehrenwerth, David Harry *lawyer*
Fawcett, David B. III *lawyer*
Fishman, Craig L. *lawyer*
Flechtner, Harry Marshal *law educator*
Flinn, Michael James *lawyer*
Frank, Ronald William *lawyer*
Frolik, Lawrence Anton *lawyer, educator, consultant*
Garraux, James D. *lawyer, metal products executive*
Goldberg, Mark Joel *lawyer*
Gormley, Kenneth Gerald *lawyer, educator*
Guadagnino, Frank T. *lawyer*
Gull, Dawn K. *lawyer*
Guter, Donald J. *law educator, former dean, career military officer*
Hackett, Mary J. *lawyer*
Hartman, Ronald G. *lawyer*
Hellman, Arthur David *law educator, consultant*
Hershey, Dale *lawyer, educator*
Hill, John Howard *retired lawyer*
Hitt, Leo N. *lawyer, educator*
Johnson, Robert Alan *lawyer*
Jones, Craig Ward *retired lawyer*
Jordan, Gregory B. *lawyer*
Kenrick, Charles William *lawyer*
Ketter, David Lee *lawyer*
King, Robert Alan *lawyer*
Knox, Charles Graham *lawyer*
Krasik, Carl *lawyer, bank executive*
Litman, Roslyn Margolis *lawyer*
Lovett, Robert G. *lawyer*
Lyncheski, John E. *lawyer*
Mahone, Glenn R. *lawyer*
McCartney, Robert Charles *retired lawyer*
McGhee, Carl Andrew *lawyer*
McGough, Walter Thomas, Jr. *lawyer*
McLaughlin, John Sherman *lawyer*
Meisel, Alan *law educator*
Murdoch, David Armor *lawyer*
Murdoch, Robert Whitten *lawyer*
Murrin, Regis Doubet *retired lawyer*
Mutterperl, William Charles *lawyer, corporate financial executive*
Norris, James Harold *lawyer*
Ober, Russell John, Jr. *lawyer*
O'Connor, Edward Gearing *lawyer*
Olson, Stephen M(ichael) *lawyer*
Parrette, Leslie Jackson *lawyer*
Phillips, Larry Edward *lawyer*
Plowman, Jack Wesley *lawyer*
Post, Peter David *lawyer*
Pudlin, Helen Pomerantz *lawyer*
Randolph, Robert DeWitt *lawyer*
Rao, Dittakavi N. *law librarian*
Raynovich, George, Jr. *retired lawyer*
Reed, W. Franklin *lawyer*
Restivo, James John, Jr. *lawyer*
Rice, Edward G. *lawyer*
Rosenberger, Bryan David *lawyer*
Scheinholtz, Leonard Louis *lawyer*
Schwendeman, Paul William *lawyer*
Segal, Frederick Leslie *lawyer*
Shuman, Joseph Duff *lawyer*
Silverman, Arnold Barry *lawyer*
Simon, Jacob Matthew *lawyer*
Sokulski, Gary A. *lawyer*
Stepanian, Steven Arvid, II, *lawyer, financial consultant*
Strader, James David *lawyer*
Stroyd, Arthur Heister, Jr. *lawyer*
Sweeney, Clayton Anthony *lawyer, business executive*
Tarasi, Louis Michael, Jr. *lawyer*
Thurman, Andrew Edward *lawyer*
Truitt, Gary R. *lawyer, insurance company executive*
Turner, Harry Woodruff *lawyer*
Ummer, James Walter *lawyer*
Van Kirk, Thomas L. *lawyer*
Vater, Charles J. *lawyer*
Veeder, Peter Greig *lawyer*
Waldo, Kurt *lawyer, metal products executive*
Walton, Jon David *lawyer, metal products executive*
Warman, Guy Lee *lawyer*
Wessels, Daniel L. *lawyer*
Wilkinson, James Allan *lawyer, healthcare executive*
Yang, Wesley *lawyer*

Plymouth Meeting
Mannino, Edward Francis *lawyer, educator*

Radnor
Gadsden, Christopher Henry *lawyer, educator*
Simon, David Frederick *lawyer*

Reading
Brightbill, David John *lawyer, former state legislator*

Saint Davids
Silverang, Kevin J. *lawyer*

Scranton
Carlson, Martin C. *prosecutor*
Gubbiotti, Christine M. *lawyer*
Haggerty, James Joseph *lawyer*

Solebury
Valentine, H. Jeffrey *legal association executive*

Southampton
Weil, Jeffrey George *lawyer*

Spring House
Rosoff, William A. *lawyer*

Springfield
Maclay, Donald Merle *retired lawyer*

Swarthmore
Elman, Gerry Jay *lawyer*

University Park
Marks, Jonathan H. *law & bioethics educator*
Whitehead, Paul *law educator, former labor union administrator*

Valley Forge
Knauss, Robert H. *lawyer, oil industry executive*

Verona
Demmler, John Henry *retired lawyer*

Villanova
Maule, James Edward *law educator*
Murphy, John Francis *law educator, consultant*

Warrington
Sigety, Elizabeth Donnem *lawyer*
Vosik, Wayne Gilbert *lawyer*

Washington
Lerner, William C. *lawyer*

Wayne
Binder, David Franklin *lawyer, writer*
Kalogredis, Vasilios J. *lawyer, healthcare management consultant*
Patterson, Scott David *lawyer*
Schoff, Dennis L. *lawyer, insurance company executive*
Silbey, Victoria E. *lawyer*
Wilson, Bruce Brighton *lawyer, retired transportation executive*

West Chester
Archbold, William Cornell, Jr. *lawyer*
Lamb, William H. *lawyer, former state supreme court justice*
Teti, Louis Nicholas *lawyer*

West Conshohocken
Odell, Herbert *lawyer*
Sager, Margaret E.W. *lawyer*
Teillon, Louis Pierre, Jr. *lawyer*

Williamsport
Carlucci, William Philip *lawyer*

York
Addison, Brian Michael *lawyer*
Buzzendore, Robert L. *lawyer*
Hoffmeyer, William Frederick *lawyer, educator*
Phillips, Amy J. *lawyer*
Schanbacher, David Charles *lawyer*

RHODE ISLAND

Barrington
Cicione, Giovanni D. *lawyer, political organization administrator*
Soutter, Thomas Douglas *retired lawyer*

Bristol
Bogus, Carl Thomas *law educator*

Cranston
Alston, Jametta O. *lawyer*

East Greenwich
Dence, Edward William, Jr. *retired lawyer, bank executive*

Jamestown
Parks, A. Lauriston *lawyer*

Little Compton
Caron, Wilfred Rene *retired lawyer*

Middletown
Gontarz, Christopher Stanley *lawyer*

Newport
McConnell, David Kelso *lawyer*

Providence
Berkelhammer, Robert Bruce *lawyer*
Bulman, John *lawyer*
Carlotti, Stephen Jon *lawyer*
Chlebus, Andrew J. *lawyer*
Conley, Patrick T. *lawyer, educator, history professor, real estate developer, writer*
Corrente, Robert Clark *lawyer, former prosecutor*
Curran, Joseph Patrick *lawyer*
Demaria, Gerald C. *lawyer*
Demopulos, Harold William *lawyer*
Fogarty, Edward Michael *lawyer*
Gasbarro, Pasco, Jr. *lawyer*
Jones, Lauren Evans *lawyer*
Kraemer, Michael Frederick *lawyer*
Ledbetter, Beverly Elizabeth *lawyer*
Lipsey, Howard Irwin *lawyer, educator*
Long, Beverly Glenn *retired lawyer*
McAndrew, Thomas Joseph *lawyer*
McCann, Gail Elizabeth *lawyer*
McElroy, Michael Robert *lawyer*
McIntyre, Jerry L. *lawyer*
O'Donnell, Terrence *lawyer, multi-industry company executive*
Olsen, Hans Peter *lawyer*
Pendergast, John Joseph III *lawyer*
Reilly, John B. *lawyer*
Roney, John M. *lawyer*
Sherman, Deming Eliot *lawyer*

Rockville
Walker, Howard Ernest *lawyer*

Westerly
Barnes, Chaplin Bradford *lawyer*

Woonsocket
Lankowsky, Zenon P. *lawyer, retail executive*
Roszkowski, Joseph John *lawyer*

SOUTH CAROLINA

Aiken
Rudnick, Irene Krugman *lawyer, educator, former state legislator*

Beaufort
Harvey, William Brantley, Jr. *lawyer, retired lieutenant governor*

Charleston
Cox, Walter Thompson III *lawyer, federal judge, educator*
Fenno, Edward Thorndike *lawyer*
Freer, Robert Elliott, Jr. *lawyer*
Grant, J. Kirkland *lawyer, educator*
Kahn, Ellis Irvin *lawyer*
Klaper, Martin Jay *lawyer*
McCullough, Ralph Clayton, II, *law educator*
Patrick, Charles William, Jr. *lawyer*
Robinson, Neil Cibley, Jr. *lawyer*
Scheman, L. Ronald *lawyer, author, bank executive*

Clemson
Cox, Headley Morris, Jr. *lawyer, educator*

Columbia
Blanton, Hoover Clarence *lawyer*
Day, Richard Earl *lawyer, educator*
Ellis, F. Earl, Jr. *lawyer*
Finkel, Gerald Michael *lawyer*
Foster, Robert Watson, Sr. *law educator*
Handel, Richard Craig *lawyer*
Harvey, Jonathan Matthew *lawyer*
Hubbard, William C. *lawyer*
Land, John Calhoun III *lawyer, South Carolina State Senator*
Matthews, Steve Allen *lawyer*
Mood, Francis P., Jr. *lawyer, utilities executive*
Nexsen, Julian Jacobs *lawyer*
Rebollo, Anthony Ernest *lawyer*
Strom, J. Preston, Jr. *lawyer*

Tate, Harold Simmons, Jr. *lawyer*
Wilkins, Walt (William Walter Wilkins III) *prosecutor*

Greenville
Ferguson, Donald Littlefield *retired lawyer*
Horton, James Wright *retired lawyer*
Hutson, Melvin Robert *lawyer*
Massey, Raymond David *lawyer*
Mauldin, John Inglis *public defender*
Oxner, George Dewey, Jr. *lawyer*
Phillips, Joseph Brantley, Jr. *lawyer*
Riley, Richard Wilson *lawyer, former United States Secretary of Education*
Sanders, Harvey Gibert, Jr. *lawyer*
Talley, Michael Frank *lawyer*
Walters, Johnnie McKeiver *lawyer*
White, Daniel Bowman *lawyer*
Wyche, Cyril Thomas *lawyer*
Wyche, Madison Baker III *lawyer*

Hilton Head Island
Becker, Karl Martin *retired lawyer*
Esposito, John Vincent *lawyer*
Hagoort, Thomas Henry *retired lawyer*
Rose, William Shepard, Jr. *lawyer*
Simons, Lawrence Brook *lawyer*

Mount Pleasant
Glenn, Edward Vernon Ferrell *lawyer, consultant*

Newberry
Partridge, William Franklin, Jr. *lawyer*

North Charleston
Heyward, Willie Bruce *lawyer, advocate*

Orangeburg
Barnwell, Charles Brison, Jr. *lawyer*

Walterboro
Cone, George Wallis *lawyer*

SOUTH DAKOTA

Britton
Farrar, Frank Leroy *lawyer, former governor*

Brookings
Beer, Betty Louise *lawyer*

Ipswich
Beck, Vaughn Peter *lawyer*

Parker
Zimmer, John Herman *lawyer*

Pierre
Gerdes, David Alan *lawyer*
Riter, Robert C., Jr. *lawyer*
Thompson, Charles Murray *lawyer*

Rapid City
Foye, Thomas Harold *lawyer*
Viken, Linda Lea Margaret *lawyer*

Sioux Falls
Jackley, Martin (Marty) J. *prosecutor*
Marshall, Mark F. *lawyer*
Tapken, Michelle G. *prosecutor*
Welk, Thomas John *lawyer*

TENNESSEE

Brentwood
Blackstock, James Fielding *lawyer*

Chattanooga
Bahner, Thomas Maxfield *lawyer*
Eason, Marcia Jean (Marcy Eason) *lawyer*

Clarksville
Smith, Gregory Dale *lawyer, judge*
Winters, David Douglas *lawyer*

Collierville
Springfield, James Francis *retired lawyer, banker*

Crossville
Marlow, James Allen *lawyer*

Fayetteville
Dickey, John Harwell *lawyer*

Franklin
Kohan, Betsy Burns *lawyer*
Rosen, William Warren *lawyer*
Seifert, Rachel A. *lawyer*

Gatlinburg
Catalfo, Alfred, Jr., (Alfio Catalfo) *lawyer*

Goodlettsville
Lanigan, Susan S. *lawyer*

Hendersonville
McCaleb, Joe Wallace *lawyer*

Johnson City
McKinney, Michael Merritt *law educator*

Kingsport
Lee, Theresa K. *lawyer, chemicals executive*

Knoxville
Coleman, Shannon DeShae *lawyer, educator*
Cone, James Christopher *lawyer*
Cremins, William Carroll *lawyer*
Dedrick, James Russell *prosecutor*
Doak, Samuel Clements *lawyer*
Giordano, Lawrence Francis *lawyer*
Hyman, Roger David *lawyer*
Jarvis, Howard E. *lawyer*
King, John K. *retired lawyer*
Ritchie, Albert *lawyer*
Vogel, Howard H. *lawyer*
Wheeler, John Watson *lawyer*
Worthington, Robert Fletcher, Jr. *lawyer*

Lenoir City
Sproul, Harvey Leonard *lawyer*

Mc Ewen
Williams, John Lee *lawyer*

Memphis
Bobango, John Allen *lawyer*
Buckner, Thomas Randolph *lawyer*
Carr, Oscar Clark III *lawyer*
Castle, Darrell *lawyer*
Clippard, Richard F. *prosecutor*
Cook, August Joseph *lawyer, accountant*
Goldsmith, Harry Louis *lawyer*
Haltom, William H. *lawyer*
Heiter, Matthew Stephen *lawyer*
Hermes, Clinton Daniel *lawyer*
Hymowitz, Steven *lawyer*
Jackson, Thomas Francis III *lawyer*
Johnson, Harry A. III *lawyer, finance company executive*
Kaput, Jim L. *lawyer*
Kustoff, David F. *lawyer, former prosecutor*
Ledbetter, Paul Mark *lawyer, writer*
Masterson, Kenneth Rhodes *lawyer*
Mc Creary, James Franklin *lawyer, mediator*
McDaniel, A. Stephen *lawyer*
Morgan, Colby Shannon, Jr. *lawyer*
Newman, Charles Forrest *lawyer*
Noel, Randall Deane *lawyer*
Norris, Charles Head *lawyer, manufacturing executive*
Pope, Thaddeus Mason *law educator*
Schuler, Walter E. *lawyer*
Scroggs, Larry Kenneth *lawyer, state legislator*
Smith, Maura Abeln *chief legal officer, paper company executive*
Steinhauer, Gillian *lawyer*
Tate, Stonewall Shepherd *lawyer*
Trammell, Bradley Ellis *lawyer*
Winchester, Richard Lee, Jr. *lawyer*

Murfreesboro
Heffington, Jack Grisham *lawyer, banker, insurance company executive, horse breeder*

Nashville
Barfield, Henry Lee, II, *lawyer*
Barnett, Bruce Edwin *lawyer*
Bass, James Orin, Sr. *lawyer*
Bostick, Charles Dent *retired lawyer*
Carlton, Thomas I., Jr. *lawyer, educator*
Cobb, Stephen A. *lawyer*
Conner, Lewis Homer, Jr. *lawyer*
Covington, Robert Newman *retired law educator*
Cowart, Richard G. *lawyer*
Ely, James Wallace, Jr. *law educator*
Griffith, James Leigh *lawyer*
Grimes, R. Dale *lawyer*
Hart, Richard Banner *lawyer*
King, David A. *lawyer*
Ledyard, Robins Heard *lawyer*
Lyon, Philip Kirkland *lawyer*
Madu, Leonard Ekwugha *lawyer, human rights advocate, columnist*
May, Joseph Leserman (Jack May) *retired lawyer*
Rubin, Edward *law educator, former dean*
Schreiber, Kurt Gilbert *lawyer*
Sims, Wilson *lawyer*
Summers, Paul G. *lawyer, former state attorney general*
Thomas, Robert Paige *lawyer*
Tuke, Robert Dudley *lawyer, educator*
Viscusi, W(illiam) Gregory Kip *law and economics educator*
Waterman, Robert A. *lawyer*
Yarbrough, Edward Meacham *prosecutor, lawyer*
Yuspeh, Alan Ralph *lawyer, health company executive*

Pulaski
Dunavant, Richard Hannah *prosecutor*

Sevierville
Waters, John B. *lawyer*

Soddy Daisy
Leitner, Paul Revere *lawyer*

Springfield
Wilks, Larry Dean *lawyer*

Trenton
Smith, Jeffrey A. *lawyer*

TEXAS

Abilene
Sartain, James Edward *lawyer*

Addison
Beck, Charles Wesley, II, *lawyer*

Amarillo
Burnette, Susan Lynn *lawyer*
Madden, Wales Hendrix, Jr. *retired lawyer*

Arlington
Goodman, Toby Ray *lawyer*
Harcrow, Edward Earl *lawyer*
Weekley, Frederick Clay, Jr. *lawyer*

Austin
Baker, Mark Bruce *lawyer, educator*
Blunck, Tedde *lawyer, engineering company executive*
Bobbitt, Philip Chase *law educator, writer*
Bode, Joyce Scruggs *lawyer*
Botsford, David L. *lawyer*
Buell, Samuel W. *law educator, lawyer*
Cannon, James Washington, Jr. *lawyer*
Clements, Jerry K. *lawyer*
Coleman, Gregory S. *lawyer*
Davis, Robert Larry *lawyer*
Demond, Walter Eugene *lawyer*
Dickie, Martha S. *lawyer*
Dyer, Cromwell Adair, Jr. *lawyer, legal association administrator*
Feazell, Vic *lawyer*
Gallerano, Andrew John *lawyer*
Golemon, Ronald Kinnan *lawyer*
Graglia, Lino Anthony *lawyer, educator*
Graham, Seldon Bain, Jr. *lawyer, engineer*
Gregory, Becky (Rebecca Ann Gregory) *lawyer, former prosecutor*
Greig, Brian Strother *lawyer*
Harrison, Richard Wayne *lawyer*
Helman, Stephen Jody *lawyer*
Hopkins, Bill Everitt *lawyer*
Hopkins, William Everitt *lawyer*
Hull, Robert Joe *lawyer*
Ikard, Frank Neville, Jr. *lawyer*
Jansen, Donald Orville *lawyer*
Jentz, Gaylord Adair *law educator*
Keys, Jerry Malcom *lawyer, educator*
Kirk, Terrence *lawyer*
Leiter, Brian R. *law and philosophy professor, writer*
Lochridge, Lloyd Pampell, Jr. *lawyer*
Lochridge, Patton G. *lawyer*
McDaniel, Myra Atwell *lawyer, former state official*
McKetta, John J. III *lawyer*
Morton, R. Steven *lawyer*
Moss, Bill Ralph *lawyer*
Moss, Logan Vansen *lawyer*
Mullenix, Linda Susan *law educator*
Nevola, Roger *lawyer*
Otto, Byron Leonard *retired lawyer, state agency administrator*
Pena, Richard *lawyer*
Richardson, James Michael *lawyer*
Roan, Forrest Calvin, Jr. *lawyer*
Rodnick, Amie Bowman *lawyer*
Rodriguez, Daniel B. *law educator*
Schuring, Elizabeth *lawyer*
Schwartz, Aaron Robert *lawyer, former state legislator*
Shapiro, David L. *lawyer*
Stephen, John Erle *lawyer, consultant*
Strauser, Robert Wayne *lawyer*
Sutton, John F., Jr. *lawyer, dean, educator*
Temple, Larry Eugene *lawyer*
Tottenham, Terry Oliver *lawyer*
Volk, William R. *lawyer*
Weddington, Sarah Ragle *lawyer, educator*
Weinberg, Louise *law educator, writer*
Weintraub, Russell Jay *lawyer, educator*
Westbrook, Jay Lawrence *law educator*
Wiese, William D. *lawyer*
Winters, Sam *lawyer*
Wood, Donald F. *lawyer*

Beaumont
Black, Robert Allen *lawyer*
Miller, Thomas Eugene *lawyer, writer*
Oxford, Hubert III *lawyer*
Scofield, Louis M., Jr. *lawyer*

Bellaire
Jacobus, Charles Joseph *lawyer, writer*

Brenham
Moorman, Richard Hal, IV, *lawyer*

Brownsville
Weisfeld, Sheldon *lawyer*

Brownwood
Bell, William Woodward *lawyer*

Bryan
Steelman, Frank (Frank Sitley) *lawyer*

Carrollton
Riggs, Arthur Jordy *retired lawyer*

Cleburne
MacLean, John Ronald *lawyer*

College Station
Godfrey, Cullen Michael *lawyer, academic administrator*

Corpus Christi
Branscomb, Harvie, Jr. *lawyer*
Klein, Melvyn Norman *lawyer, investment executive*
Leon, Rolando Luis *lawyer*
Potter, Allan L. *lawyer*
Stukenberg, Michael Wesley *lawyer*

Dallas
Acker, Rodney *lawyer*
Ackerman, Deborah *lawyer*
Adams, Carl David *lawyer*
Adams, Richard Lloyd *lawyer*
Anderson, Barbara McComas *lawyer*
Anderson, E. Karl *lawyer*
Ashley, George Edward *retired lawyer*
Beuttenmuller, Rudolf William *lawyer*
Bickel, John W., II, *lawyer*
Birkeland, Bryan Collier *lawyer*
Bliss, Robert Harms *lawyer*
Boone, Michael Mauldin *lawyer*
Boyd, Dan Stewart *lawyer*
Branson, Frank Leslie III *lawyer*
Brin, Royal Henry, Jr. *lawyer*
Bromberg, Alan Robert *lawyer, educator*
Bumpas, Stuart Maryman *lawyer*
Burke, William Temple, Jr. *lawyer*
Burns, Sandra *lawyer, educator*
Campbell, David *lawyer, utilities executive*
Cantrill, Thomas H. *lawyer*
Carpenter, Gordon Russell *retired lawyer, banker*
Case, Thomas Louis *lawyer*
Clancy, Denyse Finn *lawyer*
Coggins, Paul Edward, Jr. *lawyer*
Cowart, T(homas) David *lawyer*
Cowles, Jim E. *lawyer*
Crichton, Thomas, IV, *lawyer*
Davis, Joe A. *lawyer*
Dhillon, Uttam *lawyer, former federal agency administrator*
Doke, Marshall J., Jr. *lawyer*
Drapkin, Dennis B. *lawyer*
Dutton, Diana Cheryl *lawyer*
Dyess, Bobby Dale *lawyer*
Ellis, Alfred Wright (Al Ellis) *lawyer*
Ellis, James A., Jr. *lawyer*
Estep, Robert Lloyd *lawyer*
Everbach, Otto George *lawyer*
Falk, Robert Hardy *lawyer*
Fankhauser, Mark A. *lawyer*
Fanning, Barry Hedges *lawyer*
Feld, Alan David *lawyer*
Fenner, Suzan Ellen *lawyer*
Figari, Ernest Emil, Jr. *lawyer, educator*
Fijolek, Richard M. *lawyer*
Fillmore, Robert M. *lawyer*
Forshey, Michael S. *lawyer*
Freling, Richard Alan *lawyer*
Freytag, Sharon Nelson *lawyer*
Frisbie, Curtis Lynn, Jr. *lawyer*
Galvin, Charles O'Neill *retired law educator*
Gardner, Stephen Henry *lawyer*
Garner, Bryan Andrew *law educator, writer, consultant*
Gilchrist, Henry *lawyer*
Glendenning, Don Mark *lawyer*
Godwin, Donald Everett *lawyer*
Goodstein, Barnett Maurice *lawyer*
Goodwin, Stephen Arthur *lawyer*
Gores, Christopher Merrel *lawyer*
Gregory, Louis P. *lawyer, gas industry executive*
Hammond, Herbert J. *lawyer, arbitrator, mediator*
Hartt, Grover III *lawyer*
Helfand, Marcy Caren *lawyer*
Henkel, Kathryn Gundy *lawyer*
Hennessy, Daniel Kraft *lawyer*
Henry, Vic Houston *lawyer*
Hicks, Marion Lawrence, Jr., (Larry Hicks) *lawyer*
Hinshaw, Chester John *lawyer*
Hirschman, Karen L. *lawyer*
Hubach, Joseph F. *lawyer, electronics executive*
Huffman, Gregory Scott Combest *lawyer*
Hughes, Vester Thomas, Jr. *lawyer*
Humble, Monty Garfield *lawyer*
Hutchison, Ray Ray (E. Ray) *lawyer*
Irwin, Ivan, Jr. *lawyer*
Jayson, Melinda Gayle *lawyer*
Johnson, Madeleine Brinton *lawyer, air transportation executive*
Jordan, William Davis *lawyer*
Jung, Peter Michael *lawyer*
Keithley, Bradford Gene *lawyer*
Kemps, Steven J. *lawyer, food products executive*
Kennedy, Marc J. *lawyer*
Kent, David Charles *lawyer*
Kneese, Kyle Calvin *lawyer*
Kobdish, George Charles *lawyer*
Kohl, Kathleen Allison Barnhart Hughes *lawyer*
Kuhn, Willis Evan, II, *lawyer, mediator*
Lacy, John Ford *retired lawyer*
Lan, Donald Paul, Jr. *lawyer*
Lawson, Gary B. *lawyer*
Levin, Hervey Phillip *lawyer*
Lindley, Hamilton P. *lawyer*
Lowe, John Stanley *law educator*
Lowery, David J. *lawyer*
Makel, Larry A. *lawyer*
Mankoff, Ronald Morton *retired lawyer*
Manteuffel, Robert Lee *lawyer*
Maris, Stephen S. *lawyer, educator*
Martin, Boe Willis *lawyer*
Mason, Thomas P. *lawyer*
Massman, Richard Allan *lawyer*
McAtee, David Ray *lawyer*
McCurley, Mary Johanna *lawyer*
McDowell, John Henry, Jr. *lawyer*
Mc Elhaney, John Hess *lawyer*
McKnight, Joseph Webb *lawyer, educator, historian*
McNeil, Barry *lawyer*
McWilliams, Mike C. *lawyer*
Menges, John Kenneth, Jr. *lawyer*
Meyer, Ferdinand Charles, Jr. *lawyer*
Micciche, Daniel John *lawyer*
Mielke, Thomas J. *lawyer, health products executive*
Miers, Harriet Ellan *lawyer, former federal official*
Mighell, Kenneth John *lawyer*
Miller, Norman Richard *lawyer*
Miller, R. Terry *lawyer*
Montgomery, Will S. *lawyer*
Moore, Cheryl (Milkes) Jerome *lawyer*
Moore, Edward Warren *lawyer*
Moore, Stanley Ray *lawyer*
Mow, Robert Henry, Jr. *lawyer*
Mueller, Mark Christopher *lawyer*
Nichols, Henry Louis *retired lawyer*
Nolan, John Michael *lawyer*
O'Neil, Michelle May *lawyer*
Orwig, Matthew Dane *lawyer, former prosecutor*
Patterson, Joseph Redwine *retired lawyer*
Pennington, Karen Harder *lawyer*
Peterson, Edward Adrian *lawyer*
Peterson, Eric H. *lawyer*
Pew, John Glenn, Jr. *lawyer*
Phelan, Robin Eric *lawyer*
Pingree, Bruce Douglas *lawyer*
Pleasant, James Scott *lawyer*
Portman, Glenn Arthur *lawyer*
Powell, Michael Vance *lawyer*
Powley, Susan Elizabeth *lawyer*
Purnell, Maurice Eugene, Jr. *lawyer*
Raggio, Louise Ballerstedt *lawyer*
Raggio, Thomas Louis *lawyer*
Riddle, Michael Lee *lawyer*

Ringle, Brett Adelbert *lawyer, oil and gas industry executive, trustee*
Roberts, Harry Morris, Jr. *lawyer*
Rodgers, John Hunter *lawyer*
Roper, Richard B. III *lawyer, former prosecutor*
Ruff, Gary Kay *lawyer*
Schaeffler, Georg *lawyer, manufacturing executive*
Schreiber, Howard E. *lawyer*
Schreiber, Sally Ann *lawyer*
Selinger, Jerry Robin *lawyer*
Shepherd, Jon Glen *lawyer*
Simmons, Terry L. *lawyer*
Smith, Frank Tupper *lawyer*
Sostek, Bruce Steven *lawyer*
Stalcup, Joe Alan *retired lawyer, dean*
Steinberg, Lawrence Edward *lawyer*
Stinnett, Mark Allan *lawyer*
Stockard, James Alfred *lawyer*
Templin, Donald C. *lawyer*
Thomson, Basil Henry, Jr. *lawyer*
Thomson, Roger F. *lawyer*
Tomko, Edwin Joseph *lawyer*
True, Roy Joe *lawyer*
Tubb, James Clarence *lawyer*
Turley, Linda *lawyer*
Unterberg, Craig Scott *lawyer*
Veach, Robert Raymond, Jr. *lawyer*
Voyles, Robb Lawrence *lawyer*
Walkowiak, Vincent Steven *lawyer*
Wallace, Anderson, Jr. *lawyer, educator*
Wansbrough, Ann *legal assistant*
Warman, Lynnette R. *lawyer*
Watkins, Craig *prosecutor*
Wheatley, Seagal V. *lawyer, legal association administrator*
White, James Richard *lawyer*
Will, Clark Bradford *lawyer*
Willingham, Clark Suttles *lawyer*
Wilson, Claude Raymond, Jr. *lawyer*
Witte, Robert Jay *lawyer*
Wolin, Robert Everett *lawyer*
Woram, Brian J. *lawyer, construction executive*
Wortley, Michael D. *lawyer*
Wright, Alan *lawyer*
Yang, Emeline *lawyer*
Young, Barney Thornton *lawyer*
Zahn, Donald Jack *lawyer*

Denton
Gabriel, Eberhard John *lawyer, bank executive*
Lawhon, John III *lawyer, retired county official*

Dickinson
Neves, Kerry Lane *lawyer*

El Paso
Barfield, Lowry *lawyer*
Cross, Clinton Ferguson *lawyer*
Feuille, Richard Harlan *lawyer, director*
Gibson, Sidney Kay *retired lawyer*
Marshall, Richard Treeger *lawyer*

Ennis
Swanson, Wallace Martin *lawyer*

Euless
Paran, Mark Lloyd *retired lawyer*

Farmers Branch
Blachly, Jack Lee *lawyer*

Fort Worth
Berenson, William Keith *lawyer*
Brown, C. Harold *lawyer*
Brown, Richard Lee *lawyer*
Chalk, John Allen, Sr. *lawyer*
Dean, Beale *lawyer*
Dent, Edward Dwain *lawyer*
Elliott, Frank Wallace *lawyer, educator*
Frost, Edmund Bowen *lawyer*
Hall, Randy Jarvis *lawyer*
Harbour, Ted Ira *lawyer, construction executive*
Hart, John Clifton *lawyer*
Kelly, Raymond Boone III *lawyer*
McConnell, Michael Arthur *lawyer*
McDonald, Frank G. *lawyer, energy executive*
Munn, Cecil Edwin *lawyer*
Poole, David P. *lawyer, utilities executive*
Quinn, Francis Xavier *arbitrator, mediator, writer, law educator*
Reade, Kathleen Margaret *legal consultant, author, educator*
Searcy, Marshall Mayes, Jr. *lawyer*
Tillman, Massie Monroe *mediator, arbitrator, art gallery owner, retired judge*
Wallace, R. H., Jr. *lawyer*
Watson, Robert Francis *lawyer*
Whitehead, Elizabeth Phillips *lawyer*

Frisco
Bell, Haney Hardy III *lawyer*

Galveston
Salch, Steven Charles *lawyer, mediator, arbitrator*

Garland
Irby, Holt *lawyer*

Georgetown
Bryce, William Delf *lawyer*

Graham
Richie, Boyd Lynn *lawyer, political organization administrator*

Grapevine
Franks, Jon Michael *lawyer, mediator*

Harlingen
Pope, William L. *lawyer, judge*

Heath
Kolodey, Fred James *lawyer*

Houston
Adrogué, Sofia *lawyer*
Ajamie, Thomas Robert *lawyer*
Allender, John Roland *lawyer*
Amdur, Arthur R. *lawyer*
Anani, Tarig *lawyer, software company executive*
Asmus, David F. *lawyer*
Asselin, Heather E. *lawyer*
Atlas, Scott J. *lawyer*
Bachmann, Richard H. *lawyer, energy executive*
Baker, C. Mark *lawyer*
Baker, James Addison, III, (Jim Baker) *lawyer, former United States Secretary of State*
Baker, Robert W. *lawyer*
Ballanfant, Richard Burton *lawyer*
Bargfrede, James Allen *lawyer*
Barnett, Edward William *lawyer*
Bechtol, J. Currie *lawyer, oil industry executive*
Beirne, Martin Douglas *lawyer*
Bellatti, Lawrence Lee *lawyer*
Berg, David Howard *lawyer*
Berg, Geoffrey A. *lawyer*
Biery, Evelyn Hudson *lawyer*
Bilger, Bruce R. *lawyer*
Blackshear, A. T., Jr. *lawyer*
Bland, John Lloyd *lawyer*
Bluestein, Edwin A., Jr. *lawyer*
Boulware, Margaret A. *lawyer*
Brann, Richard R. *lawyer*
Brinson, Gay Creswell, Jr. *retired lawyer*
Buckingham, Edwin John III *lawyer*
Buckley, Vincent H. *lawyer*
Burch, Voris Reagan *mediator, arbitrator, retired lawyer*
Burgert, David Lee *lawyer*
Bux, William John *lawyer*
Caddy, Michael Douglas *lawyer*
Caldwell, Garnett Ernest *lawyer*
Caldwell, Richard H. *lawyer*
Caldwell, Rodney Kent *lawyer*
Caligur, Matthew W. *lawyer*
Campbell, Bert Louis *lawyer, arbitrator, mediator*
Carr, Edward A. *lawyer*
Carroll, James Vincent III *lawyer*
Carter, John Francis, II, *lawyer*
Carter, John Loyd *lawyer*
Caudill, William Howard *lawyer*
Cenatiempo, Michael J. *lawyer*
Chandler, Richard E., Jr. *lawyer*
Chapman, Cynthia B. *lawyer*
Chavez, J. Anthony *lawyer*
Chung, Paul W. *lawyer, energy executive*
Clarke, Robert Logan *lawyer*
Clore, Lawrence Hubert *lawyer*
Coghlan, Kelly Jack *lawyer*
Colbert, Kevin LeRoy *lawyer*
Coley, Randolph C. *lawyer*
Collings, Chris D. *lawyer*
Cook, Eugene Augustus *lawyer*
Corken, Heather Marie *lawyer*
Cornelison, Albert Otto, Jr., (Bert Cornelison) *lawyer, oil industry executive*
Cox, James Talley *lawyer*
Crain, Alan Rau, Jr. *lawyer, oil industry executive*
Crinion, Gregory Paul *lawyer*
Cruz, R. Ted (R. Edward Cruz) *lawyer*
Cunningham, Tom Alan *lawyer*
Dameris, Thad Thano *lawyer*
Day, Jonathan S. *lawyer*
DeGuerin, Dick *lawyer*
Del Valle, Teresa Jones *lawyer*
DeMent, James Alderson, Jr. *lawyer*
Dillard, Michael E. *lawyer*
Dillard, Stephen C. *lawyer*
Douglas, James Matthew *law educator, dean*
Dula, Arthur McKee III *lawyer, aerospace transportation executive*
Eiland, Gary Wayne *lawyer*
Engerrand, Kenneth G. *lawyer, educator*
Eubank, J. Thomas *lawyer*
Farenthold, Frances Tarlton *lawyer*
Farley, Andrew D. *lawyer, construction executive*
Farner, Wendy Mineau *lawyer*
Farnsworth, T. Brooke *lawyer*
Fernandes, Edward F. *lawyer*
Ford, Thomas W., Jr. *lawyer*
Foster, Charles Crawford *lawyer, educator*
Fullenweider, Donn Charles *lawyer*
Gagnon, Stewart Walter *lawyer*
Galvin, Kerry A. *lawyer, chemicals executive*
Gerachis, George Matthew *lawyer*
Gibson, Rex Hilton *lawyer*
Gonzalez, Raed *lawyer*
Goodman, Barry Michael *lawyer*
Graving, Richard John *law educator*
Gray, Robert F., Jr. *lawyer*
Gunter, Joseph Clifford III *lawyer*
Gutheinz, Stephanie Anne *legal assistant, musician*
Hall, Charles Washington *lawyer*
Hamel, Douglas E. *lawyer*
Hardin, Rusty (Russell Hardin Jr.) *lawyer*
Harper, A(lfred) J(ohn), II, *lawyer*
Harrell, Charles E. *lawyer*
Harrington, Bruce Michael *lawyer, investor*
Harvin, David Tarleton *lawyer*
Hawes, Clay Erik *lawyer*
Haynes, Richard (Racehorse Haynes) *lawyer*
Heeg, Peggy A. *lawyer, former gas industry executive*
Heinrich, Randall Wayne *lawyer*
Hewitt, Lester L. *lawyer*
Hinton, Paula Weems *lawyer*
Hlavinka, Paul Thomas *lawyer*
Hocker, Wesley Hardy *lawyer*
Hollyfield, John Scoggins *lawyer*
Holstead, John Burnham *retired lawyer*
Hoyt, Mont Powell *lawyer*
Hudson, Franklin *lawyer, real estate developer*
Hudspeth, Chalmers Mac *lawyer, educator*
Hunsaker, Barry, Jr. *lawyer*
Ivey, Jack Todd *lawyer*
Jamail, Joseph Dahr, Jr. *lawyer*
Jeske, Charles Matthew *lawyer*
Jines, Michael L. *lawyer, energy executive*
Jones, Frank Griffith *lawyer*
Jordan, Charles Milton *lawyer*
Jordan, W. Carl *lawyer*
Kay, Joel Phillip *lawyer*
Kelly, Hugh Rice *lawyer, retired energy executive*
Ketchand, Robert Lee *lawyer*
Knobloch, Charles Saron *lawyer, geophysicist, computer scientist, inventor*
Koenig, Rodney Curtis *lawyer, rancher*
Kratochvil, L(ouis) Glen *lawyer*
Krebs, Arno William, Jr. *lawyer*
Krieger, Paul Edward *lawyer*
LaFuze, William L. *lawyer*
Lake, Kathleen Cooper *lawyer*
Lanier, W. Mark *lawyer*
Lannie, Paul Anthony *lawyer, energy executive*
Larkin, Lee Roy *retired lawyer*
Lassetter, Scott D. *lawyer*
Lemmer, William C. *lawyer*
Lewis, Kevin Paul *lawyer*
Listengart, Joseph *lawyer, energy executive*
Looser, William Gregory *lawyer*
Lopez, David Tiburcio *lawyer, arbitrator, mediator, educator*
Lott, Marley *lawyer*
Love, Scott Anthony *lawyer*
Lynch, John F. *lawyer*
Marston, Edgar Jean III *lawyer*
Martin, J. Clark *lawyer*
Martin, Paul Edward *lawyer*
Mason, Dwayne L. *lawyer*
Massad, Stephen Albert *lawyer*
Masters, Claude Bivin *lawyer*
Mattox, Sharon M. *lawyer*
McCreary, Frank E. III *retired lawyer*
McDaniel, Jarrel Dave *lawyer*
McFall, Donald Beury *lawyer*
McInnis, Richard Kavin *lawyer*
McLeod, Chanse L. *lawyer*
McMahon, Catherine Driscoll *lawyer*
McQuaid, Janet *lawyer*
Melton, Stephen Reid *lawyer*
Merel, Gail *lawyer*
Miller, Barry Rixmann *lawyer*
Milliron, Nathan Joseph *lawyer*
Moehlman, Michael Scott *lawyer*
Moncure, John Lewis *lawyer*
Moore, Tim *lawyer*
Murphy, Ewell Edward, Jr. *lawyer*
Nations, Howard Lynn *lawyer*
Nelson, Joelle Grace Kenney *lawyer*
Niebruegge, Michael E. *lawyer*
Nolen, Roy Lemuel *retired lawyer*
O'Brien, Eva Fromm *lawyer*
Oldham, Darius Dudley *lawyer*
O'Quinn, John M. *lawyer*
Oshman, Gene Jay *lawyer*
Osterberg, Edward Charles, Jr. *lawyer*
O'Toole, Austin Martin *lawyer, mediator, arbitrator*
Partridge, Scott Francis *lawyer*
Pate, Stephen Patrick *lawyer*
Perich, Thomas J. *lawyer*
Pierce, Frank Powell *lawyer, judge*
Plaeger, Frederick Joseph, II, *lawyer*
Porter, Thomas William III *lawyer*
Ramsey, Michael W. *lawyer*
Ray, Hugh Massey, Jr. *lawyer*
Ray, Hugh Massey III *lawyer*
Reasoner, Harry Max *lawyer*
Rettig, Dwight W. *lawyer*
Ripley, Charlene A. *lawyer*
Roach, Robert Michael, Jr., (Randy Roach) *lawyer*
Rommel, A. Ross, Jr. *lawyer*
Rowland, Robert Alexander III *lawyer*
Rozzell, Scott Ellis *lawyer, energy executive*
Rustay, Jennifer Beth *lawyer*
Ryan, Jason Michael *lawyer*
Ryan, Stephen M. *lawyer*
Ryan, Vince *lawyer*
Sales, James Bohus *lawyer*
Sanders, Joseph *law educator*
Saunders, Charles Albert *lawyer*
Schechter, Arthur Louis *lawyer*
Schick, Robert Michael *lawyer*
Schwartz, Charles Walter *lawyer*
Schwartzel, Charles Boone *lawyer*
Schwind, William F., Jr. *lawyer, oil industry executive*
Seale, Robert Arthur *lawyer*
Secrest, George McCall, Jr., (Mac) *lawyer*
Shaddock, Carroll Sidney *lawyer*
Shannon, Margaret Barrett *lawyer*
Shouse, August Edward *lawyer*
Silva, Eugene Joseph *lawyer*
Sing, William Bender *lawyer*
Smith, Alison Leigh *lawyer*
Smith, E. Ashley *lawyer, insurance company executive*
Sonfield, Robert Leon, Jr. *lawyer*
Spalding, Andrew Freeman *lawyer*
Stewart, Pamela L. *lawyer*
Still, Charles Henry, Sr. *lawyer*
Stradley, William Jackson *lawyer*
Streng, William Paul *lawyer, educator*
Stryker, Steven Charles *lawyer*
Sullivan, John F. III *lawyer*
Sunosky, James T. *lawyer*
Susman, Stephen Daily *lawyer*
Sutton, Neal S. *lawyer*
Swan, Michael K. *lawyer*
Sydow, Michael David, Sr. *executive lawyer*
Szalkowski, Charles C. *lawyer*
Tartt, Blake *lawyer*
Thomas, Byron Andrew *lawyer*
Totten, Patricia A. *lawyer*
Van Fleet, George Allan *lawyer*
Varner, David Eugene *lawyer*
Vogel, Jennifer L. *lawyer, air transportation executive*
Wagner, Leslie *lawyer*
Wall, Kenneth E., Jr. *lawyer*
Walton, Dan Gibson *lawyer*
Webb, Jack M. *lawyer*
Weber, Fredric Alan *lawyer*
Weiner, Sanford Alan *lawyer*
Wells, Benjamin Gladney *lawyer*
Welsh, H. Ronald *lawyer*
Westby, Timothy Scott *lawyer, researcher*
Whiting, Hugh Richard *lawyer*
Whittenburg, Justin M. *lawyer*
Wilde, William Key *lawyer*
Williams, Lowell Craig *lawyer, employee relations executive*
Williamson, Peter David *lawyer*
Wilson, David Vandiver, II, *lawyer*
Wittenbraker, Rick L. *lawyer, waste management executive*
Womack, Guy Lee *lawyer, military officer*
Wood, Michael W. *lawyer*
Worthington, William Albert III *lawyer*
Wray, Thomas Jefferson *lawyer*
Yeates, Marie R. *lawyer*
Yetter, R. Paul *lawyer*
Youngdahl, Jay Thomas *lawyer*
Zeigler, Ann dePender *lawyer*

Hunt
Gambrell, James Bruton III *lawyer, educator*

Huntsville
Vaughn, Michael S. *law educator*

Irving
Beach, Charles Addison *lawyer*
Hernandez, Carlos Manuel *lawyer*
LaSala, Stephen R. *lawyer, oil industry executive*
Sudbury, David Marshall *lawyer*

Katy
Guest, Floyd Emory, Jr. *lawyer*

Kilgore
Rorschach, Richard Gordon *lawyer*

Llano
Wallis, Olney Gray *lawyer*

Lockhart
Scudday, Roy George *lawyer*

Longview
Welge, Jack Herman, Jr. *lawyer*

Lubbock
Beyer, Gerry Wayne *lawyer, educator*
Moseley, Patricia Ann *lawyer*
Phelan, Marilyn Elizabeth *law educator*
Purdom, Thomas James *lawyer*

Lufkin
McFarland, Edward T. *lawyer*

Midland
Estes, Andrew Harper *lawyer*
MacDonald, Leland Lloyd *lawyer*
Meyers, Alan Hoge *lawyer*
Taylor, Nicholas C. *lawyer, state agency administrator, energy executive*

Missouri City
Hodges, Jot Holiver, Jr. *retired lawyer, corporate financial executive*

New Braunfels
Benfield, Marion Wilson, Jr. *law educator*

North Richland Hills
Reed, Glenn W. *lawyer*

Odonnell
Saleh, John *lawyer*

Orange
Coratti, John Edward *judicial clerk*

Plano
Altabef, Peter Anthony *lawyer*
Bober, Joanne L. *lawyer, retail executive*
Dhillon, Janet L. *lawyer, retail executive*
Gordon, Storrow Moss *lawyer, information technology executive*
Markey, James Kevin *lawyer*
Mondul, Donald David *patent lawyer*

Pottsboro
Thomas, Ann Van Wynen *retired law educator*

Richardson
Conkel, Robert Dale *lawyer, consultant*
Martin, Richard Kelley *lawyer*

Round Rock
Tu, Lawrence P. *lawyer, computer company executive*

San Antonio
Armstrong, William Tucker III *lawyer*
Aycock, James J. *lawyer*
Barton, James Cary *lawyer*
Bennett, Steven Alan *lawyer, insurance company executive*
Bowers, Kim *lawyer, energy executive*
Cicconi, James William *lawyer, telecommunications industry executive*
Diaz-Dennis, Patricia *lawyer, communications executive*
Golden, Stephen L. *lawyer*
Goldstein, Gerald H. *lawyer*
Hornberger, Ronald *lawyer*
Labenz-Hough, Marlene *administrator*
Levin, Andrew W. *lawyer, communications executive*
Moynihan, John Bignell *retired lawyer*
Parrish, Charles S. *lawyer, oil industry executive*
Perry, Robert Michael *lawyer, consultant, rancher*
Pitluk, Ellen Eidelbach *lawyer, mediator*
Reams, Bernard Dinsmore, Jr. *law educator*
Reser, Don Clayton *lawyer*
Schlueter, David Arnold *law educator*
Schmutz, John Francis *lawyer*
Spears, Sally *lawyer*

Steen, John Thomas, Jr. *lawyer*

Spearman
Jarvis, Billy Britt *lawyer*

Spring
Farley, Andrew Newell *lawyer, consultant*

Sugar Land
Gross, Edmund Samuel *lawyer, oil industry executive*
Hitchcock, Bion Earl *lawyer*
Rider, Roger Alan *lawyer*

Temple
Pickle, Jerry Richard *lawyer*

Texarkana
Peck, Leonard Warren, Jr. *lawyer*

The Woodlands
Benedetto, Anthony R. *religious mediator*
Hagerman, John David *lawyer, investment advisor*
Reeves, Robert K. *lawyer, oil industry executive*

Trinidad
Conant, Allah B., Jr. *lawyer*

Tyler
Alworth, Charles Wesley *lawyer, engineer*
Ellis, Donald Lee *lawyer*
Patterson, Donald Ross *lawyer, educator*

Waco
Mackenzie, Charles Alfred *lawyer*
Mc Swain, Angus Stewart, Jr. *retired law educator*
Smith, Cullen *lawyer*

Weatherford
King, Douglas Michael *lawyer, accountant*

Wichita Falls
Briley, Stephen Morris *lawyer*
Walker, Randall Wayne *lawyer*

Wimberley
Brinsmade, Lyon Louis *retired lawyer*

Yoakum
Williams, Walter Waylon *lawyer, agricultural products supplier*

UTAH

Logan
Daines, N. George *lawyer*
West, Stephen Allan *lawyer*

Manti
Petersen, Benton Lauritz *paralegal*

Orem
Schofield, Anthony Wayne *lawyer*

Provo
Ashworth, Brent Ferrin *lawyer*
Hill, Richard Lee *lawyer*
Thomas, David Albert *law educator, director*

Saint George
Terry, Gary A. *lawyer, director, former trade association executive*

Salt Lake City
Adams, Joseph Keith *lawyer*
Barusch, Lawrence Roos *lawyer*
Baucom, Sidney George *lawyer*
Bendinger, Gary Frederick *lawyer*
Berman, Daniel Lewis *lawyer*
Bird, David R. *lawyer*
Blackburn, Michael Dale *lawyer, educator*
Bouley, Sara Elizabeth *lawyer*
Callister, Louis Henry, Jr. *lawyer*
Cassell, Paul George *law educator, former federal judge*
Christensen, Harold Graham *lawyer*
Christensen, Ray Richards *lawyer*
Cornaby, Kay Sterling *lawyer, retired state senator*
Curtis, D. Jay *lawyer*
Firmage, Edwin Brown *lawyer, educator*
Greenwood, David A. *lawyer*
Guiora, Amos Neuser *law educator*
Haslam, Dennis V. *lawyer, former professional sports team executive*
Jensen, Dallin W. *lawyer*
Jepperson, Thomas C. *lawyer*
Kirkham, John Spencer *lawyer, director*
McDermott, Kathleen E. *lawyer, corporate executive*
Mecham, Glenn Jefferson *lawyer, mayor*
Mooney, Jerome Henri *lawyer*
Moore, James R. *lawyer*
Nydegger, Rick D. *lawyer*
Scruggs, Samuel D. *lawyer, chemicals executive*
Sorenson, Stephen Jay *lawyer*
Thompson, Neil Daniel *retired lawyer*
Tolman, Brett L. *prosecutor*
Tomsic, Peggy A. *lawyer*
Zimmerman, Michael David *lawyer*

South Jordan
Larson, Bryan Alan *lawyer*

Vernal
Judd, Dennis L. *lawyer*

VERMONT

Brattleboro
Reid, David G. *lawyer*

Burlington
Berger, Ritchie Eric *lawyer*
Carleton, Ian P. *lawyer, former political organization administrator*
Coffin, Tristram J. *prosecutor*
Davis, Christopher Lee *lawyer*
Dinse, John Merrell *lawyer*
Frank, Joseph Elihu *lawyer*
Hoar, Samuel, Jr. *lawyer*
Montroll, Andrew H. *lawyer, councilman*

Lyndon Center
Downs, John Henry *lawyer*

Manchester
Eichel, Charles Richard *lawyer*

Montpelier
Diamond, M. Jerome *lawyer, retired state attorney general*
Guild, Alden *retired lawyer*
Saxman, Anna Esther *lawyer*

Newport
Pepyne, Edward Walter *lawyer, psychologist, educator*

Rutland
Crowley, Arthur Edward, Jr. *lawyer*

Saint Johnsbury
Gallagher, James C. *lawyer*
Marshall, John Henry *lawyer*

Shelburne
Canfield, Andrew Trotter *lawyer, writer*
Errecart, Joyce *lawyer, former state legislator*

South Royalton
Goodenough, Oliver Ramsdell *lawyer, educator*
Wroth, L(awrence) Kinvin *law educator*

Stowe
Whiteman, Joseph David *retired lawyer, manufacturing company executive*

Warren
Raphael, Albert Ash, Jr. *retired lawyer*

White River Junction
Kainen, Michael Roland *lawyer, state representative*

Woodstock
Zonay, Thomas A. *lawyer*

VIRGINIA

Alexandria
Buechner, Jack W(illiam) *lawyer, consultant, Former United States Representative, Missouri, educational association administrator*
Burch, John Thomas, Jr. *lawyer*
Drennan, Joseph Peter *lawyer*
Georges, Peter John *lawyer*
Goolrick, Robert Mason *legal consultant*
Harrison, Marion Edwyn *lawyer*
Hudgins, David Drake *lawyer*
Kelly, Nancy Frieda Wolicki *lawyer*
Kopp, Eugene Paul *lawyer*
Kotlarchuk, Ihor O.E. *lawyer*
McDowell, Charles Eager *lawyer, retired military officer*
McGuire, Edward David, Jr. *lawyer*
Montague, Robert Latane III *lawyer*
Mossinghoff, Gerald Joseph *lawyer, educator*
Neustadt, Arthur I. *lawyer*
Paturis, E(mmanuel) Michael *lawyer*
Pyle, Howard *lawyer, consultant*
Ritts, Leslie Sue *lawyer*
Spencer, George Henry *lawyer*
Stevens, Ron A. *lawyer, advocate, surveyor*
Straub, Peter Thornton *lawyer*
Von Drehle, Ramon Arnold *lawyer*
Williams, John Edward *lawyer*
Yamamoto, Alan H. *lawyer*

Annandale
Jollie, Susan Barbara *lawyer*
Lim, Hyunsik *lawyer*

Arlington
Anthony, Robert Armstrong *lawyer, educator*
Brenner, Edgar H. *legal association administrator*
Cohen, Sheldon Irwin *lawyer*
Crouch, Richard Edelin *lawyer*
Delaney, Raighne C. *lawyer*
Flinn, Charles Gallagher *lawyer, priest*
Gainer, Ronald Lee *lawyer*
Green, Richard Alan *retired lawyer*
Hansen, Kenneth D. *lawyer, ophthalmologist*
Johnson, Charles Owen *retired lawyer*
Kelly, John James *lawyer*
Korman, James William *lawyer*
Kosarin, Jonathan Henry *lawyer, teacher, consultant*
Leslie, Gregg P. *lawyer*
Lohr, Michael F. *lawyer*
Martin, Harry C. *lawyer*
McDermott, Francis Owen *retired lawyer*
Mellor, Chip (William H. Mellor) *lawyer*
Miller, Brian A. *lawyer, electric power industry executive*
O'Sullivan, Lynda Troutman *lawyer*
Parker, Jeffrey Scott *law educator*
Rao, Neomi *law educator*
Ray, Gilbert T. *lawyer*
Robb, Chuck (Charles Spittal Robb) *law educator, former United States Senator from Virginia*
Rousselot, Peter Frese *lawyer, consultant*
Schmidt, Paul Wickham *lawyer*
Tannenwald, Peter *lawyer*
Walker, Woodrow Wilson *retired lawyer, real estate investor, farmer*
Wilderotter, James Arthur *lawyer*

Zywicki, Todd Joseph *law educator*

Ashburn
Flaherty, Michael Paul *lawyer, investment banker*
Gold, George Myron *lawyer, editor, writer, consultant*

Burke
Bishop, Alfred Chilton, Jr. *lawyer*
Hipfel, Steven J. *lawyer*

Centreville
Fells, Robert Marshall *lawyer, business executive*

Chantilly
Becker, James Richard *lawyer*

Charlottesville
Andrews, Minerva Wilson *retired lawyer*
Bonnie, Richard Jeffrey *lawyer, educator, consultant*
Cannon, Jonathan Z. *law educator*
Chandler, Lawrence Bradford, Jr. *lawyer*
Dotson, Donald L. *lawyer*
Fitchett, Taylor *law librarian*
Fox, Charles Dunsmore, IV, *lawyer*
Goetz, Charles John *law and economics educator*
Henderson, Stanley Dale *lawyer, educator, arbitrator*
Hochberg, Bayard Zabdial *retired lawyer*
Howard, Arthur Ellsworth Dick *law educator*
Jeffries, John Calvin, Jr. *law educator, former dean*
Kennedy, Cornelius Bryant *retired lawyer*
Kensington, Andrew Justus *litigation specialist*
Lane, Mark *lawyer, educator, writer*
Meador, Daniel John *law educator*
Menefee, Samuel Pyeatt *lawyer, academic*
Middleditch, Leigh Benjamin, Jr. *lawyer, educator*
Moore, John Norton *lawyer, educator, diplomat*
Nelson, Caleb Edward *law educator*
Nelson, Krysia Carmel *lawyer*
O'Brien, David Michael *law educator*
O'Connell, Jeffrey *law educator*
O'Neil, Robert Marchant *law educator*
Schauer, Frederick Franklin *law educator*
Slaughter, Edward Ratliff, Jr. *lawyer*
Stroud, Robert Edward *lawyer*
Turner, Robert Foster *law educator, writer*
Wadlington, Walter James *law educator*
Walt, Steven David *law educator*
Wenger, Larry Bruce *law librarian, educator*
White, George Edward *lawyer, educator*
Whitehead, John Wayne *lawyer, educator, writer*

Chesapeake
Gorry, James A. III *lawyer*

Chester
Gray, Charles Robert *lawyer*

Danville
Abreu, Luis Alberto *lawyer*
Regan, Michael Patrick *lawyer*
Talbott, Frank III *lawyer*

Fairfax
Arnold, William McCauley *lawyer*
Baird, Charles Bruce *lawyer, consultant*
Bobzien, David P. *lawyer*
Codding, Frederick Hayden *lawyer*
Downey, Richard Lawrence *lawyer*
Fagan, John Ernest *lawyer*
Folk, Thomas Robert *lawyer*
McAndrews, James Patrick *retired lawyer*
McGavin, John David *lawyer*
Rieger, Michael Ira *lawyer*
Rust, John Howson, Jr. *lawyer, state legislator*
Sanderson, Douglas Jay *lawyer*
Simpson, Carter B. *lawyer*
Sturtevant, Brereton *retired lawyer, federal official*

Falls Church
Benton, Janine Schollnick *lawyer*
Boehm, Kenneth *legal association administrator*
Brady, Rupert Joseph *retired lawyer*
Clegg, Roger Burton *lawyer*
Deckelman, William L., Jr. *lawyer*
Dewey-Balzhiser, Anne Elizabeth Marie *lawyer*
Diamond, Robert Michael *lawyer*
Gallopoulos, Gregory Stratis *lawyer*
Honigberg, Carol Crossman *lawyer*
Luchini, Joseph S. *lawyer*
Melnick, John Latane *lawyer*
Meserve, Richard Andrew *lawyer, administrator*
Mugavero, Thomas Collier *lawyer*
Savner, David A. *lawyer*
Ward, Joe Henry, Jr. *retired lawyer*
Wood, John Martin *lawyer*

Fort Belvoir
Harms, John Kevin *lawyer*

Fredericksburg
Braxton, Herman Harrison, Jr. *lawyer*
Glessner, Thomas Allen *lawyer*

Front Royal
Bonzagni, Vincent Francis *lawyer*

Galax
Kapp, John Paul *lawyer, physician, educator*

Glen Allen
Levit, Jay J(oseph) *lawyer*
Newby, Michael R. *lawyer*
Weaver, Mollie Little *lawyer*

Gloucester
Hicks, C. Flippo *lawyer*

Great Falls
Cass, Ronald Andrew *lawyer, former dean*
Neidich, George *lawyer*

Grundy
McGlothlin, Michael Gordon *lawyer*

Hampton
Dildy, David Scott *lawyer*
Grierson, Kevin William *lawyer*
Smith, Stephen Mark *lawyer*

Haymarket
Frank, Jacob *lawyer*

Heathsville
McKerns, Charles Joseph *lawyer*

Hillsville
McGrady, Jonathan L. *lawyer*

Ivy
Ubben, Donald Thomas *lawyer*
Wilcox, Harvey John *lawyer*

Lexington
Wiant, Sarah Kirsten *law librarian, educator, director*

Lorton
Mastromarco, Dan Ralph *lawyer, consultant*

Lovettsville
Flannery, John Philip *lawyer*

Lynchburg
Healy, Joseph Francis, Jr. *lawyer, retired air transportation executive*
White, Kenneth Spencer, Sr. *lawyer*

Manakin Sabot
Bright, Craig Bartley *lawyer*

Mc Lean
Appler, Thomas L. *lawyer*
Aucutt, Ronald David *lawyer*
Bostrom, Robert Everett *lawyer, mortgage company executive*
Brown, Thomas Cartmel, Jr. *lawyer*
Brownlee, John Leslie *lawyer, former prosecutor*
Church, Randolph Warner, Jr. *lawyer*
Duvall, Richard Osgood *lawyer*
Finneran, John G., Jr. *lawyer, diversified financial services company executive*
Fleischer, Walter Hersch *lawyer*
Gammon, James Alan *lawyer*
Glassman, M. Melissa *lawyer*
Graham, Thomas, Jr. *lawyer*
Horan, Richard T., Jr. *lawyer*
Ingersoll, William Boley *lawyer, real estate developer*
Jackson, William Paul, Jr. *lawyer*
Knebel, John Albert *lawyer, former United States Secretary of Agriculture*
LeSourd, Nancy Susan Oliver *lawyer, writer*
Main, David C. *lawyer*
Manikas, Kyle G. *prosecutor*
Marino, Michael Frank III *lawyer*
McClure, Roger John *lawyer*
Meltzer, Steven Lee *lawyer*
Miller, David L. *lawyer*
Miller, Donald Eugene *lawyer*
Molineaux, Charles Borromeo *lawyer, arbitrator, columnist, poet*
Morris, James Malachy *lawyer*
Price, Ilene Rosenberg *lawyer*
Quinlan, J(oseph) Michael *lawyer*
Rath, Manik K. *lawyer*
Shapiro, Nelson Hirsh *lawyer*
Sirilla, George M. *lawyer*
Stump, John Sutton *retired lawyer*
Tansill, Frederick Joseph *lawyer*
Van Lare, Wendell John *lawyer, director*
Wilchins, Howard Martin *lawyer*

Mechanicsville
den Hartog, Grace Robinson *lawyer, health products executive*

Middleburg
Boardman, Harold Frederick, Jr. *lawyer, corporate executive*

Mineral
Stauffer, Ronald Eugene *lawyer, physicist*

Mount Vernon
Spiegel, H. Jay *lawyer*

Newport News
Kamp, Arthur Joseph, Jr. *lawyer*
Thro, William Eugene *lawyer, professor, university administrator*

Norfolk
Albert, Alan Dale *lawyer*
Baird, Edward Rouzie, Jr. *retired lawyer*
Bishop, Bruce Taylor *lawyer*
Bredehoft, John Michael *lawyer*
Cranford, Page Deronde *lawyer*
Crenshaw, Francis Nelson *retired lawyer*
Davis, Terry Hunter, Jr. *lawyer*
Dimino, Joseph C. *lawyer*
Drescher, John Webb *lawyer*
Hixon, James A. *lawyer, rail transportation executive*
Martin, Howard W., Jr. *lawyer*
Padgett, John David *lawyer*
Parker, Richard Wilson *lawyer, retired rail transportation executive*
Pearson, John Yeardley, Jr. *lawyer*
Poston, Anita Owings *lawyer*
Ryan, John Morgan *lawyer*
Shannon, John Sanford *lawyer, retired rail transportation executive*
Teal, Gilbert Earle, II, *lawyer, coast guard officer*
Van Buren, William Ralph III *lawyer*
Weinberg, Jerrold G. *lawyer*

Petersburg
Everitt, Alice Lubin *labor arbitrator*

Prince George
Brown, Del M. Mauhrine *lawyer, educator*

Pulaski
McCarthy, Thomas James, Jr. *lawyer*

Purcellville
Sweeny, Peter Michael *lawyer, director*

Radford
Turk, James Clinton, Jr. *lawyer*

Reston
Bredehoft, Elaine Charlson *lawyer*
Burgujian, Richard V. *lawyer*
Epstein, Gary Marvin *lawyer*
Foley, Christopher P. *lawyer*
Heleen, Mark L. *lawyer, finance company executive*
Myerson, Jay Barry *lawyer*
Plave, Lee Jonathan *lawyer*
Rau, Lee Arthur *lawyer*
Reicin, Eric David *lawyer*
Scharff, Joseph Laurent *lawyer*
Scott, Betsy Sue *lawyer*

Richmond
Allen, Jeffrey Rodgers *lawyer*
Betts, James Edward *lawyer*
Booker, Lewis Thomas *lawyer*
Broadbent, Peter Edwin, Jr. *lawyer*
Brockenbrough, Henry Watkins *retired lawyer*
Brooks, Robert Franklin, Sr. *lawyer*
Bryson, William Hamilton *law educator*
Buckley, Kevin Joseph *lawyer*
Buford, Robert Pegram *lawyer*
Burrus, Robert Lewis, Jr. *lawyer*
Catlett, Richard H., Jr. *retired lawyer*
Cogbill, John Valentine III *lawyer*
Cutchins, Clifford Armstrong, IV, *lawyer*
Davidson, C. Simon *lawyer, columnist*
Dostart, Thomas J. *lawyer*
Dray, Mark Stanley *lawyer*
Effel, Laura *lawyer*
Ellis, Andrew Jackson, Jr. *lawyer*
Fauls, Thomas E. (Ted) *lawyer*
Freeman, George Clemon, Jr. *lawyer*
Gary, Richard David *lawyer*
Gluck, Michelle H. *lawyer*
Goodpasture, Philip Henry *lawyer*
Goolsby, Allen Cunningham III *lawyer*
Grey, Robert J., Jr. *lawyer*
Hackney, Virginia Howitz *lawyer*
Hall, Stephen Charles *lawyer*
Heaton, Stuart Alan *lawyer*
Hedgebeth, Reginald D. *lawyer, retail executive*
Hettrick, George Harrison *lawyer*
Keane, Denise F. *lawyer, food products executive*
Kearfott, Joseph Conrad *lawyer*
Kilgore, Jerry Walter *lawyer, former state attorney general*
Lutz, Jacob A., III, (Jake Lutz) *lawyer*
Margolin, Eric Mitchell *lawyer*
McClard, Jack Edward *lawyer*
McFarlane, Walter Alexander *lawyer, educator*
Meath, James V. *lawyer*
Moore, Thurston Roach *lawyer*
Pagan, John Ruston *law educator*
Pearsall, John Wesley *lawyer*
Pinckney, Charles Cotesworth *lawyer*
Pollard, Overton Price *retired lawyer*
Pope, Robert Dean *lawyer*
Powell, Lewis Franklin III *lawyer*
Pulley, (J.) Waverly. (III) *lawyer*
Pusey, William Anderson *lawyer*
Rainey, Gordon Fryer, Jr. *lawyer*
Redmond, David Dudley *lawyer*
Rhoads, Mark B. *lawyer*
Rigsby, Linda Flory *lawyer, director*
Robertson, Gregory B. *lawyer*
Roday, Leon E. *lawyer, finance company executive*
Rolfe, Robert Martin *lawyer*
Schwarzschild, Jane L. *lawyer*
Sharer, John Daniel *lawyer*
Shiembob, Mark S. *lawyer*
Slater, Thomas Glascock, Jr. *lawyer*
Slaughter, Alexander Hoke *lawyer*
Smith, R. Gordon *lawyer*
Spahn, Gary Joseph *lawyer*
Starke, Harold Eugene, Jr. *lawyer*
Stone, Jacquelyn Elois *lawyer*
Strickland, William Jesse *lawyer*
Stutts, James F. *lawyer, energy executive*
Taylor, Ashley L., Jr. *lawyer*
Thompson, Paul Michael *lawyer*
Troy, Anthony Francis *lawyer*
Waddell, William Robert *lawyer*
Walsh, William Arthur, Jr. *lawyer*
Warthen, Harry Justice III *lawyer*
Watts, Stephen Hurt, II, *lawyer*
Whittemore, Anne Marie *lawyer*
Williams, Amy McDaniel *lawyer*
Witt, Walter Francis, Jr. *lawyer*
Wright, Wiley Reed, Jr. *lawyer, retired judge, mediator*

Roanoke
Anderson, Phillip Verne *lawyer*
Bates, Harold Martin *lawyer*
Dudley, Julia Campbell *prosecutor*
Fishwick, John Palmer *retired lawyer, railroad executive*
Marshall, Heman Alexander III *lawyer*
Pace, G. Michael, Jr. *lawyer*
Powell, Sarah E. *lawyer, automotive executive*
Steele, (Margaret) Anita Martin *law librarian, educator*
Stevens, Christopher Williams *lawyer*
Thomson, Paul Rice, Jr. *lawyer*

Salem
Young, James Marion *lawyer*

South Riding
Murray, Michael Patrick *lawyer*

Spotsylvania
Manthei, Richard Dale *retired lawyer, health products executive*

Springfield
Englert, Roy Theodore *lawyer*
Starrs, James Edward *retired law and forensics educator, consultant*

Vienna
Gary, Stuart Hunter *lawyer*
Mackesey, Daniel R. *lawyer*
Peters, Geoffrey Wright *lawyer, fundraising executive*
Stearns, Frank Warren *lawyer*
Titus, Bruce Earl *lawyer*
Whitaker, Thomas Patrick *lawyer*

Virginia Beach
Baldwin, Stanley Forrest *lawyer, insurance company executive*
Jones, Robert Griffith *law educator, mayor*
Pickett, Owen Bradford *lawyer, former congressman*
Rephan, Jack *lawyer*
Sekulow, Jay Alan *lawyer*
Shapiro, Richard N. *lawyer*
Shuttleworth, Thomas B., II, *lawyer*
Spitzli, Donald Hawkes, Jr. *lawyer*
Woodward, Lawrence H. *lawyer*

Ware Neck
McVey, Henry Hanna III *retired lawyer*

Warrenton
Howard, Blair Duncan *lawyer*

Williamsburg
Church, Dale Walker *lawyer*
Clark, Morton Hutchinson *lawyer*
Graham, David Browning *lawyer*
Heller, James Stephen *law librarian, educator*
Marcus, Paul *law educator*
Margolin, Robert Jeremy *lawyer*

Woodbridge
Sandler, Betty Moore *lawyer*

Woodstock
Walton, Morgan Lauck III *lawyer*

WASHINGTON

Anacortes
Cavanaugh, Michael Everett *lawyer, arbitrator, mediator*

Bellevue
Anderson, David Coryell *lawyer, automotive executive*
Santel, Patrick Francis X. *lawyer*
Schroder, Sigrid Caroline *lawyer, consultant*
Sebris, Robert, Jr. *lawyer*
Sweeney, David Brian *lawyer*

Bellingham
Anderson, David Bowen *lawyer*
Packer, Mark Barry *lawyer, financial consultant, foundation official*

Centralia
Buzzard, Steven Ray *lawyer*

Eastsound
Hoagland, Karl King, Jr. *lawyer*

Everett
Mestel, Mark David *lawyer*
Ostergaard, Joni Hammersla *lawyer*

Federal Way
McDade, Sandy D. *lawyer, paper company executive*

Gig Harbor
Thompson, Ronald Edward *lawyer*

Hoquiam
Kessler, Keith Leon *lawyer*

Issaquah
Benoliel, Joel *lawyer*
Oles, Stuart Gregory *lawyer*

Kennewick
Fearing, George B. *lawyer*

Keyport
Treacy, Gerald Bernard, Jr. *lawyer*

La Push
Krueger, Katherine Kamp *lawyer*

Mercer Island
Anderson, Peter MacArthur *retired lawyer*

Mukilteo
Edmondson, Frank Kelley, Jr. *lawyer, legal administrator*

Newcastle
Erxleben, William Charles *lawyer, data processing executive*

Olympia
Bates, Charles Walter *attorney*
Isaki, Lucy Power Slyngstad *lawyer*
Miller, Allen Terry, Jr. *lawyer*
Roe, Charles Barnett *lawyer*
Walker, Francis Joseph *lawyer*

Port Angeles
Taylor, S. Brooke *lawyer*

Seattle
Anderson, Robert T. *lawyer, educator, former federal agency administrator*
Andrews, J. David *lawyer*
Birmingham, Richard Joseph *lawyer*
Blair, M. Wayne *lawyer*
Blom, Daniel Charles *lawyer, investor, retired insurance company executive*
Blumenfeld, Charles Raban *lawyer*
Boeder, Thomas L. *lawyer*
Boggs, Paula Elaine *lawyer, beverage service company executive*
Bridge, Jonathan Joseph *lawyer, retail executive*
Bringman, Joseph Edward *lawyer*
Char, Patricia Helen *lawyer*
Chicoine, Nicole Mooney *lawyer*
Claflin, Arthur Cary *lawyer*
Clausen, Mark A. *lawyer*
Cross, Bruce Michael *lawyer*
Cunningham, Janis Ann *lawyer*
Davis, John MacDougall *lawyer*
Dial, Ellen Conedera *lawyer*
Dong, Nelson G. *lawyer*
Fischer, Thomas Covell *law educator, consultant, writer*
Fisher, Jeffrey L. *lawyer*
Foster, Susan Eileen *lawyer*
Gaffney, Joseph M. *lawyer*
Gerrard, Keith *lawyer*
Gittinger, D. Wayne *lawyer*
Gores, Thomas C. *lawyer*
Gorton, Slade (Thomas Slade Gorton III) *lawyer, lobbyist, former senator*
Grace, Ryan Thomas *lawyer*
Gradel, James D. *lawyer*
Graham, Stephen Michael *lawyer*
Gray, Marvin Lee, Jr. *lawyer*
Green, William L. *lawyer*
Haman, Raymond William *retired lawyer*
Hazelton, Penny Ann *law librarian, educator*
Hilpert, Edward Theodore, Jr. *retired lawyer*
Hopkins, Kathleen Joan *lawyer*
Huston, John Charles *law educator*
Jaffe, Robert Stanley *lawyer*
Johnson, Bruce Edward Humble *lawyer*
Kane, Alan Henry *lawyer*
Kaplan, Robert David *lawyer*
Keegan, John E. *lawyer*
Knight, W. H., Jr., (Joe Knight) *law educator, former dean*
Koehler, Reginald Stafford III *lawyer*
Landefeld, Stewart M. *lawyer*
Lemly, Thomas Adger *lawyer*
Loftus, Thomas Daniel *lawyer*
Manning, J. Richard *lawyer*
Marchese, Lisa Marie *lawyer, educator*
McCune, Philip Spear *lawyer*
McKay, John *law educator, former prosecutor*
McKay, Michael Dennis *lawyer*
Meier, R. Paul *lawyer*
Merkle, Alan Ray *lawyer*
Mesher, Barry Neal *lawyer*
Mussehl, Robert Clarence *lawyer*
Niemi, Janice *retired lawyer, state legislator, judge*
Oehler, Richard William *lawyer*
Olsen, Harold Fremont *lawyer*
Paget, Joel Hathaway *lawyer*
Palmer, Douglas S., Jr. *lawyer*
Petrie, Gregory Steven *lawyer*
Prentke, Richard Ottesen *lawyer*
Price, John R. *lawyer, educator*
Pritchard, Llewelyn George *lawyer*
Redman, Eric *lawyer*
Ritter, Daniel Benjamin *lawyer*
Robbins, Stephen J. M. *lawyer*
Robinson, Jeffery P. *lawyer*
Rosen, Jon Howard *lawyer*
Rummage, Stephen Michael *lawyer*
Samiljan, Katriana *lawyer*
Sari, Robert B. *lawyer, retail executive*
Schwab, Evan Lynn *lawyer*
Schwartz, Irwin H. *lawyer*
Smith, Scott A. *lawyer*
Squires, William Randolph III *lawyer*
Starr, Isidore *law educator*
Stoebuck, William Brees *law educator*
Stross, Cynthia *lawyer*
Sullivan, Jeffrey C. *prosecutor*
Tarleton, Earl Russell, Jr. *lawyer*
Treiger, Irwin Louis *lawyer*
Tune, James Fulcher *lawyer*
Wagoner, David Everett *lawyer, arbitrator*
Ward, Ronald R. *lawyer*
Wechsler, Mary Heyrman *lawyer*
Williams, J. Vernon *retired lawyer*
Wilson, L. Michelle (Michelle Wilson) *lawyer, information technology executive*
Wilson, Richard Randolph *lawyer*

Selah
Ring, Lucile Wiley *lawyer*

Snohomish
Ellis, Stephen Charles *lawyer*

Spokane
Connolly, Kenneth Thomas *lawyer*
Eymann, Richard Charles *lawyer*
Koegen, Roy Jerome *lawyer*
Kovacevich, Robert Eugene *lawyer*
McDevitt, James A. *prosecutor, lawyer*

Tacoma
Cloud, Douglas R. *lawyer*
George, Nicholas *lawyer, entrepreneur*
Gordon, Joseph Harold *lawyer*
Holt, William E. *lawyer, managing partner*
Krueger, James A. *lawyer*
La Fond, John Quinn *retired law educator*

Tukwila
Fitzpatrick, Thomas Mark *lawyer*

Vancouver
Karpinski, John Stanley *lawyer*

Walla Walla
Reese, John M. *lawyer*

Woodinville
Radtke, Derek Paul *lawyer*

WEST VIRGINIA

Beckley
Fragile, Stacey Lynn *lawyer*
Rhode, Marye Frances *paralegal*

Bluefield
Kantor, Isaac Norris *lawyer*

Charleston
Betts, Rebecca A. *lawyer*
Brown, James Knight *lawyer*
Casey, Nick (G. Nicholas Casey Jr.) *lawyer, political organization administrator*
Dissen, James Hardiman *lawyer*
Love, Charles Marion III *lawyer*
Miller, Charles T. *prosecutor*
Neely, Richard *lawyer*
O'Connor, Otis Leslie *retired lawyer, director*
Robinson, E. Glenn *lawyer*
Rowe, Larry Linwell *lawyer, former state senator*
Zak, Robert Joseph *lawyer*

Fairmont
Aloi, Michael John *lawyer*

Lewisburg
Ford, Richard Edmond *lawyer*

Martinsburg
Hill, Philip Bonner *lawyer*

Morgantown
Fisher, John Welton, II, *lawyer, educator, academic administrator*
Fusco, Andrew G. *lawyer*
Garrison, Michael S. *lawyer, educator, former academic administrator*
Hardesty, David Carter, Jr. *president emeritus and professor of law, former academic administrator*
Morris, William Otis, Jr. *lawyer, educator*
Ringer, Darrell Wayne (Dan) *lawyer*
Scudiere, Debra Hodges *lawyer*

Oak Hill
Hamilton, Pat R. *retired lawyer, state representative*

Weirton
Fahey, William Thomas, II, *lawyer*

Wheeling
Hill, Barry Morton *lawyer*
Potter, Sharon Lynn *prosecutor*

WISCONSIN

Black River Falls
Lister, Thomas Edward *lawyer*

Brookfield
Carter, Rodney William *lawyer*
Sprague, Charles W. *lawyer, finance company executive*
Winsten, Saul Nathan *lawyer*

Dodgeville
Angel, Timothy Luke *lawyer*

Eau Claire
Mirr, Joseph R. *lawyer*
Stoddard, Glenn McDonald *lawyer*

Elkhorn
Eberhardt, Daniel Hugo *lawyer*
Sostarich, Mark Edward *lawyer*

Grafton
Maynard, John Ralph *lawyer*

Green Bay
Wolf, Barth Joel *lawyer, energy executive*

Greendale
Vinent-Cantoral, Aida R. *mediator*

Hales Corners
Case, Karen Ann *lawyer*

Kenosha
Stern, Walter Wolf III *lawyer*

La Crosse
Sleik, Thomas Scott *lawyer*

Lake Geneva
Braden, Berwyn Bartow *lawyer*

Lancaster
Halferty, James Burkhardt *lawyer*

Madison
Barnhill, Charles Joseph, Jr. *lawyer*
Basting, Thomas J., Sr. *lawyer*
Brewster, Francis Anthony *lawyer*
Carnell, Kent I. *lawyer*
Chandler, Richard Gates *lawyer*
Curtis, Charles G., Jr. *lawyer*
Curtis, Paul David *lawyer*
Field, Henry Augustus, Jr. *lawyer*
Galanter, Marc Selig *law educator*
Greller, Jason Anthony *lawyer*

Guenther, Erik Richard *lawyer*
Hanson, David James *lawyer*
Howell, Roberta F. *lawyer*
Langer, Richard J. *lawyer*
Latta, Richard Allen *lawyer*
Lewandowski, Richard J. *lawyer*
Linstroth, Tod Brian *lawyer*
MacDougall, Priscilla Ruth *lawyer*
Marshall, Kathryn Sue *lawyer*
Melli, Marygold Shire *law educator*
Mowris, Gerald William *lawyer*
Prange, Roy Leonard, Jr. *lawyer*
Ranney, Joseph Austin *lawyer*
Sinnott, Stephen P. *former prosecutor*
Skilton, John Singleton *lawyer*
Spencer, Christopher S. *lawyer, insurance company executive*
Swan, Barbara J. *lawyer, utilities executive*
Temkin, Harvey L. *lawyer*
Vaughan, Michael Richard *lawyer*

Manitowoc
Jones, Maurice D. *lawyer*

Menomonee Falls
Schepp, Richard D. *lawyer, retail executive*

Mequon
Richman, Stephen Erik *retired lawyer, consultant*
Wallace, Harry Leland *lawyer*

Middleton
Berman, Ronald Charles *lawyer, accountant*

Milwaukee
Aaron, Gordon K. *lawyer*
Babler, Wayne E., Jr. *lawyer*
Ballman, Patricia Kling *lawyer*
Bannen, John Thomas *lawyer*
Bardenwerper, Fred Louis *lawyer*
Biller, Joel Wilson *lawyer, retired diplomat*
Biskupic, Steven M. *lawyer, former prosecutor*
Bowen, Michael Anthony *lawyer, writer*
Burke, William Ulick (Chip) *lawyer*
Busch, John Arthur *lawyer, business executive*
Cannon, David Joseph *lawyer*
Casey, John Alexander *lawyer*
Casper, Richard Henry *lawyer*
Christiansen, Keith Allan *lawyer*
Connolly, Gerald Edward *lawyer*
Cutler, Richard W. *lawyer*
Daily, Frank J(erome) *lawyer*
Daniels, John W., Jr. *lawyer*
Ellis, Dwight Holmes III *lawyer*
Emanuel, John F. *lawyer*
Erickson, Randall J. *lawyer*
Florsheim, Richard Steven *lawyer*
Fraser, Alexander Paul *lawyer*
Frauen, Kurt Herman *lawyer*
Frautschi, Timothy Clark *lawyer*
Friebert, Robert Howard *lawyer*
Friedman, James Dennis *lawyer*
Gaines, Irving David *lawyer*
Galanis, John William *lawyer*
Gallagher, Richard Sidney *lawyer*
Gauthier, Janice Lorraine *lawyer*
Gefke, Henry Jerome *lawyer*
Gemignani, Joseph Adolph *lawyer*
Geske, Janine Patricia *law educator*
Gettel, James Joseph *lawyer, consultant*
Ghiardi, James Domenic *lawyer, educator*
Goodkind, Conrad George *lawyer*
Guerin, D. Michael *lawyer*
Haberman, F. William *lawyer*
Habush, Robert Lee *lawyer*
Hoffman, Nathaniel A. *lawyer*
Holz, Harry George *lawyer*
Hunt, Kenneth Charles *lawyer*
Jackson, Tamara Nicole *lawyer*
Karp, David Barry *lawyer*
Kennedy, John Patrick *lawyer, corporate financial executive*
Kircher, John Joseph *law educator*
Kopps-Wagner, Jennifer *lawyer, insurance company executive*
Kringel, Jerome Howard *lawyer*
Krueger, Raymond Robert *lawyer*
Kubale, Bernard Stephen *lawyer*
Kushner, Beth *lawyer*
Levit, William Harold, Jr. *lawyer*
Lione, Gail Ann *lawyer, automotive executive*
Llaurado, Thadd J. *lawyer*
Lueders, Wayne Richard *lawyer*
Manista, Raymond J. *lawyer, insurance company executive*
Marquis, William Oscar *lawyer*
Masterson, Joseph Daniel *lawyer*
McGaffey, Jere D. *retired lawyer*
Melin, Robert Arthur *lawyer*
Mulcahy, Robert William *lawyer*
Okarma, Jerome D. *lawyer, manufacturing executive*
Phillips, Thomas John *lawyer*
Pindyck, Bruce Eben *lawyer, corporate financial executive*
Priebus, Reince *lawyer, political organization administrator*
Schnur, Robert Arnold *lawyer, educator*
Schott, Sarah E. *lawyer*
Sennett, Nancy J. *lawyer*
Shapiro, Robyn Sue *lawyer, educator*
Shriner, Thomas L., Jr. *lawyer*
Sturm, William Charles *lawyer*
Surridge, Stephen Zehring *lawyer, writer*
Tully, Catherine T. *lawyer*
Wiley, Edwin Packard *retired lawyer*
Williams, Allen W., Jr. *lawyer*

Oshkosh
Blankfield, Bryan J. *lawyer, automotive executive, accountant*
Curtis, George Warren *lawyer*

Racine
Coates, Glenn Richard *lawyer*
Nielsen, Mark Francis *lawyer*

Sparta
Tripp, Tyler J. *lawyer*

Sun Prairie
Eustice, Francis Joseph *lawyer*

Waukesha
Cauley, James Robert *lawyer*

Wausau
Drengler, William Allan John *lawyer*
Orr, San Watterson, Jr. *lawyer*

Wauwatosa
Heath, Robert F. *lawyer*
Savage, Thomas Ryan *lawyer*

Whitewater
Weber, Curt Michael *law educator*

WYOMING

Casper
Durham, Harry Blaine III *lawyer*
Lowe, Robert Stanley *lawyer*

Cheyenne
Carlson, Kathleen Bussart *law librarian*
Crank, Patrick J. *lawyer, former state attorney general*
Freudenthal, Steven Franklin *lawyer, political organization worker*
Rankin, Kelly Harrison *prosecutor*
Sansonetti, Thomas L. *lawyer, former federal agency administrator*
Speight, John Blain (Jack Speight) *lawyer*
White, Daniel Eugene *lawyer*

Cody
Simpson, Alan Kooi *lawyer, former senator*

Gillette
Bailey, Daniel B. *lawyer, entrepreneur*

Jackson
Schuster, Robert Parks *lawyer*
Spence, Gerry (Gerald Leonard Spence) *lawyer, writer*

Laramie
Kinney, Lisa Frances *lawyer*
Lauer, Warren A. *lawyer*

Riverton
Girard, NettaBell *lawyer*

Sheridan
Marshall, Anne Bradley *lawyer*

Wheatland
Hunkins, Raymond Breedlove *lawyer, rancher*

TERRITORIES OF THE UNITED STATES

GUAM

Hagatna
Rapadas, Leonardo M. *prosecutor*

PUERTO RICO

San Juan
Corrada del Rio, Baltasar *lawyer, retired former state supreme court justice*
Lasa-Ferrer, Armando *lawyer*
Negron-Garcia, Antonio S. *law educator, former commonwealth of Puerto Rico supreme court justice*
Rodriguez-Diaz, Juan E. *lawyer*
Rodriguez-Velez, Rosa Emilia *prosecutor*
Wexler, David B. *law educator*

VIRGIN ISLANDS

Charlotte Amalie
Feuerzeig, Henry Louis *lawyer*

Christiansted
Bland, James Theodore, Jr. *lawyer*

St Thomas
Carty, Amos W. *lawyer*
Holcombe, Justin K. *lawyer*

CANADA

ALBERTA

Calgary
McEwen, Alexander Campbell *legal association administrator, consultant, cadastral studies educator, former Canadian government official, land use planner*
Robottom, David T. *lawyer, energy executive*

BRITISH COLUMBIA

Burnaby
Wainwright, David Stanley *patent agent*

MANITOBA

Winnipeg
Schnoor, Jeffrey Arnold *lawyer*

NOVA SCOTIA

Halifax
Dexter, Robert Paul *lawyer*

ONTARIO

Kingston
Tchegus, Robert Paul *lawyer*

Markham
Gulden, Simon *lawyer, management consultant, consultant*

Ottawa
d'Aquino, Thomas *lawyer, educator, entrepreneur, global strategist*
Tassé, Roger *lawyer, former Canadian government official*
Urie, John James *retired lawyer, former Canadian federal judge*

Toronto
Arthurs, Harry William *lawyer, educator, academic administrator*
Chester, Robert Simon George *lawyer*
Farquharson, Gordon MacKay *lawyer, director*

West Toronto
Iacobucci, Frank *lawyer, judge, former academic administrator*

QUEBEC

Ile Perrot
Lalonde, Marc *lawyer, former Canadian government official*

Montreal
Gillespie, Thomas Stuart *lawyer*
Johnston, Donald James *lawyer, educator*
Popovici, Adrian *law educator, emeritus professor*
Pound, Richard William Duncan *lawyer, accountant, former academic administrator*
Robb, James Alexander *retired lawyer*

Quebec City
Dinan, Robert Michael *lawyer*
LeMay, Jacques *lawyer*
Morin, Louis *lawyer*
Prothro, Jerry Robert *lawyer*
Verge, Pierre *legal educator*

Sainte-Foy
Normand, Robert *retired lawyer*

SASKATCHEWAN

Regina
MacKay, Harold Hugh *lawyer*

Saskatoon
Ish, Daniel Russell *law educator, academic administrator*

Montreal
Jablonski, Zygmunt *lawyer*
Vachon, Jacques P. *lawyer, paper company executive*

MEXICO

Mexico City
Carreto-Chavez, Gerardo *lawyer*

ARGENTINA

Buenos Aires
Parisier, Carlos *lawyer, economist*

AUSTRIA

Linz
Strasser, Rudolf *law educator*

THE BAHAMAS

Nassau
Beck, Jan Scott *lawyer*

BANGLADESH

Kushtia
Latifur Rahaman, Rasul Boaksh *legal association administrator*

BELGIUM

Brussels
Barnum, John Wallace *lawyer*
Vinje, Thomas C. *lawyer*

BERMUDA

Hamilton
McCormick, Hugh Thomas *lawyer*
Wiegley, Roger Douglas *lawyer*

CHINA

Beijing
Christianson, Jon L. *lawyer*

Guangzhou
Wang, Jing *lawyer*

Hong Kong
Halperin, David Richard *lawyer*
Nelson, Steven Craig *lawyer*
Yu, Benita Ka Po *lawyer*

Shanghai
Cohn, David Stephen *lawyer*
Lin, Maria C.H. *lawyer*

COSTA RICA

San José
Scharf, Eric *lawyer, educator*

ENGLAND

Beverley
Edles, Gary Joel *lawyer, educator*

Bradford
Sherwin, James Terry *lawyer*

London
Batla, Raymond John, Jr. *lawyer*
Fabricant, Arthur E. *lawyer, corporate financial executive*
Glazer, Barry David *lawyer*
Gottesman, A(rthur) Edward *lawyer*
Kandel, Christopher Nelson *lawyer*
Lipworth, Sir (Maurice) Sydney *solicitor, finance company executive*
Markoski, Joseph Peter *lawyer*
Montgomery, John Warwick (Baron of Kiltartan and Lord of Morris, Comte de St. Germain de Montgommery) *law educator, theologian*
Plapinger, William A. *lawyer*
Quillen, Cecil Dyer III *lawyer*
Stevens, Robert Bocking *lawyer*
White, Walter Hiawatha, Jr. *lawyer*
Zonana, Victor *lawyer, educator*

Oxford
Raz, Joseph *philosophy and law educator*

FRANCE

Bayon
Cochran, John M. III *lawyer*

La Fossette
Barnes, Wallace Ray *retired lawyer*

Paris
Baum, Axel Helmuth *lawyer*
Cariddi, Alan Francis *lawyer*
Crawford, John Fort *lawyer*
Salans, Carl Fredric *lawyer*
Sulkowski, Hubertus Victor *lawyer*

GERMANY

Berlin
Schlink, Bernhard *law educator, writer*

Duedenbuettel
Pfennigstorf, Werner *lawyer*

Frankfurt
Bader, W(illiam) Reece *lawyer*
Herold, Karl Guenter *lawyer, consultant*
Simitis, Spiros *legal educator*

Göttingen
Starck, Christian Walter *law educator*

GREECE

Athens
Angelopoulos-Daskalaki, Gianna *lawyer, ambassador, former International Olympic Committee Executive*
Kerameus, Konstantinos D. *law educator, legal consultant*

GUATEMALA

Guatemala City
Mayora, Eduardo A. *lawyer, educator, author*

HONG KONG

Central
Roppel, Mark *lawyer*

Wen, Carson *lawyer, legislator*

Wanchai
Fung, Daniel R. (Daniel Wah-kin Fung) *lawyer, broadcasting agency administrator*

INDONESIA

Jakarta
Hsi, Edward Yang *lawyer, venture capitalist, industrialist*

ISRAEL

Be'er Sheva
Frenkel, David Arie *law professor*

ITALY

Milan
Zambelli, Angelo *lawyer*

Padua
Grossi, Francis Xavier, Jr. *lawyer, educator*

Rieti
Truini Palomba, Maria Giuseppina *supreme court lawyer, judge*

Rome
McGurn, William Barrett III *lawyer*

JAPAN

Osaka
Honnami, Shoichi *retired law educator, researcher*

Tokyo
Farrar, Stanley F. *lawyer*
Shirai, Shun *law educator, lawyer*

NETHERLANDS

The Hague
Boed, Roman A. *legal administrator*

NEW ZEALAND

Wellington
Keith, Sir Kenneth James *law commissioner, educator, judge*

NORWAY

Hosle
Drevvatne, Dag *lawyer, investor*

PHILIPPINES

Makati
Romulo, Ricardo J. *lawyer*

POLAND

Lublin
Tokarczyk, Roman Andrzej *law educator, philosopher, researcher*

REPUBLIC OF KOREA

Seoul
O'Brien, Timothy James *lawyer*
Wang, Sanghan *law educator*

ROMANIA

Bucharest
Schnecker, Niels *lawyer*

SCOTLAND

Edinburgh
Macneil, Ian Roderick *lawyer, educator*

SIERRA LEONE

Freetown
Rapp, Stephen John *international prosecutor*

SPAIN

Madrid
Garcia-Palencia, Rafael *lawyer*
Herrero Rodriguez de Miñon, Miguel *lawyer, legislator, consultant*

SWEDEN

Stockholm
Holm, Christer A. *lawyer*

SWITZERLAND

Chateau d'Oex
Berman, Joshua Mordecai *lawyer, manufacturing executive*

Vevey
Frick, David P. *lawyer*

Zurich
Hammesfahr, Robert Winter *lawyer*
Kohli, Ulrich A. *lawyer*

THAILAND

Bangkok
Russell, Paul George *lawyer*

Phucket
Pianko, Theodore A. *lawyer*

VIETNAM

Binh An Ward
Israel, Barry John *lawyer*

ADDRESS UNPUBLISHED

Abbott, Charles Favour *lawyer*
Abramson, Leslie Hope *lawyer*
Acosta, Alex (Rene Alexander Acosta) *former prosecutor, former federal agency administrator*
Adams, Arlin Marvin *lawyer, retired judge, arbitrator, mediator*
Adams, Daniel Fenton *law educator*
Adams, Thomas Lynch, Jr. *lawyer*
Aikman, Albert Edward *lawyer*
Akindemowo, Olujoke Eniola *law educator, researcher*
Akintimoye, Akindele D. *lawyer, consultant*
Alemu, Fitsum Achamyeleh *lawyer, researcher*
Alexander, George Jonathon *lawyer, educator, dean*
Alfred, Stephen Jay *retired lawyer*
Allday, Martin Lewis, Jr. *retired lawyer*
Allecta, Julie *retired lawyer*
Allen, Toni K. *lawyer*
Allen, William Hayes *lawyer, educator*
Alpern, Andrew *lawyer, architect, historian*
Altman, Louis *lawyer, author, educator*
Amar, Akhil Reed *law educator*
Ames, Marc L. *retired lawyer*
Amidon, Edwin H., Jr. *lawyer*
Andersen, David Charles *lawyer*
Anderson, Alan Stewert *lawyer*
Andrews, David Ralph *lawyer*
Ansley, Shepard Bryan *lawyer*
Areen, Judith Carol *law educator*
Armen, Margaret Meis *lawyer*
Arnold, Alanna S. Welling *lawyer*
Arnold, Charlotte S. *criminal justice agency executive, activist*
Arnold, Jerome Gilbert *lawyer*
Arthur (II), Hugh Thomas *lawyer*
Ashe, Bernard Flemming *arbitrator, lawyer, educator*
Ashton, Harris John *lawyer*
Aslakson, Kenneth Randolph *law educator*
Atkins, William Paul *lawyer*
Aubut, Marcel *lawyer, sports association official*
Auerbach, Ernest Sigmund *lawyer, insurance company executive, writer*
Aufhauser, David D. *lawyer, former federal agency administrator*
Baccini, Laurance Ellis *lawyer*
Backman, Gerald Stephen *retired lawyer*
Backus, Marcia Ellen *lawyer*
Bae, Frank S.H. *retired law librarian*
Bagley, William Thompson *lawyer*
Bailes, Katherine *lawyer, educator*
Bailey, Burck *lawyer*
Bain, William Donald, Jr. *lawyer, chemicals executive*
Baker, William Thompson, Jr. *lawyer*
Bakken, Gordon Morris *law educator*
Bakkensen, John Reser *lawyer*
Baldwin, Allen Adail *retired lawyer, writer*
Ball, James Herington *retired lawyer*
Bamberger, Phylis Skloot *lawyer, educator, retired judge*
Bandy, Jack D. *lawyer*
Barnhardt, Zeb Elonzo, Jr. *lawyer*
Barnickol, Karl R. *lawyer*
Bartz, David John *lawyer*
Baskins, Ann O'Neil *lawyer, former computer company executive*
Bateman, David Alfred *lawyer*
Battocchi, Ronald Silvio *lawyer*
Bauman, Frederick Carl *lawyer, mining executive*
Baumgarten, Jon A. *lawyer*
Begovich, Michael *criminal defense attorney, law educator*
Beldock, Myron *lawyer*
Bell, Robert Morrall *retired lawyer*
Belleville, Philip Frederick *lawyer*
Belnick, Mark Alan *lawyer, educator*
Benfield, Ann Kolb *retired lawyer*
Bennett, Bryce Hugh, Jr. *lawyer*
Bennett, Robert Thomas *lawyer, former political organization administrator, accountant*
Bergan, Edmund Paul, Jr. *lawyer*
Berger, Robert Bertram *lawyer*
Berger, Sanford Jason *retired lawyer, securities dealer, real estate broker*
Berger, Steven R. *retired lawyer, state official*
Bergstein, Daniel Gerard *lawyer*
Beringer, William Ernst *mediator, arbitrator, lawyer, retired manufacturing executive*
Berkery, Rosemary Theresa *lawyer, former diversified financial services company executive*
Berkley, Peter Lee *lawyer*
Bernstein, Merton Clay *law educator, arbitrator*
Bertram, Phyllis Ann *retired lawyer, communications executive*
Besing, Ray Gilbert *lawyer, educator*
Best, Laurence Edward *lawyer*
Bevelhymer, Darlene Pearl *lawyer, retired secondary school educator*
Bewley, Peter David *corporate director, investor*
Bey, Gwendolyn *legal association administrator*
Bidwell, James Truman, Jr. *lawyer*
Bierig, Jack R. *lawyer, educator*
Bigelow, Robert P. *lawyer, arbitrator, mediator, journalist*
Black, William Rea *lawyer*
Blackford, Robert Newton *lawyer, director*
Blackman, Jeffrey William *lawyer*
Bleicher, Samuel Abram *law professor, consultant*
Bloch, Stuart Marshall *lawyer, banker*
Bloomer, Harold Franklin, Jr. *retired lawyer*
Blow, George *lawyer*
Boal, Ellis *lawyer*
Bokat, Stephen Arthur *lawyer, former business association executive*
Bomes, Stephen D. *lawyer*
Bondi, Harry Gene *lawyer*
Bonesio, Woodrow Michael *lawyer*
Bork, Robert Heron *law educator, retired federal judge*
Borkowski, John Joseph *lawyer*
Borowitz, Albert Ira *lawyer, writer*
Bosl, Phillip L. *retired lawyer*
Boudreau, Thomas M. *lawyer, health products executive*
Boulanger, Carol Seabrook *lawyer*
Bowden, William P., Jr. *retired lawyer, finance company executive*
Bowen, Lowell Reed *retired lawyer*
Bower, Jean Ramsay *lawyer, writer*
Bowers, Christi C. *mediator, lawyer, writer*
Bradford, Mary Rosen *lawyer*
Bradley, Amelia Jane *lawyer*
Brady, Edmund Matthew, Jr. *lawyer*
Brady, Edward Thomas, Jr. *lawyer, writer*
Brady, Terrence Joseph *mediator, arbitrator, retired judge*
Brafford, William Charles *lawyer*
Bragg, Michael Ellis *lawyer, insurance company executive*
Branagan, James Joseph *lawyer*
Brantz, George Murray *retired lawyer*
Brauer, Rhonda Lyn *proxy solicitor, lawyer, corporate governance consultant*
Braun, Jerome Irwin *lawyer*
Brawner, Gerald Andre, Jr. *paralegal*
Breece, Robert William, Jr. *lawyer, investment company executive*
Brehl, James William *lawyer*
Brennan, James Joseph *lawyer, bank executive*
Brewer, Roy Edward *lawyer*
Brigden, John *lawyer*
Brodhead, David Crawmer *lawyer*
Brooke, Edward William III *lawyer, former United States Senator from Massachusetts*
Brown, B. Andrew *lawyer*
Brown, Charles Dodgson *lawyer*
Brown, David Nelson *lawyer*
Brown, Herbert Russell *lawyer, writer*
Brown, J. E. (J.E. Buster Brown) *lawyer, consultant*
Brown, John Robert *lawyer, community volunteer, librarian*
Brown Spitzmueller, Janiece Marie *lawyer*
Bruess, Charles Edward *lawyer*
Bryan, Karen Smith *lawyer*
Bryson, Nancy Southard *lawyer, former federal agency administrator*
Buchanan, William H., Jr. *retired lawyer, venture capitalist*
Buchbinder, Darrell Bruce *lawyer*
Buckley, Frederick Jean *retired lawyer*
Buda, Thaddeus J., Jr. *retired lawyer*
Bullerdick, Kim H. *lawyer, petroleum executive*
Bunn, Ronald Freeze *retired lawyer, academic administrator, political scientist*
Burack, Michael Leonard *lawyer*
Burk, Robert S. *retired lawyer*
Burke, William Thomas *lawyer, educator*
Burkey, Lee Melville, Sr. *lawyer*
Burman, Darryl Michael *lawyer*
Burnbaum, Michael William *lawyer*
Burt, Richard *lawyer*
Burton, Richard Jay *lawyer*
Bush, William Merritt *retired lawyer*
Butler, William Joseph *lawyer, educator*
Buttrey, Donald Wayne *lawyer*
Cacciatore, Ronald Keith *lawyer*
Caldera, Louis Edward *law educator, former federal official*
Campion, Thomas Francis *lawyer*
Carey, Jana Howard *lawyer*
Carlson, Theodore Joshua *lawyer, retired utilities executive*
Carroll, Joseph J(ohn) *lawyer*
Carter, Jeanne Wilmot *lawyer, publishing executive*
Cartwright, Brian Grant *lawyer*
Casella, Peter F(iore) *patent and licensing executive*
Cassidy, John Harold *lawyer*
Casson, Joseph Edward *lawyer*
Castel, Jean Gabriel *lawyer, educator, international arbitrator*
Castro, Raul Hector *lawyer, Former Governor, Arizona, ambassador*
Cazalas, Mary Rebecca Williams *lawyer, nurse*
Cerveny, David John *lawyer*
Chaifetz, David Harvey *lawyer*
Chamberlin, Michael Meade *lawyer*
Chan, Jeanette K. *lawyer*
Charles, Robert Bruce *lawyer, former federal agency administrator*
Chave, Carol *arbitrator, retired lawyer*
Cheatham, Robert William *retired lawyer*
Chen, Del-Min Amy *lawyer*
Chiara, Margaret Mary *former prosecutor, lawyer*
Chiles, Stephen Michael *retired lawyer*
Chopin, Christopher Allen *lawyer*
Christie, Christopher James *former prosecutor, lawyer*
Clark, Celia Rue *lawyer*
Clark, Donald Otis *lawyer*
Clark, Karen Heath *lawyer*
Clark, LeRoy D. *law educator*
Clark, Merrell Edward, Jr. *retired lawyer*
Clark, Ramsey (William Ramsey Clark) *lawyer, former United States Attorney General*
Closen, Michael Lee *retired law educator*
Clubb, Bruce Edwin *retired lawyer*
Coccia, Michel Andre *retired lawyer*
Cohen, Christopher B. *lawyer*
Cohen, Joel J. *lawyer, investment banker*
Colantuono, Thomas Paul *former prosecutor, state legislator*
Coleman, Robert Lee *retired lawyer*
Coleman, Robert Winston *lawyer*
Colodny, Edwin Irving *lawyer, retired air transportation executive*
Colton, Sterling Don *retired lawyer, hotel executive*
Comisky, Ian Michael *lawyer*
Compton, Robert H. *lawyer*
Condra, Allen Lee *retired lawyer, state official*
Connell, William D. *lawyer*
Conner, Lindsay Andrew *lawyer*
Connor, Laurence Davis *retired lawyer*
Cooledge, Richard Calvin *retired lawyer*
Cooper, Hal Dean *lawyer*
Cope, John R(obert) *retired lawyer*
Copeland, Robert Glenn *lawyer*
Coplin, Mark David *lawyer*
Coppotelli, Blake Albert *lawyer*
Cornish, Jeannette *lawyer*
Cowperthwait, Lindley Murray, Jr. *lawyer*
Cox, Chapman Beecher *retired lawyer, charitable organization and aerospace executive*
Cox, Marshall *lawyer*
Coyle, Martin Adolphus, Jr. *lawyer*
Cramer, John McNaight *lawyer*
Cramer, Mark Clifton *lawyer*
Crane, Roger Ryan, Jr. *lawyer*
Cranney, Marilyn Kanrek *retired lawyer*
Crary, Miner Dunham, Jr. *lawyer*
Crawford, Carol Tallman *law educator*
Crawford, Muriel Laura *lawyer, educator, writer*
Crist, Paul Grant *retired lawyer*
Crocker, Saone Baron *lawyer*
Cronson, Robert Granville *retired lawyer*
Crowe, James Joseph *lawyer*
Cumba, Mark T. *lawyer*
Cunningham, Alice Welt *law and mathematics educator*
Curtis, John Joseph *lawyer, writer*
D'Agusto, Karen Rose *lawyer*
Dahling, Gerald Vernon *retired lawyer, director*
Dailey, Dianne K. *lawyer*
Danaher, John Anthony III *prosecutor*
Daniels, Diana M. *lawyer*
Darnell, Riley Carlisle *lawyer, former state official*
Davis, C. VanLeer III *lawyer*
Davis, Clarence Clinton, Jr. *lawyer*
Davis, Roger Edwin *lawyer, retired retail executive*
Davis, Wanda Rose *lawyer*
Davis, William Allison, II, *retired lawyer*
Dawson, Suzanne Stockus *lawyer*
Day, Kahlil Amyn *mediator, lawyer*
Dean, Patricea Louise *lawyer, educator, small business owner*
De Concini, Dennis *lawyer, lobbyist, retired senator, consultant*
DeGabrielle, Donald J., Jr. *former prosecutor*
Degener, Carol M. *lawyer*
DeLaTorre, Phillip Eugene *law educator*
Delehant, Joseph Henry *lawyer*
Dellwo, Robert Dennis *lawyer*
Dempsey, Edward Joseph *lawyer*
Denneen, John Paul *lawyer*
DeVore, Daun Aline *lawyer*
DeVylder, Edgar Paul, Jr. *lawyer*
Diamond, Stuart *lawyer, educator, business executive*
Dichter, Barry Joel *lawyer*
Dickstein, Michael Ethan *mediator, arbitrator, lawyer*
Diehl, Deborah Hilda *lawyer*
Dietel, James Edwin *lawyer, consultant*
Diez de Velasco, Manuel *barrister, educator*
DiPietro, Ralph John *lawyer*
DiSalvatore, William P. *lawyer*
Dolan, Andrew Kevin *retired lawyer*
Dolan, Peter Brown *lawyer*
Dolph, Wilbert Emery *lawyer*
Domiano, Joseph Charles *lawyer*
Donlon, William James *retired lawyer*
Donohoe, Jerome Francis *lawyer*
Dorkin, Frederic Eugene *lawyer*
Dougherty, John Chrysostom III *retired lawyer*
Dowdy, Robert Alan *retired lawyer, director*
Dowling, Vincent John *retired lawyer*
Drabkin, Murray *lawyer*
Draughon, Scott *lawyer, social worker, educator*
Drechsler, Beatrice Krain *lawyer*
Driscoll, Kimberlee Marie *lawyer*
Dubin, David Meyer *lawyer, educator*
Dubin, Stephen Victor *lawyer*
Du Boff, Michael H(arold) *lawyer*
Dubuc, Carroll Edward *lawyer*
Dunn, John Francis *lawyer, state representative*
Dunn, M(orris) Douglas *lawyer*
Dunn, Robert Lawrence *lawyer*
Dutile, Fernand Neville *law educator*
Earle, Victor Montagne III *lawyer*
Early, Bert Hylton *retired lawyer, consultant*
Edmonds, Elizabeth A. *lawyer*

Edwards, Richard Alan *retired lawyer*
Elicker, Gordon Leonard *retired lawyer*
Ellenberger, Jack Stuart *law librarian*
Embry, Stephen Creston *lawyer*
Engelhardt, John Hugo *lawyer, bank executive*
English, Stephen Raymond *lawyer*
Ennis, Edgar William, Jr. *lawyer*
Erichsen, Peter Christian *lawyer*
Ernst, Daniel Pearson *lawyer*
Estes, Carl Lewis, II, *lawyer*
Etchegoyen Lynch, Martin *lawyer, consultant*
Etra, Lionel *lawyer*
Etters, Ronald Milton *retired lawyer, former government official*
Ettinger, Joseph Alan *lawyer*
Eustis, Albert Anthony *lawyer, diversified financial services company executive*
Evans, Bruce Dwight *lawyer*
Everdell, William *retired lawyer*
Ezer, Mitchel J. *lawyer*
Faber, Michael Warren *lawyer*
Fahrenkrog, Eugene Henry, Jr. *lawyer*
Fales, Haliburton, II, *lawyer*
Fanwick, Ernest *lawyer*
Faricy, John Hartnett, Jr. *lawyer*
Farmakides, John Basil *lawyer*
Farmer, Cornelia Griffin *lawyer, consultant, county hearings official*
Fay, Donald P. *lawyer*
Feigenbaum, David Louis *lawyer*
Feldkamp, John Calvin *retired lawyer, educator*
Feldman, H. Larry *lawyer*
Feldman, Roger David *lawyer*
Feldman, Shana Madigan *legal assistant*
Fenech, Joseph Charles *lawyer*
Ferguson, Bradford Lee *lawyer*
Fine, Lawrence B. *lawyer*
Fiorito, Edward Gerald *lawyer*
FitzGerald, John Edward III *lawyer*
Flanders, Robert G., Jr. *lawyer, educator, association administrator*
Fleetwood, Clifford Gene ("The Father of Philosophical Art") *lawyer, publishing and recording industry executive, author*
Fleming, Gavin John *lawyer*
Fleming, Julie A. *attorney, legal consultant*
Flick, John Edmond *retired lawyer*
Forry, John Ingram *lawyer*
Fortenbaugh, Samuel Byrod III *lawyer*
Foster, David Lee *lawyer*
Foster, Judith Christine *lawyer, writer*
Fowler, Flora Daun *retired lawyer*
Fox, Eleanor Mae Cohen *lawyer, educator, writer*
Francis, Jerome Leslie *lawyer*
Frank, Karen Susanna *lawyer*
Frankel, James Burton *retired lawyer*
French, Daniel J. *former prosecutor*
Frick, David Rhoads *lawyer, retired insurance company executive*
Fried, Charles *law educator*
Friedman, Paul Richard *lawyer*
Frisby, Herbert Russell *lawyer*
Frisch, Sidney, Jr. *lawyer, real estate and insurance broker*
Frost, Barbara Sherry *lawyer*
Frost, Sterling Newell *arbitrator, mediator, management consultant*
Frue, William Calhoun *lawyer*
Fuller, Samuel Ashby *retired lawyer, mining executive*
Gagnon, Paul Michael *former prosecutor*
Gallagher, Gerard James *maritime legal practitioner, educator, researcher*
Gardiner, Lester Raymond, Jr. *retired lawyer*
Garnjost, Kurt *lawyer*
Gary, Marc *lawyer, financial services industry executive, former telecommunications industry executive*
Gates, Stephen Frye *lawyer, retired oil industry executive*
Gatewood, Tela Lynne *lawyer*
Gavin, Donald Glenn *lawyer, educator*
Geddy, Vernon Meredith, Jr. *lawyer*
Geisler, Thomas Milton, Jr. *lawyer, educator*
Gelber, Robert Cary *retired law librarian*
Gelston, Philip A. *lawyer*
Geltzer, Robert Lawrence *lawyer, arbitrator, mediator, retired retail executive*
George, Gay *lawyer*
George, Joey Russell *lawyer*
George, Joyce Jackson *lawyer, writer, retired judge*
Geren, Gerald S. *lawyer*
Giaccio, Anthony *lawyer*
Gibbs, Frederick Winfield *lawyer, communications executive*
Gibson, William Willard, Jr. *law educator*
Gillis, John Lamb, Jr. *lawyer*
Gingold, Dennis Marc *lawyer*
Ginsberg, Ernest *lawyer, banker*
Giza, David Alan *lawyer*
Glancy, Walter John *retired lawyer*
Glasser, Ira Saul *former civil liberties organization administrator*
Glazer, Jack Henry *retired lawyer*
Golden, Joseph Aaron *lawyer*
Gomez, Larry *former prosecutor*
Goodenow, Robert W. *lawyer, former sports association administrator*
Goodman, Elizabeth Ann *retired lawyer*
Gordon, James S. *retired lawyer, director*
Gorske, Robert H. *lawyer*
Gourley, Sara J. *lawyer*
Gourvitz, Elliot Howard *lawyer*
Grace, Cynthia *lawyer, educator*
Graff, George Leonard *lawyer*
Graham, David F. *lawyer*
Gray, Jan Charles *lawyer, business owner*
Green, Carol H. *consultant, retired lawyer, journalist, educator*
Green, Carole L. *lawyer*
Greenberg, Ronald David *lawyer, educator*
Greene, John Joseph *lawyer*
Greene, Jule Blounte *lawyer*
Greenebaum, Leonard Charles *retired lawyer*
Greenfield, James Robert *lawyer*
Greenman, Jane Friedlieb *lawyer, human resources executive*
Griffin, Campbell Arthur, Jr. *retired lawyer*
Griffin, Tim (John Timothy Griffin) *former prosecutor*
Gross, Lawrence Alan *lawyer*
Gross, Mark *lawyer, food products executive*
Gross, Richard Benjamin *lawyer, film producer*
Grutman, Jewel Humphrey *lawyer, writer*
Guild, Clark Joseph, Jr. *lawyer*
Gurstel, Norman Keith *lawyer*
Gutman, Richard Edward *lawyer*
Hackel-Sims, Stella Bloomberg *lawyer, former government official*
Hackett, Robert John *lawyer*
Hackett, Wesley Phelps, Jr. *lawyer*
Hajek, Robert J., Sr. *lawyer, real estate broker*
Haley, George Brock, Jr. *retired lawyer*
Hall, James Evan *lawyer*
Hall, John Hopkins *retired lawyer*
Hall, Paul J. *lawyer*
Halleck, Charles White *lawyer, photographer, former judge*
Halpern, James Bladen *lawyer*
Hamel, Rodolphe *retired lawyer, pharmaceutical executive*
Hamilton, Dagmar Strandberg *lawyer, retired educator*
Hamilton, Robert Woodruff *retired legal association administrator, educator*
Hanaway, Catherine Lucille *lawyer, former prosecutor*
Handler, Carole Enid *lawyer, city planner*
Handler, Harold Robert *lawyer*
Hanotiau, Bernard Raoul *lawyer*
Hanson, Arnold Philip *retired lawyer*
Hardin, Hal D. *lawyer, judge, former US attorney*
Hardy, Ashton Richard *retired lawyer*
Harff, Charles Henry *retired lawyer, manufacturing executive*
Harper, Conrad Kenneth *lawyer*
Harrell, Charles Lydon, Jr. *retired lawyer*
Harris, Allen K. *lawyer*
Harvey, Marc S(an) *lawyer, historian, educator*
Hassan, Ibne *lawyer, diplomat, political philosopher, international strategist*
Hauck, Jeffrey Peter Artorius Martel *lawyer, protective services official, consultant*
Hauver, Constance Longshore *lawyer*
Hawes, Sue *lawyer*
Hawthorne, Bruce N. *lawyer, former telecommunications industry executive*
Hayes, Byron Jackson, Jr. *retired lawyer*
Hayman, Russell *lawyer*
Heath, Richard Eddy *lawyer*
Hebert, William N. *lawyer*
Heffron, Howard A. *lawyer*
Heider, Jon Vinton *retired lawyer*
Heiligenstein, Christian Enric *lawyer*
Heineman, Andrew David *retired lawyer*
Heise, John Irvin, Jr. *lawyer*
Hemingway, Richard William *law educator*
Henderson, Thomas Henry, Jr. *lawyer, former legal association executive*
Hendry, Robert Ryon *lawyer*
Hennessy, Dean McDonald *lawyer, municipal official, director*
Henry, Robert John *lawyer*
Henson, Robert Frank *retired lawyer*
Heppe, Karol Virginia *lawyer, educator*
Hermann, Donald Harold James *law educator*
Hernandez, Michelle A. *lawyer*
Hernández-Ortiz, José A. *retired lawyer, literature and language educator*
Herrell, Roger Wayne *lawyer*
Herring, Jerone Carson *retired lawyer, bank executive*
Hershatter, Richard Lawrence *lawyer, writer*
Herzog, Peter Emilius *retired legal educator*
Higginbotham, John Taylor *lawyer*
Hight, B. Boyd *retired lawyer*
Hill, David Warren *lawyer*
Hill, John Edward *lawyer*
Hirshfield, Stuart *lawyer*
Hobbs, Franklin Dean III *lawyer*
Hofer, Stephen Robert *lawyer*
Hoffheimer, Michael Harry *law educator*
Hoffman, John Fletcher *retired lawyer*
Hoffman, S. David *lawyer, engineer, military officer, educator, artist*
Hoffmann, Christoph Ludwig *lawyer*
Holl, Roger Elmo *lawyer, educator*
Holt, Marjorie Sewell *lawyer, Former United States Representative, Maryland*
Holtzschue, Karl Bressem *lawyer, author, educator*
Honaker, Jimmie Joe *lawyer, educator*
Honeystein, Karl *lawyer, media specialist*
Hopkins, William Hayes *lawyer, writer*
Horlick, Gary Norman *lawyer, educator*
Horn, Andrew Warren *lawyer*
Horton, Linda Rae *lawyer*
Horwitz, Donald Paul *lawyer*
Hough, Thomas Henry Michael *retired lawyer, educator*
Howard, Sheryl Andrea *lawyer*
Howell, Donald Lee *lawyer*
Hsu, Emilie Tien-Jung *lawyer*
Huber, David L. *retired prosecutor*
Hudkins, John W. *lawyer*
Hughes, Harry Roe *lawyer, former Governor of Maryland*
Hughes, Thomas C., Jr. *lawyer*
Humetewa, Diane J. *former prosecutor*
Humphreys, Robert Russell *lawyer, arbitrator, consultant*
Humphries, M. Clayton, Jr. *lawyer*
Hunter, Jack Duval *retired lawyer*
Hut, A. Stephen *lawyer*
Hybl, William Joseph *lawyer, foundation administrator*
Hyde, Alan Litchfield *retired lawyer*
Hynes, Brian *lawyer, lobbyist*
Iamele, Richard Thomas *retired law librarian*
Idzik, Daniel Ronald *retired lawyer*
Iklé, Richard Adolph *lawyer*
Immergut, Karin J. *prosecutor*
Jacobs, John Patrick *lawyer*
Jambor, Robert Vernon *lawyer*
Jamison, Daniel Oliver *lawyer*
Javits, Joshua Moses *lawyer*
Javitt, Gail Hannah *lawyer, educator*
Jenkins, Anthony Jerome *former prosecutor*
Jennings, Thomas Parks *lawyer*
Joelson, Mark René *lawyer*
Johanson, David Richard *lawyer*
Johns, Warren LeRoi *retired lawyer*
Johnson, Eugene Laurence *lawyer*
Johnson, James Terence *lawyer, writer, minister, educator*
Johnson, Jennifer Rose *lawyer*
Johnson, Lael Frederic *lawyer*
Johnson, Reverdy *lawyer*
Johnson, Richard Tenney *lawyer*
Johnson, Scott William *former lawyer, manufacturing executive*
Johnston, John Devereaux, Jr. *retired law educator*
Jolly, Charles Nelson *lawyer, pharmaceutical executive*
Jones, Douglas Wiley *lawyer*
Jones, Elaine R. *former legal association administrator, civil rights advocate*
Jones, John Harris *retired lawyer*
Jones, Keith Alden *lawyer*
Jones, William Rex *law educator*
Jonsen, Eric Richard *lawyer*
Jordan, Jerry Dale *lawyer, gas industry executive*
Judell, Harold Benn *lawyer*
Jungeberg, Thomas Donald *lawyer*
Jurkowitz, Daniel S. *lawyer, prosecutor, judge*
Kallgren, Edward Eugene *lawyer*
Kantor, Mark Alan *lawyer, arbitrator*
Kaplan, Helene Lois *lawyer*
Kaplan, Susan *retired lawyer*
Kapnick, Richard Bradshaw *lawyer*
Karp, Donald Mathew *lawyer, banker*
Karre, Kathleen Mary *lawyer*
Kaster, Laura A. *lawyer*
Katz, Lawrence Sheldon *lawyer*
Katz, Sanford Noah *lawyer, educator*
Kaufman, David Joseph *lawyer*
Keatinge, Robert Reed *lawyer*
Keeling, J(ohn) Michael *lawyer, trade association executive*
Keith, William Douglas *lawyer*
Kelehear, Carole Marchbanks Spann *legal assistant*
Keller, Ric (Richard A. Keller) *lawyer, former United States Representative from Florida*
Kelley, James Francis *lawyer*
Kelly, Charles Arthur *lawyer*
Kelly, Paul V. *lawyer, former sports association administrator*
Kempf, Donald G., Jr. *retired lawyer*
Kennedy, Thomas J. *lawyer*
Kenney-Baden, Linda *lawyer*
Kenny, Charles Francis *lawyer, educator*
Kenrich, John Lewis *retired lawyer*
Kent, Matthew *law clerk*
Kienitz, LaDonna Trapp *lawyer, librarian, municipal official*
Kilbourn, William Douglas, Jr. *law educator*
Killeen, Michael John *lawyer*
King, Jack A. *lawyer*
King, Michael Howard *lawyer*
King, Rebecca J. *lawyer, consultant*
King, Robert Lucien *retired lawyer*
Kirk, John Robert, Jr. *retired lawyer, consultant*
Kirwan, R. DeWitt (Kyle) *lawyer*
Klafter, Cary Ira *lawyer*
Klamon, Lawrence Paine *lawyer*
Klaus, Charles *retired lawyer*
Klein, Linda Ann *lawyer*
Klott, David Lee *lawyer*
Knapp, Thomas Joseph *lawyer*
Knight, Gary *lawyer, writer, educator*
Kolodny, Stephen Arthur *lawyer*
Kotcher, Shirley J.W. *lawyer*
Kratt, Peter George *lawyer*
Kreizinger, Loreen I. *lawyer*
Krohnke, Duane W. *retired lawyer*
Kumble, Steven Jay *lawyer*
Lackland, John *lawyer, nurseryman*
Laliberte, Brian J. *lawyer*
Lamborn, LeRoy Leslie *law educator*
Lamel, Linda Helen *lawyer, arbitrator, director, professional society and retired insurance company executive, college president*
Lamkin, Martha Dampf *lawyer, foundation executive*
Lamon, Harry Vincent, Jr. *lawyer*
Lampton, Dunn O. *retired prosecutor*
Lanahan, Daniel Joseph *lawyer*
Landau, Felix *lawyer*
Lange, William Michael *retired lawyer*
LaRobardier, Genevieve Krause *lawyer*
Laudone, Anita Helene *lawyer*
Lawless, Thomas William *lawyer*
Lea, Lorenzo Bates *lawyer*
Leary, Thomas Barrett *lawyer, former federal agency administrator*
Lederer, Peter David *lawyer*
Leibowitz, Marvin *lawyer*
Lempert, Richard Owen *lawyer, educator*
Levin, A. Leo *retired law educator, government official*
Levine, Michael E. *law educator, researcher*
Levine, Thomas Jeffrey Pello *lawyer*
Levy, David *retired lawyer, insurance company executive, consultant*
Levy, I. Richard *lawyer*
Libassi, Frank Peter *lawyer*
Licke, Wallace John *lawyer*
Lidsky, Ella *retired law librarian*
Liebman, Ronald Stanley *lawyer*
Liftin, John Matthew *lawyer*
Ligon, Duke R. *lawyer*
Liguori, Robert *lawyer, insurance company executive*
Lilly, Thomas Gerald *retired lawyer*
Lin, Jenny Mei Hwa *paralegal, painter*
Linde, Maxine Helen *lawyer, corporate financial executive, investor*
Lineen, Edward M. *lawyer, information technology executive*
Linett, David *retired lawyer*
Lipsky, Burton G. *lawyer*
Lipton, Robert Steven *lawyer*
Litman, Harry Peter *lawyer, educator*
Litvack, Sanford Martin *lawyer*
Lloyd, Robert Blackwell, Jr. *retired lawyer*
Loacker, Lynn J. *lawyer*
Long, Clarence Dickinson III *lawyer*
Longobardo, Guy Alfred *lawyer*
Loumiet, Carlos Ernesto *lawyer*
Lovisone, Sylvia Ruth *lawyer*
Lubick, Donald Cyril *lawyer*
Lucas, Paul David Mark *lawyer*
Lund, James Louis *lawyer*
Lurie, Alvin David *lawyer*
Lynch, Thomas Wimp *lawyer*
Lynch, Timothy Jeremiah-Mahoney *lawyer, educator, theologian, realtor, writer*
Lyon, Bruce Arnold *lawyer, educator*
Mabey, Ralph R. *lawyer*
MacDonald, Donald Paul *lawyer*
Macdonald, Lenna Ruth *executive lawyer, business advisor*
MacKinnon, John Alexander *lawyer*
Magid, Laurie *prosecutor*
Magurno, Richard Peter *lawyer*
Mahoney, George LeFevre *lawyer*
Maldonado, Antonio *lawyer*
Malloy, John Richard *lawyer, chemicals executive*
Mancuso, John Henry *retired lawyer, bank executive*
Manos, Christopher Lawrence *lawyer, mediator*
Marans, J. Eugene *lawyer*
Marcu, Aaron R. *lawyer*
Margolis, Daniel Herbert *lawyer*
Marinis, Thomas Paul, Jr. *lawyer*
Marker, Marc Linthacum *lawyer, investor, entrepreneur*
Marsh, Jack, Jr., (John Otho Marsh) *lawyer, former United States Representative from Virginia*
Marsh, Karyn B. *lawyer*
Martin, Alice Howze *former prosecutor*
Martin, John William, Jr. *retired lawyer, automotive executive*
Martin, Thomas MacDonald *lawyer*
Martineau, Robert John *retired law educator*
Mason, Thomas Albert *retired lawyer*
Mathis, John Prentiss *lawyer*
Matthews, Barbara Caridad *lawyer*
Matthews, Elizabeth Woodfin *law librarian*
Mayer, James Joseph *retired corporate lawyer*
Mayer, John William (Bill Mayer) *lawyer*
McAmis, Edwin Earl *retired lawyer*
McCants, William David *lawyer, writer*
McCarey, Wilma Ruth *retired lawyer*
McCarthy, J. Thomas *lawyer, educator*
McCarthy, Vincent Paul *lawyer*
Mc Clendon, William Hutchinson III *retired lawyer*
McConnell, Edward Bosworth *legal association administrator, lawyer*
McCormack, David Richard *lawyer*
Mc Cormack, Francis Xavier *lawyer, former oil company executive*
McCurley, Robert Lee, Jr. *lawyer, educator*
McDonald, Bradley G. *lawyer*
McDonnell, Joseph B. *lawyer*
McDougall, Roderick Gregory *lawyer*
McGill, Robert M. *lawyer*
McGrath, J. Paul *lawyer*
McGuffey, Carroll Wade, Jr. *lawyer*
McHenry, Barnabas *lawyer*
McIntosh, Terrie Tuckett *lawyer*
McKay, Margo Marquita *lawyer, former federal agency administrator*
McKean, Robert Jackson, Jr. *retired lawyer*
McKenna, Stephen James *retired lawyer, corporate executive*
McKeown, William P. *retired lawyer*
McLaughlin, Joseph *lawyer*
McMahon, James E. *lawyer, former prosecutor*
McManus, Richard Philip *lawyer, agricultural products executive*
McMillan, Robert Ralph *lawyer*
Mc Quade, Lawrence Carroll *lawyer, investment company executive*
Medina, Mariemma *lawyer, educator*
Meehan, Patrick Leo *former prosecutor*
Meldman, Robert Edward *lawyer*
Meltzer, Jay H. *lawyer, consultant*
Mendelson, Joan Rintel *lawyer*
Mercer, Edwin Wayne *lawyer*
Mercer, Richard James *lawyer*
Merritt, Bruce Gordon *lawyer*
Merritt, Nancy-Jo *lawyer*
Messier, Pierre *lawyer, manufacturing executive*
Messner, Robert Thomas *lawyer, bank executive*
Metcalfe, Robert Davis III *lawyer*
Meyer, Max Earl *lawyer*
Meyers, Tedson Jay *lawyer*
Meyerson, Ivan D. *lawyer, former corporate financial executive*
Miller, Gay Davis *lawyer*
Miller, Lisa Ann *lawyer*
Miller, R. Charles *lawyer*
Miller, Richard Steven *lawyer*
Millimet, Erwin *lawyer*
Milner, Irvin Myron *retired lawyer*
Minahan, Daniel Francis *lawyer, retired manufacturing executive*
Mintz, M. J. *lawyer*
Miquelon, Miriam F. *former prosecutor, lawyer*
Mitchell, David Benjamin *lawyer, arbitrator, mediator*
Mitchell, William D. (Bill Mitchell) *lawyer*
Moloney, Stephen Michael *lawyer*
Mone, Peter John *lawyer*
Monroe, Carl Dean III *lawyer*
Montoya, Regina T. *lawyer*
Moon, Barbara G. *lawyer*
Moore, Betty Jo *retired legal assistant*
Moore, Mike (Michael C.) *lawyer, former state attorney general*
Moore, Richard Hancock *lawyer, former state treasurer*
Moreno, Albert F. *lawyer, former apparel executive*
Morgan, Timi Sue *lawyer*
Morgenthaler, Alisa *lawyer*

Morof, Jeffrey W. *lawyer*
Morrison, Donald William *lawyer*
Morse, Robert Harry *lawyer*
Moya, Patrick Robert *lawyer*
Muir, J. Dapray *lawyer*
Muller, Peter *lawyer, film company and retail executive*
Munsell, Elsie Louise *retired lawyer*
Murchison, David Claudius *lawyer*
Myers, Jesse Jerome *lawyer*
Nanda, Ved Prakash *law educator, director, academic administrator*
Nash, Melvin Samuel *lawyer*
Natcher, Stephen Darlington *retired lawyer, electronics executive*
Neilson, Benjamin Reath *lawyer*
Nekritz, Edward Steven *lawyer*
Nelson, Allyson Lyn *lawyer*
Nelson, Carl Roger *retired lawyer*
Newman, Carol L. *lawyer*
Newman, Joan Meskiel *lawyer*
Newton, Francis Chandler, Jr. *lawyer*
Nolen, William Giles *lawyer, accountant*
Nonna, John Michael *lawyer*
Ober, Richard Francis, Jr. *lawyer, director, banker*
O'Brien, J. Willard *lawyer, educator*
Ockey, Ronald J. *lawyer*
O'Connor, Edward Vincent, Jr. *lawyer*
O'Connor, Marilyn Jane *paralegal*
O'Connor, Paul Daniel *lawyer*
Oles, Douglas Stuart *lawyer*
Onyido, John Chike *lawyer*
Orlebeke, William Ronald *retired lawyer, writer*
Osborn, John Edward *lawyer, pharmaceutical industry executive, government official*
O'Sullivan, Judith Roberta *lawyer, writer, artist*
Otis, Lee (Sarah) Liberman *lawyer, educator,*
Painton, Russell Elliott *retired lawyer, mechanical engineer*
Pappas, Edward Harvey *lawyer*
Parks, Patricia Jean *lawyer*
Partridge, Bruce James *lawyer, educator, writer, parliamentarian*
Pascale, Daniel Richard *lawyer*
Patrick, Victor Phillip *lawyer, manufacturing executive*
Patterson, Richard Myron *retired lawyer, editor, writer*
Paul, Eve W. *retired lawyer*
Paul, Richard Wright *lawyer*
Pavarini, Peter Alfred *lawyer*
Paye, Jean-Claude *lawyer*
Pear, Charles E., Jr. *lawyer*
Peck, Douglas Edward *lawyer*
Pereyra-Suarez, Charles Albert *lawyer*
Perkiel, Mitchel H. *lawyer*
Perotti, Rose Norma *lawyer*
Persky, Marla Susan *lawyer*
Pesch, Ellen P. *lawyer*
Peterson, Bruce D. *lawyer, energy executive*
Peterson, Erik Charles *prosecutor*
Petrillo, Leonard Philip *lawyer, retired investment company executive*
Petty, George Oliver *retired lawyer*
Phillips, Dorothy K. *lawyer*
Phillips, James Harold *retired lawyer*
Phillips, Leo Harold, Jr. *lawyer*
Pieper, Darold D. *lawyer*
Piga, Stephen Mulry *retired lawyer*
Pitcher, Griffith Fontaine *lawyer*
Pitt, George *lawyer, investment banker*
Poliakoff, Gary A. *lawyer, educator*
Polsby, Allen Isaac *retired lawyer*
Pope, John *retired law educator*
Poppe, Laurie Catherine *matrimonial lawyer, social worker, real estate executive*
Porter, John Ridgely III *lawyer*
Porter, Michael Pell *lawyer*
Portnoy, Sara S. *lawyer*
Posner, Sylvie Pérez *lawyer*
Potash, Charles *lawyer*
Pound, Frank R., Jr. *lawyer*
Powers, Elizabeth Whitmel *lawyer*
Pratt, Robert Windsor *lawyer*
Prem, F. Herbert, Jr. *retired lawyer*
Prewoznik, Jerome Frank *retired lawyer*
Price, Alfred Lee *lawyer, mining executive*
Pryer, Mary Jane *retired lawyer*
Purtle, John Ingram *lawyer, former state supreme court justice*
Pytell, Robert Henry *retired lawyer, judge*
Quarles, James Linwood III *lawyer*
Quay, Thomas Emery *lawyer*
Quaye, Sylvia Sissuh *lawyer*
Rabb, Bruce *lawyer*
Radford, R. S. *lawyer, law educator*
Ranney, George A., Jr. *lawyer*
Ratner, Michael D. *lawyer*
Ratti, Ricardo Allen *lawyer*
Rawls, Frank Macklin *lawyer*
Raymond, David Walker *lawyer*
Rea, Anne E. *lawyer*
Reath, George, Jr. *lawyer, mediator, arbitrator*
Reed, Austin F. *lawyer*
Reeder, Robert Harry *retired lawyer*
Regenstreif, Herbert *lawyer*
Reich, Laurence *lawyer*
Reiche, Frank Perley *lawyer, former federal commissioner*
Reiss, Jerome *retired lawyer*
Reiter, Glenn Mitchell *lawyer*
Reveal, Ernest Ira III *retired lawyer*
Reverdin, Bernard J. *lawyer*
Rew, Lawrence Boyd *lawyer*
Reynolds, William Bradford *lawyer*
Rhodes, Alice Graham *retired lawyer, not-for-profit community development consultant*
Rhodes, Deborah Jean Johnson *former prosecutor*
Ricciardi, Lawrence Robert *lawyer*
Rich, Michael Joseph *lawyer*
Rich, Robert Stephen *lawyer*
Richardson, John Carroll *lawyer, financial consultant*
Richardson, Margaret Milner *lawyer*
Rick, Roseleen P. *lawyer*
Ricks, Joycia Camilla *retired lawyer*
Ring, Renee Etheline *lawyer*
Rissman, Burton Richard *lawyer*
Rivlin, Rachel *lawyer*
Rizowy, Carlos Guillermo *lawyer, educator, political analyst*
Roberts, William B. *lawyer*
Roberts, William H. *lawyer*
Robinson, Davis Rowland *lawyer, international arbitrator*
Robinson, Geoffrey Laurence *lawyer*
Roditti, Esther C(laire) *lawyer, writer*
Rodnunsky, Sidney *lawyer, educator*
Rohrbach, Heidi A. *lawyer*
Romanow, Josh *lawyer*
Rose, Michael Dean *retired lawyer, educator*
Rosenn, Harold *lawyer*
Rosha, Uzi *lawyer*
Rosky, Burton Seymour *lawyer*
Ross, Michael Aaron *lawyer*
Roster, Michael *lawyer*
Roth, Michael *lawyer*
Rothenberg, Elliot Calvin *lawyer, writer*
Rothman, Howard Joel *lawyer*
Rowe, Thomas Dudley, Jr. *law educator*
Rubin, Richard Allan *lawyer*
Rubin, Zick *lawyer, writer, psychology professor*
Ruddy, Kathy Aakre *paralegal*
Rush, Sophia A. *law educator*
Rynearson, Arthur John *lawyer*
Sacripanti, Peter John *lawyer*
Sahid, Joseph Robert *lawyer*
St. Clair, Donald David *lawyer*
Saliterman, Richard Arlen *lawyer*
Salman, Robert Ronald *lawyer*
Samuels, Janet Lee *lawyer*
Santman, Leon Duane *lawyer, former federal government executive*
Sapp, John Raymond *lawyer*
Sass, Cynthia N. *lawyer*
Sattler, Bruce Weimer *lawyer*
Saunders, Lonna Jeanne *lawyer, broadcast journalist, talk host, writer*
Saunders, Terry Rose *lawyer*
Savitt, Susan Schenkel *lawyer, mediator*
Sax, Joseph Lawrence *lawyer, educator*
Sayre, John Marshall *retired lawyer, former government official*
Scharf, Michael Paul *law educator*
Scheyer, Daniel *lawyer*
Schiffman, Howard Scott *law and environmental educator*
Schmidt, Karl A. *lawyer*
Schmults, Edward Charles *lawyer*
Schneider, Carl Edward *law educator*
Schneller, Marina Velentgas *lawyer*
Schott, Donald Karl *lawyer*
Schrag, Philip Gordon *law educator*
Schram, Ronald Byard *lawyer*
Schreiber, Alan Hickman *lawyer*
Schreiber, Paul Solomon *lawyer*
Schuchard, Robert L. *lawyer*
Schulman, Alan *lawyer*
Schultz, Dennis Bernard *lawyer*
Schwab, Eileen Caulfield *lawyer, educator*
Schwartz, Bernard Julian *lawyer*
Schwerdtner, Frederick Howard *lawyer, retired police commander, real estate broker*
Scott, G. Judson, Jr. *lawyer, federal judge*
Scott, Michael Dennis *lawyer*
Sczudlo, Walter Joseph *lawyer*
Seabolt, Robert D. *lawyer*
Sears, Mary Helen *lawyer*
Seidel, Selvyn *lawyer, educator*
Sessums, T. Terrell *lawyer*
Sfekas, Stephen James *lawyer, educator*
Shaffer, Richard James *lawyer, retired manufacturing executive*
Shaffert, Kurt *retired lawyer, chemical engineer*
Shambaugh, Stephen Ward *lawyer*
Shane, Jeffrey Neil *lawyer*
Shannon, Peter Michael, Jr. *lawyer*
Shaw, Theodore Michael *former legal association administrator*
Sheeder, Robert Elwood *lawyer*
Sheldon, Terry Edwin *lawyer, investment advisor*
Shere, Dennis *lawyer, writer, retired publishing executive*
Shriver, Robert Sargent, Jr., (Sargent Shriver) *lawyer*
Shuler, Caroletta Alexis *criminal justice educator*
Shuman, Samuel Irving *lawyer, educator*
Siemer, Deanne Clemence *lawyer*
Sigety, Charles Edward *lawyer, financial planner*
Sigmond, Carol Ann *lawyer*
Simon, Robert G. *lawyer*
Sims, John R. *lawyer*
Sinor, Howard Earl, Jr. *lawyer*
Siu, Wang-Ngai *solicitor*
Skigen, Patricia Sue *lawyer*
Skol, Armand George *lawyer*
Skolnik, Barnet David *retired lawyer*
Slavitt, David Walton *retired lawyer*
Sliger, Herbert Jacquemin, Jr. *lawyer*
Slinger, Michael Jeffery *law librarian, director*
Slonaker, Norman Dale *lawyer*
Slover, William Lewis *lawyer*
Smith, Carole Dianne *retired lawyer, editor, writer, product developer*
Smith, George Patrick, II, *lawyer, educator*
Smith, Jack David *lawyer*
Smith, James A. *lawyer*
Smith, Julious Perry, Jr. *lawyer*
Smith, Kerry Clark *lawyer*
Sneeringer, Stephen Geddes *lawyer*
Snyder, John Leighton *lawyer*
Solkoff, Jerome Ira *lawyer, educator*
Solls, Mark A. *lawyer*
Sowande, Beverly Folasade *lawyer, educator*
Sparks, John Edward *lawyer*
Sparks, Robert Ronold, Jr. *lawyer*
Speers, Roland Root, II, *lawyer*
Spiegel, Jayson Leslie *lawyer, educator, professional society administrator*
Spitzberg, Irving Joseph, Jr. *lawyer*
Springer, Paul David *lawyer, film company executive*
Stansell, Leland Edwin, Jr. *lawyer, mediator, educator*
Steinberg, Craig Russell *mediator*
Steptoe, Mary Lou *lawyer*
Steptoe, Sonja *legal firm administrator*
Stern, Joseph A. *lawyer, former publishing executive*
Stern, Julian Nathaniel *lawyer, pharmaceutical executive*
Sterrett, James Kelley, II, *lawyer*
Sterrett, Samuel Black *lawyer, former judge*
Stewart, Charles Leslie *lawyer*
Stewart, Murray Baker *retired lawyer*
Stickney, John Moore *lawyer*
Stiller, Shale David *lawyer, educator*
Stillman, Elinor Hadley *retired lawyer*
Stoiber, Carlton Ray *nuclear law consultant, freelance/self-employed cartoonist*
Stojkovic, Dusan *lawyer*
Stone, Donald Raymond *lawyer*
Stone, Edward Herman *lawyer*
Strantz, Nancy Jean *law educator, consultant*
Stratton, Walter Love *lawyer*
Strodel, Robert Carl *lawyer*
Strum, Jay Gerson *retired lawyer*
Stuart, Alice Melissa *lawyer*
Surles, Richard Hurlbut, Jr. *retired law librarian*
Susman, Morton Lee *lawyer*
Sutter, Laurence Brener *lawyer*
Swanson, Victoria Clare Heldman *lawyer*
Sweeney, Deidre Ann *lawyer*
Symons, Edward Leonard, Jr. *lawyer, educator, investment advisor*
Taft, Sheldon Ashley *retired lawyer*
Taliaferro, Philip III *lawyer*
Tallman, Ann Marie *lawyer*
Tanaka, J(eannie) E. *lawyer*
Tanenbaum, Jay Harvey *lawyer*
Tanner, W(alter) Rhett *lawyer*
Taylor, Job III *lawyer*
Termini, Roseann Bridget *law educator*
Terrell, G. Irvin *lawyer*
Thackeray, Jonathan E. *lawyer*
Thiele, Howard Nellis, Jr. *lawyer*
Thigpen, Richard Elton, Jr. *retired lawyer*
Thomas, David Lindsey *lawyer, member of former state board education former state senator*
Thomas, Franklin Augustine *lawyer, consultant*
Thomas, Patricia Anne *retired law librarian*
Thompson, Holley Marker *lawyer, marketing professional, consultant*
Thompson, James Alexander, Jr. *lawyer*
Thorne, William Albert *retired lawyer*
Thurmond, J. Strom, Jr. *lawyer, former prosecutor*
Toedt, D(ell) C(harles) III *lawyer*
Tolins, Roger Alan *lawyer*
Tolman, Philip D. *lawyer, corporate financial executive*
Tondel, Lawrence C. *lawyer*
Toomey, Richard Andrew, Jr. *lawyer*
Torgerson, Larry Keith *lawyer*
Torgerson, William T. *lawyer, retired electric power industry executive*
Torre, Gary Jerome *retired lawyer*
Tract, Marc Mitchell *lawyer*
Traeger, Charles Henry III *educator and innovator*
Trechsel, Stefan *law educator*
Trimble, Phillip Richard *law educator*
Trimble, Sandra Ellingson *lawyer*
Trimble, William Cattell, Jr. *retired lawyer*
Trost, Glenn W. *lawyer*
Tucker, Laurey Dan *lawyer*
Turnage, Fred Douglas *retired lawyer*
Turner, Terry Campbell *lawyer*
Twardy, Stanley Albert, Jr. *lawyer*
Tyler, Peggy Lynne Bailey *retired lawyer*
Ufford, Charles Wilbur, Jr. *lawyer*
Uribe, Fernando, Jr. *law educator*
Vacco, Dennis C. *lawyer, former state attorney general*
van Gestel, Allan *mediator, arbitrator*
Van Gorder, John Frederic *lawyer*
Van Vleet, William Benjamin *lawyer, retired insurance company executive*
Venters, Harley Eugene *lawyer*
Voorhees, James Dayton, Jr. *lawyer*
Vosk, Ted W. *lawyer*
Wagner, Arthur Ward, Jr. *lawyer*
Walker, Linda Lee *lawyer*
Walker, Mark A. *lawyer*
Walker, Richard Henry *lawyer*
Walmer, Edwin Fitch *retired lawyer*
Wanger, Eugene Gilkison *retired lawyer*
Watson, Jack H., Jr. *lawyer, former White House chief of staff*
Watt, James Gaius *lawyer, former United States Secretary of the Interior*
Weber, Susan A. *lawyer*
Webster, Robert Kenly *lawyer*
Wegner, Harold Claus *lawyer, educator, consultant*
Weil, Peter Henry *retired lawyer*
Weinberger, Steven *lawyer, educator*
Weinstein, Philip Merrill *lawyer*
Weiss, Kenneth Andrew *lawyer, educator*
Weiss, Stephen J. *lawyer*
Weldon, Jeffrey Alan *lawyer*
Welsh, John Beresford, Jr. *retired lawyer*
Wendel, Charles Allen *retired lawyer*
Werthan, Jeffrey Michael *lawyer*
Wessling, Robert Bruce *retired lawyer*
Wetherill, Eikins *lawyer, stock exchange executive*
Whale, Arthur Richard *retired lawyer*
Wheeler, R(ichard) Kenneth *lawyer, educator*
Wheeler, Stephen Frederick *legal administrator*
Whelan, Stephen Thomas, Jr. *lawyer*
White, Jill Carolyn *lawyer*
White, Katherine Russell *lawyer*
White, Kendred Alan *lawyer*
Wiehl, Lis W. *legal analyst, educator*
Wiggins, Charles Henry, Jr. *lawyer*
Wigler, Andrew Jeffrey *lawyer*
Wilcox, Mark Dean *lawyer*
Wildhack, William August, Jr. *lawyer*
Wiley, Richard Arthur *lawyer*
Willard, Richard Kennon *lawyer, former pharmaceutical company executive*
Williams, Wesley Samuel, Jr. *lawyer*
Williamson, Douglas Franklin, Jr. *lawyer*
Wilson, Bruce Duxbury *lawyer*
Wilson, John Pasley *retired law educator*
Wilson, Rhys Thaddeus *lawyer*
Wilson, Thomas Buck *lawyer*
Wine-Banks, Jill Susan *lawyer*
Winrow, Brian Paul *law educator*
Winslow, John Franklin *lawyer*
Wiseman, Alan M(itchell) *lawyer*
Wishengrad, Marcia H. *lawyer*
Wittig, Raymond Shaffer *lawyer, intellectual property technology manager*
Wolf, Gary Wickert *retired lawyer*
Wolfen, Werner F. *lawyer*
Wolfson, Michael George *retired lawyer*
Wong-Diaz, Francisco Raimundo *lawyer, educator*
Wood, Frank Maxwell *former prosecutor, lawyer*
Wood, Robert Charles *lawyer, real estate developer*
Woodard, Joseph Lamar *law librarian, emeritus professor*
Wooldridge, William Charles *lawyer*
Worenklein, Jacob Joshua *lawyer*
Worrell, Stewart Phillip *lawyer, diversified financial services company executive*
Worthington, Bruce R. *lawyer, energy executive*
Wright, Frederick Lewis, II, *lawyer*
Wright, James Ralph *retired lawyer*
Wright, Robert Payton *lawyer*
Wruble, Bernhardt Karp *lawyer*
Wyckoff, E. Lisk, Jr. *lawyer*
Yanez, Antonio, Jr. *lawyer*
Yokubaitis, Roger T. *lawyer*
York, Gary Alan *lawyer*
Young, John Hardin *lawyer*
Young, Robert Bond *lawyer*
Young, Sherilyn Burnett *lawyer*
Zalk, Robert H. *retired lawyer*
Zarro, Janice Anne *lawyer*
Zimmer, Markus Bernhard *legal association administrator*
Zischke, Michael Herman *lawyer*
Zoeller, Donald J. *lawyer*
Zohn, Martin Steven *lawyer*
Zumpano, Carlos Antonio *lawyer*

MEDICINE *See* HEALTHCARE: MEDICINE

MILITARY

UNITED STATES

ALABAMA

Auburn
Tolbert, Clinton Jame *army officer, machinist*

Elberta
Wilkinson, Edward Anderson, Jr. *retired military officer, manufacturing executive*

Enterprise
Parker, Ellis D. *retired military officer*

Gulf Shores
Virden, Frank Stanley *naval officer*

Huntsville
Burrows, Shania Kay *civilian military employee*
Williamson, Donald Ray *retired military officer*

Madison
Parlier, Greg H. *military officer, analyst, engineer, educator, researcher*

ARIZONA

Tucson
Thurman, Robert Kenneth *retired military officer*
Wickham, John Adams, Jr. *retired army officer*

Yuma
Hudson, John Irvin *retired career officer*

ARKANSAS

Blytheville
Slowik, Richard Andrew *air force officer*

Mountain Home
Baker, Robert Leon *military officer*

CALIFORNIA

Carlsbad
Kauderer, Bernard Marvin *retired naval officer, consultant*

Edwards
Spinelli, Christopher John *military officer*

Elk Grove
Tran, Lien *military officer*

Escondido
Briggs, Edward Samuel *naval officer*

Healdsburg
Eade, George James *retired military officer, researcher*

La Jolla
Counts, Stanley Thomas *retired military officer, retired electronics executive*

Long Beach
Higginson, John *retired career officer*

Monrovia
Fannin, Daniel Paul Clark *information systems executive*

Monterey
Matthews, David Fort *career officer*
Schrady, David Alan *civilian military employee, educator*

Newport Beach
Pace, Peter *former Chairman of the Joint Chiefs of Staff, management consultant*

Orangevale
Meigel, David Walter *retired career officer, musician*

Oxnard
Kirschbaum, Alan Ira *air force officer, systems integration specialist*

San Diego
Butcher, Bobby Gene *retired military officer*
Covey, Dana Curtis *military officer, orthopaedic surgeon*
Darmstandler, Harry Max *retired military officer*
Wing, Thomas M. *military officer, systems engineer*

Santa Barbara
Conley, Philip James, Jr. *retired air force officer*

Santa Rosa
Andriano-Moore, Richard Count *retired military officer, secondary and elementary school educator*

COLORADO

Colorado Springs
Bowen, Clotilde Marion Dent *retired military officer, psychiatrist*
Caruana, Patrick Peter *retired military officer*
Renuart, Victor Eugene, Jr., (Gene Renuart) *career military officer*
Willis, Frank Edward *retired air force officer*

Dillon
Dugan, Michael Joseph *former career officer, health agency executive*

Monument
Rokke, Ervin Jerome *military officer, academic administrator*

Peterson AFB
Webster, William G., Jr. *career military officer*

U S A F Academy
Merchant, P. Glenn, Jr. *military officer, physician*

CONNECTICUT

Middletown
Fusco, George Matthew *retired military officer, engineer*

Waterford
Hinkle, Muriel Ruth Nelson *naval warfare analysis company executive*

Wilton
Burki, Arde A. *retired military officer*

DISTRICT OF COLUMBIA

Bolling AFB
Green, Charles Bruce *career military officer, surgeon*

Washington
Allen, Thad William *career military officer*
Amos, James F. *career military officer*
Austin, Lloyd J. III *career military officer*
Bradley, John A. *career military officer*
Cartwright, James E. *career military officer*
Casey, George William, Jr. *career military officer*
Chandler, Carrol H. (Howie Chandler) *career military officer*
Chiarelli, Peter W. *career military officer*
Conway, James Terry *career military officer*
Cothron, Tony L. *career military officer*
Crawford, Hunt Dorn, Jr. *retired military officer, educator, diplomat*
Cross, Terry M. *career military officer*
Cullison, Thomas R. *career military officer*
Dayzie, LaDaniel *military officer*
Donald, Admiral Kirkland H. *military officer, federal agency administrator*
Donley, Michael Bruce *civilian military employee*
DuBois, Raymond Francis, Jr. *former civilian military employee, former marketing professional*
Dyke, Charles William *retired army officer*
Fraser, William M. III *career military officer*
Gainey, Kathleen M. *career military officer*
Gavrilis, James *military officer*
Giambastiani, Edmund Peter, Jr. *retired military officer*
Ginsberg, Daniel Brian *civilian military employee*
Greenert, Jonathan W. *career military officer*
Harvey, John Collins, Jr. *career military officer*
Hawley-Bowland, Carla *career military officer*
Higgins, Paul John *career military officer*
Huston, John Wilson *military officer, historian*
Keltz, Ilean K. *military officer*
Kern, Paul John *retired military officer*
Klotz, Frank G. *career military officer*
Lamont, Thomas R. *civilian military employee, lawyer*
Lenhardt, Thomas A. *military officer*
Mabus, Raymond Edwin, Jr. *civilian military employee, former Governor of Mississippi*
McGrath, Kevin Michael *military analyst, civilian military employee, researcher*
Metz, Thomas Frederic *career military officer*
Morin, Jamie Michael *civilian military employee*
Morrison, Thomas Allen *retired military officer, lawyer, dean*
Mullen, Mike (Michael Glenn Mullen) *Chairman of the Joint Chiefs of Staff*
Paige, Kathleen K. *naval officer*
Pekoske, David Peter *career military officer*
Penn, Buddie J. (B.J. Penn) *civilian military employee*
Ralston, Joseph W. *retired military officer*
Retz, William Andrew *naval consultant, retired naval officer*
Robinson, Adam Mayfield, Jr. *career military officer, surgeon*
Robison, Victor James, Jr. *retired naval officer*
Roughead, Gary *career military officer*
Sams, Ronald F. *career military officer*
Schwartz, Norton A. *career military officer*
Sega, Ronald Michael *civilian military employee, former dean*
Selva, Paul Joseph *career military officer*
Shelton, William L. *career military officer*
Stackley, Sean Joseph *civilian military employee*
Tabb, Vandoster Langford, Sr. *retired military officer*
Tedesco, Mark J. *career military officer, physician*
Van Antwerp, Robert L., Jr. *career military officer*
Wilson, Frances C. *career military officer*
Work, Robert O. *civilian military employee, retired military officer*
Zarychta, William Alex *aviation medical officer, physician assistant*

FLORIDA

Eglin AFB
Vail, Thomas Leighton *military officer*

Fort Lauderdale
West, Allen *retired military officer, civilian military employee*

Haines City
Clement, Robert William *retired air force officer*

Hurlburt Field
Wurster, Donald C. *career military officer*

Indian Harbor Beach
Scanlon, Charles Francis *retired military officer, writer, publisher*

Jacksonville
Delaney, Kevin Francis *retired military officer, consultant*
Folk, David Wilbur *occupational health and safety administrator*

Longwood
Smyth, Joseph Patrick *retired military officer, physician*

Melbourne
Laposata, Joseph Samuel *army officer*
Simokaitis, Frank Joseph *military officer, lawyer*

Miami
Fraser, Douglas Malcolm *career military officer*

Naples
Delano, Victor *retired naval officer*
Slaff, Allan Paul *military officer, academic administrator, educator, entrepreneur*

New Port Richey
Miller, Harvey William *retired military officer*

Orlando
Limpus, Charles Everett III *non-commissioned officer*

Palm Beach Gardens
Giordano, Andrew Anthony *retired naval officer*

Pensacola
Robinson, Harold Gilbert *retired military officer, civilian military employee*

Saint Petersburg
Chrobak, Nicholas James *military officer*

Sarasota
Heiser, Rolland Valentine *former army officer, foundation administrator*

Shalimar
Burke, Kelly Howard *retired military officer, entrepreneur*

Tampa
Helmick, Frank G. *career military officer*
Odierno, Raymond T. *career military officer*
Olson, Eric Thor *career military officer*
Petraeus, David Howell *career military officer*

Weeki Wachee
Davis, Larry Michael *air force officer, healthcare manager, consultant*

West Palm Beach
Thomashow, Steven Roy *military and intelligence officer*

Windermere
Westbrook, Clinton Howard *retired military petty officer, protective services official*

GEORGIA

Atlanta
Honoré, Russel L. *retired military officer*

Columbus
Tipton, James D. *retired military officer, education educator*

Fort Benning
Gittins, Timothy Lee *military officer*
Kotwal, Russ Steven *military officer, physician*

Jonesboro
Galvin, John Rogers *retired army officer, law educator*

Stockbridge
Collins, Oliver Jack *military officer, secondary school educator*

Warner Robins
Nugteren, Cornelius *air force officer*

Woodbine
Konetzni, Albert H., Jr. *career officer*

HAWAII

Camp H M Smith
Keating, Timothy J. *career military officer*

Honolulu
Hays, Ronald Jackson *career officer*
Pollock, Gale Susan *career military officer*
Wellein, Marsha Diane Akau *military educator, director*

Pearl Harbor
Willard, Robert F. *career military officer*

Waipahu
Reyes, Arturo Pacheco *civilian military employee*

ILLINOIS

Mattoon
Phipps, John Randolph *retired army officer*

Rockford
Borling, John Lorin *military officer*

Scott Air Force Base
Lichte, Arthur J. *career military officer*
McNabb, Duncan J. *career military officer*
Rondeau, Ann E. *career military officer*

INDIANA

Madison
Jones, Richard Sheffield *veterans service officer*

KANSAS

Manhattan
Myers, Richard Bowman *former Chairman of the Joint Chiefs of Staff*

Wichita
Kenned, Kermit Lee, Jr. *retired military officer*

KENTUCKY

Fort Campbell
Griffin, Johnny Lee *military officer*
Gutheinz, Michael John *military officer, lawyer*

Richmond
Burch, John Russell *retired military officer*

MAINE

Portland
Summers, Charles E., Jr. *military officer, former state senator*

Stockton Springs
Snyder, Arnold Lee, Jr. *retired military officer, research director*

MARYLAND

Annapolis
Shey, James *military officer*
Trost, Carlisle Albert Herman *retired naval officer*
Williams, James Arthur *retired military officer, information technology executive*

Bethesda
Kem, Richard Samuel *retired army officer*
Mateczun, John Matthew *career military officer*
Nathan, Matthew Lincoln *career military officer, physician*
Schmidt, Raymond Paul *military officer, historian, government agency administrator*

Cambridge
Field, Tammy K. *civilian military employee*

Chevy Chase
Pirie, Robert Burns, Jr. *defense analyst*

Frederick
Kelsey, Ronald Grant *retired military officer, environmental engineer*

Pikesville
Wilson, Courtney B. *military officer, museum administrator*

Silver Spring
Brog, David *former air force officer, consultant*

Timonium
Sagerholm, James Alvin *retired naval officer*

Trappe
Anderson, Andrew Herbert *retired army officer*

MASSACHUSETTS

Bedford
Dyer, Joseph Wendell *retired naval officer*

Hanscom AFB
Johnson, Charles L., II, *military officer*

Natick
Miller, George David *retired military officer, not-for-profit executive*

North Oxford
Carney, Roger Francis Xavier *retired military officer*

Osterville
Schwarztrauber, Sayre Archie *former naval officer, maritime consultant*

Sharon
Parker, Harry Lee *retired army officer, academic administrator*

MINNESOTA

Edina
Leach, Bertram George *retired military officer, securities dealer*

Plymouth
Shadley, Robert D. *retired army officer*

MISSISSIPPI

Pass Christian
McCardell, James Elton *retired naval officer*

MISSOURI

Poplar Bluff
Young, William Webb *military officer, aire warfare specialist, poet*

MONTANA

Hamilton
Henley, Jack Carson *retired military officer*

NEBRASKA

Offutt AFB
Chilton, Kevin Patrick *career military officer*

NEW HAMPSHIRE

Contoocook
Held, Wayne Edward *retired navy chief*

NEW JERSEY

Eatontown
Fritch, John Kenneth *civilian military employee*

NEW MEXICO

Albuquerque
Ewers, Robert Thomas *military officer*
Flournoy, John Charles, Sr. *retired civilian military employee, officer*

Santa Fe
Anderson, William Carl *former civilian military employee, lawyer*
Sumner, Gordon, Jr. *retired military officer*

NEW YORK

Flushing
Ghazarbekian, Sahak *retired international civil servant, United Nations consultant*

Fort Drum
Youngs, Michael Theron, Jr. *non-commissioned officer*

Hamburg
Markulis, Henryk John *career military officer*

New York
Schwarzkopf, Norman (Herbert Norman Schwarzkopf Jr.) *retired military officer*

Warrensburg
Egan, Eric Omar *military officer, educator*

West Point
Chapman, Matthew A. *military officer, science educator*
Dillon, Joel *military officer*
Hann, Ronald Koy *military officer, chemistry professor*

NORTH CAROLINA

Pinehurst
Carroll, Kent Jean *retired naval officer*

Spring Hope
Hildreth, James Robert *retired air force officer*

OHIO

Brookpark
Heil, Michael Lloyd *military officer, academic administrator*

Cincinnati
Randolph, Leonard McElroy, Jr. *career officer*
Smittle, Nelson Dean *military analyst, artist*

Wright Patterson AFB
Carlson, Bruce *career military officer*
Cranston, Stewart E. *career officer*
Jackson, Jason M. *military officer, educator*

OKLAHOMA

Edmond
Hopwood, Howard Hoppy Perry *military officer*

Oklahoma City
Reimer, Dennis J. *retired career military officer*

Roosevelt
Franks, Tommy Ray *retired military officer*

Tinker AFB
Goodman, Ernest Monroe *military officer*

OREGON

Canby
Sundquist, Leah Renata *military officer*

Lake Oswego
McPeak, Merrill Anthony *retired military officer, investor, company director*

Roseburg
Little, James Stewart *military officer*

PENNSYLVANIA

Bensalem
Long, Robert C. *retired military officer, management consultant*

Clarks Green
Kubic, Charles Richard *civil engineer*

Duncansville
Shoaf, Frank Joseph *military officer*

Evans City
Pagonis, William Gus *retired army general*

Gettysburg
Coughenour, Kavin Luther *career officer, military historian*

Glenshaw
Wilkes, John Michael *military officer, auditor*

King Of Prussia
Gallis, John Nicholas *retired military officer, executive leadership training consultant*

Rutledge
Senior, Robert Thomas *retired military officer*

RHODE ISLAND

Newport
Carpenter, Stanley Dean MacDonald *military officer, educator*

Portsmouth
Bergstrom, Albion Andrew *retired military officer, educator*

SOUTH CAROLINA

Aiken
Chelberg, Robert Douglas *military officer*

Beaufort
Miller, Robert *retired military officer*

Bluffton
Pendley, William Tyler *military officer, educator*

Clemson
Clausen, Hugh Joseph *retired army officer*

Columbia
Shuler, Ellie Givan, Jr. *retired military officer, museum administrator*

Fort Jackson
Brinsfield, John Wesley *military officer, educator*

Hilton Head Island
Brown, Arthur Edmon, Jr. *retired army officer*

New Zion
Gibbons, Robert Butler, Jr. *retired military officer*

Union
Whitener, William Jackson *retired military officer, dean*

Wedgefield
McLaurin, Hugh McFaddin III *military officer, museum program director*

York
Blackwell, Paul Eugene, Sr. *military officer*

TENNESSEE

Nashville
Uzzell-Baggett, Karon Lynette *career officer*

TEXAS

Alice
Tetlie, Harold *soldier, priest*

Belton
Shoemaker, Robert Morin *retired military officer, commissioner*

College Station
Chilcoat, Richard Allen *military officer, university president*

Fort Sam Houston
Coppola, Martin Nicholas *military officer, educator*

Fort Worth
Nicholas, Nicholas Constantine *retired military officer*

Houston
Gorie, Dominic L. Pudwill *retired military officer, astronaut*
Heuser, Mark Charles *military officer, educator*
Johnson, Gregory Harold *career officer, astronaut, experimental test and fighter pilot*

Lackland AFB
Westermann, Edward Burton *military officer, analyst, educator*

Lubbock
Huffman, Walter B. *retired army officer, dean, law educator*

Mission
Eyre, Pamela Catherine *retired career officer*

Portland
Soliz, Eusebio *military officer*

Randolph AFB
Donovan, Edgardo *medical services corps officer*
Ellis, Edward R. *career officer*
Looney, William R. III *career military officer*

Sachse
Eichelberger, Charles Bell *retired career officer*

San Antonio
Czerw, Russell J. *career military officer, dentist*
Kline, John William *retired military officer, management consultant*
Reneau, Marvin Bryan *military officer, business professor*
.Rolin, Daniel Wayne, Jr. *military officer*
Sculley, Patrick David *retired army officer, director*

Schertz
Vande Hey, James Michael *retired air force officer*

Sheppard AFB
Cook, Sharla J. *career officer*

The Woodlands
Jones, Lincoln III *military officer*

UTAH

Dugway
Davis, Vernon Thomas *military officer, researcher*

Provo
Baum, Kerry Robert *retired military officer, director*

VIRGINIA

Alexandria
Adams, Ranald Trevor, Jr. *retired air force officer*
Bowman, Richard Carl *defense consultant, retired air force officer*
Brown, Frederic Joseph *military officer*
Charlip, Ralph Blair *military officer, health facility administrator*
Fedorochko, William, Jr. *retired military officer, analyst*
Gurke, Sharon McCue *career officer*
Kroesen, Frederick James *retired army officer, consultant*
Smith, Jeffrey Greenwood *retired military officer*
Wilson, Charles H. (Charles Harrison Wilson) *retired air force officer, financial planner, human resource development professional*

Arlington
Blum, Steven (H. Steven Blum) *career military officer*
DeFilippi, George *retired air force officer*
Dodgen, Larry J. *career military officer*
Gracey, James Steele *retired coast guard officer, management consultant, director*
Graves, Ernest, Jr. *retired army officer, consultant, engineer*
Hokborg, Sven-Olof *military officer*
McKinley, Craig R. *career military officer*
Nash, Anthony J. *military analyst*
Rogers, Alan Victor *former career officer*

Burke
Jeremiah, David Elmer *retired military officer*

Dulles
Eikenberry, Karl Winfrid *United States Ambassador to Afghanistan*

Fairfax
Rosenkranz, Robert Bernard *military officer*

Falls Church
Schoomaker, Eric B. *career military officer*
Underwood, Paula Kay *military officer*

Fort Belvoir
Anderson, Frank J., Jr. *retired career officer*
Crenshaw, Horace, Jr. *military officer*
Dunwoody, Ann E. *career military officer*

Great Falls
Cowhill, William Joseph *retired naval officer, consultant*

Gum Spring
Dilworth, Robert Lexow *career military officer, educator*

Hampden Sydney
Boykin, William G. (Jerry Boykin) *retired military officer*

Hampton
Abner, Harold Loyd *military officer, consultant*

Haymarket
Seely, James Michael *retired military officer, defense consultant, small business owner*

Langley AFB
Corley, John D. W. *career military officer*

Leesburg
Brown, James Robert *retired air force officer*

Lexington
Peay, J.H. Binford III *career military officer*

Lynchburg
Snead, George Murrell, Jr. *military officer, research scientist, consultant*

Mc Lean
Layman, Lawrence *naval officer*
Yarborough, William Glenn, Jr. *military officer, forester, international business executive*

Norfolk
Luttrell, William Ernest *naval officer, industrial hygienist, toxicologist, educator*
Mattis, James N. *career military officer*
Pasch, James Roy *consultant, military employee*
Train, Harry Depue, II, *retired naval officer*

Oakton
Frost, S. David *retired naval officer*

Radford
Radford, James H. *retired military officer, political science professor*

Reston
Biely, Debra Marie *retired military officer*

Round Hill
Tice, Raphael Dean *military officer*

Springfield
Ginn, Richard Van Ness *retired military officer, healthcare executive*
Hart, Herbert Michael *military officer*

Vienna
Chandler, Hubert Thomas *former army officer*

Virginia Beach
Apperson, Jack Alfonso *retired army officer, management executive*
Hopkins, Curtis L. *military officer, educator*
Stansberry, James Wesley *air force officer*

Waynesboro
Alexander, William Woodward, Jr. *military officer*

Woodbridge
Messerschmidt, William Harclerode *retired non-commissioned officer, musician*

WASHINGTON

Anacortes
Higgins, Robert (Walter) *career naval officer, physician*

Fort Lewis
Jacoby, Charles H., Jr. *career military officer*

Lynnwood
Jenes, Theodore George, Jr. *retired military officer*

MILITARY ADDRESSES OF THE UNITED STATES

EUROPE

APO
Anderson, Curtis Thorwald, II, *military officer*
Dempsey, Martin E. *career military officer*

CANADA

ONTARIO

Ottawa
de Chastelain, A(lfred) John G(ardyne) D(rummond) *Canadian army officer, diplomat*
MacKenzie, Lewis Wharton *military officer*

AUSTRALIA

Canberra
Cosgrove, P. J. *military officer*

BHUTAN

Lungtenphu
Dorji, Lam (Goongloen Gongma Lam Dorji) *military officer*

GERMANY

Damsatadt
McChrystal, Stanley A. *career military officer*
McKiernan, David D. *retired military officer*
Rodriguez, David M. *career military officer*

Stuttgart
Ward, William E. (Kip Ward) *career military officer*

Vaihingen
Stavridis, Jim (James George Stavridis) *career military officer*

JAPAN

Tokyo
Rice, Edward A., Jr. *military officer*

REPUBLIC OF KOREA

Seoul
Hwang, Seunghyeon *military officer*
Sharp, Walter L. (Skip Sharp) *career military officer*

ADDRESS UNPUBLISHED

Albright, Joseph William *management consultant*
Aldridge, Donald O'Neal *military officer*
Bagley, Ronald Laird *military officer, educator*
Barber, James Alden *navy officer, educator*
Bartrem, Duane Harvey *retired military officer, residential designer, consultant*
Baxter, Sheila R. *career military officer*
Blair, Anita K. *former civilian military employee*
Block, Emil Nathaniel, Jr. *retired air force officer*
Bolton, Claude M., Jr. *former civilian military employee, retired military officer*
Boss, Kevin Korey *military officer*
Brady, Roger A. *career military officer*
Brook, Douglas Alan *former civilian military employee*
Brownlee, Les (Romie Leslie Brownlee) *former civilian military employee*
Buker, Robert Hutchinson, Sr. *army officer, thoracic surgeon*
Büyükanit, Yasar *career military officer*
Carstens, David Henry *military officer*
Cougill, Roscoe McDaniel *retired military officer*
Crea, Vivien S. *retired military officer*
Dahouk, Abbas *military officer*
Darby, Joseph M. *reservist*
Darden, Derrick Carolyle *retired military*
Davis, Dempsie Augustus *military officer, educator, financial planner*
Davis, Harley Cleo *retired military officer*
Davis, Morris D. *retired military officer, lawyer*
Dozier, James Lee *former army officer*

Dubik, James M. *career military officer*
Dunford, James Christopher *military officer*
Eastin, Keith E. *former civilian military employee*
Elam, Fred Eldon *retired military officer*
Elgart, Edward Guerry *civilian military employee*
Fitz-Enz, David G. *retired military officer, television producer, novelist*
Floyd, Otis Henry *retired military officer, adult education educator*
Foote, Evelyn Patricia *retired military officer*
Garner, Jay Montgomery *retired military officer*
Greco, Richard, Jr. *former civilian military employee*
Gutheinz, James O'Leary *military officer, law clerk*
Haddock, Raymond Earl *retired career officer*
Hamel, Robert Arthur *military officer*
Harper, Henry H. *retired military officer*
Harris, Marcelite Jordan *retired career officer*
Harvey, Francis J. *former civilian military employee*
Herriford, Robert Levi, Sr. *retired military officer*
Hobbins, William T. *retired military officer*
Hodges, Adele E. *career military officer*
Hoover, John Elwood *former military officer, consultant, writer, educator*
James, Ronald J. *former civilian military employee, lawyer*
Johnson, Joyce *retired military officer*
Jones, David Charles *former Chairman of the Joint Chiefs of Staff*
Jones, Joshua *military officer*
Jumper, John Phillip *retired military officer*
Juskowiak, Terry Eugene *career military officer, information technology executive*
Keene-Burgess, Ruth Frances *military official*
Kiser, Colin Lee *military officer, government contractor*
Kruger, Linda Lee *retired military officer*
Kutyna, Donald Joseph *air force officer*
Leidy, Charlotte *military officer*
Lennox, William James, Jr. *retired military officer*
Less, Anthony Albert *retired naval officer*
Long, Peter Avard Chipman *retired military officer*
Lynch, Jessica *military officer*
Lyons, John W(inship) *retired civilian military employee, chemist, consultant*
Mann, Eric Louis *retired military officer, mathematics professor, researcher*
Matusiak, Frederick *military analyst, educator*
McCarthy, Michael *military officer*
Mc Fadden, George Linus *retired army officer*
McNeill, Dan K. *retired military officer*
Meigs, Montgomery Cunningham, Jr. *retired military officer, educator*
Moore, Derrick Lanier *military officer*
Mullen, William Joseph III *retired career army officer*
Nabors, Robert Lee, Sr. *military officer*
Navas, William Antonio, Jr. *former civilian military employee, retired military officer*
Netherland, Louis Victor *military officer, educator*
Netto, Amba Cecile *military officer*
North, Gary L. *career military officer*
Palmer, Dave Richard *retired military officer, academic administrator*
Parent, Rodolphe Jean *retired Canadian air force officer, pilot*
Peat, Randall Dean *military analyst, retired military officer*
Price, Robert Ira *coast guard officer*
Puddy, William Curtiss *retired military officer, not-for-profit developer*
Radzik, Albin F. *federal analyst, military consultant*
Rees, Raymond F. *military officer*
Reinike, Irma *retired civilian military employee, writer, artist, poet, lyricist*
Robinson, David Brooks *retired naval officer*
Robinson, Ronald Gene *military officer, political science professor*
Rubenstein, David Aaron *military officer, healthcare administrator*
Sanchez, Ricardo S. *retired military officer*
Sanderson, James Richard *retired naval officer, financial consultant*
San Diego, Armando G. *retired military officer, pathologist, consultant*
Scholes, Edison Earl *military officer*
Schoomaker, Peter Jan *retired military officer*
Schunicht, Shannon Anthony *retired military officer, political scientist*
Shalikashvili, John Malchase *former Chairman of the Joint Chiefs of Staff*
Shaw, John Frederick *retired naval officer*
Shelton, Hugh (Henry Hugh Shelton) *former Chairman of the Joint Chiefs of Staff*
Springer, Robert Dale *retired air force officer, consultant, lecturer*
Stein, Adam Matthew *military officer*
Teets, Peter B. *former civilian military employee*
Van Goor, Anthony Jay *retired military officer, medical executive*
Vessey, John William, Jr. *former Chairman of the Joint Chiefs of Staff*
Vincent, Hal Wellman *retired military officer, investor*
Vines, John R. *career military officer*
Walden, Joseph Lawrence *career officer*
Walsh, Patrick M. *career military officer*
Weyman, Steven Aloysius *retired military officer*
Wheeler, Albin Gray *retired military officer, educator*
Wroth, James Melvin *retired military officer*
Yeager, Chuck (Charles Elwood Yeager) *retired air force officer, test pilot*
Yeosock, John John *military officer*
Yoon, E. Yul *retired career officer*
Zuick, Ernest Ronald, Jr. *career officer, advertising executive*

REAL ESTATE

UNITED STATES

ALABAMA

Birmingham
Couch, Robert M. *real estate company executive*

Tuscaloosa
Appiah-Opoku, Seth *urban planner, educator*
McFarland, James William *real estate company executive, consultant*

ALASKA

Anchorage
Hofseth, Pauline C. *realtor*
Wolf, Dan C. *real estate company executive, broker*

Girdwood
Trautner, John James *real estate executive*

Wasilla
Cole, Brad (Bradford Cole) *real estate broker*

ARIZONA

Flagstaff
Nelson, Emily Jane *conservationist*

Mesa
Pollack, Daniel H. *real estate company executive*

Phoenix
Lewis, Orme, Jr. *real estate company executive, land use adviser*

Prescott
Masotti, Louis Henry *real estate educator, consultant*

Scottsdale
Hilton, Steven J. *real estate executive*

Tsaile
Mayer, Margaret Ann *environmentalist, educator*

Tucson
Bodinson, Holt *conservationist*
Longan, George Baker III *real estate company executive*
Tang, Esther Don *real estate developer, consultant, social worker*

CALIFORNIA

Aptos
Nicholson, Joseph Bruce *real estate developer*

Bakersfield
Chidgey, Guy Clement *marketing executive*

Berkeley
Shaheen, Susan Alison *research faculty*

Beverly Hills
Bergman, Nancy Palm *real estate investment company executive*
Tamkin, Curtis Sloane *real estate development company executive*

Brentwood
Albers, Lucia Berta *land developer*

City Of Industry
Roski, Edward P., Jr. *real estate developer, professional sports team executive*

Fountain Valley
Smith, Marie Edmonds *real estate agent, property manager*

Granite Bay
Kemper, Dorla Dean Eaton (Dorla Dean Eaton) *real estate broker*

Irvine
Bollens, Scott Alan *urban planner, educator*
Chronley, James Andrew *real estate executive*
Stack, Geoffrey Lawrence *real estate developer*
Vandell, Kerry Dean *real estate consultant, educator, director, finance educator*
Windsor, Adrian Sharon *real estate broker, literature and language professor*

La Jolla
Anthony, Harry Antoniades *retired city planner, architect, educator*
Foley, L(ewis) Michael *real estate company officer*

Laguna Beach
Hanauer, Joe Franklin *real estate company officer*

Laguna Niguel
York, James Orison *retired real estate executive*

Los Angeles
Cushman, John C. III *real estate company executive*
Linsk, Michael Stephen *real estate company executive*
Rouze, Jeffrey Alan *real estate executive*
Sterling, Donald T. *real estate mogul, professional sports team owner*
Sulentic, Robert E. *real estate company executive*
White, Brett *real estate company executive*

Lynwood
Dove, Donald Augustine *city planner, educator*

Menlo Park
Nicholas, Keri *real estate agent*

Nevada City
Chalpin-Fleitas, Susan Gail *environmental health specialist, forester*

Newport Beach
Bren, Donald L. *real estate company executive*
Fawcett, John Scott *real estate developer*
Gilchrist, Richard Irwin *real estate developer*
Kenney, William John, Jr. *real estate developer*
Matteucci, Dominick Vincent *real estate developer*
Nolan, Christopher Aloysius III *real estate developer, architect, music promotion*
Turner, Jana L. *real estate company executive*

Oakland
DiMaggio, Debbi *realtor*

Palmdale
Anderson, R(obert) Gregg *real estate company executive*

Palo Alto
Klein, Robert Nicholas, II, *real estate developer*
Moore, Cassandra Chrones *policy analyst*
Wong, Y(ing) Wood *real estate investment company executive, real estate development company executive, venture capital investment company executive*

Pebble Beach
Getreu, Sanford *retired city planner*

Penn Valley
Nix, Barbara Lois *real estate broker*

Poway
Hunt, George Wayne *real estate appraiser*

Rancho Mirage
Blixseth, Timothy *real estate developer*

Rancho Palos Verdes
Allbee, Sandra Moll *real estate broker*

Rancho Santa Fe
O'Driscoll, Margaret Millar (Peggy O'Driscoll) *real estate broker*

Ross
Nicholson, William Joseph *energy and environmental consultant*

Sacramento
Beckon, William Nelson *environmentalist*

Salida
Bawiec, John C. *real estate broker*

San Bernardino
Willis, Harold Wendt, Sr. *real estate developer*

San Diego
Oldham, Maxine Jernigan *real estate broker*

San Francisco
Bracken, Thomas Robert James *real estate investment executive*
Freund, Fredric S. *real estate broker and manager*
Shorenstein, Walter Herbert *commercial real estate development company executive*

San Jose
Rothblatt, Donald Noah *urban and regional planner, educator*

Santa Barbara
Gunner, Michael Richard *real estate manager, hotel executive*

Santa Monica
Wachs, Martin *urban planning educator, author, consultant*

Stockton
Michailoff, Ian Robert *real estate broker, land use planner*

Thousand Oaks
Wolff, Stuart *online real estate executive*

Tulare
Hefflefinger, Clarice Thorpe *real estate broker*

Twain Harte
Kinsinger, Robert Earl *property company executive, educational consultant*

Vista
Cavanaugh, Kenneth Clinton *retired real estate consultant*

Walnut Creek
Ostrander, Willis Frederick *retired real estate appraiser*

COLORADO

Aurora
Lochmiller, Kurtis L. *real estate entrepreneur*

Denver
Considine, Terry *real estate company executive*
Kroenke, E. Stanley *real estate developer, professional sports team owner*
Mandarich, David D. *real estate corporation executive*

Louisville
Schonbrun, Michael K. *senior housing developer and operator*

Vail
Kelton, Arthur Marvin, Jr. *real estate developer*

Woody Creek
Jenkins, Robert Berryman *real estate developer*

CONNECTICUT

Bethel
Kurfehs, Harold Charles *real estate executive*

Bridgeport
Pagano, Celeste Ann *retired realtor, social services coordinator*

Danbury
Anderson, Alan Reinold *real estate company and computer security firm executive, consultant*

New Haven
Alexander, Bruce Donald *real estate executive, educator*
Harrison, Henry Starin *real estate appraiser, educator, entrepreneur*

Norwalk
Soper, Jeannine *real estate agent*

Ridgefield
Bucha, Paul William *real estate consultant, management consultant, policy advisor*

Stamford
Koproski, Alexander Robert *real estate company executive*

DELAWARE

Dover
Coyle, Kevin Francis *planner*
Taylor, Suzonne Berry Stewart *real estate broker*

Lewes
Little, R. Donald *real estate entrepreneur*

DISTRICT OF COLUMBIA

Washington
Blackwelder, Brent Francis *environmentalist*
Brooks, Jane K. *real estate agent, educator*
Debele, Bekele *water resources specialist*
Grumet, Jason Seth *environmental policy adviser*
Janes, William Sargent *real estate company executive*
Stone, Roger David *environmentalist*
Train, Russell Errol *environmentalist*
Wheeler, Douglas Paul *conservationist, state agency administrator, lawyer*

FLORIDA

Cedar Key
Starnes, Earl Maxwell *retired urban and regional planner, architect, educator*

Clearwater
Zinkan, Jeffrey Patrick *real estate analyst*

Coral Gables
Balzebre, Anthony Francis, Sr. *real estate developer, investor*
Peebles, R. Donahue *real estate company executive*

Gainesville
York, Vermelle Cardwell *retired real estate broker and developer*

Howey In The Hills
Jeppesen, Richard Ferrill *real estate developer*

Hutchinson Island
Welch, Martha Lynn *environmentalist, educator*

Jacksonville
Aleschus, Justine Lawrence *retired real estate broker*
Clarkson, Charles Andrew *real estate investment executive*
Rood, John Darrell *real estate developer, former ambassador*

Lake Suzy
Ogan, Russell Griffith *real estate broker*

Longwood
Gasperoni, Emil, Sr. *realtor, real estate developer*

Lutz
Corbitt, Doris Orene *retired real estate agent, dietician*

Melbourne
Evans, Arthur Forte III *real estate developer*
Michalski, Thomas Joseph *writer, political activist, retired city planner, developer,*
Ward, William Francis, Jr. *real estate investment broker*

Miami
Bluntzer, Elena C. *real estate company executive*
Macken, Jodi *real estate company executive*
Perez, Jorge M. *real estate developer*
Raffel, Leroy B. *real estate developer*
Salvaneschi, Luigi *real estate developer, management consultant, educator*

Naples
Dorio, Martin Matthew, Jr. *real estate company executive, investor*
Dykstra, David Allen *business broker*

Nokomis
Dodderidge, Ann Thornberry *real estate agent*

Orlando
Gidel, Robert Hugh *real estate investor*

Palm Beach
Bagby, Martha L. Green *real estate holding company and publishing executive, writer*
Coudert, Dale Hokin *real estate executive, marketing consultant*
Klotsche, Charles Martin *real estate company executive, photographer, writer, financial columnist*

Palm Beach Gardens
Kleinkopf, Paul *real estate developer*

Palm Coast
Barnes, Judith Ann *real estate company executive*

Saint Petersburg
Hurley, John Kenneth *real estate company and merchant banking executive*

Saint Petersburg Beach
Hurley, Frank Thomas, Jr. *realtor*

Sarasota
McCarthy, Brian Nelson *real estate developer*

Sebring
Sherrick, Daniel Noah *real estate broker*

Sunrise
Maken, Sonny *real estate company executive, developer*

Tallahassee
Miles, Rebecca *urban planner, educator*

Vero Beach
Freeman, Donald Wilford *real estate developer, horse breeder*

Winter Park
Siry, Joseph Vincent *environmentalist, educator*

GEORGIA

Athens
Melton, Wayne Charles *real estate executive*

Atlanta
Aka, Ebenezer Osita *urban planner, educator, researcher, consultant*
Bell, Thomas Devereaux, Jr. *real estate company executive*
He, Feng *environmentalist, consultant*
Terwilliger, J. Ronald *real estate company executive*

Clarkston
Charania, Barkat *real estate consultant*

Cumming
French, James Thomas *real estate broker*

Lawrenceville
Isola, Oluwabusuyi Olabode *real estate broker, educator*

Marietta
Carnes, James Donald *real estate manager*

Newnan
Barron, Thomas Willis *real estate broker*

Toccoa
Maypole, John Floyd *real estate company executive*

Woodstock
Colgan, George Phillips *real estate developer and appraiser*

IDAHO

Donnelly
Ferensowicz, Michael Jay *real estate company executive*

Idaho Falls
Thorsen, Nancy Dain *retired real estate broker*

ILLINOIS

Champaign
Guttenberg, Albert Ziskind *planning educator*

Chicago
Berger, Miles Lee *land economist*
Bluhm, Neil Gary *real estate company executive*
Bucksbaum, John *real estate company executive*
Bucksbaum, Matthew *real estate investment trust company executive*
Daley, Vincent Raymond, Jr. *real estate company executive, consultant*
Durburg, Jack E. *real estate company executive*
Dyer, Colin *real estate services executive*
Fish, Ronda *realtor*
Kinney, James M. (Jim Kinney) *real estate company executive*
Low, David D., Jr. *real estate company executive*
Neithercut, David J. *real estate company officer*
Schaffner, Karen Ann (Karen Field) *real estate broker*
Stinton, Dale A. *real estate association executive*
Zell, Samuel *real estate company executive, publishing executive*

East Saint Louis
Thomas, Mary Lee *property manager*

Highland Park
Stein, Paula Jean Anne Barton *hotel real estate company executive, broker*

Lake Zurich
Schultz, Carl Herbert *real estate developer*

Northbrook
Levy, Arnold S(tuart) *real estate company executive*
Metz, Adam S. *real estate company executive*
Perelman, Jeffrey E. *real estate company executive*

Oak Brook
Daly, Patrick F. *real estate executive, architect*

INDIANA

Elkhart
Vite, Frank Anthony *realtor*

Fort Wayne
Glick, Anna Margaret *real estate broker, consultant*

Indianapolis
Kohart, Mary Beth *real estate company executive*
Simon, David *real estate company officer*
Simon, Herbert *real estate developer, professional sports team owner*
Simon, Melvin *real estate developer, professional sports team owner*
Sokolov, Richard Saul *real estate company executive*

Jeffersonville
Reisert, Charles Edward, Jr. *realtor, real estate developer*

KANSAS

Overland Park
Kem, Katherine Frances *urban planner*

KENTUCKY

Winchester
Cantrell, Georgia Ann *realtor*

LOUISIANA

Covington
Maurin, James E. *real estate executive*

Leesville
Thompson, Darlene Bennett *realtor, musician*

Metairie
Myers, Iona Raymer *retired real estate property manager*

MARYLAND

Baltimore
Caplan, Sharon M. *real estate company executive*
DeVito, Mathias Joseph *retired real estate company executive*
Millspaugh, Martin Laurence *real estate developer, consultant*

Berlin
Passwater, Barbara Gayhart *real estate broker*

Burtonsville
Kammeyer, Sonia Margaretha *real estate agent*

Chevy Chase
Noonan, Patrick Francis *conservation executive*

Columbia
McCuan, William Patrick *philanthropist, real estate company executive*

Frederick
Dougherty, Jennifer P. *realtor*
Whelihan, Alan Stuart *real estate developer, automotive executive*

Potomac
Dickerman, Serafina Poerio *real estate broker, consultant*
Eaves, Maria Perry *realtor*

Rockville
Frazier, Walter Ronald *real estate investment company executive*

Simpsonville
Altschuler, Ruth Phyllis *realtor, secondary school educator*

Westminster
Erb, Betty Jane *retired real estate agent*

MASSACHUSETTS

Amherst
Bentley, Richard Norcross *regional planner, writer, educator*
Larson, Joseph Stanley *environmentalist, educator*

Boston
Ahearn, Kevin J. *real estate broker*
Beal, Robert Lawrence *real estate executive*
Bushari, Elad *real estate broker*
Campion, Tracy *real estate broker*
Wigglesworth, Margaret *real estate company executive*

Cambridge
Fleming, Ronald Lee *urban planner, consultant*
Susskind, Lawrence Elliott *urban planner, mediator, educator*

Fairhaven
Hotchkiss, Henry Washington *real estate broker, financial consultant*

Gloucester
Sallah, Majeed (Jim) *retired real estate developer*

Shrewsbury
Falter, Robert Gary *real estate broker, educator*

Waltham
Nelson, Arthur Hunt *real estate company executive*

Winchester
Blackham, Ann Rosemary *realtor*

MICHIGAN

Ann Arbor
Surovell, Edward David *real estate company executive*

Grosse Ile
Smith, Veronica Latta *real estate company officer*

Newport
Cerasuolo, Jennifer Lyn *preservationist*

Niles
Tenney, Jane Morris *real estate developer*

Saginaw
Cline, Thomas William *real estate leasing company executive, management consultant*

White Lake
Clyburn, Luther Linn *real estate broker, appraiser*

MINNESOTA

Edina
Kreiser, Frank David *real estate executive*

Minneapolis
Burnet, Ralph W. *real estate company officer*

North Oaks
McDonald, Malcolm Willis *retired real estate company executive*

Saint Paul
Nerbonne, Julia Frost *environmentalist, educator*

MISSOURI

Chesterfield
Morley, Harry Thomas, Jr. *real estate executive*

Holden
Martin, Laurabelle *property manager*

Saint Joseph
Rachow, Sharon Dianne *realtor*

Saint Louis
Meissner, Edwin Benjamin, Jr. *retired real estate broker*

NEBRASKA

Lincoln
Tavlin, Michael John *real estate company and manufacturing executive*

NEVADA

Lake Tahoe
Chase, Shari *real estate company executive, broker*

Las Vegas
Barbagallo, Al T. *real estate company executive*
Barden, Don H. *real estate company officer*
Jabara, Michael Dean *real estate developer, former technology entrepreneur*
Maravich, Mary Louise *realtor*
Merrill, Wendy Jane *realtor*
Sullivan, Christopher David *real estate broker, attorney*

NEW HAMPSHIRE

Contoocook
Wood, Richard Robinson *real estate company executive*

NEW JERSEY

Berkeley Heights
Connell, Grover *real estate company executive*

Flemington
Kiovsky, Douglas George *land use planner*
Salamon, Renay *real estate broker*

Haworth
Strum, Brian J. *real estate company officer*

Manasquan
Jones, Elizabeth Harding *real estate agent, retired elementary school educator*

New Brunswick
Livingston, Lee Franklin *real estate consultant, financial consultant*

Parsippany
Hull, Anthony E. *real estate company executive*
Kunz, Thomas R. *real estate company executive*
Smith, Richard A. *real estate company executive*

Red Bank
Hovnanian, Ara K. *real estate developer*
Hovnanian, Kevork S. *real estate developer*

Teaneck
Warsawer, Harold Newton *real estate appraiser, consultant*

NEW MEXICO

Albuquerque
Davis, Betty Bourbonia *real estate company executive*
Stahl, Jack Leland *real estate company executive*

Las Cruces
Williams, Susan L. *educator*

Mora
Hanks, Eugene Ralph *real estate developer, rancher, forester, retired military officer, investor*

NEW YORK

Bridgehampton
Brennan, Paul *real estate broker*
Morabito, Enzo C. *real estate broker*
Saunders, Andrew *real estate company executive, real estate developer*

Bronx
Carter, Majora J. *urban planner*

Brooklyn
Gilmartin, MaryAnne *real estate development company executive*

Dundee
Miller, Ronald K. *real estate broker, educator*

East Greenbush
Morris, Margretta Elizabeth *conservationist*

East Hampton
DePersia, Gary R. *real estate company executive, broker*

Elmsford
Raymond, George Marc *city planner, educator*

Harrison
Strone, Michael Jonathan *real estate consultant, lawyer, art consultant*

Hunters Point
Lundgren, Richard John *real estate executive, city planner, preservationist*

Larchmont
Levi, James Harry *real estate executive, investment banker*

Long Beach
Kasner, David A. *real estate consultant, investor*

Mineola
Long, Graham E. *urban planner*

Mount Vernon
Rossini, Joseph *contracting and development corporate executive*

New York
Allee, Debra Cole *environmental consultant*
Barnett, Gary (Gershon Swiatycki) *real estate company executive*

Battle-Bey, Marva Smith *non-profit urban planning executive*
Beinecke, Frances G. *environmentalist*
Blau, Jeff T. *real estate company executive*
Boardman, Serena P. *real estate broker*
Burden, Amanda Jay Mortimer *urban planner, city official*
Close, Michael John *property manager, lawyer*
Consolo, Faith Hope *real estate company executive*
Corcoran, Barbara Anne *retired real estate company executive*
Del Nunzio, Paula *real estate company executive*
Dubin, Louis M. *real estate company executive, entrepreneur*
Farley, Katherine G. *real estate company executive*
Fascitelli, Michael Damon *real estate company executive*
Felman, Michelle *real estate investment company executive*
Field, Nikki E. *real estate broker*
Fisher, Kenneth *real estate company executive*
Garfield, Leslie Jerome *real estate executive*
Gochberg, Thomas *real estate investor, investment banker*
Grau, Marcy Beinish *real estate broker, former investment banker*
Gray, Jonathan David *real estate company executive*
Green, Stephen Lawrence *real estate developer*
Guberman, Josh *real estate company officer, real estate developer*
Hackett, Kevin R. *real estate company executive, lawyer*
Hackett, Veronica W. *real estate development company executive*
Herman, Dorothy (Dottie Herman) *real estate company executive*
Hernstadt, Judith Filenbaum *city planner, real estate and broadcast executive*
Justin, Henry *real estate developer*
Kalikow, Peter Stephen *real estate developer, former transportation and publishing executive*
Kennedy, Robert Francis, Jr. *environmentalist, radio talk show host*
Lachman, Marguerite Leanne *real estate investment advisor*
LeFrak, Richard Stone *real estate developer*
Liebman, Pamela *real estate company executive*
Macklowe, Harry B. *real estate developer*
Macklowe, William S. *real estate company executive*
Milstein, Paul *real estate developer*
Modlin, Adam D. *real estate company executive*
Mosler, Bruce Elliot *real estate company executive*
Nichols, Edie Diane *real estate broker*
Pearl, Mary Corliss *wildlife conservationist*
Petz, Edwin V. *real estate company executive, lawyer*
Quinn, Andrew Thomas *urban planner*
Rampe, Kevin M. *real estate developer*
Rosen, Aby Jacob *real estate developer*
Ross, Stephen Michael *real estate company executive, professional sports team owner*
Roth, Steven *real estate company executive*
Ruben, Lawrence *real estate developer and company executive, lawyer*
Schenker, Gregg L. *real estate company executive*
Sciame, Frank J. *real estate developer, construction executive*
Scott, Stanley DeForest *real estate company executive*
Shvo, Michael *real estate broker*
Sigety, Cornelius Edward *real estate developer, director*
Silverstein, Larry A. *real estate developer*
Sloane, Kathy *real estate broker*
Smith, Meredyth Hull *real estate broker*
Solow, Sheldon H. *real estate developer*
Speyer, Jerry I. *real estate company executive*
Srivastava, Rohit *real estate company executive, researcher*
Stacom, Darcy A. *real estate company executive*
Stacom, Tara Irene *real estate company executive*
Stern, Leonard Norman *real estate developer, former pet supply manufacturing company executive*
Sunshine, Louise Mintz *real estate marketing executive*
Swig, Kent M. *real estate company executive*
Teplitzky, Jacky *real estate broker*
Tighe, Mary Ann *real estate company executive*
Trump, Donald John *real estate developer*
Trump, Ivanka Marie *real estate company executive*
Webb, Eugene Henry *real estate company executive*
Weiss, Donald S. *real estate developer*
Yunis, Amira *real estate company officer*

Saranac Lake
Kretser, Heidi Elizabeth *conservationist, researcher*

Southampton
Sheehy, Betty Jo *real estate company executive, investment advisor*

NORTH CAROLINA

Benson
Lunn, Ronald Alan *environmentalist*

Boone
Conrad, David Paul *business broker, real estate developer, retired food service executive*

Charlotte
Taylor, Harry *real estate broker*

Greensboro
Diouf, Arona Ndoffene *environmentalist, educator*

Statesville
Redman, William Walter, Jr. *retired NC state senator, NC state utilities commissioner*

OHIO

Chagrin Falls
Stec, John Zygmunt *retired real estate company officer*

Cincinnati
Ten Eyck, Dorothea Fariss *real estate agent*

Cleveland
Canepari, Bernard Louis *environmentalist, actor*

Columbus
Coopersmith, Jeffrey Alan *real estate developer*
Pizzuti, Ronald A. *real estate developer*
Pyatt, Leo Anthony *retired real estate broker*

Dayton
Wertz, Kenneth Dean *real estate company officer*

Orange Village
Jones, Susan Dorfman *real estate broker, writer*

Shaker Heights
Solganik, Marvin *real estate executive*

Youngstown
Camacci, Michael A. *real estate broker and developer, consultant*

OKLAHOMA

Oklahoma City
Binning, Gene Barton *real estate company executive*

Tulsa
Ball, Rex Martin *urban planner, architect*

OREGON

Oakland
Lopez, Delia *real estate manager*

Pendleton
Muller, Michael *land use planner, educator*

Portland
Packard, Robert Goodale III *urban planner*

PENNSYLVANIA

Allentown
Saab, Deanne Keltum *real estate broker, appraiser*

Bala Cynwyd
Glazer, William H. *real estate developer*

Blue Bell
Deschaine, Barbara Ralph *retired real estate broker*

Bryn Mawr
Pew, Robert Anderson *retired real estate and equipment leasing corporation officer*

Erie
Gottschalk, Frank Klaus *real estate company executive*

Harrisburg
Fenstermacher, Joyce Doris *real estate agent and appraiser*

Horsham
Barzilay, Zvi *real estate developer*
Toll, Bruce Elliot *real estate developer*

Philadelphia
Barnett, Jonathan *urban planner, educator, architect*
Peck, Robert McCracken *naturalist, historian, writer*

Saint Davids
Bertsch, Frederick Charles III *appraiser, finance company executive*

State College
Porter, Richard James *real estate broker, art historian, actor, voice over artist*

York
Rebert, Jephrey Lee *urban planner, musician*

RHODE ISLAND

Warwick
Losek, Darren Thomas *property manager, sales manager*

SOUTH CAROLINA

Columbia
Carr, Edward R. *environmentalist, educator*
Hallman, Cecilia Ann *real estate consultant*
Limehouse, Harry Bancroft, Jr. *real estate developer, transportation consultant*

Hilton Head Island
Gruchacz, Robert S. *real estate company officer*
Yates-Williams, Linda Snow *real estate broker*

SOUTH DAKOTA

Rapid City
Hamilton, Douglas Warren *real estate executive*

TENNESSEE

Chattanooga
Harrison (Ingle), Bettye (Bettye Ingle) *real estate company executive*

Kingsport
Bailey, William Henry *real estate appraiser*

Nashville
van der Harst, John Jay *environmentalist*

TEXAS

Dallas
Cherry, William Speakman *real estate consultant and broker*
Doran, Mark Richard *real estate financial executive*
Marlow, Patricia Bair Bond *realtor*
McInnis, Carolyn Crawford *real estate broker*
McPherson, Gail *publishing and real estate executive*

Fort Worth
Smith, Tracey *real estate broker*

Galveston
McLeod, E. Douglas *real estate developer, lawyer*
Shelton, Kenneth R., Jr. *real estate company executive, artist*

Garland
McGrath, James Thomas *real estate investment company executive*

Granbury
Almy, Earle Vaughn, Jr., (Buddy) *real estate executive*

Houston
Blackburn, Sadie Gwin Allen *conservation executive*
Daugherty, John A., Jr. *realtor*
Duncan, Robert D. *real estate company executive*
Goldsmith, Billy Joe *real estate broker, rancher*
Heard, Larry *real estate company executive*
Morris, Malcolm Stewart *title company executive, lawyer*
Rigby, Weldon *realtor*
Untermeyer, Charles Graves (Chase Untermeyer) *real estate company executive*

Irving
Lambert-Saul, Beth *real estate company executive*

Plano
Perot, Ross (H. Ross Perot, Henry Ross Perot) *real estate company, investment company, data processing executive*
Perot, Ross, Jr., (Henry Ross Perot Jr.) *real estate developer, professional sports team executive*

Port Aransas
Turner, Elizabeth Adams Noble (Betty Turner) *real estate company executive, author*

San Antonio
Burke, Betty Jane *retired real estate manager*
Condos, Barbara Seale *real estate broker, developer, investor*

UTAH

Midvale
Teerlink, J(oseph) Leland *real estate developer*

VIRGINIA

Alexandria
Ellmore, Mark *real estate consultant*

Amissville
Hartke, Anita *real estate broker*

Appomattox
Beatson, LeGrande Guerry *environmental health specialist*

Arlington
Koury, Agnes Lillian *real estate property manager*
Watkins, Birge Swift *real estate investment executive*

Blacksburg
Dietrich, Andrea M. *environmentalist, educator*

Chesapeake
Owens, Susan Elizabeth *realtor*

Mc Lean
Nobil, James Howard, Jr. *real estate investor, developer, broker, consultant*
Talbot, Martha Hayne *conservationist, biologist*

Newport News
Goldberg, Stanley Irwin *real estate company executive*

Richmond
Chandler, Theodore Lindy, Jr. *title insurance company executive, lawyer*
Tuck, Grayson Edwin *real estate agent, gas industry executive*

Vienna
Carr, Thomas A. *real estate company executive*

Virginia Beach
Smith, Bruce *real estate company executive, retired professional football player*

WASHINGTON

Bellevue
Scott, J. Lennox *real estate company executive*

Bellingham
Bourm, Roger Michael *real estate broker, investor, property manager*

Edmonds
Bell, Nancy Lee Hoyt *real estate investor, middle school educator, volunteer*

Seattle
Blanco, Hilda J. *urban planner, educator*
Friedman, Andy *realtor*
Healey, Ada M. *real estate developer*
Kirk, Judd *real estate development executive*
Kruse, Shari *real estate agent*
McKenrick, Laurence Lee *environmentalist*
True, William L. (Bill True) *retired real estate company executive*

Spokane
Covey, Michael J. *forest products and real estate executive*

WEST VIRGINIA

Morgantown
Schaeffer, Peter (Peter Viktor Schaeffer) *urban and regional planning educator*

WISCONSIN

Appleton
Wieckert, Steven Kelly *real estate developer, former state legislator*

Beaver Dam
Butterbrodt, John Ervin *real estate company officer*

Madison
Jacobs, Harvey M. *urban planner, educator*
Moyer-Horner, Lucas *conservationist, educator*
Ring, Gerald J. *real estate developer, insurance company executive*

Mequon
Sullivan, Patricia W. (Terry Sullivan) *real estate trainer*

Wausau
Prey, Yvonne Mary *real estate broker*

CANADA

BRITISH COLUMBIA

Vancouver
Evans, John deCourcey *real estate company officer*

Victoria
Barrie, Len *real estate developer, professional sports team executive*

ONTARIO

Toronto
Carrothers, Gerald Arthur Patrick *environmental and city planning educator*
Dimma, William Andrew *real estate executive*
Eagles, Stuart Ernest *real estate company officer*
Tanenbaum, Joey *real estate developer*

BRAZIL

São Paulo
Antunes, Celina *real estate company executive*

ENGLAND

London
Hall, Sir Peter Geoffrey *urban and regional planning educator*

HONG KONG

North Point
Lee, Shau Kee *real estate developer*

INDIA

New Delhi
Singh, Kushal Pal (K.P.) *real estate developer*

KENYA

Nairobi
Maathai, Wangari *environmentalist, consultant*

MONACO

Monte Carlo
Lovett, Laurence Dow *retired real estate and steamship executive*

SPAIN

Adeje
Grindley, Bruce Alan *real estate agency executive*

UNITED ARAB EMIRATES

Dubai
Hegazy, Abdelatif M. *real estate company executive*

ADDRESS UNPUBLISHED

Anderson, Paulette Elizabeth *real estate developer, entrepreneur, retired elementary school educator*
Aulbach, George Louis *retired real estate company executive*
Barney, Austin Dunham, II, *real estate developer*
Bartlett, Arthur Eugene *real estate company executive*
Beal, Merrill David *conservationist, museum director*
Bergau, Frank Conrad *real estate, commercial and investment properties executive*
Bernhardt, Arthur Dieter *urban planner, consultant*
Blackburn, Larry H. *builder*
Bowman, Roger Manwaring *real estate company officer*
Bowne, Shirlee Pearson *real estate consultant*
Brock, Eric John *urban planner, historian, consultant*
Brooks, Michael Paul *retired urban planning educator*
Chase, J. Vincent *property manager*
Christensen, C. Lewis *real estate developer*
Citro, Yolande *real estate agent*
Corey, Kenneth Edward *urban planning and geography educator, researcher*
Crafton-Masterson, Adrienne *retired real estate company executive*
Crumbley, Esther Helen Kendrick *retired real estate agent, retired secondary school educator, councilwoman*
Cunningham, Valerie S. *historic preservationist, researcher*
Dasso, Jerome Joseph *real estate educator*
Davis, John Warren *retired real estate broker, consultant*
DeBock, Ronald Gene *real estate company executive*
Desloge, Christopher Davis, Sr. *real estate company, merchant banking and consulting executive*
DeYoung, Marilyn Brant-Chandler *retired urban planner, farmer*
Di Cecco, James *real estate company executive*
Dysart, Benjamin Clay III *conservationist, engineer, consultant*
Edwards, Kathleen *real estate broker, former educator*
Ellett, Alan Sidney *real estate developer*
Estrin, Richard William *real estate and business broker, retired editor*
Fischer, Michael Ludwig *environmental executive*
Friedman, Howard W. *retired real estate company executive*
Furlotti, Alexander Amato *real estate and investment company executive*
Galvis, Camilo Andres *real estate company executive, researcher*
Gasper, Ruth Eileen *real estate executive*
Ghebrhiwet, Freweiny Wendy *real estate broker, consultant*
Gilbert, Frederick E. *development planner, Africanist, consultant*
Glindeman, Henry Peter, Jr. *real estate developer*
Goddess, Lynn Barbara *real estate investor*
Godwin, Ralph Lee, Jr. *real estate executive*
Hakala, Karen Louise *retired real estate specialist*
Hedreen, Richard C. *real estate developer*
Heimbold, Margaret Byrne *realtor, publisher, poet, consultant*
Hero, Aphrodite S. *retired real estate developer, retired personnel director*
Hietala, Valerie Grace *alpaca rancher, realtor, environmentalist, educator*
Holleb, Doris B. *urban planner, economist*
Ingberman, Sima Blumenfeld *real estate company officer*
Jennison, Brian (Lester) *retired environmental specialist*
Kollaer, Jim C. *real estate executive, architect*
Kremer, Honor Frances (Noreen Kremer) *real estate broker, small business owner*
Lamy, M. Rebecca (Mary Rebecca Lamy) *consultant, land developer, government official*
Lax, Philip *land developer, space planner, retired*
Louargand, Marc Andrew *real estate executive, financial consultant*
Maier, Robert Henry *retired real estate executive*
Maloney, James Henry *community development executive, former congressman*
Mattano, Rebecca L. *environmentalist, educator*
Mayro, Karl R. *realtor*
McNeil, Edward Warren *real estate company executive*
Mercer, Dorothy May *real estate company executive*
Mercurio, Renard Michael *real estate company executive*
Michael, George T. *real estate manager, developer*
Page, Patricia (Patty) Newton *real estate broker, real estate company executive*
Pan, Qisheng *urban planner, educator*
Payne, Daniel Harold (Harold Payne) *real estate developer, small business owner*
Pence, Jean Virginia (Jean Pence) *retired real estate broker*
Raven, Patricia Elaine (Penny Raven) *real estate broker, developer, columnist*
Regal, Randall Nathaniel *policy analyst*
Rosen, Michael Howard *real estate executive*
Rowe-Maas, Betty Lu *real estate analyst*
Rumpakis, E. John *realtor emeritus*
Sanquist, Nancy Johnson *real estate technology consultant, educator*
Schell, Melvin Frank, Jr. *real estate agent*
Smith, Mary Louise *former real estate broker*
Snook, Paul *real estate company executive*
Stuebner, James Cloyd *real estate developer, contractor*
Sutter, Jane Elizabeth *conservationist, science educator*
Taubman, A. Alfred *real estate developer*
Toshach, Clarice Oversby *real estate developer, retired computer company executive*
VanButsel, Michael R. *real estate broker, construction executive*
Vella, Ruth Ann *real estate executive*
Voell, Richard Allen *retired private investor*
Weitz, Melissa *environmentalist*
Whaley, Ross Samuel *environmentalist, educator*
Williams, Phyllis Cutforth *retired realtor*
Wingert, Hannelore Christiane *author, realtor, chemicals executive*
Woods, Sandra Kay *real estate executive*

RELIGION

UNITED STATES

ALABAMA

Bessemer
Collins, Patricia Ann *pastor, pastoral counselor*

Birmingham
Allen, William Jere *minister*
Baker, Robert Joseph *bishop*
Dorsett, Lyle Wesley *religious studies educator*
Hull, William Edward *theology studies educator*

Florence
Barfield, Kenny Dale *religious organization administrator*
Warren, David Harold *religious studies educator*

Greensboro
Massey, James Earl *retired clergyman, educator*

Greenville
Longmire, Venus DeLoyse *minister*

Huntsville
Malm, Carl Elmer *minister, educator*

Mobile
Campbell, Stephen Frank *theology studies educator*
Lipscomb, Oscar Hugh *archbishop emeritus*
Rodi, Thomas John *archbishop*

ALASKA

Anchorage
Schwietz, Roger L. *archbishop*

Fairbanks
Kettler, Donald Joseph *bishop*

Juneau
Burns, Edward James *bishop*

ARIZONA

Flagstaff
Lapsley, James Norvell, Jr. *minister, educator*

Green Valley
Pike, George Harold, Jr. *religious organization administrator, clergyman*

Hereford
Seeland, Arthur David *bishop*

Phoenix
Dino, Gerald Nicholas *bishop*
Olmsted, Thomas James *bishop*

Sun City
Hamilton, Ronald Ray *minister*

Tempe
Barfoot, Charles Howard *theology studies educator*
Emerson, Charles LeRoy *religious studies educator*

Tucson
Ingram, Charles Owen *priest, educator*
Kicanas, Gerald Frederick *bishop*
Waterbury, Deborah Kay *minister*

ARKANSAS

Arkadelphia
Pemberton, Barbara Butler *religious studies educator*

Conway
Harris, Marjorie Jane *religious studies educator*
Leffler, Jean Riise *religious organization administrator*

Hot Springs Village
Smith, Preston *retired minister, small business owner*

Little Rock
Taylor, Anthony Basil *bishop*

Russellville
Inch, Morris Alton *theology educator*

Walnut Ridge
Gore, Kenneth Wendell, Jr. *religious studies educator*

CALIFORNIA

Angwin
Kurtz, Robert Walden *theology, philosophy, mathematics studies educator, pastor, writer*

Azusa
Adams, Jim J. *minister and higher education administrator*

Bakersfield
Frazier, Jo Frances *religious organization administrator, writer*

Baldwin Park
Driskill, James Lawrence *minister*

Berkeley
Bazian, Hatem Ahmad *religious studies educator, consultant*
Stagaman, David John *priest, theology educator*

Burbank
Bower, Richard James *minister*

Camarillo
Epperson, Stuart W. *religious raido broadcaster*

Castro Valley
Morrison, Glenn Leslie *minister*

Chula Vista
Russom, James Rayford *minister*

Claremont
Coleman, Monica Anita *theology studies educator*
Sanders, James Alvin *retired minister, retired religious studies educator*

Corona
Wood, Brenda Jean *pastor, evangelist*

Costa Mesa
Ortlund, Anne (Elizabeth Anne Ortlund) *writer, musician*
Williams, William Corey *theology educator, consultant*

El Cajon
Jammo, Sarhad Yawsip Hermiz *bishop*

Elk Grove
Vang, Timothy Teng *religious organization administrator*

Escondido
Linzey, Verna May *minister, writer*

Fountain Valley
Carter, John Frederick *missionary educator*
Einstein, Stephen Jan *rabbi*

Fresno
Steinbock, John Thomas *bishop*
Xiong, Tousu Saydangnmyang *minister, theology studies educator*

Happy Camp
Black, Barbara Ann *publisher*

Hayward
Shannon, Patricia D. *theology studies educator*

Irvine
Maas, Korey Devlin *religious studies educator*

Irwindale
Zavala, Gabino *bishop*

La Jolla
Waddy, Lawrence Heber *writer*

La Mirada
Edwards, John Kent *religious studies educator, minister*
Hayward, Douglas J. *religious studies educator*

La Quinta
Mathre, Lawrence Gerhard *minister, federal agency administrator*

Lake Forest
Warren, Rick (Richard Duane Warren) *minister, writer*

Lomita
Sartoris, Joseph Martin *bishop emeritus*

Los Angeles
Blake, Charles E. *minister, bishop*
Boyd, Malcolm *minister, writer*
Breuer, Stephen Ernest *religious organization administrator, consultant*
Chedid, John George *bishop emeritus*
Clark, Edward *bishop*
Fitzgerald, Tikhon (Lee R. H. Fitzgerald) *bishop*
Freehling, Allen Isaac *rabbi*
Mahony, Roger Michael *cardinal, archbishop*
Ogilvie, Lloyd John *clergyman*
Phillips, Keith Wendall *minister*
Price, Frederick Kenneth Cercie *minister*
Salazar, Alexander *bishop*
Shaheen, Robert Joseph *bishop*
Solis, Oscar Azarcon *bishop*
Ward, John James *bishop emeritus*

Menlo Park
DuMaine, R. Pierre *bishop emeritus*

Mission Hills
Wilkerson, Gerald Eugene *bishop*

Monterey
Garcia, Richard John *bishop*
Ryan, Sylvester Donovan *bishop emeritus*

Oakland
Cordileone, Salvatore Joseph *bishop*

Orange
Brown, Tod David *bishop*
Flores, Cirilo *bishop*
Luong, Dominic *bishop*
McFarland, Norman Francis *bishop*

Palm Desert
Ponder, Catherine *clergywoman*
Stenhouse, Everett Ray *clergy administrator*

Palm Springs
Jones, Milton Wakefield *publisher*

Pasadena
Bradley, James Edwin *religious studies educator*
Jo, Chulsu *theologian*

Portola Valley
Garsh, Thomas Burton *publisher*

Rancho Palos Verdes
Dunlop, Laurence James *religious studies educator*

Reedley
Dick, Henry Henry *minister*

Sacramento
Madera Uribe, Jose de Jesus *bishop emeritus*
Quinn, Francis Anthony *bishop emeritus*
Soto, Jaime *bishop*
Weigand, William Kenneth *Bishop Emeritus*

San Anselmo
Noel, James Anthony *religious studies educator, minister*

San Bernardino
Barnes, Gerald Richard *bishop*
Del Riego, Rutilio J. *bishop*

San Diego
Brom, Robert Henry *bishop*
Chavez, Gilbert Espinoza *bishop emeritus*
Downing, David Charles *retired minister*
Hunt, Barnabas John *priest, religious organization administrator*
Lechner, Roger A. *monsignor*

San Francisco
Justice, William J. *bishop*
Kelly, James Anthony *priest*
Niederauer, George H. *archbishop*
Quinn, John Raphael *archbishop emeritus*
Rosen, Moishe *religious organization founder*
Wang, Ignatius Chung *bishop emeritus*
Williams, Cecil *minister*

San Jose
Edmonds, Charles Henry *retired publisher*

San Leandro
Sawyer, Malcolm James, Jr. *religious studies educator*

Santa Barbara
Curry, Thomas John *bishop*
Holdrege, Barbara A. *religious studies educator*

Santa Clara
McGrath, Patrick Joseph *bishop*

Santa Clarita
Varner, William *religious studies educator*

Santa Rosa
Walsh, Daniel Francis *bishop*
Ziemann, George Patrick *bishop emeritus*

Sonora
Chandler, Edwin Russell *clergyman, writer*

Stockton
Blaire, Stephen Edward *bishop*

Studio City
Meenan, Alan John *clergyman, theology studies educator*

Thousand Oaks
Hudson, Barbara *writer, actor*

Upland
Jordan, Charles Wesley *retired bishop*

Vista
Olson, Linda Ann Salmonson *minister*

COLORADO

Aurora
Nichols, Clyde Richard *minister, consumer products company executive*

Boulder
Hoover, Stewart Mark *religious studies educator*

Colorado Springs
Dobson, James Clayton *evangelist, psychologist, author*
Hanifen, Richard Charles Patrick *bishop emeritus*
Pickle, Joseph Wesley, Jr. *religious studies educator*
Sheridan, Michael John *bishop*

Denver
Chaput, Charles J. *archbishop*
Conley, James Douglas *auxiliary bishop*
Murphy, Sister Lillian *sister, not-for-profit organization executive*
Sheeran, Michael John Leo *priest, academic administrator*

Dillon
Follett, Robert John Richard *publisher*

Fort Collins
Chorpenning, H. R. III *minister*
Rolston, Holmes III *theology studies educator, philosopher*

Greeley
Jackson, Paul Howard *minister*

Lakewood
Wilcox, Mary Marks *retired Christian education consultant, educator*

Pueblo
Tafoya, Arthur Nicholas *bishop*

CONNECTICUT

Bloomfield
Cronin, Daniel Anthony *archbishop emeritus*

Bridgeport
Lori, William Edward *bishop*

Canaan
Beizer, Lance Kurt *retired priest, lawyer*

Colchester
Nikirk, Susan Silva (Susan Silva) *minister, writer, dancer, consultant*

Greenwich
Moore, John Plunkett Dennis *publisher*

Guilford
Ogletree, Thomas Warren *retired religious studies educator*

Hamden
Forman, Charles William *religious studies educator*
Weinstein, Stanley *Buddhist studies educator*

Hartford
Hamilton, Hugh Basil *minister*
Macaluso, Christie A. *bishop*
Mansell, Henry J. *archbishop*
Mattson, Ingrid *theology studies educator, religious organization administrator*
Winter, Miriam Therese (Gloria Frances Winter) *nun, religious studies educator*

Middletown
Rockwood, Irving E., Jr. *publisher*

New Haven
Bowering, Gerhard *religious studies educator*
Rosazza, Peter Anthony *bishop*

New London
Clarke, Florence Dorothy *minister, educator*

Norwich
Cote, Michael Richard *bishop*

Plantsville
Roy, Ralph Lord *clergyman*

Redding
Begell, William *publisher*

Sharon
Tucker, Alan David *publisher*

Southport
Twiname, John Dean *minister, human services administrator*

Stamford
Chomnycky, Paul Patrick *bishop*
Losten, Basil Harry *bishop emeritus*

Storrs Mansfield
Baldwin, Carlita Rose *minister*

Wilton
Davis, Joel *publisher*

Woodstock Valley
Allaby, Stanley Reynolds *clergyman*

DELAWARE

Wilmington
Linderman, Jeanne Herron *priest*
Malooly, William Francis *bishop*
Nichols, George Leon, Jr. *minister*
Saltarelli, Michael Angelo *bishop*

DISTRICT OF COLUMBIA

Washington
Ahmed, Akbar S. *religious studies educator*
Black, Barry C. *chaplain, retired military officer*
Broglio, Timothy Paul Andrew *archbishop*
Combs, Roberta *political organization president CEO*
Coughlin, Daniel P. *chaplain*
Delio, Ilia *theology studies educator*
Di Lella, Alexander Anthony *biblical studies educator*
Dimino, Joseph Thomas *archbishop emeritus*
DuBois, Joshua *minister, federal official*
Dunn, James Milton *retired religious organization administrator*
Dunton, James Raynor *publisher*
Dyson, Michael Eric *religious studies educator, writer*
Estabrook, Joseph Walter *bishop*
Fitzmyer, Joseph Augustine *theology studies educator, priest*
Higgins, Richard Brendan *bishop*
LaHaye, Beverly *religious organization administrator*
Leckey, Dolores R. *religious organization administrator, writer*
Lustig, M. Bruce *rabbi*
Marrett, Michael McFarlene *chaplain*
Novak, Michael (John) *religion educator, author, editor*
Outlaw, Wanda Cecelia *priest*
Ross, Annie Lee *minister, counselor*
Sambi, Pietro *archbishop*
Skeris, Robert Alexander *theology and church music educator*
Smith, T. DeWitt, Jr. *religious organization administrator*
Weigel, George Shillow, Jr. *theologian*
Wogaman, John Philip *retired minister and educator*
Zikmund, Barbara Brown *minister, religious organization administrator, educator*

FLORIDA

Bartow
Meuser, Fredrick William *retired church administrator, historian*

Boca Raton
Agler, Richard Dean *rabbi*

Boynton Beach
Lessard, Raymond William *bishop emeritus*

Coral Gables
Fitzgerald, John Thomas, Jr. *religious studies educator*

Crawfordville
Brumby, James Remley, III, (Knox Brumby) *retired priest*

Daytona Beach
Bronson, Oswald Perry, Sr. *religious organization administrator, clergyman*

Fort Walton Beach
Williams, Bethtina Qubré *minister*

Jacksonville
Anthony, Yancey Lamar *minister*
David, Thompson Stuart *religious studies educator*
Galeone, Victor Benito *bishop*
Snyder, John Joseph *bishop emeritus*

Lakeland
Davis, Joseph H. *theology studies educator*
Fettke, Steven M. *religious studies educator*

Leesburg
Genzen, Gary Carl *retired minister*

Madison
Paulk, David Mitchell, II, *religious studies educator*

Miami
Noonan, John Gerard *bishop emeritus*
Rodríguez, Agustín Alejo Román *bishop emeritus*

Miami Shores
Estevez, Felipe de Jesús *bishop*
Favalora, John Clement *archbishop*
Fernández, Gilberto *bishop emeritus*

New Port Richey
O'Farrell, Mark Theodore *religious organization administrator*

Ocala
Massa, Conrad Harry *retired religious studies educator*

Orlando
Dorsey, Norbert M. *bishop emeritus*
Forbes, Daniel Merrill *minister*
Wenski, Thomas Gerard *bishop*

Palm Beach Gardens
Barbarito, Gerald Michael *bishop*
Symons, Joseph Keith *bishop emeritus*

Palmetto Bay
Weeks, Marta Joan *retired priest*

Penney Farms
Muilenburg, John Powell *minister*

Pensacola
Baldwin, Chuck (Charles O. Baldwin) *minister, radio personality*
Mountcastle, William Wallace, Jr. *retired philosophy and religion educator*
Ricard, John Huston *bishop, religious studies educator*
Stokes, Mack Boyd (Marion) *bishop*

Pompano Beach
Corsello, Lily Joann *minister, counselor, educator*

Saint Augustine
Couture, Sister Diane Rhea *sister, artist, educator*
Reeher, James Irwin *minister*

Saint Petersburg
Lemoi, Brian André *religious organization administrator, religious studies educator, writer*
Lynch, Robert Nugent *bishop*
Petty, M. S. Marty *publisher*

Sarasota
Jones, Tracey Kirk, Jr. *retired minister, educator*
McFarlin, Diane Hooten *publisher*

Venice
Dewane, Frank Joseph *bishop*
Nevins, John Joseph *bishop emeritus*

Vero Beach
Beran, Denis Carl *publisher*

West Palm Beach
Nolan, Richard Thomas *clergyman, educator*

Winter Haven
Boully, LaJuan Bonnie *minister, religious studies educator*

GEORGIA

Americus
Reckford, Jonathan Thomas More *nonprofit organization administrator*

Atlanta
Bryant, Gregory Alexander *bishop*
Gregory, Wilton Daniel *archbishop*
Keiller, James Bruce *clergyman, dean*
Massey, Denise McLain *theology studies educator*
Zarama, Luis Rafael *bishop*

Augusta
Davis, Minnie P. *minister*

Bartow
Cason, Cedric Lee *religious studies educator*

College Park
Dollar, Creflo A. *minister, religious organization administrator*

Dublin
Sapp, Peggy G. *pastor, editor, writer, speech professional*

Flintstone
Ragon, Robert Ronald *clergyman*

Lawrenceville
Brannon, Ronald Roy *retired minister*

Macon
Franklin, Roosevelt *minister*

Marietta
Slomanski, Rev. Patricia Parker *minister*

Mc Rae
Allen, Annette *minister*

Norcross
Granger, Philip Richard *minister*

Perry
Jackson, Rutha Mae *pastor, military reserve officer, secondary school educator*

Savannah
Boland, John Kevin *bishop*

Vidalia
Fountain, Edwin Byrd *minister, librarian, poet*

Woodstock
Collins, David Browning *religious institution administrator*

HAWAII

Honolulu
Silva, Clarence Richard *bishop*

Kahului
Domingo, Cora Maria Corazon Encarnacion *minister*

Kapaa
Veylanswami, Satguru Bodhinatha *head of religious order*

IDAHO

Boise
Driscoll, Michael Patrick *bishop*

Moscow
Leithart, Peter James *theologian*

Nampa
Bowes, A. Wendell *religious studies educator*
Rotz, Carol *retired theology studies educator*

ILLINOIS

Aurora
O'Donnell, Mickie Louise *religious educator*

Barrington
Hybels, Bill *Pastor*

Belleville
Braxton, Edward Kenneth *bishop*
Schlarman, Stanley Girard *bishop emeritus*
Wittenbrink, Boniface Leo *priest*

Bloomington
Skillrud, Harold Clayton *minister, retired bishop*

Chicago
Arnold, Daniel *religious studies educator*
Betz, Hans Dieter *theology studies educator*
Browning, Don Spencer *religious educator*
Chester, Stephen John *religious studies educator*
Doniger, Wendy *history of religions educator*
Farrakhan, Louis (Louis Eugene Walcott) *religious organization administrator*
Gadus, Peg *pastoral associate*
Garcia-Siller, Gustavo *bishop*
George, Francis Eugene Cardinal *cardinal, archbishop*
Goedert, Raymond Emil *bishop emeritus*
Hanson, Mark S. *bishop*
Harris, Mildred Clopton *clergy member, educator*
Hubbard, Robert Louis, Jr. *religious studies educator*
Jakubowski, Thaddeus Joseph *bishop emeritus*
Jegen, Sister Carol Frances *religious studies educator*
Kane, Francis Joseph *bishop*
Lotocky, Innocent Hilarion *bishop emeritus*
Lyne, Timothy Joseph *bishop emeritus*
Manz, John R. *bishop*
McDonald, Theresa Beatrice Pierce (Mrs. Ollie McDonald) *church official, minister*
McGinn, Bernard John *theologian, educator*
Poethig, Eunice Blanchard *clergywoman*
Reece, Beth Pauley *chaplain*
Sabatini, Lawrence *bishop emeritus*
Seminack, Richard Stephen *bishop*
Senior, Donald Paul *religious organization administrator*
Weber, Richard Martin *theology studies educator*
Wright, Jeremiah Alvesta, Jr. *retired minister*
Yu, Anthony C. *religion and literature educator*

Cicero
Paprocki, Thomas John *bishop, lawyer*

Deerfield
Harris, Dana Michelle *religious studies educator*

Elgin
Almen, Lowell Gordon *clergy, church official*
Braaten, Laurie J. *religious studies educator*

Elmhurst
Angadiath, Jacob *bishop*
Lee, Nancy C. *religious studies educator*

Evanston
Orsi, Robert *religious studies educator*

Flossmoor
Cary, William Sterling *retired church executive*

Galva
Swatos, William Henry, Jr. *priest, sociologist*

Joliet
Imesch, Joseph Leopold *bishop emeritus*
Sartain, James Peter *bishop*

Lake Forest
Feinberg, Jeffrey Enoch *religious studies educator, writer*

Libertyville
Rassas, George James *bishop*

Lincoln
Kurka, Robert Charles *minister, educator*
Mangano, Mark J. *religious studies educator*

Mahomet
Mashbern, William Allen *minister, retired religious organization administrator*

Moline
Johnson, Mary Lou *lay worker, educator*

Oak Park
Thomas, Malayilmelathethil *minister, English language educator*

Orland Park
Gorman, John Robert *bishop emeritus*

Palatine
McDonald, Andrew J. *bishop emeritus*

Peoria
Jenky, Daniel Robert *bishop*
Parsons, Donald James *retired bishop*
Saxon, Randall Lee *pastor, author, educator*

River Forest
O'Meara, Thomas Franklin *priest, educator*
Steinmann, Andrew E. *theology studies educator*
Weldon, Clodagh *theology studies educator*

Robbins
James, Marie Moody *clergywoman, musician, vocal music educator*

Rockford
Doran, Thomas George *bishop*
Gregory, Dola Bell *bishop, customer service administrator*
O'Neill, Arthur Joseph *bishop emeritus*

South Holland
Perry, Joseph Nathaniel *bishop*

Springfield
Beckwith, Peter Hess *bishop*
Bell, John Perry *minister, religious organization administrator*
Ryan, Daniel Leo *bishop emeritus*

Villa Park
Pittelko, Roger Dean *clergyman, theology studies educator*

Wauconda
Gotthardt, Mary Jane *school teacher*

Wheaton
Schwanda, Tom *religious studies educator*
Warner, William Kent, Jr. *religious organization administrator, consultant*

INDIANA

Anderson
Conrad, Harold August *retired religious pension board executive*
Shively, Fredrick Harold *religious studies educator*

Burlington
Roussakis, Peter Ellwood *minister, publisher*

Evansville
Gettelfinger, Gerald Andrew *bishop*

Fishers
Christenson, Le Roy Howard *missions mobilizer*

Fort Wayne
D'Arcy, John Michael *bishop*

Fortville
Horner, Sylvia Ann *minister, real estate broker*

Indianapolis
Brown, Frank Burch *theology studies educator, writer*
Buechlein, Daniel Mark *archbishop*
Crow, Paul Abernathy, Jr. *retired minister*
Enright, William Gerald *religious institute administrator*
Smith, Donald Archie *religious business executive, consultant*
Watkins, Harold Robert *minister*
Watkins, Sharon Elizabeth *minister, religious organization administrator*
Woodring, DeWayne Stanley *religious organization administrator*

Jasper
Brenner, Raymond Anthony *priest*

Lafayette
Higi, William Leo *bishop*
Minor, Ronald Ray *minister*

Merrillville
Tlapa, Richard Joseph *retired priest*

Noblesville
Wilson, Norman Glenn *church administrator, writer*

North Manchester
Shearer, Velma Miller *clergywoman*

Notre Dame
Davis, Stacy Nicole *religious studies educator*
Gribble, Richard Edward, Jr. *priest, educator*
Herdt, Jennifer A. *theology studies educator*
Zachman, Randall Carrington *theology studies educator*

Terre Haute
Chambers, Curtis Allen *clergyman, church administrator*

Upland
Lay, Robert Franklin *religious studies educator*

Winona Lake
Davis, John James *religion educator*
Julien, Thomas Theodore *religious denomination administrator*

IOWA

Cedar Falls
Lindberg, Duane R. *bishop, historian*

Davenport
Amos, Martin John *bishop*
Franklin, William Edwin *bishop emeritus*

Decorah
Farwell, Elwin D. *minister, consultant*

Des Moines
Charron, Joseph Leo *bishop emeritus*
Pates, Richard Edmund *bishop*

Dubuque
Hanus, Jerome George *archbishop*
Thompson, Melinda L. *theologian*

Fort Madison
Lorimer, Thomas Harold *minister*

Griswold
Blackburn, Leila Marie *pastor*

Iowa City
Smith, Frederick M. *religious studies educator*

Lamoni
Eppinger, Priscilla Elaine *religious studies educator*

Sioux City
Nickless, Ralph Walter *bishop*
Soens, Lawrence Donald *bishop emeritus*

KANSAS

Clifton
Compton, Doris Martha *lay worker*

Copeland
Birney, Walter Leroy *religious administrator*

Dodge City
Gilmore, Ronald Michael *bishop*

Kansas City
Keleher, James P. *archbishop emeritus*
Naumann, Joseph Fred *archbishop*

Lawrence
Miller, Timothy Alan *religion educator*

Lenexa
Cunningham, Paul George *minister*

Salina
Coakley, Paul Stagg *bishop*
Fitzsimons, George Kinzie *bishop emeritus*

Topeka
Marney, Brenda Joyce *reverend, computer programmer*

Wichita
Gerber, Eugene John *bishop emeritus*
Harstine, Stan D. *religious studies educator*
Jackels, Michael Owen *bishop*
Nassif, Bradley Louis *research scholar*

KENTUCKY

Crestwood
Roy, Elmon Harold *minister*

Fort Thomas
Hughes, William Anthony *bishop emeritus*

Glasgow
Whittaker, Bill Douglas *minister*

Lexington
Gainer, Ronald William *bishop*

Louisville
Boykin, Gladys *retired religious organization administrator*
Dale, Judy Ries *religious organization administrator, consultant*
Draper, Charles William *religious studies educator*
Fenner, Chris *pastor, musician*
Kelly, Thomas Cajetan *archbishop emeritus*
Kurtz, Joseph Edward *archbishop*
Zimmerman, Gideon K. *retired minister*

Owensboro
Matally, Moses *minister*
McRaith, John Jeremiah *bishop*

Richmond
Ballard, Michael Ray (Mickey Ballard) *minister, music educator*
Wright, John Daniel *minister*

Wilmore
Hiatt, Robert Jeffrey *religious studies educator*
Pohl, Christine D. *Christian ethics educator*

LOUISIANA

Alexandria
Gootee, Christy Beck *minister, educator*
Herzog, Ronald Paul *bishop*

Baton Rouge
Irvine, Stuart Andrew *religious studies educator*
Muench, Robert William *bishop*

Donaldsonville
Watson, Stanley Ellis *clergyman, small business owner*

Gilbert
Bell, Wallace Edward *minister, insurance agent*

Kenner
Carmon, Dominic *bishop emeritus*

Lafayette
Jarrell, Charles Michael *bishop*

Lake Charles
Provost, Glen John *bishop*

Speyrer, Jude *bishop emeritus*

Metairie
Hannan, Philip Matthew *archbishop emeritus*

New Orleans
Aymond, Gregory Michael *archbishop*
Fabre, Shelton Joseph *bishop*
Hughes, Alfred Clifton *Archbishop Emeritus*
Rinker, Craig Wayne *minister, educator*
Schulte, Francis B. *archbishop emeritus*

Pineville
Quarles, Charles Leland *religious studies educator, researcher*

Schriever
Jacobs, Sam Gallip *bishop*

Shreveport
Duca, Michael Gerard *bishop*

Springhill
Morgan, Larry Ronald *minister*

Tioga
Brandow, Stephen Jon *priest*

MAINE

Anson
Quimby, Janice Ann *minister*

Brunswick
Geoghegan, William Davidson *religion educator, minister*

Kingfield
Silver, Sally *minister*

Portland
Ives, Samuel Clifton *minister*
Malone, Richard Joseph *bishop*
Sawyer, Dana Waide *religious studies educator*

South Bristol
Lasher, Esther Lu *minister*

MARYLAND

Baltimore
Borders, William Donald *archbishop emeritus*
Madden, Denis James *bishop*
Mocko, George Paul *minister*
Newman, William Clifford *bishop emeritus*
O'Brien, Edwin Frederick *archbishop*
Robinson, Carrie *pastor*
Robinson, Sally Shoemaker *lay associate*
Rozanski, Mitchell Thomas *bishop*
Zaiman, Joel Hirsh *rabbi*

Chevy Chase
Zahl, Paul Francis Matthew *retired dean*

Columbia
Davis, Benjamin George *theologian, educator*

Gaithersburg
Hall, Arthur Raymond, Jr. *retired minister*

Hurlock
Shively, Bonnie Lee *pastor*

Hyattsville
González Valer, Francisco *bishop*
Holley, Rev. Martin David *bishop*
Knestout, Barry Christopher *bishop*
O'Connor, Kevin Thomas *religious organization administrator*
Wuerl, Donald William *archbishop*

La Plata
Penick, Ann Clarisse *minister, counselor*

Lanham Seabrook
Barnes, Margaret Anderson *behaviorist/minister, statistician*

Laurel
Jones, Coletta L. *minister*

Mitchellville
Brubaker, Lauren Edgar *retired minister*

Rockville
Schwarz, Sidney Howard *rabbi*

Silver Spring
Beach, Bert Beverly *clergyman*
Herbers, Tod Arthur *publisher*

MASSACHUSETTS

Amherst
Wills, David Wood *minister, educator*

Berlin
Lohr, Harold Russell *retired bishop*

Boston
Hart, John William *religion and ecology educator*
Hennessey, Robert Francis *bishop*
Lindberg, Carter Harry *retired religious studies educator*
Mason, Herbert Warren, Jr. *religion and history educator, author*

Braintree
O'Malley, Sean Patrick Cardinal *cardinal, archbishop*

Brighton
Dooher, John Anthony *bishop*

Brookline
Bustros, Cyril Salim *archbishop*

Cambridge
Graham, William Albert *religious studies and history educator*
Kaufman, Gordon Dester *theology studies educator*
Schuessler Fiorenza, Elisabeth *theology studies educator*
Wisse, Ruth R. *religious educator*

Chestnut Hill
Helmick, Raymond Glen *priest, educator*
Keenan, James F. *priest*

Fall River
Coleman, George William *bishop*

Lenox
Collins, Oral Edmond *theology educator, archaeologist*

Methuen
Elya, John Adel *bishop emeritus*
McNaughton, William John *bishop emeritus*

Natick
Edyvean, Walter James *bishop*

Northampton
Derr, Thomas Sieger *religion educator*
Donfried, Karl Paul *theologian, clergyman*

Norton
Worthley, Harold Field *retired minister, educator*

Peabody
Irwin, Francis Xavier *bishop*

South Boston
Boles, John P. *bishop emeritus*

Springfield
Dupré, Thomas Ludger *bishop emeritus*
Maguire, Joseph F. *bishop emeritus*
McDonnell, Timothy Anthony *bishop*

Squantum
Robertson, Michael Swing *minister*

Vineyard Haven
Kimball, Julie Ellis *small press publisher, humorist, writer*

Wenham
Barthold, Lauren Swayne *lay worker*
Mathewson, David *religious studies educator*

West Newton
Spitzer, Toba *rabbi*

Westford
Alluè, Emilio Simeon *bishop*

Weston
Barry, William Anthony *priest, writer*
Mc Innes, William Charles *priest, academic administrator*

Williamstown
Eusden, John Dykstra *theology studies educator, minister*

Worcester
McManus, Robert Joseph *bishop*
Parsons, Edwin Spencer *clergyman, educator*
Reilly, Daniel Patrick *bishop emeritus*

MICHIGAN

Bloomfield Hills
Mc Gehee, H. Coleman, Jr., (Harry Coleman McGhhe) *retired bishop*
Randall, Chandler Corydon *theologian*
Syme, Daniel Bailey *rabbi, institution executive*

Dearborn Heights
Ghrist, Catherine Ann *religious organization administrator*

Detroit
Anderson, Moses Bosco *bishop emeritus*
Flores, Daniel Ernest *bishop*
Gumbleton, Thomas John *bishop emeritus*
Maida, Adam Joseph Cardinal *cardinal, archbishop*
Reiss, Francis Ronald *bishop*
Vigneron, Allen Henry *archbishop*

Farmington
Penberthy, Stanley Josiah, Jr. *publisher*

Farmington Hills
Plaut, Jonathan Victor *rabbi*

Gaylord
Cooney, Patrick Ronald *bishop*

Grand Rapids
Adams, Dwayne Hurstle *religious studies educator, department chairman*
Barnes, Rosemary Lois *minister*
Beals, Paul Archer *religious studies educator*
Beeke, Joel Robert *minister, educator, writer*
Deppe, Dean Brian *theology studies educator*

DeVries, Robert K. *retired publisher, consultant*
Hurley, Walter Allison *bishop*

Harper Woods
Myhand, Cheryl *minister, educator*

Holland
Nakajima, Fumihito Andy *priest, educator*

Jackson
Popp, Nathaniel *archbishop*

Kalamazoo
Badra, Robert George *theology studies and humanities educator*
Bradley, Paul Joseph *bishop*
Donovan, Paul V. *bishop emeritus*
Murray, James A. *bishop*

Lansing
Boyea, Earl Alfred, Jr. *bishop*
Mengeling, Carl Frederick *bishop emeritus*

Marquette
Garland, James Henry *bishop emeritus*
Sample, Alexander King *bishop*
Schmitt, Mark Francis *bishop emeritus*

Northville
Davis, Lawrence Edward *church official*

Saginaw
Cistone, Joseph Robert *bishop*

Southfield
Ibrahim, Ibrahim Namo *bishop*
Willingham, Edward Bacon, Jr. *ecumenical minister, administrator*

Warren
Samra, Nicholas James *bishop emeritus*

MINNESOTA

Austin
Alcorn, Wallace Arthur *minister, writer*

Collegeville
Díaz, Miguel H. *religious studies educator, writer*

Crookston
Balke, Victor Herman *bishop emeritus*
Hoeppner, Michael Joseph *bishop*

Duluth
Worthing, Carol Marie *retired minister*

Inver Grove Heights
Koenig, Robert August *minister, educator*

Mankato
Cherrington, Janet E. *religious studies educator, researcher*
Purscell, Keith William *minister*

Minneapolis
Chemberlin, Peg *minister, religious organization administrator*
Ligocki, Lawrence Francis *religious studies educator*
McLaren, Brian *pastor, Christian activist*

New Ulm
LeVoir, John Marvin *bishop*

Rosemount
Aadland, Thomas Vernon *minister*

Roseville
McMillan, Mary Bigelow *retired minister, volunteer*

Saint Bonifacius
Gianoulis, George Christ *religious studies educator*

Saint Cloud
Kinney, John Francis *bishop*
Sowada, Alphonse Augustus *bishop emeritus*

Saint Paul
Armstrong, Chris R. *religious studies educator*
Flynn, Harry Joseph *archbishop*
Foss, Richard John *bishop*
Hopper, David Henry *theologian, educator*
Kennelly, Sister Karen Margaret *church administrator, nun, retired academic administrator*
Nienstedt, John Clayton *archbishop*
Piché, Lee Anthony *bishop*

Saint Peter
Dille, Sarah Jane *theology studies educator*
Jodock, Darrell Harland *minister, educator*

Wayzata
Roth, Robert Paul *seminary educator, writer*

Winona
Harrington, Bernard Joseph *Bishop Emeritus*
Quinn, John Michael *bishop*

MISSISSIPPI

Biloxi
Howze, Joseph Lawson Edward *bishop emeritus*
Morin, Roger Paul *bishop*

Florence
Anding, Robert Eugene *retired religion educator, minister*

Indianola
Matthews, David *clergyman*

Jackson
Carden, Alan L. *hospital chaplain*
Houck, William Russell *bishop emeritus*
Larsen, Samuel Harry *minister, educator*
Latino, Joseph Nunzio *bishop*
Waters, Guy Prentiss *theology studies educator*

Mound Bayou
Kamphefner, Pius *minister*

MISSOURI

Ballwin
Ackerson, Charles Stanley *minister, educator, social worker*

Bolivar
Fuhrman, C. Michael *religious studies educator*
Malone, Kelly Scott *theology studies educator*

Bridgeton
Hylla, Linda Kay *sister, social worker*

Excelsior Springs
Mitchell, Earl Wesley *clergyman*

Fayette
Keeling, Joe Keith *religious studies educator, retired dean*

Fenton
Meyer, Joyce *television minister, author*

Independence
Tyree, Alan Dean *clergyman*

Jefferson City
Gaydos, John Raymond *bishop*

Kansas City
Boland, Raymond James *bishop emeritus*
Diehl, James Harvey *church administrator*
Finn, Robert William *bishop*
Vogel, Arthur Anton *clergyman*

Moberly
Donaldson, Daniel J. *minister, educator*
Koutz, Tarry Alvin *religious studies educator*

Saint Joseph
Mockabee, M(arion) Eugene *minister*

Saint Louis
Barmash, Pamela *religious studies educator*
Carlson, Robert James *archbishop*
Flinn, Frank K. *religious studies educator*
Hermann, Robert Joseph *bishop*
Mahsman, David Lawrence *writer, church administrator*
Merrell, James Lee *writer, minister*
Park, Young H. *dean*
Wilkins, Addi L. *retired lay worker*

Springfield
Carson, George R. *history and religious studies educator*
Given, Mark *religious studies educator*
Johnston, James Vann, Jr. *bishop*
Leibrecht, John Joseph *bishop emeritus*
Nunnally, Waverly Earl *religious studies educator, writer*
Trout, Jacob Eugene *religious studies educator*
William, Paul Griffin *theology studies educator*

MONTANA

Billings
Barnea, Uri N. *rabbi, conductor, musician*

Great Falls
Warfel, Michael William *bishop*

Helena
Thomas, George Leo *bishop*

Kalispell
Vickers, Lee Louise *minister*

NEBRASKA

Bellevue
Milone, Anthony Michael *bishop emeritus*

Grand Island
Dendinger, William Joseph *bishop, former career officer*

Hastings
McCarthy, David Bruce *minister*

Lincoln
Allen, Edward Martin *religious studies educator*
Bruskewitz, Fabian Wendelin *bishop*
Seng, Coleen Joy *church administrator, director, former mayor*
Wiersbe, Warren Wendell *clergyman, writer, lecturer*

Omaha
Curtiss, Elden Francis *archbishop emeritus*
Lucas, George J. *archbishop*

NEVADA

Henderson
Waples, Jan Susan (Klein Waples) *priest*

Las Vegas
Freeman-Clark, J. P. Ladyhawk *vicar, underwater exploration, security and transportation executive, model*
Luckett, Byron Edward, Jr. *chaplain, retired military officer*
Pepe, Joseph Anthony *bishop*

Reno
Calvo, Randolph Roque *bishop*

NEW HAMPSHIRE

Center Sandwich
Booty, John Everitt *retired theology studies educator*

Concord
Robinson, V. Gene (The Right Reverend V. Gene Robinson) *bishop*

Loudon
Moore, Beatrice *religious organization administrator*

Manchester
Christian, Francis Joseph *bishop*
Gendron, Odore Joseph *bishop emeritus*
Gerry, Joseph John *bishop emeritus*
McCormack, John Brendan *bishop*

West Chesterfield
Garinger, Louis Daniel *retired religion educator*

NEW JERSEY

Atlantic City
Maddox, Odinga Lawrence, II, *head of religious order*

Camden
Galante, Joseph Anthony *bishop*

Chatham
Marconi, Dominic Anthony *bishop emeritus*

Cherry Hill
Bryan, Henry Collier *clergyman, retired secondary school educator*

Clifton
Rodimer, Frank Joseph *bishop emeritus*
Serratelli, Arthur Joseph *bishop*

Edison
Roskoski, John *religious studies educator, coach*

Englewood
Boteach, Shmuley *rabbi, television personality, author*

Freehold
Jawidzik, Edward Mark *priest*

Jersey City
Ashley, Willard Walden C., Sr. *minister*

Lakewood
Levovitz, Pesach Zechariah *rabbi*

Madison
Ochs, Peter Warren *religion educator*

Mahwah
Padovano, Anthony Thomas *theologian, literature educator*

Marlton
Clemens, David Allen *minister*

Medford
Hogan, Thomas Harlan *publisher*

Metuchen
Bootkoski, Paul Gregory *bishop*
Demkovitz, Russell Bernard *deacon, cemetery director*
Hughes, Edward T. *bishop emeritus*

Moorestown
Clark, Maryliz M. *retired minister*

Morris Plains
Spong, John Shelby *retired bishop, writer, columnist*

Morristown
Hastings, Mary Jane *minister*

New Brunswick
Johnson, James Turner *theology studies educator*

Newark
Arias, David *bishop emeritus*
Cruz, Manuel Aurelio *bishop*
da Cunha, Edgar Moreira *bishop*
Donato, Gaetano Aldo *bishop*
Flesey, John Walter *bishop*
Hummel, Donald Keith *priest*
McDonnell, Charles James *bishop emeritus*
Myers, John Joseph *archbishop*
Stephens, B. Consuela *minister, consultant*

Paramus
Fatica, Justin *youth minister, writer*

Pomona
Fiedler, Marcia Stein *religious studies educator*

Princeton
Armstrong, Richard Stoll *minister, educator, poet*
Belshaw, George Phelps Mellick *bishop*
Stout, Jeffrey Lee *religious studies educator*
West, Charles Converse *retired theologian*

Ridgewood
Kiernan, Richard Francis *publisher*

Rutherford
Gerety, Peter Leo *archbishop emeritus*

Teaneck
Holmes, Miriam H. *publisher*
Meno, John Peter *religious organization administrator*

Tinton Falls
Priesand, Sally J. *rabbi*

Toms River
Donaldson, Marcia Jean *lay worker*

West Caldwell
Radest, Howard Bernard *clergyman, educator*

West Milford
Stelpstra, William John *minister*

West Paterson
Pataki, Andrew *bishop emeritus*
Skurla, William Charles *bishop*

Woodbury
Doughty, A. Glenn *minister*

NEW MEXICO

Albuquerque
Sanchez, Robert Fortune *archbishop emeritus*
Sheehan, Michael Jarboe *archbishop*

Gallup
Wall, James S. *bishop*

Las Cruces
Ramirez, Ricardo *bishop*

Moriarty
Moonwalker, Tu *minister, counselor, artist*

Portales
Overton, Edwin Dean *retired campus minister, educator*

NEW YORK

Albany
Hubbard, Howard James *bishop*

Albion
Allamon, Karen Henn *minister*

Alfred
Peterson, Thomas Virgil *religious studies educator*

Angola
Green, Gerard Leo *priest, educator*

Baldwin Place
Kurian, George Thomas *publisher*

Barrytown
Wilson, Andrew Murray *religious studies educator*

Bronx
Hunt, George William *priest, magazine editor*
Reeberg, Patricia Aldora *minister, entrepreneur*
Sheridan, Patrick Joseph Thomas *bishop emeritus*

Bronxville
Bayens, Patrick James *religious studies educator*

Brooklyn
Al-Hafeez, Humza *minister, editor*
Bernard, Rev. A.R. *religious organization administrator*
Caggiano, Frank Joseph *bishop*
Catanello, Ignatius Anthony *bishop*
Cisneros, Octavio *bishop*
DiMarzio, Nicholas Anthony *bishop*
Jones, Rudolph *minister*
Mansour, Gregory John *bishop*
Sansaricq, Guy A. *bishop*
Sullivan, Joseph Martin *bishop emeritus*

Buffalo
Bang, Charles Douglas *minister*
Grosz, Edward M. *bishop*
Kmiec, Edward Urban *bishop*
Smallwood, Sandra Denise *pastor, daycare administrator*

Camillus
Jerge, Marie Charlotte *minister*

Centerport
Stevens, Martin Brian *publisher*

Cicero
Schiess, Betty Bone *priest*

Cobleskill
O'Hanlon, Carol Ann *minister*

Coxsackie
Moyna, John Lawrence *priest*

Douglaston
Daily, Thomas Vose *bishop emeritus*

Elmhurst
Brown, Ronald Joseph *religious studies educator*
Chang, Sheng-Yen *Buddhist monk, educator*
Farrell, John Thomas *priest, educator*

Farmingdale
Dunne, John C. *bishop*

Hempstead
Goodhue, Thomas Wallace *Clergyman*
Zagano, Phyllis *religious studies educator*

Ithaca
Clarkson, George Edward *theology educator, minister*

Kenmore
McLaughlin, Bernard Joseph *bishop emeritus*

Kingston
Tsirpanlis, Constantine N. *theology, philosophy, classics and history educator*

Larchmont
Rainier, Robert Paul *publisher, consultant*

Maspeth
Baltakis, Paulius Antanas *bishop*

Mexico
Halse, Frank Adams, Jr. *retired minister*

Millerton
Welsh, Donald Emory *publisher*

New York
Ahern, Patrick Vincent *bishop emeritus*
Brucato, Robert Anthony *auxiliary bishop emeritus*
Butts, Calvin O. *pastor, academic administrator*
Church, Frank Forrester *minister, writer*
Cook, Stephen Lloyd *religious studies educator, writer*
Doherty, Thomas *publisher*
Dolan, Timothy Michael *archbishop*
Forbes, Christopher (Kip Forbes) *publisher*
Friedman, J. Roger *publisher*
Giniger, Kenneth Seeman *publisher*
Ginsberg, Hersh Meier *rabbi, religious organization administrator*
Hirsch, Roseann Conte *publisher*
Hirschfield, Bradley *rabbi*
Hudson, Christopher John *publisher*
Iriondo, Josu *bishop*
Lagonegro, Dominick J. *bishop*
McCormack, William J. *bishop emeritus*
Mestice, Anthony Francis *Bishop Emeritus*
Molho, Emanuel *publisher*
Ochs, Carol Rebecca *theologian, writer, theology studies educator, philosopher*
Powers, Edward Alton *minister, educator*
Ross, Norman Alan *publisher*
Roth, Sol *rabbi*
Rubinstein, Peter J. *rabbi*
Rusch, William Graham *religious organization administrator*
Schneier, Marc *rabbi*
Sharpton, Al (Alfred Charles Sharpton Jr.) *minister, political activist, radio talk show host*
Sullivan, Dennis Joseph *bishop*
Tannenbaum, Bernice Salpeter *national religious organization executive*
Velez, Carlos *minister*
Walsh, Gerald Thomas *bishop*
Wiener, Marvin S. *rabbi, editor, executive*
Yoffie, Erich H. *religious organization administrator*
Yu, Andrew *minister*
Zapata, Angel *pastor*

Niskayuna
Nichols, Albert Myron *retired minister*

Nyack
Cozart, Helen Ray *religious studies educator, educator*
Mann, Kenneth Walker *retired minister, psychologist*
Widbin, Robert Bryan *theology studies educator*

Poughkeepsie
Glasse, John Howell *retired philosophy and theology educator*
Harmelink, Herman III *minister, writer, religious studies educator*
Moore, Deborah Dash *religion educator*

Red Hook
Pastrana, Ronald Ray *theology studies educator, earth and space science educator, department chairman, psychotherapist, retired school system administrator*

Rochester
Clark, Matthew Harvey *bishop*
Graf, William E. *religious studies educator*
Tobin, Barbara Kay *minister*

Rockville Centre
Daly, James Joseph *bishop emeritus*
Libasci, Peter A. *bishop*
Murphy, William Francis *bishop*
Wcela, Emil Aloysius *bishop*

Roosevelt
Walsh, Paul Henry *bishop*

Rushford
Devine, Stephen P. *minister, educator*

Rye
Kaufman, Shirona *cantor, educator*

Saint James
Batule, Robert John *priest, writer*

Staten Island
Pasciuto, Joseph Doria *priest*

Syracuse
Costello, Thomas Joseph *bishop emeritus*
Cunningham, Robert Joseph *bishop*
Emery, Robert Allan *minister*
Moynihan, James Michael *bishop*
Wiggins, James Bryan *religion educator*

Verbank
Berry, Maryann Paradiso *minister*

White Plains
Parker, Everett Carlton *clergyman*

Youngstown
Lamb, Charles F. *retired minister, educator*

NORTH CAROLINA

Belmont
Williams, David M. *theologian, educator*

Boiling Springs
Qualls, Paula Fontana *religious studies educator*

Buies Creek
Jonas, William Glenn, Jr. *religious studies educator, department chairman*

Cary
Slaattè, Howard Alexander *minister, philosophy educator*
Taylor, David Wyatt Aiken *retired clergyman*

Chapel Hill
Chang, Paul Kuk Won *theology educator, researcher, pastor*

Charlotte
Curlin, William George *bishop emeritus*
Graham, Billy (William Franklin Graham) *evangelist*
Graham, Franklin (William Franklin Graham III) *evangelist, missionary*
Grigg, Eddie Garman *minister, educator*
Jugis, Peter Joseph *bishop*
McKay-Wilkinson, Julie Ann *minister, marriage and family therapist*
Milton, Michael Anthony *minister, writer*
Walker, George W. C. *bishop*
Walker, Jewett Lynius *clergyman, church official*

Drexel
McCall, Maxine Cooper *publisher, minister, educator, writer*

Dunn
Wilson, Douglas Leonard *minister, educator*

Durham
Crenshaw, James L(ee) *theology educator*
Kort, Wesley Albert *religious studies educator, writer*
Meyers, Eric Mark *religion educator*

Fayetteville
Batts, Dorothy Marie *clergywoman, educator, writer*
Soderberg, Herman Albert *minister, educator*

Greenville
Jackson, Bobby Rand *minister*

Hendersonville
Trexler, Edgar Ray *minister, editor*

Hickory
Ratke, David C. *religious studies educator*

Lake Junaluska
Goodgame, Gordon Clifton *retired minister*

Liberty
Garner, M(ildred) Maxine *retired religious studies educator*

Lumberton
Johnson, Judy Van *minister, educator*
Tolar, Anne Melton *minister, music educator*

Misenheimer
Stivers, Laura A. *religious studies educator*

Monroe
Kyle, John Emery *retired religious organization administrator*

Pfafftown
Wood, Stephen Wray *minister, educator, legislator*

Raleigh
Ashmore, James Philip *minister, educator*
Burbridge, Michael Francis *bishop*
Gossman, Francis Joseph *bishop emeritus*

Snow Hill
Stevens, JoAnn A. *textile, political leader, author, minister*

Taylorsville
Ross, David Edmond *church official*

Waynesville
Hale, Joe (Joseph Rice) *church organization executive*

Weaverville
Edwards, Otis Carl, Jr. *theology studies educator*

Wilmington
Conser, Walter Hurley, Jr. *religion and philosophy educator*

Wingate
Coleman, Gillis Byrns *religious studies educator, humanities educator*

Winston Salem
Harrelson, Walter Joseph *minister, educator*
Jenkins, Barbara Alexander *pastor, overseer*
Kuhar, Edward C., Jr. *religious studies educator*
Ludolf, Marilyn Marie Keaton *lay worker*
Rights, Graham Henry *retired minister*
Spach, Jule Christian *church executive*
Winn, Albert Curry *clergyman*

NORTH DAKOTA

Bismarck
Hardy, Jayne Winifred *assistant professor theology*
Zipfel, Paul Albert *bishop*

Fargo
Aquila, Samuel Joseph *bishop*

Grand Forks
Baldwin, Gayle R. *religious studies educator*

OHIO

Akron
Malone, Alicia Jane *minister, theologian*

Ashland
Waters, Ronald W. *theology studies educator, church administrator, pastor*
Watson, JoAnn Ford *theology studies educator*

Bowling Green
Versteeg, Robert John *minister, actor, writer*

Canton
Botean, John Michael *bishop*
Mann, John Martin *minister*
Puscas, Vasile Louis *bishop emeritus*

Cincinnati
Anderson, Joan Balyeat *theology studies educator, minister*
Davis, Michael W. *theology studies educator*
Duffy, Virginia *minister*
Idinopulos, Thomas Athanasius *religious studies educator, writer*
Melcher, Sarah J. *theology studies educator*
Pilarczyk, Daniel Edward *archbishop*
Rechnitzer, Haim Otto *religious studies educator*
Sallquist, Gary Ardin *retired minister, non-profit executive*
Schnurr, Dennis Marion *archbishop*
Zola, Gary Phillip *rabbi, historian*

Cleveland
Buhrow, William Carl *religious organization administrator*
Gries, Roger William *bishop*
Lennon, Richard Gerard *bishop*
Pilla, Anthony Michael *bishop emeritus*

Columbus
Campbell, Frederick Francis *bishop*
Darling, George Curtis *minister, administrator*
Warden, Waldia Ann *retired retreat center administrator, director*
Watson, John Allan *clergyman*

Dayton
Tilley, Terrence William *religious studies educator*

Euclid
Obloy, Leonard Gerard *priest*

Findlay
Fry, Charles George *theologian, educator*
Resseguie, James Lynn *theology educator*

Holland
Matthews, Christian William, Jr. *minister*

Lakewood
Sherry, Paul Henry *minister, religious organization administrator*

Lebanon
Hartland, James Robert *retired minister*

Lorain
Quinn, Alexander James *bishop*

Marblehead
Lis, David Joseph *priest*

Oberlin
Zinn, Grover Alfonso, Jr. *retired religion educator*

Parma
Kudrick, John Michael *bishop*
Moskal, Robert M. *bishop*

Steubenville
Conlon, Robert Daniel *bishop*
Ottenweller, Albert Henry *bishop emeritus*
Sheldon, Gilbert Ignatius *bishop emeritus*

Toledo
Blair, Leonard Paul *bishop*
Donnelly, Robert William *bishop emeritus*
Gaillardetz, Richard Rene *religious studies educator, writer*

Uniontown
France, Dorothy Daniel *minister*

Wauseon
Stutzman, Donna J. *minister*

Wickliffe
Pevec, Anthony Edward *bishop emeritus*

Youngstown
Dunlap, Catherine Mary *clergywoman*
Murry, George Vance *bishop*

OKLAHOMA

Bartlesville
Sweem, Billy Don *bishop, religious organization administrator*

Bethany
Leggett, James Daniel *bishop*

Oklahoma City
Beltran, Eusebius Joseph *archbishop*
Hampton, Carol McDonald *priest, educator, historian*
Jones, Charles Edwin *historian, bibliographer, chaplain*
Ridley, Betty Ann *theology studies educator*
Taylor-White-Grigsby, Queen Deloris *minister, consultant*

Tulsa
Cox, William Jackson *retired bishop*
Lamp, Jeffrey S. *minister, educator*
Osborn, La Donna Carol *clergywoman*

OREGON

Bend
Connolly, Thomas Joseph *bishop emeritus*
Vasa, Robert Francis *bishop*

Eugene
Graziano, Margaret A. *chaplain, recreational therapist, educational consultant, volunteer*
Sanders, Jack Thomas *religious studies educator*

Portland
Bryant, Carmen Julia *missionary, educator*
Steiner, Kenneth Donald *bishop*

West Linn
Bohrer, Richard William *author, editor, educator*

PENNSYLVANIA

Akron
Dickinson, Margery Elsie *missionary, clinical psychologist*

Allentown
Barres, John O. *bishop*
Cullen, Edward Peter *bishop emeritus*

Allison Park
Jones, Carolyn Jane *minister*

Altoona
Anthony, Bertha M. *minister*

Bethlehem
Gaeta, Jane *minister*
Steffen, Lloyd Howard *minister, religious studies educator*

Blairsville
Stiffler, Erma Delores *minister, pastoral counselor, retired elementary school educator*

Camp Hill
Johnston, Thomas McElree, Jr. *retired church administrator*

Clairton
Mina, John Louis (Ivan Minea) *religious studies educator, archivist*

Drexel Hill
Thompson, William David *minister, educator*

Dunmore
Timlin, James Clifford *bishop emeritus*

Elizabethtown
Brown, Dale Weaver *clergyman, theology studies educator*
Bucher, Christina *religious studies educator*

Enola
Beatty, Robert Clinton *religious studies educator*

Erie
Trautman, Donald Walter *bishop*

Friedens
Shaffer, Brenda Joyce *minister*

Glenside
Trueman, Carl Russell *theology studies educator*

Greensburg
Bosco, Anthony Gerard *bishop emeritus*
Brandt, Lawrence Eugene *bishop*
Honeygosky, Stephen R. *priest, educator*

Harrisburg
Rhoades, Kevin Carl *bishop*

Haverford
Kee, Howard Clark *religion educator*

Hollidaysburg
Adamec, Joseph Victor *bishop*

Jenkintown
Black, Thomas Donald *retired religious organization administrator*

Johnstown
Miloro, Protopresbyter Frank *religious organization administrator, theology studies educator*
Smisko, Nicholas Richard *bishop, educator*

Lafayette Hill
Miller, Nancy Lois *senior pastor*

Lancaster
Glick, Garland Wayne *retired theological seminary president*

Latrobe
Gruber, Mark Francis *priest, educator*

Lewisburg
Jump, Chester Jackson, Jr. *clergyman, church official*

Malvern
Flynn, James R. *augusterian priest, school system administrator*

Marysville
Trigilio, John Patricio *pastor*

Merion Station
Burch, Francis Floyd *clergyman*

Phila
Pahl, Jon F. *religious studies educator*

Philadelphia
Bartlett, Allen Lyman, Jr. *retired bishop*
Beyer, Gerald John *theology educator*
Bura, John *bishop*
Cortès, Luis *religious organization administrator*
de Paulo, Craig J. N. *priest, philosopher, educator*
De Simone, Louis Anthony *bishop emeritus*
Goode, W. Wilson, Sr. *minister, former mayor*
Maginnis, Robert P. *bishop*
Marple, Dorothy Jane *retired church executive*
McFadden, Joseph Patrick *bishop*
Rigali, Justin Francis Cardinal *cardinal, archbishop*
Scullion, Mary (Sister Mary Scullion) *nun, advocate*
Senior, Timothy C. *bishop*
Shaw, William J. *religious organization administrator*
Soroka, Stefan *archbishop*
Sulyk, Stephen *archbishop emeritus*
Thomas, Daniel Edward *bishop*
Waskow, Arthur Ocean *theologian, educator*

Pittsburgh
Holder, Gerald D., Jr. *dean*
Mc Dowell, John Bernard *bishop emeritus*
Miller, William Charles *theological educator, anglican priest*
Schaub, Marilyn McNamara *theology studies educator*
Schott, Basil Myron *archbishop*
Tuell, Steven Shawn *religious studies educator, minister*
van Driel, Edwin Christiaan *theology studies educator*
Winter, William Joseph *bishop emeritus*
Zubik, David Allen *bishop*

Quarryville
Harris, Robert Laird *minister, theology educator emeritus*

Saint Peters
Detterline, Milton E., Jr. *minister*

Sayre
Bentley, Dianne H. Glover *minister, consultant*

Scranton
De Celles, Charles Edouard *theologian, educator*
Dougherty, John Martin *bishop*
Martino, Joseph F. *bishop*

Sunbury
Ely, Donald J(ean) *retired clergyman, secondary school educator*

Swarthmore
Field, Dorothy Maslin *minister*

Waynesboro
Coles, Robert Nelson, Sr. *religious organization administrator*

Wernersville
Koenig, Robert Emil *clergyman*

Willow Street
Yrigoyen, Charles, Jr. *retired church denomination executive*

Wyncote
Ehrenkrantz, Dan *rabbi*

Wynnewood
Sider, Ronald J. *theology educator, author*

RHODE ISLAND

Lincoln
Barlow, August Ralph, Jr. *minister*

Middletown
Demy, Timothy James *retired military chaplain, professor*

North Smithfield
Gelineau, Louis Edward *bishop emeritus*

Providence
Cladis, Mark S. *religious studies educator*
Frerichs, Ernest Sunley *religious studies educator*
Pearce, George Hamilton *archbishop emeritus*
Tobin, Thomas Joseph *bishop*

Warwick
Roque, Francis Xavier *bishop emeritus*

SOUTH CAROLINA

Charleston
Guglielmone, Robert Eric *bishop*
Thompson, David Bernard *bishop emeritus*

Columbia
Larkin, William John *religious studies educator*
Thomas, Latta Roosevelt *religious educator, clergy*

Darlington
Gough, Herbert Frederick, Jr. *minister*

Florence
Baroody, Albert Joseph, Jr. *pastoral counselor*

Irmo
Branham, Mack Carison, Jr. *retired religious organization administrator, minister*

Myrtle Beach
McCaffrey, Edmund F. *abbot emeritus*

Spartanburg
Bullard, John Moore *religious studies educator, church musician*

Taylors
Smith, Morton Howison *religious organization administrator, educator*

White Rock
Aull, James Stroud *retired bishop*

SOUTH DAKOTA

Rapid City
Cupich, Blase J. *bishop*

Sioux Falls
Swain, Paul Joseph *bishop*

TENNESSEE

Antioch
Worthington, Melvin Leroy *minister, writer*

Chattanooga
Stephens, Gregory D. *religious studies educator*

Collegedale
Leatherman, Donn Walter *religious studies educator*

Hendersonville
Davis, Jon C. Chris *minister*

Jackson
Dubis, Kevin Mark *religious studies educator*
Van Neste, Ray *religious studies educator, director*

Knoxville
Stika, Richard F. *bishop*

Loudon
Jones, Robert Gean *religion educator*

Memphis
Graves, William H. *minister*
Ratzlaff, David Edward *minister*
Robinson, Kenneth S. *pastor, former state agency administrator, physician*
Steib, James Terry *bishop*
Vaughn, Cary Edward *minister, director*

Nashville
Archibald, Chestina Mitchell *minister*
Bigham, Wanda Durrett *religious organization administrator*
Choby, David Raymond *bishop*
Hampton, Ralph Clayton, Jr. *pastoral studies educator, clergyman*
Land, Richard Dale *minister, religious organization administrator*
McKenzie, Vashti Murphy *bishop*
Page, Frank S. *head of religious order*
Stooksbury, William Claude *minister*
TeSelle, Eugene Arthur, Jr. *religion educator*

Sewanee
Gessell, John Maurice *minister, educator*

Signal Mountain
Hall, Thor *religion educator*

TEXAS

Abilene
Betts, Joe Delton *retired religious studies educator*
Perry, Troy D. *retired minister, religious organization administrator*

Aledo
Barton, David *religious studies educator, writer, historian, researcher*

Amarillo
Klein, Jerry Lee, Sr. *minister, philosophy educator*
Matthiesen, Leroy Theodore *bishop emeritus*
Yanta, John Walter *bishop emeritus*
Zurek, Patrick James *bishop*

Arlington
Lingerfelt, B. Eugene, Jr. *minister*

Austin
Hitchcock, Joanna *publisher*
McCarthy, John Edward *bishop emeritus*

Beaumont
Guillory, Curtis John *bishop*

Belton
Wyrick, Stephen Von *religion educator, minister*

Brownsville
Pena, Raymundo Joseph *bishop*

Brownwood
Smith, Robert Leonard *pastor, religious studies educator*

College Station
Pate, Andrew Lidden, Jr. *religious organization administrator*

Corpus Christi
Carmody, Edmond *bishop*
Gracida, Rene Henry *bishop emeritus*

Dallas
Blue, John Ronald (J. Ronald Blue) *evangelical mission executive*
Crotty, Robert Bell *religious organization administrator*
Curran, Charles Edward *theology studies educator, priest*
Daves, Don Michael *minister*
Farrell, Kevin Joseph *bishop*
Grahmann, Charles Victor *bishop emeritus*
Jakes, T(homas) D(exter) *bishop, author*
Lockridge, Deborah Ann *minister, educator, small business owner*
Morris, Henry Madison III *minister, writer, speech professional, consultant*
Pauley, Shirley Stewart *religious organization executive*
Pinson, William Meredith, Jr. *pastor, writer, administrator, professor*
Wiles, Charles Preston *minister*

Fort Worth
Gilbert, James Cayce *minister*
Hoskins, Paul Matthew *religious studies educator*
Lee, Jason K. *theology studies educator*
Vann, Kevin William *bishop*

Houston
Cooper, Valerie Gail *minister*
DiNardo, Daniel Nicholas Cardinal *cardinal, archbishop*
Fiorenza, Joseph Anthony *archbishop emeritus*
Foger, Frances Murchison *minister*
Karff, Samuel Egal *rabbi*
Montgomery, Cleothus *minister*
Nielsen, Niels Christian, Jr. *retired religious studies educator*
Osteen, Joel *minister*
Rizzotto, Vincent Michael *bishop emeritus*
Vásquez, José Stephen *bishop*

Jacksonville
Blaylock, James Carl *clergyman, librarian*

Laredo
Tamayo, James Anthony *bishop*

Lubbock
Rodriguez, Placido *bishop*

Palestine
Packard, Russell Calvert *deacon*

Plano
Oden, William Bryant *bishop, educator*

San Angelo
Pfeifer, Michael David *bishop*

San Antonio
Cantú, Oscar *bishop*
Flanagan, Thomas Joseph *bishop emeritus*
Flores, Patrick Fernandez *archbishop emeritus*
Gomez, José Horacio *archbishop*
Mc Allister, Gerald Nicholas *retired bishop, minister*

Spring
Howard, Richard Carl *minister*
Hunt, T(homas) W(ebb) *retired religion educator*
Rex, Lonnie Royce *religious organization administrator*

The Woodlands
Machle, Edward Johnstone *religious studies educator, philosopher*

Tyler
Corrada del Rio, Alvaro *bishop*

Victoria
Fellhauer, David Eugene *bishop*

Waco
Hein, Jay Forest *religious studies educator, former federal official*
Stratton, Margaret Anne *minister*
Talbert, Charles Harold *theologian, educator*

Waxahachie
Collins, William Duane *religious studies educator*

UTAH

Hyde Park
Bowen, Morgan *religious studies educator*

Ogden
Harrington, Mary Evelina Paulson (Polly) *writer, educator*

Provo
Hoskisson, Paul *religious studies educator, director*

Salt Lake City
Eyring, Henry Bennion *head of religious order*
Monson, Thomas Spencer *religious organization administrator, retired publishing executive*
Wester, John Charles *bishop*

VERMONT

Burlington
Angell, Kenneth Anthony *bishop emeritus*
Matano, Salvatore Ronald *bishop*

Colchester
Blacketor, Paul Garber *minister*

Middlebury
Ferm, Robert Livingston *religion educator*

Northfield
Wick, William Shinn *clergyman, chaplain, pastor*

Pawlet
Buechner, Carl Frederick *minister, author*

Quechee
Wood, R. Stewart, Jr. *retired bishop*

Wolcott
Fisher, Neal Floyd *religious organization administrator*

VIRGINIA

Alexandria
Devantier, Paul W. *religious organization administrator, broadcast executive*
Markham, Ian Stephen *theology studies educator, dean*

Arlington
Coe, Doug *religious organization administrator*
Loverde, Paul Stephen *bishop*

Blacksburg
Grover, Norman LaMotte *theologian, philosopher*

Charlottesville
Bouchard, Larry Drennen *religious studies educator*
Finley, Robert Van Eaton *minister*

Dinwiddie
McCray, Doris Raines *minister*

Emory
Kellogg, Frederic Richard *religious studies educator*

Fairfax
Farina, John Edward *religious studies educator*

Falls Church
Benton, Nicholas Frederick *publisher*

Front Royal
Andes, Larry Dale *minister*

Glen Allen
Anderson, James Frederick *clergyman*

Gordonsville
Wells, Mary Elizabeth Thompson *deacon, chaplain, spiritual director, iconographer*

Henrico
DiLorenzo, Francis X. *bishop*

Kents Store
Brown, Nan Marie *retired minister*

Lansdowne
Colson, Charles Wendell (Chuck Colson) *lay minister, writer*

Lynchburg
LaHaye, Timothy F. *pastor, writer*

Mechanicsville
Gerrish, Brian Albert *theologian, educator, retired minister*

Mineral
Speer, Jack Atkeson *publisher*

Norfolk
Finney, Fannie *minister, educator*

Richmond
Eakin, Frank Edwin, Jr. *religious studies educator*
Leggett, Gloria Jean *minister*
Sullivan, Walter Francis *bishop emeritus*

Springfield
Kalkwarf, Leonard V. *minister*

Yorktown
Wood, James Edward, Jr. *religion educator, author*

WASHINGTON

Des Moines
Tuell, Jack Marvin *retired bishop*

Kirkland
Kowalski, Waldemar *theology studies educator*

Langley
Le Roy, Robert Powell *retired minister, educator, writer*

Prosser
Capener, Regner Alvin *minister, electronics engineer, writer*
Cooper, Lynn Dale *retired minister, retired navy chaplain*

Seattle
Brunett, Alexander Joseph *archbishop*
Elizondo Almaguer, Eusebio L. *bishop*
Fluke, Lyla Schram (Mrs. John M. (Lyla) Fluke Sr.) *publisher*
Hunthausen, Raymond Gerhardt *archbishop emeritus*
Robb, John Wesley *religion educator*
Tyson, Joseph Jude *bishop*

Spokane
Edwards, James Robert *minister, educator*
Lee, Richard Francis James *evangelical clergyman, media consultant, lawyer*
Polley, Harvey Lee *retired missionary, math and science educator*
Skylstad, William Stephen *bishop*

Tacoma
Wiegman, Eugene William *minister, academic administrator*

University Place
Seiber, Richard Allan *retired chaplain United States Air Force*

Yakima
Sevilla, Carlos Arthur *bishop*

WEST VIRGINIA

Charleston
Prichard, John David *minister*
Scott, Olof Henderson, Jr. *priest*

Clarksburg
Payne, Johnny F. *minister*

Hurricane
Hage, Lillian C. *religious organization administrator, director, dean*

Pennsboro
Poling, Kermit William *minister*

Wheeling
Bransfield, Michael Joseph *bishop*
Michaels, James Edward *bishop emeritus*
Schmitt, Bernard William *bishop emeritus*
Thurston, Bonnie Bowman *religious studies educator, minister, poet*

WISCONSIN

Balsam Lake
Anjulis, Stanley Joseph *retired church administrator*

Bloomer
Prenzlow, Elmer John-Charles, Jr. *minister*

Boscobel
Young, Gary William *minister, educator, retired military officer*

Cottage Grove
Baird, Robert Dahlen *retired theology studies educator*

De Pere
Harris, John T., IV, *religious organization administrator*

Fitchburg
Haslanger, Philip Charles *minister*

Fond Du Lac
Schimpf, David Michael *theology studies educator, department chairman*

Green Bay
Banks, Robert J. *bishop emeritus*
Morneau, Robert Fealey *bishop*
Ricken, David Laurin *bishop*

Iola
Mishler, Clifford Leslie *publisher*

La Crosse
Listecki, Jerome Edward *bishop*

Madison
Bullock, William Henry *bishop emeritus*
Fox, Michael Vass *theology studies educator*
Morlino, Robert Charles *bishop*
Wirz, George Otto *bishop emeritus*

Merrill
Goessl, Celine *head of religious order*

Milwaukee
Callahan, William Patrick *bishop*
Lehninger, Paul David *theology studies educator*
Schaefer, Jame *religious studies educator*
Shear, Alan James *theologian*
Sklba, Richard John *bishop*
Weakland, Rembert George *archbishop emeritus*

Ogema
Giese, Robert James *minister*

Oshkosh
Barwig, Regis Norbert James *priest*

Superior
Christensen, Peter Forsyth *bishop*
Fliss, Raphael Michael *bishop emeritus*

Wauwatosa
Stubbe, Ray William *minister, writer*

Windsor
McDonald, David Michael *church administrator*

WYOMING

Cheyenne
Hart, Joseph Hubert *bishop emeritus*

TERRITORIES OF THE UNITED STATES

AMERICAN SAMOA

Pago Pago
Weitzel, John Quinn *bishop*

PUERTO RICO

San Juan
Aponte Martinez, Luis Cardinal *cardinal, archbishop emeritus*
González Nieves, Roberto Octavio *archbishop*
Torres, Daniel Fernandez *bishop*

VIRGIN ISLANDS

Charlotte Amalie
Thomas, Elliott Griffin *bishop emeritus*

St Thomas
Bevard, Herbert Armstrong *bishop*

CANADA

BRITISH COLUMBIA

Langley
Ferris, Ronald Curry *retired bishop*

Vancouver
Packer, James Innell *theology studies educator, writer*

ONTARIO

Cambridge
MacBain, William Halley *minister, theology studies educator, academic administrator*

Kitchener
Winger, Roger Elson *retired church administrator*

Ottawa
Macklem, Michael Kirkpatrick *publisher*

Thorold
O'Mara, John Aloysius *bishop emeritus*

Toronto
Finlay, Terence Edward *retired archbishop*
Novak, David *theology studies educator, rabbi*
Ryan, William Francis *priest*
Steffer, Robert Wesley *clergyman*

Unionville
Pazak, John Stephen *bishop*

Waterloo
Van Seters, John *retired biblical literature educator*

Windsor
La Rocque, Eugene Philippe *retired bishop*

QUEBEC

Montreal
Turcotte, Jean-Claude Cardinal *cardinal, archbishop*

Quebec City
Stavert, Alexander Bruce *archbishop*

Rimouski
Blanchet, Bertrand *archbishop*

Westmount
Coolidge, Robert Tytus *deacon, historian, educator*

North Hatley
Salt, Alfred Lewis *priest*

MEXICO

Guadalajara
Romano Gomez, Miguel *bishop*

Tepic
Watty Urquidi, Ricardo *bishop*

AUSTRALIA

Sydney
Clancy, Edward Bede Cardinal *cardinal, archbishop emeritus*

BANGLADESH

Dhaka
Marino, Joseph *archbishop, diplomat*

BELARUS

Minsk
Swiatek, Kazimierz Cardinal *cardinal, archbishop emeritus*

BENIN

Cotonou
Blume, Michael August *archbishop*

BRAZIL

Brasília
Falcão, José Freire Cardinal *cardinal, archbishop emeritus*

Paranagua
Novak, Alfredo Ernest *bishop emeritus*

Rio de Janeiro
Sales, Eugenio Cardinal de Araujo *cardinal, archbishop emeritus*

Salvador
Agnelo, Geraldo Majella Cardinal *archbishop*

São Paulo
Arns, Paulo Evaristo Cardinal *cardinal, archbishop emeritus*

CHINA

Hong Kong
Kwong, Peter Kong-Kit *retired archbishop*

ENGLAND

London
Carey, George Leonard (Lord Carey of Clifton) *former archbishop of Canterbury*
Murphy-O'Connor, Cormac Cardinal *cardinal, archbishop*

Malton
Habgood, John Stapylton *archbishop*

Oxford
Down, William John Denbigh *bishop*

Sturminster Newton
Seaford, John Nicholas *clergyman, retired dean*

GERMANY

Cologne
Meisner, Joachim Cardinal *cardinal, archbishop*

Munich
Langenscheidt, Florian *publisher*

St Augustin
Feldkämper, Ludger Bernhard *religious organization administrator*

Tübingen
Küng, Hans *theologian, educator*

GREECE

Thessaloniki
Rodopoulos, Panteleimon Evaggelos *clergyman*

HONDURAS

Comayaga
Scarpone Caporale, Gerald D. Joseph *bishop emeritus*

HONG KONG

Hong Kong Island
Zen Ze-kiun, Joseph Cardinal *cardinal, bishop*

INDIA

Ajmer
Menezes, Ignatius *bishop*

Alleppey
Chenaparampil, Peter Michael *bishop*

Assam
Menamparampil, Thomas S.D.B. *archbishop*

Bombay
Pimenta, Simon Ignatius Cardinal *cardinal, archbishop emeritus*

Kerala
Vithayathil, Varkey Cardinal *cardinal, archbishop*

INDONESIA

Jakarta
Darmaatmadja, Julius Riyadi Cardinal *cardinal, archbishop*

ITALY

Bologna
Biffi, Giacomo Cardinal *cardinal, archbishop emeritus*
Caffarra, Carlo Cardinal *cardinal, archbishop*

Citta del Vaticao
Harvey, James Michael *archbishop*

Genoa
Canestri, Giovanni Cardinal *cardinal, archbishop emeritus*

Naples
Giordano, Michele Cardinal *cardinal, archbishop*

Rome
Angelini, Fiorenzo Cardinal *cardinal, archbishop emeritus*
Antonelli, Ennio Cardinal *cardinal, archbishop*
Baum, William Wakefield Cardinal *cardinal, archbishop emeritus*
Benedict XVI, His Holiness Pope (Joseph Alois Ratzinger) *Pope of the Roman Catholic Church, Bishop of Rome*
Burke, Raymond Leo *archbishop*
Cordero Lanza di Montezemolo, Andrea Cardinal *cardinal, archbishop*
Di Noia, Joseph Augustine *archbishop, theologian*
Etchegaray, Roger Marie Élie Cardinal *cardinal, archbishop*
Foley, John Patrick Cardinal *cardinal, archbishop*
Herranz Casado, Julián Cardinal *cardinal, archbishop*
Kasper, Walter Cardinal *cardinal, archbishop*
Levada, William Joseph Cardinal *cardinal, archbishop emeritus*
Poupard, Paul Cardinal *cardinal, archbishop*
Sanchez, Jose Tomas Cardinal *cardinal, archbishop*
Szoka, Edmund Casimir Cardinal *cardinal, archbishop*

Turin
Bouchard, Giorgio *minister, religious organization administrator*

Vatican City
Deskur, Andrzej Maria Cardinal *cardinal, archbishop*
Dias, Ivan Cardinal *archbishop, cardinal*
Martinez Somalo, Eduardo Cardinal *cardinal, archbishop*
Martino, Renato Raffaele Cardinal *cardinal, archbishop, diplomat*
Mejia, Jorge Maria Cardinal *cardinal, archbishop*
Noe, Virgilio Cardinal *cardinal, archbishop*
Schleck, Charles Asa *archbishop emeritus*
Stafford, James Francis Cardinal *cardinal, archbishop*

JAPAN

Bunkyo
Shirayanegi, Peter Seiichi Cardinal Seiichi *cardinal, archbishop*

Mie
Kitashirakawa, Michihisa *head of religious order*

LEBANON

Beyrouth
Kolvenbach, Peter Hans *priest, head of religious order*

MOZAMBIQUE

Maputo
dos Santos, Alexandre José Maria Cardinal *cardinal, archbishop emeritus*

NEW ZEALAND

Waikanae
Williams, Thomas Stafford Cardinal *cardinal, archbishop*

Wellington
Balvo, Charles Daniel *archbishop*

NICARAGUA

Bluefields Zelaya Norte
Zywiec Sidor, David Albin *bishop*
Schmitz Simon, Pablo Ervin *bishop*

NORWAY

Oslo
Loenning, Per *bishop*

PAPUA NEW GUINEA

Mendi So Highlands
Reichert, Stephen Joseph *bishop*

PERU

Piuria
Turley Murphy, Daniel Thomas *bishop*

PHILIPPINES

Iloilo City
Lagdameo, Angel Nacorda *archbishop*

Manila
Adams, Edward Joseph *archbishop*

POLAND

Warsaw
Glemp, Jozef Cardinal *emeritus cardinal, archbishop*

SOUTH AFRICA

Pretoria
Daniel, George Francis *archbishop*
Green, James Patrick *archbishop*

SPAIN

Barcelona
Carles Gordo, Ricardo Maria Cardinal *cardinal, archbishop emeritus*

TAIWAN

Kaohsiung
Shan Kuo-hsi, Paul Cardinal *cardinal, bishop emeritus*

THAILAND

Bangkok
Kitbunchu, Michael Michai Cardinal *cardinal, archbishop emeritus*

TRINIDAD AND TOBAGO

Port of Spain
Gilbert, Edward Joseph *archbishop*
Gullickson, Thomas Edward *archbishop*

VATICAN CITY

Poggi, Luigi Cardinal *cardinal, archbishop emeritus, archivist*

ZAMBIA

Mongu
Duffy, Paul Francis *bishop*

ADDRESS UNPUBLISHED

Acker, Raymond Abijah *retired minister and army chaplain*
Allison, Andrew Marvin *church administrator*
Ambrozic, Aloysius Matthew Cardinal (His Eminence Aloysius Cardinal Ambrozic) *cardinal, archbishop emeritus*
Anderson, Hugh George *bishop*
Anderson, John Firth *retired religious organization administrator, retired librarian*
Apuron, Anthony Sablan *archbishop*
Armstrong, (Arthur) James *minister, educator, consultant, writer*
Banks, Deirdre Margaret *retired church organization administrator*
Barner, Mark E. *minister, consultant*
Batakian, Manuel *bishop*
Batdorf, Linda *administrator*
Bates, Gerald Earl *retired bishop*
Baumhart, Raymond Charles *religious organization administrator*
Beldon, Sanford T. *publisher*
Berding, Kenneth *biblical studies and biblical greek eduactor*
Berenbaum, Michael Gary *theology educator*
Bernstein, Edward Charles *rabbi*
Be Vier, William A. *retired religious studies educator*
Bevilacqua, Anthony Joseph Cardinal *cardinal, archbishop emeritus*
Bickford, Margaret Wyatt *minister*
Black, Hillel Moses *publisher*
Bodey, Richard Allen *minister, educator*
Britt, Joseph John *religious studies educator*
Brokke, Catherine Juliet *retired mission executive*
Brooks, Babert Vincent *publisher*
Bunkowske, Eugene Walter *religious studies educator*
Cacciavillan, Agostino Cardinal *cardinal, archbishop*
Carlson, Natalie Traylor *publisher*
Cash, Mary Frances *minister, retired civilian military employee*
Castle, Howard Blaine *retired religious organization administrator*
Cates, Dennis Lynn *minister*
Cedar, Paul Arnold *church executive, minister*
Chase, Lee P. *religious studies educator, consultant*
Cheatham, Carl Wade *minister, educator*
Cobb, John Boswell, Jr. *clergyman, educator*
Cook, Quentin LaMar *church leader, healthcare executive, lawyer*
Cope, Jeannette Naylor *minister*
Crawford, James Leroy *minister, retired theology studies educator*
Cummins, John Stephen *bishop emeritus*
Daniel, Elinor Perkins (Perky Daniel) *clergywoman*
DeLong, Joseph Ireland *theology studies educator*
Dipko, Thomas Earl *retired minister, religious organization administrator*
Dockstader, Deborah Ruth *minister*
Dombalis, Constantine Nicholas *minister, writer*
Donoghue, John Francis *archbishop emeritus*
Donovan, Dennis Dale *priest*
Doueihi, Stephen Hector Youssef *bishop emeritus*
Douglass, Jane Dempsey *retired theology educator*
Drey, Philip *religious studies educator*
Egan, Edward Michael Cardinal *archbishop emeritus, cardinal*
Epp, Eldon Jay *religion educator*
Epp, Menno Henry *clergyman*
Evelyn, Rev Phyllis *spiritual care administrator*
Ewing, Elisabeth Anne Rooney *priest*
Ewing, James E. *priest*
Fazio, Evelyn M. *publisher, agent*
Finnegan, Sara Anne (Sara F. Lycett) *publisher*
Fleming, Carolyn Elizabeth *religious organization administrator, interior designer*
Flory, Margaret Martha *retired religious organization administrator*
Flynt, Larry Claxton, Jr. *publisher*
Foley, David Edward *bishop emeritus*
Foys, Roger Joseph *bishop*
Frankson-Kendrick, Sarah Jane *publisher*
Frazier, Eloise M. *minister*
Friend, William Benedict *bishop emeritus*
Funk, Edith Kay *retired minister, psychotherapist, social worker*
Gemignani, Michael Caesar *clergyman, retired mathematics professor*
Godlas, Alan *religious studies educator*
Gottlieb, Michah *religious studies educator*
Gowan, Donald Elmer *religion educator*
Grady, Sandra C. *minister, counselor*
Gralla, Milton *retired publisher*
Greenberg, Irving *rabbi*
Griffin, James Anthony *bishop emeritus, academic administrator*
Griswold, Frank Tracy III *retired bishop*
Haber, Geoffrey John *rabbi*
Hagelstein, Robert Philip *publisher*
Hambidge, Douglas Walter *archbishop*
Hamilton, David Eugene *minister, educator*
Han, Eunice Myunghee *priest, educator*
Harper, Marsha Wilson *retired religious organization administrator*
Harris, Nicholas George *publisher*
Haryono, Ignatius Wibisono *writer*
Hawkes, Mary Newgeon *retired minister, educator*
Hernandez, Ramon Robert *retired minister, librarian, educator*
Hervey, Nina Fern *retired church administrator, minister*
Hickey, Barry James *archbishop*
Holle, Reginald Henry *retired bishop*
Holz, Carl Wayne *retired theologian*
Howard, Darryl E. *religious studies educator*
Huddleston, Mark *religious studies educator*
Hudnut, Robert Kilborne *clergyman, writer*
Hultstrand, Donald Maynard *bishop*
Hunter, Juanita Walters *minister*
Huras, William David *retired bishop*
Hurley, Francis T. *archbishop emeritus*
Huron, Roderick Eugene *minister, writer*
Imperato, Robert L. *religious studies educator*
Ingram, Barbara Averett *minister*
Irwin, Paul Garfield *minister, social services executive*
Jabs, Aura Lee *minister, educator*
Jerdee, Sylvia Ann *retired minister*
Johnson, Jay David *writer, consultant*
Kanarfogel, Ephraim *religious studies professor*
Katz, Colleen *publisher*
Keeler, William Henry Cardinal *cardinal, archbishop emeritus*
Kelley, Edward Allen *publisher*
Kester, Helen Mary *minister*
Kirchmeier, Emmalou Handford *minister, writer*
Krych, Margaret A. *retired religious organization administrator, educator*
Kucera, Daniel William *archbishop emeritus*
Landes, George Miller *biblical studies educator*
Landon, John William *retired minister, social worker, educator*
LaVerdiere, Claudette Marie *nun, head of religious order*
Law, Bernard Francis Cardinal *cardinal, retired archbishop*
Lazovsky, Lorna Deane *minister*
Leavy, Herbert Theodore *publisher*
Lehrman, Irving *rabbi*
Lewis, Justin Harley *religious studies educator*
Libby, Billy W. (Bill Libby) *religious studies educator*
Lohmuller, Martin Nicholas *bishop emeritus*
Lopez, Patricia Nell *minister, educator*
Loppnow, Milo Alvin *clergyman, former church official*
Lucas, Phillip Charles *religious studies educator*
Luetkehoelter, Gottlieb Werner (Lee Luetkehoelter) *retired bishop, clergyman*
Lufty, JoyBeth *minister*
Lugenbeel, Edward Elmer *publisher*
Mackey, Jeffrey Allen *priest*
Magrill, Joe Richard, Jr. *religious organization administrator, minister*
Malewski, Jennifer Jean *clergy member*
Mali, Paul *publisher, retired management educator*
Marty, Martin Emil *theology studies educator*
McCarrick, Theodore Cardinal *cardinal, archbishop emeritus*
McCoy, Gordon R. *minister*
McFadden, Lee Vernon *religious organization administrator*
McKale, Michael *religious studies educator, director*
McKinley, Ellen Bacon *priest*
McKinney, Joseph Crescent *bishop emeritus*
McMaster, Belle Miller *religious organization administrator*
Melczek, Dale Joseph *bishop*
Melvin, Billy Alfred *clergyman*
Muhammad, Claudette Marie *religious organization administrator*
Mulvee, Robert Edward *bishop emeritus*
Murdock, Larry Paul *religious studies educator, director*
Nass, Thomas P. *religious studies educator*
Norgren, William Andrew *retired religious denomination administrator*
Nottingham, William Jesse *retired religious organization administrator, minister*
Nunn, Charles Burgess *retired religious organization administrator*
Nygren, Malcolm Ernest *minister*
Ochoa, Armando Xavier *bishop*
Oh, Mark Edward *minister*
O'Hare, Joseph Aloysius *priest, editor-in-chief, former academic administrator*
Olivier, Leonard James *bishop emeritus*
Ortiz, Angel Vicente *church administrator*
Osborne, James Alfred *religious organization administrator*
Osvath, Ludovic Lajos *minister*
Otčenášek, Karel *archbishop of Roman Catholic church*
Pachal, Leah Zavin *minister, writer, interior designer, educator*
Pagels, Elaine Hiesey *theology studies educator, writer*
Palms, Roger Curtis *writer, educator, minister*
Patton-Newell, Janet Lavelle *minister*
Payne, Don J. *theology studies educator, consultant*
Payne, Sidney Stewart *retired archbishop*
Pelotte, Donald Edmond *bishop*
Phillips, Elaine Anderson *religious studies educator*
Plant, Jackson Vaughn *minister*
Popp, Bernard Ferdinand *bishop emeritus*
Post, Avery Denison *retired church official*
Pressman, Jacob *retired rabbi*
Quezada Toruño, Rodolfo Cardinal *cardinal, archbishop*
Radde-Gallwitz, Andrew *theology studies educator*
Ramey, Eudora Malois *minister*
Reece, Belynda M. *minister, military officer, consultant*
Reiss, John Charles *bishop emeritus*
Righter, Walter Cameron *retired bishop*
Robertson, LaVerne *minister*
Robinson, Howard Arthur, Jr. *minister*
Rose, Robert John *bishop emeritus*
Rueger, George Edward *bishop emeritus*
Ruof, Richard Alan *minister, poet, writer*
Rupert, Hoover *minister, writer*
Savitripriya, Swami *Hindu religious leader, author*
Scharlemann, Robert Paul *theology studies educator, minister*
Schuelke, John Paul *religious organization administrator*
Seale, James Millard *retired religious organization administrator, minister*
Shirer, Robert LLoyd *clergyman*
Shotwell, Malcolm Green *minister*
Slattery, Edward James *bishop*
Sloyan, Gerard Stephen *theology studies educator, priest*
Smetana, Pavel Amos *religious organization administrator*
Smith, John Mortimer Fourette *bishop*
Solano, Julio Rafael *priest, educator*
Spidlik, Tomas Cardinal *cardinal, priest, theologian*
Stackhouse, Max Lynn *religious studies educator*
Staggers, Mary E. *minister*
Stephens-Rich, Barbara E. *minister, educator*
Straling, Phillip Francis *bishop emeritus*
Talbot, Mary Lee *minister*
Talley, Truman Macdonald *retired publisher, editor*
Taylor, June Ruth *retired minister*
Trask, Thomas Edward *religious organization administrator*
Trussell, Jacqueline *theology studies educator*
Unsworth, Richard Preston *minister, educator, director*
Valero, René Arnold *retired bishop*
van Daalen, Albert A. *religious minister, CEO*
Vasko, Peter Theodore Frederick *priest*
Vlazny, John George *archbishop*
Vyhmeister, Nancy Jean *retired religious studies educator*
Walker, Beverly Ann *minister, health facility administrator*
Wantland, William Charles *retired bishop, lawyer*
Weber, Gloria Richie *retired minister, state legislator*
Webster, John Crosby Brown *minister, educator*
Weinkauf, Mary Louise Stanley *retired clergywoman, educator*
Welch, Richard L. *priest, lawyer*
Westerhoff, John Henry III *priest, theologian, educator*
Wharton, Margaret Mary *nun, educator*
Wilkin, Richard Edwin *clergyman, religious organization administrator*
Williams, Ervin Eugene *religious organization administrator*
Williams, James Kendrick *bishop emeritus*
Williams, Ronald Dean *minister, religious organization administrator*
Wilson, Lois M. *minister*
Winslow, David Allen *chaplain, retired military officer*
Wisehart, Mary Ruth *retired religious organization administrator*
Wooten, Cecil Aaron *retired religious organization administrator*
Zayek, Francis Mansour *archbishop, bishop emeritus*
Zirbes, Mary Kenneth *retired minister*

SCIENCE: LIFE SCIENCE

UNITED STATES

ALABAMA

Auburn
Ball, Donald Maury *agronomist, consultant*
Bell, Leonard N. *science educator*
Klesius, Phillip Harry *microbiologist, researcher*
Liu, Juncheng *research scientist*
Sorokulova, Iryna *microbiologist, educator*

Auburn University
Anderson, Christopher John *biology professor*

Bessemer
Hitchcock, Francesca Marie Oglesby *educator*

Birmingham
Black, Kelley P. *microbiologist, educator*
Braunewell, Karl-Heinz *neuroscientist*
Finley, Sara Crews *medical geneticist, educator*
Fintel, Marion Carson *biology professor*
Jun, Ho-Wook *science educator*
Korf, Bruce Richard *clinical geneticist, neurologist*
Marchase, Richard Banfield *cell biologist, educator, research administrator*
Muturi, Ephantus J. *entomologist, researcher*
Nance, Marione E. *biology educator*
Prichard, Mark Neal *virologist, educator*
Schafer, James Arthur *physiologist*
Velu, Sadanandan E. *science educator*

Chickasaw
French, Elizabeth Irene *retired biology professor, musician*

Eva
Hudson, Rhonda Ann *science educator*

Evergreen
Joyner, Daphne *biology professor*

Fayette
Estes, John Timothy *biology professor*

Florence
Rhodes, Anthony H. *retired biologist*

Huntsville
Bearden, Thomas Eugene *research scientist*
Gillani, Noor Velshi *atmospheric scientist, researcher, educator*
Nwaneri, Sam O. *science educator*
Richardson-Weninegar, Loretta Lynne *biologist, educator*
Schwinghamer, Mary Denise *veterinarian*
Sovyanhadi, Yoedono *biology professor*

Jacksonville
Goodwin, Debra Kay *science educator*

Mobile
Foster, John Wade *microbiologist, educator*

Montgomery
Dzata, Gladstone K. *biology professor*
Li, Xiaolin *science educator*
Sass, Neil Leslie *toxicologist*
Sullivan, Margaret M. *biologist, educator*

Normal
Nyochembeng, Leopold M. *plant pathologist, educator*

Sajjala, Seshadri Reddy *agronomist*
Walker, Lloyd T. *food scientist*

Troy
Magrath, Christi Lee *biology professor*

Tuskegee
Yehualaeshet, Teshome E. *microbiologist, educator*

Tuskegee Institute
Nimmanapalli, Ramadevi *veterinarian, educator*

ALASKA

Anchorage
Grant, William Stewart *geneticist*
Nielsen, Jennifer Lee *molecular ecologist, researcher*
Parker, Walter Bruce *arctic research specialist, consultant*
Peterson, Kim Moreau *biology professor*
Schoen, John W. *biologist, educator*
Wilson, Heather Marie *biologist*
Ziemba, Mary Rose *biology professor*

Fairbanks
Cysewski, Stephen David *retired science educator*
Hartman, Chris M. *science educator*
Kessel, Brina *ornithologist, educator, researcher*
Lawlor, Orion Sky *science educator*
Moelders, Carmen Nicole (Nicole Mölders) *science educator, researcher*
Zhang, Jing *science educator*

Juneau
Shepard, Beatrice L. *retired microbiologist, historian*
Siddeek, M. S.M. *marine biologist, educator*

Palmer
Ping, Chien-Lu *soil scientist, educator*

Soldotna
Jozwiak, Elizabeth Anna *biologist*

ARIZONA

Bisbee
Behney, Charles Augustus, Jr. *veterinarian*

Chandler
Angus, Patricia Jean *biology professor*

Flagstaff
Balda, Russell Paul *biologist, educator*
Cortner, Hanna Joan *retired political scientist, researcher*
Neary, Daniel George *soil scientist*
Price, Peter Wilfrid *ecology educator, researcher*
Stevens, Lawrence Edward *ecologist, curator*
Wilcoxson-Ueckert, Catherine Ann *science educator, consultant*

Glendale
Brown, Jason Andrew *science educator*
Milne, Karen Louise *retired science educator*

Maricopa
Kimball, Bruce Arnold *soil scientist*

Mesa
Bateman, Heather L. *biology professor*
Garlick, William Steven *retired biology professor*
Phelps, Norris D. *biology professor*

Payson
Stephenson, Larry Kirk *geography educator, financial planner*

Phoenix
Flejter, Wendy L. *geneticist, director*
Sima, Chao *biologist, researcher*

Scottsdale
Northey, William Thomas *microbiologist, educator*

Sun City
Joyce, Jeffrey *research scientist, consultant*

Tempe
Curtiss, Roy III *life sciences professor*
Grimm, Nancy Beth *research ecologist*
Hölldobler, Berthold Karl *zoologist*
Jacobs, Mark *biology professor, dean*
Lei, Lei *biology professor, researcher*
Page, Robert Eugene, Jr. *biology professor*
Poste, George Henry *biology professor, former pharmaceutical company executive*
Traynor, Kirsten Shoshanna *research scientist*
Uttal, William R(eichenstein) *psychology and engineering educator, research scientist*
Vannela, Raveender *biotechnologist, environmental scientist*

Thatcher
McCarthy, Michael Scott *biology professor, publishing executive*
Morris, David *science educator*

Tucson
Bandurski, Bruce Lord *retired ecologist, environmental scientist*
Bernstein, Carol *molecular biologist*
Brusca, Richard Charles *biologist, researcher, educator, administrator*
Chandler, Vicki L. *biologist, educator, director*
Erickson, Robert Porter *genetics researcher, educator, clinician*
Fleming, Sean *science educator*
Fritts, Harold Clark *botanist, educator*
Gerba, Charles Peter *microbiologist, educator*
Haynes, Caleb Vance, Jr. *geology and archaeology educator*
Hildebrand, John G(rant) *neuroscientist, educator*
Hubbard, William Bogel *planetary sciences educator*
Hull, Herbert Mitchell *botanist, researcher*
Jeter, Wayburn Stewart *retired microbiologist, educator*
Marri, Pradeep Reddy *research scientist*
Mendelson, Neil H. *microbial geneticist, educator*
Patchett, P. Jonathan *science educator*
Snyder, Richard Gerald *research scientist, administrator, educator, consultant*
VanEtten, Hans D. *plant pathologist, educator*
Yocum, Harrison Gerald *horticulturist, botanist, educator, researcher*
Zreda, Marek *science educator*

Wikieup
Brattstrom, Bayard Holmes *biology professor*

ARKANSAS

Fayetteville
Amy, Apon Weathers *science educator*
Bell, Debbie McCulley *science educator*
Brown, Avert Hayden *animal scientist, educator*
Brown, Connell Jean *retired animal science educator*
Musick, Gerald Joe *retired entomology educator*

Jefferson
Bagnyukova, Tetyana Volodymyrivna *biologist*
Hotchkiss, Charlotte Evans *veterinarian, researcher*
Leakey, Julian Edwin Arundell *toxicologist, researcher*

Lavaca
Kincade, John C. *science educator*

Little Rock
Casciano, Daniel Anthony *biologist, educator*
Gealt, Michael A. *environmental microbiologist, educator*
Hinson, Jack Allsbrook *research toxicologist, educator*
Huang, Guoliang *science educator*
Khanal, Ramesh C. *animal scientist, researcher*
Tarasenko, Olga *biologist, educator*
Yanoviak, Stephen Paul *ecologist, educator*

Paragould
Crandall, Elizabeth Diane *science educator, microbiologist*

Pocahontas
Moss, Linda Elaine *science educator*

State University
Hannigan, Robyn E. *science educator, researcher*

Stuttgart
Moldenhauer, Karen Ann Kuenzel *agriculturist, educator*

Walnut Ridge
Wheeless, Charlotte Ann *science educator*

Ward
Gray, Janet Faye Walker *science educator*

CALIFORNIA

Agoura Hills
Fox, Stuart Ira *physiologist*

Alameda
Cho, Myeong-Je *plant biologist, researcher*
Earle, Sylvia Alice *research biologist, oceanographer*

Albany
Kahlon, Talwinder Singh *research scientist*
Mills, Nicholas John *biology educator*

Aliso Viejo
Hamersley, M. Robert *environmental microbiologist professor*
Srikumar, Ramakrishnan *microbiologist, researcher*

Arcata
Black, Jeffrey M. *professor (wildlife)*
Dengler, Lori *science educator*

Atherton
Coleman, Robert Griffin *geology educator*
Eggers, Alfred John, Jr. *research corporation executive*

Bakersfield
McBride, Todd *biology professor, department chairman*

Berkeley
Arkin, Adam Paul *biology professor*
Barrett, Reginald Haughton *wildlife management educator*
Bern, Howard Alan *biologist, researcher, science educator*
Botchan, Michael R. *molecular biologist, biochemist*
Casida, John Edward *toxicology and entomology professor*
Chen, Lu *neurobiologist, biology professor*
Chiang, John Chun Hong *science educator*
Diamond, Marian Cleeves *neuroscientist, educator*
Ennals, Robert J. *research scientist*
Fleiszig, Suzanne Mariane Janete *optometry educator*
Fung, Inez Y. *science educator*
Gillespie, Rosemary *science professor, museum director*
Hoskins, Roger Allen *geneticist*
Hritonenko, Victoria *microbiologist*
King, Nicole *molecular biologist, educator*
Kohwi-Shigematsu, Terumi *research scientist*
Kremen, Claire *conservation biologist, educator*
Kuriyan, John *science educator, researcher*
Levine, Michael Steven *science educator*
Lidicker, William Zander, Jr. *zoologist, educator*
Lipps, Jere Henry *biology and geology professor*
Manga, Michael *earth science educator, geophysicist*
Marletta, Michael A. *biochemistry educator, researcher*
Mitra, Mautusi *biologist*
Power, Mary Eleanor *biology professor*
Purcell, Alexander Holmes *entomologist, educator*
Rine, Jasper *geneticist, educator*
Saraph, Prasad Vaman *research scientist, industrial engineer*
Schekman, Randy W. *molecular biology administrator, biochemist*
Scott, Eugenie Carol *science foundation director, anthropologist*
Seil, Fredrick John *retired neuroscientist*
Sen, Koushik *science educator*
Sinclair, Alistair *science educator, researcher*
Teeguarden, Dennis Earl *forest economist, educator*
Thorner, Jeremy W. *biology professor*
Wake, Marvalee Hendricks *biology professor*
Wilt, Fred *biology professor*

Bishop
Klinger, Robert Charles *ecologist*

Bodega Bay
Clegg, James Standish *physiologist, biochemist, educator*

Calimesa
Zimmermann, Muriel Madeline *retired biology professor*

Carlsbad
Prakash, Thazha Purathiyath *research scientist, chemist*

Chula Vista
Schrauzer, Gerhard Norbert *science educator, researcher*

Claremont
Hoopes, Laura L Mays *biology professor*
Phillips, M. Ian *physiologist, educator*

Cupertino
Patton, Marilyn Dilworth *english and literature educator*

Cypress
Hu, Houchun Harry *research scientist*

Davis
Ardans, Alexander Andrew *veterinarian, educator, lab administrator*
Barbour, Michael G(eorge) *botanist, educator, ecologist, consultant*
Brault, Aaron Cole *science educator*
Cech, Joseph J., Jr. *biology professor*
Day, Howard Wilman *geology educator*
Dehesh, Katayoon *science educator*
Enders, Allen Coffin *anatomy educator*
Engebrecht, JoAnne *biology professor, department chairman*
Epstein, Emanuel *plant physiologist*
Gubler, Walter Douglas *plant pathologist, educator*
Hess, Charles Edward *environmental horticulture educator*
Jones, Edward George *neuroscientist, educator*
Kado, Clarence Isao *molecular biologist*
Knoepfler, Paul *cell biologist*
Kowalczykowski, Stephen Charles *biochemist, biophysicist, microbiologist, cellular and molecular biologist, educator*
Langley, Charles Hunt *geneticist, educator*
Lucas, William John *science educator*
Morisseau, Christophe Henri Pierre *entomologist, researcher*
Moyle, Peter Briggs *marine biologist, educator*
Mukherjee, Amiya K. *metallurgy and materials science educator*
Murphy, Terence Martin *biology professor*
Qualset, Calvin O. *agronomist, educator*
Rappaport, Lawrence *plant physiology and horticulture educator*
Ronald, Pamela C. *plant pathologist, educator*
Rost, Thomas Lowell *retired botany educator*
Schank, Jeffrey Charles *science educator, researcher*
Schoener, Thomas William *ecologist, educator*
Scott, Thomas Wallace *entomologist, director*
Sillman, Arnold Joel *physiologist, educator*
Turcotte, Donald Lawson *geophysical sciences educator*
Vanderhoef, Larry Neil *biology professor, former academic administrator*
Wu, Lin L. *retired botanist, ecologist, educator*
Yilma, Tilahun Daniel *virologist, veterinarian, educator, researcher*
Zavortink, Thomas James *retired biology professor*

Del Mar
Farquhar, Marilyn Gist *cell biologist, pathologist, educator*

Duarte
Smith, Steven Sidney *molecular biologist*

El Cajon
Melahaji, Jalal Assad *science educator*

Emeryville
Houghton, Michael *geneticist*
White, Raymond Leslie *geneticist*

Encinitas
Hale, David Fredrick *biotechnology executive*

Fountain Valley
Warwick, Randall James *biology professor, writer*

Fresno
Burnett, Lynn Barkley *health science educator*
Gordus, Andrew George *ecotoxicologist*
McConnell, Charles Prescott *retired science educator*
Nakamoto, Tokumasa *science educator*
Waters, Rosemary R. *biology professor*

Fullerton
Horn, Michael H. *biologist*
Nolan-Riegle, Mary Catherine *biology professor*
Woyski, Margaret Skillman *retired geology educator*

Glendale
Ereshefsky, Larry *scientific officer, executive, psychopharmacology educator, consultant*

Goleta
Gilbert, Richard Keith *biology professor, researcher*

Grass Valley
Suri, Jasjit S. *research scientist*

Hayward
Lauzon, Carol *science educator*

Healdsburg
Vedros, Neylan Anthony *microbiologist, educator*

Hermosa Beach
Chi, Lois Wang *retired biology professor, research scientist*

Hollywood
Brooks, Lila *animal rights activist*

Hopland
Jones, Milton Bennion *retired agronomist*

Huntington Park
Gaines-Page, Rena L. *science educator*

Irvine
Ayala, Francisco José *geneticist, educator*
Baldwin, Kenneth Milton *biology professor*
Carew, Thomas James *neuroscientist, educator*
Catrakis, Haris John *science educator*
Clegg, Michael Tran *genetics educator, researcher*
Parker, Ian *science educator*
Pritt, Stacy L. *veterinarian*
Shojaeian, Parvin *research scientist, educator*
Tang, Shao-Jun *biologist, educator*
Yousefi'zadeh, Homayoun *science educator*

La Jolla
Barshop, Bruce A. *science educator*
Beutler, Bruce A. *biology professor, researcher*
Brenner, Sydney *molecular biologist, researcher*
DeFanti, Thomas Albert *retired distinguished professor*
Encalada, Sandra *biologist*
Evans, Ronald M. *microbiologist, educator*
Gilbert, James Freeman *geophysics educator*
Guillemin, Roger C.L. *physiologist, academic administrator*
Haxo, Francis Theodore *marine biologist*
Hougie, Cecil *retired science educator, retired hematologist*
Hunter, Tony (Anthony Rex) *molecular biologist, educator*
Järvinen-Pasley, Anna (Maaria Anna) *neuroscientist, researcher*
Karten, Harvey Jules *neurosciences educator*
Kooyman, Gerald Lee *physiologist, researcher*
Lakshmana, Madepalli Krishnappa *neuroscientist*
Latz, Michael I. *marine biologist, educator*
Lipton, Stuart Arthur *neuroscientist*
Liu, Shumo *molecular biologist*
Masters, Guy *science educator*
Quinton, Paul Marquis *physiologist, educator*
Rahman, Yueh-Erh *biologist*
Richman, Douglas Daniel *medical virologist, educator, internist*
Ruoslahti, Erkki *cell biologist, cancer researcher*
Scheffler, Immo Erich *molecular biologist, educator*
Schroeder, Julian Ivan *biology professor*
Seminoff, Jeffrey Aleksandr *ecologist, educator*
Sherman, Irwin William *biological sciences educator, academic administrator*
Truksa, Jaroslav *molecular biologist*
West, John Burnard *physiologist, educator*
Wilkie, Donald Walter *retired biologist, aquarium administrator*
Wood, Samuel H. *science company executive, physician, scientist*

La Mirada
Kuld, Paul *retired biology professor*
Stangl, Walter David *science educator*

Laguna Niguel
Reimer, Nona Brinkman *biology professor*

Lancaster
Suzuki-Laitila, Junko Kianna *biology professor*

Lemoore
Rogers, Joel *biology professor*

Livermore
Beller, Harry R. *microbiologist, chemist, researcher*

Loma Linda
Longo, Lawrence Daniel *physiologist, obstetrician, gynecologist, educator*
Schwab, Ernest Roe III *physiology educator, researcher, academic administrator*
Sun, Shu-Wei (Richard Sun) *science educator*
Taylor, Barry Llewellyn *microbiologist, educator*

Long Beach
Schubel, Jerry Robert *marine scientist educator, dean*
Toma, Ramses Barsoum *food science and nutrition educator*

Los Alamitos
Aberman, Harold Mark *veterinarian*

Los Altos
King, Chi-Yu *research scientist*

Los Angeles
Agnew, John A. *science educator*
Armenian, Haroutune Krikor *science educator*
Baker, Robert Frank *molecular biologist, educator*
Banerjee, Utpal *biology professor, research scientist*
Boles, Richard Gregory *clinical geneticist, researcher*
Bottjer, David John *earth science and biology educator*
Butcher, Larry L. *neuroscientist, educator*
Carmona, Victor Daniel *biology professor*
Comai, Lucio *biology professor*
Connor-Dominguez, Billie Marie *retired science information professional*
De Robertis, Edward M. F. *research scientist, educator*
Eskin, Eleazar *science educator*
Espinosa-Jeffrey, Araceli Marie *neurobiologist*
Finegold, Sydney Martin *infectious disease and microbiology researcher*
Fischer, Alfred George *geology educator*
Gasson, Judith C. *molecular biologist, research scientist*
Gilman, John Joseph *research scientist*
Goldberg, Robert B. *molecular biologist, educator*
Gordon, Malcolm Stephen *biology professor*
Grinnell, Alan Dale *neuroscientist, educator*
Guo, Wei *research scientist*
Ljubimov, Alexander V. *molecular biologist, cell biologist, researcher*
Maxson, Robert E. *biology professor*
Melnick, Michael *geneticist, educator*
O'Boyle, Christina *science educator*
Oliver, Carl Russell *science educator*
Orme, Antony Ronald *geography educator*
Rosenfeld, John Lang *geology educator*
Sachs, George *biology professor, physician*
Shackleford, Gregory M. *cancer researcher, molecular and cell biologist, educator*
Simmons, Donna Marie *neuroscientist, histotechnologist, neuroendocrine anatomist, researcher*
Slamon, Dennis Joseph *research scientist*
Szego, Clara Marian *cell biologist, educator*
Taylor, Charles Ellett *biologist, educator*
Villablanca, Jaime Rolando *neuroscientist, medical educator*
Wagar, Elizabeth Ann *microbiologist, director*
Woolf, Nancy Jean *neuroscientist, educator*
Zeng, Fan-Gang *neuroscientist*

Los Gatos
Hurtak, James J. *social scientist, consultant*

Madera
Curry, Cynthia J. R. *geneticist*

Malibu
Davis, Stephen Darrel *biology professor, researcher*
Hunt, Valerie Virginia *electrophysiologist, educator*
Martin, Karen Lynn Matthews *biology professor*

Mckinleyville
Walker, Dennis Kendon *retired botany professor*

Menlo Park
Doppalapudi, Rupa S. *cytogeneticist*
Mathews, Irimpan Ittoop *macromolecular crystallographer*
Sharma, Bhavender Paul *biotechnologist*

Merced
Albano, Valerie Dawn *biology professor*
Kallmann, Marcelo *science educator*
Yanagi, Cary *science educator*

Modesto
Mitchell, Joan LaVerne *research scientist*
Moe, Andrew Irving *veterinarian*

Moffett Field
Kittel, Peter *research scientist*
Lissauer, Jack Jonathan *astronomy educator*
Worden, Simon Pete *science administrator, career military officer*

Monrovia
Kimnach, Myron William *botanist, horticulturist*

Monterey
Boger, Dan Calvin *science professor, consultant*

Moss Landing
Bellingham, James Gladen *marine technologist, researcher*

Mountain View
Schickli, Jeanne Hlavka *virologist, researcher*

Norco
Morrison, James V. *biology professor*

North Hills
Thannickal, Thomas Chacko *neurophysiologist, researcher*

Northridge
Dudgeon, Steven Robert *biology professor*
Madelian, Vergine *biology professor*
Mehler, Ronald W. *science educator*

Novato
Yap, Clarence *biotechnology executive*

Oakland
Ames, Bruce Nathan *biochemisty and molecular biology professor*
Cherry, Lee Otis *scientific institute administrator*
Trachtenberg, Elizabeth Anne *geneticist, researcher*

Oceanside
Netsiri, Chaiyapoj *research scientist, consultant*

Orange
Wright, William Grandfield *biology professor*

Pacific Grove
Epel, David *biologist, educator*
Somero, George Nicholls *biology educator*

Palm Desert
Sausman, Karen *zoological park administrator*

Palm Springs
Petermann, Hans Jürgen *research scientist*

Palo Alto
Johnson, Noble Marshall *research scientist*
Lipsick, Joseph Steven *research scientist, medical educator*
Sanders, William John *research scientist*
Sudhof, Thomas Christian *molecular genetics educator*

Pasadena
Andersen, Richard Alan *physiologist*
Baltimore, David *microbiologist, educator, former academic administrator*
Bertani, Lillian Elizabeth Teegarden *biologist, researcher, educator*
Capponi, Agostino *research scientist*
Clauser, Francis H. *applied science educator*
Dickinson, Michael Hughes *physiologist, biotechnologist*
Elowitz, Michael *molecular biologist, educator*
Goldreich, Peter Martin *astrophysics and planetary physics educator*
Huang, Alice Shih-hou *biologist, educator, virologist*
Koch, Christof *microbiologist, educator, engineering educator*
Konishi, Masakazu *neuroscientist, educator*
Meyerowitz, Elliot Martin *biology professor*
Orphan, Victoria Jeanne *science educator*
Owen, Ray David *biology professor*
Pikov, Victor *physiologist*
Revel, Jean-Paul *biology professor*
Shaw, R. Daniel *anthropology professor*
Sternberg, Paul Warren *biologist, educator*
Varshavsky, Alexander Jacob *molecular biologist, educator*
Wasserburg, Gerald Joseph *geology and geophysics educator*
Zewail, Ahmed Hassan *chemistry and physics educator, consultant, editor*

Penn Valley
Whitsel, Richard Harry *retired biologist, entomologist*

Pomona
Venketaraman, Vishwanath *microbiologist, immunologist, educator*

Quincy
Hall, Anthony Elmitt *agriculturist, physiologist*

Rancho Cucamonga
Cosand, Diana Jeanne *biology professor*

Rancho Palos Verdes
Booth, Doris Palmer *biology professor*

Riverside
Bailey-Serres, Julia N. *geneticist, educator*
Bartnicki-Garcia, Salomon *microbiologist, educator*
Beckage, Nancy E. *physiologist, educator, entomologist*
Coffey, Michael David *plant pathologist, educator*
Ellstrand, Norman Carl *plant genetics, conservation and evolution educator*
Fairbairn, Daphne Janice *biology professor*
Hayashi, Cheryl *biologist, educator*
McHughen, Alan *geneticist, educator*
Page, Albert Lee *soil science educator, researcher*
Shouse, Peter John *soil scientist, researcher*
Van Gundy, Seymour Dean *plant pathologist, educator*

Rohnert Park
Rank, Nathan *biologist, educator*

Sacramento
Amaral, David G. *neuroscientist, educator*
Cochran, Roger *toxicologist, consultant*
Rosenberg, Dan Yale *retired plant pathologist*
Trujillo, Nicholas Lee *science educator*

Salinas
Ryder, Edward Jonas *geneticist*

San Bernardino
Michaelis, Kenneth A. *biology professor*

San Bruno
Mangano, Dennis Thomas *science educator, director*

San Diego
Albright, Thomas D. *science foundation director, educator, researcher*
Basmadjian, Edward *marine biologist*
Bernstein, Sanford Irwin *biology professor*
Bird, Lynne Marie *geneticist*
Casas, Veronica *microbiologist, educator*
Clark, Kevin Bradford *biologist*
Crutchfield, Susan Ramsey *neurophysiologist*
Dulbecco, Renato *biologist, educator*
Durrant, Barbara Susan *reproductive physiologist*
Ecker, Joseph R. *plant molecular and cellular biologist*
Eckhart, Walter *molecular biologist, educator*
Gage, Fred H. *neuroscientist, educator*
Galst, Carey Jo *biologist, educator*
Ge, Sheng *research scientist, educator*
Getis, Arthur *geography educator*
Jessen, Bart Andrew *toxicologist*
Madireddi, Mallareddy *physiologist*
Myers, Douglas George *zoological society administrator*
Nordhoff, Henry Louis (Hank Nordhoff) *biotechnology company executive, investor*
Panetta, Joseph Daniel *biotechnologist, director*
Rasochova, Lada *research scientist*
Schaechter, Moselio *microbiology educator*
Sejnowski, Terrence Joseph *science educator*
Spence, Jean Louise *biology professor, researcher*
Squire, Larry Ryan *neuroscientist, psychologist, educator*
Tozer, William Evans *entomologist, educator*
Westwick, John Keirn *molecular cell biologist*
Wilson, Darcy Benoit *science association director*

San Francisco
Alberts, Bruce Michael *cell biologist, former foundation administrator*
Blackburn, Elizabeth Helen *molecular biologist*
Chou, Fang-yu *science educator*
Clements, John Allen *physiologist*
Coughlin, Shaun R. *research scientist, medical professor*
Gruenert, Dieter C. *geneticist, educator*
Hedberg, Gail Elizabeth *registered veterinary technician, consultant*
Heyneman, Donald *parasitology and tropical medicine educator*
Horton, Jonathan Charles *neuroscientist, neuro-ophthalmologist*
Jan, Lily Yeh *physiology, biochemist*
Jiang, Xiangning *neuroscientist*
Kavanaugh, David Henry *entomologist, educator*
La Farge, Timothy *retired plant geneticist*
LeBuhn, Gretchen *biology professor*
Lisberger, Stephen G. *physiologist, educator*
Lucas, Adam Ronald *science educator*
Márquez-Magaña, Leticia Maria *biology professor*
McCormick, Frank *research scientist, biology professor*
Merzenich, Michael *neuroscientist, educator*
Miller, Walter Luther *scientist, pediatrician, educator*
Mostov, Keith Elliot *cell biologist, educator*
Randall, Janet Ann *biology professor, researcher*
Tricaro, Robert Collet *biologist, editor, poet, educator*
Vidwans, Smruti Jayant *microbiologist*
Weiner, Michael W. *neuroscientist, researcher, educator*

San Jose
Ibarra, Rufino H. *science educator*
Kim, Jong-Shik *soil microbiologist, researcher*
Silver, Steven David *science educator*

San Luis Obispo
Mann, Nancy Jean *biology professor*

San Marcos
Zhang, Xiaoyu *science educator*

San Pablo
Murphy, Thomas Patrick *science educator, researcher*

San Rafael
Coelho, Vania R. *biology professor*

Santa Barbara
Badash, Lawrence *science history educator*
Christman, Arthur Castner, Jr. *science advisor, consultant*
Crowell, John C(hambers) *geology educator, researcher*
Dunne, Thomas *geology educator*
Ji, Chen *science educator*
Jordan, Mary Ann *research biologist*
Kryter, Karl David *retired research scientist*
Lopus, Manu *biologist*
Prezelin, Barbara Berntsen *science association director, educator*
Samuel, Charles E. *virologist, biochemist, educator*
Schneider, Edward Lee *botanist, researcher*
Tucker, Shirley Lois Cotter *botanist, educator*

Santa Clara
Staples, Nathan Charles *biology professor*

Santa Cruz
Epps, Harland Warren *astronomy educator, optical design consultant*
Huskey, Harry Douglas *information and computer science educator*
Langenheim, Jean Harmon *biologist, educator*
Lay, Thorne *geosciences educator*
Shaffer, Scott A. *biology professor, researcher*
Stuart, Joshua M. *biology professor*

Santa Monica
Goldman, Charles A. *science administrator*
Salveson, Melvin Erwin *management sciences corporation chief executive, educator*

Sebastopol
Omi, Philip Nori *retired forestry professor*

South San Francisco
Andre, Patrick *biologist, director*
Barbour, Robin McDaid *research scientist, director*
Shi, Yining *biotechnologist*

Stanford
Briggs, Winslow Russell *plant biologist, educator*
Byers, Tom H. *management science and engineering educator*
Cai, James J. *biologist, researcher*
Campbell, Allan McCulloch *bacteriology educator*
Cohen, Stanley Norman *geneticist, educator*
Cork, Linda Katherine *veterinary pathologist, educator*
Dally, William J. *computer science educator*
Ehrlich, Paul Ralph *biology professor*
Falkow, Stanley *microbiologist, educator*
Grossman, Arthur R. *science educator, researcher*
Hanawalt, Philip Courtland *biology professor, researcher*
Long, Sharon Rugel *molecular biologist, educator*
Moore, Tirin *neuroscientist, educator*
Nelson, W. James *biology professor, researcher*
Salehi, Ahmad *research scientist*
Scott, Matthew Peter *biology educator*
Shapiro, Lucy *molecular biology educator*
Shatz, Carla J. *biology professor, researcher*
Shooter, Eric Manvers *retired neurobiology professor, consultant*
Sturrock, Peter Andrew *space science and astrophysics educator*
Theriot, Julie *microbiologist, medical educator*
Tiller, William Arthur *retired science educator, scientific researcher*
Yanofsky, Charles *retired biology professor*

Stockton
Ford, Shirley Griffin *science educator, pharmacist*
Ford, William Herschel *science educator*
Knudsen, Robert L. *physiologist, educator*
Stoner, Harry David-Foxe *science educator*

Sunset Beach
Pridham, Thomas Grenville *retired microbiologist*

The Sea Ranch
Hayflick, Leonard *cell biologist, biogerontologist, microbiologist, educator, writer*

Thousand Oaks
Babaeizadeh, Saeed *research scientist*
Savarin, Cecile Geraldine *science administrator*

Tujunga
Ancu, Edward Florin *veterinarian*

Union City
Mo, Jianwei *research scientist*

Van Nuys
Nakamura, Lawrence T. *microbiologist, educator*

Walnut Creek
Elliott, Margaret S. *science educator*
Kyrpides, Nikos C. *biologist*
Seaborg, David Michael *evolutionary biologist*

Westminster
Mattar, Mary Anne Y. *biology professor*

Woodland
Squires, Richard Felt *research scientist*

Yreka
Hamilton, John Bruce *biologist*

COLORADO

Arvada
Chiou, Cary Tsair *environmental scientist, hydrologist*
Powers, Christopher Sheridan *science educator, web site designer*

Aurora
Bjugstad, Kimberly Beret *neuroscientist, educator*
Dooley, J. Gordon *food scientist*
Mikulich Gilbertson, Susan Kay *science educator*
Razzaghi, Hamid *molecular biologist, researcher*
Seeds, Nicholas Warren *neuroscience educator, researcher*
Weedin, James Frank *biology professor, researcher*

Boulder
Byerly, Radford, Jr. *science administrator*
Chu, Xinzhao *science educator, researcher*
Conti, Peter Selby *astronomy educator*
Fifkova, Eva *behavioral neuroscience educator*
Guild, Nancy Ann *biology professor*
Knoelker, Michael T.F. *science observatory director*
Leland, Harry Valentine *retired biologist*
Meier, Beverly Joyce Loeffler *science educator, consultant*
Meier, Mark Frederick *research scientist, educator, artist, small business owner*
Norris, David Otto *educator*
Pace, Norman R. *science educator, microbiologist*
Snow, Theodore Peck *astrophysics educator*
Southwick, Charles Henry *zoologist, educator*
Staehelin, Lucas Andrew *cell biology professor emeritus*
Yarus, Michael *biologist, educator*

Carbondale
Cowgill, Ursula Moser *biologist, educator, environmental consultant*

Clark
Mayer, Frank Charles *math/science educator*

Colorado Springs
Ballantyne, Arnold Paul *economist, educator*
Heim, Werner G(eorge) *biology educator*

Denver
Ash, Jason Stuart *biology teaching assistant*
Ehret, Josephine Mary *retired microbiologist researcher*
Finney, Barbara Ann *biology professor*

Jones, Stephanie Lee *biologist, ornithologist, botanist*
Kappler, John W. *microbiology educator*
Kosnett, Michael J. *medical toxicologist*
Krell, Frank-Thorsten *zoologist, researcher*
McDermott, Sandra *national park administrator*
Refaeli, Yosef *biology professor*

Durango
Korb, Julie *biology professor*
Lehmer, Erin M. *biology professor*

Fort Collins
Adiku, Samuel Godfried Kwasi *soil scientist*
Bartels, Randy A. *science educator, researcher*
Fausch, Kurt Daniel *fisheries ecologist, educator*
Follett, Ronald Francis *soil scientist*
Glantz, Michelle Medora *biology professor*
Goodrich, Laurie R. *veterinarian, educator*
Johnson, Robert Britten *geology educator*
Keim, Wayne Franklin *retired agronomist, geneticist*
Kurosu, Michio *science educator*
Laituri, Melinda J. *science educator*
Lumb, William Valjean *veterinarian*
Mader, Douglas Paul *research administrator*
Mortvedt, John Jacob *soil scientist, researcher*
Newman, Steven Earl *horticulturist, educator*
Palmer, Ross Howard *veterinarian, educator*
Peterson, Gary Andrew *agronomics researcher*
Schlup, Philip *research scientist*
Seidel, George Elias, Jr. *zoology educator*
Shaner, Dale L. *weed scientist*
Skagen, Susan K. *biologist*
Stoaks, Ralph Duval *entomologist, educator, retired biotechnologist*
Theobald, David Martin *ecologist, educator*
Zhang, Shu-xin *neuroscientist*

Frisco
Janes, Donald Wallace *biologist, educator, academic administrator, consultant*

Glenwood Springs
Kelley, Robert Daryl *retired biology professor, mathematics professor*

Golden
Bettinghaus, Erwin Paul *research scientist*
Weimer, Robert Jay *geology educator, energy consultant, civic leader*
Wyman, Charles Ely *biotechnologist, research director, chemical engineer*

Littleton
Rolater, J. Rick *science association director*
Vail, Charles Daniel *veterinarian, consultant*

Longmont
Dierks, Richard Ernest *veterinarian, academic administrator*

Loveland
Armstrong, David Michael *biology professor*

Northglenn
Hemlock, Roberta Leigh *veterinary technician*

Penrose
Hilderbrand, Richard L. *science association director, consultant*

Westminster
Bennani, Farah *biology professor*

CONNECTICUT

Bethlehem
Collins, Mother Augusta *agronomist*

Coventry
Hayes, Julia Moriarty *retired science educator*

Fairfield
Fiddes, James William *biology professor*
Zavras, Eugenia T. *parasitologist, educator*

Farmington
Bronner, Felix *physiologist, biophysicist, educator, painter*
Rothfield, Lawrence I. *microbiology educator*
Shoemaker, William Joseph *neuroscientist*

Groton
Shumway, Sandra Elisabeth *shellfish biologist*

Madison
Kilbourne, Edwin Dennis *virologist, educator*
Stevenson, Robert Edwin *microbiologist, consultant*

Meriden
Lee, Henry C. *forensic scientist*

Middletown
Naegele, Janice Rae *science educator*

Milford
Perry, Dean M. *biologist*

Mystic
Ballard, Robert Duane *marine geologist*

New Britain
Penniman, Clayton *biology professor*

New Haven
Albrecht, Alice *research scientist*
Alonzo, Suzanne Henson *ecologist, educator*
Altman, Sidney *biology professor*
Anderson, John Fredric *science administrator, entomologist, researcher*
Aronson, Peter Samuel *physiologist, researcher*
Briggs, Derek Ernest Gilmor *science educator*
Brown, Thomas Huntington *neuroscientist*
Bugbee, Gregory Joseph *soil scientist, researcher*
Donoghue, Michael John *biologist, educator, museum director*
DuBois, Arthur Brooks *physiologist, educator*
Gent, Martin P.N. *agricultural scientist*
Horwich, Arthur L. *biologist, educator*
McPartland, James *research scientist*
Moczydlowski, Edward Gerard *biologist, researcher*
Monteiro, Antónia *biology professor*
Novick, Peter J. *cell biologist, educator*
Pauls, David *human geneticist, researcher*
Pollard, Thomas Dean *cell biologist, educator*
Rakic, Pasko *neuroscientist, educator*
Redmond, Donald Eugene, Jr. *neuroscientist, educator*
Rothman, James Edward *cell biologist, educator*
Schmitz, Oswald Joseph *biology professor*
State, Matthew W. *cell biologist, neuroscientist, educator*
Steitz, Thomas A. *science educator*
Summers, William Cofield *science educator*
Vermeire, Jon J. *research scientist*
Waggoner, Paul Edward *agricultural scientist*
Zito, Christina Ivins *molecular biologist, educator*

Old Saybrook
Smith, David Clark *research scientist*

Stamford
Yarish, Charles *biology professor, researcher*

Storrs Mansfield
Chazdon, Robin Lee *botanist, educator*
Devereux, Owen Francis *retired metallurgy educator*
Holsinger, Kent Eugene *biology professor, educator*
Islam, Muhammad M. *theoretical physicist*
Laufer, Hans *developmental biologist, educator*
Mulkey, Daniel K. *research scientist*
Turchin, Peter *biology professor*

Wallingford
Hartz, Richard Allen *research scientist*

DELAWARE

Dover
Hankoua, Bertrand Bachaumond *molecular biologist, educator*

Newark
Campbell, Linzy Leon *molecular biology researcher, educator*
Cornell, Howard Vernon *ecology educator*
Green, Jerry M *biologist, weed scientist*
Kennedy, Gerald L. *toxicologist, researcher*
Mason, Charles Eugene *entomologist, educator*
Sparks, Donald Lewis *soil chemistry educator*

Wilmington
Darko, Denis F. *research scientist, physician*
Hartzell, Charles R. *science foundation director, cell biologist, biochemist*
Sippel-Wetmore, Frances Marie *microbiologist, retired business owner*
Waritz, Richard Stefan *toxicologist, researcher*

DISTRICT OF COLUMBIA

Washington
Acker, Joseph G. *science association director*
Apple, Martin Allen *science executive and educator*
Ashktorab, Hassan *molecular biologist*
Bae, Insoo *science educator*
Bandows Koster, Janet *science association director*
Banks, Richard Charles *ornithologist*
Berg, Patricia Elene *molecular biologist*
Carhart, Homer Walter *retired research scientist*
Cehelsky, Marta *scientific organization executive*
Chamot, Dennis *science policy executive*
Chapman, George Bunker *biology professor*
Chiang, Peter K. *science administrator*
Coleman, Bernell *physiologist, educator*
Crandall, Frank B. *marine biologist, engineer*
Davis, Donald Ray *entomologist*
Davis, Randy Lee *soil scientist*
Eckberg, William Robert *biologist, educator, researcher*
Elias, Thomas Sam *botanist, author*
Eribo, Broderick E. *microbiologist, educator*
Fedoroff, Nina Vsevolod *research scientist, consultant, educator*
Grimes, Darrell Jay *microbiologist*
Harding, Fann *retired scientist, administrator*
Henkin, Robert Irwin *neuroscientist, internist, nuclear medicine physician, medical products executive*
Hope, William Duane *retired zoologist, curator*
Hotez, Peter Jay *parasitologist, educator*
Hudson, Kathy *microbiologist, geneticist, educator*
Hussain, Taseer S. *science educator*
Koffel, William E. *science association director, fire protection engineer*
Leshner, Alan Irvin *science administrator*
Li, Li *research scientist*
Littler, Diane Scullion *marine biologist*
Mak, I. Tong *biologist, educator*
McClung, Gwendolyn *soil microbiologist*
Meyers, Wayne Marvin *microbiologist, physician*
Moore, Donald Emerson III *zoological park administrator, curator, wildlife biologist*
Neureiter, Norman P. *science association director*
Nicolson, Dan Henry *retired plant taxonomist*
Nightingale, Elena Ottolenghi *pediatric geneticist, academic administrator, educator*
O'Grady, Richard T. *science administrator*
O'Malley, Ann S. *research scientist*
Pyke, Thomas Nicholas, Jr. *science administrator*
Sharkey, Andrew G. III *science association director*
Siegel, Frederic Richard *geology educator*
Stern, Alan (Sol Alan Stern) *science administrator, astrophysicist, researcher*
Strong, Mark Tuthill *botanist*
Studds, Colin Eastman *ecologist, researcher*
Thorington, Richard Wainwright *biologist*
Tidball, M. Elizabeth Peters *physiologist, educator*
Ucko, David Alan *science foundation official*
Wasshausen, Dieter Carl *botanist*
West, Robert MacLellan *science educator, consultant*
Wilkinson, Ronald Sterne *science administrator, historian, environmentalist*

FLORIDA

Boca Raton
Ayyanathan, Kasirajan *biology professor*
Makowski, Christopher *marine biologist, educator*
Samuels, William Mason *physiology association executive*

Bradenton
Diana, John Nicholas *physiologist*
Gauthier, Norman Leonidas *retired biology professor*
Miller, Cory D. *science educator*
Mosca-Focht, Marlene *biology professor*

Coconut Creek
Ramirez, Monica E. *science educator, dean*

Coral Gables
Lucà-Moretti, Maurizio *research scientist, nutritionist*

Davie
Abrams, Lendell Arlington *biology professor*
Arena, Paul Thomas *marine biologist, educator*
Obenauf, Steven D. *microbiologist, educator*
Stackhouse, Daniel J. *science educator*

Daytona Beach
Sen, Shukdeb *biology professor*

Delray Beach
Chavin, Walter *biological sciences educator, researcher*

Fort Lauderdale
Esiobu, Nwadiuto *biotechnologist, educator*
Yang, Rou-Ling *entomologist*

Fort Myers
Beever, James William III *biologist*
Guo, Dahai *science educator*
Schnackenberg, F. Richard *science educator, department chairman*

Fort Pierce
Calvert, David Victor *soil science educator*
Rice, Mary Esther *biologist*
Widder, Edith Anne *biologist*

Gainesville
Besch, Emerson Louis *physiologist, educator, retired dean*
Cantliffe, Daniel James *horticulture educator*
Courtenay, Walter Rowe, Jr. *biology professor, researcher*
Czarnecka-Verner, Eva *molecular biologist, educator*
Dilcher, David Leonard *paleobotany educator, researcher*
Dunn, William A., Jr. *cell biologist, educator*
Gridley, Kelly Elizabeth *biotechnologist, researcher*
Grobman, Arnold Brams *retired biology educator, academic administrator*
Hoy, Marjorie Ann *entomology educator*
Jarzen, David MacArthur *research scientist*
Levy, Julie Kay *veterinarian, educator*
Mann, Rajinder *entomologist, researcher*
Nguyen, Ru *entomologist*
Nicoletti, Paul Lee *retired veterinarian, educator*
Oppenheimer, David Gray *botanist, educator*
Pereira, Roberto M. *entomologist*
Purcifull, Dan Elwood *retired plant virologist, educator*
Quesenberry, Kenneth Hays *agronomy educator*
Schelske, Claire L. *limnologist, educator*
Schmidt-Nielsen, Bodil Mimi (Mrs. Roger G. Chagnon) *retired physiologist, educator*
Shabana, Yasser M. *plant pathologist professor, research scientist*
Smith, Matthew Denman *ecologist*
Somma, Louis A. *biologist*
Stall, William M. *weed scientist, educator*
Stehouwer, Donald J. *neuroscientist*
Teixeira, Arthur Alves *food engineer, educator, consultant*
Tumlinson, James H. III *agriculturist*
Ulanowicz, Robert Edward *science educator*
Uryasev, Stan *science educator*
Verstegen, John P.L. *theriogenologist, educator*
Vincent, Heather Ketelaar *physiologist, educator*
West-Olatunji, Cirecie *science educator*
Yamamoto, Janet Kazuko *science educator*
Yu, Simon Shyi-Jian *entomologist, educator*

Gulf Breeze
Menzer, Robert Everett *retired toxicologist, educator*

Homestead
Roberts, Larry Spurgeon *biological science educator, zoologist*

Jacksonville
Evens, Ronald Paul *biotechnologist, consultant*
Lange, Lori Jean *science professor, researcher*
Leissring, Malcolm Arthur *neuroscientist, educator*
McCarthy, Daniel Anthony *biology professor*

Jupiter
Lasmezas, Corinne Ida *neuroscientist, researcher*
Philippe, Bois Roger Jean *science educator, researcher*
Weissmann, Charles *molecular biologist, educator*

Key Biscayne
Loisel, Gerard Roland *marine biologist, educator*

Lake Alfred
Kender, Walter John *horticulturist, educator*
Nageswara Rao, Madhugiri *research scientist*

Lake Worth
Liang, Lee Z. *biology professor*

Lakeland
Chapman, Angela Marie *science educator*
Mallison, Craig T. *research scientist*

Madison
Molnar, Greg Robert *science educator*

Melbourne
Bush, Mark Bennett *ecologist, educator*
Harms, Eric A. *science educator*

Miami
Arminio, Michael, Jr. *science educator*
Bianchi, Laura *physiologist, educator*
Carraway, Kermit *cell biologist, educator*
Muench, Karl Hugo *clinical geneticist*
Pearse, Damien D. *neuroscientist, consultant*
Procop, Gary W. *microbiologist, educator, physician*
Rodriguez, Irmina Bestard *science educator*
Sadjadi, Masoud *science educator*
Scott, Troy M. *microbiologist, director*
Smeltzer, Debra Jean *botanist*

Naples
Goldman, Ralph Frederick *research physiologist, educator*

New Port Richey
Day, Peter Rodney *geneticist, educator*
Summers, Horace Kenneth *biology professor*

Okahumpka
Branham, Joseph Morhart *biologist, educator*

Orange Park
VonGruenigen, Christine Michelle *microbiologist, educator*

Orlando
Baker, Peter Mitchell *science association director, laser scientist*
Birmele, Michele Nan *biologist*
Jeanpierre, Bobby Jo *science educator*
Khalil, Mohammed K. *research scientist, medical educator*
Kincaid, John Peter *science educator*
Knowles, Patricia Marie *science educator*
Singla, Dinender K. *science educator, consultant*
Worthy, Graham Anthony James *biology professor, researcher*

Palatka
Moore, Claybourne Maunsell *biology professor*

Palm Bay
Harvey, Robert Christopher *biology professor*

Palm Beach Gardens
Khanfar, Nile Mustafa *science educator*
Mills, Christopher James *neurophysiologist, electroneurodiagnostic technologist*

Pensacola
El-Sheikh, Eman *science educator*
Petersen, Jessica M. *biology professor*

Pinellas Park
Goswami, Shashikant *veterinarian, educator*

Punta Gorda
O'Neal, Lyman Henry *biology educator*

Saint Augustine
Harvey, William Royal *physiologist, educator*
Zacharias, David Alan *biotechnologist, educator*

Saint Petersburg
Bert, Theresa M. *science educator, researcher*
Brightman, Ross I. *biology professor*
Chang, Yenhui *geneticist, director*
D'Elia, Christopher Francis *marine biologist, educator, academic administrator*

Saint Teresa
Grubbs, Ralph Dean *marine biologist*

Sarasota
Clark, Eugenie *zoologist, educator*
Mahadevan, Kumar *marine life administrator, researcher*

Tallahassee
Anderson, Theresa Ann *science educator*
DuVal, Emily H. *biology professor, researcher*
Herrick, Nathan *biologist*
Lu, Junjie *molecular biologist*
Olcese, James Michael *neuroscientist, educator*
Onokpise, Oghenekome Ukrakpo *agronomist, educator, forester, geneticist*
Park, Jin Gyu *research scientist*

Tampa
Cowell, Bruce Craig *biology educator, aquatic ecologist*
Germroth, Peter *biologist, educator*
Ghosh, Debarati *biology professor, researcher*
Kucera, Stephen D. *biology professor*
Mushinsky, Henry R. *biology professor*
Pinjari, Abdul R. *assistant professor*

Rossignol, Jean-François Armand *research scientist, medical educator*

Titusville
Rivenbark, Christine Klemenz *science educator, researcher*

West Palm Beach
Chimney, Michael John *aquatic biologist and limnologist, consultant*
Colitz, Carmen Maria Helena *veterinarian, educator*

Winter Haven
Grierson, William *retired agriculturist*

GEORGIA

Acworth
Whitmore, Michael Raymond *science educator*

Albany
Liu, May Sumei *biology professor*
Marshall, Cindy Lou *science and social studies educator*

Athens
Bacon, Charles Wilson *mycologist, educator, research scientist*
Baile, Clifton A. *biologist, researcher*
Bennetzen, Jeffrey L. *molecular biologist*
Berdanier, Lynne *science educator*
Brackett, Benjamin Gaylord *retired physiology and pharmacology educator*
Fameree, Randall Joseph, II, *physiologist, educator*
Hinton, Arthur, Jr. *microbiologist*
Kushner, Sidney Ralph *molecular genetics and biochemistry educator*
Mayo, John Arthur *microbiologist, researcher, educator*
Outcalt, Kenneth W. *ecologist, researcher*
Roellig, Dawn M. *research scientist*
Tyler, David Earl *veterinary medical educator*
Wessler, Susan R. *biologist, educator*
Williams, Susan Michelle *veterinarian, educator*

Atlanta
Ahearn, Donald G. *microbiologist, consultant, researcher*
Borek, Lois Brewer *physiologist, educator*
Capra, C. Monica *science educator*
Carey, Gerald John, Jr. *research institute director emeritus, former air force officer*
Circeo, Louis Joseph, Jr. *research scientist, civil engineer*
Clancy, Andrew Nelson *biology professor*
Cobb, Kim M. *science educator*
Cox, Nancy Jane *microbiologist*
Cox, Shanna Nakia *research scientist*
Day, Diane Elaine *science educator, researcher*
de Waal, Frans B.M. *biologist, psychology professor*
Ellis, Barbara Ann *microbiologist, epidemiologist*
Fowler, Bruce Andrew *toxicologist, researcher, public health service official*
Frey, Teryl Kenneth *biology professor, virologist*
Fridovich-Keil, Judith Lisa *molecular biology researcher, educator*
Guldiken, Rasim Oytun *research scientist*
Helms, My Nga *physiologist, researcher*
Jayaraman, Sundaresan *science educator*
Jeffery, Geoffrey Marron *medical parasitologist*
Kamio, Michiya *research scientist*
Khoury, Muin J. *geneticist, epidemiologist*
Krebs, John W. *research scientist*
Lynn, David G. *biology and chemistry professor*
Merkle, Sarah Lynn *research scientist*
Odujebe, Oladapo A. *toxicologist, educator, emergency physician*
Paul, Ketema Nnamdi *neuroscientist, educator*
Ramesh, Balasubramaniam *science educator*
Rojas, Mauricio *research scientist, educator*
Sarpong, Kwabena Dua *biology professor*
Shams, Alicia Marie *microbiologist*
Spitznagel, John Keith *retired microbiologist, immunologist, physician*
Vazirani, Vijay V. *science educator*
Yates, Jerome William *scientific administrator, researcher*
Yount, Kathryn Mary *science educator*

Augusta
Baker, Carleton Harold *physiology educator*
Kutlar, Ferdane *genetics educator, researcher*
Swenson, Gabriel J. *biology professor*

Bainbridge
Leggett, Carol Griffis *biology professor*

Carrollton
Gowens, Greg *science educator, small business owner*

Clarkston
Aliff, John Vincent *biology professor*

Decatur
Beckemeyer, Elizabeth Frances *biology professor*

Duluth
Pratt, Bonnie *science educator*

Evans
Little, Robert Colby *physiologist, educator*

Fort Valley
Yadav, Anand Krishna *biotechnologist, educator*

Gainesville
May, Sterling Randolph *biology professor, department chairman*

Griffin
Doyle, Michael Patrick *microbiologist, educator, director*

Jekyll Island
Norton, Terry M. *veterinarian, director*

Kennesaw
McCoy, R. Wesley *biology educator*

Lithonia
Baxter, Gene Francis *chemical researcher, consultant*

Macon
Bubacz, Monika *science educator*

Newnan
Culbreth, Lucretia Joy *science educator*
Krach, Dale James *science educator, athletic trainer*

Norcross
Wagner, Robert Earl *retired agronomist*

Savannah
Bose, Himangshu S. *cell biologist, educator*
Lancaster, Christopher Scott *science educator*
Saripalli, Lalitha Devi *biologist, educator*

Smyrna
Parikh, Priti P. *food scientist*

Statesboro
James, Harris Kelly *science educator, department chairman*

Tifton
Anderson, William F. *research scientist*
Hubbard, Robert K. *soil scientist*
Lewis, Wallace Joe *entomologist, researcher*

Waco
House, Janyce Elaine *science educator*

Watkinsville
Meers, Suzanne *biology professor*

Waynesboro
Byrd, Rebecca L. *science educator*

Williamson
Huckaby, Scott Allan *science educator, geologist*

Winston
Simon, Ted *toxicologist*

Woodstock
Barthlow, Michelle Jones *science educator*

HAWAII

Hilo
Crosby, Michael P. *science administrator*
Tripathi, Savarni *plant pathologist*

Honolulu
Duhamel, Solange *marine biologist*
Finucane, Melissa Lucille *research scientist*
Fok, Agnes Kwan *retired cell biologist, educator*
Gobush, Kathleen Schuyler *ecologist*
Gubler, Duane J. *virologist, educator, researcher*
Hue, Nguyen Van *soil scientist, chemist, educator*
Jarjees, Ekhlass A. *entomologist*
Jube, Sandro Lacerda Ramos *biotechnologist, researcher*
Kamemoto, Fred Isamu *retired zoologist*
Kobayashi, Donald Rikio *biologist*
Mandel, Morton *molecular biologist*
Sagawa, Yoneo *horticulturist, educator*
Vargas, Roger Irvin *entomologist, ecologist*

Kalaheo
Ragone, Carol Diane *horticulturist, ethnobotanist*

Tamc
Uyehara, Catherine Fay Takako (Yamauchi) *physiologist, educator, pharmacologist*

IDAHO

Aberdeen
Erickson, Charles *agronomist*

Boise
Morgan, Barbara R. *science educator, former astronaut*
Osguthorpe, Richard D. *science educator*
Sather, John Henry *biologist, educator, dean*
Woods, Jean Frahm *science educator*

Moscow
Roberts, Lorin Watson *botanist, educator*
Top, Eva Maria *science educator*

Twin Falls
Selelyo, Pat *biology professor*

ILLINOIS

Abbott Park
He, Yupeng *virologist, cell biologist*

Addison
Cherif, Abour Hachmi *biology and science educator*

Argonne
Schriesheim, Alan *science administrator*

Brookfield
Rabb, George Bernard *zoologist, conservationist*
Wojciechowski, Sheila *zoological park administrator*

Carbondale
Che, Dunren *science educator*
King, Sheryl S. *animal scientist, educator*
Kohler, Christopher Carl *zoology professor*
LeFebvre, Eugene Allen *zoology educator, ecologist*
Preece, John Earl *plant and soil science educator*
Rose, Gregory Mancel *neurobiologist*

Carol Stream
Cole, Kevin John *science educator*

Carterville
Krapf, Keith Alan *science educator*

Champaign
Batzli, George Oliver *ecology educator*
Cook, Paul Franklin *veterinarian, educator*
Getz, Lowell Lee *zoology educator*
Hager, Lowell Paul *biochemistry educator*
Levin, Geoffrey Arthur *botanist*

Chicago
Ashley, Mary V. *biology professor*
Banisadr, Ghazal *science educator, researcher*
Bast, Joseph L. *research organisation director*
Bell, Graeme I. *biochemistry and molecular biology educator*
Berlin, Lawrence Norman *science educator*
Cohn, Stanley Alan *cell biology educator*
Corley, Arlicia *science educator*
Coyne, Jerry Allen *ecologist, educator*
Crane, Sir Peter Robert *botanist, geologist, paleontologist, educator*
DeCoursey, Thomas Eric *physiologist, educator*
Desjardins, Claude *physiologist, dean*
Dwivedi, Yogesh *science educator*
Engeland, Christopher G. *neuroscientist, educator*
Ernest, J. Terry *ocular physiologist, educator*
Fisher, Lester Emil *retired zoo administrator*
Frederick, John Eugene *science educator*
Gettins, Peter Gregory Wolfgang *biology professor*
Gevorgyan, Vladimir *science educator, researcher*
Goodman, Steven Michael *conservation biologist*
Greenberg, Bernard *retired entomologist*
Grossi, Deann Christine *biology professor*
Hong, Seungpyo *science educator*
Jablonski, David *science educator*
Kim, Song-Jung *physiologist*
Lange, Yvonne *cell biologist, educator*
Maesen, William August *development consultant*
Mateles, Richard Isaac *biotechnologist*
McCormick, David Loyd *toxicologist, researcher, educator*
Minges Wols, Heather Ann *biology professor*
Olopade, Olufunmilayo Falusi (Funmi Olopade) *geneticist, educator, oncologist, hematologist*
Parent, Angele *research scientist*
Park, Thomas Joseph *biology researcher, educator*
Preuss, Daphne *geneticist, biology professor*
Roizman, Bernard *virologist, educator*
Spaeth, Virginia Ann *biology professor*
Strauss, Bernard S. *geneticist, educator*
Thomas, Ronald L. *science educator, director*
Vick, Linda H. *biology professor*
Yamada, Tohru *biologist, educator, researcher, director*
Zhou, Ping *research scientist*

Chicago Heights
Barrett, Reuben Edward *biology professor*

Coal City
DiGiusto, Elaine Bessie *science educator*

Deerfield
Ho Pao, Chrystal L. *biology professor*
Rentas, Angelo George *biology professor, director*

Dekalb
Bennett, (Cecil) Jack(son) *biology professor*
Zhou, Shengde *science educator, researcher*

Downers Grove
Brekke, Stewart Ernest *retired chemistry and physics educator*

Edwardsville
Watson, George William, Jr. *science educator*

Eureka
Tookey, Keith R. *computer science professor*

Evanston
Dallos, Peter John *neurobiologist, educator*
Klein, William Lee *neurobiology professor, researcher*
Lamb, Robert Andrew *molecular biologist, virologist, educator*
Novales, Ronald Richards *zoologist, educator*
Ruggero, Mario Alfredo *physiologist, educator*
Shenkar, Robert *science educator, researcher*
Weertman, Johannes *materials science educator*
Wu, Tai Te *biological sciences and engineering educator*

Glen Ellyn
Anderson, Barbara Jean *biology professor*

Granite City
Cowan, Robert Randall *science educator*

Grayslake
Coykendall, Mark Alan *biology professor, department chairman*

Great Lakes
Bienek, Diane Rose *research scientist*

Harrisburg
Maring-Sims, Mila L. *biology professor*

Jacksonville
Kasper, Carol L. *biology professor*

Joliet
Heeneman, Cheryl Lynn *biology professor*

Lincoln
Eack, Cynthia A. *science educator, department chairman*

Lisle
Ware, George Henry *botanist*

Mattoon
Hunzinger, Brenda C. *biology professor*

Maywood
Schultz, Richard Michael *biochemistry educator, researcher*

Moline
Harwood, Richard D. *science educator*

Naperville
Sukumar, Narayanasami *research scientist*

Normal
Brown, Lauren Evans *zoologist, researcher, educator*
Hattangady, Dipti Shashidhar Jyoti *microbiologist, educator*
Mockford, Edward Lee *biologist, educator*
Suh, Kyoungwon *science educator, researcher*

Northbrook
King, Robert Charles *biologist, educator*

Oswego
Riccio, Angela *science educator*

Peoria
Eller, Fred Joseph III *entomologist*
Labeda, David Paul *microbiologist*

Plainfield
Matlock, B. Jane *science educator*

Robinson
Mallard, Carrie Charlene *science educator*

Rochester
Butcher, Mark William *science educator*

Rockford
Bomgarden, Ryan D. *biotechnologist, educator*
Pantaleo, Lea *biology professor*
Raymond, Jill M. *microbiologist, educator*

Savoy
Hoffmeister, Donald Frederick *zoologist, educator*
Sinclair, James Burton *retired plant pathology educator, consultant*

Springfield
Harris, Donald Wayne *research scientist*
Munyer, Edward Arnold *zoologist*

Sugar Grove
Ashfaq, Rizwana *biology professor*

Tamms
Vellella, Christopher A. *science educator*

Urbana
Buetow, Dennis Edward *physiologist, educator*
Cann, Isaac *microbiologist, educator*
Crang, Richard Francis Earl *plant biologist, writer, research scientist*
Dawson, Jeffrey Owen *forester, educator*
Delcomyn, Fred *physiologist, educator, neurobiologist*
Feng, Albert *science educator, researcher*
Gillette, Martha U. *neuroscientist*
Heath, James Edward *retired physiology educator*
Heichel, Gary Harold *agronomist, educator*
Korban, Schuyler S. *molecular plant geneticist*
Langenheim, Ralph Louis, Jr. *geology educator*
Meyer, Richard Charles *microbiologist, educator*
Nanney, David Ledbetter *geneticist, educator*
Ra, Hyungshim Yoo *biologist, researcher*
Seigler, David Stanley *botanist, educator, chemist*
Sligar, Stephen Gary *molecular biologist, educator*
Wang, Xinlei *science educator*
Whitt, Gregory Sidney *evolution educator*
Wolfe, Ralph Stoner *microbiology educator*

Westchester
Webb, Emily *retired plant morphologist*

Woodstock
Dorn, Diane M. *science educator*

INDIANA

Anderson
Bailey, Michael John *biology professor*

Bloomington
Gest, Howard *microbiologist, educator*
Murray, Haydn Herbert *geology educator*
Ruesink, Albert William *biologist, plant sciences educator*
Taylor, Jill Bolte *neuroanatomist*
Weinberg, Eugene David *microbiologist, educator*

Chesterton
Wiemann, Marion Russell, Jr., (Baron of Camster) *biologist, ambassador general*

Gary
Schoon, Kenneth James *science educator, writer*

Greenfield
Coleman, Mark R. *research scientist*

Indianapolis
Banya, Santonino Ku'Caya *science educator*
Barman, Charles Roy *science educator*
Burr, David Bentley *anatomy educator*
Christian, Joe Clark *medical genetics researcher, educator, medical genetics researcher, educator*
Gupta, Manju *research scientist*
Ochs, Sidney *neurophysiology researcher, educator*
Packer, C. Subah *physiologist, educator*
Robertson, Michael John *internist, research scientist, educator*
Watson, David E. *toxicologist, consultant*
Wu, Min *cell biologist, researcher, educator*

Madison
Grahn, Ann Wagoner *retired science administrator*

Muncie
Hendrix, Jon Richard *biology professor*
Henzlik, Raymond Eugene *zoophysiologist, educator*
Mertens, Thomas Robert *biology professor*
Wise, Charles Davidson *science educator*

Notre Dame
D'Souza-Schorey, Crislyn *biology professor*
Fraser, Malcolm James, Jr. *biology professor*
Hager, Kristin Margaret *biology professor*
Jensen, Richard Jorg *biologist, educator*
Kulpa, Charles F. *microbiologist, educator*
Pollard, Morris *microbiologist, educator*
Shrader-Frechette, Kristin *science educator*

Rensselaer
Thomas, Jerry Arthur *retired soil scientist*

Saint Mary Of The Woods
Cadwallader, Joyce Vermeulen *biology professor*

Terre Haute
Amlaner, Charles Joseph *ecologist, department chairman*

Upland
Moore, John Morton *biology professor, consultant*

Valparaiso
Schlender, William Elmer *management sciences educator*

West Lafayette
Amstutz, Harold Emerson *veterinarian, educator*
Campanella, Osvaldo H. *biology professor*
Carlson, Gary Patrick *toxicologist, educator*
Carvajal, M. Teresa *science educator*
Dunning, John Barnard, Jr. *biology professor*
Edwards, Charles Richard *entomology and pest management educator*
Jackson, Scott Allen *biology professor*
Janick, Jules *horticultural scientist, educator*
Johannsen, Chris Jakob *agronomist, educator, administrator*
Leary, James Francis *biomedical research scientist, educator, inventor*
Le Master, Dennis Clyde *retired forester, economist, educator*
Luo, Xin *science educator*
Nelson, Philip Edwin *food scientist, educator*
Ohm, Herbert Willis *agronomy educator, agriculturist*
Thompson, Dorothea Kathleen *microbiologist*
Zheng, Wei *science educator*

IOWA

Ames
Anderson, Lloyd Lee *physiologist, educator*
Beran, George Wesley *veterinary microbiology educator*
Briggs, Robert E. *veterinarian*
Dinnes, Dana L. *agronomist*
Greve, John Henry *veterinary parasitologist, educator*
Hallauer, Arnel Roy *geneticist*
Hatfield, Jerry Lee *plant physiologist, agricultural meteorologist*
Jarecki, Marek Kazimierz *soil scientist, consultant*
Johnson, Lawrence Alan *cereal technologist, educator, administrator*
Kimura, Kayoko *veterinarian*
Lin, Zhiqun *science educator*
Lubberstedt, Thomas *plant pathologist, director*
Mengeling, William Lloyd *retired veterinarian, virologist*
Mertins, James Walter *entomologist*
Moore, Kenneth James *agronomist, educator*
O'Berry, Phillip Aaron *retired veterinarian*
Ross, Richard Francis *veterinarian, microbiologist, dean, educator*
Stabel, Judith R. *microbiologist*
Wegulo, Stephen Ngakhala *plant pathologist, researcher*
Willham, Richard Lewis *zoology educator*

Bettendorf
Dunn, Armond Russ Donald *science educator*

Cedar Falls
Waldron, Jennifer *science educator*

Cedar Rapids
Suiter, Jane *science educator*

Coralville
Koprivnjak, Tomaz *microbiologist*

Des Moines
Mitchell, Stuart *medical entomologist, consulting physician*

Dubuque
Eagleson, Gerald W. *neuroscientist, educator*

Eldridge
Downing, Paul R. *sports science educator*

Grinnell
Christiansen, Kenneth Allen *biologist, educator*
Walker, Waldo Sylvester *retired biologist, retired academic administrator*

Iowa City
Kessel, Richard Glen *zoology educator*
Lim, Ramon (Khe-Siong Lim) *neuroscience educator, researcher*
Maxson, Linda Ellen *biologist, educator*
Miller, Jordan D. *physiologist*
Stay, Barbara *zoologist, educator*
Wunder, Charles C(ooper) *physiologist, biophysicist, educator*

Ottumwa
Schindler, Fred H. *professor*

Pocahontas
Taylor, Sue Kay *science educator*

Waterloo
Mixdorf, Jon *science educator*

West Des Moines
Rosen, Matthew Stephen *retired botanist*

KANSAS

Arkansas City
Neal, Melinda K. *science educator*

Colby
Dijanic, Angela A. (Rivenshield) *toxicologist, educator*

Emporia
Sundberg, Marshall David *biology professor*

Hays
Coyne, Patrick Ivan *physiological ecologist*

Isabel
Brant, Dorris Ellen Stapleton *bacteriologist, music educator*

Kansas City
Horvat, Rebecca Thayer *microbiologist, educator*
Smith, Peter Guy *neuroscience educator, researcher*

Kiowa
Conrad, Melvin Louis *biology professor*

Lawrence
Angino, Ernest Edward *retired geology and engineering educator*
Armitage, Kenneth Barclay *retired biology professor*
Byers, George William *retired entomology educator*
Estep, Meredith E. *neuroscientist, educator*
Lichtwardt, Robert William *mycologist*
Michener, Charles Duncan *entomologist, researcher, educator*
Shankel, Delbert Merrill *microbiologist, biologist, educator*
Soberón Mainero, Jorge *former commission administrator, ecology researcher, educator*

Manhattan
Bai, Guihua *research scientist*
Bhadriraju, Subramanyam Venkata *entomologist, consultant*
Kaufman, Donald Wayne *research ecologist*
Kirkham, M. B. *plant physiologist, educator*
Stalheim-Smith, Ann *biology educator*
Tomich, John M. *biochemistry professor, science administrator*
Twiss, Page Charles *geology educator*
Walker, Charles Eugene *retired science educator*

Neosho Falls
Bader, Robert Smith *biology and zoology educator, researcher*

Olathe
Sattley, William Matthew *biology professor, researcher*

Overland Park
Follo, Judith E. *biology professor*
Goetz, Kenneth Lee *cardiovascular physiologist, research consultant, writer*

Parsons
Lomas, Lyle Wayne *agricultural research administrator, educator*

Topeka
Bayless, Kellis Matthew *biology professor*

Wichita
Dierks, Melinda Adair *science educator*
Nawrocki, Michael Alexander *veterinarian*
Park, Chan Hyung *cell biologist, physician*

KENTUCKY

Ashland
Georgas Flath, Mary Cat *biology professor*

Bowling Green
Li, Qi *science educator*

Frankfort
Huebner, Ruth A. *science educator, researcher*

Georgetown
Livingston, Tracy *biology professor*

Hazard
Currie, Paul B. *biology professor*

Lebanon
Cook, James *veterinarian*

Lexington
Chi, Young-In *science educator, researcher*
Huffman, Gerald P. *science administrator, educator*
Lai-Fook, Stephen Joseph *retired science educator*
Lodder, Robert A. *science educator*
Matveeva, Elena Aleksandrovna *microbiologist, biochemist, educator*
Palli, Subba Reddy *scientist, professor*
Sekulic, Dusan P. *science and engineering educator, researcher*
Shimojo, Masahito *science educator*
Sih, Andrew *biologist, educator*
Straus, Robert *behavioral sciences educator*
Timoney, Peter Joseph *veterinarian, educator, virologist, consultant*
Troedsson, Mats H.T. *veterinarian*

Louisville
Dobbins, Joanne Jones *microbiologist, educator*
Hu, Chuan *cell biologist*
Klotz, Martin Gunter *science educator*
Terhune, Jerry David *biology professor, researcher*
Vadhanam, Manicka V. *science educator*
Wiseman, Dennis R. *science educator*

Maysville
Quillen, Michael Duane *biology professor*

Midway
Juett, Beverly Willoughby *biology professor*

Murray
Derting, Terry L. *biology professor, researcher*

Owensboro
Caplan, Geralyn Marie *biology professor*

Princeton
Bailey, William Anthony *research scientist*

Somerset
Howard, Buford Philip *biology professor*

LOUISIANA

Baton Rouge
Albagdadi, Fakhri Abdelkareem *biology professor*
Besch, Everett Dickman *veterinarian, dean emeritus, educator*
Burns, Paul Yoder *forester, educator*
Hansel, William *biology professor*
Kang, Manjit Singh *geneticist, plant breeder*
Lehner, Luis *science educator*
Lopez, Mandi J. *veterinarian, scientist*
Pollock, David Daniel *biologist, educator, research scientist*
Superneau, Duane William *geneticist, physician*
Tipton, Kenneth Warren *retired agricultural administrator, researcher*

Centerville
Dupre, Susan V. *science educator*

Chauvin
Chesney, Edward Joseph *marine biologist, educator*
Sammarco, Paul William *ecologist, researcher*

Cut Off
Mestayer, Mary Frances *science educator*

Eunice
Vidrine, Malcolm Francis *biology educator*

Hammond
McFalls, Tiffany Beth *biology professor*

Jackson
Kondrup, John Thomas *retired research scientist*

Lafayette
Wang, Hongqing *ecologist, educator*

Monroe
Bhattacharjee, Joydeep *biology professor*

New Orleans
Barbee, Robert Wayne *cardiovascular physiologist*
Bart, Henry Leonard *biologist*
Beard, Elizabeth Letitia *physiologist, educator*
Cornelius, Mary Lynn *entomologist*
Dong, Yan *biologist*
Lesen, Amy E. *biology professor*
Mitchell, Kenneth David *physiologist, educator*
Pullikuth, Ashok K. *research scientist*
Sherry, Thomas Warren *ecologist*
Simmons, William Skip Bruce, Jr *science educator*
Surendran, Sankar *research scientist*
Susic, Dinko *physiologist*
Zhu, Dongxiao *science educator*

Prairieville
Brown, Robert Lawrence *research plant pathologist*

Shreveport
Butcher, Greg Q. *neuroscientist, educator*
Hall, Amy Matthews *science educator*

MAINE

Bangor
Merkel, Anne D. *science educator*

Bar Harbor
Coleman, Douglas *research scientist, educator*
Leiter, Edward Henry *cell biologist, researcher*
Petkov, Petko M. *geneticist, researcher*

Biddeford
Sandmire, David A. *biology professor*

Farmington
Mathews, Linnea Koons *science educator, librarian*

Kittery Point
Green, Edward Crocker *research scientist*

Mount Desert
Crawford, Richard Bradway *biologist, biochemist, educator*

Orono
Clapham, William Montgomery *plant physiologist*
Lin, Lin *research scientist*
Norton, Stephen Allen *earth sciences educator*

Portland
Bjelic, Dušan Ilija *science educator*

Topsham
Beckett, Kerrie J. *ecologist, researcher*

Waterville
Fleming, James Rodger *science historian, educator*

MARYLAND

Aberdeen Proving Ground
Kuperman, Roman Gregory *toxicologist, ecologist*
Stuebing, Edward Willis *research scientist*

Adelphi
Zheleva, Tsvetanka Spassova *scientist*

Annapolis
Miranda, Leopoldo *zoologist, director*
Pelura, James III *veterinarian, political organization administrator*
Ziegler, James F. *science educator*

Baltimore
Allen, Ronald John *astrophysics educator, researcher*
Bandaru, Veera Venkata Ratnam *research scientist, biomedical engineer*
Bensmaia, Sliman J. *neuroscientist*
Brady, Joseph Vincent *behavioral biologist, educator*
Broda-Hydorn, Susan *entomologist*
Broholm, Collin Leslie *science educator*
Brown, Richard A. *science educator*
Byun, Youngjoo *research scientist*
Chakravarti, Aravinda *geneticist*
Clemens, Mark George *physiologist*
Colwell, Rita Rossi *microbiologist, former federal agency administrator, medical educator*
Craig, Nancy L. *molecular biologist, educator, geneticist*
Davis, Guy Donald *research scientist*
Desiderio, Stephen *molecular biology educator*
Diba, Fantahun *biology professor*
Dickersin, Kay *researcher, educator*
Dickfeld, Timm-Michael *electrophysiologist, cardiologist, educator*
Eddington, Natalie Dawn *science educator, dean*
Fischer Walker, Christa Lynn *research scientist*
Galen, James Eugene *science educator*
Gall, Joseph Grafton *biologist, researcher, educator*
Gallo, Robert Charles *research scientist*
Goldberg, Alan Marvin *toxicologist, educator*
Greider, Carol Widney *molecular biologist*
Griffiths, Roland Redmond *biology educator*
Huganir, Richard Lewis *neuroscientist, educator, researcher*
Keutcha, Julienne Petnga *science educator*
Landau, Barbara *neuroscientist*
Lee, Yuan Chuan *biology professor*
Li, Albert P. *cell biologist, toxicologist*
Littlefield, John Walley *geneticist, cell biologist, pediatrician*
Moon, Cheil *neuroscientist, researcher*
Mountcastle, Vernon Benjamin *retired neuroscientist*
Permutt, Solbert *physiologist, physician*
Pittenger, David M. *aquarium administrator*
Radhakrishnan, Malathi *biologist, educator*
Ramirez Quintana, Jose Luis *research scientist*
Russell, James William *neuroscientist*
Sack, George Henry, Jr. *molecular geneticist, internist*
Sidransky, David *molecular biologist*
Singh, Om V. *biotechnologist, researcher*
Snyder, Solomon Halbert *neuroscientist, educator*
Stewart, Doris Mae *biology professor*
Tamminga, Carol Ann *neuroscientist*
Trpis, Milan *vector biologist, educator*
Trujillo, J. Roberto *virologist*
Williams, Jerry Randall *radiation biologist*
Wolman, M. Gordon *geography educator*
Wong, Guang William *physiologist, educator*
Yau, King-Wai *neuroscientist, educator*

Beltsville
Ahn, Heekwon *research biologist*
Luo, Yaguang *food scientist, researcher*
Murrell, Kenneth Darwin *microbiologist, parasitologist*
Schneider, Edwin Kahn *research scientist*

Bethesda
Adhya, Sankar L. *geneticist*
Agardy, M. Tundi *marine biologist, director*
Bennink, Jack Richard *microbiologist, researcher*
Brady, John Norris *virologist, molecular biologist*
Brady, Roscoe Owen *neurogeneticist, educator*
Brooks, Philip J. *neurobiologist*
Brown, Paul Wheeler *neuroscientist*
Citron, Bruce Alexander *geneticist, researcher*
Clore, G. Marius *biologist*

Di Paolo, Joseph Amedeo *geneticist*
Fields, Richard Douglas *neuroscientist*
Frank, Martin *physiologist, educator, medical association administrator*
Greenberg, Judith Horovitz *geneticist*
Hager, Gordon Lee *molecular biologist, researcher*
Hinnebusch, Alan Gerard *molecular geneticist*
Huntress, Wesley Theodore, Jr. *research scientist*
Jackson, Michael John *retired physiologist, association executive*
Jaquish, Cashell Elizabeth *geneticist, director*
Jen, Jin *molecular biologist, researcher*
Kutty, Raghavakurup Krishnan *research scientist*
Lebedev, Mikhail A. *neuroscientist*
Leitner, Wolfgang W. *research scientist*
Lichten, Michael J. *microbiologist, researcher*
Max, Edward Ellis *molecular biologist*
Meltzer, Paul S. *geneticist, researcher*
Mock, Beverly A. *geneticist, researcher*
Mufson, Robert Allan *cell biologist*
Nabel, Gary Jan *virologist*
Pang, Lap-Yin *molecular biologist*
Plant, Ewan P. *research scientist*
Purcell, Robert Harry *virologist, researcher*
Salmoiraghi, Gian Carlo *physiologist, educator*
Saxinger, William Carl *microbiologist*
Schlom, Jeffrey Bert *research scientist*
Sokoloff, Louis *retired physiologist, neuroscientist*
Sundaresan, Tharun *science educator*
Tatusova, Tatiana A. *research scientist*
Van Dyke, Terry Ann *geneticist, researcher*
Vydelingum, Nadarajen Ameerdanaden *cell biologist, educator, researcher, health administrator*
Winters, Thomas Andrew *microbiologist*
Yamada, Kenneth Manao *cell biologist*
Yewdell, Jonathan Wilson *cell biologist*
Zaghloul, Norann Amir *geneticist, research scientist*
Zierdt, Charles Henry *retired microbiologist*

Chevy Chase
Choppin, Purnell Whittington *science administrator*
Kandel, Eric Richard *neuroscience educator*

College Park
Ankem, Sreeramamurthy *science educator*
Bennett, Reginald Wendell *microbiologist*
Diener, Theodor Otto *plant pathologist, researcher*
Dylla, H. Frederick *science administrator, physicist*
Elliot, Elisa Louise *microbiologist*
Fanning, Delvin Seymour *soil science educator*
O'Brochta, David A. *molecular biologist, researcher*

Edgewater
Boehme, Jennifer *ecologist, oceanographer*

Ellicott City
Marra Oram, Diana Marie *microbiologist, educator*

Frederick
Gudla, Prabhakar Reddy *research scientist*
Hughes, Stephen H. *virologist, researcher*
Menotti-Raymond, Marilyn *geneticist, molecular biologist*
Reynolds, Craig W. *research scientist*
Stern, Stephan Timothy *toxicologist, researcher*
Tobin, Gregory John *biologist*
Young, Howard Alan *molecular biologist*

Gaithersburg
Chow, Laurence Chung-Lung *research scientist*
Costin, Gertrude-Emilia *toxicologist, director*
Gerard, Gary Floyd *molecular biologist*
Haque, Kashif Aziz *research scientist*

Garrett Park
Baldwin, Calvin Benham, Jr. *retired science administrator*

Germantown
Iqbal, Zafar *neuroscientist, biochemist, educator*

Jefferson
Beall, James Robert *toxicologist, consultant*

La Plata
Lauber, Kathleen P. *microbiologist, educator*
Montgomery, William E. *biology professor, department chairman*

Landover
Frederick, Amy L. *science administrator*

Laurel
Boehmer, Jamie Layne *biologist, researcher*
Hoffman, David John *physiologist, ecotoxicologist*

Montgomery Village
Narum, David L. *parasitologist*

Poolesville
Noble, Pamela Lee *primatologist*

Potomac
Khachaturian, Zaven Setrak *neuroscientist*
Myers, Lawrence Stanley, Jr. *retired radiation biologist*

Princess Anne
Chigbu, Paulinus *fisheries biologist, educator, research scientist*
Khoza, Lombuso *science educator*

Riverdale
Passoa, Steven C. *entomologist*

Rockville
Elespuru, Rosalie K. *molecular biologist and researcher*
Gluckstein, Fritz Paul *veterinarian, biomedical information specialist*
Kafka, Marian Stern *neuroscientist*
Kim, Bong-Jo *molecular biologist, researcher*
Mummaneni, Padmaja *research scientist, educator*
Nithyanandan, Pallavi *research scientist*
Ryan, Kevin William *virologist, clinical research administrator*
Slotta, Tracey *biology professor*
Smith, Hamilton Othanel *molecular biologist, educator*
Um, Ki Sung *research scientist*
Venter, J. Craig (John Craig Venter, Craig Venter) *science foundation director, geneticist*

Silver Spring
Brandt, Carl David *research virologist*
Doolan, Denise Louise *molecular biologist*
Erk, Frank Chris *biologist, educator*
Guzman, Martha Patricia *science educator*
Kant, Gloria Jean *retired neuroscientist*
Simmons, Monika *microbiologist, researcher*

Solomons
Miller, Thomas James *biology professor*
Roesijadi, Guritno *toxicology educator*

Towson
Kolagani, Rajeswari Moolathody *science educator*
Shah, Shirish Kalyanbhai *computer science, chemistry and environmental science educator*

Wye Mills
Knapp, Wesley Martin *ecologist*

MASSACHUSETTS

Amherst
Aelion, C. Marjorie *science educator*
Asker, Dalal *microbiologist, educator*
Baek, Sungmin *molecular biologist, researcher*
Jung-Lim, Lee *food scientist*
Margulis, Lynn (Lynn Alexander) *evolutionist, educator*
Michael, Dietrich *biology professor*

Auburn
Hurley, Joseph P. *science educator*

Belmont
Benes, Francine M. *neuroscientist, psychiatrist*

Boston
Altshuler, David Matthew *geneticist, endocrinologist*
Ashok, Tara Devi S. *biology professor, researcher*
Beckwith, Jonathan Roger *geneticist*
Beggs, Alan Hendrie *geneticist, researcher*
Broitman, Selwyn Arthur *microbiologist, educator, assistant dean*
Casadei, Gabriele *veterinarian, educator*
Chen, Ching-chih *information science educator, consultant*
Chen, Zheng-Yi *biologist*
Church, George McDonald *geneticist, educator, researcher*
Demidov, Vadim V. *biotechnologist, inventor, writer*
El-Baz, Farouk *science administrator, educator*
Essex, Myron Elmer *microbiology and virology educator*
Fan, Baojian *research scientist*
Foote, Warren Edgar *neuroscientist, psychologist, educator*
Golub, Todd R. *research scientist*
Goodyear, Laurie J. *physiologist, educator*
Hochedlinger, Konrad *biology professor, biomedical researcher*
Hubel, David Hunter *physiologist, science educator*
Kahn, C. Ronald *research laboratory administrator*
Kanki, Phyllis Jean *pathobiology educator*
Kariv, Ilona *molecular biologist, director*
Kucherlapati, Raju *geneticist, educator*
Levy, Stuart B. *molecular biologist, educator, science administrator, researcher*
Malicki, Jarema *research scientist*
Mela, Theofanie *physiologist*
Milunsky, Aubrey *geneticist, pediatrician, educator*
Mitchison, Timothy John *cell biologist, pharmacology educator*
O'Brien, Thomas Francis *microbiologist, director*
Onderdonk, Andrew Bruce *microbiologist*
Rouzine, Igor M. *microbiologist, educator*
Ruvkun, Gary B. *molecular geneticist*
Schwartz, Joel David *science educator*
Seidman, Jonathan G. *geneticist, educator*
Sharma, Ramaswamy *microbiologist, researcher*
Stanish, Heidi *science educator*
Struhl, Kevin *molecular biologist, educator*
Sugumaran, Manickam *biology professor*
Szostak, Jack William *molecular biologist, educator*
Talarek, Nicolas *geneticist, researcher*
Tullis, Gregory Earl *research scientist*
Vaidya, Vishal S. *biologist, educator*
Williams, Winfred W. *molecular biologist*
Wilson, Rachel I. *neurobiologist, educator*
Yang, Youxin *research scientist*

Boylston
Dixon, Anthony George *science educator*

Bridgewater
Reynolds, Ronald Foster *science educator*

Cambridge
Angert, Esther Rita *biologist, researcher*
Bell, Stephen P. *biology professor, researcher*
Berg, Howard C. *biology professor*
Bizzi, Emilio *neurophysiologist, educator*
Bomblies, Kirsten *molecular biologist, educator*
Collier, Earl Miller, Jr. *biotechnology company executive*
Dalgarno, Alexander *astronomy educator*
de Fougerolles, Antonin Robert *research scientist*
Dulac, Catherine *biology professor, researcher*
Dziewonski, Adam Marian *geologist, educator, science administrator, academic administrator*
Eggan, Kevin C. *molecular and cellular biology professor, researcher*
Erikson, Raymond Leo *biology professor*
Fee, Michale Sean *science educator*
Fink, Yoel *science educator, researcher*
Fischl, Bruce *neuroscientist, educator*
Fox, Maurice Sanford *retired molecular biologist, educator*
Gilbert, Walter *molecular biologist, educator*
Goldberg, Ray Allan *agriculturist, educator*
Grossman, Alan D. *biology educator*
Grove, Timothy Lynn *geology educator*
Hanken, James *biologist, educator, museum director*
Hastings, John Woodland *biologist, educator*
Hewitt, Jacqueline N. *astronomy educator*
Horvitz, Howard Robert *biology professor, researcher*
Hubbard, Ruth *retired biology professor*
Hynes, Richard Olding *biology researcher, educator*
Jaenisch, Rudolf *biologist, educator*
Jarosiewicz, Beata *neuroscientist*
Kanwisher, Nancy G. *neuroscientist*
Knoll, Andrew Herbert *biology professor*
Kossak, Mitchell Scott *educator, director*
Lan, Fei *biologist, researcher*
Lander, Eric Steven *geneticist, molecular biologist, mathematician*
Langmuir, Charles Herbert *geology educator*
Lauder, George V. *marine biologist*
Levi, Herbert Walter *biologist, educator*
Lin, Lih-Ling *biologist, researcher*
Lindquist, Susan Lee *biology and microbiology professor*
Losick, Richard M. *biology professor*
MacGillivray, Catherine Mary *histologist*
Marcus, Richard Sargon *research scientist*
Melton, Douglas A. *molecular and cell biology educator*
Narayan, Ramesh *astronomy educator*
Page, David C. *biologist, educator*
Pardue, Mary-Lou *biology professor*
Petersen, Ulrich *geology educator*
Prinn, Ronald G. *atmospheric science educator*
Ramme, Tina M. *biology professor, director*
Sanes, Joshua Richard *neurobiologist, researcher, educator*
Sharp, Phillip Allen *biologist, educator*
Sinha, Pawan *research scientist, educator, entrepreneur*
Tonegawa, Susumu *biology professor*
Walker, Graham Charles *biology professor*
Widnall, Sheila Evans *aeronautical educator, former secretary of air force, university official*
Wilson, Edward Osborne *biologist, educator, writer*
Wozney, John M. *research scientist*
Wurtman, Richard Jay *neuroscientist, educator, inventor*
Yannas, Ioannis Vassilios *polymer science educator*

Charlestown
Raftery, Laurel A. *research biologist, educator*
Tanzi, Rudolph Emile (Rudy Tanzi) *neuroscientist, researcher, educator*

Fall River
Corven, James M. *biology professor*

Falmouth
Saunders, John Warren, Jr. *biology professor, consultant*

Framingham
Scaria, Abraham *molecular biologist, director*

Holyoke
Clark, Lynn Laux *science educator*

Ipswich
Roberts, Richard John *molecular biologist, consultant, research director*

Jamaica Plain
Babcock, Gregory John *biotechnologist, director*

Lexington
Drouilhet, Paul Raymond, Jr. *retired science administrator, electrical engineer*
Fillios, Louis Charles *retired science educator*
Lehar, Joseph *science educator, director*

Lowell
Femia, John R. *science educator*
Liakos, Effegenia *physiologist, educator*

Medford
Oommen, Thomas *research scientist*
Sassaroli, Angelo *science educator, researcher*

Natick
Arcidiacono, Steven *microbiologist*

Needham
Lain, David Cornelius *health scientist, researcher*

New Bedford
Smietana, Walter *educational research director*

North Grafton
Costa, Lais Rosa Rodrigues *veterinarian, educator, medical researcher*
Herrmann, John *microbiologist*
Schwartz, Anthony *veterinary surgeon, educator, photographer*
Taeymans, Olivier N. *veterinarian, educator*

Peabody
Butz, Stefan Peter *science association director*

Quincy
Twining, Jonathan Emerson *biology professor*

Roxbury
Peters, Alan *anatomy educator*

Scituate
Wiley, David Nathan *biologist, researcher*

South Hadley
Townsend, Jane Kaltenbach *biologist, educator*

Waltham
Geng, Bolin *research scientist*
Nichols, Guy Warren *retired institute and utilities executive*
Partenskii, Michael B. *science educator, researcher*
Sekuler, Robert William *science educator*

Watertown
Emerson, Charles P., Jr. *research scientist*
Erhardt, Peter *research scientist*

Wellesley
Gerety, Robert John *microbiologist, researcher, pediatrician, pharmaceutical executive, drug developer*
Young, Delano Victor *cell biologist, pharmaceutical scientist, biochemist, educator*

Woods Hole
Blake, James Alan *marine biologist, educator*
Inoué, Shinya *microscopy and cell biology scientist, educator*
Melillo, Jerry M. *ecologist*
Woodwell, George Masters *ecologist, conservationist*

Worcester
Ambros, Victor R. *geneticist, educator*
Huang, Xinming *science educator*
Luna, Elizabeth (Jean) *cell biologist, educator, researcher*
Schofield, Edmund Acton, Jr. *botanist, academic administrator, conservationist, writer*
van den Berg, Bert *biology professor, researcher*

Yarmouth Port
LeBaron, Francis Newton *retired biochemistry educator*

MICHIGAN

Adrian
Husband, Robert Wayne *retired, biology educator*

Albion
Lyons-Sobaski, Sheila A. *biology professor*

Allendale
Thogerson, Mark T. *biology professor, consultant*

Alma
Oemke, Mark Paul *biology professor, researcher*

Ann Arbor
Akil, Huda *neuroscientist, educator, researcher*
Atreya, Sushil Kumar *planetary-space science educator, astrophysicist*
Cadigan, Kenneth Michael *science educator*
Clark, Noreen Morrison *behavioral science educator, researcher*
Cochran, Kenneth William *toxicologist*
Dawson, William Ryan *zoology educator*
Drach, John Charles *research scientist, educator*
Farrand, William Richard *retired geology educator*
Faulkner, John Arthur *physiologist, educator*
Fink, William Lee *ichthyologist, systematist*
Ginsburg, David *genetics educator, researcher*
Kaufman, Peter Bishop *biological sciences educator*
Kirakosyan, Ara *research scientist*
Low, Malcolm James *research scientist*
Maren, Stephen *neuroscientist, psychologist, educator*
Moore, Thomas Edwin *biologist, educator, museum director*
Petty, Elizabeth Marie *geneticist*
Richardson, Rudy James *toxicology and neurosciences educator*
Sahiner, Berkman *science administrator, educator*
Williams, John Andrew *physiology researcher, educator*
Withey, Jeffrey Howard *molecular biologist, researcher*
Zhang, Youxue *geology educator*
Zhu, Ji *science educator*

Battle Creek
Wright, Judy A. *science educator*

Dearborn
Narula, Chaitanya Kumar *research scientist*
Wang, Shengquan *science educator*

Detroit
Abu-Soud, Husam M. *science educator*
Adeyinka, Adewale *geneticist, director*
Banerjee, Amit *cell and molecular biologist*
Beierwaltes, William Howard *physiologist, educator*
Edwards, Brian Francis Peregrine *science educator*
Groves, Odessa Marie *science educator*
Heppner, Gloria Hill *research administrator, educator*
Hoffmann, Peter M. *science educator, director*
Huang, Yinlun *science educator*
Lerner, Stephen Alexander *microbiologist, physician, educator*
Pan, Zhuo-Hua *science educator*
Phillis, John Whitfield *physiologist, educator*
Rishi, Arun K. *molecular biologist, educator*
Ruden, Douglas Mark *science educator*
States, J. Christopher *molecular biology educator, researcher*
Wolf, Barry *geneticist, pediatric educator*
Zhuo, Jia Long *physiologist*

Dowagiac
Dalton, Clyde *biology professor*

East Lansing
Bromley, Stephen C. *zoology educator*
Brubaker, Robert Robinson *microbiology educator*

Bukovac, Martin John *horticulturist, educator*
Cibelli, Jose B. *research scientist, educator*
Cross, Aureal Theophilus *geology and botany educator*
Dennis, Frank George, Jr. *retired horticulture educator*
Hackel, Emanuel *science educator*
Haider, Syed Waqar *science educator*
Harrison, Tara Myers *veterinarian, educator, curator*
Kariagina, Anastasia *physiologist, educator*
McMeekin, Dorothy *botanist, plant pathologist, educator*
Petrides, George Athan *ecologist, educator*
Sparks, Harvey Vise, Jr. *physiologist*
Tiedje, James Michael *microbiologist, ecologist, educator*

Edwardsburg
Floyd, Alton David *cell biologist, consultant*

Grand Rapids
Carlotti, Ronald John *food scientist*

Grosse Pointe
Scarabelli, Tiziano Maria *molecular biologist, cardiologist, educator*

Houghton
Burton, Andrew J. *ecologist, educator*
Kerfoot, W. Charles, Jr. *biology professor*
Pickens, James B. *science educator*

Kalamazoo
Hathaway, Richard B. *science educator, researcher*
Jayasingh, Preetha *food scientist*
Kazanowski, Pawel *research and development scientist*
Marshall, Vincent de Paul *industrial microbiologist, researcher*
Port, Tamara Lynne *biology professor, writer*
Zinn, Donald Edward *biologist, researcher*

Livonia
Istephan, Asaad A. *science educator*
Steffen, Carolyn McKinnis *biology professor*
Taylor, Bonnita Kay *biology professor*

Marquette
Lehmberg, Z. Z. *educator*

Midland
Bus, James Stanley *toxicologist*
Diegel, Betsy L. *research scientist, department chairman*

Petoskey
Nicholson, William Noel *clinical neuropsychologist*

Rochester Hills
Unakar, Nalin Jayantilal *biological sciences educator*

Saline
Cruden, Robert William *botany educator*
Jeffries, Charles Dean *microbiology educator, research scientist, dean*

Sanford
Wilmot, Thomas Ray *medical entomologist, educator*

Sault Sainte Marie
Stai, Deborah *biology professor, director*

University Center
Gorte, Mary Curl *science educator*

Warren
Zavattieri, Pablo Daniel *research scientist, educator*

West Bloomfield
Barr, Martin *science educator, academic administrator*

Wilson
Harris, Mary Lynn *science educator, consultant*

Ypsilanti
Evett, Matthew *science educator*

MINNESOTA

Bloomington
Ahmad, Kashif A. *science educator, researcher*
Reutter, Michael A. *biology professor*

Brainerd
Mickelson, Paul A. *biology professor, consultant*

Crookston
Elf, Pamela Kay *biology professor*

Duluth
Johnson, Arthur Gilbert *microbiology educator*
Norberg-King, Teresa Joy *research aquatic biologist*

Mapleton
John, Hugo Herman *natural resources educator*

Minneapolis
Adams, John Stephen *geography educator*
Brooker, Robert J. *biology professor*
Danielson, James Walter *retired research microbiologist*
Dworkin, Martin *retired microbiologist*
Gorham, Eville *retired ecologist*
Gudmundson, Barbara Rohrke *ecologist*
Harris, Reuben Stewart *biology professor, researcher*
Johnson, Kenneth Harvey *veterinary pathologist*
Mangia, Silvia *science educator*
Mosley, Gregg Allen *microbiologist*
Porter, Philip Wayland *geography educator*
Ruggles, Steven *science educator*
Speedie, Marilyn Kay *microbiologist, dean, educator*
Zelazo, Philip David *science educator*

Minnetonka
Sperber, William Henry *microbiologist, writer*

Moorhead
Gee, Robert LeRoy *agriculturist, dairy farmer*

Morris
Johnson, Jane M.F. *soil scientist*
Ordway, Ellen *biologist, educator, entomologist, researcher*

Mounds View
Wang, Li *business director*

Northfield
Hawkins, Peggy Anne *veterinarian*

Rochester
Lou, Zhenkun *cell biologist, researcher*
Maher, L. James III *molecular biologist*
Ordog, Tamas *research scientist, educator*
Xu, Shang-Zhi *toxicologist, director*

Roseville
Marten, Gordon Cornelius *agronomist, educator, federal agency administrator*

Saint Cloud
Jha, Pranava K. *science educator*
Roiger, Deborah *physiologist, educator*

Saint Joseph
Kirick, Daniel John *agronomist*

Saint Paul
Barnwell, Franklin Hershel *zoology educator*
Cheng, H. H. *soil scientist, agronomic and environmental science educator emeritus*
Davis, Margaret Bryan *paleoecology researcher, educator*
Ek, Alan Ryan *forester, educator*
Kommedahl, Thor *plant pathology educator*
Leonard, Kurt John *retired plant pathologist, director*
McKinnell, Robert Gilmore *retired zoologist, biology professor, geneticist*
McNiel, Elizabeth Ann *veterinarian, educator*
Norton, Cynthia G. *biology professor*
Phillips, Ronald Lewis *plant geneticist, educator*
Roy, Robert Russell *toxicologist*
Sadowsky, Michael J. *microbiologist, educator*
Snustad, Donald Peter *geneticist, educator*
Thayanithy, Venugopal *biologist, geneticist, researcher*

White Bear Lake
Thinesen, Pamela Kay *biology faculty*

MISSISSIPPI

Diamondhead
Park, Richard A. *ecologist*

Fulton
Ewing, John Arthur *biology professor*
Milner, Michelle Leaneatrice *biology professor, department chairman*

Hattiesburg
Causey, Jana *science educator*

Itta Bena
Ikenga, Julius O. *biology professor, consultant*

Jackson
Ahmad, Hafiz Anwar *biology professor*
Ayensu, Wellington Kofi *biology professor*
Bell, Taunjah Patrease *research scientist*
Kafoury, Ramzi M. *biology and environmental health educator, researcher*
Lewis, Robert Edwin, Jr. *pathology and immunology educator, researcher*
Manning, R. Davis *physiologist, educator*
McGuire, Sarah Lea *biology professor*
Rajamohan, Kalluru R. *science educator, researcher*
Venegas-Pont, Marcia *physiologist, educator*
Yedjou, Clement Guy *science educator, researcher*

Mississippi State
Jenkins, Johnie Norton *research geneticist, research administrator*
MacGown, Joe A. *entomologist, researcher*
Reddy, Kambham Raja *botanist, educator*

Natchez
James, Lula Bonds *science educator, small business owner, apparel designer*

Oxford
Gul, Waseem *research scientist*
Keiser, Edmund Davis, Jr. *biologist, educator*

Pearl
Williams, Daniece H. *biology professor*

Perkinston
Tringle, Sarah Taylor *biology professor, department chairman*

Starkville
Topsakal, Erdem *science educator*

Stoneville
Stanturf, John Alvin, IV, *soil scientist, researcher*

Sturgis
Thomas, Charles Hill *geneticist, educator*

University
Al-Zoubi, Asem S. *science educator*
Duke, Stephen Oscar *physiologist, research scientist, educator*

Vicksburg
Gong, Ping *ecologist, researcher*

MISSOURI

Chesterfield
Williams, Luther Steward *research scientist*

Columbia
Blevins, Dale Glenn *agronomy educator*
Heflin, Colleen Marie *science educator*
Ingersoll, Christopher Glenn *toxicologist*
Manandhar, Gaurishankar *cell biologist, educator*
Men, Hongsheng *biologist, researcher*
Mitchell, Roger Lowry *retired agronomy educator*
Morehouse, Lawrence Glen *veterinarian, educator, academic administrator*
Reddy, Chada S. *toxicologist, researcher*
Roberts, R. Michael *animal scientist, biochemist, educator*
Sengupta, Shramik *science educator*
Yanders, Armon Frederick *biological sciences educator, science administrator*

Eureka
Lindsey, Susan Lyndaker *zoologist*

Fayette
Elliott, Dana Ray *biology professor, consultant*

Jefferson City
Eivazi, Frieda *biology professor*

Kansas City
Coveney, Raymond Martin, Jr. *geology educator*
Fincham, Jack Edwin *science educator*
Krumlauf, Robert Eugene *neuroscientist, educator*
Lednicky, John A. *virologist, microbiologist*
Neaves, William Barlow *cell biologist, educator*
Spigarelli, James L. *science administrator*

Kirksville
Peterson, Donald Fred *physiologist, educator*

Parkville
Bohn, Beverly *computer science professor*

Rolla
Samaranayake, V. A. *science educator, director*

Saint Louis
Bourne, Carol Elizabeth Mulligan *biology professor, phycologist*
Brudvig, Lars Andrew *ecologist*
Bruzzini, Kristen Blake *biology professor, director*
Elgin, Sarah Carlisle Roberts *biology professor, researcher*
Fraley, Robert T. *biotechnologist*
Geslani, Gemma P. *science educator, health researcher*
Green, Maurice *molecular biologist, educator, virologist*
Herzog, Erik D. *biology professor*
Martin de Camilo, Jody Elizabeth *biology professor*
Mason, Philip John *geneticist*
Miller, James Gegan *research scientist*
Mumm, Steven Robert *geneticist, educator*
Narayanan, Narayanan Narayanan *biologist, researcher*
Piwnica-Worms, Helen M. *cell biologist, educator*
Price, Joseph Levering *neuroscientist, educator*
Raven, Peter Hamilton *botanist, director*
Schaal, Barbara Anna *evolutionary biologist, educator*
Shulkina, Tatyana *botanist, researcher*
Thach, Robert Edwards *biology educator, former dean*
Wilson, Richard K. *microbiologist, researcher*

Springfield
Mathis, Alicia *biologist, department chairman*
Tenneson, Michael Gunnar *biology professor*

Villa Ridge
Laskowski, Leonard Francis, Jr. *microbiologist*

Wright City
Mabrey, Rick *science educator*

MONTANA

Bozeman
Delaney, Kevin J. *research scientist*
Patten, Duncan Theunissen *ecologist educator*
Schrag, Anne Michelle *ecologist*

Browning
McKay, Michael I. *biologist, researcher*

Great Falls
Olszewski, Chris Michael *science educator, director*

Helena
Horton, Travis B. *biologist*
Johnson, John Philip *geneticist, researcher*

Missoula
Dial, Kenneth Paul *biology professor*

NEBRASKA

Adams
Badeer, Henry Sarkis *physiology educator*

Chadron
Butterfield, Charles H. *ecologist, educator*

Crete
Muckel, Robert Dale *retired biology professor*

Hastings
Morris, Amy *biology professor*
Thorndike, Ann M. *microbiologist, educator*

Kearney
Carlson, Kimberly Ann *biology professor*
Fryda, Nicolas J. *biologist*
Hertner, John F. *biology professor, horse breeder*
Hoback, William Wyatt *biology professor*
Rothenberger, Steven John *biology professor*

Lincoln
Birla, Sohan *food scientist*
Burba, George G. *research scientist*
Dappen, Glen Eugene *retired biology professor*
Foster, John Edward *entomologist, educator*
Hanway, Donald Grant, Sr. *retired agronomist, educator*
Hoffmann, Richard John *biology professor, academic administrator*
Kren, Josef *physiology professor*
Lewis, Nancy M. *science educator*
Massengale, Martin Andrew *agronomist, educator, university president*
McVey, David Scott *veterinarian, director*
Narain, Ralph B. *biologist*
Nickerson, Kenneth Warwick *biology professor*
Osterman, John Carl *biology professor*
Pannier, Angela Kaye *science educator*
Smith, Rosemary J. *biology educator, researcher*
Stoddard, Robert H. *geography educator*
Taylor, Stephen Lloyd *toxicologist, food scientist, educator*
Vidaver, Anne Marie *plant pathology educator*
Zhang, Luwen *virologist*

Omaha
Brenneman, Rick Alan *conservation geneticist*
Gambal, David *retired biochemistry educator*
Wang, Jue *veterinarian, educator*

Papillion
Snelling, James Anthony *biology professor, technologist*

Scottsbluff
Whitaker, William L. *physiologist, educator*

Wayne
DeBoer, Buffany Dawn *biology professor*

NEVADA

Las Vegas
Alexander, John Bradfield *scientist, retired army officer*
Aulner, Dwane *biology professor*
Capanna, Albert Howard *neuroscientist, neurosurgeon, lawyer, banker*
Olsen, Dennis E. *veterinarian, director*
Ward, David Christian *science association director*

Minden
Downer, Craig *ecologist*

Reno
Gifford, Gerald Frederic *retired science educator*
Harvey, Robert Dale *physiologist and biophysicist, educator*
Yan, Wei *science association director*

Ruby Valley
Hoover, William Graham *science educator*

NEW HAMPSHIRE

Concord
Haijin, Shi *research scientist*
Palm, Jessana *biology professor*

Durham
Pistole, Thomas Gordon *microbiology professor, researcher, department chairman*
Tisa, Louis S. *microbiologist, educator*

Grantham
Callahan, Barbara Grant *toxicologist, risk assessor*

Hanover
Hoyt, Kendall *science educator*
Peart, David Ross *biology professor*
Spiegel, Evelyn Sclufer *biology professor*

Lebanon
Munck, Allan Ulf *physiologist, educator*
Ou, Lo-Chang *physiology educator*

Nashua
Rekart, Jerome Leo *science educator, researcher*

New Durham
Quimby, Fred William *retired pathology educator, veterinarian*

New London
Ourusoff, Nicholas *science educator*

NEW JERSEY

Allentown
Spreat, Susan Rogers *veterinarian*

Camden
Christman, Michael F. *geneticist, biomedical researcher*

Clifton
Yau, Edward Tintai *toxicologist, pharmacologist*

Clinton
Hulse, Robert Douglas *biotechnologist*

Cranford
Jenssen, Warren Donald *microbiologist, consultant*

Edison
Sapra, Puja *research scientist*

Franklin Lakes
Yi, Jizu *research scientist, educator*

Highlands
Psuty, Norbert Phillip *marine sciences educator*

Hoboken
Bazil, Leon A. *science educator*
Choi, Chang-Hwan *science educator*

Jersey City
Klyatis, Lev Matusovich *test and reliability scientist*

Lawrenceville
Gong, Linguo *science educator*

Madison
Demain, Arnold Lester *microbiologist, educator*

Millburn
Feng, Bo *biology professor*

Montclair
Bologna, Paul Andrew Xavier *biology professor, director*
Chinard, Francis Pierre *physiologist, consultant physician, educator*
Du, Chunguang Charles *biologist, educator*

Mountain Lakes
Wallace, MaryJean Elizabeth *science educator*

New Brunswick
Bennett, Joan Wennstrom *biology educator*
Ehrenfeld, David William *biology professor, writer*
Fisher, Hans *nutritional biochemistry educator*
Lachance, Paul Albert *food science educator, clergyman*
Maramorosch, Karl *virologist, educator*
Robson, Mark Gregory *agriculturist, educator*
Saracevic, Tefko *information science educator*
Tedrow, John Charles Fremont *soils educator*
Trivers, Robert L. *bioscience and anthropology educator, evolutionary biologist, sociobiologist*

Newark
Cheng, Mei-Fang *psychobiology educator, neuroscientist*
Ledeen, Robert Wagner *neuroscientist, educator*
Stolberg, Victor *educator*

Old Tappan
Lovitch, Joan *science educator, coach*

Paramus
Highley, Robert S. *biology professor*

Piscataway
Breslauer, Kenneth J. *science educator, researcher*
Denhardt, David Tilton *molecular and cell biology educator*
Ebright, Richard High *molecular biologist*
Essien, Francine B. *biologist, educator*
McKim, Kim S. *biology professor*
Pylyshyn, Zenon W. *science educator*
Shatkin, Aaron Jeffrey *biochemistry educator*
Sit, Ping-Fai *research scientist*
Tischfield, Jay Arnold *genetics educator*
Wadsworth, William Graham *biology professor, researcher*
Witz, Gisela *research scientist, educator*

Plainfield
Frost, David *retired biology professor, medical editor, consultant*

Pomona
Lewis, Margaret E. *biology professor*
Wood, Roger Conant *biology professor, researcher*

Port Norris
Canzonier, Walter Jude *shellfish aquaculturist*

Princeton
Altmann, Stuart Allen *biologist, educator*
Amosova, Olga *molecular biologist, consultant*
Bassler, Bonnie L. *molecular biologist*
Bhadury, Punyasloke *molecular ecologist*
Drakeman, Lisa N. *biotechnologist*
Enquist, Lynn William *molecular biologist, educator*
Gould, James L. *biology professor*
Grant, Barbara Rosemary *research scientist*
Grant, Peter Raymond *biologist, researcher, educator*
Grigger, Jane Elizabeth *earth science educator, photographer*
Mahmoud, Adel A. *physician, molecular biologist, educator*
Mauzerall, Denise L. *science educator*
Shenk, Thomas Eugene *molecular biology educator, academic administrator*
Wieschaus, Eric F. *molecular biologist, educator*
Witkin, Evelyn Maisel *retired geneticist*
Wood, Eric Franklin *earth and environmental sciences educator*
Zakian, Virginia Araxie *molecular biology professor*

Randolph
Timbilla, James Abangah *entomologist, educator*

Ridgewood
Kuiken, Diane (Dee) Marie *science educator*

River Vale
Verebey, Karl Geza *toxicologist, pharmacologist, educator*

Somerset
Tsou, Yu-Min *science administrator, chemistry researcher*

Tinton Falls
Hoelzler, Michael Gebhard *veterinarian, surgeon*

Titusville
Manji, Husseini K. *pharmaceutical company executive, neuropsychopharmacologist*

Trenton
Blando, James Douglas *research scientist*

Union
Shebitz, Daniela Joy *biology professor*

Wallington
Safira, Barabara *science educator*

Wayne
Himmelstein, Jeffrey Alan *biology professor, researcher*

West Long Branch
Zhang, Ying *science educator*

West Orange
Hwang, Karen *research scientist*
Wylie, Glenn Richard *research scientist, educator*

West Trenton
Kennen, Jonathan Gary *ecologist*

NEW MEXICO

Albuquerque
Byrd, Wyatt *microbiologist, researcher*
Deretic, Vojo Peter *cell biologist, educator*
Gibson, Ann L. *science educator, consultant*
Harris, Grant M. *biologist*
Hsi, David Ching Heng *plant pathologist, geneticist, educator*
Polley, Richard Donald *microbiologist, chemist*
Sanchez, Victoria Wagner *science educator*

Farmington
Heil, Kenneth Del *retired botanist, consultant, researcher*

Hondo
Pawley, Ray L. *retired zoological park administrator, curator, conservationist*

Las Cruces
Schemnitz, Sanford David *wildlife biology professor*
Seger, Mark *molecular biologist*
Tonn, Robert James *retired entomologist*
Whitford, Walter George *retired biology professor*
Zhang, Jinfa *geneticist, educator*

Los Alamos
Anastasio, Michael R. *science administrator*
Doggett, Norman A. *molecular biologist*
Vrugt, Jasper Alexander *research scientist*

Portales
Varela, Manuel Francisco *molecular biologist, microbiologist, biochemist*

Ruidoso
Burns, Carla D. *science educator*

Santa Fe
Guthrie, Catherine S. (Catherine S. Nicholson-Guthrie) *research scientist, consultant*
Smith, Philip Meek *science administrator, consultant*

Socorro
Axen, Gary James *geology educator*
Fu, Song *science educator, researcher*

Zuni
Tsabetsaye, Jessica L. *science educator*

NEW YORK

Albany
Cady, Nathaniel C. *biology professor, consultant*
Cohn, Douglas Lloyd *veterinarian*
Frank, Joachim *structural biologist, educator, biophysicist*
Mannella, Carmen A. *research scientist*
Mongin, Alexander Anatolievich *neuroscientist, educator*
O'Keefe, Patrick William *research scientist*
rsch, Helmut V. B. *biology professor*
Schneider, Allan Stanford *biophysics, neuroscience and pharmacology educator, biomedical research scientist*
Stevens, Roy W. *microbiologist, researcher, photographer*
Temple, Sally *neuroscientist, educator*

Alfred
Chambliss, Melvin C. *veterinarian, educator*

Apalachin
Williamson, Mark Adam *science educator*

Bay Shore
Benjaminson, Morris Aaron *microbiologist, director*

Binghamton
Klir, George Jiri *systems science educator*
Naslund, Howard Richard *geological science educator*
Sonnenfeld, Gerald *microbiology and immunology educator*

Brockport
Cook, Laurie Boivin *biology professor*
Tsubota, Stuart *biology professor*

Bronx
Chiang, I-Cheng Robert *science educator*
Fishman, Yonatan *neuroscientist*
Font, Cecilio Rafael *retired biology educator, physician*
Goodrich, James Tait *neuroscientist, neurosurgeon*
Schaller, George Beals *zoologist*
Singer, Robert H. *biology professor*
Van De Water, Thomas Roger *neuroscientist, educator*

Brooklyn
Altura, Bella T. *physiologist, educator*
Altura, Burton Myron *physiologist, educator*
Bressler, Robert Samuel *anatomy educator*
Jacobson, Leslie Sari *biologist, educator*
Kim, Jin Ryoun *science educator*
Li, Xiangdong *science educator*
Lipson, Steven Mark *virologist, microbiologist, environmental scientist, educator*
Medbury, Scot Daniel *botanical garden executive*
Okamoto, Yoshi *science educator*
Ranck, James Byrne, Jr. *neuroscience researcher, educator*
Roker, Christopher A. *microbiologist, photographer*
Schiffman, Gerald *microbiologist, educator*
Schwartz-Giblin, Susan Toby *neuroscientist, educator, dean emeritus*
Wadgaonkar, Raj *biologist, director*

Brookville
White, Stephanie *computer science educator*

Buffalo
Berezney, Ronald *molecular biologist*
Coffroth, Mary Alice *biologist, educator*
Duax, William Leo *biologist, researcher*
Elm, Lloyd Martin, Sr. *science educator*
Haase, Elaine M. *microbiologist, educator*
Pridgeon, Anthony R. *science educator*
Privitera, Gregory Joseph *neuroscientist, educator*
Skerrett, I. Martha *cell physiology professor*
You, Youngjae *science educator, researcher*
Zawicki, Joseph Leo *science educator*

Chazy
Young, Eric Otis *soil scientist, researcher, agronomist*

Cobleskill
Cronin, Thomas J. III *science educator*

Cold Spring Harbor
Hannon, Gregory J. *biology professor, researcher*
Sebat, Jonathan *geneticist, educator*
Stillman, Bruce *molecular biologist*

Cooperstown
Harman, Willard Nelson *malacologist, educator*

Deer Park
Saia, Robert Angelo *retired science educator*

Delhi
Tessier, Jack T. *biology professor*

East Aurora
Keem, Michael Dennis *veterinarian*

Fairport
Chari, Krishnan *research scientist*

Farmingdale
Chaskes, Stuart Jay *microbiologist, educator*
Ibrahim, Ahmed Zaki *science educator*

Flushing
Hoyt, Marilyn Christine *science center executive*
Muehlbauer, Esther Indelman *biology professor*
Reddy, Boojala Vijay *biology professor*
Rotenberg, Susan A. *research scientist, educator*
Seeling, Joni M. *biology professor*

Fredonia
Benton, Allen Haydon *biology professor*

Garden City
Podwall, Kathryn Stanley *biology professor*
Prabhakar, Kumkum *biology professor*

Geneseo
Beason, Robert Curtis *biologist, educator*

Geneva
Hrazdina, Geza *biochemistry educator*

Great Neck
Gabriel, Mordecai Lionel *biologist, educator*

Hempstead
Condon, Martha Ann *ecologist, biologist*

Homer
Gustafson, John Alfred *biology professor*

Hopewell Junction
Yu, Haiping *research scientist*

Houghton
Marcum, James Arthur *physiology and philosophy of science educator*

Ithaca
Adler, Kraig (Kerr) *biology professor*
Aneja, Rajindra *biotechnologist, consultant*
Ayoub, Ali *agricultural and food scientist*
Beer, Steven Vincent *plant pathologist, educator*
Confer, John L. *retired biology professor*
Crepet, William Louis *botanist, educator*
Davies, Peter John *plant physiology educator, researcher*
Dev, Chekitan *science educator*
Dhondt, André A. *zoologist, educator*
Earle, Elizabeth Deutsch *biology professor*
Eisner, Thomas *biologist, educator*
Emlen, Stephen Thompson *zoology educator*
Farnum, Cornelia Ellen *veterinarian, educator*
Fick, Gary Warren *agronomist, educator*
Grubb, David Thomas *science educator, researcher*
Hairston, Nelson George, Jr. *ecologist, educator*
Henry, Susan Armstrong *biology professor, dean*
Howarth, Robert W. *biology professor*
Jagendorf, André Tridon *physiologist*
Kennedy, Wilbert Keith, Sr. *agronomy educator, retired university official*
Kessler, Andre *ecologist, educator*
Kingsbury, John Merriam *botanist, educator*
Korf, Richard Paul *mycology educator*
Lengemann, Frederick William *retired physiology educator*
Liu, Rui Hai *science educator*
Poppensiek, George Charles *retired veterinary scientist, educator*
Rutzke, Corinne Johnson *research scientist*
Sherman, Paul W. *animal behavior educator*
Walcott, Charles *neurobiology and behavior educator*
Wasserman, Robert Harold *biology professor*
Wootton, John Francis *physiology educator*
Yu, Long-Xi *agriculturist, researcher*
Zall, Robert Rouben *food scientist, educator*

Jamaica
Cho, Seokhee *science administrator, director*

Middletown
Paradies, Michele A. *biology professor*

Millbrook
Likens, Gene Elden *biology and ecology educator*

Morrisville
Xu, Pei *agriculturist, educator*

Mount Kisco
Laster, Richard *biotechnologist, consultant*

Neponsit
Nicastri, Ann Gilbert *science educator*

New Paltz
Knapp, Ronald Gary *geography educator*

New York
Abramovich, Mark Nathan *entrepreneur, consultant*
Allis, C. David *science educator*
Anderson, Kathryn V. *developmental biologist, educator*
Bargmann, Cornelia I. *neuroscientist, science educator*
Ben Amor, Yanis *microbiologist*
Berlin, Heather Ayn *neuroscientist, philosopher, educator*
Blobel, Günter *cell biologist, educator*
Botkin, Daniel Benjamin *biologist, environmental scientist, writer*
Brenner, Menachem *science educator*
Bromage, Timothy G. *biological anthropologist, science educator*
Calame, Kathryn Lee *microbiologist, educator*
Chaganti, Raju S. *geneticist, educator, researcher*
Chalfie, Martin *biology professor*
Chan, Siu-Wai *materials science educator*
Chappell, Richard Lee *biology educator, neuroscientist*
Chen, Elizabeth Shan Shan *research scientist*
Chen, Jessie *research scientist*
Cohen, David Harris *neuroscientist, educator, academic administrator*
Cohen, Joel Ephraim *biologist, educator, demographer*
Dales, Samuel *microbiologist, virologist, educator*
Darnell, James Edwin, Jr. *molecular biologist, educator*
Davis, Jessica G. *geneticist*
de Lange, Titia *research scientist, educator*
Desnick, Robert John *human geneticist*
Di Fiore, Anthony *geneticist, educator*
Dobrof, Rose Wiesman *gerontology educator*
Fischbach, Gerald D. *science foundation director, neurobiology educator, former dean*
Godson, Godfrey Nigel *molecular geneticist, educator*
Goodman, Corey Scott *neuroscientist, biotechnologist, educator*
Greengard, Paul *neuroscientist, educator*
Grishina, Irina *science educator*
Gruzdeva, Natalia Mikhailovna *biologist, researcher*
Hall, Alan *molecular biology educator*
Hayes, Daniel Patrick *research scientist*
Hirschhorn, Rochelle *genetics educator*
Hoelz, André *biologist, researcher*
Hunter, Luke T. B. *biologist*
Joyner, Alexandra Leigh *cell biologist*
Kelley, Darcy B. *biology professor*
King, Thomas *physiologist, educator*
Li, Xiao Feng *research scientist*

Llinás, Rodolfo Riascos *neuroscientist, researcher*
Maas, Werner Karl *microbiology educator*
MacKinnon, Roderick *neuroscientist, educator*
Maddaloni, Mark A. *toxicologist*
Mishra, Bud *science educator*
Morse, Stephen Scott *virologist, epidemiologist, immunologist, educator*
Movshon, J. Anthony (Joseph Anthony Movshon) *neuroscience educator*
Mukherjee, Sushmita *science educator*
Nath, Niharika *biology professor*
Nathanielsz, Peter William *physiologist*
Old, Lloyd John *cancer biologist*
Palese, Peter M. *biology professor*
Pauluis, Olivier *science educator*
Pikitch, Ellen Karen *science educator*
Pollack, Robert Elliot *biologist, educator, writer*
Prittie, Jennifer E. *veterinarian*
Ptashne, Mark Steven *molecular biology professor*
Ravetch, Jeffrey Victor *molecular biologist, immunologist, educator*
Raynes, Jeffry *science association director*
Revenkova, Ekaterina *biologist, researcher*
Rozen, Jerome George, Jr. *entomologist, curator, professor, researcher*
Rudy, Bernardo *research scientist*
Ruggiero, David Armand *neuroscientist*
Salzer, James *biology professor*
Segal, Sheldon Jerome *biologist, educator, foundation administrator*
Shahn, Ezra *science educator*
Shapley, Robert Martin *neurophysiology and perception educator*
Silverstein, Samuel Charles *cellular biology and physiology professor, researcher*
Simon, Eric Jacob *neuroscientist, educator*
Simpson, Andrew J.G. *molecular biologist, researcher*
Stern, Yaakov *neuroscientist*
Stotzky, Guenther *microbiologist, educator*
Tall, Alan R. *molecular biologist, educator*
Tenke, Craig E. *neuroscientist, consultant*
Thaler, David Solomon *research scientist, educator*
Tierno, Philip Mario, Jr. *microbiologist, educator, researcher*
Toran-Allerand, C(laude) Dominique *neuroscientist, neurologist, educator*
Unson, Cecilia G. *science educator, researcher*
Waddell, Elizabeth Needham *research scientist, educator*
Wiesel, Torsten Nils *neurobiologist, educator*
Wisniewski, Thomas Mark *neuroscientist, neurologist, psychology professor*
Young, Michael Warren *geneticist, educator*

Newburgh
Sarro, Thomas John *biology professor*

Oakdale
Jank, David A. *educator, researcher*

Oakland Gardens
Costa, Philip Joseph *retired biology professor*

Oneonta
Pietraface, William John *biology professor*

Orangeburg
DelliPizzi, AnnMarie *biology professor*
Yaragudri, Vinod K. *neuroscientist, researcher*

Orchard Park
Urbanski, Jane F. *retired microbiologist*

Palisades
Purdy, G. Michael *observatory director*
Sanchez, Pedro Antonio *soil scientist, administrator*

Plattsburgh
Dawson, James Clifford *environmental science educator, geologist*

Potsdam
Zanta, Carolyn A. *biology professor*

Purchase
Ehrman, Lee *geneticist, educator*

Rochester
Angerer, Lynne Musgrave *biologist, researcher*
Doty, Robert William *neuroscientist, physiologist, educator*
Frisina, Robert Dana *neuroscientist, educator*
Guo, Chunlei *science educator*
Huxlin, Krystel Raluka *neuroscientist, educator*
Oberdorster, Gunter *toxicologist, educator*
Rodgers, Suzanne Hooker *physiologist, consultant*
Werren, John Haynes *biology professor*
Zhu, Donghui *research scientist*

Roslyn
Shubin, Joanna *science educator*

Rye
Sales, Mitzi S. *science educator*

Saint Albans
Norfleet, Leontine Sandra *retired biologist*

Scarsdale
Low, Murray *physiologist*

Schenectady
Fleischer, Robert Louis *geology professor*
Yu, Ting *research scientist*

Staten Island
Sánchez, Margarita María *science educator*
Scherb, Richard John *science educator*

Stony Brook
Lennarz, William Joseph *research biologist, educator*
Levinton, Jeffrey S. *biology educator, oceanographer*
Liang, Jerome Z. *science educator*
Potapova, Irina A. *cell biologist, educator*
Rohlf, F. James *biologist, educator*
Sherman, S. Murray *neuroscientist, neurobiology educator*
Sokal, Robert Reuven *biology professor, writer*

Syracuse
Hale, Sherrie LaFrance *biology professor, researcher*
Hallberg, Richard Lawrence *cell biologist, molecular biologist*
Mansouri, Nazanin *science educator*
Robinson, Joseph Edward *geology educator, petroleum engineer, consultant*
Sanger, Joseph William *cell biologist*
Shields, William Michael *biology professor, consultant*
Smith, Phillip H. *biology professor, educational association administrator*
Stevens, Richard Thomas *neuroscientist, researcher*

Troy
Bennett, Kristin Paulette *science educator*
Berg, Daniel *science and technology educator*
Ehrlich, Henry Lutz *biology professor*
Pezzolesi, Linda S.W. *science educator*
Welles, Wanda Lizak *research scientist*

Upton
Aronson, Samuel *science administrator*
Chaudhari, Praveen *science administrator, materials physicist*

Valhalla
Kang, Jian *neuroscientist, educator*

Valley Falls
Babbitt, Martha E. *retired science educator*

Victor
Morris, G. Michael *science educator*

White Plains
Estevez, Alvaro G. *biology professor, researcher*
Smith, Gerard Peter *neuroscientist*

Yorktown Heights
Wynne, James J. *research scientist*

NORTH CAROLINA

Asheboro
Jones, David M. *zoological park administrator*

Boone
Hou, Guichuan *biology professor, director*
Martin, Vicki Joan *biology professor*

Cary
Jingchun, Sun *research scientist*
Timothy, David Harry *retired biology professor*
You, Taek H. *biology professor, researcher*

Chapel Hill
Farber, Rosann Alexander *geneticist, educator*
Feduccia, J. Alan *biologist, educator*
Gherghe, Costin Marian *research scientist*
Losh, Molly *science educator*
Lundblad, Roger Lauren *biotechnology consultant*
Magnuson, Terry R. *geneticist, educator*
Maroni, Donna Farolino *biologist, researcher*
Mueller, Nancy Schneider *retired biology professor*
Pfennig, David William *biology professor*
Smithies, Oliver *geneticist, educator*
Stumpf, Walter Erich *cell biology and pharmacology professor, researcher*
Zhu, Hongtu *science educator*

Charlotte
Bullock, Sharon King *biologist, educator*
Coleman, Kent K. *science association director*

Clemmons
Jones, Marvin Lamar *histologist*

Cullowhee
Catley, Kefyn *biology professor*

Davidson
Ratchford, Joseph Thomas *science and technology policy educator, consultant*

Durham
Blum, Jacob Joseph *physiologist, educator*
Cavazos, José Enrique *neuroscientist, neurologist*
Eubanks, Mary *biologist, anthropologist*
Gillham, Nicholas Wright *geneticist, educator*
Graffagnino, Carmelo *neuroscientist, emergency physician*
Gray jr, Leon Earl *biologist, researcher*
Kashuba, Roxolana *research scientist*
Keene, Jack Donald *molecular genetics and microbiology educator*
Miller, David Sameul *physiologist*
Mudipalli, Anuradha *biologist, researcher*
Nicolelis, Miguel A. L. *neuroscientist, educator*
Pimm, Stuart L. *ecology educator*
Richardson, Curtis John *ecology educator*
Teng, Christina T. *molecular biologist, researcher*
Vogel, Steven *biologist, educator*

Elizabeth City
Blackmon, Ronald H. *biologist, science educator*
Storie, Eric Duane *science administrator*

Elon
Yap, Alexander Y. *educator, information systems, researcher, consultant*

Greensboro
Gdanitz, Robert J. *research scientist, educator*
Noble, Ralph C. *animal scientist, department chairman*
Obeng, Kofi *science educator*
Reece, Alton Davis, Jr. *science educator*
Vestal, Richard D. *biology professor*

Greenville
Carroll, Robert Graham *physiologist, educator*
Lu, Qun *cell biologist, educator*
Rheinhardt, Richard *ecologist, educator*

Hendersonville
Brittain, James Edward *science and technology educator, researcher*

Hickory
Whiteley, Emily C. *biology professor*

Morganton
McGrady, C. Nadine *science educator*
Styles, Naomi *biology professor*

Morrisville
Todd, Lori A. *toxicologist, professor*

Murfreesboro
Wethington, Amy Rene *biology professor*

Raleigh
Anderson, Norman Dean *science education educator, writer*
Aronson, Arthur Lawrence *retired veterinarian, toxicologist, educator, pharmacologist*
Breidt, Fred *microbiologist*
Brown, Robert Dale *wildlife science educator, dean*
Clauberg, Martin *research scientist*
Cook, Maurice Gayle *soil science educator, consultant*
Cooper, Arthur Wells *retired ecologist, educator*
Davey, Charles Bingham *soil scientist, educator*
Dunphy, Edward James *science educator, crop extension specialist*
Edens, Frank Wesley *physiologist*
Hardin, James W. *botanist, educator, herbarium curator*
Havlin, John Leroy *soil scientist, educator*
Hodgson, Ernest *toxicologist, educator*
Moreland, Donald Edwin *physiologist*
Pearsall, Samuel Haff III *ecologist, geographer, foundation administrator*
Stuber, Charles William *retired genetics educator, researcher, director*
Suter, Steven E. *veterinarian, educator*
Vepraskas, Michael J. *soil scientist, educator*

Research Triangle Park
Haynes, Victoria Franchetti *science administrator*
Stoker, Tammy Edwards *toxicologist, researcher*

Southern Shores
Aukland, Elva Dayton *retired biologist, educator*

Spindale
Day, Ashley Paris *biology professor*
Hoyle, Noelle L. *biology professor*

Wilmington
Alam, Shah *research scientist*
Fuller, Melvin Stuart *botany educator*
Kelley, Patricia Hagelin *geology educator*

Winston Salem
Hegde, Ashok *research scientist, educator*
Laxminarayana, Dama *geneticist, researcher, educator*

NORTH DAKOTA

Bismarck
Niksic, Gwen M. *biology professor*

Fargo
Maocheng, Yan *research scientist*
Sheridan, Mark A. *physiologist, educator*

Grand Forks
Carlson, Edward C. *anatomy educator, cell biologist, department chairman*
Melvold, Roger Wayne *microbiologist, educator*
Nilles, Matthew L. *microbiology educator, researcher*

Williston
Conway, Beverly E. *science educator*

OHIO

Akron
Fei, Juntao *research scientist*

Athens
Hicks, Kenneth H. *science educator, researcher*

Bowling Green
Zeilstra-Ryalls, Jill Helen *biology professor*

Cincinnati
Clark, Kenneth Edward *physiologist, educator*
Koehl, Joerg *microbiologist, researcher, medical educator*
Kutcher, Louis Wm. *biology professor*
Lin, Ray Y. *science educator*
Mazlack, Lawrence Joseph *science educator*
Nebert, Daniel Walter *molecular geneticist, research administrator*
Schaefer, Frank William III *microbiologist, researcher*
Silberstein, Edward Bernard *nuclear medicine educator, oncologist, hematologist, researcher*
Ward, Richard Leo *virologist*
Wray, Francis *biology professor*
Wylie, Christopher Craig *biologist, educator*

Cleveland
Blackwell, John *science educator*
Chen, Shu Guang *neuroscientist, educator, pathologist*
Dell'Osso, Louis Frank *neuroscience educator*
Durand, Dominique M. *science educator*
Ellison, Pamela Jean *science educator*
Kaltenbach, James Albert *neurobiologist, educator*
Karn, Jonathan *molecular biologist, consultant*
Lando, Jerome Burton *macromolecular science educator*
Sieg, Scott Frederick *biology educator*
Smith, Mark Anthony *neuroscientist, educator*
Taylor, Steve Henry *zoologist*
Yan, Riqiang *science educator*
Yasick, Alison L. *science educator*
Zigmond, Richard Eric *neuroscientist, researcher*

Columbus
Artsimovitch, Irina *science educator*
Balasubramaniam, V. M. *food scientist, educator*
Billman, George Edward *physiologist, educator*
Booton, Gregory Charles *geneticist, educator*
Cheesman, Kerry Lee *biology educator, researcher*
Chesebrough, David E. *science association executive*
Corbato, Charles Edward *geology educator, academic administrator*
Denlinger, David Landis *insect biology educator*
Faure, Gunter *geology educator*
Fausey, Norman Ray *soil scientist*
Foland, Kenneth A. *geological sciences educator*
Fry, Donald Lewis *physiologist, educator*
Glaser, Ronald *virologist, educator*
Hume, Elizabeth Valerie *science educator, department chairman*
Kapral, Frank Albert *microbiologist and immunology educator*
Long, Frederick *science educator*
Newsom, Gerald Higley *astronomy educator*
Peterle, Tony John *zoologist, educator*
Roth, Robert Earl *ecologist, educator*
Seoane-Vazquez, Enrique *research scientist*
Tadesse, Mesfin *botanist, biology professor, consultant, researcher*
Titterington, Lynda Carol *biology professor, researcher*
Triplehorn, Charles A. *entomologist, educator*
Wood, Jackie Dale *physiologist, educator, researcher*
Zartman, David Lester *retired zoology educator, researcher*

Dayton
Gregor, Clunie Bryan *geology educator*
Lewyanvoon, Lok C. *science educator*
Stover, David S. *science educator*
Sudkamp, Thomas *science educator*

Delaware
Iverson, Louis Robert *research ecologist*

Fairview Park
Leickly, Portia Elaine *science educator*

Hamilton
Munson, Richard Howard *horticulturist*
Werner, Laurie *science educator*

Highland Hills
Kharina, Nina Yurievna *science educator*

Kent
Evans, Melissa Rebecca *science educator*

Mentor
Fiorello, Anthony James *biology professor*

Mount Vernon
Beal, Carrie D. *biology professor*
Madtes, Paul *biology professor*

North Canton
Clevinger, Jennifer Amick *botanist*
Deakins, Donald Eugene *biology professor*

Oxford
Eshbaugh, W(illiam) Hardy *botanist, educator*
Fernandes, Joyce Juliana *science educator*
Hickey, R. James *botanist, educator*
Smart, Leonard James, Jr. *science educator*

Springfield
Welch, James M. *biology professor*

Toledo
Bullerjahn, Anne *science educator*
Chakraborty, Joana *physiologist, educator, science administrator*
Lane, Richard Durelle *neuroscientist, educator*
Stepien, Carol Ann *molecular geneticist, fisheries educator*

Twinsburg
Murphy, Kathleen S. *science educator*

Wooster
Dehority, Burk Allyn *microbiology professor*

Wright Patterson AFB
Hager, Gordon Douglas *scientist, engineering educator*
Tripp, Lloyd Dale *research scientist*

Wyoming
Cooley, William Edward *research scientist, consultant*

Yellow Springs
Webb, Paul *physiologist, educator, researcher, consultant*

Zanesville
Marks, John R. *retired science educator*
Shepherd, James Leonard *biology professor*

OKLAHOMA

Altus
Coakley, Toni M. *science educator*

Ardmore
Dixon, Richard Arthur *botanist, educator, researcher*

Midwest City
Gilbert, James Neil *science educator*

Norman
AbuBakr, Samer *microbiologist, educator*
Bluestein, Howard Bruce *meteorology educator*
Hutchison, Victor Hobbs *biologist, educator*
Mares, Michael Allen *ecologist, educator, Museum Association Administrator*

Ochelata
Hitzman, Donald Oliver *microbiologist*

Oklahoma City
Branch, John Curtis *biology professor, lawyer*
Cunningham, Madeleine White *microbiologist, immunologist*
Dubowski, Kurt Max *toxicologist, educator, consultant*
Komori, Naoka *neuroscientist, biochemist*
Sanghera, Dharambir K. *biology professor*

Park Hill
Yeager, Debra Lyn *science educator*

Pawhuska
Strahm, Samuel Edward *retired veterinarian*

Sand Springs
Quinn, Art Jay *retired veterinarian, educator*

Seminole
Helseth, David Carl *biology professor*

Stillwater
Allison, Robin W. *veterinarian, educator*
Campbell, John Roy *animal science professor, academic administrator*
Dabo, Sira Mady *science educator*
Dr. Eissa, Fahd Z. *toxicologist, educator*
Farr, Cheryl Ann *science educator, researcher*
Gilliland, Stanley Eugene *dairy-food microbiology professor*
Grischkowsky, Daniel Richard *research scientist, educator*
Rebek, Eric *entomologist, educator*

Stilwell
Doyle, Rhonda Gail *science educator*

Tulsa
Korstad, John Edward *biology professor*
Norvell, John Edmondson III *retired neuroscientist, educator*
Phillips, Mary Gutierrez *biology professor*
Stewart, Mary Tomlinson *science educator, researcher*

OREGON

Albany
Ares, Adrian *research scientist*

Arch Cape
Markham, John Charles *biologist*

Ashland
Christianson, Roger Gordon *biology professor, department chairman*
May, Richard Lee *biologist, educator*

Beaverton
Wang, Baoliang (Bob Wang) *applications scientist, researcher*

Corvallis
Anthony, Robert Gene *ecologist, educator, research scientist*
Chambers, Kenton Lee *botany educator*
Chung, Woon-Gye *toxicologist, researcher*
Frakes, Rodney Vance *plant geneticist, educator*
Henny, Charles Joseph *biologist, researcher*
Lancaster, Stephen Thomas *science educator*
Morita, Richard Yukio *microbiology and oceanography educator*
Olson, Deanna Helen *ecologist, researcher*
Qian, Michael C. *science educator, consultant*
Salafsky, Susan Rebecca *ecologist*
Sarker, Mahfuzur Rahman *microbiologist*
Tappeiner, II, John C. *forester, educator*
Waring, Richard Harvey *retired research scientist*
Waromg, Richard Harvey *ecologist, educator*
Westwood, Melvin Neil *horticulturist, pomologist*

Eugene
Matthews, Brian W. *molecular biology educator*

Florence
Marble, Duane Francis *geography educator, researcher*

Newport
Ferraro, Steven Peter *marine biologist, researcher*

Oregon City
Bown, Jennifer Porter *biology professor*

Pendleton
Klepper, Elizabeth Lee *retired physiologist*

Portland
Balkowiec, Agnieszka Zofia *science educator, researcher*
Bierzychudek, Paulette F. *biology educator*
Ebberts, Blaine Daniel *biologist*
Hagenstein, William David *forester, consultant*
Hyun, Saang-Yoon *research scientist, consultant*
Khalil, Mohammad Aslam Khan *environmental science, engineering and physics educator*
Machida, Curtis A. *research molecular neurobiologist, molecular virologist, oral biologist, educator*
Sheard, Tim *science educator*
Tobin, Allen Gerald (Jerry) *science educator*
Wall, Brian Raymond *forest economist, business consultant, researcher*

Prineville
Geisen, Michael *science educator*

Talent
MacMillen, Richard Edward *biological sciences educator, researcher*

Wilsonville
Gordon, John Charles *forestry educator*

PENNSYLVANIA

Altoona
Tormey, Brian B. *environmental geomorphologist, aerial mapping consultant*

Annville
Verhoek, Susan Elizabeth *botany educator*

Bala Cynwyd
Corliss, John Ozro *zoology educator*

Bethlehem
Guillon, Christophe *research scientist*

Bloomsburg
Srinivasan, Avinash *science educator*

Blue Bell
Earl, Judy *microbiologist, educator*
Venuti, Elaine M. *biology professor*

Bryn Mawr
Crawford, Maria Luisa Buse *geology educator*

Buffalo Mills
Duppstadt, William Homer *retired botanist, educator, lay worker*

Collegeville
Alesci, Salvatore *science association director*
Quinet, Elaine Marie *molecular biologist, researcher*

Doylestown
Mishler, John Milton (Yochanan Menashsheh ben Shaul) *science educator, artist*

Easton
Ferri, James K. *science educator*

Erie
Gauriloff, Larry Paul *biology professor, researcher*
Gilloteaux, Jacques Jean-Marie Anthime *cell biologist, researcher*
Su, Meng *science educator*

Fairview
Sorhannus, Ulf Mikael *biology professor*

Gettysburg
Hendrix, Sherman Samuel *biology professor, researcher*

Gladwyne
Silvers, Willys Kent *geneticist*

Glen Mills
Huang, Wenlin *research scientist*
O'Tanyi, Theodore J., Jr. *retired biology professor*

Harrisburg
Dennis, VanEngelsdorp *agriculturist*

Haverford
DiBerardino, Marie Antoinette *developmental biologist, educator*

Hershey
Hopper, Anita Klein *molecular genetics educator*
Undar, Akif *research scientist, biomedical engineer, educator*
Zagon, Ian Stuart *neuroscience and anatomy educator, researcher, inventor*

Horsham
Ippolito, Andrew *science educator, photographer*

Indiana
Nealen, Paul *science educator*

Johnstown
Kilpatrick, Stephen Timothy *biology professor*

Kennett Square
Long, Kimberly A. *biologist, educator*
Orsini, James A. *veterinarian, educator, author, surgeon, editor*

King Of Prussia
Lubiniecki, Anthony Stanley *microbiologist, researcher*
Thorneloe, Kevin S. *biologist*

Lancaster
Maula, Mohammad Mojibul *biology professor*

Latrobe
Koehl, Jennifer *biology professor*

Lewisburg
Pizzorno-Simpson, Marie C. *biology professor, department chairman*

Lock Haven
Jia, Dongdong *nanoscience and physics educator*

Loretto
Langer, Marian *biology professor*

Mansfield
Maris, Robert C. *biologist, educator*

Mechanicsburg
Earle, Jane I. *biologist, consultant*

Mifflinville
Farber, Phillip Andrew *retired biological and allied health sciences educator*

Narberth
Nathanson, Neal *virologist, epidemiologist, educator*

New Hope
Pelleymounter, Mary Ann *research scientist*

Newtown
Franc, Frannie *science educator, consultant*

Newtown Square
Pan, Yude *forest ecologist*

Philadelphia
Abel, Edwin George, III, (Ted Abel) *biologist, educator, researcher*
Adler, Martin William *neuropharmacologist*
Armstrong, Clay *physiology educator*
Brinster, Ralph Lawrence *biologist, educator*
Chiou, Richard Y. *science educator, researcher*
Cohen, Akiva S. *neuroscientist, educator*
Eisenstein, Toby K. *microbiology professor*
Fisher, Aron Baer *physiology educator*
Furth, John Jacob *molecular biologist, educator, pathologist*
Hammond, Benjamin Franklin *microbiologist, educator*
Hoxie, James A. *virologist, educator*
Huang, Liquan *molecular biologist, neuroscientist*
Koprowski, Hilary *microbiologist, educator*
LaFollette, Paul Sumner, Jr. *science educator*
Lambertsen, Christian James *environmental physiologist, physician, educator*
Liang, Ling L. *science educator*
Moskowitz, Robert Lawrence *biology professor*
Patrick, Ruth (Mrs. Ruth Hodge Van Dusen) *botany educator, curator*
Peachey, Lee DeBorde *biology professor*
Pepe, Frank A. *cell and developmental biology educator*
Pyeritz, Reed Edwin *geneticist, educator, medical researcher*
Raghupathi, Ramesh *neuroscientist, educator*
Rubin, Benjamin Arnold *microbiologist, immunologist, medical educator, researcher*
Rukhadze, Irma *neuroscientist*
Scandura, Joseph Michael *neuroscientist, application developer*
Schmidt, Marc F. *neuroscientist, educator*
Schultz, Richard M. *biology professor*
Schwaber, James Stephen *neuroscientist, director*
Soslau, Gerald *biochemistry professor*
Taniguchi, Tadatsugu *biology professor, researcher*
Taslidere, Ezgi *science educator*
Tavana, Madjid *science educator*
Testa, Joseph R. *geneticist, researcher, biologist*
Tsykalov, Eugene *neuroscientist, researcher*
Undieh, Ashiwel S. *science educator, department chairman*
White, Howard D. *information science educator*
Won, Chang-Hee *science educator*
Wysocky, Charles Joseph *neuroscientist*

Phoenixville
Hanlon, Barbara Jean *family and consumer sciences educator*

Pitcairn
Rose, Robert Didier *neurophysiologist*

Pittsburgh
Amara, Susan *neuroscientist*
Brumovsky, Pablo Rodolfo *neuroscientist*
Cassidy, William Arthur *geology and planetary science educator*
Cranor, Lorrie Faith *science educator, researcher*
Druzdzel, Marek Jozef *computer science educator, researcher*
Ehrlich, Garth David *molecular biologist*
Feingold, David Sidney *microbiology and biochemistry educator, researcher*
Feng, Rentian *biologist*
Garcia, Calixto Isaac *science educator*
Gollin, Susanne Merle *cell biologist, cancer researcher, geneticist*
Harrold, Ronald Thomas *research scientist*
Hatfull, Graham F. *microbiologist, educator*
Jacobson, Lewis A. *biology professor*
Jung, Kwan-Jin *science association director*
Kanade, Takeo *science educator, director*
Kiger, Robert William *botanist, science historian, educator, researcher*
LaJohn, Lawrence Anthony *research scientist*
Lennox, James G. *science educator*
Lewis, David Alan *neuroscientist, psychiatrist, educator*
Marazita, Mary Louise *genetics researcher*
Partanen, Carl Richard *biology professor*
Schatten, Gerald Phillip *stem cell biologist, reproductive biologist, educator*
Schatzkamer, Laura *biology professor*
Schwartz, Andrew B. *neuroscientist, educator*
Smith, Alan David *quantitative and natural sciences educator*
Stout, Janet E. *microbiologist, director*
Zeevi, Adriana *microbiologist, immunologist*

Reading
Weicker, Michelina Eva *biology professor, consultant*
Zervanos, Stamatis Michael (Stam Zervanos) *biology professor*

Schnecksville
Kiriposki, Marie *biology professor*

Scranton
Zwanch, Andrew V. *science educator*

Slippery Rock
Kefeli, Valentin Ilich *biologist, botanist, educator, researcher*

State College
Madjid, A. Hamid *retired science educator*
Schmalz, Robert Fowler *geology educator*

Stroudsburg
Hunt, James Christopher *marine biologist, researcher*

Swarthmore
Gilbert, Scott Frederick *biologist, educator, author*

Union City
Thomas, Paul Milton *retired science educator*

University Park
Acharya, Biswa Ranjan *biologist, researcher*
Barnes, Hubert Lloyd *geochemistry educator*
Buskirk, Elsworth Robert *physiologist, educator*
Federoff, Nina V. *biology professor, federal official*
Griffin, Kimberly Anne *educator*
Hahm, Jong-in *science educator*
Johnson, Kenneth Allen *biologist, educator*
Kim, Ke Chung *entomology, systematics, and biodiversity educator, researcher*
Nei, Masatoshi *biology professor*
Roy, Rustum *citizen scientist*
Shapiro, Beth *biology professor*

Valley Forge
Erb, Robert Allan *physical scientist*

Wayne
Krutsick, Robert Stanley *retired science center administrator*
Thelen, Edmund *research executive*

West Point
Greenwood, Susan Kay *biologist*
Renger, John Joseph *neurobiologist*
Webber, Andrea L. *research scientist*
Wise, L. David *toxicologist*

Wilkes Barre
Hayes, Wilbur Frank *retired biology professor*

Williamsport
Buckman, Debra Ann *science educator*
Kule, Chris Edward *biology professor*
Noviello, Donald *science educator*

Wyndmoor
Strobaugh, Terence Philip, Jr. *molecular biologist, microbiologist*

York
Hodgson, Elizabeth *biology professor, consultant*

Youngwood
Shafert, Tim D. *science educator*

RHODE ISLAND

Bristol
Guralnick, Lonnie J. *biology professor, dean*

Kingston
Hufnagel, Linda Ann *biology professor, researcher*
Martin, Lenore Marie *bioorganic researcher, educator*

Narragansett
Goos, Roger Delmon *retired mycologist*
Grear, Jason S. *ecologist*
Lohmann, Rainer *science educator*

Newport
Johnson, William Carter *biology professor*

Providence
Block, Bartley Cavanough *biologist, educator*
Dowben, Robert Morris *physiologist, researcher*
Fairbrother, Will *biology professor*
Janis, Christine *biology professor*
Miller, Kenneth Raymond *biologist, educator*
Wharton, Kristi Anna *biology professor*

SOUTH CAROLINA

Aiken
Bertsch, Paul M. *ecologist, director*

Anderson
Pryor, Betty Jo *biology professor*

Bluffton
Staton, Joseph L. *marine biologist, educator*

Charleston
Boger, Heather Anne *research scientist*
Harold, Antony S. *biology professor*
Knackstedt, Lori Ann *research scientist*
Machowski, Liisa Ervin Sharpes *science educator*
Meister, Howard Scott *marine biologist, educator*
Wooten-Blanks, Leslie *biologist*

Clemson
Jacobs, David P. *science educator*
Layne, Desmond R. *horticulturist, educator*
Owino, Tom Obuya *science educator, researcher*
Rajapakse, Nihal *horticulturist, educator*
Scott, Mark C. *biologist, educator*
Wheeler, Alfred George, Jr. *retired entomologist, biology professor, researcher*

Clinton
Meeker, Paige H. *science educator*

Columbia
Jabbari, Esmaiel *polymer scientist, researcher*
Janicki, Joseph S. *physiologist, educator*
Koley, Goutam *science educator*
Nachtigal, Maurice *pathology professor*
Smith, Theresa Joanne *research scientist, educator*
Wideman, Ida Devlin *science educator*

Conway
Gilman, Craig *marine science professor*

Easley
Spearman, David Hagood *retired veterinarian*

Greenville
Cureton, Claudette Hazel Chapman *retired biology professor*
Wei, Yanzhang *microbiologist, educator*

Hilton Head Island
Adams, William Hensley *ecologist, educator*
Lefer, Allan Mark *physiologist*

Lexington
Smith, John Powell *entomologist, educator*

Mc Cormick
Soni, Jayshri *science educator, director*

Myrtle Beach
Cohen, Stuart Colin *science educator*

Newberry
Horn, Charles *biology professor, department chairman*

Orangeburg
Chen, Jianguo *biology professor*
Mahroof, Rizana M. *biology professor*

Pawleys Island
Kay, Thomas Oliver *agricultural consultant*

Pendleton
Beyerlein, Anne MoYung *science educator*
Gilmour, Phillip Curtis *science educator*
Klaine, Stephen James *environmental toxicology educator*

Rock Hill
Yilma, Almaz *biology professor*

Simpsonville
Pratt, Harry Davis *retired entomologist*

Spartanburg
Leonard, Walter Raymond *retired biology professor*
Moeller, John *biology professor*

SOUTH DAKOTA

Aberdeen
Dohn, Ken W. *business educator*

Brookings
Clay, Sharon A. *science educator*
Kaushik, Radhey Shyam *microbiologist, educator, immunologist*
McFarland, Douglas C. *muscle biologist, educator*
Moldenhauer, William Calvin *soil scientist*
Rahman, Shafiqur *neuropharmacologist, scientist, professor, editor*
Schingoethe, David John *dairy cattle nutritionist*
Schumacher, Tom E. *soil scientist, educator*

Pierre
Repsys, Andrew J. *aquatic biologist, limnologist, water quality specialist, environmental biologist*

Sioux Falls
Narendranath, Neelakantam V. *microbiologist, researcher*

Vermillion
Keifer, Joyce *science association director*

TENNESSEE

Cleveland
Evans, Johnny L. *science educator*

Cordova
Bayakly, Nabil Abdulghani *biology professor*

Dyersburg
Flatt, James Lynn *biology professor*

Franklin
Thornsberry, Clyde *microbiologist*

Huntingdon
King, Tracy Lynn *science educator*

Jackson
Hayes, Robert Mac *agronomy educator*

Knoxville
Farmer, Susan Baker *taxonomic botanist*
Jones, Carl Joseph *entomologist, educator*
Schlarbaum, Scott E. *forester, educator*
Simberloff, Daniel *biologist, educator*

Lebanon
Bryan, Danny Lee *biology professor*

Memphis
Fitzgerald, Malinda E.C. *biology professor*
Freeman, Bob A. *retired microbiology educator, retired dean*
Heda, Ghanshyam Das *molecular biologist, researcher*
Howe, Martha Morgan *microbiologist, educator*
Jablonski, Monica Mary *science educator*
Leffler, Charles William *physiology and pediatrics educator*
Majumdar, Sabita *biology professor*
Pfeffer, Lawrence Marc *cell biologist*
Pruitt, Rosalyn Jolena *science educator*
Webster, Robert G. *virologist, educator*

Morristown
Bolton, Kimberly D. *biology professor*

Murfreesboro
Henderson, Ronald H. *science educator*

Nashville
Catania, Kenneth C. *neuroscientist, educator*
Ejiofor, Anthony Okechukwu *microbiologist, educator*
Fanning, Ellen *biology professor, research scientist*
Gauthier, Isabel *cognitive neuroscientist*
Hedera, Peter *neuroscientist, educator*
Pincus, Theodore *microbiologist, rheumatologist, educator*
Prince, Lawrence *science educator*
Tong, Frank *science educator*
Wang, Taylor Gunjin *science administrator, educator, astronaut*
Zald, David H. *cognitive neuroscientist*

Oak Ridge
Vishnivetskaya, Tatiana Aleksandrovna *microbiologist, researcher*
Yin, Tongming *science educator*

Sewanee
Yeatman, Harry Clay *biologist, educator*

TEXAS

Arlington
Burkart, Burke *geology educator, researcher*
Foss, Frank Wells *science educator*
Kim, Choong-Un *science educator*
Roner, Michael Robert *virologist, educator*
Smith, Charles Isaac *geology educator*

Austin
Bajaj, Chandrajit *science educator*
Biesele, John Julius *biologist, educator*
Bose, Henry Robert, Jr. *molecular biologist, educator*
Drummond Borg, Lesley Margaret *geneticist*
Eakin, Richard T. *research scientist, consultant*
Fryxell, Greta Albrecht *marine botany educator, oceanographer*
Holz, Robert Kenneth *retired geography educator*
Injo, Ok *biologist*
Jacobson, Antone Gardner *retired zoology educator*
Kirkpatrick, Mark A. *biology professor*
Mikels, Jo *science educator*
Ramirez Garza, Elizabeth Ann *biology professor, researcher*
Sessions, Alice *biology professor, department chairman*
Sutton, Harry Eldon *geneticist, educator*

Beaumont
Corbett, Robert Wayne *biology professor*
Cover, Ellen Catherine *biology professor, researcher*
Lanoue, Stephanie Anne *biology professor*
Liu, Jiangjiang *science educator*

Brenham
Dalman, Michael *science educator*

Brooks City-Base
Miller, Carolyn Lyons *microbiologist, military officer*

Brownsville
Emilio, Garrido Sanabria Rafael *science educator, researcher*
Nair, Saraswathy *molecular biologist, educator*

Bryan
Milford, Murray Hudson *retired soil science educator*

Bushland
Baumhardt, R. Louis *agronomist*
Payne, William Albert, Jr. *agronomist, educator*

College Station
Beaver, Bonnie Veryle *veterinarian, educator*
Borlaug, Norman Ernest *agricultural scientist*
Drees, Bastiaan Meijer *entomologist*
Gali, Hariprasad *research scientist*
Greenberg, Les Paul *entomologist, researcher*
Klemm, William Robert *scientist, educator*
McCrady, James David *veterinarian, educator*
Miller, Rhonda Kay *food scientist, educator*
Qin, Qing-Ming *agriculturist*
Sohrabji, Farida *neuroscientist, educator*
Stevenson, Douglass Edward *entomologist, toxicologist*
Stranges, Anthony Nicholas *science history educator*
Sweet, Merrill Henry, II, *retired biology professor*
Tai-Seale, Ming *science educator, consultant*
Wu, Guoyao *animal scientist, nutritionist, educator*

Commerce
Bertulani, Carlos A. *science educator*

Corpus Christi
McCollough, Cherie A. *science educator*

Dallas
Brown, Michael Stuart *geneticist, educator, science administrator*
German, Dwight Charles *neuroscientist, educator*
Goldstein, Joseph Leonard *molecular biologist, educator*
Mitchell, Jere Holloway *physiologist, researcher, medical educator*
Parada, Luis Fernando *science educator*
Reinert, James A. *entomology educator*
Reynolds, Jackie Susan *biology professor*
Slavine, Nikolai V. *science educator*
Thomas, Philip Jordan *science educator*
Vitetta, Ellen S. *microbiologist, immunologist, educator*

Denton
Eve, Susan Brown *science educator, dean*
Fuchs, Jannon Lou *neuroscientist, educator*
Yi, Zhixian *science educator*

Edinburg
Ahn, Seokyoung *science educator*

El Paso
Newman, Carla Ruth *science educator*
Rodriguez-Torres, Jose German *retired veterinarian*
Waissman, Naomi Assadian *biology professor*
Webb, Robert Gravem *retired biology professor*

Fort Sam Houston
Ryan, Kathy L. *physiologist, researcher*

Fort Worth
Garner, Jason W. *biology professor*
Lycan, Anthony C. *biology professor*

Galveston
Budelmann, Bernd Ulrich *zoologist, educator*
Esenaliev, Rinat Orozbekovich *science educator, lab administrator*
Ismail, Nahed *microbiologist, immunologist*
Kanuth, Michelle Susan *science educator*
Murphy, Frederick Augustus *virologist, researcher*
Srinivasan, Ganesan *molecular biologist, educator*
Thompson, Edward Ivins Bradbridge *biological chemistry and genetics educator, endocrinologist*
Torres, Alfredo Gabriel *biology professor, researcher*
Willis, William Darrell, Jr. *neuroscientist, educator*

Georgetown
Deviney, Marvin Lee, Jr. *science administrator, director*
Pierce, Benjamin Allen *biologist, educator*
Tisdell, Ronald H. *toxicologist, consultant*

Houston
Campbell, Clifford Russell *research scientist*
De Bremaecker, Jean-Claude *geophysics educator*
Dikeocha, Ndu *biology professor*
Dronamraju, Krishna Rao *geneticist*
DuMond, James Wilson, Jr. *biology professor, researcher*
Duston, Karen Lansford *biology professor*
Estes, Mary K. *virologist, researcher*
Jamrich, Milan *science educator*
Jeevarajan, Antony S. *science administrator*
Jurtshuk, Peter, Jr. *microbiologist, educator*
Khan-Mayberry, Noreen *toxicologist*
Kohli, Rajiv *science administrator*
Koo, Jaseok Peter *science educator*
Koul, Dimpy *cell biologist, educator, researcher*
Levy, Eugene Howard *planetary sciences and astrophysics educator, researcher*
Mao, Li *molecular biologist, educator*
Marriott, Susan *research scientist*
Massoud, Yehia *science educator*
Mendelson, Robert Allen *polymer scientist, rheologist*
Naeem, Rizwan C. *geneticist, educator, lab administrator, director*
Nelson, David Loren *geneticist, educator*
O'Malley, Bert William *cell biologist, educator, physician*
Papanicolaou, Andrew C. *neuroscientist, educator*
Queller, David C. *ecology and biology professor*
Sabek, Omaima M. *biology professor, director*
Snipes, Shedra Amy *research scientist*
Steele, James Harlan *retired veterinarian*
Strassmann, Joan Elizabeth *evolutionary biologist*
Uzman, James Akif *biology professor*
Wilson, Jamia Weletha *science educator*

Hurst
Eamma, Kari Ann *biology professor*
Jacaruso, Diana *biology educator*
Lindsey, Jerri Kay *biologist, educator*

Kingsville
Martinez, Alvaro Ignacio *science educator*

Kingwood
De Soignie, Roland C. *biology professor*
Morgan, Betsy Elizabeth Robison *biology professor*

La Ward
Lin, Ming T. *plant pathologist*

Lancaster
Lumbley, Sheryl Richardson *biology professor*

League City
Pandya, Utpal *microbiologist*

Levelland
Harbin, Paul B. *science educator*

Lewisville
Whitney, Sharry Jan *science educator*

Lubbock
Basu, Sukanta *science educator*
Grammas, Paula *science educator, director*
Hentges, David John *microbiology educator*
Holaday, Allan Scott *biology educator*
McGinley, Mark Alan *biology professor*
Poduslo, Shirley Ellen *neuroscientist*
Skoog, Gerald Duane *science educator*
Straus, David Conrad *microbiologist, educator*
Wendt, Charles William *soil scientist, educator*
Woodward, Jason E. *plant pathologist, educator*

Mcallen
Guerra, Luis S. *biology professor*
Snearley, Ed *biology professor*

Mission
Herbalife, Allen Henneman Ralph *science educator*

Mountain Home
Schlechte, John Warren *research scientist*

Nacogdoches
Onchoke, Kefa K. *science educator*
Wagner, Stephen C. *biology professor*

Odessa
Post, Diane *biology professor*
Sofge, Steve Wayne *biology professor*

Palestine
Nunnally, Charles Lynn *biology and agriculture professor*

Pasadena
Gilmore, Jared Raphael *science educator*
Schumacher, Barbara J *biology professor*

Pearland
Würsig, Bernd Gerhard *marine biology educator*

Plano
Helgeson, Jean Anne (Sorrels) *biology professor, consultant*

Port Aransas
Schake, Lowell Martin *zoology educator, writer*

Prairie View
Block, Harriette Howard-Lee *biology professor*
Cuero, Raul G. *microbiologist, researcher, educator*

Richardson
Atzori, Marco *neuroscientist, educator*
Dean, Denis Joseph *science educator*
Dogan, Kutsal *science educator*
Gray, Donald Melvin *molecular and cell biology educator*
McMechan, George *science educator*
Moltz, John Henry III *biology professor*

Rockport
Berkebile, Charles Alan *geology educator, hydrogeology researcher*

Round Rock
Cryer, Chad Lindsey *biology professor*

San Angelo
McCoy, J. Kelly *biology professor*

San Antonio
Bodenchuk, Michael J. *biologist, director*
Burch, James Leo *science research institute executive*
Chen, Jiguo *microbiologist, researcher*
Espey, Lawrence Lee *biology professor*
Irving, George Washington III *veterinarian, researcher, small business executive*
Jaffe, David Bendix *neuroscientist, educator*
Manchester, Lucien Caleb *biology professor*
McComas, David John *science administrator, space physicist*
McIntosh, Dennis Keith *veterinarian, consultant*
Rouse, John Wilson, Jr. *technology consultant*
Shapiro, Mark S. *neuroscientist, educator*
Wahl, Rosemarie *biologist, educator*
Wang, Yufeng *science educator*

Smithville
Scofield, Virginia Lee *research scientist*

Spring Branch
Geistfeld, James Gordon *veterinarian*

Temple
Breslin, Jerome W. *physiologist, cell biologist*
Tharakan, Binu *neuroscientist, researcher*

Texas City
Orr, Tracy Clifford *anatomy, physiology professor*

Tomball
Tynes, Alanna Marie *biology professor*

Uvalde
Kosub, Karla Ann *biology professor*
Ramsey, Frank Allen *veterinarian, retired army officer*

Vernon
Malinowski, Dariusz Piotr *horticulturist, educator*

Waco
Leidner, Dorothy E. *science educator*

Warda
Kunze, George William *retired soil scientist*

Wharton
Dees, Kevin W. *biology professor, consultant*
Jeffery, Jennifer *biology professor*

UTAH

Brookside
McMahon, James Patrick *ecologist, consultant*

Cedar City
Mayron, Lewis Walter *clinical ecology consultant*

Centerville
Schwartz, Heidi K. *science educator*

Genola
Newcomb, Helene E. *retired research scientist*

Logan
Albee-Scott, Steven Robert *biologist, educator*
Leidolf, Andreas *ecologist*
McNeal, Lyle Glen *science educator, rancher, consultant*
Rasmussen, Harry Paul *horticulture and landscape educator*
Stucker, Brent *science educator*
Tanner, David Arden *biologist, researcher*
Wagner, Dale R. *science educator*

Oakley
Silverstone, Leon Martin *neuroscientist, cardiologist, educator, research scientist*

Providence
Vest, Hyrum Grant, Jr. *retired horticultural sciences educator*

Provo
Blake, George Rowland *soil and environmental scientist, educator, researcher*
Crookston, R. Kent *agronomy educator*
Towne, Justin *biology professor, researcher*

Richmond
Funk, Cyril Reed, Jr. *agronomist, educator*

Salt Lake City
Krizaj, David *neuroscientist, ophthalmologist*
Mango, Susan E. *biologist, educator*
Olivera, Baldomero M. *biology professor*
Opitz, John Marius *clinical geneticist, pediatrician*
Salisbury, Frank Boyer *botanist, educator, writer*

VERMONT

Brattleboro
Ames, Adelbert III *neuroscientist, educator*

Burlington
Heinrich, Bernd *biologist, educator*
Kilpatrick, Charles William *biology professor*
Mintz, Keith Peter *research scientist*

Charlotte
Melby, Edward Carlos, Jr. *veterinarian*

Morrisville
Lechevalier, Hubert Arthur *microbiology educator*
Lechevalier, Mary Pfeil *retired microbiologist, educator*

Richmond
Fary, Sandra Suzanne *science educator*

South Burlington
Schaberg, Paul G. *plant physiologist*

VIRGINIA

Alexandria
Vosbeck, Elizabeth Just *retired geneticist*

Amissville
Hunter, Beverly Claire *research scientist, educator*

Annandale
Caporale, Jill Fredrica *biology professor*
Vander Maten, Mary Ann *biology professor, dean*

Arlington
Beehler, Bruce McPherson *research zoologist, ornithologist, conservationist*
Cheney, David Warren *science and technology policy analyst, executive*
Fuchs, Roland John *geography educator, academic administrator*
Giordano, James Joseph *neuroscientist, neuroethicist, pain specialist*
Heinemeier, Dan C. *science association director*
Jones, Lawrence Andrew *research scientist, retired military officer*
Lobstein, Marion Blois *biology professor*
Markessini, Joan *research scientist, psychologist*
Muller-Parker, Gisèle Thérèse *marine biologist, educator*
Olsen, Kathie Lynn *science foundation director*
Ordway, Frederick Ira III *science educator, consultant, researcher, writer*

Ashburn
Bawa, Raj *biotechnology educator, nanotechnologist*
Rao, Jagadeesh Sridhara *research scientist*
Riddiford, Lynn Moorhead *biologist, educator*

Blacksburg
Akers, Robert Michael *physiologist, educator*
Burkhart, Harold Eugene *forester, educator*
Cimini, Daniela *cell biologist, educator*
Cowles, Joe Richard *biology professor*
De Datta, Surajit Kumar *soil scientist, agronomist, educator*
Kelly, James Michael *plant and soil scientist*
Saacke, Richard George *retired biology professor*
Witonsky, Sharon *veterinarian, educator*
Yan, Jiao *marine biologist, educator*

Charlottesville
Chevalier, Roger Alan *astronomy educator, consultant*
Garrett, Reginald Hooker *biology professor, researcher*
Hammarskjold, Marie-Louise Anna *microbiologist, educator*
Mellon, DeForest, Jr. *biology professor, researcher*
Menaker, Michael *biology professor*
Molhoek, Kerrington Ramsey *research scientist*
Skrutskie, Michael F. *science educator*
Tai, Robert H. *science educator, researcher*
Tuttle, Jeremy Ballou *neuroscientist*

Dahlgren
Rayms-Keller, Alfredo *molecular biologist*

Dublin
Linzey, Juanita Bird *biology professor*

Fairfax
Sun, Donglian *meteorologist*

Falls Church
Hart, C(harles) W(illard), Jr. *zoologist, curator*
Shah, Syed-Waqar *science educator*

Front Royal
Douglas, J(ocelyn) Fielding *toxicologist, consultant*

Galax
Dunson, William Albert *biology professor, ecological consultant*

Gloucester Point
Bush, Elizabeth Olney *marine lab technician*

Hampton
Brown, Ei Ei *science educator*
Jahncke, Michael Lee *science educator, director*

Harrisonburg
Marler, Jeffrey Allen *neuroscientist*

Haymarket
Katz, Alan Charles *toxicologist*

Keswick
Rafajko, Robert Richard *science administrator*

Lansdowne
Miller, Dorothy Anne Smith *retired cytogenetics educator*

Lexington
Hickman, Cleveland Pendleton, Jr. *biology professor*
Spencer, Edgar Winston *geology educator*

Lynchburg
Offield, Martin F. *biology professor*

Manassas
Isbister, Jenefir Diane Wilkinson *microbiologist, researcher, educator, consultant*

Mc Lean
Degeorges, Paul Andre *ecologist, educator*
DeGiovanni-Donnelly, Rosalie Frances *biologist, educator*
Layson, William McIntyre *retired research consulting company executive*
Talbot, Lee Merriam *ecologist, educator, administrator*

Newport News
Cleeton, David Lawrence *economist, educational administrator*

Norfolk
Oelberg, David George *neonatologist educator, researcher*
Okpodu, Camellia Moses *biology professor, researcher*
Zalensky, Andrei O. *biology professor, researcher*

Orange
Gore, Rebecca Estes *science educator*

Portsmouth
Weiss, Ronald Dean *biology professor*

Radford
Zeakes, Samuel John *biology professor*

Reston
Shank, Fred Ross *food scientist*

Roanoke
Estabrooks, Paul *science educator*

Staunton
Deeble, Paul D. *biology professor*

Triangle
Thomas, Lindsey Kay, Jr. *research ecology biologist, educator, consultant*

Williamsburg
Guastaferro, Angelo *space science administrator, consultant*
Rahman, Zia-Ur *research scientist*
Vold, Robert Lawrence *science educator*

Wytheville
Linzey, Donald Wayne *biologist, educator, researcher*

WASHINGTON

Anacortes
Kozloff, Eugene Nicholas *zoologist, educator, author*

Bellevue
Thompson, Winston Mark Obed *entomologist, consultant, writer*
Whatmore, George Bernard *research scientist, writer, internist, neurophysiologist*

Bellingham
Acevedo-Gutierrez, Alejandro *biology professor*
Ross, June Rosa Pitt *biologist, educator*

Brinnon
Strom, Are *biologist*

Des Moines
wBarclay, Gerry *biology professor*

Longview
Foster, Virginia *retired botany educator*

Lopez Island
Brownstein, Barbara Lavin *geneticist, educator, director*

Mount Vernon
Heinze, Susanna Lynn Christie *biology professor*

Olympia
Calabria, Lalita *research scientist, educator*

Prosser
Davenport, Joan R. *agriculturist, educator*
Proebsting, Edward Louis, Jr. *retired horticulturist*

Pullman
Hassold, Terry Jon *geneticist, educator*
Jiang, Zhihua *geneticist, educator*
Keller, C. Kent *science educator*
Krueger, James Martin *physiology educator*
Pearce, Gregory *botanist*
Washida, Haruhiko *botanist*

Richland
Chikalla, Thomas David *retired science facility administrator*
Sanfilippo, Antonio *chief scientist*

Seattle
Anna, Kagley Nicole *biologist*
Aprikyan, Andranik Andrew Goorgen *molecular biologist, biomedical researcher*
Beyers, William Bjorn *geography educator*
Boersma, P. Dee *conservation biologist, educator*
Creager, Joe Scott *geology and oceanography educator*
Enders, Eva *marine biologist, researcher*
Feigl, Eric Otto *physiology educator*
Felsenstein, Joseph *science educator*
Fidel, Raya *information science educator*
Franza, B. Robert, Jr. *science association director, educator*
Franza, Bernard Robert *science association director*
Gentry, Roger Lee *research wildlife biologist*
Greenberg, E. Peter *microbiologist*
Hartwell, Leland Harrison (Lee Hartwell) *geneticist, educator*
Hauschka, Stephen Denison *developmental biologist, educator*
Hellström, Karl Erik *science educator, researcher*
Hille, Bertil *physiology educator*
Jump, Christina M. *research scientist*
Kareiva, Peter Michael *zoology educator, research ecologist*
Kenny, George Edward *pathobiology educator*
King, Ivan Robert *astronomy educator*
King, Mary-Claire *geneticist, educator*
Laing, Sharon S. *research scientist*
Ning, Xue-Han (Hsueh-Han Ning) *physiologist, researcher*
Olson, Maynard V. *science educator, researcher*
Olstad, Roger Gale *science educator*
Quinn, LeBris Smith *cell biologist*
Rand, Jim Francis *science educator*
Reh, Thomas Andrew *biologist, educator*
Roth, Mark *research scientist*
Ruggerone, Gregory T. *research scientist*
Schiffrin, Milton Julius *physiologist*
Senczuk, Anna Maria *cell biologist, researcher*
Wise, Phyllis M. *physiologist, educator*
Woods, James Sterrett *toxicologist*

Sequim
Karr, James Richard *ecologist, educator, research director*

Tacoma
Martin, Mark Owen *biology professor*

Veradale
Keating, Eugene Kneeland *animal scientist, educator*

Wenatchee
Beausoleil, Richard A. *animal scientist*
Elfving, Don C. *horticulturist, educator*

White Salmon
Chapin, F. Stuart, Jr. *science educator, director*

WEST VIRGINIA

Charleston
Gillespie, William Harry *forestry executive, geology educator*

Fairmont
McKeen, Angela Anne *science educator*

Kearneysville
Biggs, Alan Richard *plant pathologist, educator*
Brown, Eric Wayne *geneticist*

Morgantown
Carver, Jeffrey Scott *science educator*
Cochrane, Robert Lowe *biologist*
Haff, Guy Gregory *exercise science educator, researcher*
Rentch, James Spencer *forester, educator*
Siriwardane, Hema J. *science educator*
Wenger, Sharon Louise *cytogeneticist, researcher, educator*

Wheeling
Danford, Thomas R. *biology professor*

WISCONSIN

Appleton
De Stasio, Elizabeth Ann *biology educator*
Rence, Bradford G. *biology professor*

Ashland
Brouder, Mark Joseph *fishery field station supervisor, manager*
Gorman, Owen Thomas *biologist*
Saxild, Christine Ann *science educator*

Clintonville
Primmer, Lillian Juanda *science educator*

Cottage Grove
Lund, Daryl Bert *retired food science educator*

De Forest
Morjan, Wilmar *entomologist, researcher*

Eau Claire
Diggle-Dehne, Theresa A. *science educator*

Kenosha
Hegrenes, Scott Grayson *biology professor*

La Crosse
Haro, Roger John *biology professor*

Madison
Atalla, Rajai H. *science administrator, educator*
Beyer-Mears, Annette *physiologist*
Brock, Thomas Dale *retired microbiology professor*
Cassinelli, Joseph Patrick *astronomy educator*
Evert, Ray Franklin *botany educator*
Greaser, Marion Lewis *science educator*
Hood, Leroy Edward *molecular biologist, educator*
Hopen, Herbert John *horticulture educator*
Hu, Kejin *molecular and stem cell biologist*
Iltis, Hugh Hellmut *botanist, educator, environmental advocate*
Jeanne, Robert Lawrence *entomologist, educator*
Joranson, David Eric *research scientist*
Kaesberg, Paul Joseph *virology researcher*
Kang, Iksoon *research scientist*
Lan, Que *science educator*
Lorimer, Craig Gordon *ecologist, educator*
Meisner, Lorraine Faxon *geneticist*
Mertz, Janet Elaine *molecular biology researcher, educator, consultant*
Newcomb, Eldon Henry *retired botany educator*
Pella, Milton Orville *science educator*
Reps, Thomas William *science educator, small business owner*
Roseberry, James Alan *retired science educator*
Sheffield, Lewis Glosson *physiologist*
Susman, Millard *geneticist, educator*
Thomson, James Alexander *molecular biologist, educator*
Timmins, Robert *biologist*
Whitlon, Donna Sue *neuroscientist, researcher*
Wuethrich, Marcel *research scientist*

Menasha
Gonya, Teresa Joanne *biology professor*

Menomonee Falls
Janzen, Norine Madelyn Quinlan *clinical laboratory scientist*

Merton
Rheineck, Wendy Lynn *science educator*

Milwaukee
Buntin, John D. *biology professor*
Chrzanowska-Wodnicka, Magdalena B. *research scientist*
Giacinti, Louis Anthony *science educator, writer*
Munroe, Stephen H. *biology professor*
Prantil, Vincent Carl *science educator*

Oconomowoc
Stout, William E. *science educator*

Sheboygan
Abler, Ronald Francis *geography educator*

Stevens Point
Biasca, Karyn *science educator*
Long, Charles Alan *retired biology professor, museum director*
Rosenfield, Robert Norman *biology professor*

Superior
Stewart, Richard Dow *science educator*

Waukesha
Smith, Alexandra Helena *microbiologist, director*

Wautoma
Tennessen, Kenneth J. *retired entomologist*

Whitewater
Adams, Rick Alan *biologist, educator*

WYOMING

Big Horn
Canterbury, Jacqueline Lee *biology professor*

Jackson
Cox, Paul Alan *ethnobotanist, educator*

Laramie
Ford, Stephen P. *biology professor*
Lewis, Randolph Vance *molecular biologist, researcher*
Lockwood, Jeffrey Alan *entomologist*
Stefanovic, Margareta *science educator*

Teton Village
McCollister, Christopher Michael *forester*

TERRITORIES OF THE UNITED STATES

GUAM

Mangilao
Yang, Jian *food scientist, educator*

PUERTO RICO

Mayaguez
Montalvo-Rodriguez, Rafael R. *microbiologist, educator*
Pastrana, Belinda *science educator, researcher*

San Juan
Dunbar, Donald Churchill *neuroscientist, anthropologist*
Espino, Ana M. *parasitology and immunology educator, researcher*
Katar, Sri Lakshmi *science educator*

VIRGIN ISLANDS

St Thomas
King, Lillia Elise *histologist, educator*

CANADA

ALBERTA

Calgary
Jones, Geoffrey Melvill *physiology research educator*

Edmonton
Babiuk, Lorne Alan *virologist, immunologist, researcher*
Gough, Denis Ian *geophysics educator*
Stelck, Charles Richard *geology educator*

BRITISH COLUMBIA

Anmore
Ribary, Urs *neuroscientist, educator*

Sidney
Bigelow, Margaret Elizabeth Barr (M.E. Barr) *retired botany educator*
Kendrick, William Bryce *biologist, consultant, editor, writer*

Vancouver
Blair, Robert *animal science administrator, educator, researcher*
Donaldson, Edward Mossop *research scientist, marine biologist, consultant*
Jones, David Robert *retired zoology educator*
Lindsey, Casimir Charles *zoologist, educator*
Mc Lean, Donald Millis *microbiologist, educator, pathologist, pediatrician*
McNeill, John Hugh *pharmaceutical sciences educator*
Phillips, Anthony George *neurobiology researcher*
Shaw, Michael *biologist, educator*
Sinclair, Alastair James *geology educator*

White Rock
Phillips, John Edward *zoologist, educator*

MANITOBA

Winnipeg
Persaud, Trivedi Vidhya Nandan *anatomy educator, researcher, consultant*

NEWFOUNDLAND AND LABRADOR

Saint John's
Rochester, Michael Grant *geophysics educator*

NOVA SCOTIA

Halifax
Hall, Brian Keith *biology professor, writer*
Mann, Kenneth Henry *marine ecologist*

ONTARIO

Guelph
Bewley, John Derek *botany researcher, educator*

Hamilton
Blajchman, Morris Aaron *science educator, physician*

Kingston
Leggett, William C. *biology professor, academic administrator*
Wyatt, Gerard Robert *biology professor, researcher*

London
Kang, Chil-Yong *virologist, immunology educator*
Lala, Peeyush Kanti *research scientist, educator*

North York
Davey, Kenneth George *biologist, educator, academic administrator*
Regan, David *neuroscientist*

Ottawa
Baum, Bernard Rene *research scientist*
Carty, Arthur John *science policy advisor, research administrator*
Holahan, Matthew Richard *science educator*
Perry, Malcolm Blythe *biologist, researcher*
Storey, Kenneth Bruce *biology professor*
Veizer, Ján *geology educator*
Whitehead, J. Rennie *science administrator, consultant*

Richmond Hill
Liew, Choong Chin *research scientist, educator*

Scarborough
White, Calvin John *zoo executive, zoological association executive, financial manager*

Stittsville
MacLeod, Robert Angus *retired microbiology educator, researcher*

Toronto
Chandra, Ranjit Kumar *research scientist, educator, physician*
Cook, Stephen Arthur *mathematics and computer science educator*
Dunlop, David John *geophysics educator, researcher*
Liversage, Richard Albert *cell biologist, educator*
MacLennan, David Herman *research scientist, educator*
Masui, Yoshio *zoology educator*
Pawson, Anthony J. *molecular biologist*
Siminovitch, Louis *geneticist, educator, scientist*
Tobe, Stephen Solomon *zoology educator*

Waterloo
Warner, Barry Gregory *ecologist, educator*

QUEBEC

Laval
Bourget, Edwin Robert *marine ecologist, educator*
Talbot, Pierre Joseph *microbiologist, researcher*

Montreal
Carroll, Robert Lynn *biology professor, paleontologist, curator, museum director*
Chang, Thomas Ming Swi *research scientist, biotechnologist, educator*
Milic-Emili, Joseph *physiologist, educator*
Mysak, Lawrence Alexander *oceanographer, climatologist and mathematics educator*

Quebec City
Potvin, Pierre *physiologist, educator*

Saint Jean Sur Richelieu
Trudel, Marc J. *botanist, educator*

SASKATCHEWAN

Saskatoon
Huang, Pan Ming *soil science educator*

Burnaby
Alava Saltos, Juan Jose *research scientist*

Laval
Déziel, Eric *microbiologist, educator*

Sainte Anne de Bellevue
Grant, William Frederick *geneticist, biosystematist, educator*

AUSTRALIA

Hillaries
Jones, John Brian *agriculturist*

Lindfield
Morgan, Vincent Thomas *research scientist, consultant*

Sydney
Cardona, Beatriz *research scientist*
Shine, John *molecular geneticist, researcher, biochemist*

Townsville
Dobbs, Kirstin Anne *marine life administrator*

BELGIUM

Antwerp
Snyders, Dirk Johan *electrophysiologist and biophysicist educator*

Brussels
Muccioli, Giulio G. *science educator*

BRAZIL

Belém
Lainson, Ralph *parasitologist, researcher*

Pelotas
Valente, Ana Luisa Schifino *animal scientist, educator*

CAYMAN ISLANDS

Georgetown
James, Winston Clive *agriculturist, environmental services administrator, department chairman*

CHILE

Talca
Casaretto, José A. *plant biologist*

CHINA

Beijing
Liu, Yi-Xun *reproductive biologist, academician, researcher*
Yuan, Longping *agronomist*

Shenzhen
Yu, Gang *science educator*

Xi'an
Zhao, Wenming *retired biochemistry and molecular biology educator*

CROATIA

Zagreb
Kniewald, Jasna *toxicologist, educator, scientist*

CZECH REPUBLIC

Brno
Hřib, Jiří Emil *plant physiologist*

Prague
Říman, Josef *biology professor*
Sebek, Michael *research scientist, entrepreneur, educator*

ECUADOR

Quito
Del Pino, Eugenia M. *biology professor*

EGYPT

Giza
El-Mougy, Nehal Samy *plant pathologist, researcher*
Zaki, Kamal El-Din Mahmoud *veterinarian, educator*

Rossitta line
Hafez, Shireen Abdelgawad *veterinarian, educator, anatomist*

ENGLAND

Beaworthy
Richards, Sir Rex Edward *research scientist, academic administrator*

Cambridge
Baulcombe, David C. *plant scientist*
Gurdon, Sir John Bertrand *cell biologist*
Heisler, Lora Katherine *neuroscientist*
Hinde, Robert Aubrey *biologist, psychologist, educator*
Klug, Aaron *molecular biologist*
Moffatt, Henry Keith *science educator*
Rees, Martin John *astronomy educator*
Walker, John Ernest *molecular biologist, researcher*

Coventry
Feelisch, Martin *research scientist, consultant*

Kent Cranbrook
Hattersley-Smith, Geoffrey Francis *retired government research scientist*

Leeds
Phillips, Oliver *tropical forest ecologist, researcher*

Leicester
Jeffreys, Sir Alec John *geneticist, educator*

London
Evans, Christopher *biotechnologist*
Morris, Desmond (John) *zoologist, writer, artist*

Oxford
Bodmer, Sir Walter Fred *cancer research administrator*
Krebs, John Richard *zoologist, science administrator*
Nasmyth, Kim *science association director*

Saint Ives
Biggs, Peter Martin *veterinary scientist, virologist*

Southampton
Morton, Newton Ennis *human geneticist*

Sutton Bonington
Campbell, Keith H. S. *cell biologist, embryologist, educator*

ESTONIA

Tallinn
Lippmaa, Endel *science educator, researcher*

FINLAND

Helsinki
Ilus, Erkki Hannu *marine biologist, researcher*

FRANCE

Aubagne
Chermann, Jean Claude *virologist, researcher*

Compiegne
Dubuisson, Bernard Louis *science educator, administrator*

Fontenay-sous-Bois
Doucas, Vassilis *biologist, researcher*

Gif-sur-Yvette
Duplessy, Jean Claude *research scientist*

Limoges
Menier, Robert Joseph *physiologist*

Lys-Lez-Lannoy
Ledoux, Jean-Marie *veterinarian*

Paris
Bensimon, Aaron *biotechnology company executive*
De-Thé, Guy Blaudin *research scientist, educator*
Jacob, François *biologist, educator*
Kourilsky, François Michel *research scientist*
Louvard, Daniel François *cell biologist, researcher*
Montagnier, Luc Antoine *virologist*
Raharinaivo, André Léon *research scientist, educator*

Saint Etienne
Vergnaud, Jean-Maurice *science educator, researcher*

Strasbourg
van Regenmortel, Marc Hubert Victor *virologist, educator, director*

Vandoeuvre-les-Nancy
Blazy, Pierre François *science educator, consulting metallurgist*

GERMANY

Bad Nauheim
Engel, Felix Benedikt Salomon *cell biologist, researcher*

Cologne
Thiede, Walther *research scientist, consultant, writer*

Drolshagen
Arend, Peter *retired biologist, physician, allergist, lab administrator*

Halle
Parthier, Benno *biologist*

Heidelberg
Lyko, Frank *molecular biologist*

Leipzig
Pääbo, Svante *molecular biologist, biochemist*

Regensburg
Stetter, Karl Otto *microbiologist, educator*

Taunusstein
Ruppert (Metzger), Thomas Erich *cell and molecular biologist, quality assurance and regulatory professional*

GHANA

Accra
Jones, Monty P. *science administrator*

GREECE

Athens
Meletiadis, Joseph *microbiologist, educator*

GRENADA

Saint Georges
Forde, Martin S. *science educator*

HUNGARY

Szeged
Keszthelyi, Lajos *science educator*

INDIA

Karnal
Dhanker, Sultan Singh *agriculturist, researcher*

Kolkata
Patra, Amlan Kumar *animal scientist, educator*

New Delhi
Kumar, Virender *weed scientist*
Pandey, Girdhar Kumar *molecular biologist*
Srivastava, Radhey Shyam *research scientist*
Tripathy, Baishnab C. *science educator*

ISRAEL

Rehovot
Sachs, Leo *geneticist, educator*

ITALY

Rome
Levi-Montalcini, Rita *neurobiologist, researcher*

Trieste
Rao, Chintamani Nagesa Ramachandra *science educator, Indian government official, academic administrator*

JAPAN

Aichi
Kato, Nobuo *bacteriology educator*

Chiba
Arai, Toshihiko *retired microbiology and immunology educator*
Hattori, Naozo *science educator*

Kagawa
Fujita, Masayuki *biologist, educator*

Kawasaki
Yoshida, Kenichi *veterinarian, biology educator*

Saitama
Ito, Masao *neuroscience researcher*

Sanyo-Onoda
Kobayashi, Shunsuke *science educator*

Shinjuku
Ikari, Katsunori *geneticist, rheumatologist, orthopedic surgeon*

Tokyo
Fujino, Kazuo *marine geneticist*
Ishii, Akira *parasitologist, allergist, malariologist*
Kawahara, Hiroyuki *molecular cell biologist professor*
Kitani, Osamu *agriculture educator*
Kurokawa, Kaneyuki *science administrator*
Omura, Satoshi *research scientist, administrator*
Takizawa, Yukio *medical ecologist*
Togo, Hisatake *research institute administrator*
Toyoshima, Chikashi *structural biologist, educator*

Tsukuba
Akiyama, Kayo *neuroscientist, researcher*
Sutoo, Den'etsu *neuroscientist, researcher*

Yokkaichi
Tanaka, Ichirou *science educator*

KUWAIT

Kuwait
Rahman, Abdur *neuroscientist, educator*

NETHERLANDS

Haren
Alonso, David *ecologist*

PANAMA

APO
Condit, Richard Stuart *biologist*

REPUBLIC OF KOREA

Busan
Choi, Hong-Kyu *science educator*

Changwon
Lee, Youngseon *science educator, researcher*

Gyeongsan
Chang, Cheon Young *biology professor*

Jeollabuk
Chung, Ee-Yung *marine biologist, educator*

Jeonju
Chae, Jong-Chan *microbiologist, educator*

Seongnam
Seol, Dai-Wu *geneticist, educator*

Seoul
Cha, Doowon *research scientist*
Choi, Won Il *entomologist, researcher*
Chun, Jang Ho *science educator, researcher*
Kim, Baik-Ho *biology professor*
Kim, Yong-Hak *microbiologist*
Kwon, E. Hyock *science academy executive, preventive medicine physician*
Park, Sang-Dai *molecular biologist, educator*
Yoon, Kisun *food scientist, educator*

Suwon
Kim, Sung Ki *research scientist*

Yeongam
Lee, Kyung-Tae *professor, director*

ROMANIA

Bucharest
Badic, Mihai *research scientist*

RUSSIA

Archangelsk
Koubassov, Roman Victorovich *physiologist, researcher*

SINGAPORE

Singapore
Yoo, Byounghyun *research scientist*

SPAIN

Barcelona
Rissech, Carme *research scientist*

Barcelonass
Laricchia-Robbio, Leopoldo *molecular biologist, educator*

Cordoba
Vaamonde-Martin, Diana Maria *biologist, embryologist, researcher, educator*

Valencia
Docavo Alberti, Ignacio *zoology educator*

SWEDEN

Stockholm
Käll, Lukas *biotechnologist*

SWITZERLAND

Basel
Arber, Werner *microbiologist*
Gehring, Walter Jakob *biology professor, geneticist*

Geneva
Duboule, Denis *biology researcher, educator*

Zurich
Wüthrich, Kurt *molecular biologist, biophysicist, educator*

TAIWAN

Keelung
Chin-Feng, Lin *science educator*

Taipei
Lee, Hsuan-Shu *biotechnologist*
Tzyy-Jiann, Wang *science educator*

UNITED ARAB EMIRATES

Al Ain
AbuQamar, Synan F. *biology professor, researcher*

Al-Ain Abu-Dhabi
Ijaz, Muhammad Khalid Khalid *virologist, immunologist*

Dubai
Subair, Saad Osman Abdalla *science educator*

Sharjah
Abed, Farid H. *science educator*

UZBEKISTAN

Tashkent
Shakirov, Zair Saatovich *biologist, researcher*

VIETNAM

Hanoi
Nam, Ha Hai *computer science educator, researcher*

ADDRESS UNPUBLISHED

Able, Kenneth Paul *biology professor*
Abuzeineh, Alisa Amanda *research scientist*
Acker, Robert Flint *retired microbiologist*
Addo, Charles Kwame *science educator*
Agarwala, Ranjeet *science educator*
Aguirregabiria, Victor *science educator*
Ahearne, John Francis *science foundation director, researcher*
Ahrens, Franklin Alfred *veterinary pharmacology educator*
Aires, Julie H. *biology professor*
Alcantara, Adriana *science educator*
Alfano, Robert R. *science and engineering educator*
Allen, Merrill James *marine biologist*
Alroy, John *research scientist*
Althouse, Gary Carl *veterinary physiologist*
Altman, Lawrence Gene *biologist, educator*
Ancona, Kier Alexis *zoologist*
Anderson, Elaine Janet *science educator*
Arditi, Aries Robert *research scientist*
Arking, Robert *geneticist, gerontologist, educator*
Armstrong, Donald *biochemistry, pathophysiology educator*
Arnott, Howard Joseph *biology professor, dean*
Atkin, J Myron *science educator*
Au, Algie *biology professor*
Bäckman, Cristina M. *molecular biologist, biomedical researcher*
Bala, Sriram *clinical research professional*
Baltzell, Kimberly *research scientist*
Baranowski, Marcin *biology professor*
Barefoot, Aldos Cortez, Jr. *retired forester, educator*
Barnard, Donald Roy *medical and veterinary entomologist*
Barnes, Robert F *agronomist*
Bartlett, Denise Margaret *science educator*
Basu, Nikhil Kumar *research scientist*
Bathala, Neeti *science educator*
Beattie, Michael Stephen *neuroscientist, educator*
Bedigian, Dorothea *botanist*
Beggs, William H. *microbiologist, researcher*
Beiswenger, Jane Miller *retired science educator*
Belfer, Inna *research scientist, medical educator*
Benedetti, Michael M. *science educator*
Bentley, Charles Raymond *geophysics educator*
Berhe, Asmeret Asefaw *science educator*
Berka, Randy M. *molecular biologist, director*
Berra, P. Bruce *computer science educator*
Bers, Donald Martin *physiology educator*
Bhatt, Jagdish Jeyshanker *retired science educator, author*
Bick, Katherine Livingstone *neuroscientist, educator, researcher*
Bidwell, Roger Grafton Shelford *biologist, educator*
Biglaiser, Glen *science educator*
Bishop, Douglas Krumbhaar *biologist, educator*
Blackwell, James E. *retired science educator*
Blauer, Derwin Ann Taylor *educator*
Blaylock, Russell Lane *biology professor, retired neurosurgeon*
Blum, Samuel *retired research scientist*
Boardman, Paul Craig *science educator*
Bocchetta, Maurizio *molecular biologist, educator*
Bolie, Victor Wayne *molecular biologist, researcher*
Bonner, John Tyler *biology professor*
Borisy, Gary G. *science administrator, researcher, molecular biology professor*
Boyle, Tatiana Gennadievna *research scientist*
Brar, Gurdarshan Singh *soil scientist, researcher*
Breunig, Joshua Joshn *biologist, researcher*
Brown, Emery N. *neuroscientist, educator, statistician, anesthesiologist*
Brown, Jeannette Elizabeth *retired science educator*
Browne, Frederick Douglas *physiologist, educator*
Brumbaugh, Steven Gerard *biology professor*
Bryan, Billie Marie (Mrs. James A. Mackey) *retired biologist*
Bubak, Vit *research scientist*
Bullard, Ervin Trowbridge *tropical horticulturist*
Bullas, Leonard Raymond *retired microbiology professor*
Burkes, Lionel Seaton *science educator, writer, researcher*
Burton, Lawrence DeVere *agriculturist, educator*
Butler, Serena Jane Johnson *computer networking educator, small business owner*
Byrd, Isaac Burlin *retired biologist*
Caldwell, Elwood Fleming *food scientist, educator*
Caldwell, Heather Kingsley *biology professor*
Cannizzaro, Linda Ann *geneticist, researcher*
Caplan, Allan *biology professor*
Carlson, Kimberly R. *veterinarian*
Carol, Clericuzio Louise *geneticist, researcher*
Carter, Tonya M. *science educator*
Cartwright, Elizabeth *science educator*
Catherine, Anne Scine *theology educator*
Cavalli-Sforza, Luigi Luca *geneticist, educator*
Cellarius, Richard Andrew *biology professor*
Chacko, George Kuttickal *management science educator, consultant*
Chase, Peter Paul *retired science educator*
Chaudhuri, Jyoti Prakash *geneticist*
Chen, James Kenneth *chemical biology professor*
Chen, Jiangping *science educator*
Chen, Weifeng *science educator*
Cheng, Yue *molecular geneticist, pathologist*
Chitnis, Ashay *research scientist*
Chun, Asaph Y. *research scientist*
Clark-Shanks, K. Audrey *biology professor*
Clayton, David A(lvin) *biology professor*
Coffman, Diana *biology professor*
Cohen, Stanley *retired biochemistry educator*
Conover, Lloyd Hillyard *retired research scientist*
Corbett, Brooke Myers *science educator*
Costa, Fabricio *research scientist*
Coyle, Marie Bridget *retired microbiologist, lab administrator*
Craft, Suzanne *neuroscientist, educator*
Crane, Frederick Loring *biochemistry educator*
Cravats, Monroe *science educator*
Creech, John Lewis *botanist, consultant*
Cronin, Stephen Burke *science educator*
Crowell, Dring Needham *biology educator*
Crowell, Kenneth Leland *biology educator*
Curran, Tom *biology professor, researcher*
Dacus, Judy McLellan *biology professor*
Dagne, Getachew A. *biostatistician*
Dai, Qi *science educator*
D'Alesandro, Philip Anthony *parasitologist, immunologist, retired medical educator*
Daly, Benjamin *marine biologist, researcher*
Dame, Richard Franklin *marine biology educator*
Danehy, Robert Joseph *aquatic biologist*
Darzynkiewicz, Zbigniew D. *research scientist*
Daskalova, Sasha *molecular biologist*
Datta, Utpal *science educator, researcher*
Davis, John William *toxicologist*
Davis, William Edwin *retired science educator*
Deaciuc, Ion Victor *molecular biologist, researcher*
DeBakey, Lois *science administrator, educator*
Decker, Walter Johns *toxicologist*
de la Torre, Jack Carlos *clinical neuroscientist*
DeMorrow, Sharon *molecular biologist, educator*
Despommier, Dickson Donald *microbiology educator, parasitologist*
DeWoskin, Robert S. *toxicologist*
Diaz-Castillo, Carlos *research scientist*
Diefenbacher, Eric H. *science educator*
Dingman, Stanley Lawrence *retired science educator*
Dodson, Carolyn McCroskey *biology professor, consultant*
Doman, Elvira *retired science administrator*
Dorman, David Christopher *toxicologist, researcher*
Doty, Scott William *science educator*
Duenes, Annette S. *science educator, consultant*
Dugan, Patrick Raymond *microbiologist, educator, dean*
Duncombe, Tcherina Swilley *biology professor*
Dunn, Adrian John *neuroscientist*
Durbha, Surya *science educator*
Dutta, Kaushik *biologist*
Eduardo, Lau C. *molecular biologist, researcher*
Edwards, Charles *neuroscientist, educator*
Ehling, Stefan *food scientist*
Ellner, Paul Daniel *retired microbiologist*
Enroth-Cugell, Christina Alma Elisabeth *neurophysiologist, educator*
Erickson, Edward Leonard *biotechnologist, consultant*
Erives, Albert J. *biology professor*
Evans, William Lee *biologist, educator*
Faison, Edward Kerr *ecologist*
Farah, Ibrahim O. *microbiologist, biomedical researcher*
Farah, Martha J. *neuroscientist, educator*
Farkas, Daniel Frederick *food science and technology educator*
Fiedler, Carl E *retired forestry professor*
Finley, Emma Rosemary *retired science educator*
Fischer, Charlotte Froese *research scientist, educator*
Fisher, Bruce Albert *anatomy and physiology educator*
Fisher, Dale Dunbar *animal scientist, dairy nutritionist*
Fiskin, Arthur Max, Jr. *retired biologist, educator*
Fiszer-Szafarz, Berta (Berta Safars) *research scientist*
Fitch, Brooke *biology professor*
Flemming, David Paul *biologist*
Fletcher, Ronald Darling *microbiologist educator*
Fournier, R. E. Keith *retired biologist*
Fox, Michael Wilson *veterinarian, animal scientist*
Foy, Charles Daley *retired soil scientist*
Frank, Linda Maria *science educator*
Franks, Allen P. *retired research institute executive, educator*
Freeland, Stephen John *biology professor*
Freeman, Michael Elliot *science educator*
French, John Robert Putnam III *biologist*

Gabor-Hotchkiss, Magda *research scientist, librarian*
Gage, L. Patrick (Leonard Patrick Gage) *biotechnology & pharmaceutical industry consultant*
Gale, Lacey Andrews *research scientist*
Gardner, Sandi B. *retired biology professor*
Garelnabi, Mahdi Omer Hamid *research scientist*
Gatewood, George David *science educator*
Gay, William Ingalls *veterinarian, retired health science association administrator*
Gee, Glendon W. *retired soil scientist*
Gerritsen, Mary Ellen *vascular and cell biologist*
Gift, James Joseph *aquatic toxicologist*
Gilbert, Charles D. *neurobiologist*
Gillett, James Warren *retired ecotoxicology educator*
Gillette, Nancy E. *entomologist, researcher*
Glysch, Randall Lee *research scientist*
Goetsch, Peggy *biology professor*
Goffredi, Shana Kaye *marine biologist, educator*
Goldman, Bruce Dale *biology educator*
Gonzalez-Flecha, Beatriz *biology professor*
Goodall, Jane *zoologist*
Goodrich, James A. *veterinarian, researcher*
Gowans, Sir James Learmonth *retired science administrator, immunologist*
Graham, Terrence Lee *plant pathologist, educator*
Grey, Robert Dean *biology professor, former academic administrator*
Grunder, Hermann A. *science administrator, director, research scientist*
Guda, Kishore *research scientist*
Gulmahamad, Hanif *entomologist, consultant*
Guo, Jiantao *biotechnologist*
Guo, Mingruo *food scientist, educator*
Gurumurthi, Sudhanva *science educator*
Habermann, Helen *botanist, educator*
Haibach, Pamela S. *science educator*
Halder, Indrani *research scientist*
Hamdan, Lubna K. *science educator, researcher*
Hamil, Burnette Wolf *science educator*
Han, Renzhi *research scientist*
Hand, Peter James *neurobiologist, educator*
Hanks, Brian *science educator*
Harlin, Marilyn Miler *marine botany educator, researcher, consultant*
Hashemi, Shohreh S. *science educator, researcher*
Haskins, Steve *retired veterinarian*
Hatchwell, Eli *research scientist*
Hauptmann, Randal Mark *biotechnologist*
Haydel, Shelley E. *microbiologist, researcher*
He, Biyu Jade *neuroscientist*
Heinicke, Ralph Martin *science administrator, consultant*
Heintz, Michael Alfred *biology professor*
Heitzman, Deborah Ann *cell biologist*
Helgeson, John Paul *plant pathology and botany educator*
Hemmingsen, Barbara Bruff *retired microbiologist*
Henderson, Wiley Joseph *biology educator*
Hilliard, Sam Bowers *geography educator*
Hillis, William Daniel *biology professor*
Hladik, Florian *research scientist*
Holland, Branti Latessa *science educator*
Hollister, Jeffrey William *ecologist*
Honour, Lynda Charmaine *research scientist, psychotherapist, educator*
Hopkins, Robert Charles *chemistry and biophysics educator*
Hotchkiss, Andrew *biologist*
Hoty, JoAnn *biology professor*
Hou, Songming *science educator*
Howard-Peebles, Patricia N. *clinical cytogeneticist*
Hoye, Robert Earl *systems science educator*
Hunter, Malcolm Llewellyn, Jr. *biology professor*
Irwin, Nina *neuroscientist, educator*
Iyigun, Cem *science educator*
Izadjoo, Mina Jassemzadeh *microbiologist*
Izaguirre, George *retired microbiologist*
Jae-Il, Kim *research scientist*
Jangid, Kamlesh *microbiologist*
Januszewicz Ekstrom, von Lubitz Dag Konrad *scientist consultant*
Jen, Philip Hung Sun *science educator, researcher*
Jenkins, Lekelia Danielle *ecologist, researcher*
Jenkins, Stephen Philip *biology professor*
Ji, Zhenyu *cell biologist*
Joghi Thatha Gowder, Sivakumar *research scientist*
Johnson-McKee, Marian *biology professor*
Jones, Richard Hunn *biostatistician, researcher, educator*
Kaback, David Brian *molecular biologist*
Kaliski, Lucy Anne *science educator, consultant*
Kamrin, Michael Arnold *toxicology educator*
Kao, Tzu-Jen *research scientist*
Kartha, Kutty Krishnan *retired plant pathologist*
Kelder, Dorothy Mae *science educator*
Keller, Nadya Clark *retired biochemistry educator, researcher*
Kelly, Michele Patrice *neuroscientist, researcher*
Kerr, Gregory Peter *biology professor*
Kessler, Edwin *meteorology educator, consultant*
Keum, JongMin *research scientist*
Kieffer, Tara L. *virologist*
Kihega, Harold G. *biology professor*
Kimbrell, Deborah Ann *geneticist, educator*
Kirsteuer, Ernst Karl Eberhart *biologist, curator*
Klausner, Richard Daniel *cell biologist, researcher*
Klein, Marc *retired neuroscientist*
Knox, James Russell, Jr. *biophysical chemistry educator*
Ko, Jonghan *agronomist*
Koenig, Maureen Catherine *science educator*
Koka, Sai Sudha *research scientist*
Kolb, James A. *science foundation director, writer*
Kopan, Raphael *molecular biologist, consultant, medical educator, researcher*
Kozak, Elizabeth *biology professor*
Kraus, Jan P. *research scientist, educator*
Krugman, Stanley Liebert *retired science administrator, geneticist*
Krupa, Shiva *cell biologist*
Kumar, Kanagaraj Ganesh *biologist, educator*
Kumazawa, Risa *science educator*
Kung, Patrick Chung-Shu *biotechnologist*
Kushlan, James Anthony *science administrator, educator, conservationist, writer*
Kwon, Jaimyoung (Jaimie Kwon) *science educator*
Kwon, Jin-Ah *research scientist*
Kyesmu, Pius Michael *biology professor, researcher*
LaBonte, Melissa J. *biology professor*
LaCrue, Alexis Nichole *parasitologist*
Lafever, Howard Nelson *botanist, educator, geneticist*
Laksanalamai, Pongpan *microbiologist*
Lamb, Charles Franklin *biology professor, neuroscientist*
Lamb, Tiffany Dean *biology professor*
Langer, Glenn Arthur *cellular physiologist, educator*
Lansing, Elizabeth Ellen *science educator*
Lapiz-Bluhm, Maria Danet Sanchez *neuroscientist, medical/surgical nurse*
Lattanzio, Stephen Paul *astronomy educator*
Lau, Joann M. *biology professor*
Lauter, Judith Larue *neuroscientist*
Lavassani, Fereshteh *science educator*
Layne, James Nathaniel *retired vertebrate biologist*
Lazell, James Draper *biologist*
Leath, Kenneth Thomas *plant pathologist, educator, agriculturist, consultant*
Lee, Marvina Sue *science educator*
Lemke, Greg Erwin *biology professor*
Le Quéré, Jean François Marie *scientific instrumentation researcher*
Levin, Pavel *science educator, researcher*
Levins, Richard *biologist, educator*
Li, Qian *research scientist*
Li, Yawen *research scientist*
Lind, Owen Thomas *biology professor*
Liner, Ernest *biologist*
Lippincott, James Andrew *retired biochemistry and biological sciences educator*
Litscher, Eveline *biology professor*
Liu, Hongjie *biotechnologist, educator*
Livdahl, Todd Philip *biology professor*
Lotsch, Alexander *scientist*
Low, Morton David *retired neuroscientist, healthcare educator, consultant*
Lynch, John Thomas *retired science administrator, physicist*
Mandal, Prabir Kumar *biologist, educator*
Mantena, Ravi *business educator*
Mao, Weidong *science educator*
Marino, Deirdre J. *science educator*
Mark, Hon Fong Louie *cytogeneticist*
Martin, Joseph Vinson *neuroscientist, educator*
Martin, Marcia D. *science educator*
Martino, Joseph Paul *research scientist, researcher*
Matlock, John Hudson *retired science administrator, materials engineer*
Mattox, Johnny Lynn *biologist, educator*
Maunder, Addison Bruce *agronomic research company executive*
McCann, Peter Paul *biology researcher, educator*
McClellan, Roger Orville *toxicologist*
McDowell, Elizabeth Mary *retired pathology educator*
McEliece, Michelle *biology professor*
McGarvey, Daniel John *ecologist, educator*
McGhee, Laura L. *molecular biologist, researcher*
McMenamin, Sarah Kelly *biologist, educator*
McShefferty, John *retired research executive personal care, industry executive consultant*
McSwain, Byrdie Engle *laboratory scientist, immunohematologist*
Meacham, David Adam *biologist*
Menn, Julius Joel *retired research scientist, consultant*
Meyer, Robert R. *retired science educator*
Miekka, Jeanette Ann *retired science educator*
Miller, G(erson) H(arry) *science administrator, mathematician, computer scientist, chemist*
Miller, Matthew Jason *science educator, director*
Miller, Patrick William *research scientist, educator*
Minagawa, Teiichi *molecular biologist*
Mitra, Rupak *molecular biologist*
Miziorko, Henry M. *research scientist, educator*
Monjan, Andrew Arthur *retired neuroscientist*
Moon, Il-Ju *meteorologist*
Moore, Thomas Andrew *biotechnology executive*
Morden, Robert Dean *biology professor*
Morgan, Sandra *science educator*
Moritz, Chad Henry *research scientist*
Moss, Thomas Henry *science foundation director, physicist*
Mudavanhu, Blessing *research scientist*
Murarka, Shyam Prasad *science and engineering educator, administrator*
Murphy, Kimberly Ann *biology professor*
Murphy, Lesley Ryann *geneticist*
Mutale, Christian Thales *research scientist*
Naidoo, Robin *biologist, researcher*
Nanos, George Peter, Jr. *former science administrator, military officer, physicist*
Nichols, Argie Nell *science educator*
Nichols, Harvey *biology professor*
Nikaido, Hiroshi *microbiologist*
Norman, Thena Monts Durham *microbiologist, researcher, health facility administrator*
Nyberg, Stanley Eric *research scientist*
Oberste, Steve *microbiologist*
Olshan, Judd David *human ecologist*
Ölveczky, Peter Csaba *science educator*
O'Neill, Megan O. *biology professor*
Ong, Han Chuan *biology professor*
Ostlind, Dan A. *retired parasitologist*
Paganelli, Charles Victor *physiologist, educator*
Pai, Balakrishna S. *research scientist*
Pan, Ya-Hui Laurie *toxicologist, director*
Pandya, Jyotsna *biotechnologist*
Park, Inyong *science educator*
Parker, Alan John *veterinary neurologist, educator, researcher*
Pathela, Preeti *research scientist, educator*
Patterson, Laurie J. *science educator*
Pavelko, Christina Alison *biology teaching assistant*
Peeples, Mary Anne Baumann *science educator*
Penfold, Linda Margaret *reproductive physiologist, researcher*
Perschbacher, Peter Wesley *environmental science educator, research scientist*
Pervouchine, Dmitri *science educator*
Petrascheck, Michael *biologist, researcher*
Pianka, Eric Rodger *population biologist, educator*
Plotkin, Stanley Alan *virologist*
Pogue, Linda Sue *science educator*
Porter, Dan A. *biology professor, director*
Poteete, Anthony R. *molecular biologist, educator*
Pottekat, Anita *cell biologist*
Powell, Bradford Scott *research scientist, educator*
Prasad, Ashok *science educator*
Prentice, Howard Malcolm *research scientist, educator*
Proctor, Kenneth Gordon *physiology educator*
Pruitt, Robert E. *geneticist, educator*
Purves, William Kirkwood *biologist, educator*
Qu, Liangti *research scientist*
Rakkolainen, Ismo *research scientist*
Rall, Wilfrid *neuroscientist, sculptor*
Ramasamy, Shaker Gnanasekaran *science educator*
Rannala, Bruce *biology professor*
Rao, Anil Vithala *science educator*
Renner, Swen *zoologist*
Richardson, Stephen Giles *biotechnologist, research and development company executive, writer*
Riggs, Penny Kaye *molecular geneticist*
Riley, Sally Jean *retired science educator*
Rischbieter, Michael O. *biology professor*
Robb, Sarah Rainey *biology professor*
Robinson, Thomas Christopher *health science educator*
Rodecker, Stephen Bailey *science specialist, secondary school educator*
Roeller, Herbert Alfred *biology professor*
Rogers, Jack David *plant pathologist, educator*
Rogers, Ruth Frances *retired microbiologist*
Ross, Amanda Joanne *biology professor*
Rubinoff, Ira *biologist, researcher, conservationist*
Ruby, Norman F. *research scientist*
Rush, Loretta G. *biology professor*
Russell, Liane Brauch *retired geneticist*
Saalfeld, Fred Erich *science educator, researcher*
Salkind, Michael Jay *science administrator, metallurgical engineer*
Salman, Abduljabbar A. *agronomist*
Sanger, Frederick *retired molecular biologist*
Sattler, Rolf *retired plant morphologist, educator*
Schaller, Jean *geneticist*
Scherer, James R. *research scientist*
Schilling, Emily Gaenzle *research scientist*
Schlaepfer, Isabel Rubio *research scientist*
Schmaeman, Cynthia *biology professor*
Schmidt, Torrance *horticulturist*
Schoof, Rosalind *toxicologist*
Schreiber, Kai Markus *neuroscientist*
Schultz, Stanley George *physiologist, educator, dean*
Scott, Carol *science educator*
Scott, David Clinton *research scientist*
Scott, T. Gordon *chemistry and math educator, writer*
Semyonov, Oleg G. *research scientist*
Seney, Erin E. *biologist, marine biologist*
Setser, Carole Sue *food scientist, educator*
Shagam, Janet Yagoda *educator, microbiologist*
Shahied, Ishak I. *science educator*
Shanbhag, Sachin *science educator, researcher*
Shannon, Marilyn McCusker *biologist, educator*
Shaoman, Yin *research scientist*
Shaw, Helen Lester Anderson *nutrition educator, researcher, retired dean*
Shealy, Harry E., Jr. *biology professor, consultant*
Sheild, Carolyn Jean *science educator*
Shevchuk, Nikolai Alexandrovich *biologist*
Shields, Joan Marie *microbiologist, parasitologist*
Shrotriya, Vishal *research scientist*
Sigle, John Walter *science educator*
Simin, Grigory *science educator*
Simpson, Frederick James *retired science administrator*
Simpson, Michael Marcial *science and technology specialist, consultant*
Simson, Jo Anne *retired anatomy and cell biology educator*
Singh, Jatinder Pal *research scientist, consultant*
Sivacolundhu, Ramesh Kumar *veterinarian*
Sjostrand, Fritiof Stig *biologist, educator*
Slayman, Carolyn Walch *geneticist, educator*
Sloan, Anne Elizabeth *food scientist, writer*
Smarr, Larry Lee *science administrator, astrophysicist, educator*
Smith, Catherine Marie *science educator*
Smith, Erin Ann *science educator*
Smith, Janice Yoder *biology professor*
Sojka, Gary Allan *biologist, educator, academic administrator*
South, Frank Edwin *physiologist, educator*
Sperelakis, Nicholas, Sr. *retired physiology and biophysics educator, researcher*
Spiegel, Melvin *retired biology professor*
Spiess, Eliot Bruce *biologist, educator*
Staley, Airica *biologist*
Stark, Nellie May *forester, ecologist, educator*
Steiner, Heinz *science professor, researcher*
Steinhardt, Alicia Ann *biology professor, director*
Steinhauer, Josefa Melissa *biologist*
Stone, Jonathan Francis *biology professor*
Sukoff Rizzo, Stacey J. *research scientist*
Sullivan, Amanda *science educator*
Sullivan, Harry Truman *research scientist*
Sun, Yongsheng Victor *educator*
Suranovic, Steven M. *science educator*
Sutton, Lee *biology professor*
Tadros, Fawzi M. *educator*
Tadros, Mohsen Shokry *agriculturist*
Talmage, David Wilson *retired microbiologist, educator, dean*
Tan, Songxin *science educator*
Tandler, Bernard *cell biology educator*
Tarro, Giulio *virologist*
Tartir, Samir *science educator*
Tehovnik, Edward Joseph *neuroscientist*
Telford, Sam Rountree, Jr. *zoologist*
Teulé, Florence *research scientist*
Thomas, Teresa Ann *retired microbiologist, educator*
Thompson, Herbert Alden *microbiologist, public health scientist*
Thompson, Nels F. *biology professor*
Thomson, Keith Stewart *biologist, author*
Tian, Feng *biologist, researcher*
Tingus, Steven James *physiologist, researcher*
Todhunter, John Anthony *toxicologist, consultant*
Town, Terrence Christopher *research scientist*
Trammel, Denise *science educator*
Trenholm, Laurie E. *horticulturist, educator*
Troyer, Alice Kay *library and computer skills educator*
Tytler, Linda Jean *emergency manager, state legislator*
Uddin, Mohammed Rafique *biology professor*
Ullman, Edwin Fisher *biotechnologist, consultant*
Unger, Paul Walter *retired soil scientist*
Uyeda, Steven *biology professor*
Uzgoren, Eray *science educator*
Valtier, Sandra *toxicologist*
Vann, Esther Martinez *science educator*
Vavala, Domenic Anthony *medical research scientist, educator, retired military officer*
Veloso, Francisco *science educator*
Villa-Komaroff, Lydia *molecular biologist, educator, health product executive, academic administrator*
Vincent, James Louis *biotechnology company executive*
Voss, Regis Dale *agronomist, educator*
Wahome, Joseph Muriuki *zoologist, educator*
Wallace, Robert Bruce *neuroscience educator*
Wang, Yu *science educator*
Warren, Dwight William III *physiology educator*
Watabe, Norimitsu *marine biologist, educator*
Watkins, Jeffrey Clifton *neuroscientist*
Watson, James Dewey *retired molecular biologist*
Webb Girard, Amy *research scientist*
Weber, Darren Lee *neuroscientist, researcher*
Webster, Henry de Forest *neuroscientist*
Weerasinghe, Kumudini Mangala (Kelly Weise) *science educator*
Weiland, Barbara J. *neuroscientist*
Weiner, Ruth Fleischmann *science educator*
Weinstein, Michael P. *marine scientist, administrator*
Weinstein, Milton Charles *decision scientist, educator*
Weir, Sara Hart *science and health policy consultant*
Wertz, Gail Williams *microbiologist, educator*
Westring, Christian Gustav *geneticist, consultant*
Whatley, Jillian Katri *physiologist, educator*
White, Beverly Jane *retired cytogeneticist*
White, Judith Miriam *biology professor*
Wiese, Richard *explorer, field scientist, journalist*
Wilkerson, Matt *biology professor*
Wilkinson, Stanley Ralph *retired agronomist*
Williams, George Christopher *biologist, ecology and evolution educator*
Williams, Scott Matthew *science educator*
Wilmut, Ian *biologist*
Wilson, Kenneth Geddes *physics research administrator*
Wilson, Mark Stephen *research scientist*
Wiltschko, Wolfgang *zoology educator*
Winstead, Melody *science educator*
Wiseman, Patryce Avsharian *ecologist*
Witte, Owen Neil *microbiologist, molecular biologist, educator*
Woodward, James Franklin *science educator*
Wott, John Arthur *retired arboretum and botanical garden executive, horticulture educator*
Wright, Theodore Robert Fairbank *biologist, educator*
Wu, Jian Young *science educator*
Xia, Yuan-Qing *research scientist*
Xiao, Jing *science educator, researcher*
Xu, Cailin *research scientist*
Xu, Dongmei *molecular biologist, director*
Xu, Jinghai J. (Jim Xu) *toxicologist, researcher*
Yan, Wei *research scientist*
Yang, Guo-Yuan *neuroscientist*
Yard, Michael *anatomy and physiology educator, retired military officer*
Yohn, David Stewart *virologist, retired science administrator*
Young, Judith Anne *animal conservationist*
Zeng, Xianmin *science educator*
Zhang, Hongtao *research scientist, engineer*
Zhao, Li-Ru *neuroscientist, educator*
Zharikov, Sergey Ivan *biologist, researcher*
Zhdanov, Boris *research scientist*
Zhuang, Hong *food scientist*
Zima, Hans Peter *science educator*
Zughaier, Susu M. *microbiologist, researcher, immunologist*
Zwislocki, Jozef John *neuroscience educator, researcher*

SCIENCE: MATHEMATICS AND COMPUTER SCIENCE *See also* INFORMATION TECHNOLOGY

UNITED STATES

ALABAMA

Attalla
Saffels, Anna Wayne Brothers *retired mathematician, educator*

Auburn
Govil, Narendra Kumar *mathematics professor*
Nane, Erkan *mathematics professor*

Auburn University
Johnson, Peter Dexter, Jr. *mathematics professor*
Liao, Ming *mathematics professor*

Birmingham
Peeples, William Dewey, Jr. *mathematics professor*

Reilly, Kevin Denis *computer scientist, educator*
Wheeler, Ruric E. *mathematics professor*
Whigham, Mark Anthony *computer scientist*

Florence
Johnson, Johnny Ray *retired mathematics professor*

Huntsville
Freas, George Wilson, II, *computer scientist, consultant*
Zutaut, Steven Eric *systems analyst, application developer*

Montgomery
Das, Sunil R. *computer scientist, educator*

Muscle Shoals
Thompson, Bradford *mathematics professor*

ARIZONA

Fountain Hills
Israel, Robert Allan *statistician*

Phoenix
Doto, Irene Louise *statistician*
Pillalamarri, Seshasayi *computer scientist and engineer, researcher*

Prescott
Semon, Warren Lloyd *information scientist, educator*

Sierra Vista
Sizemore, Nicky Lee *computer scientist*
Smith, Barbara Jane *computer scientist, educator*

Tempe
Ericksen, Linda E. *computer science educator*
Panchanathan, Sethuraman *computer science educator*
Smith, Harvey Alvin *mathematics professor, consultant*

Tucson
Bayly, Bruce Jeremy *mathematics professor*
Gabitov, Ildar *mathematics professor*
Willoughby, Stephen Schuyler *mathematics professor*

Yuma
Hodson, Roy Goode, Jr. *retired logistician*

ARKANSAS

Arkadelphia
Nelson, Leon *retired data processing professional*

Batesville
Carius, Robert Wilhelm *mathematics professor, retired military officer*

Fayetteville
Joon Jin, Song *mathematics professor, statistics professor*
Venkatesh, Viswanath *information systems professional, educator, consultant*

Little Rock
Chiang, Chia-Chu *computer scientist, educator*

Maumelle
Bayrak, Coskun *computer scientist, researcher, educator*

CALIFORNIA

Alameda
Wu, Shuning *statistician*

Bakersfield
Fiedler, Joseph Robert *mathematician, educator*

Berkeley
Agogino, Alice Merner *computer scientist, mechanical engineer, educator*
Bajcsy, Ruzena Kucerova *computer science educator*
Chatterjee, Sourav *statistician, educator*
Chorin, Alexandre Joel *mathematician, educator*
Christ, F. Michael *mathematics professor*
Concus, Paul *mathematician, educator*
Dunlop, Neil *computer scientist, department chairman*
Eisenbud, David *mathematics professor*
Friedland, Gerald *computer scientist, researcher*
Gluss, Brian *mathematician, statistician, engineer, systems expert*
Goldberg, Evgueni *computer scientist*
Hartshorne, Robert (Robin Hartshorne) *mathematics professor*
Jones, Vaughan Frederick Randal *mathematician, educator*
Meza, Juan C. *mathematician, computer scientist*
Moore, Calvin C. *mathematics professor, academic administrator*
Rhodes, John Lewis *mathematics professor*
Schoenfeld, Alan Henry *mathematics education professor, researcher*
Simon, Horst D. *computer scientist*
Smith, Alan Jay *computer science educator, consultant*
Veklerov, Eugene *mathematician, computer scientist, educator*
Vojta, Paul Alan *mathematics professor*
Wolf, Joseph Albert *mathematician, educator*
Yu, Bin *statistician, educator*

Brea
Painchaud, Phillip Andre *metrologist*

Carson
Jones, Matthew G. *mathematics professor*
Suchenek, Marek Andrzej *computer science educator*

Castro Valley
Scherrer, Deborah King *computer scientist, educational association administrator*

Claremont
Coleman, Courtney Stafford *mathematician, educator*
Henriksen, Melvin *mathematician, educator*
Martonosi, Susan E. *mathematics professor*
Myhre, Janet *statistician, educator, consultant*
Pippenger, Nicholas John *mathematician, Computer Scientist Researcher Educator*
Schellhorn, Henry *mathematics professor*

Culver City
Alwash, Mohamad Ali *mathematics professor, researcher*

Davis
Fannjiang, Albert *mathematician, educator*
Müller, Hans-Georg *statistician*
Tracy, Craig Arnold *mathematics educator*
Walters, Richard Francis *computer science educator*

El Segundo
Macskassy, Sofus Attila *computer scientist, educator*

Fairfield
Spake, Reuben Michael *mathematics professor, researcher*

Fullerton
Suceava, Bogdan Dragos *mathematics professor, writer*

Glendale
Kay, Alan C. *computer scientist, nonprofit organization executive*

Hayward
Duncan, Doris Gottschalk *information systems educator*

Huntington Beach
McKay, David E. *mathematics professor*
Sward, Andrea Jeanne *information and computer scientist, musician*

Irvine
Barsamian, Harut *computer scientist, consultant*
Henry, Valerie *mathematics professor*
Hoffman, Donald David *cognitive and computer science educator*
Li, Peter Wai-Kwong *mathematics professor*
Nie, Qing *mathematics professor*
Saari, Donald Gene *mathematician, department chairman, economist*
Utts, Jessica Marie *statistician, educator*
Yazdi, Ahmad *computer scientist, researcher*
Zheng, Weian *mathematics professor*

La Jolla
Baouendi, M. Salah *mathematics professor*
Freedman, Michael Hartley *mathematician, educator, researcher*
Graham, Ronald Lewis *mathematician*
Martin, James John, Jr. *systems analyst, retired research and development company executive*
Micciancio, Daniele *computer scientist*
Rajasekar, Arcot *computer scientist*
Terras, Audrey Anne *mathematics professor*
Wallach, Nolan R. *mathematician, consultant*
Wulbert, Daniel Eliot *mathematician, educator*
Zyroff, Ellen Slotoroff *information scientist, classicist, educator*

Lakewood
Lestmann, Phillip Edward *mathematics educator, analyst and computer programmer*

Long Beach
Moon, Hojin *statistician, educator*
Schroeder, Arnold Leon *mathematics professor*

Los Angeles
Bekey, George Albert *computer scientist, educator*
Carleson, Lennart A(xel) E(dvard) *mathematics professor*
Cong, Jason Jingsheng *computer scientist, educator, consultant, researcher*
Gordon, Basil *retired mathematics professor*
Holt, James Franklin *retired numerical analyst, scientific programmer analyst*
Kleinrock, Leonard *computer scientist*
Pearl, Judea *computer scientist, educator*
Rosenbloom, Paul Simon *computer scientist*
Tao, Terence Chi-Shen *mathematics professor*
Waterman, Michael Spencer *mathematics and biology professor*
Zelmanowitz, Julius Martin *mathematics professor, academic administrator*

Marina Del Rey
Deelman, Ewa *computer scientist, educator*
Neuman, Clifford *computer scientist, educator*
Swartout, William R. *mathematician, educator, director*

Menlo Park
Bourne, Charles Percy *information scientist, educator*
Jarrold, William *computer scientist*
Neumann, Peter Gabriel *computer scientist*

Moffett Field
Srivastava, Ashok Narain *computer scientist, consultant*

Monterey
Brown, Gerald G. *operations research specialist, educator*
Denning, Peter James *computer scientist, engineer*
Owen, Guillermo *mathematician, educator*
Read, Robert Richard *mathematical statistics educator*

Moss Landing
Lange, Lester Henry *mathematics professor*

Mountain View
Buchheit, Paul *computer programmer, entrepreneur*
Lamport, Leslie B. *computer scientist*

Palo Alto
Barford, Lee Alton *computer scientist*
Weiss, Leonard *mathematician, consultant, writer*

Pasadena
Greenhall, Charles August *mathematician*
Holzmann, Gerard Johan *computer science researcher*
Hou, Thomas Yizhao *mathematician*
Houman, Owhadi *mathematician*
Knowles, James Kenyon *applied mathematician, educator*
Yin, Peng *computer scientist*

Pearblossom
Goldman, Gary Steven *computer scientist, consultant*

Pleasanton
Liu, Wei-Min *statistician, director*

Rancho Santa Margarita
Berta, Melissa Rose *mathematics professor*

Redding
Lund, Harold Emerson *mathematics professor*

Redwood City
Mockapetris, Paul V. *computer scientist, information technology executive*

Redwood Valley
Speed, Cynthia Agnes *retired mathematics professor*

Riverside
Kuang, Shilong *mathematics professor*
Ratliff, Louis Jackson, Jr. *mathematics professor*
Shapiro, Victor Lenard *mathematics professor*

Sacramento
Crawford, Robert Lawrence *mathematics professor*
Zhou, Kecheng *mathematics professor*

San Bernardino
Kakihara, Yuichiro *mathematics professor*

San Diego
Burgin, George Hans *computer scientist, educator*
Fernandes, Kathleen *systems analyst*
Hales, Alfred Washington *mathematics professor, consultant*
Jacobs, Gustaaf Bernardus *mathematician, mechanical engineer, aerospace engineer*
Rubin, Stuart Harvey *computer science educator, researcher*
Vaida, Florin *statistician, educator*
Van Tassel, Lowell Thomas *mathematics professor*

San Francisco
Bell, C. Gordon *computer architect and engineer, entrepreneur, researcher*
Cruse, Allan Baird *mathematician, computer scientist, educator*
Needham, Tristan *mathematics professor*

San Jose
Cho, Yushin *computer scientist*
Ho, Chungwu *mathematics professor*
Jin, Hailin *computer scientist*
Togasaki, Shinobu *computer scientist*
Wrede, Robert Clinton, Jr. *mathematician, educator*

San Luis Obispo
Hsu, John Yu-Sheng *computer scientist, educator*

San Marino
Lashley, Virginia Stephenson Hughes *retired computer science educator*

Santa Ana
Bowers, Cherie Lynn *mathematics professor*

Santa Barbara
Birnir, Bjorn *mathematics professor, director*
Minc, Henryk *mathematics professor*
Simons, Stephen *mathematics professor, researcher*

Santa Clara
Alexanderson, Gerald Lee *mathematician, educator, writer*
DeWalt, David G. *software company executive*
Klosinski, Leonard Frank *mathematics professor*
Papay, Lauri Louise *mathematics professor*

Santa Cruz
Stormes, John Max *systems analyst*
Widom, Harold *mathematician, educator*

Santa Monica
Keeler, Emmett Brown *research mathematician*

Santa Rosa
Hales, Raleigh Stanton, Jr. *retired mathematics professor, academic administrator*

South San Francisco
Su, Zheng *statistician*

Stanford
Hanrahan, Patrick M. *computer scientist*
Keller, Joseph Bishop *mathematician, educator*
Knuth, Donald Ervin *computer sciences educator*
Koller, Daphne *computer scientist*
Lai, Tze Leung *mathematician, educator*
Lambers, James Vincent *mathematician, researcher, petroleum engineer*
Liu, Tai-Ping *mathematics professor*
McCarthy, John *computer scientist, educator*
Milgram, R. James *mathematics professor*
Ullman, Jeffrey David *computer scientist, educator*
Yao, Yuan *mathematician, researcher*

Thousand Oaks
El Fattah, Yousri M. *computer scientist*

Torrance
Romanov, Volodymyr Alexeevich *computer science educator, researcher, computer science educator, researcher*

Westlake Village
Munson, John Backus *computer scientist, retired data processing executive*

Westminster
Le, Anh Quang *mathematics professor*

Yucaipa
Crise, Robert D., Jr. *mathematics professor*

COLORADO

Aurora
O'Donnell, Colin I. *statistician, researcher*

Boulder
Beylkin, Gregory *mathematician*
Glover, Fred William *information scientist, director, educator*
Mycielski, Jan *retired mathematics professor*

Colorado Springs
Simmons, George Finlay *retired mathematics professor*

Denver
Kuppireddi, Sireesh *computer scientist*
Payne, Stanley E. *mathematics professor*

Fort Collins
Estep, Donald Joseph *mathematician, educator*
Mielke, Paul William, Jr. *statistician, consultant*

Lafayette
Dowling, Thomas Allan *retired mathematics professor*

Pueblo
Barnett, Janet Heine *mathematics professor*

CONNECTICUT

Ansonia
Kerpa, Gary J. *computer science consultant*

Fairfield
Loth, Peter *mathematics professor*

Farmington
Nash, Judith Kluck *mathematics professor*

Groton
Swindell, Archie Calhoun, Jr. *statistician, consultant*

Hartford
Morin, Jared W. *computer scientist, educator, technologist*

Middletown
Linton, Fred Ernest Julius *mathematics professor, publishing executive*
Maltese, George John *mathematics professor*

New Haven
Fischer, Michael John *computer science educator*
Howe, Roger Evans *mathematician, educator*
Margulis, Gregory A. *mathematics and science professor, researcher*
McDermott, Drew Vincent *computer science educator*
Mostow, George Daniel *mathematics professor*
Silberschatz, Abraham (Avi Silberschatz) *computer scientist, educator, researcher*

Stamford
Frank, Laura Jean *computer scientist*

Storrs
Diaby, Moustapha *operations research educator*
Peters, Thomas Joseph *computer scientist, mathematician*

Storrs Mansfield
Harel, Ofer *statistician, educator*
Rajasekaran, Sanguthevar *computer science educator*
Wachman, Murray *retired mathematics professor*

Wallingford
Frisch, Michael Jay *computer scientist*

West Haven
Dausey, David James *program analyst*
Kyriakides, Tassos Constantino *biostatistician*

Wilton
Brown, James Thompson, Jr. *operations research specialist, information scientist*

DELAWARE

Newark
Colton, David Lem *mathematician, educator*
Luke, David Russell *mathematician, educator*

Wilmington
Miller, Christopher John *statistician*

DISTRICT OF COLUMBIA

Washington
Atwood, Susan Jennifer *institute administrator*
Chuang, Tze-Jer *mathematician*
Feil, Michael Bruce *statistician*
Freeman, Peter A. *dean*
Frieder, Gideon *computer scientist, educator*
Gastwirth, Joseph Lewis *statistician, educator*
Gray, Mary Wheat *statistician, lawyer*
Hedges, Harry George *retired computer scientist*
Ipatov, Sergei Ivanovich *mathematician, astronomer*
Kahlow, Barbara Fenvessy *statistician*
Kohut, Andrew *research center executive*
Mani, Inderjeet *computer scientist, educator*
McElroy, Tucker Spragye *mathematician, consultant, statistician*
Omole, Duncan Wambogo *information scientist, corporate communications specialist*
Pan, Qing *statistician, educator*
Perry, Steven Wayne *statistician*
Raphael, Louise Arakelian *mathematician, educator*
Ryan, David Alan *systems analyst*
Sadosky, Cora Susana *mathematician, educator*
Shaw, William Frederick *statistician*
Straley, Tina H. *mathematics association director*
Wittes, Janet Turk *statistician*

FLORIDA

Boca Raton
Asaduzzaman, Abu S. *computer scientist*

Bonita Springs
Powell, Robert Ellis *mathematics professor, dean*

Boynton Beach
Warga, Jack *mathematician, educator*

Daytona Beach
Seenith, Sivasundaram *mathematician, educator*

Delray Beach
Hegstrom, William Jean *retired mathematics professor*

Dunedin
Klingbiel, Paul Herman *retired information scientist*

Fort Lauderdale
Li, Wei *computer scientist*
Littman, Marlyn Kemper *information scientist, educator*

Gainesville
Agresti, Alan *statistics educator*
Dinculeanu, Nicolae *mathematician, educator*
Keesling, James Edgar *mathematics professor*
Mitchell, William John *mathematics educator*
Portier, Kenneth Michael *statistics educator*
Thompson, John Griggs *mathematician*

Jacksonville
Reid, William Hill *mathematics professor*

Lakeland
Sheppard, Albert Parker, Jr. *retired computer science educator*

Melbourne
Banerjee, Bonny *computer scientist*
Fulton, Charles Thomas *mathematics professor*
Hancock, Monte Floyd, Jr. *computer scientist*
Lakshmikantham, Vangipuram *mathematics professor*

Miami
Clarke, Peter John *computer scientist, educator, educational consultant*
España, Lourdes Maria *mathematics professor*
Ghai, Gauri L. *statistician, educator*

Orlando
Deo, Narsingh *computer scientist, educator*
Nashed, M. Zuhair *mathematics professor, editor*
Varvak, Mark *mathematician, researcher*

Patrick AFB
Kohn, Paul Franklin *mathematician*

Pensacola
Ford, Kenneth M. *computer scientist, educator*

Punta Gorda
Smith, Charles Edwin *computer science educator*

Riviera Beach
Berliner, Hans Jack *retired computer scientist*

Saint Augustine
Jurgens, Julie Graham *mathematics professor*

Sarasota
Jacobson, Melvin Joseph *mathematician, educator*

Tallahassee
Bellenot, Steven *mathematics educator, consultant*
Gilmer, Robert *mathematics professor*
Kercheval, Alec Norton *mathematician*
Kohout, Ladislav Jan *computer science educator*
Navon, Ionel Michael *mathematics professor*
Nichols, Eugene Douglas *mathematics professor*
Thompson, Daniel Ray *statistician, consultant*

Tampa
El-Hadidy, Bahaa *information scientist, educator, consultant*
Hall, Lawrence O'Higgins *computer science educator*
Kandel, Abraham *computer scientist*
Ma, Wen-Xiu *mathematician, educator*

GEORGIA

Athens
Basawa, Ishwar V. *Statistics Professor*
Stufken, John *statistician, educator*

Atlanta
Ames, William Francis *mathematician, educator*
Goodman, Seymour Evan *computer science and international studies educator, researcher, consultant*
Lim, Sung Kyu *computer scientist, educator*
Mickens, Ronald Elbert *mathematician, physics professor*
Oliker, Vladimir *mathematician, educator*
Pan, Yi *computer science educator*
Pu, Calton *computer scientist*
Thompson, Shirley Williams *mathematics professor*
Tighiouart, Mourad *statistician, researcher*
Wu, De Ting *mathematics professor, researcher, writer*
Zadeh, Javad Hamadani *mathematics professor*

Augusta
Craig, Cynthia Mae *mathematics professor*
Rempala, Grzegorz A. *mathematician, statistician, educator*

Blakely
Teal, Teresa *mathematics professor*

Columbus
Bhandary, Madhusudan *statistician, educator*

Duluth
Kimmich, Madeline P. *business operations consultant*

Jonesboro
Harris, Queen Wiggs *mathematician, educator*

Lovejoy
Onukwuli, Francis Osita *computer scientist, secondary school educator, mathematician*

Mount Berry
Taylor, Ronald D. *mathematics professor*

Savannah
Tessema, George *mathematician, educator*

HAWAII

Honolulu
Masunaga, David K. *mathematics professor*
Swanson, Richard William *retired statistician*

Paia
Loomis, James Cook *mathematician, cyberneticist, writer, educator, navigator*

IDAHO

Boise
Saltzer, Jerome Howard *computer science educator*

Moscow
Goetschel, Roy Hartzell, Jr. *mathematician, researcher*

ILLINOIS

Argonne
Lindert, Eric Alton *operations research specialist, small business owner*

Carbondale
Asoh, Derek Ajesam *information scientist, educator*
Headrick, Todd Christopher *mathematical statistician, educator*
Neuman, Edward George *mathematician, educator*
Panchapakesan, Subrahmanian *mathematics professor*

Champaign
Turquette, Atwell Rufus *logician*

Charleston
Dey, Suhrit K. *mathematician, researcher*

Chicago
Ash, J. Marshall *mathematician, educator*
Beilinson, Alexander A. *mathematics professor*
Bona, Jerry Lloyd *mathematician, educator*
Dardai, Shahid Moinuddin *computer science educator*
Drinfeld, Vladimir Gershonovich *mathematician, educator*
Filus, Lidia Z. *mathematics professor, researcher*
Giordani, Tania *mathematician, educator*
Grant, Delvin A. *management information systems educator, researcher*
Hanson, Floyd Bliss *mathematician*
Hwang, Yujong *information scientist, educator*
McDonald, Anne Leggett *mathematics professor*
Sloan, Robert Hal *computer science educator*
Smale, Stephen *mathematics professor*
Stigler, Stephen Mack *statistician, educator*
Tsay, Ruey Shiong *business and statistics educator*
Usiskin, Zalman Philip *mathematics educator*

Evanston
Jerome, Joseph Walter *mathematics professor*
Kath, William Lawrence *mathematics professor*
Matkowsky, Bernard Judah *mathematician, educator*
Olmstead, William Edward *mathematics professor*
Severini, Thomas Alan *statistician, educator*
Tanner, Martin Abba *statistician, educator*
Wilkinson, Anne Marie *mathematics professor*
Zaslow, Eric Gallant *mathematics professor*
Zelinsky, Daniel *mathematics professor*

Glen Ellyn
Cook, Joann Catherine *computer professor*
Nunamaker, Susan Sun *mathematics professor*

Godfrey
McDaniels, John Louis *retired mathematics professor*

Highland Park
Fortnow, Lance Jeremy *computer scientist, educator*
Wolfson, Ouri *computer scientist*

La Grange Park
Butler, Margaret Kampschaefer *retired computer scientist*

Lemont
Anitescu, Mihai *computer scientist, mathematician*

Lincoln
Bi, Shuwei *management information systems educator*

Macomb
Voss, David Albert *mathematics professor*

Moline
Doerder, Lowell E. *mathematics professor*

Palatine
Durian, Geoffrey P. *mathematics professor*

Romeoville
Tucker, Vicky Rose *systems analyst, director*

Springfield
Chan, Hei-Chi *mathematics professor*
Saltsgaver, Carol Madeleine *mathematics professor*

Ullin
Dillow, Rhonda L. *mathematics professor, department chairman*

University Park
Hakala, Reino William *mathematician, educator*

Urbana
Bateman, Paul Trevier *mathematician, educator*
Burkholder, Donald Lyman *mathematician, educator*
Carroll, Robert Wayne *mathematics professor*
Gropp, William Douglas *computer scientist, educator*
Ham, MyungJoo *computer scientist*
Henson, C. Ward *mathematician, educator*
Nam, Min-Young *computer scientist*
Osborn, Howard A. *retired mathematics professor*
Wang, Shaowen *information scientist, geographer, educator*

Westchester
Pavelka, Elaine Blanche *mathematics professor*

INDIANA

Bloomington
Prosser, Franklin Pierce *computer scientist*
Puri, Madan Lal *mathematics professor*
Shen, Chun-Yen *mathematics professor*
Temam, Roger M. *mathematician, educator*

Evansville
Kimberling, Clark Hershall *mathematics professor, small business owner*

Hanover
Katsov, Yefim *mathematics professor*

Indianapolis
Bleher, Pavel M. *mathematics professor*
Chiang, Alan Y. *statistician*
Cliff, Johnnie Marie *mathematics and chemistry professor*
Cowen, Carl C. *mathematics professor*
Cravens, Gary Dean *information scientist, physician*
Yovits, Marshall Clinton *information scientist, educator, dean*

Lafayette
de Branges de Bourcia, Louis *mathematics professor*

Muncie
Ali, Mir Masoom *retired statistician, educator*
East, David Harold *mathematics professor*

Notre Dame
Kogge, Peter Michael *computer scientist, educator*
Sommese, Andrew John *mathematics professor*

Terre Haute
Cochrane, Phillip *mathematics professor*

Valparaiso
Maxin, Daniel *mathematics professor*
Mundt, Marvin Glen *retired mathematics professor*

West Lafayette
Abhyankar, Shreeram Shankar *mathematics professor*
Danielli-Garofalo, Donatella *mathematics professor*
Dasgupta, Anirban *statistician, researcher*

Westville
Serwatka, Judy Ann *computer and information systems educator*

IOWA

Ames
David, Herbert Aron *retired statistician, educator*
Fuller, Wayne Arthur *statistics educator*
Gautesen, Arthur K. *mathematics professor*
Hogben, Leslie *mathematician*
Seifert, George *mathematician, educator*

Cedar Rapids
Bahadur, Birendra *displays research specialist*

Des Moines
Khots, Boris *mathematician, researcher*

Estherville
Dodge, Lynn Renee *mathematics professor*

Grinnell
Adelberg, Arnold Melvin *mathematics professor, researcher*

Iowa City
Atkinson, Kendall Eugene *mathematics professor*
Broffitt, James Drake *statistician, educator*
Hogg, Robert Vincent, Jr. *mathematical statistician, educator*
Robertson, Timothy Joel *statistician, educator*

Peosta
Dilsizian, Rick Charles *retired computer science educator*
Doffing, Timothy J. *mathematics professor*

KANSAS

El Dorado
Meyer, Ruth A. *mathematics professor*

Lawrence
Himmelberg, Charles John III *mathematics professor, researcher*
Pasik-Duncan, Bozenna Janina *mathematics professor, researcher*
Van Vleck, Fred Scott *mathematician, educator, researcher*

Overland Park
Horen, Jeffrey Harry *statistician*
Noe, James Kirby *retired computer consultant*

Shawnee Mission
Flora, Jairus Dale, Jr. *statistician*

Wichita
Isakov, Victor Michael *mathematics educator and researcher*

KENTUCKY

Bowling Green
Spraker, John Stephen *mathematician, educator*

Cynthiana
Florence, Joyce Fritz *mathematics professor*

Georgetown
Drake, Albert Estern *retired statistics educator, farming administrator*

Hazard
Cory, Cynthia Strong *mathematics professor*

Lexington
Charnigo, Richard John, Jr. *statistician, educator*
Mostert, Paul Stallings *retired mathematician*

Louisville
Das, Manabendra Nath *mathematics professor*
Datta, Susmita *statistician, bioinformatician, educator*
Eggeling da Encarnação, Luis Miguel *computer scientist, research and development company executive*
Nasraoui, Olfa *computer scientist, educator, electrical engineer*

LOUISIANA

Alexandria
Miller, Elizabeth Ann *mathematician, human services manager*

Baton Rouge
Bourdin, Blaise *mathematics professor*
Dasbach, Oliver T. *mathematician, educator*
Gudi, Thirupathi *computer scientist*
Oxley, James Grieve *mathematics professor*
Quartararo, Philip, Jr. *mathematics professor*

Dry Prong
McLain, Paul King *systems analyst*

Eunice
Hernandez, Gloria Marie *mathematician, educator*

Hammond
Merino, Dennis Iligan *mathematics educator, researcher*
Neuerburg, Kent M. *mathematics professor*

Lafayette
Dasgupta, Subrata *computer & cognitive science educator, director, writer*
Magidin, Arturo *mathematics professor*

New Orleans
Kalka, Morris *mathematics professor*
Mislove, Michael William *mathematics educator, theoretical computer scientist*

Shreveport
Spaht, Carlos G., II, *mathematics educator*

MARYLAND

Adamstown
Tidball, Charles Stanley *computer scientist, educator*

Ashton
Smith, Kent Ashton *information scientist, consultant*

Baltimore
Arsham, Hossein *operations research analyst*
Boardman, John Michael *mathematician, educator*
Choudhury, Dipa *mathematician, educator*
Goodrich, Michael Truman *computer science educator*
Lidtke, Doris Keefe *retired computer science educator*
Potra, Florian Alexander *mathematics professor*
Shiffman, Bernard *mathematician, educator*
Wierman, John Charles *mathematician, educator*

Bethesda
Lipkin, Bernice Sacks *computer scientist, educator*
Tilley, Carolyn Bittner *information scientist*

Bowie
Josyula, Darsana Purushothaman *computer scientist, educator*

College Park
Antman, Stuart Sheldon *mathematician, educator*
Hamilton, David Howard *mathematics professor*
Johnson, Raymond Lewis *mathematician*
Lucas, Henry Cameron, Jr. *information scientist, educator, writer*
Minker, Jack *computer scientist, educator*
Shneiderman, Ben Abraham *computer science educator, writer*
Stewart, Gilbert Wright *computer science educator*
Zhu, Guangyu *computer scientist, researcher*

Columbia
Gregorie, Corazon Arzalem *operations research specialist*

Fort George G Meade
Nelson, Douglas J. *mathematician*
Schmitt, Robert Lee *computer scientist*

Gaithersburg
Beichl, Isabel M. *mathematician*
Carasso, Alfred Sam *mathematician*
Rosenblatt, Joan Raup *mathematical statistician*

Hunt Valley
Igusa, Jun-Ichi *mathematician, educator*

Hyattsville
Gonzalez, Joe Fred, Jr. *mathematical statistician, educator*

Kensington
Chiazze, Leonard, Jr. *biostatistician, epidemiologist, educator*

Laurel
Maurer, Donald Eugene *mathematician*

Lexington Park
Scanlan, Robert Dennis *systems analyst*

Mount Airy
Spohn, William Gideon, Jr. *mathematician, retired musician*

North Bethesda
Moshman, Jack *statistical consultant*

Potomac
Medin, Julia Adele *mathematics professor, researcher*
Navarro, Joseph Anthony *retired statistician, consultant*
Peters, Carol Beattie Taylor (Mrs. Frank Albert Peters) *mathematician*

Princess Anne
Malik, Malik B. *mathematics professor*

Rockville
Levin, Alexander B. *mathematics professor*
Nelson, Kevin *statistician*

Silver Spring
Buenconsejo, Joan *statistician*
Sammet, Jean E. *computer scientist*
Sirken, Monroe Gilbert *statistician*

MASSACHUSETTS

Acton
Smith, Raoul Normand *computer science educator*

Belmont
Reynolds, William Francis *mathematics professor*

Boston
Boghosian, Bruce Michael *computational scientist, educator*
Boonma, Pruet *computer scientist*
D'Agostino, Ralph Benedict *mathematician, statistician, educator, consultant*
Hu, Chengcheng *biostatician, medical researcher*
Kukluk, Jacek *computer scientist*
Schoenfeld, David Alan *statistician, educator*

Burlington
Cline, Jason Alexander *computer scientist*

Cambridge
Arvind, *computer scientist, electrical engineer, educator, researcher*
Bartee, Thomas Creson *computer scientist, educator*
Boyan, Justin Andrew *computer scientist*
Colding, Tobias H. *mathematics professor*
Dennis, Jack Bonnell *computer scientist, educator*
Dudley, Richard Mansfield *mathematician, educator*
Greenspan, Harvey Philip *applied mathematician, educator*
Gross, Benedict H. *mathematician, educator, former dean*
Helgason, Sigurdur *mathematician, educator*
Jaffe, Arthur Michael *mathematician, physicist, educator*
Kac, Victor G. *mathematician, educator*
Kazhdan, David *mathematician, educator*
Kostant, Bertram *mathematician, educator*
McMullen, Curtis T. *mathematics professor*
Minsky, Marvin Lee *mathematician, educator*
Morris, Robert Tappan *computer science educator, Internet company executive*
Moses, Joel *computer scientist, educator*
Mrowka, Tomasz *mathematics professor*
Oettinger, Anthony Gervin *mathematician, educator*
Rubin, Donald Bruce *statistician, educator, research and development company executive*
Rudolph, Larry *computer science educator, researcher*
Stroock, Daniel Wyler *mathematician, educator*
Taubes, Clifford Henry *mathematician, educator*
Toomre, Alar *applied mathematician, theoretical astronomer*
Welsch, Roy Elmer *statistician, educator*
Yau, Shing-Tung *mathematics professor*

Framingham
Matheus, Christopher John *computer scientist, researcher*

Holyoke
Murphy, Eileen Bridget *retired mathematics and computer science professor*

Lincoln
LeGates, John Crews Boulton *information scientist*

Lowell
Kheifets, Alexander *mathematics professor*

Medford
Tu, Loring Wuliang *mathematics educator*

Newton
Parker, Jeff D. *operations research specialist*

North Andover
Kurzweil, Raymond C. *computer scientist, entrepreneur*

North Dartmouth
Rai, Bharatendra K. *statistician, educator*

Sharon
Zenack, Les *mathematics professor*

Waltham
Brown, Edgar Henry, Jr. *mathematician, educator*
Lian, Bong H. *mathematics professor, department chairman*
Simeonov, Simeon *computer scientist*

Watertown
Stoddard, Anne Maher *biostatistician, researcher, educator*

Westfield
Buckmore, Alvah Clarence, Jr. *computer scientist, ballistician*

Westford
Haramundanis, Katherine Leonora *information scientist, writer, astronomer, science historian*

Westport Point
Fanning, William Henry, Jr. *computer specialist*

Westwood
Smith, Denis Joseph *mathematics professor*

Williamstown
De Veaux, Richard Donald *statistician*
Hill, Victor Ernst, IV, *retired mathematics professor, musician*
Morgan, Frank *mathematics professor*
Silva, Cesar Ernestro *mathematics educator*

Worcester
Malone, Joseph James *mathematics professor, researcher*

MICHIGAN

Adrian
Lamprecht, Elizabeth Ann *mathematics professor*

Ann Arbor
Duren, Peter Larkin *mathematician, educator*
Hill, Bruce Marvin *statistician, educator*
Jonsson, Mattias *mathematics professor*
Lazarsfeld, Robert Kendall *mathematician, educator*
Woodroofe, Michael Barrett *mathematics and statistics professor*

Dearborn
Brown, James Ward *mathematician, educator, author*

Detroit
Lu, Guozhen *mathematics professor*
Rajlich, Vaclav Thomas *computer science educator, researcher, consultant*
Schreiber, Bertram Manuel *mathematics professor*
Shi, Weisong *computer scientist, educator*

East Lansing
Pichler, Shaun *statistician, educator*
Rong, Yongwu *mathematician, researcher*
Stapleton, James Hall *retired statistician, educator*

Farmington
Ginsberg, Myron *computer scientist*

Flint
Simkani, Mehrdad *mathematics professor*

Grand Rapids
Adams, Joel Cameron *computer science educator*
Becker, Robert Joseph *database consultant, application developer, educator, computer science specialist*

Kalamazoo
Yang, Li *computer scientist, educator*

Manistique
Jeffcott, Janet Bruhn *statistician, consultant*

Muskegon
Nace, Doru *mathematics professor*

Rochester
McDonald, Gary C. *mathematics professor*

Saline
Cornell, Richard Garth *biostatistics educator*

Sidney
Roy, Janice L. *mathematics professor*

Southfield
Ferguson, Roger Clark *computer science educator*
Miller, Nancy Ellen *computer scientist, consultant*

MINNESOTA

Duluth
Gallian, Joseph Anthony *mathematics professor*

Mankato
Kitsul, Pavel Ivanovich *mathematics professor, researcher*
Tung, Chia-chi *mathematics professor*

Mendota Heights
Bingham, Christopher *statistics educator*

Minneapolis
Arnold, Douglas Norman *mathematician*
Brasket, Curt Justin *systems analyst*
Chahine, Iman Chafik *mathematics professor, director*
Harris, Morton Edward *mathematics educator*
Markus, Lawrence *retired mathematics professor*
Reich, Edgar *mathematics professor*
Serrin, James Burton *mathematics professor*
Yomba, Emmanuel *mathematician, researcher, physicist*

Moorhead
Heuer, Gerald Arthur *mathematician, educator*

Northfield
Appleyard, David Frank *retired mathematics and computer science professor*
Schuster, Seymour *mathematician, educator*
Steen, Lynn Arthur *mathematician, educator*

Saint Charles
Van Norman, Willis Roger *retired computer systems researcher, consultant*

Saint Cloud
Julstrom, Bryant Arthur *computer science educator*
Olagunju, Amos Omotayo *computer science educator, consultant, computer science educator, consultant*

Saint Paul
Bressoud, David Marius *mathematics educator*

Shakopee
Eliason, Arlene F. *mathematician, educator*

Winona
Malone, Christopher John *statistician, educator*

MISSISSIPPI

Columbus
Adhikari, Dhruba Raj *mathematics professor, researcher*

Long Beach
Adan-Bante, Edith *mathematician, researcher*

Starkville
Balasubramanian, Suman *mathematician, educator*
Carino, Ricolindo L. *computer scientist, educator*

MISSOURI

Cape Girardeau
Chan, Wai *mathematics professor*

Columbia
Beem, John Kelly *retired mathematician, educator*

Kansas City
Medhi, Deepankar *computer science educator*

Maryland Heights
Han, Xiao *computer scientist, researcher*

Rolla
Grimm, Louis John *mathematician, educator*
Ingram, William Thomas III *mathematics professor*

Saint Charles
Golik, Wojciech Ludwik *mathematics professor, department chairman*

Saint Louis
Baernstein, Albert, II, *mathematician, educator*
Epner, Steven Arthur *computer consultant*
Haskins, James Leslie *mathematics professor*
Hegamin-Younger, Cecilia *statistician, consultant, educator*
Jenkins, James Allister *mathematician, educator*
Turner, Jonathan Shields *computer science educator, researcher*
Wilson, Edward Nathan *mathematician, educator*

Springfield
Don, Tosh H. *mathematics professor*

Trenton
Pushkarsky, Louis Paul *retired mathematics educator*

Union
Boehmer, Ann *mathematics professor*
Cook, Judyth W. *computer science educator*

Warrensburg
Yousef, Mahmoud *mathematics professor, computer scientist, educator*

Winona
Marshall, Lucille Ruth *retired mathematics professor*

MONTANA

Billings
Fried, Michael D. *mathematician, educator*

Bozeman
Pugesek, Bruce H. *statistician*

Missoula
Tonev, Thomas (Toma) V. *mathematics professor*

NEBRASKA

Lincoln
McCutcheon, Allan Lee *statistics educator*

Omaha
Qureshi, Sajda *information scientist, educator*

Peru
Long, Daryl Clyde *mathematics professor, science educator*

NEVADA

Ely
Daniels, Frank Emmett *mathematician, educator*

Las Vegas
Blattner, Meera McCuaig *computer scientist, educator*
Marcella, Joseph *information scientist*
Snyder, John Henry *computer science educator, consultant*

Reno
Kleinfeld, Erwin *mathematician, educator*

Yerington
Price, Thomas Munro *computer consultant, retired*

NEW HAMPSHIRE

Hanover
Kurtz, Thomas Eugene *retired mathematics professor*
Lamperti, John Williams *mathematician, educator*
McIlroy, M. Douglas *computer scientist, educator*

Keene
Jardine, Richard *mathematics professor*

Manchester
Ingraham, Alec *mathematics professor*

Nashua
Lerch, Carol M. *mathematics professor*

Plymouth
Vinogradova, Natalya *mathematician, educator*

NEW JERSEY

Bridgewater
Chiu, George *information scientist*
Shun, Zhenming *statistician, director*

Englewood
Minkoff, John *applied mathematics educator*

Florham Park
Jotshi, Arun *operations research specialist*

Fort Monmouth
Leciston, David John *computer scientist*

Hightstown
Hunter, John Stuart *statistician, consultant*

Jersey City
Aschoff, Lawrence Michael (Mick) *computer information scientist*
Metallo, Frances Rosebell *mathematics professor*
Wangiwang, Julius Bolla *mathematics professor*

Lakewood
Houle, Joseph E. *mathematics professor*

Lincroft
Ventola, Frances Ann *mathematics professor*

Matawan
Rivera-Dominguez, Alberto *mathematician, educator, mechanical engineer*

Mount Laurel
Minkiewicz, Arlene French *computer scientist*

Neptune City
DeValue, John M. *retired computer science educator*

Neshanic Station
Muckenhoupt, Benjamin *retired mathematics professor*

New Brunswick
Kantor, Paul *information scientist, educator*
Kulikowski, Casimir Alexander *computer scientist, engineer, educator*
Liu, Junfeng *statistician, educator*
Scanlon, Jane Cronin *mathematics professor*

Newark
Atluri, Vijayalakshmi *computer science educator*
Gilman, Jane Piore *mathematician*
Miura, Robert Mitsuru *mathematician, researcher, educator*
Verkhovsky, Boris *computer scientist, educator*

Ocean City
Culbertson, Jane Young *statistician*

Oradell
Tong, Mary Powderly *retired mathematician, educator*

Piscataway
Li, Yanyan *mathematician, educator*

Pomona
Carracino, Christine *mathematics professor*

Princeton
Bombieri, Enrico *mathematician, educator*
Chang, Sun-Yung Alice *mathematics professor*
Deligne, Pierre René *mathematician*
Fefferman, Charles Louis *mathematics professor*
Gear, Charles William *computer scientist*
Gunning, Robert Clifford *mathematician, educator*
Haberman, Shelby Joel *statistician, educator*
Langlands, Robert Phelan *mathematician, educator*
Levin, Simon Asher *mathematician, ecologist, educator*
Mirzakhani, Maryam *mathematician*
Nash, John Forbes, Jr. *mathematician, researcher*
Okounkov, Andrei *mathematics professor*
Sinai, Yakov G. *theoretical mathematician, educator*
Stein, Elias M. *mathematician, educator*
Voevodsky, Vladimir *mathematician*
Wiles, Andrew J. *mathematician, educator*

Rivervale
Posamentier, Alfred Steven *retired mathematics educator, dean*

Teaneck
Zwass, Vladimir *computer science and information systems educator*

Westwood
Badalamenti, Anthony Francis *mathematician, researcher*

Willingboro
Ingerman, Peter Zilahy *systems analyst, consultant*

NEW MEXICO

Albuquerque
Adair, Kristin Lynn *computer scientist, director*
Bell, Stoughton *computer scientist, mathematician, educator*
Lee, Sang-Joon *statistical professor*

Las Cruces
Salamanca-Riba, Susana Alicia *mathematics professor*
Selden, Annie *mathematics professor*
Tran, Son Cao *computer science educator*

Los Alamos
Lipnikov, Konstantin *mathematician*

Santa Fe
Kellner, Richard George *mathematician, computer scientist*

Socorro
Hossain, Anwar M. *statistician, department chairman*

NEW YORK

Albany
Hwang, Jeong-Hyon *computer scientist, educator*
Rosenkrantz, Daniel J. *computer science educator*
Willard, Dan Edward *computer scientist, educator*

Alfred
Smith, Mark Arthur *information scientist, educator*

Bayside
Chugh, Om Parkash *mathematics professor, researcher, forensics specialist*

Binghamton
Farrell, F. Thomas *mathematics professor*
Hilton, Peter John *mathematician, educator*
Zacks, Shelemyahu *mathematical sciences educator*

Bronx
Brakalova, Melkana Alexandrova *mathematician, researcher, educator*
Brenner, Terence *mathematics professor*
Koranyi, Adam *mathematics professor*
Prabhu, Vrunda P. *mathematics professor*
Rose, Israel Harold *mathematics professor*
Seltzer, William *statistician, social science administrator*
Vaninsky, Alexander Yan *mathematician, educator, researcher, financial analyst, systems analyst*

Brooklyn
Freilich, Gerald *mathematics professor*
Siegel, Stephanie S. *mathematics professor*

Buffalo
Coburn, Lewis Alan *mathematics professor*
Hauptman, Herbert Aaron *mathematician, educator, researcher*
Seitz, Mary Lee *mathematics professor*
Selman, Alan Louis *computer science educator*
Shapiro, Stuart Charles *computer scientist, educator*
Wiesenberg, Russel John *statistician*
Wilding, Gregory Edward *statistician, educator*

Clinton
Redfield, Robert Horace *mathematician, educator*

Corning
Neubauer, Dean Veral *statistician*

Flushing
Mendelson, Elliott *mathematician, educator*

Fredonia
Cox, Jonathan Andrew *mathematics professor*

Garden City
Steuer, Michael *mathematics professor*

Great Neck
Seckler, Bernard David *retired mathematics professor, translator*

Hamilton
Tucker, Thomas William *mathematics professor*

Hawthorne
Gong, Leiguang *computer scientist, researcher*
Ward, Christopher *computer scientist, researcher*
Zadrozny, Wlodek W. *computer scientist*

Hopewell Junction
Yin, Haizhou *computer scientist*

Ithaca
Barbasch, Dan Mihai *mathematics professor*
Bramble, James Henry *mathematician, educator*
Earle, Clifford John, Jr. *mathematician*
Guckenheimer, John *mathematician*
Hopcroft, John Edward *computer scientist, educator*
Kleinberg, Jon M. *computer scientist, educator*
Nerode, Anil *mathematician, educator*
Shore, Richard Arnold *mathematics professor*
Trotter, Leslie Earl *operations research specialist, educator*
Urazghildiiev, Ildar R. *mathematician*

Jamaica
Barjis, Joseph *computer scientist, educator*
DeBello, Joan Elizabeth *mathematics professor*
Ostrovskii, Mikhail Iosifovich *mathematician*

Kenmore
Kenny, John Edward *computer analyst*

Morrisville
Zbock, Jason Paul *mathematics professor*

Nesconset
Laspina, Peter Joseph *computer resource educator*

New York
Chichilnisky, Graciela *scientist mathematician, economist, educator, writer*
Edwards, Harold Mortimer *mathematics professor*
Garabedian, Paul Roesel *mathematics professor*
Gross, Jonathan Light *computer scientist, mathematician, educator*
Kurnow, Ernest *statistician, educator*
Lax, Peter David *mathematician, educator*
Marcus, Michael B. *mathematics professor*
Morawetz, Cathleen Synge *mathematician*
Mowshowitz, Abbe *computer scientist*
Newman, Charles Michael *mathematician, physicist, educator*
Nirenberg, Louis *mathematician, educator*
Nogina, Elena Y. *mathematics professor, researcher*
Pennisten, John William *computer scientist, actuary, linguist*
Rizkin, Iosif *retired systems, circuits, and computer scientist, writer*
Schulhoff, Karen L. *information specialist*
Schulzrinne, Henning G. *computer science educator*
Sellers, Peter Hoadley *mathematician, educator*
Shaw, David Elliot *computer scientist, hedge fund manager*
Silver, Nate *statistician, writer*
Sloujitel, Jacob Ben *mathematics professor, researcher*
Sohmer, Bernard *mathematics professor, administrator*
Taylor, Jean Ellen *mathematics professor, researcher*
Wallace, Robert James *mathematics and science educator*
Wright, Margaret Hagen *computer scientist, administrator*
Zeleny, Milan *management systems scientist, economist*

Ozone Park
Joanidhi, Zhani *mathematician, educator*

Pittsford
Hollingsworth, Jack Waring *mathematics professor*

Pleasantville
Knopf, Peter Martin *mathematics professor*

Port Washington
Roy, Ranja *mathematician, educator*

Poughkeepsie
Vertullo, Christina A. *mathematics professor, director*

Rochester
Alling, Norman Larrabee *mathematics professor*
Bajorski, Peter *statistician, educator*
Brooks, Bernard Peter *mathematics professor*
Kuby, Patricia J. *mathematics professor*
Oakes, David *statistician*
Raimi, Ralph Alexis *mathematics professor*
Wang, Sen *computer scientist, researcher*

Rockaway Park
Charosh, Paul Carlin *information science educator, writer*

Saint Bonaventure
Hunkins, Dalton R. *computer science professor*

Slingerlands
Zhu, Kehe *mathematician*

Stony Brook
Anderson, Michael Thomas *mathematics professor, researcher, director*
Ebin, David Gregory *mathematician, researcher, educator*
Glimm, James Gilbert *mathematician, educator*
Lawson, H(erbert) Blaine, Jr. *mathematician, educator*
Milnor, John Willard *mathematician*
Tanur, Judith Mark *statistician, sociologist, educator*
Tucker, Alan Curtiss *mathematics professor*

Syosset
Lee, Jong Pil *mathematician, educator*

Syracuse
Graver, Jack Edward *mathematics professor*
Malhotra, Yogesh *information scientist, management educator, information technology executive, management consultant, engineer*
Morris, Francis Lockwood *computer scientist*
Pardee, Otway O'Meara *computer scientist, educator*
Romeu, Jorge Luis *mathematics professor, writer*

Troy
Goel, Anuj *systems analyst, researcher*
Magdon-Ismail, Malik *computer science professor*

Valhalla
Simpson, Sean *mathematics professor*

West Hempstead
Guggenheimer, Heinrich Walter *mathematician, educator*

West Point
Beecher, Amanda I. *mathematics professor*

Westbury
Sandler, Gerald Howard *computer scientist, information technology executive, educator*

Williamsville
Berner, Robert Frank *managerial statistics educator, administrator*
Severo, Norman C. *retired statistics professor*

Yorktown Heights
Choi, Changhwan *operations research specialist*
Choi, Jong Hyuk *computer scientist*
Hoffman, Alan Jerome *mathematician, educator*
Iyengar, Arun K. *computer scientist*
Salapura, Valentina *computer science educator*

NORTH CAROLINA

Black Mountain
Dalton, Robert Edgar *retired mathematician, computer scientist*

Boone
Johnson, Phillip Eugene *mathematics professor*

Cape Carteret
Mullikin, Thomas Wilson *mathematics professor*

Chapel Hill
Brooks, Frederick Phillips, Jr. *computer scientist, educator*
Burchinal, Margaret Ruth *statistician*
Dowling, Dean Edward *information scientist, educator*
Jones, Paul McDonald *distributed information researcher, educator*
Taylor, Michael E. *mathematics professor*

Colerain
Stephens, William A. (Dean Stephens) *computer consultant*

Cullowhee
Barnes, Julia A. *mathematics professor*

Davidson
Klein, Benjamin Garrett *mathematics professor, consultant*

Dublin
Herring, Robert Dewey *mathematics professor, physics professor*

Durham
Bryant, Robert Leamon *mathematics educator*
Chang, Mou-Hsiung *mathematician*
Reif, John Henry *computer science educator*
Warner, Seth L. *mathematician, educator*

Fayetteville
Cui, Zhenlu *mathematics professor*

Gastonia
Wright, Wayne Kenneth *retired federal agency statistician*

Greenville
Khuri, Soumaya Makdissi *mathematics professor*
Pleasant, James Carroll *mathematician, computer sciences educator*

Raleigh
Chou, Wushow *retired computer scientist*
Howell, Gary Wilbur *computer scientist, mathematician, consultant*
Jing, Naihuan N. *mathematician*
Pao, Chia-Ven *mathematics professor*
Wesler, Oscar *retired mathematician, educator*
Wetsch, John Robert *information scientist*
Windham, Donald Eric *bioinformatics analyst*

Research Triangle Park
Schrager, Mindy Rae *operations management specialist*

Rocky Point
MacAskill, Lloyd Edwin *systems analyst, consultant*

Wilmington
Herman, Russell Leland *mathematics, physics professor*

Winston Salem
Sawyer, John Wesley *retired mathematics and computer science educator, consultant*

NORTH DAKOTA

Bismarck
Bruning, David Bruce *mathematics professor*

Fargo
Brennan, Joseph Patrick *mathematician*
Slator, Brian M. *computer scientist, educator*

Mayville
Champion, Kathleen Ann *mathematics professor*

OHIO

Ashtabula
Najafi, Mahmoud *mathematics professor*

Athens
Uspenskiy, Vladimir Vladimirovich *mathematics professor*
Wen, Shih-Liang *mathematics professor*

Berea
Little, Richard Allen *mathematics professor, computer science educator*

Cincinnati
Chalkley, Roger *mathematics professor*
Fei, Lin *statistician*
Jone, Wen-Ben *computer scientist, researcher*
Lindsell, Christopher J. *statistician*

Cleveland
Agayev, Nazim G. *mathematics professor*

Ballou, Ronald Herman *supply chain management educator*
Cirincione, Ross Joseph *mathematician, educator*
Flynn, James O'Donnell *statistician, educator*
Goffman, William *mathematician, educator*
Szarek, Stanislaw Jerzy *mathematics professor*

Columbus
Chandrasekaran, Balakrishnan *computer scientist, educator*
Costin, Ovidiu *mathematics professor*
Davis, Michael Walter *mathematics professor*
Feng, Wu-chi *computer science educator*
Friedman, Avner *mathematician, educator*
Golubitsky, Martin Aaron *mathematician, educator*
Muller, Mervin Edgar *computer scientist, consultant, statistician, educator*
Silverberg, Alice *mathematician, educator*
Zweben, Stuart Harvey *information scientist, educator, dean*

Dayton
Jeyaraj, Anand *information scientist*
Lair, Vickie Sue *mathematics professor*
Wang, Bin *computer scientist, educator*
Wilson, Thomas H. *mathematics professor*

Delaware
Garner, Harvey Louis *computer scientist, engineering educator, consultant*

Kent
Breitbart, Yuri *computer scientist, educator*
Varga, Richard Steven *retired mathematics professor*

Mansfield
Gregory, Thomas Bradford *mathematics professor*

Newark
Raykov, Ivan L. *mathematics professor*

Oberlin
Colley, Susan Jane *mathematician, educator*

Portsmouth
Hamilton, Virginia Mae *mathematics professor, consultant*

Steubenville
Levite, Bernard Lawrence *information scientist, educator*

Warren
He, Min *mathematics professor*

Westerville
Brombacher, Bruce E. *mathematics educator*

Wooster
Geiser, Robert Neil *computer scientist*

OKLAHOMA

Edmond
Loman, Mary LaVerne *retired mathematics professor*

Midwest City
Harrell, Beverly Ellen *mathematics professor*

Norman
Apanasov, Boris N. *mathematics professor, researcher*
Breen, Marilyn *mathematics educator*
Page, Rex L. *computer scientist, educator, software consultant*

Oklahoma City
Soderstrand, Michael Alan *mathematics professor, electrical engineer*

OREGON

Ashland
Tikekar, Rahul Vasant *computer science educator*

Corvallis
Gitelman, Alix I. *statistician, educator*
Kovchegov, Yevgeniy V. *mathematics professor*
Parks, Harold Raymond *mathematician, educator*
Petersen, Roger Gene *biometrician, educator*
Temesgen, Hailemariam *statistician, educator*

Portland
Bleiler, Steven A. *mathematician*

Tigard
DeRuntz, John A., Jr. *computer scientist*

PENNSYLVANIA

Aston
DiMarco, David *mathematician, educator*

Bethlehem
Cao, Huai-Dong *mathematician*
Caskie, Grace I. L. *statistics professor*
Schattschneider, Doris Jean *retired mathematics professor*
Terlaky, Tamás *mathematics educator*

Bryn Mawr
Ackoff, Russell Lincoln *social systems designer, educator*

East Stroudsburg
Che, Dongsheng *computer scientist, educator*

Easton
McMahon, Elizabeth Wagner *mathematician, educator*
Traldi, Lorenzo *mathematician, educator*

Indiana
Stoudt, Gary Scott *mathematics professor*

Kutztown
Vasko, Francis Joseph *mathematics professor*

Lancaster
Tien, Joy Garcia *mathematics, human development counseling professor*

Monroeville
Wagner, Greg William *computer scientist, educator*

Philadelphia
Banerji, Ranan Bihari *mathematics professor*
de Cani, John Stapley *retired statistician, educator*
Iglewicz, Boris *statistician, educator*
Kadison, Richard Vincent *mathematician, educator*
Knopp, Marvin Isadore *mathematics professor*
Mode, Charles J. *mathematician, educator*
Porter, Gerald Joseph *mathematician, educator*

Pittsburgh
Balas, Egon *mathematician, educator*
Caginalp, Gunduz *mathematician, educator, researcher*
Carbo, Toni (Toni Carbo Bearman) *information scientist, educator*
Christin, Nicolas *computer scientist, researcher*
Cox, Richard James *information science educator*
Fienberg, Stephen Elliott *statistician*
Heath, David Clay *mathematics professor, consultant*
Noll, Walter *mathematics professor*
Stoffer, David Stewart *mathematics educator*
von Ahn, Luis *computer science educator, computer scientist*
Wing, Jeannette Marie *computer science educator, consultant*

Pittston
Kupetz, James Michael *mathematics professor*

Schnecksville
Labbiento, Julianne Marie *mathematics professor*
Schillow, Ned William *mathematics professor*

State College
Simpson, Stephen George *mathematician*

Tobyhanna
Lapidus, Arnold *mathematician, educator*

University Park
Andrews, George Eyre *mathematics professor*
Barlow, Jesse Louis *computer scientist, educator*
Bressan, Alberto *mathematics professor*
Miller, Webb C. *computer scientist, biology professor*

Villanova
Beck, Robert Edward *computer scientist, educator*
Norton, Douglas Evatt *mathematician, educator*

Wallingford
Morrison, Donald Franklin *statistician, educator*

Washington
Forrest, Robert Gilliland *mathematics professor*

RHODE ISLAND

Providence
Dafermos, Constantine Michael *applied mathematics professor*
Fleming, Wendell Helms *mathematician, educator*
Freiberger, Walter Frederick *mathematics professor*
Intrator, Nathan *applied mathematician, researcher*
Kushner, Harold Joseph *mathematics professor*
McClure, Donald E. *mathematics professor, mathematical society executive*
Mumford, David Bryant *mathematics professor*
Shu, Chi-Wang *mathematics professor, researcher*
Silverman, Joseph Hillel *mathematics professor*
Zhao, Lan *mathematics professor*

SOUTH CAROLINA

Aiken
Fadimba, Koffi Baana *mathematics professor*
Reid, Thomas F. *mathematics professor*

Charleston
Rollins, John Maxwell *business professor, disc jockey*

Clemson
Brawley, Joel Vincent *mathematician, educator*

Columbia
Dilworth, Stephen James *mathematics educator*
Padgett, William Jowayne *mathematics professor, researcher*

Greenville
Higgins, Elizabeth Tate *mathematics professor, director*

Pendleton
Marshall, Gerald Lee *mathematician, educator*

Seneca
Kenelly, John Willis, Jr. *mathematician, educator*

Spartanburg
Wilde, Edwin Frederick *retired mathematics professor*

SOUTH DAKOTA

Aberdeen
Mendez, Celestino Galo *mathematics professor, dean*

Vermillion
Georgescu, Catalin *mathematician, educator*

TENNESSEE

Brownsville
Kalin, Robert *retired mathematics professor*

Chattanooga
Barioli, Francesco *mathematics professor*
Carnes, Neil Patrick *mathematics educator*
Ebiefung, Aniekan Asukwo *mathematics professor, researcher*

Columbia
Horner, Linda T. *mathematician, department chairman*

Knoxville
Abidi, Besma Roui *information scientist, educator*

Martin
Schommer, John Joseph *mathematics professor*

Memphis
Bacopulos, Dionysia Stacey *mathematics professor*
Fuller, Wayne Louis *logistics manager, retired air force officer*
Johnson, Joseph Erle *mathematician*
Kozma, Robert *mathematics professor, director*
Schelp, Richard Herbert *retired mathematics professor*

Nashville
Cooil, Bruce Kimo *mathematical statistician, statistics educator*
McCowan, Otis Blakely *mathematics professor*
Plummer, Michael David *mathematics professor*
Reed, Michael Eugene *mathematics professor*
Saff, Edward Barry *mathematics professor, dean*
Sidek, Naim *information scientist*
Williams, Marsha Rhea *computer scientist, educator, researcher, consultant*

Oak Ridge
Kim, Dongkyun *computer scientist*
Raridon, Richard Jay *retired computer scientist*

TEXAS

Alpine
Morgan, Raymond Victor, Jr. *mathematics professor*

Arlington
Dragan, Irinel Chiril *mathematics educator*
Khan, Samee Ullah *computer scientist*
Ren-Cang, Li *mathematician, educator*

Austin
Babuska, Ivo Milan *mathematics professor*
Caffarelli, Luis Angel *mathematician, educator*
Clark, Charles T(aliferro) *retired statistician*
Doyle, Marcus H. *computer technology educator*
Jones, William Richard *database administrator*
Martin, Norman Marshall *computer science educator*
Mookherjee, Reetabrata *computer scientist*
Moore, J. Strother *computer scientist, educator*
Novak, Gordon S., Jr. *computer scientist, educator*
Tate, John Torrence *mathematics professor, researcher*
Voges, Linda Kay *mathematics professor, communications engineer, educational coordinator*

Beaumont
Kemble, Joe David *mathematics professor*

Bedford
Dawes, Robert Leo *mathematician, consultant*

Brenham
Anglin, Karen Locher *mathematics professor*

Brownsville
Oudshoorn, Michael John *computer science educator*
Yi, Taeil *mathematician, educator*

Bryan
Loguinov, Dmitri *computer scientist, educator*

Coldspring
Dietterich, Thomas Glen *computer scientist, educator*

College Station
Calvin, James Arthur *statistician, educator*
Stroustrup, Bjarne *computer science and engineering professor*
Zheng, Qi *statistician, biomathematician*

Colleyville
Hennessey, Audrey Kathleen *computer researcher, educator*

Dallas
Ammari, Habib *computer science educator, researcher*
Browne, Richard Harold *statistician, consultant*
Gavish, Bezalel *computer science operations research, information systems educator*

Denton
Hays, Edith H. *mathematics educator*
Renka, Robert Joseph *computer science educator, consultant*
Thompson, Frances McBroom *mathematics professor, writer*

Edinburg
Poletaeva, Elena *mathematician, researcher*
Yagdjian, Karen *mathematics professor*

El Paso
Foged, Leslie Owen *mathematician, educator*
Leung, Ming-Ying *mathematics professor*

Fort Sam Houston
Wojcik, Barbara Elzbieta *statistician, researcher*

Fort Worth
Weaber, Terry Lee *information scientist*

Galveston
Freeman, Daniel Herbert, Jr. *biostatistician*

Hewitt
Walbesser, Henry Herman *computer science educator*

Houston
Brown, Dennison Robert *mathematician, educator*
Fernández, Ariel *mathematics educator*
Glowinski, Roland *mathematics professor*
Kakadiaris, Ioannis *computer science educator*
Kavraki, Lydia *computer scientist, educator*
Keller-McNulty, Sallie *statistician, educator, dean*
Keyfitz, Barbara Lee *mathematics educator*
Lai, Dejian *statistics educator*
Miller, Charles Rickie *systems analyst, engineering executive*
Swartz, Michael D. *statistical geneticist*
Tucker, Susan *biomathematics and computational biology professor*
Wright, Clark Phillips *computer systems specialist*
Young, John David *information systems analyst, consultant*

Irving
Cherri, Mona Y. *computer scientist, consultant, educator*

Laredo
Goonatilake, Rohitha *mathematician, educator*

Lubbock
Lakhani, Gopal *computer scientist, educator*
Sobolewski, Michael Vladyslav *computer scientist*

Mcallen
von Kuster, Lee Norman *retired mathematics professor*

Mesquite
Dennis-Monzingo, Vivian Ann *mathematics professor*
Keylon, Dorothy Marie *mathematics professor*
Lo, Timothy P. *mathematics professor*

Plano
Karr, Rosemary M. *mathematics professor*

Prairie View
Hritonenko, Natali *mathematics professor, researcher*
Michev, Dimitar Perov *mathematics professor*

Richardson
Wiorkowski, John James *mathematics professor*

San Antonio
Jimenez, Daniel Angel *computer scientist, educator*
Redfield, Carol Ann Luckhardt *computer scientist, educator*
Roy, Anuradha *statistician, educator, researcher*
Yang, Zhanbo *mathematics professor, researcher*

San Marcos
Price, Larry R. *statistician, educator*

Texas City
Robertson, Paul Francis *mathematician, educator, technologist, entrepreneur*

Tyler
Fan, Wei *operations research specialist*

Valley Mills
Odell, Patrick Lowry *retired mathematics professor*

Waco
Henderson, Johnny *mathematician, educator*
Rolf, Howard Leroy *mathematician, educator*
Sheng, Qin *mathematics professor*

UTAH

Logan
Kohler, Brynja Raquel *mathematics professor*
Symanzik, Juergen *statistician, educator*

Orem
Ling, Jun Michael *mathematics professor*
Moore, Hal G. *retired mathematician, educator*

Park City
Vance, Dianne Sanchez *mathematician, educator*

Salt Lake City
Wozniak, Steve (Stephen Gary Wozniak) *computer scientist, philanthropist*

VERMONT

Burlington
Dinitz, Jeffrey H. *mathematics professor*

Norwich
Snapper, Ernst *mathematics professor*

VIRGINIA

Alexandria
Chen, Fen *mathematician, educator, researcher*
Wasserstein, Ronald L. *statistics organization director*
Weinrich, Brian Erwin *mathematician, computer scientist*

Annandale
Walters, Karen M. *mathematics professor*

Arlington
Moris, Francisco *senior analyst*
Stoto, Michael A. *statistician, epidemiologist*
Tichenor, Charles Beckham III *operations research analyst*

Blacksburg
Arnold, Jesse Charles *retired statistician*
Hovakimyan, Naira *mathematician, educator*
Varadarajan, Srinidhi *computer scientist*

Charlottesville
Horgan, Cornelius Oliver *applied mathematics and mechanics professor, engineering educator*
Parshall, Brian J. *mathematician, educator*
Thomas, Lawrence Eldon *mathematics professor*

Chesapeake
Locke, L. Muriel *mathematician, educator*

Clifton
Hoffman, Karla Leigh *mathematician, educator*

Emory
Jones, Jerry Lee *computer educator*

Fairfax
Agnarsson, Geir *mathematics educator*
Emelianenko, Maria *mathematics professor*
Lawrence, James Franklin *mathematician, researcher*
Wegman, Edward Joseph *statistician, educator, researcher*

Falls Church
Hibbs, Ernest G. *computer scientist, engineering executive*

Fredericksburg
Hajek, Otomar *mathematician, educator*

Great Falls
Lillard, Mark Hill III *engineering consultant, retired military officer*

Hampton
Ali, Halima N. *mathematics professor, researcher*
Boonthum, Chutima *computer scientist, educator*
Jones, Opel Tamian, I, *mathematics professor, director*
Nazaryan, Hovakim *mathematician, researcher, atmospheric scientist*
Verma, Arun K. *mathematician, educator*

Harrisonburg
Taalman, Laura Anne *mathematics professor*

Herndon
Draper, William David *subject matter expert*
Khazen, Ellida Moiseyevna *mathematician*

Manassas
Bruno, Irene Evelyn *mathematician, educator*

Mc Lean
Ellison, Earl Otto *computer scientist*

Norfolk
Naik, Dayanand N. *statistician, educator*
Tolk, Andreas *computer scientist, researcher*

Petersburg
Lakew, Dejenie Alemayehu *mathematician*
Perdue, Diana S. *mathematician, educator*

Richmond
Charlesworth, Arthur Thomas *mathematics professor*
Sedaghat, Hassan *mathematician, educator*

Sterling
Martin, Roger John *computer scientist*

Vienna
Gardenier, John Stark *statistician, philosopher, researcher, writer*
Gardenier, Turkan Kumbaraci *statistician, researcher*

Virginia Beach
Cheng, George Chiwo *computer scientist*

Williamsburg
Rodman, Leiba *mathematician*

Woodbridge
Kellermann, Charles William *information scientist, educator*

Yorktown
Pinelli, Thomas Edward *information scientist*

WASHINGTON

Bellevue
Jakkula, Vikramaditya Reddy *computer scientist, researcher*

Eastsound
de Boor, Carl-Wilhelm R. *mathematician*

Kenmore
Sobolewski, John Stephen *computer scientist, director, consultant*

Kennewick
Cochran, James Alan *emeritus mathematics professor, department chairman, dean*

Olympia
Cheng, Yuk Wing *biometrician*

Orcas
Greever, John *retired mathematics professor*

Pullman
Kallaher, Michael Joseph *mathematics professor*

Redmond
Lomet, David Bruce *computer scientist*
Smith, Burton Jordan *computer designer*

Seattle
Breslow, Norman Edward *biostatistics educator, researcher*
Chalodhorn, Rawichote *computer scientist*
Devinatz, Ethan Sander *mathematics professor*
Doran, Charles Francis, Jr. *mathematician, professor*
Green, Philip P. *mathematician, educator, computer scientist*
Irving, Ron *mathematics professor*
Kalet, Ira Joseph *medical computer scientist*
Lee, John Marshall *mathematics professor*
Mason, Robert McSpadden *information scientist, educator, dean*
Michael, Ernest Arthur *mathematics professor*
Segal, Jack *mathematics professor*
Thompson, Elizabeth Alison *mathematics professor*
Urban, Nicole D. *biostatistician*
Wellner, Jon August *statistician, educator*
Yang, Yang *statistician, medical researcher*

Tacoma
Stuart, Jeffrey L. *mathematics professor, consultant*

Yakima
Lopez, George E. *mathematics professor*

WEST VIRGINIA

Bethany
Fletcher, Adam C. *mathematics professor*

Montgomery
Munasinghe, Ranjith Arachchige *mathematics professor, engineer*

Morgantown
Vatsa, Mayank *computer scientist, researcher*

West Liberty
Fliess, Robert F. *mathematics professor*

WISCONSIN

Chetek
Fossum, Robert Merle *mathematician, educator*

Green Bay
Conley, William Cleland *statistician, educator*
Kurenok, Vladimir *mathematics professor*

Madison
Askey, Richard Allen *mathematician, educator*
Beck, Anatole *mathematician, educator*
Bringmann, Kathrin *mathematician, educator*
DeWitt, David J. *computer scientist*
Draper, Norman Richard *statistician, educator*
Ferris, Michael C. *mathematics professor*
Kurtz, Thomas Gordon *mathematics professor*
Malkus, David Starr *mathematician*
Mau, Bob *statistician, evolutionary biologist*
Nagel, Alexander *mathematics professor*
Ozeki, Akichika *statistician*
Parter, Seymour Victor *computer science and mathematics educator*
Robinson, Stephen Michael *mathematician, educator*
Theron, Peter *mathematics professor*

Milwaukee
Factor, Kim A.S. *mathematics professor, educational consultant*

New Berlin
Weiner, Louis Max *retired mathematics educator*

River Falls
Ghenciu, Ioana *mathematics professor*

Whitewater
Baica, Malvina Florica *mathematics professor, researcher*
Drucker, Thomas Lyndon *mathematics professor*

Nam, Ki-Bong *mathematics professor*
Oravec, Jo Ann Rose *computing and public policy educator*

WYOMING

Casper
Wildman, Peter Roberts *mathematics professor*

TERRITORIES OF THE UNITED STATES

PUERTO RICO

Cayey
Montes-Pizarro, Errol L. *mathematician, researcher*

Mayaguez
Collins, Dennis Glenn *mathematics professor*
Jury, Mark Robert *metrologist, educator*

San Juan
Engman, Martin Feeney *mathematics professor*
Pasnicu, Cornel *mathematician, educator*

MILITARY ADDRESSES OF THE UNITED STATES

EUROPE

APO
Simpson, Sandra Kay *logistics specialist*

CANADA

BRITISH COLUMBIA

Burnaby
Brinkman, Fiona Susan *bioinformaticist, educator, molecular biologist*

Vancouver
Clark, Colin Whitcomb *mathematics professor*
Feldman, Joel Shalom *mathematician*
Granirer, Edmond Ernest *mathematician, educator*
Sion, Maurice *mathematics professor*

Victoria
Manning, Eric *computer scientist, educator, dean, researcher*
Meadow, Charles *information scientist, writer*

NEW BRUNSWICK

Saint Andrews
Anderson, John Murray *operations research specialist, consultant, retired academic administrator*

NOVA SCOTIA

Halifax
Fillmore, Peter Arthur *mathematician, educator*

ONTARIO

London
Bauer, Michael Anthony *computer scientist, educator*
Borwein, David *mathematics professor*

Ottawa
Dlab, Vlastimil *mathematics professor, researcher*
Fellegi, Ivan Peter *statistician*

Toronto
Friedlander, John Benjamin *mathematician, educator*
Gotlieb, Calvin Carl *computer scientist, educator*
Gruia, Ronald Floriano *systems analyst*
Rooney, Paul George *mathematics professor*

Waterloo
Aczél, János Dezsö *mathematician*
Paldus, Josef *mathematics professor*

QUEBEC

Montreal
Suen, Ching Yee *computer scientist, educator, researcher*

AUSTRALIA

North Ryde
Ryan, Louise *statistician, educator*

Sydenham
Marasigan, Rodel Castillo *systems analyst*

BRAZIL

Fortaleza
Teixeira, Eduardo V. *mathematics professor*

Rio de Janeiro
de Araújo, Aloisio Pessoa *mathematics professor*

BULGARIA

Sofia
Georgiev, Svetlin Georgiev *mathematics professor, researcher*
Valev, Ventzeslav Vassilev *computer scientist, educator, researcher*

CHINA

Nanjing
Han, Lixin *information scientist, educator*

Shanghai
Lu, Bao-Liang *computer scientist, educator*

CZECH REPUBLIC

Brno
Klapka, Jindřich Ludvík *mathematician, physicist, educator, researcher*

ENGLAND

Cambridge
Baker, Alan *mathematician*
Hoare, Sir Charles Antony Richard *computer scientist, researcher*
Milner, Robin *computer scientist*
Wilkes, Sir Maurice V. *computer science emeritus professor, computer scientist*

Leicestershire
Levendorskii, Serge Zakhar *mathematics educator*

London
Gelenbe, Sami Erol *computer scientist, engineering educator*
Ralston, Anthony *computer scientist, mathematician, educator*

FINLAND

Jyväskylä
Lartillot, Olivier *computer scientist, educator, researcher*

FRANCE

Nozay
Betgé-Brezetz, Stéphane *computer scientist, researcher*

Paris
Lehalle, Charles-Albert *mathematician*
Serre, Jean-Pierre *mathematician, scholar*
Yuechiming, Roger Yue Yuen Shing *mathematics professor*

Valbonne
Junker, Ulrich Martin *computer scientist, researcher*

GERMANY

Berlin
Jochmann, Frank *mathematician*

Bielefeld
Roeckner, Michael G. *mathematics professor*

Bonn
Korte, Bernhard Hermann *mathematician, researcher*

Braunschweig
Leseberg, Dieter Wolfgang Michael *mathematician*

Bremen
Wells, Raymond O'Neil, Jr. *mathematics professor, researcher*

Hamburg
Ayvazyan, Valeri *computer scientist, researcher, physicist, consultant*

INDIA

Mumbai
Sen, Pranab *computer scientist, researcher*

ISRAEL

Jerusalem
Hrushovski, Ehud *mathematics professor*

ITALY

Turin
Elia, Michele *mathematics professor*
Rossi, Guido A(ntonio) *mathematics professor, researcher*

JAPAN

Aizu-Wakamatsu
Watanabe, Shigeru *mathematician, researcher*

Gifu
Hatada, Kazuyuki *mathematician, educator*

Gunma
Hironaka, Heisuke *mathematics professor, academic administrator*

Ibaraki
Urabe, Tohsuke *mathematics professor, researcher*

Okayama
Kamiya, Hidehiko *statistics and economics professor*

Tokyo
Eto, Hajime *retired information scientist, educator*
Kato, Shuichi *information scientist, educator*
Kunii, Tosiyasu Laurence *information science educator*
Tachi, Susumu *robotics educator*
Tokoro, Mario *computer scientist*
Yaku, Takeo T. *computer scientist, educator*

MALAYSIA

Shah Alam
Zainal-Abidin, Siti-Zaleha *computer scientist, educator*

NORWAY

Oslo
Fenstad, Jens Erik *mathematics professor*

PORTUGAL

Lisbon
Campos, Luís Manuel Braga da Costa *mathematics, physics, acoustics and aeronautics educator*

REPUBLIC OF KOREA

Gyeonggi
Seo, KyungHee *computer scientist, educator*

Puchon
Kang, Hang-Bong *computer scientist, educator*

Seoul
Han, Youngmo *computer professor*
Im, Bo-Hae *mathematician, educator*
Keum, Jong-Hae *mathematician, educator*
Oh, Myoungho *computer scientist, educator*

RUSSIA

Moscow
Novikov, Sergei Petrovich *mathematician*
Romanovski, Mikhail Rem *mathematician*
Tsapenko, Nikolai Evgenievich *mathematician, educator*
Vladimirov, Vasiliy Sergeyevich *mathematician*

SCOTLAND

Edinburgh
Atiyah, Sir Michael Francis *mathematician*
Finney, David John *biometrician*

SOUTH AFRICA

Rondebosch
Ellis, George Francis Rayner *mathematics professor*

SRI LANKA

Colombo
Wirasinha, Hemamali Anushka *computer scientist, researcher*

SWEDEN

Västerås
Xiong, Ning *computer scientist*

SWITZERLAND

Lausanne
Rozza, Gianluigi *mathematician, aerospace engineer*

TURKEY

Ankara
Elbasi, Ersin *computer scientist, researcher*

Sariyer
Alkan, Emre *mathematics professor*

UKRAINE

Kiev
Reznykov, Illya Igorevich *mathematician, application developer*

ADDRESS UNPUBLISHED

Agut, Calin M. *mathematics professor*
Airoldi, Edoardo Maria *statistician, researcher, computer scientist, consultant*
Albrecht, Rebekah S. *mathematician, educator*
Ali, Kamal Mahmood *computer scientist*
Allen, Frances Elizabeth *computer scientist*
Arciniega, Armando *mathematics professor*
Arden, Bruce Wesley *retired computer scientist, engineering educator*
Arsie, Alessandro *mathematician, researcher*
Bacon, Leslie Edward *operations analysis manager*
Bagert, Donald Joseph *computer scientist, educator*
Bailar, Barbara Ann *retired statistician*
Barrett, Lida Kittrell *mathematics professor*
Beach, Michael Lindsay *statistician*
Bennett, Curtis Dwight *mathematician*
Benson, Donald Charles *mathematician, educator*
Bentley, Donald Lyon *statistics professor, minister*
Bhadra, Jayanta *computer scientist, electrical engineer*
Bhattacharya, Tilak *mathematics professor*
Bi, Jian *senior statistician, consultant*
Biswas, Pinaki *statistician*
Blair, David Clark *information scientist, educator*
Bloch, Anthony Michael *mathematician, educator*
Boardman, Elizabeth Drake *computer security professional*
Bokhari, Naila Qureshi *mathematician, educational consultant*
Bollapragada, Ramesh *information scientist, educator*
Borwein, Jonathan Michael *mathematics professor*
Bose, Sudip *statistician, educator*
Breen, Judith Snyder *mathematics professor*
Browder, Felix Earl *mathematician, educator*
Bullard, Lofton Alexander *mathematics professor*
Bush, William Read *computer scientist*
Cameron, Kirk MacGregor Drummond *statistician*
Caroleo, Linn E. *mathematics professor, writer, freelance/self-employed photographer*
Carroll, John Millar *computer science and psychology educator*
Cecil, David Rolf *mathematician, educator*
Chen, Shiping *information scientist*
Cheng, Jing-Ru C. *computer scientist, researcher*
Cherepanov, Genady Petrovich *mathematician, mechanical engineer*
Chicone, Carmen *mathematics professor*
Choi, Wooyoung *mathematics professor*
Chow, Timothy Yi-Chung *mathematician, systems engineer*
Clark, Hilary J. *mathematics professor*
Claus, Alison S. *mathematics education professor*
Clote, Peter George *computer scientist, mathematician, educator*
Cohen, Michael Paul *statistician*
Combs, Roy James, Jr. *systems analyst, researcher*
Corbett, Lenora Meade *mathematician, community college educator*
Costanza, Michael C. *retired statistics professor*
Daily, Deirdre Lynn *systems analyst*
Daquila, Richard *mathematics professor*
Davis, Brian Lee *mathematics professor*
Dittenhafer, Daniel Webster, II, *computer scientist*
Dixon, Albert Truman *mathematician, educator*
Dominguez, Alvio *mathematics professor*
Dumett, Miguel *mathematician*
Easton, Roger L. *former operations research specialist, consultant*
Edoh, Kossi *mathematics professor*
Efird, Jimmy Thomas *statistician*
Elliott, David LeRoy *mathematics and engineering educator*
Ellwanger, Steven Joseph *statistician*
Erdil, Deger Cenk *computer scientist*
Evans, Tyler Jonah *mathematics professor*
Exner, Frank Kepler *information scientist, indexer*
Fausett, Laurene Van Camp *mathematics professor*
Feng, Chengde *mathematician, educator*
Feng, Rui *statistician, educator*
Fields-Harris, Deborah Carol *mathematician, educator*
Folsom, Amanda L. *mathematician, educator*
Francis, Mildred Elaine *retired statistician, epidemiologist*
Frankston, Robert M. *computer software executive, developer*
Fukuta, Naoki *computer scientist, researcher*
Fuller, Nancy MacMurray *mathematics professor*
Gelfand, Israil Moiseievich (Izrail) *mathematician, biologist*
Gerson, Donald Jerome *computer scientist, consultant, photographer, small business owner*
Gessaman, Margaret Palmer *mathematician, educator, retired dean*
Gifford, Marjorie Fitting *mathematician, educator, consultant*
Gnanadesikan, Ramanathan *retired statistics educator, researcher*
Goldberg, Samuel *retired mathematician, foundation administrator*
Golub, Evan *computer science educator*
Greenwood, Frank *information scientist, educator*
Griffiths, Phillip A. *mathematician, retired academic administrator*
Grothendieck, Alexandre *retired mathematician*
Guild, Jeffrey K. *mathematics professor*
Gulick, Sidney (Denny) L. III *mathematics professor, writer*
Guo, Yong *statistician*
Halberstam, Heini *mathematics professor*
Hamel, Louis Reginald *retired systems analyst*
Hardie, Michael Howard *mathematician, educator*
Harnedy, Joan Catherine Holland *retired systems analyst*
Hayes, David Ryan *mathematics professor*
Hill, Michael Anthony *mathematics professor*
Holford, Theodore Richard *biostatistician, educator*
Hollis, Deborah D. *systems analyst, application developer*
Hsieh, Din-Yu *applied mathematics professor*
Hu, Hongde *mathematics professor*
Huang, Lan *statistician*
Hudachek-Buswell, Mary R. *mathematics professor*
Ismail, Ari *computer scientist*
Ivie, Evan Leon *computer science educator*
Jackson, Deborah Cheryl *mathematician*
Jahns, Angela Marie *mathematics professor*
Jasti, Srichand *statistician*
Jeffries, Clark D. *mathematician, educator*
Jin, Guohua *computer scientist, educator*
Johnstone, Iain Murray *statistician, educator, consultant*
Jones, Anita Katherine *computer scientist, educator*
Jow, Shin-Yao *mathematics professor*
Kadota, Takashi Theodore *mathematician, electrical engineer*
Kashcheyeva, Olga *mathematics professor, researcher*
Keala, Betty Ann Lyman *computer scientist*
Khuri, Marcus A. *mathematics professor*
King, Amy Cathryne Patterson *retired mathematics educator, researcher*
Kister, James Milton *retired mathematician, educator*
Krantz, Steven George *mathematics professor, writer*
Kryzhniy, Vladimir V. *mathematics professor, researcher*
Kumar, Sathish Alampalyam Poru *computer scientist, engineering educator, information technology manager*
La, Wayne H. *mathematics professor*
Lampson, Butler Wright *computer scientist*
Leach, Ronald J. *computer science educator*
Lee, Tony *analyst developer*
Li, Jichun *mathematics professor, director*
Li, Lide *mathematician, financial engineer*
Li, Xiaojie *senior research associate*
Li, Xin *computer scientist, researcher*
Llora, Xavier *computer scientist, educator*
Longstreet, John Charles *retired computer scientist*
Lotspiech, Jeffrey *computer scientist, consultant*
Lupash, Lawrence Ovidiu *computer analyst, researcher*
Lynch, Robert Emmett *mathematics professor*
Mandelbrot, Benoit B. *mathematician, research scientist, educator*
Manivannan, Dakshnamoorthy *computer scientist, educator*
March, Michael F. *propulsion systems analyst, consultant*
Mattson, Harold Frazyer, Jr. *mathematics professor*
Merritt, Susan Mary *computer science educator, dean*
Mihram, George Arthur *mathematician*
Mikhelson, Sergei *mathematician, educator*
Miller, Allen Richard *retired mathematician*
Mills, Kevin Lee *computer scientist, researcher*
Min, Misun *mathematician*
Miyake, Yasuji *computer science educator*
Moch, Peggy L. *mathematics professor*
Mohanty, Saraju P. *computer scientist, educator*
Moody, Myriam Sylvie *mathematics professor*
Murff, Elizabeth Jane Tipton *mathematician, statistician, educator*
Mysore, Shashidhar C. *computer scientist*
Nation, David Arthur *retired computer scientist, sculptor*
Naylor, Rhonda *mathematics instructor*
Nguyen, Dong *computer scientist, researcher, software engineer, educator*
Nicoara, Andreea Carina *mathematics professor*
Norton, Peter K. *retired computer utilities programmer, writer*
Oliver, Nuria Maria *computer science researcher*
Orszag, Steven Alan *applied mathematician, educator*
O'Toole, William Edward III *retired computer science and mathematics professor*
Overall, Theresa Lynne *educational technology professor*
Packer, Judith Anne *mathematics professor*
Padberg, Harriet Ann *mathematician, educator*
Pakhomov, Alexander Alexandrovich *information scientist, consultant*
Pantano, Alessandra *mathematics professor*
Pickle, Linda Williams *biostatistician*
Pilla, Venkata *systems analyst*
Pointurier, Yvan *computer scientist*
Pollock, Karen Anne *computer analyst*
Quick, Renee *mathematics professor, department chairman*
Ramos, Jorge Rafael *computer scientist, researcher*
Ratha, Nalini K. *computer scientist, researcher*
Reece, Julia Ruth *systems analyst, entrepreneur*
Reed, David Patrick *information scientist*
Reichenbach, Linda Louise *mathematician, language educator*
Reinhardt, Steven K. *computer scientist*
Rejman, Diane Louise *business analyst*
Riffenburgh, Robert Harry *biostatistician, researcher*
Robinson, Molly Jahnige *statistician, educator*
Roitman, Judith *mathematician, educator, poet*
Rosario, Bedda L. *statistician*
Rosen, Judah Ben *computer scientist*
Rotman, Joseph Jonah *mathematician, educator*
Rus, Teodor *computer scientist, educator*
Safer, Alan *statistician, educator*
Salahuddin, Parveen *information scientist, researcher*
Santhanaraman, Gopalakrishnan *computer scientist*
Schneider, Edgar Rolf Gottfried *retired mathematician, application developer, writer*
Schupp, Russ *computer professor, web site designer*
Seidman, Stephen Benjamin *dean, computer science educator*
Seleznev, Vadim Eugenjevich *mathematician, researcher*
Shan, Ying *computer scientist*
Sherman, Jimmie Lee *mathematician, educator*
Shier, Gloria Bulan *mathematics professor*
Sinha, Rakesh Kumar *computer scientist, researcher*
Sloane, Neil James Alexander *mathematician, researcher*
Solomon, Abraham Lev *mathematics professor*
Souganidis, Panagiotis Emmanuel *mathematician, educator*
Spinrad, Robert Joseph *computer scientist*
Stanley, Kenneth *statistician, educator*
Štěpánek, Petr *computer science educator*
Sultanik, Evan Andrew *computer scientist*
Suppes, Patrick *statistician, philosopher, psychologist, educator*
Tang, Irving Che-hong *mathematician, educator*
Tartakovsky, Daniel M. *applied mathematician*
Taubin, Alexander *computer scientist, educator*
Taylor, Joshua Aaron *computer scientist*
Teleman, Silviu *mathematician, educator*
Tobiassen, Barbara Sue *systems analyst, consultant, volunteer*
Tsui, Sze-Kai Jack *mathematics educator*
Tyrl, Paul *mathematics professor, researcher*
Tzeng, Jung-Ying *statistician, researcher*
Ullman, Nelly Szabo *statistician, educator*
Vasseur, Alexis Frederic *mathematics professor*
Vellanki, Gangadhar B. *information scientist, consultant*
Wallace, Linda Kay *mathematics professor*
Wang, Haiqin *computer scientist*
Wang, Ye-Yi *computer scientist*
Warma, Mahamadi Jacob *mathematics professor*
Warner, William Hamer *mathematician*
Watkins, Ann Esther *mathematics professor*
Wilding, Diane *computer scientist, consultant*
Williams, Ronald Oscar *mathematician*
Wimpffen, Otto Rudolph *mathematics professor*
Winder, Robert Owen *mathematician, computer engineer, geophysicist*
Wood, Terry Lee *mathematics educator*
Worthington, Tracy *retired operations research analyst*
Wren, Stephen Corey *mathematician, inventor*
Xie, Haiyong *computer scientist*
Xie, Lexing *computer scientist*
Yadrick, Robert Martin *operations analyst*
Yemelyanov, Alexander M. *mathematician, educator*
Yoo, Hun-Woo *information scientist, researcher*
Young, Judith A. *retired mathematics professor*
Yu, Jie *computer scientist*
Zeilberger, Doron *mathematics professor, researcher*
Zhang, Lixin *computer scientist, researcher*
Zhang, Sheng *computer scientist, researcher*
Zhao, Jianliang Leon *computer scientist, educator, computer scientist, researcher*
Zhou, Biao *computer scientist*
Zierler, Neal *retired mathematician*

SCIENCE: PHYSICAL SCIENCE

UNITED STATES

ALABAMA

Auburn
Park, Minseo *physicist, educator*

Birmingham
Chowdhury, Shafiul A. *research scientist*
Chung, Byung-Hong *retired biochemist*
Miyagawa, Ichiro *physicist*
Robinson, Edward Lee *retired physics professor, consultant*
Vyazovkin, Sergey *chemistry professor*

Huntsville
Allan, Barry David *research chemist, government official*
Burko, Lior M. *physicist, educator*
Cirtain, Jonathan W. *astrophysicist*
Costes, Nicholas Constantine *aerospace scientist, educator, retired government agency administrator*
Elsamadicy, Abdalla Mousa *physics professor*
Norman, Ralph Louis *retired physicist, consultant*
Parnell, Thomas Alfred *physicist*
Smith, Robert Earl *space scientist*
Su, Ching-Hua *materials scientist*
Vaughan, William Walton *atmospheric scientist*
Wright, John Collins *retired chemistry professor*

Irondale
Statnikov, Efim Smulevich *physicist, researcher*

Mobile
Varghese, Sakoorikal Lonappan *physicist, researcher*

Normal
Batra, Ashok K. *physics professor, researcher*

Tuscaloosa
Dixon, David Adams *chemistry professor, researcher*
Mancini, Ernest Anthony *geologist, educator, researcher*
Mankey, Gary Jay *physics professor, director*
Metzger, Robert Melville *chemistry educator*
Walock, Michael James *research assistant*

Tuskegee
Powell, Nichole Larai *chemistry professor, researcher*
Rangari, Vijaya Kumar *chemistry professor, researcher*

Tuskegee Institute
Kumar, Akshaya *research scientist, educator*

ALASKA

Fairbanks
Bhatt, Uma Suren *meteorologist, educator*
Brigham, Lawson Walter *oceanographer, researcher*
Cahill, Catherine Frances *environmental scientist, educator*
Duffy, Lawrence Kevin *biochemist, educator*
Fathauer, Theodore Frederick *meteorologist*
Kramm, Gerhard *meteorologist, researcher*
Lingle, Craig Stanley *glaciologist, educator*
Mölders, Nicole *environmental scientist, educator*
Roederer, Juan Gualterio *retired physics professor*
Royer, Thomas Clark *oceanographer*

ARIZONA

Amado
Criswell, Stephen *astronomer*

Chandler
Meieran, Eugene Stuart *materials scientist*

Flagstaff
Brumbaugh, David Scott *geophysicist, educator*
Millis, Robert Lowell *astronomer, science observatory director*
Shoemaker, Carolyn Spellman *planetary astronomer*

Glendale
Arias, Hugo Rubén *chemist, biochemist, researcher, educator*
Montague, Michelle Louise *geologist, educator*

Green Valley
Fateley, William Gene *chemist, educator, inventor*

Mesa
Hausel, William Dan *economic geologist, martial artist, public speaker, artist, writer*
Shovkovy, Igor Andriyovich *physicist, researcher*

Phoenix
Allen, John Rybolt L. *chemist, biochemist*
Crosatti, Lorenzo *research scientist*
Patel, Vimla L. *research scientist*

Prescott
Ivanova, Dorothea *physics professor, researcher*

Rio Rico
Lowell, J(ames) David *geological consultant, cattle rancher*

Scottsdale
Hu, Rusheng *research scientist*
Kinsinger, Jack Burl *chemist, educator*
Mutz, Steven *astronomer, educator*

Sierra Vista
Ponder, Herman *geologist*

Sun City
Erickson, Richard Ames *physicist, emeritus educator*

Tempe
Alford, Terry L. *materials scientist, educator*
Anselin, Luc E. *research scientist, educator*
Bauer, Ernst Georg *physicist, researcher*
Carpenter, Ray Warren *materials scientist, engineering educator, materials engineer*
Choi, Seokheun *research scientist*
Goronkin, Herbert *physicist*
Herbots, Nicole *retired physics professor*
Juvet, Richard Spalding, Jr. *chemistry professor*
Maienschein, Fred *retired physicist*
McCartney, Martha Rogers *physics professor*
McKelvy, Michael John *chemist, research scientist*
Moore, Carleton Bryant *geochemistry educator*
Pettit, George Robert *chemist, educator, cancer researcher*
Ponce, Fernando Agustin *physics professor*
Sampson, David Arthur *research scientist*
Shock, Everet *biochemist, educator*

Tucson
Angel, James Roger Prior *astronomer*
Baker, Victor Richard *geologist, hydrologist, researcher, research scientist, educator*
Barrett, Bruce Richard *physics professor*
Bloembergen, Nicolaas *physicist, researcher*
Campbell, Mary Kathryn *chemistry professor*
Chung, Gunhui *hydrologist, researcher*
De Young, David Spencer *astrophysicist, educator*
Dohm, James M. *aerospace scientist*
Dunn, Floyd *biophysics and biomedical engineering professor*
Falco, Charles Maurice *physicist, researcher*
Feng, Changjian *biochemist, chemist*
Girardeau, Marvin Denham *physics professor*
Gruhl, James *energy scientist, artist*
Hall, Henry Kingston, Jr. *chemistry professor*
Hays, James Fred *geologist, educator*
Hill, Henry Allen *physicist, researcher*
Jefferies, John Trevor *astrophysicist, director*
Karkoschka, Erich *planetary science researcher, writer*
Kohler, Sigurd H. *retired physics professor*
Lauer, Tod Richard *astronomer*
Lunine, Jonathan Irving *astronomer, educator*
Macleod, Hugh Angus McIntosh *optical science educator, physicist, consultant*
Marcialis, Robert Louis *planetary astronomer*
McNulty, Terence Patrick *metallurgist, consultant*
Mishra, Sudib Kumar *research scientist*
Mould, Jeremy Richard *astronomer*
Neugebauer, Marcia *physicist, researcher*
Oleshko, Vladimir P. *physical chemist, nanoscience researcher*
Palacios-Fest, Manuel Roberto *geologist, paleoecologist*
Pant, Ravi *research scientist*
Powers, Linda Sue *biophysicist, educator, biomedical engineer*
Prewitt, Charles Thompson *geochemist*
Rieke, Marcia J. *astronomer, educator*
Roemer, Elizabeth *retired astronomer, educator*
Thompson, Rodger Irwin *astrophysicist, educator*
Tifft, William Grant *retired physics professor, scientist*
Tuller, Markus *geophysicist, educator*
Voorakaranam, Ram *optics scientist*
Whitaker, Ewen Adair *retired astronomer*
Wong, Simon S. *environmental health scientist, educator*

ARKANSAS

Arkadelphia
Bradshaw, Joseph Earl *chemistry professor*

Conway
Burris, Debra L. *physics professor*

Fayetteville
Chakhalian, Jak *physics professor*
Kim, Jeong-Hwan *research scientist*
Kunets, Vasyl Petrovych *research scientist*
Steele, Kenneth Franklin, Jr. *hydrologist*
Wilkins, Charles L. *chemist, educator*

Fort Smith
Lee, Arthur Carson *geologist*

Little Rock
Braithwaite, Wilfred John *retired physics professor*
Darsey, Jerome Anthony (Jerry) *chemistry professor, consultant*
Karabacak, Tansel *physics professor, researcher*
Kaushal, Gur Prasad *biochemist, educator*

Pine Bluff
Walker, Richard Brian *chemistry professor*

Searcy
Province, Dennis *chemistry professor*

CALIFORNIA

Agoura Hills
Currie, Malcolm Roderick *retired aerospace and automotive executive, research scientist*

Alhambra
Im, Jaemo *research scientist*

Altadena
Mkryan, Sonya *geophysicist, educator, research scientist*

Angwin
Andrianarijaona, Vola Masoandro *physics professor, researcher*

Atherton
Fried, John H. *chemist*
Gill, Stephen Paschall *retired physicist, mathematician*

Atwater
LiWang, Andy *research scientist, educator*

Auburn
Hess, Patrick Henry *chemist, researcher*

Bayside
Cocks, George Gosson *retired chemical microscopy professor*

Berkeley
Alivisatos, Armand Paul *chemist, educator*
Attwood, David Thomas *physicist, researcher*
Berdahl, Paul Hilland *physicist*
Bergman, Robert George *chemist, educator*
Bragg, Robert Henry *physicist, researcher*
Budnitz, Robert Jay *nuclear scientist*
Calendar, Richard Lane *biochemistry educator*
Cerny, Joseph III *chemistry professor, retired dean, director*
Chew, Geoffrey Foucar *physicist*
Clarke, John *physics professor*
Daftari, Inder Krishen *physicist, researcher*
Dynes, Robert C. *physics professor, former academic administrator*
Firestone, Richard B. *nuclear scientist, researcher*
Fleming, Graham Richard *chemistry educator*
Fowler, Thomas Kenneth *physicist*
Fréchet, Jean *chemistry professor*
Frei, Heinz Markus *research scientist*
Gaillard, Mary Katharine *physicist, educator*
Glaser, Donald Arthur *physicist*
Goldhaber, Gerson *astrophysicist, researcher*
Gombocz, Erich Alfred *biochemist*
Haller, Eugene Ernest *materials scientist, educator*
Hearst, John Eugene *retired chemistry professor, consultant, researcher*
Higgins, Paul Andrew Twistington *research scientist*
Hoffman, Darleane Christian *chemistry professor*
Jackson, J(ohn) David *physicist, researcher*
Kane, Sharad Ramchandra *retired physicist*
Keasling, Jay D. *chemistry professor, research scientist*
Kerth, Leroy T. *physics professor*
Kirz, Janos *physicist*
Klein, Spencer Robert *physicist*
Klinman, Judith Pollock *biochemist, educator*
Ko, Seung Hwan *research scientist*
Kurtzman, Ralph Harold, Jr. *biochemist, researcher, consultant*
Lee, Yuan Tseh *retired chemistry professor*
Lester, William Alexander, Jr. *chemist, educator*
Linn, Stuart Michael *biochemist, educator*
Mandelstam, Stanley *physicist*
Marcy, Geoffrey W. *astronomer, physicist, educator*
Markowitz, Samuel Solomon *chemistry professor*
Miller, William Hughes *theoretical chemist, educator*
Moore, C. Bradley *chemistry professor*
Morris, John William, Jr. *metallurgy educator*
Perlmutter, Saul *astrophysicist, educator*
Perry, Dale Lynn *chemist*
Pines, Alexander *chemistry educator, researcher, consultant*
Quinn, Nigel William Trevelyan *research scientist*
Rasmussen, John Oscar *nuclear research scientist*
Raymond, Kenneth Norman *chemistry professor, researcher*
Ritchie, Robert Oliver *materials science educator, department chairman*
Romanowicz, Barbara *geology and geophysics professor*
Sessler, Andrew Marienhoff *physicist*
Shugart, Howard Alan *physicist, researcher*
Smoot, George Fitzgerald III *astrophysicist*
Somorjai, Gabor Arpad *chemist, educator*
Stapp, Henry Pierce *physicist*
Steiner, Herbert Max *physics professor*
Strauss, Herbert Leopold *chemistry professor*
Thompson, Anthony Wayne *metallurgist, educator, consultant*
Tjian, Robert Tse Nan *biochemistry educator, medical institution administrator*
Townes, Charles Hard *physics professor*
Trilling, George Henry *physicist, researcher*
Valentine, James William *paleontologist, educator, writer*
Whaley, Katharine Birgitta *chemistry professor*
Wiser, Ryan *research scientist*
Wunderer, Cornelia Beatrix *aerospace scientist*
Yang, Peidong *material science researcher*

Camarillo
Gigas, Gunter George *retired physicist, physician*

Carson
Mantravadi, Murty V. *retired optics scientist*

Castaic
Holmes, Dale Arthur *optics scientist*

Claremont
Hansch, Corwin Herman *chemistry professor*
Steinmetz, Wayne Edward *chemistry educator*

Corona Del Mar
Britten, Roy John *biophysicist*

Costa Mesa
Faridi, Abbas M. *physics professor*
Guerra, Arnold III *physics professor*

Crescent City
Carter, Neville Louis *geophysicist, educator*

Cypress
Cully, Joseph Andrew *hazard substance scientist*

Davis
Brynda, Marcin Artur *chemist, researcher*
Burtis, Kenneth C. *biochemist, educator*
Cahill, Thomas Andrew *physicist, researcher*
Calderon de la Barca Sanchez, Manuel *physicist, educator*
Chaudhari, Abhijit Jayawant *research scientist*
Choi, Hongsoo *research scientist*
Conn, Eric Edward *plant biochemist*
Fadley, Charles Sherwood *research scientist, educator*
Fuhs, G(eorg) Wolfgang *environmental research manager*
Hong, Kyung Hwa *research scientist*
Jungerman, John Albert *physics professor*
Kauzlarich, Susan Mary *chemistry educator, researcher*
La Mar, Gerd Neustadter *retired chemistry professor*
Liu, Kai *physics professor*
Medellin-Azuara, Josue *environmental scientist*
Navrotsky, Alexandra *geophysics educator*
Sergueeva, Alla Vladimirovna *materials scientist, researcher*
Shackelford, James Floyd *materials science educator, researcher*
Terning, John *physics professor, researcher*
Zhu, Xiangdong *physics professor*

Del Mar
Kenyon, Kern E. *retired oceanographer*

Duarte
Williams, Lawrence Ernest *physicist*

Edwards
Liu, Chi Tsieh *aerospace scientist, researcher*

El Dorado Hills
Bartlett, Robert Watkins *metallurgist, educator, consultant*

El Segundo
Buettner, Douglas John *physicist, astronautical engineer, director*

Emeryville
Masri, Merle Sid *biochemist, consultant*

Eureka
Kramer, Erik Daniel *physics professor*

Fountain Valley
Armstrong, Jeffrey Lee *oceanographer*

Fresno
Gruet, Karin *chemistry professor*
Kauffman, George Bernard *chemistry professor*
Wang, Zhi *environmental scientist, educator*

Fullerton
Atallah, Youssef Chahine *environmental scientist*
Lundegard, Paul *geologist, consultant*
Shapiro, Mark Howard *physicist, educator, dean*

Gardena
Martin, Melissa Carol *radiological physicist*

Glen Ellen
Berkland, James Omer *geologist*

Half Moon Bay
Lu, Adolph *physicist, researcher*

Hayward
Helgren, Erik B. *physics professor*

Hemet
Berger, Lev Isaac *physicist, researcher*

Hesperia
Fisher, Richard Paul *chemist*

Irvine
Arthur, David *research scientist*
Bullock, James Steven *physics professor*
Cho, Zang Hee *physics professor*
Clark, Bruce Robert *geologist, consultant*
Druffel, Ellen R.M. *research scientist, educator*
Dzyaloshinskii, Igor Ekhielievich *physicist*
Finlayson-Pitts, Barbara Jean *chemistry professor*
Maradudin, Alexei A. *physics professor*
McLaughlin, Calvin Sturgis *biochemistry professor*
McWilliams, Roger Dean *physicist, researcher*
Mu, Mingquan *meteorologist*
Nowick, Arthur Stanley *metallurgy and materials science educator*
Penner, Reginald Mark *chemistry professor*
Phalen, Robert Franklynn *environmental scientist*
Rose, Irwin A. (Ernie) *biochemist, educator*
Rowland, Frank Sherwood *chemistry professor*
Rynn, Nathan *physics professor, consultant*
White, Stephen Halley *biophysicist, educator*
Workman, Jerome James, Jr. *chemist*

Kensington
Appelman, Evan Hugh *retired chemist*
Connick, Robert Elwell *retired chemistry professor*

La Canada Flintridge
Baines, Kevin Hays *astronomer, planetary scientist*

La Jolla
Asmus, John Fredrich *physicist*
Backus, George Edward *theoretical geophysicist*
Berger, Wolfgang H. *oceanographer, educator, geologist*
Boger, Dale L. *chemistry professor*
Branscomb, Lewis McAdory *physicist, researcher*
Bromirski, Peter Donald *marine geophysicist, physical oceanographer*
Burbidge, E. Margaret *astronomer, educator*
Burbidge, Geoffrey *astrophysicist, educator*
Cobble, James Wikle *chemistry professor*
Crutzen, Paul Josef *research meteorologist, chemist*
Edelman, Gerald Maurice *biochemist, neuroscientist, educator*
Feher, George *biophysicist, educator*
Ginsberg, Mark H. *biomedical scientist, physician*
Grinstein, Benjamin *physicist, researcher*
Harilal, Sivanandan S. *physicist, researcher*
Heeb, Mary Jo *biochemist, researcher*
Hendrickson, David Norman *chemistry professor*
Intriligator, Kenneth *physicist, educator*
Itano, Harvey Akio *biochemistry educator*
Ivanov, Andrey V. *atmospheric chemist researcher*
Kadonaga, James Takuro *biochemist*
Kennel, Charles Frederick *atmospheric physics professor, academic administrator, government official*
Kolodner, Richard David *biochemist, educator, director*
Kozarich, John Warren *biochemist*
Krishnamurthy, Ramanarayanan *chemistry professor, researcher*
Lerner, Richard Alan *chemistry educator, scientist*
Ma, Wenxue *medical scientist*
Makhluf, Huda A. *research scientist*
Marti, Kurt *chemistry professor*
McCammon, James Andrew *chemistry professor*
Molina, Mario Jose *physical chemist, educator*
Nicolaou, Kyriacos Costa (K. C. Nicolaou) *chemistry professor*
Patton, Stuart *biochemist, educator*
Ride, Sally Kristen *physics professor, research scientist, retired astronaut*
Rotenberg, Manuel *physics professor*
Rothschild, Richard E. *astrophysicist*
Rudakov, Dmitry L. *research scientist*
Sandwell, David *geophysicist, educator*
Sham, Lu Jeu *physics professor*
Sharpless, K. Barry *chemist, educator*
Shu, Frank Hsia-San *physics professor, research scientist, educator*
Shuler, Kurt Egon *chemist, educator*

Somerville, Richard Chapin James *atmospheric scientist, educator*
Taur, Yuan *physicist, researcher*
Tsien, Roger Yonchien *chemist, cell biologist*
Tsuji, Frederick Ichiro *biochemist, molecular biologist*
Van Lint, Victor Anton Jacobus *physicist*
Wang, Lei *biochemist*
Watson, Kenneth Marshall *physics professor*
Wolynes, Peter Guy *chemistry researcher, educator*
Wong, Chi-Huey *chemistry professor*
Yoshimura, Kei *oceanographer*

Laguna Hills
Rossiter, Bryant William *chemistry consultant*

Livermore
Alder, Berni Julian *physicist, researcher*
Chernov, Alexander Alexandrovich *physicist, researcher*
Cook, Robert Crossland *chemist, researcher*
Cowgill, Donald Franklin *physicist*
Hooper, Edwin Bickford *physicist*
Karr, Thomas John *research physicist*
Kidder, Ray Edward *physicist, consultant*
Leith, Cecil Eldon *retired physicist*
Malkin, Alexander J. *biophysicist*
Nellis, William J. *physicist*
Nuckolls, John Hopkins *physicist, researcher*
Remington, Bruce A. *physics researcher*
Rescigno, Thomas Nicola *theoretical physicist*
Santer, Benjamin David *atmospheric scientist*
Tarter, Curtis Bruce *physicist, science administrator*
Trebino, Rick Peter *physicist*

Loma Linda
Mohan, Subburaman *biochemist, educator*

Long Beach
Hu, Chi Yu *retired physicist, educator*
McGaughey, Charles Gilbert *retired biochemist*
Nishino, Hitoshi *physics professor*

Los Altos
Hahn, Harold Thomas *physical chemist, chemical engineer*

Los Angeles
Barberopoulou, Aggeliki *geophysicist, educator*
Benson, Sidney William *chemistry researcher*
Bhaumik, Mani Lal *physicist*
Billig, Franklin Anthony *retired chemist*
Boyer, Paul Delos *biochemist, educator*
Coleman, Charles Clyde *physicist, educator*
Cornwall, John Michael *physics professor, consultant*
Dows, David Alan *emeritus chemistry professor*
Es-Said, Omar Salim *metallurgy educator*
Fulco, Armand John *biochemist*
Ganas, Perry Spiros *physicist*
Goda, Keisuke *research scientist*
Han, Xinhai *research scientist*
Hellwarth, Robert Willis *physicist, researcher*
Houk, Kendall Newcomb *chemistry professor*
Ingersoll, Raymond Vail *geologist, educator*
Jacoby, Neil Herman, Jr. *astronautical scientist, engineer, consultant*
Jordan, Thomas Hillman *geophysicist, educator*
Kaplan, Isaac Raymond *chemistry professor*
Kassner, Michael Ernest *materials science educator, researcher*
Kivelson, Margaret Galland *physicist*
Koga, Rokutaro (Rocky Koga) *physicist*
Krupp, Edwin Charles *astronomer*
Levine, Raphael David *chemistry professor*
Li, Yong-Gang Frank *research scientist, educator*
Lu, Jia Grace *physicist, electrical engineer, educator*
Lyons, James Richard *research scientist*
Markland, Francis Swaby, Jr. *biochemist, educator*
Naik, Vinayak Shashikant *research scientist*
Neufeld, Elizabeth Fondal *biochemist, educator*
Newman, William I. *geophysicist, astrophysicist, educator*
Olah, George Andrew *chemist, educator*
Prakash, Surya G.K. *chemistry educator*
Pritchett, Philip Lentner *physicist, researcher*
Raeder, Joachim *geophysicist*
Reisler, Emil *biochemist, educator, dean*
Reiss, Howard *chemistry professor*
Roberts, Sidney *biological chemist*
Scott, Robert Lane *chemist, educator*
Stanton, Robert James, Jr. *geologist, educator*
Stellwagen, Robert Harwood *biochemistry professor*
Stephens, Philip John *chemistry professor*
Thorne, Richard Mansergh *physicist*
Trimble, Stanley Wayne *hydrologist*
Walker, Raymond John *physicist*
West, Charles David *chemistry professor*
Whitten, Charles Alexander, Jr. *physics professor*
Woodruff, Fay *paleoceanographer, geological researcher*
Wright, Byron T. *physicist, researcher*
Wright, Edward Leonard *astronomy educator*
Zhang, Lin *research scientist*
Zou, Linhua *research scientist*

Magalia
Haard, Norman Frederick *retired chemistry professor, editor*

Malibu
Kubena, Randall L. *physicist*
Liu, David Shiao-Kung *research scientist, consultant*
Pepper, David M. *scientist, educator*
Srinivasa, Narayan *research scientist*

Marina
Shane, William Whitney *astronomer*

Mckinleyville
Peithman, Roscoe Edward *physicist, educator*

Menlo Park
Allen, Matthew Arnold *physicist*
Bernstein, Lawrence R. *inorganic chemist, pharmaceutical chemist*
Brodsky, Stanley Jerome *physics educator, consultant*
Bukry, John David *geologist*
Bynum, Gretchen Luepke *geologist*
Crosley, David Risdon *chemical physicist*
Dorfan, Jonathan Mannie *physicist, researcher*
Drell, Persis Sydney *physicist*
Drell, Sidney David *physicist, arms control and national security specialist*
Hildreth, Edward Wesley (Wes Hildreth) *geologist*
Jaros, John A. *physics professor*
Kuwabara, James Shigeru *research hydrologist*
Mankinen, Edward A. *geologist, researcher*
Michael, Andrew Jay *geophysicist*
Mill, Theodore *chemist, researcher*
Nordlund, Leif Niklas Dennis *research scientist*
Penzias, Arno Allan *astrophysicist, information scientist, researcher*
Ratcliff, Blair Norman *physicist*
Ravilisetty, Padmanabha Rao *research scientist*
Richter, Burton *physicist, educator*
Taylor, Richard Edward *physicist, researcher*
Thatcher, Wayne *geophysicist*
Winick, Herman *physicist, educator*

Merced
Davila, Lilian P. *research scientist*

Milpitas
Agarwal, Nipun *materials scientist*
Dai, Guang-ming George *optics scientist*

Moffett Field
Berenji, Hamid Reza *research scientist, educator*
Chaban, Galina M. *research scientist*
Chen, Bin *materials scientist*
D'Angelo, Gennaro *research scientist, educator*
Dholakia, Geetha Ramaswamy *physicist, researcher*
Goebel, John Henry *physicist, researcher*
Heere, Karen R. *astrophysicist*
Horikawa, Daiki *aerospace scientist*
Li, Jun *materials scientist, researcher*
Makeev, Maxim A. *physicist*
Mattioda, Andrew Lige *chemist, researcher, space scientist*

Monrovia
Andary, Thomas Joseph *biochemist, researcher*

Montague
Ryan, Daberath *chemistry professor*

Montecito
Wheelon, Albert Dewell *physicist*

Monterey
Langland, Rolf H. *meteorologist*
Maier, William Bryan, II, *physics professor*
Rice, Joseph Aubrey *physics professor, researcher*
Thompson, William Travis *physicist*

Morgan Hill
Kuster, Robert Kenneth *semi-retired scientist*

Moss Landing
Breaker, Laurence Coates *oceanographer, educator*
Brewer, Peter George *ocean geochemist*
Clague, David A. *geologist*

Mountain View
Showalter, Mark Robert *astronomer*

Murrieta
Lake, Bruce Meno *physicist*

Napa
Shin, Ernest Eun-Ho *physicist, educator, researcher*

Newark
Thissell, James Dennis *physicist*

Newbury Park
Fisk, Charles John *meteorologist, researcher, consultant*

Newport Beach
Kolyer, John McNaughton *materials scientist, retired chemist*

North Hollywood
Thomson, John Ansel Armstrong *biochemist*

Northridge
Akbarzadeh, Alireza *physicist*
Smathers, James Burton *medical physicist, educator*

Oakland
Bibel, Debra Jan *medical scientist, editor, artist*
Brust, David *physicist*
Carwell, Hattie Virginia *health physicist*
Linford, Rulon Kesler *physicist, electrical engineer*

Oceanside
L'Annunziata, Michael Frank *chemist, nuclear scientist, consultant*

Orange
Kenney, John William III *chemistry educator*

Orangevale
Gibson, Gordon Ronald *chemist*

Palo Alto
Andersen, Torben Brender *optical researcher, astronomer, software engineer*
Bratkovsky, Alexander Mikhailovich *physicist*
Fattal, David *physicist*
Huberman, Bernardo A. *physicist*
Martin, Robert Bruce *chemistry professor*
Perl, Martin Lewis *physicist, educator, chemical engineer*
Saxena, Arjun Nath *physicist*
Sleep, Norman H. *geophysics educator*
Tansey, Richard J. *research scientist*
Yang, Jianhua Joshua *materials scientist, researcher*

Palos Verdes Estates
Paulikas, George Algis *retired physicist*

Pasadena
Allen, Clarence Roderic *geologist, educator*
Andreetto, Marco *research scientist*
Barish, Barry C. *physics professor, researcher*
Barnes, Charles Andrew *physicist, researcher*
Beer, Reinhard *atmospheric scientist*
Bejczy, Antal Károly *research scientist and facility administrator*
Blake, Geoffrey Allen *chemistry professor*
Boxe, Christopher Shawn *research scientist*
Bugga, Ratnakumar Venkata *electrochemist, researcher*
Byun, Sung Hun *research scientist*
Carroll, Sean M. *physicist*
Chahine, Moustafa Toufic *atmospheric scientist*
Chan, Sunney Ignatius *retired chemistry educator*
Chang, Eng-Pi *materials scientist*
Chui, Talso C. P. *research scientist*
Coleman, Max Laurence *biogeochemist, educator, director, research scientist, lab administrator*
Cutri, Roc Michael *research scientist*
Dervan, Peter Brendan *chemistry professor*
Dressler, Alan Michael *astronomer*
Duxbury, Thomas *planetary scientist*
Eisenstein, James P. *physicist, educator*
Ellis, Richard Salisbury *astronomer, educator*
Frautschi, Steven Clark *physicist, researcher*
Freedman, Wendy Laurel *astronomer, educator, director*
Fu, Lee-Lueng *oceanographer*
Giorgini, Jon *aerospace scientist*
Golombek, Matthew Philip *research scientist, planetary geologist*
Goodstein, David Louis *physics professor*
Gray, Harry Barkus *chemistry professor*
Grotzinger, John Peter *paleontologist, educator*
Grubbs, Robert Howard *chemistry professor*
Hitlin, David George *physicist, researcher*
Kim, Joo Hyeon *astronomer*
Kitaev, Alexei *physics and computer science professor*
Lopes, Rosaly Mutel Crocce *astronomer, planetary geologist*
Marcus, Rudolph Arthur *chemist, educator*
Marsano, Joseph D. *physicist*
Massey, Richard *astrophysicist*
Mc Koy, Basil Vincent Charles *theoretical chemist, educator*
Nguyen, Hien Trong *astrophysicist, researcher*
Ouchi, Masami *astronomer*
Pieri, David C. *research scientist*
Politzer, Hugh David *physicist, educator*
Roberts, John D. *chemist, educator*
Rothemund, Paul W.K. *research scientist*
Ryan, Margaret Amy *chemist, researcher*
Sackmann, Inge-Juliana *astrophysicist*
Sandage, Allan Rex *astronomer*
Sargent, Wallace Leslie William *astronomer, educator*
Schmidt, Maarten *astronomy educator*
Schneider, Tapio *environmental scientist, educator*
Schwarz, John Henry *theoretical physicist, educator*
Shim, Changsub *research scientist*
Song, Seok Goo *geophysicist*
Spilker, Linda Joyce *aerospace scientist*
Stone, Edward C. *physicist, researcher*
Sun, Xiankai *research scientist*
Supatto, Willy *research scientist*
Talukder, Ashit *research scientist*
Tombrello, Thomas Anthony, Jr. *physics professor*
Tsurutani, Bruce Tadashi *physicist*
Vogt, Rochus Eugen *physicist, researcher*
Yeomans, Donald Keith *astronomer*

Pleasant Hill
Okosi, Nsikak Paulinus *physics professor*
Rodriguez, John M. *physics professor*

Pleasanton
Denavit, Jacques *retired physicist*
Stallings, Charles Henry *retired physicist*

Pomona
Aurilia, Antonio *physicist, researcher*
Bidlack, Wayne Ross *nutritional biochemist, toxicologist, food scientist*
Selco, Jodye Isabel *chemistry professor*

Ramona
Yoldas, Bulent Erturk *materials scientist, educator*

Rancho Santa Fe
Cuatrecasas, Pedro Martin *research biochemist, educator*

Redlands
Clopine, Gordon Alan *consulting geologist, educator*
Scott, Eric *paleontologist, educator*

Redwood City
Cremer, Jay Theodore, Jr. *research scientist*
Iverson, Charles *physics professor*

Richmond
Hommeltoft, Sven Ivar *chemist*
Onisko, Bruce Charles *mass spectroscopist*

Ridgecrest
Bennett, Harold Earl *physicist, optics researcher*
St-Amand, Pierre *geophysicist*

Riverside
Blair, Scott Craig *physics professor*
Chronister, Eric L. *chemistry professor, department chairman*
Hille, Russ *biochemist, educator*
Koo, Bonjun *environmental scientist, educator*
Maclaughlin, Douglas Earl *physicist, educator*
Pogorelov, Nikolai *physicist, researcher*
Rabenstein, Dallas Leroy *chemistry professor*
Schoeller, Wolfgang Wilhelm *chemistry educator*

Rolling Hills Estates
McCreight, Louis *retired materials scientist*

Sacramento
Natarajan, Arutselvan *chemistry professor, researcher*
Partovi, M. Hossein *physics professor, department chairman*
Purdy, James Aaron *medical physics professor*
Richardson, Michael *physics professor, department chairman*

San Clemente
Wolfram, Thomas *physicist, educator*

San Diego
Afuwape, Samuel A. *research scientist*
Cantor, Charles Robert *biochemistry professor*
German, Randall Michael *materials scientist, educator*
Harbola, Upendra *physicist*
Inchiosa, Mario Emil *physicist*
Jenkins, Scott Alan *oceanographer*
Kang, Seung Hyuk *materials scientist, electronics engineer*
Livshitz, Boris *research scientist*
Mestechkin, Mikhail Markovich *retired mathematics physicist*
Padmanabhan, Santhosh *research scientist*
Page, Eric J. *physics professor*
Rosen, Mark Daniel *chemist*
Scorcioni, Ruggero *research scientist*
Shashkin, Pavel Nikolayevich *biochemist*
Shneour, Elie Alexis *biophysicist, researcher, historian*
Vandegriff, Kim Denise *biochemist*
van der Geer, Peter *biochemist, educator*
Verma, Inder M. *biochemist*
Wamba, Kolo *physicist*

San Francisco
Aragon, Sergio R. *chemistry professor*
Batterman, Boris William *physicist, educator, academic administrator*
Burlingame, Alma Lyman *chemist, educator*
Chen, Zhigang *physics professor*
Cluff, Lloyd Sterling *earthquake geologist*
Cohen, Fred Ehrenkranz *biophysics professor*
Darling, Cynthia Lee *research professor*
DeRisi, Joseph L. *biochemist, educator*
Dill, Kenneth Austin *pharmaceutical chemistry educator*
Grodsky, Gerold Morton *biochemistry professor*
Habelitz, Stefan F. *research scientist, educator*
Hale, Victoria G. *chemist, pharmaceutical executive*
Hanahan, Douglas *biochemist, educator*
James, Thomas Larry *chemistry professor*
Johnson, Alexander D. *biochemist, molecular biologist, educator*
Julius, David *biochemist*
Lessard, Etienne *medical physicist, researcher, consultant*
Marshall, Grayson William, Jr. *materials scientist, biomedical engineer, health sciences educator, dentist*
Nguyen, Ann Cac Khue *pharmaceutical and medicinal chemist*
Omer, Selma *biochemist, educator*
Uskokovic, Vuk *research scientist*
Walter, Peter *biochemist*
Yamanaka, Shinya *stem cell scientist, educator*

San Jose
Bordenyuk, Andrey *laser scientist*
Hamill, Patrick James *physics professor, environmental scientist*
Lehman, Tobin J. *research scientist*
Madra, Satbir Singh *materials researcher, mechanical engineer*
Makasyuk, Igor *physicist, consultant*
Parkin, Stuart Stephen Papworth *materials scientist, physicist*
Rathore, Jitendra S. *chemist*
Wang, Fei *research scientist*

San Luis Obispo
Fernando, Raymond H. *chemistry professor, consultant*
Hafemeister, David Walter *physicist*

San Rafael
Pomerantz, Martin Arthur *astronomer, educator, physicist*

San Ramon
Badruzzaman, Ahmed *nuclear scientist, educator*
Su, George Shenghui (Sheng-Hui Su) *chemist, medical researcher, educator*

Santa Ana
Kropp, William Rudolph *physicist*
Micic, Miodrag *chemist, researcher*

Santa Barbara
Awramik, Stanley Michael *geology educator*
Awschalom, David Daniel *physics professor*
Bunton, Clifford Allen *chemist, educator*
Caldwell, David Orville *physics professor*
Evans, Anthony Glyn *materials scientist, educator*
Giddings, Steven B. *physics professor*
Gross, David Jonathan *physicist*
Heeger, Alan Jay *physicist, educator*
Hubbard, Arthur Thornton *chemist, educator*
Jiang, Yong *materials scientist*
Kohn, Walter *physicist, retired educator*
Macdonald, Ken Craig *geophysicist*
Marshall, Philip James *astrophysicist*
Morse, Daniel E. *biochemistry educator, science administrator*

Pilgeram, Laurence Oscar biochemist
Poulsen, Henrik Nørskov research scientist
Reich, Norbert Otto biochemist, educator
Von Weizsäcker, Ernst Ulrich environmental scientist, dean
White, Robert Stephen retired physics professor
Witherell, Michael S. physicist, educator

Santa Clara
Dafforn, Geoffrey Alan biochemist
Hayn, Carl Hugo physics professor, priest
Lee, Chan-Yun physicist, process engineer, educator
Troccoli, Mariano physicist, researcher, entrepreneur

Santa Cruz
Brown, George Stephen physics professor
Bunnett, Joseph Frederick chemist, educator
Faber, Sandra Moore astronomer, educator
Griggs, Gary Bruce oceanographer, geologist, educator, director
Kobayashi, Nobuhiko Paul materials scientist, professor
Margon, Bruce Henry astrophysicist, educator
Max, Claire Ellen physicist
Noller, Harry Francis, Jr. biochemist, educator
Sands, Matthew Linzee physicist, researcher
Shi, Chao research scientist
Williams, Quentin Christopher geophysicist, educator
Wipke, W. Todd chemistry professor
Woosley, Stanford Earl astrophysicist
Xin, Wang researcher
Young, Allan Peter physics professor

Santa Monica
Intriligator, Devrie Shapiro physicist

Santa Rosa
Yatsenko, Nikolai Afanasyevich physics researcher, educator

Solana Beach
Agnew, Harold Melvin physicist

Stanford
Alderkamp, Anne-Carlijn environmental scientist
Archer, Cristina Lozej research scientist
Baldwin, Robert Lesh biochemist, educator
Berg, Paul biochemist, educator
Bienenstock, Arthur Irwin physicist, educator, federal official
Block, Steven Michael biophysicist, educator
Boxer, Steven G. physical chemistry educator
Brauman, John I. chemist, educator
Brunger, Axel Thomas biophysicist, researcher, educator
Bube, Richard Howard retired materials scientist, educator
Cao, Linyou research scientist
Collman, James Paddock chemistry professor
Fetter, Alexander Lees theoretical physicist, educator
Fratkin, Eugene research scientist
Harbaugh, John Warvelle geologist, educator
Harbury, Pehr A.B. biochemist, educator
Harrison, Walter Ashley physicist, researcher
Hecker, Siegfried Stephen metallurgist
Hossein-Babaei, Faraz research scientist
Kennedy, Donald environmental scientist, educator, editor
Keren, Kinneret biophysicist
Kim, Na Young physicist
Klemperer, Simon Louis geophysicist, educator
Kornberg, Roger David biochemist, structural biologist
Lehman, I(srael) Robert biochemist, educator
Little, William Arthur physicist, researcher
Moerner, William Esco physical chemist, educator
Osheroff, Douglas Dean physics professor, researcher
Petrosian, Vahé astrophysicist, educator
Prasad, Manika geophysicist, researcher
Quake, Stephen R. physics professor, researcher
Ross, John physical chemist, educator
Rossing, Thomas D. physics professor
Shenker, Stephen physics professor
Silbergleit, Alexander physicist, mathematician
Solomon, Edward Ira chemistry professor, researcher
Susskind, Leonard physicist, educator
Thompson, George Albert geophysicist, educator
Trost, Barry Martin chemist, educator
Wagoner, Robert Vernon astrophysicist, educator
Walt, Martin physicist, educator
Wen, Xian-Huan hydrogeologist
Wojcicki, Stanley George physicist, researcher
Zare, Richard Neil chemistry professor

Stockton
Samoshin, Vyacheslav Vladimirovich chemistry professor, science educator, researcher
Whiteker, Roy Archie retired chemistry professor

Sunnyvale
Brozek, Tomasz research scientist
Chang, William Zhi-Ming research scientist
Cheng, Jun chemist
Das, Sandipan Kumar research scientist
Nerurkar, Shailesh B. research scientist

Temecula
Chung, Hee M. retired nuclear scientist

Thousand Oaks
Baek, Kwang-Hyun research scientist
Green, David Brian chemistry educator
Newman, Paul Richard physicist
Pincus, Howard J. geologist, engineer, educator
Remmele, Richard L., Jr. research scientist, director
Zhang, Zhongqi chemist

Torrance
Ibe, Basil Obijiaku biochemist, educator
Kim, Keehoon cybernetic scientist
Lieberman, Robert Arthur physicist
Rogers, Howard H. retired chemist

Tustin
Cruzen, Matt Earl research biochemist
Schilling, Frederick Augustus, Jr. geologist, consultant

West Sacramento
Lehman, Peggy W. oceanographer

Woodland Hills
Doi, Roy Hiroshi retired biochemist, educator

Yucaipa
Adams, Matthew Cavanaugh physics professor

COLORADO

Arvada
Mullineaux, Donal Ray geologist

Aurora
Grace, William Pershing petroleum geologist, real estate developer
Rosich, Rayner Karl physicist

Boulder
Andrews, John T. geophysicist, educator
Barry, Roger Graham climatologist, educator
Beale, Paul Drew physics professor
Cai, Huaqing meteorologist
Cech, Thomas Robert chemistry professor, former medical association administrator
Chappell, Charles Franklin meteorologist, consultant
Coffey, Michael Thomas physicist
Cooper, Owen Roger atmospheric scientist
Cornell, Eric Allin physics professor
Cumalat, John physics professor
DePuy, Charles Herbert chemist, educator
Diaz, Henry F. retired meteorologist
Diky, Vladimir chemist, researcher
Dryer, Murray physicist, educator
Dudhia, Jimy atmospheric scientist
Dye, James Eugene retired research scientist
Eriksson, Stefan space scientist
Fleming, Rex James meteorologist
Garstang, Roy Henry astrophysicist, educator
Golden, Joseph Hilary meteorologist
Gosling, John Thomas space plasma physicist, researcher
Gupta, Vijay K. hydrologist, educator
Hall, John Lewis physicist, researcher
Hermann, Allen Max physics professor
Herring, Jackson Rea physicist
Hill, Mary C. hydrologist
Hofmann, David John atmospheric science researcher, educator
Hunt, Alan James biophysicist
Hynes, James Thomas chemist, educator
Jenkins, Christopher J. research scientist
Jin, Deborah physicist, educator
Kato, Shuji chemist, researcher
Killeen, Timothy Laurence aerospace scientist, science administrator
LeMasurier, Wesley Ernest geology educator, researcher
Low, Boon Chye physicist
Lu, Chungu meteorologist, researcher, educator
Mahanthappa, Kalyana Thipperudraiah physicist, researcher
Matrosov, Sergey senior research scientist
Nesbitt, David John physics and chemistry professor
Paulson, Archie Miller geophysicist, educator
Phelps, Arthur Van Rensselaer physicist, consultant
Roellig, Leonard Oscar physics professor
Smythe, William Rodman physicist, researcher
Tatarskii, Valerian Il'Ich physics researcher
Tolbert, Bert Mills biochemist, educator
Toomre, Juri astrophysicist, educator
Trenberth, Kevin Edward atmospheric scientist
Vacek, Jaroslav chemist, researcher
Volkamer, Rainer Martin physicist, researcher, aerospace scientist
Washington, Warren Morton meteorologist
Yin, Hang chemistry professor

Colorado Springs
Abeeluck, Akheelesh Kumar physicist, researcher
Corry, Charles Elmo geophysicist, not-for-profit developer
Klipping, Robert Samuel geophysicist

Denver
Brady, Brian T. physicist, educator
Bufe, Charles Glenn geophysicist, researcher
Cobban, William Aubrey paleontologist
Delin, Geoffrey Norman hydrologist
Eaton, Gareth Richard chemistry professor, dean
Fails, Thomas Glenn geologist
Johnson, Walter Earl geophysicist
Lin, Hai chemistry professor
Madole, Richard Frank geologist, consultant
Morrison, Kendra Ann environmental scientist
Ormes, Jonathan Fairfield astrophysicist, researcher, educator
Smith, David B. geochemist, researcher
Smith, Dwight Morrell chemistry professor, academic administrator
Snee, Lawrence Warren geologist
Troutman, George William geologist

Evergreen
Haun, John Daniel petroleum geologist, educator
Heyl, Allen Van, Jr. geologist

Fort Collins
Bamburg, James Robert biochemistry professor
Borch, Thomas chemistry professor
Collett, Jeffrey Lee, Jr. environmental scientist, educator
Culver, Roger Bruce astronomer, educator
Fixman, Marshall chemist, educator
Jin, Song environmental scientist
Maciel, Gary Emmet chemistry professor, researcher
Narayanasamy, Prabagaran research scientist
Noh, Yoo-Jeong research scientist
Pagano, Rosario staff scientist
Schumm, Stanley Alfred geologist, educator
She, Chiao-Yao physics professor, researcher
Stephens, Graeme Leslie meteorologist, educator
Thurai, Merhala research scientist
Vonder Haar, Thomas H. meteorology educator
Wood, John Louis chemistry professor

Golden
Ahn, Kwang-Soon materials scientist, researcher
DeSanto, John A. physicist, educator, mathematics professor
Fude, Liu research scientist
Kim, Jin Young materials scientist
Krauss, George metallurgist
Sattel, Daniel geophysicist
Scales, John Alan physics professor
Shayer, Zeev research scientist, educator
Taylor, Philip Craig physics professor
Trefny, John Ulric retired college president
Yeatts, Frank Richard retired physics professor
Zhang, Yong physicist, researcher

Greeley
Szczyrba, Igor Nicholas mathematical physicist, consultant

Highlands Ranch
Brierley, James Alan biohydrometallurgy consultant

Lafayette
McNeill, William environmental scientist

Lakewood
Drendel, Gary environmental scientist

Littleton
Paull, Richard Allen geologist, educator

Livermore
Tkachev, Sergey Nikolayevich geophysicist

Lone Tree
Spisak, John Francis corporation executive

Louisville
Lipson, David Samuel geologist

Monument
Klazura, Gerard E. retired meteorologist

Ridgway
Lathrop, Kaye Don nuclear scientist, educator

Snowmass
Lovins, Amory Bloch physicist, energy consultant

U S A F Academy
Lu, Yalin physicist

Windsor
Mayer, Victor James geologist, educator

CONNECTICUT

East Hartford
Dardas, Zissis research scientist
Michels, H. Harvey physicist

East Lyme
Mylari, Banavara L. retired chemist

Fairfield
Block, Joel Warren geologist, educator
O'Connell, Edmond J. chemist, educator, chemist, consultant

Farmington
Osborn, Mary Jane Merten biochemist, educator

Greenwich
Davenport, Lee Losee physicist

Groton
Ebbin, Syma Alexi environmental scientist, educator
Gai, Moshe physics professor
Prakash, Chandra chemistry educator
Wallach, Morton L. scientist

Hartford
Nicaise, Olivier Jean-Charles chemistry professor

Ledyard
Chiang, Albert Chinfa polymer chemist
Harwood, Harold James, Jr. biochemist

Manchester
Galasso, Francis Salvatore materials scientist

Middletown
Sengupta, Atanu research scientist

Milford
Bowie, William Thompson chemist, educator

New Haven
Adair, Robert Kemp physicist, educator
Baltay, Charles physicist, educator
Blake, Ruth Elaine geophysicist, educator
Casten, Richard Francis physicist, educator
Curran, Lisa M. environmental scientist, educator
Gauthier, Jacques Armand geologist, educator, curator
Girvin, Steven Mark physicist, researcher, academic administrator
Jorgensen, William L. chemistry educator
Moore, Peter Bartlett biochemist, educator
Pan, Baocheng biophysicist, researcher
Reed, Mark Arthur research scientist, educator
Saunders, Martin chemistry educator, researcher
Steitz, Joan Argetsinger biochemistry professor
Thakur, Vinay V. research scientist
Urry, Meg (C. Megan Urry) physics professor
Werner, Volker Ralph physics professor
Wolf, Werner Paul physicist, researcher
Zelitch, Israel retired scientist

New Milford
Fabricand, Burton Paul physicist, researcher

North Haven
Herzenberg, Arvid physicist, researcher

Old Lyme
Carey, William Michael, Jr. research physicist, engineer

Pawcatuck
Gnanaraj, Joseph Sathiya senior scientist

Ridgefield
Busacca, Carl Alan chemist
Hammel, Heidi B. physicist, researcher, astronomer

Stamford
Chang, Ted T. chemist
Colthup, Norman Bertram retired spectroscopist

Storrs
Mueller-Westerhoff, Ulrich Theodor retired chemistry professor

Storrs Mansfield
Bartram, Ralph Herbert physicist
Do, Cuong M. research scientist
Kenny, David A. physics professor
Kessel, Quentin Cattell physicist, educator
Klemens, Paul Gustav physicist, researcher
Marcus, Harris Leon materials science educator
Narayan, Sumit research assistant
Reifsnider, Kenneth Leonard metallurgist, educator
Schulthess, Cristian P. chemistry professor
Stwalley, William Calvin physics and chemistry professor
Willis, Brian G. chemistry professor

Wallingford
Firestone, Raymond Armand chemist

West Hartford
Gould, Laurence Ira physicist

Westport
Smith, Peter Wolfgang physicist, artist

Willington
Zhang, Heng research scientist, educator

Woodbridge
Zeller, Michael Edward physicist, researcher

Woodbury
Skinner, Brian John geologist, educator

DELAWARE

Dover
Wasfi, Sadiq Hassan chemistry professor

Greenville
Rocek, Jan retired chemist

Middletown
Hall, Peter Michael physics professor, electronics engineer

Newark
Burmeister, John Luther chemistry professor, consultant
Murray, Richard Bennett retired physics professor

Wilmington
Jaycox, Gary Delmar research scientist, writer
Jezl, Barbara Ann retired chemist, automation consultant
Kaiser, Mary Agnes chemist, chemical company executive
Keating, Mimi Y. chemist
Kissa, Erik retired chemist, consultant
Kwolek, Stephanie Louise chemist, researcher
Marcali, Jean Gregory retired chemist
Parshall, George William chemist, researcher

DISTRICT OF COLUMBIA

Washington
Alexander, Joseph Kunkle, Jr. physicist
Berendzen, Richard astronomer, educator, author
Bierly, Eugene Wendell meteorologist, science foundation director
Davidson, Eugene Abraham biochemist, educator, academic administrator
DeCoster, Mark Allen research biochemist
Domning, Daryl Paul paleontologist, educator
Donohue, Joyce Morrissey biochemist, toxicologist, dietician, educator
Dutro, John Thomas, Jr. geologist, paleontologist
Egolf, David A. physics professor
El Khadem, Hassan Saad chemistry professor, researcher
Girard, James Emery chemistry professor
Goff, James Franklin physicist, consultant
Goldstein, Allan Leonard biochemist, educator
Guhathakurta, Madhulika astrophysicist
Hallgren, Richard Edwin meteorologist
Handel, Mark David atmospheric scientist, sports official
Jacobs, David Ernest environmental health scientist

Kalasinsky, Victor Frank *chemist*
Kim, Heungsoo *research scientist*
King, Michael M. *chemistry professor, department chairman*
Klein, Franz J. *physics professor*
Klimchuk, James Andrew *astrophysicist, researcher*
Klug, Christopher Aaron *physicist*
Komarov, Andrei M. *biophysicist, educator, research scientist*
Kovach, Ildiko Maria *chemistry professor, researcher*
Ledley, Robert Steven *biophysicist*
Lehman, Donald Richard *physicist, educator, academic administrator*
Lehmberg, Robert Henry *retired research physicist*
Macedo, Pedro Buarque de *physics professor, researcher*
Mamantov, Andrew *chemist*
Maran, Stephen Paul *astronomer*
Meijer, Paul Herman Ernst *physicist, educator*
Michaels, Patrick Joseph *climatologist*
Montgomery, John A. *physicist*
Morehouse, David Frank *geologist*
Ohring, George *meteorologist*
Oran, Elaine Surick *physicist*
Pauls, Thomas Albert *astrophysicist, educator*
Pecora, Louis Michael *physicist*
Phillips, Gary Wilson *physicist*
Pojeta, John, Jr. *geologist, researcher*
Press, Frank *geophysicist*
Ramaker, David E. *chemistry professor, researcher*
Read, Bill (William L. Read) *meteorologist*
Ross, Malcolm *minerals consultant*
Sáenz, Albert William *theoretical physicist, researcher, consultant*
Shukla, Deepshikha *research scientist*
Singer, Maxine Frank *retired biochemist, science association director*
Solomon, Sean Carl *geophysicist, lab administrator*
Stanley, Jean-Daniel *geoarchaeologist*
Weedman, Daniel Wilson *astronomy educator*
White, John Arnold *physics professor, research scientist*
White, Robert Mayer *meteorologist*
Zhu, Tingju *environmental scientist*

FLORIDA

Alachua
Schneider, Richard T(heodore) *optics scientist, researcher, engineer*

Boca Raton
Faulkner, John Samuel *physicist, educator*
Louda, J. William *chemist, biochemist, educator*
Párkányi, Cyril *chemistry educator*
Snyder, Patricia Ann *chemistry professor*
Weissbach, Herbert *biochemist, researcher*
Xie, Zhixiao *research scientist, educator*

Bradenton
Brunk, William Edward *astronomer*

Brooksville
McBride, Tamera Shawn Dew *geologist*

Cocoa
Bottesch, James Jonathan *research scientist, director*

Coral Gables
Beylin, Andrey *physics professor*
Einspruch, Norman Gerald *physicist, engineering educator*
Hirschberg, Joseph Gustav *physicist, educator*
Leblanc, Roger Maurice *chemistry professor*
Van Vliet, Carolyne Marina *physicist, researcher*

Dade City
Burdick, Glenn Arthur *physicist, engineering educator*

Dania Beach
Spieler, Richard Earl *oceanographer, educator*

Davie
Branly, Rolando M. *astrophysicist, educator*

Daytona Beach
Ekpo, Efremfon Frank *physicist, researcher*

Deland
Coolidge, Edwin Channing *chemistry professor*

Delray Beach
Simon, Albert *retired physicist, engineer, educator*
Zarwyn, Berthold *physicist, consultant*

Estero
Brown, Theodore Lawrence *chemistry professor*

Fort Lauderdale
Itkin, Ivan *nuclear scientist, mathematician*
Muza, Jay Phillip *oceanographer, educator, paleontologist*
Venkatachalam, Kallidaikurichi *biochemist, educator, researcher*

Fort Myers
Curtin, David Yarrow *chemist, educator*
Fauerbach, Michael *physics professor*
Horecker, Bernard Leonard *retired biochemistry professor*

Gainesville
Baigorria, Guillermo Antonio *meteorologist, researcher*
Cousins, Robert John *nutritional biochemist, educator*
Hanrahan, Robert Joseph *chemist, educator*
Kumar, Pradeep *physics professor, researcher*
Merz, Kenneth M., Jr. *chemistry professor*
Micha, David Allan *chemistry and physics professor*
Ohrn, Nils Yngve *chemistry and physics educator*
Patre, Parag *research scientist*
Perry, Vernon G. *research scientist, educator*
Rosser, Charles J. *chemistry professor*
Roy Choudhury, Kaushik *materials scientist*
Sabin, John Rogers *physics professor*
Singley, John Edward, Jr. *retired environmental scientist, consultant*
Smith, Haywood Clark, Jr. *astronomer, educator*
Thorn, Charles Behan *physics professor*

Gonzalez
Plischke, Le Moyne Wilfred *chemist, researcher*

Jacksonville
Beattie, Donald A. *aerospace scientist, consultant*
Hartman, Frederick Cooper *retired biochemist*
Mendoza, William A. *physics professor*

Jupiter
Jacobson, Jerry Irving *biophysicist, theoretical physicist, medical researcher*

Leesburg
Jones, Marcia Lynn *meteorologist, educator*

Lithia
Kulkarni, Kavita-Vibha Arun *chemist*

Longboat Key
Stapleton, Harvey James *physics professor*

Melbourne
Barua, Dilip Kumar *engineer educator*
Nelson, Gordon Leigh *chemist, educator*
Trefry, John H. III *chemical oceanographer, educator*
Turner, Niescja E. *physics professor*

Miami
Alexandrakis, George *physics professor*
Anwar, Shadab *hydrologist, researcher*
Chen, JiuHua *physicist, geophysicist, educator, materials scientist*
Dammann, W. Paul *oceanographer*
Donelan, Mark Anthony *physicist*
Fine, Rana Arnold *chemical and physical oceanographer*
Graves, Palmer *chemistry professor*
Kowalska, Maria Teresa *research scientist, educator*
Leatherman, Stephen Parker *geologist, educator, writer*
Macias, Michael *research scientist*
Mayfield, Max (Britt Mayfield) *meteorologist*
Sanchez, Danmary *research scientist*
Zhu, Yifu *physics professor*

Naples
Leitner, Alfred *retired mathematical physicist, educator, educational film producer*

Ocala
Capps, Ken Bryant *chemistry professor*

Opa Locka
Ajhar, Edward A. *astrophysicist, dean*

Orlando
Chow, Lee *physics professor*
Flinchbaugh, David Edward *physicist*
Flitsiyan, Elena S. *physicist, physics educator*
Harney, Robert Charles *laser technologist, researcher, consultant, physics educator*
Klemm, Richard Andrew *physics professor, researcher*
Liboff, Richard Lawrence *physicist, researcher*
Llewellyn, Ralph Alvin *physics professor*
Sharma, Raj Kishore *research scientist, educator*

Ormond Beach
Kanfer, Julian Norman *biochemist, educator*

Palm Beach Gardens
Levitt, George *retired chemist*

Palmetto Bay
Nakashima, Tadayoshi *retired biochemist, researcher*

Panama City
Murphy, Patrick *oceanographer*

Pensacola
Prayaga, Chandra S. *physics professor*
Zayas, Joseph M. *physics professor*

Poinciana
Williams, Donald John *physicist, researcher*

Punta Gorda
Fullman, Robert Louis *metallurgy consultant*

Saint Petersburg
Osterman, Lisa Ellen *geologist, researcher*

Sanford
Dickison, Alexander Kane *physical science educator*

Sarasota
Pierce, Richard Harry *oceanographer*

Tallahassee
Choppin, Gregory Robert *chemistry professor*
Elsner, James Brian *meteorologist, educator*
Gilmer, Penny Jane *biochemist, educator*
Gleeson, Thomas Alexander *retired meteorologist*
Hanley, Deborah Elizabeth *meteorologist, wildland firefighter*
Herz, Werner *retired chemistry professor*
Hu, Xiaolong Bill *environmental scientist, educator*
Kimel, Jacob Daniel *physics professor*
Marshall, Alan George *chemistry and biochemistry educator*
Plendl, Hans S. *retired physicist, editor*
Rikvold, Per Arne *physicist, educator*
Robson, Donald *physics professor*
Schepkin, Victor D. *biophysicist*
Schlottmann, Pedro U. J. *physics professor*
Schrieffer, John Robert *physics professor, science administrator*

Tampa
Ash, William Mason *physicist, consultant*
Binford, Jesse Stone, Jr. *chemistry professor*
Joseph, Babu *chemical educator*
Laurino, Joseph Philip *chemistry professor, consultant*
Mahmoud, Hisham *research scientist*
Martin, Dean Frederick *retired chemistry professor*
Phan, Manh-Huong *materials scientist*
Prewett, Matthew Scott *research scientist*
Zaworotko, Michael John *chemistry professor*
Zhu, Yiliang *research scientist, educator*

Titusville
Schau, Harvey Charles *physicist*

Venice
Feldmann, Edward George *pharmaceutical chemist, pharmacologist*

Wesley Chapel
Tucker, Robert C., Jr. *materials scientist, consultant*

West Palm Beach
Li, Zhongwei *hydrologist*
Ogden, John Clifton III *environmental scientist, director*
Pietro, Kathleen C. *environmental scientist*

Winter Park
Blossey, Erich Carl *chemistry professor*

GEORGIA

Acworth
Salerno, John C. *biochemist*

Albany
May, Michael *chemistry professor*
Seo, Seong S. *chemistry professor, researcher*

Alpharetta
Bridges, Alan Lynn *physicist, researcher, application developer*

Athens
Chu, Chung Kwang *medicinal chemistry professor*
Johnson, Michael Kenneth *chemistry professor*
Law, John Harold *biochemistry educator*
Rasmussen, Todd C. *hydrologist, educator*
Schaefer, Henry Frederick III *chemistry professor*
Schleyer, Paul von Ragué *chemistry educator*
Yang, Charles Qi-Xiang *chemistry educator, researcher, consultant*

Atlanta
Allison, Stuart Anthony *chemistry professor, researcher*
Anderson, Gloria Long *chemistry professor*
Borovikov, Valery *research scientist*
Cramer, Howard Ross *geologist, environmental consultant*
Declercq, Nico Felicien *research scientist*
de Heer, Walter A. *physics professor*
Dhamala, Mukesh *physics professor*
Dickinson, Robert Earl *atmospheric scientist, educator, retired science administrator*
El-Sayed, Mostafa Amr *chemistry professor*
Family, Fereydoon *physicist, researcher*
Ganesh, Thota *research scientist*
Gonzalez, Ruben Rene *biochemist, researcher, educator*
Huynh, Boi Hanh *physics professor, researcher*
Kahn, Bernd *radiochemist, educator*
Krishnamurthy, Ramesh Saligrama *environmental scientist, researcher*
Kuklenyik, Zsuzsanna *chemist, researcher*
Lewis, Lonzy James *Physics And Atmospheric Sciences Professor*
Lin, Ming-Chang *physical chemistry professor, researcher*
Mandock, Randal Lee Nicholas *geophysicist, professor*
Mani, Ramesh G. *physicist*
May, Sheldon W. *chemistry professor*
Moon, Kyoung-sik *research scientist*
Perera, Unil A.G. *physics educator, researcher*
Rahmani, Amir R. *research scientist*
Snyder, Robert Lyman *materials scientist, educator*
Sun, Qunhui *research scientist*
Valk, Henry S(nowden) *physicist, researcher*
Wilkinson, Keith D. *biochemist, educator*
Wilson, Lawrence Joseph *chemist, researcher*
Woo, Dong Hyuk *graduate research assistant*
Yun, Jaeseok *research scientist*

Barnesville
Schmude, Richard Willis, Jr. *chemistry professor*

Brunswick
Mihal, Sandra Powell *research scientist*

Clarkston
Okafor, Martin Okechukwu *physics professor, educational consultant*

Dahlonega
Formica, Sarah P. *physics professor*

Franklin Springs
Mann, Frank *physics professor*

Kennesaw
Yifru, Dawit Desalegn *environmental scientist*

Lawrenceville
Pursell, David P. *chemistry professor*

Marietta
Berryhill, Henry Lee, Jr. *retired geologist*

Mcdonough
Yang, Bong-Jun *research scientist*

Morganton
Brathovde, James Robert *chemistry professor*

Peachtree City
Roobol, Norman Richard *chemistry professor, consultant*

Savannah
Sanders, James Grady *biogeochemist*
Shin, Jong-Yeob *aerospace scientist*
Singh, Harpal *research scientist*
Walter, Paul Hermann Lawrence *chemistry professor*

Stone Mountain
Reichert, Leo Edmund, Jr. *biochemist, department chairman, endocrinologist*

Waleska
Moore, George David *physics professor, researcher*

HAWAII

Aiea
Anderson, Brooks Doran, II, *geologist, consultant*

Hawaii National Park
Swanson, Donald Alan *geologist*

Hilo
Binder, Philippe-Michel *physicist, educator*

Honolulu
Franz, Charles Norman *radar and communication scientist*
Hawke, Bernard Ray *planetary scientist, researcher*
Herbig, George Howard *astronomer, educator*
Hey, Richard Noble *marine geophysicist*
Ihrig, Judson La Moure *chemist*
Kaiser, Ralf I *chemistry professor*
Keil, Klaus *geology educator, consultant*
Khan, Mohammad Asad *geophysics educator, retired minister, former senator of Pakistan*
Lebedev, Konstantin Vladimirovich *oceanographer, researcher*
Seff, Karl *zeolite chemist, chemistry educator*
Tiwari, Atul *chemist, researcher*

Kaneohe
Dye, Stephen *physics professor*

Laie
Weber, Michael F. *physics professor*

IDAHO

Aberdeen
Liu, Keshun *food chemist*

Idaho Falls
Gertman, David I. *research scientist*
Jue, Jan-Fong *materials scientist*
Redden, George Dean *geochemist*
Sharpe, Phil *nuclear scientist*

Meridian
Swalin, Richard Arthur *scientist, company executive*

Moscow
Cole, Douglas Gene *biochemist, educator*
Hrdlicka, Patrick J. *chemistry professor*
Miller, Maynard Malcolm *geologist, educator, geoscience institute director, former state legislator*
Renfrew, Malcolm MacKenzie *chemist, educator*
Shreeve, Jean'ne Marie *chemist, educator*
Stumpf, Bernhard Josef *physicist, educator*

Pocatello
Bennett, Byron Lee *chemistry professor, researcher*
May, Matthew P. *chemist*

ILLINOIS

Abbott Park
Abad-Zapatero, Celerino *crystallographer, researcher*

Argonne
Abrikosov, Alexei Alexeyevich *physicist*
Derrick, Malcolm *physicist*
Gaffney, Jeffrey Steven *chemistry researcher*
Jellinek, Julius *scientist*
Lawson, Robert Davis *theoretical nuclear physicist*
Li, Wei *research scientist*
Ma, Shengqian *research scientist*
Mancini, Derrick Charles *physicist*
Reimer, Paul E. *physicist*
Ruscic, Branko M. *chemist, researcher*
Sizyuk, Valeryi *physicist*
Sumant, Anirudha *materials scientist, researcher*

Arlington Heights
Smith, Norman Obed *retired physical chemist, educator*

Batavia
Bardeen, William Allan *research physicist*
Bhat, Pushpalatha C. *physics professor, researcher*
Jonckheere, Alan Mathew *physicist*
Malik, Sudhir *physics professor*

Oddone, Piermaria Jorge *physicist*
Raja, Rajendran *physicist*
Rakhno, Igor *physicist*

Bolingbrook
Sabau, Carmen Sybile *retired chemist*

Bourbonnais
Monts, Stephen Lee *retired chemistry professor*
Reams, Max Warren *geology educator, researcher*

Carbondale
Anterola, Aldwin M. *biochemist, educator*
Oyana, Tonny J. *geoscientist, educator*
Tolley, Luke *chemistry professor*
Tsige, Mesfin *physicist*
Wang, Lichang *chemistry professor*
Xiao, Dong *research scientist*

Champaign
Balbach, Harold Edward *environmental scientist*
Buschbach, Thomas Charles *geologist, consultant*
Kim, Hyunjoo *research scientist*
Rebeiz, Constantin Anis *plant biochemist, lab and foundation administrator, educator*
Tao, Zhining *environmental scientist*
Wolfram, Stephen *physicist, computer company executive*

Charleston
Linton, David A. *astronomer, educator*

Chicago
Abrams, Charles B. *chemistry professor*
Batu, Vedat *senior water resources engineer*
Boccara, Nino *physicist*
Canelli, Florencia *physics professor*
Chubinskaya, Susan *biochemistry professor, researcher, scientist*
Cronin, James Watson *physicist, researcher*
Farman, Gerrie P. *research scientist*
Freed, Karl Frederick *chemistry professor*
Gangopadhyaya, Asim *physics professor, department chairman*
Goltsiker, Aleksandr Davydovich *research scientist*
Gomer, Robert *chemistry professor*
Greene Johnson, Willetta *physics professor*
Halpern, Jack *chemist, educator*
Harvey, Allison Charmaine *chemist*
Harvey, Ronald Gilbert *research chemist*
Hast, Malcolm Howard *biomedical scientist, educator*
Hildebrand, Roger Henry *astrophysicist, physicist*
Hofman, David *physics professor*
Iqbal, Zafar Mohd *biochemist, molecular biologist, pharmacologist, cancer researcher, toxicologist, consultant*
Kadanoff, Leo Philip *physicist, educator*
Khalili, Mahmoud *physics professor*
Krasnykh, Olga P. *Organic Medicinal Chemist Researcher*
Levy, Donald Harris *chemistry professor*
Liao, Shutsung *biochemist, molecular oncologist*
Makinen, Marvin William *biophysicist, educator*
Mehta, Rajendra G. *research scientist, educator*
Nambu, Yoichiro *physics professor*
Oehme, Reinhard *physicist, researcher*
Olsen, Edward John *geologist, educator, curator*
Pilcher, James Eric *physicist*
Reiffel, Leonard *physicist, consultant*
Rosner, Jonathan Lincoln *physicist, researcher*
Rosner, Robert *astrophysicist, educator*
Schroeder, Walter Andreas *physics professor*
Sibener, Steven Jay *chemistry educator*
Steiner, Donald Frederick *biochemist, physician, educator*
Stephan, Thomas *physicist, researcher*
Stroscio, Michael Anthony *physicist, researcher*
Szuchet, Sara *biochemist, educator*
Truran, James Wellington, Jr. *astrophysicist, educator*
Turner, Michael Stanley *astrophysics professor, researcher, science administrator*
Winstein, Bruce Darrell *physics professor*
Yamamoto, Hisashi *chemistry professor*
Zhiglo, Andrey *research scientist*

Cicero
Casey, Craig F. *physics professor*

Dekalb
Kevill, Dennis Neil *chemistry professor*
Kimball, Clyde William *physicist, researcher*
Yoo, Young Zo *materials scientist, researcher*

Dixon
Atchley, Charles E. *physics professor*

Downers Grove
Hubbard, Lincoln Beals *medical physicist, consultant*
Tack, Lois Catherine *biochemist, researcher*

East Peoria
Mellendorf, Kenneth Ernest *physicist, researcher*

Elk Grove Village
Jan, Chwu-Ching Hwang *environmental chemistry consultant*

Elmhurst
Ferraro, John Ralph *chemist, researcher*

Elsah
Ritter, Joseph Michael *chemistry professor, dean*

Evanston
Allred, Albert Louis *chemistry professor*
Boyang, Liu *research scientist*
Frederick, Lewis Dunbar *chemistry professor*
Goldberg, Erwin *biochemistry educator*
Hoffman, Brian M. *chemistry professor*
Ibers, James Arthur *chemist, educator*
Jang, Joon I. *physicist*
Kalogera, Vassiliki (Vicky Kalogera) *physics professor*
Lambert, Joseph Buckley *chemistry professor*
Marks, Tobin Jay *chemistry educator*
Mirkin, Chad A. *chemistry professor*
Novak, Giles Anthony *astrophysicist*
Oakes, Robert James *physics and astronomy professor*
Olson, Gregory Bruce *materials science and engineering educator, academic director*
Rasio, Frederic Armand *astrophysicist*
Schluter, Robert Arvel *physicist*
Seidman, David N(athaniel) *materials scientist, engineer, educator*
Silverman, Richard Bruce *chemist, biochemist, educator*
Stoddart, J(ames) Fraser *chemistry professor, researcher*
Wessels, Bruce W. *materials scientist, educator*

Flossmoor
Parker, Eugene Newman *retired physicist, educator*

Galesburg
Schwartzman, Peter David *environmental scientist, educator*

Glen Ellyn
Mooring, F. Paul *physics editor*
Poromanska, Margarita Kirilova *environmental scientist, educator*

Glenview
Rorig, Kurt Joachim *chemist, science association director*

Highland Park
Rivkin, William B. *physicist*

Hinsdale
Kaminsky, Manfred Stephan *physicist*

Lake Forest
Weston, Arthur Walter *chemist, consultant, retired chemicals executive*

Libertyville
Grote, Jonathan *chemist, researcher*

Lombard
McCoy, Jeanie Shearer *analytical chemist, consultant*

Macomb
Boley, Mark S. *physicist, mathematician*
Kouassi, Gilles Kouame *chemistry professor, researcher*

Naperville
Arzoumanidis, Gregory G. *chemist*
Sellers, Gregory Jude *physicist*
Sherren, Anne Terry *chemistry professor*

Normal
Throckmorton, Peter Eugene *retired organic chemist, consultant*

North Chicago
Loga, Sanda *physicist, researcher*

Northfield
Shabica, Charles Wright *retired geologist, earth science educator*

Oak Park
Johnson, Porter Wear *physics professor emeritus*

Palatine
Wilcox, C. Jayne *chemistry professor*

Peoria
Chamberlain, Joseph Miles *retired astronomer, educator*
Hojilla-Evangelista, Milagros Parker *research chemist and scientist*

Rockford
Walhout, Justine Simon *chemistry professor*

Skokie
Filler, Robert *chemist educator*

University Park
Saber, Aheda Arafat *chemistry professor*

Urbana
Beak, Peter Andrew *chemistry professor*
Bocchino, Robert Louis *research scientist*
Boulatov, Roman *chemistry professor*
Caulet, Adeline Marie *astronomer*
Cisse, Ibrahim *research scientist*
Granato, Andrew Vincent *physics professor, researcher*
Gruebele, Martin *chemistry and biophysicist professor*
Iben, Icko, Jr. *astrophysicist, educator*
Lazarus, David *physicist, researcher*
Leggett, Anthony James *physics professor, researcher*
Makri, Nancy *chemistry professor*
Martinez, Todd J. *chemistry professor*
Mintel, Richard Walter *chemistry professor*
Moore, Jeffrey Scott *chemist, materials scientist, educator*
Park, Sung-Jin *chemist, educator*
Rowland, Theodore Justin *physicist, educator, researcher*
Satterthwaite, Cameron B. *physics professor*
Snyder, Lewis Emil *astrophysicist, educator*
Song, Xiaodong *geophysicist, seismologist*
Suslick, Kenneth Sanders *chemistry professor*
Switzer, Robert Lee *biochemistry professor*
Wandelt, Benjamin Dan *physics and astronomy professor*
Woese, Carl R. *biophysicist, microbiology educator*
Wuebbles, Donald James *atmospheric scientist, educator*
Yazdani, Ali *physicist, researcher*
Zimmerman, Steven Charles *chemistry professor*

Wadsworth
Ahmad, Moghisuddin *chemist, researcher*

Washington
List, Gary Ray *chemist, consultant*

INDIANA

Bloomington
Clemmer, Wendy Renee Saffell *biochemist*
Das, Narayan Chandra *physicist, chemist, researcher*
Hattin, Donald Edward *geologist, educator*
Hites, Ronald Atlee *chemist, educator*
Kauffman, Erle Galen *geologist, paleontologist*
Letsinger, Robert Lewis *chemistry professor*
Mechref, Yehia *biochemist, director*
Merino, Enrique *retired geochemistry professor*
Ortiz, Gerardo *physicist, researcher*
Peters, Dennis Gail *chemist*
Pollock, Robert Elwood *nuclear scientist*
Serot, Brian David *physics professor*

Chesterton
Crewe, Albert Victor *physicist, researcher, artist*

Elkhart
Free, Helen Murray *retired chemist consultant*

Fort Wayne
Tahmassebi, Daryoush *chemistry professor*

Hammond
Napora, Robert Alan *physics professor*
Parashar, Neeti *physics professor, researcher*
Rowberg, Kathryn L. *chemistry professor*

Indianapolis
Bein, Frederick L. *geography educator*
Farag, Sherif Shafik *physician scientist, educator*
Irvine, Nicholas *chemist*
Mawardi, Osman Kamel *retired plasma physicist*
Mirsky, Arthur *retired geologist, educator*
Wong, David T. *biochemist, researcher*

Muncie
Harris, Joseph McAllister *retired chemist*
Hedin, Eric Robert *physics professor*

Notre Dame
Frohne, Mary Victoria *physicist, educator*
Huber, Paul William *biochemistry professor, researcher*
Meisel, Dan *chemist*
Schuler, Robert Hugo *chemist, educator*
Shephard, William Danks *physicist, educator*
Tan, Wanpeng *physicist*
Trozzolo, Anthony Marion *chemistry professor*

Valparaiso
Cook, Addison Gilbert *chemistry professor*

West Lafayette
Adelman, Steven Allen *chemist, educator*
Chang, Ching-jer *medicinal chemistry educator*
Diamond, Sidney *chemist, educator*
Evans, Dennis Hyde *chemist, educator*
Jeon, Ji-Hong *environmental and agricultural engineer, researcher*
Jiru, Teshome Edae *research scientist*
Johnston, Clifford Thomas *soil and environmental chemistry educator*
Judd, William Robert *engineering geologist, educator*
Lyanda-Geller, Yuli B. *physicist*
McMillin, David Robert *chemistry professor*
Morrison, Harry *chemistry professor*
Negishi, Ei-ichi *chemistry professor*
Overhauser, Albert Warner *physicist*
Rossmann, Michael George *biochemist, educator*
Shepson, Paul Bradford *chemistry professor*
Zwier, Timothy S. *chemistry professor*

IOWA

Ames
Barnes, Richard George *physicist, researcher*
Barton, Thomas J. *chemistry professor, researcher*
Clem, John Richard *physicist, educator*
Corbett, John Dudley *chemistry professor*
Fritz, James Sherwood *chemist, educator*
Gschneidner, Karl Albert, Jr. *metallurgist, educator, editor, consultant*
Hong, Mei *chemistry professor*
Lo, Chester C.H. *research scientist*
Randic, Milan *retired chemistry professor*
Ruedenberg, Klaus *theoretical chemist, educator*
Xu, Min *research associate*

Cedar Falls
Hanson, Roger James *physics educator*

Iowa City
Bhattacharya, Debashish *environmental scientist, educator*
Burton, Donald Joseph *chemistry professor*
Ciach, Grzegorz Jan *research scientist*
Donelson, John Everett *biochemistry professor, molecular biologist*
Folk, George Edgar, Jr. *environmental physiology educator*
Glenister, Brian Frederick *geologist, educator*
Graham, Michael M. *nuclear medicine scientist, director*
Lee, Ikjin *research scientist*
Montgomery, Rex *biochemist, educator*
Prisinzano, Thomas Edward *chemistry professor, researcher*
Titze, Ingo Roland *physics professor*

Mount Vernon
Teague, Craig M. *chemistry professor*

Panora
Hartman, James Austin *retired geologist*

West Des Moines
Lynch, David William *physicist, retired educator*

KANSAS

Concordia
Leif, Todd R. *physics professor*

Greeley
Fisher, William Ralph *retired geologist*

Hutchinson
Bowman, Larry *chemistry professor*

Kansas City
Drake, Kenneth David *geologist*

Lawrence
Ammar, Raymond George *physicist, researcher*
Dreschhoff, Gisela Auguste Marie *physicist, researcher*
Gerhard, Lee Clarence *geologist, educator*
Givens, Richard Spencer *chemist, educator*
Krishtalka, Leonard *paleontologist, educator, museum director, researcher*
Landgrebe, John Allan *chemistry professor*
Macpherson, Gwendolyn Lee *geochemist, educator*
Mitscher, Lester Allen *chemist, educator*
Schloss, John Vinton *biochemist*

Manhattan
Hammaker, Robert Michael *chemist, educator*
Klabunde, Kenneth J. *chemistry professor, researcher*
MacRitchie, Finlay *chemistry professor, consultant*
Setser, Donald Wayne *chemistry professor*
Sorensen, Christopher Michael *physics professor, researcher*
Stockli, Martin Peter *physics educator*
Thumm, Uwe *physics professor*
Wysin, Gary Matthew *physics professor*

Overland Park
Ostby, Frederick Paul, Jr. *meteorologist, retired government official, science administrator*

KENTUCKY

Bowling Green
Brett, Bolen Day *physics professor*
Cheng, Chin-Min *environmental scientist*
Slocum, Donald Warren *chemist, educator, researcher*

Danville
Montgomery, Henry Edward *chemistry professor*

Georgetown
Wiseman, Frank L., Jr. *chemistry professor*

Lexington
Brock, Carolyn Pratt *chemist, educator*
Ehmann, William Donald *chemistry professor*
Ettensohn, Frank Robert *geologist, educator*
Hamilton-Kemp, Thomas Rogers *organic chemist, educator*
Kern, Bernard Donald *retired physicist*

Louisville
Barski, Oleg Aleksandrovich *biochemist*
Belanger, William Joseph *chemist, consultant*
Gowrishetty, Usha R. *research scientist*
Johnson, Alan Arthur *physicist, educator, consultant*
Shoemaker, Gradus Lawrence *chemist, educator*
Sumanasekera, Gamini Udaya *physics professor*

Morehead
Birriel, Jennifer Jean *physics professor*
Herron, James Dudley *chemist, educator*

Murray
Cox, James Ricky *chemistry professor, researcher*

Versailles
Zourarakis, Demetrio Periferachis *natural resource scientist*

Williamsburg
Dzugan, Thomas *chemistry professor*

LOUISIANA

Baton Rouge
Beyer, Horst Reinhard *physicist*
Carman, Kevin R. *oceanographer, educator*
Chan, Julia *chemistry professor*
Dellinger, Harold Barrett Barry *chemistry professor*
Diener, Peter *astrophysicist*
Landolt, Arlo Udell *astronomer, educator*
Maverick, Andrew William *chemistry educator, researcher*
Mc Glynn, Sean Patrick *physical chemist, educator*
O'Connell, Robert Francis *physics professor*
Rau, Ravi Prakash *physics professor, researcher*
Robinson, James William *chemistry professor*
Seo, Dong Cheol *wetland biogeochemist, environmental chemist*
Shr, Mingdr *research scientist*

Sygula, Andrzej *chemist, researcher*
Traynham, James Gibson *chemist, educator*
Van Lopik, Jack Richard *geologist, educator*
Warner, Isiah Manuel *chemistry professor*
Xu, Feng *research scientist, educator*
Younathan, Ezzat Saad *retired biochemistry educator*

Covington
Vercellotti, John Raymond *chemist, researcher*

Houma
Crochet, Jared John *research scientist*

Lafayette
McNeely, Jason Bryan *research scientist*

Lake Charles
Kandalam, Anil K. *physicist, educator*

Monroe
Melder, Trevor F. *physics professor*

New Orleans
Akundi, Murty Adinarayana *research scientist, educator*
Herman, Michael F. *chemistry professor*
Jayawickramarajah, Janarthanan *chemistry professor*
Mao, Zhiqiang *physics professor*
McGuire, James Horton *physics educator*
Murrish, Charles Howard *oil and gas exploration compant executive*
Parsley, Ronald Lee *paleontology educator*
Perdew, John Paul *physics professor*
Prockop, Darwin Johnson *biochemist, medical educator*
Rosensteel, George Thomas *nuclear physicist, professor*
Tang, Jianwu *geochemist, researcher*
Tao, Jianmin *chemistry educator, researcher*
Tipler, Frank Jennings III *physicist*
Tou, Jen-sie Hsu *biochemistry educator*

Pearl River
Cantrell, Joseph Sires *chemistry professor*

Ruston
Liu, Don *researcher*

Shreveport
Huang, Shile *biochemist, educator*
Rodriguez, Juan *physics professor*

MAINE

Augusta
Huntington, Thomas Gordon *hydrologist, researcher*

Blue Hill
Katzer, James Robert *retired research scientist*

Freeport
Panish, Morton B. *retired physical chemist*

Gorham
Whitten, Maurice Mason *chemistry professor*

Lewiston
Semon, Mark David *physicist, researcher*

Orono
He, Zhongqi *chemist, researcher*

Peaks Island
Bohan, Thomas Lynch *physicist, retired lawyer*

Portland
Glucksberg, Nadia *geologist, consultant*

Windham
Ames, Ted *environmental scientist*

MARYLAND

Aberdeen Proving Ground
Carrieri, Arthur Helmut *physicist, researcher*
Kesavan, Jana *physicist, researcher*
Lenz, David E. *chemist, researcher*

Annapolis
Bontoyan, Warren Roberts *chemist, lab administrator*
Clotworthy, John Harris *oceanographic consultant*
Correll, Francis David *physics professor*
Hammer, Jacob Myer *physicist, consultant*
Mungan, Carl Edward *physics professor*
O'Sullivan, Daniel W. *chemistry professor*
Wolf, Alfred A. *physicist, educator*

Baltimore
Beer, Michael *biophysicist, educator, environmentalist*
Deutsch, Robert William *physicist*
Eichhorn, Gunther Louis *chemist, researcher*
Etter, Paul Courtney *oceanographer*
Ganem, Joseph Wilfred *physicist, writer*
Giacconi, Riccardo *astrophysicist, educator*
Goldman, Lawrence *biophysicist*
Haig, Frank Rawle *physics professor, priest*
Hauser, Michael George *astrophysicist*
Helm, Donald Cairney *geologist, retired engineer, educator*
Judd, Brian Raymond *physicist*
Kamanu, Uchemadu Chee *chemist*
Krolik, Julian Henry *astrophysicist, educator*
Lee, Yung-Keun *physicist, researcher*
Marsh, Bruce David *geologist, educator*
Mixson, Archibald James *research scientist, internist, endocrinologist*
Moos, H. Warren *physicist, educator, astronomer, director*
Moser, Ann Boody *biochemist*
Naqvi, Shahid Abbas *physicist, educator*
Posner, Gary Herbert *chemist, educator*
Riess, Adam Guy *astronomer, educator*
Roseman, Saul *biochemist, educator*
Shamoo, Adil Elias *biochemist, educator*
Sinha, Neeti *biophysicist, researcher*
Storrs, Alexander David *astronomer*
Vadakkumpadan, Fijoy *research scientist*
Weaver, Kenneth Newcomer *geologist, state agency administrator*
White, Richard Lee *astronomer*
Williams, Robert Eugene *astronomer*

Beltsville
Chaney, Rufus L. *environmental scientist*

Berlin
Brodsky, Allen *retired biophysicist*
Passwater, Richard Albert *biochemist, author*

Bethesda
Ambs, Stefan *biochemist, researcher*
Appella, Daniel *chemist, researcher*
Becker, Edwin Demuth *chemist, director*
Berger, Robert Lewis *retired biophysicist*
Chow, Carson C. *research scientist*
Fales, Henry Marshall III *chemist*
Huebner, John Stephen *geologist*
Jacobson, Kenneth Alan *chemist, researcher*
Kador, Peter Fritz *chemist*
Korn, Edward David *biochemist*
Masnyk, Ihor Jarema *chemist, director*
Murayama, Makio *biochemist*
Rice, Jerry Mercer *biochemist, consultant, pathologist*
Trus, Benes Louis *structural chemist*
Vaughan, Martha *biochemist, educator*
Weiss, George Herbert *senior scientist consultant*
Wiese, Wolfgang Lothar *physicist, researcher*
Witkop, Bernhard *chemist*
Zoon, Kathryn Christine *biochemist*

Cabin John
Townsend, John William, Jr. *physicist, retired federal agency administrator*

Calverton
DelSole, Timothy Michael *geophysicist, educator*
Hu, Zeng-Zhen *meteorologist*

Cambridge
Fisher, Thomas Richard *environmental scientist, educator*
Malone, Thomas Charleton *oceanography educator*

Chevy Chase
Sinclair, Rolf Malcolm *retired physicist*

Clarksburg
Geem, Zong Woo *interdisciplinary scientist*

College Park
Brill, Dieter Rudolf *physicist, educator*
Colombini, Marco *biophysicist*
DeFries, Ruth S. *earth system scientist, researcher*
Dusold, Laurence Richard *chemist, computer specialist*
Fenselau, Catherine Clarke *chemistry professor*
Fisher, Michael Ellis *physicist, chemist, educator, mathematician*
Gates, Sylvester James, Jr. *physics professor, researcher*
Greenberg, Oscar Wallace *physicist, researcher*
Griem, Hans Rudolf *physicist, researcher*
Gu, Jie *research scientist*
Hassouneh, Munther A. *research scientist, educator*
Kundu, Mukul Ranjan *physics and astronomy professor*
Lubkin, Gloria Becker *physicist*
Melngailis, John *physicist*
Paik, Ho Jung *physics professor*
Rabin, Herbert *physicist, educator, dean*
Rahman, Nurur *astrophysicist*
Shoushtari, Amir H. *research scientist*
Silverman, Joseph *chemistry professor*
Thirumalai, Devarajan *physical sciences researcher, educator*
Tomoya, Tatsuno *research scientist*
Veilleux, Sylvain *astrophysicist, educator*
Walters, William Ben *chemistry professor*
Williams, Ellen D. *physics professor*
Zen, E-an *research geologist, educator*

Columbia
Fisher, Dale John *retired chemist, medical investigator*
Khare, Mohan *chemist, researcher*

Dayton
Fischell, Robert Ellentuch *physicist*

Derwood
Stadtman, Thressa Campbell *biochemist*

Edgewater
McCamy, Calvin Samuel *retired optics scientist*

Elkton
Xu, Ping *chemist*

Ellicott City
Singh, Narsingh Bahadur *chemist, researcher*

Frederick
Carlson, David Emil *physicist, researcher*
DeVoe, Howard Josselyn *retired chemistry professor*
Garver, Robert Vernon *retired research physicist*
Henderson, Madeline Mary (Berry) *chemist, researcher, consultant*
McKee, Tawnya Carlene *research scientist*

Gaithersburg
Amis, Eric Jay *chemist, researcher, editor*
Caplin, Jerrold Leon *health physicist*
Caswell, Randall Smith *physicist*
Celotta, Robert James *physicist*
Clark, Charles Winthrop *physicist*
Coskuner, Orkid *research scientist, educator*
Currie, Lloyd Arthur *nuclear scientist, educator*
Hattrick-Simpers, Jason Ryan *materials scientist, researcher*
Jacox, Marilyn Esther *chemist*
Jahanmir, Said *materials scientist, mechanical engineer*
Jurchescu, Oana Diana *research scientist*
Laptev, Alexander Borisovich *physicist, researcher*
Lynn, Jeffrey Whidden *research physicist, educator*
Mighell, Alan Donald *physical chemist*
Phillips, William Daniel *physicist*
Pierce, Daniel Thornton *physicist*
Polyakov, Sergey Vladimirovich *physicist, researcher*
Reader, Joseph *physicist*
Ruckman, Mark Warren *physicist*
Savransky, Vladimir M. *research scientist*
Sengers, Johanna M. H. Levelt *physicist*
Tarrio, Charles *physicist*
Weber, Alfons *physicist*
Werner, Samuel Alfred *physicist, educator*
Wineland, David J. *physicist*

Germantown
Foulke, Judith Diane *health physicist*
Hirsch, Roland Felix *chemist, educator*

Greenbelt
Batchelor, David Allen *astrophysicist, educator*
Danchi, William C. *astrophysicist*
Day, John H. *physicist*
Gehrels, Neil (Cornelius A. Gehrels) *astrophysicist*
Jeong, Myeong-Jae *environmental scientist*
Kniffen, Donald Avery *astrophysicist, educator, researcher*
Kostiuk, Theodor *astrophysicist planetary scientist*
Kundu, Prasun Kumar *environmental scientist, physics professor*
Mather, John Cromwell *astrophysicist*
Mumma, Michael Jon *research scientist*
Rauscher, Bernard Joseph *astrophysicist*
Schmidt, Joachim Matthias *research scientist*
Shen, Bo-Wen *research scientist*
Wood, H(oward) John III *astrophysicist, astronomer*
Yang, Yuekui *atmospheric scientists*

Hagerstown
Jozik, Paul *physics professor*
Munday, John Henry *chemist, physicist, educator*

Hyattsville
Pritchett, Timothy Michael *physicist*
Ranjan, Priya *research scientist*

Lanham
Degnan, John James III *physicist*

Laurel
Blewett, David T. *astrophysicist*
Srinivasan, Rengaswamy *research scientist*

Montgomery Village
Kushner, Lawrence Maurice *physical chemist, consultant*

Mount Airy
Johnston, Josephine Rose *chemist*

New Market
Young, Russell Dawson *physicist, consultant*

North Bethesda
Edinger, Stanley Evan *clinical chemist*

Parkton
Fitzgerald, Edwin Roger *physicist, researcher*

Port Deposit
Benjamin, Francis Ellis *analytical chemist, consultant*

Potomac
Oertel, Goetz Kuno Heinrich *physicist, professional society administrator*

Prince Frederick
Beers, Richard H. *physics professor*

Pylesville
Roth, George Stanley *biochemist, physiologist, researcher*

Rockville
Buchanan, John Donald *retired nuclear scientist*
Gaunaurd, Guillermo C. *retired physicist, engineer, researcher*
Kimura, Tomohiro *biophysical and biochemical researcher*
Kruger, Jerome *materials science educator, consultant*
Loyevsky, Mark Michael *biochemist, parasitologist, researcher*
Ovanesov, Mikhail V. *biophysicist, researcher, biomedical engineer*
Pastor, Richard Walter *research chemist*
Price, Simani Mohapatra *research scientist, director*
Rao, Potarazu Krishna *environmental consultant*
Rice, Kenner Cralle *medicinal chemist*
Sansalone, William Robert *biochemist, educator, biomedical researcher*
Sarma, Dandapantula Nandakumara *senior scientist*
Schindler, Albert Isadore *physicist, researcher*
Suleiman, Orhan Hussein *radiological physicist*
Wallenmeyer, William Anton *retired physicist*

Silver Spring
Arzayus, Krisa Murray *geochemist*
Biberman, Lucien Morton *retired physicist*
Drum, Bruce Alan *physicist*
Ehrlich, Charles David *physicist*
Hudson, Ralph P. *physicist*
Shropshire, Walter, Jr. *biophysicist, pastor*
Wang, Julian XI *research scientist*
Whitmore, Frank Clifford, Jr. *retired geologist*

Suitland
Assefa, Zelalem *research scientist*

Towson
Ha, Phuoc Dai *physics professor*

Westminster
Mian, Shabbir M. *physicist, educator*

MASSACHUSETTS

Acton
Conoby, Joseph Francis *chemist*

Agawam
Kantor, Simon William *chemistry professor*

Amherst
Anber, Mohamed *research scientist*
Archer, Ronald Dean *chemist, educator*
Fadeev, Alexander Y. *chemist, researcher*
Fink, Richard David *chemist, educator*
Goldstein, Joseph Irwin *materials scientist, educator*
Hallock, Robert Bruce *physics professor*
MacKnight, William John *chemist, educator*
Metz, Ricardo Baer *chemistry professor*
Muschinski, Andreas *atmospheric physicist, educator*
O'Hara, Patricia Bernadette *chemistry professor*
Rabin, Monroe Stephen Zane *physicist*
Romer, Robert Horton *physicist, researcher*

Auburndale
Aronow, Saul *radiological physicist, consultant*

Belmont
Hauser, George *biochemist, educator*
Lyon, Richard Harold *physicist, educator*
McCann, John Joseph *research scientist, consultant*
Neumeyer, John Leopold *chemistry professor*

Beverly
Garner, Richard C. *research scientist*
Lister, Graeme George *physicist, journalist*
Qin, Shu *materials scientist*

Billerica
Gheith, Mohamed Ahmed *geology educator, consultant*

Boston
Anissimova, Svetlana Vladimirovna *physicist, researcher*
Anselme, Jean-Pierre Louis Marie *chemist*
Benneyan, James C. *research scientist*
Brecher, Kenneth *astrophysicist, educator*
Castro Neto, Antonio Helio *physics professor*
Chakrabarti, Supriya *space astrophysicist*
Cho, Sang Wan *physicist, researcher*
Cohen, Robert Sonné *physicist, philosopher, educator*
Dima, Ioana Maria *research scientist*
Edmonds, Dean Stockett, Jr. *physicist, educator, director*
Jaeger, Gregg S. *physicist, engineer*
Khismatullin, Damir Borisovich *physicist, mathematician*
Kirschner, Marc Wallace *biochemist, cell biologist*
Kornberg, Sir Hans Leo *biochemist, educator*
Lehrer, Sherwin Sam *biochemist*
Lichtenstein, Alice Hinda *nutritional biochemist*
Malenka, Bertram Julian *physicist, researcher*
Moses, Marsha Anne *biochemist, researcher*
Papisov, Mikhail I. *chemist*
Pardee, Arthur Beck *biochemist, educator*
Rao, Devulapalli Venkata *physics educator*
Rosowsky, Andre *chemist, educator*
Shabestari, Khosrow Toutounchi (T. Shabestari) *research scientist*
Sharma, Prashant *physicist, educator*
Stachel, John Jay *physicist, researcher*
Stanley, Harry Eugene *physicist, researcher*
Strominger, Jack Leonard *biochemist*
Trackman, Philip Charles *biochemist, researcher*
von Stackelberg, Katherine Ellen *environmental scientist, consultant*
Wu, Fa Yueh *retired physics professor*
Yaroslavsky, Anna *biophysicist, educator*

Brockton
Lyons, Paul Christopher *government geologist, educator*

Brookfield
Anderson, Theodore Robert *physicist, small business owner*

Brookline
Nash, Leonard Kollender *retired chemistry professor*

Burlington
Abkowitz, Stanley *research scientist*

Cambridge
Alberty, Robert Arnold *chemistry professor*
Barger, James Edwin *physicist*
Blanchet-Fincher, Graciela Beatriz *physicist*
Bradt, Hale Van Dorn *physicist, educator*
Brecher, Aviva *physicist, researcher*
Burke, Bernard Flood *physicist, researcher*
Canizares, Claude Roger *astrophysicist, educator*
Chance, Kelly *geophysicist, educator*
Chisholm, Sallie Watson *biological oceanography educator, researcher*
Clark, George Whipple *physics professor*
Corey, Elias James *chemistry professor*
Cummins, Christopher C. *chemistry professor*

Deutch, John Mark *chemistry professor, former CIA director*
Dowling, Timothy Edward *planetary science educator*
Dresselhaus, Mildred Spiewak *physics and engineering professor*
Eagar, Thomas Waddy *metallurgist, educator*
French, Anthony Philip *physicist, educator*
Frey, Frederick August *geochemist, researcher, educator*
Friedman, Jerome Isaac *physics professor, researcher*
Fu, Gregory Chung-Wei *chemistry educator*
Garland, Carl Wesley *chemist, educator*
Geller, Margaret Joan *astrophysicist, educator*
Gingerich, Owen Jay *astronomer, educator*
Glauber, Roy Jay *physics professor*
Goldstone, Jeffrey *physicist, educator*
Goodman, Alyssa Ann *astronomer, educator*
Gordon, Roy Gerald *chemistry professor*
Graessle, Dale Edward *astrophysicist*
Greene, Frederick Davis, II, *chemistry professor*
Gruen, Daniel M. *research scientist*
Halperin, Bertrand Israel *physics professor*
Han, Xinxin *chemist, researcher*
Harvey, Charles Franklin *hydrologist, educator*
Heimbach, Patrick *oceanographer*
Hernquist, Lars Eric *astronomer, educator*
Herschbach, Dudley Robert *chemistry professor*
Holton, Gerald *physicist, educator, science historian*
Huchra, John Peter *astronomer, educator*
Ivanov, Yuri Anatoly *research scientist*
Jackiw, Roman *physicist, researcher*
Janes, Daniel E. *research scientist*
Joss, Paul Christopher *astrophysicist, atmospheric physicist, educator*
Kastner, Marc Aaron *physics professor, dean*
Kerman, Arthur Kent *physicist, researcher*
Ketterle, Wolfgang *physics professor*
Khorana, Har Gobind *chemist, educator*
Klemperer, Willian *chemistry professor*
Koh, Adrian Soo Jin *research scientist*
Lenert, Andrej *research scientist*
Lewin, Walter H.G. *physics professor*
Lieber, Charles *chemistry professor, researcher, materials scientist*
Lieberman, Henry A. *research scientist*
Lipscomb, William Nunn, Jr. *retired chemistry professor*
Liu, Xiong *atmospheric physicist*
Livingston, James Duane *physicist, researcher*
Lomon, Earle Leonard *physicist, educator, consultant*
Looker, Adam *chemist*
Marsden, Brian Geoffrey *astronomer*
McElroy, Michael *physicist, researcher, educator*
Meselson, Matthew Stanley *biochemist, educator*
Milner, Richard Gerard *physicist*
Moran, James Michael, Jr. *astronomer, educator*
Murray, Cherry Ann *physicist, researcher, dean*
Myers, John *research scientist, consultant*
Negele, John William *physics professor, consultant*
Nocera, Daniel G. *chemistry professor*
O'Connell, Richard John *geophysicist, educator*
Olbert, Stanislaw *physicist*
Oppenheim, Irwin *chemical physicist, educator*
Paul, William *physicist, researcher*
Petaev, Mikhail Ivanovich *senior geologist, researcher*
Plesch, Andreas *geologist, consultant*
Ramsey, Norman F. *physicist, researcher*
Randall, Lisa *physics professor*
Reimer, Bryan *research scientist*
Robinson, Allan Richard *oceanography educator*
Roozbehani, Mardavij *research scientist*
Schlosser, C. Adam *hydrologist*
Schrock, Richard Royce *chemistry professor*
Seyferth, Dietmar *chemist, educator*
Shapiro, Irwin Ira *physicist, researcher*
Silbey, Robert James *chemistry professor, researcher, consultant*
Soljacic, Marin *physicist, educator*
Song, Xiangzhi *research scientist*
Spaepen, Frans August *physicist, educator*
Steadman, Stephen Geoffrey *physicist*
Steinfeld, Jeffrey Irwin *chemistry professor emeritus, writer*
Stern, Joel N.H. *biochemist, researcher*
Stiehl, Walter Dan *research scientist*
Strandberg, Malcom Woodrow Pershing *physicist*
Terry, James Layton, II, *research scientist*
Thaddeus, Patrick *physicist, researcher*
Ting, Samuel Chao Chung *physicist, researcher*
Tinkham, Michael *physicist, researcher*
Tofighi Niaki, Aliassghar *research scientist*
Tomasiello, Alessandro *physicist*
Valero, Henri-Pierre *research scientist*
Vessot, Robert Frederick Charles *physicist, researcher*
Walther, Philip *physicist, researcher*
Waugh, John Stewart *chemist, educator*
Weinberg, Robert Allan *biochemist, educator*
Westervelt, Robert Moore *physics educator*
Whitesides, George McClelland *chemistry professor*
Wiederschain, Dmitri *research scientist*
Wilczek, Frank Anthony *physics professor*
Wilson, Robert Woodrow *radio astronomer*
Wolk, Scott Joseph *astrophysicist*
Wood, John Armstead *planetary scientist, geological sciences educator, artist*
Yi, Wei *physicist*
Zaldarriaga, Matias *cosmologist, physics professor*
Zwierlein, Martin Wolfram *physics professor*

Concord
Horwitz, Paul *physicist*
Plummer, William Torsch *optical physicist*

Cotuit
Miller, Robert Charles *retired physicist*

Dedham
Lichtin, Norman Nahum *chemistry professor*

East Longmeadow
Skutnik, Bolesh J. *optics scientist, lay worker, lawyer*

East Orleans
Romey, William Dowden *geologist, educator*

Falmouth
Pedlosky, Joseph *geophysicist, educator*

Fitchburg
Ciottone, Judith Marino *chemistry professor*

Framingham
Dawicki, Doloretta Diane *analytical chemist, research biochemist, educator*

Gloucester
Socolow, Arthur Abraham *geologist*

Hanscom AFB
Crabtree, Peter *physicist, researcher*
Mailloux, Robert Joseph *physicist*
Rothman, Laurence Sidney *physicist*

Haverhill
DeSchuytner, Edward Alphonse *biochemist, educator*

Holyoke
Onu, Chukuemeka N. *chemistry professor, researcher*

Ipswich
Herrmann, Robert Lawrence *biochemist, educator*
Londer, Yuri Y. *biochemist*

Jamaica Plain
Valverde, Paloma *biochemist, educator*

Lexington
Cohen, Saul G. *chemist, educator*
Dionne, Gerald Francis *research physicist, educator, consultant*
Hickey, Magali B. *chemist*
Huang, Robin K. *research scientist*
Silverman, Sam Mendel *physicist, lawyer*

Lowell
Altman, Albert *retired physicist*
Karakashian, Aram Simon *physics professor*
Kegel, Gunter Heinrich Reinhard *physics professor, researcher*
Pullen, David John *physicist, researcher*
Tandel, Sujit Kashinath *physicist, researcher*
Wakim, Fahd George *physicist, researcher*

Manchester
Mack, Michael Edward *physicist*

Marlborough
Rayle, Heather Lynnette *chemist*

Medford
Kumar, Krishna *chemistry professor*
Schneps, Jack *physics professor, department chairman*

Natick
Doona, Christopher J. *research chemist*

Newburyport
Robinson, Enders Anthony *geophysicist, educator, writer*

Newton
Dunlap, William Crawford *physicist*
Golomb, Dan S. *physical chemistry educator, consultant*
Klyosov, Anatole Alex *biochemist, researcher*

North Andover
Swallow, Kathleen Clinedinst *chemistry professor*

North Dartmouth
Hsu, Jong-Ping *physicist, educator*

Northampton
Fleck, George Morrison *chemistry professor*

Northborough
Ou, Duan Li *chemist*

Peabody
Dobbs, John McGregor *physicist, mechanical engineer*

Provincetown
Giese, Graham Sherwood *oceanographer*

Randolph
Manos, Sarantos John *physics educator*

Rochester
Teal, John M. *environmental scientist*

Roxbury
Simons, Elizabeth R(eiman) *biochemist, educator*

Shrewsbury
Nixon, Eugene Ray *chemist, educator*

South Dartmouth
Mellberg, Leonard Evert *physicist*

South Hadley
Ewing Browne, Sheila *physical organic chemist, professor*
Williamson, Kenneth Lee *chemistry professor*

Springfield
Wurm, Alexander *physics professor*

Sudbury
Crooker, Nancy Uss *physicist, researcher*

Waltham
Bensinger, James Robert *physicist*
Epstein, Irving Robert *chemistry professor*
Foxman, Bruce Mayer *chemist, educator*
Newburg, David Stephen *biochemist*

Wayland
Brynjolfsson, Ari *nuclear physicist*

Wellesley
Charpie, Robert Alan *physicist, researcher*
Kato, Walter Yoneo *physicist*
Snitzer, Elias *physicist*

Westborough
Rekhi, Sandeep *geologist, physicist*

Weston
Lin, Alice Lee Lan *physicist, researcher, educator*

Williamstown
Crampton, Stuart Jessup Bigelow *physicist, researcher*
Park, David Allen *physicist, researcher*
Wobus, Reinhard Arthur *geologist, educator*

Winchester
Milburn, Richard Henry *physics professor*

Woburn
Lalgudi, Subramanian Natarajan *research scientist*
Perlovsky, Leonid Isaacovich *geophysicist, researcher*

Woods Hole
Cohen, Seymour Stanley *biochemist, educator*
Gagosian, Robert B. *chemist, educator*
Hart, Stanley Robert *geochemist, educator*
Hobbie, John Eyres *research scientist*
Limeburner, Richard *oceanographer, researcher*
Lough, Robert Gregory *oceanographer, researcher*
Poag, Claude Wylie *geologist, researcher*
Rypina, Irina I. *oceanographer*
Saito, Mak *environmental scientist*
Shimomura, Osamu *chemistry professor*
Stanley, Rachel H. R. *oceanographer*
Steele, John Hyslop *marine scientist, oceanographic institute administrator*
Uchupi, Elazar *geologist, researcher*

Worcester
Akgul, Ferit Ozan *research scientist*
Chaudhury, Sujoy Krishna *research scientist*
Downs, Timothy John *environmental scientist, educator*
Kearney, Kevin Robert *biochemist, educato, researcher*
Kerns, Christian Randolph *retired chemist*
Koehler, Stephan A. *physics professor*
Merken, Melvin *chemistry professor*

MICHIGAN

Albion
Taylor, Lawrence Dow *geologist, educator*

Allendale
Gipson, Karen *physics professor*

Alma
Beattie, Thomas Irving *physics professor*

Ann Arbor
Agranoff, Bernard William *biochemist, educator*
Akerlof, Carl William *physics professor*
Akhoury, Ratindranath *physics professor, researcher*
Barald, Katharine Francesca *developmental molecular neurobiologist, biochemist*
Bartell, Lawrence Sims *chemist, educator*
Bayatpur, Farhad *research scientist*
Bergin, Edwin Anthony *astrophysicist, educator*
Blinder, Seymour Michael *chemistry and physics professor, researcher*
Coward, James Kenderdine *chemist*
Crippen, Gordon Marvin *chemist*
Dekker, Eugene Earl *biochemistry educator*
Ewing, Rodney Charles *mineralogist, geology educator, materials scientist*
Fisk, Lennard Ayres *physicist, researcher*
Garcia-Guzman, Luis M. *research scientist, educator*
Ghannad Rezaie, Mostafa *research scientist*
Griffin, Henry Claude *retired chemistry professor*
Jones, Lawrence William *retired physicist*
Kane, Gordon Leon *physics researcher and educator*
Kesler, Stephen Edward *geology educator*
Kopelman, Raoul *chemist, physicist, educator*
Krimm, Samuel *physicist, researcher, educator, administrator*
Krisch, Alan David *physics professor*
Lin, Hai *physicist*
Longone, Daniel Thomas *chemistry professor*
Lorenzon, Wolfgang B. *physics professor, researcher*
Meyers, Philip Alan *geochemistry educator, researcher*
Nordman, Christer Eric *chemistry professor*
Nori, Franco Mauro *physicist, researcher*
Nriagu, Jerome Okon *environmental geochemist*
Pan, Xiaoqing *materials scientist, educator*
Parkinson, William Charles *physics professor, researcher*
Roe, Byron Paul *physics professor*
Saltiel, Alan Robert *biochemist*
Tomozawa, Yukio *retired physics professor*
Van der Voo, Rob *geophysicist*
Veltman, Martinus J.G. *retired physics educator*
Yen, Louis *research scientist*

Auburn Hills
Malanga, Michael Thomas *research scientist*
Wu, Ming-Cheng *research scientist*

Belleville
Wilson, David James *chemistry researcher, educator*

Chassell
Spain, James Dorris, Jr. *biochemist, educator*

Chelsea
Weinreich, Gabriel *physicist, minister, educator*

Dearborn
Chock, David P. *sustainability and environmental scientist, educator*

Detroit
Drescher, Dennis George *biochemist, researcher*
Frade, Peter Daniel *chemist, educator, administrator*
Gupta, Suraj Narayan *physicist, researcher*
M. B., Sahana *materials scientist, researcher*
Njus, David Lars *biophysicist*
Salakhutdinov, Ildar *physics professor, researcher*
Stewart, Melbourne George, Jr. *physicist, researcher*
Trimpin, Sarah *chemistry professor*

East Lansing
Austin, Sam M. *physicist, educator*
Benenson, Walter *nuclear physics professor*
Case, Eldon Darrel *materials science educator*
Chivukula, R. Sekhar *physics professor*
D'Itri, Frank Michael *environmental research chemist*
Donahue, Megan Elizabeth *astrophysicist*
Dye, James Louis *retired chemistry professor*
Harrison, Michael Jay *physicist, researcher*
Hartmann, William Morris *physics educator*
Kirkpatrick, R(obert) James *geologist, educator*
Linnemann, James Thomas *physics professor*
Preiss, Jack *biochemistry professor*
Sharkey, Thomas David *biochemist, educator*

Farmington Hills
Chapman, Gilbert Bryant, II, *physicist*

Grand Rapids
Greenfield, John Charles *biochemist, professional society administrator*
Haarsma, Deborah Joy Becker *physics professor*

Highland
Brown, Ray Kent *biochemist, physician, educator*

Holland
Gardner, Kevin Eugene *research scientist, director*
Gillmore, Jason George *chemistry professor*

Houghton
Elangovan, Shreehari *research scientist*

Kalamazoo
Holmuhamedov, Ekhson Lukmanovich *biophysicist, biochemist*

Kentwood
Yovich, Daniel John *chemist, educator*

Leland
Small, Hamish *chemist*

Midland
Chao, Marshall *chemist*
Dorman, Linneaus Cuthbert *retired chemist*

Mount Pleasant
Dietrich, Richard Vincent *geologist, educator*
Mohanty, Dillip K. *chemistry professor, researcher*
Peyrefitte, Ashton George, Jr. *meteorologist, educator*

Novi
Smith, George Wolfram *physicist, researcher*

Okemos
Burnett, Jean B. *biochemist, educator*

Rochester
Goldberg, Andrew F.X. *biochemist, educator*
Tepley, Norman *physics educator*

Romulus
Yussouff, Mohammed *retired physicist, educator*

Spring Arbor
Kuntzleman, Thomas *chemistry professor*

Sterling Heights
Kelly, Nelson Allen *chemist, researcher*

Three Rivers
Boyer, Nicodemus Elijah *chemist, consultant*

Troy
Fritzsche, Hellmut *physics professor*

University Center
Clarey, Timothy Lee *geologist, educator*
Faleski, Michael C. *physics professor*

Warren
Halalay, Ion Cornel *research scientist*
Herbst, Jan Francis *physicist, researcher*

Waterford
Anderson, Peter Stanford *physics professor*

West Bloomfield
Harwood, Julius J. *metallurgist, educator*

Ypsilanti
Barnes, James Milton *retired physics and astronomy professor*
Bhaganagar, Kiran *research scientist*
Van WIngerden, Daniel J. *retired physics professor*

MINNESOTA

Bloomington
Bekrenev, Anatoliy *physicist*

Brainerd
Vig, Pradeep Kumar *geophysics educator*

Brooklyn Park
Paulus, Eugenia *chemistry professor*

Duluth
Clarke, Margaret Jackson *physics professor, archivist*

Lakeville
Phinney, William Charles *retired geologist*

Minneapolis
Ackerman, Eugene *biophysics professor*
Carr, Peter William *chemistry professor*
Goldman, Allen Marshall *physics professor*
Gurvich, Vadim J. *chemist, director*
Halley, James Woods *physics professor*
Harris, Ilene Barmash *researcher*
Marshak, Marvin Lloyd *physicist, researcher*
Park, Eunsung *scientist, education educator*
Patterson, Steven Earl *chemistry professor, researcher*
Portoghese, Philip Salvatore *medicinal chemist, educator*
Shifman, Mikhail *physicist*
Swickrath, Michael Jacob *research scientist*
Tran, Nang Tri *research scientist, electrical engineer, entrepreneur*
Wright, Herbert E(dgar), Jr. *geologist*

Minnetonka
Wittcoff, Harold Aaron *chemist*

Moorhead
Strong, Judith Ann *retired chemist*

Northfield
Mohrig, Jerry R. *chemistry professor, researcher*

Rochester
Kao, Pai Chih *clinical chemist*
Tindall, Donald James *biological chemistry educator*
Trzasko, Joshua Damon *research scientist*

Saint Paul
Agrimson, Erick Paul *physics professor*
Fedorova, Nataliya Vasylivna *research scientist*
Gehrke, Charles William *biochemistry professor*
Krupa, Sagar *environmental scientist, educator*
Mulla, David Jamil *physicist*
Perry, James Alfred *environmental scientist, academic administrator, educator, consultant*
Pocius, Alphonsus Vytautas *physical chemist*
Schwartz, Albert Truman *chemistry professor*
Suh, Sangwon *environmental scientist, educator*
Thompson, Mary Eileen *chemistry professor*
Van Pilsum, John Franklin *biochemist, educator*

MISSISSIPPI

Bay Saint Louis
Hurlburt, Harley Ernest *ocean modeling and prediction scientist*

Cleveland
Meek, Ernest Carlysle *physics professor*

Diamondhead
Simpson, W(ilburn) Dwain *physicist, communications executive*

Fulton
Nowicki, Kenneth Robert *physics professor*

Hattiesburg
Maung, Khin Maung *physics professor*
Miao, Wujian *chemistry professor*

Jackson
Remata, Suseela Reddy *environmental science educator, researcher*

Stennis Space Center
Hou, Weilin (Will Hou) *oceanographer*
Mahoney, Kevin L. *oceanographer*

University
Breazeale, Mack Alfred *research scientist, educator*
Stolzenburg, Maribeth *research scientist*

MISSOURI

Bolivar
Kitchin, Robert Walter *chemistry professor, physics professor*

Cape Girardeau
Ghosh, Santaneel *physics professor*

Clinton
Kelsay, David Roland *chemist*

Columbia
Decker, Wayne Leroy *meteorologist, educator*
Greenlief, C. Michael *chemistry professor, director*
Guha, Suchismita *physics professor*
Havens, Timothy C. *research scientist*
Hawthorne, Marion Frederick *chemistry professor*
Hossain, Maruf *research scientist*
Johns, Williams Davis, Jr. *geologist, educator*
Kaiser, Edwin Michael *chemistry professor*
Kannan, Raghuraman *biochemist, educator*
Mashhoon, Bahram *physicist, researcher*
Randall, Douglas D. *biochemist, educator*
Randall, Linda Lea *biochemist, educator*
Sharma, Krishna Kathribail *biochemist, educator*
Weisman, Gary Andrew *biochemist*

Creve Coeur
Bockserman, Robert Julian *chemist*

Ferguson
Chubb, Charles Ray *physicist, researcher*

Fulton
Palmer, Kent Friedley *physics professor*

Independence
Lemon, Leslie Roy *radar meteorologist*

Joplin
Malzahn, Ray Andrew *chemistry professor, dean*

Kansas City
Bergman, Carla Elaine *hydrologist, consultant*
Cheng, Kuang Lu *chemist, educator*
Ching, Wai Yim *physics professor, researcher*
Dias, Jerry Ray *chemistry professor, researcher*
Kisslinger, Carl *geophysicist, educator*
Parizek, Eldon Joseph *geologist, educator, dean*
Rost, William Joseph *chemist*
Surguchov, Andrei P. *biochemist, ophthalmologist, researcher*
Wilkinson, Ralph Russell *retired biochemistry educator, toxicologist*

Kirksville
Festa, Roger Reginald *chemist, educator*

Park Hills
Scheidt, Brian R. *geologist, educator*

Rolla
Adawi, Ibrahim Hasan *physics professor*
Alexander, Ralph William, Jr. *physics professor*
Switzer, Jay A(lan) *chemistry educator*
Yan, Dongming *research scientist, educator*

Saint Louis
Agarwal, Ramesh Kumar *aeronautical scientist, researcher, educator*
Alford, Mark Gower *physicist*
Bender, Carl Martin *physics professor, consultant*
Binns, Walter Robert *astrophysics researcher*
Burgess, James Harland *physics professor, researcher*
Colletti, Ronald F. *chemist, researcher*
Concibido, Vergel C. *research and development company scientist, plant geneticist, inventor*
Cowsik, Ramanath *physics professor*
Fang, Hui *research scientist*
Feng, Paul Chi-Chia *metabolism chemist, biochemist*
Frieden, Carl *biochemist, educator*
Friedlander, Michael Wulf *physicist, researcher*
Gibbons, Patrick Chandler *physicist, researcher*
Hakkinen, Raimo Jaakko *aerospace scientist*
Handel, Peter H. *physics professor*
Holtzer, Alfred Melvin *chemistry professor*
Israel, Martin Henry *astrophysicist, educator, academic administrator*
Macias, Edward S. *chemistry professor, dean, academic administrator*
Murray, Robert Wallace *chemistry professor*
Norberg, Richard Edwin *physicist, researcher*
Rigden, John Saxby *physicist*
Roti Roti, Joseph Lee *scientist, educator*
Thacker, William D. *physics professor*
Tibi, Rigobert *seismologist, researcher*
Wang, Xue Min *biochemistry educator*
Will, Clifford Martin *physicist, researcher, educator*
Zar, David M. *research associate, consultant*

Springfield
Criswell, Charles H. (Harry Criswell) *analytical chemist, environmental and forensic consultant, executive*
Schaefer, Cheryl Plaster *physics professor*
Thompson, Clifton C. *retired chemistry professor, academic administrator*

MONTANA

Bozeman
Bayramian, Andy James *physicist, chemist, researcher*
Schmidt, Victor Hugo *physics professor, researcher*

Columbia Falls
Spade-Shenker, George Lawrence (George Shenker) *research scientist*

Dayton
von Volborth, Alex (Alexis) *geochemist, geological engineering educator*

Great Falls
Knudson, Ruthann *environmental consultant, anthropologist, archaeologist*

Kalispell
Warneke, Joel *physics professor, mining engineer*

Missoula
Jakobson, Mark John *retired physics professor*
Sears, James Walter *geologist, educator*

Monarch
Baker, David Warren *earth scientist*

Twin Bridges
Ruppel, Edward Thompson *geologist*

NEBRASKA

Crete
Wentworth, Christopher Dean *physics professor*

Hastings
Dugan, Jim *physics professor*

Kearney
Mena-Werth, Jose *physics professor*

Lincoln
Dowben, Peter Arnold *physics professor*
Eckhardt, Craig Jon *chemistry professor*
Gruverman, Alexei *physicist*
Harwood, David M. *geologist, educator*
Holmes, Mary Anne *geologist, research scientist*
Jones, Lee Bennett *chemistry professor, academic administrator*
Sellmyer, David Julian *physicist, researcher*
Treves, Samuel Blain *geologist, educator*

Omaha
Bergt, Gregory Paul *chemist, consultant*
Podariu, Iulia Anca *physics professor, researcher*
Zepf, Thomas Herman *retired physics professor*

NEVADA

Carson City
Wang, Yang *research scientist*

Henderson
Trivelpiece, Alvin William *physicist, educator, consultant*

Las Vegas
Broca, Laurent Antoine *aerospace scientist*
Chopelas, Anastasia *geophysicist, researcher*
Delgado, Carlos *physics professor*
Dufek, Janet S. *research scientist*
Holloway, Robert Wester *radiochemist*
Hua, Fred Huizhong *materials scientist*
Lledo, Haroldo Luis *geologist*
Orgill, MaryKay *chemistry professor*
Sadineni, Suresh Babu *research scientist*
Stein, David Eric *physicist, defense analyst, futurist, retired military officer*

Laughlin
Cameron, Robert Allen *geophysicist, educator*

Reno
Bauer, Bruno Steven *plasma physicist*
Phaneuf, Ronald Arthur *physics professor*
Taranik, James Vladimir *geologist, educator*

Sparks
Bonham, Harold Florian *research geologist, consultant*

NEW HAMPSHIRE

Colebrook
Gueymard, Chris A. *research scientist*

Durham
Kaufmann, Richard L. *physics professor*

Grantham
Grimley, Robert Thomas *chemistry professor*

Hanover
Doyle, William Thomas *physicist, retired educator*
Lipson, Jane Elizabeth Gotlieb *chemistry professor*
Montgomery, David Campbell *retired physics professor*

Meredith
Hatch, Frederick Tasker *research scientist*

Nashua
Hahto, Sami K. *physicist*

Salem
Simmons, Marvin Gene *retired geophysics educator*

NEW JERSEY

Annandale
Wu, Margaret *research scientist*

Basking Ridge
Morgan, Samuel P(ope) *physicist, applied mathematician*

Berkeley Heights
Geusic, Joseph Edward *physicist*
Mac Rae, Alfred Urquhart *physicist, electrical engineer*

Blackwood
Seeber, Fredrick Paul *emeritus physics professor*

Bridgewater
Albrethsen, Adrian Edysel *metallurgist, consultant*

Camden
Xue, Jinyu *physicist, medical specialist*

Edison
Garcia, Maria Luisa *biochemist, researcher*
Parisi, Angela I. *chemist*

Elizabeth
Yarasani, Venkatarama *chemist, researcher*

Glassboro
Flores, Eduardo Virgilio *physics professor*

Highland Park
Brudner, Harvey Jerome *physicist*

Hoboken
Halder, Raghunath *research scientist*
Nosonovsky, Michael *research scientist*
Roh, Heui-Seol *research scientist, educator*

Holmdel
Alferness, Rodney C. *physicist*
Doerr, Christopher Richard *research scientist*
Kang, Inuk *research scientist*

Iselin
Ilinich, Oleg *chemist, researcher*
Liu, Xinsheng *chemist*

Jackson
Arminas, Scott Arnold *chemist, poet, writer*

Kenilworth
Greenlee, William John *chemist*
Jia, Yanlin *research scientist*
Neustadt, Bernard Ray *chemist*

Lakewood
Karol, Frederick John *retired industrial chemist*

Lambertville
Beyea, Jan Edgar *physicist*

Lawrenceville
Alig, Roger Casanova *physicist, engineer*
Brill, Michael Henry *physicist, editor*

Leonia
Kurtz, Anthony David *physicist*

Maplewood
Johnson, Dewey, Jr. *retired biochemist*
Tatyrek, Alfred Frank *retired chemist, environmental engineer*

Matawan
Wang, Shuangquan *research scientist*

Middletown
Lundgren, Carl William, Jr. *physicist*

Morris Plains
Capellos, Chris Spiridon *chemist*

Morristown
Murthy, N. Sanjeeva *physicist*

Mountainside
Vice, Susan F. *medicinal chemist*

Murray Hill
Chandross, Edwin A. *chemist, consultant*

Neptune
Aguiar, Adam Martin *chemist, educator*

New Brunswick
Joshi, Amit *research scientist*
Moss, Robert Allen *chemistry professor*
Pandey, Ramesh Chandra *chemist, chemicals executive*
Robock, Alan *meteorology professor*
Strauss, Ulrich Paul *chemist, educator*

Newark
Asatryan, Rubik *chemistry professor, researcher*
Krasnoperov, Lev N. *chemistry professor*
Lanzerotti, Louis John *physicist*
Leibovich, Samuel Joseph *biochemist*
Nita, Gelu M. *physics professor, researcher*
Spruch, Grace Marmor *physics professor*

Nutley
Kong, Norman *chemist*

Oldwick
Sinfelt, John Henry *chemist*

Pennington
Nayeem, Akbar *chemist*

Piscataway
Cizewski, Jolie Antonia *physics professor, researcher*
Cohen, Morrel Herman *physicist, biologist, educator*
Glashausser, Charles Michael *physicist, researcher*
Idol, James Daniel, Jr. *chemist, educator, inventor, consultant*
Kosowsky, Arthur *physicist, educator*
Leath, Paul Larry *physicist, educator, former university official*
Lebowitz, Joel Louis *mathematical physicist, educator*
Lindenfeld, Peter *physics professor*
Lioy, Paul James *environmental health scientist*
Manowitz, Paul *biochemist, researcher, educator*
Matilsky, Terry Allen *astrophysicist, educator*
Mihalef, Viorel *research scientist*
Pan, Long *chemist*
Ransome, Ronald D. *physics professor*
Robbins, Allen Bishop *physics professor*
Wielunski, Leszek Stanislaw *materials scientist*
Wininger, Michael T. *research scientist*
Younis, Ossama *research scientist*
Zimmermann, Frank Martin *physicist, educator, research scientist*

Pomona
Sharon, Yitzhak Yaakov *physicist, educator*

Pompton Plains
Gummel, Hermann Karl *retired physicist, lab administrator*

Princeton
Adler, Stephen Louis *physicist*
Anderson, Philip W. *physicist*
Arnheim, Juliette O'Neil *chemist, librarian, consultant*
Austin, Robert Hamilton *physics professor*
Carter, Emily Ann *physical chemist, researcher, educator*
Cava, Robert J. *chemistry professor*
Chaikin, Paul M. *physicist*
Christman, Edward Arthur *physicist*
Davidson, Ronald Crosby *physicist, researcher*
Dilkhin, Stanislav S. *research scientist*
Dreizin, Edward Leonid *physicist, researcher*
Dyson, Freeman John *retired physics professor*
Fisch, Nathaniel Joseph *physicist*
Fitch, Val Logsdon *physics professor*
Florey, Klaus Georg *chemist, pharmaceutical consultant*
Fresco, Jacques Robert *biochemist, educator*
Giordmaine, Joseph Anthony *physicist*
Goldston, Robert J. *research scientist*
Grisham, Larry Richard *physicist*
Groves, John Taylor III *chemist, educator*
Halyo, Valerie *physics professor*
Hekmatshoar, Bahman *research scientist*
Jenkins, Edward Beynon *research astronomer*
Lieb, Elliott Hershel *physicist, mathematician, educator*
Long, Frank Wesley, Jr. *chemist*
Maldacena, Juan Martin *physicist, researcher*
Manabe, Syukuro *meteorologist*
Murakami, Eisuke *biochemist*
Nadeem, Tamer M. *research scientist*
Onstott, Tullis *microgeologist, geology professor*
Opaits, Dmitry Florievich *research scientist*
Oppenheimer, Michael *physicist*
Orlanski, Isidoro *meteorologist, researcher*
Ostriker, Jeremiah Paul *astrophysicist, educator*
Pechen, Alexander *theoretical physicist, researcher*
Potasek, Mary Joyce *physicist, researcher*
Royce, Barrie Saunders Hart *physicist, researcher*
Rutherford, Paul Harding *physicist*
Seiberg, Nathan *physics professor*
Smith, Arthur John Stewart *physicist, researcher*
Spiro, Thomas George *chemistry professor*
Sterzer, Fred *research physicist*
Stouffer, Ronald Jay *meteorologist*
Taylor, Edward Curtis *chemistry professor*
Taylor, Joseph Hooton, Jr. *radio astronomer, physicist*
Tomlinson, W. John *physicist, researcher*
Torquato, Salvatore *materials scientist, chemistry professor*
Villarini, Gabriele *geophysicist*
Wang, Peiyuan *scientist*
White, Roscoe Beryl *research physicist, educator*
Witten, Edward *mathematical physicist, educator*

Rahway
Imbriglio, Jason E. *chemist, researcher*
Kaczorowski, Gregory John *biochemist, researcher, science administrator*

Red Bank
Etemad, Shahab *physicist, director*

Ridgefield Park
Nagy, Christa Fiedler *biochemist*

Skillman
Diaz, Teresita Perez *chemist*

Stirling
Walsh, Peter Joseph *physics professor*

Summit
Phillips, James Charles *physicist, researcher*

Teaneck
Murthy, Vadiraja Venkatesa *retired biochemist, researcher, educator*

Trenton
Baron, Lisa Ann *environmental scientist*

Union
Pearlman, Bruce Allen *research scientist*
Zois, Constantine Nicholas Athanasios *meteorologist, educator*

West Deptford
Grasa, Gabriela Alexandra *chemist*

NEW MEXICO

Albuquerque
Busani, Tito L. *research scientist, educator*
Dickel, John Rush *physics professor*
Emin, David *physicist*
Gander, John Edward *biochemistry educator*
Ivnitski, Dmitri Markovich *bioelectrochemist*
Leeper, Ramon Joe *physicist*
Lucas, Spencer G. *paleontologist, curator, director*
Ruiz, Carlos Leon *nuclear scientist, physicist*
Shelnutt, John A. *physicist, researcher*

Kirtland AFB
Degnan, James Henry *physicist*

Las Cruces
Kemp, John Daniel *biochemist, educator*
Richardson, Albert Edward *chemistry professor, researcher*
Sohn, Hansuk *research scientist, educator*
Wang, Haobin *chemistry professor*

Los Alamos
Atcher, Robert Whitehill *chemist, educator*
Baek, Seung-Ho *research scientist*
Balick, Lee K. *research scientist, researcher*
Bdzil, John B. *research scientist, educator*
Beyerlein, Irene Jane *research scientist*
Blagoev, Krastan Blagoev *physicist, biophysicist*
Bronkhorst, Curt Allan *research scientist*
Brown, Lowell Severt *physicist, researcher*
Dai, Zhenxue *geologist, researcher, consultant*
Dion, Heather M. *chemist, researcher*
Dubey, Manvendra Krishna *environmental scientist*
Dye, Robert Craig *research scientist*
Engelhardt, Albert George *physicist*
Friar, James Lewis *physicist*
Gibson, Benjamin Franklin *physicist*
Ginocchio, Joseph Natale *physicist*
Harlow, Francis Harvey *physicist, anthropologist, research scientist, artist*
Hosemann, Peter *materials scientist*
Janecky, David Richard *geochemist*
Judd, O'Dean P. *physicist*
Lamoreaux, Steve Keith Dutch *atomic physicist, consultant*
Leddy, Johna *electrochemistry educator*
Lee, Jung-Kun *materials scientist, researcher*
Macek, Robert James *retired physicist*
Mead, William Charles *physicist*
Michaudon, André Francisque *physicist*
Mihaila, Bogdan *physicist*
Mihalas, Dimitri Manuel *astrophysicist, educator*
Misra, Amit *materials scientist, researcher*
Mitchell, Jeremy Neil *geologist, materials scientist*
Montgomery, David Scott *physicist, director*
Pack, Russell T. *retired theoretical chemist*
Picraux, Samuel Thomas *physicist, researcher*
Porch, William Morgan *physicist*
Redondo, Antonio *physicist*
Schwarz, Ricardo B. *research scientist*
Selden, Robert Wentworth *physicist, consultant*
Shao, Lin *physicist, director*
Sharp, David Howland *physicist*
Smith, James Lawrence *research physicist*
Stauffer, Philip Henry *hydrogeologist*
Terrones, Guillermo *research scientist*
Thompson, Joe D. *physicist*
Wang, Moran *physicist*
Wang, Yuejian *research scientist*
Whalen, Daniel James *astrophysicist*
Zhao, Yusheng *physicist*

Mayhill
Pastor, Stephen Daniel *chemistry professor, researcher, consultant*

Roswell
Tekut, Thomas Francis *chemistry professor*

Santa Fe
Cheetham, Alan Herbert *paleontologist*
Cowan, George Arthur *chemist, bank executive, director*
Fisher, Robert Alan *laser physicist*
Gell-Mann, Murray *theoretical physicist, educator*
Giovanielli, Damon Vincent *physicist, consultant*
Hammer, Charles F. *retired chemistry professor*
Kronberg, Philipp Paul *physicist, educator*
Louck, James Donald *physicist, researcher*
Lynn, John Eric *nuclear physicist, researcher, consultant*
Nicholls, Anthony *biophysicist, software company executive*
West, Geoffrey B. *theoretical physicist, physics professor*
White, David Hywel *physics professor, researcher*

Silver City
Buhner, Stephen Harrod *research scientist*

Socorro
Mukkamala, Srinivas *research scientist*
Simkin, Susan M. *retired astronomer*
Werbelow, Lawrence Glen *chemistry educator, researcher*

Sunspot
Keil, Stephen Lesley *astrophysicist*

NEW YORK

Albany
Brcka, Jozef *physicist, researcher*
Cole, Richard *research scientist*
Corelli, John Charles *physicist, researcher*
Fasullo, Michael Thomas *research scientist*
Hass, Martha Ann *chemistry professor*
Inomata, Akira *physics professor*
Mozhaev, Vadim *research scientist*
Wan, Shuangyi *research scientist*

Alfred
Shelby, James Elbert *materials scientist, educator*

Alfred Station
Condrate, Robert Adam, Sr. *spectroscopy educator*

Amherst
Bharadwaj, Prem Datta *physics professor*

Amityville
Citrano-Cummiskey, Debra Moira *chemist, network technician*

Auburn
Coolican, Sharon *chemistry professor*

Ballston Spa
Westbrook, Jack Hall *metallurgist, consultant*

Big Flats
Keck, Donald Bruce *physicist*

Binghamton
Coates, Donald Robert *geologist, educator*
Eisch, John Joseph *research chemist, educator, writer, consultant*
Whittingham, M(ichael) Stanley *chemist*

Brentwood
Cleland, Marshall Robert *nuclear scientist*

Brewster
Stojakovic, Dejan *metallurgist, researcher*

Briarcliff Manor
Bhargava, Rameshwar Nath *physicist*
Loudig, Olivier Daniel *biochemist*

Brockport
Finley, Kay Thomas *chemistry professor, researcher*
Tahar, Mohammed Zrendini *physics professor*

Bronx
Das, Bhaskar Chandra *chemistry professor*
Delgado-Lopez, Fernando *biochemist*
Ebose, Esokpan James *chemist*
Engelke, Charles Edward *physics professor*
Goodman, Robert M. *biochemist, educator*
Haider, Quamrul *physics professor, researcher*
Lautin, Everett Marc *radiologist, educator*
Menthena, Anuradha *research scientist*
Schramm, Vern L. *biochemist, educator*
Yalow, Rosalyn Sussman *biophysicist*

Brooklyn
Blake, Reginald Alexander *physics professor*
Boyko, Vladimir S. *physics professor, researcher*
Charton, Marvin *chemist, educator*
Choudhury, Deo Chand *physicist, educator, researcher*
Dirisu, Afusat Olayinka *research scientist*
Franco, Victor *theoretical physics educator*
Garetz, Bruce Allen *physical chemist, educator*
Goncharov, Viktor *biochemist, researcher*
Labianca, Dominick Anthony *chemist, educator*
Lange, Christopher Stephen *radiation biophysics professor*
Mook, Sarah *retired chemist*
Pearce, Eli M. *chemistry professor, academic administrator*
Shcherbakova, Estella *chemist, mathematician, educator*
Shedrinsky, Alexander Mikchail *chemistry professor, conservator, consultant*
Tsiklauri, Shalva *physics professor*
Wolf, Edward Lincoln *physicist, educator*

Buffalo
Andersen, Martha S. *biophysicist, researcher*
Bardos, Thomas Joseph *chemist, educator*
Churchill, Melvyn Rowen *chemistry professor*
Gao, Jiali *chemist, educator*
Garrick, Laura Morris *biochemistry educator*
Hui, Sek Wen *research biophysicist, educator*
Kalman, Thomas Ivan *chemistry professor, researcher*
Patel, Mulchand Shambhubhai *biochemist, researcher*
Petropoulos, Michalis *research scientist*
Pogrebnyak, Victor Alexandrovich *physicist, researcher*
Rai, Ram C. *physics professor*
Reitan, Paul Hartman *retired geologist, educator*
Srikrishnan, Thamarapu *cancer research scientist, biophysicist*
Stojkovic, Dejan B. *physicist, educator*
Taub, Mary Louise *biochemist*
Whelley, Patrick Liam *geologist*
Yen, Tingfang *research scientist*

Canandaigua
Lowther, Frank Eugene *research physicist*

Clinton
Ring, James Walter *physics professor*

Cooperstown
Peters, Theodore, Jr. *emeritus research scientist, consultant*

Corning
Miller, Roger Allen *physicist*
Williams, Jimmie Lewis *chemist, researcher*

Delmar
Matuszek, John Michael, Jr. *environmental scientist, educator, consultant*

Dunkirk
Huels, Steven Mark *physicist, mathematician, astronomer*

East Greenbush
Chen, Zewu *optics scientist*

East Hampton
Garrett, Charles Geoffrey Blythe *physicist, consultant*

Farmingdale
Nolan, Peter John *physics professor*

Flushing
Engel, Robert Ralph *chemist, educator, dean*
Goldman, Norman Lewis *chemist, educator*
Hu, Huping *biophysicist, lawyer*
Pekar, Stephen F. *geologist, paleontologist, oceanographer*

Freeport
Pullman, Maynard Edward *biochemist*

Fresh Meadows
Ravinder, Ujwala *research scientist*

Geneva
Roelofs, Wendell Lee *biochemistry professor, consultant*

Getzville
Fujia, Shigeji *physics professor*

Hamilton
Parks, Beth *physics professor*

Hannacroix
Schwebler, Stephen *retired chemist*

Hempstead
Chaiken, MarthaLeah *psychology and biology scientist*
Sobel, Sabrina G. *chemistry professor*

Ithaca
Ambegaokar, Vinay *retired physics professor*
Bassett, William Akers *retired geologist, educator*
Bauman, Dale Elton *nutritional biochemistry professor*
Butler, Thomas James *biochemist, researcher*
Csaki, Csaba *physicist*
Freed, Jack Herschel *chemist, educator*
Ginsparg, Paul *physicist*
Goldsmith, Paul Felix *astronomy and physics professor*
Hess, George Paul *biochemist, educator*
Hoffmann, Roald *chemist, educator*
Holowka, David A. *research scientist*
Howard, Scott Sheridan *research scientist*
Kinoshita, Toichiro *physicist*
Lee, David Morris *physics professor*
Lepage, Gerard Peter *physics educator*
McLafferty, Fred Warren *chemist, educator*
Oliver, Jack Ertle *geophysicist, educator*
Pikuz, Sergey *physicist, researcher*
Pohl, Robert Otto *physics professor*
Richardson, Robert Coleman *physics professor, researcher*
Rogers, Michael Bruce *physics professor*
Scheraga, Harold Abraham *retired physical chemistry professor*
Sethna, James Patarasp *physicist*
Thomas, Jacob Earl *retired physicist*
Webb, Watt Wetmore *physicist, researcher*
Widom, Benjamin *chemistry professor*

Kingston
Luke, Brian Thomas *theoretical chemist, researcher*

Larchmont
Guttenplan, Joseph B. *biochemist, educator*

Latham
Stallman, Donald Lee *environmental executive*

Lewiston
Dexter, Theodore Henry *chemist*

Manhasset
Carbon, Maren *research scientist*
Dabideen, Darrin *research scientist*

Manlius
O'Reilly, Mary *environmental scientist, educator*

Melville
Damadian, Raymond Vahan *biophysicist*

New Paltz
Lavallee, David Kenneth *chemistry professor, academic administrator*

New Rochelle
Margolin, Harold *metallurgical educator*

New York
Aleiner, Igor L. *physics professor*
Alexander, Vologodskii *biophysicist*
Baset, Salman Abdul *research scientist*
Bederson, Benjamin *physicist, researcher*
Birman, Joseph Leon *physics professor*
Borowitz, Sidney *retired physics professor*
Breslow, Esther May Greenberg *biochemistry professor, researcher*
Breslow, Ronald Charles *chemist, educator*
Briley-Saebo, Karen Catherin *physics professor*
Bronstein, Hindy *research scientist*
Brus, Louis Eugene *physical chemist*
Campbell, George, Jr. *physicist, university administrator*
Canary, James Wayne *chemist, educator*
Cao, Yifang *research scientist*
Chang, Ngee-Pong *physics educator*
Cheh, Huk Yuk *electrochemist*
Chen, Chengjun Julian *physicist, engineering educator*
Chou, Ting-Chao *inventor, educator*
Cohen, Ezechiel Godert David *physicist, researcher*
Cummins, Herman Zachary *physicist*
Danishefsky, Samuel J. *chemistry professor*
Eisenthal, Kenneth B. *physical chemistry educator*
Erlanger, Bernard Ferdinand *biochemist, educator*
Friesner, Richard A. *chemistry educator*
Fusaro, Peter C. *environmental scientist, consultant*
Gayen, Swapan Kumar *physics professor, researcher*
Goulianos, Konstantin *physicist, educator*
Green, Michael Enoch *chemistry professor*
Gutzwiller, Martin Charles *theoretical physicist, researcher*
Haines, Thomas Henry *biochemist, educator, researcher*
Han, Jefferson Y. *research scientist*
Hansen, James E. *physicist, meteorologist, federal agency administrator*
Hendrickson, Wayne A(rthur) *biochemist, educator*
Hoffert, Martin Irving *aerospace scientist, educator*
Hoffman, Linda M. *chemist, educator*
Khuri, Nicola Najib *physicist, researcher*
Khusid, Boris M. *chemical physicist*
Kim, Phillip *physics professor*
King, Edward Joseph *clinical chemist, laboratory administrator*
Krasna, Alvin Isaac *biochemist, educator*
Krulwich, Terry Ann *biochemistry researcher*

Kuo, John Tsungfen *geophysicist, educator, researcher*
Lefenfeld, Michael *chemist, materials engineer*
Levin, Janna J. *physicist, educator*
Lieberman, Seymour *biochemist, educator*
Lilja, H. *chemist, educator*
Mac Low, Mordecai-Mark *astrophysicist*
Mezentsev, Alexandre Victor *aerospace scientist, researcher*
Muir, Tom William *chemistry professor*
Muriel, Amador Cruz *physicist*
Norell, Mark Allen *paleontologist, curator*
Oinas, Valdar *aerospace scientist*
Oreskes, Irwin *biochemistry educator*
Percus, Jerome Kenneth *physicist, researcher*
Pinczuk, Aron *physicist*
Polychronakos, Alexios Pantelis *theoretical physics educator*
Pope, Martin *chemist, educator*
Porrati, Massimo *physicist, educator*
Prodan, Emil *physics professor*
Rabadan, Raul *physics professor*
Ramsay, Hamish Andrew *aerospace scientist*
Reith, Maarten Edward A. *neurochemist*
Rhodes, Yorke E(dward) *organic chemist, educator*
Robie, Daniel Cardigan *chemist*
Roeder, Robert Gayle *biochemist, molecular biologist, educator*
St. Germain, Jean Mary *medical physicist*
Sarachik, Myriam Paula Morgenstein *condensed matter physicist, educator*
Sidran, Miriam *retired physicist*
Sirlin, Alberto *physics professor*
Stork, Gilbert *chemistry professor*
Störmer, Horst Ludwig *physicist, educator*
Stroke, Hinko Henry *physicist, researcher*
Turro, Nicholas John *chemistry professor*
Tyson, Neil DeGrasse *astrophysicist, museum director*
Werthamer, Nathan Richard *physicist*

Niskayuna
Srivastava, Alok M. *research scientist*
Suzuki, Akane *metallurgist*
Varanasi, Kripa Kiran *research scientist*

Oneonta
Grimaldi, Richard Thomas, Jr. *meteorologist, educator*
Horner, Carl Matthew *chemistry professor*

Orangeburg
Helpern, Joseph Alexander *biophysicist*

Orchard Park
Amborski, Leonard Edward *retired chemist*

Palisades
Broecker, Wallace S. *geophysicist, educator*
Burckle, Lloyd Henry *geologist, researcher*
Kellogg, Herbert Humphrey *metallurgist, educator*
Kent, Dennis V. *earth scientist, educator*
Richards, Paul Granston *seismologist, geophysics educator*

Patchogue
Marr, Robert Bruce *physicist, researcher*

Pearl River
Kolb, Michael *chemist*
Verheijen, Jeroen Cunera *research scientist*

Pittsford
Goldstein, David Arthur *biophysicist, educator*
Lever, O. William, Jr. *chemist*

Plainview
Rich, Charles Anthony *hydrogeologist, consultant*

Pleasantville
Kazakov, Sergey Victorovich *chemistry professor*

Potsdam
Andreescu, E. Silvana *chemistry professor*
Islam, Muhammad Azadul *physicist, educator, researcher*
Matijevic, Egon *chemistry professor*

Poughkeepsie
Lang, William Warner *physicist*

Rensselaer
Willis, John Patrick *chemist*

Ridge
Blume, Martin *physicist*

Rochester
Boeckman, Robert Kenneth, Jr. *chemistry professor, researcher*
Cain, Burton Edward *retired chemistry professor*
Conwell, Esther Marly *physicist, researcher*
Duarte, Francisco Javier *physicist, researcher*
Eisenberg, Richard S. *chemistry professor*
Fehn, Udo *geology educator*
George, Nicholas *optics educator, researcher*
Gunter, Thomas Edgar, Jr. *biophysicist, researcher*
Houde-Walter, Susan *optics scientist, educator*
Hu, Suxing *scientist*
Kampmeier, Jack August Carlos *chemist, educator*
Kende, Andrew Steven *chemist, educator*
Knauer, James Philip *physicist*
Knox, Robert Seiple *physicist, researcher*
Kondakov, Denis *research scientist*
Kwok, Wingchi Edmund *medical physicist*
La Celle, Paul Louis *biophysics educator*
Levy, David Howard *research scientist*
Lindberg, Vern *physics professor*
Makous, Walter Leon *visual scientist, educator*
Moore, Duncan Thomas *optics scientist, educator*
Ng, Yee Seung *physicist*
Santhanam, Kalathur S. V. *chemist, researcher*
Saunders, William Hundley, Jr. *retired chemist, educator*
Sharma, Gaurav *imaging scientist, electrical engineer*
Sherman, Fred *biochemist, educator*
Thorndike, Edward Harmon *physicist*
Vorobyev, Anatoliy Y. *research scientist*
Yip, Kwok Leung *physicist, researcher*

Rouses Point
Weierstall, Richard Paul *retired pharmaceutical chemist*

Scarsdale
Porosoff, Harold *chemist, science administrator, research and development company executive*

Schenectady
Barash, Eugene *research scientist*
Faidi, Waseem *research scientist*
Finks, Robert Melvin *paleontologist, educator*
Frost, Robert Edwin *chemistry professor*
Katz, Samuel *retired geophysics educator*
Philip, A. G. Davis *astronomer, educator, editor*

Sleepy Hollow
Song, Yulin *physicist*

South Setauket
Friedlander, Gerhart *nuclear chemist*

Staten Island
Okulewicz, Steven Charles *geologist, educator*
Yang, Song-Yu *medical biochemist*

Stony Brook
Alexander, John Macmillan, Jr. *chemistry professor*
Bonner, Francis Truesdale *chemist, educator, dean*
Brown, Gerald Edward *physicist, researcher*
Geller, Marvin Alan *meteorology educator, researcher*
Goldman, Vladimir Joseph *physicist, researcher*
Kulik, Igor Orestovich *theoretical physics, researcher*
Lauher, Joseph W. *chemistry professor*
Li, Baosheng *physicist*
Swanson, Robert Lawrence *oceanographer, academic program administrator*
Weidner, Donald J. *geophysicist educator*

Syracuse
Allis, Damian Gregory *chemist, technologist, consultant*
Baldwin, John Edwin *chemistry professor*
Bickford, Marion Eugene *geologist, educator*
Gigante, Denise Mp *chemistry professor*
Honig, Arnold *physics professor, researcher*
Movileanu, Liviu *physics professor*
Prucha, John James *geologist, educator*
Schiff, Eric Allan *physics professor*
Smith, Kenneth Judson, Jr. *chemistry professor*
Teece, Mark A. *chemistry professor*
Zubieta, Jon Andoni *chemistry professor*

Troy
Ferris, James Peter *chemist, educator*
Friedman, Gerald Manfred *geologist, educator*
Giaever, Ivar *physicist*
Hatami-Marbini, Hamed *research scientist*
Intes, Xavier *research scientist*
Levinger, Joseph Solomon *physicist, researcher*
Medicus, Heinrich Adolf *physicist, researcher*
Moore, James Alfred *chemist, educator*
Schowalter, Leo John *physicist and educator*
Schroeder, John *physics professor*
Shan, Yufeng *research scientist*

Upton
Baltz, Anthony John *physicist*
Bond, Peter Danford *physicist*
Choi, Jun-Ki *research scientist*
Cotlet, Mircea *research scientist*
Damazio, Denis Oliveira *research scientist*
Fowler, Joanna S. *chemist*
Goldhaber, Maurice *physicist, researcher*
Han, Wei-Qiang *research scientist*
Hanson, Albert LeRoy *physicist, engineer*
Harbottle, Garman *chemist*
Hendrie, Joseph Mallam *physicist, nuclear engineer*
Johnson, Peter David *physicist*
Lindenbaum, S(eymour) J(oseph) *physicist*
Lowenstein, Derek Irving *physicist*
Rau, Ralph Ronald *retired physicist*
Sakaguchi, Takao *physicist*
Setlow, Jane Kellock *biophysicist*
Setlow, Richard Burton *biophysicist, researcher*
Sherman, William Benjamin *research scientist*
Tannenbaum, Michael J(ay) *physicist*
Wei, Xiangdong *physicist, researcher*
Weston, Ralph Emerson, Jr. *chemist*
Yoon, Won-Sub *materials scientist*

Vestal
Jones, Wayne Elfed, Jr. *chemist, researcher*

Victor
Merkel, Paul Barrett *chemist, consultant*

Wappingers Falls
Puttlitz, Karl Joseph, Sr. *metallurgist*

Webster
Zhang, Shengliang *materials scientist*

White Plains
Flanigen, Edith Marie *materials scientist, consultant*

Yorktown Heights
Gupta, Devendra *material scientist, engineer*
Kang, Sung Kwon *materials scientist, researcher*
Keyes, Robert W. *physicist, researcher*
Lang, Norton David *physicist*
Zitouni, Imed *research scientist*

NORTH CAROLINA

Asheville
Meyerson, Seymour *retired chemist*

Beaufort
Waggett, Rebecca Jane *research scientist*

Brevard
Foster, Edward John *engineer physicist*

Cary
Kung, Pang-Jen *materials scientist, electrical engineer*

Chapel Hill
Buck, Richard Pierson *chemistry educator, researcher*
Bursey, Maurice M. *retired chemistry professor*
Chaney, Stephen Gifford *biochemistry and biophysics educator*
Davis, Morris Schuyler *astronomer*
Forman, Donald T. *biochemist, educator*
Frampton, Paul Howard *physics researcher, educator*
Lee, Kuo-Hsiung *medicinal chemistry professor*
Ligett, Waldo Buford *chemist*
Macdonald, James Ross *physicist, researcher*
Mersini - Houghton, Laura *physicist, educator*
Merzbacher, Eugen *retired physics professor*
Messer, Jay James *environmental scientist*
Parr, Robert Ghormley *chemistry professor*
Pedersen, Lee G. *chemistry professor*
Ramsey, John Michael *chemistry professor, researcher*
Rezk, Naser Labeeb *biochemist, researcher*
Selkirk, James Kirkwood *retired biochemist*
Zhang, Jian *physics professor, researcher*

Charlotte
Burnett, John Nicholas *retired chemistry educator*
Chan, Yiumo *biochemist*
Monroe, Frederick Leroy *chemist*
Mueller, Werner Heinrich *chemical company executive*

Durham
Ciferri, Alberto *chemist, educator*
Fridovich, Irwin *biochemistry professor*
Hammes, Gordon G. *chemistry professor*
Jaszczak, Ronald Jack *physicist, researcher, consultant*
Joklik, Wolfgang Karl *biochemist, virologist, educator*
Kapadia, Anuj J. *research scientist*
Kiehart, Daniel P. *biophysicist, educator*
LaBean, Thomas Henry *chemistry professor*
Meyer, Horst *physics professor*
Mikhailov, Stepan Fedorovich *physicist, researcher*
Moss, Marcia Lynn *retired biochemist*
Pearsall, George Wilbur *materials scientist, mechanical engineer, consultant*
Pruteanu-Malinici, Iulian *research scientist*
Quin, Louis DuBose *chemist, educator*
Quinn, Jarus William *physicist, former association executive*
Socolar, Joshua E. S. *physics professor*
Suslov, Vladimir Mikhaylovich *physics professor, researcher*
Xia, Jessie Qing *research scientist*
Zhang, Qingchun *research scientist*
Zhirnov, Victor *physicist, researcher*

Elizabeth City
Bluiett, Althea G. *physics professor*

Greensboro
Sladek, Ronald John *physics professor*
Venkateswarlu, Divi *chemistry professor*

Greenville
Flood, Joseph Patrick *environmental scientist*
Hu, Xiu-Hua *biomedical physicist, biomedical engineer*
Parham, Peter Robertson *geologist*

Horse Shoe
Roskoski, Robert, Jr. *biochemist, educator, author*

Morehead City
Weber, Craig P. *meteorologist, newscaster*

Morrisville
Lopez, Rocio A. *chemist*
Shim, Woo Sub *research scientist*

Pinehurst
Huizenga, John Robert *nuclear chemist, educator*

Raleigh
Aspnes, David Erik *physicist, researcher*
Bernholc, Jerzy *physicist, educator*
Cotanch, Stephen Robert *physics educator*
Gould, Christopher Robert *physics professor*
Narayan, Jagdish *materials science educator*
Nepal, Neeraj *physicist, researcher*
Reynolds, C. Lewis, Jr. *materials scientist, educator*
Sudhakar, Nori *materials scientist, researcher*
Sun, Ying-Hsuan *research scientist*
Swaisgood, Harold Everett *biochemist, educator*
Whitten, Jerry Lynn *chemistry professor*

Research Triangle Park
Bullock, Orren Russell, Jr. *research scientist*
Iiames, John Shepherd *geologist, researcher*
Raymer, James Howard *chemist, researcher*
Reynolds, Peter James *physicist*
Subramani, Velu *chemist, researcher*
Wani, Mansukhlal Chhaganlal *chemist*

Winston Salem
Dos Santos, Patricia C. *chemistry professor*
Lee, Sang Jin *materials scientist*
Mokrasch, Lewis Carl *neurochemist, educator*
Rodgman, Alan *chemist, consultant*
Zhang, Lei *physics professor*

NORTH DAKOTA

Fargo
Rosenberg, Harry *biochemist, natural product chemist*
Tallman, Dennis Earl *professor, research scientist*

Grand Forks
Hoffmann, Mark R. *physical chemist, educator*
Kellenbenz, Dave John *meteorologist*
Kozliak, Evguenii I. *chemistry professor*
Zhang, Xiaodong *oceanographer, educator*

OHIO

Akron
Cadile, Pamela L. *chemist, sales planner*
Fleming, Paul Daniel III *chemical physicist*
Gent, Alan Neville *physicist, researcher*
Kennedy, Joseph Paul *chemist, researcher*
Olson, Byron Louis *biochemist, educator*
Piirma, Irja *chemist, educator*
Ramsey, Sally Judith Weine *chemist, research and development company executive*
Weidknecht, Marcia E. *chemistry professor*

Amelia
Tracy, David James *chemist, consultant*

Athens
Drabold, David Alan *physics professor, researcher*
Nance, Richard Damian *geologist, consultant*

Beachwood
Gatica, Norma *chemistry professor*
Krieger, Irvin Mitchell *retired chemistry professor*
Pruthi, Tarun *research scientist*

Bluffton
Rich, Ronald Lee *chemistry professor*

Bowling Green
Newman, David Stefan *chemistry professor, consultant*

Bratenahl
Dunn, Horton, Jr. *organic chemist*

Centerburg
Reynolds, Don William *geologist*

Cincinnati
Baron, Paul Andrew *research scientist*
Boolchand, Punit *physics professor*
Briskin, Madeleine *oceanographer, paleontologist*
Francis, Marion David *consulting chemist*
Goodman, Bernard *physics professor*
Jensen, Elwood Vernon *biochemist*
Meal, Larie *chemistry professor, researcher, consultant*
Russell, James Edward *physics professor*
Singh, Sandeep *research scientist*
Sullivan, James F. *physicist, researcher*
Witten, Louis *physics professor*
Yun, Yeoheung *research scientist*

Cleveland
Banerjee, Amiya Kumar *biochemist*
Barsi, Stephen *research scientist*
Carey, Paul Richard *biophysicist*
Chamis, Christos Constantinos *aerospace scientist, educator*
Chvetsov, Alexei V. *medical physicist, educator*
Colussi, Valdir Carlos *physicist*
Deissler, Robert J. *physicist*
DiCarlo, James Anthony *physicist*
Goldstein, Marvin Emanuel *aerospace scientist*
Heuer, Arthur H. *materials scientist, educator*
Klopman, Gilles *chemistry professor*
Koenig, Jack Leonard *chemist, educator*
Kowalski, Kenneth Lawrence *physicist, researcher*
Petschek, Rolfe George *physics professor*
Rogers, Charles Edwin *physical chemistry and polymer science professor*
Schuele, Donald Edward *retired physics professor, dean*
Smialek, James L. *research scientist*
Triolo, Ronald J. *research scientist, director*
Zhang, Nengli *research scientist*

Cleveland Heights
Bidelman, William Pendry *astronomer, educator*

Columbus
Adelson, Edward *physicist, educator, musician*
Behrman, Edward Joseph *biochemistry educator*
Callstrom, Matthew Raymond *chemistry educator*
Chisholm, Malcolm Harold *chemistry professor*
Chiu, Ing-Ming *biochemistry educator*
Chowdhury, Borun Dev *physicist*
Cornwell, David George *biochemist, educator*
Daehn, Glenn Steven *materials scientist*
DiMauro, Louis F. *physics professor, department chairman*
Elliot, David Hawksley *geologist, educator*
Epstein, Arthur Joseph *physics and chemistry educator*
Herbst, Eric *physicist, astronomer, chemist*
Lott, John Alfred *chemist, educator*
Miller, Terry Alan *chemistry professor*
Peters, Leonard K. *environmental scientist*
Pitzer, Russell Mosher *chemistry educator*
Reibel, Kurt *physicist, researcher*
St. Pierre, George Roland, Jr. *materials scientist, engineering executive, educator*
Shore, Sheldon G. *chemist, educator*
Soloway, Albert Herman *medicinal chemist*
Thompson, Lonnie G. *glaciologist, educator*

Wali, Mohan Kishen *environmental scientist, forester, educator*
Williams, James Case *metallurgist*
Wojcicki, Andrew Adalbert *chemist, educator*

Copley
Weil, Edward David *chemist, researcher, consultant, inventor,*

Dayton
Battino, Rubin *retired chemistry professor*
Brown, Gail Jones *physicist*
Buryachenko, Valeriy A. *research scientist*
Hangartner, Thomas Niklaus *medical physicist, educator*
Parthasarathy, Triplicane Asuri *materials scientist*
Senkov, Oleg N. *physicist, researcher, materials scientist*
Skinner, Thomas E. *physics professor*
Spokane, Robert Bruce *biophysical chemist*
Yeo, Yung Kee *physics professor*

Eastlake
Suchanek, Wojciech Lukasz *materials scientist, researcher*

Gambier
Cho, Hyun Jai *physicist*

Highland Hills
Brathwaite, Ormond Dennis *chemistry professor*

Hiram
Tur, Clarisse *physicist*

Hudson
Dowell, Michael Brendan *chemist*

Kent
Dahl, Peter Steffen *geologist, educator*
Manley, D. Mark *physics professor*
Myers, R(alph) Thomas *chemist, educator*
Tuan, Debbie Fu-Tai *chemist, educator*

Kettering
Kell, Joseph William *materials scientist*

Mansfield
Gibson, David Mark *biochemist, educator*

Marietta
Putnam, Robert Ervin *chemist, consultant*

Middletown
Marine, Susan Sonchik *analytical chemist, educator*

Milford
Dattilio, Teri A. *chemist*

Mount Vernon
Miller, Joyce Catherine *chemistry professor, research scientist*

Oberlin
Carlton, Terry Scott *retired chemist, educator*

Oxford
Crowder, Michael Wade *chemistry educator*
Gordon, Gilbert *chemist, educator*
Pechan, Michael Joseph *physics professor, researcher*

Parma
Chen, Chong *research scientist*

Sheffield Village
Herdendorf, Charles Edward III *oceanographer, limnologist, consultant*

Toledo
Azad, Abdul-Majeed *materials scientist, educator*
Bjorkman, Jon Eric *astrophysicist, educator*
Griffith, Wendell Peter *chemistry professor*
Hu, Xiche *chemistry professor*
Slama, James T. *chemistry professor, researcher*
Stierman, Donald John *geophysicist, educator*
Vijh, Uma Parvathy *astrophysicist, researcher*

Upper Arlington
Relle, Ferenc Matyas *chemist*

Wadsworth
Furry, Benjamin K. *chemist*

Warren
Del Bene, Janet Elaine *chemistry educator*

Wilberforce
Seleem, Suzanne *chemistry professor*

Willoughby
Krause, Marjorie N. *biochemist*

Wright Patterson AFB
Banda, Siva S. *research scientist*
Boeckl, John J. *research scientist*
Fernelius, Nils Conard *physicist*

Youngstown
Mettee, Howard Dawson *chemistry professor, consultant*

OKLAHOMA

Ada
Lu, Feng Hu *environmental scientist*
Stafford, Donald Gene *chemistry professor*
Wilkin, Richard Thomas *geochemist*

Alva
Batalha da Conceicao, Jose Joao *chemistry professor, researcher*

Ardmore
Monteros, Maria *biochemist and plant breeder, educator*

Edmond
Chen, Wei R. *physics professor*

Fort Towson
Pike, Thomas Harrison *plant chemist*

Norman
Cowan, John James *physicist, astronomer, educator*
Dinh, Anh Viet *research scientist*
Droegemeier, Kelvin K. *meteorologist, educator*
Edwards, Roger *meteorologist, researcher*
Fedorovich, Evgeni *geophysicist*
Strauss, Michael George *physics professor*

Oklahoma City
Alaupovic, Petar *biochemist, educator*
Blick, Kenneth Edward *clinical chemist, educator*
Botch, Sabra Ruvera *biochemist*
Broyles, Robert Herman *biochemistry and molecular biology educator*
Butnev, Viktor Yurievich *research scientist*
Copeland, Kyle A. *physicist*
Cruz-Rodz, Armando L. *chemistry professor*
Hurst, Robert Evan *biochemist, educator*
Kamm, Steven D. *physics professor*
Kasus-Jacobi, Anne *biochemist, cell biologist, researcher*

Stillwater
Das, Sumanta Kumar *research scientist, educator*
Hubbard, Todd Philip *aerospace scientist*
Sherwood, Peter Miles Anson *chemistry educator*
Waller, George Rozier, Jr. *retired biochemistry educator*
Westhaus, Paul Anthony *retired physics professor*
White, Jeffery Lane *chemistry professor, researcher*

Tulsa
Blais, Roger Nathaniel *physics professor, academic administrator*
Gregg, Elena *physics professor*
Hartman, Roger D. *physics professor*
Herr, Stephen Richard *environmental scientist, educator*

OREGON

Ashland
Abrahams, Sidney Cyril *physicist, crystallographer*
Grover, James Robb *chemist, editor*
Quainoo, George Kow *physics professor, department chairman*

Beaverton
Claycomb, Cecil Keith *biochemist, educator*
Hubbard, Robert Lane *research scientist*
Leen, Todd Kevin *physicist*

Corvallis
Dalrymple, Gary Brent *research geologist*
Drake, Charles Whitney *physicist*
Hawkes, Stephen James. *chemistry educator*
Holman, Robert Alan *oceanography educator*
Kelbert, Anna *geophysicist*
Lertsutthiwong, Monchai *research scientist*
McKinney, William Mark *retired geology educator*
Shen, Jianqiang *research scientist*
Van Holde, Kensal Edward *biochemistry educator*
Yeats, Robert Sheppard *geologist, educator*

Eugene
Crasemann, Bernd *physicist, researcher*
Csonka, Paul L. *theoretical physicist, educator*
Deshpande, Nilendra Ganesh *physics professor*
Donnelly, Russell James *physicist, educator*
Griffith, Osbie Hayes *retired chemistry professor*
Hill, Terrell Leslie *chemist, researcher, biophysicist*
Maurer, Robert Distler *retired industrial physicist*
Mazo, Robert Marc *retired chemistry professor*
Retallack, Gregory John *geologist, educator*
von Hippel, Peter Hans *chemistry professor, researcher*
Youngquist, Walter Lewellyn *geologist, consultant*

Gresham
Russell, Michael *chemistry professor*

Hillsboro
Kotlyar, Roza *research scientist*
Mudanai, Sivakumar P. *research scientist*

Myrtle Creek
Atwater, James E. *chemist, chemical engineer*

Portland
Abel, William Edward *applied physicist, consultant*
Cohen, Norm *chemist, music historian*
Gard, Gary Lee *chemistry professor, researcher*
Kim, Sunghan *research scientist*
Koenenkamp, Rolf *physics professor*
Lincoln, Sandra Eleanor *retired chemistry professor*
Mooers, Christopher Northrup Kennard *physical oceanographer, educator*
Pearson, David Petri *chemist*
Weeks, Wilford Frank *retired geophysics educator, glaciologist*

PENNSYLVANIA

Allentown
Slimmer, David Allen *physics educator*

Ambler
Veber, Daniel Frank *chemist, researcher*

Berwyn
Devlin, Thomas McKeown *biochemist, educator*
Kauffman, Joel Mervin *retired chemistry educator, researcher, consultant, medical writer*

Bethlehem
Gulick, Sean Paul Sandifer *geologist*
Heindel, Ned Duane *chemistry professor*
Herman, Richard Gerald *research chemist, consultant, educator*
Kanofsky, Alvin Sheldon *physics professor*
Kim, Yong Wook *physicist, educator*
Koel, Bruce Edward *chemist, educator, researcher*
Kovalskiy, Andriy *research scientist*
Lyman, Charles Edson *materials scientist, educator*
Smyth, Donald Morgan *chemistry professor, researcher*

Bloomsburg
Greene, Nathaniel Robert *physics professor*

Blue Bell
Wilson, H(arold) Fred(erick) *chemist, research scientist*

Bryn Mawr
Burciaga, Juan Ramon *physics professor*

Carlisle
Laws, Kenneth L. *physics professor*
Long, Howard Charles *retired physics professor*

Collegeville
Ellison, Mark *chemistry professor*
Harris, Philip A. *chemist*
Sabatucci, Joseph P. *chemist*

Easton
Bose, Ajay Kumar *chemistry professor emeritus*
Dougherty, Andrew *physics professor*

Elkins Park
Zelac, Ronald Edward *physicist*

Fogelsville
Huang, Tai-Yin *physics professor*

Harleysville
Salomon, Mark *chemist*

Harrisburg
Stanley, Edward Alexander *geologist, paleontologist, researcher, retired director, forensic specialist*

Hatfield
Shi, Hongjian *research scientist*

Haverford
Gollub, Jerry Paul *physics professor*
Noordergraaf, Abraham *biophysics educator*

Huntingdon
Schettler, Paul D. *chemistry professor*

Huntingdon Valley
Godfrey, John Carl *medicinal chemist*

King Of Prussia
Davis, Charles Baldwin *chemist*
Zajac, Matthew A. *chemist*

Lancaster
Matthews, Kelly E. *chemistry professor*

Lehman
Felty, Wayne Lee *chemist, educator*

Lewisburg
Kochel, R. Craig *geologist, educator*

Lincoln University
Major, Helen E. *physics professor, researcher*
Venerable, Grant Delbert, II, *chemist, educator, systems scientist*
Williams, Willie, Jr. *physicist, researcher*

Media
Voltz, Sterling Ernest *physical chemist, researcher*

Millersville
Dushkina, Natalia Mitkova *physicist, researcher*

Monaca
Haggerty, Denny C. *physics professor*

Monroeville
Skolnick, Herbert *geologist*

Mont Alto
Doncheski, Michael A. *physics professor*

Mount Joy
Lodde, Gordon Maynard *health physics consultant*

Nanticoke
Emelett, Stephen John *physicist, researcher*

New Holland
Papadakis, Emmanuel Philippos *physicist, consultant*

New Kensington
Ray, Siba Prasad *materials scientist, ceramics scientist*

New Wilmington
Long, Kenneth Maynard *chemistry professor*

Oakdale
Wire, Gary Lee *retired metallurgist*

Orefield
Armor, John N. *chemical company scientist, consultant, research manager*

Philadelphia
Ajzenberg-Selove, Fay *physicist, researcher*
Blumberg, Baruch Samuel *research scientist, educator*
Bortnick, Newman Mayer *research chemist*
Burstein, Elias *physicist, researcher*
Childress, Scott Julius *medicinal chemist*
Cohn, Mildred *retired biochemist, educator*
Dai, Hai-Lung *physical chemist, researcher*
Dalton, David Robert *chemistry professor*
Farren, Ann Louise *chemist, information scientist, educator*
Fitts, Donald Dennis *chemist, educator*
Girifalco, Louis Anthony *retired physics professor*
Glusker, Jenny Pickworth *chemist*
Hameka, Hendrik Frederik *chemistry professor*
Jaffe, Eileen Karen *biochemist*
Jarrett, Joseph Timothy *biochemistry educator*
Klein, Michael Lawrence *research chemist, educator*
Larson, Donald Clayton *physics professor, consultant*
Lester, Marsha I. *chemistry professor*
Lin, Liyong *physicist*
Lubensky, Tom Carl *physics professor*
Manuta, David Mark *chemist, consultant*
Mochalin, Vadym N. *research assistant professor, consultant*
Nelson, Philip Charles *physics professor*
Tahir-Kheli, Raza A. *physics professor*
Trodden, Mark *physicist*
Vitek, Vaclav *materials scientist*
Wales, Walter D. *physicist, researcher*
Yang, Shu *materials scientist*
Yilmazkuday, Hakan *assistant professor*

Pittsburgh
Arumugam, Darmindra Danaraj *research scientist*
Atthipalli, Gowtam *research scientist*
Beblo, Richard Vincent *research scientist*
Biondi, Manfred Anthony *physicist*
Bothner-By, Aksel Arnold *chemist*
Carr, Walter James, Jr. *research physicist, consultant*
Choyke, Wolfgang Justus *physicist*
Cohen, Bernard Leonard *physicist, researcher*
Collins, Terence James *chemistry professor*
Coltman, John Wesley *physicist*
Emmerich, Werner Sigmund *physicist, educator*
Feller, Robert Livingston *chemist, art conservation scientist*
Fetkovich, John G. *physics professor*
Gerjuoy, Edward *physicist*
Gilman, Frederick Joseph *physicist*
Goldstein, Bernard David *environmental scientist, educator*
Heo, Jingu *research scientist*
Janis, Allen Ira *retired physicist, educator*
Karol, Paul J *chemistry professor, consultant*
Kehwar, T. S. *physicist, educator*
Khetan, Sushil K. *chemist, researcher*
Kim, SeungJun *research scientist*
Kolmakov, German Valentinovich *physics professor, researcher*
Maher, James Vincent, Jr. *physics professor, academic administrator*
Matyjaszewski, Krzysztof *chemist, educator*
Mayer, George *materials scientist, chemist, consultant*
Münck, Eckard *chemistry professor*
Mutlu, Onur *research scientist*
Pintauer, Tomislav *chemistry professor*
Plazek, Donald John *materials scientist, educator*
Quinn, Brian Patrick *physics professor*
Rosenberg, Jerome Laib *chemist, educator*
Sashin, Donald *physicist, educator*
Sekerka, Robert Floyd *physics and mathematics professor*
Star, Alexander *chemist, educator*
Tristram-Nagle, Stephanie Ann *research scientist, educator*
Turnshek, David Alvin *physics and astronomy professor, department chairman*
Waldeck, David H. *chemistry professor*
Wallenberger, Frederick T. *fiber scientist*
White, Robert Marshall *retired physicist, educator, government official, consultant*
Widom, Michael *physicist, researcher*
Wipf, Peter *chemist*
Young, Hugh David *physics professor, writer*
Zhou, Chenming *research scientist*

Plymouth Meeting
Howitz, Konrad Theodor *biochemist*

Pottstown
Hergert, Herbert Lawrence *retired consultant and chemist*

Selinsgrove
Henry, Geneive E. *chemistry professor*

Shippensburg
Abdurrahman, Abdulmajeed Mohamed *physics professor*

South Park
Lotze, Barbara *retired physicist*

State College
Garrett, Steven Lurie *physicist*
Ren, Kailiang *materials scientist, educator*
Thompson, Stephen C. *research scientist*

Swarthmore
Bilaniuk, Oleksa Myron *physicist, researcher*
Pasternack, Robert Francis *chemistry professor*
Thornton, Edward Ralph *chemistry professor*

University Park
Allcock, Harry R. *chemistry professor*
Alley, Richard B. *geologist, educator*

Blackadar, Alfred Kimball *meteorologist, educator*
Brantley, Susan L. *geochemist, science association director*
Carlson, Toby N. *retired meteorologist*
Castleman, Albert Welford, Jr. *physical chemist, educator*
Chan, Moses Hung Wai *physicist, researcher*
Dutton, John Altnow *meteorologist, educator*
Garmire, Gordon Paul *astronomer, educator*
Garrison, Barbara Jane *chemistry professor*
Gul, Omer *chemist, researcher*
Hammes-Schiffer, Sharon *chemist, educator*
Hosler, Charles Luther, Jr. *meteorologist, educator*
Howell, Benjamin Franklin, Jr. *geophysicist, educator*
Jackman, Lloyd Miles *chemistry professor*
Jain, Jainendra Kumar *physics professor*
Kasting, James Fraser *research meteorologist, physicist*
Schuster, Stephan Christoph *biochemist, researcher*
Semouchkina, Elena *physicist, researcher*
Sen, Ayusman *chemistry professor*
Wagener, Thorsten *hydrologist, educator*
White, William Blaine *geochemist, researcher*
Winograd, Nicholas *chemist*

Villanova
Phares, Alain Joseph *physicist, researcher*
Yemelyanov, Konstantin *research scientist, educator*

Wallingford
Severdia, Anthony George *chemistry researcher*

Warminster
Gamarnik, Moisey Yankelevich *solid state physicist*

Warrington
Ulmer, Gene Carleton *geochemist, educator*

Wayne
Newman, David John *chemist*

Waynesburg
Maguire, Mildred May *retired chemistry professor*

West Chester
Falcone, James S., Jr. *chemistry professor*

West Point
Sun, Li *chemist, researcher*

Wexford
Bossart, Paul Nathaniel, Jr. *geologist, geophysicist, consultant*

Wyndmoor
Mastovska, Katerina *chemist, researcher*
Pfeffer, Philip Elliot *biophysicist*
Yadav, Madhav P. *chemist*

Wynnewood
Rosen, Gerald Harris *physicist, consultant, educator*

Yardley
Hunt, David Allen *organic chemist*

RHODE ISLAND

Narragansett
Nixon, Scott West *oceanography science educator*
Pilson, Michael Edward Quinton *oceanography educator*

Providence
Avery, Donald Hills *metallurgist, educator*
Carpenter, Gene Blakely *crystallography and chemistry educator*
Cooper, Leon N. *physicist, researcher*
Dahlberg, Albert Edward *biochemistry professor*
Estrup, Peder Jan *physics and chemistry professor*
Gerritsen, Hendrik Jurjen *physics professor, researcher*
Head, James William III *geological sciences educator*
Kosterlitz, J. Michael *physics professor*
Landsberg, Greg *physicist*
Lanou, Robert Eugene, Jr. *physicist, researcher*
Levin, Frank S. *physicist, educator*
Risen, William Maurice, Jr. *chemistry educator*
Stratt, Richard Mark *chemistry researcher, educator*
Tang, Jay X. *physics professor*
Walecki, Wojciech Jan *physicist, engineer*

Wakefield
Moore, George Emerson, Jr. *geologist, educator*

SOUTH CAROLINA

Aiken
Brisbin, I. Lehr, Jr. *retired research scientist*
Dewberry, Raymond Allen *research scientist, combat engineer*
Dickson, Paul Wesley, Jr. *physicist*

Bluffton
Croft, George T. *physicist*

Charleston
Briggs, Patrick Ray *physics professor*
Vakser, Ilya *biophysicist, educator*
Wyatt, Justin K. *chemistry professor*

Clemson
DesMarteau, Darryl Dwayne *chemistry professor*
Frugoli, Julia Alice *research scientist*
Tritt, Terry *physicist*

Columbia
Ammal, Salai Cheettu *chemist*
Datta, Timir *physicist, solid state and materials consultant*
Edge, Ronald Dovaston *physics professor*
Jeon, Donghyup *research scientist*
Preedom, Barry Mason *physicist, researcher*
Samuel, May Linda *environmental scientist*
Vogt, Thomas *physics professor, director*
Xu, Zhi-Hui *research scientist*

Gaffney
Berry, Scott D. *physics professor, director*

Greenville
Belanger, Laura Hewlette *environmental scientist, consultant*

Hopkins
Moore, Willard S. *oceanographer, educator*

Mount Pleasant
Mosier, Arvin Ray *chemist, researcher*

Orangeburg
Abdel-Kader, Wagih G. *physics professor*

Rock Hill
Sebhatu, Mesgun *physics professor*

Sumter
Amirzadeh, Jafar *physics professor*

West Columbia
Battista, Bradley Matthew *geophysicist*

SOUTH DAKOTA

Brookings
Perumal, Omathanu Pillai *research scientist, medical researcher, educator*

Freeman
Ries, Edward Richard *petroleum geologist, consultant*

Rapid City
Roggenthen, William *geologist, educator*
Smith, Paul Letton, Jr. *geophysicist*

Sioux Falls
Gerdes, Anthony Martin *research scientist, health science association administrator*
Senay, Gabriel Bogale *research scientist, educator*
Viste, Arlen Ellard *chemistry professor*

TENNESSEE

Brentwood
Heiser, Arnold Melvin *astronomer*

Chattanooga
Anderson, Larry Woodward *chemist, educator*
Symes, Steven James Kenneth *chemistry professor*

Clarksville
Blanck, Harvey F. *retired chemistry professor*
Hunley, Geene Allen *Physics Instructor*

Cookeville
Engelhardt, Robert Thomas *physicist, educator*
Kumar, Krishna *retired physics educator*
Mills, Hugh Harrison III *geologist, educator*

Jefferson City
Cordry, Sean Michael *physics professor*

Johnson City
Ahmad, Zulfiqar *biochemist, educator*
McIntosh, Cecilia Ann *biochemist, educator*

Kingsport
Weaver, Max Allen *chemist, consultant, inventor*

Knoxville
Bingham, Carrol Reid *physicist*
Chen, Chung Hqo *research scientist*
Durairaj, Baskaran *chemistry professor*
Gentry, Robert Vance *physicist, researcher, writer*
Hatcher, Robert Dean, Jr. *geologist, educator, research scientist*
Nazarewicz, Witold *nuclear scientist, educator*
Pruitt, Jonathan Neal *research scientist*
Qiu, Wulin *chemist, materials scientist, materials engineer*
Reddick, Lovett Evan *biochemist*
Schweitzer, George Keene *chemistry professor*
Wunderlich, Bernhard *retired physical chemistry professor*

Maryville
Weeks, Robert Andrew *materials science researcher, educator*

Memphis
Desiderio, Dominic Morse, Jr. *chemistry and neurochemistry professor*
Fain, John Nicholas *biochemistry educator*
Franceschetti, Donald Ralph *physicist, educator*
Li, Ying Sing *chemistry professor*
Patil, Shivaputra A. *research scientist*

Morristown
Culvern, Julian Brewer *chemist, naturalist, educator, writer, photographer*

Nashville
Bignall, Orville Newton *physicist, educator*
Chytil, Frank *biochemist*
Fort, Tomlinson *chemist, chemical engineering educator*
Gao, Benlian *biochemist*
Hamilton, Joseph Hants, Jr. *physicist, researcher*
Hanusa, Timothy P. *chemistry professor, director*
Hercules, David Michael *chemistry professor, consultant*
Hwang, Jae-Kwang *physicist, researcher*
Inagami, Tadashi *biochemistry professor*
Karim, Mohammad Rezaul *chemistry professor*
Lukehart, Charles Martin *chemistry professor*
Nagathihalli, Nagaraj *biochemist, researcher*
Osheroff, Neil *biochemist, educator*
Stassun, Keivan Guadalupe *astronomer, educator*
Surowiec, Andrew Julius *biophysicist, researcher*
Tolk, Norman Henry *physics educator*
Zavalin, Andrey I. *optics scientist, educator*

Oak Ridge
Biewer, Theodore Mathias *physicist*
Borie, Bernard Simon, Jr. *retired physicist, educator*
Cui, Xiaohui *research scientist*
Daniel, Claus *materials scientist, researcher*
Galindo-Uribarri, Alfredo *research scientist, educator*
Haire, Marvin Jonathan *nuclear scientist*
Harvey, John Arthur *nuclear physicist*
Krause, Manfred Otto *physicist*
Kronenberg, Andreas *nuclear chemist, radiochemist, nuclear technology consultant*
McFarlane, Joanna *chemist, researcher*
Melnichenko, Yuri B. *physicist*
Mirzadeh, Saed *nuclear scientist, researcher*
Mook, Herbert Arthur *research scientist*
Nephew, Edmund A. *physicist, retired mayor*
Olama, Mohammed *research scientist*
Perry, Kelly Ann *research scientist*
Plasil, Franz *physicist*
Pouchard, Line Catherine *research scientist, educator*
Read, Kenneth Francis, Jr. *physics professor, researcher*
Stracener, Daniel W. *physicist*

Pleasant Hill
Heald, Mark Aiken *physicist, educator*

Signal Mountain
Howe, Lyman Harold III *chemist, researcher*

Tullahoma
Johnson, Jacqueline Anne *physics professor*

TEXAS

Allen
Johri, Vinod B. *retired astrophysics professor, writer, researcher*

Alpine
Rohr, David Malcolm *geologist, educator*

Arlington
Armstrong, Daniel Wayne *chemist, educator*
Chen, Wei *physics professor*
Cuntz, Manfred *astrophysicist, researcher, educator, writer*
Damuth, John Erwin *marine geologist*
Mandal, Subhrangsu S. *chemistry professor, researcher*
Ray, Asok Kumar *physicist, researcher*
Reaser, Donald Frederick *retired geology educator*
Strom, E. (dwin) Thomas *chemistry professor, researcher*
Timmons, Richard Brendan *chemist, educator*
Willoughby, Sarah-Margaret C. *retired chemist, educator, chemical engineer, consultant*

Austin
Barbara, Paul Frank *chemistry professor*
Bard, Allen Joseph *chemist, educator*
Bash, Frank Ness *astronomer, educator*
Bengtson, Roger Dean *physicist, department chairman*
Boggs, James Ernest *chemistry professor*
Bowen, Sabine W. *geologist*
Chae, Chan Byoung *research scientist*
Demkov, Alexander A. *physics professor*
DeWitt-Morette, Cécile *physicist*
Duncombe, Raynor Lockwood *astronomer*
Eluru, Naveen *research scientist*
Erskine, James Lorenzo *physics professor*
Fisher, William Lawrence *geologist, educator, dean*
Folk, Robert Louis *geologist, educator*
Fonken, Gerhard Joseph *retired chemistry professor, academic administrator*
Gavenda, J(ohn) David *physicist*
Gentle, Kenneth William *physicist*
Griffy, Thomas Alan *physics professor*
Groat, Charles George *geologist, former federal agency administrator*
Hutchison, William Ray *geologist*
Lim, Sang Hyun *chemistry professor*
Mabry, Tom J. *retired biological chemistry professor*
Mark, Hans Michael *physicist, former federal agency administrator*
Petrosky, Tomio Yamakoshi *research scientist*
Stewart, Kent Kallam *analytical biochemistry educator*
Trafton, Laurence Munro *astronomer, researcher*
Udagawa, Takeshi *physicist, researcher*
Wilson, Clark R. *geophysicist, educator*
Zheng, Shuang-Cai *physics educator, researcher*

Beaumont
Bahrim, Cristian *physicist, educator, researcher*

Brownsville
Ermolinsky, Boris Sergeevich *chemist, educator*
Price, Richard H. *physics professor*

Brownwood
Bryant, Pamela L. *chemistry professor*

Bryan
McIntyre, John Armin *physics professor*

Calvert
Alemán, Marthanne Payne *environmental scientist, consultant*

Canyon
Tao, Shiquan *chemistry professor*

Cedar Hill
Wilson, Peggy Mayfield *retired chemist*

Clarendon
Wiginton, Larry Micheal *chemistry professor*

College Station
Arnowitt, Richard Lewis *retired physics professor*
Bluemel, Janet *chemistry professor*
Dessler, Alexander Jack *astrophysicist, educator*
Dominguez, Elvis *research scientist*
Duce, Robert Arthur *atmospheric chemist, oceanographer, educator*
Eaton, Gordon Pryor *geologist, consultant*
Gladysz, John Andrew *chemistry professor*
Goodman, David Wayne *research chemist, educator*
Hardy, John Christopher *physicist, researcher, educator*
Holcombe, Troy Leon *marine geologist*
Laane, Jaan *chemistry professor*
McIntyre, Peter Mastin *physicist, researcher*
Nachman, Ronald James *chemist, researcher*
O'Connor, Rod *chemist, consultant, inventor*
Pokrovsky, Valery Leonidovich *physicist, researcher*
Rumpho-Kennedy, Mary Ellen *plant biochemistry educator*
Sun, Yuefeng *research scientist, educator*
Suntzeff, Nicholas Boris *research astronomer*
Wild, James Robert *biochemistry and genetics professor*
Yapici, Murat Kaya *research scientist*

Commerce
Ni, Bukuo *chemistry professor*
Wicke, Jason *biochemist, educator*

Copper Canyon
Nickon, Alex *chemist, educator*

Dallas
Baek, Hyeonman *research scientist*
Baxter, Richard Henry Geoffrey *research scientist*
Brooks, James Elwood *geologist, educator*
Butovich, Igor A. *biochemist, educator*
Carroll, William Francis, Jr. *chemist*
Choi, Changho *physicist, educator*
Deisenhofer, Johann *biochemistry professor, researcher*
Garner, Harold Ray *experimental research physicist, biochemist*
Gibbs, James Alanson *geologist*
Harran, Patrick G. *biochemistry professor*
Marshall, John Harris, Jr. *geologist, oil industry executive*
Senkayi, Abu Lwanga *environmental scientist*
Son, Tae W. *physics professor*
Thompson, Keith F. MacKechnie *geochemist, consultant*

Denton
Anand, Aman *research scientist*
Choppali, Uma *physics professor*
Krokhin, Arkadii *physics professor*
Saleh, Farida Yousry *chemistry professor*

Edinburg
Chipara, Mircea *physicist*

El Paso
Ansari, Fariba *physics professor*
Peralta-Videa, Jose R. *environmental scientist, researcher*

Fort Worth
Caldwell, Billy Ray *geologist*
Gattis, David Robert *environmental scientist, state agency administrator*
Hull, Shelli Bigham *chemistry professor*
Matveeva, Evgenia *chemist*
Quarles, Carroll Adair, Jr. *physicist, researcher*
Reinecke, Manfred G. *chemistry professor*
Sharma, Rajendra *chemist, educator*
Wicker, Dorothy Baldwin *physicist*

Freeport
Weaver, John D. (Bert Weaver) *chemist, researcher*
Zhou, Zhe *research scientist*

Galveston
Estes, Ernest L. *geologist, educator*
Lee, James Ching *biochemistry researcher, educator*

Hewitt
Ariyasinghe, Wickramasinghe M. *physics professor*

Houston
Alauddin, Mian M. *chemist, educator*
Alavi, Mehdi *geologist*
Anderson, Richard Carl *geophysical exploration company executive*
Antignano, Angelo, IV, *geologist*
Baker, Stephen Denio *physics professor*
Bally, Albert W. *retired geologist, educator*
Bering, Edgar Andrew III *physicist, educator*
Bogard, Donald Dale *planetary geochemist*
Brotzen, Franz Richard *materials scientist, educator*
Burke, Kevin Charles Antony *geologist*
Caldwell, Tracy Ellen *surface chemist, researcher*
Carson, Daniel Douglas *biochemist, reproductive biologist*
Chu, Paul Ching-Wu *physicist, academic administrator, educator*
Cruz, Miguel Angel *biochemist, educator*
Curl, Robert Floyd, Jr. *chemistry professor*
Erdin, Serkan *physicist*
Farley, Martin Birtell *geologist*
Filiberto, Justin *geologist*

Frey, Henry Wallace *research scientist*
Galgana, Gerald Aguirre *geophysicist*
Gashawbeza, Ewenet *geophysicist*
Gibson, Everett Kay, Jr. *space scientist, geochemist*
Gorenstein, David G. *chemistry and biochemistry professor*
Howell, Kimberly *geologist, educator*
Hulet, Randall Gardner *physics professor*
Hussain, Moinuddin Syed *geologist, engineer, consultant*
Jackson, George William *research scientist, consultant*
Jeevarajan, Judith A. *chemist*
Katz, Barry Jay *geologist, researcher*
Kinsey, James Lloyd *chemist, educator*
Kouri, Donald Jack *chemist, educator*
Kuznetz, Lawrence H. *research scientist*
Lane, Neal Francis *physics professor, retired federal agency administrator*
Lewandowski, Jerome L. *physicist*
Lewis, Edward Sheldon *chemistry professor*
Li, Gang *managing consultant*
Lofgren, Gary Ernest *Planetary Scientist*
Lucid, Shannon W. *biochemist, astronaut*
Mackwell, Stephen Joseph *geophysicist, educator*
Martinez, David Roger *chemist, researcher*
McPhee, Jancy Crane *aerospace scientist*
Mohammadpour Velni, Javad *research scientist*
Ponomarev, Artem Lvovich *physicist, senior research scientist*
Rao, Nageswara Maddali *space and planetary scientist*
Reiff, Patricia Hofer *space physicist, educator*
Reso, Anthony *geologist, educator, earth resources economist*
Rong, Shu *geophysicist, researcher*
Shakir, Huzefa *research scientist*
Si, Qimiao *physics professor*
Spudich, John Lee *biochemist, molecular biologist, chemistry professor*
Stoops, James King *biochemistry researcher*
Ting, Chin-Sen *physics professor*
Villinski, Jennifer C. *geochemist*
Weinstein, Roy *physics professor*
Weisman, R(obert) Bruce *physical chemist, educator, entrepreneur*
Wilson, Thomas Leon *physicist, researcher*
Yang, Chao Yuh *biochemistry professor, medical educator*

Irving
Eaker, Charles William *chemistry professor*

Kerrville
Shaw, Alan Bosworth *geologist, retired paleontologist*

Kilgore
Buchanan, Paul Clarence *geologist, researcher*

Kingsville
Cox, Paul H. *physics professor*
Moehring, Gregory *chemistry professor, department chairman*

Laredo
Coats, Charles F. *physics and mathematics educator*

Lubbock
Bartsch, Richard Allen *chemist, educator*
Everse, Johannes *biochemist, researcher*
Lodhi, M. A.K. *physicist, educator*
Mayer, Michael Frederick *chemistry professor*

Mc Kinney
Frank, Steven Neil *chemist*

Mesquite
Justice, Mahlon G. (Jay Justice) *physics professor*

Midland
Berner, Leo De Witte, Jr. *retired oceanographer*

Nacogdoches
Markworth, Norman *astronomer, educator*
Moore, John Thomas *chemistry professor, writer*

Odessa
Stoudt, Emily Laws *geologist, educator*

Pasadena
Aquino, Dolores Catherine *chemistry professor*
Cartwright, Ann *chemistry professor, department chairman*

Prairie View
Ciftja, Orion *physicist, researcher*
Cudnik, Brian *astronomer, educator*

Richardson
Baughman, Ray Henry *materials scientist*
Cantrell, Cyrus Duncan III *physics professor, engineering educator, director*
Dasgupta, Sajib *research scientist*
Rutford, Robert Hoxie *geologist, educator*
Stern, Robert James *geologist, educator*
Yang, Duck Joo *research scientist, educator*

Rowlett
Sprague, Charles Warren *geologist*

San Antonio
Bachrach, Steven Maurice *chemistry educator*
Brancaleon, Lorenzo *biophysicist, researcher*
Budalur, Thyagarajan Subbanarayan *chemistry professor*
Cesur, Durmus *GIS expert*
Cherukuri, Ravindranath Chowdary *research scientist*
Gruber, John Balsbaugh *physics professor*
Lyle, Robert Edward *chemist*
Synek, Miroslav *physicist, chemist, world affairs consultant*
Urbach, Adam Robert *chemistry professor*

Walmsley, Judith Abrams *chemistry professor*

San Marcos
Blanda, Michael Thomas *chemist, researcher*
Feakes, Debra Arliene *chemistry professor*
Rudzinski, Walter E. *chemistry professor, department chairman*

Stafford
Corley, Larry Steven *chemist*

Sugar Land
Downs, Hartley H. III *chemist*
Goodwin, Anthony Robert Holmes *chemist, editor*
Huston, Daniel Cliff *geophysicist*

Temple
Asea, Alexzander *research scientist*

Uvalde
Graham, Robert Albert *physicist, researcher*

Waco
Cleaver, Gerald Bryan *physicist, researcher*
Goforth, Thomas Tucker *retired geophysicist*

Wichita Falls
Hallford, Randal L. *chemistry professor*

UTAH

American Fork
Zhou, Bing-Nan *chemistry professor*

Cedar City
Cotts, Laura Alford *physics professor, consultant*

Holladay
O'Halloran, Thomas Alphonsus, Jr. *retired physicist, researcher*

Logan
Cao, Yongcan *research scientist*
Zhu, Lie *physics professor*

Ogden
Berghout, Henry Laine *chemistry professor*
Carroll, Bradley W. *physics professor, department chairman*

Provo
Cheney, Brigham Vernon *physical chemist, consultant*
Henderson, Douglas James *physicist, chemist, educator, researcher*
Izatt, Reed M. *chemistry researcher*
Robins, Morris Joseph *chemistry professor, researcher*
Turley, Robert Steven *physicist, researcher*
Weber, Darrell Jack *plant biochemistry educator*

Salt Lake City
Bass, Brenda L. *biochemist, educator*
Dick, Bertram Gale, Jr. *physics professor*
Facelli, Julio Cesar *physics researcher, university administrator*
Gortatowski, Melvin Jerome *retired chemist*
Harris, Frank Ephraim *physics professor*
Hawker, Charles Davis *biochemist, director*
Louie, Janis *chemistry professor*
Mattis, Daniel Charles *physicist, researcher*
Miller, Jan Dean *metallurgy educator*
Mishchenko, Eugene *physics professor*
Picard, M(eredith) Dane *geologist*
Salomonson, Vincent Victor *meteorologist, educator*
Smith, Robert B. *geophysicist, educator*
Stang, Peter John *organic chemist*
Williams, George Abiah *physics educator*

VERMONT

Arlington
Pond, Thomas Alexander *physics professor, academic administrator*

Burlington
Kuehne, Martin Eric *chemist, educator*
Nyborg, Wesley Lemars *physics professor*
Smith, David Young *physics professor*
Wu, Junru *physics educator*

Lyndonville
Atkins, Nolan Thomas *meteorologist, educator*

Middlebury
Winkler, Paul Frank, Jr. *astrophysicist, educator*

Shelburne
White, William North *retired chemistry professor*

Thetford
Hoagland, Mahlon *biochemist, educator*

VIRGINIA

Alexandria
Bombardt, John Nicholas *research scientist*
Krall, Jonathan Francis *physicist, researcher*
Leahy, Pat (P. Patrick Leahy) *geologist, former federal official*
Lipnick, Robert Louis *chemist, toxicologist*
Masterson, Kleber Sanlin, Jr. *physicist*
Muir, Warren Roger *chemist, educator*
Romney, Carl F. *seismologist*
Toulmin, Priestley *retired geologist*

Annandale
Matuszko, Anthony Joseph *research chemist, administrator, educator*

Arlington
Bigeleisen, Jacob *chemist, educator*
Chubb, Talbot Albert *physicist, consultant*
Debney, George C. *mathematical physicist*
Erb, Karl Albert *physicist, government official*
Frederick, William George DeMott *defense company executive, consultant*
Gergely, Tomas Esteban *astronomer*
Matthews, Allan Freeman *geologist*
Shlesinger, Michael F *physicist, educator*
Whitcomb, James Hall *geophysicist, foundation administrator*

Ashburn
Rubin, Gerald Mayer *biochemistry researcher, educator*

Blacksburg
Asryan, Levon V. *physicist, electronics engineer, materials scientist*
Brewer, Karen Jenks *chemistry educator*
Cao, Yang *research scientist, educator*
Dautartas, Mino (Minodaugas) Fernand *physical chemist*
Du, Yu *research scientist*
Graybeal, Jack Daniel *chemist, educator*
Mo, Luke Wei *physicist, researcher*
Schmittmann, Beate *physics professor*

Burke
Shen, Weixing *meteorologist*

Charlottesville
Andrews, William Lester Self Self *chemistry educator*
Carter, William Walton *physicist, researcher*
Cotton, William Donaldson, Jr. *astronomer*
Fredrick, Laurence William *astronomer, educator*
Gallagher, Thomas Francis *physicist*
Gaskin, Felicia *biochemist, educator*
Good, Richard Standish *geologist*
Grimes, Russell Newell *inorganic chemist, educator*
Lo, Kwok-Yung *astronomer, educator, researcher, administrator*
Palanisamy, Prakash *research assistant*
Pearson, William Raymond *biochemist, educator*
Sabat, Michal *structural chemist*
Sackett, Charles Ackley *physicist, educator*
Sarazin, Craig Leigh *astronomer*
Sundberg, Richard Jay *chemistry professor*
Trindle, Carl *chemistry educator*
Vanden Bout, Paul Adrian *astronomer, physicist, educator*
Weber, Hans Jürgen *physics professor*
Yates, John Thomas, Jr. *chemistry professor, research scientist*

Clifton
Brooks, Matthew Wayne *agrichemical regulatory chemist, consultant*

Fairfax
Aharonov, Yakir *physicist, researcher*
Batten, Brian *research scientist*
Geller, Harold Arthur *earth and space sciences executive, educator, author*
Khan, Shahamat Ullah *environmental scientist, educator*
Manheim, Frank Tibor *oceanographer*
Morowitz, Harold Joseph *biophysicist, educator*
Trefil, James Stanley *physicist, researcher*
Yang, Chaowei Phil *research scientist, educator*

Falls Church
Akkara, Joseph Augustine *chemist, educator, researcher*

Fort Belvoir
Ratches, James Arthur *chief scientist*

Fredericksburg
Bressler, Barry Lee *physicist, systems analyst*

Hampden Sydney
Porterfield, William Wendell *chemist, educator*

Hampton
Cantrell, John Harris *physicist*
Miskolczi, Ferenc Mark *research scientist*
Nazaryan, Vahagn *physicist, medical researcher*
Tripathi, Ram Kishore *physicist, researcher*
Watson, Willie R. *research scientist*

Harrisonburg
Baker, George Harold III *physicist, educator*
Whitmeyer, Steven J. *geologist, educator*

Hartfield
Johnson, Carl Randolph *chemist, educator*

Heathsville
Winkel, Raymond Norman *aerospace scientist, consultant, retired military officer*

Herndon
Gill, Jean Kennedy *chemistry professor*
Price, James Michael *oceanographer*
Ryder, Robert T. *geologist, researcher*

Lexington
Schwab, Frederic Lyon *geologist, educator*

Mc Lean
Theon, John Speridon *meteorologist, researcher*

Newport News
Buoncristiani, A. Martin *retired physics professor*
Cardman, Lawrence Santo *physics professor, researcher*
Costa, Gerousis *physics professor*

Petersburg
Gatrone, Ralph C. *chemistry professor*

Stronach, Carey Elliott *physicist, researcher*

Radford
Zweifel, Paul Frederick *retired physics professor*

Reston
Choe, Tae Eun *research scientist*
Focazio, Michael Joseph *hydrologist, educator*
Kohlberg, Ira *physicist, mathematician*
Kramish, Arnold *physicist, historian, writer*
Naeser, Nancy Dearien *geologist, researcher*
Tucker, Robert David *geologist*
van Oss, Hendrik G. *geologist*

Richmond
Bonchev, Danail Georgiev *chemist, educator*
Carpenter, Everett E. *research scientist, educator*
Farrell, Nicholas Patrick *chemistry professor, researcher*
Fenn, John Bennett *chemist, educator*
Guney-Altay, Ozge *research scientist*
Pithawalla, Yezdi Bahadur *chemist*
Reshchikov, Michael A. *physics professor, researcher*
Sun, Qiang *scientist, educator*
Terner, James *chemistry educator*
Wang, Qian *physicist, educator*

Roanoke
Al-Zubaidi, Amer Aziz *physicist, researcher*

Salem
Fleenor, Matthew Clay *physics professor*

Springfield
Benson, William Edward (Barnes) *geologist*
Campbell, Francis James *retired chemist*
Wagner, Andrew James *retired meteorologist, elder, educator*

Staunton
Garkov, Vladimir Nikolaev *chemistry professor*

Sterling
Souw, Bernard Eng-Kie *physicist, researcher, engineer, consultant*

Vienna
Bhide, Manohar Gopal *nuclear scientist, educator*

Williamsburg
Clavero, Cesar *research scientist*
Delos, John Bernard *physicist*
Starnes, William Herbert, Jr. *chemist, educator*

Winchester
Ludwig, George Harry *retired physicist, electrical engineer*

Wise
Kellogg, Melinda Jane *physics professor*

WASHINGTON

Anacortes
Businger, Joost Alois *atmospheric scientist, educator*

Auburn
Ma, Zhenkui *remote sensing applications scientist, consultant*

Bellingham
Boudreaux, Andrew *physics professor*
Cox, David Jackson *biochemistry professor*
Matthews, Robin Adele *environmental scientist, educator*

Bothell
Soltani, Azita *director of research*

Ellensburg
Rosell, Sharon Lynn *physics and chemistry professor*

Friday Harbor
Agosta, William Carleton *chemist, educator*

Indianola
Gutsche, Carl David *chemistry professor*

Lynnwood
Olsen, Kenneth Harold *geophysicist, astrophysicist, historian*

Manchester
Fearon, Lee Charles *chemist*

Nine Mile Falls
Grubbs, Paul Alan *educator pilot*

Prosser
Harbertson, James Foster *research scientist*

Pullman
Balla, Vamsi Krishna *research scientist*
Banas, Emil Mike *physicist, researcher*
Dodgen, Harold Warren *chemistry and physics professor*
Hinman, George Wheeler *physics professor*
Stetler, Larry D. *geologist*

Redmond
Chayes, Jennifer Tour *mathematical physicist, educator*
Meshii, Masahiro *materials science educator*

Richland
Arntzen, Evan *geologist*
Bevelacqua, Joseph John *physicist, researcher*

Devarakonda, Maruthi N. *research scientist, educator*
Elderkin, Charles Edwin *retired meteorologist*
Felmy, Andrew Robert *research scientist*
Fryxell, Glen Edward *chemist, educator, materials scientist*
Hoppe, Eric W. *chemistry professor, researcher*
Kathren, Ronald *health physicist*
Kim, Jin Yong *research scientist*
Lo Presti, Charles Arthur *research scientist*
Lyubinetsky, Igor *research scientist*
Moore, Emmett Burris, Jr. *physical chemist, educator*
Murphy, Mark Kenneth *physicist, researcher*
Shin, Yongsoon *research scientist*
Xantheas, Sotiris Stavros *chemist, researcher*

Seattle
Anderson, Roger Harris *retired physics professor*
Atwater, Brian F. *geologist, educator*
Baker, David *biochemist*
Baum, William Alvin *astronomer, educator*
Bernard, Eddie Nolan *oceanographer*
Bichsel, Hans *physicist, consultant, researcher*
Bodansky, David *physicist, researcher*
Brodsky, Anatol M. *research scientist*
Brown, Robert Alan *geophysicist, educator*
Brownlee, Donald Eugene, II, *astronomer, educator*
Cahn, John Werner *metallurgist, educator*
Christian, Gary D. *chemistry professor*
Cowan, Darrel *geologist, educator*
Davidson, Ernest Roy *chemist, educator*
Durran, Dale Richard *geophysicist, educator*
Efimov, Vitaly *physicist, researcher, educator*
Evans, Bernard William *geologist, educator*
Fischer, Edmond Henri *biochemistry educator*
Gunn, John T. *oceanographer, researcher*
Halver, John Emil *nutritional biochemist*
Heath, George Ross *oceanographer*
Henley, Ernest Mark *physics professor, retired dean*
Holzworth, Robert Haviland, II, *geophysics and physics educator*
Krebs, Edwin Gerhard *biochemistry educator*
Kwiram, Alvin L. *retired chemistry professor, academic administrator*
Linnell, Albert Paul *physics and astronomy educator*
Lubatti, Henry Joseph *physicist, researcher*
McPhaden, Michael James *oceanographer, educator*
Montgomery, David R. *geologist, educator, writer*
Munch, David *retired chemistry professor*
Muy-Rivera, Martin *biochemist, researcher*
Porter, Stephen Cummings *geologist, educator*
Rabinovitch, Benton Seymour *chemist, educator emeritus*
Rehr, John J. *physicist, researcher*
Reidmiller, David R. *atmospheric chemist*
Reinhardt, William Parker *chemical physicist, educator*
Stern, Edward Abraham *physics professor*
Stoelinga, Mark Theodore *meteorologist, educator*
Suzuki, Edward M. *chemist*
Tang, Qiuhong *research scientist*
Thouless, David James *retired physicist, educator*
Tolich, Nikolai *physicist, educator*
Wei, Pax S.P. *research scientist*
Wilets, Lawrence *physicist, educator*
Wurster, Charles Frederick *environmental scientist, educator*

Spokane
Crosby, Glenn Arthur *chemistry professor*
Nawash, Jalal Mohammad *physics professor*

Tacoma
Gerganov, Bogomil E. *physics professor*
Hitz, Ralph *geologist, educator*
Rousslang, Kenneth W. *retired chemistry professor*
Tang, Kwong-Tin *physics professor, researcher*

Vancouver
Shamrell, Richard T. *physics professor*
Tang, Liang *optics scientist*

Walla Walla
Wade, Leroy Grover, Jr. *chemistry educator*

WEST VIRGINIA

Bluefield
Foster, Lewis C. *physics professor*

Charleston
Linger, Rebecca Susan *chemistry professor*

Fairmont
Swiger, Elizabeth Davis *chemist, educator*

Huntington
Babiuc-Hamilton, Maria Cristina *physics professor*
Nguyen, Que Huong *physics professor*

Montgomery
Carlson, George Theodore *physics professor*

Morgantown
Constantinescu, Adi *physicist, educator*
Spenik, James L. *research scientist*

WISCONSIN

Appleton
Cook, David Marsden *physics professor*

Eau Claire
King, Frederick W. *chemistry professor, researcher*

Fond Du Lac
Denow, Thomas D. *research scientist, educator*

Lake Geneva
Dobray, Alan Michael *theoretical physicist, research scientist*

Madison
Adler, Julius *biochemist, educator, biologist*
Anderson, Louis Wilmer, Jr. *physicist, researcher*
Barger, Amy J. *astronomer, educator*
Barger, Vernon Duane *physicist, educator*
Begum, Ayesha *astronomer, researcher*
Botez, Dan *physicist*
Bruch, Ludwig W. *physicist, researcher*
Burns, Dixie L. *astronomer, educator*
Burris, Robert Harza *biochemist, educator*
Cao, Guoping *research scientist*
Christensen, Nikolas Ivan *geophysicist, educator*
Churchwell, Edward Bruce *astronomer, educator*
Clay, Clarence Samuel *acoustical oceanographer*
Cleland, W(illiam) Wallace *biochemistry educator*
Coppersmith, Susan Nan *physicist*
Crim, Forrest Fleming, Jr. *chemist, educator*
DeWerd, Larry Albert *medical physicist, educator*
Diawara, Yacouba *physicist, researcher*
Dott, Robert Henry, Jr. *geologist, educator*
Evan, Amato Tomas *climate scientist*
Evenson, Merle Armin *chemist, educator*
Farrar, Thomas C. *chemist, educator*
Fonck, Raymond John *physicist, educator*
Gilbert, Pupa *physics professor, director*
Goll, James Gerard *chemistry professor*
Greenler, Robert George *physics professor, researcher*
Hammel, Kenneth Edward *biochemist, educator*
Han, Tao *physics professor*
Hokin, Lowell Edward *biochemist, educator*
Johnson, Clark Montgomery *geologist, educator*
Khazins, David Mikhailovich *retired research scientist*
Lagally, Max Gunter *physics professor*
Lardy, Henry A(rnold) *biochemistry professor*
Lawler, James Edward *physics professor*
Li, Fumin *research scientist*
Li, Kai *chemist, research scientist*
Li, Lingjun *chemistry professor*
Lin, Chun Chia *research physicist, educator*
Maher, Louis James, Jr. *geologist, educator*
Maynard, James Harold *chemistry professor*
Morton, Stephen Dana *chemist, consultant*
Mukerjee, Pasupati *chemistry professor*
Record, M. Thomas, Jr. *biochemist, educator*
Rodwell, John Dennis *biochemist*
Sakidja, Ridwan *research scientist*
Scherer, Victor Richard *physicist, computer scientist, musician, consultant*
Sibert, Edwin L. *chemistry professor*
Skinner, James Lauriston *chemist, educator*
Vaughan, Worth Edward *retired chemistry professor*
Zimmerman, Howard Elliot *chemist, educator*

Menomonie
Raut, Usha *physics professor*

Milwaukee
Bader, Alfred Robert *chemist*
Burch, Thaddeus Joseph, Jr. *physics professor, priest*
Buss, Daniel Frank *environmental scientist*
Cronin, Vincent Sean *geologist*
Griffith, Owen Wendell *biochemistry professor*
Haworth, Daniel Thomas *emeritus chemistry professor*
Karkheck, John Peter *physics professor, researcher*
Stockdale, Christopher *physics professor*
Tysoe, Wilfred Tjalke *chemistry professor*

Washington Island
Raup, David Malcolm *paleontology educator*

Whitefish Bay
Hendee, William Richard *medical physics educator, academic administrator, radiologist*

Whitewater
Han, Baocheng *chemistry professor, department chairman*
Kumpaty, Hephzibah J. *chemistry professor*

Williams Bay
Hobbs, Lewis Mankin *astronomer*

WYOMING

Big Horn
Schultz, Harry Pershing *chemistry researcher, retired educator*

Casper
Ptasynski, Harry *geologist, oil industry executive*
Wold, John Schiller *geologist, former congressman*

Kelly
Knowles, William Standish *retired chemist*

Laramie
Mercer, Jennifer Lynn *research scientist*
Meyer, Edmond Gerald *retired chemistry professor, energy scientist, academic administrator*

TERRITORIES OF THE UNITED STATES

PUERTO RICO

Arecibo
Friedman, Jonathan S. *environmental scientist*

Humacao
Pinto, Nicholas Joaquim *physics professor*

Mayaguez
Lopez, Gustavo E. *chemistry professor*

Ponce
Quintana-Alsina, Myriam *chemistry professor*

San Juan
Gioda, Adriana *chemistry professor*
Kumar, Ashok *research scientist, educator*
Montes, Ingrid *chemistry professor*
Saavedra-Arias, José Javier *physics professor*

CANADA

ALBERTA

Calgary
Campbell, Finley Alexander *geologist, consultant*
Milone, Eugene Frank *astronomer, educator*

Devon
Ng, Siauw-Hoi *research scientist*

Edmonton
Kay, Cyril Max *biochemist, educator*
Rutter, Nathaniel Westlund *geologist, educator*

BRITISH COLUMBIA

Delta
Russell, Richard Doncaster *geophysics educator, academic administrator*

Sidney
van den Bergh, Sidney *astronomer*

Vancouver
Affleck, Ian Keith *physics educator*
Hardy, Walter Newbold *physics professor, researcher*
Wieman, Carl E. *physics professor*

Victoria
Batten, Alan Henry *astronomer*
Best, Melvyn Edward *geophysicist*
Hutchings, John Barrie *astronomer, researcher*
Israel, Werner *physicist, educator*
Morton, Donald Charles *astronomer*
Wiles, David McKeen *chemist*

West Vancouver
Wynne-Edwards, Hugh Robert *geologist, educator, entrepreneur*

MANITOBA

Winnipeg
Smith, Ian Cormack Palmer *biophysicist*

NEWFOUNDLAND AND LABRADOR

Saint John's
Gibbons, Rex Vincent *geologist*

NOVA SCOTIA

Halifax
Matta, Chérif Farid *chemistry professor*

Tatamagouche
Roach, Margot Ruth *retired biophysicist, educator*

Wallace
Boyle, Willard Sterling *physicist, researcher*

ONTARIO

Deep River
Milton, John Charles Douglas *nuclear physicist, researcher*

Guelph
Dickinson, William Trevor *hydrologist, educator*

Hamilton
Datars, William Ross *physicist, researcher*
Schwarcz, Henry Philip *geologist, educator*
Spenser, Ian Daniel *chemistry professor*
Williams, David R. (Dafydd Rhys Williams) *research scientist, medical educator, retired astronaut*

Kingston
Stewart, Alec Thompson *physicist, educator*
Szarek, Walter Anthony *chemist, educator*

London
Bancroft, George Michael *chemical physicist, educator*
Dreimanis, Aleksis *emeritus geology educator*
Fyfe, William Sefton *geochemist, educator*
Théberge, Jean *biophysicist*

Manotick
Hobson, George Donald *retired geophysicist*

Ottawa
Alper, Howard *chemistry professor*
Halliday, Ian *astronomer*
Harington, Charles Richard *vertebrate paleontologist*
Holmes, John Leonard *chemistry professor*
Ingold, Keith Usherwood *chemist, educator*
Kates, Morris *biochemist, educator*
Mantsch, Henry Horst *chemistry professor*
St-Onge, Denis Alderic *geologist, research scientist, educator*

Toronto
Armstrong, Robin Louis *physics professor, physicist*
Bohme, Diethard Kurt *chemistry professor*
Brook, Adrian Gibbs *chemistry professor*
Goring, David Arthur Ingham *chemist, educator*
Hofmann, Theo *biochemist, educator*
Litherland, Albert Edward *physics professor*
Polanyi, John Charles *chemist, educator*
Pritchard, Huw Owen *chemist, educator*
Rowe, David John *physics professor*
Shepherd, Gordon Greeley *space physics educator, researcher*

Windsor
Thibert, Roger Joseph *clinical chemist, educator*

QUEBEC

Kirkland
Baroudy, Bahige Mourad *biochemist, researcher*

Montreal
Barrette, Jean *physicist, researcher*
Eisenberg, Adi *chemist*
Leroy, Claude *physics professor, researcher*
Li, Chao-Jun *chemistry professor, researcher*
Perlin, Arthur Saul *chemistry professor*
Podgorsak, Ervin B. *medical physicist, educator, administrator*
Sourkes, Theodore Lionel *biochemistry professor*
Taras, Paul *physicist, researcher*
Whitehead, Michael Anthony *chemistry professor*

Pointe-Claire
Bachynski, Morrel Paul *physicist*
Kaminsky, Ben *chemist*

Sherbrooke
Tremblay, André-Marie *physicist*

SASKATCHEWAN

Regina
Semenov, Andrei Yurievich *research scientist*

Saskatoon
Kerrich, Robert *geologist, educator*

Cape Ray
Harnack, Robert P. *retired professor*

Sherbrooke
Deslongchamps, Pierre *chemistry professor*

MEXICO

Jiutepec
Patino-Gomez, Carlos *hydrologist*

Mexico City
Flores-Moreno, Roberto *research scientist*

AUSTRALIA

Balmain
Jakuba, Rachel Wisniewski *environmental scientist*

Canberra
Craig, David Parker *retired chemistry professor*
Fletcher, Neville Horner *physicist*
Taylor, Stuart Ross *geochemist, writer*

Melbourne
Collis, Gavin E. *chemist*

New South Wales
Mozer, Attila Janos *materials scientist, researcher*

Southport
Mayne, Alfred R. *research scientist*

Sydney
Hora, Heinrich *physicist*

AUSTRIA

Vienna
Cetto, Ana Maria *physicist, researcher*

BELARUS

Grodno
Hrakhouskaya, Tatsiana Cheslavovna *biochemist, researcher*

Minsk
Dailyudenko, Victor *physicist, researcher*

BELGIUM

Brussels
de Duve, Christian René *chemist, educator*
Houziaux, Léo Narcisse Omer *astronomer, educator*

Liège
Mosora-Stan, Florentina Ioana *physics professor*

Sambreville
Boskovic, Bojan O. *physicist, engineer*

BRAZIL

Sorocaba
Martins, Nelson *physics professor*

CHINA

Beijing
Li, Fang-hua *physicist*
Li, Xing Zhong *physics educator*
Tu, Chuanyi *space physics educator, researcher*
Yang, Chen Ning Franklin *physicist, educator*
Yang, Guangrong *physicist, researcher, educator*
Yu, Qingjuan *astrophysicist, educator*
Zhou, Bang Rong *physicist, researcher*

Hong Kong
Che, Chi-Ming *chemist, educator*

Nanjing
Wang, Xin *geologist, researcher*
Yu, Jurong *chemist*

Shanghai
Hu, Song *oceanographer, educator*
Zhu, Xinyuan *chemistry professor*

CZECH REPUBLIC

Brno
Gröger, Roman *research scientist*

Prague
Čejka, Jiří *retired chemist, researcher*
Kotrla, Miroslav *physicist*
Kozma, Peter *physicist*

DENMARK

Copenhagen
Bohr, Aage Niels *physicist, researcher*
Kinch, Kjartan Münster *physicist*
Mottelson, Ben Roy *physicist*
Pethick, Christopher John *physicist*

ENGLAND

Birmingham
Swadener, John Gregory *mechanical engineering lecturer*

Cambridge
Buckingham, Amyand David *chemistry professor*
Cottrell, Alan *materials scientist*
Edwards, Sir Samuel Frederick *physicist, researcher*
Hawking, Stephen William *astrophysicist, mathematician, educator*
Lynden-Bell, Donald *astronomer*

Exeter
Wyatt, Adrian Frederick *physicist, researcher*

Leeds
Slechta, Jiri *theoretical physicist*

London
Davis, Brian Keith *biophysicist, researcher*
Stelle, Kellogg Sheffield *physicist*
Wallace, Bonnie Ann *biochemist, biophysicist, educator*

Macclesfield
Lovell, Sir (Alfred Charles) Bernard *astronomer, educator*

Oxford
Bell Burnell, S(usan) Jocelyn *astrophysicist, physics professor*
Dewey, John Frederick *geologist, educator*
Hirsch, Sir Peter Bernhard *metallurgist*
Johnson, Louise Napier *molecular biophysicist, educator*

Roecliffe
Hilsum, Cyril *physicist*

Surrey
Naldrett, Anthony James *geology educator*

FRANCE

Besancon
Boillat, Guy Maurice Georges *mathematical physicist*

Chatenay-Malabry
Evesque, Pierre Henri *physics researcher*

Creteil
Renoux, André *retired physicist researcher*

Gif-sur-Yvette
Cesarsky, Catherine *astrophysicist*
Rho, Mannque *theoretical physicist, researcher*

Le Vesinet
Hillion, Pierre Théodore Marie *mathematical physicist*

Mulhouse
Donnet, Jean Baptiste *physical chemist, educator, consultant*

Orleans
Price, David Cecil Long *physicist, researcher*

Orsay
Friedel, Jacques *retired physics professor*

Palaiseau
Basdevant, Jean-Louis Henri *physicist, researcher*

Paris
Cohen-Tannoudji, Claude Nessim *physics professor*
Pecker, Jean-Claude *astronomer, educator, author*

Rocquencourt
Jacquet, Philippe Pierre *research scientist, educator*

Saint Maur des Fosses
Heggy, Essam *planetary scientist*

Strasbourg
Elkomoss, Sabry Gobran *retired physicist*

Villefranche-sur-Mer
Legendre, Louis *oceanographer, educator, research scientist*

Villeurbanne
Legendre, Serge *paleontologist, researcher*

GEORGIA

Covington
Zha, Shitong *research scientist*

GERMANY

Berlin
Eichler, Hans Joachim *physics professor*
Loboda-Cackovic, Jasna *physicist, artist, sculptor, painter, research scientist*

Frankfurt
Greiner, Walter Albin Erhard *physicist*

Garching bei Muenchen
Van Hemmen, J. Leo *physics professor, researcher*

Göttingen
Oellerich, Michael *clinical chemistry professor, chemical pathologist*
Roesky, Herbert Walter *chemistry professor*
Toennies, Jan Peter *research chemical physicist*

Hamburg
Schaper, Herbert Walter August *retired chemist, researcher*

Hannover
Allen, Bruce *physicist*

Jülich
Grünberg, Peter Andreas *materials scientist*

Mainz
Binder, Kurt *physics professor*

Saarbruecken
Zhukovsky, Mikhail Andreyevich *biophysicist*

Stutensee
Barbian, Otto Alfred *physicist*

Stuttgart
Cardona, Manuel *physics professor*
Zakim, David *biochemist*

Würzburg
Manara, Jochen Walter *physicist, researcher*

GREECE

Athens
Floratos, Emmanuel *physicist, educator*
Miliotis, Demitrios *physics professor*

Piraeus
Papachristou, Costas John *physicist, researcher*

HONG KONG

Kowloon
Woo, Chia-Wei *physicist, educator*

HUNGARY

Budapest
Meszaros, Milan *astrophysicist*
Pal, Lenard *physicist*
Pungor, Ernö *chemist, educator*
Szigeti, János *physicist*
Teplán, István, Sr. *biochemist, researcher*

Debrecen
Csikai, Gyula *physicist, researcher*

INDIA

Bangalore
Kulkarni, Rahul Ravindra *research scientist*
Rao, Ramachandra U. *aerospace scientist*

Hyderabad
Raychowdhury, Subhendu *research scientist*

Kanpur
Joglekar, Satish Dinkar *physicist, educator*

New Delhi
Kaushal, Radhey Shyam *theoretical physicist, researcher*
Mitra, Asoke Nath *retired physicist, educator*

Secunderabad
Velamakanni, Gopala Krishna *geophysicist, seismologist, researcher*

INDONESIA

Jakarta
Mulhadiono, Yoga Pratomo *petroleum geologist, consultant*

IRELAND

Dublin
Fottrell, Patrick *biochemistry professor, former university president*

ISRAEL

Haifa
Ciechanover, Aaron Judah *biochemist, educator*

Netanya
Tsitverblit, Naftali Anatol *physicist, fluid mechanics engineer, researcher*

Ra'anana
Hayon, Elie M. *chemist, educator*

Rehovot
Katchalski-Katzir, Ephraim *biophysicist, educator*

ITALY

Bologna
Giacomelli, Giorgio Maria *emeritus physics professor*
Venturi, Margherita *chemistry professor, researcher*

Civitanova Marche
Rogante, Massimo *nuclear scientist, researcher*

Como
Casati, Giulio *theoretical physics professor*

Genoa
Morchio, Renzo Giulio *retired biophysicist, researcher, educator*

Padua
Piccoli, Giuliano *paleontologist, educator*

Pavia
Rubbia, Carlo *physicist*

Pisa
Mannelli, Italo Marcello *physics professor*

Ravenna
Conti, Matteo Coker *biochemist, researcher*

Rome
Maraviglia, Bruno *physicist, researcher*
Salvini, Giorgio *physicist, researcher*

Siena
Tiezzi, Enzo *physical chemistry educator*

Turin
Challet, Damien Cyrille *physicist, researcher*

JAPAN

Agatsuma
Kozai, Yoshihide *astronomer*

Aichi
Okazaki, Masaharu *chemist*

Ashikaga
Ando, Yasutaka *materials scientist, researcher*

Bunkyo
Mori, Kenji *chemistry professor*

Chiba
Matsuda, Masafumi *research scientist, educator*

Gyoda
Shibasaki, Yoshio *chemistry professor, researcher*

Hokkaido
Iida, Yoichi *chemist, molecular biologist*

Hyogo
Sugiyama, Takeharu *physical chemist*

Kashiwa
Oguchi, Takashi *geoscientist, educator*

Kobe
Kingetsu, Toshiki *retired materials physicist, researcher*
Tanaka, Ichiro *fluid mechanics scientist, educator*

Kochi
Hojo, Masashi *chemistry professor*

Oita
Higashino, Makoto *environmental scientist*

Shinjuku
Tatsuta, Kuniaki *organic chemistry educator*

Tokyo
Esaki, Leo (Esaki Leona, Esaki Reiona) *physicist, foundation executive, university president*
Iida, Shuichi *physicist, educator*
Kamimura, Hiroshi *theoretical physicist*
Kasahara, Yasushi *chemist*
Koshiba, Masatoshi *physicist, educator*
Sakurada, Yutaka *retired chemist*
Suzuki, Akira *physics professor*

Tsukuba
Tanaka, Hiroshi L. *atmospheric scientist*

Utsunomiya
Yorikawa, Hiroharu *physicist, researcher*

Yokohama
Kato, Masaharu *materials scientist, educator*
Kida, Shinichiro *oceanographer*

KAZAKHSTAN

Almaty
Mansurov, Zulkhair Aimukhametovich *chemist*

KUWAIT

Safat
Jallad, Karim N. *chemistry professor*

MOLDOVA

Kishinev
Pyshkin, Sergei L. *physics professor, researcher*

NETHERLANDS

Utrecht
't Hooft, Gerardus (Gerard) *physicist, researcher*

NORWAY

Lillestrøm
Gjessing, Dag Trygveson *physicist*

Oslo
Gjønnes, Jon Kjell *physics professor*

Trondheim
Lavrov, Alexandre Vadimovich *research scientist*

PAKISTAN

Islamabad
Qureshi, Iqbal Hussain *nuclear chemist*

Lahore
Asif, Muhammad *physicist, researcher*

PERU

Lima
Woodman, Ronald F. *aerospace scientist*

POLAND

Bydgoszcz
Czajkowski, Gerard Zygfryd *physicist, researcher*

REPUBLIC OF KOREA

Asan
Kim, Heetae *physicist, researcher*

Busan
Jung, Daiil *chemistry professor*
Kim, Kwang Ho *materials scientist, educator*
Yun, Soo In *physics professor, researcher, academic administrator*

Chungju
Lee, Joo-Woon *chemistry professor*

Geoje
Kim, Moonkoo *marine environmental chemist*

Gwangju
Moon, Deok Hyun *research scientist, educator*

Gyeongsan
Kim, Young-Il *chemistry professor*
Sohn, Youngku *chemistry professor*

Jeongeup-si
Choi, Jae-Hak *research scientist, manager*

Kyeyang
Jung, Chang Hoon *environmental scientist, educator*

Seongnam
Choi, Sang Yoon *biomedical chemist, researcher*

Seoul
Choi, Kwang-Yong *physicist*
Choi, Minha *professor*
Chung, Kyung Yoon *materials scientist*
Hong, Soon-Tae *physicist, educator*
Jyoo, Yeong-Heum *physics professor, researcher*
Kim, Chul Sung *physicist, educator*
Kim, Jeong-Geun *research scientist*
Kim, Kwang Yul *research scientist*
Min, Sun-Joon *research scientist, educator*
Yi, Seung-Ho *physicist, educator*

Suwon
Kim, Hyung-ick *postdoctoral scholar*
Oh, Sangyoon *assistant professor*

Taegu
Seok, Jaewook *materials and polymer scientist*

Ulsan
Tai, Weon-Pil *materials scientist, researcher*

Yong
Han, Moon G. *research scientist*

Yongin
Kwak, Chan *research scientist*

ROMANIA

Bucharest
Nastase, Florin *physicist, research scientist*
Zamfir, Nicolae Victor *physicist, researcher*

RUSSIA

Archangelsk
Zhilina, Ludmila *research scientist*

Kazan
Yulmetyev, Renat Muzipovich *physicist, educator*

Moscow
Ginzburg, Vitaly Lazarevich *physicist*
Klyuev, Vladimir Vladimirovitch *control systems scientist*
Zolotov, Yury Alexandrovich *chemist*

Nizhniy Novgorod
Bityurin, Nikita *physicist, researcher*

Novosibirsk
Skrinsky, Alexander Nikolaevich *physicist, researcher*
Vasilyev, Vladislav Yurievich *chemist, researcher, engineer*

Saint Petersburg
Birshtein, Tatiana Maximovna *physicist, educator, researcher*

Yurga
Apasov, Alexander Mikhailovich *physicist, educator*

SAUDI ARABIA

Riyadh
Alharbi, Abeer Ali *physics professor*

SERBIA

Belgrade
Mitrasinovic, Petar M. *chemistry professor, engineer, research scientist*

Pancevo
Trivic, Dusan Nikola *retired research scientist*

SINGAPORE

Singapore
Lau, John Hon Shing *electronics scientist*

SPAIN

Barcelona
Badell, Mariana *research scientist, consultant*

SWEDEN

Gothenburg
Svensson, Robert Charles Wilhelm *physicist, researcher*

Kiruna
Hultqvist, Bengt Karl Gustaf *physicist, educator*

Stockholm
Farahbakhshazad, Neda *research scientist*
Hallberg, Rolf Oskar *biogeochemist*

Uppsala
Laurent, Torvard Claude *biochemist, educator*
Scheicher, Ralph Hendrik *research scientist*

Örebro
Persliden, Jan R. G. *physicist*

SWITZERLAND

Bottmingen
Burger, Max Marcel *biochemist*

Geneva
Steinberger, Jack *physicist, researcher*

Yverdon-les-Bains
Egolf, Peter William *physicist*

Zurich
Dunitz, Jack David *retired chemistry educator, researcher*
Eschenmoser, Albert *chemist*
Müller, Karl Alexander (K. Alex Mueller) *physicist, researcher*
Seebach, Dieter *chemistry professor*

TAIWAN

Nankang
Shiue, Yunn-Shin Jessie *materials scientist, researcher*

Taipei
Wang, Pei-Ling *geochemist*

Yilan County
Yu, Yuan Hsiang *chemist, electronics engineer, educator*

UKRAINE

Dnipropetrovsk
Bolshakov, Vladimir Ivanovich *metallurgist, educator*

WALES

Cardiff
Jiles, David Collingwood *physicist, materials science educator*

ADDRESS UNPUBLISHED

Abella, Isaac David *physicist, researcher*
Ackermann, Bradley Lynn *research scientist*
Adsumilli, Chowdary B. *research scientist*
Afraz, Arash Seyed-Reza *research scientist*
Agapito, Luis Alberto *research scientist*
Agashe, Janhavi *research scientist*
Ahmadzadeh, Hossein *chemistry professor*
Akasheh, Osama Z. *geophysicist*
Akasofu, Syun-Ichi *geophysicist, educator*
Akbani, Rehan *research scientist*
Alessi, David Alan *research scientist*
Ames, Donald Paul *retired air research director*
An, Songon *research scientist*
Anaya, Henry Daniel *research scientist, consultant*
Anbar, Michael *biophysics professor*
Ancker-Johnson, Betsy *physicist, engineer, retired automotive executive*
Andersen, Dan Edward *physicist, entrepreneur*
Andersen, Roy Stuart *physicist*
Anglim, Paul *biochemist*
Anisimov, Victor *chemist, researcher*
Arunajatesan, Srinivasan *research scientist*
Atlas, David *meteorologist, research scientist*
Atwood, Genevieve *geologist*
Aurongzeb, Deeder *research scientist*
Avila, Charlie A. (Carlos A. Avila) *physics researcher, inventor*
Bae, Soo Hyun *research scientist*
Bahukutumbi, Radha *research scientist, educator*
Bai, He *research scientist*
Baker, D. James *oceanographer, administrator, science and management consultant*
Balázsi, Gábor *biophysicist, researcher*
Baldwin, George Curriden *physicist, researcher*
Bandyopadhyay, Aparajita *research scientist*
Bareither, Christopher *research scientist*
Barr, John Baldwin *chemist, research scientist*
Basescu, Neil *physics professor*
Bassford, Lynn Foster *physicist, engineer manager*
Basu, Sandip *research scientist*
Batteen, Mary Louise *oceanographer*
Bauer, Henry Hermann *chemistry and science educator*
Behrendt, John Charles *geophysicist, researcher, writer*
Benjamin, Arlin James *physicist*
Bennett, Charles Leonard *astrophysicist, educator*
Benson, Allen B. *chemist, educator, consultant*
Benzahra, Sidi Cherkawi *physics professor*
Berlin, Kenneth Darrell *chemistry professor, consultant, researcher*
Beuning, Penny J. *chemistry professor*
Biederman, Edwin Williams, Jr. *retired geologist*
Bikales, Norbert M. *chemist, science administrator*
Birnbaum, Milton *laser physicist, educator, researcher*
Bishop-Haynes, Aisha Suzette *materials scientist*
Bloomquist, Rodney Gordon *geologist*
Boral, Sougato *chemist, researcher*
Boschmann, Erwin *chemistry professor*
Boyer, Herbert Wayne *retired biochemist, biotechnology company executive*
Bradbeer, Clive *biochemistry educator*
Bratko, Dusan *chemistry professor, researcher*
Brennen, Reid Alyn *research scientist*
Bretthauer, Erich Walter *chemist, educator*
Brodsky, Marc Herbert *physicist, research and publishing executive*
Brown, Eric M. *research scientist*
Browne, John Charles *physicist, researcher, lab administrator*
Brunelle, Daniel J. *retired chemist*
Bucknum, Michael John *chemist, crystallographer, educator*
Budd, Ann F. *geologist, educator*
Bunyan, Ellen Lackey Spotz *retired chemist*
Bush, Brett Charles *oceanographer*
Butler, James Newton *retired chemist, educator*
Butler, Orton Carmichael *retired climatologist, educator*
Cadambe, Viveck R. *research scientist*
Cai, Chaozhong *chemist*
Cai, Ming Zhi *chemist, researcher, film producer*
Calavia, Jose Emilio *physics professor*
Calcagni, Gianluca *physicist*
Califano, Filomena *chemistry professor*
Calvert, Jack George *atmospheric chemist, educator*
Campbell, Mary Stinecipher *retired chemist*
Cannon, Steven M. *chemist*
Cao, Xinde *chemist*
Capasso, Federico *physicist*
Capiro, Natalie *research scientist*
Cardoza, David *aerospace scientist*
Caren, Robert Poston *aerospace scientist*
Carini, Gabriella *research scientist*
Carlson, Lynn Redding *astrophysicist*
Carter, Mel Keith *chemist*
Casella, Russell Carl *physicist*
Cassel, Robert Uriah *chemist*
Cathou, Renata Egone *chemist, consultant*
Cha, Byung Ho *research scientist*
Chagarov, Evgueni A. *physicist*
Chakraborty, Arpan *research scientist*
Chan, Tsz Ping *research scientist*
Chang, Byoung-Yong *chemist*
Chang, Clarence Dayton *retired chemist*
Chang, Herng-Hua *research scientist*
Chang, Ren Fang *retired physicist, researcher*
Changchun, Liu *research scientist*
Chauhan, Parth Randhir *paleontologist*
Chen, Wei *chemist, researcher, materials scientist, polymer engineer*
Chen, Yijian *research scientist*
Chibani, Omar *physicist*
Chiu, Bella Chao *astrophysicist, writer*
Chizhikov, Viktor Viktorovich *research scientist*
Choi, Eunmi *research scientist*
Choi, Stephen Sukjun *physicist*
Choi, Yoonsu *research scientist*
Chong, Andy Chinyu *research scientist*
Christensen, Lindsey *research scientist*
Christoffersen, Ralph Earl *chemist, researcher, director*
Christou, Carol Thomas *physicist, educator*
Chu, Benjamin Thomas Peng-Nien *chemistry professor*
Church, Eugene Lent *physicist, consultant*
Ciesla, Fred John *astrophysicist, meteoriticist, researcher*
Clark, Sandra Helen Becker *geologist*
Clarke, Amy J. *metallurgist*
Clarke, Kester D. *metallurgist*
Cleveland, David Michael *geologist*
Clinton, Thomas William *physicist, researcher*
Coffey, Timothy *physicist*
Coker, Ayodeji *research scientist*
Colbern, Steven Garrett *chemist, researcher*
Coletta, Nancy Joy *vision scientist, educator*
Colón Robles, Marilé *research scientist*
Colton, John P. *nuclear scientist, engineering executive*
Compton, W. Dale *physicist, researcher, engineer*
Conrath, Barney Jay *astrophysicist*
Coohill, Thomas Patrick *biophysicist, photobiologist*
Cooper, Austin Morris *chemist, engineer, researcher, consultant*
Cornish, Katrina *research scientist*
Cottam, Gene Larry *retired biochemistry educator*
Cox, Robert Hames *chemist, consultant*
Cui, Ying *research scientist*
Curott, David Richard *retired physics professor*
Curto, Paul Allen *retired research scientist*
Cusanovich, Michael Anthony *biochemist*
Dai, Shengyang *research scientist*
Damas, Marie Chantale *physicist, academic administrator*
Daniels, James Maurice *retired physicist*
Daniels, William Burton *retired physicist, educator*
Darling, Jeremy *astrophysicist, educator*
Das, Koel *research scientist*
Davids, Robert Norman *retired petroleum exploration geologist*
Davoudi, Ali *research scientist*
Day, Richard Allen *retired chemistry professor*
Dehmelt, Hans Georg *retired physicist*
de Jager, Cornelis *retired astronomer*
de Keczer, Steve A. *research scientist*
Deo, Chaitanya Suresh *materials scientist, researcher*
Dickens, Justin Kirk *nuclear physicist*
Dierolf, Volkmar *physics professor*
Dietrich, Klaus *physicist, retired professor*
Diggavi, Suhas *research scientist*
Dixon, Gordon Henry *biochemist, educator*
Dogan, Gokhan *research scientist*
Donaldson, Eva G. *chemist, writer*
Dong, Wei *research scientist*
Drahos, Sandra P. *retired chemist*
Drennan, Catherine Luschinsky *chemistry professor*
Du, Jianxin *research scientist*
Dunn, Arnold Samuel *biochemistry educator*
Dunn, Bruce Sidney *materials scientist, educator*
Dunn, Kimberly Dawn *chemist, research scientist*
Dupureur, Cynthia *chemistry professor*
Eastland, Grant *physicist*
Eck, Robert Edwin *retired physicist*
Eckelmann, Frank Donald *retired geology educator, dean*
Eichler, Duane Curtis *biochemist, educator*
Einhorn, Martin B. *physicist, educator*
Ekpenyong, Boniface Esong *physics professor*
Emery, Alan Roy *scientist, museum administrator, business executive*
Englert, Brian Carl *environmental scientist*
Engvold, Oddbjørn *astrophysics educator*
Ensminger, Luther Glenn *retired chemist*
Erdas, Andrea *physics professor*
erick, William Joseph *hydrologist*
Erickson, Mitchell Drake *chemist, environmental scientist*
Esquivel, Agerico Liwag *retired research physicist*
Estrada, Arnoldo Delfino *research scientist, consultant*
Evmenenko, Guennadi Alexandrovich *physicist*
Ewen, H. I. *physicist*
Fabiano, Nicola *physicist, researcher*
Fajardo-Acosta, Sergio *astronomer*
Fang, Haw-ren *research scientist*
Farmer, Crofton Bernard *atmospheric physicist*
Fathallah, Hassana *research scientist*
Fayngold, Moses *physics professor, researcher*
Fetter Filho, Antonio Fernando Härter *research scientist*
Fey, Willard *global environmental researcher, educator*
Finlayson, John Sylvester *retired biochemist*
Finzel, Barry Craig *research scientist*
Fleury, Paul Aimé *physicist*
Flinn, Paul Anthony *materials scientist*
Flory, Curt Alan *research physicist*
Fogleman, Guy Carroll *physicist, mathematician, educator*
Fons, Eric Wallace *physics professor*
Ford, Kenneth William *physicist*
Forlines, Clifton *research scientist*
Forster, Robert Arthur III *retired research scientist*
Fowler, Alan Bicksler *retired physicist*
Fradkin, David Milton *physicist, researcher*
Franz, John E. *bio-organic chemist, researcher*
Franz, Judy R. *physics professor*
French, Julia McAllister (Judy) *environmental consultant*
Frenkel, Alexander L. *applied mathematics professor*
Friedlander, Charles Douglas (Chuck Friedlander) *aerospace scientist, consultant*
Friedrich, Jon M. *chemistry professor*
Fu, Engang *research scientist*
Fuchs, Alan *chemistry professor*
Fukuda, Atsuo *physicist, materials science researcher, educator*
Funakoshi, Yuji *meteorologist*
Gaffin, David Morris *meteorologist, researcher*
Gai, Neville *research scientist*
Galli, John Ronald *physicist, educator*
Gao, Zhiming *research scientist*
Garcia Tormo, Xavier *physicist*
Gardner, Wilford Robert *physicist, researcher*
Garrison, Robert Frederick *astronomer, educator*
Garwin, Richard Lawrence *physicist*
Gashi, Qendrim *research scientist, mathematics professor*
Gelboin, Harry Victor *biochemistry educator, researcher*
Georg, Manfred *research scientist*
Getty, Amorette Rose Klug *research scientist*
Ghanem, Eman *biochemist*
Ghosal, Anima *research scientist*
Gimzewski, James K. *chemistry professor*
Gladysheva, Inna *biochemist, researcher*
Glashow, Sheldon Lee *physicist, researcher*
Glesk, Ivan *physicist, educator, researcher*
Godwin, Hilary A. *chemistry professor, research scientist*
Goelz, Susan *biochemist, director*
Goericke, Fabian Thomas *research scientist*
Golden, David Edward *physicist*
Goldstein, Irving Solomon *chemistry professor, consultant*
Goodland, Robert J. A. *environmental scientist*
Goodman, Charles David *physicist, researcher*
Gorbaty, Martin Leo *chemist, researcher*
Gordon, William Edwin *physicist, electrical engineer, academic administrator, educator*
Gorelik, Gennady *research scientist, writer*
Govindjee, *biophysics, biochemistry, and biology professor*
Grady, Lee Timothy *pharmaceutical chemist*
Grandy, Walter Thomas, Jr. *physicist, researcher*
Grechka, Vladimir *geophysicist*
Greene, Geoffrey Lloyd *physicist*
Grella, Luca *physicist*
Griffin, Michael Douglas *aerospace scientist, former federal agency administrator*
Guan, Yabo *research scientist*
Gudlavalleti, Seshu Kumar *research scientist*
Guo, Fulai *astrophysicist*
Guo, Yang *research scientist*
Guo, Zhichang *environmental scientist*
Guoqiang, Shu *research scientist*
Gurram, Prudhvi Krishna *research scientist*
Gurudas, Ullas *retired research scientist*
Haisch, Bernard Michael *astronomer, researcher*
Hakkila, Eero Arnold *retired nuclear safeguards technology chemist*
Hakobyan, Yeranuhi *research scientist*
Halpern, Alvin Michael *retired physicist, educator, consultant*
Hammoud, Riad *research scientist*
Harari, Haim *physicist, researcher*
Hardy, Ralph W. F. *biochemist*
Harmer, Mark A. *research scientist*
Harris, Cyril Manton *physicist, acoustical engineer, architect, educator*
Hartnett, David *physics professor, researcher*

Harwit, Martin Otto *astrophysicist, writer, educator, museum director*
Hasan, Mahbub *research scientist*
Haslett, Jared Wooddell *physicist, educator*
Hawkins, Charles Travis *retired physics professor*
He, Zhiguo *research scientist*
Heeschen, David Sutphin *astronomer, educator*
Helber, Robert William *oceanographer*
Helfand, Eugene *chemist*
Heller, Adam *chemist, researcher*
Hermann, Robert Bell *physical chemist, consultant*
Herndon, James Marvin *nuclear scientist, consultant*
Hernick, Linda VanAller *paleontologist, researcher*
Hildrum, Kirsten *research scientist*
Hinkley, Everett David, Jr. *physicist*
Hirokawa, Shoji *retired chemistry professor*
Ho, Chih-Ming *physicist, researcher*
Hodge, Ian Moir *physical chemist*
Hoefler, Torsten *research scientist*
Hoeg, Donald Francis *chemist, consultant, research and development company executive*
Holmes, Richard Brooks *mathematical physicist*
Horton, Robert Carlton *geologist*
Hou, Jianhui *chemist*
Hou, Tingjun *research scientist*
Howard, James E. *physicist, researcher*
Howard, Robert Franklin *observatory administrator, astronomer*
Hoy, Gilbert R. *retired physics educator*
Hratchian, Hrant Patrick *research scientist*
Hsieh, I-Wei *research scientist*
Huajiang, Huang *research scientist*
Hubbard, Gregory Scott *physicist*
Hudlicka, Eva *research scientist*
Huffman, John William *chemist, educator*
Hulet, Ervin Kenneth *retired nuclear chemist*
Hulse, Russell Alan *physicist*
Hunsucker, Robert Dudley *physicist, electrical engineer, educator, researcher*
Hunter, James Edward *chemist, consultant*
Huo, Jinshan *materials scientist*
Huynh, My Hang Vo *energetic materials chemist*
Hwang, Cordelia Jong *retired chemist*
Hwang, Jungseek *physics professor, researcher*
Hwang, Myun Joong *research scientist*
Idilbi, Ahmad *physicist, researcher*
Inlow, Rush Osborne *chemist*
Ivey, Elizabeth Spencer *retired physicist, educator*
Jackson, Kenneth Arthur *physicist, researcher*
Jacobson, Dale *physicist, electronics executive*
Jakubowski, Marek Krzysztof *research scientist*
Jan, Yuh Nung *biochemistry and physiology educator*
Jang, Young-Il *research and development scientist*
Jaworski, Justin W. *research scientist*
Jayaraman, Balaji *research scientist*
Jeck, Richard Kahr *research meteorologist*
Jensen, Arthur Seigfried *retired physicist*
Jiang, Bai-Chuan *optical educator*
Jin, Di *research scientist*
Johnson, Arthur William, Jr. *retired research scientist*
Johnson, Charles Minor *retired physicist*
Jordan, Nikisa S. *environmental scientist*
Jordan, Robert Reed *retired geologist, educator*
Joselyn, Jo Ann *space scientist*
Kahn, Steven Michael *astrophysicist, educator*
Kang, Kyongha *materials scientist*
Karhade, Omkar *research scientist*
Karle, Isabella L. *chemist*
Karle, Jerome *physicist, researcher*
Karoui, Abdennaceur *physics professor*
Keffer, Charles Joseph *retired physics professor, academic administrator*
Kekatpure, Rohan D. *research scientist*
Khan, Abu M. *physics professor*
Kim, Chwail *research scientist*
Kim, Do Nyeon *research scientist*
Kim, Ryoung-han *research scientist*
Kinnison, Willard Wayne *physics professor*
Kirtman, Bernard *chemistry professor*
Kistiakowsky, Vera *physical researcher, educator*
Klett, James Dean *physicist, consultant, small business owner*
Klute, Allan Aloys *retired physicist, retired economist*
Knowles, Richard Norris *chemist*
Kocherginsky, Nikolai M. *chemistry educator*
Kong, Soon-Cheol *research scientist*
Kopytine, Mikhail L. *physicist*
Korn, Jessica Susan *research scientist, educator, program manager*
Korotkova, Olga *physics professor*
Kosik, Daniel W. *physics professor*
Kounavis, Michael E. *research scientist*
Kraimer, Rebecca *environmental scientist*
Krause, Sonja *chemistry professor*
Kravitz, Rubin *chemist*
Krawetz, Stephen Andrew *molecular medicine and genetics scientist, educator*
Kribel, Robert Edward *consultant, retired physicist, academic administrator*
Krueger, Arlin James *physicist*
Krug, Edward Charles *environmental scientist*
Kuhlmann-Wilsdorf, Doris *materials scientist, inventor, retired educator*
Kulander, Byron Rodney *geologist, educator*
Kustin, Kenneth *chemist*
Kutasov, Israel Mayer *petroleum engineering and geothermics researcher, consultant*
Kuznetsova, Lyubov P. *research scientist*
Laing, Malcolm Brian *geologist, consultant*
Lande, Alexander *physicist, researcher*
Langford, Roland Everett *safety engineer, writer*
Langridge, Robert *biophysicist, educator, computational biologist*
Lanzerotti, Mary Yvonne *physicist, editor*
Laporte, Leo Frederic *geologist, educator, paleontologist*
Latchford, Wayne Harry *physics professor*
Laursen, Krista *aerospace scientist, director*
Law, Kevin *meteorologist, educator*
Law, Phillip Garth *scientist, Antarctic explorer, educationaist*
LeBlond, Paul Henri *oceanographer, educator*
Leclerc, Monique Marie Yvonne *meteorologist, educator*
Ledbetter, Hassel *research scientist, educator*
Lederman, Leon Max *physicist, researcher*
Lee, Jae-Seung *physicist, researcher*
Lee, Richard William *physicist, researcher*
Leibowitz, Jack Richard *physicist, educator*
Lessie, Douglas Louis *physics educator*
Levesque, George *research scientist*
Li, Eugene S. *physics professor*
Li, Linghong *physics professor*
Li, Xiong *geophysicist*
Li, Youzhi *research scientist*
Liang, Qing *research scientist*
Lim, Hee Chuan *physics professor, researcher*
Lin, Chengxian *research scientist*
Lin, Henry *research scientist*
Lin, Ray-Qing *physicist, researcher*
Lingren, Wesley Earl *chemistry educator*
Link, Steven Otto *environmental scientist, statistician*
Lipschutz, Michael Elazar *chemistry professor, consultant, researcher*
Liu, Huimin *physicist, educator*
Liu, Weiping *metallurgist*
Lo, Shui-yin *physicist*
Lock, Evgeniya Hristova *research scientist*
Loeser, Eric *chemist*
Logan, Joseph E. *research scientist*
Long, Harry (On-Yuen Eng) *chemist, science and technology executive, consultant*
Los, Marinus *retired agrochemical researcher*
Louie, Steven Gwon Sheng *physics professor, researcher*
Low, Philip Stewart *chemistry professor, biotechnology company executive*
Lu, Ning H. *research scientist*
Lucas, William Ray *aerospace scientist, consultant*
Luhrs, Claudia C. *materials scientist, educator*
Lukacs, Michael Edward *electro-optics researcher*
Luke, Karen *chemist, researcher*
Lussier, Alexandre *research scientist*
MacCracken, Michael Calvin *atmospheric scientist*
Maddin, Robert *metallurgist, educator*
Mahmoodian, Roza *research scientist*
Makriyannis, Alexandros *medicinal chemist, educator*
Maling, George Croswell, Jr. *physicist*
Malins, Donald Clive *biochemist, researcher*
Mansur, Louis K. *materials scientist, nuclear engineer*
Mantz, Arlan W. *physics professor*
Mao, Yuan *research scientist, educator*
Marcuse, Dietrich *retired physicist*
Mardi, Shalva Josef *research scientist*
Marineau, Eric Christian *research scientist*
Marinetti, Guido V. *biochemistry professor*
Markhotok, Anna *physics professor*
Marklin, George *physicist*
Marshall, Thomas Carlisle *retired applied physics professor*
Martin, John Carl *astronomer, educator*
Martinez-Munoz, Gloria Angelica *biochemist, researcher*
Mashnik, Stepan G. *physicist*
Masoner, Jason R. *hydrologist*
Mayo, Dana Walker *chemistry professor*
McAlexander, Melissa *chemistry professor, researcher*
McCormick, Donald Bruce *retired biochemist, educator*
McDowell, Wilbur Benedict *retired chemist consultant*
McEwen, Megan *research scientist*
McGuigan, Michael DeTurck *research scientist*
McKay, Kenneth Gardiner *retired physicist, electronics company executive*
McTague, John Paul *materials scientist, educator, chemist, researcher*
Meding, Stephen Mercer *research scientist*
Meinwald, Jerrold *retired chemistry professor*
Meisel, David Dering *retired astronomer*
Melvin, Peter Joseph *astrophysicist, educator*
Merwade, Venkatesh M. *hydrologist*
Meshejian, Wayne Kit *retired physics professor*
Mewshaw, Richard Eric *chemist*
Meyers, Robert Allen *chemist, publisher*
Michaud, Georges Joseph *physics professor*
Mihaly, Laszlo *physics professor*
Miller, John Lester *electro-optical physicist*
Miriam, Frazure Amanda *research scientist*
Mishin, Evgeny Vilenovich *physicist*
Mislow, Kurt Martin *chemist, educator*
Mitra, Abhijit *chemistry professor*
Mollenauer, Linn Frederick *retired physicist, writer*
Moncrieff, Mitchell William *atmosphere physicist researcher*
Monroe, Frederick Fales *geologist, oceanographer*
Moore, Ronald Lee *physicist*
Moreau, Nancy A. *physics professor*
Morelli, James Kevin *biochemist*
Mueller, Berndt *physics professor*
Mullis, Kary Banks *biochemist*
Munson, Ronald Alfred *retired chemist*
Murdock, John Gustaf *physics professor*
Musick, Katherine M. *research scientist*
Muthukrishnan, Swarna *research scientist*
Myers, Mark D. *geologist, former federal official*
Nadeau, Robert M. *geophysicist*
Natarajan, Sriraam *research scientist*
Nelson, Kay LeRoi *chemist, educator*
Nemec, Josef *retired organic chemist, researcher*
Neophytou, Neophytos *research scientist*
Ness, Norman Frederick *retired astrophysicist, educator, administrator*
Nevill, William Albert *chemistry professor*
Newkirk, John Burt *retired metallurgical research administrator*
Newton, Roger Gerhard *educator, physicist*
Ng, Tse Nga *research scientist*
Nirenberg, Marshall Warren *biochemist*
Nobles, Laurence Hewit *retired geology educator*
Oesterlin, Lovye Gwendolyn *retired chemist, educator, retired educational consultant*
Ogliaruso, Michael Anthony *retired chemist, educator, actor*
Ojwang, J.G.O. *research scientist*
Onton, Ann Louise Reuther *chemist*
Ooguri, Hirosi *physics professor*
Oort, Abraham Hans *meteorologist, researcher, educator*
Orbach, Raymond Lee *physicist, researcher, former federal agency administrator*
Oshchapovsky, Valentin Vladimirovich *chemist, ecologist*
O'Shea, Donald C. *physicist, educator, optical engineer*
Osterkamp, T. E. *retired physics professor*
Ostroverkhova, Oksana *physicist*
Owens, Phillip Clyde *biochemist, educator*
Page, Kelly Andrew *physics professor*
Palii, Sergiu Petru *chemist, researcher*
Pan, Liang Ru *physicist, researcher*
Pandey, Deepak K. *physicist*
Pando Zayas, Leopoldo A. *physicist*
Pannuti, Thomas Gregory *aerospace scientist, educator*
Parida, Laxmi *research scientist, educator*
Park, Daniel Sang-Won *research scientist*
Patchett, Arthur Allan *medicinal chemist, retired pharmaceutical executive*
Pathak, Siddhartha *materials scientist*
Paul, Bipul C. *senior research scientist*
Pavan, Turaga *research scientist*
Pavani, Sri Rama Prasanna *research scientist*
Pavlovska, Anastassia *physicist, researcher*
Pedersen, Thomas Sunn *physics professor*
Peebles, Lynda *chemistry professor*
Peetz, Ralf M. *chemistry professor*
Pellett, David *physics professor*
Pendyala, Ramarao *chemist, educator*
Pereira, Wellesley *research scientist*
Periaswamy, Padmini *materials scientist, researcher*
Perlman, Barry Arnold *astronomy educator*
Peterson, David Lynn *research scientist*
Phelps, Michael Edward *biophysics professor*
Phillips, Julia Mae *physicist*
Piprek, Joachim *solid state physicist*
Pirkle, Earl Charnell *retired geologist*
Pitici, Felicia *biophysicist*
Policastro, Felice *research scientist*
Pollack, Gerald Leslie *physicist, researcher, educator*
Prather, Kimberly Ann *chemistry professor*
Prawoto, Yunan *materials scientist*
Pristoop, Simon Morris *retired physicist, systems engineer, consultant*
Proctor, Richard James *geologist, consultant*
Proenza, Bill (Xavier William Proenza) *meteorologist, former federal agency administrator*
Puthoff, Harold E. *physics researcher*
Pytlewski, Laura Jean *chemistry professor*
Pytlinski, Jerzy Teodor *physicist, educator, research scientist*
Pytte, Agnar *physicist, retired academic administrator*
Qi, Li *research scientist*
Qi, Zhenyu *research scientist*
Qu, Dongxia *physicist, researcher*
Qu, Wei *research scientist*
Quitoriano, Nathaniel J. *research scientist*
Qutub, Musa Yacub *hydrogeologist, educator, consultant*
Rabinowitz, David Lincoln *research scientist*
Ragent, Boris *physicist*
Raleigh, Cecil Baring *geophysicist*
Raman, Baranidharan *research scientist*
Ravi, Sujith *environmental scientist*
Rawool-Sullivan, Mohini *research scientist*
Ray, Priyadip *research scientist*
Read, Virginia Hall *retired biochemistry professor*
Reciniello, Richard *physicist*
Reeder, Stacy Lynn *geologist*
Reucroft, Philip J. *retired materials science professor*
Rexroat, Larry P *environmental scientist*
Reynik, Robert John *retired materials scientist, science educator*
Rice, Alan R. *geophysicist*
Rice, Stuart Alan *chemist, educator*
Richardson, Charles Clifton *biochemist, educator*
Riley, Monica *microbiologist, educator*
Rinebold, Alice June *environmental scientist*
Roberts, Thomas George *retired physicist*
Robertson, John Archibald Law *nuclear scientist*
Robertson, Robert Graham Hamish *physicist*
Rodin, Eugene *aerospace scientist, researcher, engineering educator*
Rohr, Davis Charles *aerospace consultant, retired military officer*
Rohrer, Heinrich *physicist*
Roman, Nancy Grace *astronomer, consultant*
Romanowski, Thomas Andrew *physicist, educator*
Rosenberg, Eli Ira *physicist, educator*
Rosenkilde, Carl Edward *retired physicist*
Rosenthal, Joel *chemist, researcher*
Rosso, Kevin Michael *geochemist, director*
Roth, Jeffrey *geophysicist*
Roy, Biswadev *environmental scientist*
Rozenberg, Valeria *chemist, researcher*
Rybczyk, Joseph Anthony *physicist, researcher, writer, inventor*
Ryckman, Eric Michael *research scientist, educator*
Sabb, Annmarie Louise *retired chemist*
Sablik, Martin John *research physicist*
Saha, Abhijit *astronomer*
Sahai, Tuhin *research scientist*
Sahoo, Bishwabhusan *chemist*
Saini, Viney *research scientist*
Salamone, Joseph Charles *polymer chemistry professor*
Salisbury, John *chemist, researcher*
Salminen, Seppo Ossian *plant biochemist*
Sas, Robert Joseph, Jr. *geologist, researcher*
Schatz, Gottfried *biochemistry educator*
Schellman, John A. *chemistry professor*
Schmidt, Parbury P., Jr. *chemist*
Schneider, Carl Stanley *retired physics professor, researcher*
Schneider, William George *chemist, research consultant*
Schnitzer, Howard Joel *physics professor, researcher*
Schock, Robert Norman *geophysicist*
Schonhorn, Harold *chemist, researcher*
Schutz, Donald Frank *geochemist, environmental corporate executive*
Schwartz, Shirley E. *retired chemist, researcher*
Schwarz, Udo Dietmar *physicist, researcher*
Scully, Marlan Orvil *physics professor*
Seelam, Seetharami *research scientist*
Segal, Vladimir M. *retired metallurgist, researcher*
Semancik, Stephen *physicist*
Sendlinger, Shawn Crowley *chemistry professor, department chairman*
Sengupta, Abhijit *molecular and optical physicist*
Seow, Steven C. *research scientist*
Sha, William T. *senior nuclear scientist, consultant*
Shabani, Javad *research scientist*
Shackelford, Scott Addison *air force officer, retired, civilian research chemist*
Shaevitz, Joshua William *physics professor*
Shakoor, Abdul *geologist, educator*
Shan, Xi *research scientist*
Shane, Jeffrey *physics professor*
Shapoury, Alireza *research scientist*
Sharma, Brahama D. *chemistry professor*
Sharman, Robert D. *meteorologist, researcher*
Sheng, Jinhua *research scientist*
Shenoy, Sachindev Shantaram *astronomer*
Shi, Dexiu *laser and optics scientist*
Shi, Tianchen *research scientist*
Shin, Jae Cheol *research scientist*
Shin, Jaewon *research scientist*
Sidereas, Panagiotis *physicist*
Sil, Samik *geophysicist*
Silver, Lynn Leslie *research scientist, consultant*
Simpson, Joanne Malkus *meteorologist*
Simpson, Robert Homer *meteorologist, consultant*
Singleton, David Michael *chemist, researcher*
Skiff, Frederick Norman *physics educator, researcher*
Slaugh, Lynn H. *retired chemist*
Slichter, Charles Pence *physicist, researcher*
Smith, Carl Brent *retired chemist*
Smith, Charles Haddon *geologist, consultant, retired federal agency administrator*
Smith II, Leon M. *chemist*
Solomon, Susan *atmospheric chemist*
Somerville, Christopher Roland *biochemist, educator*
Souler, Benjamin Kerwin *retired research chemist, pharmacist, consultant*
Sourirajan, Karthik *research scientist*
Spangenberg, Norman Earl *retired hydrologist educator*
Spence, Joseph Thomas *biochemist*
Spong, Donald A. *physicist*
Squibb, Samuel Dexter *chemistry professor*
Srinivasan, Rangaswamy *chemical physicist*
Srivastava, Vinod K. *research scientist, educator*
Stankovich, Alla (Tsykalo) *research scientist*
Stanley, Paul *physics professor*
Stanley, Steven Mitchell *paleontologist, educator*
Steffen, Jason H. *astrophysicist*
Steinhoff, Raymond O(akley) *consulting geologist*
Stern, Robin Lauri *medical physicist*
Stetson, Robert Francis *retired metallurgist*
Stever, Horton Guyford *aerospace scientist, engineer, educator, consultant*
Stief, Louis John *chemist*
Stock, Carl William *geology educator*
Stockbauer, Roger Lewis *retired physicist, researcher*
Stringer, John *retired materials scientist*
Stroud, Robert Michael *biophysicist, educator, biotechnologist*
Strouth, Baron Howard Steven *geologist, mining engineer*
Strunz, Kai *research scientist, educator*
Stubbs, Gerald *biochemist, educator*
Sullivan, Kathryn D. *geologist, former astronaut, science association executive*
Sun, Lipeng *chemist*
Sunderman, Duane Neuman *chemist, research and development company executive*
Sutin, Norman *senior chemist emeritus, researcher*
Suttie, John Weston *biochemist*
Tai, Tsze Cheng *aerodynamicist, researcher*
Tam, Sunny Wing Yee *physicist*
Tambour, Sophie *research scientist*
Tang, Shensheng *research scientist*
Tangherlini, Frank Robert *physics educator*
Tao, Jianning *research scientist*
Tarazaga, Pablo Alberto *research scientist*
Tauc, Jan *retired physics professor*
Tay, Savas *physicist, researcher*
Tedford, Charles Franklin *biophysicist*
Tewari, Shubha *physics professor*
Thaller, Michelle Lynn *astronomer*
Thomas, John Howard *astrophysicist, mechanical engineer, educator*
Thornton, Rita Louise *environmental scientist, lawyer*
Tijardovic, Ivica *research scientist*
Tillman, Celestine *chemistry professor*
Timmins, George Emerson *physics professor*
Todorova, Valentina K. *biochemist, educator*
Tosun, Duygu *research scientist*
Tovesson, Fredrik *nuclear scientist*
Tritsch, George Leopold *retired biochemist, educator*
Tsigelny, Igor *research scientist*
Tubis, Arnold *physics professor*
Tuchman, Avraham (Avi) *physicist, researcher*
Turner, Jean L. *astronomer, educator*
Tuul, Johannes *physics professor, researcher*
Uberall, Herbert Michael Stefan *physicist, professor emeritus*
Uchrin, Christopher George *environmental engineer and scientist*
Ufimtsev, Pyotr Yakovlevich *physicist, electrical engineer, educator*
Ugorowski, Philip Brien *nuclear scientist, researcher*
Ushakov, Sergey V. *research scientist*
Usher, Timothy Dwight *physics professor*
Uysal, Ismail *research scientist*

Van Horn, Hugh M. *physicist, astronomer, educator*
Vanier, Jacques *physicist*
Vasu, Subith *research scientist*
Veeramalai, Mallika *research scientist*
Veronis, George *geophysics educator*
Vook, Frederick Ludwig *physicist, consultant*
Voorhees, Kent Jay *chemist*
Voyles, Kyle *research scientist*
Wahl, Floyd Michael *geologist*
Wallace, Jane House *retired geologist*
Walstedt, Russell Erwin *physicist*
Walters, Robert Ancil *physicist, mathematician*
Wan, Rong-Yu *metallurgist*
Wander, Joseph Day *chemist*
Wang, Gongyao *materials scientist*
Wang, Wanlin *research scientist*
Wang, Ying *chemist, researcher*
Wannier, Mario Marc-Antoine *research scientist, multi-media specialist, director*
Warnasooriya, Nilanthi *research scientist*
Watkins, George Daniels *physics professor*
Watt, William Stewart *retired physical chemist*
Webster, Harold Frank *physicist*
Webster, Owen Wright *chemist*
Weinberg, Steven *physics professor*
Weisburger, Elizabeth Kreiser *retired chemist*
Weisz, Paul B(urg) *physicist, researcher, chemical engineer*
Wellner, Marcel Nahum *research scientist, educator*
Wells, Robert Hartley *chemist, consultant*
Westerhout, Gart *retired astronomer*
Wheeler, John Oliver *retired geologist*
Wheeler, William Joe *retired research scientist*
Whitaker, Stephen Taylor *geologist, oil exploration consultant*
White, Allen Bradley *meteorologist*
Whitener, Ronnie Dale *physics professor*
Wiklind, Tommy Gert *astrophysicist*
Wilchek, Meir *biochemist, educator*
Will, Fritz G. *physical chemist, consultant*
Williams, Jean-Pierre *research scientist*
Wincheski, Russell A. *research scientist*
Winkler, Donny W. *physics professor*
Wofsy, Steven Charles *astrophysicist, researcher*
Wolff, Manfred Ernst *chemist, pharmaceutical executive*
Wong, Ah-San *planetary scientist, musician, writer*
Woo, Honguk *research scientist*
Wooton, David L. *chemist, consultant*
Workman, John Mitchell *chemist*
Wu, Man-Li C. *research scientist*
Wu, Naijun *senior fellow*
Wu, Wei *research scientist*
Wu, Yider *research scientist*
Wyrtki, Klaus *oceanography educator*
Xu, Dong *physicist, researcher*
Xu, Guangyao *research scientist*
Xu, Jingye *research scientist*
Xu, J.M. (Jimmy Xu) *physicist, educator, engineer*
Xu, Zhijie *research scientist*
Yardibi, Tarik *research scientist*
Yates, David John C. *chemist, researcher*
Yoon, Jeong Whan *research scientist, educator*
York, James Wesley, Jr. *theoretical physicist, educator*
Yu, Robert Kuan-jen *biochemistry professor*
Yuan, Junsong *research scientist*
Zabolotskaya, Evgeniya Andreevna *physicist*
Zahl, Percy *physicist, researcher*
Zaleski, Jan Franciszek *biochemist*
Zaslavsky, Leonid *research scientist*
Zavyalov, Vladimir V *physicist, educator*
Zhang, Bin *research scientist*
Zhang, Hui *aerospace scientist*
Zhang, Jun *research scientist, educator*
Zhang, Shengzhi *research scientist*
Zhang, Shiwei *physics professor, researcher*
Zhang, Yanpeng *physics professor*
Zhang, Yanwen *physicist*
Zhao, Binsheng *physicist*
Zhao, Wayne (Wei) *materials scientist, researcher, transmission electron microscopist*
Zheng, Lingyi Albert *materials scientist, researcher, materials engineer, consultant*
Zhou, Huan-Xiang *biophysicist, scientist*
Zhou, Yuyu *environmental scientist, researcher*
Zhu, Alf (Aiwu Zhu) *research scientist, educator*
Ziff, Edward Benjamin *biochemist, educator*
Zucker, Alexander *physicist, researcher*

SOCIAL SCIENCE

UNITED STATES

ALABAMA

Arab
Black, Daniel Hugh *retired social studies educator*

Auburn
Clark, Janet Eileen *retired political science professor*
Seroka, James Henry *social studies educator, academic administrator*

Birmingham
Bradley, Laurence Alan *psychologist*
English, Laura Lynn *psychologist, educator*
Nunn, Grady Harrison *retired political science professor*
Passey, George Edward *psychologist, educator*
Taub, Edward *psychology researcher*

Dothan
Wright, Burton *sociologist*

Florence
Hansen, Vagn Keith *political science educator, college administrator*

Hartselle
Slate, Joe Hutson *psychologist, educator*

Jacksonville
Chargois, Deborah Majeau *psychology professor, researcher*
Dunaway, Carolyn Bennett *retired sociology professor*

Midfield
Daniels-Rogers, LaTausha *social sciences educator, entrepreneur*

Mobile
Castello, Sergio A. *economics professor*
Shelley-Tremblay, John Fontaine *psychology professor*
Suess, James Francis *retired clinical psychologist*
Vitulli, William Francis *retired psychology educator*

Montgomery
Clark, Eddie *psychology professor*

Normal
Qureshi, Halima Akhtar *economics professor*

Troy
Rinehart, James Forrest *political science professor, department chairman*

Tuscaloosa
Baklanoff, Eric Nicholas *economist, educator*
Cramer, Dale Lewis *retired economics professor*
Fish, Mary Martha *economics professor*
Iran-Nejad, Asghar *psychology professor*

ALASKA

Fairbanks
Irish, Joel David *anthropologist*
Pippenger, Michael Kirk *economics professor, researcher*
Shier, Juliet Marie *social studies educator*

ARIZONA

Chandler
Dawson, Bennette Renee *psychologist*
Krabbenhoft, Jonna *psychologist*

Chino Valley
Walker, Winnetta Dorrean *social studies educator*

Flagstaff
Denham, Aaron Renfrew *anthropologist, educator*
Trotter II, Robert Talbot *anthropologist, educator*

Goodyear
Privette, Louise Judith *school psychologist*

Mesa
Jastrzembski, Tiffany S. *psychologist*
Nelson, Scott Bruce *psychologist*

Oro Valley
Haller, Archibald Orben *sociologist, educator*

Phoenix
Anders, Gary C. *economics professor*
Berry, JoAnn I. *psychologist*
Birnbaum Reed, Barbara Irene *psychologist*
Huelster, Jeffery James *social studies educator*
LaPointe, Gregory Vincent *psychologist*
Maneshni, Bahman *economics professor*
Masters, Jonathan Edward *clinical psychologist*
Newman, Donald Lynn *psychologist, consultant*
Reynolds, Andrew *psychologist*
Roberts, Christopher Wayne *psychologist, educational consultant*

Scottsdale
Baker, Edward Martin *engineering and industrial psychologist*
Breus, Michael J. *psychologist*
Yost, William Albert *speech and hearing science professor*

Tempe
Crnic, Keith A. *psychology professor, department chairman*
Denhardt, Robert B. *political science professor, director*
DeSerpa, Allan C. *economics professor*
Fabricius, William Van *psychology professor*
Gordon, Leonard *social sciences educator*
Hechter, Michael Norman *sociologist*
Johanson, Donald Carl *physical anthropologist*
Knox, Robert Lee *economics professor*
Li, Wei *social sciences educator*
Menjivar, Cecilia *social sciences educator*
Myint, Soe Win *geographer, educator*
Nelson, Kelly *anthropologist, educator*
O'Neil, Michael Joseph *opinion survey executive, marketing research consultant*
Prescott, Edward C. *economist, educator*
Rowley, Beverley Davies *sociologist*
Simon, Sheldon Weiss *political science professor*
Smith, V. Kerry *economics professor*
Strom, Robert Duane *psychologist, educator*
Turner, Billie Lee, II, *geographer, educator*
van der Leeuw, Sander Ernst *archaeologist, educator*
Weigend, Guido Gustav *geographer, educator*

Tuba City
Hozie, William Charles *social sciences professor*

Tucson
Axinn, George Harold *rural sociology educator*
Beattie, Bruce Robert *economics professor*
Block, Michael Kent *economics and law professor, former government official*
Breiger, Ronald Louis *social sciences educator*
Coan, Richard Welton *psychologist, educator*
Ferebee, Susan Shepherd *psychology professor*
Larwood, Laurie *psychologist, artist*
Marshall, Robert Herman *retired economics professor*
Megdal, Sharon B. *water resource educator, consultant*
Pelletier, Kenneth R. *behavioral physician, educator, author*
Reitan, Ralph Meldahl *clinical neuropsychologist, former educator*
Schwartz, Gary E. *psychologist, educator*
Schwebel, Milton *psychologist, educator*
Smith, David Wayne *retired psychologist, educator*
Soren, David *archaeologist, educator, writer, filmmaker*
Thompson, Raymond Harris *retired anthropologist, educator*
Underwood, Jane Hainline Hammons *anthropologist, educator*

Winkelman
Wilson, Maren *anthropologist, educator*

Yuma
McCarthy, Sherri Nevada *psychologist, educator, educational consultant*
Norton, Dunbar Sutton *economic developer*

ARKANSAS

Arkadelphia
Wiebers, Todd *psychology professor*

Batesville
Lankford, George Emerson III *social sciences educator*

Fayetteville
Agee, Eve *anthropologist*
Costrell, Robert Michael *economist*
Mc Gimsey, Charles Robert III *anthropologist*

Hope
Freeman, Thomas Bruce (Tom Freeman) *social studies educator*

Jonesboro
Pearce, Amy R *psychology professor*

Little Rock
Coleman, Marshia Adams *social sciences educator*
Goddard, H. Wallace *family life professor*
Kaza, Greg John *economist, educator*
Ledbetter, Calvin Reville, Jr., (Cal Ledbetter) *political science professor, legislator*

Pine Bluff
Engle, Carole Ruth *aquaculture economics professor*

Searcy
Hobby, Kenneth Lester *psychology professor*

State University
Guha, Gauri Shankar *economics professor*

CALIFORNIA

Alameda
Doerr, Robert Douglas *psychologist, educator, artist, mediator*

Anaheim
Gobar, Alfred Julian *retired economic consultant, investor, educator*

Azusa
Conover, Roger B. *economics professor*
Estrada-Lee, Christine *psychologist*
Miyake, Stephanie Ann *psychology professor, director, marriage and family therapist*

Bakersfield
Lai, Mun Sim (Nicole Lai) *economics professor*
Osterkamp, Dalene May *psychology educator, artist*

Banning
Gladden, Garnett Lee *psychologist, healthcare consultant, educator*

Benicia
Nelson, Elmer Kingsholm, Jr., (Kim Nelson) *political scientist, educator, writer, mediator, consultant*

Berkeley
Akerlof, George Arthur *economics professor*
Alhadeff, David Albert *economics professor*
Auerbach, Alan Jeffrey *economist, educator*
Bellah, Robert Neelly *sociologist, educator*
Boyarin, Daniel *social studies educator*
Brandes, Stanley Howard *anthropology educator, writer*
Cohen, Lawrence *anthropologist, writer*
Collier, David *political science professor*
Dowall, David Edmund *social sciences educator*
Hakansson, Nils Hemming *economist, educator*
Hall, Bronwyn Hughes *economics educator*
Hinshaw, Stephen P. *psychology professor, department chairman*
Joyce, Rosemary Alexandria *anthropology educator, department chairman*
Karabel, Jerome Bernard *sociologist, educator*
Kirch, Patrick Vinton *anthropology educator, archaeologist*
Lee, Ronald Demos *demographer, economist, educator*
Letiche, John Marion *economist, educator*
Maslach, Christina *psychology professor*
McFadden, Daniel Little *economist, educator*
Moskowitz, Joel M. *psychologist, researcher*
Muir, William Ker, Jr. *political science professor*
Nader, Laura *anthropologist, educator*
Nemeth, Charlan Jeanne *psychology educator*
Norgaard, Richard Bruce *ecological economist, educator, consultant*
Palmer, Stephen E. *psychology professor*
Petiet, Carole Anne *psychologist*
Powell, James L. *economics professor*
Quigley, John Michael *economist, educator*
Rausser, Gordon C(lyde) *agricultural and resource economics educator*
Reich, Robert Bernard *political economics educator, former United States Secretary of Labor*
Reiman, Amanda E. *social sciences educator*
Ring, Bonnie *psychologist, consultant, priest*
Romer, David *economics professor*
Sadoulet, Elisabeth *economics professor*
Scotchmer, Suzanne Andersen *economics professor*
Smolensky, Eugene *economics professor*
Spiller, Pablo Tomas *economics and public utilities educator*
Sternberg, Hilgard O'Reilly *geographer, educator*
Sulloway, Frank Jones *social sciences educator, historian*
Varian, Hal Ronald *economics professor*
Weir, Margaret *sociologist, political science professor*
Wilensky, Harold L. *political science professor, sociologist, researcher*
Williamson, Oliver Eaton *business economics and law professor*
Wolfinger, Raymond Edwin *retired political science professor*
Worrell, Frank Clayton *psychology professor*

Big Pine
Reynaud-Roepke, Suzanne *psychologist*

Bonita
Deane, Debbe *psychologist, journalist, editor, consultant*

Burbank
Rainwater, Carol Jean *psychology communication professor*

Burlingame
Schwantes, Robert Sidney *international relations executive*

Carlsbad
Farah, Tawfic Elias *political scientist, educator*

Carmel
Weitzman, Ronald Alfred *psychology professor*

Carmichael
Hellmuth, William Frederick *economics professor*

Carpinteria
Schmidhauser, John Richard *retired political science professor, former congressman*

Carson
Palmer, Beverly Blazey *psychologist, educator*

Castro Valley
Evans, Robert William *psychologist, theologian*

Chatsworth
Becerra Ibanez Pelliza, Julio C. *psychologist, consultant*

Chico
Smith, Valene Lucy *anthropologist, educator*

Chino Hills
Fisher, Teresa Marie *psychologist, forensic specialist*

Chula Vista
Hollowell, Daria Mae *social sciences educator*

Claremont
Bekendam, Carol Helen *psychologist*
Borcherding, Thomas Earl *economist*
Burdekin, Richard Charles Keighley *economics professor*
Csikszentmihalyi, Mihaly *psychology professor*
Halpern, Diane F. *psychology educator, professional association executive*
Jaffa, Harry Victor *political philosophy educator emeritus*
Keil, Manfred Werner *economics professor*
Lasswell, Marcia Lee *psychologist, educator*
Lipman-Blumen, Jean *public policy and organizational behavior educator*
Rossum, Ralph Arthur *political science professor*
Tao, Ran *economics professor, researcher*

Compton
Drew, Sharon Lee *sociologist*

Concord
Turnbull, Thomas Leigh *social studies educator, secondary school educator*

Culver City
Cherry, Debra Lynn *clinical psychologist*
Maltzman, Irving Myron *psychology professor*

Davis
Bryant, Brenda K. *psychologist, educator*
Cameron, A. Colin *economics professor*
Carroll, Patrick Eamonn *social sciences educator*
Coss, Richard Gerrit *psychology professor*
Groth, Alexander Jacob *political science professor*
Hoynes, Hilary Williamson *economics professor, researcher*
Mangun, George R. *psychology professor, director*
Mason, William A(lvin) *psychologist, educator, researcher*

McHenry, Henry Malcolm *anthropologist, educator*
Modjtahedi, Bagher *economist, educator*
Musolf, Lloyd Daryl *political science professor, educational association administrator*
Simonton, Dean Keith *psychology professor*
Smith, Michael Peter *social sciences educator, researcher*
Spindler, George Dearborn *anthropologist, educator, writer*

Del Mar
Quinn, Katherine Sarah *psychologist*

El Cajon
Ishmael, Wanda Shutt *psychology educator*

El Segundo
Harwick, Wayne Thomas *economist*

Emeryville
Tori, Christopher Dante *psychology professor*

Encinitas
Lougeay, Denruth Colleen *clinical psychologist, educator*

Escondido
Damsbo, Ann Marie *psychologist*

Eureka
Bowker, Lee Harrington *sociologist, educator, writer*

Fairfax
Kadoyama, Margaret *museum educator, management consultant*

Folsom
Smith, Candy *economics professor*
Textor, Alice Middle *political science professor*

Fresno
Dackawich, S. John *sociology educator, academic administrator*
Joseph, James William *political scientist, consultant, educator*

Fullerton
de Rios, Marlene Dobkin *medical anthropologist, psychotherapist*
Farka, Mira *economics professor, financial consultant*
Khalifa, Sherif Hussein *economics professor*

Glendale
Figueira-McDonough, Josefina *emeritus professor of justice studies*

Goleta
Zuk, Gerald Harvey *psychologist, consultant*

Granada Hills
Aller, Wayne Kendall *psychologist, educator, computer company executive, property manager*

Granite Bay
Hartmann, Frederick Howard *retired political science professor*

Guerneville
Mannino, J. Davis *psychologist, educator, author*

Hayward
DeVaro, Jed *economics professor*
Reevy-Manning, Gretchen Maria *psychologist, educator*
Staudohar, Paul David *economics professor, labor arbitrator*

Hemet
Frances, Carol *economics professor*

Hermosa Beach
Wickwire, Patricia Joanne Nellor *psychologist, educator*

Highland
Miller, R. Warburton *psychologist, farmer*

Hollywood
Fisher, Joel Marshall *political scientist, educator, wine consultant*

Huntington Beach
Martin, Wilfred Wesley Finny *psychologist, property owner and manager*

Idyllwild
Jones, William Lee, Jr. *psychologist, educator*

Inglewood
Barrett, Ronald Keith *psychology educator, consultant, researcher*

Irvine
Aigner, Dennis John *economics professor, consultant*
Burton, Michael Ladd *anthropology educator*
Butts, Carter Tribley *social sciences educator*
Danziger, James Norris *political science professor*
Duncan, Greg John *economics researcher*
Feldman, Martha Sue *political scientist, educator*
Feliciano, Cynthia *social sciences educator*
Greenberger, Ellen *psychologist, educator*
Herzog, Dennis Neil *psychologist, supervisor*
Huff, C(larence) Ronald *sociologist, criminologist, educator*
Jeliazkov, Ivan *economics professor*
Luce, R. Duncan (Robert Duncan Luce) *psychology professor*
Rumbaut, Rubén G., Sr. *social sciences educator*
Schonfeld, William Rost *political science professor*
Smoot, Skipi Lundquist *psychologist*
Sperling, George *psychologist, educator*
Uhlaner, Carole Jean *political science professor*
Wenzel, Lari Bea *psychologist*

La Jolla
Bardwell, Wayne Allen *psychologist, director*
Cain, William Stanley *experimental psychologist, educator, researcher*
Coburn, Marjorie Foster *psychologist, educator*
Cole, Michael *psychology professor*
Csordas, Thomas John *anthropologist, educator*
Fantino, Edmund *psychology professor*
Farson, Richard Evans *psychologist*
Fowler, James H. *political science professor*
Fowler, Raymond Dalton *psychologist, educator*
Gordon, Roger Hall *economics educator*
Harris, Philip Robert *management and space psychologist*
Jacobson, Gary Charles *political science professor*
Kutas, Marta *psychologist, educator*
Levy, Thomas Evan *anthropologist, educator*
Mandler, George *psychologist, educator*
Mandler, Jean Matter *psychologist, educator*
Margolin, Frances Mongin *clinical psychologist, educator*
Pratt, George Janes, Jr. *psychologist author*
Schneider, Benjamin *psychology professor, consultant*
Starr, Ross Marc *economist, educator*

La Quinta
Hoston, Germaine Annette *political science professor*

La Verne
Gelm, Richard Joseph *political scientist, educator*

Laguna Beach
Bent, Alan Edward *political science professor*

Lancaster
Holley, Susan L. *psychologist*

Long Beach
Baruah, Bipasha *social sciences educator*
Fiebert, Martin Stephen *psychology professor*
Nagai, Chikako *social sciences educator*

Los Altos
Green, George Reite *psychologist*

Los Altos Hills
Gibbs Stayte, Patricia Leigh *social sciences educator, researcher*

Los Angeles
Aberbach, Joel David *political science professor, writer*
Allen, Walter Recharde *sociology educator*
Allen, William Richard *retired economist*
Alvarez, Rodolfo *sociology educator, consultant*
Anawalt, Patricia Rieff *anthropologist, researcher*
Bennett, Charles Franklin, Jr. *biogeographer, educator*
Bookheimer, Susan Yost *neuropsychologist*
Cantu, Roberto *social sciences educator*
Champagne, Duane Willard *sociology educator*
Clark, Burton Robert *sociologist, educator*
Currie, Janet M. *economics professor*
Damasio, Antonio R. *psychology and neurology professor, researcher*
Damasio, Hanna *psychology and neuroscience professor, researcher*
Darby, Michael Rucker *economist, educator*
Day, Richard Hollis *economics educator*
Dekmejian, Richard Hrair *political science professor*
Dr. Phil, (Phillip Calvin McGraw) *psychologist, television personality*
Duranti, Alessandro *anthropology professor*
Elderkin-Thompson, Virginia *Neuropsychologist*
Fanselow, Michael Scott *psychology professor*
Feshbach, Seymour *psychology professor*
Forness, Steven Robert *educational psychologist*
Gatz, Margaret *psychology professor, department chairman*
Goff, Phillip Atiba *psychology professor, consultant*
Harberger, Arnold Carl *economist, educator*
Hsiao, Cheng *economics educator*
Intriligator, Michael David *economist, educator*
Irwin, Michael Ray *psychology professor, researcher*
Kahn, Matthew E. *economics professor*
Kalish-Weiss, Beth Isaacs *psychologist, psychoanalyst, consultant*
Kaplan, Robert Malcolm *health researcher, educator*
Kim, Yong Jin *economics professor*
La Force, James Clayburn, Jr. *economist, educator*
Levine, Robert Arthur *economist, educator, policy writer*
McKnight, Carl Phillip *psychologist*
Montoya, Velma *economist, consultant*
Myers, Hector *psychology professor, department chairman*
Nelson, Barbara J. *public policy professor, former dean*
Nelson, Howard Joseph *geographer, educator*
Nuechterlein, Keith H. *psychology professor*
Odell, John Stephen *political scientist*
O'Neil, Harold Francis *psychologist, educator*
Osborne, Danny *psychologist, researcher*
Pagden, Anthony Robin *political science professor, historian, writer*
Provda, Lois M. *psychologist, educator*
Raven, Bertram H(erbert) *psychology professor*
Rosenberg, Joan I. *psychologist, educator*
Sandhofer, Catherine *psychology professor*
Sears, David O'Keefe *psychology professor*
Seeman, Melvin *sociologist, educator*
Shearer, Derek Nocross *political science professor, diplomat, academic administrator*
Shelton, Samantha *psychologist*
Shieh, John Ting-chung *economics professor, department chairman*
Sklar, Richard Lawrence *political science professor*
Smith, Laurence *social sciences educator*
Squire, Molly Ann *organizational psychologist*
Steh, Bill Drago *neuropsychologist*
Telles, Cynthia Ann *psychologist*
Thompson, Richard Frederick *psychologist, neuroscientist, educator*
Turner, Ralph Herbert *sociologist, educator*
Waldinger, Roger *social studies educator*
Wilcox, Rand Roger *psychology professor*
Wong, James Bok *economist, chemical engineer, technologist, consultant*
Wood, Nancy Elizabeth *psychologist, educator*
Zaller, John Raymond *political science professor*
Zeitlin, Maurice *sociology educator*

Los Gatos
Ohanjanian, Ruzanna *clinical psychologist*

Malibu
Kim, Rebecca *social sciences educator*
Wilson, James Quinn *public policy professor*

Mckinleyville
Emenhiser, JeDon Allen *retired political science professor, dean*

Menlo Park
Fetterman, David Mark *anthropologist, educator, evaluator*
Vane, Sylvia Brakke *anthropologist, writer*

Modesto
Sawicki, Geraldine *social studies educator*

Monterey
Looney, Robert Edward *economist, educator*
Ruehsen, Moyaa *political science professor, consultant*

Moraga
Scott, Christina Lynn *psychology professor*

Moreno Valley
McLaughlin, Veronica *psychologist*

Newport Beach
Whittemore, Paul Baxter *psychologist*

North Hollywood
Totton, Carl Allen, II, *psychologist*

Northridge
Jackiewicz, Edward Louis *geographer, educator*
Mitchell, Rie Rogers *psychologist, counselor, educator*
Reagan, Janet Thompson *psychologist, educator*

Norwalk
Solomon, Namala *economics professor*

Novato
Criswell, Eleanor Camp *psychologist*
Spinrad, Michael Irwin *social studies educator*

Oakland
De Vos, George Alphonse *psychologist, anthropologist*
Preston, Elizabeth A. *psychologist*

Ojai
Griffin, John Lawrence *psychology professor*

Orange
Christian-Brougham, Ruby Rosalie *psychology professor*
Smith, Vernon Lomax *economist, educator*
Stevens, Cherita Wyman *social sciences educator, writer*

Pacific Palisades
Griver, Jeanette A. *psychologist, consultant*
Hoffenberg, Marvin *retired political science professor*
Longaker, Richard Pancoast *retired political science professor, academic administrator*

Palm Desert
Bantz, Jody Lenore *psychologist*

Palo Alto
Card, Stuart Kent *psychologist, researcher*
Flanagan, Robert Joseph *economics professor*
Moos, Rudolf H. *psychologist, researcher*
Ricardo-Campbell, Rita *retired economist educator*
Scitovsky, Anne Aickelin *economist, researcher*
Sherlock, Phyllis Krafft *psychologist*

Pasadena
Dimitrius, Jo-Ellan *trial consultant*
Goldschmidt, Walter Rochs *anthropologist*
Gorsuch, Richard Lee *psychologist, educator, minister*
Ledyard, John Odell *economics professor, consultant*
Palfrey, Thomas Rossman *economics professor, political science professor*
Scudder, Thayer *anthropologist, educator*
Shum, Matthew *social sciences educator*

Pomona
Loo, Dennis *social sciences educator*

Portola Valley
March, James Gardner *social sciences educator*

Rancho Palos Verdes
Loether, Herman John *sociologist, educator*

Redondo Beach
McWilliams, Margaret Ann *home economist, educator, writer*

Redwood City
Calvin, Allen David *psychologist, educator*
Tyson, Laura D'Andrea *economics professor, former dean*

Riverside
Calfee, Robert Chilton *psychologist, educator*
Gaffney, M. Mason *economics professor*
Griffin, Keith Broadwell *retired economics professor*
Mancilla, Faustina Ramirez *retired psychologist*
Parke, Ross Duke *psychology professor*
Petrinovich, Lewis Franklin *psychologist, educator*
Robert, Bates D. *archaeologist, educator*
Rosenthal, Robert *psychology professor*
Turk, Austin Theodore *social studies educator*

Rohnert Park
Byrne, Noel Thomas *sociologist, educator*
Steiner, John Michael *sociologist, educator*

Sacramento
Covin, David L. *retired political science professor*
Kalish, Nancy *psychology professor*
Leake, Sherrill Ann *psychologist*
Loewy, Erich H. *bioethicist educator*
Majesty, Melvin Sidney *psychologist, consultant*
Miguel, Caio F. *psychology professor*
Newland, Chester Albert *public administration educator*
Sherwood, Robert Petersen *retired social sciences educator*
Wang, Ta-Chen *economics professor*

San Bernardino
Brown-Jensen, William Ellis *psychologist*
Kaufman, James Corey *psychologist, researcher*
Paul, Margaret Lee *psychologist*

San Diego
Conroy, Stephen J. *economics professor, consultant*
Edwards, Darrel *psychologist, researcher, philosopher*
Emerick, Robert Earl *retired sociologist, educator*
Gazell, James Albert *public administration educator*
Gordon, Robert Lee *economics professor*
Hudzinski, Leonard Gerard *social sciences educator, researcher*
Lane, Sylvia *economist, educator*
Madhavan, Murugappa Chettiar *economics professor*
Reimann, Joachim Oskar Ferdinand *psychologist, public health researcher*
Robinson-Zañartu, Carol A. *psychology professor, department chairman*
Scott, Richard Malachi *psychologist*
Shedroff, Sharon D. *psychologist, anthropologist, researcher, consultant*
Sheldon-Morris, Tiffini Anne *clinical psychologist, consultative examiner*
Stoessinger, John George *political science professor*
Tayman, Jeff *retired economics professor*
Weeks, John Robert *geographer, social studies educator*

San Fernando
Shannon, George Raymond *gerontologist, educator*

San Francisco
Adler, Nancy Elinor *psychologist, educator*
Ekman, Paul *psychologist, educator*
Ellis, Linda *archaeologist, director*
Estes, Carroll Lynn *sociologist, educator*
Gemello, John Michael *economics professor, consultant, academic administrator*
Hare, Julia *educational psychologist, author, consultant*
Krippner, Stanley Curtis *psychologist*
Luft, Harold S. *health economist*
Marston, Michael *economist, consultant*
Mayer, Ronald Wesley *psychology professor*
McManis, Dena Edwy *psychologist, consultant*
Patterson, James (Jim) *economist, writer*
Rankin, Katherine Pollock *psychology professor, researcher*
Ratum, Cecilia Bangloy *retired psychologist*
Razak, Arisika *social studies educator, department chairman*
Rice, Dorothy Pechman *medical economist*
Satre, Derek Davies *psychologist, researcher*
Soh, Chunghee Sarah *anthropology educator*
Tintiangco-Cubales, Allyson Goce *social studies educator*
Zunes, Stephen *political science professor, writer*

San Jose
Cedolini, Anthony John *psychologist*
Danopoulos, Constantine P. *political science professor*
Lendl, Jennifer Lynn *psychologist*
McDowell, Jennifer *sociologist, composer, playwright*
Pinnell, Sabrina L. *political science professor*
Shao, Otis Hung-I *retired political science professor*

San Luis Obispo
Fisher, Eric O'Neill *economist*

San Marcos
Jackson, Russell Eric *psychology professor*

San Marino
Martin, Olivia Jean *social studies educator*

San Ramon
Kalicki, Jan H. *economist, political scientist, energy executive*

Santa Ana
Klassen, Margreta *clinical counseling psychologist, educator*

Santa Barbara
Altus, Grace Merriman Thompson *psychologist*
Comanor, William S. *economist, educator*
Davidson, Roger H(arry) *political science professor*
Earl, Jennifer Suzanne *sociologist, educator*
Erasmus, Charles John *anthropologist, educator*

Freudenburg, William R. *sociology educator*
Gravitz, Herbert L. *clinical psychologist, writer*
Gurven, Michael Douglas *anthropologist*
Janelle, Donald G. *geographer, researcher*
Jochim, Michael Allan *archaeologist*
Kendler, Howard H(arvard) *psychologist, educator*
Kydland, Finn E. *economics professor*
Mayer, Richard Edwin *psychology professor*
Nyborg, Vanessa Marie *psychologist, researcher, educator*
Weidemann, Celia Jean *social sciences educator, management consultant, financial consultant*

Santa Clarita
Walker, Robert F. *social studies educator*

Santa Cruz
Cheung, Yin-Wong *economics professor*
Dominguez, Virginia Rosa *anthropologist*
Pettigrew, Thomas Fraser *social psychologist, educator*
Roby, Pamela Ann *sociologist, educator*
Smith, M(ahlon) Brewster *retired psychologist, educator*
Walsh, Carl E. *economics professor*

Santa Monica
Dixon, Lloyd S. *economist*
Ellickson, Phyllis Lynn *political scientist*
Friedman, Monroe *psychologist, educator, consultant, editor, writer*
Gray, Laura B. *psychology professor, counselor*
Kurtzman, Joel Allan *economist*
Smith, James Patrick *economist*
Stiehm, Judith Hicks *political scientist*
Wolf, Charles, Jr. *economist, educator*

Santa Rosa
Lieberman, Sharon L. *retired psychology professor*
Zimmer, Richard *anthropologist, educator*

Sonora
Clarke, Paula Katherine *anthropologist, researcher, social studies educator*

Stanford
Aoki, Masahiko *economics educator*
Arrow, Kenneth Joseph *economist, educator*
Bandura, Albert *psychologist, educator*
Boskin, Michael Jay *economics professor*
Brody, Richard Alan *political science educator, researcher*
Cook, Karen S. *sociologist, professor*
Damon, William Van Buren *developmental psychologist, educator, writer*
Diamond, Larry *political scientist*
Enthoven, Alain Charles *economist, educator*
Fingar, Thomas (Charles Thomas Fingar) *political science professor, former federal official*
Fuchs, Victor Robert *economist, educator*
Granovetter, Mark *sociology educator*
Hall, Robert Ernest *economics professor*
Hansen, Peter Reinhard *economics professor*
Hickman, Bert George, Jr. *economist, educator*
Hoxby, Caroline Minter *economics professor*
Inkeles, Alex *sociology educator*
Jackson, Matthew O. *economics professor*
Krasner, Stephen David *political science educator, former federal agency administrator*
Krumboltz, John Dwight *psychologist, educator*
Kurz, Mordecai *economics professor*
Lazear, Edward Paul *economics professor*
Levin, Jonathan *economics professor*
Lewis, John Wilson *political science professor*
Martin, Joanne *social sciences educator*
McAdam, Douglas John *sociologist, educator, director*
McClelland, James Lloyd *psychologist, educator, cognitive neuroscientist*
McKinnon, Ronald Ian *retired economics professor*
Mc Lure, Charles E., Jr. *economist, consultant*
Milgrom, Paul Robert *economics educator*
Noll, Roger Gordon *economist, educator*
Rice, Condoleezza *political science professor, former United States Secretary of State*
Roberts, Donald John *economics, business professor, consultant*
Romer, Paul Michael *economics professor*
Rothwell, Geoffrey Scott *economics educator*
Sagan, Scott *political science professor*
Shultz, George Pratt *economics professor, former United States Secretary of State*
Taylor, John Brian *economist, educator*
Van Horne, James Carter *economist, educator*
Zimbardo, Philip George *psychologist, educator, writer*

Stockton
Freeman, Nina Rebecca *psychologist*
Herrin, William E. *economics professor*
Knudsen, Sondra Lynna *psychology professor*
Nagai, Nelson Kei *economics professor, history professor*

Turlock
AbuKhalil, Asad *political science professor*
Ahlem, Lloyd Harold *psychologist*

Ventura
Bowles, Walter Donald *economist, educator*
Naurath, David Allison *engineering psychologist, researcher*

Visalia
Howell, Dave *geographer, educator*

Walnut Creek
Yu, Wei *economist, researcher*

Westlake Village
Lereah, David Alan *economist*
Pingitore, Regina *psychologist, researcher*

Whittier
McKenna, Jeanette Ann *archaeologist*
Mikalson, Barbara G. *economics professor*
Prewitt, Dezzie Allen *economics professor*

Yuba City
Sheppard, Lisa Marie *psychologist*

COLORADO

Arvada
Yamamoto, Kaoru *emeritus psychology professor*

Aspen
Manosevitz, Martin *psychologist*
Newman, Ruth Gallert *psychologist*

Aurora
Doze, Maureen Adele (Maureen Adele Mee) *social studies educator*
Olson, Allison W. *social studies educator*

Boulder
Beer, Francis Anthony *political science professor emeritus*
Bourne, Lyle Eugene, Jr. *psychology professor*
Bowman, Deborah Lynn *psychologist, educator*
Greenawald, Glenn Dale *social studies trainer, curriculum developer, researcher*
Greenberg, Edward Seymour *political science professor*
Harvey, Lewis O., Jr. *psychology professor, department chairman*
Healy, Alice Fenvessy *psychology professor, researcher*
Jessor, Richard *psychologist, educator, director*
Kelso, Alec John (Jack Kelso) *anthropologist, educator*
Kintsch, Walter *retired psychology professor*
Lamping, Jennifer *economics professor*
Schneider, Vivian I. *psychologist, researcher*
Walker, Deward Edgar, Jr. *anthropologist, educator*

Broomfield
Yount-Baxley, Kathleen Ann *psychologist*

Castle Rock
Hendrick, Hal Wilmans *human factors educator*

Centennial
Dineen, Bonnie R. *social studies educator*

Colorado Springs
Brooks, Glenn Ellis *political science professor, educational association administrator*
Durham, Robert L. *psychology professor*
Farrer, Claire Anne Rafferty *anthropologist, educator*
Schmidt, Bob *psychologist*
Theobald, Rebecca Bayless *geographer, educator*
Wynn, Thomas Grant *anthropologist, educator*

Denver
Axelrod, Evan M. *psychologist, educator*
Guy, Mary Ellen Johnston *political science professor*
Kerrigan, J. Michael *psychologist*
Lefly, Dianne Louise *research psychologist*
Milliken, John Gordon *research economist*
Moorcroft, William Herbert *retired bio-psychologist, educator, researcher*
Nelson, Sarah Milledge *archaeology educator*
Padilla, Alexandre *economics professor*
Snyder, Charles Royce *sociologist, educator*
Zimet, Carl Norman *psychologist, educator*

Durango
Zeller, Christopher Lee *preservation archaeologist*

Fort Collins
Dik, Bryan J. *psychology professor, consultant*
Douglas, Aaron Jack *economist, researcher*
Morgan, George Arthur *psychologist*
Sedei Rodden, Pamela Jean *psychologist, director*

Fountain
Hazlett, David Lawrence *social studies educator*

Fruita
McCorkle, Anne Frances *social studies educator*

Golden
Petrick, Alfred, Jr. *economist, educator*

Grand Junction
Morton, Louis George *retired social sciences educator*

Greeley
Hawthorne, Barbara L. *anthropologist, educator*

Guffey
Szeliga, Victoria I. *retired social studies educator*

Lakewood
Kulkarni, Kishore Ganesh *economics professor, consultant*
Winters, Richard Allen *mineral economist*

Limon
Richards, Ann Adair *psychologist*

Littleton
Cabell, Elizabeth Arlisse *psychologist*

Longmont
Watkins, John Goodrich *psychologist, educator*

Loveland
Schmitt, Roberta J. *psychologist, educator*

Nederland
Sutton, Philip D(ietrich) *psychologist, educator*

Pine
Jones, David Milton *economist, educator*

Woodland Park
Marcantel, Keith Bernard *school psychologist, educator*

CONNECTICUT

Bethany
Bell, Wendell *sociologist, educator, futurist*

Bridgeport
Coba-Loh, Claudine Jean *psychology professor*
Maloney, Maureen Murphy *social sciences educator*

Cromwell
Barber, William Joseph *economist, educator*
Günther-Stirn, Dagmar Dorothea *retired social sciences educator*

Danbury
Tolor, Alexander *psychologist, educator*

Fairfield
Kleine, Herman *economist*
Morehouse, Sarah McCally *retired political science professor*

Farmington
Lang, Jason M. *psychology professor*

Greenwich
Fleming, Martin *economist, strategist*

Guilford
Chatt-Ellis, Allen Barrett *psychologist, neuroscientist*
Shelton, Darlene *psychologist, consultant*

Hamden
Cline, John Carroll *psychologist*
Dahl, Robert Alan *political science professor*

Hartford
Curran, Ward Schenk *economist, educator*
Gunderson, Gerald Axel *economics professor*
Vogt, Erik Michael *philosophy professor*

Higganum
de Brigard, Emilie *anthropologist, consultant*

Meriden
Crespi, Tony David *psychologist*

Middlebury
Phillips, Walter Mills III *psychologist, educator*

Middletown
Bonin, John Paul *economics professor*
Gallarotti, Giulio M. *political science professor*
Miller, Richard Alan *retired economist, educator*
Scheibe, Karl Edward *psychology professor*

Milford
Krall, Vita *psychologist*
Schwartz, Richard Edward Derecktor *retired sociologist, educator*

Mystic
Talbot, Suzanne Davidson *psychologist*

New Haven
Andrews, Donald Wilfrid Kao *economics professor*
Blatt, Sidney Jules *psychology professor, psychoanalyst, investigator*
Bracken, Paul *political science professor*
Brownell, Kelly David *psychologist, educator*
Coe, Michael Douglas *retired anthropologist*
Ember, Carol R. *anthropology educator, writer*
Ember, Melvin Lawrence *anthropologist, educator*
Hacker, Jacob Stewart *political science professor, author*
Hayes, Jonathan *psychologist*
Heninger, George Robert *psychology professor, researcher*
Johnson, Marcia K. *psychology professor, department chairman*
Kalyvas, Stathis N. *political science professor, director*
Kazdin, Alan E. *psychology professor*
Lange, Fabian *economics professor*
Marks, Lawrence Edward *psychologist, educator*
Marmor, Theodore Richard *political science professor, writer*
Mayhew, David Raymond *political science professor*
Mostaghimi, Mehdi *economist, educator*
Nelson, Alondra R. *social sciences educator*
Phillips, Peter Charles Bonest *economist, educator, researcher*
Pospisil, Leopold Jaroslav *anthropologist, law educator*
Ranis, Gustav *economist, educator*
Rosenbluth, Frances McCall *political scientist, educator*
Russett, Bruce Martin *political science professor*
Schowalter, John Erwin *child and adolescent psychiatry educator*
Schultz, T. Paul *economics professor*
Shiller, Robert James *economist*
Skowronek, Stephen Lee *political scientist, educator*
Stevens, Joseph Charles *psychology professor*
Stokes, Susan C. *political science professor*
Sutterlin, James Smyrl *political science professor, researcher*
Wagner, Allan Ray *psychology professor*
Wallerstein, Immanuel *sociologist*
Zedillo Ponce de León, Ernesto *economics professor, former president of Mexico*

New London
Dr. Zapalska, Alina M. *economics professor*

North Haven
Apter, David Ernest *political science and sociology professor*

Norwalk
Brown, William Terrel *psychology professor, educational consultant*

Plainville
Perkins-Banas, Melissa Veronica *neuropsychologist*

Shelton
DeLucia, David Ralph *psychologist*

Southbury
Atwood, Edward Charles *economist, educator*

Stamford
Dunbar, Kwamie O. *economics professor, director*
Robins, Robert Sidwar *political science professor, department chairman*

Storrs
Kiene, Susan Maria *psychologist*

Storrs Mansfield
Barnes-Farrell, Janet Lorraine *psychologist*
Katz, Leonard *psychology professor, researcher*
Leach, Colin Wayne *psychology professor*
McEachern, William Archibald *economics educator*
Michaels, Claire Farley *psychology educator*
Rickards, John Patrick *psychology professor*
Rohner, Ronald Preston *anthropology educator, psychologist*
Ross, Stephen L. *economics professor*

West Hartford
Bullock, Karen *social sciences educator*
Gitterman, Alex *social work educator*
Neace, William Phillip *psychology professor, consultant*

West Haven
Deck, Richard Allen *political scientist, consultant, writer, volunteer*

West Simsbury
Evans, Meg *psychologist*

Westport
Manley, John Frederick *political scientist, educator*

DELAWARE

Dover
Armstrong, Anthony Michael *political science professor*
Hoff, Samuel Boyer *political scientist, educator*
Pongsree, Saharat Oak *economics professor*

Georgetown
Fiedler, Clarence Wesley *psychologist*

Newark
Abrams, Burton A. *economics professor*
Bilinsky, Yaroslav *political scientist*
Butkiewicz, James Leon *economics professor, researcher, consultant*
DiRenzo, Gordon James *sociologist, psychologist, educator*
Turkel, Gerald Michael *social sciences educator*
Tynan, William Douglas *psychologist*

Wilmington
Genetta, Ann H. *psychologist, neuropsychologist*
Seidenstat, Paul *retired economics professor*

DISTRICT OF COLUMBIA

Washington
Arend, Anthony Clark *social studies educator, academic administrator*
Aschheim, Joseph *retired economist, educator*
Asfaw, Abay *economist, consultant, research scientist*
Åslund, Anders *economist*
Atkinson, Caroline *economist*
Baer, Michael Alan *political scientist, educator*
Baker, Dean *economist, think-tank executive*
Balzer, Marjorie Mandelstam *anthropology educator, editor*
Batini, Nicoletta *economist, educator*
Becker, Mary Louise *political scientist*
Begala, Paul Edward *political scientist, educator, television personality*
Bergmann, Barbara Rose *economics professor*
Besen, Stanley Martin *economist*
Bolino, August Constantino *economics professor*
Bollinger, Lori *economist*
Brainard, Lael S. *economist, writer*
Brazile, Donna L. *political strategist*
Brimmer, Andrew Felton *economist, consultant*
Brooks, Renana Esther *clinical psychologist, business and political consultant, researcher*
Brown, Nathan Jude *political scientist, educator*
Bruck, Nicholas *economist, educator*
Brzezinski, Zbigniew *political science professor, former national security advisor*
Bulir, Ales *economist*
Burtless, Gary Thomas *economist, consultant*
Calder, Kent Eyring *political science professor, federal agency administrator*
Calvert, Sandra L. *psychology professor*
Carpenter, Ted Galen *political scientist*
Choi, Woon Gyu *economist*
Cline, William Richard *economist, educator*
Coady, David Patrick *economist, educator*
Cohen, Eliot Asher *political scientist*

Conway, Kellyanne *political strategist, pollster*
Cooke, Benson George *counseling psychologist, psychology professor, consultant*
Cordes, Joseph John *economics professor, director*
Craig, John Tucker *economist, consultant*
Dang, Hai-Anh Hoang *economist, consultant*
Danziger, Raphael *political scientist, researcher*
Day, Lincoln Hubert *demographer, educator, documentary filmmaker*
Dillon, Wilton Sterling *anthropologist, foundation administrator*
Dizard, Wilson Paul, Jr. *international affairs consultant, educator*
Doran, Charles Francis *political scientist, consultant*
Downs, Anthony *economist, real estate consultant*
Eads, George Curtis *senior consultant*
Eagleburger, Lawrence Sidney *public policy advisor, former United States Secretary of State*
English, Richard Allyn *sociologist, educator*
Epstein, Gerald Lewis *technology and security policy analyst*
Ershler, William Baldwin *biogerontologist, educator*
Faux, Jeff (Geoffrey Peter Faux) *economist, writer*
Feder, Judy *political science professor*
Foust, Robert Schmertz *political science professor*
Friedman, Robert Sidney *political science professor*
Fukuyama, Francis *political scientist, educator*
Furchtgott-Roth, Harold Wilkes *economist, consultant*
Gabre-Madhin, Eleni Zaude *economist, researcher*
Galston, William Arthur *political scientist, educator*
Garfinkel, Renée Efra *psychologist*
Gillingham, Robert Fenton *economist, consultant*
Glenn, Jerome Clayton *futurist, director*
Goldgeier, James *social sciences educator*
Goldscheider, Frances K. *sociologist, educator*
Grapin, Jacqueline G. *economist*
Greenberg, Milton *political science professor*
Greenberg, Stanley B. *political strategist, pollster*
Halperin, Morton H. *political scientist*
Halperin, Samuel *education and training policy analyst*
Hannan, Timothy Hale *economist*
Haslem, John Arthur *financial economist, educator*
Helms, Robert Brake *economist*
Hess, Stephen *political scientist, writer*
Hjalmarsson, Erik *economist*
Hoffmann, Sandra Ann *economist, researcher*
Holtz-Eakin, Douglas J. *economist, former federal official*
Hudson, Michael Craig *political science professor*
Hufbauer, Gary Clyde *economist, lawyer, educator*
Hughes, Kent Higgon *economist*
Isaac, Alan G. *economics professor*
Jarmon, Charles *social sciences educator, dean*
Jaspersen, Frederick Zarr *economist*
Jensen, John Bradford *economics professor*
Joyner, Christopher Clayton *international relations educator*
Kemp, Geoffrey Thomas Howard *political scientist, consultant*
Kendrick, John Whitefield *economist, educator, consultant*
Kojm, Christopher A. *political science professor*
Kravis, Marie-Josée Drouin *economist*
Krueger, Anne *economist*
Krulfeld, Ruth Marilyn *anthropologist, educator*
Kurtzman, Howard Steven *psychologist*
Kyriakopoulos, Irene *economist, educator*
Lake, Anthony *political science professor, former national security advisor*
Lardy, Nicholas Richard *economist, educator*
Laxminarayan, Ramanan *economist*
LeoGrande, William Mark *political science professor, writer, dean*
Libin, Alexander Viktorovich *psychologist, researcher, writer*
Lieber, Robert James *political science professor*
Littig, Lawrence William *psychologist, educator*
Lyon, Andrew Bennet *economist*
Malet, David Samuel *social sciences educator*
Mann, Thomas Edward *political scientist*
Marcuss, Rosemary Daly *economist*
Martinez, Herminia S. *economist, banker*
Mattoo, Aaditya *economist*
McCabe, Brian *political strategist*
Meggers, Betty Jane *anthropologist, researcher*
Mellman, Mark Steve *public opinion researcher*
Mellor, John Williams *economist, consultant*
Miller, Aaron David *political scientist, writer*
Miller, Debra Lynn *political scientist*
Miller, Margery *psychologist, educator, speech pathology/audiology and mental health services professional, university administrator, academic administrator*
Mishra, Prachi *economist*
Mussa, Michael L. *economist, educator*
Nash, John Davidson, Jr. *economist*
Niskanen, William Arthur, Jr. *economist, retired think-tank executive*
Norquist, Grover Glenn *economist*
Nugent, Rachel A. *economist*
Oberholtzer, Lydia S. *economist, consultant*
O'Connor, Karen *political science professor, researcher, writer*
Ornstein, Norman Jay *political scientist, columnist*
Ortner, Donald J. *biological anthropologist, educator*
Osicka, Teresa D. *health economist, consultant*
Overdahl, James A. *economist*
Ozden, Caglar *economist*
Page, John Martin, Jr. *economist*
Papageorgiou, Chris *economist*
Parsons, A. Cristina *economics professor*
Perle, Richard Norman *political scientist, former federal agency administrator*
Phillips, Robert F. *economics professor, department chairman*
Preker, Alexander S. *economist*
Radin, Beryl Avis *public administration and policy educator*
Radner, Roy *economist, educator, researcher*
Rain, David Rickter *social sciences educator*
Randall, Robert L(ee) *ecological economist*
Reynolds, Robert Joel *economist, consultant*
Rich, Paul John *policy educator, consultant*
Rivlin, Alice Mitchell *economics professor, former federal official*
Roberts, Markley *economist, educator*
Rosenau, James Nathan *political scientist, educator, writer*
Rothenberg, Stuart *political scientist, columnist*
Ryn, Claes Gösta *political science professor*
Scheffman, David Theodore *economist, management educator, consultant*
Schley, Wayne Arthur *political scientist, consultant*
Schneider, Mark *political science professor*
Schorr, Lisbeth Bamberger *policy analyst*
Scott, Charneta Claudetta *psychologist, educator*
Scrivner, Ellen M. *psychologist*
Seifert, Jeffrey W. *political scientist, researcher*
Shambaugh, David Leigh *political scientist, educator, writer*
Silber, David Elliot *clinical psychologist, educator*
Snyder, Jed C. *foreign affairs specialist*
Solomon, Elinor Harris *economics professor*
Stelzer, Irwin Mark *economist*
Stent, Angela E. *political scientist, educator, director*
Stephenson, Sherry Madeline *trade economist*
Stern, Paula *international trade consultant*
Struelens, Michel Maurice Joseph Georges *political science professor, consultant*
Strum, Philippa *political science professor, researcher*
Tharp, Roland George *psychology professor*
Trachtenberg, Stephen Joel *political science professor, former academic administrator*
Trost, Robert Patrick *economist*
Tucker, Jonathan Brin *political scientist*
Turner, John Andrew *economist*
Valenzuela, Arturo Arms *political science professor, writer, consultant*
Variyam, Jayachandran N. *economist*
Voeten, Erik *political scientist, educator*
Volcker, Paul Adolph *economist, former Chairman of the Board of Governors of the Federal Reserve System*
Wehner, Peter Hermann *political scientist, former federal official*
Weinhold, Linda Lillian *psychologist, researcher*
Weintraub, Sidney *economist, educator*
Whitehurst, Grover Jay (Russ Whitehurst) *psychologist, former federal agency administrator*
Wiarda, Iêda Siqueira *political sicence educator*
Wilensky, Gail Roggin *economist, researcher*
Willner, Ann Ruth *political scientist, educator*
Willner, Dorothy *anthropologist, educator*
Winston, David *political strategist, columnist*
Wolfensberger, Donald *political scientist, columnist*
Youniss, James *psychology professor*

FLORIDA

Boca Raton
Anderson, Roxanna Marion *psychology professor*
Feinman, Ronald *social sciences educator*
Joskow, Jules *economic research company executive*
Shalom, Galit *psychologist*

Boynton Beach
Hochberg, Lois J. *retired school psychologist*
Stolzberg, Mark Elliott *psychologist*

Clearwater
Peterson, James Robert *engineering psychologist*

Coral Gables
Marcelin, Louis Herns *sociologist, educator*

Daytona Beach
Smith, Garvin *economics professor*

DeLand
King, Camille Tessitore *psychology professor*

Deerfield Beach
Panitz, Daniel R. *inventor, scientist, composer, psychologist, minister*

Delray Beach
Levinson, Harry *psychologist, educator*

Doral
Levermore, Monique A. *psychologist, educator*

Dunedin
O'Dea, J. David *psychologist, educator*

Dunnellon
Dixon, W(illiam) Robert *retired psychologist*

Estero
Routh, Donald K(ent) *psychologist, educator*

Fort Lauderdale
Cuc, Alexandru *psychology professor*
Gagnon Blodgett, Michelle Dawn *psychologist*
Hartley, Bruce A. *psychologist, educator*
Prosperi, David C. *social sciences educator*

Gainesville
Babb, Florence Evelyn *anthropologist, educator*
Brown, William Samuel, Jr. *communication sciences and disorders educator*
Conway, M. Margaret *political science professor, consultant*
Dahlgren, Robert Lawrence *social studies educator*
Dewsbury, Donald Allen *psychologist*
Harrison, Faye Venetia *anthropologist, educator, writer*
Hornberger, Robert Howard *retired psychologist*
Hozic, Aida Arfan *political science professor*
Milanich, Jerald Thomas *archaeologist, writer, curator*
Moore, John Hartwell *anthropology educator, consultant*
Oren, Ido *political science professor*
Parker, Karen F. *sociology educator*
Peck, Merton Joseph *economist, educator*
Rowland, Neil E. *psychology professor, department chairman*
Samuels, Warren Joseph *retired economics professor*
Silva, Julie *social sciences educator*
Teitelbaum, Philip *psychologist*
Thomas-Houston, Marilyn Miller *anthropologist, educator*
Thrall, Grant Ian *geography educator, software developer-consultant*
von Mering, Otto Oswald *anthropology educator*

Inverness
Holland, Brett *psychologist*

Jacksonville
Ejimofor, Cornelius Ogu *political scientist, educator*
Fisak, Brian *psychology professor*
Godfrey, John Munro *economic consultant*
Scott, Kamela Koon *psychologist, educator*

Kissimmee
Spears, Glenna Ellen *psychologist*

Lakeland
Giles, Barbara M. *political science professor*

Land O Lakes
Wilkinson, Denise V. *psychologist*

Lutz
Ellis, Leslie Elaine *psychotherapist*

Miami
Arango, Penelope Corey *psychologist, consultant*
Beltre-Sancahez, Provi *psychology professor*
Bernstein, Jeffrey Ian *economics educator, consultant*
Freshwater, Shawna Marie *neuropsychologist, clinical psychologist, cognitive neuroscientist*
Jacobson, Leonard I. *psychologist, educator*
Kanet, Roger Edward *political science professor*
Karayalcin, Cem *economics professor*
Lefley, Harriet Phillips *psychologist, educator*
Medvin, Nadeen Beth *psychologist, consultant*
Michel, Jesse Steven *psychology professor*

Miami Beach
Kalsner-Silver, Lydia *psychologist*
Palamara, Sherry A. *psychologist*

Miami Shores
Cremades, J. Gualberto *psychology professor*

Naples
Riggs, Fletcher Eugene *economist, consultant*

Ocala
Mishkin, Michael Lawrence *psychologist, educator*

Orlando
Ashe, Diane Davis *psychology professor, sport psychology consultant*
Fine, Terri Susan *political science professor*
Wenzel, Jason B. *anthropologist, educator*
Zorn, Elayne Lesley *anthropologist, educator*

Palm Beach
Murray, John Francis *psychologist*

Palm Harbor
Eberts, John Jacob *social sciences educator, department chairman*

Panama City
Roberts, Paul Craig III *economics professor, writer, columnist*

Pensacola
Arnold, Barry Raynor *philosophy educator, medical ethicist*
Killian, Lewis Martin *sociology educator*

Plantation
Costa, Paul Joseph *psychologist*

Pompano Beach
Warnath, Maxine Ammer *psychologist, arbitrator*

Ponte Vedra Beach
Wu, Hsiu Kwang *economist, educator*

Port Charlotte
Von Holden, Martin Harvey *psychologist*

Port Saint Lucie
Augelli, John Pat *geographer, educator, writer, consultant, rancher*

Quincy
Rittman, Benita Griffin *psychologist*

Saint Augustine
Henderson, Hazel *economist, writer*
Sorkin, Robert Daniel *psychologist, industrial engineer, educator*

Saint Petersburg
Janus, Nancy *human development professor*
Rosenblum, Zina Michelle Zarin *psychology professor, marketing professional, researcher*

Sanibel
Crown, David Allan *criminologist, educator*

Sarasota
Gordon, Sanford Daniel *economics professor*
Masters, John Christopher *psychologist, educator*

Stuart
Bush, Harriet *psychologist*
Grieve, William Roy *psychologist, educator, educational administrator, researcher*

Summerfield
Swanson, David Henry *retired economist, educator, consultant*

Sun City Center
Petersen, Carolyn Ashcraft *retired psychologist*

Tallahassee
Brueckheimer, William Rogers *social sciences educator*
Cockrell, Wilburn Allen *archaeologist*
Cui, Ming *social studies educator*
Davis, John Dwelle *psychology professor*
Holcombe, Randall Gregory *economics professor*
Kim, HeeMin *political science professor*
Laird, William Everette, Jr. *economics professor*
Mesev, Victor *geographer, educator*
Nam, Charles Benjamin *demographer, sociologist, educator, writer*
Reardon, Robert C. *retired psychology professor*
Standley-Burt, Nancy Vilma *retired psychologist, educator*
Thompson, Gregory Lee *social sciences educator*

Tampa
Berne, Patricia Higgins *psychologist, writer, educator*
Coleman, Rodney Albert *political scientist, consultant*
DeBoskey, Dana Stephens *psychologist, consultant*
Duda, Vaclav *social studies and biology educator, artist*
Forsythe, Robert Elliott *economics professor*
Hekkanen, Steve *psychology professor*
Horvath, Michael J. *economics professor*
Kimmel, Ellen Bishop *psychologist, educator*
Loewy, Michael *economics professor*
Lynch, Michael Joseph *criminologist, educator*
Morris, Kendall Francis *psychology professor*
Sarbacker, Donald LeRoy *economics professor*
Skvoretz, John Vincent *sociologist, educator*
Spielberger, Charles Donald *psychologist, educator*
Tan, Jun *psychology professor, researcher*
Weiner, Irving Bernard *psychologist*

Tequesta
Swets, John Arthur *psychologist, researcher*

Titusville
Fuller, Joseph Patrick *economics professor*

Velrico
Newman, Phyllis *retired counselor, therapist, hypnotist*

Venice
Delaney, Robert Finley *retired columnist, political sociologist, lecturer*
Gooding, Charles Thomas *psychologist, educator, retired academic administrator*

Vero Beach
Snook, Stover Hoffman *retired social sciences educator*

West Palm Beach
Dye, Thomas Roy *political science professor*
Gold, Bela *economist, educator*
Rakip, Anne Marie *psychology professor*

Weston
Alexander, Cynthia Louise *psychologist, educator*

Winter Haven
Scott, Sherry J. *psychologist*

Winter Park
Cook, Jo Ann Likins *psychologist*
Rock, Charles Patrick *economics professor, researcher*

Winter Springs
Smyth, Michael P. *archaeologist, educator*

GEORGIA

Albany
Ansari, Mohammed Ishaque *economics professor*
Elufiede, Babafemi Olayiwola *social sciences educator*
Stallworth, Charles Derotha, Jr. *psychologist*

Americus
Huffman, Charles M. *psychology professor*
Shapiro, Paul D. *sociologist, educator*

Athens
Allsbrook, Ogden Olmstead, Jr. *retired economics professor*
Clute, Robert Eugene *political science professor*
Dunn, Delmer Delano *political science professor*
Garbin, Albeno Patrick *sociology educator*
Johnson, Loch Kingsford *political science educator, researcher*
Kellough, J. Edward *political science professor, department chairman*
Nichols, William Curtis *psychologist, educator, marriage and family therapist, consultant*
O'Toole, Laurence Joseph *public administration and policy educator, researcher*
Pollack, Robert Harvey *psychology professor*
Reitz, Elizabeth J. *anthropologist, educator*
Sullivan, Patricia Lynne *political science professor*

Atlanta
Bahl, Roy Winford *economist, educator, consultant*
Barke, Richard P. *political science professor*
Chiang, Tze I. *economist, researcher, consultant*
Coles, Charlton J. *psychologist, educator*
Davis, Aimee Slaughter *social studies educator*
Fivush, Robyn *psychology professor, department chairman*

Fox, Mary Frank *sociology educator, researcher*
Garland, LaRetta Matthews *psychologist, nursing educator*
Gay, Robert Derril *behavioral health consultant*
Goodman, Sherryl Hope *psychology professor*
King, Preston Theodore *social sciences educator, writer, political philosopher*
Knapp, Charles Boynton *economist, former university president, educator*
Lilienfeld, Scott Owen *psychology educator*
Mialon, Sue *economics professor*
Muth, Richard Ferris *economics professor*
Nemeroff, Charles Barnet *neurobiology and psychiatry educator*
Rothbaum, Barbara Olasov *psychologist, educator*
Snarey, John Robert *psychologist, educator*
Stayton, William Ralph *psychologist, educator*
Stephan, Paula Elizabeth *economics professor, academic administrator*
Weiss, Jay M(ichael) *psychologist, educator*
Wolff, Phillip Mark *psychology professor*

Augusta
Jenks, Charles Evan *social sciences educator*

Barnesville
Borders, Michael William *psychology professor*

Carrollton
Luken, Paul Clement *social studies educator*
Stone, Sandra Smith *sociologist, academic administrator, researcher*

Clarkston
Kahiga, Mundia James *economics professor*

Claxton
Hagan, Christina M. *psychologist*
Price, Jennifer Leigh *social studies educator*

Columbus
Daniels, Michael J. *economics professor, consultant*
Langston, Vicky C. *economics professor*
Newtson, Richard L. *sociologist, educator*
Peavy, Thomas Ostine *retired psychology professor, retired education educator*

Evans
Zachert, Virginia *retired psychologist*

Fort Stewart
McCarthy, Dorothy A. (Landers) *educator*

Gainesville
Frank, Mary Lou Bryant *psychologist, educator*
Young, Douglas Parker, Jr. *social studies educator*

Griffin
Shockley, Carol Frances *psychologist, psychotherapist*

Lawrenceville
Rawson, Harve E. *psychologist, writer*

Lilburn
Neumann, Thomas William *archaeologist*

Macon
Cook, Charlotte C. *psychologist*
Mulholland, Sean *economics professor*

Marietta
Cochrane, J. La Juana *psychology professor*
Dudley, Gary Edward *psychologist*

Rock Spring
Walters, Michael W. *social sciences educator*

Roswell
Crawford, Mark E. *psychologist*

Savannah
Cebula, Richard John *economist, educator*
Martin, Grace Burkett *psychologist*
Mukhtar, Mohamed Haji *social sciences educator*
Rozantine, Gayle Stubbs *psychologist*

Statesboro
Henry, Nicholas Llewellyn *public administration educator*
Lloyd, Margaret Ann *psychologist, educator*
Yang, Bill Z. *economics professor*

Suwanee
Cox, Albert Harrington, Jr. *retired economist*

Swainsboro
Wilkes, Elaina B. *psychologist*

Toccoa Falls
Brock, Dorothy Dixon *psychologist, psychology professor*

Valdosta
Nikolov, Ivan P. *economics professor*
Whitehead, Jane Katharine *archaeologist, educator*

Young Harris
March, Boyd Lee *dean, political science professor, researcher*

HAWAII

Holualoa
Scarr, Sandra Wood *retired psychology educator, researcher*

Honolulu
Ahina, Leilani *psychologist*
Bitterman, Morton Edward *psychologist, educator*
Cho, Lee-Jay *social scientist, demographer*
Fullmer, Daniel Warren *former psychologist, educator*
Hefner, Carl J. *anthropology educator*
Kaholokula, Joseph Keaweaimoku *psychologist health disparities researcher*
Kim, Ji-Yeon *developmental psychologist*
Nordyke, Eleanor Cole *demographer, researcher, public health nurse*
Paige, Glenn Durland *political scientist, educator*
Pedersen, Paul Bodholdt *psychologist, educator*
Pinckney, Neal T. *psychologist, retired educator*
Shay, Roshani Cari *political science professor and healthcare professional*
Staats, Arthur W. *psychology professor*
Suh, Dae-Sook *political science professor*

Kailua
Tavares, Samantha *psychologist, educator*

Kaneohe
Coberly, Margaret *psychologist, educator*

Laie
Jonassen, Jon Tikivanotau Michael *political science professor, musician*

IDAHO

Boise
Guha, Bhaswati *economics professor*
Overgaard, Willard Michele *retired political scientist*
Pfouts, Ralph William *economist, consultant*
Plew, Mark G. *archaeologist, educator*
Slaughter, Richard Arthur *political scientist, economist, educator*

Caldwell
Angresano, James *political economics professor*

Mountain Home
English, Brian Patrick *social studies educator*

Pocatello
Piland, Neill Finnes *health services economist, researcher, educator*

Sandpoint
Glock, Charles Young *retired sociologist, writer*

Sun Valley
Stewart, John Todd *economist, consultant*

Twin Falls
Wright, Frances Jane *educational psychologist*

ILLINOIS

Arlington Heights
Griffin, Jean Latz *college instructor, writer, publisher*

Barrington
Chung, Joseph Sang-hoon *economics professor*

Belleville
Loehring, Brian Todd *social studies educator, department chairman*

Belvidere
Mc Nelly, Frederick Wright, Jr. *psychologist*

Bloomington
Mead, Walter Bruce *retired political science professor*

Bolingbrook
Gelin-Rodriguez, Maureen T. *psychologist*

Calumet City
Pickel, Joyce Kiley *psychologist*

Carbondale
Dai, Chifeng *economics professor*
Duram, Leslie Aileen *geographer, educator*
Primont, Daniel *economics professor*
Sutton, David E. *anthropologist, educator*
Trescott, Paul Barton *economics professor*

Champaign
Althaus, Scott L. *political science professor*
Baillargeon, Renee *psychology professor*
Carmen, Ira Harris *political scientist, educator*
Davis, James Henry *retired psychology educator*
Dulany, Donelson Edwin, Jr. *psychology professor*
Eriksen, Charles Walter *psychologist, educator*
Farmer, Helen Sweeney *psychology professor*
Irwin, David E. *psychology professor, department chairman*
Triandis, Harry Charalambos *psychologist, educator*
Xiao, Zhijie *economics educator*

Chicago
Aksikas, Jaafar *social sciences educator*
Bajich, Milena Tatic *psychologist*
Becker, Gary Stanley *economist, educator*
Bicknell-Hentges, Lindsay Pugh *psychology professor*
Bidwell, Charles Edward *sociologist, educator*
Bryant, Fred Boyd *psychology professor*
Carlton, Dennis William *economics professor*
Coase, Ronald Harry *economist, educator*
Cohler, Bertram Joseph *psychologist, educator*
Comaroff, Jean *anthropologist, educator*
Davis, Henry E. *psychologist*
Dawson, Michael C. *political science professor*
Elshtain, Jean Bethke *social sciences educator*
Epstein, Lee Joan *political science and law professor*
Fernandez, James *anthropology educator*
Fogel, Robert William *economist, historian, educator*
Freeman, Leslie Gordon *anthropologist, educator*
Freeman, Susan Tax *anthropologist, educator, culinary historian*
Gal, Susan *anthropologist, educator*
Gavrilova, Natalia S. *demographer*
Giblin, Nan J. *psychologist, educator*
Gibson, McGuire *archaeologist, educator*
Goldin-Meadow, Susan *psychology professor*
Gould, John Philip *economist, educator*
Graber, Doris Appel *political scientist, writer, editor*
Grogger, Jeffrey *economics professor*
Gupta, Mahesh P. *psychology professor*
Han, Euna *economist, researcher*
Heckman, James Joseph *economist, educator*
Heinemann, Allen W. *rehabilitation psychologist*
Hoogenboom, Carol Annette *clinical neuropsychologist*
Huttenlocher, Janellen *psychology educator, psychologist*
Kaplan, Morton A. *political science professor*
Kasule, Ssebunya Edward *political science professor*
Kroszner, Randall Scott *economics professor, former federal official*
Larson, Allan Louis *political scientist, educator, lay worker*
Laumann, Edward Otto *sociology educator*
Lima, Victor Osvaldo *economist, educator*
Liu, Ben-chieh *economist*
Lowe, Sandra Elveta *psychologist*
Lucas, Robert Emerson, Jr. *economist, educator*
Luhrmann, Tanya Marie *anthropology educator, writer*
McCloskey, Michael *social sciences, psychology, and sociology educator*
McNeill, G. David *psychologist, educator*
Mearsheimer, John Joseph *political science professor*
Morales-Pita, Antonio Evaristo *economics professor*
Murphy, Kevin M. *economics professor*
Myerson, Roger Bruce *economist, educator*
Nicholas, Ralph Wallace *anthropologist, educator*
Njoku, Mary Gloria *psychology professor, researcher*
Northcut, Terry Brumley *social sciences educator*
Peltzman, Sam *economics professor*
Prendergast, Brian *psychologist, educator*
Rosen, George *economist, educator*
Rowan, Thomas Bernard III *political science professor*
Rzepnicki, Tina L. *social sciences educator*
Sanders, Jacquelyn Seevak *psychologist, educator*
Segerstrale, Ullica Christina *social sciences educator, researcher*
Shaikh, Sabina Lee *economist, educator*
Shankman, Stewart A. *psychologist, educator*
Simons, Helen *school psychologist, psychotherapist, educator*
Simpson, Dick Weldon *political science educator*
Smith, Raymond Thomas *anthropology educator*
Smith, Stan Vladimir *economist, finance company executive*
Staller, John Edward *archaeologist, anthropologist, educator*
Swagel, Phillip L. *economics professor, former federal agency administrator*
Swonk, Diane Catherine *economist*
Taub, Richard Paul *social sciences educator*
Tezcur, Gunes Murat *political science professor*
Tolan, Patrick Henry *psychology educator*
Topel, Robert *economics professor*
Townsend, Katherine *psychologist, educator*
Uhlig, Harald *economics professor*
Walberg, Herbert John *psychologist, educator, consultant*
Wynne, Martha Ellen *psychology professor*
Zagar, Robert John *psychologist, researcher*
Zellner, Arnold *economics, econometrics and statistics professor*
Zonis, Marvin *political scientist, educator*

Decatur
Hawkin, Evyonne *social studies educator*

Deerfield
Heller, Matthew A. *psychology professor*

Dekalb
Shernoff, David Jordan *psychology professor*
Slotsve, George Aaron *economist, educator, consultant*
Un, Kheang *political scientist*
Walzer, Norman Charles *retired economics professor*

Downers Grove
Bruesch, John R. *social studies educator, department chairman*

Eureka
Staudenmeier, William John, Jr. *sociology professor*

Evanston
Brown, James Allison *anthropology educator*
Chambers, Anthony LaRoyce *psychologist, educator*
Christiano, Lawrence Joseph *economist, educator*
Eagly, Alice Hendrickson *social psychology educator*
Fong, Yuk-fai *economist, educator*
Gordon, Robert James *economics professor*
Griswold, Wendy *sociologist, educator*
Hughes, Susan L. *gerontologist, researcher*
Hurter, Arthur Patrick *economist, educator*
Kalai, Ehud *economist, researcher, educator*
Matzkin, Rosa Liliana *economics professor*
Mills, Edwin Smith *economics professor*
Oh, John Kie-Chiang *political science professor, academic administrator*
Palloni, Alberto Bruno *social sciences educator*
Spier, Kathryn Elizabeth *economist, educator*
Weisbrod, Burton Allen *economist, educator*
Whinston, Michael D. *economics professor*

Galena
Gallagher, Lynn *social sciences educator*

Galesburg
Edi, Eric *political science professor, consultant*
McAndrew, Francis Thomas *psychology professor*
Scotton, Carol Robinson *economist, educator*

Glen Carbon
Lin, Steven An-Yhi *economics professor*

Glen Ellyn
Emano, Dennis Jose Marmol *associate professor*

Glenview
Farber, Isadore E. *psychologist, educator*

Hinsdale
Dederick, Robert Gogan *economist*

Jacksonville
Green, Melinda Ann *psychologist, educator, research scientist*
Hardin, Susan Jean *social studies educator, department chairman*
Wells, Winston Raymond *political science professor*

Joliet
Zhou, Ling-Yi *psychology professor*

Kingston
Gherity, James Arthur *economics professor*

Lindenhurst
Eron, Madeline Marcus *psychologist*

Lockport
Bentley, Stephen James *psychologist, coach*

Maryville
Stark, Patricia Ann *psychologist*

Moline
Penn, J. B. *economist, former federal agency administrator*

Mundelein
Kwon, Ho-Youn *sociologist, researcher*

Naperville
Caliendo, Stephen Maynard *political science professor*
McCallum, Gerald Christopher *clinical psychologist*
Porumbescu, Doina Roxana *psychologist, educator*

Normal
Alferink, Larry Allen *psychology professor*
Lind, Nancy Susan *political science professor*
Payne, James Earl *economics professor, dean*
Titus, Janet Catherine *psychologist, researcher*

North Chicago
Kosson, David Steven *psychology professor*

Northbrook
Di Spigno, Guy Joseph *industrial psychologist, international management consultant*

Olney
Jones, Carmen Rose *social sciences educator*

Oswego
Weinstein-Blackman, Ellen Donna *school psychologist*

Palatine
Styer, Denise Marie *psychologist*

Peoria
Elmore, Donita Lynn *social studies educator*
Lewer, Joshua J. *economics professor*

River Forest
Rodgers, Jan A. *social work educator*

River Grove
Stein, Thomas Henry *social sciences educator*

Riverwoods
Kirby, Emily Baruch *psychologist, writer, academic administrator*

Rockford
Clodius, Robert LeRoy *retired economist*

Rolling Meadows
Carbonell, David *psychologist*

Schaumburg
Dore, Patricia Ann *psychologist*
Stilling, Mark *psychologist, professional football coach*

Springfield
Reyman, Jonathan Eric *archaeologist, anthropologist, researcher*
Wehrle, Leroy Snyder *economist, educator*

Tinley Park
Freitag, Carol Wilma *political scientist*

Urbana
Baer, Werner *economist, educator*
Brewer, Douglas James *anthropology professor, museum director*
Cunningham, Clark Edward *anthropology educator*
Gabriel, Michael *psychology professor*
Giles, Eugene *anthropology educator*
Gove, Samuel Kimball *retired political science professor*
Lüschen, Günther Rudolf Friedo *social sciences educator*
Nettl, Bruno *anthropologist, musicologist, educator*
Resek, Robert William *economist*

Thompson, Robert Lee *agricultural economist, educator*
Warren, Pamela A. *psychologist*
Wirt, Frederick Marshall *retired political scientist, educator*

Wheaton
Allen, Henry Lee *sociology educator, consultant*

Wilmette
Schloss, Nathan *retired economist*

Yorkville
Rytkonen, Katie *psychologist*

INDIANA

Angola
Laker, Craig William *social sciences educator*

Bloomington
Becker, William Edward *economist, consultant*
Brehm, Sharon Stephens *psychology professor, former academic administrator*
Chang, Fwu-Ranq *economics professor, researcher*
Conrad, Geoffrey Wentworth *archaeologist, educator*
Cummings, Jack Alan *psychology professor*
Guth, Sherman Leon (S. Lee) *psychologist, educator*
Jackson, Jason Baird *folklorist, director*
Leeper, Eric M. *economics professor*
O'Meara, Patrick O. *political science professor*
Ostrom, Elinor *political science professor, researcher*
Peebles, Christopher Spalding *anthropologist, educator, academic administrator*
Reingold, David Ami *sociologist, educator*
Reinisch, June Machover *psychologist, educator, researcher*
Risinger, C. Frederick *social studies educator*
Saunders, W(arren) Phillip, Jr. *economics professor, consultant, writer*
Scheiber, Laura Lee *archaeologist, educator*
Smith, Linda B. *psychology professor, department chairman*
Thorelli, Sarah V. *economist, researcher*
von Furstenberg, George Michael *economics professor, researcher*
Watson, Charles Schoff *psychology professor*

Carmel
Rychlak, Joseph Frank *psychologist, educator*

Columbus
Williams, Robert Joseph *behavioral health services executive, psychologist*

Fort Wayne
Rassuli, Ali *economist, consultant*
Sutter, Richard C. *anthropologist, educator*

Gary
Lin, Tin-Chun *economics professor, director*
Needleman, Ruth Ann *social sciences educator*

Greenwood
Hagedorn, Alan Patrick *social studies educator*

Hammond
Mitra, Amlan *economics professor, researcher*

Indianapolis
Cardwell, Sue Webb *psychology professor*
de Waal, Cornelis *philosophy professor, editor*
Divita, James J. *retired social studies educator, writer, researcher*
Gregg, Stephen Thompson *political scientist, consultant*
Grossman, Peter Zigmund *economics professor*
Harris, Robert B. *economics professor*
Kessler, Marcia Lynn *school psychologist*
Leganza, Cathleen Ann *psychologist*
Swindle, Ralph Wilson, Jr. *research psychologist*
Tatom, John Anthony *economist*
VanVoorhis, Rebecca Jane *social sciences educator, consultant*
Woods, Jeffrey George *economist, researcher*

Kendallville
Tipton, Deborah Jo *psychologist*

Kokomo
Wysong, Earl Edward *sociologist, educator*

Lafayette
Hardin, Lowell Stewart *retired economics professor*
Schönemann, Peter Hans *psychologist, educator*
Schweickert, Richard Justus *psychologist, educator*

Madison
Gotts, Edward Earl *psychologist, researcher*

Marion
Puffer, Keith Andrew *psychology professor*

Muncie
Cheng, Chu Yuan *economics professor*
Swartz, B. K., Jr., (Benjamin Kinsell Swartz Jr.) *archaeologist, educator*

North Manchester
Onyeji, Benson Chinedu *political science professor*

Notre Dame
Arnold, Peri Ethan *political scientist*
Bartell, Ernest *economist, educator, priest*
Despres, Leo Arthur *sociologist, anthropologist, educator, academic administrator*
Eberhard, Kathleen Marie *psychology educator, researcher*
Hallinan, Maureen Theresa *sociologist, educator*
Langan, Jeffrey Joseph *political science professor*
McElroy, Jerome Lathrop *economics professor*
Mirowski, Philip Edward *economics professor*
Valenzuela, Julio Samuel *sociologist, educator*
Walshe, Aubrey Peter *emeritus political science professor*
Weigert, Andrew Joseph *sociology educator*
Welch, Michael R. *sociologist, educator*

South Bend
Carrington, Michael Davis *criminal justice and security consultant*
Dowty, Alan Kent *political scientist, educator*
Trottier, Tracey *social studies educator*

Terre Haute
Leigh, Janis *clinician*

West Lafayette
Chien, Yili *economics professor*
Cicirelli, Victor George *psychologist*
Connor, John Murray *economics professor*
Davidson, James Daglish, Jr. *retired professor of sociology*
Farris, Paul Leonard *agricultural economist*
Foster, Kenneth A. *economics professor*
Gruen, Gerald Elmer *psychologist, educator*
Kadiyala, K. Rao *retired economics professor*
Loehman, Edna Tusak *economics professor*
Moghadam, Valentine M. *sociology professor*
Perrucci, Robert *sociologist, educator*
Swensen, Clifford Henrik, Jr. *psychologist, educator*
Tyner, Wallace Edward *agricultural economics educator*
Weinstein, Michael Alan *political science professor*

IOWA

Ames
Cross, Susan E. *psychologist, educator*
Harl, Neil Eugene *economist, educator, lawyer, writer*
James, Patrick *political science educator*
Kusow, Abdi M. *social sciences educator*
Lando, Harry Alan *psychology educator*
Larson, Sidner John *social sciences educator*
O'Boyle, Michael William *psychology educator*

Cedar Falls
Gilgen, Albert Rudolph *retired psychologist, educator*
van Wormer, Katherine Stuart *social work educator*

Cedar Rapids
Eichhorn, Richard Gerard *economics professor*
Sauerman, Nancy *psychology professor*

Clive
Miller, Kenneth Edward *sociologist, educator*

Davenport
Achs, Jack Horst *social studies educator*
Woodruff, Theodore Sherman *economics professor*

Dubuque
Jorgensen, Gerald Thomas *psychologist, educator, lawyer*

Grinnell
Moyer, H. Wayne *political science professor*

Iowa City
Albrecht, William Price *economist, educator, government official*
Barkan, Joel David *political science professor*
Brook, Stacey L. *economics professor*
Christensen, Alan J. *psychology professor, department chairman*
Fethke, Gary C. *economics professor, former dean*
Geweke, John Frederick *economics professor*
Honey, Rex Dean *social sciences educator*
Kim, Chong Lim *political science professor*
Levin, Irwin Paul *psychology professor*
Loewenberg, Gerhard *political science professor*
Malanson, George Patrick *geography educator*
Riezman, Raymond *economics professor*
Siebert, Calvin D. *economist, educator*
Simon, J(ennings) Richard *psychologist, educator*
Skinstad, Anne Helene *psychologist, researcher*

Keokuk
White, John David *social sciences educator*

Le Claire
Varney, Nils Roberts *neuropsychologist, researcher*

Pella
Zaffiro, James J. *political science professor*

West Burlington
Skeens, Lee Roy *psychology professor*

West Des Moines
Thompson, Gerald Everett *economics professor*

KANSAS

Fort Leavenworth
Mullis, Tony Randall *military history educator*

Goddard
Cundy, Amanda D. *psychologist*

Hays
Arano, Kathleen *economics professor*
Nassif, Carrie *psychologist, educator*

Kansas City
Lancaster, Ronnie Lyle *psychologist*
Penick, Elizabeth C. *psychologist*
Shariati, Mehdi Sezavar *social sciences educator*

Lawrence
Barnett, William Arnold *economics professor*
Chong, Kelly Haesung *sociologist*
Herlihy, Laura Hobson *anthropologist*
Kim, ChangHwan *sociologist, educator*
Pence, Ray *social studies educator*
Shaffer, Harry George *retired economics professor*
Simpson, Greg B. *psychology professor, department chairman*
Takeyama, Akiko *anthropologist, educator*

Liberal
Devinney, Carroll Lynn *economics professor*

Lindsborg
Ahlseen, Mark Jason *economics professor*
Pigge, Joyce A. *political science professor*

Manhattan
Babcock, Michael Ward *economics professor*
Barkley, Andrew Paul *economics professor*
Murray, John Patrick *psychologist, educator, researcher*
Nafziger, Estel Wayne *economics professor*
Prins, Harald Edward Lambert *anthropologist, educator*
Richter, William Louis *social sciences educator*
Wesch, Michael *anthropology educator, cultural anthropologist, media ecologist*

North Newton
Eitzen, David Stanley *sociologist, educator*

Olathe
Fales, Jennifer Lea *family and consumer sciences educator*

Overland Park
Seitter, Julie E. *psychologist*

Shawnee
Poplau, Ronald W. *social studies educator*

Topeka
Cohen, Lauren Ann *psychologist*
Jones, Carlene P. *psychologist, educator*
Smith, Loran Bradford *political science professor*
Spohn, Herbert Emil *psychologist*

Wichita
Blakeslee, Donald J. *archaeologist, writer*
Kahn, Melvin A. *political science professor*
Sommer, James Steven *psychologist*
Unruh, Susan Marie *psychologist, educator*

KENTUCKY

Bowling Green
Cangemi, Joseph Peter *psychologist, consultant, educator*

Campbellsville
Parker, Jeanette *psychology professor*

Covington
Littleton, Nan Elizabeth Feldkamp *psychologist, educator*

Danville
Anderson, David Anton *economics professor*
Johnson, Bruce Kenneth *economics professor, department chairman*

Georgetown
Cairo, Michael *political science professor*

Independence
Hopgood, James F. *anthropologist, educator*

Lexington
Garen, John Edward *economics professor*
Hall, Harry H. *agricultural economics educator*
Hillebrand, Evan Everett *economist, educator*
Hochstrasser, Donald Lee *cultural anthropologist , community health and public administrator*
Hultman, Charles William *economics professor*
Reed, Michael Robert *agricultural economist*
Rous, Beth S. *social studies educator, researcher*
Saghaian, Sayed *economics professor*
Stempel, John Dallas *international studies educator*
Stilwell, William Earle III *psychology educator, retired military officer*
Wildasin, David E(arl) *economics professor*
Worell, Judith P. *psychologist, educator*

Louisville
Davis, Charles Raymond *retired political scientist, educator*
Nahata, Babu L. *economics professor, researcher*
Stanton, Morris Duncan *psychologist, researcher, dean*
Tasman, Allan *psychiatry educator*
Zahorik, Pavel *psychology professor*

Madisonville
Florea, Jeffrey Mark *economics professor*
Price, Erica Hightower *psychologist*

Morehead
Miller, Green Russell *economist, educator*

Murray
Hassan, Seid Y. *economics professor*

Paintsville
Hovee, Mark John *psychologist*

Prestonsburg
Bell, Daniel Edwin *economics professor*

Richmond
Houston, Robert Grant, Jr. *economics professor*

Versailles
Stober, William John, II, *economics professor*

Williamsburg
Trickett, Dennis James *psychology professor*
Weaver, Susan Jeanne *sociology educator*

LOUISIANA

Alexandria
Bilotta, Warren Alexander *economics professor*

Baton Rouge
Beard, Thomas Rex *economics professor*
Cramer, Gail *economist*
Ingram, Donald Keith *psychologist, gastroenterologist*
Liu, Kam-Biu *geography educator*
Marks, Loren Dean *psychology professor*
Sandoz, George Ellis, Jr. *political science educator*

Bossier City
Paris, Norma Jean *psychologist, educational consultant*

Hammond
Lee, Sang Hyup *economics professor, researcher*

Lafayette
Brabant, Sarah Callaway *sociologist, educator*
Greco, Anthony Joseph *economics professor*
Skinner, Sarah Jackson *economics professor*

Lake Charles
Ferguson, Clarence Edward *social sciences educator*

Metairie
Falco, Maria Josephine *political scientist*
Wood, Jonathan Stuart *economist, educator*

Monroe
Parker, Tammy A. *economics professor*
Smith, Pamela LaTrice *school psychologist*
Wilson, Holly Lyn *social sciences educator, researcher*

New Orleans
Andrews, E. Wyllys *archaeologist, educator*
Balée, William L. *anthropology educator*
Boudreaux, Kenneth Justin *economist, educator*
Castaneda, Marco A. *economics professor*
Du, Shanshan *anthropologist, educator*
Jain, Prem C. *economics professor*
Kelly, Eamon Michael *economic development professor, retired university president*
Lodhi, Mahtab A. *social sciences educator*
Moely, Barbara E. *psychologist, educator*
Okorn, Nchor Bichene *political science professor*
Olson, Richard David *psychology professor*

Pineville
Thrasher, Fay C. *clinical psychologist*

Ruston
Sale, Tom S. III *financial economist*
Sarkar, Jayanta *economist, educator*

Shreveport
Staats, Thomas Elwyn *neuropsychologist*

MAINE

Alna
Russell, Clifford Springer *economics, public policy, educator*

Augusta
Nickerson, John Mitchell *political science professor*

Bath
Galleher, Gay *psychologist*

Brunswick
Fuchs, Alfred Herman *psychologist, educator*

Falmouth
Pierce, Philip Sargent *clinical psychologist*

Lewiston
Hodgkin, Douglas Irving *political science professor*
Wollman, Nathaniel *retired economics professor*

Mount Desert
Elias, Merrill Francis *neuropsychology and neuroepidemiology researcher*

Orono
Cody, Howard Hugh *political science professor*
Cohn, Steven Frederick *sociology educator, consultant*
Dalton, Timothy John *economics professor*
Goldstone, Sanford *psychologist, educator*
Kearney, Adrienne Anne *economics professor*

Unity
Lynch, Donald Frederick *psychology professor*

Waterville
Gilkes, Cheryl Louise Townsend *sociologist, educator, minister*

MARYLAND

Baltimore
Asuncion-Miller, Lana Martina *school psychologist*
Brennan, Timothy John *economics professor*
Bright, Margaret *sociologist*
Catania, A(nthony) Charles *psychologist, educator*
Cooper, Joseph *political scientist, educator*

Fakhraei, S. Hamid *economist, researcher*
Gerson, Arlene C. *psychologist*
Gindling, Thomas Henry (Tim Henry) *economics professor*
Green, Bert Franklin, Jr. *retired psychology professor*
Henderson, Lenneal Joseph, Jr. *political science professor*
Hody, Cynthia Ann *political science professor*
Karni, Edi *economics professor*
Kirkhart, Matthew Wayde *psychology professor*
Kohn, Melvin L. *sociologist*
Maccini, Louis John *economist, educator*
Melick, Clifford Francis *sociologist, researcher*
Moffitt, Robert Allen *economics educator*
Passley, Josef Antonio *psychologist, educator, writer*
Powers, David V. *psychology professor, department chairman*
Rabin, Bernard M. *psychology professor*
Salamon, Lester Milton *political science professor*
Sensenig, Arthur Lloyd *economist, consultant*
Sorkin, Alan Lowell *economist, educator*

Bethesda
Banik, Sambhu Nath *psychologist*
Cleary, Robert Edward *government and public affairs educator*
de Vries, Margaret Garritsen *economist*
Krantz, David S. *psychology educator, researcher*
Lystad, Mary Hanemann (Mrs. Robert Lystad) *sociologist, writer*
Mishkin, Mortimer *neuropsychologist*
Musil, Robert Kirkland *global environmental politics professor*
Solomon, Robert *economist*
Struyk, Raymond Jay *economist*

Bowie
Bushnell, David Sherman *social psychologist, consultant*
Sengupta, Sunando *economics professor*

Catonsville
Groninger, Lowell *psychology professor*

Chestertown
Narita, Noriko *social studies educator*
Wendel, Richard Frederick *economist, educator, consultant*

Chevy Chase
Alexander, Arthur Jacob *economist*
Krupnick, Janice Lee *psychologist, psychotherapist, educator*
Norwood, Bernard *economist*
Norwood, Janet Lippe *economist*
Sapin, Burton Malcolm *political science professor*

Clinton
Manchester, Robert W. *psychologist*

College Park
Barber, Benjamin R. *political scientist, educator*
Betancourt, Roger Rene *economist*
Destler, I. M(ac) *political scientist, foreign policy writer*
Epstein, Norman B. *psychologist, marriage and family therapist, educator*
Gaylin, Ned L. *psychologist, educator*
Hall, William Sterling *psychology educator*
Haltiwanger, John C. *economics professor*
Hill, Clara Edith *psychologist, educator*
Just, Richard Eugene *economist, consultant, agriculturist, educator*
Kearney, Melissa Schettini *economics professor*
Leathers, Howard *economics professor*
Nerlove, Marc Leon *economics professor*
Olson, Charles Eric *economist*
Presser, Harriet Betty *social studies educator*
Presser, Stanley *social sciences educator, researcher*
Quester, George Herman *political science professor*
Rubin, Kenneth H. *psychology professor, writer*
Schelling, Thomas Crombie *economist*
Schwab, Susan Carroll *public policy educator, former federal official*
Sigall, Harold Fred *psychology professor*
Soltan, Karol Edward *political science professor, director*

Cumberland
Heckert, Paul Charles *sociologist, educator*

Denton
Miller, Frank Louis *school psychologist*

Derwood
Mealy, John Burke *clinical psychologist*

Hagerstown
Harsh, Michael Gerard *social studies educator*
Moran, Suzannah *social sciences educator*

Hampstead
Dotterweich, Patrick Timothy *social studies educator*

Kensington
Oweiss, Ibrahim Mohamed *economist, educator*

La Plata
Bostwick, Catherine *psychologist*

Lanham
McClain, George Nelson *economist, lawyer*

Laurel
McConnaughey, James Walter *economist*

Lutherville
Eisenberg, Joseph Martin *psychologist, consultant*

Middletown
Robinson, Daniel N. *psychology and philosophy professor*

Mitchellville
Blasier, Cole *political scientist*
Peretz, Don *political science professor*

North Bethesda
Chapman, Janet Carter Goodrich *economist, educator*

Pomfret
Craley, Brian Scott *social sciences educator*

Potomac
Vadus, Gloria A. *scientific document examiner*
Walker, Charls Edward *economist, consultant*
Wonnacott, Paul *retired economics professor*

Princess Anne
Brockett, Ramona *criminologist, educator*

Rockville
Niewiaroski, Trudi Osmers (Gertrude) *social studies educator*
Oswald, Rudolph A. *economist*
Psotka, Joseph *psychologist*

Royal Oak
Clizbe, John Anthony *psychologist, social services administrator*

Saint Marys City
Williams, Elizabeth Nutt *psychologist, educator*

Salisbury
Anderson, Eva Klauber *psychologist, educator*
Losonczy-Marshall, Marta Elizabeth *psychologist, educator*

Shady Side
Devine, Donald J. *political science professor, consultant*

Silver Spring
Bate, Marilyn Anne *psychologist*
Glickman, Albert Seymour *psychologist, educator*
Hsueh, Chun-tu *political scientist, educator, foundation administrator, historian*
Leeworthy, Vernon Robert *economist*
Moon, Marilyn Lee *economist*
Noboa, Abdin I. *psychologist, educator*
Rayburn, Carole Ann (Mary Aida) *psychologist, researcher, writer, consultant*
Striner, Herbert Edward *economist*

Stevenson
Galbraith, Clotile Signora *psychology professor*

Towson
Muuss, Rolf Eduard *retired psychologist, author*
Nelson, H. Wayne *gerontologist, advocate*
Pomykala, Joseph Steven *economics professor*

Upper Marlboro
Greene, Monica Lynn Banks *psychologist*

Westminster
Saxton, Celeste Dawn *social studies educator, consultant*

MASSACHUSETTS

Acton
Evans, Robert, Jr. *economics professor*

Amherst
Berger, Seymour Maurice *social psychologist*
Bushouse, Brenda Kae *political science professor*
Daehler, Marvin William *psychology professor emeritus*
Gerstel, Naomi *social sciences educator*
Godfrey, Laurie Rohde *anthropologist, educator*
Haas, Peter M. *political science educator*
Hird, John A. *political science professor*
Klare, Michael Thomas *social sciences educator, director*
Pollatsek, Alexander *retired psychology professor*
Romney, Patricia Ann *psychologist, educator*
Rossi, Alice S. *sociology educator, writer*
Strickland, Bonnie Ruth *psychologist, educator*
Taubman, William Chase *political science professor, writer*
Woodbury, Richard Benjamin *anthropologist, educator*

Babson Park
Genovese, Francis Charles (Frank) *economist, educator, editor-in-chief, writer*

Barre
Reno, Brad Jeffrey *political science educator*

Belmont
Raiffa, Howard *economics educator*

Beverly
Kozyrev, Vitaly A. *political science professor, consultant*

Boston
Appley, Mortimer Herbert *psychologist, retired academic administrator*
Baicker, Katherine (Kate Baicker) *economics professor, former federal official*
Bergstresser, Daniel *economist, educator*
Bodie, Zvi *finance professor, author*
Capetillo-Ponce, Jorge Antonio *sociologist, educator*
Gary, Fireman D. *psychology professor*
Gilchrist, Simon *economics professor*
Gleason, Jean Berko *psychology professor, researcher, author*
Hammond, Norman David Curle *archaeology educator, researcher*
Haughton, Jonathan Haughton *economics professor, consultant*
Henderson, Rebecca Marta *economics professor*
Herzlinger, Regina *economist, educator, writer*
Kahn, Shulamit *economics professor*
Koenen, Karestan *psychologist, educator*
Lemi, Adugna *economics professor*
Malley-Morrison, Kathleen *psychology professor, researcher*
Manning, Peter Kirby *criminal justice educator*
Masi, Dale A. *social sciences educator, research and development company executive*
Merton, Robert C. *economist, educator*
Noor, Jawwad *economics professor*
O'Hern, Jane Susan *psychologist, educator*
Palmer, David Scott *political scientist, educator*
Plotkin, Irving H. (Irving Herman Plotkin) *economist, consultant*
Powell, Benjamin *economics professor*
Psathas, George *sociologist, educator*
Santangelo, Susan L. *psychiatry professor*
Schutt, Russell K. *social studies educator, researcher*
Smith-Doerr, Laurel A. *sociologist, educator*
Swartz, Katherine (B. Katherine Swartz) *economist, educator*
Tootell, Geoffrey Matthew Bemis *economist*
Tuerck, David George *economist, educator*

Brockton
Choquette, Keith Alan *psychologist*

Brookline
Buchin, Jacqueline Chase *psychologist*
Cromwell, Adelaide M. *sociology educator retired*

Cambridge
Allison, Graham Tillett, Jr. *political science professor, former federal agency administrator*
Alt, James Edward *political science professor*
Anderson, William Henry *psychobiology educator*
Ansolabehere, Stephen Daniel *political science professor*
Athey, Susan Carleton *economics professor*
Bailyn, Lotte *psychologist, educator*
Banaji, Mahzarin Rustum *psychology educator*
Barro, Robert Joseph *economics professor*
Bator, Francis Michel *economist, educator*
Bishop, Robert Lyle *retired economist, educator*
Bobo, Lawrence D. *sociologist, educator*
Burns, R. Nicholas (Robert Nicholas Burns, Nick Burns) *international politics professor, former ambassador*
Campbell, John Young *economics professor*
Carpenter, Daniel *political science professor*
Caves, Richard Earl *economist, educator*
Cestnick, Laurie L. *neuropsychologist, educator, scientist*
Cooper, Richard Newell *economist, educator*
Cutler, David M. *economics professor*
Dominguez, Jorge Ignacio *political scientist, educator*
Dussan V, Elizabeth B. *scientific advisor*
Eckaus, Richard Samuel *economist, educator*
Ellerman, Alfred Denny *economics professor*
Ellison, Peter Thorpe *anthropology professor*
Fash, William Leonard, Jr. *anthropologist, educator, museum director*
Feldstein, Martin Stuart *economics professor*
Forbes, Kristin J. *economics professor, former federal official*
Frankel, Jeffrey Alexander *economist, educator*
Friedman, Benjamin Morton *economics professor*
Frisch, Rose Epstein *population sciences researcher*
Fryer, Roland Gerhard *economics professor*
Fudenberg, Drew *economics professor*
Gardner, Howard Earl *psychologist, educator, writer*
Gergen, David Richmond *political science professor*
Gilbert, Daniel Todd *psychology professor*
Goldman, Marshall Irwin *economist, educator*
Gruber, Jonathan H. *economist*
Gusterson, Hugh P. *anthropology educator, writer*
Hart, Oliver D'Arcy *economics professor*
Hausmann, Ricardo *economics professor, director*
Holmstrom, Bengt R. *economics professor*
Izard, Véronique *psychologist, researcher*
Jacoby, Henry Donnan *economist, educator*
Jencks, Christopher Sandys *sociologist, educator*
Kagan, Jerome *psychologist, educator*
Kaysen, Carl *economics professor*
Kelman, Herbert Chanoch *retired psychology professor*
Keniston, Kenneth *psychologist, educator*
Kennedy, Stephen Dandridge *economist, researcher*
Keyfitz, Nathan *sociologist, demographer, educator*
King, Gary *government studies educator*
Kremer, Michael *economist, educator*
Kugler, Maurice *economics professor*
Lamberg-Karlovsky, Clifford Charles *anthropologist, archaeologist*
Lieberson, Stanley *sociologist, educator*
Mankiw, Nicholas Gregory (Gregory Mankiw) *economics professor, former federal official*
Mansbridge, Jane Jebb *political scientist, educator*
Mansfield, Harvey C., Jr. *political science professor*
McNally, Richard James *clinical psychologist, educator*
Meyer, John Robert *economist, educator*
Morgan, Marcyliena *sociologist, educator*
Newey, Whitney K. *economist, educator*
Nye, Joseph Samuel, Jr. *political science professor*
Parlee, Mary Brown *psychology educator*
Perkins, Dwight Heald *economics professor*
Pilbeam, David Roger *paleoanthropology educator, curator*
Pillay, Srinivasan *psychology professor, consultant*
Pinker, Steven Arthur *psychology professor*
Polenske, Karen Rosel *economics educator*
Poterba, James Michael *economist, educator*
Power, Samantha J. *public policy educator, writer*
Putnam, Robert D. *public policy professor*
Retsinas, Nicolas Paul *public policy educator, former federal official*
Rightmire, George Philip *anthropology educator*
Rogoff, Kenneth Saul *economics professor*
Rosovsky, Henry *economist, educator*
Samuelson, Paul Anthony *economist, educator*
Sapolsky, Harvey Morton *political scientist, educator*
Scherer, Frederic Michael *economics professor*
Schmalensee, Richard Lee *economics and management professor, former dean*
Sen, Amartya Kumar *economist, educator*
Sidanius, James H. *psychology professor*
Skolnikoff, Eugene B. *political science professor*
Snyder, James M., Jr. *political science professor, economics professor*
Solow, Robert Merton *economist, educator*
Spelke, Elizabeth Shilin *psychology professor*
Stein, Jeremy Chaim *economics professor*
Stewart, Charles Haines *political science educator*
Thompson, Dennis Frank *political science professor, consultant*
Vargas, Julie S. *behaviorologist, educator*
Verba, Sidney *political science professor, retired library director*
Vogel, Ezra F. *sociology educator*
Waters, Mary Catherine *sociology educator*
Weitzman, Martin L. *economics educator*
Willie, Charles Vert *social sciences educator*
Zeckhauser, Richard Jay *economist, educator*
Zinberg, Dorothy Shore *sociologist, educator*

Charlestown
Buckner, Randy L. *psychology professor, neuroscientist*

Chestnut Hill
Melnick, Rowell Shep *political scientist, educator*
Munnell, Alicia Haydock *economist*
Unver, M. Utku *economics professor*

Concord
Blackmer, Donald Laurence Morton *political scientist*

Dartmouth
de Sá, Maria Gloria *social sciences educator*
Sweeney, Shawna Elizabeth *political science professor, researcher*

Fitchburg
McKeon, John Joseph *economics professor*

Framingham
Coiner, Maryrose C. *psychologist*

Grafton
Marino, Michelle S. *psychologist*

Hingham
Allinson, Deborah Louise *economist*

Hull
Mathisen, Lauren J. *psychologist*

Ipswich
Jennings, Frederic Beach, Jr. *economist, saltwater flyfishing guide*

Jamaica Plain
Enggasser, Justin L. *psychologist*

Lexington
Balu, Sanjeev *pharacoeconomist*
Levine, Janice R. *clinical psychologist*
Papanek, Gustav Fritz *economist, educator*

Lowell
Benjamin, Ann Cheryl *retired psychology professor*
Das, Mitra *sociologist, educator*
Pyle, Jean L. *economist, consultant*
Sanborne, Erika L. *psychology professor*

Lynn
Berger, Harvey Robert *psychologist*

Medford
Brunye, Tad T. *psychologist*
Centner, Ryan *sociologist, educator*
Conklin, John Evan *sociology educator*
Drezner, Daniel William *political science professor*
Elkind, David *psychology professor*
Miczek, Klaus Alexander *psychology professor*
Nasr, Vali Reza *international politics professor*
Pfaltzgraff, Robert Louis, Jr. *political scientist, educator*

Natick
Adam, Gina E. *psychologist, researcher*
Sedo, Manuel Arturo *psychologist, researcher*

Newton
Burlage, Dorothy Dawson *clinical psychologist*
White, Burton Leonard *retired educational psychologist, writer, consultant*

North Dartmouth
Barrow, Clyde Wayne *social sciences educator*

North Easton
Ohanyan, Anna *political science professor*

Northampton
Dean, Dorothy G. *psychologist, social sciences educator, researcher*
Everett, Joyce E. *social sciences educator*
Reinhardt, Nola *economics educator*
Robinson, Donald Leonard *social scientist, educator*
Rose, Peter Isaac *sociologist, writer, editor*

Orleans
Rappaport, Margaret Mary Williams Ewing *psychologist, physician, writer, pilot, consultant*

Plymouth
Leonard-Zabel, Ann Marie T. *psychologist, educator*

Quincy
Spangler, Arthur Stephenson, Jr. *psychologist*

Reading
Ricci, Carla *psychologist*

Shrewsbury
Smith, Carolyn J(ane) Hostetter *psychologist, educator*

Somerville
Basáñez, Miguel Ebergenyi *political scientist, educator*

Springfield
Harnois, Veronica D'Urso *psychologist, educator*
Wronka, Joseph Michael *social policy analyst, human rights activist, educator*

Taunton
Ross, Murray David *psychologist*

Uxbridge
Iannuccilli, Janet Ann *psychologist*

Waltham
Kotchikian, Asbed *political science professor*
McCulloch, Rachel *economist, educator*
Saxe, Leonard *social psychologist, educator*
Shepard, Donald Sloane *public policy research educator*

Wellesley
Donato, Gary *political science professor*
Giddon, Donald B(ernard) *psychologist, educator*
Morant, Ricardo Bernardino *psychology professor*
Sangree, Walter Hinchman *social anthropologist, educator*
Stettner, Edward A. *political science professor*

Wellfleet
Spaniol, LeRoy *retired psychologist*

West Barnstable
Gautam, Virender *economics professor*

Westborough
Staffier, Pamela Moorman *psychologist*

Westfield
Aquino, Gabriel *social sciences educator*
Zayac, Linda Mary *sociologist, educator*

Whitinsville
Plaud, Joseph Julian *psychology educator*

Williamstown
Bolton, Roger Edwin *economist, educator*
Cramer, Phebe *psychologist*
Hastings, Philip Kay *psychology professor*
Kassin, Saul *psychology professor*
Nolan, James Lawry, Jr. *sociologist*
Sheahan, John Bernard *economist, educator*

Worcester
Benway, Gaelan Lee *sociologist, educator*
Blount, F. Alexander *psychologist, director*
Dyer-Cole, Pauline *school psychologist, educator*
Edmonds, Regina Margaret *psychology professor*
Kirschner, Suzanne R. *psychology professor*
Mathisen, Howard *psychologist, educator, minister*
Wachholtz, Amy B. *psychologist, educator*

MICHIGAN

Allegan
Gerl, Robert Raymond *psychologist, priest*

Alpena
McLarney-Vesotski, Amber Renee *psychology professor*

Ann Arbor
Arlinghaus, Sandra Judith Lach *mathematical geographer, educator*
Arnedt, John Todd *psychologist, educator*
Axelrod, Robert Marshall *political science and public policy educator*
Behling, Charles Frederick *psychologist, educator*
Brown, Donald Robert *psychology professor*
Cain, Albert Clifford *psychologist, educator*
Cohen, Malcolm Stuart *economist*
Dominguez, Kathryn Mary *economist, educator*
Eckstein, Peter Charles *retired labor union economist*
Frey, William H. *demographer, educator*
Gelman, Susan A. *psychology professor*
Haefner, Don Paul *retired psychology educator*
Himle, Joseph Alan *social sciences educator*
House, Christopher *economics professor*
House, James Stephen *social psychologist, educator*
Jackson, James Sidney *psychologist, educator*
Jackson, John Edgar *social scientist, educator, researcher*
Johnston, Lloyd Douglas *social sciences educator*
Kaplow, Julie B. *psychologist, educator*
Kelly, Raymond Case *anthropology educator*
Kim, E. Han *financial economist, educator*
Kingdon, John Wells *political science professor*
Lee, Theresa M. *psychology professor, department chairman*
Lupia, Arthur W. *political science educator*
Marcus, Joyce (Joyce Marcus Flannery) *anthropology educator*
Markovits, Andrei Steven *political science professor*
Mitchell, Edward John *economist, retired educator*
Norton, Edward C. *economist, educator*
Parsons, Jeffrey Robinson *anthropologist, educator*
Pedley, John Griffiths *archaeologist, educator*
Roberts, J. Scott *psychologist, educator*
Salant, Stephen Walter *economics professor, researcher*
Shapiro, Matthew David *economist, educator*
Shatz, Marilyn Joyce *psychologist, educator*
Shulman, Michael Eben *psychoanalyst, psychologist, consultant*
Stafford, Frank Peter, Jr. *economics professor, consultant*
Suny, Ronald Grigor *political science professor, history professor*
Tanay, Emanuel *psychiatry professor, writer*
Thornton, Arland *sociologist, educator*
Tkacheva, Olesya *political scientist*
Tsebelis, George *political science professor*
Vazquez, Delia M. *psychology professor, director*
Waltz, Susan *political scientist, educator*
Warren, Jane Carol *psychologist*
Whitman, Marina von Neumann *economist, educator*
Williams, David R. *sociologist, educator, senior research scientist*
Williams, Melvin Donald *anthropologist, educator*
Zucker, Robert A(lpert) *psychologist*

Auburn Hills
Etefia, Florence Victoria *retired school psychologist*

Berrien Springs
Hamel, Lorie Ann *psychologist*

Big Rapids
McLean, Roy L. *economics professor*

Birmingham
Auld, Frank *psychologist, educator*

Detroit
Braid, Ralph M. *economics professor*
Chasdi, Richard J. *political science professor*
Fleming, George Robert *psychologist*
Goodman, Allen Charles *economist, educator*
MacDonald, Douglas Andrew *psychologist, educator*
McArthur, Steven Francis *psychologist, educator*
Pietrofesa, John Joseph *psychologist, educator*
Sase, John Francis *economist*
Sobeck, Joanne L. *social studies educator*
Spurr, Stephen Josiah *economics professor*

Dollar Bay
Karpiak, Steven Thomas, Jr. *retired social studies educator*

East Lansing
Abeles, Norman *psychologist, educator*
Abramson, Paul Robert *political scientist, educator*
Araujo, Luis Fernando Oliveira de *economics professor*
Baillie, Richard Thomas *economist, educator*
Crewe, Nancy Moe *retired psychologist*
Dow, Steven Benjamin *social studies educator*
Ilgen, Daniel Richard *psychology professor*
Kalof, Linda Henry *sociologist, educator*
Manderscheid, Lester Vincent *agricultural economics educator*
Menchik, Paul Leonard *economist, educator*
Press, Charles *retired political science professor*
Schmid, Alfred Allan *economist*
Wiley, David Sherman *sociologist, educator*
Winder, Clarence Leland *psychologist, educator*

Farmington Hills
Klausmeier, Herbert John *psychology professor*

Grand Rapids
Abadeer, Adel S *economics professor*
Tiemstra, John Peter *economics professor*

Holland
Holmes, Jack Edward *political science professor*

Jackson
Wingblade, Loren Charles *social sciences educator*

Kalamazoo
Bridges, Cassandra Maddox *psychology professor*
Mc Allister, Lester Belden *economics professor*
Munley, Patrick H. *psychologist, educator*
Straight, Bilinda *anthropologist, educator*
Van Valey, Thomas Lee *sociologist, educator*

Midland
Luptowski, Thomas Stephen *social sciences educator*

Mount Pleasant
Oh-Lee, Justin DoHoon *psychology professor*

North Branch
Baker, Randy Thomas *social studies educator*

Northport
Thomas, Philip Stanley *economist, educator*

Okemos
Berkman, Claire Fleet *psychologist*
Solo, Robert Alexander *economist, educator*

Rochester
Cordes, Mary Kenrick *retired psychologist*
Guzik, Heather Jerrett *psychologist*

Rochester Hills
Minton, Henry Lee *psychology professor*

Southfield
Hotelling, Harold *economics professor, lawyer*
Weiner, Karen Colby (Karen Lynn Colby) *psychologist, lawyer*

Traverse City
Leuenberger, Betty Lou *psychologist, educator*

University Center
Hill, Alan Gordon *sociologist, educator*
Kolar, Marek *economics professor*

Utica
Cooper, Lindsay D. *retired social studies educator*

West Bloomfield
Marx, Thomas George *economist*

Ypsilanti
Queen, Marla Frudden *psychologist*
Weinstein, Jay A. *social sciences educator, researcher*

MINNESOTA

Bemidji
Davgun, Satish K. *social sciences educator*

Circle Pines
Paisley, John *psychologist*

Crookston
Killough, Alvin Lynard *psychology professor, consultant*

Duluth
Rapp, George Robert (Rip) *geology and archeology educator*
Tadesse, Bedassa *economics professor, researcher*

Eden Prairie
Knickerbocker, Vicky Ann *sociologist, educator*

Edina
Fenwick, Sheridan Mellon *psychologist, director*
Gottesman, Irving I. *psychologist, educator*

Forest Lake
Skrip, Cathy Lee *psychologist*

Grand Marais
Hattery, Robert Wilber *political science educator*

Mankato
Purcell, Helen Duncan *sociologist, educator*

Maple Grove
Ones, Deniz S. *psychologist, educator*

Minneapolis
Berscheid, Ellen S. *psychology professor, writer, researcher*
Brown, Robert John *social sciences educator, consultant*
Burns, Matthew Kevin *psychology professor*
Chipman, John Somerset *economist, retired educator*
Davison, Mark L. *psychology, education professor*
Gowrisankaran, Gautam *economist, educator*
Hansen, Jo-Ida Charlotte *psychology professor, researcher*
Johnson, David Wolcott *psychologist, educator*
Kiresuk, Thomas Jack *psychologist, educator*
Knoke, David Harmon *sociology educator*
Kudrle, Robert Thomas *economist, educator*
Kuncel, Nathan R. *psychology professor*
Le, Thanh Trung *economics professor*
Legge, Gordon E. *psychology professor, department chairman*
Lewis, Stephen Richmond, Jr. *economist, educator*
Maratsos, Michael Philip *psychology professor*
McConnell, Scott Rushton *educational psychology educator*
Ostrom, Don *retired political science professor*
Overmier, J. Bruce *psychology professor*
Reiss, Ira Leonard *retired sociology educator, writer*
Schreiner, John Christian *economics consultant, software publisher*
Shively, William Phillips *political scientist, educator*
Sullivan, John L. *political science professor*
Ward, David Allen *sociology educator*

Northfield
Pomponio, Xun Z. *economics professor*
Thalhammer, Kristina Emma *political science professor*

Rochester
Hauri, Peter J. *psychology professor, researcher*

Saint Joseph
Lewis, Margaret *economics professor, director*

Saint Paul
Adler, Franklin Hugh *political science professor*
Bute, Monte *social sciences educator*
Eidman, Vernon Roy *agricultural economist, educator*
Flynn, John Joseph *geographer, educator*
Fulton, Robert Lester *sociology educator*
Gavin, Eileen A. *psychology educator*
Reardon, Jack Edward *economics professor*
Rossmann, Jack Eugene *psychologist, educator*

Saint Peter
Mc Rostie, Clair Neil *economics professor*

West Saint Paul
Nightingale, Edmund Joseph *clinical psychologist, educator, consultant*

Winona
Holm, Joy Alice *goldsmith, psychology professor, artist*
Sefkow, Susan Bennett *psychology professor*

MISSISSIPPI

Brandon
Fargason, Patricia J. *psychologist*

Flora
Garbacz, Christopher *economist, researcher*

Hattiesburg
Bass, Joby *geographer, educator*
Niroomand, Farhang *economics professor, researcher*

Jackson
Freeman, Patricia Ann *economist, educator*

Mississippi State
Chi, Guangqing *demographer, educator*

Moorhead
Sanford, Kimberly Lynn *social sciences educator*

Morton
Cox, Marlina R. *social studies educator*

Tupelo
Witty, Thomas Ezekiel III *psychologist, researcher*

University
Chang, Yunhee *consumer economics professor*
Guo, Gang *political science professor*
Shughart, William Franklin, II, *economics professor, consultant*

MISSOURI

Canton
Li, Wei *psychology professor*

Cape Girardeau
Snell, William E., Jr. *psychology professor, researcher*

Columbia
Bank, Barbara J. *sociology educator*
Biddle, Bruce Jesse *social psychologist, educator*
Cowan, Nelson *cognitive psychologist, researcher*
Hoard, Mary *psychologist*
Ikerd, John E. *retired economics professor*
LoPiccolo, Joseph *psychologist, educator, author*
Monson, Michael James *economist, consultant*
Rowlett, Ralph Morgan *archaeologist, educator*

Fayette
Carter, John Jefferson *government educator, author*

Fenton
Sheble, Brian A. *psychologist, consultant, educator*

Fulton
Jaeger, Theodore Bruce *psychology professor*

Jefferson City
Markway, Barbara Gerth *psychologist, writer*

Kansas City
Forstater, Mathew *economics professor*
Johnson, Andrew T. *psychology professor*
Roosa, Jan Bertorotta *psychologist, writer*

Kirksville
Quinn, John James *political science professor*

Maryville
Kharadia, Virabhai Chelabhai *economist, educator, researcher*

Saint Joseph
Sischo, Lacey *social studies educator*

Saint Louis
Beck, Lois Grant *anthropologist, educator, author*
Browman, David L(udvig) *archaeologist*
Calvert, Randall *political scientist*
Davis, Mary Florence *psychologist*
Drake, Francis Brett *social studies educator, consultant*
Gfeller, Jeffrey D. *psychologist, educator*
Gibson, James Louis *political science professor*
Greenbaum, Stuart I. *economist, educator*
Gruenberg, Gladys Walleman *economics professor, arbitrator*
Kavanaugh, John Francis *social sciences educator, director*
Leguey-Feilleux, Jean-Robert *political scientist, educator*
Le Vine, Victor Theodore *retired political science professor*
Lindsey, Linda Lee *sociology educator*
Niblack, Tracey *social studies educator*
North, Douglass Cecil *economist, educator*
O'Connell, Daniel Craig *retired psychologist, educator*
Olney, John William *psychiatry professor*
Ozawa, Martha Naoko *social work educator*
Rank, Mark Robert *sociologist*
Roediger, Henry L. III *psychology educator*
Salisbury, Robert Holt *political science professor*
Smith, Richard Jay *anthropologist, educator, dean*
Telowitz, Marilyn Marie *English and social studies educator*
Weidenbaum, Murray Lew *economist, educator*
Weiss, Penny A. *political science professor, director*

Springfield
Branstetter, Ann Dyche *psychology professor*
Gill, Angela Sue *clinical psychologist*
Stone, Allan David *retired economics professor*

University City
Krejnik, Kelley *social studies educator*

Warrensburg
Lewandowski, Joseph D. *social studies educator, dean*

MONTANA

Billings
DeRosier, Linda Scott *psychologist, educator*

Bozeman
Christopher, John Chambers *counseling psychology educator*
Duffié, Mary Katharine *anthropologist, educator*
Gray, Philip Howard *former psychologist, writer, educator*

Butte
Ray, John Wallace III *political science professor*

Miles City
Gerber, Robin *history and social sciences educator*

Missoula
Grieves, Forest Leslie *political science professor, department chairman*
Lopach, James Joseph *political science professor*

NEBRASKA

Bellevue
Evans, Cleveland Kent *psychology professor*
Jeffrey, Mark D. *psychologist, consultant*

Grand Island
Garrelts, Deborah Louise *psychologist, educator, educational consultant*

Kearney
Miller, Richard Lee *psychology professor, department chairman*
Tenkorang, Frank A. *economist, educator*
Ziebarth-Bovill, Jane K. *social sciences educator*

Lincoln
Anderson, John Edwin *economics professor, consultant*
Auld, James S. *educational psychologist*
Deegan, Mary Jo *sociologist*
Edwards, Carolyn Pope *psychology professor*
Fuess, Scott M., Jr. *economics professor*
Spaulding, William D. *psychologist, educator*

Omaha
Boamah-Wiafe, Daniel *geographer, researcher*
Bucko, Raymond *anthropologist, educator*
Diamond, Arthur Mansfield, Jr. *economics professor*
Louisa, Angelo Joseph *social studies educator, researcher, writer*
Maydwell, Robert Mason, Jr. *social sciences educator*
Ni, Jinlan *economics professor*
Oyinlade, A. Olu *sociologist, educator*
Rush, Michael F. *human services professor*
Wilson, Daniel Richard *anthropologist, physician*
Wunsch, James Stevenson *political science professor*

Scottsbluff
Wylie, Guy Stephen *psychologist, educator*

NEVADA

Ely
Alderman, Minnis Amelia *psychologist, educator, small business owner*

Gardnerville
Griffiths, Barbara Lorraine *psychologist, marriage and family therapist, writer*

Las Vegas
Hannon, Erin E. *psychology professor*
Miller, Stephen M. *economics professor*
Numrich, Richard *economics professor*
Weeks, Gerald *psychologist, educator*

Reno
Atkinson, Glen W. *retired economics professor*
Barone, Diane *social sciences educator*
Chapman, Samuel Greeley *political science professor, criminologist*
Collier, Helen Vandivort *psychologist*
Crowley, Joseph Neil *political science professor, former academic administrator*
Cummings, Nicholas Andrew *psychologist*
Leland, Joy Hanson *retired anthropologist, researcher*
Nevins, Marybeth Eleanor *anthropologist, educator*
Piercy, Earl *social sciences educator*

Yerington
Price, Judith Holm *educational psychologist*

NEW HAMPSHIRE

Durham
Gittell, Ross Jacobs *economics and business and public policy educator*
Straus, Murray Arnold *sociology educator*
Tucker, Corinna Jenkins *social studies educator*

Exeter
Schubart, Caren Nelson *psychologist*

Goffstown
St. Pierre, Amada *psychologist, educator*

Hanover
Anthony, Denise L. *social sciences educator*
Bower, Richard Stuart *retired economist*
Hughes, Howard Clark *psychology professor, researcher*
Kleck, Robert Eldon *psychology professor*
Lyons, Gene Martin *political scientist, educator*
Masters, Roger Davis *political scientist, toxicologist, educator*
Rutter, Jeremy Bentham *archaeologist, educator*
Slaughter, Matthew J. *economics professor, former federal official*
Starzinger, Vincent Evans *political scientist, educator*
Swaine, Lucas *social sciences educator*

Henniker
Braiterman, Thea Gilda *economics professor, state legislator*

Keene
Baldwin, Peter Arthur *psychologist, educator, author, minister*
Hackett, John Thomas *retired economist and financial executive*

Lebanon
Emery, Virginia Olga Beattie *psychologist, researcher*
Skinner, Jonathan Snowden *economics educator*
Zayfert, Claudia *psychologist, educator*

Pittsfield
Pazdon, Melissa Joann *school psychologist*

Plymouth
Palmquist, Wendy Jean *psychology professor*

Portsmouth
Wener, Brian D. *psychologist*

NEW JERSEY

Boonton
Olimpio, Suzanne M. *psychologist*

Burlington
Haws, Elizabeth Anne *psychologist, director*

Caldwell
Kandel, Anatoly F. *economics professor, researcher*

Califon
Jeffers, Victoria Wilkinson *psychologist*

Camden
Worrall, John Dennis *economics professor, consultant, writer*

Chatham
Brodkin, Adele Ruth Meyer *psychologist*

Cresskill
Pappachristou, Jennifer *psychologist*

East Brunswick
Johnson, Edward Elemuel *psychologist, educator*
Midlarsky, Elizabeth Ruth *psychologist, researcher, educator*

East Orange
Severe, Kim Lynette *psychologist*

Edison
Thornton, Kirtley Elliott *psychologist*

Englewood
Puente, Tamagary *psychologist*

Englewood Cliffs
Farrell, Patricia Ann *psychologist, educator, writer*

Fair Lawn
Greenberg, Edward *psychologist*

Fanwood
Grallo, Richard Martin *research psychologist*

Freehold
Krupp, John E. *social studies educator*

Glassboro
Rosado, Maria Araya *anthropologist, educator*

Hasbrouck Heights
Lieberman, Charles *economist*
Perham, Roy Gates III *industrial psychologist*

Hillsborough
Brodie-Colontino, Patricia *psychologist*

Jackson
Leveson, Irving Frederick *economist*

Jersey City
Fong, Kai Heng Elizabeth *psychologist*
Peterson, George Anthony *psychologist, consultant*
Scott-Allen, Cynthia *psychologist*

Kendall Park
Nied, Stacey Jean *psychologist*

Lakewood
Levine, Stephen M. *psychologist, educator, consultant*

Lawrenceville
Stein, Sandra Lou *educational psychology professor emerita*

Little Ferry
Briggs, Alice *clinical child psychologist*

Lodi
Guillory, Ann Verrett *psychologist, educator, academic administrator*

Madison
Jennings, George Harold *psychology professor*

Mahwah
Harth, Marshall Stephen *psychology professor, psychotherapist*

Montville
Henn, Katherine A. *social studies educator*

Moorestown
Aziz, Tahira Hannan *psychologist*

Morristown
Boodey, Cecil Webster, Jr. *retired political science professor*
Deming, Frederick Wilson *retired economist, banker*
Wolff, Derish Michael *economist*

Mountain Lakes
Loomis, Rebecca C. *psychologist*

New Brunswick
Alexander, Robert Jackson *economist, educator*
Bronner, Stephen Eric *political science professor*
Clauss-Ehlers, Caroline S. *psychologist, educator, journalist*
Elias, Maurice Jesse *psychology educator*
Fisher, Helen E. *anthropologist, educator*
Glasser, Paul Harold *sociologist, educator, social worker, university administrator*
Leventhal, Howard *health psychology educator, researcher*
Mechanic, David *social sciences educator*
Mizrach, Bruce *economics professor*
Reock, Ernest C., Jr. *retired social studies educator, director*
Rhodes, Edward *political science professor*
Russell, Louise Bennett *economist, educator*
Shapiro, Warren *anthropologist, educator*
Tiger, Lionel *social scientist, anthropology consultant*
Toby, Jackson *sociologist, educator*

Newark
Ferguson, Yale Hicks *political scientist, educator*
Hiltz, Starr Roxanne *sociologist, educator, writer, consultant, computer scientist*
Jackson, Nancy Lee *geography educator*
Kennedy, Leslie W. *criminal justice educator, former dean*
Pagán, Gilberto, Jr. *psychologist*

Oakland
Guller, Irving Bernard *forensic and clinical psychologist, consultant, writer*

Paramus
Amato, Debra Jean *psychologist*

Paterson
Alcala, Luisa Maria *psychologist*
Geschwendt, David *psychologist*

Pennington
Cobb, Jeffrey William *psychologist*

Piscataway
Goss, Mary E. Weber *sociology educator*
Haladjian, Harry Haroutioun *psychologist*
Kilianski, Stephen *psychologist, educator*
Leslie, Alan M. *psychology professor*
Mitchell, James Kenneth *geography educator*
West, Mark Otto *psychology professor*

Pomona
Fleck, Jessica I. *psychology professor*
Lenard, Georgeann Terese *english educator*
Lester, David *psychology educator*

Princeton
Beitz, Charles R. *political scientist, educator*
Blinder, Alan Stuart *economist, educator*
Bogan, Elizabeth Chapin *economist, educator*
Bogucki, Peter Ignatius *archaeologist*
Coffey, Joseph Irving *political scientist, educator*
Cook, Michael Allan *social sciences educator*
Corr, Donald Clayton *psychologist*
Friedberg, Aaron Louis *political science professor*
Girgus, Joan Stern *psychologist, educator, director*
Gordenker, Leon *political science professor*
Grossman, Gene M. *economics professor*
Hodges, Neil *psychologist*
Hoebel, Bartley Gore *psychologist, educator*
Joyce, Carol Bertani *social studies educator*
Kahneman, Daniel *psychology professor*
Kateb, George Anthony *political science professor*
Keller, Suzanne *sociologist, psychotherapist*
Kenen, Peter Bain *economist, educator*
Keohane, Robert Owen *political scientist, educator*
Kogan, Nathan *psychologist, consultant*
Kohli, Atul *political science professor*
Krugman, Paul Robin *economics professor, columnist, writer*
Kurtzer, Daniel Charles *public policy educator, former ambassador*
Lazarus, Arnold Allan *psychologist, educator*
Lewis, Bernard *retired social studies educator*
Malkiel, Burton Gordon *economist, educator*
Maskin, Eric Stark *economics professor*
Miller, George Armitage *psychologist, educator*
Portes, Alejandro *sociologist, educator*
Quandt, Richard Emeric *economics professor*
Rauschenberger, Robert *psychologist, educator*
Rozman, Gilbert Friedell *sociologist, educator*
Shapiro, Harold Tafler *economics professor, former academic administrator*
Shear, Theodore Leslie, Jr. *archaeologist, educator*
Wallace, Walter L. *retired sociologist, educator*
Western, Bruce *sociologist, educator*
Westoff, Charles Francis *demographer, educator*
Willig, Robert Daniel *economics professor*
Willingham, Warren Willcox *psychologist*
Zelizer, Viviana *sociologist, educator*

Randolph
Goldman, Phyllis E. *psychology educator*

Red Bank
McWhinney, Madeline H. (Mrs. John Denny Dale) *economist, director*

Ridgewood
Le May, Moira Kathleen *retired psychology educator*

Saddle River
Lasser, Gail Maria *psychologist, educator*

Somerset
Lichtig, Leo Kenneth *health economist*
Rosenberg, Seymour *psychologist, educator*
Tracy, Janet Lynn *psychologist, consultant*

South Orange
Leung, Edwin Pak-wah *social studies educator, researcher*

Springfield
O'Desky, Ilyse Hope *psychologist, educator*
Shilling, A. Gary *economist, consultant*

Summit
Lovett, Juanita Pelletier *clinical psychologist*

Teaneck
Cassimatis, Peter John *economics professor*
Lipsitz, Joshua Dan *psychologist, educator*

Tenafly
Blank, Marion Sue *psychologist, educator*

Union
Adamson, Kunle Y. *economics professor, director*
Kim, Youn-Suk Ernest *economist, educator*
Norward, Josephine Norma *social work educator, consultant*

Upper Montclair
Chakraborty, Chandana *economics professor, department chairperson*

Wall
Sheprow, Matthew Warren *psychologist*

Warren
Feldman, Janie Lynn *psychologist*
O'Halloran, Patrick *psychologist*

Wayne
Campanelli-Andreopoulos, Giuliana *economics professor*

West Long Branch
Lewandowski, Gary William, Jr. *psychology professor*

Westfield
Simon, Martin Stanley *economist, consultant*

NEW MEXICO

Albuquerque
Baker, Chester Bird *agricultural economics professor*
Byers, Steven N. *anthropologist, educator, computer professional*
Condie, Carol Joy *anthropologist, science administrator*
Dutta Mazumdar, Rinita *social studies educator*
Harris, Fred R. *political scientist, educator, former United States Senator from Oklahoma*
Lamphere, Louise *anthropology and women's studies educator*
Lopez, Nancy *sociologist*
May, Philip Alan *sociologist, educator*
McCrady, Barbara Sachs *psychologist, educator*
Schwerin, Karl Henry *anthropology educator, researcher*
Singer, Beverly R. *social sciences educator, film producer*
Slate, Daniel Michael *economics professor*
Williams, Enid Roberta (Enid W. Troll) *psychologist, nurse*

El Prado
Reading, Margery Schrock *psychology professor, artist*
Young, Jon Nathan *archaeologist*

Gallup
Wilkins, Teresa J. *anthropologist, educator*

Hobbs
Steinhaus, Richard Frederick *criminologist, educator*

Las Cruces
Hunt, Darwin Paul *psychology professor*

Los Alamos
Masse, William Bruce *archaeologist*
Thompson, Lois Jean Heidke Ore *psychologist*

Santa Fe
Cordell, Linda S. *anthropologist, educator, museum director*
Sabloff, Jeremy Arac *archaeologist*
Williams, Stephen *anthropologist, educator*

Silver City
Lopez, Linda Carol *social sciences educator*

NEW YORK

Albany
Bassman, Ronald *psychologist*

Carmack, Robert Marquess *retired social sciences educator*
Glenn, Linda MacDonald *social sciences educator, state attorney general*
Kinal, Terrence *economics professor, consultant*
Kranich, Laurence Joel *economics professor*
Langer, Judith Ann *psychologist*
Ley, Ronald *psychologist, educator*
Nathan, Richard P(erle) *political science professor*
Polimeni, John Matthew *economics professor*
Theroux, P. J. *sociologist, educator*
Zimmerman, Joseph Francis *political scientist, educator*

Annandale On Hudson
Papadimitriou, Dimitri Basil *economist, educator, academic administrator*

Averill Park
Blais, Christopher R. *social studies educator*
Haines, Walter Wells *retired economics professor*

Bayside
Ohrenstein, Roman Abraham *economist, educator, rabbi*

Binghamton
Blackburn, Marcia C. *visual studies educator*
Greene, Kenneth Vincent *economics educator*
Isaacson, Robert Lee *neurobehavioral scientist, educator*
James, Gary Douglas *biological anthropologist, educator, researcher*
Lenzenweger, Mark Francis *psychologist, educator*
Levis, Donald James *psychologist, educator*
Little, Michael Alan *anthropology educator*
Masters, Stanley H. *economics professor*
Mazrui, Ali Al'Amin *political science professor, researcher*

Bloomfield
Grasso, Jonathan *psychologist*

Briarcliff Manor
Sabia, Noreen Patricia *psychologist*

Bronx
Brent, Robert John *economics educator*
Cruise, Keith R. *psychology professor*
Elkin, Jay S. *psychologist*
Hobson, Rana Dirice *psychologist*
Macklin, Ruth *bioethics educator*
McClure, Margaret McNamara *psychologist, educator*
Mitra, Sophie *economics professor*
Regan, Richard Joseph *political science professor, writer*
Rego, Simon Alexander *psychologist*
Rose, Susan Ann *psychology professor, consultant*
Senra, Jenny *psychologist*

Bronxville
Doyle, Charlotte Lackner (Mrs. James J. Doyle) *psychology educator, writer*
Mills, Nicolaus *American studies educator, writer*

Brooklyn
Doretti, Mercedes *forensic anthropologist*
Kellman, Rona J. *psychologist*
Martinez-Pons, Manuel *educational psychologist*
McSherry, J. Patrice *political science professor*
Peng, Yusheng *social sciences educator*
Salvodon-Stallings, Cynthia Judy *psychologist*
Szenberg, Michael *economics professor, editor, consultant*

Brushton
Pietropaoli, Angelo Eugene *social studies educator, musician*

Buffalo
Bateman, Derek Robert *sociologist, educator*
Bojinova, Emma D. *economics professor*
Ehrlich, Isaac *economist, educator, department chairman*
Hetzner, Donald Raymund *forensic social scientist*
Lamb, Charles Moody *political scientist, educator*
Leclaire, Joelle Julie *economics professor*
Marinaccio, Bridget C. *social sciences educator*
Salvi, Richard *psychologist, otolaryngologist, educator*
Weinberg, Thomas Stephen *social sciences educator*
Zarembka, Paul *economics professor*

Canandaigua
Jorgensen, Mia Melody *archaeologist, educator*
Principato, Amy *psychologist*

Canastota
Madle, Allen Geoffrey *economics professor*

Canton
Auster, Nancy Eileen Ross *economics professor*

Castile
Krolikowski, Gary E. *social sciences educator*

Clinton
Walker, Edward S., Jr. *political science professor, former ambassador*

Cobleskill
Braun, Mark Edward *urban studies professor*

Conesus
Dadrian, Vahakn Norair *retired sociology educator*

Copake
Schneier, Edward Vincent *political science professor*

Cortlandt Manor
Lupiani, Jennifer Lynne *school psychologist*

Dobbs Ferry
Kraetzer, Mary C. *sociologist, educator, consultant*

East Hampton
Humphrey, Craig Reed *social studies educator*

Farmingdale
Goodstone, Michael S. *psychology professor, consultant*

Flushing
Baker, A. Harvey *psychology professor*
Beveridge, Andrew Alan *sociologist, educator, consultant*
Kaufmann, Hugo M. *economics professor, director*
Rogers-Dillon, Robin *sociologist, educator*
Smith, Charles William *social sciences educator*
Steinberg, Stephen *sociologist, educator, writer*
Stinson, Sara *anthropologist, educator*

Fredonia
Croxton, Jack Sanders *psychology professor, director, consultant*

Freeport
Ferentino, Sheila Connolly *psychologist, consultant*

Garden City
Primeggia, Salvatore *sociologist, educator*
Young, Yih-Jin *sociologist, educator*

Garrison
Murray, Thomas Henry *bioethics educator, writer*

Great Neck
Christie, George Nicholas *economist, consultant*
Minkoff, Jack *retired economics professor*
Zaman, Kahkashan T. *psychologist*

Greenport
Watts, Harold Wesley *economist, educator*

Greenvale
Araoz, Daniel Leon *psychologist, educator*
Kusukawa, Akira *demographer, educator*

Groveland
Battersby, Harold Ronald *retired anthropologist, archaeologist, linguist*

Hamilton
Hansen, Bruce C. *psychology professor*

Hampton Bays
Baker, Donald Gene *social sciences educator*

Hempstead
Shafritz, Keith Michael *psychology professor*

Ithaca
Azis, Iwan Jaya *economics educator*
Barrett, Christopher B. *economics professor*
Briggs, Vernon Mason, Jr. *retired economics professor*
Darlington, Richard Benjamin *retired psychologist, educator, researcher*
Easley, David *economics professor*
Ehrenberg, Ronald Gordon *economist, educator*
Feldman, Shelley *sociologist, director*
Jarrow, Robert Alan *economist, educator*
Jordan, Kurt Anders *archaeologist, educator*
Kahn, Alfred Edward *economist, educator, government official*
Kahn, Lawrence Max *economics professor*
Kanbur, Ravi *economist*
Kennedy, Kenneth Adrian Raine *biological and forensic anthropologist*
Lyons, Thomas Patrick *economics professor*
Mueller, Betty Jeanne *social work educator*
Nishii, Lisa *psychology professor*
Pelto, Gretel H. *nutritional anthropologist, educator*
Rader, Nancy Louise de Villiers *psychology professor, consultant*
Reyna, Valerie Frances *psychologist, educator, researcher*
Smith, Robert John *anthropology educator*
Thorbecke, Erik *economics professor*
Tomek, William Goodrich *agricultural economist*
Toorawa, Shawkat M. *social studies educator*
Vanek, Jaroslav *economist, educator*
Waldman, Michael *economist, educator*

Jamaica
Brondolo, Elizabeth *psychologist, educator*
Chirico, Donna M. *psychologist, educator, researcher*
Lees, Francis *economics professor*

Katonah
Wenglowski, Gary Martin *economist*

Kingston
Clamar, Aphrodite J. *psychologist*

Larchmont
Siegel, Nathaniel Harold *sociology educator*
Zilberberg, Julie Marlene *social studies educator*

Lindenhurst
Kaufman, Susan Shiffman *psychologist*

Long Island City
Viera, Lorraine *psychologist*

Loudonville
Colesante, Robert J. *psychology professor, director*

Mahopac
Martone, Barbara *school psychologist*

Melville
Grayson, Gerald Herbert *economist, educator, arbitrator, writer*

Morrisville
Redmond, Rhonda Jean *psychologist*

Mount Vernon
Cammarosano, Joseph Raphael *economist, educator*
Scelsa, Joseph Vincent *sociologist, educator, dean*

Nesconset
Burns-Riviello, Michaela Aileen *social studies educator*

New City
Zambri, Carla Nicole *psychologist*

New Paltz
Raskin, Jonathan D. *psychologist*
Schnell, George Adam *geographer, educator, retired demographer*

New Rochelle
Salamone, Frank Anthony *anthropology educator*

New York
Aboulafia, Mitchell Stuart *liberal arts and philosophy educator*
Adrian, Tobias *economist*
Andersen, Marianne Singer *psychologist*
Banerji, Anirvan *economist, director*
Bardach, Joan Lucile *clinical psychologist*
Barnett, Robert Joseph *social sciences educator*
Barron, Susan *clinical psychologist*
Baumol, William Jack *economist, educator*
Bearman, Peter Shawn *social sciences professor*
Betts, Richard Kevin *political science professor*
Bevan, Ruth A. *political science professor, director*
Blechner, Mark Jacob *psychologist, educator*
Bowers, Patricia Eleanor Fritz *economist*
Braham, Randolph Lewis *political science professor*
Brams, Steven John *political science professor*
Bremmer, Ian *political scientist, writer*
Brunswick, Ann Finkenberg *social psychologist, health researcher*
Caraley, Demetrios James *political science professor, writer, publisher*
Clarke, Keith Charles *cartography educator*
Cohen, Stephen Frand *political scientist, writer, historian, educator, commentator*
Comitas, Lambros *anthropologist, educator*
Crapanzano, Vincent *anthropologist, educator, literary critic*
Dalton, Dennis Gilmore *retired political science professor*
Dancyger, Ida Flint *psychologist, educator*
Dave, Dhaval M. *economics professor*
Davidson, Paul *political economics educator, consultant*
DeGregorio, Carlo *social studies educator*
del Castillo, Graciana *economist, director*
deMause, Lloyd *psychologist*
Denmark, Florence Harriet Levin *psychology professor*
Denoon, David Baugh Holden *political economist, educator, consultant*
Deutsch, Morton *psychologist, educator*
Duke, Anthony Drexel *retired sociologist, educator, philanthropist*
Elinson, Jack *social sciences educator*
Erikson, Robert S. *political science professor*
Feldman, Ronald Arthur *sociologist, educator, social worker*
Fishman, Steven T. *psychologist*
Fodor, Iris Elaine *clinical psychologist, educator, psychotherapist*
Foner, Nancy *anthropologist, educator, sociologist*
Fosler, Gail D. *economist*
Galanter, Eugene *psychologist, educator*
Gangwisch, James Edward *assistant professor, researcher*
Gans, Herbert J. *sociologist, educator*
Ghilarducci, Teresa *economist, educator*
Gianaris, Nicholas Vasil *economics professor*
Gilligan, Carol *psychologist, writer*
Glanzer, Murray *psychology professor*
Goldman, George David *psychologist*
Gorenstein, Ethan Ezra *psychologist, educator*
Griffin, Anne *political scientist, educator*
Grody, Deborah *psychologist, director*
Grossman, Michael *economics professor*
Gutmann, Peter M. *economics professor*
Halper, Thomas *political science professor*
Harris, Ethan S. *economist*
Hartwig, Maria *psychology professor*
Hellerstein, Rebecca *economist*
Heyde, Martha Bennett *psychologist*
Holloway, Ralph Leslie *anthropology educator*
Hormats, Robert David *economist, investment banker*
Horsley, Heidi *psychologist, educator, radio personality*
Hoxter, Curtis Joseph *international economic advisor, public relations and communications executive*
Jacoby, Jacob *consumer psychology educator*
Jasper, James Macdonald *writer, sociology educator*
Jasso, Guillermina *sociologist, educator*
Jervis, Robert *political science professor*
Jonas, Ruth Haber *psychologist*
Joskow, Paul Lewis *economist, educator*
Kaplan, Lawrence Jay *retired economist, educator*
Karl, Kurt Erskine *economist*
Kavesh, Robert A. *economist, educator*
Kazemi, Farhad *political scientist, educator*
Kennedy, David M. *anthropologist, educator*
Korenman, Sanders *economics professor, researcher*
Krauss, Herbert Harris *psychologist*
Kurzweil, Edith *social sciences educator, editor*
Lao, Joseph R. *social sciences educator, researcher*
Lazarcik, Gregor *economist, educator, financial research company executive*
Leahey, Miles Cary *economist*
Leahy, John *economist, educator*
Lefkowitz, Joel M. *psychologist, educator*
Lehman, Edward William *social studies educator, researcher*
Levin, Henry Mordechai *economist, educator*
Levy, Marguerite F. *psychology professor emerita*
Licklider, Roy Eilers *political science educator*
Liff, Zanvel A. *psychologist*
Lipsey, Robert Edward *economist, educator*
Lothian, James Robert *economist, educator*
Lukes, Steven Michael *sociologist, educator*
Lynch, Carol *psychologist, minister*
MacLeod, William Bentley *economics, law professor*
Maldonado-Bear, Rita Marinita *economist, educator*
Marshall, Simone Verniere *psychologist, psychoanalyst*
Marty, Alvin Leonard *retired economist, educator*
McCarthy, Jonathan Paul *economist*
Mead, Lawrence Myers III *political science educator*
Mennin, Douglas Steven *psychologist*
Meyer-Bahlburg, Heino F.L. *psychology professor*
Mishkin, Frederic Stanley *economics professor, former federal official*
Moyo, Dambisa *economist, writer*
Muller, Charlotte Feldman *economist, educator*
Mundell, Robert Alexander *economist, educator*
Nadal, Kevin L. *psychology professor, director*
Naidoo, Loren Jay *psychology professor*
Nass, Martin Leo *psychology professor, psychologist*
O'Neill, June Ellenoff *economist*
Paizis, Andrew *economist, educator*
Park, Cynthia *sociology educator, consultant*
Patrick, Hugh Talbot *economist, educator*
Persell, Caroline Hodges *sociologist, educator, researcher*
Petchesky, Rosalind Pollack *social and political scientist, educator*
Phelps, Edmund Strother *economics professor*
Piven, Frances Fox *political scientist, educator*
Porzecanski, Arturo Cusiel *economist*
Proctor, Paul Wainwright *retired psychologist*
Psomiades, Harry John *political science professor*
Pye, Gordon Bruce *economist*
Raymond, Valerie *psychologist*
Redmond, Elsa M. *anthropologist*
Rehder, Bob *psychology professor*
Reisner, Steven J. *psychologist*
Riss, Eric *psychologist*
Robock, Stefan Hyman *retired economics professor*
Rosaldo, Renato Ignacio, Jr. *cultural anthropology educator*
Rosenthal, Howard Lewis *political science professor*
Roubini, Nouriel *economics professor*
Rubin, Marilyn Marks *economics professor*
Sachs, Jeffrey David *economist, educator*
Schlesinger, Stephen Cannon *foreign policy consultant*
Schonfeld, Irvin Sam *psychologist, educator*
Schotter, Andrew Roye *economics professor, consultant*
Schulman, Dennis *clinical psychologist*
Schwab, George David *social sciences educator, writer*
Schwartz, Anna Jacobson *economist*
Sheldon, Eleanor Harriet Bernert *sociologist, writer*
Shell, (Peterson) Juanita *psychologist, educator*
Shrum, Robert Matthew (Bob Shrum) *political strategist, educator, journalist*
Silver, Morris *economist, educator*
Simon, Jacqueline Albert *political scientist, writer*
Sinding, Steven William *political scientist*
Small, George LeRoy *geographer, educator*
Solecki, R. Stefan *anthropologist, educator*
Spencer, Charles S. *anthropologist*
Sperling, Gene B. *economist, former federal official*
Stein, Alexander *psychoanalyst, consultant*
Stiglitz, Joseph Eugene *economics professor, former federal official*
Sylla, Richard Eugene *economics professor*
Takooshian, Harold *social psychology educator*
Tallmer, Margot Sallop *psychologist, gerontologist, psychoanalyst*
Taylor, Lance Jerome *economics professor*
Tepper, Lynn Marsha *gerontologist, educator*
Uribe, Martin *economics professor*
van Ark, Bart (Hubertus Herman van Ark) *economist*
van der Klaauw, Wilbert H. *economics professor*
Wachtel, Paul *economist*
Wade, Estelle B. *psychologist, psychoanalyst*
Waltz, Kenneth Neal *political science educator*
Warburton, Christopher Ebun *economics professor*
Waxman, Dov *political science professor*
Weisberg-Samuels, Janet S. *psychologist*
Weisstein, Naomi *neuroscientist, psychology educator, writer*
White, Lawrence J. *economics professor*
Wilkinson, Louise Cherry *psychology professor, dean*
Williams, Joanna Pozzi *psychology professor*
Wolff, Edward Nathan *economist, educator*
Zawistowski, Stephen Louis *psychologist, educator*
Zunino, Natalia *psychologist*

Niagara University
Melnik, Mikhail *economics professor*

Niskayuna
Wright, Theodore Paul, Jr. *political science professor*

Oakdale
Sotelo-Dynega, Marlene *psychologist, professor*

Oneonta
Malhotra, Ashok Kumar *philosophy educator*

Orchard Park
Santarpia, Susan Marie *psychologist*

Oswego
Friedman, Barry A. *social sciences educator*
Lewis, Tracy K. *Spanish language and Latin American studies educator, researcher in Guarani studies*
Malgieri, Lewis Joshua *psychologist, consultant*

Oyster Bay
Landrón, Ana *school psychologist*

Pittsford
Steamer, Robert Julius *political science professor*

Plattsburgh
Bobbie, Gloria *anthropologist, educator*

Pleasant Valley
Marshall, Natalie Junemann *economics professor*

Poughkeepsie
Johnson, M(aurice) Glen *political science professor*
Scileppi, John A. *psychologist, educator*
Tavárez, David Eduardo *anthropologist, educator*

Queens
Ahmad, Dohra Khadija *psychology professor*

Rego Park
Lakah, Jacqueline Rabbat *political scientist, consultant*

Richmond Hill
Posligua-Sinnott, Ketty *psychologist*

Riverdale
Glass, David Carter *psychologist, educator*

Rochester
Ader, Robert *psychology researcher*
Bluhm, William Theodore *political scientist, educator*
Carroll, Lorrie A. *psychologist*
Deci, Edward Lewis *psychologist, educator*
Fenno, Richard Francis, Jr. *political scientist, educator*
Herbert, Andrew Mark *psychology professor*
Hopkins, Thomas Duvall *economics professor*
Johnson, Timothy J. *social work educator*
Johnston, Frank C. *psychologist*
Jones, Ronald Winthrop *economics professor*
Laties, Victor Gregory *psychologist, educator*
Long, John Broaddus, Jr. *economist, educator*
Mavromatis, John *psychology professor*
Mc Kenzie, Lionel Wilfred *economist, educator*
Niemi, Richard Gene *political science educator*
Primo, David Martin *political science professor*
Regenstreif, S(amuel) Peter *political scientist, educator*
Thomson, William *economics professor*
Vernarelli, Michael Joseph *economics professor, consultant, academic administrator*
Wagner, Aureen Pinto *psychologist, educator*
Zax, Melvin *psychologist, educator*

Rockville Centre
Lewittes, Don Jordan *psychologist*

Rye Brook
Aquino, Joseph Mario *clinical psychologist*

Scarsdale
Baruch Feldman, Caren Shein *psychologist*
Cohen, Irwin *economist*

Schenectady
Huszar, Andrew Louis *school psychologist*
Kaplan, Ilene *social sciences educator*
Lewis, Bradley Glenn *economics professor*

Selden
Schmitz, Michael *retired psychology professor*

Shoreham
Fontana, Barbara *psychologist*

Skaneateles
Garrett, Vicky P. *psychologist*

Staten Island
Franzone, Eric Scott *psychologist*
Lewis, Carla Susan *psychology educator*
Meltzer, Yale Leon *economist, educator*
Piegari, James A. *psychologist*
Xia, Ming *political science professor*

Stony Brook
Broderick, Joan Eleanor *psychologist, researcher*
Carr, Edward Gary *psychology professor*
Gagnon, John Henry *sociologist, educator*
Goldfried, Marvin Robert *psychology professor*
Leakey, Richard Erskine *paleoanthropologist, museum director*
Lodge, Milton *political science professor*
Stone, Arthur A. *psychologist, researcher*

Syracuse
Basu, Subho *social studies educator*
Birkhead, Guthrie Sweeney, Jr. *political scientist, dean*
Braungart, Richard Gottfried *political scientist, educator*
Criss, Amy H.
Kriesberg, Louis *sociologist, educator*
Mathiason, John Roland *political science professor, consultant*
Mazur, Allan Carl *sociologist, educator*
Scharoun, Susan L. *psychologist, educator*
Smith, Corinne Roth *psychologist*

Tonawanda
Brunger, Eric Geoffrey *social studies educator, coach*

Troy
Boles, David Brian *psychology educator*
Monahan, Martin J. *social studies educator*
Schechter, Stephen L. *political scientist*

Utica
Andereck, Cynthia Perry *psychologist*
Katz, David Raymond III *political science professor*
Stulmaker, Richard M. *retired social studies educator*

Waddington
Babb, Harold *psychologist, educator*

Webster
Scherer, Marcia Joslyn *psychologist, researcher, educator*

West Islip
Kaigh, Christopher Hamilton *psychologist*

West Point
Keith, Bruce Edward *sociologist*

White Plains
Rapp, Richard Tilden *economist, consultant*

Woodstock
Lieberman, Josefa Nina *retired psychologist, writer*

Yonkers
Lupiani, Donald Anthony *psychologist*
Monegro, Francisco *alternative medicine consultant, psychology professor*

NORTH CAROLINA

Andrews
Marta, Dawn Reneé *psychologist*

Asheville
Cutright, Phillips *sociologist, educator*
Dickens, Charles Henderson *retired social sciences educator*
Smith, James Finley *economist, educator*

Bakersville
Vesely, Pamela J. *social studies educator*

Belmont
Stamps, Leighton Elderkin *psychology educator*

Boone
Hill, Robert W. *psychology professor, director*
Udogu, E. Ike *social sciences educator, researcher*

Calabash
Strunk, Orlo Christopher, Jr. *psychology professor*

Carrboro
Barbarin, Oscar Anthony *psychologist*

Carthage
Osmar, Christina *psychologist*

Cary
Goodwin, Barry Kent *economics educator*
Sundstrom, Mary Chary *psychologist*

Cashiers
O'Connell, Edward James, Jr. *psychologist, educator, systems administrator, consultant*

Chapel Hill
Baroff, George Stanley *psychologist, educator*
Black, Stanley Warren III *retired economics professor*
Brown, Frank *social sciences educator*
Byrns, Ralph Truman *economics professor, writer*
Campbell, Frances Alexander *psychologist*
Elbogen, Eric B. *psychologist, educator*
Fieleke, Norman Siegfried *economist, educator*
Gray, Virginia Hickman *political science professor*
Latané, Bibb *social psychologist*
Lich-Tyler, Stephen *economics professor*
Lowman, Robert Paul *psychology professor, academic administrator*
Lysle, Donald T. *psychology professor, department chairman*
Munger, Michael Curtis *public policy educator*
Orthner, Dennis K. *social sciences educator, consultant*
Prange, Arthur Jergen, Jr. *psychology and psychiatry professor, neuroscientist*
Reichart, Karaleah S. *anthropologist, educator*
Richman, Jack M. *social sciences educator*
Schoultz, Lars *political scientist, educator*
Stenberg, Carl W. III *public administration educator, dean*
Steponaitis, Vincas Petras *archaeologist, anthropologist, educator*
Terrenato, Nicola *archaeologist, researcher*

Charlotte
Craig, Depken II A. *economics professor*
Goolkasian, Paula A. *psychologist, educator*
Lieving, Lori M. *psychologist, director*
Neel, Richard Eugene *economist, educator*
Olson, William Charles *psychology professor*
Pyle, Gerald Fredric *geographer, educator*
Shoffner, Robert L. III *economics professor*
Webster, Murray Alexander, Jr. *sociologist, educator*

Dallas
Blanton, Robert D'Alden *anthropologist, educator, history professor*

Davidson
Palmer, Edward L. *psychologist, educator, writer*

Durham
Aldrich, John Herbert *political science professor*
Bates, Robert Hinrichs *political science educator*
Behn, Robert Dietrich *public policy educator, writer*
Beresteanu, Arie *economist, educator*
Breland-Noble, Alfiee Matiese *psychologist, researcher*
Conklin, George Henry *sociologist, educator*
Echols, Laura Celeste *psychologist, consultant*
Elliot, Jeffrey M. *political science professor, department chairman*
Grabowski, Henry George *economics professor, director*
Holsti, Ole Rudolf *political scientist, educator*
Hotz, V. Joseph *economics professor*
Kelley, Allen Charles *economist, educator*
Land, Kenneth Carl *sociologist, educator, demographer*
Lifton, Walter M. *psychology and education consultant*
Lockhead, Gregory Roger *retired psychology professor*
McClain, Paula Denice *political scientist, educator*
Mickiewicz, Ellen Propper *political and social science educator*
Putallaz, Martha *psychologist, educator*
Simons, Elwyn LaVerne *physical anthropologist, primatologist, paleontologist, educator*
Strauman, Timothy J. *psychology professor, department chairman*
Surwit, Richard Samuel *psychology professor*
Swanson, Jeffrey *sociologist, researcher, educator*
Talley, Joseph Eugene *psychologist*
Tiryakian, Edward Ashod *sociologist, educator*
Treml, Vladimir Guy *economist, educator*
Williamson, Nancy E *demographer*
Wolever, Ruth Q. *psychologist, researcher*

Elizabeth City
Nwala, Kingsley *economics professor*

Gastonia
McCall, Louise Callaham *psychologist*

Greensboro
Eason, Robert Gaston *psychology professor*
Helms-VanStone, Mary Wallace *anthropology educator*
Luecht, Richard M. *psychology professor*
Ribar, David Christopher *economics professor*
Salam, A. F. *economics professor*
Wahlsten, Douglas *psychology professor*

Greenville
Bjorkman, Sylvia Johnson *psychologist*
Evans, Rand Boyd *psychologist*

Hickory
Dill, Karen Elizabeth *psychology professor, writer*

High Point
Corey, James William *political scientist, educator*
Setzler, Mark H. *political science professor*

Hillsborough
Piper, Don Courtney *political scientist, educator*

Manteo
Crites, Tara Couch *psychology professor*

Monroe
Johnson, Sarah Smith *psychologist*

Morganton
Carpenter III, Harry Everett *social sciences educator, history professor*

Pittsboro
Murdock, John Carey *economics professor, investor*
Richardson, Richard Judson *retired political science professor*

Raleigh
Allen, Steven Glen *economics and business professor*
Brooks, Jackie Daniel *social studies educator*
Cole, Kathryn Miller *psychologist, educator*
Craig, Lee A. *economics professor, consultant*
Imade, Lucky Osagie *political scientist, educator*
Newman, Slater Edmund *psychologist, educator*
Stroup, Richard Lyndell *economist, educator, writer*

Research Triangle Park
Beach, Robert Henry III *economist, educator*

Rolesville
Patierno, Alycia Lynn *school psychologist*

Salisbury
Tseng, Howard Shih Chang *economics professor, investment company executive*

Wilmington
Puente, Antonio E. *psychologist, educator, scientist*

Winston Salem
Madjd-Sadjadi, Zagros *economics professor, consultant*

NORTH DAKOTA

Dickinson
McGarva, Andrew Robert *psychology professor*

Fargo
Riley, Thomas Joseph *anthropologist, academic administrator*

Grand Forks
Russell, Sue Ann *clinical psychologist*

OHIO

Ada
Alexander, Robert M. *political science professor*
Wildman, Kenneth N. *professor emeritus of psychology*

Akron
Allen, Philip Andrew *psychology professor*
Garbrandt, Gail Elaine *political science professor, consultant*
McGuire, Robert A. *economics professor*
Nelson, Michael Arnold *economics professor, department chairman*
Noble, Allen George *geography educator*
Sterns, Harvey Leonard *psychologist, gerontologist*

Ashland
Ford, Lucille Garber *economist, educator*

Athens
McNamara, John Regis *psychology educator*
Patterson, Stephen M. *psychology professor*
Reisner, Andrew Douglas *psychologist*
Thompson, Herbert George, Jr. *economics professor, consultant*
Vedder, Richard Kent *economics professor*

Bath
Coyne, Thomas Joseph *economics and finance professor*

Berea
Miller, Dennis Dixon *economics professor*

Bowling Green
Berger, Bonnie G. *sport psychologist, educator*
Guion, Robert Morgan *psychologist, educator*
Hakel, Milton Daniel, Jr. *psychologist, educator, writer, consultant*
McCaghy, Charles Henry *retired social sciences educator*

Canton
Esber, George S. *anthropologist, educator*

Cedarville
Firmin, Michael Wayne *psychology professor*

Chillicothe
Shahrestani, Hamid *economics professor*

Cincinnati
Andritzky, Frank William *political science educator*
Ashley, Lynn *social sciences educator, consultant*
Bishop, George Franklin *political scientist, educator*
Bluestein, Venus Weller *retired psychologist, educator*
Hovanitz, Christine Anne *psychologist*
Laffitte, Larry James *industrial organizational psychologist, consultant*
Potoka, Karen *psychologist*
Tsibulsky, Vladimir Lvovich *psychologist, researcher*

Cleveland
Binstock, Robert Henry *public policy educator, writer*
Carlsson, Bo Axel Vilhelm *economics professor*
Carrol, Edward Nicholas *psychologist*
Deal, William Thomas *retired school psychologist*
Hokenstad, Merl Clifford, Jr. *social work educator*
Kolb, David Allen *psychologist, educator*
Lewine, Mark Saul *anthropology professor*
Mayland, Kenneth Theodore *economist*
McHale, Vincent Edward *political science professor*
Sibley, Willis Elbridge *anthropology educator, consultant*

Columbus
Alger, Chadwick Fairfax *political scientist, educator*
Baird, Leonard Lynn *social scientist, educator, researcher, editor*
Beck, Paul Allen *political science professor*
Bemak, Frederic Paul *psychology educator*
Brustein, William Irving *sociology educator*
Curry, Timothy Jon *sociology educator*
Everhart, Velma Vizedom *retired home economics educator, real estate agent*
Herson, Lawrence J.R. *social sciences educator, consultant*
Huber, Joan Althaus *sociology educator*
Jackson, Leslie M. *psychology professor, researcher*
Johnson, Martha Junk (Marty Johnson) *psychology professor*
Johnson, Neal Frederick *psychologist, educator*
Kessel, John Howard *political scientist, educator*
Mueller, John Ernest *political science professor, dance critic*
Naylor, James Charles *psychologist, educator*
Paxton, Pamela *social sciences educator*
Reiss, Steven *psychology professor*
Weisberg, Herbert Frank *political science professor*
Wilkinson, Deanna L. *social sciences educator*
Wiser, Vera Roubicek *psychologist*

Dayton
Bauer, John-Jack J. *psychology professor*
Shebilske, Wayne Lawrence *psychology professor, researcher*
Snipe, Tracy David *political science professor*

Findlay
Peters, Milton Eugene *retired educational psychologist*

Kent
Kaplan, David Howard *geographer, educator*
Neal-Barnett, Angela Marie *psychology professor*
Timmons-Mitchell, Jane Christina *clinical psychologist, researcher, consultant, educator, entrepreneur*
Was, Christopher A. *psychology professor*
Williams, Donald R. *social sciences educator*

Kirtland
Santos, Rolando Aguilar *economics professor*

Lima
Page, Roger Allan *retired psychology professor*

Lyndhurst
Dellas, Marie C. *retired psychology educator, consultant*

Marion
Thompson, Jo(an) *anthropologist*

Medina
Cooper, Allan D. *political science educator*

Newark
Brunell, Amy B. *psychology professor*
Federspiel, Howard M. *political science professor*

Oberlin
Kasper, Hirschel *economics educator*
Markowitz, Lawrence Peter *political science professor*
Taylor, Richard Wirth *retired political science professor*

Oxford
Bergen, Doris *psychologist, educator*
Dawisha, Adeed *political science professor*
Miller, Norman Calvin *economist*
Rejai, Mostafa *political science professor*
Shriver, Edwin R. *psychologist*
Ziegler, Melanie McClure *social sciences educator*

Painesville
Garwood, Barbara Ann *psychologist, educator*

Pataskala
Ripley, Randall Butler *political scientist, educator*

Pepper Pike
Frazier, Arthur R. *political science professor, department chairman*
Seaton, Jean Robarts *psychology educator*

Rootstown
Benshoff, Dixie L. *psychologist*
Savickas, Mark Lee *psychology professor*

Salem
Yates, Jacquelyn *political science professor*

Shaker Heights
Ludwig, L(owell) Mark *social studies educator*

Strongsville
Blumer, Frederick Elwin *retired philosophy educator*

Sugar Grove
Dombrowski, Karen S. *social studies and education educator*

Sylvania
Hountras, Peter Timothy *psychologist, educator*
Kujawa, Jean *economics professor*

Tiffin
Gridley, Mark Charles *psychologist*

Toledo
Berendt, Emil Bohdan *economist*
Brockmyer, Jeanne H. *psychology professor*
Egan, Kevin J. *economics professor*
Heintz, Carolinea Cabaniss *retired home economist, educator*
McSweeny, Austin John *psychology educator*
Wang, Leslie Tsun Chung *social sciences educator*

University Heights
Eslinger, Kenneth Nelson *social sciences educator*

University Hts
Calkins, Lindsay Noble *economics professor*

Warren
Ross, Karen Lee Hromyak *retired school psychologist*

Willoughby
Eyman, Culver Francis III *social studies educator, department chairman*

Wooster
Krain, Matthew *political science professor*
Loess, Henry Bernard *psychology professor*

Youngstown
Jackson, Cryshanna A. *social sciences educator*
Mehra, Jagdish *economics professor*

Zanesville
Earhart, Margaret V. *social studies educator*

OKLAHOMA

Edmond
Currier, Susanne *economics professor*

Lawton
Graves, Russell W. *social studies educator*
Sukar, Abdulhamid I. *economics professor*

Norman
Affleck, Marilyn *retired sociology educator*
Dalbo, Vincent James *psychologist, researcher*
Henderson, George *educational sociologist, educator*
Kondonassis, Alexander John *economist, educator*
Perkins, Edward Joseph *political science professor, retired ambassador*

Oklahoma City
Adams, Russell Lee *neuropsychologist*
Allbright, Karan Elizabeth *psychologist, consultant*
Broach, Dana *psychologist, researcher*
Craig, George Dennis *economics professor, consultant*
Henderson, J. Neil *medical anthropologist*
Morgan, Catherine Marie *psychologist, writer*
Murry, Donald Arvil *economics professor*
Myers, Densel Lee *economics professor*
Poole, Richard William *economist*
Schroeder, David J. Dean *retired psychologist*

Seminole
Jacomo, Tracy Wood *social sciences educator, consultant*
Koenig, Pamela *social sciences educator*

Stillwater
Darcy, Robert Emmett *political science and statistics professor*
Kim, Jaebeom *economics professor*
Melancon, Celinda Reese *psychologist*
Wang, Ning Lian *geographer, educator*

Tulsa
Dugger, William Mayfield *economics professor*
Hellman, Chan M. *psychology professor*

OREGON

Ashland
Bornet, Vaughn Davis *social sciences educator, historian, researcher*
Rowland, Paul Stephen *psychology professor*

Corvallis
Castle, Emery Neal *economist, educator*
Gillis, John Simon *retired psychologist, educator*

Eugene
Bichsel, Ruth J. *psychologist, educator*
Candee, Stephen M. *political science professor*
Freyd, Jennifer Joy *psychology professor*
Hunt, Elizabeth Hope *psychologist*
Jenkins, Dennis L. *archaeologist, educator*
Khang, Chulsoon *economics professor*
Kimble, Daniel Porter *psychology educator*
Littman, Richard Anton *psychologist, educator*
Moses, Louis J. *psychology professor, department chairman*
Neville, Helen J. *psychology professor, neuroscientist*
White, Patricia Marie *psychology professor, researcher*
Ziliak, James Patrick *economics educator*

Forest Grove
Nye, Tracy D. *psychologist*

Newberg
Adams, Wayne Verdun *pediatric psychologist, educator*
Warford, Patricia *psychologist*

Portland
Anastasiou, Harry *international peace and conflict studies professor*
Atkinson, Patricia Anne Webster *economics professor*
Christensen, John F. *psychologist, director*
Detweiler-Bedell, Jerusha Beth *psychology professor*
Fawls, Maurita Therese *economics professor*
Gu, Danan *demographer*
Matarazzo, Joseph Dominic *psychologist, educator*
Matarazzo, Ruth Gadbois *behavioral neuroscience and psychiatry professor emerita*
Wiens, Arthur Nicholai *psychology professor*
Wooster, Rossitza Bouneva *economics professor*

PENNSYLVANIA

Akron
Rupley, Lawrence A. *economics professor*

Allentown
Tjeltveit, Alan C. *psychology professor*

Beaver Falls
Ancil, Ralph E. *economics educator*

Bethlehem
Aronson, Jay Richard *economics professor, researcher, academic administrator*
Chisholm, Darlene Chris *economics educator*
Cordero, Lidia Estrada *psychologist, social worker*
Smolansky, Bettie Moretz *sociology educator*
Wetcher-Hendricks, Debra Elizabeth *social sciences educator*

Blue Bell
Chhatwal, Jagpreet *health economist*
May, Barbara *social sciences educator*

Bridgeville
Marcinek, Cara A. *psychologist*
Moore, Daniel Edmund *psychologist, educator, retired educational administrator*

Bryn Mawr
Anderson, Eric Edward *psychologist, consultant, healthcare executive, educator*
Porter, Judith Deborah Revitch *sociologist*
Roszkowski, Michael Joseph *psychologist*

Catawissa
Gardner, Paula J. *psychologist*

Center Valley
Hojjat, Tahereh Alavi *economics professor*

Chester
Prewitt Diaz, Joseph O. *psychologist, educator*

Clarion
Feroz, Raymond Felix *rehabilitation sciences professor*
Trejos, Sandra Roxana *economics professor*

Collegeville
Chambliss, Catherine Anne *psychologist, educator*
O'Neill, Heather Munro *economics professor*

Coopersburg
Bednar, Charles Sokol *political science professor*

Coraopolis
Beaver, William R. *sociology professor*

Dallas
Liuzzo, Anthony L. *economic educator*

Downingtown
Sweeney, Sarina Marie *psychologist, consultant*

Easton
Kincaid, John *political science professor, editor*

Edinboro
Chompalov, Ivan Mihailov *social sciences educator*

Friendsville
Bjick, Suzanne Carter *psychologist*

Glenside
Thompson, Joan Hulse *political science professor*

Greensburg
Gibson, Donald Elmer *sociologist, educator, writer*
Ramm, Douglas Robert *psychologist*

Grove City
Throckmorton, Warren *psychology professor, consultant*

Haverford
Jilani, Saleha *economics assistant professor*
McGovern, Stephen John *political scientist*

Huntingdon
Mathur, Ryan *social sciences educator*

Immaculata
Comber, George Thomas *psychology professor*

Indiana
Ciano-Federoff, Lynda *psychologist, educator*
Mc Cauley, R. Paul *criminologist, educator*
Miller, Vincent Paul, Jr. *geography and regional planning educator*
Reynolds, Virginia Edith *sociologist, anthropologist, educator, artist*

Johnstown
Errett, Daniella K. Cope *psychology professor*

Kelton
Gulick, Walter Lawrence *psychologist, educator, retired academic administrator*

Kennett Square
Smith, Virginia Eleanore *psychologist, educator*

Kutztown
Gupta, Venu Gopal *psychology professor*

Langhorne
Palladino, Christopher James *social studies educator*

Lewisburg
Candland, Douglas Keith *psychology professor*
Hauck, William Edward *retired education educator*
Nottis, Katharyn E.K. *educational psychologist, researcher*

Lincoln University
Nwachuku, Levi Akalazu *social sciences and behavioral studies educator*

Lock Haven
Forbes, Edward John, III, (Ted Forbes) *retired developmental psychologist, educator*

Meadville
Adams, Earl William, Jr. *retired economics professor*

Moon Township
Harold, Philip J. *political science professor*

Myerstown
Zimmerman, Dennis Neal *psychologist*

Nazareth
Farbod, Faramarz *political science professor*

New Alexandria
Sehring, Hope Hutchison *library science educator*

North Warren
Carlson-Johnson, Michelle Ann *psychologist, consultant*

Philadelphia
Adler, Freda Schaffer *criminologist, educator*
Ambrosini, Paul John *child psychiatry educator*
Asch, David Alan *economist, educator, healthcare educator*
Berg, Ivar Elis, Jr. *social science educator*
Bogan, Arthur Eugene *archaeologist*
Brown, Ronald Terry *psychologist, educator*
Chrysikou, Evangelia G. *psychology professor*
Cunningham, Jacqueline Lemmé *psychologist, educator, researcher*
DiIulio, John J., Jr. *political science professor*
Erdmann, James Bernard *educational psychologist*
Evan, William Martin *sociologist, educator*
Fishbein, Martin *psychologist, educator*
Foa, Edna *psychologist, educator*
Foster, Gary D. *psychologist*
Fox, Renée Claire *sociology educator*
Frankel, Francine Ruth *political science professor*
Goodenough, Ward Hunt *anthropologist, educator*
Grazian, David *sociologist, educator*
Harvey, John Adriance *psychologist, pharmacologist, researcher, educator*
Hojat, Mohammadreza *psychologist, psychological researcher*
Jemmott, Loretta Sweet *HIV/AIDS researcher, nursing educator*
Kendall, Philip C. *psychologist, educator*
Klausner, Samuel Zundel *sociologist, educator*
Klein, Lawrence Robert *economist, educator*
Krueger, Dirk *economist, educator*
Mutz, Diana C. *political science professor*
Overton, Willis F. *psychology professor*
Ozmucur, Suleyman *economics professor, researcher*
Perlman, Barry Steven *sociologist, educator*
Phelps, Charlotte DeMonte *retired economics professor*
Rescorla, Robert Arthur *psychology professor*
Rima, Ingrid Hahne *economics professor*
Romano, David Gilman *archaeologist*
Rutkowski, Duane Joseph *social studies educator*
Sankar, Pamela Lee *social sciences educator*
Schatz, Philip *psychology professor*
Shure, Myrna Beth *psychologist, educator*
Smith, Rogers Mood *political scientist, educator*
Snelbecker, Glenn Eugene *psychologist, educator*
Summers, Robert *economics professor*
Ting, Jan C. *political science professor, lawyer, consultant*
Wallace, Anthony Francis Clarke *anthropologist, educator*
Zubernis, Lynn Smith *psychologist, counselor*
Zuckerman, Marvin *retired psychologist*

Pitcairn
Wallace, Mark Alexander *social studies educator*

Pittsburgh
Ammerman, Robert Thompson *clinical psychologist*
Barry, Herbert III *psychologist, educator*
Behrmann, Marlene *psychology professor, speech pathology/audiology services professional*
Blumstein, Alfred *urban and public affairs educator*
Cagney, William Robert *psychologist*
Cohen, Sheldon *psychologist, psychology professor*
Curry, Nancy Ellen *psychologist, psychoanalyst, educator*
Dawes, Robyn Mason *psychology professor*
Drennan, Robert D. *archeology educator, researcher*
Duffy, John *economics professor*
Eaton, Joseph W. *sociology educator*
Fischhoff, Baruch *psychologist, educator*
Frazer, Jendayi Elizabeth *political science professor, former federal agency administrator*
Klatzky, Roberta Lou *psychologist, educator*
Lave, Judith Rice *economics professor*
Loewenstein, George F. *economics professor, psychology professor*
MacWhinney, Brian James *psychology professor*
McCallum, Bennett Tarlton *economist, educator*
Meltzer, Allan H. *economist, educator*
Peele, Pamela Bonifay *economics educator*
Perloff, Robert *psychologist, educator*
Shaw, Daniel Stephen *psychology professor, department chairman*
Strauss, Robert Philip *economics professor*
Sussna, Edward *economist, educator*

Radnor
Sicoli, Mary Louise Corbin *psychologist, educator*

Reading
Russell, Brenda L. *psychology professor*

Royersford
Krell-Morris, Cheri Lee *psychologist*

Rydal
Heebner, Albert Gilbert *retired economist, educator, bank executive*

Scranton
Dawoody, Alexander R. *public administrator, policy assistant professor*
Kocis, Robert A. *political science professor*
Parente, William Joseph *political science professor*

Sellersville
Alpert-Diani, Linda *psychologist*

Shippensburg
Carey, Allison C. *sociologist, educator*

Shohola
Reuder, Mary E(ileen) *retired psychology professor, retired statistician*

State College
Franklin, Paula Anne *artist, writer, psychologist*
Kirchner, Elizabeth Parsons *clinical psychologist*

Swarthmore
Hopkins, Raymond Frederick *political science educator*
Keith, Jennie *anthropology educator, academic administrator, writer*
Marecek, Jeanne *psychologist, educator*
Pryor, Frederic L. *economist, educator*

University Park
Craig, Nathan Mc Donald *anthropologist, educator*
Mark, Melvin M. *psychology professor, department chairman*
Murphy, Kevin R. *psychology professor*
Ray, William Jackson *psychologist*
Stern, Robert Morris *psychologist, gastroenterology researcher*

Valley Forge
Guttentag, Jack Mark *economist, educator*

Villanova
Hu, Bangbo *social studies educator*
Johannes, John Roland *political science professor, dean*
Langran, Robert Williams *political scientist, educator*

West Chester
Loedel, Peter Henning *political science professor*
Shaffer, Leigh S. *psychology professor*
Zandi, Mark M. *economist, financial consultant*
Zlotowski, Martin *psychologist*

Wyomissing
Genieser-DeRosa, Anya *psychologist*

York
Lehr, Donald P. *psychology professor*

RHODE ISLAND

Bristol
Krech, Shepard III *anthropology educator, museum director*

Cranston
Blessing, George Patrick *psychologist*

Kingston
McCurdy, Karen *human development professor*
Newman, Barbara Miller *psychologist, educator*
Petro, Nicolai *political science professor, consultant*
Turnbaugh, William Arthur *archaeologist, educator*
Zucker, Norman Livingston *political science professor, writer*

Narragansett
Stedman, Victoria *economics professor*

Providence
Anderson, James Alfred *cognitive science professor*
Borts, George Herbert *economist, educator*
Chafee, Lincoln Davenport *political science professor, former senator*
de Leon, Cedric *sociologist, educator*
Feldman, Allan Maurice *economist*
Gould, Richard Allan *anthropologist, archaeologist, educator*
Heath, Dwight Braley *anthropologist, educator*
Hogan, Dennis Patrick *sociology educator*
Houston, Stephen D. *anthropologist, educator*
Marsh, Robert Mortimer *sociologist, educator*
Mastropietro, Gail *psychologist, consultant*
Miller, Ivan Wilfred *psychologist, educator*
Miller, Linda B. *political scientist*
Miranda, Robert *psychologist, researcher*
Putterman, Louis G. *economics professor*
Riordan, Cornelius *sociology educator, writer, consultant*
Rueschemeyer, Marilyn Schattner *sociology educator*
Stultz, Newell Maynard *retired political science professor*
Wetle, Terrie Fox *gerontologist, educator, dean*

Smithfield
TEbaldi, Edinaldo *economics professor*

SOUTH CAROLINA

Aiken
Porca, Sanela *economics professor*

Beaufort
Saravo, Anne Cobble *clinical psychologist, mental health consultant*

Charleston
Carek, Donald J(ohn) *child psychiatry educator*
Krause, James Stuart *psychology professor, director*
Milliken, Garrett Wilson *psychology professor*
Sparks, Donals L. *economics professor*
Swenson, Cynthia Cupit *psychologist, educator*

Clemson
Benjamin, Daniel Kelly *economics professor*
Dunn, Charles Wythe *political science educator*
Haller, William John *social sciences educator*
King, Bruce Michael *psychology professor, department chairman*
Milhous, Elizabeth *social studies educator*
Sauer, Raymond D., Jr. *economics professor*

Columbia
Barbieri, Katherine *political science professor*
Glad, Betty *political scientist, educator*
Kegley, Charles William, Jr. *political science professor*
Kiker, Billy Frazier *economics professor*
Logan, Sandra Jean *retired economics and business professor*
Martin, Robert William *econometrician*
Powell, Donald Ashmore *clinical research psychologist*
Wilder, Ronald Parker *economics professor*

Conway
Stewart, Patricia Diane *psychologist*

Daniel Island
Gillespie, John David *political science educator*

Florence
Warters, T. Alissa *political science professor, director*

Gaffney
Witt, Betsy *criminologist, educator*

Greenville
Melton, Gary Bentley *psychologist, educator*
Westrope, Martha Randolph *psychologist, consultant*

Greer
McAbee, Thomas Allen *psychologist*

Mc Cormick
Zeller, Michael James *psychologist, educator*

Mount Pleasant
Bilas, Richard A. *economist*

Myrtle Beach
Cazier, James Stanley *social sciences educator, department chairman*

Orangeburg
Hooker, Ward L. *economics professor*
Kantor, Camelia Maria *geography instructor, researcher*

Rock Hill
Manetta, Ameda Avrill *social sciences educator*

Spartanburg
Krout-Watson, Tracy *psychologist*
Reback, Charles S. *economics professor*

Walterboro
Refinetti, Roberto *biopsychologist*

SOUTH DAKOTA

Aberdeen
Hedges, Mark Stephen *clinical psychologist*

Canton
Perkinson, Robert Ronald *psychologist, consultant*

Lennox
Brendtro, Larry Kay *psychologist*

Sioux Falls
Himler, Thomas Charles *psychologist*

Spearfish
Colmenero-Chilberg, Laura Elizabeth *sociology professor*
Nsiah, Christian *economics professor, consultant*

Vermillion
Clem, Alan Leland *retired political scientist, educator*

TENNESSEE

Bolivar
Boyle, Candyace *psychologist*

Chattanooga
Cothran, Dee Lisa *psychology professor*
Rabin, Alan A. *economics professor*
Wilson, Richard Lee *political science professor*

Clarksville
Wilson, Patti L. *psychologist, educator*

Franklin
Santini, Danilo John *energy economist, urban systems engineer*

Johnson City
Clements, Andrea Deason *psychology educator*
Dotterweich, Douglas Pierce *economics professor, researcher*
Fox, James J. III *psychology professor, researcher*

Knoxville
Bass, William Marvin III *anthropology educator*
Fuller, Paul *sociology educator*
Harris, Diana Koffman *sociologist, educator*
Infante, Isa Maria *political scientist, educator*

Martin
Baxter, Christopher M. *political science professor*

Mc Minnville
Grandey, Timothy Hal *social studies educator, farmer*

Memphis
Cetingok, Muammer *social sciences educator*
Geter, Jennifer L. *psychologist*
Jefferson, Daisy M. *social studies educator, english educator*
Johnson, Johnny *research psychologist, consultant*
Rubin, Rose Mohr *economics professor*

Murfreesboro
Breault, Kevin D. *social studies educator, researcher*

Nashville
Atack, Jeremy *economics professor, history professor*
Bauer, Avalyn *psychologist*
Cole, David A. *psychology professor, department chairman*
Dillehay, Tom D. *anthropologist, educator*
Gwin, Dorothy Jean Bird *retired psychology professor, dean*
Hargrove, Erwin Charles, Jr. *political science professor*
Havens, Murray Clark *political scientist, educator*
Hetherington, Marc J. *political science professor*
Hinshaw, Carroll Elton *economics professor*
Janusek, John Wayne *anthropologist, educator*
Jensen, Gary Franklin *sociology educator*
Klass, Judith Alexandra *social studies educator, writer*
Lazar, Irving *psychologist*
Li, Tong *economics professor, researcher*
McCammon, Holly *sociologist, educator*
McCarty, Richard Charles *psychology professor, dean*
Morton-Young, Tommie *psychology professor, writer*
Schoggen, Phil H(oward) *psychologist, educator*
Steiger, James Hubert *psychology professor*
Wahid, Abu N. M. *economics professor*
Westfield, Fred Meinhard *economics professor*

Oak Ridge
Colston, Freddie Charles *political science professor*
Sorokine, Alexandre *geographer, researcher*

Rockwood
Miller, Donald Eugene *anthropology educator*

Tullahoma
Cheatham, Clarence Donald *political science educator*

TEXAS

Arlington
Brainerd, Charles J(on) *psychologist, mathematics professor*
McKizzie, Robert R. *economics professor*
Ramsey, Charles Eugene *sociologist, educator*

Austin
Allen, Barbara Rothschild *retired psychology professor*
Bost, Jane Morgan *psychologist*
Buchanan, Bruce, II, *political science professor*
Burnham, Walter Dean *political science professor*
Cooper, William Wager *economics, accounting and finance professor, dean*
Davis-Floyd, Robbie Elizabeth *anthropologist, educator*
Drake, Stephen Douglas *psychologist, health facility administrator*
Dumas, Sara Lee *psychologist*
Dusansky, Richard *economist, educator*
Franklin, Cynthia Southern *psychology professor, researcher*
Galbraith, James Kenneth *economics professor*
Glade, William Patton, Jr. *economics professor*
Hinich, Melvin J. *economics professor*
Holtzman, Wayne Harold *psychologist, educator*
Kendrick, David Andrew *economist, educator*
Loehlin, John Clinton *psychologist, educator*
Lowry, Alaire Howard *psychologist*
McFadden, Dennis *psychologist, educator*
Mickenberg, Julia Lynn *American studies professor*
Muchlinski, Magdalena Natalia *anthropologist, educator*
Pangle, Thomas Lee *political scientist*
Pintar, Elizabeth *anthropologist, educator*
Pluta, Joseph Edward *economics professor*
Roach, James Robert *retired political science professor*
Sasse, Benjamin Eric *public policy educator, former federal agency administrator*
Schmandt, Jurgen A. *public affairs educator*
Schmitt, Karl Michael *retired political scientist*
Serafine, Mary Louise *psychologist, lawyer, educator*
Shapiro, Liza J. *anthropologist, educator*
Slivinske, Alec Joseph, Jr. *economics professor*
Smith, Todd Malcolm *political consultant*
Sparrow, Bartholomew Huntington *political scientist, educator*
Spelman, William *social studies educator*
Trudel, Tina M. *psychologist, educator*
Umberson, Debra *sociologist, educator*
Walter, Virginia Lee *psychologist, educator*
Williams, Anna Lassiter *psychologist, researcher*
Williams, Roberton Capell III *economics professor*

Bedford
Riggs, Audrey *psychologist*

Bellaire
Mayo, Clyde Calvin *psychologist, educator*

Belton
Erlund, Cecilia Wharton *psychology professor, small business owner*

Brenham
Drane, Clifford Conway *economics professor*

Brooks City-Base
Villarreal, Roberto Escamilla *retired political science researcher, educator, administrator*

Bryan
Van Riper, Paul Pritchard *retired political science professor*

Canyon
Thoman, Roy Edward *political scientist, educator*

College Station
Bass, George Fletcher *retired archaeology educator*
Bessler, David A *economist*
Edwards, George Charles III *political science professor, writer*
Furubotn, Eirik Grundtvig *economics professor*
Kersting, Erasmus Kristoffer *economist*
Meier, Kenneth John *political scientist*
Moroney, John Rodgers *economist, educator*
Nash, William Rhodes *retired psychology professor*
Ory, Marcia Gail *social science researcher*
Penson, John B., Jr. *economics professor, consultant*
Phillips, Charles David *gerontologist, health services researcher, public health professional*

Commerce
McBroom, James Randy *sociologist, educator*

Corpus Christi
Cohn, Edward A. *economist, educator*
Crowley, Patrick M. *economics professor, consultant*
Rabinowitz, Yaron Gil *psychologist, educator, military officer*

Dallas
Bernstein, Ira Harvey *psychology professor*
Betts, Dianne Connally *economist, educator*
Free Hosford, Mary Moore *biological and medical anthropologist*
Kemper, Robert Van *anthropologist, minister, educator*
Neeley, Beverly Evon *sociologist, consultant*
Oualline, Viola Jackson *psychologist, consultant*

Denton
Acevedo, Miguel F. *science and engineering educator*
Alexander, Jim R. *social sciences educator*
Belfiglio, Valentine John *political science professor*
Cobb, Steven Lee *economics professor*
Dadres, Susan Layne *economics professor*
Nievar, Angela M. *social sciences educator*
Preston, Michael James *social studies educator*
Seward, Rudy Ray *sociology educator*
Turner, Keith Whisnant *gerontologist, educator*
Ver Duin, D'Arlene K. *sociologist, researcher*
Yang, Philip Q. *sociologist*

Desoto
Campos, David *social sciences educator*

Edinburg
Glover-Graf, Noreen M. *social sciences educator*

Egypt
Krenek, Mary Louise *political scientist, researcher*

El Paso
Gutierrez, Richard *political science professor*
Himelstein, Philip Nathan *psychology professor*
Solórzano, Rosalía *sociologist, educator*

Fort Worth
Dees, Sandra Kay Martin *psychologist, research scientist*
Jackson, Donald Wilson *political science professor, lawyer*
Kemp, Thomas N. *economics professor*
Mullendore, Walter Edward *retired economist*
Pai, Kalpana *economics professor*
Simpson, Dennis Dwayne *psychologist, educator*
Wicker, James Eugene *retired psychologist*

Georgetown
Lopreato, Joseph *evolutionary sociologist, writer*
Nelsen, Hart Michael *sociologist, educator*
Purdy, Jesse E. *psychology professor*

Glen Rose
Lane, Willa Joan Manes *retired psychologist*

Harlingen
Lytle, Michael Allen *forensic criminologist, consultant*

Houston
Ayadi, Mary Olufemi *health economist, educator*
Bhargava, Alok *economics professor, consultant*
Black, Donna Lord *school psychology specialist*
Brito, Dagobert Llanos *economics professor*
Bryant, John Bradbury *economics professor, consultant*
Carman, Carol A. *psychologist, educator*
Condit, Linda Faulkner *retired economist*
Curry, George Evans *social sciences educator*
Cuthbertson, Gilbert Morris *political science professor*
Davidson, Chandler *sociologist, educator*
Demouy, Alyson M. *social studies educator*
Florian-Lacy, Dorothy *psychologist, educator*
Francis, James Stephen, Jr. *psychologist, educator*
Gritz, Ellen R. *behavioral scientist, educator*
Grossett, Deborah Lou *psychologist, consultant*
Gutheinz, Joseph Richard, Jr. *criminal justice educator, consultant, lawyer*
Haensly, Patricia Anastacia *psychology professor*
Hutchinson, William Kenneth *economics professor*
Jenkins, Sheila Alnita *psychologist*
Jenkins nee McKellar, Peggy Ann *psychologist, educator*
Kotarba, Joseph Anthony *sociologist, educator*
Lee, Donghyung *psychologist*
Lee, Rebecca E *psychologist, educator*
Lehrer, Kenneth Eugene *economic consulting company executive*
Medlock, Kenneth Barry *economics professor, consultant*
Miller, Janel Howell *psychologist*
Nuwal, Tara C. *economics professor*
Paul, Gordon Lee *behavioral scientist, psychologist*
Sickles, Robin C. *economics and statistics professor, consultant*
Upton, Cindy McDonough *economics professor*
von der Mehden, Fred R. *political science professor*
Wiseman, Melissa S. *economics professor*
Yatsenko, Yuri Petrovich *business professor, mathematician*

Huntsville
Joo, Hee-Jong *criminology educator*

Hurst
Mabry, Philip T. *political scientist, consultant*

Killeen
Lapierre, Coady *psychology professor, consultant*

Kingsville
Cruz Garza, Laura *psychology professor, researcher*

Lake Jackson
Pryor, Wayne David *social sciences educator*

Laredo
Mohamed Ben-Ruwin, Mohamed A. *political science professor*
Rivas, Andres Eloy *economics professor*

Lewisville
Dooley, Cristin Bevin *psychologist*

Longview
Mann, True Sandlin *psychologist, consultant*

Lubbock
Arwine, Alan Troy *political educator*
Gonzales, Alberto R. *political science professor, former United States Attorney General*
Tallent-Runnels, Mary K. *psychology professor, researcher*

Mc Kinney
Berry, Brian Joe Lobley *geographer, urban planner, political economist, educator*

Mesquite
Byrd, Kathryn Susan *psychologist, educator*
Holman, Morris H. *retired social sciences educator*

Nacogdoches
Fante-Konwinski, Rhiannon Marie *psychology professor, consultant*
Stroup, Michael D. *economics professor, dean*

Odessa
Hadjicostandi, Joanna A. *social sciences educator*

Pflugerville
Schwitters, Kathleen Chantell *school psychologist specialist*

Plano
O'Loughlin-Brooks, Jennifer L. *psychology professor*
Worsfold, Victor Leonard *retired social sciences educator*

Prairie View
Prestage, Jewel Limar *political scientist, educational consultant*

Richardson
Faria, Joao Ricardo *economist, educator*
Griffith, Daniel Alva *geography educator*
Sandler, Todd Michael *economist, political scientist, educator*
Vijverberg, Wim Petrus Maria *economics educator*

San Angelo
Butler, Michael Ward *economics professor*

San Antonio
Anderson, Anita L. *psychology professor*
Austin, Lola Houston *psychologist*
Bellows, Thomas John *political scientist, educator*
Breit, William *economist, educator, writer*
Brooks, Franklin Ramon *psychologist, military officer*
Callihan, Dorothy Jeanne *psychologist, educator*
Harris, Richard John *social sciences educator*
Katz, Martin M. *psychologist, educator*
Moore-Sickmann, Susan *psychologist*
Ribble, Ronald George *psychologist, educator, writer, behavioral consultant*
Spencer, Roger Wayne *economics professor*

San Marcos
Shields, Patricia Mary *political science professor*
Yun, Hyun Jung *political science professor*

Stephenville
Osei, Edward *economist, researcher*

Sugar Land
Fox, Lori A. *psychologist*
Harribance, Sean Lalsingh *parapsychologist*

Tomball
Fox, Clifton Robert *social studies educator*

Vernon
McCoy, Michael *economics professor*

Victoria
Harrington, Rick *psychology professor*

Waco
Ballenger, Erma Maxine *social studies educator, director*
Beaujean, Alexander A. *psychology professor*
Grinols, Earl Leroy III *economist, educator*

Waxahachie
Logue, Jeff *psychology professor, director*

UTAH

Bountiful
Mangum, Garth Leroy *retired economist*

Brigham City
Halterman, Karen Annie *psychologist*

Cedar City
White, Lynn H. *psychology professor, researcher*

Logan
Fauth, Elizabeth Braungart *human development and family studies professor*

Ogden
Elliott, Harold Marshall *geography educator*
MacKay, Kathryn Leilani *social sciences educator*

Provo
Bahr, Howard Miner *sociologist, educator*
Brown, Ralph Browning *sociologist, educator*
Creer, Thomas Laselle *psychologist, educator, writer*
Geo-Jaja, Macleans A. *economics professor, education educator*
Holt-Lunstad, Julianne *psychology professor, researcher*
Pedersen, Darhl Max *psychology professor*
Pope, C. Arden III *economics professor*
Porter, Blaine Robert Milton *sociology professor, psychology professor*

Salt Lake City
Benjamin, Lorna Smith *psychologist*
Brandon, Kathleen Virginia *retired social studies educator*
Drew, Clifford James *psychologist, educator*
Livne, Nava Levia *psychologist, researcher*
Prospero, Moises *social studies educator, director*
Shimp, Charles Patterson *psychologist, educator*
Shiptsova, Rimma *economics professor*

Sandy
Durham, Lynn Ellen *school psychologist*
Smith, Willard Grant *psychologist*
Snell, Marilyn Nelson *psychologist, researcher*

Washington
De Vany, Arthur Stacy *economics professor*

VERMONT

Arlington
Cole, Ann Harriet *psychologist, consultant*

Brandon
Farnsworth, Frank Albert *retired economics professor*

Burlington
Cutler, Stephen Joel *sociologist, educator*
Escaja, Tina *social studies educator*
Kaelber, Lutz *sociologist, educator*
Rohan, Kelly J. *psychology professor, researcher*
Shelton, Lawrence G. *social sciences educator*
Stout, Neil Ralph *retired history educator*
Thomson, Ross David *economics professor*
Vincent, Jennifer A. *economics professor, consultant*

Castleton
Roper, Scott Christopher *geographer, researcher*

Charlotte
Naylor, Thomas Herbert *economist, educator, consultant*

Colchester
Kujawa, Richard Stephen *social sciences educator*

Lyndonville
Werdenschlag, Lori B. *psychologist, educator*

Middlebury
Horlacher, David Edmund *economics professor, researcher*
Lamberti, Marjorie *retired social studies educator*
Robison, Olin Clyde *political science educator, former college president*

Newbury
Doig, Jameson Wallace *political science professor*

Northfield
Benabess, Najiba *economics professor, researcher*

Shelburne
Gilpin, Robert George, Jr. *political science professor*

South Burlington
Emery, Marla R. *geographer, researcher*

VIRGINIA

Alexandria
Cahill, Mary Beth *political strategist*
Carvalho, Julie Ann *psychologist*
Carville, James, Jr., (Chester James Carville) *political scientist, commentator*
Corrothers, Helen Gladys *criminal justice official*
Cressey, Pamela J. *archaeologist, museum director*
Johnson, Edgar McCarthy *psychologist*
Kollander, Mel *social scientist, statistician, economist*
Krueger, Gerald Peter *psychologist*
Matalin, Mary Joe *political consultant, editor*
McConville, Judy Allen *social studies educator*

Altavista
McNiel, Robyn E. *psychologist*

Arlington
Boorstein, Laurence *economist, educator*
Gunn, Joseph Ridgeway III *consulting economist*
Jehn, Christopher *economist*
Martin, Linda Gaye *demographer, economist*
Rajan, Ramkishen S. *economist, educator*
Sundquist, James Lloyd *retired political scientist*
Tolchin, Susan Jane *political science professor, writer*
Vitz, Paul Clayton *psychologist, educator*
Warshawsky, Mark Joel *public finance and labor economist, former federal policy official*

Blacksburg
Ball, Sheryl *economics professor*
Jannuzi, F. Tomasson *economics professor*

Bluemont
Kobetz, Richard William *criminologist, consultant*

Bridgewater
Porter, Lisa *sociologist, educator*

Charlottesville
Abraham, Henry Julian *retired political science professor*
Clore, Gerald L. *psychology professor*
Cornell, Dewey Gene *psychologist*
DeLoache, Judy Sprague *psychology professor*
Elzinga, Kenneth Gerald *economics professor*
Handler, Jerome Sidney *anthropology educator*
Hanft, Ruth S. Samuels *economist, consultant*
Harding, Harry *dean, political scientist, educator, consultant*
Henry, Laurin Luther *public affairs educator*
Keen, Rachel *psychology professor*
Kiewra, Gustave Paul *psychologist, educator*
Lanham, Betty Bailey *anthropologist, educator*
Olsen, Edgar Oliver *economics professor*
Pate, Robert Hewitt, Jr. *retired counselor educator*
Proffitt, Dennis R. *psychology professor, department chairman*
Reppucci, Nicholas Dickon *psychologist, educator*
Rhoads, Steven Eric *political science professor*
Sabato, Larry Joseph *political science professor, director*
Sykes, Gresham M'Cready *sociologist, educator, artist*
Wagner, Roy *anthropology educator, researcher*
Whitaker, John King *retired economics professor*
Wilson, Timothy D. *psychology professor*

Danville
Lea, Robert Lee III *social sciences educator*

Eastville
Williams, Ida Jones *consumer and home economics educator, writer*

Fairfax
Barth, Michael Carl *economist*
Bennett, James Thomas *economics professor*
Buchanan, James McGill *economist, educator*
Cowen, Tyler *economics professor*
Dennis, Rutledge M. *sociologist, educator*
Haack, Barry N. *geographer, educator*
Haines, David W. *social sciences educator*
Kash, Don Eldon *political science professor*
Katz, Mark Norman *international relations educator, consultant, author*
Lindsey, Lawrence Benjamin (Larry Lindsey) *economist, former federal official*
Nye, John Vincent Canizares *economics professor*
Parasuraman, Raja *psychology professor*
Pfiffner, James Price *political science professor*
Pruitt, Dean Garner *psychologist, educator*
Rojahn, Johannes *psychology professor*
Steele, Howard Loucks *economic development consultant, author*
Wagner, Richard E. *economist, educator*

Falls Church
Calkins, Susannah Eby *retired economist*
Crawford, Kristina S. *psychologist*
Green, James Wyche *sociologist, anthropologist, psychotherapist, consultant*
Hjort, Howard Warren *economist, consultant*
Weiss, Armand Berl *economist, association management executive*

Farmville
Dorrill, William Franklin *political scientist, educator*
Garcia, Joseph Edward *earth science and geography educator*
Lehr, David Leonard *economics professor*
Witschey, Walter Robert Thurmond *anthropologist, educator, former museum director*

Fort Belvoir
O'Kane, Barbara Lynn *research psychologist*

Fort Lee
Leppo, Lisa Marie *forensic anthropologist*

Fredericksburg
Crippen, Timothy Alan *sociology educator*
Sanford, Douglas Walker *archaeologist, educator*
Sisk, Fred Dean *retired cartographer*

Hampton
Holmes, Leonard George *psychologist*
Johnson, Leona Melissa *psychology professor, researcher*

Harrisonburg
Grayson, Joann Hess *psychology professor*
Hastedt, Glenn Peter *political science professor*
Henriques, Gregg Ros *psychology professor*

Lexington
Bang, James T. *economics professor*
Elmes, David Gordon *psychologist, educator*
Gutermuth, Karen *economics professor*
Jarrard, Leonard Everett *psychologist, educator*
Kiracofe, Clifford Attick, Jr. *political science professor*
Phillips, Charles Franklin, Jr. *retired economist*
Winfrey, John Crawford *economist, educator*

Lynchburg
Bushong, Peggy *psychology professor*
Duff, Ernest Arthur *political scientist, educator*
Lofaso, Cynthia R. *psychology professor*

Mc Lean
Auerbach, Anita L. *clinical psychologist*
Johnson, Omotunde Evan George *economist*
Nothaft, Frank Emile *economist*
Schneider, Peter Raymond *retired political scientist*
Zakheim, Dov Solomon *economist, former federal agency administrator*

Mechanicsville
Wells, Mary Julia *psychologist*

Middletown
Brumbaugh, James *economics professor*

Newington
Robertson, Jean Elizabeth *sociology educator*

Newport News
Vachris, Michelle Albert *economist, educator*

Norfolk
Ball, John David *clinical psychologist*
Cobb, Brenda *gerontological medical social worker, counselor*
Filer, Larry *economics professor*
Hubbard, Harold *political science professor*
Neumann, Serina Ann Louise *psychologist, researcher*

Portsmouth
Ojeda, Ana Maria *therapist, clinical caseworker*
Reish, Joseph E. *psychology professor*

Radford
Hiltonsmith, Robert Warren *psychology professor*
Orlov, Alexei G. *economics professor, researcher*

Reston
Payne, Roger Lee *geographer*

Richmond
Burton, Melvin Cosby, Jr. *economics professor, financial consultant*
Dhillon, Gurpreet *economics professor*
Heinicke, Craig Warren *economics professor*
McCall, Shedrick Dwight *psychologist*
McCullough, James P., Jr. *psychology professor*
Sawyer, Richard DeWight, Jr. *psychologist*
Twigg, Judyth L. *political science professor*

Roanoke
Canavan, Jane Allison *psychologist*

Springfield
de Haan, Henry John *research psychologist*

Sweet Briar
Shea, Brent Mack *social sciences educator*

Virginia Beach
Foster, Lori Ann Miller *psychologist*
Jordan, Julia Mae *psychologist*
Morrison, Jeffry H. *social sciences educator*

Warrenton
Malmgren, Harald Bernard *economist*
Pribram, Karl Harry *neuroscience and psychology educator, brain researcher*

Williamsburg
Kerns, Virginia B. *anthropologist, writer*
Lange, Carl James *retired psychology professor*
Smith, Roger Winston *retired political theory educator*

Winchester
Johnson, Carl Harold *trauma psychologist, director*

Wise
Wolny, Witold Paul *social studies educator, consultant*

Woodbridge
Tin, Jan *economist*

WASHINGTON

Battle Ground
Caltagirone, Paul John *psychologist*

Bellingham
Burdge, Rabel James *sociology educator*
Stevenson, Joan Catharine *anthropologist, educator*

Colville
Culton, Sarah Alexander *psychologist, educator*

Deer Park
Forman, Robert Edgar *retired sociology professor*

Ellensburg
Miller, Maxine Lynch *retired home economist, interior designer, educator*

Friday Harbor
MacGinitie, Walter Harold *psychologist, educator*

Hansville
Lenski, Ann Blalock *evaluation researcher, editor, writer*

Kirkland
Nelson, Matt *psychology professor*

La Conner
Garcia, John *psychologist, educator*
Knopf, Kenyon Alfred *economist, educator*

Pullman
Arthur, Linda Louise *sociologist, educator*
McSweeney, Frances Kaye *psychology professor*
Rawlins, V. Lane *economics professor, retired academic administrator*
Rosa, Eugene Anthony *sociologist, environmental scientist, educator, artist*
Warner, Dennis Allan *psychology professor*
Yan, Jia *economics professor*

Richland
Roop, Joseph McLeod *economist*

Seattle
Borgatta, Edgar F. *sociologist, educator*
Brammer, Lawrence Martin *psychologist, educator*
Chirot, Daniel *sociology and international studies educator*
Dawson, Geraldine *psychologist, educator*
Diddams, Margaret Ann DuPlissis *psychology professor, consultant*
Fiedler, Fred Edward *retired organizational psychology educator, consultant*
Greenwald, Anthony Galt *psychology educator*
Gross, Edward *retired sociologist*
Hirschman, Charles, Jr. *sociologist, educator*
MacDonald, Don *psychology educator*
Mizumori, Sheri J.Y. *psychology professor, department chairman*
Olson, David John *political science professor*
Plotnick, Robert David *economic consultant, educator*
Sarason, Irwin G. *psychology professor*
Schaie, K(laus) Warner *human development and psychology educator*
Turnovsky, Stephen John *economics professor*
Tuthill, Oliver W., Jr. *psychologist, consultant, independent film producer, director*
van den Berghe, Pierre Louis *sociologist*
Webster Stratton, Carolyn Hinde *psychology professor*

Spokane
Houseman, Gerald L. *political science professor, writer*
May, Richard B. *psychology professor*
Mays, Roy Mark, Jr., (Mark Mays) *psychologist, educator*

Tacoma
Butchart, Ronald Eugene *social foundations educator, researcher, administrator*

University Place
Bourgaize, Robert G. *economist*

Vancouver
Archer, Stephen Hunt *economist, educator*
Probst, Tahira M. *psychology professor*

WEST VIRGINIA

Fairmont
Frasure, Carl Maynard *political science professor*

Huntington
Wenzel, Loren Alvin *accounting professor*

Morgantown
Kim, Hong Nack *political science professor*
Witt, Tom *economics researcher, educator*

Parkersburg
McClung, Phil Oran *psychology professor*

Pullman
Fearn, Noelle E. *criminologist, educator*

WISCONSIN

Ashland
Joyal, Richard Dale *economics professor*

Beloit
Boros-Kazai, Andras *political science professor*
Buchanan, Gregory McClellan *psychology professor*
Davis, Harry Rex *political science professor*

Brookfield
Carter, Charlene Ann *psychologist*

Cascade
Baumann, Carol Edler *retired political scientist*

Fitchburg
Bhargava, Ashok *retired economics professor*

Green Bay
Alesch, Daniel James *social sciences educator, researcher*

Kenosha
Cyr, Arthur I. *political science and economics professor*
Mast, Joy Nystrom *biogeographer educator*

Kohler
O'Keefe, Tamra Lynn *psychologist, school system administrator, director*

La Crosse
Morehouse, Richard Edward *psychology professor*
Simpson, Steven Vincent *social sciences educator*
Vogt, Kimberly Ann *sociologist, educator*

Lancaster
Croft, Candace Ann *psychology professor, academic administrator, small business owner*

Madison
Andreano, Ralph Louis *economist, educator*
Bennett, Kenneth Alan *retired biological anthropologist*
Brock, William Allen III *economist, educator*
Chapman, Loren J. *psychology professor*
Chinn, Menzie David *economics educator*
Devine, Patricia G. *psychology professor, department chairman*
Goldberger, Arthur Stanley *economics professor*
Gooding, Diane Carol *psychology educator, researcher*
Graf, Truman Frederick *agricultural economist, educator*
Greenfield, Norman Samuel *psychologist, educator*
Hansen, W. Lee *economics professor*
Heinrich, Carolyn J. *political science professor, director*
Hester, Donald Denison *economics professor*
Jalil, Qamar *social studies educator*
Mueller, Willard Fritz *economics professor*
Rice, Joy Katharine *psychologist, education educator*
Shafer, Byron Edwin *political science professor*
Thomas, J. Mark *sociologist, educator, minister*
Wolfe, Barbara L. *economics professor, researcher*
Young, Merwin Crawford *political science professor*

Manitowoc
Bandt, Tracy Tadych *psychologist*

Menomonie
Eggert, James Edward *economics professor, writer*

Middleton
Dorner, Peter Paul *retired economist, educator*

Milwaukee
Hamlin, Christine M. *archaeologist, educator*
Kohls, Heather Lynne Hipke *economics professor, consultant*
Kuchan, Anthony Mark *psychologist, educator*
Moberg, David Oscar *sociology educator*
Paulson, Belden Henry *political scientist, educator*
Perlman, Richard Wilfred *economist, educator*
Quereshi, Mohammed Younus *retired psychology professor*
Stoiber, Karen Callan *psychologist, educator*
Warren, Richard M. *experimental psychologist, educator*

New Berlin
Marsh, Clare Teitgen *retired school psychologist*
Vissers, Michelle *psychologist*

Oconomowoc
Sieckert, Kristine Ellen *school psychologist, consultant*

Oshkosh
Gruberg, Martin *political science professor*

Pewaukee
Ostruszka, Kathleen Zelek *economics professor*
Schlei, Thomas K *social sciences educator*

Washburn
Stewart, John Miller *psychologist, educator*

Waukesha
Debrecht, Dennis Michael *economics professor, researcher*

Whitefish Bay
Hawkins, Brett William *retired political science professor*

Whitewater
Laurent, Jerome King *retired economics professor*

WYOMING

Casper
Schellberg, Thomas *economics professor*

Cheyenne
Gamst, Frederick Charles *social anthropologist*

Fairview
Luginbuehl, Marsha Lee *psychologist*

Laramie
Allen, John Logan *retired geographer*
Chai, Winberg *political science professor, foundation administrator*
Crocker, Thomas Dunstan *economics professor*
Gill, George Wilhelm *retired anthropologist*
Godby, Robert William *economics professor, department chairman*
Shaffer, Sherrill Lynn *economist*
Tschirhart, John Thomas *economist, educator*

Powell
Brophy, Dennis Richard *psychology and philosophy professor, academic administrator, minister*

TERRITORIES OF THE UNITED STATES

GUAM

Mangilao
Dames, Vivian Loyola *social sciences educator*

PUERTO RICO

Guaynabo
Guisasola Gamez, Elina *psychologist*

Rio Piedras
Hilerio, Cibel M. *psychologist, researcher*

San Juan
Folch-Serrano, Karen D. *psychologist, consultant*

CANADA

ALBERTA

Calgary
Stebbins, Robert Alan *sociology educator*

Edmonton
Keown, Lauriston Livingston, Jr. *consulting psychologist*
Mardon, Austin *geographer, writer, researcher*

Lethbridge
Los, Cornelis Albertus *economist, finance educator, risk analyst*

BRITISH COLUMBIA

Burnaby
Brantingham, Paul Jeffrey *criminologist, educator*
Kimura, Doreen *psychology professor, researcher*

Vancouver
Cynader, Max Sigmund *neuroscience professor, researcher*
Holsti, Kalevi Jacque *political scientist, department chairman*
Kesselman, Jonathan Rhys *economics professor, public policy researcher*
Laponce, Jean A. *political scientist, educator*
Marchak, Maureen Patricia *retired anthropology and sociology educator, academic administrator*
Nemetz, Peter Newman *economist, researcher, policy analysis educator*
Olsen, Inger Anna *retired psychologist*
Shearer, Ronald Alexander *economics professor*
Suedfeld, Peter *psychologist, educator*
Tees, Richard Chisholm *psychology professor emeritus*
Walker, Michael Angus *economist, director*

Victoria
Copes, Parzival *economist, researcher*

NEW BRUNSWICK

Fredericton
Kenyon, Gary Michael *gerontologist, educator*

NOVA SCOTIA

Chester Basin
Parr-Johnston, Elizabeth *economist, consultant*

Halifax
Laursen, Finn *political science professor*
Stairs, Denis Winfield *political science professor, department chairman*

ONTARIO

Hamilton
George, Peter James *economist, educator*

Kingston
Kaliski, Stephan Felix *economics professor*
MacKinnon, James Gordon *economist, educator*
Meisel, John *political scientist*
Nielsen, Morten Ørregaard *economics professor*

London
Laidler, David Ernest William *economics professor*
Wonnacott, Ronald Johnston *retired economics professor*

Niagara-on-the-Lake
Olley, Robert Edward *economist, educator*

Ottawa
Brooks, David Barry *resource economist*
Leiss, William Carl *political science professor*

Saint Catharines
Stevenson, Garth *social sciences educator*

Toronto
Dobson, Wendy Kathleen *economics professor*
Helleiner, Gerald Karl *economics professor*
Macdonald, Hugh Ian *economics professor, public policy professor, academic administrator*
Pratt, Robert Cranford *political scientist, educator*
Rose, Jeffrey Raymond *retired economist, public servant, trade unionist*

Waterloo
Fallding, Harold Joseph *sociology educator*

QUEBEC

Montreal
Brecher, Michael *political science professor*
Ikawa-Smith, Fumiko *anthropologist, educator*
Matziorinis, Kenneth N. *economist*
Melzack, Ronald *psychology professor*
Milner, Brenda Atkinson Langford *neuropsychologist*
Normandeau, Andre Gabriel *criminologist, educator*
Szabo, Denis *criminologist, educator*
Vaillancourt, Jean-Guy *sociology educator, researcher*
Waller, Harold Myron *political science professor*

Outremont
Dufour, Jean-Marie *economist, statistician, educator*

Quebec City
Belanger, Gerard *economics professor*

Sainte Croix
Grenier, Fernand *geographer, consultant*

Sainte-Foy
Tremblay, Marc Adélard *anthropologist, educator*

MEXICO

Guadalajara
Durand, Jorge *anthropologist*

Mexico City
Knaul, Felicia Marie *economist, health policy researcher*

ALBANIA

Durres
Kukeli, Agim *economics professor*

AUSTRALIA

Armadale
Neil, Sandra Eilleen Silverberg *psychologist*

CHILE

Santiago
Jimenez, Juan Pablo *economist, educator*

CHINA

Beijing
Thornton, John Lawson *economics professor, former diversified financial services company executive*

CYPRUS

Nicosia
Karageorghis, Vassos *archaeologist*

DENMARK

Risskov
Smith, Donald Frederick *psychologist, pharmacologist*

EGYPT

Cairo
Sullivan, Earl Le Roy *political science professor, former academic administrator*

ENGLAND

Bournemouth
Darvill, Timothy Charles *archaeology educator*

Bristol
Haggett, Peter *geographer, educator*

Cambridge
Renfrew, Andrew Colin (Lord Renfrew of Kaimsthorn) *archaeologist, educator, director*

Hampshire
Morris, Paul *psychologist, educator*

London
Gordon, Anthony Grant *psychologist, audiologist, independent scientist*
Kuper, Adam Jonathan *anthropologist, educator*
Maciejovsky, Boris *economist, researcher*
Portes, Richard David *economics professor*
Wainwright, Geoffrey John *archaeologist*

ESTONIA

Tallinn
Köörna, Arno *economist, educator*

FINLAND

Turku
Granö, Olavi Johannes *geography educator*

FRANCE

Paris
Allais, Maurice Felix *economist*
Cherkaoui, Mohamed *sociologist*
de Menil, Georges *economist, educator*
Fitoussi, Jean-Paul Samuel *economics professor*
Schiray, Michel *economist, research scientist, consultant*

Todorov, Tzvetan *scientific researcher*

GERMANY

APO
Adams, Julian Timothy *psychologist*

Bonn
Albach, Horst *economist*

Hamburg
Pawlik, Kurt F. *psychologist, social science educator*

Rostock
Vaupel, James W. *demographer*

GREECE

Athens
Brissimis, Sophocles Nicholas *economist*
Kalamotousakis, George John *economist, merchant banker, educator*

HONG KONG

Shatin
Mirrlees, Sir James Alexander *economics professor*

INDIA

Burdwan
Bandyopadhyay, Ranjan *sociology educator*

INDONESIA

Jakarta
Tilaar, Henry A.R. *social sciences educator*

IRELAND

Dublin
Downes, Paul Edward *psychology lecturer, research consultant*

ISRAEL

Arad
Hollander, Samuel *economist, educator*

Tel Aviv
Dekel-Tabak, Eddie *economics educator*

ITALY

Capranica VT
Liberati, Emilio *psychology doctor, sociologist, consultant*

Florence
Blondel, Jean Fernand *political science educator*

Rome
Celant, Attilio *economic geographer, educator*
Gros-Pietro, Gian Maria *economics professor*
Scognamiglio Pasini, Carlo *economics and finance professor, former senator, defense minister*
Westley, John Richard *economist*

JAPAN

Kawagoe
Maki, Atsushi *economics professor*

Kobe
Inoue, Shun *sociologist*

Machida
Miyazaki, Koichi *economics professor*

Mie
Isshiki, Masayuki *sociologist, educator, dean*

Nagoya
Kajitani, Motohisa *sociology educator*

Saitama
Muto, Takasuke *sociologist, educator*

Takarazuka
Takahashi, Yoriko *psychology professor*

Tokyo
Fukushima, Kiyohiko *economist*
Inoguchi, Takashi *political scientist, educator*
Mizuno, Atsushi *economist*
Nishiyama, Chiaki *economist, educator*
Saito, Makoto *economics professor*
Watanabe, Satoshi Patten *economist, researcher*

Tsukuba
Murayama, Yuji *geographer, science professor*

KYRGYZSTAN

Bishkek
Koichuev, Turar Koichuevich *economist, science association executive*

LEBANON

Beirut
Waterbury, John *political science professor, writer, former academic administrator*

MALAYSIA

Kuala Lumpur
Abdel-Rahim, Muddathir *political scientist, educator*

NETHERLANDS

Amsterdam
Drenth, Pieter Johan Diederik *psychology professor, consultant*

De Bilt
Van Ginkel, Johannes Auguste *geographer, educator*

Utrecht
Tielman, Rob A.P. *social sciences educator*

NORWAY

Oslo
Karlsen, Paul Johan *psychologist, researcher, writer*

PHILIPPINES

Makati
Thompson, Willard Scott (W. Scott Thompson) *social sciences educator*

POLAND

Podkowa Lesna
Kosinski, Leszek Antoni *geography educator*

REPUBLIC OF KOREA

Busan
Yoon, Seong-Min *economics professor*

Daegu
Lee, Joung-Woo *economics professor*

Seoul
Choi, Byoung Seon *economist, financial engineer, educator*
Kim, Chai-Youn *psychology professor*
Sohn, Jungyul *geographer*

Suwon
Lee, Tong Hun *economics professor*

RUSSIA

Moscow
Kotlyakov, Vladimir Mikhailovich *geographer, researcher*
Zaretskaya, Elena *social sciences educator, dean*

RWANDA

Grigoriev, Sergei Aleksandrovich *political scientist, researcher*

SCOTLAND

Aberchirder
Talbot, Nyna Lucille *psychologist, writer*

SINGAPORE

Singapore
Hong, Song-Iee *social studies educator*

SOUTH AFRICA

Rondebosch
van der Merwe, Nikolaas Johannes *archaeologist*

SPAIN

Alicante
Castejon-Costa, Juan Luis *psychologist, educator*

Barcelona
Huidobro, Fernando López *economist, biologist*

Madrid
Pérez-Díaz, Víctor Miguel *sociology educator*

TAIWAN

Pingtung
Fan, Tai-Sheng Allen *social scientist, educator*

TRINIDAD AND TOBAGO

Saint Augustine
Shaw, Timothy Milton *political science professor*

TURKEY

Ankara
Kirecci, Akif *economics professor*

Istanbul
Yamak, Sibel *social sciences educator, researcher*

ADDRESS UNPUBLISHED

Abrevaya, Jason *economics professor*
Abu-Lughod, Janet Lippman *sociologist, educator*
Acosta, Catherine *psychologist, special education educator*
Adam, Justine E. *psychologist*
Adams, James Frederick *psychologist, academic administrator, educator*
Adams, Robert McCormick *anthropologist, educator*
Adeyemi, Sele *social studies educator*
Ahrari, Ehsan M. *political science professor, dean*
Aisen, Ari *economist, researcher*
Albanese, Jay Samuel *criminologist, educator*
Albert, Gerald *retired clinical psychologist*
Aldrich, Seth F. *psychologist*
Aliber, Robert Z. *economist, educator*
Allen, Bruce Templeton *retired economics professor*
Allen, Pamela Smith *retired psychologist, writer*
Allender, Julie Ann *psychologist*
Alpher, Victor Seth *clinical psychologist, consultant*
Alshahrani, Saad Ali *economist*
Altman, Irwin *psychologist, educator*
Amoroso, Richard Louis *psychologist, educator*
Anchin, Jack C. *psychologist, educator*
Ancoli-Israel, Sonia *psychologist, researcher*
Anderson, Bernard E. *economist*
Anderson, James George *sociologist, educator, communications educator*
Andrews, Pat R. *political science professor*
Anthony-Perez, Bobbie Cotton Murphy *retired psychology professor*
Aponte, Frances *psychologist, educator*
Arakawa, Fumiyasu *archaeologist, researcher*
Ascencao, Erlete Malveira *psychologist, educator*
Astorino, Todd Anthony *exercise psychologist educator*
Aumann, Robert John *economics professor*
Aviles, Alice Alers *psychologist*
Awokuse, Titus O. *economics professor*
Axilrod, Stephen Harvey *global economic consultant, economist*
Bacolod, Marigee *economist, educator*
Bacon, Phillip *geographer, author, consultant*
Balstad, Roberta *social scientist*
Barnes, Sheila Kaye *Executive Director*
Batchelder, William Howard *psychology educator*
Bateman, Mitchell Ray *psychologist*
Bateson, Mary Catherine *retired anthropology educator, writer, lecturer*
Bavuso, Craig *psychologist*
Bayoumi, Moustafa *social studies educator*
Belgrave, Faye *social sciences educator*
Berg, Sanford Vern *economics professor, director*
Bergin, Allen Eric *clinical psychologist, educator*
Bernsen, Harold John *political scientist, educator, retired military officer*
Bernstein, Mary *sociologist, educator*
Bina, Robert W *psychologist*
Blackburn, John W. *retired psychologist*
Blalock, Carol Douglass *psychologist, educator*
Bloch, Richard M. *psychology professor, director*
Bloemen, Harmanna *economics professor*
Bloomfield, Lincoln Palmer *political scientist*
Bluth, B. J. (Elizabeth Jean Catherine Bluth) *sociologist, aerospace technologist*
Bobrow, Davis Bernard *public policy educator*
Boff, Kenneth Richard *engineering research psychologist*
Bourguignon, Erika Eichhorn *anthropologist, educator*
Bowen, Barton Richard *economics professor*
Boyarchenko, Svetlana Ivanovna *economics professor, mathematician*
Boyd, David James *retired social sciences educator*
Bracey, Earnest *political science professor*
Braen, Bernard Benjamin *retired psychology professor*
Bramson, Leon *retired social scientist, educator*
Brazelton, Garth Adam *economist*
Bredfeldt, John Creighton *economics educator, writer, retired military officer*
Bricker, Harvey Miller *retired anthropology educator*
Bricker, Victoria Reifler *anthropologist, educator*
Brill, Maria *psychologist*
Brodsky, Sheldon *economics professor, consultant*
Broyles, Jeffrey Lynn *school psychologist*
Buck, Jane Louise *retired psychology professor*
Bullard, Judith Eve *psychologist, systems engineer*
Bullock, Mary Brown *political science professor, former academic administrator*
Cacioppo, John Terrance *psychologist, educator, researcher*
Calvo, Esteban *sociologist, researcher*
Caplow, Theodore *sociologist*
Carfora, John Michael *economics professor, research and academic administrator, author*
Carliner, Geoffrey Owen *economist, director*
Carlsen, Mary Baird *clinical psychologist*
Carlson, Janet Frances *psychologist, educator*
Carlson, Roger David *psychologist, educator, minister*
Carrara, Benjamin J., II, *psychologist*
Carthey, Joseph Howard *economics professor*
Carton, Lonnie Caming *educational psychologist*
Case, Elizabeth Joy *psychology and educational assessment director*
Cassidy, Shelley *psychologist*
Cassou, Steven Peter *economics professor*
Cavin, Susan Elizabeth *sociologist, writer*
Chandra, Satish *psychologist*
Chang, Winston Wen-tsuen *economist, educator*
Chao, Ruth *psychologist, educator*
Chatterjee, Anindya *economist, researcher*
Chhaochharia, Vidhi *economics professor*
Childers, Joshua Brandon *psychologist, educator*
Chirinko, Robert S. *economics professor*
Christian, Carole Ann *psychologist, academic administrator*
Christian, James Wayne *economist*
Churchill, Ward LeRoy *social sciences educator, advocate*
Ciullo, Rosemary *psychologist*
Clark, Caleb Morgan *political scientist, educator*
Clark, William Arthur V. *geographer*
Clees, Kelly Marie *school psychologist*
Clinard, Marshall Barron *sociologist, educator*
Coberly, Elaine K. *psychologist*
Cochran, John P. *economics professor*
Cohen, Malcolm Martin *psychologist, researcher*
Colip, Olga Shearin *retired home economist, volunteer*
Collier, William Gayle *psychology professor, researcher*
Colosimo, Mary Lynn Sukurs *psychology professor*
Conrey, Thomas Joseph *psychologist*
Constantine, Madonna G. *psychology professor, researcher*
Cooper, Paula K. *psychologist*
Cotten, Annie Laura *psychologist, educator*
Crawford, Edward E. *retired psychologist*
Crisci, Pat Devita *retired psychology educator*
Currie, Robert Bruce *psychology professor*
Daniel, Coldwell III *economist, educator, entrepreneur*
Danielsen, Albert Leroy *economics professor, energy and utilities consultant*
Da Pena, Eileen *psychologist*
Darmofal, David *political scientist, educator*
Davidson, John Kenneth, Sr. *sociologist, educator, researcher, writer, consultant*
Decker, Murray Steven *social studies educator*
DeHart, Paul Robert *political science professor*
Dejud, Carlos *psychologist*
DeLeon, Richard Edward *retired political science professor*
Denevan, William Maxfield *geographer, historical ecologist, educator*
De Rosa, Eve *psychology professor*
Dey, Madan Mohan *economics professor*
Diem, Richard A. *social studies educator, educational consultant*
Dierickx, Constance Ricker *psychologist, management consultant*
di Giovanni, Julian *economist*
Dincauze, Dena Ferran *retired archaeologist, educator*
Dinwiddie, Granger *psychology professor*
DioGuardi, Richard James *psychologist, researcher*
DiRienzo, Casey *economics professor*
Dirsmith, Jessica *psychologist*
Ditton, Patricia Granville *psychologist, educator*
Dixit, Avinash Kamalakar *economics professor*
Dnes, Antony William *economist*
Dole, Arthur Alexander *former psychology professor, department chairman*
Dorvil, Judith Marie *psychologist*
Dowd, Morgan Daniel *retired political science professor, dean*
Dowling, Edward Thomas *economics professor*
Dulberg, Loretta *psychologist*
Durantini, Marta Rosa *psychology professor, researcher*
Durell, Viviane G. *psychologist, small business owner*
Dwyer, Gerald Paul, Jr. *economist, bank executive*
Earle, Timothy Keese *anthropology educator*
Eberhart, Steven Wesley *psychologist*
Eden, Benjamin *economics professor*
Ehrlich, Annette *psychologist, educator*
Eischen, Donald F. *psychologist, educator, writer*
Eisenstein, Edward Milton *psychologist, physiologist, radiologist, educator*
Ellerbrock-Bendele, Lynette *psychologist*
Endres, Kelly J. *psychologist*
Engel, Bernard Theodore *psychologist, educator*
Ericson, David Frank *political scientist, educator*
Eskew, Henry Lawrence, Jr. *economist, consultant*
Eyde, Lorraine Dittrich *psychologist, researcher*
Fararo, Thomas John *sociologist, educator*
Farley, John Edward *retired sociologist, educator, researcher*
Farmer, Roger Edward Alfred *economics professor*
Ferreira, Francisco Hollanda Guimaraes *economist, researcher*
Fishman, Joshua Aaron *sociolinguist, educator*
Fiske-Rusciano, Roberta Louise *anthropologist*
Fogel, Joshua *psychologist, researcher*
Fonseca, Christine Nel *psychologist, consultant*
Fontes, Patricia J. *psychologist*
Forsleff, Louise Stewart *psychologist, educator*
Foulkes, William David *psychologist, educator*
Fox, Robin *social studies educator*
Freedland, Kenneth E. *psychologist, educator*
French, Laurence Armand *social sciences educator*
Friedman, James Winstein *economist, educator*
Frost, Ellen Louise *political economist*
Fu, Cindy Yan *psychologist*
Funseth, Robert Lloyd Eric Martin *international consultant, retired diplomat*

Gallini, Richard psychologist, consultant
Gallucci-Breithaupt, Adrianne psychologist, social worker
Gannon, Sister Ann Ida retired philosophy educator
Gantt, Jean Wallace economics professor
Gardner, Donna L. psychologist, educator
Garrison, Steve R. political science professor
Garruto, Ralph Michael biomedical anthropologist, biologist, educator
Geertz, Hildred Storey anthropology educator
Germain, Pichop Nkengoum economics professor
Ghibesi, Jason Joseph political science professor
Ghosh, Ramya economist
Gibert, Stephen P. political scientist
Gibson, Michael Troy political science professor
Giele, Janet Zollinger sociologist, educator
Goldman, Bert Arthur retired psychology professor
Goldman, Jeri Joan psychologist
Golson, Randal L. social sciences educator, department chairman
Golub, Sharon Bramson retired psychologist, educator
Granott, Nira psychologist, researcher
Grant, Carmen Hill psychologist, psychotherapist
Greenberg, Ira Arthur psychologist
Greene, Katrina Tomar anthropologist, educator
Greenwood, Janet Kae Daly psychologist, academic administrator, marketing professional
Griffith, Heather Marie psychologist
Grimm, Dean Lain psychologist
Gross, Leon Jay psychometrician
Grühn, Daniel psychologist, educator
Gubser, Peter Anton political scientist, writer, educator
Guillet, David Wilber anthropologist, educator
Guinn, Janet Martin psychologist, consultant
Gullo, Stephen Pernice psychologist, corporate executive
Gunasekera, Hitihamy Mudiyanselage economics professor
Haber, Ralph Norman psychology consultant, researcher, educator
Hadaway, Christopher Kirk sociologist, research administrator
Hahn, Frank Horace economics professor
Haines, Richard Foster retired psychologist
Haining, Jeane psychologist
Hall, Ella Taylor clinical school psychologist
Hall, Jay social psychologist
Halpern, Joel Martin anthropologist, photographer
Hamilton, Marc C. psychologist
Hamilton, Michael Seymour political scientist, educator
Hammer, Robert Eugene psychologist
Hammond, Paul Young political science professor
Hampton, Lori Beth psychologist
Hansen, Richard Emory psychologist
Hantzis, Peter C. psychologist, educator
Hanushek, Eric Alan economics professor
Hardy, Richard Allen, Jr. psychologist, educator
Harmon-Jones, Eddie psychology professor
Harner, Michael James anthropologist, educator
Harrison, Blake Andrew social sciences educator
Hart, Karen E. psychologist, consultant
Hartzell, Irene Janofsky psychologist, mediator
Harvey, James Cardwell political science and history professor, consultant
Hayes, Robert Francis psychologist, educator
Haywood, H(erbert) Carl(ton) psychologist, educator
Hefferan, Colien Joan economist
Helfgott, Roy B. economist, educator
Herod, Charles Carteret Afro-American studies educator
Heslop, Michael George economics professor
Hidden-Dodson, Nancy retired psychologist, consultant, educator
Hilbrands, Peggy G. psychologist
Hillman, Richard Stanley retired political science professor
Hirsh-Pasek, Kathryn Ann psychology educator
Hitz, Frederick Porter public and international affairs educator
Hock, Roger R. psychology professor
Hoffman, Kevin Michael psychologist, researcher
Hollerbach, Paula Elizabeth demographer, researcher
Holmes, Paul Luther political scientist, educational consultant
Holmstrom, Lynda Lytle sociologist, educator
Holochwost, Steven John psychology professor, researcher
Holstein, Adora De Los Santos economics professor
Holzer, Harry Joseph economist, educator
Honig, Alice Sterling psychologist
Horn, Wade Frederick psychologist, former federal agency administrator
Hoskinson, Katherine Thayer school psychologist
Hough, Sigmund neuropsychologist
Howrey, Eugene Philip retired economics and statistics professor
Hudnut, William Herbert III political scientist
Hughes, Ann Hightower retired economist
Huls, Glenna L. retired sociology educator, photographer
Illukpitiya, Prabodh agriculture economist
Ingram, James Carlton economist, educator
Ioffe, Grigory geography educator, researcher
Izawa, Chizuko psychologist, researcher
Jaber, Suzanne Joy psychologist
Jacobs, Marianne anthropologist, medical/surgical nurse, educator
James, Estelle economist, educator
Jay, Corrigan R. economics professor
Jefferson, Monica Louise nueropsychologist
Jenkins, Debra psychology professor
Jett, Stephen Clinton geography and textiles educator, researcher
Jiménez, Tomás Roberto sociologist, educator
Johansen, Terri psychologist
Johnson, Albert Wesley retired political science professor, public official
Johnson, Benjamin F., VI, economist, consultant
Johnson, Charles Lavon, Jr. clinical neuropsychologist, consultant
Jones, Cleopatra Celeste retired gerontologist, sociologist, educator
Jordan, Robert Smith political science professor, civilian military employee
Juviler, Peter Henry political scientist, educator
Kahana, Eva Frost sociology educator
Kalemli-Ozcan, Sebnem economics professor
Kalkstein, Laurence Saul geography educator
Kan, Marni L. psychologist
Kane, Michael Barry social science research executive
Kanter, Jolie Lynn psychologist
Karacaovali, Baybars economics professor
Karim, Muhammad Bazlul political scientist, educator
Karson, Samuel psychologist, educator
Kaslow, Florence Whiteman psychologist, educator, family business consultant
Kavakci, Merve social sciences educator
Keller, Gail psychologist, consultant
Kelling, Angela S. psychology professor
Kellogg, Kathy psychologist
Kendrick, Budd Leroy psychologist
Kenny, Robert Wade sociology, ethics and rhetoric educator
Keohane, Nannerl Overholser political scientist, academic administrator
Kern, Martin social studies educator
Kessler, Gale Suzanne psychologist, educator
Khatena, Joe psychology professor
Kiesler, Charles Adolphus psychologist, academic administrator
Kilby, Heidi Lynn psychologist, educator
Kim, Doh-Khul economics professor
King, Rosalyn Mercita social sciences educator, psychologist, researcher
Kirkpatrick, Kent political science professor
Kist-Tahmasian, Candace Lynee psychologist
Kitchka, Jennifer Lyn psychologist
Kline, John P. psychologist, researcher
Kocel, Katherine Merle psychology professor, researcher
Koenig, Thomas Howard social studies educator
Koffler, Aviele Melissa psychologist
Komechak, Marilyn Gilbert retired psychologist, writer
Konduru, Srinivasa economics professor
Koneru, Vamsi Krishna psychologist
Koo, Shou-Eng economics professor
Kosslyn, Stephen M. psychologist, educator
Kovacs, Malcolm sociologist, educator
Kreps, Juanita Morris retired economics professor, former United States Secretary of Commerce
Kuroda, Yasumasa political science professor, researcher
Kvint, Vladimir Lev economist, strategist, mining engineer, finance educator
Laffer, Arthur Betz economist
Lancaster, Kirsten Kezar psychologist
Landon, William J. retired intelligence officer
Lann, Martha Marie psychology professor, consultant
Lasky, Richard Donald psychoanalyst, educator
La Spata, Michelle Gayle school psychologist
Lau, Stephanie economics professor
Laughlin, Louis Gene economic analyst, consultant
Lawrence, Janice Fletcher psychologist
Lazar, Zoe L. psychologist
Leach, Jim (James Albert Smith Leach) political science professor, former United States Representative from Iowa
LeBlanc, Hugh Linus political science professor, consultant
Lee, Ho Jin economist
Lee, Mordecai political scientist, educator
Lee, Tabia (T. Lee) social studies educator
Leibowitz, Rosalind psychologist, educator
Leijonhufvud, Axel Stig Bengt economics professor
Leonard, Hasse A. psychologist, educator
Leslie, Teresa Elizabeth anthropologist, educator
Lesnik, Julie anthropologist, educator
Lewis, Charles Leonard psychologist
Liang, Kathleen economics professor
Ligon, Nikimya psychologist
Lipsey, Richard George economist, educator
Lipson, Abigail psychologist
Lipson, Daniel N. political science professor
Locke, Edwin Allen III retired psychologist, educator
Loftus, Elizabeth F. psychology professor
Loge, Krista Fields psychologist
Lubotsky, Darren Howard economics professor, researcher
Luk, Debra K. psychologist
Luskin, Frederic Michael psychologist, educator
Lynton, Sandra M. psychologist
Machina, Mark Joseph economist
MacHovec, Frank J. psychologist
MacLennan, Beryce Winifred psychologist
Magana, Melanie G psychologist, consultant
Mandel, Jeffrey S. psychologist
Markovich, Patricia H. economist
Marra, Vincent J., Jr. economics professor
Marron, Donald Baird, Jr. economist
Marx, Gary T. sociologist, writer
Matheny, Adam Pence, Jr. child psychologist, educator, consultant, researcher
Matiya, Jim psychology professor
McGinnies, Elliott Morse psychologist, educator
McGough, Duane Theodore economist, consultant, retired federal official
McGuinness, Kevin Michael psychologist, director
McNealey, Billie psychologist
Mecca, Kimberly Ann psychologist
Mellins, Claude Ann psychologist
Mencher, Joan Phyllis anthropology educator
Menlove, Frances Lee psychologist
Meredith, Lisa Ann Marie literacy coach, consultant
Meschan, Lynn psychology professor
Michel, George Frederick psychology professor, researcher
Mickes, Laura psychology professor
Migue, Jean Luc economics professor
Mills-Koonce, William Roger psychologist, director
Minnich, Donna social sciences educator
Mitchell, Steve Harold psychologist
Mitra, Pritha economist
Mize, Ronald L. social studies educator
Moghimzadeh, Mahmood economics professor
Moore, Stanley Wayne retired political science professor
Morduch, Jonathan economist, educator
Morrison, Winifred Elaine Haas social sciences educator
Morse, Gayle Skawennio psychologist, consultant
Muhn, Judy Ann psychologist, genealogist, trainer
Murphy, Evelyn Frances economist
Myers, Caitlin Knowles economics professor
Myren, Richard Albert criminologist, consultant
Nadolski, Dora J. social sciences educator, researcher
Nagle, Eugenia Susan Karabacz retired sociologist, psychologist
Nampet, Wajira psychology professor
Natani, Kirmach forensic psychologist
Nathan, Gerald Dale retired psychologist, researcher, writer
Naviaux, LaRee DeVee retired psychologist, academic administrator, director
Ndibongo-Traub, Lulama economist, educator
Nearine, Robert James educational psychologist
Negron-Soto, Lizzie psychologist
Neher, Andrew W. psychologist, educator
Newborn, Jud anthropologist, writer, curator, educator, historian
Newman, Philip Robert psychologist
Nichols, Donald Arthur economist, educator
Norman, Donald Arthur psychologist, educator
O'Brien, John Wilfrid economist, educator, retired university president
Ohsfeldt, Robert L. health economist, educator
Ok, Efe A. economics professor
Onunkwo, Emmanuel Nwafor retired economics professor
O'Rourke, Sheila Gail anthropologist
Orr, Amy J. sociologist, educator
Oshinsky, James Steven psychologist
Otis, Jack social work educator
Page, Scott E. social sciences educator
Palisi, Anthony Thomas psychologist, educator
Paredes, James Anthony anthropologist
Parish, Thomas Scanlan psychology professor
Paskins, Janet Lynn psychology professor, educational consultant
Patino-Brandfon, Sylvia retired psychologist
Patterson, Samuel C. retired political science professor
Payerhin, Marek political scientist, educator
Pearson, Richard Joseph archaeologist, educator
Pearson, Scott Roberts retired economics professor
Pedersen, Knud George retired economics professor, academic administrator
Pence, Kris political science professor
Pepper, Joline Romano psychologist, educator
Pepper, Pamela Poe psychologist
Peretti, Peter Oral psychology professor, researcher
Peterson, Bruce Ernest social studies educator
Petranovich, Danilo political science professor
Petri, Peter Alexander economist, educator, director
Pezeshk, Violet psychologist, educator
Phelps, Charles Elliott economics professor, director
Pilisuk, Marc psychology educator
Pine, Charles Joseph clinical psychologist
Pineyro, Michele psychologist
Pirchner, Herman, Jr. foreign policy specialist
Pitts, Roger L. psychologist
Pollack, Gerald Alexander economist, educator, federal agency administrator
Pollack, Jonathan Duker political science professor
Polomsky, Michael Douglas psychology professor
Pope, Kenneth Sayle psychologist
Poser, Ernest George psychologist, educator
Pounds, Kevin D. social studies educator
Prado, William Manuel psychologist, educator
Premack, David psychologist
Procter, Robert J. economics professor, consultant
Radulović, Novak Aleksandar economist, composer
Rajan, Raghuram economist, educator
Ramsay, J. Russell psychologist
Randall, Richard Rainier geographer
Randazzo, Marisa R. psychologist
Raschke, Jeanne M. psychologist
Redlo, Mitchell economics professor, consultant
Reed, Adam Victor psychologist, engineer, information scientist
Reese, Hayne Waring psychologist, educator
Reichard, Ulrich H. anthropologist, educator
Reichs, Kathy (Kathleen Joan Toelle Reichs) forensic anthropologist, educator, writer
Reinleitner, Katherine Mindlin psychologist, foundation administrator
Reis, Ricardo economics professor
Relyea, Harold Clarence political scientist, writer
Reynolds, Lloyd George economist, educator
Richard, N. Landers psychology professor
Richard, Robert Carter psychological consultant
Richardson, Laurel Walum sociology educator
Rickel, Annette Urso psychology and psychiatry researcher, educator
Rips, Lance Jeffrey psychology professor
Robinson, James Arthur political scientist
Robinson, Marguerite Stern anthropologist, educator, consultant
Roche de Coppens, Peter George sociologist, educator
Rogers, Frederic Halsey economist
Romanucci-Ross, Lola anthropologist, educator
Romes, Rekina psychologist
Rosales, Monica D. social studies educator
Rosicki, Maria Trzetrzewinska-Trett clinical psychologist
Roussel, Lee Dennison economist
Rove, Karl Christian political analyst, former federal official
Rubenstein, Judith Louise psychologist
Rubner, Michael international relations educator, university administrator
Rudd, Ann Talton psychologist, artist
Rudolph, James Robert psychologist
Rumpf, Ann psychologist
Russell, Mason Webster economist, consultant
Rutherfurd, Lisa school psychologist
Ruttenberg, Ruth A. economist
Sabodash, Vladlena economics professor, researcher
Sade, Donald Stone anthropology educator
Salava, Jennifer Anne psychologist
Salins, Peter D. political science professor, academic administrator
Sammons, Morgan Taylor psychologist
Sargent, Thomas Andrew retired political science professor
Saumell, Eileen Mary psychologist
Scheff, Thomas Joel sociologist, educator
Scheffler, Linda Weingarten psychologist, educator
Schegloff, Emanuel Abraham social studies educator
Schein, Virginia Ellen psychologist
Scheinman, Nancy Jane psychologist
Schexnider, Virginia Reeves school psychologist
Schlesinger, James Rodney economist, former United States Secretary of Defense
Schmandt-Besserat, Denise archaeologist, educator
Schmidt, Harvey Martin economist, educator, financial analyst, consultant
Schneider, Allen Morris psychology professor
Schoen, Robert demographer
Schulhofer-Wohl, Samuel economics professor
Schultz, Caitlin G. psychologist, educator
Schwartz, Eliezer psychologist, educator
Schwendinger, Julia Rosalind Siegel sociology researcher
Scott, Lesli psychologist
Sebastian, Peter political scientist, consultant, retired diplomat
Seck, Ousmane economics professor
Seeborg, Michael C. economics professor
Selders, Jean E. retired psychology professor
Sentell-Perez, Jo psychologist
Serling, Joel Martin educational psychologist
Seyon, Patrick L. N. social sciences educator, educational consultant
Shapiro, Leo J. social researcher
Shapiro, Perry economics educator
Sharpe, William Forsyth economics professor
Shaw, Richard Thomas humanitarian, retired federal agent, retired military officer
Shelor, Belva Jean psychologist
Shepp, Bryan Eugene psychologist, educator
Sherry, George Leon political science professor
Shields, Andrea Lyn psychologist, coach, educator
Shields, Stephanie psychology professor
Silberling, Louise Stillman sociologist, writer, editor
Silverman, Jerry Mark political science professor, consultant
Simon, Adam F. political science professor
Simon, Norma Plavnick psychologist
Sims, Kent Otway economist
Sinai, Allen Leo economist, educator
Singh, Madhu social studies educator
Sisk, Jane Elizabeth economist, educator
Skenderian, Jessica Josephine psychologist
Smelser, Neil Joseph sociologist
Smith, David Horton social science researcher-theorist, writer, consultant, nonprofit organization founder, internet business founder
Smith, Vme Edom (Verna Mae Smith) social sciences educator, freelance photographer, writer
Smoot, Julianna political fundraiser
Snyder, Marvin neuropsychologist
Soileau, Monica Marie economist
Spelman, Nancy Latting developmental psychologist
Spiro, Herbert John political scientist, ambassador
Spitzer, Eliot Laurence political science professor, former Governor of New York
Spitzer, John J. retired economics professor
Splane, Richard Beverley social work educator
Spraggins, Johnnie David sociology and cultural studies educator
Spring, Anita anthropologist, educator
Spring, Bonnie Joan preventive medicine professor
Springer, Debra Ann psychologist
Sprinthall, Norman Arthur psychology educator
Stamm, Brad economics professor
Steiner, Robert L. economist
Sternheimer, Karen sociologist, writer
Stetz, Melba Del Carmen psychologist
Stevens, Rebecca Ann sociologist, educator
Stevenson, Joyce R.L. retired psychologist
Stiles, Beverly Lynn sociologist, educator
Stoeckel, Luke Edward psychologist, researcher
Stoytcheva, Petia economics professor
Striker, Cecil Leopold archaeologist, educator
Stryker, Robin social sciences educator
Stryker, Sheldon sociologist, educator
Stultz, Cilla Holmes psychologist
Sun, Jiaming social sciences educator
Suraci, Patrick Joseph clinical psychologist
Sussman, Gerald social sciences educator
Sussman, Janet I. social sciences educator
Swanstrom, Thomas Evan economist
Swartz, Jon David psychologist, educator
Switzer, Janet psychologist administrator
Taylor, Leslie Ronald psychologist
Taylor, Ronald Lewis sociology educator
Teeters, Nancy Hays economist
Tenhagen, Allison Mae psychologist
Textor, Robert Bayard cultural anthropology educator, writer, consultant
Thayer, Jane Hillis psychologist
Thiessen, Delbert Duane psychologist
Thompson, Alan Eric economics professor
Tiburcio, Nelson Jose criminologist, consultant
Tideman, T. Nicolaus economics educator
Timmermann, Allan Gilling management and economics professor
Tishman, Lynn P. psychologist, psychoanalyst
Tobias, Veronica Ann (Roni Tobias) psychologist
Topaloglu, Zeynep economics professor
Townsend, Tiffany G. psychology professor
Traynham, Earle Campbell retired economics professor, dean
Tripp, Amanda psychologist
Trotter, Suzanne Michelle psychologist
Trzcinski, Eileen social studies educator, director
Tschoepe, Gary Joseph retired political science professor
Tyler, John Duke psychologist, educator
Ulfelder, Jay political scientist, director

Upshaw, Harry Stephan *psychologist, educator*
Valdivia, Annarella *psychologist*
Vallier, Nanette *psychologist*
Vandeputte, Dixie Dianne *retired psychologist, educator*
Vanderlinde, Roger *social sciences educator*
Van Dyk, Frederick Theodore *political scientist, writer*
Van Houten, Ronald *psychology professor*
Van Inwegen, Patrick F. *political science professor*
Varakin, Donald Alexander *psychology professor*
Vasconcelos, Marco *psychologist*
Vaux, Henry James, Jr. *economics professor*
Vayalakkara, Jyothi *neuropsychologist, director, educator*
Vernon, Margaret Katherine *psychologist*
Vojnovic, Igor Zoran *geographer, urban planner, educator*
von Wachter, Till Marco *economics professor*
Wadden, Thomas Antony *psychologist, educator*
Wadkins, Theresa A. *psychology professor, researcher*
Waggoner, Cheri *psychologist*
Wagner, Antonin *economics professor*
Waldkoetter, Raymond Oliver *psychologist, consultant*
Walker, Clarence Eugene *psychology professor*
Walker, Ronald Edward *psychologist, educator*
Walsh Mitchell, Diana *school psychologist, consultant*
Wang, Mo *psychology professor*
Wang, Yung-Ho Ophelia *geographer, educator*
Ward, Jeannette Poole *retired psychologist, educator*
Warne, William Robert *economist*
Watson, Patty Jo *anthropology educator*
Watters, Ann Oliva *psychologist, educator*
Waud, Roger Neil *economist, educator*
Webel, Charles Peter *human science and psychology educator*
Weckler, Nora *retired psychology educator, psychotherapist*
Wehner, André *psychologist, educator*
Weil, Rolf Alfred *economist, retired university president*
Weiner, Ferne *psychologist*
Weiner, Max *psychology professor*
Weissenburger, David Allen *psychologist, educator, consultant*
Wellisz, Stanislaw *economics professor*
Werner-Jacobsen, Emmy Elisabeth *developmental psychologist*
Wertlieb, Donald Lawrence *psychologist, educator*
Whitehead, Tanya Dianne Grubbs *psychologist, educator, researcher*
Wieand, Lou Ann *psychology educator, psychotherapist*
Wilkinson, Doris *medical sociology educator*
Wilkinson, Richard H. *archaeologist, educator*
Wilson, Melinda J. *psychologist*
Wilson, Scott Thomas *psychologist, researcher*
Wilson, Wayne Jerome *psychology professor*
Witte, Ann Dryden *economics educator*
Wolfe, Gregory Baker *international relations educator*
Wolman, William *economist, journalist, broadcaster*
Wolynez, Allen Lawrence *psychology professor*
Wonders, William Clare *geography educator*
Worth, John Eugene *anthropologist, educator*
Wright, John W. *social studies educator*
Wrong, Dennis Hume *retired sociologist, educator*
Wu, Hong *economics professor*
Yamanouchi-Rynn, Midori *retired social sciences educator*
Yang, Li *geography and tourism educator*
Yankey, Kofi *economics professor*
York, Joan Elizabeth Smith *psychologist*
Zavala, Albert *research psychologist*
Zelek, Charles Andrew *economist*
Zielke, Julie Faye *psychologist*
Zimet, Lloyd *sport psychologist, health educator, program planner and administrator*
Zirkel, Raymond Elliot *psychologist, educator*
Zola, Joshua *psychologist*
Zuckerman, Harriet *sociologist, educator*